CHAMBERS

Dictionary of
Quotations

CHAMBERS

Dictionary of
Quotations

Editor
Alison Jones

with the assistance of
Stephanie Pickering
Megan Thomson

CHAMBERS

CHAMBERS

An imprint of Chambers Harrap Publishers Ltd
7 Hopetoun Crescent, Edinburgh EH7 4AY
Larousse Kingfisher Chambers Inc.
95 Madison Avenue, New York, New York 10016

First published by Chambers Harrap 1996

10 9 8 7 6 5 4 3 2 1

British Library Cataloguing in Publication Data
for this book is available from the British Library

ISBN 0-550-21019-9

Cover illustration: *The Bookworm*
Courtesy of Image Select

Typeset in Great Britain by Cambridge University Press
Printed in France

Contents

Introduction

This new dictionary takes a fresh look at what a quotation is, and sees it as not just a literary nugget in the traditional manner but as any recorded piece of spoken or written language that expresses an idea or thought in an interesting and memorable way, and throws light on the life and times of its author ('author' used here in the widest possible sense). Users will find all the expected quotations from great writers past and present, as well as many that are less expected. In addition, they will find quotations from many other walks of life including, for example, sport. Bill Shankly (former manager of Liverpool Football Club) is in his own way as quotable as Shakespeare: *Me having no education, I had to use my brains.*

This is then an entirely new collection, compiled by over forty specialist researchers who have gone back to original texts to verify the form of quotations wherever possible. As well as the usual writers, critics, politicians and journalists, we have sought out architects, entertainers, scientists, fashion designers, youth icons, activists, musicians, travellers, those involved in sports, psychologists, feminists, industrialists, and many more, as a reflection of the wide diversity of modern life. A higher proportion of women has been included, and the coverage is truly international, extending to other varieties of English and to other languages of the world where these provide material that is readily quotable in English. Quotations from languages using the Roman alphabet are given in the original with a translation. Where the translation is not specified, we have aimed to give a good working English version.

Quotations are arranged alphabetically by author, and chronologically (as far as possible) within each author entry, with the year of the quotation put first when this is known. We have been concerned throughout to place quotations in their biographical and historical context, drawing on Chambers' extensive reference resources to provide brief biographies and contextual notes in order to enhance the reader's understanding and appreciation of the quotations. This arrangement also gives a sense of the development of the philosophy and style of an author or speaker, and we believe it is one of the key features that makes this work much more than a collection of *bons mots*. (In exceptional cases, a different arrangement has seemed sensible; for example, the books of the Bible follow the traditional ordering for ease of reference.)

A dependable source for each quotation is given whenever possible; sometimes however quotations are known from many secondary sources with no traceable primary source, and these are said to be 'attributed'.

We have added a comprehensive index which refers the user to the author, the page number on which the quotation occurs, and the number of the quotation on the page. Quotations are numbered from 1 to 99 and then start again at 1. So a reference to BACON 55:27 points to the quotation by Francis Bacon numbered 27 on page 55. Cross-references in the text use the same system.

The people that fill the pages of this book have, in various ways, influenced our world and our awareness of it with their words. We have aimed at presenting the most memorable comments on all aspects of human experience throughout the ages. However, no selection can be definitive, and the editors would welcome suggestions for inclusion in future editions. We believe users will find the *Chambers Dictionary of Quotations* to be not only a valuable and authoritative reference tool, but also a source of lasting enjoyment.

The Editors

Abbreviations

b	born
bk.	book
c	century (in dates, eg 18c)
c.	*circa* (about)
ch.	chapter
d	died
fl.	floruit
l.	line
pt.	part
sc.	scene

Names of months are shortened to their first three letters

Contributors

Editors
Alison Jones
Stephanie Pickering
Megan Thomson

Publishing Director
Robert Allen

Subject Contributors

Katherine Acheson	Children's literature in English
	Canadian literature
	16th- and 17th-century English literature
Julia Carlson	Fashion
	Food and Drink
	19th-century US literature
John Robert Colombo	Canadian affairs
Ingrid Cranfield	Travel and travel literature
José Garcia	Spanish and Latin-American literature
Graham Giles	Mathematics
	New Age
W Eric Gustafson	Biography
	Business
	Economics
	Sociology
Bruce Henstell	Science and technology
David Horspool	Military history
Dean Juniper	Psychology
Victoria Keller	Art
Grace Kenny	Architecture
	Education
Michael Kinsella	18th- and 19th-century English literature
Paul Maloney	Opera/operetta lyrics
	West European history
Kenny Mathieson	19th- and 20th-century US literature
	20th-century British literature
	Jazz
Kevin McGinley	Old English and medieval European literature
Jim Orton	Australian literature, history and culture
Patricia Perilli	Cinema
Michael Petheram	Media
	Philosophy
David Pickering	Law
	Medicine
	Music
James Robertson	Scottish literature, history and culture

Adrian Room	People and places
Donald Rutherford	Economics
D W D Shaw	Christian theology and literature
Sean Sheehan	South East Asian literature, history and culture
Jane Stewart	Commonwealth literature
	Feminism
Susan Stiles	French and German literature
Onno van Nijf	Ancient history and classical studies

Political consultant
Kenneth Baker

North American consultant
Rev James B Simpson

Administrative and editorial staff
Trevor Anderson
Elaine McAdam
Nicolas McDowell
Louise McGinnity
Robin McMorran
Patricia Marshall
Lucy Morison
Amber Roome
Nicholas Shearing
Elizabeth Small
Alice Stoakley de Palomino

Computing
Ilona Bellos-Morison

The Publishers would like to acknowledge the contribution of
Min Lee to the early stages of this project

Quotations

Abbott, Diane Julie 1953–

British Labour politician, who became the first black woman Member of Parliament in 1987.

1 Forests of middle-aged men in dark suits…all slightly redfaced from eating and drinking too much…a nightmare of elderly white males.
1988 Of the House of Commons.
In the *New York Times*, 3 Jun.

Abelard, Peter 1079–1142

French ecclesiast and theologian. At the age of 38, he fell in love with his 17-year-old pupil Héloïse; when the affair was discovered, he was castrated by her relatives. He became a monk and went on to found the monastic school of the Paraclete and to serve as Abbot of St Gildas-de-Rhuys, Brittany. Declared a heretic by his adversaries, he died on his way to defend himself.

2 *Non enim facile de his, quos plurimum diligimus, turpitudinem suspicamur.*

We do not easily suspect evil of those whom we love most.
c.1132 *Historia Calamitatum*, ch.6.

3 *Cum itaque membris his vilissimis, quæ pro summæ turpitudinis exercitio pudenda vocantur, nec proprium sustinent nomen, me divina gratia mundavit potios quam privavit, quid aliud egit quam ad puritatem munditiæ conservandem sordida removit et vitia.*

When divine grace cleansed rather than deprived me of those most vile members which from their grossly depraved activity are called 'pudenda' ['shameful'], having no proper name of their own, what else did it do but remove filth and foulness so as to preserve unblemished purity?
c.1135 Of his castration. Second letter to Héloïse.

4 *O quanta qualia sunt illa sabbata,*
Quae semper celebrat superna curia.

O what their joy and their glory must be,
Those endless sabbaths the blessèd ones see.
Hymnarius Paraclitensis, bk.1, no.29, 'Sabbato. Ad Vesperas' (translated by J M Neale).

Abercrombie, Lascelles 1881–1938

English poet and critic. He wrote several volumes of poetry in the Georgian manner, and a number of works of academic literary criticism.

5 The poet's business is not to describe things to us, or to tell us about things, but to create in our minds the very things themselves.
1932 *Poetry: Its Music and Meaning*, introduction.

Abse, Dannie 1923–

Welsh writer and physician, specialist at a London chest clinic since 1954. Best-known as a poet, he has also written novels, plays and autobiographical works, including *A Poet in the Family* (1974) and *A Strong Dose of Myself* (1982).

6 I know the colour rose, and it is lovely,
But not when it ripens in a tumour;
And healing greens, leaves and grass, so springlike,
In limbs that fester are not springlike.
1968 'Pathology of Colours'.

7 So in the simple blessing of a rainbow,
In the bevelled edge of a sunlit mirror,
I have seen visible, Death's artifact
Like a soldier's ribbon on a tunic tacked.
1968 'Pathology of Colours'.

8 The theme of Death is to Poetry what Mistaken Identity is to Drama.
1984 Journal entry, Feb, collected in *Journals from the Ant-Heap* (1986).

9 We British are an aggressive nation. We seem to have become more violent this last decade: look how we drive fast and furious, with fists clenched; listen, at the stadiums, how the crowds shout, 'Kick his fuckin' head in,' or to the sirens of police cars and ambulances in the shoddy streets of Brixton or Liverpool.
1986 *Journals from the Ant-Heap*, 'Appendix 1: Authors Take Sides'.

Abu 'l-'Alá Al-Ma'arri 973–1058

Syrian poet and scholar. He was blinded by smallpox in childhood and devoted himself to study, memorizing the manuscripts of Syrian libraries. As well as poems, he wrote philosophical and mystical works.

10 We live ignorant and die in errancy as we lived.
c.1000 *Luzùmiyyàt*, stanza 4 (translated by R A Nicholson in *Studies in Islamic Poetry*, 1921).

11 The world's best moment is a calm hour passed In listening to a friend who can talk well.
c.1000 *Luzùmiyyàt*, stanza 32 (translated by R A Nicholson in *Studies in Islamic Poetry*, 1921).

12 We flee from Death's bitter cup; he follows, loving and fain.
c.1000 *Luzùmiyyàt*, stanza 36 (translated by R A Nicholson in *Studies in Islamic Poetry*, 1921).

13 Life is a malady whose one medicine is Death.

> **c.1000** *Luzùmiyyàt*, stanza 41 (translated by R A Nicholson in *Studies in Islamic Poetry*, 1921).

14 Consider every moment past
    A thread from life's frayed mantle cast.

> **c.1100** *Luzùmiyyàt*, stanza 57 (translated by R A Nicholson in *Studies in Islamic Poetry*, 1921).

Abzug, Bella originally *Bella Savitzky* 1920–98

US Congresswoman, lawyer and writer. She is one of the key figures of the modern feminist movement.

15 Richard Nixon self-impeached…[and] gave us General Ford as his revenge.

> **1976** In *Rolling Stone*, 2 Dec.

Accius 170–c.86 BC

Roman poet and playwright.

16 *Oderint, dum metuant.*

Let them hate, so long as they fear.

> Quoted in Seneca *Dialogues*, 'De Ira'.

Ace, Goodman 1899–1982

US humorist, best known for his radio shows such as *The Easy Aces* (1928–45), with his wife Jane Epstein Ace. He also wrote for television comedians from 1952.

17 Derived from the words Terrible Vaudeville… We call it a medium because nothing's well done.

> **1954** Of TV. Letter to Groucho Marx. Collected in *The Groucho Letters* (1967).

Achebe, Chinua originally *Albert Chinualumogo* 1930–

Nigerian novelist, poet and essayist. His novel *Things Fall Apart* (1958) explores tensions in 19c African society. Other works include *Anthills of the Savannah* (1987, short-listed for the Booker Prize).

18 Among the Ibo the art of conversation is regarded very highly, and proverbs are the palm-oil with which words are eaten.

> **1958** *Things Fall Apart*, ch.1. The title is taken from Yeats's poem 'The Second Coming'.

19 Even now they have not found the mouth with which to tell of their suffering.

> **1958** *Things Fall Apart*, ch.20.

20 Whenever people have asked me which among my novels is my favourite I have always evaded a direct answer, being strongly of the mind that in sheer invidiousness that question is fully comparable to asking a man to list his children in the order in which he loves them. A paterfamilias worth his salt will, if he must, speak about the peculiar attractiveness of each child.

> **1974** *Arrow of God*, preface to 2nd edn.

Acheson, Dean Gooderham 1893–1971

US lawyer and politician. As Under-Secretary (1945–7) and then Secretary of State (1949–53) in the Truman administration, he helped to establish the Marshall Plan (1947) and the North Atlantic Treaty Organization.

21 I will undoubtedly have to seek what is happily known as gainful employment, which I am glad to say does not describe holding public office.

> **1952** On resigning as Secretary of State to resume his career as a lawyer. In *Time*, 22 Dec.

22 Diplomatic problems used to be discussed by ambassadors… Foreign Ministers were called…somebody thought of the summit meetings… We are nearing the moment when political meetings will be held at a divine level.

> **1959** Comment to reporters in Florence, Sep. Recalled in *This Vast External Realm* (1973).

23 The institution of the throne is an anachronistic, feudal institution perfectly adapted to the use of anachronistic feudal-minded groups.

> Opposing US Ambassador Joseph Grew's recommendation for the Emperor's retention in postwar Japan. Quoted in Lee Giovanitti and Fred Freed *The Decision to Drop the Atomic Bomb* (1960).

24 He still had his glorious sense of words drawn from the special reservoir from which Lincoln also drew, fed by Shakespeare and those Tudor critics who wrote the first Prayer Book of Edward VI and their Jacobean successors who translated the Bible.

> **1961** Of Winston Churchill. *Sketches from Life of Men I Have Known.*

25 The old house carried an assurance, typically Portuguese, that nothing was urgent.

> **1961** On the US Embassy residence in Lisbon. *Sketches from Life of Men I Have Known.*

26 He wanted to be independent of the vagaries of butlers.

> **1961** Of Winston Churchill, who liked to keep a champagne bottle next to his plate. *Sketches from Life of Men I Have Known.*

27 He smiled with the spontaneity of a mechanical tiger.

> **1961** Of Soviet Foreign Minister V M Molotov. *Sketches from Life of Men I Have Known.*

28 He struck me as looking like a pear on top of two toothpicks.

> **1962** Of Charles de Gaulle, 22 Oct, after a visit during the Cuban missile crisis. Quoted in David S McLellan and David C Acheson (eds) *Among Friends: Personal Letters of Dean Gooderham Acheson* (1980).

29 Great Britain has lost an Empire and not yet found a role. The attempt to play a separate power role—that is, a role apart from Europe, based on a special relationship with the United States, on being the head of the Commonwealth—is about to be played

out. Her Majesty's Government is now attempting, wisely in my opinion, to re-enter Europe.

1962 Speech at West Point military academy, 5 Dec. According to the *New York Times*, 23 Nov 1969, Prime Minister Harold Wilson later countered, 'Mr Acheson is a distinguished figure who has lost a State Department and not yet found himself a role'.

30 Fumbling silence in the White House seeps out over the country like a cold fog over a river bed where no stream runs.

1963 Letter to Harry S Truman, 28 May, alluding to the Eisenhower administration. Quoted in David S McLelland and David C Acheson (eds) *Among Friends: Personal Letters of Dean Gooderham Acheson* (1980).

31 A real Centaur—part man, part horse's ass. A rough appraisal, but curiously true.

1968 Of President Johnson. 13 Apr.

32 Like finding oneself pregnant and trying to fall in love as quickly as possible.

On the weekend of Richard M Nixon's inauguration. Quoted in Douglas Brinkley *Dean Acheson: The Cold War Years 1953–71* (1992).

33 I had shown my colors. Those who took their red straight, without a chaser of white and blue, were not mollified.

1969 *Present at the Creation.*

34 The enormity of the task…[was] just a bit less formidable than that described in the first chapter of Genesis.

1969 Of postwar restructuring. *Present at the Creation.*

35 The first requirement of a statesman is that he be dull.

1970 In *The Observer*, 21 Jun.

36 Much in life cannot be affected…but must be borne…without complaint, because complaints are a bore…and undermine the serenity essential to endurance.

Quoted in Gaddis Smith *American Secretaries of State* (1972).

37 Neither action nor style could have accomplished the result alone. Both were needed.

1975 Of Winston Churchill's charisma. *Grapes from Thorns.*

38 His speeches were prepared with that infinite capacity for taking pains, which is said to be genius.

1975 Of Winston Churchill. *Grapes from Thorns.*

39 Courageous and loyal to the tips of his stubby fingers.

1975 Of British Foreign Secretary Ernest Bevin. *Grapes from Thorns.*

40 Breathless and bewildered like an old lady at a busy intersection.

On the State Dept under Cordell Hull. Quoted in David S McLellan *Dean Acheson: The State Department Years* (1976).

41 Our name for problems is significant. We call them

headaches. You take a powder and they are gone.

Quoted in David S McLellan *Dean Acheson: The State Department Years* (1976).

42 You can't argue with a river, it is going to flow. You can dam it up…put it to useful purposes…deflect it, but you can't argue with it.

On the fruitlessness of keeping Russian fishermen from waters that should be off limits. Quoted in David S McLellan *Dean Acheson: The State Department Years* (1976).

43 A memorandum is written not to inform the reader but to protect the writer.

1977 In the *Wall Street Journal*, 8 Sep.

44 The Canadians seem to be held together with string and safety pins.

Quoted in David S McLellan and David C Acheson (eds) *Among Friends: Personal Letters of Dean Gooderham Acheson* (1980).

45 Trust him as much as you would a rattlesnake with a silencer on its rattle.

1980 Advice to President Truman on J Edgar Hoover. Quoted in David S McLellan and David C Acheson (eds) *Among Friends: Personal Letters of Dean Gooderham Acheson* (1980).

46 How gently, wisely, and justly G M Young deals with him. That is not the way to write biography.

Collected in David S McClellan and David C Acheson (eds) *Among Friends: Personal Letters of Dean Gooderham Acheson* (1980). On Young's biography *Stanley Baldwin* (1952).

47 Homage to plain dumb luck.

Of the effectiveness of the US blockade of Soviet ships bringing missiles to Cuba. Quoted in Walter Isaacson and Evan Thomas *The Wise Men* (1986).

48 The Iraqi is really not whacky
Toady, perhaps, even tacky.
When they gave *him* the word
He gave *us* the bird
And joined with the Arabs, by cracky!

Limerick written during dull meeting of Foreign Ministers. Quoted in Walter Isaacson and Evan Thomas *The Wise Men* (1986).

49 Charm never made a rooster.

Of poorly-organized attempts to maintain peace by good intentions. Quoted in James B Reston *Deadline* (1991).

50 It is just as full of propaganda as a dog is full of fleas. In fact, I say it's all fleas and no dog.

Of Russian Foreign Minister Andre Vishinsky's proposal that the US should withdraw from postwar Europe. Quoted in James B Reston *Deadline* (1991).

51 With a nation, as with a boxer, one of the greatest assurances of safety is to add reach to power.

Alluding to US bases in Europe. Quoted in James B Reston *Deadline* (1991).

52 If the best minds in the world had set out to find us the worst possible location in the world to fight this damnable war, politically and militarily, the unanimous choice would have been Korea.

On the Korean War. Quoted in Joseph Goulden *Korea* (1992).

Ackerman, Diane 1948–

US poet and writer. Her poetry is published in many journals and books, which include *Wife of Light* (1978) and *Lady Faustus* (1983). She has published non-fiction and is a staff writer at the *New Yorker*.

53 An occasion, catalyst, or tripwire…permits the poet to reach into herself and haul up whatever nugget of the human condition distracts her at the moment, something that can't be reached in any other way.
Quoted in the *New York Times*, 10 Mar 1991.

Ackroyd, Peter 1949–

English writer. He has written a number of erudite and playful novels and scholarly biographies, including studies of Dickens and T S Eliot.

54 And the smell of the library was always the same— the musty odour of old clothes mixed with the keener scent of unwashed bodies, creating what the chief librarian had once described as 'the steam of the social soup'.
1987 *Chatterton*, ch.5.

55 No poet is ever completely lost. He has the secret of his childhood safe with him, like some secret cave in which he can kneel. And, when we read his poetry, we can join him there.
1987 *Chatterton*, ch.10.

56 He had a fear of the dead, and of all inanimate things, rising up around him to claim him; it is the fear of the pre-eminently solitary child and solitary man.
1990 Of Charles Dickens. *Dickens*, prologue.

57 Is it possible to be nostalgic about old fears?
1992 *English Music*, ch.1.

58 Yes, I have inherited the past because I have acknowledged it at last… And, now that I have come to understand it, I no longer need to look back.
1992 *English Music*, ch.19.

Acton, John Emerich Edward Dalberg, 1st Baron Acton of Aldenham 1834–1902

English historian. He sat as a Liberal MP (1859–64) and was created baron by Gladstone in 1869. In 1895 he was appointed Professor of Modern History at Cambridge.

59 Power tends to corrupt, and absolute power corrupts absolutely. Great men are almost always bad men. There is no worse heresy than that the office sanctifies the holder of it.
1887 Letter to Bishop Mandell Creighton, 3 Apr.

Adamov, Arthur 1908–70

Russian-born French playwright. A leading exponent of the Theatre of the Absurd, he was the author of such plays

as *Le Professeur Taranne* (1953), *Le Ping Pong* (1955) and *Le Printemps '71* (1961).

60 The reason why Absurdist plays take place in No Man's Land with only two characters is primarily financial.
1962 Speech at Edinburgh, 13 Sep.

Adams, Abigail 1744–1818

US first lady, wife of President John Adams, and early feminist.

61 In the new code of laws which I suppose it will be necessary for you to make I desire you would remember the ladies, and be more generous and favourable to them than your ancestors. Do not put such unlimited power into the hands of the husbands. Remember all men would be tyrants if they could.
1776 Letter to John Adams, 31 Mar.

62 It is not in the still calm of life, or the repose of a pacific station, that great characters are formed… Great necessities call out great virtues.
1780 Letter to John Quincy Adams, 19 Jan.

Adams, Arthur Henry 1872–1936

New Zealand-born journalist, poet and playwright, whose first collection was *Maoriland: and Other Verses* (1899). His *London Streets* (1906) is a colonist's portrayal of the city. He returned to Sydney, Australia, as editor of *Bulletin* and *Lone Hand*.

63 The land lies desolate and stripped;
Across its waste has thinly strayed
A tattered host of eucalypt.
From whose gaunt uniform is made
A ragged penury of shade.
1913 'Written in Australia', in *The Collected Verses of Arthur H Adams*.

Adams, Charles Francis 1807–86

US diplomat and writer, congressman from Massachusetts (1858–61) and Minister to Britain during the American Civil War (1861–8).

64 It would be superfluous in me to point out to your lordship that this is war.
1863 Despatch to Earl Russell during the Civil War, 5 Sep. Quoted in C F Adams *Charles Francis Adams* (1900), ch.17.

Adams, Douglas Noël 1952–

English novelist and scriptwriter. His radio serial *The Hitch-Hiker's Guide to the Galaxy* was a cult success, and its sequels were also successful novels.

65 Don't Panic.
1979 *The Hitch-Hiker's Guide to the Galaxy*, preface. These words are said to be written in large friendly letters on the cover of the Guide.

66 The Answer to the Great Question Of...Life, the Universe and Everything...Is...Forty-two.
1979 *The Hitch-Hiker's Guide to the Galaxy*, ch.27.

67 'The first ten million years were the worst,' said Marvin, 'and the second ten million years, they were the worst too. The third ten million I didn't enjoy at all. After that I went into a bit of a decline.'
1980 Marvin, the paranoid android. *The Restaurant at the End of the Universe*, ch.18.

68 So Long, and Thanks for All the Fish.
1984 Title of novel.

69 It can hardly be a coincidence that no language on earth has ever produced the expression 'as pretty as an airport'.
1988 *The Long Dark Tea-Time of the Soul*, ch.1.

70 Kate's spirits sank to the very bottom of her being and began to prowl around there making a low growling noise.
1988 *The Long Dark Tea-Time of the Soul*, ch.1.

Adams, Henry Brooks 1838–1918

US historian, son of Charles Francis Adams and grandson of John Quincy Adams. His historical works include *Mont Saint Michel and Chartres* (1904), and his autobiography *The Education of Henry Adams* (published privately 1907, publicly 1918) won the 1919 Pulitzer Prize.

71 Some day science may have the existence of mankind in its power and the human race commit suicide by blowing up the race.
1862 Letter to Charles Francis Adams, Jr, 11 Apr.

72 Politics, as a practice, whatever its professions, has always been the systematic organization of hatreds.
1907 *The Education of Henry Adams*, ch.1.

73 All experience is an arch to build on.
1907 *The Education of Henry Adams*, ch.6.

74 A friend in power is a friend lost.
1907 *The Education of Henry Adams*, ch.7.

75 These questions of taste, of feeling, of inheritance, need no settlement. Everyone carries his own inch-rule of taste, and amuses himself by applying it, triumphantly, wherever he travels.
1907 *The Education of Henry Adams*, ch.12.

76 Chaos often breeds life, when order breeds habit.
1907 *The Education of Henry Adams*, ch.16.

77 A teacher affects eternity; he can never tell where his influence stops.
1907 *The Education of Henry Adams*, ch.20, 'Failure'.

78 One friend in a lifetime is much; two are many; three are hardly possible. Friendship needs a certain parallelism of life, a community of thought, a rivalry of aim.

1907 *The Education of Henry Adams*, ch.20.

79 What one knows is, in youth, of little moment; they know enough who know how to learn.
1907 *The Education of Henry Adams*, ch.21.

80 He had often noticed that six months' oblivion amounts to newspaper death, and that resurrection is rare. Nothing is easier, if a man wants it, than rest, profound as the grave.
1907 *The Education of Henry Adams*, ch.22.

81 Practical politics consists in ignoring the facts.
1907 *The Education of Henry Adams*, ch.22.

82 American art, like the American language and American education, was as far as possible sexless.
1907 *The Education of Henry Adams*, ch.25, 'The Dynamo and the Virgin'.

83 No one means all he says, and yet very few say all they mean, for words are slippery and thought is viscous.
1907 *The Education of Henry Adams*, ch.31, 'The Grammar of Science'.

Adams, John 1735–1826

US statesman and second President, a leader of resistance to Britain and central figure in the Declaration of Independence (1776). He became the first US Vice-President under Washington (1789), and later President (1796–1800).

84 A government of laws, and not of men.
1774 In the *Boston Gazette*, no.7. The phrase was later incorporated into the Massachusetts Constitution (1780).

85 I agree with you that in politics the middle way is none at all.
1776 Letter to Horatio Gates, 23 Mar.

86 The second day of July 1776 will be the most memorable epoch in the history of America. It ought to be solemnised with pomp and parade, with shows, games, sports, guns, bells, bonfires and illuminations from one end of this continent to the other—from this time forward, for ever more.
1776 Letter to his wife, 3 Jul, on the vote of Congress for independence from Britain.

87 You and I ought not to die before we have explained ourselves to each other.
1813 Letter to Thomas Jefferson, 15 Jul.

88 What a poor, ignorant, malicious, short-sighted, crapulous mass is Tom Paine's common sense.
1819 Letter to Thomas Jefferson, 22 Jun, referring to the Republican's treatise on independence entitled *Common Sense*.

Adams, John Quincy 1767–1848

US politician and sixth President. Ambassador to Europe and Secretary of State under Monroe, he negotiated the acquisition of Florida from Spain, before becoming President (1825). He failed to win re-election but continued to oppose slavery as a congressman.

89 *Fiat justitia, pereat coelum.* My toast would be, may our country be always successful, but whether successful or otherwise, always right.
1816 Letter to John Adams, 1 Aug.
▷ See Decatur 311:71, Ferdinand I 385:13.

90 The American continents, by the free and independent condition that they have assumed and maintain, are henceforth not to be considered as subjects for future colonisation by any European powers… In the wars of the European powers in matters relating to ourselves, we have never taken any part; nor does it comport with our policy to do so.
1823 The Monroe Doctrine, 2 Dec.

91 I inhabit a weak, frail, decayed tenement; battered by the winds and broken in on by the storms, and, from all I can learn, the landlord does not intend to repair.
1848 Attributed, as he lay on his deathbed. Quoted in Clifton Fadiman *The Faber Book of Anecdotes* (1985).

Adams, Judge Richard 1846–1908

Irish judge. After a Law degree, he became a journalist in Cork until he was called to the Irish Bar in 1873. From 1894 he was Judge of the County Court, Limerick.

92 Look here, sir, tell me no more unnecessary lies. Such lies as your attorney advised you are necessary for the presentation of your fraudulent case I will listen to though I shall decide against you whatever you swear, but if you tell me another unnecessary lie, I'll put you in the dock.
Presiding over Limerick County Court. Quoted in A M Sullivan *Old Ireland.*

93 You have been acquitted by a Limerick jury, and you may now leave the dock without any other stain upon your character.
Quoted in Maurice Healy *The Old Munster Circuit.*

Adams, Samuel 1722–1803

Political leader in the American Revolution, who signed the Declaration of Independence. Clerk of the lower house of Massachusetts legislature, he was involved in the Boston Tea Party.

94 What a glorious morning is this.
1775 On hearing gunfire at Lexington, 19 Apr. Quoted in J K Hosmer *Samuel Adams* (1886), ch.19.

Adamson, Harold 1906—80

US lyricist.

95 Comin' in on a wing and a prayer.

1943 Title of song. The phrase was taken from the words of a fighter pilot from his battered jet to ground control.

Adcock, (Karen) Fleur 1934–

New Zealand poet who settled in Britain in 1963. Her works include *The Eye of the Hurricane* (1964), *The Incident Book* (1986), *Time-Zones* (1991) and *Selected Poems* (1983).

96 Do not ask me for charity now:
Go away until your bones are clean.
1983 *Selected Poems,* 'Advice to a Discarded Lover'.

Addison, Joseph 1672–1719

English poet, playwright and essayist. After a Grand Tour of Europe (1699–1704), he entered Parliament as a Whig in 1708. He contributed numerous essays to the *Tatler* and was co-founder with Richard Steele of the *The Spectator* (1711).

97 Music, the greatest good that mortals know,
And all of heaven we have below.
1694 'A Song for St Cecilia's Day'.

98 For wheresoe'er I turn my ravished eyes,
Gay gilded scenes and shining prospects rise,
Poetic fields encompass me around,
And still I seem to tread on classic ground.
1704 *A Letter from Italy.*

99 A painted meadow, or a purling stream.
1704 *A Letter from Italy.*

1 'Twas then great Marlbro's mighty soul was proved.
1705 *The Campaign*, 1.279.

2 And, pleased th' Almighty's orders to perform,
Rides in the whirl-wind, and directs the storm.
1705 *The Campaign*, 1.291–2.

3 And those who paint 'em truest praise 'em most.
1705 *The Campaign*, 1.476.

4 This republic has been much more powerful than it is at present, as it is still likelier, to sink than increase in its dominions.
1705 On Venice. *Remarks on Several parts of Italy.*

5 I remember when our whole island was shaken with an earthquake some years ago, there was an impudent mountebank who sold pills which (as he told the country people) were very good against an earthquake.
1710 In *The Tatler*, no.240, 21 Oct.

6 A reader seldom peruses a book with pleasure until he knows whether the writer of it be a black man or a fair man, of a mild or choleric disposition, married or a bachelor.
1711 In *The Spectator*, no.1, 1 Mar.

7 Thus I live in the world rather as a Spectator of mankind, than as one of the species, by which

means I have made myself a speculative statesman, soldier, merchant, and artisan, without ever meddling with any practical part of life.
1711 In *The Spectator*, no.1, 1 Mar.

8 Nothing is capable of being well set to music that is not nonsense.
1711 In *The Spectator*, no.18.

9 A perfect tragedy is the noblest production of human nature.
1711 In *The Spectator*, no.39.

10 In all thy humours, whether grave or mellow,
Thou'rt such a touchy, testy, pleasant fellow;
Hast so much wit, and mirth, and spleen about thee,
There is no living with thee, nor without thee.
1711 In *The Spectator*, no.68, 18 May.

11 As Sir Roger is landlord to the whole congregation, he keeps them in very good order, and will suffer nobody to sleep in it [the church] besides himself; for if by chance he has been surprised into a short nap at sermon, upon recovering out of it, he stands up, and looks about him; and if he sees anybody else nodding, either wakes them himself, or sends his servant to them.
1711 In *The Spectator*, no.112, 9 Jul.

12 Sir Roger told them, with the air of a man who would not give his judgement rashly, that much might be said on both sides.
1711 In *The Spectator*, no.122, 20 Jul.

13 It was a saying of an ancient philosopher, which I find some of our writers have ascribed to Queen Elizabeth, who perhaps might have taken occasion to repeat it, that a good face is a letter of recommendation.
1711 In *The Spectator*, no.221, 13 Nov.

14 I have often thought, says Sir Roger, it happens very well that Christmas should fall out in the Middle of Winter.
1712 In *The Spectator*, no.269, 8 Jan.

15 A true critic ought to dwell rather upon excellencies than imperfections, to discover the concealed beauties of a writer, and communicate to the world such things as are worth their observation.
1712 In *The Spectator*, no.291, 2 Feb.

16 These widows, Sir, are the most perverse creatures in the world.
1712 In *The Spectator*, no.335, 25 Mar.

17 Mirth is short and transient, cheerfulness fixed and permanent... Mirth is like a flash of lightning that breaks through a gloom of clouds, and glitters for a moment: cheerfulness keeps up a kind of day-light in the mind, and fills it with a steady and perpetual serenity.
1712 In *The Spectator*, no.381, 17 May.

18 The Knight in the triumph of his heart made several reflections on the greatness of the British Nation; as, that one Englishman could beat three Frenchmen; that we could never be in danger of Popery so long as we took care of our fleet; that the Thames was the noblest river in Europe; that London Bridge was a greater piece of work than any of the Seven Wonders of the World; with many other honest prejudices which naturally cleave to the heart of a true Englishman.
1712 In *The Spectator*, no.383, 20 May.

19 Wide and undetermined prospects are as pleasing to the fancy, as the speculations of eternity or infinitude are to the understanding.
1712 In *The Spectator*, no.412, 23 Jun.

20 Through all Eternity to Thee
A joyful Song I'll raise,
For oh! Eternity's too short
To utter all thy Praise.
1712 In *The Spectator*, no.453, 9 Aug.

21 We have in England a particular bashfulness in every thing that regards religion.
1712 In *The Spectator*, no.458, 15 Aug.

22 The spacious firmament on high,
With all the blue ethereal sky,
And spangled heavens, a shining frame,
Their great Original proclaim.
Th' unwearied sun from day to day
Does his Creator's power display;
And publishes to every land
The work of an Almighty hand.
1712 In *The Spectator*, no.465, 23 Aug.

23 In Reason's ear they all rejoice,
And utter forth a glorious voice,
For ever singing, as they shine:
'The hand that made us is divine.'
1712 In *The Spectator*, no.465, 23 Aug.

24 A woman seldom asks advice before she has bought her wedding clothes.
1712 In *The Spectator*, no.475, 4 Sep.

25 Our disputants put me in mind of the skuttle fish, that when he is unable to extricate himself, blackens all the water about him, till he becomes invisible.
1712 In *The Spectator*, no.476, 5 Sept.

26 If we may believe our logicians, man is distinguished from all other creatures by the faculty of laughter.
1712 In *The Spectator*, no.494, 26 Sep.

27 An account of it would have been thought
fabulous, were not the Wall itself extant.
1712 Commenting on the Great Wall of China, *The Spectator*,
no.415, 26 Jun.

28 'Tis not in mortals to command success,
But we'll do more, Sempronius; we'll deserve it.
1713 *Cato*, act 1, sc.2, l.43–4.

29 'Tis pride, rank pride, and haughtiness of soul;
I think the Romans call it stoicism.
1713 *Cato*, act 1, sc.4, l.82–3.

30 Were you with these, my prince, you'd soon forget
The pale, unripened beauties of the north.
1713 *Cato*, act 1, sc.4, l.134–5.

31 The woman that deliberates is lost.
1713 *Cato*, act 4, sc.1, l.31.

32 Curse on his virtues! they've undone his country.
Such popular humanity is treason.
1713 *Cato*, act 4, sc.1, l.205–6.

33 What a pity is it
That we can die but once to serve our country!
1713 *Cato*, act 4, sc.1, l.258–9.

34 Content thyself to be obscurely good.
When vice prevails, and impious men bear sway,
The post of honour is a private station.
1713 *Cato*, act 4, sc.1, l.319–21.

35 It must be so—Plato, thou reason'st well!—
Else whence this pleasing hope, this fond desire,
This longing after immortality?
Or whence this secret dread, and inward horror,
Of falling into naught? Why shrinks the soul
Back on herself, and startles at destruction
'Tis the divinity that stirs within us;
'Tis heaven itself, that points out an hereafter,
And intimates eternity to man.
Eternity! thou pleasing, dreadful thought!
1713 *Cato*, act 5, sc.1, l.1–10.

36 From hence, let fierce contending nations know
What dire effects from civil discord flow.
1713 *Cato*, act 5, sc.1, closing words.

37 'We are always doing,' says he, 'something for
Posterity, but I would fain see Posterity do
something for us.'
1714 In *The Spectator* no.583, 20 Aug.

38 There is sometimes a greater judgement shewn in
deviating from the rules of art, than in adhering to
them; and...there is more beauty in the works of a
great genius who is ignorant of all the rules of art,
than in the works of a little genius, who not only
knows but scrupulously observes them.
1714 In *The Spectator*, no.592, 10 Sep.

39 I should think myself a very bad woman, if I had
done what I do for a farthing less.
1716 *The Drummer*, act 1, sc.1.

40 See in what peace a Christian can die.
1719 Last words, to his stepson Lord Warwick. Quoted in
Edward Young *Conjectures on Original Composition* (1759).

41 Hunting is not a proper employment for a thinking
man.
Quoted in Colin Jarman *The Guinness Dictionary of Sports
Quotations* (1990).

Ade, George 1866–1944
US humorist and dramatist.

42 R-E-M-O-R-S-E!
Those dry Martinis did the work for me;
Last night at twelve I felt immense,
Today I feel like thirty cents.
My eyes are blurred, my coppers hot,
I'll try to eat, but I cannot.
It is no time for mirth and laughter,
The cold, grey dawn of the morning after.
1903 *The Sultan of Sulu*, act 2.

Adelman, Kenneth Lee 1946–
US political scientist, director of the US Arms Control
and Disarmament Agency (1983–8). His works include
*The Great Universal Embrace: Arms Summitry—a skeptic's
account* (1989).

43 The history of arms control is a history of great
visions eventually mugged by reality.
1986 In *Newsweek*, 1 Dec.

Adenauer, Konrad 1876–1967
German statesman. Dismissed by the Nazis (1933), he
founded the Christian Democratic Union (1945) and
became first Chancellor of the Federal Republic of
Germany (1949–63).

44 We must free ourselves from thinking in terms of
nation states. The countries of western Europe are
no longer in a position to protect themselves
individually. Not one of them is any longer in a
position to salvage Europe's culture.
1953 Speech, May.

Adler, Jerry 1949–
US journalist, editor of *Newsweek*.

45 She...happens to stick out a foot just as history is
rushing by.
1988 Of Fawn Hall, the secretary who helped Col Oliver
North to dispose of top-secret papers, 'the archetype of the
Accidental Celebrity'. In *Newsweek*, 9 Mar.

46 Norman Rockwell, the Brueghel of the 20th
century bourgeoisie, the Holbein of Jell-O ads and

magazine covers; by common assent, the most American artist of all.

1993 On the opening of the Norman Rockwell Museum at Stockbridge, Massachusetts. In *Newsweek*, 12 Apr.

47 The widespread belief that Yuppies as a class would perish from Brie-cheese poisoning turned out to be over-optimistic.

1995 'The Rise of the Overclass', in *Newsweek*, 31 Jul.

Adler, Larry (Lawrence Cecil) 1914–

US musician and virtuoso on the harmonica. He emigrated to Britain after being blacklisted in the US.

48 His first choice had been Yehudi Menuhin; he was lucky he got me. Menuhin on the mouth-organ is a mess.

1984 On Henry Koster's casting for the film *Music for Millions* (1944).

Adler, Polly 1900–62

US writer.

49 A House is not a Home.

1954 Title of a book.

Adorno, Theodor 1903–69

German social philosopher and musicologist, who emigrated to the US in 1934. His *Negative Dialectics* (1966) expounds his complex theories, but he also wrote more accessible mass-culture works.

50 In psychoanalysis nothing is true except the exaggerations.

1966 *Negative Dialectics*.

Aelius Aristides AD 117–189

Greek orator. He spent much of his life giving rhetorical demonstrations throughout Asia Minor. He is best known for his encomium of Rome and his 'Sacred Teachings', an account of his dreams while seeking a cure in the temple of Asclepius.

51 As the character is, such is the speech.

Pros Platona Peri Rhetorikes, bk.2, 1.392.

St Aelred of Riveaulx d.1167

English writer, historian and Cistercian monk. Raised at the court of David I of Scotland, he became Abbot of Revesby (1143) and Riveaulx (1147). He aided the England–France alliance in support of Pope Alexander II against Emperor Frederick III.

52 *Invenis fateor in rege monachum, claustrum in curia, in palatio monasterii disciplinam.*

I confess that I found in the king a monk, in the court a cloister, and in the palace the discipline of a monastery.

?c.1160 Lament for David I, King of Scotland. Quoted in John Fordoun *Chronicle of Scotland* (c.1384), bk.5, ch.43.

Aeschylus c.525–c.456 BC

Greek dramatist, who served in the Athenian army at Marathon (490 BC) and probably in the navy at Salamis (480 BC). He won 13 first prizes in the dramatic contests of Athens from 484 to 458 BC, but only seven of his many works have survived.

53 Ship-destroyer, man-destroyer, city-destroyer.

Of Helen. *Agamemnon*, 1.689.

54 Unworthy was what he did to her, worthy was what he suffered.

Clytemnestra speaks of Agamemnon's sacrifice of their daughter Iphigeneia. *Agamemnon*, 1.1527–8 (translated by H Lloyd-Jones).

55 For by the will of the gods Fate hath held sway since ancient days.

Persae, 1.102 (translated by H Weir Smyth).

56 Now you battle for your all.

Persae, 1.402–5 (translated by H Weir Smyth).

57 Once to die is better than length of days in sorrow without end.

Prometheus Vinctus, 1.750–1.

58 It's a man's job—no place for women's plans here!— what lies outside. Stay home and cause no trouble.

Septem contra Thebas, 1.200–1 (translated by C M Dawson).

59 Obedience, you know, is Good Luck's mother, wedded to Salvation, they say.

Septem contra Thebas, 1.224–5 (translated by C M Dawson).

60 Remember to be submissive, thou art an alien, a fugitive, and in need.

Supplices, 1.202 (translated by H Weir Smyth).

Agassiz, (Jean) Louis (Rodolphe) 1807–73

Swiss-born US zoologist and geologist. A professor of natural history at Neuchâtel, he came to the US (1846) to teach at Harvard University. His works include a study of fossil fish and a *Natural History of the United States* (1857–62).

61 The student must remember, for his consolation…that his failures are almost as important to the cause of science and to those who follow him in the same road, as his successes. It is much to know what we cannot do in any given direction—the first step, indeed, toward the accomplishment of what we can do.

1896 *Geological Sketches*.

62 The study of nature is interwoven with the highest mind. You should never trifle with nature.

Attributed.

Agate, James 1877–1947

English theatre critic. He wrote for *The Sunday Times* from 1923 until his death and also published a notable nine-part autobiography, *Ego* (1935–47).

63 Happy is the country which has no history, and happier still is that musical comedy about which one can find nothing to say.

1920 In *The Sunday Times*.

64 I don't know very much, but what I do know I know better than anybody, and I don't want to argue about it. I know what I think about an actor or an actress, and am not interested in what anybody else thinks. My mind is not a bed to be made and re-made.

1943 Journal entry, 9 Jun. Collected in *Ego 6* (1944).

65 Long experience has taught me that in England nobody goes to the theatre unless he or she has bronchitis.

Attributed.

66 She had a heart as big as Waterloo Station.

Of Marie Lloyd. Attributed.

Agawa, Hiroyuki 1920–

Japanese novelist. His *Citadel in Spring* is the semi-autobiographical story of a young man fighting on the losing side of World War II. Much of the story is set in Hiroshima, the city of his birth.

67 It quickly swelled into the shape of a gigantic question mark, the middle of which was a vivid crimson, and as this thunderhead-like column billowed upward through the sky, she could see a red ball of fire at its core.

1949 Of the atomic explosion, Hiroshima. *Haru no shiro* (*Citadel in Spring*, translated by Lawrence Rogers), ch.9.

Agnew, Spiro T(heodore) 1918–96

US Republican politician. As liberal Governor of Maryland he introduced anti-racial-discrimination legislation, but by 1968 had become much more conservative. He was Nixon's running mate in the 1968 election, and Vice-President (1969–73).

68 To some extent, if you've seen one city slum, you've seen them all.

1968 Election campaign speech, Detroit, 18 Oct.

69 A spirit of national masochism prevails, encouraged by an effete corps of impudent snobs who characterize themselves as intellectuals.

1969 Of media pundits. Speech, New Orleans, 19 Oct.

70 In the United States today we have more than our fair share of the nattering nabobs of negativism. They have formed their own Four H Club—the hopeless, hysterical, hypochondriacs of history.

1970 Of media pundits. Speech, San Diego, 11 Sep.

71 I was…one of the worst complications he could have had.

1980 On the effect of his no-contest plea to income-tax evasion and subsequent resignation upon Richard M Nixon. *Go Quietly or Else*.

Agustini, Delmira 1886–1914

Uruguayan poet, who was murdered by her estranged husband, who then committed suicide. Her bold sincerity and impassioned lyrics rank her among the most outstanding early modernist poets.

72 *Por todos los senderos de la noche han venido
a llorar en mi lecho.
¡Fueron tantos, son tantos!
Yo no sé cuáles viven, yo no sé cuál ha muerto.
Me lloraré a mí misma para llorarlos todos.*

They have came from all of night's pathways
to cry in my bed.
They were so many, they are so many!
I don't know who lives, I don't know who has died.
I'll cry for myself so that I can cry for all.

1924 *El rosario de Eros*, 'Mis amores' ('My lovers').

St Aidan c.600–651

Irish monk, known as the Apostle of Northumbria. He was summoned from Iona by King Oswald to evangelize the north and established a community on Lindisfarne. He died in the church he had built in Bamburgh.

73 *Nam tibi carior est ille filius equae quam ille filius Dei?*

Is this son of a mare dearer to you, then, than that son of God?

c.645 To King Oswin of Deira, who had objected when Aidan gave to a beggar a horse which he had received as a gift from the king. Quoted in Bede *Historia Ecclesiastica Gentis Anglorum* (731), bk.3, ch.14.

Akers, John Fellows 1934–

American businessman. Joined IBM as a sales trainee in 1960 and rose to become Chairman 1986–93.

74 Each school can, once again, become what it was always meant to be—a building that has four walls with tomorrow inside.

1991 In the *Wall Street Journal*, 20 Mar.

Akins, Zoë 1886–1958

US poet and playwright. Her works include the play *The Greeks Had a Word for It* (1930) and the Pulitzer Prize-winning stage adaptation of Edith Wharton's novel *The Old Maid* (1935).

75 The Greeks Had a Word for It.

1930 Title of play.

Alain (Émile-Auguste Chartier) 1868–1951

French philosopher, writer and poet.

76 *Rien n'est plus dangereux qu'une idée, quand on n'a qu'une idée.*

Nothing is more dangerous than an idea, when you have only one idea.

1938 Propos sur la religion, no.74.

Alan of Lille also known as 'Alanus de Insulis'
c.1114–1202

French writer and scholar. His major literary works include *De Planctu Natura* and *Anticlaudianus*.

77 *Omni mundi creatura*
    Quasi liber et pictura
    Nobis est, et speculum.

    Each creature of the world
    Is as a book, a picture,
    And a mirror to us.
    c.1170 *De Incarnatione Christi* (*Rhythmus Alter*), l.1–3.

78 *Post nubila maxima, Phoebus.*

    After the greatest clouds, the sun.
    1175 *Liber Parabolarum*, ch.1, l.33.

79 *Qui jacet in terra non habe unde cadet.*

    He who is lying on the ground has nowhere to fall.
    1175 *Liber Parabolarum*, ch.2, l.18.

80 *Mille viae ducunt homines per sæcula Romam.*

    Throughout the ages, a thousand roads lead to Rome.
    1175 *Liber Parabolarum*, ch.3, l.56.

Alba, Duke of, Ferdinand Alvarez de Toledo 1508–82

Spanish soldier, made a general at 26 and Commander-in-Chief at 30. He led successful campaigns against the Netherlands and Portugal.

81 I have tamed men of iron in my day, shall I not easily crush these men of butter?
    1567 On his appointment as Lieutenant-General to the Netherlands. Quoted in J L Motley *The Rise of the Dutch Republic* (1889), vol.2.

Albee, Edward Franklin, III 1928–

US dramatist, influenced by the Theatre of the Absurd, whose plays address the moral ambiguities of US middle-class life. His best known work is *Who's Afraid of Virginia Woolf?* (1962), but *A Delicate Balance* (1966) and *Seascape* (1975) both won Pulitzer Prizes.

82 JERRY: I have learned that neither kindness or cruelty by themselves, or independent of each other, create any effect beyond themselves.
    1958 *The Zoo Story.*

83 JERRY: When you're a kid you use the cards as a substitute for a real experience, and when you're older you use real experience as a substitute for the fantasy.
    1958 On pornographic playing cards. *The Zoo Story.*

84 BESSIE: I am sick of the disparity between things as they are and as they should be. I'm tired. I'm tired of the truth and I'm tired of lying about the truth.
    1960 *The Death of Bessie Smith.*

85 Who's Afraid of Virginia Woolf?
    1962 Title of play.

86 MARTHA: I have a fine sense of the ridiculous, but no sense of humour.
    1962 *Who's Afraid of Virginia Woolf?*, act 1.

87 GEORGE: By God, you gotta have a swine to show you where the truffles are.
    1962 *Who's Afraid of Virginia Woolf?*, act 2.

88 I am a Doctor.
    A.B....M.A....PH.D....ABMAPHID!...a wasting disease of the frontal lobes.
    1962 Spoken by a college professor. *Who's Afraid of Virginia Woolf?*

89 American critics are like American universities...both have dull and half-dead faculties.
    1969 Speech to the New York Cultural League. Reported in news summaries, 6 Nov.

90 People would rather sleep their way through life than stay awake for it.
    Quoted in Joseph F McCrindle (ed) *Behind the Scenes* (1971).

Prince Albert 1819–61

Prince Consort of Queen Victoria, son of the Duke of Saxe-Coburg-Gotha. A patron of the arts and science, he planned the Great Exhibition of 1851. He died of typhoid.

91 I have had wealth, rank and power, but, if these were all I had, how wretched I should be.
    1861 Attributed last words.

Alberti, Leon Battista 1404–72

Italian architect, musician, painter and humanist, dubbed 'Alberti the all-sided' by the historian Burckhardt. His work *De re aedificatoria* (c.1450), is considered the first modern work on architecture.

92 Perhaps the artist who seeks dignity above all in his 'historia', ought to represent very few figures; for as paucity of words imparts majesty to a prince, provided his thoughts and orders are understood, so the presence of only the strictly necessary numbers of bodies confers dignity on a picture.
    1436 *On Painting* (translated by Cecil Grayson).

93 I prefer you to take as your model a mediocre sculpture rather than an excellent painting, for from painted objects we train our hand only to make a likeness, whereas from sculptures we learn to represent both likeness and correct incidence of light.
    1436 *On Painting* (translated by Cecil Grayson).

94 I am really persuaded that if we were to inquire of all the Cities which within the Memory of Man have fallen by Siege into the Power of new Masters, who it was that subjected and overcame them, they would tell you, the Architect; and that they were strong enough to have despised the armed Enemy, but not to withstand the Shocks of the Engines, the Violence of the Machines and the Force of other Instruments of War with which the Architect, distressed, demolished and ruinated them. On the contrary, they would inform you that their greatest Defense lay in the Art and Assistance of the Architect.
1451–2 *Architecttura* (translated by James Leoni, 1755).

Alcaeus c.620–c.580 BC

Greek lyric poet. He lived in Mytilene on Lesbos, and was a contemporary of Sappho. Only fragments remain of his 10 books of *Odes*.

95 Brave men are a city's strongest tower of defence.
c.600 BC Attributed.

Alcott, Louisa May 1832–88

US writer. Her children's classic *Little Women* (1868) drew on her own experiences. She completed a sequel, *Good Wives*, in 1869 and wrote other novels, including *Little Men* (1871) and *Jo's Boys* (1886).

96 Christmas won't be Christmas without any presents.
1868 *Little Women*, pt.1, ch.1.

97 Conceit spoils the finest genius…and the great charm of all power is modesty.
1868 *Little Women*, pt.1, ch.7.

98 Housekeeping ain't no joke.
1868 *Little Women*, pt.1, ch.11.

99 She had a womanly instinct that clothes possess an influence more powerful over many than the worth of character or the magic of manners.
1869 *Little Women*, pt.2, ch.34.

1 Girls are so queer you never know what they mean. They say no when they mean yes, and drive a man out of his wits just for the fun of it.
1869 *Little Women*, pt.2, ch.35.

2 What *do* girls do who haven't any mothers to help them through their troubles?
1869 *Little Women*, pt.2, ch.46.

Alcuin 735–804

English cleric and scholar. In 771 Charlemagne summoned him to his court as tutor of the royal family. In 778 he became master of his old school at York. His numerous works include treatises on rhetoric, ethics, and theology.

3 *Nec audiendi qui solent dicere, vox populi, vox Dei, quum tumultuositas vulgi semper insaniae proxima sit.*

We should not listen to those who like to affirm that the voice of the people is the voice of God, for the tumult of the masses is truly close to madness.
800 Letter to Charlemagne.

Aldington, Richard pseudonym of *Edward Godfree* 1892–1962

English poet, novelist and biographer. He married fellow Imagist poet Hilda Doolittle ('H.D.'). His best-known work is the novel *Death of a Hero* (1929).

4 Patriotism is a lively sense of collective responsibility. Nationalism is a silly cock crowing on its own dunghill.
1931 *The Colonel's Daughter*, pt.1, ch.6.

Aldiss, Brian Wilson 1925–

English science-fiction writer and novelist. Early novels include *The Hand-Reared Boy* (1970) and *A Soldier Erect* (1971), but his major work has been in science fiction, as a writer, critic and compiler of anthologies.

5 Science fiction is no more written for scientists than ghost stories are written for ghosts.
1961 *Penguin Science Fiction*, introduction.

6 Keep violence in the mind
Where it belongs.
1969 *Barefoot in the Head*, 'Charteris'.

7 The feat represents immense achievement for the neotenic ape, species homo sapiens. But behind this lie two old attributes of the ape—tribalism and inquisitiveness.
1969 On space flight, in *The Guardian*.

8 Hubris clobbered by Nemesis.
1975 His definition of science fiction. *Science Fiction Art*, introduction.

Aldrich, Henry 1647–1710

English cleric, Dean of Christ Church, Oxford. He designed the Peckwater Quadrangle and wrote the popular catch 'Hark, the bonny Christ-Church Bells', but is best remembered for his *Artis Logicae Compendium* (1691).

9 If all be true that I do think,
There are five reasons why men drink,
Good wine, a friend, or being dry,
Or lest we should be by-and-by,
Or any other reason why.
1689 'Five Reasons for Drinking'.

Aldrin, Edwin E(ugene) Jr known as *'Buzz'* 1930–

US astronaut, a crew member on Apollo 11 and the second man to walk on the moon.

10 Houston, Tranquillity Base here. The Eagle has landed.

1969 Radio transmission from the moon, 20 Jul. These were the first words uttered by a human on the moon's surface.

11 Beautiful! Beautiful! Magnificent desolation.

1969 Spoken as he stepped out of the Eagle to join Neil Armstrong on the first moon walk, 20 Jul.

Alembert, Jean le Rond d' 1717–83

French mathematician and philosopher. He wrote a major work on *Dynamics* (1743) and pioneered studies on the mechanics of rigid bodies, the motions of fluids and vibrating strings.

12 Day by day natural science accumulates new riches…
The true system of the World has been recognized,
developed and perfected… Everything has been
discussed and analyzed, or at least mentioned.

1759 *Elements of Philosophy*.

Alexander the Great 356–323 BC

King of Macedonia. He succeeded his father Philip at the age of 20, and set out to conquer the Persian Empire, campaigning as far as Afghanistan and the Indus valley. He died of a fever in Babylon, and his empire was divided between his generals.

13 Truly, if I were not Alexander, I would be Diogenes.

Quoted in Plutarch *Alexander*, 14.3.

▷ See Diogenes of Sinope 331:60.

14 The end and object of conquest is to avoid doing
the same thing as the conquered.

Quoted in Plutarch *Alexander*, 40.2.

Alexander I 1777–1825

Tsar of Russia (1801–25), grandson of Catherine the Great. He spent much of his reign fighting Napoleon and founded the Holy Alliance (1815) to exclude the House of Bonaparte from power in France.

15 Napoleon thinks that I am a fool, but he who
laughs last laughs longest.

1808 Letter to his sister, 8 Oct.

Alexander II known as 'the Liberator'
1818–81

Tsar of Russia (1855–81). His reign was marked by the emancipation of the serfs (1861), political and military reform, the expansion of the Russian Empire into Asia and the defeat of Turkey (1877–8). He was assassinated.

16 It is better to abolish serfdom from above than to
wait for it to abolish itself from below.

1856 Speech, 30 Mar.

Alexander, Cecil Frances 1818–95

Irish hymnwriter and poet.

17 All things bright and beautiful,
All creatures great and small,

All things wise and wonderful,
The Lord God made them all.

1848 'All Things Bright and Beautiful'.

18 The rich man in his castle,
The poor man at his gate,
God made them, high or lowly,
And ordered their estate.

1848 'All Things Bright and Beautiful'.

19 Once in royal David's city
Stood a lowly cattle-shed,
Where a mother laid her baby
In a manger for his bed.
Mary was that mother mild,
Jesus Christ her little child.

1848 'Once in Royal David's City'.

20 There is a green hill far away,
Without a city wall,
Where the dear Lord was crucified,
Who died to save us all.

1848 'There is a Green Hill Far Away'

21 I bind into myself today
The strong name of the Trinity,
By invocation of the same
The Three in One and One in Three.

1889 'St Patrick's Breastplate', his translation from the Irish.

Alexander, Sir William c.1567–1640

Scottish courtier and poet.

22 The weaker sex, to piety more prone.

1637 Of women. 'Doomsday', Fifth Hour.

Algren, Nelson 1909–81

US novelist, a journalist in Chicago and a migrant worker during the Depression. His hard-bitten, realist novels include *The Man with the Golden Arm* (1949).

23 A Walk on the Wild Side.

1956 Title of novel.

24 Never play cards with a man called Doc. Never eat
at a place called Mom's. And never, ever, no matter
what else you do in your whole life, never sleep with
anyone whose troubles are worse than your own.

1956 In *Newsweek*, 2 Jul. Algren claimed that these were his only principles, taught him by 'a nice old Negro lady'.

25 I went out there for a thousand a week, and I
worked Monday, and I got fired Wednesday. The
guy that hired me was out of town Tuesday.

In Malcolm Crowley (ed) *Writers at Work* (1958).

26 The hard necessity of bringing the judge on the
bench down into the dock has been the peculiar
responsibility of the writer in all ages of man.

1961 Preface to re-print of *Chicago: City On The Make* (first published 1951).

Ali, Muhammad formerly *Cassius Clay*
1942–

US boxer. World heavyweight champion in 1964, he was stripped of his title after refusing military service on religious grounds (he was a Black Muslim). His title was restored in 1970, lost to Joe Frazier the next year and regained in 1974 and 1978. He retired in 1981.

27 I am the greatest!
1962 In the *Louisville Times*, 16 Nov. This became his catchphrase.

28 Float like a butterfly, sting like a bee.
c.1964 Of his boxing style. Quoted in G Sullivan *Cassius Clay* (1964), ch.8.

Allainval, Abbé d' 1700–53
French dramatist.

29 *L'embarras des richesses.*

The Embarrassment of Riches.
1726 Title of play.

Allen, Henry Southworth 1941–
US journalist. He is a reporter and editor for the *Washington Post* (1970–).

30 They are a great tradition…gliding in and out of the corridors of power with the opulent calm of angelfish swimming through an aquarian castle.
1989 Of presidential advisers. In the *Washington Post*, 3 Jan.

31 He long ago learned to eschew the little turf-dances of human encounter.
1989 Of Brent Scowcroft, National Security Council adviser to George Bush. In the *Washington Post*, 3 Jan.

32 It is unlikely that anyone will write his biography, but he will be enshrined in 10,000 indexes.
1989 Of Brent Scowcroft, National Security Council adviser to George Bush. In the *Washington Post*, 3 Jan.

33 Doesn't she know that numberless women have walked past mirrors hoping for a hint of Bacall's slinkiness?
1994 Of Lauren Bacall at age 70. In the *Washington Post*, 27 Oct.

34 Edward Hopper is the great painter of American hell in the 20th century, the limner-laureate of the beauty, poignance, eternity and bone-ache disquietude of life.
1995 In the *Washington Post*, 25 Jun.

Allen, Woody pseudonym of *Allen Stewart Konigsberg* 1935–
US film-maker and writer. He is best known for his comic films, which focus on the neuroses of urban life and relationships, and he has also published collections of essays and stories.

35 I think crime pays. The hours are good, you travel a lot.
1969 *Take the Money and Run.*

36 Not only is there no God, but try getting a plumber on weekends.
1969 'My Philosophy', in *The New Yorker*, 27 Dec.

37 TB or not TB, that is the congestion.
1972 *Everything You Always Wanted to Know about Sex.*

38 The lion and the calf shall lie down together but the calf won't get much sleep.
1974 'The Scrolls', in *The New Republic*, 31 Aug.

39 It's not that I'm afraid to die. I just don't want to be there when it happens.
1975 *Death: A Comedy in One Act.*

40 It immediately doubles your chances for a date on Saturday night.
1975 On bisexuality. In the *New York Times*, 1 Dec.

41 My one regret in life is that I am not someone else.
Quoted as epigraph in Eric Lax *Woody Allen and His Comedy* (1975).

42 Death is an acquired trait.
Quoted in Eric Lax *Woody Allen and His Comedy* (1975), ch.11.

43 I don't want to achieve immortality through my work… I want to achieve it through not dying.
Quoted in Eric Lax *Woody Allen and His Comedy* (1975), ch.12.

44 And my parents finally realize that I'm kidnapped and they snap into action immediately: they rent out my room.
Quoted in Eric Lax *Woody Allen and His Comedy* (1975).

45 On the plus side, death is one of the few things that can be done as easily lying down.
1976 *Without Feathers*, 'Early Essays'.

46 Money is better than poverty, if only for financial reasons.
1976 *Without Feathers*, 'Early Essays'.

47 That was the most fun I ever had without laughing.
1977 Of sex. *Annie Hall* (with Marshall Brickman).

48 Don't knock masturbation. It's sex with someone I love.
1977 *Annie Hall* (with Marshall Brickman).

49 I'm old fashioned. I don't believe in extra-marital relationships. I think people should mate for life, like pigeons or Catholics.
1979 *Manhattan* (with Marshall Brickman).

50 More than at any other time in history, mankind faces a crossroads. One path leads to despair and utter hopelessness. The other, to total extinction. Let us pray we have the wisdom to choose correctly.
1980 *Side Effects*, 'My Speech to the Graduates'.

51 Eighty percent of success is showing-up.
Quoted in Thomas J Peters and Robert H Waterman *Among Friends* (1982).

Allingham, Margery Louise 1904–66

English writer, creator of the fictional detective Albert Campion. She wrote a series of elegant and witty detective novels, such as *Flowers for the Judge* (1936) and *The China Governess* (1968).

52 Once sex rears its ugly 'ead it's time to steer clear.
1936 *Flowers for the Judge*, ch.4.

Allingham, William 1824–89

Irish poet and editor of *Fraser's Magazine* (from 1874). His *Diary* (published 1907) is a rich recollection of Victorian literary life. Other works include *Day and Night Songs* (1855), illustrated by Dante Gabriel Rossetti and Millais.

53 Up the airy mountain,
Down the rushy glen,
We daren't go a-hunting,
For fear of little men;
Wee folk, good folk,
Trooping all together;
Green jacket, red cap,
And white owl's feather!
1850 'The Fairies'.

54 Four ducks on a pond,
A grass-bank beyond,
A blue sky of spring,
White clouds on the wing;
What a little thing
To remember for years—
To remember with tears!
1888 'A Memory'.

Allsop, (Harold) Bruce 1912–

English architect, author, publisher and artist. He retired from lecturing in 1977. His many books include *A Modern Theory of Architecture* (1977) and *Should Man Survive?* (1982).

55 For the normal business of living man is most at ease on the ground.
1977 *A Modern Theory of Architecture*.

56 The phenomenon of architecture is a development of the phenomenon of man.
1977 *A Modern Theory of Architecture*.

Almeida, Manuel Antônio de 1831–61

Brazilian writer, translator and journalist, killed in a shipwreck off the Brazilian coast while on a newspaper assignment. His *Memórias de um sargento de milícias* is considered the first great novel in Brazilian literature.

57 *Espiar a vida alheia, inquirir dos escravos o que se passava no interior das casas, era naquele tempo coisa tão comum e enraizada nos costumes, que ainda hoje, depois de passados tantos anos, restam grandes vestígios dêsse belo hábito.*

Spying on other people's lives, asking slaves what was going on inside their houses was then so common and such a part of our customs that today, after so many years have passed, we have many remnants of such a beautiful habit.
1853 *Memórias de um sargento de milícias* (*Memoirs of a Militia Sergeant*, 1959), ch.3.

Alsop, Stewart 1914–74

US political columnist.

58 A fashionable gentleman who much concerns himself with the fashions of gentlemen is neither fashionable nor a gentleman.
1975 In *Newsweek*, 30 Jun.

Alther, Lisa née Reed 1944–

US novelist. She achieved success with her comic novel *Kinflicks* (1976), and explored the themes of personal and sexual identity in several subsequent books.

59 If this was adulthood, the only improvement she could detect in her situation was that now she could eat dessert without eating her vegetables.
1976 *Kinflicks*, ch.2.

60 There was nothing wrong with her that a vasectomy of the vocal chords wouldn't fix.
1976 *Kinflicks*, ch.4.

61 I happen to feel that the degree of a person's intelligence is directly reflected by the number of conflicting attitudes she can bring to bear on the same topic.
1976 *Kinflicks*, ch.7.

62 He picked her up out of the dirt and turned her into the clod she was today.
1981 *Original Sins*, pt.4, ch.1.

Amado, Jorge 1912–

Brazilian novelist, born on a cacao plantation in Ferradas. He was imprisoned several times and exiled for leftist activities. Most of his novels are picaresque, ribald tales of lower-class Bahian city life.

63 *Ninguém no cais tem um nome só. Todos têm também um apelido ou abreviam o nome, ou o aumentam, ou lhe acrescentam qualquer coisa que recorde uma história, uma luta, um amor.*

No one on the docks has just one name. Everybody has a nickname too, or the name is shortened, or lengthened, or something is added that recalls a tale, a fight, a woman.
1936 *Mar morto* (*Sea of Death*, 1984), 'Iemanjá'.

St Ambrose c.339–97 AD

Bishop of Milan. He was much admired by St Augustine.

64 *Ubi Petrus, ibi ergo ecclesia.*

Where Peter is, there, accordingly, is the Church.
Explanatio psalmi 40.

American Library Association

65 The computer is a fast idiot, it has no imagination; it cannot originate action. It is, and will remain, only a tool to man.

1964 Statement of the American Library Association regarding the Univac computer exhibited at the New York World's Fair, 1964.

Amerine, Maynard Andrew 1911–98

US oenologist, Professor at the University of California. His works on viniculture include *Wine: An Introduction for Americans* (1965) and *Introduction to Food Science and Technology* (1973).

66 The fine wine leaves you with something pleasant; the ordinary wine just leaves.

Quoted in Clifton Fadiman *The New Joy of Wine* (1990).

Amery, Leo(pold) Charles Maurice Stennett 1873–1955

English Conservative politician. After working on *The Times* for 10 years he became an MP and served as Colonial Secretary (1919–29) and Secretary of State for India and Burma.

67 For twenty years he has held a season ticket on the line of least resistance and has gone wherever the train of events has carried him, lucidly justifying his position at whatever point he happened to find himself.

1914 Of Herbert Asquith, in *Quarterly Review*, Jul.

68 Speak for England, Arthur!

1939 Shouted to Arthur Greenwood, Labour Opposition spokesman, 2 Sep, as Greenwood began a House of Commons speech calling for the resignation of Prime Minister Neville Chamberlain, immediately preceding the declaration of World War II.

69 Cromwell said to the Long Parliament when he thought it was no longer fit to conduct the affairs of the nation, 'You have sat too long here for any good you have been doing. Depart, I say, and let us have done with you. In the name of God, go!'

1940 Remark addressed to Prime Minister Neville Chamberlain, House of Commons, 7 May.

Amin (Dada), Idi 1925–

Ugandan soldier and politician, an army commander who seized power in 1971 and was proclaimed President. He was deposed by exiled Ugandans with the help of the Tanzanian army in 1979 and fled to Libya.

70 Your experience will be a lesson to all of us men to be careful not to marry ladies in very high positions.

1978 Unsolicited advice to Lord Snowdon on the ending of his marriage to Princess Margaret, quoted in A Barrow *International Gossip* (1983).

Amis, Sir Kingsley 1922–95

English novelist and poet. He achieved success with his irreverent novel *Lucky Jim* (1954), and went on to write a substantial body of novels, poetry and non-fiction.

71 The light did him harm, but not as much as looking at things did; he resolved, having done it once, never to move his eyeballs again. A dusty thudding in his head made the scene before him beat like a pulse. His mouth had been used as a latrine by some small creature of the night, and then as its mausoleum.

1953 *Lucky Jim*, ch.6.

72 He thought what a pity it was that all his faces were designed to express rage or loathing. Now that something had happened that really deserved a face, he'd none to celebrate it with. As a kind of token, he made his Sex Life in Ancient Rome face.

1953 *Lucky Jim*, ch.25.

73 Man's love is of man's life a thing apart; Girls aren't like that.

1956 'A Bookshop Idyll'.

▷ See Byron 222:36.

74 Politics is a thing that only the unsophisticated can really go for.

1957 'Socialism and the Intellectuals'.

75 Work was like cats were supposed to be: if you disliked and feared it and tried to keep out if its way, it knew at once and sought you out and jumped on your lap and climbed all over you to show how much it loved you. Please God, he thought, don't let me die in harness.

1960 *Take A Girl Like You*, ch.5.

76 More will mean worse.

1960 On expanding university intake, in *Encounter*, Jul.

77 Outside every fat man there was an even fatter man trying to close in.

1963 *One Fat Englishman*, ch.3.

▷ See also Connolly 283:75.

78 He was of the faith chiefly in the sense that the church he currently did not attend was Catholic.

1963 *One Fat Englishman*, ch.8.

79 It was no wonder that people were so horrible when they started life as children.

1963 *One Fat Englishman*, ch.14.

80 I was never an Angry Young Man. I am angry only when I hit my thumb with a hammer.

1979 Dissociating himself from that literary grouping, in *The Eton College Chronicle*, Jun.

81 The rewards for being sane may not be very many but knowing what's funny is one of them.
1984 *Stanley and the Women*, ch.2.

82 Alun's life was coming to consist more and more exclusively of being told at dictation speed what he knew.
1986 *The Old Devils*, ch.7.

83 Booze, of course, and then curtains.
1986 His response to being asked how he would spend his Booker Prize cheque, 22 Oct.

Amis, Martin Louis 1949–

English novelist, son of Kingsley Amis. His novels, characterized by realistic dialogue, vivid descriptive passages and a disturbing blend of wit and despair, include *The Rachel Papers* (1974), *London Fields* (1989), *Time's Arrow* (1991) and *The Information* (1995).

84 The middle-management of Manhattan stared on, their faces as thin as credit cards.
1984 *Money*.

85 His name was Shadow, short for Shadow That Comes in Sight, an old Indian name, Apache or Cheyenne. I very much approved of this. You don't want dogs called Spot or Pooch. You don't want dogs called Nigel or Keith. The names of dogs should salute the mystical drama of the animal life. *Shadow*—that's a *good* name.
1984 *Money*.

86 My theory is—we don't really go that far into other people, even when we think we do. We hardly ever go in and bring them out. We just stand at the jaws of the cave, and strike a match, and ask quickly if anybody's there.
1984 *Money*.

87 New York is a jungle, they tell you. You could go further, and say that New York is a jungle. New York *is a jungle*. Beneath the columns of the old rain forest, made of melting macadam, the mean Limpopo of swamped Ninth Avenue bears an angry argosy of crocs and dragons, tiger fish, noise machines, sweating rainmakers.
1984 *Money*.

88 My belief is that everything that's written about you is actually secondary showbiz nonsense, and you shouldn't take any notice of it.
1985 Quoted in John Haffenden *Novelists in Interview* (1985).

89 When success happens to an English writer, he acquires a new typewriter. When success happens to an American writer, he acquires a new life.
1986 *The Moronic Inferno*, 'Kurt Vonnegut'.

90 Most writers need a wound, either physical or spiritual.
1987 *The Observer*, 30 Aug.

91 How do we prevent the use of nuclear weapons? By threatening to use nuclear weapons. And we can't get rid of nuclear weapons, because of nuclear weapons.
1987 *Einstein's Monsters*, introduction.

92 Someone watches over us when we write. Mother. Teacher. Shakespeare. God.
1989 *London Fields*, ch.1.

93 And meanwhile time goes about its immemorial work of making everyone look and feel like shit.
1989 *London Fields*, ch.2.

94 But we mustn't go too far back…in anybody's life… Because if we do…then nobody is to blame for anything, and nothing matters, and everything is allowed.
1989 *London Fields*, ch.10.

95 Insects are what neurosis would sound like, if neurosis could make a noise with its nose.
1995 *The Information*, pt.3.

96 You see tragedy requires persons of heroic stature. It works on the principle of people being more than human—super-human—and also being only too human. But there just aren't many great figures around now, so the tragic mechanisms can't work.
1995 Explaining why only comedy can reflect contemporary reality. Quoted in an interview in *The Scotsman*, 7 Apr.

Ammianus Marcellinus c.330–390 AD

Roman historian, born of Greek parents in Antioch. After a military career he moved to Rome, and devoted himself to literature. He wrote in Latin a history of the Roman Empire.

97 *Etiam parietes arcanorum soli conscii timebantur.*

Even the walls, the only sharers of secrets, were feared.
History, 14.1.7 (translated by J C Rolfe). This became a proverbial expression in the medieval tradition: 'parietes habent aures' (the walls have ears).

Amundsen, Roald Engelbregt Gravning 1872–1928

Norwegian explorer. In 1903–6 he sailed the Northwest Passage in the smack *Gjöa*. Hearing of a British expedition to the South Pole, he made as if sailing for the Arctic but instead turned south. His party beat that of Captain Scott to the South Pole by one month.

98 Beg leave to inform you proceeding Antarctica. Amundsen.
1910 Cable sent from Madeira to Captain Robert F Scott in Melbourne, 12 Oct.

Anaxagoras c.500–428 BC

Greek philosopher. He taught in Athens, and Pericles and Euripides were among his pupils. He denied the divine nature of the celestial bodies, was banned from Athens for impiety, and died in Lampsacus.

99 The sun provides the moon with its brightness.

Fragment in Plutarch *De facie in orbe lunae*, 929b.

Anderson, Admiral George, Jr ?–1992

US Chief of Naval Operations in the Cuban missile crisis, 1962. On retirement from the Navy he served as US Ambassador to Portugal.

1 Now, Mr Secretary, if you and your deputy will go back to your offices, the Navy will run the blockade.

1962 On brandishing a manual of procedures to Pentagon officials at the time of the Cuban missile crisis. Recalled on his death, 4 Mar 1992.

Anderson, John Edward 1917–

US businessman.

2 You need enough cash cows to feed your pigs.

1994 On financing. In *Forbes*, 17 Oct.

Anderson, Dame Judith née Frances Margaret Anderson-Anderson 1898–1992

Australian actress. She achieved fame in the theatre, but is best remembered for her screen role as Mrs Danvers in Alfred Hitchcock's *Rebecca* (1940). In 1984 a Broadway theatre was named after her.

3 I find myself wearing gloves more often.

On how being made a Dame of the British Empire had changed her. Attributed.

Anderson, Lindsay 1932–94

Indian-born British stage and film director. During the 1950s he made documentary films and won an Oscar for his short film *Thursday's Children*. His feature film credits include *This Sporting Life* (1963), *If* (1968) and *The Whales of August* (1987).

4 Perhaps the tendency is to treat the films of one's own country like the prophets—with less than justice.

1947 Comment, quoted in Ian Christie *Arrows of Desire*.

Anderson, Maxwell 1888–1959

US dramatist. He wrote a large number of plays in both prose and verse, many on historical subjects.

5 What Price Glory?

1924 Title of play (with Lawrence Stallings).

6 But it's a long, long while
From May to December;
And the days grow short
When you reach September.

1938 'September Song' (music by Kurt Weill).

Anderson, Poul William 1926–

US science fiction and fantasy writer, author of numerous novels and short stories.

7 I have yet to see any problem, however complicated, which, when you looked at it in the right way, did not become still more complicated.

1969 In the *New Scientist*, 25 Sep.

Anderson, Robert Woodruff 1917–

US dramatist and novelist. His plays, confronting the difficulties of human relationships, include *Tea and Sympathy* (1953, filmscript 1956) and *I Never Sang for My Father* (1968), and he also wrote several filmscripts and a novel, *After* (1973).

8 All you're supposed to do is every once in a while give the boys a little tea and sympathy.

1953 On the duties of a headmaster's wife. *Tea and Sympathy*, act 1.

Anderson, Sherwood 1876–1941

US author, who left a lucrative job as manager of a paint factory to write full-time. His *Winesburg, Ohio* (1919) is a naturalistic study of small-town America in 23 stories.

9 The moment one of the people took one of the truths to himself, called it his truth, and tried to live his life by it, he became a grotesque and the truth he embraced a falsehood.

1919 *Winesburg, Ohio*, 'The Book of the Grotesque'.

Andrade, Carlos Drummond de 1902–87

Brazilian modernist poet. Although trained in pharmacy, he turned to writing and journalism. A friend of Neruda, he shared his devotion to socialism. His writing is characteristically low-key and ironic, focusing on everyday subjects.

10 *O marciano encontrou-me na rua*
e teve medo de minha impossiblidade humana.
Como pode existir, penseu consigo, um ser
que no existir põe sem tamanha anulação de
*   existência?*

The Martian met me in the streets
and was frightened by my human impossibility.
He wondered how such a being could exist
who could not exist without unmaking so much
    existence.

1961 *Lição de coisas*, 'Science Fiction'.

Andrade, Mário de 1893–1945

Brazilian modernist writer. His works reflect a deep interest in Brazilian folk culture, and his highly individual prose style imitates colloquial Brazilian speech.

11 *Os guerreiros de cá não buscam mavórticas damas*
para o enalce epitóelamico; mas antes as preferem
dóceis e facilmente trocáveis por pequeninas e voláteis

fôlhas de papel a que o vulgo chamará dinheiro—o 'curriculum vitae' da Civilização.

The warriors here do not seek out mettlesome women for epithalamic conjunction, but prefer them docile and willing to exchange with ease their favors for those small and deliquescent leaves of paper which the masses call dough—the *curriculum vitae* of Civilization.

1928 *Macunaíma* (*O Herói sem nenhum caráter*) (*Macunaima,* 1984), ch.9.

Andreas Capellanus fl. late 12c

French priest and writer, possibly chaplain to the court of Champagne. *De Amore* is his only known work.

12 *Liquide constet inter virum et uxorem amorem sibi locum vindicare non posse.*

It is clearly certain that between man and wife love can claim no place.

c.1185 *De Amore,* bk.1, ch.6, section 7.

Andrewes, Lancelot 1555–1626

English ecclesiastic, renowned for his memorable sermons. He became Bishop of Chichester, then Ely and finally Winchester.

13 It was no summer progress. A cold coming they had of it, at this time of the year; just, the worst time of the year, to take a journey, and specially a long journey, in. The ways deep, the weather sharp, the days short, the sun farthest off *in solstitio brumali,* the very dead of winter.

1622 *Of the Nativity,* sermon 15.

▷ See Eliot 369:3.

14 The nearer the Church, the further from God.

1622 *Of the Nativity,* sermon 15.

Andrews, Julie originally *Julia Elizabeth Wells* 1935–

British singer and actress. She starred in several long-running Broadway musicals, notably *My Fair Lady* (1956) and *Camelot* (1960). Her most popular films have been *Mary Poppins* (1964) and *The Sound of Music* (1965).

15 I'd like to thank all those who made this possible—especially Jack Warner

1965 Speech at the Oscar ceremony when she won an Academy Award for her role in *Mary Poppins,* 5 Apr. Warner had rejected her for the screen role of Eliza in *My Fair Lady,* although she had played it to great acclaim on the stage, preferring Audrey Hepburn whose singing had to be dubbed. Andrews had instead taken the part in *Mary Poppins.*

Angelou, Maya originally *Maya Johnson* 1928–

Black US writer. A sexual assault on her in childhood left her mute for several years. She was a singer and dancer before becoming a successful writer with her multi-volume autobiography.

16 If growing up is painful for the Southern Black girl, being aware of her displacement is the rust on the razor that threatens the throat.

1969 *I Know Why The Caged Bird Sings,* opening section.

17 Children's talent to endure stems from their ignorance of alternatives.

1969 *I Know Why The Caged Bird Sings,* ch.17.

18 The quality of strength lined with tenderness is an unbeatable combination, as are intelligence and necessity when unblunted by formal education.

1970 *I Know Why The Caged Bird Sings,* ch.29.

19 At fifteen life had taught me undeniably that surrender, in its place, was as honorable as resistance, especially if one had no choice.

1970 *I Know Why The Caged Bird Sings,* ch.31.

20 The fact that the adult American Negro female emerges a formidable character is often met with amazement, distaste and even belligerence. It is seldom accepted as an inevitable outcome of the struggle won by survivors, and deserves respect if not enthusiastic acceptance.

1970 *I Know Why The Caged Bird Sings,* ch.34

21 Most plain girls are virtuous because of the scarcity of opportunity to be otherwise.

1970 *I Know Why The Caged Bird Sings,* ch.35

22 It is a historical truth. No man can know where he is going unless he knows exactly where he has been and exactly how he arrived at his present place.

1972 On Africa. In the *New York Times,* 16 Apr.

23 There is a kind of strength that is almost frightening in black women. It's as if a steel rod runs right through the head down to the feet.

1973 Television interview, 21 Nov. Collected in *Conversations with Maya Angelou* (1989).

24 We had won… I thought if war did not include killing, I'd like to see one every year. Something like a festival.

1974 On the end of World War II. *Gather Together In My Name,* prologue.

25 Self-pity in its early stage is as snug as a feather mattress. Only when it hardens does it become uncomfortable.

1974 *Gather Together In My Name,* ch.6.

26 The sadness of the women's movement is that they don't allow the necessity of love. See, I don't personally trust any revolution where love is not allowed.

1975 Interview in *California Living,* 14 May. Collected in *Conversations with Maya Angelou* (1989).

27 Oh, the holiness of always being the injured party. The historically oppressed can find not only sanctity but safety in the state of victimization. When access to a better life has been denied often enough, and successfully enough, one can use the rejection as an excuse to cease all efforts.

1976 *Singin' and Swingin' and Getting Merry Like Christmas*, ch.9.

28 Life loves the liver of it.

1977 Interview in *Black Scholar*, Jan–Feb. Collected in *Conversations with Maya Angelou* (1989).

29 Something made greater by ourselves and in turn that makes us greater.

1977 Defining work. Interview in *Black Scholar*, Jan–Feb. Collected in *Conversations with Maya Angelou* (1989).

30 There is an awesome reality to Rent Day. It comes trumpeting, forcing the days before it into a wild scramble.

1981 *The Heart of a Woman*, ch.3.

31 The cliché of whites being ignorant of blacks was not only true, but understandable. Oh, but we knew them with the intimacy of a surgeon's scalpel.

1981 *The Heart of a Woman*, ch.12.

32 Genet had been right at least about one thing. Blacks should be used to play whites. For centuries we had probed their faces, the angles of their bodies, the sounds of their voices and even their odors. Often our survival had depended on the accurate reading of a white man's chuckle or the disdainful wave of a white woman's hand.

1981 *The Heart of a Woman*, ch.12.

33 Poetry is music written for the human voice.

1989 In 'The Power of the Word', Public Broadcasting Service, 15 Sep.

34 Wouldn't Take Nothing for my Journey Now.

1994 Title of book.

Annan, Noël Gilroy, Baron 1916–

35 He cultivated to perfection the sneer which he used like an oyster-knife, inserting it into the shell of his victim, exposing him with a quick-turn of the wrist, and finally flipping him over and inviting his audience to discard him as tainted and inedible.

1991 On the critic F R Leavis. *English Intellectuals Between the World Wars*.

Anne, Queen 1665–1714

36 Cricket is not illegal, for it is a manly game.

1710 Quoted in Colin Jarman *The Guinness Dictionary of Sports Quotations* (1990).

37 I have changed my Ministers but I have not changed my measures. I am still for moderation, and I will govern by it.

1711 Addressing her new Tory administration, Jan.

Anne Elizabeth Alice Louise 1950–

38 It could be said that the AIDS pandemic is a classic own-goal scored by the human race against itself.

1988 In the *Daily Telegraph*, 27 Jan.

Annenberg, Walter H 1908–

39 Only when you are moved by a painting should you buy it. Being moved is what collecting is all about.

1991 In *Connoisseur*, Feb.

40 You are asking me to sell members of my family.

1991 In the *New York Times*, 12 Mar. Rejecting a billion-dollar Japanese offer for his art collection.

Anonymous

41 Either with it or upon it.

Traditionally said by a Spartan mother while handing her son his shield when he went to war; he should either return with it (ie as a victor) or on it (ie dead). Plutarch *Lacaenarum Apophthegmata*, 241f.

42 *Cave canem!*

Beware of the dog!

Famous expression, found in mosaics and inscriptions in Pompeii and other Roman towns. See also Petronius *Satyricon*, 29.1: *Ad sinistram enim intrantibus no longe ab ostiarii cella canis ingens, catena vinctus, in pariete erat pictus superque quadrata littera scriptum cave canem* (For on the left hand as you went in, not far from the porter's office, a great dog on a chain was painted on the wall, and over him was written in large letters: 'Beware of the dog'. Translation by W H D Rouse).

43 Not everyone can sail to Corinth.

ie, not everybody has the same opportunities. Greek proverb, which is also mentioned by Horace *Epistulae*, 1. 17.36: 'Non cuivis homini contingit adire Corinthum'.

44 Nothing in excess.

Famous motto in Antiquity. According to Plato, the text was a temple inscription in Delphi (*Hipparchus*, 228e).

45 *Patria est ubicumque est bene.*

One's country is wherever one does well.

Quoted as proverbial by Cicero in *Tusculanes Disputationes*, 5. 108. The saying was attributed to the mythical figure Teucer, ancestor of the Trojans, by the Roman tragedian Pacuvius (220–c.130 BC).

46 *Ave Caesar, morituri te salutant!*

Hail Caesar, we who are about to die salute you!

Traditional formula for gladiators saluting the emperor. One source for the expression is Suetonius *Claudius* 21: 'Ave Imperator, morituri te salutant', ('Hail Emperor, we salute you, we who are about to die!').

47 *Candida me docuit nigras odisse puellas. Odero si potero. Si non, invitus amabo.*

A white girl instructed me to hate black girls. I shall hate them if I can. If not, I shall love them— against my will.

c.1c AD Graffito found in Pompeii. In *Corpus Inscriptionum Latinarum* IV, 1520.

48 *Fures fores, frugi intro!*

Thieves out, profit in!

c.1c AD Graffito found in Pompeii. In *Corpus Inscriptionum Latinarum* IV, 4278.

49 *Fullones ululamque cano, non arma virumque.*

Of fullers and their wailing, I sing, not of arms and the man.

c.1c AD Graffito found in Pompeii. In *Corpus Inscriptionum Latinarum* IV, 9131. This is a parody of the famous opening line of Virgil's *Aeneid* 1.1: 'Arma virumque cano'.

50 Enjoy another glass, for you see what the end is.

c.2c AD Epitaph from Cos for a certain Chrysogonos. Quoted in W Peek *Griechische Versinschriften*, vol.1, no.378.

51 The glory of God is man, and the glory of man is his dress.

c.450 *Babylonian Talmud.* Quoted in Barton Stevenson (ed) *The Macmillan Book of Proverbs, Maxims, and Famous Phrases* (1948).

52 *Gæth a wyrd swa hio scel.*

Fate always goes as it must.

c.800 *Beowulf*, l.455.

53 *Wyrd oft nereth*
unfægne eorl thonne his ellen deah.

Fate often preserves
the undoomed warrior when his courage holds firm.

c.800 *Beowulf*, l.572–3.

54 *Oft seldan hwær*
æfter leodhyre lytle hwile
bongar bugeth.

It is very rare that,
after the fall of a prince,
the deadly spear rests for long.

c.800 *Beowulf*, l.2029–31.

55 He is joyful with swift movement when a mouse sticks in his sharp paw.
I too am joyful when I understand a dearly loved difficult problem.

c.820 'Me and Pangur Bán', by an unidentified cat-owning scholar, translated in Gerard Murphy *Early Irish Lyrics* (1956), no.1.

56 *Lytle hwile leof beoth grene*
thonne hie eft fealewiath, feallath on eorthan
and forweorniath weorthiath to duste.

For a little while the leaves are green.
Then they turn yellow, fall to the ground,
and perish, turning to dust.

c.900 *Second Dialogue of Solomon and Saturn*, l.136–8.

57 *Widgongel wif word gespringeth.*

A roving woman gives rise to gossip.

c.900 *Maxims I*, l.64.

58 *Feoh byth frofur fira gehwylcum*
Sceal theah manna gehwylc miclun hyt dælan.

Money is a comfort to each man,
But everyone should nevertheless give it away freely.

?c.900 *The Rune Poem*, l.1–2.

59 *Ear byth egle eorla gehwylcun.*

The grave is ghastly to every man.

?c.900 *The Rune Poem*, l.90.

60 Thought shall be the harder, heart the keener,
courage the greater, as our might lessens.

c.1000 *The Battle of Maldon* (translated by R K Gordon).

61 *La flur de France as perdut.*

The flower of France is lost.

c.1110 *Chanson de Roland*, l.2445.

62 *Mult ad apris ki bien conuist ahan.*

He who has suffered much learns much.

c.1110 *Chanson de Roland*, l.2524.

63 *Man sol sô vrouwen ziehen…*
das si üppeclîche sprüche lasen under wegen.

Women should be trained in such a way
that they avoid idle chatter.

c.1200 *Das Nibelungenlied*, ch.14, l.193–4.

64 And nowe in the winter, when men kill the fat swine
They get the bladder and blow it great and thin,
With many beans and peason put within:
It ratleth, soundeth, and shineth clere and fayre
While it is throwen and caste up in the ayre,
Each one contendeth and hath a great delite
With foote and with hands the bladder for to smite;
If it fall to grounde, they lifte it up agayne,

But this waye to labour they count in no payne.

Medieval verse, one of the earliest descriptions of football in England.

65 *Graeca non leguntur.*

Things in Greek are not read.

Term used by medieval '*glossatores*' (commentators) of the *Corpus Iuris*, indicating that the parts in Greek should be skipped. It became a traditional comment to indicate ignorance.

66 Al night by the rose, rose,
Al night by the rose I lay,
Dorst ich nought the rose stele,
And yet I bar the flour away.

c.1210–40 Untitled lyric.

67 Sumer is icumen in,
Lhude sing cuccu!
Groweth sed, and bleweth med,
And springth the wude nu.

c.1250 'Sumer is icumen in', l.1–4.

▷ See also Pound 785:51.

68 Quhen Alysaunder oure kyng wes dede,
That Scotland led in lauche and le,
Away wes sons of alle and brede,
Off wyne and wax, of gamyn and gle;
Oure gold wes changyd in to lede.
Cryst, borne in to virgynyte,
Succour Scotland, and remede,
That stad is in perplexyte.

c.1286 Lines said to have been written after the death of Alexander II of Scotland, the earliest extant piece of Scottish verse. Quoted in the *Original Chronicle of Andrew Wyntoun* (c.1420), bk.7.

69 Lenten is come with love to toune.

c.1300 'Lenten is come', l.1.

70 *Quamdiu centum viui remanserint, nuncquam*
Anglorum dominio aliquatenus volumus subjugari.

As long as one hundred of us shall remain alive, we shall never consent to subject ourselves in any degree to English dominion.

1320 *Declaration of Arbroath*, a letter sent by the barons of Scotland to Pope John XXII, asserting Scotland's independence from England and their right to defend that independence with or without the support of their sovereign.

71 Not what thou arte, ne what thou hast ben,
beholdeth God with his mercyful iye; bot that thou
woldest be.

c.1370 *The Cloud of Unknowing*, ch.75.

72 *Patience is a poynt, thagh it displese ofte.*

Patience is a virtue, though it often displeases.

c.1370 *Patience*, l.1.

73 *Ay wolde man of happe more hente*
Then moghte by ryght upon hem cleven.

Man always desires to seize more of happiness,

Than rightfully belongs to him.

c.1370 *Pearl*, l.1195–6.

74 *Of alle chevalry to chose, the chef thyng alosed*
Is the lel layk of luf, the lettrure of armes.

Choosing from all chivalrous actions, the chief things to praise
Are the loyal sport of love and the lore of arms.

c.1370 *Sir Gawain and the Green Knight*, l.1512–3.

75 *Yif thou wolte lyve frely, lerne to dye gladly.*

c.1375 *The Art of Dieing.*

76 Young men a wooing, for God that you bought,
Be well ware of wedding and think in your
thought:
'Had I wist' is a thing, it serves of nought.

c.1425 *The Second Shepherd's Play*, part of the York cycle of Mystery Plays, l.91–3.

77 *Now why that erthe luves erthe, wondere me thinke,*
Or why that erthe for erthe sholde other swete or
swinke:
For when that erthe upon erthe es broghte within
brinke,
Thane shall erthe of erthe have a foulle stinke.

Now, why earth loves earth, I wonder to think,
Or why earth for earth should either sweat or
labour:
For when earth upon earth comes within the grave's
brink,
Then earth upon earth shall have a foul stink.

c.1450 'Erthe oute of erthe', l.19–22.

78 I wyll that my son manhede take
For reson wyll that there be thre—
A man, a madyn, and a tre.
Man for man, tre for tre,
Madyn for madyn; thus shall it be.

?c.1450 God the Father explains how Christ will atone for Adam's sin. *Towneley Annunciation Play*, l.30–5.

79 *Pees maketh plente;*
Plente maketh pride;
Pride make plee;
Plee maketh povert;
Povert maketh pees.

Peace makes plenty;
Plenty makes pride;
Pride makes lawsuits;
Lawsuits make poverty;
Poverty makes peace.

c.1470 Untitled lyric.

80 O God in Heaven, on you we call,
Kyrie eleison,
Help us seize our priests and kill them all,
Kyrie eleison.

1476 Satirical chant. Quoted in Gerald Strauss *Manifestations of Discontent in Germany on the Eve of the Reformation* (1971).

81 Everyman, I will go with thee, and be thy guide.
In thy most need to go by thy side.
c.1485 Knowledge speaks to Everyman. *Everyman*, l.522–3.

82 In youth open your mind, And let all learning in;
Words the head does not shape Are worthless, out
and in.
Words wit has not salted, No nearer the heart than
the lip,
Are nothing more than wind, A puppy's insolent
yelp.
c.1500 'To a Boy'. Translated from the Irish by Michael
O'Donovan ('Frank O'Connor').

83 Westron winde, when wilt thou blow,
The smalle raine downe can raine?
Christ if my love were in my armes,
And I in my bed againe.
c.1500 Untitled lyric.

84 Back and side go bare, go bare,
Both foot and hand go cold;
But, belly, God send thee good ale enough,
Whether it be new or old.
c.1575 Song, included in the play *Gammer Gurton's Needle*, act
2. William Stevenson (c.1530–75) and John Still (1543–1608)
have both been credited with authorship of the play, but the
song probably predates it.

85 I cannot eat but little meat,
My stomach is not good;
But sure I think that I can drink
With him that wears a hood.
c.1575 Song, included in the play *Gammer Gurton's Needle*, act
2. 'Him that wears a hood' is either a monk or a scholar.

86 And Tib my wife, that as her life
Loveth well good ale to seek,
Full oft drinks she, till ye may see
The tears run down her cheeks.
c.1575 Song, included in the play *Gammer Gurton's Needle*,
act 2.

87 Though raging stormes movis us to shake,
And wind makis waters overflow;
We yield thereto bot dois not break
And in the calm bent up we grow.

So baneist men, though princes rage,
And prisoners, be not despairit.
Abide the calm, whill that it 'suage,
For time sic causis has repairit.
1582 *The Maitland Manuscript*, 'The Reeds in the Loch Sayis'.

88 Brissit brawnis and broken banis
Stryfe discorde and waistis wanis
Crukit in eild, syne halt withal,
This are the bewteis of the fute-ball.
1582 *The Maitland Manuscript*, 'The Bewteis of the Fute-ball'.

89 *Flavit deus et dissipati sunt*

God blew and they were scattered.
1588 Inscription on medallion to commemorate the English
defeat of the Spanish Armada.

90 The rose is red, the leaves are green,
God save Elizabeth, our noble queen.
1589 Lines written by a Westminster schoolboy in the margin
of his copy of *Julius Caesar*. Quoted in P W Hasler (ed) *The
House of Commons, 1558–1603* (vol.1), p.474.

91 My Love in her attire doth show her wit,
It doth so well become her;
For every season she hath dressings fit,
For winter, spring, and summer.
No beauty she doth miss
When all her robes are on;
But beauty's self she is
When all her robes are gone.
'Madrigal'. Collected in F Davison (ed) *Poetical Rhapsody*
(1602).

92 Nose, nose, jolly red nose,
Who gave thee this jolly red nose?…
Nutmegs and ginger, cinnamon and cloves,
And they gave me this jolly red nose.
Quoted in Francis Beaumont and John Fletcher *The Knight of the
Burning Pestle* (1609) but thought to be a rhyme of earlier origin.

93 Even when the courtesan farts
She does it as a favour
c.1616–1853 Collected in R H Blyth *Senryō: Japanese Satirical
Verses Translated and Explained* (1949).

94 Possession is nine points of the law.
Proverb, quoted in T Draxe *Adages* (1616) no.163.

95 Too many cooks spoil the broth.
Quoted in Sir Balthazar Gerbier *Three Chief Principles of
Magnificent Building* (1665).

96 O he's a ranting roving blade!
O he's a brisk and a bonnie lad!
Betide what may, my heart is glad
To see my lad wi' his white cockade.
18c 'The White Cockade'.

97 O this is no my ain house,
I ken by the biggin o't.
18c 'This is no my ain house'.

98 A good rider may often be thrown from his horse,
And climb on once again to face forward his course,
Which is how I went forward myself on my way,
And come, Christ, and give me my true judgment
day.
18c Traditional Irish poem. Translated by Owen Dudley
Edwards.

99 And wasna he a roguey,
A roguey, a roguey,
And wasna he a roguey,
The piper o' Dundee?
18c 'The Piper o' Dundee'.

1 The Campbells are comin', O-ho, O-ho!

c.1715 'The Campbells are comin'. Although its origins are uncertain, this song may date from John Campbell, Duke of Argyll's attack on the Jacobite army at Sheriffmuir (1715).

2 Cam ye ower frae France?
Cam ye doun by Lunnon?
Saw ye Geordie Whelps
And his bonnie woman?
Were ye at the place
Ca'd the Kittle Housie?
Saw ye Geordie's grace
Ridin' on a goosie?

c.1715 'Cam Ye Ower Frae France?', stanza 1. This Jacobite song alludes to George I and his reputed fondness for visiting brothels.

3 It made Gay Rich and Rich Gay.

c.1728 Alluding to the phenomenal success of *The Beggar's Opera*, written by John Gay and produced by John Rich.

4 O ye'll tak the high road, and I'll tak the low road,
And I'll be in Scotland afore ye,
But me and my true love will never meet again
On the bonnie, bonnie banks o' Loch Lomond
By yon bonnie banks and by yon bonnie braes,
Where the sun shines bright on Loch Lomond.

1746 'The Bonnie Banks o' Loch Lomond', chorus and stanza 1. The author was a Jacobite imprisoned in Carlisle.

5 Whaur's yer Wullie Shakespeare noo?

1756 Shout from an enthusiastic member of the audience at the first production of John Home's *Douglas* at the Canongate Theatre, Edinburgh.

6 Boston, Boston, Boston!
Thou hast naught to boast on,
But a Grand Sluice, and a high steeple;
A proud conceited ignorant people,
And a coast where souls are lost on.

1766 Comment by visitor at the opening of the Grand Sluice, Boston, Lincolnshire, 15 Oct. Quoted in Jennifer Westwood *Albion* (1985), ch. 6, 'English Shires'.

7 Some hae meat and canna eat
And some wad eat that want it;
But we hae meat and we can eat,
And sae the Lord be thankit.

c.1790 'The Selkirk Grace', sometimes attributed to Robert Burns.

8 I challenge all the men alive
To say they e'er were gladder,
Than boys all striving,
Who should kick most wind out of the bladder.

1794 Charterhouse public school song, celebrating football.

9 Here's tae us; wha's like us?
Gey few, and they're a' deid.

19c Scottish toast of uncertain origin. 'Damn' and other variations are sometimes substituted for 'gey'.

10 This stone commemorates the exploit of William Webb Ellis, who, with a fine disregard for the rules of football as played in his time, first took the ball in his arms and ran with it, thus originating the distinctive feature of the Rugby game. AD1823.

Plaque at Rugby School.

11 What can be more palpably absurd than the prospect held out of locomotives travelling twice as fast as stagecoaches?

1825 *Quarterly Review*, Mar.

12 There was a girl in our town,
Silk an' satin was her gown,
Silk an' satin, gold an' velvet,
Guess her name, three times I've telled it.

Quoted in James Orchard Halliwell *The Nursery Rhymes of England* (1842). The answer, of course, is 'Ann'.

13 The deceased Gentleman was, we are informed, a native of Ashbourn, Derbyshire, at which place he was born in the Year of Grace, 217, and was consequently in the 1643rd year of his age. For some months the patriotic Old Man had been suffering from injuries sustained in his native town, so far back as Shrovetide in last year; he was at once removed (by appeal) to London, where he lingered in suspense till the law of death put its icy hand upon him, and claimed as another trophy to magisterial interference one who had long lived in the hearts of the people.

1860 'Death of the Right Honourable Game Football', as published in a court circular. There had been recent attempts in the courts to ban the riotous custom of 'Shrovetide football' pursued at Ashbourne, Derbyshire, and other villages.

14 What happens when a game of football is proposed at Christmas among a party of young men assembled from different schools? Alas!… The Eton man is enamoured of his own rules, and turns up his nose at Rugby as not sufficiently aristocratic; while the Rugbeian retorts that 'bullying' and 'sneaking' are not to his taste, and he is not afraid of his shins, or of a 'maul' or 'scrimmage'. On hearing this the Harrovian pricks up his ears, and though he might previously have sided with Rugby, the insinuation against the courage of those who do not allow 'shinning' arouses his ire, and causes him to refuse to lay with one who has offered it. Thus it is found impossible to get up a game.

1861 Editorial in *The Field* newspaper, illustrating the confusion before the codification of the rules of football and rugby.

15 Well-informed people know it is impossible to transmit the voice over wires and that were it possible to do so, the thing would be of no practical value.

1865 Editorial in the *Boston Post*.

16 It is a good plan, if it can previously be so arranged, to have one side with striped jerseys of one colour, say red; and the other with another, say blue. This prevents confusion and wild attempts to run after and wrest the ball from your neighbour. I have often seen this done, and the invariable apology—'I beg your pardon, I thought you were on the opposite side'.
1867 In *Routledge's Handbook of Football.*

17 In affectionate remembrance of English cricket, which died at the Oval on 29th August, 1882. Deeply lamented by a large circle of sorrowing friends and acquaintances. RIP. NB The body will be cremated and the ashes taken to Australia.
1882 Notice in *The Sporting Times*, 2 Sep, after the England cricket team's defeat by the Australians.

18 The climate of Manitoba consists of seven months of Arctic weather and five months of cold weather.
1882 *Settler's Guide to the North-West*, issued by the Northern Pacific Railway Company, New York.

19 The British 'Sphere of Influence'—the cricket ball.
Mr Punch's Book of Sport.

20 £1 per week should be ample remuneration for the best professional footballer that ever existed.
1886 In *The Field* newspaper.

21 To the Glorious, Pious, and Immortal Memory of King William the Third, Prince of Orange, who delivered us from Popes and Popery, Knaves and Knavery, Slaves and Slavery, Brass Money, and Wooden Shoes, and He that Will Not Take this Toast May He Be Damn'd, Cramm'd, and Jamm'd Down the Great Gun of Athlone, and the Gun Fired in the Pope's Belly, and the Pope Fired in the Devil's Belly, and the Devil Fired into Hell, and the Door Lock'd, and the Key Forever in the Pocket of a Stout Orangeman. And Here's a Fart for the Bishop of Cork!
c.1890 'The Orange Toast', traditional Protestant Irish.

22 These Ibsen creatures are 'neither men nor women, they are ghouls', vile, unlovable, morbid monsters, and it were well indeed for society if all such went and drowned themselves at once.
1891 In *The Gentlewoman*. Review of Henrik Ibsen's *Rosmersholm.*

23 How different, how very different, from the home life of our own dear Queen!
c.1892 Overheard from a member of the audience when Sarah Bernhardt appeared in the role of Cleopatra.

24 I don't know, darlin', but I think it was somethin' he did against the English.
1895 Unidentified Irish nurse in the US answering an infant's question on the cause of Oscar Wilde's imprisonment, reported by Kenneth Wiggins Porter.

25 The ordinary 'horseless-carriage' is at present a luxury for the wealthy; and although the price will probably fall in the future, it will never, of course, come into as common use as the bicycle.
1899 *Literary Digest*, 14 Oct.

26 Far away from where I am now there is a little gap in the hills, and beyond it the sea; and 'tis there I do be looking the whole day long, for it's the nearest thing to yourself that I can see.
c.1900 Letter from an unidentified Irish postboy to his beloved, quoted in Maurice Healy *The Old Munster Circuit.*

27 *Citius, altius, fortius.*

Swifter, higher, stronger.
Motto of the Olympic Games, c.1908. It was apparently adopted by Baron de Coubertin after he spotted it over the doorway of a French lycée, though it has also been attributed to Reverend Father Didon.

28 Skegness is so bracing.
from 1909 Slogan in railway advertisements promoting Skegness, Lincolnshire, as a holiday resort. Quoted in Nigel Rees *Dictionary of Popular Phrases* (1990).

29 That the automobile has practically reached the limit of its development is suggested by the fact that during the past year no improvements of a radical nature have been introduced.
1909 *Scientific American*, 2 Jan.

30 Your country needs you!
1914 First use of British World War I recruiting slogan.

31 Berlin by Christmas.
1914 British press.

32 Say it ain't so, Joe.
1919 Attributed words of a young fan, to US baseball star 'Shoeless Joe' Jackson (1887–1951) who was accused of accepting bribes to throw the 1919 World Series (the 'Black Sox' scandal). Jackson always maintained his innocence, but he and seven other players were barred from baseball for life.

33 Four and twenty Yankees, feeling very dry,
Went across the border to get a drink of rye.
When the rye was opened, the Yanks began to sing,
'God bless America, but God save the King!'
c.1919 Ditty current in Canada, referring to Americans crossing the border to drink during Prohibition. The Duke of Windsor, later Edward VIII, heard it during his tour of Canada (1919) and repeated it to his father, George V, on his return, as he recalled in *A King's Story* (1951).

34 The cure of the id by the odd.
c.1920 Popular definition of psychology.

35 Dear Sir, your astonishment's odd:
I am always about in the Quad.
And that's why the tree
Will continue to be
Since observed by Yours faithfully, God.
c.1924 Reply to Ronald Knox's limerick. The limericks summarise Bishop George Berkeley's philosophy that everything is dependent at all times on the will of God.
▷ See Knox 567:61.

36 There is no woman who does not dream of being dressed in Paris.

1925 Catalogue of the 1925 Paris Exhibition. Quoted in Colin McDowell *McDowell's Directory of Twentieth Century Fashion* (1984), ch.1.

37 There was a faith-healer of Deal
Who said, 'Although pain isn't real,
If I sit on a pin
And it punctures my skin,
I dislike what I fancy I feel.'

Collected in *The Week-End Book* (1925).

38 Let's get out of these wet clothes and into a dry martini.

c.1925 The origin of this line is disputed; it has been attributed to Billy Wilder, Charles Butterworth, Alexander Woollcott and Robert Benchley's press agent. It was used by Mae West in *Every Day's a Holiday* (1937 film) and by Benchley in *The Major and the Minor* (1942 film).

39 Can't act. Can't sing. Slightly bald. Can dance a little.

c.1930 Studio executive's assessment of Fred Astaire on his first screen test.

40 *Ein Reich, ein Volk, ein Führer.*

One realm, one people, one leader.

1934 German Nazi slogan.

41 Sticks nix hick pix

1935 Headline from *Variety*, 17 Jul. A famous example of the US trade paper's idiosyncratic form of English, referring to the unpopularity of films with rural themes in rural areas.

42 Who dares, wins.

1940s Motto of the British Special Air Service regiment.

43 A bayonet is a weapon with a worker at each end.

1940 British pacifist slogan during World War II.

44 A neurotic builds castles in the air, but a psychotic lives in them.

c.1940 Popular saying.

45 *Arbeit macht frei.*

Work liberates.

c.1940 Legend over the gates of the concentration camp at Auschwitz, Poland.

46 Export or die.

1940s British Board of Trade.

47 Walls have ears.

1940s British war slogan.

48 Coughs and sneezes spread diseases. Trap the germs in your handkerchief.

1942 British Government health slogan, quoted in J Darracott and B Loftus *Second World War Posters* (1972).

49 Went the day well?

Title of an anthology of tributes to men and women killed in the war, used for the title of Cavalcanti's 1942 film about German soldiers invading an English village.

50 No girls, no legs, no jokes, no chance.

1943 Review of the Rodgers and Hammerstein musical *Oklahoma!* wired to theatre critic Walter Winchell by one of his informants after its pre-Broadway tryout in New Haven. Quoted in Peter Hay *Broadway Anecdotes* (1989).

51 If only we might fall
Like cherry blossoms in the spring
So pure and radiant.

c.1945 Quoted in Ivan Morris *The Nobility of Failure* (1975).

52 I like Ike.

1947 Campaign slogan for Dwight D Eisenhower's presidential bid. Irving Berlin presented a song with this title, based on *They Like Ike* from his Broadway musical *Call Me Madam*, to an Eisenhower rally at Madison Square Garden, 8 Feb 1952.

53 Whose finger do you want on the trigger?

1952 Headline in the *Daily Mirror*, 21 Sep, reflecting popular mistrust of both Labour and Conservative leadership in the light of the new destructive potential of the atomic bomb.

54 Masserman, the cat man,
Makes cats neurotic.
Are cats and humans
Similarly symptotic?

1952 Popular jingle. Dr Jules Massermann conducted some bizarre, behavioural experiments into animal neurosis.

55 No pain—no gain.

Bodybuilding motto. The catchphrase may have had its origins in Adlai Stevenson's slogan 'There are no gains without pain', first voiced when accepting the Democratic nomination in 1952.

56 Piping Pebworth, Dancing Marston,
Haunted Hillborough, Hungry Grafton,
Dodging Exhall, Papist Wixford,
Beggarly Broom, and Drunken Bidford.

'Traditional Rhyme on the Vale of Avon Place-Names', quoted in Arnold Silcock, *Verse and Worse* (1952), 'Whimsies'.

57 Madly for Adlai.

1952 Campaign slogan for Adlai Stevenson's presidential bid.

58 Ban the Bomb.

1953 Used by US nuclear disarmament movement from 1953.

59 Psychology? When my daughter needs psychology I fetch her a skelp across her backside, which lifts her nigh six inches in t'air.

1955 Young Yorkshire mother's response on being asked by a local education psychologist how she felt psychology might assist her in the upbringing of her difficult daughter.

60 Cambridge has always tried to be more typical and less exotic than the other place.

1958 In *The Listener*, 14 Aug. 'The other place' has traditionally come to be used of Cambridge from an Oxford viewpoint and vice versa.

61 Life's better with the Conservatives...don't let Labour ruin it.

1959 Conservative Party general election slogan.

62 A chair should be judged by one's pants, a jewel by

the light in a lady's eyes, a typewriter by the hovering fingers.

1959 On good design. In *Time Magazine*, 12 Jan.

63 Nature's way of telling you to slow down.

Of death. Quoted in *Newsweek*, 25 Apr 1960.

64 Let's get America moving again.

1960 John F Kennedy's presidential election slogan.

65 GIGO: Garbage in, garbage out.

c.1960 The great and seemingly most basic principle of the computer, coined anonymously sometime early in its development.

66 I have to say Miss Brown, that your methods are outdated and incorrect. But the children love you and are learning well. Do not on any account make any changes.

c.1960 Unknown school inspector, quoted in Antony Garrard Newton Flew *Shephard's Warning. Setting schools back on course* (1994).

67 Would you buy a used car from this man?

1960 Democratic slogan to disparage Richard M Nixon in the 1960 presidential campaign. Nixon had come across badly in television debates, in contrast to the charismatic John F Kennedy.

68 Stop The World, I Want to Get Off.

1961 From the musical by Leslie Bricusse and Anthony Newley.

69 Never again.

1960s Jewish Defence League.

70 Stretch pants—the garment that made skiing a spectator sport.

1961 In *Time Magazine*, 23 Feb.

71 All the egg heads are in one basket.

1961 Of President Kennedy's advisers. Quoted by Harold Macmillan in a letter to the Queen, 12 Apr.

72 That Was The Week That Was.

1962–3 Title of satirical BBC TV series.

73 Our little bit of grandeur is gone.

1963 Heard on a Dublin bus shortly after the assassination of John Fitzgerald Kennedy, 22 Nov, reported by Sheila O'Sullivan.

74 Make love, not war.

Flower Power movement, mid-1960s.

75 Thirteen wasted years.

1964 Labour Party general election slogan.

76 Don't report what he says, report what he means.

1964 Unwritten reporters' rule for covering Senator Barry Goldwater's campaign for presidential nomination. Quoted in Robert MacNeil *The Right Place at the Right Time* (1982).

77 Hearts and minds.

c.1965 Used by US Defence Department official with regard to winning public support for its Vietnam policy.

78 An important senior faun.

Description of Prime Minister Harold Macmillan's appearance. Quoted in John Gunther *Procession* (1965).

79 Hey, hey, LBJ! How many kids did you kill today?

1966 US anti-Vietnam war demonstrators.

80 Black is beautiful.

1966 US black civil rights movement.

81 Black power.

1966 US black civil rights slogan coined by Stokely Carmichael.

82 Magnificent magpiety.

1966 Of the art collection of cosmetic manufacturer Helena Rubinstein. *Time Magazine*, 29 Apr.

83 Bombs away with Curtis LeMay.

1967 Used by US anti-Vietnam demonstrators.

84 Burn, baby, burn!

1967 Radical cry in racial riots and fire-raising in Watts, California and Newark, New Jersey. Quoted in *Time*, 11 Aug.

85 It became necessary to destroy the town to save it.

1968 Statement issued by the US army, referring to Ben Tre in Vietnam. In the *New York Times*, 8 Feb.

86 I'm Backing Britain.

1968 Coined by publisher Robert Maxwell to encourage the public to buy British-made goods.

87 Culture is dead, now let us start creating.

1968 Graffito by Parisian students on the School of Architecture walls, May.

88 My mother thinks Vietnam is somewhere near Panama.

c.1968 The last words of a US soldier fatally wounded during the Vietnam War, quoted by Australian film-maker John Pilger in his 1978 film *Do you remember Vietnam?*

89 Who Else but Nelse?

1968 Campaign slogan for Nelson Rockefeller's presidential bid.

90 When you've got it, flaunt it.

1969 Braiff Airlines slogan.

91 Power to the people.

1969 US Black Panther movement slogan.

92 Out of the closets and into the streets.

1969 US Gay rights movement slogan.

93 Here men from the planet Earth first set foot upon the moon, July 1969 AD. We came in peace for all mankind.

1969 Text of the plaque left on the moon by the first astronauts to walk there, Buzz Aldrin and Neil Armstrong, 20 Jul.

94 Burn your bra!

1970 US feminists' slogan.

95 Yesterday's men.

1970 Labour Party general election slogan, referring to the Conservative leadership.

96 Send them a message.

1972 Governor George Wallace's presidential election slogan.

97 Nice one, Cyril.

1972 Buy-line in TV advertisement for Wonderloaf. It was adopted in 1973 as the title of a pop song by the Cockerel Chorus, addressed to Tottenham Hotspur left-back Cyril Knowles.

98 The abominable no-man.

Of Sherman Adams, Eisenhower's Chief of Staff. Quoted in William Safire *Before the Fall* (1975).

99 The Grin Will Win.

1976 Campaign slogan for Jimmy Carter's presidential bid.

1 He who has not travelled does not know the value of a man.

Arab proverb. Quoted in Ingrid Cranfield *The Challengers* (1976), preface.

2 Hypochondria is the only disease I haven't got.

1978 Graffito seen in New York.

3 Just when you thought it was safe to get back into the water.

c.1978 Publicity slogan for *Jaws 2*.

4 Sick as a parrot.

c.1978 Football cliché. The phrase may have started life as 'sick as a pierrot', an allusion to the sadfaced French Pierrot character of the 18th century, but similar phrases appear in literature as early as the 17th century.

5 To err is human; to blame it on the other party is politics.

1979 In the *Washingtonian*, Nov.

6 Labour isn't working.

1979 Used by the Conservative Party in its general election campaign, referring to high unemployment under the then Labour Government.

7 On yer bike!

1981 Catchphrase derived from Norman Tebbit's Conservative Party conference speech.

8 The Great Communicator.

1981 Tag coined for President Reagan, who was renowned for his ability to put a good spin on speeches prepared for him.

9 Britain is a Morris Minor country, but with Rolls Royce diplomacy.

1982 Remark made during the Falklands crisis by a UN delegate, Apr. Quoted in The Sunday Times Insight Team *The Falklands War* (1982).

10 See Freddy before he sees you!

1984 Publicity for *A Nightmare on Elm Street*.

11 It's morning again in America.

1984 Campaign slogan for Ronald Reagan's presidential campaign. Quoted in Hedrick Smith *The Power Game* (1988).

12 A desk is a dangerous place from which to view the world.

1985 Sign on desk of American Express president Louis Gerstner. Quoted in the *New York Times*, 26 Jun.

13 Cannes…is 10,000 people looking for 10 people who really count.

1986 Unknown French publicist speaking on the Cannes Film Festival. Quoted in the *New York Times*, 17 May.

14 Art comes to you proposing to give nothing but the highest quality to your moments as they pass.

Inscription on wall of entrance gallery at Dallas' Lloyd Paxton Art and Antiques. Quoted in *Architectural Digest*, May 1986.

15 Save something for the Third Act.

Show business adage applied by President Reagan to his final months in the White House. Quoted in *Time*, 16 Mar 1987.

16 The future ain't what it used to be.

1987 Anonymous Iowa farmer quoted by President Bush on NBC TV, 10 May.

17 There are checks and balances in government—the checks go to candidates and the balance to the people.

Quoted in *Sunday Morning*, CBS TV broadcast, 17 May 1987.

18 Bill was a tropical fish. His native habitat was hot water.

1987 Of William J Casey of the CIA and his role in the Iran arms sales. Quoted in the *New York Times*, 19 Jul.

19 I know one thing we did right
Was the day we started to fight,
Keep your eye on the prize,
Hold on, hold on!

Civil rights song, quoted in Juan Williams *Eye on the Prize* (1987).

20 Skinny cooks can't be trusted.

1987 Quoted by David Cobb Craig in 'Home Cooking Away From Home', *Life*, Jul.

21 Global double zero.

1987 In *Time Magazine*, 3 Aug. This arms control term was applied to Mikhail Gorbachev's agreement for mutual elimination of intermediate and shorter-range missiles in Asia and Europe.

22 Don't die of ignorance.

1987 AIDS awareness campaign slogan.

23 To go to school and finish my schooling without getting pregnant.

1987 15-year old Detroit girl's definition of the American dream. Reported in *Newsweek*, 29 Jan.

24 Mr Elbows and Knees.

1988 Of Democratic presidential nominee Michael S Dukakis. Quoted in *Time*, 21 Nov.

25 We loved your play. We only have problems with your main character, the second act and the ending.

1988 Fan's comment to playwright Wendy Wasserstein on *The Heidi Chronicles*. Quoted in the *New York Times*, 24 Jan 1991.

26 No duties, only opportunities.

Motto of Princeton, NJ, Institute for Advanced Study. Quoted in Ed Regis *Who Got Einstein's Office?* (1988).

27 Before you save the world, you've got to save your
    seat.
    1989 On the need for legislators to keep in close touch with
    their constituents. Quoted in the *New York Times*, 2 Jan.

28 Life is a sexually transmitted disease.
    Graffito, quoted in D J Enright *Faber Book of Fevers and Frets*
    (1989).

29 We're kuwaiting.
    1990 NBC TV broadcast, 16 Aug. The speaker was a US
    serviceman posted to the Gulf after Iraq's invasion of Kuwait.

30 Don't iron while the strike is hot.
    1991 Women's liberation slogan, quoted in PBS broadcast, 26
    Jan.

31 We're here,
    We're queer.
    Get used to it.
    1991 Motto of the homosexual liberation movement, Queer
    Nation, which rejected use of the term 'gay'. Quoted in the *New
    York Times*, 6 Apr.

32 Twelve drawers full of political cancer.
    1991 FBI agent referring to the files of J Edgar Hoover. Quoted
    in *Newsweek*, 23 Sep.

33 A fatheaded, boneheaded, dunderheaded,
    blunderheaded, muttonheaded, knuckleheaded,
    chuckleheaded, puddingheaded, jobernowled
    wash-out of a cock-up.
    1991 Journalist speaking of the poll tax introduced by
    Margaret Thatcher. Quoted in *The Economist*, 3 Dec 1994.

34 He who hath the gold maketh the rule.
    1991 Inscription on plaque in Armand Hammer's bedroom.
    Quoted in *Regardie's*, Feb.

35 Polyester…the most valuable word to come out of
    the 70s, the one that defines tacky for all time.
    1991 'Prettier Poly', *New York Times* editorial, 21 Mar.

36 The heraldic equivalent of a pair of furry dice
    bouncing around in the back of a state coach.
    1992 On the title of Countess of Finchley bestowed on former
    Prime Minister Margaret Thatcher. In the *New Yorker*, 6 Jan.

37 The economy, stupid!
    1992 Sign in the Clinton campaign headquarters which
    became a by-word for the central issue of the 1992 presidential
    campaign. Quoted in *Fortune*, 19 Oct.

38 It's easier to get a photograph of the Pope in the
    shower than a picture of her.
    1993 On Hillary Rodham Clinton's low profile in the period
    between her husband's election and inauguration. In *Newsweek*,
    25 Jan.

39 Behold the turtle, it only makes progress when it
    sticks its neck out.
    Favourite saying of Harvard's president James B Conant.
    Quoted in James G Hershberg *James B Conant* (1993).

40 From the cradle to the grave,

Even if I misbehave,
There's a place for me
On government subsidy.
Quoted by a caller from Baltimore on Station WAMU,
Washington, 15 Jun 1993.

41 Artists and poets are the raw nerve ends of
    humanity. By themselves they can do little to save
    humanity. Without them there would be little
    worth saving.
    Inscription on headstone in Green River Cemetery, Springs NY
    where Jackson Pollock, Elaine de Kooning, and other artists are
    buried. Quoted in the *New York Times*, 17 Aug 1993.

42 To have one's credit cards cancelled is now akin to
    being excommunicated by the medieval church.
    1993 In *Reader's Digest*, Sep.

43 Complete the mission, though I be the lone
    survivor. Never leave a fallen comrade to fall into
    the hands of the enemy.
    1993 *The Ranger's Creed*, quoted in the *New York Times*, 25
    Oct. The Rangers, a US Army unit, had stayed to guard the
    body of a pilot fatally caught in a downed helicopter in Somalia.

44 A potato candidate. The best part of him is
    underground.
    1994 Of Adlai Stevenson and his respectable ancestors. In the
    Washington Post, 9 Jan.

45 I don't know if Mr Kissinger is a great writer, but
    anyone finishing this book is a great reader.
    1994 Unidentified book reviewer quoted by Henry Kissinger
    on the publication of his 900-page *Diplomacy*. In the
    Washington Post, 11 Apr.

46 The castor oil of the Palestinian peace movement.
    1994 Of PLO Chair Yassir Arafat. In NPR broadcast, 4 Jul.

47 He looks like a homeless man in a thousand dollar
    suit.
    1994 On Senator Edward M Kennedy's campaign for re-
    election at age 62. In the *Washington Post*, 1 Oct.

48 If you are not the lead dog, the view never changes.
    Paperweight on the desk of Richard Scott, chief executive
    officer, Hospital Corp of America. Quoted in *Forbes*, 10 Oct
    1994.

49 The President is a walking dead man. He just
    doesn't know it yet.
    1994 Senior legislator on President Clinton's political future as
    he entered the second half of his term of office. In *Nightline*,
    ABC TV broadcast, 6 Dec.

50 Running a cemetery is just like being President:
    you got a lot of people under you and nobody's
    listening.
    Quoted by Bill Clinton, 10 Jan 1995.

51 Has he reconnected with the angry middle?
    1995 Listener's question on Clinton's rapport with the middle
    class after the State of the Union speech. In NPR broadcast, 26
    Jan.

52 I'm spending my children's inheritance.
Bumper sticker alluding to the economics of Social Security. Quoted in the *New York Times*, 24 Feb 1995.

53 Louisianans don't tolerate corruption; they demand it.
1995 In the *New York Times*, 5 Mar.

54 Welfare should be a safety-net, not a hammock.
1995 In NPR broadcast, 12 Mar.

55 To avoid criticism, say nothing, do nothing, be nothing.
Inscription on a pillow given Claudia ('Lady Bird') Johnson by her staff. Quoted in *Life*, Apr 1995.

56 Hussein isn't just sitting on the fence; he *is* the fence.
1995 Unknown US diplomat on Jordan's King Hussein prior to making peace with Palestine. Quoted in *The Times*, 22 Jul.

57 The French want to attack, the Americans want to bomb, and the British want to have another meeting.
1995 US diplomat commenting on the war in Bosnia. Quoted by William Safire in the *New York Times*, 27 Jul.

58 You can't expect the Rapid Reaction Force to be ready immediately.
1995 On the British force being sent to Bosnia. Military spokesperson interviewed on BBC Radio 4's *Today* programme.

59 Craft is the handprint of all culture.
1995 On exhibit of metal and ceramic work displayed at the White House. In *Sunday Morning*, CBS TV, 30 Apr.

60 An apple a day keeps the doctor away.
Proverb.

61 It's 105 degrees in Saigon and rising.
Prearranged coded signal for US citizens and their dependents to assemble at evacuation points during Vietnam War. Quoted in Walter Isaacson *Kissinger* (1992).

62 It's what's in the grooves that counts.
Slogan of Tamla Motown Records.

63 Let no-one enter who does not know his geometry.
Inscription at the entrance of Plato's Academy. Reported by commentators on Aristotle (Elias *In Aristotelis categorias commentarium*, 18, 118, 18).

64 Twelve Highlanders and a bagpipe make a rebellion.
Scottish proverb.

65 Wha daur meddle wi' me?
Scots paraphrase of the Scottish royal motto, 'Nemo me impune lacessit' ('No one provokes me with impunity').

66 When the world was made, the rubbish was sent to Stockport.
Quoted in Wolfgang Mieder *Investigations of Proverbs, Proverbial Expressions, Quotations and Clichés* (1984), in turn taken from *Notes and Queries* (1871).

67 *Resta viator et lege!*
Stand still, traveller, and read!
Corpus Inscriptionum Latinarum III, 371 (From Cyzicus in Mysia).

68 *Salud, Dinero, Amor…y Tiempo.*
Health, Wealth, Love…and Time to enjoy them.
Traditional Spanish wedding toast.

Anouilh, Jean 1910–87
French playwright. The author of light comedies, historical pieces and tragedies, his plays include *Antigone* (1944), *Ring Round the Moon* (1947) and *Becket, or the Honour of God* (1959).

69 *Faire l'amour avec une femme qui ne vous plaît pas, c'est aussi triste que de travailler.*
To make love with a woman whom you do not like is as sad as going to work.
1931 *L'Hermine*, act 1.

70 *Je sais de quelles petitesses meurent les plus grandes amours.*
I know how pettiness ruins the greatest loves.
1931 *L'Hermine*, act 2.

71 *Nous voulons tous louer à l'année et nous ne pouvons jamais louer que pour une semaine ou pour un jour. C'est l'image de la vie.*
We would all like to lease for a year and we can only lease for a week or from day to day. That is the image of life.
1937 *Le Rendez-vous de Senlis*, act 1.

72 *Il y aura toujours un chien perdu quelque part qui m'empêchera d'être heureux.*
There will always be a lost dog somewhere that will prevent me being happy.
1938 *La Sauvage*, act 3.

73 *La mort ne fait jamais mal. La mort est douce… Ce qui fait souffrir avec certains poisons, certaines blessures maladroites, c'est la vie. C'est le reste de vie. Il faut se confier franchement à la mort comme une amie.*
Death never hurts. Death is sweet… Life is what makes us suffer with its poisons and awkward injuries. That's what remains of life. We must confide freely in death as we would in a friend.
1941 *Eurydice*, act 1.

74 *C'est bon pour les hommes de croire aux idées et de mourir pour elles.*
It is good for people to believe in ideas and die for them.
1944 *Antigone*.

75 *C'est plein de disputes, un bonheur.*
Happiness is full of strife.
1944 *Antigone*.

76 *Rien n'est vrai que ce qu'on ne dit pas.*

Nothing is true except that which is unsaid.
1944 *Antigone.*

77 *Chacun de nous a un jour, plus ou moins triste, plus ou moins lointain, où il doit enfin accepter d'être un homme.*

There will come a day for each of us, more or less sad, more or less distant, when we must accept the condition of being human.
1944 *Antigone.*

78 *Mourir, ce n'est rien. Commence donc par vivre. C'est moins drôle et c'est plus long.*

To die is nothing. Begin by living. It's less funny and lasts longer.
1946 *Roméo et Jeannette*, act 3.

79 *Vous savez bien que l'amour, c'est avant tout le don de soi!*

Above all, you must understand that love is the gift of oneself!
1949 *Ardèle.*

80 *Dieu est avec tout le monde... Et, en fin de compte, il est toujours avec ceux qui ont beaucoup d'argent et de grosses armées.*

God is on everyone's side... And, in the last analysis, he is on the side with plenty of money and large armies.
1953 *L'Alouette (The Lark).*

St Anselm 1033–1109

Italian cleric, scholar and scholastic philosopher, author of numerous philosophical and devotional treatises. In 1078 he became Abbot of Bec, in Normandy, and in 1093 was appointed Archbishop of Canterbury.

81 *Neque enim quaero ut credem, sed credo ut intelligam.*

For I do not seek to understand so that I may believe; but I believe so that I may understand.
1078 *Proslogion*, ch.1 (translated by M J Charlesworth).

82 *Id quod mains non cogitari potest.*

That than which a greater cannot be thought.
1078 Of God. *Proslogion*, ch.3. His famous ontological argument for the existence of God. Since a being that exists is necessarily greater than a being that does not, God must by this definition exist.

Antheil, George 1900–59

US composer, of Polish descent. His controversial modernistic works included the *Jazz Symphony* (1925) and the *Ballet Mécanique* (1927), written for 10 pianos and a variety of eccentric percussion instruments.

83 Art cannot hold its breath too long without dying.
1945 *Bad Boy of Music.*

Anthony, Susan B(rownell) 1820–1906

US social reformer and women's suffrage leader. A campaigner in temperance and anti-slavery movements, she co-founded the National Women's Suffrage Association with Elizabeth Cady (1869).

84 The true Republic: men, their rights and nothing more; women, their rights and nothing less.
1868–70 On the front of her newspaper, *The Revolution.*

85 There will never be complete equality until women themselves help to make laws and to elect lawmakers.
In *The Arena.*

Antiphon 5c BC

Greek philosopher and sophist. Only fragments survive of his works.

86 The greatest cost, namely time.
Quoted in Plutarch *Antonius*, 28.

Apelles 4c BC

Greek painter, probably born in Colophon on the Ionian coast of Asia Minor.

87 *Ne supra crepidam sutor iudicaret.*

Let the cobbler stick to his last.
Quoted in Pliny *Naturalis Historia*, 35.36.85. A cobbler who had criticized Apelles' way of rendering a sandal in one of his paintings, proceeded to criticize the rest of the painting as well. The expression became proverbial.

Apollinaire, Guillaume originally *Wilhelm Apollinaris de Kostrowitzki* 1880–1918

French poet and author of Polish–Italian parentage. Associated with avant-garde literary groups, he is said to have invented the word 'surrealism'.

88 *Et toi mon coeur pourquoi bats-tu*
Comme un guetteur mélancolique
J'observe la nuit et la mort.

And you my heart why do you pound
Like some melancholy watchman
I watch the night and death.
1899 *Le Guetteur mélancolique*, préface.

89 *Avant tout, les artistes sont des hommes qui veulent devenir inhumains.*

Above all, artists are men who want to become inhuman.
1913 *Les Peintres cubistes*; *Méditations esthétiques*, 'Sur la peinture, 1'.

90 *Un Picasso étudie un objet comme un chirurgien dissèque un cadavre.*

A Picasso studies an object like a surgeon dissects a corpse.
1913 *Les Peintres cubistes*; *Méditations esthétiques*, 'Sur la peinture, 2'.

91 *La géométrie est aux arts plastiques ce que la grammaire est à l'art de l'écrivain.*

Geometry is to sculpture what grammar is to the art of the writer.

1913 *Les Peintres cubistes; Méditations esthétiques,* 'Sur la peinture, 3'.

92 *Sous le pont Mirabeau coule la Seine.*
Et nos amours, faut-il qu'il m'en souvienne?
La joie venait toujours après la peine.

Under Mirabeau Bridge flows the Seine.
And our loves, must I remember them?
Joy always came after pain.

1913 *Les Alcools,* 'Le Pont Mirabeau'.

93 *Vienne la nuit sonne l'heure*
Les jours s'en vont je demeure.

Let night come, ring out the hour,
The days go by, I remain.

1913 *Les Alcools,* 'Le Pont Mirabeau'.

94 *Je connais gens de toutes sortes*
Ils n'égalent pas leur destin.

I know people of all sorts
They do not measure up to their destiny.

1913 *Les Alcools,* 'Marizibill'.

95 *L'art, de plus en plus, aura une patrie.*

Art, more and more, will have a country.

1913 'L'Esprit nouveau et les poètes', *Mercure de France.*

96 *Il est grand temps de rallumer les étoiles.*

It's high time we relit the stars.

1917 *Les Mamelles de Tirésias,* prologue.

97 *Perdre*
Mais perdre vraiment
Pour laisser place à la trouvaille
Perdre
La vie pour trouver la Victoire.

To lose
But really to lose
And make room for discovery
To lose
Life so as to discover Victory.

1918 *Calligrammes,* 'Toujours'.

Appleton, Sir Edward Victor 1892–1965

English physicist, Professor at London University (1924) and Cambridge (1936). He discovered the Appleton layer of electrically charged particles in the Earth's upper atmosphere, and was awarded the 1947 Nobel Prize for Physics.

98 You must not miss Whitehall. At one end you will find a statue of one of our kings who was beheaded; at the other, a monument to the man who did it. That is just one example of our attempts to be fair to everybody.

1948 Speech, Stockholm, 1 Jan.

99 I do not mind what language an opera is sung in so long as it is a language I don't understand.

1955 In *The Observer,* 28 Aug.

Appleton, Thomas Gold 1812–84

US man of letters and wit, the brother-in-law of Henry Wadsworth Longfellow. His own literary output consisted of formal poetry and pleasant essays and is collected in *Faded Leaves* (1872) and *A Sheaf of Papers* (1875).

1 Good Americans, when they die, go to Paris.

Quoted in Oliver Wendell Holmes *The Autocrat at the Breakfast Table* (1858), ch.6. Although the speaker in Holmes's book is not identified by name, he is generally identified as Appleton.

2 Boston is a state of mind.

Attributed. This quotation has also been attributed to Ralph Waldo Emerson and Mark Twain.

3 A Boston man is the east wind made flesh.

Attributed.

Aquinas, St Thomas 1225–74

Italian Dominican monk and leading scholastic theologian, known as The Angelic Doctor. He was the first to attempt a complete theological system, and as Doctor of the Church his work is particularly respected in the Roman Catholic tradition.

4 *Pulchitrudo enim creaturae nihil est aliud quam similitudo divinae pulchritudinis in rebus partecipita.*

The beauty of creatures is nothing other than an image of the divine beauty in which things participate.

c.1260 *Commentarium in Dionysii De Divinibus Nominibus,* bk.4, ch.5.

5 *Pangue, lingua, gloriosi*
Corporis mysterium,
Sanguinisque pretiosi,
Quem in mundi pretium
Fructus ventris generosi
Rex effudit gentium.

Now, my tongue, the mystery telling
Of the glorious Body sing,
And the Blood, all price excelling,
Which the Gentiles' Lord and King,
In a Virgin's womb once dwelling,
Shed for this world's ransoming.

1263 *Pangue Lingua Gloriosi,* known as the Corpus Christi hymn (translated by J M Neale et al).

6 *Tantum ergo sacramentum*
Veneremur cernui;
Et antiquum documentum
Novo cedat ritui.

Therefore we, before him bending,
This great Sacrament revere;
Types and shadows have their ending,

For the newer rite is here.

1263 *Pangue Lingua Gloriosi*, known as the Corpus Christi hymn (translated by J M Neale et al).

7 *Solus homo delectatur in ipsa pulchitrudine sensibilium secundum seipsam.*

Only man delights in the beauty of sense objects for their own sake.

c.1268 *Summa Theologia*, bk.1, question 91, article 3.

8 *Ars autem deficit ab operatione naturae.*

Art pales when compared to the workings of nature.

c.1272 *Summa Theologia*, bk. 3, question 66, article 4.

Arbuthnot, John 1667–1735

Scottish physician and writer, who published five satirical pamphlets against the Duke of Marlborough in 1712, under the title *The History of John Bull.*

9 Law is a bottomless pit.

1712 *The History of John Bull*, title of pamphlet.

10 Hame's hame, be it never so hamely.

1712 *The History of John Bull*, 'John Bull Still in His Senses', ch.3.

11 Curle (who is one of the new terrors of Death) has been writing letters to every body for memoirs of his life.

1733 Letter to Jonathan Swift, 13 Jan.

Archer, Jeffrey Howard, Lord 1940–

English politician and writer. A Conservative MP (1969–74), he resigned from the Commons after a financial disaster and turned to fiction, becoming a best-selling author of political potboilers.

12 Not a Penny More, Not a Penny Less.

1975 Title of novel.

13 First Among Equals.

1984 Title of novel.

Archimedes c.287–212 BC

Greek mathematician, whose innovations included siege-engines and the Archimedean screw for water raising. He was killed at the Roman siege of Syracuse.

14 Give me a firm spot on which to stand, and I shall move the earth.

Traditionally attributed to Archimedes; a variation can be found in Plutarch *Marcellus*, 14.

15 Eureka, Eureka! (I found it, I found it!).

Vitruvius 9.9.10. Attributed, on discovering the principle of upthrust on a floating body while having a bath. Archimedes had been given the task of establishing whether there was the proper weight of gold in the crown of Hieron of Syracuse. One day when entering his bath he noticed the water which flowed over the sides as he entered and he correctly perceived that the weight of the water displaced was that of the weight of his body.

Arenas, Reinaldo 1943–90

Cuban novelist. He held several minor positions in Cuba before leaving the country in 1980 for the US. He committed suicide in New York while suffering from AIDS.

16 *Nuestro portero descubrió, o creyó descubrir, que su labor no se podía limitar a abrir la puerta del edificio, sino que él, el portero, era el señalado, el elegido, el indicado…para mostrarles a todas aquellas personas una puerta más amplia y hasta entonces invisible o inaccesible; puerta que era la de sus propias vidas.*

Our doorman discovered (or thought he had discovered) that his tasks could not be limited to just opening the door of the building—but that he, the doorman, was the one *chosen, elected, singled out*…to show everyone who lived there a wider door, until then either invisible or inaccessible: the door to their own lives.

1989 *El portero* (*The Doorman*, 1961), pt.1, ch.1.

Aretino, Pietro 1492–1557

Italian poet, illegitimate son of a nobleman. Banished from his native town, he wandered through Italy. His wit secured the favour of Pope Leo X, subsequently lost with the salacious *Sonetti Lussuriosi*. Later patrons included Giovanni de Medici, Francis I and Charles V. He reputedly died by falling from a stool while laughing.

17 I am a free man, I do not need to copy Petrarch or Boccaccio. My own genius is enough. Let others worry themselves about style and so cease to be themselves. Without a master, without a model, without a guide, without artifice, I go to work and earn my living, my well-being, and my fame. What do I need more? With a goose quill and a few sheets of paper I mock the universe.

Quoted in J H Plumb (ed) *The Horizon Book of the Renaissance* (1961, new edn by Penguin, 1982).

Arguedas, José María 1911–69

Peruvian fiction writer and ethnologist. His works reflect the tensions that underlie Peruvian society, in the marginalization of native peoples. He committed suicide.

18 *¿Dónde está la patria, amigo? Ni en el corazón ni en la saliva.*

Where is the country, my friend? It is not in the heart or in the saliva.

1971 *El zorro de arriba y el zorro de abajo* ('The Upper and the Lower Fox'), ch.3.

Ariosto, Ludovico 1474–1533

Italian poet. He joined the court of Cardinal Ippolito d'Este at Ferrara in 1503, where he produced his most famous work, the Roland epic, *Orlando Furioso* (completed 1516, enlarged 1532). He also wrote comedies, satires and sonnets.

19 *Natura il fece, e poi roppe la stampa.*

Nature made him, and then broke the mould.
1516 *Orlando Furioso, canto 10, stanza 84.*

Aristophanes c.448–c.388 BC

Greek comic poet. Only 11 comedies survive of his 54 plays; they are characterized by exaggeration, parody and satire of contemporary political and cultural life.

20 Who brings owls to Athens?
Avae (The Birds), l.301. This ancient proverb, quoted by various authors, is the equivalent of 'to carry coals to Newcastle'.

21 Old age is second childhood.
Nubes (The Clouds), l.1417.

22 Till the wolf and the lamb be united.
On the impossibility of peace between sworn enemies. *Pax*, l.1076.

Aristotle 384–322 BC

Greek philosopher, scientist and physician, a student of Plato and tutor to Alexander the Great. His philosophical works include *Metaphysics, Politics, Rhetoric* and *Poetics*. His influence has been incalculable; in medieval Europe he was known simply as 'The Philosopher'.

23 All men naturally desire knowledge.
Metaphysics, bk.1, ch.1, 980a (translated by H Tredennick).

24 It is through wonder that men now begin and originally began to philosophize; wondering in the first place at obvious perplexities, and then by gradual progression raising questions about the greater matters too.
Metaphysics, bk.1, ch.2, 982 (translated by H Tredennick).

25 Every art and every inquiry, and similarly every action and pursuit, is thought to aim at some good; and for this reason the good has rightly been declared to be that at which all things aim.
Nicomachean Ethics, bk.1, ch.1, 1093 (translated by Sir David Ross).

26 Human good turns out to be activity of soul exhibiting excellence, and if there is more than one sort of excellence, in accordance with the best and most complete. For one swallow does not make a summer, nor does one day; and so too one day, or a short time, does not make a man blessed and happy.
Nicomachean Ethics, bk.1, ch.7, 1098 (translated by Sir David Ross).

27 Virtue, then, is a state of character concerned with choice, lying in a mean...it is a mean between two vices, that which depends on excess and that which depends on defect.
Nicomachean Ethics, bk.2, ch.6, 1006 (translated by Sir David Ross).

28 For man, therefore, the life according to reason is best and pleasantest, since reason more than anything else *is* man.
Nicomachean Ethics, bk.10, ch.7, 1178 (translated by Sir David Ross).

29 Tragedy is thus a representation of an action that is worth serious attention, complete in itself and of some amplitude...by means of pity and fear bringing about the purgation of such emotions.
c.330BC *Poetics*, ch.6.

30 Now a whole is that which has a beginning, a middle, and an end.
c.330BC *Poetics*, ch.7, referring to tragedy.

31 Man is by nature a political animal; it is his nature to live in a state.
c.330BC *Politics*, bk.1, ch.2, 1253a (translated by T A Sinclair).

32 Nature, as we say, does nothing without some purpose; and for the purpose of making man a political animal she has endowed him alone among the animals with the power of reasoned speech.
c.330BC *Politics*, bk.1, ch.2, 1253b (translated by T A Sinclair).

33 It is a bad thing that many from being rich should become poor; for men of ruined fortunes are sure to stir up revolutions.
c.330BC *Politics*, bk.4.

34 The flute is not an instrument that has a good moral effect—it is too exciting.
c.330 BC *Politics*.

35 For that which has become habitual, becomes as it were natural.
Rhetorica, 1370a (translated by J H Freese).

36 *Amicus Plato, sed magis amica veritas.*

Plato is dear to me, but dearer still is truth.
Proverbial expression, traditionally attributed to Aristotle, going back to a passage in the *Ethica Nicomachea*, 1069a.

Arlott, (Leslie Thomas) John 1914–91

English cricket commentator and writer, a police detective before joining the BBC in 1945. His voice became the epitome of radio cricket commentary.

37 The Master: records prove the title good:
Yet figures fail you, for they cannot say
How many men whose names you never knew
Are proud to tell their sons they saw you play.

They share the sunlight of your summer day
Of thirty years; and they, with you, recall
How, through those well-wrought centuries, your hand
Reshaped the history of bat and ball.
1952 'To John Berry Hobbs on his Seventieth Birthday'.

38 Cricket, like the novel, is great when it presents men in the round, when it shows the salty quality of human nature.

1953 Quoted in Colin Jarman *The Guinness Dictionary of Sports Quotations* (1990).

39 Most games are skin-deep, but cricket goes to the bone.

1977 *Arlott and Trueman on Cricket.*

40 Cricket is a game of the most terrifying stresses with more luck about it than any other game I know. They call it a team game, but in fact it is the loneliest game of all.

Another Word from Arlott.

Arlt, Roberto 1900–42

Argentinian fiction writer, dramatist and journalist. The son of German immigrants, his works emphasize the anger and disillusionment of the urban middle class.

41 ¡Y yo, yo, Señor, no tendré nunca una querida tan linda como esa querida que lucen los cromos de los libros viciosos!

And I, Sir, I'll never have a mistress as beautiful as those in the pictures of obscene books!

1926 *El juguete rabioso* ('The Rabid Toy'), ch.2.

Armey, Dick (Richard Keith) 1940–

US congressman and former economics lecturer, majority leader of the House of Representatives.

42 It is like relying on the Flintstones for an understanding of the Stone Age.

1994 On economic data from the Congressional Budget Office. In *Time*, 25 Nov.

43 Entitlement spending—the politics of greed wrapped in the language of love.

1994 On President Johnson's legacy to his party. In the *US News & World Report*, 12 Dec.

Armistead, Lewis Addison 1777–1863

Confederate general. Commissioned in the US army from Virginia, he resigned when that state seceded. He took part in Picket's charge at Gettysburg, where he was killed.

44 Give them the cold steel, boys!

1863 Attributed, during the American Civil War.

Armstrong, Louis known as Satchmo 1900–71

US jazz trumpeter and singer, the first major jazz virtuoso. He led studio groups such as the Hot Five and the Hot Seven as well as working with many big bands, and as a singer introduced the scat style. He toured extensively and appeared in over 50 films as a musician and entertainer.

45 Musicians don't retire; they stop when there's no more music in them.

1968 Quoted in *The Observer*, 21 Apr.

46 If you still have to ask…shame on you.

Habitual response when asked what is jazz? Quoted in M Jones *Salute to Satchmo* (1970).

47 All music is folk music. I ain't never heard no horse sing a song.

Quoted in the *New York Times*, 7 Jul 1971.

48 A lotta cats copy the Mona Lisa, but people still line up to see the original.

Alluding to his many imitators. Quoted in David Pickering *Brewer's Twentieth Century Music* (1994).

Armstrong, Neil A(lden) 1930–

US astronaut. A former fighter pilot, he commanded Gemini 8 (1966) and in 1969 was a crew member of Apollo 11, and the first man to walk on the moon.

49 That's one small step for a man, one giant leap forward for mankind.

1969 His words on becoming the first man to walk on the moon, 20 Jul. Armstrong claimed to have said 'That's one small step for a man…', but tape-recordings seem to confirm that he omitted the 'a', thereby causing some confusion among his listeners.

50 I believe every human has a finite number of heartbeats. I don't intend to waste any of mine running around doing exercises.

Quoted in Colin Jarman *The Guinness Dictionary of Sports Quotations* (1990).

Armstrong, Robert, Baron Armstrong of Ilminster 1927–

English civil servant. In 1970 he became principal private secretary to Prime Minister Edward Heath, and later Secretary to the Cabinet and Head of the Home Civil Service under Margaret Thatcher.

51 It contains a misleading impression, not a lie. It was being economical with the truth.

1986 On a letter, during cross-examination at the 'Spycatcher' trial, New South Wales, Australia, quoted in the *Daily Telegraph*, 19 Nov.

Arnald Amaury d.1225

French clergyman. Abbot of Citeaux (1202–12), he was the first inquisitor against the Albigensian heresy. In 1212 as Bishop of Narbonne he crusaded against the Moors in Spain.

52 Kill them all. God will recognize his own.

1209 Quoted in Caeserius of Heisterbach *Dialogus Miraculorum* (c.1233), bk.5, ch.21. Cited and translated in Jonathon Sumpton *The Albigensian Crusade* (1978), ch.6.

Arnold, Matthew 1822–88

English poet and critic. His poems, mainly elegiac in mood and on pastoral themes, include 'The Forsaken Merman' (1849), 'The Scholar-Gypsy' (1853) and 'Thyrsis' (1867). His critical works include *Essays in Criticism* (1865, 1888) and *Culture and Anarchy* (1869).

53 Come, dear children, let us away;
Down and away below!
1849 *The Strayed Reveller, and Other Poems*, 'The Forsaken Merman', l.1–2.

54 Now the great winds shorewards blow;
Now the salt tides seawards flow;
Now the wild white horses play,
Champ and chafe and toss in the spray.
1849 *The Strayed Reveller, and Other Poems*, 'The Forsaken Merman', l.4–7.

55 Sand-strewn caverns, cool and deep,
Where the winds are all asleep;
Where the spent lights quiver and gleam;
Where the salt weed sways in the stream.
1849 *The Strayed Reveller, and Other Poems*, 'The Forsaken Merman', l.35–8.

56 Where great whales come sailing by,
Sail and sail, with unshut eye,
Round the world for ever and aye.
1849 *The Strayed Reveller, and Other Poems*, 'The Forsaken Merman', l.43–5.

57 Not deep the Poet sees, but wide.
1849 *The Strayed Reveller, and Other Poems*, 'Resignation', l.214.

58 Yet they, believe me, who await
No gifts from chance, have conquered fate.
1849 *The Strayed Reveller, and Other Poems*, 'Resignation', l.247–8.

59 Not milder is the general lot
Because our spirits have forgot,
In action's dizzying eddy whirled,
The something that infects the world.
1849 *The Strayed Reveller, and Other Poems*, 'Resignation', l.275–8.

60 Others abide our question. Thou art free.
We ask and ask: Thou smilest and art still,
Out-topping knowledge.
1849 *The Strayed Reveller, and Other Poems*, 'Shakespeare'.

61 And thou, who didst the stars and sunbeams know,
Self-schooled, self-scanned, self-honoured, self-secure,
Didst tread on Earth unguessed at.—Better so!
All pains the immortal spirit must endure,
All weakness which impairs, all griefs which bow,
Find their sole speech in that victorious brow.
1849 *The Strayed Reveller, and Other Poems*, 'Shakespeare'.

62 Who saw life steadily, and saw it whole:
The mellow glory of the Attic stage;
Singer of sweet Colonus, and its child.
1849 Of Sophocles. *The Strayed Reveller, and Other Poems*, 'To a Friend'.

63 France, famed in all great arts, in none supreme.
1849 *The Strayed Reveller, and Other Poems*, 'To a Republican Friend—Continued'.

64 The sea of faith
Lay like the folds of a bright girdle furled.
But now I only hear
Its melancholy, long, withdrawing roar,
Retreating, to the breath
Of the night-wind, down the vast edges drear
And naked shingles of the world.
1851 'Dover Beach', stanza 3.

65 And we are here as on a darkling plain
Swept with confused alarms of struggle and flight,
Where ignorant armies clash by night.
1851 'Dover Beach', stanza 4.

66 Be neither saint nor sophist-led, but be a man.
1852 'Empedocles on Etna', act 1, sc.2, l.136.

67 Is it so small a thing
To have enjoyed the sun,
To have lived light in the spring,
To have loved, to have thought, to have done.
1852 'Empedocles on Etna', act 1, sc.2, l.397–400.

68 Because thou must not dream, thou needst not then despair!
1852 'Empedocles on Etna', act 1, sc.2, l.426.

69 And we forget because we must
And not because we will.
1852 *Empedocles on Etna and Other Poems*, 'Absence'.

70 Only—but this is rare—
When a beloved hand is laid in ours,
When, jaded with the rush and glare
Of the interminable hours,
Our eyes can in another's eyes read clear,
When our world-deafened ear
Is by the tones of a loved voice caressed—
A bolt is shot back somewhere in our breast,
And a lost pulse of feeling stirs again.
The eye sinks inward, and the heart lies plain,
And what we mean, we say, and what we would, we know.
1852 *Empedocles on Etna and Other Poems*, 'The Buried Life', l.77–87.

71 Come to me in my dreams, and then
By day I shall be well again!
For then the night will more than pay
The hopeless longing of the day.
1852 *Empedocles on Etna and Other Poems*, 'Longing' (later published as 'Faded Leaves' in *Poems: Second Series*, 1855).

72 Calm soul of all things! make it mine
To feel, amid the city's jar,
That there abides a peace of thine,
Man did not make, and cannot mar.
1852 *Empedocles on Etna and Other Poems*, 'Lines written in Kensington Garden'.

73 He spoke, and loosed our heart in tears.
    He laid us as we lay at birth
    On the cool flowery lap of earth.
    1852 Of William Wordsworth. *Empedocles on Etna and Other Poems*, 'Memorial Verses, April 1850', l.47–9.

74 With aching hands and bleeding feet
    We dig and heap, lay stone on stone;
    We bear the burden and the heat
    Of the long day, and wish 'twere done.
    Not till the hours of light return,
    All we have built do we discern.
    1852 *Empedocles on Etna and Other Poems*, 'Morality'.

75 Say, has some wet bird-haunted English lawn
    Lent it the music of its trees at dawn?
    1852 *Empedocles on Etna and Other Poems*, 'Parting', l.19–20.

76 Resolve to be thyself: and know, that he
    Who finds himself, loses his misery.
    1852 *Empedocles on Etna and Other Poems*, 'Self-Dependence', l.31–2.

77 Ah! two desires toss about
    The poet's feverish blood.
    One drives him to the world without,
    And one to solitude.
    1852 *Empedocles on Etna and Other Poems*, 'Stanzas in Memory of the Author of 'Obermann'', l.93–6.

78 Still bent to make some port he knows not where,
    Still standing for some false impossible shore.
    1852 *Empedocles on Etna and Other Poems*, 'A Summer Night', l.68–9.

79 Yes! in the sea of life enisled,
    With echoing straits between us thrown,
    Dotting the shoreless watery wild,
    We mortal millions live alone.
    1852 *Empedocles on Etna and Other Poems*, 'To Marguerite—Continued', l.1–4.

80 A God, a God their severance ruled!
    And bade betwixt their shores to be
    The unplumbed, salt, estranging sea.
    1852 *Empedocles on Etna and Other Poems*, 'To Marguerite—Continued', l.22–4.

81 I am past thirty, and three parts iced over.
    1853 Letter to Arthur Hugh Clough, 12 Feb

82 Hark! ah, the Nightingale!
    The tawny-throated!
    Hark! from that moonlit cedar what a burst!
    What triumph! hark—what pain!
    1853 *Poems: A New Edition*, 'Philomela', l.1–4.

83 Eternal Passion!
    Eternal Pain!
    1853 *Poems: A New Edition*, 'Philomela', l.31–2.

84 Her cabined ample Spirit,

It fluttered and failed for breath.
Tonight it doth inherit
The vasty hall of death.
1853 *Poems: A New Edition*, 'Requiescat'.

85 Go, for they call you, Shepherd, from the hill.
    1853 *Poems: A New Edition*, 'The Scholar-Gipsy', l.1.

86 All the live murmur of a summer's day.
    1853 *Poems: A New Edition*, 'The Scholar-Gipsy', l.20.

87 Tired of knocking at Preferment's door.
    1853 *Poems: A New Edition*, 'The Scholar-Gipsy', l.35.

88 Crossing the stripling Thames at Bab-lock-hithe,
    Trailing in the cool stream thy fingers wet,
    As the slow punt swings round.
    1853 *Poems: A New Edition*, 'The Scholar-Gipsy', l.74–6.

89 Rapt, twirling in thy hand a withered spray,
    And waiting for the spark from heaven to fall.
    1853 *Poems: A New Edition*, 'The Scholar-Gipsy', l.119–20.

90 The line of festal light in Christ-Church hall.
    1853 *Poems: A New Edition*, 'The Scholar-Gipsy', l.129.

91 Thou waitest for the spark from heaven! and we,
    Light half-believers in our casual creeds…
    Who hesitate and falter life away,
    And lose tomorrow the ground won today—
    Ah, do not we, Wanderer, await it too?
    1853 *Poems: A New Edition*, 'The Scholar-Gipsy', l.171–4.

92 O born in days when wits were fresh and clear,
    And life ran gaily as the sparkling Thames:
    Before this strange disease of modern life,
    With its sick hurry, its divided aims,
    Its heads o'ertaxed, its palsied hearts, was rife—
    Fly hence, our contact fear!
    1853 *Poems: A New Edition*, 'The Scholar-Gipsy', l.201–6.

93 Still nursing the unconquerable hope,
    Still clutching the inviolable shade.
    1853 *Poems: A New Edition*, 'The Scholar-Gipsy', l.211–12.

94 Curled minion, dancer, coiner of sweet words!
    1853 *Poems: A New Edition*, 'Sohrab and Rustum', l.458.

95 No horse's cry was that, most like the roar
    Of some pained desert lion, who all day
    Hath trailed the hunter's javelin in his side,
    And comes at night to die upon the sand.
    1853 *Poems: A New Edition*, 'Sohrab and Rustum', l.501–4.

96 Truth sits upon the lips of dying men.
    1853 *Poems: A New Edition*, 'Sohrab and Rustum', l.656.

97 But the majestic river floated on,
    Out of the mist and hum of that low land,
    Into the frosty starlight.
    1853 *Poems: A New Edition*, 'Sohrab and Rustum', l.875–7.

98 Oxus, forgetting the bright speed he had
    In his high mountain cradle in Pamere,
    A foiled circuitous wanderer—till at last
    The longed-for dash of waves is heard, and wide
    His luminous home of waters opens, bright
    And tranquil, from whose floor the new-bathed
        stars
    Emerge, and shine upon the Aral Sea.
    1853 *Poems: A New Edition*, 'Sohrab and Rustrum', l.886–92.

99 Cruel, but composed and bland,
    Dumb, inscrutable and grand,
    So Tiberious might have sat,
    Had Tiberius been a cat.
    1855 *Poems: Second Series*, 'Poor Matthias', l.40–3.

1   For rigorous teachers seized my youth,
    And other its faith, and trimmed its fire,
    Showed me the high, white star of Truth,
    There bade me gaze, and there aspire.
    1855 *Poems: Second Series*, 'Stanzas from the Grande Chartreuse', l.67–70.

2   Wandering between two worlds, one dead,
    The other powerless to be born,
    With nowhere yet to rest my head,
    Like these, on earth I wait forlorn.
    1855 *Poems: Second Series*, 'Stanzas from the Grande Chartreuse', l.85–8.

3   What helps it now, that Byron bore,
    With haughty scorn which mocked the smart,
    Through Europe to the Aetolian shore
    The pageant of his bleeding heart?
    That thousands counted every groan,
    And Europe made his woe her own?
    1855 *Poems: Second Series*, 'Stanzas from the Grande Chartreuse', l.133–8.

4   This truth—to prove, and make thine own:
    'Thou hast been, shalt be, art, alone.'
    1857 'Isolation. To Marguerite', l.29-30.

5   Wordsworth says somewhere that wherever Virgil
    seems to have composed 'with his eye on the
    object', Dryden fails to render him. Homer
    invariably composes 'with his eye on the object',
    whether the object be moral or a material one: Pope
    composes with his eye on his style, into which he
    translates his object, whatever it is.
    1861 *On Translating Homer*, lecture 1.

6   Of these two literatures [French and German], as of
    the intellect of Europe in general, the main effort,
    for now many years, has been a critical effort; the
    endeavours, in all branches of knowledge—
    theology, philosophy, history, art, science—to see
    the object as in itself it really is.
    1861 *On Translating Homer*, lecture 2.

7   [The translator] will find one English book and one
    only, where, as in the *Illiad* itself, perfect plainness
    of speech is allied with perfect nobleness; and that
    book is the Bible.
    1861 *On Translating Homer*, lecture 3.

8   Nothing has raised more questioning among my
    critics than these words—noble, the grand style... I
    think it will be found that the grand style arises in
    poetry, when a noble nature, poetically gifted,
    treats with simplicity or with severity a serious
    subject.
    1862 *On Translating Homer; Last Words*.

9   Nothing could moderate, in the bosom of the great
    English middle class, their passionate, absorbing,
    almost blood-thirsty clinging to life.
    1865 *Essays in Criticism First Series*, preface.

10 Beautiful city! so venerable, so lovely, so unravaged
    by the fierce intellectual life of our century, so
    serene!...whispering from her towers the last
    enchantments of the Middle Age... Home of lost
    causes, and forsaken beliefs, and unpopular names,
    and impossible loyalties!
    1865 Of Oxford. *Essays in Criticism First Series*, preface.

11 I am bound by my own definition of criticism: a
    disinterested endeavour to learn and propagate the
    best that is known and thought in the world.
    1865 *Essays in Criticism First Series*, 'The Function of Criticism at the Present Time'.

12 Philistinism!—We have not the expression in
    English. Perhaps we have not the word because we
    have so much of the thing.
    1865 *Essays in Criticism First Series*, 'Heinrich Heine'.

13 The great apostle of the Philistine, Lord Macaulay.
    1865 *Essays in Criticism First Series*, 'Joubert'.

14 The signal-elm, that looks on Ilsley downs,
    The Vale, the three lone weirs, the youthful
        Thames.
    1866 *New Poems*, 'Thyrsis', l.14–15. The poem is an elegy for his friend Arthur Hugh Clough, who drowned in 1861.

15 And that sweet City with her dreaming spires,
    She needs not June for beauty's heightening.
    1866 Of Oxford. *New Poems*, 'Thyrsis', l.19–20.

16 So have I heard the cuckoo's parting cry,
    From the wet field, through the vext garden trees,
    Come with the volleying rain and tossing breeze:
    'The bloom is gone, and with the bloom go I.'
    1866 *New Poems*, 'Thyrsis', l.57-60.

17 Too quick despairer, wherefore wilt thou go?
    Soon will the high Midsummer pomps come on,
    Soon will the musk carnations break and swell.
    1866 *New Poems*, 'Thyrsis', l.61–3.

18 For Time, not Corydon, hath conquered thee.
   1866 *New Poems*, 'Thyrsis', l.80.

19 The foot less prompt to meet the morning dew,
   The heart less bounding at emotion new,
   And hope, once crushed, less quick to spring
      again.
   1866 *New Poems*, 'Thyrsis', l.138–40.

20 It is not in the outward and visible world of
   material life that the Celtic genius of Wales or
   Ireland can at this day hope to count for much; it is
   in the inward world of thought and science. What
   it *has* been, what is *has* done, what it will be or will
   do, as a matter of modern politics.
   1867 'On the Study of Celtic Literature'.

21 Let us reunite ourselves with our better mind and
   with the world through science; and let it be one of
   our angelic revenges on the Philistines, who among
   their other sins are the guilty authors of Fenianism,
   to found at Oxford a chair of Celtic, and to send,
   through the gentle ministration of science, a
   message of peace to Ireland.
   1867 'On the Study of Celtic Literature'.

22 Creep into thy narrow bed,
   Creep, and let no more be said!
   Vain thy onset! all stands fast.
   Thou thyself must break at last.
   Let the long contention cease!
   Geese are swans, and swans are geese.
   Let them have it how they will!
   Thou art tired; best be still.
   1867 *New Poems*, 'The Last Word'.

23 Coldly, sadly descends
   The autumn evening. The field
   Strewn with its dank yellow drifts
   Of withered leaves, and the elms,
   Fade into dimness apace,
   Silent;—hardly a shout
   From a few boys late at their play!
   1867 *New Poems*, 'Rugby Chapel, November 1857'.

24 Our society distributes itself into Barbarians,
   Philistines, and Populace; and America is just
   ourselves, with the Barbarians quite left out, and
   the Populace nearly.
   1869 *Culture and Anarchy*, preface.

25 The pursuit of perfection, then, is the pursuit of
   sweetness and light… He who works for sweetness
   and light united, works to make reason and the will
   of God prevail.
   1869 *Culture and Anarchy*, ch.1.

26 The men of culture are the true apostles of equality.
   1869 *Culture and Anarchy*, ch.1.

27 That vast portion…of the working-class which, raw
   and half-developed has long lain half-hidden amidst
   its poverty and squalor, and is now issuing from its
   hiding-place to assert an Englishman's heaven-born
   privilege of doing as he likes, and is beginning to
   perplex us by marching where it likes, meeting
   where it likes, bawling what it likes, breaking what
   it likes—to this vast residuum we may with great
   propriety give the name of Populace.
   1869 *Culture and Anarchy*, ch.3.

28 Hebraism and Hellenism—between these two
   points of influence moves our world.
   1869 *Culture and Anarchy*, ch.4.

29 'He knows' says Hebraism, 'his Bible!'—whenever
   we hear this said, we may, without any elaborate
   defence of culture, content ourselves with
   answering simply: 'No man, who knows nothing
   else, knows even his Bible.'
   1869 *Culture and Anarchy*, ch.5.

30 Culture, the acquainting ourselves with the best
   that has been known and said in the world, and
   thus with the history of the human spirit.
   1873 *Literature and Dogma*, preface.

31 Culture is the passion for sweetness and light, and
   (what is more) the passion for making them prevail.
   1873 *Literature and Dogma*, preface.

32 The true meaning of religion is thus not simply
   morality, but morality touched with emotion.
   1873 *Literature and Dogma*, ch.1.

33 Conduct is three-fourths of our life and its largest
   concern.
   1873 *Literature and Dogma*, ch.1.

34 The eternal *not ourselves* that makes for righteousness.
   1873 *Literature and Dogma*, ch.8.

35 But there remains the question: what righteousness
   really is. The method and secret and sweet
   reasonableness of Jesus.
   1873 *Literature and Dogma*, ch.12.

36 So we have the Philistine of genius in religion—
   Luther; the Philistine of genius in politics—
   Cromwell; the Philistine of genius in
   literature—Bunyan.
   1879 *Mixed Essays*, 'Lord Falkland'.

37 The theatre is irresistible: organise the theatre.
   1882 *Irish Essays*, 'The French Play in London'.

38 In poetry, no less than in life, he is 'a beautiful and
   ineffectual angel, beating in the void his luminous
   wings in vain'.
   1888 Of Shelley. *Essays in Criticism Second Series*, 'Shelley'. The
   phrase is a quotation from his own work on Byron.

39 More and more mankind will discover that we have to turn to poetry to interpret life for us, to console us, to sustain us. Without poetry, our science will appear incomplete; and most of what now passes with us for religion and philosophy will be replaced by poetry.
1888 *Essays in Criticism Second Series*, 'The Study of Poetry'.

40 The difference between genuine poetry and the poetry of Dryden, Pope, and all their school, is briefly this: their poetry is conceived and composed in their wits, genuine poetry is conceived and composed in the soul.
1888 *Essays in Criticism Second Series*, 'Thomas Gray'.

41 Poetry is at bottom a criticism of life.
1888 *Essays in Criticism Second Series*, 'Wordsworth'.

42 His expression may often be called bald…but it is bald as the bare mountain tops are bald, with a baldness full of grandeur.
1888 *Essays in Criticism Second Series*, 'Wordsworth'.

Arnold, Thomas 1795–1842

British educator and historian, educational reformer who introduced mathematics, modern languages, and modern history into the curriculum of his day.

43 My object will be, if possible, to form Christian men, for Christian boys I can scarcely hope to make.
1828 Letter to Rev John Tucker, 2 Mar, on being appointed headmaster of Rugby School.

44 Rather than have it the principal thing in my son's mind, I would gladly have him think that the sun went around the earth, and that the stars were so many spangles set in the bright blue firmament.
1836 Letter to Dr Greenhill, 9 May.

Arnold, Thurman Wesley 1891–1969

US lawyer, Professor at Yale (1930–8), Assistant Attorney General in charge of anti-trust enforcement (1938–43) and Associate Justice at the Court of Appeals (1943–5).

45 We must protect big business from domination by fat-minded men whose principal business policy is to avoid a competitive race for efficiency… They believe in a system of soft enterprise,—soft in the way that an octopus is soft, with tentacles that stifle and suffocate.
1942 'The Abuse of Patents', in *Atlantic Monthly*, Jul.

Aron, Raymond Claude Ferdinand 1905–83

French sociologist and journalist, editor of *La France Libre* in London (1940–4).

46 To customs and beliefs, the very ones we hold sacred, sociology ruthlessly attaches the adjective 'arbitrary'.

1971 *Politics and History.*

47 In a way, all sociologists are akin to Marxists because of their inclination to settle everyone's accounts but their own.
1971 *Politics and History.*

Arras, Jean d' also known as Jean Blondel fl.c.1375

French writer. He collaborated with Antoine du Val and Fouquart de Cambrai on the *Évangèle des Quenouilles*, which provides much information on life at the time.

48 *Bonté vaut mieux que beauté.*

Kindness is worth more than beauty.
c.1393 *Melusine.*

Asahi Shimbun

The leading mass-circulation newspaper of Japan.

49 Are we correct to have changed as much as we have? Or is Yokoi correct not to have changed at all?
1972 Editorial comment, 28 Jan, on the discovery of World War II survivor Sergeant Yokoi in the Pacific jungles.

Ascham, Roger 1515–68

English humanist, Protestant and scholar, reader in Greek at Cambridge, and tutor to Princess Elizabeth. He published a defence of archery, *Toxophilus*, in 1545, and is most famous for his treatise on humanist education, *The Schoolmaster* (1570).

50 He that will write well in any tongue, must follow this counsel of Aristotle, to speak as the common people do, to think as wise men do; and so should every man understand him, and the judgment of wise men allow him.
1545 *Toxophilus*, 'To all Gentlemen and Yeomen of England'.

51 Young children [are] sooner allured by love than driven by beating to attain good learning.
1570 *The Schoolmaster*, 'A Preface to the Reader'.

52 For [the] quick in wit and light in manners be either seldom troubled or very soon weary, in carrying a very heavy purse.
1570 *The Schoolmaster*, bk.2.

Ashbery, John Lawrence 1927–

US poet, critic and novelist. Poetry collections include the award-winning *Self-Portrait in a Convex Mirror* (1976).

53 Darkness falls like a wet sponge.
1956 *Some Trees*, 'The Picture of Little J. A. in a Prospect of Flowers', opening line.

54 And it is the colour of sand,

The darkness, as it sifts through your hand.
1962 *The Tennis Court Oath*, 'How Much Longer Will I Be Able To Inhabit The Divine Sepulcher…'.

55 Self-portrait in a Convex Mirror.
1976 Title of book.

56 Slated for demolition.
1979 Complete text of poem entitled 'The Cathedral Is', in *As We Know*.

57 Still I enjoy
The long sweetness of the simultaneity, yours and
  mine, ours and mine,
The mosquitoey summer night light.
1981 *Shadow Train*, 'Here Everything Is Still Floating'.

58 My name has gotten to be a household word—at least in certain households. I think there are now people who know my name, but don't know what I do. I'm famous for being famous.
1985 Interview in *PN Review*, no.46.

59 There is the view that poetry should improve your life. I think people confuse it with the Salvation Army.
1989 In the *International Herald Tribune*, 2 Oct.

Ashdown, Paddy (Jeremy John Durham)
1941–

British politician. After working with the Royal Marines (1959–71) and the diplomatic service (1971–6), he was elected to Parliament in 1983 and became leader of the Social and Liberal Democratic Party on its formation in 1988.

60 Neil Kinnock has travelled the road to Damascus so often, I hear that he has decided to buy himself a season ticket.
1990 At the Liberal Democratic Party conference, Sep.

61 The ringmaster has altered, but the circus remains the same.
1990 On John Major's election as Conservative Party leader, in *The Observer*, 2 Dec.

62 I have learnt from bitter experience that when the armchair theorists and the Whitehall generals start talking of a surgical war, it is time to run for cover.
1991 Referring to plans for the Gulf War. In the *Sunday Times*, 27 Jan.

Ashford, Daisy Mary Margaret   1881–1972

English writer. She wrote her only book, *The Young Visiters*, in 1890, and published the manuscript in 1919. Its childish idiosyncrasies made it a best-seller, and it was adapted for the stage in 1920, and as a musical in 1968.

63 Mr Salteena was an elderly man of 42 and was fond of asking peaple to stay with him.
1890 *The Young Visiters, or Mr Salteena's Plan*, ch.1.

64 You look rather rash my dear your colors don't quite match your face.
1890 *The Young Visiters, or Mr Salteena's Plan*, ch.2.

65 Bernard always had a few prayers in the hall and some whiskey afterwards as he was rather pious but Mr Salteena was not very addicted to prayers so he marched up to bed.
1890 *The Young Visiters, or Mr Salteena's Plan*, ch.3.

66 Oh I see said the Earl but my own idear is that these things are as piffle before the wind.
1890 *The Young Visiters, or Mr Salteena's Plan*, ch.5.

67 I am very fond of fresh air and royalties.
1890 *The Young Visiters, or Mr Salteena's Plan*, ch.5.

68 The bearer of this letter is an old friend of mine not quite the right side of the blanket as they say in fact he is the son of a first rate butcher but his mother was a decent family called Hyssopps of the Glen so you see he is not so bad and is desireus of being the correct article.
1890 *The Young Visiters, or Mr Salteena's Plan*, ch.5.

69 My life will be sour grapes and ashes without you.
1890 *The Young Visiters, or Mr Salteena's Plan*, ch.8.

70 Oh Bernard muttered Ethel this is so sudden. No no cried Bernard and taking the bull by both horns he kissed her violently on her dainty face.
1890 *The Young Visiters, or Mr Salteena's Plan*, ch.9.

71 She had very nice feet and plenty of money.
1890 *The Young Visiters, or Mr Salteena's Plan*, ch.12.

Asimov, Isaac   1920–92

Russian-born US science-fiction novelist and popular scientist. A distinguished biochemist and hugely popular writer, he became a familiar media figure. His works include the 'Foundation' series (1951–3). He coined the term 'robotics'.

72 Science fiction writers foresee the inevitable, and although problems and catastrophes may be inevitable, solutions are not.
1975 'How Easy To See The Future', in *Natural History*, Apr.

73 If there is a category of human being for whom his work ought to speak for itself, it is the writer.
1976 Comment in D L Fitzpatrick (ed) *Contemporary Novelists*.

74 It is change, continuing change, inevitable change, that is the dominant factor in our society today… This, in turn, means that our statesmen, our businessmen, our everyman must take on a science fictional way of thinking.
1978 'My Own View', in R Holdstock (ed) *Encyclopedia of Science Fiction* (1978).

Aslet, Clive William 1955–

English journalist, editor of *Country Life* (1993–).

75 Biography is now more or less a branch of psychiatry.

1994 In *Country Life*, 10 Nov, reviewing Jonathan Dimbleby *The Prince of Wales: A Biography* (1994).

76 We expect the ticking movement of the human timepiece to be revealed.

1994 In *Country Life*, 10 Nov, reviewing Jonathan Dimbleby *The Prince of Wales: A Biography* (1994).

Asquith, Herbert Henry, 1st Earl of Oxford and Asquith 1852–1928

British Liberal politician and Prime Minister. He became an MP (1886), Home Secretary (1892–5), Chancellor (1906) and Prime Minister (1908–16). His period in office was marked by the introduction of old age pensions, the Parliament Act of 1911, the declaration of war (1914) and the Sinn Féin rebellion (1916). A coalition with Conservatives hastened his resignation. He wrote *Memories and Reflections* (1928).

77 We shall never sheath the sword which we have not lightly drawn until Belgium recovers in full measure all and more than all that she has sacrificed, until France is adequately assured against the menace of aggression, until the rights of the smaller nationalities of Europe are placed upon an unassailable foundation and until the military domination of Prussia is wholly and finally destroyed.

1914 Speech at the Guildhall, London, 9 Nov.

78 It is fitting that we should have buried the unknown Prime Minister by the side of the Unknown Soldier.

1923 Remark at the Westminster Abbey funeral of Bonar Law, 5 Nov.

79 One to mislead the public, another to mislead the Cabinet, and the third to mislead itself.

Of the three sets of figures kept by the War Office. Quoted in Alistair Horne *Price of Glory* (1962).

Asquith, Margot 1864–1945

Scottish society figure and wit, wife of Herbert Asquith (married 1894). Her group 'The Souls' advocated greater freedom for women. She continued her extravagant lifestyle through the war, and when Asquith was forced to resign (1916) wrote two sensational autobiographies.

80 If Kitchener is not a great man, he is, at least, a great poster.

Quoted in P Magnus *Kitchener: Portrait of an Imperialist*. Lady Asquith uses the phrase in her *Memories* (1933), but attributes it to her daughter Elizabeth.

81 She tells enough white lies to ice a wedding cake.

Of Lady Desborough. Quoted in *The Listener*, 11 Jun 1953.

82 David Lloyd George could not see a belt without hitting underneath it.

1953 *The Listener*, 11 Jun 1953.

83 Stafford Cripps has a brilliant mind, until he makes it up.

Quoted in *The Wit of the Asquiths* (published 1974).

84 F E Smith is very clever, but sometimes he lets his brains go to his head.

Quoted in *The Wit of the Asquiths* (published 1974).

85 The t is silent, as in Harlow.

Attributed riposte to Jean Harlow who was having trouble pronouncing her name. The line may actually have been spoken by Margot Grahame, an English actress in Hollywood in the 1930s.

86 I have no face, only two profiles clapped together.

Attributed.

Asquith of Yarnbury, (Helen) Violet Bonham-Carter, Baroness 1887–1969

English Liberal politician and publicist, daughter of Herbert Asquith. A prominent society figure, she was president of the Liberal Party Organization (1944–5) and governor of the BBC (1941–6).

87 Harold Macmillan held his party together by not allowing his left wing to see what his right wing was doing.

Attributed.

Astell, Mary 1668–1731

English writer, the 'first British feminist'. Orphaned in 1684, she moved alone to London in about 1686. In *A Serious Proposal to the Ladies* (1694) she argues for the education of women. *Some Reflections Upon Marriage* (1700, 2nd edn 1706) highlights the disadvantages of marriage for women.

88 Your glass will not do you half so much service as a serious reflection of your own minds.

1694 *A Serious Proposal to the Ladies For the Advancement of their True and Greatest Interest*, 'By a Lover of Her Sex', pt.1.

89 Women are from their very Infancy debarred those advantages, with the want of which they are afterwards reproached, and nursed up in those vices which will hereafter be upbraided to them. So partial are men as to expect brick where they afford no straw.

1694 *A Serious Proposal to the Ladies For the Advancement of their True and Greatest Interest*, 'By a Lover of Her Sex', pt.1.

90 Fetters of gold are still fetters, and the softest lining can never make them so easy as liberty.

1696 An Essay in Defence of the Female Sex.

91 If absolute sovereignty be not necessary in a State, how comes it to be so in a family?

1706 Some Reflections upon Marriage Occasion'd by the Duke and Duchess of Mazarine's Case which is also consider'd, preface (1706 edn).

92 If all men are born free, how is it that all women are born slaves? as they must be if the being subjected to the inconsistent, uncertain, unknown, arbitrary will of men, be the perfect condition of slavery? and if the essence of freedom consists, as our masters say it does, in having a standing rule to live by? And why is slavery so much condemned and strove against in one case, and so highly applauded, and held so necessary and so sacred in another?

1706 Some Reflections upon Marriage Occasion'd by the Duke and Duchess of Mazarine's Case which is also consider'd, preface (1706 edn).

93 But if marriage be such a blessed state, how comes it, may you say, that there are so few happy marriages? Now in answer to this, is it not to be wondered that so few succeed, we should rather be surprized to find so many do, considering how imprudently men engage, the motive they act by, and the very strange conduct they observe throughout.

1706 Some Reflections upon Marriage Occasion'd by the Duke and Duchess of Mazarine's Case which is also consider'd, preface (1706 edn).

94 A woman indeed can't properly be said to choose, all that is allowed her, is to refuse or accept what is offered.

1706 Some Reflections upon Marriage Occasion'd by the Duke and Duchess of Mazarine's Case which is also consider'd, preface (1706 edn).

Astley, Sir Jacob 1579–1652

English Royalist commander, leader of Charles I's last remaining army which surrendered in March 1646.

95 O Lord! Thou knowest how busy I must be this day: if I forget thee, do not thou forget me.

1642 Prayer before the Battle of Edgehill, 23 Oct. Quoted in Sir Philip Warwick Memoires (1702).

96 You have now done your work and may go play, unless you will fall out amongst yourselves.

1646 Remark to his Parliamentarian captors, Mar. Quoted in Samuel Rawson Gardiner History of the Great Civil War, 1642–9 (1911), vol.3.

Astor (of Hever Castle), Nancy Witcher Astor, Viscountess née Langhorne

1879–1964

US-born British politician, the first woman MP to sit in the House of Commons. She was especially interested in social problems, including women's rights and temperance.

97 I married beneath me. All women do.

1951 Speech, Oldham.

98 You will never get on in politics, my dear, with *that* hair.

Attributed remark addressed to Shirley Williams.

Asturias, Miguel Ángel 1889–1974

Guatemalan poet, novelist and diplomat, winner of the Nobel Prize for Literature in 1967 and the Soviet Union's Lenin Peace Prize in 1966.

99 *Como te decía al principio, nadie hace nada y, naturalmente, soy yo, es el Presidente de la República el que lo tiene que hacer todo, aunque salga como el cohetero. Con decir que si no fuera por mí no existiría la fortuna, ya que hasta de diosa ciega tengo que hacer en la lotería.*

But, as I told you, nobody ever does a thing, and so naturally it is I, the President of the Republic, who has to do everything, and take all the blame as well. You might almost say that if it weren't for me Fortune wouldn't exist, as I have even to take the part of the blind goddess in the lottery.

1946 El señor presidente (The President, 1963), pt.3, ch.37.

Atatürk, Mustapha Kemal 1880–1938

Turkish soldier and statesman, founder and first President (1923–38) of the Turkish Republic. In the subsequent social and political revolution he encouraged westernization. He took the title Atatürk, 'Father of the Turks', in 1935.

1 It was necessary to abolish the fez, emblem of ignorance, negligence, fanaticism and hatred of progress and civilization, to accept in its place the hat—the headgear worn by the whole civilized world.

1927 From his six-day speech to the Turkish Assembly, Oct.

Atkinson, Brooks 1894–1984

US journalist and theatre critic.

2 After each war there is a little less democracy to save.

1951 Once Around the Sun.

3 Thanks for tomorrow, thanks for last week, thanks for next Friday—in fact thanks for everything except last night.

Reviewing Le Roy Bailey's *Thanks for Tomorrow*. Quoted in the *New York Times*, 14 Jan 1984.

Atkinson, Ron 1939–

English football manager. He played for Oxford United until 1971 and subsequently managed West Bromwich

Albion, Atlético Madrid, Manchester United, Sheffield Wednesday, Aston Villa and Coventry City.

4 It's bloody tough being a legend.

1983 Quoted in Peter Ball and Phil Shaw *The Book of Football Quotations* (1989).

Atlas, Charles 1894–1972

US bodybuilder.

5 You too can have a body like mine!

c.1922 Advertising slogan.

Atlas, James 1949–

US writer and critic, Editor of the *New York Times* magazine (1988–).

6 A penumbra of somber dignity has descended over his reputation.

1985 Of Edmund Wilson. In the *New York Times*, 28 Jul, reviewing David Castronovo *Edmund Wilson* (1984).

7 To read Wilson…is to be instructed and amused in the highest sense—that is educated.

1985 Of Edmund Wilson. In the *New York Times*, 28 Jul, reviewing David Castronovo *Edmund Wilson* (1984).

Attlee (of Walthamstow), Clement (Richard) Attlee, 1st Earl 1883–1967

English Labour politician, Deputy Prime Minister in Churchill's war cabinet (1942–5) and Prime Minister (1945–51). During his administration the National Health Service was established and India and Burma were given independence.

8 We believe in a League system in which the whole world should be ranged against an aggressor… We do not think that you can deal with national armaments by piling up national armaments in other countries.

1935 House of Commons, 11 Mar.

9 We have seen today a gallant, civilized and democratic people betrayed and handed over to a ruthless despotism.

1938 House of Commons speech on Czechoslovakia, 3 Oct.

10 I count our progress by the extent to which what we cried in the wilderness five and thirty years ago has now become part of the assumptions of the ordinary man and woman… It is better to argue from what has been done to what may be done, rather than to suggest that very little has been accomplished.

1944 Of the Labour Party. Letter to Harold J Laski, 1 May.

11 I have been very happy…serving in a state of life to which I had never expected to be called.

1954 *As It Happened.*

12 Few thought he was even a starter

There were many who thought themselves smarter
But he ended PM
CH and OM
An earl and a knight of the garter.

1956 A limerick on himself, in a letter to Tom Attlee, 8 Apr.

13 Russian communism is the illegitimate child of Karl Marx and Catherine the Great.

1956 Speech, Aarhus University, 11 Apr.

14 Democracy means government by discussion, but it is only effective if you can stop people talking.

1957 Speech, Oxford, 14 Jun.

15 The House of Lords is like a glass of champagne that has stood for five days.

Attributed.

Atwood, Margaret Eleanor 1939–

Canadian writer and poet. Her first book of poetry, *The Circle Game* (1966), won the Governor General's Award. Later works include poetry such as *The Journals of Susanna Moodie* (1970), *Two-Headed Poems* (1978) and *True Stories* (1981) and novels such as *The Edible Woman* (1969), *Cat's Eye* (1988) and *The Robber Bride* (1993). She has also published short stories, essays and criticism.

16 (The photograph was taken
the day after I drowned.
I am in the lake, in the center
of the picture, just under the surface.)

1966 *The Circle Game*, 'This is a Photograph of Me'.

17 we flounder, the air
ungainly in our new lungs
with sunlight streaming merciless on the shores of morning

1966 *The Circle Game*, 'Pre-Amphibian'.

18 He stood, a point
on a sheet of green paper
proclaiming himself the center,
with no walls, no borders
anywhere; the sky no height
above him, totally un-
enclosed
and shouted:
Let me out!

1968 *The Animals in that Country*, 'Progressive Insanities of a Pioneer'.

19 Marriage is not
a house or even a tent
it is before that, and colder.

1970 *Procedures from Underground*, 'Habitation'.

20 If the national mental illness of the United States is megalomania, that of Canada is paranoid schizophrenia.

1970 *The Journals of Susanna Moodie: Poems by Margaret Atwood*, afterword.

21 We are all immigrants to this place even if we were born here: the country is too big for anyone to inhabit completely, and in the parts unknown to us we move in fear, exiles and invaders.
    1970 Writing of Canada and Canadians in *The Journals of Susanna Moodie: Poems by Margaret Atwood*, afterword.

22 Possibly the symbol for America is the Frontier… The corresponding symbol for England is the Island… The central symbol for Canada…is undoubtedly Survival, *la Survivance*.
    1972 *Survival: a Thematic Guide to Canadian Literature*, ch.1, 'Survival'.

23 This above all, to refuse to be a victim. Unless I can do that I am nothing.
    1972 *Surfacing*.

24 Mirrors
    are the perfect lovers.
    1974 *You are Happy*, 'Tricks with Mirrors'.

25 You are suspended in me
    beautiful and frozen, I
    preserve you, in me you are safe.
    1974 *You Are Happy*, 'Tricks with Mirrors'.

26 To live in prison is to live without mirrors. To live without mirrors is to live without the self.
    1978 *Two-headed Poems*, 'Marrying the Hangman'.

27 I would like to be the air
    that inhabits you for a moment
    only. I would like to be that unnoticed
    and that necessary.
    1981 *True Stories*, 'Variation on the Word *Sleep*'.

28 At some time during that hour, though not for the whole hour, I forgot what things were called and saw instead what they are.
    1983 *Murder in the Dark*, 'Strawberries'.

29 Canada was open for business. And closed for everything else.
    1988 Essay on censorship in *The Globe and Mail*, 'The Porn Patrol', 18 Feb. Collected in Douglas Fetherling (ed) *Best Canadian Essays* (1989).

30 Who knows what evil lurks in the hearts of men? An older woman knows. But how much older do you have to get before you acquire that kind of wisdom?
    1993 *The Robber Bride*, ch.48.

Auber, Daniel-François-Esprit 1782–1871

French composer of operas. His best-known works are *La Muette de Portici*, usually entitled *Masaniello* (1828), and *Fra Diavolo* (1830).

31 Well, there's no help for it. Ageing seems to be the only available way to live a long time.
    Attributed, when a friend lamented that they were both getting older. Quoted in Clifton Fadiman *The Faber Book of Anecdotes* (1985).

Aubrey, John 1626–97

English antiquary. Only his credulous *Miscellanies* (1696) of folklore and ghost stories were printed in his lifetime, and his colourful biographical anecdotes were later collected as *Brief Lives* (or *Letters by Eminent Persons*) 1813.

32 How these curiosities would be quite forgot, did not such idle fellows as I am put them down.
    1693 *Brief Lives* (published 1813), 'Venetia Digby'.

33 He had read much, if one considers his long life; but his contemplation was much more than his reading. He was wont to say that if he had read as much as other men, he should have known no more than other men.
    1693 Of Thomas Hobbes. *Brief Lives* (published 1813), 'Thomas Hobbes'.

34 His harmonical and ingenious soul did lodge in a beautiful and well proportioned body. He was a spare man…. He was so fair that they called him the *lady* of Christ's College.
    1693 Of Milton. *Brief Lives* (published 1813), 'John Milton'.

35 Sir Walter, being strangely surprised and put out of his countenance at so great a table, gives his son a damned blow over the face. His son, as rude as he was, would not strike his father, but strikes over the face the gentleman that sat next to him and said 'Box about: 'twill come to my father anon.'
    1693 *Brief Lives* (published 1813), 'Sir Walter Raleigh'.

36 When he killed a calf he would do it in a high style, and make a speech.
    1693 *Brief Lives* (published 1813), 'William Shakespeare'. Aubrey had been misinformed that Shakespeare's father was a butcher. He was in fact a glover.

37 The first sense he had of God was when he was eleven years old at Chigwell being retired into a chamber alone: he was so suddenly surprised with a sense of inward comfort and (as he thought) an external glory in the room that he had many times said that from thence he has the Seal of Divinity and Immortality, that there was a God and that the soul of man was capable of enjoying his divine communications.
    1693 Of William Penn, early Quaker. *Brief Lives* (published 1813).

Auchincloss, Louis Stanton 1917–

US writer and critic, who studied law. His works chronicle the life of New York City and its inhabitants, particularly the aristocracy. His works include *Venus in Sparta* (1958) and *Pursuit of the Prodigal* (1960).

38 Perfection irritates as well as it attracts, in fiction as in life.
1965 *Pioneers and Caretakers: A Study of Nine American Women Novelists.*

39 A neurotic can perfectly well be a literary genius, but his greatest danger is always that he will not recognize when he is dull.
1965 *Pioneers and Caretakers: A Study of Nine American Women Novelists.*

40 The glittering structure of her cultivation sits on her novels like a rather showy icing that detracts from the cake beneath.
1965 Of Edith Wharton. *Pioneers and Caretakers: A Study of Nine American Women Novelists.*

41 I would rather see the old reservoir on Forty-second Street or the original Madison Square Garden than I would any of the lost wonders of the ancient world.
Quoted in Carol Gelderman *Louis Auchincloss* (1993).

Auden, W(ystan) H(ugh) 1907–73

English-born US poet. His early work reflects his concern with social problems of the 1930s and his left-wing commitment. His conversion from liberal humanism to Anglo-Catholicism informs his later work. He collaborated with Christopher Isherwood in three plays and *Journey to a War* (1939).

42 Harrow the house of the dead; look shining at New styles of architecture, a change of heart.
1930 'Sir, No Man's Enemy'.

43 Private faces in public places
Are wiser and nicer
Than public faces in private places.
1932 *The Orators*, dedication.

44 What do you think about England, this country of ours where nobody is well?
1932 *The Orators*, 'Address for a Prize Day'.

45 To ask the hard question is simple.
1933 *Poems*, no.27.

46 The sky is darkening like a stain;
Something is going to fall like rain,
And it won't be flowers.
1935 'The Witness'.

47 This is the Night Mail crossing the border
Bringing the cheque and the postal order.
1936 'Night Mail', pt.1, written to accompany a documentary by the Post Office Film Unit.

48 And none will hear the postman's knock
Without a quickening of the heart.
For who can bear to feel himself forgotten?

1936 'Night Mail', written to accompany a documentary by the Post Office Film Unit.

49 And make us as Newton was, who in his garden watching
The apple falling towards England, became aware
Between himself and her of an eternal tie.
1936 *Look, Stranger*, no.1.

50 Out on the lawn I lie in bed,
Vega conspicuous overhead.
1936 *Look, Stranger*, no.2.

51 Look, stranger, at this island now
The leaping light for your delight discovers.
1936 *Look, Stranger*, no.5.

52 A shilling life will give you all the facts.
1936 *Look, Stranger*, no.13.

53 August for the people and their favourite islands.
Daily the steamers sidle up to meet
The effusive welcome of the pier.
1936 *Look, Stranger*, no.30.

54 I dread this like the dentist, rather more so:
To me Art's subject is the human clay,
And landscape but a background to a torso;
All Cézanne's apples I would give away
For one small Goya or a Daumier.
1936 'Letter to Byron', pt.3, stanza 20, collected in *Poems, Essays, Dramatic Writings 1927–1939* (1977).

55 The stars are dead. The animals will not look:
We are left alone with our day, and the time is short, and
History to the defeated
May say Alas but cannot help nor pardon.
1937 *Spain*.

56 The desires of the heart are as crooked as corkscrews,
Not to be born is the best for man;
The second-best is a formal order,
The dance's pattern; dance while you can.
1937 'Letter to William Coldstream, Esq', in *Letter from Iceland* (with Louis MacNeice).

57 All the others translate: the painter sketches
A visible world to love or reject.
1938 'The Composer' (XXXIV), collected in *The English Auden. Poems 1936–39* (1977).

58 Stop all the clocks, cut off the telephone,
Prevent the dog from barking with a juicy bone,
Silence the pianos and with muffled drum
Bring out the coffin, let the mourners come.
1939 'Stop all the clocks', Collected Poems, Faber. Featured in the 1994 film *Four Weddings and a Funeral.*

59 About suffering they were never wrong,
The Old Masters: how well they understood

Its human position; how it takes place
While someone else is eating or opening a window
or just walking dully along.
1940 'Musée des Beaux Arts'.

60 I'll love you dear, I'll love you
Till China and Africa meet
And the river jumps over the mountain
And the salmon sing in the street,
I'll love you till the ocean
Is folded and hung up to dry
And the seven stars go squawking
Like geese about the sky.
1940 'As I Walked Out One Evening'.

61 But all the clocks in the city
Began to whirr and chime:
'O let not Time deceive you,
You cannot conquer Time.'
1940 'As I Walked Out One Evening'.

62 O tell me the truth about love.
When it comes, will it come without warning
Just as I'm picking my nose?
Will it knock on my door in the morning,
Or tread in the bus on my toes?
1940 'Twelve Poems', sect.12.

63 Encased in talent like a uniform,
The rank of every poet is well known;
They can amaze us like a thunderstorm,
Or die so young, or live for years alone.
1940 'The Novelist'.

64 Our researchers into Public Opinion are content
That he held the proper opinions for the time of
year;
When there was peace, he was for peace; when
there was war, he went.
1940 'The Unknown Citizen'.

65 Was he free? Was he happy? The question is absurd:
Had anything been wrong, we should certainly
have heard.
1940 'The Unknown Citizen'.

66 Perfection, of a kind, was what he was after,
And the poetry he invented was easy to understand.
1940 'Epitaph On A Tyrant'.

67 When he laughed, respectable senators burst with
laughter,
And when he cried the little children died in the
streets.
1940 'Epitaph On A Tyrant'.

68 To us he is no more a person
Now but a whole climate of opinion.
1940 'In Memory of Sigmund Freud', stanza 17.

69 O all the instruments agree

The day of his death was a dark cold day.
1940 'In Memory of W.B. Yeats', pt.1.

70 You were silly like us: your gift survived it all;
The parish of rich women, physical decay,
Yourself; mad Ireland hurt you into poetry.
Now Ireland has her madness and her weather still,
For poetry makes nothing happen.
1940 'In Memory of W.B. Yeats', pt.2.

71 Earth receive an honoured guest;
William Yeats is laid to rest:
Let the Irish vessel lie
Emptied of its poetry.
1940 'In Memory of W.B. Yeats', pt.3.

72 In the nightmare of the dark
All the dogs of Europe bark,
And the living nations wait,
Each sequestered in its hate.
1940 'In Memory of W.B. Yeats', pt.3.

73 In the deserts of the heart
Let the healing fountain start,
In the prison of his days
Teach the free man how to praise.
1940 'In Memory of W.B. Yeats', pt.3.

74 Lay your sleeping head, my love,
Human on my faithless arm;
Time and fevers burn away
Individual beauty from
Thoughtful children, and the grave
Proves the child ephemeral:
But in my arms till break of day
Let the living creature lie,
Mortal, guilty, but to me
The entirely beautiful.
1940 'Lullaby'.

75 I and the public know
What all schoolchildren learn,
Those to whom evil is done
Do evil in return.
1940 'September 1, 1939'.

76 There is no such thing as the State
And no one exists alone;
Hunger allows no choice
To the citizen or the police;
We must love one another or die.
1940 'September 1, 1939'.

77 To the man-in-the-street, who, I'm sorry to say,
Is a keen observer of life,
The word 'Intellectual' suggests straight away
A man who's untrue to his wife.
1940 *New Year Letter* (published 1941), note to l.1277.

78 And by ocean's margin this innocent virgin

Constructed an organ to enlarge her prayer,
And notes tremendous from her great engine
Thundered out on the Roman air.

Blonde Aphrodite rose up excited,
Moved to delight by the melody,
White as an orchid she rode quite naked
In an oyster shell on top of the sea.
1941 'Anthem for St Cecilia's Day'.

79 Blessed Cecilia, appear in visions
To all musicians, appear and inspire:
Translated Daughter, come down and startle
Composing mortals with immortal fire.
1941 'Anthem for St Cecilia's Day'.

80 Sob, heavy world,
Sob as you spin
Mantled in mist, remote from the happy.
1944–46 *The Age of Anxiety*, pt.4, 'The Dirge'.

81 In our anguish we struggle
To elude Him, to lie to Him, yet His love observes
His appalling promise; His predilection
As we wander and weep is with us to the end,
Minding our meanings, our least matter dear to
    Him.
1944–46 *The Age of Anxiety*, pt.6, Epilogue.

82 Altogether elsewhere, vast
Herds of reindeer move across
Miles and miles of golden moss,
Silently and very fast.
1951 'The Fall of Rome'.

83 There is no love;
There are only the various envies, all of them
    sad.
1951 'In Praise of Limestone', l.58–9.

84 To save your world you asked this man to die:
Would this man, could he see you now, ask why?
1955 'Epitaph for the Unknown Soldier'.

85 No good opera plot can be sensible, for people do
not sing when they are feeling sensible.
Quoted in *Time*, 29 Dec 1961.

86 It is a sad fact about our culture that a poet can earn
much more money writing or talking about his art
than he can by practising it.
1963 *The Dyer's Hand*, foreword.

87 Pleasure is by no means an infallible critical guide,
but it is the least fallible.
1963 *The Dyer's Hand*, 'Reading'.

88 Between the ages of twenty and forty we are
engaged in the process of discovering who we are,
which involves learning the difference between
accidental limitations which it is our duty to

outgrow and the necessary limitations of our nature
beyond which we cannot trespass with impunity.
1963 *The Dyer's Hand*, 'Reading'.

89 Some books are undeservedly forgotten; none are
undeservedly remembered.
1963 *The Dyer's Hand*, 'Reading'.

90 No poet or novelist wishes he were the only one
who ever lived, but most of them wish they were
the only one alive, and quite a number fondly
believe that their wish has been granted.
1963 *The Dyer's Hand*, 'Writing'.

91 It takes little talent to see clearly what lies under
one's nose, a good deal of it to know in which
direction to point that organ.
1963 *The Dyer's Hand*, 'Writing'.

92 The true men of action in our time, those who
transform the world, are not the politicians and
statesmen, but the scientists… When I find myself
in the company of scientists, I feel like a shabby
curate who has strayed by mistake into a drawing
room full of dukes.
1963 *The Dyer's Hand*, 'The Poet and the City'.

93 Man is a history-making creature who can neither
repeat his past nor leave it behind.
1963 *The Dyer's Hand*, 'D.H. Lawrence'.

94 The image of myself which I try to create in my
own mind in order that I may love myself is very
different from the image which I try to create in the
minds of others in order that they may love me.
1963 *The Dyer's Hand*, 'Hic et Ille'.

95 Among those whom I like or admire, I can find no
common denominator, but among those whom I
love, I can: all of them make me laugh.
1963 *The Dyer's Hand*, 'Notes on the Comic'.

96 Geniuses are the luckiest of mortals because what
they must do is the same as what they most want to
do.
1964 Foreword to Dag Hammarskjöld, *Markings*.

97 Some thirty inches from my nose
The frontier of my Person goes,
And all the untilled air between
Is private *pagus* or demesne.
Stranger, unless with bedroom eyes
I beckon you to fraternize,
Beware of rudely crossing it:
I have no gun, but I can spit.
1966 'Prologue: The Birth of Architecture', postscript.

98 Youth may be forgiven when it is brash or noisy,
but this does not mean that brashness and noise are
virtues.
1966 *Collected Shorter Poems 1927–1957*, introduction.

99 Political history is far too criminal and pathological to be a fit subject of study for the young. Children should acquire their heroes and villains from fiction.
1970 *A Certain World.*

1 All sin tends to be addictive, and the terminal point of addiction is what is called damnation.
1970 *A Certain World,* 'Hell'.

2 Of course, Behaviourism 'works'. So does torture. Give me a no-nonsense, down-to-earth behaviourist, a few drugs, and simple electrical appliances, and in six months I will have him reciting the Athanasian Creed in public.
1970 *A Certain World,* 'Behaviourism'

3 To my generation no other English poet seemed so perfectly to express the sensibility of a male adolescent. If I do not now turn to him very often, I am eternally grateful to him for the joy he gave me in my youth.
1972 Of A E Housman. 'A Worcestershire Lad', collected in *Forewords and Afterwords* (1973).

4 Music is the best means we have of digesting time.
Quoted in Robert Craft *Stravinsky: Chronicle of a Friendship* (1972).

5 That singular command,
I do not understand,
Bless what there is for being,
What else am I for,
Agreeing or disagreeing?
'Precious Fire', in *Collected Poems* (1976).

6 Thou shall not sin
With statisticians nor commit
A social science.
'Under Which Lyre'.

7 My face looks like a wedding-cake left out in the rain.
Quoted in Humphrey Carpenter *W H Auden* (1981), pt.2, ch.6.

St Augustine originally *Aurelius Augustinus*
AD 354–430

Bishop of Hippo from 395. The son of Numidian Roman citizens (from modern Tunisia), he was converted to Christianity in 386. His works include his *Confessions* and *The City of God.*

8 *Da mihi castitatem et continentiam, sed noli modo.*

Grant me chastity and continence, but not yet.
AD **397** *Confessions,* bk.8, ch.7 (translated by Henry Chadwick).

9 *Tolle, lege, tolle, lege.*

Pick up and read, pick up and read.
AD **397** *Confessions,* bk.8, ch.12.

10 *Sero te amavi, pulchritudo tam antiqua et tam nova, sero te amavi!*

Late have I loved you, beauty so old and so new: late have I loved you.
AD **397** *Confessions,* bk.10, ch.27.

11 *Continentiam iubes; da quod iubes et iube quod vis.*

You command continence; give what you command and command what you will.
AD **397** *Confessions,* bk.10, ch.29.

12 *Quid est ergo tempus? Si nemo ex me quaerat, scio; si quaerenti explicare velim, nescio.*

What, then, is time? I know well enough what it is, provided that nobody asks me; but if I am asked what it is and try to explain, I am baffled.
AD **397** *Confessions,* bk.11, ch.14 (translated by R S Pine-Coffin).

13 *Multi quidem facilius se abstinent ut non utantur, quam temperent ut bene utantur.*

For many, total abstinence is easier than perfect moderation.
AD **401** *On the Good of Marriage,* ch.21.

14 *Dilige et quod vis fac.*

Love, and do what you like
AD **413** *In Epistolam Joannis ad Parthos,* tractatus 7, section 8.

15 What varieties man has found out in buildings, attires, husbandry, navigation, sculpture and imagery! What perfection has he shown, in the shows of theatres, in taming, killing, and catching wild beasts! What millions of inventions has he against others, and for himself in poisons, arms, engines, stratagems, and the like! What thousands of medicines for the health, of meats for the throat, of means and figures to persuade, of elegant phrases to delight, of verses for pleasure, of musical inventions and instruments! What excellent inventions are geography, arithmetic, astrology, and the rest! How large is the capacity of man, if we should stand upon particulars!
AD **427** *The City of God.*

16 All the devastation, the butchery, the plundering, the conflagrations, and all the anguish which accompanied the recent disaster at Rome were in accordance with the general practice of warfare.
AD **427** *City of God,* vol.1, ch.1, section 8.

17 If you don't believe it, you won't understand it.
Quoted in Erasmus *De Libero Arbitrio* (1523).

18 Do not plan long journeys, because whatever you believe in you have already seen. When a thing is everywhere, the way to find it is not to travel but to love.
Quoted in Ingrid Cranfield *The Challengers* (1976).

Augustus originally *Caius Iulius Caesar Octavianus* 63 BC–AD 14

First Roman emperor, a senator's son adopted by Caesar in his will (44 BC). With Marcus Antonius and Lepidus he secured power after the battle of Philippi (42 BC) but the triumvirate collapsed and after Actium (31 BC) Caesar was sole ruler of the Roman Empire. He took the title Augustus in 27 BC and expanded the empire until the loss of three legions in Germany (AD 9).

19 *Quintili Vare, legiones redde.*

Quintilius Varus, give me back my legions.
Quoted in Suetonius, *Augustus*, section 23.

20 *Festina lente.*

Hurry slowly.
Quoted in Suetonius *Augustus*, section 25 (originally quoted in Greek, but better known in the Latin form).

21 *Acta est fabula.*

The play is over.
AD **14** Last words, attributed. In Suetonius *Augustus*, section 99.1, the scene of his death-bed is described: 'He summoned a group of friends and asked: 'Have I played my part in the farce of life well enough?' adding the verse: 'If it was any good, please applaud for the play, and send us with pleasure on our way'.'

Aung San Suu Kyi 1945–

Burmese human rights activist and a leading campaigner for the National League for Democracy before being detained in 1989 by the country's ruling military junta. In 1994 she was involved in meetings with the government, and was released in July 1995.

22 There is nothing new in Third World governments seeking to justify and perpetuate authoritarian rule by denouncing liberal democratic principles as alien.
1989 *Freedom From Fear*, 'In Quest of Democracy'.

23 Regimented minds cannot grasp the concept of confrontation as an open exchange of major differences with a view to settlement through genuine dialogue.
1989 *Freedom From Fear*, 'In Quest of Democracy'.

Aurelius, Marcus Aurelius Antoninus AD 121–80

Roman emperor. He was consul from 140 to 161, when he succeeded Antoninus Pius to the throne. His *Meditations*, written in Greek, consist of notes made throughout his life.

24 A little flesh, a little breath, and a Reason to rule all—that is myself.
c.AD **170–80** *Meditations*, bk.2, no.2 (translated by M Staniforth).

25 Nowhere can a man find a quieter or more untroubled retreat than in his own soul.
c.AD **170–180** *Meditations*, bk.4, no.3 (translated by M Staniforth).

26 Soon you will have forgotten the world, and the world will have forgotten you.
c.AD **170–180** *Meditations*, bk.7, no.21 (translated by M Staniforth).

27 To live each day as though one's last, never flustered, never apathetic, never attitudinizing—here is perfection of character.
c.AD **170–180** *Meditations*, bk.7, no.69 (translated by M Staniforth).

Austen, Jane 1775–1817

English novelist. Her works satirized fashionable society, exploring the role of women. *Sense and Sensibility* (1811), *Pride and Prejudice* (1813), *Mansfield Park* (1814) and *Emma* (1815) were published anonymously; *Persuasion* and *Northanger Abbey* were both published posthumously (1818).

28 It was too pathetic for the feelings of Sophia and myself—we fainted alternately on the sofa.
1790 *Love and Freindship*, 'Letter the 8th'.

29 She was nothing more than a mere good-tempered, civil and obliging young woman; as such we could scarcely dislike her—she was only an Object of Contempt.
1790 *Love and Freindship*, 'Letter the 13th'.

30 We met…Dr Hall in such very deep mourning that either his mother, his wife, or himself must be dead.
1799 Letter to Cassandra Austen, 17 May.

31 On every formal visit a child ought to be of the party, by way of provisions for discourse.
1811 *Sense and Sensibility*, vol.2, ch.6.

32 It is not time or opportunity that is to determine intimacy; it is disposition alone. Seven years would be insufficient to make some people acquainted with each other, and seven days are more than enough for others.
1811 *Sense and Sensibility*, vol.2, ch.12.

33 It is a truth universally acknowledged, that a single man in possession of a good fortune, must be in want of a wife.
1813 *Pride and Prejudice*, ch.1, opening lines.

34 Her mind was less difficult to develop. She was a woman of mean understanding, little information, and uncertain temper.
1813 Of Mrs Bennet. *Pride and Prejudice*, ch.1.

35 Happiness in marriage is entirely a matter of chance.
1813 *Pride and Prejudice*, ch.6.

36 May I ask whether these pleasing attentions proceed from the impulse of the moment, or are the result of previous study?
1813 *Pride and Prejudice*, ch.14.

37 Mr Wickham is blessed with such happy manners as may ensure his making friends—whether he may be equally capable of retaining them, is less certain.
1813 *Pride and Prejudice*, ch.18.

38 From this day you must be a stranger to one of your parents.—Your mother will never see you again if you do *not* marry Mr Collins, and I will never see you again if you *do*.
1813 *Pride and Prejudice*, ch.20.

39 Without thinking highly either of men or matrimony, marriage had always been her object; it was the only honourable provision for well-educated young women of small fortune, and however uncertain of giving happiness, must be their pleasantest preservative from want.
1813 *Pride and Prejudice*, ch.22.

40 Next to being married, a girl likes to be crossed in love a little now and then. It is something to think of, and gives her a sort of distinction among her companions.
1813 *Pride and Prejudice*, ch.24.

41 What are men to rocks and mountains? Oh! what hours of transport we shall spend! And when we do return, it shall not be like other travellers, without being able to give one accurate idea of anything. We will know where we have gone—we will recollect what we have seen. Lakes, mountains, and rivers, shall not be jumbled together in our imaginations; nor, when we attempt to describe any particular scene, will we begin quarrelling about its relative situation.
1813 *Pride and Prejudice*, ch.27.

42 You ought certainly to forgive them as a Christian, but never to admit them in your sight, or allow their names to be mentioned in your hearing.
1813 *Pride and Prejudice*, ch.57.

43 For what do we live, but to make sport for our neighbours, and laugh at them in our turn?
1813 *Pride and Prejudice*, ch.57.

44 There is not one in a hundred of either sex who is not taken in when they marry. Look where I will, I see that it is so; and I feel that it must be so, when I consider that it is, of all transactions, the one in which people expect most from others, and are least honest themselves.
1814 *Mansfield Park*, ch.5.

45 Selfishness must always be forgiven you know, because there is no hope for a cure.
1814 *Mansfield Park*, ch.7.

46 We do not look in great cities for our best morality.
1814 *Mansfield Park*, ch.9.

47 Let us have no ranting tragedies. Too many characters—Not a tolerable woman's part in the play.
1814 *Mansfield Park*, ch.14.

48 A large income is the best recipe for happiness I ever heard of. It certainly may secure all the myrtle and turkey part of it.
1814 *Mansfield Park*, ch.22.

49 Shakespeare one gets acquainted with without knowing how. It is part of an Englishman's constitution. His thoughts and beauties are so spread abroad that one touches them everywhere, one is intimate with him by instinct.
1814 *Mansfield Park*, ch.34.

50 I must have a London audience. I could never preach, but to the educated; to those who were capable of estimating my composition.
1814 *Mansfield Park*, ch.34.

51 I think I may boast myself to be, with all possible vanity, the most unlearned and uninformed female who ever dared to be an authoress.
1815 Letter to Rev James Clarke, quoted in Justin Wintle and Richard Kenin (eds) *The Dictionary of Biographical Quotation* (1978).

52 She would not have him really suspect such a circumstance as her not being thought perfect by every body.
1816 *Emma*, ch.1.

53 A real, honest, old-fashioned Boarding-school, where a reasonable quantity of accomplishments were sold at a reasonable price, and where girls might be sent to be out of the way and scramble themselves into a little education, without any danger of coming back prodigies.
1816 *Emma*, ch.3.

54 One half of the world cannot understand the pleasures of the other.
1816 *Emma*, ch.9.

55 The sooner every party breaks up the better.
1816 *Emma*, ch.25.

56 I do not know whether it ought to be so, but certainly silly things do cease to be silly if they are done by sensible people in an impudent way. Wickedness is always wickedness, but folly is not always folly. It depends upon the character of those

who handle it.
1816 *Emma*, ch.26.

57 Surprises are foolish things. The pleasure is not enhanced, and the inconvenience is often considerable.
1816 *Emma*, ch.26.

58 One has no great hopes from Birmingham. I always say there is something direful in the sound.
1816 Mrs Elton speaking. *Emma*, ch. 36.

59 Goldsmith tells us, when a lovely woman stoops to folly, she has nothing to do but die; and when she stoops to be disagreeable, it is equally to be recommended as a clearer of ill-fame.
1816 *Emma*, ch.45.
▷ See Goldsmith 434:5.

60 What should I do with your strong, manly, spirited sketches, full of variety and glow?——How could I possibly join them on to the little bit (two inches wide) of ivory on which I work with so fine a brush, as produces little effect after much labour?
1816 Letter to J Edward Austen, 16 Dec.

61 Single women have a dreadful propensity for being poor——which is one very strong argument in favour of matrimony.
1817 Letter to Fanny Knight, 13 Mar.

62 Pictures of perfection as you know make me sick and wicked.
1817 Of heroines in novels. Letter to Fanny Knight, 23 Mar.

63 Oh! it is only a novel!...only some work in which the most thorough knowledge of human nature, the happiest delineation of its varieties, the liveliest effusions of wit and humour are conveyed to the world in the best chosen language.
1818 *Northanger Abbey*, ch.5.

64 But history, real solemn history, I cannot be interested in...it tells me nothing that does not vex or weary me...the men all so good for nothing, and hardly any women at all.
1818 *Northanger Abbey*, vol.1, ch.14.

65 Where people wish to attach, they should always be ignorant. To come with a well informed mind, is to come with an inability of administering to the vanity of others, which a sensible person would always wish to avoid. A woman especially, if she have the misfortune of knowing anything, should conceal it as well as she can...imbecility in females is a great enhancement of their personal charms.
1818 *Northanger Abbey*, ch.14.

66 Vanity was the beginning and the end of Sir Walter Elliot's character; vanity of person and of situation.
1818 *Persuasion*, ch.1.

67 'My idea of good company, Mr Elliot, is the company of clever, well-informed people, who have a great deal of conversation; that is what I call good company.' 'You are mistaken,' said he gently, 'that is not good company, that is the best.'
1818 *Persuasion*, ch.16.

68 We cannot help ourselves. We live at home, quiet, confined, and our feelings prey upon us. You are forced on exertion. You have always a profession, pursuits, business of some sort or other, to take you back into the world immediately, and continual occupation and change soon weaken impressions.
1818 Of the difference between women and men. *Persuasion*, ch.23.

69 Men have every advantage of us in telling their story. Education has been theirs in so much higher a degree; the pen has been in their hands.
1818 *Persuasion*, ch.23.

70 All the privilege I claim for my own sex (it is not a very enviable one, you need not covet it) is that of loving longest, when existence or when hope is gone.
1818 *Persuasion*, ch.23.

Auster, Paul pseudonym of *Paul Benjamin* 1947–

US novelist, poet and essayist. He is best known for his novels, which include the *New York Trilogy* (1985–7) and *The Music of Chance* (1991).

71 We construct a narrative for ourselves, and that's the thread we follow from one day to the next. People who disintegrate as personalities are the ones who lose that thread.
1989 In *The Sunday Times*, 16 Apr.

Austin, Alfred 1835–1913

English poet. Appointed Poet Laureate in 1896, he was the author of *The Season; a Satire* (1861), *The Human Tragedy* (1862), *The Conversion of Winckelmann* (1862), several volumes of poetry and an autobiography (1911).

72 Along the electric wires the message came: 'He is no better, he is much the same.'
1910 'On the Illness of the Prince of Wales'. There is some doubt about the authorship of this satiric poem, but it is usually credited to Austin.

Austin, Mary Hunter 1868–1934

US novelist, short story writer and suffragist, best known for her fiction about the American West and portraits of Native American life. Her works include *The Land of Little Rain* (1903), *A Woman of Genius* (1912) and her autobiography, *Earth Horizon* (1932).

73 When a woman ceases to alter the fashion of her hair, you guess that she has passed the crisis of her experience.
1903 *The Land of Little Rain*, 'The Basket Maker'.

Austin, Warren R(obinson) 1877–1962

US lawyer and diplomat, a Senator (1931–46) and subsequently US representative at the United Nations (1947–53).

74 It is better that aged diplomats be bored than for young men to die.
On soporifically lengthy debates at the United Nations.

75 Jews and Arabs should settle their differences like good Christians.
Attributed.

Avison, Margaret 1918–

Canadian poet. She has worked as a librarian, lecturer, social worker and embassy secretary. Her first book of poems *Winter Sun* (1960) was followed by *The Dumbfounding* (1966) and *Sunblue* (1978).

76 Purpose apart, perched like an umpire, dozes,
Dreams golden balls whirring through indigo.
Clay blurs the whitewash but day still encloses
The albinos, bonded in their flick and flow.
Playing in musicked gravity, the pair
Score liquid Euclids in foolscaps of air.
1960 *Winter Sun*, 'Tennis'.

Ayer, Sir Alfred Jules 1910–89

English philosopher, professor at Oxford (1947–59). His first book *Language, Truth and Logic* (1936) was an iconoclastic attack on metaphysical speculation. He wrote many more works, and was knighted in 1970.

77 The traditional disputes of philosophers are, for the most part, as unwarranted as they are unfruitful.
1936 *Language, Truth and Logic*, ch.1.

78 We shall maintain that no statement which refers to a 'reality' transcending the limits of all possible sense-experience can possibly have any literal significance.
1936 *Language, Truth and Logic*, ch.1.

79 The criterion which we use to test the genuineness of apparent statements of fact is the criterion of verifiability. We say that a sentence is factually significant to any given person, if, and only if, he knows how to verify the proposition which it purports to express — that is, if he knows what observations would lead him, under certain conditions, to accept the proposition as being true, or reject it as being false.
1936 *Language, Truth and Logic*, ch.1

80 Sentences which simply express moral judgements do not say anything. They are pure expressions of feeling and as such do not come under the category of truth and falsehood.
1936 *Language, Truth and Logic*, ch.6.

81 It appears, then, that ethics, as a branch of knowledge, is nothing more than a department of psychology and sociology.
1936 *Language, Truth and Logic*, ch.6.

82 But if science may be said to be blind without philosophy, it is true also that philosophy is virtually empty without science.
1936 *Language, Truth and Logic*, ch.8.

Ayres, Pam 1947–

English poet. She established a reputation as a popular versifier, reading her own poems on everyday themes on British television in the 1970s.

83 Medicinal discovery,
It moves in mighty leaps,
It leapt straight past the common cold
And gave it us for keeps.
1976 *Some of Me Poetry*, 'Oh no, I got a cold'.

Aytoun, Sir Robert 1570–1638

Scottish poet and courtier at the court of James VI and I in London. He wrote lyrics in English and Latin, and is credited with the prototype of 'Auld Lang Syne'.

84 I loved thee once; I'll love no more—
Thine be the grief as is the blame;
Thou art not what thou wast before,
What reason I should be the same?
'To an Inconstant Mistress', stanza 1.

Aytoun, William Edmonstoune 1813–65

Scottish lawyer and humorist, who contributed many parodies and burlesque reviews to *Blackwood's*. His best-known work was *Lays of the Scottish Cavaliers and other Poems* (1848).

85 Fhairshon swore a feud
Against the clan M'Tavish;
Marched into their land
To murder and to ravish;
For he did resolve
To extirpate the vipers,
With four-and-twenty men
And five-and-thirty pipers.
1845 'The Massacre of the Macpherson', stanza 1.

86 'He is coming! he is coming!'
Like a bridegroom from his room,
Came the hero from his prison
To the scaffold and the doom.
1848 *Lays of the Scottish Cavaliers and other Poems*, 'The Execution of Montrose', stanza 14.

87 They bore within their breasts the grief
That fame can never heal—
The deep, unutterable woe
Which none save exiles feel.
1848 *Lays of the Scottish Cavaliers and other Poems*, 'The Island of the Scots', stanza 12.

Babbage, Charles 1792–1871

English mathematician, inventor and scientific theoretician, who developed the programmable 'analytical engine', which was able to perform computations.

88 Perhaps the most important principle on which the economy of a manufacture depends, is the division of labour amongst the persons who perform the work.

1832 *On the Economy of Machinery and Manufactures.*

Babbitt, Bruce Edward 1938–

US lawyer, Governor of Arizona (1978–87), a Democrat and noted conservationist.

89 There is room in the west for wolves.

1995 Statement at Yellowstone National Park in Wyoming, 12 Jan, to the House of Representatives Natural Resources Committee, on the controversial restoration of wildlife.

Babel, Isaac 1894–c.1939

Russian short-story writer.

90 No iron can stab the heart with such force as a full stop put just at the right place.

1932 *Guy de Maupassant.*

Babeuf, François Noël 1760–97

French communist. As 'Gracchus Babeuf' during the French Revolution, he plotted to destroy the Directory (1796) and institute a communist state, but he was discovered and guillotined.

91 The French Revolution is merely the herald of a far greater and much more solemn revolution, which will be the last... The hour has come for founding the Republic of equals—that great refuge open to every man.

Conjuration des Égaux.

Bach, Johann Sebastian 1685–1750

German composer and organist, whose polyphonic works greatly influenced the course of Western music. He composed over 200 cantatas, the *Saint John Passion* (1723), the *Saint Matthew Passion* (1729), the *Mass in B Minor* (1733), and Christmas and Easter Oratorios, as well as much keyboard and instrumental music.

92 There is nothing to it. You only have to hit the right notes at the right time and the instrument plays itself.

Of the organ. Quoted in K Geiringer *The Bach Family* (1954).

93 An agreeable harmony for the honour of God and the permissible delights of the soul.

His definition of music. Quoted in Derek Watson *Music Quotations* (1991).

Bach, Richard 1936–

US author, formerly a military pilot. His *Jonathan Livingston Seagull* (1970), about a seagull's passion for flying, was followed by *Illusions* (1977), *The Bridge Across Forever* (1984) and *One* (1988).

94 Heaven is not a place, and it is not a time. Heaven is being perfect.

1970 *Jonathan Livingston Seagull.*

95 The gull sees farthest who sees highest.

1970 *Jonathan Livingston Seagull.*

96 'To begin with,' he said heavily, 'you've got to understand that a seagull is an unlimited idea of freedom, an image of the Great Gull, and your whole body, from wingtip to wingtip, is nothing more than your thought itself.'

1970 *Jonathan Livingston Seagull.*

97 There is no such thing as a problem without a gift for you in its hands. You seek problems because you need their gifts.

1977 *Illusions.*

98 Argue for your limitations, and sure enough, they're yours.

1977 *Illusions.*

99 'I don't know they're true,' he said. 'I believe them because it's fun to believe them.'

1977 *Illusions.*

Bacon, Francis, Viscount St Albans 1561–1626

English philosopher and statesman. Educated as a scholar and a lawyer, he entered the service of the crown and eventually became Lord Chancellor. Key works include *Essays* (1597–1625), *The Advancement of Learning* (1605), *Novum Organum* (1620) and *The New Atlantis* (1627).

1 I have taken all knowledge to be my province.

1592 Letter to Lord Burghley.

2 Knowledge is power

1597 *Meditationes sacrae*, 'De Haresibus' (Of Heresies).

3 Opportunity makes a thief.

1598 Letter to the Earl of Essex.

4 For all knowledge and wonder (which is the seed of knowledge) is an impression of pleasure in itself.

1605 *The Advancement of Learning*, bk.1, ch.1, section 3.

5 So let great authors have their due, as time, which is the author of authors, be not deprived of his due, which is further and further to discover the truth.

1605 *The Advancement of Learning*, bk.1, ch.4, section 12.

6 If a man will begin with certainties, he shall end in doubts; but if he will be content to begin with doubts, he shall end in certainties.

1605 *The Advancement of Learning*, bk.1, ch.5, section 8.

7 Learned men…do many times fail to observe decency and discretion in their behaviour and carriage, so as the vulgar sort of capacities do make a judgment of them in greater matters by that which they find them wanting in smaller.
1605   *The Advancement of Learning*, bk.1.

8 Martin Luther…was enforced to awake all antiquity and to call former times to his succour to make a party against the present time, so that the ancient authors both in divinity and in humanity which had long time slept in libraries began generally to be read and revolved.
1605   *The Advancement of Learning*, bk.1.

9 Vain matter is worse than vain words.
1605   *The Advancement of Learning*, bk.1.

10 Time seemeth to be of the nature of a river or stream, which carrieth down to us that which is light and blown up, and sinketh and drowneth that which is weighty and solid.
1605   *The Advancement of Learning*, bk.1.

11 Antiquities are history defaced, or some remnants of history which have casually escaped the shipwreck of time.
1605   *The Advancement of Learning*, bk.2, ch.2, section 1.

12 [Poesy] was ever thought to have some participation of divineness, because it doth raise and erect the mind, by submitting the shows of things to the desires of the mind; whereas reason doth buckle and bow the mind unto the nature of things.
1605   *The Advancement of Learning*, bk.2, ch.4, section 2.

13 The knowledge of man is as the waters, some descending from above, and some springing from beneath; the one informed by the light of nature, the other inspired by divine revelation.
1605   *The Advancement of Learning*, bk.2, ch.5, section 1.

14 They are ill discoverers that think there is no land, when they can see nothing but sea.
1605   *The Advancement of Learning*, bk.2, ch.7, section 5.

15 A dance is a measured pace, as a verse is a measured speech.
1605   *The Advancement of Learning*, bk.2, ch.16, section 5.

16 But men must know, that in this theatre of man's life it is reserved only for God and angels to be lookers on.
1605   *The Advancement of Learning*, bk.2, ch.20, section 8.

17 We are much beholden to Machiavel and others, that write what men do, and not what they ought to do.
1605   *The Advancement of Learning*, bk.2, ch.21, section 9.

18 Did not one of the fathers in great indignation call poesy *vinum daemonum*?
1605   *The Advancement of Learning*, bk.2, ch.22, section 13. The Latin translates as 'the wine of the devils'.

19 All good moral philosophy is but an handmaid to religion.
1605   *The Advancement of Learning*, bk.2, ch.22, section 14.

20 Of knowledge there is no satiety.
1605   *The Advancement of Learning*, bk.2.

21 It is not granted to man to love and to be wise.
1605   *The Advancement of Learning*, bk.2.

22 Tennis is a game of no use in itself.
1605   *The Advancement of Learning*, bk.2.

23 Man seeketh in society comfort, use, and protection.
1605   *The Advancement of Learning*, bk.2.

24 Fortunes…come tumbling into some men's laps.
1605   *The Advancement of Learning*, bk.2.

25 It is in life as it is in ways, the shortest way is most commonly the foulest, and surely the fairer way is not much about.
1605   *The Advancement of Learning*, bk.2, ch.23, section 45.

26 Empires and old women are more happy many times in their cures than learned physicians, because they are more exact and religious in holding to the composition and confection of tried medicines.
1605   *The Advancement of Learning*, bk.4, ch.2.

27 The subtlety of nature is greater many times over than the subtlety of the senses and understanding.
1620   *Novum Organum*, bk.1, aphorism 10.

28 *Quod enim mavult homo verum esse, id potius credit.*

For what a man would like to be true, that he more readily believes.
1620   *Novum Organum*, bk.1, aphorism 49.

29 Those who have handled sciences have been either men of experiment or men of dogmas. The men of experiment are like the ant; they only collect and use; the reasoners resemble spiders, who make cobwebs out of their own substance. But the bee takes a middle course; it gathers its material from the flowers of the garden and of the field, but transforms and digests by a power of its own. Not unlike this is the true business of philosophy.
1620   *Novum Organum* bk.1, aphorism 95.

30 *Vim et virtutem et consequentias rerum inventarum notare juvat; quae non in aliis manifestius occurrunt, quam in illis tribus quae antiquis incognitae, et quarum primordia, licet recentia, obscura et ingloria*

sunt: Artis nimirum Imprimendi, Pulveris Tormentarii, et Acus Nauticae. Haec enim tria rerum faciem et statum in orbe terrarum mutaverunt.

It is well to observe the force and virtue and consequence of discoveries, and these are to be seen nowhere more conspicuously than in those three which were unknown to the ancients, and of which the origin, though recent, is obscure and inglorious; namely, printing, gunpowder and the magnet [ie the compass]. For these three have changed the whole face and state of things throughout the world.
1620 *Novum Organum*, bk.1, aphorism 129 (translated by James Spedding).

31 *Natura enim non imperatur, nisi parendo.*

For we cannot command Nature except by obeying her.
1620 *Novum Organum*, bk.1, aphorism 129.

32 It would be unsound fancy and self-contradictory to expect that things which have never yet been done can be done except by means which have never yet been tried.
1620 *Novum Organum.*

33 The lame man who keeps the right road outstrips the runner who takes a wrong one. Nay, it is obvious that when a man runs the wrong way, the more active and swift he is the further he will go astray.
1620 *Novum Organum.*

34 *Divitiae bona ancilla, pessima domina.*

Riches are a good handmaid, but the worst mistress.
1623 *De Dignitiate et Augmentis Scientiarum*, Antitheta no.6 (translated by Gilbert Watts, 1640).

35 The voice of the people hath some divineness in it, else how should so many men agree to be of one mind?
1623 *De Dignitiate et Augmentis Scientiarum*, Antitheta no.9 (translated by Gilbert Watts, 1640).

36 *Silentium, stultorum virtus.*

Silence is the virtue of fools.
1623 *De Dignitiate et Augmentis Scientiarum*, Antitheta no.31 (translated by Gilbert Watts, 1640).

37 The end of our foundation is the knowledge of causes, and secret motions of things; and the enlarging of the bounds of human Empire, to the effecting of all things possible.
1624 *New Atlantis* (published posthumously, 1627).

38 Wise nature did never put her precious jewels into a garret four stories high: and therefore...exceeding tall men had ever very empty heads.
1625 *Apophthegms.*

39 Hope is a good breakfast, but it is a bad supper.
1625 *Apophthegms.*

40 What is truth? said jesting Pilate; and would not stay for an answer.
1625 *Essays*, no.1, 'Of Truth'.

41 The inquiry of truth, which is the love-making, or wooing of it, the knowledge of truth, which is the presence of it, and the belief of truth, which is the enjoying of it, is the sovereign good of human nature.
1625 *Essays*, no.1, 'Of Truth'.

42 For it is a true Rule that Love is ever rewarded, either with the reciproque, or with an inward and secret contempt.
1625 *Essays*, no.10, 'Of Love'.

43 Men fear death as children fear to go in the dark; and as that natural fear in children is increased with tales, so is the other.
1625 *Essays*, no.2, 'Of Death'.

44 There is no passion in the mind of man so weak, but it mates and masters the fear of death. And therefore death is no such terrible enemy, when a man hath so many attendants about him that can win the combat of him. Revenge triumphs over death; love slights it; honour aspireth to it; grief flieth to it.
1625 *Essays*, no.2, 'Of Death'.

45 It is as natural to die as to be born; and to a little infant, perhaps, the one is as painful as the other.
1625 *Essays*, no.2, 'Of Death'.

46 Death...openeth the gate to good fame, and extinguisheth envy.
1625 *Essays*, no.2, 'Of Death'.

47 All colours will agree in the dark.
1625 *Essays*, no.3, 'Of Unity in Religion'.

48 Revenge is a kind of wild justice, which the more man's nature runs to, the more ought law to weed it out.
1625 *Essays*, no.4, 'Of Revenge'.

49 The virtue of prosperity, is temperance; the virtue of adversity, is fortitude.
1625 *Essays*, no.5, 'Of Adversity'.

50 Prosperity is the blessing of the Old Testament, adversity is the blessing of the New.
1625 *Essays*, no.5, 'Of Adversity'.

51 Prosperity is not without many fears and distastes; and adversity is not without comforts and hopes.
1625 *Essays*, no.5, 'Of Adversity'.

52 Prosperity doth best discover vice, but adversity doth best discover virtue.

1625 *Essays*, no.5, 'Of Adversity'.

53 Let judges also remember that Solomon's throne was supported by lions on both sides; let them be lions, but yet lions under the throne.
1625 *Essays*, no.6, 'Of Judicature'.

54 The joys of parents are secret, and so are their griefs and fears.
1625 *Essays*, no.7, 'Of Parents and Children'.

55 Children sweeten labours, but they make misfortunes more bitter.
1625 *Essays*, no.7, 'Of Parents and Children'.

56 He that hath wife and children hath given hostages to fortune; for they are impediments to great enterprises, either of virtue or mischief. Certainly the best works, and of greatest merit for the public, have proceeded from the unmarried or childless men, which both in affection and means have married and endowed the public.
1625 *Essays*, no.8, 'Of Marriage and the Single Life'.

57 There are some other that account wife and children but as bills of charge.
1625 *Essays*, no.8, 'Of Marriage and the Single Life'.

58 The most ordinary cause of a single life is liberty, especially in certain self-pleasing and humorous minds, which are so sensible of every restraint, as they will go near to think their girdles and garters to be bonds and shackles.
1625 *Essays*, no.8, 'Of Marriage and the Single Life'.

59 Unmarried men are best friends, best masters, best servants, but not always best subjects, for they are light to run away, and almost all fugitives are of that condition.
1625 *Essays*, no.8, 'Of Marriage and the Single Life'.

60 Certainly wife and children are a kind of discipline of humanity; and single men, though they be many times more charitable, because their means are less exhaust, yet…they are more cruel and hardhearted (good to make severe inquisitors), because their tenderness is not so oft called upon.
1625 *Essays*, no.8, 'Of Marriage and the Single Life'.

61 Wives are young men's mistresses, companions for middle age, and old men's nurses.
1625 *Essays*, no.8, 'Of Marriage and the Single Life'.

62 He was reputed one of the wise men that made answer to the question when a man should marry? 'A young man not yet, an elder man not at all.'
1625 *Essays*, no.8, 'Of Marriage and the Single Life'.

63 It is often seen that bad husbands have very good wives; whether it be that it raiseth the price of their husband's kindness when it comes, or that the wives take a pride in their patience. But this never fails, if the bad husbands were of their own choosing, against their friends' consent; for then they will be sure to make good their own folly.
1625 *Essays*, no.8, 'Of Marriage and the Single Life'.

64 I had rather believe all the fables in the legend, and the Talmud, and the Alcoran, than that this universal frame is without a mind.
1625 *Essays*, no.9, 'Of Atheism'.

65 It is true, that a little philosophy inclineth Man's mind to atheism; but depth in philosophy bringeth men's minds about to religion.
1625 *Essays*, no.9 'Of Atheism'.
▷ See Berkeley 95:53.

66 The speaking in perpetual hyperbole is comely in nothing but love.
1625 *Essays*, no.10, 'Of Love'.

67 All rising to great place is by a winding stair.
1625 *Essays*, no.11, 'Of Great Place'.

68 Men in great place are thrice servants: servants of the sovereign or state, servants of fame, and servants of business.
1625 *Essays*, no.11, 'Of Great Place'.

69 It is a strange desire to seek power and to lose liberty.
1625 *Essays*, no.11, 'Of Great Place'.

70 The rising unto place is laborious, and by pains men come to greater pains; and it is sometimes base, and by indignities men come to dignities. The standing is slippery, and the regress is either a downfall, or at least an eclipse, which is a melancholy thing: *Cum non sis qui fueris, non esse cur velis vivere.*
1625 *Essays*, no.11, 'Of Great Place'. The Latin is taken from Cicero's *Familiar Letters*, and translates as: 'When you are not what you were, there is no reason to live.'

71 Certainly great persons had need to borrow other men's opinions to think themselves happy; for if they judge by their own feeling, they cannot find it; but if they think with themselves what other men think of them, and that other men would fain be as they are, then they are happy.
1625 *Essays*, no.11, 'Of Great Place'.

72 Men in great fortunes are strangers to themselves.
1625 *Essays*, no.11, 'Of Great Place'.

73 Merit and good works is the end of man's motion, and conscience of the same is the accomplishment of man's rest.
1625 *Essays*, no.11, 'Of Great Place'.

74 The vices of authority are chiefly four: delays, corruption, roughness, and facility.
1625 *Essays*, no.11, 'Of Great Place'.

75 All great rising is by a winding stair.
1625 *Essays*, no.11, 'Of Great Place'.

76 In civil business; What first? Boldness; What second, and third? Boldness. And yet boldness is a child of ignorance and baseness.
1625 *Essays*, no.12, 'Of Boldness'.

77 There is in human nature generally more of the fool than of the wise.
1625 *Essays*, no.12, 'Of Boldness'.

78 Mahomet made the people believe that he would call a hill to him, and from the top of it offer up his prayers for the observers of his law. The people assembled: Mahomet called the hill to come to him again and again; and when the hill stood still he was never a whit abashed, but said, 'If the hill will not come to Mahomet, Mahomet will go to the hill.'
1625 *Essays*, no.12, 'Of Boldness'.

79 New nobility is but the act of power, but ancient nobility is the act of time.
1625 *Essays*, no.14, 'Of Nobility'.

80 The surest way to prevent seditions…is to take away the matter of them.
1625 *Essays*, no.15, 'Of Seditions and Troubles'.

81 Money is like muck, not good except it be spread.
1625 *Essays*, no.15, 'Of Seditions and Troubles'.

82 The remedy is worse than the disease.
1625 *Essays*, no.15, 'Of Seditions and Troubles'.

83 It were better to have no opinion of God at all than such an opinion as is unworthy of him.
1625 *Essays*, no.17, 'Of Superstition'.

84 In all superstition wise men follow fools.
1625 *Essays*, no.17, 'Of Superstition'.

85 There is a superstition in avoiding superstition.
1625 *Essays*, no.17, 'Of Superstition'. This is directed against Puritan reformers, who decried both Catholic and Anglican rites as 'superstitious'.

86 It is a miserable state of mind to have few things to desire and many things to fear.
1625 *Essays*, no.19, 'Of Empire'.

87 In things that are tender and unpleasing, it is good to break the ice by some whose words are of less weight, and to reserve the more weighty voice to come in as by chance.
1625 *Essays*, no.22, 'Of Cunning'.

88 Nothing doth more hurt in a state than that cunning men pass for wise.
1625 *Essays*, no.22, 'Of Cunning'.

89 Be so true to thyself as thou be not false to others.
1625 *Essays*, no.23, 'Of Wisdom for a Man's Self'.

90 It is a poor centre of a man's actions, himself.
1625 *Essays*, no.23, 'Of Wisdom for a Man's Self'.

91 It is the nature of extreme self-lovers, as they will set a house on fire, and it were but to roast their eggs.
1625 *Essays*, no.23, 'Of Wisdom for a Man's Self'.

92 It is the wisdom of the crocodiles, that shed tears when they would devour.
1625 *Essays*, no.23, 'Of Wisdom for a Man's Self'.

93 As the births of living creatures at first are ill-shapen, so are all innovations, which are the births of time.
1625 *Essays*, no.24, 'Of Innovations'.

94 He that will not apply new remedies must expect new evils; for time is the greatest innovator.
1625 *Essays*, no.24, 'Of Innovations'.

95 To choose time is to save time.
1625 *Essays*, no.25, 'Of Dispatch'.

96 The French are wiser than they seem, and the Spaniards seem wiser than they are.
1625 *Essays*, no.26, 'Of Seeming Wise'.

97 It had been hard for him that spake it to have put more truth and untruth together, in a few words, than in that speech: 'Whosoever is delighted in solitude is either a wild beast, or a god.'
1625 *Essays*, no.27, 'Of Friendship'.

98 A crowd is not company, and faces are but a gallery of pictures, and talk but a tinkling cymbal, where there is no love.
1625 *Essays*, no.27, 'Of Friendship'.
▷ See Bible 150:62.

99 [Friendship] redoubleth joys, and cutteth griefs in half.
1625 *Essays*, no.27, 'Of Friendship'.

1 As if you would call a physician, that is thought good for the cure of the disease you complain of but is unacquainted with your body, and therefore may put you in the way for a present cure but overthroweth your health in some other kind; and so cure the disease and kill the patient.
1625 *Essays*, no.27, 'Of Friendship'.

2 Riches are for spending; and spending for honour and good actions.
1625 *Essays*, no.28, 'Of Expense'.

3 Neither will it be, that a people overlaid with taxes should ever become valiant and martial.
    1625 *Essays*, no.29, 'Of the True Greatness of Kingdoms'.

4 Suspicions amongst thoughts are like bats amongst birds, they ever fly by twilight.
    1625 *Essays*, no.31, 'Of Suspicion'.

5 There is nothing makes a man suspect much, more than to know little.
    1625 *Essays*, no.31, 'Of Suspicion'.

6 If you dissemble sometimes your knowledge of that you are thought to know, you shall be thought, another time, to know that you know not.
    1625 *Essays*, no.32, 'Of Discourse'.

7 When the world was young it begat more children; but now it is old it begets fewer: for I may justly account new plantations to be the children of former kingdoms.
    1625 *Essays*, no.33, 'Of Plantations'.

8 If you plant where savages are, do not only entertain them with trifles and jingles, but use them justly and graciously.
    1625 *Essays*, no.33, 'Of Plantations'.

9 Nature is often hidden, sometimes overcome, seldom extinguished.
    1625 *Essays*, no.38, 'Of Nature in Men'.

10 Chiefly the mould of a man's fortune is in his own hands.
    1625 *Essays*, no.40, 'Of Fortune'.

11 If a man look sharply, and attentively, he shall see Fortune; for though she be blind, yet she is not invisible.
    1625 *Essays*, no.40, 'Of Fortune'.

12 Beauty is as summer-fruits, which are easy to corrupt, and cannot last.
    1625 *Essays*, no.43, 'Of Beauty'.

13 Virtue is like a rich stone, best plain set.
    Essays, no.43, 'Of Beauty'.

14 That is the best part of beauty, which a picture cannot express.
    1625 *Essays*, no.43, 'Of Beauty'.

15 There is no excellent beauty that hath not some strangeness in the proportion.
    1625 *Essays*, no.43, 'Of Beauty'.

16 God Almighty first planted a garden; and indeed, it is the purest of human pleasures.
    1625 *Essays*, no.46, 'Of Gardens'.

17 It is generally better to deal by speech than by letter.
    1625 *Essays*, no.47, 'Of Negotiating'.

18 It is better dealing with men in appetite, than with those that are where they would be.
    1625 *Essays*, no.47, 'Of Negotiating'.

19 If you would work any man, you must either know his nature and fashions, and so lead him; or his ends, and so persuade him; or his weakness and disadvantages, and so awe him, or those that have interest in him, and so govern him.
    1625 *Essays*, no.47, 'Of Negotiating'.

20 There is little friendship in the world, and least of all between equals.
    1625 *Essays*, no.48, 'Of Followers and Friends'.

21 To spend too much time in studies is sloth; to use them too much for ornament is affectation; to make judgment wholly by their rules is the humour of a scholar.
    1625 *Essays*, no.50, 'Of Studies'.

22 Read not to contradict and confute, nor to believe and take for granted, nor to find talk and discourse, but to weigh and consider.
    1625 *Essays*, no.50, 'Of Studies'.

23 Some books are to be tasted, others to be swallowed, and some few to be chewed and digested; that is, some books are to be read only in parts; others to be read but not curiously; and some few to be read wholly, and with diligence and attention. Some books also may be read by deputy, and extracts made of them by others.
    1625 *Essays*, no.50, 'Of Studies'.

24 If a man write little, he had need have a great memory; if he confer little, he had need have a present wit; and if he read little he had need have much cunning, to seem to know that he doth not.
    1625 *Essays*, no.50, 'Of Studies'.

25 Histories make men wise; poets, witty; the mathematics, subtle; natural philosophy, deep; moral, grave; logic and rhetoric, able to contend.
    1625 *Essays*, no.50, 'Of Studies'.

26 Light gains make heavy purses.
    1625 *Essays*, no.52, 'Of Ceremonies and Respects'.

27 A wise man will make more opportunities than he finds.
    1625 *Essays*, no.52, 'Of Ceremonies and Respects'.

28 It was prettily devised of Aesop, 'The fly sat upon the axletree of the chariot-wheel and said, what a dust do I raise.'
    1625 *Essays*, no.54, 'Of Vain-Glory'.

29 In the youth of a state arms do flourish; in the middle age of a state, learning; and then both of

them together for a time; in the declining age of a state, mechanical arts and merchandise.

1625 *Essays*, no.58, 'Of Vicissitude of Things'.

30 I bequeath my soul to God… For my name and memory, I leave it to men's charitable speeches, and to foreign nations, and the next age.

1626 From his will.

31 God's first Creature, which was Light.

New Atlantis (published 1627).

32 The end of our foundation is the knowledge of causes, and secret motions of things; and the enlarging of the bounds of human Empire, to the effecting of all things possible.

1627 Of Solomon's House, the centre of Bacon's scientific utopia. *New Atlantis* (published 1627).

33 No man can tickle himself.

Sylva Sylvarum (published 1627), bk.8.

34 Generally music feedeth that disposition of the spirits which it findeth.

Sylva Sylvarum (published 1627).

35 The world's a bubble; and the life of man
Less than a span.

The World (published 1629).

36 Books must follow sciences, and not sciences books.

A Proposition…Touching Amendment of the Laws of England (published 1657).

37 The government of a woman has been a rare thing at all times; felicity in such government a rarer thing still; felicity and long continuance together the rarest thing of all.

Quoted in J E Neale *The Age of Catherine de Medici and Essays in Elizabethan History* (1963), p.217.

Bacon, Francis 1909–92

Irish-born painter, who settled in England in 1928 and began painting without formal training. His work draws on surrealism and motion photography, often evoking angst. He was a technical perfectionist, and destroyed much of his work.

38 I think of myself as a kind of pulverizing machine into which everything I look at and feel is fed. I believe that I am different from the mixed-media jackdaws who use photographs etc. more or less literally.

On the use of photographs in his art. Quoted in John Russell *Francis Bacon* (1979).

39 Who can I tear to pieces, if not my friends?… If they were not my friends, I could not do such violence to them.

Quoted in John Russell *Francis Bacon* (1979).

Bacon, Martha 1917–81

US educator and author

40 She soothed and solaced and celebrated, destroying her gift by maiming it to suit her hearers.

1965 On Phillis Wheatley. In *Christian Science Monitor*, 24 Jun.

Bacon, Roger known as *Doctor Mirabilis*
c.1214–c.1292

English philosopher, scientist and alchemist, closely associated with Oxford. His major works include the *Opus Majus*, *Opus Minor* and *Opus Tertium*. He became a Franciscan, but was rejected and persecuted for heresy.

41 All science requires mathematics…the knowledge of mathematical things is almost innate in us…this is the easiest of sciences. A fact which is obvious in that no one's brain rejects it. For laymen and people who are utterly illiterate know how to count and reckon.

1267 *Opus Majus*, pt.4, ch.1 (translated by Robert Belle Burke, 1928).

42 Mathematics is the door and key to the sciences.

1267 *Opus Majus*, pt.4, ch.1 (translated by Robert Belle Burke, 1928).

43 There are two modes of acquiring knowledge, namely, by reasoning and experience. Reasoning draws a conclusion and makes us grant the conclusion, but does not make the conclusion certain, nor does it remove doubt so that the mind may rest on the intuition of truth unless the mind discovers it by the path of experience.

1267 *Opus Majus* (translated by Robert Belle Burke, 1928).

Baden-Powell, Robert Stephenson Smyth, 1st Baron 1857–1941

English soldier. He became a hero for his defence of Mafeking (1899–1900) during the Boer War but is usually remembered as the founder of the Boy Scout movement in 1908 and for his book *Scouting for Boys* (1908).

44 The scouts' motto is founded on my initials, it is: BE PREPARED, which means, you are always to be in a state of readiness in mind and body to do your DUTY.

1908 *Scouting for Boys*.

45 Football, in itself, is a grand game for developing a lad physically and also morally…but it is a vicious game when it draws crowds of lads away from playing the game themselves to be merely onlookers at a few paid players.

1908 *Scouting for Boys*.

Baedeker, Karl 1801–59

German editor and publisher, famous for his foreign travel guides. The first, for Coblenz, appeared in 1829, and they continued to be published after his death.

46 On arrival at a Syrian port the traveller's passport is sometimes asked for, but an ordinary visiting-card will answer the purpose equally well.

1876 *Palestine and Syria*, 'Passports and Custom House'.

47 Oxford is on the whole more attractive than Cambridge to the ordinary visitor; and the traveller is therefore recommended to visit Cambridge first, or to omit it altogether if he cannot visit both.

1887 *Great Britain*, Route 30: 'From London to Oxford'.

Baer, George Frederick 1842–1914

US lawyer and industrialist, who led the resistance to the strike by the United Mine Workers of America in 1902.

48 The rights and interests of the laboring man will be protected and cared for, not by the labor agitators, but by the Christian men to whom God, in his infinite wisdom, has given control of the property interests of the country.

1902 Letter to the press during the Pennsylvanian miners' strike.

Bagehot, Walter 1826–77

British economist and journalist. His *English Constitution* (1867) is still considered a standard work, and *Physics and Politics* (1872), applying evolution theories to politics, greatly influenced 19c thought.

49 The essence of Toryism is enjoyment…but as far as communicating and establishing your creed are concerned—try a little pleasure. The way to keep up old customs is, to enjoy old customs; the way to be satisfied with the present state of things is, to enjoy that state of things.

1856 Essay on *Macaulay*.

50 No real English gentleman, in his secret soul, was ever sorry for the death of a political economist.

1858 *Estimates of Some Englishmen and Some Scotchmen*, 'The First Edinburgh Reviewers'.

51 Writers, like teeth, are divided into incisors and grinders.

1858 *Estimates of Some Englishmen and Some Scotchmen*, 'The First Edinburgh Reviewers'.

52 It is said that England invented the phrase, 'Her Majesty's Opposition'; that it was the first government which made a criticism of administration as much a part of the polity as administration itself.

1867 *The English Constitution*, ch.2, 'The Cabinet'.

53 *The Times* has made many ministries.

1867 *The English Constitution*, ch.2, 'The Cabinet'.

54 The fancy of the mass of men is incredibly weak; it can see nothing without a visible symbol, and there is much that it can scarcely make out with a symbol.

55 The order of nobility is of great use, too, not only in what it creates, but in what it prevents. It prevents the rule of wealth—the religion of gold. This is the obvious and natural idol of the Anglo-Saxon… From this our aristocracy preserves us. There is no country where a 'poor devil of a millionaire is so ill off as in England'. The experiment is tried every day, and every day it is proved that money alone—money *pur et simple*—will not buy 'London Society'.

1867 *The English Constitution*, ch.4, 'The House of Lords'.

56 A severe though not unfriendly critic of our institutions said that the cure for admiring the House of Lords was to go and look at it.

1867 *The English Constitution*, ch.4, 'The House of Lords'.

57 The great offices, whether permanent or parliamentary, which require mind now give social prestige, and almost only those. An Under-Secretary of State with £2,000 a year is a much greater man than the director of a finance company with £5,000, and the country saves the difference.

1867 *The English Constitution*, ch.4, 'The House of Lords'.

58 Nations touch at their summits.

1867 *The English Constitution*, ch.4, 'The House of Lords'.

59 The best reason why monarchy is a strong government is, that it is an intelligible government. The mass of mankind understand it, and they hardly anywhere in the world understand any other.

1867 *The English Constitution*, ch.6, 'The Monarchy'.

60 Throughout the greater part of his life George III was a kind of 'consecrated obstruction'.

1867 *The English Constitution*, ch.6, 'The Monarchy'.

61 Above all things our royalty is to be reverenced, and if you begin to poke about it you cannot reverence it… Its mystery is its life. We must not let in daylight upon magic.

1867 *The English Constitution*, ch.6, 'The Monarchy (continued)'.

62 Political economy traces in an abstract way the effects of the desire to be rich; and nations must nowadays abound in that passion if they are to have much power or respect in the world.

1876 'Preliminaries of Political Economy', collected in *Economic Studies* (1880).

63 Men of business have a solid judgment, a wonderful guessing power of what is going to happen, each in his own trade, but they have never practised themselves in reasoning out their judgments and in supporting their guesses by argument; probably if they did so, some of the finer and correcter parts of their anticipations would vanish.

1876 'Postulates of English Political Economy', in *Economic Studies* (1880).

64 Who can tell without instruction what is likely to be the effect of the new loans of England to foreign nations? We press upon half-finished and half-civilized communities incalculable sums; we are to them what the London money-dealers are to students at Oxford and Cambridge.

1876 'Postulates of English Political Economy', in *Economic Studies* (1880).

65 No man has come so near to our definition of a constitutional statesman—the powers of a first-rate man and the creed of a second-rate man.

1881 *Biographical Studies*, 'The Character of Sir Robert Peel'.

66 A constitutional statesman is in general a man of common opinion and uncommon abilities.

1881 *Biographical Studies*, 'The Character of Sir Robert Peel'.

Bailey, Francis Lee 1933–

US criminal lawyer, who founded his own detective agency at Harvard. He defended the Boston Strangler among others, and his works include *The Defense Never Rests* (1971).

67 When you see a lawyer trying to pick a smart jury, you know he's got a strong case.

1972 In the *Los Angeles Times*, 9 Jan.

68 The guilty never escape unscathed. My fees are sufficient punishment for anyone.

1972 In the *Los Angeles Times*, 9 Jan.

69 I think my grandmother actually smelled like a cookie and that's enough to get any child's attention.

Quoted by Phyllis Hanes in *Christian Science Monitor*, 15 Jun 1988.

Bailey, Nathan d.1742

English lexicographer, best known for *An Universal Etymological English Dictionary* (1721), which gives word origins as well as definitions.

70 LONDON…the Metropolis of *Great-Britain*, founded before the City of *Rome*, walled by *Constantine* the Great, no ways inferior to the greatest in *Europe* for Riches and Greatness.

1721 *An Universal Etymological English Dictionary*.

Bailey, Philip James 1816–1902

English poet, father of the Spasmodic school. His great work *Festus* (1839) was expanded in 1889 to incorporate previously published volumes: *The Angel World* (1850), *The Mystic* (1855) and *Universal Hymn* (1867).

71 America, thou half-brother of the world;

With something good and bad of every land.

1839 *Festus*, sc.10.

Baillie, Robert 1599–1662

Scottish Presbyterian leader, an opponent of Archbishop Laud and of episcopacy. He was selected by the Scottish Church to invite Charles II to accept the covenant and crown of Scotland.

72 The Parliament of England cannot have on earth so strong pillars and pregnant supporters of all their privileges as free protestant assemblies established by law, and kept in their full freedom from the lowest to the highest—from the congregational eldership to the general synod of the nation.

A Dissuasive from the Errors of Time, 1645–6.

Bainbridge, Beryl Margaret 1934–

English novelist and playwright. She worked as an actress and publisher's clerk before publishing *A Weekend with Claude* (1967). Her work is marked by a caustic wit and a finely turned prose style.

73 I am of the firm belief that everybody could write books and I never understand why they don't. After all, everybody speaks. Once the grammar has been learnt it is simply talking on paper and in time learning what not to say.

1976 In D L Kirkpatrick (ed) *Contemporary Novelists*.

74 Being constantly with children was like wearing a pair of shoes that were expensive and too small. She couldn't bear to throw them out, but they gave her blisters.

1977 *Injury Time*, ch.4.

75 We are essentially fragile. We don't have to wait for the sword or some other equally sensational weapon to strike us down… There are so many ways of us dying it's astonishing any of us choose old age.

1978 *Young Adolf*, ch.12.

76 I haven't the humility to find anything beneath me.

1989 *An Awfully Big Adventure*, ch.3.

77 It's all changed now, which is why it mattered to those young men from Liverpool that they should be there to support their team. What other group is going to troop their colours for them, present them with scarves and emblems? To what other section of society should they owe allegiance? Not to country; we're going into Europe. Not to community; we're all isolated, shut in little boxes, high-rise or low, watching another box. Not to God; science has got rid of him. Not to guilt; Freud shoved that out of the window.

1989 After the Hillsborough football disaster. Quoted in David Pickering *The Cassell Soccer Companion* (1994).

78 The vital accessories to my work are my reference
    books, such as the complete Shakespeare and a
    prayer book, and a large refuse bin.
    1991 In *The Guardian*, 8 Aug.

Bairnsfather, Bruce 1888–1959

British cartoonist, a soldier in World War I and cartoonist
with US troops in World War II. His works include
Fragments from France (1916), *Bullets and Billets* (1917)
and *Jeeps and Jests* (1943).

79 Well, if you knows of a better 'ole, go to it.
    1915 Caption to cartoon in *Fragments from France*. The
    speaker, Ol' Bill, is waist-deep in mud on the Somme. The
    phrase was used as the title for a 1926 US film based on the
    character, *The Better 'Ole*.

Baker, Howard Henry, Jr 1925–

US public official, Republican senator from Tennessee
and a member of the Watergate Committee (1973). He
became Senate Leader and White House Chief of Staff
(1987–8) under Reagan.

80 Never speak more clearly than you think.
    1987 On becoming President Reagan's third Chief of Staff. In
    the *New York Times*, 6 Sep.

Baker, James Addison, III 1930–

US lawyer and government official. He managed the
campaigns of Ford (1976) and Bush (1980, 1988). As
Secretary of State (1989–92) he initiated a round of
Middle East peace talks.

81 Sometimes you move publicly, sometimes privately.
    Sometimes quietly, sometimes at the top of your
    voice. And sometimes an active policy is best
    advanced by doing nothing until the right time—
    or never.
    1990 Of statesmanship. In *Time*, 19 Mar.

Baker, John Austin 1928–

English cleric and theologian, Bishop of Salisbury
(1982–93).

82 The crucified Jesus is the only accurate picture of
    God the world has ever seen.
    1970 *The Foolishness of God*.

Baker, Kenneth (Wilfred), Rt. Hon. 1934–

English Conservative politician and writer. He was
Secretary of State for the Environment (1985) and
introduced a controversial education reform bill as
Secretary of State for Education (1986-9) under Margaret
Thatcher. He was Home Secretary under John Major
(1990–2).

83 If Conservative Backbench MPs want to get on in
    politics they will have to find a foothold in the
    narrow strip of land that lies between sycophancy
    and rebellion.
    1979 Queen's Speech in the House of Commons.

Baker, Russell Wayne 1925–

US newspaper columnist and humorist, writing
principally for the *Baltimore Sun* and the *New York Times*.
In 1962 he began writing for the *Observer* and has since
published best-selling works of humour. He won a
Pulitzer Prize for distinguished commentary (1979).

84 So there he is at last. Man on the moon. The poor
    magnificent bungler! He can't even get to the office
    without undergoing the agonies of the damned,
    but give him a little metal, a few chemicals, some
    wire and twenty or thirty billion dollars and vroom!
    there he is, up on a rock a quarter of a million miles
    up in the sky.
    1969 Editoral pages, the *New York Times*, 21 Jul.

85 What is it about sociology that instantly bogs us
    down in fens of jargon?
    1990 In the *New York Times*, 15 Dec.

86 California's power to cloud men's minds must never
    be forgot. Under its spell we submitted for eight
    years to the governance of Ronald Reagan, who had
    trouble distinguishing history from old movie
    plots.
    1995 'Don't Look Back', in the *New York Times*, 1 Aug.

Bakunin, Mikhail Alekseyevich 1814–76

Russian anarchist. He was sent to Siberia in 1855 but
escaped, and became an advocate of anarchism, speaking
against Marx at the First Communist International
(1868), until he was outvoted and expelled at the Hague
Congress (1872).

87 From each according to his faculties, to each
    according to his needs; that is what we wish,
    sincerely and energetically.
    1870 Anarchists' declaration, signed by the 47 defendants after
    the failed uprising in Lyons.
    ▷ See Marx 661:24.

Balazs, Bela originally *Hubert Bauer*
1884–1949

Hungarian writer who wrote *Theory of the Film: Character
and Growth of a New Art*.

88 Film art has a greater influence on the minds of the
    general public than any other art.
    1953 *Theory of the Film: Character and Growth of a New Art*
    (translated by Edith Bone).

Balcon, Michael 1896–1977

British film producer.

89 In the absence of money, we'll have to make do
with talent.

> Quoted in David Puttnam *Michael Balcon: The Pursuit of British
> Cinema* (1984), preface.

90 Well if you fellows feel so strongly in favour, on my
head be it.

> Quoted in David Puttnam *Michael Balcon: The Pursuit of British
> Cinema* (1984), preface.

Baldwin, James Arthur 1924–87

US writer and civil rights activist. His often autobiographical novels include *Go Tell it on the Mountain*
(1954) and *Just Above My Head* (1979).

91 At the root of the American Negro problem is the
necessity of the American white man to find a way
of living with the Negro in order to be able to live
with himself.

> **1953** 'Stranger in a Village', in *Harper's*, Oct.

92 It seems to be typical of life in America, where
opportunities, real and fancied, are thicker than
anywhere else on the globe, that the second
generation has no time to talk to the first.

> **1955** *Notes of a Native Son*, 'Notes of a Native Son'.

93 I learned in New Jersey that to be a Negro meant,
precisely, that one was never looked at but was
simply at the mercy of the reflexes the color of one's
skin caused in other people.

> **1955** *Notes of a Native Son*, 'Notes of a Native Son'.

94 The writer's greed is appalling. He wants, or seems
to want, everything and practically everybody; in
another sense, and at the same time, he needs no
one at all.

> **1961** *Nobody Knows My Name*, 'Alas, Poor Richard'.

95 Children have never been very good at listening to
their elders, but they have never failed to imitate
them. They must, they have no other models.

> **1961** *Nobody Knows My Name*, 'Fifth Avenue, Uptown'.

96 Anyone who has ever struggled with poverty knows
how extremely expensive it is to be poor.

> **1961** *Nobody Knows My Name*, 'Fifth Avenue, Uptown'.

97 Freedom is not something that anybody can be
given; freedom is something people take and
people are as free as they want to be.

> **1961** *Nobody Knows My Name*, 'Notes for a Hypothetical
> Novel'.

98 Money, it turned out, was exactly like sex, you
thought of nothing else if you didn't have it and
thought of other things if you did.

> **1961** 'Black Boy Looks at the White Boy', in *Esquire*, May.

99 If the concept of God has any validity or any use, it
can only be to make us larger, freer, and more

loving. If God cannot do this, then it is time we got
rid of Him.

> **1962** 'Down at the Cross', in *The New Yorker*, 17 Nov.

1 The Fire Next Time.

> **1963** Title of book of essays. Baldwin took the phrase from the
> traditional spiritual, 'Home in the Rock'.

2 It comes as a great shock around the age of five, six
or seven to discover that the flag to which you have
pledged your allegiance, along with everybody else,
has not pledged its allegiance to you. It comes as a
shock to see Gary Cooper killing off the Indians
and, although you are rooting for Gary Cooper,
that the Indians are you.

> **1965** Speech at Cambridge Union, 17 Feb, arguing for the
> motion that 'The American Dream is at the expense of the
> American Negro'.

3 If they take you in the morning, they will be
coming for us that night.

> **1971** 'Open Letter to my Sister, Angela Davis', in *The New
> York Review of Books*, 7 Jan.

Baldwin, Stanley, 1st Earl Baldwin of Bewdley 1867–1947

English Conservative politician, Chancellor (1922–3)
and Prime Minister (1923, 1924–9 and 1935–7). His
period of office was marked by the abdication of Edward
VIII in 1936.

4 A lot of hard-faced men who look as if they had
done very well out of the war.

> **1918** Of the first post-World War I Parliament. Quoted in J M
> Keynes *Economic Consequences of the Peace* (1919).

5 I met Curzon in Downing Street, and received the
sort of greeting a corpse would give an undertaker.

> **1923** Of his rival for the premiership, Lord Curzon, on the
> death of Bonar Law. Attributed.

6 A platitude is simply a truth repeated until people
get tired of hearing it.

> **1924** Speech in the House of Commons, 29 May.

7 There are three classes which need sanctuary more
than others—birds, wild flowers, and Prime
Ministers.

> **1925** In *The Observer*, 24 May.

8 The work of a Prime Minister is the loneliest job in
the world.

> **1927** Speech, 9 Jan.

9 The papers conducted by Lord Rothermere and
Lord Beaverbrook are not newspapers in the
ordinary acceptance of the term. They are engines
of propaganda for the constantly-changing policies,
desires, personal wishes, and personal likes and
dislikes of two men... What the proprietorship of
those papers is aiming at is power, and power

without responsibility—the prerogative of the harlot throughout the ages.

1931 Speech, 18 Mar. Rudyard Kipling, Baldwin's cousin, is alleged to be the original author of this famous phrase. Harold Macmillan claimed that the Duke of Devonshire (his father-in-law) responded 'Good God, that's done it, he's lost us the tarts.'

10 I think it is well also for the man in the street to realize that there is no power on earth that can protect him from being bombed. Whatever people will tell him, the bomber will always get through. The only defence is in offence, which means that you have to kill more women and children more quickly than the enemy if you want to save yourselves.

1932 Speech in the House of Commons, 10 Nov.

11 When you think about the defence of England, you no longer think of the chalk cliffs of Dover. You think of the Rhine. That is where our frontier lies today.

1934 House of Commons, 30 Jul.

12 There is a wind of nationalism and freedom blowing round the world, and blowing as strongly in Asia as elsewhere.

1934 Speech, Dec.

13 I shall be but a short time tonight. I have seldom spoken with greater regret, for my lips are not yet unsealed. Were these troubles over I would make a case, and I guarantee that not a man would go into the lobby against us.

1935 Speech in the House of Commons, 10 Dec, speaking on the Abyssinian crisis. This is often misquoted as 'My lips are sealed'.

14 You will find in politics that you are much exposed to the attribution of false motives. Never complain and never explain.

1943 Advice to Harold Nicholson.

15 When the call came for me to form a Government, one of my first thoughts was that it should be a Government of which Harrow would not be ashamed.

Attributed.

Balfour, Arthur James Balfour, 1st Earl

1848–1930

Scottish Conservative politician and Prime Minister (1902–5). As Chief Secretary for Ireland (1887–91) his policy of suppression earned him the name 'Bloody Balfour', and as Foreign Secretary (1916–19) he was responsible for the Balfour Declaration, which promised Zionists a national home in Palestine.

16 I look forward to a time when Irish patriotism will as easily combine with British patriotism as Scottish patriotism combines now.

1889 Speech, Glasgow, Dec.

17 His Majesty's Government looks with favour upon the establishment in Palestine of a national home for the Jews.

1917 The Balfour Declaration, made in a letter to Lord Rothschild, 2 Nov.

18 The General Strike has taught the working classes more in four days than years of talking could have done.

1926 Speech in the House of Commons, 7 May.

19 I thought that he was a young man of promise, but it appears that he is a young man of promises.

Of Winston Churchill. Quoted in Churchill *My Early Life* (1930), ch. 17.

20 Herbert Asquith's clarity is a great liability because he has nothing to say.

Quoted by George Will in *Newsweek*, 9 Sep 1991.

21 Nothing matters very much, and very few things matter at all.

Attributed.

22 I would rather be an opportunist and float, than go to the bottom with my principles around my neck.

Attributed.

23 It has always been desirable to tell the truth, but seldom if ever necessary to tell the whole truth.

Attributed.

Ball, George Wildman 1909–94

US lawyer and diplomat. As Under-Secretary of State (1961–6) he played a major part in foreign policy, particularly in the Trade Agreements of 1962. He opposed the war in Vietnam, and left government for banking in 1966.

24 Once on the tiger's back, we cannot be sure of picking the place to dismount.

1964 Memo to Secretary of Defense Robert S McNamara, 5 Oct, on the escalation of the Vietnam War. It became known as 'the tiger's back memo'. Quoted in Deborah Shapley *Promise and Power* (1993).

25 Like giving the keys of the world's largest liquor store to a confirmed alcoholic.

On oil profiteering that permitted an arms-buying spree by Mohammed Reza Pahlavi, last shah of Iran. Quoted in William Shawcross *The Shah's Last Ride* (1988).

26 Never to be bored, never to be frustrated, never to be alone.

Defining what John F Kennedy wanted from the presidency. *President Kennedy* (1993).

Ball, John d.1381

English priest, one of the leaders of the Peasant's Revolt of 1381. He was executed for his part in these events.

27 When Adam delved and Eve span,

Who was then a gentleman?

1381 Sermon on the eve of the Peasant's Revolt. Quoted in George Holmes *The Later Middle Ages, 1272–1485* (1962), ch.7.

Ballads

28 'Oh, mother, mother, mak my bed,
    And mak it saft and narrow;
    My love has died for me to-day,
    I'll die for him tomorrow.'
    'Barbara Allen'.

29 It fell about the Lammas tide,
    When the muir-men win their hay,
    The doughty Douglas bound him to ride
    Into England, to drive a prey.
    'The Battle of Otterbourne', opening lines.

30 There was twa sisters in a bower,
    Binnorie, O Binnorie;
    There came a knight to be their wooer,
    By the bonnie mill-dams o' Binnorie.
    'Binnorie', stanza 1.

31 Ye Highlands and ye Lawlands,
    O where hae ye been?
    They hae slain the Earl of Murray
    And laid him on the green.
    'The Bonnie Earl of Murray', stanza 1.

32 He was a braw gallant,
    And he play'd at the ba';
    And the bonnie Earl of Murray
    Was the flower amang them a'.

    He was a braw gallant,
    And he play'd at the glove;
    And the bonnie Earl of Murray,
    O he was the Queen's luve.

    O lang will his lady
    Look owre the castle Doune,
    Ere she sees the Earl of Murray
    Come sounding thro' the toun.
    'The Bonnie Earl of Murray'.

33 O the broom, the bonnie, bonnie broom,
    The broom of Cowdenknowes;
    I wish I were with my dear swain,
    With his pipe and my yowes.
    'The Broom of Cowdenknowes', opening lines.

34 'A bed, a bed,' Clerk Sanders said,
    'A bed for you and me!'
    'Fye na, fye na,' said may Margaret,
    'Till anes we married be!'
    'Clerk Sanders'

35 Is there any room at your head, Sanders?
    Is there any room at your feet?

Or any room at your twa sides,
Where fain, fain I would sleep?

There is nae room at my head, Margaret,
There is nae room at my feet;
My bed it is the cold, cold grave;
Among the hungry worms I sleep.
'Clerk Sanders'.

36 She hadna sailed a league, a league,
    A league but barely three,
    When dismal grew his countenance
    And drumlie grew his e'e.
    They hadna sailed a league, a league,
    A league but barely three,
    Until she espied his cloven foot,
    And she wept right bitterlie.
    'The Demon Lover'.

37 Late at e'en, drinkin' the wine,
    And ere they paid the lawin',
    They set a combat them between,
    To fight it at the dawin'.

    'O stay at hame, my noble lord,
    O stay at hame, my marrow!
    My cruel brother will you betray
    On the dowie houms o' Yarrow!'
    'The Dowie Houms o' Yarrow'.

38 'Yestreen I dreamed a dolefu' dream;
    I ken'd here wad be sorrow!
    I dreamed I pu'd the heather green,
    On the dowie banks o' Yarrow.'

    She gaed up yon high, high hill—
    I wat she gaed wi' sorrow—
    An' in the den spied nine dead men,
    On the dowie houms o' Yarrow.
    'The Dowie Houms o' Yarrow'.

39 'Why dois your brand sae drap wi' bluid,
    Edward, Edward,
    Why dois your brand sae drap wi' bluid,
    And why sae sad gang ye O?'
    'Edward', opening lines.

40 Then up and started our gudewife,
    Gied three skips on the floor:
    'Gudeman, ye've spoken the foremost word,
    Get up and bar the door.'
    'Get Up and Bar the Door'.

41 I wish I were where Helen lies,
    Night and day on me she cries;
    O that I were where Helen lies,
    On fair Kirkconnell lea!
    'Helen of Kirkconnell', opening lines.

42 'It's I, Jamie Telfer o' the fair Dodhead,

And a harried man I think I be!
There's naething left at the fair Dodhead
But a waefu' wife and bairnies three.'
'Jamie Telfer'.

43 'Will ye gang wi' me, Lizzy Lindsay,
Will ye gang to the Highlands wi' me?
Will ye gang wi' me, Lizzy Lindsay.
My bride and my darling to be?'
'Lizzy Lindsay', opening lines.

44 This ae nighte, this ae nighte,
—*Every nighte and alle,*
Fire and fleet and candle-lighte,
And Christe receive thy saule.
'A Lyke-Wake Dirge', opening lines.

45 Marie Hamilton's to the kirk gane,
Wi' ribbons in her hair;
The king thought mair o' Marie Hamilton
Than ony that were there.
'Marie Hamilton', opening lines.

46 'Yestreen the queen had four Maries,
The night she'll hae but three;
There was Marie Seaton, and Mari Beaton,
And Marie Carmichael, and me.'
'Marie Hamilton'.

47 The king sits in Dunfermline town,
Drinking the blude-red wine;
'O whare will I get a skeely skipper,
To sail this new ship of mine?'
'Sir Patrick Spens', opening lines.

48 'I saw the new moon late yestreen,
Wi' the auld moon in her arm;
And if we gang to sea, master,
I fear we'll come to harm.'
'Sir Patrick Spens'.

49 And lang, lang may the ladyes sit,
Wi' their fans into their hand,
Before they see Sir Patrick Spens
Come sailing to the strand!
'Sir Patrick Spens'.

50 Half-owre, half-owre to Aberdour,
'Tis fifty fathoms deep,
And there lies gude Sir Patrick Spens,
Wi' the Scots lords at his feet.
'Sir Patrick Spens'.

51 'O I forbid you, maidens a',
That wear gowd on your hair,
To come or gae by Carterhaugh,
For young Tam Lin is there.

'There's nane that gaes by Carterhaugh,
But they leave him a wad.
Either their rings or green mantles,

Or else their maidenhead.'

Janet has kilted her green kirtle
A little aboon her knee,
And she has braided her yellow hair
A little aboon her bree,
And she's awa' to Carterhaugh
As fast as she can hie.
'Tam Lin', opening stanzas.

52 True Thomas lay on Huntlie bank,
A ferlie he spied wi' his e'e,
And there he saw a ladye bright,
Come riding down by the Eildon Tree.
'Thomas the Rhymer', opening lines.

53 And see ye not yon braid, braid road,
That lies across the lily leven?
That is the path of Wickedness,
Though some call it the Road to Heaven.
'Thomas the Rhymer'.

54 There were three ravens sat on a tree,
They were as black as they might be.
The one of them said to his make,
'Where shall we our breakfast take?'
'The Three Ravens'.

55 As I was walking all alane,
I heard twa corbies making a mane;
The tane unto the tother say,
'Where sall we gang and dine to-day?'

'In behint yon auld fail dye,
I wot there lies a new-slain knight;
And naebody kens that he lies there,
But his hawk, his hound, and his lady fair.

'His hound is to the hunting gane,
His hawk to fetch the wild-fowl hame,
His lady's ta'en another mate,
So we may mak our dinner sweet.'
'The Twa Corbies', opening stanzas.

56 O'er his white banes, when they are bare,
The wind sall blaw for evermair.
'The Twa Corbies'.

57 O waly, waly up the bank,
And waly, waly doun the brae,
And waly, waly yon burn-side
Where I and my love wont to gae.

I lean'd my back unto an aik,
I thocht it was a trustie tree;
But first it bow'd, and syne it brake—
Sae my true love did lichtlie me.

O waly, waly, gin love be bonnie
A little time while it is new;
But when 'tis auld it waxeth cauld
And fades awa' like morning dew.

O wherefore should I busk my heid,
O wherefore should I kame my hair?
For my true love has me forsook,
And says he'll never lo'e me mair.
pre-1566 'Waly, Waly', opening stanzas.

58 But had I wist, before I kiss'd,
That love had been sae ill to win.
I'd lock'd my heart in a case o' gowd,
And pinn'd it wi' a siller pin.
'Waly, Waly', stanza 4.

59 Tom Pearce, Tom Pearce, lend me your grey mare,
All along, down along, out along lee.
For I want for to go to Widdicombe Fair,
Wi' Bill Brewer, Jan Stewer, Peter Gurney, Peter
   Davey, Dan'l Whiddon, Harry Hawk,
Old Uncle Tom Cobleigh and all.
'Widdicombe Fair'.

60 There lived a wife at Usher's Well,
And a wealthy wife was she;
She had three stout and stalwart sons,
And sent them o'er the sea.
'The Wife of Usher's Well', opening lines.

61 The cock doth craw, the day doth daw,
The channerin' worm doth chide.
'The Wife of Usher's Well'.

Ballard, J(ames) G(raham) 1930–

British novelist and science-fiction writer, born in China. His novel *Empire of the Sun* draws on his childhood experiences in wartime Shanghai, then occupied by Japan.

62 The only truly alien planet is Earth.
1962 'Which Way to Inner Space', in *New Worlds*, May.

63 He believes that science fiction is the apocalyptic
literature of the 20th century, the authentic
language of Auschwitz, Eniwetok and
Aldermaston. He also believes that inner space, not
outer, is the real subject of science fiction.
1965 Author's statement contained in a biographical note to *The Drowned World*.

64 Science and technology multiply around us. To an
increasing extent they dictate the languages in
which we speak and think. Either we use those
languages, or we remain mute.
1974 *Crash*.

Balliett, Whitney 1926–

US writer. He is jazz critic of *The New Yorker*, and has written several books on music.

65 The Sound of Surprise.
1959 Title of book, much cited as a definition of jazz.

66 A bundle of biases held loosely together by a sense
of taste.

1962 His definition of a critic. *Dinosaurs in the Morning*, introductory note.

Balzac, Honoré de 1799–1850

French writer, one of the great 19c realist novelists. He created a world of characters whose lives are interwoven in his *Comédie humaine*.

67 *Un homme n'a jamais pu élever sa maîtresse jusqu'à
lui; mais une femme place toujours son amant aussi
haut qu'elle.*

A man can never elevate his mistress to his rank,
but a woman can always place her lover as high as
she.
1829 *Physiologie du mariage*.

68 *Le mariage doit incessamment combattre un monstre
qui dévore tout: l'habitude.*

Marriage should always combat the monster that
devours everything: habit.
1829 *Physiologie du mariage*.

69 *La femme mariée est un esclave qu'il faut savoir
mettre sur un trône.*

A married woman is a slave whom one must put on
a throne.
1829 *Physiologie du mariage*.

70 *Un mari, comme un gouvernement, ne doit jamais
avouer de faute.*

A husband, like a government, never needs to
admit a fault.
1829 *Physiologie du mariage*.

71 *En toute chose, nous ne pouvons être jugés que par nos
pairs.*

In all things, we should only be judged by our
peers.
1830 *La Maison du chat-qui-pelote*.

72 *Dans ces grandes crises, le coeur se brise ou se bronze.*

In times of crisis, the heart either breaks or boldens.
1830 *La Maison du chat-qui-pelote*.

73 *Le bonheur engloutit nos forces, comme le malheur
éteint nos vertus.*

Happiness engulfs our strength, just as misfortune
extinguishes our virtues.
1831 *La Peau de chagrin*.

74 *La haine est un tonique, elle fait vivre, elle inspire la
vengeance; mais la pitié tue, elle affaiblit encore notre
faiblesse.*

Hatred is a tonic, it makes one live, it inspires
vengeance; but pity kills, it weakens our weaknesses
still further.
1831 *La Peau de chagrin*.

75 *Beaucoup d'hommes ont un orgueil qui les pousse à cacher leurs combats et à ne se montrer que victorieux.*

Many men have pride that causes them to hide their combats and to only show themselves victorious.
1831 *La Recherche de l'absolu.*

76 *A lui la foi, à elle le doute, à elle le fardeau le plus lourd: la femme ne souffre-t-elle pas toujours pour deux?*

For him, faith; for her, doubt and for her the heavier load: does not the woman always suffer for both?
1831 *La Recherche de l'absolu.*

77 *L'amour n'est pas seulement un sentiment, il est un art aussi.*

Love is not only a feeling; it is also an art.
1831 *La Recherche de l'absolu.*

78 *L'amour a son instinct, il sait trouver le chemin du coeur comme le plus faible insecte marche à sa fleur avec une irrésistible volonté qui ne s'épouvante de rien.*

Love has its own instinct. It knows how to find the road to the heart just as the weakest insect moves toward its flower by an irresistible will which fears nothing.
1832 *La Femme de trente ans.*

79 *Le coeur d'une mère est un abîme au fond duquel se trouve toujours un pardon.*

A mother's heart is an abyss at the bottom of which there is always forgiveness.
1832 *La Femme de trente ans.*

80 *Les faits ne sont rien, ils n'existent pas, il ne subsiste de nous que des Idées.*

Deeds are nothing. They do not exist. Only our ideas survive.
1832 *Louis Lambert.*

81 *Nos beaux sentiments ne sont-ils pas les poésies de la volonté?*

Aren't our best feelings poetry of the will?
1835 *Le Père Goriot.*

82 *La passion est toute l'humanité. Sans elle, la religion, l'histoire, le roman, l'art seraient inutiles.*

Passion is all of humanity. Without it, religion, history, the novel and art would be useless.
1842 *La Comédie humaine*, foreword.

83 *L'homme n'est ni bon ni méchant, il naît avec des instincts et des aptitudes.*

Man is neither good nor evil; he is born with instincts and abilities.
1842 *La Comédie humaine*, foreword.

84 *L'avarice commence où la pauvreté cesse.*

Greed begins where poverty ends.
1843 *Illusions perdues*, 'Les deux poètes'.

85 *Les dettes sont jolies chez les jeunes gens de vingt-cinq ans, plus tard, personne ne les leur pardonne.*

Debts are becoming for 25-year-olds; after this, no one forgives them.
1843 *Illusions perdues*, 'Un Grand homme de province'.

Banda, Hastings Kamuzu 1898–1997

Malawiian statesman, Prime Minister (1963) and President (1966; Life President from 1971).

86 I wish that I could bring Stonehenge to Nyasaland, to show that there was a time when Britain had a savage culture.
1963 In *The Observer*, 10 Mar.

Bandeira, Manuel 1886–1968

Brazilian poet, literary historian, translator and educator. He achieved enormous popularity and national acclaim.

87 *Estou farto do lirismo comedido*
Do lirismo bem comportado
Do lirismo funcionário público com livro de ponto expediente protocolo e manifestações de apreço ao Sr diretor
Estou farto do lirismo que pára e vai averiguar no dicionário o cunho vernáculo de um vocábulo

Abaixo os puristas

I'm sick of cautious lyricism
of well-behaved lyricism
of a civil servant lyricism complete with time card office hours set procedures and expressions of esteem for Mr Boss, Sir.
I'm sick of the lyricism that has to stop in midstream to look up the precise meaning of a word.

Down with purists!
1930 *Libertinagem*, 'Poética' (translated as 'Poetics', 1989).

Bankhead, Tallulah 1903–68

US actress. She made her New York début in 1918 and subsequently played a range of classical and contemporary roles, attracting notoriety for her scandalous private life. She wrote an autobiography, *Tallulah* (1952).

88 There is less in this than meets the eye.
1922 Attending a revival of Maeterlinck's play *Aglavaine and Selysette*. Quoted in Alexander Woollcott *Shouts and Murmurs* (1923), ch.4.

89 Cocaine habit-forming? Of course not. I ought to know. I've been using it for years.
1939 In conversation at the first night party of Lillian Hellman's *Little Foxes*. Recalled in *Tallulah* (1952), ch.4.

90 I'm as pure as the driven slush.

Quoted by Maurice Zolotow, in *The Saturday Evening Post*, 12 Apr 1947.

91 Darling, they've absolutely ruined your perfectly dreadful play!

1957 Greeting Tennessee Williams at the film premiere of his play *Orpheus Descending*. Quoted in Peter Hay *Broadway Anecdotes*.

92 Only good girls keep diaries. Bad girls don't have time.

Recalled on her death, 12 Dec 1968.

93 Nobody can be exactly like me. Sometimes even I have trouble doing it.

Attributed.

Banks, Iain Menzies 1954–

Scottish writer of semi-fantastic novels including *The Wasp Factory* (1984) and *The Bridge* (1986).

94 They are, after all, a language; they do not so much say things about as, they are what is said.

1986 Of clothes. *The Bridge*, ch.2.

95 'You're not upset, are you, Orr?' Brooke says, pouring wine into my glass.
'Merely sober. The symptoms are similar.'

1986 *The Bridge*, ch.3.

96 The choice is not between dream and reality; it is between two different dreams.

1986 *The Bridge*, coda.

97 It was the day my grandmother exploded.

1992 *The Crow Road*, ch.1, opening words.

98 Mr Blawke always reminded me of a heron; I'm not sure why. Something to do with a sense of rapacious stillness, perhaps, and also the aura of one who knows time is on his side.

1992 Of the family lawyer. *The Crow Road*, ch.1.

99 The belief that we somehow moved on to something else—whether still recognisably ourselves, or quite thoroughly changed—might be a tribute to our evolutionary tenacity and our animal thirst for life, but not to our wisdom.

1992 On the idea of life after death. *The Crow Road*, ch.18.

Banks, Lynne Reid 1929–

English novelist and playwright. Her best-known novel is her first, *The L-Shaped Room* (1960). She has also written plays for radio and television and fiction for children.

1 Jane Austen is the only novelist I know whose peculiar genius lies in taking perfectly ordinary people through ordinary situations, and transmogrifying them into fascinating fiction.

1991 In her entry in *Contemporary Novelists*, 5th edn.

Bannister, Sir Roger Gilbert 1929–

English athlete and neurologist. In 1954 he ran the first 'four-minute mile' (3 mins 59.4 secs). He was knighted in 1975. After a distinguished medical career, he was appointed Master of Pembroke College, Oxford (1985).

2 I leapt at the tape like a man taking his last spring to save himself from the chasm that threatens to engulf him.

1955 Of the end of his record-breaking run. *First Four Minutes*.

3 I sometimes think that running has given me a glimpse of the greatest freedom a man can ever know, because it results in the simultaneous liberation of both body and mind.

1955 *First Four Minutes*.

Banting, Frederick Grant 1891–1941

Canadian physician and discoverer of insulin.

4 Diabetus. Ligate pancreatic ducts of dog. Keep dogs alive till acini degenerate leaving Islets. Try to isolate the internal secretion of these to relieve glycosuria.

1920 Note scribbled in his journal, 2.00am, 31 Oct. This led to the discovery of insulin for the treatment of diabetes, as recorded in Michael Bliss *The Discovery of Insulin* (1982).

Barach, Alvan Leroy 1895–1977

US physician. He was Professor of Medicine at Columbia University and a pioneer in respiratory therapy.

5 An alcoholic has been lightly defined as a man who drinks more than his own doctor.

1962 In the *Journal of the American Medical Association*, vol.181, p.393.

Baraka, Amiri adopted name of *LeRoi (Everett Leroy) Jones* 1934–

US poet, playwright and prose writer. He adopted a Muslim identity in 1967 after establishing his reputation as a radical and outspoken black voice.

6 Preface to a Twenty Volume Suicide Note.

1961 Title of poetry collection.

7 A rich man told me recently that a liberal is a man who tells other people what to do with their money.

1962 'Tokenism', in *Kulchur*, spring issue.

8 A man is either free or he is not. There cannot be any apprenticeship for freedom.

1962 'Tokenism', in *Kulchur*, spring issue.

9 But when a man who sees the world one way becomes the slave of a man who interprets the world in exactly the opposite way, the result is, to my mind, the *worst* possible kind of slavery.

1963 *Blues People*, ch.1.

Barbellion, W(illiam) N(ero) P(ilate),

pseudonym of *Bruce Frederick Cummings*

1889–1919

English diarist. He was a self-taught biologist, and worked for the British Museum. His principal work is the self-critical *Journal of A Disappointed Man* (1919).

10 I can remember wondering as a child if I were a young Macaulay or Ruskin and secretly deciding that I was. My infant mind even was bitter with those who insisted on regarding me as a normal child and not as a prodigy.

1919 *Journal of A Disappointed Man*, 23 Oct.

11 Give me the man who will surrender the whole world for a moss or a caterpillar, and impracticable visions for a simple human delight.

1919 *Enjoying Life and Other Literary Remains*, 'Crying for the Moon'.

Barbirolli, Sir John 1899–1970

British conductor and cellist, conductor of the New York Philharmonic in 1937 and of the Hallé Orchestra in Manchester (1943–58). In 1950 he was awarded the Gold Medal of the Royal Philharmonic Society, and he became principal conductor of the Hallé in 1958.

12 Three farts and a raspberry, orchestrated.

Of modern music. Quoted in M Kennedy *Barbirolli, Conductor Laureate* (1971).

13 I want you to sound like 22 women having babies without chloroform.

To a chorus. Quoted in M Kennedy *Barbirolli, Conductor Laureate* (1971).

Barbour, John c.1316–95

Scottish poet, prelate and scholar, the 'father of Scottish poetry'. His national epic, *The Brus*, is a narrative poem on the life of Robert I, the Bruce. He served as Archdeacon of Aberdeen from c.1357 until his death.

14 Storyss to rede ar delitabill,
Supposs that thai be nocht but fabill.

c.1375 *The Brus*, bk.1, l.1–2.

15 A! fredome is a noble thing!
Fredome mayss man to haiff liking,
Fredome all solace to man giffis:
He levys at ess that frely levys!

c.1375 *The Brus*, bk.1, l.225–8.

16 Luff is off sae mekill mycht,
That it all paynis makis lycht.

c.1375 *The Brus*, bk.2, l.520–1.

Barker, George Granville 1913–91

English poet, novelist and playwright. He was associated with Dylan Thomas and the New Apocalyptic group, but his poetry retained a distinctively individual quality.

17 Sitting as huge as Asia, seismic with laughter,
Gin and chicken helpless in her Irish hand.

1944 'To My Mother'.

18 Honouring itself the clay rears up
To praise its pottering purposes,
But, oh, much sorrow shall it sup
Before fulfilment is.

1954 'Goodman Jacksin and the Angel'.

19 When the guns begin to rattle
And the men to die
Does the Goddess of the Battle
Smile or sigh?

1962 'Battle Hymn of the New Republic'.

Barkley, Alben William 1877–1956

US lawyer and Democratic politician, Vice President under Truman (1949–53).

20 The best audience is intelligent, well-educated and a little drunk.

Recalled on his death, 30 Apr 1956.

Barlow, Joel 1754–1812

US poet. He is best remembered for his mock-heroic salute to the humble hasty-pudding (a dish of boiled Indian meal), although he considered his turgid epic *The Colombiad* (1807) his major work.

21 I sing the sweets I know, the charms I feel,
My morning incense, and my evening meal,
The sweets of Hasty-Pudding. Come, dear bowl,
Glide o'er my palate, and inspire my soul.

1796 'The Hasty-Pudding', canto 1

Barnard, Frederick R

22 One picture is worth ten thousand words.

1927 In *Printer's Ink*, 10 Mar.

Barnes, Clive 1927–

English theatre critic. He has written for the *New York Post* since 1978, directing much of his venom against the commercial Broadway stage.

23 This is the kind of show to give pornography a bad name.

1969 Reviewing *Oh, Calcutta!*, *New York Times*, 18 Jun.

Barnes, Djuna 1892–1982

US writer, who spent a large part of her life in Europe. She is best known for her novel *Nightwood* (1936).

24 New York is the meeting place of the peoples, the only city where you can hardly find a typical American.

1916 'Greenwich Village As It Is', in *Pearson's Magazine*, Oct.

25 After all, it is not where one washes one's neck that counts but where one moistens one's throat.
1916 'Greenwich Village As It Is', in *Pearson's Magazine*, Oct.

26 Sleep demands of us a guilty immunity. There is not one of us who, given an eternal incognito, a thumbprint nowhere set against our souls, would not commit rape, murder and all abominations.
1936 Doctor. *Nightwood*, ch.5.

27 Dreams have only the pigmentation of fact.
1936 Doctor. *Nightwood*, ch.5.

28 I'm a fart in a gale of wind, a humble violet under a cow pat.
1936 Doctor. *Nightwood*, ch.5.

Barnes, Julian Patrick 1946–

English novelist, formerly a lexicographer and journalist. His best known work is *Flaubert's Parrot* (1984), a meditation on fiction and biography.

29 We'd both been to the country and found it disappointingly empty.
1981 *Metroland*, pt.1, ch.4.

30 You can have your cake and eat it: the only trouble is you get fat.
1984 *Flaubert's Parrot*, ch.7.

31 The writer must be universal in sympathy and an outcast by nature: only then can he see clearly.
1984 *Flaubert's Parrot*, ch.10.

32 Do not imagine that Art is something which is designed to give gentle uplift and self-confidence. Art is not a *brassière*. At least, not in the English sense. But do not forget that *brassière* is the French for life-jacket.
1984 *Flaubert's Parrot*, ch.10.

33 Books are where things are explained to you; life is where things aren't… Books make sense of life. The only problem is that the lives they make sense of are other people's lives, never your own.
1984 *Flaubert's Parrot*, ch.13.

34 Women were brought up to believe that men were the answer. They weren't. They weren't even one of the questions.
1986 *Staring At The Sun*, pt.2.

35 Does history repeat itself, the first time as tragedy, the second time as farce? No, that's too grand, too considered a process. History just burps, and we taste again that raw-onion sandwich it swallowed centuries ago.
1989 *A History of the World in 10¹/₂ Chapters*, 'Parenthesis'.

36 I've always thought you are what you are and you shouldn't pretend to be anyone else. But Oliver

used to correct me and explain that you are whoever it is you're pretending to be.
1991 *Talking It Over*, ch.2.

37 Love is just a system for getting someone to call you darling after sex.
1991 *Talking It Over*, ch.16.

Barnum, P(hineas) T(aylor) 1810–91

US showman. He introduced freak shows, including General Tom Thumb (1842), in his New York museum, and in 1881 co-founded the Barnum and Bailey Circus, 'the greatest show on earth'.

38 There's a sucker born every minute.
Attributed.

Barr, Alfred Hamilton, Jr 1902–81

US art historian, first Director of the Museum of Modern Art, New York. His many works include *Cubism and Abstract Art* (1936).

39 Except the American woman, nothing interests the eye of American man more than the automobile, or seems so important to him as an object of aesthetic appreciation.
1963 In news summaries, 31 Dec.

Barrer, Bruce

40 She endured a five-year marriage to Ernest Hemingway that roughly coincided with and bore more than a passing resemblance to World War II.
1993 Of Martha Gelhorn. In the *Wall Street Journal*, 9 Mar.

Barrie, Sir J(ames) M(atthew) 1860–1937

Scottish novelist and dramatist. After journalism and several autobiographical works, he turned to playwriting in 1890, with such works as *The Admirable Crichton* (1902), *Peter Pan* (1904) and *What Every Woman Knows* (1908, published 1918).

41 The life of every man is a diary in which he means to write one story, and writes another; and his humblest hour is when he compares the volume as it is with what he vowed to make it.
1891 *The Little Minister*, vol.1, ch.1.

42 That is ever the way. 'Tis all jealousy to the bride and good wishes to the corpse.
1901 *Quality Street* (published 1913), act 1.

43 When the first baby laughed for the first time, the laugh broke into a thousand pieces and they all went skipping about, and that was the beginning of fairies.
1904 *Peter Pan* (published 1928), act 1.

44 Every time a child says 'I don't believe in fairies' there is a little fairy somewhere that falls down dead.
1904 *Peter Pan* (published 1928), act 1.

45 To die will be an awfully big adventure.
1904 *Peter Pan* (published 1928), act 3.

46 Charm…it's a sort of a bloom on a woman. If you have it, you don't need to have anything else; and if you don't have it, it doesn't much matter what else you have.
1908 *What Every Woman Knows* (published 1918), act 1.

47 My lady, there are few more impressive sights in the world than a Scotsman on the make.
1908 *What Every Woman Knows* (published 1918), act 2.

48 I have always found that the man whose second thoughts are good is worth watching.
1908 *What Every Woman Knows* (published 1918), act 3.

49 Every man who is high up loves to think that he has done it all himself; and the wife smiles, and lets it go at that. It's our only joke. Every woman knows that.
1908 *What Every Woman Knows* (published 1918), act 4.

50 One's religion is whatever he is most interested in, and yours is Success.
1921 *The Twelve-Pound Look.*

51 I bowl so slow that if after I have delivered the ball and don't like the look of it, I can run after it and bring it back.
Quoted in Colin Jarman *The Guinness Dictionary of Sports Quotations* (1990).

52 What a polite game tennis is. The chief word in it seems to be 'sorry' and admiration of each other's play crosses the net as frequently as the ball.
Quoted in Colin Jarman *The Guinness Dictionary of Sports Quotations* (1990).

53 I am glad you have asked me. I should like you to convey when you are acting it that the man you portray has a brother in Shropshire who drinks port.
Responding to a young actor's urgent request for advice as to how he should play a minor part in one of Barrie's plays. Attributed.

Barrington, Jonah 1941–

English squash player. He was British Open Champion six years in succession (1967–73).

54 Squash is boxing with racquets.
Quoted in Colin Jarman *The Guinness Dictionary of Sports Quotations* (1990).

Barry, Marion Shepilov, Jr 1936–

US politician, Mayor of Washington, DC (1979–91). He was arrested and charged with possession of cocaine in 1990.

55 There are two kinds of truth…real truths and made-up truths.
1990 Of the drug charges lodged against him. In the *Washington Post*, 13 May.

Barrymore, Ethel 1879–1959

US actress, one of the most prominent members of the Drew-Barrymore acting dynasty. She made her New York début in 1901 and went on to excel both in contemporary dramas and in Shakespearean roles. New York's Barrymore Theatre was opened in her honour in 1928.

56 For an actress to be a success she must have the face of Venus, the brains of Minerva, the grace of Terpsichore, the memory of Macaulay, the figure of Juno, and the hide of a rhinoceros.
Quoted in George Jean Nathan *The Theatre in the Fifties* (1953).

57 I never let them cough. They wouldn't dare.
1956 Of her audiences. In the *New York Post*, 7 Jun.

Barrymore, John 1882–1942

US actor of the Drew-Barrymore dynasty. He made his stage début in 1903 and distinguished himself in Shakespearean and other roles before turning to films. Renowned for his chaotic private life, he suffered increasingly from alcoholism.

58 Die? I should say not, old fellow. No Barrymore would allow such a conventional thing to happen to him.
1942 Quoted in Lionel Barrymore *We Barrymores* (1951), ch.26.

59 My only regret in the theatre is that I could never sit out front and watch me.
Quoted in Eddie Cantor *The Way I See It* (1959), ch.2.

60 Method acting? There are quite a few methods. Mine involves a lot of talent, a glass, and some cracked ice.
Quoted in *Actors about Acting, Loving, Living, Life* (1972).

Barrymore, Lionel 1848–1954

US actor, brother of Ethel and John Barrymore. He gave up a successful stage career for the cinema in 1925, finding fame as Dr Gillespie in a series of *Dr Kildare* films (from 1938).

61 How like father—a curtain call!
1905 Attributed comment, when his father's coffin had to be raised up again after it had snagged on being lowered into the grave.

62 I've played everything but the harp.
Attributed, when asked to suggest his own epitaph.

Barth, John Simmons 1930–

US novelist. His books are much concerned with the processes of story-telling and the making of myths, explored in a rich, highly literary mix of realism, fantasy and often arcane erudition.

63 Everyone is necessarily the hero of his own life story.
1958 *The End of the Road*, ch.1.

64 Every life has a Scheherazadesworth of stories.
1994 *Once Upon A Time*, 'Program Note'.

Barth, Karl 1886–1968

Swiss Reformed theologian, champion of neo-orthodoxy and influential in founding the German Confessing Church, which opposed Nazism. His extensive theological output proved highly influential in 20c Christian theology.

65 Jesus Christ, as he is attested to us in Holy Scripture, is the one Word of God whom we have to hear, and whom we have to trust and obey in life and in death.
1934 *The Barmen Declaration* adopted by the Confessing Church in Germany (translated by D S Bax, 1984).

66 Humanity in its basic form is co-humanity.
1948 *Kirchliche Dogmatik* vol.3, pt.2 (translated by H Knight as *Church Dogmatics*, 1960).

67 Basically and comprehensively, therefore, to be human is *to be with God*.
1948 *Kirchliche Dogmatik* vol.3, pt.2 (translated by H Knight as *Church Dogmatics*, 1960).

68 It is a bad sign when Christians are frightened by 'political' sermons—as if Christian preaching could be anything but political.
1954 *Gegen den Strom* (translated by E M Delacourt and S Godwin as 'The Christian Community and the Civil Community' in *Against the Stream*, 1954).

69 Whether the angels play only Bach in praising God I am not quite sure; I am sure, however, that *en famille* they play Mozart.
1968 Quoted in the *New York Times*.

Barthelme, Donald 1931–89

US novelist and short story writer.

70 The distinction between children and adults, while probably useful for some purposes, is at bottom a specious one, I feel. There are only individual egos, crazy for love.
1964 *Come Back, Dr Caligari*, 'Me and Miss Mandible'.

71 We like books that have a lot of *dreck* in them, matter which presents itself as not wholly relevant (or indeed, at all relevant), but which, carefully attended to, can supply a kind of 'sense' of what is going on. This 'sense' is not to be obtained by reading between the lines (for there is nothing there, in those white spaces), but by reading the lines themselves—looking at them, and so arriving at a feeling not of satisfaction exactly, that is too much to expect, but of having read them; of having 'completed' them.
1967 *Snow White*.

72 'Some people', Miss R. said, 'run to conceits or wisdom but I hold to the hard, brown, nutlike word. I might point out that there is enough aesthetic excitement here to satisfy anyone but a damned fool.'
1968 *Unspeakable Practices, Unnatural Acts*, 'The Indian Uprising'.

73 Endings are elusive, middles are nowhere to be found, but worst of all is to begin, to begin, to begin.
1968 *Unspeakable Practices, Unnatural Acts*, 'The Dolt'.

74 Doubt is a necessary precondition to meaningful action. Fear is the great mover in the end.
1972 *Sadness*, 'The Rise of Capitalism'.

75 The self cannot be escaped, but it can be, with ingenuity and hard work, distracted.
1972 *Sadness*, 'Daumier'.

76 Let me point out, if it has escaped your notice, that what an artist does, is fail.
1972 *Sadness*, 'The Sandman'.

77 The world is sagging, snagging, scaling, spalling, pilling, pinging, pitting, warping, checking, fading, chipping, cracking, yellowing, leaking, stalling, shrinking, and in dynamic unbalance.
1974 *Guilty Pleasures*, 'Down the Line with the Annual'.

78 No tale ever happened in the way we tell it. But the moral is always correct.
1975 *The Dead Father*, ch.6.

Barthes, Roland 1915–80

French literary critic, and major theorist of semiology. He developed a modernist school of criticism which argues for the 'death' of the author, and the need for the reader to recreate the text.

79 *Je crois que l'automobile est aujourd'hui l'équivalent assez exact des grandes cathédrales gothiques: je veux dire une grande création d'époque, conçue passionnément par des artistes inconnus, consommée dans son image, sinon dans son usage, par un peuple entier qui s'approprie en elle un objet parfaitement magique.*

Cars today are almost the exact equivalent of the great Gothic cathedrals…the supreme creation of an era, conceived with passion by unknown artists, and consummated in image if not in usage by a whole population which appropriates them as a purely magical object.

1957 *Mythologies*, 'La nouvelle Citroën'.

80 *Le toucher est le plus démystificateur de tous les sens, à la différence de la vue, qui est le plus magique.*

Touch is the most demystifying of all senses, different from sight which is the most magical.

1957 *Mythologies*, 'La nouvelle Citroën'.

81 *Tout refus du langage est une mort.*

Any refusal of language is a death.

1957 *Mythologies*, 'Le mythe, aujourd'hui'.

82 *L'endroit le plus érotique d'un corps n'est-il pas là où le vêtement bâille?*

Is not the most erotic part of the body wherever the clothing affords a glimpse?

1973 *Le Plaisir du texte.*

83 *L'amoureux qui n'oublie pas quelquefois meurt par excès, fatigue et tension de mémoire (tel Werther).*

The lover who does not forget *sometimes* dies from excess, fatigue, and the strain of memory (like Werther).

1977 *Fragments d'un discours amoureux.*

84 *Le langage est une peau: je frotte mon langage contre l'autre.*

Language is a skin; I rub my language against another language.

1977 *Fragments d'un discours amoureux*, 'Déclaration'.

85 *Tout ce qui est anachronique est obscène.*

Everything anachronistic is obscene.

1977 *Fragments d'un discours amoureux*, 'Obscène'.

Bartley, Robert Leroy 1937–

US journalist. He joined the *Wall Street Journal* in 1962 as a staff writer, and rose to become Editor (1979–) and Vice-President (1983–). He won a Pulitzer Prize for editorial writing in 1980.

86 You can't beat the market because it's smarter than you are. Intellectually, the only task is trying to determine what the market is telling you.

1992 *The Seven Fat Years*, ch.3.

87 The mystery is why we even collect these figures; if we kept similar statistics for Manhattan Island, Park Avenue could lay awake at night worrying about its trade deficit.

1992 On the balance of payments record. *The Seven Fat Years.*

Bartók, Béla 1881–1945

Hungarian composer and pianist. Much influenced by European folk music, he wrote works for piano and strings as well as music for ballet and opera. He died in poverty in the US, having emigrated in 1940.

88 The trouble is that I have to go with so much still to say.

1945 Spoken on his deathbed. Quoted in David Pickering *Brewer's Twentieth Century Music* (1994).

89 I cannot conceive of music that expresses absolutely nothing.

Quoted in Machlis *Introduction to Contemporary Music* (1963).

Baruch, Bernard Mannes 1870–1965

US financier and statesman. He became a powerful political influence, 'the adviser of presidents', and served on many commissions, including the American Atomic Energy Commission.

90 Let us not be deceived—we are today in the midst of a cold war.

1947 Address to the South Carolina legislature, 16 Apr, using an expression suggested to him by editor Herbert Bayard Swope.

91 The cold war is getting warmer.

1948 Address to a Senate committee.

92 To me old age is always fifteen years older than I am.

1955 In *Newsweek*, 29 Aug.

Barzun, Jacques 1907–

French-born US scholar, Professor of History at Columbia University (1945) and Dean and Provost there (1958–67). His works include *Darwin, Marx, Wagner* (1941) and *The Use and Abuse of Art* (1974).

93 Teaching is not a lost art, but the regard for it is a lost tradition.

1955 In *Newsweek*, 5 Dec.

94 The test and use of man's education is that he finds pleasure in the exercise of the mind.

1958 'Science and the Humanities', in the *Saturday Evening Post*, 3 May.

95 If it were possible to talk to the unborn, one could never explain to them how it feels to be alive, for life is washed in the speechless real.

1959 *The House of Intellect.*

96 Science is an all-pervasive energy, for it is at once a mode of thought, a source of strong emotion, and a faith as fanatical as any in history.

1964 *Science, The Glorious Entertainment.*

97 Whoever wants to know the heart and mind of America had better learn baseball.

Quoted in Michael Novak *The Joy of Sport* (1976), pt 1.

98 Baseball is a kind of collective chess with arms and legs in full play under sunlight.

Quoted in Colin Jarman *The Guinness Dictionary of Sports Quotations* (1990).

99 To watch a football game is to be in prolonged
neurotic doubt as to what you're seeing. It's more
like an emergency happening at a distance than a
game.

    Quoted in Colin Jarman *The Guinness Dictionary of Sports
Quotations* (1990).

Basho, Matsuo   1644–94

Japanese poet, regarded as the founder of *haiku* as a
significant poetic form, and influenced by Zen
Buddhism.

1 An old pond
    A frog jumps in
    The sound of water

    c.1689 Quoted in Hugh Cortazzi *The Japanese Achievement*
(1990).

2 Year by year,
    the monkey's mask
    reveals the monkey

    c.1689 *On Love and Barley: Haiku of Basho*, no.3 (translated by
Lucien Stryk).

3 Year's end—
    still in straw hat
    and sandals

    c.1689 *On Love and Barley: Haiku of Basho*, no.126 (translated
by Lucien Stryk).

4 Orchid—breathing
    incense into
    butterfly's wings

    c.1689 *On Love and Barley: Haiku of Basho*, no.166 (translated
by Lucien Stryk).

5 Friends part
    forever—wild geese
    lost in cloud

    c.1689 *On Love and Barley: Haiku of Basho*, no.219 (translated
by Lucien Stryk).

6 Learn about a pine tree from a pine tree, and about
a bamboo stalk from a bamboo stalk.

    Attributed, quoted in *On Love and Barley: Haiku of Basho*
(translated by Lucien Stryk), introduction.

Baskin, Leonard   1922–

US sculptor and graphic artist, also an influential teacher.
His powerful works include *Man with a Dead Bird*.

7 Pop art is the inedible raised to the unspeakable.

    1965 In *Publisher's Weekly*, 5 Apr.

    ▷ See Wilde 1077:66.

Bastard, Thomas   1566–1618

English poet.

8 Age is deformed, youth unkind,
    We scorn their bodies, they our mind.

    1598 *Chrestoleros*, bk.7, epigram 9.

Bates, H(erbert) E(rnest)   1905–74

English novelist, playwright and short-story writer. His
most popular publications include *Fair Stood the Wind for
France* (1944), *The Jacaranda Tree* (1949) and *The
Darling Buds of May* (1958).

9 Perfick.

    1958 Pa Larkin's characteristic summation. *The Darling Buds
of May*, ch.1 and passim.

Bates, Katharine Lee   1859–1929

US educator, author and poet. Her works include *College
Beautiful and Other Poems* (1887), *Sunshine and Other
Verses for Children* (1890), *Hermit Island* (1891) and *Fairy
Gold* (1916).

10 O beautiful for spacious skies,
    For amber waves of grain,
    For purple mountain majesties
    Above the fruited plain!
    America! America!
    God shed His grace on thee.
    And crown thy good with brotherhood
    From sea to shining sea.

    1893 'America the Beautiful', opening lines.

Bateson, Gregory   1904–80

English-born US social scientist, with interests in
anthropology and psychology.

11 Information is any difference that makes a
difference.

    1984 Quoted in *Scientific American*, no.41, Sep.

Batman, John   1801–39

Australian explorer, generally accepted as the founder of
Melbourne, the site of which he bought from a local
Aboriginal group for trinkets.

12 This will be the place for a Village.

    1835 Journal entry, Jun. The phrase is often quoted as 'a fine
place for a Village'.

Battelle, Phyllis   1922–

US columnist.

13 Where great-grandmothers dread to grow old.

    1958 Of Hollywood. In the *Journal-American*, 15 Mar.

Baudelaire, Charles   1821–67

French Symbolist poet and critic. He is best-known for
his collection *Les Fleurs du mal* (1857), for which author,
printer and publisher were prosecuted for impropriety,
but was praised by critics and has exerted an influence far
into the 20c.

14 *Hypocrite lecteur,—mon semblable,—mon frère!*

    Hypocrite reader—my fellow man—my brother!

    1857 *Les Fleurs du mal*, 'Au lecteur'.

    ▷ See Eliot 368:84.

15 *Je sais la douleur est la noblesse unique*
   Où ne mordront jamais la terre et les enfers.

I know that pain is the one nobility
upon which Hell itself cannot encroach.
1857 *Les Fleurs du mal*, 'Bénédiction' (translated by Richard
Howard, 1982).

16 *Le Poète est semblable au prince des nuées*
   Qui hante la tempête et se rit de l'archer;
   Exilé sur le sol au milieu des huées,
   Ses ailes de géant l'empêchent de marcher.

The Poet is like that prince of the clouds
Who haunts the storms and laughs at the archer;
Exiled to the ground in the midst of jeers,
His giant wings prevent him from walking.
1857 *Les Fleurs du mal*, 'L'Albatros'—'Spleen et idéal', no.2.

17 *Les parfums, les couleurs et les sons se répondent.*

Scents, colors, and sounds echo one another.
1857 *Les Fleurs du mal*, 'Correspondances'.

18 *O douleur! ô douleur! Le Temps mange ma vie.*

Oh pain! Oh pain! time is eating away my life.
1857 *Les Fleurs du mal*, 'L'Ennemi'.

19 *Homme libre, toujours tu chériras la mer.*

Free man! You shall always cherish the sea.
1857 *Les Fleurs du Mal*, 'L'Homme et la mer'.

20 *Quand notre coeur a fait une fois sa vendange,*
   Vivre est un mal.

Once our heart has been harvested once,
Life becomes miserable.
1857 *Les Fleurs du Mal*, 'Semper eadem'.

21 *Ne cherchez plus mon coeur; les bêtes l'ont mangé.*

Don't search any further for my heart; wild beasts
ate it.
1857 *Les Fleurs du Mal*, 'Causerie'.

22 *Là, tout n'est qu'ordre et beauté,*
   Luxe, calme et volupté.

There where all is order and beauty.
Lush, calm and voluptuous.
1857 *Les Fleurs du Mal*, 'L'Invitation au Voyage'.

23 *J'ai plus de souvenirs que si j'avais mille ans.*

I have more memories than if I were one thousand
years old.
1857 *Les Fleurs du Mal*, 'Spleen'.

24 *Souviens-toi que le Temps est un joueur avide*
   Qui gagne sans tricher, à tout coup! c'est la loi.

Remember! Time, that tireless gambler, wins
on every turn of the wheel: that is the law.
1857 *Les Fleurs du Mal*, 'L'Horloge' (translated by Richard
Howard, 1982).

25 *Certes, je sortirai quant à moi satisfait*
   D'un monde où l'action n'est pas la soeur du rêve.

Indeed, for my part, I shall be happy to leave
A world where action is not sister to the dream.
1857 *Les Fleurs du Mal*, 'Le Reniement de Saint-Pierre'.

26 *Ah! Seigneur! donnez-moi la force et le courage*
   De contempler mon coeur et mon corps sans dégoût.

Lord! give me the strength and the courage
To see my heart and my body without disgust.
1857 *Les Fleurs du Mal*, 'Un Voyage à Cythère'.

27 *Amer savoir, celui qu'on tire du voyage!*

Bitter is the knowledge gained in travelling.
1857 *Les Fleurs du Mal*, 'Le Voyage'.

28 If photography is allowed to stand in for art in
some of its functions it will soon supplant or
corrupt it completely thanks to the natural support
it will find in the stupidity of the multitude. It
must return to its real task, which is to be the
servant of the sciences and the arts, but the very
humble servant, like printing and shorthand which
have neither created nor supplanted literature.
1859 'Salon of 1859', sect.2, in *Curiosités Esthétiques* (1868).

29 Woe betide the man who goes to antiquity for the
study of anything other than ideal art, logic and
general method!
c.1860 Letter, published in *The Painter of Modern Life* (1863).

30 *Il est l'heure de s'enivrer! Pour n'être pas les esclaves*
   martyrisés du Temps, enivrez-vous sans cesse! De vin,
   de poésie ou de vertu, à votre guise.

This is the time for drunkenness! Be not the
martyred slaves of Time, drink without stopping!
Drink wine, poetry, or virtue, as you please.
1869 *Le Spleen de Paris*, 'Enivrez-vous'.

31 *Parce que le Beau est toujours étonnant, il serait*
   absurde de supposer que ce qui est étonnant est
   toujours beau.

Just because the beautiful is *always* shocking, it
would be absurd to suppose that that which is
shocking is *always* beautiful.
1869 *Le Spleen de Paris*, 'Salon de 1859', pt.2.

32 *L'imagination est la reine du vrai, et le possible est un*
   des provinces du vrai.

Imagination is the queen of the truth and the
possible is one of the provinces of the truth.
1869 *Le Spleen de Paris*, 'Salon de 1859', pt.3.

33 *Comme l'imagination a créé le monde, elle le*
   gouverne.

Because imagination created the world, it governs
it.
1869 *Le Spleen de Paris*, 'Salon de 1859', pt.4.

34 *Le mal se fait sans effort, naturellement, par fatalité;*
le bien est toujours le produit d'un art.

Evil is done without effort, *naturally*, it's destiny;
good is always a product of art.
1869 *Le Spleen de Paris*, 'Le Peintre de la vie moderne', pt.11.

35 *L'art moderne a une tendance essentiellement*
démoniaque.

Modern art tends towards the demonic.
1869 *L'Art romantique.*

36 *Quand même Dieu n'existerait pas, la religion serait*
encore sainte et divine—Dieu est le seul être qui, pour
régner, n'ai même pas besoin d'exister.

Even if God did not exist, religion would still be
holy and divine. God is the only being who, in
order to reign, need not even exist.
1875 *Journaux intimes.* 'Fusées', no.1.

37 *La volupté unique et suprême de l'amour gît dans la*
certitude de faire le mal.

The unique, supreme pleasure of love consists in
the certainty of doing *evil.*
1875 *Journaux intimes.* 'Fusées', no.2.

38 *La femme est naturelle, c'est-à-dire abominable.*

Woman is *natural,* that is, abominable.
1887 *Mon coeur mis à nu,* pt.5.

39 *Le Dandy doit aspirer à être sublime, sans*
interruption. Il doit vivre et dormir devant un miroir.

The dandy must aspire to be sublime at all times.
He must live and sleep in front of a mirror.
1887 *Mon coeur mis à nu,* pt.5.

40 *Etre un homme utile m'a paru toujours quelque chose*
de bien hideux.

To be useful has always seemed to me quite
hideous.
1887 *Mon coeur mis à nu,* pt.9.

41 *Il faut travailler sinon par goût, au moins par*
désespoir, puisque, tout bien vérifié, travailler est
moins ennuyeux que s'amuser.

We should work: if not by preference, at least out of
despair. All things considered, work is less boring
than amusement.
1887 *Mon coeur mis à nu,* pt.18.

42 *Il y a dans tout homme, à toute heure, deux*
postulations simultanées, l'une vers Dieu, l'autre vers
Satan.

Every man at every moment has two simultaneous
tendencies: one toward God, the other toward
Satan.
1887 *Mon coeur mis à nu,* pt.19.

43 *Il n'existe que trois êtres respectables: le prêtre, le*
guerrier, le poète. Savoir, tuer et créer.

There are only three respectable beings: priest,
warrior, poet. To know, to kill and to create.
1887 *Mon coeur mis à nu,* pt.22.

44 *L'être le plus prostitué, c'est l'être par excellence, c'est*
Dieu, puisqu'il est
l'ami suprême pour chaque individu, puisqu'il est le
réservoir commun,
inépuisable de l'amour.

The most prostituted being, the Being par
excellence, is God, since he is
supreme friend to every individual, since he is the
common, inexhaustible
reservoir of love.
1887 *Mon coeur mis à nu,* pt.46.

45 *Je ne comprends pas qu'une main pure puisse toucher*
un journal sans une convulsion de dégoût.

I cannot imagine how a pure hand can touch a
newspaper without disgust.
1887 *Mon coeur mis à nu,* pt.81.

46 At its best a poem full of space and reverie.
Of portraits. Quoted in the *New York Times,* 1 Jan 1995.

47 *Il faut épater le bourgeois.*

One must astound the bourgeois.
Attributed.

Baughan, Blanche Edith 1870–1958

New Zealand writer and penal reformer, born in England
where she published *Verses* (1898). She emigrated in
1900 and wrote popular verse with an increasingly local
flavour.

48 Well, I'm leaving the poor old place, and it cuts as
keen as a knife;
The place that's broken my heart—the place where
I've lived my life.
1903 *Reuben and Other Poems,* 'The Old Place'.

Baxter, Sir Beverley (Arthur) 1891–1964

British politician and journalist. Canadian-born, he
joined the Daily Express in London in 1920 and was
editor-in-chief from 1929-33. He became MP for Wood
Green 1935-45, and 1945-50 and MP for Southgate from
1950 until his death.

49 Beaverbrook is so pleased to be in the Government
that he is like the town tart who has finally married
the mayor.
1940 Remark attributed to Baxter in Sir Henry Channon
Chips: the Diaries (1967), entry for 12 Jun.

50 A great many persons are able to become
Members of this House without losing their
insignificance.
1946 Speech, House of Commons.

Baxter, Richard 1615–91

English Nonconformist clergyman. Chaplain to Cromwell's army in the English Civil War, he became Royal Chaplain in 1660, but was imprisoned in 1685 for sedition in his *Paraphrase on the New Testament*.

51 Watch against inordinate sensual delight in even the lawfullest of sports. Excess of pleasure in any such vanity doth very much corrupt and befool the mind.

1678 *A Christian Directory*.

Bazelitz, Georg

52 I have trouble with beauty.

1995 On the effects of witnessing suffering as a child in Dresden during the war. In the *New York Times*, 21 May.

Beachcomber

▷ See J B Morton

Bearden, Romare 1914–88

US painter, whose bright, bold works deal with the experience of black Americans.

53 The canvas was always saying no to me.

Of early attempts to perfect his medium. Recalled on his death in the *Washington Post*, 14 Mar 1988.

Beasant, Dave 1959–

English goalkeeper, who played for Wimbledon, Newcastle United and Chelsea. He became the first goalkeeper to captain a team to victory in the FA Cup, 1988.

54 I was a bit disappointed. I should have caught it really.

1988 Of the save that made him the first goalkeeper to stop a penalty in an FA Cup Final. Quoted in Peter Ball and Phil Shaw *The Book of Football Quotations* (1989).

Beattie, Ann 1947–

US writer and art critic. Her works include *Distortions* (1976) and *What Was Mine* (1991).

55 There are things that get whispered about that writers are there to overhear.

1987 *Best American Short Stories*, introduction.

Beattie, James 1735–1803

Scottish philosopher and poet, professor of moral philosophy at Aberdeen. He attacked Hume's scepticism in his *Essay on the Nature and Immutability of Truth* (1770), and wrote an autobiographical poem, *The Minstrel* (1771–4).

56 Some deemed him wondrous wise, and some believed him mad.

1771 *The Minstrel*, bk.1, stanza 16.

57 In the deep windings of the grove no more

The hag obscene, and grisly phantom dwell;
Nor in the fall of mountain-stream, or roar
Of winds, is heard the angry spirit's yell.

1774 *The Minstrel*, bk.2, stanza 47.

Beatty, David, 1st Earl Beatty 1871–1936

British Admiral. After serving in Egypt and Sudan he became Rear Admiral in 1910. Early successes in World War I were followed by a major role in the Battle of Jutland. He commanded the fleet (1916–19) and was First Sea Lord (1919–27).

58 There's something wrong with our bloody ships today, Chatfield.

1916 Comment at the Battle of Jutland, which ended in stalemate, 31 May. Quoted in Winston Churchill *The World Crisis 1916–1918* (1927), pt.1.

Beaumarchais, Pierre Augustin Caron de 1732–99

French writer who led a colourful life as artisan, member of the royal household, music teacher to Louis XV's daughter, speculator, secret agent in England, and munitions runner for the American colonies.

59 *Aujourd'hui, ce qui ne vaut pas la peine d'être dit, on le chante.*

Today, what is not worth being said is sung.

1775 *Le Barbier de Séville*, act 1, sc.2.

60 *Je me presse de rire de tout, de peur d'être obligé d'en pleurer.*

I am quick to laugh at everything so as not to be obliged to cry.

1775 *Le Barbier de Séville*, act 1, sc.2.

61 *On s'intéresse guère aux affaires des autres que lorsqu'on est sans inquiétude sur les siennes.*

We hardly interest ourselves in the affairs of others when things are going well for ourselves.

1775 *Le Barbier de Séville*.

62 *Les vices, les abus, voilà ce qui ne change point, mais se déguise en mille formes sous le masque des moeurs dominantes: leur arracher ce masque et les montrer à découvert, telle est la noble tâche de l'homme qui se voue au théâtre.*

Vices, indulgences, these are the things which never change but which disguise themselves in a thousand forms beneath the mask of prevailing morals: to lift off this mask and expose them, this is the noble task of the person who devotes himself to the theatre.

1784 *Le Mariage de Figaro*, préface.

63 *De toutes les choses sérieuses, le mariage étant la plus bouffonne.*

Of all serious things, marriage is the most farcical.

1784 *Le Mariage de Figaro*, act 1, sc.9.

64 *Boire sans soif et faire l'amour en tout temps,*
Madame, il n'y a que ça qui nous distingue des autres
bêtes.

We drink when we are not thirsty and make love at
any time, Madam. These are the only things which
distinguish us from other animals.
1784 *Le Mariage de Figaro,* act 2, sc.21.

65 *Les Anglais, à la vérité, ajoutent par ci, par là,*
quelques autres mots en conversant; mais il est bien
aisé de voir que God-dam *est le fond de la langue.*

In truth, the English do add here and there other
words when speaking, but it is obvious that
Goddamn is the base of their language.
1784 *Le Mariage de Figaro,* act 3, sc.5.

Beaumont, Sir Francis c. 1584–1616

English dramatist, a friend of Ben Jonson and his circle,
particularly John Fletcher, with whom he wrote at least 10
plays. *The Woman Hater* (1605) and *The Knight of the
Burning Pestle* (c.1607) are thought to be mainly
Beaumont's work.

66 What things have we seen,
Done at the Mermaid! heard words that have been
So nimble, and so full of subtil flame,
As if that every one from whence they came,
Had meant to put his whole wit in a jest,
And had resolv'd to live a fool, the rest
Of his dull life.
1605 *Letter to Ben Jonson,* verses prefacing Jonson's *Volpone.*

67 She's private to herself, and best of knowledge
Whom she will make so happy as to sigh for.
c.1607 *The Knight of the Burning Pestle,* act 1.

Beaumont, Sir Francis and Fletcher, John

c.1584–1616, c.1578–1625

English dramatists.

68 It is always good
When a man has two irons in the fire.
1608 *The Faithful Friends,* act 1.

69 PHILASTER: Oh, but thou dost not know
What 'tis to die.
BELLARIO: Yes, I do know, my Lord:
'Tis less than to be born; a lasting sleep;
A quiet resting from all jealousy,
A thing we all pursue; I know besides,
It is but giving over of a game,
That must be lost.
1609 *Philaster* (published 1620), act 3, sc.1.

70 All your better deeds
Shall be in water writ, but this in marble.
1609 *Philaster* (published 1620), act 5.

71 Kiss till the cow comes home.
c.1610 *The Scornful Lady* (published 1616), act 2, sc.2.

72 There is no other purgatory but a woman.
c.1610 *The Scornful Lady* (published 1616), act 3.

73 Upon my buried body lay
Lightly gentle earth
1610–11 *The Maid's Tragedy,* act 2, sc.1.

74 Those have most power to hurt us that we love.
1610–11 *The Maid's Tragedy,* act 5.

75 The terror of his name has stretched itself
Wherever there is sun.
1611 *A King and No King,* act 2, sc.2.

76 What art thou that dost creep into my breast
And dar'st not see my face? Show forth thyself.
I feel a pair of fiery wings displayed
Hither, from thence. You shall not tarry there;
Up and begone. If thou beest love, begone.
1611 *A King and No King,* act 3, sc.1.

77 I see there's truth in no man, nor obedience
But for his own ends.
1611 *A King and No King,* act 4, sc.2.

78 You are no better than you should be.
1612 *The Coxcomb,* act 4, sc.3.

Beaverbrook, Max (William Maxwell Aitken), 1st Baron 1879–1964

Canadian-born British newspaper magnate and
politician. After entering politics in 1910, he bought the
Daily Express (1916) and made it the world's most widely
read newspaper, founding the *Sunday Express* (1921). He
was Minister of Supply and Lord Privy Seal during World
War II.

79 Churchill on top of the wave has in him the stuff of
which tyrants are made.
1928–32 *Politicians and the War.*

80 He has all the qualities that go to the making of a
leader of the Conservative Party. He is not stupid,
but he is very dull. He is not eloquent, but he talks
well. He is not honest, politically, but he is most
evangelical. He has a little money, but not much.
He always conforms to the party policy.
1935 Commenting on Sir Samuel Hoare's appointment as
Foreign Secretary.

81 Our cock won't fight.
1936 Of Edward VIII. Comment to Winston Churchill during
the abdication crisis. Quoted in Francis Donaldson *Edward
VIII* (1974).

82 I run the paper purely for the purpose of making
propaganda, and with no other motive.
1947 Evidence to the Royal Commission on the Press.

83 With the publication of his private papers in 1952, he committed suicide 25 years after his death.
    1956 Of Earl Haig. *Men and Power: 1917–1918*.

84 He did not seem to care which way he travelled providing he was in the driver's seat.
    1963 Of Lloyd George. *The Decline and Fall of Lloyd George*, ch.7.

85 I am now in my eighty-fourth year and that is approaching the moment when I must bring out my Late Night Final.
    c.1963 Quoted in A J P Taylor *Beaverbrook* (1972), ch.13.

86 Here I must say, in my eighty-sixth year, I do not feel greatly different from when I was eighty-five. This is my final word. It is time for me to become an apprentice once more. I have not settled in which direction. But somewhere, sometime soon.
    1964 Address at a farewell banquet in London, hosted for him by Roy Thomson, Lord Thomson of Fleet, 25 May. He died two weeks later.

87 *News, Opinion and Advertisment must all come under the head of Entertainment to a reasonable extent—or they will not be read.* People do not read to be bored. Unless a newspaper can make its material in every department interesting it simply is not read.
    Publicity handout for the *Daily Express*, quoted in A J P Taylor *Beaverbrook* (1972), ch.8.

88 Success never depended on pandering to the public taste. It has always been founded on simplicity.
    Quoted in A J P Taylor *Beaverbrook* (1972), ch.13.

Becker, Gary Stanley 1930–

US economist, Professor of Economics and Sociology at the University of Chicago. He won the Nobel Prize for Economics (1992).

89 They talk a good game, but economists hardly know enough about business cycles to figure out where they come from, let alone where they're going.
    1989 'How Bad Will the Next Downturn Be?', in *Business Week*, 10 Apr.

Beckett, Samuel 1906–89

Irish author and playwright who lived mostly in France. His best-known play, *En Attendant Godot* (*Waiting for Godot*, 1956), exemplifies his absurdist view of the human condition. He was awarded the Nobel Prize for Literature (1969).

90 *Je ne supporterai plus d'être un homme, je n'essaierai plus.*

    I can no longer bear to be human and I will no longer try.
    1951 *Molloy, Malone Meurt*.

91 There is man in his entirety, blaming his shoe when his foot is guilty.
    1955 *Waiting for Godot*, act 1.

92 Nothing happens, nobody comes, nobody goes, it's awful!
    1955 *Waiting for Godot*, act 1.

93 He can't think without his hat.
    1955 Of Lucky. *Waiting for Godot*, act 1.

94 VLADIMIR: That passed the time.
    ESTRAGON: It would have passed in any case.
    VLADIMIR: Yes, but not so rapidly.
    1955 *Waiting for Godot*, act 1.

95 I am like that. I either forget right away or I never forget.
    1955 *Waiting for Godot*, act 2.

96 You overdo it with your carrots.
    1955 *Waiting for Godot*, act 2.

97 We are not saints, but we have kept our appointment. How many people can boast as much?
    1955 *Waiting for Godot*, act 2.

98 We are all born crazy. Some remain that way.
    1955 *Waiting for Godot*, act 2.

99 They give birth astride of a grave, the light gleams an instant, then it's night once more.
    1955 *Waiting for Godot*, act 2.

1 If I had the use of my body, I would throw it out of the window.
    1958 *Malone Dies*.

2 *Tout est faux, il n'y a personne…il n'y a rien.*

    Everything is false. There is no one…there is nothing.
    1958 *Nouvelles et textes pour rien*.

3 CLOV: Do you believe in the life to come?
    HAMM: Mine was always that.
    1958 *Endgame*.

4 *Bien choisir son moment et se taire, serait-ce le seul moyen d'avoir être et habitat?*

    To carefully choose one's moment and keep quiet, is this the only way one can be and live?
    1958 *Nouvelles et textes pour rien*.

5 Joyce was a synthesizer, trying to bring in as much as he could. I am an analyzer, trying to leave out as much as I can.
    1981 In the *New York Times*, 19 Apr.

6 I was in hospital once. There was a man in another ward, dying of throat cancer. In the silence, I could

hear his screams continually. That's the only kind of form my work has.

Attributed, in conversation with Harold Pinter.

Becket, Thomas à, Saint 1118–70

English churchman and martyr. Appointed Chancellor of England by Henry II in 1155, in 1162 he became Archbishop of Canterbury. He proved troublesome to Henry, opposing his remarriage, and was murdered in Canterbury Cathedral by four of the king's soldiers.

7 You will soon hate me as much as you love me now, for you assume an authority in the affairs of the church to which I shall never assent.

c.1160 Remark to Henry II. Quoted in J R Green *A Short History of the English People* (1915), vol.1, ch.2, section 8.

Bede known as 'the Venerable' 673–735

English Benedictine monk, scholar and historian. His numerous works include saints' lives, hymns, grammatical treatises and biblical commentaries. His *Historia Ecclesiastica Gentis Anglorum* is the single most valuable source for early English history.

8 *Talis, inquiens, mihi videtur, rex, vita hominum praesens in terris, ad comparationem eius, quod nobis incertum est, temporis, quale cum te residente, ad caenam cum ducibus ac ministris tuis tempore brumale…adveniens unus passerum domum citissime, pervolaverit; qui cum per unum ostium ingrediens, mox per aliud exierit. Ipso quidem tempore, quo intus est, hiemis tempestate non tangitur, sed tamen parvissimo spatio serenitatis ad momentum excurso, mox de hieme in hiemem regrediens, tuis oculis elabitur. Ita haec vita hominum ad modicum apparet; quid autem sequatur, quidve praecesserit, prorsus ignoramus.*

'Such,' he said, 'O King, seems to me the present life of men on earth, in comparison with that time which to us is uncertain, as if when on a winter's night you sit feasting with your ealdormen and thegns—a single sparrow should fly swiftly into the hall, and coming in at one door, instantly fly out through another. In that time in which it is indoors it is indeed not touched by the fury of the winter, and yet, this smallest space of calmness being passed almost in a flash, from winter going into winter again, it is lost to your eyes. Somewhat like this appears the life of man; but of what follows or what went before, we are utterly ignorant.'

731 *Historia Ecclesiastica Gentis Anglorum* (*Ecclesiastical History of the English People*, translated by B Colgrave, 1969), bk.2, ch.13 .

Bee, Barnard Elliot 1823–61

Confederate General, killed at the First Battle of Bull Run.

9 There is Jackson with his Virginians, standing like a stone wall. Let us determine to die here, and we will conquer.

1861 Of General Thomas J Jackson, whose resistance stopped the Union advance at Bull Run, 21 Jul. Quoted in B Perley Poore *Perley's Reminiscences* (1886), vol.2, ch.7. 'Stonewall Jackson' became a popular nickname for the General.

Beecham, Sir Thomas 1879–1961

British conductor and impresario, famed for his outspokenness and wit, and for a dashing and romantic style of performance. He conducted frequently at Covent Garden from 1910, and founded several orchestras, including the London Philharmonic (1932) and the Royal Philharmonic (1947), with whom he made many recordings.

10 A musicologist is a man who can read music but can't hear it.

1930 Quoted in H Proctor-Gregg *Beecham Remembered* (1976).

11 The English may not like music—but they absolutely love the noise it makes.

Quoted in L Ayre *The Wit of Music* (1930).

12 It is far too large. It ought to be removed.

1940 On his first visit to Sydney, in 1940, being asked by a local journalist his opinion of the Harbour Bridge. Quoted in Gerald Moore *Am I too Loud?* (1962).

13 Good music is that which penetrates the ear with facility and quits the memory with difficulty. Magical music never leaves the memory.

1953 Television broadcast, 17 Nov.

14 Hark! The herald angels sing!
    Beecham's Pills are just the thing,
    Two for a woman, one for a child,
    Peace on earth and mercy mild!

Quoted in Neville Cardus *Sir Thomas Beecham* (1961). Sir Thomas was heir to the Beecham pharmaceutical company.

15 The musical equivalent of the towers of St Pancras Station.

Of Elgar's First Symphony. Quoted in Neville Cardus *Sir Thomas Beecham* (1961).

16 There are two golden rules for an orchestra: start together and finish together. The public doesn't give a damn what goes on in between.

Quoted in Harold Atkins and Archie Newman *Beecham Stories* (1978).

17 Like two skeletons copulating on a corrugated tin roof.

Of the harpsichord's sound. Quoted in Harold Atkins and Archie Newman *Beecham Stories* (1978).

18 British music is in a state of perpetual promise. It might almost be said to be one long promissory note.

Quoted in Harold Atkins and Archie Newman *Beecham Stories* (1978).

19 The function of music is to release us from the tyranny of conscious thought.
Quoted in Harold Atkins and Archie Newman *Beecham Stories* (1978).

20 You have between your legs the most sensitive instrument known to man, and all you can do is scratch it.
Attributed rebuke to a female cellist. Quoted in Ian Crofton and Donald Fraser *A Dictionary of Musical Quotations* (1985).

Beerbohm, Sir (Henry) Max(imilian)
1872–1956

English writer, caricaturist and theatre critic, of Lithuanian extraction, who succeeded George Bernard Shaw as drama critic of the *Saturday Review*. His criticism was collected in *Around Theatre* (1953) and *More Theatres* (1968). He also wrote a novel, *Zuleika Dobson* (1911), an ironic romance about Oxford student life.

21 Most women are not so young as they are painted.
1894 *The Yellow Book*, vol.1.

22 Fate wrote her a most tremendous tragedy, and she played it in tights.
1894 Of Queen Caroline of Brunswick. *The Yellow Book*, vol.3.

23 There is always something rather absurd about the past.
1895 *The Yellow Book*, vol.4

24 To give an accurate and exhaustive account of the period would need a far less brilliant pen than mine.
1895 *The Yellow Book*, vol.4.

25 I have the satiric temperament: when I am laughing at anyone I am generally rather amusing, but when I am praising anyone, I am always deadly dull.
1898 In *The Saturday Review*, 28 May.

26 [At school] I was a modest, good-humoured boy. It is Oxford that has made me insufferable.
1899 *More*, 'Going Back To School'.

27 When a public man lays his hand on his heart and declares that his conduct needs no apology, the audience hastens to put up its umbrellas against the particularly severe downpour of apologies in store for it. I won't give the customary warning. My conduct shrieks aloud for apology, and you are in for a thorough drenching.
1906 'A Straight Talk' (parody of George Bernard Shaw), in the *Saturday Review*, 22 Dec.

28 She was one of those born to make chaos cosmic.
1911 *Zuleika Dobson*, ch.2.

29 Zuleika, on a desert island, would have spent most of her time in looking for a man's footprint.

30 The dullard's envy of brilliant men is always assuaged by the suspicion that they will come to a bad end.
1911 *Zuleika Dobson*, ch.4.

31 Women who love the same man have a kind of bitter freemasonry.
1911 *Zuleika Dobson*, ch.4.

32 You will find that the woman who is really kind to dogs is always one who has failed to inspire sympathy in men.
1911 *Zuleika Dobson*, ch.6.

33 Beauty and the lust for learning have yet to be allied.
1911 *Zuleika Dobson*, ch.7.

34 You will think me lamentably crude: my experience of life has been drawn from life itself.
1911 *Zuleika Dobson*, ch.7.

35 She was one of the people who say 'I don't know anything about music really, but I know what I like.'
1911 *Zuleika Dobson*, ch.9.

36 You cannot make a man by standing a sheep on its hind-legs. But by standing a flock of sheep in that position you can make a crowd of men.
1911 *Zuleika Dobson*, ch.9.

37 The Socratic method is not a game at which two can play.
1911 *Zuleika Dobson*, ch.15.

38 I looked out for what the metropolitan reviewers would have to say. They seemed to fall into two classes: those who had little to say and those who had nothing.
1919 *Seven Men*, 'Enoch Soames'.

39 I have known no man of genius who had not to pay, in some affliction or defect either physical or spiritual, for what the gods had given him.
1920 *And Even Now*, 'The Pines'.

40 Not philosophy, after all, not humanity, just sheer joyous power of song, is the primal thing in poetry.
1920 *And Even Now*, 'The Pines'.

41 One might well say that mankind is divisible into two great classes: hosts and guests.
1920 *And Even Now*, 'Hosts and Guests'.

42 I maintain that though you would often in the fifteenth century have heard the snobbish Roman say, in a would-be off-hand tone, 'I am dining with the Borgias tonight,' no Roman ever was able to say, 'I dined last night with the Borgias.'
1920 *And Even Now*, 'Hosts and Guests'.

43 The critic who justly admires all kinds of things simultaneously cannot love any one of them.
1946 'George Moore', in the *Saturday Review*, c.1912.

44 The thought of him has always slightly irritated me. Of course he was a wonderful all-round man, but the act of walking round him has always tired me.
1956 Of William Morris. Letter to Sam Behrman, Feb.

45 Only mediocrity can be trusted to be always at its best.
Quoted in S N Behrman *Conversations with Max* (1960), but also attributed elsewhere to Jean Giraudoux and W Somerset Maugham.

46 The one art-form that has been invented in England.
Of the pantomime. Attributed.

47 Reminds me of a Christmas-tree decorated by a Pre-Raphaelite.
Of the actress Ellen Terry. Attributed.

48 They were a tense and peculiar family, the Oedipuses, weren't they?
Attributed.

Beethoven, Ludwig van 1770–1827

German composer. His prolific output included two masses, the opera *Fidelio*, nine symphonies, five piano concertos, piano sonatas and string quartets. Increasing deafness affected him and his music deeply. His influence, especially on the Romantics, was immense.

49 The immortal god of harmony.
1801 Of Bach. Letter to Christoph Breitkopf.

50 I must confess that I live a miserable life… I live entirely in my music.
1801 Letter to F G Wegeler.

51 *Muß es sein? Es muß sein! Es muß sein!*

Must it be? It must be! It must be!
1826 Written above the opening bars of the String Quartet in F Major, Op 135, his last work.

52 I still hope to create a few great works and then like an old child to finish my earthly course somewhere among kind people.
1826 Letter to F G Wegeler.

53 *Plaudite, amici, comedia finita est.*

Applaud, my friends, the comedy is over.
1827 Quoted in Ian Crofton and Donald Fraser *A Dictionary of Musical Quotations* (1985), quoting the last words of Augustus as he lay dying.
▷ See Augustus 50:21.

54 I shall hear in heaven.
1827 Attributed last words. Quoted in Ian Crofton and Donald Fraser *A Dictionary of Musical Quotations* (1985).

Beeton, Isabella Mary née Mayson
1836–65

English writer on cookery. Her *Book of Household Management* (1859-60) was published in serial form in a woman's magazine founded by her husband, the publisher Samuel Orchard Beeton.

55 There is no more fruitful source of family discontent than a housewife's badly-cooked dinners and untidy ways.
1861 *The Book of Household Management*, preface.

56 A place for everything and everything in its place.
1861 *The Book of Household Management*, ch.2.

Behan, Brendan Francis 1923–64

Irish playwright, twice imprisoned for IRA activities. He was released by general amnesty (1946), but was rearrested and deported in 1952. His works include *The Quare Fellow* (1956), *The Hostage* (1958) and an autobiography, *Borstal Boy* (1958).

57 When I came back to Dublin, I was courtmartialled in my absence and sentenced to death in my absence, so I said they could shoot me in my absence.
1958 *The Hostage*, act 1.

58 My name is Behan, Brendan Behan, after Saint Brendan, who got into one of our little Irish boats called a curragh one day in the sixth century and sailed across the Atlantic and found America, and when he'd found it, like a sensible man he turned around and sailed back and left it where it fuckin' well was.
1962 Speech in New York.

59 Bless you, Sister. May all your sons be bishops!
1964 Addressing a nursing nun taking his pulse shortly before he died. Attributed.

60 Critics are like eunuchs in a harem. They're in there every night, they see how it should be done every night, but they can't do it themselves.
Quoted in Gyles Brandreth *Great Theatrical Disasters* (1983).

61 I am a daylight atheist.
Quoted in Daniel Farson *Sacred Monsters*, 'Rousting in Dublin' (1988).

62 Other people have a nationality. The Irish and the Jews have a psychosis.
Richard's Cork Leg (1961).

Behn, Aphra née Amis 1640–89

English writer. She had an adventurous life, growing up in Surinam and acting as a professional spy in Antwerp.

Perhaps the first professional woman author in England, her works include *Oroonoko* (1688), *The Forced Marriage* (1670) and *The Rover* (1678).

63 Variety is the soul of pleasure.
    1678 *The Rover*, pt.2, act 1.

64 Come away; poverty's catching.
    1678 *The Rover*, pt.2, act 1.

65 Money speaks sense in a language all nations understand.
    1678 *The Rover*, pt.2, act 3, sc.1.

66 A brave world, Sir, full of religion, knavery, and change: we shall shortly see better days.
    1682 *The Roundheads*, act 1, sc.1.

67 Be just, my lovely swain, and do not take
    Freedoms you'll not to me allow;
    Or give Amynta so much freedom back
    That she may rove as well as you.

    Let us then love upon the honest square,
    Since interest neither have designed.
    For the sly gamester, who ne'er plays me fair,
    Must trick for trick expect to find.
    1684 *Poems upon Several Occasions*, 'To Lysander, on some Verses he writ, and asking more for his Heart than 'twas worth'.

68 Faith, Sir, we are here to-day, and gone to-morrow.
    1686 *The Lucky Chance*, act 4.

69 Love ceases to be a pleasure, when it ceases to be a secret.
    1686 *The Lover's Watch*, 'Four o'Clock. General Conversation'.

70 Oh, what a dear ravishing thing is the beginning of an Amour!
    1687 *The Emperor of the Moon*, act 1, sc.1.

71 They represented to me an absolute idea of the first state of innocence, before man knew how to sin.
    1688 Of the Indians of Surinam. *Oroonoko, or the Royal Slave*.

72 Simple Nature is the most harmless, inoffensive, and virtuous mistress.
    1688 *Oroonoko, or the Royal Slave*.

73 And though she had some decays in the face, she had none in her sense and wit.
    1688 *Oroonoko, or the Royal Slave*.

74 Since Man with that inconstancy was born,
    To love the absent, and the present scorn.
    Why do we deck, why do we dress
    For such a short-liv'd happiness?
    1688 *Lycidus*, 'To Alexis in Answer to his Poem against Fruition,' stanza 3.

75 The soft, unhappy sex.
    1698 *The Wandering Beauty*.

Behrman, S(amuel) N(athaniel)
1893–1973

US playwright, known for sophisticated comedies such as *No Time for Comedy* (1939) and *Lord Pengo* (1962). Other works include screenplays and biographies.

76 Early in life, Duveen…noticed that Europe had plenty of art and America had plenty of money, and his entire astonishing career was the product of that simple observation.
    1952 *Duveen*, ch.1. Joseph Duveen was a highly successful US art dealer.

Belasco, David stagename of David Valasco
1859–1931

US actor-manager and dramatist. Nicknamed the 'Bishop of Broadway', he adapted many successful plays for the theatres he managed in New York.

77 Boxing is show-business with blood.
    Quoted in Colin Jarman *The Guinness Dictionary of Sports Quotations* (1990).

Bell, Alexander Melville 1819–1905
Language instructor, father of Alexander Graham Bell.

78 Yes, Alec, it is I, your father, speaking.
    1876 The first words spoken and heard on the world's first long-distance telephone call, from Alexander Melville Bell in Brantford, Ontario, Canada, to his son Alexander Graham Bell in nearby Paris, 13 km away, 10 Aug.

Bell, Bernard Iddings 1886–1958
US cleric, chaplain at the University of Chicago.

79 A good education is not so much one which prepares a man to succeed in the world, as one which enables him to sustain a failure.
    1950 In *Life*, 16 Oct.

Bell, (Arthur) Clive Howard 1881–1964
English critic of art and literature, an influential member of the Bloomsbury set, husband of Vanessa Bell. His aesthetic theory emphasized form over content in art.

80 It would follow that 'significant form' was form behind which we catch a sense of ultimate reality.
    1914 *Art*, pt.1, ch.3.

81 Art and Religion are, then, two roads by which men escape from circumstance to ecstasy.
    1914 *Art*, pt.2, ch.1.

82 I will try to account for the degree of my aesthetic emotion. That, I conceive, is the function of the critic.
    1914 *Art*, pt.3, ch.3.

83 Materially make the life of the artist sufficiently miserable to be unattractive, and no one will take

to art save those in whom the divine daemon is absolute.
1914 *Art*, pt.5, ch.1.

84 Comfort came in with the middle classes.
1928 *Civilization*, ch.4.

85 Only reason can convince us of those three fundamental truths without a recognition of which there can be no effective liberty: that what we believe is not necessarily true; that what we like is not necessarily good; and that all questions are open.
1928 *Civilization*, ch.5.

Bell, Vanessa née *Stephen* 1879–1961

English painter and designer, sister of Virginia Woolf. She married the critic Clive Bell (1907) but left him in 1916 to live with Duncan Grant.

86 Rather lovely descriptions of scenery, don't you think?
1928 Remark to Robert Medley and Rupert Doone, when asked what she thought of D H Lawrence's *Lady Chatterley's Lover*. Recalled in Robert Medley *Drawn from the Life: a Memoir* (1983), p.91.

Bellay, Joachim du 1522–60

French poet famous for his sonnets. He was a founding member of the Pléiade and wrote its manifesto, *La défense et illustration de la langue française.*

87 *Rome de Rome est le seul monument,*
Et Rome Rome a vaincu seulement.

Rome is the only monument left of Rome,
And only Rome vanquished Rome.
1558 *Antiquitez de Rome*, no.5.

88 *Rome seule pouvait à Rome ressembler,*
Rome seule pouvait Rome fait trembler.

Only Rome can resemble Rome,
And Rome alone can make Rome fall.
1558 *Antiquitez de Rome*, no.6.

89 *France, mère des arts, des armes et des lois.*

France, mother of arts, of weapons and of laws.
1558 *Les Regrets*, no.9.

90 *Heureux, qui comme Ulysse, a fait un beau voyage,*
Ou comme cestuy là qui conquit la toison,
Et puis est retourné, plein d'usage et raison,
Vivre entre ses parents le reste de son aage!

Happy is he who, like Ulysses, has taken a wondrous journey
Or has won the Golden Fleece,
And then returns home wise and useful
To live in his homeland the rest of his days.
1558 *Les Regrets*, no.31.

91 *Celuy vit seulement, lequel vit aujourdhuy.*

Only the person who lives for today lives at all.
1558 *Les Regrets*, no.65.

92 *Je n'écris point d'amour, n'estant point amoureux,*
Je n'écris de beauté, n'aiant belle maistresse,
Je n'écris de douceur, n'esprouvant que rudesse,
Je n'écris de plaisir, me trouvant douloureux.

I cannot write of love, as I am not in love,
I cannot write of beauty, as I have no beautiful mistress,
I cannot write of sweetness, as I experience nothing but hardship,
I cannot write of pleasure, as I am always in pain.
1558 *Les Regrets*, no.79.

Belli, Carlos Germán 1927–

Peruvian poet, translator and journalist. He travelled widely in South America, Spain, Italy and the United States. His poems are noted for their nihilistic outlook and an orderly precision of language.

93 *De los libros el luminoso plectro*
diríase que pasa
a ser lía del recto,
pues después de tanto leer sin tasa
nada ha quedado en casa.

The luminous plectrum of books
can be said to become
a portion of the rectum,
since after so much eager reading
not a thing remains at home.
1961 *¡Oh hada cibernética!*, 'Cuando el seso tiene la altura de un grano de arena' ('When the brain is as high as a grain of sand').

Bellini, Mario

Italian architect.

94 A design career is a process of learning better and better what you know instinctively.
1987 In the *New York Times*, 25 Jun.

95 I designed a bench in a few moments. But, of course, it took me 25 years to do it.
1987 In the *New York Times*, 25 Jun.

Belloc, (Joseph) Hilaire Pierre 1870–1953

French-born British writer, poet, Roman Catholic apologist and Liberal MP (1906–10). His works include *The Servile State* (1912), travel books, historical studies and religious books. He is best known for his comic and nonsensical verse for children.

96 Child! do not throw this book about;
Refrain from the unholy pleasure
Of cutting all the pictures out!
Preserve it as your chiefest treasure.
1896 *The Bad Child's Book of Beasts*, dedication.

97 A manner rude and wild

Is common at your age.
1896 *The Bad Child's Book of Beasts*, introduction.

98 When people call this beast to mind,
They marvel more and more
At such a little tail behind,
So large a trunk before.
1896 *The Bad Child's Book of Beasts*, 'The Elephant'.

99 I shoot the Hippopotamus
With bullets made of platinum,
Because if I use the leaden ones
His hide is sure to flatten 'em.
1896 *The Bad Child's Book of Beasts*, 'The Hippopotamus'.

1 Mothers of large families (who claim to common
sense)
Will find a Tiger will repay the trouble and
expense.
1896 *The Bad Child's Book of Beasts*, 'The Tiger'.

2 The Microbe is so very small
You cannot make him out at all.
1897 *More Beasts for Worse Children*, 'The Microbe'.

3 Whatever happens, we have got
The Maxim Gun, and they have not.
1898 *The Modern Traveller*, bk.6.

4 I am a Catholic. As far as possible I go to Mass
every day. As far as possible I kneel down and tell
these beads every day. If you reject me on account
of my religion, I shall thank God that he has spared
me the indignity of being your representative.
1906 Election campaign speech, Salford.

5 The chief defect of Henry King
Was chewing little bits of string.
1907 *Cautionary Tales*, 'Henry King'.

6 Physicians of the utmost fame
Were called at once, but when they came
They answered, as they took their fees,
'There is no cure for this disease.'
1907 *Cautionary Tales*, 'Henry King'.

7 'Oh, my friends, be warned by me,
That breakfast, dinner, lunch, and tea
Are all the human frame requires…'
With that the wretched child expires.
1907 *Cautionary Tales*, 'Henry King'.

8 And always keep a hold of Nurse
For fear of finding something worse.
1907 *Cautionary Tales*, 'Jim'.

9 We had intended you to be
The next Prime Minister but three:
The stocks were sold; the Press was squared;
The Middle Class was quite prepared.
But as it is!…My language fails!
1907 *Cautionary Tales*, 'Jim'.

Go out and govern New South Wales!
1907 *Cautionary Tales*, 'Jim'.

10 Matilda told such Dreadful Lies,
It made one Gasp and Stretch one's Eyes;
Her Aunt, who, from her Earliest Youth,
Had kept a Strict Regard for Truth,
Attempted to Believe Matilda:
The effort very nearly killed her.
1907 *Cautionary Tales*, 'Matilda'.

11 She was not really bad at heart,
But only rather rude and wild;
She was an aggravating child.
1907 *Cautionary Tales*, 'Rebecca'.

12 Her funeral sermon (which was long
And followed by a sacred song)
Mentioned her virtues, it is true,
But dwelt upon her vices too.
1907 *Cautionary Tales*, 'Rebecca'.

13 It is the best of trades, to make songs, and the
second best to sing them.
1909 *On Everything*.

14 I said to Heart, 'How goes it?' Heart replied:
'Right as a Ribstone Pippin!' But it lied.
1910 'The False Heart'.

15 When I am living in the Midlands
That are sodden and unkind.
1910 'The South Country'.

16 Everywhere the sea is a teacher of truth. I am not
sure that the best thing I find in sailing is not this
salt of reality.
c.1910 *The Cruise of the Nona*.

17 Do you remember an Inn,
Miranda?
Do you remember an Inn,
And the tedding and the spreading
Of the straw for a bedding,
And the fleas that tease in the High Pyrenees
And the wine that tasted of the tar?
1923 'Tarantella'.

18 When I am dead, I hope it may be said,
'His sins were scarlet, but his books were read.'
1923 'On His Books'.

19 And even now, at twenty-five,
He has to WORK to keep alive!
Yes! All day long from 10 till 4!
For half the year or even more;
With but an hour or two to spend
At luncheon with a city friend.
1930 *New Cautionary Tales*, 'Peter Goole'.

20 I am a sundial, and I make a botch

Of what is done much better by a watch.
1938 'On a Sundial'.

21 Statistics are the triumph of the quantitative method, and the quantitative method is the victory of sterility and death.
1940 *The Silence of the Sea.*

Bellow, Saul 1915–

Canadian-born US writer. He moved to Chicago in 1924, and was educated there. His best novels examine Jewish-American identity and the dilemma of liberal humanist values in a fast-changing world. He won the Nobel Prize for Literature in 1975.

22 Everyone knows there is no fineness or accuracy of suppression. If you hold down one thing you hold down the adjoining.
1953 *The Adventures of Augie March*, ch.1.

23 Of course, in an age of madness, to expect to be untouched by madness is a form of madness. But the pursuit of sanity can be a form of madness, too.
1959 *Henderson The Rain King*, ch.3.

24 If I am out of my mind, it's all right with me, thought Moses Herzog.
1961 *Herzog*, opening words.

25 A man may say, 'From now on I'm going to speak the truth.' But the truth hears him and runs away and hides before he's even done speaking.
1961 *Herzog.*

26 I feel that art has something to do with the achievement of stillness in the midst of chaos.
1965 Interview in *The Paris Review*, no.37, winter issue.

27 No wonder the really powerful men in our society, whether politicians or scientists, hold writers in contempt. They do it because they get no evidence from modern literature that anybody is thinking about any significant question.
1965 Interview in *The Paris Review*, no.37, winter issue.

28 I am more stupid about some things than about others; not equally stupid in all directions; I am not a well-rounded person.
1969 *Mr Sammler's Planet*, ch.2.

29 Conquered people tend to be witty.
1969 *Mr Sammler's Planet*, ch.2.

30 Mr Sammler with his screwy visions! He saw the increasing triumph of Enlightenment—Liberty, Equality, Adultery!
1969 *Mr Sammler's Planet*, ch.3.

31 There is much to be said for exotic marriages. If your husband is a bore, it takes years longer to discover.

1969 *Mr Sammler's Planet*, ch.6.

32 I think that New York is not the cultural centre of America, but the business and administrative centre of American culture.
1969 In radio interview, reported in *The Listener*, 22 May.

33 The idea, anyway, was to ward off trouble. But now the moronic inferno had caught up with me.
1975 *Humboldt's Gift*. Martin Amis used the phrase *The Moronic Inferno* as the title for a book of essays on the US (1986).

34 The only real distinction at this dangerous moment in human history and cosmic development has nothing to do with medals and ribbons. Not to fall asleep is distinguished. Everything else is mere popcorn.
1975 *Humboldt's Gift.*

35 After all these years wallowing in low seriousness— low seriousness, you understand, is high seriousness that's failed.
1975 Interview in *The Sunday Times*, 12 Jan.

36 The feeling individual appeared weak—he felt only his own weakness. But if he accepted his weakness and his separateness and descended into himself, intensifying his loneliness, he discovered his solidarity with other isolated creatures.
1976 Nobel Prize Lecture, Stockholm, 12 Dec.

37 A novel is balanced between a few true impressions and the multitude of false ones that make up most of what we call life.
1976 Nobel Prize Lecture, Stockholm, 12 Dec.

38 Tears may be intellectual, but they can never be political. They save no man from being shot, no child from being thrown alive into the furnace.
1982 *The Dean's December*, ch.12.

39 As a rule Corde avoided cemeteries and never went near the graves of his parents. He said it was just as easy for your dead to visit you, only by now he would have to hire a hall.
1982 *The Dean's December*, ch.15.

40 The secret motive of the absent-minded is to be innocent while guilty. Absent-mindedness is spurious innocence.
1987 *More Die of Heartbreak.*

41 Erotic practices have become diversified. Sex used to be a single-crop farming, like cotton or wheat; now people raise all kinds of things.
1987 *More Die of Heartbreak.*

42 The modern reader (or viewer, or listener: let's include everybody) is perilously overloaded. His

attention is, to use the latest lingo, 'targeted' by powerful forces... Our consciousness is a staging area, a field of operations for all kinds of enterprises, which make free use of it.
1989 *Something To Remember Me By*, preface.

43 But Fonstein belonged to an even more advanced category...their aim is to convert weaknesses and secrets into burnable energy. A first-class man subsists on the matter he destroys, just as the stars do.
1989 *Something To Remember Me By*, 'The Bellarosa Connection'.

Bemelmans, Ludwig 1898–1962

US writer and restaurateur. He wrote food and travel books, and is best remembered for his 'Madeline' series for children.

44 In an old house in Paris
that was covered with vines
lived twelve little girls in two straight lines.
1939 *Madeline*.

45 And nobody knew so well
How to frighten Miss Clavell.
1939 *Madeline*.

46 Serves you right, you horrid brat
For what you did to that poor cat.
1956 *Madeline and the Bad Hat*.

Benaud, Richie (Richard) 1930–

Australian cricketer and broadcaster. He played in 63 Test matches (28 as captain), scoring 2201 Test runs and taking 248 wickets.

47 Cricket is a batsman's game.
1961 *Way of Cricket*.

Benchley, Robert Charles 1889–1945

US humorist and critic, a member of the famous circle of New York wits and writers known as the Algonquin Round Table. He was drama critic of *Life* and the *New Yorker*, and appeared in cameo roles in many films.

48 In America there are two classes of travel—first class, and with children.
1925 *Pluck and Luck*.

49 The surest way to make a monkey of a man is to quote him.
1936 *My Ten Years in a Quandary*.

50 I haven't been abroad in so long that I almost speak English without an accent now.
1938 *After 1903—What?*

51 One square foot less and it would be adulterous.

On the tiny office he shared with Dorothy Parker, quoted in the *New Yorker*, 5 Jan 1946.

52 My only solution for the problem of habitual accidents...is to stay in bed all day. Even then, there is always the chance that you will fall out.
1949 *Chips Off the Old Benchley*, 'Safety Second'.

53 A great many people have come up to me and asked how I manage to get so much work done and still keep looking so dissipated.
1949 *Chips Off the Old Benchley*, 'How To Get Things Done'.

54 So who's in a hurry?
On being told that the particular drink he was drinking was slow poison. Quoted in Nathaniel Benchley *Robert Benchley* (1955), ch.1.

55 STREETS FLOODED. PLEASE ADVISE.
Telegraph message to the US on arriving in Venice. Quoted in R E Drennan (ed) *Wits End* (1973).

56 Opera is where a guy gets stabbed in the back, and instead of dying, he sings.
Quoted in Ian Crofton and Donald Fraser *A Dictionary of Musical Quotations* (1985).

Bendix, Reinhard 1916–

German-born US sociologist, Professor at the University of California, Berkeley.

57 In retrospect it always seems as if everything had to develop just the way it did. I call this view the fallacy of retrospective determinism—which looks at the modern world as a victory of the children of light over the children of darkness if we approve of the development, and of darkness over light if we condemn it.
1984 *Force, Fate, and Freedom: On Historical Sociology*.

Benedetti, Mario 1920–

Uruguayan fiction writer, poet and essayist, who lived in Cuba in the late 1960s. After returning to Uruguay, he helped establish a leftist coalition for future elections. With the military takeover of 1973 he was forced to leave the country.

58 *está demás decirte que a esta altura
no creo en predicadores ni en generales
ni en las nalgas de miss universo
ni en el arrepentimiento de los verdugos
ni en el catecismo del confort
ni en el flaco perdón de dios.*

It's not useless to tell you that, at this stage,
I don't believe in preachers or generals
or in Miss Universe's buttocks
or in the executioner's repentance
or in the catechism of comfort
or in God's slim forgiving.
1974 *Poemas de otros*, 'Credo' ('Creed').

Benét, Stephen Vincent 1898–1943

US poet and novelist. He wrote many evocative poems on the history and national identity of America, of which 'American Names' is the most famous.

59 I have fallen in love with American names,
    The sharp, gaunt names that never get fat,
    The snakeskin-titles of mining-claims,
    The plumed war-bonnet of Medicine Hat,
    Tucson and Deadwood and Lost Mule Flat.
    1927 'American Names'.

60 There are English counties like hunting-tunes
    Played on the keys of a postboy's horn,
    But I will remember where I was born.
    1927 'American Names'.

61 I will get me a bottle of Boston sea
    And a blue-gum nigger to sing me blues.
    I am tired of loving a foreign muse.
    1927 'American Names'.

62 I shall not rest quiet in Montparnasse.
    I shall not lie easy at Winchelsea.
    You may bury my body in Sussex grass,
    You may bury my tongue at Champmédy.
    I shall not be there, I shall rise and pass.
    Bury my heart at Wounded Knee.
    1927 'American Names'. *Bury My Heart At Wounded Knee* was used by Dee Brown as the title of a book on the Indian genocide (1971).

63 One cannot balance tragedy in the scales
    Unless one weighs it with the tragic heart.
    1928 'John Brown's Body'.

64 We thought we were done with these things but we
        were wrong.
    We thought, because we had power, we had
        wisdom.
    1935 'A Litany for Dictatorships'.

Benn, Tony (Anthony Neil Wedgwood) 1925–

English Labour politician. He became an MP (1950–60), and renounced his hereditary title to be re-elected to the Commons. He held various government posts, and as a left-wing representative unsuccessfully challenged Neil Kinnock for the leadership of the Labour Party in 1988.

65 The House of Lords is the British Outer Mongolia for retired politicians.
    1962 Speech made during his campaign to disclaim his hereditary peerage, 11 Feb.

66 It is as wholly wrong to blame Marx for what was done in his name, as it is to blame Jesus for what was done in his.
    Quoted in Alan Freeman *The Benn Heresy* (1982).

67 It is beginning to dawn on people that the influence of a nation is not measured by the size of its military budget, but by its industrial strength.
    1991 In *The Independent*, 18 Apr.

68 The dependence of London on Washington for the supply of our so-called independent nuclear weapons is all that remains of the 'special relationship' and…it is really a ball and chain limiting our capacity to play a more positive role in the world.
    1991 In *The Independent*, 18 Apr.
    ▷ See Churchill 265:31.

69 It is the same each time with progress. First they ignore you, then they say you are mad, then dangerous, then there's a pause, and then you can't find anyone who disagrees.
    1991 Speech at the Labour Party Conference, Oct.

Bennard, George 1873–1958

70 I will cling to the old rugged cross,
    And exchange it some day for a crown.
    1913 'The Old Rugged Cross'.

Bennett, Alan 1934–

English writer. He came to prominence as an actor and writer in *Beyond the Fringe* (1960), and went on to write wry, mordant plays and monologues for stage and screen. He adapted his play *The Madness of George III* as an Oscar-winning film (*The Madness of King George*, 1995).

71 Life is rather like a tin of sardines—we're all of us looking for the key.
    1960 *Beyond the Fringe*.

72 I've never understood this liking for war. It panders to instincts already catered for within the scope of any respectable domestic establishment.
    1968 *Forty Years On* (published 1969), act 1.

73 Memories are not shackles, Franklin, they are garlands.
    1968 *Forty Years On* (published 1969), act 2.

74 The Breed never dies. Sapper, Buchan, Dornford Yates, practitioners in that school of Snobbery with Violence that runs like a thread of good-class tweed through twentieth-century literature.
    1968 *Forty Years On* (published 1969), act 2. *Snobbery With Violence* was used as a book title by Colin Wilson (1971).

75 It's the one species I wouldn't mind seeing vanish from the face of the earth. I wish they were like the White Rhino—six of them left in the Serengeti National Park, and all males.
    1971 Of dogs. *Getting On* (published 1972), act 1.

76 The longer I practise medicine, the more convinced I am there are only two types of cases: those that involve taking the trousers off and those that don't.
1973 *Habeas Corpus.*

77 One of the few things I have learned in life is that there is invariably something odd about women who wear ankle socks.
1977 *The Old Country*, act 1.

78 We were put to Dickens as children but it never took. That unremitting humanity soon had me cheesed off.
1977 *The Old Country*, act 2.

79 There is no such thing as a good script, only a good film, and I'm conscious that my scripts often read better than they play.
1984 *A Private Function*, introduction to published screenplay.

80 I'm going to throw caution to the winds and have a sweet sherry.
1984 Spoken by Maggie Smith as Joyce Chilvers in *A Private Function*.

81 I want a future that will live up to my past.
1984 Spoken by Maggie Smith as Joyce Chilvers in *A Private Function*.

82 They're going to have to be made to sit up and take notice. They're going to have to be made to realise who we are. My father had a chain of dry cleaners.
1984 *A Private Function*.

83 I'm not good at precise, coherent argument. But plays are suited to incoherent argument, put into the mouths of fallible people.
1991 In *The Sunday Times*, 24 Nov.

84 My claim to literary fame is that I used to deliver meat to a woman who became T. S. Eliot's mother-in-law.
1992 In *The Observer*, 26 Apr. The lady in question was the mother of Eliot's wife Valerie Fletcher; Bennett's father was the butcher in the same Yorkshire village.

Bennett, (Enoch) Arnold 1867–1931

English novelist. He was also a journalist, and lived in Paris for ten years. His best known books are those set in the pottery-making heartland of the Five Towns in the Midlands, notably the *Clayhanger* trilogy.

85 Essential characteristic of the really great novelist: a Christ-like, all-embracing compassion.
1896 Journal entry, 15 Oct.

86 'Bah!', she said, 'With people like you, love only means one thing.' 'No,' he replied. 'It means twenty things, but it doesn't mean nineteen.'
1904 Journal entry, 20 Nov.

87 My general impression is that Englishmen act better than Frenchmen, and Frenchwomen better than Englishwomen.
1909 *Cupid and Commonsense*, preface.

88 His opinion of himself, having once risen, remained at 'set fair'.
1911 *The Card*, ch.1.

89 'Ye can call it influenza if ye like,' said Mrs Machin. 'There was no influenza in my young days. We called a cold a cold.'
1911 *The Card*, ch.8.

90 A cause may be inconvenient, but it's magnificent. It's like champagne or high heels, and one must be prepared to suffer for it.
1918 *The Title*, act 1.

91 Being a husband is a whole-time job. That is why so many husbands fail. They cannot give their entire attention to it.
1918 *The Title*, act 1.

92 Journalists say a thing that they know isn't true, in the hope that if they keep on saying it long enough it will be true.
1918 *The Title*, act 2.

93 Mr Lloyd George spoke for 17 minutes, in which period he was detected only once in the use of an argument.
1921 *Things That Have Interested Me.*

94 A test of a first-rate work, and a test of your sincerity in calling it a first-rate work, is that you finish it.
1921 *Things That Have Interested Me*, 'Finishing Books'.

95 In the meantime alcohol produces a delightful social atmosphere that nothing else can produce.
1921 *Things That Have Interested Me*, 'For and Against Prohibition'.

96 Pessimism, when you get used to it, is just as agreeable as optimism.
1921 *Things That Have Interested Me*, 'Slump Into Pessimism'.

97 The price of justice is eternal publicity.
1923 *Things That Have Interested Me* (2nd series), 'Secret Trials'.

98 Between thirty and forty a man may have reached the height of discretion without having tumbled over the top and into the feather-bed of correctitude.
1930 In the *Evening Standard*, 29 May.

99 Good taste is better than bad taste, but bad taste is better than no taste, and men without individuality have no taste—at any rate no taste that they can impose on their publics.
1930 In the *Evening Standard*, 21 Aug.

1 The thing is to produce an impression on the reader—the best you can, the truest you can, but some impression. The newest despisers of form and conventionalization produce no impression at all.
   1931 Journal entry, 11 Sep.

2 The saxophone is the embodied spirit of beer.
   Quoted in Derek Watson *Music Quotations* (1991).

Bennett, James Gordon, Snr 1795–1872

Scots-born US journalist. In 1835 he started the *New York Herald*, pioneering many journalistic innovations.

3 The Press is the living Jury of the Nation.
   1831 In the *Courier and Enquirer*, 6 Aug.

4 An editor must always be with the people—think with them—feel with them—and he need fear nothing, he will always be right—always be strong—always *free*.
   1831 In the *Courier and Enquirer*, 12 Nov.

5 This is the editorial age, and the most intellectual of all ages.
   1831 In the *Courier and Enquirer*, 12 Nov.

6 What is to prevent a daily newspaper from being made the greatest organ of social life? Books have had their day—the theatres have had their day— the temple of religion has had its day. A newspaper can be made to take the lead of all these in the great movements of human thought and of human civilisation. A newspaper can send more souls to Heaven, and save more from Hell, than all the churches or chapels in New York—besides making money at the same time.
   1836 In the *New York Herald*, 19 Aug.

7 I have infused life, glowing eloquence, philosophy, taste, sentiment, wit, and humor into the daily newspaper… Shakespeare is the great genius of the drama—Scott of the novel—Milton and Byron of the poem—and I mean to be the genius of the daily newspaper press.
   c.1836 Quoted in Oliver Carlson *The Man Who Made News: James Gordon Bennett* (1942), ch.10.

Bennis, Warren Gameliel 1925–

US economist and business administrator.

8 Leaders are people who do the right things. Managers are people who do things right…a profound difference.
   1994 In *Fortune*, 19 Sep.

Benson, A(rthur) C(hristopher) 1862–1925

English academic writer. He wrote a number of critical studies and biographies of eminent literary Victorians, and is remembered now for his patriotic poem 'Land of Hope and Glory', set to music by Elgar.

9 Land of Hope and Glory, Mother of the Free, How shall we extol thee who are born of thee? Wider still and wider shall thy bounds be set; God who made thee mighty, make thee mightier yet.
   1902 'Land of Hope and Glory'.

10 If the dullest person in the world would only put down sincerely what he or she thought about his or her life, about work and love, religion and emotion, it would be a fascinating document.
   1906 'From A College Window'.

Benson, Stella 1892–1933

English novelist. Her diary was published long after her death from tuberculosis.

11 Call no man foe, but never love a stranger.
   1917 *This is the End.*

Bentham, Jeremy 1748–1832

English philosopher, jurist and writer. His works include *A Fragment of Government* (1776) and *Introduction to the Principles of Morals and Legislation* (1789), which expounds his theory of hedonistic utilitarianism.

12 The community is a fictitious *body*, composed of the individual persons who are considered as constituting as it were its *members*. The interest of the community then, is what? The sum of the interests of the several members who compose it.
   1789 *An Introduction to the Principles of Morals and Legislation*, ch.1.

13 The greatest happiness of the greatest number is the foundation of morals and legislation.
   1789 *An Introduction to the Principles of Morals and Legislation*, ch.1.
   ▷ See Hutcheson 506:42.

14 All punishment is mischief: all punishment in itself is evil.
   1789 *An Introduction to the Principles of Morals and Legislation*, ch.13.

15 Every law is an evil, for every law is an infraction of liberty.
   1789 *An Introduction to the Principles of Morals and Legislation*.

16 An absolute and unlimited right over any object of property would be the right to commit nearly every crime. If I had such a right over the stick I am about to cut, I might employ it as a mace to knock down the passengers, or I might convert it into a sceptre as an emblem of royalty, or into an idol to offend the national religion.

Principles of the Civil Code, pt.1, ch.13, final note. Collected in John Bowring (ed) *Works* (1838–43), vol.1.

17 Natural rights is simple nonsense: natural and imprescriptable rights, rhetorical nonsense—nonsense upon stilts.

Anarchical Fallacies. Collected in J Bowring (ed) *Works* (1838–43), vol.2.

18 Publicity is the very soul of justice. It is the keenest spur to exertion, and the surest of all guards against improbity.

Draught of a code for the organization of the judicial establishment in France. Collected in John Bowring (ed) *Works* (1838–43), vol.4.

19 He rather hated the ruling few than loved the suffering many.

Of James Mill. Quoted in *Memories of Old Friends, being Extracts from the Journals and Letters of Caroline Fox* (1882).

20 Prose is when all the lines except the last go on to the end. Poetry is when some of them fall short of it.

Quoted in M St J Packe *The Life of John Stuart Mill* (1954), bk.1, ch.2.

21 To be the most effectively benevolent man who ever lived.

His ambition. Quoted in Mary Peter Mack *International Encyclopedia of the Social Sciences* (1968), vol.2.

Bentley, Edmund Clerihew 1875–1956

English writer and journalist. His books include *Biography for Beginners* (1905), *Baseless Biography* (1939) and the classic detective novel *Trent's Last Case* (1913). He is best known for his humorous verse form, named the clerihew after him.

22 The art of Biography
Is different from Geography.
Geography is about Maps,
But Biography is about Chaps.

1905 *Biography for Beginners*, introduction.

23 What I like about Clive
Is that he is no longer alive.
There is a great deal to be said
For being dead.

1905 *Biography for Beginners*, 'Clive'.

24 Sir Christopher Wren
said, 'I am going to dine with some men.
If anybody calls
Say I am designing St Paul's.'

1905 *Biography for Beginners*, 'Sir Christopher Wren'.

25 Sir Humphrey Davy
Abominated gravy.
He lived in the odium
Of having discovered sodium.

1905 *Biography for Beginners*, 'Sir Humphrey Davy'.

26 John Stuart Mill,
By a mighty effort of will,
Overcame his natural *bonhomie*
And wrote 'Principles of Political Economy'.

1905 *Biography for Beginners*, 'John Stuart Mill'.

27 Henry the Eighth
Took a thuctheththion of mateth.
He inthithted that the monkth
Were a lathy lot of thkunkth.

1929 *More Biography*, 'Henry the Eighth'.

28 George the Third
Ought never to have occurred.
One can only wonder
At so grotesque a blunder.

1929 *More Biography*, 'George the Third'.

29 When their lordships asked Bacon
How many bribes he had taken
He had at least the grace
To get very red in the face.

1939 *Baseless Biography*, 'Bacon'.

Bentley, Nicholas Clerihew 1907–78

English artist and writer, son of Edmund Clerihew Bentley. He was best known for his cartoons, and illustrations to works such as T S Eliot's *Old Possum's Book of Practical Cats* (1939). He edited several editions of *Pick of Punch* (1955–60).

30 Henry Campbell-Bannerman is remembered chiefly as the man about whom all is forgotten.

1974 *An Edwardian Album*.

Bentsen, Lloyd Millard, Jr 1921–

US politician, senator from Texas (1971–93). He was the Democratic nominee for Vice-President in the 1988 elections.

31 America has just passed through…an eight-year coma in which slogans were confused with solutions and rhetoric passed for reality.

1988 Recalling the Reagan administration as he accepted the Democratic nomination for Vice President, 21 Jul.

32 Senator, I served with Jack Kennedy. I knew Jack Kennedy. Jack Kennedy was a friend of mine. Senator, you're no Jack Kennedy.

1988 On his opponent Dan Quayle's contention that his congressional experience equalled that of President Kennedy when he sought the presidency. Reported in the *New York Times*, 9 Oct.

Benuzzi, Felice 1910–

Italian diplomat, lawyer and athlete. In Jan 1943 he and two friends escaped from a POW camp at Nanyuki to climb Mt Kenya with minimal equipment and provisions, before breaking back into the camp again and giving themselves up to the British commandant.

33 I emerged at last, stumbled a few steps in the mud and then I saw it: an ethereal mountain emerging from a tossing sea of clouds framed between two dark barracks—a massive, blue-black tooth of sheer rock inlaid with azure glaciers, austere yet floating fairy-like on the near horizon. It was the first 17,000-foot peak I had ever seen.
I stood gazing until the vision disappeared among the shifting cloud banks.
For hours afterwards I remained spell-bound.
I had definitely fallen in love.
1952 *No Picnic on Mount Kenya.*

34 To remember is far worse than to forget.
1952 On being a Prisoner of War. *No Picnic on Mount Kenya.*

Berdyaev, Nicholas 1874–1948

Russian philosopher. He originally supported the communist revolution but subsequently found that Marxism lacked a spiritual element and abandoned it. He founded the Academy of the Philosophy of Religion in Berlin (later transferred to Paris).

35 Man found his form and his identity under the action of religious principles and energies; the confusion in which he is losing them cannot be re-ordered by purely human efforts.
1923 'Konets Rennesansa' in *Sofiya* (translated as 'The End of the Renaissance' in the *Slavonic Review*, Jun/Dec 1925).

Berendt, John 1939–

US writer and editor. He is a columnist for *Esquire* magazine and was a Pulitzer Prize finalist for general non-fiction in 1995 for *Midnight in the Garden of Good and Evil.*

36 In Atlanta, the first question is 'What's your business?' In Macon, it is 'Where do you go to church?' In Augusta they want your grandmother's maiden name. But in Savannah, the first question is 'What would you like to drink?'
1994 *Midnight in the Garden of Good and Evil.*

Berenson, Bernard 1865–1959

Lithuanian-born US art critic. An authority on the Renaissance, he could identify Italian masterworks by style and technique. His works include *Venetian Painters of the Renaissance* (1894) and *Rumor and Reflection* (1952).

37 I earn it by enjoying such authority and prestige that people will not buy expensive Italian pictures without my approval.
Comment on his income, addressed to the Internal Revenue Service. Quoted in *The Making of a Legend* (1987).

Beresford, Lord Charles 1846–1919

British politician.

38 Very sorry can't come. Lie follows by post.
Telegraph to the Prince of Wales, declining a dinner invitation. Quoted in Ralph Nevill *The World of Fashion 1837–1922* (1923), ch.5.

Berg, Alban 1885–1935

Austrian composer, best known for his opera *Wozzeck* (1925), his violin concerto and the *Lyric Suite* for string quartet.

39 Why is Schoenberg's Music so Hard to Understand?
1924 Title of essay.

Berger, Bennett Maurice 1926–

US sociologist, Professor at the University of California, San Diego (from 1973). His works include *Looking for America* (1971).

40 Oversimplification is now a common term of reproach in academic discussions; everyone is against oversimplification. But there is no parallel term nearly as frequently used to describe the opposite phenomenon, which surely occurs as often, if not more so.
1990 *Authors of their Own Lives* (edited by Berger), introduction.

Berger, John Peter 1926–

English writer and art critic. His writing has been strongly influenced by Marxism, and he caused a sensation by denouncing the Booker Corporation in his acceptance speech when awarded the Booker Prize for his novel *G* in 1972.

41 The five senses within whose pentagon each man is alone.
1972 *G*, pt.3, ch.5.

42 If we could all live a thousand years…we would each, at least once during that period, be considered a genius.
1972 *G*, pt.3, ch.6.

43 The camera relieves us of the burden of memory.
1978 *New Statesman*, 17 Aug.

44 It is not usually possible in a poem or a story to make the relationship between particular and universal fully explicit. Those who try to do so end up writing parables.
1979 *Pig Earth*, 'Historical Afterward'.

45 Photography, because it stops the flow of life, is always flirting with death.
1983 In the *New Statesman*, 22/29 Dec.

46 All weddings are similar but every marriage is different. Death comes to everyone but one mourns alone.
1985 *The White Bird*, 'The Storyteller'.

47 Every city has a sex and age which have nothing to do with demography.
1987 In *The Guardian*, 27 Mar.

48 Every painted image of something is also about the absence of the real thing. All painting is about the presence of absence.
1988 In *New Statesman and Society*, 15 Jul.

Bergreen, Laurence 1950–

49 He was not fit for marriage, only for work. A major writer, he conceded, required major torment.
1984 Of James Agee. *James Agee*.

Berkeley, George 1685–1753

Irish idealist philosopher and Anglican Bishop of Cloyne (1734–52). His philosophical works, such as *A Treatise Concerning the Principles of Human Knowledge* (1710), argue that things in the material world only exist when perceived in the mind.

50 I am inclined to think that the far greater part, if not all, of those difficulties which have hitherto amused philosophers, and blocked up the way to knowledge, are entirely owing to ourselves—that we have first raised a dust and then complain we cannot see.
1710 *A Treatise Concerning the Principles of Human Knowledge*, introduction.

51 Some truths there are so near and obvious to the mind that a man need only open his eyes to see them. Such I take this important one to be, viz. that all the choir of heaven and furniture of the earth, in a word all those bodies which compose the mighty frame of the world, have not any subsistence without a mind—that their *being* is *to be perceived or known*.
1710 *A Treatise Concerning The Principles Of Human Knowledge*, pt.1, section 6.

52 Whatever is immediately perceived is an idea: and can any *idea* exist out of the mind?
1713 *Three Dialogues between Hylas And Philonous*, first dialogue.

53 The same principles which at first lead to scepticism, pursued to a certain point bring men back to common sense.
1734 *Three Dialogues between Hylas and Philonous*, dialogue 3.
▷ See Bacon 57:65.

54 Whose fault is it if poor Ireland still continues poor?
1737 *The Querist*, pt.3.

55 Truth is the cry of all, but the game of the few.
1744 *Siris*.

56 It is impossible that a man who is false to his friends and neighbours should be true to the public.
1750 *Maxims Concerning Patriotism*.

Berlin, Irving originally *Israel Baline* 1888–1989

Russian-born US composer, who began as a singing waiter. He wrote lyrics and music for over 900 songs including 'Alexander's Ragtime Band' and 'White Christmas'. The musical *Annie Get Your Gun* (1946) marked the peak of his career.

57 Come on and hear,
Come on and hear
Alexander's Ragtime Band
1911 'Alexander's Ragtime Band', opening lines, featured in the 1938 film of the same title.

58 A pretty girl is like a melody
That haunts you night and day.
1919 'A Pretty Girl is Like a Melody'.

59 The song is ended
But the melody lingers on.
1927 Song from *Ziegfeld Follies*.

60 I'm puttin' on my top hat
Tyin' up my white tie
Brushin' off my tails
1935 'Top Hat, White Tie and Tails', performed by Fred Astaire in *Top Hat*.

61 There may be trouble ahead
But while there's moonlight and music and love and romance
Let's face the music and dance
1936 'Let's Face the Music and Dance', in the film *Follow the Fleet*.

62 I'm dreaming of a white Christmas,
Just like the ones I used to know,
Where the tree-tops glisten
And children listen
To hear sleigh bells in the snow.
1942 'I'm Dreaming of a White Christmas', in the film *Holiday Inn*.

63 There's No Business Like Show Business.
1946 Title of song from the film *Annie Get Your Gun*.

64 Listen kid, take my advice—never hate a song that has sold half a million copies.
Comment to the young Cole Porter, attributed.

65 No, for prosperity.
Attributed, when asked whether he wrote his songs for posterity.

Berlin, Sir Isaiah 1907–97

Russian-born British philosopher and historian of ideas. He was Professor of Social and Political Theory at Oxford (1957–67) and President of Wolfson College (1966–75). He served as a diplomat to Russia and the US in World War II.

66 Liberty is liberty, not equality or fairness or justice or human happiness or a quiet conscience.
1958 *Two Concepts of Liberty*, note.

67 The desire not to be impinged upon, to be left to oneself, has been the mark of high civilisation both on the part of individuals and communities.
1959 *Four Essays on Liberty.*

68 Man cannot live without seeking to describe and explain the universe.
1962 In the *Sunday Times.*

69 No perfect solution is, not merely in practice, but in principle, possible in human affairs, and any determined attempt to produce it is likely to lead to suffering, disillusionment and failure.
1978 *The Crooked Timber of Humanity,* 'The Decline of Utopian Ideals in the West'.

70 Pluralism—that is, the conception that there are many different ends that men may seek and still be fully rational, fully men, capable of understanding each other and sympathising and deriving light from each other.
1978 *The Crooked Timber of Humanity,* 'The Pursuit of the Ideal'.

Bernanos, Georges 1888–1948

French novelist who explored the role of the devil and sin in modern society. A fervent opponent of Fascism, he lost favour with conservative Catholics after publishing polemical tracts against Franco.

71 *Le désir de la prière est déjà une prière.*

The wish for prayer is already a prayer.
1936 *Le Journal d'un curé de campagne,* ch.2 (translated by P Morris as *Diary of a Country Priest,* 1937).

72 *L'enfer, Madame, c'est de ne plus aimer.*

Hell, Madam, is to no longer love.
1936 *Journal d'un curé de campagne,* ch.2.

Bernard of Chartres d. c.1130

French divine and scholar. He taught logic and grammar at Chartres school from 1114, becoming Chancellor in 1119. In 1124 he began teaching at Paris. Only fragments of his three philosophical treatises survive.

73 *Nanos gigantiun humeris insidentes.*

Dwarfs standing on the shoulders of giants.
c.1128 Of modern scholars in relation to their ancient predecessors. Quoted in John of Salisbury *Metalogicon* (1159), bk.3, ch.4.

St Bernard of Clairvaux 1090–1153

Theologian and reformer, first abbot (1115) of the newly-founded Cistercian monastery of Clairvaux, Champagne. Renowned for his studious, ascetic life and eloquence (he spoke in support of the Second Crusade, 1146), he founded over 70 monasteries.

74 *Omnes nimirum, ex quo monachi sumus, infirmos stomachos habemus, et tam necessarium Apostoli de utendo vino consilium merito non negligimus. Modico, tamen quod ille praemissit, nescio cur praetermisso.*

Being monks, we all naturally have a weak stomach, and we therefore justly attend to the Apostle's advice to use wine. He adds, however, the words 'a little'; I can't think why I have omitted them.
c.1124 *Apologia ad Guillelmum,* ch.9, section 21.

75 You have been called to hold a high position, but not a safe one; a sublime position, but not a secure one. How terrible, how very terrible is the place you hold!
c.1145 Letter to Eugenius III shortly after he had became Pope, on the dangers of the growth of papal power. Collected in B S James (ed and trans) *The Letters of St Bernard of Clairvaux* (1953).

76 *Aiunt non vos esse papam, sed me.*

They say it is not you who are pope, but me.
c.1145 Of his own influence within the Cistercian order. Letter to Pope Eugenius III.

77 You ordered. I obeyed... I opened my mouth; I spoke; and at once the Crusaders have multiplied to infinity. Villages and towns are now deserted. You will scarcely find one man for every seven women. Everywhere you see widows whose husbands are still alive.
1146 Letter to Pope Eugenius III describing the effects of preaching the Second Crusade. Collected in J P Migne (ed) *Patrologia Latina,* vol.182, letter no.247.

78 *Liberavi animam meam.*

I have freed my soul.
c.1147 Letter to Abbot Suger.

Bernard, Claude 1813–78

French scientist, considered the founder of contemporary experimental medicine on account of his work on the digestive process and on the vasomotor mechanism.

79 In science, the best precept is to alter and exchange our ideas as fast as science moves ahead.
1865 *An Introduction to the Study of Experimental Medicine,* vol.1, ch.1, section 3 (translated by H C Greene).

80 Science rejects the indeterminate.
1865 *An Introduction to the Study of Experimental Medicine,* vol.1, ch.1, section 3 (translated by H C Greene).

81 True science teaches us to doubt and, in ignorance, to refrain.
1865 *An Introduction to the Study of Experimental Medicine,* vol.1, ch.1, section 3 (translated by H C Greene).

82 Particular facts are never scientific; only generalization can establish science.
1865 *An Introduction to the Study of Experimental Medicine,* vol.1, ch.1, section 3 (translated by H C Greene).

83 Science does not permit exceptions.
    1855–56 *Lesions of Experimental Pathology.*

Bernardin de Saint-Pierre, Jacques-Henri
1737–1814

French novelist, friend of Rousseau and enemy of many others, naturalist and precursor of the Romantics. He travelled widely in Martinique, Russia and Madagascar.

84 *Les hommes ne veulent connaître que l'histoire des grands et des rois, qui ne sert à personne.*

    Men wish to hear no stories but those about the great and powerful, which are no use to anyone.
    1788 *Paul et Virginie.*

85 *Après le rare bonheur de trouver une compagne qui nous soit bien assortie, l'état le moins malheureux de la vie est sans doute de vivre seul.*

    After the rare happiness of finding a companion with whom we are well matched, the least unpleasant state of life is without doubt to live alone.
    1788 *Paul et Virginie.*

86 *La solitude rétablit aussi bien les harmonies du corps que celles de l'âme.*

    Solitude restores the harmonies of the body no less than those of the soul.
    1788 *Paul et Virginie.*

87 *On se fait une idée précise de l'ordre, mais non pas du désordre. La beauté, la vertu, le bonheur, ont des proportions; la laideur, le vice, et le malheur, n'en ont point.*

    We can form a precise idea of order, but not of disorder. Beauty, virtue, happiness, all have their proportions; ugliness, vice and unhappiness have none.
    1788 *Paul et Virginie.*

88 *Le parfum de mille roses ne plaît qu'un instant; mais la douleur que cause une seule de leurs épines dure longtemps après la piqûre.*

    The perfume of a thousand roses pleases only for an instant; but the pain caused by a single one of their thorns lasts a long time after the prick.
    1788 *Paul et Virginie.*

89 *La mort, mon fils, est un bien pour tous les hommes; elle est la nuit de ce jour inquiet qu'on appelle la vie.*

    Death, my son, is a good for all; it is the night of this worrisome day that one calls life.
    1788 *Paul et Virginie.*

90 *Artistes, poètes, écrivains, si vous copiez toujours, on ne vous copiera jamais.*

Artists, poets, writers, if you copy others all the time, no one will copy you.
1790 *Mémoires sur la ménagerie.*

Bernays, Edward 1891–1995

US pioneer public relations consultant, born in Vienna. His many books include *Crystallizing Public Opinion* (1923) and *The Engineering of Consent* (1955).

91 The engineering of consent.
    1955 His definition of public relations, the field he was credited with founding. *The Engineering of Consent.*

Berners, Dame Juliana or *Juliana Barnes*
fl.14c

English nun, traditionally Prioress of Sopwell convent, St Albans. She was the author of the *Treatyse perteynynge to Hawkynge, Huntynge, Fyshynge, and Coote Armiris* (1486).

92 A greyhound should be heeded lyke a snake,
    And neckyd lyke a drake,
    Backed lyke a bream,
    Footed lyke a catte,
    Taylled lyke a ratte.
    1486 *Treatyse perteynynge to Hawkynge, Huntynge, Fyshynge, and Coote Armiris.*

93 The Salmon is the most stately fish that any man may angle to in fresh water.
    1486 *Treatyse perteynyne to Hawkynge, Huntynge, Fyshynge, and Coote Armiris.*

Bernhardt, Sarah stage-name of *Sarah Henriette Rosine Bernard* 1844–1923

French actress. Hailed internationally as one of the leading theatrical performers of her generation, she made her stage début in 1862 and went on to play many of the great tragic roles in Shakespeare, Racine, Hugo, Rostand, Sardou and others.

94 *J'adore ce cricket; c'est tellement Anglais.*

    I do so love cricket—it's so very English.
    c.1905 On being taken to see a game of football in Manchester. Quoted in R Buckle *Nijinsky* (1971).

95 For the theatre one needs long arms; it is better to have them too long than too short. An *artiste* with short arms can never, never make a fine gesture.
    1907 *Memories of My Life.*

Bernini, Gianlorenzo 1598–1680

Italian sculptor, painter and architect, one of the key figures of Italian Baroque art.

96 Sometimes, in order to imitate the original, it is necessary to put something that is not in the original into a portrait in marble.
    Attributed remark made to Paul Fréart, in *Diary of Cavalier Bernini's Journey in France* (1665).

Bernstein, Leonard 1918–90

US conductor, pianist and composer. He achieved fame in 1943 as conductor with the New York Philharmonic. His compositions include three symphonies, a television opera and the musical *West Side Story* (1958).

97 It would be nice to hear someone accidentally whistle something of mine, somewhere, just once.
1960 *The Joy of Music.*

Berra, Yogi Lawrence Peter 1925–

US baseball player and coach. A star with the New York Yankees, he took part in a record 14 World Series (1946–63). He went on to manage the New York Yankees, the New York Mets and the Houston Astros.

98 If the people don't want to come out to the park, nobody's gonna stop them.
Quoted in Colin Jarman *The Guinness Dictionary of Sports Quotations* (1990).

99 He made too many wrong mistakes.
Quoted in Colin Jarman *The Guinness Dictionary of Sports Quotations* (1990).

1 You can observe a lot just by watching.
Quoted in Colin Jarman *The Guinness Dictionary of Sports Quotations* (1990).

2 You can't think and hit at the same time.
Quoted in Colin Jarman *The Guinness Dictionary of Sports Quotations* (1990).

3 It ain't over 'til it's over.
Attributed.

Berry, Chuck (Charles Edward Anderson) 1926–

US black rock 'n' roll singer, whose influential hits included 'Maybelline' (1955), 'School Days' (1957), and 'Johnny B Goode' (1958). In 1959 he was charged with transporting a minor over state lines for immoral purposes and jailed for two years (1962).

4 You know my temperature's risin',
The juke box's blowin' a fuse,
My heart's beatin' rhythm,
My soul keeps a singin' the blues—
Roll over Beethoven,
Tell Tchaikovsky the news.
1956 'Roll over Beethoven'.

Berryman, John originally John Allyn Smith 1914–72

US poet and novelist. His reputation rests on his complex, often obscure poetry, collected in *The Dispossessed* (1948), *Homage to Mistress Bradstreet* (1953) and the extended sequence of *Dream Songs* (1964).

5 We must travel in the direction of our fears.
1942 'A Point of Age'.

6 He is learning, well behind his desperate eyes,
The epistemology of loss, how to stand up
Knowing what every man must one day know
And most know many days, how to stand up.
1942 'The Ball Poem'.

7 The moon came up late and the night was cold,
Many men died—although we know the fate
Of none, nor of anyone, and the war
Goes on, and the moon in the breast of man is cold.
1948 'The Moon and the Night and the Men'.

8 Mountainous, woman not breaks and will bend:
sways God nearby: anguish comes to an end.
Blossomed Sarah, and I
blossom. Is that thing alive? I hear a famisht howl.
1953 'Homage to Mistress Bradstreet', stanza 21.

9 Pioneering is not feeling well,
not Indians, beasts.
Not all their riddling can forestall
one leaving.
1953 'Homage to Mistress Bradstreet', stanza 23.

10 Headstones stagger under great draughts of time
after heads pass out, and their world must reel
speechless, blind in the end
about its chilling star
1953 'Homage to Mistress Bradstreet', stanza 55.

11 Life, friends, is boring. We must not say so.
1964 'Dream Song No.14'.

12 And moreover my mother taught me as a boy
(repeatedly) 'Ever to confess you're bored
means you have no
Inner Resources.' I conclude now I have no
inner resources, because I am heavy bored.
1964 'Dream Song No.14'.

13 There sat down, once, a thing on Henry's heart
so heavy, if he had a hundred years
& more, & weeping, sleepless, in all them time
Henry could not make good.
1964 'Dream Song No.29'.

14 I seldom go to films. They are too exciting
said the Honourable Possum.
1964 'Dream Song No.53'.

15 Bats have no bankers and they do not drink
and cannot be arrested and pay no tax
and, in general, bats have it made.
1964 'Dream Song No.63'.

16 A lone letter from a young man: that is fame.
1968 'Dream Song No.342'.

17 My girls suffered during this month or so,

so did my seminars & lectures &
my poetry even. To be a *critic*, ah,
how deeper and more scientific.
1971 'Olympus'.

18 The artist is extremely lucky who is presented with
the worst possible ordeal which will not actually
kill him.
1972 Interview in *The Paris Review*, winter issue.

19 He crusht a cigarette out. Crusht him out
Surprising God, at last, in a wink of time.
His soul was forwarded.
Adressat unbekannt.
1977 'Henry's Fate'.

Berton, Pierre 1920–

Canadian writer, journalist and broadcaster. His many
works include *The Mysterious North* (1956) and *Why We
Act Like Canadians* (1982).

20 A Canadian is somebody who knows how to make
love in a canoe.
1973 Interviewed by Dick Brown in *The Canadian*, 22 Dec.

Bethell, (Mary) Ursula 1874–1945

New Zealand poet, born in England. Her works,
celebrating detail in nature, include *From a Garden in the
Antipodes* (1929) and *Day and Night: Poems 1924–1935*
(1939).

21 But beside it I have planted a green Bay-tree,
—A sweet Bay, an Olive, and a Turkey Fig,
—A Fig, an Olive, and a Bay.
1929 *From a Garden in the Antipodes*, 'Detail'.

Bethmann Hollweg, Theobald von
1856–1921

German statesman, Imperial Chancellor (1909–17), who
played an important part in events leading to war in
1914. Anxious for a negotiated peace, he was forced from
office in 1917.

22 Just for a word 'neutrality'—a word which in
wartime has so often been disregarded—just for a
scrap of paper Great Britain is going to make war
on a kindred nation who desires nothing better
than to be friends with her.
1914 On Britain's reaction to the German invasion of neutral
Belgium, 4 Aug. Quoted in *British Documents on the Origins of
the War 1898–1914* (1926), vol.11.

23 If the iron dice roll, may God help us.
1914 Speech in the Reichstag.

Bethune, Norman 1890–1939

Canadian physician and revolutionary.

24 The function of the artist is to disturb. His duty is
to arouse the sleeper, to shake the complacent

pillars of the world. He reminds the world of its
dark ancestry, and shows the world its present, and
points the way to its new birth. He is at once the
product and the preceptor of his time.
1937 Letter from Madrid, 5 May. Quoted in Ted Allen and
Sydney Gordon *The Scalpel, The Sword* (1952).

Betjeman, Sir John 1906–84

English poet, writer and broadcaster, whose nostalgic
light verse, often masking an underlying melancholy,
achieved great popularity. Appointed Poet Laureate in
1972, he was also a defender of traditional architecture
and a perceptive social critic.

25 Oh! Chintzy, chintzy cheeriness,
Half dead and half alive.
1930 'Death in Leamington', first published in the *London
Mercury*.

26 Sing on, with hymns uproarious,
Ye humble and aloof,
Look up! and oh, how glorious
He has restored the roof!
1931 *Mount Zion*, 'Hymn'.

27 Broad of Church and broad of Mind,
Broad before and broad behind,
A keen ecclesiologist,
A rather dirty Wykehamist.
1931 *Mount Zion*, 'The Wykehamist'.

28 Ghastly Good Taste, or a depressing story of the
rise and fall of English architecture.
1933 Title and sub-title of book.

29 He sipped at the weak hock and seltzer
As he gazed at the London skies
Through the Nottingham lace of the curtains
Or was it his bees-winged eyes?
1937 *Continual Dew*, 'The Arrest of Oscar Wilde at The
Cadogan Hotel'.

30 Spirits of well-shot woodcock, partridge, snipe,
Flutter and bear him up the Norfolk sky:
In that red house in a red mahogany book-case
The stamp collection waits with mounts long dry.
1937 *Continual Dew*, 'Death of King George V'.

31 Come, friendly bombs, and fall on Slough
It isn't fit for humans now
There isn't grass to graze a cow
Swarm over, Death!
1937 *Continual Dew*, 'Slough'.

32 Pam, I adore you, Pam, you great mountainous
sports girl,
Whizzing them over the net, full of the strength of
five:
That old Malvernian brother, you zephyr and khaki
shorts girl,
Although he's playing for Woking,

Can't stand up to your wonderful backhand drive.

1940 *Old Lights for New Chancels,* 'Pot Pourri from a Surrey Garden'.

33 Think of what our Nation stands for,
Books from Boots' and country lanes,
Free speech, free passes, class distinction,
Democracy and proper drains.
Lord, put beneath Thy special care
One-eighty-nine Cadogan Square.

1940 *Old Lights for New Chancels,* 'In Westminster Abbey'.

34 The test of an abstract picture, for me, is not my
first reaction to it, but how long I can stand it
hanging on the wall of a room where I am living.

1944 *John Piper.*

35 Miss J. Hunter Dunn, Miss J. Hunter Dunn,
Furnish'd and burnish'd by Aldershot sun,
What strenuous singles we played after tea,
We in the tournament—you against me!

1945 *New Bats in Old Belfries,* 'A Subaltern's Love-Song'.

36 Miss Joan Hunter Dunn, Miss Joan Hunter Dunn,
I can hear from the car-park the dance has begun.
Oh! full Surrey twilight! importunate band!
Oh! strongly adorable tennis-girl's hand!

1945 *Old Lights for New Chancels,* 'A Subaltern's Love-Song'.

37 For a full spring-tide of blossom seethed and
departed hence,
Leaving land-locked pools of jonquils by sunny
garden fence.

1945 *Old Lights for New Chancels,* 'May-Day Song for North Oxford'.

38 And low the mists of evening lie
And lightly skims the midge.

1945 *Old Lights for New Chancels,* 'Henley-on-Thames'.

39 Rumbling under blackened girders, Midland,
bound for Cricklewood,
Puffed its sulphur to the sunset where that Land of
laundries stood.

1945 *Old Lights for New Chancels,* 'Parliament Hill Fields'.

40 Up the hill where stucco houses in Virginia creeper
drown—
And my childish wave of pity, seeing children
carrying down
Sheaves of drooping dandelions to the courts of
Kentish Town.

1945 *Old Lights for New Chancels,* 'Parliament Hill Fields'.

41 Bournemouth is one of the few English towns one
can safely call 'her'.

1949 Radio talk, later collected in *First and Last Loves* (1952), 'Bournemouth'.

42 St Endellion! St Endellion! The name is like a ring
of bells.

1950 Radio talk, later collected in *First and Last Loves* (1952), 'St Endellion'.

43 Imagine the position of the modern architect.
Picture the young fellow to be put into a
'profession' because trade is considered beneath
him (another antiquarian prejudice). The young
fellow hasn't exactly got a legal mind, like father;
he's not much good at essays, so he can't write; he
faints at the sight of blood so can't be a doctor.
What is there for him to do? Architecture of course.

1952 *First and Last Loves.*

44 Oh prams on concrete balconies, what will your
children see?

1952 *First and Last Loves.*

45 History must not be written with bias, and both
sides must be given, even if there is only one side.

1952 *First and Last Loves.*

46 And girls in slacks remember dad,
And oafish louts remember Mum.

1954 *A Few Late Chrysanthemums,* 'Christmas'.

47 And is it true? And is it true,
This most tremendous tale of all,
Seen in a stained-glass window's hue,
A Baby in an ox's stall?
The Maker of the stars and sea
Become a Child on earth for me?

1954 *A Few Late Chrysanthemums,* 'Christmas'.

48 Gaily into Ruislip Gardens
Runs the red electric train
With a thousand Ta's and Pardon's
Daintily alights Elaine.

1954 *A Few Late Chrysanthemums,* 'Middlesex'.

49 Then Harrow-on-the-Hill's a rocky island
And Harrow churchyard full of sailor's graves,
And the constant click and kissing of the trolley
busses hissing
Is the level to the Wealdstone turned to waves.

1954 *A Few Late Chrysanthemums,* 'Harrow-on-the-Hill'.

50 But I'm dying now and done for,
What on earth was all the fun for?
I am ill and old and terrified and tight.

1954 *A Few Late Chrysanthemums,* 'Sun and Fun—Song of a Night-club Proprietress'.

51 Does Mum, the Persil-user, still believe
That there's no Devil and that youth is bliss?
As certain as the sun behind the Downs
And quite as plain to see, the Devil walks.

1954 *A Few Late Chrysanthemums,* 'Original Sin on the Sussex Coast'.

52 Phone for the fish knives, Norman

As Cook is a little unnerved;
You kiddies have crumpled the serviettes
And I must have things daintily served.
1954 *A Few Late Chrysanthemums*, 'How To Get On In Society'.

53 In the licorice fields at Pontefract
My love and I did meet
And many a burdened licorice bush
Was blooming round our feet;
Red hair she had and golden skin,
Her sulky lips were shaped for sin,
Her sturdy legs were flannel-slack'd,
The strongest legs in Pontefract.
1954 *A Few Late Chrysanthemums*, 'The Licorice Fields at Pontefract'.

54 In the Garden City Café with its murals on the wall
Before a talk on 'Sex and Civics' I meditated on the Fall.
1954 *A Few Late Chrysanthemums*, 'Huxley Hall'.

55 It's awf'lly bad luck on Diana
Her ponies have swallowed their bits;
She fished down their throats with a spanner
And frightened them all into fits.
1954 *A Few Late Chrysanthemums*, 'Hunter Trails'.

56 Oh wasn't it naughty of Smudges?
Oh, Mummy, I'm sick with disgust.
She threw me in front of the Judges
And my silly old collarbone's bust.
1954 *A Few Late Chrysanthemums*, 'Hunter Trails'.

57 I heard the church bells hollowing out the sky
Deep beyond deep, like never-ending stars.
1960 *Summoned By Bells*, ch.1.

58 Childhood is measured out by sounds and smells
And sights, before the dark of reason grows.
1960 *Summoned By Bells*, ch.4.

59 The dread of beatings! Dread of being late!
And, greatest dread of all, the dread of games!
1960 *Summoned by Bells*, ch.7.

Beuys, Joseph 1921–86

German avant-garde artist. Professor of Sculpture at Düsseldorf Academy (1961–71), his works were typically 'assemblages' of rubbish, deliberately anti-formal. He co-founded the German Green Party.

60 A total work of art is only possible in the context of the whole of society. Everyone will be a necessary co-creator of a social architecture, and, so long as anyone cannot participate, the ideal form of democracy has not been reached. Whether people are artists, assemblers of machines or nurses, it is a matter of participating in the whole.
1972 From an interview with G Jappe (translated by J Wheelwright), in *Studio International*, vol.184, no.950, Dec.

Quoted in C Harrison and P Wood (eds) *Art in Theory 1900–1990* (1992).

Bevan, Aneurin 1897–1960

Welsh Labour politician, a miner who took a leading part in the 1926 General Strike, and a brilliant, irreverent orator. He entered politics in 1929 and joined the Labour Party (1931). As Minister of Health (1945–51), he introduced the National Health Service (1948).

61 The worst thing I can say about democracy is that it has tolerated the right honourable gentleman [Neville Chamberlain] for four and a half years.
1929 House of Commons, 23 Jul.

62 We have been the dreamers. We have been the sufferers. Now we are the builders. We want the complete political extinction of the Tory Party— and 25 years of Labour Government, for we cannot do in five years what requires to be done.
1945 Labour Party conference, Blackpool, 18 May.

63 This island is made mainly of coal and surrounded by fish. Only an organizing genius could produce a shortage of coal and a shortage of fish at the same time.
1945 Speech at Blackpool. Reported in the *Daily Herald*, 25 May.

64 No amount of cajolery, and no attempts at ethical or social seduction, can eradicate from my heart a deep and burning hatred for the Tory Party that inflicted those experiences on me. So far as I am concerned, they are lower than vermin.
1948 Speech on the inter-war depression, made at the inauguration of the National Health Service, 5 Jul.

65 In Place of Fear.
1952 Title of his book about disarmament.

66 We know what happens to people who stay in the middle of the road. They get run over.
1953 In *The Observer*, Dec.

67 A man suffering from petrified adolescence.
Of Winston Churchill. Quoted in Vincent Brome *Aneurin Bevan* (1953).

68 I am not going to spend any time whatsoever attacking the Foreign Secretary. Quite honestly, I am beginning to feel extremely sorry for him. If we complain about the tune, there is no reason to attack the monkey when the organ grinder is present.
1957 Expressing his wish to address Prime Minister Harold Macmillan rather than Selwyn Lloyd on the Suez crisis in the House of Commons, May.

69 If you carry this resolution, you will send a Foreign Secretary—whoever he may be—naked into the conference chamber. You call that statesmanship. I call it an emotional spasm.

1957 Labour Party conference speech against unilateral disarmament, Oct.

70 I read the newspapers avidly. It is my one form of continuous fiction.

1960 In *The Times,* 29 Mar.

71 Politics is a blood sport.

Quoted in Jennie Lee *My Life with Nye* (1980).

Beveridge, William Henry Beveridge, 1st Baron 1879–1963

British economist, administrator and social reformer, Director of the London School of Economics (1919–37). His *Report on Social Insurance and Allied Services* (The Beveridge Report, 1942) helped to create the Welfare State.

72 The trouble in modern democracy is that men do not approach to leadership until they have lost the desire to lead anyone.

1934 In *The Observer,* 15 Apr.

73 The object of government in peace and in war is not the glory of rulers or of races, but the happiness of the common man.

1942 *Social Insurance and Allied Services,* pt.7.

74 The most urgent tasks in Britain, once war is over, are, on the one hand, the making of a common attack on the giant evils of Want, Disease, Ignorance and Squalor, and on the other hand, the re-equipping of British industry.

1944 *Full Employment in a Free Society.*

75 The state is or can be master of money, but in a free society it is master of very little else.

1948 *Voluntary Action,* ch.12.

Bevin, Ernest 1881–1951

English Labour politician. He formed the National Transport and General Workers' Union, becoming its General Secretary (1921–40), then entered politics. He was appointed Minister of Labour and National Service in the coalition, and later Foreign Secretary (1945–51).

76 The most conservative man in the world is the British trade unionist, when you want to change him.

1927 Speech to Trade Union Congress, 8 Sep.

77 If you open that Pandora's box, you never know what Trojan 'orses will appear.

1948 Expressing doubts about the value of the newly formed Council of Europe. Recalled by his secretary Sir Roderick Barclay in Michael Charlton *The Price of Victory* (1983).

78 Well you know, Chris, we've got to give them something and I think we'll give them this talking shop in Strasbourg—the Council of Europe.

1948 Comment to Christopher Mayhew. Quoted in Michael Charlton *The Price of Victory* (1983).

79 A turn-up in a million.

On himself. Quoted in his entry by Baron Francis-Williams in the *Dictionary of National Biography* (1951–60).

80 Anything you make a mistake about, I will get you out of, and anything you do well I will take the credit for.

Attributed, to a subordinate. Quoted in A J P Taylor *From the Boer War to the Cold War: Essays on Twentieth-Century Europe* (1995).

Bhagavad Gita

81 I am become Death, the shatterer of worlds.

J R Oppenheimer, the nuclear physicist, recalled this line while watching an atomic cloud billow across the landscape in the moments following the first successful test of an atomic bomb, 16 Jul 1945.

Bible (Old Testament)

All quotations are taken from the King James, or Authorized, translation of the Bible (1611).

82 In the beginning God created the heaven and the earth. And the earth was without form, and void; and darkness was upon the face of the deep. And the spirit of God moved upon the waters.

Genesis 1:1–2.

83 And God said, Let there be light: and there was light.

Genesis 1:3.

84 And God called the light Day and the darkness he called Night. And the evening and morning were the first day.

Genesis 1:5.

85 And God saw that it was good.

Genesis 1:10.

86 And God said, Let us create man in our image, after our likeness: and let them have dominion over the fish of the sea, and over the fowl of the air, and over the cattle, and over all the earth, and over every creeping thing that creepeth upon the earth. So God created man in his own image, in the image of God created he him; male and female created he them. And God blessed them, and God said unto them, Be fruitful and multiply, and replenish the earth, and subdue it: and have dominion over the fish of the sea, and over the fowl of the air, and over every living thing that moveth upon the earth.

Genesis 1:26–8.

87 And on the seventh day God ended his work which he had made, and he rested on the seventh day from all his work which he had made. And God blessed the seventh day and sanctified it: because that in it he had rested from all his work which God created and made.

Genesis 2:2–3.

88 And the LORD God formed man out of the dust of the ground, and breathed into his nostrils the breath of life; and man became a living soul.

Genesis 2:7.

89 And the LORD God planted a garden eastwards in Eden; and there he put the man whom he had formed. And out of the ground made the LORD God to grow every tree that is pleasant for the sight, and good for food; the tree of life also in the midst of the garden, and the tree of knowledge of good and evil.

Genesis 2:8–9.

90 And the LORD God took the man and put him into the garden of Eden to dress it and to keep it. And the LORD God commanded the man, saying, Of every tree of the garden thou mayest freely eat: But of the tree of the knowledge of good and evil, thou shalt not eat of it: for in the day that thou eatest thereof thou shalt surely die.

Genesis 2:15–17.

91 And the LORD God said, It is not good that the man should be alone; I will make him an help meet for him.

Genesis 2:18.

92 And the LORD God caused a deep sleep to fall on Adam, and he slept: and he took one of his ribs, and closed up the flesh instead thereof; And the rib, which the LORD God had taken from man, make he a woman, and brought her unto the man. And Adam said, This is now bone of my bones, and flesh of my flesh: she shall be called Woman, because she was taken out of Man. Therefore shall a man leave his father and his mother, and shall cleave unto his wife: and they shall be one flesh. And they were both naked, the man and his wife, and were not ashamed.

Genesis 2:21–5.

93 Now the serpent was more subtil than any beast of the field which the LORD God had made.

Genesis 3:1.

94 And the serpent said unto the woman, Ye shall not surely die: For God doth know that in the day ye eat thereof, then your eyes shall be opened, and ye shall be as gods, knowing good and evil.

Genesis 3:4–5.

95 And when the woman saw that the tree was good for food, and that it was pleasant to the eyes, and a tree to be desired to make one wise she took of the fruit thereof, and did eat, and gave also to her husband with her; and he did eat. And the eyes of them both were opened, and they knew that they were naked; and they sewed fig leaves together, and made themselves aprons. And they heard the voice of the LORD God walking in the garden in the cool of the day: and Adam and his wife hid themselves from the presence of the LORD God amongst the trees of the garden.

Genesis 3:6–8. In the Geneva Bible of 1560, the word 'aprons' was rendered 'breeches', and the version was therefore known as the Breeches Bible.

96 And he said, I heard thy voice in the garden, and I was afraid, because I was naked; and I hid myself. And he said, Who told thee that thou wast naked? Hast thou eaten of the tree, whereof I commanded thee that thou shouldst not eat?

Genesis 3:10–11.

97 And the man said, The woman whom thou gavest to be with me, she gave me of the tree, and I did eat. And the LORD God said unto the woman, What is this that thou hast done? And the woman said, The serpent beguiled me, and I did eat.

Genesis 3:12–13.

98 And the LORD God said unto the serpent, Because thou hast done this, thou art cursed above all cattle, and above every beast of the field; upon thy belly thou shalt go, and dust shalt thou eat all the days of thy life: And I will put enmity between thy seed and her seed; it shall bruise thy head, and thou shalt bruise his heel.

Genesis 3:14–15.

99 Unto the woman he said, I will greatly multiply thy sorrow and conception; in sorrow thou shalt bring forth children; and thy desire shall be for thy husband, and he shall rule over thee.

Genesis 3:16.

1 And unto Adam he said, Because thou hast hearkened unto the voice of thy wife, and hast eaten of the tree, of which I commanded thee, saying, Thou shalt not eat of it: cursed is the ground for thy sake; in sorrow shalt thou eat of it all the days of thy life.

Genesis 3:17.

2 In the sweat of thy face shalt thou eat bread, till thou return to the ground; for out of it wast thou taken: for dust thou art, and unto dust shalt return.

Genesis 3:19.

3 And the LORD God said, Behold, the man is become as one of us, to know good and evil: and now, lest he put forth his hand, and take also of the tree of life, and eat, and live for ever: Therefore the LORD God sent him forth from the garden of Eden, to till the ground from whence he was taken. So he drove out the man; and he placed at the east of the

garden of Eden Cherubims, and a flaming sword which turned every way, to keep the tree of life.
Genesis 3:21–4.

4 And Adam knew Eve his wife; and she conceived and bare Cain, and said, I have gotten a man from the LORD.
Genesis 4:1.

5 And the LORD said unto Cain, Where is Abel thy brother? And he said, I know not: Am I my brother's keeper? And he said, What hast thou done? the voice of thy brother's blood crieth unto me from the ground.
Genesis 4:9.

6 My punishment is greater than I can bear.
Cain. Genesis 4:10.

7 And the LORD said unto him, Therefore whoever slayeth Cain, vengeance shall be taken on him sevenfold. And the LORD set a mark upon Cain lest any finding him should kill him.
Genesis 4:15.

8 And Cain went out from the presence of the LORD, and dwelt in the land of Nod, on the east of Eden.
Genesis 4:16.

9 And all the days of Methuselah were nine hundred sixty and nine years; and he died.
Genesis 5:27.

10 They went in two and two unto Noah into the ark, the male and the female, as God had commanded Noah.
Genesis 7:9.

11 But the dove found no rest for the sole of her foot.
Genesis 8:9.

12 And the dove came to him in the evening; and, lo, in her mouth was an olive leaf pluckt off: so Noah knew that the waters were abated from off the earth.
Genesis 8:11.

13 I will not again curse the ground any more for man's sake; for the imagination of man is evil from his youth; neither will I again smite any more every thing living, as I have done. While the earth remaineth, seedtime and harvest, and cold and heat, and summer and winter, and day and night shall not cease.
Genesis 8:21–2.

14 At the hand of every man's brother will I require the life of man. Whoso sheddeth man's blood, by man shall his blood be shed: for in the image of God made he man.
Genesis 9:5–6.

15 I do set my bow in the cloud, and it shall be for a token of a covenant between me and the earth.
Genesis 9:13.

16 He was a mighty hunter before the LORD: wherefore it is said, Even as Nimrod the mighty hunter before the LORD.
Genesis 10:9.

17 And the LORD came down to see the city and the tower, which the children of men builded. And the LORD said, Behold, the people is one, and they all have one language; and this they begin to do: and now nothing will be restrained from them, which they have imagined to do. Go to, let us go down, and there confound their language, that they may not understand one another's speech. So the LORD scattered them abroad from thence upon the face of all the earth: and they left off to build the city. Therefore is the name of it called Babel; because the LORD did there confound the language of all the earth: and from thence did the LORD scatter them abroad upon the face of all the earth.
Genesis 11:5–9.

18 Now the LORD had said unto Abram, Get thee out of thy country, and from thy kindred, and from thy father's house, unto a land that I will shew thee: And I will make of thee a great nation, and I will bless thee, and make thy name great; and thou shalt be a blessing: And I will bless them that bless thee, and curse him that curseth thee: and in thee shall all families of the earth be blessed.
Genesis 12:1–3.

19 But the men of Sodom were wicked and sinners before the LORD exceedingly.
Genesis 13:13.

20 Thou shalt be buried in a good old age.
Genesis 15:15.

21 Behold, thou art with child, and shalt bear a son, and shalt call his name Ishmael; because the LORD hath heard thy affliction. And he will be a wild man; his hand will be against every man, and every man's hand against him; and he shall dwell in the presence of all his brethren.
Genesis 16:11–12.

22 And when Abram was ninety years old and nine, the LORD appeared to Abram, and said unto him, I am the Almighty God: walk before me, and be thou perfect.
Genesis 17:1.

23 And I will establish my covenant between me and thee and thy seed after thee in their generations for an everlasting covenant, to be a God unto thee, and to thy seed after thee. And I will give unto thee, and

to thy seed after thee, the land wherein thou art a stranger, all the land of Canaan, for an everlasting possession; and I will be their God.... Every man child among you shall be circumcised.
Genesis 17:7–10.

24 Shall not the Judge of all the earth do right.
Genesis 18:25.

25 Then the LORD rained upon Sodom and upon Gomorrah brimstone and fire from the LORD out of heaven.
Genesis 19:24.

26 But his wife looked back from behind him, and she became a pillar of salt.
Genesis 19:26.

27 Take now thy son, thine only son Isaac, whom thou lovest.
Genesis 22:2.

28 My son, God will provide himself a lamb for a burnt offering.
Genesis 22:8.

29 Esau sells his birthright for a mess of pottage.
1560 Chapter heading for Genesis 25 (in the Geneva Bible).

30 And the boys grew: and Esau was a cunning hunter, a man of the field; and Jacob was a plain man, dwelling in tents.
Genesis 25:27.

31 Esau said, Behold, I am at the point to die: and what profit shall this birthright do to me? And Jacob said, Swear to me this day: and he sware unto him: and he sold his birthright unto Jacob. Then Jacob gave Esau bread and pottage of lentiles; and he did eat and drink, and rose up, and went his way: thus Esau despised his birthright.
Genesis 25:32–4.

32 And Jacob said to Rebekah his mother, Behold, Esau my brother is a hairy man, and I am a smooth man.
Genesis 27:11.

33 Thy brother came with subtilty, and hath taken away thy blessing.
Genesis 27:35.

34 And he dreamed and behold a ladder set up on the earth, and the top of it reached to heaven: and behold the angels of God ascending and descending on it.
Genesis 28:12.

35 And Jacob awaked out of his sleep, and he said, Surely the LORD is in this place; and I knew it not.
Genesis 28:16.

36 And Jacob served seven years for Rachel; and they seemed unto him but a few days, for the love he had to her.
Genesis 29:20.

37 The LORD watch between me and thee, when we are absent one from another.
Genesis 31:49.

38 I will not let thee go, except thou bless me.
Genesis 32:26.

39 Now Israel loved Joseph more than all his children, because he was the son of his old age: and he made him a coat of many colours.
Genesis 37:3.

40 And they said to one another, Behold, this dreamer cometh.
Genesis 37:19.

41 And all his sons and all his daughters rose up to comfort him; but he refused to be comforted; and he said, For I will go down into the grave unto my son mourning. Thus his father wept for him.
Genesis 37:35.

42 And Onan knew that the seed should not be his; and it came to pass, when he went in unto his brother's wife, that he spilled it on the ground, lest that he should give seed to his brother.
Genesis 38:9.

43 And she caught him by his garment, saying, Lie with me: and he left his garment in her hand, and fled, and got him out.
Genesis 39:12.

44 And the seven thin ears devoured the seven rank and full ears. And Pharaoh awoke, and, behold, it was a dream.
Genesis 41:7.

45 Ye are spies; to see the nakedness of the land ye are come.
Genesis 42:9.

46 And he said, My son shall not go down with you; for his brother is dead, and he is left alone: if mischief befall him by the way in the which ye go, then shall ye bring down my gray hairs with sorrow to the grave.
Genesis 42:38.

47 And the famine was sore in the land.
Genesis 43:1.

48 I will give you the good of the land of Egypt, and ye shall eat the fat of the land.
Genesis 45:18.

49 So he sent his brethren away, and they departed: and he said unto them, See that ye fall not out by the way.
Genesis 45:24.

50 And Jacob said unto Pharaoh, The days of the years of my pilgrimage are an hundred and thirty years: few and evil have the days of the years of my life been, and have not attained unto the days of the years of the life of my fathers in the days of their pilgrimage.
Genesis 47:9.

51 Unstable as water, thou shalt not excel.
Genesis 49:4.

52 And he said, Who made thee a prince and a judge over us? intendest thou to kill me, as thou killedst the Egyptian?
Exodus 2:14.

53 And the angel of the LORD appeared unto him in a flame of fire out of the midst of a bush: and he looked, and, behold, the bush burned with fire, and the bush was not consumed.
Exodus 3:2.

54 And he said, Draw not nigh hither: put off thy shoes from off thy feet, for the place whereon thou standest is holy ground.
Exodus 3:5.

55 And Moses hid his face; for he was afraid to look upon God.
Exodus 3:6.

56 And I am come down to deliver them out of the land of the Egyptians, and to bring them up out of that land unto a good land and a large, unto a land flowing with milk and honey.
Exodus 3:8.

57 And God said unto Moses, I AM THAT I AM.
Exodus 3:14.

58 But I am slow of speech, and of a slow tongue.
Exodus 4:10.

59 Let my people go.
Exodus 7:16.

60 Your lamb shall be without blemish, a male of the first year.
Exodus 12:5.

61 And thus shall ye eat it; with your loins girded, your shoes on your feet, and your staff in your hand; and ye shall eat it in haste: it is the LORD's passover. For I will pass through the land of Egypt this night, and will smite all the firstborn in the land of Egypt, both man and beast; and against all the gods of Egypt I will execute judgment: I am the LORD.
Exodus 12:11–12.

62 And Pharaoh rose up in the night, he and all his servants, and all the Egyptians; and there was a great cry in Egypt; for there was not a house where there was not one dead.
Exodus 12:30.

63 And the Egyptians were urgent upon the people, that they might send them out of the land in haste; for they said, We be all dead men.
Exodus 12:33.

64 And the LORD went before them by day in a pillar of a cloud, to lead them the way; and by night in a pillar of fire, to give them light; to go by day and night.
Exodus 13:21.

65 The LORD is a man of war: the LORD is his name.
Exodus 15:3.

66 And the children of Israel said unto them, Would to God we had died by the hand of the LORD in the land of Egypt, when we sat by the flesh pots, and when we did eat bread to the full; for ye have brought us forth to this wilderness, to kill this whole assembly with hunger.
Exodus 16:3.

67 And it came to pass, when Moses held up his hand, that Israel prevailed: and when he let down his hand, Amalek prevailed.
Exodus 17:11.

68 And God spake all these words, saying, I am the LORD thy God, which have brought thee out of the land of Egypt, out of the house of bondage.
Thou shalt have no other gods before me.
Thou shalt not make unto thee any graven image, or any likeness of any thing that is in heaven above, or that is in the earth beneath, or that is in the water under the earth:
Thou shalt not bow down thyself to them, nor serve them: for I the LORD thy God am a jealous God, visiting the iniquity of the fathers upon the children unto the third and fourth generation of them that hate me;
And shewing mercy unto thousands of them that love me, and keep my commandments.
Thou shalt not take the name of the LORD thy God in vain; for the LORD will not hold him guiltless that taketh his name in vain.
Remember the sabbath day, to keep it holy. Six days thou shalt labour and do all thy work: But the seventh day is the sabbath of the LORD thy God:

in it thou shalt not do any work, thou, nor thy son, nor thy daughter, thy manservant, nor thy maidservant, nor thy cattle, nor thy stranger that is within thy gates:

For in six days the LORD made heaven and earth, the sea, and all that in them is, and rested the seventh day: wherefore the LORD blessed the sabbath day, and hallowed it.

Honour thy father and thy mother: that thy days may be long upon the land which the LORD thy God giveth thee.

Thou shalt not kill.

Thou shalt not commit adultery.

Thou shalt not steal.

Thou shalt not bear false witness against thy neighbour.

Thou shalt not covet thy neighbour's house, thou shalt not covet thy neighbour's wife, nor his manservant, nor his maidservant, nor his ox, nor his ass, nor any thing that is thy neighbour's.

Exodus 20:1–17.

69 And if any mischief follow, then thou shalt give life for life, Eye for eye, tooth for tooth, hand for hand, foot for foot. Burning for burning, wound for wound, stripe for stripe.

Exodus 21:23–4.

70 And thou shalt put in the breastplate of judgment the Urim and the Thummim; and thy shall be upon Aaron's heart, when he goeth in before the LORD: and Aaron shall bear the judgment of the children of Israel upon his heart before the LORD continually.

Exodus 28:30.

71 And he received them at their hand, and fashioned it with a graving tool, after he had made it a molten calf: and they said, These be thy gods, O Israel, which brought thee up out of the land of Egypt.

Exodus 32:4.

72 And the LORD said unto Moses, I have seen this people, and, behold, it is a stiffnecked people.

Exodus 32:9.

73 Who is on the LORD's side? let him come unto me.

Exodus 32:26.

74 And the LORD spake unto Moses face to face, as a man speaketh unto his friend.

Exodus 33:11.

75 And he said, My presence shall go with thee, and I will give thee rest. And he said unto him, If thy presence go not with me carry us not up hence.

Exodus 33:14–15.

76 And he said, I beseech thee, shew me thy glory.

Exodus 33:18.

77 And he said, I will make all my goodness pass before thee… And he said, Thou canst not see my face: for there shall no man see me, and live. And the LORD said, Behold, there is a place by me, and thou shalt stand upon a rock: And it shall come to pass, while my glory passeth by, that I will put thee in a clift of the rock, and will cover thee with my hand while I pass by: And I will take away mine hand, and thou shalt see my back parts: but my face shall not be seen.

Exodus 33:19–23.

78 For I am the LORD your God: ye shall therefore sanctify yourselves, and ye shall be holy; for I am holy: neither shall ye defile yourselves with any manner of creeping thing that creepeth upon the earth.

Leviticus 11:44.

79 But the goat, on which the lot fell to be the scapegoat, shall be presented alive before the LORD, to make an atonement with him, and to let him go for a scapegoat into the wilderness.

Leviticus 16:10.

80 Thou shalt not avenge, nor bear any grudge against the children of thy people, but thou shalt love thy neighbour as thyself: I am the LORD.

Leviticus 19:18.

81 The LORD bless thee, and keep thee:
The LORD make his face shine upon thee, and be gracious unto thee:
The LORD lift up his countenance upon thee, and give thee peace.

Numbers 6:24–6.

82 The land through which we have gone to search it, is a land that eateth up the inhabitants thereof; and all the people that we saw in it are men of a great stature. And there we saw the giants, the sons of Anak, which come of the giants: and we were in our own sight as grasshoppers, and so we were in their sight.

Numbers 13:32–33.

83 The rod of Aaron for the house of Levi was budded, and brought forth buds, and bloomed blossoms, and yielded almonds.

Numbers 17:8.

84 And Moses made a serpent of brass, and put it upon a pole, and it came to pass, that if a serpent had bitten any man, when he beheld the serpent of brass, he lived.

Numbers 21:9.

85 And the LORD opened the mouth of the ass, and she said unto Balaam, What have I done unto thee, that thou hast smitten me these three times?

Numbers 22:28.

86 God is not a man, that he should lie; neither the son of man, that he should repent: hath he said, and shall he not do it? or hath he spoken, and shall he not make it good?
Numbers 23:19.

87 What hath God wrought!
Numbers 23:23. These words were transmitted by Samuel Morse on 24 May 1844, the first electronic telegraph message.

88 Be sure your sin will find you out.
Numbers 32:23.

89 I call heaven and earth to witness against you this day.
Deuteronomy 4:26.

90 Hear, O Israel: the LORD our God is one LORD: And thou shalt love the LORD thy God with all thy soul, and with all thy might. And these words, which I command thee this day, shall be in thine heart: And thou shalt teach them diligently unto thy children, and shalt talk of them when thou sittest in thine house, and when thou walkest by the way, and when thou liest down, and when thou risest up. And thou shalt bind them for a sign upon thine hand, and they shall be as frontlets between thine eyes. And thou shalt write them upon the posts of thy house, and on thy gates.
Deuteronomy 6:4–9.

91 Ye shall not go after other gods, of the gods of the people which are round about you; (For the LORD thy God is a jealous God among you).
Deuteronomy 6:14–15.

92 And he humbled thee, and suffered thee to hunger, and fed thee with manna, which thou knewest not, neither did thy fathers know; that he might make thee know that man doth not live by bread only, but by every word that proceedeth out of the mouth of the LORD doth man live.
Deuteronomy 8:3.

93 Speak not thou in thine heart, after that the LORD thy God hath cast them out from before thee, saying, For my righteousness the LORD hath brought me in to possess this land: but for the wickedness of these nations the LORD doth drive them out from before thee.
Deuteronomy 9:4.

94 If there arise among you a prophet, or a dreamer of dreams, and giveth thee a sign or a wonder... Thou shalt not hearken.
Deuteronomy 13:1–3.

95 When thou cuttest down thine harvest in thy field, and hast forgot a sheaf in the field, thou shalt not go again to fetch it: it shall be for the stranger, for the fatherless, and for the widow: that the LORD thy God may bless thee in all the work of thine hands.
Deuteronomy 24:19.

96 Thou shalt not muzzle the ox when he treadeth out the corn.
Deuteronomy 25:4.

97 Cursed be he that removeth his neighbour's landmark. And all the people shall say, Amen.
Deuteronomy 27:17.

98 The secret things belong unto the LORD our God; but those things which are revealed belong unto us and our children for ever, that we may do all the words of this law.
Deuteronomy 29:29.

99 I call heaven and earth to record this day against you, that I have set before you life and death, blessing and cursing: therefore choose life, that both thou and thy seed may live.
Deuteronomy 30:19.

1 Give ear, O ye heavens, and I will speak: and hear, O earth, the words of my mouth. My doctrine shall drop as the rain, my speech shall distil as the dew, as the small rain upon the tender herb, and as the showers upon the grass.
Deuteronomy 32:1–2.

2 He found him in a desert land, and in the waste howling wilderness; he led him about, he instructed him, he kept him as the apple of his eye.
Deuteronomy 32:10.

3 Thou art waxen fat, thou art grown thick, thou art covered with fatness.
Deuteronomy 32:15.

4 As thy days, so shall thy strength be.
Deuteronomy 33:25.

5 The eternal God is thy refuge, and underneath are the everlasting arms.
Deuteronomy 33:27.

6 So Moses the servant of the LORD died there in the land of Moab... but no man knoweth of his sepulchre unto this day.
Deuteronomy 34:5–6.

7 There shall not any man be able to stand before thee all the days of thy life: as I was with Moses, so I will be with thee: I will not fail thee, nor forsake thee.
Joshua 1:5.

8 Have I not commanded thee? Be strong and of a good courage: be not afraid, neither be thou

dismayed: for the LORD thy God is with thee whithersoever thou goest.
Joshua 1:9.

9 Behold, when we come into the land, thou shalt bind this line of scarlet thread in the window which thou didst let us down by.
Joshua 2:18.

10 So the people shouted when the priests blew with the trumpets: and it came to pass, when the people heard the sound of the trumpet, and the people shouted with a great shout, that the wall fell down flat, so that the people went up into the city, every man straight before him, and they took the city.
Joshua 6:20.

11 I am going the way of all the earth.
Joshua 23:14.

12 Choose you this day whom ye will serve… but as for me and my house, we will serve the LORD.
Joshua 24:15.

13 Then Jael Heber's wife took a nail of the tent, and took an hammer in her hand, and went softly unto him and smote the nail into his temples, and fastened it into the ground: for he was fast asleep and weary. So he died.
Judges 4:21.

14 He asked for water, and she brought him milk; she brought forth butter in a lordly dish. She put her hand to the nail, and her right hand to the workmen's hammer; and with the hammer she smote Sisera, she smote off his head, when she had pierced and stricken through his temples. At her feet he bowed, he fell, he lay down: at her feet he bowed he fell: where he bowed, there he fell down dead. The mother of Sisera looked out at a window, and cried through the lattice, Why is his chariot so long in coming? why tarry the wheels of his chariots?
Judges 5:25–8.

15 The sword of the LORD, and of Gideon.
Judges 7:18.

16 Then said they unto him, Say now Shibboleth: and he said Sibboleth: for he could not frame to pronounce it right. Then they took him, and slew him.
Judges 12:6.

17 And he said unto them, Out of the eater came forth meat, and out of the strong came forth sweetness. And they could not in three days expound the riddle.
Judges 14:14.

18 If ye had not plowed with my heifer, ye had not found out my riddle.
Judges 14:18.

19 He smote them hip and thigh.
Judges 15:8.

20 With the jawbone of an ass, heaps upon heaps, with the jaw of an ass have I slain a thousand men.
Judges 15:15–16.

21 And she said, The Philistines be upon thee, Samson. And he awoke out of his sleep, and said, I will go out as at other times before, and shake myself. And he wist not that the LORD was departed from him. But the Philistines took him, and put out his eyes, and brought him down to Gaza, and bound him with fetters of brass; and he did grind in the prison house.
Judges 16:19–21.

22 And Samson said, Let me die with the Philistines. And he bowed himself with all his might; and the house fell upon the lords, and upon all the people that were therein. So the dead which he slew at his death were more than they which he slew in his life.
Judges 16:29–30.

23 In those days there was no king in Israel, but every man did that which was right in his own eyes.
Judges 17:6.

24 The people arose as one man.
Judges 20:8.

25 Intreat me not to leave thee, or to return from following after thee: for whither thou goest, I will go; and where thou lodgest, I will lodge: thy people shall be my people, and thy God my God: Where thou diest, will I die, and there will I be buried: the LORD do so to me, and more also, if ought but death part thee and me.
Ruth 1:16–17.

26 Now the Lord saith, Be it far from me; for them that honour me I will honour, and they that despise me shall be lightly esteemed.
1 Samuel 2:30.

27 The LORD called Samuel: and he answered, Here am I. And he ran unto Eli, and said, Here am I; for thou calledst me. And he said, I called not; lie down again.
1 Samuel 3:4–5.

28 Speak, LORD; for thy servant heareth.
1 Samuel 3:9.

29 Behold, I will do a thing in Israel, at which both the ears of every one that heareth it shall tingle.
1 Samuel 3:11.

30 Be strong, and quit yourselves like men.
1 Samuel 4:9.

31 And it came to pass, when he made mention of the ark of God, that he fell from off the seat backward by the side of the gate, and his neck brake, and he died: for he was an old man, and heavy.
1 Samuel 4:18.

32 Behold, thou art old, and thy sons walk not in thy ways: now make us a king to judge us like all the nations.
1 Samuel 8:5.

33 God save the king.
1 Samuel 10:24.

34 But now thy kingdom shall not continue: the LORD hath sought him a man after his own heart, and the LORD hath commanded him to be captain over his people.
1 Samuel 13:14.

35 Hath the LORD as great delight in burnt offerings and sacrifices, as in obeying the voice of the LORD? Behold, to obey is better than sacrifice, and to hearken than the fat of rams. For rebellion is as the sin of witchcraft, and stubbornness is as iniquity and idolatry.
1 Samuel 15:22–3.

36 Look not on his countenance, or on the height of his stature; because I have refused him: for the LORD seeth not as man seeth; for man looketh on the outward appearance, but the LORD looketh on the heart.
1 Samuel 16:7.

37 Now he was ruddy, and withal of a beautiful countenance, and goodly to look to. And the LORD said, Arise, anoint him: for this is he.
1 Samuel 16:12.

38 I know thy pride, and the naughtiness of thine heart.
1 Samuel 17:28.

39 David said moreover, The LORD that delivered me out of the paw of the lion, and out of the paw of the bear, he will deliver me out of the hand of this Philistine. And Saul said unto David, Go, and the LORD be with thee.
1 Samuel 17:37.

40 And he took his staff in his hand, and chose him five smooth stones out of the brook.
1 Samuel 17:40.

41 And the Philistine said unto David, Am I a dog, that thou comest to me with staves?
1 Samuel 17:43.

42 Saul hath slain his thousands, and David his ten thousands.
1 Samuel 18:7.

43 Behold, I have played the fool, and have erred exceedingly.
1 Samuel 26:21.

44 Saul and Jonathan were lovely and pleasant in their lives, and in their death they were not divided: they were swifter than eagles, they were stronger than lions…. I am distressed for thee, my brother Jonathan: very pleasant hast thou been unto me: thy love to me was wonderful, passing the love of women. How are the mighty fallen, and the weapons of war perished!
2 Samuel 1:23–7.

45 And David danced before the LORD with all his might.
2 Samuel 6:14.

46 Set ye Uriah in the forefront of the hottest battle, and retire ye from him, that he may be smitten, and die.
2 Samuel 11:15.

47 But the poor man had nothing, save one little ewe lamb
2 Samuel 12:3.

48 Thou art the man.
2 Samuel 12:7.

49 For we must needs die, and are as water spilt on the ground, which cannot be gathered up again: neither doth God respect any person.
2 Samuel 14:14.

50 And when Ahithophel saw that his counsel was not followed, he saddled his ass, and arose, and gat him home to his house, to his city, and put his household in order, and hanged himself.
2 Samuel 17:23.

51 And the king was much moved, and went up to the chamber over the gate, and wept: and as he went, thus he said, O my son Absalom, my son, my son Absalom! would God I had died for thee, O Absalom, my son, my son!
2 Samuel 18:33.

52 Nay: but I will surely buy it of thee at a price: neither will I offer burnt offerings unto the Lord my God of that which dost cost me nothing.
2 Samuel 24:24.

53 Now king David was old and stricken in years; and they covered him with clothes, but he gat no heat.
1 Kings 1:1.

54 I go the way of all the earth: be thou strong therefore, and shew thyself a man.
1 Kings 2:2.

55 I am but a little child: I know not how to go out or come in.
1 Kings 3:7.

56 But if ye shall at all turn from following me… Then will I cut off Israel out of the land which I have given them; and this house, which I have hallowed for my name, will I cast out of my sight; and Israel shall be a proverb and a byword among all people.
1 Kings 9:6–7.

57 And when the queen of Sheba heard of the fame of Solomon concerning the name of the LORD, she came to prove him with hard questions.
1 Kings 10:1.

58 I believed not the words, until I came, and mine eyes had seen it: and, behold, the half was not told me.
1 Kings 10:7.

59 But king Solomon loved many strange women.
1 Kings 11:1.

60 My little finger shall be thicker than my father's loins. And now whereas my father did lade you with a heavy yoke, I will add to your yoke: my father hath chastised you with whips, but I will chastise you with scorpions.
1 Kings 12:10–11.

61 He slept with his fathers.
1 Kings 14:20.

62 And the ravens brought him bread and flesh in the morning, and bread and flesh in the evening; and he drank of the brook.
Of Elijah. 1 Kings 17:6–7.

63 Elijah came unto all the people, and said, How long halt ye between two opinions? if the LORD be God, follow him: but if Baal, then follow him. And the people answered him not a word.
1 Kings 18:21.

64 Cry aloud: for he is a god; either he is talking, or is pursuing, or he is in a journey, or peradventure he sleepeth, and must be wakened.
1 Kings 18:27.

65 There is a sound of abundance of rain.
1 Kings 18:41.

66 Behold, there ariseth a little cloud out of the sea, like a man's hand.
1 Kings 18:44.

67 Elijah…girded up his loins, and ran before Ahab.
1 Kings 18:46.

68 But he himself went a day's journey into the wilderness, and came and sat down under a juniper tree: and he requested for himself that he might die; and said, It is enough, now, O LORD, take away my life; for I am not better than my fathers.
1 Kings 19:4.

69 And, behold, the LORD passed by, and a great and strong wind rent the mountains, and brake in pieces the rocks before the LORD; but the LORD was not in the wind: and after the wind an earthquake; but the LORD was not in the earthquake: And after the earthquake a fire; but the LORD was not in the fire: and after the fire a still small voice.
1 Kings 19:11–12.

70 Elijah passed by him and cast his mantle upon him.
1 Kings 19:19.

71 In the place where dogs licked the blood of Naboth shall dogs lick thy blood, even thine. And Ahab said to Elijah, Hast thou found me, O mine enemy?
1 Kings 21:20.

72 A certain man drew a bow at a venture, and smote the king of Israel between the joints of the harness.
1 Kings 22:34.

73 Behold there appeared a chariot of fire, and horses of fire, and parted them both asunder; and Elijah went up by a whirlwind into heaven. And Elisha saw it, and he cried, My father, my father, the chariot of Israel, and the horsemen thereof.
2 Kings 2:11–12.

74 The spirit of Elijah doth rest on Elisha.
2 Kings 2:15.

75 Go up, thou bald head.
2 Kings 2:23.

76 Say unto her, Is it well with thee? is it well with thy husband? is it well with the child? And she answered, It is well.
2 Kings 4:26.

77 Let him come now to me, and he shall know that there is a prophet in Israel.
2 Kings 5:8.

78 Is it peace? and Jehu said, What hast thou to do with peace? turn thee behind me.
2 Kings 9:18.

79 The driving is like the driving of Jehu the son of Nimshi; for he driveth furiously.
2 Kings 9:20.

80 And when Jehu was come to Jezreel, Jezebel heard of it; and she painted her face, and tired her head, and looked out at a window.
2 Kings 9:30.

81 And he lifted up his face to the window, and said, Who is on my side? who? And there looked out to him two or three eunuchs.
2 Kings 9:32.

82 So they threw her down: and some of her blood was sprinkled on the wall, and on the horses: and he trode her under foot.
2 Kings 9:33.

83 And they went to bury her: but they found no more of her than the skull, and the feet, and the palms of her hands.
2 Kings 9:35.

84 Now, behold, thou trustest upon the staff of this bruised reed, even upon Egypt, on which if a man lean, it will go into his hand, and pierce it: so is Pharaoh king of Egypt unto all that trust on him.
2 Kings 18:21.

85 And when they came unto the threshingfloor of Chidon, Uzza put forth his hand to hold the ark; for the oxen stumbled. And the anger of the LORD was kindled against Uzza, and he smote him, because he put his hand to the ark: and there he died before God.
1 Chronicles 13:9–10.

86 But who am I, and what is my people, that we should be able to offer so willingly after this sort? for all things come of thee, and of thine own have we given thee. For we are strangers before thee, and soujourners, as were all our fathers: our days on the earth are as a shadow, and there is none abiding.
1 Chronicles 29:14–15.

87 And he died in a good old age, full of days, riches, and honour: and Solomon his son reigned in his stead.
1 Chronicles 29:28.

88 And king Solomon gave to the queen of Sheba all her desire, whatsoever she asked, beside that which she had brought unto the king.
2 Chronicles 9:12.

89 For the eyes of the LORD run to and fro throughout the whole earth, to shew himself strong in the behalf of them whose heart is perfect toward him. Herein thou hast done foolishly: therefore from henceforth thou shalt have wars.
2 Chronicles 16:9.

90 Be not afraid nor dismayed by reason of this great multitude; for the battle is not yours, but God's.
2 Chronicles 20:15.

91 They which builded on the wall, and they that bare burdens, with those that laded, every one with one of his hands wrought in the work, and with the other hand held a weapon.
Nehemiah 4:17–18.

92 Go your way, eat the fat, and drink the sweet, and send portions unto them for whom nothing is prepared: for this day is holy unto our Lord; neither be ye sorry; for the joy of the LORD is your strength.
Nehemiah 8:10.

93 So will I go in unto the king, which is not according to the law: and if I perish, I perish.
Esther 4:16.

94 And the LORD said unto Satan, Whence comest thou? Then Satan answered the LORD, and said, From going to and fro in the earth, and from walking up and down in it.
Job 1:7.

95 Naked came I out of my mother's womb, and naked shall I return thither: the LORD gave, and the LORD hath taken away; blessed be the name of the LORD.
Job 1:21.

96 Skin for skin, yea, all that a man hath will he give for his life. But put forth thine hand now, and touch his bone and his flesh, and he will curse thee to thy face.
Job 2:4–5.

97 And he took him a potsherd to scrape himself withal; and he sat down among the ashes. Then said his wife unto him, Dost thou still retain thine integrity? curse God, and die.
Job 2:8–9.

98 Let the day perish wherein I was born, and the night in which it was said, There is a man child conceived.
Job 3:2–3.

99 There the wicked cease from troubling, and there the weary be at rest.
Job 3:17.

1 Shall mortal man be more just than God? shall a man be more pure than his maker?
Job 4:17.

2 Yet man is born unto trouble, as the sparks fly upward.
Job 5:7.

3 My days are swifter than a weaver's shuttle
Job 7:6.

4 Wherefore then hast thou brought me forth out of the womb? Oh that I had given up the ghost, and no eye had seen me!
Job 10:18.

5 Canst thou by searching find out God? canst thou find out the Almighty unto perfection? It is as high as heaven; what thou do? deeper than hell; what canst thou know? The measure thereof is longer than the earth, and broader than the sea.
Job 11:7–9.

6 No doubt but ye are the people, and wisdom shall die with you.
Job 12:2.

7 With the ancient is wisdom; and in length of days understanding.
Job 12:12.

8 Though he slay me, yet will I trust in him: but I will maintain mine own ways before him.
Job 13:15.

9 Man that is born of a woman is of few days, and full of trouble. He cometh forth like a flower, and is cut down: he fleeth also as a shadow, and continueth not.
Job 14:1–2.

10 I have heard many such things: miserable comforters are ye all.
Job 16:1–2.

11 I am escaped with the skin of my teeth.
Job 19:20.

12 For I know that my redeemer liveth, and that he shall stand at the latter day upon the earth: And though after my skin worms destroy this body, yet in my flesh shall I see God.
Job 19:25–7.

13 But ye should say, Why persecute we him, seeing the root of the matter is found in me?
Job 19:28.

14 Behold, my desire is, that the Almighty would answer me, and that mine adversary had written a book.
Job 31:35.

15 Great men are not always wise: neither do the aged understand judgment.
Job 32:9.

16 Therefore doth Job open his mouth in vain; he multiplieth words without knowledge.
Job 35:16.

17 Who is this that darkeneth counsel by words without knowledge? Gird up now thy loins like a man; for I will demand of thee, and answer thou me. Where wast thou when I laid the foundations of the earth? declare, if thou hast understanding.
Job 38:2–4.

18 When the morning stars sang together, and all the sons of God shouted for joy.
Job 38:7.

19 Hitherto shalt thou come, but no further: and here shall thy proud waves be stayed.
Job 38:2–11.

20 Hath the rain a father? or who hath begotten the drops of dew?
Job 38:28.

21 Canst thou bind the sweet influences of Pleiades, or loose the bands of Orion?
Job 38:31.

22 Hast thou given the horse strength? hast thou clothed his neck with thunder? Canst thou make him afraid as a grasshopper? the glory of his nostrils is terrible. He paweth in the valley and rejoiceth in his strength: he goeth on to meet the armed men.
Job 39:19–21.

23 He swalloweth the ground with fierceness and rage: neither believeth he that it is the sound of the trumpet. He saith among the trumpets, Ha, ha, and he smelleth the battle afar off, the thunder of the captains, and the shouting.
Job 39:24–5.

24 Behold now behemoth, which I made with thee; he eateth grass as an ox.
Job 40:15.

25 The shady trees cover him with their shadow; the willows of the brook compass him about. Behold, he drinketh up a river, and hasteth not: he trusteth that he can draw up Jordan into his mouth.
Job 40:22–3.

26 Canst thou draw out leviathan with an hook?
Job 41:1.

27 I have heard of thee by the hearing of the ear: but now mine eye seeth thee. Wherefore I abhor myself, and repent in dust and ashes.
Job 42:5–6.

28 So the LORD blessed the latter end of Job more than his beginning.
Job 42:12.

29 Blessed is the man that walketh not in the counsel of the ungodly, nor standeth in the way of sinners, nor sitteth in the seat of the scornful. But his delight is in the law of the LORD; and in his law doth he meditate day and night. And he shall be like a tree planted by the rivers of water, that bringeth forth his fruit in his season; his leaf also shall not wither; and whatsoever he doeth shall

prosper. The ungodly are not so: but are like the chaff which the wind driveth away.
Psalms 1:1–14.

30 Why do the heathen rage, and the people imagine a vain thing?
Psalms 2:1.

31 He that sitteth in the heavens shall laugh: the LORD shall have them in derision.
Psalms 2:4.

32 Thou art my Son: this day have I begotten thee. Ask of me, and I shall give thee the heathen for thine inheritance, and the uttermost parts of the earth for thy possession. Thou shalt break them with a rod of iron; thou shalt dash them in pieces like a potter's vessel.
Psalms 2:8–9.

33 Stand in awe, and sin not: commune with your own heart upon your bed, and be still.
Psalms 4:4.

34 O LORD our Lord, how excellent is thy name in all the earth! who hast set thy glory above the heavens. Out of the mouth of babes and sucklings hast thou ordained strength because of thine enemies, that thou mightest still the enemy and the avenger.
Psalms 8:1–2.

35 When I consider thy heavens, the work of thy fingers, the moon and the stars, which thou hast ordained; What is man, that thou art mindful of him? and the son of man, that thou visitest him? For thou hast made him a little lower than the angels, and hast crowned him with glory and honour. Thou madest him to have dominion over the works of thy hands; thou hast put all things under his feet.
Psalms 8:3–9.

36 The fool hath said in his heart, There is no God.
Psalms 14:1–2.

37 They are all gone aside, they are all together become filthy: there is none that doeth good, no, not one.
Psalms 14:4.

38 LORD, who shall abide in thy tabernacle? who shall dwell in thy holy hill? He that walketh uprightly, and worketh righteousness, and speaketh the truth in his heart.
Psalms 15:1–2.

39 The lines are fallen unto me in pleasant places; yea, I have a goodly heritage.
Psalms 16:6.

40 For thou wilt not leave my soul in hell; neither wilt thou suffer thine Holy One to see corruption.
Psalms 16:10.

41 Keep me as the apple of the eye, hide me under the shadow of thy wings.
Psalms 17:8.

42 For by thee I have run through a troop; and by my God have I leaped over a wall.
Psalms 18:29.

43 He maketh my feet like hinds' feet, and setteth me upon my high places.
Psalms 18:33.

44 The heavens declare the glory of God; and the firmament sheweth his handywork. Day unto day uttereth speech, and night unto night sheweth knowledge. There is no speech nor language, where their voice is not heard. Their line is gone out through all the earth, and their words to the end of the world. In them hath he set a tabernacle for the sun, Which is as a bridegroom coming out of his chamber, and rejoiceth as a strong man to run a race. His going forth is from the end of the heaven, and his circuit unto the ends of it: and there is nothing hid from the heat thereof.
Psalms 19:1–6.

45 The law of the LORD is perfect, converting the soul: the testimony of the LORD is sure, making wise the simple. The statutes of the LORD are right, rejoicing the heart: the commandment of the LORD is pure, enlightening the eyes. The fear of the LORD is clean, enduring for ever: the judgments of the LORD are true and righteous altogether. More to be desired are they than gold, yea, than much fine gold: sweeter also than honey and the honeycomb.
Psalms 19:7–10.

46 Some trust in chariots, and some in horses: but we will remember the name of the LORD our God.
Psalms 20:7.

47 My God, my God, why hast thou forsaken me? why art thou so far from helping me, and from the words of my roaring?
Psalms 22:1.

48 But I am a worm, and no man; a reproach of men, and despised of the people. All they that see me laugh me to scorn: they shoot out the lip, they shake the head, saying, He trusted on the LORD that he would deliver him: let him deliver him, seeing he delighted in him.
Psalms 22:6–8.

49 I am poured out like water, and all my bones are out of joint: my heart is like wax; it is melted in the

midst of my bowels. My strength is dried up like a potsherd; and my tongue cleaveth to my jaws; and thou hast brought me into the dust of death. For dogs have compassed me: the assembly of the wicked have inclosed me: they pierced my hands and my feet. I may tell all my bones: they look *and* stare upon me. They part my garments among them, and cast lots upon my vesture.
Psalms 22:14–18.

50 The LORD is my shepherd; I shall not want. He maketh me to lie down in green pastures: he leadeth me beside the still waters. He restoreth my soul: he leadeth me in the paths of righteousness for his name's sake. Yea, though I walk through the valley of death, I will fear no evil: for thou art with me; thy rod and thy staff they comfort me. Thou preparest a table before me in the presence of mine enemies: thou anointest my head with oil; my cup runneth over. Surely goodness and mercy shall follow me all the days of my life: and I will dwell in the house of the LORD for ever.
Psalms 23:1–6.

51 The earth is the LORD's, and the fulness thereof; the world, and they that dwell therein.
Psalms 24:1.

52 Lift up your heads, O ye gates; and be ye lift up, ye everlasting doors; and the King of glory shall come in. Who is this King of glory? The LORD strong and mighty, the LORD mighty in battle.
Psalms 24:7–8.

53 Remember not the sins of my youth, nor my transgressions.
Psalms 25:7.

54 The LORD is my light and my salvation; whom shall I fear? the LORD is the strength of my life; of whom shall I be afraid?
Psalms 27:1.

55 Though an host should encamp against me, my heart shall not fear: though war should rise against me, in this will I be confident. One thing have I desired of the LORD, that will I seek after; that I may dwell in the house of the LORD all the days of my life, to behold the beauty of the LORD, and to inquire in his temple.
Psalms 27:3–4.

56 Thou hast turned for me my mourning into dancing: thou hast put off my sackcloth, and girded me with gladness.
Psalms 30:11.

57 Into thine hand I commit my spirit: thou hast redeemed me, O LORD God of truth.
Psalms 31:5.

58 For this shall every one that is godly pray unto thee in a time when thou mayest be found: surely in the floods of great waters they shall not come nigh unto him. Thou *art* my hiding place; thou shalt preserve me from trouble; thou shalt compass me about with songs of deliverance. Selah.
Psalms 32:6–7.

59 I will instruct thee and teach thee in the way which thou shalt go: I will guide thee with mine eye. Be ye not as the horse, or as the mule, which have no understanding: whose mouth must be held in with bit and bridle, lest they come near unto thee.
Psalms 32:8–9.

60 I sought the LORD, and he heard me, and delivered me from all my fears.
Psalms 34:4.

61 O taste and see that the LORD is good: blessed is the man that trusteth in him. O fear the LORD, ye his saints: for there is no want to them that fear him. The young lions do lack, and suffer hunger: but they that seek the LORD shall not want any good thing.
Psalms 34:8–10.

62 The children of men put their trust under the shadow of thy wings.
Psalms 36:7.

63 Delight thyself also in the LORD, and he shall give thee the desires of thine heart. Commit thy way unto the LORD; trust also in him; and he shall bring *it* to pass.
Psalms 37:4–5.

64 But the meek shall inherit the earth; and shall delight themselves in the abundance of peace.
Psalms 37:11.

65 I have been young and now am old; yet have I not seen the righteous forsaken, nor his seed begging bread.
Psalms 37:25.

66 I waited patiently for the LORD, and he inclined unto me, and heard my cry. He brought me up also out of an horrible pit, out of the miry clay, and set my feet upon a rock, and established my goings.
Psalms 40:1–2.

67 Yea, mine own familiar friend, in whom I trusted, which did eat of my bread, hath lifted up his heel against me.
Psalms 41:9.

68 As the hart panteth after the water brooks, so panteth my soul after thee, O God. My soul

thirsteth for God, for the living God: when shall I come and appear before God?
Psalms 42:1–2.

69 Why art thou cast down, O my soul? and why art thou disquieted in me? hope thou in God: for I shall yet praise him for the help of his countenance.
Psalms 42:5.

70 Deep calleth unto deep at the noise of thy waterspouts: all thy waves and thy billows are gone over me.
Psalms 42:7.

71 Yea, for thy sake are we killed all the day long; we are counted as sheep for the slaughter.
Psalms 44:22.

72 God is our refuge and strength, a very present help in trouble. Therefore will not we fear, though the earth be removed, and though the mountains be carried into the midst of the sea.
Psalms 46:1–2.

73 There is a river, the streams whereof shall make glad the city of God, the holy place of the tabernacles of the most High. God is in the midst of her; she shall not be moved: God shall help her, and that right early.
Psalms 46:4–5.

74 He maketh wars to cease unto the end of the earth; he breaketh the bow, and cutteth the spear in sunder; he burneth the chariot in the fire.
Be still, and know that I am God: I will be exalted among the heathen, I will be exalted in the earth.
Psalms 46:9–10.

75 Great is the LORD, and greatly to be praised in the city of our God, in the mountain of his holiness. Beautiful for situation, the joy of the whole earth, is mount Zion, on the sides of the north, the city of the great King.
Psalms 48:1–2.

76 For I acknowledge my transgressions: and my sin is ever before me. Against thee, thee only, have I sinned, and done this evil in thy sight: that thou mightest be justified when thou speakest, and be clear when thou judgest. Behold, I was shapen in iniquity; and in sin did my mother conceive me.
Psalms 51:3–5.

77 Behold, thou desirest truth in the inward parts: and in the hidden part thou shalt make me to know wisdom. Purge me with hyssop, and I shall be clean: wash me, and I shall be whiter than snow.
Psalms 51:6–7.

78 Create in me a clean heart, O God; and renew a right spirit within me. Cast me not away from thy presence; and take not thy holy spirit from me. Restore unto me the joy of thy salvation; and uphold me with thy free spirit. Then will I teach transgressors thy ways; and sinners shall be converted unto thee.
Psalms 51:10–13.

79 Deliver me from bloodguiltiness, O God, thou God of my salvation: and my tongue shall sing aloud of thy righteousness. O Lord, open thou my lips; and my mouth shall shew forth thy praise. For thou desirest not sacrifice; else would I give it: thou delightest not in burnt offering. The sacrifices of God are a broken spirit: a broken and a contrite heart, O God, thou wilt not despise.
Psalms 51:14–17.

80 Oh that I had wings like a dove! for then would I fly away, and be at rest.
Psalms 55:6.

81 Lead me to the rock that is higher than I.
Psalms 61:2.

82 Truly my soul waiteth upon God: from him cometh my salvation. He only is my rock and my salvation; he is my defence; I shall not be greatly moved.
Psalms 62:1–2.

83 O God, thou art my God; early will I seek thee: my soul thirsteth for thee, my flesh longeth for thee in a dry and thirsty land, where no water is.
Psalms 63:1.

84 Thou crownest the year with thy goodness; and thy paths drop fatness.
Psalms 65:11.

85 God be merciful unto us, and bless us; and cause his face to shine upon us; Selah. That thy way may be known upon earth, thy saving health among all nations. Let the people praise thee, O God; let all the people praise thee.
Psalms 67:1–3.

86 Sing unto God, sing praises to his name: extol him that rideth upon the heavens by his name JAH, and rejoice before him. A father of the fatherless, and a judge of the widows, is God in his holy habitation. God setteth the solitary in families: he bringeth out those which are bound with chains: but the rebellious dwell in a dry land.
Psalms 68:4–6.

87 Thou hast ascended on high, thou hast led captivity captive: thou hast received gifts for men; yea, for the rebellious also, that the LORD God might dwell among them.
Psalms 68:18.

88 In thee, O Lord, do I put my trust: let me never be put to confusion.
Psalms 71:1.

89 Truly God is good to Israel, even to such as are of a clean heart. But as for me, my feet were almost gone; my steps had well nigh slipped. For I was envious at the foolish, when I saw the prosperity of the wicked.
Psalms 73:1–3.

90 When I thought to know this, it was too painful for me; Until I went into the sanctuary of God; then understood I their end.
Psalms 73:16–17.

91 Nevertheless I am continually with thee: thou hast holden me by my right hand. Thou shalt guide me with thy counsel, and afterward receive me to glory. Whom have I in heaven but thee? and there is none upon earth that I desire beside thee. My flesh and my heart faileth: but God is the strength of my heart, and my portion for ever.
Psalms 73:23–6.

92 I am the Lord thy God, which brought thee out of the land of Egypt: open thy mouth wide, and I will fill it.
Psalms 81:10.

93 How amiable are thy tabernacles, O Lord of hosts! My soul longeth, yea, even fainteth for the courts of the Lord: my heart and my flesh crieth out for the living God.
Yea, the sparrow hath found an house, and the swallow a nest for herself, where she may lay her young, even thine altars, O Lord of hosts, my King, and my God.
Psalms 84:1–3.

94 Who passing through the valley of Baca make it a well; the rain also filleth the pools.
They go from strength to strength, every one of them in Zion appeareth before God.
Psalms 84:6–7.

95 For a day in thy courts is better than a thousand. I had rather be a doorkeeper in the house of my God, than to dwell in the tents of wickedness.
Psalms 84:10.

96 Glorious things are spoken of thee, O city of God.
Psalms 87:1–3.

97 Lord, thou hast been our dwelling place in all generations. Before the mountains were brought forth, or ever thou hadst formed the earth and the world, even from everlasting to everlasting, thou art God.
Psalms 90:1–2.

98 For a thousand years in thy sight are but as yesterday when it is past, and as a watch in the night.
Psalms 90:4.

99 The days of our years are threescore years and ten; and if by reason of strength they be fourscore years, yet is their strength labour and sorrow; for it is soon cut off, and we fly away.
Psalms 90:10.

1 So teach us to number our days that we may apply our hearts unto wisdom.
Psalms 90:12.

2 Surely he shall deliver thee from the snare of the fowler, and from the noisome pestilence.
He shall cover thee with his feathers, and under his wings shalt thou trust: his truth shall be thy shield and buckler.
Thou shalt not be afraid for the terror by night; nor for the arrow that flieth by day;
Nor for the pestilence that walketh in darkness; nor for the destruction that wasteth at noonday.
A thousand shall fall at thy side, and ten thousand at thy right hand, but it shall not come nigh thee.
Psalms 91:3–7.

3 Because thou hast made the Lord, which is my refuge, even the most high, thy habitation.
Psalms 91:9.

4 They shall still bring forth fruit in old age; they shall be fat and flourishing.
Psalms 92:14.

5 He that planted the ear, shall he not hear? he that formed the eye, shall he not see?
Psalms 94:9.

6 O come let us sing unto the Lord: let us make a joyful noise to the rock of our salvation. Let us come before his presence with thanksgiving, and make a joyful noise unto him with psalms.
Psalms 95:1–2.

7 Harden not your heart, as in the provocation, and as in the day of temptation in the wilderness: When your fathers tempted me, proved me, and saw my work. Forty years long was I grieved with this generation, and said, It is a people that do err in their heart, and they have not known my ways: Unto whom I sware in my wrath that they should not enter into my rest.
Psalms 95:8–11.

8 O worship the Lord in the beauty of holiness: fear before him, all the earth.
Psalms 96:9.

9 Make a joyful noise unto the LORD, all ye lands. Serve the LORD with gladness: come before his presence with singing. Know ye that the LORD he is God: it is he that hath made us, and not we ourselves; we are his people, and the sheep of his pasture. Enter into his gates with thanksgiving, and into his courts with praise: be thankful unto him, and bless his name. For the LORD is good; his mercy is everlasting; and his truth endureth to all generations.
Psalms 100:1–5.

10 Of old hast thou laid the foundation of the earth: and the heavens are the work of thy hands.
Psalms 102:25.

11 Bless the LORD, O my soul: and all that is within me, bless his holy name. Bless the LORD, O my soul, and forget not all his benefits: Who forgiveth all thine iniquities; who healeth all thy diseases; Who redeemeth thy life from destruction; who crowneth thee with loving kindness and tender mercies; Who satisfieth thy mouth with good things; so that thy youth is renewed like the eagle's.
Psalms 103:1–5.

12 The LORD is merciful and gracious, slow to anger, and plenteous in mercy. He will not always chide: neither will he keep his anger for ever. He hath not dealt with us after our sins; nor rewarded us according to our iniquities.
Psalms 103:8–10.

13 For as the heaven is high above the earth, so great is his mercy toward them that fear him. As far as the east is from the west, so far hath he removed our transgressions from us.
Psalms 103:11–12.

14 Like as a father pitieth his children, so the LORD pitieth them that fear him. For he knoweth our frame; he remembereth that we are dust.
Psalms 103:13–14.

15 As for man, his days are as grass: as a flower of the field, so he flourisheth. For the wind passeth over it, and it is gone; and the place thereof shall know it no more.
Psalms 103:15–16.

16 He causeth the grass to grow for the cattle, and herb for the service of man: that he may bring forth food out of the earth; And wine that maketh glad the heart of man, and oil to make his face to shine, and bread which strengtheneth man's heart.
Psalms 104:14–15.

17 Man goeth forth unto his work and to his labour until the evening.
Psalms 104:23.

18 So is this great and wide sea, wherein are things creeping innumerable, both small and great beasts. There go the ships: there is that leviathan, whom thou hast made to play therein.
These wait all upon thee; that thou mayest give them their meat in due season.
Psalms 104:25–7.

19 Their soul abhorreth all manner of meat; and they draw near unto the gates of death.
Psalms 107:18.

20 They that go down to the sea in ships, that do business in great waters;
These see the works of the LORD, and his wonders in the deep.
Psalms 107:23–4.

21 They reel to and fro, and stagger like a drunken man, and are at their wit's end.
Psalms 107:27.

22 The LORD said unto my Lord, Sit thou at my right hand, until I make thine enemies thy footstool.
Psalms 110:1.

23 The LORD hath sworn, and will not repent, Thou art a priest for ever after the order of Melchizedek.
Psalms 110:4.

24 The fear of the LORD is the beginning of wisdom.
Psalms 111:10.

25 For thou hast delivered my soul from death, mine eyes from tears, and my feet from falling. I will walk before the LORD in the land of the living. I believed, therefore have I spoken: I was greatly afflicted: I said in my haste, All men are liars.
Psalms 116:8–11.

26 Precious in the sight of the LORD is the death of his saints.
Psalms 116:15.

27 The stone which the builders refused is become the head stone of the corner. This is the LORD's doing; it is marvellous in our eyes. This is the day which the LORD hath made; we will rejoice and be glad in it.
Psalms 118:22–4.

28 Blessed be he that cometh in the name of the LORD: we have blessed you out of the house of the LORD.
Psalms 118:26.

29 Wherewithal shall a young man cleanse his way? by taking heed thereto according to thy word.
Psalms 119:9.

30 Thy word have I hid in mine heart, that I might not sin against thee.
Psalms 119:11.

31 I have more understanding than all my teachers: for thy testimonies are my meditation.
Psalms 119:99.

32 How sweet are thy words unto my taste! yea, sweeter than honey to my mouth!
Psalms 119:103.

33 Thy word is a lamp unto my feet, and a light unto my path.
Psalms 119:105.

34 The entrance of thy words giveth light; it giveth understanding unto the simple.
Psalms 119:130.

35 Great peace have they which love thy law: and nothing shall offend them.
Psalms 119:165.

36 I will lift up mine eyes unto the hills, from whence cometh my help. My help cometh from the LORD, which made heaven and earth. He will not suffer thy foot to be moved: he that keepeth thee will not slumber. Behold, he that keepeth Israel shall neither slumber nor sleep. The LORD is thy keeper: the LORD is thy shade upon thy right hand. The sun shall not smite thee by day, nor the moon by night. The LORD shall preserve thee from all evil: he shall preserve thy soul. The LORD shall preserve thy going out and thy coming in from this time forth, and even for evermore.
Psalms 121:1–8.

37 I was glad when they said unto me, Let us go into the house of the LORD.
Psalms 122:1.

38 Pray for the peace of Jerusalem: they shall prosper that love thee. Peace be within thy walls, and prosperity within thy palaces.
Psalms 122:6–7.

39 They that trust in the LORD shall be as mount Zion, which cannot be removed, but abideth for ever.
Psalms 125:1.

40 They that sow in tears shall reap in joy. He that goeth forth and weepeth, bearing precious seed, shall doubtless come again with rejoicing, bringing his sheaves with him.
Psalms 126:5–6.

41 Except the LORD build the house, they labour in vain that build it: except the LORD keep the city, the watchman waketh but in vain. It is vain for you to rise up early, to sit up late, to eat the bread of sorrows: for so he giveth his beloved sleep.
Psalms 127:1–2.

42 Lo, children are an heritage of the LORD: and the fruit of the womb is his reward. As arrows are in the hand of a mighty man; so are children of the youth. Happy is the man that hath his quiver full of them: they shall not be ashamed, but they shall speak with the enemies in the gate.
Psalms 127:3–5.

43 Thy wife shall be as a fruitful vine by the sides of thine house: thy children like olive plants round about thy table.
Psalms 128:3.

44 Out of the depths have I cried unto thee, O LORD. Lord, hear my voice: let thine ears be attentive to the voice of my supplications. If thou, LORD, shouldest mark iniquities, O LORD, who shall stand? But, there is forgiveness with thee, that thou mayest be feared.
Psalms 130:1–4.

45 Behold, how good and how pleasant it is for brethren to dwell together in unity! It is like the precious ointment upon the head, that ran down upon the beard, even Aaron's beard: that went down to the skirts of his garments; As the dew of Hermon, and as the dew that descended upon the mountains of Zion: for there the LORD commanded the blessing, even life for evermore.
Psalms 133:1–3.

46 O give thanks unto the LORD; for he is good: for his mercy endureth for ever.
Psalms 136:1.

47 By the rivers of Babylon, there we sat down, yea, we wept, when we remembered Zion. We hanged our harps upon the willows in the midst thereof. For there they that carried us away captive required of us a song; and they that wasted us required of us mirth, saying, Sing us one of the songs of Zion. How shall we sing the LORD's song in a strange land?
Psalms 137:1–4.

48 O LORD, thou hast searched me, and known me. Thou knowest my downsitting and mine uprising, thou understandest my thought afar off. Thou compassest my path and my lying down, and art acquainted with all my ways. For there is not a word in my tongue, but, lo, O LORD, thou knowest it altogether. Thou hast beset me behind and before, and laid thine hand upon me. Such knowledge is too wonderful for me; it is high, I cannot attain unto it.
Psalms 139:1–6.

49 Whither shall I go from thy spirit? or whither shall I flee from thy presence?
    If I ascend up into heaven, thou art there: if I make my bed in hell, behold, thou art there.
    If I take the wings of the morning, and dwell in the uttermost parts of the sea;
    Even there shall thy hand lead me, and thy right hand shall hold me.
    If I say, Surely the darkness shall cover me; even the night shall be light about me.
    Yea, the darkness hideth not from thee; but the night shineth as the day: the darkness and the light are both alike to thee.
    Psalms 139:7–12.

50 I will praise thee; for I am fearfully and wonderfully made: marvellous are thy works; and that my soul knoweth right well. My substance was not hid from thee, when I was made in secret, and curiously wrought in the lowest parts of the earth. Thine eyes did see my substance, yet being unperfect; and in thy book all my members were written, which in continuance were fashioned, when as yet there was none of them.
    Psalms 139:14–16.

51 Search me, O God, and know my heart: try me, and know my thoughts: And see if there be any wicked way in me, and lead me in the way everlasting.
    Psalms 139:23–4.

52 Set a watch, O LORD, before my mouth; keep the door of my lips.
    Psalms 141:3.

53 The eyes of all wait upon thee; and thou givest them their meat in due season. Thou openest thine hand, and satisfiest the desire of every living thing.
    Psalms 145:15–16.

54 He telleth the number of the stars; he calleth them all by their names.
    Psalms 147:4.

55 Let the high praises of God be in their mouth, and a two-edged sword in their hand.
    Psalms 149:6.

56 Wisdom crieth without; she uttereth her voice in the streets.
    Proverbs 1:20.

57 Trust in the LORD with all thine heart; and lean not unto thine own understanding. In all thy ways acknowledge him, and he shall direct thy paths.
    Proverbs 3:5–6.

58 For whom the LORD loveth he correcteth; even as a father the son in whom he delighteth.
    Proverbs 3:12.

59 Wisdom is the principal thing; therefore get wisdom: and with all thy getting get understanding.
    Proverbs 4:7.

60 Happy is the man that findeth wisdom, and the man that getteth understanding. For the merchandise of it is better than the merchandise of silver, and the gain thereof than fine gold. She is more precious than rubies: and all the things thou canst desire are not to be compared unto her. Length of days is in her right hand; and in her left hand riches and honour. Her ways are ways of pleasantness, and all her paths are peace. She is a tree of life to them that lay hold upon her: and happy is every one that retaineth her.
    Proverbs 3:13–18.

61 For the lips of a strange woman drop as an honeycomb, and her mouth is smoother than oil: But her end is bitter as wormwood, sharp as a two-edged sword. Her feet go down to death; her steps take hold on hell.
    Proverbs 5:3–5.

62 Let thy fountain be blessed: and rejoice with the wife of thy youth. Let her be as the loving hind and pleasant roe; let her breasts satisfy thee at all times; and be thou ravished always with her love.
    Proverbs 5:18–19.

63 Go to the ant, thou sluggard; consider her ways, and be wise.
    Proverbs 6:6.

64 Yet a little sleep, a little slumber, a little folding of the hands to sleep: So shall thy poverty come as one that travelleth, and thy want as an armed man.
    Proverbs 6:10–11.

65 Can a man take fire in his bosom and his clothes not be burned? Can one go upon hot coals, and his feet not be burned?
    Proverbs 6:27–8.

66 Wisdom hath builded her house, she hath hewn out her seven pillars.
    Proverbs 9:1.

67 Stolen waters are sweet, and bread eaten in secret is pleasant.
    Proverbs 9:17.

68 The rich man's wealth is his strong city: the destruction of the poor is their poverty.
    Proverbs 10:15.

69 A false balance is abomination to the LORD: but a just weight is his delight.

Proverbs 11:1.

70 He that is surety for a stranger shall smart for it: and he that hateth suretiship is sure.
Proverbs 11:15.

71 A virtuous woman is a crown to her husband: but she that maketh ashamed is as rottenness in his bones.
Proverbs 12:4.

72 A wise son heareth his father's instruction: but a scorner heareth not rebuke.
Proverbs 13:1.

73 Hope deferred maketh the heart sick: but when the desire cometh, it is a tree of life.
Proverbs 13:12.

74 He that spareth his rod hateth his son: but he that loveth him chasteneth him betimes.
Proverbs 13:24.

75 There is a way which seemeth right unto a man, but the end thereof are the ways of death.
Proverbs 14:12.

76 The poor is hated even of his own neighbour: but the rich hath many friends.
Proverbs 14:20.

77 In all labour there is profit: but the talk of the lips tendeth only to penury.
Proverbs 14:23.

78 A soft answer turneth away wrath: but grievous words stir up anger.
Proverbs 15:1.

79 A merry heart maketh a cheerful countenance.
Proverbs 15:13.

80 Better is little with the fear of the LORD than great treasure and trouble therewith. Better is a dinner of herbs where love is, than a stalled ox and hatred therewith.
Proverbs 15:16–17.

81 A word spoken in due season, how good is it!
Proverbs 15:23.

82 A good report maketh the bones fat.
Proverbs 15:30.

83 Commit thy works unto the LORD, and thy thoughts shall be established.
Proverbs 16:3.

84 Pride goeth before destruction, and an haughty spirit before a fall.
Proverbs 16:18.

85 Children's children are the crown of old men; and the glory of children are their fathers.
Proverbs 17:6.

86 A friend loveth at all times, and a brother is born for adversity.
Proverbs 17:17.

87 A merry heart doeth good like a medicine: but a broken spirit drieth the bones.
Proverbs 17:22.

88 The name of the LORD is a strong tower: the righteous runneth into it, and is safe.
Proverbs 18:10.

89 A man that hath friends must shew himself friendly: and there is a friend that sticketh closer than a brother.
Proverbs 18:24.

90 He that hath pity upon the poor lendeth unto the LORD; and that which he hath given will he pay him again.
Proverbs 19:17.

91 The king's heart is in the hand of the LORD, as the rivers of water: he turneth it whithersoever he will.
Proverbs 20:1.

92 Every way of a man is right in his own eyes: but the LORD pondereth the hearts.
Proverbs 21:2.

93 It is better to dwell in a corner of the housetop, than with a brawling woman in a wide house.
Proverbs 21:9.

94 Train up a child in the way he should go: and when he is old, he will not depart from it.
Proverbs 22:6.

95 Wilt thou set thine eyes upon that which is not? for riches certainly make themselves wings; they fly away as an eagle toward heaven.
Proverbs 23:5.

96 Remove not the old landmark; and enter not into the fields of the fatherless.
Proverbs 23:10.

97 If thou faint in the day of adversity, thy strength is small.
Proverbs 24:10.

98 A word fitly spoken is like apples of gold in pictures of silver.
Proverbs 25:11.

99 Confidence in an unfaithful man in time of trouble is like a broken tooth, and a foot out of joint.
Proverbs 25:19.

1 If thine enemy be hungry, give him bread to eat; and if he be thirsty, give him water to drink: For thou shalt heap coals of fire upon his head, and the LORD shall reward thee.
Proverbs 25:21–2.

2 As a dog returneth to his vomit, so a fool returneth to his folly.
Proverbs 26:11.

3 The slothful man saith, There is a lion in the way; a lion is in the streets.
Proverbs 26:13.

4 Where no wood is, there the fire goeth out: so where there is no talebearer, the strife ceaseth.
Proverbs 26:20.

5 Boast not thyself of tomorrow; for thou knowest not what a day may bring forth.
Proverbs 27:1.

6 Wrath is cruel, and anger is outrageous; but who is able to stand before envy?
Proverbs 27:4.

7 Open rebuke is better than secret love. Faithful are the wounds of a friend; but the kisses of an enemy are deceitful.
Proverbs 27:5–6.

8 A continual dropping in a very rainy day and a contentious woman are alike.
Proverbs 27:15.

9 Hell and destruction are never full; so the eyes of man are never satisfied.
Proverbs 27:20.

10 A fool uttereth all his mind: but a wise man keepeth it in till afterwards.
Proverbs 29:11.

11 Where there is no vision, the people perish: but he that keepeth the law, happy is he.
Proverbs 29:18.

12 Who can find a virtuous woman? for her price is far above rubies.
Proverbs 31:10.

13 Favour is deceitful, and beauty is vain: but a woman that feareth the LORD, she shall be praised.
Proverbs 31:30.

14 Vanity of vanities, saith the Preacher, vanity of vanities; all is vanity. What profit hath a man of all his labour which he taketh under the sun? One generation passeth away, and another generation cometh: but the earth abideth for ever.
Ecclesiastes 1:2–4.

15 All the rivers run into the sea; yet the sea is not full; unto the place from whence the rivers come, thither they return again.
Ecclesiastes 1:7.

16 The thing that hath been, it is that which shall be; and that which is done is that which shall be done: and there is no new thing under the sun.
Ecclesiastes 1:9.

17 For in much wisdom is much grief: and he that increaseth knowledge increaseth sorrow.
Ecclesiastes 1:18.

18 I said of laughter, It is mad: and of mirth, What doeth it?
Ecclesiastes 2:2.

19 To every thing there is a season, and a time to every purpose under the heaven:
A time to be born, and a time to die; a time to plant, and a time to pluck up that which is planted;
A time to kill, and a time to heal; a time to break down, and a time to build up;
A time to weep, and a time to laugh; a time to mourn, and a time to dance:
A time to cast away stones, and a time to gather stones together; a time to embrace, and a time to refrain from embracing;
A time to get, and a time to lose; a time to keep, and a time to cast away;
A time to rend, and a time to sew; a time to keep silence, and a time to speak;
A time to love, and a time to hate; a time of war, and a time of peace.
Ecclesiastes 3:1–8.

20 I know that there is no good in them, but for a man to rejoice, and to do good in his life. And also that every man should eat and drink, and enjoy the good of all his labour, it is the gift of God. I know that, whatsoever God doeth, it shall be for ever: nothing can be put to it, nor any thing taken from it: and God doeth it, that men should fear before him. That which hath been is now; and that which is to be hath already been; and God requireth that which is past.
Ecclesiastes 3:12–15.

21 Wherefore I perceive that there is nothing better, than that a man should rejoice in his own works; for that is his portion: for who shall bring him to see what shall be after him?
Ecclesiastes 3:22.

22 Wherefore I praise the dead which are already dead more than the living which are yet alive.
Ecclesiastes 4:2.

23 Two are better than one; because they have a good reward for their labour. For if they fall, the one will lift up his fellow: but woe to him that is alone when he falleth; for he hath not another to help him up.
Ecclesiastes 4:9–10.

24 And if one prevail against him, two shall withstand him; and a threefold cord is not quickly broken.
Ecclesiastes 4:12.

25 Better is a poor and a wise child than an old and foolish king, who will no more be admonished.
Ecclesiastes 4:13.

26 Be not rash with thy mouth, and let not thine heart be hasty to utter any thing before God: for God is in heaven, and thou upon earth: therefore let thy words be few.
Ecclesiastes 5:2.

27 For as the crackling of thorns under a pot, so is the laughter of a fool: this also is vanity.
Ecclesiastes 7:6.

28 Better is the end of a thing than the beginning thereof: and the patient in spirit is better than the proud in spirit.
Ecclesiastes 7:8.

29 Say not thou, What is the cause that the former days were better than these? for thou dost not inquire wisely concerning this.
Ecclesiastes 7:10.

30 There is no man that hath power over the spirit to retain the spirit; neither hath he power in the day of death: and there is no discharge in that war; neither shall wickedness deliver those that are given to it.
Ecclesiastes 8:8.

31 Then I commended mirth, because a man hath no better thing under the sun, than to eat, and to drink, and to be merry: for that shall abide with him of his labour the days of his life, which God giveth him under the sun.
Ecclesiastes 8:15.

32 For to him that is joined to all the living there is hope: for a living dog is better than a dead lion. For the living know that they shall die: but the dead know not any thing, neither have they any more a reward; for the memory of them is forgotten.
Ecclesiastes 9:4–5.

33 Go thy way, eat thy bread with joy, and drink thy wine with a merry heart; for God now accepteth thy works.
Ecclesiastes 9:7.

34 Whatsoever thy hand findeth to do; do it with thy might; for there is no work, nor device, nor knowledge, nor wisdom, in the grave, whither thou goest.
Ecclesiastes 9:10.

35 I returned, and saw under the sun, that the race is not to the swift, nor the battle to the strong, neither yet bread to the wise, nor yet riches to men of understanding, nor yet favour to men of skill; but time and chance happeneth to them all.
Ecclesiastes 9:11

36 Dead flies cause the ointment of the apothecary to send forth a stinking savour: so doth a little folly him that is in reputation for wisdom and honour.
Ecclesiastes 10:1.

37 He that diggeth a pit shall fall into it; and whoso breaketh an hedge, a serpent shall bite him.
Ecclesiastes 10:8.

38 A feast is made for laughter, and wine maketh merry: but money answereth all things.
Ecclesiastes 10:19.

39 Curse not the king, no not in thy thought; and curse not the rich in thy bedchamber: for a bird of the air shall carry the voice, and that which hath wings shall tell the matter.
Ecclesiastes 10:20.

40 Cast thy bread upon the waters: for thou shalt find it after many days.
Ecclesiastes 11:1.

41 Rejoice, O young man, in thy youth; and let thy heart cheer thee in the days of thy youth, and walk in the ways of thine heart, and in the sight of thine eyes: but know thou, that for all these things God will bring thee into judgment.
Ecclesiastes 11:9.

42 Remember now thy Creator in the days of thy youth, while the evil days come not, nor the years draw nigh, when thou shalt say, I have no pleasure in them;
While the sun, or the light, or the moon, or the stars, be not darkened, nor the clouds return after the rain:
In the day when the keepers of the house shall tremble, and the strong men shall bow themselves, and the grinders cease because they are few, and those that look out of the windows be darkened,
And the doors shall be shut in the streets, when the sound of the grinding is low, and he shall rise up at the voice of the bird, and all the daughters of musick shall be brought low:
Also when they shall be afraid of that which is high, and fears shall be in the way, and the almond tree

shall flourish, and the grasshopper shall be a burden, and desire shall fail: because man goeth to his long home, and mourners go about the streets: Or ever the silver cord be loosed, or the golden bowl be broken, or the pitcher be broken at the fountain, or the wheel broken at the cistern. Then shall the dust return to the earth as it was: and the spirit shall return unto God who gave it.
Ecclesiastes 12:1–7.

43 And further, by these, my son, be admonished: of making many books there is no end; and much study is a weariness of the flesh.
Ecclesiastes 12:12.

44 Fear God, and keep his commandments: for this is the whole duty of man.
Ecclesiastes 12:13.

45 The song of songs, which is Solomon's.
Song of Solomon 1:1.

46 I am the rose of Sharon, and the lily of the valleys. As the lily among thorns, so is my love among the daughters.
Song of Solomon 2:1–2.

47 He brought me to the banqueting house, and his banner over me was love.
Song of Solomon 2:4.

48 I charge you, O ye daughters of Jerusalem, by the roes, and by the hinds of the field, that ye stir not up, nor awake my love, till he please.
Song of Solomon 2:7.

49 My beloved spake, and said unto me, Rise up, my love, my fair one, and come away. For lo, the winter is past, the rain is over and gone.
Song of Solomon 2:10–11.

50 My beloved is mine, and I am his: he feedeth among the lilies.
Song of Solomon 2:16.

51 Behold, thou art fair, my love; behold, thou art fair; thou hast doves' eyes within thy locks: thy hair is as a flock of goats, that appear from mount Gilead. Thy teeth are like a flock of sheep that are even shorn, which came up from the washing; whereof every one bear twins, and none is barren among them. Thy lips are like a thread of scarlet, and thy speech is comely: thy temples are like a piece of a pomegranate within thy locks. Thy neck is like the tower of David builded for an armoury, whereon there hang a thousand bucklers, all shields of mighty men. Thy two breasts are like two young roes that are twins, which feed among the lilies. Until the day break, and the shadows flee away, I will get me to the mountain of myrrh, and to the hill of frankincense. Thou art all fair, my love; there is no spot in thee.
Song of Solomon 4:1–7.

52 A garden inclosed is my sister, my spouse; a spring shut up, a fountain sealed.
Song of Solomon 4:12.

53 My beloved put in his hand by the hole of the door, and my bowels were moved for him.
Song of Solomon 5:4.

54 How fair and how pleasant art thou, O love, for delights!
Song of Solomon 7:6.

55 Love is strong as death; jealousy is cruel as the grave: the coals thereof are coals of fire, which hath a most vehement flame. Many waters cannot quench love, neither can the floods drown it: if a man would give all the substance of his house for love, it would utterly be contemned.
Song of Solomon 8:6–7.

56 Come now, and let us reason together, saith the LORD: though your sins be as scarlet, they shall be as white as snow; though they be red like crimson, they shall be as wool.
Isaiah 1:17–18.

57 They shall beat their swords into plowshares, and their spears into pruninghooks: nation shall not lift up sword against nation, neither shall they learn war any more.
Isaiah 2:4.

58 What mean ye that ye beat my people to pieces, and grind the faces of the poor? saith the Lord GOD of hosts.
Isaiah 3:15.

59 Woe unto them that rise up early in the morning, that they may follow strong drink; that continue until night, till wine inflame them!
Isaiah 5:11.

60 In the year that king Uzziah died I saw also the Lord sitting upon a throne, high and lifted up, and his train filled the temple. Above it stood the seraphims: each one had six wings; with twain he covered his face, and with twain he covered his feet, and with twain he did fly. And one cried unto another, and said, Holy, holy, holy, is the LORD of hosts: the whole earth is full of his glory. And the posts of the door moved at the voice of him that cried, and the house was filled with smoke.
Isaiah 6:1–4.

61 Then said I, Woe is me! for I am undone; because I am a man of unclean lips, and I dwell in the midst

of a people of unclean lips; for mine eyes have seen the King, the LORD of hosts. Then flew one of the seraphims unto me, having a live coal in his hand, which he had taken with the tongs from off the altar: And he laid it upon my mouth, and said, Lo, this hath touched thy lips; and thine iniquity is taken away, and thy sin purged. Also I heard the voice of the Lord, saying, Whom shall I send, and who will go for us? Then said I, Here am I; send me.
Isaiah 6:5–8.

62 Then said I, Lord, how long?
Isaiah 6:11.

63 Therefore the Lord himself shall give you a sign; Behold, a virgin shall conceive, and bear a son, and shall call his name Immanuel.
Isaiah 7:14.

64 And he shall be for a sanctuary; but for a stone of stumbling and for a rock of offence to both the houses of Israel, for a gin and for a snare to the inhabitants of Jerusalem.
Isaiah 8:14.

65 The people that walked in darkness have seen a great light: they that dwell in the land of the shadow of death, upon them hath the light shined.
Isaiah 9:2.

66 For unto us a child is born, unto us a son is given: and the government shall be upon his shoulder: and his name shall be called Wonderful, Counseller, The mighty God, The everlasting Father, The Prince of Peace. Of the increase of his government and peace there shall be no end, upon the throne of David, and upon his kingdom, to order it, and to establish it with judgment and with justice from henceforth even for ever. The zeal of the LORD of hosts will perform this.
Isaiah 9:6–7.

67 And there shall come forth a rod out of the stem of Jesse, and a Branch shall grow out of his roots: And the spirit of the LORD shall rest upon him, the spirit of wisdom and understanding, the spirit of counsel and might, the spirit of knowledge and of the fear of the LORD.
Isaiah 11:1–2.

68 The wolf also shall dwell with the lamb, and the leopard shall lie down with the kid; and the calf and the young lion and the fatling together; and a little child shall lead them. And the cow and the bear shall feed; their young ones shall lie down together: and the lion shall eat straw like the ox. And the sucking child shall play on the hole of the asp, and the weaned child shall put his hand on the cockatrice' den. They shall not hurt nor destroy in all my holy mountain for the earth shall be full of the knowledge of the LORD, as the waters cover the sea.
Isaiah 11:6–9.

69 Therefore with joy shall ye draw water out of the wells of salvation.
Isaiah 12:3.

70 How art thou fallen from heaven, O Lucifer, son of the morning!
Isaiah 14:12.

71 And behold joy and gladness, slaying oxen, and killing sheep, eating flesh, and drinking wine: let us eat and drink; for to morrow we shall die.
Isaiah 22:13.

72 The earth shall reel to and fro like a drunkard, and shall be removed like a cottage; and the transgression thereof shall be heavy upon it; and it shall fall, and not rise again.
Isaiah 24:20.

73 He will swallow up death in victory; and the Lord GOD will wipe away tears from off all faces; and the rebuke of his people shall he take away from off all the earth: for the LORD hath spoken it.
Isaiah 25:8.

74 Thou wilt keep him in perfect peace, whose mind is stayed on thee.
Isaiah 26:3–4.

75 For precept must be upon precept, precept upon precept; line upon line, line upon line; here a little, and there a little:
For with stammering lips and another tongue will he speak to this people.
Isaiah 28:10–11.

76 We have made a covenant with death, and with hell are we at agreement.
Isaiah 28:15.

77 Behold, I lay in Zion for a foundation a stone, a tried stone, a precious corner stone, a sure foundation: he that believeth shall not make haste. Judgment also will I lay to the line, and righteousness to the plummet: and the hail shall sweep away the refuge of lies, and the waters shall overflow the hiding place.
Isaiah 28:16–17.

78 Forasmuch as this people draw near me with their mouth, and with their lips do honour me, but have removed their heart far from me, and their fear toward me is taught by the precept of men.
Isaiah 29:13.

79 In returning and rest shall ye be saved; in quietness and in confidence shall be your strength: and ye would not.
Isaiah 30:15.

80 And thine ears shall hear a word behind thee, saying, This is the way, walk ye in it, when ye turn to the right hand, and when ye turn to the left.
Isaiah 30:21.

81 And a man shall be as an hiding place from the wind, and a covert from the tempest; as rivers of water in a dry place, as the shadow of a great rock in a weary land.
Isaiah 32:2.

82 Then the eyes of the blind shall be opened, and the ears of the deaf shall be unstopped. Then shall the lame man leap as an hart, and the tongue of the dumb sing: for in the wilderness shall waters break out, and streams in the desert. And the parched ground shall become a pool, and the thirsty land springs of water: in the habitation of dragons, where each lay, shall be grass with reeds and rushes.
Isaiah 35:5–7.

83 And an highway shall be there, and a way, and it shall be called The way of holiness; the unclean shall not pass over it; but it shall be for those: the wayfaring men, though fools shall not err therein.
Isaiah 35:8.

84 Lo, thou trusted in the staff of this broken reed, on Egypt; whereon if a man lean, it will go into his hand, and pierce it: so is Pharaoh king of Egypt to all that trust in him.
Isaiah 36:5–6.

85 Comfort ye, comfort ye my people, saith your God.
Speak ye comfortably to Jerusalem, and cry unto her, that her warfare is accomplished, that her iniquity is pardoned: for she hath received of the LORD'S hand double for all her sins.
The voice of him that crieth in the wilderness, Prepare ye the way of the LORD, make straight in the desert a highway for our God.
Every valley shall be exalted, and every mountain and hill shall be made low: and the crooked shall be made straight, and the rough places plain:
And the glory of the LORD shall be revealed, and all flesh shall see it together: for the mouth of the LORD hath spoken it.
The voice said, Cry. And he said, What shall I cry?
All flesh is grass, and all the goodliness thereof is as the flower of the field:
The grass withereth, the flower fadeth: because the spirit of the LORD bloweth upon it: surely the people is grass. The grass withereth, the flower

fadeth: but the word of our God shall stand for ever.
Isaiah 40:1–8.

86 He shall feed his flock like a shepherd: he shall gather the lambs with his arm, and carry them in his bosom, and shall gently lead those that are with young.
Isaiah 40:11.

87 Who hath measured the waters in the hollow of his hand, and meted out heaven with the span, and comprehended the dust of the earth in a measure, and weighed the mountains in scales, and the hills in a balance?
Isaiah 40:12.

88 Behold, the nations are as a drop of a bucket, and are counted as the small dust of the balance: behold, he taketh up the isles as a very little thing.
Isaiah 40:14–15.

89 To whom then will ye liken God? or what likeness will ye compare unto him?
Isaiah 40:18.

90 Have ye not known? have ye not heard? hath it not been told you from the beginning? have ye not understood from the foundations of the earth?
Isaiah 40:21.

91 Even the youths shall faint and be weary, and the young men shall utterly fall: But they that wait upon the LORD shall renew their strength; they shall mount up with wings as eagles; they shall run, and not be weary; and they shall walk, and not faint.
Isaiah 40:30–31.

92 A bruised reed shall he not break, and the smoking flax shall he not quench: he shall bring forth judgment unto truth.
Isaiah 42:3.

93 Fear not: for I have redeemed thee, I have called thee by thy name; thou art mine. When thou passest through the waters, I will be with thee; and through the rivers, they shall not overflow thee: when thou walkest through the fire, thou shalt not be burned; neither shall the flame kindle upon thee.
Isaiah 43:1–5.

94 Woe unto him that striveth with his Maker! Let the potsherd strive with the potsherds of the earth. Shall the clay say to him that fashioneth it, What makest thou? or thy work, He hath no hands?
Isaiah 45:9.

95 Can a woman forget her suckling child, that she should not have compassion on the son of her

womb? yea, they may forget, yet will I not forget thee.

Isaiah 49:15.

96 How beautiful upon the mountains are the feet of him that bringeth good tidings, that publisheth peace; that bringeth good tidings of good, that publisheth salvation; that saith unto Zion, Thy God reigneth! Thy watchmen shall lift up the voice; with the voice together shall they sing: for they shall see eye to eye, when the LORD shall bring again Zion.

Isaiah 52:7–8.

97 Break forth into joy, sing together, ye waste places of Jerusalem: for the LORD hath comforted his people, he hath redeemed Jerusalem. The LORD hath made bare his holy arm in the eyes of all the nations; and all the ends of the earth shall see the salvation of our God.

Isaiah 52:9–10.

98 As many were astonished at thee; his visage was so marred more than any man, and his form more than the sons of men: So shall he sprinkle many nations; the kings shall shut their mouths at him: for that which had not been told them shall they see; and that which they had not heard shall they consider.

Isaiah 52:14–15.

99 Who hath believed our report? and to whom is the arm of the LORD revealed? For he shall grow up before him as a tender plant, and as a root out of a dry ground: he hath no form nor comeliness; and when we shall see him, there is no beauty that we should desire him. He is despised and rejected of men; a man of sorrows, and acquainted with grief: and we hid as it were our faces from him; he was despised, and we esteemed him not. Surely he hath borne our griefs, and carried our sorrows.

Isaiah 53:1–4.

1 But he was wounded for our transgressions, he was bruised for our iniquities: the chastisement of our peace was upon him; and with his stripes we are healed. All we like sheep have gone astray; we have turned every one to his own way; and the LORD hath laid on him the iniquity of us all. He was oppressed, and he was afflicted, yet he opened not his mouth: he is brought as a lamb to the slaughter, and as a sheep before her shearers is dumb, so he openeth not his mouth.

Isaiah 53:5–7.

2 He was cut off out of the land of the living: for the transgression of my people was he stricken. And he made his grave with the wicked, and with the rich

in his death; because he had done no violence, neither was any deceit in his mouth.

Isaiah 53:8–9.

3 Ho, every one that thirsteth, come ye to the waters, and he that hath no money; come ye, buy, and eat; yea, come, buy wine and milk without money and without price. Wherefore do ye spend money for that which is not bread? and your labour for that which satisfieth not? hearken diligently unto me, and eat ye that which is good, and let your soul delight itself in fatness.

Isaiah 55:1–3.

4 Seek ye the LORD while he may be found, call ye upon him while he is near.

Isaiah 55:6.

5 For my thoughts are not your thoughts, neither are your ways my ways, saith the LORD. For as the heavens are higher than the earth, so are my ways higher than your ways, and my thoughts than your thoughts.

Isaiah 55:8–9.

6 For as the rain cometh down, and the snow from heaven, and returneth not thither, but watereth the earth, and maketh it bring forth and bud, that it may give seed to the sower, and bread to the eater: So shall my word be that goeth forth out of my mouth: it shall not return unto me void, but it shall accomplish that which I please, and it shall prosper in the thing whereto I sent it.

Isaiah 55:10–11.

7 For ye shall go out with joy, and be led forth with peace: the mountains and the hills shall break forth before you into singing, and all the trees of the field shall clap their hands.

Isaiah 55:12.

8 Instead of the thorn shall come up the fir tree, and instead of the brier shall come up the myrtle tree: and it shall be to the LORD for a name, for an everlasting sign that shall not be cut off.

Isaiah 55:13.

9 Peace, peace to him that is far off, and to him that is near, saith the LORD; and I will heal him.

Isaiah 57:19.

10 There is no peace, saith my God, to the wicked.

Isaiah 57:21.

11 Arise, shine; for thy light is come, and the glory of the LORD is risen upon thee.

Isaiah 60:1–3.

12 The Spirit of the Lord GOD is upon me; because the LORD hath anointed me to preach good tidings unto the meek; he hath sent me, to bind up the

brokenhearted, to proclaim liberty to the captives, and the opening of the prison to them that are bound; To proclaim the acceptable year of the LORD, and the day of vengeance of our God; to comfort all that mourn; To appoint unto them that mourn in Zion, to give unto them beauty for ashes, the oil of joy for mourning, the garment of praise for the spirit of heaviness; that they might be called trees of righteousness, the planting of the LORD, that he might be glorified.
Isaiah 61:1–3.

13 But we are all as an unclean thing, and all our righteousnesses are as filthy rags; and we all do fade as a leaf; and our iniquities, like the wind, have taken us away.
Isaiah 64:6.

14 Stand by thyself, come not near to me; for I am holier than thou.
Isaiah 65:5.

15 For, behold, I create new heavens and a new earth: and the former shall not be remembered, nor come into mind.
Isaiah 65:17.

16 The wolf and the lamb shall feed together, and the lion shall eat straw like the bullock: and dust shall be the serpent's meat. They shall not hurt nor destroy in all my holy mountain, saith the LORD.
Isaiah 65:25.

17 Behold, I have put my words in thy mouth. See, I have this day set thee over the nations and over the kingdoms, to root out, and to pull down, and to destroy, and to throw down, to build, and to plant.
Jeremiah 1:9–10.

18 They have forsaken me the fountain of living waters, and hewed them out cisterns, broken cisterns, that can hold no water.
Jeremiah 2:13.

19 They were as fed horses in the morning: every one neighed after his neighbour's wife.
Jeremiah 5:8.

20 But this people hath a revolting and a rebellious heart; they are revolted and gone.
Jeremiah 5:23.

21 Saying, Peace, peace; when there is no peace.
Jeremiah 6:13–14.

22 Is this house, which is called by my name, become a den of robbers in your eyes?
Jeremiah 7:11.

23 The harvest is past, the summer is ended, and we are not saved.
Jeremiah 8:20.

24 Is there no balm in Gilead; is there no physician there?
Jeremiah 8:22.

25 Can the Ethiopian change his skin, or the leopard his spots? then may ye also do good, that are accustomed to do evil.
Jeremiah 13:23.

26 The heart is deceitful above all things, and desperately wicked: who can know it? I the LORD search the heart, I try the reins.
Jeremiah 17:9–10

27 The LORD hath appeared of old unto me, saying, Yea, I have loved thee with an everlasting love: therefore with lovingkindness have I drawn thee.
Jeremiah 31:3.

28 A voice was heard in Ramah, lamentation, and bitter weeping; Rachel weeping for her children refused to be comforted for her children, because they were not.
Jeremiah 31:15.

29 How doth the city sit solitary, that was full of people! how is she become as a widow! she that was great among the nations, and princess among the provinces, how is she become tributary!
Lamentations 1:1.

30 Is it nothing to you, all ye that pass by? behold, and see if there be any sorrow like unto my sorrow.
Lamentations 1:12.

31 And I said, My strength and my hope is perished from the LORD: Remembering mine affliction and my misery, the wormwood and the gall.
Lamentations 3:18–19.

32 It is of the LORD'S mercies that we are not consumed, because his compassions fail not. They are new every morning: great is thy faithfulness.
Lamentations 3:21–3.

33 It is good for a man that he bear the yoke in his youth.
Lamentations 3:27.

34 The appearance of the wheels and their work was like unto the colour of a beryl: and they four had one likeness: and their appearance and their work was as it were a wheel in the middle of a wheel.
Of his vision in exile. Ezekiel 1:15–16.

35 For thou art not sent to a people of a strange speech and of an hard language, but to the house of Israel; Not many people of a strange speech and of an hard language, whose words thou canst not

understand. Surely, had I sent thee to them, they would have hearkened unto thee.
Ezekiel 3:5–6.

36 And I will give them one heart, and I will put a new spirit within you; and I will take the stony heart out of their flesh, and will give them an heart of flesh.
Ezekiel 11:19.

37 Son of man, eat thy bread with quaking, and drink thy water with trembling and with carefulness.
Ezekiel 12:18.

38 The fathers have eaten sour grapes, and the children's teeth are set on edge.
Ezekiel 18:2.

39 I will accept you with your sweet savour, when I bring you out from the people, and gather you out of the countries wherein you have been scattered; and I will be sanctified in you before the heathen. And ye shall know that I am the LORD, when I shall bring you into the land of Israel, into the country for the which I lifted up mine hand to give it to your fathers. And there shall ye remember your ways, and all your doings, wherein ye have been defiled; and ye shall loath yourselves in your own sight for all your evils that ye have committed.
Ezekiel 20:41–3.

40 As I live, saith the Lord GOD, I have no pleasure in the death of the wicked; but that the wicked turn from his way and live: turn ye, turn ye from your evil ways; for why will ye die, O house of Israel?
Ezekiel 33:11.

41 The hand of the LORD was upon me, and carried me out in the spirit of the LORD, and set me down in the midst of the valley which was full of bones.
Ezekiel 37:1.

42 Son of man, can these bones live?
Ezekiel 37:3.

43 Prophesy upon these bones, and say unto them, O ye dry bones, hear the word of the LORD. Thus saith the Lord GOD unto these bones; Behold, I will cause breath to enter into you, and ye shall live: And I will lay sinews upon you, and will bring up flesh upon you, and cover you with skin, and put breath in you, and ye shall live; and ye shall know that I am the LORD. So I prophesied as I was commanded: and as I prophesied, there was a noise, and behold a shaking, and the bones came together, bone to his bone. And when I beheld, lo, the sinews and the flesh came up upon them, and the skin covered them above: but there was no breath in them. Then said he unto me, Prophesy unto the wind, prophesy, son of man, and say to the wind, Thus saith the Lord GOD; Come from the four winds, O breath, and breathe upon these slain, that they may live. So I prophesied as he commanded me, and the breath came into them, and they lived, and stood up upon their feet, an exceeding great army.
Ezekiel 37:4–10.

44 Then he said unto me, Son of man, these bones are the whole house of Israel: behold, they say, Our bones are dried, and our hope is lost: we are cut off for our parts. Therefore prophesy and say unto them, Thus saith the Lord GOD; Behold, O my people, I will open your graves, and cause you to come up out of your graves, and bring you into the land of Israel.
Ezekiel 37:11–12.

45 Thou, O king, sawest, and behold a great image. This great image, whose brightness was excellent, stood before thee; and the form thereof was terrible. This image's head was of fine gold, his breast and his arms of silver, his belly and his thighs of brass. His legs of iron, his feet part of iron and part of clay. Thou sawest till that a stone was cut out without hands, which smote the image upon his feet that were of iron and clay, and brake them to pieces.
Daniel 2:31–34.

46 Then Nebuchadnezzar the king was astonied, and rose up in haste, and spake, and said unto his counsellors, Did not we cast three men bound into the midst of the fire? They answered and said unto the king, True, O king. He answered and said, Lo, I see four men loose, walking in the midst of the fire, and they have no hurt; and the form of the fourth is like the Son of God. Then Nebuchadnezzar came near to the mouth of the burning fiery furnace, and spake, and said, Shadrach, Meshach, and Abednego, ye servants of the most high God, come forth, and come hither. Then Shadrach, Meshach, and Abednego, came forth of the midst of the fire.
Daniel 3:24–6.

47 The same hour was the thing fulfilled upon Nebuchadnezzar: and he was driven from men, and did eat grass as oxen, and his body was wet with the dew of heaven, till his hairs were grown like eagles' feathers, and his nails like birds' claws.
Daniel 4:33.

48 In the same hour came forth fingers of a man's hand, and wrote over against the candlestick upon the plaister of the wall of the king's palace: and the king saw the part of the hand that wrote.
Daniel 5:5.

49 And this is the writing that was written, MENE, MENE, TEKEL, UPHARSIN. This is the interpretation of the thing: MENE; God hath numbered thy kingdom, and finished it, TEKEL; Thou art weighed in the balances, and art found wanting. PERES; Thy kingdom is divided, and given to the Medes and Persians.

Daniel 5:25–8.

50 I saw in the night visions and, behold, one like the Son of man came with the clouds of heaven, and came to the Ancient of days, and they brought him near before him.

Daniel 7:13.

51 And they that be wise shall shine as the brightness of the firmament; and they that turn many to righteousness as the stars for ever and ever. But thou, O Daniel, shut up the words, and seal the book, even to the time of the end: many shall run to and fro, and knowledge shall be increased.

Daniel 12:1–4.

52 For they have sown the wind, and they shall reap the whirlwind.

Hosea 8:7.

53 When Israel was a child, then I loved him, and called my son out of Egypt.

Hosea 11:1.

54 And I will restore to you the years that the locust hath eaten, the cankerworm, and the caterpiller, and the palmerworm, my great army which I sent among you.

Joel 2:25.

55 And it shall come to pass afterward, that I will pour out my spirit upon all flesh, and your sons and your daughters shall prophesy, your old men shall dream dreams, your young men shall see visions.

Joel 2:28.

56 Beat your plowshares into swords, and your pruninghooks into spears: let the weak say, I am strong.

Joel 3:10.

57 Can two walk together, except they be agreed?

Amos 3:3.

58 The lion hath roared, who will not fear? the Lord GOD hath spoken, who can but prophesy?

Amos 3:8.

59 Therefore thus will I do unto thee, O Israel: and because I will do this unto thee, prepare to meet thy God, O Israel.

Amos 4:12.

60 Shall not the day of the LORD be darkness, and not light? even very dark, and no brightness in it?

Amos 5:20.

61 Behold, the days come, saith the Lord GOD, that I will send a famine in the land, not a famine of bread, nor a thirst for water, but of hearing the words of the LORD: And they shall wander from sea to sea, and from the north even to the east, they shall run to and fro to seek the word of the LORD, and shall not find it.

Amos 8:11–12.

62 But thou, Bethlehem, Ephratah, though thou be little among the thousands of Judah, yet out of thee shall he come forth unto me that is to be ruler in Israel.

Micah 5:2.

63 O LORD, revive thy work in the midst of the years, in the midst of the years make known; in wrath remember mercy.

Habakkuk 3:2.

64 He that earneth wages earneth wages to put it into a bag with holes.

Haggai 1:6.

65 I lifted up mine eyes again, and looked, and behold a man with a measuring line in his hand. Then said I, Whither goest thou? And he said unto me, To measure Jerusalem, to see what is the breadth thereof, and what is the length thereof.

Zechariah 2:1–2.

66 For thus saith the LORD of hosts; After the glory hath he sent me unto the nations which spoiled you: for he that toucheth you toucheth the apple of his eye.

Zechariah 2:8.

67 Then he answered and spake unto me, saying, This is the word of the LORD unto Zerubbabel, saying, Not by might, nor by power, but by my spirit, saith the LORD of hosts.

Zechariah 4:6.

68 And I said unto them, If ye think good, give me my price; and if not, forbear. So they weighed for my price thirty pieces of silver.

Zechariah 11:12.

69 Have we not all one father, hath not one God created us? why do we deal treacherously every man against his brother, by profaning the covenant of our fathers?

Malachi 2:10.

70 Bring ye all the tithes into the storehouse, that there may be meat in mine house, and prove me now herewith, saith the LORD of hosts, if I will not open you the windows of heaven, and pour you out a blessing, that there shall not be room enough to receive it.

Malachi 3:10.

71 Then they that feared the LORD spake often one to another: and the LORD hearkened, and heard it, and a book of remembrance was written before him for them that feared the LORD, and that thought upon his name.
Malachi 3:16.

72 For, behold, the day cometh, that shall burn as an oven; and all the proud, yea, and all that do wickedly, shall be stubble: and the day that cometh shall burn them up, saith the LORD of hosts, that it shall leave them neither root nor branch. But unto you that fear my name shall the Sun of righteousness arise with healing in his wings; and ye shall go forth, and grow up as calves of the stall.
Malachi 4:1–2.

73 Behold, I will send you Elijah the prophet before the coming of the great and dreadful day of the LORD: And he shall turn the heart of the fathers to the children, and the heart of the children to their fathers, lest I come and smite the earth a curse.
Malachi 4:5–6.

Bible (Apocrypha)

74 The first wrote, Wine is the strongest. The second wrote, The king is strongest. The third wrote, Women are strongest: but above all things Truth beareth away the victory.
1 Esdras 3:10–12.

75 By this also ye must know that women have dominion over you: do ye not labour and toil, and give and bring all to the woman? Yea, a man taketh his sword, and goeth his way to rob and to steal, to sail upon the sea and upon rivers; And looketh upon a lion, and goeth in the darkness; and when he hath stolen, spoiled, and robbed, he bringeth it to his love.
1 Esdras 4:22–4.

76 Then were the entrances of this world made narrow, full of sorrow and travail: they are but few and evil, full of perils, and very painful. For the entrances of the elder world were wide and sure, and brought immortal fruit. If then they that live labour not to enter these strait and vain things, they can never receive those that are laid up for them.
2 Esdras 7:12–14.

77 For the world hath lost his youth, and the times begin to wax old.
2 Esdras 14:10.

78 Be not greedy to add money to money: but let it be as refuse in respect of our child.
Tobit 5:18.

79 For the ear of jealousy heareth all things: and the noise of murmurings is not hid.
Wisdom of Solomon 1:10.

80 Nevertheless through envy of the devil came death into the world: and they that do hold of his side do find it.
Wisdom of Solomon 2:24.

81 But the souls of the righteous are in the hand of God, and there shall no torment touch them. In the sight of the unwise they seemed to die: and their departure is taken for misery, And their going from us to be utter destruction: but they are in peace. For though they be punished in the sight of men, yet is their hope full of immortality. And having been a little chastised, they shall be greatly rewarded: for God proved them, and found them worthy for himself.
Wisdom of Solomon 3:1–5.

82 And in the time of their visitation they shall shine, and run to and fro like sparks among the stubble.
Wisdom of Solomon 3:7.

83 For the bewitching of naughtiness doth obscure things that are honest; and the wanderings of concupiscence doth undermine the simple mind. He being made perfect in a short time, fulfilled a long time.
Wisdom of Solomon 4:12–13.

84 Even so we in like manner, as soon as we were born, began to draw to our end, and had no sign of virtue to shew; but were consumed in our own wickedness. For the hope of the ungodly is like dust that is blown away with the wind; like a thin froth that is driven away with the storm; like as the smoke which is dispersed here and there with a tempest, and passeth away as the remembrance of a guest that tarrieth but a day.
Wisdom of Solomon 5:13–14.

85 For all men have one entrance into life, and the like going out.
Wisdom of Solomon 7:6.

86 For thou hast power of life and death: thou leadest to the gates of hell, and bringest up again.
Wisdom of Solomon 16:13.

87 My son, if thou come to serve the Lord, prepare thy soul for temptation.
Ecclesiasticus 2:1.

88 Saying, We will fall into the hands of the Lord, and not into the hands of men: for as his majesty is, so is his mercy.
Ecclesiasticus 2:18.

89 Be not curious in unnecessary matters: for more things are shewed unto thee than men understand.
Ecclesiasticus 3:23.

90 Be not ignorant of any thing in a great matter or a small.
Ecclesiasticus 5:15.

91 A faithful friend is the medicine of life; and they that fear the Lord shall find him.
Ecclesiasticus 6:16.

92 Laugh no man to scorn in the bitterness of his soul: for there is one which humbleth and exalteth.
Ecclesiasticus 7:11.

93 Miss not the discourse of the elders: for they also learned of their fathers, and of them thou shalt learn understanding, and to give answer as need requireth.
Ecclesiasticus 8:9.

94 Open not thine heart to every man, lest he requite thee with a shrewd turn.
Ecclesiasticus 8:19.

95 Give not thy soul unto a woman to set her foot upon thy substance.
Ecclesiasticus 9:2.

96 Forsake not an old friend; for the new is not comparable to him: a new friend is as new wine; when it is old, thou shalt drink it with pleasure.
Ecclesiasticus 9:10.

97 Many kings have sat down upon the ground; and one that was never thought of hath worn the crown.
Ecclesiasticus 11:5.

98 Judge none blessed before his death: for a man shall be known in his children.
Ecclesiasticus 11:28.

99 He that toucheth pitch shall be difiled therewith; and he that hath fellowship with a proud man shall be like unto him.
Ecclesiasticus 13:1.

1 Burden not thyself above thy power while thou livest; and have no fellowship with one that is mightier and richer than thyself: for how agree the kettle and the earthen pot together? for if the one be smitten against the other, it shall be broken.
Ecclesiasticus 13:2.

2 All flesh waxeth old as a garment: for the covenant from the beginning is, Thou shalt die the death.
Ecclesiasticus 14:17.

3 Desire not a multitude of unprofitable children, neither delight in ungodly sons.
Ecclesiasticus 16:1.

4 Be not made a beggar by banqueting upon borrowing, when thou hast nothing in thy purse: for thou shalt lie in wait for thine own life, and be talked on.
Ecclesiasticus 18:33.

5 A labouring man that is given to drunkenness shall not be rich: and he that contemneth small things shall fall by little and little.
Ecclesiasticus 19:1.

6 Wine and women will make men of understanding to fall away: and he that cleaveth to harlots will become impudent.
Ecclesiasticus 19:2.

7 If thou hast heard a word, let it die with thee; and be bold, it will not burst thee.
Ecclesiasticus 19:10.

8 As the climbing up a sandy way is to the feet of the aged, so is a wife full of words to a quiet man.
Ecclesiasticus 25:20.

9 The stroke of the whip maketh marks in the flesh: but the stroke of the tongue breaketh the bones. Many have fallen by the edge of the sword: but not so many as have fallen by the tongue.
Ecclesiasticus 28:17–18.

10 Envy and wrath shorten the life, and carefulness bringeth age before the time.
Ecclesiasticus 30:24.

11 Leave off first for manners' sake; and be not unsatiable, lest thou offend.
Ecclesiasticus 31:17.

12 Wine is as good as life to a man, if it be drunk moderately: what life is then to a man that is without wine? for it was made to make men glad.
Ecclesiasticus 31:27.

13 Let thy speech be short, comprehending much in few words; be as one that knoweth and yet holdeth his tongue.
Ecclesiasticus 32:8.

14 In all thy works keep to thyself the preeminence; leave not a stain in thine honour.
Ecclesiasticus 33:22.

15 Honour a physician with the honour due unto him for the uses which ye may have of him: for the Lord hath created him. For of the most High cometh healing, and he shall receive honour of the king.
Ecclesiasticus 38:1–2.

16 The wisdom of a learned man cometh by opportunity of leisure: and he that hath little

business shall become wise. How can he get wisdom that holdeth the plough, and that glorieth in the goad, that driveth oxen, and is occupied in their labours, and whose talk is of bullocks?
Ecclesiasticus 38:24–5.

17 Let us now praise famous men, and our fathers that begat us.
Ecclesiasticus 44:1.

18 Their bodies are buried in peace; but their name liveth for evermore.
Ecclesiasticus 44:14.

19 Here then will we begin the story: only adding thus much to that which hath been said, that it is a foolish thing to make a long prologue, and to be short in the story itself.
Maccabees 2:32.

20 And when he was at the last gasp, he said, Thou like a fury takest us out of this present life, but the King of the world shall raise us up, who have died for his laws, unto everlasting life.
Maccabees 7:9.

Bible (New Testament)

21 And she shall bring forth a son, and thou shalt call his name JESUS: for he shall save his people from their sins.
St Matthew 1:21.

22 Now all this was done, that it might be fulfilled which was spoken of the Lord by the prophet, saying, Behold, a virgin shall be with child, and shall bring forth a son, and they shall call his name Emmanuel, which being interpreted is, God with us.
St Matthew 1:22–3

23 Now when Jesus was born in Bethlehem of Judaea in the days of Herod the king, behold, there came wise men from the east to Jerusalem, Saying, Where is he that is born King of the Jews? for we have seen his star in the east, and are come to worship him.
St Matthew 2:1–2.

24 And when they were come into the house, they saw the young child with Mary his mother, and fell down, and worshipped him: and when they had opened their treasures, they presented unto him gifts; gold, and frankincense, and myrrh.
St Matthew 2:11.

25 And saying, Repent ye: for the kingdom of heaven is at hand. For this is he that was spoken of by the prophet Esaias, saying, The voice of one crying in the wilderness, Prepare ye the way of the Lord, make his paths straight.
St Matthew 3:2–3.

26 And the same John had his raiment of camel's hair, and a leathern girdle about his loins; and his meat was locusts and wild honey.
St Matthew 3:4.

27 But when he saw many of the Pharisees and Sadducees come to his baptism, he said unto them, O generation of vipers, who hath warned you to flee from the wrath to come?
St Matthew 3:7.

28 And Jesus, when he was baptized, went up straightway out of the water: and, lo, the heavens were opened unto him, and he saw the Spirit of God descending like a dove, and lighting upon him: And lo a voice from heaven, saying, This is my beloved Son, in whom I am well pleased.
St Matthew 3:16–17.

29 Then was Jesus led up of the spirit into the wilderness to be tempted of the devil. And when he had fasted forty days and forty nights, he was afterward an hungred. And when the tempter came to him, he said, If thou be the Son of God, command that these stones be made bread. But he answered and said, It is written, Man shall not live by bread alone, but by every word that proceedeth out of the mouth of God.
St Matthew 4:1–4.

30 Jesus said unto him, It is written again, Thou shalt not tempt the Lord thy God.
St Matthew 4:7.

31 Again, the devil taketh him up into an exceeding high mountain, and sheweth him all the kingdoms of the world, and the glory of them; And saith unto him, All these things will I give thee, if thou wilt fall down and worship me. Then saith Jesus unto him, Get thee hence, Satan: for it is written, Thou shalt worship the Lord thy God, and him only shalt thou serve.
St Matthew 4:8–10.

32 The people which sat in darkness saw great light; and to them which sat in the region and shadow of death light is sprung up.
St Matthew 4:16.

33 And he saith unto them, Follow me, and I will make you fishers of men.
St Matthew 4:19.

34 And seeing the multitudes, he went up into a mountain: and when he was set, his disciples came unto him:

And he opened his mouth, and taught them, saying,

Blessed are the poor in spirit: for theirs is the kingdom of heaven.

Blessed are they that mourn: for they shall be comforted.

Blessed are the meek: for they shall inherit the earth.

Blessed are they which do hunger and thirst after righteousness: for they shall be filled.

Blessed are the merciful: for they shall obtain mercy.

Blessed are the pure in heart: for they shall see God.

Blessed are the peacemakers: for they shall be called the children of God.

Blessed are they which are persecuted for righteousness' sake: for theirs is the kingdom of heaven.

Blessed are ye, when men shall revile you, and persecute you, and shall say all manner of evil against you falsely, for my sake.

Rejoice, and be exceeding glad: for great is your reward in heaven: for so persecuted they the prophets which were before you.
St Matthew 5:1–12.

35 Ye are the salt of the earth: but if the salt have lost his savour, wherewith shall it be salted? it is thenceforth good for nothing, but to be cast out, and to be trodden under foot of men.
St Matthew 5:13.

36 Ye are the light of the world. A city that is set on an hill cannot be hid. Neither do men light a candle, and put it under a bushel, but on a candlestick; and it giveth light unto all that are in the house. Let your light so shine before men, that they may see your good works and glorify your Father which is in heaven.
St Matthew 5:14–16.

37 Think not that I am come to destroy the law, or the prophets: I am not come to destroy, but to fulfil. For verily I say unto you, Till heaven and earth pass, one jot or one tittle shall in no wise pass from the law, till all be fulfilled.
St Matthew 5:17–18.

38 For I say unto you, That except your righteousness shall exceed the righteousness of the scribes and Pharisees, ye shall in no case enter into the kingdom of heaven.
St Matthew 5:20.

39 But I say unto you, That whosoever is angry with his brother without a cause shall be in danger of the judgment: and whosoever shall say to his brother, Raca, shall be in danger of the council: but

whosoever shall say, Thou fool, shall be in danger of hell fire.
St Matthew 5:22.

40 Ye have heard that it was said by them of old time. Thou shalt not commit adultery: But I say unto you. That whosoever looketh on a woman to lust after her hath committed adultery with her already in his heart.
St Matthew 5:27–8.

41 And if thy right eye offend thee, pluck it out, and cast it from thee: for it is profitable for thee that one of thy members should perish, and not that thy whole body should be cast into hell. And if thy right hand offend thee, cut it off, and cast it from thee: for it is profitable for thee that one of thy members should perish, and not that thy whole body should be cast into hell.
St Matthew 5:29–30.

42 Ye have heard that it hath been said, An eye for an eye, and a tooth for a tooth: But I say unto you, That ye resist not evil: but whosoever shall smite thee on thy right cheek, turn to him the other also.
St Matthew 5:38–9.

43 And whosoever shall compel thee to go a mile, go with him twain.
St Matthew 5:41.

44 Ye have heard that it hath been said, Thou shalt love thy neighbour, and hate thine enemy. But I say unto you, Love your enemies, bless them that curse you, do good to them that hate you, and pray for them which despitefully use you, and persecute you.
St Matthew 5:43–4.

45 That ye may be the children of your Father which is in heaven: for he maketh his sun to rise on the evil and on the good, and sendeth rain on the just and on the unjust.
St Matthew 5:45.

46 Be ye therefore perfect, even as your Father which is in heaven is perfect.
St Matthew 5:48.

47 Therefore when thou doest thine alms, do not sound a trumpet before thee, as the hypocrites do in the synagogues and in the streets, that they may have glory of men, Verily I say unto you, They have their reward. But when thou doest alms, let not thy left hand know what thy right hand doeth: That thine alms may be in secret: and thy Father which seeth in secret himself shall reward thee openly.
St Matthew 6:2–4.

48 But thou, when thou prayest, enter into thy closet, and when thou hast shut thy door, pray to thy Father which is in secret; and thy Father which seeth in secret shall reward thee openly. But when ye pray, use not vain repetitions, as the heathen do: for they think that they shall be heard for their much speaking.
St Matthew 6:6–7.

49 After this manner therefore pray ye: Our Father which art in heaven, Hallowed be thy name. Thy kingdom come. Thy will be done in earth, as it is in heaven. Give us this day our daily bread. And forgive us our debts, as we forgive our debtors. And lead us not into temptation, but deliver us from evil: For thine is the kingdom, and the power, and the glory, for ever. Amen.
St Matthew 6:9–13

50 Lay not up for yourselves treasures upon earth, where moth and rust doth corrupt, and where thieves break through and steal: But lay up for yourselves in heaven, where neither moth nor rust doth corrupt, and where thieves do not break through nor steal: For where your treasure is, there will your heart be also.
St Matthew 6:19–21.

51 No man can serve two masters: for either he will hate the one, and love the other; or else he will hold to the one, and despise the other. Ye cannot serve God and mammon.
St Matthew 6:24.

52 Behold the fowls of the air: for they sow not, neither do they reap, nor gather into barns; yet your heavenly Father feedeth them. Are ye not much better than they? Which of you by taking thought can add one cubit unto his stature? And why take ye thought for raiment? Consider the lilies of the field, how they grow; they toil not, neither do they spin: And yet I say unto you, That even Solomon in all his glory was not arrayed like one of these.
St Matthew 6:26–9.

53 But seek ye first the kingdom of God, and his righteousness; and all these things shall be added unto you. Take therefore no thought for the morrow: for the morrow shall take thought for the things of itself. Sufficient unto the day is the evil thereof.
St Matthew 6:33–4

54 Judge not, that ye be not judged. For with what judgment ye judge, ye shall be judged: and with what measure ye mete, it shall be measured to you again.
St Matthew 7:1–2.

55 And why beholdest thou the mote that is in thy brother's eye, but considerest not the beam that is in thine own eye?
St Matthew 7:3.

56 Give not that which is holy unto the dogs, neither cast ye your pearls before swine, lest they trample them under their feet, and turn again and rend you.
St Matthew 7:6.

57 Ask, and it shall be given you; seek, and ye shall find; knock, and it shall be opened unto you: For every one that asketh receiveth; and he that seeketh findeth; and to him that knocketh it shall be opened.
St Matthew 7:7–8.

58 Or what man is there of you, whom if his son ask bread, will he give him a stone? Or if he ask a fish, will he give him a serpent? If ye then, being evil, know how to give good gifts unto your children, how much more shall your Father which is in heaven give good things to them that ask him?
St Matthew 7:9–11.

59 Enter ye in at the strait gate: for wide is the gate, and broad is the way, that leadeth to destruction, and many there be which go in thereat: Because strait is the gate, and narrow is the way, which leadeth unto life, and few there be that find it.
St Matthew 7:13–14.

60 Beware of false prophets, which come to you in sheep's clothing, but inwardly they are ravening wolves.
St Matthew 7:15.

61 Wherefore by their fruits ye shall know them.
St Matthew 7:20.

62 Not every one that saith unto me, Lord, Lord, shall enter into the kingdom of heaven; but he that doeth the will of my Father which is in heaven.
St Matthew 7:21.

63 Therefore whosoever heareth these sayings of mine, and doeth them, I will liken him unto a wise man, which built his house upon a rock: And the rain descended, and the floods came, and the winds blew, and beat upon that house; and it fell not: for it was founded upon a rock. And every one that heareth these sayings of mine, and doeth them not, shall be likened unto a foolish man, which built his house upon the sand: And the rain descended, and the floods came, and the winds blew, and beat upon that house; and it fell: and great was the fall of it.
St Matthew 7:24–7.

64 The centurion answered and said, Lord, I am not worthy that thou shouldest come under my roof: but speak the word only, and my servant shall be healed. For I am a man under authority, having soldiers under me: and I say to this man, Go, and he goeth; and to another, Come, and he cometh; and to my servant, Do this, and he doeth it. When Jesus heard it, he marvelled, and said to them that followed, Verily I say unto you, I have not found so great faith, no, not in Israel.
St Matthew 8:8–10.

65 But the children of the kingdom shall be cast out into outer darkness: there shall be weeping and gnashing of teeth.
St Matthew 8:12.

66 And Jesus saith unto him, The foxes have holes, and the birds of the air have nests; but the Son of man hath not where to lay his head.
St Matthew 8:20.

67 But Jesus said unto him, Follow me; and let the dead bury their dead.
St Matthew 8:22.

68 And his disciples came to him, and awoke him, saying, Lord, save us: we perish. And he saith unto them, Why are ye fearful, O ye of little faith? Then he arose, and rebuked the winds and the sea; and there was a great calm. But the men marvelled, saying, What manner of man is this, that even the winds and the sea obey him!
St Matthew 8:25–7.

69 And as Jesus passed forth from thence, he saw a man, named Matthew, sitting at the receipt of custom: and he saith unto him, Follow me. And he arose, and followed him.
St Matthew 9:9.

70 But when Jesus heard that, he said unto them, They that be whole need not a physician, but they that are sick. But go ye and learn what that meaneth, I will have mercy, and not sacrifice: for I am not come to call the righteous, but sinners to repentance.
St Matthew 9:12–13.

71 No man putteth a piece of new cloth unto an old garment, for that which is put in to fill it up taketh from the garment, and the rent is made worse. Neither do men put new wine into old bottles: else the bottles break, and the wine runneth out, and the bottles perish: but they put new wine into new bottles, and both are preserved.
St Matthew 9:16–17.

72 But the Pharisees said, He casteth out devils through the prince of the devils.
St Matthew 9:34.

73 But go rather to the lost sheep of the house of Israel.
St Matthew 10:6.

74 Heal the sick, cleanse the lepers, raise the dead, cast out devils: freely ye have received, freely give.
St Matthew 10:8.

75 And whosoever shall not receive you, nor hear your words, when ye depart out of that house or city, shake off the dust of your feet.
St Matthew 10:14.

76 Behold, I send you forth as sheep in the midst of wolves: be ye therefore wise as serpents, and harmless as doves.
St Matthew 10:16.

77 The disciple is not above his master, nor the servant above his lord.
St Matthew 10:24.

78 Are not two sparrows sold for a farthing? and one of them shall not fall on the ground without your Father. But the very hairs of your head are all numbered. Fear ye not therefore, ye are of more value that many sparrows.
St Matthew 10:29–31.

79 Think not that I am come to send peace on earth: I came not to send peace, but a sword.
St Matthew 10:34.

80 He that loveth father or mother more than me is not worthy of me: and he that loveth son or daughter more than me is not worthy of me. And he that taketh not his cross, and followeth after me, is not worthy of me. He that findeth his life shall lose it: and he that loseth his life for my sake shall find it.
St Matthew 10:37–9.

81 And whosoever shall give to drink unto one of these little ones a cup of cold water only in the name of a disciple, verily I say unto you, he shall in no wise lose his reward.
St Matthew 10:42.

82 And said unto him, Art thou he that should come, or do we look for another?
St Matthew 11:3.

83 Jesus answered and said unto them, Go and shew John again those things which ye do hear and see: The blind receive their sight, and the lame walk, the lepers are cleansed, and the deaf hear, the dead are raised up, and the poor have the gospel preached to them.
St Matthew 11:4–5.

84 And as they departed, Jesus began to say unto the multitudes concerning John, What went ye out into the wilderness to see? A reed shaken with the wind? But what went ye out for to see? A man clothed in soft raiment? behold, they that wear soft clothing are in kings' houses. But what went ye out for to see? A prophet? yea, I say unto you, and more than a prophet. For this is he, of whom it is written, Behold, I send my messenger before thy face, which shall prepare thy way before thee.
St Matthew 11:7–10.

85 He that hath ears to hear, let him hear.
St Matthew 11:15.

86 And saying, We have piped unto you, and ye have not danced; we have mourned unto you, and ye have not lamented.
St Matthew 11:17.

87 But wisdom is justified of her children.
St Matthew 11:19.

88 Come unto me, all ye that labour and are heavy laden, and I will give you rest. Take my yoke upon you, and learn of me; for I am meek and lowly in heart: and ye shall find rest unto your souls. For my yoke is easy, and my burden is light.
St Matthew 11:28–30.

89 A bruised reed shall he not break, and smoking flax shall he not quench, till he send forth judgment unto victory.
St Matthew 12:20.

90 He that is not with me is against me: and he that gathereth not with me scattereth abroad.
St Matthew 12:30.

91 Wherefore I say unto you, All manner of sin and blasphemy shall be forgiven unto men: but the blasphemy against the Holy Ghost shall not be forgiven unto men.
St Matthew 12:31.

92 O generation of vipers, how can ye, being evil, speak good things? for out of the abundance of the heart the mouth speaketh.
St Matthew 12:34.

93 But he answered and said unto them, An evil and adulterous generation seeketh after a sign; and there shall no sign be given to it, but the sign of the prophet Jonas: For Jonas was three days and three nights in the whale's belly; so shall the Son of man be three days and three nights in the heart of the earth.
St Matthew 12:39–40.

94 The queen of the south shall rise up in the judgment with this generation, and shall condemn it: for she came from the uttermost parts of the earth to hear the wisdom of Solomon; and, behold, a greater than Solomon is here.
St Matthew 12:42.

95 When the unclean spirit is gone out of a man, he walketh through dry places, seeking rest, and findeth none. Then he saith, I will return into my house from whence I came out; and when he is come, he findeth it empty, swept, and garnished. Then goeth he, and taketh with himself seven other spirits more wicked than himself, and they enter in and dwell there: and the last state of that men is worse than the first. Even so shall it be also unto this wicked generation.
St Matthew 12:43–5.

96 And he stretched forth his hand toward his disciples, and said, Behold my mother and my brethren! For whosoever shall do the will of my Father which is in heaven, the same is my brother, and sister, and mother.
St Matthew 12:49–50.

97 And he spake many things unto them in parables, saying, Behold, a sower went forth to sow; And when he sowed, some seeds fell by the wayside, and the fowls came and devoured them up: Some fell upon stony places, where they had not much earth: and forthwith they sprung up, because they had no deepness of earth: And when the sun was up, they were scorched; and because they had no root, they withered away. And some fell among thorns; and the thorns sprung up, and choked them: But others fell into good ground, and brought forth fruit, some an hundredfold, some sixtyfold, some thirtyfold.
St Matthew 13:3–8.

98 He also that received seed among the thorns is he that heareth the word; and the care of this world, and the deceitfulness of riches, choke the word, and he becometh unfruitful.
St Matthew 13:22.

99 But he that received seed into the good ground is he that heareth the word, and understandeth it; which also beareth fruit, and bringeth forth, some an hundredfold, some sixty, some thirty.
St Matthew 13:23.

1 But while men slept, his enemy came and sowed tares among the wheat, and went his way.
St Matthew 13:25.

2 He said unto them, An enemy hath done this. The servants said unto him, Wilt thou then that we go and gather them up?
St Matthew 13:28.

3 Another parable put he forth unto them, saying, The kingdom of heaven is like to a grain of mustard seed which a man took, and sowed in his field: Which indeed is the least of all seeds: but when it is grown, it is the greatest among herbs, and becometh a tree, so that the birds of the air come and lodge in the branches thereof.
St Matthew 13:31–2.

4 Again the kingdom of heaven is like unto a merchant man, seeking goodly pearls: Who, when he had found one pearl of great price, went and sold all that he had, and bought it.
St Matthew 13:45–6.

5 And they were offended in him. But Jesus said unto them, A prophet is not without honour, save in his own country, and in his own house.
St Matthew 13:57.

6 And they say unto him, We have here but five loaves, and two fishes.
St Matthew 14:17.

7 And in the fourth watch of the night Jesus went unto them, walking on the sea. And when the disciples saw him walking on the sea, they were troubled, saying, It is a spirit; and they cried out for fear. But straightway Jesus spake unto them, saying, Be of good cheer; it is I; be not afraid.
St Matthew 14:25–7.

8 And immediately Jesus stretched forth his hand, and caught him, and said unto him, O thou of little faith, wherefore didst thou doubt?
St Matthew 14:31.

9 Not that which goeth into the mouth defileth a man; but that which cometh out of the mouth, this defileth a man.
St Matthew 15:11.

10 Let them alone: they be blind leaders of the blind. And if the blind lead the blind, both shall fall into the ditch.
St Matthew 15:14.

11 And she said, Truth, Lord: yet the dogs eat of the crumbs which fall from their masters' table.
St Matthew 15:27.

12 He answered and said unto them, When it is evening, ye say, It will be fair weather: for the sky is red. And in the morning, It will be foul weather to day: for the sky is red and lowring. O ye hypocrites, ye can discern the face of the sky; but can ye not discern the signs of the times?
St Matthew 16:2–3.

13 And Simon Peter answered and said, Thou art the Christ, the Son of the living God. And Jesus

answered and said unto him, Blessed art thou, Simon Barjona: for flesh and blood hath not revealed it unto thee, but my Father which is in heaven. And I say also unto thee, That thou art Peter, and upon this rock I will build my church; and the gates of hell shall not prevail against it. And I will give unto thee the keys of the kingdom of heaven: and whatsoever thou shalt loose on earth shall be loosed in heaven.
St Matthew 16:16–19.

14 From that time forth began Jesus to shew unto his disciples, how that he must go unto Jerusalem, and suffer many things of the elders and the chief priests and scribes, and be killed, and be raised again the third day. Then Peter took him, and began to rebuke him, saying, Be it far from thee, Lord: this shall not be unto thee. But he turned, and said unto Peter, Get thee behind me, Satan: thou art an offence unto me: for thou savourest not the things that be of God, but those that be of men.
St Matthew 16:21–3.

15 Then said Jesus unto his disciples, If any man will come after me, let him deny himself, and take up his cross, and follow me. For whosoever will save his life shall lose it: and whosoever will lose his life for my sake shall find it. For what is a man profited, if he shall gain the whole world, and lose his own soul? or what shall a man give in exchange for his soul?
St Matthew 16:24–6.

16 And Jesus said unto them, Because of your unbelief: for verily I say unto you, If ye have faith as a grain of mustard seed, ye shall say unto this mountain, Remove hence to yonder place; and it shall remove; and nothing shall be impossible unto you.
St Matthew 17:20.

17 And said, Verily I say unto you, Except ye be converted, and become as little children, ye shall not enter into the kingdom of heaven.
St Matthew 18:3

18 And whoso shall receive one such little child in my name receiveth me. But whoso shall offend one of these little ones which believe in me, it were better for him that a millstone were hanged about his neck, and that he were drowned in the depth of the sea.
St Matthew 18:5–6.

19 Wherefore if thy hand or thy foot offend thee, cut them off, and cast them from thee: it is better for thee to enter into life halt or maimed, rather than having two hands or two feet to be cast into everlasting fire. And if thine eye offend thee, pluck

it out, and cast it from thee: it is better for thee to enter into life with one eye, rather than having two eyes to be cast into hell fire.
St Matthew 18:8–9.

20 Again I say unto you, That if two of you shall agree on earth as touching any thing that they shall ask, it shall be done for them of my Father which is in heaven. For where two or three are gathered together in my name, there am I in the midst of them.
St Matthew 18:19–20.

21 Then came Peter to him, and said, Lord, how oft shall my brother sin against me, and I forgive him? till seven times? Jesus saith unto him, I say not unto thee, Until seven times: but, Until seventy times seven.
St Mattthew 18:21–2.

22 And said, For this cause shall a man leave father and mother, and shall cleave to his wife: and they twain shall be one flesh? Wherefore they are no more twain, but one flesh What therefore God hath joined together, let not man put asunder.
St Matthew 19:5–6.

23 Then were there brought unto him little children, that he should put his hands on them, and pray: and the disciples rebuked them. But Jesus said, Suffer little children, and forbid them not, to come unto me: for of such is the kingdom of heaven. And he laid his hands on them, and departed thence.
St Matthew 19:13–15.

24 Jesus said unto him, If thou wilt be perfect, go and sell that thou hast, and give to the poor, and thou shalt have treasure in heaven: and come and follow me. But when the young man heard that saying, he went away sorrowful: for he had great possessions.
St Matthew 19:21–2.

25 And again I say unto you, It is easier for a camel to go through the eye of a needle, than for a rich man to enter into the kingdom of God.
St Matthew 19:24.

26 When his disciples heard it, they were exceedingly amazed, saying, Who then can be saved? But Jesus beheld them, and said unto them, With men this is impossible; but with God all things are possible.
St Matthew 19:25–6.

27 But many that are first shall be last; and the last shall be first.
St Matthew 19:30.

28 And about the eleventh hour he went out, and found others standing idle, and saith unto them, Why stand ye here all the day idle?
St Matthew 20:6.

29 Is it not lawful for me to do what I will with mine own? Is thine eye evil, because I am good? So the last shall be first, and the first last: for many be called, but few chosen.
St Matthew 20:15–16.

30 And a very great multitude spread their garments in the way; others cut down branches from the trees, and strawed them in the way. And the multitudes that went before, and that followed, cried, saying, Hosanna to the Son of David: Blessed is he that cometh in the name of the Lord; Hosanna in the highest.
St Matthew 21:8–9.

31 And Jesus went into the temple of God, and cast out all them that sold and bought in the temple, and overthrew the tables of the moneychangers, and the seats of them that sold doves, And said unto them, It is written, My house shall be called the house of prayer; but ye have made it a den of thieves.
St Matthew 21:12–13.

32 Render therefore unto Caesar the things which are Caesar's; and unto God the things that are God's.
St Matthew 22:21.

33 For in the resurrection they neither marry, nor are given in marriage, but are as the angels of God in heaven.
St Matthew 22:30.

34 Jesus said unto him, Thou shalt love the Lord Thy God with all thy heart, and with all thy soul, and with all thy mind. This is the first and great commandment. And the second is like unto it, Thou shalt love thy neighbour as thyself. On these two commandments hang all the law and the prophets.
St Matthew 22:37–40.

35 Ye blind guides, which strain at a gnat, and swallow a camel.
St Matthew 23:24.

36 Woe unto you, scribes and Pharisees, hypocrites! for ye are like unto whited sepulchres, which indeed appear beautiful outward, but are within full of dead men's bones, and of all uncleanness.
St Matthew 23:27.

37 And ye shall hear of wars and rumours or wars: see that ye be not troubled: for all these things must come to pass, but the end is not yet. For nation shall rise against nation, and kingdom against kingdom: and there shall be famines, and pestilences, and earthquakes, in divers places.
St Matthew 24:6–7.

38 Verily I say unto you. This generation shall not pass, till all these things be fulfilled. Heaven and earth shall pass away, but my words shall not pass away.
St Matthew 24:34–5.

39 For as in the days that were before the flood they were eating and drinking, marrying and giving in marriage, until the day that Noe entered into the ark.
St Matthew 24:38.

40 Watch therefore: for ye know not what hour your Lord doth come. But know this, that if the goodman of the house had known in what watch the thief would come, he would have watched, and would not have suffered his house to be broken up.
St Matthew 24:42–3.

41 His lord said unto him, Well done, thou good and faithful servant: thou hast been faithful over a few things, I will make thee ruler over many things: enter thou into the joy of thy lord.
St Matthew 25:21.

42 For unto every one that hath shall be given, and he shall have abundance: but from him that hath not shall be taken away even that which he hath. And cast ye the unprofitable servant into outer darkness: there shall be weeping and gnashing of teeth.
St Matthew 25:29–30.

43 When the Son of man shall come in his glory, and all the holy angels with him, then shall he sit upon the throne of his glory: And before him shall be gathered all nations: and he shall separate them one from another, as a shepherd divideth his sheep from the goats: And he shall set the sheep on his right hand, but the goats on the left.
St Matthew 25:31–3.

44 Then shall the King say unto them on his right hand, Come, ye blessed of my Father, inherit the kingdom prepared for you from the foundation of the world: For I was an hungred, and ye gave me meat: I was thirsty, and ye gave me drink: I was a stranger, and ye took me in: Naked, and ye clothed me: I was sick, and ye visited me: I was in prison, and ye came unto me.
St Matthew 25:34–6.

45 And the King shall answer and say unto them, Verily I say unto you, Inasmuch as ye have done it unto one of the least of these my brethren, ye have done it unto me.
St Matthew 25:40.

46 For ye have the poor always with you; but me ye have not always.
St Matthew 26:11.

47 Then one of the twelve, called Judas Iscariot, went unto the chief priests, And said unto them, What will ye give me, and I will deliver him unto you? And they covenanted with him for thirty pieces of silver.
St Matthew 26:14–15.

48 And as they were eating, Jesus took bread, and blessed it, and brake it, and gave it to the disciples, and said, Take, eat; this is my body. And he took the cup, and gave thanks, and gave it to them, saying, Drink ye all of it; For this is my blood of the new testament, which is shed for many for the remission of sins.
St Matthew 26:26–8.

49 Jesus said unto him, Verily I say unto thee, That this night, before the cock crow, thou shalt deny me thrice. Peter said unto him, Though I should die with thee yet will I not deny thee. Likewise also said all the disciples.
St Matthew 26:34–5.

50 And he went a little further, and fell on his face, and prayed, saying, O my Father, if it be possible, let this cup pass from me: nevertheless not as I will, but as thou wilt.
St Matthew 26:39.

51 Watch and pray, that ye enter not into temptation: the spirit indeed is willing, but the flesh is weak.
St Matthew 26:41.

52 Then said Jesus unto him, Put up again thy sword into his place: for all they that take the sword shall perish with the sword.
St Matthew 26:52.

53 When Pilate saw that he could prevail nothing, but that rather a tumult was made, he took water, and washed his hands before the multitude, saying I am innocent of the blood of this just person: see ye to it. Then answered all the people, and said, His blood be on us, and on our children.
St Matthew 27:24–5.

54 He saved others; himself he cannot save. If he be the King of Israel, let him now come down from the cross, and we will believe him.
St Matthew 27:42.

55 And about the ninth hour Jesus cried with a loud voice, saying Eli, Eli, lama sabachthani? that is to say, My God, my God, why hast thou forsaken me?
St Matthew 27:46.

56 Jesus, when he had cried again with a loud voice, yielded up the ghost. And behold, the veil of the temple was rent in twain from the top to the

bottom; and the earth did quake, and the rocks rent; And the graves were opened; and many bodies of the saints which slept arose.
St Matthew 27:50–2.

57 He is not here: for he is risen, as he said. Come, see the place where the Lord lay. And go quickly, and tell his disciples that he is risen from the dead; and, behold, he goeth before you into Galilee; there shall ye see him: lo, I have told you.
St Matthew 28:6–7.

58 And Jesus came and spake unto them, saying, All power is given unto me in heaven and in earth. Go ye therefore, and teach all nations, baptizing them in the name of the Father, and of the Son, and of the Holy Ghost: Teaching them to observe all things whatsoever I have commanded you: and, lo, I am with you alway, even unto the end of the world. Amen.
St Matthew 28:18–20.

59 When Jesus heard it, he saith unto them, They that are whole have no need of the physician, but they that are sick: I came not to call the righteous, but sinners to repentance.
St Mark 2:17.

60 And he said unto them, The sabbath was made for man, and not man for the sabbath: Therefore the Son of man is Lord also of the sabbath.
St Mark 2:27–8.

61 And if a kingdom be divided against itself, that kingdom cannot stand. And if a house be divided against itself, that house cannot stand. And if Satan rise up against himself, and be divided, he cannot stand, but hath and end. No man can enter into a strong man's house, and spoil his goods, except he will first bind the strong man; and then he will spoil his house.
St Mark 3:24–7.

62 And he said unto them, He that hath ears to hear, let him hear.
St Mark 4:9.

63 And he said unto them, Take heed what ye hear: with what measure ye mete, it shall be measured to you: and unto you that hear shall more be given.
St Mark 4:24.

64 And he asked him, What is thy name? And he answered, saying, My name is Legion: for we are many.
St Mark 5:9.

65 And Jesus, immediately knowing in himself that virtue had gone out of him, turned him about in the press, and said, Who touched my clothes?
St Mark 5:30.

66 And were beyond measure astonished, saying, He hath done all things well: he maketh both the deaf to hear, and the dumb to speak.
St Mark 7:37.

67 And he looked up, and said, I see men as trees, walking.
St Mark 8:24.

68 And straightway the father of the child cried out, and said with tears, Lord, I believe; help thou mine unbelief.
St Mark 9:24.

69 But when Jesus saw it, he was much displeased, and said unto them, Suffer the little children to come unto me, and forbid them not: for of such is the kingdom of God.
St Mark 10:14.

70 And there came a certain poor widow, and she threw in two mites, which make a farthing. And he called unto him his disciples, and saith unto them, Verily I say unto you, That this poor widow hath cast more in, than all they which have cast into the treasury: For all they did cast in of their abundance; but she of her want did cast in all that she had, even all her living.
St Mark 12:42–4.

71 And when the centurion, which stood over against him, saw that he so cried out, and gave up the ghost, he said, Truly this man was the Son of God.
St Mark 15:39.

72 And he said unto them, Go ye into all the world, and preach the gospel to every creature.
St Mark 16:15.

73 And the angel came in unto her, and said, Hail, thou that art highly favoured, the Lord is with thee: blessed art thou among women. And when she saw him, she was troubled at his saying, and cast in her mind what manner of salutation this should be.
St Luke 1:28–9.

74 And Mary said, Behold the handmaid of the Lord; be it unto me according to thy word. And the angel departed from her.
St Luke 1:38.

75 And Mary said,
My soul doth magnify the Lord,
And my spirit hath rejoiced in God my Saviour.
For he hath regarded the low estate of his
  handmaiden: for, behold, from henceforth all
  generations shall call me blessed.
For he that is mighty hath done to me great things;
  and holy is his name.

And his mercy is on them that fear him from generation to generation.

He hath shewed strength with his arm; he hath scattered the proud in the imagination of their hearts.

He hath put down the mighty from their seats, and exalted them of low degree.

He hath filled the hungry with good things; and the rich he hath sent empty away.

St Luke 1:46–53.

76 And it came to pass in those days, that there went out a decree from Caesar Augustus, that all the world should be taxed.
St Luke 2:1.

77 And so it was, that, while they were there, the days were accomplished that she should be delivered. And she brought forth her firstborn son, and wrapped him in swaddling clothes, and laid him in a manger; because there was no room for them in the inn.
St Luke 2:6–7.

78 And there were in the same country shepherds abiding in the field, keeping watch over their flock by night. And, lo, the angel of the Lord came upon them, and the glory of the Lord shone round about them: and they were sore afraid. And the angel said unto them, Fear not: for, behold, I bring you good tidings of great joy, which shall be to all people. For unto you is born this day in the city of David a Saviour, which is Christ the Lord. And this shall be a sign unto you; Ye shall find the babe wrapped in swaddling clothes, lying in a manger. And suddenly there was with the angel a multitude of the heavenly host praising God, and saying, Glory to God in the highest, and on earth peace, good will toward men. And it came to pass, as the angels were gone away from them into heaven, the shepherds said one to another, Let us now go even unto Bethlehem, and see this thing which is come to pass, which the Lord hath made known unto us.
St Luke 2:8–15.

79 Lord, now lettest thou thy servant depart in peace, according to thy word: For mine eyes have seen thy salvation, Which thou hast prepared before the face of all people; A light to lighten the Gentiles, and the glory of thy people Israel.
St Luke 2:29–32.

80 And Jesus increased in wisdom and stature, and in favour with God and man.
St Luke 2:52.

81 And he said unto them, Ye will surely say unto me this proverb, Physician, heal thyself: whatsoever we have heard done in Capernaum, do also here in thy country.
St Luke 4:23.

82 Woe unto you, when all men shall speak well of you! for so did their fathers to the false prophets.
St Luke 6:26.

83 Give, and it shall be given unto you; good measure, pressed down, and shaken together, and running over, shall men give into your bosom. For with the same measure that ye mete withal it shall be measured to you again.
St Luke 6:38.

84 Wherefore I say unto thee, Her sins, which are many, are forgiven; for she loved much: but to whom little is forgiven, the same loveth little.
St Luke 7:47.

85 And he said to them all, If any man will come after me, let him deny himself, and take up his cross daily, and follow me.
St Luke 9:23.

86 And Jesus said unto him, No man, having put his hand to the plough, and looking back, is fit for the kingdom of God.
St Luke 9:62.

87 And into whatsoever house ye enter, first say, Peace be to this house. And if the son of peace be there, your peace shall rest upon it: if not, it shall turn to you again. And in the same house remain, eating and drinking such things as they give: for the labourer is worthy of his hire. Go not from house to house.
St Luke 10:5–7.

88 And he said unto them, I beheld Satan as lightning fall from heaven.
St Luke 10:18.

89 And Jesus answering said, A certain man went down from Jerusalem to Jericho, and fell among thieves, which stripped him of his raiment, and wounded him, and departed, leaving him half dead. And by chance there came down a certain priest that way: and when he saw him, he passed by on the other side.
St Luke 10:30–31.

90 But a certain Samaritan, as he journeyed, came where he was: and when he saw him, he had compassion on him, And went to him, and bound up his wounds, pouring in oil and wine, and set him on his own beast, and brought him to an inn, and took care of him. And on the morrow when he departed, he took out two pence, and gave them to the host, and said unto him, Take care of him; and

whatsoever thou spendest more, when I come again, I will repay thee.
St Luke 10:33–5.

91 And he said, He that shewed mercy on him. Then said Jesus unto him, Go, and do thou likewise.
St Luke 10:37

92 But Martha was cumbered about much serving, and came to him, and said, Lord, dost thou not care that my sister hath left me to serve alone? bid her therefore that she help me.
And Jesus answered and said unto her, Martha, Martha, thou art careful and troubled about many things:
But one thing is needful: and Mary hath chosen that good part, which shall not be taken away from her.
St Luke 10:40–2.

93 Woe unto you, lawyers! for ye have taken away the key of knowledge: ye entered not in yourselves, and them that were entering in ye hindered.
St Luke 11:52.

94 And he said, This will I do: I will pull down my barns, and build greater; and there will I bestow all my fruits and my goods. And I will say to my soul, Soul, thou hast much goods laid up for many years; take thine ease, eat, drink, and be merry. But God said unto him, Thou fool, this night thy soul shall be required of thee: then whose shall those things be, which thou hast provided? So is he that layeth up treasure for himself, and is not rich toward God.
St Luke 12:18–21.

95 For which of you, intending to build a tower, sitteth not down first, and counteth the cost, whether he have sufficient to finish it?
St Luke 14:28.

96 What man of you, having an hundred sheep, if he lose one of them, doth not leave the ninety and nine in the wilderness, and go after that which is lost, until he find it? And when he hath found it, he layeth it on his shoulders, rejoicing.
St Luke 15:4–5.

97 Either what woman having ten pieces of silver, if she lose one piece, doth not light a candle, and sweep the house, and seek diligently till she find it? And when she hath found it, she calleth her friends and her neighbours together, saying, Rejoice with me; for I have found the piece which I had lost. Likewise, I say unto you, there is joy in the presence of the angels of God over one sinner that repenteth.
St Luke 15:8–10.

98 And not many days after the younger son gathered all together, and took his journey into a far country, and there wasted his substance with riotous living.
St Luke 15:13.

99 And he would fain have filled his belly with the husks that the swine did eat: and no man gave unto him. And when he came to himself, he said, How many hired servants of my father's have bread enough and to spare, and I perish with hunger! I will arise and go to my father, and will say unto him, Father, I have sinned against heaven, and before thee, And am no more worthy to be called thy son: make me as one of thy hired servants.
St Luke 15:16–19.

1 And he arose, and came to his father. But when he was yet a great way off, his father saw him, and had compassion, and ran, and fell on his neck, and kissed him. And the son said unto him, Father, I have sinned against heaven, and in thy sight, and am no more worthy to be called thy son. But the father said to his servants, Bring forth the best robe, and put it on him; and put a ring on his hand, and shoes on his feet: And bring hither the fatted calf, and kill it: and let us eat, and be merry: For this my son was dead, and is alive again; he was lost, and is found. And they began to be merry.
St Luke 15:20–4.

2 It was meet that we should make merry, and be glad: for this thy brother was dead, and is alive again; and was lost, and is found.
St Luke 15:32.

3 And the lord commended the unjust steward, because he had done wisely: for the children of this world are in their generation wiser than the children of light.
St Luke 16:8.

4 And I say unto you, Make to yourselves friends of the mammon of unrighteousness; that, when ye fail, they may receive you into everlasting habitations.
St Luke 16:9.

5 He that is faithful in that which is least is faithful also in much: and he that is unjust in the least is unjust also in much.
St Luke 16:10.

6 There was a certain rich man, which was clothed in purple and fine linen, and fared sumptuously every day: And there was a certain beggar named Lazarus, which was laid at his gate, full of sores, And desiring to be fed with the crumbs which fell from the rich man's table: moreover the dogs came and licked his sores.
St Luke 16:19–21.

7 And it came to pass, that the beggar died, and was carried by the angels into Abraham's bosom: the rich man also died, and was buried; And in hell he lift up his eyes, being in torments, and seeth Abraham afar off, and Lazarus in his bosom. And he cried and said, Father Abraham, have mercy on me, and send Lazarus, that he may dip the tip of his finger in water, and cool my tongue; for I am tormented in this flame.
St Luke 16:22–4.

8 And beside all this, between us and you there is a great gulf fixed: so that they which would pass from hence to you cannot; neither can they pass to us, that would come from thence.
St Luke 16:26.

9 Neither shall they say, Lo here! or, lo there! for, behold, the kingdom of God is within you.
St Luke 17:21.

10 Remember Lot's wife.
St Luke 17:32.

11 Two men went up into the temple to pray, the one a Pharisee, and the other a publican. The Pharisee stood and prayed thus with himself, God, I thank thee, that I am not as other men are, extortioners, unjust, adulterers, or even as this publican. I fast twice in the week, I give tithes of all that I possess. And the publican, standing afar off, would not lift up so much as his eyes unto heaven, but smote upon his breast, saying, God be merciful to me a sinner. I tell you, this man went down to his house justified rather than the other: for every one that exalteth himself shall be abased; and he that humbleth himself shall be exalted.
St Luke 18:10–14.

12 And he answered and said unto them, I tell you that, if these should hold their peace, the stones would immediately cry out.
St Luke 19:40.

13 In your patience possess ye your souls.
St Luke 21:19.

14 Saying, Father, if thou be willing, remove this cup from me: nevertheless not my will, but thine, be done.
St Luke 22:42.

15 And the Lord turned, and looked upon Peter. And Peter remembered the word of the Lord, how he had said unto him, Before the cock crow, thou shalt deny me thrice.
St Luke 22:61.

16 Then said Jesus, Father, forgive them; for they know not what they do. And they parted his raiment, and cast lots.
St Luke 23:34.

17 And he said unto Jesus, Lord, remember me when thou comest into thy kingdom. And Jesus said unto him, Verily I say unto thee, To day shalt thou be with me in paradise.
St Luke 23:42–3.

18 And the sun was darkened, and the veil of the temple was rent in the midst.
St Luke 23:45.

19 And when Jesus had cried with a loud voice, he said, Father, into thy hands I commend my spirit: and having said thus, he gave up the ghost.
St Luke 23:46.

20 And as they were afraid, and bowed down their faces to the earth, they said unto them, Why seek ye the living among the dead? He is not here, but is risen: remember how he spake unto you when he was yet in Galilee.
St Luke 24:5–6.

21 And their words seemed to them as idle tales, and they believed them not.
St Luke 24:11.

22 And they said one to another, Did not our heart burn within us, while he talked with us by the way, and while he opened to us the scriptures?
St Luke 24:32.

23 And they gave him a piece of a broiled fish, and of an honeycomb.
St Luke 24:42.

24 In the beginning was the Word, and the Word was with God, and the Word was God. The same was in the beginning with God. All things were made by him; and without him was not anything made that was made.
St John 1:1–3.

25 In him was life; and the life was the light of men. And the light shineth in darkness; and the darkness comprehended it not.
St John 1:4–5.

26 That was the true Light, which lighteth every man that cometh into the world. He was in the world, and the world was made by him, and the world knew him not.
St John 1:9–10.

27 And the Word was made flesh, and dwelt among us, (and we beheld his glory, the glory as of the only begotten of the Father,) full of grace and truth.
St John 1:14.

28 The next day John seeth Jesus coming unto him, and saith, Behold the Lamb of God, which taketh away the sin of the world.
St John 1:29.

29 And Nathanael said unto him, Can there any good thing come out of Nazareth? Philip saith unto him, Come and see.
St John 1:46.

30 Jesus saith unto her, Woman, what have I to do with thee? mine hour is not yet come.
St John 2:4.

31 When the ruler of the feast had tasted the water that was made wine, and knew not whence it was: (but the servants which drew the water knew;) the governor of the feast called the bridegroom, And saith unto him, Every man at the beginning doth set forth good wine; and when men have well drunk, then that which is worse: but thou hast kept the good wine until now.
St John 2:9–10.

32 Jesus answered and said unto him, Verily, verily, I say unto thee, Except a man be born again, he cannot see the kingdom of God. Nicodemus saith unto him, How can a man be born when he is old? can he enter the second time into his mother's womb, and be born?
St John 3:3–4.

33 Marvel not that I said unto thee, Ye must be born again. The wind bloweth where it listeth, and thou hearest the sound thereof, but canst not tell whence it cometh, and whither it goeth: so is every one that is born of the Spirit.
St John 3:7–8.

34 For God so loved the world, that he gave his only begotten Son, that whosoever believeth in him should not perish, but have everlasting life.
St John 3:16.

35 For God sent not his Son into the world to condemn the world; but that the world through him might be saved. He that believeth on him is not condemned: but he that believeth not is condemned already, because he hath not believed in the name of the only begotten Son of God. And this is the condemnation, that light is come into the world, and men loved darkness rather than light, because their deeds were evil.
St John 3:17–19.

36 He must increase, but I must decrease.
St John 3:30.

37 But the hour cometh, and now is, when the true worshippers shall worship the Father in spirit and in truth: for the Father seeketh such to worship him. God is a Spirit: and they that worship him must worship him in spirit and in truth.
St John 4:23–4.

38 Say not ye, There are yet four months, and then cometh harvest? behold, I say unto you, Lift up your eyes, and look on the fields; for they are white already to harvest.
St John 4:35.

39 Jesus saith unto him, Rise, take up thy bed, and walk.
St John 5:8.

40 He was a burning and a shining light; and ye were willing for a season to rejoice in his light.
Of John the Baptist. St John 5:35.

41 Search the scriptures; for in them ye think ye have eternal life: and they are they which testify of me.
St John 5:39.

42 There is a lad here, which hath five barley loaves, and two small fishes: but what are they among so many?
St John 6:9.

43 And Jesus said unto them, I am the bread of life: he that cometh to me shall never hunger; and he that believeth on me shall never thirst.
St John 6:35.

44 All that the Father giveth me shall come to me; and him that cometh to me I will in no wise cast out.
St John 6:37.

45 Verily, verily, I say unto you, He that believeth on me hath everlasting life. I am that bread of life. Your fathers did eat manna in the wilderness, and are dead. This is the bread which cometh down from heaven, that a man may eat thereof, and not die. I am the living bread which came down from heaven: if any man eat of this bread, he shall live for ever: and the bread that I will give is my flesh, which I will give for the life of the world.
St John 6:47–51.

46 It is the spirit that quickeneth; the flesh profiteth nothing: the words that I speak unto you, they are spirit, and they are life.
St John 6:63.

47 So when they continued asking him, he lifted up himself, and said unto them, He that is without sin among you, let him first cast a stone at her.
St John 8:7.

48 Then spake Jesus again unto them, saying, I am the light of the world: he that followeth me shall not walk in darkness, but shall have the light of life.
St John 8:12.

49 And ye shall know the truth, and the truth shall make you free.
St John 8:32.

50 If the Son therefore shall make you free, ye shall be free indeed.
St John 8:36.

51 Ye are of your father the devil, and the lusts of the father ye will do. He was a murderer from the beginning, and abode not in the truth, because there is no truth in him. When he speaketh a lie, he speaketh of his own: for he is a liar, and the father of it.
St John 8:44.

52 Whether he be a sinner or no, I know not: one thing I know, that, whereas I was blind, now I see.
St John 9:25.

53 The thief cometh not, but for to steal, and to kill, and to destroy: I am come that they might have life, and that they might have it more abundantly.
St John 10:10.

54 I am the good shepherd: the good shepherd giveth his life for the sheep. But he that is an hireling, and not the shepherd, whose own the sheep are not, seeth the wolf coming, and leaveth the sheep, and fleeth: and the wolf catcheth them, and scattereth the sheep. The hireling fleeth, because he is an hireling, and careth not for the sheep. I am the good shepherd, and know my sheep, and am known of mine. As the Father knoweth me, even so know I the Father: and I lay down my life for the sheep. And other sheep I have which are not of this fold: them also must I bring, and they shall hear my voice; and there shall be one fold, and one shepherd.
St John 10:11–16.

55 I am the resurrection, and the life: he that believeth in me, though he were dead, yet shall he live.
St John 11:25.

56 Jesus wept.
This is the shortest verse in the Bible. St John 11:35.

57 For the poor always ye have with you; but me ye have not always.
St John 12:8.

58 That thou doest, do quickly.
Jesus to Judas. St John 13:27.

59 A new commandment I give unto you, That ye love one another; as I have loved you, that ye also love one another. By this shall all men know that ye are my disciples, if ye have love one to another.
St John 13:34–5.

60 Let not your heart be troubled: ye believe in God, believe also in me.
St John 14:1.

61 In my Father's house are many mansions: if it were not so, I would have told you. I go to prepare a place for you. And if I go and prepare a place for you, I will come again, and receive you unto myself; that where I am, there ye may be also.
St John 14:2–3.

62 Jesus saith unto him, I am the way, the truth, and the life: no man cometh unto the Father, but by me.
St John 14:6.

63 Peace I leave with you, my peace I give unto you: not as the world giveth, give I unto you, Let not your heart be troubled, neither let it be afraid.
St John 14:27.

64 This is my commandment, That ye love one another, as I have loved you. Greater love hath no man than this, that a man lay down his life for his friends.
St John 15:12–13.

65 I have yet many things to say unto you, but ye cannot bear them now.
St John 16:12.

66 These things I have spoken unto you, that in me ye might have peace. In the world ye shall have tribulation: but be of good cheer; I have overcome the world.
St John 16:33.

67 While I was with them in the world, I kept them in thy name: those that thou gavest me I have kept, and none of them is lost, but the son of perdition; that the scripture might be fulfilled.
St John 17:12.

68 Pilate saith unto him, What is truth?
St John 18:38.

69 Then said the chief priests of the Jews to Pilate, Write not, The King of the Jews; but that he said, I am King of the Jews. Pilate answered, What I have written I have written.
St John 19:21–2.

70 When Jesus therefore saw his mother, and the disciple standing by, whom he loved, he saith unto his mother, Woman, behold thy son! Then saith he to the disciple, Behold thy mother! And from that hour that disciple took her unto his own home.
St John 19:26–7.

71 He said It is finished: and he bowed his head, and gave up the ghost.

St John 19:28–30.

72 But one of the soldiers with a spear pierced his side, and forthwith came there out blood and water.
St John 19:34.

73 The first day of the week cometh Mary Magdalene early, when it was yet dark, unto the sepulchre, and seeth the stone taken away from the sepulchre.
St John 20:1–2.

74 So they ran both together: and the other disciple did outrun Peter, and came first to the sepulchre.
St John 20:4.

75 Jesus saith unto her, Woman, why weepest thou? whom seekest thou? She, supposing him to be the gardener, saith unto him, Sir, if thou have borne him hence, tell me where thou hast laid him, and I will take him away. Jesus saith unto her, Mary. She turned herself, and saith unto him, Rabboni; which is to say, Master. Jesus saith unto her, Touch me not; for I am not yet ascended to my Father: but go to my brethren, and say unto them, I ascend unto my Father, and your Father; and to my God, and your God.
St John 20:15–17. The Latin Vulgate translation of the Bible, ascribed to St Jerome, famously renders the phrase 'Do not touch me' as 'Noli me tangere'.

76 Except I shall see in his hands the print of the nails, and put my finger into the print of the nails, and thrust my hand into his side, I will not believe.
Thomas. St John 20:24–5.

77 Be not faithless, but believing. And Thomas answered and said unto him, My Lord and my God. Jesus saith unto him, Thomas, because thou hast seen me, thou hast believed: blessed are they that have not seen, and yet have believed.
St John 20:27–9.

78 When thou wast young, thou girdest thyself, and walkedst whither thou wouldest: but when thou shalt be old, thou shalt stretch forth thy hands, and another shall gird thee, and carry thee whither thou wouldest not.
St John 21:18.

79 It is not for you to know the times or the seasons, which the Father hath put in his own power. But ye shall receive power, after that the Holy Ghost is come upon you: and ye shall be witnesses unto me both in Jerusalem, and in all Judea, and in Samaria, and unto the uttermost part of the earth.
Acts of the Apostles 1:7–8.

80 Ye men of Galilee, why stand ye gazing up into heaven? this same Jesus, which is taken up from you into heaven, shall so come in like manner as ye have seen him go into heaven.
Acts of the Apostles 1:11.

81 And when the day of Pentecost was fully come, they were all with one accord in one place. And suddenly there came a sound from heaven as of a rushing mighty wind, and it filled all the house where they were sitting. And there appeared unto them cloven tongues like as of fire, and it sat upon each of them. And they were all filled with the Holy Ghost, and began to speak with other tongues, as the Spirit gave them utterance.
Acts of the Apostles 2:1–4.

82 Silver and gold have I none; but such as I have give I thee: In the name of Jesus Christ of Nazareth rise up and walk.
Acts of the Apostles 3:6.

83 And he leaping up stood, and walked, and entered with them into the temple, walking, and leaping, and praising God.
Acts of the Apostles 3:8.

84 Neither is there salvation in any other: for there is none other name under heaven given among men, whereby we must be saved.
Acts of the Apostles 4:12.

85 We ought to obey God rather than men.
Acts of the Apostles 5:29.

86 Then the twelve called the multitude of the disciples unto them, and said, It is not reason that we should leave the word of God, and serve tables.
Acts of the Apostles 6:2–4.

87 And the witnesses laid down their clothes at a young man's feet, whose name was Saul.
Acts of the Apostles 7:57–8.

88 Understandest thou what thou readest? And he said, How can I, except some man should guide me?
Acts of the Apostles 8:30–1.

89 Saul, Saul, why persecutest thou me? And he said, Who art thou, Lord? And the Lord said, I am Jesus whom thou persecutest: it is hard for thee to kick against the pricks.
Acts of the Apostles 9:3–5.

90 Tabitha, which by interpretation is called Dorcas: this woman was full of good works.
Acts of the Apostles 9:36.

91 And saw heaven opened, and a certain vessel descending unto him, as it had been a great sheet knit at the four corners, and let down to the earth: Wherein were all manner of fourfooted beasts of the earth, and wild beasts, and creeping things, and

fowls of the air. And there came a voice to him, Rise, Peter; kill, and eat.
Acts of the Apostles 10:11–13.

92 What God hath cleansed, that call not thou common.
Acts of the Apostles 10:15.

93 Of a truth I perceive that God is no respecter of persons: But in every nation he that feareth Him, and worketh righteousness, is accepted with Him.
Acts of the Apostles 10:34–5.

94 The gods are come down to us in the likeness of men.
Acts of the Apostles 14:11.

95 Sirs, why do ye these things? We also are men of like passions with you, and preach unto you that ye should turn from these vanities unto the living God, which made heaven, and earth, and the sea, and all things that are therein.
Acts of the Apostles 14:15.

96 Sirs, what must I do to be saved? And they said, Believe on the Lord Jesus Christ, and thou shalt be saved, and thy house.
Acts of the Apostles 16:30–1.

97 But the Jews which believeth not, moved with envy, took unto them certain lewd fellows of the baser sort, and gathered a company, and set all the city on an uproar.
Acts of the Apostles 17:5.

98 These that have turned the world upside down are come hither also.
Acts of the Apostles 17:6.

99 What will this babbler say?
Acts of the Apostles 17:18.

1 Ye men of Athens, I perceive that in all things ye are too superstitious. For as I passed by, and beheld your devotions, I found an altar with this inscription, TO THE UNKNOWN GOD. Whom therefore ye ignorantly worship, him declare I unto you.
Acts of the Apostles 17:22–3.

2 God that made the world and all things therein, seeing that he is Lord of heaven and earth, dwelleth not in temples made with hands; Neither is worshipped with men's hands, as though he needed any thing, seeing he giveth to all life, and breath, and all things.
Acts of the Apostles 17:24–5.

3 For in him we live, and move and have our being.
Acts of the Apostles 17:28.

4 And the times of this ignorance God winked at; but now commandeth all men every where to repent.
Acts of the Apostles 17:30.

5 Have ye received the Holy Ghost since ye believed? And they said unto him, We have not so much as heard whether there be any Holy Ghost.
Acts of the Apostles 19:2.

6 It is more blessed to give than to receive.
Acts of the Apostles 20:35.

7 I am a man which am a Jew of Tarsus, a city in Cilicia, a citizen of no mean city.
Acts of the Apostles 21:39.

8 The chief captain answered, With a great sum obtained I this freedom. And Paul said, But I was free born.
Acts of the Apostles 22:27–8.

9 Paul, thou art beside thyself; much learning doth make thee mad.
Acts of the Apostles 26:24.

10 Almost thou persuadest me to be a Christian.
Acts of the Apostles 26:28.

11 For I am not ashamed of the gospel of Christ: for it is the power of God unto salvation to every one that believeth; to the Jew first, and also to the Greek. For therein is the righteousness of God revealed from faith to faith: as it is written, The just shall live by faith.
Romans 1:16–17.

12 Who changed the truth of God into a lie, and worshipped and served the creature more than the Creator.
Romans 1:25.

13 For when the Gentiles, which have not the law, do by nature the things contained in the law, these, having not the law, are a law unto themselves.
Romans 2:14.

14 God forbid: yea, let God be true, but every man a liar.
Romans 3:4.

15 For all have sinned, and come short of the glory of God.
Romans 3:23.

16 Because the law worketh wrath: for where no law is, there is no transgression.
Romans 4:15.

17 Who against hope believed in hope, that he might become the father of many nations.
Romans 4:18.

18 While we were yet sinners, Christ died for us.
Romans 5:8.

19 Where sin abounded, grace did much more abound.
Romans 5:20.

20 What shall we say then? Shall we continue in sin, that grace may abound? God forbid. How shall we, that are dead to sin, live any longer therein?
Romans 6:1–2.

21 Knowing that Christ being raised from the dead dieth no more; death hath no more dominion over him.
Romans 6:9.

22 For the wages of sin is death; but the gift of God is eternal life through Jesus Christ our Lord.
Romans 6:23.

23 To will is present with me; but how to perform that which is good I find not. For the good that I would I do not: but the evil which I would not, that I do.
Romans 7:19.

24 O wretched man that I am! who shall deliver me from the body of this death? I thank God through Jesus Christ our Lord. So then with the mind I myself serve the law of God; but with the flesh the law of sin.
Romans 7:22–5.

25 There is therefore now no condemnation to them which are in Christ Jesus, who walk not after the flesh, but after the Spirit.
Romans 8:1.

26 For they that are after the flesh do mind the things of the flesh; but they that are after the Spirit the things of the Spirit. For to be carnally minded is death; but to be spiritually minded is life and peace.
Romans 8:5–6.

27 For ye have not received the spirit of bondage again to fear; but ye have received the Spirit of adoption, whereby we cry, Abba, Father. The Spirit itself beareth witness with our spirit, that we are the children of God:
And if children, then heirs; heirs of God, and joint-heirs with Christ; if so be that we suffer with him, that we may be also glorified together.
Romans 8:15–17.

28 For we know that the whole creation groaneth and travaileth in pain together until now.
Romans 8:22.

29 And we know that all things work together for good to them that love God, to them who are the called according to his purpose.
Romans 8:28.

30 If God be for us, who can be against us?
Romans 8:31.

31 I am persuaded, that neither death, nor life, nor angels, nor principalities, nor powers, nor things present, nor things to come, Nor height, nor depth, nor any other creature, shall be able to separate us from the love of God, which is in Christ Jesus our Lord.
Romans 8:38–9.

32 Nay but, O man, who art thou that repliest against God? Shall the thing formed say to him that formed it, Why hast thou made me thus? Hath not the potter power over the clay, of the same lump to make one vessel unto honour, and another unto dishonour?
Romans 9:20–1.

33 I beseech you therefore, brethren, by the mercies of God, that ye present your bodies a living sacrifice, holy, acceptable unto God, which is your reasonable service.
And be not conformed to this world: but be ye transformed by the renewing of your mind, that ye may prove what is that good, and acceptable, and perfect, will of God.
Romans 12:1–2.

34 Not slothful in business; fervent in spirit; serving the Lord.
Romans 12:11.

35 Rejoice with them that do rejoice, and weep with them that weep.
Romans 12:15.

36 Mind not high things, but condescend to men of low estate. Be not wise in your own conceits. Recompense to no man evil for evil. Provide things honest in the sight of all men. If it be possible, as much as lieth in you, live peaceably with all men. Dearly beloved, avenge not yourselves, but rather give place unto wrath: for it is written, Vengeance is mine; I will repay, saith the Lord.
Romans 12:16–19.

37 Be not overcome of evil, but overcome evil with good.
Romans 12:21.

38 Let every soul be subject unto the higher powers. For there is no power but of God: the powers that be are ordained of God.
Romans 13:1.

39 Render therefore to all their dues: tribute to whom tribute is due; custom to whom custom; fear to whom fear; honour to whom honour. Owe no man any thing, but to love one another: for he that loveth another hath fulfilled the law.
Romans 13:7–8.

40 Love worketh no ill to his neighbour: therefore love is the fulfilling of the law.
Romans 13:10.

41 Doubtful disputations.
Romans 14:1.

42 Whether we live therefore, or die, we are the Lord's.
Romans 14:8.

43 Salute one another with an holy kiss.
Romans 16:16.

44 For after that in the wisdom of God the world by wisdom knew not God, it pleased God by the foolishness of preaching to save them that believe.
1 Corinthians 1:21.

45 But God hath chosen the foolish things of the world to confound the wise; and God hath chosen the weak things of the world to confound the things which are mighty.
1 Corinthians 1:27.

46 But as it is written, Eye hath not seen, nor ear heard, neither have entered into the heart of man, the things which God hath prepared for them that love him. But God hath revealed them unto us by his Spirit: for the Spirit searcheth all things, yea, the deep things of God.
1 Corinthians 2:9–10.

47 I have planted, Apollos watered; but God gave the increase.
1 Corinthians 3:6.

48 We are made a spectacle unto the world, and to angels, and to men.
1 Corinthians 4:9.

49 What? know ye not that your body is the temple of the Holy Ghost which is in you, which ye have of God, and ye are not your own? For ye are bought with a price: therefore glorify God in your body, and in your spirit, which are God's.
1 Corinthians 6:19–20.

50 It is better to marry than to burn.
1 Corinthians 7:9.

51 For the unbelieving husband is sanctified by the wife.
1 Corinthians 7:14.

52 But he that is married careth for the things that are of the world, how he may please his wife.
1 Corinthians 7:33.

53 I am made all things to all men, that I might by all means save some.
1 Corinthians 9:22.

54 Know ye not that they which run in a race run all, but one receiveth the prize? So run, that ye may obtain.
1 Corinthians 9:24.

55 Wherefore let him that thinketh he standeth take heed lest he fall.
1 Corinthians 10:12.

56 All things are lawful for me, but all things are not expedient: all things are lawful for me, but all things edify not.
1 Corinthians 10:23.

57 For the earth is the Lord's, and the fulness thereof.
1 Corinthians 10:26.

58 If a man have long hair, it is a shame unto him. But if a woman have long hair, it is a glory to her: for her hair is given her for a covering.
1 Corinthians 11:15.

59 The Lord Jesus the same night in which he was betrayed took bread: And when he had given thanks, he brake it, and said, Take, eat: this is my body, which is broken for you: this do in remembrance of me. After the same manner also he took the cup, when he had supped, saying, This cup is the new testament in my blood: this do ye, as oft as ye drink it, in remembrance of me. For as often as ye eat this bread, and drink this cup, ye do shew the Lord's death till he come.
1 Corinthians 11:23–6.

60 No man can say that Jesus is the Lord, but by the Holy Ghost.
1 Corinthians 12:3.

61 Now there are diversities of gifts, but the same Spirit. And there are differences of administrations, but the same Lord. And there are diversities of operations, but it is the same God which worketh all in all.
1 Corinthians 12:4–6.

62 Though I speak with the tongues of men and of angels, and have not charity, I am become as sounding brass, or a tinkling cymbal. And though I have the gift of prophecy, and understand all mysteries, and all knowledge; and though I have all faith, so that I could remove mountains, and have not charity, I am nothing. And though I bestow all my goods to feed the poor, and though I give my body to be burned, and have not charity, it profiteth me nothing. Charity suffereth long, and is kind; charity envieth not; charity vaunteth not itself, is not puffed up, Doth not behave itself unseemly, seeketh not her own, is not easily provoked, thinketh no evil; Rejoiceth not in iniquity, but rejoiceth in the truth; Beareth all

things, believeth all things, hopeth all things,
endureth all things. Charity never faileth: but
whether there be prophecies, they shall fail;
whether there be tongues, they shall cease; whether
there be knowledge, it shall vanish away. For we
know in part, and we prophesy in part. But when
that which is perfect is come, then that which is in
part shall be done away. When I was a child, I spake
as a child, I understood as a child, I thought as a
child: but when I became a man, I put away
childish things. For now we see through a glass,
darkly; but then face to face: now I know in part;
but then shall I know even as also I am known. And
now abideth faith, hope, charity, these three; but
the greatest of these is charity.
1 Corinthians 13:1–13.

63 For if the trumpet give an uncertain sound, who
shall prepare himself to the battle?
1 Corinthians 14:8.

64 Let all things be done decently and in order.
1 Corinthians 14:40.

65 And last of all he was seen of me also, as of one
born out of due time. For I am the least of the
apostles, that am not meet to be called an apostle,
because I persecuted the church of God.
But by the grace of God I am what I am.
1 Corinthians 15:8–9.

66 If in this life only we have hope in Christ, we are of
all men most miserable.
1 Corinthians 15:19.

67 But now is Christ risen from the dead, and become
the firstfruits of them that slept.
For since by man came death, by man came also the
resurrection of the dead.
For as in Adam all die, even so in Christ shall all be
made alive.
1 Corinthians 15:20–2.

68 He must reign, till he hath put all enemies under
his feet. The last enemy that shall be destroyed is
death.
1 Corinthians 15:26.

69 What advantageth it me, if the dead rise not? let us
eat and drink; for tomorrow we die.
1 Corinthians 15:32.
▷ See Parker 754:9.

70 Evil communications corrupt good manners.
1 Corinthians 15:33.

71 The first man is of the earth, earthy.
1 Corinthians 15:47.

72 Behold, I shew you a mystery; We shall not all
sleep, but we shall all be changed, In a moment, in

the twinkling of an eye, at the last trump: for the
trumpet shall sound, and the dead shall be raised
incorruptible, and we shall be changed.
1 Corinthians 15:51–2.

73 O death, where is thy sting? O grave, where is thy
victory?
1 Corinthians 15:55.

74 Watch ye, stand fast in the faith, quit you like men,
be strong.
1 Corinthians 16:13.

75 Not that we are sufficient of ourselves to think any
thing as of ourselves; but our sufficiency is of God;
Who also hath made us able ministers of the new
testament; not of the letter, but of the spirit: for the
letter killeth, but the spirit giveth life.
2 Corinthians 3:5–6.

76 But we have this treasure in earthen vessels.
2 Corinthians 4:7.

77 We are troubled on every side, yet not distressed;
we are perplexed, but not in despair.
2 Corinthians 4:8.

78 For we know that if our earthly house of this
tabernacle were dissolved, we have a building of
God, an house not made with hands, eternal in the
heavens.
2 Corinthians 5:1.

79 For we walk by faith, not by sight.
2 Corinthians 5:7.

80 Therefore if any man be in Christ, he is a new
creature: old things are passed away; behold, all
things are become new.
2 Corinthians 5:17.

81 Now then we are ambassadors for Christ.
2 Corinthians 5:20.

82 For he saith, I have heard thee in a time accepted,
and in the day of salvation have I succoured thee:
behold, now is the accepted time; behold, now is
the day of salvation.
2 Corinthians 6:2.

83 As unknown, and yet well known; as dying, and,
behold, we live; as chastened, and not killed; As
sorrowful, yet alway rejoicing; as poor, yet making
many rich; as having nothing, and yet possessing all
things.
2 Corinthians 6:9–10.

84 So let him give; not grudgingly, or of necessity: for
God loveth a cheerful giver.
2 Corinthians 9:7.

85 For ye suffer fools gladly, seeing ye yourselves are wise.
2 Corinthians 11:19.

86 And lest I should be exalted above measure through the abundance of the revelations, there was given to me a thorn in the flesh, the messenger of Satan to buffet me.
2 Corinthians 12:7.

87 My grace is sufficient for thee: for my strength is made perfect in weakness. Most gladly therefore will I rather glory in my infirmities, that the power of Christ may rest upon me. Therefore I take pleasure in infirmities, in reproaches, in necessities, in persecutions, in distresses for Christ's sake: for when I am weak, then am I strong.
2 Corinthians 12:9–10.

88 They gave to me and Barnabas the right hands of fellowship.
Galatians 2:9.

89 There is neither Jew nor Greek, there is neither bond nor free, there is neither male nor female: for ye are all one in Christ Jesus.
Galatians 3:28.

90 Ye are fallen from grace.
Galatians 5:4.

91 But the fruit of the Spirit is love, joy, peace, longsuffering, gentleness, goodness, faith, Meekness, temperance: against such there is no law.
Galatians 5:22–3.

92 Be not deceived; God is not mocked: for whatsoever a man soweth, that shall he also reap.
Galatians 6:7.

93 Let us not be weary in well doing: for in due season we shall reap, if we faint not.
Galatians 6:9.

94 See what a large letter I have written unto you with mine own hand.
Galatians 6:11.

95 And came and preached peace to you which were afar off, and to them that were nigh.
Ephesians 2:17.

96 Now therefore ye are no more strangers and foreigners, but fellow citizens with the saints, and of the household of God.
Ephesians 2:19.

97 Unto me, who am less than the least of all saints, is this grace given, that I should preach among the Gentiles the unsearchable riches of Christ.
Ephesians 3:8.

98 That he would grant you, according to the riches of his glory, to be strengthened with might by his Spirit in the inner man; That Christ may dwell in your hearts by faith; that ye, being rooted and grounded in love, May be able to comprehend with all saints what is the breadth, and length, and depth, and height; And to know the love of Christ, which passeth knowledge, that ye might be filled with all the fulness of God.
Ephesians 3:16–19.

99 Now unto him that is able to do exceeding abundantly above all that we ask or think, according to the power that worketh in us, Unto him be glory in the church by Christ Jesus throughout all ages, world without end. Amen.
Ephesians 3:20–1.

1 Wherefore putting away lying, speak every man truth with his neighbour: for we are members one of another. Be ye angry, and sin not: let not the sun go down upon your wrath.
Ephesians 4:25–6.

2 Redeeming the time, because the days are evil.
Ephesians 5:16.

3 Be not drunk with wine, wherein is excess; but be filled with the Spirit.
Ephesians 5:18.

4 Ye fathers, provoke not your children to wrath.
Ephesians 6:4.

5 Not with eyeservice, as menpleasers; but as the servants of Christ, doing the will of God from the heart;
With good will doing service, as to the Lord, and not to men.
Ephesians 6:6–7.

6 Finally, my brethren, be strong in the Lord, and in the power of his might. Put on the whole armour of God, that ye may be able to stand against the wiles of the devil. For we wrestle not against flesh and blood, but against principalities, against powers, against the rulers of the darkness of this world, against spiritual wickedness in high places. Wherefore take unto you the whole armour of God, that ye may be able to withstand in the evil day, and having done all, to stand. Stand therefore, having your loins girt about with truth, and having on the breastplate of righteousness; And your feet shod with the preparation of the gospel of peace; Above all, taking the shield of faith, wherewith ye shall be able to quench all the fiery darts of the wicked. And take the helmet of salvation, and the sword of the Spirit, which is the word of God.
Ephesians 6:10–17.

7 For to me to live is Christ, and to die is gain.
Philippians 1:21.

8 Let this mind be in you, which was also in Christ
Jesus: Who, being in the form of God, thought it
not robbery to be equal with God: But made
himself of no reputation, and took upon him the
form of a servant, and was made in the likeness of
men: And being found in fashion as a man, he
humbled himself, and became obedient unto
death, even the death of the cross. Wherefore God
also hath highly exalted him, and given him a name
which is above every name: That at the name of
Jesus every knee should bow, of things in heaven,
and things in earth, and things under the earth;
And that every tongue should confess that Jesus
Christ is Lord, to the glory of God the Father.
Philippians 2:5–11.

9 Work out your own salvation with fear and
trembling.
Philippians 2:12.

10 Circumcised the eighth day, of the stock of Israel,
of the tribe of Benjamin, an Hebrew of the
Hebrews; as touching the law, a Pharisee.
Paul lists his religious credentials. Philippians 3:5

11 But what things were gain to me, those I counted
loss for Christ.
Philippians 3:7.

12 Forgetting those things which are behind, and
reaching forth unto those things which are before, I
press toward the mark for the prize of the high
calling of God in Christ Jesus.
Philippians 3:13–14.

13 Whose end is destruction, whose God is their belly,
and whose glory is in their shame, who mind
earthly things.
Philippians 3:19.

14 Rejoice in the Lord alway: and again I say, Rejoice.
Let your moderation be known unto all men. The
Lord is at hand. Be careful for nothing; but in every
thing by prayer and supplication with thanksgiving
let your requests be made known unto God. And
the peace of God, which passeth all understanding,
shall keep your hearts and minds through Christ
Jesus.
Philippians 4:4–7.

15 Finally, brethren, whatsoever things are true,
whatsoever things are honest, whatsoever things are
just, whatsoever things are pure, whatsoever things
are lovely, whatsoever things are of good report; if
there be any virtue, and if there be any praise, think
on these things.
Philippians 4:8.

16 I have learned, in whatsoever state I am, therewith
to be content.
Philippians 4:11.

17 I can do all things through Christ which
strengtheneth me.
Philippians 4:13.

18 My God shall supply all your need according to his
riches in glory by Christ Jesus.
Philippians 4:19.

19 Beware lest any man spoil you through philosophy
and vain deceit, after the tradition of men, after the
rudiments of the world, and not after Christ.
Colossians 2:8.

20 Set your affection on things above, not on things
on the earth.
Colossians 3:2.

21 Lie not one to another, seeing that ye have put off
the old man with his deeds; And have put on the
new man, which is renewed in knowledge after the
image of him that created him: Where there is
neither Greek nor Jew, circumcision nor
uncircumcision, Barbarian, Scythian, bond nor
free: but Christ is all, and in all.
Colossians 3:9–11.

22 Husbands, love your wives, and be not bitter
against them.
Colossians 3:19.

23 Let your speech be alway with grace, seasoned with
salt, that ye may know how ye ought to answer
every man.
Colossians 4:6.

24 Study to be quiet, and to do your own business,
and to work with your own hands, as we
commanded you.
1 Thessalonians 4:11.

25 For the Lord himself shall descend from heaven with
a shout, with the voice of the archangel, and with the
trump of God: and the dead in Christ shall rise first:
Then we which are alive and remain shall be caught
up together with them in the clouds, to meet the
Lord in the air: and so shall we ever be with the Lord.
1 Thessalonians 4:16–17.

26 Prove all things; hold fast that which is good.
1 Thessalonians 5:21.

27 If any would not work, neither should he eat.
2 Thessalonians 3:10.

28 This is a faithful saying, and worthy of all
acceptation, that Christ Jesus came into the world
to save sinners; of whom I am chief.
1 Timothy 1:15.

29 If a man desire the office of a bishop, he desireth a good work. A bishop then must be blameless, the husband of one wife, vigilant, sober, of good behaviour, given to hospitality, apt to teach; Not given to wine, no striker, not greedy of filthy lucre; but patient, not a brawler, not covetous.
1 Timothy 3:1–3.

30 But refuse profane and old wives' fables, and exercise thyself rather unto godliness. For bodily exercise profiteth little: but godliness is profitable unto all things.
1 Timothy 4:7–8.

31 Let no man despise thy youth.
1 Timothy 4:12.

32 Drink no longer water, but use a little wine for thy stomach's sake and thine often infirmities.
1 Timothy 5:23.

33 For we brought nothing into this world, and it is certain we can carry nothing out. And having food and raiment let us be therewith content.
1 Timothy 6:7–8.

34 For the love of money is the root of all evil.
1 Timothy 6:10.

35 Fight the good fight of faith.
1 Timothy 6:12.

36 For God hath not given us the spirit of fear; but of power, and of love, and of a sound mind.
2 Timothy 1:7.

37 I know whom I have believed, and am persuaded that he is able to keep that which I have committed unto him against that day.
2 Timothy 1:12.

38 Hold fast the form of sound words, which thou hast heard of me.
2 Timothy 1:13.

39 All scripture is given by inspiration of God, and is profitable of doctrine, for reproof, for correction, for instruction in righteousness.
2 Timothy 3:16.

40 Preach the word; be instant in season, out of season.
2 Timothy 4:2.

41 I have fought a good fight, I have finished my course, I have kept the faith.
2 Timothy 4:7.

42 The Cretans are always liars, evil beasts, slow bellies.
Titus 1:12.

43 Unto the pure all things are pure: but unto them that are defiled and unbelieving is nothing pure; but even their mind and conscience is defiled.
Titus 1:15.

44 God, who at sundry times and in divers manners spake in time past unto the fathers by the prophets, Hath in these last days spoken unto us by his Son, whom he hath appointed heir of all things, by whom he also made the worlds: Who being the brightness of his glory, and the express image of his person, and upholding all things by the word of his power, when he had by himself purged our sins, sat down on the right hand of the Majesty on high.
Hebrews 1:1–3.

45 For the word of God is quick, and powerful, and sharper than any twoedged sword, piercing even to the dividing asunder of soul and spirit.
Hebrews 4:12.

46 Ye have need that one teach you again which be the first principles of the oracles of God; and are become such as have need of milk, and not of strong meat.
Hebrews 5:12.

47 Without shedding of blood is no remission.
Hebrews 9:22.

48 It is appointed unto men once to die, but after this the judgment.
Hebrews 9:27.

49 It is a fearful thing to fall into the hands of the living God.
Hebrews 10:31.

50 Now faith is the substance of things hoped for, the evidence of things not seen.
Hebrews 11:1.

51 These all died in faith, not having received the promises, but having seen them afar off, and were persuaded of them, and embraced them, and confessed that they were strangers and pilgrims on the earth.
Hebrews 11:13.

52 But now they desire a better country, that is, an heavenly: wherefore God is not ashamed to be called their God: for he hath prepared for them a city.
Hebrews 11:16.

53 Of whom the world was not worthy.
Hebrews 11:38.

54 Wherefore seeing we also are compassed about with so great a cloud of witnesses, let us lay aside every

weight, and the sin which doth so easily beset us, and let us run with patience the race that is set before us, Looking unto Jesus the author and finisher of our faith; who for the joy that was set before him endured the cross, despising the shame, and is set down at the right hand of the throne of God.
Hebrews 12:1–2.

55 For whom the Lord loveth he chasteneth.
Hebrews 12:6.

56 For our God is a consuming fire.
Hebrews 12:29.

57 Be not forgetful to entertain strangers: for thereby some have entertained angels unawares.
Hebrews 13:1–2.

58 Jesus Christ the same yesterday, and to day, and for ever.
Hebrews 13:8.

59 He that wavereth is like a wave of the sea driven with the wind and tossed. For let not that man think that he shall receive any thing of the Lord. A double minded man is unstable in all his ways.
James 1:7–8.

60 Every good gift and every perfect gift is from above, and cometh down from the Father of lights, with whom is no variableness, neither shadow of turning.
James 1:17.

61 Be ye doers of the word, and not hearers only, deceiving your own selves. For if any be a hearer of the word, and not a doer, he is like unto a man beholding his natural face in a glass: For he beholdeth himself, and goeth his way, and straightway forgetteth what manner of man he was.
James 1:22–4.

62 If any man among you seem to be religious, and bridleth not his tongue, but deceiveth his own heart, this man's religion is vain.
James 1:26.

63 Pure religion and undefiled before God and the Father is this, To visit the fatherless and widows in their affliction, and to keep himself unspotted from the world.
James 1:27.

64 Thou believest that there is one God; thou doest well: the devils also believe, and tremble.
James 2:19.

65 Faith without works is dead.
James 2:20.

66 Even so the tongue is a little member, and boasteth great things. Behold, how great a matter a little fire kindleth!
James 3:5.

67 And the tongue is a fire, a world of iniquity: so is the tongue among our members, that it defileth the whole body, and setteth on fire the course of nature; and it is set on fire of hell.
James 3:6.

68 Out of the same mouth proceedeth blessing and cursing. My brethren, these things ought not so to be. Doth a fountain send forth at the same place sweet water and bitter?
James 3:10–11.

69 Submit yourselves therefore to God, Resist the devil, and he will flee from you. Draw nigh to God, and he will draw nigh to you.
James 4:7–8.

70 What is your life? It is even a vapour, that appeareth for a little time, and then vanisheth away. For that ye ought to say, If the Lord will, we shall live, and do this, or that.
James 4:14–15.

71 Grudge not one against another, brethren, lest ye be condemned: behold, the judge standeth before the door.
James 5:9.

72 Swear not, neither by heaven, neither by the earth, neither by any other oath: but let your yea be yea; and your nay, nay.
James 5:12.

73 The effectual fervent prayer of a righteous man availeth much.
James 5:16.

74 He which converteth the sinner from the error of his way shall save a soul from death, and shall hide a multitude of sins.
James 5:20.

75 Wherefore gird up the loins of your mind, be sober, and hope to the end for the grace that is to be brought unto you at the revelation of Jesus Christ.
1 Peter 1:13.

76 For all flesh is as grass, and all the glory of man as the flower of grass. The grass withereth, and the flower thereof falleth away.
1 Peter 1:24.

77 As newborn babes, desire the sincere milk of the word, that ye may grow thereby: If so be you have tasted that the Lord is gracious.
1 Peter 2:2.

78 But ye are a chosen generation, a royal priesthood, an holy nation, a peculiar people; that ye should shew forth the praises of him who hath called you out of darkness into his marvellous light.
1 Peter 2:9.

79 Honour all men. Love the brotherhood. Fear God. Honour the king.
1 Peter 2:17

80 For ye were as sheep going astray; but are now returned unto the Shepherd and Bishop of your souls.
1 Peter 2:25.

81 Giving honour unto the wife, as unto the weaker vessel.
1 Peter 3:7.

82 And above all things have fervent charity among yourselves: for charity shall cover the multitude of sins.
1 Peter 4:8.

83 Casting all your care upon him; for he careth for you.
1 Peter 5:6–7.

84 Be sober, be vigilant; because your adversary the devil, as a roaring lion, walketh about, seeking whom he may devour.
1 Peter 5:8.

85 The dog is turned to his own vomit again; and the sow that was washed to her wallowing in the mire.
2 Peter 2:22.

86 One day is with the Lord as a thousand years, and a thousand years as one day.
2 Peter 3:8–9.

87 But the day of the Lord will come as a thief in the night.
2 Peter 3:10–11.

88 If we say that we have no sin, we deceive ourselves, and the truth is not in us. If we confess our sins, he is faithful and just to forgive us our sins, and to cleanse us from all unrighteousness.
1 John 1:8–9.

89 If any man sin, we have an advocate with the Father, Jesus Christ the righteous.
1 John 2:1.

90 Behold, what manner of love the Father hath bestowed upon us, that we should be called the sons of God.
1 John 3:1.

91 But whoso hath this world's good, and seeth his brother have need, and shutteth up his bowels of compassion from him, how dwelleth the love of God in him?
1 John 3:17.

92 Beloved, let us love one another: for love is of God; and every one that loveth is born of God, and knoweth God. He that loveth not knoweth not God; for God is love.
1 John 4:7–8.

93 Herein is love, not that we loved God, but that he loved us, and sent his Son to be the propitiation for our sins.
1 John 4:10.

94 There is no fear in love; but perfect love casteth out fear.
1 John 4:18.

95 If a man say, I love God, and hateth his brother, he is a liar: for he that loveth not his brother whom he hath seen, how can he love God whom he hath not seen?
1 John 4:20.

96 John to the seven churches which are in Asia: Grace be unto you, and peace, from him which is, and which was, and which is to come.
Revelation 1:4.

97 Behold, he cometh with clouds; and every eye shall see him, and they also which pierced him: and all kindreds of the earth shall wail because of him. Even so, Amen.
Revelation 1:7.

98 I was in the Spirit on the Lord's day, and heard behind me a great voice, as of a trumpet, Saying, I am Alpha and Omega, the first and the last: and, What thou seest, write in a book, and send it unto the seven churches which are in Asia.
Revelation 1:10–11.

99 And in the midst of the seven candlesticks one like unto the Son of man, clothed with a garment down to the foot, and girt about the paps with golden girdle.
His head and his hairs were white like wool, as white as snow; and his eyes were as a flame of fire;
And his feet like unto fine brass, as if they burned in a furnace; and his voice as the sound of many waters.
And he had in his right hand seven stars: and out of his mouth went a sharp two-edged sword: and his countenance was as the sun shineth in his strength.
And when I saw him, I fell as his feet as dead.
Revelation 1:13–17.

1 I am he that liveth, and was dead; and, behold, I
am alive for evermore, Amen; and have the keys of
hell and of death.
Revelation 1:18.

2 I have somewhat against thee, because thou hast
left thy first love.
Revelation 2:4.

3 Be thou faithful unto death, and I will give thee a
crown of life.
Revelation 2:10.

4 And he shall rule them with a rod of iron; as the
vessels of a potter shall they be broken to shivers.
Revelation 2:27.

5 Behold, I have set before thee an open door, and no
man can shut it: for thou hast a little strength, and
hast kept my word, and hast not denied my name.
Revelation 3:8.

6 I know thy works, that thou art neither cold nor
hot: I would thou wert cold or hot. So then because
thou art lukewarm, and neither cold nor hot, I will
spew thee out of my mouth.
Revelation 3:15–16.

7 Behold, I stand at the door, and knock: if any man
hear my voice, and open the door, I will come in to
him, and will sup with him, and he with me.
Revelation 3:20.

8 And before the throne there was a sea of glass like
unto crystal: and in the midst of the throne, and
round about the throne, were four beasts full of
eyes before and behind. And the first beast was like
a lion, and the second beast like a calf, and the third
beast had a face as man, and the fourth beast was
like a flying eagle.
Revelation 4:6–7.

9 And the four beasts had each of them six wings
about him; and they were full of eyes within: and
they rest not day and night, saying, Holy, holy,
holy, Lord God Almighty, which was, and is, and is
to come.
Revelation 4:8.

10 Cast their crowns before the throne, saying, Thou
art worthy, O Lord, to receive glory and honour
and power: for thou hast created all things, and for
thy pleasure they are and were created.
Revelation 4:10–11.

11 Who is worthy to open the book, and to loose the
seals thereof? And no man in heaven, nor in earth,
neither under the earth, was able to open the book,
neither to look thereon. And I wept much, because
no man was found worthy to open and to read the
book, neither to look thereon.
Revelation 5:2–4.

12 And I looked, and behold a pale horse: and his
name that sat on him was Death, and Hell followed
with him.
Revelation 6:8.

13 And said to the mountains and rocks, Fall on us,
and hide us from the face of him that sitteth on the
throne, and from the wrath of the Lamb: For the
great day of his wrath is come; and who shall be
able to stand?
Revelation 6:16–17.

14 A great multitude, which no man could number, of
all nations, and kindreds, and people, and tongues,
stood before the throne, and before the Lamb,
clothed with white robes, and palms in their hands
Revelation 7:9.

15 These are they which came out of great tribulation,
and have washed their robes, and made them white
in the blood of the Lamb. Therefore are they before
the throne of God, and serve him day and night in
his temple: and he that sitteth on the throne shall
dwell among them. They shall hunger no more,
neither thirst any more; neither shall the sun light
on them nor any heat. For the Lamb which is in the
midst of the throne shall feed them, and shall lead
them unto living fountains of waters: and God
shall wipe away all tears from their eyes.
Revelation 7:14–17.

16 And when he had opened the seventh seal, there
was silence in heaven about the space of half an
hour.
Revelation 8:1.

17 I saw a star fall from heaven unto the earth: and to
him was given the key of the bottomless pit.
Revelation 9:1.

18 And there were stings in their tails.
Revelation 9:10.

19 I took the little book out of the angel's hand, and
ate it up; and it was in my mouth sweet as honey:
and as soon as I had eaten it, my belly was bitter.
Revelation 10:9–10.

20 And there appeared a great wonder in heaven; a
woman clothed with the sun, and the moon under
her feet, and upon her head a crown of twelve stars.
Revelation 12:1.

21 And there was war in heaven: Michael and his
angels fought against the dragon; and the dragon
fought and his angels, And prevailed not; neither
was their place found any more in heaven. And the
great dragon was cast out, that old serpent, called

the Devil, and Satan, which deceiveth the whole world: he was cast out into the earth, and his angels were cast out with him.
Revelation 12:7–9.

22 And that no man might buy or sell, save he that had the mark, or the name of the beast, or the number of his name. Here is wisdom. Let him that hath understanding count the number of the beast: for it is the number of a man; and his number is Six hundred threescore and six.
Revelation 13:17–18.

23 The same shall drink of the wine of the wrath of God, which is poured out without mixture into the cup of his indignation; and he shall be tormented with fire and brimstone in the presence of the holy angels, and in the presence of the Lamb: And the smoke of their torment ascendeth up for ever and ever: and they have no rest day nor night, who worship the beast and his image, and whosoever receiveth the mark of his name.
Revelation 14:10–11.

24 Blessed are the dead which die in the Lord from henceforth: Yea, saith the Spirit, that they may rest from their labours; and their works do follow them.
Revelation 14:13.

25 And I saw as it were a sea of glass mingled with fire.
Revelation 15:2.

26 Behold, I come as a thief. Blessed is he that watcheth, and keepeth his garments, lest he walk naked, and they see his shame. And he gathereth them together into a place called in the Hebrew tongue Armageddon.
Revelation 16:15–16.

27 Come hither; I will shew unto thee the judgment of the great whore that sitteth upon many waters.
Revelation 17:1.

28 I saw a woman sit upon a scarlet coloured beast, full of names of blasphemy, having seven heads and ten horns. And the woman was arrayed in purple and scarlet colour, and decked with gold and precious stones and pearls, having a golden cup in her hand full of abominations and filthiness of her fornication: And upon her forehead was a name written, MYSTERY, BABYLON THE GREAT, THE MOTHER OF HARLOTS AND ABOMINATIONS OF THE EARTH. And I saw the woman drunken with the blood of the saints, and with the blood of the martyrs of Jesus: and when I saw her, I wondered with great admiration.
Revelation 17:3–6.

29 And a mighty angel took up a stone like a great millstone, and cast it into the sea, saying, Thus with violence shall that great city Babylon be thrown down, and shall be found no more at all.
Revelation 18:21.

30 And I saw heaven opened, and behold a white horse; and he that sat upon him was called Faithful and True, and in righteousness he doth judge and make war.
Revelation 19:11.

31 And he hath on his vesture and on his thigh a name written, KING OF KINGS, AND LORD OF LORDS.
Revelation 19:16.

32 And he laid hold on the dragon, that old serpent, which is the Devil, and Satan, and bound him a thousand years, And cast him into the bottomless pit, and shut him up, and set a seal upon him, that he should deceive the nations no more, till the thousand years should be fulfilled: and after that he must be loosed a little season.
Revelation 20:2–3.

33 And I saw a great white throne, and him that sat on it, from whose face the earth and the heaven fled away; and there was found no place for them. And I saw the dead, small and great, stand before God; and the books were opened: and another book was opened, which is the book of life: and the dead were judged out of those things which were written in the books, according to their works. And the sea gave up the dead which were in it; and death and hell delivered up the dead which were in them: and they were judged every man according to their works. And death and hell were cast into the lake of fire. This is the second death. And whosoever was not found written in the book of life was cast into the lake of fire.
Revelation 20:11–15.

34 And I saw a new heaven and a new earth: for the first heaven and the first earth were passed away; and there was no more sea. And I John saw the holy city, new Jerusalem, coming down from God out of heaven, prepared as a bride adorned for her husband.
Revelation 21:1–2.

35 Behold, the tabernacle of God is with men, and he will dwell with them, and they shall be his people, and God himself shall be with them, and be their God. And God shall wipe away all tears from their eyes; and there shall be no more death, neither sorrow, nor crying, neither shall there be any more pain: for the former things are passed away. And he that sat upon the throne said, Behold, I make all things new. And he said unto me, Write: for these words are true and faithful.
Revelation 21:3–5.

36 I will give unto him that is athirst of the fountain of the water of life freely.
Revelation 21:6.

37 And the street of the city was pure gold, as it were transparent glass.
Revelation 21:21.

38 And the gates of it shall not be shut at all by day: for there shall be no night there.
Revelation 21:25.

39 And he shewed me a pure river of water of life, clear as crystal, proceeding out of the throne of God and of the Lamb. In the midst of the street of it, and on either side of the river, was there the tree of life, which bare twelve manner of fruits, and yielded her fruit every month: and the leaves of the tree were for the healing of the nations.
Revelation 22:1–2.

40 He which testifieth these things saith, Surely I come quickly. Amen. Even so, come, Lord Jesus. The grace of our Lord Jesus Christ be with you all. Amen.
Revelation 22:20–1.

Bible (Vulgate)

A 4c translation of the Bible into Latin, commissioned by Pope Damasus and undertaken by Jerome (382–405). It became known as the *versio vulgata*, the 'common translation', and is still an official text of the Roman Catholic Church. The quotations given here are those that are well known in their Latin form.

41 *Dominus illuminatio mea, et salus mea, quem timebo?*

The Lord is the source of my light and my safety, so whom shall I fear?
Psalm 26:1.

42 *Asperges me hyssopo, et mundabor; lavabis me, et super nivem dealbabor.*

You will sprinkle me with hyssop, and I shall be made clean; you will wash me and I shall be made whiter than snow.
Psalm 50:9 (Psalm 51:7 Authorized Version).

43 *Cantate Domino canticum novum, quia mirabilia fecit.*

Sing to the Lord a new song, because he has done marvellous things.
Psalm 97:1 (Psalm 98:1 Authorized Version).
▷ See Book of Common Prayer 176:69.

44 *Jubilate Deo, omnis terra; servite Domino in laetitia.*

Sing joyfully to God, all the earth; serve the Lord with gladness.
Psalm 99:2 (Psalm 100:2 Authorized Version).
▷ See Book of Common Prayer 177:89.

45 *Beatus vir qui timet Dominum, in mandatis ejus volet nimis!*

Happy is the man who fears the Lord, who is only too willing to follow his orders.
Psalm 111:1 (Psalm 112:1 Authorized Version).

46 *Non nobis, Domine, non nobis; sed nomini tuo da gloriam.*

Not unto us, Lord, not unto us; but to thy name give glory.
Psalm 113 (second part):1 (Psalm 115:1 Authorized Version).

47 *Laudate Dominum, omnes gentes; laudate eum, omnes populi.*

Praise the Lord, all nations; praise him, all people.
Psalm 116:1 (Psalm 117:1 Authorized Version).

48 *Nisi Dominus aedificaverit domum, in vanum laboraverunt qui aedificant eam.*
Nisi Dominus custodierit civitatem, frustra vigilat qui custodit eam.

Unless the Lord has built the house, its builders have laboured in vain. Unless the Lord guards the city, the watchman watches in vain.
Psalm 126:1 (Psalm 127:1 Authorized Version).

49 *De profundis clamavi ad te, Domine; Domine exaudi vocem meam.*

Up from the depths I have cried to thee, Lord; Lord, hear my voice.
Psalm 129:1 (Psalm 130:1 Authorized Version).

50 *Vanitas vanitatum, dixit Ecclesiastes; vanitas vanitatum, et omnia vanitas.*

Vanity of vanities, said the preacher; vanity of vanities, and everything is vanity.
Ecclesiastes 1:2.
▷ See Bible (Old Testament) 122:14.

51 *Rorate, coeli, desuper, et nubes pluant Justum; aperiatur terra, et germinet Salvatorem.*

Drop down dew, heavens, from above, and let the clouds rain down righteousness; let the earth be opened, and a saviour spring to life.
Isiah 45:8.

52 *Benedicite, omnia opera Domini, Domino; laudate et superexaltate eum in secula.*

Bless the Lord, all the works of the Lord; praise him and exalt him above all things for ever.
Daniel 3:57.

53 *Magnificat anima mea Dominum; et exsultavit spiritus meus in Deo salutari meo.*

My soul doth magnify the Lord: and my spirit hath rejoiced in God my Saviour.
St Luke 1:46.

▷ See Bible (New Testament) 141:75.

54 *Esurientes implevit bonis, et divites dimisit inanes.*

He hath filled the hungry with good things: and the rich he hath sent empty away.
St Luke 1.53.

▷ See Bible (New Testament) 141:75.

55 *Nunc dimittis servum tuum, Domine, secundum verbum tuum in pace.*

Lord, now lettest thou thy servant depart in peace: according to thy word.
St Luke 2:29.

▷ See Bible (New Testament) 142:79.

56 *Pax Vobis.*

Peace be unto you.
St Luke 24:36.

57 *Quo vadis?*

Where are you going?
St John 16:5.

58 *Ecce homo.*

Behold the man.
St John 19:5.

59 *Noli me tangere.*

Do not touch me.
St John 20:17.

▷ See Bible (New Testament) 147:75.

Bickerstaffe, Isaac c.1735–c.1812

Irish playwright. An officer of marines, he was dismissed from the service and later forced to flee the country. He is credited with establishing the comic opera in English theatre.

60 And this the burthen of his song,
  For ever used to be,
  I care for nobody, not I,
  If no one cares for me.
1762 *Love in a Village*, act 1, sc.2.

61 'Tis a sure sign that work goes on merrily, when folks sing at it.
1765 *The Maid of the Mill*, act 1, sc.1.

62 Perhaps it was right to dissemble your love,

But—why did you kick me downstairs?
1789 'An Expostulation'.

Biddle, Francis Beverley 1886–1968

US lawyer, Solicitor General (1940) and Attorney General (1941–5). He served as US judge on the Nuremberg trials of war criminals.

63 The Constitution has never greatly bothered any wartime President.
1962 *In Brief Authority.*

Bierce, Ambrose Gwinett 1842–c.1914

US writer and journalist, best known for his *Cynic's Word Book* (1906, retitled *The Devil's Dictionary*, 1911). His collection of stories *Tales of Soldiers and Civilians* (1892) coincided with his divorce and the death of his son in a gunfight. He is thought to have died in Mexico.

64 Accordion, n. An instrument in harmony with the sentiments of an assassin.
1906 *The Cynic's Word Book.* Retitled *The Devil's Dictionary* (1911).

65 Acquaintance, n. A person whom we know well enough to borrow from, but not well enough to lend to.
1906 *The Cynic's Word Book.* Retitled *The Devil's Dictionary* (1911).

66 Advice, n. The smallest current coin.
1906 *The Cynic's Word Book.* Retitled *The Devil's Dictionary* (1911).

67 Alliance, n. In international politics, the union of two thieves who have their hands so deeply inserted in each other's pocket that they cannot separately plunder a third.
1906 *The Cynic's Word Book.* Retitled *The Devil's Dictionary* (1911).

68 Ambition, n. An overmastering desire to be vilified by enemies while living and made ridiculous by friends when dead.
1906 *The Cynic's Word Book.* Retitled *The Devil's Dictionary* (1911).

69 Applause, n. The echo of a platitude.
1906 *The Cynic's Word Book.* Retitled *The Devil's Dictionary* (1911).

70 Battle, n. A method of untying with the teeth a political knot that would not yield to the tongue.
1906 *The Cynic's Word Book.* Retitled *The Devil's Dictionary* (1911).

71 Bore, n. A person who talks when you wish him to listen.
1906 *The Cynic's Word Book.* Retitled *The Devil's Dictionary* (1911).

72 Brain, n. An apparatus with which we think that we think.

1906 *The Cynic's Word Book.* Retitled *The Devil's Dictionary* (1911).

73 Calamities are of two kinds: misfortune to ourselves, and good fortune to others.
1906 *The Cynic's Word Book.* Retitled *The Devil's Dictionary* (1911).

74 Circumlocution, n. A literary trick whereby the writer who has nothing to say breaks it gently to the reader.
1906 *The Cynic's Word Book.* Retitled *The Devil's Dictionary* (1911).

75 Conservative, n. A statesman who is enamoured of existing evils, as distinguished from the Liberal, who wishes to replace them with others.
1906 The Cynic's Word Book. Retitled *The Devil's Dictionary* (1911).

76 Consult, v. t. To seek another's approval of a course already decided upon.
1906 *The Cynic's Word Book.* Retitled *The Devil's Dictionary* (1911).

77 Corporation, n. An ingenious device for obtaining individual profit without individual responsibility.
1906 *The Cynic's Word Book.* Retitled *The Devil's Dictionary* (1911).

78 Cynic, n. A blackguard whose faulty vision sees things as they are, not as they ought to be.
1906 *The Cynic's Word Book.* Retitled *The Devil's Dictionary* (1911).

79 Diplomacy, n. The patriotic art of lying for one's country.
1906 *The Cynic's Word Book.* Retitled *The Devil's Dictionary* (1911).

80 Education, n. That which discloses to the wise and disguises from the foolish their lack of understanding.
1906 *The Cynic's Word Book.* Retitled *The Devil's Dictionary* (1911).

81 Egotist, n. A person of low taste, more interested in himself than in me.
1906 *The Cynic's Word Book.* Retitled *The Devil's Dictionary* (1911).

82 Faith, n. Belief without evidence in what is told by one who speaks, without knowledge, of things without parallel.
1906 *The Cynic's Word Book.* Retitled *The Devil's Dictionary* (1911).

83 Fashion, n. A despot whom the wise ridicule and obey.
1906 *The Cynic's Word Book.* Retitled *The Devil's Dictionary* (1911).

84 Future, n. That period of time in which our affairs prosper, our friends are true and our happiness is assured.
1906 *The Cynic's Word Book.* Retitled *The Devil's Dictionary* (1911).

85 History, n. An account, mostly false, of events, mostly unimportant, which are brought about by rulers, mostly knaves, and soldiers, mostly fools.
1906 *The Cynic's Word Book.* Retitled *The Devil's Dictionary* (1911).

86 Ink, n. A villainous compound…chiefly used to facilitate the infection of idiocy and promote intellectual crime.
1906 *The Cynic's Word Book.* Retitled *The Devil's Dictionary* (1911).

87 Marriage, n. The state or condition of a community consisting of a master, a mistress and two slaves, making in all, two.
1906 *The Cynic's Word Book.* Retitled *The Devil's Dictionary* (1911).

88 Mayonnaise, n. One of the sauces which serve the French in place of a state religion.
1906 *The Cynic's Word Book.* Retitled *The Devil's Dictionary* (1911).

89 Painting, n. The art of protecting flat surfaces from the weather and exposing them to the critic.
1906 *The Cynic's Word Book.* Retitled *The Devil's Dictionary* (1911).

90 Patience, n. A minor form of despair, disguised as a virtue.
1906 *The Cynic's Word Book.* Retitled *The Devil's Dictionary* (1911).

91 Peace, n. In international affairs, a period of cheating between two periods of fighting.
1906 *The Cynic's Word Book.* Retitled *The Devil's Dictionary* (1911).

92 Philosophy, n. A route of many roads leading from nowhere to nothing.
1906 *The Cynic's Word Book.* Retitled *The Devil's Dictionary* (1911).

93 Piano, n. A parlour utensil for subduing the impenitent visitor. It is operated by depressing the keys of the machine and the spirits of the audience.
1906 *The Cynic's Word Book.* Retitled *The Devil's Dictionary* (1911).

94 Positive, adj. Mistaken at the top of one's voice.
1906 *The Cynic's Word Book.* Retitled *The Devil's Dictionary* (1911).

95 Prejudice, n. A vagrant opinion without visible means of support.
1906 *The Cynic's Word Book.* Retitled *The Devil's Dictionary* (1911).

96 Saint, n. A dead sinner revised and edited.

1906 *The Cynic's Word Book.* Retitled *The Devil's Dictionary* (1911).

97 Talk, v.t. To commit an indiscretion without temptation, from an impulse without purpose.

1906 *The Cynic's Word Book.* Retitled *The Devil's Dictionary* (1911).

98 Vote, n. The instrument and symbol of a freeman's power to make a fool of himself and a wreck of his country.

1906 *The Cynic's Word Book.* Retitled *The Devil's Dictionary* (1911).

99 That sovereign of insufferables.

1882 *Wasp*, alluding to Oscar Wilde.

Biko, Stephen 1946–77

South African black civil rights activist, founder of the Black Consciousness Movement. In 1973 he was placed under a banning order, and detained four times. He died in police custody, allegedly as a result of beatings.

1 Whites must be made to realise that they are only human, not superior. It's the same with Blacks. They must be made to realise that they are also human, not inferior.

1977 In the *Boston Globe*, 26 Oct.

Billings, Josh pseudonym of *Henry Wheeler Shaw* 1818–85

US humorist. He became a popular success with *Josh Billings, His Sayings* (1865).

2 Man was kreated a little lower than the angells and has bin gittin a little lower ever since.

1865 *Josh Billings, His Sayings*, ch.28.

3 It ain't often that a man's reputashun outlasts his munny.

1865 *Josh Billings, His Sayings*, ch.39.

4 Mi advise to them who are about tu begin, in arnest, the jurney ov life, is tu take their harte in one hand and a club in the other.

1865 *Josh Billings, His Sayings*, ch.71.

5 Love iz like the meazles; we kant have it bad but onst, and the latter in life we hav it the tuffer it goes with us.

1874 *Josh Billings' Wit and Humour*.

Binyon, (Robert) Laurence 1869–1943

English poet and art critic. He worked at the British Museum (1913–33) and was Norton Professor of Poetry at Harvard (1933–4). He is best remembered for his patriotic elegy 'For The Fallen', which Elgar set to music.

6 With proud thanksgiving, a mother for her children,

England mourns for her dead across the sea.
Flesh of her flesh they were, spirit of her spirit,
Fallen in the cause of the free.

1914 'For the Fallen', in *The Times*, 21 Sep.

7 They shall not grow old, as we that are left grow old:
Age shall not weary them, nor the years condemn.
At the going down of the sun and in the morning
We will remember them.

1914 'For the Fallen', in *The Times*, 21 Sep.

8 Now is the time for the burning of the leaves.

1942 'The Burning of the Leaves'.

9 Rootless hope and fruitless desire are there;
Let them go to the fire, with never a look behind.
The world that was ours is a world that is ours no
   more.

1942 'The Burning of the Leaves'.

10 Earth cares for her own ruins, naught for ours.
Nothing is certain, only the certain spring.

1942 'The Burning of the Leaves'.

Bioy Casares, Adolfo 1914–99

Argentinian fiction writer, known for his life-long association with Jorge Luis Borges, with whom he published several anthologies and works of fiction. His own writings are examples of fantastic literature.

11 *La eternidad rotativa puede parecer atroz al espectador; es satisfactoria para sus individuos. Libres de malas noticias y de enfermedades, viven siempre como si fuera la primera vez, sin recordar las anteriores.*

A circular eternity may seem atrocious to the spectator, but it is satisfactory to individuals inside. Free from bad news and disease, they always live as if it were the first time, and do not remember previous times.

1940 *La invención de Morel (The Invention of Morel*, 1964).

Bird, Isabella married name *Isabella Bishop* 1831–1904

English traveller. She travelled and climbed in Australasia, America and the East; then returned to England to marry. When her husband died in 1886, she set off for Tibet and in 1890 travelled between Persia and the Black Sea. In 1894–7 she again visited the Far East, founding hospitals and orphanages, and her last journey was to Africa.

12 A man who any woman might love, but who no sane woman would marry.

1879 Of Rocky Mountain Jim, her guide on her travels on horseback through the Rockies. *A Lady's Life in the Rocky Mountains*.

13 One eye was entirely gone, and the loss made one side of the face repulsive, while the other might have been modelled in marble. 'Desperado' was written in large letters all over him. I almost repented of having sought his acquaintance.

1879 Of Rocky Mountain Jim, her guide on her travels on horseback through the Rockies. *A Lady's Life in the Rocky Mountains.*

14 I am well as long as I live on horseback…sleep out-of-doors, or in a log cabin, and lead in all respects a completely unconventional life. But each time for a few days…I have become civilised, I have found myself rapidly going down again.

1879 *A Lady's Life in the Rocky Mountains.*

15 Japan offers as much novelty perhaps as an excursion to another planet.

1880 *Unbeaten Tracks in Japan: An Account of Travels on Horseback in the Interior 1880* (published 1885).

16 Appropriating the fruits of Christian civilisation, but rejecting the tree from which they spring.

1880 *Unbeaten Tracks in Japan: An Account of Travels on Horseback in the Interior 1880* (published 1885).

17 It is singular that the Japanese, who rarely commit a solecism in taste in their national costume, architecture, or decorative art, seem to be perfectly destitute of perception when they borrow ours.

1880 *Unbeaten Tracks in Japan: An Account of Travels on Horseback in the Interior 1880* (published 1885).

Birkenhead, F(rederick) E(dwin) Smith, 1st Earl of 1872–1930

English Conservative politician and lawyer, a brilliant orator. In the Irish crisis (1914) he opposed Home Rule, but helped to negotiate the Settlement of 1921. He resigned after criticism over his conduct as Secretary of State for India (1924–8) to pursue commerce.

18 The world continues to offer glittering prizes to those who have stout hearts and stout swords.

1923 Rectorial address, Glasgow University, 7 Nov.

19 We have the highest authority for believing that the meek shall inherit the Earth; though I have never found any particular corroboration of this aphorism in the records of Somerset House.

1924 *Contemporary Personalities,* 'Marquess Curzon'.

20 As a matter of fact, we both are, and the only difference between us is that I am trying to be, and you can't help it.

In response to a judge's observation that Smith was being 'extremely offensive'. Quoted in 2nd Earl of Birkenhead *Frederick Edwin Earl of Birkenhead,* vol.1, ch.9 (1933).

21 It is not for me, Your Honour, to attempt to fathom the inscrutable workings of Providence.

In reply to a judge's testy inquiry 'What do you suppose I am on the Bench for, Mr Smith?'. Quoted in 2nd Earl of Birkenhead *F. E.: The Life of F. E. Smith, First Earl of Birkenhead,* ch. 9 (1959).

22 Possibly not, My Lord, but far better informed.

In reply to a judge who had complained 'I have read your case, Mr Smith, and I am no wiser now than I was when I started'. Quoted in 2nd Earl of Birkenhead *F. E.: The Life of F. E. Smith, First Earl of Birkenhead,* ch. 9 (1959).

23 I do not deal with subtleties; I am only a lawyer.

Quoted in Richard Fountain *The Wit of the Wig* (1968).

24 He has devoted the best years of his life to preparing his impromptu speeches.

Of Winston Churchill. Attributed.

Birney, Earle 1904–95

Canadian poet, Professor at the universities of Toronto and, after World War II, British Columbia. His first work was *David and Other Poems* (1942).

25 And now he could only
bar himself in and wait
for the great flint to come singing into his heart.

1952 'Bushed'.

26 Through the cold time
she holds me
with evergreen
devotion
she bears up my whiteness.

1977 'She Is'.

Birns, Harold

New York City Buildings Commissioner.

27 OG = PLR × AEB: the opportunity for graft equals the plethora of legal requirements multiplied by the number of architects, engineers and builders.

1963 Formula for bribery in building and housing codes. In the *New York Times,* 2 Oct.

Biro, Lajos 1880–1948

Hungarian screenwriter. He worked for Alexander Korda during the 1930s on various films, including *The Private Life of Henry VIII* (1933) and *The Four Feathers* (1939).

28 The things I've done for England.

1933 Line delivered by Charles Laughton as Henry VIII to Else Lanchester as Anne of Cleves in *The Private Life of Henry VIII* (with Arthur Wimperis).

Bishop, Elizabeth 1911–79

US poet. Her work is highly regarded for its precision, elegance and imagination.

29 The ship's ignored. The iceberg rises
and sinks again; its glassy pinnacles
correct elliptics in the sky.
This is a scene where he who treads the boards
is artlessly rhetorical.

1946 'The Imaginary Iceberg'.

30 The armoured cars of dreams, contrived to let us do

so many a dangerous thing.
1946 'Sleeping Standing Up'.

31 All the untidy activity continues,
awful but cheerful.
1955 'The Bight'.

32 Come like a light in the white mackerel sky,
come like a daytime comet
with a long unnebulous train of words,
from Brooklyn, over the Brooklyn Bridge, on this
fine morning,
please come flying.
1955 'Invitation to Miss Marianne Moore'.

33 What childishness is it that while there's breath of
life
in our bodies, we are determined to rush
to see the sun the other way round?
1965 'Questions of Travel'.

34 Oh, must we dream our dreams
and have them, too?
1965 'Questions of Travel'.

35 The art of losing isn't hard to master;
so many things seem filled with the intent
to be lost that their loss is no disaster.
1969 'One Art'.

Bishop, Jim 1907–87

US Syndicated columnist.

36 A good writer is not, per se, a good book critic. No
more so than a good drunk is automatically a good
bartender.
1957 In the *Journal-American*, 26 Nov.

37 The peeping Tom of the sciences…men who care
not where they are going: they merely want to
know where everyone else has been.
1961 Of archaeology. In the *Journal American*, 14 Mar.

Bismarck, Otto Edward Leopold, Fürst von (Prince of) 1815–98

Prussian statesman, Prime Minister of Prussia. He
expanded territory at the expense of Denmark and
Austria, forming a new German Empire of which he was
Chancellor (1871–90) until he resigned, disapproving of
the policies of the new Kaiser, Wilhelm II.

38 The great questions of our day cannot be solved by
speeches and majority votes but by iron and blood.
1862 Speech to the Prussian Chamber, 30 Sep. He later altered
the concluding words to the more commonly quoted 'blood and
iron'.

39 Politics is not an exact science.
1863 Speech to the Prussian Chamber, 18 Dec.

40 Anyone who has ever looked into the glazed eyes of
a soldier dying on the battlefield will think hard
before starting a war.
1867 Speech, Berlin, Aug.

41 If we are to negotiate, I envisage that we shall play
an essentially modest role; that of an honest broker
who really intends to do business.
1878 Speech to the Reichstag, 19 Feb, on preventing war in
Europe.

42 If there is ever another war in Europe, it will come
out of some damned silly thing in the Balkans.
1898 Attributed deathbed remark. Quoted in the House of
Commons, 16 Aug 1945.

43 My map of Africa lies in Europe. Here lies Russia
and here lies France, and we are in the middle. That
is my map of Africa.
Remarking on his preoccupation with European, as opposed to
colonial territorial concerns. Quoted in A J P Taylor *The
Struggle for Mastery in Europe 1848–1918* (1954), p.294.

Bissell, Claude T(homas) 1916–

Canadian scholar and university administrator, President
of the University of Toronto (1958–71).

44 It's ironical that the first people to demand free
speech are the first people to deny it to others.
1969 Of student protesters who disrupted the appearance of
Clark Kerr, former President of Berkeley, at the University of
Toronto, 5 Feb. Recalled in *Halfway up Parnassus* (1974).

Black, Arthur 1943–

Canadian broadcaster and humorist.

45 I predict that ashtrays will become as obsolete as
spitoons in our lifetime.
1989 *That Old Black Magic*, 'Smoking Can be Dangerous to
Your Health'.

Black, Conrad 1944–

Canadian newspaper proprietor. He acquired the *Daily
Telegraph* group in 1985. His works include *A Life in
Progress* (1994).

46 Journalists as a group, unlike all other powerful
groups, require some protection from themselves,
and from their own excesses.
Speech, Annual Dinner of the Canadian Press, 20 Apr, reported
in the *Globe and Mail* the following day.

Black, Hugo LaFayette 1886–1971

US lawyer, senator (1927–37) and Associate Justice of the
US Supreme Court (1937–71). He strongly supported
civil liberties.

47 Without deviation, without exception, without any
ifs, buts, or whereases, freedom of speech means
you shall not do something to people for views they
have, express, speak, or write.

Quoted in Irving Dillard (ed) *One Man's Stand for Freedom* (1963).

Blacker, Valentine 1728–1823

Anglo-Irish soldier.

48 Put your trust in God, my boys, and keep your powder dry.

'Oliver's Advice', collected in E Hayes *Ballads of Ireland* (1856), vol.1, p.192. The words are sometimes attributed to Oliver Cromwell.

▷ See Forgy 397:25.

Blackstone, Sir William 1723–80

English jurist. Called to the bar in 1746, he became King's Counsel and MP (both 1761), Solicitor-General (1763) and a judge of the court of common pleas (1770). He published *Commentaries on the Laws of England* (1765–9).

49 It is better that ten guilty persons escape than one innocent suffer.

1769 *Commentaries on the Laws of England*, vol.4, ch. 27. A puzzled visitor is apocryphally said to have remarked, 'Better for whom?'

Blainey, Geoffrey Norman 1930–

Australian economic historian and social commentator. He showed in *The Tyranny of Distance* (1966) how geographical isolation had shaped Australian history and people.

50 The Tyranny of Distance.

1966 Title of book.

Blair, Hamish pseudonym of *Andrew James Fraser Blair* 1872–1935

Scottish author and journalist. He moved from England to India where he founded *Empire* (1906) and the *Eastern Bureau* (1912). He wrote a number of short stories as well as articles, sketches and light verse.

51 This bloody town's a bloody cuss—
No bloody trains, no bloody bus,
And no one cares for bloody us—
In bloody Orkney.

1952 'The Bloody Orkneys', stanza 1. First published in Arnold Silcock *Verse and Worse*, 'Queer People'.

52 Best bloody place is bloody bed,
With bloody ice on bloody head,
You might as well be bloody dead,
In bloody Orkney.

1952 'The Bloody Orkneys', last stanza. First published in Arnold Silcock *Verse and Worse*, 'Queer People'.

Blair, Tony (Anthony Charles Lynton) 1953–

Scottish-born Labour politician and barrister, elected Prime Minister in 1997.

53 Labour is the Party of law and order in Britain today—tough on crime and tough on the causes of crime.

1993 Speech as Shadow Home Secretary, Labour Party Conference, Sep.

Blake, Eubie James Hubert 1883–1983

US jazz musician.

54 If I'd known I was gonna live this long, I'd have taken better care of myself.

1983 Quoted in *The Observer*, 13 Feb. He died 5 days after his 100th birthday.

Blake, William 1757–1827

English poet, painter, engraver and mystic. His works range from the lyrical *Songs of Innocence* (1789) and *Songs of Experience* (1794) to the mystical poems of *The Marriage of Heaven and Hell* (1791). His best-known engravings are in *The Illustrations to the Book of Job* (1826).

55 Whether on Ida's shady brow,
Or in the chambers of the East,
The chambers of the sun that now
From ancient melody have ceased.

1783 *Poetical Sketches*, 'To The Muses'.

56 How have you left the ancient love
That bards of old enjoyed in you!
The sound is forced, the notes are few!

1783 *Poetical Sketches*, 'To The Muses'.

57 The hills tell each other, and the listening
Valleys hear; all our longing eyes are turned
Up to thy holy feet visit our clime.
Come o'er the eastern hills and let our winds
Kiss thy perfumed garments; let us taste
Thy morn and evening breath. Scatter thy pearls
Upon our love-sick land that mourns for thee.

1783 *Poetical Sketches*, 'To Spring'.

58 O thou who passest through our valleys in
Thy strength, curb thy fierce steeds, ally the heat
That flames from their large nostrils! thou, O Summer,
Beneath our oaks hast slept while we beheld
With joy thy ruddy limbs and flourishing hair.

1783 *Poetical Sketches*, 'To Summer'.

59 O Autumn, laden with fruit, and stained
With the blood of grape, pass not, but sit
Beneath my shady roof; there thou may'st rest,
And tune thy jolly voice to my fresh pipe,
And all the daughters of the year shall dance!
Sing now the lusty song of fruits and flowers

1783 *Poetical Sketches*, 'To Autumn'.

60 O Winter! bar thine adamantine doors.

The north is thine— there hast thou built thy dark
Deep-founded habitation. Shake not thy roofs,
Nor bend thy pillars with thine iron car.
1783 *Poetical Sketches*, 'To Winter'.

61 Does the eagel know what's in the pit
Or wilt thou go ask the mole?
Can wisdom be put in a silver rod,
Or Love in a golden bowl.
1789 Thel's Motto. *The Book of Thel*.

62 Piping down the valleys wild,
Piping songs of pleasant glee,
On a cloud I saw a child,
And he laughing said to me,
'Pipe a song about a lamb!'
So I piped with merry cheer.
'Piper, pipe that song again!'
So I piped. He wept to hear.
1789 *Songs of Innocence*, 'Introduction'.

63 Little lamb, who made thee?
Dost thou know who made thee?
Gave thee life and bid thee feed
By the stream and o'er the mead;
Gave thee clothing of delight,
Softest clothing, woolly, bright;
Gave thee such a tender voice,
Making all the vales rejoice?
Little lamb, who made thee?
Dost thou know who made thee?
1789 *Songs of Innocence*, 'The Lamb'.

64 My mother bore me in the southern wild,
And I am black, but O! my soul is white;
White as an angel is the English child,
But I am black as if bereaved of light.
1789 *Songs of Innocence*, 'The Little Black Boy'.

65 And all must love the human form,
In heathen, Turk or Jew;
Where mercy, Love and Pity dwell
There God is dwelling too.
1789 *Songs of Innocence*, 'The Divine Image'.

66 When my mother died I was very young,
And my father sold me while yet my tongue
Could scarcely cry weep weep weep weep.
So your chimneys I sweep, and in soot I sleep.
1789 *Songs of Innocence*, 'The Chimney Sweep'.

67 'Father! father! where are you going?
O do not walk so fast.
Speak, father, speak to your little boy,
Or else I shall be lost.'
1789 *Songs of Innocence*, 'The Little Boy Lost'.

68 He kissed the hand and by the hand led
And to his mother brought,

Who in sorrow pale, through the lonely dale,
Her little boy weeping sought.
1789 *Songs of Innocence*, 'The Little Boy Found'.

69 For Mercy has a human heart
Pity a human face:
And Love, the human form divine,
And Peace, the human dress.
1789 *Songs of Innocence*, 'The Divine Image'.

70 Then cherish pity, lest you drive an angel from your
door.
1789 *Songs of Innocence*, 'Holy Thursday'.

71 Without contraries is no progression. Attraction
and repulsion, reason and energy, love and hate, are
necessary to human existence.
1790 *The Marriage of Heaven and Hell*, 'The Argument'.

72 Energy is Eternal Delight.
1790 *The Marriage of Heaven and Hell*, 'The Voice of the
Devil'.

73 The road of excess leads to the palace of wisdom.
1790 *The Marriage of Heaven and Hell*, 'Proverbs of Hell'.

74 He who desires and acts not, breeds pestilence.
1790 *The Marriage of Heaven and Hell*, 'Proverbs of Hell'.

75 Eternity is in love with the productions of time.
1790 *The Marriage of Heaven and Hell*, 'Proverbs of Hell'.

76 Prisons are built with stones of Law, brothels with
bricks of Religion.
1790 *The Marriage of Heaven and Hell*, 'Proverbs of Hell'.

77 The tygers of wrath are wiser than the horses of
instruction.
1790 *The Marriage of Heaven and Hell*, 'Proverbs of Hell'.

78 The Pride of the peacock is the glory of God.
The lust of the goat is the bounty of God.
The wrath of the lion is the wisdom of God.
The nakedness of woman is the work of God.
1790 *The Marriage of Heaven and Hell*, 'Proverbs of Hell'.

79 Sooner murder an infant in its cradle than nurse
unacted desires.
1790 *The Marriage of Heaven and Hell*, 'Proverbs of Hell'.

80 If the doors of perception were cleansed everything
would appear to man as it is, infinite.
1790 *The Marriage of Heaven and Hell*, 'A Memorable Fancy',
plate 14. Aldous Huxley used this phrase as the title of his work
The Doors of Perception (1954).

81 Mutual forgiveness of each vice,
Such are the Gates of Paradise.
1793 *The Gates of Paradise*, prologue.

82 He who binds to himself a Joy

Doth the winged life destroy;
But he who kisses the Joy as it flies
Lives in Eternity's sunrise
1793 *MS Notebooks*, p.105.

83 Never pain to tell thy love
Love that never told can be;
For the gentle wind does move
Silently, invisably.
1793 *MS Notebooks*, p.115.

84 Hear the voice of the Bard!
Who presents, past and future sees.
1794 *Songs of Experience*, 'Introduction'.

85 Love seeketh not itself to please,
Nor for itself hath any care,
But for another gives its ease,
And builds a heaven in hell's despair.
1794 *Songs of Experience*, 'The Clod and the Pebble'.

86 Love seeketh only self to please,
To bind another to its delight,
Joys in another's loss of ease
And builds a hell in heaven's despite.
1794 *Songs of Experience*, 'The Clod and the Pebble'.

87 Ah, sunflower, weary of time,
Who countest the steps of the sun,
Seeking after that sweet golden clime
Where the traveller's journey is done;
Where the youth pined away with desire
And the pale virgin shrouded in snow
Arise from their graves, and aspire
Where my sunflower wishes to go.
1794 *Songs of Experience*, 'Ah! Sunflower'.

88 O rose, thou art sick!
The invisible worm
That flies in the night,
In the howling storm,
Has found out thy bed
Of crimson joy,
And his dark secret love
Does thy life destroy.
1794 *Songs of Experience*, 'The Sick Rose'.

89 Is this a holy thing to see
In a rich fruitful land,
Babes reduced to misery,
Fed with cold and usurous hand?
1794 *Songs of Experience*, 'Holy Thursday'.

90 I went to the Garden of Love,
And saw what I never had seen:
A chapel was built in the midst
Where I used to play on the green.
1794 *Songs of Experience*, 'The Garden of Love'.

91 And I saw it was filled with graves,

And tomb-stones where flowers should be;
And priests in black gowns were walking their
rounds,
And blinding with briars my joys and desires.
1794 *Songs of Experience*, 'The Garden of Love'.

92 I wander through each charter'd street,
Near where the charter'd Thames does flow,
And mark in every face I meet
Marks of weakness, marks of woe.
1794 *Songs of Experience*, 'London'.

93 I was angry with my friend:
I told my wrath, my wrath did end.
I was angry with my foe:
I told it not, my wrath did grow.
1794 *Songs of Experience*, 'A Poison Tree'.

94 My mother groaned! my father wept.
Into the dangerous world I leapt,
Helpless, naked, piping loud
Like a fiend hid in a cloud.
1794 *Songs of Experience*, 'Infant Sorrow'.

95 Tyger! Tyger! burning bright
In the forests of the night,
What immortal hand or eye
Could frame thy fearful symmetry?
1794 *Songs of Experience*, 'The Tyger'.

96 When the stars threw down their spears,
And watered heaven with their tears,
Did he smile his work to see?
Did he who made the Lamb make thee?
1794 *Songs of Experience*, 'The Tyger'.

97 Dear Mother, dear Mother, the Church is cold,
But the Ale-house is healthy and pleasant and
warm.
1794 *Songs of Experience*, 'The Little Vagabond'.

98 O why was I born with a different face?
Why was I not born like the rest of my race?
1803 Letter to Thomas Butts, 16 Aug.

99 Mock on, mock on, Voltaire Rousseau;
Mock on , mock on, 'tis all in vain!
You throw the sand against the wind,
And the wind clows it back again.
1800–3 *MS Notebooks*, p.7.

1 To see a world in a grain of sand,
And heaven in a wild flower,
Hold infinity in the palm of your hand,
And eternity in an hour.
c.1803 *Auguries of Innocence*, l.1-4.

2 A robin red breast in a cage
Puts all Heaven in a rage.
c.1803 *Auguries of Innocence*, l.5–6.

3 Man was made for Joy and Woe,
  And when this we rightly know,
  Thro' the world we safely go.
  Joy and Woe are woven fine,
  A clothing for the soul divine.
  c.1803 *Auguries of Innocence*, l. 56–60.

4 The strongest poison ever known
  Came from Ceasar's laurel crown.
  c.1804 *Auguries of Innocence*, l.97–8.

5 The whore and gambler, by the state
  Licensed build that nation's fate.
  The harlot's cry from street to street
  Shall weave old England's winding sheet.
  c.1804 *Auguries of Innocence*, l.113–6.

6 We are led to believe a Lie
  When we see with, not thro' the Eye.
  c.1803 *Auguries of Innocence*, l.125–6

7 The fields from Islington to Marybone,
  To Primrose Hill and Saint John's Wood,
  Were builded over with pillars of gold;
  And there Jerusalem's pillars stood.
  c.1804–7 *Jerusalem*, plate 27.

8 He who would do good to another man must do it
    in Minute Particulars.
  General Good is the plea of the scoundrel,
    hypocrite, and flatterer;
  For Art and Science cannot exist but in minutely
    organized Particulars.
  1804–7 *Jerusalem*, plate 55.

9 I gave you the end of the golden string;
  Only wind it into a ball,
  It will lead you in at Heaven's gate,
  Built in Jerusalem's wall.
  c.1804–7 *Jerusalem*, plate 77.

10 I care not whether a man is good or evil; all that I
    care
  Is whether he is a wise man is a fool. Go! put off
    Holiness,
  And put on intellect, or my thunderous hammer
    shall drive thee,
  To wrath which thou condemnest, till thou obey
    my voice.
  c.1804–7 *Jerusalem*, plate 91.

11 Painters are noted for being dissipated and wild.
  c.1808 *Annotations to Sir Joshua Reynolds' Discourses.*

12 The man who never in his mind and thoughts
  travelled to heaven is no artist.
  c.1808 *Annotations to Sir Joshua Reynolds' Discourses.*

13 What has Reasoning to do with the Art of Painting?
  c.1808 *Annotations to Sir Joshua Reynolds' Discourses.*

14 Knowledge of ideal beauty is not to be acquired. It
  is born with us. Innate ideas are in every man, born
  with him; they are truly himself.
  c.1808 *Annotations to Sir Joshua Reynolds' Discourses.*

15 When Sir Joshua Reynolds died
  All Nature was degraded;
  The King dropp'd a tear into the Queen's ear,
  And all his pictures faded.
  c.1808 *Annotations to Sir Joshua Reynolds' Discourses.*

16 Thy friendship oft has made my heart to ache:
  Do be my enemy—for friendship's sake.
  1808–11
  MS Notebooks, 'To H[ayley]', p.37.

17 And did those feet in ancient time
  Walk upon England's mountains green?
  And was the holy Lamb of God
  On England's pleasant pastures seen?
  1809 *Milton*, preface. Stanza 1.

18 And did the Countenance Divine
  Shine forth upon our clouded hills?
  And was Jerusalem builded here
  Among these dark Satanic mills?
  1809 *Milton*, preface. Stanza 2.

19 Bring me my bow of burning gold!
  Bring me my arrows of desire!
  Bring me my spear! O clouds, unfold!
  Bring me my chariot of fire!
  1809 *Milton*, preface. Stanza 3.

20 I will not cease from mental fight,
  Nor shall my sword sleep in my hand,
  Till we have built Jerusalem
  In England's green and pleasant land.
  1809 *Milton*, preface. Stanza 4.

21 God appears and God is light
  To those poor souls who dwell in night,
  But does a human form display
  To those who dwell in realms of day.
  1809 *Milton*, 'And Did Those Feet In Ancient Time'.

Blanch, Lesley 1907–

English biographer, traveller and cookery writer.

22 She was an Amazon. Her whole life was spent
  riding at breakneck speed towards the wilder shores
  of love.
  1954 *The Wilder Shores of Love*, pt.2, ch.1.

Blanchflower, Danny (Robert Dennio)
1926–93

Northern Ireland-born footballer. He won numerous
titles as captain of Tottenham Hotspur in the early 1960s

and collected a total of 56 caps playing for Northern Ireland before retiring to become a noted football commentator and columnist.

23 We try to equalize before the others have scored.
    1958 Explaining his tactics as captain of Northern Ireland. Quoted in Colin Jarman *The Guinness Dictionary of Sports Quotations* (1990).

24 The great fallacy is that the game is first and last about winning. It's nothing of the kind. The game is about glory. It's about doing things in style, with a flourish, about going out and beating the other lot, not waiting for them to die of boredom.
    Quoted in Hunter Davis *The Glory Game* (1972).

Blass, Bill (William Ralph) 1922–

US fashion designer.

25 When in doubt wear red.
    1982 In news summaries, 31 Dec.

Blavatsky, Helena Petrovna 1831–91

Russian-born mystic, founder of the Theosophical Society. Her books include *The Secret Doctrine* and *Isis Unveiled*.

26 'Theosophy' is the essence of all religion and of absolute truth, a drop of which only underlies every creed.
    1889 *The Key to Theosophy.*

27 Theosophy, on earth, is like the white ray of the spectrum, and each religion only one of the seven colours.
    1889 *The Key to Theosophy.*

Blest Gana, Alberto 1830–1920

Chilean novelist and Ambassador to France and England. He lived in Paris until the end of his career. He pioneered the documentary social novel in Spanish American literature.

28 *Entre nosotros el dinero ha hecho desaparecer más preocupaciones de familia que en las viejas sociedades europeas. En éstas hay lo que llaman aristocracia de dinero, que jamás alcanza con su poder…a hacer olvidar enteramente la oscuridad de la cuna, al paso que en Chile…todo va cediendo su puesto a la riqueza.*

    Among us, money has dissolved more worries than among ancient European societies. The latter have what they call the moneyed aristocracy, which, despite all its power, never gets to forget its humble origins; on the other hand, in Chile everything yields to wealth.
    1862 *Martín Rivas*, ch.2 (translated 1918).

Blinder, Alan 1945–

US economist, Professor at Princeton University and Vice Chair of the Federal Reserve System Board.

29 Economists have the least influence on policy where they know the most and are most agreed…the most influence on policy where they know the least and disagree most.
    1987 *Hard Heads, Soft Hearts.*

30 If you try to give an on-the-one-hand-or-the-other-hand answer, only one of the hands tends to get quoted.
    1995 On economic forecasting. In the *Wall Street Journal*, 23 Jun.

Bliss, Sir Arthur 1891–1975

English composer, music director of the BBC (1942–4) and Master of the Queen's Musick (from 1953). His compositions, sometimes avant-garde, included ballets, an opera, chamber music and film scores.

31 The jazz band can be used for artificial excitement and aphrodisiac purposes, but not for spreading eternal truths.
    1941 'Music Policy'.

Blixen, Karen, Baroness pseudonym
Isak Dinesen 1885–1962

Danish novelist and story teller. Her book *Out of Africa* (1938) is set on the Kenyan coffee plantation she managed with her husband (also cousin) Baron Bror Blixen. She was divorced in 1921, and returned to Denmark in 1931.

32 What is man, when you come to think upon him, but a minutely set, ingenious machine for turning, with infinite artfulness, the red wine of Shiraz into urine?
    1934 *Seven Gothic Tales*, 'The Dreamers'.

33 The true aristocracy and the true proletariat of the world are both in understanding with tragedy. To them it is the fundamental principle of God, and the key, the minor key, to existence. They differ in this way from the bourgeoisie of all classes, who deny tragedy, who will not tolerate it, and to whom the word tragedy means in itself unpleasantness.
    1937 *Out of Africa*, pt.5, ch.1.

Bloom, Allan 1930–92

US writer and educator, Professor of Political Science at the University of Chicago. His best-known work is *The Closing of the American Mind* (1987).

34 The liberally educated person is one who is able to resist the easy and preferred answers, not because he is obstinate but because he knows others worthy of consideration.
    1987 *The Closing of the American Mind*, preface.

35 Education is the taming or demonstration of the soul's raw passions—not suppressing them or

excising them, which would deprive the soul of its energy—but forming and informing them as art.

1987 *The Closing of the American Mind.*

Bloom, André Borisovich, Anthony, Metropolitan of Sourozh 1914–

Russian churchman and writer, Head of the Russian Orthodox Church in Great Britain and Ireland.

36 It is not the constant thought of their sins, but the vision of the holiness of God that makes the saints aware of their own sinfulness.

1966 *Living Prayer.*

37 A miracle is not the breaking of the laws of the fallen world. It is the re-establishment of the laws of the kingdom.

1966 *Living Prayer.*

Bloom, Harold 1930–

US literary critic and writer, Professor of English (1965–77) and Humanities (1974–) at Yale. His many works include *The Breaking of the Vessels* (1981).

38 The most beautiful prose paragraph yet written by any American.

1991 On the opening of ch.19 of Mark Twain's *Huckleberry Finn*. *The Western Canon.*

Blough, Roger M(iles) 1904–85

US industrialist.

39 Steel prices cause inflation like wet sidewalks cause rain.

1967 In *Forbes*, 1 Aug.

Blunden, Edmund Charles 1896–1974

English poet and critic. He served in World War I, an experience reflected both in his poetry and in his prose work *Undertones of War* (1928), but is essentially a nature poet.

40 All things they have in common, being so poor, And their one fear, Death's shadow at the door. Each sundown makes them mournful, each sunrise Brings back the brightness in their failing eyes.

1920 'Almswomen'.

41 And night this toppling reed, still as the dead The great pike lies, the murderous patriarch, Watching the water-pit shelving and dark Where through the plash his lithe bright vassals tread.

1920 'The Pike'.

42 Unrecorded, unrenowned, Men from whom my ways begin, Here I know you by your ground But I know you not within—

There is silence, there survives Not a moment of your lives.

1922 'Forefathers'.

43 Then is not death at watch Within those secret waters? What wants he but to catch Earth's heedless sons and daughters?

1925 'The Midnight Skaters'.

44 Dance on this ball-floor thin and wan, Use him as though you love him; Court him, elude him, reel and pass, And let him hate you through the glass.

1925 'The Midnight Skaters'.

45 Cuinchy…was a slaughter yard… Who that had been there for but a few hours could ever forget the sullen sorcery and mad lineaments of Cuinchy?

1928 *Undertones of War*, 'IV. The Sudden Depths'. Cuinchy, near Arras, was the scene of heavy fighting in 1914.

46 This was my country and it may be yet, But something flew between me and the sun.

1928 'The Resignation'.

47 I have been young, and now am not too old; And I have seen the righteous forsaken, His health, his honour and his quality taken. This is not what we were formerly told.

1929 'Report On Experience'.

48 Mastery in poetry consists largely in the instinct for not ruining or smothering or tinkering with moments of vision.

1930 'Leigh Hunt'.

49 I am for the woods against the world, But are the woods for me?

1931 'The Kiss'.

50 Cricket to us was more than play, It was a worship in the summer sun.

'Pride of the Village'. Quoted in Alan Ross (ed) *The Penguin Cricketer's Companion* (1978).

Blythe, Ronald George 1922–

English writer. He is best known for his book *Akenfield*, a portrait of an English village told in interviews with linking commentary.

51 As for the British churchman, he goes to church as he goes to the bathroom, with the minimum of fuss and with no explanation if he can help it.

1963 *The Age of Illusion*, ch.12.

52 An industrial worker would sooner have a £5 note but a countryman must have praise.

1969 *Akenfield*, ch.5.

53 Suffolk used to worship Sunday, not God.

1969 *Akenfield*, ch.6.

54 One of the reasons why old people make so many journeys into the past is to satisfy themselves that it is still there.

1979 *The View in Winter*, introduction.

Boccioni, Umberto 1882–1916

Italian artist, futurist painter and sculptor. A key figure in the drafting of the Futurist Manifesto (1910), he later turned to sculpture, attempting to convey motion and light in three-dimensional form.

55 It is necessary to destroy the pretended nobility, entirely literary and traditional, of marble and bronze… The sculptor can use twenty different materials, or even more, in a single work, provided that the plastic emotion requires it.

1912 In the *Technical Manifesto of Futurist Sculpture* (11 Apr, Milan).

Bodenheim, Maxwell 1892–1954

US writer and critic.

56 Poetry is the impish attempt to paint the color of the wind.

Quoted in Ben Hecht's play *Winkelberg* (1958).

Boethius, Anicius Manlius Severinus c.480–524 AD

Roman philosopher and statesman. Under Theodoric he became consul and later chief minister, but was accused of treason and executed. While in prison he wrote *De consolatione philosophiae* (*The Consolation of Philosophy*).

57 *Nam in omni adversitate fortunae infelicissimum est genus infortunii, fuisse felicem.*

In all adversity of fortune, the most wretched kind is once to have been happy.

523 *De consolatione philosophiae*, bk.2, pt.4 (translated by V E Watts).

Bogan, Louise 1897–1970

US poet and critic, poetry editor of the *New Yorker* for many years. Her work is intense and deeply personal.

58 Women have no wideness in them
They are provident instead,
Content in the tight hot cell of their hearts
To eat dusty bread.

1923 'Women'.

59 But childhood prolonged cannot remain a fairyland. It becomes a hell.

1940 On Katherine Mansfield. 'Childhood's False Eden'.

60 The intellectual…is the fine nervous flower of the bourgeoisie.

1943 'Some Notes on Popular and Unpopular Poetry'.

Bogart, John B 1848–1921

US journalist, an early editor of the *New York Sun*.

61 When a dog bites a man, that is not news, because it happens so often. But if a man bites a dog, that is news.

Quoted in F M O'Brien *The Story of the Sun* (1918), ch.10. The phrase is often attributed to Charles A Dana.

Bohlen, Charles Eustis 1904–74

US diplomat and Soviet specialist, Ambassador to Russia (1953–7, 1959–61).

62 A non-Communist premier with Communist ministers would be like a woman trying to stay half pregnant.

Of Winston Churchill's suggestion that the West share spheres of influence with Joseph Stalin in the post-war development of the Balkans. Quoted in Walter Isaacson and Evan Thomas *The Wise Men* (1986).

63 There are two ways you can tell when a man is lying…when he says he can drink champagne all night and not get drunk…[and] when he says he understands Russians.

Quoted in the *New York Times*, 26 Dec 1993.

Boileau (Despréaux), Nicolas 1636–1711

French critic. His works include satires (1660–6), epistles, critical dissertations (particularly the influential *L'Art poétique*, 'The Art of Poetry', 1674), epigrams and translations.

64 *Si j'écris quatre mots, j'en effacerai trois.*

If I write four words, I strike out three of them.

1665 *Satire no.2 A M. Molière*.

65 Often, the fear of one evil leads us into inflicting one that is worse.

1674 *L'Art poétique*.

Bok, Derek 1930–

US educator, President of Harvard University (1971–91) and Professor Emeritus there from 1991. His works include *Beyond the Ivory Tower: Social Responsibilities of the Modern University* (1982).

66 If you think education is expensive—try ignorance.

1979 In *Town and Country*, May.

Bold, Alan 1943–

Scottish poet, biographer and critic, a prolific full-time writer and anthologizer since 1967. He wrote an award-winning biography of Hugh MacDiarmid (1989).

67 In Scotland, land of the omnipotent No.

1969 'A Memory of Death'.

68 That which once united man

Now drives him apart. We are not helpless
Creatures crashing onwards irresistibly to doom.
There is time for everything and time to chose
For everything. We are that time, that choice.
Everybody gets what he deserves.

1969 'June 1967 at Buchenwald'.

69 The poet lives as long as his lines are imprinted on
the minds of his readers.

1989 *MacDairmid*, epilogue.

Bolingbroke, Henry St John, 1st Viscount
1678–1751

English Jacobite statesman, joint leader of the Tory Party.
On the death of Queen Anne he fled to France, where he
wrote *Reflections on Exile* (1714). He also wrote the
influential *Idea of a Patriot King* (1749).

70 What a world is this, and how does fortune banter
us!

1714 Letter to Jonathan Swift, 3 Aug.

71 Faction is to party what the superlative is to the
positive. Party is a political evil, and faction is the
worst of all parties.

1738 *Idea of a Patriot King*. Published in 1749.

Bolívar, Simón   1783–1830

Venezuelan soldier and statesman. He led revolutions
against Spanish rule in New Granada (Colombia), Peru
and Upper Peru (Bolivia). He became President of
Colombia (1821–30) and of Peru (1823–9), and was a
gifted prose writer.

72 *Más grande es el odio que nos ha inspirado la
Península, que el mar que nos separa de ella; menos
difícil es unir los dos continentes, que reconciliar los
espíritus de ambos países.*

The hate that the Iberian peninsula has inspired in
us is broader than the sea which separates us from
it; it is less difficult to join both continents than to
join both countries' souls.

1815 'Carta de Jamaica' (translated as *The Jamaica Letter*,
1977).

Bolles, Richard Nelson   1927–

US writer and Episcopal clergyman.

73 What Color is Your Parachute?

1972 Title of a vocational guidance book published annually.

Bolt, Robert Oxton   1924–95

English playwright and screenwriter. His best-known
work is the play *A Man for All Seasons* (1960). His
screenplays include *Dr Zhivago* (1965) and *The Mission*
(1986).

74 A Man for All Seasons.

1960 Play title, originally said by Robert Whittington about
his contemporary Sir Thomas More, the central character in
Bolt's play.

75 It profits a man nothing to give his soul for the
whole world...
But for Wales—!

1960 *A Man for All Seasons*, act 2.

76 To be human at all, we must stand fast a little, even
at the risk of being heroes.

1960 Thomas More. *A Man for all Seasons*.

77 The courts of Europe are a jungle, compared to
which your jungles here are a well-kept garden.

1986 Line delivered by Ray McAnally as Cardinal Altamirano
in *The Mission*.

Bonavia, David   1940–88

British journalist and Editor of the *Far East Economic
Review*. His main field of interest was China.

78 Their civilization is based on the most forthrightly
materialistic value system in the history of
mankind. If they see pie in the sky, they
immediately start figuring out how to get it down
onto the dinner table.

1961 *The Chinese*.

Bond, Carrie Jacobs   1862–1946

US songwriter and lyricist.

79 When you come to the end of a perfect day,
And you sit alone with your thought,
While the chimes ring out with a carol gay
For the joy that the day has brought,
Do you think what the end of a perfect day
Can mean to a tired heart,
When the sun goes down with a flaming ray,
And the dear friends have to part?

1910 'A Perfect Day'.

Bone, Sir David   1874–1959

Scottish novelist. He was a high-ranking sailor, and wrote
novels about the sea.

80 It's 'Damn you, Jack—I'm all right!' with you
chaps.

1910 *The Brassbounder*, ch.3.

Bonhoeffer, Dietrich   1906–45

German Lutheran pastor and theologian, executed for
implication in a plot against Hitler. His theology,
especially his plea for 'religionless Christianity', was
influential in mid- and late-20c theology.

81 The Church knows nothing of a sacredness of war.
The Church which prays 'Our Father' asks God
only for peace.

1932 Draft of a new Catechism with F Hildebrandt, in *Gesammelte Schriften*, vol.3 (1947, translated by E Robinson and J Bowden in *No Rusty Sword*, 1965).

82 The cross is God's truth about us, and therefore it is the only power that can make us truthful. When we know the cross we are no longer afraid of the truth.
1937 *Nachfolge* (translated as *The Cost of Discipleship*).

83 *Billige Gnade ist Gnade ohne Nachfolge, Gnade ohne Kreuz, Gnade ohne den lebendigen, menschgewordenen Jesus Christus.*

Cheap grace is grace without discipleship, grace without the cross, grace without Jesus Christ, living and incarnate.
1937 *Nachfolge* (translated as *The Cost of Discipleship*).

84 If religion is only a garment of Christianity—and even this garment has looked very different at different times—then what is religionless Christianity?
1944 Letter to Eberhardt Bethge, 30 Apr. Collected in *Widerstand und Ergebung* (1951, translated 1953).

85 Death is the supreme Festival on the road to freedom.
1945 Letter, collected in *Widerstand und Ergebung* (1951, translated 1953).

86 *Es ist der Vorzug und das Wesen der Starken, daß sie die großen Entscheidungsfragen stellen und zu ihnen klar Stellung nehmen können. Die Schwachen müssen sich immer zwischen Alternativen entscheiden, die nicht die ihren sind.*

It is the nature, and the advantage, of strong people that they can bring out the crucial questions and form a clear opinion about them. The weak always have to decide between alternatives that are not their own.
1951 *Widerstand und Ergebung*, 'Ein paar Gedanken über Verschiedenes' (translated 1953).

87 *Ein Gott, der sich von uns beweisen ließe, wäre ein Götze.*

A God who let us prove his existence would be an idol.
'Glaubst du, so hast du'. Versuch eines Lutherischen Katchismus ('If you believe it, you have it'. Attempt at a Lutheran Catechism). Quoted in E Robinson and J Bowden *No Rusty Sword* (1965).

Book of Common Prayer

The idea of a new prayer book was developed initially by Thomas Cranmer during the reigns of Edward VI and Elizabeth I. The final text was published in 1662.

88 Dearly beloved brethren, the Scripture moveth us in sundry places to acknowledge and confess our manifold sins and wickedness.
Morning Prayer, Sentences of the Scriptures.

89 We have erred and strayed from thy ways like lost sheep. We have followed too much the devices and desires of our own hearts. We have offended against thy holy laws. We have left undone those things which we ought to have done. And we have done those things which we ought not to have done. And there is no health in us.
Morning Prayer, General Confession.

90 A godly, righteous, and sober life.
Morning Prayer, General Confession.

91 And forgive us our trespasses, As we forgive them that trespass against us.
Morning Prayer, the Lord's Prayer.

92 Glory be to the Father, and to the Son: and to the Holy Ghost;
As it was in the beginning, is now and ever shall be: world without end. Amen.
Morning Prayer, Gloria.

93 Lord God of Sabaoth.
Morning Prayer, Te Deum.

94 I believe in God the Father Almighty, Maker of heaven and earth: And in Jesus Christ his only Son our Lord, Who was conceived by the Holy Ghost, Born of the Virgin Mary, Suffered under Pontius Pilate, Was crucified, dead, and buried: He descended into hell; The third day he rose again from the dead; He ascended into heaven, And sitteth on the right hand of God the Father Almighty; From thence he shall come to judge the quick and the dead. I believe in the Holy Ghost; The holy Catholick Church; The Communion of Saints; The Forgiveness of sins; The Resurrection of the body, And the life everlasting. Amen.
Morning Prayer, Apostle's Creed.

95 Give peace in our time, O Lord.
Morning Prayer, versicle.

96 The author of peace and lover of concord, in knowledge of whom standeth our eternal life, whose service is perfect freedom.
Morning Prayer, Second Collect, for Peace.

97 Neither run into any kind of danger.
Morning Prayer, Third Collect, for Grace.

98 Pour upon them the continual dew of thy blessing.
Morning Prayer, Prayer for the Clergy and People.

99 O God, from whom all holy desires, all good counsels, and all just works do proceed: Give unto thy servants that peace which the world cannot give.
Evening Prayer, Second Collect.

1 Lighten our darkness, we beseech thee, O Lord; and by thy great mercy defend us from all perils and dangers of this night.
Evening Prayer, Third Collect, for Aid against Perils.

2 Whosoever will be saved: before all things it is necessary that he hold the Catholic Faith.
Athanasian Creed.

3 And yet they are not three Gods: but one God.
Athanasian Creed.

4 O God the Father of heaven: have mercy upon us miserable sinners.
Litany.

5 From envy, hatred, and malice, and all uncharitableness, Good Lord, deliver us.
Litany.

6 All sorts and conditions of men.
Prayer for all Conditions of Men.

7 All who profess and call themselves Christians.
Prayer for all Conditions of Men.

8 We bless thee for our creation, preservation, and all the blessings of this life; but above all for thine inestimable love in the redemption of the world by our Lord Jesus Christ; for the means of grace, and for the hope of glory.
General Thanksgiving.

9 Almighty God, give us grace that we may cast away the works of darkness, and put upon us the armour of light, now in the time of this mortal life.
Collects, 1st Sunday in Advent.

10 Hear them, read, mark, learn, and inwardly digest them.
Of all the holy Scriptures. *Collects*, 2nd Sunday in Advent.

11 Have mercy upon all Jews, Turks, Infidels, and Hereticks, and take from them all ignorance, hardness of heart, and contempt of thy word.
Collects, Good Friday.

12 Lord of all power and might, who art the author and giver of all good things.
Collects, 7th Sunday after Trinity.

13 Serve thee with a quiet mind.
Collects, 21st Sunday after Trinity.

14 Lord, we beseech thee to keep thy household the Church in continual godliness.
Collects, 22nd Sunday after Trinity.

15 The glory that shall be revealed.
Collects, St Stephen's Day.

16 Almighty God, unto whom all hearts be open, all desires known, and from whom no secrets are hid:

Cleanse the thoughts of our hearts by the inspiration of thy Holy Spirit, that we may perfectly love thee, and worthily magnify thy holy Name; through Christ our Lord. Amen.
Holy Communion, Collect.

17 For I the Lord thy God am a jealous God, and visit the sins of the fathers upon the children unto the third and fourth generation of them that hate me, and shew mercy unto thousands in them that love me and keep my commandments.
Holy Communion, Second Commandment.

18 All things visible and invisible.
Holy Communion, Nicene Creed.

19 Very God of very God, Begotten, not made, Being of one substance with the Father, By whom all things were made: Who for us men and for our salvation came down from heaven.
Holy Communion, Nicene Creed.

20 And I believe in the Holy Ghost, The Lord and giver of life, Who proceedeth from the Father and Son, Who with the Father and the Son together is worshipped and glorified, Who spake by the Prophets.
Holy Communion, Nicene Creed.

21 And I believe one Catholick and Apostolick Church.
Holy Communion, Nicene Creed.

22 Let us pray for the whole state of Christ's Church militant here in earth.
Holy Communion, Introduction to Prayer for the Church militant.

23 Draw near with faith.
Holy Communion, Invitation.

24 Ye that do truly and earnestly repent you of your sins, and are in love and charity with your neighbours, and intend to lead a new life.
Holy Communion, Invitation.

25 We acknowledge and bewail our manifold sins and wickedness, Which we from time to time most grievously have committed, By thought, word, and deed, Against thy Divine Majesty, Provoking most justly thy wrath and indignation against us.
Holy Communion, General Confession.

26 Hear what comfortable words our Saviour Christ saith unto all that truly turn to him.
Holy Communion, Words of Encouragement.

27 It is meet and right so to do.
Holy Communion, versicles and responses.

28 Therefore with Angels, and Archangels, and with all the company of heaven, we laud and magnify

thy glorious Name; evermore praising thee, and saying: Holy, holy, holy, Lord God of hosts, heaven and earth are full of thy glory: Glory be to thee, O Lord most High. Amen.
Holy Communion, Praise.

29　A full, perfect, and sufficient sacrifice, oblation, and satisfaction, for the sins of the whole world.
Holy Communion, Prayer of Consecration.

30　We do not presume to come to this thy Table, O merciful Lord, trusting in our own righteousness, but in thy manifold and great mercies. We are not worthy so much as to gather up the crumbs under thy Table. But thou art the same Lord, whose property is always to have mercy: Grant us therefore, gracious Lord, so to eat the flesh of thy dear Son Jesus Christ, and to drink his blood, that our sinful bodies may be made clean by his body, and our souls washed through his most precious blood, and that we may evermore dwell in him, and he in us. Amen.
Holy Communion, Prayer of Humble Access.

31　The Body of our Lord Jesus Christ, which was given for thee, preserve thy body and soul unto everlasting life: Take and eat this in remembrance that Christ died for thee, and feed on him in thy heart by faith with thanksgiving.
Holy Communion.

32　The Blood of our Lord Jesus Christ, which was shed for thee, preserve thy body and soul unto everlasting life: Drink this in remembrance that Christ's Blood was shed for thee, and be thankful.
Holy Communion.

33　The peace of God, which passeth all understanding, keep your hearts and minds in the knowledge and love of God, and of his Son Jesus Christ our Lord: And the blessing of God Almighty, the Father, the Son, and the Holy Ghost, be amongst you and remain with you always. Amen.
Holy Communion, Blessing.

34　O merciful God, grant that the old Adam in this Child may be so buried, that the new man may be raised up in him. Amen.
Publick Baptism of Infants, Blessing.

35　We receive this Child into the Congregation of Christ's flock, and do sign him with the sign of the Cross, in token that hereafter he shall not be ashamed to confess the faith of Christ crucified, and manfully to fight under his banner against sin, the world, and the devil, and to continue Christ's faithful soldier and servant unto his life's end. Amen.

Publick Baptism of Infants, Reception of the Child.

36　I should renounce the devil and all his works, the pomps and vanity of this wicked world, and all the sinful lusts of the flesh.
Catechism.

37　To keep my hands from picking and stealing, and my tongue from evil-speaking, lying, and slandering.
Catechism.

38　To learn and labour truly to get mine own living, and to do my duty in that state of life, unto which it shall please God to call me.
Catechism.

39　An outward and visible sign of an inward and spiritual grace given unto us.
Catechism.

40　Children being now come to the years of discretion.
Confirmation, Preface.

41　If any of you know cause or just impediment, why these two persons should not be joined together in holy Matrimony, ye are to declare it. This is the first time of asking.
Solemnization of Matrimony, the Banns.

42　Dearly beloved, we are gathered together here in the sight of God, and in the face of this Congregation, to join together this man and this woman in holy Matrimony; which is an honourable estate, instituted of God.
Solemnization of Matrimony, Exhortation.

43　Therefore is not by any to be enterprized, nor taken in hand, unadvisedly, lightly, or wantonly, to satisfy men's carnal lusts and appetites, like brute beasts that have no understanding; but reverently, discreetly, advisedly, soberly, and in the fear of God.
Solemnization of Marriage, Exhortation.

44　First, It was ordained for the procreation of children, to be brought up in the fear and nurture of the Lord, and to the praise of his holy Name.
Solemnization of Marriage, Exhortation.

45　Thirdly, It was ordained for the mutual society, help, and comfort, that the one ought to have of the other, both in prosperity and adversity. Into which holy estate these two persons present come now to be joined.
Solemnization of Marriage, Exhortation.

46　Therefore if any man can shew any just cause, why they may not lawfully be joined together, let him now speak, or else hereafter for ever hold his peace.
Solemnization of Marriage, Exhortation.

47 Wilt thou have this woman to thy wedded wife, to live together after God's ordinance in the holy estate of Matrimony? Wilt thou love her, comfort her, honour, and keep her, in sickness and in health; and, forsaking all other, keep thee only unto her, so long as ye both shall live?
Solemnization of Marriage, Betrothal.

48 Wilt thou have this man to thy wedded husband, to live together after God's ordinance in the holy estate of Matrimony? Wilt thou obey him, and serve him, love, honour and keep him, in sickness and in health; and, forsaking all other, keep thee only unto him, so long as ye both shall live?
Solemnization of Marriage, Betrothal.

49 To have and to hold from this day forward, for better for worse, for richer for poorer, in sickness and in health, to love and to cherish, till death us do part, according to God's holy ordinance; and thereto I plight thee my troth.
Solemnization of Marriage, Betrothal.

50 To love, cherish, and to obey.
Solemnization of Marriage, Betrothal. This is the bride's form of the oath.

51 With this ring I thee wed, with my body I thee worship, and with all my worldly goods I thee endow.
Solemnization of Marriage, Wedding.

52 Those whom God hath joined together let no man put asunder.
Solemnization of Marriage, Priest's Declaration.

53 Consented together in holy wedlock.
Solemnization of Marriage, Minister's Declaration.

54 Peace be to this house.
Visitation of the Sick.

55 Almighty God, the fountain of all goodness.
Morning Prayer, Prayer for the Royal Family.

56 Man that is born of a woman hath but a short time to live, and is full of misery.
Burial of the Dead, Anthem.

57 In the midst of life we are in death.
Burial of the Dead, Anthem.

58 We therefore commit his body to the ground; earth to earth, ashes to ashes, dust to dust; in sure and certain hope of the Resurrection to eternal life, through our Lord Jesus Christ.
Burial of the Dead, Committal.

59 Why do the heathen so furiously rage together, and why do the people imagine a vain thing? The kings of the earth stand up, and the rulers take counsel together, against the Lord, and against his Anointed.
Psalm 2:1–2.

60 The Lord will abhor both the blood-thirsty and deceitful man.
Psalm 5:6.

61 Make thy way plain before my face.
Psalm 5:8.

62 Let them perish through their own imaginations.
Psalm 5:11.

63 Up, Lord, and let not man have the upper hand.
Psalm 9:19.

64 But they are all gone out of the way, they are altogether become abominable: there is none that doeth good, no not one.
Psalm 14:4.

65 The lot is fallen unto me in a fair ground: yea, I have a goodly heritage.
Psalm 16:7.
▷ See Kipling 563:93.

66 The heavens declare the glory of God: and the firmament sheweth his handywork. One day telleth another: and one night certifieth another. There is neither speech nor language: but their voices are heard among them. Their sound is gone out into all lands: and their words into the ends of the world.
Psalm 19:1-4.

67 Thou shalt prepare a table before me against them that trouble me: thou hast anointed my head with oil, and my cup shall be full.
Psalm 23:5.

68 Into thy hands I commend my spirit.
Psalm 31:6.

69 Sing unto the Lord a new song: sing praises lustily unto him with a good courage.
Psalm 33:3.

70 I myself have seen the ungodly in great power, and flourishing like a green bay-tree. I went by, and lo, he was gone: I sought him, but his place could no where be found. Keep innocency, and take heed unto the thing that is right: for that shall bring a man peace at the last.
Psalm 37:36–8.

71 Lord, let me know mine end, and the number of my days: that I may be certified how long I have to live.
Psalm 39:5.

72 My bones are smitten asunder as with a sword: while mine enemies that trouble me cast me in the

teeth; Namely, while they say daily unto me: Where is now thy God?
Psalm 42:12-13.

73 Instead of thy fathers thou shalt have children, whom thou mayest make princes in all lands.
Psalm 45:17.

74 He maketh wars to cease in all the world: he breaketh the bow, and knappeth the spear in sunder, and burneth the chariots in the fire. Be still then, and know that I am God.
Psalm 46:9-10.

75 God is gone up with a merry noise: and the Lord with the sound of the trump.
Psalm 47:5.

76 And I said, O that I had wings like a dove: for then would I flee away, and be at rest.
Psalm 55:6.

77 Be merciful unto me, O God, be merciful unto me, for my soul trusteth in thee: and under the shadow of thy wings shall be my refuge, until this tyranny be over-past.
Psalm 57:1.

78 They are as venomous as the poison of a serpent: even like the deaf adder that stoppeth her ears; Which refuseth to hear the voice of the charmer: charm he never so wisely.
Psalm 58:4–5.

79 They go to and fro in the evening: they grin like a dog, and run about through the city.
Psalm 59:6.

80 He is the God that maketh men to be of one mind in an house, and bringeth the prisoners out of captivity: but letteth the runagates continue in scarceness.
Psalm 68:6.

81 Why hop ye so, ye high hills? this is God's hill, in the which it pleaseth him to dwell: yea, the Lord will abide in it for ever.
Psalm 68:16.

82 Thou art gone up on high, thou hast led captivity captive, and received gifts for men.
Psalm 68:18.

83 Thy rebuke hath broken my heart; I am full of heaviness: I looked for some to have pity on me, but there was no man, neither found I any to comfort me. They gave me gall to eat: and when I was thirsty they gave me vinegar to drink.
Psalm 69:21–2.

84 So the Lord awaked as one out of sleep: and like a giant refreshed with wine.
Psalm 78:66.

85 O how amiable are thy dwellings, thou Lord of hosts!
Psalm 84:1.

86 Lord, thou hast been our refuge from one generation to another. Before the mountains were brought forth, or ever the earth and the world were made: thou art God from everlasting, and world without end.
Psalm 90:1-2.

87 O come, let us sing unto the Lord; let us heartily rejoice in the strength of our salvation. Let us come before his presence with thanksgiving; and shew ourselves glad in him with psalms. For the Lord is a great God; and a great King above all gods. In his hand are all the corners of the earth; and the strength of the hills is his also. The sea is his, and he made it; and his hands prepared the dry land. O come, let us worship and fall down, and kneel before the Lord our Maker. For he is the Lord our God; and we are the people of his pasture, and the sheep of his hand.
Psalm 95:1-7.

88 Today if ye will hear his voice, harden not your hearts: as in the provocation, and as in the day of temptation in the wilderness; When your fathers tempted me: proved me, and saw my works.
Psalm 95:8–9.

89 O be joyful in the Lord, all ye lands: serve the Lord with gladness, and come before his presence with a song.
Psalm 100:1.

90 Whose feet they hurt in the stocks: the iron entered into his soul.
Psalm 105:18.

91 Their soul abhorred all manner of meat: and they were even hard at death's door.
Psalm 107:18.

92 Lord, I am not high-minded: I have no proud looks.
Psalm 131:1.

93 Such knowledge is too wonderful and excellent for me: I cannot attain unto it.
Psalm 139:5.

94 I will give thanks unto thee, for I am fearfully and wonderfully made: marvellous are thy works, and that my soul knoweth right well.
Psalm 139:13.

95 O put not your trust in princes, nor in any child of man: for there is no help in them.
Psalm 146:2.

96 We therefore commit his body to the deep, to be turned into corruption, looking for the resurrection of the body, (when the Sea shall give up her dead.)

Forms of Prayer to be Used at Sea, At the Burial of their Dead at Sea.

97 Holy Scripture containeth all things necessary to salvation.

Articles of Religion, VI Of the Sufficiency of the holy Scriptures for Salvation.

98 A fond thing vainly invented.

Articles of Religion, XXII of Purgatory.

99 The Bishop of *Rome* hath no jurisdiction in this Realm of *England*.

Articles of Religion, XXXVII Of the Civil Magistrates.

1 It is lawful for Christian men, at the commandment of the Magistrate, to wear weapons, and serve in the wars.

Articles of Religion, XXXVII Of the Civil Magistrates.

2 A Man may not marry his Grandmother.

Table of Kindred and Affinity.

Bookchin, Murray pseudonym of Lewis Herber 1921–

US writer on social, ecological and environmental issues.

3 Once regarded as the herald of enlightenment in all spheres of knowledge, science is now increasingly seen as a strictly instrumental system of control. Its use as a system of manipulation and its role in restricting human freedom now parallel in every detail its use as a means of natural manipulation.

1982 *The Ecology of Freedom*.

Booth, John Wilkes 1839–65

US actor, usually remembered as the assassin of President Abraham Lincoln. He was hunted down and shot several days after the killing.

4 *Sic semper tyrannis!* The South is avenged!

1865 Attributed, as he shot Lincoln at Ford's Theatre, Washington DC, 14 Apr. 'Sic semper tyrannis', *Thus always to tyrants*, is the motto of the Commonwealth of Virginia.

Booth, Junius Brutus 1796–1852

English-born US actor, a leading rival of Edmund Kean in London, particularly admired as Shylock and Richard III. He continued his success after emigrating in 1821, but succumbed to alcohol-induced melancholia.

5 Where's the stage and what's the play?

Attributed, on being found drunk backstage shortly before making his first entrance.

Booth, Martin 1944–

English writer educated in Hong Kong. *The Dragon and the Pearl* (1994) is an account of life there.

6 At any one time, 15 per cent of the buildings of Hong Kong are being either demolished or rebuilt, renovated or restructured.

1994 *The Dragon and the Pearl*, foreword.

Boothby, Sir Robert John Graham, 1st Baron Boothby of Buchan and Rattray Head 1900–86

Scottish Conservative politician, Parliamentary Secretary to Winston Churchill (1926–9) and an original member of the Council of United Europe. His works include *The New Economy* (1943) and *I Fight to Live* (1947).

7 Of all the pygmies, Samuel Hoare was the pygmiest.

Attributed.

Borah, William Edgar 1865–1940

US Republican politician. Elected Senator for Idaho in 1906, he advocated disarmament and, as a convinced isolationist, was instrumental in blocking US entry into the League of Nations.

8 A democracy must remain at home in all matters that affect the nature of her institutions. They are of a nature to call for the undivided attention and devotion of the entire nation. We do not want the racial antipathies or national antagonisms of the Old World transformed to this continent—as they will, should we become a part of European politics. The people of this country are overwhelmingly for a policy of neutrality.

1936 Radio broadcast, 22 Feb.

Borelli, Giovanni Alfonso 1608–79

Italian mathematician and astronomer, who reasoned that celestial objects follow parabolic paths.

9 No sensible person will deny that the works of Nature are in the highest degree simple, necessary and as economical as possible. Therefore machines devised by mankind will doubtlessly likewise attain most success if they are as far as possible modelled on works of Nature.

1680 *De moto animalium*.

Borges, Jorge Luis 1899–1986

Argentinian writer. He returned to Argentina from Europe in 1921, introducing avant-garde Ultraist theories in essays and poems before publishing his intricate and fantasy-woven short stories in the 1940s. He lost his sight in the 1950s.

10 *Los metafísicos de Tlön no buscan la verdad ni siquiera la verosimilitud: buscan el asombro. Juzgan*

que la metafísica es una rama de la literatura fantástica.

The metaphysicians of Tlön do not seek for the truth or even for verisimilitude, but rather for the astounding. They judge that metaphysics is a branch of fantastic literature.
1941 *Ficciones*, 'Tlön, Uqbar, Orbis Tertius' (1963).

11 *Quizá la historia universal es la historia de la diversa entonación de algunas metáforas.*

It may be that universal history is the history of the different intonations given a handful of metaphors.
1952 *Otras inquisiciones*, 'La esfera de Pascal' (translated as 'The Fearful Sphere of Pascal', 1964).

12 *En vano te hemos prodigado el océano,*
En vano el sol, que vieron los maravillados ojos de
   Whitman;
Has gastado los años y te has gastado,
Y todavía no has escrito el poema.

We have lavished the ocean on you in vain,
in vain the sun that was seen by Whitman's
   astounded eyes;
You have spent your years and you have spent
   yourself,
But you haven't written the poem yet.
1964 *El otro, el mismo*, 'Mateo XXV, 30' ('Matthew 25:30').

13 While we are asleep in this world, we are awake in another one; in this way, every man is two men.
Quoted in John Russell *The Meaning of Modern Art* (1974).

14 Canada is so far away it hardly exists.
1974 Response to the question 'What do you think of when you think of Canada?', when interviewed in Buenos Aires by Canadian poet and broadcaster Robert Zend, 4 Oct.

15 The Falklands thing was a fight between two bald men over a comb.
1983 In *Time*, 14 Feb.

Borgia, Cesare 1476–1507

Italian soldier, illegitimate son of Pope Alexander VI. He served in the papal army and was created Duke of Romagna, but was defeated in 1506 under Pope Julius II. Macchiavelli praised him as a model prince, but he was commonly perceived as a cruel dictator.

16 *Aut Caesar, aut nihil.*

Either Caesar or nothing.
Motto. It goes back to a couplet composed in 1507, after Borgia's death, by Fausto Maddalena Romano: 'Borgia Caesar erat, factis et nomine Caesar, /aut nihil, aut Caesar dixit: utrumque fuit.' (Borgia was Caesar: he was Caesar in name and in fact. He said /Either Caesar, or nothing: he was both.)

Borman, Frank 1928–

US astronaut, later President of Eastern Airlines.

17 Capitalism without bankruptcy is like Christianity without hell.
1986 In *US*, 21 Apr.

Born, Max 1882–1970

German-born British physicist, Professor of Physics at Göttingen until forced to leave by the Nazis. He won the Nobel Prize (1954) for his insights into quantum mechanics.

18 There are two objectionable types of believers: those who believe the incredible and those who believe that 'belief' must be discarded and replaced by 'the scientific method'.
1951 *Natural Philosophy of Cause and Chance.*

19 Science…is so greatly opposed to history and tradition that it cannot be absorbed by our civilization.
1968 *My Life and Views.*

Borotra, Jean 1898–1994

French tennis player. He won the men's singles title at Wimbledon in 1924 and other titles.

20 The only possible regret I have is the feeling that I will die without having played enough tennis.
Quoted in Colin Jarman *The Guinness Dictionary of Sports Quotations* (1990).

Borovoy, A Alan 1932–

General Counsel of the Canadian Civil Liberties Association.

21 I would renounce, therefore, the attempt to create heaven on earth, and focus instead on reducing the hell.
1988 *When Freedoms Collide: A Case for Our Civil Liberties.* His personal maxim.

22 I don't ask employers, for example, to *like* blacks or Jews or native people; I ask employers to *hire* the qualified members of these groups whether they like them or not.
1988 *When Freedoms Collide: A Case for our Civil Liberties.*

Borrow, George Henry 1803–81

English writer and traveller. His part fictional, part factual books reflect his interest in languages and his love of Romany lore. They include *The Bible in Spain* (1843), *Lavengro* (1851), *The Romany Rye* (1857) and *Wild Wales* (1862).

23 There's night and day, brother, both sweet things; sun, moon, and stars, brother, all sweet things: there's likewise a wind on the heath. Life is very sweet, brother; who would wish to die?
1851 *Lavengro*, ch.25.

24 Fear God, and take your own part.
1857 *The Romany Rye*, ch.16.

25 I never saw such a place for merched anllad [wanton women] as Northampton.
1862 *Wild Wales*, ch.34.

26 'Scotland! a queer country that, your honour!' 'So it is,' said I; 'a queerer country I never saw in all my life.' 'And a queer set of people, your honour.' 'So they are,' said I; 'a queerer set of people than the Scotch you would scarcely see in a summer's day.'
1862 *Wild Wales*, ch.83.

Bosquet, Pierre 1810–61

French soldier, General during the Crimean War.

27 *C'est magnifique, mais ce n'est pas la guerre.*

It is magnificent, but it isn't war.
1854 On seeing the Charge of the Light Brigade at the Battle of Balaclava, 25 Oct. Quoted in Cecil Woodham Smith *The Reason Why* (1953), ch.12.

Bossidy, John Collins 1860–1928

US doctor and versifier.

28 And this is good old Boston,
The home of the bean and the cod,
Where the Lowells talk to the Cabots
And the Cabots talk only to God.
1910 Toast delivered at Holy Cross alumni dinner, Boston. ·

Boswell, James 1740–95

Scottish man of letters and biographer of Dr Johnson, whom he first met in 1763. Their great friendship led, after Johnson's death, to Boswell's literary masterpiece, the *Life of Samuel Johnson* (1791).

29 I think there is a blossom about me of something more distinguished than the generality of mankind.
1763 Journal entry, 20 Jan. Collected in F A Pottle (ed) *Boswell's London Journal* (1950).

30 JOHNSON: Well, we had a good talk.
BOSWELL: Yes, Sir; you tossed and gored several persons.
1768 Conversation, summer, recorded in *The Life of Samuel Johnson*, vol.2.

31 I am, I flatter myself, completely a citizen of the world. In my travels through Holland, Germany, Switzerland, Italy, Corsica, France, I never felt myself from home.
1773 *Journal of a Tour to the Hebrides* (ed F A Pottle, 1936), entry for 14 Aug.

32 A man, indeed, is not genteel when he gets drunk; but most vices may be committed very genteelly: a man may debauch his friend's wife genteelly: he may cheat at cards genteelly.
1775 *The Life of Samuel Johnson*, vol.2, entry for 6 Apr.

Botha, P(ieter) W(illem) 1932–

South African statesman, Prime Minister (1978–84) and President (1984–9). His attempts at limited constitutional reform were met with a right-wing defection from his ruling National Party (1982).

33 We simply could not go on with policies that were a failure economically and internationally, and which we could not morally justify. To allocate rights and privileges on the basis of a physical characteristic was tantamount to sinning against God.
1991 Interviewed by Donald Woods, BBC TV, Feb.

Botham, Ian Terence 1955–

English cricketer. He established a record number of Test wickets (373) and scored 5,057 runs in Tests for England, including 14 Test centuries.

34 Cricket is full of theorists who can ruin your game in no time.
1980 *Ian Botham on Cricket.*

35 I want to stress again one aspect of the game which is most important. *Never argue with an umpire.*
1980 *Ian Botham on Cricket.*

Bottomley, Gordon 1874–1948

English poet and playwright. His interest in Celtic folklore is reflected in much of his work, and he is best remembered for his *Poetry of Thirty Years* (1925) and some of his plays.

36 When you destroy a blade of grass
You poison England at her roots;
Remember no man's foot can pass
Where evermore no green life shoots.
1912 'To Ironfounders and Others'.

37 Your worship is your furnaces
Which, like old idols, lost obscenes,
Have molten bowels; your vision is
Machines for making more machines.
1912 'To Ironfounders and Others'.

Boucicault, Dion(ysus Lardner)
originally *Dionysius Lardner Bursiquot*
c. 1820–1890

Irish playwright, actor and director. His many works include popular melodramas such as *The Corsican Brothers* (1852), *The Colleen Bawn* (1860) and *The Shaughraun* (1875). He also promoted theatrical reforms, including the box set.

38 Men talk of killing time, while time quietly kills them.
1841 *London Assurance*, act 2, sc.1.

39 It's a mighty pleasant thing to die like this, once in a way, and hear all the good things said about ye

afther you're dead and gone, when they can do you no good.

1874 Aside by Conn. *The Shaughraun*, act 3, sc.2.

40 His first holiday.

His own suggested epitaph. Attributed.

Boulanger, Nadia 1887–1979

French musician and teacher. She studied at the Paris Conservatoire (1879–1904) and wrote many vocal and instrumental works.

41 Do not take up music unless you would rather die than not do so.

Advice to her pupils. Quoted in Alan Kendall *The Tender Tyrant: Nadia Boulanger* (1976).

Boulding, Kenneth Ewart 1910–93

British-born US economist and social philosopher (or 'social ecologist'), president of the American Economic Association and professor at the Universities of Michigan and Colorado.

42 We know very little about what it is that moves great masses of men to action, and until we know more about this it is fitting for the social scientist to maintain a becoming modesty in the presence of a great deal to be modest about.

1966 *The Impact of the Social Sciences.*

43 Science might almost be redefined as the process of substituting unimportant questions which can be answered for important questions which cannot.

1969 *The Image.*

44 Almost the whole pollution–environmental problem is summed up in the proposition that all goods are generally produced jointly with bads.

1972 In Sam H Schurr (ed) *Energy, Economic Growth, and the Environment* (1972).

Boulton, Sir Harold Edwin 1859–1935

English songwriter. He compiled and wrote many collections of national songs, including the well-known 'Glorious Devon' (1902) and 'Skye Boat Song' (1908).

45 When Adam and Eve were dispossessed
Of the garden hard by Heaven,
They planted another one down in the west,
'Twas Devon, glorious Devon!

1902 'Glorious Devon'.

46 Speed, bonnie boat, like a bird on the wing,
'Onward!' the sailors cry;
Carry the lad that's born to be king
Over the sea to Skye.

1908 'Skye Boat Song'. The date and authorship of the original song are uncertain, but this is certainly now the most famous version.

Bourassa, Henri 1868–1952

Canadian politician. He entered the Commons as an Independent Liberal (1896) and founded the Quebec Nationalist party, opposing involvement with Britain and the US. He was founding editor of *Le Devoir*, a Montreal newspaper.

47 Our special task, as French Canadians, is to insert into America the spirit of Christian France.

1918 *La Langue, Gardienne de la Foi.*

Bourdillon, F(rancis) W(illiam) 1852–1951

English poet.

48 The night has a thousand eyes,
And the day but one;
Yet the light of the bright world dies,
With the dying sun.

The mind has a thousand eyes,
And the heart but one;
Yet the light of a whole life dies,
When love is done.

1878 *Among the Flowers*, 'Light'.

▷ See Lyly 620:62.

Bowen, Catherine Shober née *Drinker* 1897–1973

US writer, biographer and essayist, whose many books include *The Lion and the Throne* (biography of Sir Edward Coke, 1957) and *Miracle at Philadelphia* (1966).

49 In writing biography, fact and fiction shouldn't be mixed. And if they are, the fiction parts should be printed in red ink, the fact parts in black ink.

1958 In *Publisher's Weekly*, 24 Mar. Bowen's biographies were frequently partly fictionalized.

Bowen, Frank Charles 1894–

50 *Irish hurricane*, a flat calm with drizzling rain.

1929 *Sea Slang, a Dictionary of the Old-Timers' Expressions and Epithets.*

Bowie, David real name *David Robert Jones* 1947–

English rock singer, known for his extravagant stage images. He has also acted in films, including *The Man Who Fell To Earth* (1976).

51 You must understand that this is not a woman's dress I'm wearing. It's a man's dress.

Quoted in Maxim Jakubowski *The Wit and Wisdom of Rock and Roll* (1983).

Bowles, Paul Frederick 1910–

US novelist, poet, travel writer, translator and composer. He studied music in Paris, and began writing fiction after

World War II. He lived in Tangier from 1952, and much of his work is set there.

52 The Sheltering Sky.
    1947 Title of novel.

53 Too much importance is given the writer and not enough to his work. What difference does it make who he is and what he feels, since he's merely a machine for transmission of ideas. In reality he doesn't exist—he's a cipher, a blank. A spy sent into life by the forces of death. His main objective is to get the information across the border, back into death.
    1966 Letter to James Leo Herlihy, 30 Apr.

54 The wind howls and the countryside is the colour of a lion. For a week the cicadas have been screaming; I think by now most of them have burst, for there are far fewer.
    1969 Letter to Ned Rorem, 20 Aug.

55 It was an experiment, and I think a successful one, in communal living. It worked largely because Auden ran it; he was exceptionally adept at getting the necessary money out of us when it was due.
    1972 On an artist's house in New York. *Without Stopping; An Autobiography*, ch.12.

56 My curiosity about alien cultures was avid and obsessive. I had a placid belief that it was good for me to live in the midst of people whose motives I did not understand; this unreasoned conviction was clearly an attempt to legitimize my curiosity.
    1972 *Without Stopping; An Autobiography*, ch.14.

57 The act of living had been enjoyable; at some point when I was not paying attention, it had turned into a different sort of experience, to whose grimness I had grown so accustomed that I now took it for granted.
    1972 *Without Stopping; An Autobiography*, ch.17.

58 I envy you if you're able to sustain a uniform degree of interest throughout *Ulysses*. People are always saying they do. People also claim to be clairvoyant and to levitate.
    1981 Letter to Millicent Dillon, 1 Jul.

59 The only effort worth making is the one it takes to learn the geography of one's own nature.
    1989 In *The Sunday Times*, 23 Jul.

Boycott, Geoff 1940–
English cricketer, who made 108 appearances for England. He scored a total of 8,114 Test runs.

60 To have some idea what it's like, stand in the outside lane of a motorway, get your mate to drive his car at you at 95 mph and wait until he's 12 yards away, before you decide which way to jump.

    1989 Of the experience of facing fast bowlers. Quoted in Helen Exley *Cricket Quotations* (1992).

Boyd, LM
US journalist.

61 Most business meetings are staged to supply people who'd rather talk than work with people who'd rather listen than work.
    1990 'Grab Bag', in the *San Francisco Chronicle*, 7 Apr.

Boyd, William Andrew Murray 1952–
Scottish writer, born in Ghana. A lecturer in English at Oxford (1980–3) and TV critic with the *New Statesman*, he then concentrated on fiction, with novels such as *A Good Man in Africa* (1981) and *Brazzaville Beach* (1990).

62 Like Rome, Nkongsamba was built on seven hills, but there all similarity ended. Set in undulating tropical rain forest, from the air it resembled nothing so much as a giant pool of crapulous vomit on somebody's expansive unmown lawn.
    1981 *A Good Man in Africa*, ch.1.

63 Morgan liked to imagine the town as some immense yeast culture, left in a deep cupboard by an absent-minded lab technician, festering uncontrolled, running rampant in the ideal growing conditions.
    1981 *A Good Man in Africa*, ch.1

64 My first act on entering this world was to kill my mother.
    1988 *The New Confessions*, opening words.

65 The natural world is full of irregularity and random alteration, but in the antiseptic, dust-free, shadowless, brightly lit, abstract realm of the mathematicians they like their cabbages spherical, please.
    1990 *Brazzaville Beach*, 'Cabbages Are Not Spheres'.

66 It seems to me that there are statements about the world and our lives that have no need of formal proof procedures.
    1990 *Brazzaville Beach*, 'Fermat's Last Theorem II'.

Boyer, Charles 1899–1978
French actor who moved to Hollywood in 1929 and was particularly successful in romantic roles. His appearances include *The Garden of Allah* (1936), *Mayerling* (1937), *Love Affair* (1939) and *All This and Heaven Too* (1940).

67 Come with me to the Casbah.
    1938 Although he never actually spoke this line, it was popularly associated with him as Pepe in the film *Algiers*.

Boyer, Eugene L
President of the Carnegie Foundation for Advancement of Teaching.

68 A poor surgeon hurts one person at a time. A poor teacher hurts 30.
    1986 In *People*, 17 Mar.

Boyle, Peter G

69 They are the last drops of vintage wine from a musty old bottle.
    Of Winston Churchill's letters to President Eisenhower. Quoted in Peter G Boyle (ed) *The Churchill-Eisenhower Correspondence 1953–1955* (1990).

Bracken, Peg 1918–

US writer and humorist. Her books include *The I Hate to Cook Book* (1960) and *I Didn't Come Here to Argue* (1969).

70 Cheese for dessert is rather like *Paradise Lost* in that everyone thinks he *ought* to like it, but still you don't notice too many people actually curling up with it.
    1960 *The I Hate to Cook Book*, ch.9.

Bracken, Thomas 1843–98

New Zealand poet, journalist and politician, born in Ireland. He emigrated in 1869. His work, characterized by Victorian sentimentality, includes *Lays and Lyrics: God's Own Country and Other Poems* (1893).

71 Oh, God! that men would see a little clearer,
    Or judge less harshly where they cannot see;
    Oh, God! that men would draw a little nearer
    To one another, they'd be nearer Thee,
    And understood.
    1905 *Not Understood, and Other Poems*, 'Not Understood'.

Bradbury, Malcolm Stanley 1932–

English novelist, critic and teacher. His novels include *The History Man* (1975) and *Rates of Exchange* (1982).

72 It had always seemed to Louis that a fundamental desire to take postal courses was being sublimated by other people into sexual activity.
    1959 *Eating People Is Wrong*, ch.5.

73 I like the English. They have the most rigid code of immorality in the world.
    1959 *Eating People Is Wrong*, ch.5.

74 Reading someone else's newspaper is like sleeping with someone else's wife. Nothing seems to be precisely in the right place, and when you find what you are looking for, it is not clear then how to respond to it.
    1965 *Stepping Westward*, bk.1, ch.1.

75 My experience of ships is that on them one makes an interesting discovery about the world. One finds one can do without it completely.
    1965 *Stepping Westward*, bk.1, ch.2.

76 They don't spend themselves in relationships until they know what the odds are; long hours spent as babies lying in the rain outside greengrocers' shops have made them tough.
    1965 *Stepping Westward*, bk.2, ch.4.

77 English history is all about men liking their fathers, and American history is all about men hating their fathers and trying to burn down everything they ever did.
    1965 *Stepping Westward*, bk.2, ch.5.

78 The English are polite by telling lies. The Americans are polite by telling the truth.
    1965 *Stepping Westward*, bk.2, ch.5.

79 'We stay together, but we distrust each other.'
    'Ah, yes,…but isn't that a definition of marriage?'
    1975 *The History Man*, ch.3.

80 If God had meant us to have group sex, I guess he'd have given us all more organs.
    1976 *Who Do You Think You Are?*, 'A Very Hospitable Person'.

81 The British have long had a taste for bad books, but they like them well written.
    1981 In *The Observer*, 25 Oct.

82 In Slaka, sex is just politics with the clothes off.
    1983 *Rates of Exchange*, pt.4, ch.3.

83 Here we have a saying: a good friend is someone who visits you when you are in prison. But a *really* good friend is someone who comes to hear your lectures.
    1983 *Rates of Exchange*, pt.4, ch.3.

84 Conversation is never easy for the British, who are never keen to express themselves to strangers or, for that matter, anyone, even themselves.
    1983 *Rates of Exchange*, pt.5, ch.3.

85 You probably know, the better class of Briton likes to send his children away to school until they're old and intelligent enough to come home again. Then they're too old and intelligent to want to.
    1983 *Rates of Exchange*, pt.5, ch.3.

86 There were moments when Henry was glad he was a writer, for writers could live in their own minds and didn't have to go out at all.
    1987 *Cuts*.

87 The modern novel has been many things, and functioned at many levels. It would keep D.H. Lawrence poor, and make Jilly Cooper and Jeffrey Archer rich.
    1993 *The Modern British Novel*, preface.

88 The post-war period has not been marked by a great aesthetic debate about the novel comparable to that of the earlier half of the century, in part because the role of the writer and critic divided, the writer going off to the marketplace and the critic to the university (which eventually turned out to be much the same thing).

1993 *The Modern British Novel*, preface.

Bradbury, Ray(mond Douglas) 1920–

US science-fiction writer, one of the earliest writers in the genre to be recognized for his literary merits. His short story collections include *The Martian Chronicles* (1950).

89 The Day it Rained Forever.

1959 Title of story.

90 Where robot mice and robot men, I said, run round in robot towns.

1977 *Where Robot Mice and Robot Men Run Round In Robot Towns*, prologue.

Bradley, Francis Herbert 1846–1924

Welsh philosopher, who spent most of his life at Oxford, a central figure of the 19c British Idealist movement. His important works are *Ethical Studies* (1876) and *Appearance and Reality* (1893).

91 Metaphysics is the finding of bad reasons for what we believe upon instinct, but to find these reasons is no less an instinct.

1893 *Appearance and Reality*, preface.

92 Where everything is bad it must be good to know the worst.

1893 *Appearance and Reality*, preface.

Bradley, Omar Nelson 1893–1981

US soldier. He played a prominent part in World War II, especially in Tunisia and Sicily. Chairman of the joint Chiefs-of-Staff in 1949, he was promoted to General in 1950.

93 We have grasped the mystery of the atom and rejected the Sermon on the Mount.

1948 Speech, 10 Nov, commemorating Armistice Day.

94 The wrong war, at the wrong place, at the wrong time—and with the wrong enemy.

1951 At the Senate inquiry into proposals to escalate the Korean war into China, May.

Bradman, Sir Don(ald George) 1908–

Australian cricketer and stockbroker. He played for Australia (1928–48, Captain 1936–48), scoring the highest aggregate and largest number of centuries in Tests against England. In 1949 he became the first Australian cricketer to be knighted.

95 It's hard to bat with tears in your eyes.

1948 When bowled for a duck in his final Test innings. Quoted in Colin Jarman *The Guinness Dictionary of Sports Quotations* (1990).

96 There is probably a greater premium on temperament for a batsman than for any player in any branch of sport.

1958 *The Art of Cricket*.

97 May cricket continue to flourish and spread its wings. The world can only be richer for it.

1958 *The Art of Cricket*.

98 Every ball is for me the first ball, whether my score is 0 or 200, and I never visualize the possibility of anybody getting me out.

Quoted in Colin Jarman *The Guinness Dictionary of Sports Quotations* (1990).

Bradstreet, Anne née Dudley 1612–72

English-born American Puritan poet. She emigrated to New England with her husband, a non-Comformist minister, later Governor of Massachusetts. Her first collection was published in London by her brother-in-law without her knowledge.

99 In Criticks hands, beware thou dost not come;
And take thy way where yet thou art not known,
If for thy Father askt, say, thou hadst none:
And for thy Mother, she alas is poor,
Which caus'd her thus to send thee out of door.

1650 *The Tenth Muse Lately Sprung Up In America*, 'The Author to Her Book'.

1 I am obnoxious to each carping tongue
Who says my hand a needle better fits,
A poet's pen all scorn I should thus wrong
For such despite they cast on female wits;
If what I do prove well, it won't advance,
They'll say it's stolen, or else, it was by chance.

1678 *Several Poems Compiled with Great Variety of Wit and Learning*, 'The Prologue'.

2 If ever two were one, then surely we.

1678 *Several Poems Compiled with Great Variety of Wit and Learning*, 'To My Dear and Loving Husband'.

Brady, Nicholas Frederick 1930–

US financier and politician, Secretary of the Treasury (1988–93) under Bush.

3 If you want to be vice president, stand out here in the rain in your underwear and let everybody see what you're made of.

1988 On the need to strip the secrecy from selection of vice presidential candidates instead of having surprise choices such as Dan Quayle. In the *Washington Post*, 28 Aug.

4 We have a habit in this country of correcting things just as they are about to correct themselves.

1989 In the *New York Times*, 1 Feb.

Bragg, Melvyn 1939–

English novelist. He has written a number of novels in the realist tradition, and is well known as a television presenter, notably of the arts series *The South Bank Show*.

5 Patriotism is seen not only as the last refuge of the scoundrel but as the first bolt-hole of the hypocrite.
1976 *Speak For England*, introduction.

▷ See Johnson 529:73.

Brahms, Johannes 1833–97

German composer. His compositions include four symphonies and several concertos, a large body of songs, chamber music and music for piano, and *A German Requiem* (1869).

6 When I feel the urge to compose, I begin by appealing directly to my Maker and I first ask Him the three most important questions pertaining to our life here in this world—whence, wherefore, whither.
Quoted in A Hopkins *Music All Around Me* (1967).

Bramante, Donato 1444–1514

Italian High Renaissance architect.

7 The dome of the Pantheon over the vault of the Temple of Peace.
c.1505 Description of his design for St Peter's, Rome. Quoted in Vincent Cronin *The Flowering of the Renaissance* (1969).

Bramston, James c.1694–1744

English cleric and poet.

8 What's not destroyed by Time's devouring hand? Where's Troy, and where's the Maypole in the Strand?
1729 *The Art of Politics*.

Brando, Marlon 1924–

US film and stage actor, trained in 'method acting'. He found fame in a stage (1947) and screen (1951) production of *A Streetcar Named Desire*, and went on to play a wide variety of roles. He refused an Academy Award for *The Godfather* (1972) in protest at the film industry's treatment of Native Americans.

9 Sometimes you just get the feeling that here it is 11 o'clock in the morning and you're not in school.
1959 On playing in Western films. In the *New York Post*, 11 May.

10 An actor is a kind of guy who if you ain't talking about him ain't listening.
Quoted in Bob Thomas *Brando* (1973), ch.8.

Braque, Georges 1882–1963

French painter, a developer of Fauvism, and later under the influence of Picasso, of Cubism. He was badly injured in World War I.

11 *L'Art est fait pour troubler, la Science rassure.*

Art was made to disturb, science reassures.
Notebook entry. Collected in *Le Jour et la nuit: Cahiers 1917–52*.

12 *La vérité existe; on n'invente que le mensonge.*

Truth exists; only lies are invented.
Notebook entry. Collected in *Le Jour et la nuit: Cahiers 1917–52*.

Brasch, Charles 1909–73

New Zealand poet. His works include *The Land and Other People* (1939), *Ambulando* (1964) and *Home Ground* (1974). A posthumous book of *Collected Poems* was published in 1984.

13 The ruby and amethyst eyes of anemones Glow through me, fiercer than stars.
Home Ground (1974), 'Night Cries, Wakari Hospital: Winter Anemones'.

Brathwaite, Edward Kamau originally
Lawson Edward Brathwaite 1930–

West Indian poet and historian, born in Barbados. His best-known work *The Arrivants: A New World Trilogy* (1973) consists of three earlier long poems, exploring different aspects of Caribbean culture and identity.

14 It is not enough
to be pause, to be hole
to be void, to be silent
to be semicolon, to be semicolony;
1969 *Islands*, no.3 'Rebellion', pt.6 'Negus', collected as *The Arrivants: A New World Trilogy* (1973).

Bratton, John W

British songwriter.

15 If you go down in the woods today
You're sure of a big surprise
If you down in the woods today
You'd better go in disguise.
For every Bear that ever there was
Will gather there for certain because,
Today's the day the Teddy Bears have their Picnic.
1932 'The Teddy Bear's Picnic' (with James B Kennedy).

Braudy, Leo Beal 1941–

US scholar, Professor of Literature at the University of Southern California.

16 People are looking to other lives for answers to questions of their own.
1987 On the increasing popularity of biography. Quoted by Alvin P Sarnoff in *US News and World Report*, 3 Aug.

Braun, Wernher von 1912–77

German-born US rocket scientist and engineer who helped develop the liquid-fuel rocket for the Nazis, and later switched his allegiance to the US. He became technical adviser to the US rocket program and later director of development operations at NASA where he was responsible for development of the Saturn V launch vehicle.

17 Our sun is one of 100 billion stars in our galaxy. Our galaxy is one of billions of galaxies populating the universe. It would be the height of presumption to think that we are the only living things in that enormous immensity.
1960 In the *New York Times*, 29 Apr.

Brautigan, Richard 1935–84

US fabulist and poet, an icon of the 1960s counter-culture movement. His seemingly whimsical fables were also literary experiments. He committed suicide.

18 Language does not leave fossils, at least not until it has become written.
1967 *Trout Fishing In America*, 'Prelude to the Mayonnaise Chapter'.

19 The time is right to mix sentences with dirt and the sun with punctuation and rain with verbs.
1968 *Please Plant This Book*, 'Squash'.

20 If you get hung up on everybody else's hangups, then the whole world's going to be nothing more than one huge gallows.
1970 *The Abortion: An Historical Romance*.

21 Loading Mercury with a Pitchfork.
1976 Title of poetry collection.

22 They used language concentrating emotion, detail and image until they arrived at a form of dew-like steel.
1978 On Japanese poets. *June 30th–June 30th*.

Brecher, Irving 1914–

US screenwriter and director. He wrote the scripts for two of the Marx Brothers later films—*At the Circus* (1939) and *Go West* (1940).

23 I'll bet your father spent the first year of your life throwing rocks at the stork.
1939 *At the Circus*.

Brecht, Bertolt Eugen Friedrich 1898–1956

German poet, playwright and theatre director, an innovator of epic theatre and the alienation effect. He fled Nazi Germany when Hitler came to power and returned to settle in East Berlin in 1947, where he directed the *Berliner Ensemble* theatre. His works include *The Threepenny Opera* (1928, with Kurt Weill), *The Life of Galileo* (1938), *Mother Courage and her Children* (1939) and *The Caucasian Chalk Circle* (1945).

24 *Und der Haifisch, der hat Zähne*
Und die trägt er im Gesicht

Und Macheath, der hat ein Messer
Doch das Messer sieht man nicht.

Oh, the shark has pretty teeth, dear,
And he shows them pearly white.
Just a jack-knife has Macheath, dear,
And he keeps it out of sight.
1928 *Die Dreigroschenoper* (The Threepenny Opera), prologue (translated by Ralph Manheim and John Willett, 1970).

25 *Erst kommt das Fressen, dann kommt die Moral.*

Food comes first, then morals.
1928 *Die Dreigroschenoper* (The Threepenny Opera), act 2, sc.3 (translated by Ralph Manheim and John Willett, 1970).

26 *Von der Wiege bis zur Bahre, zuerst die Wäsche.*

From the cradle to the grave, underwear first, last and all the time.
1928 *Die Dreigroschenoper* (The Threepenny Opera), act 2, sc.5 (translated by Ralph Manheim and John Willet, 1970).

27 *Angesichts von Hindernissen mag die kürzeste Linie zwischen zwei Punkten die krumme sein*

When it comes to obstacles, the shortest line between two points may be the crooked one.
1938 *Leben des Galilei* (The Life of Galileo), sc 14 (translated by Howard Benton, 1980).
▷ See Lessing 599:12.

28 *Die Wissenschaft kennt nur ein Gebot: den wissenschaftlichen Beitrag.*

Science knows only one commandment: contribute to science.
1938 *Leben des Galilei* (The Life of Galileo), sc.14 (translated by Howard Brenton, 1980).

29 *Weil ich ihm nicht traue, sind wir befreundet.*

Because I don't trust him, we are friends.
1939 *Mutter Courage und ihre Kinder* (Mother Courage and her Children), sc.3.

30 *Die schönsten Pläne sind schon zuschanden geworden durch die Kleinlichkeit von denen, wo sie ausführen sollten, denn die Kaiser selber können ja nix machen.*

The finest plans have always been spoiled by the littleness of those who should carry them out. Even emperors cannot do it all by themselves.
1939 *Mutter Courage und ihre Kinder* (Mother Courage and her Children), sc.6.

31 *Der Krieg findet immer einen Ausweg.*

War always finds a way.
1939 *Mutter Courage und ihre Kinder* (Mother Courage and her Children), sc.6.

Brenan, Gerald 1894–1987

English travel writer, born in Malta. After an itinerant early life he settled in Spain, producing *South from Granada* (1957) and *The Spanish Labyrinth* (1943) among other works.

32 Religions are kept alive by heresies, which are really sudden explosions of faith. Dead religions do not produce them.

1978 *Thoughts in a Dry Season.*

Brennan, William J(oseph), Jr 1906–97

US jurist, Associate Justice of the US Supreme Court (1956–90). He took an active role in liberal decisions handed down under Chief Justice Earl Warren.

33 Sex and obscenity are not synonymous.

1967 Ruling that established a new legal standard for obscenity, 24 Jun.

34 Death is an unusually severe and degrading punishment.

1972 Ruling to outlaw states' right to impose capital punishment, 29 Jun.

Brennus

Gallic king who captured Rome, 390 BC.

35 *Vae victis.*

Down with the defeated!

390 BC His cry on capturing Rome. Quoted in Livy *Ab urbe condita*, bk.5, ch.48, section 9.

Breslin, Jimmy 1930–

US sports journalist and writer, host of a TV series, *Jimmy Breslin's People* (1986). His works include *Can't Anybody Here Play This Game?* (1963).

36 They're killing the game with this phoney mystique—telling people that a guy needs the abilities of a brain surgeon to play left-guard for the Colts. Football is simply a game to keep the coalminers off the streets.

Quoted in Colin Jarman *The Guinness Dictionary of Sports Quotations* (1990).

37 Rage is the only quality which has kept me, or anybody I have ever studied, writing columns for newspapers.

1990 In *The Times*, 9 May.

Brewster, Kingman, Jr 1919–88

US educator, Professor of Law at Harvard (1950–60) and President of Yale (1963–77). He was US Ambassador to Britain (1977–81), and stayed on there as the representative of a US law firm.

38 The most fundamental value of a liberal education is that it makes life more interesting.

Recalled on his death in the *New York Times*, 9 Nov 1988.

Brezhnev, Leonid Ilyich 1906–82

Russian politician. As General Secretary of the Soviet Communist Party Central Committee after Khrushchev (1964), he became the most powerful Soviet leader, the first to hold simultaneously the position of General Secretary and President of the Supreme Soviet (1977–82).

39 She is trying to wear the trousers of Winston Churchill.

1979 Of Margaret Thatcher. Speech.

40 Whatever may divide us, Europe is our common home. A common fate has linked us through the centuries, and it continues to link us today.

1981 Speech while visiting the Federal Republic of Germany, 23 Nov.

Bricker, John W. 1893–1986

US Senator. He was Governor of Ohio (1939–45) and then Senator (1945–49). He ran as Republican vice-presidential candidate in 1944.

41 Joe, you're a dirty son of a bitch but there are times when you've got to have a son of a bitch around, and this is one of them.

c.1953 Comment to Senator Joseph R McCarthy on rescuing Republic prominence by pressing charges of Communism in government. Recalled in *This Fabulous Century* (1970).

Bridges, Robert Seymour 1844–1930

English Poet Laureate and hymn writer, who qualified and practised as a doctor, a friend of Gerard Manley Hopkins. As wartime Poet Laureate he compiled an anthology *The Spirit of Man* (1916) to lift the nation's spirits.

42 So sweet love seemed that April morn,
When first we kissed beside the thorn,
So strangely sweet, it was not strange
We thought that love could never change.

But I can tell—let truth be told—
That love will change in growing old;
Though day by day is nought to see,
So delicate his motions be.

1894 'So Sweet Loved Seemed'.

43 All my hope on God is founded
He does still my trust renew,
Me through change and chance he guideth,
Only good and only true.
God unknown,
He alone
Calls my heart to be his own.

1899 Hymn.

44 And I replied unto all these things which encompass the door of my flesh, 'Ye have told me of my god, that ye are not he: tell me something of him'. And they cried all with a great voice, 'He made us'. My questioning them was my mind's desire, and their Beauty was their answer.

1916 *The Spirit of Man: The Confessions of St Augustine.*

Bridges, (Henry) Styles 1898–1961

US Senator. He was Republican Governor of New Hampshire (1935–37) and then Senator (1937–61). He opposed the New Deal and was a supporter of Joseph McCarthy.

45　China asked for a sword, and we gave her a dull paring knife.

Of China's collapse to Communism. Quoted in David Halberstam *The Fifties* (1993).

Bridie, James pseudonym of *Osborne Henry Mavor* 1888–1951

Scottish playwright and doctor. Founder of the Glasgow Citizens' Theatre, he enjoyed considerable success with such plays as *The Anatomist* (1930) and *Daphne Laureola* (1949).

46　I sat through the first act and heard my lovely lines falling like cold porridge on a damp mattress.

1939 *One Way of Living*, alluding to a performance of his play *Marriage is no Joke*.

Bright, John 1811–89

British radical statesman and orator, a leading member of the Anti-Corn League (1839), MP from 1843 and an enormous influence on the Unionist party. A member of the Peace Society, he denounced the Crimean War (1854).

47　The Angel of Death has been abroad throughout the land. You may almost hear the beating of his wings.

1855 Of the Crimean War. Speech, House of Commons, 23 Feb.

48　This regard for the liberties of Europe, this care at one time for the protestant interest, this excessive love for the balance of power, is neither more nor less than a gigantic system of outdoor relief for the aristocracy of Great Britain.

1858 Speech, Birmingham, 29 Oct.

49　England is the mother of Parliaments.

1865 Speech, Birmingham, 18 Jan.

50　There is no nation on the continent of Europe that is less able to do harm to England, and there is no nation on the continent of Europe to whom we are less able to do harm, than Russia. We are so separate that it seems impossible that the two nations, by the use of reason or common sense at all, could possibly be brought into conflict with each other.

1878 Speech, Birmingham, 13 Jan.

Brillat-Savarin, Jean Anthelme 1755–1826

French politician, gastronome and writer, Mayor of Belley in 1793. During the French Revolution he took refuge in Switzerland and America. His *Physiologie du goût* is an elegant and witty compendium of the art of dining.

51　*Dis-moi ce que tu manges, je te dirai ce que tu es.*

Tell me what you eat and I will tell you what you are.

1825 *Physiologie du goût*, aphorism 4 (translated by Anne Drayton, 1970).

52　*La découverte d'un mets nouveau fait plus pour le bonheur du genre humain que la découverte d'une étoile.*

The discovery of a new dish does more for the happiness of mankind than the discovery of a star.

1825 *Physiologie du goût*, aphorism 9 (translated by Anne Drayton, 1970).

53　*La volaille est pour la cuisine ce qu'est la toile pour les peintres.*

Fowls are to the kitchen what his canvas is to the painter.

1825 *Physiologie du goût*, pt.1, ch.6, section 34 (translated by Anne Drayton, 1970).

54　*La truffe n'est point un aphrodisiaque positif; mais elle peut, en certaines occasions, rendre les femmes plus tendres et les hommes plus aimables.*

The truffle is not a true aphrodisiac; but in certain circumstances it can make women more affectionate and men more attentive.

1825 *Physiologie du goût*, pt.1, ch.6, section 44 (translated by Anne Drayton, 1970).

55　*L'alcool est le monarque des liquides, et porte au dernier degré l'exaltation palatale.*

Alcohol is the prince of liquids, and carries the palate to its highest pitch of exaltation.

1825 *Physiologie du goût*, pt.1, ch.9, section 53 (translated by Anne Drayton, 1970).

56　*C'est aussi de tous les arts celui qui nous a rendu le service le plus important pour la vie civile.*

It is also of all arts the one which has done the most to advance the cause of civilization.

1825 Of cooking. *Physiologie du goût*, pt.1, ch.27, section 123 (translated by Anne Drayton, 1970).

Brinkley, David McClure 1920–

US news commentator, best known for the nightly *Huntley–Brinkley Report* (1956–70), co-hosted with Chet Huntley.

58 If you turn on your set and see nothing is
    happening…do not call a serviceman. You have
    tuned in the US Senate.
    1986 On ABC TV broadcast, 1 Jun.

59 A cavalry commander…said he had just been given
    a thousand new men who had never seen a horse
    and a thousand horses who had never seen a man.
    1988 On World War II. *Washington Goes to War.*

60 [They] will fearlessly commit both parties to favor
    mother love and the protection of the whooping
    crane, and to oppose the man-eating shark and the
    more unpopular forms of sin.
    Of party platforms. Quoted in Marc Gunther *The House That
    Roone Built* (1994).

Brisbane, Arthur 1864–1936

US newspaper editor and writer. Editor of the *New York
Herald*, which was owned by William Randolph Hearst,
he was a proponent of 'sensationalist' journalism.

61 Never forget that if you don't hit a newspaper
    reader between the eyes with your first sentence,
    there is no need of writing a second one.
    c.1900 Quoted in Oliver Carlson *Brisbane: a Candid Biography*
    (1937), ch.5.

62 Hang your idea on a peg that all can read.
    c.1907 Quoted in Oliver Carlson *Brisbane: a Candid Biography*
    (1937), ch.7.

Britten, Baron (Edward) Benjamin, of Aldeburgh 1913–76

English composer, pianist and conductor, a student of
John Ireland and Frank Bridge. His extensive output
includes the opera *Peter Grimes* (1945) and other operas,
songs, chamber music and orchestral works, and the *War
Requiem* (1961), written for the reopening of Coventry
Cathedral. With Peter Pears, he founded the Aldeburgh
Festival (1948), at which much of his work was first
performed.

63 I remember the first time I tried the result looked
    rather like the Forth Bridge.
    1964 Of his first attempts at composition. Quoted in the
    Sunday Telegraph.

Brock, Sir Isaac 1768–1812

British soldier, commander of the British and militia
forces in the War of 1812.

64 Push on, brave York Volunteers!
    1812 Last command before succumbing to a sniper's bullet in
    the Battle of Queenston Heights, Niagara peninsula, Upper
    Canada (modern Ontario), 13 Oct. Quoted in C P Stacey
    'Brock's Muniments', in *Books in Canada* (Aug–Sep 1980).

Brodber, Erna 1940–

Jamaican writer and critic. Her works include sociological
studies on women and children in Jamaica, books on

Caribbean literature, and novels including *Jane and
Louisa Will Soon Come Home* (1980) and *Myal* (1988), on
colonial education.

65 Different rhymes for different times
    Different styles for different climes
    Someday them rogues in Whitehall
    Be forced to change their tune.
    1988 *Myal*, ch.15.

Brodkey, Harold 1930–96

US writer and journalist, a victim of AIDS.

66 Nothing I have ever written has been admired as
    much as the announcement of my death.
    Remark about his articles tracing the course of his illness in the
    New Yorker. Quoted in his obituary in *The Scotsman*, 29 Jan
    1996.

Brodsky, Ioseph 1940–96

Russian-born US poet. Exiled from Russia as a 'social
parasite', he took US citizenship in 1977 and was awarded
the Nobel Prize in 1987. He has latterly written in
English, and has translated his earlier Russian poems.

67 Illness and death…the only things that a tyrant has
    in common with his subjects… In this sense alone,
    a nation profits from being run by an old man.
    1986 *Less Than One*, 'On Tyranny'.

68 The dusty catastrophe of Asia. Green only on the
    banner of the Prophet. Nothing grows here except
    mustaches.
    1986 *Less Than One*, 'Flight From Byzantium'.

69 Racism? But isn't it only a form of misanthropy?
    1986 *Less Than One*, 'Flight From Byzantium'.

70 Snobbery? But it's only a form of despair.
    1986 *Less Than One*, 'Flight From Byzantium'.

71 A big step for me, and a small step for mankind.
    1987 Response on hearing of his Nobel Prize award. Quoted in
    his obituary in *The Scotsman*, 29 Jan 1996.
    ▷ See Armstrong 35:49.

72 Were we to choose our leaders on the basis of their
    reading experience and not their political
    programs, there would be much less grief on earth.
    I believe—not empirically, alas, but only
    theoretically—that for someone who has read a lot
    of Dickens to shoot his like in the name of an idea
    is harder than for someone who has read no
    Dickens.
    1987 Nobel Prize Acceptance Speech.

73 There are worse crimes than burning books. One
    of them is not reading them.
    1991 Comment at a press conference in Washington, DC, 15
    May, on accepting the US poet laureateship.

74 Russia is my home…and for everything that I have in my soul I am obligated to Russia and its people. And—this is the main thing—obligated to its language.
1992 In the *New York Times*, 1 Oct.

75 They should be in every room in every motel in the land.
1992 Of poetry books. In the *New York Times*, 1 Oct.

Brody, Hugh 1943–
Canadian ecologist and writer.

76 Resources left in the ground are saved, not lost.
1981 *Maps and Dreams: Indians and the British Columbia Frontier.*

Bronowski, Jacob 1908–74
Polish-born British mathematician, poet and humanist. He was a popular broadcaster, particularly on the BBC's *Brains Trust* and *The Ascent of Man* (1973).

77 Dissent is the native activity of the scientist, and it has got him into a good deal of trouble in the last years. But if that is cut off, what is left will not be a scientist. And I doubt whether it will be a man.
1953 'The Sense of Human Dignity', lecture at Massachusetts Institute of Technology, 19 Mar.

78 Science has nothing to be ashamed of, even in the ruins of Nagasaki. The shame is theirs who appeal to other values than the human imaginative values which science has evolved.
1953 'The Sense of Human Dignity', lecture at Massachusetts Institute of Technology, 19 Mar.

79 At bottom, the society of scientists is more important than their discoveries. What science has to teach us here is not its techniques but its spirit: the irresistible need to explore.
1956 *Science and Human Values.*

80 Man masters nature not by force but by understanding. This is why science has succeeded where magic failed: because it has looked for no spell to cast on nature.
1956 *Universities Quarterly*, vol.10, issue 3.

81 Sooner or later every one of us breathes an atom that has been breathed before by anyone you can think of who has lived before us—Michelangelo or George Washington or Moses.
1966 Quoted in the *New York Times*, 13 Oct 1969.

82 No science is immune to the infection of politics and the corruption of power.
1971 In *The Listener*.

83 The world can only be grasped by action, not by contemplation… The hand is the cutting edge of the mind.

1973 *The Ascent of Man*, ch.3.

84 That is the essence of science: ask an impertinent question and you are on the way to a pertinent answer.
1973 *The Ascent of Man*, ch.4.

85 Man is a singular creature. He has a set of gifts which make him unique among the animals, so that unlike them he is not a figure in the landscape—he is the shaper of the landscape.
1979 In *The Listener*.

Brontë, Anne 1820–49
English novelist and poet, younger sister of Charlotte and Emily. Her first novel *Agnes Grey* (1847) was published under the pseudonym Acton Bell. She also wrote *The Tenant of Wildfell Hall* (1848).

86 To think a soul so near divine,
   Within a form, so angel fair,
   United to a heart like thine,
   Has gladdened once our humble sphere.
1846 'A Reminiscence', in *Poems by Currer, Ellis and Acton Bell.*

87 My soul is awakened, my spirit is soaring
   And carried aloft on the wings of the breeze;
   For above and around me the wild wind is roaring,
   Arousing to rapture the earth and the seas.
1846 'Line Composed in a Wood on a Windy Day', in *Poems by Currer, Ellis and Acton Bell.*

88 All true histories contain instruction; though in some, the treasure may be hard to find, and when found, so trivial in quantity that the dry, shrivelled kernel scarcely compensates for the trouble of cracking the nut.
1847 *Agnes Grey*, ch.1.

89 He'll be all right when he's married, as Mama says; and reformed rakes make the best husbands, everybody knows. I only wish he were not so ugly—that's all I think about—but then there's no choice here in the country.
1847 *Agnes Grey*, ch.13.

90 What is it that constitutes virtue, Mrs Graham? Is it the circumstance of being able and willing to resist temptation; or that of having no temptation to resist?
1848 *The Tenant of Wildfell Hall*, ch.3.

Brontë, Charlotte 1816–55
English novelist and poet, elder sister of Emily and Anne. Her four novels are *Jane Eyre* (1847), *Shirley* (1849), *Villette* (1853) and *The Professor* (1857).

91 We wove a web in childhood,
   A web of sunny air;
   We dug a spring in infancy

Of water pure and fair;
We sowed in youth a mustard seed,
We cut an almond rod;
We are now grown up to riper age—
Are they withered in the sod?
1835 'We Wove a Web in Childhood'.

92 But two miles more and then we rest!
Well, there is still an hour of day,
And long the brightness of the west
Sit then, awhile, here in this wood
So total is the solitude,
We safely may delay.
1846 'Regret', in *Poems by Currer, Ellis and Acton Bell.*

93 Women are supposed to be very calm generally: but
women feel just as men feel: they need exercise for
their faculties, and a field for their efforts as much
as their brothers do; they suffer from too rigid a
restraint, too absolute a stagnation, precisely as
men would suffer…it is thoughtless to condem
them, or laugh at them, if they seek to do more
than custom has pronounced necessary for their
sex.
1847 *Jane Eyre*, ch.12.

94 I grant an ugly woman is a blot on the fair face of
creation; but as to the gentleman, let them be
solicitous to possess only strength and valour: let
their motto be:—Hunt, shoot, and fight: the rest is
not worth a flip.
1847 *Jane Eyre* ch.17.

95 The soul fortunately, has an interpreter—often an
unconscious, but still a truthful interpreter—in the
eye.
1847 *Jane Eyre*, ch.28.

96 Reader, I married him.
1847 *Jane Eyre*, ch.38.

97 Conventionality is not morality. Self-righteousness
is not religion. To attack the first is not to assail the
last. To pluck the mask from the face of the
Pharisee, is not to lift an impious hand to the
Crown of Thorns.
1848 *Jane Eyre* (2nd edn), preface.

98 Of late years an abundant shower of curates has
fallen upon the north of England.
1849 *Shirley*, ch.1.

99 I describe imperfect characters. Every character in
this book will be found to be more or less
imperfect, my pen refusing to draw anything in the
model line.
1849 *Shirley*, ch.5.

1 Old maids like the houseless and unemployed
poor, should not ask for a place and an occupation

in the world: the demand disturbs the happy and
the rich.
1849 *Shirley*, ch.22.

2 Liberty lends us her wings and Hope guides us by
her star.
1853 *Villette*, ch.6.

3 Out of association grows adhesion, and out of
adhesion amalgamation.
1853 *Villette*, ch.25.

4 What animal magnetism drew thee and me
together—I know not.
1857 *The Professor*, ch.1.

5 Unlawful pleasure, trenching on another's rights, is
delusive and envenomed pleasure—its hollowness
disappoints at the time, its poison cruelly tortures
afterwards, its effects deprave forever.
1857 *The Professor*, ch.20.

Brontë, Emily Jane 1818–48

English novelist and poet, sister of Anne and Charlotte.
Her poems were first published under the pseudonym
Ellis Bell. Her only novel is the intense and powerful
Wuthering Heights (1847).

6 The night is darkening round me,
The wild winds coldly blow;
But a tyrant spell has bound me
And I cannot, cannot go.
1837 'The Night is Darkening Round Me'.

7 The winter wind is loud and wild,
Come close to me, my darling child;
Forsake thy books, and mateless play;
And, while the night is gathering grey,
We'll talk its pensive hours away.
1846 'Faith and Despondency', in *Poems by Currer, Ellis and
Acton Bell.*

8 No coward soul is mine,
No trembler in the world's storm-troubled sphere:
I see Heaven's glories shine,
And faith shines equal, arming me from fear.
1846 'No Coward Soul is Mine', in *Poems by Currer, Ellis and
Acton Bell.*

9 Cold in the earth—and the deep snow piled above
thee,
Far, far, removed, cold in the dreary grave!
Have I forgot, my only Love, to love thee,
Severed at last by Time's all-serving wave?
1846 'Rememberance', in *Poems by Currer, Ellis and Acton Bell.*

10 I've dreamt in my life dreams that have stayed with
me ever after, and changed my ideas; they've gone
through and through me, like wine through water,
and altered the colour of my mind.
1847 *Wuthering Heights*, ch.9.

11 As different as a moonbeam from lightning, or frost
from fire.
1847 *Wuthering Heights*, ch.9.

12 My love for Linton is like the foliage in the woods.
Time will change it, I'm well aware, as winter
changes the trees. My Love for Heathcliff resembles
the eternal rocks beneath—a source of little visible
delight but necessary. Nelly, I *am* Heathcliff.
1847 *Wuthering Heights*, ch.9.

13 He might as well plant an oak in a flower-pot, and
expect it to thrive, as imagine he can restore her to
vigour in the soil of his shallow cares!
1847 *Wuthering Heights*, ch.14.

14 The more the worms writhe, the more I yearn to
crush out their entrails!
1847 Heathcliff. *Wuthering Heights*, ch.14.

15 I lingered around them, under the benign sky;
watched the moths fluttering among the heath and
hare-bells; listened to the soft wind breathing
through the grass; and wondered how anyone
could ever imagine unquiet slumbers, for the
sleepers in that quiet earth.
1847 *Wuthering Heights*, ch.34, closing words.

Brooke, Frances née *Moore* 1724–89

English writer. In Canada (1763–8) with her minister
husband, she produced 'Canada's first novel', *The History
of Emily Montague* (1769). She wrote other novels and
plays, and edited a periodical *The Old Maid.*

16 I no longer wonder the elegant arts are unknown
here; the rigor of the climate suspends the very
powers of the understanding; what then must
become of those of the imagination?… Genius will
never mount high, where the faculties of the mind
are benumbed half the year.
1769 *The History of Emily Montague*, 'Letter 49'.

Brooke, Rupert Chawner 1887–1915

English poet, icon of the World War I 'lost generation'.
His early verse was published in 1911, and his reputation
was established by the posthumous publication of *1914
and Other Poems*. He died of blood poisoning on Skyros.

17 Breathless, we flung us on the windy hill.
Laughed in the sun, and kissed the lovely grass.
1910 'Sonnet'.

18 But there's wisdom in women, of more than they
have known,
And thoughts go blowing through them, are wiser
than their own.
1913 'There's Wisdom in Women', written Jun.

19 Then, the cool kindliness of sheets, that soon
Smooth away trouble; and the rough male kiss

Of blankets
1914 'The Great Lover'.

20 The benison of hot water; furs to touch;
The good smell of old clothes.
1914 'The Great Lover'.

21 If I should die, think only this of me:
That there's some corner of a foreign field
That is for ever England.
There shall be
In that rich dust a richer dust concealed;
A dust whom England bore, shaped, made aware,
Gave, once, her flowers to love, her ways to roam,
A body of England's, breathing English air,
Washed by the rivers, blest by suns of home.
1914 'The Soldier'.

22 In hearts at peace, under an English heaven.
1914 'The Soldier'.

23 Blow out, you bugles, over the rich Dead!
There's none of these so lonely and poor of old,
But, dying, has made us rarer gifts than gold.
1914 'The Dead'.

24 Naught broken save this body, lost but breath;
Nothing to shake the laughing heart's long peace
there
But only agony, and that has ending;
And the worst friend and enemy is but Death.
1914 'Peace'.

25 Here tulips bloom as they are told;
Unkempt about those hedges blows
An English unoffical rose.
1915 'The Old Vicarage, Grantchester'.

26 And spectral dance, before the dawn,
A hundred Vicars down the lawn;
Curates, long dust, will come and go
On lissom, clerical, printless toe;
And oft between the boughs is seen
The sly shade of a Rural Dean.
1915 'The Old Vicarage, Grantchester'.

27 God! I will pack, and take a train,
And get me to England once again!
For England's the one land, I know,
Where men with Spendid Hearts may go.
1915 'The Old Vicarage, Grantchester'.

28 For Cambridge people rarely smile,
Being urban, squat, and packed with guile.
1915 'The Old Vicarage, Grantchester'.

29 They love the Good; they worship Truth;
They laugh uproariously in youth;
(And when they get to feeling old,
They up and shoot themselves, I'm told).
1915 'The Old Vicarage, Grantchester'.

30   Stands the Church clock at ten to three?
     And is there honey still for tea?
     1915 'The Old Vicarage, Grantchester'.

31   Fish (fly-replete, in depth of June,
     Dawdling away their wat'ry noon).
     1915 'Heaven'.

32   Fish say, they have their stream and pond;
     But is there anything beyond?
     1915 'Heaven'.

33   But somewhere, beyond Space and Time
     Is wetter water, slimier slime!
     1915 'Heaven'.

34   Unfading moths, immortal flies,
     And the worm that never dies.
     And in that heaven of all their wish,
     There shall be no more land, say fish.
     1915 'Heaven'.

Brookner, Anita 1928–

English novelist and art historian. A spare, elegant stylist, she won the Booker Prize in 1984 for her novel *Hôtel Du Lac*.

35   It is best to marry for purely selfish reasons.
     1981 *A Start in Life*.

36   It is my contention that Aesop was writing for the tortoise market…hares have no time to read.
     1984 *Hôtel Du Lac*, ch.2.

37   Good women always think it is their fault when someone else is being offensive. Bad women never take the blame for anything.
     1984 *Hôtel Du Lac*, ch.7.

38   Blanche Vernon occupied her time most usefully in keeping feelings at bay.
     1986 *Misalliance*, ch.1.

39   I think you always feel braver in another language.
     1988 In *The Observer*, 7 Aug.

40   They were privileged children…they would always expect to be greeted with smiles.
     1989 *Lewis Percy*, ch.9.

41   Satire is dependent on strong beliefs, and on strong beliefs wounded.
     1989 In *The Spectator*, 23 Mar.

42   I reflected how easy it is for a man to reduce women of a certain age to imbecility. All he has to do is give an impersonation of desire, or better still, of secret knowledge, for a woman to feel herself a source of power.
     1993 *A Family Romance*, ch.7.

Brooks, Louise 1906–85

US film actress, embodiment of the flapper age, renowned for her innocent sexuality and natural screen presence.

43   Every actor has a natural animosity toward every other actor, present or absent, living or dead.
     1982 *Lulu in Hollywood*.

Brooks, Mel pseudonym of *Melvin Kaminsky* 1926–

US director, writer and actor. His successful comedies have included *The Producers* (1968), *Blazing Saddles* (1974) and *Young Frankenstein* (1974).

44   That's it baby. If you've got it, flaunt it.
     1968 *The Producers*.

Brooks, Van Wyck 1886–1963

US author and critic. He wrote biographical studies of Mark Twain (1920), Henry James (1925) and Emerson (1932). His works, which attacked materialism, also include *The Flowering of New England* (1936, Pulitzer Prize).

45   It is not that the French are not profound, but they all express themselves so well that we are led to take their geese for swans.
     1958 *From A Writer's Notebook*.

Brougham, Henry Peter, 1st Baron Brougham and Vaux 1778–1868

Scottish jurist and politician. He was called to the English bar in 1808 and entered parliament in 1810. Noted for his eloquence, he became Lord Chancellor in 1830 and promoted the passage of the Reform Bill.

46   A legal gentleman who rescues your estate from your enemies, and keeps it himself.
     His definition of a lawyer. Quoted in Richard Fountain *The Wit of the Wig* (1968).

Broun, (Matthew) Heywood Campbell 1888–1939

US journalist, humorist and novelist.

47   Except that right side is up is best, there is not much to learn about holding a baby. There are one hundred and fifty-two distinctly different ways— and all are right! At least, all will do.
     1921 *Seeing Things at Night*, 'Holding a Baby'.

48   The tragedy of life is not that man loses, but that he almost wins.
     1922 *Pieces of Hate, and Other Enthusiasms*, 'Sport for Art's Sake'.

49   Just as every conviction begins as a whim so does every emancipator serve his appreticeship as a crank. A fanatic is a great leader who is just entering the room.
     1928 In *New York World*, 6 Feb.

50 The tradition of baseball always has been agreeably free of chivalry. The rule is 'Do anything you can get away with'.

Quoted in Colin Jarman *The Guinness Dictionary of Sports Quotations* (1990).

51 Sports do not build character. They reveal it.

Quoted in Colin Jarman *The Guinness Dictionary of Sports Quotations* (1990).

Brown, Pat (Edmund Gerald, Sr) 1905–96

US lawyer and politician, Governor of California (1959–66).

52 Why, this is the worst disaster since my election.

1965 Of the Watts riots. Recalled in the *New York Times*, 21 Aug 1994.

Brown, John 1800–59

US militant abolitionist. In 1859 he led an unsuccessful raid on the US Armory at Harper's Ferry, Virginia, and was convicted of treason and hanged. He was twice married and had 20 children.

53 I am as content to die for God's eternal truth on the scaffold as in any other way.

1859 Letter to his children on the eve of his execution, 2 Dec.

Brown, John Mason 1900–69

US theatre critic. He wrote long-running theatre columns in the *New York Post* and *Saturday Review* as well as publishing several books on the theatre.

54 Tallulah Bankhead barged down the Nile last night as Cleopatra—and sank.

1937 In the *New York Post*, 11 Nov.

55 To many, dramatic criticism must seem like an attempt to tattoo soap bubbles.

1963 *Stagebill.*

56 He has ears he likes to bathe in sound.

1963 Of playwright Maxwell Anderson. *Dramatis Personae.*

Brown, Olympia 1835–1900

US religious leader, the first woman ordained in the US.

57 The more we learn of science, the more we see that its wonderful mysteries are all explained by a few simple laws so connected together and so dependent upon each other, that we see the same mind animating them all.

1895 Sermon in Wisconsin, c.13 Jan.

Brown, Rita Mae 1944–

US writer and feminist, a campaigner for gay rights. She is the author of a number of popular novels.

58 No government has the right to tell its citizens when or whom to love. The only queer people are those who don't love anybody.

1982 Speech, 28 Aug, at the opening ceremony of the Gay Olympics, San Francisco.

59 If Michaelangelo were a heterosexual, the Sistine Chapel would have been painted basic white and with a roller.

1988 In the *New York Times*, 15 May.

60 I think the reward for conformity is that everyone likes you except yourself.

1988 *Bingo*, ch.35.

Brown, Thomas 1663–1704

English satirical writer.

61 I do not love thee, Dr Fell.
The reason why I cannot tell;
But this I know, and know full well,
I do not love thee, Dr Fell.

Composed while an undergraduate at Christ Church, Oxford, under the Deanship of Dr Fell.

Brown, Walter fl.15c

Scottish poet. *Letters of Gold* is his only known surviving poem.

62 Grit riches and prosperitie
Upfosteris vyce.

15c *Letters of Gold*, l.131–2.

Browne, Sir Thomas 1605–82

English writer and physician. His meditative *Religio Medici* appeared in an authorized version in 1643. Other works include *Pseudodoxia Epidemica, or Enquiries into…Vulgar and Common Errors* (1646) and *Hydriotaphia* (Urn Burial) (1658).

63 For my religion, though there be several circumstances that might persuade the world I have none at all—as the general scandal of my profession, the natural course of my studies, the indifferency of my behaviour and discourse in matters of religion, neither violently defending one, nor with that common ardour and contention opposing another—yet in despite hereof I dare without usurpation assume the honourable style of a Christian.

1634–5 *Religio Medici* (published 1643), pt 1, section 1.

64 My common conversation I do acknowledge austere, my behaviour full of rigor, sometimes not without morosity; yet at my devotion I love to use the civility of my knee, my hat, and hand, with all those outward and sensible motions which may express or promote my invisible devotion.

1634–5 *Religio Medici* (published 1643), pt 1, section 3.

65 Those vulgar heads that look asquint on the face of truth.
  1634–5 *Religio Medici* (published 1643), pt 1, section 3.

66 In brief, where the Scripture is silent, the church is my text; where that speaks, 'tis but my comment; where there is a joint silence of both, I borrow not the rules of my religion from Rome or Geneva, but the dictates of my own reason.
  1634–5 *Religio Medici* (published 1643), pt 1, section 5.

67 Where we desire to be informed, 'tis good to contest with men above ourselves; but to confirm and establish our opinions, 'tis best to argue with judgements below our own, that the frequent spoils and victories over their reasons may settle in ourselves an esteem and confirmed opinion of our own.
  1634–5 *Religio Medici* (published 1643), pt 1, section 6.

68 Every man is not a proper champion for truth, nor fit to take up the gauntlet in the cause of verity.
  1634–5 *Religio Medici* (published 1643), pt 1, section 6.

69 Every man's own reason is his best Oedipus.
  1634–5 Oedipus here means riddle-solver. *Religio Medici* (published 1643), pt 1, section 6.

70 For indeed heresies perish not with their authors, but like the river Arethusa, though they lose their currents in one place, they rise up again in another.
  1634–5 *Religio Medici* (published 1643), pt 1, section 6.

71 Men are lived over again; the world is now as it was in ages past.
  1634–5 *Religio Medici* (published 1643), pt 1, section 6.

72 Methinks there be not impossibilities enough in religion for an active faith.
  1634–5 *Religio Medici* (published 1643), pt 1, section 6.

73 I desire to exercise my faith in the difficultest points, for to credit ordinary and visible objects is not faith but persuasion.
  1634–5 *Religio Medici* (published 1643), pt 1, section 6.

74 I love to lose myself in a mystery, to pursue my reason to an *O altitudo!*
  1634–5 *Religio Medici* (published 1643), pt 1, section 9.

75 Who can speak of eternity without a solecism, or think thereof without an ecstasy? Time we may comprehend, 'tis but five days elder than ourselves.
  1634–5 *Religio Medici* (published 1643), pt 1, section 11.

76 We carry with us the wonders we seek without us: there is all Africa and her prodigies in us.
  1634–5 *Religio Medici* (published 1643), pt 1, section 15.

77 We are that bold and adventurous piece of nature which he that studies wisely learns in a compendium what others labour at in a divided piece and endless volume.
  1634–5 *Religio Medici* (published 1643), pt 1, section 15.

78 Nature is not at variance with art nor art with nature, they both being the servants of his providence: art is the perfection of nature.
  1634–5 *Religio Medici* (published 1643), pt 1, section 16.

79 All things are artificial, for nature is the art of God.
  1634–5 *Religio Medici* (published 1643), pt 1, section 16.

80 Obstinacy in a bad cause, is but constancy in a good.
  1634–5 *Religio Medici* (published 1643), pt 1, section 25.

81 Persecution is a bad and indirect way to plant religion.
  1634–5 *Religio Medici* (published 1643), pt 1, section 25.

82 There are many…canonized on earth, that shall never be Saints in Heaven.
  1634–5 *Religio Medici* (published 1643), pt 1, section 26.

83 I am not so much afraid of death, as ashamed thereof.
  1634–5 *Religio Medici* (published 1643), pt 1, section 40.

84 Certainly there is no happiness within this circle of flesh, nor is it in the optics of these eyes to behold felicity; the first day of our Jubilee is death.
  1634–5 *Religio Medici* (published 1643), pt 1, section 44.

85 I have tried if I could reach that great resolution…to be honest without a thought of Heaven or Hell.
  1634–5 *Religio Medici* (published 1643), pt 1, section 47.

86 To believe only in possibilities, is not faith, but mere Philosophy.
  1634–5 *Religio Medici* (published 1643), pt 1, section 48.

87 There is no road or ready way to virtue.
  1634–5 *Religio Medici* (published 1643), pt 1, section 55.

88 The world was before the creation and at an end before it had a beginning; and thus was I dead before I was alive. Though my grave be England, my dying place was Paradise, and Eve miscarried of me before she conceived of Cain.
  1634–5 *Religio Medici* (published 1643), pt 1, section 59.

89 All places, all airs make unto me one country; I am in England, everywhere, and under any meridian.
  1634–5 *Religio Medici* (published 1643), pt 2, section 1.

90 It is the common wonder of all men, how among so many millions of faces, there should be none alike.
  1634–5 *Religio Medici* (published 1643), pt 2, section 1.

91 I could be content that we might procreate like trees, without conjunction, or that there were any

way to perpetuate the World without this trivial and vulgar way of coition: it is the foolishest act a wise man commits in all his life.
1634–5 *Religio Medici* (published 1643), pt 2, section 9.

92 We all labour against our own cure, for death is the cure of all diseases.
1634–5 *Religio Medici* (published 1643), pt 2, section 9.

93 Whilst I study to find how I am a microcosm of little world, I find myself something more than the great. There is surely a piece of divinity in us; something that was before the elements, and owes no homage unto the sun.
1634–5 *Religio Medici* (published 1643), pt 2, section 11.

94 Old mortality, the ruins of forgotten times.
1658 *Hydriotaphia* (Urn Burial), Epistle Dedicatory.

95 Were the happiness of the next world as closely apprehended as the felicities of this, it were a martyrdom to live.
1658 *Hydriotaphia* (Urn Burial), ch.4.

96 The long habit of living indisposeth us for dying.
1658 *Hydriotaphia* (Urn Burial), ch.5.

97 Adversity stretcheth our days.
1658 *Hydriotaphia* (Urn Burial), ch.5.

98 We cannot hope to live so long in our names as some have done in their persons.
1658 *Hydriotaphia* (Urn Burial), ch.5.

99 'Tis too late to be ambitious.
1658 *Hydriotaphia* (Urn Burial), ch.5.

1 There is no antidote against the opium of time.
1658 *Hydriotaphia* (Urn Burial), ch.5.

2 To be nameless in worthy deeds exceeds an infamous history… Who would not rather have been the good thief than Pilate?
1658 *Hydriotaphia* (Urn Burial), ch.5.

3 Man is a noble animal, splendid in ashes, and pompous in the grave.
1658 *Hydriotaphia* (Urn Burial), ch.5.

4 Life is a pure flame, and we live by an invisible sun within us.
1658 *Hydriotaphia* (Urn Burial), ch.5.

5 Life itself is but the shadow of death, and souls departed but the shadows of the living. All things fall under this name. The sun itself is but the dark *simulacrum*, and light but the shadow of God.
1658 *The Garden of Cyrus*, ch.2.

6 The quincunx of heaven runs low, and 'tis time to close the five parts of knowledge.

1658 *The Garden of Cyrus*, ch.5.

7 All things began in order, so shall they end, and so shall they begin again; according to the ordainer of order and mystical mathematics of the city of heaven.
1658 *The Garden of Cyrus*, ch.5.

8 Nor will the sweetest delight of gardens afford much comfort in sleep; wherein the dullness of that sense shakes hands with delectable odours; and though in the bed of Cleopatra, can hardly with any delight raise up the ghost of a rose.
1658 *The Garden of Cyrus*, ch.5.

Browne, William 1692–1774
English physician and poet.

9 The King to Oxford sent a troop of horse,
For Tories own no argument but force;
With equal skill to Cambridge books he sent,
For Whigs admit no force but argument.
Literary Anecdotes.

Browning, Elizabeth née *Barrett* 1806–61
English poet, who married Robert Browning (1846). Her early work includes her *Essay on Mind, and other Poems* which was published anonymously when she was 19. Her other writing include *Poems* (1884), translations of Aeschylus's *Prometheus Bound* (1833 and a new translation in her *Poems* of 1850), the long narrative poem *Aurora Leigh* (1856), *Sonnets from the Portuguese* (also published in *Poems*, 1850) which were not translations but express her own love, and *Casa Guidi Windows* (1851) on the theme of Italian Liberation. *Last Poems* was published posthumously in 1862.

10 Thou large-brained woman and large-hearted man.
1844 *Poems*, 'To George Sand. A Desire', l.1.

11 And because I was a poet, and because the public praised me,
With their critical deductions for the modern writer's fault;
I could sit at rich men's tables,—though the courtesies that raise me,
Still suggested clear between us, the pale spectrum of the salt.
1844 *Poems*, 'Lady Geraldine's Courtship', stanza 9.

12 And the rolling anapaestic
Curled, like vapour over shrines.
1844 *Poems*, 'Wine of Cyprus', stanza 10.

13 I am floated along, as if I should die
Of Liberty's exquisite pain
1849 'The Runaway Slave at Pilgrim's Point', stanza 36.

14 Straightway I was 'ware

So weeping, how a mystic shape did move
Behind me, and drew me backward by the hair
And a voice said in mastery while I strove…
'Guess now who holds thee!'—'*Death*', I said, but
there
The silver answer rang…'Not Death, but Love.'
1850 *Poems*, 'Sonnets from the Portuguese', sonnet 1.

15 If thou must love me, let it be for naught
Except for love's sake only.
1850 *Poems*, 'Sonnets from the Portuguese', sonnet 14.

16 When our two souls stand up erect and strong,
Face to face, silent, drawing nigh and nigher,
Until their lengthening wings break into fire
At either curvèd point,…what bitter wrong,
Can the earth do to us, that we should not long
Be here contented?
1850 *Poems*, 'Sonnets from the Portuguese', sonnet 22.

17 Let the world's sharpness like a clasping knife
Shut in upon itself, and do no harm
In this close hand of love.
1850 *Poems*, 'Sonnets from the Portuguese', sonnet 24.

18 First time he kissed me, but only kissed
The fingers of this hand wherewith I write,
And ever since it grew more clean and white…
1850 *Poems*, 'Sonnets from the Portuguese', sonnet 38.

19 How do I love thee? Let me count the ways!—
I love thee to the depth and breadth and height
My soul can reach, when feeling out of sight
For the ends of Being and Ideal Grace.
I love thee to the level of everyday's
Most quiet need, by the sun and candlelight—
I love thee freely, as men strive for Right,—
I love thee purely, as they turn from Praise;
I love thee with the passion, put to use
In my old griefs,…and with my childhood's faith:
I love thee with the love I seemed to lose
With my lost Saints,—I love thee with the breath
Smiles, tears, of all my life!—and, if God choose,
I shall but love thee better after death.
1850 *Poems*, 'Sonnets from the Portuguese', sonnet 43.

20 God answers sharp and sudden on some prayers,
And thrusts the thing we have prayed for in our
face,
A gauntlet with a gift in't.
1856 *Aurora Leigh*, bk.2.

21 The music soars within the little lark,
And the lark soars.
1856 *Aurora Leigh*, bk.3.

22 Since when was genius found respectable?
1856 *Aurora Leigh*, bk.6.

23 Earth's crammed with heaven,

And every common bush afire with God.
1856 *Aurora Leigh*, bk.7.

Browning, Robert 1812–89

English poet. His poetry offers a wide range of characters, dramatic situations, and a rich variety of forms and rhythms. His work includes *Men and Women* (1855), *Dramatis Personae* (1864) and *The Ring and the Book* (1868–9).

24 God is the perfect poet,
Who in his person acts his own creations.
1835 *Paracelsus*, pt.2, l.648–9.

25 The year's at the spring,
And days at the morn;
Morning's at seven;
The hill-side's dew-pearled;
The lark's on the wing;
The snail's on the thorn;
God's in His heaven—
All's right with the world.
1841 *Pippa Passes*, pt.1.

26 Like a god going thro' his world there stands
One mountain, for a moment in the dusk,
Whole brotherhoods of cedars on its brow
1841 *Pippa Passes*, pt.2.

27 There's a great text in Galatians,
Once you trip on it, entails
Twenty-nine distinct damnations,
One sure, if another fails.
1842 *Dramatic Lyrics*, 'Soliloquy of the Spanish Cloister'.

28 My scrofulous French novel
On grey paper with blunt type!
1842 *Dramatic Lyrics*, 'Soliloquy of the Spanish Cloister'.

29 The moth's kiss, first!
Kiss me as if you made believe
You were not sure, this eve,
How my face, your flower, had pursed
Its petals up.
1842 *Dramatic Lyrics*, 'In a Gondola'.

30 What's become of Waring
Since he gave us all the slip?
1842 *Dramatic Lyrics*, 'Waring'. The first line was used as the title of a novel by Anthony Powell.

31 Hamelin Town's in Brunswick,
By famous Hanover city;
The river Weser, deep and wide,
Washes its wall on the southern side;
A pleasanter spot you never spied.
1842 *Dramatic Lyrics*, 'The Pied Piper of Hamlin'.

32 Rats!
They fought the dogs and killed the cats,
And bit the babies in the cradles.

And ate the cheeses out of the vats.
1842 *Dramatic Lyrics*, 'The Pied Piper of Hamlin'.

33 I sprang to the stirrup, and Joris, and he;
I galloped, Dirck galloped, we galloped all three.
1845 *Dramatic Romances and Lyrics*, 'How they brought the Good News from Ghent to Aix'.

34 Just for a handful of silver he left us,
Just for a riband to stick in his coat.
1845 Of Wordsworth. *Dramatic Romances and Lyrics*, 'The Lost Leader'.

35 Never glad confident morning again!
1845 *Dramatic Romances and Lyrics*, 'The Lost Leader'.

36 Oh, to be in England
Now that April's there,
And whoever wakes in England
Sees, some morning, unaware,
That the lowest boughs and the brushwood sheaf
Round the elm-tree bole are in tiny leaf,
While the chaffinch sings on the orchard bough
In England—now!
1845 *Dramatic Romances and Lyrics*, 'Home-Thoughts, from Abroad'.

37 That's the wise thrush; he sings each song twice over,
Lest you think he never could recapture
The first fine careless rapture!
1845 *Dramatic Romances and Lyrics*, 'Home-Thoughts, from Abroad'.

38 'Here and here did England help me: how can I help England?'—say.
1845 *Dramatic Romances and Lyrics*, 'Home-Thoughts, from the Sea'.

39 And then how I shall lie through centuries,
And hear the blessed mutter of the mass,
And see God made and eaten all day long,
And feel the steady candle-flame, and taste
Good strong thick stupefying incense-smoke!
1845 *Dramatic Romances and Lyrics*, 'The Bishop Orders his Tomb'.

40 A tap at the pane, the quick sharp scratch
And blue spurt of a lighted match,
And a voice less loud, through its joys and fears,
Than the two hearts beating each to each!
1845 *Dramatic Romances and Lyrics*, 'Meeting at Night'.

41 There may be heaven; there must be hell.
1845 *Dramatic Romances and Lyrics*, 'Time's Revenges'.

42 In the natural fog of the good man's mind.
1850 'Christmas Eve'.

43 Where the quiet-coloured end of evening smiles,
Miles and miles.
1855 *Men and Women*, 'Love among the Ruins'.

44 If you get simple beauty and naught else,
You get about the best thing God invents.
1855 *Men and Women*, 'Fra Lippo Lippi'.

45 This world's no blot for us
Nor blank; it means intensely, and means good:
To find its meaning is my meat and drink.
1855 *Men and Women*, 'Fra Lippo Lippi'.

46 Hark—the dominant's persistence till it must be answered to!
1855 *Men and Women*, 'A Toccata of Galuppi's'.

47 What of soul was left, I wonder, when the kissing had to stop?
1855 *Men and Women*, 'A Toccata of Galuppi's'.

48 Dear, dead woman, with such hair, too—what's become of all the gold
Used to hang and brush their bosoms? I feel chilly and grown old.
1855 *Men and Woman*, 'A Toccata of Galuppi's'.

49 'Tis the Last Judgement's fire must cure this place,
Calcine its clods and set my prisoners free.
1855 *Men and Women*, 'Childe Roland to the Dark Tower Came'.

50 As for the grass, it grew as scant as hair in leprosy—
thin dried blades pricked the mud which
underneath looked kneaded up with blood.
One stiff blind horse, his every bone a-stare, stood stupefied.
1855 *Men and Women*, 'Childe Roland to the Dark Tower Came'.

51 I never saw a brute I hated so;
He must be wicked to deserve such pain.
1855 *Men and Women*, 'Childe Roland to the Dark Tower Came'.

52 It was roses, roses, all the way.
1855 *Men and Women*, 'The Patriot'.

53 And find a poor devil has ended his cares
At the foot of your rotten-runged rat-riddled stairs?
Do I carry the moon in my pocket?
1855 *Men and women*, 'Master Huges of Saxe–Gotha'.

54 Just when we are safest, there's a sunset-touch,
A fancy from a flower-bell, some one's death,
A chorus-ending from Euripides, —
And that's enough for fifty hopes and fears
As old and new at once as Nature's self,
To rap and knock and enter in our soul.
Take hands and dance there, a fantastic ring,
Round the ancient idol, on his base again,—
The grand Perhaps.
1855 *Men and Women*, 'Bishop Blougram's Apology'.

55 All we have gained then by our unbelief
   Is a life of doubt diversified by faith,
   For one of faith diversified by doubt:
   We called the chess-board white,—we call it black.
   1855 *Men and Women*, 'Bishop Blougram's Apology'.

56 You, for example, clever to a fault,
   The rough and ready man who write apace,
   Read somewhat seldomer, think perhaps even less.
   1855 *Men and Women*, 'Bishop Blougram's Apology'.

57 No, when the fight begins within himself,
   A man's worth something.
   1855 *Men and Women*, 'Bishop Blougram's Apology'.

58 He said true things but called them by wrong
   names.
   1855 *Men and Women*, 'Bishop Blougram's Apology'.

59 Ah, did you once see Shelley plain,
   And did he stop to speak to you
   And did you speak to him again?
   How strange it seems, and new!
   1855 *Men and Women*, 'Memorabilia'.

60 So free we seem, so fretted fast we are!
   1855 *Men and Women*, 'Andrea del Sarto'.

61 Ah, but a man's reach should exceed his grasp,
   Or what's a heaven for?
   1855 *Men and Women*, 'Andrea del Sarto', l.97–8.

62 Your ghost will walk, you lover of trees,
   (If love remains)
   In an English lane.
   1855 *Men and Women*, 'De Gustibus'.

63 Open your heart and you will see
   graved inside of it, 'Italy.'
   Such lovers old are I and she;
   So it always was, so it still shall be!
   1855 *Men and Women*, 'De Gustibus'.

64 Stand still, true poet that you are!
   I know you; let me try and draw you.
   Some night you'll fail us: when afar
   You rise, remember one man saw you,
   Knew you, and named a star!
   1855 *Men and Women*, 'Popularity'.

65 I would that you were all to me,
   You that are just so much, no more.
   1855 *Men and Women*, ' Two in the Campagna'.

66 Only I discern—
   Infinite passion, and the pain
   Of finite hearts that yearn.
   1855 *Men and Women*, ' Two in the Campagna'.

67 There they are, my fifty men and women

Naming me the fifty poems finished!
Take them, Love, the book and me together.
Where the heart lies, let the brain lie also.
1855 *Men and Women*, 'One Word More. To E.B.B.', stanza 1.

68 Suddenly, as rare things will, it vanished.
   1855 *Men and Women*, 'One Word More. To E.B.B.', stanza 4.

69 Dante, who loved well because he hated,
   Hated wickedness that hinders loving.
   1855 *Men and Women*, 'One Word More. To E.B.B.', stanza 5.

70 Proves she like some portent of an iceberg
   Swimming full upon the ship it founders
   Hungry with huge teeth of splintered crystals?
   1855 *Men and Women*, 'One Word More. To E.B.B.', stanza 17.

71 What's come to perfection perishes.
   Things learned on earth, we shall practise in
      heaven.
   Work done least rapidly, Art most cherishes.
   1855 *Men and Women*, 'One Word More. To E.B.B.', stanza 17.

72 God be thanked, the meanest of his creatures
   Boasts two soul-sides, one to face the world with,
   One to show a woman when he loves her!
   1855 *Men and Women*, 'One Word More. To E.B.B.', stanza 18.

73 Wrote one song—and in my brain I sing it,
   Drew one angel—borne, see, on my bosom!
   1855 *Men and Women*, 'One Word More. To E.B.B.', closing lines.

74 But God has a few of us to whom he whispers in
      the ear;
   The rest may reason and welcome; 'tis we musicians
      know.
   1864 *Dramatis Personae*, 'Abt Vogler'.

75 Grow old along with me!
   The best is yet to be,
   The last of life, for which the first was made:
   Our times are in His hand
   Who saith, 'A whole I planned,
   Youth shows but half; trust God:
   See all nor be afraid!'
   1864 *Dramatis Personae*, 'Rabbi ben Ezra', stanza 1.

76 Time's wheels runs back or stops: Potter and clay
   endure.
   1864 *Dramatis Personae*, 'Rabbi ben Ezra', stanza 27.

77 My times be in Thy hand!
   Perfect the cup as planned!
   Let age approve of youth, and
   Death complete the same!
   1864 *Dramatis Personae*, 'Rabbi ben Ezra', stanza 32.

78 Stung by the splendour of a sudden thought.
   1864 *Dramatis Personae*, 'A Death in the Desert'.

79 For I say, this is death and the sole death,
   When a man's loss comes to him from his gain,
   Darkness from light, from knowledge ignorance,
   And lack of love from love made manifest.
   1864 *Dramatis Personae*, 'A Death in the Desert'.

80 Progress, man's distinctive mark alone,
   Not God's, and not the beasts'; God is, they are,
   Man partly is and wholly hopes to be.
   1864 *Dramatis Personae*, 'A Death in the Desert'.

81 And it is good to cheat the pair, and gibe,
   Letting the rank tongue blossom into speech.
   Setebos, Setebos, and Setebos!
   Thinketh, He dwelleth i' the cold o' the moon.
   Thinketh He made it, with the sun to match,
   But not the stars; the stars came otherwise.
   1864 *Dramatis Personae*, 'Caliban upon Setebos', stanza 1.

82 Let twenty pass, and stone the twenty-first,
   Loving not, hating not, just choosing so.
   1864 *Dramatis Personae*, 'Caliban upon Setebos', stanza 1.

83 We loved, sir—used to meet:
   How sad and bad and mad it was—
   But then, how it was sweet!
   1864 *Dramatis Personae*, 'Confessions', stanza 9.

84 There's more hateful form of foolery—
   The social sage's, Solomon of saloons
   And philosophic diner-out.
   1864 *Dramatis Personae*, 'Mr Sludge, The Medium', stanza 1.

85 Well, British Public, ye who like me not,
   (God love you!)
   1868–9 *The Ring and the Book*, bk.1, l.410

86 'Go get you manned by Manning and new-
   manned
   By Newman and, mayhap, wise-manned to boot
   By Wiseman.'
   1868–9 *The Ring and the Book*, bk.1, l.444–6.

87 Youth means love,
   Vows can't change nature, priests are only men.
   1868–9 *The Ring and the Book*, bk.1, l.1056–7.

88 O lyric love half angel and half bird
   And all a wonder and a wild desire.
   1868–9 *The Ring and the Book*, bk.1, l.1391–2.

89 In the great right of an excessive wrong.
   1868–9 *The Ring and the Book*, bk.3, l. 1055.

90 Faultless to a fault.
   1868–9 *The Ring and the Book*, bk.9, l.1175.

91 Why comes temptation but for a man to meet
   And master and make crouch beneath his foot,
   And so be pedestalled in triumph?
   1868–9 *The Ring and the Book*, bk.10, l.1184–6.

92 White shall not neutralize the black, nor good
   Compensate bad in man, absolve him so:
   Life's business being just the terrible choice.
   1868–9 *The Ring and the Book*, bk.10, l.1235–7.

93 There's a new tribunal now
   Higher than God's,—the educated man's!
   1868–9 *The Ring and the Book*, bk.10, l.1975–6.

94 Into that sad obscure sequestered state
   Where God unmakes but to remake the soul
   He else made first in vain; which must not be.
   1868–9 *The Ring and the Book*, bk.10, l.2129–31.

95 It is the glory and good of Art,
   That Art remains the one way possible
   Of speaking truth, to mouths like mine, at least.
   1868–9 *The Ring and the Book*, bk.12, l.838–40.

96 But, thanks to wine-less and democracy,
   We've still our stage where truth calls spade a spade!
   1875 'Aristophanes' Apology', stanza 1.

97 Ignorance is not innocence but sin.
   1875 *The Inn Album*, canto 5.

98 I want to know a butcher paints,
   A baker rhymes for his pursuit,
   Candlestick-maker much acquaints
   His soul with song, or, haply mute,
   Blows out his brains upon the flute.
   1876 'Shop', stanza 21.

99 Good, to forgive;
   Best, to forget!
   Living, we fret;
   Dying, we live.
   1878 *La Saisiaz*, prologue.

1 At midnight in the silence of the sleep-time,
   When you set your fancies free.
   1889 *Asolando*, epilogue.

2 One who never turned his back but marched breast
   forward,
   Never doubted clouds would break,
   Never dreamed, though right were worsted, wrong
   would triumph,
   Held we fall to rise, are baffled to fight better,
   Sleep to wake.
   1889 *Asolando*, epilogue.

3 Greet the unseen with a cheer!
   1889 *Asolando*, epilogue.

Broyard, Anatole

4 She has always ridden the passions as if they were a
   magnificent horse.
   1978 On Edna O'Brien. In the *New York Times*, 1 Jan.

5 Such a fatigue of adjectives, a drone of alliterations, a huffing of hyphenated words hurdling the meter like tired horses. Such a faded upholstery of tears, stars, bells, bones, flood and blood…a thud of consonants in tongue, night, dark, dust, seed, wound and wind.
   1974 On Dylan Thomas's poetry. *Aroused by Books.*

6 I remember a table in *Barchester Towers* that had more character than the combined heroes of three recent novels I've read.
   1974 *Aroused by Books.*

7 When Harriet goes to bed with a man, she always takes her wet blanket with her.
   1974 On a character in Iris Owen's *After Claude* (1973). *Aroused by Books.*

8 Chic is a convent for unloved women.
   1988 In the *New York Times*, 10 Jan.

Brummel, George Bryan called *Beau* Brummell 1778–1840
English dandy, a leader of 19c fashionable society. A close friend of the Prince Regent (later George IV), he quarrelled with him in 1813, and was later forced to flee to Calais with gambling debts. He died a pauper in a lunatic asylum.

9 Who's your fat friend?
   c.1813 Of the Prince Regent. Remark addressed to his companion, whom the Prince had acknowledged while studiously ignoring Brummell. Quoted in Jesse *Life of George Brummell* (1844), vol.1.

Brunet, Michel 1917–
Canadian historian.

10 The thing which amazes me is that I know perfectly well, as a historian, that there is corruption in any government—there's always corruption. It's bad when it's more than fifteen percent.
   Interviewed by Ramsay Cook in Eleanor Cook (ed) *The Craft of History* (1973).

Brunner, John Kilian Houston 1934–95
English science-fiction writer, an important contributor to the more literary aspirations of the genre. *Stand On Zanzibar* is his best-known work.

11 POPULATION EXPLOSION Unique in human experience, an event which happened yesterday but which everyone swears won't happen until tomorrow.
   1969 *Stand On Zanzibar*, 'The Hipcrime Vocab'.

Bruno, Frank(lin Roy) 1961–
English boxer. He won the European heavyweight title in 1985, and the World Championship in 1995. He later lost this to Mike Tyson, and failed to regain it in 1996.

12 Know what I mean, Harry?
   Catchphrase, addressed to sports commentator Harry Carpenter.

Bryan, Richard H 1937–
US politician, Governor of Nevada (1982–9) and Senator (1989–).

13 Being chairman of the Senate Ethics Committee is like jumping off a cliff. The thrill is very short.
   1993 NPR broadcast, 2 Nov.

Bryan, William Jennings 1860–1925
US lawyer, Democratic politician and pacifist. Elected to Congress in 1890, he ran unsuccessfully in two presidential elections (1896, 1900). Appointed Secretary of State by Woodrow Wilson (1913), he resigned in 1915 over the US's second *Lusitania* note to Germany.

14 There are two ideas of government. There are those who believe that, if you will only legislate to make the well-to-do prosperous, their prosperity will leak through on those below. The Democratic idea, however, has been that if you legislate to make the masses prosperous, their prosperity will find its way up through every class which rests upon them.
   1896 Speech at the Democratic National Convention, 10 Jul.

15 What shall we say of the intelligence, not to say religion, of those who are so particular to distinguish between fishes and reptiles and birds, but put a man with an immortal soul in the same circle with the wolf, the hyena, and the skunk? What must be the impression made upon children by such a degradation of man?
   Statement issued in Dayton, Tennessee, 28 Jul, 1925, by Mrs. W J Bryan, shortly after the end of the Scopes trial and her husband's death.

Bryant, David 1931–
English bowls player. He won the World Championship title in 1966 and 1980.

16 I'm not an athlete, more a gymnast and golfer, soldered together.
   Quoted in Colin Jarman *The Guinness Dictionary of Sports Quotations* (1990).

17 Bowls is a young man's game which old men can play.
   Quoted in Colin Jarman *The Guinness Dictionary of Sports Quotations* (1990).

Bryant, William Cullen 1794–1878
US writer and journalist. Originally a lawyer, after the success of *Thanatopsis* (1817) he turned increasingly to prose and verse writing, becoming editor of the New York *Evening Post* (1829).

18 All that tread

The globe are but a handful to the tribes
That slumber in its bosom.
1817 'Thanatopsis', in the *North American Review*, Sep.

19 These are the gardens of the Desert, these
The unshorn fields, boundless and beautiful,
For which the speech of England has no name—
The Prairies.
1832 *Poems*, 'The Prairies'.

Buber, Martin 1878–1965

Austrian Jewish theologian and philosopher, founding editor of *Der Jude* (1916–24, The Jew), known for his important studies in Hasidism and Existentialism. Professor at Frankfurt (1923–33), he fled Germany for Palestine in 1938, becoming Professor of the Sociology of Religion in Jerusalem.

20 Egos appear by setting themselves apart from other egos. Persons appear by entering into relation with other persons.
1923 *Ich und Du* (translated by R G Smith as *I and Thou*, 1936).

21 *Jedes geeinzelte Du ist ein Durchblick zu ihm. Durch jedes geeinzelte Du spricht das Grundwort das Ewige an.*

Every particular *Thou* is a glimpse through to the eternal *Thou*; by means of every particular *Thou* the primary word addresses the eternal *Thou*.
1923 *Ich und Du* (translated by R G Smith as *I and Thou*, 1936).

Buchan, John, 1st Baron Tweedsmuir
1875–1940

Scottish author and statesman, best known for his fast-moving adventure stories, particularly *The Thirty-Nine Steps* (1915). He was Governor-General of Canada from 1935 until his death.

22 You think that a wall as solid as the earth separates civilisation from barbarism. I tell you the division is a thread, a sheet of glass.
1916 *The Power-House*, ch.3, 'Tells of a Midsummer Night'.

23 Civilisation is a conspiracy.
1916 *The Power-House*, ch.3, 'Tells of a Midsummer Night'.

24 It's a great life if you don't weaken.
1919 *Mr Standfast*, ch.5.

25 Look at the Irish! They are the cleverest propagandists extant, and managed to persuade most people that they were a brave, generous, humorous, talented, warm-hearted race, cruelly yoked to a dull mercantile England, when, God knows, they were exactly the opposite.
1924 *The Three Hostages*.

26 To live for a time close to great minds is the best kind of education.

1940 *Memory Hold-the-Door*, ch.2.

27 An atheist is a man who has no invisible means of support.
1943 Quoted in H E Fosdick *On Being a Real Person*, ch.10.

Buchanan, James 1791–1868

US statesman and 15th President (1857–61). A Democrat, he tried to maintain a balance between pro-slavery and anti-slavery factions, but was unable to avert the Civil War (1861–5).

28 All the friends that I loved and wanted to reward are dead, and all the enemies that I hated and I had marked out for punishment are turned to my friends.
1857 On finally achieving his country's highest political office at the age of 65.

29 If you are as happy, my dear Sir, on entering this house as I am on leaving it and returning home, you are the happiest man in the country.
1861 Said on welcoming his successor, Abraham Lincoln, to the White House.

Buchman, Sidney 1902–75

US film writer and producer. His films include *Mr Smith Goes to Washington* (1939), *Here Comes Mr Jordan* (1941) and *The Group* (1966).

30 I wouldn't give you two cents for all your fancy rules if, behind them, they didn't have a little bit of plain, ordinary kindness—and a little looking out for the other fella, too.
1939 Line delivered by James Stewart in *Mr Smith Goes to Washington*.

Buchwald, Art 1925–

US writer and humorist. He won a Pulitzer Prize for outstanding commentary (1982).

31 This is not an easy time for humorists because the government is far funnier than we are.
1987 Speech to international meeting of satirists and cartoonists. Reported in the *New York Times*, 28 Jun.

Buck, Gene (Edward Eugene) 1885–1957

US songwriter.

32 That Shakespearian rag,—
Most intelligent, very elegant.
1912 'That Shakespearian Rag' (with Herman Ruby).
▷ See Eliot 368:86.

Buck, Pearl née Sydenstricker 1892–1973

US novelist, brought up in China and later a teacher and missionary there. Her works include *The Good Earth* (1931), set in China. She won the Nobel Prize for Literature in 1938.

33 Race prejudice is not only a shadow over the colored—it is a shadow over all of us, and the shadow is darkest over those who feel it least and allow its evil effects to go on.
1943 *What America Means To Me*, ch.1.

34 None who have always been free can understand the terrible fascinating power of the hope of freedom to those who are not free.
1943 *What America Means To Me*, ch.4.

35 Every great mistake has a halfway moment, a split second when it can be recalled and perhaps remedied.
1943 *What America Means To Me*, ch.10.

36 Praise out of season, or tactlessly bestowed, can freeze the heart as much as blame.
1967 *To My Daughters, With Love*, 'First Meeting'.

37 Nothing and no one can destroy the Chinese people. They are relentless survivors… They yield, they bend to the wind, but they never break.
1972 *China, Past and Present*, ch.1.

Bucke, Richard Maurice 1837–1902
Canadian psychiatrist and author. His works include *Cosmic Consciousness: A Study in the Evolution of the Human Mind* (1901).

38 Cosmic consciousness.
1894 Phrase first used in a paper read by Bucke to the American Medico-Psychological Association, Philadelphia, 18 May. He defined it as 'a higher form of consciousness than that possessed by the ordinary man'.

Buckingham, George Villiers, 2nd Duke of 1628–87
English statesman, exiled after the Royalist defeat in the Civil War. He became a member of Charles II's cabal after the Restoration, and was instrumental in Clarendon's downfall (1667), but lost power and was dismissed in 1674.

39 Ay, now the plot thickens very much upon us.
1672 *The Rehearsal*, act 3, sc.1.

40 The world is made up for the most part of fools and knaves.
'To Mr Clifford, on his *Humane Reason*', collected in *The Dramatic Works* (1715), vol.2.

Buechner, Carl Frederick 1926–
US clergyman, novelist, poet and essayist. His works include *Lion Country* (1971) and *Godric* (1980).

41 Glory is to God what style is to an artist… To behold God's glory, to sense his style, is the closest you can get this side of Paradise, just as to read King Lear is the closest you can get to Shakespeare.
1973 *Wishful Thinking*.

42 There is no event so commonplace but that God is present in it, always hiddenly, always leaving you room to recognize him or not to recognize him… Listen to your life. See it for the fathomless mystery it is. In the boredom and pain of it no less than in the excitement and gladness: touch, taste, smell your way to the heavenly and hidden heart of it because in the last analysis all moments are key moments, and life itself is grace.
1983 *Now and Then*.

Buffett, Warren Edward 1930–
US investment broker and corporate executive.

43 It is better to be approximately right than precisely wrong.
1994 In *Fortune*, 4 Apr.

Buford, Bill (William Holmes) 1954–
US-born editor and writer who spent much of his career in Britain (editing *Granta* until 1995), and has later been fiction and literary editor of the *New Yorker* (1995–).

44 I found myself growing increasingly irritated with the notion of a British novel, which was really an irritation with the word British, a grey, unsatisfactory, bad-weather kind of word, a piece of linguistic compromise.
1994 Editorial, *Granta*, no.43.

Bukowski, Charles 1920–94
German-born US poet and writer. His spare, sardonic writing evoked a seamy, low-life urban netherworld in poems, short stories and novels.

45 Show me a man who lives alone and has a perpetually clean kitchen, and 8 times out of 9 I'll show you a man with detestable spiritual qualities.
1967 *Tales of Ordinary Madness*, 'Too Sensitive'.

46 You begin saving the world by saving one man at a time; all else is grandiose romanticism or politics.
1967 *Tales of Ordinary Madness*, 'Too Sensitive'.

47 Erections, Ejaculations, Exhibitions and General Tales of Ordinary Madness.
1972 Title of book.

48 Love is a Dog from Hell.
1977 Title of book.

49 Play the Piano Drunk Like a Percussion Instrument Until the Fingers Begin to Bleed a Bit.
1979 Title of book.

Buller, A H Reginald 1874–1944
Canadian botanist, Professor of Botany at the University of Manitoba.

50 There was a young lady named Bright

Whose speed was far faster than light;
She set out one day
In a relative way
And returned on the previous night.

1923 'Relativity', published anonymously in *Punch*, 19 Dec. Buller's claim to authorship is recorded in W S Baring-Gould *The Lure of the Limerick* (1968).

Bullock, Alan Louis Charles, Baron Bullock 1914–

British historian, notably of 20c Europe. He was Master of St Catherine's College, Oxford (1960–80).

51 Hitler showed surprising loyalty to Mussolini, but it never extended to trusting him.

1952 *Hitler: A Study in Tyranny.*

52 The people Hitler never understood, and whose actions continued to exasperate him to the end of his life, were the British.

1952 *Hitler: A Study in Tyranny.*

Bulmer-Thomas, Ivor 1905–93

British politician and writer. He joined *The Times* (1930–7) and was later deputy editor of the *Daily Telegraph* (1953–4). He entered parliament as a Labour MP in 1942, turning Conservative in 1949.

53 If he ever went to school without any boots, it was because he was too big for them.

1949 At the Conservative Party conference, responding to remarks by Harold Wilson about his humble upbringing.

▷ See Wilson 1085:27.

Bülow, Prince Bernhard Heinrich von 1849–1929

German statesman, Chancellor (1900–9), Foreign Secretary (1897), Count (1899) and Prince (1905). He wrote *Imperial Germany* (translated 1916) and Memoirs (translated 1931–2).

54 *Mit einem Worte: wir wollen niemand in den Schatten stellen aber wir verlangen auch unseren Platz an der Sonne.*

In a word, we desire to throw no one into the shade, but we also demand our own place in the sun.

1897 Speech to the Reichstag, 6 Dec.

Bulwer-Lytton, Edward George Lytton, 1st Baron Lytton 1803–73

English writer and politician, known for historical novels such as *The Last Days of Pompeii* (1834), poetry and several plays. A Reform MP (1831–41), he returned as a Conservative in 1852.

55 Beneath the rule of men entirely great, the pen is mightier than the sword.

1839 *Richelieu*, act 2, sc.2.

Bunting, Basil 1900–85

English poet. He was encouraged by Pound and worked with Ford Madox Ford on *The Transatlantic Review*, but never found a wide audience. The long poem *Briggflatts* is his best-known work.

56 Our doom
is, to be sifted by the wind,

heaped up, smoothed down like silly sands.
We are less permanent than thought.

1925 *Villon*, pt.1.

57 Name and date
split in soft slate
a few months obliterate.

1966 *Briggflatts.*

58 It looks well enough on the page, but never well enough.

1966 *Briggflatts.*

59 Clear Cymric voices carry well this Autumn night,
Aneurin and Taliesin, cruel owls
for whom it is never altogether dark
before the rules made poetry a pedant's game.

1966 *Briggflatts.*

60 Who
swinging his axe
to fell kings,
guesses
where we go?

1966 *Briggflatts*, coda.

Buñuel, Luis 1900–83

Spanish film director, who was successful with early surrealist experiments in collaboration with Dali. His work is characterized by a poetic, often erotic, use of imagery, black humour and a hatred of Catholicism.

61 *Grâce à Dieu, je suis toujours athée.*

Thanks be to God, I am still an atheist.

1959 In *Le Monde*, 16 Dec.

62 *Le Charme discret de la bourgeoisie.*

The Discreet Charm of the Bourgeoisie.

1972 Title of film.

Bunyan, John 1628–88

English writer and preacher. His father was a tinker and he received little formal education. His works, including an autobiography *Grace Abounding to the Chief of Sinners* (1666) and probably most of *The Pilgrim's Progress* (1st part 1678, 2nd part 1684), were written while imprisoned for nonconformity.

63 Oh, the diligence of Satan! Oh, the desperateness of man's heart!

1666 *Grace Abounding to the Chief of Sinners.*

64 This miry slough, is such a place as cannot be mended: It is the descent whither the scum and filth that attends conviction for sin doth continually run, and therefore is it called the Slough of Despond.
1678 *The Pilgrim's Progress*, pt.1.

65 The valley of Humiliation.
1678 *The Pilgrim's Progress*, pt.1.

66 It beareth the name of Vanity-Fair, because the town where 'tis kept, is lighter than vanity.
1678 *The Pilgrim's Progress*, pt.1.

67 Hanging is too good for him, said Mr Cruelty.
1678 *The Pilgrim's Progress*, pt 1.

68 Now Giant Despair had a wife, and her name was Diffidence.
1678 *The Pilgrim's Progress*, pt.1.

69 Sleep is sweet to the labouring man.
1678 *The Pilgrim's Progress*, pt.1.

70 So I awoke, and behold it was a dream.
1678 *The Pilgrim's Progress*, pt.1.

71 A man that could look no way but downwards, with a muckrake in his hand.
1684 *The Pilgrim's Progress*, pt.2.

72 For though when he was here, he was Fool in every man's mouth, yet now he is gone he is highly commended of all.
1684 *The Pilgrim's Progress*, pt.2.

73 He that is down needs fear no fall,
    He that is low no pride.
    He that is humble ever shall
    Have God to be his guide.
1684 *The Pilgrim's Progress*, pt.2.

74 My Sword, I give to him that shall succeed me in my Pilgrimage, and my Courage and Skill, to him that can get it. My Marks and Scars I carry with me, to be a witness for me, that I have fought his Battles, who now will be my Rewarder... As he went, he said, Death, where is thy Sting? And as he went down deeper, he said, Grave where is thy Victory? So he passed over, and the Trumpets sounded for him on the other side.
1684 Mr Valiant-for-Glory. *The Pilgrim's Progress*, pt.2.

75 He that lives in sin and looks for happiness hereafter is like him that soweth cockle and thinks to fill his barn with wheat or barley.
1684 *The Pilgrim's Progress*, pt.2.

Burbank, Luther 1849–1926
US plant breeder and natural scientist.

76 Science is knowledge arranged and classified according to truth, facts, and the general laws of nature.
1926 Interview in the *San Francisco Bulletin*, 22 Jan.

Burchard, Samuel Dickinson 1812–91
US Presbyterian minister and staunch Republican supporter.

77 The party whose antecedents are rum, Romanism, and rebellion.
1884 Of the Democratic party. Speech at the Fifth Avenue Hotel, New York City, 29 Oct.

Burgess, Anthony real name *John Anthony Burgess Wilson* 1917–94
English writer. He is widely regarded as among the most important novelists of his generation, notably for his controversial dystopian novel *A Clockwork Orange* (1962).

78 Who ever heard of a clockwork orange? Then I read a malenky bit out loud in a sort of very high type preaching goloss: 'The attempt to impose upon man, a creature of growth and capable of sweetness, to ooze juicily at the last round the bearded lips of God, to attempt to impose, I say, laws and conditions appropriate to a mechanical creation, against this I raise my sword-pen.'
1962 *A Clockwork Orange*.

79 He said it was artificial respiration, but now I find I am to have his child.
1963 *Inside Mr Enderby*, pt.1, ch.4.

80 Bath twice a day to be really clean, once a day to be passably clean, once a week to avoid being a public menace.
1963 *Inside Mr Enderby*, pt.2, ch.1.

81 Rome's just a city like anywhere else. A vastly overrated city, I'd say. It trades on belief just as Stratford trades on Shakespeare.
1963 *Inside Mr Enderby*, pt.2, ch.1.

82 *Pax Romana*. Where they made a desolation they called it a peace. What absolute nonsense! It was a nasty, vulgar sort of civilization, only dignified by being hidden under a lot of declensions.
1963 *Inside Mr Enderby*, pt.2, ch.2.

83 Keep away from physicians. It is all probing and guessing and pretending to them. They leave it to Nature to cure in her own time, but they take the credit. As well as very fat fees.
1964 *Nothing Like the Sun*.

84 The possession of a book becomes a substitute for reading it.
1966 In the *New York Times Book Review*, 4 Dec.

85 A sure sign of an amateur is too much detail to compensate for too little life.
1971 In the *Times Literary Supplement*, 18 Jun.

86 Death comes along like a gas bill one can't pay—and that's all one can say about it.
1974 Interview in *Playboy*.

87 There is usually something wrong with writers the young like.
1974 Interview in *Playboy*.

88 It was the afternoon of my eighty-first birthday, and I was in bed with my catamite when Ali announced that the archbishop had come to see me.
1980 The opening lines of *Earthly Powers*.

89 Reality is what I see, not what you see.
1983 In the *Sunday Times Magazine*, 18 Dec.

90 God was good on the physical and emotional sides and a great one for hate. He generously spilled his own hate into his dearest creation.
1984 *Enderby's Dark Lady*.

91 If Freud had worn a kilt in the prescribed Highland manner he might have had a very different attitude to genitals.
1986 In *The Observer*, 24 Aug.

92 Death, like the quintessence of otherness, is for others.
1987 *Little Wilson and Big God*, ch.6.

93 Music says nothing to the reason: it is a kind of closely structured nonsense.
1989 In *The Observer*, 23 Jul.

94 I could see now that a literary education did not fit one for the popular novelist's trade. Once you had started using words like flavicomous or acroamatic, because you liked the sound of them, you were lost.
1990 *You've Had Your Time*, ch.1.

Burgon, John William 1813–88
English cleric, Dean of Chichester from 1876.

95 Match me such marvel, save in Eastern clime,— A rose-red city—'half as old as Time'!
1845 *Petra*.

Burke, Edmund 1729–97
Anglo-Irish statesman and political philosopher. He became Secretary for Ireland (1759) and an MP (1765). His works include *Reflections on the French Revolution* (1790).

96 No passion so effectually robs the mind of all its powers of acting than fear.
1757 *On the Sublime and Beautiful*, pt.2, section 2.

97 Custom reconciles us to everything.
1757 *On the Sublime and Beautiful*, pt.4, section 18.

98 It is a general popular error to imagine the loudest complainers for the public to be the most anxious for its welfare.
1769 *Observations on a late Publication on the Present State of the Nation*, 2nd edn.

99 To complain of the age we live in, to murmur at the present possessors of power, to lament the past, to conceive extravagant hopes of the future, are the common dispositions of the greatest part of mankind.
1770 *Thoughts on the Cause of the Present Discontents*.

1 When bad men combine, the good must associate; else they will fall, one by one, an unpitied sacrifice in a contemptible struggle.
1770 *Thoughts on the Cause of the Present Discontents*.

2 It is therefore our business carefully to cultivate in our minds, to rear to the most perfect vigour and maturity, every sort of generous and honest feeling that belongs to our nature. To bring the dispositions that are loved in private life into the service and conduct of the commonwealth; so to be patriots, as not to forget we are gentlemen.
1770 *Thoughts on the Cause of the Present Discontents*.

3 The greater the power, the more dangerous is the abuse.
1771 Speech on the Middlesex Election, House of Commons, 7 Feb.

4 Parliament is a deliberative assembly of one nation. You choose a Member indeed; but when you have chosen him, he is not the Member for Bristol, but he is a Member of Parliament.
1774 Speech to Bristol voters.

5 The concessions of the weak are the concessions of fear.
1775 *On Conciliation with America*.

6 The use of force alone is but temporary. It may subdue for a moment; but it does not remove the necessity of subduing again; and a nation is not governed, which is perpetually to be conquered.
1775 *On Conciliation with America*.

7 Nothing less will content me, than *whole America*.
1775 *On Conciliation with America*.

8 All Protestantism, even the most cold and passive, is a sort of dissent. But the religion most prevalent in our northern colonies is a refinement on the principle of resistance; it is the dissidence of dissent, and the Protestantism of the Protestant religion.
1775 *On Conciliation with America*.

9 It is not, what a lawyer tells me I may do; but what humanity, reason, and justice, tells me I ought to do.
1775 *On Conciliation with America.*

10 Freedom and not servitude is the cure of anarchy; as religion, and not atheism, is the true remedy for superstition.
1775 *On Conciliation with America.*

11 Slavery they can have anywhere. It is a weed that grows in every soil.
1775 *On Concilation with America.*

12 It is the love of the people; it is their attachment to their goverment, from the sense of the deep stake they have in such a glorious institution, which gives you your army and your navy, and infuses into both that liberal obedience, without which your army would be a base rabble, and your navy nothing but rotten timber.
1775 *On Concilation with America.*

13 A great empire and little minds go ill together.
1775 *On Conciliation with America.*

14 All government, indeed every human benefit and enjoyment, every virtue and every prudent act, is founded on compromise and barter.
1775 *On Conciliation with America.*

15 Between craft and credulity, the voice of reason is stifled.
1777 *Letter to the Sheriffs of Bristol.*

16 Liberty too must be limited in order to be possessed.
1777 *Letter to the Sheriffs of Bristol.*

17 Among a people generally corrupt, liberty cannot long exist.
1777 *Letter to the Sheriffs of Bristol.*

18 If any man ask me what a free government is, I answer that for any practical purpose, it is what the people think it so.
1777 *Letter to the Sheriffs of Bristol.*

19 People crushed by law have no hope but from power. If laws are their enemies, they will be enemies to laws; and those, who have to hope and nothing to lose, will always be dangerous, more or less.
1777 *Letter to Charles James Fox, 8 Oct.*

20 Individuals pass like shadows, but the Commonwealth is fixed and stable.
1780 Speech, House of Commons, 11 Feb.

21 The people are the masters.

1780 Speech, House of Commons, 11 Feb.

22 Bad laws are the worst sort of tyranny.
1780 Speech, Bristol.

23 He was not merely a chip off the old block, but the old block itself.
1781 Commenting on William Pitt the Younger's maiden speech in the House of Commons, 26 Feb.

24 The people never give up their liberties but under some delusion.
1784 Speech, Buckinghamshire.

25 Whenever our neighbours house is on fire, it cannot be amiss for the engines to play a little on our own.
1790 *Reflections on the Revolution in France.*

26 A state without the means of some change is without the means of its conservation.
1790 *Reflections on the Revolution in France.*

27 People will not look forward to posterity, who never look backward to their ancestors.
1790 *Reflections on the Revolution in France.*

28 Those who attempt to level never equalize.
1790 *Reflections on the Revolution in France.*

29 Whatever each man can separately do, without trespassing upon others, he has a right to do for himself; and he has a right to a fair portion of all which society, with all its combination of skill and force, can do in his favour.
1790 *Reflections on the Revolution in France.*

30 Government is a contrivance of human wisdom to provide for human wants.
1790 *Reflections on the Revolution in France.*

31 The age of chivalry is gone.—That of sophisters, economists, and calculators, has succeeded; and the glory of Europe is extinguished for ever.
1790 *Reflections on the Revolution in France.*

32 The unbought grace of life, the cheap defence of nations, the nurse of manly sentiment and heroic enterprise is gone! it is gone, that sensibility of principle, that chasity of honour, which felt a stain like a wound, which ennobled whatever it touched, and under which vice itself lost half its evil, by losing all its grossness.
1790 *Reflections on the Revolution in France.*

33 In the groves of their academy, at the end of every vista, you see nothing but the gallows.
1790 *Reflections on the Revolution in France.*

34 Kings will be tyrants from policy when subjects are rebels from principle.
1790 *Reflections on the Revolution in France.*

35 Man is by his constitution a religious animal; atheism is against not only our reason, but our instincts.
1790 *Reflections on the Revolution in France.*

36 Society is indeed a contract…it becomes a partnership not only between those who are living, but between those who are living, those who are dead, and those who are to be born.
1790 *Reflections on the Revolution in France.*

37 Superstition is the religion of feeble minds.
1790 *Reflections on the Revolution in France.*

38 Our patience will achieve more than our force.
1790 *Reflections on the Revolution in France.*

39 By hating vices too much, they come to love men too little.
1790 *Reflections on the Revolution in France.*

40 We begin our public affection in our families. No cold relation is a zealous citizen.
1790 *Reflections on the Revolution in France.*

41 Good order is the foundation of all good things.
1790 *Reflections on the Revolution in France.*

42 The only infallible criterion of wisdom to vulgar judgements—success.
1791 *Letter to a Member of the National Assembly.*

43 Tyrants seldom want pretexts.
1791 *Letter to a Member of the National Assembly.*

44 Somebody has said, that a king may make a nobleman but he cannot make a gentleman.
1795 Letter to William Smith, 29 Jan.

45 And having looked to government for bread, on the very first scarcity they will turn and bite the hand that fed them. To avoid that evil, government will redouble the causes of it; and then it will become inveterate and incurable.
1795 *Thoughts and Details on Scarcity,* Nov (published 1800).

46 To innovate is not to reform.
1796 *A Letter to a Noble Lord.*

47 All men that are ruined are ruined on the side of their natural propensities.
1796 *Two Letters on the Proposals for Peace with the Regicide Directory,* 9th edn.

48 Example is the school of mankind, and they will learn at no other.
1796 *Two Letters on the Proposals for Peace with the Regicide Directory,* 9th edn.

49 Never, no never, did Nature say one thing and Wisdom say another.

1797 *Third Letter…on the Proposals for Peace with the Regicide Directory.*

Burke, Johnny 1908–64

US lyricist.

50 Every time it rains, it rains
Pennies from heaven.
1936 'Pennies from Heaven'.
▷ See also Thatcher 1007:14.

51 Like Webster's dictionary, we're Morocco bound.
1942 Title song in *Road to Morocco,* sung by Bing Crosby and Bob Hope. Music by Jimmy Van Heusen.

52 Or would you like to swing on a star
Carry moonbeams home in a jar
And be better off than you are
Or would you rather be a fish?
1944 *Swinging on a Star,* sung by Bing Crosby in the film *Going My Way.* Music by Jimmy Van Heusen.

Burke, Kenneth 1897–1986

US music and literary critic. His theory of literature as 'symbolic action' was very influential.

53 Any performance is discussable from the standpoint of what it *attains* or what it *misses.* Comprehensiveness can be discussed as superficiality, intensiveness as stricture, tolerance as uncertainty—and the poor *pedestrian* abilities of a fish are clearly explainable in terms of his excellence as a *swimmer.* A way of seeing is also a way of not seeing.
1936 *Permanence and Change.*

Burke, Tim(othy) c.1942–

Canadian newspaper columnist.

54 There are no lapsed Catholics after a Christmas concert by Pavarotti.
1987 In *The Montreal Gazette,* 8 Dec.

Burns, Ken Lauren 1953–

US filmmaker and historian. He has won numerous awards for documentary and historical films on aspects of American life.

55 We are a people starved for self-definition.
1991 On the success of his 11-hour television documentary *The Civil War.* In *People,* 7 Jan.

Burns, Robert 1759–96

Scottish poet and songwriter, the son of a farmer. The Kilmarnock edition (1786) of his poems made his name, and his skill at providing lyrics for old Scottish airs assured his place as one of the world's most popular poets and as his country's national bard. His influence in promoting Scots in literature was enormous.

56 Green grow the rashes, O;
   Green grow the rashes, O;
   The sweetest hours that e'er I spend,
   Are spent amang the lasses, O.
   1784 'Green grow the Rashes. A Fragment', chorus

57 What signifies the life o' man,
   An 'twere na for the lasses, O.
   1784 'Green grow the Rashes. A Fragment', stanza 1.

58 If honest Nature made you *fools*,
   What sairs your grammars.
   1785 'Epistle to J. Lapraik, An Old Scotch Bard, 1 April 1785', stanza 11.

59 They *gang* in Stirks, and *come out* Asses,
   Plain truth to speak;
   An' syne they think to climb Parnassus
   By dint o' Greek!
   1785 'Epistle to J. Lapraik, An Old Scotch Bard, 1 April 1785', stanza 12.

60 Gie me ae spark o' Nature's fire,
   That's a' the learning I desire.
   1785 'Epistle to J. Lapraik, An Old Scotch Bard, 1 April 1785', stanza 13.

61 O Thou that in the heavens does dwell!
   Wha, as it pleases best Thysel,
   Sends ane to heaven, an' ten to hell,
   A' for Thy glory,
   And no for ony gude or ill
   They've done before Thee!
   1785 'Holy Willie's Prayer', stanza 1.

62 My curse upon your whunstane hearts,
   Ye Enbrugh Gentry!
   The tythe o' what ye waste at *cartes*
   Wad stow'd his pantry!
   1785 'To W. Simpson, Ochiltree', stanza 4, referring to the poet Robert Fergusson, who died a pauper in the Edinburgh bedlam in 1774 at the age of 24, and whom Burns considered 'my elder brother in misfortune, by far my elder brother in the muse.'

63 Some books are lies frae end to end,
   And some great lies were never penn'd.
   1785 'Death and Doctor Hornbook. A True Story', stanza 1.

64 I was na fou, but just had plenty.
   1785 'Death and Doctor Hornbook. A True Story', stanza 3.

65 There's some are fou o' *love divine*,
   There's some are fou o' *brandy*.
   1785 'The Holy Fair', stanza 27.

66 From scenes like these, old SCOTIA's grandeur springs,

That makes her lov'd at home, rever'd abroad:
Princes and lords are but the breath of kings,
'An honest man's the noble work of GOD'.
1785 'The Cotter's Saturday Night', stanza 19. The last line is in fact a misquotation of Pope; 'noble' was corrected to 'noblest' in the 1794 edition of Burns' poems.
▷ See Pope 781:50.

67 Wee, sleeket, cowrin, tim'rous *beastie*,
   O, what a panic's in thy breastie!
   Thou need na start awa sae hasty
   Wi' bickering brattle!
   I wad be laith to rin an' chase thee,
   Wi' murd'ring *pattle!*
   1785 'To A Mouse, On turning her up in her Nest with the Plough, November, 1785', stanza 1.

68 The best-laid schemes o' *Mice* an' *Men*
   Gang aft a-gley.
   1785 'To A Mouse, On turning her up in her Nest with the Plough, November, 1785', stanza 7.

69 A fig for those by law protected!
   Liberty's a glorious feast!
   Courts for Cowards were erected,
   Churches built to please the Priest.
   c.1786 'The Jolly Beggars', or 'Love and Liberty, a Cantata', chorus to a song to the tune 'Jolly Mortals, fill your glasses'.

70 His lockèd, letter'd, braw brass-collar,
   Show'd him the *gentleman* an' *scholar.*
   1786 'The Twa Dogs'.

71 The tither was a *ploughman's collie*,
   A rhyming, ranting, raving billie.
   1786 'The Twa Dogs'.

72 FREEDOM and WHISKY gang thegither,
   Tak aff your *dram!*
   1786 'The Author's Earnest Cry and Prayer, to the Right Honorable and Honorable, the Scotch Representatives in the House of Commons', stanza 30.

73 O Thou, whatever title suit thee!
   Auld Hornie, Satan, Nick, or Clootie.
   1786 'Address to the Deil', stanza 1.

74 An' now, auld *Cloots*, I ken ye're thinkan,
   A certain *Bardie's* rantin, drinkin,
   Some luckless hour will send him linkan,
   To your black pit;
   But faith! he'll turn a corner jinkan,
   An' cheat you yet.
   1786 'Address to the Deil', stanza 20.

75 But *Facts* are cheels that winna ding,
   And downa be disputed.
   1786 'A Dream', stanza 4.

76 Man's inhumanity to Man
   Makes countless thousands mourn!
   1786 'Man was made to Mourn, A Dirge', stanza 7.

77 O wad some Pow'r the giftie gie us
To see oursels as ithers see us!
It wad frae monie a blunder free us
An' foolish notion.
1786 'To a Louse, On Seeing one on a Lady's Bonnet at Church', stanza 8.

78 It was upon a Lammas night,
When corn rigs are bonie,
Beneath the moon's unclouded light,
I held awa to Annie.
1786 'Song, The Rigs o' Barley', or 'Corn Rigs Are Bonie', stanza 1.

79 I hae been blythe wi' Comrades dear;
I hae been merry drinking.
1786 'Song, The Rigs o' Barley', or 'Corn Rigs Are Bonie', stanza 4.

80 Corn rigs, an' barley rigs,
An' corn rigs are bonie:
I'll ne'er forget that happy night,
Amang the rigs wi' Annie.
1786 'Song, The Rigs o' Barley', or 'Corn Rigs Are Bonie', chorus.

81 Now westlin winds, and slaught'rin guns
Bring Autumn's pleasant weather.
1786 'Song, composed in August', stanza 1.

82 O ye wha are sae guid yoursel,
Sae pious and sae holy,
Ye've nought to do but mark and tell
Your Neebours' fauts an folly!
1786 'Address to the Unco Guid, or the Rigidly Righteous', stanza 1.

83 Then gently scan your brother Man,
Still gentler sister Woman;
Tho' they may gang a kennin wrang,
To step aside is human.
1786 'Address to the Unco Guid, or the Rigidly Righteous', stanza 7.

84 Fair fa' your honest, sonsie face,
Great Chieftain o' the Puddin-race!
Aboon them a' ye tak your place,
Painch, tripe, or thairm:
Weel are ye wordy of a *grace*
As lang's my arm.
1786 'To a Haggis', stanza 1.

85 Auld Scotland wants nae skinking ware That jaups
in luggies;
But, if ye wish her gratefu' prayer,
Gie her a *Haggis!*
1786 'To a Haggis', stanza 8.

86 Edina! *Scotia's* darling seat,
All hail thy palaces and tow'rs,
Where once beneath a monarch's feet

Sat Legislation's sov'reign pow'rs.
1786 'Address to Edinburgh', stanza 1.

87 There was a lad was born in Kyle,
But what na day o' what na style.
I doubt it's hardly worth the while
To be sae nice wi' Robin.
1787 'There was a lad', or 'Rantin' Rovin' Robin', stanza 1.

88 Robin was a rovin' Boy,
Rantin' rovin', rantin', rovin',
Robin was a rovin' Boy,
Rantin' rovin' Robin.
1787 'There was a lad', or 'Rantin' Rovin' Robin', chorus.

89 There was three kings into the east,
Three kings both great and high,
And they hae sworn a solemn oath
John Barleycorn should die.
1787 'John Barleycorn. A Ballad', stanza 1.

90 Bony lassie will ye go
To the birks of Aberfeldey.
1787 'The Birks of Aberfeldey', chorus.

91 Sae rantingly, sae wantonly,
Sae dauntingly gae'd he:
He play'd a spring, and danc'd it round
Below the gallows-tree.
1788 'McPherson's Farewell', chorus.

92 O rattlin, roarin Willie,
O he held to the fair;
An' for to sell his fiddle
And buy some other ware.
1788 'Rattlin, roarin Willie', stanza 1.

93 Rattlin, roarin Willie,
Ye're welcome hame to me!
1788 'Rattlin, roarin Willie', stanza 3.

94 Should auld acquaintance be forgot
And never brought to mind?
Should auld acquaintance be forgot,
And auld lang syne!
1788 'Auld Lang Syne', stanza 1. This is the most familiar version of an older, traditional song, reworked by Burns.

95 For auld lang syne, my jo,
For auld lang syne,
We'll tak a cup o' kindness yet
For auld lang syne.
1788 'Auld Lang Syne', chorus. This is the most familiar version of an older, traditional song, reworked by Burns.

96 And there's a hand, my trusty fiere!
And gie's a hand o' thine!
1788 'Auld Lang Syne', stanza 5. This is the most familiar version of an older, traditional song, reworked by Burns.

97 Go fetch to me a pint o' wine,
And fill it in a silver tassie,

That I may drink, before I go,
A service to my bonie lassie.
1788 'My Bonie Mary', stanza 1.

98 Of a' the airts the wind can blaw,
I dearly like the West;
For there the bonie Lassie lives,
The Lassie I lo'e best.
1788 'Of a' the airts the wind can blaw', or 'I Love my Jean',
stanza 1.

99 Flow gently, sweet Afton, among thy green braes,
Flow gently, I'll sing thee a song in thy praise.
1789 'Afton Water', stanza 1.

1 The golden Hours, on angel wings,
Flew o'er me and my Dearie;
For dear to me as light and life
Was my sweet Highland Mary.
1789 'Highland Mary', stanza 2.

2 We are na fou, we're nae that fou,
But just a drappie in our e'e;
The cock may craw, the day may daw,
And ay we'll taste the barley bree.
1789 'Willie brew'd a peck o' maut', chorus.

3 Ay waukin, O,
Waukin still and weary:
Sleep I can get nane,
For thinkin on my Dearie.
1790 'Ay waukin O', chorus.

4 My love she's but a lassie yet,
My love she's but a lassie yet;
We'll let her stand a year or twa,
She'll no be half sae saucy yet.
1790 'My love she's but a lassie yet', chorus

5 My heart's in the Highlands, my heart is not here,
My heart's in the Highlands a chasing the deer;
Chasing the wild deer, and following the roe;
My heart's in the Highlands, wherever I go.
1790 'My heart's in the Highlands', chorus.

6 John Anderson my jo, John,
When we were first acquent;
Your locks were like the raven,
Your bonie brow was brent;
But now your brow is beld, John,
Your locks are like the snaw;
But blessings on your frosty pow,
John Anderson my jo.
1790 'John Anderson my Jo', stanza 1.

7 An ye had been whare I hae been,
Ye wad na been sae canty, O;
An ye had seen what I hae seen,
I' th' braes o' Killiecrankie, O.
1790 'Killiecrankie', chorus.

8 When chapman billies leave the street,
And drouthy neebors, neebors meet,
As market-days are wearing late,
An' folk begin to tak the gate.
1790 'Tam o' Shanter. A Tale'.

9 Whare sits our sulky sullen dame,
Gathering her brows like gathering storm,
Nursing her wrath to keep it warm.
1790 'Tam o' Shanter. A Tale'.

10 Auld Ayr, wham ne'er a town surpasses,
For honest men and bonny lasses.
1790 'Tam o' Shanter. A Tale'.

11 Ah! gentle dames! it gars me greet,
To think how mony counsels sweet,
How mony lengthen'd sage advices,
The husband frae the wife despises!
1790 'Tam o' Shanter. A Tale'.

12 Tam lo'ed him like a vera brither;
They had been fou for weeks thegither.
1790 'Tam o' Shanter. A Tale'.

13 The storm without might rair and rustle,
Tam did na mind the storm a whistle.
1790 'Tam o' Shanter. A Tale'.

14 Kings may be blest but Tam was glorious,
O'er a' the ills o' life victorious!
1790 'Tam o' Shanter. A Tale'.

15 But pleasures are like poppies spread,
You seize the flower, its bloom is shed;
Or like the snow falls in the river,
A moment white—then melts for ever.
1790 'Tam o' Shanter. A Tale'.

16 Nae man can tether time or tide;
The hour approaches Tam maun ride;
That hour, o' night's black arch the key-stane,
That dreary hour Tam mounts his beast in.
1790 'Tam o' Shanter. A Tale'.

17 Inspiring, bold John Barleycorn!
What dangers thou canst make us scorn!
Wi' tippenny, we fear nae evil;
Wi' usquabae, we'll face the devil!
1790 'Tam o' Shanter. A Tale'. 'Usquabae' = whisky.

18 Five tomahawks, wi' blude red-rusted;
Five scymitars, wi' murder crusted.
1790 'Tam o' Shanter. A Tale'.

19 As Tammie glowr'd, amaz'd, and curious,
The mirth and fun grew fast and furious:
The piper loud and louder blew;
The dancers quick and quicker flew.
1790 'Tam o' Shanter. A Tale'.

20 Ah, Tam! Ah, Tam! thou'll get thy fairin!

In hell they'll roast thee like a herrin!
1790 'Tam o' Shanter. A Tale'.

21 Whene'er to drink you are inclin'd,
Or cutty sarks run in your mind,
Think, ye may buy the joys o'er dear—
Remember Tam o' Shanter's mare.
1790 'Tam o' Shanter. A Tale'.

22 Ye banks and braes o' bonie Doon,
How can ye bloom sae fresh and fair;
How can ye chant, ye little birds,
And I sae weary fu' o' care!
1791 'The Banks o' Doon' (second version), stanza 1.

23 And my fause Luver staw my rose,
But, ah! he left the thorn wi' me.
1791 'The Banks o' Doon' (second version), stanza 2.

24 Ae fond kiss, and then we sever!
Ae fareweel, and then for ever!
Deep in heart-wrung tears I'll pledge thee,
Warring sighs and groans I'll wage thee.
1791 'Ae Fond Kiss', stanza 1.

25 Had we never lov'd sae kindly,
Had we never lov'd sae blindly!
Never met—or never parted,
We had ne'er been broken-hearted.
1791 'Ae Fond Kiss', stanza 4.

26 Fare-thee-weel, thou first and fairest!
Fare-thee-weel, thou best and dearest!
Thine be ilka joy and treasure,
Peace, Enjoyment, Love and Pleasure!
1791 'Ae Fond Kiss', stanza 5.

27 Ye Jacobites by name, give an ear, give an ear!
Ye Jacobites by name, give an ear.
1792 'Ye Jacobites by name', stanza 1.

28 Sic a wife as Willie's wife,
I wad na gie a button for her.
1792 'Willie Wastle', or 'Sic a wife as Willie's wife', stanza 1.

29 Willie Wastle dwalt on Tweed,
The spot they ca'd it Linkumdoddie.
1792 'Willie Wastle', or 'Sic a wife as Willie's wife', stanza 1.

30 Fareweel to a' our Scottish fame,
Fareweel our ancient glory.
1792 'Such a parcel of rogues in a nation', stanza 1.

31 Now Sark rins o'er the Solway sands,
An' Tweed rins to the ocean,
To mark where England's province stands,
Such a parcel of rogues in a nation!
1792 'Such a parcel of rogues in a nation', stanza 1.

32 We're bought and sold for English gold,

Such a parcel of rogues in a nation!
1792 'Such a parcel of rogues in a nation', stanza 3.

33 The deil cam fiddlin thro' the town,
And danc'd awa wi' th' Exciseman;
And ilka wife cries, auld Mahoun,
I wish you luck o' the prize, man!
1792 'The Deil's awa wi' th' Exciseman', stanza 1.

34 There's threesome reels, there's foursome reels,
There's hornpipes and strathspeys, man,
But the ae best dance e'er cam to the Land
Was, the deil's awa wi' th' Exciseman.
1792 'The Deil's awa wi' th' Exciseman', stanza 3.

35 When o'er the hill the eastern star
Tells bughtin-time is near, my jo,
And owsen frae the furrowed field
Return sae dowf and weary O.
1792 'My ain kind dearie', or 'The Lea-rig', stanza 1.

36 I'll meet thee on the lea-rig,
My ain kind Dearie, O.
1792 'My ain kind dearie', or 'The Lea-rig', stanza 1.

37 Scots, wha hae wi' Wallace bled,
Scots, wham Bruce has aften led,
Welcome to your gory bed,—
Or to victorie!—
Now's the day, and now's the hour;
See the front o' battle lour;
See approach proud Edward's power,
Chains and Slaverie!
1793 'Bruce's Address at Bannockburn', stanza 1.

38 Liberty's in every blow!
Let us do or die!
1793 'Bruce's Address at Bannockburn', stanza 3.

39 Though this was fair, and that was braw,
And yon the toast of a' the town,
I sigh'd, and said amang them a',
'Ye are na Mary Morison.'
1793 'Mary Morison', stanza 2.

40 O my Luve's like a red, red rose
That's newly sprung in June;
O my luve's like the melodie
That's sweetly play'd in tune.
As fair art thou, my bonie lass,
So deep in luve am I;
And I will luve thee still, my Dear,
Till a' the seas gang dry.
Till a' the seas gang dry, my Dear,
And the rocks melt wi' the sun:
O I will love thee still, my Dear,
While the sands o' life shall run.
1794 'A red, red rose'.

41 Ca' the yowes to the knowes,

Ca' them whare the heather grows,
Ca' them whare the burnie rowes,
My bonie Dearie!
1794 'Ca' the yowes to the knowes' (second version), chorus.

42 Is there for honest Poverty
That hings his head, and a' that;
The coward-slave, we pass him by,
We dare be poor for a' that!
For a' that, and a' that,
Our toils obscure, and a' that,
The rank is but the guinea's stamp,
The man's the gowd for a' that.
1795 'For a' that and a' that', stanza 1.

43 A man's a man for a' that.
1795 'For a' that and a' that', stanza 2.

44 For a' that, and a' that,
It's comin' yet for a' that,
That Man to Man the warld o'er
Shall brothers be, for a' that.
1795 'For a' that and a' that', stanza 5.

45 Gin a body meet a body
Comin thro' the rye,
Gin a body kiss a body
Need a body cry?
1796 'Comin thro' the rye', stanza 2.

46 An' Charlie he's my darling, my darling, my
darling,
Charlie he's my darling, the young Chevalier.
1796 'Charlie he's my darling', chorus.

47 It was a' for our rightfu' king,
We left fair Scotland's strand.
1796 'It was a' for our rightfu' king', stanza 1.

48 Now a' is done that men can do,
And a' is done in vain.
1796 'It was a' for our rightfu' king', stanza 2.

49 He turn'd him right and round about,
Upon the Irish shore,
And gae his bridle reins a shake,
With, Adieu for evermore, my dear,
And Adieu for evermore!
1796 'It was a' for our rightfu' king', stanza 3.

50 Oh wert thou in the cauld blast,
On yonder lea, on yonder lea;
My plaidie to the angry airt,
I'd shelter thee, I'd shelter thee.
1796 'Oh wert thou in the cauld blast', stanza 1.

51 There's death in the cup—sae beware!
Nay, more—there is danger in touching;
But wha can avoid the fell snare?
The man and his wine's sae bewitching!
1796 'Inscription on a Goblet'.

Burroughs, Edgar Rice 1875–1950

US novelist. He was a hugely successful writer of popular fiction, much of it in the science fiction and fantasy genres, and is best known as the creator of Tarzan. The much-quoted line 'Me Tarzan, you Jane', does not appear in any story, and is a misattribution by actor Johnny Weissmuller.

52 Tarzan of the Apes.
1912 Title of story.

Burroughs, William S(eward) 1914–97

US writer. He wandered through the US and Europe after graduating from Harvard, becoming a heroin addict in New York (1944). His novels draw on his experiences, establishing him as a spokesman of the 'beat' generation.

53 The face of 'evil' is always the face of total need.
1959 *The Naked Lunch*, introduction.

54 I think there are innumerable gods. What we on
earth call God is a little tribal God who has made
an awful mess.
1965 In *Paris Review*, Fall.

55 After one look at this planet any visitor from outer
space would say 'I WANT TO SEE THE MANAGER.'
1985 *The Adding Machine*, 'Women: A Biological Mistake'.

56 You can't fake quality any more than you can fake a
good meal.
1987 *The Western Lands*, ch.2.

57 No problems can be solved, and all solutions lead
to more problems.
Comment to Allen Ginsberg. Quoted in Barry Miles *Ginsberg* (1989), ch.17.

58 Nothing exists until or unless it is observed. An
artist is making something exist by observing it.
1992 *Painting and Guns*, 'The Creative Observer'.

59 Virtue is simply happiness, and happiness is a by-
product of function. You are happy when you are
functioning.
1992 *Painting and Guns*, 'The Creative Observer'.

Burt, Benjamin Hapgood 1880–1950

US songwriter.

60 All Dressed Up and No Place to Go.
1913 Song title, *The Beauty Shop* (music by Silvio Hein).

61 One evening in October, when I was one-third
sober,
An' taking home a 'load' with manly pride;
My poor feet began to stutter, so I lay down in the
gutter,
And a pig came up an' lay down by my side.
Then we sang 'It's all fair weather when good
fellows get together,'

Till a lady passing by was heard to say:
'You can tell a man who boozes by the company he
 chooses',
And the pig got up and slowly walked away.
1933 'The Pig Got Up and Slowly Walked Away', song.

Burton, C L 1876–1961

Canadian businessman.

62 I hold no brief for private enterprise. But I have
unshakeable faith in individual enterprise.
1952 *A Sense of Urgency: Memoirs of a Canadian Merchant.*

63 Life, if you have a bent for it, is a beautiful thing. It
consists, I do believe, of having a sense of urgency.
1952 *A Sense of Urgency: Memoirs of a Canadian Merchant.*

Burton, Robert pseudonym *Democritus Junior*
1577–1640

English writer and clergyman. Educated at Oxford, he
remained at Christ Church for life. His *Anatomy of
Melancholy* (1621) is a vast, witty compendium of
Jacobean knowledge and superstition about the 'disease'
of melancholy, which went through several editions in his
lifetime.

64 All my joys to this are folly,
Naught so sweet as melancholy.
1621 *Anatomy of Melancholy*, 'The Author's Abstract of
Melancholy'.

65 A loose, plain, rude writer…I call a spade a spade.
1621 *Anatomy of Melancholy*, 'Democritus to the Reader'.

66 All poets are mad.
1621 *Anatomy of Melancholy*, 'Democritus to the Reader'.

67 I may not here omit those two main plagues, and
common dotages of human kind, wine and
women, which have infatuated and besotted
myriads of people. They go commonly together.
1621 *Anatomy of Melancholy*, pt.1, section 2, member 3,
subsection 13.

68 *Hinc quam sit calamus saevior ense patet.*

From this it is clear how much the pen is worse
than the sword.
1621 *Anatomy of Melancholy*, pt.1, section 2, member 4,
subsection 4.

69 See one promontory (said Socrates of old), one
mountain, one sea, one river, and see all.
1621 *Anatomy of Melancholy*, pt.1, section 2, member 4,
subsection 7.

70 One was never married, and that's his hell; another
is, and that's his plague.
1621 *Anatomy of Melancholy*, pt.1, section 2, member 4,
subsection 7.

71 Who cannot give good counsel? 'tis cheap, it costs
them nothing.
1621 *Anatomy of Melancholy*, pt.2, section 3, member 1,
subsection 1.

72 What is a ship but a prison?
1621 *Anatomy of Melancholy*, pt.2, section 3, member 4,
subsection 1.

73 Tobacco, divine, rare, superexcellent tobacco,
which goes far beyond all their panaceas, potable
gold, and philosopher's stones, a sovereign remedy
to all diseases… But, as it is commonly abused by
most men, which take it as tinkers do ale, 'tis a
plague, a mischief, a violent purger of goods, lands,
health, hellish, devilish, and damned tobacco, the
ruin and overthrow of body and soul.
1621 *Anatomy of Melancholy*, pt.2, section 4, member 2,
subsection 1.

74 But this love of ours is immoderate, inordinate, and
not to be comprehended in any bounds. It will not
contain itself within the union of marriage or apply
to one object, but is a wandering, extravagant, a
domineering, a boundless, an irrefragable, a
destructive passion.
1621 *Anatomy of Melancholy*, pt.3, section 2, member 1,
subsection 2.

75 No cord nor cable can so forcibly draw, or hold so
fast, as love can do with a twined thread. The
scorching beams under the equinoctial or extremity
of cold within the circle Arctic, where the very seas
are frozen, cold or torrid zone cannot avoid or expel
this heat, fury, and rage of mortal men.
1621 *Anatomy of Melancholy*, pt.3, section 2, member 1,
subsection 2.

76 Of women's unnatural, unsatiable lust, what
country, what village doth not complain?
1621 *Anatomy of Melancholy*, pt.3, section 2, member 1,
subsection 2.

77 A passion of the brain, as all other melancholy, by
reason of corrupt imagination.
1621 Of love. *Anatomy of Melancholy*, pt.3, section 2, member
1, subsection 2.

78 One religion is as true as another.
1621 *Anatomy of Melancholy*, pt.3, section 4, member 2,
subsection 1.

79 Be not solitary, be not idle.
1621 *Anatomy of Melancholy*, closing words.

Buruma, Ian

British writer.

80 Isherwood did not so much find himself in Berlin
as reinvent himself; Isherwood became a fiction, a
work of art.
1986 Of Christopher Isherwood. In the *New Republic*, 4 Nov.

81 A nation of people longing to be 12-year-olds or even younger.
   1994 Of Japan. *The Wages of Guilt.*

82 German memory was like a massive tongue seeking out, over and over, a sore tooth.
   1994 *The Wages of Guilt.*

Busby, Sir Matt(hew) 1909–94

Scottish football player and manager. He led Manchester United to glory in the 1950s, and successfully rebuilt the team after the Munich air crash in 1958 to win the European Cup in 1968.

83 The theory that the League and Cup double will never be done in modern times is nonsense. I realize no one has done it for sixty years, but there is a simple explanation for that. No club has been good enough.
   1957 Attributed, four years before Tottenham Hotspur won both the League Championship and the FA Cup.

Bush, Barbara Pierce 1925–

Former US First Lady. The daughter of a wealthy New York publisher, she married George Bush (1945), who became President in 1989.

84 No other single building is so much a part of the American consciousness.
   1992 At the 200th anniversary of the laying of the White House cornerstone. Reported in the *Washington Times*, 24 Jan.

85 I wrote in my diaries about…good meals that I have eaten and am wearing today.
   1994 *Barbara Bush: A Memoir.*

Bush, George Herbert Walker 1924–

US Republican politician and 41st President. After losing to Reagan for the Republican candidacy in the 1980 elections, he became his Vice-President and later President (1989–92). He presided over the US-led UN coalition to defeat Iraq in the Gulf War.

86 The United States is the best and fairest and most decent nation on the face of the earth.
   1988 Speech, May.

87 Read my lips: no new taxes.
   1988 Accepting the Republican presidential nomination, 19 Aug.

Bush, George W 1948–

US businessman and politician, son of George Herbert Walker Bush. Governor of Texas (1994–).

88 I've inherited 100 per cent of his enemies and only 50 per cent of his friends.
   1994 Of his father, former President George Bush's influence on the governatorial campaign. In the *Washington Times*, 12 Oct.

Bush, Vannevar 1890–1974

US electrical engineer and physicist, education and Dean of Engineering at the Massachusetts Institute of Technology. He later led the US Office of Scientific Research.

89 To pursue science is not to disparage things of the spirit.
   1953 Speech at the Massachusetts Institute of Technology, 5 Oct.

90 It was through the Second World War that most of us suddenly appreciated for the first time the power of man's concentrated efforts to understand and control the forces of nature. We were appalled by what we saw.
   1967 *Science is Not Enough.*

91 Science has a simple faith, which transcends utility. Nearly all men of science, all men of learning for that matter, and men of simple ways too, have it in some form and in some degree. It is the faith that it is the privilege of man to learn to understand, and that this is his mission. If we abandon that mission under stress we shall abandon it forever, for stress will not cease. Knowledge for the sake of understanding, not merely to prevail, that is the essence of our being. None can define its limits, or set its ultimate boundaries.
   1967 *Science is Not Enough.*

Busoni, Ferruccio Benvenuto 1866–1924

Italian pianist and composer. An infant prodigy, he taught and played throughout Europe and wrote four operas. His pupils included Kurt Weill.

92 Music is the art of sounds in the movement of time.
   1923 *The Essence of Music.*

Bussy-Rabutin, Comte de 1618–93

French soldier and poet.

93 *L'absence est à l'amour ce qu'est au feu le vent;*
   Il éteint le petit, il allume le grand.

   Absence is to love what wind is to fire;
   It extinguishes the small, it kindles the great.
   1665 *Histoire Amoureuse des Gaules. Maximes d'Amour*, pt.2.

94 *Comme vous savez, Dieu est d'ordinaire pour les gros escadrons contre les petits.*

   As you know, God is usually on the side of the big squadrons against the small.
   1677 Letter to the Comte de Limoges, 18 Oct.

Butler, Joseph 1692–1752

English moral philosopher, cleric and Christian apologist. Originally a dissenter, he joined the Church of England and became Bishop of Bristol, and later of Durham.

95 But to us, probability is the very guide of life.
   1736   *The Analogy of Religion*, introduction.

96 Sir, the pretending to extraordinary revelations and
   gifts of the Holy Ghost is a horrid thing, a very
   horrid thing.
   Comment to John Wesley. Quoted in John Wesley Works, *pt.13.*

Butler (of Saffron Walden), R(ichard) A(usten) Butler, Baron   1902–82

British Conservative politician. He became Chancellor of
the Exchequer, Home Secretary and Deputy Prime
Minister, and narrowly lost the premiership to Alec
Douglas-Home, becoming Foreign Secretary (1963–4).

97 After all, it is not every man who nearly becomes
   Prime Minister of England.
   1957   On being passed over as Harold Macmillan's successor in
   favour of Alec Douglas-Home, Jan.

98 Politics is the art of the possible.
   1971   *The Art of the Possible.*
   ▷ See Galbraith 411:78.

99 The best Prime Minister we've got.
   *Attributed comment on Harold Macmillan, on a train going to
   the Party Conference in Brighton.*

Butler, Samuel   1612–80

English satirist, who served in noble households and in
government. His *Hudibras* (1663–78), a burlesque satire
on Puritanism, was a special favourite of Charles II.
Despite royal favour, he died in penury.

1 A client is fain to hire a lawyer to keep from the
   injury of other lawyers—as Christians that travel in
   Turkey are forced to hire Janissaries, to protect
   them from the insolencies of other Turks.
   1660   *Prose Observations.*

2 But here our authors make a doubt
   Whether he were more wise or stout.
   Some hold the one and some the other;
   But howsoe'er they make a pother,
   The difference was so small his brain
   Outweighed his rage but half a grain;
   Which made some take him for a tool
   That knaves do work with, called a fool.
   1663   *Hudibras*, pt.1, canto 1, l.29–36.

3 We grant, although he had much wit,
   He was very shy of using it;
   As being loath to wear it out,
   And therefore bore it not about,
   Unless on holidays, or so,
   As men their best apparel do.
   1663   *Hudibras*, pt.1, canto 1, l.45–50.

4 'Tis known he could speak Greek

As naturally as pigs squeak.
1663   *Hudibras*, pt.1, canto 1, l.51–2.

5 He was in logic a great critic,
   Profoundly skilled in analytic.
   He could distinguish and divide
   A hair 'twixt south and southwest side.
   1663   *Hudibras*, pt.1, canto 1, l.65–8.

6 For every *why* he had a *wherefore*.
   1663   *Hudibras*, pt.1, canto 1, l.132.

7 He knew what's what, and that's as high
   As metaphysic wit can fly.
   1663   *Hudibras*, pt.1, canto 1, l.149–50.

8 And with as delicate a hand
   Could twist as tough a rope of sand;
   And weave fine cobwebs, fit for skull
   That's empty when the moon is full;
   Such as take lodgings in a head
   That's to be let unfurnishèd.
   1663   *Hudibras*, pt.1, canto 1, l.155–60.

9 And still be doing, never done:
   As if Religion were intended
   For nothing else but to be mended.
   1663   *Hudibras*, pt.1, canto 1, l.202–4.

10 For rhyme the rudder is of verses,
   With which like ships they steer their courses.
   1663   *Hudibras*, pt.1, canto 1, l.457–8.

11 Great actions are not always true sons
   Of great and mighty resolutions.
   1663   *Hudibras*, pt.1, canto 1, l.877–8.

12 Ay me! what perils do environ
   The man that meddles with cold iron!
   1663   *Hudibras*, pt.1, canto 3, l.1–2.
   ▷ See Spenser, *The Faerie Queen*, bk.1, canto 8, stanza 1

13 I'll make the fur
   Fly 'bout the ears of the old cur.
   1663   *Hudibras*, pt.1, canto 3, l.277–8.

14 I am not now in fortune's power
   He that is down can fall no lower.
   1663   *Hudibras*, pt.1, canto 3, l.871–2.

15 Learning, that cobweb of the brain,
   Profane, erroneous, and vain.
   1663   *Hudibras*, pt.1, canto 3, l.1339–40.

16 She that with poetry is won
   Is but a desk to write upon.
   1664   *Hudibras*, pt.2, canto 1, l.591–2.

17 Love is a boy, by poets styled,
   Then spare the rod, and spoil the child.
   1664   *Hudibras*, pt.2, canto 1, l.843–4.

18 Oaths are but words, and words but wind.
    1664 *Hudibras*, pt.2, canto 2, l.107.

19 For saints may do the same things by
    The spirit, in sincerity,
    Which other men are tempted to.
    1664 *Hudibras*, pt.2, canto 2, l.235–7.

20 Doubtless the pleasure is as great
    Of being cheated, as to cheat.
    As lookers-on feel most delight,
    That least perceive a juggler's sleight,
    And still the less they understand,
    The more th' admire his sleight of hand.
    1664 *Hudibras*, pt.2, canto 3, l.1–6.

21 For in what stupid age or nation
    Was marriage ever out of fashion?
    1678 *Hudibras*, pt.3, canto 1, l.817–18.

22 What makes all doctrines plain and clear?
    About two hundred pounds a year.
    And that which was prov'd true before,
    Prove false again? Two hundred more.
    1678 *Hudibras*, pt.3, canto 1, l.1277–80.

23 For if it be but half denied,
    'Tis half as good as justified.
    1678 *Hudibras*, pt.3, canto 2, l.803–4.

24 For, those that fly, may fight again,
    Which he can never do that's slain.
    1678 *Hudibras*, pt.3, canto 3, l.243–4.

25 He that complies against his will
    Is of his own opinion still.
    1678 *Hudibras*, pt.3, canto 3, l.547.

26 Neither have the heart to stay,
    Nor wit enough to run away.
    1678 *Hudibras*, pt.3, canto 3, l.569–60.

27 For money has a power above
    The stars and fate, to manage love.
    1678 *Hudibras*, pt.3, canto 3, l.1279–80.

Butler, Samuel 1835–1902

English writer and parliamentary secretary. His Utopian satire *Erewhon* (1872) and its supplement *Erewhon Revisited* (1901) deal with the origins of religious belief. His autobiographical novel *The Way of All Flesh* was published posthumously (1903).

28 I am forgetting myself into admiring a mountain which is of no use for sheep. This is wrong. A mountain here is only beautiful if it has good grass on it.
    1863 Of Mt Cook. *A First Year in Canterbury Settlement.*

29 The wish to spread those opinions that we hold conducive to our own welfare is so deeply rooted in the English character that few of us can escape its influence.
    1872 *Erewhon.*

30 Exploring is delightful to look forward to and back upon, but it is not comfortable at the time, unless it be of such an easy nature as not to deserve the name.
    1872 *Erewhon.*

31 A hen is only an egg's way of making another egg.
    1877 *Life and Habit*, ch.8.

32 It was very good of God to let Carlyle and Mrs Carlyle marry one another and so make only two people miserable instead of four.
    1884 Letter to Miss E M A Savage, 21 Nov.

33 Life is like playing a violin solo in public and learning the instrument as one goes on.
    1895 Speech at the Somerville Club, 27 Feb.

34 It has been said that although God cannot alter the past, historians can; it is perhaps because they can be useful to Him in this respect that He tolerates their existence.
    1901 *Erewhon Revisited*, ch.14.

35 All animals, except man, know that the principal business of life is to enjoy it.
    1903 *The Way of All Flesh*, ch.19.

36 The advantage of doing one's praising for oneself is that one can lay it on so thick and exactly in the right places.
    1903 *The Way of All Flesh*, ch.34.

37 Young as he was, his instinct told him that the best liar is he who makes the smallest amount of lying go the longest way.
    1903 *The Way of All Flesh*, ch.39.

38 A man's friendships are, like his will, invalidated by marriage.
    1903 *The Way of All Flesh*, ch.75.

39 'Getting into the key of C sharp,' he said, 'is like an unprotected female travelling on the Metropolitan Railway, and finding herself at Shepherd's Bush, without quite knowing where she wants to go to. How is she ever to get safe back to Clapham Junction?'
    1903 *The Way of All Flesh.*

40 There's many a good tune played on an old fiddle.
    1903 *The Way of All Flesh.*

41 As soon as any art is pursued with a view to money, then farewell, in ninety-nine cases out of a hundred, all hope of genuine good work.
    Collected in H F Jones (ed) *The Notebooks of Samuel Butler* (1912).

42 Justice is being allowed to do whatever I like. Injustice is whatever prevents my doing it.

Collected in H F Jones (ed) *The Notebooks of Samuel Butler* (1912).

43 An apology for the Devil: It must be remembered that we have only heard one side of the case. God has written all the books.

Collected in H F Jones (ed) *The Notebooks of Samuel Butler* (1912), ch.14.

44 Handel is so great and so simple that no one but a professional musician is unable to understand him.

Collected in H F Jones (ed) *The Notebooks of Samuel Butler* (1912).

45 The healthy stomach is nothing if not conservative. Few radicals have good digestions.

Collected in H F Jones (ed) *The Notebooks of Samuel Butler* (1912).

46 Science, after all, is only an expression for our ignorance of our own ignorance.

Collected in H F Jones (ed) *The Notebooks of Samuel Butler* (1912).

47 To live is like to love—all reason is against it, and all healthy instinct for it.

Collected in H F Jones (ed) *The Notebooks of Samuel Butler* (1912).

48 The three most important things a man has are, briefly, his private parts, his money, and his religious opinions.

Collected in *Further Extracts from the Notebooks* (1934).

49 Jesus! with all thy faults I love thee still.

Collected in *Further Extracts from the Notebooks* (1934).

50 A lawyer's dream of heaven: every man reclaimed his own property at the resurrection, and each tried to recover it from all his forefathers.

Collected in *Further Extracts from the Notebooks* (1934).

Butler, William 1535–1618

51 Doubtless God could have made a better berry, but doubtless God never did.

Of the strawberry. Quoted in Izaak Walton *The Compleat Angler* (3rd edn, 1661), pt.1, ch.5.

Butterfield, Sir Herbert 1900–79

English historian, Professor of Modern History at Cambridge.

52 We can do worse than remember the principle which both gives us a firm Rock and leaves us the maximum elasticity for our minds—Hold to Christ, and for the rest be totally uncommitted.

1949 *Christianity and History.*

53 In a profound sense we may say that the crucifixion, however else we may interpret it, accuses human nature, accuses all of us in the very things that we think are our righteousness.

1951 *History and Human Relations.*

Byatt, Dame A(ntonia) S(usan) née Drabble 1936–

English writer and critic, sister of Margaret Drabble. Her works include critical studies of Iris Murdoch (1965 and 1976) and an edition of George Eliot (1979), and novels including *Possession* (Booker Prize, 1990), which explores the experience of women in 20c society.

54 There is something both gratifying and humiliating in watching a man who has taken you for a routinely silly woman begin to take you seriously.

1985 *Still Life*, ch.18, 'Hic Ille Raphael'.

55 Autobiographies tell more lies than all but the most self-indulgent fiction.

1987 'The Day That E.M. Forster Died'.

56 He's one of those men who argues by increments of noise—so that as you open your mouth he says another, cleverer, louder thing.

1990 *Possession*, ch.15.

Byrd, William 1543–1623

English composer and organist. A firm Catholic, prosecuted as a recusant, he wrote music for both Catholic and Anglican services, as well as madrigals, songs and music for strings.

57 The exercise of singing is delightful to nature and good to preserve the health of Man.

1588 *Psalmes, Sonets and Songs.*

Byron, George Gordon, 6th Baron Byron of Rochdale 1788–1824

English Romantic poet. Lame from birth, he later dramatized himself as a gloomy, romantic man of mystery, the 'Byronic hero'. Suspected of an incestuous affair with his half-sister, he left for Venice, where he wrote *Beppo* (1818) and *Don Juan* (1819–24). He died fervently supporting the Greek war of independence against the Turks.

58 Yet, when confinement's lingering hour was done,
Our sport, our studies, and our souls were one:
Together we impell'd the flying ball;
Together waited in our tutor's hall;
Together join'd in cricket's manly toil.

1807 *Hours of Idleness*, 'Childish Recollections'. Of his childhood days at Harrow public school.

59 I'll publish, right or wrong:
Fools are my theme, let satire be my song.

1809 *English Bards and Scotch Reviewers*, l.5–6.

60 A man must serve his time to every trade
   Save censure—critics all are ready made.
   Take hackneyed jokes from Miller, got by rote,
   With just enough of learning to misquote.
   1809 *English Bards and Scotch Reviewers*, l.63–6.

61 Be warm, but pure; be amorous, but be chaste.
   1809 *English Bards and Scotch Reviewers*, l.306.

62 The petrifactions of a plodding brain.
   1809 *English Bards and Scotch Reviewers*, l.416.

63 Then let Ausonia, skilled in every art
   To soften manners, but corrupt the heart,
   Pour her exotic follies o'er the town,
   To sanction Vice, and hunt Decorum down.
   1809 *Engish Bards and Scotch Reviewers*, l.618–21.

64 Let simple Wordsworth chime his childish verse,
   And brother Coleridge lull the babe at nurse.
   1809 *English Bards and Scotch Reviewers*, l.917–18.

65 And glory, like the phoenix midst her fires,
   Exhales her odours, blazes, and expires.
   1809 *English Bards and Scotch Reviewers*, l.959–60.

66 A land of meanness, sophistry and mist.
   1812 Of Scotland. 'The Curse of Minerva', l.138.

67 Each breeze from foggy mount and marshy plain
   Dilutes with drivel every drizzly brain,
   Till, burst at length, each wat'ry head o'er flows,
   Foul as their soil, and frigid as their snows.
   1812 Of Scotland and the Scots. 'The Curse of Minerva',
   l.139–42.

68 The laughing dames in who he did delight,
   Whose large blue eyes, fair locks, and snowy hands,
   Might shake the saintship of an anchorite.
   1812–18 *Childe Harold's Pilgrimage*, canto 1, stanza 11.

69 Adieu, adieu! my native shore
   Fades o'er the waters blue.
   1812–18 *Childe Harold's Pilgrimage*, canto 1, stanza 13.

70 Here all were noble, save Nobility.
   1812–18 *Childe Harold's Pilgrimage*, canto 1, stanza 85.

71 None are so desolate but something dear,
   Dearer than self, possesses or possessed
   A thought, and claims the homage of a tear.
   1812–18 *Childe Harold's Pilgrimage*, canto 2, stanza 24.

72 Oh, lovely Spain! renown'd, romantic land!
   1812–18 *Childe Harold's Pilgrimage*, canto 2, stanza 35.

73 Dark Sappho! could not verse immortal save
   That beast imbued with such immortal fire?
   Could she not live who life eternal gave?
   1812–18 *Childe Harold's Pilgrimage*, canto 2, stanza 39.

74 Fair Greece! sad relic of departed worth!
   Immortal, though no more! though fallen, great!
   1812–18 *Childe Harold's Pilgrimage*, canto 2, stanza 73.

75 Hereditary bondsmen! know ye not
   Who would be free themselves must strike the
   blow?
   1812–18 *Childe Harold's Pilgrimage*, canto 2, stanza 76.

76 And yet how lovely in thine age of woe,
   Land of lost gods and godlike men! art thou!
   1812–18 Of Greece. *Childe Harold's Pilgrimage*, canto 2,
   stanza 85.

77 Art, Glory, Freedom fail, but Nature still is fair.
   1812–18 *Childe Harold's Pilgrimage*, canto 2, stanza 87.

78 What is the worst of woes that wait on age?
   What stamps the wrinkle deeper on the brow?
   To view each loved one blotted from life's page,
   And be alone on earth, as I am now.
   1812–18 *Childe Harold's Pilgrimage*, canto 2, stanza 98.

79 Once more upon the waters! yet once more!
   And the waves bound beneath me as a steed
   That knows his rider.
   1812–18 *Childe Harold's Pilgrimage*, canto 3, stanza 2.

80 The wandering outlaw of his own dark mind.
   1812–18 *Childe Harold's Pilgrimage*, canto 3, stanza 3.

81 Years steal
   Fire from the mind as vigour from the limb;
   And life's enchanted cup but sparkles near the
   brim.
   1812–18 *Childe Harold's Pilgrimage*, canto 3, stanza 8.

82 Where rose the mountains, there to him were
   friends;
   Where rolled the ocean, thereon was his home;
   Where a blue sky, and glowing clime, extends,
   He had the passion and the power to roam.
   1812–18 *Childe Harold's Pilgrimage*, canto 3, stanza 13.

83 The very knowledge that he lived in vain,
   That all was over on this side the tomb,
   Had made Despair a smilingness assume.
   1812–18 *Childe Harold's Pilgrimage*, canto 3, stanza 16.

84 There was a sound of revelry by night,
   And Belgium's capital had gathered then
   Her beauty and her chivalry, and bright
   The lamps that shone o'er fair women and brave
   men;
   A thousand hearts beat happily; and when
   Music arose with its voluptuous swell,
   Soft eyes looked love to eyes which spake again,
   And all went merry as a marriage bell;
   But hush! hark! a deep sound strikes like a rising
   knell!
   1812–18 *Childe Harold's Pilgrimage*, canto 3, stanza 21.

85 He rushed into the field, and, foremost fighting, fell.
   1812–18 *Childe Harold's Pilgrimage*, canto 3, stanza 23.

86 Quiet to quick bosoms is a hell.
   1812–18 *Childe Harold's Pilgrimage*, canto 3, stanza 42.

87 I live not in myself, but I become
   Portion of that around me; and to me,
   High mountains are a feeling, but the hum
   Of human cities torture.
   1812–18 *Childe Harold's Pilgrimage*, canto 3, stanza 72.

88 His love was passion's essence:—as a tree
   On fire by lightning, with ethereal flame
   Kindled he was, and blasted.
   1812–18 *Childe Harold's Pilgrimage*, canto 3, stanza 78.

89 Sapping a solemn creed with solemn sneer.
   1812–18 Of Edward Gibbon. *Childe Harold's Pilgrimage*, canto 3, stanza 107.

90 I have not loved the world, nor the world me.
   1812–18 *Childe Harold's Pilgrimage*, canto 3, stanza 113.

91 I stood
   Among them, but not of them; in a shroud
   Of thoughts which were not their thoughts.
   1812–18 *Childe Harold's Pilgrimage*, canto 3, stanza 113.

92 I stood in Venice, on the Bridge of Sighs;
   A palace and a prison on each hand:
   I saw from out the wave her structures rise
   As from the stroke of the enchanter's wand:
   A thousand years their cloudy wings expand
   Around me, and a dying Glory smiles
   O'er the far times, when many a subject land
   Look'd to the winged Lion's marble piles,
   Where Venice sate in state, thron'd on her hundred
     isles!
   1812–19 *Childe Harold's Pilgrimage*, canto 4, stanza 1.

93 Fair Italy!
   Thou art the garden of the world, the home
   Of all Art yields, and Nature can decree;
   Even in thy desert, what is like to thee?
   1812–18 *Childe Harold's Pilgrimage*, canto 4, stanza 26.

94 The moon is up, and yet it is not night;
   Sunset divides the sky with her—a sea
   Of glory streams along the Alpine height
   Of blue Friuli's mountains; Heaven is free
   From clouds, but of all colours seems to be
   Melted to one vast Iris of the West,
   Where the day joins the past eternity.
   1812–18 *Childe Harold's Pilgrimage*, canto 4, stanza 27.

95 Italia! oh Italia! thou who hast
   The fatal gift of beauty.
   1812–18 *Childe Harold's Pilgrimage*, canto 4, stanza 42.

96 Oh Rome! my country! city of the soul!
   1812–18 *Childe Harold's Pilgrimage*, canto 4, stanza 78.

97 From mighty wrongs to petty perfidy
   Have I not seen what human things could do?
   From the loud roar of foaming calumny
   To the small whisper of the asp paltry few,
   And subtler venom of the reptile crew,
   The Janus glance of whose significant eye,
   Learning to lie with silence, would seem true,
   And without utterance, save the shrug or sigh,
   Deal round to happy fools its speechless obloquy.
   1812–18 *Childe Harold's Pilgrimage*, canto 4, stanza 136.

98 But I have lived, and have not lived in vain:
   My mind may loose its force, my blood its fire,
   And my frame perish even in conquering pain;
   But there is that within me which shall tire
   Torture and Time, and breathe when I expire.
   Something unearthly, which they deem not of,
   Like the remembered tone of a mute lyre,
   Shall on their softened spirits sink, and move
   In hearts all rocky now the late remorse of love.
   1812–18 *Childe Harold's Pilgrimage*, canto 4, stanza 137.

99 The seal is set.—Now welcome, thou dread power!
   Nameless, yet thus omnipotent, which here
   Walk'st in the shadow of the midnight hour
   With a deep awe, yet all distinct from fear;
   Thy haunts are ever where the dead walls rear
   Their ivy mantles, and the solemn scene
   Derives from thee a sense so deep and clear
   That we become a part of what has been,
   And grow unto the spot, all-seeing but unseen.
   1812–18 *Childe Harold's Pilgrimage*, canto 4, stanza 138.

1 There were his young barbarians all at play,
   There was their Dacian mother—he, their sire,
   Butchered to make a Roman holiday.
   1812–18 *Childe Harold's Pilgrimage*, canto 4, stanza 141.

2 A ruin—yet what ruin! from its mass
   Walls, palaces, half-cities, have been reared.
   1812–18 *Childe Harold's Pilgrimage*, canto 4, stanza 143.

3 While stands the Coliseum, Rome shall stand;
   When falls the Coliseum, Rome shall fall;
   And when Rome falls—the World.
   1812–18 *Childe Harold's Pilgrimage*, canto 4, stanza 145.

4 Oh! that desert were my dwelling-place,
   With one fair spirit for my minister,
   That I might all forget the human race,
   And, hating no one, love but only her!
   1812–18 *Childe Harold's Pilgrimage*, canto 4, stanza 177.

5 There is a pleasure in the pathless woods,
   There is a rapture on the lonely shore,
   There is society, where none intrudes,

By the deep sea, and music in its roar:
I love not man less, but nature more.
1812–18 *Childe Harold's Pilgrimage*, canto 4, stanza 178.

6 Roll on, thou deep and dark blue Ocean—roll!
Ten thousand fleets sweep over thee in vain;
Man marks the earth with ruin—his control
Stops with the shore.
1812–18 *Childe Harold's Pilgrimage*, canto 4, stanza 179.

7 When for a moment, like a drop of rain,
He sinks into thy depths with bubbling groan,
Without a grave, unkindled, uncoffined, and
    unknown.
1812–18 *Childe Harold's Pilgrimage*, canto 4, stanza 179.

8 Dark-heaving;—boundless, endless, and
    sublime—
The image of eternity.
1812–18 Of the sea. *Childe Harold's Pilgrimage*, canto 4, stanza 183.

9 Never under the most despotic of infidel
Governments did I behold such squalid
wretchedness as I have seen since my return, in the
very heart of a Christian country. And what are
your remedies? After months of inaction, and
months of action worse than inactivity, at length
comes forth the grand specific—the never-failing
nostrum of all state physicians from the days of
Draco to the present time; death. Is there not blood
enough upon your penal code that more must be
poured forth to ascend to Heaven and testify
against you?
1812 Maiden speech, House of Lords, 27 Feb, against a proposal to introduce the death penalty for machine-wrecking.

10 Such hath it been—shall be—beneath the sun
The many still must labour for the one.
1814 *The Corsair*, canto 1, stanza 8.

11 There was a laughing devil in sneer,
That raised emotions both of rage and fear;
And where his frown of hatred darkly fell,
Hope withering fled, and Mercy sighed farewell!
1814 *The Corsair*, canto 1, stanza 9.

12 Deep in my soul that tender secret dwells,
Lonely and lost to light for evermore,
Save when to thine my heart responsive swells,
Then trembles into silence as before.
1814 *The Corsair*, 'Medora's Song', canto 1, stanza 14.

13 The spirit burning but unbent
May writhe, rebel—the weak alone repent!
1814 *The Corsair*, canto 2, stanza 10.

14 Oh! too convincing—dangerously dear—
In woman's eye the unanswerable tear!
1814 *The Corsair*, canto 2, stanza 15.

15 Shakespeare's name, you may depend upon it,
stands absurdly too high and will go down. He had
no invention as to stories, none whatever. He took
all his plots from old novels, and threw their stories
into dramatic shape… That he threw over whatever
he did write some flashes of genius, nobody can
deny; but this was all.
1814 Letter to James Hogg, 24 Mar.

16 She walks in beauty like the night
Of cloudless climes and starry skies;
And all that's best of dark and bright
Meet in her aspect and her eyes:
Thus mellowed to that tender light
Which heaven to gaudy day denies.
1815 'She Walks in Beauty'.

17 There's not a joy the world can give like that it takes
away.
1816 'Stanzas for Music'.

18 The mind can make
Substance, and people planets of its own
With beings brighter than have been, and give
A breath to forms which can outlive all flesh.
1816 *The Dream*, stanza 1.

19 Sorrow is knowledge: they who know the most
Must mourn the deepest o'er the fatal truth,
The tree of knowledge is not that of Life.
1817 *Manfred*, act 1, sc.1.

20 How beautiful is all this visible world!
How glorious in its action and itself!
But we, who name ourselves its sovereigns, we,
Half dust, half deity, alike unfit
To sink or soar, with our mixed essence make
A conflict of its elements, and breathe
The breath of degradation and of pride.
1817 *Manfred*, act 1, sc.2.

21 In short he was a perfect cavaliero,
And to his very valet seemed a hero.
1818 *Beppo*, stanza 33.

22 His heart was one of those which most enamour us,
Wax to receive, and marble to retain.
1818 *Beppo*, stanza 34.

23 Our cloudy climate, and our chilly women.
1818 *Beppo*, stanza 49.

24 Old man! 'tis not so difficult to die.
1819 *Manfred* (2nd edn), act 3, sc.4.

25 And Coleridge, too, has lately taken wing,
But, like a hawk encumbered with his hood,
Explaining metaphysics to the nation—
I wished he would explain his explanation.
1819–24 *Don Juan*, canto 1, dedication, stanza 2.

26 But—Oh! ye lords of ladies intellectual,
Inform us truly, have they not hen-pecked you all?.
1819–24 *Don Juan*, canto 1, stanza 22.

27 Married, charming, chaste, and twenty-three.
1819–24 *Don Juan*, canto 1, stanza 59.

28 What men call gallantry, and gods adultery,
Is much more common where the climate's sultry.
1819–24 *Don Juan*, canto 1, stanza 63.

29 Christians have burnt each, other quite persuaded
That all the Apostles would have done as they did.
1819–24 *Don Juan*, canto 1, stanza 83.

30 He thought about himself, and the whole earth,
Of man the wonderful, and of the stars,
And how the deuce they ever could have birth;
And then he thought of earthquakes, and of wars,
How many miles the moon might have in girth,
Of air-balloons, and of the many bars
To perfect knowledge of the boundless skies;
And then he thought of Donna Julia's eyes.
1819–24 *Don Juan*, canto 1, stanza 92.

31 A little still she strove, and much repented,
And whispering 'I will ne'er consent'—consented.
1819–24. *Don Juan*, canto 1, stanza 117.

32 Sweet is revenge—especially to women.
1819–24 *Don Juan*, canto 1, stanza 124.

33 'Tis sweet to win, no matter how, one's laurels
By blood or ink; 'tis sweet to put an end
To strife; 'tis sometimes sweet to have our quarrels,
Particularly with a tiresome friend;
Sweet is old wine in bottles, ale in barrels;
Dear is the helpless creature we defend
Against the world; and dear the schoolboy spot
We ne'er forget, though there we are forgot.
1819–24 *Don Juan*, canto 1, stanza 126.

34 But sweeter still than this, than these, than all,
Is first and passionate love—it stands alone,
Like Adam's recollection of his fall;
The tree of knowledge hath been pluck'd—all's
known
And life yields nothing further to recall
Worthy of this ambrosial sin, so shown,
No doubt in fable, as the unforgiven
Fire which Prometheus filch'd for us from heaven.
1819–24 *Don Juan*, canto 1, stanza 127.

35 Pleasure's a sin, and sometimes sin is a pleasure.
1819–24 *Don Juan*, canto 1, stanza 133.

36 Man's love is of man's life a thing apart,
'Tis woman's whole existence.
1819–24 *Don Juan*, canto 1, stanza 194.
▷ See Amis 16:73.

37 If ever I should condescend to prose,
I'll write poetical commandments, which
Shall supersede beyond all doubt all those
That went before; in these I shall enrich
My text with many things that no one knows,
And carry precept to the highest pitch:
I'll call the work 'Longinus o'er a Bottle,
Or, Every Poet his own Aristotle'.
1819–24 *Don Juan*, canto 1, stanza 204.

38 Thou shall believe in Milton, Dryden, Pope;
Thou shalt not set up Wordsworth, Coleridge,
Southey;
Because the first is crazed beyond all hope,
The second drunk, the third so quaint and
mouthey:
With Crabbe it may be difficult to cope,
And Campbell's Hippocrene is somewhat drouthy:
Thou shalt not steal from Samuel Rogers, nor
Commit flirtation with the muse of Moore.
1819–24 *Don Juan*, canto 1, stanza 205.

39 So for a good old-gentlemanly vice,
I think I must take up with avarice.
1819–24 *Don Juan*, canto 1, stanza 216.

40 There's nought, no doubt, so much the spirit calms
As rum and true religion.
1819–24 *Don Juan*, canto 2, stanza 34.

41 It was a wild and breaker-beaten coast,
With cliffs above, and a broad sandy shore,
Guarded by shoals and rocks as by an host,
With here and there a creek, whose aspect wore
A better welcome to the tempest-tost;
And rarely ceased the haughty billow's roar,
Save on the dead long summer days, which make
The outstretch'd ocean glitter like a lake.
1819–24 *Don Juan*, canto 2, stanza 177.

42 Few things surpass old wine; and they may preach
Who please,—the more because they preach in
vain,
Let us have wine and woman, mirth and laughter,
Sermons and soda water the day after.
1819–24 *Don Juan*, canto 2, stanza 178.

43 Man, being reasonable, must get drunk;
The best of Life is but intoxication.
Glory, the grape, love, gold, in these are sunk
The hopes of all men, and of every nation.
1819 *Don Juan*, canto 2, stanza 179.

44 They looked up to the sky, whose floating glow
Spread like a rosy ocean, vast and bright;
They gazed upon the glittering sea below,
Whence the broad moon rose circling into sight;
They heard the wave's splash, and the wind so low,
And saw each other's dark eyes darting light

Into each other—and, beholding this,
Their lips drew near, and clung to a kiss.
1819–24 *Don Juan*, canto 2, stanza 185.

45 In her first passion woman loves her lover,
In all the others all she loves is love.
1819–24 *Don Juan*, canto 3, stanza 3.

46 'Tis melancholy, and a fearful sign
Of human frailty, folly, also crime,
That love and marriage rarely can combine,
Although they both are born in the same clime;
Marriage from love, like vinegar from wine
A sad, sour, sober beverage—by time
Is sharpened from its high celestial flavour,
Down to a very homely household savour.
1819–24 *Don Juan*, canto 3, stanza 5.

47 Think you, if Laura had been Petrach's wife,
He would have written sonnets all his life?
1819–24 *Don Juan*, canto 3, stanza 8.

48 All tragedies are finished by a death,
All comedies are ended by a marriage;
The future states of both are left to faith.
1819–24 *Don Juan*, canto 3, stanza 9.

49 He was the mildest mannered man
That ever scuttled ship or cut a throat,
With such true breeding of a gentleman,
You never could divine his real thought.
1819–24 *Don Juan*, canto 3, stanza 41.

50 The mountains look on Marathon—
And Marathon looks on the sea;
And musing there an hour alone,
I dreamed that Greece might still be free.
1819–24 *Don Juan*, canto 3, stanza 86.

51 And if I laugh at any mortal thing
'Tis that I may not weep.
1819–24 *Don Juan*, canto 4, stanza 4.

52 But after being fired at once or twice,
The ear becomes more Irish, and less
nice.
1819–24 *Don Juan*, canto 4, stanza 41.

53 I have a passion for the name of 'Mary,'
For once it was a magic sound to me;
And still it half calls up the realms of fairy,
Where I beheld what never was to be.
1819–24 *Don Juan*, canto 5, stanza 4.

54 There is a tide in the affairs of women,
Which taken at the flood, leads—God knows
where.
1819–24 *Don Juan*, canto 6, stanza 2.

55 Gaunt Famine never shall approach the throne.

Though Ireland starve, great George weighs twenty
stone.
1823 *Don Juan*, canto 8, stanza 126.

56 And, after all what is a lie? 'Tis but
The truth in masquerade.
1819–24 *Don Juan*, canto 11, stanza 37.

57 Now hatred is by far the longest pleasure;
Men love in haste, but they detest at leisure.
1819–24 *Don Juan*, canto 13, stanza 4.

58 The English winter—ending in July,
To recommence in August.
1819–24 *Don Juan*, canto 13, stanza 42.

59 Society is now one polished horde,
Formed of two mighty tribes, the Bores and Bored.
1819–24 *Don Juan*, canto 13, stanza 95.

60 'Tis strange but true; for truth is always stranger;
Stranger than fiction.
1819–24 *Don Juan*, canto 14, stanza 101.

61 All present life is but an interjection,
An 'Oh!' or 'Ah!' of joy or misery,
Or a 'Ha! ha!' or 'Bah!'—a yawn or 'Pooh!'
Of which perhaps the latter is most true.
1819–24 *Don Juan*, canto 15, stanza 1.

62 Between two worlds life hovers like a star,
'Twixt night and morn, upon the horizon's verge.
How little do we know that which we are!
How less what we may be!
1819–24 *Don Juan*, canto 15, stanza 99.

63 There's music in the sighing of a reed;
There's music in the gushing of a rill;
There's music in all things, if men had ears:
Their earth is but an echo of the spheres.
1819–24 *Don Juan*, canto 15, stanza 5.

64 Eat, drink, and love; the rest's not worth a fillip.
1821 *Sardanapalus*, act 1, sc.2.

65 Oh, talk not to me of a name great in story;
The days of our youth are the days of our glory;
And the myrtle and ivy of sweet two-and-twenty
Are worth all your laurels, though ever so plenty.
1821 'Stanzas Written on the Road between Florence and Pisa,
November 1821'.

66 The angels all were singing out of tune,
And hoarse with having little else to do,
Excepting to wind up the sun and moon,
Or curb a runaway young star or two.
1822 *The Vision of Judgement*, stanza 2.

67 As he drew near, he gazed upon the gate
Ne'er to be entered more by him or Sin,
With such a glance of supernatural hate,
As made Saint Peter wish himself within;

He pattered with his keys at a great rate,
And sweated through his apostolic skin:
Of course his perspiration was but ichor,
Or some such other spiritual liquor.
1822 *The Vision of Judgement*, stanza 25.

68 And when the tumult dwindled to a calm,
I left him practising the hundredth psalm.
1822 *The Vision of Judgement*, stanza 106.

69 For what were all these country patriots born?
To hunt, and vote, and raise the price of corn?
1823 *The Age of Bronze*, stanza 14.

70 I awoke one morning and found myself famous.
Of the instant popularity of *Childe Harolde*. Quoted in Thomas
Moore *Letters and Journals of Lord Byron* (1830), vol.1.

Byron, Henry James 1834–84

English playwright and actor. His most successful plays
included *Our Boys* (1874) and the comedies *War to the
Knife* (1865) and *A Hundred Thousand Pounds* (1866), as
well as numerous burlesques and extravaganzas.

71 Life's too short for chess.
1874 *Our Boys.*

Byron, Robert 1905–41

English traveller, critic of art and architecture and
historian, who travelled extensively in Europe and Asia.
His best-known book is *The Road to Oxiana* (1937). He
drowned in 1941 when his ship to the Mediterranean was
torpedoed.

72 The existence of St Sophia is atmospheric; that of
St Peter's, overpowering, imminently substantial.
One is a church to God; the other a salon for his
agents. One is consecrated to reality, the other to
illusion. St Sophia, in fact, is large, and St Peter's is
vilely, tragically small.
1929 *The Byzantine Achievement.*

73 *Herat, 8 December.* What a day it was! God save me
from any more adventures on a drained stomach.
1937 *The Road to Oxiana.*

74 I shall have warmonger put on my passport.
c.1938 Comment in response to the rise of Nazism, opposing
the policy of appeasement. Quoted in Bruce Chatwin's
introduction to *The Road to Oxiana* (1980 edn).

Cabell, James Branch 1879–1958

US novelist and critic. *Jurgen* (1919) is the best known of a
sequence of 18 novels, collectively known as *Biography of
Michael.* His *Preface to the Past* (1936) is a book of criticism.

75 I am willing to taste any drink once.
1919 *Jurgen*, ch.1.

76 A man possesses nothing certainly save a brief loan
of his own body.

1919 *Jurgen*, ch.20.

77 I shall marry in haste and repeat at leisure.
1919 *Jurgen*, ch.26.
▷ See Congreve 280:99

78 Drunkenness is a joy reserved for the Gods: so do
men partake of it impiously, and so are they very
properly punished for their audacity.
1919 *Jurgen*, ch.28.

79 Poetry is man's rebellion against being what he is.
1919 *Jurgen.*

80 The optimist proclaims that we live in the best of all
possible worlds; and the pessimist fears this is true.
1926 *The Silver Stallion*, bk.4, ch.26.

Cabrera Infante, Guillermo 1929–

Cuban novelist, film critic and diplomat. He supported
Castro's revolutionary forces initially, but later left the
country and settled in London (1965), becoming a
British subject. *Tres tristes tigres* is full of puns, neologisms
and humorous word play.

81 *Hablando siempre y siempre contando chismes y
haciendo chistes y siempre y también filosofando o
estetizando o moralizando, siempre: la cuestión era
hacer ver como que no trabajábamos porque en La
Habana, Cuba, esa es la única manera de ser gente
bien.*

Talking all the time and telling jokes or gossiping
all the time and always and also philosophizing or
aestheticizing or moralizing, but always: the thing
was to make it look like we didn't have to work
because in Havana, Cuba, this is the only way to be
high society …
1967 *Tres tristes tigres* (*Three Trapped Tigers*, 1971), 'Bachata'.

Caesar, Irving 1895–1996

US librettist and lyricist.

82 Tea for two, and two for tea.
1924 *No! No! Nanette*, 'Tea for Two' (with Otto Harbach.
Music by Vincent Youmans).

Caesar, Gaius Julius 100/102–44 BC

Roman general and statesman. As consul (59 BC) and
proconsul (58–50 BC) he extended Roman power in Gaul
and Britain. Refusing to disband his army, he came into
conflict with the Senate, supported by Pompey, whom
Caesar defeated in the civil war that followed. He became
dictator for life, but was assassinated in 44 BC. His works
include the *Commentarii* ('War Commentaries'), *De Bello
Gallico* ('On the Gallic War', 7 vols) and *De Bello Civili*
('On the Civil War', 3 vols).

83 *Gallia est omnis divisa in partes tres.*

Gaul as a whole is divided into three parts.
51 BC *De Bello Gallico*, bk.1, section 1, opening words.

84 *Fere libenter homines id quod volunt credunt.*

Men are nearly always willing to believe what they wish.

51 BC *De Bello Gallico*, bk.3, section 18.

85 Caesar's wife must be above suspicion.

Attributed. Based on an episode in Plutarch *Caesar* 10.6, which tells that Caesar divorced his wife after accusations of impiety, although he defended her in court.

86 *Iacta est alea.*

The die is cast.

49 BC Comment on crossing the river Rubicon (the border between his province and Italy) with his troops, thereby committing himself to civil war. Quoted in Suetonius *Lives of the Twelve Caesars*, 'Divus Iulius', section 32.

87 *Veni, vidi, vici.*

I came, I saw, I conquered.

46 BC Said to have been written on a *titulus* (placard) carried along in Caesar's triumph after a campaign in Pontus (Asia Minor) during the civil war (46 BC). Quoted in Suetonius *Lives of the Twelve Caesars*, 'Divus Iulius', section 37. Another source reports that Caesar used this expression in a letter to the Senate after the same campaign (cf. Plutarch, *Caesar* 50, 3-4).

88 *Et tu, Brute?*

You too, Brutus?

Attributed last words, when struck by his murderers, Cassius and Brutus. The tradition is based on Suetonius *Divus Iulius*, 82: 'Some say that when he saw Marcus Brutus about to deliver the second blow, he reproached him in Greek with: 'You too, my son?' (the Greek is 'kai su, teknon').

Cage, John 1912–92

US ultra-modernist composer. His experiments included 'aleatory' music, in which the role of chance determines how a piece will develop. His books include *Silence* (1961), *M* (1973), and *Empty Works* (1979).

89 Which is more musical, a truck passing by a factory or a truck passing by a music school?

1961 *Silence.*

90 I have nothing to say
and I am saying it and that is poetry.

1961 'Lecture on Nothing'.

Cagney, James 1899–1986

US film actor. A leading role in *Public Enemy* (1931) established him as the quintessential screen gangster. He won an Academy Award for his performance in *Yankee Doodle Dandy* (1942).

91 Look Ma—top of the world.

1949 Line delivered in *White Heat* (screenplay by Ivan Goff and Ben Roberts).

Cain, James M(allahan) 1892–1977

US crime writer.

92 The Postman Always Rings Twice.

1934 Title of novel.

93 Double Indemnity.

1943 Title of novel.

Calas, Nicolas 1907–88

Greek-born art critic and poet, who associated with the Surrealists in Paris in the 1930s. He moved to the United States in 1939.

94 Art is a form of communication that insinuates. We *expect* the artist to have more to say than what he communicated and *suspect* that what he said was a subterfuge for hiding something.

1968 *Art in the Age of Risk.*

Caldwell, Philip 1920–

US company executive, Chairman of the Ford Motor Co (1980–5).

95 We redesigned everything but the air in the tires.

1995 Of the development of the Taurus, which was to become America's best-selling car. In *Fortune*, 3 Apr.

Calhoun, John Caldwell 1782–1850

US statesman and orator, Vice-President under John Q Adams and then Andrew Jackson. His *Address to the People of South Carolina* (1831) set forth his theory of state rights.

96 The Government of the absolute majority, instead of the Government of the people, is but the Government of the strongest interests; and when not efficiently checked, it is the most tyrannical and oppressive that can be devised.

1833 Speech, US Senate, 15 Feb.

Caligula properly *Gaius Julius Caesar Germanicus* AD 12–41

Roman Emperor (AD 37–41), nicknamed Caligula as a child from his little soldier's boots (*caligae*). His extravagant, autocratic, vicious and mentally unstable behaviour resulted in his assassination.

97 *Utinam populus Romanus unam cervicem haberet!*

Would that the Roman people had but one neck!

c.40 AD Quoted in Suetonius's *Lives of the Caesars* 'Gaius Caligula', section 30.

Callaghan (of Cardiff), (Leonard) James Callaghan, Baron 1912–

English Labour politician. As Chancellor of the Exchequer he introduced controversial corporation and selective employment taxes. He was Home Secretary (1967–70), Foreign Secretary (1974–6) and Prime Minister (1976–9).

98 Britain has lived for too long on borrowed time, borrowed money, and even borrowed ideas.

1976 Quoted in *The Observer*, 3 Oct.

99 There is no virtue in producing socially well adjusted members of society who are unemployed because they do not have the skills. Nor at the other extreme must they be technically efficient robots.

1976 Speech at Ruskin College, Oxford, reprinted in the *Times Higher Education Supplement*, 15 Oct. This speech began the so-called 'Great Debate' on education.

1 A lie can travel halfway round the world before the truth has got its boots on.

1976 Speech in the House of Commons, Nov.

▷ See Spurgeon 961:64

2 Either back us or sack us.

1977 Speech, Labour Party Conference, 5 Oct.

3 Crisis? What crisis?

1979 Headline in *The Sun*, 11 Jan, alluding to his remark on returning from the Guadaloupe summit to be confronted by widespread strikes. His actual words were, 'I don't think that other people in the world would share the view that there is mounting chaos.'

Callanan, Jeremiah John 1795–1829

Irish poet. Born in Cork and sent by his parents to study for the priesthood, he developed instead his interest in lyrical poetry. He supported himself by teaching and writing. He gained general celebrity with *Gougane Barra*.

4 There grows the wild ash; and a time-stricken willow
Looks chidingly down on the mirth of the billow,
As, like some gay child that sad monitor scorning,
It lightly laughs back to the laugh of the morning.

1826 'Gougane Barra'.

Calonne, Charles Alexandre de 1734–1802

French politician. Appointed Controller-General in 1783, he was exiled in 1787 when he failed to provide a statement of accounts to explain the treasury deficit. Napoleon I permitted his return in 1802.

5 *Madame, si c'est possible, c'est fait; impossible? cela se fera.*

Madam, if a thing is possible, consider it done; the impossible? that will be done.

Quoted in J Michelet *Histoire de la Révolution Française* (1847), vol.1, pt.2. This has been adapted as the slogan of the US army: 'The difficult we do immediately; the impossible takes a little longer.'

Calvino, Italo 1923–85

Italian modernist writer and journalist, born in Cuba. A fascist under compulsion, he later joined the Resistance (1943) and wrote for the Communist *L'unità* in the 1940s. His novels combine fantasy with a hard satirical wit.

6 *Lo sguardo dei cani che non capiscono e non sanno che possono aver ragione a non capire.*

The gaze of dogs who don't understand and who don't know that they may be right not to understand.

1957 *Il Barone Rampante*, ch.10.

Cambronne, Pierre, Baron de 1770–1842

French general in the Napoleonic wars.

7 *La Garde meurt, mais ne se rend pas.*

The Guards die but do not surrender.

1815 Attributed, when called upon to surrender at the Battle of Waterloo, 18 Jun.

Campbell, Donald Malcolm 1921–67

English speedboat racer. Son of Sir Malcolm Campbell, he broke all his father's land and water speed records, but was killed when his hydroplane *Bluebird* crashed on Lake Coniston at about 300mph.

8 There is no hope of bailing out of a speedboat. You hit the water and become so much pulp.

Quoted in Douglas Young-James *Donald Campbell: An Informal Biography* (1968).

Campbell, Kim originally *Avril Phaedra Campbell* 1947–

Canadian politician. She entered the Commons in 1988 as a Progressive Conservative, becoming Canada's first woman Prime Minister (Jun–Dec, 1993); she lost her parliamentary seat in the 1993 election.

9 Charisma without substance is a dangerous thing.

1986 Speech, while unsuccessfully contesting the leadership of the Social Credit Party of British Columbia, 22 Oct.

Campbell, Mrs Patrick née *Beatrice Rose Stella Tanner* 1865–1940

English actress. Famed for her stage presence and incisive wit, she made her début in 1888. She corresponded with George Bernard Shaw, who wrote *Pygmalion* especially for her.

10 When you were quite a little boy somebody ought to have said 'hush' just once.

1912 Letter to George Bernard Shaw, 1 Nov.

11 The deep, deep peace of the double-bed after the hurly-burly of the chaise-longue.

Her definition of marriage, quoted in Alexander Woollcott *While Rome Burns*, 'The First Mrs Tanqueray' (1934).

12 It doesn't matter what you do in the bedroom as long as you don't do it in the street and frighten the horses.

Quoted in Daphne Fielding *The Duchess of Jermyn Street* (1964), ch.2. Sometimes attributed to Edward VII.

13 Watching Tallulah Bankhead on the stage is like watching somebody skating on very thin ice—and

the English want to be there when she falls
through.
Quoted in *The Times*, 13 Dec 1968.

Campbell, (Ignatius) Roy Dunnachie

1901–57

South African poet, who spent much of his life in Britain. He moved from an early liberalism to outspoken right-wing Catholicism, and is best remembered for his early lyric poems.

14 South Africa, renowned both far and wide
For politics and little else besides.
1928 'The Wayzgoose'.

15 You praise the firm restraint with which they
    write—
I'm with you there, of course:
They use the snaffle and the curb all right,
But where's the bloody horse?
1930 'On Some South African Novelists'.

16 Of all the clever people round me here
I most delight in Me—
Mine is the only voice I care to hear,
And mine the only face I like to see.
1930 'Home Thoughts in Bloomsbury'.

17 Write with your spade, and garden with your pen,
Shove your couplets to their long repose.
And type your turnips down the field in rows.
1931 'The Georgiad', pt.2.

18 Burn, with Athens and with Rome,
A sacred city of the mind.
1936 'Toledo, July 1936'.

19 I will go stark: and let my meanings show
Clear as a milk-white feather in a crow
Or a black stallion on a field of snow.
1936 'A Good Resolution'.

20 He shouldered high his voluntary Cross,
Wrestled his hardships into forms of beauty,
And taught his gorgon destinies to sing.
1943 'Luis de Camões'.

21 Giraffes!—a People
Who live between the earth and skies,
Each in his own religious steeple,
Keeping a light-house with his eyes.
1946 'Dreaming Spires'.

22 Translations, like wives, are seldom faithful if they
are in the least attractive.
1949 *The Poetry Review*, Jun/Jul.

23 I hate 'Humanity' and all such abstracts: but I love
people. Lovers of 'Humanity' generally hate *people
and children*, and keep parrots or puppy dogs.
1951 *Light On A Dark Horse*, ch.13.

Campbell, Thomas   1777–1844

Scottish poet and journalist, Editor from 1820 to 1830 of *The New Monthly Magazine,* to which he contributed many poems. He is buried in Westminster Abbey.

24 On the green banks of Shannon, when Sheelah was
    nigh,
No blithe Irish lad was so happy as I;
No harp like my own could so cheerily play,
And wherever I went was my poor dog Tray.
1799 'The Harper', stanza 1.

25 'Tis distance lends enchantment to the view,
And robes the mountain in its azure hue.
1799 *The Pleasures of Hope*, pt.1, l.7–8.

26 Hope, for a season, bade the world farewell,
And Freedom shrieked—as Kosciusko fell!
1799 *The Pleasures of Hope*, pt.1, l.381–2.

27 What millions died—that Caesar might be great!
1799 *The Pleasures of Hope*, pt.2, l.174.

28 What though my wingèd hours of bliss have been,
Like angel-visits, few and far between?
1799 *The Pleasures of Hope*, pt.2, l.375–6.

29 A chieftain to the Highlands bound
Cries 'Boatman, do not tarry!
And I'll give thee a silver pound
To row us o'er the ferry.'
1809 'Lord Ullin's Daughter', stanza 1.

30 And yet, amidst that joy and uproar,
Let us think of them that sleep,
Full many a fathom deep,
By thy wild and stormy steep,
Elsinore!
1809 'The Battle of the Baltic', stanza 8.

31 To-morrow let us do or die!
1809 'Gertrude of Wyoming', pt.3, stanza 37.

32 An original something, fair maid you would win
    me
To write—but how shall I begin?
For I fear I have nothing original in me—
Excepting Original Sin.
1843 'To a Young Lady, Who Asked Me to Write Something
Original for Her Album'.

33 Now Barabbas was a publisher.
Attributed. Quoted in Samuel Smiles *A Publisher and his
Friends: Memoir and Correspondence of the late John Murray*
(1891), vol.1, ch.14. The quote is sometimes attributed to
Byron.

Campion, Jane   1954–

New Zealand film director and writer. Her films include the dramatization of Janet Frame's autobiography *An Angel at My Table* (1990) and *The Piano* (1993).

34 Remember your own childhood. That complete
certainty you had, looking at the grown-ups, that
you would never be like that. It was a lonely feeling,
but euphoric, too.
1994 Interview with Sarah Gristwood in *The Times Magazine*,
1 Jan, 'Jane Campion: A Childhood'.

Campion, Thomas 1567–1620

English physician, poet and composer. As well as poetry
in Latin and English he wrote four *Books of Airs* for voice
and lute (1601–17) and *Observations in the Art of English
Poesie* (1602), defending classical structures.

35 My sweetest Lesbia, let us live and love,
And though the sager sort our deeds reprove,
Let us not weigh them. Heaven's great lamps do
    dive
Into their west, and straight again revive,
But soon as once set is our little light,
Then must we sleep one ever-during night.
1601 *A Book of Airs*, no.1, 'My Sweetest Lesbia', translation of a
song by Catullus.
▷ See Catullus 245:59.

36 As her lute doth live or die,
Led by her passion, so must I:
For when of pleasure she doth sing,
My thoughts enjoy a sudden spring,
But if she doth of sorrow speak,
Ev'n from my heart the strings do break.
1601 *A Book of Airs*, no.6, 'When to Her Lute Corinna Sings'.

37 I care not for these ladies that must be wooed and
    prayed.
Give me kind Amaryllis, the wanton country maid.
1601 *A Book of Airs*, 'I Care Not for These Ladies'.

38 Rose-cheeked Laura, come,
Sing thou smoothly with thy beauty's
Silent music, either other
Sweetly gracing.
1602 *Second Book of Airs*, 'Rose-Cheeked Laura'.

39 There is a garden in her face,
Where roses and white lilies grow,
A heavenly paradise is that place,
Wherein all pleasant fruits do flow.
There cherries grow, which none may buy
Till 'Cherry ripe!' themselves do cry.
1617 *Fourth Book of Airs*, 'There is a Garden in her Face'.

40 Fain would I wed a fair young man that night and
    day could please me,
When my mind or body grieved that had the power
    to ease me.
Maids are full of longing thoughts that breed a
    bloodless sickness,
And that, oft I hear men say, is only cured by
    quickness.
1617 *Fourth Book of Airs*, 'Fain Would I Wed'.

41 Yet I would not die a maid, because I had a mother,
As I was by one brought forth, I would bring forth
    another.
1617 *Fourth Book of Airs*, 'Fain Would I Wed'.

Campo, Estanislao de 1834–80

Argentinian soldier, political journalist and gaucho
(pampas cowboy) poet. *Fausto,* a long poetic dialogue in
six episodes, relates a gaucho's impressions of a
performance of Gounod's *Faust* in Buenos Aires.

42 *Por hembras yo no me pierdo.
La que me empaca su amor
pasa por el cernidor
y…si te vi, no me acuerdo.*

I make no fuss about females.
The one who gives me her love
Gets sifted in my private sieve
and…I don't think we ever met.
1866 *Fausto*, pt.3 (translated as *Faust*, 1943).

Camus, Albert 1913–60

French writer. Active in the French Resistance, he found
fame with his Existentialist novel *L'Étranger* (The
Stranger, 1942). Other works include *La Peste* (The
Plague, 1947), *La Chute* (The Fall, 1956), plays and
political writings. He was awarded a Nobel Prize in 1957
and he died in a car accident.

43 *Intellectuel = celui qui se dédouble.*

Intellectual: someone whose mind watches itself.
Carnets, 1935–42 (published 1962).

44 *La politique et le sort des hommes sont formés par des
hommes sans idéal et sans grandeur. Ceux qui ont une
grandeur en eux ne font pas de politique.*

Politics and the fate of mankind are shaped by men
without ideals and without greatness. Those who
have greatness within them do not go in for
politics.
Carnets, 1935–42 (published 1962).

45 *L'absurde est la notion essentielle et la première vérité.*

The absurd is the fundamental idea and the first
truth.
1942 *Le Mythe de Sisyphe* (*The Myth of Sisyphus*, 1955).

46 *Il n'y a qu'un problème philosophique vraiment
sérieux: c'est le suicide. Juger que la vie vaut ou ne
vaut pas la peine d'être vécue, c'est répondre à la
question fondamentale de la philosophie.*

There is but one truly serious philosophical
problem, and that is suicide. Judging whether life is
or is not worth living amounts to answering the
fundamental question of philosophy.

1942 *Le Mythe de Sisyphe* (*The Myth of Sisyphus*, 1955), 'Absurdity and Suicide'.

47 *L'homme se trouve devant l'irrationnel. Il sent en lui son désir de bonheur et de raison. L'absurde naît de cette confrontation entre l'appel humain et le silence déraisonnable du monde.*

Man stands face to face with the irrational. He feels within him his longing for happiness and for reason. The absurd is born of this confrontation between the human need and the unreasonable silence of the world.
1942 *Le Mythe de Sisyphe* (*The Myth of Sisyphus*, 1955), 'The Absurd Walls'.

48 *Il n'est pas de destin que ne se surmonte par le mépris.*

There is no fate that cannot be surmounted by scorn.
1942 *Le Mythe de Sisyphe* (*The Myth of Sisyphus*, 1955).

49 *La lutte elle-même vers les sommets suffit à remplir un cœur d'homme. Il faut imaginer Sisyphe heureux.*

The struggle itself towards the heights is enough to fill a human heart. One must imagine that Sisyphus is happy.
1942 *Le Mythe de Sisyphe* (*The Myth of Sisyphus*, 1955).

50 *Aujourd'hui, maman est morte. Ou peut-être hier, je ne sais pas.*

Mother died today. Or perhaps it was yesterday, I don't know.
1942 *L'Etranger*.

51 *Peut-on être un saint sans Dieu: C'est le seul problème concret que je connaisse aujourd'hui.*

Can one become a saint without God? That is the only concrete problem I know of today.
1947 *La Peste*.

52 *Il y a dans les hommes plus de choses à admirer que de choses à mépriser.*

There are more things to admire in people than to despise.
1947 *La Peste*.

53 *Qu'est-ce qu'un homme révolté? Un homme qui dit non.*

What is a rebel? A man who says no.
1951 *L'Homme révolté*.

54 *Toutes les révolutions modernes ont abouti à un renforcement de l'Etat.*

All modern revolutions have ended in a reinforcement of the State.
1951 *L'Homme révolté*.

55 *Tout révolutionnaire finit en oppresseur ou en hérétique.*

Every revolutionary ends as an oppressor or a heretic.
1951 *L'Homme révolté*.

56 *Le style, comme la popeline, dissimule trop souvent de l'eczéma.*

Style, like sheer silk, too often hides eczema.
1956 *La Chute*, ch.1 (translated by Stuart Gilbert).

57 *Vous savez ce qu'est le charme: une manière de s'entendre répondre oui sans avoir posé aucune question claire.*

You know what charm is: a way of getting the answer yes without having asked any clear question.
1956 *La Chute*, (translated by Stuart Gilbert).

58 *Chacun exige d'être innocent, à tout prix, même si, pour cela, il faut accuser le genre humain et le ciel.*

Everyone insists on his or her innocence, at all costs, even if it means accusing the rest of the human race and heaven.
1956 *La Chute*, (translated by Stuart Gilbert).

59 *C'est si vrai que nous nous confions rarement à ceux qui sont meilleurs que nous.*

It is true that we seldom confide in those who are better than ourselves.
1956 *La Chute*, (translated by Stuart Gilbert).

60 *N'attendez pas le jugement dernier. Il a lieu tous les jours.*

Do not wait for the last judgment. It happens every day.
1956 *La Chute*, (translated by Stuart Gilbert).

61 *Combien de crimes commis simplement parce que leur auteur ne pouvait supporter d'être en faute!*

How many crimes are committed merely because their authors could not endure being wrong!
1956 *La Chute*, (translated by Stuart Gilbert).

62 *La vérité, comme la lumière, aveugle. Le mensonge, au contraire, est un beau crépuscule qui met chaque objet en valeur.*

Truth, like light, blinds. A lie, on the contrary, is a beautiful twilight which shows the value of each object.
1956 *La Chute*, (translated by Stuart Gilbert).

63 All that I know surely about morality and the obligations of man, I owe to football.
1957 'What I owe to Football', in *France Football*. In his youth, Camus kept goal for the Oran football club in Algiers.

64 A novel is never anything but a philosophy put into images.
Recalled on his death, 4 Jan 1960.

Canmore, Malcolm d.1093

King of Scotland. The son of Duncan (who was killed by Macbeth), he spent his youth in Northumbria and returned in 1057 to take the throne after Macbeth's death.

65 *Excellentioris personæ semper casus in vitium, minoris lapsum, comparatione scandali multe longius antecedit.*

The scandal of an exalted person's fall into vice, when compared to the lapse of one lesser, always far exceeds it.

c.1057 Quoted in John Fordun's *Chronicle of Scotland* (c.1384), bk.5, ch.4.

Cannadine, David

66 Prince Albert…discovered the impotence of being earnest.

1991 Of Queen Victoria's consort. *The Pleasure of the Past.*

67 Neville Chamberlain had greatness thrust upon him—and in trying to prove he could bear it, collapsed under the weight.

1991 *The Pleasure of the Past.*

Cannan, Edwin 1861–1935

English economist, Professor at the London School of Economics. He was editor of the standard edition of Adam Smith's *Wealth of Nations* in 1904.

68 It often happens that a man of considerable eminence in his own profession, but without the smallest acquaintance with the fundamentals of economics, will make a suggestion which is precisely on a level with the proposition that the locomotive would be much more efficient if its weight were taken off the driving wheels so that they could revolve more easily. The editor of an important magazine accepts with joy the contribution in which he develops his ideas, and the public feebly thinks that there may be something in it, and is confirmed in this view by the fact that professional economists are as disinclined to publish a refutation of it as the Astronomer Royal is to answer the theorists who declare that the world is flat.

1914 *Wealth*, ch.6.

Canning, George 1770–1827

English statesman. He became Foreign Secretary in 1822 on the death of his political opponent Castlereagh, and began a programme of liberalization. On Liverpool's resignation in 1827, he formed his own administration but died the same year.

69 Pitt is to Addington
As London is to Paddington.

c.1803 'The Oracle'. Henry Addington, first Viscount Sidmouth (1757–1844) was Prime Minister (1801–4) and a political rival of Pitt, who served in his administrations.

70 And finds, with keen discriminating sight,
Black's not so black;—nor white so very white.

1821 'New Morality', l.199–200.

71 Give me the avowed, erect and manly foe;
Firm I can meet, perhaps return the blow;
But of all plagues, good Heaven, thy wrath can send,
Save me, oh, save me, from the candid friend.

1821 'New Morality', l.207–8.

72 In matters of commerce
The fault of the Dutch
Is offering too little
And asking too much.

1826 Dispatch enciphered to Sir Charles Bagehot, English ambassador at The Hague, 31 Jan.

73 I called the New World into existence, to redress the balance of the Old.

1826 Speech to the Commons, on Portugal, 12 Dec.

Cantillon, Richard c.1680–1734

Irish-born banker and economist who made a fortune in Paris after the collapse of the Mississippi Company. His single surviving work is *Essai sur la nature du Commerce en Général* (Essay on the Nature of Trade, published 1755).

74 If all the Labourers in a Village breed up several Sons to the same work there will be too many Labourers to cultivate the Lands belonging to the Village, and the surplus Adults must go to seek a livelihood elsewhere, which they generally do in Cities.

1730–4 *Essay on the Nature of Trade.*

75 The Crafts which require the most Time in training or most Ingenuity and Industry must necessarily be the best paid.

1730–4 *Essay on the Nature of Trade.*

76 Men multiply like Mice in a barn if they have unlimited Means of Subsistence.

1730–4 *Essay on the Nature of Trade.*

Capote, Truman 1924–84

US novelist. His best-known works include the semi-documentary novel *In Cold Blood* (1966), *Breakfast at Tiffany's* (1958) and *Music for Chameleons* (1980).

77 Other Voices, Other Rooms.

1948 Title of novel.

78 None of these people have anything interesting to say, and none of them can write, not even Mr Kerouac. What they do isn't writing at all—it's typing.

1959 On the Beat novelists. Television discussion, reported in the *New Republic*, 9 Feb.

79 Venice is like eating an entire box of chocolate liqueurs in one go.
1961 In *The Observer*, 26 Nov.

80 Even an attorney of modest talent can postpone doomsday year after year, for the system of appeals that pervades American jurisprudence amounts to a legalistic wheel of fortune, a game of chance, somewhat fixed in the favor of the criminal, that the participants play interminably.
1965 *In Cold Blood*, ch.4.

81 Buddy, it's fruitcake weather!
1966 Of December in Alabama. *A Christmas Memory*.

82 I don't care what anybody says about me as long as it isn't true.
Quoted in David Frost *The Americans* (1970), 'When Does A Writer Become A Star'.

83 Writing has laws of perspective, of light and shade, just as painting does, or music. If you are born knowing them, fine. If not, learn them. Then rearrange the rules to suit yourself.
1974 Interview in *Paris Review*, Summer.

84 When God hands you a gift, he also hands you a whip; and the whip is intended for self-flagellation solely.
1979 In *Vogue*, Dec. Collected in *Music for Chameleons* (1980) 'Music for Chameleons'.

85 Writing stopped being fun when I discovered the difference between good writing and bad, and then made an even more terrifying discovery—the difference between very good writing and true art: it is subtle, but savage.
1979 In *Vogue*, Dec.

86 Great fury, like great whisky, requires long fermentation.
1980 *Music for Chameleons*, 'Handcarved Coffins'.

87 Finishing a book is just like you took a child out in the yard and shot it.
Quoted in Linda Botts (ed) *Loose Talk* (1980).

88 The chic old blue-haired ladies…chew in mute chandeliered isolation.
Of elderly residents of the Ritz. *Answered Prayers* (published 1986).

89 The morals of a baboon and the guts of a butterfly.
Of Kenneth Tynan. Quoted in Gerald Clarke *Capote* (1988).

90 The better the actor the more stupid he is.
Attributed.

Capp, Al originally *Alfred Gerald Caplin* 1909–79

US cartoonist, best known for his strip 'L'il Abner' (1934–77), which satirized current affairs with a hillbilly cast of characters in Dogpatch.

91 A product of the untalented, sold by the unprincipled to the utterly bewildered.
1963 Of abstract art. In the *National Observer*, 1 Jul.

Capra, Frank 1897–1991

Italian-born US film director. He became renowned for his films celebrating the common man, such as *You Can't Take It With You* (1938).

92 There are no rules in filmmaking. Only sins. And the cardinal sin is dullness.
Recalled on his death in *People*, 16 Sep 1991.

Caraway, Hattie Wyatt 1878–1950

US politician. In 1932, she was the first woman to be elected to the US Senate.

93 The windows need washing.
1932 On arriving in the Senate. Recalled on her death, 21 Dec 1950.

94 I haven't the heart to take a minute from the men. The poor dears love it so.
Explaining why she never made a speech during 13 years as the first woman in the US Senate. Quoted in David Brinkley *Washington Goes to War* (1988).

Carballido, Emilio 1925–

Mexican short-story writer and dramatist. He is one of the most popular Latin American playwrights

95 *Es usted un homo sapiens, mamífero vertebrado… Se encuentra en el periodo de domesticación, y sería colocado en una jaula al menor síntoma de ferocidad. En la escuela, en los laboratorios o en las oficinas de gobierno sabemos todo cuanto puede saberse de usted, de sus semejantes o de los otros seres en la escala zoológica.*

You are a homo sapiens, a vertebrate mammal… You are currently being tamed, and you would be put in a cage if you showed any sign of fierceness. At school, in the laboratories and in government offices we know as much as can be known about you, about your fellow beings and about the other beings in the zoological scale.
1960 *El día que se soltaron los leones* ('The Day When They Let the Lions Loose'), act 1.

Cardoria, Brigadier General Sherian Grace

US soldier, Brigadier General and the highest-ranking black woman in the US military.

96 By act of Congress, male officers are gentlemen,
but by act of God, we are ladies.
1989 In *US News and World Report*, 13 Feb.

Cardus, Sir Neville 1889–1975

English critic and journalist. He joined the *Manchester Guardian* as a music critic (1916), later becoming a cricket writer, and wrote several books on his two passions.

97 Pussycats.
1938 Of Bruch's violin concertos. In the *Manchester Guardian*.

98 Sawdust and spangles.
1938 Of Liszt's Second Piano Concerto. In the *Manchester Guardian*.

99 Like the British constitution, cricket was not made: it has 'grown'.
1945 *English Cricket*.

1 The opera…is the only one in existence that might conceivably have been composed by God.
1961 Of Mozart's *The Magic Flute*. In the *Manchester Guardian*.

2 The laws of cricket tell of the English love of compromise between a particular freedom and a general orderliness, or legality.
Quoted in Sir Rupert Hart-Davis *Cardus on Cricket* (1977).

3 Cricket more than any other game is inclined towards sentimentalism and cant.
Quoted in Sir Rupert Hart-Davis *Cardus on Cricket* (1977).

4 There ought to be some other means of reckoning quality in this the best and loveliest of games; the scoreboard is an ass.
1981 *A Fourth Innings with Cardus*.

5 It is far more than a game, this cricket.
1981 *A Fourth Innings with Cardus*.

6 The elements are cricket's presiding geniuses.
1981 *A Fourth Innings with Cardus*.

Carew, Thomas 1595–1639

English Cavalier poet, courtier and statesman. His most notable works include 'Rapture', 'To Ben Jonson' and an elegy for John Donne.

7 Why should the follies of this dull age
Draw from thy pen such an immodest rage
As seems to blast thy else-immortal bays,
When thine own tongue proclaims thy itch of
    praise?
Such thirst will argue drought.
1631 'To Ben Jonson, Upon occasion of his Ode of Defiance annexed to his play of *The New Inn*'.

8 The wiser world doth greater thee confess
Than all men else, than thy self only less.
1631 'To Ben Jonson, Upon occasion of his Ode of Defiance annexed to his play of *The New Inn*'.

9 Can we not force from widowed poetry,
Now thou art dead, great Donne, one elegy
To crown thy hearse?
1633 'An Elegy upon the Death of the Dean of Paul's, Dr. John Donne'.

10 Unkneaded dough-baked prose.
1633 'An Elegy upon the Death of the Dean of Paul's, Dr. John Donne'.

11 You committed holy rapes upon our will.
1633 'An Elegy upon the Death of the Dean of Paul's, Dr. John Donne'.

12 The Muses' garden, with pedantic weeds
O'erspread, was purged by thee; the lazy seeds
Of servile imitation thrown away,
And fresh invention planted.
1633 'An Elegy upon the Death of the Dean of Paul's, Dr. John Donne'.

13 Here lies a king, that ruled as he thought fit
The universal monarchy of wit
1633 'An Elegy upon the Death of the Dean of Paul's, Dr. John Donne'.

14 And so our souls that cannot be embraced
Shall the embraces of our bodies taste.
1640 'A Rapture'.

15 I'll seize the rosebuds in their perfumed bed,
The violet knots, like curious mazes spread
O'er all the garden, taste the ripened cherry,
The warm, firm apple, tipped with coral berry.
Then will I visit with a wandering kiss
The vale of lilies and the bower of bliss,
And where the beauteous region doth divide
Into two milky ways, my lips shall slide
Down those smooth alleys, wearing as I go
A track for lovers on the printed snow.
1640 'A Rapture'.

16 All things are lawful there that may delight
Nature or unrestrainèd appetite.
1640 'A Rapture'.

17 Then tell me why
This goblin Honour which the world adores
Should make men atheists and not women whores.
1640 'A Rapture'.

18 Ask me no more whither dost haste
The nightingale when May is past;
For in your sweet dividing throat
She winters, and keeps warm her note.
1640 'A Song'.

19 Ask me no more if east or west

The Phoenix builds her spicy nest;
For unto you at last she flies,
And in your fragrant bosom dies.
1640 'A Song'.

20 Give me more love or more disdain;
The torrid or the frozen zone:
Bring equal ease unto my pain;
The temperate affords me none.
1640 'Mediocrity in Love Rejected'.

21 So though a virgin, yet a bride
To every Grace, she justified
A chaste polygamy, and died.
1640 'Inscription on the Tomb of Lady Mary Wentworth'.

Carey, John 1934–

English literary critic, Professor of English Literature at Oxford (1976–).

22 Given the state of the planet, humans, or some humans, must now be categorized as vermin.
1992 *The Intellectuals and the Masses*, postscript.

Carey, Peter 1943–

Australian novelist and short story writer. He was awarded the Booker Prize for *Oscar and Lucinda* (1988).

23 Glass is a thing in disguise, an actor, is not solid at all, but a liquid…an old sheet of glass will not only take on a royal and purplish tinge but will reveal its true liquid nature by having grown fatter at the bottom and thinner at the top, and… It is invisible, solid, in short a joyous and paradoxical thing, as good a material as any to build a life from.
1988 *Oscar and Lucinda*, ch.32, 'Prince Rupert's Drops'.

24 The declared meaning of a spoken sentence is only its overcoat, and the real meaning lies underneath its scarves and buttons.
1988 *Oscar and Lucinda*, ch.43 'Leviathan'.

Carleton, William 1794–1869

Irish writer, the youngest of 14 children born to peasant parents. His sketches were collected as *Traits and Stories of the Irish Peasantry* (1830, 2nd series 1833). Other works include *The Squanders of Castle Squander* (1852).

25 I remember on one occasion, when she was asked to sing the English version of the touching melody 'The Red-Haired Man's Wife', she replied, 'I will sing it for you; but the English words and the air are like a quarrelling man and wife; *the Irish melts into the tune*, but the English doesn't.'
1830 *Traits and Stories of the Irish Peasantry*, introduction.

Carlyle, Jane Baillie née *Jane Baillie Welsh*
1801–66

Wife of Thomas Carlyle. She married Carlyle in 1826, supporting him loyally through his depressions and ill-health, though resisting his suggestions that she write herself. After her death, Carlyle wrote a memoir of her in *Reminiscences* (1881) and edited her letters and diaries.

26 I am not at all the sort of person you and I took me for.
1822 Letter to Thomas Carlyle, 2 May.

27 Medical men all over the world having merely entered into a tacit agreement to call all sorts of maladies people are liable to, in cold weather, by one name; so that one sort of treatment may serve for all, and their practice thereby be greatly simplified.
1837 Letter to John Welsh, 4 Mar.

28 When I think of what I is
And what I used to was,
I gin to think I've sold myself
For very little cas.
1855 Journal entry, 5 Nov. Collected in James Anthony Froude (ed) *Letters and Memorials of Jane Welsh Carlyle*, vol.2 (1883).

29 I scorched my intellect into a cinder of stolidity.
Quoted in Alexander Carlyle (ed) *New Letters and Memorials of Jane Welsh Carlyle*, 'Mrs Carlyle's Notebook' (1903).

30 If you hate a man, though only in secret, never trust him, because hate is hardly to be hidden.
Quoted in Alexander Carlyle (ed) *New Letters and Memorials of Jane Welsh Carlyle*, 'Mrs Carlyle's Notebook' (1903).

Carlyle, Thomas 1795–1881

Scottish historian and essayist. His best-known work, *Sartor Resartus*, on social philosophy, appeared in 1833–4. In 1834 he moved to London, where his major works included *The French Revolution* (3 vols, 1837) and *Frederick the Great* (6 vols, 1858–65).

31 His fellow creatures are still objects of reverence and love, though their basenesses are plainer to no eye than to his. To reconcile these contradictions is the task of all good men.
1824 *Goethe*, introduction to German Romance, vol.4.

32 A mind that has seen, and suffered, and done, speaks to us of what it has tried and conquered.
1824 *Goethe*, introduction to German Romance, vol.4.

33 The true Church of England, at this moment, lies in the Editors of the newspapers.
1829 *Signs of the Times*.

34 It is no very good symptom either of nations or individuals, that they deal much in vaticination.
1829 *Signs of the Times*.

35 Seldom can the unhappy be persuaded that the evil of the day is sufficient for it; and the ambitious will not be content with the present splendour, but paints yet more glorious triumphs, on the cloud curtain of the future.
1829 *Signs of the Times.*

36 Meanwhile, we too admit that the present is an important time… We were wise indeed, could we discern truly the signs of our own time; and by knowledge of its wants and advantages, wisely adjust our own position in it.
1829 *Signs of the Times.*

37 Were we required to characterise this age of ours by any single epithet, we should be tempted to call it, not an Heroical, Devotional, Philosophical, or Moral Age, but above all others, the Mechanical Age. It is the Age of Machinery, in every outward and inward sense of the word.
1829 *Signs of the Times.*

38 We remove mountains, and make seas our smooth highway; nothing can resist us. We war with rude Nature; and, by our resistless engines, come off always victorious, and loaded with spoils.
1829 *Signs of the Times.*

39 Wealth has more and more increased, and at the same time gathered itself more and more into masses, strangely altering the old relations, and increasing the distance between the rich and the poor.
1829 *Signs of the Times.*

40 Men are grown mechanical in head and in the heart, as well as in the hand. They have lost faith in individual endeavour, and in natural force of any kind.
1829 *Signs of the Times.*

41 By our skill in Mechanism, it has come to pass, that in the management of external things we excel all other ages; while in whatever respects the pure mortal nature, in true dignity of soul and character, we are perhaps inferior to most civilised ages.
1829 *Signs of the Times.*

42 We are Giants in physical power: in a deeper than metaphorical sense, we are Titans, that strive, by heaping mountain on mountain, to conquer Heaven also.
1829 *Signs of the Times.*

43 Philosophers…stand among us not to do, nor to create anything, but as a sort of Logic-mill to grind out the true causes and effects of all that is done and created.
1829 *Signs of the Times.*

44 We have a faith in the imperishable dignity of man; in the high vocation to which, throughout this his earthly history, he has been appointed.
1829 *Signs of the Times.*

45 To reform a world, to reform a nation no wise man will undertake; and all but foolish men know, that the only solid, though a far slower reformation, is what each begins and perfects on himself.
1829 *Signs of the Times.*

46 No man who has once heartily and wholly laughed can be altogether irreclaimably bad.
1833–4 *Sartor Resartus*, bk.1, ch.4.

47 He who first shortened the labour of copyists by device of *Movable Types* was disbanding hired armies, and cashiering most Kings and Senates, and creating a whole new democratic world: he had invented the art of printing.
1833–4 *Sartor Resartus*, bk.1, ch.5.

48 Man is a tool-using animal… Without tools he is nothing, with tools he is all.
1833–4 *Sartor Resartus*, bk.1, ch.5.

49 Whoso has sixpence is sovereign (to the length of sixpence) over all men; commands cooks to feed him, philosophers to teach him, kings to mount guard over him,—to the length of sixpence.
1833–4 *Sartor Resartus*, bk.1, ch.5.

50 Man's earthly interests, 'are all hooked and buttoned together, and held up, by Clothes.'
1833–4 *Sartor Resartus*, bk.1, ch.8.

51 Be not the slave of words.
1833–4 *Sartor Resartus*, bk.1, ch.8.

52 Language is called the garment of thought: however, it should rather be, language is the flesh-garment, the body, of thought.
1833–4 *Sartor Resartus*, bk.1, ch.11.

53 The end of man is an action and not a thought, though it were the noblest.
1833–4 *Sartor Resartus*, bk.2, ch.6.

54 The everlasting No.
1833–4 *Sartor Resartus*, bk.2, ch.7, title.

55 Most true it is, as a wise man teaches us, that 'doubt of any sort cannot be removed except by Action.' On which ground, too, let him who gropes painfully in darkness or in uncertain light, and prays vehemently that the dawn may ripen into day, lay this other precept well to heart, which to me was of invaluable service: *'Do the Duty which lies nearest thee'*, which thou knowest to be a Duty! Thy second duty will already have become clearer.
1833–4 *Sartor Resartus*, bk.2, ch.9.

56 Man's unhappiness, as I construe, comes of his greatness; it is because there is an Infinite in him, which with all his cunning he cannot quite bury under the Finite.
1833–4 *Sartor Resartus*, bk.2, ch.9.

57 Be no longer a chaos, but a world, or even worldkin. Produce! Produce! Were it but the pitifullest infinitesimal fraction of a product, produce it in God's name! 'Tis the utmost thou hast in thee: out with it, then.
1833–4 *Sartor Resartus*, bk.2, ch.9.

58 Friends! trust not the heart of that man for whom Old Clothes are not venerable.
1833–4 *Sartor Resartus*, bk.3, ch.6.

59 How great a Possibility, how small a realized Result.
1834 Of Samuel Taylor Coleridge. Letter to Emerson, 12 Aug.

60 The public is an old woman. Let her maunder and mumble.
1835 Journal entry.

61 Hope ushers in a Revolution—as earthquakes are preceded by bright weather.
1837 *History of the French Revolution*, vol.1, bk.2, ch.1.

62 A whiff of grapeshot.
1837 *History of the French Revolution*, vol.1, bk.5, ch.3.

63 Under all the roofs of this distracted City is the nodus of a drama, not untragical, crowding towards solution.
1837 *History of the French Revolution*, vol.1, bk.5, ch.6.

64 How true it is, that there is nothing dead in this Universe; that what we call dead is only changed, its forces working in inverse order! 'The leaf that lies rotting in moist winds,' says one, 'has still force; else how could it rot?'
1837 *History of the French Revolution*, vol.2, bk.3, ch.1.

65 The difference between Orthodoxy or My-doxy and Heterodoxy or Thy-doxy.
1837 *History of the French Revolution*, vol.2, bk.4, ch.2.

66 The seagreen Incorruptible.
1837 Of Robespierre. *History of the French Revolution*, vol.2, bk.4, ch.4.

67 Pity is lost in rage and fear.
1837 *History of the French Revolution*, vol.3, bk.2, ch.7.

68 France was long a despotism tempered by epigrams.
1837 *History of the French Revolution*, vol.3, bk.7, ch.7.

69 Aristocracy of the Moneybag.
1837 *History of the French Revolution*, vol.3, bk.7, ch.7.

70 The 'golden-calf of self-love'.
1838 *Critical and Miscellaneous Essays*, 'Burns'.

71 For, strictly considered, what is all knowledge too but recorded experience, and a product of history; of which, therefore, reasoning and belief, no less than action and passion are essential materials?
1838 *Critical and Miscellaneous Essays*, 'History'.

72 History is the essence of innumerable biographies.
1838 *Critical and Miscellaneous Essays*, 'History'.

73 When the oak-tree is fallen, the whole forest echoes with it; but a hundred acorns are planted silently by some unnoticed breeze.
1838 *Critical and Miscellaneous Essays*, 'History'.

74 Laws themselves, political Constitutions, are not our Life; but only the house wherein our Life is led.
1838 *Critical and Miscellaneous Essays*, 'History'.

75 History is philosophy teaching by experience.
1838 *Critical and Miscellaneous Essays*, 'History'.

76 A well-written life is almost as rare as a well-spent one.
1838 *Critical and Miscellaneous Essays*, 'Jean Paul Fredrich Richter'.

77 There is no life of a man, faithfully recorded, but is a heroic poem of its sort, rhymed or unrhymed.
1838 *Critical and Miscellaneous Essays*, 'Sir Walter Scott'.

78 Under all speech there lies a silence that is better. Silence is deep as Eternity; speech is shallow as Time.
1838 *Critical and Miscellaneous Essays*, 'Sir Walter Scott'.

79 A feeling generally exists that the condition and disposition of the Working Class is a rather ominous matter at present; that something ought to be said, something ought to be done, in regard to it.
1839 *Chartism*, ch.1.

80 A witty statesman said, you might prove anything by figures.
1839 *Chartism*, ch.2.

81 To believe practically that the poor and luckless are here only as a nusiance to be abraded and abated, and in some permissable manner made away with, and swept out of sight, is not an amiable faith.
1839 *Chartism*, ch.3.

82 A man willing to work, and unable to find work, is perhaps the saddest sight that fortune's inequality exhibits under the sun.
1839 *Chartism*, ch.4

83 Surely of all 'rights of man', this right of the ignorant man to be guided by the wiser, to be, gently or forcibly, held in the true course by him, is the indisputablest.
1839 *Chartism*, ch.6.

84 In epochs when cash payment has become the sole nexus of man to man.
1839 *Chartism*, ch.6.

85 The English are used to suffrage; it is their panacea for all that goes wrong with them.
1839 *Chartism*, ch.9.

86 Books are written by martyr-men, not for rich men alone but for all men. If we consider it, every human being has, by the nature of the case, a *right* to hear what other wise human beings have spoken to him. It is one of the Rights of Men; a very cruel injustice if you deny it to a man!
1840 Letter to John Sterling, collected in *New Letters of Carlyle* (1904), vol.1.

87 It is well said, in every sense, that a man's religion is the chief fact with regard to him.
1841 *On Heroes, Hero-Worship and the Heroic in History*, 'The Hero as Divinity' (published 1897).

88 Worship is transcendent wonder.
1841 *On Heroes, Hero-Worship, and the Heroic*, 'The Hero as King'.

89 I hope we English will long maintain our *grand talent pour le silence.*
1841 *On Heroes, Hero-Worship, and the Heroic*, 'The Hero as King'.

90 In books lies the soul of the whole Past Time; the articulate audible voice of the Past, when the body and material substance of it has altogether vanished like a dream.
1841 *On Heroes, Hero-Worship, and the Heroic*, 'The Hero as Man of Letters'.

91 The true University these days is a collection of books.
1841 *On Heroes, Hero-Worship, and the Heroic*, 'The Hero as Man of Letters'.

92 Adversity is sometimes hard upon a man; but for one man who can stand prosperity, there are a hundred that will stand adversity.
1841 *On Heroes, Hero-Worship, and the Heroic*, 'The Hero as Man of Letters'.

93 Heaven's splendour over his head, Hell's darkness under his feet.
1843 *Past and Present*, bk.2, ch.15.

94 Work earnestly at anything, you will by degrees learn to work at all things.
1843 *Past and Present*, bk.3, ch.2.

95 Captains of Industry.
1843 *Past and Present*, bk.4, ch.4, title.

96 Respectable Professors of the Dismal Science.
1850 *Latter-Day Pamphlets*, no.1, 'The Present Time'.

97 Nature admits no lie.
1850 *Latter-Day Pamphlets*, no.5.

98 A Parliament speaking through reporters to Buncombe and the twenty-seven millions mostly fools.
1850 *Latter-Day Pamphlets*, no.6, 'Parliaments'.

99 Transcendental moonshine.
1851 Of the romantic impulses that had led Sterling to the priesthood. *The Life of John Sterling*, pt.1, ch.15.

1 Maid-servants, I hear people complaining, are getting instructed in the 'ologies'.
1866 Inaugural address as Rector of Edinburgh University, 2 Apr.

2 All reform except a moral one will prove unavailing.
1872 *Critical and Miscellaneous Essays*, 'Corn Law Rhymes'.

3 If Jesus Christ were to come today, people would not even crucify him. They would ask him to dinner, and hear what he had to say, and make fun of it.
Quoted in D A Wilson *Carlyle at his Zenith* (1927).

Carman, (William) Bliss 1861–1929

Canadian poet. His vivid and optimistic poetry includes *Songs from Vagabondia* (with Richard Hovey, 1894, 1896 and 1901) and *Pipes of Pan* (1902–5).

4 Have little care that Life is brief,
And less that art is long.
Success is in the silences,
Though fame is in the song.
1923 *Ballads and Lyrics*, 'Envoi'. These lines are reproduced on the plaque erected in his honour at the University of New Brunswick, Fredericton, Canada.

Carnegie, Andrew 1835–1919

Scottish-born US steel magnate and philanthropist. He emigrated with his family in 1848, investing his savings in oil lands as a youth and amassing a vast fortune, with which he endowed numerous institutions and good causes.

5 The man who dies rich…dies disgraced.
1889 'The Gospel of Wealth', in the *North American Review*, Jun.

6 While the law [of competition] may be sometimes hard for the individual, it is best for the race, because it insures the survival of the fittest in every department. We accept and welcome, therefore, as conditions to which we must accommodate ourselves, great inequality of environment, the concentration of business, industrial and commercial, in the hands of a few, and the law of competition between these, as being not only beneficial, but essential to the future progress of the race.

1889 'The Gospel of Wealth', in the *North American Review*, Jun.

Carnegie, Dale originally *Dale Carnagey* 1888–1955

US lecturer and writer, a pioneer of self-help psychology.

7 How to Win Friends and Influence People.
1930 Title of book.

Carpentier, Alejo 1904–80

Cuban novelist, musicologist and journalist, Ambassador to Europe for a considerable period of Castro's regime. His style has been called neo-Baroque.

8 *A tal punto me hunden mis palabras, como dichas por otro, por un juez que yo llevara dentro sin saberlo y se valiera de mis propios medios físicos para expresarse, que me aterro, al oírme, de lo difícil que es volver a ser hombre cuando se ha dejado de ser hombre.*

As though they were coming from the lips of another, from a judge I carried within me without knowing it, and who made use of my own faculties to express himself, my words took such hold upon me that it frightened me to realize, as I listened to myself, how hard it is to become a man when one has ceased to be a man.
1953 *Los pasos perdidos* (translated as *The Lost Steps*, 1956), ch.1, pt.2.

Carr, E(dward) H(allet) 1892–1982

English political scientist and historian. In the diplomatic service until 1936, he was Assistant Editor of *The Times* (1941–6) and wrote several important historical texts, including biographies of Marx (1934) and Bakunin (1937).

9 The unending dialogue between the present and the past.
Of biography. Quoted in James G Hershberg *James B Conant* (1993).

Carr, Emily 1871–1945

Canadian painter and writer, who recorded the lives of west-coast native Canadians in words and paintings. Her first book *Klee Wyck* (1941) won the Governor-General's Award.

10 The outstanding event was the *doing* which I am still at. Don't pickle me away as done.
c.1940 Quoted in Ira Dilworth's foreword to *Klee Wyck* (1951 edn).

11 There was neither horizon, cloud, nor sound; of that pink, spread silence even I had become part, belonging as much to sky as to earth.
1941 *Klee Wyck*, ch.17, 'Salt Water'.

Carr, J(ames) L(loyd) 1912–

English novelist. His best known work is *A Month in the Country* (1980), which was also filmed.

12 'I've never been spoken to like this before in all my thirty years' experience,' she wails. '*You* have not had thirty years' experience, Mrs Grindle-Jones,' he says witheringly. '*You* have had one year's experience 30 times.'
1972 *The Harpole Report*, ch.21.

13 In rural England, people live wrapped tight in a cocoon; only their eyes move to make sure that nobody gets more than themselves.
1975 *How Steeple Sinderby Wanderers Won the FA Cup*, pt.2.

14 You must understand, James, that their English God is not so dominant a business institution as ours.
1985 On the US version of God. *The Battle of Pollocks Crossing*.

Carrà, Carlo 1881–1966

Italian painter, involved first in *Pittura Metafisica* and then in Futurism.

15 *The painting of sounds, noises and smells calls for:*
1. Reds, rrrrreds, the rrrrrreddest rrrrrrreds that shouuuuuuut.
2. Greens, that can never be greener, greeeeeeeeeeeeens that screeeeeeeam, yellows, as violent as can be: polenta yellows, saffron yellows, brass yellows.
1913 In the *Manifesto of Futurist Painting*, quoted in *Futurismo e Futurismi* (1986).

16 This is the truth! In order to achieve this *total painting*, which requires the active cooperation of all the senses, *a painting which is a plastic state of mind of the universal*, you must paint, as drunkards sing and vomit, sounds, noises and smells!
1913 In the *Manifesto of Futurist Painting*, quoted in *Futurismo e Futurismi* (1986).

Carracci, Annibale 1560–1609

Italian painter, one of a family of artists from Bologna.

17 Poets paint with words, painters speak with works.
Attributed rebuke to his brother Agostino. Quoted in G P Bellori *Vite* (1672).

Carrigan, Jim Richard 1929–

US lawyer, judge at the US Court of Appeals.

18 It is all too rare today to hear the clear, clean ring of a really original insult.
1987 In *Time*, 28 Aug.

Carroll, Lewis pseudonym of *Rev Charles Lutwidge Dodgson* 1832–98

English poet, mathematician and logician. A shy man with a stammer, he was most comfortable in the company of children. He is best known for his children's books *Alice's Adventures in Wonderland* (1865) and *Through the Looking-Glass* (1871).

19 'And what is the use of a book,' thought Alice, 'without pictures or conversations?'
 1865 *Alice's Adventures in Wonderland*, ch.1, 'Down the Rabbit-Hole'.

20 'Even if my head *would* go through,' thought poor Alice, 'it would be of very little use without my shoulders.'
 1865 *Alice's Adventures in Wonderland*, ch.1,'Down the Rabbit-Hole'.

21 'Curiouser and curiouser!' cried Alice (she was so much surprised, that for the moment she quite forgot how to speak good English).
 1865 *Alice's Adventures in Wonderland*, ch.2, 'The Pool of Tears'.

22 How doth the little crocodile
 Improve his shining tail,
 And pour the waters of the Nile
 On every golden scale!

 How cheerfully he seems to grin,
 How neatly spreads his claws,
 And welcomes little fishes in,
 With gently smiling jaws!
 1865 *Alice's Adventures in Wonderland*, ch.2, 'The Pool of Tears'.

23 'I'll be judge, I'll be jury,' said cunning old Fury; 'I'll try the whole cause, and condemn you to death.'
 1865 *Alice's Adventures in Wonderland*, ch.3, 'A Caucus-Race and a Long Tale', told by the Dormouse.

24 'You are old, Father William,' the young man said, 'And your hair has become very white;
 And yet you incessantly stand on your head—
 Do you think, at your age, it is right?'

 'In my youth,' Father William replied to his son, 'I feared it might injure the brain;
 But now that I'm perfectly sure I have none,
 Why, I do it again and again.'
 1865 *Alice's Adventures in Wonderland*, ch.5, 'Advice from a Caterpillar'.
 ▷ See Southey 954:29.

25 'If everybody minded their own business,' the Duchess said, in a hoarse growl, 'the world would go round a deal faster than it does.'
 1865 *Alice's Adventures in Wonderland*, ch.6, 'Pig and Pepper'.

26 Speak roughly to your little boy,
 And beat him when he sneezes:
 He only does it to annoy,
 Because he knows it teases.
 1865 The Duchess's lullaby. *Alice's Adventures in Wonderland*, ch.6, 'Pig and Pepper'.

27 'All right,' said the Cat; and this time it vanished quite slowly, beginning with the end of the tail, and ending with the grin, which remained some time after the rest of it had gone.
 1865 The disappearance of the Cheshire Cat. *Alice's Adventures in Wonderland*, ch.6, 'Pig and Pepper'.

28 'Then you should say what you mean,' the March Hare went on.
 'I do,' Alice hastily replied; 'at least—at least I mean what I say—that's the same thing, you know.'
 'Not the same thing a bit!' said the Hatter. 'Why, you might just as well say that 'I see what I eat' is the same thing as 'I eat what I see!'
 1865 *Alice's Adventures in Wonderland*, ch.7, 'A Mad Tea-Party'.

29 Twinkle, twinkle, little bat!
 How I wonder what you're at!
 Up above the world you fly!
 Like a teatray in the sky.
 1865 *Alice's Adventures in Wonderland*, Ch. 7, 'A Mad Tea-Party'.

30 'Take some more tea,' the March Hare said to Alice, very earnestly.
 'I've had nothing yet,' Alice replied in an offended tone, 'so I can't take more.'
 'You mean you can't take *less*,' said the Hatter: 'It's very easy to take *more* than nothing.'
 1865 *Alice's Adventures in Wonderland*, ch.7, 'A Mad Tea-Party'.

31 Off with her head!
 1865 The Queen of Hearts. *Alice's Adventures in Wonderland*, ch.8, 'The Queen's Croquet Ground'.

32 Everything's got a moral, if only you can find it.
 1865 The Duchess. *Alice's Adventures in Wonderland*, ch.9, 'The Mock Turtle's Story'.

33 Take care of the sense, and the sounds will take care of themselves.
 1865 The Duchess. *Alice's Adventures in Wonderland*, ch.9, 'The Mock Turtle's Story'.

34 'Just about as much right,' said the Duchess, 'as pigs have to fly.'
 1865 *Alice's Adventures in Wonderland*, ch.9, 'The Mock Turtle's Story'.

35 'That's the reason they're called lessons,' the Gryphon remarked: 'because they lessen from day to day.'
 1865 *Alice's Adventures in Wonderland*, ch.9, 'The Mock Turtle's Story'.

36 'I only took the regular course.'
 'What was that?' inquired Alice.
 'Reeling and Writhing, of course, to begin with,' the Mock Turtle replied; 'and then the different branches of Arithmetic—Ambition, Distraction, Uglification, and Derision.'

1865 *Alice's Adventures in Wonderland*, ch.9, 'The Mock Turtle's Story'.

37 The Drawling-master was an old conger-eel, that used to come once a week: *he* taught us Drawling, Stretching, and Fainting in Coils.
1865 *Alice's Adventures in Wonderland*, ch.9, 'The Mock Turtle's Story'.

38 'Will you walk a little faster?' said a whiting to a snail,
'There's a porpoise close behind us and he's treading on my tail.'
1865 *Alice's Adventures in Wonderland*, ch.10, 'The Lobster-Quadrille'.

39 Will you, won't you, will you, won't you, will you join the dance?
1865 *Alice's Adventures in Wonderland*, ch.10, 'The Lobster-Quadrille'.

40 Beautiful Soup, so rich and green,
Waiting in a hot tureen!
Who for such dainties would not stoop?
Soup of the evening, beautiful Soup!
1865 Song of the Mock Turtle. *Alice's Adventures in Wonderland*, ch.10.

41 'Tis the voice of the lobster; I heard him declare,
'You have baked me too brown, I must sugar my hair.'
1865 *Alice's Adventures in Wonderland*, ch.10, 'The Lobster-Quadrille'.

42 The Queen of Hearts, she made some tarts,
All of a summer day:
The Knave of Hearts, he stole those tarts
And took them quite away!
1865 *Alice's Adventures in Wonderland*, ch.11, 'Who Stole the Tarts?'.

43 'Where shall I begin, please your Majesty?' he asked.
'Begin at the beginning,' the King said, gravely, 'and go on till you come to the end; then stop.'
1865 *Alice's Adventures in Wonderland*, ch.12, 'Alice's Evidence'.

44 'That's not a regular rule: you invented it just now.'
'It's the oldest rule in the book,' said the King.
'Then it ought to be Number One,' said Alice.
1865 *Alice's Adventures in Wonderland*, ch.12, 'Alice's Evidence'.

45 'No, no!' said the Queen. 'Sentence first—verdict afterwards.'
1865 *Alice's Adventures in Wonderland*, ch.12, 'Alice's Evidence'.

46 'Why,' said the Dodo, 'the best way to explain it is to do it.'
1865 *Alice's Adventures in Wonderland*, ch.3, 'A Caucus-Race and a Long Tale'.

47 'Twas brillig, and the slithy toves
Did gyre and gimble in the wabe;
All mimsy were the borogoves,

And the mome raths outgrabe.
'Beware the Jabberwock, my son!
The jaws that bite, the claws that catch!
Beware the Jubjub bird, and shun
The frumious Bandersnatch!'
He took his vorpal sword in hand:
Long time the manxome foe he sought—
So rested he by the Tumtum tree,
And stood a while in thought.
And, as in uffish thought he stood,
The Jabberwock, with eyes of flame,
Came whiffling through the tulgey wood,
And burbled as it came!
One, two! One, two! And through and through
The vorpal blade went snicker-snack!
He left it dead and with its head
He went galumphing back.
'And hast thou slain the Jabberwock?
Come to my arms, my beamish boy!
Oh frabjous day! Callooh! Callay!'
He chortled in his joy.
1871 *Through the Looking-Glass* ch.1, 'Looking-Glass House'.

48 Curtsey while you're thinking what to say. It saves time.
1871 *Through the Looking-Glass*, ch.2, 'The Garden of Live Flowers'.

49 'When you say "hill," the Queen interrupted, 'I could show you hills, in comparison with which you'd call that a valley.'
'No, I shouldn't,' said Alice, surprised into contradicting her at last: 'a hill *can't* be a valley, you know. That would be nonsense—'
The Red Queen shook her head. 'You may call it 'nonsense' if you like,' she said, 'but *I've* heard nonsense, compared with which that would be as sensible as a dictionary!'
1871 *Through the Looking-Glass*, ch.2, 'The Garden of Live Flowers'.

50 Now, *here*, you see, it takes all the running *you* can do, to keep in the same place. If you want to get somewhere else, you must run at least twice as fast as that!
1871 *Through the Looking-Glass*, ch.2, 'The Garden of Live Flowers'.

51 Speak in French when you can't think of the English for a thing—turn out your toes as you walk—and remember who you are!
1871 The Red Queen's advice to Alice as she begins the chess game. *Through the Looking-Glass*, ch.2, 'The Garden of Live Flowers'.

52 'You shouldn't make jokes,' Alice said, 'if it makes you so unhappy.'
1871 Alice to the gnat. *Through the Looking-Glass*, ch.3, 'Looking-Glass Insects'.

53 Tweedledum and Tweedledee

Agreed to have a battle;
For Tweedledum said Tweedledee
Had spoilt his nice new rattle.
1871 *Through the Looking-Glass*, ch.4, 'Tweedledum and Tweedledee'.

54 'Contrariwise,' continued Tweedledee, 'if it was so, it might be; and if it were so, it would be: but as it isn't it ain't. That's logic.'
1871 *Through the Looking-Glass*, ch.4, 'Tweedledum and Tweedledee'.

55 The sun was shining on the sea,
Shining with all his might:
He did his very best to make
The billows smooth and bright—
And this was odd, because it was
The middle of the night.
1871 Tweedledee. *Through the Looking-Glass*, ch.4, 'Tweedledum and Tweedledee'.

56 The Walrus and the Carpenter
Were walking close at hand;
They wept like anything to see
Such quantities of sand:
'If this were only cleared away,'
They said, 'it would be grand!'
1871 Tweedledee. *Through the Looking-Glass*, ch.4, 'Tweedledum and Tweedledee'.

57 'The time has come,' the Walrus said,
'To talk of many things:
Of shoes—and ships—and sealing-wax—
Of cabbages—and kings—
And why the sea is boiling hot—
And whether pigs have wings.'
1871 Tweedledee. *Through the Looking-Glass*, ch.4, 'Tweedledum and Tweedledee'.

58 'You know,' he said very gravely, 'it's one of the most serious things that can possibly happen to one in a battle—to get one's head cut off.'
1871 *Through the Looking-Glass*, ch.4, 'Tweedledum and Tweedledee'.

59 The rule is, jam to-morrow and jam yesterday—but never jam to-day.
1871 The White Queen. *Through the Looking-Glass*, ch.5, 'Wool and Water'.

60 'It's a poor sort of memory that only works backwards,' the Queen remarked.
1871 *Through the Looking-Glass*, ch.5, 'Wool and Water'.

61 Consider anything, only don't cry!
1871 *Through the Looking-Glass*, ch.5, 'Wool and Water'.

62 Alice laughed. 'There's no use trying,' she said: 'one can't believe impossible things.'
'I daresay you haven't had much practice,' said the Queen. 'When I was your age, I always did it for half-an-hour a day. Why, sometimes I've believed as many as six impossible things before breakfast.'
1871 *Through the Looking-Glass*, ch. 5, 'Wool and Water'.

63 'It's *very* provoking,' Humpty Dumpty said after a long silence, looking away from Alice as he spoke, 'to be called an egg—*very*!'
1871 *Through the Looking-Glass*, ch.6, 'Humpty Dumpty'.

64 With a name like yours you might be any shape, almost.
1871 *Through the Looking-Glass*, ch.6, 'Humpty Dumpty'.

65 'They gave it me,' Humpty Dumpty continued thoughtfully…'for an un-birthday present.'
1871 *Through the Looking-Glass*, ch.6, 'Humpty Dumpty'.

66 'The question is,' said Humpty Dumpty, 'which is to be master—that's all.'
1871 *Through the Looking-Glass*, ch.6, 'Humpty Dumpty'.

67 'That's a great deal to make one word mean,' Alice said in a thoughtful tone.
'When I make a word do a lot of work like that,' said Humpty Dumpty, 'I always pay it extra.'
1871 *Through the Looking-Glass*, ch.6, 'Humpty Dumpty'.

68 'Slithy' means 'lithe and slimy'… You see it's like a portmanteau—there are two meanings packed up into one word.
1871 Humpty Dumpty explaining the *Jabberwock* poem. *Through the Looking-Glass*, ch.6, 'Humpty Dumpty'.

69 'I can repeat poetry as well as other folk if it comes to that—'
'Oh, it needn't come to that!' Alice hastily said.
1871 *Through the Looking-Glass*, ch.6, 'Humpty Dumpty'.

70 'There's glory for you!'
'I don't know what you mean by 'glory',' Alice said.
'I meant, 'there's a nice knock-down argument for you!'
'But 'glory' doesn't mean 'a nice knock-down argument',' Alice objected.
'When I use a word,' Humpty Dumpty said in a rather scornful tone, 'it means just what I choose it to mean—neither more nor less.'
1871 *Through the Looking-Glass*, ch.6, 'Humpty Dumpty'.

71 The Lion and the Unicorn were fighting for the crown:
The Lion beat the Unicorn all round the town.
Some gave them white bread, some gave them brown;
Some gave them plum-cake and drummed them out of town.
1871 *Through the Looking-Glass*, ch.7, 'The Lion and the Unicorn'.

72 He's an Anglo-Saxon Messenger—and those are Anglo-Saxon attitudes.
1871 *Through the Looking-Glass*, ch.7, 'The Lion and the Unicorn'.

73 The Lion looked at Alice wearily. 'Are you
   animal—or vegetable—or mineral?' he said,
   yawning at every other word.
   1872 *Through the Looking-Glass*, ch.7, 'The Lion and the
   Unicorn'.

74 I must have *two* you know—to come and go. One
   to come, and one to go.
   1872 The King speaking of his messengers. *Through the
   Looking-Glass*, ch.7, 'The Lion and the Unicorn'.

75 It's as large as life and twice as natural!
   1872 *Through the Looking-Glass*, ch.7, 'The Lion and the
   Unicorn'.

76 'It's long,' said the Knight, 'but it's very, *very*
   beautiful. Everybody that hears me sing it—either
   it brings the *tears* into their eyes, or else—'
   'Or else what?' said Alice, for the Knight had made
   a sudden pause.
   'Or else it doesn't, you know.'
   1871 *Through the Looking-Glass*, ch.8, 'It's My Own
   Invention'.

77 I'll tell thee everything I can:
   There's little to relate.
   I saw an aged, aged man,
   A-sitting on a gate.
   1872 *Through the Looking-Glass*, ch.8, 'It's My Own
   Invention'.

78 Or madly squeeze a right-hand foot
   Into a left-hand shoe.
   1872 *Through the Looking-Glass*, ch.8, 'It's My Own
   Invention'.

79 Un-dish-cover the fish, or dishcover the riddle.
   1872 *Through the Looking-Glass*, ch.9, 'Queen Alice'.

80 'Fan her head!' the Red Queen anxiously
   interrupted. 'She'll be feverish after so much
   thinking.'
   1871 *Through the Looking-Glass*, ch.9, 'Queen Alice'.

81 'Do you know Languages? What's the French for
   fiddle-de-dee?'
   'Fiddle-de-dee's not English,' Alice replied gravely.
   'Who ever said it was?' said the Red Queen.
   Alice though she saw a way out of the difficulty this
   time. 'If you'll tell me what language 'fiddle-de-dee'
   is, I'll tell you the French for it!' she exclaimed
   triumphantly.
   But the Red Queen drew herself up rather stiffly,
   and said 'Queens never make bargains.'
   1871 *Through the Looking-Glass*, ch.9, 'Queen Alice'.

82 What I tell you three times is true.
   1876 *The Hunting of the Snark*, 'Fit the First: The Landing'.

83 He would answer to 'Hi!' or to any loud cry,

Such as 'Fry me!' or 'Fritter-my-wig!'
   1876 *The Hunting of the Snark*, 'Fit the First: The Landing'.

84 His intimate friends called him 'Candle-ends',
   And his enemies, 'Toasted-cheese'.
   1876 *The Hunting of the Snark*, 'Fit the First: The Landing'.

85 'What's the good of Mercator's North Poles and
      Equators,
   Tropics, Zones and Meridian lines?'
   So the Bellman would cry: and the crew would
      reply,
   'They are merely conventional signs!'
   1876 *The Hunting of the Snark*, 'Fit the Second: The Bellman's
   Speech'.

86 But the principle failing occurred in the sailing,
   And the Bellman, perplexed and distressed,
   Said he *had* hoped, at least, when the wind blew
      due East,
   That the ship would *not* travel due West!
   1876 *The Hunting of the Snark*, 'Fit the Second: The Bellman's
   Speech'.

87 They sought it with thimbles, they sought it with
      care;
   They pursued it with forks and hope;
   They threatened its life with a railway-share;
   They charmed it with smiles and soap.
   1876 *The Hunting of the Snark*, 'Fit the Fifth: The Beaver's
   Lesson'.

88 He thought he saw an Elephant,
   That practised on a fife:
   He looked again, and found it was
   A letter from his wife.
   'At length I realize,' he said
   'The bitterness of life!'
   1889 *Sylvie and Bruno*, ch.5.

89 He thought he saw a Rattlesnake
   That questioned him in Greek,
   He looked again and found it was
   The Middle of Next Week.
   'The one thing I regret,' he said,
   'Is that it cannot speak!'
   1889 *Sylvie and Bruno*, ch.6.

Carson, Edward Henry, Baron 1854–1935

Irish Unionist politician, Solicitor General in the
Conservative Government 1900–5. He successfully
defended the Marquis of Queensberry against Oscar
Wilde's libel suit in 1895. In 1912, he forced the
Government to exclude Ulster from the Home Rule
settlement. During World War I, he served as Attorney
General (1915), First Lord of the Admiralty (1916–17)
and a member of the war cabinet (1917–18).

90 A sentence of death with a stay of execution for six
   years.

1914 On the British Government's compromise terms by which Ireland was to be allowed to defer Home Rule for six years. Speech, Mar.

91 My only great qualification for being put at the head of the navy is that I am wholly at sea.

c.1916 Quoted in I Colvin *Life of Lord Carson* (1936), vol.3, ch.23.

Carter, Angela Olive 1940–92

English novelist and essayist, whose works combine fantasy and genre pastiche. They include *The Magic Toyshop* (1967) and *The Sadeian Woman* (1979).

92 Clothes are our weapons, our challenges, our visible insults.

1967 'Notes for a Theory of Sixties Style', in *New Society* (1967). Collected in *Nothing Sacred* (1982).

93 Solitude and melancholy, that is a woman's life.

1977 *The Passion of New Eve*, ch.9.

94 Myth deals in false universals, to dull the pain of particular circumstances.

1979 *The Sadeian Woman*, 'Polemical Preface'.

95 What is marriage but prostitution to one man instead of many?

1985 *Nights at the Circus*, 'London 2'.

96 I notice that I'm getting more sentimental as I get older; I feel I owe it to myself somehow.

1985 Quoted in John Haffenden *Novelists in Interview* (1985).

97 He was a man with a great future behind him, already.

1991 *Wise Children*, ch.3.

98 She looked like a million dollars, I must admit, even if in well-used notes.

1991 *Wise Children*, ch.5.

Carter, Jimmy (James Earl) 1924–

US Democratic politician and 39th President (1977–81). He helped to effect the Egypt–Israel peace treaties (1979), but after the taking of US hostages in Iran and the Soviet invasion of Afghanistan he was defeated by Reagan in the 1980 elections.

99 Why not the best?

1976 Presidential campaign slogan.

1 I am convinced that UFOs exist, because I have seen one.

1976 TV interview, 16 Jun.

2 We become not a melting pot but a beautiful mosaic. Different people, different beliefs, different yearnings, different hopes, different dreams.

1976 Speech at Pittsburgh, 27 Oct.

3 I have looked on a lot of women with lust. I have committed adultery in my heart many times. God recognizes I will do that, and forgives me.

1976 *Playboy* interview, Nov.

4 The experience of democracy is like the experience of life itself—always changing, infinite in its variety, sometimes turbulent and all the more valuable for having been tested by adversity.

1978 Address to the Parliament of India, 2 Jun.

5 If you fear making anyone mad, then you ultimately probe for the lowest common denominator of human achievement.

1978 Address to the Future Farmers of America, Kansas City, 9 Nov.

6 All of you have met another Democratic President. I've never had that opportunity yet.

1991 On greeting former Presidents Bush, Reagan, Ford and Nixon at the dedication of the Reagan Library. Reported in the *New York Times*, 5 Nov.

7 My role is one of filling vacuums.

1994 On his work with 105 countries since leaving the White House. Broadcast on ABC TV, 13 Dec.

8 I feel truer to myself…more of a missionary than a politician.

1995 On the Carter Library as a centre for the study of international issues. In *Life*, Nov.

Carter, Lillian 1898–1983

Mother of President Jimmy Carter.

9 Sometimes when I look at my children, I say to myself, 'Lillian, you should have stayed a virgin.'

1977 In *Woman* magazine, 9 Apr.

Cartier, Jacques 1491–1557

French navigator and explorer in North America, discoverer of the St Lawrence river.

10 In fine I am rather inclined to believe that this is the land God gave to Cain.

1534 Of Canada, as he sailed past the bleak northern shore of the Gulf of St Lawrence. Journal entry, summer. Quoted in H P Biggar (ed) *The Voyages of Jacques Cartier* (1924).

Cartland, Dame (Mary) Barbara Hamilton 1901–

English romantic novelist. A prolific writer of popular romances, she became a media celebrity for her garish dress and well-honed sense of social status.

11 At fifty you have the choice of keeping your face or your figure and it's *much* better to keep your face.

1981 In *The Daily Mail*, 10 Jul.

12 I answer 20,000 letters a year and so many couples are having problems because they are not getting the right proteins and vitamins.

> **1986** Quoted in *The Observer*, 31 Aug.

Cartwright, John 1740–1824

English reformer, 'The Father of Reform', and political writer.

13 One man shall have one vote.

> **1780** *The People's Barrier Against Undue Influence*, ch.1, 'Principles, maxims, and primary rules of politics'.

Caruso, Enrico 1873–1921

Italian operatic tenor renowned for the power and musical purity of his voice.

14 You know whatta you do when you shit? Singing, it's the same thing, only up!

> Quoted in H Brown *Whose Little Boy Are You?* (1983).

Cary, (Arthur) Joyce Lunel 1888–1957

English novelist. His best known books are *Mister Johnston* (1939), set in Africa, and *The Horse's Mouth* (1944), the final work in a trilogy exploring the pretensions of the art world.

15 This is not to pretend that reading is a passive act. On the contrary, it is highly creative, or re-creative; itself an art.

> **1939** *Mister Johnston*, preface.

16 I ain't complaining—it's a duty laid down upon us by God—but the Pax Britannia takes a bit of keeping up—with 'arf the world full of savages and 'arf the other 'arf just getting in the way.

> **1939** *Mister Johnston*.

17 She had a mannish manner of mind and face, able to feel hot and think cold.

> **1940** *Herself Surprised*, ch.7.

18 It is the misfortune of an old man that though he can put things out of his head he can't put them out of his feelings.

> **1942** *To Be A Pilgrim*, ch.8.

19 Sara could commit adultery at one end and weep for her sins at the other, and enjoy both at once.

> **1944** *The Horse's Mouth*, ch.8.

20 Remember I'm an artist. And you know what that means in a court of law. Next worse to an actress.

> **1944** *The Horse's Mouth*, ch.14.

21 To a real anarchist a poke in the eye is better than a bunch of flowers. It makes him see stars.

> **1944** *The Horse's Mouth*, ch.16.

22 The only good government…is a bad one in a hell of a fright.

> **1944** *The Horse's Mouth*, ch.32.

23 It is the tragedy of the world that no one knows what he doesn't know; and the less a man knows, the more sure he is that he knows everything.

> **1958** *Art and Reality*, introduction.

Casal, Julián del 1863–93

Cuban poet, forerunner of the *modernista* movement, influenced by Baudelaire and the Parnassian poets. He was a chronic invalid and frequently took a morbid view of life.

24 *Tengo el impuro amor de las ciudades,*
y a este sol que ilumina las edades
prefiero yo del gas las claridades.

I have an impure love for cities,
and I prefer the light coming from gaslamps
rather than this sun that lights the ages.

> **1893** *Bustos y rimas*, 'En el campo' ('In the Countryside').

Casals, Pablo 1876–1973

Spanish cellist, conductor and composer. In 1936 he emigrated because of the Civil War.

25 The most perfect technique is that which is not noticed at all.

> Quoted in Julian Lloyd Webber *The Song of the Birds* (1985).

Cassini, Oleg Lolewski 1913–

French-born US fashion designer, raised in Italy.

26 I imagined her as an ancient Egyptian princess.

> **1987** On designing for Jacqueline Kennedy as First Lady. *In My Own Fashion*.

27 Fashion anticipates, and elegance is a state of mind.

> **1987** *In My Own Fashion*.

Casson, Sir Hugh Maxwell 1910–

English architect and artist, Director of Architecture for the Festival of Britain (1948–51). His works include a series, *Hugh Casson's London* (1983), *Oxford* (1988) and *Cambridge* (1992).

28 Architecture cannot be understood without some knowledge of the society it serves.

> **1948** *An Introduction to Victorian Architecture*.

29 The Victorians expected every building, like every painting, to tell a story, and preferably to point to a moral as well.

> **1948** *An Introduction to Victorian Architecture*.

Castle, Ted (Edward Cyril, Baron Castle of Islington) 1907–79

English journalist, Assistant Editor (1944–50) and Editor (1951–2) of *Picture Post*.

30 In Place of Strife.

1969 Title of a White Paper on industrial relations, 17 Jan, suggested by Castle to his wife Barbara Castle, Secretary of State for Employment and Productivity.

Castro (Ruz), Fidel 1927–

Cuban revolutionary. He landed in Cuba in 1956 with a small band of insurgents. In 1958 Batista was forced to flee and Castro became Prime Minister (1959–76) and President (1976–), instituting a Marxist–Leninist programme.

31 *La historia me absolverá.*

History will absolve me.

1953 Title of propaganda pamphlet.

32 We are not politicians. We made our revolution to get the politicians out.

1961 Speech on assuming the presidency, two years after overthrowing the Batista regime.

33 A man who does not believe in human beings is not a revolutionary.

1967 Speech, 29 Jan.

34 I was a man lucky enough to have discovered a political theory, a man who was caught up in the whirlpool of Cuba's political crisis long before becoming a fully-fledged communist. Discovering Marxism was like finding a map in a forest.

1971 Speech, Chile, 18 Nov.

Caswall, Edward 1814–78

English hymnwriter and translator.

35 Jesu, the very thought of Thee
With sweetness fills the breast.

1849 *Hymns and Poems*, 'Jesu, the Very Thought of Thee' (a translation from 12c Latin, often attributed to St Bernard).

36 When morning gilds the skies.

1854 Title and first line of hymn.

37 See amid the winter's snow,
Born for us on earth below,
See, the Lamb of God appears,
Promised from eternal years!

Hail thou ever-blessèd morn!
Hail, redemption's happy dawn!
Sing through all Jerusalem:
Christ is born in Bethlehem!

1858 'See Amid the Winter's Snow'.

Cather, Willa Sibert 1873–1947

US novelist, poet and journalist. Her best-known books are the trilogy on pioneering life, *O Pioneers!* (1913), *The Song of the Lark* (1915) and *My Antonia* (1918).

38 The history of every country begins in the heart of a man or a woman.

1913 *O Pioneers!*, pt.1, ch.5.

39 Isn't it queer: there are only two or three human stories, and they go on repeating themselves as fiercely as if they had never happened before; like the larks in this country, that have been singing the same five notes over for thousands of years.

1913 *O Pioneers!*, p.2, ch.4.

40 I like trees because they seem more resigned to the way they have to live than other things do.

1913 *O Pioneers!*, pt.2, ch.8.

41 Artistic growth is, more than it is anything else, a refining of the sense of truthfulness.

1915 *The Song of the Lark*, pt.6, ch.11.

42 Winter lies too long in country towns; hangs on until it is stale and shabby, old and sullen.

1918 *My Antonia*, bk.2, ch.7.

43 The dead might as well speak to the living as the old to the young.

1922 *One of Ours*, bk.2, ch.6.

44 When it has left a place where we have always found it, it is like shipwreck; we drop from security into something malevolent and bottomless.

1926 Of kindness. *My Mortal Enemy*.

45 Oh, the Germans classify, but the French arrange.

1927 *Death Comes to the Archbishop*, prologue.

46 The irregular and intimate quality of things made entirely by the human hand.

1927 *Death Comes to the Archbishop*, bk.1, ch.3.

47 Most of the basic material a writer works with is acquired before the age of fifteen.

Quoted in René Rapin *Willa Cather* (1930).

48 Only solitary men know the full joys of friendship. Others have their family—but to a solitary and an exile his friends are everything.

1931 *Shadows On The Rock*, bk.3, ch.5.

49 Religion and art spring from the same root and are close kin. Economics and art are strangers.

1936 In *Commonweal*, 17 Apr.

50 Every fine story must leave in the mind of the sensitive reader an intangible residuum of pleasure, a cadence, a quality of voice that is exclusively the writer's own, individual, unique.

1936 *Not Under Forty*, 'Miss Jewett'.

Catiline full name *Lucius Sergius Catilina* c.108–62 BC

Roman conspirator, from an obscure senatorial family. In 63 BC, he plotted to murder Cicero and other hostile senators, and to seize power, but was arrested and executed.

51 *Idem velle atque idem nolle, ea demum firma*
amicitia est.

Agreements in likes and dislikes—this, and only
this is what constitutes true friendship.
Quoted in Sallust *De Catilinae coniuratione*, bk.20, pt.4
(translated by J C Rolfe).

Cato full name *Marcus Porcius Cato* (known as 'the Elder' or 'the Censor') 234–149 BC

Roman statesman and orator, renowned for his strict
morality and conservatism. Appointed *censor* in 184 BC,
he discharged his duties rigorously. He was sent on a
mission to Carthage in 175 BC.

52 All mankind rules its women, and we rule all
mankind, but our women rule us.
Criticizing the prevalent domination of women. Quoted (in
Greek) in Plutarch *Regum et imperatorum apophthegmata*,
pt.198d (translated by F C Babbitt).

53 *Orator vir bonus dicendi peritus.*

An orator is a good man, skilled in speaking.
Quoted in Quintilian *Institutio Oratoria*, bk.12, pt.1, section 1
(translated by H E Butler).

54 *Rem tene, verba sequentur.*

Stick to your subject, and words will follow.
Attributed advice to orators. Quoted in Gaius Julius Victor *Ars
Rhetorica*, 'De inventione'.

55 *Delenda est Carthago.*

Carthage must be destroyed.
Attributed. Quoted in Florus *Epitome*, bk.1, pt.31 ('Cato
inexpiabili odio delendam esse Carthaginem, et cum de alio
consuleretur, pronuntiabat') and Pliny *Naturalis Historia*, bk.15,
ch.74.

Cattell, Raymond Bernard 1905–

British psychologist, designer of intelligence and
personality tests. Associated with the eugenics movement
in the 1930s, he believed that the large size and low IQs of
lower-class families would undermine the nation's
intellect.

56 The Fight for our National Intelligence.
1937 Title of book.

Catto, Henry Edward 1930–

US government official, chief of protocol at the White
House (1974–6) and Ambassador to the UN (1976–7)
and the UK (1989–91).

57 Like being the captain of a mine-sweeper, if you do
your job well, nobody notices. If you don't, there's a
hell of an explosion.
1988 On his role as chief of protocol. In the *Washington Post*,
22 Mar.

Catullus full name *Gaius Valerius Catullus*
c.84–c.54 BC

Latin poet, mainly known for his passionate love poems
for Lesbia. Her true name was Clodia, and she was
probably the sister of Cicero's enemy P Clodius Pulcher.

58 *Cui dono lepidum novum libellum*
arida modo pumice expolitum?
Corneli, tibi.

Who shall I give my nice new little book to,
my little book polished with dry pumice? To you,
Cornelius.
Dedication to Cornelius Nepos, the biographer.
Carmina, no.1, l.1–3.

59 *Vivamus, mea Lesbia, atque amemus,*
rumoresque senum severiorum
omnes unius aestimemus assis.

Let us live, my Lesbia, and let us love!
Let us not give one penny if old men
protest and disapprove.
Carmina, no.5, l.1–3.
▷ See Campion 228:35.

60 *Quaeris, quot mihi basiationes*
tuae, Lesbia, sint satis superque?

You ask me, Lesbia, how many kisses
it will take to make me fully satisfied?
Carmina, no.7, l.1-2.

61 *Nam risu inepto res ineptior nulla est.*

For there is nothing more ridiculous than a
ridiculous laugh.
Carmina, no.39.

62 *Ille mi par esse Deo videtur,*
ille, si fas est, superare Divos,
qui sedens adversus identidem te
*   spectat et audit*
dulce ridentem.

He seems to me to be like a god,
even superior to the Gods, if it is
permitted to say so, the man who sits
gazing on you all day and listens to
your sweet laughter.
Carmina, no.51, l.1–5.

63 *Otium et reges prius et beatas*
*   perdidit urbes.*

Often has leisure ruined great kings and fine cities.
Carmina, no.51, l.15–16.

64 *Odi et amo. quare id faciam, fortasse requiris.*
nescio sed fieri sentio et excrucior.

I hate and I love. You ask me to explain, perhaps.
I don't know. But I feel it happen and the pain is
dreadful.
Carmina, no.85.

Causley, Charles 1917–

English poet of verse for adults and children, much of it set in his native Cornwall.

65 You must take off your clothes for the doctor
And stand as straight as a pin,
His hand of stone on your white breastbone
Where the bullets all go in.
1953 'Recruiting Drive'.

66 Timothy Winters comes to school
With eyes as wide as a football pool,
Ears like bombs and teeth like splinters:
A blitz of a boy is Timothy Winters.
1957 'Timothy Winters'.

67 Who is the smiling stranger
With hair as white as gin,
What is he doing with the children
And who could have let him in?
1961 'Innocent's Song'.

Cavafy, Constantine pseudonym of Konstantínos Pétron Kaváfis 1863–1933

Egyptian-born Greek poet who spent much of his life working as a civil servant in Alexandria. Most of his work was published posthumously, including in English translation *Poems* (1951) and *Complete Poems* (1961).

68 And now, what will become of us without any
barbarians?
Those people were a kind of solution.
1904 'Waiting for the Barbarians' (translated by E Keeley and P Sherrard).

69 Have Ithaka always in your mind
Your arrival there is what you are destined for.
1911 'Ithaka' (translated by E Keeley and P Sherrard).

70 New places you will not find, you will not find
another sea
The city will follow you.
1911 'The Town' (translated by E Keeley and P Sherrard).

Cavell, Edith Louisa 1865–1915

English nurse, matron of a Red Cross hospital in Brussels during World War I. She was arrested by the Germans in 1915, charged with helping Allied soldiers escape to Holland, and executed when she did not deny the charges.

71 Standing, as I do, in view of God and eternity, I
realize that patriotism is not enough. I must have
no hatred or bitterness towards anyone.
1915 On the eve of her execution. Reported in *The Times*, 23 Oct.

Cavendish, Margaret, Duchess of Newcastle 1624–74

English writer and playwright. She was a maid of honour at the court of Charles I, and married the Duke of Newcastle in 1645. They lived in exile in Europe during the Civil War.

72 Marriage is the grave or tomb of wit.
1662 *Plays*, 'Nature's Three Daughters', pt.2, act 5, sc.20.

73 If Nature had not befriended us with beauty, and
other good graces, to help us to insinuate our selves
into men's affections, we should have been more
enslaved than any other of Nature's creatures she
hath made.
1664 *Sociable Letters*.

Cecil, Lord (Edward Christian) David Gascoyne 1902–86

English literary critic and essayist, Professor of English Literature at Oxford (1948-70) and a respected literary biographer. His traditional approach to literary criticism earned him the scorn of F R Leavis.

74 It does not matter that Dickens's world is not life-
like; it is alive.
1934 *Early Victorian Novelists*.

75 The primary object of a student of literature is to
be delighted.
1949 *Reading as One of the Fine Arts*.

76 Funny you should ask. As a matter of fact I did
have a light temperature when I set out.
Response to a Berlin nightclubber's ambiguous question, 'Sind Sie normal?'. Quoted in Jonathan Keates 'The Delightful Lord David', in the *Times Literary Supplement*, 1 Mar 1991. Keates also describes how Cecil had confessed that, had he visited Sodom and Gomorrah, he would probably only have noticed the cathedral.

Cecil, Robert Arthur James Gascoyne, 5th Marquis of Salisbury 1893–1972

English Conservative statesman. Opposition Leader in the Lords (1945–51), he became Secretary of State for Commonwealth Relations in Churchill's Government and Leader of the Lords (1951–7).

77 The Colonial Secretary [Iain Macleod] has been too
clever by half. I believe that he is a very fine bridge
player. It is not considered immoral, or even bad
form, to outwit one's opponent at bridge. It almost
seems to me as if the Colonial Secretary, when he
abandoned the sphere of bridge for the sphere of
politics, brought his bridge technique with him.
1961 Speech, House of Lords.

Cecil, Robert Arthur Talbot Gascoyne, 3rd Marquis of Salisbury 1830–1903

English Conservative statesman and three times Prime Minister (1885–6, 1886–92, 1895–1902), often serving as his own Foreign Secretary. He remained as head of government during the Boer War (1899–1902), and then retired.

78 Peace without honour is not only a disgrace, but, except as a temporary respite, it is a chimera.
1864 In the *Quarterly Review*, Apr.

79 Under a more heroic Minister, and in a less self-seeking age, it is probable that England would have preferred the risk, whatever its extent, to the infamy of betraying an ally whom she had enticed into peril. But our Ministry is not heroic; and our generation, though not indifferent to glory, prefers it when it is safe and cheap.
1864 On Palmerston's failure to defend Denmark against Prussia, in the *Quarterly Review*, Jul.

80 Horny-handed sons of toil.
1873 In the *Quarterly Review*, Oct.

81 English policy is to float lazily downstream, occasionally putting out a diplomatic boathook to avoid collisions.
1877 Letter to Lord Lytton, 9 Mar.

82 The commonest error in politics is sticking to the carcasses of old policies.
1877 Speech, Hatfield, 25 May.

83 Randolph and the Mahdi have occupied my thoughts about equally. The Mahdi pretends to be half mad, but is very sane in reality. Randolph occupies exactly the converse position.
1884 Of Lord Randolph Churchill. Letter to Lady John Manners, May.

84 We are part of the community of Europe, and we must do our duty as such.
1888 Speech, Caernarvon, 10 Apr.

85 It is a superstition of an antiquated diplomacy that there is any necessary antagonism between Russia and Great Britain.
1896 Speech, London Guildhall, 9 Nov.

Céline, Louis-Ferdinand pseudonym of *Louis Ferdinand Destouches* 1894–1961

French novelist, author of *Journey to the End of Night* (1932), and other misanthropic works. He wrote anti-Semitic tracts before World War II and collaborated with the Germans. He escaped to Denmark after the war, but returned to France in 1951.

86 *Entre le pénis et les mathématiques…il n'existe rien. Rien!*

Between the penis and mathematics…there's nothing. Nothing!
1932 *Voyage au bout de la nuit* (*Journey to the End of Night*, translated by John H P Marks, 1960).

87 *Voyager, c'est bien utile, ça fait travailler l'imagination. Tout le reste n'est que déceptions et fatigues. Notre voyage à nous est entièrement imaginaire. Voilà sa force.*

To travel is useful. It engages the imagination. Everything else is deceitful and boring. Our own voyage is entirely imaginary. And therein lies its force.
1932 *Voyage au bout de la nuit* (*Journey to the End of Night*, translated by John H P Marks, 1960).

88 *Quand on a pas d'imagination, mourir c'est peu de chose, quand on en a, mourir c'est trop.*

For those who have no imagination, death means little. For those who have one, death is often too much.
1932 *Voyage au bout de la nuit* (*Journey to the End of Night*, translated by John H P Marks, 1960).

89 *C'est l'actuel qui compte. Invoquer sa postérité, c'est faire un discours aux asticots.*

It is the present that counts. To invoke one's posterity is to make a speech to maggots.
1932 *Voyage au bout de la nuit* (*Journey to the End of Night*, translated by John H P Marks, 1960).

90 *La plupart des gens ne meurent qu'au dernier moment; d'autres commencent et s'y prennent vingt ans d'avance et parfois davantage. Ce sont les malheureux de la terre.*

Most people only die at the last moment; others begin early and take twenty years and sometimes more. These are the most miserable people on earth.
1932 *Voyage au bout de la nuit* (*Journey to the End of Night*, translated by John H P Marks, 1960).

91 *Des pauvres, c'est-à-dire des gens dont la mort n'intéresse personne.*

The poor—that is, the people whose death interests no one.
1932 *Voyage au bout de la nuit* (*Journey to the End of Night*, translated by John H P Marks, 1960).

92 *Les Anglais, c'est drôle quand même comme dégaine, c'est mi-curé, mi-garçonnet.*

The English are funny and peculiar, half-clergymen and half-little boys.
1936 *Mort à crédit*.

Cellini, Benvenuto 1500–71

Italian goldsmith and sculptor, known for his autobiography as much as for his art.

93 A painting is merely the image of a tree, a man, or any other object reflected in a fountain. The difference between a painting and sculpture is the difference between a shadow and the thing which casts it.
1547 Letter to Benedetto Varchi.

Cennini, Cennino c.1370–c.1440

Florentine painter and writer, best remembered for his *Il Libro dell'Arte*, a practical guide for the art student.

94 Do not fail, as you go on, to draw something every day, for no matter how little it is it will be well worth while, and it will do you a world of good.
c.1400 *Il Libro dell'Arte* (The Craftsman's Handbook).

95 There is another cause which, if you indulge it, can make your hand so unsteady that it will waver more, and flutter far more, than leaves do in the wind, and this is indulging too much in the company of women.
c.1400 *Il Libro dell'Arte* (The Craftsman's Handbook).

Cervantes, Miguel de 1547–1616

Spanish writer, best known for his novel *Don Quixote* (in two parts 1605, 1615), the first part of which is thought to have been written in prison in La Mancha. Other works include *La Galatea* (1585), a pastoral romance, and many plays, only two of which survive.

96 *La mejor salsa del mundo es el hambre.*

Hunger is the best sauce in the world.
1615 *Don Quixote*, pt.2, ch.5.

97 *El pan comido y la compañia deshecha.*

With the bread eaten, the company breaks up.
1615 *Don Quixote*, pt.2, ch.7.

98 Well, now, there's a remedy for everything except death.
1615 *Don Quixote*, pt.2, ch.10.

99 *Dos linajes sólo hay en el mundo, como decía una abuela mía, que son el tener y el no tener.*

There are but two families in the world, as my grandmother used to say—the Haves and the Havenots.
1615 *Don Quixote*, pt.2, ch.20.

1 *Digo, paciencia y barajar.*

What I say is, patience, and shuffle the cards.
1615 *Don Quixote*, pt.2, ch.23.

Césaire, Aimé Fernand 1913–

Caribbean poet known for his visionary, surrealist style and as a Marxist and anti-colonialist.

2 *Ma bouche sera la bouche des malheurs qui n'ont point de bouche, ma voix, la liberté de celles qui s'affaissent au cachot du désespoir.*

My voice will be the voice of those who suffer and have no voice. My voice, the freedom of those weakened in the dungeon of despair.
1939 *Cahier d'un retour au pays natal.*

3 *Je vois l'Afrique multiple et une verticale dans la tumultueuse péripétie avec ses bourrelets, ses nodules,*

un peu à part, mais à portée du siècle, comme un coeur de réserve.

I see several Africas and one vertical in the tumultuous event with its screens and nodules, a little separated, but within the century, like a heart in reserve.
1960 *Ferrements*, 'Pour saluer le Tiers-Monde'.

Cézanne, Paul 1839–1906

French Post-Impressionist painter, a friend of Zola who persuaded him to go to Paris to paint in 1862. His paintings foreshadow Cubism, emphasizing underlying forms with glowing colours.

4 May I repeat what I told you here: treat nature by the cylinder, the sphere, the cone, everything in perspective.
1904 Letter to Emile Bernard, 15 Apr.

5 The Louvre is the book in which we learn to read.
1905 Letter to Emile Bernard.

6 Monet is only an eye, but my God what an eye!
Attributed, in conversation with Ambroise Vollard. Quoted in Cooper *Claude Monet* (1957).

7 I wished to copy nature but I could not. But I was satisfied when I discovered that the sun could not be reproduced but that it must be represented by something else—colour.
Quoted in D Hooker (ed) *Art of the Western World* (1989).

Ch'in Chia c.150 BC

Chinese poet and civil servant about whom very little is known. He wrote a series of three poems on his separation from his wife, the result of a posting to Beijing.

8 I sent a carriage to bring you back
But it went empty, and empty it returned.
c.150 BC 'To My Wife 1', collected in *A Book of Chinese Verse* (translated by N L Smith and R H Kotewall).

9 Sorrow comes as in a circle
And cannot be rolled up like a map.
c.150 BC 'To My Wife 2', collected in *A Book of Chinese Verse* (translated by N L Smith and R H Kotewall).

10 One separation breeds ten thousand regrets.
c.150 BC 'To My Wife 2', collected in *A Book of Chinese Verse* (translated by N L Smith and R H Kotewall).

Chalmers, Patrick Reginald 1872–1942

English writer and banker, an authority on field sports.

11 What's lost upon the roundabouts we pulls up on the swings!
1912 *Green Days and Blue Days*, 'Roundabouts and Swings'.

Chamberlain, Sir (Joseph) Austen

1863–1937

English Conservative politician, successively Chancellor of the Exchequer, Secretary for India, Unionist leader, Foreign Secretary and First Lord of the Admiralty. He received the 1925 Nobel Peace Prize for negotiating the Locarno Pact.

12 I yield to no one in my devotion to this great League of Nations, but not even for this will I destroy that smaller but older league of which my own country was the birthplace, and of which it remains the centre… Beware how you so draw tight the bonds, how you so pile obligation on obligation and sanction on sanction, lest at last you find that you are not living nations but dead states.

1927 Speech, League of Nations Assembly, Geneva, 9 Sep.

Chamberlain, Joseph 1836–1914

English Liberal politician. He was President of the Board of Trade, but resigned over Gladstone's Home Rule bill (1880). Leader of the Liberal Unionists from 1889, he was also Secretary of State for the Colonies (1895), and retired in 1903.

13 Lord Salisbury constitutes himself the spokesman of a class, of the class to which he himself belongs, who 'toil not neither do they spin'.

1883 Speech, 30 Mar.

14 Provided that the City of London remains, as it is at present, the clearing-house of the world, any other nation may be its workshop.

1904 Speech at the Guildhall, 19 Jan.

15 The day of small nations has passed away. The day of Empires has come.

1904 Speech at Birmingham, 12 May, advocating preferential trade within the British Empire as a means of ensuring Britain's security.

Chamberlain, (Arthur) Neville 1869–1940

English politician, who played a leading part in the formation of the National Government (1931). As Prime Minister (1937–40) he advocated appeasement of Italy and Germany. He resigned as a result of criticism of his war leadership.

16 In war, whichever side may call itself the victor, there are no winners, but all are losers.

1938 Speech at Kettering, 3 Jul.

17 How horrible, fantastic, incredible it is that we should be digging trenches and trying on gas-masks here because of a quarrel in a far away country between people of whom we know nothing.

1938 Radio broadcast, 27 Sep, referring to Germany's annexation of the Sudetenland.

18 This morning I had another talk with the German Chancellor, Herr Hitler, and here is the paper that bears his name upon it as well as mine: 'We regard the agreement signed last night and the Anglo-German naval agreement, as symbolic of the desire of our two people never to go to war with one another again.'

1938 Speech on the signing of the Munich Agreement, Heston airport, 30 Sep.

19 My good friends, this is the second time in our history that there has come back from Germany to Downing Street peace with honour. I believe it is peace for our time. Go home and have a nice, quiet sleep.

1938 Speech from the window of No. 10 Downing Street to the crowds outside, 30 Sep, having returned that day from signing the Munich Agreement. The earlier peace referred to was the Treaty of Berlin which Beaconsfield brought back in 1878.

▷ See also Disraeli 333:23.

20 We should seek by all means in our power to avoid war, by analysing possible causes, by trying to remove them, by discussion in a spirit of collaboration and good will. I cannot believe that such a programme would be rejected by the people of this country, even if it does mean the establishment of personal contact with the dictators.

1938 Speech in the House of Commons, 6 Oct.

21 This morning, the British ambassador in Berlin handed the German Government a final note stating that, unless we heard from them by 11 o'clock, that they were prepared at once to withdraw their troops from Poland, a state of war would exist between us. I have to tell you that no such undertaking has been received, and that consequently this country is at war with Germany.

1939 Radio broadcast, 3 Sep.

22 Whatever may be the reason—whether it was that Hitler thought he might get away with what he had got without fighting for it, or whether it was that after all the preparations were not sufficiently complete—however, one thing is certain—he missed the bus.

1940 Speech at Central Hall, Westminster, 4 Apr.

Chamberlain, Wilt(on Norman) 1936–

US basketball player. Over seven feet tall, he set many individual scoring records.

23 Nobody roots for Goliath.

1967 Quoted in Colin Jarman *The Guinness Dictionary of Sports Quotations* (1990).

Chamfort, Sébastian-Roch Nicolas

1741–94

French writer. He joined the Jacobins at the outbreak of the French Revolution, but his remarks on the terror brought him into disfavour. Threatened with arrest, he attempted suicide, dying several days later.

24 *Guerre aux châteaux, paix aux chaumières.*

War to the castles, peace to the cottages.
1790 Motto for the Revolution.

25 Society is composed of two large classes; those who have more dinners than appetites, and those with more appetites than dinners.
Maximes et Pensées (published 1795), ch.1.

26 *Vivre est une maladie dont le sommeil nous soulage toutes les 16 heures. C'est un palliatif. La mort est le remède.*

Living is an illness to which sleep provides relief every 16 hours. It's a palliative. Death is the remedy.
Maximes et Pensées (published 1795), ch.2.

27 *Sois mon frère, ou je te tue.*

Be my brother, or I kill you.
His interpretation of the motto 'Fraternité ou la mort'. Quoted in P R Angus (ed) *Oeuvres Complètes* (1824), vol.1.

Chandler, Raymond 1888–1959

US crime writer, brought up in England. He returned to America and lived in California. He is best known for his creation of Philip Marlowe, a cynically philosophical, wise-cracking private detective whose career is closely involved with a series of beautiful and seductive *femmes fatales.*

28 I was neat, clean, shaved and sober, and I didn't care who knew it.
1939 Philip Marlowe. *The Big Sleep*, ch.1.

29 The General spoke again, slowly, using his strength as carefully as an out-of-work showgirl uses her last good pair of stockings.
1939 *The Big Sleep*, ch.2.

30 He looked about as inconspicuous as a tarantula on a slice of angel food.
1940 Of Moose Malloy. *Farewell, My Lovely*, ch.1.

31 It was a blonde. A blonde to make a bishop kick a hole in a stained glass window.
1940 *Farewell, My Lovely*, ch.13.

32 She gave me a smile I could feel in my hip pocket.
1940 *Farewell, My Lovely*, ch.18

33 Down these mean streets a man must go who is not himself mean, who is neither tarnished nor afraid.
1944 'The Simple Art of Murder'. In *Atlantic Monthly*, Dec.

34 The English may not always be the best writers in the world, but they are incomparably the best dull writers.
1944 'The Simple Art of Murder'. In *Atlantic Monthly*, Dec.

35 If my books had been any worse, I should not have been invited to Hollywood, and if they had been any better, I should not have come.
1945 Letter to Charles W Morton, 12 Dec.

36 Just don't get too complicated Eddie. When a guy gets too complicated he's unhappy. And when he's unhappy—his luck runs out.
1945 *The Blue Dahlia.*

37 Would you convey my compliments to the purist who reads your proofs and tell him or her that I write in a sort of broken-down patois which is something like the way a Swiss waiter talks, and that when I split an infinitive, God damn it, I split it so it will stay split.
1947 Letter to Edward Weeks at *Atlantic Monthly*, 18 Jan.

38 By the way, do you ever read the Bible? I suppose not very often, but I had occasion to the other night and believe me it is a lesson in how not to write for the movies. The worst kind of overwriting. Whole chapters that could have been said in one paragraph. And the dialogue!
1947 Letter to Edgar Carter, 28 Mar.

39 It wasn't exactly carelessness; her knowledge of literate English contained such vast areas of desert that she took it for granted that half of what she wrote would be meaningless to her.
1947 On the shortcomings of his ex-secretary. Letter to Erle Stanley Gardner, 1 Jul.

40 California, the department-store state. The most of everything and the best of nothing.
1949 *The Little Sister*, ch.13.

41 A big hard-boiled city with no more personality than a paper cup.
1949 Of Los Angeles. *The Little Sister*, ch.26.

42 It is pretty obvious that the debasement of the human mind caused by a constant flow of fraudulent advertising is no trivial thing. There is more than one way to conquer a country.
1951 Letter to Carl Barndt, 15 Nov.

43 Some people are better off dead—like your wife and my father for instance.
1951 Line delivered by Robert Walker as Bruno in the film *Strangers on a Train* (with Czenzi Ormonde), based on the novel by Patricia Highsmith.

44 A preoccupation with words for their own sake is fatal to good film-making. It's not what films are for.
1951 Chandler to Dale Warren, 7 Nov.

45 If people could deal with each other honestly, they would not need agents.
1952 'Ten Per Cent of Your Life', in *Atlantic Monthly*, Feb.

46 Alcohol is like love... The first kiss is magic, the second is intimate, the third is routine. After that you take the girl's clothes off.

1953 *The Long Good-Bye*, ch.4.

47 A dead man is the best fall guy in the world. He never talks back.

1953 *The Long Good-Bye*, ch.10.

48 By his standards anyone who noticed how many walls the room had would be observant.

1953 On an interviewer. Letter to Roger Machell, 15 Mar.

49 I suppose all writers are crazy, but if they are any good, I believe they have a terrible honesty.

1957 Letter to Edgar Carter, 3 Jun.

50 Dashiell Hammett took murder out of the Venetian vase and dropped it into the alley.

On the moving of murder mysteries from the English country house to more realistic areas. Quoted in *Contemporary Authors* (1979).

51 As elaborate a waste of human intelligence as you can find outside an advertising agency.

Of chess. Quoted in Colin Jarman *The Guinness Dictionary of Sports Quotations* (1990).

52 The streets were dark with something more than night.

Quoted in the *Smithsonian*, May 1994.

Chanel, Gabrielle known as *Coco* 1883–1971

French couturier. In the 1920s she came to prominence with designs notable for simple elegance and comfort, such as her 'chemise' dress and collarless cardigan jacket. She also developed a perfume, Chanel No.5.

53 Fashion is made to become unfashionable.

1957 In *Life*, 19 Aug.

54 Youth is something very new: twenty years ago no one mentioned it.

Quoted in Marcel Haedrich *Coco Chanel: Her Life, Her Secrets* (1972), ch.1 (translated by Charles Lam Markmann).

55 A fashion for the young? That is a pleonasm: there is no fashion for the old.

Quoted in Marcel Haedrich *Coco Chanel: Her Life, Her Secrets* (1972), ch.1 (translated by Charles Lam Markmann).

56 Nature gives you the face you have when you are twenty. Life shapes the face you have at thirty. But it is up to you to earn the face you have at fifty.

Quoted in Marcel Haedrich *Coco Chanel: Her Life, Her Secrets* (1972), ch.1 (translated by Charles Lam Markmann).

▷ See Orwell 745:63, Cartland 242:11.

57 Fashion is architecture: it is a matter of proportions.

Quoted in Marcel Haedrich *Coco Chanel: Her Life, Her Secrets* (1972), ch.1 (translated by Charles Lam Markmann).

58 You ask if they were happy. This is not a characteristic of a European. To be contented— that's for the cows.

Quoted in A Madsen *Coco Chanel* (1990), ch.35.

Channing, Carol Elaine 1921–

US comedienne. A star of US cabaret, she has made occasional appearances in films, notably in *Thoroughly Modern Millie* (1967).

59 Laughter is much more important than applause. Applause is almost a duty. Laughter is a reward. Laughter means they trust and like you.

Attributed.

60 I am terribly shy, but of course no one believes me. Come to think of it, neither would I.

Attributed.

Channon, Sir Henry 1897–1958

English Conservative politician. He became an MP in 1935, becoming a parliamentary private secretary in 1938. He kept a witty diary recording the political and society figures of the time.

61 This afternoon I slept for two hours in the Library of the House of Commons. A deep House of Commons sleep. There is no sleep to compare with it—rich, deep, and guilty.

Attributed.

62 I love the House of Commons so passionately that were I to be offered a peerage, I should be tempted to refuse it. Only tempted, of course.

Attributed.

Chao AD 168–89

Chinese poet. Little is known of him and only fragments of his poetry have survived.

63 Obsequiousness is glorified:
While honest worth must wait outside.

c.180 AD 'Poems of Disgust, no.1', collected in *A Golden Treasury of Chinese Poetry* (translated by John Turner, 1976).

Chaplin, Charlie (Sir Charles Spencer)
1889–1977

English film actor and director. He developed his skill in comedy under Fred Karno and moved to Hollywood in 1914. His early short comedies were extremely popular. His feature films included *Modern Times* (1936), *The Great Dictator* (1940) and *Limelight* (1952).

64 They are spoiling the oldest art in the world—the art of pantomime. They are ruining the great beauty of silence.

1929 Of the advent of talking pictures. Interview in *Motion Picture Magazine*, May.

65 All I need to make a comedy is a park, a policeman and a pretty girl.
   1964 *My Autobiography*, ch.10.

Chapman, Arthur 1873–1935

US poet and author, best known for his long poem *Out Where The West Begins* (1916).

66 Out where the handclasp's a little stronger,
   Out where the smile dwells a little longer,
   That's where the West begins.
   1916 *Out Where the West Begins*, stanza 1.

Chapman, (Anthony) Colin Bruce 1928–82

English motor racing manager, founder of the Lotus racing team.

67 Money is how we keep the score in motor racing nowadays.
   1974 Quoted in Colin Jarman *The Guinness Dictionary of Sports Quotations* (1990).

Chapman, George c.1559–1634

English dramatist, poet and translator. His plays include *The Blind Beggar of Alexandria* (1595) and *Bussy d'Ambois* (1607). In 1598 he wrote a continuation of Marlowe's unfinished *Hero and Leander*, and he made important translations of Homer (1598–1624).

68 Man is a torch borne in the wind; a dream
   But of a shadow, summed with all his substance.
   1607 *Bussy d'Ambois*, act 1, sc.1.

69 Who to himself is law, no law doth need,
   Offends no law, and is a king indeed.
   1607 *Bussy d'Ambois*, act 1, sc.1.

70 Perfect happiness, by princes sought,
   Is not with birth born, nor exchequers bought.
   1611 *The Iliads of Homer Prince of Poets*, 'Epistle Dedicatory'.

71 Fate's such a shrewish thing.
   1611 *The Iliads of Homer Prince of Poets*, bk.4, l.21.

72 We have watered our houses in Helicon.
   1611 *May-Day*, act 3, sc.3. This is sometimes misquoted as 'We have watered our horses in Helicon'.

73 A poem, whose subject is not truth, but things like truth.
   1613 *The Revenge of Bussy d'Ambois*, dedication.

74 Danger, the spur of all great minds.
   1613 *The Revenge of Bussy d'Ambois*, act 5, sc.1.

75 I know an Englishman
   Being flattered, is a lamb; threatened, a lion.
   Alphonsus, Emperor of Germany (published posthumously, 1654), act 1. Although this is credited to Chapman, his authorship is doubtful.

76 I am ashamed the law is such an ass.
   Revenge for Honour (published posthumously, 1654), act 3, sc.2. Although this is credited to Chapman, his authorship is doubtful.
   ▷ See Dickens 321:42.

Chapman, John 1900–

US theatre critic.

77 It is three and a half hours long, four characters wide, and a cesspool deep.
   1962 In the *New York Daily News*, 15 Oct, reviewing Edward Albee's *Who's Afraid of Virginia Woolf?*

Chardin, Jean-Baptiste-Siméon 1699–1779

French painter of genre scenes and still-life.

78 The man who has not realized the difficulty of art never does anything worthwhile; the man who realizes it too soon does nothing at all.
   1765 Quoted in Frank Elgar *Mondrian* (1968).

Chargaff, Erwin 1905–

Czech-born US biochemist. He settled at Columbia University in 1935, where his pioneering research on nucleic acids laid the foundations for modern molecular biology.

79 What counts…in science is to be not so much the first as the last.
   1971 In *Science*, vol.172.

Charles, Elizabeth 1828–96

British writer.

80 To know how to say what others only know how to think is what makes men poets or sages; and to dare to say what others only dare to think makes men martyrs or reformers—or both.
   Chronicle of the Schönberg-Cotta Family.

Charles I 1600–49

King of Scotland and England. His marriage to the Catholic French princess, Henrietta Maria, his expensive foreign wars and his high-handed treatment of Parliament (he dismissed three parliaments and ruled for 11 years without one) culminated in the Civil War and his execution.

81 A rule that may serve for a statesman, a courtier, or a lover—never make a defence or an apology before you be accused.
   1636 Letter to Lord Wentworth, 3 Sep.

82 I see all the birds are flown.
   1642 After his unsuccessful attempt to arrest the Five Members in the House of Commons, 4 Jan.

83 I tell you (and I pray God it be not laid to your charge) that I am the martyr of the people.
   1649 Speech upon the scaffold.

Charles II 1630–85

King of Scotland and England. Exiled during the Civil War, on the execution of his father Charles I (1649) he was proclaimed king in Edinburgh but was not recalled as king to England until 1660. His childless marriage produced a succession crisis and contributed to much political and religious tension.

84 Whereas, women's parts in plays have hitherto been acted by men in the habits of women…we do permit and give leave for the time to come that all women's parts be acted by women.

1662 Royal licence, sanctioning the appearance of actresses on the English stage.

85 Better than a play.

1670 Commenting on the debates in the House of Lords over the Divorce Bill. Quoted in A Bryant *King Charles II* (1931).

86 This is very true—for my words are my own, and my actions are my Ministers'.

Riposte to 'The King's Epitaph'.

▷ See Rochester 817:66.

87 Let not poor Nelly starve.

c.1685 Worrying on his deathbed about his mistress, Nell Gwynn. Quoted in Bishop Gilbert Burney *History of My Own Time* (1724), vol.1, bk.2.

Charles V 1500–58

Holy Roman Emperor (1519–58) and King of Spain (1516–56), founder of the Habsburg dynasty. His wars against France led to the formation of the Holy League against him. After numerous wars, he divided his Empire between his son and brother and retired to a monastery in Spain.

88 I came, I saw, God conquered.

1547 Attributed remark after the Battle of Muhlberg, 23 Apr.

▷ See also Caesar 225:87, John III Sobieski 522:30.

89 Remember, the prince is like a mirror exposed to the eyes of all his subjects who continually look to him as a pattern on which to model themselves, and who in consequence without much trouble discover his vices and virtues.

1555 *Instructions à Philippe II son Fils* (*Advice To His Son*, translated 1788). Quoted in G R Elton *Renaissance and Reformation, 1300–1648* (2nd edn, 1968), p.137.

90 To God I speak Spanish, to women Italian, to men French, and to my horse—German.

Attributed.

Charles, Prince of Wales 1948–

HRH The Prince of Wales, son of Elizabeth II.

91 What is proposed is like a monstrous carbuncle on the face of a much-loved and elegant friend.

1984 On the proposed extension to the National Gallery, London. Speech at the 150th anniversary of the Royal Institute of British Architects, 30 May.

Charlton, Sir Bobby (Robert) 1937–

English footballer. He won 106 caps for England and played in the victorious World Cup team of 1966.

92 Some people tell me that we professional players are soccer slaves. Well, if this is slavery, give me a life sentence.

1960 Quoted in Peter Ball and Phil Shaw *The Book of Football Quotations* (1989).

93 They know on the Continent that European football without the English is like a hot dog without the mustard.

1988 Quoted in Peter Ball and Phil Shaw *The Book of Football Quotations* (1989). There was at the time a European ban in force against English clubs.

Charlton, Jack (John) 1935–

English footballer, brother of Bobby Charlton. He played in the victorious World Cup team of 1966, and subsequently became manager of the Republic of Ireland team.

94 Soccer is a man's game; not an outing for mamby-pambies.

1967 *For Leeds and England.*

95 I have a little black book with two players in it, and if I get a chance to do them I will. I will make them suffer before I pack this game in. If I can kick them four years over the touch-line, I will.

1970 Remark to reporters, which led to severe trouble with the soccer authorities. Quoted in Colin Jarman *The Guinness Dictionary of Sports Quotations* (1990).

Charpak, Georges 1924–

French physicist, born in Poland. He was awarded the Nobel Prize for Physics in 1992.

96 I can buy a new pair of shoes this afternoon.

1992 On being awarded $1.2 million for his work on atom smashers. In the *Washington Post*, 15 Oct.

Chase, Edna Woolman 1877–1954

US fashion journalist, editor of *Vogue* (1914–52).

97 Fashion can be bought. Style one must possess.

1954 *Always in Vogue*, ch.12.

Chatwin, Bruce 1940–89

English travel writer and novelist. His travels in the Sudan, Patagonia and Australia converted him to nomadic asceticism. His prize-winning books are a mixture of documentary, fiction, anthropology and philosophy.

98 That will not bring back the things we love: the high, clear days and the blue icecaps on the mountains; the lines of white poplars fluttering in the wind, and the long white prayer flags… Nor shall we get back the smell of the beanfields; the sweet, resinous smell of deodar wood burning, or

the whiff of a snow leopard at 14,000 feet. Never.
Never. Never.
1980 Introduction to Robert Byron's *The Road to Oxiana*.

99 Being lost in Australia gives you a lovely feeling of
security.
1987 *The Songlines*, ch.10.

1 Tyranny sets up its own echo-chamber.
1988 *Utz*.

2 Like all self-possessed people, he was prey to doubt.
1989 *What Am I Doing Here*, 'Heavenly Horses'.

Chaucer, Geoffrey c.1345–1400

English poet. He served in the King's household,
travelling extensively on state business. Much influenced
by Boccaccio, his spirited and often humorous poetry
established the literary language of English. He lost his
offices in 1386 and fell on hard times, but in 1399 was
awarded a pension.

3 Ful craftier to pley she was
Than Athalus, that made the game
First of the ches, so was his name.
c.1370 *The Book of the Duchess*, l.662–4.

4 That lyf so short, the craft so long to lerne,
Th'assay so hard, so sharp the conquerynge.
c.1380 *The Parliament of Fowls*, l.1–2.

5 But love a womman that she woot it nought,
And she wol quyte it that thow shalt nat fele;
Unknowe, unkist, and lost, that is unsought.
c.1385 *Troilus and Criseyde*, bk.1, l.807–9.

6 So longe mote ye lyve, and alle proude,
Til crowes feet be growen under youre yë.
c.1385 *Troilus and Criseyde*, bk 2, l.402–3.

7 It is nought good a slepyng hound to wake.
c.1385 *Troilus and Criseyde*, bk.3, l.764.

8 For I have seyn of a ful misty morwe
Folowen ful ofte a myrie someris day.
c.1385 *Troilus and Criseyde*, bk.3, l.1060–1.

9 Right as an aspes leef she gan to quake.
c.1385 *Troilus and Criseyde*, bk.3, l.1200.

10 For of fortunes sharpe adversitee
The worst kynde of infortune is this,
A man to han ben in prosperitee,
And it remembren, whan it passed is.
c.1385 *Troilus and Criseyde*, bk.3, l.1625–8.

11 Oon ere it herde, at tother out it went.
c.1385 *Troilus and Criseyde*, bk.4, l.434.

12 For tyme ylost may nought recovered be.
c.1385 *Troilus and Criseyde*, bk.4, l.1283.

13 Ek gret effect men write in place lite;

Th'entente is al, and nat the lettres space.
c.1385 *Troilus and Criseyde*, bk.5, l.1629–30.

14 Go, litel bok, go, litel myn tragedye,
Ther God thi makere yet, er that he dye,
So sende myght to make in som comedye!
c.1385 *Troilus and Criseyde*, bk.5, l.1786–8.

15 And for ther is so gret diversite
In Englissh and in writing of oure tonge,
So prey I God that non myswrite the,
Ne the mysmetre for defaute of tonge.
And red wherso thow be, or elles songe,
That thow be understonde, God I biseche!
c.1385 *Troilus and Criseyde*, bk.5, l.1793–8.

16 Whan that Aprill with his shoures soote
The droghte of March hath perced to the roote.
1387 *Canterbury Tales*, 'General Prologue', l.1–2.

17 And smale foweles maken melodye,
That slepen al the nyght with open ye
(So priketh hem nature in hir corages);
Thanne longen folk to goon on pilgrimages.
1387 *Canterbury Tales*, 'General Prologue', l.9–12.

18 He loved chivalrie,
Trouthe and honour, fredom and curteisie.
1387 *Canterbury Tales*, 'General Prologue', l.45–6.

19 He was a verray, parfit gentil knyght.
1387 *Canterbury Tales*, 'General Prologue', l.72.

20 Ful weel she soong the service dyvyne,
Entuned in hir nose ful semely,
And Frenssh she spak ful faire and fetisly,
After the scole of Stratford atte Bowe,
For Frenssh of Parys was to hire unknowe.
1387 *Canterbury Tales*, 'General Prologue', l.122–6.

21 A Clerk ther was of Oxenford also,
That unto logyk hadde longe ygo.
As leene was his hors as is a rake.
1387 *Canterbury Tales*, 'General Prologue', l.285–7.

22 But al be that he was a philosophre,
Yet hadde he but litel gold in cofre.
1387 *Canterbury Tales*, 'General Prologue', l.298–9.

23 Nowher so bisy a man as he ther nas,
and yet he semed bisier than he was.
1387 *Canterbury Tales*, 'General Prologue', l.321–2.

24 And thries hadde she been at Jerusalem;
She hadde passed many a straunge strem;
At Rome she hadde been, and at Boloigne,
In Galice at Seint-Jame, and at Coloigne.
1387 *Canterbury Tales*, 'General Prologue', l.463–6.

25 If gold ruste, what shall iren do?
1387 *Canterbury Tales*, 'General Prologue', l.500.

26 But Cristes lore, and his apostles twelve,
He taughte, but first he folwed it him-selve.
1387 *Canterbury Tales*, 'General Prologue', l.527–8.

27 And therefore, at the kynges court, my brother,
Ech man for hymself, ther is noon oother.
1387 *Canterbury Tales*, 'The Knight's Tale'. l.1181–2.

28 Ther is no newe gyse that it nas old.
1387 *Canterbury Tales*, 'The Knight's Tale', l.1267.

29 The bisy larke, messager of day.
1387 *Canterbury Tales*, 'The Knight's Tale'. l.1491.

30 Pitee renneth soone in gentil herte.
1387 *Canterbury Tales*, 'The Knight's Tale', l.1761.

31 The smylere with the knyf under the cloke.
1387 *Canterbury Tales*, 'The Knight's Tale', l.1999.

32 What is this world? what asketh men to have?
Now with his love, now in his colde grave.
1387 *Canterbury Tales*, 'The Knight's Tale', l.2777–8.

33 This world nys but a thurghfare ful of wo,
And we been pilgrymes, passynge to and fro.
1387 *Canterbury Tales*, 'The Knight's Tale', l. 2847–8.

34 'The gretteste clerkes been noght wisest men.'
1387 *Canterbury Tales*, 'The Reeve's Tale', l.4054.

35 Yblessed be god that I have wedded fyve!
Welcome the sixte, whan that evere he shal.
1387 *Canterbury Tales*, 'The Wife of Bath's Prologue', l.44–5.

36 Crist wole we clayme of him oure gentilleesse,
Nat of oure eldres for hire old richesse.
1387 *Canterbury Tales*, 'The Wife of Bath's Tale', l.1117–8.

37 Love wol nat been constreyned by maistrye.
Whan maistrie comth, the God of Love anon
Beteth his wynges, and farewel he is gon!
1387 *Canterbury Tales*, 'The Franklin's Tale', l.764–6.

38 Wommen, of kynde, desiren libertee,
And nat to been constreyned as a thral;
And so doon men, if I sooth seyen shal.
1387 *Canterbury Tales*, 'The Franklin's Tale', l.768–70.

39 Til that the brighte sonne loste his hewe;
For th'orisonte hath reft the sonne his lyght;
This is as muche to seye as it was nyght!
1387 *Canterbury Tales*, 'The Franklin's Tale', l.1016–8.

40 Trouthe is the hyest thyng that man may kepe.
1387 *Canterbury Tales*, 'The Franklin's Tale', l.1479.

41 O wombe! O bely! O stynkyng cod
Fulfilled of dong and of corrupcioun!
1387 *Canterbury Tales*, 'The Pardoner's Tale', l.534–5.

42 'By God,' quod he, 'for pleynly, at a word,

Thy drasty rymyng is nat worth a toord!'
1387 *Canterbury Tales*, 'Sir Thopas', l.929–30.

43 What is bettre than gold? Jaspre. What is bettre
than jaspre? Wisedoom.
1387 *Canterbury Tales*, 'The Tale of Melibee', l.1106–7.

44 And what is bettre than wisedoom? Womman. And
What is bettre than a good womman? Nothyng.
1387 *Canterbury Tales*, 'The Tale of Melibee', l.1107–8.

45 His coomb was redder than the fyn coral,
And batailled as it were a castle wal;
His byle was blak, and as the jeet it shoon;
Lyk asure were his legges and his toon;
His nayles whitter than the lylye flour,
And lyk the burned gold was his colour.
1387 Of Chauntecleer. *Canterbury Tales*, 'The Nun's Priest's Tale,' l.2859–64.

46 Mordre wol out, that see we day by day.
1387 *Canterbury Tales*, 'The Nun's Priest's Tale', l.3052.

47 Thou shalt make castels thanne in Spayne,
And dreme of joye, all but in vayne.
The Romaunt of the Rose, l.2573. This translation of the *Roman de la Rose* has been attributed to Chaucer but it is thought now to be the work of several authors, including Chaucer.

Cheever, John William 1912–82

US short-story writer and novelist. He sold his first short story, 'Expelled', after being thrown out of school at the age of 17, and became a regular contributor to the *New Yorker*, writing lyrical tales of alcoholism, adultery and loss. His novels include *The Wapshot Chronicle* (1957) and *Falconer* (1977).

48 The city is old, out of step with the century, but age
only seems to have quickened its elements… Relics
from the past continually pierce the present. Some
dream of love survives the sandstone apartment
houses.
1934 Of Boston. Letter to Elizabeth Ames.

49 When the beginnings of self-destruction enter the
heart it seems no bigger than a grain of sand.
1952 Collected in *The Journals*, 'The Late Forties and Fifties'.

50 Wisdom we know is the knowledge of good and
evil—not the strength to choose between the
two.
1956 Collected in *The Journals*, 'The Late Forties and Fifties'.

51 Neither you nor I nor anyone else can describe the
volcanic landscapes a poor girl strays into when she
marries a literary man.
1965 Letter to Frederick Exley, 16 Jun.

52 A lonely man is a lonesome thing, a stone, a bone, a
stick, a receptacle for Gilbey's gin, a stooped figure

sitting at the edge of a hotel bed, heaving copious sighs like the autumn wind.

1966 Collected in *The Journals*, 'The Sixties'.

53 We travel by plane, oftener than not, and yet the spirit of our country seems to have remained a country of railroads.

1969 On the US. *Bullet Park*, pt.1, ch.1.

54 My veins are filled once a week with a Neapolitan carpet cleaner distilled from the Adriatic and I am as bald as an egg. However I still get around and am mean to cats.

1982 On his cancer treatment. Letter to Philip Roth, 10 May.

55 Yevtushenko has…an ego that can crack crystal at a distance of 20 feet.

Recalled on Cheever's death, 18 Jun 1982.

56 Trust your editor, and you'll sleep on straw.

Favourite axiom, quoted in Susan Cheever *Home Before Dark* (1984).

Chekhov, Anton 1860–1904

Russian playwright and short-story writer. His first play, *The Seagull* (1896), failed initially but was revived in Moscow in 1898. Others include *Uncle Vanya* (1897), *The Three Sisters* (1901) and *The Cherry Orchard* (1904).

57 Brevity is the sister of talent.

1889 Letter to Alexander Chekhov, 11 Apr.

58 MEDVEDENKO: Why do you wear black all the time? MASHA: I'm in mourning for my life.

1896 *The Seagull*, act 1.

59 Women can't forgive failure.

1896 *The Seagull*, act 2.

60 The chief thing, my dear fellows, is to play it simply, without any theatricality: just very simply. Remember that they are all ordinary people.

1896 Attributed advice to actors, during a rehearsal of *The Seagull*.

61 A woman can become a man's friend only in the following stages—first an acquaintance, next a mistress, and only then a friend.

1897 *Uncle Vanya*, act 2.

62 When a woman isn't beautiful, people always say, 'You have lovely eyes, you have lovely hair.'

1897 *Uncle Vanya*, act 3.

63 If a lot of cures are suggested for a disease, it means that the disease is incurable.

1904 *The Cherry Orchard*, act 1 (translated by Elisaveta Fen).

64 To begin to live in the present, we must first atone for our past and be finished with it, and we can only atone for it by suffering, by extraordinary, unceasing exertion.

1904 *The Cherry Orchard*, act 2 (translated by Elisaveta Fen).

Chelmsford, Frederick John Napier Thesiger, 1st Viscount 1868–1933

English colonial administrator, Governor of Queensland (1905–9) and of New South Wales (1909–13), Viceroy of India (1916–21) and First Lord of the Admiralty (1924).

65 We have here an educated class 95 per cent of whom hate us.

1918 Of the situation in India. Letter to George V.

Chereskin, Alvin 1928–

US advertising executive, founder and president of AC&R Advertising (later affiliated with Saatchi & Saatchi).

66 Sex! What is that but *life*, after all? We're all of us selling sex, because we're all selling life.

1986 In the *New Yorker*, 15 Sep.

Chernow, Ron 1949–

US journalist, a columnist with *The Wall Street Journal* (1990–).

67 Capitalism requires people to be pious souls in the workplace, wild pagans at the cash register.

1993 In *The Wall Street Journal*, 31 Aug.

Cherry-Garrard, Apsley 1886–1959

Polar explorer and a member of Scott's last expedition. His group found the bodies of Scott and his companions in 1912.

68 At once the cleanest and most isolated way of having a bad time which has ever been devised.

1952 Of polar exploration. Recalled in *The Worst Journey in the World*.

Chesnut, Mary Boykin Miller 1823–86

US diarist, daughter of a South Carolina senator and wife of the heir to a large plantation. Her diary of the Civil War, *A Diary from Dixie*, was published in 1905.

69 Mrs. Stowe did not hit the sorest spot. She makes Legree a bachelor.

1861 Diary entry, 26 Aug, recording the conversation of a group of southern white women on the subject of men and slavery. The reference is to the principal slaveholder in Harriet Beecher Stowe's *Uncle Tom's Cabin*.

Chesnutt, Charles Waddell 1858–1932

US writer, the first black fiction writer to gain national acclaim when his stories were published in the *Atlantic Monthly* in the 1880s. He also wrote a biography of Frederick Douglass (1899).

70 Those who set in motion the forces of evil cannot always control them afterwards.

1901 *The Marrow of Tradition*, ch.35.

Chesterfield, Philip Dormer Stanhope, 4th Earl of 1694–1773

English statesman and orator, a member of the Pelham ministry (1744), Irish Lord-Lieutenant (1745) and Secretary of State (1746–8). His *Letters to his Son* (published 1774) are a worldly guide to manners and success.

71 The difference in this case between a man of sense and a fop, is, that the fop values himself upon his dress; the man of sense laughs at it, at the same time that he knows he must not neglect it.
1745 Letter to his son, 19 Nov.

72 Whatever is worth doing at all is worth doing well.
1746 Letter to his son, 10 Mar.

73 An injury is much sooner forgotten than an insult.
1746 Letter to his son, 9 Oct.

74 I recommend you to take care of the minutes, for hours will take care of themselves.
1747 Letter to his son, 6 Nov.

75 Advice is seldom welcome; and those who want it the most always like it the least.
1748 Letter to his son, 29 Jan.

76 Wear your learning, like your watch in a private pocket: and do not merely pull it out and strike it, merely to show that you have one.
1748 Letter to his son, 22 Feb.

77 There is nothing so illiberal and so ill-bred, as audible laughter.
1748 Letter to his son, 9 Mar.

78 It must be owned, that the Graces do not seem to be natives of Great Britain; and I doubt, the best of us here have more of rough than polished diamond.
1748 Letter to his son, 11 Nov.

79 Style is the dress of thoughts.
1749 Letter to his son, 24 Nov.

80 Fashion is more tyrannical at Paris than in any other place in the world; it governs even more absolutely than their king, which is saying a great deal. The least revolt against it is punished by proscription. You must observe and conform to all the minutiae of it, if you will be in fashion there yourself; and if you are not in fashion, you are nobody.
1750 Letter to his son, 30 Apr.

81 The chapter of knowledge is very short, but the chapter of accidents is a very long one.
1753 Letter to Solomon Dayrolles, 16 Feb.

82 In matters of religion and matrimony I never give any advice; because I will not have anybody's

torments in this world or the next laid to my charge.
1765 Letter to Arthur Charles Stanhope, 12 Oct.

83 In case my godson Philip Stanhope shall at anytime keep or be concerned in keeping any racehorse or pack of hounds, or reside one night at Newmarket, that infamous seminary of iniquity and ill-manners, during the course of the races there, or shall resort to the said races or shall lose in one day at any game or bet whatsoever the sum of £500 then in any of the cases aforesaid it is my express will that he, my said godson, shall forfeit and pay out of my estate the sum of £50,000 to and for the use of the Dean and Chapter of Westminster.
1773 Clause in his will.

84 David, you are an actor everywhere but upon the stage.
Attributed, in conversation with the actor David Garrick.

85 The pleasure is momentary, the position ridiculous, and the expense damnable.
Of sex. Attributed.

Chesterton, G(ilbert) K(eith) 1874–1936

English critic, novelist and poet, one of the most colourful and provocative writers of his day. His amiable detective-priest Father Brown first appeared in *The Innocence of Father Brown* (1911). Many of his essays and articles were published in his own *G. K.'s Weekly*.

86 I share all your antipathy to the noisy Plebeian excursionist. A visit to Ramsgate during the season and the vision of the crowded, howling sands has left in me feelings which all my Radicalism cannot allay. At the same time I think that the lower orders are seen unfavourably when enjoying themselves. In labour and trouble they are more dignified and less noisy.
1891 Letter to E C Bentley. Collected in Maisie Ward *Gilbert Keith Chesterton* (1943).

87 With monstrous head and sickening cry
And ears like errant wings,
The devil's walking parody
Of all four-footed things.
1900 'The Donkey'.

88 Fools! For I also had my hour;
One far fierce hour and sweet:
There was a shout about my ears,
And palms before my feet.
1900 'The Donkey'.

89 Literature is a luxury; fiction is a necessity.
1901 *The Defendant*, 'Defence of Penny Dreadfuls'.

90 All slang is metaphor, and all metaphor is poetry.
1901 *The Defendant*, 'Defence of Slang'.

91 'My country right or wrong', is a thing that no patriot would think of saying except in a desperate case. It is like saying, 'My mother, drunk or sober'.
1901 *The Defendant*, 'Defence of Patriotism'
▷ See Decatur 311:71.

92 The human race, to which so many of my readers belong, has been playing at children's games from the beginning, and will probably do it till the end, which is a nuisance for the few people who grow up.
1904 *The Napoleon of Notting Hill*, ch.1.

93 The word 'orthodoxy' not only no longer means being right; it practically means being wrong.
1905 *Heretics*, ch.1.

94 There is no such thing on earth as an uninteresting subject; the only thing that can exist is an uninterested person.
1905 *Heretics*, ch.3.

95 In the case of Smith, the name is so poetical that it must be an arduous and heroic matter for the man to live up to it… Yet our novelists call their hero 'Aylmer Valence', which means nothing, or 'Vernon Raymond', which means nothing, when it is in their power to give him this sacred name of Smith—this name of iron and flame… If you think the name of 'Smith' prosaic, it is not because you are practical and sensible; it is because you are too much affected with literary refinements. The name shouts poetry at you.
1905 *Heretics*, ch.3.

96 Charity is the power of defending that which we know to be indefensible. Hope is the power of being cheerful in circumstances which we know to be desperate.
1905 *Heretics*, ch.12.

97 A good novel tells us the truth about its hero; but a bad novel tells us the truth about its author.
1905 *Heretics*, ch.15.

98 The artistic temperament is a disease that afflicts amateurs. It is a disease which arises from men not having sufficient power of expression to utter and get rid of the element of art in their being.
1905 *Heretics*, ch.17.

99 Bigotry may be roughly defined as the anger of men who have no opinions.
1905 *Heretics*, ch.20.

1 Science in the modern world has many uses; its chief use, however, is to provide long words to cover the errors of the rich.
1905 *Heretics*, ch13.

2 There is a great man who makes every man feel small. But the real great man is the man who makes every man feel great.
1906 *Charles Dickens*, ch.1.

3 The madman is not the man who has lost his reason. The madman is the one who has lost everything except his reason.
1908 *Orthodoxy*, ch.2.

4 Poets do not go mad; but chess players do.
1908 *Orthodoxy*, ch.2.

5 The men who really believe in themselves are all in lunatic asylums.
1908 *Orthodoxy*, ch.2.

6 It is an act of faith to assert that our thoughts have any relation to reality at all.
1908 *Orthodoxy*, ch.3.

7 Tradition means giving votes to the most obscure of all classes, our ancestors. It is the democracy of the dead.
1908 *Orthodoxy*, ch.4.

8 All conservatism is based upon the idea that if you leave things alone you leave them as they are. But you do not. If you leave a thing alone you leave it to a torrent of change.
1908 *Orthodoxy*, ch.7.

9 Angels can fly because they take themselves lightly.
1908 *Orthodoxy*, ch.7.

10 Thieves respect property. They merely wish the property to become their property that they may more perfectly respect it.
1908 *The Man who was Thursday*, ch.4.

11 An adventure is only an inconvenience rightly considered. An inconvenience is only an adventure wrongly considered.
1908 *All Things Considered*, 'On Running After One's Hat'.

12 No animal ever invented anything so bad as drunkenness—or so good as drink.
1908 *All Things Considered*, 'Wine When It Is Red'.

13 Lying in bed would be an altogether perfect and supreme experience if only one had a coloured pencil long enough to draw on the ceiling.
1909 'On Lying In Bed'.

14 He desired all beautiful things—even God.
1909 Of Oscar Wilde. In the *Daily News*, 19 Oct.

15 The Christian ideal has not been tried and found wanting. It has been found difficult; and left untried.
1910 *What's Wrong with the World*, ch.1, 'The Unfinished Temple'.

16 Compromise used to mean that half a loaf was
better than no bread. Among modern statesmen, it
really seems to mean that half a loaf is better than a
whole loaf.
1910 *What's Wrong with the World*, ch.3.

17 She was maintaining the prime truth of woman,
the universal mother…that if a thing is worth
doing, it is worth doing badly.
1910 *What's Wrong with the World*, pt.4, 'Folly and Female
Education'.

18 I tell you naught for your comfort,
Yea, naught for your desire,
Save that the sky grows darker yet
And the sea rises higher.
1911 *Ballad of the White Horse*, bk.1.

19 For the great Gaels of Ireland
Are the men that God made mad,
For all their wars are merry,
And all their songs are sad.
1911 *Ballad of the White Horse*, bk.2.

20 There is always a forgotten thing,
And love is not secure.
1911 *Ballad of the White Horse*, bk.3.

21 When all philosophies shall fail,
This word alone shall fit;
That a sage feels too small for life,
And a fool too large for it.
1911 *Ballad of the White Horse*, bk.8.

22 He could not think up to the height of his own
towering style.
1912 Of Tennyson. *The Victorian Age in Literature*, ch.3.

23 And Noah he often said to his wife when he sat
down to dine.
'I don't care where the water goes if it doesn't get
into the wine.'
1914 *The Flying Inn*, ch.5, stanza 1. Collected as 'Wine and
Water' in *Wine, Water and Song* (1915).

24 The rich are the scum of the earth in every country.
1914 *The Flying Inn*, ch.15.

25 Tea is like the East he grows in,
A great yellow Mandarin
With urbanity of manner
And unconsciousness of sin.
1914 *The Flying Inn*, ch.18, stanza 2. Collected as 'The Song of
Right and Wrong' in *Wine, Water and Song* (1915).

26 When red wine had brought red ruin
And the death-dance of our times,
Heaven sent us Soda Water
As a torment for our crimes.
1914 *The Flying Inn*, ch.18, stanza 4. Collected as 'The Song of
Right and Wrong' in *Wine, Water and Song* (1915).

27 The folk that live in Liverpool, their heart is in
their boots;
They go to hell like lambs, they do, because the
hooter hoots.
1914 'Me Heart'.

28 They haven't got no noses,
The fallen sons of Eve.
1914 'Song of Quoodle'.

29 And goodness only knowses
The Noselessness of Man.
1914 'Song of Quoodle'.

30 Tea, although an Oriental,
Is a gentleman at least;
Cocoa is a cad and coward,
Cocoa is a vulgar beast.
1914 'Song of Right and Wrong'.

31 Before the Roman came to Rye or out to Severn
strode,
The rolling English drunkard made the rolling
English road.
1914 'Rolling English Road'.

32 A merry road, a mazy road, and such as we did
tread
The night we went to Birmingham by way of
Beachy Head.
1914 'Rolling English Road'.

33 For there is good news yet to hear and fine things to
be seen,
Before we go to Paradise by way of Kensal Green.
1914 'Rolling English Road'.

34 To be clever enough to get all that money, one must
be stupid enough to want it.
1914 *The Wisdom of Father Brown*, 'Paradise of Thieves'.

35 Journalism largely consists in saying 'Lord Jones
Dead' to people who never knew Lord Jones was
alive.
1914 *The Wisdom of Father Brown*, 'The Purple Wig'.

36 We only know the last sad squires ride slowly
towards the sea,
And a new people takes the land: and still it is not we.
1915 'The Secret People'.

37 The souls most fed with Shakespeare's flame
Still sat unconquered in a ring,
Remembering him like anything.
1915 'Shakespeare Memorial'.

38 John Grubby, who was short and stout
And troubled with religious doubt,
Refused about the age of three
To sit upon the curate's knee.
1915 'The New Freethinker'.

39 And I dream of the days when work was scrappy,
And rare in our pockets the mark of the mint,
When we were angry and poor and happy,
And proud of seeing our names in print.
1915 'Song of Defeat'.

40 The gallows in my garden, people say,
Is new and neat and adequately tall.
1915 'Ballade of Suicide'.

41 The strangest whim has seized me... After all
I think I will not hang myself today.
1915 'Ballade of Suicide'.

42 They died to save their country and they only saved
the world.
1922 'English Graves'.

43 Democracy means government by the uneducated,
while aristocracy means government by the badly
educated.
1931 In the *New York Times*, 1 Feb.

44 A great deal of contemporary criticism reads to me
like a man saying: 'Of course I do not like green
cheese: I am very fond of brown sherry'.
1933 *All I Survey*, 'On Jonathan Swift'.

45 Why do you rush through the fields in trains,
Guessing so much and so much.
Why do you flash through the flowery meads,
Fat-head poet that nobody reads;
And why do you know such a frightful lot
About people in gloves and such?
1933 'The Fat White Woman Speaks', a response to Frances
Cornford's poem.
▷ See Cornford 288:58.

46 It isn't that they can't see the solution. It is that they
can't see the problem.
1935 *The Scandal of Father Brown*, 'Point of a Pin'.

47 Am in Market Harborough. Where ought I to be?
Attributed. Chesterton remarks in his *Autobiography* (1936),
ch.16, 'I cannot remember whether this story is true; but it is
not unlikely, or, I think, unreasonable.'

48 Music with dinner is an insult both to the cook and
the violinist.
Quoted in *The New York Times*, 16 Nov 1967.

49 I regard golf as an expensive way of playing marbles.
Quoted in Colin Jarman *The Guinness Dictionary of Sports
Quotations* (1990).

Chiang Kai-Shek 1887–1975
Chinese general and nationalist, defeated by Mao
Zedong's forces. In 1948 he was forced to withdraw to
Taiwan where he retained the office of President.

50 The sky cannot have two suns.
c.1945 Quoted in Ross Merrill *Mao* (1993) ch.10.

Child, Julia McWilliams 1912–
US cookery expert.

51 Life itself is the proper binge.
1980 In *Time Magazine*, 7 Jan.

52 The view of history that we get through the kitchen
window is a more gentle view, not of war and
politics, but of family and community and sharing.
1993 On studying cookbooks dating back to the 1400s in the
Library of Congress. In *Memory and Imagination*, PBS TV, 15
Aug.

Chirico, Giorgio de 1888–1978
Italian painter, born in Greece, the developer of
'metaphysical painting', based on semi-abstract geometric
figures. In the 1930s he renounced his earlier work and
returned to an academic style.

53 If a work of art is to be truly immortal, it must pass
quite beyond the limits of the human world,
without any sign of common sense and logic. In
this way the work will draw nearer to dream and to
the mind of a child.
Quoted in Saranne Alexandrian *Surrealist Art* (1970).

Chisholme, Caroline née Jones 1808–77
English-born Australian social worker and philanthropist.
She married an army officer and settled in New South
Wales in 1838, where she worked with impoverished
immigrant women and children. Her petition to Earl
Grey helped persuade the British Government to grant
free passage to the families of convicts.

54 If Her Majesty's Government be really desirous of
seeing a well-conducted community spring up in
these Colonies, the social wants of the people must
be considered... For all the clergy you can
despatch, all the schoolmasters you can appoint, all
the churches you can build, and all the books you
can export, will never do much good without what
a gentleman in that Colony very appropriately
called 'God's police'—wives and little children—
good and virtuous women.
1847 *Emigration and Transportation Relatively Considered; in a
Letter, Dedicated, by Permission, to Earl Grey*, 17 Jun. The phrase
'God's police' was adopted by Australian feminist Anne
Summers in her feminist critique of Australian culture, *Damned
Whores and God's Police*, (1975).
▷ See Clark 267:86.

Chocano, José Santos 1875–1934
Peruvian poet, teacher, editor and diplomat. He visited
almost every Central and South American country, often
being expelled for political intrigue. He was assassinated
in Chile.

55 *Soy el cantor de América autóctono y salvaje;
mi lira tiene un alma, mi canto un ideal.
Mi verso no se mece colgado de un ramaje
con un vaivén pausado de hamaca tropical.*

I am the aboriginal and savage singer of America;
my lyre has a soul, my song has an ideal.
My poetry does not swing from the branches
with the slow movement of a tropical hammock.
1906 *Alma América*, 'Blasón' (translated as 'Blazon', 1935).

Chomsky, (Avram) Noam 1928–

US linguist and social critic. His theories revolutionized the study of language and remain controversial. In the political arena, he has criticized many aspects of US foreign policy.

56 An obscenity, a depraved act by weak and miserable men, including all of us, who have allowed it to go on and on with endless fury.
1969 Of US involvement in the war in Vietnam. *American Power and the New Mandarins*.

57 As soon as questions of will or decision arise, human science is at a loss.
1978 Television interview, 30 Mar, reported in *The Listener*, 6 Apr.

58 The military system is, to a substantial extent, a method whereby the population provides a subsidy to the high technology industry.
1988 Interview, Public Broadcasting System, 4 Nov.

Chopin, Kate (Katherine) née O'Flaherty
1851–1904

US novelist and short story writer. After the death of her husband she began to write sketches of Creole life, including *Bayou Folk* (1894). Her novel *The Awakening* (1899) was harshly condemned for its frank treatment of female sexuality.

59 The voice of the sea speaks to the soul. The touch of the sea is sensuous, enfolding the body in its soft, close embrace.
1899 *The Awakening*, ch.6.

60 The past was nothing to her... The future was a mystery which she never attempted to penetrate. The present alone was significant.
1899 *The Awakening*, ch.15.

61 She was becoming herself and daily casting aside that fictitious self which we assume like a garment with which to appear before the world.
1899 *The Awakening*, ch.19.

62 The artist must possess the courageous soul that dares and defies.
1899 *The Awakening*, ch.39.

63 I trust I will not be giving away professional secrets to say that many readers would be surprised, perhaps shocked, at the questions which some newspaper editors will put to a defenseless woman under the guise of flattery.

1899 'On Certain Brisk Days', in the *St Louis Post–Dispatch*, 26 Nov.

Christiansen, Arthur 1904–63

British journalist, Editor of the *Daily Express* (1933–58).

64 Whenever possible print a woman's age.
1957 Quoted in Francis Williams *Dangerous Estate*.

65 The people who lived behind those clean lace curtains in row after row of identical boxes were newspaper readers, and every word in at any rate *my* newspaper must be clear and comprehensible to them, must be interesting to them, must encourage them to break away from littleness, stimulate their ambition, help them to want to build a better land.
1961 *Headlines all my Life*, ch.1.

66 Remember the people in the back streets of Derby.
1961 *Headlines all my Life*, ch.1.

67 Show me a contented newspaper editor and I will show you a bad newspaper.
1961 *Headlines all my Life*, ch.15.

68 No matter how many media for the dissemination of news are created, there is one rule that should never be broken: TELL THE PEOPLE!
1961 *Headlines all my Life*, ch.18.

69 My approach to newspapers was based on the idea that when you looked at the front page you said: 'Good heavens', when you looked at the middle page you said: 'Holy smoke', and by the time you got to the back page—well, I'd have to utter a profanity to show how exciting it was.
1961 *Headlines all my Life*, ch.19.

Christie, Dame Agatha Mary Clarissa
née *Miller* 1890–1976

English author, who wrote more than 70 classic detective novels including *The Mysterious Affair at Styles* (1920), *Murder on the Orient Express* (1934) and *Death on the Nile* (1937).

70 He tapped his forehead. 'These little grey cells. It is up to them—as you say over here.'
1920 *The Mysterious Affair at Styles*, ch.10.

71 Life nowadays is dominated and complicated by the remorseless Zip. Blouses zip up, skirts zip down, ski-ing suits zip everywhere... Why? Is there anything more deadly than a Zip that turns nasty on you?
1946 *Come, Tell Me How You Live*, ch.1.

72 Here, in the west of Ireland, the Romans had never marched, tramp, tramp, tramp: had never fortified a camp: had never built a well-ordered, sensible, useful road. It was a land where common sense and an orderly way of life were unknown.

Hercule Poirot looked down at the tips of his patent-leather shoes and sighed. He felt forlorn and very much alone. The standards by which he lived were here not appreciated.

1947 *The Labours of Hercules.*

73 War settles *nothing*…to *win* a war is as disastrous as to lose one.

1977 *An Autobiography*, ch.10.

Christine de Pisan 1364–1430

Italian-born French writer. Taken to the court of Charles V as a child, married at 15 and widowed at 25, she became the first professional woman poet and official biographer of Charles V. Other works include lyrics and essays on politics and the status of women in society.

74 *Ne la hauteur ou abaissement des gens ne gist mie es corps selonc le sexe, mais en la perfeccion des meurs et vertus.*

The dignity or baseness of a person lies not in their body according to the sex, but in the perfection of behaviour and virtues.

1405 *Cité des Dames*, bk.1, ch.9.

75 *De tant comme femmes ont le corps plus delie que les hommes, plus foible et moins habille a plusieurs choses faire, de tant ont elles l'entendement plus a delivre et plus agu ou elles s'appliquent.*

Just as women's bodies are more delicate than men's, weaker and less able for many things, so, where they apply themselves, their understanding is freer and sharper.

1405 *Cité des Dames*, bk.1, ch.27.

Christopher, Warren Miner 1925–

US lawyer and government official, Secretary of State (1993–). In 1980 he negotiated for the release of US hostages in Iran.

76 I wish the meeting had been as good as the lunch.

1994 On beginning talks in Beijing with China's Prime Minister. In the *New York Times*, 13 Mar.

77 Sometimes you have to learn how to give the right answer to the wrong question.

1994 On Syrian President Hafez Assad's complaint that he had been put off by a hostile question in a news conference shared with President Clinton. In *US News and World Report*, 19 Dec.

Church, Richard 1893–1972

English author, known for his poems, novels, literary criticism, travel books and children's stories.

78 We have to accept the verbal portraits, as indeed we have to accept paintings and sculptures, as well as photographs, of the immortals whose influence on our lives is often greater than that of our own family members.

In praise of biography. Quoted in *Christian Science Monitor*, 30 Apr 1963.

79 He delights to expose the raw nerves of evil, showing it as a force in the world, a skeletonlike figure working visible mischief in the ordinary everyday affairs of men and women and children.

Of Graham Greene. Recalled on Greene's death in the *New York Times*, 4 Apr 1991.

Churchill, Charles 1731–64

English satirical poet. His works savagely attacked many well-known figures of his time, including Samuel Johnson, Tobias Smollett and William Hogarth. He is best known for *The Rosciad* (1761).

80 A pert, prim Prater of the northern race,
Guilt in his heart, and famine in his face.

1761 Of the Scottish-born judge Alexander Wedderburn, later Lord Loughborough. *The Rosciad*, l.75–6.

81 Fashion—a word which knaves and fools may use,
Their knavery and folly to excuse.

1761 *The Rosciad*, l.455–6.

82 So much they talked, so very little said.

1761 *The Rosciad*, l.550.

83 But, spite of all the criticizing elves,
Those who would make us feel, must feel themselves.

1761 *The Rosciad*, l.961–2.

84 Keep up appearances; there lies the test;
The world will give thee credit for the rest.
Outward be fair, however foul within;
Sin if thou wilt, but then in secret sin.

1762 *Night*, l.311–12.

85 Just to the windward of the law.

1763 *The Ghost*, bk.3, l.56.

86 A joke's a very serious thing.

1763 *The Ghost*, bk.3, l.1386.

87 Apt Alliteration's artful aid.

1763 *The Prophecy of Famine*, l.86.

88 The danger chiefly lies in acting well;
No crime's so great as daring to excel.

1763 *An Epistle to William Hogarth*, l.51–2.

89 Be England what she will,
With all her faults, she is my country still.

1764 *The Farewell*, l.27–8.

90 It can't be Nature, for it is not sense.

1764 *The Farewell*, l.200.

Churchill, Jeanette née *Jeanette Jerome*

1852–1921

US-born wife of Lord Randolph Henry Spencer Churchill, daughter of a prominent New York businessman.

91 There is no such thing as a moral dress… It's people who are moral or immoral.

1921 'That Moral Dress', in the *Daily Chronicle*, 16 Feb.

Churchill, Lord Randolph Henry Spencer

1849–95

British politician, the leader of a guerrilla band of Conservatives known as the 'Fourth Party' (from 1880) and father of Sir Winston Churchill. He was Chancellor of the Exchequer and leader of the House of Commons (1886).

92 Ulster will not be a consenting party. Ulster, at the proper time, will resort to the supreme arbitrament of force; Ulster will fight and Ulster will be right.

1886 Public letter, 7 May.

93 This monstrous mixture of imbecility, extravagance and political hysteria, better known as the Bill for the future government of Ireland—this farrago of superlative nonsense, is to be put in motion for this reason and no other: to gratify the ambition of an old man in a hurry.

1886 Pamphlet attacking Gladstone's Home Rule Bill, Jun.

94 I could never make out what those damned dots meant.

Of decimal points. Quoted in Winston Churchill *Lord Randolph Churchill* (1906).

95 The duty of an Opposition is to oppose.

Remark attributed by his son, Winston Churchill. The phrase was used earlier by Edward Stanley, 14th Earl of Derby, who attributed it to Mr Tierney (4 Jun 1841).

Churchill, Sir Winston Leonard Spencer

1874–1965

English statesman, Prime Minister (1940–5, 1951–2) and writer. He became a Conservative MP in 1900 but turned Liberal in 1904 and was made First Lord of the Admiralty (1911), and Chancellor of the Exchequer (1924–9). He returned to the Conservative Party in 1929 and on Chamberlain's defeat formed a coalition government to pursue the war with Germany.

96 Business carried on as usual during alterations on the map of Europe.

1914 Of the British people's view of World War I. Speech at the Guildhall, London, 9 Nov.

97 In war: resolution. In defeat: defiance. In victory: magnanimity. In peace: goodwill.

c.1918 *The Second World War* (1948), vol.1, epigraph. According to Sir Edward Marsh, in *A Number of People* (1939), the phrase occurred to Churchill shortly after the end of World War I. Some sources attribute it to Marsh himself.

98 Of all tyrannies in history, the Bolshevik tyranny is the worst, the most destructive, the most degrading. Every British and French soldier killed last year was really done to death by Lenin and Trotsky—not in fair war, but by the treacherous desertion of an ally without parallel in the history of the world.

1919 Speech, London, 11 Apr.

99 The community lacks goods and a million and a quarter people lack work. It is certainly one of the highest functions of national finance and credit to bridge the gap between the two.

1925 Letter to Otto Niemeyer, 22 Feb. Collected in D E Moggridge *Maynard Keynes* (1992).

1 The day must come when the nation's whole scale of living must be reduced. If that day comes, Parliament must lay the burden equally on all classes.

1925 Speech as Chancellor of the Exchequer, House of Commons, 7 Aug.

2 Jellicoe was the only man on either side who could lose the war in an afternoon.

1927 On Admiral Jellicoe, commander of the Grand Fleet in World War I. *The World Crisis*, pt.1, ch.5.

3 The loss of India would mark and consummate the downfall of the British Empire. That great organism would pass at a stroke out of life into history. From such a catastrophe there could be no recovery.

1930 Speech to the Indian Empire Society, London, 12 Dec.

4 Mr Gladstone read Homer for fun, which I thought served him right.

1930 *My Early Life*.

5 Those who can win a war well can rarely make a good peace, and those who could make a good peace would never have won the war.

1930 *My Early Life*.

6 The War was decided in the first twenty days of fighting, and all that happened afterwards consisted in battles which, however formidable and devastating, were but desparate and vain appeals against the decision of Fate.

1930 His preface to E L Spears *Liaison 1914*.

7 I remember, when I was a child, being taken to the celebrated Barnum's circus, which contained an exhibition of freaks and monstrosities, but the exhibit on the programme which I most desired to see was the one described as 'The Boneless Wonder'. My parents judged that the spectacle would be too revolting and demoralizing for my youthful eyes, and I have waited 50 years to see the boneless wonder sitting on the Treasury Bench.

1931 Alluding to Ramsay Macdonald. Speech in the House of Commons, 28 Jan.

8 It is alarming and odious to see Mr Gandhi, a seditious Middle Temple lawyer, now posing as a fakir of a type well-known in the East, striding half-naked up the steps of the vice-regal palace, while he is still conducting a defiant campaign of civil disobedience, to parley on equal terms with the representative of the King-Emperor.

1931 Speech, 23 Feb.

9 That long frontier from the Atlantic to the Pacific oceans, guarded only by neighbourly respect and honourable obligations, is an example to every country and a pattern for the future of the world.

1939 Address at the Canada Club, London, 20 Apr.

10 This is no war for domination or imperial aggrandisement or material gain... It is a war...to establish, on impregnable rocks, the rights of the individual and it is a war to establish and revive the stature of man.

1939 Speech in the House of Commons, 3 Sep, on the declaration of war against Germany by Britain and France.

11 I cannot forecast to you the action of Russia. It is a riddle wrapped inside a mystery inside an enigma. But perhaps there is a key; that key is Russian national interest.

1939 Radio broadcast, 1 Oct.

12 You ask what is our aim. I can answer in one word—victory. Victory at all costs, victory in spite of all terror, victory, however long and hard the road may be.

1939 Radio broadcast, 1 Oct.

13 I have nothing to offer but blood, toil, tears and sweat.

1940 Speech in the House of Commons on assuming the premiership, 13 May.

14 We shall not flag or fail. We shall go on to the end. We shall fight in France, we shall fight on the seas and oceans, we shall fight with growing confidence and growing strength in the air, we shall defend our island whatever the cost may be. We shall fight on the beaches, we shall fight on the landing grounds, we shall fight in the fields and in the streets, we shall fight in the hills. We shall never surrender.

1940 Speech in the House of Commons, 4 Jun, after the Dunkirk evacuation.

15 Let us therefore brace ourselves to our duties, and so bear ourselves that, if the British Empire and its Commonwealth last for a thousand years, men will still say: 'This was their finest hour.'

1940 Speech, 18 Jun. Quoted in A J P Taylor *English History 1914–45*, p.491.

16 Never in the field of human conflict has so much been owed by so many, to so few.

1940 On the Battle of Britain pilots. Speech, House of Commons, 20 Aug.

17 No one can guarantee success in war, but only deserve it.

1940 Letter to Lord Wavell, 26 Nov. Quoted in Winston Churchill *The Second World War* (1949), vol.2, ch.27.

18 Here is the answer that I will give to President Roosevelt...Give us the tools, and we will finish the job.

1941 Radio broadcast, 9 Feb.

19 No one has been a more consistent opponent of Communism than I have for the last 25 years. I will unsay no word that I have spoken about it, but all that fades away before the spectacle that is now unfolding. The past, with its crimes, its follies, and its tragedies, flashes away. I see the Russian soldiers standing on the threshold of their native land, guarding the fields that their fathers have tilled from time immemorial. Any man or state who fights on against Nazidom will have our aid. Any man or state who marches with Hitler is our foe.

1941 Radio broadcast on the German invasion of Russia, 22 Jun.

20 When I warned the French that Britain would fight on alone, General Weygand told their Prime Minister and his divided Cabinet that in three weeks England will have her neck wrung like a chicken. Some chicken, some neck!

1941 Speech to the Canadian Parliament, 30 Dec.

21 What kind of people do they think we are?

1941 Of the Japanese. Speech to Congress, Dec.

22 Commanders and senior officers should die with troops. The honour of the British Empire and the British Army is at stake.

1942 Telegram to Wavell, the commander in chief of armed forces in Singapore, 10 Feb, after being told that a Japanese victory was inevitable. Recalled in *The Second World War*, vol.4 (1951).

23 The latest refinements of science are linked with the cruelties of the Stone Age.

1942 Speech, 26 Mar, in devastated war-time London.

24 Now this is not the end. It is not even the beginning of the end. But it is, perhaps, the end of the beginning.

1942 Speech at the Mansion House, London, 10 Nov, referring to the Battle of Egypt.

25 I have not become the King's First Minister in order to preside over the liquidation of the British Empire.

1942 Speech at the Mansion House, London, 10 Nov.

26 We make this wide encircling movement in the Mediterranean, having for its primary object the recovery of the command of that vital sea, but also having for its object the exposure of the under-belly of the Axis, especially Italy, to heavy attack.
1942 Speech in the House of Commons, 11 Nov.

27 There is no finer investment for any community than putting milk into babies. Healthy citizens are the greatest asset any country can have.
1943 Speech on BBC radio, 21 Mar.

28 The Bomb brought peace, but man alone can keep that peace.
1945 House of Commons, 16 Aug.

29 If this is a blessing, it is certainly very well disguised.
1945 On his defeat in the first post-war general election, quoted in Richard Nixon *Memoirs* (1978).

30 From Stettin in the Baltic to Trieste in the Adriatic, an iron curtain has descended across the Continent.
1946 Speech at Fulton, Missouri, 5 Mar. He had used the phrase in a telegraph to President Trueman, 12 May 1945, when he said of the Russian-held territories that 'An iron curtain is drawn down upon their front'.

31 Would a special relationship between the United States and the British Commonwealth be inconsistent with our overriding loyalty to the world organisation?
1946 Speech at Fulton, Missouri, Mar.

32 No one pretends that democracy is perfect or all-wise. Indeed, it has been said that democracy is the worst form of Government except all those other forms that have been tried from time to time.
1947 Speech in the House of Commons, 11 Nov.

33 Science bestowed immense new powers on man, and, at the same time, created conditions which were largely beyond his comprehension and still more beyond his control.
1949 Speech, Massachusetts Institute of Technology, 31 Mar.

34 I am ready to meet my maker. Whether my maker is ready for the ordeal of meeting me is another matter.
1949 Speech, Nov.

35 I have only one purpose—the destruction of Hitler, and my life is much simplified thereby. If Hitler invaded Hell, I would at least make a favourable reference to the Devil in the House of Commons.
Recalled in *The Second World War*, vol.3 (1950), ch.20.

36 Perhaps it is better to be irresponsible and right than to be responsible and wrong.
1950 Radio broadcast, 26 Aug.

37 If you recognize anyone, it does not mean that you like him. We all, for instance, recognize the honourable Member for Ebbw Vale.
1952 Of Aneurin Bevan, in a House of Commons debate on 1 Jul on British recognition of communist China.

38 I have lived 78 years without hearing of bloody places like Cambodia.
1953 Comment, 28 Apr. Quoted in Lord Moran *Winston Churchill, The Struggle for Survival* (1966).

39 Talking jaw is better than going to war.
1954 White House speech, 26 Jun. His comment is often rendered 'To jaw-jaw is always better than to war-war.'

40 An appeaser is someone who feeds a crocodile, hoping it will eat him last.
1954 Attributed. Quoted in *Reader's Digest*, Dec.

41 I have never accepted what many people have kindly said—that I inspired the nation. It was the nation and the race living around the globe that had the lion heart. I had the luck to be called upon to give the roar.
1954 Speech to both Houses of Parliament in Westminster Hall, Nov, on the occasion of his 80th birthday.

42 Scientists should be on tap, but not on top.
Quoted in Randolph S Churchill *Twenty-One Years* (1965).

43 I am so bored with it all.
Attributed last words.

44 An empty taxi arrived at 10 Downing Street, and when the door was opened Attlee got out.
Attributed. Quoted in Kenneth Harris *Attlee* (1982), ch.16.

45 An ineffectual attempt to direct an uncontrollable sphere into an inaccessible hole with instruments ill-adapted for the purpose.
Quoted in Michael Hobbs *The Golf Quotations Book* (1992).

46 All I wanted was compliance with my wishes after reasonable discussion.
Attributed. Quoted in A J P Taylor *From the Boer War to the Cold War: Essays on Twentieth-Century Europe* (1995).

47 In defeat unbeatable: in victory unbearable.
Of Montgomery. Quoted in Sir Edward Howard Marsh *Ambrosia and Small Beer*, ch.5.

48 Do not criticize your Government when out of the country. Never cease to do so when at home.
Attributed.

49 There, but for the grace of God, goes God.
Of Sir Stafford Cripps. Attributed.

Ciardi, John 1916–85

US poet, critic and translator. His translation of Dante's *Inferno* is much admired.

50 This island rock in space turns flowering endlessly

To peaks of cloud still mounting where you took
Your last high passage and your faltering luck.
1947 'Elegy for Kurt Porjescz, Missing in Action, 1 April, 1945'.

51 At the next vacancy for God, if I am elected,
I shall forgive last the delicately wounded
who, having been slugged no harder than anyone else,
never got up again, neither to fight back,
nor to finger their jaws in painful admiration.
1959 'In Place of a Curse'

52 You don't have to suffer to be a poet. Adolescence is enough.
1962 In the *Saturday Review*, Fall issue.

Cibber, Colley 1671–1757

English actor and dramatist. He worked for most of his career at the Theatre Royal in Drury Lane, and in 1696 established himself as both playwright and actor with his first comedy, *Love's Last Shift*. From 1730 he was Poet Laureate.

53 One had as good be out of the World, as out of the Fashion.
1696 *Love's Last Shift: or, The Fool in Fashion*, act 2, sc.1.

54 Perish the thought!
1700 *Richard III*, act 5 (his adaptation of Shakespeare's play).

55 Stolen sweets are best.
1709 *The Rival Fools*, act 1.

Cicero full name *Marcus Tullius Cicero*
106–43 BC

Roman orator and statesman, exiled after his unconstitutional execution of the Catiline conspirators. Although recalled by the people (57 BC) he lost the respect of both Caesar and Pompey by his vacillations. He wrote most of his major works on rhetoric and philosophy in retirement in Rome. His speeches against Mark Antony after Caesar's death (*The Philippics*) cost him his life.

56 *Quo usque tandem abutere, Catilina, patientia nostra?*
In heaven's name, Catiline, how long will you abuse our patience?
63 BC Opening line of the first of four speeches against the conspirator L Sergius Catilina, 8 Nov. *In Catilinam* 1.1.

57 *O tempora, o mores!*
What times! what morals!
63 BC Favourite phrase, used on various occasions. See *In Catilinam*, 1.1, *In Verrem*, 4.25 and *Pro rege Deiotaro* 11.31.

58 *Salus populi suprema est lex.*
The good of the people is the chief law.
52 BC *De Legibus*, bk.3, ch.3.

59 *Silent enim leges inter arma.*

For laws are silent in time of war.
51 BC *Pro Milone*, ch.11.

60 *Cui bono?*
Who benefits?
51 BC *Pro Milone*, ch.12 (and elsewhere).

61 *Nervos belli, pecuniam infinitam.*
The sinews of war, unlimited money.
44 BC *Fifth Philippic*, ch.5.

62 *Nihil tam absurde dici potest quo non dicatur ab aliquo philosophorum.*
There is nothing so absurd that it has not been said by some philosopher.
c.44 BC *De Divinatione*, bk.2, section 58.

63 *Civis Romanus sum.*
I am a Roman citizen.
In Verrem 5.147. This is a reference to the tradition that Roman citizens in foreign courts could often expect preferential treatment. The Roman governor Verres, whom Cicero was prosecuting, had ignored this fact altogether, even executing Roman citizens.

64 *Cedant arma togae, concedant laurea laudi.*
Let war yield to peace, laurels to paeans.
De Officiis, bk.1, ch.77.

65 *Mens cuiusque is est quisque: non ea figura quae digito demonstrari potest.*
The mind is the true self, not the person that can be pointed to with the finger.
De Republica bk.6, ch.24.

66 *O fortunatam natam me consule Romam!*
O lucky Rome, born when I was consul!
Cicero was consul in 63 BC. His only extant line of poetry, quoted in Juvenal, *Satires* 10, l.122.

Cisneros, Henry 1947–

US politician, Secretary of Housing and Urban Development (1993–7).

67 Like piles of dry wood with red-hot coals underneath.
1993 Of US cities, rife with racial tension. In *US News and World Report*, 19 Apr.

68 We have to be honest, we have to be truthful and speak to the one dirty secret in American life, and that is racism.
1993 In *US News and World Report*, 19 Apr.

Cixous, Hélène 1937–

French feminist author and critic who has argued that women write differently from men by virtue of their bodies.

69 *On dit que la vie et la mort sont au pouvoir de la langue.*

It is said that life and death are under the power of language.
1969 *Dedans.*

70   *La seule différence incontestable n'est pas celle des sexes ou des âges ou des forces, mais celle des vifs et des morts.*

The only incontestable difference is not that of sex or age or strength, but that of the living and the dead.
1969 *Dedans.*

71   *J'ai peu de mots. Mon père qui les avait tous, est parti si précipitamment, qu'il n'a pas eu le temps de me les donner.*

I have few words. My father, who had all of them, left so suddenly that he did not have the time to give them all to me.
1969 *Dedans.*

72   *Le temps et le monde et la personne ne se rencontrent qu'une seule fois.*

Time, the world and the person only encounter one another once.
1969 *Dedans.*

73   *Je me cherche à travers les siècles et je ne me vois nulle part.*

I have searched for myself across time and have not found myself anywhere.
1974 *Prénoms du soleil* (translated by Morag Shiach in *Hélène Cixous: A Politics of Writing*).

74   *Des mots sont arrachés vivants à la langue défunte.*

Words are taken alive from a defunct language.
1976 *La.*

75   *On ne s'éveille qu'au contact de l'amour. Et avant ce temps, on n'est que jardins sans douleurs, espaces fourmillant de corps érotiques, champs de mers poissonneuses, chairs sans soucis.*

One wakes only to the touch of love. Before then, we are only gardens without sorrows, spaces swarming with erotic bodies, landscapes of seas full of fish, flesh without cares.
1976 *La.*

76   *Quand je n'écris pas, c'est comme si j'étais morte.*

When I do not write, it's as though I'm dead.
Quoted in Jean-Louis Rambures *Comment travaillent les écrivains* (1978).

77   *Je ne suis pas innocente. L'innocence est une science du sublime. Et je ne suis qu'au tout début de l'apprentissage.*

I am not innocent. Innocence is a science of the sublime. And I am only at the very beginning of the apprenticeship.
1979 *Vivre l'orange / To Live the Orange* (bilingual text, translated by Ann Liddle and Sarah Cornell).

78   *Je voudrais tant être une femme sans y penser.*

I would like so much to be a woman without thinking about it.
1983 *Le Livre de Promethea.*

Clare, John   1793–1864

English poet, whose work reflects the harsh rural world of the 19c. He became mentally unstable in 1823 and spent the last 23 years of his life in a lunatic asylum.

79   When badgers fight and everyone's a foe.
1836 'Badger'.

80   A quiet, pilfering, unprotected race.
1841 'The Gipsy Camp'.

81   The present is the funeral of the past,
     And man the living sepulchre of life.
1845 'The present is the funeral of the past'.

82   I am—yet what I am, none cares or knows;
     My friends forsake me like a memory lost:
     I am the self-consumer of my woes.
1848 'I Am'.

83   I long for scenes where man hath never trod
     A place where woman never smiled or wept
     There to abide with my Creator God
     And sleep as I in childhood sweetly slept,
     Untroubling and untroubled where I lie
     The grass below, above, the vaulted sky.
1848 'I Am'.

84   He could not die when the trees were green,
     For he loved the time too well.
'The Dying Child' (published 1873).

Clark, Eleanor   1913–

US writer, wife of Robert Penn Warren. Her works include *Eyes, Etc.* (1977), on her experience of blindness. She won the National Book Award, 1965 for *The Oysters of Locmariaquer.*

85   If you don't love life you can't enjoy an oyster.
1964 *The Oysters of Locmariaquer,* ch.1.

Clark, Ralph

British lieutenant of the First Fleet to Australia.

86   The damned whores the moment that they got below fell a fighting amongst one and another and Capt Meridith order the Sergt. not to part them but to let them fight it out.
c.1789 *The Journal and Letters of Lt Ralph Clark 1787–1792.* The phrase 'damned whores' was adopted by Australian feminist Anne Summers in her feminist critique of Australian culture, *Damned Whores and God's Police* (1975).

▷ See Chisholme 260:54

Clark, Ramsey 1927–

US lawyer, appointed Attorney General (1967–9), known for his staunch defence of civil liberties and his opposition to the Vietnam War.

87 A right is not what someone gives you; it's what no one can take from you.
1977 In the *New York Times*, 2 Oct.

Clarke, Sir Arthur C(harles) 1917–

English author, a prolific and entertaining writer of works of science fiction, popular science, mysticism and speculative thought. His story 'The Sentinel' was the basis of Stanley Kubrick's film *2001: A Space Odyssey.*

88 Overhead without any fuss the stars were going out.
1958 'The Nine Billion Names of God'.

89 Any sufficiently advanced technology is indistinguishable from magic.
1962 *Profiles of the Future*, introduction.

90 When a distinguished but elderly scientist states that something is possible he is almost certainly right. When he states that something is impossible, he is very probably wrong.
1962 *Profiles of the Future.*

Claudel, Paul 1868–1955

French dramatist, poet and diplomat, whose writing reflects his mystical Catholicism. He was ambassador to Japan (1921–7), the US (1927–33) and Belgium (1933–35). His works include the play *Tidings Brought to Mary* (1912) and *Five Great Odes* (1910).

91 You explain nothing, O poet, but thanks to you all things become explicable.
Recalled on his death, 23 Feb 1955.

92 A cocktail is to a glass of wine as rape is to love.
Quoted by William Grimes in 'The American Cocktail', *Americana*, Dec 1992.

Claudius Caecus, Appius 4c–3c BC

Roman statesman and lawgiver. He oversaw the construction of Rome's first aqueduct, the Aqua Appia. He later became blind, hence his surname, Caecus.

93 *Faber est suae quisque fortunae.*

Each man is the architect of his own fate.
Sallust Ad Caesarem Senem de Re Publica Oratio, ch.1, sect.2.

Clausewitz, Karl Philip Gottlieb von
1780–1831

Prussian general, Director of the Prussian army school in Berlin (1818–30) and Gneisenau's Chief-of-Staff. His treatise *Vom Kriege* ('On War', 1833) had a major impact on strategic studies.

94 Battles decide everything.
1812 *Principles of War* (translated by J J Graham).

95 Only the study of military history is capable of giving those who have no experience of their own a clear picture of what I have just called the friction of the whole machine.
1812 *Principles of War* (translated by J J Graham).

96 *Der Krieg ist nichts als eine Fortsetzung des politischen Verkehrs mit Einmischung anderer Mittel.*

War is merely the continuation of policy with the admixture of other means.
1833 *Vom Kriege*, bk.8, ch.6, section b. The phrase is commonly rendered 'War is the continuation of politics by other means.'

Clavell, James du Maresq 1924–94

Australian-born US novelist. His first novel, *King Rat* (1962), is set in Singapore's Changi prison, where the Japanese kept prisoners of war (1942–5). Clavell was himself a prisoner of war in Java.

97 These men too were criminals. Their crime was vast. They had lost a war. And they had lived.
1962 *King Rat.*

Cleaver, Eldridge 1935–98

US political activist.

98 You're either part of the solution, or you're part of the problem.
1968 Speech, San Francisco.

Cleese, John 1939–

British actor, comedian and writer, best known for his contribution to the satirical televison series, *Monty Python's Flying Circus.*

99 Loving your neighbour as much as yourself is practically bloody impossible… You might as well have a commandment that states, 'Thou shalt fly'.
1993 In *The Times.*

Clemenceau, Georges 1841–1929

French statesman, leader of the extreme left, known as 'The Tiger'. He was Premier (1906–9, 1917–20) and presided at the 1919 Peace Conference.

1 *La guerre, c'est une chose trop grave pour la confier à des militaires.*

War is too serious a business to be left to generals.
Quoted in Hampden Jackson *Clemenceau and the Third Republic* (1946), but also attributed elsewhere to others.

2 He died as he had lived—like a second lieutenant.
1891 On the death of General Boulanger, who had shot himself on the grave of his mistress, who had died two months earlier. In *La Justice*. Quoted in Edgar Holt *The Tiger: The Life of Georges Clemenceau 1841–1929* (1976).

3 Your verdict, gentlemen, will be less upon us than upon yourselves. We appear before you. You appear before history.

   1898 Addressing the jury as a member of the defence at Zola's trial, 22 Feb, following the publication of *J'Accuse*.

4 *Politique intérieure, je fais la guerre; politique extérieure, je fais toujours la guerre. Je fais toujours la guerre.*

   My home policy? I wage war. My foreign policy? I wage war. Always, everywhere, I wage war.

   1918 Speech to the Chamber of Deputies, 8 Mar.

5 *Il est plus facile de faire la guerre que la paix.*

   It is far easier to make war than to make peace.

   1919 Speech at Verdun, 20 Jul.

6 America is the only country in history that miraculously has gone directly from barbarism to decadence without the usual interval of civilization.

   Attributed. This has also been attributed to George Bernard Shaw.

7 We have won the war. Now we have to win the peace—and that may be more difficult.

   Quoted in David R Watson *George Clemenceau; A Political Biography* (1974).

Cleveland, (Stephen) Grover 1837–1908

22nd and 24th US President (1885–9, 1893–7). He supported civil service reform and lower tariffs, and in his second term he took a strong stance against Britain in its boundary dispute with Venezuela.

8 I have considered the pension list of the republic a roll of honour.

   1888 Veto of the Dependent Pension Bill, 5 Jul.

Cleveland, John 1613–1658

English poet, a satirical propagandist for the Royalists in the Civil War, and for a time a political prisoner. Two collections of his poems were published during his lifetime, one in 1651 and the other in 1653.

9 Had Cain been Scot, God would have changed his doom
   Nor forced him wander, but confined him home.

   1647 'The Rebel Scot'.

10 Mystical grammar of amorous glances,
    Feeling of pulses the physic of love,
    Rhetorical courtings, and musical dances;
    Numbering of kisses arithmetic prove.

    1651 'Mark Antony'.

11 Virtue's no more in womankind
    But the green sickness of the mind.
    Philosophy, their new delight,
    A kind of charcoal appetite.

    1653 'The Antiplatonic'.

12 Give me a lover bold and free,
    Not eunuched with formality.

    1653 'The Antiplatonic'.

13 Like an ambassador that beds a queen
    With the nice caution of a sword between.

    1653 'The Antiplatonic'.

Clifford, Clark 1906–98

US lawyer.

14 The amiable dunce.

    Of Ronald Reagan. Quoted in Haynes Johnson *Sleep-Walking Through History* (1991).

Clinton, Bill (William) 1946–

US Democratic politician and 42nd President. He was elected state Attorney General (1976) then Governor of Arkansas (1978, the youngest person ever to hold that office), and served for five terms (1979–81 and 1983–92). In 1992 he was elected the first Democratic President for 12 years.

15 Cash for trash.

    1992 On tabloid payments to his alleged mistress Gennifer Flowers. On ABC TV, 23 Jan.

16 On this day with high hopes and brave hearts, in massive numbers, the American people have voted to make a new beginning.

    1992 Accepting victory in the election, 3 Nov.

17 When somebody tells you it is not a money problem, they're talking about somebody else's money.

    1992 In *USA Today*, 20 Dec.

18 That hallowed piece of earth, that land of light and revelation, is the home to the memories and dreams of Jews, Muslims and Christians throughout the world.

    1993 On the signing of Palestinian–Israeli peace accord at the White House, 13 Sep.

19 I have had a drill to the tooth of America for the last two years.

    1994 Of painful political decisions. In the *US News & World Report*, 13 Feb.

20 I can't stop being President.

    1994 Comment after a suicide plane attack and two incidents of gunfire on the White House. Reported in the *New York Times*, 18 Dec.

21 If something makes you cry, you have to do something about it. That's the difference between politics and guilt.

    On what makes a liberal. Quoted in Meredith Oakley *On the Make* (1994).

22 Half the time when I see the evening news, I wouldn't be for me, either.

    1995 Comment, 2 Jun.

Clinton, Hillary Rodham 1947–

US politician and lawyer, wife of President Bill Clinton. As a lawyer she specialized in family issues and children's rights, and after her husband's election was appointed head of his Health Care Task Force.

23 I suppose I could have stayed home, baked cookies, and had teas.

1992 Rejecting charges of a conflict of interest between politics and her legal career. In the *New York Times*, 18 May.

24 I'd be a terrific governor…a terrific president.

1992 Statement during her husband's presidential campaign. Reported in the *Washington Post*, 22 Feb 1995.

25 It is time for us to say here in Beijing, and the world to hear, that it is no longer acceptable to discuss women's rights as separate from human rights.

1995 Addressing the 4th World Conference on Women. Reported in the *New York Times*, 6 Sep.

Clive, Kitty 1711–85

English comic actress. Though she longed to be a tragic actress, she excelled in light comedy under the management of David Garrick at Drury Lane. She retired in 1769.

26 Damn him, he could act a gridiron.

On watching a performance by David Garrick. Quoted in William Archer's introduction to *Dramatic Essays of Leigh Hunt*.

Clive, Robert, 1st Baron of Plassey
1725–74

English soldier and administrator in India, who defeated a large Indian–French force at Plassey (1757). After a spell in Parliament in Britain he returned to Calcutta (1765) to reform the civil service and the military, but was criticized for his drastic measures.

27 It is scarcely hyperbole to say that tomorrow the whole Moghul Empire is in our power.

1757 Letter, 24 Jun, following victory at Plassey the previous day.

28 By God, Mr Chairman—at this moment I stand astonished at my own moderation!

1773 At a parliamentary inquiry into his rapacious policies on India.

Clough, Arthur Hugh 1819–61

English poet. A friend of Ruskin, Arnold and Carlyle, he experienced a religious crisis in Oxford which pervades much of his writing.

29 Sesquipedalian blackguard.

1848 *The Bothie of Tober-na-Vuolich*, pt.2, l.223.

30 Grace is given of God, but knowledge is bought in the market.

1848 *The Bothie of Tober-na-Vuolich*, pt.4, l.159.

31 What shall we do without you? Think where we are. Carlyle has led us all out into the desert, and he has left us there.

1848 Parting words to Ralph Waldo Emerson, 15 Jul. Quoted in E E Hale *James Russell Lowell and his Friends*, ch.9.

32 Say not the struggle naught availeth
The labour and the wounds are vain,
The enemy faints not, nor faileth,
And as things have been, things remain.

If hopes were dupes, fears may be liars;
It may be, in yon smoke concealed,
Your comrades chase e'en now the fliers,
And, but for you, possess the field.

For the tired waves, vainly breaking,
Seem here no painful inch to gain,
Far back, through creeks and inlets making
Comes silent, flooding in, the main.

And not by eastern windows only,
When daylight comes, comes in the light,
In front the sun climbs slow, how slowly,
But westward, look, the land is bright.

1849 'Say Not the Struggle Naught Availeth'.

33 Afloat. We move: Delicious! Ah,
What else is like the gondola?

1850 *Dipsychus* (published 1865), sc.5.

34 This world is bad enough maybe;
We do not comprehend it;
But in one fact can all agree
God won't, and we can't mend it.

1850 *Dipsychus* (published 1865), sc.5.

35 'There is no God', the wicked saith,
'And truly it's a blessing,
For what he might have done with us
It's better only guessing.'

1850 *Dipsychus* (published 1865), sc.6.

36 And almost every one when age,
Disease, or sorrow strike him,
Inclines to think there is a God,
Or something very like him.

1850 *Dipsychus* (published 1865), sc.6.

37 'Tis better to have fought and lost,
Than never to have fought at all.

1854 'Peschiera'.

▷ See Tennyson 999:30.

38 Rome, believe me, my friend, is like its own Monte Testaceo,
Merely a marvellous mass of broken and castaway wine-pots.

1858 *Amours de Voyage*, canto 1, pt.2.

39 The horrible pleasure of pleasing inferior people.

1858 *Amours de Voyage*, canto 1, pt.11.

40 Am I prepared to lay down my life for the British
   female?
   Really, who knows?…
   Ah, for a child in the street I could strike; for the
   full-blown lady—
   Somehow, Eustace, alas! I have not felt the
   vocation.
   1858 *Amours de Voyage*, canto 2, pt.4.

41 I do not like being moved: for the will is excited;
   and action
   Is a most dangerous thing: I tremble for something
   factitious,
   Some malpractice of heart and illegitimate process;
   We are so prone to these things with our terrible
   notions of duty.
   1858 *Amours de Voyage*, canto 2, pt.11.

42 But for his funeral train which the bridegroom sees
   in the distance,
   Would he so joyfully, think you, fall in with the
   marriage-procession?
   1858 *Amours de Voyage*, canto 3, pt.6.

43 Allah is great, no doubt, and Juxtaposition his
   prophet.
   1858 *Amours de Voyage*, canto 3, pt.6.

44 Mild monastic faces in quiet collegiate cloisters.
   1858 *Amours de Voyage*, canto 3, pt.9.

45 Whither depart the souls of the brave that die in
   the battle,
   Die in the lost, lost fight, for the cause that perishes
   with them?
   1858 *Amours de Voyage*, canto 5, pt.6.

46 Thou shalt have one God only: who
   Would be at the expense of two?
   1862 *The Latest Decalogue.*

47 Thou shalt not kill; but need'st not strive
   Officiously to keep alive.
   1862 *The Latest Decalogue.*

48 Do not adultery commit;
   Advantage rarely comes of it.
   1862 *The Latest Decalogue.*

49 Thou shalt not steal; an empty feat,
   When it's so lucrative to cheat.
   1862 *The Latest Decalogue.*

50 Thou shalt not covet; but tradition
   Approves all forms of competition.
   1862 *The Latest Decalogue.*

Clough, Brian 1935–

English football player and manager. As a player, he set a
postwar goal-scoring record of 254 goals, and also won

two England caps. He went on to become a controversial
and outspoken but highly successful manager.

51 Football hooligans? Well, there are 92 club
   chairmen for a start.
   Quoted in Colin Jarman *The Guinness Dictionary of Sports
   Quotations* (1990).

52 Say nowt, win it, then—talk your head off.
   Summarizing his managerial style. Quoted in Colin Jarman *The
   Guinness Dictionary of Sports Quotations* (1990).

Cobbett, William 1762–1835

English radical politician and journalist. His pioneering
essays on the the conditions of the rural poor were
collected in his best-known work *Rural Rides* (1830).

53 Protestations of impartiality I shall make none.
   They are always useless and are besides perfect
   nonsense, when used by a news-monger.
   1797 In the first issue of *Porcupine's Gazette*, 4 Mar, 'Address to
   the public'.

54 All Middlesex is *ugly*, notwithstanding the millions
   upon millions which it is continually sucking up
   from the rest of the kingdom.
   1822 *Rural Rides* (published 1830), entry for 25 Sep.

55 DEAL is a most villanous place. It is full of filthy-
   looking people. Great desolation of abomination
   has been going on here.
   1823 On Deal, Kent. *Rural Rides* (published 1830), entry for 3
   Sep.

56 The town of GUILDFORD, which (taken with its
   environs) I, who have seen so many, many towns,
   think the prettiest, and, taken all together, the most
   agreeable and most happy-looking, that I ever saw
   in my life.
   1825 On Guildford, Surrey. *Rural Rides* (published 1830),
   entry for 23 Oct.

57 WESTBURY, a nasty odious *rotten-borough*, a
   really *rotten* place.
   1826 On Westbury, Wiltshire. *Rural Rides* (published 1830),
   entry for 3 Sep.

58 From a very early age, I had imbibed the opinion,
   that it was every man's duty to do all that lay in his
   power to leave his country as good as he had found
   it.
   1832 *Political Register*, 22 Dec.

Cobden, Richard 1804–65

English economist and politician, known as 'The Apostle
of Free Trade'. In 1838 he co-founded the Anti-Corn
League, and as MP from 1841 he spoke in support of the
cause, bringing about the repeal of the Corn Laws in
1846.

59 Are we to be the Don Quixotes of Europe—to go about fighting for every cause where we find that someone has been wronged?

1854 Referring to the Crimean War, House of Commons, 22 Dec.

Cockburn, Alison née *Rutherford* 1713–94

Scottish poet, whose best-known lyric 'The Flowers of the Forest' commemorates a calamity in Ettrick Forest. Walter Scott was her protégé.

60 I've seen the smiling of Fortune beguiling,
I've felt all its favours and found its decay;
Sweet was its blessing, kind its caressing,
But now it is fled, fled far, far away.

1765 'The Flowers of the Forest'.

61 O fickle Fortune, why this cruel sporting?
Why thus torment us poor sons of day?
Nae mair your smiles can cheer me, nae mair your frowns can fear me,
For the flowers of the forest are a' wade away.

1765 'The Flowers of the Forest'. wade = weeded. The last line is often rendered 'For the flowers of the forest are withered away'.

Cocteau, Jean 1889–1963

French poet, playwright and film director, a key figure in Surrealism and Dadaism, elected to the French Academy in 1955. His works explore the problems of adolescence and family relationships.

62 *Le tact dans l'audace c'est de savoir jusqu'où on peut aller trop loin.*

Being tactful in audacity is knowing how far one can go too far.

1918 *Le Coq et l'Arlequin.*

63 *Le pire drame pour un poète, c'est d'être admiré par malentendu.*

The worst tragedy for a poet is to be admired through being misunderstood.

1918 *Le Coq et l'Arlequin.*

64 *S'il faut choisir un crucifié, la foule sauve toujours Barabbas.*

If it has to choose who is to be crucified, the crowd will always save Barabbas.

1918 *Le Coq et l'Arlequin.*

65 *Vivre est une chute horizontale.*

Life is a horizontal fall.

1930 *Opium.*

66 Art produces ugly things which frequently become beautiful with time. Fashion, on the other hand, produces beautiful things which always become ugly with time.

1960 In the *New York World-Telegram and Sun*, 21 Aug.

Coffee, Lenore 1900–84

US screenwriter.

67 What a dump!

1949 Spoken by Bette Davis in *Beyond the Forest.*

Coffinhal, Jean Baptiste 1754–94

Presiding judge at the trial of chemist Antoine Lavoisier.

68 The Republic has no need for scientists.

1794 Quoted in the *Encyclopedia Britannica* (1911), vol.16.

Cohan, George M(ichael) 1878–1942

US actor-manager and playwright. Having started out in vaudeville, he became one of the great Broadway personalities, appearing in plays by himself and others at his own George M Cohan Theatre from 1911.

69 I'm a Yankee Doodle Dandy
A Yankee Doodle, do or die;
A real live nephew of my Uncle Sam's,
Born on the fourth of July.

1904 'Yankee Doodle Boy'.

70 I don't care what you say about me, as long as you say *something* about me, and as long as you spell my name right.

Quoted in John McCabe *George M Cohan, The Man Who Owned Broadway*, ch.13.

Coke, Sir Edward 1552–1634

English jurist, prosecutor of Essex, Raleigh and the Gunpowder conspirators. After 1606 he vindicated national liberties against the royal prerogative. Dismissed in 1617, he led the popular party in Parliament from 1620 and instigated the Petition of Right (1628).

71 How long soever it hath continued, if it be against reason, it is of no force in law.

1628 *The First Part of the Institutes of the Laws of England*, bk.1, ch.10, sect.80.

72 We have a saying in the House of Commons; that old ways are the safest and surest ways.

1628 Speech, London, 8 May.

73 A man's house is his castle.

1628 *The Third Part of the Institutes of the Laws of England*, ch.73.

Coke, F T Desmond 1879–1931

English novelist. A schoolmaster, he wrote several popular novels set in English public schools and universities, notably *The Bending of a Twig* (1906) and *Sandford of Merton* (1908).

74 His blade struck the water a full second before any other...until, as the boats began to near the winning post his own was dipping in the water twice as fast as any other.

1908 *Sandford of Merton*, ch.12. Often misquoted as 'All rowed fast but none so fast as stroke'.

Cole, Mac

Founder, Cole Carnival Shows.

75 The first carnival person was Christopher Columbus. When he sailed, he didn't know where he was going. When he got there, he didn't know where he was. And when he got back, he didn't know where he'd been.
1989 In the *Washington Times*, 18 Aug.

Cole, W Sterling 1904–88

Chair, Joint Committee on Atomic Energy.

76 It is more sinful to conceal the power of the atom than it is to reveal it.
1954 Statement, 9 Mar, endorsed by Winston Churchill in a letter to President Eisenhower. Quoted in Peter G Boyle (ed) *The Churchill-Eisenhower Correspondence 1953–55*.

Cole, William 1919–

US children's writer. His output consists chiefly of humorous verse, such as *A Boy Named Mary Jane* (1975). He has also edited many poetry and verse collections.

77 Said Jerome K. Jerome to Ford Madox Ford,
  'There's something, old boy, that I've always
    abhorred:
  When people address me and call me 'Jerome',
  Are they being standoffish, or too much at home?'
  Said Ford, 'I agree;
  It's the same thing with me.'
'Mutual Problem', collected in *The Oxford Book of American Light Verse* (1979).

Coleman, Ornette 1930–

US jazz saxophonist and composer. A controversial figure when he first appeared in New York in the late 1950s, he went on to become a key figure in the development of Free Jazz, and beyond.

78 The creation of music is just as natural as the air we breathe. I believe music is really a free thing, and any way you can enjoy it, you should.
1958 Sleeve-note, *Something Else!*

79 Many people apparently don't trust their reactions to art or to music unless there is a verbal *explanation* for it. In music the only thing that matters is whether you *feel* it or not.
1959 Sleeve-note, *Change of the Century*.

80 When I have them working together, it's like a beautiful kaleidoscope.
1981 On the music of his band Prime Time. Quoted in John Litweiler *The Freedom Principle* (1984).

Coleridge, Samuel Taylor 1772–1834

English poet, with Wordsworth one of the founders of the Romantic movement. Among his best known poems are 'The Rime of the Ancient Mariner' (1798), 'Christabel' (1816) and 'Kubla Khan' (1816).

81 So for the mother's sake the child was dear,
  And dearer was the mother for the child.
1797 'Sonnet to a Friend Who Asked Me How I Felt When the Nurse First Presented My Infant to Me'.

82 No sound is dissonant which tells of life.
1797 'This Lime-Tree Bower my Prison'.

83 It is an ancient Mariner,
  And he stoppeth one of three.
  'By thy long grey beard and glittering eye,
  Now wherefore stopp'st thou me?'
1789 'The Rime of the Ancient Mariner', pt.1.

84 He holds him with his glittering eye—
  The Wedding-Guest stood still,
  And listens like a three years' child:
  The Mariner hath his will.
  The Wedding-Guest sat on a stone:
  He cannot choose but hear;
  And thus spake on that ancient man,
  The bright-eyed Mariner.
1798 'The Rime of the Ancient Mariner', pt.1.

85 'God save thee, ancient Mariner!
  From the fiends that plague thee thus!
  Why look'st thou so?'—With my cross-bow
  I shot the Albatross.
1798 'The Rime of the Ancient Mariner', pt.1.

86 We were the first that ever burst
  Into that silent sea.
1798 'The Rime of the Ancient Mariner', pt.2.

87 As idle as a painted ship
  Upon a painted ocean.
1798 'The Rime of the Ancient Mariner', pt.2.

88 Water, water, everywhere,
  Nor any drop to drink.
  The very deep did rot: O Christ!
  That ever this should be!
  Yes, slimy things did crawl with legs
  Upon the slimy sea.
1798 'The Rime of the Ancient Mariner', pt.2.

89 I fear thee ancient Mariner!
  I fear thy skinny hand!
  And thou art long, and lank, and brown,
  As is the ribbed sea-sand.
1798 'The Rime of the Ancient Mariner', pt.4.

90 And a thousand thousand slimy things
  Lived on; and so did I.
1798 'The Rime of the Ancient Mariner', pt.4.

91 A spring of love gushed from my heart,
And I blessed them unaware.
1798 'The Rime of the Ancient Mariner', pt.4.

92 We were a ghastly crew.
1798 'The Rime of the Ancient Mariner', pt.5.

93 Like one, that on a lonesome road
Doth walk in fear and dread,
And having once turned round walks on,
And turns no more his head;
Because he knows, a frightful fiend
Doth close behind him tread.
1798 'The Rime of the Ancient Mariner', pt.6.

94 No voice, but oh! the silence sank
Like music on my heart.
1798 'The Rime of the Ancient Mariner', pt.6.

95 He prayeth well, who loveth well
Both man and bird and beast.
He prayeth best, who loveth best
All things both great and small.
1798 'The Rime of the Ancient Mariner', pt.7.

96 He went like one that hath been stunned,
And is of sense forlorn:
A sadder and wiser man,
He rose the morrow morn.
1798 'The Rime of the Ancient Mariner', pt.7.

97 O let me be awake, my God!
Or let me sleep alway.
1798 'The Rime of the Ancient Mariner', pt.7.

98 The frost performs its secret ministry,
Unhelped by any wind.
1798 'Frost at Midnight'.

99 Bells, the poor man's only music.
1798 'Frost at Midnight'.

1 And hark! the Nightingale begins its song,
'Most musical, most melancholy' bird!
A melancholy bird?…his song
Should make all Nature lovelier, and itself
Be loved like Nature!
1798 'The Nightingale'.

2 Belovèd, what are names but air?
Choose thou whatever suits the line;
Call me Sappho, call me Chloris,
Call me Lalage or Doris,
Only, only call me Thine.
1799 'Names', a translation from G E Lessing's German original (first published in the *Morning Post*, 1803).

3 All thoughts, all passions, all delights
Whatever stirs this mortal frame,
All are but ministers of Love,

And feed his sacred flame.
1799 'Love'.

4 Those sounds which oft have raised me, whilst they awed,
And sent my soul abroad,
Might now perhaps their wonted impulse give,
Might startle this dull pain, and make it move and live!
1802 'Dejection: An Ode', stanza 1.

5 I may not hope from outward forms to win
The passion and the life, whose fountains are within.
1802 'Dejection: An Ode', stanza 3.

6 Ah! from the soul itself must issue forth
A light, a glory, a fair luminous cloud
Enveloping the Earth—
And from the soul itself must there be sent
A sweet and potent voice, of its own birth
Of all sweet sounds the life and element!
1802 'Dejection: An Ode', stanza 4.

7 O pure of heart! thou need'st not ask of me
What this strong music in the soul may be!
What, and wherein it doth exist,
This light, this glory, this fair luminous mist,
This beautiful and beauty-making power.
1802 'Dejection: An Ode', stanza 5.

8 'Alas!' said she, 'we ne'er can be
Made happy by compulsion!'
1809 'The Three Graves', pt.4, stanza12.

9 What is an Epigram? a dwarfish whole,
Its body brevity, and wit its soul.
1809 'Epigram'.

10 Alas! they had been friends in youth;
But whispering tongues can poison truth;
And constancy lives in realms above;
And life is thorny; and youth is vain;
And to be wroth with one we love
Doth work like madness on the brain.
1816 'Christabel', pt.2.

11 On awaking he…instantly and eagerly wrote down the lines that are here preserved. At this moment he was unfortunately called out by a person on business from Parlock.
1816 Preliminary note to 'Kubla Khan', explaining the reasons for the fragmented end of the poem.

12 In Xanadu did Kubla Khan
A stately pleasure-dome decree:
Where Alph, the sacred river, ran
Through caverns measureless to man
Down to a sunless sea.
1816 'Kubla Khan', opening lines.

13 A savage place! as holy and enchanted
    As e'er beneath a waning moon was haunted
    By woman wailing for her demon-lover!
    1816 'Kubla Khan'.

14 And from this chasm, with ceaseless turmoil
       seething,
    As if this earth in fast thick pants were breathing,
    A mighty fountain momently was forced.
    1816 'Kubla Khan'.

15 It was a miracle of rare device,
    A sunny pleasure-dome with caves of ice!
    1816 'Kubla Khan'.

16 Through wood and dale the sacred river ran,
    Then reached the caverns measureless to man,
    And sank in tumult to a lifeless ocean:
    And 'mid this tumult Kubla heard from far
    Ancestral voices prophesying war!
    1816 'Kubla Khan'.

17 A damsel with a dulcimer
    In a vision once I saw:
    It was an Abyssinian maid,
    And on her dulcimer she played,
    Singing of Mount Abora.
    1816 'Kubla Khan'.

18 And all who heard should see them there,
    And all should cry, Beware! Beware!
    His flashing eyes, his floating hair!
    Weave a circle round him thrice,
    And close your eyes with holy dread,
    For he on honey-dew hath fed,
    And drunk the milk of Paradise.
    1816 'Kubla Khan'.

19 Until you understand a writer's ignorance, presume
    yourself ignorant of his understanding.
    1817 *Biographia Literaria*, ch.12.

20 That willing suspension of disbelief for the
    moment, which constitutes poetic faith.
    1817 *Biographia Literaria*, ch.14.

21 Kean is original; but he copies from himself. His
    rapid descents from the hyper-tragic to the infra-
    colloquial, though sometimes productive of great
    effect, are often unreasonable. To see him act, is like
    reading Shakespeare by flashes of lightning.
    1823 Of Edmund Kean. *Table Talk* (published 1835), entry for
    27 Apr.

22 He who begins by loving Christianity better than
    Truth will proceed by loving his own sect or church
    better than Christianity, and end by loving himself
    better than all.
    1825 *Aids to Reflection: Moral and Religious Aphorisms*.

23 Summer has set in with its usual severity.

1826 Letter to Vincent Novello, 9 May.

24 Prose = words in their best order;—poetry = the
    best words in the best order.
    1827 *Table Talk* (published 1835), entry for 12 Jul.

25 The man's desire is for the woman; but the woman's
    desire is rarely other than for the desire of the man.
    1827 *Table Talk* (published 1835), entry for 23 Jul.

26 In Köhln, a town of monks and bones,
    And pavements fang'd with murderous stones
    And rags, and hags, and hideous wenches;
    I counted two and seventy stenches,
    All well defined, and several stinks!
    Ye Nymphs that reign o'er sewers and sinks,
    The river Rhine, it is well known,
    Doth wash your city of Cologne;
    But tell me, Nymphs, what power divine
    Shall henceforth wash the river Rhine?
    1828 'Cologne', first published in *Friendship's Offering* (1834),
    as 'Lightheartedness in Rhyme', no.4.

27 If men could learn from history, what lessons it
    might teach us! But passion and party blind our
    eyes, and the light which experience gives is a
    lantern on the stern, which shines only on the
    waves behind us!
    1831 *Table Talk* (published 1835), entry for 18 Dec.

28 Farce is nearer tragedy in its essence than comedy
    is.
    1833 *Table Talk* (published 1835), entry for 25 Aug.

29 Of no age—nor of any religion, or party or
    profession. The body and substance of his works
    came out of the unfathomable depths of his own
    oceanic mind.
    1834 Of Shakespeare. *Table Talk* (published 1835), entry for
    15 Mar.

30 Iago's soliloquy—the motive-hunting of motiveless
    malignity.
    The Literary Remains of Samuel Taylor Coleridge (published
    1836), bk.2, 'Notes on the Tragedies of Shakespeare: Othello'.

Colette full name *Sidonie Gabrielle Colette*
1873–1954

French writer. Her first husband, Henri Gauthier-Villars,
published her early *Claudine* series under his pen-name
'Willy'. Her writing is marked by its exploration of the
sensual. Later works include *Chéri* (1920) and *Gigi*
(1945).

31 *Quand elle lève ses paupières, on dirait qu'elle se
    déshabille.*

    When she raises her eyelids it's as if she were taking
    off all her clothes.
    1903 *Claudine et Annie*, ch.3 (translated by Antonia White).

32 *Il découvrait... le monde des émotions qu'on nomme, à la légère, physiques.*

He was discovering... the world of the emotions that are so lightly called physical.
1923 *Le Blé en herbe.*

33 *Ne porte jamais de bijoux artistiques, ça déconsidère complètement une femme.*

Don't ever wear artistic jewelry; it wrecks a woman's reputation.
1944 *Gigi.*

Collingwood, Cuthbert, Baron 1748–1810

English admiral. He rose from midshipman to become second-in-command to Nelson at Trafalgar, on board the *Royal Sovereign.*

34 Now, gentlemen, let us do something today which the world may talk of hereafter.
1805 Remark to troops before the Battle of Trafalgar, 21 Oct. Quoted in G L Newnham Collingwood (ed*)* *A Selection from the Correspondence of Lord Collingwood* (1828), vol.1.

Collingwood, R(obin) G(eorge) 1889–1943

British philosopher and historian, with a strong archaeological interest. He wrote widely on the philosophy of history although his work was not well known until well after his death.

35 Perfect freedom is reserved for the man who lives by his own work and in that work does what he wants to do.
1924 *Speculum Mentis.*

36 A man ceases to be a beginner in any given science and becomes a master in that science when he has learned that... he is going to be a beginner all his life.
1942 *New Leviathan,* pt.1 ch.1.

Collins, Charles 1874–1926

English songwriter. He wrote rapid patter songs for use by music-hall stars of the day such as Harry Champion.

37 Any old iron, any old iron,
Any any old old iron?
You look neat
Talk about a treat,
You look dapper from your napper to your feet.
Dressed in style, brand new tile,
And your father's old green tie on,
But I wouldn't give you tuppence for your old watch chain;
Old iron, old iron?
1911 'Any old iron' (with E A Sheppard and Fred Terry). The second line is commonly rendered 'Any any any old iron?'.

38 My old man said, 'Follow the van,
Don't dilly-dally on the way!'

Off went the cart with the home packed in it,
I walked behind with my old cock linnet.
But I dillied and dallied, dallied and dilled,
Lost the van and don't know where to roam.
You can't trust the 'specials' like the old time 'coppers'
When you can't find your way home.
1919 'Don't Dilly-Dally on the Way' (with Fred Leigh).

Collins, Michael 1890–1922

Irish patriot and leader of the IRA. He signed the treaty of 1921 giving Ireland dominion status, believing it the best possible at the time, and after attempting to form a government under the terms of the treaty was killed in an ambush by hardline republicans.

39 Think—what I have got for Ireland? Something which she has wanted these past seven hundred years. Will anyone be satisfied with the bargain? Will anyone? I tell you this—early this morning I signed my death warrant. I thought at the time how odd, how ridiculous—a bullet may just as well have done the job five years ago.
1921 Letter, written after signing the peace treaty with Great Britain, 6 Dec.

Collins, Michael 1930–

Italian-born US astronaut who as a crew member of Apollo 11 piloted the spacecraft during its historic mission to the moon (1969). He orbited the moon alone in the command unit while Neil Armstrong and Buzz Aldrin made the first manned lunar landing.

40 I knew I was alone in a way that no earthling has ever been before.
1972 In *Times Magazine,* Dec 11, 1972.

Collins, William 1721–59

English poet, first published at the age of 17. His poetry, which is original and even experimental for the day, includes the 'Ode to Simplicity', 'Dirge in Cymbeline', 'Ode to Evening' and 'How Sleep the Brave'.

41 Too nicely Jonson knew the critic's part,
Nature in him was almost lost in Art.
1743 'Verses addressed to Sir Thomas Hanmer'.

42 To fair Fidele's grassy tomb
Soft maids and village hinds shall bring
Each opening sweet of earliest bloom,
And rifle all the breathing spring.
1744 'Dirge in Cymbeline'.

43 How sleep the brave, who sink to rest,
By all their country's wishes blest!
1746 'How Sleep the Brave' (published 1748), no.1.

44 By fairy hands their knell is rung,
By forms unseen their dirge is sung.
1746 'How Sleep the Brave' (published 1748), no.2.

45 O thou, the friend of man assigned,
   With balmy hands his wounds to bind,
   And charm his frantic woe:
   When first Distress with dagger keen
   Broke forth to waste his destined scene,
   His wild unsated foe!

   1747 *Odes on Several Descriptive and Allegoric Subjects*, 'Ode to Pity', no.1.

46 Ah Fear! Ah frantic Fear!
   I see, I see thee near.

   1747 *Odes on Several Descriptive and Allegoric Subjects*, 'Ode to Fear', l.5–6.

47 Though taste, though genius bless
   To some divine excess,
   Faints the cold work till thou inspire the whole;
   What each, what all supply
   May court, may charm our eye,
   Thou, only thou can'st raise the meeting soul!

   1747 *Odes on Several Descriptive and Allegoric Subjects*, 'Ode to Simplicity', no.8.

48 Now air is hushed, save where the weak-eyed bat
   With short shrill shriek flits by on leathern wing,
   Or where the beetle winds
   His small but sullen horn,
   As oft he rises midst the twilight path,
   Against the pilgrim borne in heedless hum.

   1747 *Odes on Several Descriptive and Allegoric Subjects*, 'Ode to Evening', l.9–14.

49 While Spring shall pour his showers, as oft he
        wont,
   And bathe thy breathing tresses, meekest Eve!
   While Summer loves to sport
   Beneath thy lingering light;
   While sallow Autumn fills thy lap with leaves,
   Or Winter, yelling through the troublous air,
   Affrights thy shrinking train,
   And rudely rends thy robes.

   1747 *Odes on Several Descriptive and Allegoric Subjects*, 'Ode to Evening', l.41–8.

50 With eyes up-raised, as one inspired,
   Pale Melancholy sate retired,
   And from her wild sequestered seat,
   In notes by distance made more sweet,
   Poured thro' the mellow horn her pensive soul.

   1747 'The Passions, An Ode for Music', l.57–61.

51 Love of peace, and lonely musing,
   In hollow murmurs died away.

   1747 'The Passions, An Ode for Music', l.67–8.

Colombo, John Robert 1936–

Canadian editor and poet.

52 Canada could have enjoyed:

English government,
French culture,
And American know-how.
Instead it ended up with:
English know-how,
French government,
And American culture.

1965 'O Canada', collected in Al Purdy (ed) *The New Romans* (1968).

Colton, Charles Caleb 1780–1832

British clergyman and writer. He was also a successful sportsman and was known for his gambling, which eventually led to his financial ruin and suicide.

53 Men will wrangle for religion; write for it; fight for it—anything but live for it.

   1820 *Lacon*, vol.1, no.25.

54 When you have nothing to say, say nothing.

   1820 *Lacon*, vol.1, no.183.

55 Imitation is the sincerest form of flattery.

   1820 *Lacon*, vol.1, no.217.

56 Examinations are formidable even to the best prepared, for the greatest fool may ask more than the wisest man can answer.

   1820 *Lacon*, vol.1, no.322.

57 If you would be known, and not know, vegetate in a village; if you would know, and not be known, live in a city.

   1820 *Lacon*, vol.1, no.334.

Coltrane, John 1926–67

US jazz saxophonist. He was the most influential tenor and soprano saxophonist of the post-war era.

58 The main thing a musician would like to do is to give a picture to the listener of the many wonderful things he knows and senses in the universe.

   1966 Quoted in sleeve-note to the re-issue of *Coltrane's Sound* (originally published 1961).

Colum, Padraic 1881–1972

Irish poet, playwright, novelist, biographer, critic and children's writer, a central figure in the Irish Literary Renaissance. Reflecting a peasant background, his work was realistic rather than romantic. His collections include *Wild Earth* (1907).

59 Sunset and silence! A man: around him earth
        savage, earth broken;
   Beside him two horses—a plough!

   Earth savage, earth broken, the brutes, the dawn-
        man there in the sunset,
   And the Plough that is twin to the Sword, that is
        founder of cities!

   1907 *Wild Earth*, 'The Plougher'.

60 My young love said to me, 'My brothers won't
   mind,
   And my parents won't slight you for your lack of
   kind.'
   Then she stepped away from me, and this she did
   say,
   'It will not be long, love, till our wedding day.'

   She stepped away from me and she moved through
   the fair
   And fondly I watched her go here and go there,
   Then she went her way homeward with one star
   awake,
   As the swan in the evening moves over the lake.

   The people were saying no two were ere wed
   But one had a sorrow that never was said,
   And I smiled as she passed with her goods and her
   gear,
   And that was the last that I saw of my dear.

   I dreamt it last night that my young love came in,
   So softly she entered, her feet made no din;
   She came close beside me, and this she did say,
   'It will not be long, love, till our wedding day.'
   1907 *Wild Earth*, 'She moved through the Fair'.

61 Then the wet, winding roads,
   Brown bogs with black water;
   And my thoughts on white ships
   And the King o' Spain's daughter.
   1907 'A Drover'.

62 Oh, to have a little house!
   To own the hearth and stool and all!
   The heaped-up sods upon the fire,
   The pile of turf against the wall!
   To have a clock with weights and chains
   And a pendulum swinging up and down,
   A dresser filled with shining delph,
   Speckled and white and blue and brown!
   c.1907 'An Old Woman of the Roads'.

Columbus, Christopher Spanish name
Cristóbal Colón 1451–1506

Genoese explorer, and discoverer of the New World
(1492). His *Carta del descubrimiento* is the first European
historical document about America.

63 *Toda la cristiandad debe tomar alegría y hacer
   grandes fiestas, y dar gracias solemnes a la Santa
   Trinidad, con muchas oraciones solemnes por el tanto
   ensalzamiento que habrán, en tornándose tantos
   pueblos a nuestra Santa Fe, y después por los bienes
   temporales que no solamente a la España, mas a todos
   los cristianos tendrán aquí refigerio y ganancia.*

   All Christendom ought to feel joyful and make
   great celebrations and give solemn thanks to the
   Holy Trinity with many solemn prayers for the

great exaltation which it will have, in the turning of
so many people to our holy faith, and afterwards
for material benefits, since not only Spain but all
Christians will hence have refreshment and profit.
1493 *Carta del descubrimiento* (translated as *The Letter in
Spanish of Christopher Columbus*, 1889).

Comden, Betty pseudonym of *Elizabeth Cohen*
1919–

US screenwriter and lyricist, who worked with Adolph
Green on a number of musicals. Her scripts include *On
the Town* (1949), *Singin' in the Rain* (1952) and *Bells are
Ringing* (1960).

64 I can stand anything but failure.
   1953 Line delivered by Oscar Levant in *The Band Wagon*.

65 The party's over, it's time to call it a day.
   1956 'The Party's Over' (with Adolphe Green, music by Jule
   Styne).

Commoner, Barry 1917–

US biologist closely associated with issues of ecology,
public health and environmental policy.

66 Science is triumphant with far-ranging success, but
   its triumph is somehow clouded by growing
   difficulties in providing for the simple necessities of
   human life on earth.
   1966 *Science and Survival*.

67 The gap between brute power and human need
   continues to grow, as the power fattens on the same
   faulty technology that intensifies the need.
   1972 'The Closing Circle', in *Technology*, 1972.

Comnena, Anna 1083–1153

Byzantine princess and historian, daughter of Emperor
Alexius I. She retired to a convent to write an account of
her father's reign after failing to secure the imperial throne
for her husband, Nicephorus Bryennius.

68 A mounted Kelt is irresistible; he would bore his
   way through the walls of Babylon.
   c.1148 Her description of the Frankish knights who passed
   through Constantinople on the First Crusade, 1097. *The
   Alexiad of Anna Comnena*, bk.13, ch.8 (translated by E R A
   Sewter).

Compton-Burnett, Dame Ivy 1892–1969

English novelist. Her novels, which explore the nuances
of human relationships, include *Pastors and Masters*
(1925), *Brothers and Sisters* (1929), *More Women than
Men* (1933) and *Mother and Son* (1955).

69 'Well, of course, people are only human,' said
   Dudley to his brother, as they walked to the house
   behind the women. 'But it really does not seem
   much for them to be.'

1939 *A Family and A Fortune*, ch.2.

70 People don't resent having nothing nearly as much as too little.
   1939 *A Family and A Fortune*, ch.4.

71 It will be a beautiful family talk, mean and worried and full of sorrow and spite and excitement. I cannot be asked to miss it in my weak state. I should only fret.
   1939 *A Family and A Fortune*, ch.10.

72 As regards plots I find real life no help at all. Real life seems to have no plots.
   1945 *Orion*, no.1, 'A Conversation'.

73 And people in life hardly seem definite enough to appear in print. They are not good or bad enough, or clever or stupid enough, or comic or pitiful enough.
   1945 *Orion*, no.1, 'A Conversation'.

74 We must use words as they are used, or stand aside from life.
   1955 *Mother and Son*, ch.9.

75 There is more difference within the sexes than between them.
   1955 *Mother and Son*, ch.10.

76 When I die people will say it is the best thing for me. It is because they know it is the worst. They want to avoid the feeling of pity.
   1961 *The Mighty and Their Fall*, ch.4.

77 There are different kinds of wrong. The people sinned against are not always the best.
   1961 *The Mighty and Their Fall*, ch.7.

78 There's not much to say. I haven't been at all deedy.
   1969 When asked about her life. In *The Times*, 30 Aug.

Comte, Auguste Isidore Marie Françoise
1798–1857

French social scientist, mathematician and philosopher of social science, whose work in logical positivism laid the foundations for contemporary social science.

79 To understand a science it is necessary to know its history.
   1851–4 *Système de Politique positive* (*Positive Philosophy*).

Conant, James Bryant 1893–1978

US educator, President of Harvard University (1933–53).

80 There is only one proved method of assisting the advancement of pure science—that of picking men of genius, backing them heavily, and leaving them to direct themselves.

1945 Letter to the *New York Times*, 13 Aug.

81 It seems as though I were in a lunatic asylum, but I am never sure who is the attendant and who the inmate.
   1950 Of Washington. Letter to Bernard Baruch, Feb. Quoted in James G Hershberg *James B Conant* (1993).

82 A Harvard education consists of what you learn at Harvard while you are not studying.
   Quoted in *Time Magazine*, 29 Sep 1986.

Condon, Richard 1915–96

US writer. He made his reputation with his successful novel of political intrigue, *The Manchurian Candidate* (1959).

83 In Mexico the gods ruled, the priests interpreted and interposed, and the people obeyed. In Spain, the priests ruled, the king interpreted and interposed, and the gods obeyed. A nuance in an ideological difference is a wide chasm.
   1961 *A Talent for Loving*, bk.1, ch.6.

84 He was an unzipped fly caught in forever amber.
   1967 *The Ecstasy Business*, ch.1.

85 What is art is not likely to be decided for decades or longer after the work has been produced—and then is often redecided—so we must not think badly if we regard literature as entertainment rather than as transcendent enlightenment.
   1976 Comment in D L Fitzpatrick (ed) *Contemporary Novelists*.

86 She felt sexual urgings towards Yvonne in the manner that politicians feel an enormous sexual pull towards mirrors.
   1978 *Bandicoot*, ch.21.

Confucius or *K'ung Fu-tse*, 'The Master K'ung'
551–479 BC

Chinese philosopher. He was Governor of Chung-tu, Minister of Works and later Minister of Justice. Although his social reform measures were popular, his enemies forced him into exile. His sayings are collected in the *Confucian Analects*, compiled by his pupils after his death.

87 Man has three ways of acting wisely. First, on meditation; that is the noblest. Secondly, on imitation; that is the easiest. Thirdly, on experience; that is the bitterest.
   c.479 BC *The Analects*.

88 The people may be made to follow a course of action, but they may not be made to understand it.
   c.479 BC *The Analects*.

89 When you meet someone better than yourself, turn your thoughts to becoming his equal. When you meet someone not as good as you are, look within and examine your own self.

c.479 BC *The Analects*, p.413.

90 When I have pointed out one corner of a square to anyone and he does not come back with the other three, I will not point it out to him a second time.

c.479 BC *The Analects*, p.449.

91 He that in his studies wholly applies himself to labour and exercise, and neglects meditation, loses his time, and he that only applies himself to meditation, and neglects labour and exercise, only wanders and loses himself.

Quoted in Colin Jarman *The Guinness Dictionary of Sports Quotations* (1990).

Congreve, William 1670–1729

English dramatist and poet. His first publication was a novel (1692), and he translated Juvenal and wrote original verse. He is best remembered for his witty plays, including *Love for Love* (1698) and *The Way of the World* (1700).

92 I am always of the opinion with the learned, if they speak first.

1692 *Incognita.*

93 In my conscience I believe the baggage loves me, for she never speaks well of me herself, nor suffers any body else to rail at me.

1693 Bellemore to Sharper. *The Old Bachelor*, act 1, sc.3.

94 Man was by Nature Woman's cully made: We never are, but by ourselves, betrayed.

1693 Lucy to Silvia. *The Old Bachelor*, act 3, sc.1.

95 Bilbo's the word, and slaughter will ensue.

1693 Bluffe to Sir Joseph. *The Old Bachelor*, act 3, sc.7.

96 Ask all the tyrants of thy sex, if their fools are not known by this part-coloured livery—I am melancholy when thou art absent; look like an ass when thou art present; wake for thee, when I should sleep, and even dream of thee, when I am awake; sigh much, drink little, eat less, court solitude, am grown very entertaining to my self, and (as I am informed) very troublesome to everybody else. If this be not love, it is madness, and then it is pardonable—Nay yet a more certain sign of all this; I give thee my money.

1693 Heartwell to Sylvia. *The Old Bachelor*, act 3, sc.10.

97 Eternity was in that moment.

1693 Bellmore to Laetitia. *The Old Bachelor*, act 4, sc.7.

98 Now am I slap-dash down in the mouth.

1693 Sir Joseph to Bluffe. *The Old Bachelor*, act 4, sc.9.

99 Thus grief still treads upon the heels of pleasure:

Married in haste, we may repent at leisure.

1693 Sharper to Setter. *The Old Bachelor*, act 5, sc.1.

1 Some by experience find those words mis-placed: At leisure married, they repent in haste.

1693 Setter to Sharper. *The Old Bachelor*, act 5, sc.1.

2 I could find it in my heart to marry thee, purely to be rid of thee.

1693 Belinda to Bellmore. *The Old Bachelor*, act 5, sc.10.

3 Courtship to marriage, as a very witty prologue to a very dull play.

1693 Bellmore to Belinda. *The Old Bachelor*, act 5, sc.10.

4 It is the business of a comic poet to paint the vices and follies of human kind.

1693 *The Double Dealer*, epistle dedicatory.

5 Retired to their tea and scandal, according to their ancient custom.

1693 Mellefont to Charles. *The Double Dealer*, act 1, sc.1.

6 There is nothing more unbecoming a man of quality than to laugh; Jesu, 'tis such a vulgar expression of the passion!

1693 Lord Froth to Brisk. *The Double Dealer*, act 1, sc.4.

7 Tho' marriage makes man and wife one flesh, it leaves 'em still two fools.

1693 Cynthia to Mellefont. *The Double Dealer*, act 2, sc.3.

8 She lays it on with a trowel.

1693 Brisk to Lord Froth. *The Double Dealer*, act 3, sc.10.

9 See how love and murder will out.

1693 *The Double Dealer*, act 4, sc.6.

10 No mask like open truth to cover lies, As to go naked is the best disguise.

1693 *The Double Dealer*, act 5, sc.6.

11 Has he not a rogue's face?…a haunting-look to me…has a damned Tyburn-face, without the benefit o' the Clergy.

1695 Of Sir Sampson. *Love for Love*, act 2, sc.7.

12 I came upstairs into the world; for I was born in a cellar.

1695 Jeremy. *Love for Love*, act 2, sc.7.

13 I know that's a secret, for it's whispered every where.

1695 Tattle to Scandal. *Love for Love*, act 3, sc.3.

14 He that first cries out stop thief, is often he that has stolen the treasure.

1695 Scandal to Mrs Foresight. *Love for Love*, act 3, sc.14.

15 Women are like tricks by sleight of hand, which, to admire, we should not understand.

1695 Valentine. *Love for Love*, act 4, sc.21.

16 A branch of one of your antediluvian families, fellows that the flood could not wash away.
1695 Sir Sampson to Angelica. *Love for Love*, act 5, sc.2.

17 To find a young fellow that is neither a wit in his own eye, nor a fool in the eye of the world, is a very hard task.
1695 Sir Sampsom to Angelica. *Love for Love*, act 5, sc.2.

18 Aye, 'tis well enough for a servant to be bred at an University. But the education is a little too pedantic for a gentleman.
1695 Tattle to Jeremy. *Love for Love*, act 5, sc.3.

19 Nay, for my part I always despised Mr Tattle of all things; nothing but his being my husband could have made me like him less.
1695 Mrs Frail to Mrs Foresight. *Love for Love*, act 5, sc.11.

20 I confess freely to you, I could never look long upon a Monkey, without very Mortifying Reflections.
1695 Letter to John Dennis, 10 Jul.

21 Music hath charms to soothe a savage breast, To soften rocks, or bend a knotted oak.
1697 Almeria to Leonora. *The Mourning Bride*, act 1, sc.1.

22 Heaven has no rage, like love to hatred turned, Nor Hell a fury, like a woman scorned.
1697 Zara. *The Mourning Bride*, act 3, sc.8.

23 Is he then dead?
What, dead at last, quite, quite for ever dead!
1697 Almeria to Leonora. *The Mourning Bride*, act 5, sc.11.

24 They come together like the Coroner's Inquest, to sit upon the murdered reputations of the week.
1700 Fainall to Mirabell. *The Way of the World*, act 1, sc.1.

25 She once used me with that insolence that in revenge I took her to pieces; sifted her, and separated her failings; I studied 'em, and got 'em by rote. The catalogue was so large that I was not without hopes, one day or other, to hate her heartily: to which end I so used myself to think of 'em that at length, contrary to my design and expectation, they gave me every hour less and less disturbance, till in a few days it became habitual to me to remember 'em without being displeased. They are now grown as familiar to me as my own frailties, and in all probability in a little time longer I shall like 'em as well.
1700 *The Way of the World*, act 1, sc.3.

26 Ay, ay, I have experience: I have a wife, and so forth.
1700 Fainall to Mirabell. *The Way of the World*, act 1, sc.3.

27 FAINALL: 'Tis for the honour of England that all Europe should know that we have blockheads of all ages.
MIRABELL: I wonder there is not an Act of Parliament to save the credit of the nation, and prohibit the exportation of fools.
1700 *The Way of the World*, act 1, sc.5.

28 A wit should no more be sincere than a woman constant; one argues a decay of parts, as t'other of beauty.
1700 *The Way of the World*, act 1, sc.6.

29 What, he speaks unseasonable truths sometimes, because he has not wit enough to invent an evasion.
1700 *The Way of the World*, act 1, sc.6.

30 I always take blushing either for a sign of guilt, or of ill breeding.
1700 Petulant to Mirabell. *The Way of the World*, act 1, sc.9.

31 To pass over youth in dull indifference, to refuse the sweets of life because they once must leave us, is as preposterous as to wish to have been born old, because we one day may be old. For my part, my youth may wear and waste, but it shall never rust in my possession.
1700 *The Way of the World*, act 2, sc.1.

32 Say what you will, 'tis better to be left than never to have been loved.
1700 Mrs Warwood to Mrs Fainall. *The Way of the World*, act 2, sc.1.

33 WITWOUD: Madam, do you pin up your hair with all your letters?
MILLAMANT: Only with those in verse, Mr Witwoud. I never pin up my hair with prose.
1700 *The Way of the World*, act 2, sc.4.

34 Beauty is the lover's gift.
1700 Mirabell. *The Way of the World*, act 2, sc.4.

35 Here she comes i' faith full sail, with her fan spread and streamers out, and a shoal of fools for tenders.
1700 Of Mirabell. *The Way of the World*, act 2, sc.5.

36 Nobody knows how to write letters; and yet one has 'em, one does not know why.—They serve one to pin up one's hair.
1700 *The Way of the World*, act 2, sc.5.

37 To please a fool is some degree of folly.
1700 *The Way of the World*, act 2, sc.6.

38 A fellow that lives in a windmill has not a more whimsical dwelling than the heart of a man that is lodged in a woman.
1700 *The Way of the World*, act 2, sc.7.

39 A little disdain is not amiss; a little scorn is alluring.
1700 Lady Wishfort to Foible. *The Way of the World*, act 3, sc.5.

40 Love's but the frailty of the mind,
When 'tis not with ambition joined;
A sickly flame, which if not fed expires;
And feeding, wastes in self-consuming fires.
1700 *The Way of the World*, act 3, sc.12.

41 Marriage is honourable, as you say; and if so,
wherefore should cuckoldom be a discredit, being
derived from so honourable a root?
1700 *The Way of the World*, act 3, sc.12.

42 I confess I have deserted the high place I once held
of sighing at your feet.
1700 *The Way of the World*, act 3, sc.12.

43 O, nothing is more alluring than a levee from a
couch in some confusion.
1700 Lady Wishfort to Foible. *The Way of the World*, act 4, sc.1.

44 Don't let us be familiar or fond, nor kiss before
folks, like my Lady Fadler and Sir Francis: nor go to
Hyde-Park together the first Sunday in a new
chariot, to provoke eyes and whispers, and then
never be seen there together again; as if we were
proud of one another the first week, and ashamed
of one another ever after... Let us be very strange
and well-bred: Let us be as strange as if we had been
married a great while, and as well-bred as if we were
not married at all.
1700 Millimant to Mirabell. *The Way of the World*, act 4, sc.5.

45 These articles subscribed, if I continue to endure
you a little longer, I may by degrees dwindle into
wife.
1700 Millimant to Mirabell. *The Way of the World*, act 4, sc.5.

46 I hope you do not think me prone to any iteration
of nuptials.
1700 Lady Wishfort to Whitwell disguised as Sir Roland. *The Way of the World*, act 4, sc.12.

47 Music alone with sudden charms can bind
The wand'ring sense, and calm the troubled
mind.
c.1701 'Hymn to Harmony'.

48 Would I were free from this restraint,
Or else had hopes to win her;
Would she could make of me a saint,
Or I of her a sinner.
'Pious Selinda Goes to Prayers'.

Conklin, Edwin G(rant) 1863–1952

Professor of Embryology at Princeton. He was a specialist
in the embryology of marine organisms.

49 Wooden legs are not inherited but wooden heads
may be.
Recalled on his death, 21 Nov 1952.

Connally, John Bowden 1917–

US politician and lawyer. He was Governor of Texas
(1963–9).

50 A chess tournament disguised as a circus.
1964 Of US political conventions. In the *National Observer*.
Quoted in Edwin A Roberts Jr *Elections 1964*.

51 It's not a sin to be rich anymore—it's a miracle.
1988 In *Time*, 18 Jan.

52 All hat and no cattle.
1989 Responding to George Bush's claim to be a Texan. In the
New York Times, 14 Feb.

Connally, Tom (Thomas Terry) 1877–1963

US Congressman and lawyer. He was Representative for
Texas (1917–29) and a Senator (1929–53). A Democrat,
he supported southern business interests and opposed
anti-lynching legislation. He was a strong supporter of the
UN and NATO.

53 Don't you ever shake that lanky Yankee finger at
me.
1963 To Senator Charles Tobey. Reported in *Time*, 8 Nov.

Connell, James 1852–1929

Irish socialist and songwriter.

54 The people's flag is deepest red;
It shrouded oft our martyred dead.
And ere their limbs grew stiff and cold,
Their heart's blood dyed its every fold.
Then raise the scarlet standard high!
Within its shade we'll live or die.
Tho' cowards flinch and traitors sneer,
We'll keep the red flag flying here.
1889 'The Red Flag', official anthem of the Labour Party.

Connolly, Cyril Vernon 1903–74

English author and journalist. He founded and edited the
influential cultural journal *Horizon* (1939–50). His best
known books are *Enemies of Promise* (1938) and *The
Unquiet Grave* (1944).

55 Better to write for yourself and have no public,
than to write for the public and have no self.
1933 In the *New Statesman*, 25 Feb.

56 Destroy him as you will, the bourgeois always
bounces up—execute him, expropriate him, starve
him out *en masse*, and he reappears in your
children.
1937 In *The Observer*, 7 Mar.

57 A great writer creates a world of his own and his
readers are proud to live in it. A lesser writer may
entice them in for a moment, but soon he will
watch them filing out.
1938 *Enemies of Promise*, ch.1.

58 Literature is the art of writing something that will be read twice; journalism what will be read once.
1938 *Enemies of Promise*, ch.3.

59 As repressed sadists are supposed to become policemen or butchers, so those with an irrational fear of life become publishers.
1938 *Enemies of Promise*, ch.10

60 I should like to see the custom introduced of readers who are pleased with a book sending the author some small cash token… Not more than a hundred pounds—that would be bad for my character—not less than half a crown—that would do no good to yours.
1938 *Enemies of Promise*, ch.13.

61 Whom the gods wish to destroy they first call promising.
1938 *Enemies of Promise*, ch.13

62 There is no more sombre enemy of good art than the pram in the hall.
1938 *Enemies of Promise*, ch.14.

63 All charming people have something to conceal, usually their total dependence on the appreciation of others.
1938 *Enemies of Promise*, ch.16.

64 Humorists are not happy men. Like Beachcomber or Saki or Thurber they burn while Rome fiddles.
1938 *Enemies of Promise*, ch.16.

65 A private school has all the faults of a public school without any of its compensations.
1938 *Enemies of Promise*, ch.19.

66 I have called this style the Mandarin style… It is the style of those writers whose tendency is to make their language convey more than they mean or more than they feel, it is the style of most artists and all humbugs.
1938 *Enemies of Promise*, ch.20.

67 Were I to deduce any system from my feelings on leaving Eton, it might be called *The Theory of Permanent Adolescence.*
1938 *Enemies of Promise*, ch.24.

68 The more books we read, the sooner we perceive that the only function of a writer is to produce a masterpiece. No other task is of any consequence.
1944 *The Unquiet Grave*, pt.1.

69 There is no fury like an ex-wife looking for a new lover.
1944 *The Unquiet Grave*, pt.1.

70 In the sex war thoughtlessness is the weapon of the male, vindictiveness of the female.
1944 *The Unquiet Grave*, pt.1.

71 Life is a maze in which we take the wrong turning before we have learnt to walk.
1944 *The Unquiet Grave*, pt.1.

72 Everything is a dangerous drug to me except reality, which is unendurable.
1944 *The Unquiet Grave*, pt.1.

73 The civilization of one epoch becomes the manure of the next.
1944 *The Unquiet Grave*, pt.2.

74 The disasters of the world are due to its inhabitants not being able to grow old simultaneously.
1944 *The Unquiet Grave*, pt.2.

75 Imprisoned in every fat man a thin one is wildly signalling to be let out.
1944 *The Unquiet Grave*, pt.2.

76 The true index of a man's character is the health of his wife.
1944 *The Unquiet Grave*, pt.2.

77 We are all serving a life-sentence in the dungeon of self.
1944 *The Unquiet Grave*, pt.2.

78 Our memories are card-indexes consulted, and then put back in disorder by authorities whom we do not control.
1944 *The Unquiet Grave*, pt.2.

79 It is closing time in the gardens of the West and from now on an artist will be judged only by the resonance of his solitude or the quality of his despair.
1949 *Horizon*, no.120–1, Dec 1949–Jan 1950 (double issue, the final issue of the journal).

80 A romantic interest in our own sex, not necessarily carried as far as physical experiments, was the intellectual fashion.
Of Oxford during his student days. Quoted in Peter Quennell *The Marble Foot* (1977).

Connolly, James 1868–1916

Irish Labour leader and insurgent. He organized the Irish Socialist Republican party and founded *The Workers' Republic*, the first Irish socialist paper. He lectured in the US and organized strikes in Ireland, and was executed for his part in the 1916 Easter rebellion.

81 It is an axiom enforced by all the experience of the ages, that they who rule industrially will rule politically.
1909 *Socialism Made Easy.*

82 Don't be 'practical' in politics. To be practical in that sense means that you have schooled yourself to

think along the lines, and in the grooves that those who rob you would desire you to think.

1909 *Socialism Made Easy.*

83 The day has passed for patching up the capitalist system; it must go. And in the work of abolishing it the Catholic and the Protestant, the Catholic and the Jew, the Catholic and the Freethinker, the Catholic and the Buddhist, the Catholic and the Mahometan will co-operate together, knowing no rivalry but the rivalry of endeavour toward an end beneficial to all. For, as we have said elsewhere, Socialism is neither Protestant nor Catholic, Christian nor Freethinker, Buddhist, Mahometan, nor Jew; it is only HUMAN.

1910 *Labour, Nationality, and Religion.*

84 The worker is the slave of capitalist society, the female worker is the slave of that slave.

1915 *The Re-conquest of Ireland.*

Connor, Sir William Neil pseudonym
Cassandra 1909–67

English journalist, a columnist with the *Daily Mirror* from 1935 until his death.

85 As I was saying when I was interrupted, it is a powerful hard thing to please all of the people all of the time.

1946 On resuming his Cassandra column in the *Daily Mirror,* Sep, after the end of World War II.

Conrad, Joseph originally *Jozef Teodor Konrad Nalecz Korzeniowski* 1857–1924

Polish-born British novelist who joined an English merchant ship in 1878, and was naturalized in 1884 as a master mariner. The sea provided the background for much of his work, notably *Heart of Darkness* (1899) and *Lord Jim* (1900).

86 It is only those who do nothing that make no mistakes, I suppose.

1896 *An Outcast of the Islands,* pt.3, ch.2.

87 Any work that aspires, however humbly, to the condition of art should carry its justification in every line.

1897 *The Nigger of the Narcissus,* preface.

88 My task which I am trying to achieve is, by the power of the written word to make you hear, to make you feel—it is, before all, to make you *see*. That—and no more, and it is everything.

1897 *The Nigger of the Narcissus,* preface.

89 The conquest of the earth, which mostly means the taking it away from those who have a different complexion or slightly flatter noses than ourselves,

is not a pretty thing when you look into it too much. What redeems it is an idea only.

1899 *Heart of Darkness,* pt.1 (first published in *Blackwood's Magazine,* collected in *Youth: A Narrative, and Two Other Stories,* 1902).

90 We live, as we dream—alone.

1899 *Heart of Darkness,* pt.1 (first published in *Blackwood's Magazine,* collected in *Youth: A Narrative, and Two Other Stories,* 1902).

91 Exterminate all the brutes!

1899 *Heart of Darkness,* pt.2 (first published in *Blackwood's Magazine,* collected in *Youth: A Narrative, and Two Other Stories,* 1902).

92 He cried in a whisper at some image, at some vision—he cried out twice, a cry that was no more than a breath: 'The horror! The horror!'

1899 Kurtz's final words. *Heart of Darkness,* pt.3 (first published in *Blackwood's Magazine,* collected in *Youth: A Narrative, and Two Other Stories,* 1902).

93 Mistah Kurtz—he dead.

1899 *Heart of Darkness,* pt.3 (first published in *Blackwood's Magazine,* collected in *Youth: A Narrative, and Two Other Stories,* 1902).

94 A man that is born falls into a dream like a man who falls into the sea… The way is to the destructive element submit yourself, and with the exertions of your hands and feet in the water make the deep, deep sea keep you up.

1900 *Lord Jim,* ch.20.

95 You shall judge a man by his foes as well as by his friends.

1900 *Lord Jim,* ch.34.

96 Suddenly a puff of wind, a puff faint and tepid and laden with strange odours of blossoms, of aromatic wood, comes out of the still night—the first sigh of the east on my face.

1902 'Youth'.

97 The mysterious East, perfumed like a flower, silent like death, dark like a grave.

1902 'Youth'.

98 I remember my youth and the feeling that it will never come back any more—the feeling that I could last for ever, outlast the sea, the earth, and all men; the deceitful feeling that lures us on to joys, to perils, to love, to vain effort—to death; the triumphant conviction of strength, the heat of life in the handful of dust, the glow in the heart that with every year grows dim, grows cold, grows small, and expires— and expires, too soon, too soon—before life itself.

1902 'Youth'.

99 Action is consolatory. It is the enemy of thought and the friend of flattering illusions.

1904 *Nostromo*, pt.1, ch.6.

1 Liberty of the imagination should be the most precious possession of a novelist.
1905 'Books'.

2 To be hopeful in an artistic sense it is not necessary to think that the world is good. It is enough to believe that there is no impossibility of it being made so.
1905 'Books'.

3 Of all the inanimate objects, of all men's creations, books are the nearest to us, for they contain our very thoughts, our ambitions, our indignations, our illusions, our fidelity to truth, and our persistent leaning towards error. But most of all they resemble us in their precarious hold on life.
1905 'Books'.

4 The terrorist and the policeman both come from the same basket.
1907 *The Secret Agent*, ch.4.

5 Some kind of moral discovery should be the object of every tale.
1911 *Under Western Eyes*, prologue.

6 Words, as is well known, are the great foes of reality.
1911 *Under Western Eyes*, prologue.

7 The scrupulous and the just, the noble, humane, and devoted natures; the unselfish and the intelligent may begin a movement—but it passes away from them. They are not the leaders of a revolution. They are its victims.
1911 *Under Western Eyes*, pt.2, ch.3.

8 A belief in a supernatural source of evil is not necessary; men alone are quite capable of every wickedness.
1911 *Under Western Eyes*, pt.2, ch.4.

9 All ambitions are lawful except those which climb upwards on the miseries or credulities of mankind.
1912 *Some Reminiscences*, preface.

10 On the contrary, the mere fact of dealing with matters outside the general run of everyday experience laid me under the obligation of a more scrupulous fidelity to the truth of my own sensations. The problem was to make unfamiliar things credible.
1915 *Within the Tides*, preface.

11 Thinking is the great enemy of perfection. The habit of profound reflection, I am compelled to say, is the most pernicious of all the habits formed by civilized man.
1915 *Victory*, author's note.

12 It is not the clear-sighted who rule the world. Great achievements are accomplished in a blessed, warm fog.
1915 *Victory*, author's note.

13 It was amazing to think that in those miles of human habitations there was not probably half a dozen pounds of nails.
1917 Of Bangkok. *The Shadow-Line*.

14 In plucking the fruit of memory one runs the risk of spoiling its bloom.
1920 *The Arrow of Gold*, author's note.

Conran, Shirley Ida née *Pearce* 1932–
English designer and fashion editor, first wife of Sir Terence Conran. She is the author of several best-selling books, including *Superwoman* (1975) and *Lace* (1982).

15 Our motto: Life is too short to stuff a mushroom.
1975 *Superwoman*, epigraph.

Conroy, (Donald) Pat(rick) 1945–
US writer.

16 It was like walking down the street with the Statue of Liberty.
1995 On walking in Manhattan with the instantly recognizable Barbra Streisand. In *WAMU*, 4 Sep.

Constable, John 1776–1837
English landscape painter. With Turner, one of Britain's most important and best-loved landscape painters.

17 A gentleman's park is my aversion. It is not beauty because it is not nature.
1822 In R B Beckett (ed) *Constable's Correspondence*, Suffolk Records Society (1962–70).

18 In Claude's landscape all is lovely—all amiable—all is amenity and repose;—the calm sunshine of the heart.
1836 Lecture, 2 Jun. Quoted in C R Leslie *Memoirs of the Life of John Constable* (1843).

19 When I set down to make a sketch from nature, the first thing I try to do is to forget that I have ever seen a picture.
Quoted in C R Leslie *Memoirs of the Life of John Constable* (1843).

20 There is nothing ugly; *I never saw an ugly thing in my life*: for let the form of an object be what it may—light, shade and perspective will always make it beautiful.
Quoted in C R Leslie *Memoirs of the Life of John Constable* (1843).

21 He seems to paint with tinted steam.
Of Turner. Quoted in *Treasures of the Fitzwilliam Museum* (1982).

Constant (de Rebecque), (Henri) Benjamin 1767–1830

French novelist and politician. He supported the Revolution in Paris (1795) and was banished (1802) for opposing Napoleon. On his return in 1814 he became leader of the liberal opposition. His best-known novel *Adolphe* (1816) is based on his relationship with Mme de Staël.

22 *L'art pour l'art, sans but, car tout but dénature l'art. Mais l'art atteint au but qu'il n'a pas.*

Art for art's sake, with no purpose, for any purpose perverts art. But art achieves a purpose which is not its own.

1804 *Journal intime*, 11 Feb, quoted in the *Revue Internationale*, 10 Jan 1887.

Constantine full name *Flavius Valerius Aurelius Constantinus* c.274–337 AD

Roman Emperor, who adopted Christianity c.312 AD. He founded a royal residence at Byzantium (Constantinople), an act of great historical importance.

23 *In hoc signo vinces.*

In this sign thou shalt conquer.

AD 312 'Constantine's Vision', quoted in Eusebius *Life of Constantine*.

Cook, Arthur James 1883–1931

Welsh miners' leader, General Secretary of the national union and a key figure in the General Strike of 1926.

24 Not a penny off the pay; not a second on the day.

1926 Miners' strike slogan, coined in a speech, 3 Apr. It is often rendered 'not a minute on the day'.

Cook, Captain James 1728–79

English navigator. He undertook expeditions to the Pacific, the Antarctic and the west coast of North America, charting all these regions. He was killed in Hawaii by natives as he landed to recover a stolen boat.

25 As to a Southern Continent, I do not believe any such thing exists, unless in a high altitude.

1768–71 *Captain Cook's Journal during his First Voyage Round the World made in H. M. Bark 'Endeavour'.*

26 Curse the scientists, and all science into the bargain.

Quoted in J C Beaglehole (ed) *The Voyage of the Resolution* (1961).

Cook, Peter 1937–94

English comedian. He appeared in revue at Cambridge University and went on to write and star in the revue *Beyond the Fringe* (1960).

27 I go to the theatre to be entertained. I don't want to see plays about rape, sodomy and drug addiction— I can get all that at home.

Comedy routine. Also used as a cartoon caption in *The Observer*, 8 Jul 1962.

28 We exchanged many frank words in our respective languages.

1961 Impersonation of Harold Macmillan. *Beyond the Fringe*.

Cooke, (Alfred) Alistair 1908–

English-born US journalist and broadcaster, best known for his 'Letter from America', first broadcast by the BBC in 1946.

29 All Presidents start out pretending to run a crusade, but after a couple of years they find they are running something much less heroic, much more intractable: namely, the Presidency.

1963 In *The Listener*.

30 An episode out of George Orwell rewritten by Charles Dickens.

1979 Of Gerald R Ford's succession to the US presidency on Richard M Nixon's resignation. *The Americans*.

31 Like a christening, a wedding, a graduation ceremony, a holy war, a revolution even…a fireworks display, a gaudy promise of what life ought to be, not life itself.

1979 Of elections. *The Americans*.

32 But after all it's not the winning that matters, is it? Or is it? It's—to coin a word—the amenities that count: the smell of the dandelions, the puff of the pipe, the click of the bat, the rain on the neck, the chill down the spine, the slow, exquisite coming on of sunset and dinner and rheumatism.

Quoted in Helen Exley *Cricket Quotations* (1992).

33 Canned music is like audible wallpaper.

Quoted in David Pickering *Brewer's Twentieth Century Music* (1994).

Coolidge, (John) Calvin 1872–1933

US Republican politician and 30th President (1923–9). A strong supporter of US business interests, he was re-elected in 1924 but refused renomination in 1928.

34 Civilization and profits go hand in hand.

1920 Speech, New York, 27 Nov.

35 There is no right to strike against the public safety by anybody, anywhere, at any time.

1919 Telegram to the President of the American Federation of Labour, while Coolidge was Governor of Massachusetts during the Boston police strike.

36 The chief business of the American people is business.

1925 Speech to the Society of Newspaper Editors, Washington, 17 Jan.

37 Prosperity is only an instrument to be used, not a deity to be worshipped.

1928 Speech, Boston, 11 Jun.

38 Perhaps one of the most important
    accomplishments of my Administration has been
    minding my own business.
    1929 Press conference, Mar.

39 Patriotism is easy to understand in America. It
    means looking out for yourself while looking out
    for your country.
    Attributed.

Cooper, Dame Gladys 1888–1971

English actress. She made her stage début in 1905 and
subsequently achieved stardom with her performance in
Pinero's *The Second Mrs Tanqueray* (1922).

40 If this is what virus pneumonia does to one, I really
    don't think I shall bother to have it again.
    1971 Last words.

Cooper, James Fenimore 1789–1851

US writer, a prolific novelist and essayist. He is now
chiefly remembered for his 5-volume *Leatherstocking
Tales*, which includes *The Last of the Mohicans* (1826).

41 The tendency of democracies is, in all things, to
    mediocrity.
    1838 *The American Democrat*, 'On the Disadvantages of
    Democracy'.

42 Equality of condition is incompatible with
    civilization, and is found only to exist in those
    communities that are but slightly removed from
    the savage state. In practice, it can only mean a
    common misery.
    1838 *The American Democrat*, 'On the Disadvantages of a
    Monarchy'.

43 Individuality is the aim of political liberty.
    1838 *The American Democrat*, 'Individuality'.

44 It is a misfortune that necessity has induced men to
    accord greater license to this formidable engine, in
    order to obtain liberty, than can be borne with less
    important objects in view; for the press, like fire, is
    an excellent servant, but a terrible master.
    1838 *The American Democrat*, 'On the Press'.

Cooper, William pseudonym of *Harry Huff*
1910–

English novelist. A barbed and witty satirist, he was a
forerunner of the 'angry young man' school of the 1950s.

45 I would gladly have thrashed her for it.
    Unfortunately, thrashing your young woman
    doesn't make her admire you more as a novelist.
    1950 *Scenes from Provincial Life*, pt.3, ch.1.

46 If girls aren't ignorant, they're cultured… You can't
    avoid suffering.
    1950 *Scenes from Provincial Life*, pt.3, ch.2.

47 The trouble about finding a husband for one's
    mistress, is that no other man seems quite good
    enough.
    1950 *Scenes from Provincial Life*, pt.3, ch.5.

Coover, Robert Lowell 1932–

US novelist, short-story writer and playwright, best
known for the experimental stories.

48 The narrative impulse is always with us; we couldn't
    imagine ourselves through a day without it.
    1986 In *Time Out*, 7 May.

Cope, Wendy 1945–

English poet.

49 I used to think all poets were Byronic—
    Mad, bad and dangerous to know.
    And then I met a few.
    1986 'Triolet'.
    ▷ See Lamb 576:4.

50 In April one seldom seems cheerful:
    Dry stones, sun and dust make me fearful;
    Clairvoyantes distress me,
    Commuters depress me—
    Met Stetson and gave him an earful.
    1986 *Making Cocoa for Kingsley Amis*, 'Waste Land Limericks'
    pt.1.
    ▷ See Eliot 368:81.

51 There are so many kinds of awful men—
    One can't avoid them all. She often said
    She'd never make the same mistake again:
    She always made a new mistake instead.
    1986 'Rondeau Redoublé'.

52 It's nice to meet serious people
    And hear them explain their views:
    Your concern for the rights of women
    Is especially welcome news.
    I'm sure you'd never exploit one;
    I expect you'd rather be dead;
    I'm thoroughly convinced of it—
    Now can we go to bed?
    1986 'From June to December'.

53 Bloody men are like bloody buses—
    You wait for about a year
    And as soon as one approaches your stop
    Two or three others appear.
    1992 *Serious Concerns*, 'Bloody Men', stanza 1.

54 My heart has made its mind up
    And I'm afraid it's you.
    1992 *Serious Concerns*, 'Valentine'.

Copland, Aaron 1900–90

US composer. His early works employed jazz idioms, and he later drew on US folk tradition, as in the ballets *Billy the Kid* (1938) and *Appalachian Spring* (1944). He also composed film scores, operas and symphonies.

55 The whole problem can be stated quite simply by asking, 'Is there a meaning to music?' My answer would be, 'Yes'. And 'Can you state in so many words what the meaning is?' My answer to that would be 'No'.
1939 *What to Listen for in Music.*

56 The difference between Beethoven and Mahler is the difference between watching a great man walk down the street and watching a great actor act the part of a great man walking down the street.
Quoted in the *Wall Street Journal*, 9 Jun 1995.

Cornford, Frances née Darwin 1886–1960

English poet, the granddaughter of Charles Darwin. She lived most of her life in Cambridge, and her poetry deals with the minute details of emotion.

57 A young Apollo, golden-haired,
Stands dreaming on the verge of strife,
Magnificently unprepared
For the long littleness of life.
1910 Of Rupert Brooke. 'Youth'.

58 O fat white woman whom nobody loves,
Why do you walk through the fields in gloves,
When the grass is soft as the breast of doves
And shivering-sweet to the touch?
Oh why do you walk through the fields in gloves,
Missing so much and so much?
1910 'To a Fat Lady Seen From a Train'
▷ See Chesterton 260:45.

59 Now we know nothing, nothing is richer now
Because of all he was. O friend we have loved
Must it be thus with you?—and if it must be
How can men bear laboriously to live?
1915 'Rupert Brooke'.

60 I hope to meet my Maker brow to brow
And find my own the higher.
1954 'Epitaph for a Reviewer'.

Cornforth, Sir John Warcup 1917–

Australian organic chemist. Despite being totally deaf from childhood, he pioneered the study of enzyme stereochemistry and was awarded a Nobel Prize for Chemistry in 1975.

61 In a world where it is so easy to neglect, deny, pervert and suppress the truth, the scientist may find his discipline severe. For him, truth is so seldom the sudden light that shows new order and beauty; more often, truth is the uncharted rock that sinks his ship in the dark.
1975 Nobel Prize speech.

Corwin, Thomas 1794–1865

US politician, Governor of Ohio (1840–2), Senator (1845–50) and Secretary of the Treasury (1850–3) under President Fillmore.

62 If I were a Mexican, I would tell you, 'Have you not enough room in your own country to bury your dead men? If you come into mine, we will greet you with bloody hands and hospitable graves.'
1846 Speech to the Senate against the American–Mexican War, 11 Feb.

Cory, William originally William Johnson 1823–92

English academic, translator and poet. He was assistant master at Eton (1845–72), when he wrote the 'Eton Boat Song', but he resigned over controversy about his friendships with pupils. He also tutored Mary Coleridge (1861–1907).

63 They told me, Heraclitus, they told me you were dead,
They brought bitter news to hear, and bitter tears to shed.
I wept as I remembered how often you and I
Had tired the sun with talking and sent him down the sky.
1858 *Ionica, Poems*, 'Heraclitus', his translation of an epigram by Callimachus.

64 A handful of grey ashes, long long ago at rest.
1858 *Ionica, Poems*, 'Heraclitus', his translation of an epigram by Callimachus.

65 You promise heavens free from strife,
Pure truth, and perfect change of will;
But sweet, sweet is this human life,
So sweet, I fain would breathe it still;
Your chilly stars I can forgo,
This warm kind world is all I know.
1858 *Ionica, Poems*, 'Mimnermus in Church.'

66 All beauteous things for which we live
By laws of space and time decay.
But Oh, the very reason why
I clasp them, is because they die.
1858 *Ionica, Poems*, 'Mimnermus in Church.'

67 Jolly boating weather
And a hay-harvest breeze,
Blade on the feather,
Shade off the trees;
Swing, swing together,
With your body between your knees.
1865 *Eton Boat Song.*

Coryate, Thomas c.1577–1617

English traveller and wit. In 1608 he set out on a journey on foot through central Europe, later travelling east as far as India. In 1611 he published *Coryat's Crudities Hastily gobled up in five Moneths' travells.*

68 Of all the pleasures in the world, travel is (in my opinion) the sweetest and most delightful.

    1611 *Coryat's Crudities Hastily gobled up in five Moneths' travells.*

Cotman, John Sell 1782–1842

English landscape painter and etcher, best-known for his work in watercolour.

69 Three quarters of mankind, you know, mind more what is represented than how it is done.

    Quoted in William Vaughn *Romantic Art* (1978).

Coubertin, Pierre de, Baron 1863–1937

French educationalist. He revived the Olympic Games at Athens in 1896, in the hope that they would foster national and international understanding through sport.

70 Women have but one task, that of crowning the winner with garlands.

    1902 Quoted in Colin Jarman *The Guinness Dictionary of Sports Quotations* (1990).

71 The most important thing in the Olympic games is not winning but taking part—just as the most important thing in life is not the triumph but the struggle. The essential thing in life is not conquering but fighting well.

    1908 Speech to Olympic Games officials, London, 24 Jul.

Coué, Émile 1857–1926

French pharmacist, pioneer of 'auto-suggestion'. He opened a free clinic in Nancy in 1910 and 'Couéism' subsequently attracted followers all round the world.

72 *Tous les jours, à tous points de vue, je vais de mieux en mieux.*

  Every day, in every way, I am getting better and better.

    1915 *De la suggestion et de ses applications.* Maxim recommended by Coué to his patients, to be repeated several times over on rising and on going to bed.

Coupland, Douglas 1961–

Canadian novelist. His *Generation X: Tales for an Accelerated Culture* (1991) was a cult novel defining the angst of the children of the baby boomers.

73 Generation X

    From the title of his satiric novel *Generation X: Tales for an Accelerated Culture*. The phrase refers to young people born in the mid-1960s who are in no hurry to 'find themselves'.

74 MCJOB: A low-pay, low-prestige, low-dignity, no-future job in the service sector. Frequently considered a satisfying career choice for people who have never held one.

    1991 *Generation X,* 'The Sun is Your Enemy'.

75 HISTORICAL OVERDOSING: To live in a period of time when too much seems to happen.

    1991 *Generation X,* 'The Sun is Your Enemy'.

76 HISTORICAL SLUMMING: the act of visiting locations such as diners, smokestack industrial sites, rural villages—locations where time appears to have been frozen many years back—so as to experience relief when one returns back to 'the present'.

    1991 *Generation X,* 'Our Parents Had More'.

77 BRAZILIFICATION: The widening gulf between the rich and the poor and the accompanying disappearance of the middle classes.

    1991 *Generation X,* 'Our Parents Had More'.

78 CONSENSUS TERRORISM: The process that decides in-office attitudes and behavior.

    1991 *Generation X,* 'Quit Recycling the Past'.

79 Marketing is essentially about feeding the poop back to diners fast enough to make them think they're still getting real food.

    1991 *Generation X,* 'Quit Your Job'.

80 Shopping is Not Creating.

    1991 *Generation X,* chapter heading.

81 Their talk was endless, compulsive, and indulgent, sometimes sounding like the remains of the English language after having been hashed over by nuclear war survivors for a few hundred years.

    1991 *Generation X,* 'It Can't Last'.

82 I want to tell them that I envy their upbringings that were so clean, so free of *futurelessness.* And I want to throttle them for blithely handing over the world to us like so much skid-marked underwear.

    1991 Claire speaking of her parents. *Generation X,* 'Eat Your Parents'.

83 BRADYISM: A multisibling sensibility derived from having grown up in large families...symptoms of *Bradyism* include a facility for mind games, emotional withdrawal in situations of overcrowding, and a deeply felt need for a well-defined personal space.

    1991 *Generation X,* 'Define Normal'.

84 STRANGELOVE REPRODUCTION: Having children to make up for the fact that one no longer believes in the future.

    1991 *Generation X,* 'Define Normal'.

85 PERSONALITY TITHE: A price paid for becoming a couple; previously amusing human beings become boring: *'Thanks for inviting us, but*

Noreen and I are going to look at flatware catalogs tonight. Afterward we're going to watch the shopping channel.'
1991 *Generation X*, 'MTV Not Bullets'.

86 NOSTALGIA IS A WEAPON
1991 *Generation X*, 'Welcome Home from Vietnam, Son'.

Cousins, Norman 1915–90

US editor and activist. As director of the *Saturday Review* (1942–71, 1973–7), he broadened its scope and circulation, campaigning on issues such as nuclear disarmament. His works include *Who Speaks for Man?* (1953).

87 The poet reminds men of their uniqueness and it is not necessary to possess the ultimate definition of this uniqueness. Even to speculate is a gain.
1978 In the *Saturday Review*, 15 Apr.

88 President Nixon's motto was, if two wrongs don't make a right, try three.
1979 In the *Daily Telegraph*, 17 Jul.

Cousteau, Jacques Yves 1910–97

French underwater explorer, who helped develop the Aqua-Lung (1943) and later became famous for a series of documentaries about the world's oceans.

89 The sea is the universal sewer.
1971 Testimony before the House Committee on Science and Astronautics, 28 Jan.

Coventry, Thomas, 1st Baron 1578–1640

English judge.

90 The dominion of the sea, as it is an ancient and undoubted right of the crown of England, so it is the best security of the land... The wooden walls are the best walls of this kingdom.
1635 Speech to the Star Chamber, 17 Jun. 'Wooden walls' refers to ships.

Coward, Sir Noël Pierce 1899–1973

English playwright, actor, director, composer and singer. His witty, stylish and sometimes biting plays include *Hay Fever* (1925), *Private Lives* (1930), *Blithe Spirit* (1941) and *Present Laughter* (1943). His films include the Academy Award-winning *In Which We Serve* (1941).

91 Poor Little Rich Girl.
1925 Title of song.

92 There's sand in the porridge and sand in the bed,
And if this is pleasure we'd rather be dead.
1928 'The English Lido' (song).

93 I believe that since my life began
The most I've had is just
A talent to amuse.

Heigho, if love were all!
1929 'If Love Were All'.

94 Very flat, Norfolk.
1930 *Private Lives*, act 1.

95 Extraordinary how potent cheap music is.
1930 *Private Lives*, act 1.

96 Certain women should be struck regularly, like gongs.
1930 *Private Lives*, act 3.

97 Mad dogs and Englishmen
Go out in the midday sun.
1931 'Mad Dogs and Englishmen' (song).

98 In the Philippines, there are lovely screens
To protect you from the glare.
1931 'Mad Dogs and Englishmen' (song).

99 Mad about the boy,
It's pretty funny but I'm mad about the boy.
He has a gay appeal
That makes me feel
There may be something sad about the boy.
1932 'Mad About the Boy' (song).

1 People are wrong when they say the opera isn't what it used to be. It is what it used to be. That's what's wrong with it.
1933 *Design for Living*.

2 Don't put your daughter on the stage, Mrs Worthington,
Don't put your daughter on the stage.
1935 'Mrs Worthington' (song).

3 The stately homes of England,
How beautiful they stand,
To prove the upper classes
Have still the upper hand.
1938 'The Stately Homes of England' (song).

4 Dear Mrs A,
Hooray, hooray,
At last you are deflowered.
On this as every other day
I love you—Noël Coward.
1940 Telegram sent to Gertrude Lawrence the day after her marriage, quoted in Gertrude Lawrence *A Star Danced* (1945).

5 It's discouraging to think how many people are shocked by honesty and how few by deceit.
1941 *Blithe Spirit*.

6 Don't Let's Be Beastly to the Germans.
1943 Song title.

7 Speak clearly, don't bump into people, and if you must have motivation think of your pay packet on Friday.

1962 Speech, Gallery First-Nighters' Club, sharing his advice to young actors. On other occasions he repeated it in the form 'Just say your lines and don't trip over the furniture'.

8 Squash—that's not exercise, it's flagellation.

Quoted in Colin Jarman *The Guinness Dictionary of Sports Quotations* (1990).

9 I never realised before that Albert married beneath him.

c.1964 Quoted in Kenneth Tynan *Tynan on Theatre* (1964), alluding to the performance of a particular actress in the role of Queen Victoria.

10 I love criticism just so long as it's unqualified praise.

Attributed.

11 Two things should have been cut. The second act and that youngster's throat.

After watching a play featuring a 14-year-old child star (sometimes identified as Bonnie Langford). Attributed.

12 He must have been a marvellously good shot.

On hearing that an impresario he disliked had blown his brains out. Attributed.

Cowley, Abraham 1618–67

English poet, essayist and Royalist. He served Queen Henrietta Maria in exile during the Civil War, and only returned to England permanently at the Restoration. His works include a lyric collection *Poetical Blossomes* (1633) and the epic *Davideis* (1656).

13 The world's a scene of changes, and to be Constant, in Nature were inconstancy.

1647 *The Mistress*, 'Inconstancy'.

14 Such were the numbers which could call
The stones into the Theban wall.
Such miracles are ceased, and now we see
No towns or houses raised by poetry.

1656 *Poems*, 'Ode: Of Wit'.

15 Ye fields of Cambridge, our dear Cambridge, say,
Have ye not seen us walking every day?
Was there a tree about which did not know
The love betwixt us two?

1656 'On the Death of Mr William Harvey'.

16 Life is an incurable disease.

1656 'To Dr. Scarborough', stanza 6.

17 Fill all the glasses there, for why
Should every creature drink but I,
Why, man of morals, tell me why?

1656 'Drinking'.

18 God the first garden made, and the first city Cain.

1668 *Essays, in Verse and Prose*, 'The Garden'.

19 This only grant me, that my means may lie
Too low for envy, for contempt too high.

1668 *Essays, in Verse and Prose*, 'Of Myself'.

Cowley, Hannah 1743–1809

English playwright and poet, an early exponent of the comedy of manners. She also wrote long narrative verses (1780–94).

20 But what is woman?—only one of Nature's agreeable blunders.

1779 *Who's the Dupe?*, act 2.

21 Five minutes! Zounds! I have been five minutes too late all my life-time!

1780 *The Belle's Stratagem*, act 1, sc.1.

Cowley, Malcolm 1898–1989

US writer and critic, known for his studies of US expatriate writers in the 1920s and for his works on William Faulkner.

22 A new generation does not appear every 30 years. It appears when writers of the same age join in a common revolt against the fathers and when, in the process of adopting a new life style, they find their own models and spokesmen.

Quoted in the *New York Times*, 29 Mar 1989.

23 I…chopped the manuscript down to size, or sawed it into fireplace lengths.

Quoted in the *New York Times*, 29 Mar 1989.

24 Going back to Hemingway's work after several years is like going back to a brook where you had often fished and finding the woods as deep and cool as they used to be.

Quoted in Pete Hamill *A Drinking Life* (1994).

Cowper, William 1731–1800

English poet, whose work reflects the evangelical revival. Regarded as a precursor of Wordsworth, he wrote *The Task* (1785), a long rural poem, and a collection of moral satires, *Poems* (1782).

25 Damned below Judas; more abhorred than he was.

c.1774 Of himself. 'Hatred and Vengeance, my eternal portion'.

26 O make this heart rejoice or ache;
Decide this doubt for me;
And if it be not broken, break—
And heal it if it be.

1779 *Olney Hymns*, 'The Contrite Heart'.

27 God moves in a mysterious way
His wonders to perform;
He plants his footsteps in the sea,
And rides upon the storm.

1779 *Olney Hymns*, 'Light Shining out of Darkness'.

28 Blind unbelief is sure to err,

And scan his work in vain;
God is his own interpreter,
And he will make it plain.
1779 *Olney Hymns*, 'Light Shining out of Darkness'.

29 Behind a frowning providence
He hides a smiling face.
1779 *Olney Hymns*, 'Light Shining out of Darkness'.

30 Oh! for a closer walk with God,
A calm and heav'nly frame;
A light to shine upon the road
That leads me to the Lamb!
1779 *Olney Hymns*, 'Walking with God'.

31 A tale should be judicious, clear, succinct;
The language plain, and incidents well linked;
Tell not as new what ev'ry body knows,
And new or old, still hasten to a close.
1782 *Poems*, 'Conversation', l.235–8.

32 The pipe with solemn interposing puff,
Makes half a sentence at a time enough;
The dozing sages drop the drowsy strain,
Then pause, and puff—and speak, and pause
  again.
1782 *Poems*, 'Conversation', l.245–8.

33 His wit invites you by his looks to come,
But when you knock it never is at home.
1782 *Poems* 'Conversation', l.303–4.

34 The discumbered Atlas of the state.
1782 *Poems*, 'Retirement'.

35 He likes the country, but in truth must own,
Most likes it, when he studies it in town.
1782 *Poems*, 'Retirement'.

36 Religion Caesar never knew
Thy posterity shall sway,
Where his eagles never flew,
None as invincible as they.
1782 *Poems*, 'Boadicea: an Ode'.

37 Rome shall perish—write that word
In the blood that she has spilt.
1782 *Poems*, 'Boadicea: an Ode'.

38 I am monarch of all I survey,
My right there is none to dispute;
From the centre all round to the sea,
I am lord of the fowl and the brute.
O Solitude! where are the charms
That sages have seen in thy face?
Better dwell in the midst of alarms,
Than reign in this horrible place.
1782 *Poems*, 'Verses Supposed to be Written by Alexander Selkirk, During His Solitary Abode in the Island of Juan Fernandez'.

39 I am out of humanity's reach.
1782 *Poems*, 'Verse Supposed to be Written by Alexander Selkirk, During His Solitary Abode in the Island of Juan Fernandez'.

40 When I think of my own native land,
In a moment I seem to be there;
But alas! recollection at hand
Soon hurries me back to despair.
1782 *Poems*, 'Verse Supposed to be Written by Alexander Selkirk, During His Solitary Abode in the Island of Juan Fernandez'.

41 Grief is itself a med'cine
1782 *Poems*, 'Charity', l.159.

42 He found it inconvenient to be poor.
1782 *Poems*, 'Charity', l.189.

43 Spare the poet for his subject sake.
1782 *Poems*, 'Charity', l.636.

44 The man that hails you Tom or Jack,
And proves by thumps upon your back
How he esteems your merit,
Is such a friend, that one had need
Be very much his friend indeed
To pardon or to bear it.
1782 *Poems*, 'Friendship', l.169–74.

45 Remorse, the fatal egg by pleasure laid.
1782 *Poems*, 'The Progress of Error', l.239.

46 As creeping ivy clings to wood or stone,
And hides the ruin that it feeds upon,
So sophistry, cleaves close to, and protects
Sin's rotten trunk, concealing its defects.
1782 *Poems*, 'The Progress of Error', l.285–8.

47 How much a dunce that has been sent to roam
Excels a dunce that has been kept at home.
1782 *Poems*, 'The Progress of Error', l.415–6.

48 Laugh at all you trembled at before.
1782 *Poems*, 'The Progress of Error', l.592.

49 Our severest winter, commonly called the spring.
1783 Letter to Rev William Unwin, 8 Jun.

50 There is a mixture of evil in everything we do;
indulgence encourages us to encroach, while
we exercise the rights of children, we become
childish.
1783 Letter to Rev William Unwin, 7 Sep.

51 Thus first necessity invented stools,
Convenience next suggested elbow-chairs,
And luxury the accomplished sofa last.
1785 *The Task*, bk.1, 'The Sofa', l.86–8.

52 God made the country, and man made the town.
1785 *The Task*, bk.1, 'The Sofa', l.749.

53 At eve
    The moonbeam, sliding softly in between
    The sleeping leaves, is all the light they wish,
    Birds warbling all the music.
    1785 *The Task*, bk.1, 'The Sofa'.

54 England, with all thy faults I love thee still—
    My country!
    1785 *The Task*, bk.2, 'The Timepiece', l.206–7.

55 There is a pleasure in poetic pains
    Which only poets know.
    1785 *The Task*, bk.2, 'The Timepiece', l.285–6.

56 Variety's the spice of life,
    That gives it all its flavour.
    1785 *The Task*, bk.2, 'The Timepiece', l.606–7.

57 Defend me, therefore, common sense, say I,
    From reveries so airy, from the toil
    Of dropping buckets into empty wells,
    And growing old in drawing nothing up!
    1785 *The Task*, bk.3, 'The Garden', l.187–90.

58 Detested sport,
    That owes its pleasure to another's pain.
    1785 Of hunting. *The Task*, bk.3, 'The Garden', l.326–7.

59 Studious of laborious ease.
    1785 *The Task*, bk.3, 'The Garden', l.361.

60 Now stir the fire, and close the shutters fast,
    Let fall the curtains, wheel the sofa round,
    And, while the bubbling and loud-hissing urn
    Throws up a steamy column, and the cups,
    That cheer but not inebriate, wait on each,
    So let us welcome peaceful evening in.
    1785 *The Task*, bk.4, 'The Winter Evening', l.34–9.

61 But war's a game, which, were their subjects wise,
    Kings should not play at. Nations would do well
    To extort their truncheons from the puny hands
    Of heroes, whose infirm and baby minds
    Are gratified with mischief, and who spoil,
    Because men suffer it, their toy the world.
    1785 *The Task*, bk.5, 'The Winter Morning Walk', l.187–92.

62 Knowledge dwells
    In heads replete with thoughts of other men;
    Wisdom in minds attentive to their own.
    1785 *The Task*, bk.6, 'The Winter Walk at Noon', l.89–91.

63 Knowledge is proud that he has learned so much;
    Wisdom is humble that he knows no more.
    1785 *The Task*, bk.6, 'The Winter Walks at Noon', l.96–7.

64 Nature is but a name for an effect,
    Whose cause is God.
    1785 *The Task*, bk.6, 'The Winter Walk at Noon', l.223.

Crabbe, George 1754–1832

English poet and clergyman, whose early career was spent in poverty until Edmund Burke befriended him. His best-known poem, *The Village* (1783), is a bleak account of rural life.

65 Lo! the poor toper whose untutored sense,
    Sees bliss in ale, and can with wine dispense;
    Whose head proud fancy never taught to steer,
    Beyond the muddy ecstasies of beer.
    1775 *Inebriety, a Poem*, pt.1, l.132–5.

66 With awe, around these silent walks I tread;
    These are the lasting mansions of the dead.
    1781 *The Library* (published 1808), l.105–6.

67 Lo! all in silence, all in order stand,
    And mighty folios first, a lordly band:
    Then quartos their well-ordered ranks maintain,
    And light octavos fill a spacious plain;
    See yonder, ranged in more frequented rows,
    A humbler band of duodecimos.
    1781 *The Library* (published 1808), l.128–33.

68 Fashion, though Folly's child, and guide of fools,
    Rules e'en the wisest, and in learning rules.
    1781 *The Library* (published 1808), l.167–8.

69 Coldly profane and impiously gay.
    1781 *The Library* (published 1808), l.265.

70 Yes, thus the Muses sing of happy swains,
    Because the Muses never knew their pains:
    They boast their peasants' pipes, but peasants now
    Resign their pipes and plod behind the plough.
    1783 *The Village*, bk.1, l.21–4.

71 I grant indeed that fields and flocks have charms,
    For him that gazes or for him that farms.
    1783 *The Village*, bk.1, l.39–40.

72 I paint the cot,
    As truth will paint it, and as bards will not.
    1783 *The Village*, bk.1, l.53–4.

73 Where Plenty smiles—alas! she smiles for few,
    And those who taste not, yet behold her store,
    Are as the slaves that dig the golden ore,
    The wealth around them makes them doubly poor.
    1783 *The Village*, bk.1, l.136–9.

74 The cold charities of man to man.
    1783 *The Village*, bk.1, l.245.

75 A potent quack, long versed in human ills,
    Who first insults the victim whom he kills;
    Whose murd'rous hand a drowsy bench protect,
    And whose most tender mercy is neglect.
    1783 *The Village*, bk.1, l.282.

76 The murmuring poor, who will not fast in peace.
    1785 *The Newspaper*, l.158.

77 A master passion is the love of news.
1785 *The Newspaper*, l.279.

78 Our farmers round, well pleased with constant
gain,
Like other farmers, flourish and complain.
1807 *Poems*, 'The Parish Register', pt.1, l.273–4.

79 'What is a church?'—Our honest sexton tells,
''Tis a tall building, with a tower and bells.'
1810 *The Borough*, letter 2, 'The Church', l.11–12.

80 Virtues neglected then, adored become,
And graces slighted, blossom on the tomb.
1810 *The Borough*, letter 2, 'The Church', l.133–4.

81 Ye Lilies male! think (as your tea you sip,
While the Town small-talk flows from lip to lip;
Intrigues half-gathered, conversation-scraps,
Kitchen-cabals, and nursery-mishaps),
If the vast world may not some scene produce,
Some state where your small talents might have
use.
1810 *The Borough*, letter 3, 'The Vicar', l.69–74.

82 Habit with him was all the test of truth,
'It must be right: I've done it from my youth.'
1810 *The Borough*, letter 3, 'The Vicar', l.138–9.

83 There anchoring, Peter chose from man to hide,
There hang his head, and view the lazy tide
In it hot slimy channel slowly glide;
Where the small eels that left the deeper way
For the warm shore, within the shallows play;
Where gaping mussels, left upon the mud,
Slope their slow passage to the fallen flood.
1810 *The Borough*, letter 22, 'Peter Grimes', l.185–91.

84 He nursed the feelings these dull scenes produce,
And loved to stop beside the opening sluice;
Where the small stream, confined in narrow
bound,
Ran with a dull, unvaried, sad'ning sound;
Where all presented to the eye or ear,
Oppressed the soul! with misery, grief, and fear.
1810 *The Borough*, letter 22, 'Peter Grimes', l.194–9.

85 That all was wrong because not all was right.
1812 *Tales*, 'The Convert', l.313.

86 He tried the luxury of doing good.
1819 *Tales of the Hall*, 'Boys at School', l.139.

87 'The game,' said he, 'is never lost till won.'
1819 *Tales of the Hall*, 'Gretna Green', l.334.

88 The face the index of a feeling mind.
1819 *Tales of the Hall*, 'Lady Barbara', l.124.

89 Secrets with girls, like loaded guns with boys,
Are never valued till they make a noise.
1819 *Tales of the Hall*, 'The Maid's Story', l.84–5.

Craik, Dinah Maria née Mulock 1826–87

English novelist, essayist and poet. She published over 20
novels, the best-known being *John Halifax, Gentleman*
(1858). Although sentimental, her work emphasizes the
self-reliance of women.

90 Leonora, Leonora,
How the word rolls—*Leonora*—
Lion-like, in full-mouthed sound,
Marching o'er the metric ground
With a tawny tread sublime;
So your name moves, Leonora,
Down my desert rhyme.
1881 *Collected Poems*, 'Leonora'.

Crane, (Harold) Hart 1899–1932

US poet. He was an alcoholic who led a troubled life
which ended in suicide. He has come to be regarded as
one of the most important US poets of the century.

91 The Cross alone has flown the wave.
But since the Cross sank, much that's warped and
cracked
Has followed in its name, has heaped its grave.
1920 'The Mermen', in *The Dial*, no.85, Jul.

92 The bottom of the sea is cruel.
1926 *White Buildings*, 'Voyages', pt.1.

93 And onwards, as bells off San Salvador
Salute the crocus lustres of the stars,
In these poinsettia meadows of her tides.
1926 *White Buildings*, 'Voyages', pt.2.

94 Bequeath us no earthly shore until
Is answered in the vortex of our grave
The seal's wide spindrift gaze toward paradise.
1926 *White Buildings*, 'Voyages', pt.2.

95 Light wrestling there incessantly with light,
Star kissing star through wave on wave unto
Your body rocking!
1926 *White Buildings*, 'Voyages', pt.3.

96 Slow tyranny of moonlight, moonlight loved
And changed.
1926 *White Buildings*, 'Voyages', pt.5.

97 O Sleepless as the river under thee,
Vaulting the sea, the prairies' dreaming sod,
Unto us lowliest sometime sweep, descend
And of the curveship lend a myth to God.
1927 'To Brooklyn Bridge', in *The Dial*, Jun.

98 You who desired so much—in vain to ask—
Yet fed your hunger like an endless task,
Dared dignify the labor, bless the quest—
Achieved that stillness ultimately best,
Being, of all, least sought for: Emily, hear!
1929 'To Emily Dickinson', in *The Nation*, 29 Jun.

99 The last bear, shot drinking in the Dakotas
    Loped under wires that span the mountain stream.
    Keen instruments, strung to a vast precision
    Bind town to town and dream to ticking dream.
    1930 *The Bridge*, 'The River'.

1 Hobo-trekkers that forever search
    An empire wilderness of freight and rails.
    1930 *The Bridge*, 'The River'.

2 Dead echoes! But I knew her body there,
    Time like a serpent down her shoulder, dark,
    And space, an eaglet's wing, laid on her hair.
    1930 *The Bridge*, 'The River'.

3 Few evade full measure of their fate.
    1930 *The Bridge*, 'The River'.

4 Thin squeaks of radio static,
    The captured fume of space foams in our ears.
    1930 *The Bridge*, 'Cape Hatteras'.

5 Stars scribble on our eyes the frosty sagas,
    The gleaming cantos of unvanquished space.
    1930 *The Bridge*, 'Cape Hatteras'.

6 Cowslip and shad-blow, flaked like tethered foam
    Around bared teeth of stallions, bloomed that
       spring
    When first I read thy lines, rife as the loam
    Of prairies, yet like breakers cliffward leaping!
    1930 Of Walt Whitman. *The Bridge*, 'Cape Hatteras'.

7 Our Meistersinger, thou set breath in steel;
    And it was thou who on the boldest heel
    Stood up and flung the span on even wing
    Of that great Bridge, our Myth, whereof I sing.
    1930 On Whitman and Brooklyn Bridge. *The Bridge*, 'Cape
    Hatteras'.

8 Our tongues recant like beaten weather vanes.
    1930 *The Bridge*, 'The Tunnel'.

9 The phonographs of hades in the brain
    Are tunnels that re-wind themselves, and love
    A burnt match skating in a urinal.
    1930 *The Bridge*, 'The Tunnel'.

10 The bell-rope that gathers God at dawn
    Dispatches me as though I dropped down the knell
    Of a spent day.
    1932 'The Broken Tower', in the *New Republic*, 8 Jun.

Crane, Stephen 1871–1900

11 The Red Badge of Courage
    1895 Title of novel.

12 'It is bitter—bitter,' he answered;
    'But I like it
    Because it is bitter,
    And because it is my heart.'
    1895 *The Black Riders*, 'The Heart'. The speaker is a 'naked,
    bestial' creature which the narrator sees eating its heart in the
    desert.

13 None of them knew the color of the sky.
    1898 *The Open Boat*.

14 A man said to the universe:
    'Sir, I exist!'
    'However,' replied the universe,
    'The fact has not created in me
    A sense of obligation.'
    1899 *A Man Said to the Universe*.

Cranfield, Ingrid 1945–

15 To Hunt an 'assault' on the mountain merely
    meant a concerted, military-style operation;
    whereas to Shipton 'assault' sounded more like a
    criminal offence.
    1978 Of the contrast in approach to the climbing of Mt
    Everest between Eric Shipton, originally appointed as leader of
    the 1953 expedition, and John Hunt, who replaced him. In
    Expedition, vol.8, no.4, Jul.

Cranmer, Thomas 1489–1556

16 This hath offended! Oh this unworthy hand!
    1556 Last words at the stake, referring to the hand which had
    signed several recantations, later withdrawn.

Crashaw, Richard c.1613–49

17 *Nympha pudica Deum vidit, et erubuit.*

    The conscious water saw its God, and blushed.
    1634 Of the water which Jesus turned into wine at Cana.
    Epigrammata Sacra, 'Aquae in Vinum Versae' (translated by
    Dryden).

18 Wellcome, all Wonders in one sight!
    Eternity shut in a span.
    Summer in Winter, Day in Night.
    Heaven in Earth and God in Man.
    1646 'Hymn of the Nativity' (published 1652), l.79.

19 I would be married, but I'd have no wife,
    I would be married to a single life.
    1646 'On Marriage'.

20 Th' have left thee naked, Lord, O that they had!
    This garment too I would they had denied.
    Thee with thyself they have too richly clad,
    Opening the purple wardrobe of thy side.
    O never could be found garments too good
    For thee to wear, but these, of thine own blood.
    1646 'On Our Crucified Lord, Naked and Bloody'.

21 And now where'er he strays
    Among the Galilean mountains
    Or more unwelcome ways,
    He's followed by two faithful fountains;
    Two walking baths; two weeping motions;
    Portable and compendious oceans.
    1646 'Saint Mary Magdalene, or The Weeper'.

22 What heaven-entreated heart is this,
    Stands trembling at the gate of bliss,
    Holds fast the door, yet dares not venture
    Fairly to open it, and enter?
    1646 'To the Noblest and best of Ladies, the Countess of
    Denbigh'.

23 Say, lingering fair! why comes the birth
    Of your brave soul so slowly forth?
    1646 'To the Noblest and best of Ladies, the Countess of
    Denbigh'.

24 What yet fantastic bands
    Keep the free heart from its own hands!
    1646 'To the Noblest and best of Ladies, the Countess of
    Denbigh'.

25 Yield, then, O yield, that love may win
    The fort at last, and let life in.
    1646 'To the Noblest and best of Ladies, the Countess of
    Denbigh'.

26 In love's field was never found
    A nobler weapon than a wound.
    'The Flaming Heart Upon the Book and Picture of Saint Teresa',
    collected in *Carmen Deo Nostro* (published posthumously,
    1652).

27 All thy brim-filled bowls of fierce desire
    'The Flaming Heart Upon the Book and Picture of Saint Teresa',
    collected in *Carmen Deo Nostro* (published posthumously,
    1652).

Craster, Mrs Edmund d.1874

28 The centipede was happy quite,
    Until the toad in fun
    Asked him which leg went after which,
    Which drove him into such a pitch
    He lay distracted in a ditch,

Considering how to run.
Attributed.

Crawford, Joan originally *Lucille Fay le Sueur*
1904–77

US film actress. Originally a nightclub dancer, she began
in silent films in 1925 and found fame in the 1930s and
1940s.

29 I found that incredible thing, a public.
    Quoted in Alexander Walker *Joan Crawford* (1983).

Cripps, Arthur S(hearly) 1869–1952

English clergyman. He was the writer of occasional verse,
mainly on rural or religious themes.

30 England has greater counties—
    Their peace to hers is small;
    Low hills, rich fields, calm rivers,
    In Essex seek them all.
    Quoted in S P B Mais and Tom Stephenson (eds) *Lovely Britain*
    (c.1930).

Cripps, Sir (Richard) Stafford 1889–1952

English Labour politician and economist, expelled from
the Party for his opposition to appeasement (1939). In
1945 he was readmitted and subsequently became
Chancellor of the Exchequer, with a successful austerity
policy.

31 There is only a certain sized cake to be divided up,
    and if a lot of people want a larger slice they can
    only take it from others who would, in terms of real
    income, have a smaller one.
    1948 Speech, Trades Union Congress, 7 Sep.

Crisp, Quentin 1908–

English writer. He achieved notoriety with the
publication of *The Naked Civil Servant*, an account of his
experiences growing up as a flamboyant homosexual in
England.

32 Keeping up with the Joneses was a full-time job
    with my mother and father. It was not until many
    years later when I lived alone that I realized how
    much cheaper it was to drag the Joneses down to
    my level.
    1968 *The Naked Civil Servant*, ch.1.

33 As soon as I stepped out of my mother's womb on
    to dry land, I realized that I had made a
    mistake…but the trouble with children is that they
    are not returnable.
    1968 *The Naked Civil Servant*, ch.2.

34 This woman did not fly to extremes, she lived
    there.
    1968 *The Naked Civil Servant*, ch.3.

35 I don't hold with abroad and think that foreigners speak English when our backs are turned.
1968 *The Naked Civil Servant*, ch.4.

36 If one is not going to take the necessary precautions to avoid having parents, one must undertake to bring them up.
1968 *The Naked Civil Servant*, ch.5.

37 There was no need to do any housework after all. After the first four years the dirt doesn't get any worse.
1968 *The Naked Civil Servant*, ch.15.

38 Life was a funny thing that happened to me on the way to the grave.
1968 *The Naked Civil Servant*, ch.18.

39 I became one of the stately homos of England.
1968 *The Naked Civil Servant*, ch.24.

40 An autobiography is an obituary in serial form with the last instalment missing.
1968 *The Naked Civil Servant*, ch.29.

41 In England, the system is benign and the people are hostile. In America, the people are friendly—and the system is brutal!
1985 In *The Guardian*, 23 Oct.

Critchfield, Richard Patrick 1931–

US journalist. His books include *The Long Charade: Political Subversion in the Vietnam War* (1968) and *An American Looks at Britain* (1990).

42 What people read most of the time should be as worth mentioning as what they read almost none of the time.
1990 *An American Looks at Britain*.

Critchley, Julian Michael Gordon 1930–

English Conservative MP, writer and broadcaster, known for his acerbic and witty comments on Westminster life.

43 I was told when a young man that the two occupational hazards of the Palace of Varieties were alcohol and adultery. The hurroosh that follows the intermittent revelation of the sexual goings-on of an unlucky MP has convinced me that the only safe pleasure for a parliamentarian is a bag of boiled sweets.
1982 In *The Listener*, 10 Jun.

44 She has been beastly to the Bank of England, has demanded that the BBC 'set its house in order' and tends to believe the worst of the Foreign and Commonwealth Office. She cannot see an institution without hitting it with her handbag.
1982 Profile of Margaret Thatcher in *The Times*, 21 Jun.

Critias c.460–403 BC

Athenian aristocrat and politician, one of the 30 tyrants who ruled Athens after the Peloponnesian war (404 BC). He was killed in the democratic revolution of 404/3. Only fragments of his poetry and tragedies survive.

45 Is not living at all not better than living badly?
Fragment, quoted in H Diels and W Kranz (eds) *Die Fragmente der Vorsokratiker* (1952), vol.2, 385, no.23.

Croker, John Wilson 1780–1857

Irish politician and essayist, known for his satires on the Irish stage and Dublin society. He became an MP (1807) and helped found the *Quarterly Review* (1809).

46 We are now, as we have always been, decidedly and conscientiously attached to what is called the Tory, and which might with more propriety be called the Conservative party.
1830 *Quarterly Review*, Jan.

Cromer, Evelyn Baring, Earl 1841–1917

English colonial administrator.

47 It is well that Gordon should be under my orders, but a man who habitually consults the prophet Isaiah when he is in difficulty is not apt to obey the orders of anyone.
Of General Charles George Gordon. Quoted in Charles Chevenix Trench *Charley Gordon* (1978).

Crompton, Richmal originally *Richmal Samuel Lamburn* 1890–1969

English writer, a Classics teacher until she contracted polio in 1923. Her best-known children's books are those in the 'William' series, beginning with *Just William* (1922).

48 I'll thcream and thcream and thcream until I'm thick.
1925 Violet Elizabeth. *Still—William*, ch.8.

Cromwell, Oliver 1599–1658

English soldier and Puritan statesman. In the Civil War he led his New Model Army to victory at Naseby (1645). After the execution of Charles I, he established a Commonwealth, and later, on dissolving the Rump Parliament (1653) and refusing the crown, a Protectorate.

49 A few honest men are better than numbers.
1643 Letter to Sir William Spring, Sep. Quoted in Thomas Carlyle *Letters and Speeches of Oliver Cromwell* (1845).

50 I had rather had a plain, russet-coated Captain, that knows what he fights for, and loves what he knows, than that which you call a Gentle-man and is nothing else.
1643 Letter to Sir William Spring, Sep. Quoted in Thomas Carlyle *Letters and Speeches of Oliver Cromwell* (1845).

51 The state, in choosing men to serve it, takes no notice of their opinions. If they be willing faithfully to serve it, that satisfies.
1644 Said before the Battle of Marston Moor, 2 Jul.

52 EARL OF MANCHESTER: If we beat the King ninety-nine times, yet he is King still so will his posterity be after him; but if the King beat us once we shall be hanged, and our posterity made slaves.
OLIVER CROMWELL: My Lord, if this be so, why did we take up arms at first? This is against fighting hereafter. If so, let us make peace, be it never so base.
1644 Recorded in *The Calendar of State Papers*, 10 Nov.

53 I beseech you, in the bowels of Christ, think it possible you may be mistaken.
1650 Letter to the General Assembly of the Church of Scotland, 3 Aug.

54 Mr Lely, I desire you would use all your skill to paint my picture truly like me, and not flatter me at all; but remark all these roughnesses, pimples, warts, and everything as you see me, otherwise I will never pay a farthing for it.
1650 Remark to Sir Peter Lely, who was about to paint his portrait. Quoted in H Walpole *Anecdotes of Painting in England*, vol.3 (1763).

55 You have sat too long here for any good you have been doing. Depart, I say, and let us have done with you. In the name of God, go!
1653 On dismissing the Rump Parliament, 20 Apr.

56 Take away that fool's bauble—the Mace.
1653 On dismissing the Rump Parliament, 20 Apr.

57 My desire is to make what haste I can to be gone.
1658 Last words. Quoted in John Morley *Oliver Cromwell* (1900), bk.5, ch.10.

Cronenberg, David 1943–

Canadian director of horror films.

58 More blood! More blood!
Characteristic on-set declaration. Quoted in Neil Gaiman and Kim Newman *Ghastly Beyond Belief* (1985).

59 I don't have a moral plan. I'm a Canadian.
Quoted in Leslie Halliwell *Halliwell's Filmgoer's and Video Viewer's Companion* (9th edn, 1988).

Cronyn, Hume 1911–

Canadian-born actor, writer and director. He married Jessica Tandy, with whom he acted many times.

60 The most magical moment in the theater is a silence so complete that you can't even hear people breathe. It means that you've got them.
1990 In *Time*, 2 Apr.

Crosby, Bing originally *Harry Lillis Crosby*
1904–77

US film actor and singer. His many successful films include the *Road to* series with Bob Hope and Dorothy Lamour.

61 That was a great game of golf.
1977 Last words, as he finished play at the 18th hole before suffering a heart attack.

62 He was an average guy who could carry a tune.
Suggesting his own epitaph. Quoted in David Pickering *Brewer's Twentieth Century Music* (1994).

Cross, Douglas

US songwriter.

63 I Left my Heart in San Francisco.
1954 Title of song.

Crossman, Richard Howard Stafford
1907–74

British Labour politician. He chronicled his ministerial career and the workings of government in a series of diaries, begun in 1952, which were published in four volumes (1975–81), despite attempts to suppress them.

64 My Minister's room is like a padded cell, and in certain ways I am like a person who is suddenly certified a lunatic and put safely into this great, vast room, cut off from real life. Of course they don't behave *quite* like nurses, because the Civil Service is profoundly deferential—'Yes, Minister! No, Minister! If you wish it, Minister!'
1964 *The Diaries of a Cabinet Minister*, vol.1 (1975), 22 Oct.

Crowley, (Edward) Aleister 1875–1947

English writer and occultist. He founded his own order and became notorious for rumours of orgies, drugs and the sacrifice of babies in the course of black magic ceremonies.

65 Do what thou wilt shall be the whole of the Law.
1909 *Book of the Law*.

Cruyff, Johann 1947–

Dutch footballer, European Footballer of the Year (1973, 1974).

66 I am no longer a footballer. I am an industry.
1973 On being transferred from Ajax to Barcelona for a record £922,000. Quoted in Peter Ball and Phil Shaw *The Book of Football Quotations* (1989).

Cullen, Countee 1903–46

Black US poet and novelist, an important figure in the Harlem Renaissance of the 1920s.

67 She even thinks that up in heaven

Her class lies late and snores,
While poor black cherubs rise at seven
To do celestial chores.
1925 *On These I Stand*, 'For a Lady I Know'.

68 What is Africa to me:
Copper sun or scarlet sea,
Jungle star or jungle track,
Strong bronzed men, or regal black
Women from whose loins I sprang
When the birds of Eden sang?
1925 *On These I Stand*, 'Heritage'.

69 One three centuries removed
From the scenes his fathers loved,
Spicy grove, cinnamon tree,
What is Africa to me?
1925 *On These I Stand*, 'Heritage'.

70 So I lie, whose fount of pride,
Dear distress, and joy allied,
Is my somber flesh and skin,
With the dark blood dammed within.
1925 *On These I Stand*, 'Heritage'.

71 Ever at Thy glowing altar
Must my heart grow sick and falter,
Wishing He I served were black
1925 *On These I Stand*, 'Heritage'.

72 Lord, forgive me if my need
Sometimes shapes a human creed.
1925 *On These I Stand*, 'Heritage'.

cummings, e e pen name of *Edward Estlin Cummings* 1894–1962

US writer and painter, best known as an eccentric innovator in lyrical poetry, using idiosyncratic typography. He also wrote a novel, plays, and essays.

73 He had no nose, properly speaking, but a large beak of preposterous widthlessness, which gave his whole face the expression of falling gravely downstairs, and quite obliterated the unimportant chin.
1922 *The Enormous Room*, ch.3.

74 Subconsciously every one was, of course, fearful that he himself would go nuts—everyone with the exception of those who had already gone nuts, who were in the wholly pleasant situation of having no fear.
1922 *The Enormous Room*, ch.5.

75 To create is first of all to destroy…there is and can be no such thing as authentic art until the *bons trucs* (whereby we are taught to see and imitate on canvas and in stone and by words this so-called world) are entirely and thoroughly and perfectly annihilated by that vast and painful process of

Unthinking which may result in a minute bit of purely personal Feeling. Which minute bit is Art.
1922 *The Enormous Room*, ch.12.

76 The tall, impossibly tall, incomparably tall, city shoulderingly upwards into hard sunlight leaned a little through the octaves of its parallel edges, leaningly strode upwards into firm, hard, snowy sunlight; the noises of America nearingly throbbed with smokes and hurrying dots which are men and which are women and which are things new and curious and hard and strange and vibrant and immense, lifting with a great ondulous stride firmly into immortal sunlight…
1922 *The Enormous Room*, ch.13, closing words.

77 spring
when the world is puddle wonderful
1923 *Tulips and Chimneys*, 'Chanson Innocente'.

78 the Cambridge ladies who live in furnished souls
are unbeautiful and have comfortable minds
1923 *Tulips and Chimneys*, 'Sonnets-Realities', no.1.

79 Buffalo Bill's
defunct
—who used to
—ride a watersmooth-silver
——stallion
and break onetwothreefourfive pigeonsjustlike
   that
1923 Tulips and Chimneys, 'Portraits', no.8.

80 Humanity i love you because you
are perpetually putting the secret of
life in your pants and forgetting
it's there and sitting down
on it.
1925 *XLI Poems*, no.2, 'La Guerre'.

81 who knows if the moon's
a balloon, coming out of a keen city
in the sky—filled with pretty people?
1925 'Seven Poems, VII'. David Niven used the phrase for his autobiography, *The Moon's a Balloon* (1975).

82 If a poet is anybody, he is somebody to whom things made matter very little—somebody who is obsessed by Making.
1926 *is 5*, foreword.

83 'next to of course god america i
love you land of the pilgrims' and so forth oh
say can you see by the dawn's early my
country 'tis of centuries come and go
and are no more what of it we should worry
in every language even deafanddumb
they sons acclaim you glorious name by gorry
by jingo by gee by gosh by gum
1926 *is 5*, 'Two, III'.

84 why talk of beauty what could be more beautiful than these heroic happy dead
who rushed like lions to the roaring slaughter
they did not stop to think they died instead
then shall the voices of liberty be mute?

He spoke. And drank rapidly a glass of water.
1926 *is 5*, 'Two, III'.

85 America makes prodigious mistakes, America has
colossal faults, but one thing cannot be denied:
America is always on the move. She may be going
to Hell, of course, but at least she isn't standing still.
1927 'Why I Like America', in *Vanity Fair*, May.

86 nobody, not even the rain, has such small hands
1931 *w*, 'somewhere I have never travelled'.

87 unless statistics lie he was
more brave than me: more blond than you
1931 *w*, 'i sing of Olaf glad and big'.

88 What about the world, Mr Cummings?
I live in so many: which one do you mean?
1934 Introduction to revised edition of *The Enormous Room*.

89 my father moved through dooms of love
through sames of am through haves of give,
singing each morning out of each night
my father moved through depths of height
1940 *50 poems*, 'my father moved through dooms of love'.

90 because my father lived his soul
love is the whole and more than all
1940 *50 poems*, 'my father moved through dooms of love'.

91 a politician is an arse upon
which everyone has sat except a man
1944 *1x1*, no.10.

92 pity this busy monster, manunkind,
not. Progress is a comfortable disease.
1944 *1x1*, no.14.

93 We doctors know
a hopeless case if—listen: there's a hell
of a good universe next door; let's go
1944 *1x1*, no.14.

94 anyone lived in a pretty how town
(with up so floating many bells down)
spring summer autumn winter
he sang his didn't he danced his did
1949 *50 poems*, no.29.

95 Knowledge is a polite word for dead but not buried
imagination.
1951 'Jottings', in *Wake*, no.10.

96 for whatever we lose (like a you or a me)
it's always ourselves we find in the sea
'maggie and milly and molly and may'.

97 Humane, but not human.
On Ezra Pound. Recalled on Cummings' death, 3 Sep 1962.

98 A draftsman of words.
Self-description. Quoted in the *New York Times*, 30 Oct 1963.

Cunningham, Allan 1784–1842
Scottish poet, friend and acquaintance of James Hogg and
Walter Scott.

99 A wet sheet and a flowing sea,
A wind that follows fast,
And fills the white and rustling sail,
And bends the gallant mast
1825 'A Wet Sheet and a Flowing Sea', stanza 1.

1 Wha the deil hae we got for a King,
But a wee, wee German lairdie!
1847 *Poems and Songs*, 'The Wee, Wee German Lairdie', stanza 1.

Cunningham, Roseanna 1951–
Scottish advocate and nationalist politician. Her family
emigrated to Australia in 1960 but she returned in 1976,
becoming MP for Perth and Kinross (1995).

2 Until a woman is free to be as incompetent as the
average male then she will never be completely
equal.
1995 By-election campaign speech, May.

Cuomo, Mario Matthew 1932–
US lawyer and Democratic politician, Governor of New
York (1983–94).

3 We propose it, we massage it, and we often have to
ram it.
1988 Of legislation. In the *US News and World Report*, 25 Jan.

4 If there's a plastic surgeon who claims to be
responsible for this face, then New York State will
decertify him immediately.
1991 On reports that he had undergone plastic surgery. In
Newsweek, 11 Nov.

5 President Bush...seems to think that the ship [of
state] will be saved by imperceptible undercurrents,
directed by the invisible hand of some cyclical
economic god, that will gradually move the ship so
that at the last moment it will miraculously glide
past the rocks to safer shores.
1992 Address nominating Bill Clinton as Democratic
presidential candidate, 15 Jul.

6 It is as if Homer not only chronicled the siege of
Troy, but conducted the siege as well. As if
Shakespeare set his play writing aside to lead the
English against the Armada.
1992 Tribute to Lincoln's literary and political genius. In the
New York Times, 18 Nov.

7 Commitment seems to live more in the poetry of our aspirations than in the prose of the realities we have created.

1992 In the *New York Times*, 18 Nov.

8 Ever since the Republican landslide on Nov 8, it's been getting dark outside a little earlier every day. You notice that?

1994 In the *New York Times*, 17 Dec.

9 Dog eat dog produces, inevitably, just one dog.

1994 In the *New York Times*, 31 Dec.

Cupitt, Don 1934–

English radical theologian, Dean of Emmanuel College, Cambridge (1966–91).

10 A belief is made religious, not so much by its content, as rather by the way it is held.

1984 *The Sea of Faith*.

11 It is hardest of all to give up the last slivers and shreds of objectivity, but only by doing so can faith finally free itself from all that is outworn and become as fully voluntary, creative and courageous as it is required to be today.

1984 *The Sea of Faith*.

Curie, Marie originally *Marya Sklodowska* 1867–1934

Polish-born French chemist, who shared a 1903 Nobel Prize with her husband Pierre and with Henri Becquerel for research on radioactivity. In 1911 she again won the Nobel Prize for the discovery of radium and polonium.

12 In science, we must be interested in things, not in persons.

Quoted in Eve Curie *Madame Curie* (1937), ch.16 (translated by Vincent Sheean, 1943).

Curnow, (Thomas) Allen Munro 1911–

New Zealand poet and critic, whose works focus on his country's past and its quest for national identity.

13 Fluent in all the languages dead or living, the sun comes up with a word of worlds all spinning in a world of words.

1979 *An Incorrigible Music*, 'A Balanced Bait in Handy Pellet Form'.

Curran, Charles

US journalist.

14 One of nature's Balkans.

Of his friend and fellow journalist, Rebecca West. Quoted by V S Prichett in the *New Yorker*, 21 Dec 1987.

15 [She] has several skins fewer than any other human being…a kind of psychological haemophilia, which is one reason why she writes so well, and

why she is so vulnerable.

Of his friend and fellow journalist, Rebecca West. Quoted by V S Prichett in the *New Yorker*, 21 Dec 1987.

Curran, John Philpot 1750–1817

Irish judge and orator, called to the Irish bar in 1775. He entered Parliament in 1783, and although a staunch Protestant strongly opposed the Union.

16 The condition upon which God hath given liberty to man is eternal vigilance; which condition if he break, servitude is at once the consequence of his crime, and the punishment of his guilt.

1790 Speech, Dublin, 10 Jul.

17 Like the silver plate on a coffin.

Of Sir Robert Peel's smile. Quoted by Daniel O'Connell in the House of Commons, 26 Feb 1835.

18 But as in wailing there's nought availing, And Death unfailing will strike the blow, Then for that reason, and for a season, Let us be merry before we go.

?1773 'Let Us Be Merry Before We Go'.

Currie, Edwina 1946–

English Conservative politician. She was appointed Health Minister (1986–8), and she attracted notoriety for her outspoken comments on various health issues.

19 My message to the businessmen of this country when they go abroad on business is that there is one good thing above all they can take with them to stop them catching AIDS—and that is the wife.

1987 Speech as Health Minister, 12 Feb.

20 The strongest possible piece of advice that I could give to any young woman is: Don't screw around and don't smoke.

1988 In *The Observer*, 3 Apr.

21 Most of the egg production in this country, sadly, is now infected with salmonella.

1988 Radio interview as junior Health Minister, 3 Dec, which outraged both the domestic poultry industry and those of her own Back-Benchers who represented agricultural constituencies, forcing her resignation two weeks later.

Curtis, Charles P

22 Literature is a power line and the motor, mark you, is the reader.

1957 *A Commonplace Book*.

Curtis, Lionel 1872–1955

British writer.

23 In private conversation he tries on speeches like a man trying on ties in his bedroom, to see how he would look in them.

1912 Of Winston Churchill. Letter to Nancy Astor.

Curtis, Richard Whalley Anthony 1956–

British writer for film and television, best known for the TV series *Blackadder* and for the film *Four Weddings and a Funeral* (1994).

24 Whatever your script is like, no matter how much stewing and rewriting—if the punters don't want to sleep with the star, you may never be asked to write another one.

1994 Introduction to the published script of *Four Weddings and a Funeral.*

Curtis, Tony pseudonym of *Bernie Schwartz* 1925–

US film actor.

25 Like kissing Hitler.

Of working with Marilyn Monroe on *Some Like It Hot*. Attributed.

Curtiz, Michael originally *Mihaly Kertesz* 1888–1962

Hungarian-born film director.

26 Bring on the empty horses!

1936 Instructions during the filming of *The Charge of the Light Brigade*, subsequently used by David Niven for the title of one of his books. Curtiz's less-than-perfect English was renowned for producing such felicitious phrases.

Curzon (of Kedleston), Lord George Nathaniel 1859–1925

English statesman. As Viceroy of India from 1898 he introduced many social and political reforms and partitioned Bengal. He resigned after a disagreement with Kitchener (1905), but returned to politics as Lord Privy Seal (1915) and Foreign Secretary (1919–24).

27 It is only when you get to see and realise what India is—that she is the strength and the greatness of England—that you feel that every nerve a man may strain, every energy he may put forward, cannot be devoted to a nobler purpose than keeping tight the cords that hold India to ourselves.

1893 Speech at Southport, 15 May.

28 I hesitate to say what the functions of the modern journalist may be, but I imagine that they do not exclude the intelligent anticipation of the facts even before they occur.

1898 House of Commons, 29 Mar.

29 To fight for the right, to abhor the imperfect, the unjust, or the mean, to swerve neither to the right hand nor the left, to care nothing for flattery or applause or odium or abuse—it is so easy to have any of them in India—never to let your enthusiasm be soured or your courage grow dim but to remember that the Almighty has placed your hand on the greatest of his ploughs, in whose furrow the nations of the future are germinating and taking shape, to drive the blade a little forward in your time and to

feel that somewhere among those millions you have left, a little justice, or happiness or prosperity, a sense of manliness or moral dignity, a spring of patriotism, a dawn of intellectual enlightenment or a stirring of duty where it did not exist before—that is enough, that is the Englishman's justification in India. It is good enough for his watchword while he is here, for his epitaph when he has gone. I have worked for no other aim. Let India be my judge.

1906 Farewell speech on departing from Bombay as Viceroy of India.

30 I never knew that the lower classes had such white skins.

c.1915 Remark made during a visit of front-line British troops in World War I, after observing some of them bathing in old beer barrels.

31 Gentlemen do not take soup at luncheon.

Attributed. Quoted in E L Woodward *Short Journey* (1942), ch.7.

St Cyprian full name *Thascius Caecilius Cyprianus* c.200–258 AD

Christian martyr and Father of the Church. Probably born in Carthage, he became a bishop and theologian. Excommmunicated for his views on baptism, he was beheaded in Valerian's reign.

32 *Habere non potest Deum patrem qui ecclesiam non habet matrem.*

He cannot have God for his father who has not the church for his mother.

AD 251 *De Ecclesiae Catholicae Unitate*, ch 6.

33 *Salus extra ecclesiam non est.*

There is no salvation outside the church.

AD 256 *Letters*, no.73.

Cyrano de Bergerac, Savinien de 1619–55

French poet and soldier, famous as a duellist. Student of Gassendi, who influenced him in the philosophy of free-thinking.

34 *Peut-on être innocent, lorsqu'on aime un coupable?*

Can one be innocent when one loves a guilty person?

1653 *La Mort d'Agrippine*, act 5, sc.5.

35 *Un Philosophe doit juger le vulgaire, et non pas juger comme le vulgaire.*

A philosopher should judge the masses and should not judge like the masses.

1654 *Lettres diverses, Contre les sorciers* (later published as *Voyage dans la lune*).

36 *Non, non, si ce Dieu visible éclaire l'homme, c'est par accident, comme le flambeau du roi éclaire par accident au crocheteur qui passe par la rue.*

No, no, if this manifest God enlightens men, it is purely by accident, just as the king's torch throws its light upon a labourer who passes him in the street.

1656 *L'Autre Monde, ou, Les Estats et empires de la lune* (later published as *Voyage dans la lune*).

Daché, Lilly 1904–

French-born US milliner. Her autobiography, *Talking Through My Hats*, was published in 1946.

37 Glamour is what makes a man ask for your telephone number. But it also is what makes a woman ask for the name of your dressmaker.

1955 'Lilly Daché's Secrets of Lifelong Glamour Book', in *Woman's Home Companion*, vol.82, Jul.

Dafoe, John W 1866–1944

Canadian publisher and editor.

38 A journalist is hardly an authority upon anything—unless perhaps upon the appraisal of the drift of public opinion.

1923 Convocation address at the University of Manitoba, Winnipeg, May. Quoted in Murray Donnelly *Dafoe of the Free Press* (1968).

39 There are only two kinds of government, the scarcely tolerable and the absolutely unbearable.

Characteristic remark, quoted in Murray Donnelly *Dafoe of the Free Press* (1968).

Daily Express

40 Britain will not be involved in a European war this year, or next year either.

1938 Headline, 30 Sep. The newspaper used similar phrases frequently, up to 11 Aug 1939, three weeks before the outbreak of World War II.

Daily Mirror

41 Whose finger do you want on the trigger?

1951 Headline, 21 Sep, referring to the atom bomb.

Dalai Lama originally Tenzin Gyatso 1935–

Spiritual and temporal leader of Tibet. He negotiated an autonomy agreement for Tibet with the Chinese in 1951 but went into exile after the suppressed nationalist uprising in 1959. Now living in India, he continues to move for Tibetan independence.

42 Frankly speaking, it is difficult to trust the Chinese. Once bitten by a snake, you feel suspicious even when you see a piece of rope.

1981 Quoted in the *Observer Colour Magazine*, 5 Apr.

Dalglish, Kenny 1951–

Scottish footballer and manager. As manager of Liverpool, he won the League and Cup double in 1986.

43 The saddest and most beautiful sight I have ever seen.

1989 Of the display of flowers and club scarfs that were piled on Liverpool's Anfield pitch in memory of those who died in the Hillsborough football disaster. Quoted in Peter Ball and Phil Shaw *The Book of Football Quotations* (1989).

Dalí, Salvador 1904–89

Spanish painter, graphic artist and sculptor, the most flamboyant of the Surrealist artists. His work draws on the symbolism of dreams and, later, religion.

44 At the age of six I wanted to be a cook. At seven I wanted to be Napoleon. And my ambition has been growing steadily ever since.

1948 *The Secret Life of Salvador Dalí*, prologue.

45 I do not paint a portrait to look like the subject, rather does the person grow to look like his portrait.

Quoted in Esar *A Treasury of Humorous Quotations* (1951).

46 The first man to compare the cheeks of a young woman to a rose was obviously a poet; the first to repeat it was possibly an idiot.

1968 *Dialogues with Marcel Duchamp*, preface.

47 The famous soft watches are nothing else than the tender, extravagant, solitary, paranoic-critical camembert of time and space.

1969 *Conquest of the Irrational.*

48 Every good painter who aspires to the creation of genuine masterpieces should first of all marry my wife.

Quoted in Saranne Alexandrian *Surrealist Art* (1970).

49 *Le surréalisme, c'est moi.*

I am surrealism.

Quoted in Saranne Alexandrian *Surrealist Art* (1970), ch.5.

▷ See Louis XIV 614:47.

Dallek, Robert 1934–

US historian, Professor at the University of California, Los Angeles.

50 What makes war interesting for Americans is that we don't fight war on our soil, we don't have direct experience of it, so there's an openness about the meanings we give it.

1991 In the *New York Times*, 24 Feb.

Daly, Daniel 1874–1937

US gunnery sergeant in World War I.

51 Come on you sons of bitches! Do you want to live forever?

1918 Attributed, to his troops at Belleau Wood, 4 Jun.

▷ See Frederick the Great 403:24.

Daly, Mary 1928–

US feminist theorist and theologian. She advocates a feminist spirituality in *Beyond God the Father* (1973) and *Gyn/Ecology: the Metaethics of Radical Feminism* (1978).

52 Mister-ectomy n.: guaranteed solution to The Contraceptive Problem, tried and true and therefore taboo birth control method, recommended by Gyn/Ecologists, insisted upon by spinsters.

1987 *Webster's First New Intergalactic Wickedary of the English Language* (with Jane Caputi), Word Web 2.

St Peter Damian or *Pietro Damiani* 1007–72

Italian cleric and saint. A swineherd in his youth, he rose to become Bishop of Ostia and a Cardinal. He was active in attempts to reform the clergy in order to correct immorality.

53 *Sanctum Satanum meum.*

My holy Satan.

c.1070 Of Hildebrand, later Pope Gregory VII. Letter to Pope Alexander II and Cardinal Archdeacon Hildebrand.

Damrosch, Walter Johannes 1862–1950

German-born US conductor and composer. Having established a reputation as a conductor of Wagner, he became a champion of works by contemporary composers.

54 If a young man at the age of twenty-three can write a symphony like that, in five years he will be ready to commit murder.

1925 After conducting Aaron Copland's *Symphony for Organ and Orchestra.* Quoted in Machlis *Introduction to Contemporary Music* (1963).

Dana, Charles Anderson 1819–97

US newspaper editor. From 1848 to 1862 he edited the New York *Tribune*. From 1863 to the end of the Civil War he was assistant-secretary of war. In 1867 he purchased the New York *Sun*.

55 I have always felt that whatever Divine Providence permitted to occur I was not too proud to report.

1888 *The Art of Newspaper Making*, 'The Modern American Newspaper'.

56 Get the news, get all the news, and nothing but the news.

1888 *The Art of Newspaper Making*, 'The Modern American Newspaper'.

57 The invariable law of the newspaper is to be interesting.

1888 *The Art of Newspaper Making*, 'The Making of a Newspaper Man'.

Danforth, John Claggett 1936–

US lawyer and politician, Senator from Missouri (1976–).

58 It has locked candidates into ridiculous positions because only ridiculous positions can be compacted into 30-second commercials.

1990 Of television in politics. In the *New York Times*, 18 Mar.

Dangarembga, Tsitsi 1959–

Zimbabwean writer. Her novel *Nervous Conditions* (1988) portrays the effect of white values on black African society, especially women. She has also published a play *She No Longer Weeps* (1987).

59 This business of womanhood is a heavy burden… And these days it is worse, with the poverty of blackness on one side and the weight of womanhood on the other.

1988 *Nervous Conditions*, ch.1.

Dangerfield, George

60 Ireland is one of the few countries—perhaps the last—where the boundaries between politics and art have never been fixed.

1935 *The Strange Death of Liberal England.*

Daniel, Samuel 1562–1619

English poet and dramatist. A private tutor and courtier, he wrote masques, plays and epistles. His poetic works include the sonnet sequence *Delia* (1592) and the epic *Civil Wars Between the Two Houses of Lancaster and York* (1594–1609).

61 I that have loved thee thus before thou fadest,
My faith shall wax, when thou art in thy waning.
The world shall find this miracle in me,
That fire can burn when all the matter's spent.

1592 *Delia*, sonnet 33.

62 Care-charmer Sleep, son of the sable Night,
Brother to Death, in silent darkness born,
Relieve my languish and restore the light;
With dark forgetting of my care return.
And let the day be time enough to mourn
The shipwreck of my ill adventured youth:
Let waking eyes suffice to wail their scorn
Without the torment of the night's untruth.

1592 *Delia*, sonnet 54.

63 O thou whom envy ev'n is force t'admire!

1594 'To the Right Honourable, the Lady Mary, Countess of Pembroke'. Daniel was part of the group of writers who met at Wilton, which also included Jonson and Drayton, and he tutored Pembroke's son.

64 Unless above himself he can
Erect himself, how poor a thing is man!

1594 'To the Lady Margaret, Countess of Cumberland'.

65 Custom that is before all law, Nature that is above all art.

1603 *A Defence of Rhyme.*

66 But years hath done this wrong,
    To make me write too much, and live too long.
    1605 *Philotas*, 'To the Prince', dedication.

Dante Alighieri originally *Durante*
1265–1321

Italian poet and scholar, author of *The Divine Comedy* (a poet's journey through hell, purgatory and paradise, begun c.1307). A White Guelf, he was exiled from his native Florence when the Black Guelfs triumphed in 1309. He died in Ravenna.

67 *Nel mezzo cammin di nostra vita*
    mi ritrovai per una selva oscura
    che la diritta via era smarrita.

    In the middle of the journey of our life
    I found myself in a dark wood
    where the straight path was lost.
    c.1320 *Divina Commedia*, 'Inferno', canto 1, l.1–3.

68 *Lasciate ogni speranza voi ch'entrate.*

    Abandon all hope ye who enter here.
    c.1320 Inscription above the gates of Hell. *Divina Commedia*, 'Inferno', canto 3, l.9.

69 *Nessun maggior dolore,*
    Che ricordarsi del tempo felice
    Nella miseria.

    There is no greater pain than to remember a happy time when one is in misery.
    c.1320 *Divina Commedia*, 'Inferno', canto 5, l.121–3.

70 *E quindi uscimmo a riveder le stelle.*

    Thence we came forth to see the stars again.
    c.1320 *Divina Commedia*, 'Inferno', canto 34, l.139.

71 *Lì si vedrà la superbia ch'assette,*
    che fa lo Scotto et l'Inghilese folle,
    sì ch no può soffrir dentro a sua meta.

    There shall you see the pride which causes thirst,
    which makes the Scots and the English mad,
    so that they cannot remain within their boundaries.
    c.1320 *Divina Commedia*, 'Paradiso', canto 1, l.121–3.

72 *E'n la sua voluntade è nostra pace.*

    In His will is our peace.
    c.1320 *Divina Commedia*, 'Paradiso', canto 3, l.85.

73 *L'amor che move ile sole e l'altre stelle.*

    The love that moves the sun and the other stars.
    c.1320 *Divina Commedia*, 'Paradiso', canto 33, l.145.

Danton, Georges Jacques 1759–94

French revolutionary leader. As Minister of Justice (1792) he voted for the king's death. He tried to moderate the severity of the Revolutionary Tribunal, but lost the leadership to Robespierre and was executed for conspiracy.

74 *De l'audace, et encore de l'audace, et toujours de l'audace!*

    Boldness, and again boldness, and always boldness!
    1792 Speech to the Legislative Committee of General Defence, 2 Sep.

Darío, Rubén pseudonym of *Félix Rubén García Sarmiento* 1867–1916

Nicaraguan poet, journalist and diplomat. From 1886 he travelled extensively throughout Latin America and Europe. A key figure of Spanish-American Modernism, he experimented with rhythm, metre and imagery.

75 *Si hay poesía en nuestra América, ella está en las cosas viejas: en Palenke y Uatlán, en el indio legendario y el inca sensual y fino y en el gran Moctezuma de la silla de oro. Lo demás es tuyo, demócrata Walt Whitman.*

    If there is poetry in our America, it is in ancient items: in Palenke and Uatlán, in the legendary Indian and in the sensuous and elegant Inca and the great Moctezuma. The rest is yours, democratic Walt Whitman.
    1896 *Prosas profanas*, 'Palabras liminares'.

76 *Yo persigo una forma que no encuentra mi estilo,*
    botón de pensamiento que busca ser la rosa;
    se anuncia con un beso que en mis labios se posa
    al abrazo imposible de la Venus de Milo.

    I seek a form that my style cannot discover,
    a bud of thought that wants to be a rose;
    it is heralded by a kiss that is placed on my lips
    in the impossible embrace of the Venus de Milo.
    1896 *Prosas profanas*, 'Yo persigo una forma…' (translated as 'I seek a form…', 1922).

77 *Dichoso el árbol que es apenas sensitivo,*
    y más la piedra dura porque ésa ya no siente,
    pues no hay dolor más grande que el dolor de ser vivo,
    ni mayor pesadumbre que la vida consciente.

    Blessed is the almost insensitive tree,
    more blessed is the hard stone that doesn't feel,
    for no pain is greater than the pain of being alive,
    and no sorrow more intense than conscious life.
    1901 *Cantos de vida y esperanza*, 'Lo fatal' ('Fatalism').

Dark, Eleanor née *O'Reilly* pseudonym *Patricia O'Rane* 1901–85

Australian novelist and poet. Her works include the historical trilogy *The Timeless Land* (1941), *Storm of Time* (1948) and *No Barrier* (1953).

78 Silence ruled this land. Out of silence mystery comes, and magic, and the delicate awareness of unreasoning things.
    1941 *The Timeless Land*, pt.1, '1788'.

Darman, Richard Gordon 1943–

US government official, a former investment banker, director of office management and the budget in President Bush's Cabinet (1987–92).

79 I am now celebrating the 20th anniversary of the first request for my resignation. I look forward to many more.

Address to the White House press room. Quoted in Brian Kelly *Adventures in Porkland* (1992).

Darnell, Bill c.1940–

Canadian ecologist and activist, one of the original founders of the Greenpeace Foundation in Vancouver, British Columbia.

80 Make it a *green* peace.

1970 Quoted in Robert Hunter *Warriors of the Rainbow* (1979).

Darrow, Clarence Seward 1857–1938

US lawyer. He undertook the defence of John T Scopes (1925) for the teaching of Darwinism in school.

81 I do not pretend to know where many ignorant men are sure—that is all that agnosticism means.

1925 Speech in defence of John T Scopes, 15 Jul.

Darwin, Charles Robert 1809–82

English naturalist. He joined the HMS *Beagle* scientific survey (1831–6) to South America and Australasia, which led eventually to his theory of evolution and the publication of many scientific works, including *The Origin of Species by Means of Natural Selection* (1859).

82 The naturalist in England, in his walks, enjoys a great advantage over others in frequently meeting with something worthy of attention; here he suffers a pleasant nuisance in not being able to walk a hundred yards without being fairly tied to the spot by some new and wondrous creature.

1832 In Brazil. *Journey of Researches into the Geology and Natural History of the Various Countries Visited during the Voyage of HMS 'Beagle' Round the World* (published 1839).

83 I have called this principle, by which each slight variation, if useful, is preserved, by the term of Natural Selection, in order to mark its relation to man's power of selection.

1859 *The Origin of Species by Means of Natural Selection*, ch.3.

84 From the war of nature, from famine and death, the most exalted object which we are capable of conceiving, namely, the production of the higher animals, directly follows. There is grandeur in this view of life.

1859 *The Origin of Species by Means of Natural Selection*, ch.14.

85 Great is the power of steady misrepresentation—but the history of science shows how, fortunately, this power does not long endure.

1859 *The Origin of Species by Means of Natural Selection.*

86 I have tried lately to read Shakespeare, and found it so intolerably dull that it nauseated me.

1860 Autobiography.

87 False facts are highly injurious to the progress of science, for they often long endure; but false views, if supported by some evidence, do little harm, as every one takes a salutary pleasure in proving their falseness.

1871 *The Descent of Man and Selection in Relation to Sex*, ch.13.

88 The chief distinction in the intellectual powers of the two sexes is shewn by man's attaining to a higher eminence in whatever he takes up, than can woman—whether requiring deep thought, reason, or imagination, or merely the use of the senses and hands.

1871 *The Descent of Man and Selection in Relation to Sex*, ch.19.

89 We must however acknowledge, as it seems to me, that man with all his noble qualities...still bears in his bodily frame the indelible stamp of his lowly origin.

1871 *The Descent of Man and Selection in Relation to Sex*, ch.21.

90 I must begin with a good body of facts and not from a principle (in which I always suspect some fallacy) and then as much deduction as you please.

1874 Letter to J Fiske, 8 Dec.

91 A mathematician is a blind man in a dark room looking for a black cat which isn't there.

Quoted in John D Barrow *Pie in the Sky, Counting, Thinking and Being* (1992).

Darwin, Sir Francis 1848–1925

English botanist, son of Charles Darwin. He became a Reader in Botany at Oxford (1888) and produced his father's *Life and Letters* (1887–1903).

92 In science the credit goes to the man who convinces the world, not to the man to whom the idea first occurs.

1914 'Francis Galton', in *Eugenics Review*, vol.6, issue 1, Apr.

Daugherty, Harry Micajah 1860–1941

US politician, manager of Warren G Harding's political career from 1902. He was tried and acquitted (1927) on fraud charges.

93 A group of senators, bleary eyed for lack of sleep, will have to sit down at about two o'clock in the morning around a table in a smoke-filled room in some hotel, and decide the nomination.

1920 On the Republicans' failure to choose a presidential candidate at their convention.

David, Hal 1921–

US lyricist and brother of Mack David. He frequently worked with Burt Bacharach.

94 Raindrops Keep Fallin' on my Head.

1969 Title of song. (Music by Burt Bacharach.)

Davidson, John 1857–1909

Scottish poet and writer. He moved to London in 1885, publishing *Fleet Street Eclogues* (1893) and *Ballads and Songs* (1894). He committed suicide by drowning himself at Penzance.

95 The difficultest job a man can do,
    is to come it brave and meek with thirty bob a
       week,
    and feel that that's the proper thing for you.

1894 *Ballads and Songs*, 'Thirty Bob a Week', stanza 15.

96 It's naked child against hungry wolf;
    it's playing bowls upon a splitting wreck;
    it's walking on a string across a gulf
    with millstones fore-and-aft about your neck;
    but the thing is daily done by many and many a
       one;
    and we fall, face forward, fighting, on the deck.

1894 *Ballads and Songs*, 'Thirty Bob a Week', stanza 16.

97 In anguish we uplift
    A new unhallowed song:
    The race is to the swift,
    The battle to the strong.

1899 'War Song', stanza 1.
▷ See Bible 123:35.

98 And blood in torrents pour
    In vain—always in vain,
    For war breeds war again.

1899 'War Song', stanza 7.

99 When the pods went pop on the broom, green
       broom,
    And apples began to be golden-skinned,
    We harboured a stag in the Priory coomb.

1906 *Holiday and other Poems*, 'A Runnable Stag', stanza 1.

1 A stag of warrant, a stag, a stag,
   A runnable stag, a kingly crop,
   Brow, bay and tray and three on top,
   A stag, a runnable stag.

1906 *Holiday and other Poems*, 'A Runnable Stag', stanza 1.

Davie, George Elder 1912–

Scottish philosopher, a pioneer in studies of the Scottish Enlightenment.

2 The Democratic Intellect.

1961 Title of book.

Davies, (Sarah) Emily 1830–1921

English feminist and educational reformer who campaigned vigorously for equal opportunities for women in education.

3 If neither governesses or mothers *know*, how can they teach? So long as education is not provided *for* them, how can it be provided *by* them?

1868 Paper read at the Annual Meeting of the National Association for the Promotion of Social Sciences, published in *Thoughts on some Questions Relating to Women 1860–1908*.

4 We have persuaded ourselves that Englishmen of the present day are such a nervously excitable race, that the only chance for their descendants is to keep the mothers in a state of coma. The fathers, we think are incurable.

1868 Paper read at the Annual Meeting of the National Association for the Promotion of Social Sciences, published in *Thoughts on some Questions Relating to Women 1860–1908*.

Davies, Sir John 1569–1626

English poet and civil servant. He held high office in Ireland where he supported severe repressive measures and was nominated chief justice (1626). His poems include *Orchestra, or a Poem of Dancing* (1596) and *Hymns to Astrea* (1599).

5 Dancing is a frenzy and a rage.

1596 *Orchestra, or a Poem of Dancing*, stanza 16.

6 This wondrous miracle did Love devise,
   For dancing is love's proper exercise.

1596 *Orchestra, or a Poem of Dancing*, stanza 18.

7 Learn then to dance, you that are princes born,
   And lawful lords of earthly creatures all;
   Imitate them, and thereof take no scorn,
   (For this new art to them is natural)
   And imitate the stars celestial.
   For when pale death your vital twist shall sever,
   Your better parts must dance with them forever.

1596 *Orchestra, or a Poem of Dancing*, stanza 60.

8 Skill comes so slow, and life so fast doth fly,
   We learn so little and forget so much.

1599 *Nosce Teipsum*, stanza 19.

9 I know my life's a pain and but a span,
   I know my sense is mocked in every thing;
   And to conclude, I know myself a man,
   Which is a proud and yet a wretched thing.

1599 *Nosce Teipsum*, stanza 45.

10 Wedlock, indeed, hath oft compared been
    To public feasts where meet a public rout,
    Where they that are without would fain go in
    And they that are within would fain go out.

1608 'A Contention Betwixt a Wife, a Widow, and a Maid for Precedence', l.193–6.

Davies, Ray(mond Douglas) 1944–

British songwriter and rock musician, founder of The Kinks (1963). His lyrics are noted for their lightly satirical commentary.

11 One week he's in polka-dots, the next week he's in stripes
'Cos he's a dedicated follower of fashion.
1966 'Dedicated Follower of Fashion'.

Davies, Robertson 1913–95

Canadian novelist, playwright, critic and essayist. After the Deptford trilogy (1970–5) he wrote another trilogy, *What's Bred in the Bone* (1985), shortlisted for the Booker Prize.

12 There is more to marriage than four bare legs under a blanket.
1957 *Love and Libel.*

13 'Mary, what made you do it?'
She looked him honestly in the face and gave the answer that became famous in Deptford: 'He was very civil, 'Masa. And he wanted it so badly.'
1970 Mrs. Dempster explains to her parson husband why she had sex with a tramp. *Fifth Business*, pt.1, ch.10.

14 I saw corpses, and grew used to their unimportant look, for a dead man without any of the panoply of death is a desperately insignificant object.
1970 Of World War I. *Fifth Business*, pt.2, ch.1.

15 When a man is down on his luck he seems to consume all he can get of coffee and doughnuts.
1970 *Fifth Business*, pt.4, ch.1.

16 He was killed by the usual cabal: by himself, first of all; by the woman he knew; by the woman he did not know; by the man who granted his inmost wish; and by the inevitable fifth, who was keeper of his conscience and keeper of the stone.
1970 *Fifth Business*, pt.6, ch.8.

17 Canada is not really a place where you are encouraged to have large spiritual adventures.
1972 Interviewed by Peter C Newman, 'The Master's Voice', in *Maclean's*, Sep.

18 The ideal companion in bed is a good book.
Interviewed by Terence M Green, recorded in J Madison Davis (ed) *Conversations with Robertson Davies* (1989).

Davies, W(illiam) H(enry) 1871–1940

British poet, who emigrated to the US at the age of 22. He lost a leg there while jumping a train and returned to England, where he lived as a tramp until his poetry found a public. He also wrote novels and autobiographical works.

19 It was the Rainbow gave thee birth,
And left thee all her lovely hues.
1910 'The Kingfisher'.

20 What is this life if, full of care,
We have no time to stand and stare?
1911 'Leisure'.

21 A rainbow and a cuckoo's song
May never come together again;
May never come
This side the tomb.
1914 'A Great Time'.

22 And hear the pleasant cuckoo, loud and long—
The simple bird that thinks two notes a song.
1916 'April's Charms'.

da Vinci, Leonardo

▷ See Leonardo da Vinci

Davis, Adelle 1904–74

US nutritionist.

23 People in nutrition do get the idea that they are going to live to be 150. And they never do.
1973 Quoted in Daniel Yergin's 'Supernutritionist', *New York Times* magazine, 20 May.

Davis, Bette originally *Ruth Elizabeth Davis* 1908–89

US film actress. She made her screen début in 1931 and in the late 1930s and 1940s starred in a string of romantic melodramas such as *The Old Maid* (1939) and *Now Voyager* (1942).

24 Mother of three; divorcee; American. Twenty years experience as an actress in motion pictures. Mobile still and more affable than rumour would have it. Wants steady employment in Hollywood. (Has had Broadway). References upon request.
1962 Advertisement placed in the Hollywood trade papers.

25 Evil people…you never forget them. And that's the aim of any actress—never to be forgotten.
1966 On her favourite character roles. In the New York State Theater programme, Jun.

26 The best time I ever had with Joan Crawford was when I pushed her down the stairs in *Whatever Happened to Baby Jane?*
Quoted in Doug McClelland *Star Speak* (1987).

27 I have eyes like a bullfrog, a neck like an ostrich and long, limp hair. You just have to be good to survive with that equipment.
Attributed.

28 She's the original good time who was had by all.
On an anonymous starlet. Attributed.

Davis, Jefferson 1808–89

US statesman. He led the Senate's extreme State Rights Party, supported slavery, and was President of the rebel

Confederate States during the Civil War (1861–5). Later imprisoned, he was never brought to trial.

29 All we ask is to be let alone.
1861 Inaugural address, 18 Feb.

Davis, Miles Dewey, III 1926–91

US jazz trumpeter and composer. A leading figure in post-war jazz, he also won wide acceptance with rock audiences in the 1970s and 1980s.

30 An artist's first responsibility is to himself.
1961 *Ebony*, Jan.

31 You could be a great musician, an innovative and important artist, but nobody cared if you didn't make the white people who were in control some money.
1989 *Autobiography*, ch.10.

Davis, Sammy, Jnr 1925–90

US jazz musician, actor, dancer and comedian.

32 Being a star has made it possible for me to get insulted in places where the average Negro could never hope to go and get insulted.
1965 *Yes I Can*, pt.3, ch.23.

Davis, Steve 1957–

English snooker player. Between 1980 and 1985 he won three world titles.

33 Billiards is very similar to snooker, except there are only three balls and no one watches it.
1988 Quoted in Colin Jarman *The Guinness Dictionary of Sports Quotations* (1990).

Davis, Stuart 1894–1964

US Cubist painter.

34 An artist who has travelled on a steam train, driven an automobile, or flown in an airplane doesn't feel the same way about form and space as one who has not.
1940 'Is There a Revolution in the Arts?', in *Bulletin of America's Town Meeting of the Air*, vol.5, no.19 (19 Feb.).

35 It has been often said, even by proponents of those pictures known in aesthetic slang as Cubist and Abstract, that they have no subject matter. Such a statement is equivalent to saying that life has no subject matter.
1943 'The Cube Root', in *Art News*, vol.41, 1 Feb.

Davis, Thomas Osborne 1814–45

Irish poet and politician, head of the Young Ireland Movement. He cofounded the weekly *Nation* in 1842,

and wrote patriotic verses which became anthems of the Sinn Féin movement.

36 'Did they dare, did they dare, to slay Owen Roe
     O'Neil?'
   'Yes, they slew with poison him they feared to meet
     with steel.'
   'May God wither up their hearts! May their blood
     cease to flow!
   May they walk in living death, who poisoned
     Owen Roe!'
1842 'Lament for the Death of Owen Roe O'Neil'.

37 Sagest in the council was he, kindest in the hall:
   Sure we never won a battle—'twas Owen won them
     all.
   Had he lived, had he lived, our dear country had
     been free;
   But he's dead, but he's dead, and 'tis slaves we'll ever
     be.
1842 'Lament for the Death of Owen Roe O'Neil'.

38 They fought as they revelled, fast, fiery, and true,
   And, though victors, they left on the field not a
     few;
   And they who survived fought and drank as of
     yore,
   But the land of their heart's hope they never saw
     more,
   For in far, foreign fields, from Dunkirk to Belgrade
   Lie the soldiers and chiefs of the Irish Brigade.
1845 *The Spirit of the Nation*, 'The Battle-Eve of the Brigade'.

39 Our colonel comes from Brian's race,
   His wounds are in his breast and face.
1845 *The Spirit of the Nation*, 'Clare's Dragoons'.

40 Viva la the New Brigade!
   Viva la the Old One, too!
   Viva la, the Rose shall fade,
   And the Shamrock shine for ever new!
1845 *The Spirit of the Nation*, 'Clare's Dragoons'.

41 Come in the evening, or come in the morning,
   Come when you're looked for, or come without
     warning.
1846 'The Welcome'.

Davison, Emily Wilding 1872–1913

English militant suffragette, who campaigned fiercely for women's emancipation. She was frequently imprisoned, and died after running in front of the King's horse at the 1913 Derby.

42 As I am a woman and women do not count in the State, I refuse to be counted. Rebellion against tyrants is obedience to God.
1911 Comment on uncompleted Census paper, quoted in Gertrude Colmore *The Life of Emily Wilding Davison* (1913).

Dawkins, Richard 1941–

British zoologist, Professor at Oxford. He has done much to popularize the theories of Charles Darwin, most notably in his work *The Selfish Gene* (1976).

43 We are survival machines—robot vehicles blindly programmed to preserve the selfish molecules known as genes. This is a truth which still fills me with astonishment.
1976 *The Selfish Gene*, ch.2.

44 It has no vision, no foresight, no sight at all. If it can be said to play the role of watchmaker in nature, it is the *blind* watchmaker.
1986 Of natural selection. *The Blind Watchmaker*, ch.1.
▷ See Paley 751:65.

45 However many ways there may be of being alive, it is certain that there are vastly more ways of being dead.
1986 *The Blind Watchmaker*, ch.1.

Day, Clarence Shepard 1874–1935

US humorist, best known for his writings in the *New Yorker* and for his autobiographical sketches in *Life With Father*.

46 The poets of each generation seldom sing a new song. They turn themes men always have loved, and sing them in the mode of their times.
1921 *The Crow's Nest*, 'Humpty-Dumpty and Adam'.

47 The real world is not easy to live in. It is rough; it is slippery. Without the most clear-eyed adjustments we fall and get crushed. A man must stay sober: not always, but most of the time.
1921 *The Crow's Nest*, 'In His Baby Blue Ship'.

48 I meant to be prompt, but it never occurred to me that I had better try to be early.
1935 *Life With Father*, 'Father teaches me to be prompt'.

49 Imagine the Lord talking French! Aside from a few odd words in Hebrew, I took it for granted that God had never spoken anything but the most dignified English.
1935 *Life With Father*, 'Father interferes'.

50 'If you don't go to other men's funerals,' he told Father stiffly, 'they won't go to yours.'
1935 *Life With Father*, 'Father interferes'.

51 Father declared he was going to buy a new plot in the cemetery, a plot all for himself. 'And I'll buy one on a corner,' he added triumphantly, 'where I can get out.'
1935 *Life With Father*, penultimate paragraph.

Day, Doris originally Doris Kappelhoff 1924–

US singer and film actress, whose sunny personality and girl-next-door image made her a star of 1950s musicals.

52 The really frightening thing about middle age is the knowledge that you'll grow out of it.
Quoted in A E Hotchner *Doris Day* (1978).

Dayan, Moshe 1915–81

Israeli soldier and politician. He left the Labour Party in 1966 to set up the Rafi Party with Ben Gurion. His heavily-outnumbered forces were successful in the 'Six-Day War' (1967), and as Foreign Minister he helped secure peace with Egypt (1977).

53 Whenever you accept our views, we shall be in full agreement with you.
Remark to US envoy Cyrus Vance during the Arab–Israeli negotiations, quoted in *The Observer*, 14 Aug 1977.

Day-Lewis, Cecil 1904–72

Irish poet and critic. Professor at Oxford (1951–6) and Harvard (1964–5), he became Poet Laureate in 1968. As well as poetry he wrote criticism, translation and, under the pseudonym Nicholas Blake, detective novels.

54 Tempt me no more; for I
Have known the lightning's hour,
The poet's inward pride,
The certainty of power.
1933 *The Magnetic Mountain*, pt.3, no.24.

55 You that love England, who have an ear for her music,
The slow movement of clouds in benediction,
Clear arias of light thrilling over her uplands,
Over the chords of summer sustained peacefully.
1933 *The Magnetic Mountain*, pt.4, no.32.

56 Do not expect again a phoenix hour,
The triple-towered sky, the dove complaining,
Sudden the rain of gold and heart's first ease
Traced under trees by the eldritch light of sundown.
1935 'From Feathers to Iron'.

57 Now we lament one
Who danced on a plume of words,
Sang with a fountain's panache,
Dazzled like slate roofs in sun
After rain, was flighty as birds
And alone as a mountain ash.
The ribald, inspired urchin
Leaning over the lip
Of his world, as over a rock pool
Or a lucky dip,
Found everything brilliant and virgin.
1953 'In Memory of Dylan Thomas'.

Dean, John 1938–

US government official. As White House adviser to President Nixon, he was implicated in the Watergate scandal.

58 I am convinced that we are going to make the whole road and put this thing in the funny pages of the history books.
1973 Taped conversation with the President, Feb.

59 We have a cancer within, close to the presidency, that is growing. It is growing daily.
1973 Taped conversation with the President, Mar.

60 Doing time is like climbing a mountain wearing roller skates.
1977 On conviction after the Watergate scandal. In *Newsweek*, 4 Jul.

de Beauvoir, Simone 1906–86

French philosopher, feminist and writer, who maintained a lifelong association with fellow-existentialist Jean-Paul Sartre. Her *Le deuxième sexe* (The Second Sex, 1949–50) is a pioneering feminist text.

61 There is a good case for showing that airplanes, machines, the telephone and the radio do not make men of today happier than those of former times.
1948 *Ethics of Ambiguity.*

62 *On ne naît pas femme: on le devient.*

One is not born a woman: one becomes a woman.
1949 *Le deuxième sexe* (The Second Sex), bk.2, pt.1, ch.1.

63 *Ce n'est guère que dans les asiles que les coquettes gardent avec entêtement une foi entière en des regards absents; normalement, elles réclament des témoins.*

Women fond of dress are hardly ever entirely satisfied not to be seen, except among the insane; usually they want witnesses.
1949 *Le deuxième sexe* (The Second Sex), bk.2, pt.5, ch.18 (translated by H M Parshley, 1952).

64 *La femme…sait que quand on la regarde on ne la distingue pas de son apparence: elle est jugée, respectée, désirée à travers sa toilette.*

Woman…knows that when she is looked at she is not considered apart from her appearance: she is judged, respected, desired, by and through her toilette.
1949 *Le deuxième sexe* (The Second Sex), bk.2, pt.7, ch.25 (translated by H M Parshley, 1952).

65 *Si l'on vit assez longtemps, on voit que toute victoire se change un jour en défaite.*

If you live long enough, you'll find that every victory turns into a defeat.
1955 *Tous les hommes sont mortels* (All Men Are Mortal).

Debussy, Claude Achille 1862–1918

French composer. His writing for piano was described as 'musical Impressionism'. He translated it to the orchestra in *La Mer* (1905), to his opera, *Pelléas et Mélisande*, and to other works.

66 The colour of my soul is iron-grey and sad bats wheel about the steeple of my dreams.
1894 Letter.

67 That old poisoner.
1896 Letter, alluding to Wagner.

68 People don't very much like things that are beautiful—they are so far from their nasty little minds.
1900 Letter.

69 A pink bonbon stuffed with snow.
1903 Of the music of Edvard Grieg. *Gil Blas.*

70 A century of aeroplanes deserves its own music. As there are no precedents, I must create anew.
1913 Quoted in *La Revue S.I.M.*

Decatur, Stephen 1779–1820

US naval officer, who distinguished himself in the war with Tripoli (1801–5) and fought against Britain, capturing the frigate *Macedonian* (1812), but surrendering in 1814.

71 Our country! In her intercourse with foreign nations, may she always be in the right; but our country, right or wrong.
1816 Speech made in Norfolk, Virginia, Apr.
▷ See Adams 6:89, Chesterton 258:91.

Deffand, Marquise du 1697–1780

French noblewoman, famous for her wit and beauty. Her salon was frequented by leading figures in Paris literary society, including Voltaire, Montesquieu and D'Alembert.

72 The distance does not matter; it is only the first step that counts.
1763 Letter, 7 Jul.

Defoe, Daniel 1660–1731

English writer, best known for his novels *Robinson Crusoe* (1719) and *Moll Flanders* (1722), and for his partly factual *Journal of the Plague Year* (1724). He also wrote a travel book, *A Tour Thro the Whole Island of Great Britain* (1724–7).

73 The soul is placed in the body like a rough diamond, and must be polished, or the lustre of it will never appear.
1697 *An Essay Upon Projects*, 'Of Academies: An Academy for Women'.

74 The best of men cannot suspend their fate:
The good die early, and the bad die late.
1697 'Character of the late Dr Annesley'.

75 Wherever God erects a house of prayer,
The Devil always builds a chapel there;
And 'twill be found, upon examination,
The latter hast the largest congregation.
1701 *The True-Born Englishman*, pt.1, l.1–4.

76 From this amphibious ill-born mob began
That vain, ill-natured thing, an Englishman.
1701 *The True-Born Englishman*, pt.1, l.132–3.

77 Your Roman-Saxon-Danish-Norman English.
1701 *The True-Born Englishman*, pt.1, l.139.

78 His lazy, long, lascivious reign.
1701 Of Charles II. *The True-Born Englishman*, pt.1, l.236.

79 Actions receive their tincture from the times,
And as they change are virtues made or crimes.
1703 *A Hymn to the Pillory*, l.29–30.

80 It happened one day, about noon, going towards
my boat, I was exceedingly surprised with the print
of a man's naked foot on the shore, which was very
plain to be seen in the sand. I stood like one
thunderstruck, or as if I had seen an apparition.
1719 *Robinson Crusoe*.

81 My man Friday.
1719 *Robinson Crusoe*.

82 Vice came in always at the door of necessity, not at
the door of inclination.
1721 *Moll Flanders*.

83 Manchester, one of the greatest, if not really the
greatest mere village in England.
1724–7 *A Tour Thro the Whole Island of Great Britain*, letter 10.

84 Here is a pleasant situation, and yet nothing
pleasant to be seen. Here is a harbour without
ships, a port without trade, a fishery without nets, a
people without business; and, that which is worse
than all, they do not seem to desire business, much
less do they understand it.
1724–7 Of Kirkcudbright, Scotland. *A Tour Thro the Whole Island of Great Britain*, letter 12.

85 A very fine city; the four principal streets are the
fairest for breadth, and the finest built that I have
ever seen in one city together… In a word, 'tis the
cleanest and beautifullest, and best built city in
Britain, London excepted.
1724–7 Of Glasgow. *A Tour Thro the Whole Island of Great Britain*, letter 12.

86 Pleasure is a *thief* to business.
1725 *The Complete English Tradesman*, vol.1, ch.9.

87 Things as certain as death and taxes, can be more
firmly believed.
1726 *History of the Devil*, bk.2, ch.6.
▷ See also Franklin 402:12.

De Forest, Lee 1873–1961

US inventor, pioneer in the development of wireless telegraphy and radio.

88 While theoretically and technically television may
be feasible, commercially and financially I consider
it an impossibility, a development of which we
need waste little time dreaming.
1926 In the *New York Times*.

Degas, (Hilaire Germain) Edgar
1834–1917

French artist. After a trip to Italy, where he was influenced by Renaissance painters, he returned to Paris and exhibited with the Impressionists (1874–86).

89 Art does not expand, it repeats itself.
1872 Letter to Paul Frölich, 27 Nov.

90 It is essential to do the same subject over again, ten
times, a hundred times.
1886 Letter to Bartholomé, 17 Jan.

91 Aren't all beautiful things made by renunciation?
Quoted in P Lafond *Degas* (1918–9).

92 Drawing is not the form; it is the way of seeing the
form.
Quoted in P Valéry *Degas, danse, dessin* (1938).

93 Art cannot be made with an intent to please.
Quoted in R H Ives Gammell *The Shop-Talk of Edgar Degas* (1961).

94 It is all very well to copy what you see; it is much
better to draw what you see only in memory.
Quoted in R H Ives Gammell *The Shop-Talk of Edgar Degas* (1961).

95 Everybody has talent at twenty-five. The difficult
thing is to have it at fifty.
Quoted in R H Ives Gammell *The Shop-Talk of Edgar Degas* (1961).

de Gaulle, Charles 1890–1970

French general. Leader of the 'Free French' during World War II, he became head of the provisional government, and later Prime Minister (1958). As President of the Fifth Republic, he implemented an assertive foreign policy, but in 1969 resigned after the defeat of his referendum proposals for senate and regional reforms.

96 Nothing great will ever be achieved without great
men—and men only become great if they are
determined to be so.
1934 *Le Fil de l'Épée*.

97 *La France a perdu une bataille! Mais la France n'a pas
perdu la guerre!*

France has lost a battle! But France has not lost the
war!

1940 Proclamation, 18 Jun. Collected in *Discours, Messages et Declarations de General de Gaulle* (1941).

98   *Puisque ceux qui avaient le devoir de manier l'épée de la France l'ont laissée tomber brisée, moi, j'ai ramassé le tronçon du glaive.*

Since those whose duty it was to wield the sword of France have let it fall shattered to the ground, I have taken up the broken blade.
1940 Speech, 13 Jul.

99   The French will only be united under the threat of danger. How else can one govern a country that produces 246 different types of cheese?
1951 Speech. Quoted in *Les Mots du Général* (1962).

1   *Les traités, voyez-vous, sont comme les jeunes filles et comme les roses: ça dure ce que ça dure.*

Treaties are like girls and roses—they last while they last.
1963 Speech at the Elysée Palace, 2 Jul. Quoted in Brian Crozier *De Gaulle the Statesman* (1973).

2   I myself have become a Gaullist only little by little.
1963 In *The Observer*, 29 Dec.

3   I respect only those who resist me, but I cannot tolerate them.
1966 In the *New York Times*, 12 May.

4   Vive le Québec! Vive le Québec libre! Vive le Canada français! Vive la France!
1967 Address to the crowd before Montreal's City Hall, 24 Jul. The slogan 'Québec libre' was identified with the separatist cause.

5   When I want to know what France thinks, I ask myself.
Sons of France.

6   In order to become the master, the politician poses as the servant.
Attributed.

7   Politics is too important to be left to the politicians.
Attributed.

Dekanahwideh   fl.c.1450

Native American leader, traditional founder of the Six Nations Confederacy.

8   I, Dekanahwideh, and the Confederated Chiefs, now uproot the tallest pine tree, and into the cavity thereby made we cast all weapons of war… Thus shall the Great Peace be established.
Traditional words from the Six Nations Confederacy (present-day Ontario and the Northeastern United States), one of the world's oldest constitutions, quoted in Paul A W Wallace *The White Roots of Peace* (1946).

Dekker, Thomas   c.1570–c.1641

English dramatist. He wrote dramas for both public and private stages, masques, pageants and topical pamphlets, and was imprisoned for debt for three years. He frequently collaborated with other dramatists.

9   Ill is the weather that bringeth no gain.
1600 *The Shoemaker's Holiday*, 'The First Three-men's Song'.

10   Dost thou not know that love respects no blood, Cares not for difference of birth or state?
1600 *The Shoemaker's Holiday*, act 5, sc.5.

11   Golden slumbers kiss your eyes,
Smiles awake you when you rise;
Sleep, pretty wantons, do not cry,
And I will sing a lullaby,
Rock them, rock them, lullaby.
1603 *The Pleasant Comedy of Patient Grisill*, act 4, sc.2.

12   That great fishpond.
1604 Of the seas. *The Honest Whore*, pt.1, act 1, sc.2.

13   This wench we speak of strays so from her kind, Nature repents she made her; 'tis a mermaid Has tolled my son to shipwreck
1611 *The Roaring Girl* (with Thomas Middleton), act 1, sc.2.

14   'Tis the maddest fantasticalest girl. I never knew so much flesh and so much nimbleness put together.
1611 *The Roaring Girl* (with Thomas Middleton), act 2, sc.2.

15   I have no humour to marry; I love to lie o' both sides of the bed myself; and again, o' th' other side.
1611 *The Roaring Girl* (with Thomas Middleton), act 2, sc.2.

16   I have the head now of myself, and am man enough for a woman.
1611 *The Roaring Girl* (with Thomas Middleton), act 2, sc.2.

17   Thou'rt one of those
That thinks each woman thy fond flexible whore.
1611 *The Roaring Girl* (with Thomas Middleton), act 3, sc.1.

de Kooning, Willem   1904–97

Dutch-born US painter, who emigrated to the US in 1926 and became a leader of Abstract Expressionism, especially in action painting. His works, which focus on the human form, include the controversial series *Woman I–V* (1952–3).

18   Style is a fraud. I always felt the Greeks were hiding behind their columns.
1949 'A Desperate View', lecture given in New York.

19   Flesh was the reason why oil painting was invented.
1980 In *Bulletin*, Pittsburgh International Museum.

Delacroix, (Ferdinand Victor) Eugène
1798–1863

French Romantic painter, whose loose drawing and vivid colour aroused controversy. He continued to experiment with non-classical techniques and the use of colour.

20 What makes men of genius, or rather, what they
make, is not new ideas, it is that idea—possessing
them—that what has been said has still not been
said enough.
1824 *The Journal of Eugène Delacroix* (translated by W Pach,
1948), entry for 15 May.

21 I live in company with a body, a silent companion,
exacting and eternal. He it is who notes that
individuality which is the seal of the weakness of
our race. My soul has wings, but the brutal jailer is
strict.
1824 *The Journal of Eugène Delacroix* (translated by W Pach,
1948), entry for 4 Jun.

22 A taste for simplicity cannot endure for long.
1847 *The Journal of Eugène Delacroix* (translated by W Pach,
1948).

23 Painters who are not colourists produce
illumination and not painting.
1852 *The Journal of Eugène Delacroix* (translated by W Pach,
1948).

De La Mare, Walter 1873–1956

English poet and novelist. He worked for an oil company
until 1908, when he became a full-time writer. His work
included volumes of verse, novels, prose fantasy, and short
stories for both children and adults.

24 Oh, no man knows
Through what wild centuries
Roves back the rose.
1912 'All That's Past'.

25 'Is there anybody there?' said the Traveller,
Knocking on the moonlit door;
And his horse in the silence champed the grasses
Of the forest's ferny floor.
1912 'The Listeners'.

26 'Tell them I came, and no one answered,
That I kept my word,' he said.
1912 'The Listeners'.

27 Aye, they heard his foot upon the stirrup,
And the sound of iron on stone,
And how the silence surged softly backward,
When the plunging hoofs were gone.
1912 'The Listeners'.

28 He is crazed with the spell of far Arabia,
They have stolen his wits away.
1912 'Arabia'.

29 But beauty vanishes; beauty passes;
However rare—rare it be;
And when I crumble, who will remember
This lady of the West Country?
1912 'Epitaph'.

30 Ann, Ann!
Come! quick as you can!
There's a fish that *talks*
In the frying pan.
1913 'Alas, Alack'.

31 Slowly, silently, now the moon
Walks the night in her silver shoon.
1913 'Silver'.

32 A face peered. All the grey night
In chaos of vacancy shone;
Nought but vast Sorrow was there—
The sweet cheat gone.
1918 'The Ghost'.

33 When I lie where shades of darkness
Shall no more assail mine eyes.
1918 'Fare Well'.

34 Look thy last on all things lovely,
Every hour. Let no night
Seal thy sense in deathly slumber
Till to delight
Thou have paid thy utmost blessing.
1918 'Fare Well'.

35 Too late for fruit, too soon for flowers.
Attributed, when asked, while ill, if he would prefer fruit or
flowers. Quoted in Clifton Fadiman *The Faber Book of Anecdotes*
(1985).

Delaney, Shelagh 1939–

English playwright and screenwriter, whose best-known
play, *A Taste of Honey* (produced 1958) was written when
she was 17.

36 Women never have young minds. They are born
three thousand years old.
1957 *A Taste of Honey*, act 1, sc.2.

DeLillo, Don 1936–

US novelist. His ambitious dissection of modern cultural
codes in novels such as *White Noise* (1985) and *Libra*
(1988) have made him an important voice in modern
fiction.

37 I've come to think of Europe as a hardcover book,
America as the paperback version.
1982 Owen Brademas. *The Names*, ch.1.

38 Tourism is the march of stupidity.
1982 James Axton. *The Names*, ch.3.

39 If I were a writer, how I would enjoy being told the
novel is dead. How liberating to work in the
margins, outside a central perception. You are the
ghoul of literature. Lovely.
1982 Owen Brademas. *The Names*, ch.4.

40 To a writer, madness is a final distillation of self, a final editing down. It's the drowning out of false voices.
1982 Owen Brademas. *The Names*, ch.5.

41 Men with secrets tend to be drawn to each other, not because they want to share what they know but because they need the company of the like-minded, the fellow-afflicted.
1988 Walter Everett, Jr. *Libra*, pt.1, '17 April'.

42 A conspiracy is everything that ordinary life is not. It's the inside game, cold, sure, undistracted, forever closed off to us. We are the flawed ones, the innocents, trying to make some rough sense of the daily jostle. Conspirators have a logic and a daring beyond our reach.
1988 *Libra*, pt.2, 'In Dallas'.

Delius, Frederick 1862–1934

English composer of German-Scandinavian descent. He settled in France in 1890, establishing himself as a prolific and highly original composer. In 1924 he became paralysed and blind, but continued to work with the help of his amanuensis Eric Fenby.

43 It is only that which cannot be expressed otherwise that is worth expressing in music.
1920 'At the Crossroads'.

Deming, W(illiam) Edwards 1900–93

US statistician, inventor of modern quality control.

44 What's the aim of the school of business, for example? They teach students how business is conducted today and how to perpetuate it. Any wonder we're in trouble? They ought to be preparing students for the future, not for the past.
1990 Interview in the *Wall Street Journal*, 4 Jun.

Democritus c.460–c.370 BC

Greek philosopher. Only fragments of his extensive work on ethics have survived.

45 Nothing exists except atoms and empty space; everything else is opinion.
Diogenes Laertius, vol.9.

46 Strength and beauty are the blessings of youth; temperance, however, is the flower of old age.
Fragment quoted in H Diels and W Kranz (eds) *Die Fragmente der Vorsokratiker*, vol.2 (1952), no.294.

Dempsey, Jack (William Harrison) 1895–1983

US boxer. He won the world heavyweight title in 1919 and lost it to Gene Tunney in 1926. He retired in 1940 and became a successful restaurateur.

47 Honey, I forgot to duck.

1926 Attributed, to his wife after he was knocked out by Gene Tunney. US President Ronald Reagan repeated the phrase to his wife when wounded in an attempted assassination, 1981.

48 When you're fighting, you're fighting for one thing—money.
Quoted in Colin Jarman *The Guinness Dictionary of Sports Quotations* (1990).

Deng Xiaoping 1904–97

Chinese political leader who rose to power (1978) after disgrace during the Cultural Revolution. His international esteem suffered after he sanctioned the Tiananmen Square massacre of pro-democracy supporters, Jun 1989.

49 It doesn't matter whether the cat is black or white, as long as it catches mice.
1962 Speech at Communist Youth League conference, Jul.

50 A fundamental contradiction does not exist between socialism and a market economy.
1985 Address to US businessmen organized by *Time* magazine, 18 Dec.

51 Even if they're functioning out of ignorance, they are still participating and must be suppressed. In China, even one million people can be considered a small sum.
1989 Of pro-democracy demonstrators. In *The Times*, 5 Jun.

Denham, Sir John 1615–69

Irish poet and Royalist, who undertook secret missions for Charles I and Charles II during the Civil War and Protectorate, and was knighted in 1661. He is credited with introducing to English verse the couplet form which later dominated 18c poetry.

52 Can knowledge have no bound, but must advance So far, to make us wish for ignorance?
1642 *Cooper's Hill*, l.145-6.

53 O could I flow like thee, and make thy stream My great example, as it is my theme! Though deep, yet clear, though gentle, yet not dull, Strong without rage, without o'erflowing full.
1642 Of the Thames. *Cooper's Hill*, l.189-92

54 Such is our pride, our folly, or our fate, That few, but such as cannot write, translate.
1648 'To Richard Fanshaw'.

55 Old Mother Wit, and Nature gave Shakespeare and Fletcher all they have; In Spenser, and in Jonson, Art Of slower Nature got the start.
1667 'On Mr Abraham Cowley'.

56 Youth, what man's age is like to be doth show; We may our ends by our beginnings know.
1668 'Of Prudence', l.225-6.

Deniehy, Daniel Henry 1828–65

Australian lawyer, politician, orator and writer, who formed his own famous library.

57 A Bunyip Aristocracy.

1853 Quoted in *The Australian Dictionary of Biography*, vol 4. The bunyip is a mythical, chimerical animal of Australian folklore.

Denis, Maurice 1870–1943

French painter and art theorist, associated with the Nabis group ('prophets' influenced by Gauguin), and Symbolism.

58 Remember that a painting—before it is a battlehorse, a nude woman, or some anecdote—is essentially a flat surface covered with colours assembled in a certain order.

1912 *Théories: 1890–1910*.

Denman, Thomas, 1st Baron 1779–1854

English jurist. Whig MP (1818–26), he was Attorney-General in Earl Grey's administration (1830–2), and Lord Chief Justice (1832–50).

59 Trial by jury itself, instead of being a security to persons who are accused, will be a delusion, a mockery, and a snare.

1844 Judgement in *O'Connell* v *The Queen*, 4 Sep.

Denning, Alfred Thompson, Lord 1899–1999

English judge. As Master of the Rolls (1962–82), he earned a reputation for his outspoken opinions.

60 A wrong decision can make me very miserable. But I have trust in God. If you have this trust you don't have to worry, as you don't have the sole responsibility.

1982 Speech on his retirement.

Dennis, C(larence Michael) J(ames) 1876–1938

Australian poet and journalist. His poems have been popular for their vernacular humour.

61 Me pal 'e trots 'er up an' does the toff—
'E allus wus a bloke fer showin' off.
'This 'ere's Doreen,' 'e sez. 'This 'ere's the Kid.'
I dips me lid.

1915 *Songs of a Sentimental Bloke* , 'The Intro'. Bill persuades his friend to introduce him to a girl.

Dennis, John 1657–1734

English playwright and critic. He was among the most famous critics of his day, but his own plays met with little success and he was one of the targets of Alexander Pope's satire in *The Dunciad*.

62 Damn them, see how the rascals use me! They will not let my play run, and yet they steal my thunder!

1709 Attributed, when watching a production of *Macbeth* that featured a thunder machine he had designed for use in his own play *Appius and Virginia*, which had been denied a long run. Said to be the origin of the phrase 'to steal one's thunder'.

63 A man who could make so vile a pun would not scruple to pick a pocket.

Of Dennis. In the *Gentleman's Magazine* 1781, editorial note.

De Quincey, Thomas 1785–1859

English writer. He ran away from school in 1802, lived with a prostitute in London, became an opium addict at Oxford, lived for a time in the Lake District and moved to Edinburgh in 1828.

64 A duller spectacle this earth of ours has not to show than a rainy Sunday in London.

1821 *Confessions of an English Opium Eater* (originally serialized in the *London Magazine*, published 1822).

65 Thou hast the keys of Paradise, oh just, subtle, and mighty opium!

1821 *Confessions of an English Opium Eater* (originally serialized in the *London Magazine*, published 1822).

66 Books, we are told, propose to *instruct* or to *amuse*. Indeed!… The true antithesis to knowledge, in this case, is not *pleasure*, but *power*. All that is literature seeks to communicate power; all that is not literature, to communicate knowledge.

1823 *Letters to a Young Man whose Education has been Neglected*, no.3, in the London Magazine, Jan–Jul.

67 Murder Considered as One of the Fine Arts.

1827 Title of essay, in *Blackwood's Magazine*, Feb.

68 If once a man indulges himself in murder, very soon he comes to think little of robbing; and from robbing he comes next to drinking and sabbath-breaking, and from that to invicility and procrastination.

1839 'On Murder Considered as One of the Fine Arts' (supplementary paper), in *Blackwood's Magazine*, Nov.

Derby, Edward Geoffrey Smith Stanley, 14th Earl of 1799–1869

English statesman and Conservative Prime Minister (1852, 1858–9, 1866–8), formerly a Whig. He entered the Lords in 1844 and headed the Protectionists from 1846, the year he became Party leader.

69 The foreign policy of the noble Earl, Lord Russell, may be summed up in two truly expressive words: meddle and muddle.

1884 Speech in the House of Lords, Feb, referring to the Prime Minister's policy on the American Civil War.

Desai, Anita née Mazumbar 1937–

Indian novelist, who writes for children and adults. Her *The Clear Light of Day* (1980) and *In Custody* (1984) were both shortlisted for the Booker Prize.

70 Do you know anyone who would—secretly,
    sincerely, in his innermost self—*really* prefer to
    return to childhood?
    1980 *The Clear Light of Day*, ch.1.

Desbiens, Jean-Paul 1927–

Canadian writer and educator.

71 Education is impossible without love, without
    loving a few of the great men of the past.
    1965 *For Pity's Sake* (translated by Frédéric Côte).

Desbordes-Valmore, Marceline 1786–1859

French poet. She worked in the theatre and published
children's stories before turning to poetry. Her poems are
written in an open, informal style, often as dialogues.

72 *Par toi tout le bonheur que m'offre l'avenir*
    Est dans mon souvenir.

    Through you, all the happiness that the future
    offers
    Is in my memory.
    1819 *Elegies, Marie et romances*, 'Le Souvenir'.

73 *Ce qu'on donne à l'amour est à jamais perdu.*

    What one gives in love is forever lost.
    1830 *Poésies*, 'L'Isolement'.

74 *J'ai vécu d'aimer, j'ai donc vécu de larmes.*

    I lived to love. I lived, therefore, in tears.
    1860 *Poésies posthumes*, 'Rêve intermittent d'une nuit triste'.

Descartes, René 1596–1650

French philosopher and mathematician. He travelled
widely before settling in Holland and writing his major
works (both popular, in French, and scholarly, in Latin);
the *Discours de la méthode* (1637), *Meditationes de prima
philosophia* (1641), and *Principia philosophiae* (1644).

75 *La lecture de tous les bons livres est comme une
    conversation avec les plus honnêtes gens des siècles
    passés, qui en ont été les auteurs, et même une
    conversation étudiée en laquelle ils ne nous découvrent
    que les meilleures de leurs pensées.*

    The reading of good books is like a conversation
    with the best men of past centuries—in fact like a
    prepared conversation, in which they reveal their
    best thoughts.
    1637 *Discours de la méthode* (*Discourse on method*), 1st
    discourse (translated by G E M Anscombe and Peter Geach).

76 *Le bon sens est la chose du monde la mieux partagée:
    car chacun pense en être si bien pourvu, que ceux
    même qui sont les plus difficiles à contenter en toute
    autre chose n'ont point coutume d'en désirer plus qu'ils
    ont. En quoi il n'est pas vraisemblable que tous se
    trompent; mais plutôt cela témoigne que la puissance
    de bien juger et distinguer le vrai d'avec le faux, qui*

*est proprement ce qu'on nomme le bon sens ou la
raison, est naturellement égale en tous les hommes.*

Good sense is the most fairly distributed thing in
the world; for everyone thinks himself so well
supplied with it, that even those who are hardest to
satisfy in every other way do not usually desire
more of it than they already have. In this matter it
is not likely that everybody is mistaken; it rather
goes to show that the power of judging well and
distinguishing truth from falsehood, which is what
we properly mean by good sense or reason, is
naturally equal in all men.
1637 *Discours de la méthode* (*Discourse on method*), 1st
discourse (translated by G E M Anscombe and Peter Geach)

77 *Pour ce qu'alors je désirais vaquer seulement à la
    recherche de la vérité, je pensai qu'il fallait que
    je…rejetasse comme absolument faux tout ce en quoi
    je pourrais imaginer le moindre doute, afin de voir s'il
    ne resterait point, après cela, quelque chose en ma
    créance qui fût entièrement indubitable.*

    Since my present aim was to give myself up to the
    pursuit of truth alone, I thought I must…reject as
    if absolutely false anything as to which I could
    imagine the least doubt, in order to see if I should
    not be left at the end believing something that was
    absolutely indubitable.
    1637 *Discours de la méthode* (*Dicourse on method*), 4th
    discourse (translated by G E M Anscombe and Peter Geach).

78 *Je pris garde que, pendant que je voulais ainsi penser
    que tout était faux, il fallait nécessairement que moi,
    qui le pensais, fusse quelque chose.*

    I noticed that while I was trying to think
    everything false, it must needs be that I, who was
    thinking this, was something.
    1637 *Discours de la méthode* (*Discourse on method*), 4th
    discourse (translated by G E M Anscombe and Peter Geach).

79 *Je pense, donc je suis.*

    I think, therefore I am.
    1637 *Discours de la méthode* (*Discourse on method*), 4th
    discourse (translated by G E M Anscombe and Peter Geach).
    Often quoted as 'Cogito, ergo sum', but Descartes wrote the
    French version before the Latin.

80 *Je pouvais prendre pour règle générale, que les choses
    que nous concevons fort clairement et fort
    distinctement sont toutes vraies.*

    I could take it as a general rule that whatever we
    conceive very clearly and very distinctly is true.
    1637 *Discours de la méthode* (*Discourse on method*), 4th
    discourse (translated by G E M Anscombe and Peter Geach).

81 *Animadverti jam ante aliquot annos quam multa,
    ineunte aetate, falsa pro veris admiserim, et quam
    dubia sint quaecunque istis postea superextruxi, ac
    proinde funditus omnia semel in vita esse evertenda,
    atque a primis fundamentis denno inchoandum, si*

quid aliquando firmum et mansurum cupiam in scientiis stabilire.

Some years ago now I observed the multitude of errors that I had accepted as true in my earliest years, and the dubiousness of the whole superstructure I had since then reared on them; and the consequent need of making a clean sweep for once in my life, and beginning again from the very foundations, if I would establish some secure and lasting result in science.

1641 *Meditationes*, 1st meditation (translated by G E M Anscombe and Peter Geach).

82 *Supponam igitur non optimum Deum, fontem veritatis, sed genium aliquum malignum, eundemque summe potentem et callidum, omnem suam industriam in eo posuisse, ut me falleret.*

I will suppose then, not that there is a supremely good God, the source of truth; but that there is an evil spirit, who is supremely powerful and intelligent, and does his utmost to deceive me.

1641 *Meditationes*, 1st meditation (translated by G E M Anscombe and Peter Geach).

83 *Agnoscam fieri non posse ut existam talis naturae qualis sum, nempe ideam Dei in me habens, nisi revera Deus etiam existeret, Deus, inquam, ille idem cujus idea in me est.*

I could not possibly exist with the nature I actually have, that is, one endowed with the idea of God, unless there really is a God; the very God, I mean, of whom I have an idea.

1641 *Meditationes*, 3rd meditation (translated by G E M Anscombe and Peter Geach)

Deschamps, Eustache c.1345–1406
French poet, soldier and courtier.

84 *Rien ne se peut comparer à Paris.*

Nothing can compare to Paris.
c.1370 'Ballade de Paris', refrain.

Deschamps, Yvon 1935–
Canadian entertainer, known for his separatist allegiances.

85 All we want is an independent Quebec within a strong and united Canada.
Quoted by Peter C Newman in *Maclean's*, 13 Nov 1978. This has become the classic formulation of Quebec's national and political aspirations.

Destouches, Philippe originally Néricault
1680–1754
French playwright, a diplomat in England (1717–23). His early comedies are undistinguished, but his masterpiece is *Le Glorieux* (The Boaster, 1732).

86 *Les absents ont toujours tort.*

The absent are always in the wrong.
1717 *L'Obstacle imprévu*, act 1, sc.6.

De Valera, Éamon 1882–1975
Irish statesman, born in the US. He narrowly escaped execution for his part in the 1916 Easter Rebellion, and became leader of Sinn Féin (1917–26). He was Prime Minister (1932–48, 1951–4, 1957–9) and President (1959–73).

87 Why doesn't he use a spoon?
1921 On being told that David Lloyd George had said talking to him was like trying to pick up mercury with a fork.

Devlin, Denis 1908–59
Irish poet and diplomat, born in Scotland. His poetry, which assimilates Christian iconography into cosmopolitan settings, was not appreciated until after his death.

88 And sad, Oh sad, that glen with one thin stream
He met his death in; and a farmer told me
There was but one small bird to shoot: it sang
'Better Beast and know your end, and die
Than Man with murderous angels in his head.'
c.1956 'The Tomb of Michael Collins'.

De Voto, Bernard 1897–1955
US historian and writer, known for 'The Easy Chair' in *Harper's Magazine* from 1935. His works include the historical trilogy beginning with *The Year of Decision: 1846* (1943) and he edited Twain's work.

89 The proper union of gin and vermouth is a great and sudden glory; it is one of the happiest marriages on earth, and one of the shortest lived.
1949 In *Harper's Magazine*, Dec.

90 Novelists, whatever else they may be besides, are also children talking to children—in the dark.
1950 *The World of Fiction.*

91 When evening quickens in the street, comes a pause in the day's occupation that is known as the cocktail hour.
1951 *The Hour.*

92 You can no more keep a martini in the refrigerator than you can keep a kiss there.
1951 *The Hour.*

De Vries, Peter 1910–93
US novelist and humorist, best known for his *The Tunnel of Love* (1954).

93 It is the final proof of God's omnipotence that he need not exist in order to save us.
1958 *The Mackerel Plaza*, ch.1.

94 Look at it this way: Psychoanalysis is a permanent fad.
1973 *Forever Panting.*

Dewey, John 1859–1952

US philosopher and educator. A leading pragmatist, he developed an influential philosophy of education which stressed learning through experience. His writings include *The Quest for Certainty* (1929) and *The Child and the Curriculum* (1902).

95 When physics, chemistry, biology, medicine, contribute to the detection of concrete human woes and to the development of plans for remedying them and relieving the human estate, they become moral; they become part of the apparatus of moral inquiry or science… When the consciousness of science is fully impregnated with the consciousness of human value, the greatest dualism which now weighs humanity down, the split between the material, the mechanical and the scientific and the moral and ideal will be destroyed.
1920 *Reconstruction in Philosophy.*

96 The function of criticism is the reeducation of perception of works of art… The conception that its business is to appraise, to judge in the legal and moral sense, arrests the perception of those who are influenced by the criticism that assumes this task.
1934 *Art as Experience.*

De Wolfe, Elsie 1865–1950

English actress, interior decorator and hostess, the wife of the British diplomat, Sir Charles Mendl.

97 Beige! Just my color.
On seeing the Acropolis for the first time. Quoted in Nina Campbell and Caroline Seebohm *Elsie de Wolfe: A Decorative Life* (1992), ch.1.

Diaghilev, Sergei 1872–1929

Russian impresario. His Ballets Russes company, formed in 1911, created a sensation throughout Europe and launched the careers of such dancers as Balanchine, Fokine, Nijinsky and Pavlova.

98 *Étonne-moi!*

Astonish me!
1912 Attributed, when Jean Cocteau complained that he was getting insufficient direction when designing the scenario for a new ballet. Quoted in Wallace Fowlie (ed) *Journals of Jean Cocteau* (1956), ch.1.

Diana, Princess of Wales 1961–97

She married Charles, Prince of Wales, in 1981 and they were divorced in 1996.

99 I'm as thick as a plank.
Remark quoted in *Sunday Today*, 25 Jan 1987.

1 There were three of us in this marriage, so it was a bit crowded.
1995 Of her marriage to Charles, Prince of Wales and his relationship with Camilla Parker-Bowles. BBC *Panorama* broadcast, 20 Nov.

Díaz, Jorge 1930–

Chilean dramatist born in Argentina. He has lived in Spain since 1965. His plays are influenced by the theatre of the absurd and other avant-garde experimental movements.

2 ¡Pero la verdad es que estoy cansada, horriblemente cansada de ser la esposa femenina de ese animal masculino que se rasca, pierde el pelo sistemáticamente y canta tangos pasados de moda!…
Quisiera…quisiera engordar, fumar un puro y enviudar de una manera indolora y elegante.

The truth is, I'm tired, frightfully tired of being the feminine spouse to the masculine animal who scratches himself, systematically loses his hair and sings outdated tangos!… I'd like… I'd like to get fat, to smoke cigars and to become a widow in a painless and elegant fashion.
1961 *El cepillo de dientes* (*The Toothbrush*), act 1 .

Diaz, Porfirio 1830–1915

President of Mexico. He supported Juarez in the War of the Reform and gained the presidency through rebellion in 1877.

3 Poor Mexico, so far from God and so close to the United States.
1846 Attributed, at the beginning of the American–Mexican War (1846–8).

Dibdin, Charles 1745–1814

English songwriter, who wrote his first operetta (*The Shepherd's Artifice*, performed at Covent Garden 1762) as a boy. He wrote nearly 100 sea songs and 70 dramatic pieces.

4 For a soldier I listed, to grow great in fame,
And be shot at for sixpence a day.
1791 'Charity'.

5 Did you ever hear of Captain Wattle?
He was all for love, and a little for the bottle.
1797 'Captain Wattle and Miss Roe'.

6 Then trust me, there's nothing like drinking
So pleasant this side of the grave;
It keeps the unhappy from thinking,
And makes e'en the valiant more brave.
'Nothing Like Grog'. First published 1803.

7 What argufies pride and ambition?
Soon or late death will take us in tow:
Each bullet has got its commission,
And when our time's come we must go.
'Each Bullet Has Got Its Commission'. First published 1803.

Dick, Philip K(indred) 1928–82

US science-fiction writer. His output was prolific, marked by a strong literary sensibility as well as a powerful, often chilling imagination and humour.

8 Dr Bloodmoney, Or How We Got Along After The Bomb.
1965 Title of novel.

9 I mean, after all; you have to consider that we're only made out of dust. That's admittedly not much to go on and we shouldn't forget that. But even considering, I mean, it's sort of a bad beginning, we're not doing too bad. So I personally have faith that even in this lousy situation we're faced with we can make it. You get me?
1966 *The Three Stigmata of Palmer Eldritch*, closing words.

10 Do Androids Dream Of Electric Sheep?
1968 Title of novel, later the basis for the film *Blade Runner*.

11 Reality is that which, when you stop believing in it, doesn't go away.
1972 Quoted in introduction to *I Hope I Shall Arrive Soon* (1986).

12 Drug misuse is not a disease, it is a decision, like the decision to step out in front of a moving car. You would call that not a disease but an error of judgement.
1977 *A Scanner Darkly*, author's note.

13 The basic tool for the manipulation of reality is the manipulation of words. If you can control the meaning of words, you can control the people who must use the words.
1986 *I Hope I Shall Arrive Soon*, 'How To Build A Universe That Doesn't Fall Apart Two Days Later'.

Dickens, Charles John Huffam 1812–70

English novelist. After a childhood of poverty and hardship, during which his parents were sent to a debtors' prison, he became one of England's most popular and prolific novelists, exposing the inhumanities of the 19c with an idiosyncratic blend of wit and sentimentality and a gallery of memorable characters.

14 Grief never mended no broken bones, and as good people's wery scarce, what I says is, make the most on 'em.
1836–7 *Sketches by Boz*, 'Gin Shops'.

15 We shall never forget the mingled feelings of awe and respect with which we used to gaze on the exterior of Newgate in our schoolboy days…[the doors] looking as if they were made for the express purpose of letting people in, and never letting them out again.
1836–7 *Sketches by Boz*, 'Criminal Courts'.

16 Heads, heads, take care of your heads… Five children—mother—tall lady, eating sandwiches—forgot the arch—crash—knock—children look round—mother's head off—sandwich in her hand—no mouth to put it in—head of a family off—shocking, shocking!

1836–7 Jingle. *Pickwick Papers*, ch.2.

17 'I am ruminating,' said Mr Pickwick, 'on the strange mutability of human affairs.' 'Ah, I see—in at the palace door one day, out at the window the next. Philosopher, Sir?' 'An observer of human nature, sir,' said Mr Pickwick.
1836–7 *Pickwick Papers*, ch.2.

18 Kent, sir—everyone knows Kent—apples, cherries, hops, and women.
1836–7 Jingle. *Pickwick Papers*, ch.2.

19 There was a fine gentle wind, and Mr Pickwick's hat rolled sportively before it. The wind puffed, and Mr Pickwick puffed, and the hat rolled over and over as merrily as a living porpoise in a strong tide.
1836–7 *Pickwick Papers*, ch.4.

20 I wants to make your flesh creep.
1836–7 The Fat Boy. *Pickwick Papers*, ch.8.

21 'It's always best on these occasions to do what the mob do.' 'But suppose there are two mobs?' suggested Mr Snodgrass. 'Shout with the largest,' replied Mr Pickwick.
1836–7 *Pickwick Papers*, ch.13.

22 And a wery good name it is—only one I know, that ain't got a nickname to it.
1836–7 Sam Weller comments on Job Trotter's Christian name. *Pickwick Papers*, ch.16.

23 Poverty and oysters always seem to go together.
1836–7 Sam Weller. *Pickwick Papers*, ch.22.

24 Dumb as a drum vith a hole in it, sir.
1836–7 Sam Weller. *Pickwick Papers*, ch.25.

25 Our noble society for providing the infant negroes in the West Indies with flannel waistcoats and moral pocket handkerchiefs.
1836–7 Mr Stiggins. *Pickwick Papers*, ch.27.

26 Poetry's unnat'ral; no man ever talked in poetry 'cept a beadle on boxin' day, or Warren's blackin' or Rowland's oil, or some o' them low fellows; never you let yourself down to talk poetry, my boy.
1836–7 Sam Weller's father. *Pickwick Papers*, ch.33.

27 It's my opinion, sir, that this meeting is drunk, sir!
1836–7 Mr Stiggins. *Pickwick Papers*, ch.33.

28 'Yes, I have a pair of eyes,' replied Sam, 'and that's just it. If they wos a pair o' patent double million magnifyin' gas microscopes of hextra power, p'raps I might be able to see through a flight o' stairs and a deal door; but bein' only eyes, you see my wision's limited.'

1836–7 *Pickwick Papers*, ch.34.

29 Miss Bolo rose from the table considerably agitated, and went straight home, in a flood of tears and a sedan chair.
1836–7 *Pickwick Papers*, ch.35.

30 We know, Mr. Weller—we, who are men of the world—that a good uniform must work its way with the women, sooner or later.
1836–7 The Gentleman in Blue. *Pickwick Papers*, ch.37.

31 It's a regular holiday to them–all porter and skittles.
1836–7 *Pickwick Papers,* ch.41.

32 Anythin' for a quiet life, as the man said wen he took the sitivation at the lighthouse.
1836–7 Sam Weller. *Pickwick Papers*, ch.43.

33 The fact is, that there was considerable difficulty in inducing Oliver to take upon himself the office of respiration—a troublesome practice, but one which custom has rendered necessary to our easy existence—and for some time he lay gasping on a little flock mattress, rather unequally poised between this world and the next, the balance being decidedly in favour of the latter. Now, if during this period, Oliver had been surrounded by careful grandmothers, anxious aunts, experienced nurses, and doctors of profound wisdom, he would most inevitably and indubitably have been killed in no time.
1837–9 *Oliver Twist*, ch.1.

34 Please, sir, I want some more.
1837–9 Oliver. *Oliver Twist*, ch.2.

35 It was a nice sickly season just at this time. In commercial phrase, coffins were looking up.
1837–9 *Oliver Twist*, ch.6.

36 What a fine thing capital punishment is! Dead men never repent; dead men never bring awkward stories to light. Ah, it's a fine thing for the trade! Five of 'em strung up in a row; and none left to play booty, or turn white-livered!
1837–9 Fagin. *Oliver Twist*, ch.9.

37 'Hard,' replied the Dodger. 'As nails,' added Charley Bates.
1837–9 *Oliver Twist*, ch.9.

38 There is a passion for hunting something deeply implanted in the human breast.
1837–8 *Oliver Twist*, ch.10.

39 I'll eat my head.
1837–9 Mr Grimwig. *Oliver Twist*, ch.14.

40 I only know two sorts of boys. Mealy boys, and beef-faced boys.

1837–9 Mr Grimwig. *Oliver Twist*, ch.14.

41 This ain't the shop for justice.
1837–9 The Artful Dodger. *Oliver Twist*, ch.43.

42 'If the law supposes that,' said Mr Bumble…'the law is a ass—a idiot.'
1837–9 *Oliver Twist*, ch.51.

43 United Metropolitian Improved Hot Muffin and Crumpet Baking and Punctual Delivery Company.
1838–9 *Nicholas Nickleby*, ch.2.

44 EDUCATION.—At Mr Wackford Squeers's Academy, Dotheboys Hall, at the delightful village of Dotheboys, near Greta Bridge in Yorkshire, Youth are boarded, clothed, booked, furnished with pocket-money, provided with all necessaries, instructed in all languages living and dead, mathematics, orthography, geometry, astronomy, trigonometry, the use of the globes, algebra, single stick (if required), writing, arithmetic, fortification, and every other branch of classical literature. Terms, twenty guineas per annum. No extras, no vacations, and diet unparalleled.
1838–9 *Nicholas Nickleby*, ch.3.

45 He had but one eye, and the popular prejudice runs in favour of two.
1838–9 *Nicholas Nickleby*, ch.4.

46 Subdue your appetites, my dears, and you've conquered human nature.
1838–9 *Nicholas Nickleby*, ch.5.

47 There are only two styles of portrait painting; the serious and the smirk.
1838–9 Mrs Squeers. *Nicholas Nickleby*, ch.10.

48 Oh! They're too beautiful to live, much too beautiful!
1938–9 Mrs Kenwigs. *Nicholas Nickleby*, ch. 14.

49 Sir, My pa requests me to write to you, the doctors considering it doubtful whether he will ever recuvver the use of his legs which prevents his holding a pen.
1838–9 Fanny Squeers. *Nicholas Nickleby*, ch.15.

50 'It's very easy to talk,' said Mrs Mantalini. 'Not so easy when one is eating a demnition egg,' replied Mr Mantalini; 'for the yolk runs down the waistcoat, and yolk of egg does not match any waistcoat but a yellow waistcoat, demmit.'
1838–9 *Nicholas Nickleby*, ch.17.

51 Language was not powerful enough to describe the infant phenomenon.
1838–9 *Nicholas Nickleby*, ch.23.

52 I am a demd villain! I will fill my pockets with change for a sovereign in half-pence and drown

myself in the Thames…I will become a demd, damp, moist, unpleasant body.
1838–9 Mr Mantalini. *Nicholas Nickleby*, ch.34.

53 Every baby born into the world is a finer one than the last.
1838–9 *Nicholas Nickleby*, ch.36.

54 Bring in the bottled lightning, a clean tumbler, and a corkscrew.
1838–9 The Gentleman in the Small-Clothes. *Nicholas Nickleby*, ch.49.

55 All is gas and gaiters.
1838–9 The Gentleman in the Small-Clothes. *Nicholas Nickleby*, ch.49.

56 My life is one demd horrid grind!
1838–9 Mr Mantalini speaking. *Nicholas Nickleby*, ch.64.

57 What is the odds so long as the fire of soul is kindled at the taper of conwiviality, and the wing of friendship never moults a feather!
1840–1 Dick Swiveller. *The Old Curiosity Shop*, ch.2.

58 Fan the sinking flame of hilarity with the wing of friendship; and pass the rosy wine.
1840–1 Dick Swiveller. *The Old Curiosity Shop*, ch.7.

59 And don't you think you must be a very wicked little child…to be a waxwork child at all.?
1840–1 Miss Monflathers to Nell. *The Old Curiosity Shop*, ch.31.

60 'Did you ever taste beer?'
'I had a sip of it once,' said the small servant.
'Here's a state of things!' cried Mr. Swiveller, raising his eyes to the ceiling. 'She *never* tasted it—it can't be tasted in a sip!'
1840–1 *The Old Curiosity Shop*, ch.57.

61 They moved so gently, that their footsteps made no noise; but there were sobs from among the group, and sounds of grief and mourning.
1840–1 The death of little Nell. *The Old Curiosity Shop*, ch.71.

62 Something will come of this. I hope it mayn't be human gore.
1841 Simon Tappertit. *Barnaby Rudge*, ch.4.

63 Polly put the kettle on, we'll all have tea.
1841 Grip. *Barnaby Rudge*, ch.17.

64 'There are strings', said Mr Tappertit, 'in the human heart that had better not be wibrated.'
1841 Mr Tappertit. *Barnaby Rudge*, ch.22.

65 Oh gracious, why wasn't I born old and ugly?
1841 Miss Miggs. *Barnaby Rudge*, ch.70.

66 Was there ever such a sunny street as this Broadway! The pavement stones are polished with the tread of feet until they shine again… Heaven

save the ladies, how they dress! We have seen more colours in these ten minutes, than we should have seen elsewhere, in as many days. What various parasols! what rainbow silks and satins! what pinking of thin stockings and pinching of thin shoes, and fluttering of ribbons and silk tassels, and display of rich cloaks with gaudy hoods and linings!
1842 *American Notes.*

67 Politics are much discussed, so are banks, so is cotton. Quiet people avoid the question of the Presidency…the great constitutional feature of this institution being, that directly the acrimony of the last election is over, the next one begins.
1842 *American Notes.*

68 'The name of those fabulous animals (pagan, I regret to say) who used to sing in the water, has quite escaped me.' Mr George Chuzzlewit suggested 'Swans'. 'No,' said Mr Pecksniff. 'Not swans. Very like swans, too. Thank you.' The nephew…propounded 'Oysters'. 'No', said Mr Picksniff…'nor oysters. But by no means unlike oysters…wait. Sirens! Dear me! sirens, of course.'
1843–4 *Martin Chuzzlewit*, ch.4.

69 Any man may be in good spirits and good temper when he's well dressed. There an't much credit in that. If I was very ragged and very jolly, then I should begin to feel I had gained a point, Mr. Pinch.
1843–4 Mark Tapley. *Martin Chuzzlewit*, ch.5.

70 His moral character…was full of promise but of no performance.
1843–4 Of Mr Pecksniff. *Martin Chuzzlewit*, ch.5.

71 Affection beaming in one eye, and calculation shining out of the other.
1843–4 Of Mrs Todgers. *Martin Chuzzlewit*, ch.8.

72 Let us be moral. Let us contemplate existence.
1843–4 Mr Pecksniff. *Martin Chuzzlewit*, ch.9.

73 Here's the rule for bargains: 'Do other men, for they would do you.' That's the true business precept.
1843–4 Jonas Chuzzlewit. *Martin Chuzzlewit*, ch.11.

74 Buy an annuity cheap, and make your life interesting to yourself and everybody else that watches the speculation.
1843–4 *Martin Chuzzlewit*, ch.18.

75 'Mrs Harris,' I says, 'leave the bottle on the chimley-piece, and don't ask me to take none, but let me put my lips to it when I am so dispoged.'
1843–4 Mrs Gamp. *Martin Chuzzlewit*, ch.19.

76 Features are an index to the heart.

77 At the same moment a peculiar fragrance was borne upon the breeze, as if a passing fairy had hiccoughed, and had previously been to a wine-vaults.
    1843–4 At Mrs Gamp's entrance. *Martin Chuzzlewit*, ch.25.

78 Gamp would certainly have drunk its little shoes right off its feet, as with our precious boy he did, and arterwards send the child a errand to sell his wooden leg for any money it would fetch as matches in the rough, and bring it home in liquor.
    1843–4 Mrs Gamp. *Martin Chuzzlewit*, ch.25.

79 She's the sort of woman…one would almost feel disposed to bury for nothing: and do it neatly, too!
    1843–4 Mould speaking about Mrs Gamp. *Martin Chuzzlewit*, ch.25.

80 He'd make a lovely corpse.
    1843–4 Mrs Gamp speaking of Jonas Chuzzlewit. *Martin Chuzzlewit*, ch.25.

81 We never knows wot's hidden in each other's hearts; and if we had glass winders there, we'd need keep the shutters up, some on us, I do assure you!
    1843–4 Mrs Gamp. *Martin Chuzzlewit*, ch.29.

82 A lane was made; and Mrs Hominy…came slowly up it in a procession of one.
    1843–4 *Martin Chuzzlewit*, ch.34.

83 'Mind over matter,' said the lady in the wig, 'glide swift into the vortex of immensity. Howls the sublime and softly sleeps the calm Ideal, in the whispering chambers of Imagination.'
    1843–4 *Martin Chuzzlewit*, ch.34.

84 Farewell! Be the proud bride of a ducal coronet, and forget me!…Unalterably, never yours, Augustus.
    1843–4 Augustus Moddle. *Martin Chuzzlewit*, ch.34.

85 'Bah!' said Scrooge, 'Humbug!'
    1843 *A Christmas Carol*, stave 1.

86 'You are fettered,' said Scrooge, trembling. 'Tell me why?'
    'I wear the chain I forged in life,' replied the Ghost. 'I made it link by link, and yard by yard; I girded it on, of my own free will I wore it.
    1843 *A Christmas Carol*, stave 1.

87 'God bless us every one!' said Tiny Tim, the last of all.
    1843 *A Christmas Carol*, stave 3.

88 But however and whenever we part from one another, I am sure we shall none of us forget poor Tiny Tim.

89 It was a turkey! He could never have stood upon his legs, that bird. He would have snapped 'em off short in a minute, like sticks of sealing-wax.
    1843 *A Christmas Carol*, stave 5.

90 The earth was made for Dombey and Son to trade in, and the sun and moon made to give them light. Rivers and seas were formed to float their ships; rainbows gave them promise of fair weather; winds blew for or against their enterprise; stars and planets circled in their orbits, to preserve inviolate a system of which they were the centre.
    1846–8 *Dombey and Son*, ch.1.

91 Dombey and Son had often dealt in hides, but never in hearts. They left that fancy ware to boys and girls, and boarding-schools and books.
    1846–8 *Dombey and Son*, ch.1.

92 As to Mr Feeder, B.A., Doctor Blimber's assistant, he was a kind of human barrel-organ, with a little list of tunes at which he was continually working, over and over again, without any variation.
    1846–8 *Dombey and Son*, ch.11.

93 What the waves were always saying.
    1846–8 *Dombey and Son*, ch.16.

94 Train up a fig-tree in the way it should go, and when you are old sit under the shade of it.
    1846–8 Captain Cuttle. *Dombey and Son*, ch.19.

95 Cows are my passion.
    1846–8 Mrs Skewton. *Dombey and Son*, ch.21.

96 Say, like those wicked Turks, there is no What's-his-name but Thingummy, and What-you-may-call-it is his prophet!
    1846–8 Mrs Skewton. *Dombey and Son*, ch.27.

97 If you could see my legs when I take my boots off, you'd form some idea of what unrequited affection is.
    1846–8 Mr Toots. *Dombey and Son*, ch.48.

98 David Copperfield from head to foot! Calls a house a rookery when there's not a rook near it and takes the birds on trust because he sees the nests!
    1849–50 Betsey Trotwood of David's father. *David Copperfield*, ch.1.

99 Bewitching Mrs Copperfield's incumbrance?
    1849–50 Mr Quinion of David. *David Copperfield*, ch.2.

 1 Brooks of Sheffield.
    1849–50 Mr Murdstone of David. *David Copperfield*, ch.2.

 2 I am a lone lorn creetur…and everythink goes contrairy with me.
    1849–50 Mrs Gummidge. *David Copperfield*, ch.3.

3 I'd better go into the house, and die and be a riddance!
   1849–50 Mrs Gummidge. *David Copperfield*, ch.3.

4 Barkis is willin'.
   1849–50 Barkis's proposal of marriage to Peggotty. *David Copperfield*, ch.5.

5 I never will desert Mr Micawber.
   1849–50 Mrs Micawber. *David Copperfield*, ch.12.

6 Annual income twenty pounds, annual expenditure nineteen nineteen six, result happiness. Annual income twenty pounds, annual expenditure twenty pounds ought and six, result misery.
   1849–50 Mr Micawber. *David Copperfield*, ch.12.

7 I am well aware that I am the 'umblest person going... My mother is likewise a very 'umble person. We live in a numble abode.
   1849–50 Uriah Heep. *David Copperfield*, ch.16.

8 We are so very 'umble.
   1849–50 Uriah Heep. *David Copperfield*, ch.17.

9 'Orses and dorgs is some men's fancy. They're wittles and drink to me—lodging, wife, and children—reading, writing and 'rithmetic—snuff, tobacker, and sleep.
   1849–50 Man on the Canterbury coach. *David Copperfield*, ch.19.

10 I only ask for information.
    1849–50 Rosa Dartle. *David Copperfield*, ch.20.

11 'It was as true', said Mr Barkis, '...as taxes is. And nothing's truer than them.'
    1849–50 *David Copperfield*, ch.21.

12 What a world of gammon and spinnage it is, though, ain't it?
    1849–50 Miss Mowcher. *David Copperfield*, ch.22.

13 Other things are all very well in their way, but give me Blood!
    1849–50 Mr Waterbrook. *David Copperfield*, ch.25.

14 Accidents will occur in the best-regulated families.
    1849–50 Mr Micawber. *David Copperfield*, ch.28.

15 'People can't die, along the coast,' said Mr Peggotty, 'except when the tide's pretty nigh out. They can't be born, unless it's pretty nigh in—not properly born, till flood. He's a going out with the tide.'
    1849–50 *David Copperfield*, ch.30.

16 Mrs Crupp had indignantly assured him that there wasn't room to swing a cat there; but, as Mr Dick justly observed to me... 'You know, Trotwood, I don't want to swing a cat. I never do swing a cat. Therefore, what does that signify to me!'
    1849–50 *David Copperfield*, ch.35.

17 'No better opening anywhere,' said my aunt, 'for a man who conducts himself well, and is industrious.'
    1849–50 Of Mr Micawber's prospects in Australia. *David Copperfield*, ch.52.

18 Fog everywhere. Fog up the river, where it flows among green aits and meadows; fog down the river, where it rolls defiled among the tiers of shipping and the waterside pollutions of a great (and dirty) city. Fog on the Essex marshes, fog on the Kentish heights. Fog creeping into the cabooses of collier-brigs; fog lying out on the yards and hovering in the rigging of great ships... And hard by Temple Bar, in Lincoln's Hall, at the very heart of the fog, sits the Lord High Chancellor in his High Court of Chancery.
    1852–3 *Bleak House*, ch.1.

19 But Jarndyce and Jarndyce still drags its dreary length before the court, perennially hopeless.
    1852–3 *Bleak House*, ch.1.

20 The evil of it is that it is a world wrapped up in too much jeweller's cotton and fine wool, and cannot hear the rush of the larger worlds, and cannot see them as they circle round the sun. It is a deadened world, and its growth is sometimes unhealthy for want of air.
    1852–3 Of the Court of Chancery. *Bleak House*, ch.2.

21 This is a London particular...A fog, miss.
    1852–3 Mr Guppy to Esther. *Bleak House*, ch.3.

22 I expect a judgement. Shortly.
    1852–3 *Bleak House*, ch.3. The judgement predicted, in the case of *Jarndyce* v *Jarndyce*, fails to materialize for many years.

23 The wind's in the east... I am always conscious of an uncomfortable sensation now and then when the wind is blowing in the east.
    1852–3 Mr Jarndyce. *Bleak House*, ch.6.

24 It is said that the children of the poor are not brought up, but dragged up.
    1852–3 Mr Jarndyce. *Bleak House*, ch.6.

25 An oyster of the old school whom nobody can open.
    1852–3 Of Mr Tulkinghorn. *Bleak House*, ch.10.

26 I don't feel any vulgar gratitude to you. I almost feel as if *you* ought to be grateful to *me*, for giving you the opportunity of enjoying the luxury of generosity...For anything I can tell, I may have come into the world expressly for the purpose of increasing your stock of happiness.
    1852–3 Harold Skimpole. *Bleak House*, ch.6.

27 He wos wery good to me, he wos!
1852–3 Joe speaking of Nemo. *Bleak House*, ch.11.

28 'For I don't,' says Joe, 'I don't know nothink.'
1852–3 *Bleak House*, ch.16.

29 You are a human boy, my young friend. A human
boy. O glorious to be a human boy!…
O running stream of sparkling joy
To be a soaring human boy!
1852–3 Mr Chadband. *Bleak House*, ch.19.

30 Jobling, there *are* chords in the human mind.
1852–3 Mr Guppy. *Bleak House*, ch.20.

31 'It is,' says Chadband, 'the ray of rays, the sun of
suns, the moon of moons, the star of stars. It is the
light of Terewth.'
1852–3 *Bleak House*, ch.25.

32 'Old girl,' said Mr Bagnet, 'give him my opinion.
You know it.'
1852–3 *Bleak House*, ch.27.

33 It is a melancholy truth that even great men have
their poor relations.
1852–3 *Bleak House*, ch.28.

34 Never have a mission.
1852–3 Mr Jellyby. *Bleak House*, ch.30.

35 The one great principle of the English law is, to
make business for itself. There is no other principle
distinctly, certainly, and consistently maintained
through all its narrow turnings.
1852–3 *Bleak House*, ch.39.

36 He is not a genuine foreign-grown savage; he is the
ordinary home-made article. Dirty, ugly,
disagreeable to all the senses, in body a common
creature of the common streets, only in soul a
heathen.
1852–3 Of Joe. *Bleak House*, ch.47.

37 Dead, your Majesty, Dead, my lords and
gentlemen. Dead, Right Reverends and Wrong
Reverends of every Order. Dead, men and women,
born with heavenly compassion in your hearts. And
dying thus around us every day.
1852–3 On the death of Joe. *Bleak House*, ch.47.

38 Now what I want is, Facts… Facts alone are wanted
in life.
1854 Mr Gradgrind. *Hard Times*, bk.1, ch.1.

39 The speaker, and the schoolmaster, and the third
grown person present, all backed a little, and swept
with their eyes the inclined plane of little vessels
then and there arranged in order, ready to have
imperial gallons of facts poured into them until
they were full to the brim.
1854 *Hard Times*, bk.1, ch.1.

40 'Bitzer' said Thomas Gradgrind. 'Your definition of
a horse.'
'Quadruped. Graminivorous. Forty teeth, namely
twenty-four grinders, four eye-teeth, and twelve
incisive. Sheds coat in the spring; in marshy
countries, sheds hoofs, too. Hoofs hard, but
requiring to be shod with iron. Age known by
marks in mouth.' Thus (and much more) Bitzer.
'Now girl number twenty,' said Mr Gradgrind.
'You know what a horse is.'
1854 *Hard Times*, bk.1, ch.2.

41 It was a town of red brick…unnatural red and
black as the painted face of a savage.
1854 Of Coketown. *Hard Times*, bk.1, ch.5.

42 Coketown…ugly citadel, where Nature was as
strongly bricked out as killing airs and gases were
bricked in.
1854 *Hard Times*, bk.1, ch.10.

43 I see traces of the turtle soup, and venison, and gold
spoon in this.
1854 Mr Bounderby. *Hard Times*, bk.1, ch.11.

44 Ah, Rachel, aw a muddle! Fro' first to last, a
muddle!
1854 Stephen Blackpool. *Hard Times*, bk.3, ch.6.

45 People mutht be amuthed. They can't be alwayth a
learning, nor yet they can't be alwayth a working,
they an't made for it.
1854 Mr Sleary. *Hard Times*, bk.3, ch.8.

46 Whatever was required to be done, the
Circumlocution Office was beforehand with all the
public departments in the art of perceiving—How
Not To Do It.
1855–7 *Little Dorrit*, bk.1, ch.10.

47 Take a little time—count five-and-twenty,
Tattycoram.
1855–7 Mr Meagles. *Little Dorrit*, bk.1, ch.16.

48 In company with several other old ladies of both
sexes.
1855–7 *Little Dorrit*, bk.1, ch.17.

49 It was not a bosom to repose upon, but it was a
capital bosom to hang jewels upon.
1855–7 *Little Dorrit*, bk.1, ch.21.

50 You can't make a head and brains out of a brass
knob with nothing in it.
1855–7 Mr F's Aunt. *Little Dorrit*, bk.1, ch.23.

51 I revere the memory of Mr F. as an estimable man
and most indulgent husband, only necessary to
mention Asparagus and it appeared or to hint at

any little delicate thing to drink and it came like magic in a pint bottle, it was not ecstasy but it was comfort.

1855–7 Flora Finching. *Little Dorrit*, bk.1, ch.24.

52 As to marriage on the part of a man, my dear, Society requires that he should retrieve his fortunes by marriage. Society requires that he should gain by marriage. Society requires that he should found a handsome establishment by marriage. Society does not see, otherwise, what he has to do with marriage.

1855–7 Mrs Merdle. *Little Dorrit*, bk.1, ch.33.

53 Father is rather vulgar, my dear. The word Papa, besides, gives a pretty form to the lips. Papa, potatoes, poultry, prunes, and prism, are all very good words for the lips: especially prunes and prism.

1855–7 Mrs General. *Little Dorrit*, bk.2, ch.5.

54 That it is at least as difficult to stay a moral infection as a physical one; that such a disease will spread with the malignity and rapidity of the plague; that the contagion, when it has once made head, will spare no pursuit or condition, but will lay hold on people in the soundest health, and become developed in the most unlikely constitutions; is a fact as firmly established by experience as that we human creatures breathe an atmosphere.

1855–7 *Little Dorrit*, bk.2, ch.13.

55 The land of Shakespeare, Milton, Bacon, Newton, Watt, the land of a host of past and present abstract philosophers, natural philosophers, and subduers of Nature and Art in their myriad forms, called to Mr Sparkler to come and take care of it, lest it should perish. Mr Sparkler, unable to resist the agonised cry from the depths of his country's soul, declared that he must go.

1855–7 *Little Dorrit*, bk.2, ch.15.

56 Mr Dorrit stood firmly rooted to the carpet, a statue of mystification.

1855–7 *Little Dorrit*, bk.2, ch.17.

57 Once a gentleman, and always a gentleman.

1855–7 Rigaud. *Little Dorrit*, bk.2, ch.28.

58 It was the best of times, it was the worst of times, it was the age of wisdom, it was the age of foolishness, it was the epoch of belief, it was the epoch of incredulity, it was the season of Light, it was the season of Darkness, it was the spring of hope, it was the winter of despair, we had everything before us, we had nothing before us, we were all going direct to Heaven, we were all going direct the other way.

1859 *A Tale of Two Cities*, bk.1, ch.1.

59 I pass my whole life, miss, in turning an immense pecuniary Mangle.

1859 Mr Lorry. *A Tale of Two Cities*, bk.1, ch.4.

60 If it was ever intended that I should go across salt water, do you suppose Providence would have cast my lot in an island?

1859 Miss Pross. *A Tale of Two Cities*, bk.1, ch.4.

61 If you must go flopping yourself down, flop in favour of your husband and child, and not in opposition to 'em.

1859 Jerry Cruncher. *A Tale of Two Cities*, bk.2, ch.1.

62 I care for no man on earth, and no man on earth cares for me.

1859 Mr Carton. *A Tale of Two Cities*, bk.2, ch.4.

63 It is a far, far better thing that I do, than I have ever done; it is a far, far better rest that I go to, than I have ever known.

1859 Sydney Carton. *A Tale of Two Cities*, bk.3, ch.15.

64 Cleanliness is next to Godliness, and some people do the same by their religion.

1860–1 *Great Expectations*, ch.4.

65 I was always treated as if I had insisted on being born in opposition to the dictates of reason, religion, and morality.

1860–1 Pip. *Great Expectations*, ch.4.

66 Your sister is given to government.

1860–1 Joe Gargery. *Great Expectations*, ch.7.

67 In the little world in which children have their existence, whosoever brings them up, there is nothing so finely perceived and so finely felt, as injustice.

1860–1 *Great Expectations*, ch.8.

68 I had cherished a profound conviction that her bringing me up by hand, gave her no right to bring me up by jerks.

1860–1 *Great Expectations*, ch.8.

69 It is a most miserable thing to feel ashamed of home.

1860–1 *Great Expectations*, ch.14.

70 Probably every new and eagerly expected garment ever put on since clothes came in, fell a trifle short of the wearer's expectation.

1860–1 *Great Expectations*, ch.19.

71 You wouldn't mind being at once introduced to the Aged, would you?

1860–1 Wemmick introduces Pip to his father. *Great Expectations*, ch.25.

72 'Have you seen anything of London, yet?' 'Why, yes, Sir—but we didn't find that it come up to its

likeness in the red bills—it is there drawd too architectooralooral.'

1860–1 Herbert questions Joe Gargery. *Great Expectations*, ch.27.

73 I loved Estella... I loved her against reason, against promise, against peace, against hope, against happiness, against all discouragement that could be.

1860–1 *Great Expectations*, ch.29.

74 'Halloa! Here's a church!...Let's go in!...Here's Miss Skiffins! Let's have a wedding.'

1860–1 *Great Expectations*, ch.55.

75 There was a curious mixture in the boy, of uncompleted savagery, and uncompleted civilisation.

1864–5 Of Mortimer. *Our Mutual Friend*, bk.1, ch.2.

76 Mrs Boffin...is a highflyer at Fashion.

1864–5 *Our Mutual Friend*, bk.1, ch.5.

77 A literary man—with a wooden leg.

1864–5 Mr Boffin speaking of Silas Wegg. *Our Mutual Friend*, bk.1, ch.5.

78 Professionally he declines and falls, and as a friend he drops into poetry.

1864–5 Mr Boffin speaking of Silas Wegg. *Our Mutual Friend*, bk.1, ch.5.

79 These two ignorant and unpolished people had guided themselves so far on in their journey of life, by a religious sense of duty and desire to do right.

1864–5 Of Mr and Mrs Boffin. *Our Mutual Friend*, bk.1, ch.9.

80 Mr Podsnap was well to do, and stood very high in Mr Podsnap's opinion.

1864–5 *Our Mutual Friend*, bk.1, ch.11.

81 Mr Podsnap settled that whatever he put behind him he put out of existence...'I don't want to know about it; I don't choose to discuss it; I don't admit it!'

1864–5 *Our Mutual Friend*, bk.1, ch.11.

82 There is in the Englishman a combination of qualities, a modesty, an independence, a responsibility, a repose, combined with an absence of everything calculated to call a blush into the cheek of a young person, which one would seek in vain among the Nations of the Earth.

1864–5 Mr Podsnap. *Our Mutual Friend*, bk.1, ch.11.

83 Why christened Pleasant, the late Mrs Riderhood might possibly have been able at some time to explain, and possibly not. Her daughter had no information on that point. Pleasant she found herself, and she couldn't help it. She had not been consulted on the question.

1864–5 *Our Mutual Friend*, bk.1, ch.29.

84 I think...that it is the best club in London.

1864–5 Mr Tremlow's description of the House of Commons. *Our Mutual Friend*, bk.2, ch.3.

85 Come up and be dead! Come up and be dead!

1864–5 Jenny Wren. *Our Mutual Friend*, bk.2, ch.5.

86 A slap-up gal in a bang-up chariot.

1864–5 The scout's description of Bella. *Our Mutual Friend*, bk.2, ch.8.

87 I want to be something so much worthier than the doll in the doll's house.

1864–5 Bella. *Our Mutual Friend*, bk.4, ch.5.

88 Stranger, pause and ask thyself the question, Canst thou do likewise? If not, with a blush retire.

1870 *Edwin Drood*, ch.4.

89 The delights—the ten thousand million delights of a pantomime.

Attributed.

Dickinson, Emily Elizabeth 1830–86

US poet who spent her life in seclusion in Massachusetts, writing over 1000 intensely lyrical and personal poems, few of which were published during her lifetime.

90 Success is counted sweetest
By those who ne'er succeed.

c.1859 *Complete Poems*, no.67 (first published 1890).

91 Can I expound the skies?
How still the Riddle lies!

c.1859 *Complete Poems*, no.89 (first published 1890).

92 Surgeons must be very careful
When they take the knife!
Underneath their fine incisions
Stirs the culprit—*Life*!

c.1859 *Complete Poems*, no.108 (first published 1891).

93 To fight aloud, is very brave,
But gallanter, I know,
Who charge within the bosom
The Cavalry of Woe.

c.1859 *Complete Poems*, no.126 (first published 1890).

94 Musicians wrestle everywhere—
All day—among the crowded air
I hear the silver strife—
And—waking—long before the morn—
Such transport breaks upon the town
I think it that 'New Life!'

c.1860 *Complete Poems*, no.157 (first published 1891).

95 'Faith' is a fine invention
When Gentlemen can *see*—
But *Microscopes* are prudent
In an Emergency.

c.1860 *Complete Poems*, no.185 (first published 1891).

96 Inebriate of Air—am I—
And Debauchee of Dew—
Reeling—thro endless summer days—
From inns of Molten Blue—
c.**1860** *Complete Poems*, no.214 (first published 1861).

97 'Hope' is the thing with feathers—
That perches in the soul—
And sings the tune without the words—
And never stops—at all—
c.**1860** *Complete Poems*, no.254 (first published 1891).

98 Some keep the Sabbath going to Church—
I keep it, staying at Home—
With a Bobolink for a Chorister—
And an Orchard, for a Dome—
c.**1860** *Complete Poems*, no.324 (first published 1864).

99 After great pain, a formal feeling comes—
The Nerves sit ceremonious, like Tombs.
c.**1862** *Complete Poems*, no.341 (first published 1929).

1 Much Madness is divinest Sense—
To a discerning Eye—
Much Sense—the starkest Madness—
c.**1862** *Complete Poems*, no.435 (first published 1890).

2 They shut me up in Prose—
As when a little girl
They put me in the Closet—
Because they liked me 'still'.
1862 *Complete Poems*, no.613 (first published 1935).

3 The Brain—is wider than the Sky.
c.**1862** *Complete Poems*, no.632 (first published 1896).

4 I cannot live with You—
It would be Life—
And Life is over there—
Behind the Shelf.
c.**1862** *Complete Poems*, no.640 (first published 1890).

5 One need not be a Chamber—to be Haunted—
One need not be a House—
The brain has Corridors—surpassing
Material Place—
c.**1863** *Complete Poems*, no.670 (first published 1891).

6 Because I could not stop for Death—
He kindly stopped for me—
The carriage held but just Ourselves—
And Immortality.
c.**1863** *Complete Poems*, no.712 (first published 1890).

7 Ample make this Bed—
Make this Bed with Awe—
In it wait till Judgement break
Excellent and Fair.
c.**1864** *Complete Poems*, no.829 (first published 1891).

8 Of Consciousness, her awful Mate

The soul cannot be rid—
As easy the secreting her
Behind the Eyes of God
c.**1864** *Complete Poems*, no.894 (first published 1945).

9 Faith—is the Pierless Bridge
Supporting what We see
Unto the Scene that We do not.
c.**1864** *Complete Poems*, no.915 (first published 1929).

10 Death is a dialogue between
The Spirit and the Dust.
c.**1864** *Complete Poems*, no.976 (first published 1890).

11 Tell all the Truth but tell it slant—
Success in Circuit lies
Too bright for our infirm Delight
The Truth's superb surprise.
c.**1868** *Complete Poems*, no.1129 (first published 1945).

12 A word is dead
When it is said,
Some say.
I say it just
Begins to live
That day.
?1872 *Complete Poems*, no.1212 (first published 1894).

13 The abdication of Belief
Makes the Behavior small—
Better an ignis fatuus
Than no illume at all.
c.**1882** *Complete Poems*, no.1551 (first published 1945).

14 He ate and drank the precious Words,
His Spirit grew robust;
He knew no more that he was poor,
Nor that his frame was Dust.
c.**1883** *Complete Poems*, no.1587 (first published 1890).

15 The Pedigree of Honey
Does not concern the Bee—
A Clover, any time, to him,
Is Aristocracy—
c.**1884** *Complete Poems*, no.1627 (first published 1890).

16 'Eternity' is there,
We say, as of a station.
Meanwhile, he is so near,
He joins me in my Ramble—
Divides abode with me—
No Friend have I that so persists
As this Eternity.
Complete Poems, no.1684 (first published 1914).

17 Parting is all we know of heaven,
And all we need of hell.
Complete Poems, no.1732 (first published 1896).

18 Rearrange a 'Wife's' affection!

When they dislocate my Brain!
Amputate my freckled Bosom!
Make me bearded like a man!
1862 *Complete Poems*, no.1737 (first published 1891).

19 The distance that the dead have gone
Does not at first appear—
Their coming back seems possible
For many an ardent year.
Complete Poems, no.1742 (first published 1896).

20 Let us go in; the fog is rising.
Last words, attributed.

Dickinson, John 1732–1808

US revolutionary statesman, leader of conservative opposition to the British. His draft formed the basis of the Articles of Confederation.

21 Then join hand in hand, brave Americans all—
By uniting we stand, by dividing we fall.
1768 'The Liberty Song'.

22 We have counted the cost of this contest, and find nothing so dreadful as voluntary slavery… Our cause is just, our union is perfect.
1775 Declaration of reasons for taking up arms against Britain, 8 Jul, presented to Congress. Quoted in C J Stille *The Life and Times of John Dickinson* (1891), ch.5.

Diderot, Denis 1713–84

French philosopher, novelist, essayist, playwright and critic. A leading figure in the Enlightenment, he is best remembered for his ambitious *Encyclopédie* (1751–72). Other writings include sentimental dramas and theoretical studies of the theatre.

23 *Il ne faut point donner d'esprit à ses personnages; mais savoir les placer dans des circonstances qui leur en donnent.*

You should not give a mind to your characters, but know instead how to put them in situations which will give it to them.
1757 *Entretiens sur le fils naturel*, pt.2.

24 *Les passions détruisent plus de préjugés que la philosophie. Et comment le mensonge leur résisterait-il? Elles ébranlent quelquefois la vérité.*

Passions destroy more prejudices than philosophy. And how do passions resist lies? They burn sometimes with truth.
1757 *Entretiens sur le fils naturel*, pt.2.

25 *Les beautés ont, dans les arts, le même fondement que les vérités dans la philosophie. Qu'est-ce que la vérité? La conformité de nos jugements avec les êtres. Qu'est-ce que la beauté d'imitation? La conformité de l'image avec la chose.*

Beauty in art has the same base as truth in philosophy. What is the truth? The conformity of our judgements with that of others. What is a beautiful imitation? The conformity of the image with the thing.
1757 *Entretiens sur le fils naturel*, pt.3.

26 *Une danse est un poème.*

A dance is a poem.
1757 *Entretiens sur le fils naturel*, pt.3.

27 *Soit donc que vous composiez, soit donc que vous jouiez, ne pensez non plus au spectateur que s'il n'existait pas. Imaginez sur le bord du théâtre, un grand mur qui vous sépare du parterre; jouez comme si la toile ne se levait pas.*

Whether you compose or act, think no more of the spectator than if he did not exist. Imagine at the edge of the stage a large wall which separates you from the orchestra; act as if the curtain never rose.
1758 *Discours sur la poésie dramatique* (On Dramatic Poetry), introducing the theatrical concept of the 'fourth wall'.

28 *Le génie se sent; mais il ne s'imite point.*

Genius is felt, but it is not imitated.
1758 *Discours sur la poésie dramatique* (On Dramatic Poetry).

29 *En général, plus un peuple est civilisé, poli, moins ses moeurs sont poétiques; tout s'affaiblit en s'adoucissant.*

In general, the more a people is civilized, refined, the less its morals are poetic; everything weakens and turns mild.
1758 *Discours sur la poésie dramatique* (On Dramatic Poetry).

30 *La poésie veut quelque chose d'énorme, de barbare et de sauvage.*

Poetry needs something on the scale of the grand, the barbarous, the savage.
1758 *Discours sur la poésie dramatique* (On Dramatic Poetry).

31 *Le public ne sait pas toujours désirer le vrai.*

The public does not always know how to desire the truth.
1758 *Discours sur la poésie dramatique* (On Dramatic Poetry).

32 *Le rôle d'un auteur est un rôle assez vain; c'est celui d'un homme qui se croit en état de donner des leçons au public. Et le rôle du critique? Il est bien plus vain encore; c'est celui d'un homme qui se croit en état de donner des leçons à celui qui se croit en état d'en donner au public.*

The role of the author is vain enough; it is that of a person who considers himself able to give lessons to the public. And the role of the critic? It is vainer still; it is that of a person who considers himself able to give lessons to he who considers himself able to give them to the public.
1758 *Discours sur la poésie dramatique* (On Dramatic Poetry).

33 *Ce n'est que par la mémoire que nous sommes un même individu pour les autres et pour nous-mêmes. Il ne me reste peut-être pas, à l'âge que j'ai, une seule molécule du corps que j'apportai en naissant.*

It is only in memory that we are the same person for others and for ourselves. At the age I am now, there is probably not a single molecule of my body that I had when born.

1758 *Discours sur la poésie dramatique* (On Dramatic Poetry).

34 *Mes pensées sont mes catins.*

My thoughts are my prostitutes.

1761–74 *Le Neveu de Rameau.*

35 *Rien ne dissemble plus de lui que lui-même.*

Nothing resembles him less than himself.

1761–74 *Le Neveu de Rameau.*

36 *Voyez-vous cet oeuf. C'est avec cela qu'on renverse toutes les écoles de théologie, et tous les temples de la terre.*

See this egg. It is with this that all the schools of theology and all the temples of the earth are to be overturned.

1769 *Le Rêve de d'Alembert* (published 1830), pt.1.

37 *Tous les jours on couche avec des femmes qu'on n'aime pas, et l'on ne couche pas avec des femmes qu'on aime.*

We sleep with women we do not love every day and and never with the women we love.

c.1771–80 *Jacques le fataliste et son maître.*

38 *L'esprit de l'escalier.*

Staircase wit.

1773–8 That is, the witty reply that comes to mind after leaving the company, while descending the stairs. *Paradoxe sur le Comédien* (published 1830).

39 Two qualities essential for the artist: morality and perspective.

1776–81 *Pensées détachées sur la peinture.*

40 One composition is meagre, though it has many figures; another is rich, though it has few.

1776–81 *Pensées détachées sur la peinture.*

41 Paint as they spoke in Sparta.

1776–81 *Pensées détachées sur la peinture.*

42 *L'homme est né pour la société; séparez-le, isolez-le, ses idées se désuniront, son caractère se tournera, mille affections ridicules s'élèveront dans son coeur; des pensées extravagantes germeront dans son esprit, comme les ronces dans une terre sauvage.*

Man is born to live in society: separate him, isolate him, and his ideas disintegrate, his character changes, a thousand ridiculous affectations rise up in his heart; extreme thoughts take hold in his mind, like the brambles in a wild field.

1796 *La Religieuse.*

Didion, Joan 1934–

US writer, a respected essayist on US life and culture. Her best-known novels are *A Book of Common Prayer* (1977) and *Democracy* (1984).

43 Innocence ends when one is stripped of the delusion that one likes oneself.

1961 'On Self Respect', collected in *Slouching Towards Bethlehem* (1968).

44 Was there ever in anyone's life span a point free in time, devoid of memory, a night when choice was any more than the sum of all the choices gone before?

1963 *Run River*, ch.4.

45 New York was no mere city. It was instead an infinitely romantic notion, the mysterious nexus of all love and money and power, the shining and perishable dream itself. To think of 'living' there was to reduce the miraculous to the mundane; one does not 'live' at Xanadu.

1967 'Goodbye To All That', collected in *Slouching Towards Bethlehem* (1968).

46 We tell ourselves stories in order to live.

1979 *The White Album*, 'The White Album, 1'.

47 Everything was unmentionable but nothing was unimaginable.

1979 Of Los Angeles in 1968–9. *The White Album*, 'The White Album, 10'.

48 To believe in 'the greater good' is to operate, necessarily, in a certain ethical suspension.

1979 *The White Album*, 'The Woman's Movement'.

Dietz, Howard 1896–1983

US writer and lyricist.

49 That's Entertainment.

1953 Title of song reputedly written by Dietz and Arthur Schwartz for the film *The Band Wagon* in less than an hour.

50 More stars than there are in heaven.

MGM slogan.

Dillard, Annie 1945–

US writer. She is best known for her essay collection *Pilgrim at Tinker Creek* (1974), and has also written poetry and fiction.

51 It was a bitter birthday present from evolution.

1974 Of self-consciousness. *Pilgrim at Tinker Creek*, ch.6.

52 I don't know what it is about fecundity that so appals. I suppose it is the teeming evidence that birth and growth, which we value, are ubiquitous and blind, that life itself is so astonishingly cheap, that nature is as careless as it is bountiful, and that with extravagance goes a crushing waste that will one day include our own cheap lives.

1974 *Pilgrim at Tinker Creek*, ch.10.

53 I think the dying pray at the last not please but thank you as a guest thanks his host at the door.
1974 *Pilgrim at Tinker Creek*, ch.15.

Dillingham, Charles 1868–1934
US theatre producer.

54 I bet you, Ziggie, a hundred bucks that he ain't in here.
1926 Attributed whisper to Florenz Ziegfeld as they acted as pall-bearers at the funeral of escapologist Harry Houdini.

Dillon, Wentworth c.1633–1685
Irish poet and critic.

55 Choose an author as you choose a friend.
1684 *Essay on Translated Verse*, l.96.

56 Immodest words admit of no defence,
For want of decency is want of sense.
1684 *Essay on Translated Verse*, l.113.

DiMaggio, Joe (Joseph Paul) 1914–99
US baseball player. A powerful and elegant centre fielder and hitter, he played for 15 seasons with the New York Yankees, voted Most Valuable Player three times. In 1954 he married (briefly) Marilyn Monroe.

57 There's no skill involved. Just go up there and swing at the ball.
Of baseball. Quoted in Colin Jarman *The Guinness Dictionary of Sports Quotations* (1990).

58 It's no fun being married to an electric light.
Of his marriage to Marilyn Monroe. Quoted in Colin Jarman *The Guinness Dictionary of Sports Quotations* (1990).

Dimbleby, Richard 1913–65
English broadcaster, best known for his commentaries on state occasions. He joined the BBC's news team in 1936, becoming its first war correspondent (1939).

59 The moment of the Queen's crowning is come.
1953 Commentary on the coronation at Westminster Abbey, 2 Jun.

Dinesen, Isak
▷ See Blixen, Karen, Baroness

Diogenes of Sinope c.410–c.320 BC
Greek Cynic philosopher and moralist, student of Antisthenes.

60 Yes…stand out of my sun a little.
His reply when asked by Alexander the Great if he lacked anything. Quoted in Plutarch *Parallel Lives*, 'Alexander'.
▷ See Alexander 13:13.

61 I am looking for an honest man.
His reply when asked why he was wandering the streets of Athens during the day with a lantern.

Dior, Christian 1905–57
French couturier who founded his own Paris house in 1947 and achieved worldwide fame with his 'New Look' in the same year.

62 Women are most fascinating between the ages of thirty-five and forty, after they have won a few races and know how to pace themselves. Since few women ever pass forty, maximum fascination can continue indefinitely.
1955 In *Collier's Magazine*, 10 Jun.

63 In the world today *haute couture* is one of the last repositories of the marvellous, and the *couturiers* the last possessors of the wand of Cinderella's Fairy Godmother.
Dior by Dior (translated by Antonia Fraser, 1957).

Dirksen, Everett McKinley 1896–1969
US Republican politician.

64 The oil can is mightier than the sword.
1964 In *Life*, 5 Jun.

65 I am a man of fixed and unbending principles, the first of which is to be flexible at all times.
Recalled on his death, 7 Sep 1969.

66 A billion here, a billion there. Pretty soon it runs into real money.
1979 Quoted in 'Half a Trillion in Real Money', editorial in the *New York Times*, 2 Dec.

Disch, Thomas M(ichael) 1940–
US writer, best known for his sophisticated, politically conscious science fiction, eg *Camp Concentration* (1968). He has also written several volumes of poetry.

67 Mankind Under The Leash.
1966 Title of novel.

68 A predilection for genre fiction is symptomatic of a kind of arrested development.
1986 In *The Face*, Mar.

69 Science fiction, like Brazil, is where the nuts come from.
1987 In *The Observer*, 23 Aug.
▷ See Thomas 109:47.

Disney, Walt(er Elias) 1901–66
US artist and film producer. His animated characters such as Mickey Mouse (1928) featured in *Silly Symphonies* (from 1929) and later full-length animated films.

70 Fancy being remembered around the world for the invention of a mouse!

c.1966 Comment to his wife during his last illness. Quoted in Leonard Mosley *Disney's World* (1985).

Disraeli, Benjamin, 1st Earl of Beaconsfield 1804–81

British statesman, first known for his political novels *Coningsby* (1844) and *Sybil* (1846). He became a Tory MP in 1837, Chancellor of the Exchequer (1852, 1858–9 and 1866), and Prime Minister (1868, 1874–80). His second administration (1874–80) was notable both for diplomacy and social reform.

71 Experience is the child of Thought, and Thought is the child of Action. We cannot learn men from books.
1826–7 *Vivian Grey*, bk.5, ch.1.

72 I repeat…that all power is a trust—that we are accountable for its exercise—that, from the people, and for the people, all springs, and all must exist.
1826–7 *Vivian Grey*, bk.6, ch.10.

73 A good eater must be a good man; for a good eater must have a good digestion, and a good digestion depends upon a good conscience.
1831 *Young Duke*, bk.1, ch.14.

74 'The age of chivalry is past', said May Dacre. 'Bores have succeeded to dragons.'
1831 *The Young Duke*, bk.2, ch.5.

75 Read no history: nothing but biography, for that is life without theory.
1832 *Contarini Fleming*, pt.1, ch.23.

76 The practice of politics in the East may be defined by one word—dissimulation.
1832 *Contarini Fleming*, pt.5, ch.10.

77 Time is the great physician.
1837 *Henrietta Temple*, bk.6, ch.9.

78 Though I sit down now, the time will come when you will hear me.
1837 On being barracked during his overly ornate maiden speech in the House of Commons, 7 Dec.

79 The Continent will not suffer England to be the workshop of the world.
1838 House of Commons, 15 Mar.

80 No Government can be long secure without a formidable Opposition.
1844 *Coningsby*, bk.2, ch.1.

81 Conservatism discards Prescription, shrinks from Principle, disavows Progress; having rejected all respect for antiquity, it offers no redress for the present, and makes no preparation for the future.
1844 *Coningsby*, bk.2, ch.5.

82 Youth is a blunder; Manhood a struggle; Old Age a regret.
1844 *Coningsby*, bk.3, ch.1.

83 It seems to me a barren thing this Conservatism— an unhappy cross-breed, the mule of politics that engenders nothing.
1844 *Coningsby*, bk.3, ch.5.

84 What Art was to the ancient world, Science is to the modern.
1844 *Coningsby*, bk.4, ch.1.

85 The depository of power is always unpopular.
1844 *Coningsby*, bk.4, ch.13.

86 Man is only truly great when he acts from the passions.
1844 *Coningsby*, bk.4, ch.13.

87 Consider Ireland. Thus you have a starving population, an absentee aristocracy, and an alien Church—and in addition, the weakest executive in the world. That is the Irish Question.
1844 Speech, House of Commons, 16 Feb.

88 I am neither a Whig nor a Tory. My politics are described in one word, and that word is England.
1844 Speech, House of Commons.

89 To do nothing and get something, formed a boy's ideal of a manly career.
1845 *Sybil*, bk.1, ch.5.

90 'Two nations; between whom there is no intercourse and no sympathy; who are as ignorant of each other's habits, thoughts and feelings, as if they were dwellers in different zones, or inhabitants of different planets; who are formed by a different breeding, are fed by a different food, are ordered by different manners, and are not governed by the same laws.' 'You speak of—' said Egremont, hesitatingly. 'THE RICH AND THE POOR.'
1845 *Sybil*, bk.2, ch.5.

91 Little things affect little minds.
1845 *Sybil*, bk.3, ch.2.

92 The Youth of a Nation are the trustees of Posterity.
1845 *Sybil*, bk.6, ch.13

93 The right honourable gentleman caught the Whigs bathing and walked away with their clothes.
1845 House of Commons speech, 28 Feb, attacking Prime Minister Sir Robert Peel for bullying his back-benchers into supporting the Government's action in intercepting the private mail of radical MPs.

94 A Conservative government is an organized hypocrisy.
1845 Speech, House of Commons, 17 Mar.

95 A majority is always the best repartee.

1847 *Tancred*, bk.2, ch.14.

96 London is a modern Babylon.
1847 *Tancred*, bk.5, ch.5.

97 Justice is truth in action.
1851 Speech, House of Commons, 11 Feb.

98 He has to learn that petulance is not sarcasm, and that insolence is not invective.
1852 Of Sir Charles Wood. Speech, House of Commons, 16 Dec.

99 England does not love coalitions.
1852 Speech, House of Commons, 17 Dec.

1 The blue ribbon of the turf.
1852 Of the Derby race. *Life of Lord George Bentinck*, ch.26.

2 If a traveller were informed that such a man was Leader of the House of Commons, he may well begin to comprehend how the Egyptians came to worship an insect.
1852 Of Lord John Russell. Attributed.

3 His temper, naturally morose, has become licentiously peevish. Crossed in his Cabinet, he insults the House of Lords and plagues the most eminent of his colleagues with the crabbed malice of a maundering witch.
1855 Of Lord Aberdeen, whose disagreements with his Whig–Peelite coalition over the Crimean War eventually forced his resignation.

4 Finality is not the language of politics.
1859 Speech, House of Commons, 28 Feb.

5 I hold that the characteristic of the present age is craving credulity.
1864 Speech, Oxford, 25 Nov.

6 Party is organized opinion.
1864 Speech, Oxford, 25 Nov.

7 The question is this: is man an ape or an angel? I am on the side of the angels.
1864 Speech, Oxford, 25 Nov.

8 Assassination has never changed the history of the world.
1865 Speech, House of Commons, 1 May, paying tribute to US President Abraham Lincoln who had been assassinated in Washington, 14 Apr.

9 I have climbed to the top of the greasy pole.
1868 On becoming Prime Minister.

10 The pursuit of science leads only to the insoluble.
1870 *Lothair*, ch.17.

11 A Protestant, if he wants aid or advice on any matter, can only go to his solicitor.
1870 *Lothair*, ch.27.

12 When a man fell into his anecdotage it was a sign for him to retire from the world.
1870 *Lothair*, ch.28.

13 Every woman should marry—and no man.
1870 *Lothair*, ch.30.

14 You know who the critics are? The men who have failed in literature and art.
1870 *Lothair*, ch.35.

15 'My idea of an agreeable person,' said Hugo Bohun, 'is a person who agrees with me.'
1870 *Lothair*, ch.35.

16 Increased means and increased leisure are the two civilizers of man.
1872 Speech at Manchester, 3 Apr.

17 A University should be a place of light, of liberty, and of learning.
1873 Speech, House of Commons, 11 Mar.

18 An author who speaks about his own books is almost as bad as a mother who talks about her own children.
1873 Rectorial address, Glasgow, 19 Nov.

19 Upon the education of the people of this country the fate of this country depends.
1874 Speech, House of Commons, 15 Jun.

20 Posterity will do justice to that unprincipled maniac Gladstone—an extraordinary mixture of envy, vindictiveness, hypocrisy and superstition and with one commanding characteristic. Whether Prime Minister or Leader of the Opposition, whether preaching, praying , speechifying, or scribbling—never a gentleman. He is so vain that he wants to figure in history as the settler of all the great questions; but a parliamentary Constitution is not favourable to such ambitions. Things must be done by parties, not by persons using parties as tools.
c.1874 Letter.

21 I am dead: dead, but in the Elysian fields.
1876 On his elevation to the House of Lords.

22 Gladstone, like Richelieu, cannot write. Nothing can be more unmusical, more involved, or more uncouth than all his scribblement.
1877 Letter, 3 Oct.

23 Lord Salisbury and myself have brought you peace—but a peace, I hope, with honour.
1878 Declaration, 16 Jul, on returning from the Berlin Congress with the guarantees it had produced of continuing peace in Europe.
▷ See also Chamberlain 249:19.

24 A sophistical rhetorician inebriated with the exuberance of his own verbosity.
1878 Of Gladstone. Speech reported in *The Times*, 29 Jul.

25 His Christianity was muscular.
1880 *Endymion*, ch.14.

26 You must dress according to your age, your pursuits, your object in life.
1880 *Endymion*, ch.23.

27 What all men should avoid is the 'shabby genteel'. No man ever gets over it... You had better be in rags.
1880 *Endymion*, ch.23

28 'Sensible men are all the same religion.' 'And pray what is that?' inquired the prince. 'Sensible men never tell.'
1880 Waldershire. *Endymion*, ch.81.

29 I believe they went out, like all good things, with the Stuarts.
1880 *Endymion*, ch.99.

30 I will not go down to posterity talking bad grammar.
1881 On correcting proofs of his last parlimentary speech, 31st Mar. Quoted in Robert Blake *Disraeli*, ch.32.

31 There are three kinds of lies: lies, damned lies and statistics.
Attributed. Quoted in Mark Twain *Autobiography*, vol.1 (published 1924).

32 Millstones around our neck.
Of the colonies. Quoted in Robert Blake *The Conservative Party from Peel to Churchill* (1970).

33 England is unrivalled for two things—sport and politics.
Quoted in Colin Jarman *The Guinness Dictionary of Sports Quotations* (1990).

Dobson, (Henry) Austin 1840–1921
English poet. He published several volumes of carefully crafted, often humorous verse, and prose studies of famous writers.

34 Time goes, you say? Ah no!
Alas, Time stays, we go.
1877 'Paradox of Time'.

35 Fame is a food that dead men eat,
I have no stomach for such meat.
1906 'Fame is a Fool'.

Dobzhansky, Theodosius G 1900–75
Russian-born US geneticist, Professor at Columbia University and the University of California at Davis.

36 Nature's stern discipline enjoins mutual help at least as often as warfare. The fittest may also be the gentlest.
1962 *Mankind Evolving*.

Docherty, Tommy (Thomas Henderson)
1928–
Scottish footballer and manager. In a tempestuous career he played for Scotland and managed ten clubs, including Manchester United and Queen's Park Rangers, and was briefly manager of Scotland (1971–2).

37 The ideal board of directors should be made up of three men—two dead and the other dying.
1977 Quoted in Colin Jarman *The Guinness Dictionary of Sports Quotations* (1990).

38 Our strikers couldn't score in a brothel.
1985 Of the forwards at Wolverhampton Wanderers. Quoted in Peter Ball and Phil Shaw *The Book of Football Quotations* (1989).

Doctorow, E(dgar) L(awrence) 1931–
US novelist, best known for *Ragtime* (1975) and *Billy Bathgate* (1989).

39 A few professional alienists understood his importance, but to most of the public he appeared as some kind of German sexologist, an exponent of free love who used big words to talk about dirty things. At least a decade would have to pass before Freud would have his revenge and see his ideas begin to destroy sex in America forever.
1975 *Ragtime*, ch.5.

40 There is no longer any such thing as fiction or non-fiction; there's only narrative.
1988 In the *New York Times Book Review*, 27 Jan.

41 Like art and politics, gangsterism is a very important avenue of assimilation into society.
1990 In the *International Herald Tribune*, 1 Oct.

Dodd, Christopher J 1944–
US Democratic politician.

42 Time is the 101st Senator...the ally of the people who want to do nothing.
1994 On the difficulty of passing President Clinton's health program when legislators were longing for vacation. In the *New York Times*, 26 Aug.

Dodd, Ken(neth) 1931–
English stand-up comedian, singer and actor.

43 The trouble with Freud is that he never had to play the old Glasgow Empire on a Saturday night after Rangers and Celtic had both lost.

1965 Television interview, discussing Freud's theory of catharsis through laughter, whereby jokes produce a feeling of elation.

Doddridge, Philip 1702–51

English non-conformist minister and hymn-writer.

44 Hark, the glad sound! The Saviour comes,
The Saviour promised long;
Let every heart exult with joy,
And every voice be song!
Hymns, 'Hark, The Glad Sound' (published 1755).

45 O God of Bethel! by whose hand
Thy people still are fed,
Who through this weary pilgrimage
Hast all our fathers led:
Hymns, 'O God of Bethel' (published 1755).

46 Ye servants of the Lord,
Each in his office wait,
Observant of the heavenly word,
And watchful at his gate.
Hymns, 'Ye Servants of the Lord' (published 1755).

47 Father of Peace, and God of love!
We own Thy power to save,
That power by which our Shepherd rose
Victorious o'er the grave.
Hymns, 'Father of Peace' (published 1755).

Dole, Elizabeth Hanford 1936–

US lawyer and government official.

48 Sometimes I think we're the only two lawyers in Washington who trust each other.
1987 On her marriage to Senator Robert Dole. In *Newsweek*, 3 Aug.

Dole, Robert Joseph 1923–

US Republican politician. He ran unsuccessfully for presidential nomination in 1980 and 1988.

49 George Meany could run for President, but then why should he step down?
1976 On Meany's status as president of the American Federation of Labor. In the *Wall Street Journal*, 7 Sep.

50 It is inside work with no heavy lifting.
1988 On the vice presidency. ABC TV broadcast, 24 Jul.

51 Contrary to reports that I took the loss badly, I slept like a baby—every two hours I woke up and cried.
1988 On losing presidential nomination. ABC TV broadcast, 14 Aug.

52 Putting a majority together is like a one-armed man wrapping cranberries.
Quoted in Hedrick Smith *The Power Game* (1988).

53 This President will go down in history as the only President who raised taxes before he took office and cut spending after he left office.
1993 On Bill Clinton's retroactive tax increases and promises of future spending cuts. In the *Los Angeles Times*, 16 Feb.

54 I thought about it a lot and I think every country ought to have a President.
1995 To television host David Letterman on decision to seek high office. Reported in *Time*, 13 Feb.

55 We really win if we win. But we may even win if we lose.
1995 On the prospect of gaining popularity by reintroducing a balanced budget amendment. In the *New York Times*, 2 Mar.

Domínguez Camargo, Hernando 1606–59

Colombian epic poet. A Jesuit, he probably abandoned this calling at the end of his life. His major work, the unfinished *Poema heroyco*, is a long, ambitious narrative in a highly Baroque style.

56 *¡En tantas de la muerte librerías,
los cuerpos de esos huesos, mal seguro,
estudia, Julio; y en su letra advierte,
que son abecedarios de la muerte!*

Julio, in those libraries of death
study the bodies of those bones—an assured evil;
and learn from those characters
that they form the abecedary of death!
1666 *San Ignacio de Loyola, Poema heroyco* ('Heroic Poem of Saint Ignatius of Loyola'), bk.4, canto 6.

Donahue, Phil 1935–

US broadcaster, host of the day-time talk show *Donahue* (1967–). His books include *Donahue* (1979) and *The Human Animal* (1985).

57 The breasts, the hallmark of our culture. You cannot sell anything in America without the breasts.
1990 On NBC TV, Aug.

Donald, David Herbert 1920–

US historian and writer, Professor at Harvard (1973–91, emeritus from 1991). His many works include *Charles Sumner and the Coming of the Civil War* (1960, Pulitzer Prize).

58 Their correspondence was something like a duet between a tuba and a piccolo.
1987 On letters of Thomas Wolfe and Aline Bernstein. *Look Homeward: A Life of Thomas Wolfe*.

Donleavy, J(ames) P(atrick) 1926–

US-born Irish writer, best known for his picaresque novel *The Ginger Man* (1955).

59 To marry the Irish is to look for poverty.
1955 *The Ginger Man*, ch.2.

60 But Jesus, when you don't have any money the
problem is food. When you have money, it's sex.
When you have both it's health, you worry about
getting ruptured or something. If everything is
simply jake then you're frightened of death.
1955 *The Ginger Man*, ch.5.

61 When I die I want to decompose in a barrel of
porter and have it served in all the pubs in Dublin.
I wonder would they all know it was me?
1955 *The Ginger Man*, ch.31.

62 I got disappointed in human nature as well and
gave it up because I found it too much like my
own.
1973 *A Fairy Tale of New York*, ch.18.

63 Writing is turning one's worst moments into
money.
1979 In *Playboy*, May.

Donne, John c.1572–1631

English priest and poet. He converted from Catholicism
to Anglicanism, becoming Dean of St Paul's.

64 Shall I leave all this constant company,
And follow headlong, wild uncertain thee?
1594–5 *Satires*, no.1.

65 For if one eat my meat, though it be known
The meat was mine, the excrement is his own.
1594–5 *Satires*, no.2.

66 Kind pity chokes my spleen.
1594–5 *Satires*, no.3.

67 On a huge hill,
Cragged, and steep, Truth stands, and he that will
Reach her, about must, and about must go.
1594–5 *Satires*, no.3.

68 Are not your kisses then as filthy, and more,
As a worm sucking an envenomed sore?
Doth not thy fearful hand in felling quake,
As one which gathering flowers, still fears a snake?
Is not your last act harsh, and violent,
As when a plough a stony ground doth rent?
c.1595 *Elegies*, no.8, 'The Comparison'.

69 Filled with her love, may I be rather grown
Mad with much heart than idiot with none.
c.1595 *Elegies*, no.10, 'The Bracelet'.

70 I will not look upon the quickening sun,
But straight her beauty to my sense shall run;
The air shall note her soft, the fire most pure;
Water suggest her clear, and the earth sure;
Time shall not lose our passages.
c.1595 *Elegies*, no.12, 'His Parting from Her'.

71 Come, madam, come, all rest my powers defy,

Until I labour, I in labour lie.
The foe oft-times having the foe in sight,
Is tired with standing though he never fight.
Off with that girdle, like heaven's zone glistering,
But a far fairer world encompassing.
Unpin that spangled breastplate which you wear,
That busy fools may be stopped there.
Unlace yourself, for that harmonious chime
Tells me from you that now 'tis your bed time.
c.1595 *Elegies*, no.19, 'To His Mistress Going to Bed'.

72 License my roving hands, and let them go
Before, behind, between, above, below.
O my America! my new-found-land,
My kingdom, safeliest when with one man
manned.
c.1595 *Elegies*, no.19, 'To His Mistress Going to Bed'.

73 I wonder, by my troth, what thou and I
Did, till we loved? were we not weaned till then?
But sucked on country pleasures, childishly?
c.1595–1605 'The Good Morrow', collected in *Songs and
Sonnets* (1633).

74 Now thou hast loved me one whole day,
Tomorrow when thou leav'st, what wilt thou say?
c.1595–1605 'Woman's Constancy', collected in *Songs and
Sonnets* (1633).

75 Go, and catch a falling star,
Get with child a mandrake root,
Tell me, where all past years are,
Or who cleft the Devil's foot.
c.1595–1605 'Song: Go and catch a falling star', collected in
Songs and Sonnets (1633).

76 Sweetest love I do not go,
For weariness of thee,
Nor in hope the world can show
A fitter Love for me;
But since that I
Must die at last, 'tis best,
To use myself in jest
Thus by feigned deaths to die.
c.1595–1605 'Song: Sweetest love I do not go', collected in
Songs and Sonnets (1633).

77 Busy old fool, unruly sun,
Why dost thou thus,
Through windows, and through curtains, call on
us?
Must to thy motions lovers' seasons run?
Saucy pedantic wretch, go chide
Late schoolboys, and sour prentices,
Go tell court-huntsmen that the King will ride,
Call country ants to harvest offices;
Love, all alike, no season knows, nor clime,
Nor hours, days, months, which are the rags of
time.

c.1595–1605 'The Sun Rising', collected in *Songs and Sonnets* (1633).

78 She's all states, and all princes I,
Nothing else is.
Princes do but play us; compared to this,
All honour's mimic, all wealth alchemy.
c.1595–1605 'The Sun Rising', collected in *Songs and Sonnets* (1633).

79 For god's sake, hold your tongue, and let me love,
Or chide my palsy, or my gout,
My five grey hairs, or ruined fortune flout,
With wealth your state, your mind with arts
  improve,
Take you a course, get you a place,
Observe his honour, or his grace,
Or the King's real, or his stamped face
Contemplate; what you will, approve,
So you will let me love.
c.1595–1605 'The Canonization', collected in *Songs and Sonnets* (1633).

80 Alas, alas, who's injured by my love?
What merchant's ships have my sighs drowned?
Who says my tears have overflowed his ground?
When did my colds a forward spring remove?
When did the heats which my veins fill
Add one more to the plaguey bill?
Soldiers find wars, and lawyers find out still
Litigious men, which quarrels move,
Though she and I do love.
c.1595–1605 'The Canonization', collected in *Songs and Sonnets* (1633).

81 'Tis the year's midnight, and it is the day's.
c.1595–1605 'Nocturnal upon St Lucy's Day', collected in *Songs and Sonnets* (1633).

82 I sing the progress of a deathless soul.
c.1595–1605 'The Progress of the Soul', stanza 1, collected in *Songs and Sonnets* (1633).

83 Nature's great masterpiece, an Elephant.
c.1595–1605 'The Progress of the Soul', stanza 39, collected in *Songs and Sonnets* (1633).

84 I am two fools, I know,
For loving, and for saying so
In whining poetry.
c.1595–1605 'The Triple Fool', collected in *Songs and Sonnets* (1633).

85 Twice or thrice had I loved thee,
Before I knew thy face or name;
So in a voice, so in a shapeless flame
Angels affect us oft, and worshipped be;
Still when, to where thou wert, I came,
Some lovely glorious nothing did I see.
c.1595–1605 'Air and Angels', collected in *Songs and Sonnets* (1633).

86 He which hath business, and makes love, doth do
Such wrong, as when a married man doth woo.
c.1595–1605 'Break of Day', collected in *Songs and Sonnets* (1633).

87 O more than moon,
Draw not up seas to drown me in thy sphere,
Weep me not dead, in thine arms, but forbear
To teach the sea what it may do too soon.
c.1595–1605 'A Valediction: Of Weeping', collected in *Songs and Sonnets* (1633).

88 Mark but this flea, and mark in this
How little that which thou deny'st me is;
It sucked me first, and now sucks thee,
And in this flea our two bloods mingled be.
c.1595–1605 'The Flea', collected in *Songs and Sonnets* (1633).

89 Come live with me, and be my love,
And we will some new pleasures prove
Of golden sands, and crystal brooks:
With silken lines, and silver hooks.
c.1595–1605 'The Bait', collected in *Songs and Sonnets* (1633).
▷ See Marlowe 655:31, Raleigh 800:12.

90 As virtuous men pass mildly away,
And whisper to their souls, to go,
Whilst some of their sad friends do say,
The breath goes now, and some say, no:

So let us melt, and make no noise,
No tear-floods, nor sigh-tempests move;
'Twere profanation of our joys
To tell the laity of our love.
c.1595–1605 'A Valediction: Forbidding Mourning', collected in *Songs and Sonnets* (1633).

91 Our two souls therefore, which are one,
Though I must go, endure not yet
A breach, but an expansion,
Like gold to airy thinness beat.
c.1595–1605 'A Valediction: Forbidding Mourning', collected in *Songs and Sonnets* (1633).

92 Thy firmness makes my circle just,
And makes me end, where I begun.
c.1595–1605 'A Valediction: Forbidding Mourning', collected in *Songs and Sonnets* (1633).

93 Where, like a pillow on a bed,
A pregnant bank swelled up, to rest
The violet's reclining head,
Sat we two, one another's best.
c.1595–1605 'The Ecstasy', collected in *Songs and Sonnets* (1633).

94 Our eye-beams twisted, and did thread
Our eyes, upon one double string.
c.1595–1605 'The Ecstasy', collected in *Songs and Sonnets* (1633).

95 So to engraft our hands, as yet

Was all the means to make us one,
And pictures in our eyes to get
Was all our propagation.

And whilst our souls negotiate there,
We like sepulchral statues lay;
All day, the same our postures were,
And we said nothing all the day.
c.1595–1605 'The Ecstasy', collected in *Songs and Sonnets* (1633).

96 I had rather owner be
Of thee one hour, than all else ever.
c.1595–1605 'A Fever', collected in *Songs and Sonnets* (1633).

97 To what a cumbersome unwieldiness
And burdenous corpulence my love had grown,
But that I did, to make it less,
And keep it in proportion,
Give it a diet, made it feed upon
That which love worst endures, *discretion*.
?1595–1605 'Love's Diet', collected in *Songs and Sonnets* (1633).

98 And seeing the snail, which everywhere doth roam,
Carrying his own house still, still is at home,
Follow (for he is easy paced) this snail,
Be thine own palace, or the world's thy gaol.
1597–8 'To Sir Henry Wotton'.

99 More than kisses, letters mingle souls
1597–8 'To Sir Henry Wotton'.

1 John Donne, Anne Donne, Un-done.
1602 Letter to his wife from prison. Quoted in Izaak Walton *The Life of Doctor Donne* (1640).

2 Immensity cloistered in thy dear womb.
1609 *La Corona*, 'Nativity'.

3 At the round earth's imagined corners, blow
Your trumpets, angels, and arise, arise
From death, you numberless infinities
Of souls, and to your scattered bodies go.
c.1610–15 *Holy Sonnets*, no.7.

4 Death be not proud, though some have called thee
Mighty and dreadful, for thou art not so,
For those, whom thou think'st thou dost overthrow,
Die not, poor death, nor yet canst thou kill me.
From rest and sleep, which but thy pictures be,
Much pleasure, then from thee much more must flow,
And soonest our best men with thee do go,
Rest of their bones and soul's delivery.
c.1610–15 *Holy Sonnets*, no.10.

5 One short sleep past, we wake eternally,
And Death shall be no more: Death, thou shalt die!
c.1610–15 *Holy Sonnets*, no.10.

6 Oh let me then His strange love still admire.
c.1610–15 *Holy Sonnets*, no.11.

7 Batter my heart, three-personed God; for You
As yet but knock, breathe, shine, and seek to mend.
c.1610–15 *Holy Sonnets*, no.14.

8 Take me to You, imprison me, for I,
Except You enthrall me, never shall be free,
Nor ever chaste, except You ravish me.
c.1610–15 *Holy Sonnets*, no.14.

9 I am a little world made cunningly
Of elements and an angelic sprite.
c.1610–15 *Holy Sonnets*, no.15.

10 What if this present were the world's last night?
c.1610–15 *Holy Sonnets*, no.19.

11 And new philosophy calls all in doubt,
The element of fire is quite put out;
The sun is lost, and th'earth, and no man's wit
Can well direct him, where to look for it.
1611 'An Anatomy of the World: The First Anniversary'.

12 If man were anything, he's nothing now.
1611 'An Anatomy of the World: The First Anniversary'.

13 'Tis all in pieces, all coherence gone.
1611 'An Anatomy of the World: The First Anniversary'.

14 She, she is dead; she's dead; when thou know'st this,
Thou know'st how dry a cinder this world is.
1611 'An Anatomy of the World: The First Anniversary'.

15 Verse hath a middle nature: heaven keeps souls,
The grave keeps bodies, verse the fame enrols.
1611 'An Anatomy of the World: The First Anniversary'.

16 Let man's soul be a sphere, and then, in this,
The intelligence that moves, devotion is.
'Good Friday, 1613. Riding Westward', published 1635.

17 It comes equally to us all, and makes us all equal
when it comes. The ashes of an oak in the chimney
are no epitaph of that oak, to tell me how high or
how large that was; it tells me not what flocks it
sheltered while it stood, nor what men it hurt when
it fell…and when a whirlwind hath blown the dust
of the churchyard into the church, and the man
sweeps out the dust of the church into the
churchyard, who will undertake to sift those dusts
again, and to pronounce, This is the Patrician, this
the noble flower, and this the yeomanly, this the
Plebeian bran.
c.1621 Of death. Sermon, 8 Mar.

18 Since I am coming to that holy room
Where, with Thy choir of saints forevermore,
I shall be made Thy Music, as I come
I tune the instrument here at the door,

And what I must do then, think now before.
c.1623 'Hymn to God my God, in my Sickness'.

19 Wilt thou forgive that sin, where I begun,
    Which is my sin, though it was done before?
    Wilt thou forgive those sins through which I run
    And do them still, though still I do deplore?
    When thou hast done, thou hast not done,
    For I have more.
    c.1623 'Hymn to God the Father'.

20 It is too little to call man a little world; except God,
    man is a diminutive to nothing.
    1624 *Devotions Upon Emergent Occasions*, Meditation no.4.

21 But I do nothing upon my self,
    and yet I am mine own executioner.
    1624 *Devotions Upon Emergent Occasions*, Meditation no.12.

22 No man is an island, entire of itself; every man is a
    piece of the continent, a part of the main.
    1624 *Devotions Upon Emergent Occasions*, Meditation no.17.

23 Any man's death diminishes me, because I am
    involved in mankind; and therefore never send to
    know for whom the bell tolls; it tolls for thee.
    1624 *Devotions Upon Emergent Occasions*, Meditation no.17.

24 My God, my God, thou art a direct God, may I not
    say a literal God…But thou art also…a figurative, a
    metaphorical God too: a God in whose words there
    is such a height of figures, such voyages, such
    peregrinations to fetch remote and precious
    metaphors, such extensions, such spreadings, such
    curtains of allegories, such third heavens of
    hyperboles, so harmonious elocutions, so retired
    and so reserved expressions, so commanding
    persuasions, so persuading commandments, such
    sinews even in thy milk, and such things in thy
    words, as all profane authors seem of the seed of the
    serpent that creeps; thou art the dove that flies.
    1624 *Devotions Upon Emergent Occasions*, Expostulation 19,
    'The Language of God'.

25 The air is not so full of motes, of atoms, as the
    church is of mercies.
    1624 *Sermons*, 'Christmas Day, 1624'.

26 He brought light out of darkness, not out of a lesser
    light; he can bring thy summer out of winter,
    though thou have no spring… God comes to thee,
    not as in the dawning of the day, not as in the bud
    of the spring, but as the sun at noon to illustrate all
    shadows, as the sheaves in harvest to fill all
    penuries. All occasions invite his mercies, and all
    times are his seasons.
    1624 *Sermons*, 'Christmas Day, 1624'.

27 All the four Monarchies, with all their thousands of
    years, and all the powerful Kings and all the
    beautiful Queens of this world, were but as a bed of
    flowers, some gathered at six, some at seven, some
    at eight, all in one morning, in respect to this day.
    1626 On eternity. Sermons, 30 Apr.

28 I throw myself down in my Chamber, and I call in,
    and invite God, and his Angels thither, and when
    they are there, I neglect God and his Angels, for the
    noise of a fly, for the rattling of a coach, for the
    whining of a door.
    1626 'Sermon preached at the Funeral of Sir William
    Cockayne', 12 Dec.

29 How imperfect is all our knowledge!
    1626 'Sermon preached at the Funeral of Sir William
    Cockayne', 12 Dec.

30 Young men mend not their sight by using old men's
    spectacles.
    1626 'Sermon preached at the Funeral of Sir William
    Cockayne', 12 Dec.

31 And if there be any addition to knowledge, it is
    rather a new knowledge than a greater knowledge;
    rather a singularity in a desire of proposing
    something that was not known at all before than an
    improving, an advancing, a multiplying of former
    inceptions; and by that means, no knowledge
    comes to be perfect.
    1626 'Sermon preached at the Funeral of Sir William
    Cockayne', 12 Dec.

32 He that purchases a manor will think to have an
    exact survey of the land, but who thinks of taking
    so exact a survey of his conscience, how that money
    was got that purchased that manor? We call that a
    man's means, which he hath; but that is truly his
    means, what way he came by it.
    1626 'Sermon preached at the Funeral of Sir William
    Cockayne', 12 Dec.

33 The world is a great volume, and man the index of
    that book.
    1626 'Sermon preached at the Funeral of Sir William
    Cockayne', 12 Dec.

34 And into the gate they shall enter, and in that house
    they shall dwell, where there shall be no Cloud nor
    Sun, no darkness nor dazzling, but one equall light,
    no noyse nor silence, but one equall musick, no
    fears nor hopes, but one equall possession, no foes
    nor friends, but one equall communion and
    Identity, no ends nor beginnings, but one equall
    eternity.
    1687 *Sermons*, 29 Feb.

Donoghue, Denis 1928–

Irish literary critic, Professor at New York University.

35 If there is a distinctive Irish experience, it is one of
    division, exacerbated by the fact that division in a

country so small seems perverse. But the scale doesn't matter.

1986 *We Irish.*

Donoso, José 1924–

Chilean novelist. After teaching at several universities in Chile and the US, he moved to Spain. *El obsceno pájaro de la noche*, his masterpiece, presents a hallucinatory and grotesque vision of Chilean society.

36 *Los servidores acumulan los privilegios de la miseria…conservan los instrumentos de la venganza porque van acumulando en sus manos ásperas y verrugosas esa otra mitad de sus patrones, la mitad inútil, descartada, lo sucio y lo feo que ellos . . . les han ido entregando con el insulto de cada enagua gastada que les regalan.*

Servants accumulate the privileges of misery… They save up the instruments of vengeance because their coarse warty hands collect, bit by bit, that other sides of their employers—the useless, discarded side, the filth and the sordidness that…they've been putting into their servants' hands with the insult of each shabby skirt they gave them.

1970 *El obsceno pájaro de la noche*, ch.4 (translated as *The Obscene Bird of Night*, 1973).

Doolittle, James Harold 1896–1993

US air force officer. He was the Commanding General, US 8th Air Force, in the ETO (European Theatre of Operations) in 1944.

37 Next to a letter from home, Captain Miller, your organization is the greatest morale builder in the ETO.

1944 Of Glenn Miller's wartime band. Comment on stage after a concert for the troops at Wycombe Abbey, 29 Jul. The words were later attributed to General Eisenhower in the publicity for the film *The Glenn Miller Story* (1954).

Doram-Smith, Sir Reginald Hugh 1899–1977

Irish-born British politician, a former army colonel who became an MP in 1935, Minister of Agriculture and Fisheries (1939–40) and Governor of Burma (1941–6).

38 Let 'Dig for Victory' be the motto of everyone with a garden and of every able-bodied man and woman capable of digging an allotment in their spare time.

1939 Radio broadcast, 3 Oct.

Dorgan, Tad (Thomas Aloysius) 1877–1929

US cartoonist and sportswriter. He was known for his satiric cartoons and colourful use of slang.

39 Yes, We Have No Bananas.

1922 Cartoon caption, later used as the title of a song by Irving Conn and Frank Silver (1923) and as an advertising slogan for Elders and Fyffes, British banana importers.

Dos Passos, John Roderigo 1896–1970

US novelist, playwright, travel writer and poet. He is best known for his novels such as *Manhattan Transfer* (1925) and the massive, formally experimental epic trilogy *U.S.A* (1930–6).

40 U.S.A. is the slice of a continent. U.S.A. is a group of holding companies, some aggregations of trade unions, a set of laws bound in calf, a radio network, a chain of moving picture theatres, a column of stock quotations rubbed out and written in by a Western Union boy on a black-board, a publiclibrary full of old newspapers and dogeared historybooks with protests scrawled in the margins in pencil. U.S.A. is the world's greatest rivervalley fringed with mountains and hills. U.S.A. is a set of bigmouthed officials with too many bankaccounts. U.S.A. is a lot of men buried in their uniforms in Arlington Cemetery. U.S.A. is the letters at the end of an address when you are away from home. But mostly U.S.A. is the speech of the people

1938 *U.S.A.*, 'U.S.A.' (new prologue to collected trilogy).

41 People don't choose their careers. They are engulfed by them.

1959 In the *New York Times*, 25 Oct.

Dostoevsky, Fyodor Mikhailovitch 1825–81

Russian novelist. He was condemned to death in 1849 for his revolutionary connections, but was instead sent to hard labour in Siberia until 1859.

42 The formula 'Two and two is five' is not without its attractions.

1864 *Notes from Underground.*

43 All people seem to be divided into 'ordinary' and 'extraordinary'. The ordinary people must lead a life of strict obedience and have no right to transgress the law because…they are ordinary. Whereas the extraordinary people have the right to commit any crime they like and transgress the law in any way just because they happen to be extraordinary.

1866 *Crime and Punishment*, pt.3, ch.5 (translated by David Magarshak).

44 Power is given only to him who dares to stoop and take it…one must have the courage to dare.

1866 *Crime and Punishment*, pt.5, ch.4 (translated by David Magarshak).

45 If you were to destroy in mankind the belief in immortality, not only love but every living force

maintaining the life of the world would at once be dried up.
1879–80 *The Brothers Karamazov*, bk.2, ch.6.

46 If the devil doesn't exist, but man has created him, he has created him in his own image and likeness.
1879–80 *The Brothers Karamazov*, bk.5, ch.4.

47 So long as man remains free he strives for nothing so incessantly and so painfully as to find someone to worship.
1879–80 *The Brothers Karamazov*, bk.5, ch.5.

48 Love all God's creation, the whole of it and every grain of sand in it. Love every leaf, every ray of God's lights. Love the animals, love the plants, love everything. If you love everything, you will perceive the divine mystery in things.
1879–80 *The Brothers Karamazov*, bk.6, ch.3.

Douglas, Lord Alfred Bruce 1870–1945

English poet. He is remembered chiefly for his relationship with Oscar Wilde, which precipitated Wilde's downfall.

49 I am the love that dare not speak its name.
1894 'Two Loves'.

50 All good poetry is forged slowly and patiently, link by link, with sweat and blood and tears.
1919 *Collected Poems*, introduction.

Douglas, Charles 1840–74

New Zealand explorer, who travelled over much uncharted territory in the South Island of New Zealand.

51 I am perfectly aware that the mosquito and sandfly have a purpose in this world, but why don't they attend to it? Their destiny is to keep down microscopic insects…but their sphere of use is when they are in the grub state. Why don't they stick at that and not trouble innocent unoffending prospectors who can't carry a curtain? The mosquitoes are worse this season than ever I saw them, and make a fellow think irreverently of Old Noah, if he gave them a passage in the ark, in early days.
1891 Quoted in J Pascoe (ed) *Mr Explorer Douglas* (1957).

52 I believe the reason I escaped, both this time and on other occasions, was the idea of perishing never entered my head. Nothing is so bad as terror for lowering a man's stamina.
1891 Quoted in J Pascoe (ed) *Mr Explorer Douglas* (1957).

Douglas, Gavin c.1474–1522

Scottish poet and, from 1515, Bishop of Dunkeld. His translation of Virgil's *Aeneid* is considered to be one of the greatest achievements of Scots vernacular literature.

53 First I protest, beau schiris, by your leif

Beis weill adivisit my werk or ye reprief;
Consider it warely, read ofter than anis,
Weill, at ane blenk, slee poetry nocht ta'en is.
c.1513 *Eneados*, bk.1, prologue.

54 Riveris ran reid on spate with water broun,
And burnis hurlis all their bankis doun.
c.1513 *Eneados*, bk.7, prologue.

55 And all small fowlys singis on the spray:
Welcum the lord of lycht and lamp of day.
c.1513 *Eneados*, bk.12, prologue.

Douglas, Keith Castellian 1920–44

English poet. Only one volume of his poems was published in his lifetime, and he was killed in action shortly after the D-Day landings in Normandy.

56 Remember me when I am dead
and simplify me when I'm dead.
1941 'Simplify Me When I'm Dead'.

57 For here the lover and killer are mingled
who had one body and one heart.
And death, who had the soldier singled
has done the lover mortal hurt.
1943 'Vergissmeinnicht'.

58 If at times my eyes are lenses
through which the brain explores
constellations of feeling
my ears yielding like swinging doors
admit princes to the corridors
into the mind, do not envy me.
I have a beast on my back.
1944 'Bête Noire'.

59 And all my endeavours are unlucky explorers
come back, abandoning the expedition;
the specimens, the lilies of ambition
still spring in their climate, still unpicked;
but time, time is all I lacked
to find them, as the great collectors before me.
1944 'On a Return from Egypt, 1943–44' (published 1946).

Douglas, (George) Norman 1868–1952

Scottish novelist, travel writer and essayist. His works include *Siren Land* (1911), an account of his travels in Italy, and the novel *South Wind* (1917).

60 Bouillabaisse is only good because cooked by the French, who, if they cared to try, could produce an excellent and nutritious substitute out of cigar stumps and empty matchboxes.
1911 *Siren Land*, 'Rain on the Hills'.

61 Don Francesco was a fisher of men, and of women. He fished *ad maiorem Dei gloriam*, and for the fun of the thing. It was his way of taking exercise.
1917 *South Wind*, ch.2

62 You can tell the ideals of a nation by its advertisements.
1917 *South Wind*, ch.6

63 Many a man who thinks to found a home discovers that he has merely opened a tavern for his friends.
1917 *South Wind*, ch.20

64 It is the drawback of all sea-side places that half the landscape is unavailable for purposes of human locomotion, being covered by useless water.
1921 *Alone*, 'Mentone'.

65 As to abuse—I thrive on it. Abuse, hearty abuse, is a tonic to all save men of indifferent health.
1928 *Some Limericks*.

66 Education is a state-controlled manufactory of echoes.
1929 *How About Europe?*

67 To find a friend one must close one eye. To keep him—two.
1941 *Alamanc*.

68 A child of eight is many-sided. By eighteen most of his auspicious angles have been polished away; he is standardised; transformed, perhaps into the perfect citizen. Your perfect citizen may be a fine fellow, but he is not the perfect man.
1946 *Late Harvest*.

Douglas, William Orville 1898–1980

US lawyer, Associate Justice of the US Supreme Court (1939–80). His consistently liberal decisions were occasionally controversial, such as the stay of execution granted to the Rosenbergs, convicted spies, in 1953.

69 It is procedure that spells much of the difference between rule by law and rule by whim or caprice.
1951 Ruling to strike the Joint Anti-Fascist Refugee Committee and two other organizations from the Attorney General's list of subversive groups until final adjudication, 30 Apr.

70 We are a religious people whose institutions presuppose a Supreme Being.
1952 Ruling to allow the release of public schools students for religious instruction, 28 Apr.

71 If the individual is no longer to be sovereign, if the police can pick him up whenever they do not like the cut of his jib…we enter a new regime.
1968 Dissenting opinion in ruling to uphold the police right 'to stop and frisk', 10 Jun.

Douglass, Frederick originally Frederick Augustus Washington Bailey 1817–95

US abolitionist. Born a slave, in 1838 he escaped and changed his name. He lectured on slavery in Great Britain

(1845–47) and £150 was collected so that he could purchase his freedom.

72 The white man's happiness cannot be purchased by the black man's misery.
1849 'The Destiny of Colored Americans' in *The North Star*, 16 Nov.

73 To imagine that we shall ever be eradicated is absurd and ridiculous. We can be remodified, changed, and assimilated, but never extinguished.
1849 'The Destiny of Colored Americans' in *The North Star*, 16 Nov.

74 Where justice is denied, where poverty is enforced, where ignorance prevails, and where one class is made to feel that society is an organized conspiracy to oppress, rob, and degrade them, neither persons nor property will be safe.
1886 Speech in Washington DC, commemorating the 24th anniversary of emancipation.

75 No man can point to any law in the U.S. by which slavery was originally established. Men first make slaves and then make laws.
1889 Speech, Bethel Literary and Historical Association, Washington DC, Apr.

Dove, Rita Frances 1952–

US writer, poet and editor. Her poetry collections include *Thomas and Beulah* (1986, Pulitzer Prize) and *Grace Notes* (1989).

76 A good poem is like a bouillon cube. It's concentrated and it nourishes you when you need it.
1989 In *Time Magazine*, 18 Oct.

Dowd, Maureen

US newspaper columnist.

77 President Clinton returned today…to the university where he didn't inhale, didn't get drafted, and didn't get a degree.
1994 On President Clinton's visit to Oxford where as a Rhodes Scholar he had tried marijuana, avoided conscription, and left to attend Yale Law School. In the *New York Times*, 9 Jun.

78 Don't write anything down, but save everything that anyone else writes down.
1995 Advice for political survival in Washington. In the *US News and World Report*, 9 Jan.

Dowland, John 1563–1626

English lutenist and song-writer. Having failed, as a Catholic, to win a place at the court of Elizabeth I, he made his name in Europe before returning home. His *First Book of Songes* appeared in 1597 and ran to five editions by 1613.

79 Who loves not music and the heavenly muse,

That man God hates.

1614 Commendatory poem to William Leighton's *Teares or Lamentations of a Sorrowfull Soule*.

Downey, Dr Richard 1881–1953

English prelate, Bishop of Liverpool.

80 If Stalin had learned to play cricket, the world might now be a better place.

1948 Quoted in Colin Jarman *The Guinness Dictionary of Sports Quotations* (1990).

Dowson, Ernest 1867–1900

English poet. A member of the 'decadent' school, he studied at Oxford and became part of the Rhymers' Club. He developed friendships with W B Yeats and Arthur Symons and lived in France, where he died of alcoholism.

81 I have forgot much, Cynara! Gone with the wind,
Flung roses, roses, riotously with the throng,
Dancing, to put thy pale, lost lilies out of mind;
But I was desolate and sick of an old passion,
Yea, all the time, because the dance was long:
I have been faithful to thee, Cynara! in my
   fashion.

1896 *Verses*, 'Non Sum Qualis Eram Bonae Sub Regno Cynarae'.

82 They are not long, the days of wine and roses:
Out of a misty dream
Our path emerges for a while, then closes
Within a dream.

1896 'Vitae Summa Brevis'.

Doyle, Sir Arthur Conan 1859–1930

Scottish physician and writer. His stories of the brilliant and resourceful detective Sherlock Holmes and his assistant, Dr Watson, are among the most enduringly popular works of crime fiction ever written. He also wrote historical romances and other novels.

83 London, that great cesspool into which all the loungers and idlers of the Empire are irresistibly drained.

1887 *A Study in Scarlet*, ch.1.

84 It is a capital mistake to theorize before one has all the evidence. It biases the judgement.

1887 *A Study in Scarlet*, ch.3.

85 Where there is no imagination there is no horror.

1887 *A Study in Scarlet*, ch.5.

86 It is a mistake to confound strangeness with mystery.

1887 *A Study in Scarlet*, ch.7.

87 Our ideas must be as broad as Nature if they are to interpret Nature.

1887 *A Study in Scarlet*, ch.7.

88 Detection is, or ought to be, an exact science, and should be treated in the same cold and unemotional manner. You have attempted to tinge it with romanticism, which produces much the same effect as if you worked a love-story or an elopement into the fifth proposition of Euclid.

1890 *The Sign of Four*, ch.1.

89 The most winning woman I ever knew was hanged for poisoning three little children for their insurance money.

1890 *The Sign of Four*, ch.2.

90 I never make exceptions. An exception disproves the rule.

1890 *The Sign of Four*, ch.2.

91 How often have I said to you that when you have eliminated the impossible, whatever remains, *however improbable*, must be the truth?

1890 *The Sign of Four*, ch.6.

92 You know my methods. Apply them.

1890 *The Sign of Four*, ch.6.

93 'It is the unofficial force—the Baker Street irregulars.' As he spoke, there came a swift pattering of naked feet upon the stairs, a clatter of high voices, and in rushed a dozen dirty and ragged little street Arabs.

1890 *The Sign of Four*, ch.8.

94 The bow was made in England,
Of true wood, of yew wood,
The wood of English bows.

1891 *The White Company*, 'Song of the Bow'.

95 Singularity is almost invariably a clue. The more featureless and commonplace a crime is, the more difficult it is to bring it home.

1892 *The Adventures of Sherlock Holmes*, 'The Boscombe Valley Mystery'.

96 You know my method. It is founded upon the observance of trifles.

1892 *The Adventures of Sherlock Holmes*, 'The Boscombe Valley Mystery'.

97 It has long been an axiom of mine that the little things are infinitely the most important.

1892 *The Adventures of Sherlock Holmes*, 'A Case of Identity'.

98 Depend upon it, there is nothing so unnatural as the commonplace.

1892 *The Adventures of Sherlock Holmes*, 'A Case of Identity'.

99 The case has, in some respects, been not entirely devoid of interest.

1892 *The Adventures of Sherlock Holmes*, 'A Case of Identity'.

1 It is quite a three-pipe problem, and I beg that you won't speak to me for fifty minutes.

1892 *The Adventures of Sherlock Holmes*, 'The Red-Headed League'.

2 To Sherlock Holmes she is always *the* woman. I have seldom heard him mention her under any other name. In his eyes she eclipses and predominates the whole of her sex.
1892 Of Irene Adler. *The Adventures of Sherlock Holmes*, 'Scandal in Bohemia'.

3 You see, but you do not observe.
1892 *The Adventures of Sherlock Holmes*, 'Scandal in Bohemia'.

4 A man should keep his little brain attic stocked with all the furniture that he is likely to use, and the rest he can put away in the lumber room of his library, where he can get it if he wants it.
1892 *The Adventures of Sherlock Holmes*, 'The Five Orange Pips'.

5 It is my belief, Watson, founded upon my experience, that the lowest and vilest alleys in London do not present a more dreadful record of sin than does the smiling and beautiful countryside.
1892 *The Adventures of Sherlock Holmes*, 'The Copper Beeches'.

6 Crime is common. Logic is rare. Therefore it is upon the logic rather than upon the crime that you should dwell.
1892 *The Adventures of Sherlock Holmes*, 'The Copper Beeches'.

7 A long shot, Watson; a very long shot!
1894 *The Memoirs of Sherlock Holmes*, 'Silver Blaze'.

8 Ex-Professor Moriarty of mathematical celebrity…is the Napoleon of crime, Watson.
1894 *The Memoirs of Sherlock Holmes*, 'The Final Problem'.

9 'Excellent!', I cried.
'Elementary', said he.
1894 *The Memoirs of Sherlock Holmes*, 'The Crooked Man'. The famous phrase 'Elementary, my dear Watson' does not in fact appear in any of the Conan Doyle books. It may have originated with a review of the film *The Return of Sherlock Holmes* in the *New York Times*, 19 Oct 1929.

10 They were the footprints of a gigantic hound!
1902 *The Hound of the Baskervilles*, ch.2.

11 A study of family portraits is enough to convert a man to the doctrine of reincarnation.
1902 *The Hound of the Baskervilles*, ch.13.

12 You mentioned your name as if I should recognise it, but I assure you that, beyond the obvious facts that you are a bachelor, a solicitor, a Freemason, and an asthmatic, I know nothing whatever about you.
1905 *The Return of Sherlock Holmes*, 'The Norwood Butler'.

13 Now, Watson, the fair sex is your department.

1905 *The Return of Sherlock Holmes*, 'The Second Stain'.

14 It is horrible, yet fascinating, this struggle between a set purpose and an utterly exhausted frame.
1908 Of the final moments of the 1908 Olympic marathon, in which the Italian runner Dorando Pietri had to be helped over the finishing line and was thus disqualified. Quoted in Colin Jarman *The Guinness Dictionary of Sports Quotations* (1990).

15 'I am inclined to think—' said I.
'I should do so,' Sherlock Holmes remarked, impatiently.
1915 *The Valley of Fear*, ch.1.

16 Mediocrity knows nothing higher than itself, but talent instantly recognises genius.
1915 *The Valley of Fear*, ch.1.

17 All other men are specialists, but his specialism is omniscience.
1917 *His Last Bow*, 'Bruce-Partington Plans'.

18 Good old Watson! You are the one fixed point in a changing age.
1917 *His Last Bow*, title story.

19 There is but one step from the grotesque to the horrible.
1917 *His Last Bow*, 'Wisteria Lodge'

20 Matilda Briggs…was a ship which is associated with the giant rat of Sumatra, a story for which the world is not yet prepared.
1927 *The Case-Book of Sherlock Holmes*, 'The Sussex Vampire'.

Doyle, Charles 1928–

New Zealand poet, primarily of the city and suburbs. His collections include *A Splinter of Glass* (1956) and *Messages for Herod* (1965).

21 If only to be born were being invented
Merely, or, better still, to concoct oneself
From an antique alembic, a receipt. How splendid
To take the phial cleanly from its shelf;

Powders and liquids, all one's favourite hues
Making the being one would be, the looker at stars
Or storks on the spires of Denmark, drinker of dews,
Or an eye simply.
'Phials', collected in *Quadrant*, 1964.

Drabble, Margaret 1939–

English writer. Her novels often deal with the experiences and difficulties of educated young women.

22 Sometimes it seems the only accomplishment my education ever bestowed on me was the ability to think in quotations.
1963 *A Summer Birdcage*, ch.1.

23 Perhaps the rare and simple pleasure of being seen for what one is compensates for the misery of being it.

1963 *A Summer Birdcage*, ch.7.

24 What fools middle-class girls are to expect other people to respect the same gods as themselves and E M Forster.

1963 *A Summer Birdcage*, ch.11.

25 Lord knows what incommunicable small terrors infants go through, unknown to all.

1965 *The Millstone.*

26 England's not a bad country… It's just a mean, cold, ugly, divided, tired, clapped-out, post-imperial, post-industrial slag-heap covered in polystyrene hamburger cartons.

1989 *A Natural Curiosity.*

Drake, Sir Francis c.1540–96

Elizabethan seaman, the first Englishman to circumnavigate the world. In 1585 he sailed on a successful expedition to the Spanish Indies. He commanded the fleet that defended England against the Spanish Armada in 1588.

27 The singeing of the King of Spain's beard.

1587 His description of an expedition to Cadiz, quoted in Francis Bacon *Considerations touching a war with Spain* (1629).

28 The advantage of time and place in practical actions is half the victory; which being lost is irrecoverable.

1588 Letter to Elizabeth I, 13 Apr.

29 There is plenty of time to win this game, and to thrash the Spaniards too.

1588 Attributed, while finishing a game of bowls at Plymouth Hoe, 20 Jul, before sailing to meet the Armada. Quoted in the *Dictionary of National Biography* (1917–), vol.5, p.1342.

Drapeau, Jean 1916–

Canadian politician, Mayor of Montreal (1954–57, 1960–86).

30 The Montreal Olympics can no more have a deficit than a man can have a baby.

1973 Comment at press conference, Montreal, 29 Jan. The games went well over budget.

Drayton, Michael 1563–1631

English poet and dramatist. After his first work *The Harmony of the Church* (1591) was condemned by the Church, he turned to pastoral and historical themes. *Polyolbion* (1616–22) is a topographical survey of Britain. Only one play survives, *The First Part of Sir John Oldcastle* (1600).

31 She ware a frock of frolic green.

1593 *Idea, the Shepherd's Garland*, 'The Eighth Eclogue'.

32 So in all humours sportively I range;
My muse is rightly of the English strain,
That cannot long one fashion entertain.

1594 *Ideas Mirrour*, 'To the Reader of these Sonnets'.

33 Dear, why should you command me to my rest,
When now the night doth summon all to sleep?
Methinks this time becometh lovers best;
Night was ordained together friends to keep.

1594 *Ideas Mirrour*, sonnet 37.

34 When Time shall turn those amber locks to grey,
My verse again shall gild and make them gay.

1597 *England's Heroic Epistles*, 'Henry Howard, Earl of Surrey, to the Lady Geraldine'.

35 Fair stood the wind for France
When we our sails advance,
Nor now to prove our chance
Longer will tarry.

1606 *Poems Lyrick and Pastorall*, 'To the Cambro-Britons and Their Harp, His Ballad of Agincourt', describing Henry V's expedition to France, 1415.

36 Upon Saint Crispin's day
Fought was this noble fray,
Which fame did not delay
To England to carry;
Oh, when shall English men
With such acts fill a pen,
Or England breed again
Such a King Harry?

1606 Of the Battle of Agincourt. *Poems Lyrick and Pastorall*, 'To the Cambro-Britons and Their Harp, His Ballad of Agincourt'.

37 But she, good sir,
Did not prefer
You, for that I was ranging;
But for that she
Found faith in me
And she loved to be changing.

1606 *Poems Lyrick and Pastorall*, 'To His Rival'.

38 That shire which we the Heart of England well may call.

1612–22 Of Warwickshire. *Polyolbion*, song 13, l.2.

39 Neat Marlowe, bathed in the Thespian springs,
Had in him those brave translunary things
That the first poets had; his raptures were
All air and fire, which made his verses clear,
For that fine madness still he did retain
Which rightly should possess a poet's brain.

1619 'To My Most Dearly Loved Henry Reynolds, Esquire, of Poets and Poesie'.

40 Since there's no help, come let us kiss and part;

Nay, I have done, you get no more of me,
And I am glad, yea glad with all my heart
That thus so cleanly I myself can free;
Shake hands forever, cancel all our vows,
And when we meet at any time again,
Be it not seen in either of our brows
That we one jot of former love retain.
Now at the last gasp of love's latest breath,
When, his pulse failing, passion speechless lies,
When faith is kneeling by his bed of death,
And innocence is closing up his eyes,
Now if thou wouldst, when all have given him over,
From death to life thou mightst him yet recover.
1619 *Idea*, sonnet 61.

41 The walls of spiders' legs are made,
Well mortised and finely laid;
He was the master of his trade
It curiously builded;
The windows of the eyes of cats,
And for the roof, instead of slats,
Is covered with the skins of bats,
With moonshine that are gilded.
1627 *Nymphidia, The Court of Fairy.*

Drennan, William 1754–1820

Irish patriot and poet.

42 Nor one feeling of vengeance presumed to defile
The cause, or the men, or the Emerald Isle.
1795 *Erin*, stanza 3.

Drexler, Arthur

US art administrator, Director of Architecture and Design at the Metropolitan Museum of Art, New York.

43 History is written for the victors and what they leave out is the losers.
1975 In the *New York Review*, 27 Nov.

Driberg, Tom (Thomas Edward Neil), Baron of Bradwell 1905–76

English journalist, broadcaster and politician. On the editorial staff of the *Daily Express* (1928–43), he became an independent (1942) then Labour (1945) MP and was created a life peer in 1975.

44 Sincerity is all that counts is a widespread modern heresy. Think again. Bolsheviks are sincere. Fascists are sincere. Lunatics are sincere. People who believe that the earth is flat are sincere. They can't all be right. Better make certain first that you have something to be sincere about, and with.
1937 In the *Daily Express.*

Drucker, Peter Ferdinand 1909–

Austrian-born US management consultant, Professor at Claremont Graduate School, California.

45 Entrepreneurship can be learned, but it can't be taught, so schools are not much good.
1988 Interviewed in 'Adam Smith' *The Roaring '80s* (1988), ch.2.

46 If you ever run into an industry that says it needs better people, sell its shares. There *are* no better people. You have to use ordinary, every-day people and make them capable of doing the work.
1991 In the *Los Angeles Times*, 17 Sep.

Drummond, Thomas 1797–1840

Scottish engineer and statesman, developer of the Drummond Light (lime-light). He was appointed Under-Secretary for Ireland in 1835.

47 Property has its duties as well as its rights.
1838 Letter to the Earl of Donoughmore, 22 May.

Dryden, John 1631–1700

English poet, critic and playwright. His satirical verses such as *Absalom and Achitophel* (1681) were highly regarded, and he was made Poet Laureate in 1668. Among his best plays are *Marriage-à-la-Mode* (1673) and *All for Love* (1678); his works were prefaced with critical essays, including the seminal *Essay of Dramatic Poesy* (1668). He became a Catholic in 1685 and on refusing to swear allegiance to William and Mary was deprived of his laureateship.

48 An horrid stillness first invades the ear,
And in that silence we the tempest fear.
1660 *Astraea Redux*, l.7–8.

49 His colours laid so thick on every place,
As only showed the paint, but hid the face.
1660 Epistle 'To my honoured friend Sir Robert Howard', l.75–6.

50 I strongly wish for what I faintly hope:
Like the day-dreams of melancholy men,
I think and think on things impossible,
Yet love to wander in that golden maze.
1664 *The Rival Ladies*, act 3, sc.1.

51 And love's the noblest frailty of the mind.
1665 *The Indian Emperor*, act 2, sc.2.

52 Repentance is the virtue of weak minds.
1665 *The Indian Emperor*, act 3, sc.1.

53 For all the happiness mankind can gain
Is not in pleasure, but in rest from pain.
1665 *The Indian Emperor*, act 4, sc.1.

54 By viewing nature, nature's handmaid art,
Makes mighty things from small beginnings grow:
Thus fishes first to shipping did impart,
Their tail the rudder, and their head the prow.
1667 *Annus Mirabilis*, st.155.

55 For secrets are edged tools,

And must be kept from children, and from fools.
1667 *Sir Martin Mar-All*, act 2, sc.2.

56 I am resolved to grow fat and look young till forty,
and then slip out of the world with the first wrinkle
and the reputation of five-and-twenty.
1668 *The Maiden Queen*, act 3, sc.1.

57 Every age has a kind of universal genius, which
inclines those that live in it to some particular
studies.
1668 *An Essay of Dramatic Poesy.*

58 A thing well said will be wit in all languages
…though it may lose something in the translation.
1668 *An Essay of Dramatic Poesy*, 'The Wit of the Ancients: The
Universal'.

59 Shakespeare…was the man who of all modern,
and perhaps ancient poets, had the largest and
most comprehensive soul. All images of Nature
were still present to him, and he drew them, not
laboriously, but luckily; when he describes
anything, you more than see it, you feel it too.
Those who accuse him to have wanted learning,
give him the greater commendation: he was
naturally learned; he needed not the spectacles
of books to read Nature; he looked inwards,
and found her there… He is many times flat,
insipid; his comic wit degenerating into clenches,
his serious swelling into bombast. But he is always
great.
1668 *An Essay of Dramatic Poesy*, 'Shakespeare and Ben Jonson
Compared'.

60 He invades authors like a monarch; and what
would be theft in other poets, is only victory in
him.
1668 Of Ben Jonson. *An Essay of Dramatic Poesy*, 'Shakespeare
and Ben Jonson Compared'.

61 If by the people you understand the multitude, the
hoi polloi, 'tis no matter what they think; they are
sometimes in the right, sometimes in the wrong:
their judgement is a mere lottery.
1668 *An Essay of Dramatic Poesy.*

62 One cannot say he wanted wit, but rather that he
was frugal of it.
1668 Of Ben Jonson. *An Essay of Dramatic Poesy*, 'Shakespeare
and Ben Jonson Compared'.

63 You seldom find him making love in any of his
scenes or endeavouring to move the passions; his
genius was too sullen and saturnine to do it
gracefully, especially when he knew he came
after those who had performed both to such an
height.
1668 Of Ben Jonson. *An Essay of Dramatic Poesy*, 'Shakespeare
and Ben Jonson Compared'.

64 If I would compare [Jonson] with Shakespeare, I
must acknowledge him the more correct poet, but
Shakespeare the greater wit.
1668 *An Essay of Dramatic Poesy*, 'Shakespeare and Ben Jonson
Compared'.

65 Shakespeare was the Homer, or father of our
dramatic poets; Jonson was the Virgil, the pattern
of elaborate writing; I admire him, but I love
Shakespeare.
1668 *An Essay of Dramatic Poesy*, 'Shakespeare and Ben Jonson
Compared'.

66 And he, who servilely creeps after sense,
Is safe, but ne'er will reach an excellence.
1669 *Tyrannic Love*, prologue.

67 All delays are dangerous in war.
1669 *Tyrannic Love*, act 1, sc.1.

68 Pains of love be sweeter far
Than all other pleasures are.
1669 *Tyrannic Love*, act 4, sc.1.

69 I am as free as nature first made man,
Ere the base laws of servitude began,
When wild in woods the noble savage ran.
1670 *The Conquest of Granada*, pt.1, act 1, sc.1.

70 Forgiveness to the injured does belong;
But they ne'er pardon, who have done the wrong.
1670 *The Conquest of Granada*, pt.2, act 1, sc.2.

71 Thou strong seducer, opportunity!
1670 *The Conquest of Granada*, pt.2, act 4, sc.3.

72 I am to be married within these three days; married
past redemption.
1672 *Marriage-à-la-Mode*, act 1, sc.1.

73 The very Janus of poets; he wears almost
everywhere two faces; and you have scarce begun to
admire the one, ere you despise the other.
1672 Of Shakespeare. *Essay on the Dramatic Poetry of the Last
Age.*

74 So poetry, which is in Oxford made
An art, in London only is a trade.
1673 'Prologue to the University of Oxon…at the Acting of
The Silent Woman'.

75 Sure the poet…spewed up a good lump of clotted
nonsense at once.
1674 *Notes and Observations on the Empress of Morocco*, 'The
First Act'.

76 Death, in itself, is nothing; but we fear,
To be we know not what, we know not where.
1675 *Aureng-Zebe*, act 4, sc.1.

77 None would live past years again,
Yet all hope pleasure in what yet remain;
And, from the dregs of life, think to receive,

What the first sprightly running could not give.
1675 *Aureng-Zebe*, act 4, sc.1.

78 They, who would combat general authority with particular opinion, must first establish themselves a reputation of understanding better than other men.
1677 'The Author's Apology for Heroic Poetry and Heroic Licence', an essay prefacing *State of Innocence*, a libretto based on *Paradise Lost*.

79 Virgil and Horace [were] the severest writers of the severest age.
1677 'The Author's Apology for Heroic Poetry and Heroic Licence', an essay prefacing *State of Innocence*, a libretto based on *Paradise Lost*.

80 A propriety of thoughts and words; or, in other terms, thought and words elegantly adapted to the subject.
1677 Definition of wit. 'The Author's Apology for Heroic Poetry and Heroic Licence', an essay prefacing *State of Innocence*, a libretto based on *Paradise Lost*.

81 All human things are subject to decay,
And, when fate summons, monarchs must obey.
1678 *MacFlecknoe* (published 1682), l.1–2.

82 Shadwell alone, of all my sons, is he
Who stands confirmed in full stupidity.
1678 Richard Flecknoe selects Shadwell as heir to the kingdom of dullness. *MacFlecknoe* (published 1682), l.17–18.

83 The rest to some faint meaning make pretence,
But Shadwell never deviates into sense.
Some beams of wit on other souls may fall,
Strike through and make a lucid interval;
But Shadwell's genuine night admits no ray,
His rising fogs prevail upon the day.
1678 *MacFlecknoe* (published 1682), l.19–24.

84 Thy genius calls thee not to purchase fame
In keen iambics, but mild anagram:
Leave writing plays, and choose for thy command
Some peaceful province in Acrostic Land.
There thou mayest wings display and altars raise,
And torture one poor word ten thousand ways.
1678 *MacFlecknoe* (published 1682), l.203–8.

85 Errors, like straws, upon the surface flow;
He who would search for pearls must dive below.
1678 *All for Love, or The World Well Lost*, prologue.

86 Then he defies the world and bids it pass.
1678 Of Antony. *All for Love, or The World Well Lost*, act 1.

87 Virtue's his path; but sometimes 'tis too narrow
For his vast soul; and then he starts out wide,
And bounds into a vice.
1678 Of Antony. *All for Love, or The World Well Lost*, act 1.

88 Sure there's contagion in the tears of friends.
1678 *All for Love, or The World Well Lost*, act 1.

89 My love's a noble madness.
1678 Cleopatra to Iris. *All for Love, or The World Well Lost*, act 2, sc.1.

90 Give, you gods,
Give to your boy, your Caesar,
The rattle of a globe to play withal,
This gewgaw world, and put him cheaply off:
I'll not be pleased with less than Cleopatra.
1678 Anthony. *All for Love, or The World Well Lost*, act 2, sc.1.

91 Moderate sorrow
Fits vulgar love, and for a vulgar man:
But I have lov'd with such transcendent passion,
I soar'd, at first, quite out of reason's view,
And now am lost above it.
1678 *All for Love, or The World Well Lost*, act 2.

92 O that faint word, *respect*! how I disdain it!
1678 *All for Love, or The World Well Lost*, act 2.

93 My heart's so full of joy,
That I shall do some wild extravagance
Of love in public; and the foolish world,
Which knows not tenderness, will think me mad.
1678 *All for Love, or The World Well Lost*, act 2.

94 We were so clos'd within each other's breasts
The rivets were not found that join'd us first.
That does not reach us yet: we were so mix'd,
As meeting streams, both to ourselves were lost;
We were one mass; we could not give or take,
But from the same; for he was I, I he!
1678 Antony speaking of his friendship with Dollabella. *All for Love, or The World Well Lost*, act 3.

95 What I have left is from my native spring;
I've still a heart that swells, in scorn of fate,
And lifts me to my banks.
1678 *All for Love, or The World Well Lost*, act 3.

96 The worst your malice can,
Is but to say the greatest of mankind
Has been my slave. The next, but far above him
In my esteem, is he whom law calls yours,
But whom his love made mine.
1678 Cleopatra boasts to Octavia of her conquest of Caesar and Antony. *All for Love, or The World Well Lost*, act 3.

97 Men are but children of a larger growth;
Our appetites as apt to change as theirs,
And full as craving too, and full as vain.
1678 Dollabella. *All for Love, or The World Well Lost*, act 4, sc.1.

98 Nature meant me
A wife, a silly, harmless, household dove,
Fond without art, and kind without deceit;
But Fortune, that has made a mistress of me,
Has thrust me out to the wide world, unfurnish'd
Of falsehood to be happy.
1678 Cleopatra. *All for Love, or The World Well Lost*, act 4.

99 Welcome, thou kind deceiver!
Thou best of thieves; who with an easy key,
Dost open life, and, unperceived by us,
Even steal us from ourselves.

1678 Cleopatra speaking of Love. *All for Love, or The World Well Lost*, act 5, sc.1.

1 My whole life
Has been a golden dream of love and friendship.

1678 *All for Love, or The World Well Lost*, act 5.

2 All the learn'd are cowards by profession.

1678 *All for Love, or The World Well Lost*, act 5.

3 Politicians neither love nor hate.

1681 *Absalom and Achitophel, l.223*

4 In pious times, ere priestcraft did begin,
Before polygamy was made a sin.

1681 *Absalom and Achitophel*, pt.1, l.1–2.

5 Whate'er he did was done with so much ease,
In him alone, 'twas natural to please.

1681 *Absalom and Achitophel*, pt.1, l.27–8.

6 His motions all accompanied with grace;
And paradise was opened in his face.

1681 *Absalom and Achitophel*, pt.1, l.29–30.

7 The Jews, a headstrong, moody, murmuring race.

1681 *Absalom and Achitophel*, pt.1, l.45.

8 But when to sin our biased nature leans,
The careful Devil is still at hand with means;
And providently pimps for ill desires.

1681 *Absalom and Achitophel*, pt.1, l.79–81.

9 Then Israel's monarch, after Heaven's own heart,
His vigorous warmth did, variously, impart
To wives and slaves: and, wide as his command,
Scattered his Maker's image through the land.

1681 *Absalom and Achitophel*, pt.1, l.7–10. An oblique reference to Charles II, who had no legitimate, but many illegitimate, children.

10 Plots, true or false, are necessary things,
To raise up commonwealths and ruin kings.

1681 Alluding to the alleged Popish plot to murder the king, which brought about the Exclusion crisis. *Absalom and Achitophel*, pt.1, l.83–4.

11 Some truth there was, but dashed and brewed with lies,
To please the fools, and puzzle all the wise.

1681 *Absalom and Achitophel*, pt.1, l.114.

12 Pleased with the danger, when the waves went high
He sought the storms; but for a calm unfit,
Would steer too nigh the sands to boast his wit.

1681 Alluding to Anthony Ashley Cooper, first Earl of Shaftesbury, leader of the Exclusion forces. *Absalom and Achitophel*, pt.1, l.160–2.

13 Great wits are sure to madness near allied,
And thin partitions do their bands divide.

1681 *Absalom and Achitophel*, pt.1, l.163–4

14 Why should he, with wealth and honour blest,
Refuse his age the needful hours of rest?
Punish a body which he could not please;
Bankrupt of life, yet prodigal of ease?
And all to leave what with his toil he won
To that unfeathered two-legged thing, a son.

1681 *Absalom and Achitophel*, pt.1, l.165–70.

15 In friendship false, implacable in hate:
Resolved to ruin or to rule the state.

1681 *Absalom and Achitophel*, pt.1, l.173–4.

16 He stood at bold defiance with his prince;
Held up the buckler of the people's cause
Against the crown, and skulked behind the laws.

1681 *Absalom and Achitophel*, pt.1, l.205–7.

17 The people's prayer, the glad diviner's theme,
The young men's vision and the old men's dream!

1681 *Absalom and Achitophel*, pt.1, l.238–9.
▷ See Bible 130:55.

18 What cannot praise effect in mighty minds,
When flattery soothes, and when ambition blinds!

1681 *Absalom and Achitophel*, pt.1, l.303–4.

19 Desire of power, on earth a vicious weed,
Yet, sprung from high, is of celestial seed:
In God 'tis glory; and when men aspire,
'Tis but a spark too much of heavenly fire.

1681 *Absalom and Achitophel*, pt.1, l.305.

20 All empire is no more than power in trust.

1681 *Absalom and Achitophel*, pt.1, l.411.

21 Better one suffer, than a nation grieve.

1681 *Absalom and Achitophel*, pt.1, l.416.

22 But far more numerous was the herd of such
Who think too little and who talk too much.

1681 *Absalom and Achitophel*, pt.1, l.533–4.

23 A man so various that he seemed to be
Not one, but all mankind's epitome.
Stiff in opinions, always in the wrong;
Was everything by starts, and nothing long:
But, in the course of one revolving moon,
Was chemist, fiddler, statesman, and buffoon.

1681 *Absalom and Achitophel*, pt. 1, l.545–60.

24 In squandering wealth was his peculiar art:
Nothing went unrewarded, but desert.
Beggared by fools, whom still he found too late:
He had his jest, and they had his estate.

1681 *Absalom and Achitophel*, pt.1, l.559–62.

25 Youth, beauty, graceful action seldom fail:

But common interest always will prevail:
And pity never ceases to be shown
To him, who makes the people's wrongs his own.
1681 *Absalom and Achitophel,* pt.1, l.723–6.

26 For who can be secure of private right,
If sovereign sway may be dissolved by might?
Nor is the people's judgement always true:
The most may err as grossly as the few.
1681 *Absalom and Achitophel,* pt.1, l.779–82.

27 Government itself at length must fall
To nature's state, where all have right to all.
1681 *Absalom and Achitophel,* pt.1, l.793.

28 The court he practised, not the courtier's art:
Large was his wealth, but larger was his heart.
1681 Of the loyalist James Butler, Duke of Ormond. *Absalom and Achitophel,* pt.1, l.825–6.

29 Swift was the race, but short the time to run.
1681 *Absalom and Achitophel,* pt.1, l.837.

30 Never was patriot yet, but was a fool.
1681 *Absalom and Achitophel,* pt.1, l.968.

31 From plots and treasons Heaven preserve my years,
But save me most from my petitioners.
Unsatiate as the barren womb or grave;
God cannot grant so much as they can crave.
1681 *Absalom and Achitophel,* pt.1, l.985–8.

32 Beware the fury of a patient man.
1681 *Absalom and Achitophel,* pt.1, l.1005.

33 For lawful power is still superior found,
When long driven back, at length it stands the
ground.
1681 *Absalom and Achitophel,* pt.1, l.1024–5.

34 Doeg, though without knowing how or why,
Made still a blund'ring kind of melody;
Spurred boldly on, and dashed through thick and
thin,
Through sense and nonsense, never out nor in;
Free from all meaning, whether good or bad,
And in one word, heroically mad.
1681 *Absalom and Achitophel,* pt.2, l.412–17.

35 Rhyme is the rock on which thou art to wreck.
1681 *Absalom and Achitophel,* pt.2, l.486.

36 But 'tis the talent of our English nation,
Still to be plotting some new reformation.
1681 *Sophonisba* (2nd edn).

37 There is a pleasure sure,
In being mad, that none but madmen know!
1681 *The Spanish Friar,* act 1, sc.1.

38 And, dying, bless the hand that gave the blow.
1681 *The Spanish Friar,* act 2, sc.2.

39 We loathe our manna, and we long for quails.
1682 *The Medal,* l.131.

40 But treason is not owned when 'tis descried;
Successful crimes alone are justified.
1682 *The Medal,* l.207–8.

41 And this unpolished rugged verse I chose
As fittest for discourse and nearest prose.
1682 *Religio Laici,* l.453–4.

42 Farewell, too little, and too lately known,
Whom I began to think and call my own.
1684 'To the Memory of Mr Oldham'. John Oldham was the author of *Satires upon the Jesuits* (1681).

43 Bold knaves thrive without one grain of sense,
But good men starve for want of impudence.
1684 *Constantine the Great,* epilogue.

44 Mute and magnificent, without a tear.
1685 *Threnodia Augustalis,* stanza 2.

45 Freedom which in no other land will thrive,
Freedom an English subject's sole prerogative.
1685 *Threnodia Augustalis,* stanza 10.

46 Her pencil drew whate'er her soul designed,
And oft the happy draft surpassed the image in her
mind.
1686 'To the Pious Memory of the Accomplished Young Lady Mrs Anne Killigrew'.

47 O double sacrilege on things divine,
To rob the relic, and deface the shrine!
1686 'To the Pious Memory of the Accomplished Young Lady Mrs Anne Killigrew'. Killigrew had died of smallpox.

48 And doomed to death, though fated not to die.
1687 *The Hind and the Panther,* pt.1, l.8.

49 For truth has such a face and such a mien
As to be loved needs only to be seen.
1687 *The Hind and the Panther,* pt.1, l.33–4.

50 My thoughtless youth was winged with vain
desires,
My manhood, long misled by wandering fires,
Followed false lights; and when their glimpse was
gone
My pride struck out new sparkles of her own...
Good life be now my task: my doubts are done;
(What more could fright my faith than Three in
One?)
1687 *The Hind and the Panther,* pt.1, l.71–6.

51 Reason to rule, but mercy to forgive:
The first is law, the last prerogative.
1687 *The Hind and the Panther,* pt.1, l.261–2.

52 Either be wholly slaves or wholly free.

1687 *The Hind and the Panther*, pt.2, l.285.

53 Much malice mingled with a little wit
    Perhaps may censure this mysterious writ.
    1687 *The Hind and the Panther*, pt.3, l.1–2.

54 For present joys are more to flesh and blood
    Than a dull prospect of a distant good.
    1687 *The Hind and the Panther*, pt.3, l.364–5.

55 By education most have been misled;
    So they believe, because they so were bred.
    The priest continues what the nurse began,
    And thus the child imposes on the man.
    1687 *The Hind and the Panther*, pt.3, l.389–92.

56 T'abhor the makers, and their laws approve,
    Is to hate traitors and the treason love.
    1687 *The Hind and the Panther*, pt.3, l.706–7.

57 For those whom God to ruin has designed,
    He fits for fate, and first destroys their mind.
    1687 *The Hind and the Panther*, pt.3, l..1093–4.

58 Three poets, in three distant ages born,
    Greece, Italy, and England did adorn.
    The first in loftiness of thought surpassed,
    The next in majesty, in both the last:
    The force of Nature could no farther go;
    To make a third, she joined the former two.
    1688 'Epigram on Milton', engraved on the frontispiece to the
    1688 edition of *Paradise Lost*. The three poets are Homer, Virgil
    and Milton.

59 That fairy kind of writing which depends only
    upon the force of imagination.
    1691 *King Arthur*, dedication.

60 War is the trade of kings.
    1691 *King Arthur*, act 2, sc.2.

61 Fairest Isle, all isles excelling,
    Seat of pleasures, and of loves;
    Venus here will choose her dwelling,
    And forsake her Cyprian groves.
    1691 *King Arthur*, act 5, 'Song of Venus'.

62 Music, Music for a while
    Shall all your cares beguile.
    1692 *Oedipus* (with Nathaniel Lee).

63 How easy it is to call rogue and villain, and that
    wittily! But how hard to make a man appear a fool,
    a blockhead, or a knave, without using any of those
    opprobrious terms! To spare the grossness of the
    names, and to do the thing yet more severely, is to
    draw a full face, and to make the nose and cheeks
    stand out, and yet not to employ any depth of
    shadowing.
    1693 *A Discourse Concerning the Original and Progress of Satire*,
    'The Art of Satire'.

64 A man may be capable, as Jack Ketch's wife said of
    his servant, of a plain piece of work, a bare hanging;
    but to make a malefactor die sweetly was only
    belonging to her husband.
    1693 *A Discourse Concerning the Original and Progress of Satire*,
    'The Art of Satire'.

65 Ovid, the soft philosopher of love.
    1694 *Love Triumphant*, act 2, sc.1.

66 Thou tyrant, tyrant Jealousy,
    Thou tyrant of the mind!
    1694 *Love Triumphant*, act 3, sc.1, 'Song of Jealousy'.

67 Happy, happy, happy, pair!
    None but the brave,
    None but the brave,
    None but the brave deserves the fair.
    1697 *Alexander's Feast*, l.4–7.

68 With ravished ears
    The monarch hears,
    Assumes the god,
    Affects to nod,
    And seems to shake the spheres.
    1697 *Alexander's Feast*, l.42–6.

69 Drinking is the soldier's pleasure;
    Rich the treasure;
    Sweet the pleasure;
    Sweet is pleasure after pain.
    1697 *Alexander's Feast*, l.57–60.

70 Fallen from his high estate,
    And welt'ring in his blood:
    Deserted at his utmost need
    By those his former bounty fed;
    On the bare earth expos'd he lies,
    With not a friend to close his eyes.
    1697 *Alexander's Feast*, l.78–83.

71 Revolving in his altered soul
    The various turns of chance below.
    1697 *Alexander's Feast*, l.85-86.

72 War, he sung, is toil and trouble;
    Honour but an empty bubble.
    Never ending, still beginning,
    Fighting still, and still destroying,
    If the world be worth thy winning,
    Think, oh think, it worth enjoying.
    1697 *Alexander's Feast*, l.97–102.

73 Sighed and looked, and sighed again.
    1697 *Alexander's Feast*, l.120.

74 Let old Timotheus yield the prize,
    Or both divide the crown:
    He raised a mortal to the skies;
    She drew an angel down.
    1697 Of 'Divine Cecilia'. *Alexander's Feast*, l.177–80.

75 We must beat the iron while it is hot, but we may polish it at leisure.
1697 *Aeneis* (his translation of Virgil's *Aeneid*), dedication.

76 Arms, and the man I sing, who, forced by fate,
And haughty Juno's unrelenting hate,
Expelled and exiled, left the Trojan shore.
1697 *Aeneis* (his translation of Virgil's *Aeneid*), bk.1, l.1–3.

77 What judgement I had increases rather than diminishes; and thoughts, such as they are, come crowding in so fast upon me, that my only difficulty is to choose or reject; to run them into verse or give them the other harmony of prose.
1700 *Fables Ancient and Modern*, preface.

78 We can only say that he lived in the infancy of our poetry, and that nothing is brought to perfection at the first.
1700 *Fables Ancient and Modern*, preface, 'In Praise of Chaucer'.

79 [Chaucer] must have been a man of a most wonderful comprehensive nature, because, as it has been truly observed of him, he has taken into the compass of his *Canterbury Tales* the various manners and humours of the whole English nation in his age.
1700 *Fables Ancient and Modern*, preface, 'In Praise of Chaucer'.

80 A perpetual fountain of good sense.
1700 Of Chaucer. *Fables Ancient and Modern*, preface.

81 'Tis sufficient to say, according to the proverb, that here is God's plenty.
1700 Of the *Canterbury Tales*. *Fables Ancient and Modern*, preface, 'In Praise of Chaucer'.

82 One of our great poets is sunk in his reputation, because he could never forgive any conceit which came in his way; but swept like a drag-net, great and small. There was plenty enough, but the dishes were ill-sorted; whole pyramids of sweetmeats, for boys and women; but little of solid meat for men.
1700 Of Abraham Cowley. *Fables Ancient and Modern*, preface.

83 Refined himself to soul, to curb the sense
And made almost a sin of abstinence.
1700 'The Character of a Good Parson', l.10–11.

84 He trudged along unknowing what he sought,
And whistled as he went, for want of thought.
1700 *Cymon and Iphigenia*, l.84–5.

85 She hugged the offender, and forgave the offence.
1700 *Cymon and Iphigenia*, l.367.

86 Of seeming arms to make a short essay,
Then hasten to be drunk, the business of the day.
1700 *Cymon and Iphigenia*, l.407–8.

87 Better to hunt in fields, for health unbought,
Than fee the doctor for a nauseous draught.
The wise, for cure, on exercise depend;
God never made his work, for man to mend.
1700 Epistle, 'To my honoured kinsman John Driden', l.92–5.

88 Even victors are by victories undone.
1700 Epistle, 'To my honoured kinsman John Driden', l.164.

89 But love's a malady without a cure.
1700 *Palamon and Arcite*, bk.2, l.110.

90 Fool, not to know that love endures no tie,
And Jove but laughs at lovers' perjury.
1700 *Palamon and Arcite*, bk.2, l.148–9.

91 And Antony, who lost the world for love.
1700 *Palamon and Arcite*, bk.2, l.607.

92 Repentance is but want of power to sin.
1700 *Palamon and Arcite*, bk.3, l.813.

93 Since every man who lives is born to die,
And none can boast sincere felicity,
With equal mind, what happens, let us bear,
Nor joy nor grieve too much for things beyond our care.
Like pilgrims to th'appointed place we tend;
The world's an inn, and death the journey's end.
1700 *Palamon and Arcite*, bk.3, l.883–8.

94 A virgin-widow, and a mourning bride.
1700 *Palamon and Arcite*, bk.3, l.927.

95 A very merry, dancing, drinking,
Laughing, quaffing, and unthinking time.
1700 *The Secular Masque*, l.39–40.

96 Joy ruled the day, and Love the night.
1700 *The Secular Masque*, l.81.

97 All, all of a piece throughout;
Thy chase had a beast in view;
Thy wars brought nothing about;
Thy lovers were all untrue.
'Tis well an old age is out,
And time to begin a new.
1700 *The Secular Masque*, l.92–7.

Dubin, Al 1891–1945

Swiss-born US lyricist.

98 Come and meet those dancing feet
On the avenue I'm taking you to
Forty Second Street
1932 From the title song, *Forty-Second Street*. Music by Harry Warren.

99 You're Getting to be a Habit with Me.
1932 Title of song in *Forty-Second Street*. Music by Harry Warren.

1 We're in the money, We're in the money
We've got a lot of what it takes to get along.
1933 From the song 'We're in the Money' featured in *Gold Diggers of 1933*. Music by Harry Warren.

2 I Only Have Eyes For You
1934 Title of song from the film *Dames*. Music by Harry Warren.

3 You may not be an angel
Cause angels are so few
But until the day that one comes along
I'll string along with you
1934 From the song 'I'll String Along With You' in *Twenty Million Sweethearts*. Music by Harry Warren.

4 Come on along and listen to
The Lullaby of Broadway
The hip hooray and bally hoo
The Lullaby of Broadway
1935 From the song 'Lullaby of Broadway' in *Gold Diggers of 1935*. Music by Harry Warren.

Du Bois, W(illiam) E(dward) B(urghardt) 1868–1963

US writer. He became a leading figure in and spokesman for the black community, and wrote a number of pioneering books on black life and social reform.

5 The problem of the twentieth century is the problem of the colour line.
1900 Address to the Pan-African Conference, London.

6 To be a poor man is hard, but to be a poor race in a land of dollars is the very bottom of hardships.
1903 *The Souls of Black Folk*, ch.1.

7 Herein lies the tragedy of the age: not that men are poor…not that men are wicked…but that men know so little of men.
1903 *The Souls of Black Folk*, ch.12.

8 If there is anybody in this land who thoroughly believes that the meek shall inherit the earth they have not often let their presence be known.
1924 *The Gift of Black Folk*, ch.9.

9 Today I see more clearly than yesterday that back of the problem of race and color, lies a greater problem which both obscures and implements it: and that is the fact that so many civilized persons are willing to live in comfort even if the price of this is poverty, ignorance and disease of the majority of their fellowmen; that to maintain this privilege men have waged war until today war tends to become universal and continuous, and the excuse for this war continues largely to be color and race.
Preface to re-print of *The Souls of Black Folk* (1969).

10 One thing alone I charge you. As you live, believe in life! Always human beings will live and progress to a greater, broader and fuller life. The only possible death is to lose belief in this truth simply because the great end comes slowly, because time is long.
1957 Written 26 Jun, and read as an oration at his funeral.

Du Bos, Jean-Baptiste 1670–1742

French critic, whose work influenced aesthetic theory.

11 *Les larmes d'un inconnu nous émeuvent même avant que nous sachions le sujet qui le fait pleurer.*

The tears of someone we do not know move us even before we know the reason why he weeps.
1719 *Réflexions critiques sur la poésie et la peinture.*

12 *Le sentiment enseigne bien mieux si l'ouvrage touche que toutes les dissertations composées par les critiques.*

Feeling teaches much more that all the writing of critics if the work touches us.
1719 *Réflexions critiques sur la poésie et la peinture.*

Dudek, Louis 1918–

Canadian poet and aphorist, whose works attempt to liberate Candian poetry from its British influences. His early lyric poetry was followed by longer poems such as *En Mexico* (1958).

13 Aphorisms give you more for your time and money than any other literary form. Only the poem comes near to it, but then most good poems either start off from an aphorism or arrive at one… Aphorisms and epigrams are the corner-stones of literary art.
Collected in *Notebooks 1960–1994* (1994).

14 Fame is based on what people say about you, reputation on what they think of you.
Collected in *Notebooks 1960–1994* (1994).

15 If there is a heaven it's no doubt already filled— with horses, chickens, lambs, and other poor creatures. People will simply not get in.
Collected in *Notebooks 1960–1994* (1994).

16 All the ills of mankind spring from belonging to a race, a nation, a city, a group of some kind. The ideal would be to belong to none, and to care for all—but who is capable of that?
Collected in *Notebooks 1960–1994* (1994).

17 Intellectually, most people never wash. They never free their minds of the accumulated rubbish of centuries.
Collected in *Notebooks 1960–1994* (1994).

18 Imagination should be integrated with life, not turned into a separate activity, art, that monopolizes one's whole existence.
Collected in *Notebooks 1960–1994* (1994).

19 Hatred is generalized, but love is for the particular.
Collected in *Notebooks 1960–1994* (1994).

20 The twentieth century had a wonderful capacity for seeing nothing as the sum of everything.
Collected in *Notebooks 1960–1994* (1994).

Duell, Charles H

US government official, Commissioner of the Office of Patents.

21 Everything that can be invented has been invented.
1899 Letter to President William McKinley, suggesting that an Office of Patents was no longer necessary.

Duesenberry, James Stemble 1918–

US economist, Professor at Harvard.

22 Economics is all about how people make choices. Sociology is all about why they don't have any choices to make.
1960 In the National Bureau of Economic Research's *Demographic and Economic Change in the Developed World*.

Duffield, George 1818–88

US Presbyterian minister and hymnwriter.

23 Stand Up! Stand Up For Jesus!
1858 *The Psalmist*, title of hymn. Duffield's inspiration for the hymn came from the dying words of the evangelist Dudley Atkins Tyng to him: 'Tell them to stand up for Jesus.'

Dugommier, General Jean François Coquille 1736–94

General of the French Republic.

24 *Récompensez, avancez ce jeune homme; car, si l'on était ingrat envers lui, il s'avancerait de lui-même.*

Reward that young man, promote him; for if his services are not recognised, he will promote himself.
1794 Comment to the Minister for War, speaking of the 24-year-old Napoleon Bonaparte, after the siege of Toulon. Quoted in John Julius Norwich *Venice* (1981).

Dulles, John Foster 1888–1959

US Republican politician, Secretary of State from 1953 until his resignation just a week before his death. His vigorous diplomacy led to many personal conferences with statesmen in other countries.

25 You have to take chances for peace, just as you must take chances in war… The ability to get to the verge without getting into the war is the necessary art. If you try to run away from it, if you are scared to go to the brink, you are lost.
1956 Quoted in 'How Dulles Averted War', in *Life* magazine, 16 Jan. His biographer Peter Grose in *Gentleman Spy* (1994) claims Dulles 'never actually used the word '*brinkmanship*', but the label stuck to him as the legacy of a diplomatic strategy that was reckless for the nuclear age'.

26 The Soviets sought not a place in the sun, but the sun itself. Their objective was the world. They would not tolerate compromise on goals, only on tactics.
Comment to his brother Allen. Quoted in Peter Grose *Gentleman Spy* (1994).

Dumas, Alexandre, *père* 1802–70

French novelist and playwright. He began writing plays, but turned to travelogues and historical novels, including *Le Comte de Monte Cristo* (The Count of Monte Cristo, 1844–5).

27 *Tous pour un, un pour tous.*

All for one, one for all.
1844 *Les Trois Mousquetaires*, ch.9.

28 *Cherchons la femme.*

Let us look for the woman.
1854–5 *Les Mohicans de Paris*.

Dumas, Alexandre, *fils* 1824–95

French writer, illegitimate son of Dumas père. In addition to his novel *La Dame aux camélias* (1848), he produced many brilliant dramas, essays, letters and speeches, and may have aided George Sand with her work for the stage.

29 The demi-monde does not represent the crowd of courtesans, but the class of declassed women… It is divided from that of honest women by public scandal, and divided from that of the courtesans by money.
1855 On the first performance of his play *La Dame aux camélias*, 20 Mar, the first recorded use of the phrase. Quoted in Joanna Richardson *The Courtesans* (1967), p.227.

30 All generalizations are dangerous, even this one.
Attributed.

Du Maurier, Dame Daphne 1907–89

English novelist and short-story writer.

31 Last night I dreamt I went to Manderley again.
1938 *Rebecca*, opening words.

32 Every book is like a purge; at the end of it one is empty…like a dry shell on the beach, waiting for the tide to come in again.
1956 In the *Ladies Home Journal*, Nov.

Dunbar, Paul Laurence 1872–1906

US poet, the son of escaped slaves. He wrote several volumes of poetry in dialect, including *Lyrics of Lowly Life* (1896).

33 We wear the mask that grins and lies, It hides our cheeks and shades our eyes.
1895 'We Wear the Mask', stanza 1.

34 I know why the caged bird sings!

1895 'Sympathy', stanza 3. This was used by Maya Angelou as the title of her autobiography in 1970.

Dunbar, William c.1460–c.1520

Scottish poet, thought to have graduated from St Andrew's University in 1479. He was a courtier of James IV, and wrote many short poems, remarkable for their range of style and subject.

35 He that may be but sturt or stryfe,
And leif ane lusty plesand lyfe,
And syne with mariege dois him mell,
And bindis him with ane wicket wyfe,
He wirkis sorrow to him sell.

early 16c 'Ane His Awin Ennemy', l.6–10.

36 Now of wemen this I say for me,
Off erthly thingis nane may bettir be;
Thay suld haif wirschep and great honoring
Off men, aboif all uthir erthly thing.

early 16c 'In Prais of Wemen', lines 1–4.

37 Be riche in patience, gif thow in gudis be pure;
Quho levis mirry, he levis michtely:
Without glaidnes availis no tresour.

early 16c 'No Tressour Availis without Glaidnes', l.22–4.

38 Be courtly ay in clething and costly arrayit,
That hurtis yow nought worth a hen; yowr
husband pays for all.

early 16c The Tua Mariit Wemen and the Wedo, l.268–9.

39 London, thou art of townes *A per se*.
Soveraign of cities, someliest in sight,
Of high renoun, riches, and royaltie;
Of lordis, barons, and many goodly knyght;
Of most delectable lusty ladies bright;
Of famous prelatis in habitis clericall;
Of merchauntis full of sybstaunce and myght;
London, thou art the flour of Cities all.

c.1501 'To the City of London', attributed to 'A Rhymer of Scotland'. Dunbar was a member of the Scots party negotiating the marriage of James IV to Margaret Tudor, and is popularly attributed with the verse.

40 I that in heill wes and gladnes
Am trublit now with gret seiknes
And feblit with infermite:
Timor mortis conturbat me.

c.1505 'Lament for the Makaris', stanza 1. The Latin is from the Office for the Dead: 'The fear of death disturbs me'.

41 Sen for the deid remeid is none,
Best is that we for dede dispone
Eftir our deid that lif may we:
Timor morits conturbat me.

c.1505 'Lament for the Makaris', stanza 25.

42 In to thir dirk and drublie dayis,

Quhone sabill all the hevin arrayis
With mystie vapouris, cluddis and skyis,
Nature all curage me denyis
Off sangis, ballattis, and of playis.

'Meditatioun in Wyntir', stanza 1.

Duncan, Isadora 1878–1927

US dancer. She was hailed as one of the most innovative dancers of her day, espousing a free-flowing interpretative style of dance that was quite distinct from conventional ballet.

43 *Adieu, mes amis. Je vais à la gloire!*

Farewell, my friends. I am going to glory!

1927 Last words, shortly before she broke her neck when her long scarf caught in the wheels of her open-topped Bugatti sportscar. Quoted in Mary Desti *Isadora Duncan's End*, ch.25.

Duncan, Robert Edwards originally *Edward Howard Duncan* 1919–88

US poet. He was associated with the Black Mountain Poets including Charles Olsen and Robert Creeley.

44 Among my friends love is a payment.
It is an old debt for a borrowing foolishly spent.

1946 Early Poems 1939–46, 'Among My Friends Love Is A Great Sorrow'.

45 Neither our vices nor our virtues
further the poem.

1960 The Opening of the Field, 'Poetry, A Natural Thing'.

46 Noble men in the quiet of morning hear
Indians singing the continent's violent requiem.

1960 The Opening of the Field, 'A Poem Beginning With A Line By Pindar'.

47 Desire paces Eternity as if it had bounds, craving
death.
The Word climbs upward into Its crown.

1964 Roots and Branches, 'Structure of Rime XVII'.

48 I would be a falcon and go free.
I tread her wrist and wear the hood,
Talking to myself, and would draw blood.

1968 Bending The Bow, 'My Mother Would Be A Falconress'.

49 The great house of our humanity
No longer stands.

1984 Ground Work: Before The War, 'Bring It Up From The Dark'.

Dunlop, Ian 1925–

English art historian.

50 The Shock of the New: seven historic exhibitions
of modern art.

1972 Title of book.

Dunn, Douglas Eaglesham 1942–

Scottish poet, essayist and anthologizer. A librarian at Hull University, he was encouraged by Philip Larkin. He is one of Scotland's most respected contemporary poets.

51 This masculine invisibility makes gods of them,
A pantheon of boots and overalls.
1969 'Men of Terry Street'.

52 And all their lives, like that, they'll have to rush
Forwards in reverse, always holding their caps.
1979 'Glasgow Schoolboys, Running Backwards'.

53 Snow has begun to fall on the guilty secrets of
Europe.
1981 'The Deserter'.

54 I shall sieve through our twenty years, until
I almost reach the sob in the intellect,
The truth that waits for me with its loud grief,
Sensible, commonplace, beyond understanding.
1985 *Elegies*, 'The Clear Day'.

55 Only the mind sliding against events
And the antiseptic whiff of destiny.
1985 *Elegies*, 'Second Opinion'.

56 Best friend and love, my true contemporary,
She taught me how to live, then how to die,
And I curate her dreams and gallery.
1985 *Elegies*, 'Writing with Light'.

57 I shiver in the memory
And sculpt my foolish poetry
From thwarted life and snapped increase.
Cancer's no metaphor.
1985 *Elegies*, 'Anniversaries'.

58 A genius who invents a noise
Adds to the store of sonic toys
That *Homo ludens* in his wisdom
Accepts into his playful system.
1988 'An Address to Adolphe Sax in Heaven'.

59 Nationalism, and its chum, patriotism, encourage
unedifying hyperbole.
1992 'Language and Liberty', introduction to the *Faber Book of Twentieth Century Scottish Poetry*.

Dunne, Finley Peter 1867–1936

US humorist, editor of the *Chicago Journal* (1897–1900). His philosopher-bartender Mr Dooley became the exponent of Irish-American topical satire.

60 Glory Be, whin Business gets above sellin' tinpinny
nails in a brown paper cornucopy, 'tis hard to tell it
fr'm murther.
1901 *Mr Dooley's Opinions*, 'On Wall Street'.

61 Even an Englishman was niver improved by bein'
blown up.

'Revolution'. Collected in Louis Filler (ed) *The World of Mr Dooley* (1962).

Dunne, Philip 1908–

US screenwriter. His films include *Suez* (1938), *How Green was My Valley* (1941), *Forever Amber* (1947) and *The Robe* (1953).

62 A perfumed parlor snake.
1947 Daniel Gregg's description of Miles Fairley in *The Ghost and Mrs Muir*.

Dunning, John 1731–1820

British lawyer and politician.

63 The influence of the Crown has increased, is
increasing, and ought to be diminished.
1780 Motion passed by the House of Commons.

Duplessis, Maurice 1890–1959

Canadian statesman, Premier of Quebec (1936–9, 1944–59).

64 The bishops eat from my hand.
Characteristic remark, recalled in Conrad Black *Duplessis* (1977).

Durant, William James 1885–1981

US historian and essayist. He wrote a series of popular works culminating in the massive *Story of Civilization* (11 vol, 1935–67), written with his wife.

65 There is nothing in Socialism that a little age or a
little money will not cure.
Attributed.

Dürer, Albrecht 1471–1528

German painter and engraver. He travelled widely (1490–4) and in 1498 published his first major series of woodcuts, illustrations of the Apocalypse. He was employed by Emperor Maximilian I and later Charles V.

66 The art of painting cannot be truly judged save by
such as are themselves good painters; from others
verily it is hidden even as a strange tongue.
c.1512 Quoted in William Martin Conway *Literary Remains of Albrecht Dürer* (1889).

67 He that would be a painter must have a natural
turn thereto. Love and delight are better teachers
of the Art of Painting than compulsion is.
c.1512 *On Painting*. Quoted in William Martin Conway *Literary Remains of Albrecht Dürer* (1889).

Durkheim, Émile 1858–1917

French sociologist, appointed to the first chair of sociology in France in 1913.

68 The economic services that it can render are picayune compared to the moral effect that it produces, and its true function is to create in two or more persons a feeling of solidarity.

1893 Of labour. *The Division of Labor in Society* (translated by George Simpson, 1933).

69 The division of labor does not present individuals to one another, but social functions.

1893 *The Division of Labor in Society* (translated by George Simpson, 1933).

70 Our excessive tolerance of suicide is due to the fact that, since the state of mind from which it springs is a general one, we cannot condemn it without condemning ourselves; we are too saturated with it not partly to excuse it.

1897 *Suicide: a Study in Sociology* (translated by John A Spaulding and George Simpson, 1952).

71 All known religious beliefs, whether simple or complex, present one common characteristic: they presuppose a classification of all things, real and ideal, of which men think, into two classes or opposed groups, generally designated...*profane* and *sacred*.

1912 *The Elementary Forms of the Religious Life* (translated by Joseph Ward Swain, 1965).

72 If the idea of society were extinguished in individual minds and the beliefs, traditions and aspirations of the group were no longer felt and shared by individuals, society would die. We can say of it what we just said of divinity: it is real only in so far as it has a place in the human consciousness, and this place is whatever we may give it. We now see the real reason why the gods cannot do without their worshippers any more than these can do without their gods; it is because society, of which the gods are only a symbolic expression, cannot do without individuals any more than these can do without society.

1912 *The Elementary Forms of the Religious Life* (translated by Joseph Ward Swain, 1965).

Durocher, Leo 1906–91

US baseball manager, noted for his toughness.

73 Nice guys finish last.

1946 When asked if he regretted beating the New York Giants, who had been described as a 'nice bunch of guys'. He later used this as a book title, 1975.

74 Show me a good loser and I'll show you an idiot.

1950 Attributed.

Durranc, Edouard

75 How beautiful the Republic was—under the Empire.

Quoted in Edgar Holt *The Tiger: The Life of Georges Clemenceau 1841–1929* (1976).

Durrell, Lawrence George 1912–90

English novelist, poet, travel writer and playwright, born in India. His best known works are the novel sequences *The Alexandria Quartet* (1957–60) and *The Avignon Quincunx* (1974–85).

76 I love to feel events overlapping each other, crawling over one another like wet crabs in a basket.

1958 *Balthazar*, pt.1

77 No one can go on being a rebel too long without turning into an autocrat.

1958 *Balthazar*, pt.2.

78 Poggio's, where people go to watch each other watch each other.

1968 *Tunc*, ch.1

79 History is the endless repetition of the wrong way of living, and it'll start again tomorrow, if it's moved from here today.

1978 In *The Listener*, 20 Apr.

Dürrenmatt, Friedrich 1921–90

Swiss writer. After several novels he established an international reputation as a playwright with works such as *The Physicists* (1962) and *Play Strindberg* (1969).

80 What was once thought can never be unthought.

1962 *The Physicists*.

Dury, Ian 1942–

British rock singer, associated with the punk era of the late 1970s.

81 Sex 'n' drugs 'n' rock 'n' roll.

1977 Title of song.

Dvořák, Antonin 1841–1904

Czech composer and organist. His work, basically classical but with colourful Slavonic motifs, became increasingly popular throughout Europe.

82 I have composed too much.

Letter to Sibelius.

Dworkin, Andrea 1946–

US radical feminist, civil-rights activist and writer, whose work examines the relationship between male power and pornography. In 1983 she made an unsuccessful attempt to define pornography as sexual discrimination under law.

83 A man wants what a woman has—sex. He can steal it (rape), persuade her to give it away (seduction), rent it (prostitution), lease it over the long term (marriage in the United States), or own it outright (marriage in most societies).

1976 In *Ms*, vol.5, no.6, Dec. Collected as 'Phallic Imperialism: why economic recovery will not work for us' in *Letters from a War Zone* (1988).

84 The power of money is a distinctly male power. Money speaks, but it speaks with a male voice. In the hands of women, money stays literal, count it out, it buys what it is worth or less. In the hands of men, money buys women, sex, status, dignity, esteem, recognition, loyalty, all manner of possibility.

1981 *Pornography: Men Possessing Women*.

85 One of the differences between marriage and prostitution is that in marriage you only have to make a deal with one man.

1984 In *The A.B.C.s of Reading*, winter issue. Collected as 'Feminism: An Agenda' *in Letters from a War Zone* (1988).

86 Violation is a synonym for intercourse.

1987 *Intercourse*, 'Occupation/Collaboration'.

Dyer, Sir Edward c.1545–1607

English poet, diplomat and courtier, a friend of Sir Philip Sidney. Only a few of his poems survive.

87 My mind to me a kingdom is;
Such perfect joy therein I find
That it excels all other bliss
That world affords or grows by kind.
Though much I want which most men have,
Yet still my mind forbids to crave.

1588 'In Praise of a Contented Mind'.

88 No princely pomp, no wealthy store,
No force to win the victory,
No wily wit to salve a sore,
No shape to feed each gazing eye;
To none of these I yield as thrall.
For why my mind doth serve for all.

1588 'In Praise of a Contented Mind'.

89 Some weigh their pleasure by their lust,
Their wisdom by their rage of will,
Their treasure is their only trust;
And cloakèd craft their store of skill.
But all the pleasure that I find
Is to maintain a quiet mind.

1588 'In Praise of a Contented Mind'.

90 My wealth is health and perfect ease;
My conscience clear my chief defence;
I neither seek by bribes to please,
Nor by deceit to breed offense.
Thus do I live; thus will I die.
Would all did so well as I!

1588 'In Praise of a Contented Mind'.

Dylan, Bob pseudonym of *Robert Allen Zimmerman* 1941–

US singer and song-writer. His early acoustic, folk-influenced songs such as 'Blowin' in the Wind' were succeeded in 1965 by rock 'n' roll, with 'Mr Tambourine Man' and 'Like a Rolling Stone'.

91 How many roads must a man walk down
Before you can call him a man?…
The answer, my friend, is blowin' in the wind,
The answer is blowin' in the wind.

1962 'Blowin' in the Wind'.

92 But I can't think for you,
You'll have to decide,
Whether Judas Iscariot
Had God on his side.

1963 'With God on our Side'.

93 Ah, but I was so much older then,
I'm younger than that now.

1964 'My Back Pages'.

94 The Times They Are A' Changing.

1964 Title of a song.

95 The motorcycle black madonna
Two-wheeled gypsy queen.

1965 'Gates of Eden'.

96 Money doesn't talk, it swears.

1965 'It's Alright, Ma (I'm Only Bleeding)'.

97 Hey! Mr Tambourine Man, play a song for me.
I'm not sleepy and there is no place I'm going to.

1965 'Mr Tambourine Man'.

98 Folk music is a bunch of fat people.

Quoted in David Pickering *Brewer's Twentieth Century Music* (1994).

Dyson, Freeman J(ohn) 1923–

English-born US theoretical physicist, a nuclear weapons designer who has subsequently undertaken major work in arms control and disarmament.

99 For insight into human affairs I turn to stories and poems rather than to sociology. This is the result of my upbringing and background. I am not able to make use of the wisdom of the sociologists because I do not speak their language.

1979 *Disturbing the Universe*, ch.1.

1 Science and technology, like all original creations of the human spirit, are unpredictable. If we had a reliable way to label our toys good and bad, it would be easy to regulate technology wisely. But we can rarely see far enough ahead to know which road leads to damnation. Whoever concerns himself with big technology, either to push it forward or to stop it, is gambling in human lives.

1979 *Disturbing the Universe*, ch.1.

Dyson, Will(iam Henry) 1880–1938

Australian-born radical cartoonist of the London *Daily Herald*.

2 Curious! I seem to hear a child weeping.

1919 Cartoon caption in the *Daily Herald*, 17 May. French minister Clemenceau is shown leaving the Palais de Versailles with Woodrow Wilson and Lloyd George after signing the peace treaty with Germany. The 'child' is the generation of 1940.

Eagleton, Terry 1943–

English literary critic, a leading exponent of Marxist criticism and Professor at Linacre College, Oxford.

3 Homosexuality was the badge of the upper class and the sign of a revolt against it; and it is small wonder that someone locked for a lifetime in this impossible contradiction should end up with cirrhosis of the liver.

1993 Review of Sean French's *Patrick Hamilton: a Life* (1993). In the *London Review of Books*, 2 Dec.

4 If there are indeed any iron laws of history, one of them is surely that in any major crisis of the capitalist system, a sector of the liberal middle class will shift to the left, and then shift smartly back again once the crisis has blown over.

1993 In the *London Review of Books*, 2 Dec.

Eastwood, Clint 1930–

US actor and director. He achieved fame initially from his roles in westerns, later for more modern brutal roles.

5 You've got to ask yourself a question. Do I feel lucky. Well do you punk?

1971 As Harry Callahan in *Dirty Harry* (screenplay by Harry Julian Fink, Rita M Fink and Dean Riesner).

6 Nothing wrong with shooting so long as the right people get shot.

1973 As Harry Callahan in *Magnum Force* (screenplay by John Milius and Michael Cimino).

Eban, Abba originally *Aubrey Solomon* 1915–

Israeli diplomat and politician, born in South Africa. He was Israeli UN representative (1948), Ambassador to Washington (1950–9) and Foreign Minister (1966–74), but was unexpectedly defeated in the 1989 general election.

7 History teaches us that men and nations behave wisely once they have exhausted all other alternatives.

1970 Speech, London, 16 Dec.

Ebbinghaus, Hermann 1850–1909

German experimental psychologist. He carried out pioneering research on memory to investigate higher mental processes, and published his findings in *Über das Gedächtnis* (1885).

8 Psychology has a long past, but only a short history.

1885 *Summary of Psychology*.

Eberhart, Richard Ghormley 1904–

US poet and academic.

9 If I could only live at the pitch that is near madness
   When everything is as it was in my childhood
   Violent, vivid and of infinite possibility.

1947 'If I Could Only Live at the Pitch that is Near Madness'.

10 You would think the fury of aerial bombardment
    Would rouse God to relent; the infinite spaces
    Are still silent. He looks on shock-pried faces.
    History, even, does not know what is meant.

1951 'The Fury of Aerial Bombardment'.

11 Was man made stupid to see his own stupidity?
    Is God by definition indifferent, beyond us all?
    Is the eternal truth man's fighting soul
    Wherein the Beast ravens in its own avidity?

1951 'The Fury of Aerial Bombardment'.

Eberts, Jake 1941–

Canadian-born film producer. In 1977 he founded Goldcrest Films which made *Chariots of Fire* and *Local Hero*.

12 My Indecision Is Final.

1990 Title of his book on Goldcrest Films.

Echeverría, Esteban 1805–51

Argentinian poet and fiction writer. An opponent of the dictator Rosas, he was exiled in 1839 and lived in Uruguay until his death. He was the innovator of the Romantic school in Spanish American literature.

13 *A pesar de que la mía es historia, no la empezaré por el arca de Noé y la genealogía de sus ascendientes como acostumbraban hacerlo los antiguos historiadores españoles de América, que deben ser nuestros prototipos.*

I'm going to tell a true story, but I won't start with Noah's Ark and the genealogy of his forefathers, as is usual among the ancient Spanish historians of America, who we consider our prototypes.

1838 *El matadero* (*The Slaughter-House*, 1959).

The Economist

British journal, founded in 1843.

14 Michael Harrington…was America's leading socialist; a position, one might have thought, that almost epitomized marginality.

1989 *The Economist*, 12 Aug.

15 Corruption is more than a poison afflicting Chinese business life. It *is* Chinese business life.

1994 *The Economist*, 29 Jan.

16 One of the saddest features of the real world is that goods do not spontaneously present themselves for distribution.
1994 *The Economist*, 5 Nov.

Eddington, Sir Arthur Stanley 1882–1944

English astronomer and physicist, Professor of Astronomy (from 1913) and Director of the Observatory (from 1914) at Cambridge University.

17 Let us draw an arrow arbitrarily. If as we follow the arrow we find more and more of the random element in the world, then the arrow is pointing towards the future; if the random element decreases the arrow points towards the past... I shall use the phrase 'time's arrow' to express this one-way property of time which has no analogue in space.
1928 *The Nature of the Physical World*, ch.4. Martin Amis used the phrase 'Time's Arrow' for the title of his 1991 novel.

18 I ask you to look both ways. For the road to a knowledge of the stars leads through the atom; and important knowledge of the atom has been reached through the stars.
1928 *Stars and Atoms*, lecture 1.

19 I think it is something of the same sort of security we should seek in our relationship with God. The most flawless proof of the existence of God is no substitute for it; and if we have that relationship, the most convincing disproof is turned aimlessly aside. If I may say it with reverence, the soul and God laugh together over so odd a conclusion.
1929 *Science and the Unseen World.*

20 I believe that there are 15,747,724,136,275,002,577,605,653,961,181, 555,468,044,717,914,527,116,709,366,231,425, 076,185,631,031,296 protons in the universe, and the same number of electrons.
1938 Tarner Lecture.

Eden, Sir (Robert) Anthony, 1st Earl of Avon 1897–1977

Anglo-Irish politician and Conservative Prime Minister (1955–7). He ordered British forces to occupy the Suez Canal Zone (1956), an action which caused widespread condemnation.

21 Everybody is always in favour of general economy and particular expenditure.
1956 In *The Observer*, 17 Jun.

22 We best avoid wars by taking even physical action to stop small ones. Everybody knows that the United Nations is not in a position to do that... We must face the fact that the United Nations is not yet the internal equivalent of our own legal system and rule of law. Police action must be to

separate the belligerents and to prevent a resumption of hostilities.
1956 House of Commons, 1 Nov.

23 We are not at war with Egypt. We are in armed conflict.
1956 On the Suez crisis, House of Commons, 4 Nov.

Eden, Lady Clarissa 1920–

Wife of Sir Anthony Eden.

24 During the past few weeks, I felt sometimes that the Suez canal was flowing through my drawing room.
1956 Speech, Nov.

Edgeworth, Maria 1768–1849

Anglo-Irish novelist, whose novels reflect the rhythms of Irish country speech in their wry observation and humour. She is best remembered for *Castle Rackrent* (1800) and *The Absentee* (1812).

25 Possessed, as are all the fair daughters of Eve, of an hereditary propensity, transmitted to them undiminished through succeeding generations, to be 'soon moved with the slightest touch of blame'; very little precept and practice will confirm them in the habit, and instruct them all the maxims, of self-justification.
1795 *Letters for Literary Ladies*, 'An Essay on the Noble Science of Self-Justification'.

26 Man is to be held only by the *slightest* chains; with the idea that he can break them at pleasure, he submits to them in sport.
1795 *Letters for Literary Ladies*, 'Letters of Julia and Caroline', no.1.

27 Sir Patrick died that night—just as the company rose to drink his health with three cheers, he fell down in a sort of fit, and was carried off—they sat it out, and were surprised, on enquiry, in the morning, to find it was all over with poor Sir Patrick.
1800 *Castle Rackrent*, 'An Hibernian Tale'.

28 Sir Patrick Rackrent lived and died a monument of old Irish hospitality.
1800 *Castle Rackrent*, 'An Hibernian Tale'.

29 I've a great fancy to see my funeral before I die.
1800 Sir Cody to Thady. *Castle Rackrent*, 'History of Sir Conolly Rackrent'.

30 Did the Warwickshire militia, who were chiefly artisans, teach the Irish to drink beer, or did they learn from the Irish how to drink whiskey?
1800 *Castle Rackrent*, 'History of Sir Conolly Rackrent'.

31 Come when you're called;

And do as you're bid;
Shut the door after you;
And you'll never be chid.
1804 *The Contrast*, ch.1.

32 What a misfortune it is to be born a woman!…
Why seek for knowledge, which can prove only
that our wretchedness is irremediable? If a ray of
light break in upon us, it is but to make darkness
more visible; to show us the new limits, the Gothic
structure, the impenetrable barriers of our prison.
1806 *Leonora*, letter 1.

33 There need, at all events, be none of this, if people
would but live upon their own estates, and kill their
own mutton.
1812 Sir Terenece O'Fay. *The Absentee*, ch.5.

34 Those enemies to Ireland—those cruel absentees!
1812 Count O'Halloran. *The Absentee*, ch.8.

35 Deeds, not words.
1812 Sir James Brooke's motto. *The Absentee*, ch.9.

36 Let me not, even in my own mind, commit the
injustice of taking a speck for the whole.
1812 *The Absentee*, ch.11.

37 Her son saw that the *Londonmania* was now
stronger than ever upon her.
1812 *The Absentee*, ch.14.

38 In marrying, a man does not, to be sure, marry his
wife's mother; and yet a prudent man, when he
begins to think of the daughter, would look sharp
at the mother; ay, and back to the grandmother
too, and along the whole female line of ancestry.
1812 Count O'Halloran's advice to Lord Colambare. *The
Absentee*, ch.15.

Edinburgh, Prince Philip, Duke of 1921–

Consort of Elizabeth II, son of Prince Andrew of Greece
and Princess Alice of Battenberg. He entered the Royal
Navy in 1939, became a naturalized British subject in
1947, and was created Duke of Edinburgh on the eve of
his marriage (20 Nov). In 1956 he began the Duke of
Edinburgh Award Scheme to foster the leisure activities of
young people.

39 I have very little experience of self-government. In
fact, I am one of the most governed people in the
world.
1959 In the *New York Times*, 30 Dec.

40 We are suffering a national defeat comparable to
any lost military campaign, and what is more, it is
self-inflicted… It is about time that we pulled our
fingers out… The rest of the world most certainly
does not owe us a living.
1961 Speech to British industrialists, London, 17 Oct.

41 There is a widely held and quite erroneously held
belief that cricket is just another game.
1975 In *Wisden: Cricketers' Almanack*, 'The Pleasures of
Cricket'.

42 The grouse are in no danger at all from people who
shoot grouse.
1988 Quoted in *Private Eye*, no.693, 8 Jul.

Edison, Thomas Alva 1847–1931

US inventor, one of the most productive of his time.
Among his inventions were the gramophone and the
motion picture.

43 The phonograph…is not of any commercial value.
c.1860 Comment to his assistant, Samuel Insull. Edison hoped
that his invention would find a place in businesses and offices,
rather than in the entertainment world. Quoted in Robert A
Conot *A Streak of Luck: The Life and Legend of Thomas Edison*
(1979).

44 Genius is one per cent inspiration, ninety-nine per
cent perspiration.
c.1903 Quoted in *Harper's Monthly Magazine*, Sep 1932.

Edmeston, John 1721–1867

English architect and hymnwriter.

45 Lead us, Heavenly Father, lead us
O'er the world's tempestuous sea.
1821 *Sacred Lyrics, Set 2*, 'Lead us, Heavenly Father'.

Edward II 1284–1327

King of England (from 1307). His invasion of Scotland
resulted in defeat by Robert the Bruce at Bannockburn
(1314). He was eventually murdered.

46 Forasmuch as there is great noise in the city caused
by hustling over large balls, from which many evils
may arise, which God forbid, we command and
forbid on behalf of the King, on pain of
imprisonment, such game to be used in the city in
future.
1314 Royal proclamation, banning football from the streets of
London.

Edward III 1312–77

King of England (from 1327). He started hostilities
against France in 1337 and assumed the title of King of
France in 1340. Victories at Crecy (1346) and Poitiers
(1356) led to a large concession of territory by the French.
He also invaded Scotland.

47 Also say to them, that they suffre hym this day to
wynne his spurres, for if god be pleased, I well this
journey be his, and the honoure thereof.
1346 Of his 16-year-old son, Edward the Black Prince. Quoted
in the *Chronicle of Froissart* (translated by Sir John Bourchier,
Lord Berners, 1523–5), ch.130.

48 *Honi soit qui mal y pense.*

Evil be to him that evil thinks.

c.1348 Motto of the Order of the Garter. Said to have been uttered by Edward when adjusting the Countess of Salisbury's garter, which had slipped down.

Edward VII 1841–1910

King of the UK (from 1901), son of Queen Victoria. In 1863 he married Alexandra of Denmark. His scandalous behaviour as Prince of Wales led to his exclusion from affairs of state, but as king he made several visits to improve international relations.

49 Because a man has a black face and a different religion from ours, there is no reason why he should be treated as a brute.

1875 Letter from India to Lord Granville, 30 Nov.

Edward VIII 1894–1972

King of the UK (1936). He succeeded his father George V in 1936, but abdicated (11 Dec) because of his proposed marriage to divorcee Mrs Wallis Simpson. As Duke of Windsor, he lived in Paris except during his governorship of the Bahamas (1940–5).

50 These works brought all these people here. Something should be done to get them at work again.

1936 Comment while viewing the derelict Dowlais Iron and Steel Works, 18 Nov. It is often rendered 'Something must be done'.

51 I have found it impossible to carry the heavy burden of responsibility, and to discharge my duties as King as I would wish, without the help and support of the woman I love.

1936 Radio broadcast to the nation, 11 Dec, following his abdication to marry Wallis Simpson.

Edwards, Bob (Robert Chambers) 1864–1922

Canadian publisher and writer.

52 One can always tell when one is getting old and serious by the way that holidays seem to interfere with one's work.

1913 In *Eye Opener*, 20 Dec.

Edwards, Oliver 1711–91

English lawyer, an acquaintance of Samuel Johnson.

53 You are a philosopher, Dr Johnson. I have tried too in my time to be a philosopher; but, I don't know how, cheerfulness was always breaking in.

1778 In conversation with Dr Johnson, 17 Apr. Quoted in James Boswell *Life of Samuel Johnson* (1791).

Edwards, Otis C(arl) Jr 1928–

US theologian and educator, ordained into the Episcopal Church in 1954. After serving in several churches as curate and rector, he taught at Nashotah House

(1969–74) before being appointed Dean of Seabury-Western Theological Seminary (1974–83).

54 To be loose with grammar is to be loose with the worst woman in the world.

1966 New Testament lecture, Nashotah House, 10 Jan.

Egan, Pierce 1772–1849

English sporting writer. A London journalist, he wrote *Boxiana: or Sketches of Ancient and Modern Pugilism* (1812–13), and is best remembered for *Life in London* (1821), a description of the life of a 'man about town'.

55 Here lies, bowl'd out by Death's unerring ball,
A cricketer renowned, by name John Small;
But though his name was small, yet great was his fame,
For nobly did he play the 'noble game'.
His life was like his innings—long and good;
Full ninety summers had Death withstood,
At length the ninetieth winter came—when (Fate
Not leaving him one solitary mate)
This last of Hambledonians, old John Small,
Gave up his bat and ball—his leather, wax and all.

1832 Epitaph on cricketer John Small. *Pierce Egan's Book of Sports.*

Ehrlich, Paul Ralph 1932–

US biologist, Professor at Stanford University.

56 The first rule of intelligent tinkering is to save all the parts.

1971 In the *Saturday Review*, 5 Jun.

Ehrlichman, John 1925–99

US government official, Special Counsel to the Nixon White House, implicated in the Watergate scandal.

57 He's the Big Enchilada.

1973 On the possibility of pinning the blame for Watergate on Attorney General John Mitchell. Taped conversation, 27 Mar.

58 I think we ought to let him hang there. Let him twist slowly, slowly in the wind.

1973 Of Patrick Gray, regarding his nomination as director of the FBI. Taped conversation with John Dean, reported in the *Washington Post*, 27 Jul.

Eichelbaum, Samuel 1894–1969

Argentinian playwright and fiction writer. He began writing in a naturalistic style, but later adopted an emotional realism to show the effect of social environment on the individual.

59 '¡No hay políticos malos! Y buenos, tampoco, ¡qué caray! Los políticos no son ni buenos ni malos. Son hombres de oficio. Como los carpinterios y los albañiles'.

'There are no bad politicians! There aren't any good ones either, damn it! Politicians are neither bad nor good. They are professionals, like carpenters or masons.'

1940 *Un guapo del 900* ('A Handsome Man from the Nineteen Hundreds'), act 1.

Einstein, Albert 1879–1955

German-born theoretical physicist, who took Swiss (1901) and US (1940) citizenship. His early work on the photoelectric effect pioneered quantum theory and won him the 1921 Nobel Prize. He is best known for his special (1905) and general (1916) theories of relativity. After Hitler's rise to power he lectured in the US, and later urged international control of atomic weapons.

60 $E = mc^2$

1905 *Zur Elektrodynamik bewegter Körper* (The Electrodynamics of Moving Bodies).

61 *Raffiniert ist der Herrgott, aber böshaft ist er nicht.*

God is subtle, but he is not malicious.

1921 Said on a visit to Princeton University, May, and later carved above a fireplace there.

62 *Jedenfalls bin ich überzeugt, daß der nicht würfelt.*

Anyway, I am sure that he [God] does not play dice.

1926 Letter to Max Born, 4 Dec.

▷ See Hawking 461:62.

63 One of the strongest motives that lead people to give their lives to art and science is the urge to flee from everyday life, with its drab and deadly dullness and thus to unshackle the chains of one's own transient desires, which supplant one another in an interminable succession so long as the mind is fixed on the horizon of daily environment.

1933 Prologue to Max Planck *Where is Science Going?* (1933).

64 I think and think for months and years. Ninety-nine times, the conclusion is false. The hundredth time I am right.

1934 *The World as I See It.*

65 It may be possible to set up a nuclear reaction in uranium by which vast amounts of power could be released… This new phenomenon would also lead to the construction of…extremely powerful bombs of a new type.

1939 Letter to President Franklin D Roosevelt.

66 Science without religion is lame, religion without science is blind.

1941 *Science, Philosophy and Religion: A Symposium*, ch.13.

67 The most beautiful emotion we can experience is the mystical. It is the power of all true art and science. He to whom this emotion is a stranger, who can no longer wonder and stand rapt in awe, is as good as dead. To know that what is impenetrable to us really exists, manifesting itself as the highest wisdom and the most radiant beauty, which our dull faculties can comprehend only in their most primitive forms—this knowledge, this feeling, is at the center of true religiousness. In this sense, and in this sense only, I belong to the rank of devoutly religious men.

Quoted in Philipp Frank *Einstein: His Life and Times* (1947), ch.12, section 5.

68 Science can only state what is, not what should be.

1950 *Out of my Later Years.*

69 Perfections of means and confusion of goals seem—in my opinion—to characterize our age.

1950 *Out of my Later Years.*

70 The man of science is a poor philosopher.

1950 *Out of my Later Years.*

71 The whole of science is nothing more than a refinement of everyday thinking.

1950 *Out of my Later Years.*

72 If *A* is success in life, then *A* equals *x* plus *y* plus *z*. Work is *x*; *y* is play; and *z* is keeping your mouth shut.

1950 In *The Observer*, 15 Jan.

73 The most incomprehensible thing about the world is that it is comprehensible.

1950 In *Life Magazine.*

74 If only I had known, I would have become a watchmaker.

1955 On his part in developing the atom bomb. In the *New Statesman*, 16 Apr.

75 The grand aim of all science is to cover the greatest number of empirical facts by logical deduction from the smallest number of hypotheses or axioms.

1970 Quoted in *Life Magazine*, 9 Jan.

76 As far as the laws of mathematics refer to reality, they are not certain, and as far as they are certain, they do not refer to reality.

Quoted in Fritjof Capra *The Tao of Physics* (1975), ch.2.

77 Everything should be made as simple as possible, but not simpler.

Quoted in *Newsweek*, 16 Apr 1979.

Eisenhower, Dwight D(avid) 1890–1969

US soldier and Republican politician, whose success as Supreme Commander of Allied forces during World War II and later of NATO swept him to victory as 34th US President (1953–61). His main concerns were foreign policy and anti-communism.

78 The eyes of the world are upon you. The hopes and prayers of liberty-loving people everywhere march with you.

1944 Despatch to US forces on D-Day, 6 Jun.

79 Neither a wise man nor a brave man lies down on the tracks of history to wait for the train of the future to run over him.
1952 In *Time*, 6 Oct.

80 I shall go to Korea, to try to end the war.
1952 Presidential campaign pledge, Oct.

81 A soldier's pack is not so heavy a burden as a prisoner's chains.
1953 Inaugural address, 20 Jan.

82 History does not long entrust the care of freedom to the weak or the timid.
1953 Inaugural address, 20 Jan.

83 I just won't get into a pissing contest with that skunk.
1953 Comment to his brother Milton, refusing to publicly contend with Senator Joseph R McCarthy. Quoted in Piers Brandon *Ike* (1986).

84 You have a row of dominoes set up. You knock over the first one, and what will happen to the last is that it will go over very quickly.
1954 Explaining the domino theory in relation to SE Asia, 7 Apr.

85 There can be no law if we were to invoke one code of international conduct for those who oppose us and another for our friends.
1956 Speech on the Suez crisis, 31 Oct.

86 If the United Nations once admits that international disputes can be settled by using force, we will have destroyed the foundation of the organization and our best hope of establishing a world order.
1957 Address to the nation on Israel's invasion of Egypt, 20 Feb.

87 Now, on Friday noon, I am to become a private citizen. I am proud to do so. I look forward to it.
1961 Concluding his farewell address to the nation, 17 Jan.

88 In the councils of government, we must guard against the acquisition of unwarranted influence, whether sought or unsought, by the military-industrial complex. The potential for the disastrous rise of misplaced powers exists and will persist.
1961 Farewell address, Jan.

89 I want…the $60 GI job and no medals on my chest.
1963 To President Truman, 25 Nov. Quoted in Michael R Beschloss *Eisenhower* (1990).

90 There's one thing to be said about being President—nobody can tell you when to sit down.
1964 Speech.

91 A fine man who, in the middle of a stormy lake, knows nothing of swimming.
His initial impression of President Harry S Truman while he was military chief of staff. Quoted in Michael R Beschloss *Eisenhower* (1990).

92 Just what does he think the Presidency *is?*
On being warned by a doctor to avoid 'irritation, frustration, anxiety, fear, and above all else, anger'. Quoted in Michael R Beschloss *Eisenhower* (1990).

93 This embattled shore, portal of freedom, is forever hallowed by the ideals, the valor and the sacrifices of our fellow countrymen.
Inscription at US cemetery near St-Laurent. Quoted in the *New York Times*, 5 Jun 1994.

Eisenstaedt, Alfred 1898–1995

German-born US photographer and photojournalist, renowned for his candid pictures of both everyday life and historic occasions.

94 The most important thing about photographing people is not clicking the shutter…it is clicking with the subject.
1966 *Witness to Our Time.*

95 I want to be a mouse in a mousehole.
1995 On the unobtrusiveness of the photographer. In NPR broadcast, 24 Aug.

Elgar, Sir Edward 1857–1934

British composer. His *Enigma Variations* (1899) and the oratorio *The Dream of Gerontius* (1900) established his reputation as the leading English composer of his generation. He was Master of the King's Musick from 1924.

96 To my friends pictured within.
1899 Dedication to the *Enigma Variations.*

97 My idea is that there is music in the air, music all around us, the world is full of it and you simply take as much as you require.
Quoted in R J Buckley *Sir Edward Elgar* (1905), ch.4.

Elgin, James Bruce 1811–63

British government official. In 1860 he was in China, enforcing the treaty of Tientsin (1858), and his actions included the burning of the Summer Palace in Beijing.

98 You can scarcely imagine the beauty and magnificence of the buildings we burnt.
1860 Letter, 18 Aug. Quoted in Nigel Cameron *Barbarians and Mandarins* (1989) ch.16.

Eliot, George pseudonym of Mary Ann Evans 1819–80

English novelist, renowned for her powers of observation and characterization. Her novels include *Adam Bede*

(1854), *The Mill on the Floss* (1860), *Silas Marner* (1861) and her masterpiece, *Middlemarch* (1871–2).

99 Life is too precious to be spent in this weaving and unweaving of false impressions, and it is better to live quietly under some degree of misrepresentation than to attempt to remove it by the uncertain process of letter-writing.
1856 Letter to Mrs Peter Taylor, 8 Jun. Collected in G S Haight (ed) *The George Eliot Letters* (1954), vol.2.

1 In every parting there is an image of death.
1858 *Scenes of Clerical Life*, ch.10.

2 Errors look so very ugly in persons of small means—one feels they are taking quite a liberty in going astray; whereas people of fortune may naturally indulge in a few delinquencies.
1858 *Scenes of Clerical Life*, ch.25.

3 He knew two kinds of Methodists—the ecstatic and the bilious.
1859 *Adam Bede*, ch.2.

4 We are apt to be kinder to the brutes that love us than to the women that love us. Is it because the brutes are dumb?
1859 *Adam Bede*, ch.4.

5 Young souls, in such pleasant delirum as hers, are as unsympathetic as butterflies sipping nectar.
1859 Of Hetty. *Adam Bede*, ch.9.

6 I aspire to give no more than a faithful account of men and things as they have mirrored themselves in my mind.
1859 *Adam Bede*, ch.17.

7 Our deeds determine us, as much as we determine our deeds; and until we know what has been or will be the peculiar combination of outward with inward facts, which constitute a man's critical actions, it will be better not to think ourselves wise about his character.
1859 *Adam Bede*, ch.29.

8 A maggot must be born i' the rotten cheese to like it.
1859 *Adam Bede*, ch.32.

9 There's no pleasure i' living, if you're to be corked up for iver, and only dribble your mind out by the sly, like a leaky barrel.
1859 Mrs Poyster. *Adam Bede*, ch.32.

10 He was like a cock who thought the sun had risen to hear him crow.
1859 *Adam Bede*, ch.33.

11 Deep, unspeakable suffering may well be called a baptism, a regeneration, the initiation into a new state.

1859 *Adam Bede*, ch.42

12 We hand folks over to God's mercy, and show none ourselves.
1859 *Adam Bede*, ch.42.

13 The mother's yearning, that completest type of the life in another life which is the essence of real human love, feels the presence of the cherished child even in the debased, degraded man.
1859 *Adam Bede*, ch.43.

14 If art does not enlarge men's sympathies, it does nothing morally.
1859 Letter to Charles Bray, 5 Jul.

15 He would punish everyone who deserved it: why, he wouldn't have minded being punished himself if he deserved it; but, then, he never did deserve it.
1860 Of Tom Tulliver. *The Mill on the Floss*, bk.1. ch.5.

16 Anger and jealousy can no more bear to lose sight of their objects than love.
1860 *The Mill on the Floss*, bk.1, ch.10.

17 The Catholics, bad harvests, and the mysterious fluctuations of trade—three evils mankind had to fear.
1860 *The Mill on the Floss*, bk.1, ch.12.

18 In a mind charged with an eager purpose and an unfinished vindictiveness, there is no room for new feelings.
1860 *The Mill on the Floss*, bk.4, ch.3.

19 Our life is determined for us—and it makes the mind very free when we give up wishing and only think of bearing what is laid upon us and doing what is given us to do.
1860 *The Mill on the Floss*, bk.5, ch.1.

20 The dead level of provincial existence.
1860 *The Mill on the Floss*, bk.5, ch.3.

21 The happiest women, like the happiest nations, have no history.
1860 *The Mill on the Floss*, bk.6, ch.3.

22 I should like to know what is the proper function of women, if it is not to make reasons for husbands to stay at home, and still stronger reasons for bachelors to go out.
1860 *The Mill on the Floss*, bk.6, ch.6.

23 'Character' says Novalis, in one of his questionable aphorisms, 'character is destiny.'
1860 *The Mill on the Floss*, bk.6, ch.6.

24 Half the sorrows of women would be averted if they could repress the speech they know to be useless; nay, the speech they have resolved not to make.
1866 *Felix Holt*, ch.2.

25 There is no private life which has not been determined by a wider public life.
1866 *Felix Holt*, ch.3.

26 An election is coming. Universal peace is declared, and the foxes have a sincere interest in prolonging the lives of the poultry.
1866 *Felix Holt*, ch.5.

27 Speech is often barren; but silence also does not necessarily brood over a full nest. Your still fowl, blinking at you without remark, may all the while be sitting on one addled egg; and when it takes to cackling will have nothing to announce but that addled delusion.
1866 *Felix Holt*, ch.15.

28 A woman can hardly ever choose…she is dependent on what happens to her. She must take meaner things, because only meaner things are within her reach.
1866 *Felix Holt*, ch.27.

29 There's many a one who would be idle if hunger didn't pinch him; but the stomach sets us to work.
1866 *Felix Holt*, ch.30.

30 Women were expected to have weak opinions; but the great safeguard of society and of domestic life was, that opinions were not acted on. Sane people did what their neighbours did, so that if any lunatics were at large, one might know and avoid them.
1871–2 *Middlemarch*, bk.1, ch.1.

31 A woman dictates before marriage in order that she may have an appetite for submission afterwards.
1871–2 *Middlemarch*, bk.1, ch.9.

32 He said he should prefer not to know the sources of the Nile, and that there should be some unknown regions preserved as hunting-grounds for the poetic imagination.
1871–2 *Middlemarch*, bk.1, ch.9.

33 Among all forms of mistake, prophecy is the most gratuitous.
1871–2 *Middlemarch*, bk.1, ch.10.

34 Plain women he regarded as he did the other severe facts of life, to be faced with philosophy and investigated by science.
1871–2 *Middlemarch*, bk.1, ch.11.

35 Any one watching keenly the stealthy convergence of human lots, sees a slow preparation of effects from one life on another, which tells like a calculated irony on the indifference or the frozen stare with which we look at our unintroduced neighbour.

1871–2 *Middlemarch*, bk.1, ch.11.

36 To point out other people's errors was a duty that Mr Bulstrode rarely shrank from.
1871–2 *Middlemarch*, bk.2, ch.13.

37 If we had a keen vision and feeling of all ordinary human life, it would be like hearing the grass grow and the squirrel's heart beat, and we should die of that roar which lies on the other side of silence.
1871–2 *Middlemarch*, bk.2, ch.20.

38 We do not expect people to be deeply moved by what is not unusual. That element of tragedy which lies in the very fact of frequency, has not yet wrought itself into the coarse emotion of mankind.
1871–2 *Middlemarch*, bk.2, ch.20.

39 A woman, let her be as good as she may, has got to put up with the life her husband makes for her.
1871–2 *Middlemarch*, bk.3, ch.25.

40 It is an uneasy lot at best, to be what we call highly taught and yet not to enjoy: to be present at this great spectacle of life and never to be liberated from a small hungry shivering self.
1871–2 *Middlemarch*, bk.3, ch.29.

41 A man is seldom ashamed of feeling that he cannot love a woman so well when he sees a certain greatness in her: nature having intended greatness for men.
1871–2 *Middlemarch*, bk.4, ch.39.

42 Gossip is a sort of smoke that comes from the dirty tobacco-pipes of those who diffuse it: it proves nothing but the bad taste of the smoker.
1876 *Daniel Deronda*, bk.2, ch.13.

43 A difference of taste in jokes is a great strain on the affections.
1876 *Daniel Deronda*, bk.2, ch.15.

44 There is a great deal of unmapped country within us which would have to be taken into account in an explanation of our gusts and storms.
1876 *Daniel Deronda*, bk.3, ch.24.

45 Friendships begin with liking or gratitude—roots that can be pulled up.
1876 *Daniel Deronda*, bk.4, ch.32.

Eliot, T(homas) S(tearns) 1888–1965

US-born English poet, dramatist and critic, whose work enshrined the disillusionment of the post-World War I generation and the advance of modernism. His most significant poetic works are *The Waste Land* (1922) and *Four Quartets* (1944). In 1948 he was awarded the Nobel Prize for Literature.

46 Let us go then, you and I,

When the evening is spread out against the sky
Like a patient etherized upon a table.
1915 'The Love Song of J Alfred Prufrock' (first published in
Poetry magazine, collected in *Prufrock and Other Observations*,
1917), opening lines.

47 In the room the women come and go
Talking of Michelangelo.
1915 'The Love Song of J Alfred Prufrock' (first published in
Poetry magazine, collected in *Prufrock and Other Observations*,
1917).

48 Should I, after tea and cakes and ices,
Have the strength to force the moment to its crisis?
1915 'The Love Song of J Alfred Prufrock' (first published in
Poetry magazine, collected in *Prufrock and Other Observations*,
1917), l.79–80.

49 For I have known them all already, known them
all—
Have known the evenings, mornings, afternoons,
I have measured out my life with coffee spoons;
I know the voices dying with a dying fall
Beneath the music from a farther room.
1915 'The Love Song of J Alfred Prufrock' (first published in
Poetry magazine, collected in *Prufrock and Other Observations*,
1917).

50 I should have been a pair of ragged claws
Scuttling across the floors of silent seas.
1915 'The Love Song of J Alfred Prufrock' (first published in
Poetry magazine, collected in *Prufrock and Other Observations*,
1917).

51 I am no prophet—and here's no great matter;
I have seen the moment of my greatness flicker,
And I have seen the eternal Footman hold my coat,
and snicker,
And in short, I was afraid.
1915 'The Love Song of J Alfred Prufrock' (first published in
Poetry magazine, collected in *Prufrock and Other Observations*,
1917).

52 No! I am not Prince Hamlet, nor was meant to be;
Am an attendant lord, one that will do
To swell a progress, start a scene or two,
Advise the prince.
1915 'The Love Song of J Alfred Prufrock' (first published in
Poetry magazine, collected in *Prufrock and Other Observations*,
1917).

53 I grow old...I grow old...
I shall wear the bottoms of my trousers rolled.
1915 'The Love Song of J Alfred Prufrock' (first published in
Poetry magazine, collected in *Prufrock and Other Observations*,
1917), l.120-21.

54 Do I dare to eat a peach?
1915 'The Love Song of J Alfred Prufrock' (first published in
Poetry magazine, collected in *Prufrock and Other Observations*,
1917), l.122.

55 I have heard the mermaids singing, each to each.

I do not think that they will sing to me.
1915 'The Love Song of J Alfred Prufrock' (first published in
Poetry magazine, collected in *Prufrock and Other Observations*,
1917).

56 The winter evening settles down
With smell of steaks in passageways
Six o'clock.
The burnt-out ends of smoky days.
1917 *Prufrock and Other Observations*, 'Preludes', 1.

57 The morning comes to consciousness
Of faint stale smells of beer
From the sawdust-trampled street.
1917 *Prufrock and Other Observations*, 'Preludes', pt.2.

58 Held in a lunar synthesis,
Whispering lunar incantations
Dissolve the floors of memory
And all its clear relations
Its divisions and precisions.
1917 *Prufrock and Other Observations*, 'Rhapsody On a Windy
Night'.

59 Midnight shakes the memory
As a madman shakes a dead geranium.
1917 *Prufrock and Other Observations*, 'Rhapsody On a Windy
Night'.

60 Stand on the highest pavement of the stair—
Lean on a garden urn—
Weave, weave the sunlight in your hair.
1917 *Prufrock and Other Observations*, 'La Figlia Che Piange'.

61 Sometimes these cogitations still amaze
The troubled midnight and the noon's repose.
1917 *Prufrock and Other Observations*, 'La Figlia Che Piange'.

62 I am aware of the damp souls of housemaids
Sprouting despondently at area gates.
1917 *Prufrock and Other Observations*, 'Morning At The
Window'.

63 Webster was much possessed by death
And saw the skull beneath the skin;
And breastless creatures under ground
Leaned backward with a lipless grin.
1919 'Whispers of Immortality'.

64 Uncorseted, her friendly bust
Gives promise of pneumatic bliss.
1919 'Whispers of Immortality'.

65 Polyphiloprogenitive
The sapient sutlers of the Lord
Drift across the window-panes
In the beginning was the Word.
1919 'Mr Eliot's Sunday Morning Service'.

66 Apeneck Sweeney spreads his knees
Letting his arms hang down to laugh,
The zebra stripes along his jaw

Swelling to maculate giraffe.
1919 'Sweeney Among The Nightingales'.

67 And let their liquid siftings fall
To stain the stiff dishonoured shroud.
1919 'Sweeney Among The Nightingales'.

68 Here I am, an old man in a dry month,
Being read to by a boy, waiting for rain.
1919 'Gerontion'.

69 Signs are taken for wonders. 'We would see a sign!'
The word within the word, unable to speak a word,
Swaddled with darkness. In the juvescence of the
year
Came Christ the tiger.
1919 'Gerontion'.

70 After such knowledge, what forgiveness? Think
now
History has many cunning passages, contrived
corridors
And issues, deceives with whispering ambitions,
Guides us by vanities.
1919 'Gerontion'.

71 Neither fear nor courage saves us. Unnatural vices
Are fathered by our heroism. Virtues
Are forced upon us by our impudent crimes.
1919 'Gerontion'.

72 Tenants of the house,
Thoughts of a dry brain in a dry season.
1919 'Gerontion'.

73 Where are the eagles and the trumpets?
Buried beneath some snow-deep Alps.
Over buttered scones and crumpets
Weeping, weeping multitudes
Droop in a hundred A.B.C.'s.
1920 'Cooking Egg'.

74 The emotion of art is impersonal.
1920 *The Sacred Wood*, 'Tradition and Individual Talent'.

75 Poetry is not a turning loose of emotion, but an
escape from emotion; it is not the expression of
personality but an escape from personality.
1920 *The Sacred Wood*, 'Tradition and Individual Talent'.

76 The only way of expressing emotion in the form of
art is by finding an 'objective correlative'…such
that when the external facts, which must terminate
in sensory experience, are given, the emotion is
immediately evoked.
1920 *The Sacred Wood*, 'Hamlet and his Problems'.

77 The bad poet dwells partly in a world of objects
and partly in a world of words, and he never can get
them to fit.
1920 *The Sacred Wood*, 'Swinburne as a Poet'.

78 Immature poets imitate; mature poets steal; bad
poets deface what they take, and good poets make
it into something better, or at least something
different.
1920 *The Sacred Wood*, 'Philip Massinger'.

79 In the seventeenth century a dissociation of
sensibility set in from which we have never
recovered; and this dissociation, as is natural, was
due to the influence of the two most powerful poets
of the century, Milton and Dryden.
1921 *Selected Essays* (1932), 'The Metaphysical Poets'.

80 When a poet's mind is perfectly equipped for its
work, it is constantly amalgamating disparate
experience…in the mind of the poet these
experiences are always forming new wholes.
1921 *Selected Essays* (1932), 'The Metaphysical Poets'.

81 April is the cruellest month, breeding
Lilacs out of the dead land, mixing
Memory and desire, stirring
Dull roots with spring rain.
1922 *The Waste Land*, pt.1, 'The Burial of the Dead'.

82 And I will show you something different from either
Your shadow at morning striding behind you
Or your shadow at evening rising to meet you;
I will show you fear in a handful of dust.
1922 *The Waste Land*, pt.1, 'The Burial of the Dead'.

83 Unreal City,
Under the brown fog of a winter dawn,
a crowd flowed over London Bridge, so many,
I had not thought death had undone so many.
1922 *The Waste Land*, pt.1, 'The Burial of the Dead'.

84 'You! hypocrite lecteur!—mon semblable,—mon
frère!'
1922 *The Waste Land*, pt.1, 'The Burial of the Dead'.
▷ See Baudelaire 76:14.

85 The Chair she sat in, like a burnished throne,
Glowed on the marble.
1922 *The Waste Land*, pt.2, 'A Game of Chess'.
▷ See Shakespeare 905:68.

86 O O O O that Shakespeherian Rag—
It's so elegant
So intelligent.
1922 *The Waste Land*, pt.2, 'A Game of Chess'.

87 Hurry up please it's time.
1922 *The Waste Land*, pt.2, 'A Game of Chess'.

88 Sweet Thames, run softly till I end my song,
Sweet Thames, run softly, for I speak not loud or
long.
But at my back in a cold blast I hear
The rattle of the bones, and chuckle spread from
ear to ear.

1922 *The Waste Land*, pt.3, 'The Fire Sermon'.
▷ See Marvell 658:73.

89 I Tiresias, old man with wrinkled dugs
Perceived the scene, and foretold the rest—
I too awaited the expected guest.
He, the young man carbuncular, arrives,
A small house agent's clerk, with one bold stare,
One of the low on whom assurance sits
As a silk hat on a Bradford millionaire.
1922 *The Waste Land*, pt.3, 'The Fire Sermon'.

90 When lovely woman stoops to folly and
Paces about her room again, alone,
She smoothes her hair with automatic hand,
And puts a record on the gramophone.
1922 *The Waste Land*, pt.3, 'The Fire Sermon'.
▷ See Goldsmith 432:5.

91 A current under sea
Picked his bones in whispers.
1922 *The Waste Land*, pt.4, 'Death By Water'.

92 O you who turn the wheel and look to windward,
Consider Phlebas, who was once handsome and tall
  as you.
1922 *The Waste Land*, pt.4, 'Death By Water'.

93 He who was living is now dead
We who were living are now dying
With a little patience.
1922 *The Waste Land*, pt.5, 'What The Thunder Said'.

94 Who is the third who walks always beside you?
When I count, there are only you and I together
But when I look ahead up the white road
There is always another one walking beside you.
1922 *The Waste Land*, pt.5, 'What The Thunder Said'.

95 In this decayed hole among the mountains
In the faint moonlight, the grass is singing
Over the tumbled graves.
1922 *The Waste Land*, pt.5, 'What The Thunder Said'.

96 The awful daring of a moment's surrender
Which an age of prudence can never retract.
1922 *The Waste Land*, pt.5, 'What The Thunder Said'.

97 These fragments I have shored against my ruins.
1922 *The Waste Land*, pt.5, 'What The Thunder Said'.

98 We are the hollow men
We are the stuffed men
Leaning together
Headpiece filled with straw. Alas!
1925 'The Hollow Men'.

99 This is the dead land
This is cactus land
Here the stone images
Are raised, here they receive
The supplication of a dead man's hand

Under the twinkle of a fading star.
1925 'The Hollow Men'.

1 Between the idea
And the reality
Between the motion
And the act
Falls the shadow.
1925 'The Hollow Men'.

2 This is the way the world ends
Not with a bang but a whimper.
1925 'The Hollow Men', closing lines.

3 A cold coming we had of it,
Just the worst time of the year
For a journey, and such a long journey:
The ways deep and the weather sharp,
The very dead of winter.
1927 'The Journey of the Magi'.

4 But set down
This, set down
This: were we led all that way for
Birth or Death? There was a Birth, certainly,
We had evidence and no doubt. I had seen birth
  and death
But had thought they were different; this Birth was
Hard and bitter agony for us, like Death, our
  death.
We returned to our places, these Kingdoms,
But no longer at ease here, in the old dispensation,
With an alien people clutching their gods.
I should be glad of another death.
1927 'The Journey of the Magi'.

5 All great poetry gives the illusion of a view of life.
1927 'Shakespeare and the Stoicism of Seneca'.

6 We know too much and are convinced of too little.
Our literature is a substitute for religion, and so is
  our religion.
1928 'A Dialogue on Dramatic Poetry', collected in *Selected
Essays* (1932).

7 Genuine poetry can communicate before it is
understood.
1929 *Dante*.

8 Because I do not hope to turn again
Because I do not hope
Because I do not hope to turn.
1930 'Ash Wednesday'.

9 Because these wings are no longer wings to fly
But merely vans to beat the air
The air which is now thoroughly small and dry
Smaller and dryer than the will.
1930 'Ash Wednesday'.

10 Teach us to care and not to care

Teach us to sit still.
1930 'Ash Wednesday'.

11 Lady, three white leopards sat under a juniper-tree
    In the cool of the day.
    1930 'Ash Wednesday', pt.2.

12 Birth, and copulation, and death.
    That's all the facts when you come to brass tacks:
    Birth, and copulation, and death.
    I've been born, and once is enough.
    1932 *Sweeney Agonistes*, 'Fragment of an Agon'.

13 Any man has to, needs to, wants to
    Once in a lifetime, do a girl in.
    1932 *Sweeney Agonistes*, 'Fragment of an Agon'.

14 The people which ceases to care for its literary
    inheritance becomes barbaric; the people which
    ceases to produce literature ceases to move in
    thought and sensibility.
    1933 *The Use of Poetry and the Use of Criticism*.

15 Poetry is not a career, but a mug's game.
    1933 *The Use of Poetry and the Use of Criticism*.

16 But the essential advantage for a poet…is to be able
    to see beneath both beauty and ugliness; to see the
    boredom, and the horror, and the glory.
    1933 *The Use of Poetry and the Use of Criticism*.

17 Where is the Life we have lost in living?
    Where is the wisdom we have lost in knowledge?
    Where is the knowledge we have lost in
      information?
    1934 *The Rock*, pt.1.

18 And the wind shall say: 'Here were decent godless
      people:
    Their only monument the asphalt road
    And a thousand lost golf balls.'
    1934 *The Rock*, pt.1

19 What life have you if you have not life together?
    There is not life that is not in community,
    And no community not lived in praise of God.
    1934 *The Rock*.

20 A book is not harmless merely because no one is
    consciously offended by it.
    1935 *Religion and Literature*.

21 Those who talk of the Bible as a 'monument of
    English prose' are merely admiring it as a
    monument over the grave of Christianity.
    1935 *Religion and Literature*.

22 Time present and time past
    Are both perhaps present in time future,
    And time future contained in time past.
    1935 *Four Quartets*, 'Burnt Norton', pt.1.

23 Footfalls echo in the memory
    Down the passage which we did not take
    Towards the door we never opened
    Into the rose-garden. My words echo
    Thus, in your mind.
    1935 *Four Quartets*, 'Burnt Norton', pt.1.

24 Go, go, go, said the bird: human kind
    Cannot bear very much reality.
    1935 *Four Quartets*, 'Burnt Norton', pt.1.

25 At the still point of the turning world. Neither flesh
      nor fleshless;
    Neither from nor towards; at the still point, there
      the dance is,
    But neither arrest nor movement.
    1935 *Four Quartets*, 'Burnt Norton', pt.2.

26 Time past and time future
    Allow but a little consciousness.
    1935 *Four Quartets*, 'Burnt Norton', pt.2.

27 Only through time time is conquered.
    1935 *Four Quartets*, 'Burnt Norton', pt.2.

28 Time and the bell have buried the day,
    The black cloud carries the sun away.
    1935 *Four Quartets*, 'Burnt Norton', pt.4.

29 After the kingfisher's wing
    Has answered light to light, and is silent, the light is
      still
    At the still point of the turning world.
    1935 *Four Quartets*, 'Burnt Norton', pt.5.

30 Or say that the end precedes the beginning,
    And the end and the beginning were always there
      before the beginning and after the end.
    And all is always now.
    1935 *Four Quartets*, 'Burnt Norton', pt.5.

31 Words strain,
    Crack and sometimes break, under the burden,
    Under the tension, slip, slide, perish,
    Decay with imprecision, will not stay in place,
    Will not stay still.
    1935 *Four Quartets*, 'Burnt Norton', pt.5.

32 Yet we have gone on living,
    Living and partly living.
    1935 *Murder in the Cathedral*, pt.1.

33 The last temptation is the greatest treason:
    To do the right deed for the wrong reason.
    1935 *Murder in the Cathedral*, pt.1.

34 Clear the air! clean the sky! wash the wind! take the
    stone from the stone, take the skin from the arm,
    take the muscle from bone, and wash them.
    1935 *Murder in the Cathedral*, pt.2.

35 Forgive us, O Lord, we acknowledge ourselves

as type of the common man,
Of the men and women who shut the door
and sit by the fire;
Who fear the blessing of God, the loneliness
of the night of God, the surrender required,
the deprivation inflicted;
Who fear the injustice of men less than the
justice of God;
Who fear the hand at the window, the fire
in the thatch, the fist in the tavern,
the push into the canal
Less than we fear the love of God.
1935 *Murder in the Cathedral.*

36 How unpleasant to meet Mr Eliot!
With his features of clerical cut,
And his brow so grim
And his mouth so prim.
1936 'Five-Finger Exercises'.

37 Success is relative:
It is what we can make of the mess we have made of
things.
1939 *The Family Reunion*, pt.2, sc.3.

38 Round and round the circle
Completing the charm
So the knot be unknotted
The cross be uncrossed
The crooked be made straight
And the curse be ended.
1939 *The Family Reunion*, pt.2, sc.3.

39 At first you may think I'm as mad as a hatter
When I tell you a cat must have THREE DIFFERENT
NAMES.
1939 *Old Possum's Book of Practical Cats*, 'The Naming of
Cats'.

40 When you notice a cat in profound meditation
The reason, I tell you, is always the same:
His mind is engaged in a rapt contemplation
Of the thought, of the thought, of the thought of
his name:
His ineffable effable
Effanineffable
Deep and inscrutable singular name.
1939 *Old Possum's Book of Practical Cats*, 'The Naming of
Cats'.

41 Macavity, Macavity, there's no one like Macavity,
There never was a Cat of such deceitfulness and
suavity.
He always has an alibi, and one or two to
spare:
At whatever time the deed took place—MACAVITY
WASN'T THERE!
1939 *Old Possum's Book of Practical Cats*, 'Macavity: The
Mystery Cat'.

42 No *vers* is *libre* for the man who wants to do a good
job.
1940 Introduction to Ezra Pound *Poems.*

43 In my beginning is my end.
1940 *Four Quartets*, 'East Coker', pt.1.

44 I said to my soul, be still, and wait without hope
For hope would be hope for the wrong thing; wait
without love
For love would be love of the wrong thing; there is
yet faith
But the faith and the hope and the love are all in
the waiting.
Wait without thought, for you are not ready for
thought,
So the darkness shall be the light and the stillness
the dancing.
1944 *Four Quartets*, 'East Coker', pt.1.

45 A periphrastic study in a worn-out poetical fashion,
Leaving one still with the intolerable wrestle
With words and meanings.
1940 *Four Quartets*, 'East Coker', pt.1.

46 There is, it seems to us,
At best, only a limited value
In the knowledge derived from experience.
1940 *Four Quartets*, 'East Coker', pt.2.

47 Do not let me hear
Of the wisdom of old men, but rather of their folly,
1940 *Four Quartets*, 'East Coker', pt.2.

48 The only wisdom we can hope to acquire
Is the wisdom of humility: humility is endless.
1940 *Four Quartets*, 'East Coker', pt.2.

49 O dark dark dark. They all go into the dark,
The vacant interstellar spaces, the vacant into the
vacant,
1940 *Four Quartets*, 'East Coker', pt.3.

50 And what you do not know is the only thing you
know
And what you own is what you do not own
And where you are is where you are not.
1940 'East Coker', pt.3.

51 The wounded surgeon plies the steel
That questions the distempered part;
Beneath the bleeding hands we feel
The sharp compassion of the healer's art
Resolving the enigma of the fever chart.
1940 *Four Quartets*, 'East Coker', pt.4.

52 The dripping blood our only drink,
The bloody flesh our only food:
In spite of which we like to think
That we are sound, substantial flesh and blood—
Again, in spite of that, we call this Friday good.
1940 *Four Quartets*, 'East Coker', pt.4.

53 And so each venture
Is a new beginning, a raid on the inarticulate
With shabby equipment always deteriorating
In the general mess of imprecision of feeling,
Undisciplined squads of emotion.
1940 *Four Quartets*, 'East Coker', pt.5.

54 There is only the fight to recover what has been lost
And found and lost again and again: and now,
under conditions
That seem unpropitious. But perhaps neither gain
nor loss.
For us, there is only the trying. The rest is not our
business.
1940 *Four Quartets*, 'East Coker', pt.5.

55 Home is where one starts from. As we grow older
The world becomes stranger, the pattern more
complicated
Of dead and living.
1940 *Four Quartets*, 'East Coker', pt.5.

56 Love is most nearly itself
When here and now cease to matter.
1940 *Four Quartets*, 'East Coker', pt.5.

57 I do not know much about gods; but I think that
the river
Is a strong brown god—sullen, untamed and
intractable,
1941 *Four Quartets*, 'The Dry Salvages', pt.1.

58 The river is within us, the sea is all about us.
1941 *Four Quartets*, 'The Dry Salvages', pt.1.

59 The tolling bell
Measures time not our time, rung by the unhurried
Ground swell, a time
Older than the time of chronometers.
1941 *Four Quartets*, 'The Dry Salvages', pt.1.

60 We had the experience but missed the meaning,
And approach to the meaning restores the
experience
In a different form, beyond any meaning
We can assign to happiness.
1941 *Four Quartets*, 'The Dry Salvages', pt.2.

61 Time the destroyer is time the preserver.
1941 *Four Quartets*, 'The Dry Salvages', pt.2.

62 You cannot face it steadily, but this thing is sure,
That time is no healer: the patient is no longer
here.
1941 *Four Quartets*, 'The Dry Salvages', pt.3.

63 And right action is freedom
From past and future also.
1941 *Four Quartets*, 'The Dry Salvages', pt.5.

64 For most of us, there is only the unattended

Moment, the moment in and out of time.
1941 *Four Quartets*, 'The Dry Salvages', pt.5.

65 These are only hints and guesses,
Hints followed by guesses; and the rest
Is prayer, observance, discipline, thought and
action.
The hint half guessed, the gift half understood, is
Incarnation.
1941 *Four Quartets*, 'The Dry Salvages', pt.5.

66 Here the impossible union
Of spheres of existence is actual,
Here the past and future
Are conquered, and reconciled.
1941 *Four Quartets*, 'The Dry Salvages', pt.5.

67 Midwinter Spring is its own season
Sempiternal though sodden towards sundown,
Suspended in time, between pole and tropic.
1942 *Four Quartets*, 'Little Gidding', pt.1.

68 And glow more intense than blaze of branch, or
brazier,
Stirs the dumb spirit: no wind, but pentecostal fire
In the dark time of the year. Between melting and
freezing
The soul's sap quivers.
1942 *Four Quartets*, 'Little Gidding', pt.1.

69 And what you thought you came for
Is only a shell, a husk of meaning
From which the purpose breaks only when it is
fulfilled
If at all. Either you had no purpose
Or the purpose is beyond the end you figured
And is altered in fulfilment.
1942 *Four Quartets*, 'Little Gidding', pt.1.

70 And what the dead had no speech for, when living,
They can tell you, being dead: the communication
Of the dead is tongued with fire beyond the
language of the living.
1942 *Four Quartets*, 'Little Gidding', pt.1.

71 Dust in the air suspended
Marks the place where a story ended.
1942 *Four Quartets*, 'Little Gidding', pt.2.

72 In the uncertain hour before the morning
Near the ending of interminable night
At the recurrent end of the unending.
1942 *Four Quartets*, 'Little Gidding', pt.2.

73 Since our concern was speech, and speech impelled
us
To purify the dialect of the tribe
And urge the mind to aftersight and foresight.
1942 *Four Quartets*, 'Little Gidding', pt.2.

74 From wrong to wrong the exasperated spirit

Proceeds, unless restored by that refining fire
Where you must move in measure, like a dancer.
1942 _Four Quartets_, 'Little Gidding', pt.2.

75 History may be servitude,
History may be freedom.
1942 _Four Quartets_, 'Little Gidding', pt.3.

76 This is the use of memory:
For liberation—not less of love but expanding
Of love beyond desire, and so liberation
From the future as well as the past.
1942 _Four Quartets_, 'Little Gidding', pt.3.

77 The dove descending breaks the air
With flame of incandescent terror
Of which the tongues declare
The one discharge from sin and error.
1942 _Four Quartets_, 'Little Gidding', pt.4.

78 We shall not cease from exploration
And the end of all our exploring
Will be to arrive where we started
And know the place for the first time.
1942 _Four Quartets_, 'Little Gidding', pt.4.

79 What we call the beginning is often the end
And to make an end is to make a beginning.
The end is where we start from.
1942 _Four Quartets_, 'Little Gidding', pt.5.

80 A people without history
Is not redeemed from time, for history is a
pattern
Of timeless moments.
1942 _Four Quartets_, 'Little Gidding', pt.5.

81 And all shall be well and
All manner of thing shall be well
When the tongues of flame are in-folded
Into a crowned knot of fire
And the fire and the rose are one.
1942 _Four Quartets_, 'Little Gidding', pt.5.

82 Culture may even be described simply as that
which makes life worth living.
1948 _Notes Towards a Definition of Culture_, ch.1.

83 You've missed the point completely, Julia:
There _were_ no tigers. _That_ was the point.
1950 _The Cocktail Party_, act 1, sc.1, opening lines.

84 What is hell?
Hell is oneself,
Hell is alone, the other figures in it
Merely projections. There is nothing to escape
from
And nothing to escape to. One is always alone.
1950 _The Cocktail Party_, act 1, sc.3.

Elizabeth I 1533–1603

Queen of England (from 1558), daughter of Henry VIII and Anne Boleyn. Imprisoned by her Catholic half-sister Mary (later Mary I), she ascended the throne as a Protestant ruler on Mary's death. After several conspiracies she had Mary, Queen of Scots executed (1587) and her subsequent persecution of Catholics led Philip of Spain to send an Armada, which was defeated (1588). Elizabeth never married.

85 If I am to disclose to you what I should prefer if I
follow the inclination of my nature, it is this:
beggar-woman and single, far rather than queen
and married!
1563 Attributed reply to an imperial envoy. Quoted in J E Neale _Queen Elizabeth I_ (1979).

86 Though I be a woman yet I have as good a courage
answerable to my place as ever my father had. I am
your anointed queen. I will never be by violence
constrained to do anything. I thank God I am
indeed endued with such qualities that if I were
turned out of the realm in my petticoat I were able
to live in any place of Christendom.
1566 Speech to a parliamentary delegation, 5 Nov. Quoted in Christopher Haigh _Elizabeth I_ (1988).

87 The doubt of future foes exiles my present joy.
c.1568 'The Doubt of Future Foes'.

88 No foteball player be used or suffered within the
City of London and the liberties thereof upon pain
of imprisonment.
1572 Royal proclamation, banning football from the streets of London.

89 My care is like my shadow in the sun,
Follows me flying, flies when I pursue it,
Stands and lies by me, doth what I have done.
c.1582 'On Monsieur's Departure'.

90 I know that I have the body of a weak and feeble
woman, but I have the heart and stomach of a
king—and a king of England too; and think foul
scorn that Parma or Spain, or any Prince of Europe,
should dare to invade the borders of my realm.
1588 Address at Tilbury on the approach of the Spanish Armada.

91 My lord, we make use of you, not for your bad legs,
but for your good head.
c.1590 To her gout-stricken courtier William Cecil. Quoted in F Chamberlain _Sayings of Queen Elizabeth_ (1923).

92 To be a King and to wear a crown is a thing more
glorious to them that see it than it is pleasant to
them that bear it.
1601 Address to parliament. Quoted in G R Elton _Renaissance and Reformation 1300–1648_ (2nd edn, 1968), p.134.

93 Little man, little man! The word 'must' is not to be
used to princes!

1603 To Robert Cecil when, during her last illness, he told her that she must go to bed. Quoted in Christopher Haigh *Elizabeth I* (1988), p.24.

94 Like strawberry wives, that laid two or three great strawberries at the mouth of their pot, and all the rest were little ones.

Of the Commission of Sales. Quoted in Francis Bacon *Apophthegms New and Old* (1625), no.54.

Elizabeth II 1926–

Queen of the UK and Head of the Commonwealth, daughter of George VI. She was proclaimed Queen on 6 February 1952, and crowned on 2 June 1953. She married Philip, Duke of Edinburgh, in 1947.

95 I think that people will concede that, on this of all days, I should begin my speech with the words, 'My husband and I'.

1972 Speech at a banquet to celebrate her silver wedding anniversary, 20 Nov.

96 Experience shows that great enterprises seldom end with a tidy and satisfactory flourish. Together, we are doing our best to re-establish peace and civil order in the Gulf region, and to help those members of civil and ethnic minorities who continue to suffer through no fault of their own. If we succeed, our military success will have achieved its true objective.

1991 Commenting on the aftermath of the Gulf War in the first address by a British monarch to Congress, 16 May.

Elizabeth, Queen, the Queen Mother

1900–

Queen Consort of King George VI, mother of Elizabeth II. Until her marriage to the King in 1923, she was Lady Elizabeth Bowes-Lyon.

97 I'm glad we've been bombed. It makes me feel I can look the East End in the face.

1940 Comment to a London policeman, 13 Sep. Quoted in John Wheeler-Bennet *King George VI* (1948), pt.3, ch.6.

Elkin, Stanley Lawrence 1930–95

US novelist and short-story writer, Professor of US Literature from 1969. His novels include *Boswell* (1964), *The Magic Kingdom* (1985) and *The MacGuffin* (1991).

98 All books *are* the Book of Job, high moral tests and tasks set in fairy tales, landmined and unforgiving as golf greens, as steeplechase and gameboard and obstacle course.

1991 'The Future of the Novel', in the *New York Times*, 17 Feb.

99 Story is just just deserts…man in the crucible like jack in the box.

1991 'The Future of the Novel', in the *New York Times*, 17 Feb.

Ellerton, John 1826–93

English cleric, hymnologist, hymnwriter and translator.

1 God the Omnipotent! King, who ordainest
   Great winds Thy clarions, lightnings Thy sword.
   1866 Hymn (with Henry Fothergill Chorley, 1808–72).

2 The day thou gavest, Lord, is ended,
   The darkness falls at Thy behest.
   1870 *A Liturgy for Missionary Meetings*, 'The Day Thou Gavest'.

Ellington, Duke (Edward Kennedy)

1899–1974

US composer, band-leader and pianist. He founded his first regular group in New York in 1924 and became a key figure in orchestral jazz. He composed about 2000 works, including 'Mood Indigo' and 'Sophisticated Lady'.

3 Playing bop is like playing Scrabble with all the vowels missing.
   1954 In *Look*, 10 Aug.

4 When it sounds good, it *is* good.
   1957 *Such Sweet Thunder*, programme note.

5 Bubber was the first man I heard use the expression, 'it don't mean a thing if it ain't got that swing.' Everything, and I repeat, everything had to swing.
   1965 Of trumpeter Bubber Miley. 'The Most Essential Instrument', in *Jazz Journal*, Dec.

6 New music? Hell, there's been no new music since Stravinsky.
   1970 Quoted in D Jewell *Duke* (1977).

7 Music is my mistress, and she plays second fiddle to none.
   1973 *Music Is My Mistress*.

Elliot, Jean also known as *Jane Elliot*

1727–1805

Scottish poet and songwriter, whose only surviving work, based on traditional versions, was written as a lament for the Battle of Flodden.

8 I've heard the lilting at our yowe-milking,
   Lasses a-lilting before the dawn o' day;
   But now they are moaning on ilka green loaning:
   'The Flowers of the Forest are a' wede away'.
   1769 'The Flowers of the Forest', stanza 1.
   ▷ See Cockburn 272:61.

Elliott, Charlotte 1789–1871

English religious poet and hymnwriter.

9 Just as I am, without one plea

But that Thy blood was shed for me,
And that Thou bid'st me come to Thee,
O Lamb of God, I come!
1834 *Invalid's Hymn Book*, 'Just As I Am'.

Elliott, Sir Claude Aurelius 1888–1973

English schoolmaster, head and Provost of Eton College.

10 I've often thought I should like to have a set of postcards printed: 'Dear Sir or Madam, Thank you for your communication. Go to hell. Yours sincerely.'
Quoted in the *Times Literary Supplement*, 22 Jan 1988.

Ellis, George 1753–1815

British poet, born in the West Indies. He co-founded the Tory *Anti-Jacobin* (1797) and made important translations of Middle English verse.

11 Snowy, Flowy, Blowy,
Showery, Flowery, Bowery,
Hoppy, Croppy, Droppy,
Breezy, Sneezy, Freezy.
'The Twelve Months'.

Ellison, Harlan Jay 1934–

US novelist, essayist, critic, and editor. He has written mainly in the genres of science fiction and fantasy, where he has been a radical and outspoken contributor.

12 I Have No Mouth And I Must Scream.
1967 Title of story collection.

13 The reason men are greater than animals isn't because we can dream of the stars…it's because we have something they haven't. Greed.
1970 *The Glass Teat*, introduction.

14 Our childhoods are sowing the wind, our adulthoods are reaping the whirlwind.
1974 *Approaching Oblivion*, introduction.

15 All The Lies That Are My Life.
1989 Title of autobiography.

Ellison, Ralph Waldo 1914–94

US novelist, best known for his classic account of black urban existence, *Invisible Man*, his only completed novel. He also wrote essays on music and culture.

16 I am an invisible man. No, I am not a spook like those who haunted Edgar Allen Poe; nor am I one of your Hollywood-movie ectoplasms. I am a man of substance, of flesh and bone, fibre and liquids— and I might even be said to possess a mind. I am invisible, understand, simply because people refuse to see me… When they approach me they see only my surroundings, themselves, or figments of their imagination—indeed, everything and anything except me.
1952 *Invisible Man*, prologue.

17 I was never more hated than when I tried to be honest… On the other hand, I've never been more loved and appreciated than when I tried to 'justify' and affirm someone's mistaken beliefs; or when I've tried to give my friends the incorrect, absurd answers they wished to hear.
1952 *Invisible Man*, epilogue.

18 All novels are about certain minorities: the individual is a minority.
1955 Interview in *Paris Review*, Spring.

19 Part of the problem for the invisible man was that he was invisible to himself, that he didn't grasp his own complexity.
1992 Quoted by Keith Botsford in Ellison's obituary, 18 Apr 1994, in the *Independent*.

Ellwood, David T 1953–

US economist, Professor at Kennedy School, Harvard University.

20 The chief source of economic insecurity in America used to be growing old; now it's being born into or raised in a single-parent family.
1991 In the *Washington Post*, 22 Feb.

Eltit, Diamela 1949–

Chilean novelist. Her novels are complex and experimental, but she has found a devoted readership among intellectuals and feminist circles.

21 *Para decirlo de otra manera, no es la herida la que causó el grito, sino exactamente a la inversa; para herirse es preciso el grito, todo lo demás es un pretexto.*

In other words, it was not the wound that caused the scream, but precisely the opposite: to get wounded one needs the scream; the rest is only a pretext.
1983 *Lumpérica*, 1

Elton, Sir Geoffrey Rudolph 1921–

British historian, Professor at Cambridge University.

22 When I meet a historian who cannot think that there have been great men, great men moreover in politics, I feel myself in the presence of a bad historian; and there are times when I incline to judge all historians by their opinion of Winston Churchill—whether they can see that, no matter how much better the details, often damaging, of man and career become known, he still remains, quite simply, a great man.
1970 *Political History*, ch.2.

Eluard, Paul pseudonym of *Eugène Grindel*
1895–1952

French writer, a founder of the Surrealist movement with which he later parted (1938). He was active in political affairs, in the Resistance and the Communist party.

23 *Le poète est celui qui inspire bien plus que celui qui est inspiré.*

The poet is more the inspirer than the one who is inspired.
1936 *L'Evidence poétique.*

24 *Je suis né pour te connaître
Pour te nommer
Liberté.*

I was born to know you
To give you your name:
Freedom.
1942 *Poésie et Vérité*, 'Liberté'.

25 *Adieu tristesse
Bonjour tristesse.*

Farewell sadness
Hello sadness.
1942 *Poésie et Vérité*, 'La vie immédiate'.

Emerson, Ralph Waldo 1803–82

US philosopher and poet, a central figure of the transcendentalist movement. He was a minister in the Unitarian church, but resigned after a controversy over his belief in spiritual independence.

26 By the rude bridge that arched the flood,
Their flag to April's breeze unfurled,
Here once the embattled farmers stood
And fired the shot heard around the world.
1837 'Concord Hymn', opening lines. This poem was sung on 4 Jul 1837 at the dedication of the battle monument commemorating the battle of 19 Apr 1775.

27 This time, like all times, is a very good one, if we but know what to do with it.
1837 'The American Scholar', lecture at Harvard University.

28 All are needed by each one;
Nothing is fair or good alone.
1839 'Each and All', l.11-12.

29 The only gift is a portion of thyself.
1841 *Essays: Second Series*, 'Gifts'.

30 In every work of genius we recognize our own rejected thoughts: they come back to us with a certain alienated majesty.
1841 *Essays: First Series*, 'Self-Reliance'.

31 Every Stoic was a Stoic; but in Christendom where is the Christian?
1841 *Essays: First Series*, 'Self-Reliance'.

32 Whoso would be a man must be a nonconformist.
1841 *Essays: First Series*, 'Self-Reliance'.

33 A foolish consistency is the hobgoblin of little minds, adored by little statesmen and philosophers and divines. With consistency a great soul has simply nothing to do.
1841 *Essays: First Series*, 'Self-Reliance'.

34 To be great is to be misunderstood.
1841 *Essays: First Series*, 'Self-Reliance'.

35 Nothing can bring you peace but yourself.
1841 *Essays: First Series*, 'Self-Reliance'.

36 The dice of God are always loaded.
1841 *Essays: First Series*, 'Compensation'.

37 There is properly no history; only biography.
1841 *Essays: First Series*, 'History'.

38 All mankind love a lover.
1841 *Essays: First Series*, 'Love'.

39 A friend may well be reckoned the masterpiece of nature.
1841 *Essays: First Series*, 'Friendship'.

40 The only reward of virtue is virtue; the only way to have a friend is to be one.
1841 *Essays: First Series*, 'Friendship'.

41 In skating over thin ice, our safety is in our speed.
1841 *Essays: First Series*, 'Prudence'.

42 People wish to be settled: only as far as they are unsettled is there any hope for them.
1841 *Essays: First Series*, 'Circles'.

43 Nothing great was ever achieved without enthusiasm.
1841 *Essays: First Series*, 'Circles'.

44 Though we travel the world over to find the beautiful, we must carry it with us, or we find it not.
1841 *Essays: First Series*, 'Art'.

45 In sculpture, did ever anybody call the Apollo a fancy piece? Or say of the Laocoön how it might be made different? A masterpiece of art has in the mind a fixed place in the chain of being, as much as a plant or a crystal.
1841 'Thoughts on Art', in *The Dial*, vol.1, no.3, Jan.

46 Have I a lover
Who is noble and free?
I would he were nobler
Than to love me.
1841 'The Sphinx', stanza 12.

47 The reward of a thing well done is to have done it.

1844 'New England Reformers', lecture to the Society, 3 Mar.

48 It is not metres, but a metre-making argument, that makes a poem.
1844 *Essays: Second Series*, 'The Poet'.

49 Let the Stoics say what they please, we do not eat for the good of living, but because the meat is savory and the appetite is keen.
1844 *Essays: Second Series*, 'Nature'.

50 The only gift is a portion of thyself.
1844 *Essays: Second Series*, 'Gifts'.

51 Every man is wanted, and no man is wanted much.
1844 *Essays: Second Series*, 'Nominalist and Realist'.

52 Things are in the saddle,
And ride mankind.
1847 *Poems*, 'Ode', dedicated to W H Channing.

53 Belief consists in affirming the affirmations of the soul; unbelief, in denying them.
1850 *Representative Men*, 'Montaigne; or, The Skeptic'.

54 Is not marriage an open question, when it is alleged, from the beginning of the world, that such as are in the institution wish to get out; and such as are out wish to get in.
1850 *Representative Men*, 'Montaigne; or, The Skeptic'.

55 Keep cool: it will be all one a hundred years hence.
1850 *Representative Men*, 'Montaigne; or, The Skeptic'.

56 I can reason down or deny everything, except this perpetual Belly: feed he must and will, and I cannot make him respectable.
1850 *Representative Men*, 'Montaigne; or, The Skeptic'.

57 The world is upheld by the veracity of good men: they make the earth wholesome.
1850 *Representative Men*, 'Uses of Great Men'.

58 Every hero becomes a bore at last.
1850 *Representative Men*, 'Uses of Great Men'.

59 Perpetual modernness is the measure of merit in every work of art.
1850 *Representative Men*, 'Plato'.

60 Men's actions are too strong for them. Show me a man who has acted, and who has not been the victim and slave of his action.
1850 *Representative Men*, 'Goethe'.

61 The aristocrat is the democrat ripe, and gone to seed.
1850 *Representative Men*, 'Napoleon, The Man of the World'.

62 As long as our civilization is essentially one of property, of fences, of exclusiveness, it will be

mocked by delusions. Our riches will leave us sick; there will be bitterness in our laughter; and our wine will burn our mouth.
1850 *Representative Men*, 'Napoleon, The Man of the World'.

63 They have in themselves what they value in their horses, mettle and bottom.
1856 Of Englishmen. *English Traits*, 'Manners'.

64 If the red slayer think he slays,
Or if the slain think he is slain,
They know not well the subtle ways
I keep, and pass, and turn again.
1857 'Brahma'. Collected in *May Day* (1867).
▷ See Lang 579:67.

65 A person seldom falls sick, but the bystanders are animated with a faint hope that he will die.
1860 *The Conduct of Life*, 'Considerations by the Way'.

66 Art is a jealous mistress, and if a man have a genius for painting, poetry, music, architecture, or philosophy, he makes a bad husband and an ill provider.
1860 *The Conduct of Life*, 'Wealth'.

67 We are born believing. A man bears beliefs as a tree bears apples.
1860 *The Conduct of Life*, 'Worship'.

68 Immortality will come to such as are fit for it, and he who would be a great soul in future must be a great soul now.
1860 *The Conduct of Life*, 'Worship'.

69 The louder he talked of his honour, the faster we counted our spoons.
1860 *The Conduct of Life*, 'Worship'.

70 The revelation of Thought takes men out of servitude into freedom.
1860 *The Conduct of Life*, 'Fate'.

71 He has not learned the lesson of life who does not every day surmount a fear.
1870 *Society and Solitude*, 'Courage'.

72 Raphael paints wisdom; Handel sings it, Phidias carves it, Shakespeare writes it, Wren builds it, Columbus sails it, Luther preaches it, Washington arms it, Watt mechanizes it.
1870 *Society and Solitude*, 'Art'.

73 Hitch your wagon to a star.
1870 *Society and Solitude*, 'Civilization'.

74 We boil at different degrees.
1870 *Society and Solitude*, 'Eloquence'.

75 Can anybody remember when the times were not hard, and money was not scarce?
1870 *Society and Solitude*, 'Works and Days'.

76 We do not count a man's years, until he has nothing
    else to count.
    1870 *Society and Solitude*, 'Old Age'.

77 America is a country of young men.
    1870 *Society and Solitude*, 'Old Age'.

78 A rogue alive to the ludicrous is still convertible. If
    that sense is lost, his fellow-men can do little for
    him.
    1876 *Letters and Social Aims*, 'The Comic'.

79 Music is the poor man's Parnassus.
    1876 *Letters and Social Aims*, 'Poetry and Imagination'.

Emery, Jane

80 As thin and neat as a furled umbrella.
    1992 On Rose Macaulay. *Rose Macaulay*.

Emmet, Robert 1778–1803

Irish patriot, member of the United Irishmen. In 1803 he
plotted an insurrection against the English, and was
hanged after returning from the Wicklow Mountains for a
last meeting with his sweetheart.

81 I have but one request to make at my departure
    from this world, it is—the charity of its silence. Let
    no man write my epitaph; for as no man who
    knows my motives, dare now vindicate them, let no
    prejudice or ignorance asperse them. Let them rest
    in obscurity and peace! Let my memory be left in
    oblivion, and my tomb remain uninscribed, until
    other times and other men can do justice to my
    character. When my country takes her place among
    the nations of the earth, *then*, and *not till then*, let
    my epitaph be written.
    1803 Speech before being sentenced.

Empson, Sir William 1906–84

English critic and poet. He established his reputation with
his first book on textual criticism, *Seven Types of
Ambiguity* (1930, revised 1947). An edition of *Collected
Poems* was published in 1955.

82 Seven Types of Ambiguity.
    1930 Title of book.

83 Slowly the poison the whole blood stream fills.
    It is not the effort or the failure tires.
    The waste remains, the waste remains and kills.
    1935 'Missing Dates'.

84 Ripeness is all; her in her cooling planet
    Revere; do not presume to think her wasted.
    1935 'To An Old Lady'.

85 But as to risings, I can tell you why.
    It is on contradiction that they grow.
    It seemed the best thing to be up and go.

Up was the heartening and the strong reply.
The heart of standing is we cannot fly.
    1935 'Aubade'.

86 Waiting for the end, boys, waiting for the end.
    What is there to be or do?
    What's become of me or you?
    1940 'Just a Smack at Auden'.

Engels, Friedrich 1820–95

German socialist philosopher, founder of 'scientific
socialism'. He first met Karl Marx in Brussels in 1844,
collaborated with him on the *Communist Manifesto*
(1848), and later edited and translated Marx's writings.

87 [The] English proletariat is becoming more and
    more bourgeois, so that this most bourgeois of all
    nations is apparently aiming ultimately at the
    possession of a bourgeois aristocracy and a
    bourgeois proletariat *as well as* a bourgeoisie. For a
    nation which exploits the whole world this is of
    course to a certain extent justifiable.
    1858 Letter to Karl Marx, 7 Oct.

88 *Der Staat wird nicht 'abgeschafft', er stirbt ab.*

    The state is not 'abolished'; it withers away.
    1878 *Anti-Dühring*, pt.3, ch.2.

89 The British Labour movement is today, and for
    many years has been, working in a narrow circle of
    strikes that are looked upon, not as an expedient,
    and not as a means of propaganda, but as an
    ultimate aim.
    1878 Letter to Eduard Bernstein, 17 Jul.

90 The society that will organize production on the
    basis of a free and equal association of the
    producers will put the whole machinery of the state
    where it will then belong: into the museum of
    antiquities, by the side of the spinning wheel and
    the bronze axe.
    1884 *The Origin of the Family, Private Property, and the State.*

Engle, Paul Hamilton 1908–91

US poet, novelist and critic, whose writing is formal,
elegant and accessible. He ran courses in literature and
writing in his native Iowa.

91 Poetry—tries to tell you about a vision in the
    unvisionary language of farm, city and love.
    1956 In *Life*, 28 May.

Ennius, Quintus Ennius c.239–169 BC

Roman poet, probably of Greek extraction. He was a
friend of Scipio Africanus the Elder, and he introduced
the hexameter into Latin. Only fragments have survived
of his work.

92 *Quod est ante pedes nemo spectat, caeli scrutantur
    plagas.*

No one regards the things before his feet, but views with care the regions of the sky.

Fragment of *Iphigeneia*, quoted in Cicero *De Divinatione*, bk.2 (translated by W A Falconer, 1979).

93 How like us is that ugly brute, the ape!

Quoted in Cicero *De Divinatione*, bk.50 (translated by H Rackham, 1942).

Enright, D(ennis) J(oseph) 1920–

English poet, critic and literary journalist. He has held posts in universities around the world (1947–80), although his humanistic work rejects academic politics.

94 Metaphysical lederhosen.

On the murky philosophizing and cumbrous symbolism of German novels. Quoted by John Gross in the *New York Times*, 20 Jan 1987.

Ephorus of Cumæ c.400–330 BC

Greek historian.

95 Music was invented to deceive and delude mankind.

History, preface.

Ephron, Nora 1941–

US screenwriter and director.

96 I always say that a successful parent is one who raises a child so that they can pay for their own psychoanalysis.

1995 In *The Guardian*, 26 Jun.

Epstein, Julius J 1909–

US screenwriter, twin brother of Philip Epstein. The two worked as a screenwriting team for many years on films such as *Casablanca* (1942) and *My Foolish Heart* (1949).

97 Of all the gin joints in all the towns in all the world, she walks into mine.

1942 Humphrey Bogart as Rick in *Casablanca* (with Philip G Epstein and Howard Koch).

98 If she can stand it, I can. Play it!

1942 Humphrey Bogart as Rick in *Casablanca* (with Philip G Epstein and Howard Koch). The line is commonly rendered 'Play it again, Sam', a conflation with an earlier line of Ingrid Bergman, 'Play it, Sam. Play *As Time Goes By*.'

99 Here's looking at you, kid.

1942 Humphrey Bogart as Rick in *Casablanca* (with Philip G Epstein and Howard Koch).

1 I'm no good at being noble, but it doesn't take much to see that the problems of three little people don't amount to a hill of beans in this crazy world.

1942 Humphrey Bogart as Rick in *Casablanca* (with Philip G Epstein and Howard Koch).

2 If that plane leaves the ground and you're not with him, you'll regret it. Maybe not today, maybe not tomorrow, but soon and for the rest of your life.

1942 Humphrey Bogart as Rick in *Casablanca* (with Philip G Epstein and Howard Koch).

3 Major Strasser has been shot. Round up the usual suspects.

1942 Claude Rains as Captain Louis Renault in *Casablanca* (with Philip G Epstein and Howard Koch).

4 A woman is beautiful only when she is loved.

1944 *Mr Skeffington* (with Philip Epstein).

5 Honeymoon's over—time to get married.

1972 *Pete 'n Tillie*.

6 When you've reached my age, and your friends are beginning to worry about you, blind dates are a way of life.

1972 *Pete 'n Tillie*.

7 Dear J W, have the bank president finish the script.

Response to a note from Jack Warner which had read 'Railroad presidents get in at nine o'clock, bank presidents get in at nine o'clock, read your contract, you're coming in at nine o'clock.' Quoted in Aljean Harmetz *Round Up the Usual Suspects* (1993).

Erasmus, Desiderius originally Gerrit Gerritszoon 1466–1536

Dutch humanist and scholar, author of the satire *Encomium Moriae* (The Praise of Folly, 1509) and *Colloquia familiaria* (1519), an audacious treatment of Church abuses. Other works include the first translation of the Greek New Testament.

8 *In regione caecorum rex est luscus.*

In the country of the blind the one-eyed man is king.

c.1500 *Adages*, bk.3, century 4, no.96.

9 Let a king recall that it is better to improve his realm than to increase his territory.

1517 *Querela Pacis*.

Ernst, Max 1891–1976

German-born artist, a founder of the Dada group and later a key figure of Surrealism. He settled in the US in 1941 but returned to France in 1953.

10 The artist is a spectator, indifferent or impassioned, at the birth of his work, and observes the phases of its development.

Quoted in Saranne Alexandrian *Surrealist Art* (1970).

11 Collage is a supersensitive and scrupulously accurate instrument, similar to a seismograph, which is able to record the exact amount of the possibility of human happiness at any period.

Quoted in Saranne Alexandrian *Surrealist Art* (1970).

Ertz, Susan pseudonym of *Mrs Ronald McCrindle* c.1894–1985

US novelist, born in England. She was the author of a great many popular novels.

12 Someone has somewhere commented on the fact that millions long for immortality who don't know what to do with themselves on a rainy Sunday afternoon.
1943 *Anger in the Sky*, ch.5.

Etherege, Sir George c.1635–1692

English dramatist, who spent most of his life in royal service abroad. Inspired by Molière, he founded the comedy of intrigue in English literature.

13 Like dancers on the ropes poor poets fare,
Most perish young, the rest in danger are.
1676 *The Man of Mode or, Sir Fopling Flutter*, prologue.

14 What a dull, insipid thing is a billet-doux written in cold blood, after the heat of the business is over!
1676 *The Man of Mode or, Sir Fopling Flutter*, act 1, sc.1.

15 Next to the coming to a good understanding with a new mistress, I love a quarrel with an old one.
1676 *The Man of Mode or, Sir Fopling Flutter*, act 1, sc.1.

16 I know he is a devil, but he has something of the angel yet undefaced in him, which makes him so charming and agreeable that I must love him, be he never so wicked.
1676 *The Man of Mode or, Sir Fopling Flutter*, act 2, sc.2.

17 We are not masters of our own affections; our inclinations daily alter: now we love pleasure, and anon we shall dote on business. Human frailty will have it so, and who can help it?
1676 *The Man of Mode or, Sir Fopling Flutter*, act 2, sc.2.

18 When love grows diseased, the best thing we can do is to put it to a violent death. I cannot endure the torture of a lingering and consumptive passion.
1676 *The Man of Mode or, Sir Fopling Flutter*, act 2, sc.2.

19 I must confess I am a fop in my heart; ill customs influence my very senses, and I have been so used to affectation that without the help of the air of the court what is natural cannot touch me.
1688 Letter to Mr Poley, 12 Jan.

Euclid 4c BC

Greek mathematician, best known for his 13-volume work *The Elements*, dealing with plane and solid geometry and arithmetic.

20 That which was to be proved.
c.300 BC *Elementa*, bk.1, proposition 5. Although originally written in Greek, this phrase is usually quoted in its Latin form, 'Quod erat demonstrandum', sometimes abbreviated to 'QED'.

21 There is no 'royal road' to geometry.
c.300 BC Response to Ptolemy I, when asked if there were an easier way to solve theorems. Quoted in Proclus *Commentary on the First Book of Euclid's Elementa*, prologue.

Eudamidas 4c BC

King of Sparta, the brother of Agis I whom he succeeded in 331/330 BC.

22 The speech is admirable, but the speaker is not to be trusted; for he has never been amid the blare of trumpets.
Of a philosopher who had claimed that philosophers were the only good generals. Quoted in Plutarch *Apophthegmata Laconica*, 220E (translated by F C Babbitt, 1931).

Euripides 480 or 484–406 BC

Greek dramatist. Of more than 80 plays only 18 survive complete. He won the tragic prize only five times, but his plays gained popularity after his death.

23 Regard this day's life as yours, but all else as Fortune's.
Alcestis, l.788-9 (translated by D Kovacs, 1994).

24 I have found nothing stronger than Necessity.
Alcestis, l.965 (translated by D Kovacs, 1994).

25 Nothing else that a wife may suffer, equals this: if she loses her husband, she loses her life.
Andromacha, l.375-6.

26 Women's love is for their men, not for their children.
Electra, l.265.

27 None wise dares hopeless venture.
Helena, l.811 (translated by A S Way, 1959).

28 The life of men is painful.
Hippolytus, l.190.

29 It is necessary for mortals to be worn with toil.
Hippolytus, l.207.

30 Your very silence is your confession.
Clytaemnestra to Agamemnon, realizing that he plans to sacrifice their daughter, Iphigenia, to secure favourable winds during the Greek expedition against Troy. *Iphigenia Aulidensis*, l.1142.

31 The meanest life is better than the most glorious death.
Iphigeneia Aulidensis, l.1252 (translated by W S Merwin and G E Dimock Jr, 1978).

32 Wrath brings mortal men their gravest hurt.
Medea, l.1080 (translated by D Kovacs, 1994).

33 A change is always nice.
Orestes, l.234 (translated by M L West, 1987).

34 Lucky is the man who has been successful with his children and not got ones who are notorious disasters.

Orestes, l.542–3 (translated by M L West, 1987).

35 And wealth abides not, it is but for a day.

Phoenissae, l.558.

Eusebius c.264–340 AD

Greek Christian writer, bishop of Caesarea in Palestine. His many works include a *Chronicon* (History of the World), an ecclesiastical history and a biography of Constantine.

36 *In hoc signo vinces.*

In this sign you shall be victorious.

His translation of a Greek description of the sign which appeared to Constantine before the battle of the Milvian bridge in 312, which led to his conversion to Christianity. *Vita Constantini*, 1.28.

Evans, Bergen 1904–78

US scholar and literary critic, Professor of English at Indiana University.

37 It was said of Metternich that he was so conservative that had *he* been present at the Creation, he would have begged God to have retained Chaos.

1968 Note in his *Dictionary of Quotations*.

Evans, Dame Edith 1888–1976

English actress, best remembered for her starchy Lady Bracknell in Oscar Wilde's *The Importance of Being Earnest* (1939), which she also played on film.

38 People always ask me the most ridiculous questions. They want to know, 'How do you approach a role?' Well, I don't know. I approach it by first saying yes, then getting on with the bloody thing.

Attributed.

Evans, George Essex 1863–1909

Australian poet, born in England. A journalist and literary editor, he is best known for his patriotic ceremonial verse.

39 Not as the songs of other lands
Her song shall be.

'An Australian Symphony', in *Collected Verse* (1920).

Evans, Walker 1903–75

US photographer, chronicler of the harsh life in the rural South during the Great Depression of the 1930s. His photographs appear in James Agee's *Let Us Now Praise Famous Men* (1941).

40 People out of work are not given to talking much about the one thing on their minds. You only sense by indirection, degrees of anger, shades of humiliation and echoes of fear.

Quoted in *Fortune*, 11 Feb 1980.

Evelyn, John 1620–1706

English diarist. His *Diary*, which covers the years 1641–1706, offers an insight into life in post-Restoration England.

41 This knight was indeed a valiant Gent: but not a little given to romance, when he spake of himself.

1651 Diary entry, 6 Sep.

42 I saw *Hamlet Prince of Denmark* played, but now the old plays begin to disgust this refined age.

1661 Diary entry, 26 Nov.

Ewart, Gavin Buchanan 1916–95

Scottish-born poet. His poems are often humorous or scatological in nature, and frequently mimic comic popular forms like the limerick. He published his first book of poems in 1939.

43 Miss Twye was soaping her breasts in the bath
When she heard behind her a meaning laugh
And to her amazement she discovered
A wicked man in the bathroom cupboard.

1939 'Miss Twye'.

44 Sex suppressed will go berserk,
But it keeps us all alive.
It's a wonderful change from wives and work
And it ends at half past five.

1966 'Office Friendships'.

45 Would you rather live in lively London
or where a young penguin lies screaming?

1977 *Where a Young Penguin Lies Screaming*, epigraph.

46 He's very popular among his mates.
I think I'm Auden, he thinks he's Yeats.

1986 'Seamus Heaney'.

47 On the Last Day the wrecks will surface over the sea.

1986 'Resurrection'.

Ewer, William Norman 1885–1976

British writer.

48 How odd
Of God
To choose
The Jews.

1924 In *The Week-End Book*.

Fackenheim, Emil L 1916–

Jewish rabbi and philosopher, Professor at the University of Toronto.

49 Had every Christian in Hitler's Europe followed the example of the king of Denmark and decided to put on the yellow star, there would be today neither despair in the church nor talk of the death of God.

1968 *Quest for Past and Future.*

Fadiman, Clifton 1904–99

US writer, literary critic and lecturer. He worked as a book reviewer for the *New Yorker*.

50 Liquor is not a necessity. It is a means of momentarily sidestepping necessity.

1955 *Party of One*, 'From My Notebooks'.

51 The mama of dada.

1955 Of Gertrude Stein. *Party of One.*

52 Cheese, milk's leap toward immortality.

1957 *Any Number Can Play*, 'The Cheese Stands Alone'.

53 The police dog of American fiction, except that his hatred is not the result of mere crabbedness but of an eye that sees too deep for comfort.

Of US writer Ring Lardner. Quoted in Scott Meredith *George S Kaufman and His Friends* (1974).

54 Poetry in a bottle.

1985 Of wine. In *Manhattan Inc*, Jul.

Falkland, Lucius Cary, Viscount 1610–43

English statesman and writer, whose house at Tew attracted the brightest intellects of Oxford and London. A Royalist during the Civil War, he was Secretary of State in 1642 and was killed at the first Battle of Newbury.

55 When it is not necessary to change, it is necessary not to change.

1641 Speech, House of Commons, 22 Nov. Collected as 'A Speech concerning Episcopacy' in *Discourses of Infallibility* (1660).

Faludi, Susan 1960–

US journalist and writer, staff writer with the *Wall Street Journal*. Her controversial and award-winning study *Backlash* (1991) argues that there is a male reaction against feminism in contemporary society.

56 The more women are paid, the less eager they are to marry.

1992 *Backlash* (UK edn), ch.2, 'Man Shortages and Barren Wombs'.

57 Social scientists *could* supply plenty of research to show that one member of the family, at least, is happier and more well adjusted when mum stays home and looks after the children. But that person is dad—a finding of limited use to backlash publicists.

1992 *Backlash* (UK edn), ch.2, 'Man Shortages and Barren Wombs'.

58 A backlash against women's rights is nothing new. Indeed, it's a recurring phenomenon: it returns every time women begin to make some headway towards equality, a seemingly inevitable early frost to the brief flowerings of feminism.

1992 *Backlash* (UK edn), ch.3, 'Backlashes Then and Now.'

Fanon, Frantz Omar 1925–61

French West Indian psychoanalyst and social philosopher, editor of *El Moudjahid* in Tunis and Ambassador to Ghana. He is best remembered for his critiques of colonialism.

59 *Aux colonies, l'infrastructure économique est également une superstructure. La cause est conséquence: on est riche parce que blanc, on est blanc parce que riche.*

In the colonies the economic substructure is also a superstructure. The cause is the consequence; you are rich because you are white, you are white because you are rich.

1961 *Les Damnés de la terre* (The Wretched of the Earth, translated by Constance Farrington, 1965), ch.1, 'Concerning Violence'.

60 *Le colonialisme ne se satisfait pas d'enserrer le peuple dans ses mailles, de vider le cerveau colonisé de toute forme et de tout contenu. Par une sorte de perversion de la logique, il s'oriente vers le passé du peuple opprimé, le distort, le défigure, l'anéantit.*

Colonialism is not satisfied merely with holding a people in its grip and emptying the native's brain of all form and content. By a kind of perverted logic, it turns to the past of the oppressed people, and distorts, disfigures and destroys it.

1961 *Les Damnés de la terre* (The Wretched of the Earth, translated by Constance Farrington, 1965), ch.4, 'On National Culture'.

61 *Le colonialisme accule le peuple dominé à se poser constamment la question: 'Qui suis-je en réalité?'*

Colonialism forces the people it dominates to ask themselves the question constantly: 'In reality, who am I?'

1961 *Les Damnés de la terre* (The Wretched of the Earth, translated by Constance Farrington, 1965), ch.5, 'Colonial War and Mental Disorders'.

Farjeon, Eleanor 1881–1965

English children's writer. Her copious output comprises stories, poems, recountings, fables, saints' lives and prayers, and includes *Nursery Rhymes of London Town* (1916) and 'A Morning Song' (1957).

62 Morning has broken

Like the first morning,
Blackbird has spoken
Like the first bird.
Praise for the singing!
Praise for the morning!
Praise for them springing
Fresh from the Lord!

1957 *Children's Bells*, 'A Morning Song'.

63 There's Carol like a rolling car,
And Martin like a flying bird,
And Adam like the Lord's First Word,
And Raymond like the Harvest Moon,
And Peter like a piper's tune,
And Alan like the flowing on
Of water. And there's John, like John.

1958 *Then There Were Three*, 'Boys' Names'.

Farjeon, Herbert 1887–1945

English actor, theatre manager and critic.

64 I've danced with a man, who's danced with a girl,
who's danced with the Prince of Wales.

1927 *The Picnic*.

Farquhar, George c.1677–1707

Irish playwright, who turned to soldiering after an early career as an actor. His comic plays include *Love and a Bottle* (1698), *The Recruiting Officer* (1706) and, most famously, *The Beaux' Stratagem* (1707).

65 Poetry's a mere drug, Sir.

1698 *Love and a Bottle*, act 3, sc.2.

66 I hate all that don't love me, and slight all that do.

1699 *The Constant Couple*, act 1, sc.2.

67 Crimes, like virtues, are their own reward.

1702 *The Inconstant*, act 4, sc.2.

68 Hanging and marriage, you know, go by destiny.

1706 *The Recruiting Officer*, act 3, sc.2.

69 Sir, you shall taste my Anno Domini.

1707 *The Beaux' Stratagem*, act 1, sc.1.

70 I have fed purely upon ale; I have eat my ale, drank my ale, and I always sleep upon ale.

1707 *The Beaux' Stratagem*, act 1, sc.1.

71 There is no scandal like rags, nor any crime so shameful as poverty.

1707 *The Beaux' Stratagem*, act 1, sc.1.

72 Since a woman must wear chains, I would have the pleasure of hearing 'em rattle a little.

1707 *The Beaux' Stratagem*, act 2, sc.2.

73 No woman can be a beauty without a fortune.

1707 *The Beaux' Stratagem*, act 2, sc.2.

Farragut, David Glasgow 1801–70

US Admiral. He served in the War of 1812, and had minor commands in the American-Mexican War before leading a Union fleet in the Civil War. He was the US navy's first Vice-Admiral (1864) and Admiral (1866).

74 Damn the torpedoes! Full speed ahead.

1864 At the Battle of Mobile Bay, 5 Aug. Quoted in A T Mahan *Great Commanders: Admiral Farragut* (1892), ch.10.

Faulkner, William Harrison 1897–1962

US novelist, known for his experiments in literary form and style and for his treatment of social and racial problems in the US South in a series of novels beginning with *Sartoris* (1929). He was awarded the Nobel Prize for Literature in 1949.

75 *Yes*, he thought, *between grief and nothing I will take grief.*

1939 Wilborne. *The Wild Palms*, 'Wild Palms', no.5.

76 No man can cause more grief than that one clinging blindly to the vices of his ancestors.

1948 *Intruder in the Dust*, ch.3.

77 He must teach himself that the basest of all things is to be afraid and, teaching himself that, forget it forever, leaving no room in his workshop for anything but the old verities and truths of the heart, the old universal truths lacking which any story is ephemeral and doomed—love and honour and pity and compassion and sacrifice.

1950 Nobel Prize acceptance speech.

78 I believe man will not merely endure, he will prevail. He is immortal, not because he, alone among creatures, has an inexhaustible voice but because he has a soul, a spirit capable of compassion and sacrifice and endurance.

1950 Nobel Prize acceptance speech.

79 Maybe the only thing worse than having to give gratitude constantly all the time, is having to accept it.

1951 *Requiem For A Nun*, act 2, sc.1.

80 Since his capacity to do is forced into channels of evil through environment and pressures, man is strong before he is moral. The world's anguish is caused by people between twenty and forty.

1956 Interview in *Paris Review*, Spring.

81 An artist is a creature driven by demons.

1956 Interview in *Paris Review*, Spring.

82 The writer's only responsibility is to his art. He will be completely ruthless if he is a good one.

1956 Interview in *Paris Review*, Spring.

83 If a writer has to rob his mother, he will not hesitate; the *Ode on a Grecian Urn* is worth any number of old ladies.

1956 Interview in *Paris Review*, Spring.

84 The aim of every artist is to arrest motion, which is life, by artificial means and hold it fixed so that a hundred years later, when a stranger looks at it, it moves again since it is life.

> **1956** Interview in *Paris Review*, Spring.

85 All of us failed to match our dreams of perfection. So I rate us on the basis of our splendid failure to do the impossible.

> **1956** On his generation of writers. Interview in *Paris Review*, Spring.

86 If I were reincarnated, I'd want to come back as a buzzard. Nothing hates him or envies him or wants him or needs him. He is never bothered or in danger, and he can eat anything.

> **1956** Interview in *Paris Review*, Spring.

87 Success is feminine and like a woman; if you cringe before her she will override you. So the way to treat her is to show her the back of your hand. Then maybe she will do the crawling.

> **1956** Interview in *Paris Review*, Spring

88 No man can write who is not first a humanitarian.

> **1957** In *Time*, 25 Feb.

89 The last sound on the worthless earth will be two human beings trying to launch a homemade spaceship and already quarreling about where they are going next.

> **1959** Speech to UNESCO Commission, in the *New York Times*, 3 Oct.

90 But a man shouldn't fool with booze until he's fifty; then he's a damn fool if he doesn't.

> Quoted in Webb and Wigfall Green *William Faulkner of Oxford* (1965).

Fauré, Gabriel Urbain 1845–1924

French composer. Director of the Conservatoire (1905–20), he is remembered chiefly for his songs and instrumental music, and for his *Requiem*.

91 If that was music, I have never understood what music was.

> **1902** After attending the première of Debussy's *Pelléas et Mélisande*. Quoted in R Orledge *Gabriel Fauré* (1979).

Favre, Jules Claude Gabriel 1809–80

French lawyer and politician. He took part in the July Revolution (1830), becoming a Republican leader and, after the fall of Napoleon III, Foreign Minister. He negotiated the Treaty of Frankfurt (1871).

92 Not an inch of our territory or a stone of our fortresses.

> **1870** Reply to Bismark's demands for concessions, 18 Sep, following France's defeat in the Franco-Prussian War. Quoted in A J P Taylor *The Struggle for Mastery in Europe 1848–1918* (1954), p.212.

Fawcett, Percy Harrison 1867–c.1925

English explorer. After military service he made several expeditions to Brazil (1906–25) in search of traces of ancient civilizations, disappearing with his son and a companion in the Mato Grosso region. Their fate is a mystery.

93 There, I believed, lay the greatest secrets of the past yet preserved in our world of today. I had come to the turn of the road; and for better or worse I chose the forest path.

> **1911** Of South America. Collected in Brian Fawcett (ed) *Exploration Fawcett* (1953).

94 You need have no fear of any failure.

> **1925** Last words written to his wife. Collected in Brian Fawcett (ed) *Exploration Fawcett* (1953).

Fawkes, Guy 1570–1606

English conspirator. He converted to Catholicism at an early age, and served in the Spanish army in the Netherlands (1593–1604). He was involved in the Gunpowder Plot, and was caught red-handed and hanged.

95 A desperate disease requires a dangerous remedy.

> **1605** When questioned after his arrest on 5 Nov.

Feibleman, Peter

US author and literary executor of Lillian Hellmann. His novels include *A Place Without Twilight* and *Daughters of Necessity*. With Lillian Hellmann he wrote *Eating Together*.

96 The biggest difference between Lillian as a grown-up and Lillian as a child was that she was taller.

> **1988** On Lillian Hellman. *Lily*.

Feiffer, Jules 1929–

US cartoonist and writer. His early cartoons in *Village Voice* (1956) were followed by *Little Murders* (a black comedy, 1965), a novel *Harry: The Rat with Women* (1963) and a screenplay, *Carnal Knowledge* (1971).

97 I used to think I was poor. Then they told me I wasn't poor, I was needy. They told me it was self-defeating to think of myself as needy, I was deprived. Then they told me under-privilege was over-used. I was disadvantaged. I still don't have a dime. But I have a great vocabulary.

> **1956** Cartoon caption.

98 As a matter of racial pride we want to be called *blacks*. Which has replaced the term *Afro-American*. Which replaced *Negroes*. Which replaced *colored people*. Which replaced *darkies*. Which replaced *blacks*.

> Quoted in William Safire *Language Maven Strikes Again* (1990).

Feininger, Lyonel 1871–1956

US Cubist painter, also associated with the German painters of the Blaue Reiter.

99 Each individual work serves as an expression of our most personal state of mind at that particular moment and of the inescapable, imperative need for release by means of an appropriate act of creation: in the rhythm, form, colour and mood of a picture.
1917 Letter to Paul Westheim, quoted in Wolf-Dieter Dube *The Expressionists* (1972).

Fenton, James 1949–

English satirical poet and critic, formerly a war correspondent.

1 It is not what they built. It is what they knocked down.
It is not the houses. It is the spaces between the houses.
It is not the streets that exist. It is the streets that no longer exist.
It is not your memories which haunt you.
It is not what you have written down.
It is what you have forgotten, what you must forget.
What you must go on forgetting all your life.
1981 'A German Requiem'.

2 And I'm afraid, reading this passage now,
That everything I knew has been destroyed
By those whom I admired but never knew;
The laughing soldiers fought to their defeat
And I'm afraid most of my friends are dead.
1982 'In a Notebook'.

3 Oh let us not be condemned for what we are.
It is enough to account for what we do.
1983 'Children in Exile'.

Fenwick, Millicent Hammond 1910–93

US politician and diplomat, congresswoman from New Jersey (1975–83). She compiled the *Vogue Book of Etiquette* (1948).

4 The gentle and respectful ways of saying 'To hell with you' are being abandoned.
Recalled on her death, 16 Sep 1993.

Ferber, Edna 1887–1968

US writer. She wrote a number of novels and short stories, and is remembered as the writer of *Show Boat* (1926), which inspired the successful musical.

5 Mother Knows Best.
1923 Title of story.

6 I am not belittling the brave pioneer men but the sunbonnet as well as the sombrero has helped to settle this glorious land of ours.
1929 *Cimarron*, ch.23.

7 America—rather, the United States—seems to me to be the Jew among the nations. It is resourceful, adaptable, maligned, envied, feared, imposed upon. It is warm-hearted, overfriendly; quick-witted, lavish, colorful; given to extravagant speech and gestures; its people are travellers and wanderers by nature, moving, shifting, restless; swarming in Fords, in ocean liners; craving entertainment; volatile.
1939 *A Peculiar Treasure*, ch.1.

8 It was part of the Texas ritual… We know about champagne and caviar but we talk hog and hominy.
1952 *Giant*, ch.2.

9 A woman can look both moral and exciting—if she also looks as if it was quite a struggle.
1954 In *Reader's Digest*, Dec.

10 Science had married the wilderness and was taming the savage shrew.
1958 Of Alaska. *Ice Palace*.

11 Being an old maid is like death by drowning, a really delightful sensation after you cease to struggle.
Quoted in 'Completing the Circle', in R E Drennan *Wit's End* (1973).

12 Dinner parties are for eating, not mating.
Reminder to hostesses who only invite people in pairs. In the *New York Times*, 25 Sep 1984.

Ferdinand I 1503–64

Holy Roman Emperor from 1558, heir to his elder brother, Charles V, whom he joined in battling against Ottoman incursions. He was mainly responsible for the compromise at Augsburg (1555) which ended the religious wars.

13 *Fiat justitia et pereat mundus.*

Let justice be done, though the world may perish.
Motto.
▷ See Watson 1055:54.

Ferguson, Sir Samuel 1810–86

Irish poet and Celtic scholar, president of the Royal Irish Academy and a key figure in the study of early Irish art. His spirited poetry draws on Irish myth.

14 Wider comprehensions, deeper insights to the dead belong:—
Since for Love thou wakest not, sleeper, yet awake for sake of Song!
c.1864 'The Tain-Quest'.

Fergusson, Robert 1750–74

Scottish poet, much admired by Burns. He wrote primarily of Edinburgh life and died in its lunatic asylum aged 24.

15 For thof ye had as wise a snout on

As Shakespeare or Sir Isaac Newton,
Your judgement fouk wou'd hae a doubt on,
I'll tak my aith,
Till they cou'd see ye wi' a suit on
O' gude Braid Claith.
1772 'Braid Claith', stanza 9.

16 Wanwordy, crazy, dinsome thing,
As e'er was fram'd to jow or ring,
What gar'd them sic in steeple hing
They ken themsel',
But weel wat I they coudna bring
Waur sounds frae hell.
1772 'To the Tron-Kirk Bell', stanza 1.

17 Auld Reikie! wale o' ilka town
That Scotland kens beneath the moon;
Whare couthy chiels at e'ening meet
Their bizzing craigs and mous to weet.
1773 'Auld Reikie, A Poem'.

18 Now gae your wa's—Tho' anes as gude
As ever happit flesh and blude,
Yet part we maun—the case sae hard is,
Amang the writers and the bardies
That lang they'll brook the auld I trow,
Or neibours cry, 'Weel brook the new'.
1773 'To My Auld Breeks'.

Ferlinghetti, Lawrence 1919–

US poet and publisher. A member of the Beat Generation of poets, he founded the important radical bookstore and publishing house, City Lights, in San Francisco.

19 A Coney Island of the Mind.
1958 Title of book.

20 the poet like an acrobat
climbs on rime
to a high wire of his own making.
1958 'A Coney Island of the Mind', section 15.

21 I have a feeling I'm falling
on rare occasions
but most of the time I have my feet on the ground
I can't help it if the ground itself is falling.
1973 'Mock Confessional'.

22 For even bad poetry has relevance
for what it does not say
for what it leaves out.
1988 'Uses of Poetry'.

23 As I get older I perceive
Life has its tail in its mouth.
1988 'Poet as Fisherman'.

Fermat, Pierre de 1601–65

French lawyer, mathematician, and founder of number theory. A great deal of his fame stems from Fermat's Last Theorem.

24 To divide a cube into two other cubes, a fourth power or in general any power whatever into two powers of the same denomination above the second is impossible, and I have assuredly found an admirable proof of this, but the margin is too narrow to contain it.
Scribbled note in the margins of his copy of Diophantus's *Arithmetica*. He did not live to provide the promised proof, and the conjecture became famous as Fermat's Last Theorem. In 1993 Andrew Wiles, a British mathematician, claimed to have discovered the proof.

Fermi, Enrico 1901–54

Italian-born US physicist, discoverer of the element neptunium and winner of the 1938 Nobel Prize. In 1942 he created the first self-sustaining chain reaction in uranium, which led to the atomic bomb.

25 Whatever Nature has in store for mankind, unpleasant as it may be, men must accept, for ignorance is never better than knowledge.
Quoted in Laura Fermi *Atoms in the Family* (1954).

Fern, Fanny née Willis 1811–72

US writer, whose witty sketches were collected in *Fern Leaves from Fanny's Portfolio* (1853). When he made his famous attack on women writers, Nathaniel Hawthorne was careful to exempt her.

26 Well, it is a humiliating reflection, that the straightest road to a man's heart is through his palate.
1854 *Fern Leaves from Fanny's Port-Folio, Second Series*, 'Hungry Husbands'. Often quoted as 'The way to a man's heart is through his stomach.'

Fernández, Macedonio 1874–1952

Argentinian philosopher, poet and novelist. He lived a secluded life, reluctant to publish his manuscripts. His philosophical postulates anticipate the work of later writers such as Borges and Bioy Casares.

27 *Todo se ha escrito, todo se ha dicho, todo se ha hecho, oyó Dios que le decían y aún no había creado el mundo, todavía no había nada. También eso ya me lo han dicho, repuso quizá desde la vieja, hendida Nada. Y comenzó.*

Everything has been written, everything has been said, everything has been made: that's what God heard before creating the world, when there was nothing yet. I have also heard that one, he may have answered from the old, split Nothingness. And then he began.
1967 *Museo de la novela de la Eterna* (The Museum of Eternity's Novel), 'Prólogo a la eternidad'.

Ferré, Rosario 1943–

Puerto Rican novelist and critic, who has lived and taught in both Puerto Rico and the US.

28 *Dios sólo nos tiene aquí prestados, en este valle de lágrimas no estamos más que de paso. Si llegara algún día a pensar que ha perdido a su hija para el mundo de los hombres, la habrá ganado para el de los ángeles.*

God has us here only on loan, we are transitory in this vale of tears. If you ever come to think that you have lost your daughter to the world of men, think also that you have given her to that of the angels.

1976 *La Bella Durmiente* (Sleeping Beauty).

Ferrier, Kathleen 1912–53

English contralto. The range and richness of her voice, together with her remarkable technical control, rapidly won her a great reputation until her early death from cancer.

29 Now I'll have eine kleine pause.

1953 Last words. Quoted in Gerald Moore *Am I Too Loud?* (1962).

Feuerbach, Ludwig 1829–80

German philosopher, famous for his interpretation of Christian doctrine in secular terms and for its adaptation by Karl Marx.

30 While Socrates empties the cup of poison with unshaken soul, Christ exclaims, 'If it is possible, let this cup pass from me'. Christ in this respect is the self-confession of human sensibility.

1841 *Das Wesen des Christentums* (translated by Marian Evans (George Eliot) as *The Essence of Christianity*, 1854).

31 The power of miracle is the power of imagination.

1841 *Das Wesen des Christentums* (translated by Marian Evans (George Eliot) as *The Essence of Christianity*, 1854).

32 *Der Mensch ist, was er ißt.*

Man is what he eats.

Quoted in Jacob Moleschott *Lehre der Nahrungsmittel: Für das Volk* (1850).

Feynman, Richard P(hillips) 1918–88

US physicist who shared (1965) the Nobel Prize in Physics for his work on quantum electrodynamics.

33 We have a habit in writing articles published in scientific journals to make the work as finished as possible, to cover up all the tracks, to not worry about the blind alleys or describe how you had the wrong idea first, and so on. So there isn't any place to publish, in a dignified manner, what you actually did in order to do the work.

1966 Nobel Lecture.

34 You know how it always is, every new idea, it takes a generation or two until it becomes obvious that there's no real problem. I cannot define the real problem, therefore I suspect there's no real problem, but I'm not sure there's no real problem.

1982 Explaining his feelings on quantum mechanics. In the *International Journal of Theoretical Physics*, vol.21.

35 If I could explain it to the average person, I wouldn't have been worth the Nobel Prize.

1985 In *People Magazine*, 22 Jul.

36 For a successful technology, reality must take precedence over public relations, for nature cannot be fooled.

1988 *What do YOU Care what Other People Think?*

Fiedler, Leslie A(aron) 1917–92

US critic and novelist. His reputation rests on his influential and often controversial books on US 'literary anthropology', of which *Love and Death in the American Novel* is the best known.

37 Come Back To The Raft Again, Huck Honey!

1955 Title of essay on the repressed homoerotic undercurrent in US writing.

38 To be an American (unlike being English or French or whatever) is precisely to *imagine* a destiny rather than to inherit one; since we have always been, insofar as we are Americans at all, inhabitants of myth rather than history.

1969 'Cross the Border—Close The Gap', in *Playboy*, Dec.

Field, Barron 1786–1846

Australian jurist, born in London. He went to Sydney in 1817 as Judge of the New South Wales Supreme Court and published the first collection of Australian verse, *First Fruits of Australian Poetry* (1819).

39 Kangaroo, Kangaroo!
Thou Spirit of Australia,
That redeems from utter failure.
From perfect desolation,
And warrants the creation
Of this fifth part of the Earth.

1819 *First Fruits of Australian Poetry*, 'The Kangaroo'.

Field, Eugene 1850–95

US writer and theatre critic. A columnist for the *Chicago Morning News*, he achieved a reputation as a humorist and poet with his column 'Sharps and Flats'. He also published several books of children's verse.

40 Mr Creston Clarke played King Lear at the Tabor Grand last night. All through five acts of Shakespeare's tragedy he played the king as though under momentary apprehension that someone else was about to play the ace.

c.1880 Attributed review in the *Denver Post*.

41 Wynken, Blynken, and Nod one night
Sailed off in a wooden shoe—
Sailed on a river of crystal light,
Into a sea of dew.

1889 'Wynken, Blynken, and Nod'.

42 I never lost a little fish. Yes, I am free to say.
  It always was the biggest fish I caught that got away.
  Attributed.

Field, Frank 1942–

English Labour politician. Director of the Child Poverty Action Group (1969–79) and the Low Pay Unit (1974–80), he became an MP in 1979 and has campaigned strenuously for social justice.

43 The House of Lords is a model of how to care for the elderly.
  1981 In *The Observer*, 24 May.

Fielding, Henry 1707–54

English novelist and playwright. After the introduction of the Theatrical Licensing Act in 1737 he turned to fiction, with works such as *The Adventures of Joseph Andrews* (1742) and *Amelia* (1751). He died in Lisbon.

44 Love and scandal are the best sweeteners of tea.
  1728 *Love in Several Masques*, act 4, sc.11.

45 Map me no maps, sir, my head is a map, a map of the whole world.
  1730 *Rape upon Rape*, act 2, sc.5.

46 Oh! The roast beef of England,
  And old England's roast beef!
  1731 *Grub Street Opera*, act 3, sc.3.

47 All Nature wears one universal grin.
  1731 *Tom Thumb the Great*, act 1, sc.1.

48 I am as sober as a Judge.
  1734 *Don Quixote in England*, act 3, sc.14.

49 He in a few minutes ravished this fair creature, or at least would have ravished her, if she had not, by a timely compliance, prevented him.
  1743 *Jonathan Wild*, bk.3, ch.7.

50 Thwackum was for doing justice, and leaving mercy to heaven.
  1749 *Tom Jones*, bk.3, ch.10.

51 What is commonly called love, namely the desire of satisfying a voracious appetite with a certain quantity of delicate white human flesh.
  1749 *Tom Jones*, bk.6, ch.1.

52 His designs were strictly honourable, as the phrase is; that is, to rob a lady of her fortune by way of marriage.
  1749 *Tom Jones*, bk.11, ch.4.

53 It hath been often said, that it is not death, but dying, which is terrible.
  1751 *Amelia*, bk.3, ch.4.

54 One fool at least in every married couple.
  1751 *Amelia*, bk.9, ch.4.

Fields, Dorothy 1905–74

US author and lyricist, daughter of comedian Lew Fields. She wrote the books and lyrics for many Broadway shows and films, often with Jimmy McHugh or Jerome Kern.

55 Grab your coat, and get your hat,
  Leave your worry on the doorstep,
  Just direct your feet
  To the sunny side of the street.
  1930 'On the Sunny Side of the Street'.

56 I might as well play bridge with my old maid aunts
  I haven't got a chance
  This is a fine romance.
  1934 'A Fine Romance', song featured in the film *Swing Time* (music by Jerome Kern).

Fields, W C originally *William Claude Dukenfield* 1879–1946

US comedian. He wrote and performed in several classic comedies including *The Bank Dick* (1940), *My Little Chickadee* (1940) and *Never Give a Sucker an Even Break* (1940).

57 It ain't a fit night out for man or beast.
  1932 *The Fatal Glass of Beer*.

58 Women are like elephants to me. I like to look at them, but I wouldn't want to own one.
  1935 *Mississippi*.

59 Egbert, is it true that married people live longer? No, it just seems longer.
  1940 *The Bank Dick*.

60 Never Give a Sucker an Even Break.
  1941 Title of film, but an earlier catch-phrase of Fields's that may have originated in the 1923 film *Poppy*.

61 I was in love with a beautiful blonde once, dear. She drove me to drink. That's the one thing I'm indebted to her for.
  1941 *Never Give a Sucker an Even Break*.

62 Anybody who hates children and dogs can't be all bad.
  Attributed.

63 Fish fuck in it.
  Attributed, his reason for not drinking water.

Fierstein, Harvey Forbes 1954–

US playwright and actor. He began as a female impersonator and played several stage and screen roles before writing the semi-autobiographical *Torch Song Trilogy* (produced 1982).

64 I assume everyone is gay, unless told otherwise.
  1994 In *Life*, Jan.

Findley, Timothy 1931–

Canadian writer and actor. His novels include *The Wars* (1977), *The Telling of Lies: A Mystery* (1986) and *Headhunter* (1993). He has received the Governor General's Award (1978) and is an Officer of the Order of Canada (1986).

65 He did the thing that no one else would even dare to think of doing. And that to me's as good a definition of a 'hero' as you'll get. Even when the thing that's done is something of which you disapprove.
   1977 Juliet D'Orsey. *The Wars*, pt.1, section 3.

66 Dead men are serious.
   1977 *The Wars*, pt.1, section 20.

67 Any man whose love of horses is stronger than his fear of being an absurdity is all right with me.
   1977 Rodwell. *The Wars*, pt.2, section 8.

Firbank, (Arthur Annesley) Ronald
1886–1926

English novelist. Solitary and somewhat eccentric, he wrote slight but witty and innovative novels. His works include *Valmouth* (1919) and *Prancing Nigger* (1924).

68 There was a pause—just long enough for an angel to pass, flying slowly.
   1915 *Vainglory*, ch.6.

69 The world is disgracefully managed, one hardly knows to whom to complain.
   1915 *Vainglory*, ch.10.

70 All millionaires love a baked apple.
   1915 *Vainglory*, ch.13.

71 She stands, I fear, poor thing, now, for something younger than she looks.
   1919 *Valmouth*, ch.1.

72 'I know of no joy,' she airily began, 'greater than a cool white dress after the sweetness of confession.'
   1919 *Valmouth*, ch.4.

73 There was really no joy in pouring out one's sins while he sat assiduously picking his nose.
   1919 *Valmouth*, ch.6.

74 His Weariness the Prince entered the room in all his tinted orders.
   1923 *The Flower Beneath the Foot*, ch.1.

75 'O! help me heaven,' she prayed, 'to be decorative and to do right!'
   1923 *The Flower Beneath the Foot*, ch.2.

76 Beneath the strain of expectation even the little iced sugar cakes upon the tea-table looked green with worry.
   1923 *The Flower Beneath the Foot*, ch.3.

77 Looking back, I remember the average curate at home as something between a eunuch and a snigger.
   1923 *The Flower Beneath the Foot*, ch.4.

78 'Basta!' his master replied with all the brilliant glibness of the Berlitz-school.
   1923 *The Flower Beneath the Foot*, ch.5.

79 She looks at other women as if she would inhale them.
   1923 *The Flower Beneath the Foot*, ch.5.

80 'I've never travelled,' Dona Consolation blandly confessed, 'but I dare say, dear, you can't judge Egypt by Aïda.'
   1926 *Concerning the Eccentricities of Cardinal Pirelli*, ch.9.

Fisher, Geoffrey Francis, Baron Fisher of Lambeth 1887–1972

English prelate and Archbishop of Canterbury (1945–61). He officiated at the coronation of Elizabeth II in Westminster Abbey (1953).

81 The long and distressing controversy over capital punishment is very unfair to anyone meditating murder.
   1957 In *The Sunday Times*, 24 Feb.

Fisher, H(erbert) A(lbert) L(aurens)
1865–1940

English historian. As Education Minister (1916–22) he sponsored the Fisher Act (1918). He wrote on Napoleon, and is best known for his *History of Europe* (1936).

82 Men wiser and more learned than I have discerned in history a plot, a rhythm, a predetermined pattern. Those harmonies are concealed from me. I can see only one emergency following upon another, as wave follows upon wave; only one real fact with respect to which, since it is unique, there can be no generalizations. Only one safe rule for the historian: that he should recognize in the development of human destinies the play of the contingent and the unforeseen.
   1936 *History of Europe*, introduction.

83 Purity of race does not exist. Europe is a continent of energetic mongrels.
   1936 *History of Europe*, ch.1.

Fisher, M F K 1908–

US cookery writer.

84 Sharing food with another human being is an intimate act that should not be indulged in lightly.
   1949 *An Alphabet for Gourmets*, 'A Is for Dining Alone'.

85 In America we eat, collectively, with a glum urge for food to fill us. We are ignorant of flavor. We are as a nation taste-blind.
1976 *The Art of Eating.*

Fiske, John 1842–1901

English historian, tutor and librarian at Harvard. He wrote many popular books on US history, Spencerian philosophy and Darwinism.

86 The element of chance...is expelled. Nobody would now waste his time in theorizing about a fortuitous concourse of atoms. We have so far spelled out the history of creation as to see that all has been done in strict accordance with law. The method has been the method of evolution, and the more we study it the more do we discern in it intelligible coherence.
1900 *Through Nature to God.*

Fitzgerald, Edward 1809–83

English scholar, poet and translator, a friend of Thackeray, Carlisle and Tennyson. His translation of the *Rubáiyát of Omar Khayyam* was first published anonymously in 1859.

87 Awake! for Morning in the bowl of night
Has flung the stone that puts the stars to flight:
And Lo! the Hunter of the East has caught
The Sultan's turret in a noose of light.
1859 *The Rubáiyát of Omar Khayyam of Naishapur,* stanza 1.

88 Here with a loaf of bread beneath the bough,
A flask of wine, a book of verse—and Thou
Beside me singing in the wilderness—
And wilderness is paradise enow.
1859 *The Rubáiyát of Omar Khayyam of Naishapur,* stanza 12. In the 1879 edn this was changed to 'A Book of Verses underneath the Bough, / A Jug of Wine, a loaf of Bread—and Thou / Beside me singing in the Wilderness— / Oh, Wilderness were Paradise enow!'

89 The moving finger writes; and, having writ,
Moves on: nor all thy piety nor wit
Shall lure it back to cancel half a line,
Nor all thy tears wash out a word of it.
1859 *The Rubáiyát of Omar Khayyam of Naishapur,* stanza 51.

90 Drink! for you know not whence you came, nor why:
Drink! for you know not why you go nor where.
1859 *The Rubáiyát of Omar Khayyam of Naishapur,* stanza 74.

91 And when Thyself with shining foot shall pass
Among the guests star-scattered on the grass,
And in thy joyous errand reach the spot
Where I made one—turn down an empty glass!
1859 *The Rubáiyát of Omar Khayyam of Naishapur,* stanza 75. In the 1879 edition this was changed to 'And when like her, O Saki, you shall pass...'.

Fitzgerald, F(rancis) Scott Key 1896–1940

US novelist who epitomized the Jazz Age in his best-known book *The Great Gatsby* (1925). He wrote about US expatriates in *Tender is the Night* (1934).

92 At eighteen our convictions are hills from which we look; at forty-five they are caves in which we hide.
1920 'Bernice Bobs Her Hair', in the *Saturday Evening Post*, 1 May.

93 The wise writer, I think, writes for the youth of his own generation, the critics of the next, and the schoolmasters of ever afterward.
1920 Interview in the *New York Tribune,* 7 May.

94 She had once been a Catholic, but discovering that priests were infinitely more attentive when she was in process of losing or regaining faith in Mother Church, she maintained an enchantingly wavering attitude.
1921 Of Beatrice Blaine. *This Side of Paradise,* bk.1, ch.1.

95 If I start to hold somebody's hand they laugh at me, and *let* me, just as if it wasn't part of them. As soon as I get hold of a hand they sort of disconnect it from the rest of them.
1921 *This Side of Paradise,* bk.1, ch.1.

96 The Beautiful and the Damned.
1922 Title of novel.

97 Personality is an unbroken series of successful gestures.
1925 *The Great Gatsby,* ch.1.

98 One of those men who reach such an acute limited excellence at twenty-one that everything afterward savors of anti-climax.
1925 Of Tom Buchanan. *The Great Gatsby,* ch.1.

99 In his blue gardens, men and girls came and went like moths among the whisperings and the champagne and the stars.
1925 *The Great Gatsby,* ch.3.

1 Everyone suspects himself of at least one of the cardinal virtues, and this is mine: I am one of the few honest people that I have ever known.
1925 Nick Carraway, the narrator. *The Great Gatsby,* ch.3.

2 There are only the pursued, the pursuing, the busy, and the tired.
1925 *The Great Gatsby,* ch.4.

3 Reach me a rose, honey, and pour me a last drop into that there crystal glass.
1925 *The Great Gatsby,* ch.4.

4 Her voice is full of money.
1925 *The Great Gatsby,* ch.7.

5 They were careless people, Tom and Daisy—they smashed up things and creatures and then retreated

back into their money or their vast carelessness, or whatever it was that kept them together, and let other people clean up the mess they had made.
1925 *The Great Gatsby*, ch.9.

6 And as the moon rose higher the unessential houses began to melt away until gradually I became aware of the old island here that flowered once for Dutch sailor's eyes—a fresh, green breast of the new world... For a transitory enchanted moment man must have held his breath in the presence of this continent, compelled into an aesthetic contemplation he neither understood nor desired, face to face for the last time in history with something commensurate to his capacity for wonder.
1925 *The Great Gatsby*, ch.9.

7 Gatsby believed in the green light, the orgiastic future that year by year recedes before us. It eluded us then, but that's no matter—to-morrow we will run faster, stretch out our arms further... And one fine morning... So we beat on, boats against the current, borne back ceaselessly into the past.
1925 *The Great Gatsby*, ch.9.

8 Let me tell you about the very rich. They are different from you and me.
1926 *All The Sad Young Men*, 'The Rich Boy'. Hemingway published an ironic rejoinder in 'The Snows of Kilimanjaro'; 'Yes, they have more money'.
▷ See Hemingway 471:3.

9 Though the Jazz Age continued, it became less and less of an affair of youth. The sequel was like a children's party taken over by the elders.
1931 'Echoes of the Jazz Age', *Scribner's Magazine*, Nov.

10 Mostly, we authors repeat ourselves—that's the truth.
1933 'One Hundred False Starts', in the *Saturday Evening Post*, 4 Mar.

11 Tender is the Night.
1934 Title of novel.

12 When people are taken out of their depths they lose their heads, no matter how charming a bluff they may put up.
1934 *Tender Is The Night*, bk.3, ch.12.

13 The test of a first-rate intelligence is the ability to hold two opposed ideas in the mind at the same time, and still retain the ability to function.
1936 'The Crack-Up', in *Esquire*, Feb.

14 In a real dark night of the soul, it is always three o'clock in the morning, day after day.
1936 'Handle With Care', in *Esquire*, Mar.

15 Often I think writing is a sheer paring away of

oneself leaving always something thinner, barer, more meagre.
1940 Letter, 27 Apr.

16 The faces of most American women over thirty are relief maps of petulant and bewildered unhappiness.
1940 Letter, 5 Oct.

17 It's not a slam at *you* when people are rude—it's a slam at the people they've met before.
1941 *The Last Tycoon*, ch.1.

18 No grand idea was ever born in a conference, but a lot of foolish ideas have died there.
Note Books, E, in Edmund Wilson (ed) *The Crack-Up* (1945).

19 Show me a hero and I will write you a tragedy.
Note Books, E, in Edmund Wilson (ed) *The Crack-Up* (1945).

20 Great art is the contempt of a great man for small art.
Note Books, L, in Edmund Wilson (ed) *The Crack-Up* (1945).

21 When the first-rate author wants an exquisite heroine or a lovely morning, he finds that all the superlatives have been worn shoddy by his inferiors. It should be a rule that bad writers must start with plain heroines and ordinary mornings, and, if they are able, work up to something better.
Note Books, L, in Edmund Wilson (ed) *The Crack-Up* (1945).

Fitzgerald, Penelope Mary 1916–

English novelist and biographer. She won the Booker Prize in 1979 for *Offshore*.

22 Patience is passive, resignation is active.
1986 *Innocence*.

Flanagan, Bud stage name of *Robert Winthrop* 1896–1968

English comedian. He was immensely popular both as one of the Crazy Gang of comedians and in a duo with Chesney Allen.

23 Underneath the Arches,
I dream my dreams away,
Underneath the Arches,
On cobble-stones I lay.
1932 'Underneath the Arches' (song).

24 No dog can go as fast as the money you bet on him.
Quoted in Colin Jarman *The Guinness Dictionary of Sports Quotations* (1990).

Flanders, Michael and Donald Swann 1922–75, 1923–

English songwriting team, who made their name with *At the Drop of a Hat* (1956).

25 Mud! Mud! Glorious mud!
Nothing quite like it for cooling the blood.

So follow me, follow,
Down to the hollow,
And there let us wallow
In glorious mud.
1952 'The Hippopotamus'.

26 Eating people is wrong!
1956 'The Reluctant Cannibal'. Malcolm Bradbury took the phrase as the title of his 1959 novel.

27 Ma's out, Pa's out—let's talk rude:
Pee, po, belly, bum, drawers.
c.1956 'P**, P*, B****, B**, D******'.

28 The English, the English, the English are best!
I wouldn't give tuppence for all of the rest!
1963 'Song of Patriotic Prejudice'.

Flaubert, Anne Justine Caroline 1793–1872

Mother of Gustave Flaubert.

29 Your mania for sentences has dried up your heart.
To her son. Quoted in D J Enright *A Mania for Sentences* (1983), p.101.

Flaubert, Gustave 1821–80

French novelist, master of the realistic novel. He studied law at Paris before turning to writing. His works include *Madame Bovary* (1857) and *Trois contes* (1877). He intended to include a *Dictionnaire des idées reçues* in the second volume of *Bouvard et Pécuchet*.

30 *Je suis autant Chinois que Français.*

I am as much Chinese as French.
1846 Letter to Mme Louise Colet, 8 Aug.

31 *L'Idée seule est éternelle et nécessaire.*

The idea alone is eternal and necessary.
1846 Letter to Mme Louise Colet, 9 Aug.

32 *Il ne faut pas toujours croire que le sentiment soit tout. Dans les arts, il n'est rien sans la forme.*

You must not think that feeling is everything. Art is nothing without form.
1846 Letter to Mme Louise Colet, 12 Aug.

33 *On fait de la critique quand on ne peut pas faire de l'art, de même qu'on se met mouchard quand on ne peut pas être soldat.*

Someone is a critic when he cannot be an artist in the same way that a man becomes an informer when he cannot be a soldier.
1846 Letter to Mme Louise Colet, 22 Oct.

34 My kingdom is as wide as the universe and my wants have no limits. I go forward always, freeing spirits and weighing words, without fear, without compassion, without love, without God. I am called science.
1874 *The Temptation of St Antony*.

35 *Les oeuvres les plus belles sont celles où il y a le moins de matière; plus l'expression se rapproche de la pensée, plus le mot colle dessus et disparaît, plus c'est beau. Je crois que l'avenir de l'art est dans ces voies.*

The most beautiful works are those that have the least content; the closer the expression is to the thought, the more indistinguishable the word from the content, the more beautiful is the work. I believe that the future of art lies in this direction.
1852 Letter to Mme Louise Colet, 16 Jan.

36 *La courtisane est un mythe. Jamais une femme n'a inventé une débauche.*

The courtesan is a myth. No woman has ever invented any new sensual pleasure.
1852 Letter to Mme Louise Colet, Aug.

37 *L'amour, croyait-elle, devait arriver tout à coup, avec de grands éclats et des fulgurations.*

She believed that love should appear instantaneously, with the brilliance of a lightning storm.
1857 *Madame Bovary*, pt.1, ch.8.

38 *La parole humaine est comme un chaudron fêlé où nous battons des mélodies à faire danser les ours, quand on voudrait attendrir les étoiles.*

Human speech is like a cracked kettle on which we beat out tunes for bears to dance to, when all the time we are longing to move the stars to pity.
1857 *Madame Bovary*, pt.1, ch.12.

39 *Le charme de la nouveauté, peu à peu tombant comme un vêtement, laissait voir à nu l'éternelle monotonie de la passion, qui a toujours les mêmes formes et le même langage.*

The charm of novelty, falling little by little like a robe, revealed the eternal monotony of passion, which has always the same forms and the same language.
1857 *Madame Bovary*, pt.2, ch.12.

40 *Il faut écrire pour soi, avant tout. C'est seule chance de faire beau.*

It is necessary to write for oneself, above all. It is the only hope of creating something beautiful.
1858 Letter to Mlle Leroyer de Chantepie, 11 Jul.

41 *Un romancier, selon moi, n'a pas le droit de dire son avis sur les choses de ce monde. Il doit, dans sa vocation, imiter Dieu dans la sienne, c'est-à-dire faire et se taire.*

A novelist, in my opinion, does not have the right to give advice on the affairs of the world. He must, in his occupation, imitate God in His; that is to say, create and keep quiet.
1866 Letter to Mlle Bosquet.

42 *Axiome: la haine du bourgeois est le commencement de la vertu.*

Axiom: Hatred of the bourgeois is the beginning of wisdom.
1867 Letter to George Sand, 10 May.

43 *Il tournait dans son désir, comme un prisonnier dans son cachot.*

He was circling in his desire, like a prisoner in his dungeon.
1869 *L'Education sentimentale*, pt.1, ch.5.

44 *Antiquité. —en tout ce qui s'y rapporte: Est poncif, embêtant! etc.*

Antiquity. And everything to do with it, clichéd and boring.
Bouvard et Pécuchet avec un choix des scénarios, du Sottisier, L'Album de la Marquise et Le Dictionnaire des idées reçues. (published 1881, translated by Geoffrey Wall, 1994).

45 *Homère. Célèbre par sa façon de rire: rire homérique. N'a jamais existé.*

Homer. Famous for his laugh. 'Homeric laughter'. Never existed.
Bouvard et Pécuchet avec un choix des scénarios, du Sottisier, L'Album de la Marquise et Le Dictionnaire des idées reçues. (published 1881, translated by Geoffrey Wall, 1994).

46 *Latin. Langage naturel de l'homme. Gâte l'écriture. Est seulement utile pour comprendre les inscriptions des fontaines publiques. Il faut se méfier des citations en Latin; elles cachent toujours quelque chose de leste.*

Latin. Man's natural language. Spoils your style. Useful only for reading the inscriptions on public fountains. Beware of quotations in Latin: they always conceal something improper.
Bouvard et Pécuchet avec un choix des scénarios, du Sottisier, L'Album de la Marquise et Le Dictionnaire des idées reçues. (published 1881, translated by Geoffrey Wall, 1994).

Flecker, James Elroy 1884–1915

English poet. He studied Oriental languages and joined the consular service, symptoms of a fascination with the East which is reflected in much of his verse.

47 O friend unseen, unborn, unknown,
Student of our sweet English tongue,
Read out my words at night, alone:
I was a poet, I was young.
1910 'To a Poet A Thousand Years Hence'.

48 We who with songs beguile your pilgrimage
And swear that Beauty lives though lilies die,
We Poets of the proud old lineage
Who sing to find your hearts, we know not why—
What shall we tell you? Tales, marvellous tales
Of ships and stars and isles where good men rest.
1913 'The Golden Journey to Samarkand', epilogue.

49 For lust of knowing what should not be known,
We take the Golden Road to Samarkand.
1913 'The Golden Journey to Samarkand', epilogue.

50 How splendid in the morning glows the lily; with
what grace he throws
His supplication to the rose.
1913 'Yasmin'.

51 The dragon-green, the luminous, the dark, the
serpent-haunted sea.
1913 'The Gates of Damascus'.

52 For pines are gossip pines the wide world through
And full of runic tales to sigh or sing.
1913 'Brumana'.

53 Half to forget the wandering and pain,
Half to remember days that have gone by,
And dream and dream that I am home again!
1913 'Brumana'.

54 West of these out to seas colder than the Hebrides
I must go
Where the fleet of stars is anchored and the young
Star captains glow.
1913 'The Dying Patriot'.

55 A ship, an isle, a sickle moon—
With few but with how splendid stars
The mirrors of the sea are strewn
Between their silver bars!
1913 'A Ship, an Isle, a Sickle Moon'.

56 I have seen old ships sail like swans asleep.
1915 'The Old Ships'.

Fleming, Ian Lancaster 1908–64

English novelist. He is best known for his creation of the hugely popular secret service agent, James Bond.

57 Live and Let Die.
1954 Title of novel.

58 From Russia with Love.
1957 Title of novel.

59 I would like a medium Vodka dry Martini—with a
slice of lemon. Shaken and not stirred, please. I
would prefer Russian or Polish vodka.
1958 *Dr No*, ch.14.

Fleming, Marjory 1803–11

Scottish child writer, the subject of an essay by Dr John Brown which popularized her image as 'Pet Marjorie' and invented an affectionate relationship with her distant relative Walter Scott.

60 The most Devilish thing is 8 times 8 and 7 times 7
it is what nature itselfe cant endure.
1810 'Journal 2' in F Sidgwick (ed) *The Complete Marjory Fleming* (1934).

61 Many girls have not the advantage I have and I
[am] very very glad that satan has not geven me
boils and many other Misfortunes.

> **1810** 'Journal 2' in F Sidgwick (ed) *The Complete Marjory Fleming* (1934).

62 To Day I pronunced a word which should never
come out of a ladys lips it was that I called John a
Impudent Bitch.

> **1810** 'Journal 2' in F Sidgwick (ed) *The Complete Marjory Fleming* (1934).

63 I would rather have a man dog then a women dog
because they do not bear like women dogs, it is a
hard case it is shoking.

> **1810** 'Journal 2' in F Sidgwick (ed) *The Complete Marjory Fleming* (1934).

64 I hope I will be religious again but as for reganing
my charecter I despare for it.

> **1810** 'Journal 2' in F Sidgwick (ed) *The Complete Marjory Fleming* (1934).

65 An annibaptist is a thing I am not a member of:—I
am a Pisplikan just now & a Prisbeteren at
Kercaldy my native town which thugh dirty is clein
in the country.

> **1811** 'Journal 3' in F Sidgwick (ed) *The Complete Marjory Fleming* (1934).

66 Love is a very papithatick thing as well as
troublesom & tiresome but O Isabella forbid me to
speak about it.

> **1811** 'Journal 3' in F Sidgwick (ed) *The Complete Marjory Fleming* (1934).

Fletcher, Andrew of Saltoun 1655–1716

Scottish patriot, fierce opponent of Stuart policy and of
union with England. After the Union he retired in disgust
and devoted himself to agriculture.

67 This will be the issue of that darling Plea, of being
one and not two; it will be turned upon the Scots
with a Vengeance; and their 45 Scots Members may
dance round to all Eternity, in this Trap of their
own making.

> **1706** *State of the Controversy betwixt United and Separate Parliaments*, a critique of the proposed Union.

68 It is only fit for the slaves who sold it.

> **1707** Of Scotland, on leaving it after the signing of the Treaty of Union. Quoted in G W T Ormond *Fletcher of Saltoun* (1897).

Fletcher, John 1579–1625

English dramatist, who collaborated with Beaumont until
the latter's marriage in 1613, and also with Shakespeare,
Jonson, Middleton, Massinger and Rowley, as well as
writing on his own. He died of plague.

69 Care-charming Sleep, thou easer of all woes,
Brother to Death.

> **c.1610–14** *Valentinian*, act 5, sc.7.

70 Best while you have it use your breath,
There is no drinking after death.

> **1616** *The Bloody Brother*, act 2, sc.2, song (with Ben Jonson, George Chapman and Philip Massinger).

71 And he that will go to bed sober,
Falls with the leaf still in October.

> **1616** *The Bloody Brother*, act 2, sc.2, song (with Ben Jonson, George Chapman and Philip Massinger).

72 We are stark naught all, bad's the best of us.

> **1616** *The Bloody Brother*, act 4, sc.2 (with Ben Jonson, George Chapman and Philip Massinger).

73 We are beasts now, and the beasts are our masters.

> **c.1621** *The Wild Goose-Chase*, act 1, sc.1.

74 Blush at your faults.

> **c.1621** *The Wild Goose-Chase*, act 1, sc.1.

75 Give me the plump Venetian, fat, and lusty,
That meets me soft and supple, smiles upon
   me
As if a cup of full wine leaped to kiss me.

> **c.1621** *The Wild Goose-Chase*, act 1, sc.2.

76 Health and an able body are two jewels.

> **c. 1621** *The Wild Goose-Chase*, act 2, sc.1.

77 Nothing is thought rare
Which is not new and follow'd, yet we know
That what was worne some twenty yeare agoe,
Comes into grace againe.

> **c.1623** *The Noble Gentleman*, prologue.

78 Are you at ease now? Is your heart at rest?
Now you have got a shadow, an umbrella
To keep the scorching world's opinion
From your fair credit.

> **1624** *Rule a Wife and Have a Wife*, act 3, sc.1.

Florio, John c.1553–1625

English scholar, writer and translator, born of Italian
Protestant family in London. His most famous work is his
translation of Montaigne's *Essays* (1603); he also
published an Italian–English dictionary, *A World of Words*
(1598), and two compendiums of Italian proverbs.

79 England is the paradise of women, the purgatory of
men, and the hell of horses.

> **1591** *Second Frutes*, ch.12.

Flynn, Errol 1909–59

Hollywood actor born in Tasmania. He starred in
historical swashbucklers such as *Captain Blood* (1935),
The Adventures of Robin Hood (1938) and *The Sea Hawk*
(1940). His off-screen reputation for drinking, drug-

taking and womanizing became legendary and eventually affected his career.

80 The public has always expected me to be a playboy and a decent chap never lets his public down.
Quoted in Gary Herman *The Book of Hollywood Quotes* (1979).

81 Inside this Hollywood playboy is a someway decent actor waiting for a chance to prove it. But, since Hollywood will never give me that chance, I drink to obliviate that decent actor.
Quoted in Michael Wilding and Pamela Wilcox *Apple Sauce* (1982).

Fo, Dario 1926–

Italian playwright and actor-manager, whose often controversial plays and revues deal with political themes. His plays include *Accidental Death of an Anarchist* (1970) and *Trumpets and Raspberries* (1984).

82 *Non si paga, non si paga.*

We won't pay, we won't pay.
1974 Play title, translated into English in 1981 as *Can't pay? Won't pay!*

Foch, Ferdinand 1851–1929

French Marshal, born in Tarbes. He taught at the École de Guerre, and proved himself a great strategist at the Battles of the Marne and Ypres. He commanded the Allied armies in 1918.

83 *Mon centre cède, ma droite recule, situation excellente, j'attaque.*

My centre is giving way, my right is retreating, situation excellent, I am attacking.
1914 Message sent during the first Battle of the Marne, Sep. Quoted in R Recouly *Foch* (1919), ch.6.

84 *Ce n'est pas un traité de paix, c'est un armistice de vingt ans.*

This is not a peace treaty, it is an armistice for twenty years.
1919 At the signing of the Treaty of Versailles. Quoted in Paul Reynaud *Memoires* (1963), vol.2.

Fontenelle, Bernard le Bovier de 1657–1757

French writer, the nephew of Corneille. He introduced mathematics and the natural sciences into the conversation of the salons, and expressed scientific ideas through literature. He was secretary of the *Académie des Sciences* (1699–1741).

85 *Ah! si l'on ôtait les chimères aux hommes, quel plaisir leur resterait?*

Oh! If man were robbed of his fantasies, what pleasure would be left him?
1683 *Dialogue des Morts.*

86 *L'univers…je l'en estime plus depuis que je sais qu'il ressemble à une montre; il est surprenant que l'ordre de la nature, tout admirable qu'il est, ne roule que sur des choses si simples.*

I have come to esteem the universe more now that I know it resembles a watch; it is surprising that the order of nature, as admirable as it is, only runs on such simple things.
1686 *Entretiens sur la pluralité des mondes.*

87 *Les mouvements les plus naturels, et les plus ordinaires, sont ceux qui se font le moins sentir; cela est vrai jusque dans la morale. Le mouvement de l'amour-propre nous est si naturel que, le plus souvent, nous ne le sentons pas.*

The most natural and ordinary movements are those which are the least felt; this is also true in morals. Self-love is so natural to us that, most often, we never feel it.
1686 *Entretiens sur la pluralité des mondes, Premier soir.*

88 *Leibniz n'était point marié; il y avait pensé à l'âge de cinquante ans; mais la personne qu'il avait en vue voulut avoir le temps de faire ses réflexions. Cela donne à Leibniz le loisir de faire aussi les siennes, et il ne se maria point.*

Leibniz never married; he had considered it at the age of fifty, but the person he had in mind desired time to think about it. This gave Leibniz time to reflect, also, and he didn't marry
Eloge des académiciens, Leibniz.

89 *Les vrais philosophes sont comme les éléphants, qui en marchant ne posent jamais le second pied à terre que le premier ne soit bien affermi.*

True philosophers are like elephants who when walking never place their second foot on the ground until the first is steady.
1686 *Entretiens sur la pluralité des mondes, Sixième soir.*

90 *Un grand obstacle au bonheur, c'est de s'attendre à un trop grand bonheur.*

The greatest obstacle to happiness is the expectation of too great a happiness.
1724 *Du bonheur.*

Foot, Michael Mackintosh 1913–

English Labour politician. He resigned the leadership of the Labour party in 1983, after a heavy defeat in the general election. A pacifist and CND supporter, his prolific writings include a two-volume biography of Aneurin Bevan.

91 The only man I knew who could make a curse sound like a caress.
1962 Of Aneurin Bevan. *Aneurin Bevan 1897–1945*, vol.1.

92 The members of our secret service have apparently spent so much time looking under the bed for Communists that they haven't had time to look in the bed.
1963 Attributed comment on the Profumo scandal.

93 A Royal Commission is a broody hen sitting on a china egg.
1964 Speech, House of Commons.

94 Men of power have not time to read; yet men who do not read are unfit for power.
1980 *Debts of Honour.*

Foote, Samuel 1720–77

English actor-manager and playwright. Dubbed the 'English Aristophanes', he excelled in satirical comedy at the Haymarket Theatre, which he managed. He won a limited theatrical patent as compensation when he lost a leg in a practical joke involving the Duke of York. His plays include *The Englishman in Paris* (1753) and *The Minor* (1760).

95 So she went into the garden to cut a cabbage-leaf, to make an apple-pie; and at the same time a great she-bear coming up the street, pops its head into the shop. 'What! no soap?' So he died and she very imprudently married the barber; and there were present the Picninnies, and the Joblillies, and the Garynlies, and the Grand Panjandrum himself, with the little round button at top; and they all fell to playing the game of catch-as-catch-can till the gunpowder ran out of the heels of their boots.
Responding to a challenge from the actor Charles Macklin that there was no speech he could not repeat from memory after just one hearing. Macklin had to acknowledge defeat. Foote's phrases 'no soap' and 'the grand Panjandrum' became widely adopted. Quoted in Maria Edgeworth *Harry and Lucy* (1825), vol.2.

Forbes, Malcolm Stevenson, Jr 1947–

US publisher. He joined Forbes Inc in 1970, becoming Chairman of Forbes Newspapers in 1989.

96 People who never get carried away, should be.
1976 In *Town and Country*, Nov.

97 It is unfortunate we can't buy many business executives for what they are worth and sell them for what they think they are worth.
Quoted in David Mahoney *Confessions of a Street-Smart Manager* (1988).

Ford, Ford Madox originally Ford Hermann Hueffer 1873–1939

English writer and editor. He was associated with the modernist movement, and launched *The English Review* and later *The Transatlantic Review*. His best known novels are *The Good Soldier* and the *Parade's End* tetralogy.

98 God knows that the lesson we learn from life is that our very existence in the nature of things is a perpetual harming of somebody else—if only because every mouthful of food that we eat is a mouthful taken from somebody else.
1911 *Ancient Lights*, dedication.

99 I should say that Rossetti was a man without principles at all, who earnestly desired to find salvation along the lines of least resistance.
1911 Of Dante Gabriel Rossetti. *Memories and Impressions.*

1 You cannot be absolutely dumb when you live with a person unless you are an inhabitant of the North of England or the State of Maine.
1915 *The Good Soldier*, pt.3, ch.4.

2 Alas, it does indeed seem a monstrous thing, but after all, what is chaste in Constantinople may have the aspect of lewdness in Liverpool, and what in Liverpool may pass for virtue in Constantinople is frequently regarded as vice.
1915 Letter to John Lane, 17 Dec.

3 Only two classes of books are of universal appeal. The very best and the very worst.
1924 *Joseph Conrad, A Personal Remembrance*, pt.1.

4 We used to say that a passage of good style began with a fresh, usual word, and continued with fresh, usual words to the end; there was nothing more to it.
1924 *Joseph Conrad, A Personal Remembrance*, pt.3.

5 We agreed that the novel is absolutely the only vehicle for the thought of our day.
1924 *Joseph Conrad, A Personal Remembrance*, pt.3.

6 I have always had the greatest contempt for novels written with a purpose. Fiction should render, not draw morals. But…I sinned against my gods to the extent of saying that I was going—to the level of the light vouchsafed me—to write a work that should have for its purpose the obviating of all future wars.
1934 On *Parade's End.*

Ford, Henry 1863–1947

US automobile engineer and manufacturer. In 1903 he started the Ford Motor Company, pioneering 'assembly line' mass-production techniques for his famous Model T (1908–9), 15 million of which were produced up to 1928.

7 History is more or less bunk. It's tradition.
1916 Interview, *Chicago Tribune*, May.

8 Any color—so long as it's black.
Of the Model T Ford. Quoted in Allan Nevins *Ford* (1957), vol.2.

9 Exercise is bunk. If you are healthy, you don't need

it: if you are sick, you shouldn't take it.
Attributed.

Ford, Henry 1917–87

US businessman, grandson of Henry Ford, president of the Ford Motor Co from 1945 and Chairman from 1960. He introduced many modernizing measures.

10 My name is on the building.
His habitual justification for having the last word. Recalled on his death, 29 Sep 1987.

Ford, John c.1586–c.1640

English dramatist, who collaborated with Dekker, Fletcher, Rowley and Webster. His works include *The Broken Heart* (1633), *'Tis Pity She's a Whore* (1633) and *Perkin Warbeck* (1634), a historical play.

11 I am…a mushroom
On whom the dew of heaven drops now and then.
1633 *The Broken Heart*, act 1, sc.3.

12 The joys of marriage are the heaven on earth,
Life's paradise, great princess, the soul's quiet,
Sinews of concord, earthly immortality,
Eternity of pleasures; no restoratives
Like to a constant woman.
1633 *The Broken Heart*, act 2, sc.2.

13 He hath shook hands with time.
1633 *The Broken Heart*, act 5, sc.2.

14 Nice philosophy
May tolerate unlikely arguments,
But heaven admits no jest.
1633 *'Tis Pity She's a Whore*, act 1, sc.1.

15 'Tis my destiny
That you must either love, or I must die.
1633 *'Tis Pity She's a Whore*, act 1, sc.2.

16 Busy opinion is an idle fool.
1633 *'Tis Pity She's a Whore*, act 5, sc.3.

17 Why, I hold fate
Clasped in my fist, and could command the course
Of time's eternal motion, hadst thou been
One thought more steady than an ebbing sea.
1633 *'Tis Pity She's a Whore*, act 5, sc.4.

18 Of one so young, so rich in nature's store,
Who could not say, 'tis pity she's a whore?
1633 *'Tis Pity She's a Whore*, act 5, sc.6.

19 Tell us, pray, what devil
This melancholy is, which can transform
Men into monsters.
1638 *The Lady's Trial*, act 3, sc.1.

Ford, Lena Guilbert 1870–1916

British songwriter.

20 Keep the Home-fires burning,
While your hearts are yearning,
Though your lads are far away
They dream of Home.
There's a silver lining
Through the dark clouds shining;
Turn the dark cloud inside out,
Till the boys come Home.
1914 'Till the Boys Come Home', a war-time anthem (music by Ivor Novello).

Ford, Richard 1944–

US writer. He has written several novels, of which the best known is *The Sportswriter* (1986), and short stories, and edited the *Granta Book of the American Short Story* (1991).

21 If there's another thing that sportswriting teaches you, it is that there are no transcendent themes in life. In all cases things are here and they're over, and that has to be enough.
1986 *The Sportswriter*, ch.1.

22 Married life requires shared mystery even when all the facts are known.
1986 *The Sportswriter*, ch.5.

23 Leaving reminds us what we can part with and what we can't, then offers us something new to look forward to, to dream about.
1992 'An Urge for Going', in *Harper's*, Feb.

Foreman, George 1948–

US boxer, world heavyweight champion (1973–4).

24 A boxer never sees the big one that hits him.
Quoted in Colin Jarman *The Guinness Dictionary of Sports Quotations* (1990).

Forgy, Howell Maurice 1908–83

US naval chaplain.

25 Praise the Lord and pass the ammunition.
1941 At Pearl Harbor, 7 Dec. Reported in the *New York Times*, 1 Nov 1942, and used as a song title by Frank Loesser, 1942.
▷ See Blacker 165:48.

Formby, George 1904–61

English entertainer. He developed a music-hall act featuring a ukulele and comic songs which translated well to film, and became one of Britain's most popular pre-war stars.

26 When I'm Cleaning Windows.
1936 Title of song (with Harry Gifford and Fred E Cliffe), first featured in the film *Keep Your Seats Please*.

27 It's me Auntie Maggie's home-made remedy
Guaranteed never to fail
Now that's the stuff that will do the trick
It's sold at ev'ry chemist for 'one and a kick'.

1941 'Auntie Maggie's Remedy' (with Eddie Latta), song featured in the film *Turned Out Nice Again*.

Forster, E(dward) M(organ)   1879–1970

English novelist and critic, a member of the Bloomsbury circle. His novels include *Howards End* (1910) and *A Passage To India* (1924). *Maurice* (written 1913–14), on homosexuality, was published posthumously in 1971. He was a prolific essayist and critic.

28 Here is the heart of our island: the Chilterns, the North Downs, the South Downs radiate hence. The fibres of England unite in Wiltshire, and did we condescend to worship her, here should we erect our national shrine.
1907   *The Longest Journey*, ch.13.

29 A Room with a View.
1908   Title of novel.

30 They are our gates to the glorious and the unknown. Through them we pass out into adventure and sunshine, to them, alas! we return.
1910   On railway terminii. *Howards End*, ch.2.

31 It will be generally admitted that Beethoven's Fifth Symphony is the most sublime noise that has ever penetrated into the ear of man.
1910   *Howards End*, ch.5.

32 He believed in sudden conversion, a belief which may be right, but which is peculiarly attractive to the half-baked mind.
1910   *Howards End*, ch.6.

33 She felt that those who prepared for all the emergencies of life beforehand may equip themselves at the expense of joy.
1910   *Howard's End*, ch.7.

34 The poor cannot always reach those whom they want to love, and they can hardly ever escape from those whom they no longer love.
1910   *Howards End*, ch.7.

35 Personal relations are the important thing for ever and ever, and not this outer life of telegrams and anger.
1910   *Howards End*, ch.19.

36 Only connect! That was the whole of her sermon. Only connect the prose and the passion, and both will be exalted, and human love will be seen at its height. Live in fragments no longer.
1910   *Howards End*, ch.22.

37 Death destroys a man: the idea of death saves him.
1910   *Howards End*, ch.27.

38 There is much to be said for apathy in education.
1913–14   *Maurice* (published 1971), ch.1.

39 Religion is far more acute than science, and if it only added judgement to insight, would be the greatest thing in the world.
1913–14   *Maurice* (published 1971), ch.44.

40 'I don't think I understand people very well. I only know whether I like or dislike them.' 'Then you are an Oriental.'
1924   *A Passage To India*, ch.2.

41 The so-called white races are really pinko-grey.
1924   *A Passage To India*, ch.7.

42 Nothing in India is identifiable, the mere asking of a question causes it to disappear or to merge in something else.
1924   *A Passage to India*, ch.8.

43 The echo began in some indescribable way to undermine her hold on life. Coming at a moment when she chanced to be fatigued, it had managed to murmur, 'Pathos, piety, courage—they exist, but are identical, and so is filth. Everything exists, nothing has value.'
1924   *A Passage To India*, ch.14.

44 Yes—oh dear yes—the novel tells a story.
1927   *Aspects of the Novel*, ch.2.

45 *Ulysses*…is a dogged attempt to cover the universe with mud, an inverted Victorianism, an attempt to make crossness and dirt succeed where sweetness and light failed, a simplification of the human character in the interests of Hell.
1927   Of James Joyce's 1922 novel. *Aspects of the Novel*, ch.6.

46 They go forth into a world…of men who are as various as the sands of the sea; into a world of whose richness and subtlety they have no conception. They go forth into it with well-developed bodies, fairly developed minds, and undeveloped hearts.
1936   On public schoolboys. *Abinger Harvest*, 'Notes on English Character'.

47 It is not that the Englishman can't feel—it is that he is afraid to feel.
1936   *Abinger Harvest*, 'Notes on English Character'.

48 It is frivolous stuff, and how rare, how precious is frivolity! How few writers can prostitute all their powers! They are always implying 'I am capable of higher things.'
1936   *Abinger Harvest*, 'Ronald Firbank'.

49 The historian must have a third quality as well: some conception of how men who are not historians behave. Otherwise he will move in a world of the dead.
1936   *Abinger Harvest*, 'Captain Edward Gibbon'.

50 Works of art, in my opinion, are the only objects in the material universe to possess internal order, and that is why, though I don't believe that only art matters, I do believe in Art for Art's sake.
1951 *Two Cheers for Democracy*, 'Art for Art's Sake'.

51 I do not believe in Belief... Lord I disbelieve—help thou my unbelief.
1951 *Two Cheers for Democracy*, 'What I Believe'.

52 I hate the idea of causes, and if I had to choose between betraying my country and betraying my friend, I hope I should have the guts to betray my country.
1951 *Two Cheers for Democracy*, 'What I Believe'.

53 So two cheers for democracy: one because it admits variety and two because it permits criticism. Two cheers are quite enough: there is no occasion to give three. Only Love the Beloved Republic deserves that.
1951 *Two Cheers for Democracy*, 'What I Believe'. The phrase 'Love the Beloved Republic' is taken from Swinburne's poem 'Hertha'.

54 Think before you speak is criticism's motto; speak before you think creation's.
1951 *Two Cheers for Democracy*, 'Raison d'être of Criticism'.

55 Creative writers are always greater than the causes that they represent.
1951 *Two Cheers for Democracy*, 'Gide and George'.

56 I would suggest that the only books that influence us are those for which we are ready, and which have gone a little farther down our particular path than we have yet got ourselves.
1951 *Two Cheers for Democracy*, 'Books That Influenced Me'.

57 One was left, too, with a gap in Christianity: the canonical gospels do not record that Christ laughed or played. Can a man be perfect if he never laughs or plays? Krishna's jokes may be vapid, but they bridge a gap.
1953 *The Hill of Devi*, 'Gokul Ashtami'.

Foster, Sir George 1847–1931
Canadian politician.

58 These somewhat troublesome days when the great Mother Empire stands splendidly isolated in Europe.
1896 Speech in the House of Commons, 16 Jan. *The Times* reported the speech under the heading of 'Splendid Isolation', 22 Jan.

Foster, Stephen Collins 1826–64
US songwriter. His 125 compositions include 'The Old Folks at Home', 'Camptown Races' and 'Jeannie with the Light Brown Hair', but despite their success, he died in poverty and obscurity.

59 Gwine to run all night,
Gwine to run all day,
I'll bet my money on de bob-tail nag,
Somebody bet on de bay.
1850 'Camptown Races', chorus.

60 Way down upon the Swanee River,
Far, far away,
There's where my heart is turning ever;
There's where the old folks stay.
1851 'The Old Folks at Home'.

61 I dream of Jeannie with the light brown hair,
Floating, like a vapour, on the soft summer air.
1854 'Jeannie with the Light Brown Hair'.

62 Beautiful dreamer, wake unto me,
Starlight and dewdrop are waiting for thee.
1864 'Beautiful Dreamer'.

Foster, Vince(nt W, Jr)
Deputy Counsel, Clinton White House.

63 I was not meant for the spotlight of public life in Washington. Here running people down is considered sport.
1993 Note found after his suicide. Reported in the *New York Times*, 13 Aug.

Fowles, John Robert 1926–
English novelist. He scored a cult success with *The Magus* (1965, revised 1977), and consolidated his reputation as an ambitious experimental writer with *The French Lieutenant's Woman* (1969).

64 All perfect republics are a perfect nonsense. The craving to risk death is our last great perversion. We come from night, we go into night. Why live in night?
1965 *The Magus*, ch.19.

65 And if you are wise you will never pity the past for what it did not know, but pity yourself for what it did.
1965 *The Magus*, ch.24.

66 That is the great distinction between the sexes. Men see objects, women see the relationship between objects... It is an extra dimension of feeling which we men are without and one that makes war abhorrent to all real women—and absurd.
1965 *The Magus*, ch.52.

67 In essence the Renaissance was simply the green end of one of civilization's hardest winters.
1969 *The French Lieutenant's Woman*, ch.10.

68 We all write poems; it is simply that poets are the ones who write in words.

1969 *The French Lieutenant's Woman*, ch.19.

69 The more abhorrent a news item the more comforting it was to be the recipient since the fact that it had happened elsewhere proved that it had not happened here, was not happening here, and would therefore never happen here.

1974 *The Ebony Tower*, 'Poor Koko'.

70 Cricket remains for me the game of games, the sanspareil, the great metaphor, the best marriage ever devised of mind and body...For me it remains the Proust of pastimes, the subtlest and most poetic, the most past-and-present; whose beauty can lie equally in days, in a whole, or in one tiny phrase, a blinding split second.

Quick Singles, 'Vain Memories'. Quoted in Helen Exley *Cricket Quotations* (1992).

Fox, Charles James 1749–1806

English Liberal statesman. He formed an administration with Lord North in 1783, and on its failure became Pitt's leading parliamentary adversary. He was a strong apponent of the war with France, and an advocate of non-intervention.

71 How much the greatest event it is that ever happened in the world—and how much the best.

1779 On the fall of the Bastille. Letter to Richard Fitzpatrick, 30 Jul.

72 The worst of a revolution is a restoration.

1785 House of Commons, 10 Dec.

73 I die happy.

1806 Last words. Quoted in Lord John Russell *Life and Times of C J Fox*, vol.3 (1860), ch.9.

Fox, George 1624–90

English itinerant Puritan preacher and writer, who was imprisoned for dissent. He was the founder of Society of Friends (known as 'Quakers').

74 One morning, as I was sitting by the fire, a great cloud came over me, and a temptation beset me, and I sate still... And I sate still under it and let it alone, a living hope rose in me, and a true voice arose in me which cried: There is a living God who made all things. And immediately the cloud and temptation vanished away, and the life rose over it all, and my heart was glad, and I praised the living God.

1648 *Journal of George Fox*.

75 Walk cheerfully over the world, answering that of God in everyone.

1656 *Journal of George Fox*.

Frame, Janet Paterson also known as *Jean Paterson Frame* 1924–

New Zealand poet and writer. She was misdiagnosed as schizophrenic, and spent eight years in psychiatric hospitals. Her autobiographical trilogy *To the Is-land* (1982), *An Angel at my Table* (1984) and *The Envoy from Mirror City* (1985) was made into an award-winning film by Jane Campion.

76 What use the green river, the gold place, if time and death pinned human in the pocket of my land not rest from taking underground the green all-willowed and white rose and bean flower and morning-mist picnic of song in pepper-pot breast of thrush?

1961 *Owls Do Cry*, pt.1, ch.4.

77 From the first place of liquid darkness, within the second place of air and light, I set down the following record with its mixture of fact and truths and memories of truths and its direction always toward the Third Place, where the starting point is myth.

1982 *To the Is-land*, ch.1, 'In the Second Place'.

78 I was born...with ready-made parents and a sister and brother who had already begun their store of experience, inaccessible to me except through their language and the record, always slightly different, of our mother and father, and as each member of the family was born, each, in a sense with memories on loan, began to supply the individual furnishings of each Was-land, each Is-land, and the hopes and dreams of the Future.

1982 *To the Is-land*, ch.1, 'In the Second Place'.

79 The word *permanent*...had its own kind of revenge on those who misused it, for the Bible said that nothing was permanent and everything came and went.

1982 *To the Is-land*, ch.2, 'Toward the Is-Land'.

France, Anatole pseudonym of *Jacques Anatole François Thibault* 1844–1924

French novelist, poet and essayist, who won the Nobel Prize for literature in 1921. Along with Emile Zola, he championed the cause of Dreyfus.

80 *Le bon critique est celui qui raconte les aventures de son âme au milieu des chefs-d'oeuvres.*

The good critic is one who recognizes the adventures of his own soul in great works of art.

1892 *La Vie littéraire*, préface.

81 *Le livre est l'opium de l'Occident.*

Books are the opium of the West.

1892 *La Vie littéraire*, préface.

▷ See Marx 660:6.

82 *La faim et l'amour sont les deux axes du monde.*

Hunger and love are the two axes of the world.
1892 *La Vie littéraire*, pt.3.

83 *L'histoire est condamnée, par un vice de nature, au mensonge.*

History is condemned, by a defect of nature, to lies.
1892 *La Vie littéraire*, pt.17.

84 *Les vérités découvertes par l'intelligence demeurent stériles.*

Truths discovered by intelligence are sterile.
1892 *La Vie littéraire*, pt.21.

85 *Je tiens à mon imperfection comme à ma raison d'être.*

I hold on to my imperfection as tightly as my reason for being.
1894 *Le Jardin d'Epicure.*

86 *Il y a toujours un moment où la curiosité devient un péché, et le diable s'est toujours mis du côté des savants.*

There is always a moment when curiosity becomes a sin and the devil is always on the side of the learned.
1894 *Le Jardin d'Epicure.*

87 *L'histoire n'est pas une science, c'est un art. On n'y réussit que par l'imagination.*

History is not a science. It is an art. One only can succeed in it through the imagination.
1894 *Le Jardin d'Epicure.*

88 To disarm the strong and arm the weak would be to change the social order which it's my job to preserve. Justice is the means by which established injustices are sanctioned.
1901 *Crainquebille.*

89 *Le poireau, c'est l'asperge du pauvre.*

The leek is the asparagus of the poor.
1906 *Crainquebille.*

90 *La majestueuse égalité des lois, qui interdit au riche comme au pauvre de coucher sous les ponts, de mendier dans les rues et de voler du pain.*

The majestic equality of laws forbids the rich as well as the poor to sleep under bridges, to beg in the streets and to steal bread.
1910 *Le Lys rouge.*

St Francis of Assisi c.1181–1226

Italian monk and saint, founder of the Franciscan order. The son of a wealthy merchant, in 1206 he renounced his patrimony and became a hermit, attracting followers who rejected all forms of property. His works include sermons, ascetic treatises and hymns.

91 Lord, make me an instrument of Your peace.
Where there is hatred, let me sow love;
Where there is injury, pardon;
Where there is doubt, faith;
Where there is despair, hope;
Where there is darkness, light;
Where there is sadness, joy.

O divine Master, grant that I may not so much
  seek
To be consoled as to console;
To be understood as to understand;
To be loved as to love.
For it is in giving that we receive;
It is in pardoning that we are pardoned;
And it is in dying that we are born to eternal life.
Attributed prayer, traditionally known as the 'Prayer of St Francis'.

92 *Bene veniat soror mea mors.*

Welcome, my sister Death.
1226 Last words. Quoted in Thomas of Celano *Life of St Francis* (c.1245), bk.2, ch.163.

Francis, Dick (Richard Stanley) 1920–

English jockey and writer. In the Grand National of 1956 he was on the point of winning when his horse collapsed. Subsequently he became a writer of popular thrillers with a racing background.

93 I approach chapter One each year with a deeper foreboding than I ever felt facing Becher's.
Quoted in Colin Jarman *The Guinness Dictionary of Sports Quotations* (1990).

Francis I 1494–1547

King of France (1515–47) after his father-in-law Louis XII. The chief feature of his reign was his military conflict with Emperor Charles V.

94 *De toutes choses ne m'est demeuré que l'honneur et la vie qui est saulve.*

Of all I had, only honour and life have been spared.
1525 Letter to his mother, Louise of Savoy, after his defeat and capture by Charles V at Pavia, 24 Feb. Collected in *Collection des documents inedits sur l'histoire de France* (1847), vol.1.

95 *Souvent femme varie,*
Mal habil qui s'y fie

Woman is often fickle,
Foolish the man who trusts her.
Couplet scratched by the king on the glass of a window at Chambord. Quoted in Vincent Cronin *Louis XIV* (1964), p.175.

96 But is he a patriot for me?
On being assured of the loyalty of a candidate for high office. The phrase was later used as a title by John Osborne for his 1965 play.

Frankenthaler, Helen 1928–

US artist, a key figure in the Abstract Expressionism school. Her innovative, colourful works include *The Human Edge* (1967).

97 A picture that is beautiful, or that comes off, or that works, looks as if it was all made at one stroke.

   1972 Quoted in Ian Crofton (ed) *A Dictionary of Art Quotations* (1988).

98 I follow the rules until I go against them all.

   1993 On translating her large, lyrical abstracts from paintings to prints. In the *Washington Times*, 16 Apr.

Franklin, Benjamin 1706–90

US statesman, author and scientist, whose popular *Poor Richard's Almanack* first appeared in 1732. He proved that lightning and electricity are identical and suggested that buildings should be protected by lightning conductors. He was involved in the Declaration of Independence (1775), and helped secure British recognition (1783).

99 The body of
   Benjamin Franklin, printer,
   (Like the cover of an old book,
   Its contents worn out,
   And stripped of its lettering and gilding)
   Lies here, food for worms!
   Yet the work itself shall not be lost,
   For it will, as he believed, appear once more
   In a new
   And more beautiful edition,
   Corrected and amended
   By its Author!

   1728 Proposed epitaph for himself.

1 To lengthen thy Life, lessen thy Meals.

   1733 *Poor Richard's Almanack*, Jun.

2 He that drinks fast, pays slow.

   1733 *Poor Richard's Almanack*, Aug.

3 Necessity never made a good bargain.

   1735 *Poor Richard's Almanack*, Apr.

4 Nothing but Money,
   Is sweeter than Honey.

   1735 *Poor Richard's Almanack*, Jun.

5 Time is money.

   1748 *Advice to a Young Tradesman.*

6 Fond Pride of Dress is sure an Empty Curse;
   E'er Fancy you consult, consult your Purse.

   1751 *Poor Richard Improved*, May.

7 A little neglect may breed mischief...for want of a nail, the shoe was lost; for want of a shoe, the horse was lost; and for want of a horse the rider was lost.

   1758 *Poor Richard's Almanack*, preface.

8 Some punishment seems preparing for a people who are so ungratefully abusing the best Constitution and the best king that any nation was ever blessed with.

   1768 Speech in London during the Wilkes riots, May.

9 There never was a good war or a bad peace.

   1773 Letter, 11 Sep.

10 We must indeed all hang together or, most assuredly, we shall all hang separately.

   1776 On signing the Declaration of Independence, 4 Jul.

11 Furnished as all Europe is with Academies of Science, with nice instruments and the spirit of experimentation, the progress of human knowledge will be rapid and discoveries made of which we have at present no conception. I begin to be almost sorry I was born since I cannot have the happiness of knowing what will be known a hundred years hence.

   1783 Letter to Sir Joseph Banks, President of the Royal Society, 27 Jul.

12 In this world nothing can be said to be certain, except death and taxes.

   1789 Letter to Jean Baptiste Le Roy, 13 Nov.

   ▷ See Defoe 312:87

13 What is the use of a new-born child?

   Reply when questioned as to the use of a new invention. Quoted in J Parton *Life and Times of Benjamin Franklin* (1864), pt.4, ch.17.

Franklin, (Stella Marian Sarah) Miles
pseudonym *Brent of Bin Bin* 1879–1954

Australian novelist, journalist and feminist. After writing *My Brilliant Career* (1901), she moved to the US (1906) then England (1915), returning to Australia in 1927. Other work includes the *Brent of Bin* series (1928), the autobiographical *My Career Goes Bung* (1946) and critical essays.

14 This was life—my life—my career, my brilliant career!

   1901 *My Brilliant Career*, ch.5.

15 Grannie remarked that I might have the spirit of an Australian but I had by no means the manners of a lady.

   1901 *My Brilliant Career*, ch.19.

16 I am proud that I am an Australian, a daughter of the Southern Cross, a child of the mighty bush. I am thankful I am a peasant, a part of the bone and muscle of my nation, and earn my bread by the sweat of my brow, as man was meant to do. I rejoice I was not born a parasite, one of the blood-suckers

who loll on velvet and satin, crushed from the proceeds of human sweat and blood and souls.
1901 *My Brilliant Career*, ch.38.

Franz Josef I 1830–1916

Emperor of Austria (1848) and King of Hungary (1867).

17 Farewell youth!
1848 On signing the document that made him Emperor, following the abdication of Ferdinand. Attributed, quoted in A J P Taylor *From Napoleon to the Second International* (1993).

Fraser, George MacDonald 1925–

English writer of historical fiction.

18 I have observed, in the course of a dishonest life, that when a rogue is outlining a treacherous plan, he works harder to convince himself than to move his hearers.
1969 *Flashman*.

Fraser, Major Sir Keith Alexander
1867–1935

British politician. After his army career he became MP for Leicestershire (1918-23) and a Justice of the Peace for Ross and Cromarty.

19 I never met anyone in Ireland who understood the Irish question, except one Englishman who had been there only a week.
1919 House of Commons, May.

Fraser, (John) Malcolm 1930–

Australian politician. He became an MP in 1955 and leader of the Liberals in 1975. He formed a caretaker government until becoming Prime Minister (Dec). Defeated in the 1983 elections, he retired soon afterwards.

20 Life is not meant to be easy.
1971 The Deakin Lecture, Melbourne, 20 Jul.

Frayne, Trent 1918–

Canadian sportswriter.

21 It is an axiom of sports that the legs go first. For sportswriters, it's the enthusiasm.
1990 *The Tales of an Athletic Supporter*.

Frederick II 1194–1250

Holy Roman Emperor, last of the Hohenstaufen line. His plans to consolidate his power in Italy were frustrated by the Lombard cities and the popes. During the Fifth Crusade in 1228 he took possession of Jerusalem, and crowned himself king there (1229).

22 Our work is to present things that are as they are.
De Ate Venandi cum Avibus

Frederick II, the Great 1712–86

King of Prussia from 1740. He fought against the Austrians in the War of the Austrian Succession (1740–8) and seized Silesia in 1741. In 1772 he shared in the first partition of Poland. By the time of his death, Prussia had become a world power.

23 Troops always ready to act, my well-filled treasury, and the liveliness of my disposition—these were my reasons for making war on Maria Theresa.
1741 Letter to Voltaire.

24 Rascals, would you live for ever?
1757 Attributed, to hesitant guards at the Battle of Kolin, 18 Jun.
▷ See Daly 303:51.

25 *Chassez les préjugés par la porte, ils rentreront par la fenêtre.*

Drive out prejudices through the door, and they will return through the window.
1771 Letter to Voltaire, 19 Mar.

26 *Vanité des Vanités; Vanité de la géométrie.*

Vanity of vanities! Vanity of mathematics!
1778 Letter to Voltaire, 25 Jan, protesting against the increasing use of mathematical calculation in engineering projects, which he saw as theory triumphing over practical experience.

27 My people and I have come to an agreement that satisfies us both. They are to say what they please, and I am to do what I please.
Attributed.

Freed, Arthur pseudonym of Arthur Grossman
1894–1973

US producer and lyricist. He came to Hollywood in 1929 and worked for MGM, producing many well-known musicals. As a lyricist he frequently worked with composer Nacio Herb Brown.

28 I'll walk down the lane with a happy refrain
And singin' just singin' in the rain.
1929 'Singin' in the Rain' featured in *Hollywood Revue of 1929* and other films, including the famous musical of the same title (music by Nacio Herb Brown).

29 You Are My Lucky Star.
1935 Title of song featured in *Broadway Melody of 1936* (music by Nacio Herb Brown).

Freeman, Bud (Lawrence) 1906–91

US jazz saxophonist. He was a leading figure in the evolution of the Chicago style in the 1920s and 1930s.

30 I think audiences come to hear older musicians like me just to see if we can pick up a horn without falling over.
1989 *Crazeology: The Autobiography of a Chicago Jazzman* (as told to Robert Wolf), ch.9.

Freeman, Edward Augustus 1823–92

English historian, Regius Professor of Modern History at Oxford. Among his prolific output were his *History of Federal Government* (1863) and *History of the Norman Conquest* (1867–76).

31 This would be a grand land if only every Irishman would kill a negro, and be hanged for it.
1881 Of America. Letter to F H Dickinson from New Haven, 4 Dec.

32 Nobody can't do nothing never at all for Ireland— you can't help people against their will; that's what it comes to—let it go, let it go.
1882 Letter to Edith Thompson, 29 Jan.

33 History is past politics, and politics is present history.
1886 *Methods of Historical Study.*

Freeman, John 1880–1929

English poet.

34 In that sharp light the fields did lie
Naked and stone-like; each tree stood
Like a tranced woman, bound and stark,
Far off the wood
With darkness ridged the riven dark.
1916 'Stone Trees'.

35 Than these November skies
Is no sky lovelier. The clouds are deep;
Into their grey the subtle spies
Of colour creep,
Changing their high austerity to delight,
Till ev'n the leaden interfolds are bright.
1916 'November Skies'.

36 It was the lovely moon—she lifted
Slowly her white brow among
Bronze cloud-waves that ebbed and drifted
Faintly, faintlier afar.
1916 'It Was the Lovely Moon'.

Freleng, Friz born *Isadore Freleng* 1905–95

US cartoon director.

37 That's all folks!
Porky Pig's stammered trademark, sign-off line for Warner Brothers' *Looney Tunes.*

French, Marilyn 1929–

US writer and feminist scholar. She enjoyed a huge success with her best-selling first novel, *The Woman's Room* (1977), and has written further novels and feminist studies.

38 'I hate discussions of feminism that end up with who does the dishes,' she said. So do I. But at the end, there are always those damned dishes.
1977 *The Women's Room,* bk.1, ch.21.

39 Whatever they may be in public life, whatever their relations with men, in their relations with women, all men are rapists, and that's all they are. They rape us with their eyes, their laws, and their codes.
1977 *The Women's Room,* bk.5, ch.19.

Freud, Sigmund 1856–1939

Austrian neurologist, founder of psychoanalysis. He published his controversial but influential ideas in such works as *The Interpretation of Dreams* (1900), *The Psychopathology of Everyday Life* (1904) and *Ego and Id* (1923).

40 I am actually not at all a man of science... I am by temperament nothing but a conquistador, an adventurer.
1900 Letter to Wilhelm Fliess, Feb.

41 Congratulations and bouquets keep pouring in, as if the role of sexuality had been suddenly recognised by His Majesty, the interpretation of dreams confirmed by the Council of Ministers, and the necessity of the psychoanalytic therapy of hysteria carried by a two-thirds majority in Parliament.
1902 Letter to Wilhelm Fliess, 11 Mar, describing the public enthusiasm in Vienna that greeted his appointment to an associate professorship at the age of 45.

42 The principal task of civilisation, its actual raison d'être, is to defend us against nature.
1903 *Introductory Lectures.*

43 A woman who is very anxious to get children always reads 'storks' for 'stocks'.
1904 *Psychopathology of Everyday Life.*

44 *Die Anatomie ist das Schicksal.*

Anatomy is destiny.
1924 *Collected Works,* vol.5.

45 At bottom God is nothing more than an exalted father.
1927 *The Future of an Illusion.*

46 The more the fruits of knowledge become accessible to men, the more widespread is the decline of religious belief.
1927 *The Future of an Illusion.*

Friday, Nancy 1937–

US feminist and writer, whose works include *My Secret Garden* (1973), *My Mother, My Self* (1977) and *Women on Top* (1991).

47 If you believe in the maternal instinct and fail at mother love, you fail as a woman. It is a controlling idea that holds us in an iron grip.
1977 *My Mother, My Self,* ch.1.

48 The older I get, the more of my mother I see in myself.

1977 *My Mother, My Self,* ch.1.

Friedan, Betty (Elizabeth) Naomi née Goldstein 1921–

US feminist and writer, founder of the National Organization for Women (1966) and author of the seminal feminist text *The Feminine Mystique* (1963).

49 The problem lay buried, unspoken, for many years in the minds of American women. It was a strange stirring, a sense of dissatisfaction, a yearning that women suffered in the middle of the twentieth century in the United States. Each suburban wife struggled with it alone. As she made the beds, shopped for groceries, matched slipcover material, ate peanut butter sandwiches with her children, chauffeured Cub Scouts and Brownies, lay beside her husband at night—she was afraid to ask even of herself the silent question—'Is this all?'

1963 *The Feminine Mystique,* ch.1, 'The Problem that has no Name'.

50 Women, even though they are almost too visible as sex objects in this country, are invisible people.

1969 Speech at First National Conference for Repeal of Abortion Laws, Chicago.

51 Motherhood will only be a joyous and responsible human act when women are free to make, with full conscious choice and full human responsibility, the decisions to become mothers.

1969 Speech at First National Conference for Repeal of Abortion Laws, Chicago.

Friedman, Milton 1912–

US economist. A leading monetarist, his work includes the permanent income theory of consumption, and the role of money in determining events, particularly the US Great Depression. He was awarded the Nobel Prize for Economics in 1976.

52 Economics as a positive science is a body of tentatively accepted generalizations about economic phenomena that can be used to predict the consequences of changes in circumstances.

1953 'The Methodology of Positive Economics' in *Essays in Positive Economics.*

53 There is no such thing as a free lunch.

1973 Lecture. The phrase is thought to have been coined anonymously, perhaps referring to the 19c US tradition of supplying food in bars to patrons buying drinks.

54 The price that the market sets on the services of our resources is similarly affected by a bewildering mixture of chance and choice. Frank Sinatra's voice was highly valued in twentieth century United States. Would it have been highly valued in twentieth-century India, if he had happened to be born and to live there?

1981 *Free to Choose* (with Rose Friedman).

55 No major institution in the US has so poor a record of performance over so long a period as the Federal Reserve, yet so high a public reputation.

1988 'The Fed Has No Clothes', in *The Wall Street Journal,* 15 Apr.

Friedrich, Carl

Historian.

56 To be an American is an ideal, while to be a Frenchman is a fact.

1987 In *Time,* 9 Nov.

Friedrich, Caspar David 1774–1840

German painter, who depicted landscape as vast and desolate expanses in which man is a melancholy spectator.

57 Just as the pious man prays without speaking a word and the Almighty hearkens unto him, so the artist with true feelings *paints* and the sensitive man understands and recognizes it.

Quoted in S Hinz *Caspar David Friedrich in Briefen und Bekenntnissen* (1968).

58 The Divine is everywhere, even in a grain of sand, here I have represented it in bull-rushes.

Remark to the German artist Peter Cornelius, quoted in S Hinz *Caspar David Friedrich in Briefen und Bekenntnissen* (1968).

59 Close your bodily eye, so that you may see your picture first with the spiritual eye. Then bring to the light of day that which you have seen in the darkness so that it may react on others from the outside inwards.

Quoted in *Caspar David Friedrich 1774–1840,* Tate Gallery (1972).

60 Despite what even many artists appear to believe, art is not and should not be merely a skill. It should actually be completely and utterly the language of our feelings, our frame of mind; indeed, even of our devotion and our prayers.

Quoted in *Caspar David Friedrich 1774–1840,* Tate Gallery (1972).

61 The artist should not only paint what he sees before him, but also what he sees within him. If, however, he sees nothing within him, then he should also omit to paint that which he sees before him.

Quoted in *Caspar David Friedrich 1774–1840,* Tate Gallery (1972).

62 Every true work of art must express a distinct feeling.

Quoted in William Vaughn *Romantic Art* (1978).

Frisch, Max Rudolph 1911–91

Swiss writer, novelist and playwright. His novels include *I'm Not Stiller* (1954), *Homo Faber* (1957), and *A Wilderness of Mirrors* (1964). His plays include *The Firebugs* (1953) and *Andorra* (1961, translated 1962).

63 *Ich kann nur berichten, was ich weiß.*

I can only report on what I know.
1957 *Homo Faber*, pt.1.

64 *Technik…Kniff, die Welt so einzurichten, daß wir sie nicht erleben müssen.*

Technology…the knack of so arranging the world that we don't have to experience it.
1957 *Homo Faber*, pt.2.

65 *Kein Mensch, wenn er die Welt sieht, die sie ihm hinterlassen, versteht seine Eltern.*

No person, upon seeing the world pass behind him, understands his parents.
1961 *Andorra*, sc.9.

66 *Ich habe kein Gemüt, sondern Angst.*

I have no comfort, only anxiety.
1961 *Andorra*, sc.9.

67 *Man kann sich seinen Vater nicht wählen.*

A person cannot choose his father.
1961 *Andorra*, 10.

68 *Ich gehe ins Theater ja auch nicht als Voyeur.*

I do not go into the theater as a voyeur.
1967 *Biographie.*

Frohman, Charles 1860–1915

US theatre manager. Among his many successful productions were several plays by J M Barrie.

69 Why fear death? It's the most beautiful adventure in life.
1915 Last words, paraphrasing a line in J M Barrie's *Peter Pan*, said to the actress Rita Jolivet as the *Lusitania* went down after being torpedoed by a German submarine, 7 May.

Fromm, Erich 1900–80

German-born US psychoanalyst and author, who emigrated in 1934 to the US, where he practised psychoanalysis and lectured at various institutions.

70 The pace of science forces the pace of technique. Theoretical physics forces atomic energy on us; the successful production of the fission bomb forces upon us the manufacture of the hydrogen bomb. We do not choose our problems, we do not choose our products; we are pushed, we are forced—by what? By a system which has no purpose and goal transcending it, and which makes man its appendix.
1955 *The Sane Society.*

Frost, Robert Lee 1874–1963

US poet, whose work is rooted in New England. He established his reputation with *A Boy's World* (1913) and *North of Boston* (1914) and won Pulitzer Prizes in 1924, 1931, 1937 and 1943.

71 Most of the change we think we see in life Is due to truths being in and out of favour.
1914 *North of Boston*, 'The Black Cottage'.

72 Something there is that doesn't love a wall, That sends the frozen-ground-swell under it, And spills the upper boulders in the sun; And makes gaps even two can pass abreast.
1914 *North of Boston*, 'Mending Wall'.

73 Before I built a wall I'd ask to know What I was walling in or walling out, And to whom I was like to give offence.
1914 *North of Boston*, 'Mending Wall'.

74 Part of a moon was falling down the west, Dragging the whole sky with it to the hills.
1914 *North of Boston*, 'The Death of the Hired Man'.

75 'Home is the place where, when you have to go there,
They have to take you in.'
'I should have called it
Something you somehow haven't to deserve.'
1914 *North of Boston*, 'The Death of the Hired Man'.

76 A sentence is a sound in itself on which sounds called words may be strung.
1914 Letter to John Bartlett, 22 Feb.

77 I shall be telling this with a sigh Somewhere ages and ages hence: Two roads diverged in a wood, and I— I took the one less travelled by, And that has made all the difference.
1916 'The Road Not Taken'.

78 We love the things we love for what they are.
1916 'Hyla Brook'.

79 The question that he frames in all but words Is what to make of a diminished thing.
1916 'The Oven Bird'.

80 I'd like to go by climbing a birch tree And climb black branches up a snow-white trunk *Toward* heaven, till the tree could bear no more, But dipped its top and set me down again. That would be good both going and coming back. One could do worse than be a swinger of birches.
1916 'Birches'.

81 They listened at his heart.
Little—less—nothing!—and that ended it.
No more to build on there. And they, since they
Were not the one dead, turned to their affairs.

1916 'Out, Out—'.

82 No wonder poets sometimes have to *seem*
So much more businesslike than businessmen.
Their wares are so much harder to get rid of.
1923 'New Hampshire'.

83 He knew too well for any earthly use
The line where man leaves off and nature starts,
And never overstepped it save in dreams.
1923 'New Hampshire'.

84 Never tell me that not one star of all
That slip from heaven at night and softly fall
Has been picked up with stones to build a wall.
1923 'A Star in a Stoneboat'.

85 Some say the world will end in fire,
Some say in ice.
From what I've tasted of desire
I hold with those who favour fire.
But if I had to perish twice,
I think I know enough of hate
To say that for destruction ice
Is also great
And would suffice.
1923 'Fire and Ice', complete poem.

86 The woods are lovely, dark and deep.
But I have promises to keep,
And miles to go before I sleep,
And miles to go before I sleep.
1923 'Stopping by Woods on a Snowy Evening'.

87 I have been one acquainted with the night.
1928 'Acquainted with the Night'.

88 It is this backward motion toward the source,
Against the stream, that most we see ourselves in.
The tribute of the current to the source.
1928 'West-Running Brook'.

89 The land may vary more;
But wherever the truth may be—
The water comes ashore,
And the people look at the sea.
1928 'Neither Far Out Nor in Deep'.

90 A poet is a person who thinks there is something
special about a poet and about his loving one
unattainable woman. You'll usually find he takes
the physical out on whores. I am defining a
romantic poet—and there is no other kind. An
unromantic poet is a self-contradiction.
1930 Letter to Louis Untermeyer, 6 Jun.

91 Writing free verse is like playing tennis with the net
down.
1935 Address at Milton Academy, Mass, 17 May.

92 What brought the kindred spider to that height,

Then steered the white moth thither in the night?
What but design of darkness to appall?—
If design govern in a thing so small.
1936 'Design'.

93 I never dared be radical when young
For fear it would make me conservative when old.
1936 'Ten Mills, 1. Precaution'.

94 Like a piece of ice on a hot stove the poem must
ride on its own melting. A poem may be worked
over once it is in being, but may not be worried
into being.
1939 'The Figure a Poem Makes', preface to *Collected Poems*.

95 Happiness Makes up in Height for What it Lacks
in Length.
1942 Title of poem.

96 The land was ours before we were the land's.
She was our land more than a hundred years
Before we were her people.
1942 'The Gift Outright'.

97 And were an epitaph to be my story
I'd have a short one ready for my own.
I would have written of me on my stone:
I had a lover's quarrel with the world.
1942 'The Lesson for Today'.

98 We dance round in a ring and suppose,
But the Secret sits in the middle and knows.
1942 'The Secret Sits', complete poem.

99 I have never started a poem yet whose end I knew.
Writing a poem is discovering.
1955 In *The New York Times*, 7 Nov.

1 Forgive, O Lord, my little jokes on Thee
And I'll forgive Thy great big one on me.
1959 'The Preacher', complete poem.

2 Poetry is a way of taking life by the throat.
Quoted in Elizabeth S Sargeant *Robert Frost: The Trail By Existence* (1960).

3 Summoning artists to participate
In the august occasions of the state
Seems something artists ought to celebrate.
1961 'For John F Kennedy: His Inauguration', 20 Jan. Snow-blindness prevented the aged poet from reading beyond the first three lines on the occasion.

4 Courage is in the air in bracing whiffs.
1961 'For John F Kennedy: His Inauguration', 20 Jan.

5 Education is... hanging around until you've caught
on.
Recalled on his death, 29 Jan 1963.

6 The mind skating circles around itself as it moves
forward.
His definition of style. Recalled on his death, 29 Jan 1963.

7 The right reader of a good poem can tell the moment it strikes him that he has taken an immortal wound—that he will never get over it.
Recalled on his death, 29 Jan 1963.

8 Poetry is what is lost in translation. It is also what is lost in interpretation.
Quoted in Louis Untermeyer *Robert Frost: A Backward Look* (1964).

Froude, James Anthony 1818–94

English writer and historian, who resigned his Oxford fellowship after controversy over his early novels. He wrote a *History of England from the Fall of Wolsey to the Spanish Armada* (12 vols, 1856–69).

9 Wild animals never kill for sport. Man is the only one to whom the torture and death of his fellow-creatures is amusing in itself.
1886 *Oceana.*

Fry, C(harles) B(urgess) 1872–1956

English all-round sportsman, who represented his country in athletics, cricket and soccer. As a cricketer, he played 26 Tests for England, some as captain. After World War II he served as India's delegate to the League of Nations and declined an offer of the throne of Albania.

10 It is a standing insult to sportsmen to have to play under a rule which assumes that players intend to trip, hack and push their opponents, and to behave like cads of the most unscrupulous kidney. The lines marking a penalty area are a disgrace to the playing fields of a public school.
1907 Quoted in Colin Jarman *The Guinness Dictionary of Sports Quotations* (1990).

11 In football it is widely acknowledged that if both sides agree to cheat, cheating is fair.
1911 Quoted in Colin Jarman *The Guinness Dictionary of Sports Quotations* (1990).

12 The game is so full of plot-interest and drama.
Of rugby union. Quoted in E H D Sewell *Rugger: The Man's Game* (1950).

Fry, Christopher pseudonym of Christopher Harris 1907–

English playwright. His early poetic drama was succeeded by comedies and tragi-comedies such as *A Phoenix Too Frequent* (1946) and *Venus Observed* (1950).

13 The Lady's not for Burning.
1949 Play title, subsequently reworked by Margaret Thatcher in the form 'The lady's not for turning' at the Conservative Party Conference, 1980.

14 What after all
Is a halo? It's only one more thing to keep clean.
1949 *The Lady's not for Burning*, act 1.

15 Where in this small-talking world can I find
A longitude with no platitude?
1949 *The Lady's not for Burning*, act 3.

16 I hope
I've done nothing so monosyllabic as to cheat.
A spade is never so merely a spade as the word Spade would imply.
1950 *Venus Observed*, act 1.

17 The Dark is Light Enough.
1954 Title of play.

Fry, Roger Eliot 1866–1934

English artist and art critic, who championed modern artists such as Cézanne, organizing the first London exhibition of Post-Impressionists in 1910. He devised an aesthetic theory of 'significant form'.

18 The trouble with Moore is that he knows what a work of art is, and is trying to make one.
c.1930 Of Henry Moore. Quoted in Robert Medley *Drawn from the Life: a Memoir* (1983).

19 Art is significant deformity.
Quoted in Virginia Woolf *Roger Fry* (1940), ch.8.

Frye, Northrop 1912–91

Canadian literary critic and Episcopalian priest. His influential *Anatomy of Criticism* (1957) explores the common motifs and myths underlying literature.

20 Literature is a human apocalypse, man's revelation to man, and criticism is not a body of adjudications, but the awareness of that revelation, the last judgment of mankind.
1963 *The Educated Imagination*, 'The Keys of Dreamland'.

21 Literature is conscious mythology: as society develops, its mythical stories become structural principles of story-telling, its mythical concepts, sun-gods and the like, become habits of metaphoric thought. In a fully mature literary tradition the writer enters into a structure of traditional stories and images.
1971 *The Bush Garden*, 'Conclusion'.

22 Where is here?
'Haunted by Lack of Ghosts', in David Staines (ed) *The Canadian Imagination* (1977).

23 Most of my writing consists of an attempt to translate aphorisms into continuous prose.
Quoted in Richard Kostelanetz, 'The Literature Professors' Literature Professor', in *The Michigan Quarterly Review*, Fall 1978.

24 The knowledge that you can have is inexhaustible, and what is inexhaustible is benevolent. The knowledge that you cannot have is of the riddles of birth and dead, of our future destiny and the

purposes of God. Here there is no knowledge, but illusions that restrict freedom and limit hope. Accept the mystery behind knowledge: It is not darkness but shadow.

1988 Address, Metropolitan United Church, Toronto, 10 Apr, quoted by Alexandra Johnston in *Vic Report*, spring 1991.

25　Even the human heart is slightly left of centre.

Quoted by Paul Wilson in 'Growing Up with Orwell', in *The Idler*, Jul-Aug 1989.

Fuentes, Carlos　1928–

Mexican novelist and playwright, press secretary with the UN and Ambassador to France (1975–7). His first collection of short stories, *Los dias enmascarados* (The Masked Days, 1964) was followed by *Terra Nostra* (1975).

26　*Yo soy un artista. El placer de la carne le resta fuerzas a mi vocación pictórica, prefiero sentir que los jugos de mi sexo fluyen hacia un cuadro, lo irrigan, lo fertilizan, lo realzan; cástrame el goce de la carne, satisfáceme el goce del arte.*

I am an artist. The pleasure of the flesh robs strength from my artistic vocation, I prefer to feel my sexual juices flow toward a painting, wash over it, fertilize it, realize it; the delights of the flesh castrate me, the delights of art satisfy me.

1975 *Terra Nostra* (1976), 'El cronista'.

27　What America does best is to understand itself. What it does worst is to understand others.

1986 In *Time*, 16 Jun.

Fulbright, J(ames) William　1905–95

US Democratic politician, lawyer and author. As Chairman of the Senate Committee on Foreign Relations, he became a major critic of the Vietnam War (1964–75).

28　We have the power to do any damn fool thing we want to do, and we seem to do it every 10 minutes.

1952 In *Time*, 4 Feb.

29　In a democracy dissent is an act of faith. Like medicine, the test of its value is not in its taste, but its effects.

1966 Speech to the US Senate, 21 Apr.

30　Fearful and hostile behavior is not rational but neither is it uncommon, either to individuals or to nations, including our own.

1995 On the 'arrogance of power' of US policy on Vietnam. In the *New Yorker*, 6 Mar.

Fulford, Robert　1932–

Canadian cultural commentator.

31　My generation of Canadians grew up believing that, if we were very good or very smart, or both, we would someday *graduate* from Canada.

1970 'Notebook', in *Saturday Night*, Oct.

Fuller, (Sarah) Margaret, Marchioness Ossoli　1810–50

US feminist and literary critic. She edited *Dial* (a transcendentalist journal, 1840–2) and moved to New York (1844) then Italy (1847), where she married Marquis Ossoli and was involved in the Revolution. She was shipwrecked returning to New York.

32　Beware of over-great pleasure in being popular or even beloved.

1840 Letter to her brother, 20 Dec. Collected in Alice Rossi *The Feminist Papers* (1973).

33　As the friend of the negro assumes that one man cannot, by right, hold another in bondage, should the friend of woman assume that man cannot, by right, lay even well-meant restrictions on woman.

1843 'The Great Lawsuit', in *Dial*, vol.4, Jul.

34　It is well known that of every strong woman they say she has a masculine mind.

1843 'The Great Lawsuit', in *Dial*, vol.4, Jul.

Fuller, Peter　1947–90

English art critic, writer and founder of the magazine *Modern Painters*.

35　It is only a mild exaggeration to say that now no one wants Fine Artists, except Fine Artists, and that neither they nor anyone else have the slightest idea what they should be doing, or for whom they should be doing it.

1981 *Beyond the Crisis in Art*.

Fuller, R(ichard) Buckminster　1895–1983

US architect, inventor, engineer and philosopher, whose revolutionary technological designs reflect his personal vision of a better-designed and more efficient future. In 1962 he became Norton Professor of Poetry at Harvard.

36　God, to me, it seems,
is a verb
not a noun
proper or improper.

1940 Poem, published in *No More Secondhand God* (1963).
▷ See Hugo 502:79.

37　I just invent, then wait until man comes around to needing what I've invented.

1964 On his innovative geodesic domes. In *Time Magazine*, 10 Jun.

38　Either war is obsolete or men are.

1966 In the *New Yorker*, 8 Jan.

39　I am a passenger on the spaceship, Earth.

1969 *Operating Manual for Spaceship Earth*, ch.1.

40　Now there is one outstandingly important fact regarding Spaceship Earth, and that is that no instruction book came with it.

1969 *Operating Manual for Spaceship Earth*, ch.4.

41 If we do more with less, our response will be
adequate to take care of everybody.
1972 In *Playboy*.

Fuller, Roy Broadbent 1912–91

English poet and novelist. His work is marked by careful
construction and acute observation.

42 As horrible thoughts,
Loud fluttering aircraft slope above his head
At dusk.
The ridiculous empires break like biscuits.
1942 'The Middle of a War'.

43 The poets get a quizzical ahem.
They reflect time, I am the very ticking.
1944 'A Wry Smile'.

44 Anyone happy in this age and place
Is daft or corrupt. Better to abdicate
From a material and spiritual terrain
Fit only for barbarians.
1954 'Translation'.

Fuller, Thomas 1608–61

English antiquarian and divine. His 11-volume *Church
History of Britain* (1655) was attacked as a 'rhapsody'. The
unfinished *Great Worthies of England*, a biographical
miscellany, was published by his son in 1661.

45 Know most of the rooms of thy native country
before thou goest over the threshold thereof.
1642 *The Holy and Profane State*, bk.2, ch.4, 'Of Travelling'.

46 *Mon Mam Cymbry.* That is, Anglesea is the Mother
of Wales.
1662 *History of the Worthies of England*, 'Anglesea'. The saying is
an old one, meaning that Anglesey's corn is enough to sustain all
Wales.

Fuller, Thomas 1654–1734

English physician and writer.

47 Bacchus hath drowned more men than Neptune.
Gnomologia, no.830.

48 Borrowed garments never fit well.
Gnomologia, no.1008.

49 Eat-well is drink-well's brother.
Gnomologia, no.1357.

50 Fine cloth is never out of fashion.
Gnomologia, no.1537.

51 God sends meat, and the devil sends cooks.
Gnomologia, no.1687.

52 Good clothes open all doors.
Gnomologia, no.1705.

53 It is in vain to mislike the current fashion.

Gnomologia, no.2968.

54 The present fashion is always handsome.
Gnomolgia, no.4718.

55 Often drunk, and seldom sober
Falls like the leaves in October.
Gnomologia, no.6219.

56 It signifies nothing to play well and lose.
1732 Quoted in Colin Jarman *The Guinness Dictionary of
Sports Quotations* (1990).

Furthman, Jules 1888–1966

US screenwriter. His credits include *Shanghai Express*
(1932), *Mutiny on the Bounty* (1935), *To Have and Have
Not* (1945) and *The Big Sleep* (1946).

57 You know you don't have to act with me, Steve. You
don't have to say anything and you don't have to do
anything. Not a thing. Oh, maybe just whistle. You
know how to whistle, don't you, Steve? You just put
your lips together—and blow.
1945 Lauren Bacall as Slim to Humphrey Bogart (Steve) in *To
Have and Have Not* (with William Faulkner).

Fuseli, Henry 1741–1825

Swiss-born, but active mainly in England. He was a key
figure of the Romantic movement, as painter,
draughtsman and writer on art.

58 Art, like love, excludes all competition and absorbs
the man.
1789 *Aphorisms on Art*, no.3 (published 1831).

59 The superiority of the Greeks seems not so much
the result of climate and society, as of the simplicity
of their end and the uniformity of their means.
1789 *Aphorisms on Art*, no.148 (published 1831).

60 Art among a religious race produces reliques;
among a military one, trophies, among a
commercial one, articles of trade.
1789 *Aphorisms on Art*, no.149 (published 1831).

61 The forms of virtue are erect, the forms of pleasure
undulate.
1789 *Aphorisms on Art*, no.194 (published 1831).

62 Selection is the invention of the landscape painter.
1789 *Aphorisms on Art*, number 237, (published 1831).

Fyffe, Will 1885–1947

Scottish comedian, singer and actor. He wrote several
sketches for Harry Lauder and when they were rejected
performed them himself, thereby launching a long and
successful career on stage and in film.

63 I belong to Glasgow
Dear old Glasgow town!

But what's the matter with Glasgow?
For it's going round and round.
I'm only a common old working chap,
As anyone can see,
But when I get a couple of drinks on a Saturday,
Glasgow belongs to me.
1921 'I Belong to Glasgow', chorus.

Gabor, Dennis 1900–79

British physicist born in Hungary. Gabor left Germany in 1933 to become professor of electronics at Imperial College, London. He did important work on the electronic microscope and is generally recognized as the main contributor to the discovery of holography.

64 Till now man has been up against Nature: from now on he will be up against his own nature.
1964 *Inventing the Future.*

65 The most important and urgent problems of the technology of today are no longer the satisfactions of the primary needs or of archetypal wishes, but the reparation of the evils and damages wrought by the technology of yesterday.
1970 *Innovations.*

Gabor, Zsa Zsa 1919–

Hungarian-born US actress, sister of Eva Gabor. Her films include *Moulin Rouge* (1953), *Touch of Evil* (1958) and *Arrivederci Baby* (1966).

66 I never hated a man enough to give him diamonds back.
Quoted in *The Observer*, 28 Aug 1957.

67 A girl must marry for love and keep on marrying until she finds it.
Attributed.

Gagarin, Yuri A(lekseyevich) 1934–68

Soviet cosmonaut, the first person to achieve orbital space flight on 12 Apr, 1961.

68 I could have gone on flying through space forever.
1961 In the *New York Times*, 14 Apr.

Gainsborough, Thomas 1727–88

English portrait and landscape painter.

69 I wish you would recollect that Painting and Punctuality mix like Oil and Vinegar, and that Genius and regularity are utter Enemies and must be to the end of time.
1772 Letter to Edward Stratford, 1 May, excusing himself for not yet finishing the portrait of him and his wife.

70 We are all going to heaven, and Vandyke is of the company.

1788 Last words (attributed), quoted in William B Boulton *Thomas Gainsborough* (1905), ch.9.

Gaitskell, Hugh 1906–63

English Labour politician, Leader of the Opposition (1955–63). He opposed Eden's Suez action (1956), and refused to accept a narrow conference vote for unilateral disarmament (1960), surviving the subsequent leadership challenge.

71 Some of us will fight and fight again to save the party we love. We will fight and fight again to bring back sanity and honesty and dignity, so that our party, with its great past, may retain its glory and its greatness.
1960 Denouncing unilateralists trying to gain control of the party. National conference speech, Oct.

72 Let us not forget that we can never go farther than we can persuade at least half the people to go.
1961 Labour party conference speech, Oct.

73 It does mean the end of Britain as an independent European state. It means the end of a thousand years of history.
1962 On Britain joining the European Community. Labour party conference speech.

Galbraith, John Kenneth 1908–

Canadian-born US economist and diplomat, Professor at Harvard (1949–75), Ambassador to India (1961–3) and advisor to Presidents Kennedy and Johnson.

74 The charge that an idea is radical, impractical, or long-haired is met by showing that a prominent businessman has favored it... an additional tactic in this strategy of defense... is to assert that Winston Churchill once sponsored the particular idea. If one is challenged, a sufficiently careful investigation will show that he did.
1955 *Economics and the Art of Controversy.*

75 Few things are as immutable as the addiction of political groups to the ideas by which they have once won office.
1958 *The Affluent Society.*

76 In the affluent society, no useful distinction can be made between luxuries and necessities.
1958 *The Affluent Society.*

77 It takes a certain brashness to attack the accepted economic legends but none at all to perpetuate them. So they are perpetuated.
1960 *The Liberal Hour.*

78 Politics is not the art of the possible. It consists in choosing between the disastrous and the unpalatable.
1962 Letter to John F Kennedy, 2 Mar.
▷ See Butler 216:98.

79 The line dividing the state from what is called private enterprise, or at least from the highly organized part of it, is a traditional fiction.
1967 *The New Industrial State.*

80 The real accomplishment of modern science and technology consists in taking ordinary men, informing them narrowly and deeply and then, through appropriate organization, arranging to have their knowledge combined with that of other specialized but equally ordinary men. This dispenses with the need for genius. The resulting performance, though less inspiring, is far more predictable.
1967 *The New Industrial State.*

81 There are times in politics when you must be on the right side and lose.
1968 In *The Observer*, 11 Feb.

82 It is the good fortune of the affluent country that the opportunity cost of economic discussion is low and hence it can afford all kinds.
1971 *Economics, Peace, and Laughter.*

83 In a world where for pedagogic and other purposes a very large number of economists is required, an arrangement which discourages many of them from rendering public advice would seem to be well conceived.
1971 *Economics, Peace, and Laughter.*

84 Much discussion of money involves a heavy overlay of priestly incantation.
1975 *Money*, p.4.

85 Much of the world's work, it has been said, is done by men who do not feel quite well. Marx is a case in point.
1977 *The Age of Uncertainty*, ch.3.

86 We have escapist fiction...why not escapist biography?
1980 In the *New York Times*, 27 Jul.

87 Speeches in our culture are the vacuum that fills a vacuum.
1984 Speech at the American University, Washington DC. Quoted in *Time* magazine, 18 Jun.

Galeano, Eduardo 1940–

Uruguayan writer and journalist. He left his job as a newspaper editor when he went into exile in Chile in 1973. He lived in Spain (1976–84) and now lives back in Uruguay. His books include *Days and Nights of Love and War* (1978) and *Song of Ourselves* (1975). Both books won the Cuban Casa de la Americas prize.

88 In the house of words was a table of colors. They offered themselves in great fountains and each poet took the color he needed: lemon yellow or sun yellow, ocean blue or smoke blue, crimson red, blood red, wine red.
1991 *The Book of Embraces.*

Galen or *Claudius Galenus* c.130–c.201AD

Greek physician, imperial physician to Marcus Aurelius, Commodus and Severus. He wrote extensively on medical and philosophical matters, and his theories have been highly influential.

89 Much music marreth men's manners.
Quoted in Roger Ascham *Toxophilus* (1545).

Galilei, Galileo 1564–1642

Italian astronomer, mathematician and physicist, credited with anticipating Newton's laws of motion. He constructed the first astronomical telescope, and controversially argued that the earth revolved around the sun.

90 *Eppur si muove.*

Nevertheless, it moves.
1632 Attributed muttered remark, after being compelled to publicly renounce his arguments against a geocentric universe. This famous quotation is almost certainly an invention.

Gallico, Paul William 1897–1976

US journalist, novelist and short-story writer. His works include *The Snow Goose* (1941) and *The Poseidon Adventure* (1969).

91 College football today is one of the last great strongholds of genuine old-fashioned American hypocrisy.
1938 *Farewell to Sport.*

92 When in Doubt—Wash.
1950 *Jennie*, ch.5, chapter title. Peter, having turned into a cat, is taught the proper etiquette.

93 I have covered boxing, promoted boxing, watched it, thought about it, and after long reflection I cannot find a single thing that is good about it either from the point of view of participant or spectator.
Quoted in Edith Summerskill *The Ignoble Art* (1956).

94 No one can be as calculatedly rude as the British, which amazes Americans, who do not understand studied insult and can only offer abuse as a substitute.
1962 In the *New York Times*, 14 Jan.

Galloway, Janice 1956–

Scottish writer. She worked as a teacher, but became a full-time writer after the success of her first novel (chronicling a mental breakdown) and short stories in *Blood* (1991).

95 The Trick is to Keep Breathing.
1989 Title of first novel.

96 I write because I hate being told HOW IT IS. I didn't realise that for a long while. I thought it was LIFE I hated: that the unfairnesses that were explained as JUST HOW IT IS were JUST HOW IT IS. BUT HOW IT IS wasn't.
1993 'Objective Truth and the Grinding Machine'. In Brown and Munro (eds) *Writers Writing* (1993).

97 Quiet book-learning in monasteries and ethereal music, sonnets and courtly love—that stuff is all fantasy and veneer… You couldn't afford to let the beauty of the thing seduce you too far or you forgot the truth and the truth was always hard as iron bloody bars.
1994 *Foreign Parts*, ch.7.

Gallup, George Horace   1901–84

US statistician and public opinion expert. He developed the Gallup polls for testing public opinion, which proved their worth by correctly predicting Franklin Roosevelt's 1936 election victory.

98 Polling is merely an instrument for gauging public opinion. When a president or any other leader pays attention to poll results, he is, in effect, paying attention to the views of the people. Any other interpretation is nonsense.
1979 NBC news, 1 Dec.

99 I could prove God statistically.
Attributed.

Galsworthy, John   1867–1933

English novelist and playwright, best known for his series of novels *The Forsyte Saga* (1906–28). His plays, including *Strife* (1909), illustrate his interest in social and ethical issues. He was awarded the Nobel Prize in 1932.

1 From all *I* can learn, he's got no business, no income, and no connection worth speaking of; but then, I know nothing—nobody tells me anything.
1906 *The Man of Property*, pt.1, ch.1.

2 When a Forsyte was engaged, married, or born, the Forsytes were present; when a Forsyte died—but no Forsyte had as yet died; they did not die; death being contrary to their principles, they took precautions against it, the instinctive precautions of highly vitalised persons who resent encroachments on their property.
1906 *The Man of Property*, pt.1, ch.1.

3 It is not good enough to spend time and ink in describing the penultimate sensations and physical movements of people getting into a state of rut, we all know them so well.

1914 On D H Lawrence's *Sons and Lovers*, in a letter to Edward Garnett, 13 Apr.

4 He was afflicted by the thought that where Beauty was, nothing ever ran quite straight, which, no doubt, was why so many people looked on it as immoral.
1920 *In Chancery*, pt.1, ch.13.

5 When we began this fight, we had clean hands— are they clean now? What's gentility worth if it can't stand fire?
1920 *The Skin Game*, act 3.

6 Slang is vigorous and apt. Probably most of our vital words were once slang.
1927 *Castles in Spain and Other Screeds*.

Galt, John   1779–1839

Scottish novelist and Canadian pioneer. After a failed business venture in London he travelled in the Levant (1809–11) and later turned to writing.

7 In a word, man in London is not quite so good a creature as he is out of it.
1821 *The Ayrshire Legatees*, ch.7, 'Discoveries and Rebellions', letter 22.

8 From the lone shieling of the misty island
Mountains divide us, and the waste of seas—
Yet still the blood is strong, the heart is Highland,
And we in dreams behold the Hebrides!
Fair these broad meads, these hoary woods are
    grand;
But we are exiles from our fathers' land.
1829 'Canadian Boat Song', a translation from the Gaelic attributed to Galt, published in *Blackwood's Magazine*, Sep. It has also been attributed to Walter Scott.

Galtieri, Leopoldo Fortunato   1926–

Argentinian soldier and politician, President of Argentina (1981–3). In 1982, he ordered the invasion of the disputed Malvinas (Falkland) Islands; their recovery by Britain led to his downfall.

9 Why are you telling me this? The British won't fight.
1982 Responding to a warning from US Secretary of State Alexander Haig about the consequence of the invasion.

Galton, Sir Francis   1822–1911

English scientist. He travelled widely in Africa and wrote *The Art of Travel*, which became the explorer's standard handbook.

10 There are even times when any assumption of dignity becomes ludicrous, and the traveller must, as Mungo Park once had to do, 'lay down as a rule to make himself as useless and as insignificant as possible, as the only means of recovering his liberty'.
1855 *The Art of Travel*.

Gandhi, Indira (Priyadarshini) 1917–84

Indian politician and Prime Minister (1966–77, 1980–4). Although a leader of the developing nations, she failed to suppress sectarian violence at home and was assassinated by Sikh extremists, members of her bodyguard.

11 Even if I die in the service of this nation, I would be proud of it. Every drop of my blood, I am sure, will contribute to the growth of this nation and make it strong and dynamic.

1984 Speech at Orissa, 31 Oct, the day before her assassination.

Gandhi, Mohandas Karamchand known as Mahatma [great souled] 1869–1948

Indian nationalist leader, who advocated peaceful non-cooperation to achieve independence, but was jailed for conspiracy (1922–4) following his civil disobedience campaign. After independence (1947), his attempts to stop the Hindu–Muslim conflict in Bengal led to his assassination by a Hindu fanatic.

12 I claim that in losing the spinning wheel we lost our left lung. We are, therefore, suffering from galloping consumption. The restoration of the wheel arrests the progress of the…disease.

1921 Speech, 13 Oct.

13 Non-violence is the first article of my faith. It is also the last article of my creed.

1922 Speech at Shahi Bag, 18 Mar.

14 Non-violence is not a garment to be put on and off at will. Its seat is in the heart, and it must be an inseparable part of our very being.

1926 *War or Peace*, 'Young India'.

15 What do I think of Western civilization? I think that it would be a good idea.

Attributed.

Garbo, Greta pseudonym of Greta Lovisa Gustafsson 1905–90

Swedish-born actress who went to the US in 1925 with director Mauritz Stiller. Her films at MGM during the 1930s include *Queen Christina* (1933), *Anna Karenina* (1936) and *Ninotchka* (1939). She retired in 1941.

16 I want to be alone.

1932 The media has famously attributed these words to Garbo although she always denied she said them. In the film *Grand Hotel* (1932) Grusinskaya (played by Garbo) says 'I want to be left alone'.

17 One day, there's a hand that goes over the face and changes it. You look like an apple that isn't young anymore.

1994 In *Vanity Fair*, Feb.

García Márquez, Gabriel 1928–

Colombian novelist and journalist, awarded the Nobel Prize for Literature (1982). His fiction, typically set in the imaginary village of Macondo, tends to magical realism.

18 *No se le había ocurrido pensar hasta entonces que la literatura fuera el mejor juguete que se había inventado para burlarse de la gente.*

It had never occurred to him until then to think that literature was the best plaything that had ever been invented to make fun of people.

1967 *Cien años de soledad* (translated as *One Hundred Years of Solitude*, 1970).

Garcilaso de la Vega, Inca 1539–1616

Peruvian soldier, translator and historian, son of a Spanish father and an Inca princess. He went to Spain in 1560 and became a soldier. His historical compositions draw on both indigenous sources and imagination.

19 *Porque allá los españoles y las otras naciones…como tienen historias divinas y humanas, saben por ellas cuándo empezaron a reinar sus Reyes y los ajenos…todo esto y mucho más saben por sus libros. Empero vosotros, que carecéis de ellos, ¿Qué memoria tenéis de vuestras antiguallas?, ¿Quién fue el primero de nuestros Incas?*

Over there Spaniards and other nations know from their divine and human history when their Kings and other peoples' Kings began their reigns… Their books teach them all of this, and much more. But you, who have no books, what memories do you have of your ancient past? Who was our first Inca?

1609 *Comentarios reales* (the *Royal Commentaries of Peru*, 1688), bk.1, ch.15.

Gardner, Ava originally Lucy Johnson 1922–90

US film actress. Signed for MGM as a teenager, she achieved fame in *The Killers* (1946) and later *The Barefoot Contessa* (1954) and *Night of the Iguana* (1964). She was married to Mickey Rooney, Artie Shaw and Frank Sinatra.

20 *On the Beach* is a story about the end of the world, and Melbourne sure is the right place to film it.

1959 Alleged comment to Australian journalist Neil Jillett of the Melbourne *Age* at the shooting of a film based on the book by British-Australian novelist Nevil Shute.

21 What I'd really like to say about stardom is that it gave me everything I never wanted.

1990 *Ava: My Story*.

Gardner, John William 1912–77

US public official, Secretary of Health, Education and Welfare (1965–8). In 1970 he founded the citizens' lobby Common Force, which he chaired until his death.

22 We are all faced with a series of great
opportunities—brilliantly disguised as insoluble
problems.
Quoted in *Reader's Digest*, Mar 1966.

23 We get richer and richer in filthier and filthier
communities until we reach a final stage of affluent
misery—a crocus on a garbage heap.
1969 In the *New York Times*, 9 Oct.

Garibaldi, Giuseppe 1807–82

Italian patriot, twice forced to flee the country for his
revolutionary activities. He returned in 1859 for Italy's
war of liberation, leading his thousand 'red shirts',
conquering Sicily and Naples for the unified kingdom of
Italy.

24 England is a great and powerful nation, foremost in
human progress, enemy to despotism, the only safe
refuge for the exile, friend of the oppressed. If ever
England should be so circumstanced as to require
the help of any ally, cursed be the Italian who
would not step forward with me in her defence.
1854 Letter, 12 Apr.

25 *Soldati, io esco da Roma. Chi vuole continuare la
guerra contro lo straniero venga con me. Non posso
offrigli né onori né stipendi; gli offro fame, sete,
marcie forzate, battaglie e morte. Chi ama la patria
me segua.*

Soldiers, I'm getting out of Rome. Anyone who
wants to carry on the war against the outsiders,
follow me. I can offer you neither honours nor
wages, I offer you hunger, thirst, forced marches,
battles and death. Anyone who loves his country,
follow me.
Quoted in Giuseppe Guerzoni *Garibaldi* (1882), vol.1.

Garland, (Hamilton) Hamlin 1860–1940

US writer. He is remembered chiefly for his stories of
Midwest farm life in books including *Main-Travelled
Roads* and *Prairie Folks* (1892), but also wrote novels,
essays and memoirs.

26 Like the main-travelled road of life it is traversed by
many classes of people, but the poor and the weary
predominate.
1890 *Main-Travelled Roads*, 'The Main-Travelled Road of the
West'.

27 There is no gilding of setting sun or glamor of
poetry to light up the ferocious and endless toil of
the farmers' wives.
1899 *Boy Life on the Prairie*, 'Melons and Early Frost'.

Garner, John Nance 1868–1967

US lawyer and politician, Speaker of the House (1931–3)
and Vice-President under President Roosevelt (1933–41).

He opposed Roosevelt's third-term candidacy and retired
in 1941.

28 Worst damnfool mistake I ever made was letting
myself be elected Vice President of the United
States. Should have stuck…as Speaker of the
House… Gave up the second most important job
in Government for eight long years as Roosevelt's
spare tire.
1963 In the *Saturday Evening Post*, 2 Nov.

29 The vice-presidency isn't worth a pitcher of warm
piss. It doesn't amount to a hill of beans.
Quoted in O C Fisher *Cactus Jack* (1978), ch.11.

Garrick, David 1717–79

English actor and theatre manager. He revolutionized
acting with his naturalistic Shakespearean heroes and in
1747 became manager of the Drury Lane theatre,
introducing many theatrical reforms.

30 Here lies Nolly Goldsmith, for shortness called
Noll,
Who wrote like an angel, but talked like poor Poll.
1773 Of Oliver Goldsmith. 'Impromptu Epitaph'.

31 Are these the choice dishes the Doctor has sent us?
Is this the great poet whose works so content us?
This Goldsmith's fine feast, who has written fine
books?
Heaven sends us fine meat, but the Devil sends
cooks.
1777 'On Doctor Goldsmith's Characteristical Cookery'.

32 Comedy is a very serious thing.
Attributed, in conversation with the actor Jack Bannister.

Gaskell, Mrs Elizabeth Cleghorn née
Stevenson 1810–65

English novelist. She is best known for her novels of social
realism, including *North and South* (1855), in which she
criticized the conditions in English factories, and
Cranford (1851–3).

33 Their dress is very independent of fashion; as they
observe, 'What does it signify how we dress here at
Cranford, where everybody knows us?' And if they
go from home, their reason is equally cogent,
'What does it signify how we dress here, where
nobody knows us?'
1851–3 Of the Cranford ladies. *Cranford*, ch.1.

34 A man…is *so* in the way in the house!
1851–3 *Cranford*, ch.1.

Gass, William H(oward) 1924–

US novelist, literary theorist and philosopher, best known
for his experimental story collection *In The Heart of the
Heart of the Country* (1968). He has also written novels
and works of criticism and aesthetics.

35 I love metaphor the way some people love junk food.
1977 Interview in *Paris Review*, Summer.

36 One's complete sentences are attempts, as often as not, to complete an incomplete self with words.
1977 Interview in *Paris Review*, Summer.

Gates, Bill (William Henry III) 1955–

US businessman, who founded the Microsoft Corporation with Paul Allen in 1974. In 1980 the company bought an operating system and adapted it for the IBM personal computer; the company is now the world's chief software producer for personal computers.

37 I think business is very simple. Profit. Loss. Take the sales, subtract the costs, you get this big positive number. The math is quite straightforward.
1993 Quoted in the *US News and World Report*, 15 Feb.

Gauguin, Paul 1848–1903

French Post-Impressionist painter, printmaker and sculptor.

38 There are noble tones, ordinary ones, tranquil harmonies, consoling ones, others which excite by their vigor.
1885 Letter to Emile Schuffenecker.

39 Some advice: do not paint too much after nature. Art is an abstraction; derive this abstraction from nature while dreaming before it, and think more of the creation which will result than of nature.
1888 Letter to Emile Schuffenecker.

40 You may dream freely when you listen to music as well as when you look at painting. When you read a book you are the slave of the author's mind.
c.1888 *Notes Synthétiques*, quoted in J Rewald *Gauguin* (1938).

Gautier, Théophile 1811–72

French poet, novelist and critic. He propounded the theory of 'art for art's sake', and was honoured by Baudelaire. His many novels include the celebrated *Mademoiselle de Maupin* (1835).

41 *Virginité, mysticisme, mélancolie! Trois mots inconnus, trois maladies nouvelles apportées par le Christ.*

Virginity, mysticism, melancholy! Three unknown words, three new illnesses brought by Christ.
1835 *Mademoiselle de Maupin*.

42 *Hélas! Les femmes n'ont lu que le roman de l'homme et jamais son histoire.*

Alas, women have read only the novel of mankind, not the history.
1835 *Mademoiselle de Maupin*.

43 *L'orgueil sort du cœur le jour où l'amour y entre.*

Pride leaves the heart the moment love enters it.
1835 *Mademoiselle de Maupin*.

44 The religion of money is today the only one which has no unbelievers.
1860s On the France of the Second Republic. Quoted in Joanna Richardson *The Courtesans* (1967), p.2.

Gavarni real name Guillaume Sulpice Chevalier 1804–88

French lithographer.

45 *Les Enfants Terribles.*

The Little Terrors.
1842 Title of a series of prints.

Gay, James 1810–91

Canadian poet, the self-styled 'Poet Laureate of Canada'.

46 Hail our Great Queen in her regalia;
One foot in Canada, the other in Australia.
Attributed to Gay by William Arthur Deacon in *The Four Jameses* (1927).

Gay, John 1685–1732

English poet, best known for his extraordinarily popular *The Beggar's Opera* (1728), set to music by Pepusch. In his final years he lived chiefly with his patrons, the Duke and Duchess of Queensberry.

47 Praising all alike, is praising none.
1714 'A Letter to a Lady', l.114.

48 Life is a jest; and all things show it.
I thought so once; but now I know it.
1720 'My Own Epitaph'.

49 A woman's friendship ever ends in love.
1720 *Dione*, act 4, sc.6.

50 And when a lady's in the case,
You know, all other things give place.
1727 *Fables*, 'The Hare and Many Friends', l.41.

51 She who trifles with all
Is less likely to fall
Than she who but trifles with one.
1727 'The Coquet Mother and the Coquet Daughter'.

52 How, like a moth, the simple maid
Still plays around the flame!
1728 *The Beggar's Opera*, act 1, sc.4, air 4.

53 Do you think your mother and I should have lived comfortably so long together, if ever we had been married?
1728 *The Beggar's Opera*, act 1, sc.8.

54 Money, wife, is the true fuller's earth for reputations, there is not a spot or a stain but what it can take out.

1728 *The Beggar's Opera*, act 1, sc.9.

55 The comfortable estate of widowhood, is the only hope that keeps up a wife's spirits.
1728 *The Beggar's Opera*, act 1, sc.10.

56 If with me you'd fondly stray
Over the hills and far away.
1728 *The Beggar's Opera*, act 1, sc.13, air 16.

57 I must have women. There is nothing unbends the mind like them.
1728 *The Beggar's Opera*, act 2, sc.3.

58 To cheat a man is nothing; but the woman must have fine parts indeed who cheats a woman!
1728 *The Beggar's Opera*, act 2, sc.4.

59 How happy I could be with either,
Were t'other dear charmer away!
1728 *The Beggar's Opera*, act 2, sc.13.

60 Music might tame and civilize wild beasts, but 'tis evident it never yet could tame and civilize musicians.
1729 *Polly*.

61 From wine what sudden friendship springs!
1738 *Fables*, 'The Squire and his Cur', l.4.

Gay, Noel pseudonym of *Richard Moxon Armitage* 1898–1954

British songwriter who wrote for stage and screen. His song *Leaning on a Lamp-Post* became one of George Formby's greatest successes.

62 I'm leaning on a lamp-post at the corner of the street
In case a certain little lady comes by.
1937 Song sung by George Formby, featured in the film *Feather Your Nest*.

Geddes, Sir Eric Campbell 1875–1937

British politician, a member of the War Cabinet in 1918. He presided over the 'Geddes Axe' committee on national expenditure in 1922.

63 The Germans, if this Government is returned, are going to pay every penny. They are going to be squeezed as a lemon is squeezed—until the pips squeak. My only doubt is not whether we can squeeze hard enough, but whether there is enough juice.
1918 Speech at Cambridge Guildhall, 10 Dec.

Gee, Maggie 1948–

English novelist. She has written a number of highly regarded literary novels.

64 There are people not spoken about, people not written about, people whose name is a way of

saying they are not there. *Hibakusha*, atomic victims—the scarred who carry our scars.
1983 Of the victims of the bombing of Hiroshima and Nagasaki. *The Burning Book*, ch.1.

65 The alcohol made the present enough, it held her in its golden hand, where past and future were comprehended, where nothing mattered, nothing was lost, where everything could be known and forgiven, where she herself could be whole at last.
1994 *Lost Children*, ch.35.

Geldof, Sir Bob (Robert) 1954–

Irish rock musician and philanthropist, founder of the Boomtown Rats (1975–86). He established the pop charity Bandaid in 1984 for African famine relief, and organized simultaneous Live Aid concerts in Philadelphia and London in 1985.

66 Irish Americans are about as Irish as Black Americans are African.
1986 In *The Observer*, 22 Jun.

67 Rock 'n' roll is instant coffee.
Quoted in David Pickering *Brewer's Twentieth Century Music* (1994).

Gellhorn, Martha Ellis 1908–98

US journalist and novelist. She covered numerous wars throughout the world between 1936 and 1985 and also wrote essays and fiction. Her first husband (1940–5) was Ernest Hemingway.

68 I see mysteries and complications wherever I look, and I have never met a steadily logical person.
1959 *The Face of War*, introduction.

69 It would be a bitter cosmic joke if we destroy ourselves due to atrophy of the imagination.
1959 *The Face of War*, introduction.

70 Gradually I came to realize that people will more readily swallow lies than truth, as if the taste of lies was homey, appetizing: a habit.
1959 *The Face of War*, introduction.

71 You define your own horror journey, according to your taste. My definition of what makes a journey wholly or partially horrible is boredom. Add discomfort, fatigue, strain in large amounts to get the purest-quality horror, but the kernel is boredom. I offer that as a universal test of travel; boredom, called by any other name, is why you yearn for the first available transport out. But what bores whom?... The threshold of boredom must be like the threshold of pain, different in all of us.
1979 *Travels with Myself and Another*.

72 We savaged them, though they had never hurt us, and we cannot find it in our hearts, our honor, to give them help—because the government of

Vietnam is Communist. And perhaps because they won.

1986 On the Vietnamese. *The Face of War* (rev edn), 'The War in Vietnam—Vietnam Again, 1986'

Genet, Jean 1910–86

French playwright, author and poet who spent much of his youth in jail. Once his literary talent was discovered, many, including Sartre, came to champion his cause even dubbing him 'Saint Genet'.

73 *Jean Cocteau me croit un mauvais voleur. C'est parce qu'auprès de lui je suis d'abord un écrivain. Les voleurs me croient un mauvais écrivain.*

Jean Cocteau thinks that I am poor thief. That's because next to him I am primarily a writer. Thieves think that I am a poor writer.

1949 *Journal du voleur.*

74 *L'artiste n'a pas—ou le poète—pour fonction de trouver la solution pratique des problèmes du mal.*

It is not up to the artist or to the poet to find practical solutions to the problems of evil.

1956 *Le Balcon*, 'Avertissement'.

75 *Prisons, cachots, lieux bénis où le mal est impossible, puisqu'ils sont le carrefour de toute la malédiction du monde. On ne peut pas commettre le mal dans le mal.*

Prison, dungeons, blessed places where evil is impossible because they are the crossroads of all the evil in the world. One cannot commit evil in hell.

1956 *Le Balcon*, 'Deuxième tableau'.

76 *Ce qu'il nous faut, c'est la haine. D'elle naîtront nos idées.*

Hatred is what we need. Ideas are born from hatred.

1958 *Les Nègres*, épigraphe.

77 *Dans les villes actuelles, le seul lieu,—hélas encore vers la périphérie—où un théâtre pourrait être construit, c'est le cimetière.*

In today's cities, the only place—unfortunately on the outskirts—to construct a theater is a cemetery.

1959 *L'étrange mort d'...*

Genghis Khan originally Temujin

c.1167–1227

Mongol conqueror. Leader of the Mongols from 1206, he conquered widely throughout Asia, penetrating Persia and Eastern Europe as far as the Dnieper River. His empire was divided between his sons and grandsons on his death.

78 Happiness lies in conquering one's enemies, in driving them in front of oneself, in taking their property, in savouring their despair, in outraging their wives and daughters.

c.1210 Quoted in Witold Rodzinski *The Walled Kingdom: A History of China* (1979).

Geoffrey de Breteuil fl.12c

French ecclesiastic.

79 *Claustrum sine armario quasi castrum sine armamentario. Ipsum armarium nostrum est armamenturium.*

A cloister without a library is like a castle without an armoury. For the library is our armoury.

c.1165 Letter to Peter Mangot.

George II 1683–1760

King of Great Britain and Ireland (1727–60) and Elector of Hanover, last British king to command in the field, at Dettingen, 1743. His reign saw the Jacobite defeat at Culloden (1746), British involvement in India after Plassey (1757) and the onset of the Seven Years War.

80 Oh! he is mad is he? Then I hope he will *bite* some of my other generals.

c.1759 Replying to remarks made about General James Wolfe by the Duke of Newcastle. Quoted in Henry Beckles Wilson *Life and Letters of James Wolfe* (1909), ch.17.

George III 1738–1820

King of Great Britain and Ireland (1760–1820). In the 1770s he was blamed with North for the loss of the American colonies. In 1783 he called Pitt (the Younger) to office, ending the supremacy of the old Whig families. As a result of his supposed insanity (now believed to have been porphyria), his son George was made Regent.

81 I can never suppose this country so far lost to all ideas of self-importance as to be willing to grant America independence; if that could ever be adopted, I shall despair of this country being ever preserved from a state of inferiority, and consequently falling into a very low class among the European states.

1780 Letter to Lord North, 7 Mar.

82 I was the last to consent to the separation, but the separation having been made, and having become inevitable, I have always said that I would be the first to meet the friendship of the United States as an independent power.

1785 Letter to John Adams, first US Ambassador to England, 1 Jun.

George V 1865–1936

King of Great Britain (1910–36). He served in the navy and travelled widely in the Empire. His reign saw the Union of South Africa (1910), World War I (1914–18), the Irish Free State Settlement (1922) and the General Strike (1926).

83 I have many times asked myself whether there can be more potent advocates of peace on earth

through the years to come than this massed multitude of silent witnesses to the desolation of war.

1922 Message read at the Terlincthun Cemetery, Boulogne, 13 May.

84 Today 23 years ago, dear Grandmama died. I wonder what she would have thought of a Labour government.

1924 Of Queen Victoria. Diary entry, 22 Jan, on having invited Ramsay Macdonald to form the first Labour Administration.

85 Bugger Bognor.

1929 or 1936 Reply to a courtier who had remarked 'Cheer up, your Majesty, you will soon be at Bognor again', either during his convalescence or on his deathbed. Quoted in Kenneth Rose *King George V* (1983), ch.9.

86 I will not have another war. If there is another and we are threatened with being brought into it, I will go to Trafalgar Square and wave a red flag myself sooner than allow this country to be brought in.

1935 To David Lloyd George, 10 May.

87 Golf always makes me so damned angry.

Quoted in Colin Jarman *The Guinness Dictionary of Sports Quotations* (1990).

George VI 1895–1952

King of Great Britain (1936–52). After ascending the throne (on the abdication of his elder brother, Edward VIII), he remained in bomb-damaged Buckingham Palace during World War II and delivered many broadcasts, mastering a speech impediment.

88 The British Empire has advanced to a new conception of autonomy and freedom, to the idea of a system of British nations, each freely ordering its own individual life, but bound together in unity by allegiance to one Crown, and co-operating in all that concerns the common weal.

1927 Opening, as Duke of York, the first Australian Parliament to assemble in Canberra, 9 May.

89 Abroad is bloody.

Quoted in W H Auden *A Certain World* (1970), 'Royalty'.

George, Chief Dan 1899–1981

Canadian native spokesperson.

90 The heart never knows the colour of the skin.

1974 *My Heart Soars.*

George, Daniel pseudonym of D G Bunting 1890–1967

British author and critic.

91 O Freedom, what liberties are taken in thy name!

1963 *The Perpetual Pessimist.*

George-Brown, George (Alfred) Brown, Baron 1914–85

English Labour politician. He was Vice-Chairman and Deputy Leader of the party (1960–70), and unsuccessfully contested Harold Wilson for party leadership in 1963.

92 Most British statesman have either drunk too much or womanised too much. I never fell into the second category.

1974 In *The Observer*, Nov.

93 Lovely creature in scarlet, dance with me!

Drunken invitation to a red-robed apostolic delegate. Attributed.

Geracimos, Ann

94 Washington is a town where more people probably contemplate writing a book than finish reading one.

1989 In the *Washington Times*, 29 Mar.

Gerald of Wales c.1146–1243

Welsh bishop and historian. He wrote 17 books and planned several others, all in Latin. His best-known works are *The History and Topography of Ireland* (1185) and *Journey through Wales* (1191).

95 Among the smaller islands there is one of fair size that is now called the Isle of Man… There was a great controversy in antiquity concerning the question: to which of the two countries should the island properly belong? Eventually, however, the matter was settled. All agreed that since it allowed poisonous reptiles to live in it, it should belong to Britain.

1185 *The History and Topography of Ireland*, pt.2 (translated by John J O'Meara, 1951).

Gerbert later *Pope Sylvester II* 940–1003

French divine and scholar, whose chemical, mathematical and philosophical expertise led to claims that he was in league with the Devil. In 982 he became Abbot of Bobbio, and was appointed Archbishop of Ravenna in 988. He was elected Pope in 999. He opposed the separatist tendencies of the French Church.

96 *Cum studio bene vivendi semper conjuncxi studium bene dicendi.*

I have always combined the study of how to live well with the study of how to speak well.

985 Letter to Ebrard, Abbot of Tours.

97 *An quicquam melius amicas divinitas mortalibus concesserit nescio.*

I do not know if the divinity has provided mortals with anything better than friends.

985 Letter to Abbot Gerald of Aurillac.

98 *Delegimus certum otium studiorum, quam incertum negotium bellorum.*

We have opted for the certain leisure of study, rather than the uncertain business of war.

985 Letter to Monk Raymond.

Gergen, David Richmond 1942–

US government official, an assistant and later adviser to Presidents Nixon, Ford, Reagan and Clinton. He was Managing Editor of the *US News and World Report* (1985–6).

99 About the time you are writing a line that you have written so often that you want to throw up, that is the first time the American people will hear it.

1993 On working as a speech-writer in the Nixon White House. In the *New York Times*, 31 Oct.

1 A naked moment in politics.

1993 On the vulnerability of the President. In the *New York Times*, 31 Oct.

2 We are making politics a spectator sport in which our only duty is to vote somebody into office and then retire to the grandstands.

1993 In *US News and World Report*, 10 May.

Gerhardie, William Alexander 1895–1977

English novelist, born and educated in St Petersburg. His best-known books are the novels *Futility* (1922) and *Polyglots* (1925).

3 She even sighed offensively…as if she meant to charge me with the necessity of doing so.

1922 *Futility*, pt.3, ch.3.

4 There are as many fools at a university as anywhere… But their folly, I admit, has a certain stamp—the stamp of university training, if you like. It is trained folly.

1925 *Polyglots*, ch.7.

5 We are like icebergs in the ocean: one-eighth part consciousness and the rest submerged beneath the surface of articulate apprehension.

1925 *Polyglots*, ch.14.

Gershwin, George 1898–1937

US composer. His early works are Broadway musicals, such as *Lady Be Good* (1924), written with his brother Ira. Other works include the opera *Porgy and Bess*, *Rhapsody in Blue* (a concert piece in the jazz idiom) and *An American in Paris*.

6 Not many composers have ideas. Far more of them know how to use strange instruments which do not require ideas.

1930 'The Composer in the Machine Age'.

7 Jazz is the result of the energy stored up in America.

Quoted in D Morgenstern *Composers on Music* (1958).

Gershwin, Ira originally *Israel Gershowitz* 1896–1983

US lyricist. He worked exclusively with his brother George Gershwin until George died, and then with other composers including Kurt Weill and Jerome Kern.

8 I got rhythm,
I got music,
I got my man—
Who could ask for anything more.

1930 'I Got Music' featured in the film *Girl Crazy*, (music by George Gershwin).

9 Away with the music of Broadway!
Be off with your Irving Berlin!
Oh, I'd give no quarter
to Kern or Cole Porter
and Gershwin keeps pounding on tin.
How can I be civil
when hearing this drivel?
It's only for night-clubbing souses.
Oh, give me the free 'n' easy
waltz that is Viennesey
And go tell the band
if they want a hand
the waltz must be Strauss's!

1936 'By Strauss'.

10 The way you wear your hat,
The way you sip your tea,
The mem'ry of all that—
No, no! They can't take that away from me!

1937 'They Can't Take That Away from Me', song from the film musical *Shall We Dance?* (music by George Gershwin).

11 The way your smile just beams
The way you sing off key
The way you haunt my dreams
No, no! They can't take that away from me!

1937 'They Can't Take That Away from Me', song from the film musical *Shall We Dance?* (music by George Gershwin).

12 You say potato and I say po-tah-to
You say tomato and I say to-mah-to…
Let's call the whole thing off!

1937 'Let's call the whole thing off', song from the film musical *Shall We Dance?* (music by George Gershwin).

13 A foggy day in London Town
Had me low and had me down.

1937 'A Foggy Day', song from the musical *Damsel in Distress* (music by George Gershwin).

14 Holding hands at midnight
'Neath a starry sky,
Nice work if you can get it,
And you can get it if you try.

1937 'Nice Work If You Can Get It', song from the musical *Damsel in Distress* (music by George Gershwin).

15 In time the Rockies may crumble

Gibraltar may tumble
They're only made of clay,
But our love is here to stay.

1938 'Love is here to stay', sung by Kenny Baker in *The Goldwyn Follies* (music by George Gershwin).

Getty, Jean Paul 1892–1976

US oil executive, multi-millionaire and art collector. He entered the oil business in his early 20s, and merged his father's fortune with his own in 1930. Despite his legendary wealth, he acquired a reputation for miserliness.

16 Some people find oil, some don't.

His entire submission when asked by a magazine editor to submit an article entitled 'The Secret of My Success'. Quoted by L M Boyd in the *San Francisco Chronicle*, 2 Mar 1991.

Giacosa, Giuseppe 1847–1906

Italian librettist.

17 *Che gelida manina.*

Your tiny hand is frozen.

1896 Rodolpho to Mimi. *La Bohème* (with Luigi Illica, music by Puccini).

Gibbon, Edward 1737–94

English historian. After a visit to Rome (1764) he embarked on a history of the Roman Empire. He became an MP in 1774, and the first volume of *The Decline and Fall of the Roman Empire* appeared in 1776. Lord Sheffield published his *Miscellaneous Works* (1796), including his autobiography.

18 If a man were called to fix the period in the history of the world during which the condition of the human race was most happy, and prosperous, he would, without hesitation, name that which elapsed from the death of Domitian to the accession of Commodus.

1776–88 *The Decline and Fall of the Roman Empire*, ch.3.

19 The principles of a free constitution are irrevocably lost when the legislative power is nominated by the executive.

1776–88 *The Decline and Fall of the Roman Empire*, ch.3.

20 In every age and country, the wiser, or at least the stronger, of the two sexes, has usurped the powers of the state, and confined the other to the cares and pleasures of domestic life.

1776–88 *The Decline and Fall of the Roman Empire*, ch.6.

21 Corruption, the most infallible symptom of constitutional liberty.

1776–88 *The Decline and Fall of the Roman Empire*, ch.21.

22 The Huns…chanted a funeral song to the memory of a hero, glorious in his life, invincible in his death, the father of his people, the scourge of his enemies, and the terror of the world.

1776–88 Description of the funeral of Attila the Hun. *The Decline and Fall of the Roman Empire*, ch.35.

23 The Rhine is not more impassable than the Nile or Euphrates, and the Arabian fleet might have sailed without a naval combat into the mouth of the Thames. Perhaps the interpretation of the Koran would now be taught in the schools of Oxford, and her pupils might demonstrate to a circumcised people the sanctity and truth of the revelation of Mahomet.

1776–88 *The Decline and Fall of the Roman Empire*, ch.52.

24 Persuasion is the resource of the feeble; and the feeble can seldom persuade.

1776–88 *The Decline and Fall of the Roman Empire*, ch.68.

25 All that is human must retrograde if it does not advance.

1776–88 *The Decline and Fall of the Roman Empire*, ch.71.

26 To the University of Oxford I acknowledge no obligation; and she will as cheerfully renounce me for a son, as I am willing to disclaim her for a mother. I spent fourteen months at Magdalen College: they proved the fourteen months the most idle and unprofitable of my whole life.

Memoirs of my Life (published 1796), ch.3.

27 It was here that I suspended my religious inquiries (aged 17).

Memoirs of my Life (published 1796), ch.4.

28 I sighed as a lover, I obeyed as a son.

On his enforced visit to Lausanne, leaving behind Suzanne Curchod. *Memoirs of my Life* (published 1796), ch.4. This passage was inserted (from a draft) by Lord Sheffield.

29 It was at Rome, on the fifteenth of October 1764, as I sat musing amidst the ruins of the Capitol, while the barefooted friars were singing vespers in the temple of Jupiter, that the idea of writing the decline and fall of the City first started to my mind.

Memoirs of my Life (published 1796), ch.6, note. Variations of the lines can be found in the various drafts of Gibbon's autobiography and in the last lines of the *Decline and Fall:* 'It was among the ruins of the Capitol that I first conceived the idea of a work which has amused and exercised near twenty years of my life, and which, however inadequate to my own wishes, I finally deliver to the curiosity and candour of the public' (vol.6, ch.71).

30 My English text is chaste, and all licentious passages are left in the obscurity of a learned language.

Memoirs of my Life (published 1796), ch.8.

Gibbons, Kaye

31 I read about writers' lives with the fascination of

one slowing down to get a good look at an automobile accident.

1990 In the *New York Times*, 7 Jan.

Gibbons, Orlando 1583–1625

English composer and organist of Westminster Abbey (from 1623). He wrote little, but some of his anthems, services and madrigals are regarded as masterpieces.

32 The silver swan, who living had no note.
When death approached, unlocked her silent
   throat;
Leaning her breast against the reedy shore,
Thus sung her first and last, and sung no more:
'Farewell, all joys; Oh death, come close mine eyes;
More geese than swans now live, more fools than
   wise.'

1612 *The First Set of Madrigals and Motets of Five Parts*, 'The Silver Swan'.

Gibbons, Stella Dorothea 1902–89

English writer. She worked as a journalist, and wrote novels, poetry and short stories. Her reputation rests on her famous parody of rural fiction, *Cold Comfort Farm*.

33 The life of the journalist is poor, nasty, brutish and short. So is his style.

1932 *Cold Comfort Farm*, foreword.

34 And when the spring comes her hour is upon her again. 'Tes the hand of Nature and we women cannot escape it.

1932 Judith Starkadder, of Meriam. *Cold Comfort Farm*, ch.5.

35 Something nasty in the woodshed.

1932 Aunt Ada Doom. *Cold Comfort Farm*, ch.10.

36 He said that, by god, D. H. Lawrence was right when he had said there must be a dumb, dark, dull, bitter belly-tension between a man and a woman, and how else could this be achieved save in the long monotony of marriage?

1932 Mr Mybug, proposing to Rennett. *Cold Comfort Farm*, ch.20.

Gibbs, Wolcott 1902–58

US journalist and critic.

37 Backward ran sentences until reeled the mind.

1936 Parody of *Time* magazine's literary style. 'Time…Fortune…Life…Luce', in the *New Yorker*, 28 Nov.

Gibran, Kahlil 1883–1931

Syrian mystic, author and artist, whose most famous work is *The Prophet* (1923).

38 Your children are not your children.
They are the sons and daughters of Life's longing
   for itself.
They came through you but not from you

And though they are with you yet they belong not
   to you.
You may give them your love but not your
   thoughts,
For they have their own thoughts.
You may house their bodies, but not their souls,
For their souls dwell in the house of tomorrow,
   which you cannot visit, not even in your dreams.
You may strive to be like them, but not seek to
   make them like you,
For life goes not backward, nor tarries with
   yesterday.
You are the bows from which your children as
   living arrows are sent forth.

1923 *The Prophet*, 'On Children'.

Gibson, Wilfred Wilson 1878–1962

English poet. He was a prolific writer of both poetry and plays, rooted in the reality of everyday life.

39 But we, how shall we turn to little things
And listen to the birds and winds and streams
Made holy by their dreams,
Nor feel the heart-break in the heart of things?

1918 'Lament'.

Gibson, William Ford 1948–

US science-fiction writer, best-known as the author of *Necromancer* (1984) which spawned the genre of cyberpunk fiction.

40 Cyberspace. A consensual hallucination experienced daily by billions of legitimate operators, in every nation, by children being taught mathematical concepts… A graphical representation of data abstracted from the banks of every computer in the human system. Unthinkable complexity. Lines of light ranged in the non-space of the mind, clusters and constellations of data. Like city lights, receding.

1984 *Necromancer*. This is the first recorded use of the term 'cyberspace'.

41 Cyberspace is where you are when you're on the telephone.

1994 In the *US News and World Report*, 21 Jun.

Gide, André Paul Guillaume 1869–1951

French writer of fiction, poetry, plays, criticism, biography and translations. His novels focus on the conflict between the spiritual and the physical. He won the Nobel Prize for Literature in 1947.

42 *Nous avons bâti sur le sable*
   Des cathédrales impérissables.

We have built immovable cathedrals
In the sand.

1895 *Paludes.*

43 *Que mon livre t'enseigne à t'intéresser plus à toi qu'à lui-même—puis à tout le reste plus qu'à toi.*

May my book teach you to be more interested in yourself than in it—then, in everyone else more than yourself.
1897 *Les Nourritures terrestres*, pt.1.

44 *La sagesse n'est pas dans la raison, mais dans l'amour.*

Wisdom comes not from reason but from love.
1897 *Les Nourritures terrestres*, pt.1.

45 *Familles! je vous hais! Foyers clos; portes refermées; possessions jalouses du bonheur.*

Families! I hate you! Enclosed hallways, shut doors, jealous possessions of happiness.
1897 *Les Nourritures terrestres*, pt.4.

46 *Chaque instant de notre Vie est essentiellement irremplaçable: sache parfois t'y concentrer uniquement.*

Every instant of our lives is essentially irreplaceable: you must know this in order to concentrate on life.
1897 *Les Nourritures terrestres*, pt.4.

47 *C'est avec de beaux sentiments qu'on fait de la mauvaise littérature.*

Bad literature is written with beautiful sentiments.
1928 Letter to François Mauriac.

48 *Le bonheur de l'homme n'est pas dans la liberté, mais dans l'acceptation d'un devoir.*

Man's happiness does not come from freedom but in the acceptance of a task.
1932 Journal entry, 8 Feb.

Gielgud, Sir (Arthur) John 1904–

English actor and producer. A leading Shakespearian actor, he has also appeared in many films, notably as Cassius in *Julius Caesar* (1952) and as the valet in *Arthur* (1981).

49 Daniel Day Lewis has what every actor in Hollywood wants: talent. And what every actor in England wants: looks.
1995 In *The Independent*, 13 May.

50 Being another character is more interesting than being yourself.
Attributed.

Gilbert, Sir Humphrey 1537–83

English navigator and explorer. He took Newfoundland for the crown in 1583, establishing a colony at St John's. He was drowned on the journey home.

51 We are as near to heaven by sea as by land!
1583 Dying words as his frigate *Squirrel* sank in the Atlantic Ocean near the Azores, 5 Aug. Quoted in Richard Hakluyt *Third and Last Volume of the Voyages…of the English Nation* (1600).

Gilbert, Sir W(illiam) S(chwenck)
1836–1911

English parodist and librettist. His humorous verse was collected in 1869 as the *Bab Ballads*. His partnership with Sir Arthur Sullivan, from 1871, produced a succession of light operas, from *Trial by Jury* (1875) to *The Grand Duke* (1896).

52 So I fell in love with a rich attorney's Elderly, ugly daughter.
1875 *Trial by Jury.*

53 She may very well pass for forty-three In the dusk with a light behind her!
1875 *Trial by Jury.*

54 I'm called little Buttercup—dear Little Buttercup, Though I could never tell why.
1878 *HMS Pinafore*, act 1.

55 CAPT:Bad language or abuse,
I never, never use,
Whatever the emergency;
Though 'Bother it' I may
Occasionally say,
I never use a big, big D—
ALL: What, never?
CAPT: No, never!
ALL: What *never*?
CAPT: Well, hardly ever!
ALL: Hardly ever swears a big, big D—
Then give three cheers, and one cheer more,
For the well-bred Captain of the *Pinafore*!
1878 *HMS Pinafore.*

56 I am the monarch of the sea,
The Ruler of the Queen's Navee,
Whose praise Great Britain loudly chants
And we are his sisters, and his cousins, and his aunts!
1878 *HMS Pinafore.*

57 In spite of all temptations
To belong to other nations,
He remains an Englishman!
1878 *HMS Pinafore.*

58 When I was a lad I served a term
As office boy to an attorney's firm.
I cleaned the windows and I swept the floor,
And I polished up the handle of the big front door.
I polished up that handle so carefullee
That now I am the Ruler of the Queen's Navee!
1878 *HMS Pinafore*, act 1.

59 Climbing over rocky mountain,
Skipping rivulet and fountain.
1879 Girls' chorus, *The Pirates of Penzance*, act 1.

60 It is, it is a glorious thing
To be a Pirate King.
1879 Pirate King's song, *The Pirates of Penzance*, act 1.

61 Oh, is there not one maiden here
Whose homely face and bad complexion
Have caused all hopes to disappear
Of ever winning man's affection?
1879 Frederick's Song, *The Pirates of Penzance*, act 1.

62 I am the very model of a modern Major-General,
I've information vegetable, animal and mineral,
I know the kings of England, and I quote the fights
historical,
From Marathon to Waterloo, in order categorical.
1879 The Major-General's Song, *The Pirates of Penzance*, act 1.

63 I can hum a fugue of which I've heard the music's
din afore,
And whistle all the airs from that infernal nonsense
Pinafore.
1879 The Major-General's Song, *The Pirates of Penzance*, act 1.

64 Stay, Frederic, stay!
Nay, Mabel, nay!
1879 Mabel and Frederic's duet, *The Pirates of Penzance*, act 2.

65 When a felon's not engaged in his employment
Or maturing his felonious little plans
His capacity for innocent enjoyment
Is just as great as any honest man's—
Ah! When constabulary duty's to be done
A policeman's lot is not a happy one.
1879 Sergeant's Song, *The Pirates of Penzance*, act 2.

66 And everyone will say,
As you walk your mystic way,
'If this young man expresses himself in terms too
deep for me,
Why, what a very singularly deep young man this
deep young man must be!'
1881 Bunthorne's song, *Patience*, act 1.

67 Sing 'Booh to you—
Pooh, pooh to you'—
And that's what I shall say!
1881 Jane and Bunthorne's duet, *Patience*, act 2.

68 A commonplace young man,
A matter-of-fact young man,
A steady and stolid-y, jolly Bank-Holiday
Every-day young man!
1881 Bunthorne and Grovesnor's duet. *Patience*, act 2.

69 A Japanese young man,
A blue and white young man,

Francesca di Rimini, miminy, piminy,
Je-ne-sais-quoi young man.
1881 Bunthorne and Grovesnor's duet. *Patience*, act 2.

70 A Chancery Lane young man,
A Somerset House young man,
A very delectable, highly respectable,
Threepenny-bus young man!
A pallid and thin young man,
1881 Bunthorne and Grovesnor's duet. *Patience*, act 2.

71 A haggard and lank young man,
A greenery-yallery, Grovesnor Gallery,
Foot-in-the-grave young man!
A Sewell & Cross young man,
A Howell & James young man,
A push-ing young par-ti-cle—
'What's the next ar-ti-cle?'—
Wa-ter-loo House young man!
1881 Bunthorne and Grovesnor's duet. *Patience*, act 2.

72 Bow, bow, ye lower middle classes!
Bow, bow, ye tradesmen, bow ye masses!
1882 Chorus, *Iolanthe*, act 1 (first performed 25 Nov,
simultaneously in London and New York).

73 The Law is the true embodiment
Of everything that's excellent.
It has no kind of fault or flaw,
And I, my Lords, embody the Law.
1882 *Iolanthe*, act 1.

74 When I went to the Bar as a very young man,
(Said I to myself—said I),
I'll work on a new and original plan,
(Said I to myself—said I).
1882 *Iolanthe*, act 1.

75 I often think it's comical
How Nature always does contrive
That every boy and every gal
That's born into the world alive
Is either a little Liberal
Or else a little Conservative!
1882 Private Willis's Song, *Iolanthe*, act 2.

76 The House of Peers, throughout the war,
Did nothing in particular,
And did it very well:
Yet Britain set the world ablaze
In good King George's glorious days!
1882 Lord Mountarat's Song, *Iolanthe*, act 2.

77 When you're lying awake with a dismal headache,
and repose is taboo'd by anxiety,
I conceive you may use any language you choose to
indulge in, without impropriety.
1882 Lord Chancellor's Nightmare Song, *Iolanthe*, act 2.

78 On fire that glows

With heat intense
I turn the hose
Of common sense,
And out it goes,
At small expense!...
Oh, Captain Shaw!
Type of true love kept under!
Could thy Brigade
With cold cascade
Quench my great love, I wonder!
1882 The Fairy Queen's song, *Iolanthe*, act 2.

79 Expressive glances
Shall be our lances
And pops of Sillery
Our light artillery.
1884 Trio, *Princess Ida*, act 1.

80 I've an irritating chuckle, I've a celebrated sneer,
I've an entertaining snigger, I've a fascinating leer.
To everybody's prejudice I know a thing or two;
I can tell a woman's age in half a minute—and I do.
But although I try to make myself as pleasant as I
can,
Yet everybody says I'm such a disagreeable man!
1884 Gama's Song, *Princess Ida*, act 1.

81 Oh, doughty sons of Hungary!
May all success
Attend and bless
Your warlike ironmongery!
1884 Chorus, *Princess Ida*, act 3.

82 A wandering minstrel I—
A thing of shreds and patches
Of ballads, songs and snatches
And dreamy lullaby!
1885 Nanki-Poo's Song, *The Mikado*, act 1.

83 As in a month you've got to die
If Ko-Ko tells us true,
'Twere empty compliment to cry
'Long life to Nanki-Poo!'
But as one month you have to live
As fellow-citizen,
This toast with three times three we'll give—
'Long life to you—till then!'
1885 Pooh-Bah's solo, *The Mikado*, act 1.

84 As some day it may happen that a victim must be
found,
I've got a little list—I've got a little list
Of society offenders who might well be
underground,
And who never would be missed— who never
would be missed!
There's the pestilential nuisances who write for
autographs—

All people who have flabby hands and irritating
laughs.
1885 Ko-Ko's Song, *The Mikado*, act 1.

85 The idiot who praises, with enthusiastic tone,
All centuries but this, and every country but his
own;
And the lady from the provinces, who dresses like a
guy,
And who 'doesn't think she dances, but would
rather like to try';
And that singular anomaly, the lady novelist—
I don't think she'd be missed—I'm *sure* she'd not be
missed!
1885 Ko-Ko's Song, *The Mikado*, act 1.

86 Defer, defer,
To the Lord High Executioner!
1885 Chorus, *The Mikado*, act 1.

87 Three little maids from school are we,
Pert as a school-girl well can be
Filled to the brim with girlish glee.
1885 Trio for Yum-yum, Peep-Bo and Pitti Sing, with Chorus
of Girls, *The Mikado*, act 1.

88 To sit in solemn silence in a dull, dark dock,
In a pestilential prison, with a life-long lock,
Awaiting the sensation of a short, sharp shock,
From a cheap and chippy chopper on a big black
block!
1885 Trio, *The Mikado*, act 1.

89 Here's a how-de-do!
1885 Trio, *The Mikado*, act 2.

90 My object all sublime
I shall achieve in time—
To let the punishment fit the crime.
1885 The Mikado's Song, *The Mikado*, act 2.

91 And there he plays extravagant matches
In fit–less fin–ger stalls
On a cloth un–true
With a twist–ed cue
And ellip–ti–cal bil–liard balls.
1885 The doom of the billiard sharp. *The Mikado*, act 2.

92 On a tree by a river a little tom-tit
Sang 'Willow, titwillow, titwillow!'
1885 Ko-Ko's Song, *The Mikado*, act 2.

93 This particularly rapid unintelligable patter
Isn't generally heard, and if it is it doesn't
matter!
1887 *Ruddigore*, act 2.

94 For I have a song to sing, O!...
It is sung to the moon
By a love-lorn loon,
Who fled from the mocking throng, O!

It's the song of a merryman moping mum,
Whose soul was sad and whose glance was glum
Who sipped no sup and who craved no crumb,
As he sighed for the love of a ladye!

1888 Jack Point's Song, *The Yeomen of the Guard.*

95 In enterprise of martial kind,
When there was any fighting,
He led his regiment from behind—
He found it less exciting.
But when away his regiment ran,
His place was at the fore, O—
That celebrated,
Cultivated
Underrated
Nobleman,
The Duke of Plaza-Toro!

1889 Duke's Song, *The Gondoliers*, act 1.

96 I am a courtier grave and serious
Who is about to kiss your hand:
Try to combine a pose imperious
With a demeanour nobly bland.

1889 *The Gondoliers*, act 2.

97 Take a pair of sparkling eyes.

1889 Marco's Song, *The Gondoliers*, act 2.

98 Funny without being vulgar.

1893 Of Sir Henry Beerbohm Tree's performance as Hamlet. Attributed.

99 Do you know how they are going to decide the Shakespeare–Bacon dispute? They are going to dig up Shakespeare and dig up Bacon; they are going to get Tree to recite *Hamlet* to them. And the one who turns in his coffin will be the author of the play.

Letter.

1 My dear chap! Good isn't the word!

To an actor who had just given a very weak performance. Attributed.

Gill, Brendan 1914–97

US writer and critic of film, theatre and architecture. His works include *The Day the Money Stopped* (1957) and *A New York Life: of friends and others* (1990). He received the national Book Award for *The Trouble of One House* (1951).

2 In the later nineteenth century, the tops of skyscrapers often took the shape of domes, surmounted by jaunty gilded lanterns; later came ziggurats, mausoleums, Alexandrian lighthouses, miniature Parthenons. These charming follies contained neither royal corpses nor effigies of gods and goddesses; rather they contained large wooden tanks filled with water.

1982 Quoted in Laura Rosen *Top of the City: New York's hidden rooftop world* (1990), foreword.

3 He stared the assorted meannesses and failed promises of American life straight in the face, and they stared back.

1990 On Walker Evans' photographs for James Agee's book on the destitute South. *A New York Life.*

4 The big houses sat in self-congratulatory propinquity on their level green lawns…stout matrons seated elbow to elbow, implacably chaperoning a ball.

1990 On a residential boulevard of Rochester, New York. *A New York Life.*

5 A vain attempt to subdue that unsubduable country.

1990 Of Cromwell's settlement of Scots in the north of Ireland. *A New York Life.*

Gill, (Arthur) Eric Rowton 1882–1940

English artist, type designer and writer.

6 That state is a state of Slavery in which a man does what he likes to do in his spare time and in his working time that which is required of him.

1929 *Art-nonsense and Other Essays*, 'Slavery and Freedom'.

7 The artist is not a special kind of man but every man a special kind of artist.

1934 *Art*, introduction.

8 Man cannot live on the human plane, he must be either above or below it.

1940 *Autobiography*, closing words.

9 Science is analytical, descriptive, informative. Man does not live by bread alone, but by science he attempts to do so. Hence the deadliness of all that is purely scientific.

'Art'. Collected in *Essays* (1948).

Gillespie, Dizzy (John Birks) 1917–93

US jazz trumpeter, composer and bandleader. A leading exponent of bebop in the 1940s, he formed several big bands and led an international touring orchestra (1956).

10 It's taken me all my life to learn what not to play.

Quoted in N Hentoff *Jazz Is* (1978).

11 When I first heard Charlie Parker, I said, 'That's how our music should be played.'… After we got it together, yeah, I knew we were making something new. It was magic. Nobody on the planet was playing like that but us.

1991 On bebop. In the *San Francisco Chronicle*, 25 May.

12 Now, our music is universal. It shares the rhythmic content of African music, music of the Western Hemisphere and various lands of the East, and has merged this rhythm with European harmonies, the soul of the slaves, the blues, and the spirituals to create jazz.

1979 *Dizzy–To Be Or Not To Bop* (with Al Fraser), 'Evolutions'.

Gillette, King Camp 1855–1932

US inventor of the safety razor (c.1895), founder of the Gillette Safety Razor Company (1901).

13 To be successful in business, you should produce something cheap, habit-forming, and consumed by use.
    Attributed.

Gilman, Charlotte Anna pen names *Charlotte Perkins Gilman* and *Charlotte Perkins Stetson* 1860–1935

US feminist and writer. She lectured on women's and other social issues, and her *Women and Economics* (1898) is regarded as a feminist landmark. Her fiction includes the story 'The Yellow Wall-Paper' (1892), a feminist study of madness.

14 The economic status of women generally depends on that of men generally, and…the economic status of women individually depends upon that of men individually, those men to whom they are related.
    1898 *Women and Economics: A Study of the Economic Relation between Men and Women as a factor in Social Evolution,* ch.1.

15 The labor of women in the house, certainly, enables men to produce more wealth than they otherwise could; and in this way [they] are economic factors in society. But so are horses.
    1898 *Women and Economics: The Study of the Economic Relation between Men and Women as a factor in Social Evolution,* ch.1.

16 Whatever the economic value of the domestic industry of women is, they do not get it. The women who do the most work get the least money, and the women who have the most money do the least work.
    1898 *Women and Economics: The Study of the Economic Relation between Men and Women as a factor in Social Evolution,* ch.1.

17 His dominance is not that of one chosen as best fitted to rule…but it is sovereignty based on the accident of sex.
    1898 *Women and Economics: The Study of the Economic Relation between Men and Women as a factor in Social Evolution,* ch.1.

Gilmore, Dame Mary Jean née *Mary Jean Cameron* 1865–1962

Australian writer and poet. She sailed to Paraguay in 1893 to help establish the New Australia Movement Utopian community, and when this failed returned to Australia (1902), becoming a journalist. A life-long supporter of aboriginal rights, in 1936 she was awarded the DBE.

18 I span and Eve span
    A thread to bind the heart of man!
    1918 *The Passionate Heart and Other Poems,* 'Eve-song'.

19 Lone, lone, and lone I stand,

With none to hear my cry,
As the black feet of the night
Go walking down the sky.
1932 *Under the Wilgas,* 'The Myall in Prison'.

Gilmour, Sir Ian 1926–

English Conservative politician, Secretary of State for defence (1970–4) and Lord Privy Seal (1979–81).

20 It does no harm to throw the occasional man overboard, but it does not do much good if you are steering full speed ahead for the rocks.
    1981 In *The Times,* after he was sacked by Margaret Thatcher for publicly criticizing her anti-European stance.

Gingold, Hermione 1897–1987

English actress. A star of intimate revue, she also appeared with success in plays by Noël Coward and in musicals by Stephen Sondheim.

21 I got all the schooling any actress needs. That is, I learned to write enough to sign contracts.
    Attributed.

Gingrich, Newt(on Leroy) 1943–

US politician. Originally a history professor, he became representative from Georgia in 1978 and subsequently Leader of conservative Republicans in the House. He became Speaker of the House in 1995.

22 One reason I try to get people to call me Newt is to break down barriers. It's a whole lot easier for someone to say, 'Newt, you've got a spot on your tie,' than it is to say 'Congressman'.
    1979 Attributed comment.

Ginsberg, Allen 1926–97

US poet, a key member of the 'Beat' movement with Jack Kerouac and William Burroughs. Despite his anti-establishment views, he was a popular poet and performer. His works include *Kaddish and Other Poems* (1961).

23 A naked lunch is natural to us,
    we eat reality sandwiches.
    But allegories are so much lettuce.
    Don't hide the madness.
    1954 'On Burroughs' Work'.

24 The madman bum and angel beat in Time,
    unknown, yet putting down here
    what might be left to say in time come after death
    1956 *Howl and Other Poems,* 'Howl, I'.

25 Moloch whose mind is pure machinery! Moloch whose blood is running
    money! Moloch whose fingers are ten armies!
    Moloch whose breast
    is a cannibal dynamo! Moloch whose ear is a smoking tomb!
    1956 *Howl and Other Poems,* 'Howl, II'.

26 You were never no locomotive, Sunflower, you were
a sunflower!
And you Locomotive, you are a locomotive, forget
me not!
1956 *Howl and Other Poems*, 'Sunflower Sutra'.

27 America I've given you all and now I'm nothing.
1956 *Howl and Other Poems*, 'America'.

28 America I'm putting my queer shoulder to the
wheel.
1956 *Howl and Other Poems*, 'America'.

29 Democracy! Bah! When I hear that word I reach for
my feather Boa!
1960 Journal entry, Oct. Collected in *Journals: Early Fifties
Early Sixties*, 'New York City'.

30 and poets should stay out of politics or become
monsters
I have become monsterous with politics.
1961 *Kaddish and Other Poems*, 'Death to Van Gogh's Ear!'

31 A very unique cat…a French Canadian Hinayana
Buddhist Beat Catholic savant.
1970 Of Jack Kerouac. *This Fabulous Century 1950–1960*.

32 What if someone gave a war & Nobody came?
Life would ring the bells of Ecstasy and Forever be
Itself again.
1973 *The Fall of America*, 'Graffiti 12th Cubicle Men's Room
Syracuse Airport'.
⊳ See Sandburg 841:71.

33 All this time [San Francisco, from 1955] I realized
we were involved as a community with a historical
change of consciousness and some kind of cultural
revolution… I thought it was really in some
respects a contest between further liberation or
1984 authoritarianism, police state; that it was
creeping police state or creeping socialism-
libertarianism.
1984 Quoted in Gordon Ball (ed) *Allen Ginsberg: Journals
Mid-Fifties* (1995), 'Meditations on Record Keeping by Poet,
Transcribed by Editor'.

34 Poetry is not an expression of the party line. It's that
time of night, lying in bed, thinking what you
really think, making the private world public, that's
what the poet does.
Quoted in Barry Miles *Ginsberg* (1989), ch.5.

Giovanni, Nikki née *Yolande Cornelia*
Giovanni, Jr 1943–

US poet, a significant voice in the development of black
consciousness. Her early work was more radical in tone
than subsequent more introspective volumes.

35 Mistakes are a fact of life
It is the response to error that counts.
1968 *Black Judgement*, 'Of Liberation', stanza 16.

36 and I really hope no white person ever has cause to
write about me
because they never understand Black love is Black
wealth and they'll
probably talk about my hard childhood and never
understand that
all the while I was quite happy
1968 *Black Judgement*, 'Nikki–Rosa'.

37 its a sex object if you're pretty
and no love
or love and no sex if you're fat
1968 *Black Judgement*, 'Woman Poem'.

38 White people really deal more with God and black
people with Jesus.
1971 Conversation with James Baldwin, London, 4 Nov.
Collected in *A Dialogue* (1973).

39 A white face goes with a white mind. Occasionally
a black face goes with a white mind. Very seldom a
white face will have a black mind.
1971 Conversation with James Baldwin, London, 4 Nov.
Collected in *A Dialogue* (1973).

Gipp, George 1895–1920

US American football player. His success on the field
inspired Notre Dame to two unbeaten seasons (1919 and
1920), though his career was cut short by his death from
pneumonia.

40 Some time, Rock, when the team's up against it,
when things are wrong and the breaks are beating
the boys–tell them to go in there with all they've
got and win just one for the Gipper.
1920 Last words, to coach Knute Rockne. Rockne told the
team about Gipp's request in 1928, when their fortunes were
low, and inspired the squad to new efforts. 'Win one for the
Gipper' subsequently became a catchphrase throughout US
sport.

Giraudoux, (Hippolyte) Jean 1882–1944

French writer, head of propaganda in World War II. He is
best known for his poetic plays, including *La Guerre de
Troie n'aura pas Lieu* (1935, translated as *The Tiger at the
Gates*, 1955) and *Pour Lucrèce* (1953, translated as *Duel of
Angels*, 1958).

41 *Le plagiat est la base de toutes les littératures, excepté
de la première, qui d'ailleurs est inconnue.*

Plagiarism is the base of all literature except the first
text which, however, is unknown.
1922 *Siegfried et le Limousin*.

42 *L'humanité est…une entreprise surhumaine.*

Humanity is…a superhuman undertaking.
1933 *Intermezzo*, act 1, sc.6.

43 A golf course is the epitome of all that is purely
transitory in the universe, a space not to dwell in,
but to get over as quickly as possible.

1933 Quoted in Colin Jarman *The Guinness Dictionary of Sports Quotations* (1990).

44 *Nous savons tous ici que le droit est la plus puissante des écoles de l'imagination. Jamais poète n'a interprété la nature aussi librement qu'un juriste la réalité.*

We all know here that the law is the most powerful of schools for the imagination. No poet ever interpreted nature as freely as a lawyer interprets the truth.

1935 *La Guerre de Troie n'aura pas Lieu*, act 2, sc.5.

45 *Il n'est pas très prudent d'avoir des dieux et des légumes trop dorés.*

It is not wise to have either your gods or your vegetables too gilded.

1935 *La Guerre de Troie n'aura pas lieu*, act 2, sc.13.

46 *C'est de là que vient tout le mal: Dieu est un homme.*

All evil comes from this fact: God was a man.

1937 *Sodome et Gomorrhe*, act 1, sc.2.

Girondo, Oliverio 1891–1967

Argentinian poet, who travelled extensively in Europe and Africa and had close contact with the French avant garde. He edited the Ultraist manifiesto in the avant-garde magazine *Martín Fierro* (1924).

47 *Cansado,*
sobre todo,
de estar siempre conmigo,
de hallarme cada día,
cuando termina el sueño,
allí, donde me encuentre,
con las mismas narices
y con las mismas piernas

Tired,
above all,
of being always with myself,
of finding myself everyday,
when the dream comes to an end,
wherever I am,
with the same old nose
and with the same old legs.

1942 *Persuasión de los días*, 'Cansancio' ('Fatigue').

Giscard d'Estaing, Valéry 1926–

French politician, born in Germany. A Resistance worker during World War II, he was Finance Minister (1962–6) before launching the National Federation of Independent Republicans. He defeated Mittervand to become President (1974–81).

48 During my seven years in office, I was in love with seventeen million French women... I know this declaration will inspire irony and that English language readers will find it very French.

1988 *Le Pouvoir et la Vie.*

Gitlin, Todd

US associate professor of sociology, University of California (Berkeley). He has written on culture, politics and the media. He is also a published poet.

49 There is a misunderstanding by marketers in our culture about what freedom of choice is. In the market, it is equated with multiplying choice. This is a misconception. If you have infinite choice, people are reduced to passivity.

1990 In the *New York Times*, 14 Feb.

Gladstone, W(illiam) E(wart) 1809–98

English Liberal statesman. He entered Parliament as a Conservative (1832), and in 1867 became leader of the Liberal Party. As Prime Minister (1868–74, 1880–5, 1886, 1892–4) he established a system of national education (1870), introduced parliamentary reforms aimed at universal male suffrage and argued for Irish Home Rule.

50 It is upon those who say that it is necessary to exclude forty-nine fiftieths of the working classes [from the vote] to show cause, and I venture to say that every man who is not presumably incapacitated by some consideration of personal unfitness or of political danger, is morally entitled to come within the pale of the Constitution.

1864 House of Commons, 11 May.

51 One cannot fight against the future. Time is on our side.

1866 Speech on the Reform Bill, House of Commons, 27 Apr.

52 Remember the rights of the savage, as we call him. Remember that the happiness of his humble home, remember that the sanctity of life in the hill villages of Afghanistan, among the winter snows, is as inviolable in the eye of Almighty God as can be your own.

1879 Speech at Edinburgh Foresters' Hall, during the Midlothian Campaign, 26 Nov.

53 England's foreign policy should always be inspired by the love of freedom. There should be a sympathy with freedom, a desire to give it scope, founded not upon visionary ideas but upon the long experience of many generations within the shores of this happy isle, that in freedom one lays the firmest foundations both of loyalty and order.

1879 Speech, West Calder, 27 Nov.

54 All the world over, I will back the masses against the classes.

1886 Speech, Liverpool, 28 Jun.

55 We are part of the community of Europe, and we must do our duty as such.

1888 Speech, 10 Apr.

56 What that Sicilian mule was to me, I have been to the Queen.

1894 Memorandum on his relationship with Queen Victoria, 20 Mar.

57 It is not a Life at all. It is a Reticence, in three volumes.

Of J W Cross's *Life of George Eliot.* Quoted in E F Benson *As We Were* (1930), ch.6.

Glasgow, Ellen Anderson Gholson
1874–1945

US novelist. Much of her fiction was set in the South. She won a Pulitzer Prize in 1941 for *In This Our Life.*

58 It was not the matter of the work, but the mind that went into, that counted—and the man who was not content to do small things well would leave great things undone.

1900 *The Voice of the People,* bk.2, ch.4.

59 Women like to sit down with trouble as if it were knitting.

1932 *The Sheltered Life,* pt.3, section 3.

60 No matter how vital experience might be while you lived it, no sooner was it ended and dead than it became as lifeless as the piles of dry dust in a school history book.

1941 *In This Our Life,* pt.3, ch.9.

Gleick, James 1954–

US writer and software designer.

61 The Internet has taken shape with startlingly little planning… The most universal and indispensable network on the planet somehow burgeoned without so much as a board of directors, never mind a mergers-and-acquisitions department. There is a paradoxical lesson here for strategists. In economic terms, the great corporations are acting like socialist planners, while old-fashioned free-market capitalism blossoms at their feet.

1994 In the *New York Times Magazine,* 1 May.

Gloucester, William Henry, 1st Duke of
1743–1805

62 Another damned, thick, square book! Always scribble, scribble, scribble! Eh! Mr Gibbon?

1781 Attributed, when presented with the second volume of *The Decline and Fall of the Roman Empire.* These words have also been attributed to George III and the Duke of Cumberland.

Godard, Jean-Luc 1930–

French film critic and director. His first feature *A Bout de Souffle* (1959) established him as one of the leading members of the 'New Wave'. Other notable films include *Pierrot Le Fou* (1965), *Alphaville* (1965) and *Week-end* (1967).

63 *La photographie, c'est la vérité. Le cinéma: la vérité vingt-quatre fois par seconde.*

Photography is truth. And cinema is truth twenty-four times a second

1960 Line in *Le Petit Soldat.*

Goebbels, (Paul) Joseph 1897–1945

German Nazi official. In 1926 Hitler appointed him district party leader for Berlin and in 1928 he entered the Reichstag. As Minister for propaganda from 1933 he was a vociferous and virulent anti-Semite. He killed his family and committed suicide as Berlin fell in 1945.

64 *Ohne Butter werden wir fertig, aber nicht beispielsweise ohne Kanonen. Wenn wir einmal überfallen werden, dann können wir uns nicht mit Butter, sondern nur mit Kanonen verteidigen.*

We can manage without butter but not, for example, without guns. If we are attacked, we can only defend ourselves with guns not butter.

1936 Speech in Berlin, 17 Jan.

65 *Wenn das deutsche Volk die Waffen niederlegte, würden die Sowjets…ganz Ost- und Südosteuropa zuzüglich des größten Teiles des Reiches besetzen. Vor diesem einschließlich der Sowjetunion riesigen Territorium würde sich sofort ein eiserner Vorhang heruntersenken.*

Should the German people lay down their arms, the Soviets…would occupy all eastern and south-eastern Europe together with the greater part of the Reich. Over all this territory, which with the Soviet Union would be of enormous extent, an iron curtain would at once descend.

1945 In *Das Reich,* a Nazi propaganda weekly, quoted in *The Times* and the *Manchester Guardian* on 23 Feb.

▷ See also Churchill 265:30.

Goering, or Göring, Hermann Wilhelm
1893–1946

German soldier and Nazi leader, commander of the Hitler storm troopers, and head of the Gestapo. He was sentenced to death at the Nuremberg Trials, but committed suicide.

66 Our movement took a grip on cowardly Marxism, and from it, extracted the meaning of socialism. It also took from the cowardly, middle-class parties their nationalism. Throwing both into the cauldron of our way of life there emerged, as clear as crystal, the synthesis—German National Socialism.

1933 Speech, Berlin, 9 Apr.

67 Would you rather have butter or guns? …preparedness makes us powerful. Butter merely makes us fat.

1936 Speech, Hamburg.

▷ See Goebbels 430:64.

68 I hereby commission you to carry out all the preparations with regard to…a total solution of the Jewish question, in those territories of Europe that are under German influence.

1941 Directive to the Nazi High Command, 31 Jul, quoted in William Shirer *The Rise and Fall of the Third Reich* (1962).

Goethe, Johann Wolfgang von 1749–1832

German poet, dramatist and scientist. His early nationalistic, 'Sturm und Drang' dramas were followed by lyric poetry and poetical drama. His masterpiece was *Faust*, on which he worked for most of his life.

69 English plays,
    Atrocious in content,
    Absurd in form,
    Objectionable in action,
    Execrable English Theatre!

1749 Attributed.

70 For a woman, she has extraordinary talent. One must look for what she does, not what she fails to do.

1786–8 Of the painter Angelica Kauffman. *Italienische Reise* (published 1816–17, translated by W H Auden and Elizabeth Mayer as *Italian Journey*, 1962).

71 *Wenn es eine Freude ist das Gute zu geniessen, so ist es eine grössere das Bessere zu empfinden, und in der Kunst ist das Beste gut genug.*

As it is a joy to enjoy what is good, so it is a greater joy to experience what is better, and in art the best is good enough.

1787 *Italienische Reise* 3 Mar. (published 1816–17, translated by W H Auden and Elizabeth Mayer as *Italian Journey*, 1962).

72 *Wer nie sein Brot mit Tränen aß,*
    Wer nie die kummervollen Nächte,
    Auf seinem Bette weinen saß,
    Der kennt euch nicht, ihr himmlischen Mächte.

Who never ate his bread in sorrow,
Who never spent the darksome hours
Weeping and watching for the morrow
He knows ye not, ye heavenly powers.

1795–6 *Wilhelm Meisters Lehrjahre,* (translated by Carlyle in 1824 as *Wilhelm Meister's Apprenticeship*).

73 *Es irrt der Mensch, so lang er strebt.*

Man will err while yet he strives.

1808 *Faust,* pt.1, 'Prolog im Himmel'.

74 *Grau, teurer Freund, ist alle Theorie.*
    Und grün des Lebens goldner Baum.

All theory, dear friend, is grey, but the golden tree of actual life springs ever green.

1808 *Faust,* pt.1, 'Studierzimmer'.

75 *Alles Gescheite ist schon gedacht worden; man muß nur versuchen, es noch einmal zu denken.*

Everything clever has been thought of before. We must try to think it again.

1819 *Sprüche in Prosa, Maximen und Reflexionen*, pt.1.

76 *Der Aberglaube ist die Poesie des Lebens.*

Superstition is the poetry of life.

1819 *Sprüche in Prosa, Maximen und Reflexionen*, pt.3.

77 *Neuere Poeten tun viel Wasser in die Tinte.*

Modern poets mix a lot of water with their ink.

1819 *Sprüche in Prosa, Maximen und Reflexionen*, pt.6.

78 *Das Erste und Letzte, was vom Genie gefordert wird, ist Wahrheitsliebe.*

The first and the last thing demanded of genius is the love of truth.

1819 *Sprüche in Prosa, Maximen und Reflexionen*, pt.6.

79 *Klassisch ist das Gesunde, romantisch das Kranke.*

The classical period was healthy; the romantic diseased.

1819 *Sprüche in Prosa, Maximen und Reflexionen*, pt.7.

80 Lord Byron is only great as a poet; as soon as he reflects he is a child.

1825 Eckermann's *Conversations with Goethe*, 18 Jan.

81 *Ich kenne mich auch nicht und Gott soll mich auch davor behuten.*

I do not know myself, and God forbid that I should.

1829 Eckermann's *Conversations with Goethe*, 10 Apr.

82 *Mehr Licht!*

More light!

1832 Last words.

83 *Ach du ich irrte, hatt ich viel Gespielen,*
    Da ich dich kenne, bin ich fast allein.

Ah! while I erred I had many friends.
Now that I know you, I am alone.

Gedichte, Zuneigung (published 1910).

Goheen, Robert F(rancis) 1919–

US classical scholar and educator, born in India. He joined Princeton University in 1948, and became President there (1957–72). He was Ambassador to India (1977–80).

84 If you feel that you have both feet planted on level ground, then the university has failed you.

1961 Baccalaureate address. Reported in *Time* magazine, 23 Jun.

Golding, Sir William (Gerald) 1911–93

English novelist. He achieved fame with his first novel *Lord of the Flies* (1954), and was awarded the Nobel Prize for Literature in 1983.

85 Ralph wept for the end of innocence, the darkness
of man's heart, and the fall through the air of a true,
wise friend called Piggy.
1954 *Lord of the Flies*, ch.12.

86 Sleep is when all the unsorted stuff comes flying
out as from a dustbin upset in a high wind.
1956 *Pincher Martin*, ch.6.

87 Philip is a living example of natural selection. He
was as fitted to survive in this modern world as a
tapeworm in an intestine.
1959 *Free Fall*, ch.2.

88 Eighteen is a good time for suffering. One has all
the necessary strength, and no defences.
1967 *The Pyramid.*

89 With lack of sleep and too much understanding I
grow a little crazy, I think, like all men at sea who
live too close to each other and too close thereby to
all that is monstrous under the sun and moon.
1980 *Rites of Passage*, closing words.

90 The theme defeats structuralism, for it is an
emotion. The theme of *Lord of the Flies* is grief,
sheer grief, grief, grief, grief.
1982 'Moving Target'.

91 It really means nothing in this country
whatsoever—but then being a writer here means
nothing either.
1983 On winning the Nobel Prize. Quoted in *The Observer*, 31
May.

92 Life should serve up its feast of experience in a
series of courses.
1987 *Close Quarters.*

Goldman, William 1931–

US screenwriter, best known for the script of *Butch
Cassidy and the Sundance Kid* for which he won an
Academy Award.

93 Boy, I got vision. The rest of the world wears
bifocals.
1969 Anachronistic line delivered by Paul Newman in *Butch
Cassidy and the Sundance Kid.*

Goldmark, Peter Carl 1940–

US government official, President of the Rockefeller
Foundation (1988–).

94 Welfare is hated by those who administer it;
misused by those who pay for it; and held in
contempt by those who receive it.
1977 In the *New York Times*, 24 May.

Goldsmith, Oliver 1728–74

Irish novelist, poet, and playwright. After studying
medicine and attempting to join the Church, he began a
literary career. He is best known for the novel *The Vicar of
Wakefield* (1766), the poem *The Deserted Village* (1770)
and the play *She Stoops to Conquer* (1773).

95 The doctor found, when she was dead,
Her last disorder mortal.
1759 'Elegy on Mrs Mary Blaize'.

96 Where'er I roam, whatever realms to see,
My heart untravelled fondly turns to thee;
Still to my brother turns with ceaseless pain,
And drags at each remove a lengthening chain.
1764 *The Traveller*, l.7–10.

97 Such is the patriot's boast, where'er we roam,
His first, best country ever is, at home.
1764 *The Traveller*, l.73–4.

98 Laws grind the poor, and rich men rule the law.
1764 *The Traveller*, l.386.

99 How small, of all that human hearts endure,
That part which laws or kings can cause or cure!
1764 *The Traveller*, l.429–30.

1 I was ever of the opinion, that the honest man who
married and brought up a large family, did more
service than he who continued single and only
talked of population.
1766 *The Vicar of Wakefield*, ch.1.

2 Let us draw upon content for the deficiencies of
fortune.
1766 *The Vicar of Wakefield*, ch.3.

3 Conscience is a coward, and those faults it has not
strength enough to prevent it seldom has justice
enough to accuse.
1766 *The Vicar of Wakefield*, ch.13.

4 It seemed to me pretty plain, that they had more of
love than of matrimony in them.
1766 *The Vicar of Wakefield*, ch.16.

5 When lovely woman stoops to folly
And finds too late that men betray,
What charm can soothe her melancholy,
What art can wash her guilt away?
1766 *The Vicar of Wakefield*, ch.29.

6 Friendship is a disinterested commerce between
equals; love, an abject intercourse between tyrants
and slaves.
1768 *The Good-Natured Man*, act 1.

7 Silence is become his mother tongue.
1768 *The Good-Natured Man*, act 2.

8 Sweet Auburn, loveliest village of the plain,
Where health and plenty cheered the labouring
swain.
1770 *The Deserted Village*, l.1–2.

9   How often have I paused on every charm,
    The sheltered cot, the cultivated farm,
    The never-failing brook, the busy mill,
    The decent church that topped the neighbouring
      hill.
    1770 *The Deserted Village*, l.9–12.

10 Ill fares the land, to hastening ills a prey
    Where wealth accumulates and men decay:
    Princes and lords may flourish or may fade;
    A breath can make them, as a breath has made;
    But a bold peasantry, their country's pride,
    When once destroyed, can never be supplied.
    1770 *The Deserted Village*, l.51–6.

11 The village preacher's modest mansion rose.
    A man he was to all the country dear,
    And passing rich with forty pounds a year.
    1770 *The Deserted Village*, l.140–2.

12 The village master taught his little school;
    A man severe he was and stern to view;
    I knew him well, and every truant knew;
    Well had the boding tremblers learned to trace
    The day's disasters in his morning face;
    Full well they laughed, with counterfeited glee,
    At all his jokes, for many a joke had he.
    1770 *The Deserted Village*, l.196–202.

13 In arguing too, the parson owned his skill,
    For e'en though vanquished, he could argue still;
    While words of learned length, and thund'ring
      sound
    Amazed the gazing rustics ranged around,
    And still they gazed, and still the wonder grew,
    That one small head could carry all he knew.
    1770 *The Deserted Village*, l.211–16.

14 And, even while fashion's brightest arts decoy,
    The heart distrusting asks, if this be joy.
    1770 *The Deserted Village*, l.263–4.

15 The rich man's joys increase, the poor's decay,
    'Tis yours to judge how wide the limits stand
    Between a splendid and a happy land.
    1770 *The Deserted Village*, l.266–8.

16 Thus fares the land, by luxury betrayed.
    1770 *The Deserted Village*, l.295.

17 In all the silent manliness of grief.
    1770 *The Deserted Village*, l.384.

18 I see the rural virtues leave the land.
    1770 *The Deserted Village*, l.398.

19 Though very poor, may still be very blest.
    1770 *The Deserted Village*, l.426.

20 I love everything that's old: old friends, old times,
    old manners, old books, old wine.
    1773 *She Stoops to Conquer*, act 1, sc.1.

21 Is it one of my well-looking days, child? Am I in
    face to-day?
    1773 *She Stoops to Conquer*, act 1, sc.1.

22 Let school-masters puzzle their brain,
    With grammar, and nonsense, and learning;
    Good liquor, I stoutly maintain,
    Gives genius a better discerning.
    1773 *She Stoops to Conquer*, act 1, sc.2.

23 I'll be with you in a squeezing of a lemon.
    1773 *She Stoops to Conquer*, act 1, sc.2.

24 It's a damned long, dark, boggy, dirty, dangerous
    way.
    1773 *She Stoops to Conquer*, act 1, sc.2.

25 The first blow is half the battle.
    1773 *She Stoops to Conquer*, act 2, sc.1.

26 But there's no love lost between us.
    1773 *She Stoops to Conquer*, act 4, sc.1.

27 Our Garrick's a salad; for in him we see
    Oil, vinegar, sugar, and saltness agree.
    1774 *Retaliation*, l.11–12.

28 Who, too deep for his hearers, still went on
      refining,
    And thought of convincing, while they thought of
      dining;
    Though equal to all things, for all things unfit,
    Too nice for a statesman, too proud for a wit.
    1774 Of Edmund Burke. *Retaliation*, l.29–32.

29 On the stage he was natural, simple, affecting;
    'Twas only that when he was off he was acting.
    1774 Of Garrick. *Retaliation*, l.101–2.

30 When they talked of their Raphaels, Correggios,
      and stuff,
    He shifted his trumpet, and only took snuff.
    1774 Of Reynolds. *Retaliation*, l.145–6.

Goldwater, Barry M(orris) 1909–98

US politician, Senator from Arizona (1952–64, 1969–87)
and leader of the extreme right Republican wing. He was
defeated in the 1964 presidential election by Lyndon B
Johnson.

31 Extremism in the defence of liberty is no vice, and
    moderation in the pursuit of justice is no virtue.
    1964 Speech to the Republican convention, 16 Jul.

32 In your heart, you know I'm right.
    1964 Presidential campaign slogan.

33 He had probably been vaccinated with a
    phonograph needle.

1979 On the windy presidential candidate Hubert Humphrey. *With No Apologies.*

34 You don't need to be 'straight' to fight and die for your country. You just need to shoot straight.
1993 On homosexuals in the military. In *Life*, Dec.

Goldwyn, Sam(uel) originally *Schmuel Gelbfisz* 1882–1974

Polish-born US film producer. In 1917 he founded Goldwyn Pictures Corporation and in 1925 the Metro-Goldwyn-Mayer Company. His films include *Wuthering Heights* (1939), *The Little Foxes* (1941) and *Guys and Dolls* (1955). He is credited with many artless Goldwynisms, most probably apocryphal.

35 I'll cable Hitler and ask him to shoot around you.
1939 Remark to David Niven, Sep, when Niven left Hollywood to return to England. Quoted in David Niven *Bring on the Empty Horses* (1975).

36 I don't care if it doesn't make a nickel. I just want every man, woman and child in America to see it!
1946 Of *The Best Years of Our Lives*. Quoted in Leslie Halliwell *Halliwell's Filmgoer's and Video Viewer's Companion* (9th edn, 1989).

37 Any man who goes to a psychiatrist should have his head examined.
Quoted in Norman Zierold *Moguls* (1969), ch.3.

38 Please write music like Wagner, only louder.
Note to a composer of a forthcoming film soundtrack. Recalled on his death, 1974.

39 You ought to take the bull between the teeth.
Recalled on his death, 31 Jan 1974.

40 Now why did you name your baby 'John'? Every Tom, Dick and Harry is named 'John'.
Attributed. Quoted in Fred Metcalf (ed) *The Penguin Dictionary of Humorous Quotations* (1986).

41 I seriously object to seeing on the screen what belongs in the bedroom.
Attributed maxim. Quoted in Leslie Halliwell *Halliwell's Filmgoer's and Video Viewer's Companion* (9th edn, 1989).

42 What we want is a story that starts with an earthquake and works its way up to a climax.
Quoted in Leslie Halliwell *Halliwell's Filmgoer's and Video Viewer's Companion* (9th edn, 1989).

43 A verbal contract isn't worth the paper it's written on.
Attributed. Quoted in A Scott Berg *Goldwyn* (1989).

44 I'll give you a definite maybe.
Attributed. Quoted in A Scott Berg *Goldwyn* (1989).

45 Include me out.
Attributed. Quoted in A Scott Berg *Goldwyn* (1989).

46 We are dealing in facts, not realities.
Attributed. Quoted in A Scott Berg *Goldwyn* (1989).

47 You gotta take the sour with the bitter.
Remark allegedly said to Billy Wilder when one of his films flopped. Quoted in A Scott Berg *Goldwyn* (1989).

48 The most important thing in acting is honesty. Once you've learned to fake that, you're in.
Attributed.

49 The only reason so many people showed up at his funeral was because they wanted to make sure he was dead.
Of Louis B Mayer. Attributed.

Gomez, Vernon Louis known as 'Lefty' 1908–89

US baseball player, pitcher for the New York Yankees in the 1930s.

50 Tell you what, you keep the salary and pay me the cut.
When asked to take a cut in salary from $20,000 to $7,500 following a poor season. Quoted in Colin Jarman *The Guinness Dictionary of Sports Quotations* (1990).

Goncharov, Ivan Alexandrovich 1812–91

Russian novelist. He led an uneventful life in the civil service and produced *Oblomov* (1857, translated 1915), one of the greatest works of Russian realism.

51 The trouble is that no devastating or redeeming fires have ever burnt in my life… My life began by flickering out.
1859 *Oblomov*, pt.2, ch.4 (translated by David Magarshak).

52 You lost your ability for doing things in childhood… It all began with your inability to put on your socks and ended by your inability to live.
1859 *Oblomov*, pt.4, ch.2 (translated by David Magarshak).

González Prada, Manuel 1848–1918

Peruvian reformer, journalist and poet. Nationalistic, pro-Indian, anti-Spanish and anti-clerical, he was a virtuoso in the vocabulary of invective, combining intensity of emotion with a pervasive sense of form.

53 *Aunque chillen los pedantes*
y arruguen todos el ceño,
lo declaro yo: Cervantes
suele producirme sueño

Pedants may cry out loud
or frown at me,
but I must say it: Cervantes
usually puts me to sleep.
1937 *Grafitos*, 'Hombres y libros' ('Men and Books').

Gooch, George Peabody 1873–1968

English historian and politician. He wrote several works on political and diplomatic history.

54 We can now look forward with something like confidence to the time when war between civilised nations will be considered as antiquated as a duel.
1911 *History of Our Time 1855–1911.*

Goodall, John 1863–1942

English footballer, captain of Preston North End. He also captained England, winning a total of 14 caps. He subsequently played cricket at county level for Derbyshire.

55 The one passion of my life has been football—the most exhilarating game I know, and the strongest protest against selfishness, without sermonizing, that was ever put before a thoughtful people.
Quoted in Andrew Ward and Anton Rippon *The Derby County Story* (1983).

Gorbachev, Mikhail Sergeyevich 1931–

Russian politician, President of the Supreme Soviet of the USSR (1988–90) and first executive President of the USSR. Despite his historic achievements as the father of *glasnost* (openness of information) and *perestroika* (a radical reform programme), which ended the Cold War, he was forced to resign on 25 Dec 1991. He was awarded the Nobel Peace Prize in 1990.

56 Some comrades apparently find it hard to understand that democracy is just a slogan.
1987 In *The Observer*, 1 Feb.

57 If the Russian word 'perestroika' has easily entered the international lexicon, it is due to more than just interest in what is going on in the Soviet Union. Now the whole world needs restructuring; that is, progressive development, a fundamental change.
1987 *Perestroika: New Thinking for our Country and the World.*

58 The Soviet people want full-blooded and unconditional democracy.
1988 Speech, Jul.

59 Life is making us abandon established stereotypes and outdated views; it is making us discard illusions.
1988 Speech, United Nations, 7 Dec.

60 Mitterrand has 100 lovers. One has AIDS, but he doesn't know which one. Bush has 100 bodyguards. One is a terrorist, but he doesn't know which one. Gorbachev has 100 economic advisers. One is smart, but he doesn't know which one.
1990 In *The Sunday Times*, 9 Dec.

Gordon, Adam Lindsay 1833–70

Australian poet, born in the Azores. A series of personal tragedies led to a mental breakdown, and he committed suicide.

61 Question not, but live and labour

Till yon goal be won,
Helping every feeble neighbour,
Seeking help from none;
Life is mostly froth and bubble,
Two things stand like stone:
KINDNESS in another's trouble,
COURAGE in your own.
1866 'Ye Wearie Wayfarer: Hys Ballad. In Eight Fyttes', in *Bell's Life in Victoria*, Nov 1866, collected *in Sea Spray and Smoke Drift* (1867).

62 I would that with sleepy, soft embraces
The sea would fold me—would find me rest
In luminous shades of her secret places,
In depths where her marvels are manifest;
So the earth beneath her should not discover
My hidden couch—nor the heaven above her—
As a strong love shielding a weary lover,
I would have her shield me with shining breast.
'The Swimmer', stanza 5, collected in *Bush Ballads and Galloping Rhymes* (1870).

63 A little season of love and laughter,
Of light and life, and pleasure and pain,
And horror of outer darkness after,
And dust returneth to dust again.
Then the lesser life shall be as the greater,
And the lover of life shall join the hater,
And the one thing cometh sooner or later,
And no one knoweth the loss or gain.
'The Swimmer', stanza 10, collected in *Bush Ballads and Galloping Rhymes* (1870).

Gordon, Mack 1904–59

Polish-born US lyricist.

64 Pardon me boy is that the Chattanooga Choo-choo,
Track twenty nine,
Boy you can give me a shine.
1941 Song 'Chattanooga Choo Choo', featured in *Sun Valley Serenade* (music by Harry Warren).

65 Dinner in the diner
nothing could be finer
than to have your ham'n eggs in Carolina.
1941 Song 'Chattanooga Choo Choo', featured in *Sun Valley Serenade* (music by Harry Warren).

Gordon, Ruth 1896–1985

US actress and playwright, best known for the screenplays she wrote with her husband Garson Kanin, *Adam's Rib* (1949) and *Pat and Mike* (1952). She won an Oscar for her performance in *Rosemary's Baby* (1968).

66 MAX: Say, is it too early for a drink?
POLLY: What's early about it? It's tomorrow in Europe and yesterday in China.
1943 *Over Twenty-One*, act 3.

Gore, Al(bert, Jr) 1948—

US Vice-President (1993).

67 You get all the French-fries the President can't get to.

1994 On being Vice President. In the *New York Times*, 8 Apr.

Gorostiza, José 1901–73

Mexican poet and diplomat. The most famous member of the avant-garde *Contemporáneos* group, his published poems are few but complex.

68 *¡Oh inteligencia, soledad en llamas,*
   que todo lo concibe sin crearlo!

   Oh intelligence, flaming solitude,
   envisioning all without creating!

   1939 *Muerte sin fin*, pt.1 (translated as *Death without End*, 1969).

Gorostiza, Manuel Eduardo de 1789–1851

Mexican dramatist and diplomat. He spent his youth in Spain, returning to Mexico in 1833 where he fought in the US invasion. He was a key figure in Latin American neoclassical theatre.

69 *Yo no digo por eso que el té no sea saludable…cuando*
   duelen las tripas…pero al cabo no pasa de ser agua
   caliente; sólo podía habernos venido de Inglaterra, que
   como allí son herejes, ni tendrán vino, ni bueyes
   cebones.

   I'm not saying that tea is not healthy…when you have a stomach ache…but, all in all, it is only hot water; it could only come from the English, who, being heretics as they are, probably have no wine or good beer.

   1833 *Contigo pan y cebolla*, act 1.

Gosse, Sir Edmund 1849–1928

English critic and translator. He wrote biographies of many notable literary figures, and translated the plays of Henrik Ibsen.

70 A sheep in sheep's clothing.

Of Sturge Moore, a poet. Quoted in F Greenslet *Under the Bridge* (1943), ch.10.

71 We were as nearly bored as enthusiasm would permit.

Of a play by Algernon Swinburne. Quoted in C Hassall *Biography of Edward Marsh*.

Gottfried von Strassburg fl.c.1200

German poet. His major work is the version of the Tristan and Isolde legend, *Tristan*, but his appraisals of the works of other writers are a striking early example of literary criticism.

72 *Wan swelh wip tugendet wider ir art,*

diu gerne wider ir art bewart
ir lop, ir êre, under ire lip,
diu ist niwan mit namen ein wip
und ist ein man mit muote.

When a woman grows in virtue despite her nature
and gladly preserves the integrity
of her honour, her reputation, and her person,
she is only a woman in name:
in spirit she is a man.

c.1210 *Tristan*, l.17971–3.

Gottlieb, Adolph 1903–74

US painter, one of the leaders of Abstract Expressionism.

73 Certain people always say we should go back to nature. I notice they never say we should go forward to nature. It seems to me they are more concerned that we should go back, than about nature.

1947 In *Tiger's Eye*, vol.1, no.2, Dec, quoted in C Harrison and Paul Wood (eds) *Art in Theory 1900–1990*, (1992).

Gould, Glenn 1932–82

Pianist and musical theorist. He performed his last live concert in 1964, thereafter confining himself to recording.

74 The concert is dead.

Quoted in Richard Kostelanetz *Master Minds* (1969).

75 The purpose of art is the lifelong construction of a state of wonder.

Quoted by Lorraine Monk at the Commencement Address, York University, Toronto, 6 Nov 1982.

Gould, Stephen Jay 1941–

US palaeontologist and science writer, Professor at Harvard University since 1967.

76 A man does not attain the status of Galileo merely because he is persecuted, he must also be right.

1977 *Ever Since Darwin*.

77 Science must be understood as a social phenomenon, a gutsy, human enterprise, not the work of robots programmed to collect pure information.

1981 *The Mismeasure of Man*.

78 Science is an integral part of culture. It's not this foreign thing, done by an arcane priesthood. It's one of the glories of the human intellectual tradition.

1990 In *The Independent*, 24 Jan.

Gounod, Charles François 1818–93

French composer. His works include operas, masses, hymns and oratorio, and he was popular as a songwriter. He fled to England in the Franco-Prussian war (1870), becoming a commander of the Legion of Honour in 1877.

79 **God grant me a failure like that!**

1861 Of Wagner's opera *Tannhäuser*, after the disastrous première of its revised version at the *Opéra*, 13 Mar, when it was withdrawn after only three performances. Quoted in Joanna Richardson *La Vie Parisienne* (1971).

▷ See Mérimée 674:17.

Gourmont, Rémy de 1858–1915

French writer and critic, leader of the Symbolist movement. He founded the periodical *Le Mercure de France*, and wrote essays, literary criticism and novels.

80 **Science is the only truth and it is the great lie. It knows nothing, and people think it knows everything. It is misrepresented. People think that science is electricity, automobilism, and dirigible balloons. It is something very different. It is life devouring itself. It is the sensibility transformed into intelligence. It is the need to know stifling the need to live. It is the genius of knowledge vivisecting the vital genius.**

1905 *Promenades Philosophiques* (translated by Glen S Burne, 1966).

Gowers, Sir Ernest Arthur 1880–1966

English civil servant, called to the bar in 1906. His *Plain Words* (1948) and *ABC of Plain Words* (1951) is a guide for officials in writing clear English. He revised Fowler's *Dictionary of Modern English Usage* (1965).

81 **It is not easy nowadays to remember anything so contrary to all appearances as that officials are the servants of the public; and the official must try not to foster the illusion that it is the other way round.**

1948 *Plain Words*, ch.3.

82 **Sociology is a new science concerning itself not with esoteric matters outside the comprehension of the layman, as the older sciences do, but with the ordinary affairs of ordinary people. This seems to engender in those who write about it a feeling that the lack of any abstruseness in their subject matter demands a compensatory abstruseness in their language.**

1965 'Sociologese', in H F Fowler *A Dictionary of Modern English Usage* (2nd rev edn).

Goya, Francisco de 1746–1828

Spanish painter and graphic artist, perhaps best known for his series of etchings *The Disasters of War*.

83 **But where do they find these lines in nature? Personally I only see forms that are lit up and forms that are not, planes which advance and planes which recede, relief and depth. My eye never sees outlines or particular features or details. I do not** count the hairs in the beard of the man who passes by any more than the buttonholes on his jacket attract my notice. My brush should not see better than I do.

Quoted in Enriqueta Harris *Goya* (1969).

Grace, W(illiam) G(ilbert) 1848–1915

English cricketer and physician. He made his début in first-class cricket in 1864; by the time he retired in 1908 he had scored 126 first-class centuries and 54,896 runs, and taken 2,864 wickets.

84 **Let's be getting at them before they get at us.**

His reason for always choosing to bat first if his team won the toss. Quoted in Colin Jarman *The Guinness Dictionary of Sports Quotations* (1990).

85 **They haven't come to see you umpiring, they have come to see me bat.**

On refusing to leave the crease after an umpire gave him out before he had scored, attributed. Other versions of the story have the umpire refusing to call out on the first ball, explaining to the outraged bowler that the crowd had paid not to see him bowl, but to see Grace bat.

Graham, Harry 1874–1936

English writer of light verse. His blackly comic rhymes in *Ruthless Rhymes for Heartless Homes* (1899) and the later *More Ruthless Rhymes* (1930) won widespread popularity.

86 **Aunt Jane observed, the second time**
   She tumbled off a bus,
   'The step is short from the Sublime
   To the Ridiculous.'

1899 *Ruthless Rhymes for Heartless Homes*, 'Equanimity'.

87 **O'er the rugged mountain's brow**
   Clara threw the twins she nursed,
   And remarked, 'I wonder now
   Which will reach the bottom first?'

1899 *Ruthless Rhymes for Heartless Homes*, 'Calculating Clara'.

88 **Billy, in one of his nice new sashes,**
   Fell in the fire and was burnt to ashes;
   Now, although the room grows chilly,
   I haven't the heart to poke poor Billy.

1899 *Ruthless Rhymes for Heartless Homes*, 'Tender-Heartedness'.

89 **Weep not for little Léonie**
   Abducted by a French *Marquis*!
   Though loss of honour was a wrench
   Just think how it's improved her French.

1930 *More Ruthless Rhymes for Heartless Homes*, 'Compensation'.

Grahame, Kenneth 1859–1932

Scottish children's writer and Secretary of the Bank of England (1898–1908). He wrote essays and country tales but is best remembered for *The Wind in the Willows* (1908).

90 Believe me, my young friend, there is *nothing*— absolutely nothing—half so much worth doing as simply messing about in boats.
1908 *The Wind in the Willows*, ch.1.

91 The poetry of motion! The *real* way to travel! The *only* way to travel! Here today—in next week tomorrow! Villages skipped, towns and cities jumped—always somebody else's horizon!
1908 Toad rhapsodizes about the motor car. *The Wind in the Willows*, ch.2.

92 The smell of buttered toast simply talked to Toad, and with no uncertain voice; talked of warm kitchens, of breakfasts on bright frosty mornings, of cosy parlour firesides on winter evenings, when one's ramble was over and slippered feet were propped on the fender; of the purring of contented cats, and the twitter of sleepy canaries.
1908 *The Wind in the Willows*, ch.8.

93 The clever men at Oxford
Know all that there is to be knowed.
But they none of them know one half as much
As intelligent Mr Toad.
1908 *The Wind in the Willows*, ch.10.

Gramm, Philip L 1942–

US Senator and economist.

94 If I had to decide today, I would run. But I may come to my senses.
1994 On seeking presidential nomination. In *Time*, 26 Sep.

95 I didn't come to Washington to be loved and I haven't been disappointed.
1995 In NPR broadcast, 24 Feb.

96 Sophia Loren is not a citizen.
1995 On being asked if he would choose a woman as a running mate. In *Newsweek*, 13 Mar.

97 I have the most reliable friend that you can have in American politics—ready money.
1995 On seeking presidential nomination. In the *New York Times*, 23 Apr.

Grand, Sarah pen name *Frances Elizabeth Clarke* later *McFall* 1854–1943

British novelist and feminist, born in Ireland. She was Mayoress of Bath (1923, 1925–9), and is best known for her novels which explore sexual double standards.

98 Both the cow-woman and the scum-woman are well within range of the comprehension of the Bawling Brotherhood, but the new woman is a little above him, and he never thought of looking up to where she has been sitting apart in silent contemplation all these years.
1894 *North American Review*, 'The New Aspect of the Woman Question', Mar.

Grant, Cary pseudonym of *Archibald Leach* 1904–86

English-born US film star. He made his film début in 1932 and developed a reputation as a suave, debonair performer in sophisticated light comedy. His films include *Bringing up Baby* (1938), *His Girl Friday* (1940), *An Affair to Remember* (1957) and *North by Northwest* (1959).

99 Not only will I not play it, but if Rex Harrison doesn't do it, I won't even go to see it.
c.1963 Response when offered the role of Professor Henry Higgins in the film of *My Fair Lady*. Attributed.

1 Old Cary Grant fine. How you?
His response to a journalist's terse cable to his press agent, 'How old Cary Grant?' Attributed.

Grant, George P 1918–

Canadian philosopher and teacher.

2 We listen to others to discover what we ourselves believe.
Quoted in *CBC Times*, 18 Feb 1959.

Grant, Hugh 1960–

British actor, who became an international star after starring in *Four Weddings and a Funeral* (1994).

3 I play the sort of character who would sell his grandmother for career advancement, something I've come across a lot with actors.
1994 On his role in *Restoration*. In *Screen International*, 2 Sep.

4 If *Pulp Fiction* had been set in the Sussex countryside—and I'm sure it could have worked— then things might have turned out very differently.
1995 Contrasting *Four Weddings and a Funeral* with a notoriously violent urban US drama. Speech at the British Academy of Film and Television Arts award ceremony, reported in *Screen International*, 28 Apr.

Grant, Sir Robert 1779–1838

English lawyer and politician, Advocate-General and Governor of Bombay.

5 O worship the King, all glorious above;
O gratefully sing his power and his love:
Our Shield and Defender, the Ancient of Days,
Pavilioned in splendour, and girded with praise.
1833 'O worship the King, all glorious above', collected in *Sacred Poems* (1839).

6 O tell of his might, O sing of his grace,
  Whose robe is the light, whose canopy space.
  His chariots of wrath the deep thunder-clouds
     form,
  And dark is his path on the wings of the storm.

  1833 'O worship the King, all glorious above', collected in
  Sacred Poems (1839).

Grant, Ulysses S(impson) 1822–85

US soldier and 18th President (1869–77), Union general
in the Civil War, who accepted the Confederate surrender
at Appomattox Court House (1865). He presided over
the reconstruction of the South, but his administration
was marred by scandal and corruption.

7 No terms except unconditional and immediate
  surrender can be accepted. I propose to move
  immediately upon your works.

  1862 Message to Simon Bolivar Buckner, besieged at Fort
  Donelson, 16 Feb. Quoted in P C Headley *The Life and
  Campaigns of General U. S. Grant* (1869), ch.6.

8 I purpose to fight it out on this line, if it takes all
  summer.

  1864 Despatch to Washington from Spottsylvania, 11 May.
  Quoted in P C Headley *The Life and Campaigns of U. S. Grant*
  (1869), ch.23.

9 I know no method to secure the repeal of bad or
  obnoxious laws so effective as their stringent
  execution.

  1869 Inaugural address, 4 Mar.

10 I only know two tunes. One of them is 'Yankee
   Doodle', and the other isn't.

   Attributed. Quoted in Derek Watson *Music Quotations* (1991).

Grass, Günter Wilhelm 1927–

German novelist, poet and playwright who served briefly
in the German army before apprenticing as a stonemason.
His novels explore social and political questions.

11 *Ich bin Schriftsteller von Beruf. Ich versuche, gegen
   die vergehende Zeit anzuschreiben, damit das
   Vergangene nicht unbekannt bleibt.*

   I am a writer by profession. I seek in my writing to
   hold back time so that the present is not forgotten.

   1978 *Denkzettel: Politische Reden und Aufsètze.*

12 *Ich sei nicht nur als Autor, sondern auch als Mann
   betroffen. Und zwar irgendwie schuldhaft.*

   I am moved, not only as an author, but as a person.
   And feel somehow guilty.

   1977 *Der Butt* (translated as *The Flounder*, 1978).

13 We of the long tails! We of the presentient whiskers!
   We of the perpetually growing teeth! We, the
   serried footnotes to man, his prolifating
   commentary. We, indestructible!

   1987 *Die Ratten* (*The Rat*, 1987).

Grattan, Henry 1746–1820

Irish statesman. He abansoned law for politics in 1775,
leading the fight for independence. Unable to prevent the
Act of Union, he sat at Westminster until his death.

14 She hears the ocean protesting against separation,
   but she hears the sea protesting against union. She
   follows therefore her physical destination when she
   protests against the two situations, both equally
   unnatural—separation and union.

   Of Ireland. Quoted in Conor Cruise O'Brien *Parnell and his
   Party* (1957).

Graves, Robert von Ranke 1895–1985

English writer. He lived abroad for much of his adult life.
His works include novels, poems, essays, studies of
mythology, criticism, and his autobiography, *Goodbye To
All That* (1929).

15 His eyes are quickened so with grief,
   He can watch a grass or a leaf
   Every instant grow.

   1921 'Lost Love'.

16 Love shall come at your command
   Yet will not stay.

   1923 'Song of Contrariety'.

17 Children are dumb to say how hot the day is,
   How hot the scent is of the summer rose.

   1927 'The Cool Web'.

18 Goodbye to All That.

   1929 Title of autobiography.

19 Take your delight in momentariness,
   Walk between dark and dark—a shining space
   With the grave's narrowness, though not its peace.

   1938 'Sick Love'.

20 In fear begotten, I begot in fear.
   Would you have had me cast fear out
   So that you should not be?

   1938 'Parents to Child'.

21 What, then, was war?
   No mere discord of flags
   But an infection of the common sky
   That sagged ominously upon the earth
   Even when the season was the airiest May?

   1938 'Recalling War'.

22 To evoke posterity
   Is to weep on your own grave,
   Ventriloquizing for the unborn.

   1938 'To Evoke Posterity'.

23 To bring the dead to life
   Is no great magic.
   Few are wholly dead:
   Blow on a dead man's embers
   And a live flame will start.

   1938 'To Bring the Dead to Life'.

24 Truth-loving Persians do not dwell upon
The trivial skirmish fought near Marathon.
1945 'The Persian Version'.

25 Stirring suddenly from long hibernation,
I knew myself once more a poet
Guarded by timeless principalities
Against the worm of death.
1945 'Mid-Winter Waking'.

26 To be a poet is a condition rather than a profession.
1946 Response to a questionnaire from the editor of *Horizon*.

27 The function of poetry is religious invocation of
the Muse; its use is the experience of mixed
exaltation and horror that her presence excites.
1948 *The White Goddess*, foreword.

28 For a woman to have a *liaison* is almost always
pardonable, and occasionally, when the lover
chosen is sufficiently distinguished, even
admirable.
1950 *Occupation: Writer*, 'Lars Porsena'.

29 In love as in sport, the amateur status must be
strictly maintained.
1950 *Occupation: Writer*, 'Lars Porsena'.

30 Counting the slow heart beats,
The bleeding to death of time in slow heart beats,
Wakeful they lie.
1951 'Counting the Beats'.

31 Prose books are the show dogs I breed and sell to
support my cat.
1958 On writing novels to support his love of writing poetry.
In the *New York Times*, 13 Jul.

32 Why have such scores of lovely, gifted girls
Married impossible men?
1958 'A Slice of Wedding Cake'.

33 Julia: how Irishly you sacrifice
Love to pity, pity to ill-humour,
Yourself to love, still haggling at the price.
'Reproach to Julia', collected in *Collected Poems* (1959).

34 Love is a universal migraine
A bright stain on the vision
Blotting out reason.
1961 'Symptoms of Love'.

35 A well-chosen anthology is a complete dispensary
of medicine for the more common mental
disorders, and may be used as much for prevention
as cure.
1962 *On English Poetry*, 'Definitions'.

36 Nine-tenths of English poetic literature is the result
either of vulgar careerism, or of a poet trying to

keep his hand in. Most poets are dead by their late
twenties.
1962 In *The Observer*, 11 Nov.

37 If there's no money in poetry, neither is there
poetry in money.
1963 Speech at London School of Economics, 6 Dec.

38 The remarkable thing about Shakespeare is that he
is really very good—in spite of all the people who
say he is very good.
1964 Attributed.

39 The poet is the unsatisfied child who dares to ask
the difficult question which arises from the
schoolmaster's answer to his simple question, and
then the still more difficult question which arises
from that.
Recalled on his death, 7 Dec 1985.

40 Love without hope, as when the young bird-catcher
Swept off his tall hat to the Squire's own daughter,
So let the imprisoned larks escape and fly
Singing about her head, as she rode by.
'Love without Hope'.

Gray, Alasdair James 1934–

Scottish novelist, painter and playwright. His novel
Lanark (1981) is an inventive semi-fantasy based in
Glasgow. He has subsequently written and illustrated
several equally unconventional novels.

41 Of course in nature the only ending is death, but
death hardly ever happens when people are at their
best. That is why we like tragedies. They show men
energetically with their wits about them and
deserving to do it.
1981 *Lanark*, bk.1, interlude.

42 Art is the only work open to people who can't get
along with others and still want to be special.
1981 *Lanark*, bk.3, ch.1.

43 Glasgow, the sort of industrial city where most
people live nowadays but nobody imagines living.
1981 *Lanark*, bk.3, ch.11.

Gray, Alexander 1882–1968

Scottish economist, Professor at Aberdeen and Edinburgh
Universities.

44 The services of a menial servant, taking him as an
example of unproductive labour, 'generally perish
in the very instant of their performance'—and
forthwith into this galley, along with the menial
servant, goes the sovereign, accompanied by all the
army, the navy, and the civil service, followed by
churchmen, lawyers, buffoons and opera dancers.
All these—and it is a hard saying—render services

which perish in the very instant of their performance.

1931 *The Development of Economic Doctrine.*

Gray, Thomas 1716–71

English poet. In 1742 he wrote his *Ode on a Distant Prospect of Eton College* (1747) and began the famous *Elegy written in a Country Churchyard* (1751). He declined the Laureateship (1757), and became Professor of History and Modern Languages at Cambridge (1768).

45 Ye distant spires, ye antique towers,
    That crown the wat'ry glade.

1742 *Ode on a Distant Prospect of Eton College* (published 1747), l.1–2.

46 Still as they run they look behind,
    They hear a voice in every wind,
    And snatch a fearful joy.

1742 *Ode on a Distant Prospect of Eton College* (published 1747), l.38–40.

47 Alas, regardless of their doom,
    The little victims play!
    No sense have they of ills to come,
    Nor care beyond to-day.

1742 *Ode on a Distant Prospect of Eton College* (published 1747), l.51–4.

48 To each his suff'rings, all are men,
    Condemned alike to groan;
    The tender for another's pain,
    Th' unfeeling for his own.

    Yet ah! why should they know their fate?
    Since sorrow never comes too late,
    And happiness too swiftly flies.
    Thought would destroy their paradise.
    No more; where ignorance is bliss,
    'Tis folly to be wise.

1742 *Ode on a Distant Prospect of Eton College* (published 1747), l.91–100.

49 The language of the age is never the language of poetry, except among the French, whose verse, where the thought or image does not support it, differs in nothing from prose.

1742 Letter to Richard West, 8 Apr. Collected in H W Starr (ed) *Correspondence of Thomas Gray* (1971).

50 Demurest of the tabby kind,
    The pensive Selima reclined,
    Gazed on the lake below.

1747 *Ode on the Death of a Favourite Cat, Drowned in a Tub of Gold Fishes*, l.4–6.

51 The velvet of her paws,
    Her coat that with the tortoise vies,
    Her ears of jet and emerald eyes,
    She saw; and purred applause.

1747 *Ode on the Death of a Favourite Cat, Drowned in a Tub of Gold Fishes*, l.9–12.

52 What female heart can gold despise?
    What cat's averse to fish?

1747 *Ode on the Death of a Favourite Cat, Drowned in a Tub of Gold Fishes*, stanza 4.

53 A fav'rite has no friend!

1747 *Ode on the Death of a Favourite Cat, Drowned in a Tub of Gold Fishes*, stanza 6.

54 Not all that tempts your wandering eyes
    And heedless hearts, is lawful prize;
    Nor all that glisters gold.

1747 *Ode on the Death of a Favourite Cat, Drowned in a Tub of Gold Fishes*, l.40–3.

55 The Attic warbler pours her throat,
    Responsive to the cuckoo's note,
    The untaught harmony of spring.

1748 *Ode on the Spring*, l.5–7.

56 Where'er the oak's thick branches stretch
    A broader browner shade;
    Where'er the rude and moss-grown beech
    O'er-canopies the glade,
    Beside some water's rushy brink
    With me the Muse shall sit, and think.

1748 *Ode on the Spring*, l.11–16.

57 How low, how little are the proud,
    How indigent the great!

1748 *Ode on the Spring*, l.19–20.

58 The insect youth are on the wing,
    Eager to taste the honeyed spring,
    And float amid the liquid noon:
    Some lightly o'er the current skim,
    Some show their gaily-gilded trim
    Quick-glancing to the sun.

1748 *Ode on the Spring*, l.25–30.

59 Methinks I hear in accents low
    The sportive kind reply:
    Poor moralist! and what art thou?
    A solitary fly!

1748 *Ode on the Spring*, l.41–4.

60 Shame of the versifying tribe!
    Your history whither are you spinning?
    Can you do nothing but describe?

1750 *A Long Story*, l.17–20.

61 To celebrate her eyes, her air—
    Coarse panegyrics would but tease her.
    Melissa is her nom de guerre.
    Alas, who would not wish to please her!

1750 *A Long Story*, l.33–6.

62 The curfew tolls the knell of parting day,

The lowing herd wind slowly o'er the lea,
The ploughman homeward plods his weary way,
And leaves the world to darkness and to me.

Now fades the glimmering landscapes on the sight,
And all the air a solemn stillness holds,
Save where the beetle wheels his droning flight,
And drowsy tinklings lull the distant folds.
1751 *Elegy Written in a Country Churchyard*, l.1–8.

63 Save that from yonder ivy-mantled tower
The moping owl does to the moon complain.
1751 *Elegy Written in a Country Churchyard*, l.9–10.

64 Beneath those rugged elms, that yew-tree's shade,
Where heaves the turf in many a mouldering heap,
Each in his narrow cell for ever laid,
The rude forefathers of the hamlet sleep.

The breezy call of incense-breathing Morn,
The swallow twitt'ring from the straw-built shed,
The cock's shrill clarion, or the echoing horn,
No more shall rouse them from their lowly bed.
1751 *Elegy Written in a Country Churchyard*, l.13–20.

65 For them no more the blazing hearth shall burn,
Or busy housewife ply her evening care:
No children run to lisp their sire's return,
Or climb upon his knees the envied kiss to share.
1751 *Elegy Written in a Country Churchyard*, l.21–4.

66 Let not Ambition mock their useful toil,
Their homely joys and destiny obscure;
Nor Grandeur hear, with a disdainful smile,
The short and simple annals of the poor.

The boast of heraldry, the pomp of power,
And all that beauty, all that wealth e'er gave,
Awaits alike th' inevitable hour,
The paths of glory lead but to the grave.
1751 *Elegy Written in a Country Churchyard*, l.29–36.

67 Can storied urn or animated bust
Back to its mansion call the fleeting breath?
Can Honour's voice provoke the silent dust,
Or Flattery soothe the dull cold ear of Death?
1751 *Elegy Written in a Country Churchyard*, l.41–4.

68 But knowledge to their eyes her ample page
Rich with the spoils of time did ne'er unroll;
Chill Penury repressed their noble rage,
And froze the genial current of the soul.
1751 *Elegy Written in a Country Churchyard*, l.49–52.

69 Full many a gem of purest ray serene
The dark unfathomed caves of ocean bear:
Full many a flower is born to blush unseen
And waste its sweetness on the desert air.
1751 *Elegy Written in a Country Churchyard*, l.52–6.

70 Some mute inglorious Milton here may rest,

Some Cromwell guiltless of his country's blood.
1751 *Elegy Written in a Country Churchyard*, l.59–60.

71 Their lot forbad: nor circumscribed alone
Their growing virtues, but their crimes confined:
Forbad to wade through slaughter to a throne,
And shut the gates of mercy on mankind.
1751 *Elegy Written in a Country Churchyard*, l.65–8.

72 Far from the madding crowd's ignoble strife
Their sober wishes never learned to stray;
Along the cool sequestered vale of life
They kept the noiseless tenor of their way.
1751 *Elegy Written in a Country Churchyard*, l.73–76. Thomas
Hardy popularized the phrase as the title of his novel *Far From
the Madding Crowd* (1874).

73 Their name, their years, spelt by the unlettered
    muse,
The place of fame and elegy supply:
And many a holy text around she strews,
That teach the rustic moralist to die.
1751 *Elegy Written in a Country Churchyard*, l.81–4.

74 For who to dumb Forgetfulness a prey,
This pleasing anxious being e'er resigned,
Left the warm precincts of the cheerful day,
Nor cast one longing ling'ring look behind?
1751 *Elegy Written in a Country Churchyard*, l.85–8.

75 Mindful of the unhonoured dead.
1751 *Elegy Written in a Country Churchyard*, l.93.

76 Oft have we seen him at the peep of dawn
Brushing with hasty steps the dews away
To meet the sun upon the upland lawn.
1751 *Elegy Written in a Country Churchyard*, l.98–100.

77 Here rest his head upon the lap of earth
A youth to fortune and to fame unknown.
Fair Science frowned not on his humble birth,
And Melancholy marked him for her own.
1751 *Elegy Written in a Country Churchyard*, l.117–20, 'The
Epitaph'.

78 No farther seek his merits to disclose,
Or draw his frailties from their dread abode,
(There they alike in trembling hope repose)
The bosom of his Father and his God.
1751 *Elegy Written in a Country Churchyard*, l.125–8, 'The
Epitaph'.

79 Ruin seize thee, ruthless King!
Confusion on thy banners wait,
Tho' fanned by Conquest's crimson wing
They mock the air with idle state.
1757 *The Bard. A Pindaric Ode*, l.1–4.

80 To save thy secret soul from nightly fears.
1757 *The Bard. A Pindaric Ode*, l.6.

81 Loose his beard, and hoary hair

Streamed, like a meteor, to the troubled air.
1757 *The Bard. A Pindaric Ode*, l.19–20.

82 Cold is Cadwallon's tongue,
That hushed the stormy main.
1757 *The Bard. A Pindaric Ode*, l.29–30.

83 Dear as the light that visits these sad eyes,
Dear as the ruddy drops that warm my heart,
Ye died amidst your dying country's cries.
1757 *The Bard. A Pindaric Ode*, l.40–2.

84 Weave the warp, and weave the woof,
The winding-sheet of Edward's race.
Give ample room, and verge enough
The characters of hell to trace.
1757 *The Bard. A Pindaric Ode*, l.49–52.

85 Mighty victor, mighty lord,
Low on his funeral couch he lies!
No pitying heart, no eye, afford
A tear to grace his obsequies.
1757 *The Bard. A Pindaric Ode*, l.63–6.

86 Fair laughs the morn and soft the zephyr blows,
While proudly riding o'er the azure realm
In gallant trim the gilded vessel goes;
Youth on the prow, and Pleasure at the helm;
Regardless of the sweeping whirlwind's sway,
That, hushed in grim repose, expects his evening
prey.
1757 *The Bard. A Pindaric Ode*, l.71–6.

87 In buskined measures move
Pale Grief and pleasing Pain,
With Horror, tyrant of the throbbing breast.
1757 *The Bard. A Pindaric Ode*, l.128–30.

88 'Be thine despair and sceptred care;
To triumph, and to die, are mine.'
He spoke, and headlong from the mountain's
height
Deep in the roaring tide he plunged to endless
night.
1757 *The Bard. A Pindaric Ode*, l.141–4.

89 Far from the sun and summer-gale,
In thy green lap was Nature's darling laid.
1757 Of William Shakespeare. *The Progress of Poesy*, l.83–4.

90 Nor second he, that rode sublime
Upon the seraph-wings of ecstasy,
The secrets of th' abyss to spy.
He passed the flaming bounds of place and time:
The living throne, the sapphire-blaze,
Where angels tremble, while they gaze,
He saw; but blasted with excess of light,
Closed his eyes in endless night.
1757 Of Milton. *The Progress of Poesy*, l.95–102.

91 Thoughts, that breathe, and words, that burn.

1757 *The Progress of Poesy*, l.110.

92 Beyond the limits of a vulgar fate,
Beneath the good how far—but far above the great.
1757 *The Progress of Poesy*, l.122–3.

93 It has been usual to catch a mouse or two (for
form's sake) in public once a year.
1757 On refusing the Laureateship. Letter to William Mason,
19 Dec.

94 Too poor for a bribe, and too proud to importune,
He had not the method of making a fortune.
1761 'Sketch of his own Character'.

95 I shall be but a shrimp of an author.
1768 Letter to Horace Walpole, 25 Feb.

96 Any fool may write a most valuable book by
chance, if he will only tell us what he heard and saw
with veracity.
1768 Letter to Horace Walpole, 25 Feb.

Grayser, Stephen A

US marketing expert, Professor of Marketing at Harvard
Business School.

97 The poets of commerce.
1987 Of advertising copywriters. In the *New York Times*, 28
Apr.

Greeley, Horace 1811–72

US journalist, founding editor of the *New York Tribune*.

98 Go West, young man, and grow up with the
country.
1850 *Hints Toward Reforms*.

Greenberg, Clement 1909–

US art critic.

99 When you don't like something the words come
more readily.
1991 Aged 82, on the relative ease of negative criticism over
positive. In the *New York Times*, 3 Oct.

1 For every good art critic there may be ten great
artists.
1991 In the *New York Times*, 3 Oct.

Greene, (Henry) Graham 1904–91

English writer. His writings included novels (which he
divided into 'entertainments' and more serious works),
short stories, essays, plays, biography, criticism, travel
books and two volumes of autobiography.

2 At one with the One, it didn't mean a thing beside a
glass of Guinness on a sunny day.
1938 *Brighton Rock*, pt.1, ch.1.

3 He trailed the clouds of his own glory after him; hell lay about him in his infancy. He was ready for more deaths.
1938 *Brighton Rock*, pt.2, ch.2.
▷ See Wordsworth 1098:51.

4 I couldn't eat, just went on drinking coffee, and sweating it out again. Liquid had no time to be digested; it came through the pores long before it reached the stomach. I lay wet through with sweat for four hours—it was very nearly like happiness.
1939 In Mexico. *The Lawless Roads* (published in the US as *Another Mexico*).

5 There is always one moment in childhood when the door opens and lets the future in.
1940 *The Power and the Glory*, pt.1, ch.1.

6 A virtuous man can almost cease to believe in Hell, but he carried Hell about with him. Sometimes at night he dreamed of it… Evil ran like malaria in his veins.
1940 *The Power and the Glory*, pt.3, ch.1.

7 They had been corrupted by money, and he had been corrupted by sentiment. Sentiment was the more dangerous, because you couldn't name its price.
1948 *The Heart of the Matter*, bk.1, pt.1, ch.2, iii.

8 He felt the loyalty we all feel to unhappiness—the sense that that is where we really belong.
1948 *The Heart of the Matter*, bk.2, pt.2, ch.1, i.

9 His hilarity was like a scream from a crevasse.
1948 *The Heart of the Matter*, bk.3, pt.1, ch.1, i.

10 Of those four winters which I passed in Indo-China opium has left the happiest memory.
1955 *The Quiet American*, introduction.

11 That feeling of exhilaration which a measure of danger brings to the visitor with a return ticket.
1955 *The Quiet American*, introduction.

12 Death was the only absolute value in my world. Lose life and one would lose nothing again for ever… Death was far more certain than God, and with death there would no longer be the daily possibility of love dying.
1955 *The Quiet American*, pt.1, ch.3.

13 Our Man in Havana.
1958 Title of novel.

14 Hail Mary, quite contrary!
1958 *Our Man in Havana*, pt.1, ch.2.

15 Those who marry God…can become domesticated too—it's just as humdrum a marriage as all the others.
1961 *A Burnt-Out Case*, ch.1.

16 Fame is a powerful aphrodisiac.
1964 In the *Radio Times*, 10 Sep.

17 His slang…was always a little out of date, as though he had studied in a dictionary of popular usage, but not in the latest edition.
1966 *The Comedians*, pt.1, ch.1.

18 The man who offers a bribe gives away a little of his own importance; the bribe once accepted, he becomes the inferior, like a man who has just paid for a woman.
1966 *The Comedians*, pt.1, ch.4.

19 We musn't complain too much of being comedians—it's an honourable profession. If only we could be good ones the world might gain at least a sense of style.
1966 *The Comedians*, pt.2, ch.5.

20 An autobiography is only 'a sort of life'—it may contain less errors of fact than a biography, but it is of necessity even more selective: it begins later and it ends prematurely.
1971 *A Sort of Life*, preface.

21 And the motive for recording these scraps of the past? It is much the same motive that has made me a novelist: a desire to reduce a chaos of experience to some sort of order, and a hungry curiosity.
1971 *A Sort of Life*, preface.

22 I put the muzzle of the revolver into my right ear and pulled the trigger… I was out by one. I remember an extraordinary sense of jubilation, as if carnival lights had been switched on in a drab street. My heart knocked in its cage, and life contained an infinite number of possibilities.
1971 Recalling a game of Russian roulette with his brother's revolver in 1923. *A Sort of Life*, ch.6, pt.2.

23 He would certainly have despised Christ for being the son of a carpenter, if the New Testament had not proved in time to be such a howling commercial success.
1980 *Dr Fischer of Geneva*, ch.7.

24 Writing a novel does not become easier with practice.
1980 *Ways of Escape*, ch.5.

25 Writing is a form of therapy; sometimes I wonder how all these people who do not write, compose or paint can manage to escape the madness, the melancholia, the panic fear which is inherent in the human situation.
1980 *Ways of Escape*, ch.9.

26 Perhaps we are all fictions, father, in the minds of God.
1982 *Monsignor Quixote*, pt.1, ch.1.

27 The believer will fight another believer over a shade of difference: the doubter fights only with himself.
    1982 *Monsignor Quixote*, pt.1, ch.4.

28 A solitary laugh is often a laugh of superiority.
    1982 *Monsignor Quixote*, pt.1, ch.9.

29 The world is not black and white. More like black and grey.
    1982 Quoted in 'Sayings of the Year', *The Observer*, Dec.

30 What's the good of a lie if it's seen through? When I tell a lie no-one can tell it from the gospel truth. Sometimes I can't even tell it myself.
    1988 The Captain. *The Captain and the Enemy*, pt.1, ch.1.

Greene, Robert 1558–92

English dramatist. His many plays and romances include the prose romance *Pandosto* (1588) and the comedy *Friar Bacon and Friar Bungay* (c.1589). He laid the foundations of English drama.

31 Love taught me that your honour did but jest.
    c.1589 *Friar Bacon and Friar Bungay* (published 1594), sc.8.

32 Only your hearts be frolic, for the time
    Craves that we taste of naught but jouissance.
    c.1589 *Friar Bacon and Friar Bungay* (published 1594), sc.16.

33 For there is an upstart crow, beautified with our feathers, that with his tiger's heart wrapped in a player's hide, supposes he is as well able to bombast out a blank verse as the best of you; and being an absolute *Iohannes fac totum*, is in his own conceit the only Shake-scene in a country.
    1592 Of Shakespeare. *The Groatsworth of Wit, Bought with a Million of Repentance. Iohannes fac totum* = 'Jack-of-all-trades'.

Greenspan, Alan 1926–

US financier and economist, Chairman of the Board of Governors of the Federal Reserve System.

34 Since I've become a central banker, I've learned to mumble with great coherence… If I seem unduly clear to you, you must have misunderstood what I said.
    1987 Address to Congress, Sep. Quoted by Jonathan Marshall in the *San Francisco Chronicle*, 9 Jun 1995.

35 The buck starts here.
    Sign on his desk. Quoted in Bob Woodward *The Agenda* (1994).
    ▷ See Truman 1030:33.

36 The gut-feel of the 55-year old trader is more important than the mathematical elegance of the 25-year old genius.
    1995 In the *New York Times*, 6 Mar, shortly after the collapse of Barings in Singapore brought about by a young derivatives trader.

37 I worry incessantly that I might be too clear.
    1995 In the *New York Times*, 25 Jun.

Greer, Germaine 1939–

Australian feminist, author and lecturer. Her first book *The Female Eunuch* (1970) challenges male dominance and the misrepresentation of female sexuality, which she attributes to Freud.

38 A full bosom is actually a millstone around a woman's neck.
    1970 *The Female Eunuch*, 'Body: Curves'.

39 Freud is the father of psychoanalysis. It had no mother.
    1970 *The Female Eunuch*, 'Soul: The Psychological Sell'.

40 If women understand by emancipation the adoption of the masculine role then we are lost indeed.
    1970 *The Female Eunuch*, 'Soul: Womanpower'.

41 English children have lost their innocence, for their first lessons have been in the exploitation of their adult slave.
    1970 Of the mother's subjugation to her family's demands. *The Female Eunuch*, 'Love: Family'.

42 Many a housewife staring at the back of her husband's newspaper, or listening to his breathing in bed is lonelier than any spinster in a rented room.
    1970 *The Female Eunuch*, 'Love: Security'.

43 Libraries are reservoirs of strength, grace and wit, reminders of order, calm and continuity, lakes of mental energy, neither warm nor cold, light nor dark.
    1991 In the *New York Times*, 24 Mar.

Pope Gregory I known as 'the Great'
540–604

Italian divine. He resigned as Praetor of Rome in 575, distributing his wealth to the poor, and entered a monastery. Reluctantly elected Pope in 590, he carried out many reforms. He wrote numerous Biblical commentaries and homilies.

44 *Non Angli, sed angeli.*

    Not Angles, but angels.
    c.580 Reference to Angle slave children seen by Gregory in Rome, which inspired him with the desire to convert Britain to Christianity. Quoted in Bede *Historia Ecclesiastica gentis Anglorum* (c.731), bk.2, ch.1. His exact words according to Bede were 'Nam et angelicam habent faciem, et tales angelorum in caelis decet esse coheredes' ('Since they have the faces of angels, they should be the co-heirs of the angels in heaven').

45 *Scriptura sacre mentis oculis quasi quoddam speculum opponitur, ut interna nostra facies in ipsa videatur.*

    Holy scripture is placed before the eyes of our mind like a mirror, so that we may view our inner face therein.
    c.582 *Moralia in Job*, bk.2, ch.1, section 1.

Pope Gregory VII also known as *Hildebrand*
c.1020–1085

Italian cleric. He was appointed Cardinal by Leo IX and as Pope from 1073 instituted many reforms to the clergy. He asserted the right of the Pope to direct temporal authorities, and conflicted violently with Emperor Henry IV, who appointed an anti-Pope (Clement III) and seized Rome (1084).

46 *Dilexi iustitiam et odi iniquitatem, propterea morior in exilio.*

I have loved righteousness and hated iniquity, and therefore I die in exile.

1085 Last words. Quoted in Christopher Brooke *Europe in the Central Middle Ages 962–1154* (1964), ch.15.

Gregory, Lady Isabella Augusta née *Persse*
1852–1932

Irish playwright. After marrying Sir William Gregory, Governor of Ceylon (1880), she founded with W B Yeats Dublin's Abbey Theatre. Her plays include *Spreading the News* (1904), and she also wrote Irish legends and translated Molière.

47 His eyesight has always been weak, a sort of film over the eyes. A doctor advised him not to read, but he said, 'Then I should be ignorant', and he refused an operation because there was a thousandth chance he might go blind and so remain ignorant.

1924 Of Sean O'Casey. Journal entry, 8 Jun.

Gregory, John Walter 1864–1932

British-born geologist, geographer and explorer, Professor of Geology at Melbourne University (1900–4), and then at Glasgow. In 1932 he joined an expedition to Peru, where he was drowned on a canoeing trip.

48 The Dead Heart of Australia.

1906 Title of book, dealing with the central deserts of Australia.

Grellet, Stephen 1773–1855

French-born missionary to America.

49 I expect to pass through this world but once. Any good thing, therefore, that I can do, or any kindness that I can show to any fellow-creature, let me do it now…for I shall not pass this way again.

Attributed.

Grenfell, Joyce née *Phipps* 1910–79

English comedienne. She starred in intimate revue in the 1940s and developed a fine line in the art of comic monologues; occasional film appearances included parts in such comedies as *Laughter in Paradise* (1951) and *The Belles of St Trinian's* (1954).

50 George—don't do that.

Catchphrase from one of her comic monologues, also the title of her autobiography, 1977.

51 Stately as a galleon, I sail across the floor,
Doing the Military Two-step, as in the days of yore.

1978 'Stately as a Galleon' (song).

Grenfell, Julian Henry Francis 1888–1915

English poet, killed in action during World War I. He is largely remembered for his patriotic poem 'Into Battle'.

52 And life is colour and warmth and light
And a striving evermore for these;
And he is dead, who will not fight;
And who dies fighting has increase.

1915 'Into Battle', in *The Times*, 27 May.

Grenfell, Sir Wilfred 1865–1940

English medical missionary and writer.

53 The service we render to others is really the rent we pay for our room on this earth.

1938 *A Labrador Logbook.*

Grenville, George 1712–70

English statesman. He became Prime Minister in 1763, and his period of office was marked by the prosecution of John Wilkes and the passing of the American Stamp Act before his resignation in 1765.

54 It is clear that both England and America are now to be governed by the mob.

1765 On the repeal of the Stamp Act, Jul.

Grey of Fallodon, Edward Grey, 1st Viscount 1862–1933

British statesman. He was Liberal MP for Berwick-on-Tweed (1885–1916), and Secretary for Foreign Affairs (1905–16), distinguishing himself in the Balkans peace negotiations (1913) and on the outbreak of World War I in 1914. He was subsequently Ambassador to Washington (1919–20) and Chancellor of Oxford University from 1928.

55 It is the lees left by Bismarck that still foul the cup.

1906 On the duplicity of international diplomacy as practised in the early 20c. Letter to President Roosevelt, Dec. Quoted in G M Trevelyan *Grey of Fallodon* (1937).

56 If there is war, there will be Labour Governments in every country—and quite right too.

1914 In conversation with the Italian Ambassador, Jul.

57 The lamps are going out all over Europe. We shall not see them lit again in our lifetime.

1914 Remark made on the eve of World War I, 3 Aug, in his room at the Foreign Office, recounted in *Twenty-Five Years* (1925), vol.2, ch.18.

58 In 1914, Europe had arrived at a point at which every country except Germany was afraid of the present, and Germany was afraid of the future.

1924 House of Lords, 24 Jul.

Grieg, Edvard Hagerup 1843–1907

Norwegian composer, whose works, much influenced by folk heritage, include orchestral suites, incidental music for Ibsen's *Peer Gynt*, choral music and piano pieces.

59 I am sure my music has a taste of codfish in it.

1903 Speech. Quoted in Ian Crofton and Donald Fraser *A Dictionary of Musical Quotations* (1985).

Griffith, D(avid Lewelyn) W(ark) 1874–1948

US film director. He began as an actor and short-story writer before entering the infant film industry, learning his trade in hundreds of short films. He is best known for *The Birth of a Nation* (1915) and *Intolerance* (1916).

60 Viewed as a drama, the war is somewhat disappointing.

c.1915 Comment on World War I. Quoted in Leslie Halliwell *Halliwell Filmgoer's Companion* (1984).

61 Out of the cradle, endlessly rocking.

1916 *Intolerance*.

Grillparzer, Franz 1791–1872

Austrian politician, poet and playwright. He was prone to hypochondria and depression.

62 *Es binden Sklavenfesseln nur die Hände,*
Der Sinn, er macht den Freien und den Knecht.

The chains of slavery can only bind the hands.
The mind makes us either free or enslaved.
1818 *Sappho*, act 2, sc.4.

63 *Gold schenkt die Eitelkeit, der rauhe Stolz*
Die Freundschaft und die Liebe schenken Blumen.

Gold is the gift of vanity and pride,
Friendship and love offer flowers.
1818 *Sappho*, act 2, sc.4.

64 *Ich süchste dich und habe mich gefunden.*

I sought you and I found myself.
1818 *Sappho*, act 5, sc.6.

Grimaldi, Joseph 1778–1837

English comedian, of Italian descent. His Clown figure transformed English pantomime, though his career was virtually over by 1824 as a result of the injuries he suffered in slapstick routines on stage.

65 Here we are again!

c.1800 His customary greeting to the audience on making his entrance as Clown, later adopted as a catchphrase by clowns everywhere.

Griswold, Alfred Whitney 1906–63

US educator, President of Yale University (1950–63).

66 A Socrates in every classroom.

1951 On his hopes for the Yale faculty. In *Time Magazine*, 11 Jun.

67 Could Hamlet have been written by a committee, or the *Mona Lisa* painted by a club? Could the New Testament have been composed as a conference report?

1957 Baccalaureate address, 9 Jun.

68 Self-respect…comes to us when we are alone, in quiet moments in quiet places when we suddenly realize that, knowing the good, we have done it; knowing the beautiful, we have served it; knowing the truth, we have spoken it.

1957 Baccalaureate address, 9 Jun.

Gromyko, Andrei Andreevich 1909–89

Soviet politician, notorious for his austere and humourless demeanour. As Foreign Minister (1957–85) he influenced Soviet relations with the West during the Cold War. President in 1985, he was replaced by Gorbachev.

69 Every night, whisper 'Peace' in your husband's ear.

1984 Said to Nancy Reagan at a White House reception, 28 Sep.

70 This man, Comrades, has a nice smile, but he has iron teeth.

1985 Speech to the Supreme Soviet on proposing Mikhail Gorbachev as the new party leader.

Grossmith, George 1847–1912

English comedian and entertainer. He took leading parts in Gilbert and Sullivan operettas (1877–89) and with his brother, Weedon, wrote *The Diary of A Nobody*, first serialized in *Punch* (published 1892).

71 What's the good of a home if you are never in it?

1892 *The Diary of a Nobody* (with Weedon Grossmith), ch.1.

72 I left the room with silent dignity, but caught my foot in the mat.

1892 *The Diary of a Nobody* (with Weedon Grossmith), ch.7.

Grosvenor, Gilbert M 1875–1966

US geographer and editor, Director then President of the National Geographic Society (1899–1954) and editor of its magazine. He pioneered the use of colour photography, and encouraged conservation and wildlife protection.

73 If you don't know where you are, you're nowhere.

On the NGS's establishment of a $20-million foundation to fight ignorance of geography. Quoted in *The Washington Post*, 14 Jan 1988.

Guedalla, Philip 1889–1944

English historian and biographer, known for his irreverent wit. His books include *Supers and Supermen* (1920),

Palmerston (1926), a biography of Wellington, *The Duke* (1931), and *Mr Churchill* (1941).

74 The work of Henry James has always seemed divisible by a simple dynastic arrangement into three reigns: James I, James II, and the Old Pretender.
1920 *Supers and Supermen*, 'Some Critics'.

75 History repeats itself. Historians repeat each other.
1920 *Supers and Supermen*, 'Some Historians'.

76 The Crimean War is one of the bad jokes of history.
1943 *The Two Marshals*.

Guibert of Nogent c.1097

Medieval historian.

77 God has instituted in our time holy wars, so that the order of knights and the crowd running in their wake, who following the example of the ancient pagans have been engaged in slaughtering one another, might find a new way of gaining salvation.
c.1097 *Gesta Dei per Francos*, in *Receuil des Historiens de Croisades Occidentaux*, edited by L'Academie des Inscriptions et Belles-Lettres (1847–95), vol.4, p.124.

Guillén, Nicolás 1902–89

Cuban poet, of mixed African and European descent, a leader of the Afro-Cuban movement. An outspoken member of the Communist Party, he was active in Castro's regime.

78 *Según un yanqui que debe*
ser todo un derrochador,
es Cuba donde mejor
se come siempre y se bebe.

According to a gringo who must
be a true spendthrift,
Cuba is always the best place
to eat and to drink.
1953 *Sátira política*, 'Depende' ('It Depends').

Guimarães Rosa, João 1908–67

Brazilian novelist. He practised medicine in his native area, then joined the foreign service. *Grande Sertão* is derived from the oral tradition of the hinterland of Brazil.

79 *Um está sempre no escuro, só no último derradeiro é*
que clareiam a sala.

One is always in the dark, and it is only at the last moment that they turn on the lights in the room.
1956 *Grande Sertão: Verédas* (translated as *The Devil to Pay in the Backlands*, 1963).

Guiraldes, Ricardo 1886–1927

Argentinian poet and novelist, renowned for his masterful blending of the gaucho (cowboy) tale with modernist techniques.

80 *Si sos gaucho en de veras, no has de mudar, porque*
andequiera que vayas irás con tu alma por delante.

If you're really a gaucho, you can't change, because wherever you go, you'll go with your soul leading the way.
1926 *Don Segundo Sombra* (1935), ch.26.

Guitry, Sacha 1885–1957

French actor and playwright. Born in Russia, he established himself as a popular light comedian as well as writing a number of screenplays and directing several films.

81 The others were only my wives. But you, my dear, will be my widow.
Attributed reply to his fifth wife, when she expressed jealousy of her predecessors.

Gulbenkian, Nubar Sarkis 1896–1972

British industrialist and philanthropist. He worked with his father in the oil business, advising on Middle East oil negotiations (1926–8, 1948–54), and was honourary counsellor at the Turkish embassy (1966–72).

82 The best number for a dinner party is two—myself and a damn good head waiter.
1965 In the *Daily Telegraph*, 14 Jan.

Gullit, Ruud 1962–

Dutch footballer. He transferred to the Italian club AC Milan for a record £6 million in 1987.

83 If I'd wanted to be an individual, I'd have taken up tennis.
Quoted in Colin Jarman *The Guinness Dictionary of Sports Quotations* (1990).

Gunn, Jeannie known as Mrs Aeneas Gunn 1870–1961

Australian writer. In 1901 she married Aeneas James Gunn and went with him to Elsey Station, Northern Territory. When her husband died in 1903 she returned to Melbourne and wrote of her experiences in the outback.

84 There's time enough for everything in the Never-Never.
1908 *We of the Never-Never*, ch.5.

Gunn, Thom(son William) 1929–

English poet. He has lived in the US since 1954. He is recognized as one of the major poets of his generation.

85 I saw that lack of love contaminates,
You know I know you know I know you know.
1954 'Carnal Knowledge'.

86 At worst, one is in motion; and at best,

Reaching no absolute, in which to rest,
One is always nearer by not keeping still.
1957 'On the Move'.

Gunther, John 1901–70

US author and journalist. He established his reputation with the best-selling *Inside Europe* (1939), and followed it with a series of *Inside* books.

87 Bright grayness. Both the clothes and hair were neat and gray. The gray-framed spectacles magnified the gray hazel eyes, but there was no grayness in the mind.
Of Harry S Truman. Quoted in David McCullough *Truman* (1992).

Gurney, Dorothy Frances 1858–1932

English poet and hymnwriter.

88 The kiss of the sun for pardon,
The song of the birds for mirth,
One is nearer God's Heart in a garden
Than anywhere else on earth.
1913 'God's Garden'.

Gurney, Ivor 1890–1937

English poet and composer, especially renowned for his war poems.

89 The songs I had are withered
Or vanished clean.
Yet there are bright tracks
Where I have been.
1922 'The Songs I Had'.

90 I paid the prices of life
Standing where Rome immortal heard October's strife,
A war poet whose right of honour cuts falsehood like a knife.
c.1922 'Poem for End'.

Gurney, John Hampden 1802–62

English clergyman and hymnwriter.

91 Ye holy angels bright,
Who wait at God's right hand,
Or through the realms of light
Fly at your Lord's command,
Assist our song,
Or else the theme too high doth seem
For mortal tongue.
1838 'Ye Holy Angels Bright', based on a poem by Richard Baxter (1615–91).

Gustavus II (Adolphus) 1594–1632

King of Sweden (1611), who entered the Thirty Years War by invading Poland in 1621. His armies conquered much

of Germany in 1631, and he was killed at the Battle of Lützen, 1632.

92 All the wars that are now afoot in Europe have been fused together, and have become a single war.
1630 Letter to Axel Oxenstierna, referring to the Thirty Years War, 1618–48.

Guston, Philip 1912–80

Canadian-born painter. He moved with his family to California in 1916. His early paintings combine realism with surrealism and his later work is characterised by its cartoon-like style.

93 I go to my studio every day, because one day I may go and the angel will be there. What if I don't go and the angel came?
1991 Quoted by Gail Godwin in the *Washington Post*, 7 Mar.

Guthrie, Woody (Woodrow Wilson) 1912–67

US folk-singer, songwriter and author. His songs draw on traditional country music and blues themes and reflect his social and political concerns.

94 This land is your land, this land is my land,
From California to the New York Island.
From the redwood forest to the Gulf Stream waters
This land was made for you and me.
1956 'This Land is Your Land'.

95 You can't write a good song about a whore-house unless you been in one.
1964 Quoted in *Broadside*.

Guy, Ray 1939–

Canadian columnist.

96 Pity the poor creatures in warmer countries where the seasons never change. Where summer is eternal and they never know the pain of waiting and the joy at last when summer comes.
1976 *That Far Greater Bay*, 'Catching Conners'.

Gwyn, Nell 1650–87

English actress. Originally an orange-seller at Drury Lane, she became a popular performer in comedies; her admirers included Charles II, whose mistress she became in about 1669. She retired from the stage in 1670.

97 Pray, good people, be civil; I am the Protestant whore.
1675 Attributed, when angry crowds pressed round her carriage in the belief that she was Charles II's unpopular Catholic mistress Louise de Kérouaille.

Haas, Ernst Bernard 1921–

Austrian photographer and author. Known for his early black and white photojournalism (particularly his 'Returning Prisoners of War' story in 1949), he was a pioneer of early colour, and his work on colour-blur made his fame. His film assignments include *The Misfits, Moby Dick, West Side Story* and *Heaven's Gate*.

98 Beauty pains, and when it pained most, I shot.

1955 In *Life*, 1 Aug. 'The Glow of Paris'.

Habington, William 1605–54

English writer, one of the metaphysical followers of Donne. He published a book of lyrics, *Castara* (1634), a play, *The Queen of Aragon* (1640) and *The History of Edward the Fourth* (1640).

99 O empty boast of flesh.

1634 *Castara*, 'Upon Beauty'.

1 'Cause some make forfeit of their name,
  And slave themselves to man's desire;
  Shall the sex free
  From guilt, damn'd to the bondage be?

1634 *Castara*, 'Against Them Who Lay Unchastity to the Sex of Women'.

Haeckel, Ernst Heinrich 1834–1919

German biologist and philosopher, who popularized Darwinism in the German-speaking world. He became Professor of Comparative Anatomy at the University of Jena.

2 God…a gaseous vertebrate.

1899 *Welträtsel* (The Riddle of the Universe).

Hagen, Walter 1892–1969

US golfer. The first great professional US golfer, he won the US Open twice and the British Open four times.

3 Give me a man with big hands and big feet and no brains and I'll make a golfer out of him.

Quoted in Michael Hobbs *The Golf Quotation Book* (1992).

Haggai, Thomas

US businessman.

4 Cast your bread upon the waters, but wait until the tide is coming in to do it.

1988 In *Fortune*, 7 Nov.

Haggard, Sir (Henry) Rider 1856–1925

English novelist. He travelled to Natal and the Transvaal (1875–9) before embarking on a literary life. His first successful novel was *King Solomon's Mines* (1885), followed by *She* (1887) and *Ayesha* (1905), among others.

5 A little while and I will be gone from among you, whither I cannot tell. From nowhere we came, into nowhere we go. What is Life? It is a flash of a firefly in the night. It is a breath of a buffalo in the winter time. It is as the little shadow that runs across the grass and loses itself in the sunset.

1885 Dying words of the African chief Umbopa in *King Solomon's Mines*. John Peter Turner in *The North-West Mounted*

Police (1950) credited them to Crowfoot (c.1830–90), chief of the Blackfoot Indians, who died in his teepee overlooking the Bow River, Alberta, 25 Apr 1890, and this attribution gained popular acceptance.

6 She who must be obeyed.

1887 *She*, ch.6, and passim.

7 What a terrifying reflection it is, by the way, that nearly all our deep love for women who are not our kindred depends—at any rate, in the first instance—upon their personal appearances. If we lost them, and found them again dreadful to look on, though otherwise they were the very same, should we still love them?

1887 *She*, ch.26 'What We Saw', narrator's note.

Haig, Alexander Meigs, Jr 1924–

US soldier and Republican politician, White House Chief of Staff at the end of Nixon's presidency and Supreme NATO Commander. He was Secretary of State under Reagan (1981–2), and unsuccessfully sought presidential nomination in 1988.

8 As of now, I am in control here in the White House.

1981 Said immediately after the attempted assassination of President Reagan, 30 Mar, in Vice-President George Bush's absence from Washington DC.

9 I take it as a compliment when an agent of the largest and most heinous bully of the century, the Soviet Union, accuses me of being a bully.

1995 On how he was seen as US Secretary of State by former Soviet Ambassador Anatoly Dobrynin. In the *Washington Post*, 27 Oct.

Haig, Douglas, 1st Earl Haig of Bemersyde 1861–1928

Scottish field marshal. He became Commander of the British Expeditionary Force in 1915. His war of attrition was costly and widely criticized; he led the final successful offensive of World War I in Aug 1918.

10 Every position must be held to the last man: there must be no retirement. With our backs to the wall, and believing in the justice of our cause, each one of us must fight on until the end.

1918 Order to British troops facing the German offensive across the Somme battlefields, 12 Apr. Quoted in A Duff Cooper *Haig* (1936), vol.2, ch.23.

Haile Selassie originally Prince Ras Tafari Makonnen 1891–1975

Emperor of Ethiopia (1930–6, 1941–74), leader of the revolution against Lij Yasu (1916). He was exiled after the Italian conquest of Abyssinia (1935–6), and restored after British liberation. Although deposed after the famine of 1973, he is still much revered, notably by Rastafarians.

11 Throughout history it has been the inaction of those who could have acted, the indifference of those who should have known better, the silence of the voice of justice when it mattered most, that has made it possible for evil to triumph.

1963 Address to a special session of the UN General Assembly, 4 Oct, making him the first head of state to address both that organization and the League of Nations.

Hailsham, Quintin (McGarel) Hogg, Baron Hailsham of St Marylebone, 2nd Viscount 1907–

English Conservative politician. After succeeding to his title (1950), he held a number of senior state posts. In 1963 he renounced his peerage in an unsuccessful bid to become Leader of the Conservative Party. He was later Lord Chancellor.

12 Conservatives do not believe that the political struggle is the most important thing in life… The simplest of them prefer fox-hunting, the wisest religion.

1947 *The Case for Conservatism*, pt.1.

13 A great party ought not to be brought down because of a squalid affair between a woman of easy virtue and a proved liar.

1963 On the Profumo affair, BBC TV, 13 Jun.

14 If the British public falls for this, I say that it will be stark, staring bonkers.

1964 Press conference on the Labour election manifesto, 12 Oct.

Halberstam, David 1934–

US journalist and author, staff writer and correspondent for the *New York Times* (1960–7). His books include *The Powers That Be* (1979) and *The Next Century* (1991).

15 He has seen the future and it is hamburgers.

1993 On Ray Kroc's decision to buy and expand the original McDonald's. *The Fifties*.

Haldane, J(ohn) B(urdon) S(anderson) 1892–1964

Anglo-Indian biologist. He wrote many popular books on biology and genetics, and was Chairman of the *Daily Worker* (1940–9), but left the Communist Party in 1956.

16 Bad as our urban conditions often are, there is not a slum in the country which has a third of the infantile death-rate of the royal family in the middle ages.

1924 *Daedalus, or Science and the Future*.

17 Now, my own suspicion is that the universe is not only queerer than we suppose, but queerer than we *can* suppose.

1927 *Possible Worlds and Other Papers*, 'Possible Worlds'.

18 I believe that the scientist is trying to expand absolute truth and the artist absolute beauty, so that I find in art and science, and in an attempt to live a good life, all the religion I want.

1931 *Living Philosophies*.

19 My final word, before I'm done,
Is 'Cancer can be rather fun'.
Thanks to the nurses and Nye Bevan
The NHS is quite like heaven
Provided one confronts the tumour
With a sufficient sense of humour.
I know that cancer often kills,
But so do cars and sleeping pills;
And it can hurt one till one sweats,
So can bad teeth and unpaid debts.

1964 'Cancer's a Funny Thing'.

Hale, Nathan 1755–76

American revolutionary soldier. In 1776 he volunteered to penetrate British lines on Long Island and procure intelligence for Washington, but was detected and hanged as a spy.

20 I only regret that I have but one life to lose for my country.

1776 At his execution, 22 Sep.

Hale, Robert Beverly 1901–85

US artist, teacher and curator. He has permanent collections in the Whitney, the Metropolitan Museum of Art, New York City, and in many private collections. He was curator at the Metropolitan (1949–85) and lectured at Pennsylvania Academy of Fine Arts (1968–85) and Columbia University. He wrote, edited and translated books on art.

21 New artists must break a hole in the subconscious and go fishing there.

1960 In *Time*, 11 Apr.

Hale, Sarah Josepha née Buell 1788–1879

US writer. In 1828 she became editor of the *Ladies' Magazine* in Boston. She wrote a novel, *Northwood* (1827), and *Poems for Our Children* (1830).

22 Mary had a little lamb,
Its fleece was white as snow,
And everywhere that Mary went
The lamb was sure to go.

1830 *Poems for Our Children*, 'Mary's Little Lamb'.

Hales, Stephen 1677–1761

English clergyman and physiologist, considered the founder of plant physiology. His investigations are reported in his work *Statickal Essays*, the first of which, *Vegetable Staticks*, was published in 1727.

23 Since we are assured that the all-wise Creator has observed the most exact proportions of number, weight and measure in the make of all things, the most likely way therefore to get any insight into the nature of those parts of the Creation which come within our observation must in all reason be to number, weigh and measure.

1727 *Vegetable Staticks.*

Haliburton, Thomas Chandler 1796–1865

Canadian lawyer and satirist. In 1835 he began a series of satiric sketches later enlarged as *The Clockmaker; or The Sayings and Doings of Samuel Slick* (1836). His *The Old Judge; or Life in a Colony* (1849) combines social history and satire.

24 I was always well mounted. I am fond of a horse, and always piqued myself on having the fastest trotter in the Province. I have made no great progress in the world. I feel doubly, therefore, the pleasure of not being surpassed on the road.

1836 *The Clockmaker* (first series), 'The Trotting Horse'.

25 If a chap seems bent on cheatin' himself, I like to be neighbourly and help him to do it.

1838 *The Clockmaker* (second series), 'A Cure for Smuggling'.

Halifax, Edward Frederick Lindley Wood, 1st Earl of 1881–1959

English Conservative politician, Viceroy of India (1926–31). He was Foreign Secretary (1938–40) under Neville Chamberlain, whose 'appeasement' policy he implemented, and Ambassador to the US (1941–6).

26 I often think how much easier the world would have been to manage if Herr Hitler and Signor Mussolini had been at Oxford.

1937 Speech, York, 4 Nov.

Halifax, George Savile, 1st Marquis of 1633–95

English statesman, created viscount (1668) at the Restoration. Under James II, he was dismissed as President of the Council for opposing the repeal of the Test and Habeas Corpus Acts. He gave allegiance to William of Orange, but joined the Opposition in 1689.

27 Men are not hanged for stealing horses, but that horses may not be stolen.

c.1687 *Political Thoughts and Reflections*, 'Of Punishment'.

28 Anger is never without an argument, but seldom with a good one.

c.1687 *Political Thoughts and Reflections*, 'Of Anger'.

29 Malice is of a low stature, but it hath very long arms.

c.1687 *Political Thoughts and Reflections*, 'Of Malice and Envy'.

30 The best way to suppose what may come, is to remember what is past.

c.1687 *Political Thoughts and Reflections*, 'Miscellaneous Experience'.

31 When the people contend for their liberty, they seldom get anything by their victory but new masters.

c.1687 *Political Thoughts and Reflections*, 'Of Prerogative, Power and Liberty'.

32 Most men's anger about religion is as if two men should quarrel for a lady they neither of them care for.

Collected in *Complete Works* (published 1912).

Hall, Charles 1745–1825

English physician educated in Holland, best known for his socialist work *The Effects of Civilization on the People in European States* (1805). In 1805 he was impoverished by a lawsuit and, refusing aid, later died in prison determined to show that he had been unjustly treated.

33 The effect of trade and commerce with respect to most civilized states is to send out of their countries what the poor, that is, the great mass of mankind, have occasion for, and to bring back, in return, what is consumed almost wholly by a small part of those nations, viz. the rich. Hence it appears that the greater part of manufactures, trade and commerce is highly injurious to the poor as being the chief means of depriving them of the necessaries of life.

1805 *The Effects of Civilization on the People in European States.*

Hall, J C (Joyce Clyde) 1891–1982

US businessman, founder of Hallmark Cards Inc.

34 The art of the masses.

Of illustrated greetings cards. Recalled on his death, quoted in *The Annual Obituary 82* (1983).

Halsey, W(illiam) F(rederick) known as 'Bull' Halsey 1882–1959

US naval officer, commander at the Battle of Leyte Gulf (1944) and others. He received the formal Japanese surrender on his flagship, the USS *Missouri*, on 2 Sep 1945.

35 The Third Fleet's sunken and damaged ships have been salvaged and are retiring at high speed toward the enemy.

1944 Comment, 14 Oct, on hearing claims that the Japanese had virtually annihilated the US fleet. Quoted in E B Potter *Bull Halsey* (1985), ch.17.

Hamer, Robert 1911–63

British film director and screenwriter. Best known for *It Always Rains on Sunday* (1947), *Kind Hearts and Coronets* (1949, with John Dighton) and *School for Scoundrels* (1960).

36 I shot an arrow in the air. She fell to earth in Berkeley Square.
1949 *Kind Hearts and Coronets* (with John Dighton).

37 Every lunch time I went to see how my inheritance was proceeding. Sometimes the deaths column brought good news. Sometimes the births column brought bad. The advent of twin sons to the Duke was a terrible blow. Fortunately an epidemic of diphtheria restored the status quo almost immediately.
1949 *Kind Hearts and Coronets* (with John Dighton).

38 I always say that my west window has all the exuberance of Chaucer without, happily, any of the concomitant crudities of his period.
1949 *Kind Hearts and Coronets* (with John Dighton).

Hamilton, Alexander c.1755–1804

US statesman, Washington's aide-de-camp in the American Revolution and later a congressman. As Secretary of the Treasury (1789–95) he restored the country's finances, but he was killed in a duel with a rival.

39 A national debt, if it is not excessive, will be to us a national blessing.
1781 Letter to Robert Morris, 30 Apr.

40 To model our political systems upon speculations of lasting tranquillity is to calculate on the weaker springs of the human character.
1787–8 *The Federalist Papers*.

Hamilton, Edith 1867–1963

German-born US classicist, whose popular works include *The Greek Way* (1930).

41 To be able to be caught up into the world of thought—that is educated.
Quoted in the *Saturday Evening Post*, 27 Sep 1958.

Hammarskjöld, Dag Hjalmar Agne Carl 1905–61

Swedish statesman. As Secretary-General of the United Nations from 1953 he took part in conciliation moves in the Middle East. He was awarded the Nobel Peace Prize posthumously, after he was killed in an air crash while involved in the Congo crisis.

42 For what has been—thanks!
For what shall be—yes!
1950 *Vägmarken* (translated by L Sjöberg and W H Auden as *Markings*, 1964).

43 God does not die on the day when we cease to believe in a personal deity, but we die on the day when our lives cease to be illumined by the steady radiance, renewed daily, of a wonder, the source of which is beyond all reason.

44 Before Thee in humility, with Thee in faith, in Thee in peace.
1955 *Vägmarken* (translated by L Sjöberg and W H Auden as *Markings*, 1964).

45 The 'men of the hour', the self-assured who strut among us in the jingling harness of their success and importance, how can you let yourself be irritated by them. Let them enjoy their triumph— on the level to which it belongs.
1956 *Vägmarken* (translated by L Sjöberg and W H Auden as *Markings*, 1964).

46 I didn't know Who—or what—put the question, I don't know when it was put. I don't even remember answering. But at some moment I did answer Yes to Someone—or Something—and from that hour I was certain that existence is meaningful and that, therefore, my life, in self-surrender, had a goal.
1961 *Vägmarken* (translated by L Sjöberg and W H Auden as *Markings*, 1964).

47 Weep
If you can,
Weep,
But do not complain—
And you must be thankful.
1961 *Vägmarken* (translated by L Sjöberg and W H Auden as *Markings*, 1964).

48 Never let success hide its emptiness from you; achievement its nothingness; toil its desolation. Keep alive the incentive to push on further, that pain in the soul that drives us beyond ourselves. Do not look back, and do not dream about the future either. It will neither give you back the past, nor satisfy your other daydreams. Your duty, your reward, your destiny are here and now.
1961 *Vägmarken* (translated by L Sjöberg and W H Auden as *Markings*, 1964).

Hammer, Armand 1898–1990

US business executive and art collector.

49 The art world is a jungle echoing to the calls of vicious jealousies and ruthless combat between dealers and collectors; but I have been walking in the jungles of business all my life, and fighting tooth and nail for pictures comes as a form of relaxation to me.
1987 *Hammer, Witness to History*, his autobiography.

50 My Van Gogh is better than *Irises*. I have the whole garden.
On ranking his own Van Gogh, *Hospital at Saint-Rémy*, over the *Irises* that brought £53.9 million at auction. In *Connoisseur*, Jan 1991.

Hammerstein, Oscar II 1895–1960

US lyricist–librettist. In collaboration with composer Richard Rodgers he wrote such hit musicals as *Oklahoma!* (1943), *South Pacific* (1949) and *The Sound of Music* (1959).

51 Fish got to swim and birds got to fly
I got to love one man till I die
Can't help lovin' dat man of mine.
1927 Song from *Show Boat* (music by Jerome Kern).

52 Ol' Man River.
1927 Title of song from *Show Boat* (music by Jerome Kern).

53 When I grow too old to dream
Your love will live in my heart.
1935 Song from *The Night is Young* (music by Sigmund Romberg).

54 As you walk through the storm,
Hold your head up high,
And don't be afraid of the dark,
At the end of the storm,
Is a golden sky,
And the sweet silver song of the lark,
Walk on through the wind,
Walk on through the rain,
Though your dreams be tossed and blown.
Walk on, walk on,
With hope in your hearts,
And you'll never walk alone,
You'll never walk alone.
1945 *Carousel*, 'You'll never walk alone' (music by Richard Rodgers). The song was subsequently released in a pop version by Gerry and the Pacemakers in 1963 and adopted as a club song by Liverpool football club.

55 I'm Gonna Wash That Man Right Outa My Hair.
1949 Title of song sung by Mitzi Gaynor in *South Pacific* (music by Richard Rodgers).

56 You've got to be taught to be afraid
Of people whose eyes are oddly made,
Of people whose skin is a different shade.
You've got to be carefully taught

You've got to be taught before it's too late,
Before you are six or seven or eight,
To hate all the people your relatives hate.
You've got to be carefully taught.
1949 'You've Got to be Carefully Taught', song from *South Pacific* (music by Richard Rodgers).

57 The hills are alive with the sound of music
With the songs they have sung
For a thousand years.
1959 *The Sound of Music*, title song (music by Richard Rodgers).

Hammett, (Samuel) Dashiell 1894–1961

US crime writer. He joined the Pinkerton Detective Agency as an operator, and later translated his experiences into literature. He suffered from alcohol abuse, which broke his health, and like his partner Lillian Hellman, came into conflict with McCarthy in the anti-Communist trials.

58 He looked rather pleasantly like a blond satan.
1930 Of Sam Spade. *The Maltese Falcon*, 'Spade and Archer'.

59 'I mean that you paid us more than if you'd been telling the truth,' he explained blandly, 'and enough more to make it all right.'
1930 *The Maltese Falcon*, 'The Black Bird'.

60 I distrust a man that says when. If he's got to be careful not to drink too much it's because he's not to be trusted when he does.
1930 *The Maltese Falcon*, 'The Fat Man'.

61 Murder doesn't round out anybody's life except the murdered's and sometimes the murderer's.
1932 *The Thin Man*, ch.31.

Hampton, Christopher 1946–

English playwright. He established his reputation with such plays as *The Philanthropist* (1970) and *Savages* (1973). He adapted *Les Liaisons Dangereuses* (1986) from the novel by Laclos.

62 Masturbation is the thinking man's television.
1970 *The Philanthropist*.

63 I always divide people into two groups. Those who live by what they know to be a lie, and those who live by what they believe, falsely, to be the truth.
1970 *The Philanthropist*.

64 If I had to give a definition of capitalism, I would say: the process whereby American girls turn into American women.
1974 *Savages*, sc.16.

65 Asking a working writer what he thinks about critics is like asking a lamp-post how it feels about dogs.
Attributed.

Hancock, Lang(ley George) 1909–92

Australian mining industrialist, who discovered iron ore in the Pilbara region with his light aircraft. His various claims, including Rhodes Ridge, made him one of Australia's richest men.

66 The best way to help the poor is not to become one of them.
Quoted in R W Kent (ed) *Money Talks* (1985).

Hand, (Billings) Learned 1872–1961

US jurist, senior judge at the US Court of Appeals for the Second Circuit (1924–51). His legal judgements had enormous influence on the Supreme Court.

67 The spirit of liberty is the spirit which is not too sure that it is right.

1944 Address at 'I Am An American Day' in New York's Central Park, recalled on his death, 18 Aug 1961.

Handel, George Frideric 1685–1759

German-born English composer. He settled in England in 1712, becoming first Director of the Royal Academy of Music (1720). He turned from opera to oratorio in 1739, notably *Messiah* (1742). Other works include *Water Music* and *Music for the Royal Fireworks*.

68 Whether I was in my body or out of my body as I wrote it I know not. God knows.

Of the 'Hallelujah Chorus' in his *Messiah*. Quoted in Romain Rolland *Essays on Music* (1948).

Handy, Charles Brian 1932–

Irish management teacher. His works include *The Making of Managers* (1988) and *The Age of Unreason* (1991).

69 Words are the bugles of social change.

1991 *The Age of Unreason*.

Hankey, Katherine 1834–1911

English evangelist and hymnwriter.

70 Tell me the old, old story,
Of unseen things above.

1866 *The Story Wanted*, 'Tell Me the Old, Old Story'.

Hansberry, Lorraine Vivian 1930–65

US playwright. Her semi-autobiographical *A Raisin in the Sun* (1959), the first Broadway play written by a black woman, dealt with the problems facing a black family in a white neighbourhood.

71 Though it be a thrilling and marvelous thing to be merely young and gifted in such times, it is doubly so—doubly dynamic—to be young, gifted and black.

1969 Speech to entrants in the United Negro College Fund writers competition, reported in the *New York Times*, 25 May. The phrase was later used as the title of her biography *Young, Gifted and Black* (1969).

Harburg, E(dgar) Y(ip) 1898–1981

US lyricist–librettist, born in New York, who contributed to many Broadway shows. Best known for the songs in *The Wizard of Oz*.

72 Brother can you spare a dime?

1932 Title of song.

73 Say, it's only a paper moon,
Sailing over a cardboard sea.

1933 'It's Only a Paper Moon' (with Billy Rose, music by Harold Arlen).

74 Lydia The Tattooed Lady.

1939 Title of song featured in the Marx Brothers film *At the Circus* (music by Harold Arlen).

75 Somewhere over the Rainbow.
Way up high
There's a land that I heard of
Once in a lullaby.

1939 'Over the Rainbow', sung by Judy Garland in *The Wizard of Oz* (music by Harold Arlen).

Hardie, (James) Keir 1856–1915

Scottish Labour politician, a former miner. He founded and edited the *Labour Leader*, and was Chairman of the Independent Labour Party and of the Labour Party (1906–8), which he helped to found. He was a strong pacifist, and lost his seat opposing the Boer War.

76 From his childhood onward this boy will be surrounded by sycophants and flatterers by the score, and will be taught to believe himself as of a superior creation. A line will be drawn between him and the people whom he is to be called upon some day to reign over. In due course, following the precedent which has already been set, he will be sent on a tour round the world, and probably rumours of a morganatic alliance will follow, and the end of it all will be that the Country will be called upon to pay the bill.

1894 Speech in the House of Commons, 28 Jun, opposing an Address of Congratulation to the Queen being passed in the House of Commons, on the birth of a son (the future Edward VIII) to the Duke and Duchess of York.

77 Can a Man be a Christian on a Pound a Week?

1901 Title of pamphlet.

Hardie, Robert 1904–73

Scottish doctor who, when Singapore fell in 1942, became one of the 61,000 Allied prisoners of war forced by the Japanese to work on the Burma–Siam railway. He kept a secret diary while a prisoner.

78 This is the last day of 1943, a year to be said goodbye to without regret, holding as it did nothing beyond captivity and depression, weary waiting, and above all the sight of immeasurable human misery, suffering and death.

1943 Diary entry, 31 Dec.

Harding, Warren G(amaliel) 1865–1923

US politician and 29th President. A successful journalist, he emerged as a power in the Republican Party, won its nomination and became President (1920–3) when he campaigned against US membership of the League of Nations.

79 America's present need is not heroics but healing; not nostrums but normalcy; not revolution but restoration.

1920 Speech, Boston, Jun.

Hardwicke, Sir Cedric 1893–1964

English actor and director. He made his stage début in 1912 and appeared in plays by George Bernard Shaw, Emlyn Williams and Shakespeare among others, appearing to acclaim on both sides of the Atlantic.

80 I can't act. I have never acted. And I shall never act. What I do is suspend my audience's power of judgement till I've finished.
1945 Attributed.

81 When in doubt, shout—that's the motto.
Attributed, repeating advice that was given to him as a young actor.

Hardy, Godfrey Harold 1877–1947

English mathematician, professor at Oxford and Cambridge. With Srinivasa Ramanujan, he found an exact formula for the partition function, which expresses the number of ways a number can be written as a sum of smaller numbers.

82 Beauty is the first test: there is no permanent place in the world for ugly mathematics.
1941 *A Mathematician's Apology.*

83 A science is said to be useful if its development tends to accentuate the existing inequities in the distribution of wealth, or more directly promotes the destruction of human life.
1941 *A Mathematician's Apology.*

Hardy, Thomas 1840–1928

English novelist and poet. His novels include *The Mayor of Casterbridge* (1886), *Tess of the D'Urbervilles* (1891) and *Jude the Obscure* (1896). His poetry was collected in *Wessex Poems* (1898), and he also wrote a drama, *The Dynasts* (1903–8).

84 Good, but not religious-good.
1872 *Under the Greenwood Tree*, ch.2.

85 That man's silence is wonderful to listen to.
1872 *Under the Greenwood Tree*, ch.14.

86 No man likes to see his emotions the sport of a merry-go-round of skittishness.
1874 *Far from the Madding Crowd*, ch.4.

87 Men thin away to insignificance and oblivion quite as often by not making the most of good spirits when they have them as by lacking good spirits when they are indispensable.
1874 *Far from the Madding Crowd*, ch.22.

88 He was moderately truthful towards men, but to women lied like a Cretan.
1874 Of Sergeant Troy. *Far from the Madding Crowd*, ch.25.

89 It is hard for a woman to define her feelings in language which is chiefly made by men to express theirs.

1874 *Far from the Madding Crowd*, ch.81.

90 Human beings, in their generous endeavour to construct a hypothesis that shall not degrade a First Cause, have always hesitated to conceive a dominant power of a lower moral quality than their own.
1878 *The Return of the Native*, bk.6, ch.1.

91 There was a natural instinct to abjure man as the blot on an otherwise kindly universe.
1886 *The Mayor of Casterbridge*, ch.1.

92 Her bygone simplicity was the art that conceals art.
1886 *The Mayor of Casterbridge*, ch.15.

93 Sex had never before asserted itself in her so strongly, for in former days she had perhaps been too impersonally human to be distinctively feminine.
1886 Of Miss Newson. *The Mayor of Casterbridge*, ch.15.

94 Her occasional pretty and picturesque use of dialect words—those terrible marks of the beast to the truly genteel.
1886 *The Mayor of Casterbridge*, ch.20.

95 It is not by what is, in this life, but by what appears, that you are judged.
1886 *The Mayor of Casterbridge*, ch.25.

96 She whose youth had seemed to teach that happiness was but the occasional episode in a general drama of pain.
1886 *The Mayor of Casterbridge*, ch.45.

97 It was one of those sequestered spots outside the gates of the world.
1887 *The Woodlanders*, ch.1.

98 Why it was that upon this beautiful feminine tissue, sensitive as gossamer, and practically blank as snow as yet, there should have been traced such a coarse pattern as it was doomed to receive; why so often the coarse appropriates the finer thus, the wrong man the woman, the wrong woman the man, many thousand years of analytical philosophy have failed to explain to our sense of order.
1891 *Tess of the D'Urbervilles*, ch.11.

99 'Justice' was done, and the President of the Immortals (in Aeschylean phrase) had ended his sport with Tess.
1891 *Tess of the D'Urbervilles*, ch.59.

1 A novel is an impression, not an argument.
1892 *Tess of the D'Urbervilles*, preface to 5th edn.

2 His face wearing the fixity of a thoughtful child's who has felt the pricks of life somewhat before his time.
1896 *Jude the Obscure*, pt.1, ch.1.

3 What was good for God's birds was bad for God's gardener.
1896 *Jude the Obscure*, pt.1, ch.2.

4 It was better to love a woman than to be a graduate, or a parson; ay, or a pope!
1896 *Jude the Obscure*, pt.1, ch.7.

5 Cruelty is the law pervading all nature and society; and we can't get out of it if we would!
1896 *Jude the Obscure*, pt.5, ch.8.

6 Done because we are too menny.
1896 The note left by Jude's young son, who had hanged his siblings and himself. *Jude the Obscure*, pt.6, ch.2.

7 An aged thrush, frail, gaunt and small,
In blast-beruffled plume,
Had chosen thus to fling his sail
Upon the growing gloom.

So little cause for carollings
Of such ecstatic sound
Was written on terrestrial things
Afar or nigh around,
That I could think there trembled through
His happy good-night air
Some blessed Hope, whereof he knew
And I was unaware.
1902 'The Darkling Thrush'.

8 If way to the Better there be, it exacts a full look at the worst.
1902 'De Profundis'.

9 What we gain by science is, after all, sadness, as the Preacher saith. The more we know of the laws and nature of the Universe the more ghastly a business we perceive it all to be—and the non-necessity of it.
1902 Letter to Edward Clodd, 27 Feb.

10 A local thing called Christianity.
1904 *The Dynasts*, pt.1, act 1, sc.6.

11 War makes rattling good history; but Peace is poor reading.
1904 *The Dynasts*, pt.1, act 2, sc.5.

12 Woman much missed, how you call to me, call to me,
Saying that now you are not as you were
When you had changed from the one who was all to me,
But as at first, when our day was fair.
1914 'The Voice'.

13 This is the weather the cuckoo likes,
And so do I;
When showers betumble the chestnut spikes,
And nestlings fly:

And the little brown nightingale bills his best,
And they sit outside at 'The Travellers' Rest',
And maids come forth sprig-muslin drest,
And citizens dream of the south and west,
And so do I.
1922 *Late Lyrics and Earlier*, 'Weathers'.

14 Well, World, you have kept faith with me,
Kept faith with me;
Upon the whole you have proved to be
Much as you said you were.
1928 *Winter Words*, 'He Never Expected Much'.

Hargreaves, W F 1846–1919

English songwriter. Married to US singer Ella Shields, he wrote such music-hall standards as 'I must go home tonight'.

15 I acted so tragic the house rose like magic,
The audience yelled, 'You're sublime'.
They made me a present of Mornington Crescent,
They threw it a brick at a time.
'The Night I appeared as Macbeth' (song).

Harington, Sir John 1561–1612

English courtier and writer, godson of Elizabeth I. He translated Ariosto's *Orlando Furioso* (1591) and published the satiric *The Metamorphosis of Ajax* (1596), which contained the first design of a flushing toilet. His government work in Ireland inspired *A Short View of the State of Ireland* (1605).

16 When I would make a feast
I would my guests should praise it, not the cooks.
1618 *Epigrams*, bk.1, no.5, 'Against Writers that Carp at Other Men's Books'.

17 Treason doth never prosper, what's the reason?
For if it prosper, none dare call it treason.
1618 *Epigrams*, bk.4, no.5.

Harkin, Thomas 1939–

US politician, Democratic Senator from Iowa.

18 The Gulf War was like teenage sex. We got in too soon and we got out too soon.
1991 Quoted in the *Independent on Sunday*, 29 Sep.

Harkness, Richard Long 1907–77

US radio and television news commentator. He was also a journalist and government official. As the Washington correspondent for NBC (1943–72) he covered the Roosevelt–Churchill war conferences, as well as UN sessions, NATO and domestic political campaigns.

19 A group of the unwilling, picked from the unfit, to do the unnecessary.
1960 Definition of a committee. In the *New York Herald Tribune*, 15 Jun.

Harlech, William David Ormsby Gore, 5th Baron 1918–85

English Conservative politician and businessman. British Ambassador in Washington (1961–5). On his return he obtained the franchise for Harlech Television (1967). He was President of the British Board of Film Censors at a time of increasing permissiveness.

20 It would indeed be the ultimate tragedy if the history of the human race proved to be nothing more noble than the story of an ape playing with a box of matches on a petrol dump.
   1960 In the *Christian Science Monitor*, 25 Oct.

Harlow, Jean pseudonym of *Harlean Carpentier* 1911–37

US actress, best known for her roles as a fast-talking wisecracking blonde in *Hell's Angels* (1930), *Red Dust* (1932) and *Libelled Lady* (1936). She died young from cerebral oedema.

21 Excuse me while I slip into something more comfortable.
   1930 Line delivered in *Hell's Angels* (screenplay by Howard Estabrook and Harry Behn).

Harold II c.1019–66

Earl of Wessex and King of England (1066). Shipwrecked in Normandy, he swore an oath to support Duke William's claim to the English throne. When he was elected king, William invaded, and Harold was killed at Hastings.

22 He will give him seven feet of English ground, or as much more as he may be taller than other men.
   1066 His offer to the invading Norse King Harald Hardrada, quoted in Snorri Sturluson *Heimskringla* (c.1260), 'King Harald's Saga', section 91 (translated by Samuel Laing as *History of the Norse Kings*, 1844).

Harpur, Charles 1813–68

Australian poet. He used traditional, ornate 18c English verse patterns, overlaid with pastoral Australian imagery, in an attempt to create an appropriate colonial style.

23 Stale is their gladness who were never sad.
   'Sonnet XIII', collected in C W Salier (ed) *Rosa: Love Sonnets to Mary Doyle* (1949).

Harrington, James 1611–77

English political theorist. Although a republican, he was an attendant of Charles I and was with him at the scaffold. His semi-romance *The Commonwealth of Oceana* (1656) proposed a commonwealth based on property. He was arrested and imprisoned in 1661.

24 No man can be a politician except he first be an historian or a traveller; for except he can see what must be, or what may be, he is no politician.
   1656 *The Commonwealth of Oceana.*

Harrington, Michael 1928–89

US political activist and writer. In 1973 he set up the Democratic Socialist Organizing Committee. His *The Other America: Poverty in the United States* (1962) is an indictment of poverty in the US.

25 If there is technological advance without social advance, there is, almost automatically, an increase in human misery, in impoverishment.
   1962 *The Other America: Poverty in the United States*, ch.1.

26 Clothes make the poor invisible too: America has the best-dressed poverty the world has ever known.
   1962 *The Other America: Poverty in the United States*, ch.1.

Harris, Joel Chandler 1848–1908

US author, who worked for the Atlanta *Constitution* (1876–1900). His reputation rests on his Uncle Remus stories, told in dialect. They include *Uncle Remus: His Songs and His Sayings* (1880) and *Nights with Uncle Remus* (1883).

27 Tar-Baby, she stay still, en Brer Fox, he lay low.
   1880 *Uncle Remus: His Songs and His Sayings*, 'The Wonderful Tar-Baby Story'.

28 Bred en bawn in a brier-patch!
   1880 *Uncle Remus: His Songs and His Sayings*, 'How Mr. Rabbit Was Too Sharp for Mr. Fox'.

29 Licker talks mighty loud w'en it git loose fum de jug.
   1880 *Uncle Remus: His Songs and His Sayings*, 'Plantation Proverbs'.

30 Hongry rooster don't cackle w'en he fine a wum.
   1880 *Uncle Remus: His Songs and His Sayings*, 'Plantation Proverbs'.

31 Watch out w'en you'er gittin all you want. Fattenin' hogs ain't in luck.
   1880 *Uncle Remus: His Songs and His Sayings*, 'Plantation Proverbs'.

32 When folks git ole en strucken wid de palsy, dey mus' speck ter be laff'd at.
   1883 *Nights with Uncle Remus*, 'Mr. Man Has Some Meat'.

33 All by my own-alone self.
   1883 *Nights with Uncle Remus*, 'Brother Wolf Falls a Victim'.

Harris, Rolf 1930–

Australian entertainer and artist. He went to London in 1952 to study art, and began working with the BBC children's department.

34 Tie Me Kangaroo Down, Sport
   1950s Title and chorus of song, passim in BBC children's programme.

Harris, (Theodore) Wilson pseudonym of *Kona Waruk* 1921–

British novelist, born in Guyana. His best-known work is *The Guyana Quartet* (1960–3).

35 The dark notes rose everywhere, so dark, so
    sombre, they broke into a fountain—light as the
    rainbow—sparkling and immaterial as invisible
    sources and echoes. The savannahs grew lonely as
    the sea and broke again into a wave and forest. Tall
    trees with black marching boots and feet were clad
    in the spurs and sharp wings of a butterfly.
    1960 *The Palace of the Peacock*, ch.11.

Harrison, Tony 1937–

English poet. His work has focused on giving voice to
working class culture. His best-known work is the
inflammatory poem *V*, a denunciation of contemporary
British life.

36 Articulation is the tongue-tied's fighting.
    1978 'On Not Being Milton'.

37 This pen's all I have of magic wand.
    1985 *V.*

38 I have always disliked the idea of an arts ghetto in
    which poetry is kept on a life-support system.
    1989 In *The Observer*, 23 Jul.

Harrison, Wallace K(irkman) 1895–1981

US architect, whose best-known designs include the UN
Secretariat building and the Metropolitan Opera House,
both in New York. He married into the Rockefeller
dynasty.

39 When we started the UN we were not trying to
    make a monument. We were building a
    workshop—a workshop for world peace. And we
    tried to make it the best damn workshop we could.
    1952 In *Time*, 22 Sep.

Harrod, Sir Roy 1900–78

English economist, Professor at Oxford (1922–67), noted
for his work on international economics and economic
growth.

40 The most basic law of economics…that one cannot
    get something for nothing.
    1948 *Towards a Dynamic Economics.*

41 No economy ever stands still.
    1963 *The British Economy*

Hart, Gary originally *Hartpence* 1936–

US lawyer and Democrat politician. He entered the
Senate in 1974, and was narrowly defeated for the
presidential nomination by Walter Mondale in 1980. He
made a further unsuccessful bid for the presidency in
1984.

42 You can get awful famous in this country in seven
    days.

    1984 Rueful comment after reports of his marital infidelity
    ended his presidential campaign. In the *New York Times*, 7 Oct.

43 This is one Hart that you will not leave in San
    Francisco.
    1984 Said after his failed bid for the presidential nomination at
    the Democratic National Convention in San Francisco.

Hart, Lorenz 1895–1943

US songwriter.

44 When love congeals
    It soon reveals
    The faint aroma of performing seals,
    The double-crossing of a pair of heels.
    I wish I were in love again!
    1937 'I Wish I Were in Love Again' (music by Richard
    Rodgers), from *Babes in Arms*.

45 I get too hungry for dinner at eight.
    I like the theater, but never come late.
    I never bother with people I hate.
    That's why the lady is a tramp.
    1937 'The Lady is a Tramp' (music by Richard Rodgers), from
    Babes in Arms.

46 I'm wild again
    Beguiled again
    A simpering, whimpering child again,
    Bewitched, bothered and bewildered am I.
    1941 'Bewitched' (music by Richard Rodgers), from *Pal Joey*.

Hart, Moss 1904–65

US playwright and author. He won a Pulitzer Prize for
You Can't Take It With You (1937) and a Perry award for
directing his own play *My Fair Lady* (1957). He also
wrote *Once in a Lifetime* (1930).

47 A play for me never really takes on an aspect of
    reality until it has left the dry air of the study and
    begins to sniff the musty breezes of a bare stage.
    1959 *Act One.*

48 The four most dramatic words in the English
    language: 'Act One, Scene One.'
    1959 *Act One.*

Harte, Francis Bret 1836–1902

US writer, who wrote sketches of California miners in
works such as 'The Luck of Roaring Camp' (1868).
Secretary of the US Mint in San Francisco (1864–70), he
became US consul at Krefeld (1878–80) and Glasgow
(1880–5).

49 I reside at Table Mountain, and my name is
        Truthful James;
    I am not up to small deceit or any sinful games.
    1868 'The Society upon the Stanislaus', stanza 1.

50 Which I wish to remark—

And my language is plain—
That for ways that are dark
And for tricks that are vain,
The heathen Chinee is peculiar,
Which the same I would rise to explain.

1870 'Plain Language from Truthful James', stanza 1. The poem became popularly known as 'That Heathen Chinee'.

51 We are ruined by Chinese cheap labour.

1870 'Plain Language from Truthful James', stanza 7.

52 And on that grave where English oak and holly
And laurel wreaths entwine,
Deem it not all a too presumptuous folly,
This spray of Western pine!

1870 On the death of Charles Dickens. 'Dickens in Camp', stanza 10.

53 If, of all words of tongue and pen,
The saddest are, 'It might have been,'

More sad are these we daily see:
'It is, but hadn't ought to be.'

1871 'Mrs. Judge Jenkins'.

Hartley, L(eslie) P(oles) 1895–1972

English writer. His early published works were short stories of a macabre turn. He went on to write successful novels of considerable psychological acuity.

54 The past is a foreign country: they do things differently there.

1953 *The Go-Between*, prologue.

Harvey, William 1578–1657

English physician and scientist, who established the foundations of modern medicine. He was the first to demonstrate the function of the heart and the complete circulation of the blood.

55 Nature is nowhere accustomed more openly to display her secret mysteries than in cases where she shows tracings of her workings apart from the beaten paths; nor is there any better way to advance the proper practice of medicine than to give our minds to the discovery of the usual law of nature, by careful investigation of cases of rarer forms of disease.

1657 Letter to John Vlackveld, 24 Apr.

Haskell, Molly

56 The propaganda arm of the American Dream machine.

1973 Of Hollywood. *From Reverence to Rape: the treatment of women in the movies.*

Haskins, Minnie Louise 1875–1951

English author and educationist.

57 And I said to the man who stood at the gate of the year:
'Give me a light that I may tread safely into the unknown.'
And he replied:
'Go out into the darkness and put your hand into the hand of God. That shall be to you better than light and safer than a known way.'

1908 *Desert*, 'God Knows'. Quoted by King George VI, Christmas address, 25 Dec 1939.

Hattersley, Roy Sydney George
Hattersley, Baron 1932–

English Labour politician. He became an MP in 1964 and served in the Callaghan Government.

58 As a boy I genuinely believed in the man who never ate bacon because its red and white stripes reminded him of Sheffield United—indeed in my blue and white Wednesday heart I applauded and supported his loyalty.

1976 *Goodbye to Yorkshire.*

Haughey, Charles James 1925–

Irish politician and Prime Minister (1979–81, 1982, 1987–92). He became a Fianna Fáil MP (1957), but was dismissed from his post in 1970 after a quarrel with the Prime Minister, Jack Lynch. He was succeeded as Prime Minister by Albert Reynolds in 1992.

59 It seems that the historic inability in Britain to comprehend Irish feelings and sensitivities still remains.

1988 In *The Observer*, Feb.

Havel, Václav 1936–

Czechoslovakian playwright and politician. He was a co-founder of Charter '77, President of Czechoslovakia (1989–1992) and President of the Czech Republic (1993–).

60 The worst thing is that we live in a contaminated moral environment. We fell morally ill because we became used to saying something different from what we thought.

1990 First speech as Czech President, 1 Jan.

Hawes, Hampton 1928–77

US jazz pianist. He was an important (but often undervalued) figure in West Coast jazz.

61 The worst thing that can happen to old good music is that it might become dated for a while, but watch out, in twenty years it will come drifting back like bell-bottoms and W. C. Fields movies.

1974 *Raise Up Off Me* (with Don Asher), ch.22.

Hawking, Stephen William 1942–

British theoretical physicist, theorist of the astronomical bodies known as black holes. His *A Brief History of Time*

(1988) is a successful popular account of modern cosmology. From the 1960s he has suffered from a progressive motor neurone disease.

62 God not only plays dice. He also sometimes throws the dice where they cannot be seen.
1975 In *Nature*, vol.257.
▷ See Einstein 363:62.

63 If we find the answer to that, it would be the ultimate triumph of human reason—for then we would know the mind of God.
1988 He is referring to the question of why we and the universe exist. *A Brief History of Time*, ch.11.

Hawthorn, Mike 1929–59

English racing driver. Driving for Ferrari, he won the Formula One World Championship in 1958 but then retired from the sport, only to be killed in a road accident a few months later.

64 Motor racing is dangerous; but what is danger? It is dangerous to climb a mountain. It is dangerous to cross main roads. It is dangerous to explore a jungle. One cannot frame regulations to make everything safe.
1959 Shortly before his death. Quoted in Colin Jarman *The Guinness Dictionary of Sports Quotations* (1990).

Hawthorne, Nathaniel 1804–64

US novelist, who worked in the Salem custom house and was Consul at Liverpool (1853–7). Between 1850 and 1852 he lived in Lenox near Herman Melville, where he wrote *The Scarlet Letter* (1850) and *The House of the Seven Gables* (1851).

65 We sometimes congratulate ourselves at the moment of waking from a troubled dream: it may be so the moment after death.
c.1836 *The American Notebooks*, ch.1.

66 The love of posterity is a consequence of the necessity of death. If a man were sure of living forever here, he would not care about his offspring.
1840 *The American Notebooks* (published 1868), ch.3.

67 Bees are sometimes drowned in the honey which they collect—so some writers are lost in their collected learning.
1842 *The American Notebooks* (published 1868), ch.5.

68 Human nature will not flourish, any more than a potato, if it be planted and replanted, for too long a series of generations, in the same worn-out soil.
1850 *The Scarlet Letter*, 'The Custom-House'.

69 The founders of a new colony, whatever Utopia of human virtue and happiness they might originally project, have invariably recognized it among their earliest practical necessities to allot a portion of the virgin soil as a cemetery, and another portion as the site of a prison.
1850 *The Scarlet Letter*, ch.1.

70 Let men tremble to win the hand of woman, unless they win along with it the utmost passion of her heart!
1850 *The Scarlet Letter*, ch.15.

71 No man, for any considerable period, can wear one face to himself, and another to the multitude, without finally getting bewildered as to which may be the true.
1850 *The Scarlet Letter*, ch.20.

72 When a writer calls his work a Romance, it need hardly be observed that he wishes to claim a certain latitude, both as to its fashion and material, which he would not have felt himself entitled to assume had he professed to be writing a Novel.
1851 *The House of the Seven Gables*, preface.

73 Life is made up of marble and mud.
1851 *The House of the Seven Gables*, ch.2.

74 Life, within doors, has few pleasanter prospects than a neatly arranged and well-provisioned breakfast-table.
1851 *The House of the Seven Gables*, ch.7

75 The world, that grey-bearded and wrinkled profligate, decrepit, without being venerable.
1851 *The House of the Seven Gables*, ch.12.

76 The world owes all its onward impulse to men ill at ease. The happy man inevitably confines himself within ancient limits.
1851 *The House of the Seven Gables*, ch.20.

77 In the depths of every heart, there is a tomb and a dungeon, though the lights, the music, and revelry above may cause us to forget their existence, and the buried ones, or prisoners whom they hide.
1851 *Twice-Told Tales*, 'The Haunted Mind'.

78 The greatest obstacle to being heroic is the doubt whether one may not be going to prove one's self a fool; the truest heroism is to resist the doubt; and the profoundest wisdom, to know when it ought to be resisted and when to be obeyed.
1852 *The Blithedale Romance*, ch.2.

79 America is now wholly given over to a d—d mob of scribbling women.
1855 Quoted in Caroline Ticknor *Hawthorne and His Publisher* (1913).

80 The present is burthened too much with the past.
1856 Entry for 27 Mar at the British Museum, collected in *The English Notebooks* (1870).

81 Nobody has any conscience about adding to the improbabilities of a marvelous tale.
1860 *The Marble Faun*, ch.4.

82 How is it possible to say an unkind or irreverential word of Rome? The city of all time, and of all the world!

1860 *The Marble Faun,* ch.12.

83 Dr Johnson's morality was as English an article as a beefsteak.

1863 *Our Old Home.*

Hay, Ian pseudonym of *Major-General John Hay Beith* 1876–1952

Scottish novelist and dramatist. His light popular novels (eg *Pip,* 1907) were followed by war books, including *The First Hundred Thousand* (1915). His best-known comedies are *Tilly of Bloomsbury* (1919) and *The Housemaster* (1936).

84 What do you mean, funny? Funny peculiar, or funny ha-ha?

1936 *The Housemaster,* act 3.

Hayakawa, S(amuel) I(chiye) 1906–92

Canadian-born US philologist and politician. His semantics works include *Language in Action* (1941, later retitled *Language in Thought and Action*). He was president of San Francisco State College (1968-73) and entered the House as Senator for California (1977-83).

85 In a real sense, people who have read good literature have lived more than people who cannot or will not read.

1941 *Language in Action.*

86 It's ours. We stole it fair and square.

Of the Panama Canal Zone. Attributed.

Haydn, Franz Joseph 1732–1809

Austrian composer. Kapellmeister to the Esterházy family from 1761, he twice visited England and several works were first performed in London. His works include piano music, string quartets, concertos, symphonies, masses and choral works such as the oratorio *The Creation* (1798).

87 But all the world understands my language.

1790 Reply to Mozart, who had advised him against visiting England because he could not speak the language. Quoted in Ian Crofton and Donald Fraser *A Dictionary of Musical Quotations* (1985).

Haydon, Benjamin Robert 1786–1846

English historical painter. He was twice imprisoned for debt, and, after a number of bitter disappointments, shot himself.

88 The French had a more martial air than the English. There seemed to be a species of military instinct in all classes. No young man appeared to have finished his education till after a bloody campaign… They were at this singular period,

without the least exaggeration, a century behind us in notions of legal and moral responsibility.

Autobiography (published 1847).

Hayek, Friedrich August von 1899–1992

Austrian-born British political economist and libertarian moral philosopher. Professor at the London School of Economics (1932–50), Chicago (1950–72) and Freiburg (1962–5) and a guru of the New Right, in 1974 he was awarded the Nobel Prize for Economics with Gunnar Myrdal.

89 The more the state 'plans' the more difficult planning becomes for the individual.

1944 *The Road to Serfdom.*

90 We are only beginning to understand on how subtle a communication system the functioning of an advanced industrial society is based—a communications system which we call the market and which turns out to be a more efficient mechanism for digesting dispersed information than any that man has deliberately designed.

1978 *New Studies in Philosophy, Politics, Economics and the History of Ideas,* 'The Pretence of Knowledge'.

91 [There is] a delusion that macro-economics is both viable and useful (a delusion encouraged by its extensive use of mathematics, which must always impress politicians lacking any mathematical education, and which is really the nearest thing to the practice of magic that occurs among professional economists).

1989 *The Fatal Conceit: The Errors of Socialism,* ch.6.

Hayes, J Milton 1884–1940

British author.

92 There's a one-eyed yellow idol to the north of Khatmandu,
There's a little marble cross below the town,
There's a broken-hearted woman tends the grave of Mad Carew,
And the Yellow God forever gazes down.

1911 *The Green Eye of the Yellow God.*

Hayes, Rutherford B(irchard) 1822–93

US Republican statesman and 19th President (1877–81). Under his presidency, the country recovered commercial prosperity, and his policy included the reform of the civil service and the conciliation of the Southern states.

93 He serves his party best who serves his country best.

1877 Inaugural address, 5 Mar.

Hayward, Thomas Bibb 1924–

US admiral, Chief of Operations in the US Navy (1978–83). He served in both Korea and Vietnam.

94 We are…a one-and-a-half ocean navy with a three-ocean commitment.

1982 Congressional testimony, reported in the *New York Times*, 11 Apr.

Hazlitt, William 1778–1830

English essayist, whose controversial and witty work ranges from theatre and literature to politics and even sports. His various collections of essays include *Table Talk* (1821) and *Spirit of the Age, or Contemporary Portraits* (1825).

95 There is in Kean, an infinite variety of talent, with a certain monotony of genius.

1815 Of the actor Edmund Kean. In *The Examiner*, 10 Dec.

96 Mr Kemble sacrifices too much to decorum. He is chiefly afraid of being contaminated by too close an identity with the character he represents. This is the greatest vice in an actor, who ought never to *bilk* his part.

1816 Of John Philip Kemble's performance as Sir Giles Overreach in Massinger's *A New Way to Pay Old Debts*. In *The Examiner*, 5 May.

97 There is nothing good to be had in the country, or if there is, they will not let you have it.

1817 *The Round Table*, 'Observation on Mr Wordsworth's Poem *The Excursion*'.

98 The art of pleasing consists in being pleased.

1817 *The Round Table*, 'On Manner'.

99 He talked on for ever; and you wished him to talk on for ever.

1818 Of Coleridge. *Lectures on the English Poets*, 'On the Living Poets'.

1 Fashion constantly begins and ends in the two things it abhors most, singularity and vulgarity.

1818 'On Fashion', in the *Scots Magazine*.

2 The love of liberty is the love of others; the love of power is the love of ourselves.

1819 *Political Essays*, 'The Times Newspaper'.

3 Those who make their dress a principal part of themselves, will, in general, become of no more value than their dress.

1819 *Political Essays*, 'On the Clerical Character'.

4 You will hear more good things on the outside of a stagecoach from London to Oxford than if you were to pass a twelvemonth with the undergraduates, or heads of colleges, of that famous university.

1821 *Table Talk*, vol.1, 'The Ignorance of the Learned'.

5 We can scarcely hate any one that we know.

1822 *Table Talk*, vol.2, 'On Criticism'.

6 Give me the clear blue sky over my head, and the green turf beneath my feet, a winding road before me, and a three hours' march to dinner—and then to thinking! It is hard if I cannot start some game on these lone heaths.

1822 *Table Talk*, vol.2, 'On Going a Journey'.

7 *The Times* is, we suppose, entitled to the character it gives of itself, of being the 'leading journal of Europe', and is perhaps the greatest engine of temporary opinion in the world.

1823 In the *Edinburgh Review*, May.

8 It is a commercial paper, a paper of business, and it is conducted on principles of trade and business. It floats with the tide: it sails with the stream. It has no other principle.

1823 Of *The Times*. In the *Edinburgh Review*, May.

9 It takes up no falling cause; fights no uphill battle; advocates no great principle; holds out a helping hand to no oppressed or obscure individual. It is 'ever strong upon the stronger side'.

1823 Of *The Times*. In the *Edinburgh Review*, May.

10 Paris is a beast of a city to be in—to those who cannot get out of it. Rousseau said well, that all the time he was in it, he was only trying how he should leave it… The continual panic in which the passenger is kept, the alarm and the escape from it, the anger and the laughter at it, must have an effect on the Parisian character, and tend to make it the whiffling, skittish, snappish, volatile, inconsequential, unmeaning thing it is.

1824 *Notes on a Journey through France and Italy* (published 1856).

11 He is a kind of *fourth estate* in the politics of the country.

1825 Of the journalist and reformer William Cobbett. *Spirit of the Age*, 'Mr. Cobbett'.

12 Death cancels everything but truth; and strips a man of everything but genius and virtue. It is a sort of natural canonization.

1825 *Spirit of the Age*, 'Lord Byron'.

13 The present is an age of talkers, and not of doers; and the reason is, that the world is growing old. We are so far advanced in the Arts and Sciences, that we live in retrospect, and dote on past achievement.

1825 *Spirit of the Age*, 'Mr Coleridge'.

14 He writes as fast as they can read, and he does not write himself down… His worst is better than any other person's best… His works (taken together) are almost like a new edition of human nature. This is indeed to be an author!

1825 *Spirit of the Age*, 'Sir Walter Scott'.

15 Mr Wordsworth's genius is a pure emanation of the Spirit of the Age. Had he lived in any other period of the world, he would never have been heard of.
    1825 *Spirit of the Age*, 'Mr Wordsworth'.

16 The dupe of friendship, and the fool of love; have I not reason to hate and to despise myself? Indeed I do; and chiefly for not having hated and despised the world enough.
    1826 *The Plain Speaker*, 'On the Pleasure of Hating'.

17 His sayings are generally like women's letters; all the pith is in the postscript.
    1826–7 Of Charles Lamb. *Conversations of James Northcote*.

18 The origin of all science is in the desire to know causes; and the origin of all false science and imposture is in the desire to accept false causes rather than none; or, which is the same thing, in the unwillingness to acknowledge our own ignorance.
    1829 In *The Atlas*, 15 Feb.

19 So have I loitered my life away, reading books, looking at pictures, going to plays, hearing, thinking, writing on what pleased me best. I have wanted only one thing to make me happy, but wanting that have wanted everything.
    Literary Remains (published 1836), 'My First Acquaintance with Poets'.

20 But of all footmen the lowest class is *literary footmen.*
    Sketches and Essays (published 1839), 'Footmen'.

21 A nickname is the heaviest stone that the devil can throw at a man.
    Sketches and Essays (published 1839), 'Nicknames'.

22 The greatest offence against virtue is to speak ill of it.
    Sketches and Essays (published 1839), 'On Cant and Hypocrisy'.

23 There is an unseemly exposure of mind, as well as of the body.
    Sketches and Essays (published 1839), 'On Disagreeable People'.

24 Rules and models destroy genius and art.
    Sketches and Essays (published 1839), 'On Taste'.

25 All is without form and void. Someone said of his landscapes that they were pictures of nothing and very like.
    Of Turner's painting, quoted in J Lindsay *Turner: The Man and his Art* (1985).

26 Well, I've had a happy life.
    1830 Last words. Quoted in W C Hazlitt *Memoirs of William Hazlitt* (1867).

Hazzard, Shirley 1931–

Australian-born US novelist. Her works include short stories, the satirical *People in Glass Houses* (1967) and a novel, *The Transit of Venus* (1980).

27 Nothing…makes a more fanatical official than a Latin. Organization is alien to their natures, but once they get the taste for it they take to it like drink.
    1967 *People in Glass Houses*, 'Official Life'.

Healey, Denis Winston Healey, Baron 1917–

English Labour politician, Secretary of State for Defence (1964–70) and Chancellor of the Exchequer (1974–9). Unsuccessful in the Labour leadership contests of 1976 and 1980, he became Deputy Leader (1980–3) and shadow Foreign Secretary (1980–7).

28 That part of his speech was rather like being savaged by a dead sheep.
    1978 Responding to a speech by Chancellor of the Exchequer Sir Geoffrey Howe, House of Commons, Jun.

29 For the past few months, [Margaret Thatcher] has been charging around like some bargain-basement Boadicea.
    1982 In *The Observer*, 7 Nov.

30 The great She-elephant, the great She-who-must-be-obeyed, the Catherine the Great of Finchley.
    1985 Of Margaret Thatcher. Comment when Trade Union recognition was withdrawn for employees working in GCHQ.

Heaney, Seamus Justin 1939–

Irish poet and critic, born in Northern Ireland. He moved to Dublin in 1976 and became Professor of Poetry at Oxford (1989–). His works include *Death of a Naturalist* (1966) and *The Haw Lantern* (1987). He won the Nobel Prize for Literature, 1996.

31 Between my finger and my thumb
    The squat pen rests.
    I'll dig with it.
    1966 *Death of a Naturalist*, 'Digging'.

32 My father worked with a horse-plough,
    His shoulders globed like a full sail strung
    Between the shafts and the furrow.
    1966 *Death of a Naturalist*, 'Follower'.

33 Love, you shall perfect for me this child
    Whose small imperfect limits would keep breaking:
    Within new limits now, arrange the world
    And square the circle: four walls and a ring.
    1966 *Death of a Naturalist*, 'Poem: For Marie'.

34 My poor scapegoat,

    I almost love you
    but would have cast, I know,
    the stones of silence.
    1975 *North*, 'Punishment'.

35 I hold my lady's head
    like a crystal

    and ossify myself
    by gazing: I am screes
    on her escarpments,
    a chalk giant

    carved upon her downs.
    Soon my hands, on the sunken
    fosse of her spine
    move towards the passes.
    1975 *North*, 'Bone Dreams', no.4.

36 He had gone miles away
    For he drank like a fish
    Nightly, naturally
    Swimming towards the lure
    Of warm lit-up places.
    1979 *Field Work*, 'Casualty'.

37 How culpable was he
    That last night when he broke
    Our tribe's complicity?
    'Now you're supposed to be
    An educated man,'
    I hear him say. 'Puzzle me
    The right answer to that one.'
    1979 *Field Work*, 'Casualty'. On a man killed breaking the
    curfew.

38 Don't be surprised,
    If I demur, for, be advised,
    My passport's green.
    No glass of ours was ever raised
    To toast *The Queen*.
    1983 'An Open Letter to Blake and Andrew, Editors,
    Contemporary British Verse, Penguin Books, Middlesex'.
    Heaney was complaining at his inclusion in the book edited by
    Blake Morrison and Andrew Motion on the grounds of his Irish
    nationality.

39 Need I go on? I hate to bite
    Hands that led me to the limelight
    In the Penguin book, I regret
    The awkwardness.
    But British, no, the name's not right.
    Yours truly, Seamus.
    1983 'An Open Letter to Blake and Andrew, Editors,
    Contemporary British Verse, Penguin Books, Middlesex'.
    Heaney was complaining at his inclusion in the book edited by
    Blake Morrison and Andrew Motion on the grounds of his Irish
    nationality.

40 The riverbed, dried-up, half full of leaves.
    Us, listening to a river in the trees.
    1987 *The Haw Lantern*, 'For Bernard and Jane McCabe',
    complete poem.

41 When I landed in the republic of conscience

it was so noiseless when the engines stopped
I could hear a curlew high above the runway.
1987 *The Haw Lantern*, 'From the Republic of Conscience',
p.1, stanza 1.

42 Their embassies, he said, were everywhere
    but operated independently
    and no ambassador would ever be relieved.
    1987 *The Haw Lantern*, 'From the Republic of Conscience',
    p.3, stanza 4.

43 She taught me what her uncle once taught her:
    How easily the biggest coal block split
    If you got the grain and hammer angled right.

    The sound of that relaxed alluring blow,
    Its co-opted and obliterated echo,
    Taught me to hit, taught me to loosen,

    Taught me between the hammer and the block
    To face the music. Teach me now to listen,
    To strike it rich behind the linear black.
    1987 *The Haw Lantern*, 'Clearances: In Memoriam M.K.H.,
    1911–1984'.

Hearst, William Randolph 1863–1951

US newspaper proprietor. He revolutionized journalism
with innovations such as the banner headline, in papers
such as the *Chicago Examiner*, *Boston American*,
Cosmopolitan and *Harper's Bazaar*.

44 You furnish the pictures and I'll furnish the war.
    1898 Telegram to the artist Frederic Remington at the
    beginning of the Spanish–American War in Cuba, Mar. This
    may be apocryphal, but it inspired a famous line of dialogue in
    Orson Welles's film *Citizen Kane*.

Heat Moon, William Least originally
William Trogdon 1939–

US writer. He made his name with *Blue Highways: A
Journey Into America*, a travelogue of America which, like
Prairyerth (1991), also explored his Native American
heritage.

45 Beware thoughts that come in the night. They
    aren't turned properly; they come in askew, free of
    sense and restriction, deriving from the most
    remote of sources.
    1983 *Blue Highways: A Journey Into America*, opening words.

46 There are two kinds of adventurers: those who go
    truly hoping to find adventure and those who go
    secretly hoping they won't.
    1983 *Blue Highways: A Journey Into America*, pt.2, ch.4.

47 To say nothing is out here is incorrect; to say the
    desert is stingy with everything except space and
    light, stone and earth is closer to the truth.
    1983 *Blue Highways: A Journey Into America*, pt.4, ch.80.

48 Motels can be big, but never grand.
    1983 *Blue Highways: A Journey Into America*, pt.5, ch.2.

49 Whoever the last true cowboy in America turns out
to be, he's likely to be an Indian.
1983 *Blue Highways: A Journey Into America*, pt.5, ch.2.

Heath, Sir Edward Richard George 1916–

English Conservative politician, chief negotiator for
Britain's entry into the European Common Market, and
Prime Minister (1970–4). He was replaced as leader by
Margaret Thatcher, whose policies he openly criticized.

50 We are the trade union for pensioners and children;
the trade union for the disabled and the sick; the
trade union for the nation as a whole.
1970 Election campaign speech, 20 Feb.

51 This would, at a stroke, reduce the rise in prices,
increase productivity, and reduce unemployment.
1970 Statement on proposed tax cuts and a price freeze by
nationalized industries, 16 Jun. These words were contained in a
press release, and were never actually spoken by Heath.

52 It is the unpleasant and unacceptable face of
capitalism, but one should not suggest that the
whole of British industry consists of practices of
this kind.
1973 House of Commons, 15 May, referring to the Lonrho
tax-avoidance scandal involving 'Tiny' Rowland, owner of
Harrods and the London and Rhodesia company.

53 If you want to see the acceptable face of capitalism,
go out to an oil rig in the North Sea.
1974 Election campaign speech, 18 Feb.

54 Ocean racing is like standing under a cold shower
tearing up £5 notes.
Quoted in Colin Jarman *The Guinness Dictionary of Sports
Quotations* (1990).

Hebbel, Friedrich 1813–63

German dramatist, whose plays typically have a legendary
or historical setting, exploring the conflict between the
individual and humanity as a whole.

55 *Dies Oesterreich ist eine kleine Welt,*
In der die grosse ihre Probe hält.

Austria is a little world in which the big one holds
its tryouts.
On the social and political disintegration affecting the Austro-
Hungarian Empire in the late 1890s. Quoted in Heinrich
Benedikt (ed) *Geschichte der Republik Oesterreich* (1954).

Heber, Reginald 1783–1826

English divine and hymnwriter, Bishop of Calcutta from
1823.

56 Brightest and best of the sons of the morning!
Dawn on our darkness and lend us Thine aid!
1811 In the *Christian Observer*, Nov.

57 By cool Siloam's shady rill

How sweet the lily grows!
1812 In the *Christian Observer*, Apr.

58 From Greenland's icy mountains,
From India's coral strand,
Where Afric's sunny fountains
Roll down their coral strand.
1819 Quoted in the *Christian Observer*, Feb 1823.

59 Holy, Holy, Holy! Lord God Almighty!
Early in the morning our song shall rise to Thee:
Holy, Holy, Holy! merciful and mighty!
God in Three Persons, blessèd Trinity.
1826 'Holy, Holy, Holy!'.

Hecht, Ben 1894–1964

US writer. A journalist in Chicago, he began to write
novels, plays and filmscripts. From 1946 he was dedicated
to the Zionist cause.

60 The movie-makers are able to put more reality into
a picture about the terrors of life at the ocean
bottom than into a tale of two Milwaukeeans in
love.
1954 In news reports, 13 Jun.

Hedin, Sven Anders 1865–1952

Swedish explorer and geographer, who travelled in
unexplored regions of central Asia, where he made the
first detailed map (1908). He was outspoken in his
political beliefs, including sympathy for Nazi Germany.

61 But the adventure, the conquest of an unknown
country, the struggle against the impossible, all
have a fascination which draws me with an
irresistible force.
1926 *My Life as an Explorer*.

Hegel, Georg Wilhelm Friedrich
1770–1831

German idealist philosopher. His first major work
Phänomenologie des Geistes (The Phenomenology of the
Mind, 1807) attacked romantic intuitionism. Other
works include *Enzyklopädie der philosophischen
Wissenschaften* (Encyclopedia of the Philosophical
Sciences, 1817), in which he set out his tripartite system
of logic, philosophy of nature and of mind.

62 In England, even the poorest of people believe that
they have rights; that is very different from what
satisfies the poor in other lands.
1821 *The Philosophy of Right*.

63 Experience and history teach...that nations and
governments have never learned anything from
history, or acted upon any lessons they might have
drawn from it.
1830 *Lectures on the Philosophy of World History*, introduction.

64 Political genius consists in identifying oneself with a principle.
Constitution of Germany.

Heidegger, Martin 1889–1976

German philosopher, student of Husserl and Professor of Philosophy at Freiburg. He was an important theoretician of phenomenology. His major work is *Being and Time* (1927).

65 The essence of technology is by no means anything technological.
1949 'The Question Concerning Technology', collected in *Basic Writings* (1977).

66 The mathematical is that evident aspect of things within which we are always already moving and according to which we experience them as things at all, and as such things. The mathematical is this fundamental position we take toward things by which we take up things as already given to us, and as they must and should be given. Therefore, the mathematical is the fundamental presupposition of the knowledge of things.
'Modern Science, Metaphysics and Mathematics', collected in *Basic Writings* (1977).

Heifetz, Jascha 1901–87

US violinist of Russo-Polish birth. A child prodigy, he settled in the US after the Russian Revolution, becoming a citizen in 1924. He first appeared in Britain in 1920.

67 I occasionally play works by contemporary composers and for two reasons. First, to discourage the composer from writing any more, and secondly to remind myself how much I appreciate Beethoven.
1961 In *Life.*

Heine, Heinrich 1797–1856

German poet and critic, who lived most of his life in Paris. An incurable spinal disease left him bedridden from 1848. He became a prominent radical political journalist, writing essays on French and German culture and composing satirical verse.

68 *Alle kräftige Menschen lieben das Leben*

All great, powerful souls love life.
1835 *Idéen, Das Buch Le Grand*, pt.3.

69 *Das Leben ist der Güter höchstes, und das schlimmste Uebel ist der Tod.*

Life is the greatest of blessings, and death the worst of evils.
1835 *Idéen, Das Buch Le Grand*, pt.3.

70 *Ich glaube sogar, durch Leidenskämpfe könnten die Tiere zu Menschen werden.*

I believe that by suffering even animals could be made human.
1836 *Französische Zustände.*

71 Nothing is more futile than theorizing about music. No doubt there are laws, mathematically strict laws, but these laws are not music; they are only its conditions… The essence of music is revelation.
1837 *Letters on the French Stage.*

72 *Ich kenn es wohl, dein Mißgeschick:*
Verfehltes Leben, verfehlte Liebe!

I know it well, your mishap:
A missed life, a missed love!
1840–4 *Neue Gedichte, Unterwelt*, pt.5.

73 *Dieu me pardonnera. C'est son métier.*

God will forgive me. It is his trade.
1856 Attributed, on his deathbed.

Heinse, Wilhelm 1745–1803

German novelist and art critic, whose work influenced the writers and artists of the Romantic movement.

74 Drawing is only a necessary evil, proportions are easily determined: colour is the goal, the beginning and end of art.
1787 *Ardinghello.*

75 The best subjects for artists, surely, are animals and plants, grasses and trees; these they can represent, but human beings they ought to leave to poets.
1787 *Ardinghello.*

76 Every form is individual, there exists none which is abstract.
Quoted in J J W Heinse *Sämmtliche Werke* (1903–25).

Heisenberg, Werner 1901–76

German physicist, a founder of quantum theory. His 'uncertainty principle' states that it is impossible to determine both the position and momentum of a subatomic particle. He received the 1932 Nobel Prize for Physics.

77 Natural science does not simply describe and explain nature; it is part of the interplay between nature and ourselves; it describes nature as exposed to our method of questioning.
1959 *Physics and Philosophy.*

78 Unless you stake your life, life will not be won.
1969 *Der Teil und das Ganze*, translated by A J Pomerans as *Physics and Beyond* (1971).

79 An expert is someone who knows some of the worst mistakes that can be made in his subject and who manages to avoid them.
1969 *Der Teil und das Ganze*, translated by A J Pomerans as *Physics and Beyond* (1971), ch.17.

Heller, Joseph 1923–

US novelist. He drew on his wartime experience for his black comedy *Catch-22* (1961), which became an international bestseller. Later books include *Something Happened* (1974), *God Knows* (1984) and *Picture This* (1988).

80 He was a self-made man who owed his lack of success to nobody.
1961 Of Colonel Cargill. *Catch-22*, ch.3.

81 He had decided to live forever or die in the attempt, and his only mission each time he went up was to come down alive.
1961 Of Yossarian. *Catch-22*, ch.3.

82 There was only one catch and that was Catch-22, which specified that a concern for one's safety in the face of dangers that were real and immediate was the process of a rational mind. Orr was crazy and could be grounded. All he had to do was ask; and as soon as he did, he would no longer be crazy and would have to fly more missions. Orr would be crazy to fly more missions and sane if he didn't, but if he was sane he had to fly them. If he flew them he was crazy and didn't have to; but if he didn't want to he was sane and had to. Yossarian was moved very deeply by the absolute simplicity of this clause of Catch-22, and let out a respectful whistle. 'That's some catch, that Catch-22,' he observed. 'It's the best there is,' Doc Daneeka agreed.
1961 *Catch-22*, ch.5.

83 'Yossarian? Is that his name? Yossarian? What the hell kind of a name is Yossarian?' Lieutenant Scheisskopf had the facts at his finger tips. 'It's Yossarian's name, sir,' he explained.
1961 *Catch-22*, ch.8, 'Lieutenant Scheisskopf'.

84 Hungry Joe collected lists of fatal diseases and arranged them in alphabetical order so that he could put his finger without delay on any one he wanted to worry about.
1961 *Catch-22*, ch.17.

85 Frankly, I'd like to see the government get out of the war altogether and leave the whole field to private industry.
1961 Milo Minderbinder. *Catch-22*, ch.24.

86 Success and failure are both difficult to endure. Along with success come drugs, divorce, fornication, bullying, travel, meditation, medication, depression, neurosis and suicide. With failure comes failure.
1975 Interview in *Playboy*, Jun.

87 If Richard Nixon was second-rate, what in the world *is* third-rate?
1979 *Good As Gold*, ch.6.

88 And a man who lay with a beast, said the Lord, would surely die. And if he doesn't lie with a beast, I would have countered, he won't die?
1984 King David. *God Knows*, ch.2.

89 Mankind is resilient: the atrocities that horrified us a week ago become acceptable tomorrow.
1988 *Picture This*, ch.37.

Heller, Walter Wolfgang 1915–

Chairman of the US Council of Economic Advisers to the President under Kennedy.

90 An economist is someone who, when he finds something which works in practice, wonders if it will work in theory.
1992 Attributed.

Hellman, Lillian Florence 1907–84

US playwright, whose plays include *The Children's Hour* (1934) and *The Little Foxes* (1939). In 1952 she came before McCarthy's House Un-American Activities Committee. She lived for many years with Dashiell Hammett.

91 That's cynical. [Smiles.] Cynicism is an unpleasant way of saying the truth.
1939 Ben. *The Little Foxes*, act 1.

92 It's an indulgence to sit in a room and discuss your beliefs as if they were a juicy piece of gossip.
1941 Sara. *Watch On The Rhine*, act 2.

93 I do not like subversion or disloyalty in any form and if I had ever seen any I would have considered it my duty to have reported it to the proper authorities. But to hurt innocent people whom I knew many years ago in order to save myself is to me inhuman and indecent and dishonorable.
1952 Letter to John S Wood, 19 May, on being asked to give information for the McCarthy trials. Collected in *US Congress Committee Hearing on Un-American Activities* (1952), pt.8.

94 I cannot and will not cut my conscience to fit this year's fashions, even though I long ago came to the conclusion that I was not a political person and could have no comfortable place in any political group.
1952 Letter to John S Wood, 19 May, on being asked to give information for the McCarthy trials. Collected in *US Congress Committee Hearing on Un-American Activities* (1952), pt.8.

95 That's what you always said, success isn't everything but it makes a man stand straight, and you were right.
1960 Julian. *Toys in the Attic*, act 1.

96 Well, people change and forget to tell each other. Too bad—causes so many mistakes.
1960 Anna. *Toys in the Attic*, act 3.

97 If I had to give young writers advice, I would say don't listen to writers talking about writing or themselves.

1960 In the *New York Times*, 21 Feb.

98 Intellectuals can tell themselves anything, sell themselves any bill of goods, which is why they were so often patsies for the ruling classes in nineteenth-century France and England, or twentieth-century Russia and America.

1967 Journal entry, 30 Apr. Collected in *An Unfinished Woman* (1969), ch.13

99 It is a mark of many famous people that they cannot part with their brightest hour.

1973 *Pentimento*, 'Theatre'.

1 The English don't raise their voices, Arthur, although they may have other vulgarities.

1973 *Pentimento*, 'Arthur W. A. Cowan'.

2 I am suspicious of guilt in myself and in other people: it is usually a way of not thinking, or of announcing one's own fine sensibilities the better to be rid of them.

1976 *Scoundrel Time*.

3 He was getting over a four-day drunk, and I was getting over a 4-year marriage.

1985 On meeting Dashiell Hammett. In the *Christian Science Monitor*, 13 Oct.

Helmholtz, Hermann Ludwig Ferdinand von 1821–94

German scientist and investigator of thermodynamics and electrodynamics. He was Professor of Physics at the University of Berlin.

4 Whoever, in the pursuit of science, seeks after immediate practical utility may rest assured that he seeks in vain.

1862 Lecture at Heidelberg, collected in *Popular Lectures on Scientific Subjects* (1873).

Helmsley, Leona (Mindy) neé Rosenthal 1920–

US businesswoman. Convicted of tax evasion in 1989, she received a four-year jail sentence, but avoided jail until 1992. She was released in 1994.

5 We don't pay taxes. Only the little people pay taxes.

1989 Remark to a former hotel housekeeper which became a byword of her trial and conviction for tax fraud. Reported in the *New York Times*, 13 Jul.

Héloïse 1101–64

French abbess. At 17 she had a child by her tutor, Peter Abelard. After Abelard was castrated by her family, she entered the convent of Argenteuil, becoming prioress there, and later became abbess at the Paraclete, founded by Abelard.

6 *Et si uxoris nomen sanctius ac validius videtur, dulcius mihi semper exstitit amicæ vocabulum; aut si non indigneris, concubinæ vel scorti.*

If the name of wife seems more blessed or more binding, always sweeter to me will be the word lover, or if I may, concubine or whore.

c.1135 First letter to Peter Abelard.

7 *Non enim quo quisque ditior sive potentior, ideo et melior: fortunae illud est, hoc virtutis.*

To be wealthier or more powerful is not necessarily to be worthier: the former are products of fortune, the latter stems from virtue.

c.1135 First letter to Peter Abelard.

8 *Non enim rei effectus, sed efficientis affectus in crimine est. Nec quæ fiunt, sed quo animo fiunt, æquitus pensat.*

Crime lies not in the deed, but in the doer's intention: it is not what was done, but the spirit in which it was done that justice should consider.

c.1135 First letter to Peter Abelard.

Helpmann, Sir Robert Murray 1909–86

Australian dancer, actor and choreographer. He débuted in Adelaide (1923), studied with Pavlova and in 1931 went to Britain. Star of the new Sadler's Wells Ballet (1933–50), he danced in many films and also acted with the Royal Shakespeare Company. His choreographic work includes *Hamlet* (1942) and *Miracle in the Gorbals* (1944).

9 You see there are portions of the human anatomy which would keep swinging after the music had finished.

c.1968 Disagreeing with the suggestion that there might be a future for nudity in dance. Quoted in Elizabeth Salter *Helpmann* (1978), ch.21. It is sometimes quoted as a comment on the opening night of the musical *Oh, Calcutta!*, as 'The trouble with nude dancing is that not everything stops when the music stops.'

Hemans, Felicia neé Browne 1793–1835

English poet.

10 The stately homes of England,
   How beautiful they stand!
   Amid their tall ancestral trees,
   O'er all the pleasant land.

1849 'The Homes of England'.

▷ See Coward 290:3.

11 The boy stood on the burning deck
   Whence all but he had fled;
   The flame that lit the battle's wreck
   Shone round him o'er the dead.

1849 'Casablanca'.

Hemingway, Ernest Millar 1899–1961

US novelist, short-story writer and journalist, whose terse prose style was much imitated. He was a legendary figure known for his drinking, big-game hunting, and deep-sea fishing. He won the Nobel Prize for Literature in 1954. Depressed by his failing powers, he later committed suicide.

12 Switzerland is a small, steep country, much more up and down than sideways, and is all stuck over with large brown hotels built on the cuckoo clock style of architecture.
1922 In the *Toronto Star Weekly*, 4 Mar.

13 A man's got to take a lot of punishment to write a really funny book.
1924 Letter, 6 Dec.

14 God knows people who are paid to have attitudes toward things, professional critics, make me sick: camp-following eunuchs of literature.
1925 Letter to Sherwood Anderson, 23 May.

15 Don't you like to write letters? I do because it's such a swell way to keep from working and yet feel you've done something.
1925 Letter to F Scott Fitzgerald, 1 Jul.

16 Soon I was alone and began cursing the bloody bible because there were no titles in it—although I found the source of practically every good title you ever heard of. But the boys, principally Kipling, had been there before me and swiped all the good ones so I called the book Men Without Women hoping it would have a large sale among the fairies and old Vassar Girls.
1927 Letter to F Scott Fitzgerald, 15 Sep.

17 I did not say anything. I was always embarrassed by the words sacred, glorious and sacrifice and the expression in vain. We had heard them, sometimes standing in the rain almost out of earshot, so that only the shouted words came through, and had read them, on proclamations that were slapped up by billposters over other proclamations, now for a long time, and I had seen nothing sacred, and the things that were glorious had no glory and the sacrifices were like the stock-yards at Chicago if nothing was done with the meat except to bury it.
1929 Frederic Henry. *A Farewell to Arms*, ch.27.

18 I had the paper but I did not read it because I did not want to read about the war. I was going to forget the war. I had made a separate peace.
1929 Frederic Henry. *A Farewell to Arms*, ch.34.

19 The world breaks everyone and afterwards many are strong at the broken places. But those that will not break it kills. It kills the very good and the very gentle and the very brave impartially. If you are

none of these you can be sure it will kill you too but there will be no special hurry.
1929 Frederic Henry. *A Farewell to Arms*, ch.34.

20 I mean grace under pressure.
1929 His definition of 'guts'. Interview with Dorothy Parker in the *New Yorker*, 30 Nov.

21 Hail nothing full of nothing, nothing is with thee.
1932 End of the older waiter's 'nada' prayer. *Winner Take Nothing*, 'A Clean, Well-Lighted Place'.

22 When you have shot one bird flying you have shot all birds flying. They are all different and they fly in different ways but the sensation is the same and the last one is as good as the first.
1932 *Winner Take Nothing*, 'Fathers and Sons'.

23 About morals, I know only that what is moral is what you feel good after and what is immoral is what you feel bad after.
1932 *Death in the Afternoon*, ch.1.

24 Bullfighting is the only art in which the artist is in danger of death and in which the degree of brilliance in the performance is left to the fighter's honor.
1932 *Death in the Afternoon*, ch.9.

25 There is no lonelier man in death, except the suicide, than the man who has lived many years with a good wife and then outlived her. If two people love each other there can be no happy end to it.
1932 *Death in the Afternoon*, ch.11.

26 Madame, all stories, if continued far enough, end in death, and he is no true story-teller who would keep that from you.
1932 *Death in the Afternoon*, ch.11.

27 The great thing is to last and get your work done, and see and hear and understand and write when there is something that you know and not before and not too damn much after.
1932 *Death in the Afternoon*, ch.16.

28 The hardest thing to do is to write straight honest prose on human beings.
1934 'Old Newsman Writes', in *Esquire*, Dec.

29 All modern American literature comes from one book by Mark Twain called *Huckleberry Finn*. American writing comes from that. There was nothing before. There has been nothing good since.
1935 *The Green Hills of Africa*, ch.1.

30 The only time it isn't good for you is when you write or when you fight. You have to do that cold. But it always helps my shooting. Modern life, too,

is often a mechanical oppression and liquor is the only mechanical relief.
1935 Of whisky. Letter to Ivan Kashkin, 19 Aug.

31 He remembered poor Julian and his romantic awe of them and how he had started a story once that began, 'The very rich are different from you and me.' And somebody had said to Julian, 'Yes, they have more money.'
1936 'The Snows of Kilimanjaro', in *Esquire*, Aug. In the original version 'Julian' was named as F Scott Fitzgerald, but the pseudonym was used for book publication in *The Fifth Column and Other Stories* (1938).
▷ See Fitzgerald 391:8.

32 'A man…ain't got no hasn't got any can't really isn't any way out… One man alone ain't got…no chance.
1937 Harry Morgan's dying words. *To Have and Have Not.*

33 'Oh,' she said, 'I die each time. Do you not die?' 'No. Almost. But did thee feel the earth move?' 'Yes. As I died. Put thy arm around me, please.'
1940 *For Whom The Bell Tolls*, ch.7.

34 He was just a coward and that was the worst luck any man could have.
1940 *For Whom The Bell Tolls*, ch.30.

35 Cowardice, as distinguished from panic, is almost always simply a lack of ability to suspend the functioning of the imagination.
1942 Introduction to *Men At War.*

36 It wasn't by accident that the Gettysburg address was so short. The laws of prose writing are as immutable as those of flight, of mathematics, of physics.
1945 Letter, 23 Jul.

37 I started out very quiet and I beat Mr Turgenev. Then I trained hard and I beat Mr De Maupassant. I've fought two draws with Stendhal, and I think I had an edge in the last one. But nobody's going to get me in any ring with Mr Tolstoy unless I'm crazy or I keep getting better.
1950 In the *New Yorker*, 13 May.

38 Writing and travel broaden your ass if not your mind and I like to write standing up.
1950 Letter, 9 Jul.

39 All the contact I have had with politics has left me feeling as though I had been drinking out of spittoons.
1950 In the *New York Times*, 17 Sep.

40 A man can be destroyed but not defeated.
1952 *The Old Man and the Sea.*

41 It is because we have had such great writers in the past that a writer is driven out far past where he can go, out to where no one can help him.
1954 Nobel Prize Acceptance Speech, 10 Dec.

42 No classic resembles any previous classic, so do not be discouraged.
1956 Advice to young writers, in *McCall's*, May.

43 Once writing has become your major vice and greatest pleasure only death can stop it.
1958 Interview in the *Paris Review*, Spring.

44 Under the black hat, when I had first seen them, the eyes had been those of an unsuccessful rapist.
1964 Of Percy Wyndham-Lewis. *A Moveable Feast*, ch.12 (published posthumously).

45 I always try to write as good as the best picture that was ever painted.
Quoted in the *Saturday Review*, 9 May 1964.

46 Never confuse movement with action.
Quoted in A E Hotchner *Papa Hemingway* (1966), pt.1, ch.1.

47 Hesitation increases in relation to risk in equal proportion to age.
Quoted in A E Hotchner *Papa Hemingway* (1966), pt.1, ch.3.

48 To be a successful father, there's one absolute rule: when you have a kid, don't look at it for the first two years.
Quoted in A E Hotchner *Papa Hemingway* (1966), pt.2, ch.5.

49 Wearing underwear is as formal as I ever hope I get.
Quoted in A E Hotchner *Papa Hemingway* (1988).

50 My writing is nothing, my boxing is everything.
Quoted in Colin Jarman *The Guinness Dictionary of Sports Quotations* (1990).

Hempstone, Smith 1929–

US journalist, writer and diplomat, Ambassador to Kenya (1989–93). His works include *Africa, Angry Young Giant* (1961).

51 If you liked Beirut, you'll love Mogadishu.
1992 To US Marines in Somalia some years after the Corps' losing battle against Kenyan terrorists. Reported in the *Guardian Weekly*, 19 Dec.

52 It will take five years to get Somalia not on its feet but just on its knees.
1992 Reported in the *Guardian Weekly*, 19 Dec.

Henderson, Leon 1895–1986

US economist.

53 Having a little inflation is like being a little pregnant.
Attributed.

Henderson, Sir Nevile Meyrick 1882–1942

English diplomat. He served as Minister to Yugoslavia (1929–35) and as Ambassador to Argentina (1935–7) and to Germany until the outbreak of World War II.

54 When I go to see Herr Hitler I give him the Nazi salute because that is the normal thing. It carries no hint of approval of anything he or his regime may do. And, if I do it, why should you or your team object?

1938 When asked for advice by the England football team in 1938 about giving the Nazi salute before a match in Berlin against Germany. The England team gave the salute, and thereby attracted considerable notoriety at home.

Hendrix, Jimi (James Marshall) 1942–70

US rock guitarist and singer, based in Britain from 1966. Born into poverty, he taught himself guitar and became one of rock music's most innovative and influential instrumentalists before drugs and alcohol caused his death.

55 Purple haze is in my brain
Lately things don't seem the same.
1967 'Purple Haze'.

56 You can't mess with people's heads, that's for sure. But that's what music's all about, messing with people's heads.

Quoted in Nat Shapiro *An Encyclopedia of Quotations about Music* (1978).

Henley, W(illiam) E(rnest) 1849–1903

English poet, playwright, critic and editor. He collaborated with his friend R L Stevenson in four plays. He edited the *Scots Observer* (1889), renaming it *The National Observer*. The best known of his poetry collections is *In Hospital* (1903).

57 In the fell clutch of circumstance,
I have not winced nor cried aloud:
Under the bludgeonings of chance
My head is bloody but unbowed.
1888 'Invictus', collected in *In Hospital* (1903).

58 It matters not how strait the gate,
How charged with punishments the scroll,
I am the master of my fate:
I am the captain of my soul.
1888 'Invictus', collected in *In Hospital* (1903).

59 What have I done for you,
England, my England?
1900 'Pro Rege Nostro'.

Henri, Adrian Maurice 1932–

English poet, associated with the Mersey poets of the 1960s.

60 Beautiful boys with bright red guitars
In the spaces between the stars.
1967 'Mrs Albion You've Got a Lovely Daughter'.

61 Love is a fanclub with only two fans.
1967 'Love Is…'.

62 I wanted your soft verges
But you gave me the hard shoulder.
1967 'Song of a Beautiful Girl Petrol-pump Attendant'.

Henry II 1133–89

King of England from 1154. He instituted numerous political reforms aimed at diminishing the power of the barons and of the Church.

63 Will no one rid me of this turbulent priest?
1170 Of Thomas à Becket. Quoted in W L Warren *Henry II*, p508. Four of Henry's soldiers took his words to heart and proceeded to Canterbury, where they murdered Becket in the cathedral.

Henry V 1387–1422

King of England from 1413. He won a famous victory against the French at Agincourt in 1415, despite numerical disadvantage.

64 War has three handmaidens ever waiting on her, Fire, Blood, and Famine, and I have chosen the meekest maid of the three.
1418 Comment during the English army's siege of Rouen. Quoted in J R Green *A Short History of the English People*, vol.1 (1915), ch.5, section 6.

Henry VIII 1491–1547

King of England (1509–47). His desire to divorce his first wife, Catherine of Aragon, against papal decree led to ecclesiastical revolution, with Henry as sole head of the Church of England. In all he married six wives. His reign also saw the judicial murder of Sir Thomas More and others who dared to oppose him.

65 We at no time stand so highly in our estate royal as in the time of Parliament, wherein we as head, and you as members, are conjoined and knit together into one body politic, so as whatsoever offence or injury is offered to the meanest member of the House is to be judged as done against our person and the whole Court of Parliament.
1543 Address to a deputation from the House of Commons, 31 Mar.

Henry, Philip 1631–96

English clergyman.

66 All this, and heaven too!
Quoted in Matthew Henry *Life of Mr Philip Henry* (1698), ch.5.

Henryson, Robert c.1425–c.1508

Scottish poet, usually designated 'schoolmaster of Dunfermline', whose surviving poems include *The Testament of Cresseid* and metrical versions of Aesop's fables.

67 For to be yong I wald not, for my wis,

Off all this warld to mak me lord and king:
The more of age, the nerar hevynnis blis.
c.1460 'The Praise of Age', l.5–9.

68 The man that will nocht quhen he may
Sall haif nocht quhen he wald.
c.1460 'Robene and Makeyne', l.91–2.

69 The nuttis schell, thocht it be hard and teuch,
Haldis the kirnell, sueit and delectabill;
Sa lyis thair ane doctrine wyse aneuch
And full of frute vnder ane fenyeit fabill.
c.1470 *Moral Fables*, prologue, l.15–19.

70 Ane bow that is ay bent
Worthis ay unsmart and dullis on the string;
Sa dois the mynd that is ay diligent
In ernistfull thochtis and in studying.
c.1470 *Moral Fables*, prologue, l.21–5.

71 Best thing in eird, I say for me,
Is merry hart with small possessioun.
c.1470 *Moral Fables*, 'The Two Mice', l.387–8.

72 Louers be war and tak gude heid about
Quhome that ye lufe, for quhome ye suffer paine.
I lat yow wit, thair is richt few thairout
Quhome ye may traist to haue trew lufe agane.
c.1470 *The Testament of Cresseid*, l.561–4.

73 Nocht is your fairnes bot ane faiding flour,
Nocht is your famous laud and hie honour
Bot wind inflat in uther mennis eiris.
c.1470 *The Testament of Cresseid*, stanza 65

Henze, Hans Werner 1926–

German composer. His stage works, often reflecting his socialist commitment, include the operas *Der Junge Lord* (1965) and *The English Cat* (1983). He has also composed orchestral, chamber, vocal and piano music.

74 There is no such thing as an unmusical person.
1969 'Does Music have to be Political?'

75 My profession…consists of bringing truths nearer to the point where they explode.
1982 *Music and Politics*.

Hepburn, Katharine 1909–

US film and stage actress. She made her professional stage début in *The Czarina* (1928). Her films include *Bringing up Baby* (1938) and *The African Queen* (1951). *The Lion in Winter* (1968) and *On Golden Pond* (1981) both won her Academy Awards. She was the professional and personal partner of Spencer Tracy.

76 The average Hollywood film star's ambition is to be admired by an American, courted by an Italian, married to an Englishman and have a French boyfriend.
1954 In the *Journal American*, 22 Feb.

77 When a man says he likes a woman in a skirt, I tell him to try one.
1994 WETA TV broadcast, Washington, 27 Jun.

78 She gave him sex and he gave her class.
Explaining the success of the Fred Astaire and Ginger Rogers partnership. Attributed.

Hepworth, Barbara 1903–75

English sculptor. She was an important figure in the development of British abstract art.

79 Carving is interrelated masses conveying an emotion: a perfect relationship between the mind and the colour, light and weight which is the stone, made by the hand which feels.
1934 *Unit One.*

80 There is an inside and an outside to every form.
1970 *A Pictorial Autobiography.*

81 My left hand is my thinking hand. The right is only a motor hand.
1970 *A Pictorial Autobiography.*

Heraclitus fl.500 BC

Greek philosopher, born in Ephesus. Only fragments survive of his book 'On Nature', which was written in an aphoristic style.

82 All is flux, nothing is stationary.
c.500 BC Quoted in Aristotle *De caelo*, bk.3, pt.1.18.

83 Education is another sun to the educated.
Fragment quoted in H Diels and W Kranz (eds) *Die Fragmente der Vorsokratiker*, vol.1 (1951), 181, no.134.

84 The path up and down is one and the same.
c.500 BC Quoted in Kirk, Raven and Schofield (eds) *The Presocratic Philosophers* (1957), ch.6.

85 Upon those that step into the same rivers different and different waters flow. They scatter and gather, come together and flow away, approach and depart.
c.500 BC Quoted in Kirk, Raven and Schofield (eds) *The Presocratic Philosophers* (1957), ch.6. Often quoted as 'It is not possible to step into the same river twice', from Plato, *Cratylus* 402a.

86 The world is an ever-living fire.
c.500 BC Quoted in Kirk, Raven and Schofield (eds) *The Presocratic Philosophers* (1957), ch.6.

87 You would not find out the boundaries of the soul, even by travelling along every path: so deep a measure does it have.
c.500 BC Quoted in Kirk, Raven and Schofield (eds) *The Presocratic Philosophers* (1957), ch.6.

88 If you do not expect the unexpected, you will not find it; for it is hard to be sought out, and difficult.

Collected in Charles H Kahn *The Art and Thought of Heraclitus* (1979).

89 The fairest order in the world is a heap of random sweepings.

Collected in Charles H Kahn *The Art and Thought of Heraclitus* (1979).

Herbert, Sir A(lan) P(atrick) 1890–1971

English writer and politician. He was called to the bar but never practised, having established himself as a humorist. His 'Misleading Cases' were accounts of unusual trials, in such collections as *Uncommon Law* (1935). He was an MP from 1935–50.

90 Don't tell my mother I'm living in sin,
Don't let the old folks know.

1925 'Don't Tell My Mother I'm Living in Sin'.

91 Don't let's go to the dogs tonight
For mother will be there.

1926 'Don't Let's Go to the Dogs Tonight'.

92 Not huffy, or stuffy, not tiny or tall,
But fluffy, just fluffy, with no brains at all.

1927 Of women. 'I Like Them Fluffy'.

93 Let's find out what everyone is doing
And then stop everyone from doing it.

1930 'Let's Stop Somebody From Doing Something'.

94 As my poor father used to say
In 1863,
Once people start on all this Art
Goodbye, moralitee!

1930 'Lines for a Worthy Person'.

95 Other people's babies—
That's my life!
Mother to dozens,
And nobody's wife.

1930 'Other People's Babies'.

96 Well, fancy giving money to the Government!
Might as well have put it down the drain.
Fancy giving money to the Government!
Nobody will see the stuff again.

1931 'Too Much!'.

97 For Kings and Governments may err
But never Mr Baedeker.

1931 'Mr Baedeker, or Britons Abroad'.

98 Holy Deadlock.

1934 Title of novel

99 Milord, in that case an Act of God was defined as 'something which no reasonable man could have expected'.

1935 *Uncommon Law*, 'Act of God'.

1 People must not do things for fun. We are not here for fun. There is no reference to fun in any Act of Parliament.

1935 *Uncommon Law*, 'Is it a Free Country?'

2 The Common Law of England has been laboriously built about a mythical figure—the figure of 'The Reasonable Man'.

1935 *Uncommon Law*, 'The Reasonable Man'.

3 The critical period in matrimony is breakfast-time.

1935 *Uncommon Law*, 'Is Marriage Lawful?'

4 The Englishman never enjoys himself except for a noble purpose.

1935 *Uncommon Law*, 'Fox-Hunting Fun'.

5 It may be life, but ain't it slow?

1941 'It May be Life'.

6 Nothing is wasted, nothing is in vain:
The seas roll over but the rocks remain.

c.1949 From an operetta, *Tough at the Top*, published in *My Life and Times* (1970), ch.7.

Herbert, George 1593–1633

English metaphysical poet and clergyman. His religious lyrics are collected in *The Temple, Sacred Poems and Private Ejaculations*, published posthumously in 1633.

7 Drink not the third glasse, which thou canst not tame,
When once it is within thee.

'The Church-porch', collected in *The Temple, Sacred Poems and Private Ejaculations*, l.25–6 (published posthumously, 1633).

8 A broken Altar, Lord, thy servant rears,
Made of a heart, and cemented with tears.

'The Altar', collected in *The Temple, Sacred Poems and Private Ejaculations* (published posthumously, 1633).

9 Avoid, Profaneness; come not here:
Nothing but holy, pure, and clear,
Or that which groaneth to be so,
May at his peril further go.

'Superliminare', collected in *The Temple, Sacred Poems and Private Ejaculations* (published posthumously, 1633).

10 Let all the world in ev'ry corner sing
My God and King.

'Antiphon', collected in *The Temple, Sacred Poems and Private Ejaculations* (published posthumously, 1633).

11 I got me flowers to strew Thy way,
I got me boughs off many a tree;
But Thou wast up by break of day,
And brought'st Thy sweets along with Thee.

'Easter Song', collected in *The Temple, Sacred Poems and Private Ejaculations* (published posthumously, 1633).

12 A servant with this clause

Makes drudgery divine;
Who sweeps a room as for Thy laws
Makes it and th' action fine.

'The Elixir', collected in *The Temple, Sacred Poems and Private Ejaculations* (published posthumously, 1633).

13 Teach me, my God and King,
In all things Thee to see,
And what I do in any thing
To do it as for Thee.

'The Elixir', collected in *The Temple, Sacred Poems and Private Ejaculations* (published posthumously, 1633).

14 Whereas my birth and spirit rather took
The way that takes the town;
Thou didst betray me to a lingering book,
And wrap me in a gown.

'Affliction (1)', collected in *The Temple, Sacred Poems and Private Ejaculations* (published posthumously, 1633).

15 Sorrow was all my soul; I scarce believed,
Till grief did tell me roundly, that I lived.

'Affliction (1)', collected in *The Temple, Sacred Poems and Private Ejaculations* (published posthumously, 1633).

16 I read, and sigh, and wish I were a tree;
For sure then I should grow
To fruit or shade: at least some bird would trust
Her household to me, and I should be just.

'Affliction (1)', collected in *The Temple, Sacred Poems and Private Ejaculations* (published posthumously, 1633).

17 Love bade me welcome: yet my soul drew back;
Guilty of dust and sin.
But quick-ey'd Love, observing me grow slack
From my first entrance in,
Drew nearer to me, sweetly questioning
If I lacked any thing.

'Love', collected in *The Temple, Sacred Poems and Private Ejaculations* (published posthumously, 1633).

18 'You must sit down,' says Love, 'and taste my meat,'
So I did sit and eat.

'Love', collected in *The Temple, Sacred Poems and Private Ejaculations* (published posthumously, 1633).

19 I know the ways of Pleasure, the sweet strains,
The lullings and the relishes of it.

'The Pearl', collected in *The Temple, Sacred Poems and Private Ejaculations* (published posthumously, 1633).

20 King of glory, King of peace
I will love Thee
And that love may never cease,
I will move Thee.

'Praise', collected in *The Temple, Sacred Poems and Private Ejaculations* (published posthumously, 1633).

21 My God, I heard this day,
That none doth build a stately habitation,
But that he means to dwell therein.

What house more stately hath there been,
Or can be, than is Man? to whose creation
All things are in decay.

'Man', collected in *The Temple, Sacred Poems and Private Ejaculations* (published posthumously, 1633).

22 Man is all symmetry,
Full of proportions, one limb to another.

'Man', collected in *The Temple, Sacred Poems and Private Ejaculations* (published posthumously, 1633).

23 O mighty love! Man is one world, and hath
Another to attend him.

'Man', collected in *The Temple, Sacred Poems and Private Ejaculations* (published posthumously, 1633).

24 Who says that fictions only and false hair
Become a verse? Is there in truth no beauty?
Is all good structure in a winding stair?

'Jordan (1)', collected in *The Temple, Sacred Poems and Private Ejaculations* (published posthumously, 1633).

25 I sought out quaint words, and trim invention;
My thoughts began to burnish, sprout, and swell,
Curling with metaphors a plain intention,
Decking the sense, as if it were to sell.

'Jordan (2)', collected in *The Temple, Sacred Poems and Private Ejaculations* (published posthumously, 1633).

26 So did I weave my self into the sense.

'Jordan (2)', collected in *The Temple, Sacred Poems and Private Ejaculations* (published posthumously, 1633).

27 I struck the board, and cried, 'No more.
I will abroad.'
What? shall I ever sigh and pine?
My lines and life are free; free as the road,
Loose as the wind, as large as store.

'The Collar', collected in *The Temple, Sacred Poems and Private Ejaculations* (published posthumously, 1633).

28 Sure there was wine
Before my sighs did dry it; there was corn
Before my tears did drown it.

'The Collar', collected in *The Temple, Sacred Poems and Private Ejaculations* (published posthumously, 1633).

29 My crooked winding ways, wherein I live.

'A Wreath', collected in *The Temple, Sacred Poems and Private Ejaculations* (published posthumously, 1633).

30 The soul in paraphrase.

'Prayer (1)', collected in *The Temple, Sacred Poems and Private Ejaculations* (published posthumously, 1633).

31 O that thou shouldst give dust a tongue
To cry to thee,
And then not hear it crying!

'Denial', collected in *The Temple, Sacred Poems and Private Ejaculations* (published posthumously, 1633).

32 Sweet day, so cool, so calm, so bright,

The bridal of the earth and sky:
The dew shall weep thy fall tonight,
For thou must die.

'Virtue', collected in *The Temple, Sacred Poems and Private Ejaculations* (published posthumously, 1633).

33　Joy, I did lock thee up; but some bad man
Hath let thee out again.

'The Bunch of Grapes', collected in *The Temple, Sacred Poems and Private Ejaculations* (published posthumously, 1633).

34　When God at first made man,
Having a glass of blessings standing by,
'Let us,' said he, 'pour on him all we can:
Let the world's riches, which dispersèd lie,
Contract into a span.

'The Pulley', collected in *The Temple, Sacred Poems and Private Ejaculations* (published posthumously, 1633).

35　Let him be rich and weary, that at least,
If goodness lead him not, yet weariness
May toss him to My breast.

'The Pulley', collected in *The Temple, Sacred Poems and Private Ejaculations* (published posthumously, 1633).

36　Farewell, sweet phrases, lovely metaphors:
But will ye leave me thus? when ye before
Of stews and brothels only knew the doors,
Then did I wash you with my tears, and more,
Brought you to church well-dressed and clad:
My God must have my best, even all I had.

'The Forerunners', collected in *The Temple, Sacred Poems and Private Ejaculations* (published posthumously, 1633).

37　Throw away thy rod,
Throw away thy wrath:
O my God,
Take the gentle path.

'Discipline', collected in *The Temple, Sacred Poems and Private Ejaculations* (published posthumously, 1633).

38　He that makes a good war makes a good peace.

1640 *Outlandish Proverbs*, no.420.

39　Music helps not the toothache.

1640 *Jacula Prudentum*. This is probably an older proverb.

40　God's mill grinds slow, but sure.

1651 *Jacula Prudentum*.

41　He that will learn to pray, let him go to sea.

1651 *Jacula Prudentum*.

Herbert, Xavier 1901–84

Australian writer. His novel *Capricornia* won the Sesquicentennial Literary Prize (1938) and the 1939 Australian Literary Society Gold Medal.

42　Since no normal humble man can help but feel magnificent in a brand-new suit of clothes, it is not surprising that those who don a fresh suit of bright white linen every day should feel magnificent always. Nor is it surprising that a normal humble head should swell beneath a solar topee, since a topee is more a badge of authority than a hat, as is the hat of a soldier.

1938 *Capricornia*, 'Psychological Effect of a Solar Topee'.

Herfindahl, Orris C 1918–

US economist.

43　Conservation of one resource may entail the sacrifice of another resource which others want to conserve.

1974 *Resource Economics: Selected Writings*, p.6.

Hernández, Felisberto 1902–64

Uruguayan novelist and pianist. He led an obscure life and wrote stories describing banal events with fantastic resolutions. His surrealistic sense of humour paved the way for literary experiments in Latin America and beyond.

44　*Se ha hecho para los vivos y no para los muertos el porqué metafísico y las reflexiones sobre la vida y la muerte, pero no les hace falta aclarar todo el misterio, les hace falta distraerse y soñar en aclararlo.*

Metaphysical questions and reflections on life and death were created for people alive and not for the dead. However, they do not have to solve all mystery; it is enough for them to create some distraction and to dream that they clarify.

1929 *Libro sin tapas*, 'La piedra filosofal' ('The Philosopher's Stone').

Hernández, José 1834–86

Argentinian poet. He had little formal education and was a gaucho (pampas cowboy) in his youth, later becoming a soldier in the civil wars, a newspaper editor and a minor government official.

45　*Yo he conocido cantores*
que era un gusto el escuchar;
mas no quieren opinar
y se divierten cantando;
pero yo canto opinando,
que es mi modo de cantar.

I have known singers
it was a pleasure to listen to;
they amuse themselves singing
and don't care to give opinions;
but I sing giving opinions
and that's my kind of song.

1879 *La vuelta de Martín Fierro*, pt.1 (translated as *Martín Fierro*, 1923).

46　*Hay hombres que de su ciencia*
tienen la cabeza llena;
hay sabios de todas menas,
mas digo, sin ser muy ducho:

es mejor que aprender mucho
el aprender cosas buenas.

There are some men who have their heads
full up with the things they know.
Wise men come in all sizes,
but I don't need so much sense to say
that better than learning a lot of things
is learning things that are good.
1879 *La vuelta de Martín Fierro*, pt.32.

Herodotus c.485 BC–c.425 BC

Greek historian. His *Histories* deal with the wars between
the Persians and the Greeks. He is often called 'The
Father of History'.

47 In peace, children inter their parents; war violates
the order of nature and causes parents to inter their
children.
c.440 BC *The Histories of Herodotus*, bk.1, ch.87 (translated by
Aubrey de Selincourt).

Herr, Michael 1940–

US journalist and war correspondent.

48 Vietnam was what we had instead of happy
childhoods.
1977 *Dispatches*, 'Colleagues', section 3.

49 All the wrong people remember Vietnam. I think
all the people who remember it should forget it,
and all the people who forgot it should remember
it.
1989 In the *Observer*, 15 Jan.

Herrick, Robert 1591–1674

English poet and clergyman, a Royalist who lost his living
during the Civil War. His writing, both secular and
religious, is collected in *Hesperides* and *Noble Numbers*
(both 1648).

50 I write of *Hell*; I sing (and ever shall)
Of *Heaven*, and hope to have it after all.
1648 *Hesperides*, 'The Argument of His Book'.

51 I sing of brooks, of blossoms, birds, and bowers:
Of April, May, of June, and July-flowers.
I sing of May-poles, Hock-carts, wassails, wakes,
Of bride-grooms, brides, and of their bridal-cakes.
1648 *Hesperides*, 'The Argument of His Book'.

52 Is there no way to beget
In my limbs their former heat?
Aeson had (as *Poets* fain)
Baths that made him young again:
Find that *Medicine* (if you can)
For your dry-decrepit man:
Who would but fain his strength renew,
Were it but to pleasure you.

1648 'To His Mistress'.

53 But ah! if empty dreams so please,
Love give me more such nights as these.
1648 'The Vision to *Electra*'.

54 But thou liv'st fearless; and thy face ne'er shows
Fortune when she comes, or goes.
1648 'A Country Life: To His Brother, *M. Tho. Herrick*'.

55 Wealth cannot make a life, but Love.
1648 'A Country Life: To His Brother, *M. Tho. Herrick*'.

56 Soul of my lie, and fame!
Eternal lamp of love! whose radiant flame
Out-glares the Heav'ns *Osiris*; and thy gleams
Out-shine the splendour of his mid-day beams.
1648 'The Welcome to Sack'.

57 'Tis thou, alone, who with thy mystic fan,
Work'st more than Wisdom, Art, or Nature can,
To rouse the sacred madness; and awake
The frost-bound-blood, and spirits; and to make
Them frantic with thy raptures, flashing through
The soul, like lightning, and as active too.
1648 'His Fare-well to Sack'.

58 Let others drink thee freely; and desire
Thee and their lips espous'd; while I admire,
And love thee; but not taste thee. Let my Muse
Fail of thy former helps; and only use
Her inadult'rate strength: what's done by me
Hereafter, shall smell of the lamp, not thee.
1648 'His Fare-well to Sack'.

59 Her legs were such *Diana* shows,
When tuckt up she a hunting goes;
With buskins shortened to descry
The happy dawning of her thigh.
1648 'The Vision'.

60 Get up, get up for shame, the blooming morn
Upon her wings presents the god unshorn.
1648 'Corinna's Going a Maying'.

61 See how *Aurora* throws her fair
Fresh-quilted colours through the air:
Get up, sweet-slug-a-bed, and see
The dew-bespangling herb and tree.
1648 'Corinna's Going a Maying'.

62 So when or you or I are made
A fable, song, or fleeting shade;
All love, all liking, all delight
Lies drowned with us in endless night.
Then while time serves, and we are but decaying;
Come, my *Corinna*, come, let's go a Maying.
1648 'Corinna's Going a Maying'.

63 Gather ye rose-buds while ye may,

Old Time is still a flying:
And this same flower that smiles to day,
Tomorrow will be dying.

1648 'To the Virgins, to Make Much of Time'.

64　Go happy rose, and interwove
With other flowers, bind my love.
Tell her too, she must not be,
Longer flowing, longer free,
That so oft has fetter'd me.

1648 'To the Rose: Song'

65　Then come on, come on, and yield
A savour like unto a blessed field,
When the bedabbled morn
Washes the golden ears of corn.

1648 'A Nuptial Song, or Epithalamion, on Sir Clipseby Crew and His Lady'.

66　Her eyes, the glow-worm lend thee,
The shooting stars attend thee;
And the elves also,
Whose little eyes glow,
Like the sparks of fire, befriend thee.

1648 'The Night-piece, to Julia', written for his young daughter.

67　When as in silks my *Julia* goes,
Then, then (me thinks) how sweetly flows
That liquefaction of her clothes.

1648 'Upon Julia's Clothes'.

68　A sweet disorder in the dress
Kindles in clothes a wantonness:
A lawn about the shoulders thrown
Into a fine distraction…
A careless shoe-string, in whose tie
I see a wild civility:
Do more bewitch me, than when Art
Is too precise in every part.

1648 'Delight in Disorder'.

69　Where we such clusters had,
As made us nobly wild, not mad;
And yet each verse of thine
Out-did the meat, out-did the frolic wine.

1648 'An Ode for [Ben Jonson]'.

Herriot, James pseudonym of *J Alf Wight* 1916–95

Scottish-born veterinary surgeon and writer of a series of highly popular novels on the adventures of a country vet.

70　I have long held the notion that if a vet can't catch his patient there's nothing much to worry about.

1976 *Vet in Harness*.

Hersey, John Richard 1914–93

US author, born in China. As Far East correspondent for *Time* magazine, his most famous piece was his eye-witness report in the *New Yorker* (31 Aug 1946) of the bombing of Hiroshima. His novels include *A Bell for Adano* (1944) and *The Walnut Door* (1977).

71　A gifted glassblower of language.

1988 On the British poet and critic I A Richards. In the *New Yorker*, 18 Jul.

Herzen, Alexander Ivanovich 1812–70

Russian political thinker and writer, a revolutionary socialist active in the Paris revolution of 1848. He settled in London (1851), producing propagandist novels and treatises, and smuggling into Russia his journal *Kolokol* ('The Bell', 1857–67).

72　Science, which cuts its way through the muddy pond of daily life without mingling with it, casts its wealth to right and left, but the puny boatmen do not know how to fish for it.

1855 Notebook entry, collected in *Byloe i dumy* (*My Past and Thoughts*), vol.3 (published 1861–7, translated by Constance Garnett, 1924).

73　There are those who prefer to get away *inwardly*, some with the help of a powerful imagination and an ability to abstract themselves from their surroundings…some with the help of opium or alcohol… I prefer shifting my whole body to shifting my brain, and going round the world to letting my head go round.

1861–7 *Byloe i dumy* (*My Past and Thoughts*, translated by Constance Garnett, 1924).

74　There is a certain basis of truth in the fear that the Russian government is beginning to have of communism, for communism is Tsarist autocracy turned upside down.

1861–7 *Byloe i dumy* (*My Past and Thoughts*, translated by Constance Garnett, 1924).

Herzl, Theodor 1860–1904

Zionist leader. He graduated in law but wrote essays and plays until the anti-Semitism aroused by the Dreyfus trial (1894) roused him to political action and he convened the First Zionist Congress (1897).

75　Do you know out of what the German Empire arose? Out of dreams, songs, fantasies and black-red-gold ribbons… Bismark merely shook the tree that fantasies had planted.

Quoted in Carl E Schorske *Fin-de-Siècle Vienna* (1961), p.165.

Herzog, Maurice 1919–

French engineer and mountaineer. He led the French Himalayan Expedition of 1950, which made the first ascent of Annapurna, losing several fingers and toes through frostbite. *Annapurna* was dictated during his subsequent three-year period in hospital.

76　The mountains were there and so was I.

1952 His reason for becoming a mountain climber. Quoted in

Annapurna: Conquest of the First 8000-metre Peak (1952, translated by Nea Morin and Janet Adam Smith).

77 Annapurna, to which we had gone empty-handed, was a treasure on which we should live the rest of our lives. With this realization we turn the page: a new life begins.
There are other Annapurnas in the lives of men.
1952 Quoted in *Annapurna: Conquest of the First 8000-metre Peak* (translated by Nea Morin and Janet Adam Smith).

Heseltine, Michael Ray Dibdin 1933–

British Conservative politician. He was Defence Secretary under Margaret Thatcher, and resigned on the issue of the takeover of Westland Helicopters (1986). Defeated by John Major in the 1990 leadership contest, he became Secretary of State for the Environment (1990–2) and for Trade and Industry (1992–5). He was Deputy Prime Minister from 1995 to 1997.

78 It is the only time that I can ever remember the Prime Minister reading out the conclusions of a meeting that did not take place. They were already written before it started.
1986 Of the Cabinet meeting, Jan, on the Westland affair at which he resigned as Defence Minister.

79 I can foresee no circumstance in which I would allow my name to be put forward for the leadership of the Conservative Party.
1990 Said on numerous occasions in the autumn.

80 I am persuaded now that I have a better prospect than Mrs Thatcher of leading the Conservatives to a fourth electoral victory and preventing the ultimate calamity of a Labour Government.
1990 On announcing his decision to stand for the leadership, Nov.

Hesiod c.8c BC

One of the earliest Greek poets, best known for *Works and Days*, which depicts rural life in archaic Greece, and *Theogony*.

81 Potter is piqued with potter, joiner with joiner, beggar begrudges beggar, and singer singer.
Of a quarrel within a village. *Opera et dies*, 25 (translated by M L West, 1988).

82 The ill design is most ill for the designer.
Opera et dies, 266 (translated by M L West, 1988).

83 Inhibition is no good provider for a needy man, inhibition, which does men great harm and great good,
inhibition attaches to poverty, boldness to wealth.
Opera et dies, 317–9 (translated by M L West, 1988).

Hess, Moses 1812–75

German political writer, and an early friend of Marx.

84 Imagine Rousseau, Voltaire, Holbach, Lessing, Heine, and Hegel united in one person—I say united, not lumped together—and you have Dr Marx.
Quoted in AJP Taylor's introduction to the Penguin edition of *The Communist Manifesto* (1967).

Hewart, Gordon, (1st Viscount) 1870–1943

British barrister. He was called to the Bar in 1902 and attended the Paris Peace Conference in 1919 as Attorney-General. He was made Lord Chief Justice of England (1922–40).

85 Justice should not only be done, but should manifestly and undoubtedly be seen to be done.
1923 Case of *Rex v. Sussex Justices*, 9 Nov.

Hewett, Dorothy Coade later *Davies* and *Lilley* 1923–

Australian playwright and poet. Her poetic works include *Windmill Country* (1965) and *Rapunzel in Suburbia* (1979), and her plays include *The Chapel Perilous* (1971) and *This Old Man Comes Rolling Home* (1976).

86 I had a tremendous world in my head and more than three-quarters of it will be buried with me.
1971 Sally Banner. *The Chapel Perilous*, act 2.

Hewett, Sylvia Ann

US economist.

87 What we've done in this country in the past few decades is socialize the cost of growing old and privatize the cost of childhood.
1991 In the *Washington Post*, 22 Feb.

Heyerdahl, Thor 1914–

Norwegian anthropologist and adventurer, best known for his voyages and journeys, particularly the *Kon-Tiki* and *Ra* expeditions, which reproduce the methods and materials used by early peoples.

88 Just occasionally you find yourself in an odd situation. You get into it by degrees and in the most natural way, but when you are right in the midst of it you are suddenly astonished and ask yourself how in the world it all came about.
If, for example, you put to sea on a wooden raft with a parrot and five companions, it is inevitable that sooner or later you will wake up one morning out at sea, perhaps a little better rested than ordinarily, and begin to think about it.
1948 *The Kon-Tiki Expedition: By Raft Across the South Seas* (translated by F H Lyon).

Heyward, Du Bose 1885–1940

US lyricist.

89 Summer time an' the livin' is easy,

Fish are jumpin' an' the cotton is high.
Oh, yo' daddy's rich, and yo' ma is good-lookin',
So hush, little baby, don' yo' cry.
1935 'Summertime' from *Porgy and Bess* (with Ira Gershwin, music by George Gershwin).

90 It ain't necessarily so,
De t'ings dat yo' li'ble
To read in the Bible
It ain't necessarily so.
1935 'It Ain't Necessarily So' from *Porgy and Bess* (with Ira Gershwin, music by George Gershwin).

Heywood, Thomas c.1574–1641

English dramatist, poet and actor. He claimed to have contributed to 220 plays, but much of his work has been lost, including his unpublished 'Lives of All the Poets…'.

91 Content's a kingdom, and I wear that crown.
c.1607 *A Woman Killed With Kindness*, sc.7.

92 That Time could turn up his swift sandy glass,
To untell the days.
c.1607 *A Woman Killed With Kindness*, sc.13.

93 With this kiss I wed thee once again.
c.1607 *A Woman Killed With Kindness*, sc.16.

Hicks, Sir Edward Seymour 1871–1949

English actor-manager and author. A popular light comedian, he appeared in many successful plays written by himself.

94 You will recognize, my boy, the first sign of old age: it is when you go out into the streets of London and realize for the first time how young the policemen look.
Quoted in C R D Pulling *They Were Singing* (1952), ch.7.

Hicks, Sir John Richard 1904–89

English economist, Professor of Political Economy at Manchester (1938–46) and Oxford (1952–65). He laid the foundation of modern welfare economics, and was awarded the Nobel Prize for Economics in 1972 with Kenneth Arrow.

95 The best of all monopoly profits is a quiet life.
1935 *Econometrica*, 'The Theory of Monopoly'.

96 We ought to define a man's income as the maximum value which he can consume during a week, and still expect to be as well off at the end of the week as he was at the beginning.
1946 *Value and Capital* (2nd edn).

97 Weapons grow rusty if unused, and a Union which never strikes may lose the ability to organise a formidable strike, so that its threats become less effective.
1963 *The Theory of Wages* (2nd edn).

98 There is much of economic theory which is pursued for no better reason than its intellectual attraction; it is a good game.
1979 *Causality in Economics*.

Hickson, William Eward 1803–70

British educator and writer on singing.

99 If at first you don't succeed,
Try, try again.
'Try and Try Again'.

Higley, Brewster

US songwriter.

1 Oh give me a home where the buffalo roam,
Where the deer and the antelope play,
Where seldom is heard a discouraging word
And the skies are not cloudy all day.
c.1873 'Home on the Range'.

Hill, (Norman) Graham 1929–75

English racing driver. He won the Formula One World Championship in 1962 in a BRM. In 1967 he rejoined Lotus and won the world title for a second time (1968). He retired in 1975 and was killed in an air crash a few months later.

2 It is like balancing an egg on a spoon while shooting the rapids.
On motor racing. Quoted in Colin Jarman *The Guinness Dictionary of Sports Quotations* (1990).

Hill, Joe originally *Joel Hägglund* 1879–1915

US labour leader and songwriter.

3 You will eat, by and by,
In that glorious land above the sky;
Work and pray, live on hay,
You'll get pie in the sky when you die.
1911 *Songs of the Workers*, 'Preacher and the Slave'.

Hill, Rowland 1744–1833

English popular preacher. He helped to found the Religious Tract Society and the London Missionary Society, and in 1801 published the popular *Village Dialogues*.

4 I do not see any reason why the devil should have all the good tunes.
Quoted in E W Broome *The Rev. Rowland Hill* (1881), ch.7.

Hillaby, John 1917–

English writer, naturalist and prodigious walker. He has journeyed on foot, usually alone, through Africa, across Europe and across the length of Britain.

5 Walking is a way of being somewhere, rather than striving to arrive.
1964 *Journey to the Jade Sea*.

6 Fortunately for poets and those who like to walk about in the open air, the beauty of landscape is not something that can be reduced easily to basic geology or a few ready-wrapped phrases about what places are used for. Preference and prejudice creep in.

1968 *Journey through Britain.*

Hillary, Sir Edmund Percival 1919–

New Zealand mountaineer and explorer. He was a member of John Hunt's Everest expedition, and reached the summit with Sherpa Tenzing Norgay on 29 May 1953. He was appointed New Zealand High Commissioner to India in 1984.

7 We knocked the bastard off!

1953 On returning from the summit of Everest, Jun. Quoted in his autobiography *Nothing Venture, Nothing Win* (1975), ch.10.

8 Better if he had said something natural like, 'Jesus, here we are.'

1974 Criticizing Neil Armstrong's premeditated words on first stepping onto the moon. Quoted in the *Sunday Times*.

▷ See Armstrong 35:49.

Hillebrand, Fred 1893–

US musical comedy actor and songwriter. He wrote *Ghosts of Broadway* for television and *Southlands*, an American opera.

9 Home James, and Don't Spare the Horses.

1934 Title of song.

Hillingdon, Lady 1857–1940

10 I am happy now that Charles calls on my bedchamber less frequently than of old. As it is, I now endure but two calls a week and when I hear his steps outside my door I lie down on my bed, close my eyes, open my legs, and think of England.

1912 Journal entry. Quoted in J Gathorne-Hardy *The Rise and Fall of the British Nanny* (1972), ch.3. The phrase is often rendered 'Lie back and think of England'.

Hilton, James 1900–54

English novelist. Several of his books have been filmed, including *Lost Horizon* (1933), *Goodbye, Mr Chips* (1934) and *Random Harvest* (1941).

11 Nothing really wrong with him—only anno domini, but that's the most fatal complaint of all, in the end.

1934 *Goodbye, Mr Chips*, ch.1.

Hindemith, Paul 1895–1963

German composer. His early neo-classical compositions gave way to chromatic works such as *Konzertmusik*

(1930–3). His symphony *Mathis der Maler* (1934) was banned by the Nazis and he emigrated to Turkey then Britain, where he continued composing.

12 Tonality is a natural force, like gravity.

1937 *The Craft of Musical Composition.*

13 There are only two things worth aiming for: good music and a clean conscience.

1938 Letter to Willy Strecker.

14 There are only twelve notes. You must treat them carefully.

Quoted in Derek Watson *Music Quotations* (1991).

Hippocrates c.460 BC–c.370 BC

Greek physician, the 'father of medicine', associated with the profession's 'Hippocratic oath'. He practised on Cos. The 'Hippocratic Corpus' is a collection of 72 medical and surgical treatises, but were probably not written by him.

15 *Ars longa vita brevis.*

The craft so long [to learn], the life so short.

Quoted in Seneca *De brevitate vitae*, 1. The original was in Greek.

16 Science is the father of knowledge, but opinion breeds ignorance.

The Canon, vol. 4 (translated by John Chadwick).

Hirohito 1901–89

Emperor of Japan during World War II. In 1945 he announced the Japanese surrender in a broadcast to his people and called for their support.

17 We declared war on America and Britain out of Our sincere desire to ensure Japan's self-preservation and the stabilisation of East Asia.

1945 Declaration, 15 Aug. Quoted in Edward Behr *Hirohito* (1989).

18 Endure what is difficult to endure and to suffer what is difficult to suffer.

1945 Declaration, 15 Aug. Quoted in Hugh Cortazzi *The Japanese Achievement* (1990).

19 It was not clear to me that our course was unjustified. Even now I am not sure how historians will allocate the responsibility for the war.

1945 Remark to General MacArthur, quoted in Edward Behr *Hirohito* (1989), introduction.

Hirsch, E(ric) D(onald), Jr 1928–

US educational reformer, Professor of English at the University of Virginia from 1989. His works include *Cultural Literacy: What Every American Needs to Know* (1987), and he was co-editor of *A Dictionary of Cultural Literacy* (1988).

20 Cultural literacy is the oxygen of social intercourse.

1987 *Cultural Literacy: What Every American Needs to Know*, introduction.

Hirschfeld, Al   1903–

US artist, theatrical caricaturist for the *New York Times* for over 55 years.

21 I was a sculptor. But that's really drawing—a drawing you fall over in the dark, a three-dimensional drawing.

1988 In the *New York Times*, 21 Jun. 85th birthday interview.

22 The opening-night audience is mostly friends of the cast and backers of the show, and they come to applaud their money.

1988 In the *New York Times*, 21 Jun.

23 Writers who drew, they all seemed to draw the same way. They managed to keep that childlike creativity in their line.

Of Edward Lear and James Thurber. Quoted in Neil A Grauer *Remember Laughter* (1994).

Hitchcock, Sir Alfred Joseph   1899–1980

English film director, a master of suspense thrillers. His films include (in Britain) *The Thirty Nine Steps* (1935) and *The Lady Vanishes* (1938), (in Hollywood) *Rebecca* (1940), *Psycho* (1960) and many others.

24 If I made *Cinderella*, the audience would immediately be looking for a body in the coach.

1956 In *Newsweek*, 11 Jun.

25 Television has brought back murder into the home—where it belongs.

1965 In *The Observer*, 19 Dec.

26 The more successful the villain, the more successful the picture.

Quoted in François Truffaut *Hitchcock* (1968).

27 Actors are cattle. Disney probably has the right idea. He draws them and if he doesn't like them he tears them up.

Quoted in Doug McClelland *Star Speak* (1987).

Hitler, Adolf   1889–1945

German dictator, Leader of the Third Reich for 12 years. He was defeated by the Allies in World War II, during which over six million people were killed by the Nazis in concentration camps. He died in a Berlin bunker in 1945.

28 *Die breite Masse eines Volkes…einer großen Lüge leichter zum Opfer fällt als einer kleinen.*

The broad mass of a nation…will more easily fall victim to a big lie than to a small one.

1925 *Mein Kampf* (*My Struggle*, 1939), ch.10.

29 *Wer in Europa die Brandfackel des Krieges erhebt, kann nur das Chaos wünschen.*

Whoever lights the torch of war in Europe can wish for nothing but chaos.

1935 Speech in the Reichstag, Berlin, 21 May.

30 *Ich gehe mit traumwandlerischer Sicherheit den Weg, den mich die Vorsehung gehen heißt.*

I go the way that Providence dictates with the assurance of a sleepwalker.

1936 Speech in Munich, 14 March, in Max Domarus (ed.) *Hitler: Reden und Proklamationen 1932–1945* (1962), p.606.

31 *Es ist die letzte territoriale Forderung, die ich Europa zu stellen habe, aber es ist die Forderung, von der ich nicht abgehe, und die ich, so Gott will, erfüllen werde.*

It is the last territorial claim which I have to make in Europe, but it is the claim from which I will not recede and which, God-willing, I will make good.

1938 On the Sudetenland. Speech in Berlin, 26 Sep. In Max Domarus (ed.) *Hitler: Reden und Proklamationen 1932–1945* (1962), p.927.

32 *In bezug auf das sudetendeutsche Problem meine Geduld jetzt zu Ende ist!*

With regard to the problem of the Sudeten Germans, my patience is now at an end!

1938 Speech in Berlin, 26 Sep, in Max Domarus (ed.) *Hitler: Reden und Proklamationen 1932–1945* (1962), p.932.

Ho Chi-Minh, Nguyen Van Thann   1892–1969

Vietnamese political leader, who became President of North Vietnam in 1954. He led his country, first in the independence movement against the French (1946–54) and later in the war against US-backed South Vietnam in the 1960s.

33 Let him who has a rifle use his rifle, let him who has a sword use his sword! And let those who have no sword take up pick-axes and sticks.

1946 Rallying call, Dec. Quoted in J Facouture *Ho Chi-Minh*.

34 It is better to sniff France's dung for a while than eat China's all our lives.

1946 Attributed. Quoted in J Facouture *Ho Chi-Minh*.

Hobbes, Thomas   1588–1679

English political philosopher. He wrote several works on government, and at the exiled English court in Paris wrote his major work on political philosophy, *Leviathan* (1651), combining metaphysics, psychology and political philosophy. In 1652 he returned to England and submitted to Cromwell.

35 Science [is] knowledge of the truth of Propositions and how things are called.

1650 *Human Nature*, ch.6.

36 In Geometry (which is the only science that it hath pleased God hitherto to bestow on mankind) men begin at settling the significations of their words; which…they call Definitions.

1651 *Leviathan*, pt.1, ch.4.

37 Science is the knowledge of consequences and the

dependence of one fact upon another.
1651 *Leviathan*, pt.1, ch.5.

38 The value, or worth of a man, is as of all other things, his price; that is to say, so much as would be given for the use of his power.
1651 *Leviathan*, pt.1, ch.10.

39 I put for a general inclination of all mankind, a perpetual and restless desire of power after power, that ceaseth only in death.
1651 *Leviathan*, pt.1, ch.11.

40 Whatsoever therefore is consequent to a time of war, where every man is enemy to every man; the same is consequent to the time wherein men live without other security than what their own strength, and their own invention shall furnish them withall. In such condition, there is no place for industry; because the fruit thereof is uncertain: and consequently no culture of the earth; no navigation, nor use of the commodities that may be imported by sea; no commodious building; no instruments of moving, and removing such things as require much force; no knowledge of the face of the Earth; no account of Time; no Arts; no Letters; no Society; and which is worst of all, continual fear, and danger of violent death; and the life of man, solitary, poor, nasty, brutish, and short.
1651 *Leviathan*, pt.1, ch.13.

41 They that are discontented under monarchy call it tyranny; and they that are displeased with aristocracy call it oligarchy; so also, they which find themselves grieved under a democracy call it anarchy, which signifies the want of government; and yet I think no man believes that want of government is any new kind of government.
1651 *Leviathan*, pt.2, ch.19.

42 A Free Man is he, that in those things, which by his strength and wit he is able to do, is not hindered to do what he has a will to.
1651 *Leviathan*, pt.2, ch.21.

43 The Enemy has been here in the night of our natural ignorance, and sown the tares of spiritual errors.
1651 *Leviathan*, pt.4, ch.44.

Hobhouse, John Cam, 1st Baron Broughton 1786–1869

British statesman. He wrote *Journey through Albania* with Lord Byron (1813), entered Parliament as a radical in 1820, and after succeeding to his baronetcy held several cabinet posts.

44 It is said to be hard on His Majesty's Ministers to raise objections to this proposition. For my part, I think it no more hard on his Majesty's Opposition to compel them to take this course.
1826 House of Commons, 27 Apr. This is the first recorded use of the term 'His Majesty's Opposition'.

Hobsbawn, E(ric John Ernest) 1917–

English economist, Professor at the University of London and former lecturer at Cambridge. He is the author of a number of works of history including *Bandits* (1969).

45 There is not much that even the most socially responsible scientists can do as individuals, or even as a group, about the social consequences of their activities.
1970 In the *New York Review of Books*, 18 Nov.

Hobson, John Atkinson 1858–1940

English economist. An unorthodox figure, he believed 'under-consumption' to be the cause of unemployment. His works include an autobiography, *Confessions of an Economic Heretic* (1938).

46 Organised outdoor sports for the old ruling classes.
1902 On 'militarism and colonialism'. *Imperialism.*

Hoby, Sir Edward 1560–1617

English politician.

47 On the 5th November we began our Parliament, to which the King should have come in person but refrained, through a practice but that morning discovered. The plot was to have blown up the King…at one instant to have ruined the whole estate and kingdom of England.
1605 Letter to the British Ambassador to Brussels, describing the Gunpowder Plot, 19 Nov.

Hockney, David 1937–

British painter, photographer, set designer and printmaker.

48 It's a myth that if you're liked by only four people it must be good. It might also be very bad: they might be your mother, your brother, your uncle and your aunt.
1978 *David Hockney.*

Hodgson, Ralph 1871–1962

English poet. He published three volumes of Georgian poems, on the themes of nature and England (1907–17). After lecturing in Japan, he settled in the US.

49 Time, you old gipsy man,
    Will you not stay,
    Put up your caravan
    Just for one day?
1917 'Time, You Old Gipsy Man'.

50 I climbed a hill as light fell short,

And rooks came home in scramble sort,
And filled the trees and flapped and fought
And sang themselves to sleep.
1917 'Song of Honour'.

51 I stood upon that silent hill
And stared into the sky until
My eyes were blind with stars and still
I stared into the sky.
1917 'Song of Honour'.

52 When stately ships are twirled and spun
Like whipping tops and help there's none
And mighty ships ten thousand ton
Go down like lumps of lead.
1917 'Song of Honour'.

53 'Twould ring the bells of heaven
The widest peal for years,
If Parson lost his senses
And people came to theirs,
And he and they together
Knelt down with angry prayers
For tamed and shabby tigers
And dancing dogs and bears,
And wretched, blind, pit ponies,
And little hunted hares.
1917 'Bells of Heaven'.

Hoffer, Eric 1902–83

Migratory farm labourer, box factory worker and later longshoreman in San Francisco, who turned to writing social philosophy. His most influential work was *The True Believer* (1951), on mass movements in politics.

54 Where there is the necessary technical skill to move mountains, there is no need for the faith that moves mountains.
1955 *The Passionate State of Mind.*

Hoffman, Abbie 1936–89

US radical activist and writer. In 1968 he helped organize violent anti-Vietnam war demonstrations in Chicago, and was prominent in the 'Chicago Seven' trial in 1969. He was active in public demonstrations until 1986.

55 I always held my flower in a clenched fist.
1980 On his social activism as a 1960s flower child. *Soon to Be a Major Motion Picture.*

Hoffman, Dustin 1937–

US actor. He made his Broadway début in 1961 and after a modest start achieved fame in the cinema with *The Graduate* (1967). He subsequently won Oscars for *Kramer vs Kramer* (1979) and *Rain Man* (1988).

56 If I'd seen me at a party, I'd never have gone up and met me.
1995 In *Dateline*, NBC TV broadcast, 8 Mar.

Hoffman, Hans 1880–1966

German-born US painter, who emigrated to the US in 1930. His work is characterized by bold, clashing colours.

57 The ability to simplify means to eliminate the unnecessary so that the necessary may speak.
1967 *Search for the Real.*

Hoffmann, Heinrich 1809–94

German physician and children's writer. His character Struwwelpeter is a slovenly, naughty boy who features in a book of cautionary tales written for his four-year-old son. He also wrote poetry, satire and medical works.

58 Augustus was a chubby lad;
Fat, ruddy cheeks Augustus had:
And everybody saw with joy
The plump and hearty, healthy boy.
He ate and drank as he was told,
And never let his soup get cold.
But one day, one cold winter's day,
He screamed out, 'Take the soup away!
O take the nasty soup away!
I won't have any soup today'.
1845 *Struwwelpeter*, 'Augustus'.

59 Look at little Johnny there,
Little Johnny Head-in-Air!
1845 *Struwwelpeter*, 'Johnny Head-in-Air'.

60 The door flew open, in he ran,
The great, long, red-legged scissor-man.
1845 *Struwwelpeter*, 'The Little Suck-a-Thumb'.

Hofstadter, Douglas R(ichard) 1945–

US cognitive scientist and writer, Professor of Computer Science at the University of Indiana. His *Godel, Escher, Bach* is a series of ruminations on computers and cognition.

61 Hofstadter's Law: It always takes longer than you expect, even when you take into account Hofstadter's Law.
1979 *Godel, Escher, Bach.*

Hofstadter, Richard 1916–70

US historian, Professor at Columbia University (1946–70). He applied theories of natural selection and ideology to the study of US capitalism and politics in works such as *The Age of Reform* (1955).

62 The nation seems to slouch onward into its uncertain future like some huge inarticulate beast, too much attainted by wounds and ailments to be robust, but too strong and resourceful to succumb.
Quoted in Hedrick Smith *The Power Game* (1988).

63 It has been our fate as a nation not to have ideologies but to be one.
Quoted in the *New York Times*, 2 Jul 1989.

Hogarth, William 1697–1764

English painter and engraver. He is known for his moral paintings and prints of low life (such as the *Industry and Idleness* series, 1747).

64 Simplicity, without variety, is wholly insipid.
    1753 *The Analysis of Beauty.*

Hogg, James 1770–1835

Scottish poet and novelist. The self-taught 'Ettrick Shepherd' divided his time between literary Edinburgh and his native Borders countryside. His best-known work is the psychological novel *The Private Memoirs and Confessions of a Justified Sinner.*

65 Lock the door, Lariston, lion of Liddesdale;
    Lock the door, Lariston, Lowther comes on;
    The Armstrongs are flying,
    The widows are crying,
    The Castletown's burning, and Oliver's gone!
    c.1810 'Lock the Door, Lariston', stanza 1.

66 'What a wonderful boy he is!' said my mother.
    'I'm feared he turn out to be a conceited gowk,' said
    old Barnet, the minister's man.
    1824 *The Private Memoirs and Confessions of a Justified Sinner.*

67 Where the pools are bright and deep,
    Where the grey trout lies asleep,
    Up the river and o'er the lea,
    That's the way for Billy and me.
    1831 'A Boy's Song', stanza 1. From *A Poetic Mirror* 1829–31.

Hoggart, Simon David 1946–

English political commentator and broadcaster, political columnist with *Punch* (1979–85) and parliamentary reporter with *The Guardian* (1993–).

68 The nanny seemed to be extinct until 1975, when, like the coelacanth, she suddenly and unexpectedly reappeared in the shape of Margaret Thatcher.
    1983 In *Vanity Fair*, Aug.

Holland, Henry Scott 1847–1918

English clergyman and theologian, renowned for his eloquent preaching.

69 Death is nothing at all; it does not count. I have only slipped away into the next room.
    1910 Sermon, Whit Sunday.

Hollander, Anne 1930–

US art historian. She explores the connections between fashion and art in *Seeing Through Clothes* (1975).

70 Dress is a form of visual art, a creation of images with the visible self as its medium.
    1975 *Seeing Through Clothes*, ch.5.

Hollinghurst, Alan 1954–

English novelist. He scored a critical success with his frank account of gay life, *The Swimming Pool Library* (1988).

71 My life was a strange one that summer, the last summer of its kind there was ever to be. I was riding high on sex and self-esteem—it was my time, my *belle époque*—but all the while with a faint flicker of calamity, like flames around a photograph, something seen out of the corner of the eye.
    1988 *The Swimming Pool Library*, ch.1.

Holman, James 1786–1857

English naval officer. Although blind from the age of 25 he continued travelling, firstly to the Continent (1819–22), then to the Russian Empire and later to Brazil, South Africa, South Asia, Tasmania, New South Wales and New Zealand.

72 On the summit of the precipice and in the deep green woods emotions as palpable and as true have agitated me as if I were surveying them with the blessing of sight. There was an intelligence in the winds of the hills and in the solemn stillness of the buried foliage that could not be misleading. It entered into my heart and I could have wept, not that I did not see, but that I could not portray all I felt.
    1834 *A Voyage round the World.*

Holme, Richard 1936–

British electoral reformer and writer. He is chairman of the all–party Constitutional Reform Centre and a former President of the Liberal Party.

73 She is the Enid Blyton of economics. Nothing must be allowed to spoil her simple plots.
    1980 Of Margaret Thatcher. Speech at the Liberal Party Conference, 10 Sep.

Holmes, John Clellon 1926–88

US writer. He is credited with first use of the phrase 'The Beat Generation'. His own novels include *Go* (1952) and *The Horn* (1958).

74 To Walden the saxophone was, at once, his key to the world in which he found himself, and the way by which that world was rendered impotent to brand him either a failure or madman or Negro or saint.
    1958 *The Horn*, 'Chorus: Walden'.

75 Jazz music has haunted America for seventy years. It has tempted us out of our lily-white reserve with its black promise of untrammeled joy.
    1979 Preface to reprint of *The Horn.*

76 Some books accrete things to themselves like a magnet. The writer risks sterility by subjecting the

mysterious power of imagination to the devices of mere comprehension.

1979 Preface to reprint of *The Horn*.

Holmes, Oliver Wendell 1809–94

US physician and writer, who in 1842 discovered that puerperal fever was contagious. His essays in the *Atlantic Monthly* were collected in four volumes, including *The Autocrat of the Breakfast Table* (1857–8) and *The Professor at the Breakfast Table* (1858–9). He also published three novels and several volumes of poetry.

77 Man wants but little drink below,
But wants that little strong.
1848 'A Song of Other Days'.

78 And, when you stick on conversation's burrs,
Don't strew your pathway with those dreadful *urs*.
1848 'A Rhymed Lesson'.

79 A moment's insight is sometimes worth a life's experience.
1857–8 *The Autocrat of the Breakfast Table*.

80 They are the brute beasts of the intellectual domain.
1857–8 Of facts. *The Autocrat of the Breakfast Table*, ch.1.

81 A thought is often original, though you have uttered it a hundred times.
1857–8 *The Autocrat of the Breakfast Table*, ch.1.

82 When one has had *all* his conceit taken out of him, when he has lost *all* his illusions, his feathers will soon soak through, and he will fly no more.
1857–8 *The Autocrat of the Breakfast Table*, ch.1.

83 Some of the sharpest men in argument are notoriously unsound in judgment.
1857–8 *The Autocrat of the Breakfast Table*, ch.1.

84 Put not your trust in money, but put your money in trust.
1857–8 *The Autocrat of the Breakfast Table*, ch.2.

85 Build thee more stately mansions, O my soul,
As the swift seasons roll!
Leave thy low-vaulted past!
1857–8 *The Autocrat of the Breakfast Table*, ch.4, 'The Chambered Nautilus'.

86 Truth is tough. It will not break, like a bubble, at a touch; nay, you may kick it about all day like a football, and it will be round and full at evening.
1857–8 *The Autocrat of the Breakfast Table*, ch.5

87 Sin has many tools, but a lie is the handle which fits them all.
1857–8 *The Autocrat of the Breakfast Table*, ch.6.

88 Boston State-House is the hub of the solar system. You couldn't pry that out of a Boston man, if you had the tire of all creation straightened out for a crowbar.
1857–8 *The Autocrat of the Breakfast Table*, ch.6.

89 The world's great men have not commonly been great scholars, nor its great scholars great men.
1857–8 *The Autocrat of the Breakfast Table*, ch.6.

90 Talk about those subjects you have had long in your mind, and listen to what others say about subjects you have studied but recently. Knowledge and timber shouldn't be much used till they are seasoned.
1857–8 *The Autocrat of the Breakfast Table*, ch.6.

91 Shabby gentility has nothing so characteristic as its hat.
1857–8 *The Autocrat of the Breakfast Table*, ch.8.

92 Have you heard of the wonderful one-hoss shay
That was built in such a logical way,
It ran a hundred years to a day.
1857–8 *The Autocrat of the Breakfast Table*, ch.11, 'The Deacon's Masterpiece'.

93 Nothing is so common-place as to wish to be remarkable.
1857–8 *The Autocrat of the Breakfast Table*, ch.12.

94 Fate tried to conceal him by calling him Smith.
1858 Of Samuel Francis Smith. 'The Boys'.

95 Depart,—be off,—excede,—evade,—erump!
1858 'Aestivation'.

96 Apology is only egotism wrong side out.
1858–9 *The Professor at the Breakfast Table*.

97 Fashion is only the attempt to realize Art in living forms and social intercourse.
1858–9 *The Professor at the Breakfast Table*.

98 Lord of all being, throned afar,
Thy glory flames from sun and star;
Centre and soul of every sphere,
Yet to each loving heart how near!
1858–9 *The Professor at the Breakfast Table*.

99 We must have a weak spot or two in a character before we can love it much.
1858–9 *The Professor at the Breakfast Table*.

1 It is the province of knowledge to speak, and it is the privilege of wisdom to listen.
1872 *The Poet at the Breakfast Table*, ch.10.

2 To be seventy years young is sometimes far more cheerful and hopeful than to be forty years old.
1879 Letter to Julia Ward Howe, 27 May.

3 The morning cup of coffee has an exhilaration about it which the cheering influence of the

afternoon or evening cup of tea cannot be expected to reproduce.

1891 *Over the Teacups*, ch.1.

Holmes, Oliver Wendell, Jr 1841–1935

US lawyer, Professor at Harvard Law School, Justice of the US Supreme Court for 30 years.

4 For the rational study of the law the blackletter man may be the man of the present, but the man of the future is the man of statistics and the master of economics.

1897 'The Path of the Law', in the *Harvard Law Review*, 10:469.

Holst, Gustav Theodore 1874–1934

British composer, of Swedish origin. Prevented by neuritis in his hand from becoming a concert pianist, he learned the trombone and taught music before establishing himself as a composer.

5 Never compose anything unless the not composing of it becomes a positive nuisance to you.

1921 Letter to W G Whittaker.

Holt, Harold Edward 1908–67

Australian politician. He succeeded Robert Menzies as Prime Minister in 1966 but disappeared while swimming in the sea off Victoria the following year. He was a supporter of US policy in Vietnam.

6 All the Way with LBJ.

1966 Speech, Washington DC, Jun.

Homans, George C 1910–89

US sociologist, Professor at Harvard University.

7 It is really intolerable that we can say only one thing at a time; for social behavior displays many features at the same time, and so in taking them up one by one we necessarily do outrage to its rich, dark, organic unity.

1961 *Social Behavior: its Elementary Forms*.

8 The rule of distributive justice is a statement of what ought to be, and what people say ought to be is determined in the long run and with some lag by what they find in fact to be the case.

1974 *Social Behavior: its Elementary Forms* (rev edn).

Home of the Hirsel, Baron Alec (Alexander Frederick) Douglas-Home
1903–95

Scottish Conservative statesman. An MP from 1931, he was Chamberlain's secretary during negotiations with Hitler and Mussolini (1937–9). He succeeded as 14th Earl of Home (1951), but after Macmillan's resignation

he renounced his peerage and became Prime Minister (1963–4).

9 As far as the fourteenth earl is concerned, I suppose Mr Wilson, when you come to think of it, is the fourteenth Mr Wilson.

1963 Response to Harold Wilson's claim that the democratic process had 'ground to a halt with a fourteenth earl' when Home won the premiership. Reported in the *Daily Telegraph*, 22 Oct.

10 There are two problems in my life. The political ones are insoluble, and the economic ones are incomprehensible.

1964 Speech, Jan.

11 When I read economic documents, I have to have a box of matches and start moving them into position, to illustrate and simplify the points to myself.

1965 *The Making of the Prime Minister*.

12 Fishing is undoubtedly a form of madness but, happily for the once-bitten, there is no cure.

1976 Quoted in Colin Jarman *The Guinness Dictionary of Sports Quotations* (1990).

13 My wife had an uncle who could never walk down the nave of his abbey without wondering whether it would take spin.

In *The Twentieth Century Revisited*, BBC TV programme, 1982.

14 Oh God, if there be cricket in heaven, let there also be rain.

Quoted in Helen Exley *Cricket Quotations* (1992).

Home, Henry, Lord Kames 1696–1782

Scottish judge, philosopher and agricultural improver, a central figure of the Scottish Enlightenment.

15 Fare ye a' weel, ye bitches!

1782 His alleged words on taking leave of his fellow judges in the Court of Session. He died eight days later. Quoted in Robert Chambers *Traditions of Edinburgh* (1824), 'The Parliament House'.

Homer 8c BC

Greek epic poet, in antiquity said to have been blind, to whom are attributed the *Iliad* (dealing with episodes in the Trojan War) and the *Odyssey* (dealing with the subsequent wanderings of Odysseus). Scholars now date the poems to the eighth century BC, as the culmination of an oral tradition dating back to the Bronze Age.

16 He who battles with the immortals does not live long, nor do his children prattle about his knees when he has returned from battle.

c.700 BC *Iliad*, bk.5, l.407 (translated by Martin Hammond).

17 Like that of leaves is a generation of men.

c.700 BC *Iliad*, bk.6, l.146 (translated by Martin Hammond).

18 Always to be best, and to be distinguished above
the rest.
c.700 BC Motto of the hero Glaucus. *Iliad*, bk.6, l.208
(translated by Martin Hammond).

19 Victory switches from man to man.
c.700 BC *Iliad*, bk.6, l.339 (translated by Martin Hammond).

20 One omen is best of all—to fight for your country.
c.700 BC *Iliad*, bk.7, l.243 (translated by Martin Hammond).

21 Tribeless, lawless, homeless is he who loves the
horror of civil war.
c.700 BC *Iliad*, bk.9, l.63–4 (translated by Martin
Hammond).

22 This is the best portent, to fight in defence of one's
country.
c.700 BC *Iliad*, bk.12, l.243 (translated by Martin Hammond).

23 It is no shame for a man to die fighting for his
country.
c.700 BC *Iliad*, bk.15, l.496 (translated by Martin Hammond).

24 Tell me, Muse, of the man of many ways, who was
driven
far journeys, after he had sacked Troy's sacred
citadel.
Many were they whose cities he saw, whose minds
he learned of,
many the pains he suffered in his spirit on the wide
sea,
struggling for his own life and the homecoming of
his companions.
c.700 BC *Odyssey*, bk.1, l.1–5 (translated by Richmond
Lattimore). Opening lines.

Homer, Winslow 1836–1910

US painter, known for his watercolours of rural and
domestic scenes and especially for his seascapes after
1881.

25 The life that I have chosen gives me my full hours
of enjoyment for the balance of my life. The sun
will not rise, or set, without my notice, and
thanks.
1895 Letter to his brother, Charles, 23 Feb.

26 I regret very much that I have painted a picture that
requires any description.
On being asked about the meaning of a painting by a dealer.
Quoted by Andrea Bennett in the *New York Times Book Review*,
15 Sep 1991.

Honegger, Arthur 1892–1955

French composer of Swiss descent. One of the group of
Parisian composers known as *Les Six*, he established his
reputation with the oratorio *King David* (1921).
Subsequent works include the dramatic oratorio *Joan of
Arc at the Stake* (1936).

27 The modern composer is a madman who persists in
manufacturing an article which nobody wants.
1951 *I am a Composer.*

28 Composing is not a profession. It is a mania—a
harmless madness.
1951 *I am a Composer.*

29 To write music is to raise a ladder without a wall to
lean it against. There is no scaffolding: the building
under construction is held in balance only by the
miracle of a kind of internal logic, an innate sense
of proportion.
1951 *I am a Composer.*

30 The public doesn't want new music: the main thing
it demands of a composer is that he be dead.
1951 *I am a Composer.*

Honorius of Autun fl.1106–35

French ecclesiastic, and the author of numerous
philosophical, theological and devotional works.

31 *Universitas in modo citharae sit disposita, in qua
diversa genera in modo chordarum sit consonantia.*

The universe is arranged like a cithera, in which
different kinds of things sound together
harmoniously, just as they do in a chord.
c.1120 *Liber Duodecim Questionum*, ch.2.

32 *Quid confert animae pugna Hectoris, vel disputatio
Platonis, aut carmina Maronis, vel neniae Nasonis?*

Of what benefit to the soul are the struggles of
Hector, the disputations of Plato, the songs of
Virgil, or the dirges of Ovid?
c.1130 *Gemma Animae*, prologue.

Hood, Thomas 1799–1845

English poet and journalist. His collection *Odes and
Addresses* (1825) was followed by several volumes of
humorous verse and political poems such as *The Story of
the Shirt* (1843).

33 I saw old Autumn in the misty morn
Stand shadowless like Silence, listening
To silence
1823 'Ode: Autumn'.

34 Ben Battle was a soldier bold,
And used to war's alarms:
But a cannon-ball took off his legs,
So he laid down his arms!
1826 'Faithless Nelly Gray'.

35 For here I leave my second leg,
And the Forty-second Foot!
1826 'Faithless Nelly Gray'.

36 The love that loves a scarlet coat

Should be more uniform.
1826 'Faithless Nelly Gray'.

37 I remember, I remember,
The house where I was born,
The little window where the sun
Came peeping in at morn;
He never came a wink too soon,
Nor brought too long a day,
But now, I often wish the night
Had borne my breath away!
1826 'I Remember'.

38 I remember, I remember,
The fir trees dark and high;
I used to think their slender tops
Were close against the sky:
It was a childish ignorance,
But now 'tis little joy
To know I'm farther off from heav'n
Than when I was a boy.
1826 'I Remember'.

39 She stood breast high amid the corn,
Clasped by the golden light of morn,
Like the sweetheart of the sun,
Who many a glowing kiss had won.
1827 'Ruth'.

40 The sedate, sober, silent, serious, sad-coloured sect.
1839 Of the Quakers. *Comic Annual*, 'The Doves and the Crows'.

41 'Extremes meet', as the whiting said with its tail in its mouth.
1839 *Comic Annual*, 'The Doves and the Crows'.

42 Holland...lies so low they're only saved by being dammed.
1840 *Up the Rhine*, 'Letter from Martha Penny to Rebecca Page'.

43 Home-made dishes that drive one from home.
1841–3 *Miss Kilmansegg and her Precious Leg*, 'Her Misery'.

44 When Eve upon the first of Men
The apple pressed with specious cant,
Oh! what a thousand pities then
That Adam was not Adamant!
1842 'A Reflection'.

45 With fingers weary and worn,
With eyelids heavy and red,
A woman sat, in unwomanly rags
Plying her needle and thread—
Stitch! stitch! stitch!
In poverty, hunger, and dirt.
And still with a voice of dolorous pitch
She sang the 'Song of the Shirt'.
1843 'The Song of the Shirt'.

46 O! men with sisters dear,
O! men with mothers and wives!
It is not linen you're wearing out,
But human creatures' lives!
1843 'The Song of the Shirt'.

47 Oh! God! that bread should be so dear,
And flesh and blood so cheap!
1843 'The Song of the Shirt'.

48 Take her up tenderly,
Lift her with care;
Fashioned so slenderly,
Young, and so fair!
1844 'The Bridge of Sighs'.

49 Mad from life's history,
Glad to death's mystery,
Swift to be hurled—
Anywhere, anywhere,
Out of the world!
1844 'The Bridge of Sighs'.

50 But evil is wrought by want of thought,
As well as want of heart!
1844 'The Lady's Dream'.

51 No sun—no moon!
No morn—no noon
No dawn—no dusk—no proper time of day.
1844 'No'.

52 No warmth, no cheerfulness, no healthful ease,
No comfortable feel in any member—
No shade, no shine, no butterflies, no bees,
No fruits, no flowers, no leaves, no birds,—
November!
1844 'No'.

53 What is a modern poet's fate?
To write his thoughts upon a slate;
The critic spits on what is done,
Gives it a wipe—and all is gone.
1897 'A Joke'. Collected in Hallam Tennyson *Alfred Lord Tennyson* (vol.2, ch.3).

Hooker, Richard 1554–1600

English theologian, writer of an extensive treatise on the basis of Church government, which had a powerful influence on Anglican doctrine.

54 See we not plainly that obedience of creatures unto the law of nature is the stay of the whole world?
1594 *Laws of Ecclesiastical Polity*.

55 Man doth seek a triple perfection: first a sensual, consisting in those things which very life itself requireth either as necessary supplements, or as beauties and ornaments thereof; then an intellectual, consisting in those things which none underneath man is either capable of or acquainted

with; lastly a spiritual and divine, consisting in those things whereunto we tend by supernatural means here, but cannot here attain unto them.
1594 *Laws of Ecclesiastical Polity.*

56 They must have hearts very dry and tough, from whom the melody of psalms doth not sometime draw that wherein a mind religiously affected delighteth.
1594 *Laws of Ecclesiastical Polity.*

Hoover, Herbert Clark 1874–1964

US Republican politician. As 31st President (1929–33), his opposition to direct assistance for the unemployed in the recession led to defeat by Roosevelt in 1932. He assisted with various US–European economic relief programmes after World War II.

57 The grass will grow in the streets of a hundred cities, a thousand towns; the weeds will overrun the fields of millions of farms if [tariff protection] is taken away.
1923 Presidential campaign speech, 22 Oct.

58 We are nearer today to the ideal of the abolition of poverty and fear from the lives of men and women than ever before in any land.
1923 Presidential campaign speech, 22 Oct.

59 The American system of rugged individualism.
1928 Speech, New York City, 22 Oct.

60 People moved in hushed and anxious hours while his life lingered on. It was thus I learned that some great man was at the helm of our country.
1951 On President Garfield's assassination, 2 Jul 1881. *The Memoirs of Herbert Hoover,* vol 1.

61 I should have been glad to have humanity forget all about stray alcoholic drinks…but in the present stage of human progress, this vehicle of joy could not be generally suppressed by federal law.
1951 On prohibition. *The Memoirs of Herbert Hoover,* vol.1.

62 All men are equal before a fish.
1951 Quoted in Colin Jarman *The Guinness Dictionary of Sports Quotations* (1990).

63 Democracy is not a polite employer… The only way out of elective office is to get sick or die or get kicked out.
1952 *The Memoirs of Herbert Hoover,* vol.2.

64 The White House…a palace more comfortable than that of most kings.
1952 *The Memoirs of Herbert Hoover,* vol.2.

65 A chameleon on plaid.
On his opponent Franklin D Roosevelt. Quoted in James MacGregor Burns *The Lion and the Fox* (1956).

66 Honour is not the exclusive property of any political party.
1964 In *Christian Science Monitor,* 21 May.

67 Sportsmanship, next to the Church, is the greatest teacher of morals.
Quoted in John Rickards Betts *America's Sporting Heritage: 1850–1950* (1974).

68 Dewey has no inner reserve of knowledge on which to draw for his thinking. A man couldn't wear a moustache like that without having it affect his mind.
Quoted in Richard Norton Smith *An Uncommon Man* (1984).

Hoover, J(ohn) Edgar 1895–1972

US public servant, director of the Federal Bureau of Investigation (1924–72). He remodelled it, making it more efficient, but his vendettas against liberal activists in later years were criticized.

69 We of the FBI are powerless to act in cases of oral–genital intimacy, unless it has in some way obstructed interstate commerce.
Quoted in the *New York Times,* 6 Oct 1980.

70 You are honored by your friends…distinguished by your enemies. I have been very distinguished.
Address to the House Sub-Committee on Appropriations. Quoted in Curt Gentry *J Edgar Hoover* (1991).

Hope, A(lec) D(erwent) 1907–

Australian poet and critic. He retired from academic life in 1972 to concentrate on poetry. Works include *The Wandering Isles* (1955), *The Drifting Continent* (1979) and *The Tragical History of Dr Faustus* (1982).

71 Historians spend their lives and lavish ink
Explaining how great commonwealths collapse
From great defects of policy—perhaps
The cause is sometimes simpler than they think.
…Have more states perished, then,
For having shackled the enquiring mind,
Than those who, in their folly not less blind,
Trusted the servile womb to breed free men?
1965 'Advice to Young Ladies', in *Collected Poems 1930–1970* (1972).

72 They call her a young country, but they lie:
She is the last of lands, the emptiest,
A woman beyond her change of life, a breast
Still tender but within the womb is dry.
'Australia', in *Collected Poems 1930–1970* (1972).

Hope, Sir Anthony Hawkins 1863–1933

English novelist. His novel *The Prisoner of Zenda* (1894), a romantic adventure set in fictitious Ruritania, established him as one of the most popular of all Victorian writers.

73 Oh, for an hour of Herod!

1904 On witnessing the first performance of J M Barrie's children's play *Peter Pan*. Quoted in Denis Mackail *Story of JMB* (1941), ch.17. Records exist of something similar having been said by the English actress Dorothea Jordan when watching the child actor William Betty and his imitators in the early 19c.

Hope, Bob originally *Leslie Townes Hope*
1903–

English-born US actor and humorist. With Bing Crosby and Dorothy Lamour he appeared in the successful *Road to...* comedies (1940–52). An entertainer of troops in World War II and a noted golfer and humanitarian, he became a showbusiness institution.

74 If you watch a game, it's fun. If you play it, it's recreation. If you work at it, it's golf.
   Quoted in the *Reader's Digest*, Oct 1958.

75 I don't know what people have got against Jimmy Carter. He's done nothing.
   1980 Campaign speech for Ronald Reagan, 2 Nov.

76 Fish don't applaud.
   1989 When asked why he didn't retire and go fishing, in the *New York Times*, 28 Sep.

Hopkins, Gerard Manley 1844–89

English poet and Jesuit priest. His work is characterized by religious subjects and the use of natural imagery. His poems include 'The Wreck of the Deutschland' (1876), 'Pied Beauty' (1877) and 'The Windhover' (1877). His poetry was written in secret, only published 30 years after his death.

77 I have desired to go
   Where springs not fail,
   To fields where flies no sharp and sided hail
   And a few lilies blow
   And I have asked to be
   Where no storms come,
   Where the green swell is in the havens dumb,
   And out of the swing of the sea.
   1864 'Heaven-Haven'.

78 Crystal sincerity hath found no shelter but in a fool's cap.
   1864 'Floris in Italy'. Collected in H House and G Storey (eds) *The Journals and Papers of Gerard Manley Hopkins* (1959), p.42.

79 Elected Silence, sing to me
   And beat upon my whorled ear,
   Pipe me to pastures still and be
   The music that I care to hear.
   1866 'The Habit of Perfection'.

80 Palate, the hutch of tasty lust,
   Desire not to be rinsed with wine:
   The can must be so sweet, the crust
   So fresh that come in fasts divine!
   1866 'The Habit of Perfection'.

81 I did say yes

O at lightning and lashed rod;
Thou heardst me truer than tongue confess
Thy terror, O Christ, O God.
1876 'The Wreck of the Deutschland', pt.1, stanza 2.

82 The world is charged with the grandeur of God.
   It will flame out like shining from shook foil...
   Generations have trod, have trod, have trod;
   And all is seared with trade; bleared, smeared with toil;
   And wears man's smudge and shares man's smell: the soil
   Is bare now, nor can foot feel, being shod.
   1877 'God's Grandeur'.

83 Because the Holy Ghost over the bent
   World broods with warm breast and with ah! bright wings.
   1877 'God's Grandeur'.

84 Glory be to God for dappled things.
   1877 'Pied Beauty'.

85 All things counter, original, spare, strange;
   Whatever is fickle, freckled (who knows how?)
   With swift, slow; sweet, sour; adazzle, dim;
   He fathers-forth whose beauty is past change:
   Praise him.
   1877 'Pied Beauty'.

86 The glassy peartree leaves and blooms, they brush
   The descending blue; that blue is all in a rush
   With richness.
   1877 'Spring'.

87 Look at the stars! look, look up at the skies!
   O look at all the fire-folk sitting in the air!
   The bright boroughs, the circle-citadels there!
   1877 'The Starlight Night'.

88 I caught this morning morning's minion, kingdom of
   Daylight's dauphin, dapple-dawn-drawn Falcon.
   1877 'The Windhover'.

89 My heart in hiding
   Stirred for a bid,—the achieve of, the mastery of the thing!
   1877 'The Windhover'.

90 Towery city and branchy between towers;
   Cuckoo-echoing, bell-swarmèd, lark-charmèd, rook-racked, river-rounded.
   1879 Of Oxford. 'Duns Scotus's Oxford', published 1918.

91 Ten or twelve, only ten or twelve
   Strokes of havoc unselve
   The sweet especial scene
   Rural scene, a rural scene
   Sweet especial rural scene.
   1879 'Binsey Poplars'.

92 Margaret, are you grieving
 Over Goldengrove unleaving?
 1880 'Spring and Fall: to a young child'.

93 Ah! as the heart grows older
 It will come to such sights colder
 By and by, not spare a sigh
 Though worlds of wanwood leafmeal lie;
 And yet you *will* weep and know why.
 1880 'Spring and Fall: to a young child'.

94 It is the blight man was born for,
 It is Margaret you mourn for.
 1880 'Spring and Fall: to a young child'.

95 I can scarcely fancy myself to ask a superior to
 publish a volume of my verse and I own that
 humanly there is very little likelihood of that ever
 coming to pass. And to be sure if I chose to look at
 things on one side and not the other I could of
 course regret this bitterly. But there is more peace
 and it is the holier lot to be unknown than to be
 known.
 1881 Letter to Richard Watson Dixon, 29 Oct. Collected in C
 C Abbott (ed) *The Correspondence of Gerard Manley Hopkins
 and Richard Watson Dixon* (1935).

96 What would the world be, once bereft
 Of wet and wildness? Let them be left,
 O let them be left, wildness and wet;
 Long live the weeds and the wilderness yet.
 1881 'Inversnaid'.

97 Time has three dimensions and one positive pitch
 or direction. It is therefore not so much like any
 river or any sea as like the Sea of Galilee, which has
 the Jordan running through it and giving a current
 to the whole.
 1881 'Creation and Redemption The Great Sacrifice'.
 Collected in C Devlin (ed) *The Sermons and Devotional Writings
 of Gerard Manley Hopkins* (1959), ch.8.

98 God...is so great that all things give him glory if
 you mean they should.
 1882 'The Principle or Foundation', closing words. Collected
 in G Roberts (ed) *Gerard Manley Hopkins. Selected Prose* (1980).

99 Wild air, world-mothering air,
 Nestling me everywhere.
 1883 'The Blessed Virgin Compared to the Air We Breathe'.

1 Not, I'll not, carrion comfort, Despair, not feast on
 thee;
 Not untwist—slack they may be—these last
 strands of man
 In me or, most weary, cry *I can no more*. I can;
 Can something, hope, wish day come, not choose
 not to be.
 1885 'Carrion Comfort'.

2 That night, that year

Of now done darkness I wretch lay wrestling with
 (my God!) my God.
 1885 'Carrion Comfort'.

3 No worst, there is none. Pitched past pitch of grief,
 More pangs will, schooled at forepangs, wilder wring.
 Comforter, where, where is your comforting?
 1885 'No worst, there is none'.

4 O the mind, mind has mountains; cliffs of fall
 Frightful, sheer, no-man-fathomed. Hold them
 cheap
 May who ne'er hung there.
 1885 'No worst, there is none'.

5 Here! creep,
 Wretch, under a comfort serves in a whirlwind: all
 Life death does end and each day dies with sleep.
 1885 'No worst, there is none'.

6 The fine pleasure is not to do a thing but to feel
 that you could... If I could but get on, if I could
 but produce a work I should not mind its being
 buried, silenced, and going no further; but it kills
 me to be time's eunuch and never to beget.
 1885 Letter to Robert Bridges, 1 Sep. Collected in C C Abbott
 (ed) *The Correspondence of Gerard Manley Hopkins and Robert
 Bridges* (1935).

7 I am all at once what Christ is, since he was what I
 am, and
 This Jack, joke, poor potsherd, patch, matchwood,
 immortal diamond,
 Is immortal diamond.
 1888 'That Nature is a Heraclitean Fire'.

8 Thou art indeed just, Lord, if I contend
 With thee; but, sir, so what I plead is just.
 Why do sinners' ways prosper? and why must
 Disappointment all I endeavour end?
 1889 'Thou art indeed just, Lord'.

9 Birds build—but not I build; no, but strain,
 Time's eunuch, and not breed one work that wakes.
 Mine, O thou lord of life, send my roots rain.
 1889 'Thou art indeed just, Lord'.

10 The male quality is the creative gift.
 Quoted in C C Abbott (ed) *Correspondence of Gerard Manley
 Hopkins and Richard Watson Dixon* (1935).

11 I always knew in my heart Walt Whitman's mind to
 be more like my own than any other man's living.
 Quoted in Denis Donoghue *England, their England* (1988).

Hopkins, J Castell 1864–1923
Canadian editor and writer.

12 Canada only needs to be known in order to be
 great.
 1901 *The Story of the Dominion*, preface.

Hopper, Edward 1882–1967

US painter, known for his haunting, atmospheric paintings of empty streets and houses. His works include *Early Sunday Morning* (1930).

13 A nation's art is greatest when it most reflects the character of its people.

Quoted in Anatole Broyard *Aroused by Books* (1974).

14 It's probably a reflection of my own, if I may say, loneliness. I don't know. It could be the whole human condition.

On the mood and content of his paintings. Quoted in the *Washington Post*, 25 Jun 1995.

Hopper, Grace Murray 1906–92

US computer scientist and naval officer, developer of the Cobol computer language.

15 Life was simple before World War II. After that, we had systems.

Quoted in the OCLC Newsletter, no.167, Mar/Apr, 1987.

16 We've tended to forget that no computer will ever ask a new question.

Quoted in the OCLC Newsletter, no.167, Mar/Apr, 1987.

17 A ship in port is safe but that's not what ships are built for.

1987 Address at Trinity College, Washington. Reported in *Time*, 22 Jun.

Horace full name *Quintus Horatius Flaccus*

65 BC–8 BC

Roman poet of the Augustan age. His works, which survive in their entirety, include the *Satires* (c.35 BC), *Odes* (c.23–13 BC), *Epistles* (c.19 BC) and the *Ars Poetica* (c.19 BC). His poetry is characterized by an urbane sociability and a love of the country.

18 *Carpe diem.*

Seize the day.

Odes, bk.1, no.11, l.8.

19 *Nunc est bibendum!*

Now is the time to drink!

Odes, bk.1, no.37, l.1.

20 *Eheu fugaces, Postume, Postume, labuntur anni.*

Oh, my Postumus, Postumus, the fleeting years are slipping by.

Odes, bk.2, no.14, l.1.

21 *Odi profanum vulgus et arceo;*
Favete linguis; carmina non prius
Audita Musarum sacerdos
Virginibus puerisque canto.

I despise the uninitiated mob and I warn them off: keep your tongues well-omened; I, priest of the

Muses, am singing songs, never heard before, to girls and boys.

Odes, bk.3, no.1, l.1–5 (translated by G Williams).

22 *Dulce et decorum est pro patria mori.*

It is a sweet and seemly thing to die for one's country.

Odes, bk.3, no.2, l.13.
▷ See Owen 748:13.

24 *Exegi monumentum, aere perennius.*

I have completed a memorial more lasting than bronze.

Odes, bk.3, no.30, l.1.

25 *Vixere fortes ante Agamemnona*
Multi; sed omnes illacrimabiles
Urgentur ignotique longa
Nocte, carent quia vate sacro.

Many brave men lived before Agamemnon's time; but they are all unmourned and unknown, covered by the long night, because they lack their sacred poet.

Odes, bk.4, no.9, l.25–8.

26 *Dulce est desipere in loco.*

Frivolity is sweet, at the right time.

Odes, bk.4, no.12, l.28.

27 *Quo semel est imbuta recens servabit odorem testa diu.*

The first scent you pour in a jar lasts for years.

Epistulae, bk.1, no.2, l.69.

28 *Concordia discors.*

Harmony in discord.

Epistulae, bk.1, no.12, l.7.

29 *Graecia capta ferum victorem cepit et artes*
Intulit agresti Latio.

Captive Greece overcame her savage conqueror and brought the arts into rustic Latium.

Epistulae, bk.2, no.1, l.156.

30 *Brevis esse laboro, Obscurus fio.*

I try hard to be succinct, and am merely obscure.

Ars Poetica, 25.

31 *Si vis me flere, dolendum est,*
Primum ipse tibi.

If you wish me to shed tears
You must first feel pain yourself.

Ars Poetica, 102.

32 *Parturiunt montes; nascetur ridiculus mus.*

The mountains are in labour, and there will be born an absurd little mouse.

Ars Poetica, 139.

33 *Omne tulit punctum, qui miscuit utile dulci.*

The man who has mixed profit with pleasure wins everyone's approval.
Ars Poetica, 343.

34 *Indignor quandoque bonus dormitat Homerus.*

I am vexed when the worthy Homer nods.
Ars Poetica, 359.

35 *Est modus in rebus.*

There is a measure in things.
Satirae, bk.1, no.1, l.106.

Horner, Dr Jack

Curator of Palaeontology, Museum of the Rockies.

36 In the lifetime of one person, we went from figuring out where we came from to figuring out how to get rid of ourselves.
1993 On the 80-year period from Darwin's *Origin of Species* to the first nuclear bomb. In *Time*, 26 Apr.

Hornung, Ernest William 1866–1921

English novelist. Brother-in-law of Arthur Conan Doyle, he created Raffles the gentleman burglar, hero of *The Amateur Cracksman* (1899), *Mr Justice Raffles* (1909) and many other adventure stories.

37 'Cricket,' said Raffles, 'like everything else, is a good enough sport until you discover a better. As a source of excitement it isn't in it with other things you wot of Bunny, and the involuntary comparison becomes a bore. What's the satisfaction of taking a man's wicket when you want his spoons?'
1899 *The Amateur Cracksman.*

Horsley, Samuel 1733–1806

English prelate, most famous for his theological controversy (1783–9) with Joseph Priestly over the uncreated divinity of Christ. He published several scientific works.

38 In *this* country, my Lords…the individual subject…has nothing to do with the laws but to obey them.
1795 Speech in the House of Lords, 13 Nov.

Housman, A(lfred) E(dward) 1859–1936

English scholar and poet. He was a distinguished classical scholar, and is known primarily for his poetry, particularly *A Shropshire Lad* (1896), an anti-pastoral view of country life which was widely popular after an initially cool reception.

39 Loveliest of trees, the cherry now
Is hung with bloom along the bough,
And stands about the woodland ride
Wearing white for Eastertide.
1896 *A Shropshire Lad*, no.2.

40 Now, of my threescore years and ten,
Twenty will not come again,
And take from seventy springs a score,
It only leaves me fifty more.
1896 *A Shropshire Lad*, no.2.

41 And since to look at things in bloom
Fifty springs are little room,
About the woodlands I will go
To see the cherry hung with snow.
1896 *A Shropshire Lad*, no.2.

42 Clay lies still, but blood's a rover;
Breath's a ware that will not keep.
Up, lad: when the journey's over
There'll be time enough to sleep.
1896 *A Shropshire Lad*, no.4.

43 And naked to the hangman's noose
The morning clocks will ring
A neck God made for other use
Than strangling in a string.
1896 *A Shropshire Lad*, no.9.

44 When I was one-and-twenty
I heard a wise man say,
'Give crowns and pounds and guineas
But not your heart away;
Give pearls away and rubies,
But keep your fancy free.'
But I was one-and-twenty
No use to talk to me.
1896 *A Shropshire Lad*, no.13.

45 Oh, when I was in love with you,
Then I was clean and brave,
And miles around the wonder grew
How well I did behave.
1896 *A Shropshire Lad*, no.18.

46 And now the fancy passes by,
And nothing will remain,
And miles around they'll say that I
Am quite myself again.
1896 *A Shropshire Lad*, no.18.

47 And silence sounds no worse than cheers
After dying has stopped the ears.
1896 *A Shropshire Lad*, no.19.

48 Twice a week the winter through
Here I stood to keep the goal:
Football then was fighting sorrow
For the young man's soul.
1896 *A Shropshire Lad*, no.21.

49 In summertime in Bredon
The bells they sound so clear;
Round both the shires they ring them
In steeples far and near,

A happy noise to hear.
1896 *A Shropshire Lad*, no.21.

50 Here of a Sunday morning
My love and I would lie,
And see the coloured counties,
And hear the larks so high
About us in the sky.
1896 *A Shropshire Lad*, no.21.

51 'Come all to church, good people,'—
Oh, noisy bells, be dumb;
I hear you, I will come.
1896 *A Shropshire Lad*, no.21.

52 The lads in their hundreds to Ludlow come in for
the fair,
There's men from the barn and the forge and the
mill and the fold,
The lads for the girls and the lads for the liquor are
there,
And there with the rest are lads that will never be
old.
1896 *A Shropshire Lad*, no.23.

53 On Wenlock Edge the wood's in trouble;
His forest fleece the Wrekin heaves;
The wind it plies the saplings double,
And thick on Severn snow the leaves.
1896 *A Shropshire Lad*, no.31.

54 The gale, it plies the saplings double,
It blows so hard, 'twill soon be gone:
To-day the Roman and his trouble
Are ashes under Uricon.
1896 *A Shropshire Lad*, no.31.

55 From far, from eve and morning
And yon twelve-winded sky,
The stuff of life to knit me
Blew hither: here am I.
1896 *A Shropshire Lad*, no.32.

56 Speak now, and I will answer;
How shall I help you, say;
Ere to the wind's twelve quarters
I take my endless way.
1896 *A Shropshire Lad*, no.32.

57 Into my heart an air that kills
From yon far country blows:
What are those blue remembered hills,
What spires, what farms are those?
1896 *A Shropshire Lad*, no.40.

58 That is the land of lost content,
I see it shine plain,
The happy highways where I went
And cannot come again.
1896 *A Shropshire Lad*, no.40.

59 And bound for the same bourn as I,
On every road I wandered by,
Trod beside me, close and dear,
The beautiful and death-struck year.
1896 *A Shropshire Lad*, no.41.

60 Clunton and Clunbury,
Clungunford and Clun,
Are the quietest places
Under the sun.
1896 *A Shropshire Lad*, no.50, epigraph.

61 With rue my heart is laden
For golden friends I had,
For many a rose-lipt maiden
And many a lightfoot lad.
1896 *A Shropshire Lad*, no.54.

62 By brooks too broad for leaping
The lightfoot boys are laid;
The rose-lipt girls are sleeping
In fields where roses fade.
1896 *A Shropshire Lad*, no.54.

63 Say, for what were hop-yards meant,
Or why was Burton built on Trent?
Oh many a peer of England brews
Livelier liquor than the Muse,
And malt does more than Milton can
To justify God's ways to man.
Ale, man, ale's the stuff to drink
For fellows whom it hurts to think.
1896 *A Shropshire Lad*, no.62.

64 Oh I have been to Ludlow fair
And left my necktie God knows where,
And carried half-way home, or near,
Pints and quarts of Ludlow beer.
1896 *A Shropshire Lad*, no.62.

65 Then the world seemed none so bad,
And I myself a sterling lad;
And down in lovely muck I've lain,
Happy till I woke again.
1896 *A Shropshire Lad*, no.62.

66 I tell the tale that I heard told.
Mithridates, he died old.
1896 *A Shropshire Lad*, no.62.

67 This great College, of this ancient University, has
seen some strange sights. It has seen Wordsworth
drunk and Porson sober. And here am I, a better
poet than Porson, and a better scholar than
Wordsworth, betwixt and between.
1911 Speech on taking up the Chair of Latin at Trinity College,
Cambridge.

68 Pass me the can, lad; there's an end of May.
1922 *Last Poems*, no.9.

69 May will be fine next year as like as not:
Oh, ay, but then we shall be twenty-four.
1922 *Last Poems*, no.9.

70 We for a certainty are not the first
Have sat in taverns while the tempest hurled
Their hopeful plans to emptiness, and cursed
Whatever brute and blackguard made the world.
1922 *Last Poems*, no.9.

71 The troubles of our proud and angry dust
Are from eternity, and shall not fail.
Bear them we can, and if we can we must.
Shoulder the sky, my lad, and drink your ale.
1922 *Last Poems*, no.9.

72 But men at whiles are sober
And think by fits and starts,
And if they think, they fasten
Their hands upon their hearts.
1922 *Last Poems*, no.10.

73 The laws of God, the laws of man,
He may keep that will and can;
Not I: let God and man decree
Laws for themselves and not for me;
And if my ways are not as theirs
Let them mind their own affairs.
1922 *Last Poems*, no.12.

74 And how am I to face the odds
Of man's bedevilment and God's?
I, a stranger and afraid
In a world I never made.
1922 *Last Poems*, no.12.

75 The candles burn their sockets,
The blinds let through the day,
The young man feels his pockets
And wonders what's to pay.
1922 *Last Poems*, no.21.

76 To think that two and two are four
And neither five nor three
The heart of man has long been sore
And long 'tis like to be.
1922 *Last Poems*, no.35.

77 These, in the day when heaven was falling,
The hour when earth's foundations fled,
Followed their mercenary calling
And took their wages and are dead.
1922 *Last Poems*, no.37, 'Epitaph on an Army of Mercenaries'.

78 Their shoulders held the sky suspended;
They stood, and earth's foundations stay;
What God abandoned, these defended,
And saved the sum of things for pay.
1922 *Last Poems*, no.37, 'Epitaph on an Army of Mercenaries'.

79 For nature, heartless, witless nature,

Will neither care nor know
What stranger's feet may find the meadow
And trespass there and go,
Nor ask amid the dews of morning
If they are mine or no.
1922 *Last Poems*, no.40.

80 Experience has taught me, when I am shaving of a
morning, to keep watch over my thoughts, because,
if a line of poetry strays into my memory, my skin
bristles so that the razor ceases to act.
1933 'The Name and Nature of Poetry', Lecture at Cambridge,
9 May.

81 The seat of this sensation is the pit of the stomach.
1933 'The Name and Nature of Poetry', Lecture at Cambridge,
9 May.

82 The stroke of midnight ceases,
And I lie down alone.
1936 *More Poems*, no.11.

83 Life, to be sure, is nothing much to lose;
But young men think it is, and we were young.
1936 *More Poems*, no.36.

84 Good-night. Ensured release
Imperishable peace,
Have these for yours,
While earth's foundations stand
And sky and sea and land
And heaven endures.
1936 *More Poems*, no.48.

85 That is indeed very good. I shall have to repeat that
on the Golden Floor!
1936 Remark made to his doctor after the latter had told him a
risqué story on his death-bed.

86 The Grizzly bear is huge and wild;
He has devoured the infant child.
The infant child is not aware
He has been eaten by the bear.
'Infant Innocence', collected *The Oxford Book of Light Verse*
(1938).

87 Oh who is that young sinner with the handcuffs on
    his wrist?
And what has he been after that they groan and
    shake their fists?
And wherefore is he wearing such a conscience-
    stricken air?
Oh they're taking him to prison for the colour of
    his hair.
'Additional Poems', no.18, in *Collected Poems* (1939).

88 'Tis a shame to human nature, such a head of hair
    as his;
In the good old time 'twas hanging for the colour
    that it is;

Though hanging isn't bad enough and flaying
would be fair
For the nameless and abominable colour of his hair.

'Additional Poems', no.18, in *Collected Poems* (1939).

89 Now hollow fires burn out to black
And lamps are guttering low. .
Square your shoulders, lift your pack,
And leave your friends and go.

Oh, never fear, man, nought's to dread
Look not left nor right.
In all the endless road you tread,
There's nothing but the night.

Quoted in Bernard Levin *Hannibal's Footsteps* (1985).

How, William Walsham 1823–97

English churchman and religious writer, the first Bishop
of Wakefield.

90 For all the Saints who from their labours rest,
Who Thee by faith before the world confess'd,
Thy name, O Jesu, be for ever blest,
Alleluia!

1864 'For All the Saints', in Earl Nelson *Hymns for Saints' Days*.

91 From earth's wide bounds, from ocean's farthest
coast,
Through gates of pearl streams in the countless
host,
Singing to Father, Son, and Holy Ghost,
Alleluia!

1864 'For All the Saints', in Earl Nelson *Hymns for Saints' Days*.

Howard, Thomas, Earl of Surrey and 2nd Duke of Norfolk 1443–1524

English nobleman and soldier. He fought for Richard III
at Bosworth (1485) and was imprisoned by Henry VII,
but regained his estates and led successful campaigns
against the Scots, including Flodden (1513).

92 He was my crowned King, and if the Parliamentary
authority of England set the crown upon a stock, I
will fight for that stock: And as I fought then for
him, I will fight for you, when you are established
by the said authority.

1485 Explaining before the future Henry VII his reasons for
siding with Richard III at Bosworth, 22 Aug. Quoted in
William Camden *Remains Concerning Britain* (1605).

Howe (of Aberavon), (Richard Edward) Geoffrey Howe, Baron 1926–

English Conservative politician. In 1989 he became
Deputy Prime Minister, Lord President of the Council
and Leader of the House of Commons. His resignation
from Margaret Thatcher's Government in Nov 1990, and
his subsequent resignation speech, were instrumental in
her downfall.

93 Megaphone diplomacy leads to a dialogue of the
deaf.

1985 Quoted in *The Observer*, 29 Sep.

94 How on earth are the Chancellor of the Exchequer
and the Governor of the Bank of England…to be
taken seriously against that kind of background
noise? It is rather like sending your opening
batsmen to the crease, only for them to find, the
moment the first balls are bowled, that their bats
have been broken before the game by the team
captain.

1990 Personal statement on his resignation, House of
Commons, 13 Nov.

95 If some of my former colleagues are to be believed,
I must be the first Minister in history to have
resigned because he was in full agreement with
Government policy.

1990 Personal statement on his resignation, House of
Commons, 13 Nov.

Howe, Gordie (Gordon) 1928–

Canadian hockey player.

96 All pro athletes are bilingual. They speak English
and profanity.

Dismissing Canadian bilingualism. Quoted by George
Gamester in *The Toronto Star*, 27 May 1975.

Howe, Joseph 1804–73

Anglo-Canadian journalist and statesman.

97 A wise nation preserves its records, gathers up its
muniments, decorates the tombs of its illustrious
dead, repairs its great public structures, and fosters
national pride and love of country, by perpetual
references to the sacrifices and glories of the past.

1871 Address at Framingham, Massachusetts, 31 Aug.
Collected in *Poems and Essays* (1874).

Howe, Julia Ward 1819–1910

US feminist and writer, influential in suffragette and
Unitarian causes. Her poetry collections include *Passion
Flowers* (1854). She made history as the first woman
member of the American Academy.

98 Mine eyes have seen the glory of the coming of the
Lord:
He is tramping out the vintage where the grapes of
wrath are stored.
He hath loosed the fatal lightning of his terrible
swift sword:
His truth is marching on.

1862 'Battle Hymn of the Republic'.

Howe, Louis McHenry 1871–1936

US diplomat.

99 You can't adopt politics as a profession and hope to remain honest.
1933 Speech, Columbia University, 17 Jan.

Hoyle, Edmond 1672–1769

English authority on card games. He published manuals on whist, backgammon, brag, quadrille, piquet and chess.

1 When in doubt, win the trick.
A Short Treatise on the Game of Whist (first published 1742, this edn edited by Charles Jones, 1790). This may be an addition by Jones.

Hoyle, Sir Fred 1915–

English astronomer and mathematician, one of the first to apply modern physics to cosmology. He was knighted in 1972.

2 To take an almost religious view, this earth is nothing very special. There have probably been millions of earths just like ours each producing a particular intelligent species. That is not to say that they all developed well, that they all achieved some sort of perfection. And if the planner made lots of them and some of them chose to destroy themselves, then we can only suppose that the planner is a hard and practical man.
1974 In the *Daily Mail.*

Hubbard, Elbert Green 1856–1915

US writer, editor and printer.

3 Life is just one damned thing after another.
1909 In *The Philistine,* Dec.

4 Little minds are interested in the extraordinary; great minds in the commonplace.
1911 *Thousand and One Epigrams.*

5 One machine can do the work of fifty ordinary men. No machine can do the work of one extraordinary man.
1911 *Thousand and One Epigrams,* no.46.

6 Editor: a person employed by a newspaper, whose business it is to separate the wheat from the chaff, and to see that the chaff is printed.
1914 *The Roycroft Dictionary.*

7 College football is a sport that bears the same relation to education that bullfighting does to agriculture.
Quoted in Colin Jarman *The Guinness Dictionary of Sports Quotations* (1990).

Hubble, Edwin Powell 1889–1953

US astronomer. In 1929 he formulated Hubble's law: galaxies recede with speeds directly proportionate to their distance from us, confirming that the universe is expanding. The space telescope launched in 1990 was named in his honour.

9 We measure shadows, and we search among ghostly errors of measurement for landmarks that are scarcely more substantial.
Quoted in Dennis Overbye *Lonely Hearts of the Cosmos* (1991).

Hügel, Friedrich von, Baron 1852–1925

Austrian-born British theologian and Bible critic, son of the Austrian Ambassador in Italy. He settled in England in 1871. His works include *The Mystical Element in Religion* (1908–9) and *The Reality of God* (published 1931).

10 I take these to be the seven great facts and doctrines concerning God—his richness; his double action, natural and supernatural; his perfect freedom; his delightfulness; his otherness; his adorableness and his prevenience.
The Life of Prayer (published 1927).

11 Christianity has taught us to care. Caring is the greatest thing, caring matters most.
Letter to his niece.

Hugh of St Victor c.1096–1141

German divine and scholar, who entered the Augustinian order despite his parents' objections. In 1115 he was sent to the Abbey of St Victor in Paris, where he completed his vows, later becoming master of the school. He composed many treatises on theological, philosophical and devotional subjects.

12 *Delicatus illi est adhuc cui patria dulcis est. Fortis autem jam qui omne solum patria est, perfectus vero evi mundus totus exsilium est.*

He whose own homeland is sweet to him is a mere beginner. He to whom every soil is as his native land is strong. But he to whom the whole world is a place of exile has achieved perfection.
c.1127 *Didascalicon,* bk.3, ch.20.

Hughes, Howard Robard 1905–76

US millionaire businessman, film producer and aviator. Known as an eccentric, he left Hollywood in 1932 to design, build and fly aircraft before returning to film production. After 1966 he lived in complete seclusion.

13 That man's ears make him look like a taxi-cab with both doors open.

Of Clark Gable. Quoted in Charles Higham and Joel Greenbert *Celluloid Muse* (1969).

Hughes, (James Mercer) Langston
1902–67

US poet, a leading figure of the Harlem Renaissance, whose poetry and sketches reflect folk culture, jazz, blues, and colloquial speech. His works include *Weary Blues* (1926) and the autobiographical *The Big Sea* (1940).

14 I, too, sing America.

I am the darker brother.
They send me to eat in the kitchen
When company comes.
But I laugh
And eat well,
And grow strong.

1925 'I, Too', in *Survey Graphic*, Mar.

15 Tomorrow
I'll sit at the table
when company comes
Nobody'll dare
Say to me,
'Eat in the kitchen'
Then.

1925 'I, Too', in *Survey Graphic*, Mar.

16 Swaying to and fro on his rickety stool
He played that sad raggy tune like a musical fool.
Sweet blues!

1926 'The Weary Blues'.

17 I swear to the Lord,
I still can't see,
Why Democracy means,
Everybody but me.

1943 'The Black Man Speaks'.

18 What happens to a dream deferred?

Does it dry up
like a raisin in the sun?

1951 'Dream Deferred'. Lorraine Hansberry used the phrase for the title of her play *A Raisin in the Sun* (1959).

19 Maybe it just sags
like a heavy load.

Or does it explode?

1951 'Dream Deferred'.

20 You are white—
yet a part of me, as I am a part of you.
That's American.

1951 'Theme for English B'.

21 A wonderful time—the War:

when money rolled in
and blood rolled out.

1951 'Green Memory'.

22 'It's powerful,' he said.
'What?'
'That one drop of negro blood—because *just* one drop of black blood makes a man coloured. *One* drop—you are a Negro!'

1953 *Simple Takes a Wife*.

Hughes, Richard Arthur Warren 1900–76

English novelist. He is best known for his adventure tale *A High Wind in Jamaica* (1929, entitled *The Innocent Voyage* in the US). Other works include *Hazard: A Sea Story* (1938), *The Fox in the Attic* (1961) and *The Wooden Shepherdess* (1972).

23 Nature is as wasteful of promising young men as she is of fish-spawn. It's not just getting them killed in wars: mere middle age snuffs out ten times more talent than ever wars and sudden death do.

1961 *The Fox in the Attic*, bk.1, ch.18.

24 For a politician rises on the backs of his friends (that's probably all they're good for), but it's through his enemies he'll have to govern afterwards.

1961 *The Fox in the Attic*, bk.2, ch.20.

25 Do your bit to save humanity from lapsing back into barbarity by reading all the novels you can.

1975 Speech at Foyle's Literary Luncheon, London, in honour of his 75th birthday.

Hughes, Robert Studley Forrest 1938–

Australian-born US art critic, writer with *Time* magazine (1970–). His works include *The Art of Australia* (1966), *Fatal Shores* (1987) and *Nothing If Not Critical* (1990).

26 Lentil-soup colors.

1981 Of the paints used by French realists. In *Time*, 13 Apr.

27 The protein of our cultural imagination.

1984 Of the US Museum of Modern Art. In *Time*, 14 May.

28 Close by the Hudson, in MANHATTAN'S TOWN,
The iron palaces of Art glare down
On such as, wandering in the streets below,
Perambulate in glamorous SoHo,
A spot acclaimed by savant and by bard
As forcing chamber of the Avant-Garde.

1984 'The SoHoiad', in the *New York Review of Books*.

29 Popular in our time, unpopular in his. So runs the stereotype of rejected genius.

1985 On a Caravaggio exhibition. In *Time*, 11 Mar.

30 Landscape is to American painting what sex and
psychoanalysis are to the American novel.
1985 In *Time*, 30 Dec.

31 [A Gustave Courbet] portrait of a trout…has more
death in it than Rubens could get in a whole
Crucifixion.
1986 In *Time*, 15 Sep.

32 Its clones have hung on so many suburban walls
over the decades that it has become the *Mona Lisa*
of the vegetable world.
1987 On Vincent van Gogh's *Sunflowers*. In *Time*, 13 Apr.

33 The self is now the sacred cow of American culture,
self-esteem is sacrosanct, and so we labour to turn
arts education into a system in which no one can
fail. In the same spirit, tennis could be shorn of its
elitist overtones: you just get rid of the net.
1994 *Culture of Complaint: The Fraying of America*.

34 America came up with the idea of therapeutic
avant-gardism, and built museums in its name.
These temples stood on two pillars. The first was
aestheticism… The second was the familiar one of
social benefit.
1994 *Culture of Complaint: The Fraying of America*

Hughes, Ted (Edward James) 1930–98

English poet. His elemental, highly symbolic works
include *The Hawk in the Rain* (1957) and *Crow* (1970).
He was appointed Poet Laureate in 1984.

35 The world rolls under the long thrust of his heel.
Over the cage floor the horizons come.
1957 'The Jaguar'.

36 It took the whole of Creation
To produce my foot, my each feather:
Now I hold Creation in my foot.
1960 'Hawk Roosting'.

37 Nothing has changed since I began.
My eye has permitted no change.
I am going to keep things like this.
1960 'Hawk Roosting'.

38 Pike, three inches long, perfect
Pike in all parts, green tigering the gold.
Killers from the egg: the malevolent aged grin.
1960 'Pike'.

39 The gash in its throat was shocking, but not
pathetic.
1960 'View of a Pig'.

40 The deeps are cold:
In that darkness camaraderie does not hold:
Nothing touches but, clutching, devours.
1960 'Relic'.

41 The brassy wood-pigeons
Bubble their colourful voices, and the sun
Rises upon a world well-tried and old.
1967 'Stealing Trout on a May Morning'.

42 No, the serpent did not
Seduce Eve to the apple.
All that's simply
Corruption of the facts.

Adam ate the apple.
Eve ate Adam.
The serpent ate Eve.
This is the dark intestine.

The serpent, meanwhile,
Sleeps his meal off in Paradise—
Smiling to hear
God's querulous calling.
1967 'Theology'.

43 Who owns the whole rainy, stony earth? *Death*.
Who owns all of space? *Death*.
1970 'Examination at the Womb-door'.

44 But who is stronger than death?
Me, evidently.
1970 'Examination at the Womb-door'.

45 And he shivered with the horror of Creation.
1970 'Crow Alights'.

46 But Oedipus he had the luck
For when he hit the ground
He bounced up like a jackinabox
And knocked his Daddy down.
1970 'Song for a Phallus'.

47 And the elephant sings deep in the forest-maze
About a star of deathless and painless peace
But no astronomer can find where it is.
1972 'Crow's Elephant Totem Song'.

48 Black village of gravestones.
1979 'Heptonstall'.

49 Only the rain never tires.
1979 'Heptonstall'.

Hughes, Thomas 1822–96

English reformer and novelist. Called to the bar in 1848,
a Liberal MP (1865–74), and a county court judge
(1882), he is best remembered for his semi-
autobiographical classic, *Tom Brown's Schooldays* (1856).

50 Life isn't all beer and skittles—but beer and skittles,
or something better of the same sort, must form a
good part of every Englishman's education.
1856 *Tom Brown's Schooldays*, pt.1, ch.2.

51 He never wants anything but what's right and fair,
only when you come to settle what's right and fair,

it's everything that he wants and nothing that you want. And that's his idea of a compromise. Give me the Brown compromise when I'm on his side.
1856 *Tom Brown's Schooldays*, pt.2, ch.2.

52 It's more than a game. It's an institution.
1856 Of cricket. *Tom Brown's Schooldays*, pt.2, ch.7.

Hughes, William Morris 1864–1952

Welsh-born Australian statesman. He emigrated in 1884 and became Minister for External Affairs (1904) in the first Labour Government and subsequently Prime Minister (1915–23). He founded the United Australian party.

53 Mr President, I speak for sixty thousand dead!
1919 Reply to Woodrow Wilson at the Versailles Peace Conference, Jan, referring to the ANZAC fatalities in World War I. Wilson had asked 'Mr Hughes, I speak for very many millions of people. For whom do you speak?'.

54 Without the Empire we should be tossed like a cork in the cross current of world politics. It is at once our sword and our shield.
1926 Speech, Melbourne.

Hugo, Victor Marie 1802–85

French poet, dramatist, and novelist. His great epics are *The Hunchback of Notre Dame* (1831) and *Les Misérables* (1862). His writings and theories were enormously influential.

55 *Le beau n'a qu'un type; le laid en a mille.*

Beauty has only one form; ugliness has a thousand.
1827 *Cromwell*, préface.

56 *Les temps primitifs sont lyriques, les temps antiques sont épiques, les temps modernes sont dramatiques.*

The primitive era was lyrical, the classical era was epic and the modern era is dramatic.
1827 *Cromwell*, préface.

57 *Il n'y a ni règles ni modèles; ou plutôt il n'y a d'autres règles que les lois générales de la nature qui planent sur l'art tout entier, et les lois spéciales qui, pour chaque composition, résultent des conditions d'existence propres à chaque sujet.*

There are no rules or models; that is, there are no rules except general laws of nature which hover over the entire earth and special laws which apply to specific conditions.
1827 *Cromwell*, préface.

58 *La vérité de l'art ne saurait jamais être…la réalité absolue. L'art ne peut donner la chose même.*

The truth of art should never be…*absolute reality.* Art should not show the thing itself.
1827 *Cromwell*, préface.

59 *Le but de l'art est presque divin: ressusciter, s'il fait de l'histoire; créer, s'il fait de la poésie.*

The goal of art is almost divine: to resuscitate, if it concerns history; to create, if it concerns poetry.
1827 *Cromwell*, préface.

60 *Le vers est la forme optique de la pensée. Voilà pourquoi il convient surtout à la perspective scénique.*

Verse is the optical form of thought. That is the reason a scenic perspective suits it.
1827 *Cromwell*, préface.

61 *La langue française n'est point fixée et ne se fixera point.*

French is not a *static* language and will never become static.
1827 *Cromwell*, préface.

62 *Sois donc ami sincère ou sincère ennemi,*
Et ne reste pas traître et fidèle à demi.

Be either a sincere friend or a sincere enemy,
And never be half-traitor and half-faithful.
1827 *Cromwell*, act 1, sc.1.

63 *L'Angleterre toujours sera sœur de la France.*

England will always be the sister of France.
1827 *Cromwell*, act 2, sc.2.

64 *Vous me manquez, je suis absente de moi-même.*

I miss you, I am estranged from myself.
1830 *Hernani*, act 1, sc.2.

65 *Nos pères avaient un Paris de pierre, nos fils auront un Paris de plâtre.*

Our fathers had a Paris made of stone; our sons will have a Paris made of plaster.
1831 *Notre-Dame de Paris*, pt.3, ch.2.

66 *Rêver, c'est le bonheur; attendre, c'est la vie.*

To dream is happiness; to wait is life.
1831 *Les Feuilles d'automne*, no.27, 'A mes amis L.B. et S.-B.'.

67 *Au banquet du bonheur bien peu sont conviés.*

Few are invited to the banquet of happiness.
1831 *Les Feuilles d'automne*, no.32, 'Pour les pauvres'.

68 *Mêlez toute votre âme à la création!*

Involve all of your soul in creation!
1831 *Les Feuilles d'automne*, no.38, 'Pan'.

69 *O Virgile! ô poète! ô mon maître divin!*

Oh Virgil! Oh poet! Oh my divine master!
1837 *Les Voix intérieures*, no.7, 'A Virgile'.

70 *Le drame tient de la tragédie par la peinture des passions et de la comédie par la peinture des caractères. Le drame est la troisième grande forme de l'art.*

In drama, tragedy paints the passions and comedy paints characters. Drama is the third great form of art.
1838 *Ruy Blas*, préface.

71 *Je ne veux pas tomber, non, je veux disparaître.*

I do not want to fall; I want to disappear.
1838 *Ruy Blas*, act 1, sc.1.

72 *Visage de traître!*
Quand la bouche dit oui, le regard dit peut-être.

Face of a traitor!
When the mouth says yes, the look says maybe.
1838 *Ruy Blas*, act 1, sc.2.

73 *Sous l'habit d'un valet, les passions d'un roi.*

Beneath the clothing of a manservant, the passions of a king.
1838 *Ruy Blas*, act 1, sc.3.

74 *Les femmes aiment fort à sauver qui les perd.*

Women try hard to save those who damn them.
1838 *Ruy Blas*, act 1, sc.4.

75 *Dieu s'est fait homme; Soit! Le diable s'est fait femme.*

God made himself a man. So be it! The devil made himself a woman.
1838 *Ruy Blas*, act 2, sc.5.

76 *Tout se fait par intrigue et rien par loyauté.*

Everything is done by intrigue, not by loyalty.
1838 *Ruy Blas*, act 3, sc.2.

77 *Ah! toute nation bénit qui la délie.*

Ah! every nation blesses what undoes it.
1838 *Ruy Blas*, act 3, sc.5.

78 *La popularité? c'est la gloire en gros sous.*

Popularity? It is glory in large coins.
1838 *Ruy Blas*, act 3, sc.5.

79 *Le mot, c'est le Verbe, et le Verbe, c'est Dieu.*

The word is the Verb, and the Verb is God.
1856 *Contemplations*, bk.1, no.8.

80 *Cette cloison qui nous sépare du mystère des choses et que nous appelons la vie.*

Life is a screen which separates us from the mystery of things.
1862 *Les Misérables*, vol.1, bk.1, ch.2.

81 *Ce génie particulier de la femme qui comprend l'homme mieux que l'homme ne se comprend.*

A woman's particular talent is to understand a man better than he understands himself.
1862 *Les Misérables*, vol.1, bk.1, ch.9.

82 *Les livres sont des amis froids et sûrs.*

Books are cold and certain friends.

1862 *Les Misérables*, vol.1, bk.5, ch.3.

83 *Conscience déchirée entraîne vie décousue.*

A torn conscience brings about a disconnected life.
1862 *Les Misérables*, vol.2, bk.1, ch.16.

84 *La symétrie, c'est l'ennui, et l'ennui est le fond même du deuil. Le désespoir bâille.*

Symmetry is boredom and boredom is the foundation of grief. Despair yawns.
1862 *Les Misérables*, vol.2, bk.4, ch.1.

85 *Personne ne garde un secret comme un enfant.*

No one keeps a secret like a child.
1862 *Les Misérables*, vol.2, bk.7, ch.8.

86 *Respirer Paris, cela conserve l'âme.*

To inhale Paris preserves the soul.
1862 *Les Misérables*, vol.3, bk.1, ch.6.

87 *On jugerait bien plus sûrement un homme d'après ce qu'il rêve que d'après ce qu'il pense.*

We would judge a man more certainly according to his dreams than to his thoughts.
1862 *Les Misérables*, vol.3, bk.5, ch.5.

88 *On a voulu, à tort, faire de la bourgeoisie une classe. La bourgeoisie est tout simplement la portion contentée du peuple. Le bourgeois, c'est l'homme qui a maintenant le temps de s'asseoir. Une chaise n'est pas une caste.*

Wrongly, one wanted to make the bourgeoisie a class. The bourgeoisie is simply a contented section of the public. A bourgeois is a man who now has the time to sit down. A chair is not a caste.
1862 *Les Misérables*, vol.4, bk.1, ch.2.

89 *La première égalité, c'est l'équité.*

The first equality is equity.
1862 *Les Misérables*, vol.4, bk.1, ch.4.

90 *Le premier symptôme de l'amour vrai chez un jeune homme, c'est la timidité, chez une jeune fille, c'est la hardiesse.*

The first symptom of true love in a young man is timidity; in a young woman, it is boldness.
1862 *Les Misérables*, vol.4, bk.3, ch.6.

91 *Le dix-neuvième siècle est grand, mais le vingtième sera heureux.*

The nineteenth century is great, but the twentieth will be happy.
1862 *Les Misérables*, vol.5, bk.1, ch.4.

92 *Le suicide, cette mystérieuse voie de fait sur l'inconnu.*

Suicide: that mysterious route towards the unknown.
1862 *Les Misérables*, vol.5, bk.3, ch.10.

93 *Jésus a pleuré, Voltaire a souri; c'est de cette larme divine et de ce sourire humain qu'est faite la douceur de la civilisation actuelle.*

Jesus wept; Voltaire smiled. Of that divine tear and of that human smile the sweetness of present civilisation is composed.

1878 Speech on Voltaire's centenary, 30 May.

94 Science says the first word on everything and the last word on nothing.

Things of the Infinite (translated by L O'Rouke, 1907).

Huidobro, Vicente 1893–1948

Chilean poet, who wrote in French as well as Spanish. He created the movement known as *creacionismo*, which abandons traditional descriptive poetry.

95 *Que se rompa el andamio de los huesos
Que se desrrumben las vigas del cerebro
Y arrastre el huracán los trozos a la nada al otro lado
En donde el viento azota a Dios*

Smash the scaffold of the bones
Pull down the rafters of the brain
Let the hurricane drag the pieces to the nothing on the other side
Where the wind thrashes God

1931 *Altazor o el viaje en paracaídas*, canto 1 (translated as *Altazor, or, A Voyage in a Parachute*, 1988).

Humboldt, Alexander Freiherr, Baron von

1769–1859

German naturalist and traveller. He travelled through Central and South America (1799–1804), and his observations laid the foundations for the sciences of physical geography and meteorology.

96 In the sphere of natural investigation, as in poetry and painting, the delineation of that which appeals most strongly to the imagination, derives its collective interest from the vivid truthfulness with which the individual features are portrayed.

1897 *Cosmos*, vol.1.

97 The great and solemn spirit that pervades the intellectual labor (of science) arises from the sublime consciousness of striving toward the infinite, and of grasping all that is revealed to us amid the boundless and inexhaustible fullness of creation, development and being.

1897 *Cosmos*, vol.3.

Hume, David 1711–76

Scottish philosopher and historian. His most important work, the empiricist *A Treatise of Human Nature*, was published anonymously (1739–40). He published a five-volume *History of England* (1754–62) and was secretary to the British Ambassador in Paris (1763–5).

98 Let us fix our attention out of ourselves as much as possible; let us chase our imagination to the heavens, or to the utmost limits of the universe; we never really advance a step beyond ourselves, nor can conceive any kind of existence, but those perceptions, which have appeared in that narrow compass.

1739 *A Treatise of Human Nature*, bk.1, pt.2, section 6.

99 We have no other notion of cause and effect, but that of certain objects, which have been *always conjoined* together, and which in all past instances have been found inseparable.

1739 *A Treatise of Human Nature*, bk.1, pt.3, section 6.

1 For my part, when I enter most intimately into what I call *myself*, I always stumble on some particular perception or other, of heat or cold, light or shade, pain or pleasure. I never can catch *myself* at any time without a perception, and never can observe anything but the perception.

1739 *A Treatise of Human Nature*, bk.1, pt.4, section 6.

2 In all the events of life, we ought still to preserve our scepticism. If we believe that fire warms, or water refreshes, it is only because it costs us too much pains to think otherwise.

1739 *A Treatise of Human Nature*, bk.1, pt.4, section 7.

3 Reason is, and ought only to be the slave of the passions, and can never pretend to any other office than to serve and obey them.

1739 *A Treatise of Human Nature*, bk.2, pt.3, section 3.

4 It is not contrary to reason to prefer the destruction of the whole world to the scratching of my finger.

1739 *A Treatise of Human Nature*, bk.2, pt.3, section 3.

5 It is not, therefore, reason, which is the guide of life, but custom.

1739 *A Treatise of Human Nature*, abstract.

6 Art may make a suit of clothes; But nature must produce a man.

1741 *Essays Moral, Political and Literary*, 'The Epicurean'.

7 It cannot reasonably be doubted, but a little miss, dressed in a new gown for a dancing-school ball, receives as complete enjoyment as the greatest orator, who triumphs in the splendour of his eloquence, while he governs the passions and resolutions of a numerous assembly.

1741 *Essays Moral, Political and Literary*, 'The Sceptic'.

8 All the objects of human reason or enquiry may naturally be divided into two kinds, to wit, *Relations of Ideas*, and *Matters of Fact*.

1748 *An Enquiry Concerning Human Understanding*, section 4, pt.1.

9 A wise man proportions his belief to the evidence.

1748 *An Enquiry Concerning Human Understanding*, section 10, pt.1.

10 When we run over libraries, persuaded of these principles, what havoc must we make? If we take in our hand any volume; of divinity or school metaphysics, for instance; let us ask, *Does it contain any abstract reasoning concerning quantity or number?* No. *Does it contain any experimental reasoning concerning matter of fact or existence?* No. Commit it then to the flames: for it can contain nothing but sophistry and illusion.

1748 *An Enquiry Concerning Human Understanding*, section 12, pt.3.

11 The increase of riches and commerce in any one nation, instead of hurting, commonly promotes the riches and commerce of all its neighbours.

1752 *Essays Moral, Political and Literary*, 'Of the Jealousy of Trade'.

12 Never literary attempt was more unfortunate than my Treatise of Human Nature. It fell *dead-born from the press*, without reaching such distinction, as even to excite a murmur among the zealots.

1777 *My Own Life*, ch.1.

Humphrey, Hubert Horatio 1911–78

US politician. He served as Vice-President under Lyndon B Johnson but failed to win the Democratic candidature in 1968.

13 There are not enough jails, not enough policemen, not enough courts to enforce a law not supported by the people.

1965 Speech, 1 May.

Humphry, Derek

Founder of the Hemlock Society, which supported euthanasia for the terminally ill.

14 We're not lawbreakers, we're law reformers.

1992 In *Time*, 28 Dec.

Hunt, G W 1829–1904

British composer, lyricist and painter.

15 We don't want to fight, but by Jingo if we do, We've got the ships, we've got the men, we've got the money too!

1878 Music hall song, inspired by Disraeli's speech of 9 Nov 1876 threatening Russia with war if it sent volunteers into Servia and Montenegro. This is the origin of 'jingoism'.

Hunt, Johnnie B(ryan) 1924–

US businessman of poor origins.

16 I was hungry once and once you're hungry, you're different.

1992 In *Forbes*, 19 Oct.

Hunt, Lamar 1932–

US owner of the Kansas City Chiefs American football club.

17 My definition of utter waste is a coachload of lawyers going over a cliff, with three empty seats.

Quoted in Colin Jarman *The Guinness Dictionary of Sports Quotations* (1990).

Hunt, (James Henry) Leigh 1784–1859

English poet, critic and essayist. With his brother he edited *The Examiner* (1808–21) and popularized Keats and Shelley. His house in Hampstead was a literary meeting-place, and he was caricatured by Dickens as Harold Skimpole in *Bleak House*.

18 Never lay yourself open to what is called conviction: you might as well open your waist-coat to receive a knock-down blow.

1808 'Rules for the Conduct of Newspaper Editors', in *The Examiner*, 6 Mar.

19 A playful moderation in politics is just as absurd as a remonstrative whisper to a mob.

1808 'Rules for the Conduct of Newspaper Editors', in *The Examiner*, 6 Mar.

20 She can overpower, astonish, afflict, but she cannot win; her majestic presence and commanding features seem to disregard love, as a trifle to which they cannot descend.

1808 Of Sarah Siddons. *Critical Essays on the Performers of the London Theatres.*

21 The two divinest things this world has got, A lovely woman in a rural spot! **1816** 'The Story of Rimini', canto 3, l.257–8.

22 The laughing queen that caught the world's great hands.

1818 Of Cleopatra. 'The Nile'.

23 Stolen sweets are always sweeter, Stolen kisses much completer, Stolen looks are nice in chapels, Stolen, stolen, be your apples.

1830 'Song of Fairies Robbing an Orchard'.

24 Poetry, in the most comprehensive application of the term, I take to be the flower of any kind of experience, rooted in truth, and issuing forth into beauty.

1832 *The Story of Rimini*, preface to rev edn.

25 The pretension is nothing; the performance everything. A good apple is better than an insipid peach.

1832 *The Story of Rimini*, preface to rev edn.

26 'No love,' quoth he, 'but vanity, sets love a task like that.'

1836 'The Glove and the Lions'.

27 Abou Ben Adhem (may his tribe increase!)
Awoke one night from a deep dream of peace.
1838 'Abou Ben Adhem'.

28 I pray thee then,
Write me as one that loves his fellow-men.
1838 'Abou Ben Adhem'.

29 Jenny kissed me when we met,
Jumping from the chair she sat in;
Time, you thief, who love to get
Sweets into your list, put that in:
Say I'm weary, say I'm sad,
Say that health and wealth have missed me,
Say I'm growing old, but add,
Jenny kissed me.
1838 'Rondeau'.

30 That man must be very much absorbed in
reflection, or stupid, or sulky, or unhappy, or a
mere hog at his trough, who is not moved to say
something when he dines.
1851 *Table-Talk*, 'Table-Talk'.

31 If you are ever at a loss to support a flagging
conversation, introduce the subject of eating.
1851 *Table-Talk*, 'Eating'.

Hunt, Sir Rex 1926–

Governor of the Falkland Islands.

32 It is very uncivilised to invade British territory. You
are here illegally.
1982 Attributed remark to an Argentinian general. Quoted in
Life, Jan 1983.

Hunter, William 1718–83

Scottish anatomist and obstetrician, appointed physician-
extraordinary to Queen Charlotte Sophia (1764) and first
Professor of Anatomy to the Royal Academy (1768). His
Hunterian Museum was bequeathed to Glasgow
University.

33 Some physiologists will have it that the stomach is a
mill;—others, that it is a fermenting vat;—others
again that it is a stew-pan;—but in my view of the
matter, it is neither a mill, a fermenting vat, nor a
stew-pan—but a *stomach*, gentlemen, a *stomach*.
1824 Quoted in J A Paris *A Treatise on Diet*, epigraph, from a
note made by Hunter on one of his lectures.

Hupfeld, Herman 1894–1951

US composer of popular songs, best known for 'Sing
Something Simple' and 'As Time Goes By'.

34 You must remember this, a kiss is still a kiss,
A sigh is just a sigh;

The fundamental things apply,
As time goes by.
1931 'As Time Goes By', sung by Dooley Wilson in the film
Casablanca (1943).

Hussein, ibn Talal 1935–99

King of Jordan (1952–99), four times married. The
longest-serving Arab leader, pro-Western in attitude, he
moved towards democracy in Jordan.

35 After all the doors were shut, our region is facing a
deep abyss after the turning of the Gulf crisis into
an imminent catastrophe. We have not left a door
that we did not knock on, or a road that we did not
take to find a political settlement of this crisis.
1991 On his attempts to intercede for peace in the Gulf War,
Jan.

Hussein, Saddam 1937–

Iraqi politician, a key figure in Iraq's 1968 revolution and
later President (from 1979). He engaged in the Iran–Iraq
War (1980–8) and in 1990 invaded Kuwait and was
repulsed by a coalition of Western and Arab forces. He
made further raids on Iran in 1993, defying UN ceasefire
resolutions.

36 The devil Bush and his treacherous gang, with
criminal Zionism, have begun the great showdown,
the mother of all battles between good and evil.
1991 Speech in Baghdad, 6 Jan, describing Operation Desert
Storm. Quoted in the *Sunday Times*, 27 Jan.

37 There is no other course but the one we have
chosen, except the course of humiliation and
darkness, after which there will be no bright sign in
the sky or brilliant light on earth... All this will
make us more patient and steadfast, and better
prepared for the battle which God blesses and
which good men support. Then there will only be a
glorious conclusion, where a brilliant sun will clear
the dust of battle, and where the clouds of battles
will be dispelled.
1991 Baghdad radio broadcast, 21 Feb.

Huston, John 1906–87

US actor, screenwriter and director, son of Walter
Huston. He made his directorial début with *The Maltese
Falcon* (1941). Other successes include *Key Largo* (1948),
The African Queen (1951), *Moulin Rouge* (1952) and *The
Man Who Would Be King* (1975).

38 You're good, you're real good.
1941 Line delivered by Humphrey Bogart in *The Maltese
Falcon*.

39 A work of art doesn't dare you to realize it. It
germinates and gestates by itself.
1982 Reply to a tribute from the Directors Guild of America.
Reported in *Variety*, 26 Apr.

Hutchens, John Kennedy 1905–

US journalist and editor. He was theatre critic with the *New York Times* (1929–32, 1934–8), editor of the *New York Times Book Review* (1946–8), and was on the editorial board of the Book-of-the-Month Club (1963–88).

40 A writer and nothing else: a man alone in a room with the English language, trying to get human feelings right.

1961 On Stephen Crane. In the *New York Herald Tribune*, 10 Sep.

Hutcheson, Francis 1694–1746

Scottish philosopher, born in Ulster, a Professor of Moral Philosophy at Glasgow (1729–46) and exponent of the theory of moral sense. His ideas were later expanded by David Hume and taken up by the Utilitarians.

41 Wisdom denotes the pursuing of the best ends by the best means.

1725 *An Inquiry into the Original of our Ideas of Beauty and Virtue*, treatise 1, sect.5.

42 That action is best, which procures the greatest happiness for the greatest numbers.

1725 *An Inquiry into the Original of our Ideas of Beauty and Virtue*, treatise 2, sect.3. This is the classic exposition of pragmatism.

▷ See Bentham 92:13.

Hutchins, Robert M 1899–1977

US educationalist, Chancellor of the University of Chicago.

43 On the principle laid down by Gilbert and Sullivan that when everybody is somebody, nobody is anybody; if everybody is abnormal, we don't need to worry about anybody.

1951 Farewell address to students at University of Chicago. Recalled at his memorial service, Santa Barbara, California, 20 May 1989.

44 Whenever I feel like exercise, I lie down until the feeling passes.

Quoted in Colin Jarman *The Guinness Dictionary of Sports Quotations* (1990).

Huxley, Aldous Leonard 1894–1963

English novelist and essayist. His satirical novels *Crome Yellow* (1921) and *Antic Hay* (1923) established his reputation, and his best-known work is the dystopian novel *Brave New World* (1932). Other works include *Eyeless in Gaza* (1936) and *Time Must Have a Stop* (1944).

45 I can sympathize with people's pains, but not with their pleasures. There is something curiously boring about somebody else's happiness.

1920 *Limbo*, 'Cynthia'.

46 The proper study of mankind is books.

1921 *Crome Yellow*, ch.28.

▷ See Pope 780:42.

47 There are few who would not rather be taken in adultery than in provincialism.

1923 *Antic Hay*, ch.10.

48 Mr Mercaptan went on to preach a brilliant sermon on that melancholy sexual perversion known as continence.

1923 *Antic Hay*, ch.18.

49 Lady Capricorn, he understood, was still keeping open bed.

1923 *Antic Hay*, ch.21.

50 I'm afraid of losing my obscurity. Genuineness only thrives in the dark. Like celery.

1925 *Those Barren Leaves*, pt.1, ch.1.

51 Science has 'explained' nothing: the more we know the more fantastic the world becomes and the profounder the surrounding darkness.

1925 *Views of Holland*.

52 Facts do not cease to exist because they are ignored.

1927 *Proper Studies*, 'Note on Dogma'.

53 That all men are equal is a proposition to which, at ordinary times, no sane human being has ever given his assent.

1927 *Proper Studies*, 'The Idea of Equality'.

54 Those who believe that they are exclusively in the right are generally those who achieve something.

1927 *Proper Studies*, 'Note on Dogma'

56 Several excuses are always less convincing than one.

1928 *Point Counter Point*, ch.1.

57 A bad book is as much of a labour to write as a good one; it comes as sincerely from the author's soul.

1928 *Point Counter Point*, ch.13.

58 There is no substitute for talent. Industry and all the virtues are of no avail.

1928 *Point Counter Point*, ch.13.

59 Brought up in an age when ladies apparently rolled along on wheels, Mr Quarles was peculiarly susceptible to calves.

1928 *Point Counter Point*, ch.20.

60 Parodies and caricatures are the most penetrating of criticisms.

1928 *Point Counter Point*, ch.28.

61 Happiness is like coke—something you get as a by-product in the process of making something else.

1928 *Point Counter Point*, ch.30.

62 Too much consistency is as bad for the mind as it is for the body. Consistency is contrary to nature, contrary to life.
1929 *Do What You Will*, 'Wordsworth in the Tropics'.

63 After silence, that which comes nearest to expressing the inexpressible is music.
1931 *Music At Night*.

64 Experience is not what happens to a man; it is what a man does with what happens to him.
1932 *Texts and Pretexts*, introduction.

65 Only man behaves with such gratuitous folly. It is the price he has to pay for being intelligent but not, as yet, quite intelligent enough.
1932 *Texts and Pretexts*, 'Amor Fati'.

66 The escalator from the Social Predestination Room… One circuit of the cellar at ground level, one on the first gallery, half on the second, and on the two hundred and sixty-seventh morning, daylight in the Decanting Room. Independent existence—so called.
1932 *Brave New World*, ch.1.

67 Our Ford…had been the first to reveal the appalling dangers of family life.
1932 *Brave New World*, ch.3.

68 Oh, she's a splendid girl. Wonderfully pneumatic.
1932 *Brave New World*, ch.3.

69 The sexophones wailed like melodious cats under the moon.
1932 *Brave New World*, ch.5.

70 The real pitch lake is simply about two hundred asphalt tennis courts, in very bad condition, set in the midst of some gently undulating green meadows. I am inclined to ask for my money back.
1934 On the Trinidad Pitch Lake. *Beyond the Mexique Bay*.

71 Official dignity tends to increase in inverse ratio to the importance of the country in which the office is held.
1934 *Beyond the Mexique Bay*.

72 'Death,' said Mark Staithes. 'It's the only thing we haven't succeeded in completely vulgarizing.'
1936 *Eyeless in Gaza*, ch.31.

73 The end cannot justify the means, for the simple and obvious reason that the means employed determine the nature of the ends produced.
1937 *Ends and Means*, ch.1.

74 We are living now, not in the delicious intoxication induced by the early successes of science, but in a rather grisly morning-after, when it has become apparent that what triumphant science has done

hitherto is to improve the means for achieving unimproved or actually deteriorated ends.
1937 *Ends and Means*, ch.1.

75 So long as men worship the Caesars and Napoleons, Caesars and Napoleons will duly arise and make them miserable.
1937 *Ends and Means*, ch.8.

76 What is science? Science is angling in the mud—angling for immortality and for anything else that may happen to turn up.
1939 *After Many a Summer Dies the Swan*.

77 The quality of moral behaviour varies in inverse ratio to the number of human beings involved.
1941 *Grey Eminence*, ch.10.

78 There's only one corner of the universe you can be certain of improving, and that's your own self.
1945 *Time Must Have a Stop*, ch.7.

79 You learn to love by loving—by paying attention and doing what one thereby discovers has to be done.
1945 *Time Must Have a Stop*, ch.30.

80 Facts are ventriloquist's dummies. Sitting on a wise man's knee they may be made to utter words of wisdom; elsewhere they say nothing, or talk nonsense.
1945 *Time Must Have a Stop*.

81 Most human beings have an infinite capacity for taking things for granted.
1950 'Variations on a Philosopher'.

82 We participate in a tragedy; at a comedy we only look.
1952 *The Devils of Loudun*, ch.11.

83 I was seeing what Adam had seen on the morning of his creation—the miracle, moment by moment, of naked existence.
1954 *The Doors of Perception*.

84 I have spoken so far only of the blissful visionary experience… But visionary experience is not always blissful. It's sometimes terrible. There is hell as well as heaven.
1956 *Heaven and Hell*.

85 'Bed,' as the Italian proverb succinctly puts it, 'is the poor man's opera.'
1956 *Heaven and Hell*.

86 The most distressing thing that can happen to a prophet is to be proved wrong. The next most distressing thing is to be proved right.
1956 'Brave New World Revisited', in *Esquire*.

87 But liberty, as we all know, cannot flourish in a country that is permanently on a war footing, or even a near-war footing. Permanent crisis justifies permanent control of everybody and everything by the agencies of central government.
1956 'Brave New World Revisited', in *Esquire.*

88 But some of us still believe that, without freedom, human beings cannot become fully human and that freedom is therefore supremely valuable.
1956 'Brave New World Revisited', in *Esquire.*

89 That men do not learn very much from the lessons of history is the most important of all the lessons that history has to teach.
1959 'A Case of Voluntary Ignorance'.

90 Science is the reduction of the bewildering diversity of unique events to manageable uniformity within one of a number of symbol systems, and technology is the art of using these symbol systems so as to control and organize unique events. Scientific observation is always a viewing of things through the refracting medium of a symbol system, and technological praxis is always handling of things in ways that some symbol system has dictated. Education in science and technology is essentially education on the symbol level.
1962 In *Daedalus*, spring issue.

91 Idealism is the noble toga that political gentlemen drape over their will to power.
Quoted in his *New York Herald Tribune* obituary, 24 Nov 1963.

92 The propagandist's purpose is to make one set of people forget that certain other sets of people are human.
1937 *The Olive Tree.*

Huxley, Sir Julian Sorell 1887–1975

English biologist and humanist, grandson of T H Huxley. He was the first Director-General of UNESCO, and formulated a pragmatic ethical theory of 'evolutionary humanism'.

93 We all know how the size of sums of money appears to vary in a remarkable way according as they are being paid in or paid out.
1923 *Essays of a Biologist*, ch.5.

94 Operationally, God is beginning to resemble not a ruler but the last fading smile of a cosmic Cheshire cat.
1957 *Religion Without Revelation* (rev edn), ch.3.

Huxley, T(homas) H(enry) 1825–95

English biologist, who made significant contributions to palaeontology and comparative anatomy. He famously supported Darwin's controversial theory of evolution by natural selection, and the term 'agnostic' has been attributed to him.

95 The generalizations of science sweep in ever-widening circles, and more aspiring flights, through a limitless creation.
1859 Letter to *The Times*, 26 Dec.

96 Sit down before fact as a little child, be prepared to give up every preconceived notion, follow humbly wherever and to whatsoever abysses Nature leads, or you shall learn nothing.
1860 Letter to Charles Kingsley.

97 Most of my colleagues were -*ists* of one sort or another; and however kind and friendly they might be, I, the man without a rag of a label to cover himself with, could not fail to have some of the uneasy feelings which must have beset the historical fox when, after leaving the trap in which his tail remained, he presented himself to his normally elongated companions. So I took thought, and invented what I conceived to be the appropriate title of 'agnostic'.
1869 *Science and Christian Tradition.*

98 The central propositions [of Descartes]…are these: There is a path that leads to the truth so surely that any one who will follow it must needs reach the goal… And there is one guiding rule by which a man may always find this path…give unqualified assent to no propositions but those the truth of which is so clear and distinct that they cannot be doubted.
1870 *Lay Sermons, Addresses, and Reviews.*

99 The great tragedy of Science—the slaying of a beautiful hypothesis by an ugly fact.
1870 'Biogenesis and Abiogenesis', in the *British Association Annual Report.*

1 Our reverence for the nobility of manhood will not be lessened by the knowledge that man is in substance and in structure, one with the brutes; for he alone possesses the marvelous endowment of intelligible and rational speech whereby…he has slowly accumulated and organized the experience which is almost wholly lost with the cessation of individual life in other animals; so that he now stands raised above it as on a mountain-top, far above the level of his humble fellows, and transfigured from his grosser nature by reflecting, here and there, a ray from the infinite source of truth.
1880 *Man's Place in Nature.*

2 It is the customary fate of new truths to begin as heresies and to end as superstitions.
1880 *Science and Culture and Other Essays*, 'The Coming of Age of the Origin of the Species'.

3 Irrationally held truths may be more harmful than reasoned errors.

1880 *Science and Culture and Other Essays*, 'The Coming of Age of the Origin of the Species'.

4 Science is nothing but trained and organized common sense, differing from the latter only as a veteran may differ from a raw recruit: and its methods differ from those of common sense only as far as the guardman's cut and thrust differ from the manner in which a savage wields his club.

1893–4 *Collected Essays*, no.4, 'The Method of Zadig'.

5 Some experience of popular lecturing had convinced me that the necessity of making things plain to uninstructed people was one of the very best means of clearing up the obscure corners in one's own mind.

1894 *Man's Place in Nature* (rev edn), preface.

6 Next to being right in this world, the best of all things is to be clearly and definitely wrong. If you go buzzing about between right and wrong, vibrating and fluctuating, you come out nowhere; but if you are absolutely and thoroughly and persistently wrong you must, some of these days, have the extreme good fortune of knocking your head against a fact, and that sets you all straight again.

Attributed.

Huxtable, Ada Louise née *Landman*

c.1921–

US architectural critic. In her columns for the *New York Times*, she denounced new buildings and property speculation which spoiled American cities. Her work helped promote the preservation of historic buildings. She won a Pulitzer Prize for criticism in 1970.

7 I got a terrible case of the Fountainblues.

1970 On Miami Beach. In the *New York Times*, 15 Oct.

8 America the beautiful,
Let me sing of thee;
Burger King and Dairy Queen
From sea to shining sea.

1971 'Goodbye History, Hello Hamburger', in the *New York Times*, 21 Mar.

9 New York, thy name is irreverence and hyperbole. And grandeur.

1975 In the *New York Times*, 20 Jul.

Hyde, Robin pseudonym of *Iris Guiver Wilkinson* 1906–39

New Zealand novelist, poet and journalist, born in South Africa. She was one of the few women career journalists of the 1930s. Brief affairs led to the births of two sons; the first, whose name she adopted, was still-born. Her works include the autobiographical novel *The Godwits Fly* (1938).

10 Something there had been, something delicate, wild and far away. But it was shut out behind the doors of yesterday, lost beyond the hills.

1938 *The Godwits Fly*, ch.3.

11 You were English and not English. It took time to realize that England was far away.

1938 *The Godwits Fly*, ch.3.

12 We live half our lives in England…there can't have been anything quite like this since the Roman colonists settled in Britain: not the hanging on with one hand, and the other hand full of seas.

1938 *The Godwits Fly*, ch.8.

13 Having a lover isn't much to write home about.

1938 *The Godwits Fly*, ch.17.

14 She stands an instant in the sun
Athwart her harsh land's red and green—
Hands of a serf, and warrior eyes
Of some flame-sceptred Irish queen.
…As if she does not care that life
Has reft the jewels from her hair—
But grieves that menial needs and base
Were those that left her palace bare.

1938 *The Godwits Fly*, ch.23. This poem is an adaptation of 'The Farmer's Wife', first published in *The Desolate Star* (1929).

Hyde-White, Wilfred 1903–91

British film actor.

15 The suaveness isn't born of confidence; it's born of fright.

Quoted in his obituary, in the *San Francisco Chronicle*, 7 May 1991.

Iacocca, Lee (Lido Anthony) 1924–

US businessman, president of the Ford Motor Company and later head of Chrysler Corporation.

16 People want economy and they will pay any price to get it.

1974 In the *New York Times*, 13 Oct.

17 If you want to continue being leaders in the world, start by getting some of that [Federal] debt off your backs. Debtors can't be leaders. It's the guy holding the IOUs who can call the shots; the other guy is called a hostage.

1992 Quoted in the *New York Times*, 26 May.

Ibarruri Gomez, Dolores known as *La Pasionaria* 1895–1989

Spanish writer and politician, a founder of the Spanish Communist Party (1920). She urged the fight against the

Fascist forces, and left for the USSR when Franco came to power. On returning to Spain in 1977, she was re-elected to the National Assembly.

18 It is better to die on your feet than live on your knees. *No pasarán!*

1936 Speech in Paris, 3 Sep, at the onset of the Spanish Civil War, imploring the people to defend the Republic against the Fascist uprising. 'No pasarán', associated with the World War I battle of Verdun, was to become the battlecry of the Republican cause.

▷ See Pétain 767:4.

Ibn Battuta 1304–68

Arab traveller and geographer, who spent 30 years visiting parts of Africa, Asia and southern Europe. He then settled in Fez and wrote the history of his journeys.

19 Never to travel any road a second time.

14c His guiding principle. *Travels in Asia and Africa 1325–1354* (translated by H A R Gibb, 1929).

Ibsen, Henrik Johan 1828–1906

Norwegian playwright, the founder of modern prose drama. His realistic plays on sensitive social issues revolutionized modern European drama. They include *En dukkehjem* (A Doll's House, 1879), *Vildanden* (The Wild Duck, 1884) and *Hedda Gabler* (1890).

20 *Flertallet har aldrig retten på sin side. Aldrig, siger jeg! Det er en af disse samfundsløgnere, som en fri, tænkende mand må gøre oprør imod. Hvem er det, som udgør flertallet af beboerne i et land? Er det de kloge folk, eller er det dè dumme? Jeg tænker, vi får være enige om, at dumme mennesker er tilstede i en ganske forskrækkelig overvældende majoritet rundt omkring på den hele vide jord.*

The majority never has right on its side. Never, I say! That is one of the social lies that a free, thinking man is bound to rebel against. Who makes up the majority in any given country? Is it the wise men or the fools? I think we must agree that the fools are in a terrible overwhelming majority, all the wide world over.

1882 *En folkefiende* ('An Enemy of the People'), act 4.

21 *En skulde aldrig ha' sine bedste buxer på, nå r en er ude og strider for frihed og sandhed.*

You should never have your best trousers on when you turn out to fight for freedom and truth.

1882 *En folkefiende* ('An Enemy of the People'), act 5.

22 *Luftslotter,—de er så nemme at ty ìnd i, de. Og nemme at bygge også.*

Castles in the air—they are so easy to take refuge in. And so easy to build, too.

1892 *The Master Builder*, act 3.

23 On the contrary!

1906 Last words, refuting a nurse's suggestion that he was feeling better.

I Ching c.2000 BC

I Ching (The Book of Changes) is reputed to have been composed by a Chinese king and his son under guidance from a Taoist sage. It is a compendium of observations and advice regarding the rise and fall of individuals and their power groups and was later annotated by Confucius.

24 It is unlucky to sound off about happiness.

c.2000 BC *I Ching*, no.16 (translated by Thomas Cleary).

25 Change proves true on the day it is finished.

c.2000 BC *I Ching*, no.49 (translated by Thomas Cleary).

26 Cultured people practice self-examination with trepidation and fear.

c.2000 BC *I Ching*, no.51 (translated by Thomas Cleary).

Ignatieff, Michael 1947–

Canadian author and broadcaster.

27 The medium's gaze is brief, intense, and promiscuous. The shelf life of the moral causes it makes its own is brutally short.

1988 'Is Nothing Sacred? The Ethics of Television', in *Daedalus: Journal of the American Academy of Arts and Sciences*, Fall.

Ignatow, David 1914–97

US poet and academic. He published several volumes of poetry, much of it highly autobiographical in content.

28 Faster and faster it rolled,
with me running after it
bent low, gritting my teeth,
and I found myself doubled over
and rolling down the street
head over heels, one complete somersault
after another like a bagel
and strangely happy with myself.

1968 *Rescue The Dead*, 'The Bagel'.

29 To love is to be a fish.
My boat wallows in the sea.
You who are free,
rescue the dead.

1968 *Rescue The Dead*, 'Rescue The Dead'.

Ihimaera, Witi Tame 1944–

New Zealand writer and diplomat. His novel *Tangi* (1973), about a son's return home to his father's funeral and to his Maori roots, was the first written by a Maori to have been published. In addition, he has written *The Matriarch* (1986), a spiritual odyssey through history for Maori identity.

30 The sunlight falls across the country, lighting up the greenstone years of a boy with his father.

1973 *Tangi*, ch.14.

31 *Titiro ki te rangi tahuri rawa ake, Kahore he whenua
    e…Kua riro*: We looked up to heaven and before we
    knew where we were there was no land left…gone.
    1986 *The Matriarch*, ch.3.

Illich, Ivan 1926–

Austrian-born US social critic, resident of Mexico.

32 Current nationalism is merely the affirmation of
    the right of colonial elites to repeat history and
    follow the road traveled by the rich toward the
    universal consumption of internationally marketed
    packages, a road which can ultimately lead only to
    universal pollution and universal frustration.
    1970 *Celebration of Awareness*, ch.12.

33 In both rich and poor nations consumption is
    polarized while expectation is equalized.
    1970 *Celebration of Awareness*, ch.12.

34 In a consumer society there are inevitably two
    kinds of slaves: the prisoners of addiction and the
    prisoners of envy.
    1973 *Tools for Conviviality*, ch.3.

Inge, William Ralph 1860–1954

English prelate and theologian, known as 'The Gloomy
Dean' for his pessimistic sermons as Dean of St Paul's
(1911–34). His books include *Outspoken Essays* (1919,
1922), *Lay Thoughts of a Dean* (1926, 1931) and more
serious theological works.

35 It takes in reality only one to make a quarrel. It is
    useless for the sheep to pass resolutions in favour of
    vegetarianism, while the wolf remains of a different
    opinion.
    1919 *Outspoken Essays* (first series), 'Patriotism'.

36 A man may build himself a throne of bayonets, but
    he cannot sit on it.
    1923 *Philosophy of Plotinus*, vol.2, lecture 22.

37 Many people believe that they are attracted by
    God, or by Nature, when they are only repelled by
    man.
    1931 *More Thoughts of a Lay Dean*, pt.4, ch.1.

38 The enemies of freedom do not argue; they shout
    and they shoot.
    1948 *The End of an Age*, ch.4.

39 The effect of boredom on a large scale in history is
    underestimated. It is a main cause of revolutions,
    and would soon bring to an end all the static
    Utopias and the farmyard civilization of the
    Fabians.
    1948 *The End of an Age*, ch.6.

40 A nation is a society united by a delusion about its
    ancestry and by a common hatred of its
    neighbours.
    Sagittarius and George.

Ingersoll, Robert 1833–99

US lawyer, orator, and free-thinker, called 'The Great
Agnostic' for his anti-religious views.

41 The hope of science is the perfection of the human
    race. The hope of theology is the salvation of a few
    and the damnation of almost everybody.
    1867 *The Age of Reason*, Mar.

42 An honest God is the noblest work of man.
    1876 *The Gods*, pt.1.
    ▷ See Pope 781:50.

43 In nature there are neither rewards nor
    punishments—there are consequences.
    1881 *Some Reasons Why*, pt.8, 'The New Testament'.

Ingram, John Kells 1823–1907

Irish economist and poet, Professor of Oratory then of
Greek at Trinity College, Dublin. In 1847 he co-founded
the Dublin Statistical Society, attempting in his works to
formulate a social rather than purely mathematical science
of economics.

44 Who fears to speak of Ninety-Eight?
    Who blushes at the name?
    When cowards mock the patriot's fate,
    Who hangs his head for shame?
    He's all a knave or half a slave
    Who slights his country thus:
    But a *true* man, like you, man,
    Will fill your glass with us.
    1845 *The Spirit of the Nation*, 'The Memory of the Dead'.

Ingrams, Richard Reid 1937–

English writer, former editor of the satirical magazine
Private Eye.

45 I have come to regard the law courts not as a
    cathedral but rather as a casino.
    1977 Referring to libel suits against him. Quoted in *The
    Guardian*, 30 Jul.

Ingres, Jean Auguste Dominique
1780–1867

French painter, leading exponent of the Classical tradition
in 19c France. He painted many of his famous nudes
while living in Rome (1806–20).

46 Is there anyone among the great men who has not
    imitated? Nothing is made with nothing.
    1821 Quoted in Henri Delaborde *Ingres, sa vie, ses travaux, sa
    doctrine* (1870).

47 What do these so-called artists mean when they preach the discovery of the 'new'? Is there anything new? Everything has been done, everything has been discovered.

1821 Quoted in Henri Delaborde *Ingres, sa vie, ses travaux, sa doctrine* (1870).

48 Anti-classic art, if it may even be called an art, is merely the art of the idle. It is the doctrine of those who desire to produce without working, to know without learning.

1821 Quoted in Henri Delaborde *Ingres, sa vie, ses travaux, sa doctrine* (1870).

49 Make copies, young man, many copies. You can only become a good artist by copying the masters.

1855 Attributed comment to Degas. Quoted in A Vollard *Souvenirs d'un marchand de tableaux* (1937).

50 They have let the wolf into the sheepfold!

1859 Attributed remark on hearing that Delacroix had been elected to the Academy. Quoted in P Amaury-Duval *L'atelier d'Ingres* (1878).

51 One must go after the modelling like a fly crawling over a piece of paper.

Attributed aphorism. Quoted in P Valéry *Degas, Danse, Dessin* (1938).

Innis, Harold Adams 1894–1952

Canadian political economist.

52 Canadian nationalism was systematically encouraged and exploited by American capital. Canada moved from colony to nation to colony.

1948 'Great Britain, the United States and Canada', collected in Mary Quayle Innis (ed) *Essays in Canadian Economic History* (1956).

53 Property like incest holds the family together.

Quoted in William Christian (ed) *The Idea File of Harold Adams Innis* (1980).

Pope Innocent III originally *Lotario de' Conti di Segni* 1160–1216

Italian prelate and scholar, elected Pope in 1198. He asserted the authority of the papacy over secular princes, and strongly promoted the Fourth Crusade.

54 *Omnis cupidus at avarus contra naturam nititur et molitur. Natura namque pauperem adducit in mundum; natura pauperem reducit a mundo.*

Every covetous and avaricious man struggles and strives against nature. For nature brings him into the world poor, and takes him out of it poor.

1195 *De Miseraria Condicionis Humane*, bk.2, ch.12.

55 *Gule carum tributem exigit, sed vilissimum reddit, quia quanto sunt delicaciora cibavia, tanto fetidiora sunt stercora.*

Gluttony demands a heavy tribute but gives the basest returns: the more delicate the food, the more reeking the dung.

1195 *De Miseraria Condicionis Humane*, bk.2, ch.20.

56 This [Magna Carta] has been forced from the King. It constitutes an insult to the Holy See, a serious weakening of the royal power, a disgrace to the English nation, a danger to all Christendom, since this civil war obstructs the crusade. Therefore…we condemn the charter and forbid the King to keep it, or the barons and their supporters to make him do so, on pain of excommunication.

1215 Papal Bull, 24 Aug.

Inouye, Daniel Ken 1924–

US politician, Democratic senator from Hawaii since 1962. He served on the committees investigating Watergate (1973–4) and (as Chairman) the Iran-Contra affair (1987).

57 No times were more dangerous than when our country was born, when revolution was our midwife.

1987 Response to Adm John M Poindexter and Lt Col Oliver L North's contention that their actions were greatly influenced by 'a dangerous world'. In the *New York Times*, 24 Jul.

58 These hearings will be remembered longest not for the facts they elicited, but for the extraordinary and extraordinarily frightening views of government they exposed.

1987 On the Iran-Contra hearings. In the *New York Times*, 24 Jul.

59 A great nation betrayed the principles which have made it great, and thereby became hostage to hostage-takers.

1987 Of the Iran-Contra scandal. In the *New York Times*, 24 Jul.

Irigaray, Luce

French feminist literary critic who has applied Lacan's psychoanalytic writings to the question of the difference between women's and men's writing.

60 *Il faut renouveler le langage.*

We must re-invent language.

1981 *Corps-à-corps avec la mère.*

Irving, Washington 1783–1859

US essayist. Under the pseudonym 'Geoffrey Crayon' he wrote *The Sketch Book* (1819–20) which included 'Rip Van Winkle' and 'The Legend of Sleepy Hollow'. Several collections are devoted to his European travels, including *Tales of a Traveller* (1824). He was US Ambassador to Spain (1842–6).

61 What is history, in fact, but a kind of Newgate calendar, a register of the crimes and miseries that man has inflicted on his fellow-man?
1809 *A History of New York*, bk.4, ch.1.

62 My native country was full of youthful promise; Europe was rich in the accumulated treasures of age.
1819–20 *The Sketch Book*, 'The Author's Account of Himself'.

63 A tart temper never mellows with age, and a sharp tongue is the only edged tool that grows keener with constant use.
1819–20 *The Sketch Book*, 'Rip Van Winkle'.

64 A woman's whole life is a history of the affections.
1819–20 *The Sketch Book*, 'The Broken Heart'.

65 Whenever a man's friends begin to compliment him about looking young, he may be sure that they think he is growing old.
1822 *Bracebridge Hall*, 'Bachelors'.

66 I am always at a loss to know how much to believe of my own stories.
1824 *Tales of a Traveller*, 'To the Reader'.

67 There is a certain relief in change, even though it be from bad to worse… I have often found in travelling in a stage-coach, that it is often a comfort to shift one's position, and be bruised in a new place.
1824 *Tales of a Traveller*, 'To the Reader'.

68 The almighty dollar, that great object of universal devotion throughout our land.
1855 *Wolfert's Roost*, 'The Creole Village'.

Isaacs, Jorge 1837–95

Colombian novelist. He worked variously as a journalist, businessman, government official and consul to Chile. His much-imitated romantic novel *María* is notable for its idyllic descriptions of nature.

69 *Las grandes bellezas de la creación no pueden a un tiempo ser vistas y cantadas: es necesario que vuelvan a el alma empalidecidas por la memoria infiel.*

The most beautiful things on earth cannot be seen and sung at the same time: they must return to the soul weakened by unfaithful memory.
1867 *María*, ch.2 (translated as *María: A South American Romance*, 1977).

Isaacson, Walter Seff 1952–

US magazine editor and writer. He joined *Time* as a staff writer in 1978 and worked his way up to Managing Editor (1996–). His works include *The Wise Men* (1986) and *Kissinger: A Biography* (1992).

70 He was something between an epitome and a parody.

1992 On Harvard Professor William Elliott, Kissinger's mentor. *Kissinger: A Biography*.

71 No one could shine his shoes, much less fill them.
1992 On President Nixon's self-image at the time of his resignation. *Kissinger: A Biography*

Isherwood, Christopher William Bradshaw 1904–86

English novelist. He collaborated with Auden in the 1930s. He moved to California in 1939, and became a US citizen in 1946.

72 I am a camera with its shutter open, quite passive, recording, not thinking… Some day, all this will have to be developed, carefully printed, fixed.
1930 'A Berlin Diary', in *Goodbye to Berlin* (1939).

73 Like Shelley and like Baudelaire it may be said of him that he suffered, in his own person, the neurotic ills of an entire generation.
1937 Of T E Lawrence, 'Lawrence of Arabia'. Collected in *Exhumations* (1966).

74 They share the insult of each other's presence.
1962 On characters in his novels. *Down There on a Visit*.

Ishiguro, Kazuo 1954–

British novelist, born in Japan. His first book, *A Pale View of Hills* (1982), was set in Japan, but later works have been English in tone and subject, notably *The Remains of the Day*.

75 An Artist of the Floating World.
1988 Title of novel.

76 A 'great' butler can only be, surely, one who can point to his years of service and say that he has applied his talents to serving a great gentleman— and through the latter, to serving humanity.
1989 *The Remains of the Day*, 'Day Two—Afternoon'.

77 Perhaps it is indeed time that I began to look at this whole matter of bantering more enthusiastically. After all, when we think about it, it is not such a foolish thing to indulge in—particularly if it is the case that in bantering lies the key to human warmth.
1989 *The Remains of the Day*, 'Day Six—Evening'.

Ising, Rudolf C d.1992

78 That's all folks!
Porky Pig's stammered trademark, sign-off line for Warner Brothers' *Looney Tunes*. Recalled on his death in the *New York Times*, 23 Jul 1992.

Issigonis, Sir Alec (Alexander Arnold Constantine) 1906–88

Turkish-born British car designer. He came to the English Midlands where he designed some of Britain's most popular and influential cars, including the Morris Minor and the Mini.

79 All creative people hate mathematics. It's the most uncreative subject you can study.
Recalled on his death. Quoted in *The Australian*, 5 Oct 1988.

80 Styling is designing for obsolescence.
Recalled on his death. Quoted in *The Australian*, 5 Oct 1988.

81 A camel is a horse designed by a committee.
Attributed to him in *The Guardian*, 14 Jan 1991.

Ito, Lance Allan 1950–

US jurist, presiding judge at the Los Angeles Superior Court (1989–). His most famous case is the O J Simpson murder trial (1994–5).

82 Rule 1: Be cautious, careful and when in doubt, keep your mouth shut.
Rule 2: When tempted to say something, take a deep breath and refer to Rule 1.
1994 In the *New York Times*, 23 Jul.

Ivan IV known as Ivan the Terrible 1530–84

Grand Prince of Moscow (1533–84), the first to assume the title of 'tsar' (Latin *Caesar*). In 1564 he began a reign of terror, directed mainly at the aristocracy.

83 To shave the beard is a sin that the blood of all the martyrs cannot cleanse. It is to deface the image of man created by God.
Quoted in David Maland *Europe in the Seventeenth Century* (1968).

Ives, Charles Edward 1874–1954

US composer. His innovative, experimental works were unappreciated for most of his life, but in 1947 he was awarded a Pulitzer Prize for his 3rd symphony (composed 1911).

84 Please don't try to make things nice! All the wrong notes are *right*… I want it that way.
c.1914 Note to the copyist of *The Fourth of July*.

Jackson, Jesse Louis 1941–

US clergyman and Democratic politician, organizer of Operation PUSH (People United to Save Humanity, 1971). In 1984 and 1988 he sought nomination for the presidency, the first black American to be a serious candidate for the office.

85 I cast my bread on the waters long ago. Now it's time for you to send it back to me—toasted, and buttered on both sides.
1984 Addressing black voters, New York, 30 Jan.

86 My constituency is the desperate, the damned, the disinherited, the disrespected, and the despised.
1984 Speech at the Democratic National Convention, San Francisco, 17 Jul.

87 Our flag is red, white and blue, but our nation is a rainbow—red, yellow, brown, black and white—and we are all precious in God's sight… America is not like a blanket—one piece of unbroken cloth, the same colour, the same texture, the same size. America is more like a quilt—many patches, many pieces, many colors, many sizes; all woven and held together by a common thread.
1984 Launching his 'rainbow coalition' at the Democratic National Convention, San Francisco, 17 Jul.

Jackson, Robert Houghwout 1892–1954

US jurist, Associate Justice of the US Supreme Court (1941–54). He took leave to be US chief counsel at the Nuremberg war trials (1945–6). His decisions upheld freedom of speech and religion.

88 We are not final because we are infallible, but we are infallible only because we are final.
1953 Ruling to uphold the Supreme Court as the bench of last appeal, 9 Feb.

89 He who must search a haystack for a needle is likely to end up with the attitude that the needle is not worth the search.
1953 Ruling to uphold the Supreme Court as the bench of last appeal, 9 Feb.

Jacobs, Andrew, Jr 1932–

US lawyer and Democratic politician.

90 It's like saying that the patient died but the good news is that he's eating less.
1982 Of the Reagan administration's claim to have reduced inflation. In the *Washington Post*, 6 Jun.

Jacobs, Herman

Pharmaceutical store supplier.

91 It is not the mouse who is the thief, it is the hole that allows the mouse in.
1994 His interpretation of Talmudic principles applied in business. In *Forbes*, 21 Nov.

Jacobs, Joe 1896–1940

US boxing manager. He was manager of boxer Max Schmeling.

92 We wuz robbed!
1932 After Schmeling's unexpected defeat by Jack Sharkey, 21 Jun. Quoted in Peter Heller *In this Corner* (1975). Jack Dempsey in 1927 claimed 'I was robbed of the championship' when he lost to Gene Tunney. The cry was subsequently widely adopted by aggrieved losers.

Jacobs, W(illiam) W(ymark) 1863–1943

English short-story writer. He specialized in colourful yarns about the watermen on the Thames, and macabre stories.

93 'Dealing with a man,' said the night-watchman, 'is
as easy as a teetotaller walking along a nice wide
pavement; dealing with a woman is like the same
teetotaller, after four or five whiskies, trying to get
up a step that ain't there.'
1919 *Deep Waters*, 'Husbandry'.

Jagger, Mick and *Richards, Keith* both
1943–

English rock musicians, who with Bill Wyman, Charlie
Watts and Brian Jones formed The Rolling Stones (1961).
Their rebellious image and controversial lifestyles added
to the extraordinary success of their music.

94 I can't get no satisfaction
I can't get no girl reaction.
1966 '(I Can't Get No) Satisfaction'.

95 Mother needs something today to calm her down,
And though she's not really ill,
There's a little yellow pill:
She goes running for the shelter
Of a mother's little helper,
And it helps her on her way,
Gets her through her busy day.
1966 'Mother's Little Helper'.

96 Please allow me to introduce myself
I'm a man of wealth and taste.
I've been around for a long, long year
Stole many a man's soul and faith.
And I was around when Jesus Christ
Had his moments of doubt and pain,
Made damn sure that Pilate
Washed his hands and sealed his fate.
Pleased to meet you, hope you guess my name
But what's puzzling you
Is the nature of my game.
1968 'Sympathy for the Devil'.

97 I shouted out, 'Who killed the Kennedys?'
When after all it was you and me.
1968 'Sympathy for the Devil'.

98 It's Only Rock and Roll.
1974 Title of song.

James I 1394–1437

King of Scotland (from 1424). He was imprisoned by the
English for 18 years before returning to Scotland to take
the throne. His measures to curb the nobles' power led
to his murder. *The Kingis Quair*, his only surviving work,
is thought to have introduced Chaucerian style to
Scotland.

99 The bird, the beste, the fisch eke in the see,
They lyve in fredome, euerich in his kynd,
And I, a man, and lakkith libertee!
c.1435 *The Kingis Quair*, stanza 27.

James IV 1473–1513

King of Scotland (from 1488). His marriage to Margaret
Tudor, daughter of Henry VII of England, led ultimately
to the union of the crowns. He was defeated and killed at
Flodden.

1 It is statute and ordained that in na place of the
Realme there be used Fute-ball, Golfe, or uther sik
unproffitable sportes.
1491 Royal decree.

James V 1512–42

King of Scotland (from 1513). He succeeded to the
throne as an infant, amid quarrelling pro-French and pro-
English factions. As an adult he ruled with a mixture of
good judgement and vindictiveness, strengthening the
Crown's power and revenues.

2 Adieu, Farewell, it came with a lass, it will pass with
a lass.
1542 Said on his death-bed, 14 Dec, on hearing of the birth of his
daughter Mary, referring to the Crown of Scotland passing from
the Stewarts. Quoted in Robert Lindsay of Pitscottie (c.1532–80)
The Historie and Cronicles of Scotland (published 1728), vol.1.

James, Alice 1848–92

US diarist, sister of Henry and William James. She spent
her childhood travelling with her family in Europe. A
semi-invalid for much of her life, she lived in England to
be near her brother, Henry. Her diary was published
posthumously.

3 How heroic to be able to suppress one's vanity to
the extent of confessing that the game is too hard.
1889 On suicide. Diary entry, 5 Aug.

4 When will women begin to have the first glimmer
that above all other loyalties is the loyalty to Truth,
i.e., to yourself, that husband, children, friends and
country are as nothing to that.
1889 Diary entry, 19 Nov.

5 How sick one gets of being 'good', how much I
should respect myself if I could burst out and make
every one wretched for 24 hours.
1889 Diary entry, 11 Dec.

6 I suppose one has a greater sense of intellectual
degradation after an interview with a doctor than
from any human experience.
1890 Diary entry, 27 Sep.

James, Clive Vivian Leopold 1939–

Australian journalist, writer and broadcaster, famous as a
witty and perceptive cultural commentator.

7 A country so precipitously convoluted that the
rivers flowing through it look like the silver trails of
inebriated slugs.
1978 'Postcard from Japan', in the *Observer* magazine, 4 Jun.

8 She sounded like the book of Revelations read out over a railway station public-address system by a headmistress of a certain age wearing calico knickers.
1979 Of Margaret Thatcher. In the *Observer*.

James, C(yril) L(ionel) R(obert) 1901–89

Trinidadian writer, lecturer and political activist. Arguing for the freedom of blacks through Marxism and revolution, he was deported from the US and placed under house arrest in Trinidad.

9 Body-line was not an incident, it was not an accident, it was not a temporary aberration. It was the violence and ferocity of our age expressing itself in cricket.
1963 *Beyond the Boundary.*

James, Henry 1843–1916

US-born British novelist, brother of William and Alice James. He took British citizenship in 1915. Many of his novels explore his 'international theme', including *The Ambassadors* (1903) and *The Golden Bowl* (1904). His critical theory is defined in 'The Art of Fiction' (1884).

10 It's a complex fate, being an American, and one of the responsibilities it entails is fighting against a superstitious valuation of Europe.
1872 Letter to Charles Eliot Norton, 4 Feb.

11 It takes a great deal of history to produce a little literature.
1879 *Hawthorne*, ch.1.

12 It is, I think, an indisputable fact that Americans are, as Americans, the most self-conscious people in the world, and the most addicted to the belief that the other nations of the earth are in a conspiracy to under value them.
1879 *Hawthorne*, ch.6.

13 Cats and monkeys—monkeys and cats—all human life is there!
1879 *The Madonna of the Future*, vol.1. The *News of the World* took 'All human life is there' as its slogan from the late 1950s.

14 There are few hours in life more agreeable than the hour dedicated to the ceremony known as afternoon tea.
1881 *The Portrait of a Lady*, ch.1.

15 An Englishman's never so natural as when he's holding his tongue.
1881 Isabel Archer. *The Portrait of a Lady*, ch.10.

16 Money's a horrid thing to follow, but a charming thing to meet.
1881 Gilbert Osmond. *The Portrait of a Lady*, ch.35.

17 Art derives a considerable part of its beneficial exercise from flying in the face of presumptions.

1884 'The Art of Fiction', collected in *Partial Portraits* (1988).

18 The only obligation to which in advance we may hold a novel, without incurring the accusation of being arbitrary, is that it be interesting.
1884 'The Art of Fiction', collected in *Partial Portraits* (1888).

19 Experience is never limited, and it is never complete; it is an immense sensibility, a kind of huge spider-web of the finest silken threads suspended in the chamber of consciousness, and catching every air-borne particle in its tissue.
1884 'The Art of Fiction', collected in *Partial Portraits* (1888).

20 Try to be one of the people on whom nothing is lost!
1884 'The Art of Fiction', collected in *Partial Portraits* (1888).

21 What is character but the determination of incident? What is incident but the illustration of character?
1884 'The Art of Fiction', collected in *Partial Portraits* (1888).

22 The superiority of one man's opinion over another's is never so great as when the opinion is about a woman.
1890 *The Tragic Muse*, ch.9.

23 We work in the dark—we do what we can—we give what we have. Our doubt is in our passion and our passion is our task. The rest is madness.
1893 Dencombe speaking of the artist. 'The Middle Years', in *Scribner's Magazine*, May.

24 The time-honored bread-sauce of the happy ending.
1894–5 *Theatricals, Second Series*, preface.

25 Most English talk is a quadrille in a sentry box.
1899 The Duchess. *The Awkward Age*, bk.5, ch.4.

26 People talk about the conscience, but it seems to me one must just bring it up to a certain point and leave it there. You can let your conscience alone if you're nice to the second housemaid.
1899 Nanda Brookenham. *The Awkward Age*, bk.6, ch.3.

27 Live all you can; it's a mistake not to. It doesn't so much matter what you do in particular, so long as you have your life. If you haven't had that what *have* you had?
1903 Lambert Strether. *The Ambassadors*, bk.5, ch.11.

28 In art economy is always beauty.
1909 Preface for revised New York edition of *The Altar of the Dead* (first published 1895).

29 The terrible *fluidity* of self-revelation.
1909 Preface for revised New York edition of *The Ambassadors* (1903).

30 I'm glad you like adverbs—I adore them; they are the only qualifications I really much respect.

1912 Letter to Miss M Bentham Edwards, 5 Jan, quoted in Percy Lubbock (ed) *The Letters of Henry James* (1920).

31 Summer afternoon—summer afternoon; to me those have always been the two most beautiful words in the English language.
Quoted in Edith Wharton *A Backward Glance* (1934), ch.10, section 6.

32 So here it is at last, the distinguished thing!
Quoted in Edith Wharton *A Backward Glance* (1934), ch.14, section 3. According to Wharton, these were James's last words.

33 I hate American simplicity. I glory in the piling up of complications of every sort.
Remark to his niece. Quoted in Leon Edel *The Letters of Henry James* (1953–72), vol.4, introduction.

James, P(hyliss) D(orothy) 1920–

English writer. She specializes in carefully detailed crime fiction.

34 I thought that writing a detective story would be a wonderful apprenticeship because, whatever people tell you, a crime novel is not easy to write well. As I continued with my craft I became increasingly fascinated by the form and realized that you can use the formula to say something true about men and women and the society in which they live.
1991 'Series Detectives', collected in Brown and Munro (eds) *Writers Writing* (1993).

35 Murder is a unique crime for which we can never make reparation.
1991 'Series Detectives', collected in Brown and Munro (eds) *Writers Writing* (1993).

James, William 1842–1910

US philosopher and psychologist, brother of Henry and Alice James. A 'radical empiricist', he is often considered the founder of pragmatism. His *Principles of Psychology* (1890) places psychology on a physiological basis. Other works include *The Will to Believe* (1907) and *Pragmatism* (1907).

36 Man lives by science as well as bread.
1875 *Vivisection.*

37 Metaphysics means nothing but an unusually obstinate effort to think clearly.
1890 *The Principles of Psychology*, ch.6.

38 But facts are facts, and if we only get enough of them they are sure to combine.
1890 *The Principles of Psychology*, ch.7.

39 The aim of science is always to reduce complexity to simplicity.
1890 *The Principles of Psychology*, ch.9.

40 Consciousness, then, does not appear to itself chopped up in bits. Such words as 'chain' or 'train'

do not describe it fitly as it presents itself in the first instance. It is nothing jointed; it flows. A 'river' or a 'stream' are the metaphors by which it is most naturally described. *In talking of it hereafter, let us call it the stream of thought, of consciousness, or of subjective life.*
1890 *The Principles of Psychology*, ch.9. This is the coining of the phrase 'stream of consciousness', later applied to the narrative technique used by Joyce and others.

41 The baby, assailed by eyes, ears, nose, skin, and entrails at once, feels it all as one great blooming, buzzing confusion.
1890 *The Principles of Psychology*, ch.13.

42 As the art of reading (after a certain stage in one's education) is the art of skipping, so the art of being wise is the art of knowing what to overlook.
1890 *The Principles of Psychology*, ch.22.

43 Man is essentially *the* imitative animal. His whole educability and in fact the whole history of civilization depend on this trait, which his strong tendencies to rivalry, jealousy, and acquisitiveness reinforce.
1890 *The Principles of Psychology*, ch.24.

44 If this life be not a real fight, in which something is eternally gained for the universe by success, it is no better than a game of private theatricals from which one may withdraw at will.
1897 *The Will to Believe.*

45 Sobriety diminishes, discriminates, and says no; drunkenness expands, unites, and says yes.
1902 *The Varieties of Religious Experience*, 'Mysticism'.

46 The philosophy which is so important in each of us is not a technical matter; it is our more or less dumb sense of what life honestly and deeply means... it is our individual way of just seeing and feeling the total push and pressure of the cosmos.
1907 *Pragmatism*, lecture 1.

47 Tender-minded and tough-minded.
1907 His terms for two kinds of philosophical temperament. *Pragmatism*, lecture 1.

48 You must bring out of each word its practical cash-value, set it at work within the stream of your experience.
1907 *Pragmatism*, lecture 2.

49 First, you know, a new theory is attacked as absurd; then it is admitted to be true, but obvious and insignificant; finally it is seen to be so important that its adversaries claim that they themselves discovered it.
1907 *Pragmatism*, lecture 6.

50 'The true' to put it very briefly, is only the expedient in the way of our thinking, just as 'the right' is only the expedient in the way of our behaving.
1907 *Pragmatism*, lecture 6.

51 Many persons nowadays seem to think that any conclusion must be very scientific if the arguments in favor of it are derived from twitching of frogs' legs–especially if the frogs are decapitated—and that—on the other hand—any doctrine chiefly vouched for by the feelings of human beings–with heads on their shoulders—must be benighted and superstitious.
1907 *Pragmatism*.

52 Hogamus, higamous
Man is polygamous
Higamous, hogamous
Woman monogamous.
Quoted in the *Oxford Book of Marriage* (1990).

Janeway, Elizabeth Hall 1913–
US author and critic.

53 As long as mixed grills and combination salads are popular, anthologies will undoubtedly continue in favor.
Quoted in Helen Hull (ed) *The Writer's Book* (1950), ch.32.

Janowitz, Tama 1957–
US writer. She has written novels and short stories, and scored a cult success with the story collection *Slaves of New York* (1986).

54 Long after the bomb falls and you and your good deeds are gone, cockroaches will still be here, prowling the streets like armoured cars.
1986 *Slaves of New York*, 'Modern Saint 271'.

55 With publicity comes humiliation.
1992 In the *International Herald Tribune*, 8 Sep.

Jarrell, Randall 1914–65
US poet and critic. A passionate poet and incisive critic, he also wrote one satirical novel, *Pictures From An Institution*, and children's books. He committed suicide.

56 I felt quite funny when Freud died. It was like having a continent disappear.
1939 Letter to Allen Tate, Sep.

57 Six miles from earth, loosed from its dream of life, I woke to black flak and the nightmare fighters. When I died they washed me out of the turret with a hose.
1945 'The Death of the Ball Turret Gunner'.

58 A good poet is someone who manages, in a lifetime of standing out in thunderstorms, to be struck by lightning five or six times; a dozen or two dozen times and he is great.
1953 *Poetry and the Age*, 'The Obscurity of the Poet'.

59 President Robbins was so well adjusted to his environment that sometimes you could not tell which was the environment and which was President Robbins.
1954 *Pictures From An Institution*, pt.1, ch.4.

60 To Americans, English manners are far more frightening than none at all.
1954 *Pictures From An Institution*, pt.1, ch.4.

61 She looked at me the way you'd look at a chessman if it made its own move.
1954 *Pictures From An Institution*, pt.2, ch.1.

62 It's better to entertain an idea than to take it home to live with you for the rest of your life.
1954 *Pictures From An Institution*, pt.4, ch.9.

63 You Americans do not rear children, you *incite* them; you give them food and shelter and applause.
1954 *Pictures From An Institution*, pt.4, ch.10.

64 Is an institution always a man's shadow shortened in the sun, the lowest common denominator of everybody in it?
1954 *Pictures From An Institution*, pt.5, ch.9.

65 One of the most obvious facts about grown-ups, to a child, is that they have forgotten what it is like to be a child.
Introduction to Christina Stead *The Man Who Loved Children* (1965).

Jarry, Alfred 1873–1907
French playwright and humorist, best known for the creation of the petty tyrant in *Ubu Roi*, a play first written when he was only 15.

66 *Quant à l'action, elle se passe en Pologne, c'est à dire, nulle part.*

The action takes place in Poland; in other words, nowhere.
1896 *Ubu Roi*, introduction.

67 *Mère Ubu, tu es bien laide aujourd'hui. Est-ce parce que nous avons du monde?*

Mother Ubu, you are very ugly today. Is it because we have company?
1896 *Ubu Roi*, act 1, sc.1.

68 *La mort n'est que pour les médiocres.*

Death is only for the mediocre.
1898 *Gestes et opinions du Docteur Faustroll Pataphysicien*, vol.8, pt.37.

69 *Dieu est le point tangent de zéro et de l'infini.*

God is the tangential point of zero and the infinite.

1898 *Gestes et opinions du Docteur Faustroll Pataphysicien*, vol.8, pt.41.

70 *S'apercevoir que sa mère est vierge.—Les 36 situations dramatiques trente-septième situation.*

The thirty-seventh dramatic situation: To become aware that one's mother is a virgin.
1899 *L'Amour absolu*, pt.3, épigraphe.

Jaurès, (Auguste Marie Joseph) Jean
1859–1914

French socialist leader, writer and orator. He co-founded the socialist paper *L'Humanité* (1904), and was central in the founding of the French Socialist Party. He was assassinated in Paris.

71 There is, then, over the affairs of the army a universal conspiracy of silence, of childlike mysteries, of clannishness, routine and intrigue.
1910 *L'Armée Nouvelle.*

Jay, Sir Antony Rupert 1930–

English writer and television producer. He joined the BBC in 1955, editing *Tonight* (1962–3) and co-writing the successful *Yes, Minister* and *Yes, Prime Minister* (1980–8). He was knighted in 1988.

72 From now on you can keep the lot.
    Take every single thing you've got,
    Your land, your wealth, your men, your dames,
    Your dream of independent power,
    And dear old Konrad Adenauer,
    And stick them up your Eiffel Tower.
1963 On France's rejection of British membership of the Common Market, in *Time*, 8 Feb.

73 The great modern corporations are so similar to independent or semi-independent states of the past that they can only be fully understood in terms of political or constitutional history, and management can only be properly studied as a branch of government.
1967 *Management and Machiavelli.*

74 Efficiency…is measured at the extremities. You do not find the efficiency of an army at headquarters, nor of a firm in head office. It is at the remotest point—the private soldier or humble legionary on the distant frontier, the girl at the counter or the branch-office junior salesman—that the really decisive test of an army or a firm is made. It is there that all the instruction and knowledge of relevant facts and procedural disciplines bear fruit—or wither on the tree.
1967 *Management and Machiavelli.*

75 The bigger the organization, the fewer the jobs worth doing.
1967 *Management and Machiavelli.*

Jay, Peter 1937–

British economist, broadcaster and diplomat, Ambassador to the US (1977–9), later economics editor at the BBC (1990–).

76 [Prince Charles] is entitled to be as underwhelmed by the prospect of reigning over a fourth-class nation as the rest of us are by the prospect of living in it.
1986 Of Prince Charles. In the *London Illustrated News*, Apr.

Jeffers, (John) Robinson 1887–1962

US poet and dramatist. A number of his works drew on themes from biblical stories and Greek drama. His veneration of nature often went hand in hand with a contempt for the works of humanity.

77 While this America settles in the mould of its vulgarity, heavily
    thickening to empire
1924 *Tamar and Other Poems*, 'Shine, Perishing Republic'.

78 And boys, be in nothing so moderate as in love of man, a clever servant,
    insufferable master.
1924 *Tamar and Other Poems*, 'Shine, Perishing Republic'.

79 The poet as well
    Builds his monument mockingly;
    For man will be blotted out, the blithe earth die, the brave sun
    Die blind, his heart blackening:
    Yet stones have stood for a thousand years, and pained
    thoughts found
    The honey peace in old poems.
1924 *Tamar and Other Poems*, 'To The Stone-Cutters'.

80 Stone-cutters fighting time with marble, you foredefeated
    Challengers of oblivion
1925 *Roan Stallion, Tamar and Other Poems*, 'To The Stone-Cutters'.

81 The wing trails like a banner in defeat,
    No more to use the sky forever but live with famine
    And pain a few days
1928 *Cawdor*, 'Hurt Hawks'.

82 He is strong and pain is worse to the strong, incapacity is worse.
1928 *Cawdor*, 'Hurt Hawks'.

83 The wild God of the world is sometimes merciful to those
    That ask mercy, not often to the arrogant.
    You do not know him, you communal people, or you have forgotten him;
    Intemperate and savage, the hawk remembers him;
    Beautiful and wild, the hawks, and men that are dying, remember him.
1928 *Cawdor*, 'Hurt Hawks'.

84 I'd sooner, except the penalties, kill a man than a
hawk
1928 *Cawdor*, 'Hurt Hawks'.

85 This wild swan of a world is no hunter's game.
Better bullets than yours would miss the white
breast,
Better mirrors than yours would crack in the flame.
1935 *Solstice*, 'Love the Wild Swan'.

86 Praise life, it deserves praise, but the praise of life
That forgets the pain is a pebble
Ruttled in dry ground.
1948 *The Double Axe and Other Poems*.

Jefferson, Thomas 1743–1826

US statesman, third President (1801–9). Prominent in
the first Continental Congress (1774), he drafted the
Declaration of Independence. His administration saw war
with Tripoli, the Louisiana Purchase (1803) and the
prohibition of the slave trade.

87 We hold these truths to be sacred and undeniable;
that all men are created equal and independent; that
from that equal creation they derive rights inherent
and inalienable, among which are the preservation
of life, and liberty, and the pursuit of happiness.
c.1776 Draft of the American Declaration of Independence.
Collected in J P Boyd et al *Papers of Thomas Jefferson* (1950), vol.1.

88 Were it left to me to decide whether we should have
a government without newspapers, or newspapers
without a government, I should not hesitate a
moment to prefer the latter.
1787 Letter to Col Edward Carrington, 16 Jan.

89 A little rebellion now and then is a good thing.
1787 Letter to James Madison, 30 Jan.

90 The tree of liberty must be refreshed from time to
time with the blood of patriots and tyrants. It is its
natural manure.
1787 Letter to W S Smith, 13 Nov.

91 A bill of rights is what the people are entitled to
against every Government on earth, general or
particular, and what no just government should
refuse or rest on inference.
1787 Letter to James Madison, 20 Dec.

92 I have seen enough of one war never to wish to see
another.
1794 Letter to John Adams, 25 Apr.

93 I am for encouraging the progress of science in all
its branches; and not for…awing the human mind
by stories of raw-head and bloody bones to a
distrust of its own vision and to repose implicitly
on that of others.
1799 Letter, 26 Jan.

94 Equal and exact justice to all men…freedom of
religion, freedom of the press, freedom of the
person under the protection of the habeas corpus;
and trial by juries impartially selected—these
principles form the bright constellation that has
gone before us.
1801 Inaugural address, 4 Mar.

95 When a man assumes a public trust, he should
consider himself as public property.
1807 Letter to Baron von Humboldt.

96 Some men look at Constitutions with
sanctimonious reverence and deem them like the
Ark of the Covenant—too sacred to be touched.
1816 Letter to Samuel Kercheval, 12 Jul.

97 Games played with the ball, and others of that
nature, are too violent for the body, and stamp no
character on the mind.
Quoted in Colin Jarman *The Guinness Dictionary of Sports
Quotations* (1990).

Jeffrey, Lord Francis 1773–1850

Scottish critic, lawyer and judge, founder of the
Edinburgh Review.

98 This will never do.
1814 Of Wordsworth's *The Excursion* (1814). In the *Edinburgh
Review*, Nov.

Jenkins, David Edward 1925–

English churchman, Bishop of Durham (1984–94). He
became notorious for his radical and often controversial
views.

99 A conjuring trick with bones only proves that it is
as clever as a conjuring trick with bones… A
resuscitated corpse might be a resuscitated corpse
and might be the sign of something, but there is
still the question of what it is the symbol of.
1984 Of the Christian doctrine of Christ's physical
resurrection. 'Poles Apart', BBC radio broadcast, 4 Oct.

1 Christians are not called to win battles, but to find
ways of being in battles.
1988 *Spirituality for Conflict*.

Jensen, Albert D

US soldier, colonel in the Air Force.

2 We're going faster and lower than anything out
there. And we can bomb the knot off a tree.
1987 On the capabilities of the B-1 bomber 10 years after its
initial development. In the *New York Times*, 4 Jul.

Jerome, Jerome K(lapka) 1859–1927

English humorous novelist and playwright. He became
joint editor of *The Idler* (1892) and started his own

weekly, *To-Day*. He is best known for his classic *Three Men in a Boat* (1899).

3   It is impossible to enjoy idling thoroughly unless one has plenty of work to do.
    1886 *Idle Thoughts of an Idle Fellow*, 'On Being Idle'.

4   Love is like the measles; we all have to go through it.
    1886 *Idle Thoughts of an Idle Fellow*, 'On Being in Love'.

5   We drink one another's healths, and spoil our own.
    1886 *Idle Thoughts of an Idle Fellow*, 'On Eating and Drinking'.

6   It is a most extraordinary thing, but I never read a patent medicine advertisement without being impelled to the conclusion that I am suffering from the particular disease therein dealt with in its most virulent form.
    1889 *Three Men in a Boat*, ch.1.

7   But there, everything has its drawbacks, as the man said when his mother-in-law died, and they came down upon him for the funeral expenses.
    1889 *Three Men in a Boat*, ch.3.

8   I like work: it fascinates me. I can sit and look at it for hours. I love to keep it by me: the idea of getting rid of it nearly breaks my heart.
    1889 *Three Men in a Boat*, ch.15.

9   It is always the best policy to speak the truth—unless, of course, you are an exceptionally good liar.
    1892 In *The Idler* (edited by Robert Barr and Jerome), Feb.

10 I want a house that has got over all its troubles; I don't want to spend the rest of my life bringing up a young and inexperienced house.
    1909 *They and I*, ch.11.

11 I did not know I was a humorist. I have never been sure about it. In the middle ages, I should probably have gone about preaching and got myself burned or hanged.
    1926 *My Life and Times*, ch.6.

Jerome, William   1865–1932
US songwriter.

12 Any Old Place I can Hang my Hat is Home Sweet Home to Me.
    1901 Title of song.

Jerrold, Douglas William   1803–57
English author, dramatist and wit. His works include the play *Black-ey'd Susan* (1829), various comedies and a series of novels. He wrote for *Punch* under the pseudonym 'Q' and edited several magazines.

13 Religion's in the heart, not in the knees.
    1830 *The Devil's Ducat*, act 1, sc.2.

14 Earth is here so kind, that just tickle her with a hoe and she laughs with a harvest.
    Of Australia. *The Wit and Opinions of Douglas Jerrold* (published 1859), 'A Land of Plenty'.

15 Love's like the measles—all the worse when it comes late in life.
    The Wit and Opinions of Douglas Jerrold (published 1859), 'Love'.

16 The best thing I know between France and England is—the sea.
    The Wit and Opinions of Douglas Jerrold (published 1859), 'The Anglo-French Alliance'.

17 If an earthquake were to engulf England tomorrow, the English would manage to meet and dine somewhere among the rubbish, just to celebrate the event.
    Quoted in Blanchard Jerrold *The Life and Remains of Douglas Jerrold* (1859), ch.14.

18 The only athletic sport I mastered was backgammon.
    Quoted in W Jerrold *Douglas Jerrold*, vol.1, ch.1 (1914).

Jevons, William Stanley   1835–82
English economist, Professor of Political Economy at University College London (1876–81).

19 Economics, if it is to be a science at all, must be a mathematical science.
    1871 *The Theory of Political Economy*.

20 The point of equilibrium will be known by the criterion that an infinitely small amount of commodity exchanged in addition, at the same rate, will bring neither gain nor loss of utility.
    1871 *The Theory of Political Economy*.

21 Labour once spent has no influence on the future value of any article; it is gone and lost for ever. In commerce bygones are for ever bygones; and we are always starting clear at each moment, judging the values of things with a view to future utility.
    1871 *The Theory of Political Economy*.

22 All classes of society are trade unionists at heart, and differ chiefly in the boldness, ability, and secrecy with which they pursue their respective interests.
    1882 *The State in Relation to Labour*, introduction.

23 It is requisite from time to time to remind one generation of the experience which led a former generation to important legislative actions.
    1882 *The State in Relation to Labour*.

Jiang Qing or Chiang Ch'ing   1914–91
Chinese politician, third wife of Mao Zedong. After Mao's death in 1976 she was arrested—as one of the 'gang

of four'—and sentenced to death in 1980, later commuted to life imprisonment. She committed suicide.

24 Sex is engaging in the first rounds but what sustains interest in the long run is power.

c.1970 Quoted in Ross Merrill *Mao* (1993), ch.10.

25 Man's contribution to human history is nothing more than a drop of sperm.

1984 In *Newsweek*, 20 Feb.

26 Today the revolution has been stolen by the revisionist clique of Deng.

1991 Remark, May. Quoted in Ross Merrill *Mao* (1993), introduction.

St Joan of Arc 1412–31

French patriot and saint. As a 13-year-old peasant she heard saintly voices bidding her to free Paris from the English, and in 1429 she led troops into Orleans and successfully raised the siege. She was later sold to the English, who burned her as a witch.

27 And as for you, archers, soldiers, gentlemen, and all others who are besieging Orleans, depart in God's name to your own country... I assure you that wherever I find your people in France I shall fight them, and pursue them, and expel them from here, whether they will or not.

1429 Letter to the English at Poitiers, 22 Mar. Quoted in *Les Procès de Jeanne d'Arc* (translated by C Larrington), p.33.

28 *Si je ny y suis, Dieu m'y veuille mettre; et si je y suis, Dieu m'y veuille tenir.*

If I am not in grace, may God set me there; and if I am, may God keep me there.

1431 Quoted in the record of her trial at Rouen, 24 Feb.

St John of the Cross originally *Juan de Ypes y Alvarez* 1542–91

Spanish Christian mystic, founder of the Order of Discalced Carmelites.

29 God passes through the thicket of the world, and wherever his glance falls he turns all things to beauty.

Cántico espiritual (translated by K Kavanaugh and O Rodriguez as *The Spiritual Canticle*).

John III of Poland (Sobieski) 1624–96

King of Poland (from 1674), elected after a distinguished military career. He formed the Holy League alliance with Pope Innocent XI and the Holy Roman Emperor, Leopold I, in 1688, campaigning against the Turks.

30 I came, I saw, God conquered.

1683 Message sent to the Pope after the defeat of the Turks at the Battle of Vienna, 12 Sep.

▷ See Caesar 225:87, Charles V 253:88.

Pope John XXIII originally *Angelo Giuseppe Roncalli* 1881–1963

Italian prelate, Pope (1958–63). He convened the 21st Ecumenical Council and in 1963 issued the encyclical *Pacem in Terris* (Peace on Earth), advocating reconciliation between East and West.

31 In order to imbue civilization with sound principles and enliven it with the spirit of the gospel, it is not enough to be illumined with the gift of faith and enkindled with the desire of forwarding a good cause. For this end it is necessary to take an active part in the various organizations and influence them from within. And since our present age is one of outstanding scientific and technical progress and excellence, one will not be able to enter these organizations and work effectively from within unless he is scientifically competent, technically capable and skilled in the practice of his own profession.

1963 *Encyclical*, 'Pacem in Terris', 10 Apr.

32 If civil authorities legislate for or allow anything that is contrary to that order and therefore contrary to the will of God, neither the laws made or the authorizations granted can be binding on the consciences of the citizens, since God has more right to be obeyed than man.

1963 *Encyclical*, 'Pacem in Terris', 10 Apr.

33 The social progress, order, security and peace of each country are necessarily connected with the social progress, order, security and peace of all other countries.

1963 *Encyclical*, 'Pacem in Terris', 10 Apr.

Pope John Paul II originally *Karol Jozef Wojtyła* 1920–

Polish priest and theologian. He became Archbishop and Metropolitan of Cracow in 1964, was elected Cardinal (1967) and then Pope (1978), the first non-Italian pope in 456 years.

34 It is unbecoming for a cardinal to ski badly.

c.1968 Attributed, responding to criticism that it was unbecoming for him, then a cardinal, to be seen skiing.

35 The command 'Thou shall not kill' must be binding on the conscience of humanity if the terrible tragedy and destiny of Cain is not to be repeated.

1979 Speech at Drogheda, Ireland, 29 Sep.

36 Violence is a lie, for it goes against the truth of our faith, the truth of our humanity... Violence is a crime against humanity, for it destroys the very fabric of society. On my knees I beg you to turn away from the paths of violence.

1979 Speech at Drogheda, Ireland, 29 Sep.

37 Commitment to the poor is based on the Gospel: it does not have to rely on some political manifesto.
1979 Speech at the Third Conference of Latin American Bishops, Puebla.

38 A process of genocide is being carried out before the eyes of the world.
1989 Of the situation in Beirut. In the *Independent*, 16 Aug.

John, Gwen 1876–1939

Welsh painter, sister of Augustus John. From 1904 she worked in Paris as an artist's model, becoming Rodin's mistress. She converted to Roman Catholicism in 1913 and became increasingly reclusive.

39 My religion and my art—they are all my life.
Quoted in K Petersen and J J Wilson *Women Artists* (1979).

Johns, Jasper 1930–

US painter and sculptor, a pioneer of Pop Art in the US. He challenged the relationship between art and reality, painting ordinary objects in a deliberately banal style (eg *Flag*, 1954).

40 Things that are seen but not looked at.
1988 Defining the subject of his art. Quoted by Deborah Solomon in 'The Unflagging Artistry of Jasper Johns', in the *New York Times*, 19 Jun.

Johnson, Ben 1961–

Jamaican-born Canadian sprinter.

41 I have never, ever knowingly taken illegal drugs, and I would never embarrass my family, my friends, my country, and the kids who love me.
1988 Statement at press conference, Toronto, 4 Oct. Johnson tested positive to the use of banned substances, was stripped of his Olympic gold medal, and subsequently admitted using anabolic steroids.

Johnson, Claudia Alta Taylor known as Lady Bird 1912–

US First Lady (1963–9), the widow of President Lyndon B Johnson. She was active in conservation and improvement programmes. After the presidency she wrote *A White House Diary*.

42 We had a delicious dinner of too much.
1970 On dining at Manhattan's Plaza Hotel. *A White House Diary*.

43 Somehow that was one of the most poignant sights—that immaculate woman, exquisitely dressed, and caked in blood.
1970 On Jacqueline Kennedy after her husband's assassination. *A White House Diary*.

44 I face the prospect of another campaign like an open-ended stay in a concentration camp.
1970 *A White House Diary*.

45 Mrs Kennedy is going to marry Aristotle Socrates Onassis!… I feel strangely freer! No shadow walks behind me down the halls of the White House.
1970 *A White House Diary*.

46 We were distant. But that suited both of us.
1995 On her relationship with Jacqueline Kennedy Onassis. In the *Washington Post*, 23 Mar.

47 This country needs to be united. And sadly, sadly, he wasn't the man who could do it.
1995 On Lyndon B Johnson's decision not to seek a second term during the Vietnam War. In the *Washington Post*, 23 Mar.

Johnson, Hiram Warren 1866–1945

US politician. He entered the Senate from California (1917–45) and as a founder of the Progressive Party was Theodore Roosevelt's running mate in his unsuccessful 1912 campaign. He outspokenly opposed the League of Nations.

48 The first casualty when war comes is truth.
1917 Speech, US Senate.

Johnson, Lyndon B(aines) also called LBJ 1908–73

US politician, 36th President (1963–9). He came to power after Kennedy's assassination, and was returned with a huge majority in 1964. He presided over the Civil Rights Act (1964) and the Voting Rights Act (1965), but the Vietnam War made him unpopular.

49 I am a free man, an American, a United States Senator, and a Democrat, in that order.
1958 *Texas Quarterly*, winter issue.

50 I want to be progressive without getting both feet off the ground at the same time…a progressive who is prudent.
1964 Interview, 16 Mar.

51 You let a bully come into your front yard, and the next day he'll be on your porch.
1964 In *Time*, Apr.

52 We are not about to send American boys 9,000 or 10,000 miles away from home to do what Asian boys ought to be doing for themselves.
1964 On the war in Vietnam. Speech at Akron University, 21 Oct.

53 Better to have him inside the tent pissing out, than outside pissing in.
Of J Edgar Hoover. Quoted in David Halberstam *The Best and the Brightest* (1971), ch.20.

54 I want loyalty. I want him to kiss my ass in Macy's window at high noon and tell me it smells like roses. I want his pecker in my pocket.

Of a potential assistant. Quoted in David Halberstam *The Best and the Brightest* (1971), ch.20.

55 So dumb he can't fart and chew gum at the same time.

Of Gerald Ford. Quoted in Richard Reeves *A Ford, not a Lincoln.* (1975), ch.2.

56 Let's press the flesh.

Of shaking voters' hands. Quoted in Alistair Cooke *The Americans* (1980).

57 I want every family in America to have a carpet on the floor and a picture on the wall. After bread, you've got to have a picture on the wall.

On visiting Pittsburgh's Polish–Czech area. Quoted in Alistair Cooke *The Americans* (1980).

58 I don't believe I'll ever get credit for anything I do in foreign affairs, no matter how successful it is, because I didn't go to Harvard.

1980 To columnist Hugh Sidey. Quoted in Alistair Cooke *The Americans* (1980).

59 I can teach it round or flat.

When asked by a school board about the shape of the earth. Quoted in Tom Wicker *One of Us* (1991).

Johnson, Pauline 1861–1913

Native Canadian poet and patriot.

60 The Dutch may have their Holland, the Spaniard have his Spain,
The Yankee to the south of us must south of us remain;
For not a man dare lift a hand against the men who brag
That they were born in Canada beneath the British flag.

1903 'Canadian Born', collected in *Flint and Feather* (1912).

Johnson, Philander Chase 1866–1939

US journalist.

61 Cheer up—the worst is yet to come.

1920 In *Everybody's Magazine*, May.

Johnson, Philip Cortelyou 1906–

US architect, best known for his book *The International Style* (1932). His designs include the Lincoln Center (1964) and the American Telephone and Telegraph Headquarters Building (1978) in New York city.

62 American megalomania is largely responsible for the growth of the Skyscraper School.

1931 'The Skyscraper School of Modern Architecture', in *Arts*, XVII (May). Collected in *Writings* (1979).

63 They say a building is good architecture if it works. Of course, this is poppycock. All buildings work

…You expect any architect, a graduate of Harvard or not, to be able to put the kitchen in the right place.

1954 'The Seven Crutches of Architecture', informal talk to students, School of Architectural Design, Harvard University, 7 Dec. Published in *Perspecta 3* (1955).

64 It's got to be clear, back in your own mind, that serving the client is one thing and the art of architecture another.

1954 'The Seven Crutches of Architecture', informal talk to students, School of Architectural Design, Harvard University, 7 Dec. Published in *Perspecta 3* (1955).

65 Surely architecture is the organization for pleasure of enclosed space. And what more magnificent enclosure than a town, a *place*, a place where the spirit is cuddled, made serene, made proud, happy, or excited depending on the ceremony, the day, the hour.

1954 'The Seven Crutches of Architecture', informal talk to students, School of Architectural Design, Harvard University, 7 Dec. Published in *Perspecta 3* (1955).

66 You can't learn architecture any more than you can learn a sense of music or of painting. You shouldn't talk about art, you should do it.

1954 'The Seven Crutches of Architecture', informal talk to students, School of Architectural Design, Harvard University, 7 Dec. Published in *Perspecta 3* (1955).

67 The automobile is the greatest catastrophe in the entire history of City architecture.

1955 'The Town and the Automobile or the Pride of Elm Street', published in *Writings* (1979).

68 The delicate operation of separating an American from the four-wheeled part of him has to be performed with tact.

1955 'The Town and the Automobile or the Pride of Elm Street', published in *Writings* (1979).

69 Some of the opera houses in Italy had to be burnt down because people could *neither* see nor hear. They gave up seeing years ago, but they did enjoy the music.

1960 Informal talk, Architectural Association School of Architecture, 28 Nov. Collected in *Writings* (1979).

70 Architecture is the art of how to waste space.

1964 In the *New York Times*, 27 Dec.

71 I'm about four skyscrapers behind.

Excusing himself from a dinner party. Quoted in the *Wall Street Journal*, 20 Jun 1984.

Johnson, Samuel known as *Dr Johnson*
1709–84

English lexicographer, critic, poet and conversationalist, best known for his *Dictionary of the English Language* (1747–55) and an edition of Shakespeare (1765). In 1773 he toured Scotland with James Boswell, and wrote *A Journey to the Western Isles of Scotland* (1775). Other works include *Rasselas* (1759) and *Lives of the English Poets* (1779–81).

72 Sir, we are a nest of singing birds.

1730 Of Pembroke College, Oxford. Quoted in James Boswell *The Life of Samuel Johnson* (1791), vol.1.

73 It is incident to physicians, I am afraid, beyond all other men, to mistake subsequence for consequence.

1734 Review of Dr Lucas's *Essay on Waters*, 25 Nov.

74 It is not easy to forbear reflecting with how little reason these men profess themselves the followers of Jesus, who left this great characteristick to his disciples, that they should be known by loving one another, by universal and unbounded charity and benevolence.

1735 Of the Jesuit missionaries in Abyssinia. Johnson's preface to Fr. J de Lobo's *Voyage to Abyssinia*.

75 Unmoved though witlings sneer and rivals rail;
Studious to please, yet not ashamed to fail.

c.1737 *Irene*, prologue (first produced 1749).

76 A thousand horrid Prodigies foretold it.
A feeble government, eluded Laws,
A factious Populace, luxurious Nobles,
And all the maladies of stinking states.

c.1737 *Irene*, act 1, sc.1 (first produced 1749).

77 There Poetry shall tune her sacred voice,
And wake from ignorance the Western World.

c.1737 *Irene*, act 4, sc.1 (first produced 1749).

78 For who would leave, unbrib'd, *Hibernia's* Land,
Or change the rocks of *Scotland* for the *Strand*?

1738 *London: a Poem*, l.9–10.

79 By numbers here from shame or censure free,
All crimes are safe, but hated poverty.
This, only this, the rigid law pursues,
This, only this, provokes the snarling muse.

1738 *London: a Poem*, l.158–61.

80 The stage but echoes back the public voice.
The drama's laws the drama's patrons give,
For we, who live to please, must please to live.

1747 Prologue, written for David Garrick on the occasion of the opening of his management of the Theatre Royal, Drury Lane.

81 Let observation with extensive view,
Survey mankind, from China to Peru.

1749 *The Vanity of Human Wishes*, l.1–2.

82 Yet hope not life from grief or danger free,
Nor think the doom of man reversed for thee:
Deign on the passing world to turn thine eyes,
And pause awhile from letters, to be wise;

There mark what ills the scholar's life assail,
Toil, envy, want, the patron and the jail.

1749 *The Vanity of Human Wishes*, l.155–60.

83 Enlarge my life with multitude of days,
In health, in sickness, thus the suppliant prays;
Hides from himself his state, and shuns to know,
That life protracted is protracted woe.
Time hovers o'er, impatient to destroy,
And shuts up all the passages of joy.

1749 *The Vanity of Human Wishes*, l.255–60.

84 Must helpless man, in ignorance sedate,
Roll darkling down the torrent of his fate?

1749 *The Vanity of Human Wishes*, l.345–6.

85 Still raise for good the supplicating voice,
But leave to heaven the measure and the choice.

1749 *The Vanity of Human Wishes*, l.351–2.

86 A man may write at any time, if he will set himself doggedly to it.

1750 Comment, Mar. Quoted in James Boswell *The Life of Samuel Johnson* (1791), vol.1.

87 I'll come no more behind your scenes, David: for the silk stockings and white bosoms of your actresses excite my amorous propensities.

1750 In conversation with the actor-manager David Garrick. Quoted in James Boswell *The Life of Samuel Johnson* (1791), vol.1.

88 There are minds so impatient of inferiority, that their gratitude is a species of revenge, and they return benefits, not because recompense is a pleasure, but because obligation is a pain.

1750–2 In *The Rambler*.

89 No place affords a more striking conviction of the vanity of human hopes, than a public library.

1750–2 In *The Rambler*.

90 Wit, you know, is the unexpected copulation of ideas, the discovery of some occult relation between images in appearance remote from each other.

1750–2 In *The Rambler*.

91 Almost every man wastes part of his life in attempt to display qualities which he does not possess, and to gain applause which he cannot keep.

1750–2 In *The Rambler*.

92 The love of life is necessary to the vigorous prosecution of any undertaking.

1750–2 In *The Rambler*.

93 I have laboured to refine our language to grammatical purity, and to clear it from colloquial barbarisms, licentious idioms, and irregular combinations.

1750–2 In *The Rambler*.

94 A fly, Sir, may sting a stately horse and make him wince; but one is but an insect, and the other is a horse still.

1754 Of Edwards' criticism of Thomas Warburton. Quoted in James Boswell *The Life of Samuel Johnson* (1791), vol.1.

95 They teach the morals of a whore, and the manners of a dancing master.

1754 Of Lord Chesterfield's letters. Quoted in James Boswell *The Life of Samuel Johnson* (1791), vol.1.

96 This man I thought had been a Lord among wits; but, I find, he is only a wit among Lords.

1754 Of Lord Chesterfield. Quoted in James Boswell *The Life of Samuel Johnson* (1791), vol.1.

97 Ignorance, madam, pure ignorance.

1755 Reply to a lady who had asked why he had defined *pastern* as the 'knee' of a horse. Quoted in James Boswell *The Life of Samuel Johnson* (1791), vol.1.

98 I had done all I could; and no man is well pleased to have his all neglected, be it ever so little.

1755 Letter to Lord Chesterfield, 7 Feb. Quoted in James Boswell *The Life of Samuel Johnson* (1791), vol.1.

99 Is not a Patron, my lord, one who looks with unconcern on a man struggling for life in the water, and, when he has reached ground, encumbers him with help? The notice which you have been pleased to take of my labours, had it been early, had been kind; but it has been delayed till I am indifferent, and cannot enjoy it; till I am solitary, and cannot impart it; till I am known, and do not want it.

1755 Letter to Lord Chesterfield, 7 Feb. Quoted in James Boswell *The Life of Samuel Johnson* (1791), vol.1.

1 There are two things which I am confident I can do very well: one is an introduction to a literary work, stating what it is to contain, and how it should be executed in the most perfect manner; the other is a conclusion, shewing from various causes why the execution has not been equal to what the author promised to himself and to the public.

1755 Quoted in James Boswell *The Life of Samuel Johnson* (1791), vol.1.

2 If a man does not make a new acquaintance as he advances through life, he will soon find himself left alone. A man, Sir, should keep his friendship in constant repair.

1755 Quoted in James Boswell *The Life of Samuel Johnson* (1791), vol.1.

3 Change is not made without inconvenience, even from worse to better.

1755 *A Dictionary of the English Language*, preface.

4 It is the fate of those who toil at the lower employments of life...to be exposed to censure, without hope of praise; to be disgraced by

miscarriage or punished for neglect... Among these unhappy mortals is the writer of dictionaries... Every other author may aspire to praise; the lexicographer can only hope to escape reproach.

1755 *A Dictionary of the English Language*, preface.

5 I am not yet so lost in lexicography as to forget that words are the daughters of earth, and that things are the sons of heaven. Language is only the instrument of science, and words are but the signs of ideas: I wish, however, that the instrument might be less apt to decay, and that signs might be permanent, like the things which they denote.

1755 *A Dictionary of the English Language*, preface.

6 I have protracted my work till most of those whom I wished to please have sunk into the grave; and success and miscarriage are empty sounds.

1755 *A Dictionary of the English Language*, preface.

7 Every quotation contributes something to the stability or enlargement of the language.

1755 *A Dictionary of the English Language*, preface.

8 But these were the dreams of a poet doomed at last to wake a lexicographer.

1755 *A Dictionary of the English Language*, preface.

9 If the changes we fear be thus irresistible, what remains but to acquiesce with silence, as in the other insurmountable distresses of humanity? It remains that we retard what we cannot repel, that we palliate what we cannot cure.

1755 *A Dictionary of the English Language*, preface.

10 *Dull.* To make dictionaries is dull work.

1755 *A Dictionary of the English Language*.

11 *Excise.* A hateful tax levied upon commodities.

1755 *A Dictionary of the English Language*.

12 *Lexicographer.* A writer of dictionaries, a harmless drudge.

1755 *A Dictionary of the English Language*.

13 *Net.* Anything reticulated or decussated at equal distances, with interstices between the intersections.

1755 *A Dictionary of the English Language*.

14 *Oats.* A grain, which in England is generally given to horses, but in Scotland supports the people.

1755 *A Dictionary of the English Language*.

15 *Patron.* Commonly a wretch who supports with insolence, and is paid with flattery.

1755 *A Dictionary of the English Language*.

16 *Pension.* Pay given to state hireling for treason to his country.

1755 *A Dictionary of the English Language.*

17 The only end of writing is to enable the readers
better to enjoy life, or better to endure it.
1757 Reviewing Soame Jenyns *A Free Inquiry into the Nature
and Origin of Evil*, in the *Literary Magazine*, Apr–Jul.

18 To us, who are regaled every morning and evening
with intelligence, and are supplied from day to day
with materials for conversation, it is difficult to
conceive how man can subsist without a
newspaper.
1758 In *The Idler*, no.7, 27 May.

19 When two Englishmen meet, their first talk is of
the weather.
1758 In *The Idler*, no.11, 24 Jun.

20 To these compositions is required neither genius
nor knowledge, neither industry nor spriteliness,
but contempt of shame, and indifference to truth
are absolutely necessary.
1758 Of journalistic reporting. In *The Idler*, no.31, 11 Nov.

21 Among the calamities of War may be justly
numbered the diminution of the love of truth, by
the falsehoods which interest dictates and credulity
encourages.
1758 In *The Idler*, no.31, 11 Nov.

22 Nothing is more hopeless than a scheme of
merriment.
1759 In *The Idler*, no.58, 26 May.

23 The Europeans have scarcely visited any coast, but
to gratify avarice, and extend corruption; to
arrogate dominion without right, and practice
cruelty without incentive... But there is reason to
hope...that the light of the gospel will at last
illuminate the sands of Africa, and the deserts of
America, though its progress cannot but be slow
when it is so much obstructed by the lives of
Christians.
1759 Introduction to *The World Displayed.*

24 Marriage has many pains, but celibacy has no
pleasures.
1759 *Rasselas*, ch.26.

25 No man will be a sailor who has contrivance
enough to get himself into jail; for being in a ship is
being in a jail, with the chance of being drowned...
A man in a jail has more room, better food, and
commonly better company.
1759 Remark, 16 Mar. Quoted in James Boswell *The Life of
Samuel Johnson* (1791), vol.1.

26 Liberty is, to the lowest rank of every nation, little
more than the choice of working or starving.
1760 'The Bravery of the English Common Soldier', in *The
British Magazine*, Jan.

27 The notion of liberty amuses the people of
England, and helps to keep off the taedium vitae.
When a butcher tells you that his heart bleeds for
his country he has, in fact, no uneasy feeling.
1763 Remark, 16 May. Quoted in James Boswell *The Life of
Samuel Johnson* (1791), vol.1.

28 Yes, Sir, many men, many women, and many
children.
1763 Remark, 16 May, on being asked if any man of a modern
age could have written *Ossian*. Quoted in James Boswell *The
Life of Samuel Johnson* (1791), vol.1.

29 The noblest prospect which a Scotchman ever sees,
is the high road that leads him to England!
1763 Remark, 6 Jul. Quoted in James Boswell *The Life of
Samuel Johnson* (1791), vol.1.

30 A man ought to read just as inclination leads him;
for what he reads as a task will do him little good.
1763 Remark, 14 Jul. Quoted in James Boswell *The Life of
Samuel Johnson* (1791), vol.1.

31 But if he does really think that there is no
distinction between virtue and vice, why, Sir, when
he leaves our houses, let us count our spoons.
1763 Remark, 14 Jul. Quoted in James Boswell *The Life of
Samuel Johnson* (1791), vol.1.

32 A man with a good coat upon his back meets with a
better reception than he who has a bad one.
1763 Remark, 20 Jul. Quoted in James Boswell *The Life of
Samuel Johnson* (1791), vol.1.

33 All the arguments which are brought to represent
poverty as no evil, show it to be evidently a great
evil. You never find people labouring to convince
you that you may live very happily upon a plentiful
fortune.
1763 Remark, 20 Jul. Quoted in James Boswell *The Life of
Samuel Johnson* (1791), vol.1.

34 Truth, Sir, is a cow, that will yield such people no
more milk, and so they are gone to milk the bull.
1763 Of sceptics. Remark, 21 Jul. Quoted in James Boswell
The Life of Samuel Johnson (1791), vol.1.

35 Young men have more virtue than old men; they
have more generous sentiments in every respect.
1763 Remark, 21 Jul. Quoted in James Boswell *The Life of
Samuel Johnson* (1791), vol.1.

36 In my early years I read very hard. It is a sad
reflection, but a true one, that I knew almost as
much at eighteen as I do now.
1763 Remark, 21 Jul. Quoted in James Boswell *The Life of
Samuel Johnson* (1791), vol.1.

37 Your levellers wish to level down as far as
themselves; but they cannot bear levelling up to
themselves.
1763 Remark, 21 Jul. Quoted in James Boswell *The Life of
Samuel Johnson* (1791), vol.1.

38 It is burning a farthing candle at Dover, to shew light at Calais.

1763 Summarizing the influence of the plays of Thomas Sheridan upon English literature, 28 Jul. Quoted in James Boswell *The Life of Samuel Johnson* (1791), vol.1.

39 Sir, a woman's preaching is like a dog walking on its hinder legs. It is not done well; but you are surprised to find it done at all.

1763 Remark, 31 Jul. Quoted in James Boswell *The Life of Samuel Johnson* (1791), vol.1.

40 He who does not mind his belly will hardly mind any thing else.

1763 Remark, 5 Aug. Quoted in James Boswell *The Life of Samuel Johnson* (1791), vol.1.

41 'I refute it *thus*.'

1763 Johnson refutes Bishop Berkeley's theory of the non-existence of matter by kicking a large stone, 6 Aug. Quoted in James Boswell *The Life of Samuel Johnson* (1791), vol.1.

42 Nature has given women so much power that the law has very wisely given them little.

1763 Letter to John Taylor, 18 Aug.

43 A very unclubbable man.

1764 Of Sir John Hawkins. Remark quoted in James Boswell *The Life of Samuel Johnson* (1791), vol.1.

44 Nothing can please many, and please long, but just representations of general nature.

1765 *Plays of William Shakespeare*, preface.

45 He that tries to recommend him by select quotations, will succeed like the pedant in Hierocles, who, when he offered his house to sale, carried a brick in his pocket as a specimen.

1765 Of Shakespeare. *Plays of William Shakespeare*, preface.

46 Love is only one of many passions.

1765 *Plays of William Shakespeare*, preface.

47 Notes are often necessary, but they are necessary evils.

1765 *Plays of William Shakespeare*, preface.

48 That all who are happy, are equally happy, is not true. A peasant and a philosopher may be equally satisfied, but not equally happy. Happiness consists in the multiplicity of agreeable consciousness.

1766 Remark, Feb. Quoted in James Boswell *The Life of Samuel Johnson* (1791), vol.2.

49 It is our first duty to serve society, and, after we have done that, we may attend wholly to the salvation of our own souls. A youthful passion for abstracted devotion should not be encouraged.

1766 Remark, Feb. Quoted in James Boswell *The Life of Samuel Johnson* (1791), vol.2.

50 Our tastes greatly alter. The lad does not care for the child's rattle, and the old man does not care for the young man's whore.

1766 Quoted in James Boswell *The Life of Samuel Johnson* (1791), vol.2.

51 It was not for me to bandy civilities with my sovereign.

1767 Remark, Feb. Quoted in James Boswell *The Life of Samuel Johnson* (1791), vol.2.

52 Now, sir, there is the liberty of the press, which you know is a constant topic. Suppose you and I and two hundred more were restrained from printing our thoughts: what then? What proportion would that restraint upon us bear to the private happiness of the nation?

1768 Remark, May. Quoted in James Boswell *The Life of Samuel Johnson* (1791), vol.2.

53 Sir, if a man has a mind to *prance*, he must study at Christ-Church and All-Souls.

1769 Remark, Autumn. Quoted in James Boswell *The Life of Samuel Johnson* (1791), vol.2.

54 We know our will is free, and there's an end on't.

1769 Remark, 16 Oct. Quoted in James Boswell *The Life of Samuel Johnson* (1791), vol.2.

55 It matters not how a man dies, but how he lives. The act of dying is not of importance, it lasts so short a time.

1769 Remark, 26 Oct. Quoted in James Boswell *The Life of Samuel Johnson* (1791), vol.2.

56 That fellow seems to me to possess but one idea, and that is a wrong one.

1770 Quoted in James Boswell *The Life of Samuel Johnson* (1791), vol.2.

57 The triumph of hope over experience.

1770 On a friend's second marriage shortly after the death of his first, troublesome, wife. Quoted in James Boswell *The Life of Samuel Johnson* (1791), vol.2.

58 I do not care to speak ill of any man behind his back, but I believe the gentleman is an *attorney*.

1770 Quoted in James Boswell *The Life of Samuel Johnson* (1791), vol.2.

59 Every man has a lurking wish to appear considerable in his native place.

1771 Letter to Sir Joshua Reynolds, 17 Jul. Quoted in James Boswell *The Life of Samuel Johnson* (1791), vol.2.

60 I would not give half a guinea to live under one form of government rather than another. It is of no moment to the happiness of an individual.

1772 Remark, 31 Mar. Quoted in James Boswell *The Life of Samuel Johnson* (1791), vol.2.

61 There is more knowledge of the heart in one letter of Richardson's, than in all *Tom Jones*.

1772 Remark, 6 Apr. Quoted in James Boswell *The Life of Samuel Johnson* (1791), vol.2.

62 Grief is a species of idleness.

1773 Letter to Mrs Thrale, whose son had just died, 17 Mar.

63 He has, indeed, done it very well; but it is a foolish thing well done.

1773 Of Oliver Goldsmith, who had responded to Thomas Evans's uncomplimentary open letter with a physical assault, and then published an apology in the *London Chronicle*. Remark, 3 Apr. Collected in James Boswell *The Life of Samuel Johnson* (1791), vol.2.

64 Read over your compositions, and where ever you meet with a passage which you think is particularly fine, strike it out.

1773 Remark, 30 Apr, quoting an old college tutor. Collected in James Boswell *The Life of Samuel Johnson* (1791), vol.2.

65 A lawyer has no business with the justice or injustice of the cause which he undertakes, unless his client asks his opinion, and then he is bound to give it honestly. The justice or unjustice of the cause is to be decided by the judge.

1773 Remark, 15 Aug. Quoted in James Boswell *The Journal of the Tour of the Hebrides* (1785).

66 I inherited a vile melancholy from my father, which has made me mad all my life, at least not sober.

1773 Remark, 16 Sep. Quoted in James Boswell *The Journal of a Tour to the Hebrides* (1785).

67 I am always sorry when any language is lost, because languages are the pedigrees of nations.

1773 Remark, 18 Sep. Quoted in James Boswell *The Journal of a Tour to the Hebrides* (1785).

68 A cucumber should be well sliced, and dressed with pepper and vinegar, and then thrown out, as good for nothing.

1773 Remark, 5 Oct. Quoted in James Boswell *The Journal of a Tour to the Hebrides* (1785).

69 At seventy-seven it is time to be in earnest.

1775 *A Journey to the Western Isles of Scotland*, 'Col'.

70 There are few ways in which a man can be so innocently employed than in getting money.

1775 Remark, 27 Mar. Collected in James Boswell *The Life of Samuel Johnson* (1791), vol.2. This is sometimes rendered 'A man is seldom so innocently occupied as when he is making money.'

71 It is wonderful, when a calculation is made, how little the mind is actually employed in the discharge of any profession.

1775 Remark, 6 Apr. Collected in James Boswell *The Life of Samuel Johnson* (1791), vol.2.

72 The greatest part of a writer's time is spent in reading, in order to write: a man will turn over half a library to make one book.

1775 Remark, 6 Apr. Collected in James Boswell *The Life of Samuel Johnson* (1791), vol.2.

73 Patriotism is the last refuge of a scoundrel.

1775 Remark, 7 Apr. Collected in James Boswell *The Life of Samuel Johnson* (1791), vol.2.

74 Knowledge is of two kinds. We know a subject ourselves, or we know where we can find information upon it.

1775 Remark, 18 Apr. Quoted in James Boswell *The Life of Samuel Johnson* (1791), vol.2.

75 Politics are now nothing more than means of rising in the world.

1775 Remark, 18 Apr. Quoted in James Boswell *The Life of Samuel Johnson* (1791), vol.2.

76 Players, Sir! I look upon them as no better than creatures set upon tables and joint stools to make faces and produce laughter, like dancing dogs.

1775 Letter to James Macpherson.

77 How is it that we hear the loudest yelps for liberty among the drivers of negroes?

1775 *Taxation No Tyranny*.

78 In lapidary inscriptions a man is not upon oath.

1775 Quoted in James Boswell *The Life of Samuel Johnson* (1791), vol.2.

79 There is nothing which has yet been contrived by man, by which so much happiness is produced as by a good tavern or inn.

1776 Remark, 21 Mar. Quoted in James Boswell *The Life of Samuel Johnson* (1791), vol.2.

80 Marriages would in general be as happy, and often more so, if they were all made by the Lord Chancellor, upon a due consideration of characters and circumstances, without the parties having any choice in the matter.

1776 Remark, 22 Mar. Quoted in James Boswell *The Life of Samuel Johnson* (1791), vol.2.

81 I had often wondered why young women should marry, as they have so much more freedom, and so much more attention paid to them while unmarried, than when married.

1776 Remark, 25 Mar. Quoted in James Boswell *The Life of Samuel Johnson* (1791), vol.2.

82 Fine clothes are good only as they supply the want of other means of procuring respect.

1776 Remark, 27 Mar. Quoted in James Boswell *The Life of Samuel Johnson* (1791), vol.2.

83 Consider, Sir, how should you like, though conscious of your innocence, to be tried before a jury for a capital crime, once a week.

1776 Remark, 3 Apr. Quoted in James Boswell *The Life of Samuel Johnson* (1791), vol.3.

84 We would all be idle if we could.

> **1776** Remark, 3 Apr. Quoted in James Boswell *The Life of Samuel Johnson* (1791), vol.3.

85 No man but a blockhead ever wrote, except for money.

> **1776** Remark, 5 Apr. Quoted in James Boswell *The Life of Samuel Johnson* (1791), vol.3.

86 It is better that some should be unhappy than that none should be happy, which would be the case in a general state of equality.

> **1776** Remark, 7 Apr. Quoted in James Boswell *The Life of Samuel Johnson* (1791), vol.3.

87 A man who has not been in Italy, is always conscious of an inferiority, from his not having seen what it is expected a man should see.

> **1776** Remark, 11 Apr. Quoted in James Boswell *The Life of Samuel Johnson* (1791), vol.3.

88 Every man of any education would rather be called a rascal, than accused of deficiency in the graces.

> **1776** Remark, May. Quoted in James Boswell *The Life of Samuel Johnson* (1791), vol.3.

89 Sir, you have but two topics, yourself and me. I am sick of both.

> **1776** Remark, May. Quoted in James Boswell *The Life of Samuel Johnson* (1791), vol.3.

90 If I had no duties, and no reference to futurity, I would spend my life in driving briskly in a post-chaise with a pretty woman.

> **1777** Remark, 19 Sep. Quoted in James Boswell *The Life of Samuel Johnson* (1791), vol.3.

91 Depend upon it, Sir, when a man knows he is to be hanged in a fortnight, it concentrates his mind wonderfully.

> **1777** Remark, 19 Sep, alluding to the forthcoming execution of Dr Dodd. Quoted in James Boswell *The Life of Samuel Johnson* (1791), vol.3.

92 When a man is tired of London, he is tired of life; for there is in London all that life can afford.

> **1777** Remark, 20 Sep. Quoted in James Boswell *The Life of Samuel Johnson* (1791), vol.3.

93 All argument is against it; but all belief is for it.

> **1778** Remark, 31 Mar, on the existence of ghosts. Quoted in James Boswell *The Life of Samuel Johnson* (1791), vol.3.

94 Seeing Scotland, Madam, is only seeing a worse England.

> **1778** Remark quoted in a letter to Boswell, 7 Apr. Quoted in James Boswell *The Life of Samuel Johnson* (1791), vol.3.

95 The more contracted that power is, the more easily it is destroyed. A country governed by a despot is an inverted cone.

> **1778** Remark, 14 Apr. Quoted in James Boswell *The Life of Samuel Johnson* (1791), vol.3.

96 As the Spanish proverb says, 'He, who would bring home the wealth of the Indies, must carry the wealth of the Indies with him.' So it is in travelling; a man must carry knowledge with him, if he would bring home knowledge.

> **1778** Remark, 17 Apr. Quoted in James Boswell *The Life of Samuel Johnson* (1791), vol.3.

97 Sir, the insolence of wealth will creep out.

> **1778** Remark, 18 Apr. Quoted in James Boswell *The Life of Samuel Johnson* (1791), vol.3.

98 Wine makes a man better pleased with himself. I do not say that it makes him more pleasing to others.

> **1778** Remark, 28 Apr. Quoted in James Boswell *The Life of Samuel Johnson* (1791), vol.3.

99 BOSWELL: There is more learning in their [Chinese] language than in any other, from the immense number of their characters.
JOHNSON: It is only more difficult from its rudeness, as there is more labour in hewing down a tree with a stone than with an axe.

> **1778** Conversation, 8 May. Quoted in James Boswell *The Life of Samuel Johnson* (1791), vol.3.

1 Were it not for imagination, sir, a man would be as happy in the arms of a chambermaid as of a Duchess.

> **1778** Remark, 9 May. Quoted in James Boswell *The Life of Samuel Johnson* (1791), vol.3.

2 A man who exposes himself when he is intoxicated, has not the art of getting drunk.

> **1779** Remark, 24 Apr. Quoted in James Boswell *The Life of Samuel Johnson* (1791), vol.3.

3 Claret is the liquor for boys; port, for men; but he who aspires to be a hero [smiling] must drink brandy.

> **1779** Remark, 7 Aug. Quoted in James Boswell *The Life of Samuel Johnson* (1791), vol.3.

4 Remember that all tricks are either knavish or childish.

> **1779** Letter to Boswell, 9 Sep. Quoted in James Boswell *The Life of Samuel Johnson* (1791), vol.3.

5 BOSWELL: Is not the Giant's Causeway worth seeing?
JOHNSON: Worth seeing? Yes, but not worth going to see.

> **1779** Conversation, 12 Oct. Quoted in James Boswell *The Life of Samuel Johnson* (1791), vol.3.

6 If you are idle, be not solitary; if you are solitary, be not idle.

> **1779** Letter to Boswell, 27 Oct. Quoted in James Boswell *The Life of Samuel Johnson* (1791), vol.3.

7 Trade could not be managed by those who manage it, if it had much difficulty.
   1779 Letter to Hester Thrale, 16 Nov.

8 The true genius is a mind of large general powers, accidentally determined to some particular direction.
   1779–81 *Lives of the English Poets*, 'Cowley'.

9 The father of English criticism.
   1779–81 Of Dryden. *Lives of the English Poets*, 'Dryden'.

10 To charge all unmerited praise with the guilt of flattery, and to suppose that the encomiast always knows and feels the falsehood of his assertions, is surely to discover great ignorance of human nature and human life. In determinations depending not on rules, but on experience and comparison, judgement is always to some degree subject to affection. Very near to admiration is the wish to admire.
   1779–81 *Lives of the English Poets*, 'Halifax'.

11 It...had the effect, as was ludicrously said, of making Gay *rich*, and Rich *gay*.
   1779–81 Of the *Beggar's Opera*, written by Gay and produced by Rich. *Lives of the English Poets*, 'John Gay'.

12 An exotic and irrational entertainment.
   1779–81 Of Italian opera. *Lives of the English Poets*, 'Hughes'.

13 I am disappointed by that stroke of death, which has eclipsed the gaiety of nations, and impoverished the public stock of harmless pleasure.
   1779–81 His tribute to the recently-deceased actor David Garrick. *Lives of the English Poets*, 'Life of Edmund Smith'.

14 Every man has a right to utter what he thinks truth, and every other man has a right to knock him down for it. Martyrdom is the test.
   1780 Quoted in James Boswell *The Life of Samuel Johnson* (1791), vol.4.

15 Depend upon it, said he, that if a man talks of his misfortunes there is something in them that is not disagreeable to him; for where there is nothing but pure misery, there never is any recourse to the mention of it.
   1780 Quoted in James Boswell *The Life of Samuel Johnson* (1791), vol.4.

16 A wise Tory and a wise Whig, I believe, will agree. Their principles are the same, though their modes of thinking are different.
   1781 Written note given to Boswell, May. Quoted in James Boswell *The Life of Samuel Johnson* (1791), vol.4.

17 Classical quotations is the parole of literary men all over the world.
   1781 Remark, 8 May. Quoted in James Boswell *The Life of Samuel Johnson* (1791), vol.4.

18 Sir, I have two very cogent reasons for not printing any list of subscribers;—one, that I have lost all the names,—the other, that I have spent all the money.
   1781 Remark, May. Quoted in James Boswell *The Life of Samuel Johnson* (1791), vol.4.

19 Why, that is, because, dearest, you're a dunce.
   1781 To Lady Corke, who had said that she was affected by Sterne's writings. Quoted in James Boswell *The Life of Samuel Johnson* (1791), vol.4.

20 Always, Sir, set a high value on spontaneous kindness. He whose inclination prompts him to cultivate your friendship of his own accord, will love you more than one whom you have been at pains to attract to you.
   1781 Remark, May. Quoted in James Boswell *The Life of Samuel Johnson* (1791), vol.4.

21 I hate a fellow whom pride, or cowardice, or laziness drives into a corner, and who does nothing when he is there but sit and growl; let him come out as I do, and bark.
   1782 Remark, 10 Oct, alluding to Jeremiah Markland. Quoted in James Boswell *The Life of Samuel Johnson* (1791), vol.4.

22 Resolve not to be poor; whatever you have, spend less. Poverty is a great enemy to human happiness; it certainly destroys liberty, and it makes some virtues impracticable, and others extremely difficult.
   1782 Letter to Boswell, 7 Dec. Quoted in James Boswell *The Life of Samuel Johnson* (1791), vol.4.

23 How few of his friends' houses would a man choose to be at when he is sick.
   1783 Quoted in James Boswell *The Life of Samuel Johnson* (1791), vol.4.

24 There is a wicked inclination in most people to suppose an old man decayed in his intellects. If a young or middle-aged man, when leaving a company, does not recollect where he laid his hat, it is nothing; but if the same inattention is discovered in an old man, people will shrug up their shoulders, and say, 'His memory is going.'
   1783 Quoted in James Boswell *The Life of Samuel Johnson* (1791), vol.4.

25 Sir, there is no settling the point of precedency between a louse and a flea.
   1783 On the relative merits of two minor poets. Quoted in James Boswell *The Life of Samuel Johnson* (1791), vol.4.

26 My dear friend, clear your mind of cant... You may talk in this manner; it is a mode of talking in Society: but don't think foolishly.
   1783 Remark, 15 May. Quoted in James Boswell *The Life of Samuel Johnson* (1791), vol.4.

27 It is as bad as bad can be: it is ill-fed, ill-killed, ill-kept, and ill-drest.

1783 Of the roast mutton he was served at an inn, 3 Jun. Quoted in James Boswell *The Life of Samuel Johnson* (1791), vol.4.

28 As I know more of mankind I expect less of them, and am ready now to call a man a good man, upon easier terms than I was formerly.

1783 Remark, Sep. Quoted in James Boswell *The Life of Samuel Johnson* (1791), vol.4.

29 Milton, Madam, was a genius that could cut a Colossus from a rock; but could not carve heads upon cherry-stones.

1784 Remark to Hannah More, 13 Jun, who had commented with surprise that Milton's sonnets failed to compare with his epic *Paradise Lost*. Quoted in James Boswell *The Life of Samuel Johnson* (1791), vol.4.

30 Talking of the Comedy of 'The Rehearsal', he said 'It has not enough wit to keep it sweet.' This was easy;—he therefore caught himself, and pronounced a more rounded sentence; 'It has not vitality enough to preserve it from putrefaction.'

1784 Remark, Jun. Quoted in James Boswell *The Life of Samuel Johnson* (1791), vol.4.

31 Sir, I have found you an argument; but I am not obliged to find you an understanding.

1784 Remark, Jun. Quoted in James Boswell *The Life of Samuel Johnson* (1791), vol.4.

32 No man is a hypocrite in his pleasures.

1784 Remark, Jun. Quoted in James Boswell *The Life of Samuel Johnson* (1791), vol.4.

33 Dictionaries are like watches, the worst is better than none, and the best cannot be expected to go quite true.

1784 Letter to Francesco Sastres, 21 Aug. Quoted in James Boswell *The Life of Samuel Johnson* (1791), vol.4.

34 Sir, I look upon every day to be lost, in which I do not make a new acquaintance.

1784 Remark, Nov. Quoted in James Boswell *The Life of Samuel Johnson* (1791), vol.4.

35 I will be conquered; I will not capitulate.

1784 Of his increasing ill health, Nov. Quoted in James Boswell *The Life of Samuel Johnson* (1791), vol.4.

36 An odd thought strikes me:—we shall receive no letters in the grave.

1784 Remark, Dec. Quoted in James Boswell *The Life of Samuel Johnson* (1791), vol.4.

37 Difficult do you call it, sir? I wish it were impossible.

Of the playing of a famous violinist. Quoted in G B Hill *Johnsonian Miscellanies*, vol.2 (1784).

38 It is the only sensual pleasure without vice.

1784 Of music. Quoted in Sir John Hawkins *Johnsoniana* (1787).

39 I would rather see the portrait of a dog that I know, than all the allegorical paintings they can show me in the world.

Quoted in Mrs Piozzi *Anecdotes of the Late Samuel Johnson* (1786).

40 Corneille is to Shakespeare...as a clipped hedge is to a forest.

Quoted in Mrs Piozzi *Anecdotes of the Late Samuel Johnson* (1786).

41 It is very strange, and very melancholy, that the paucity of human pleasures should persuade us ever to call hunting one of them.

Quoted in Mrs Piozzi *Anecdotes of the Late Samuel Johnson* (1786).

42 Of all noises I think music the least disagreeable.

Quoted in *The Morning Chronicle*, 1816.

43 Fly fishing may be a very pleasant amusement; but angling or float fishing I can only compare to a stick and a string, with a worm at one end and a fool at the other.

Quoted in Hawker *Instructions to Young Sportsmen* (1859). The attribution is doubtful, and Swift has also been credited with the remark.

44 The use of travelling is to regulate imagination by reality, and instead of thinking how things may be, to see them as they are.

Attributed.

Johnston, Brian 1913–94

English cricket commentator.

45 The bowler's Holding, the batsman's Willey.

1976 Radio commentary, during a Test match between England and the West Indies.

46 Turner looks a bit shaky and unsteady, but I think he's going to bat on—one ball left!

Radio commentary, during an England Test match after batsman Glenn Turner was hit on the box by a cricket ball on the fifth ball of the over.

Johst, Hanns 1890–1978

German dramatist.

47 *Wenn ich Kultur höre...entsichere ich meinen Browning!*

When I hear anyone talk of culture...I take off the safety catch on my Browning!

1933 *Schlageter*, act 1, sc.1. The phrase is often attributed to Hermann Goering, in the form 'Whenever I hear the word culture, I reach for my gun!'

Jolson, Al pseudonym of *Asa Yoelson*

1886–1950

Russian-born US actor and singer. He emigrated to the US in 1893 and made his stage début in *The Children of the Ghetto* (1899). He was the star of the first talking picture *The Jazz Singer* in 1927.

48 You Ain't Heard Nothin' Yet.

1919 Title of a song, allegedly taken from an earlier impromptu remark in a café in which Jolson was performing. It is popularly recognized as a line from *The Jazz Singer* (screenplay by Alfred Cohn), the first major film with sound.

Jonas, George 1935–

Hungarian-born Canadian author.

49 There are many wrongs in the world, but none that could be righted by the terrorist's program.

1987 *Crocodiles in the Bathtub and Other Perils.*

50 Maybe that's what is crazy: to want to be free. A lot of people wouldn't cross the street for it.

1989 *A Passion Observed: The Story of a Motorcycle Racer.*

Jones, Bobby (Robert Tyre) 1902–71

US golfer. He won the US Open four times, the British Open three times, the US Amateur Championship five times and the British Amateur Championship once. In 1930 he won the 'Grand Slam', and retired from competitive golf.

51 Golf is a game that is played on a five inch course— the distance between your ears.

Quoted in Colin Jarman *The Guinness Dictionary of Sports Quotations* (1990).

Jones, Henry Arthur 1851–1929

English playwright. His early melodramas were followed by more realistic plays and social comedies.

52 O God! Put back Thy universe and give me yesterday.

1907 *The Silver King* (with Henry Herman), act 2, sc.4.

Jones, James 1921–77

US writer. He is best known for his novel set in the run-up to the bombing of Pearl Harbor, *From Here To Eternity*, and its sequel, *The Thin Red Line* (1962).

53 From Here To Eternity.

1951 Title of novel.

54 I therefore solemnly declare to all young men trying to be writers that they do not actually have to become drunkards first.

1959 Interview in the *Paris Review*, Winter.

55 To me politics is like one of those annoying and potentially dangerous, but generally just painful, chronic diseases that you just have to put up with all your life if you happen to have contracted it. Politics is like having diabetes.

1959 Interview in the *Paris Review*, Winter.

56 Conversation is more often likely to be an attempt at deliberate evasion, deliberate confusion, rather than communication. We're all cheats and liars, really.

1959 Interview in the *Paris Review*, Winter.

Jones, John Paul 1747–92

US admiral. He fought the English fleet in the American Revolution, and later became rear-admiral in the Russian navy.

57 Sir, I have not yet begun to fight.

1779 His reply to a request for surrender when his ship was sinking, 23 Sep. He lashed his ship to his enemy's and boarded it, accepting the enemy captain's surrender. Quoted in Anna de Koven *Life and Letters of John Paul Jones* (1913).

Jones, Quincy Delight 1933–

Jazz trumpeter and songwriter, leader of his own orchestra from 1960. His many albums include *Body Heat* (1974) and *The Dude* (1981). As Vice-President of Mercury Records he promoted Frank Sinatra and Michael Jackson among others.

58 Jazz has always been a man telling the truth about himself.

Quoted in Alan Kendall *The Tender Tyrant: Nadia Boulanger* (1976).

59 To try to talk to the young people who will run the future—in ten minutes—is a little like trying to put a cantaloupe in a coke bottle.

1995 At Claremont College commencement. Reported in the *New York Times*, 29 May.

Jong, Erica née Mann 1942–

US novelist and poet. She achieved notoriety with her controversial first novel, *Fear of Flying*.

60 Everyone has talent. What is rare is the courage to follow the talent to the dark place where it leads.

1972 'The Artist As Housewife', in *The First Ms. Reader.*

61 If sex and creativity are often seen by dictators as subversive activities, it's because they lead to the knowledge that you own your own body (and with it your own voice), and that's the most revolutionary insight of all.

1972 'The Artist As Housewife', in *The First Ms. Reader.*

62 Women are the only exploited group in the world who have been idealized into powerlessness.

1978 In *Time.*

63 The zipless fuck is absolutely pure. It is free of ulterior motives. There is no power game. The man is not 'taking' and the woman is not 'giving'. No one is attempting to cuckold a husband or humiliate a wife. No one is trying to prove

anything or get anything out of anyone. The zipless fuck is the purest thing there is. And it is rarer than the unicorn. And I have never had one.
1973 *Fear of Flying*, ch.1.

64 Solitude is un-American.
1973 *Fear of Flying*, ch.1.

65 Gossip is the opiate of the oppressed.
1973 *Fear of Flying*, ch.6.

66 Horrible as successful artists often are, there is nothing crueller or more vain than a failed artist.
1973 *Fear of Flying*, ch.9.

67 Jealousy is all the fun you think they had.
1973 *Fear of Flying*.

68 Advice is what we ask for when we already know the answer but wish we didn't.
1977 *How To Save Your Own Life*, 'A Day in the Life…'.

69 Friends *love* misery, in fact. Sometimes, especially if we are too lucky or too successful or too pretty, our misery is the only thing that endears us to our friends.
1977 *How To Save Your Own Life*, 'A Day in the Life…'.

70 Every country gets the circus it deserves. Spain gets bullfights. Italy gets the Catholic Church. America gets Hollywood.
1977 *How To Save Your Own Life*, 'Take the Red-Eye…'.

71 Fear of Fifty.
1994 Title of memoir.

Jonson, Ben 1572–1637

English dramatist. Imprisoned for killing a man in a duel, he became a Catholic but later recanted. His plays reject romantic comedy for a more realistic mode and include *Volpone* (1606), *The Silent Woman* (1609) and *The Alchemist* (1610). He was regarded as superior to Shakespeare in his day.

72 GENT: He hath been beyond-sea, once, or twice.
CARL: As far as *Paris*, to fetch over a fashion, and come back again.
1600 *Every Man Out of His Humour*, act 2, sc.2.

73 Well, I will scourge those apes,
And to these courteous eyes oppose a mirror,
As large as is the stage whereon we act;
Where they shall see the time's deformity
Anatomised in every nerve, and sinew,
With constant courage, and contempt of fear.
1600 *Every Man Out Of His Humour*, Induction.

74 Good morning to the day; and next, my gold!
1609 *Volpone*, act 1, sc.1.

75 Yet I glory
More in the cunning purchase of my wealth
Than in the glad possession.
1609 *Volpone*, act 1, sc.1.

76 What should I do,
But cocker up my genius, and live free
To all delights my fortune calls me to?
1609 *Volpone*, act 1, sc.2.

77 Hood an ass with reverend purple,
So you can hide his two ambitious ears,
And he shall pass for a cathedral doctor.
1609 *Volpone*, act 1, sc.3.

78 Give 'em words;
Pour oil into their ears, and send them hence.
1609 *Volpone*, act 1, sc.4.

79 He has no faith in physic. He does think
Most of your doctors are the greater danger,
And worse disease, t'escape.
1609 *Volpone*, act 1, sc.4.

80 'Fore heaven, I wonder at the desperate valour
Of the bold English, that they dare let loose
Their wives to all encounters!
1609 *Volpone*, act 1, sc.5.

81 Calumnies are answered best with silence.
1609 *Volpone*, act 2, sc. 2.

82 Ay, a plague on't,
My conscience fools my wit!
1609 *Volpone*, act 2, sc.7.

83 Success hath made me wanton.
1609 *Volpone*, act 3, sc.1.

84 All my house,
But now, steamed like a bath with her thick breath.
A lawyer could not have been heard; nor scarce
Another woman, such a hail of words
She has let fall.
1609 Of Lady Politic Would-be. *Volpone*, act 3, sc.5.

85 Come, my Celia, let us prove,
While we can, the sports of love,
Time will not be ours for ever,
He, at length, our good will sever;
Spend not then his gifts in vain:
Suns that set may rise again;
But if once we lose this light,
'Tis with us perpetual night.
Why should we defer our joys?
Fame and rumour are but toys.
1609 *Volpone*, 'Song', act 3, sc.7.

86 His soul moves in his fee.

1609 Of the lawyer. *Volpone*, act 4, sc.5.

87 I'd have your tongue, sir, tipped with gold for this.
    1609 *Volpone*, act 4, sc.6.

88 A pox of her autumnal face, her pieced beauty!
    1609–10 *Epicoene*, act 1, sc.1.

89 Still to be neat, still to be drest,
    As you were going to a feast;
    Still to be powdered, still perfumed,
    Lady, it is to be presumed,
    Though art's hid causes are not found,
    All is not sweet, all is not sound.

    Give me a look, give me a face,
    That makes simplicity a grace;
    Robes loosely flowing, hair as free:
    Such sweet neglect more taketh me,
    Than all the adulteries of art;
    They strike mine eyes, but not my heart.
    1609–10 *Epicoene*, act 1, sc.1.

90 Let me see: all discourses but mine own afflict me;
    they seem harsh, impertinent, and irksome.
    1609–10 *Epicoene*, act 2, sc.1.

91 A man of your head and hair should owe more to
    that reverend ceremony, and not mount the
    marriage bed like a town-bull, or a mountain-goat;
    but stay the due season and ascend it then with
    religion and fear.
    1609–10 *Epicoene*, act 3, sc.5.

92 Fortune, that favours fools.
    1610 *The Alchemist*, act 1, sc.4.

93 [The play] is like to be a very conceited scurvy one,
    in plain English.
    1614 *Bartholomew Fair*, 'Induction'.

94 WIN LITTLEWIT: Come, indeed, la, you are such a
    fool, still!
    LITTLEWIT: No, but half a one, Win; you are the
    t'other half: man and wife make one fool, Win.
    1614 *Bartholomew Fair*, act 1, sc.1.

95 He is a fellow of a most arrogant and invincible
    dullness, I assure you.
    1614 *Bartholomew Fair*, act 1, sc.1.

96 There is a doing of right out of wrong, if the ways
    be found.
    1614 *Bartholomew Fair*, act 2, sc.2.

97 I see compassion may become a justice, though it
    be a weakness, I confess, and nearer a vice than a
    virtue.
    1614 *Bartholomew Fair*, act 4, sc.2.

98 There's reason good, that you good laws should
    make:

Men's manners ne'er were viler, for your sake.
1616 *Epigrams*, 'To the Parliament'.

99 Nor shall our cups make any guilty men:
    But, at our parting, we will be, as when
    We innocently met. No simple word,
    That shall be utter'd at our mirthful board,
    Shall make us sad next morning: or affright
    The liberty, that we'll enjoy tonight.
    1616 *Epigrams*, 'On Inviting a Friend to Supper'.

1 Thou art not, Penshurst, built to envious show
   Of touch or marble, nor canst boast a row
   Of polished pillars, or a roof of gold;
   Thou hast no lantern whereof tales are told,
   Or stair, or courts; but standst an ancient pile,
   And these grudged at, art reverenced the
   while.
   1616 *The Forest*, 'To Penshurst'.

2 Then hath thy orchard fruit, thy garden flowers,
   Fresh as the air, and new as are the hours.
   The early cherry, with the later plum,
   Fig, grape, and quince, each in his time doth
   come:
   The blushing apricot, and woolly peach
   Hang on thy walls, that every child may reach.
   1616 *The Forest*, 'To Penshurst'.

3 Freedom doth with degree dispense.
   1616 *The Forest*, 'To Sir Robert Wroth'.

4 Nor for my peace will I go far,
   As wanderers do, that still do roam,
   But make my strengths, such as they are,
   Here in my bosom, and at home.
   1616 *The Forest*, 'To the World'.

5 Drink to me, only, with thine eyes,
   And I will pledge with mine;
   Or leave a kiss but in the cup,
   And I'll not look for wine.
   1616 *The Forest*, 'To Celia'.

6 'Tis grown almost a danger to speak true
   Of any good mind, now: There are so few.
   1616 *The Forest*, 'Epistle to Katherine, Lady Aubigny'.

7 Rest in soft peace, and, asked, say here doth lie
   Ben Jonson his best piece of poetry.
   1616 'On My First Son'.

8 Soul of the Age!
   The applause, delight, the wonder of our stage!
   1623 'To the Memory of My Beloved, The Author, Mr.
   William Shakespeare, and What He Hath Left Us'.

9 Thou hadst small Latin, and less Greek.
   1623 'To the Memory of My Beloved, The Author, Mr.
   William Shakespeare, and What He Hath Left Us', prefatory
   dedication to the first folio of Shakespeare's plays.

10 He was not of an age, but for all time!

1623 'To the Memory of My Beloved, The Author, Mr. William Shakespeare, and What He Hath Left Us'.

11 Sweet Swan of Avon! What a sight it were
To see thee in our waters yet appear,
And make those flights upon the banks of Thames
That so did take Eliza, and our James!

1623 'To the Memory of My Beloved, The Author, Mr. William Shakespeare, and What He Hath Left Us'.

12 O rare Ben Jonson.

1637 His epitaph in Westminster Abbey. It is thought that the words were inscribed on his gravestone at the order of a certain Sir John Young, possibly in error for 'Orare Ben Jonson' ('Pray for Ben Jonson').

13 For Love's sake, kiss me once again,
I long, and should not beg in vain,
Here's none to spy, or see;
Why do you doubt, or stay?
I'll taste as lightly as the Bee,
That doth but touch his flower, and flies away.
Once more, and (faith) I will be gone:
Can he that loves, ask less than one?

The Underwood, 'A Celebration of Charis', no.7 (published 1640).

14 Minds that are great and free,
Should not on fortune pause,
'Tis crown enough to virtue still, her own applause.

The Underwood, 'An Ode To Himself' (published 1640).

15 Helen, did Homer never see
Thy beauties, yet could write of thee?

The Underwood, 'An Ode' (published 1640).

16 Come, let us here enjoy the shade;
For love in shadow best is made.
Though envy oft his shadow be,
None brooks the sunlight worse than he.

The Underwood, 'A Song' (published 1640).

17 'Tis true, I'm broke! Vows, oaths, and all I had
Of credit lost. And I am now run mad,
Or do upon my self some desperate ill;
This sadness makes no approaches, but to kill.

The Underwood, 'An Elegy', no.40 (published 1640).

18 Wisdom without honesty is mere craft and cozenage. And therefore the reputation for honesty must first be gotten; which cannot be but by living well. A good life is a main argument.

Timber: or Discoveries made upon Men and Matter (published 1640).

19 Poetry in this latter age hath proved but a mean mistress to such as have wholly addicted themselves to her, or given their names up to her family. They who have but saluted her on the by, and now and then tendered their visits, she hath done much for, and advanced in the way of their own professions (both the law and the gospel) beyond all they could

have hoped, or done for themselves without her favour.

Timber: or Discoveries made upon Men and Matter (published 1640).

20 I remember that the players have often mentioned it as an honour to Shakespeare that in his writing, whatsoever he penned, he never blotted out a line. My answer hath been, Would he had blotted a thousand: which they thought a malevolent speech…[but] I loved the man and do honour his memory, on this side idolatry, as much as any.

Timber: or Discoveries made upon Men and Matter (published 1640).

21 There was ever more in him to be praised than to be pardoned.

Of Shakespeare. *Timber: or Discoveries made upon Men and Matter* (published 1640).

22 The fear of every man that heard him was, lest he should make an end.

Of Francis Bacon. *Timber: or Discoveries made upon Men and Matter* (published 1640).

23 For a man to write well, there are required three necessaries: to read the best authors, observe the best speakers, and much exercise of his own style.

Timber: or Discoveries made upon Men and Matter (published 1640).

24 Ready writing makes not good writing, but good writing brings on ready writing.

Timber: or Discoveries made upon Men and Matter (published 1640).

25 Custom is the most certain mistress of language, as the public stamp makes the current money.

Timber: or Discoveries made upon Men and Matter (published 1640).

26 Our composition must be more accurate in the beginning and end than in the midst, and in the end more than in the beginning; for through the midst the stream bears us.

Timber: or Discoveries made upon Men and Matter (published 1640).

27 Our style should be as a skein of silk, to be carried and found by the right thread, not ravelled and perplexed; then all is a knot, a heap.

Timber: or Discoveries made upon Men and Matter (published 1640).

Jordan, June 1936–

US poet, essayist, political activist and writer for children. Her work has been marked by a strong commitment to black consciousness.

28 Body and soul, Black America reveals the extreme questions of contemporary life, questions of freedom and identity: *How can I be who I am?*

1969 'Black Studies: Bringing Back the Person', in the

29 We do not deride the fears of prospering white America. A nation of violence and private property has every reason to dread the violated and the deprived.
1969 'Black Studies: Bringing Back the Person', in the *Evergreen Review*, Oct.

30 To rescue our children we will have to let them save us from the power we embody: we will have to trust the very difference that they forever personify.
1978 Keynote address for Child Welfare League of America. Collected as 'Old Stories: New Lives' in *Moving Towards Home* (1989).

31 I am a feminist, and what that means to me is much the same as the meaning of the fact that I am Black: it means that I must undertake to love myself as though my very life depends upon self-love and self-respect.
1978 Address to Black Writers Conference, Howard University. Collected as 'Where Is The Love?' in *Moving Towards Home* (1989).

Joseph of Exeter fl.12c
English poet.

32 The youths at cricks did play
Throughout the merry day.
1180 Quoted in Ivor Brown *A Book of England* (1958). This is thought to be the first mention of the game of cricket in English literature.

Joseph II 1741–90
Holy Roman Emperor (1756–90), known as 'the revolutionary emperor' for his programme of modernization. He suppressed papal power and in 1781 published an Edict of Toleration for Protestants and Greeks.

33 As I have just come from making my Easter confession on Good Friday and have forgiven all those who trespass against me, I cannot harbour any thoughts of revenge, only contempt for an arrant shit who is bursting with pride, although he is simply being taken for a ride by his women.
1786 Of the senior dignitary of the Holy Roman Empire, the Elector-Archbishop of Mainz. Letter to Trauttmansdorff (his representative at Mainz), 14 Apr. Quoted in T C W Blanning *Joseph II* (1994), p.148.

34 Here lies a prince whose intentions were pure, but who had the misfortune to see all his plans collapse.
Epitaph for himself. Quoted in T C W Blanning *Joseph II* (1994), p.1.

Josephus, Flavius AD 37–100
Jewish historian and soldier, commander of Galilee. He surrendered to the Romans rather than commit suicide, and later won imperial patronage and lived in Rome. His works include *The Antiquities of the Jews*.

35 Their exercises are unbloody battles, and their battles bloody exercises.
c.75–9 AD Of the Romans. *A History of the Jewish War*, bk.3, ch.5, section 1 (translated by William Whiston).

Jourdan, Louis originally Louis Gendre 1921–
French-born actor. He appeared in French films 1940–6, then came to the USA. His many American and European film credits since include *Gigi* (1958), *Can Can* (1960) and *Octopussy* (1983).

36 In New York people don't go to the theater—they go to see hits.
1950 In the *New York Herald Tribune*, 1 Jan.

Jouvet, Louis 1887–1951
French actor and director. Appointed director of the Comédie des Champs-Élysées in 1922, he had a profound impact on the development of French theatre between the wars, making many reforms.

37 The one thing constant in a changing world is the avant-garde.
Attributed.

Jovanovich, William 1920–
US publisher. He joined Harcourt Brace Jovanovich Inc in 1947, eventually becoming President and Director.

38 The most important single thing in publishing is the English sentence, and the editor who cannot contemplate it again and again with a sense of wonder has not yet gained respect for the complexity of learning.
1964 *Now, Barabbas*.

Jowett, Benjamin 1817–93
English classical scholar, Professor of Greek at Oxford (1855–93), ordained as an Anglican priest in 1845.

39 One man is as good as another until he has written a book.
Quoted in Evelyn Abbott and Lewis Campbell (eds) *Life and Letters of Benjamin Jowett* (1897), vol.1.

40 Nowhere probably is there more true feeling, and nowhere worse taste, than in a churchyard.
Quoted in Evelyn Abbott and Lewis Campbell (eds) *Letters of Benjamin Jowett* (1899), ch.6.

Joyce, James Augustine Aloysius
1882–1941
Irish writer who lived in exile on the Continent and was plagued for most of his life with deteriorating eyesight. His fiction includes *Dubliners* (1914), *Ulysses* (1922), one of the most influential works of twentieth-century fiction, and *Finnegans Wake* (1939).

41 'O, pa!' he cried. 'Don't beat me, pa! And I'll…I'll say a *Hail Mary* for you… I'll say a *Hail Mary* for you, pa, if you don't beat me.'
1914 *Dubliners*, 'Counterparts'.

42 His soul swooned slowly as he heard the snow falling faintly through the universe and faintly falling, like the descent of their last end, upon all the living and the dead.
1914 *Dubliners*, 'The Dead'.

43 The fellows were practising long shies and bowling lobs and slow twisters. In the soft grey silence he could hear the bump of the balls: and from here and from there through the quiet air the sound of the cricket bats: pick, pack, pock, puck: like drops of water in a fountain falling softly in the brimming bowl.
1916 *A Portrait of the Artist as a Young Man*.

44 At the door Dante turned round violently and shouted down the room, her cheeks flushed and quivering with rage:
—Devil out of hell! We won! We crushed him to death! Fiend!
The door slammed behind her.
Mr Casey, freeing his arms from his holders, suddenly bowed his head on his hands with a sob of pain.
—Poor Parnell! he cried loudly. My dead king!
1916 *A Portrait of the Artist as a Young Man*.

45 The snotgreen sea. The scrotumtightening sea.
1922 *Ulysses*.

46 It is a symbol of Irish art. The cracked lookingglass of a servant.
1922 *Ulysses*.

47 When I makes tea I makes tea, as old mother Grogan said. And when I makes water I makes water... *Begob, ma'am*, says Mrs. Cahill, *God send you don't make them in the one pot.*
1922 *Ulysses*.

48 History, Stephen said, is a nightmare from which I am trying to awake.
1922 *Ulysses*.

49 Lawn Tennyson, gentleman poet.
1922 *Ulysses*.

50 Come forth, Lazarus! And he came fifth and lost the job.
1922 *Ulysses*.

51 A man of genius makes no mistakes. His errors are volitional and are the portals of discovery.
1922 *Ulysses*.

52 Greater love than this, he said, no man hath that a man lay down his wife for his friend. Go thou and do likewise. Thus, or words to that effect, saith Zarathustra, sometime regius professor of French letters to the university of Oxtail.
1922 *Ulysses*.

53 Mr. Leopold Bloom ate with relish the inner organs of beasts and fowls. He liked thick giblet soup, nutty gizzards, a stuffed roast heart; liver slices fried with crustcrumbs, fried hencod's roes. Most of all he liked grilled mutton kidneys which gave to his palate a fine tang of faintly scented urine.
1922 *Ulysses*, pt.2.

54 A woman loses a charm with every pin she takes out.
1922 *Ulysses*, pt.2.

55 Heavenly weather. If life was always like that. Cricket weather. Sit around under sunshades. Over after over. Out. They can't play it here. Still, Captain Buller broke a window in Kildare Street Club with a slog to square leg.
1922 *Ulysses*. Legend has it that W G Grace performed the feat of breaking the Kildare Street Club window while playing at the distant College Park in the 1870s.

56 Her crocus dress she wore, lowcut, belongings on show.
1922 *Ulysses*, pt.2.

57 yes and how he kissed me under the Moorish wall and I thought well as well him as another and then I asked him with my eyes to ask again yes and then he asked me would I yes to say yes my mountain flower and first I put my arms around him yes and drew him down to me so he could feel my breasts all perfume yes and his heart was going like mad and yes I said yes I will Yes.
1922 *Ulysses*, last words.

58 I read the first 2 pages of the usual sloppy English and [Stuart Gilbert] read me a lyrical bit about nudism in the wood and the end which is a piece of propaganda in favour of something which, outside of D. H. L.'s country at any rates, makes all the propaganda for itself.
1931 On D H Lawrence's *Lady Chatterly's Lover*. Letter to Harriet Weaver, 17 Dec.

59 That ideal reader suffering from an ideal insomnia.
1939 *Finnegans Wake*.

60 Gentes and laitymen, fullstoppers and semicolonials, hybreds and lubberds!
1939 *Finnegans Wake*.

61 All moanday, tearsday, wailsday, thumpsday, frightday, shatterday till the fear of the Law.
1939 *Finnegans Wake*.

Joyce, Nora d.1951
Wife of James Joyce.

62 Well, Jim, I haven't read any of your books but I'll have to someday because they must be good

considering how well they sell.

To her husband James Joyce. Recalled on her death, 12 Apr 1951.

Joyce, William known as *Lord Haw Haw*

1906–46

British traitor. He fled to Germany before World War II, from where he broadcast anti-British propaganda in his upper-class drawl until captured at Flensburg and executed.

63 The Twenty Thousand Thieves.

c.1941 Of the Australian 9th Division troops who were besieged at Tobruk, North Africa. Radio broadcast from Nazi Germany.

Juana Inés de la Cruz, sor   1651–95

Mexican intellectual, nun and poet. After she took her vows at the age of 16, attempts were made to stop her writing. Two years after writing her defence, *Respuesta a sor Filotea*, she sold her books and devoted herself to religion.

64 *En perseguirme, Mundo, ¿Qué interesas?*
¿En qué te ofendo, cuando sólo intento
poner bellezas en mi entendimiento
y no mi entendimiento en las bellezas?

World, in hounding me, what do you gain?
How can it harm you if I choose, astutely,
rather to stock my mind with things of beauty,
than waste its stock on every beauty's claim?

1688 *Poesía, teatro y prosa*, 'Quéjase de la suerte' (translated as 'She Complains about her Fate', 1985).

65 *Aprendamos a ignorar,*
pensamiento, pues hallamos
que cuanto añado al discurso,
tanto le usurpo a los años.

Thought, let's learn not to know,
since so plainly it appears
that whatever we add to our minds
we take away from our years.

1688 *A Sor Juana Anthology*, 'Acusa la hidropesía de mucha ciencia' (translated as 'She condemns the bloatedness of much learning', 1985).

66 *Este natural impulso que Dios puso en mí...su*
Majestad sabe por qué y para qué; y sabe que le he
pedido que apague la luz de mi entendimiento
dejando sólo lo que baste para guardar su Ley, pues lo
demás sobra, (según algunos) en una mujer; y aun hay
quien dice que daña.

This natural impulse which God has implanted in me...only His Majesty knows why and wherefore and His Majesty also knows that I have prayed to Him to extinguish the light of my mind, only leaving sufficient to keep His Law, since any more is overmuch, so some say, in a woman, and there are even those who say it is harmful.

1691 *Poesía, teatro y prosa*, 'Respuesta a sor Filotea' ('An Answer to Sister Filotea', 1982).

Julian of Norwich known as *Lady Julian*

c.1342–1416

English anchoress, who spent much of her life enclosed in a cell attached to the Church of St Julian, Norwich. In 1373 she experienced a series of religious visions which she set down in her *Revelations of Divine Love*.

67 He shewed a little thing, the quantitie of an haselnott, lying in the palme of my hand, as me semide, and it was as rounde as a balle. I looked theron with the eye of my understanding, and thought, What may this be. And it was answered generaelly thus: It is all that is made... It lasteth and ever shall, for god loueth it.

1373–c.1393 *Revelations of Divine Love*, ch.5 (transcribed by D Harford, 1925).

68 Pray inwardly, even though you do not enjoy it. It does good though you feel nothing, even though you think you are doing nothing.

1373–c.1393 *Revelations of Divine Love* (transcribed by D Harford, 1925).

69 It is true that sin is the cause of all this pain; but all shall be well, and all shall be well, and all manner of things shall be well.

1373–c.1393 *Revelations of Divine Love*, ch.27 (transcribed by D Harford, 1925).

Jumblatt, Walid   1949–

Lebanese politician and hereditary Druze chieftain, who succeeded his father Jumblatt on the latter's assassination in 1977.

70 Here, even the law of the jungle has broken down.

1985 Of the situation in Beirut, in the *Sunday Times*, 29 Dec.

Jung, Carl Gustav   1875–1961

Swiss psychiatrist. After collaborating with Sigmund Freud he published *The Psychology of the Unconscious* (1911–12), departing from Freud's psychosexual emphasis. Subsequently he developed analytical psychology and the concept of the 'collective unconscious'.

71 The pendulum of the mind oscillates between sense and nonsense, not between right and wrong.

1962 *Memories, Dreams and Reflections*.

72 Show me a sane man and I will cure him for you.

Quoted in *The Observer*, 19 Jul 1975.

'Junius' possibly the pseudonym of *Sir Philip Francis* (1740–1818)

The identity of Junius, whose scathing political letters were printed in the *Public Advertiser* between 1769 and 1771 and collected in 1772, has never been established. Sir Philip Francis is a favourite candidate.

73 There is a holy mistaken zeal in politics as well as in religion. By persuading others, we convince ourselves.
1769 *Public Advertiser*, 19 Dec, Letter 35.

74 Let it be impressed upon your minds, let it be instilled into your children, that the liberty of the press is the *Palladium* of all the civil, political, and religious rights of an Englishman.
1772 *Letters*, Dedication to the Authorized Edition.

Just, Ward Swift 1935–

US journalist and writer. He was a correspondent with *Newsweek* (1963–5) and the *Washington Post* (1965–70), before turning full time to fiction with works such as *The American Blues* (1984).

75 The place where bulls and foxes dine very well, but lambs end up head down on the hook.
1988 Of Chicago. *Jack Gance*.

Justinian I AD 482–565

Emperor of the East Roman Empire (from 527). His reign saw the restoration of the Roman Empire to its ancient limits and many legal reforms, collected in the *Corpus Juris Civilis*, which had a considerable influence on European law.

76 Justice is the constant and perpetual wish to render to every one his due.
533 *Institutiones*, pt.1.

Juvenal full name *Decimus Iunius Iuvenalis*
c.55–c.140 AD

Roman lawyer and satirist. He was banished to Egypt for some years by Domitian for his 16 verse satires (c.100–128 AD), which deal with the corruption and immorality of the times.

77 *Difficile est saturam non scribere.*

It is difficult not to write satire.
Satirae, no.1, l.30.

78 *Quis tulerit Gracchos de seditione querentes?*

Who can bear the Gracchi deploring revolution?
Satirae, no.2, l.24. The brothers Caius and Tiberius Sempronius Gracchus (2c BC) attempted radical agrarian reforms, and were both killed by political opponents.

79 *Nil habet infelix paupertas durius in se*
Quam quod ridiculos homines facit.

The hardest thing to bear in poverty is the fact that it makes men ridiculous.
Satirae, no.3, l.152–3 (translated by Peter Green).

80 *Cantabit vacuus coram latrone viator.*

Travel light and you can sing in the robber's face.
Satirae, no.10, l.22.

81 *Nam qui dabat olim*
imperium, fasces, legiones, omnia, nunc se
continet atque duas tantum res anxius optat,
panem et circenses.

Time was when their plebiscite elected generals, Heads of State, commanders of legions: but now they've pulled in their horns, there's only two things that concern them: bread and games.
Of the people of Rome. *Satirae*, no.10, l.78–81 (translated by Peter Green).

82 *Orandum est ut sit mens sana in corpore sano.*

One should pray to have a sound mind in a sound body.
Satirae, no.10, l.356.

83 *Maxima debetur puero reverentia, si quid*
turpe paras.

If you are planning any misdeed, never forget that a child has a first claim on your respect.
Satirae, no.14, l.47 (translated by Peter Green).

Kafka, Franz 1883–1924

Czech novelist and short-story writer who wrote in German. After studying law he worked in Prague at a worker's accident insurance company. He is best known for his bleak studies of the absurdity of the human condition.

84 *Ich glaube, mann sollte überhaupt nur solche Bücher lesen, die einen beißen und stechen.*

I think we ought to read only the kind of books that wound and stab us.
1904 Letter to Oskar Pollack. Collected in Richard and Clara Winston (ed and trans) *Letters to Friends, Family, and Editors* (1977).

85 *Ist es schwer und kann es ein Außenseiter begreifen, daß man eine Geschichte von ihrem Anfang in sich erlebt, vom fernen Punkt bis zu der heranfahrenden Lokomotive aus Stahl, Kohl und Dampf, sie aber auch jetzt noch nicht verläßt, sondern von ihr gejagt wird und aus eigenem Schwung vor ihr läuft, wohin sie nur stößt und wohin man sie lockt.*

It is so difficult and can an outsider understand that you experience a story within yourself from its beginning, from the distant point up to the approaching locomotive of steel, coal and steam, and you don't abandon it even now, but want to be pursued by it and have time for it, therefore are pursued by it and of your own volition run before it wherever it may thrust and wherever you may lure it.
1911 Diary entry, Aug. Collected in Max Brod (ed) *The Diaries of Franz Kafka, 1910–1913* (1948).

86 *Als Gregor Samsa eines Morgens aus unruhigen Träumen erwachte, fand er sich in seinem Bett zu einem ungeheueren Ungeziefer verwandelt.*

When Gregor Samsa awoke one morning from uneasy dreams he found himself transformed in his bed into a gigantic insect.
1915 *Metamorphosis*, ch.1.

87 *Es ist oft besser, in Ketten als frei zu sein.*

It is often safer to be in chains than to be free.
1925 *Der Prozess* (The Trial).

88 *Ich bin so weit, daß ich Gewißheit gar nicht haben will.*

I have reached the stage where I no longer wish to have certainty.
'Der Bau', collected in Nahum N Glatzer (ed) *The Complete Stories* (1971).

89 *Er lächelte und sagte: 'Von mir willst du den Weg erfahren?' 'Ja,' sagte ich, 'da ich ihn selbst nich finden kann.' 'Gibs auf, gibs auf,' sagte er und wandte sich mit einem grossen Schwunge ab, so wie Leute, die mit ihrem Lachen allein sein wollen.*

He smiled and said: 'You asking me the way?' 'Yes,' I said, 'since I cannot find it myself.' 'Give it up! Give it up!' said he, and turned with a sudden jerk, like someone who wants to be alone with his laughter.
'Gibs Auf!', collected in Nahum N Glatzer (ed) *The Complete Stories* (1971).

Kahn, Gus 1886–1941

US lyricist and author. He supplied the lyrics for many classic hit songs of the 1920s and 1930s, among them 'Toot, Toot, Tootsie', 'Carolina in the Morning', 'Yes Sir, That's My Baby', and 'Makin' Whoopee'.

90 There's nothing surer,
The rich get rich and the poor get children.
In the meantime, in between time,
Ain't we got fun.
1921 'Ain't We Got Fun' (with Raymond B Egan).

91 All God's Chillum got Rhythm.
1937 Title of song.

Kaiko, Takeshi 1930–89

Japanese novelist. His first novel to be translated into English was *Darkness in Summer* (1972).

92 I don't trust anybody who's never eaten bread with the salt of tears.
1963 'The Laughing Stock', in *Five Thousand Runaways* (translated by Cecilia Segawa Seigle).

93 Late one morning, I awoke in the capital of a certain country and found myself—not changed overnight into a large brown beetle, nor feeling

exactly on top of the world—merely ready to go home.
1978 'The Crushed Pellet', in *Five Thousand Runaways* (translated by Cecilia Segawa Seigle).

Kandinsky, Wassily 1866–1944

Russian-born painter and writer on art. He was an important pioneer of abstract art. With Franz Marc, the editor of the *Blaue Reiter Almanac*.

94 The force that propels the human spirit on the clear way forward and upward is the abstract spirit.
1912 'On the Question of Form', in *Blaue Reiter Almanac*.

95 We should never make a god out of form. We should struggle for form only as long as it serves as a means of expression for the inner sound.
1912 'On the Question of Form', in *Blaue Reiter Almanac*.

96 Every work of art is the child of its time, often it is the mother of our emotions.
1912 *Concerning the Spiritual in Art*.

97 In general, therefore, color is a means of exerting a direct influence upon the soul. Color is the keyboard. The eye is the hammer. The soul is the piano, with its many strings.
Quoted in K C Lindsay and P Vergo (eds and trans) *Kandinsky: Complete Writings on Art* (1982).

Kant, Immanuel 1724–1804

German philosopher, Professor of Logic and Metaphysics at Konigsberg (1770), who developed a theory of knowledge depending on perception, and propounded the 'moral argument' for the existence of God. His great work is the *Kritik der reinen Vernunft* (Critique of Pure Reason, 1781).

98 *Der Verstand vermag nichts anzuschauen, und die Sinne nichts zu denken. Nur daraus, daß sie sich vereinigen, kann Erkenntnis entspringen.*

The understanding can intuit nothing, the senses can think nothing. Only through their union can knowledge arise.
1781 *Kritik der reinen Vernunft* (*Critique of Pure Reason*), B75 (translated by N Kemp Smith).

99 *Ich habe also demnach keine Erkenntnis von mir, wie ich bin, sondern bloß, wie ich mir selbst erscheine. Das Bewußtsein seiner selbst ist also noch lange nicht eine Erkenntnis seiner selbst.*

I have no *knowledge* of myself as I am but merely as I appear to myself. The consciousness of myself is thus very far from being a knowledge of the self.
1781 *Kritik der reinen Vernunft* (*Critique of Pure Reason*), B158 (translated by N Kemp Smith).

1 *Eben darin Philosophie besteht, seine Grenzen zu kennen.*

It is precisely in knowing its limits that philosophy consists.

1781 *Kritik der reinen Vernunft* (*Critique of Pure Reason*), B755 (translated by N Kemp Smith).

2 *Sapere aude*, have the courage to know: that is the motto of enlightenment.

1783 His reply to a newspaper's challenge to define enlightenment. Quoted in *The Economist*, 16 Mar 1996.

3 *Aus so krummen Holze, als woraus der Mensch gemacht ist, kann nichts ganz Gerades gezimmert werden.*

Out of the crooked timber of humanity, no straight thing can ever be made.

1784 *Idee zu einer allgemeinen Geschichte in weltbürgerlicher Absicht* (*Idea for a General History with a Cosmopolitan Purpose*), prop.6.

4 *Ich solle niemals anders verfahren, als so, daß ich auch wollen könne, meine Maxime solle ein allgemeines Gesetz werden.*

I ought never to act except in such a way *that I can also will that my maxim should become a universal law.*

1785 *Grundlagen zur Metaphysik der Sitten* (*Groundwork to a Metaphysic of Morals*), ch.1 (translated by H J Paton).

5 *Handle so, daß du die Menschheit, so wohl in deiner Person eines jeden andern, jederzeit zugleich als Zweck, niemals bloß als Mittel brauchest.*

Act in such a way that you always treat humanity, whether in your own person or in the person of any other, never simply as a means, but always at the same time as an end.

1785 *Grundlagen zur Metaphysik der Sitten* (*Groundwork to a Metaphysic of Morals*), ch.2 (translated by H J Paton).

6 *Ich mußte also das Wissen aufheben, um zum Glauben Platz zu bekommen.*

I have therefore found it necessary to deny *knowledge*, in order to make room for *faith.*

1787 *Kritik der reinen Vernunft* (*Critique of Pure Reason*), preface to 2nd edn (translated by N Kemp Smith).

7 *Zwei Dinge erfüllen das Gemüt mit immer neuer und zunehmender Bewunderung und Ehrfurcht, je öfter und anhaltender sich das Nachdenken damit beschäftigt: der bestirnte Himmel über mir, und das moralische Gesetz in mir.*

Two things fill the mind with ever new and increasing admiration and awe, the oftener and more steadily we reflect on them: *the starry heavens above me and the moral law within.*

1788 *Kritik der praktischen Vernunft* (*Critique of Practical Reason*) (translated by T K Abbott).

Kapitsa, Peter Leonidovich 1894–1984

Soviet physicist who studied in Britain under Ernest Rutherford. Director of the Institute of Physical Problems, he was dismissed by Stalin for refusing to work on an atomic bomb, but was later reinstated.

8 Theory is a good thing but a good experiment lasts forever.

1980 *Experiment, Theory, Practice.*

Karloff, Boris originally *William Henry Pratt* 1887–1969

English-born US film star. He went to Canada and the US aiming at a diplomatic career, but turned to acting, finding fame as the monster in *Frankenstein* (1931) and other horror roles.

9 The monster was indeed the best friend I could ever have.

1991 On his success as Frankenstein's monster. Quoted in *Connoisseur*, Jan.

Karr, Alphonse 1808–90

French writer and journalist.

10 *Plus ça change, plus c'est la même chose.*

The more things change, the more they stay the same.

1849 *Les Guêpes*, Jan.

Karsh, Yousuf 1908–

Turkish-born Canadian portrait photographer.

11 I said, 'Forgive me, sir,' and plucked the cigar out of his mouth. By the time I got back to my camera, he looked so belligerent he could have devoured me. It was at that instant that I took the photograph. The silence was deafening.

1983 Recalling how he snapped the celebrated 'bulldog' photograph of Sir Winston Churchill in the Speaker's Chambers, House of Commons, Ottawa, on 30 Dec 1941. *Karsh: A Fifty-Year Retrospective.*

Kaufman, George S(imon) 1889–1961

US playwright, director and journalist, a member of the Algonquin Round Table circle of literary wits. He collaborated on several successful comedies with Moss Hart, notably *The Man Who Came to Dinner* (1939), and also worked with Edna Ferber and George Gershwin.

12 Am sitting in the last row. Wish you were here.

1932 Telegram sent during a performance of *Of Thee I Sing* to the actor William Gaxton, who was taking various liberties with Kaufman's lines while playing the leading role.

13 Massey won't be satisfied until he's assassinated.

1938 Of Raymond Massey in the title role of *Abe Lincoln in Illinois*. Recalled on Kaufman's death, 2 Jun 1961.

14 Satire is what closed Saturday night.

Quoted in Howard Teichmann *George S Kaufman* (1972).

15 I saw his play under bad conditions. The curtain was up.

Of Alexander Woollcott. Quoted in Scott Meredith *George S Kaufman and His Friends* (1974).

16 Like the Arabs, I fold my tens and silently steal away.

On winning at poker. Quoted in Scott Meredith *George S Kaufman and His Friends* (1974).

▷ See Longfellow 611:4.

17 It's what God would have done if he'd had the money.

On visiting Pocantico Hills, the Rockefeller family's 3,000-acre Hudson River estate. Quoted in Michael Kramer and Sam Roberts *I Never Wanted to be Vice-President of Anything!* (1976).

18 God finally caught his eye.

Epitaph for a deceased waiter. Quoted in Jon Winokur *The Portable Curmudgeon* (1987).

19 Close the play and keep the store open nights.

Reply when asked by one of his backers, the owner of Bloomingdale's department store, how the premiere of Kaufman's latest play had gone. Attributed.

20 Over my dead body.

Suggestion for his own epitaph. Attributed.

21 There was scattered laughter in the rear of the theatre, leading to the belief that somebody was telling jokes back there.

Play review.

Kaufmann, Christoph

German author and critic.

22 *Sturm und Drang.*

Storm and stress.

c.1775 Suggested title for a romantic historical play of F M Klinger, adopted as the defining term for late-18c German drama.

Kaunitz-Rietberg, Wenzel Anton, Prince von 1711–94

Austrian statesman, Ambassador to the French court (1750–2). Appointed Chancellor in 1753, he directed Austrian politics for almost 40 years. Active in the ecclesiastical reforms of Joseph II, he was a liberal patron of arts and sciences.

23 That was very good of him.

1790 Attributed, on hearing that Joseph II had died. Quoted in T C W Blanning *Joseph II* (1994), p.198.

Kavanagh, P(atrick) J(oseph Gregory) 1931–

English poet and novelist. His works include the autobiographical *The Perfect Stranger*, (1966) and his *Collected Poems* (1987).

24 Charlie Parker...always filled me with a kind of despair, because he played the way I would have

liked to write, and this wasn't possible for me or anyone else. He made poetry seem word-bound.

1966 *The Perfect Stranger*, ch.5.

25 Try not to despise yourself too much—it's only a conceit.

1968 *A Song and Dance*, ch.6.

26 But years ago he had decided never to be afraid of the deafeningly obvious, it is always news to somebody.

1968 *A Song and Dance*, ch.6.

27 Mary lived by wondering what lay round the corner. I lived by knowing there was no corner.

1973 *A Happy Man*, ch.12.

Kazantzakis, Nikos 1883–1957

Greek writer, best known for his novel *Zorba the Greek* (1946, filmed 1964) and the long autobiographical narrative poem, *The Odyssey, a Modern Sequel* (1938).

28 My entire soul is a cry, and all my work is a commentary on that cry.

1965 *Report to Greco.*

Kazin, Alfred 1915–98

US writer, best known for influential books of literary criticism such as *On Native Grounds* (1942) and the autobiographical *A Walker in the City* (1951).

29 In a very real sense, the writer writes in order to teach himself, to understand himself, to satisfy himself; the publishing of his ideas, though it brings gratifications, is a curious anti-climax.

1963 In *Think*, Feb.

30 Only power can get people into a position where they may be noble.

Quoted in M Korda *Power in the Office* (1976).

Keating, Paul John 1944–

Australian Republican politician. He became President of the New South Wales Labor Party (1979–83) and in 1991 was elected Leader of the Australian Labor Party. He was Prime Minister from 1991–6.

31 A banana republic.

1986 On Australia's balance-of-payments crisis and cycle of recession. Radio broadcast, Radio 2GB, Sydney, 14 May.

Keats, John 1795–1821

English Romantic poet. His long mythological poem *Endymion* (1818) was fiercely criticized but *Lamia and Other Poems* (1820), containing the romances 'The Eve of St Agnes' and 'Lamia', the epic 'Hyperion' and his major odes, was better received. He died of tuberculosis in Rome.

32 Much have I travell'd in the realms of gold.
   1815 'On first looking into Chapman's Homer', l.1.
   (Published in The Examiner 1816.)

33 Then felt I like some watcher of the skies
   When a new planet swims into his ken;
   Or like stout Cortez when with eagle eyes
   He star'd at the Pacific—and all his men
   Look'd at each other with a wild surmise—
   Silent, upon a peak in Darien.
   1815 'On first looking into Chapman's Homer', l.9–14.
   (Published in The Examiner 1816.)

34 Sweetly they slept
   On the blue fields of heaven, and then there crept
   A little noiseless noise among the leaves,
   Born of the very sign that silence heaves.
   1816 'I Stood Tip-Toe Upon a Little Hill', l.9–12.

35 Here are sweet peas, on tiptoe for a flight,
   With wings of gentle flush o'er delicate white.
   1816 'I Stood Tip-Toe Upon a Little Hill', l.57–8.

36 Morality
   Weighs heavily on me like unwilling sleep.
   1817 'On Seeing the Elgin Marbles'.

37 Yet the sweet converse of an innocent mind,
   Whose words are images of thoughts refined,
   Is my soul's pleasure; and it sure must be
   Almost the highest bliss of human-kind,
   When to thy haunts two kindred spirits flee.
   1817 'O Solitude! if I must with thee dwell'.

38 Stop and consider! life is but a day;
   A fragile dew-drop on its perilous way
   From a tree's summit; a poor Indian's sleep
   While his boat hastens to the monstrous steep
   Of Montmorenci.
   1817 'Sleep and Poetry', l.85–9.

39 O for ten years, that I may overwhelm
   Myself in poesy; so I may do the deed
   That my own soul has to itself decreed.
   1817 'Sleep and Poetry', l.96–8.

40 They swayed about upon a rocking horse,
   And thought it Pegasus.
   1817 'Sleep and Poetry', l.186–7.

41 And they shall be accounted poet kings
   Who simply tell the most heart-easing things.
   1817 'Sleep and Poetry', l.267–8.

42 It keeps eternal whisperings around
   Desolate shores—and with its mighty swell
   Gluts twice ten thousand Caverns.
   1817 'On the Sea'.

43 I had a dove and the sweet dove died;

And I have thought it died of grieving:
O, what could it grieve for? Its feet were tied,
With a silken thread of my own hands' weaving.
1817 'I had a Dove and the Sweet Dove Died'.

44 A long poem is a test of invention which I take to
   be the Polar star of poetry, as fancy is the sails, and
   imagination the rudder.
   1817 Letter to Benjamin Bailey, 8 Oct.

45 I am certain of nothing but the holiness of the
   heart's affections and the truth of the
   imagination—what the imagination seizes as
   beauty must be truth—whether it existed before or
   not.
   1817 Letter to Benjamin Bailey, 22 Nov.

46 O for a life of sensations rather than of thoughts!
   1817 Letter to Benjamin Bailey, 22 Nov.

47 Negative Capability; that is, when a man is capable
   of being in uncertainties, mysteries, doubts,
   without any irritable reaching after fact and reason.
   1817 Letter to G and T Keats, 21 Dec.

48 Souls of Poets dead and gone
   What Elysium have ye known,
   Happy field or mossy cavern,
   Choicer than the Mermaid Tavern?
   1818 'Lines on the Mermaid Tavern'

49 When I have fears that I may cease to be
   Before my pen has gleaned my teeming brain,
   Before high-piled books, in charactery,
   Hold like rich garners the full ripened grain;
   1818 'When I Have Fears that I may Cease to Be'.

50 When I behold, upon the night's starred face
   Huge cloudy symbols of a high romance,
   And think that I may never live to trace
   Their shadows, with the magic hand of chance;
   And when I feel, fair creature of an hour,
   That I shall never look upon thee more,
   Never have relish in the faery power
   Of unreflecting love;—then on the shore
   Of the wide world I stand alone, and think
   Till love and fame to nothingness so sink.
   1818 'When I Have Fears that I may Cease to Be'.

51 If poetry comes not as naturally as leaves to a tree it
   had better not come at all.
   1818 Letter to John Taylor, 27 Feb.

52 Scenery is fine—but human nature is finer.
   1818 Letter to Benjamin Bailey, 13 Mar.

53 It is impossible to live in a country which is
   continually under hatches... Rain! Rain! Rain!
   1818 Letter to J H Reynolds, 10 Apr.

54 I think I shall be among the English Poets after my
death.
1818 Letter to George and Georgiana Keats, 14 Oct.

55 The imagination of a boy is healthy, and the
mature imagination of a man is healthy; but there
is a space of life between, in which the soul is in a
ferment, the character undecided, the way of life
uncertain, the ambition thick-sighted: thence
proceeds mawkishness.
1818 *Endymion*, preface.

56 A thing of beauty is a joy for ever:
Its loveliness increases; it will never
Pass into nothingness; but still will keep
A bower quiet for us, and a sleep
Full of sweet dreams, and health, and quiet
breathing.
1818 *Endymion*, bk.1, l.1–5.

57 The grandeur of the dooms
We have imagined for the mighty dead.
1818 *Endymion*, bk.1, l.20–1.

58 They always must be with us, or we die.
1818 *Endymion*, bk.1, l.33.

59 Who, of men, can tell
That flowers would bloom, or that green fruit
would swell
To melting pulp, that fish would have bright mail,
The earth its dower of river, wood, and vale,
The meadows runnels, runnels pebble-stones,
The seed its harvest, or the lute its tones,
Tones ravishments, or ravishment its sweet,
If human souls did never kiss and greet?
1818 *Endymion*, bk.1, l.835–42.

60 Here is wine,
Alive with sparkles—never, I aver,
Since Ariadne was a vintager,
So cool a purple.
1818 *Endymion*, bk.2, l.441–4.

61 To Sorrow,
I bade good-morrow,
And thought to leave her far away behind;
But cheerly, cheerly,
She loves me dearly
She is so constant to me, and so kind.
1818 *Endymion*, bk.4, l.173–8.

62 Their smiles,
Wan as primroses gathered at midnight
By chilly fingered spring.
1818 *Endymion*, bk.4, l.969–71.

63 Turn the key deftly in the oiled wards,
And seal the hushed Casket of my Soul.
1819 'To Sleep'.

64 I have met with women whom I really think would
like to be married to a poem, and to be given away
by a novel.
1819 Letter to Fanny Brawne, 8 Jul.

65 I have two luxuries to brood over in my walks,
your loveliness and the hour of my death. O that
I could have possession of them both in the same
minute.
1819 Letter to Fanny Brawne, 25 Jul.

66 My friends should drink a dozen of Claret on my
Tomb.
1819 Letter to Benjamin Bailey , 14 Aug.

67 Give me books, fruit, french wine and fine weather
and a little music out of doors, played by somebody
I do not know.
1819 Letter to Fanny Keats, 29 Aug.

68 Fanatics have their dreams, wherewith they weave
A paradise for a sect.
1819 'The Fall of Hyperion', l.1–2.
(Published 1856.)

69 'None can usurp this height,' returned that shade,
'But those to whom the miseries of the world
Are misery, and will not let them rest.'
1819 'The Fall of Hyperion', l.147–9.
(Published 1856.)

70 The poet and the dreamer are distinct,
Diverse, sheer opposite, antipodes.
The one pours out a balm upon the world,
The other vexes it.
1819 'The Fall of Hyperion', l.199–202.
(Published 1856.)

71 Call the world if you please 'The vale of soul-
making'.
1819 Letter to George and Georgiana Keats, 14 Feb.

72 Oh what can ail thee, knight at arms
Alone and palely loitering;
The sedge is wither'd from the lake,
And no birds sing.
1820 'La Belle Dame Sans Merci', stanza 1.

73 She found me roots of relish sweet,
And honey wild, and manna dew;
And sure in language strange she said,
I love thee true.
1820 'La Belle Dame Sans Merci', stanza 7.

74 I saw pale kings, and princes too,
Pale warriors, death-pale were they all;
Who cry'd—'La belle Dame sans merci
Hath thee in thrall!'
1820 'La Belle Dame Sans Merci', stanza 10.

75 She was a gordian shape of dazzling hue,

Vermilion-spotted, golden, green, and blue;
Striped like a zebra, freckled like a pard,
Eyed like a peacock, and all crimson barr'd.
1820 *Lamia, Isabella, The Eve of St. Agnes and Other Poems,*
'Lamia', pt.1, l.47–50.

76 Real are the dreams of Gods, and smoothly pass
Their pleasures in a long immortal dream.
1820 *Lamia, Isabella, The Eve of St. Agnes and Other Poems,*
'Lamia', pt.1, l.127–8.

77 Love in a hut, with water and a crust,
Is—Love, forgive us!—cinders, ashes, dust;
Love in a palace is perhaps at last
More grievous torment than a hermit's fast.
1820 *Lamia, Isabella, The Eve of St. Agnes and Other Poems,*
'Lamia', pt.2, l.1–4.

78 That purple-lined palace of sweet sin.
1820 *Lamia, Isabella, The Eve of St. Agnes and Other Poems,*
'Lamia', pt.2, l.31.

79 In pale contented sort of discontent.
1820 *Lamia, Isabella, The Eve of St. Agnes and Other Poems,*
'Lamia', pt.2, l.135.

80 Do not all charms fly
At the mere touch of cold philosophy?
There was an awful rainbow once in heaven:
We know her woof, her texture; she is given
In the dull catalogue of common things.
Philosophy will clip an Angel's wings.
1820 *Lamia, Isabella, The Eve of St. Agnes and Other Poems,*
'Lamia', pt.2, l.229–34.

81 Why were they proud? again we ask aloud,
Why in the name of Glory were they proud?
1820 *Lamia, Isabella, The Eve of St. Agnes and Other Poems,*
'Isabella; or, The Pot of Basil', stanza 16.

82 So the two brothers and their murdered man
Rode past fair Florence.
1820 *Lamia, Isabella, The Eve of St. Agnes and Other Poems,*
'Isabella; or, The Pot of Basil', stanza 27.

83 And she forgot the stars, the moon, and sun,
And she forgot the blue above the trees,
And she forgot the dells where waters run,
And she forgot the chilly autumn breeze;
She had no knowledge when the day was done,
And the new morn she saw not: but in peace
Hung over her sweet Basil evermore,
And moistened it with tears unto the core.
1820 *Lamia, Isabella, The Eve of St. Agnes and Other Poems,*
'Isabella; or, The Pot of Basil', stanza 53.

84 'For cruel 'tis,' said she,
'To steal my Basil-pot away from me.'
1820 *Lamia, Isabella, The Eve of St. Agnes and Other Poems,*
'Isabella; or, The Pot of Basil', stanza 62.

85 St. Agnes' Eve—Ah, bitter chill it was!

The owl, for all his feathers, was a-cold;
The hare limped trembling through the frozen
grass,
And silent was the flock in woolly fold.
1820 *Lamia, Isabella, The Eve of St. Agnes and Other Poems,*
'The Eve of St. Agnes', stanza 1.

86 The silver, snarling trumpets 'gan to chide.
1820 *Lamia, Isabella, The Eve of St. Agnes and Other Poems,*
'The Eve of St. Agnes', stanza 4.

87 And soft adorings from their loves receive
Upon the honeyed middle of the night.
1820 *Lamia, Isabella, The Eve of St. Agnes and Other Poems,*
'The Eve of St. Agnes', stanza 6.

88 The music, yearning like a God in pain.
1820 *Lamia, Isabella, The Eve of St. Agnes and Other Poems,*
'The Eve of St. Agnes', stanza 7.

89 Sudden a thought came like a full-blown rose,
Flushing his brow, and in his painted heart
Made purple riot.
1820 *Lamia, Isabella, The Eve of St. Agnes and Other Poems,*
'The Eve of St. Agnes', stanza 16.

90 A poor, weak, palsy-stricken, churchyard thing.
1820 *Lamia, Isabella, The Eve of St. Agnes and Other Poems,*
'The Eve of St. Agnes', stanza 18.

91 A casement high and triple-arched there was,
All garlanded with carven imag'ries
Of fruits, and flowers, and bunches of knot-
grass,
And diamonded with panes of quaint device,
Innumerable of stains and splendid dyes,
As are the tiger-moth's deep-damasked wings.
1820 *Lamia, Isabella, The Eve of St. Agnes and Other Poems,*
'The Eve of St. Agnes', stanza 24.

92 Full on this casement shone the wintry moon,
And threw warm gules on Madeleine's fair breast,
As down she knelt for heaven's grace and boon;
Rose-bloom fell on her hands, together prest,
And on her silver cross soft amethyst,
And on her hair a glory like a saint:
She seemed a splendid angel, newly drest,
Save wings, for heaven.
1820 *Lamia, Isabella, The Eve of St. Agnes and Other Poems,*
'The Eve of St. Agnes', stanza 25.

93 By degrees
Her rich attire creeps rustling to her knees.
1820 *Lamia, Isabella, The Eve of St. Agnes and Other Poems,*
'The Eve of St. Agnes', stanza 25.

94 As though a rose should shut, and be a bud
again.
1820 *Lamia, Isabella, The Eve of St. Agnes and Other Poems,*
'The Eve of St. Agnes', stanza 27.

95 And still she slept an azure-lidded sleep,

In blanched linen, smooth, and lavendered,
While he from forth the closet brought a heap
Of candied apple, quince, and plum, and gourd;
With jellies soother than the creamy curd,
And lucent syrops, tinct with cinnamon;
Manna and dates, in argosy transferred
From Fez; and spiced dainties, every one,
From silken Samarcand to cedared Lebanon.

1820 *Lamia, Isabella, The Eve of St. Agnes and Other Poems,*
'The Eve of St. Agnes', stanza 30.

96 He played an ancient ditty, long since mute,
In Provence called, 'La belle dame sans mercy'.

1820 *Lamia, Isabella, The Eve of St. Agnes and Other Poems,*
'The Eve of St. Agnes', stanza 33.

97 And the long carpets rose along the gusty floor.

1820 *Lamia, Isabella, The Eve of St. Agnes and Other Poems,*
'The Eve of St. Agnes', stanza 40.

98 And they are gone: aye, ages long ago
These lovers fled away into the storm.

1820 *Lamia, Isabella, The Eve of St. Agnes and Other Poems,*
'The Eve of St. Agnes', stanza 42.

99 Deep in the shady sadness of a vale
Far sunken from the healthy breath of morn,
Far from the fiery noon and eve's one star,
Sat gray-haired Saturn, quiet as a stone,
Still as the silence round about his lair.

1820 *Lamia, Isabella, The Eve of St. Agnes and Other Poems,*
'Hyperion', bk.1, l.1–5.

1 Where the dead leaf fell, there did it rest.

1820 *Lamia, Isabella, The Eve of St. Agnes and Other Poems,*
'Hyperion', bk.1, l.10.

2 But oh! How unlike marble was that face.

1820 *Lamia, Isabella, The Eve of St. Agnes and Other Poems,*
'Hyperion', bk.1, l.34.

3 That large utterance of the early Gods.

1820 *Lamia, Isabella, The Eve of St. Agnes and Other Poems,*
'Hyperion', bk.1, l.51.

4 Season of mists and mellow fruitfulness,
Close bosom-friend of the maturing sun;
Conspiring with him how to load and bless
With fruit the vines that round the thatch-eaves run.

1820 *Lamia, Isabella, The Eve of St. Agnes and Other Poems,* 'To
Autumn', stanza 1.

5 Where are the songs of Spring? Ay, where are they?
Think not of them, thou hast thy music too.

1820 *Lamia, Isabella, The Eve of St. Agnes and Other Poems,* 'To
Autumn', stanza 3.

6 Thou still unravished bride of quietness,
Thou foster-child of silence and slow time.

1820 *Lamia, Isabella, The Eve of St. Agnes and Other Poems,*
'Ode on a Grecian Urn', stanza 1.

7 What men or Gods are these? What maidens loth?

What mad pursuit? What struggle to escape?
What pipes and timbrels? What wild ecstasy?

1820 *Lamia, Isabella, The Eve of St. Agnes and Other Poems,*
'Ode on a Grecian Urn', stanza 1.

8 Heard melodies are sweet, but those unheard
Are sweeter; therefore, ye soft pipes, play on;
Not to the sensual ear, but, more endeared,
Pipe to the spirit ditties of no tone.

1820 *Lamia, Isabella, The Eve of St. Agnes and Other Poems,*
'Ode on a Grecian Urn', stanza 2.

9 She cannot fade, though thou hast not thy bliss,
For ever wilt thou love, and she be fair!

1820 *Lamia, Isabella, The Eve of St. Agnes and Other Poems,*
'Ode on a Grecian Urn', stanza 2.

10 O Attic shape! Fair attitude!

1820 *Lamia, Isabella, The Eve of St. Agnes and Other Poems,*
'Ode on a Grecian Urn', stanza 5.

11 Thou, silent form, dost tease us out of thought
As doth eternity: Cold Pastoral!

1820 *Lamia, Isabella, The Eve of St. Agnes and Other Poems,*
'Ode on a Grecian Urn', stanza 5.

12 'Beauty is truth, truth beauty,'—that is all
Ye know on earth, and all ye need to know.

1820 *Lamia, Isabella, The Eve of St. Agnes and Other Poems,*
'Ode on a Grecian Urn', stanza 5.

13 My heart aches, and a drowsy numbness pains
My sense, as though of hemlock I had drunk,
Or emptied some dull opiate to the drains
One minute past, and Lethe-wards had sunk:
'Tis not through envy of thy happy lot,
But being too happy in thine happiness
That thou, light-winged Dryad of the trees,
In some melodious plot
Of beechen green, and shadows numberless,
Singest of summer in full-throated ease.

1820 *Lamia, Isabella, The Eve of St. Agnes and Other Poems,*
'Ode to a Nightingale', stanza 2.

14 O, for a draught of vintage! that hath been
Cooled a long age in the deep-delved earth,
Tasting of Flora and the country green,
Dance, and Provençal song, and sunburnt mirth!
O for a beaker full of the warm South,
Full of the true, the blushful Hippocrene,
With beaded bubbles winking at the brim,
And purple-stained mouth;
That I might drink, and leave the world unseen,
And with thee fade away into the forest dim.

1820 *Lamia, Isabella, The Eve of St. Agnes and Other Poems,*
'Ode to a Nightingale', stanza 2.

15 Fade far away, dissolve, and quite forget
What thou among the leaves hast never known,
The weariness, the fever, and the fret
Here, where men sit and hear each other groan;

Where palsy shakes a few, sad, last grey hairs,
Where youth grows pale, and spectre-thin, and dies;
Where but to think is to be full of sorrow
And leaden-eyed despairs.
1820 *Lamia, Isabella, The Eve of St. Agnes and Other Poems,*
'Ode to a Nightingale', stanza 3.

16 Already with thee! tender is the night.
1820 *Lamia, Isabella, The Eve of St. Agnes and Other Poems,*
'Ode to a Nightingale', stanza 4.

17 Fast fading violets covered up in leaves;
And mid-May's eldest child,
The coming musk-rose, full of dewy wine,
The murmurous haunt of flies in summer eves.
1820 *Lamia, Isabella, The Eve of St. Agnes and Other Poems,*
'Ode to a Nightingale', stanza 5.

18 Darkling I listen; and, for many a time
I have been half in love with easeful Death,
Called him soft names in many a musèd
  rhyme,
To take into the air my quiet breath;
Now more than ever seems it rich to die,
To cease upon the midnight with no pain,
While thou art pouring forth thy soul abroad
In such an ecstasy!
1820 *Lamia, Isabella, The Eve of St. Agnes and Other Poems,*
'Ode to a Nightingale', stanza 6.

19 Thou wast not born for death, immortal Bird!
1820 *Lamia, Isabella, The Eve of St. Agnes and Other Poems,*
'Ode to a Nightingale', stanza 7.

20 Forlorn! the very word is like a bell
To toll me back from thee to my sole self!
Adieu! the fancy cannot cheat so well
As she is famed to do, deceiving elf.
1820 *Lamia, Isabella, The Eve of St. Agnes and Other Poems,*
'Ode to a Nightingale', stanza 8.

21 I know the colour of that blood; it is arterial
blood; I cannot be deceived in that colour; that
drop of blood is my death-warrant—I must die.
1821 On examining a drop of blood that fell from his mouth as
he lay dying from tuberculosis. Quoted in John Sutherland *The
Oxford Book of Literary Anecdotes* (1975).

22 Here lies one whose name was writ in water.
Epitaph for himself. Quoted in Richard Monckton Milnes *Life,
Letters and Literary Remains of John Keats* (1848), vol.2.

Keble, John 1792–1866

English churchman, the father of the Tractarian movement. He was also influential in the Oxford Movement
after J H Newman's secession to Rome.

23 New every morning is the love
Our wakening and uprising prove.
1827 *The Christian Year*, 'Morning'.

Keenan, Brian 1947–

Irish–British teacher. He was kidnapped on 11 April 1986
while working at the American University of Beirut by
Iranian terrorists and held hostage for four years.

24 I'm going to visit every country in the world, eat all
the food of the world, drink all the drink of the
world—and, I hope, make love to every woman in
the world. Then I might get a good night's sleep.
1990 Said on his release, BBC TV, 25 Aug.

Keillor, (Gary Edward) Garrison 1942–

US humorous writer and broadcaster. In 1974 he began
his live radio show, *A Prairie Home Companion*, telling
tales of small-town Minnesota set in fictional Lake
Wobegon. His works include *Lake Wobegon Days* (1985).

25 Where all the women are strong, all the men are
good-looking, and all the children are above
average.
from 1974 His description of the fictional mid-Western town
Lake Wobegon, used regularly in *A Prairie Home Companion*.

26 Peanut butter has survived everything that has been
done to improve it.
1990 In NPR broadcast, 29 Dec.

27 Public radio is a ghetto of good taste.
1991 In National Public Radio broadcast, 9 Feb.

28 March is the month that God designed to show
those who don't drink what a hangover is like.
1991 In NPR broadcast, 1 Dec.

29 It's a play that after you've been there for a short
while, you wonder how long this is going to take.
1995 Of Edward Albee's *Three Tall Women*. In *New York*, 2 Jan.

Keller, Helen Adams 1880–1968

US writer. She became deaf and blind at 19 months, but
educated by Anne Sullivan she learned to speak,
graduated in 1904 and became a distinguished lecturer
and writer.

30 As the eagle was killed by the arrow winged with its
own feather, so the hand of the world is wounded
by its own skill.
1912 In the *American Magazine*, Dec.

Kelman, James 1946–

Scottish novelist, whose novels and short stories set in
working-class Glasgow are characterized by an
uncompromising vernacular style and vocabulary. In
1994 his novel *How late it was, how late* won the Booker
Prize.

31 Theoretical webs, dirty webs, fusty webs, old and
shrivelling away into nothingness, a fine dust. Who
needs that kind of stuff. Far far better getting out
into the open air and doing it, actually doing it,

something solid and concrete and unconceptualisable.

1989 *A Disaffection.*

32 Yes, they say, go and write whatever story you want, but don't use whatever language is necessary... By implication those in authority ask the writer to censor and suppress her or his own work. They demand it. If you don't comply then your work isn't produced.

1992 *Some Recent Attacks*, 'The Importance of Glasgow in My Work'.

33 My culture and my language have the right to exist, and no one has the authority to dismiss that.

1994 Speech at the Booker Prize award ceremony, 11 Oct.

34 Ye wake in a corner and stay there hoping yer body will disappear, the thoughts smothering ye; these thoughts; but ye want to remember and face up to things, just something keeps ye from doing it, why can ye no do it; the words filling yer head: then the other words; there's something far far wrong; ye're no a good man, ye're just no a good man.

1994 *How late it was, how late*, opening words.

Kelvin, William Thomson, 1st Baron
1824–1907

Irish-born Scottish physician and mathematician, who developed the temperature scale named after him.

35 At what time does the dissipation of energy begin?

When his wife proposed an afternoon walk. Quoted in A Fleming *Memories of a Scientific Life*.

Kemble, Charles 1775–1854

English actor-manager. A celebrated comic actor, he became manager of Covent Garden in 1822 but subsequently ran into financial difficulties, mitigated in the early 1830s when he presented his daughter Fanny Kemble's stage début.

36 Sir, I now pay you this exorbitant charge, but I must ask you to explain to Her Majesty that she must not in future look upon me as a source of income.

When reluctantly obliged to pay overdue income tax. Attributed.

Kemble, John Philip 1757–1823

English actor-manager, brother of Sarah Siddons and Charles Kemble. A successful tragic actor, he was manager of the Theatre Royal, Drury Lane and subsequently of Covent Garden, where riots greeted his decision to raise ticket prices.

37 Ladies and gentlemen, unless the play is stopped, the child cannot possibly go on.

Addressing the audience during a performance that was being much disrupted by a child crying. Attributed.

Kempis, St Thomas à c.1380–1471

German monk and author. In 1400 he entered the Augustinian convent of Agnetenberg, near Zwolle, where he was Sub-Prior at the time of his death.

38 *Vere magnus est, qui magnam habet caritatem.*

He is truly great who has great charity.

c.1413 *De Imitatione Christi*, bk.1, ch.4, section 6.

39 *Quam cito transit gloria mundi.*

How quickly the glory of the world passes.

c.1413 *De Imitatione Christi*, bk.1, ch.4, section 6.

40 *Homo proponit, sed Deus disponit.*

Man proposes, but God disposes.

c.1413 *De Imitatione Christi*, bk.1, ch.19, section 2.

41 *Nemo secure præcipit, nisi qui bene obedire didicit.*

Nobody rules safely, but he who has learned well how to obey.

c.1413 *De Imitatione Christi*, bk.1, ch.20, section 2.

42 *Transeunt omnia, et tu cum eis pariter.*

All things perish, and you along with them.

c.1413 *De Imitatione Christi*, bk.2, ch.1, section 4.

43 *Gloria boni hominis, testimonium bonæ conscientiæ.*

The testimony of a good conscience is the good man's glory.

c.1413 *De Imitatione Christi*, bk.2, ch.6, section 1.

44 *In cruce salus, in cruce vita.*

In the cross is salvation, in the cross is life.

c.1413 *De Imitatione Christi*, bk.2, ch.12, section 2.

45 *Si libenter crucem portas, portabit te.*

If you bear your cross willingly, it will bear you.

c.1413 *De Imitatione Christi*, bk.2, ch.12, section 5.

46 *De duobos malis minus est semper eligendum.*

Of two evils the lesser should always be chosen.

c.1413 *De Imitatione Christi*, bk.3, ch.12, section 2.

Ken, Thomas 1637–1711

English churchman and royal chaplain. He became Bishop of Bath and Wells (1685), and was deposed in 1691 when he refused to take the oath of allegiance to William III.

47 Awake my soul, and with the sun
Thy daily stage of duty run.

1709 *Manual of Prayers for the use of the Scholars of Winchester College.*

48 Praise God, from whom all blessings flow,
Praise Him, all creatures here below,
Praise Him above, ye heavenly host,
Praise Father, Son, and Holy Ghost.

1709 *Manual of Prayers for the use of the Scholars of Winchester College.*

Kendall, Henry Clarence 1839–82

Australian poet who worked variously as a civil servant, freelance writer, timber merchant and inspector of forests. His great love of the Australian countryside is evident in his collections *Poems and Songs* (1862), *Leaves from Australian Forests* (1869), and *Songs from the Mountains* (1880).

49 Through breaks of the cedar and sycamore bowers
   Struggles the light that is love to the flowers;
   And, softer than slumber and sweeter than singing,
   The notes of the bell-birds are running and ringing.
   The silver-voiced bell-birds, the darlings of daytime!
   They sing in September their songs of the May-time.

   1869 *Leaves from Australian Forests*, 'Bell-Birds'.

Kennan, George Frost 1904–

US diplomat and historian, adviser to Secretary of State Dean Acheson (1949–52) and John Foster Dulles and US Ambassador in Moscow and Yugoslavia. Initially in favour of 'containment' of the USSR, he later called for US disengagement from Europe.

50 The best that an American can look forward to is the lonely pleasure of one who stands at long last on a chilly and inhospitable mountain top where few have been, where few can follow, and where few will consent to believe that he has been.

   On negotiating with the Soviets. Quoted in Walter Isaacson and Evan Thomas *The Wise Men* (1986).

51 A guest of one's time and not a member of the household.

   Of the feeling of being viewed as a pragmatist. Quoted in Walter Isaacson and Evan Thomas *The Wise Men* (1986).

52 Fig leaves of democratic procedure to hide the nakedness of Stalinist dictatorship.

   Of postwar agreements to govern Eastern Europe. Quoted in Walter Isaacson and Evan Thomas *The Wise Men* (1986).

Kennedy, A(lison) L 1965–

Scottish novelist. Her short stories and novels have established her as a leading writer of her generation.

53 Night Geometry and the Garscadden Trains.

   1990 Title of short story collection.

54 Words just say what you want them to; they don't know any better.

   1990 'The Role of Notable Silences in Scottish History'.

55 4. The chosen and male shall go forth unto professions while the chosen and female shall be homely, fecund, docile and slightly artistic.

   1993 *Looking for the Possible Dance*, 'The Scottish Method for the Perfection of Children'.

56 7. Joy is fleeting, sinful and the forerunner of despair.

   1993 *Looking for the Possible Dance*, 'The Scottish Method for the Perfection of Children'.

57 We all have it in us to be an opium for every conceivable mass.

   1995 *So I Am Glad*, ch.1.

58 I am not calm, I am unspontaneous. When something happens to me, I don't know how to feel.

   1995 *So I Am Glad*, ch.1.

Kennedy, Edward M(oore) 1932–

US Democratic politician, son of Joseph and brother of John and Robert. His political career was dogged by his involvement in a car accident at Chappaquidick in 1969, in which a female companion was drowned, and he withdrew as presidential candidate in 1980.

59 I don't mind not being President. I just mind that someone else is.

   1986 Speech, Washington, 22 Mar.

60 Sunlight is the best disinfectant.

   1990 On sponsoring legislation for the disclosure of graduation rates and crime figures on campuses. In the *New York Times*, 8 Oct.

Kennedy, John F(itzgerald) 1917–63

US Democratic politician, 35th President. His *Profiles in Courage* (1956) won the Pulitzer Prize. The first Catholic, and the youngest person, to be elected President (1961–3), he initiated education and civil rights reform and induced the USSR to withdraw its missiles from Cuba (1962). He was assassinated, allegedly by Lee Harvey Oswald, while being driven in an open car through Dallas, Texas.

61 We stand today on the edge of a new frontier. But the new frontier of which I speak is not a set of promises. It is a set of challenges. It sums up not what I intend to offer the American people, but what I intend to ask of them. It appeals to their pride, not their pocketbook—it holds out the promise of more sacrifice instead of more security.

   1960 On accepting the Democratic Convention's presidential nomination, 15 Jul.

62 Let us never negotiate out of fear, but let us never fear to negotiate. Together let us explore the stars.

   1961 Inaugural address, Washington, 20 Jan.

63 All this will not be finished in the first 100 days, nor will it be finished in the first 1,000 days, nor in the life of this Administration—nor even, perhaps, in our lifetime on this planet. But let us begin.

   1961 Inaugural address, Washington, 20 Jan.

64 Let the word go forth from this time and place, to friend and foe alike, that the torch has been passed to a new generation of Americans, born in this

century, tempered by war, disciplined by a hard and bitter peace, proud of our ancient heritage, and unwilling to witness or permit the slow undoing of those human rights to which this nation has always been committed, and to which we are committed today at home and around the world. Let every nation know, whether it wishes us well or ill, that we shall pay any price, bear any burden, meet any hardship, support any friend, oppose any foe, to assure the survival and success of liberty.
1961 Inaugural address, Washington, 20 Jan.

65 And so, my fellow Americans, ask not what your country can do for you. Ask what you can do for your country.
1961 Inaugural address, Washington, 20 Jan.

66 I believe that this nation should commit itself to achieving the goal, before this decade is out, of landing a man on the moon and returning him safely to earth.
1961 State of the Union message to Congress, May.

67 Now we have a problem in making our power credible, and Vietnam is the place.
1961 Attributed remark to journalist James Reston, following Kennedy's meeting with Khrushchev, Jun.

68 A form of atomic blackmail.
1961 On the Soviet decision to resume nuclear testing, 31 Aug.

69 The cold reaches of the universe must not become the new area of an even colder war.
1961 Address to the United Nations, 25 Sep.

70 Mankind must put an end to war or war will put an end to mankind.
1961 Address to the United Nations, 25 Sep.

71 Those who make peaceful revolution impossible will make violent revolution inevitable.
1962 Speech to Latin American diplomats, 12 Mar.

72 This is the most extraordinary collection of talent, of human knowledge, that has ever been gathered in the White House—with the possible exception of when Thomas Jefferson dined alone.
1962 Address at a dinner for 49 Nobel laureates, 29 Apr.

73 The cost of freedom is always high, but Americans have always paid it. And one path we shall never choose, and that is the path of surrender, or submission.
1962 Address to the nation, 22 Oct.

74 If you take the wrong course…the President bears the burden of the responsibility quite rightly. The advisers may move on—to new advice.
1962 Comment to White House Special Counsel Theodore C Sorensen, Dec, after the ill-fated Bay of Pigs invasion of Cuba.

75 His stately ship of life, having weathered the severest storms of a troubled century, is anchored in tranquil waters, proof that courage and faith and zest for freedom are truly indestructible. The record of his triumphant passage will inspire free hearts all over the globe.
1963 On conferring honorary US citizenship on Winston Churchill, 9 Apr.

76 [Winston Churchill] mobilized the English language and sent it into battle.
1963 On conferring honorary US citizenship on Winston Churchill, 9 Apr.

77 Equality of opportunity does not mean equality of responsibility.
1963 Address at Vanderbilt University, 19 May.

78 Man is still the most extraordinary computer of all.
1963 Speech, 21 May.

79 History teaches us that enmities between nations…do not last forever. We must conduct our affairs in such a way that it becomes in the communists' interests to agree on a genuine peace…to let each nation choose its own future, so long as that choice does not interfere with the choices of others. If we cannot now end our differences, at least we can help make the world safe for diversity.
1963 Speech, American University, Washington DC, 10 Jun.

80 The rights of every man are diminished when the rights of one man are threatened.
1963 On sending national guardsmen to ensure peaceful integration at the University of Alabama. Address to the nation, 11 Jun.

81 He [John Hoban] believed by incorporating several features of the Dublin style he would make it more home-like for any President of Irish descent. It was a long wait, but I appreciate his efforts.
1963 On the Irish-American architect's design of the White House. Speech to the Irish Parliament reported in the *New York Times*, 19 Jun.

82 Let it not be said of this Atlantic generation that we left ideals and visions to the past, nor purpose and determination to our adversaries. We have come too far, we have sacrificed too much to disdain the future now.
1963 Speech to the West German Parliament, Frankfurt, 25 Jun.

83 There are many people in the world who really don't understand, or say they don't, what is the great issue between the free world and the Communist world. Let them come to Berlin!
1963 Address in Berlin's Rudolf Wilde Platz, 26 Jun, 22 months after the erection of the wall dividing the city.

84 We have never had to put a wall up to keep our people in, to prevent them from leaving us.

1963 Address in Berlin's Rudolf Wilde Platz, 26 Jun, 22 months after the erection of the wall dividing the city.

85 All free men, wherever they may live, are citizens of Berlin, and therefore, as a free man, I take pride in the words, 'Ich bin ein Berliner.' I am a Berliner!

1963 Speech at West Berlin City Hall, Rudolf Wilde Platz, 26 Jun. Unfortunately for Kennedy, his phrase translated into colloquial German as 'I am a doughnut.'

86 For the first time, we have been able to reach an agreement which can limit the dangers of this age.

1963 On the ratification of a treaty to limit nuclear testing, 7 Oct.

87 The highest duty of the writer, the composer, the artist is to remain true to himself… In serving his vision of the truth, the artist best serves his nation.

1963 At the dedication of Amherst College Robert Frost Library, 25 Oct.

88 When power leads man towards arrogance, poetry reminds him of his limitations. When power narrows the area of man's concern, poetry reminds him of the richness and diversity of existence. When power corrupts, poetry cleanses.

1963 At the dedication of Amherst College Robert Frost Library, 25 Oct.

89 I look forward to…a future in which our country will match its military strength with our moral restraint; its wealth with our wisdom; its power with our purpose.

1963 Last major public speech, Amherst College, 26 Oct.

90 The definition of happiness of the Greeks…is full use of your powers along lines of excellence. I find, therefore, the Presidency provides some happiness.

1963 News conference, 31 Oct.

91 We're heading into nut country today.

1963 Spoken to his wife in Fort Worth a few hours before the assassination in Dallas. Quoted in William Manchester *The Death of a President* (1967).

92 We in this country, in this generation, are—by destiny, rather than choice—the watchmen on the walls of the world.

1963 Address prepared for Dallas luncheon on the day he was assassinated, 22 Nov.

93 What your government believes is its own business; what it does in the world is the world's business.

Letter to Nikita Khrushchev. Quoted in Theodore C Sorensen *Kennedy* (1965).

94 The three most overrated things in the world are the state of Texas, the FBI, and hunting trophies.

Quoted in William Manchester *The Death of a President* (1967).

95 You don't fire God.

Expressing reluctance to replace FBI Director J Edgar Hoover. Reported after Kennedy's death in Senate committee findings on US intelligence activities, 1976.

96 You never know what's hit you. A gunshot is the perfect way.

Comment on methods of assassination. Quoted in Peter Collier and David Horowitz *The Kennedys* (1984).

Kennedy, Joseph Patrick 1888–1969

US businessman and diplomat, a supporter of Roosevelt and the 'New Deal'. The grandson of an Irish immigrant, he placed his fortune at the political disposal of his nine children, all of whom except the eldest son, killed in a flying accident, achieved international fame.

97 With the money I spent I could have elected my chauffeur.

Of his contributions to John F Kennedy's presidential campaign. Quoted in Nigel Hamilton *JFK: Reckless Youth* (1992).

98 Don't get mad, get even.

Attributed.

Kennedy, Joseph P(atrick) II 1952–

US Democratic politician and congressman.

99 I've had a tough time learning how to act like a Congressman. Today I accidentally spent some of my own money.

1987 In *Newsweek*, 9 Feb.

Kennedy, Robert F(rancis) 1925–68

US politician, son of Joseph. Manager of his brother John's presidential campaign, he became Attorney-General (1961–4) and Senator for New York from 1965. In 1968 he was assassinated after winning the California primary election.

1 Courage is the most important attribute of a lawyer.

1962 Speech at the University of San Francisco Law School, 29 Sep.

2 One fifth of the people are against everything all the time.

1964 In *The Observer*, May.

3 My thanks to you all—and now it's on to Chicago, and let's win there.

1968 Last public remark after winning the Californian primary for the Democratic presidential nomination in Los Angeles, before being assassinated as he left the rally, 4 Jun.

4 It isn't the first step that concerns me, but both sides escalating to the fourth or fifth step—and we don't go to the sixth because there is no one around to do so.

On the possibility of initiating nuclear warfare. *Thirteen Days* (published 1969).

5 Many times…I had heard the military take positions which, if wrong, had the advantage that no one would be around at the end to know.

1969 Recalling discussions on Soviet placement of nuclear missiles in Cuba. *Thirteen Days* (published 1969).

6 Well, we Kennedys, we eat Rockefellers for breakfast.

Quoted in Peter Collier and David Horowitz *The Rockefellers* (1976).

Kennedy, Roger George 1926–

Director, National Park Service. Before working in finance he was a correspondent for NBC. He has written books on architecture, houses and historic America.

7 How do you put a price on the Washington Monument?

1995 On presenting his annual budget to Congress and being asked to produce a price list setting a market value on each of the nation's 368 park units. Reported in the *US News and World Report*, 3 Apr.

Kent, Bruce 1929–

British cleric and peace campaigner, Chairman (1987–90) and Vice-President (1990–) of the Campaign for Nuclear Disarmament.

8 Preparing for suicide is not a very intelligent means of defence.

1989 Speech.

Kent, Corita known as 'Sister Corita' 1918–86

US artist, best remembered for her prints and her 'Love' postage stamp (1985).

9 Women's liberation is the liberation of the feminine in the man and the masculine in the woman.

1974 In the *Los Angeles Times*, 11 Jul.

Kent, Rockwell 1882–1971

US artist and writer, best known for his stark woodcuts, often accompanying his travel writing. His major works include the paintings *Toilers of the Sea* and *Winter* and writings such as *Wilderness* (1921).

10 Sledgehammer sentimentality.

Of his wholesome depiction of contemporary America. Quoted in the *Washington Post*, 6 Jun 1993

Kerouac, Jack (John) 1922–69

US novelist. His fast-moving, stream of consciousness novel *On The Road* became the quintessential text of the Beat Generation.

11 All of life is a foreign country.

1949 Letter, 24 Jun.

12 But then they danced down the street like dingledodies, and I shambled after as I've been doing all my life after people who interest me, because the only people for me are the mad ones, the ones who are mad to live, mad to talk, mad to be saved, desirous of everything at the same time, the ones who never yawn or say a commonplace thing, but burn, burn, burn, like fabulous yellow roman candles exploding like spiders across the stars and in the middle you see the blue centerlight pop and everybody goes 'Awww!'

1957 *On The Road*, pt.1, ch.1.

13 I have nothing to offer anybody except my own confusion.

1957 *On The Road*, pt.2, ch.3.

14 The road is life.

1957 *On the Road.*

15 John Clellon Holmes…and I were sitting around trying to think up the meaning of the Lost Generation and the subsequent Existentialism and I said, 'You know, this is really a beat generation' and he leapt up and said 'That's it, that's right!'

1959 Interview in *Playboy*, Jun.

16 Desolation Angels.

1965 Title of novel.

Kerr, Jean née Collins 1923–

US playwright. Her works include successful Broadway plays and humorous autobiographies. She collaborated with her husband Walter Kerr on several projects, including an adaptation of Werfel's *Song of Bernadette* (1946).

17 Even though a number of people have tried, no one has yet found a way to drink for a living.

1964 *Poor Richard*, act 1.

Kesey, Ken Elton 1935–

US novelist. He achieved a major success with his novel *One Flew Over the Cuckoo's Nest*, set in a mental hospital, and became a hero of the US counter-culture in the 1960s.

18 One Flew Over the Cuckoo's Nest.

1962 Title of novel, derived from a traditional rhyme.

19 But it's the truth even if it didn't happen.

1962 *One Flew Over The Cuckoo's Nest*, pt.1.

20 I'd rather be a lightning rod than a seismograph.

Quoted in Tom Wolfe *The Electric Kool-Aid Acid Test* (1968), ch.1.

21 We are always acting on what just finished happening. It happened at least 1/30th of a second ago. We think we're in the present, but we aren't. The present we know is only a movie of the past.

Quoted in Tom Wolfe *The Electric Kool-Aid Acid Test* (1968), ch.11.

22 You don't lead by pointing and telling people some place to go. You lead by going to that place and making a case.

1970 Interview in *Esquire*, Jun.

Kethe, William d. c.1608

English divine, army chaplain and hymnwriter. His hymns are characteristically written in metre, like psalms.

23 All people that on earth do dwell,
Sing to the Lord with cheerful voice;
Him serve with fear, His praise forth tell,
Come ye before Him, and rejoice.

1560 *Daye's Psalter*, 'All People That on Earth Do Dwell'.

Key, Francis Scott 1779–1843

US lawyer and poet, best known for his devotional verse and prose. His poem 'The Star-Spangled Banner' was officially adopted as the national anthem of the US in 1931.

24 O say, can you see, by the dawn's early light,
What so proudly we hailed at the twilight's last gleaming—
Whose broad stripes and bright stars, through the clouds of the fight,
O'er the ramparts we watched were so gallantly streaming!
And the rocket's red glare, the bombs bursting in air,
Gave proof through the night that our flag was still there;
O! say, does that star-spangled banner yet wave
O'er the land of the free, and the home of the brave?

1814 'The Star-Spangled Banner', originally published as 'The Defence of Fort M'Henry' in the *Baltimore Patriot*, 20 Sep; it commemorates the bombardment of Fort McHenry, Baltimore, by the British, 13–14 Sep.

Keynes (of Tilton), John Maynard, 1st Baron 1883–1946

English economist. His major works, *A Treatise on Money* (1930) and the revolutionary *General Theory of Employment, Interest and Money* (1936), were inspired by the unemployment crisis. His views influenced Roosevelt's 'New Deal' administration and underpin modern macroeconomics.

25 I work for a government I despise for ends I think criminal.

1917 Letter to Duncan Grant, 15 Dec.

26 Like Odysseus, the President looked wiser when he was seated.

1919 Of Woodrow Wilson. *The Economic Consequences of the Peace*, ch.3.

27 Lenin was right. There is no subtler, no surer means of overturning the existing basis of society than to debauch the currency. The process engages all the hidden forces of economic law on the side of destruction, and does it in a manner which not one man in a million is able to diagnose.

1919 *The Economic Consequences of the Peace*.

28 England still stands outside Europe. Europe's voiceless tremors do not reach her. Europe is apart, and England is not of her flesh and body.

1919 *The Economic Consequences of the Peace*

29 The *long run* is a misleading guide to current affairs. *In the long run*, we are all dead. Economists set themselves too easy, too useless a task if in tempestuous seasons they can only tell us that when the storm is long past the ocean is flat again.

1923 *A Tract on Monetary Reform*, ch.3.

30 If Enterprise is afoot, Wealth accumulates whatever may be happening to Thrift; and if Enterprise is asleep, Wealth decays, whatever Thrift may be doing.

1930 *A Treatise on Money*.

31 A 'sound' banker, alas! is not one who foresees danger and avoids it, but one who, when he is ruined, is ruined in a conventional and orthodox way along with his fellows, so that no one can really blame him.

1931 *Essays in Persuasion*.

32 It is *not* a correct deduction from the Principles of Economics that enlightened self-interest always operates in the public interest… Experience does *not* show that individuals when they make up a social unit are always less clear-sighted than when they act separately.

1931 *Essays in Persuasion*.

33 I agree that our methods of control are unlikely to be sufficiently delicate or sufficiently powerful to maintain continuous full employment. I should be quite content with a reasonable approximation to it, and in practice I should probably relax my expansionist measures a little before technical full employment had actually been reached.

1936 Letter to E F M Durbin, 30 Apr.

34 It might have been supposed that competition between expert professionals, possessing judgement and knowledge beyond that of the average private investor, would correct the vagaries of the ignorant individual left to himself. It happens, however, that the energies and skills of the professional investor and speculator are mainly occupied elsewhere. For most of these persons are, in fact, largely concerned, not with making superior long-term

forecasts of the probable yield on an investment over its whole life, but with foreseeing changes in the conventional bias of valuation a short time ahead of the general public... This battle of wits to anticipate the basis of conventional valuation a few months hence, rather than the prospective yield of an investment over a long term of years, does not even require gulls amongst the public to feed the maws of the professional; it can be played by professionals amongst themselves.
1936 *The General Theory of Employment, Interest, and Money.*

35 Speculators may do no harm as bubbles on a steady stream of enterprise. But the position is serious when enterprise becomes the bubble on a whirlpool of speculation. When the capital development of a country becomes a by-product of the activities of a casino, the job is likely to be ill-done.
1936 *The General Theory of Employment, Interest, and Money.*

36 If the Treasury were to fill old bottles with banknotes, bury them at suitable depths in disused coalmines which are then filled up to the surface with town rubbish, and leave it to private enterprise on well-tried principles of *laissez-faire* to dig the notes up again...there need be no more unemployment and, with the help of the repercussions, the real income of the community, and its capital wealth also, would probably become a good deal greater than it actually is. It would, indeed, be more sensible to build houses and the like; but as there are political and practical difficulties in the way of this, the above would be better than nothing.
1936 *The General Theory of Employment, Interest and Money.*

37 The ideas of economists and political philosophers, both when they are right and when they are wrong, are more powerful than is commonly understood. Indeed the world is ruled by little else. Practical men, who believe themselves to be quite exempt from any intellectual influences, are usually the slaves of some defunct economist. Madmen in authority, who hear voices in the air, are distilling their frenzy from some academic scribbler of a few years back. I am sure the power of vested interests is vastly exaggerated compared with the gradual encroachment of ideas.
1936 *The General Theory of Employment, Interest and Money.*

38 The outstanding faults of the economic society in which we live are its failure to provide for full employment and its arbitrary and inequitable distribution of wealth and incomes.
1936 *The General Theory of Employment, Interest, and Money.*

39 We take it as a fundamental psychological rule of any modern community that, when its real income

is increased, it will not increase its consumption by an equal absolute amount.
1936 *The General Theory of Employment, Interest, and Money.*

40 Worldly wisdom teaches us that it is better for the reputation to fail conventionally than to succeed unconventionally.
1936 *The General Theory of Employment, Interest and Money.*

41 I believe that there is social and psychological justification for significant inequalities of incomes and wealth, but not for such large disparities as exist today.
1936 *The General Theory of Employment, Interest and Money.*

Khayyám, Omar c.1050–c.1123

Persian poet and scholar. Born in Nishapur, he was summoned to Merv by the sultan, where he reformed the Muslim calendar. A renowned astronomer, he also composed mathematical treatises, and is best remembered for his *Rubáiyát*.

42 Know yourself as a snowdrift on the sand
Heaped for two days, or three, then thawed and gone.
c.1100 *Rubáiyát*, stanza 16 (translated by Robert Graves and Omar Ali-Shah, 1972).

43 Never anticipate tomorrow's sorrow;
Live always in this paradisal now.
c.1100 *Rubáiyát*, stanza 21 (translated by Robert Graves and Omar Ali-Shah, 1972).

44 The cheerful bird of youth flutters away—
I hardly noticed how it came or went.
c.1100 *Rubáiyát*, stanza 103 (translated by Robert Graves and Omar Ali-Shah, 1972).

Khomeini, Ayatollah Ruhollah 1900–89

Iranian religious and political leader. Exiled in 1964, he returned to Iran in 1979 after the collapse of the Shah's government and became virtual head of state. He instigated a fundamentalist 'Islamic Revolution'.

45 Music is no different from opium. Music affects the human mind in a way that makes people think of nothing but music and sensual matters... Music is a treason to the country, a treason to our youth, and we should cut out all this music and replace it with something instructive.
1979 Ramadan speech, 23 Jul. Quoted in Lebrecht *Discord* (1982).

Khrushchev, Nikita Sergeyevich
1894–1971

Soviet politician. On the death of Stalin he became First Secretary of the Communist Party (1953–64), and subsequently denounced Stalinism. His period of office was marked by the 1956 Poznan riots, the Hungarian uprising, and the Cuban missile crisis (1962).

46 Those who wait for the USSR to reject Communism must wait until a shrimp learns to whistle.
1955 Speech in Moscow, 17 Sep.

47 Whether you like it not, history is on our side. We will bury you.
1956 Remark to Western diplomats at the Kremlin, 18 Nov. Khrushchev later claimed that he had meant 'We will overtake you [economically]', rather than this more sinister version.

48 Politicians are the same all over. They promise to build a bridge even where there is no river.
1960 Press conference, New York, Oct.

49 When you are skinning your customers, you should leave some skin on to grow so that you can skin them again.
1961 Speech to British industrialists, May.

50 They talk about who won and who lost. Human reason won. Mankind won.
1962 Of the ending of the Cuban missile crisis. In the *Observer*, 11 Nov.

51 We had no use for the teachings of the Gospels; if someone slaps you, just turn the other cheek. We had shown that anyone who slapped us on our cheek would get his head kicked off.
1970 *Khrushchev Remembers*. This biography, published in the West, is of dubious authenticity.

52 What the scientists have in their briefcases is terrifying.
Attributed.

Kierkegaard, Sören Aabye 1813–55

Danish philosopher and religious thinker, who attacked dogmatism and the established Lutheran church and foreshadowed Existentialism.

53 The thing is to find a truth *for me*, to find *the idea for which I can live and die*.
1835 Journal entry (translated by Alexander Dru, 1938).

54 There are many people who reach their conclusions about life like schoolboys; they cheat their master by copying the answer out of a book without having worked out the sum for themselves.
1837 Journal entry (translated by Alexander Dru, 1938).

55 Without risk there is no faith.
1846 *Concluding Unscientific Postscript*, bk.2, pt.2, ch.2 (translated by Swenson and Lowrie).

56 If a man in truth *will* the Good then he must be willing to suffer *for* the Good.
1846 *Purity Of Heart Is To Will One Thing* (translated by D Steere, 1938).

57 It is perfectly true, as philosophers say, that life must be understood backwards. But they forget the other proposition, that it must be lived forwards.

And if one thinks over that proposition it becomes more and more evident that life can never really be understood in time simply because at no particular moment can I find the necessary resting-place from which to understand it—backwards.
Journal entry (translated by Alexander Dru, 1938).

58 Father in Heaven, when the thought of Thee wakes in our hearts, let it not awaken like a frightened bird that flies about in dismay, but like a child waking from its sleep with a heavenly smile.
Journal entry (translated by Alexander Dru, 1938).

59 Most people really believe that the Christian commandments (e.g. to love one's neighbour as oneself) are intentionally a little too severe—like putting the clock on half an hour to make sure of not being late in the morning.
Journal entry (translated by Alexander Dru, 1938).

60 The bird on the branch, the lily in the meadow, the stag in the forest, the fish in the sea, the countless joyful creatures sing, God is Love. But beneath all these sopranos, as it were a sustained bass part, is the *De profundis* of the Sacrificed, God is Love.
Journal entry (translated by Alexander Dru, 1938).

61 The ethical reality of the individual is the only reality.
1846 *Concluding Unscientific Postscript*, bk.2, pt.2, ch.3 (translated by Swenson and Lowrie).

Killy, Jean-Claude 1944–

French ski racer. He won the downhill and combined gold medals at the World Championship in Chile in 1966 and a further three gold medals in the Winter Olympics in 1968, after which he turned professional.

62 Skiing is a battle against yourself, always to the frontiers of the impossible. But most of all, it must give you pleasure. It is not an obligation but a joy.
1968 In *Sports Illustrated*, 18 Nov.

Kilmer, Joyce 1886–1918

US poet.

63 I think that I shall never see
A poem lovely as a tree.
1914 'Trees'.

Kilpatrick, James J 1920–

US writer and broadcaster.

64 A whore may be *naked*, but a mistress is *nude*. We are talking class.
1993 *Fine Print: Reflections on the Writing Art*.

Kim Il Sung 1912–94

North Korean soldier and political leader. After proclaiming his country a Republic in 1948 he remained in political control until his death. Within his country he was regarded with awe by the majority of citizens.

65 Everything is decided by a person's thoughts and if he is ideologically motivated, there is nothing he cannot do.

1969 Speech, 20 Apr. Collected in *Selected Works* (1992), vol.1, 'Work with Artists Should be Carried Out in Line with Political Principles'.

Kimball, Donald M

US business executive.

66 There's no place where success comes before work, except in the dictionary.

1986 In *USA Today*, 21 Apr.

Kincaid, Jamaica originally *Elaine Potter Richardson* 1949–

Antiguan writer; living in the US. Her works include *At the Bottom of the River* (1983), the autobiographical novel *Annie John* (1985), and a critique of colonialism and tourism, *A Small Place* (1988).

67 There was nothing noble-minded men could not do when they discovered they could slap time on their wrists just like that.

1988 *A Small Place.*

68 A tourist is an ugly human being.

1988 *A Small Place.*

King, Billie Jean née *Moffitt* 1943–

US tennis player, who won a record 20 titles at Wimbledon (1965–80).

69 Ask Nureyev to stop dancing, ask Sinatra to stop singing, then you can ask me to stop playing.

1982 Quoted in Colin Jarman *The Guinness Dictionary of Sports Quotations* (1990).

70 If you're up against a girl with big boobs, bring her to the net and make her hit backhand volleys.

1982 *Billie Jean King.*

King, Carlyle 1907–

Canadian political scientist and socialist.

71 The main business of socialist parties is not to form governments but to change minds.

Attributed, 1940s.

King, Don 1932–

US boxing promoter.

72 Only in America could a Don King happen.

Quoted in Colin Jarman *The Guinness Dictionary of Sports Quotations* (1990). King adopted 'Only in America' as a catchphrase, billing himself as Don 'Only in America' King.

King, Martin Luther Jr 1929–68

US civil rights leader. He advocated passive resistance to segregation and led a boycott (1955–6) against segregated

bus lines in Montgomery, Alabama. In 1964 he received both the Kennedy and Nobel Peace Prizes. He was assassinated by James Earl Ray.

73 He who passively accepts evil is as much involved in it as he who helps to perpetuate it.

1958 *Strides Towards Freedom.*

74 It may be true that the law cannot make a man love me, but it can keep him from lynching me, and I think that's pretty important.

1962 Speech at Cornell College, Mt Vernon, Iowa. Reported in the *Wall Street Journal*, 13 Nov.

75 Injustice anywhere is a threat to justice everywhere.

1963 Letter from Birmingham jail, Alabama, 16 Apr.

76 I have a dream. I have a dream that my four little children will one day live in a nation where they will not be judged by the colour of their skin but by the content of their character.

1963 Washington civil rights rally, 15 Jun.

77 If a man hasn't discovered something he will die for, he isn't fit to live.

1963 Speech in Detroit, 23 Jun.

78 When the architects of our republic wrote the magnificent words of the Constitution and the Declaration of Independence, they were signing a promissory note to which every American was to fall heir… America has defaulted on this promissory note insofar as her citizens of color are concerned.

1963 Speech at the Lincoln Memorial, 28 Aug, during the March on Washington.

79 We have…come to this hallowed spot to remind America of the fierce urgency of now.

1963 Speech at the Lincoln Memorial, 28 Aug, during the March on Washington.

80 Let us not seek to satisfy our thirst for freedom by drinking from the cup of bitterness and hatred…[nor] allow our creative protests to degenerate into physical violence.

1963 Speech at the Lincoln Memorial, 28 Aug, during the March on Washington.

81 You have been the victim of creative suffering.

1963 Speech at the Lincoln Memorial, 28 Aug, during the March on Washington.

82 I have a dream that one day…the sons of former slaves and the sons of former slave owners will be able to sit together at the table of brotherhood.

1963 Speech at the Lincoln Memorial, 28 Aug, during the March on Washington.

83 We have genuflected before the god of science only to find that it has given us the atomic bomb,

producing fears and anxieties that science can never mitigate.

1963 *Strength to Love*, ch.13.

84 The church must be reminded that it is not the master or servant of the state, but rather the conscience of the state.

1963 *Strength to Love*.

85 Discrimination is a hellhound that gnaws at negroes in every waking moment of their lives, to remind them that the lie of their inferiority is accepted as truth in the society dominating them.

1967 Speech at the Christian leadership conference, Atlanta, 16 Aug.

86 I've been to the mountain top. I've looked over, and I've seen the promised land. I may not get there with you, but I want you to know tonight that we as a people will get to the promised land. So, I'm happy tonight. Mine eyes have seen the glory of the coming of the Lord.

1968 Speech at Memphis, 3 Apr, the day before he was assassinated.

87 Love is the only force capable of transforming an enemy into a friend.

Attributed, collected in *The Words of Martin Luther King*.

King, William Lyon Mackenzie 1874–1950

Canadian Liberal politician, Prime Minister 1921–6, 1926–30 and 1935–48. His view that the dominions should be autonomous within the British Empire resulted in the Statute of Westminster (1931).

88 If some countries have too much history, we have too much geography.

1936 Address to the House of Commons, Ottawa, 18 Jun.

Kingsley, Charles 1819–75

English writer. Among his best-known works are the historical novels *Westward Ho!* (1855), and the children's book *The Water Babies* (1863). A Christan Socialist, he also published an immense number of articles on current topics.

89 'Oh Mary, go and call the cattle home,
And call the cattle home,
And call the cattle home,
Across the sands of Dee.'
The western wind was wild and dank with foam,
And all alone went she.

1850 *Alton Locke*, ch.26, 'The Sands of Dee'.

90 Come; and strong within us
Stir the Vikings' blood;
Bracing brain and sinew;
Blow, thou wind of God!

1857 'Ode to the North-East Wind'.

91 Be good, sweet maid, and let who will be clever;
Do noble things, do not dream them, all day long:
And so make life, death, and that vast for-ever
One grand, sweet song.

1858 'A Farewell'.

92 Once upon a time there was a little chimney-sweep, and his name was Tom.

1863 *The Water-Babies*, ch.1.

93 The great elm-trees in the gold-green meadows were fast asleep above, and the cows fast asleep beneath them; nay, the few clouds which were about were fast asleep likewise, and so tired that they had lain down on the earth to rest, in long white flakes and bars, among the stems of the elm-trees, and along the tops of the alders by the stream.

1863 *The Water-Babies*, ch.1.

94 When all the world is young, lad,
And all the trees are green;
And every goose a swan, lad,
And every lass a queen;
Then hey for boot and horse, lad,
And round the world away:
Young blood must have its course, lad,
And every dog his day.

1863 Song. *The Water Babies*, ch.2.

95 He was as thorough an Englishman as ever coveted his neighbour's goods... [He was] chief professor of Necrobioneopalaeonthydrochthonanthropopithek-ology.

1863 Professor Ptthmllnsprts. *The Water-Babies*, ch.4.

96 The healthiest situation in England, on Easthampstead Plain. Free run of Windsor Forest. *The Times* every morning. A double-barrelled gun and pointers, and leave to shoot three Wellington College boys a week (not more) in case black game was scarce.

1863 The reward for criminal lunacy. *The Water-Babies*, ch.4.

97 I am the ugliest fairy in the world, and I shall be till people behave themselves as they ought to do. And then I shall grow as handsome as my sister... Mrs Doasyouwouldbedoneby.

1863 Mrs Bedonebyasyoudid. *The Water-Babies*, ch.5.

98 How long would it take a school-inspector of average activity to tumble head over heels from London to York?

1863 *The Water-Babies*, ch.8.

99 So Tom went home with Ellie...and he is now a great man of science...and knows everything about everything, except why a hen's egg don't turn into a crocodile, and two or three other little things which no one will know till the coming of the

Cocqcigrues. And all this from what he learnt when he was a water-baby, underneath the sea.
'And of course, Tom married Ellie?'
My dear child, what a silly notion! Don't you know that no one ever marries in a fairy tale, under the rank of a prince or a princess?
1863 *The Water-Babies*, ch.8.

1 We have used the Bible as if it was a constable's handbook—an opium-dose for keeping beasts of burden patient while they are being overloaded.
Letters to the Chartists, no.2.

2 To be discontented with the divine discontent, and to be ashamed with the noble shame, is the very germ and first upgrowth of all virtue.
1874 *Health and Education*.

Kingsley, Mary Henrietta 1862–1900

English writer and traveller. After the death of her invalid parents she travelled to West Africa (1893 and 1895), living among the natives, and wrote accounts of both journeys. She died of enteric fever while serving as a nurse in the second Boer War.

3 A certain sort of friendship soon arose between the Fans and me. We each recognized that we belonged to that same section of the human race with whom it is better to drink than to fight. We knew we would each have killed the other, if sufficient inducement were offered, and so we took a certain amount of care that the inducement should not arise.
1893 *Travels in West Africa* (published 1899).

4 It is at these times that you realise the blessings of a good thick skirt… Save for a good many bruises, here I was with the fulness of my skirt tucked under me, sitting on nine ebony spikes some twelve inches long, in comparative comfort.
1893 *Travels in West Africa* (published 1899).

5 The sooner the Crown Colony system is removed from the sphere of practical politics and put under a glass case in the South Kensington Museum, labelled 'Extinct', the better for everyone.
1899 *West African Studies*.

6 West Africa today is just a quarry of paving stones for Hell, and those stones were cemented in place with men's blood mixed with wasted gold.
1899 *West African Studies*.

Kington, Miles 1941–

British writer. He is best known as a humorist, and also writes on jazz.

7 Nobody has ever been able to define jazz satisfactorily. This is probably because anyone who was capable of doing so never really wanted to,

knowing how much you would have to leave out of the definition.
1992 *The Jazz Anthology*, ch.1

Kinnock, Neil Gordon 1942–

Welsh Labour politician. In 1983 he succeeded Michael Foot as Party leader, and united the Party under moderate policies, but resigned after the 1992 election defeat.

8 We cannot remove the evils of capitalism without taking its source of power: ownership.
1975 In *Tribune*.

9 I want to retire at 50. I want to play cricket in the summer and geriatric football in the winter, and sing in the choir.
1980 In *The Times*, 28 Jul.

10 Like Brighton Pier—all right as far as it goes, but inadequate for getting to France.
1981 On Conservative European policy, House of Commons, 2 Feb.

11 It's a pity others had to leave theirs on the ground at Goose Green to prove it.
1983 Reply to a heckler who had said Mrs Thatcher had shown 'guts' in the Falklands Crisis. Quoted in *The Times*, 6 Jun.

12 If Margaret Thatcher wins on Thursday, I warn you not to be ordinary, I warn you not to be young, I warn you not to fall ill, I warn you not to get old.
1983 Speech one day before polling, Jun.

Kinsella, W(illiam) P(atrick) 1935–

Canadian novelist.

13 There was silence in the room. Then a voice, stunning as thunder, clear and common as a train whistle—the voice of a ball-park announcer: 'If you build it, he will come.'
1980 'Shoeless Joe Jackson Comes to Iowa', a short story later expanded into the novel *Shoeless Joe* (1982) and filmed as *Field of Dreams* (1989).

Kipling, (Joseph) Rudyard 1865–1935

English writer, born in Bombay, who lived for several years in India. His verse both celebrated and satirized the British Imperial presence, and won him widespread popularity, while the stories in *The Jungle Book* are considered classics of their kind. He also wrote novels and a biography, and was awarded the Nobel Prize in 1907.

14 The toad beneath the harrow knows
Exactly where each tooth-point goes;
The butterfly upon the road
Preaches contentment to that toad.
1886 'Pagett, MP'.

15 Never praise a sister to a sister, in the hope of your compliments reaching the proper ears.
1888 *Plain Tales from the Hills*, 'False Dawn'.

16 Take my word for it, the silliest woman can manage a clever man; but it takes a very clever woman to manage a fool.
1888 *Plain Tales from the Hills*, 'Three and—an Extra'.

17 Every one is more or less mad on one point.
1888 *Plain Tales from the Hills*, 'On the Strength of a Likeness'.

18 The Man who Would be King.
1888 *Wee Willie Winkie*, title of short story.

19 Being kissed by a man who didn't wax his moustache was—like eating an egg without salt.
1888 *The Story of the Gadsbys*, 'Poor Dear Mamma'.

20 Down to Gehenna or up to the Throne,
He travels fastest who travels alone.
1888 *The Story of the Gadsbys*, 'L'Envoi'. The poem was later renamed 'The Winners' (1912).

21 A man lives well and happily until he begins to feel unwell. Then he feels worse because the climate allows him no chance of pulling himself together—and then he dies.
1889 Of life in Singapore. *From Sea to Sea*.

22 We're poor little lambs who've lost our way,
Baa! Baa! Baa!
We're little black sheep who've gone astray,
Baa-aa-aa!
Gentlemen-rankers out on the spree,
Damned from here to eternity
God ha' mercy on such as we,
Baa! Yah! Bah!
1889 'The Gentlemen-Rankers'.

23 Oh, East is East, and West is West, and never the twain shall meet,
Till earth and sky stand presently at God's great Judgement seat;
But there is neither East nor West, Border, nor Breed, nor Birth,
When two strong men stand face to face, tho' they come from the ends of the earth.
1889 'The Ballad of East and West'.

24 The Japanese should have no concern with business.
1889 *From Sea to Sea*.

25 Moulmein is situated up the mouth of a river which ought to flow through South America.
1889 *From Sea to Sea*.

26 Come you back to Mandalay,
Where the old flotilla lay:
Can't you 'ear their paddles chunkin' from Rangoon to Mandalay?
On the road to Mandalay,
Where the flyin'-fishes play,

An' the dawn comes up like thunder outer China 'crost the Bay!
1890 'Mandalay'.

27 Ship me somewhere east of Suez, where the best is like the worst,
Where there aren't no Ten Commandments an' a man can raise a thirst.
1890 'Mandalay'.

28 By the old Moulmein Pagoda, lookin' eastward to the sea,
There's a Burma girl a-settin', and I know she thinks o' me;
For the wind is in the palm trees, an' the temple bells they say:
'Come you back, you British soldier'; come you back to Mandalay!'
1890 'Mandalay'.

29 For they're hangin' Danny Deever, you can hear the Dead March play,
The regiment's in 'ollow square—they're hangin' him to-day;
They've taken of his buttons off an' cut his stripes away,
An' they're hangin' Danny Deever in the mornin'.
1890 'Danny Deever'.

30 O it's Tommy this, an' Tommy that, an' 'Tommy, go away';
But it's 'Thank you, Mister Atkins,' when the band begins to play.
1890 'Tommy'.

31 Then it's Tommy this, an' Tommy that, and 'Tommy 'ow's yer soul?'
But it's 'Thin red line of 'eroes' when the drums begin to roll.
1890 'Tommy'.
▷ See Russell 834:44.

32 For it's Tommy this, an' Tommy that, and 'Chuck him out, the brute!'
But it's 'Saviour of 'is country' when the guns begin to shoot.
1890 'Tommy'.

33 When you're wounded and left on Afghanistan's plains
And the women come out to cut up what remains
Just roll to your rifle and blow out your brains
An' go to your Gawd like a soldier.
1890 'The Young British Soldier'.

34 So 'ere's *to* you, Fuzzy-Wuzzy, at your 'ome in the Soudan;
You're a pore benighted 'eathen but a first-class fightin' man;

An' 'ere's *to* you, Fuzzy-Wuzzy, with your 'ayrick
  'ead of 'air—
You big black boundin' beggar—for you broke a
  British square!
1890 'Fuzzy-Wuzzy'.

35 The uniform 'e wore
    Was nothin' much before,
    An' rather less than 'arf o' that be'ind.
    1890 'Gunga Din'.

36 Though I've belted you and flayed you,
    By the livin' Gawd that made you,
    You're a better man than I am, Gunga Din!
    1890 'Gunga Din'.

37 'Ave you 'eard o' the Widow at Windsor
    With a hairy gold crown on 'er 'ead?
    She 'as ships on the foam—she 'as millions at 'ome,
    An' she pays us poor beggars in red.
    1890 'The Widow at Windsor'.

38 An' I seed her first a-smokin' of a whackin' white
      cheroot,
    An' a-wastin' Christian kisses on an 'eathen idol's
      foot.
    1890 'Mandalay'.

39 And the talk slid north, and the talk slid south,
    With the sliding puffs from the hookah-mouth.
    Four things greater than all things are,—
    Women and Horses and Power and War.
    1890 'The Ballad of the King's Jest'.

40 When the flush of a new-born sun fell first on
      Eden's green and gold,
    Our father Adam sat under the Tree and scratched
      with a stick in the mould;
    And the first rude sketch that the world had seen
      was joy to his mighty heart,
    Till the Devil whispered behind the leaves, 'It's
      pretty, but is it Art?'
    1892 'The Conundrum of the Workshops'.

41 We know that the tail must wag the dog, for the
      horse is drawn by the cart;
    But the Devil whoops, as he whooped of old: 'It's
      clever, but is it Art?'
    1892 'The Conundrum of the Workshops'.

42 Winds of the World, give answer! They are
      whimpering to and fro—
    And what should they know of England who only
      England know?—
    The poor little street-bred people that vapour and
      fume and brag.
    1891 'The English Flag'.

43 If I were damned of body and soul,
    I know whose prayers would make me whole,

Mother o' mine, O mother o' mine.
1891 *The Light That Failed*, dedication.

44 There ain't twelve hundred people in the world
    who understand pictures. The others pretend and
    don't care.
    1891 *The Light That Failed.*

45 And the end of the fight is a tombstone white, with
      the name of the late deceased,
    And the epitaph drear: 'A fool lies here who tried to
      hustle the East.'
    1892 *The Naulahka*, ch.5.

46 For the sin ye do by two and two ye must pay for
      one by one!
    1892 'Tomlinson'.

47 There be triple ways to take, of the eagle or the
      snake,
    Or the way of a man with a maid;
    But the sweetest way to me is a ship's upon the sea
    In the heel of the North-East Trade.
    1892 'The Long Trail'.

48 There are nine and sixty ways of constructing tribal
      lays,
    And—every—single—one—of—them—is—
      right!
    1892 'In the Neolithic Age'.

49 A man-cub is a man-cub, and he must learn *all* the
    Law of the Jungle.
    1894 *The Jungle Book*, 'Kaa's Hunting'.

50 'We be one blood, thou and I', Mowgli answered. 'I
    take my life from thee to-night. My kill shall be thy
    kill if ever thou art hungry, O Kaa.'
    1894 *The Jungle Book*, 'Kaa's Hunting'.

51 Brother, thy tail hangs down behind!
    1894 *The Jungle Book*, 'The Road Song of the Bandar-Log'.

52 Now this is the Law of the Jungle—as old and as
      true as the sky;
    And the Wolf that shall keep it may prosper, but
      the Wolf that shall break it must die.
    1895 *The Second Jungle Book*, 'The Law of the Jungle'.

53 Keep ye the law—be swift in all obedience—
    Clear the land of evil, drive the road and bridge the
      ford.
    Make ye sure to each his own
    That he reap where he hath sown;
    By the peace among our peoples let men know we
      serve the Lord!
    1896 'A Song of the English'.

54 We have fed our sea for a thousand years

And she calls us, still unfed,
Though there's never a wave of all her waves
But marks our English dead.
1896 'A Song of the Dead'.

55 If blood be the price of admiralty
Lord God, we ha' paid in full!
1896 'A Song of the Dead'.

56 I've taken my fun where I've found it,
An' now I must pay for my fun,
For he more you 'ave known o' the others
The less will you settle for one;
1896 'The Ladies'.

57 For the Colonel's Lady an' Judy O'Grady
Are sisters under their skins!
1896 'The Ladies'.

58 The 'eathen in 'is blindness bows down to wood an'
stone;
'E don't obey no orders unless they is 'is own.
1896 'The 'Eathen'.

59 The 'eathen in 'is blindness must end where 'e
began.
But the backbone of the Army is the non-
commissioned man!
1896 'The 'Eathen'.

60 And only the master shall praise us, and only the
Master shall blame;
And no one shall work for money, and no one shall
work for fame,
But each for the joy of working, and each, in his
separate star,
Shall draw the Thing as he sees It for the God of
Things as They are!
1896 'When Earth's Last Picture is Painted'.

61 The tumult and the shouting dies—
The captains and the kings depart—
Still stands Thine ancient Sacrifice,
An humble and a contrite heart.
Lord God of Hosts, be with us yet,
Lest we forget—lest we forget!
1897 'Recessional'.
▷ See Bible 116:79.

62 If, drunk with sight of power, we loose
Wild tongues that have not Thee in awe—
Such boasting as the Gentiles use,
Or lesser breeds without the Law.
1897 'Recessional'.

63 What the horses o' Kansas think to-day, the horses
of America will think tomorrow; an' I tell *you* that
when the horses of America rise in their might, the
day o' the Oppressor is ended.
1898 *The Day's Work*, 'A Walking Delegate'.

64 Take up the White Man's burden—
Send forth the best ye breed—
Go, bind your sons to exile
To serve your captives' need.
1899 'The White Man's Burden'.

65 Your new-caught, sullen peoples,
Half devil and half child.
1899 'The White Man's Burden'.

66 By all ye will or whisper,
By all ye leave or do,
The silent sullen peoples
Shall weigh your God and you.
1899 'The White Man's Burden'.

67 When you've shouted 'Rule Britannia', when you've
sung 'God save the Queen'—
When you've finished killing Kruger with your
mouth—
Will you kindly drop a shilling in my little
tambourine
For a gentleman in *Kharki* ordered South?
1899 *The Absent-Minded Beggar*.

68 Mr Raymond Martin, beyond question, was born
in the gutter, and bred in a Board-School, where
they played marbles. He was further (I give the
barest handful from great store) a Flopshus Cad, an
Outrageous Stinker, a Jelly-bellied Flag-flapper
(this was Stalky's contribution), and several other
things which it is not seemly to put down.
1899 *Stalky & Co.*

69 Being human, she must have been afraid of
something, but one never found out what it was.
c.1900 Of Mary Kingsley (1862–1900), the enterprising
English traveller in West Africa. Attributed.

70 Little Friend of all the World.
1901 Kim's nickname. *Kim*, ch.1.

71 Men are as chancy as children in their choice of
playthings.
1901 *Kim*, ch.10.

72 One does not own to the possession of money in
India.
1901 *Kim*, ch.11.

73 'Noble and generous cetacean, have you ever tasted
Man?' 'No,' said the Whale. 'What is it like?'
'Nice,' said the small 'Stute Fish. 'Nice but nubbly.'
1902 *Just So Stories*, 'How the Whale Got His Throat'.

74 You must not forget the Suspenders, Best Beloved.
1902 *Just So Stories*, 'How the Whale Got His Throat'.

75 He had his Mummy's leave to paddle, or else he
would never have done it, because he was a man of
infinite-resource-and-sagacity.

1902 *Just So Stories*, 'How the Whale Got His Throat'.

76 The camel's hump is an ugly lump
    Which well you may see at the Zoo;
    But uglier yet is the hump we get
    From having too little to do.
    1902 *Just So Stories*, 'How the Camel Got His Hump'.

77 The cure for this ill is not to sit still,
    Or frowst with a book by the fire;
    But to take a large hoe and a shovel also,
    And dig till you gently perspire.
    1902 *Just So Stories*, 'How the Camel Got His Hump'.

78 Most 'scruciating idle.
    1902 *Just So Stories*, 'How the Camel Got His Hump'.

79 'Humph yourself!'
    And the Camel humphed himself.
    1902 *Just So Stories*, 'How the Camel Got His Hump'.

80 There lived a Parsee from whose hat the rays of the
    sun were reflected in more-than-oriental-
    splendour.
    1902 *Just So Stories*, 'How the Rhinoceros Got His Skin'.

81 But there was one Elephant—a new Elephant—an
    Elephant's Child—who was full of 'satiable
    curiosity, and that means he asked ever so many
    questions.
    1902 *Just So Stories*, 'The Elephant's Child'.

82 The great grey-green, greasy Limpopo River, all set
    about with fever-trees.
    1902 *Just So Stories*, 'The Elephant's Child'.

83 Led go! You are hurtig be!
    1902 *Just So Stories*, 'The Elephant's Child'.

84 And I'd like to roll to Rio
    Some day before I'm old!
    1902 *Just So Stories*, 'The Beginning of the Armadilloes'.

85 'You are making my spots ache,' said Painted
    Jaguar.
    1902 *Just So Stories*, 'The Beginning of the Armadillos'.

86 But the wildest of all the wild animals was the Cat.
    He walked by himself, and all places were alike to
    him.
    1902 *Just So Stories*, 'The Cat That Walked By Himself'.

87 And he went back through the Wet Wild Woods,
    waving his wild tail and walking by his wild lone.
    But he never told anybody.
    1902 *Just So Stories*, 'The Cat That Walked By Himself'.

88 He would surprise them out of their jumpsome
    lives.
    1902 *Just So Stories*, 'How the Leopard Got His Spots'.

89 Something lost behind the Ranges.

1903 *The Five Nations*, 'The Explorer'.

90 Who hath desired the Sea?—the sight of salt water
    unbounded—
    The heave and the halt and the hurl and the crash
    of the comber wind-hounded?
    The sleek-barrelled swell before storm, grey,
    foamless, enormous, and growing—
    Stark calm on the lap of the Line or the crazy-eyed
    Hurricane blowing.
    1903 'The Sea and the Hills'.

91 And here the sea-fogs lap and cling
    And here, each warning each,
    The sheep-bells and the ship-bells ring
    Along the hidden beach.
    1903 'Sussex'.

92 God gives all men all earth to love,
    But since man's heart is small,
    Ordains for each one spot shall prove
    Belovèd over all.
    1903 'Sussex'.

93 Each to his choice, and I rejoice
    The lot has fallen to me
    In a fair ground—in a fair ground—
    Yea, Sussex by the sea!
    1903 'Sussex'.
    ▷ See Book of Common Prayer 176:65.

94 Then ye returned to your trinkets; then ye
    contented your souls
    With the flannelled fools at the wicket or the
    muddied oafs at the goals.
    1903 'The Islanders'.

95 An' it all goes into the laundry
    But it never comes out in the wash.
    1903 'Stellenbosh'.

96 'Tisn't beauty, so to speak, nor good talk necessarily.
    It's just It. Some women'll stay in a man's memory
    if they once walked down a street.
    1904 *Traffics and Discoveries*, 'Mrs Bathurst'.

97 The God who Looks after Small Things had caused
    the visitor that day to receive two weeks' delayed
    mails in one.
    1904 *Traffics and Discoveries*, 'The Captive'

98 Of all the trees that grow so fair,
    Old England to adorn,
    Greater are none beneath the Sun,
    Than Oak, and Ash, and Thorn.
    1906 *Puck of Pook's Hill*, 'Tree Song'.

99 England shall bide till Judgement Tide
    By Oak, and Ash, and Thorn.
    1906 *Puck of Pook's Hill*, 'Tree Song'.

1 What is a woman that you forsake her,
And the hearth-fire and the home-acre,
To go with the old grey Widow-maker?
1906 *Puck of Pook's Hill*, 'Harp Song of the Dane Women'.

2 If you wake at midnight, and hear a horse's feet,
Don't go drawing back the blind, or looking in the
street,
Them that asks no questions isn't told a lie.
Watch the wall, my darling, while the Gentlemen
go by!
1906 *Puck of Pook's Hill*, 'Smuggler's Song'.

3 Land of our birth, we pledge to thee
Our love and toil in the years to be;
When we are grown and take our place,
As men and women with our race.
1906 *Puck of Pook's Hill*, 'Children's Song'.

4 Teach us delight in simple things
And mirth that has no bitter springs;
Forgiveness free of evil done,
And love to all men 'neath the sun!
1906 *Puck of Pook's Hill*, 'Children's Song'.

5 But I consort with long-haired things
In velvet collar-rolls,
Who talk about the Aims of Art,
And 'theories' and 'goals',
And moo and coo with women-folk
About their blessed souls.
1909 'In Partibus'.

6 There is sorrow enough in the natural way
From men and women to fill our day;
But when we are certain of sorrow in store,
Why do we always arrange for more?
Brothers and Sisters, I bid you beware
Of giving your heart to a dog to tear.
1909 'The Power of the Dog'.

7 They shut the road through the woods
Seventy years ago.
Weather and rain have undone it again,
And now you would never know
There was once a road through the woods.
1910 *Rewards and Fairies*, 'Way Through the Woods'.

8 If you can keep your head when all about you
Are losing theirs and blaming it on you;
If you can trust yourself when all men doubt
you,
But make allowance for their doubting too;
If you can wait and not be tired by waiting,
Or being lied about, don't deal in lies,
Or being hated, don't give way to hating,
And yet don't look too good, nor talk too wise;
If you can dream—and not make dreams your
master;

If you can think—and not make thoughts your
aim,
If you can meet with Triumph and Disaster
And treat those two imposters just the same.
1910 *Rewards and Fairies*, 'If—'.

9 If you can talk with crowds and keep your virtue,
Or walk with Kings—nor lose the common touch,
If neither foes nor loving friends can hurt you,
If all men count with you, but none too much;
If you can fill the unforgiving minute
With sixty seconds' worth of distance run,
Yours is the Earth and everything that's in it.
And—which is more—you'll be a Man, my son!
1910 *Rewards and Fairies*, 'If—'.

10 One man in a thousand, Solomon says,
Will stick more close than a brother.
1910 *Rewards and Fairies*, 'The Thousandth Man'

11 It is always a temptation to a rich and lazy nation.
To puff and look important and to say:-
'Though we know we should defeat you, we have
not the time to meet you,
We will therefore pay you cash to go away.'

And that is called paying the Dane-geld;
But we've proved it again and again,
That if once you have paid him the Dane-geld
You never get rid of the Dane.
1911 'Dane-Geld'.

12 'Oh, where are you going to, all you Big Steamers,
With England's own coal, up and down the salt
seas?
'We are going to fetch you your bread and your
butter,
Your beef, pork, and mutton, eggs, apples and
cheese.'
1911 'Big Steamers'.

13 Our England is a garden that is full of stately views,
Of borders, beds and shrubberies and lawns and
avenues,
With statues on the terraces and peacocks strutting
by;
But the Glory of the Garden lies in more than
meets the eye.
1911 'The Glory of the Garden'.

14 Our England is a garden, and such gardens are not
made
By singing:—'Oh, how beautiful!' and sitting in
the shade,
While better men than we go out and start their
working lives
At grubbing weeds from gravel paths with broken
dinner-knives.
1911 'The Glory of the Garden'.

15 Oh, Adam was a gardener, and God who made him
    sees
  That half a proper gardener's work is done upon his
    knees,
  So when your work is finished, you can wash your
    hands and pray
  For the Glory of the Garden that it may not pass
    away!
  1911 'The Glory of the Garden'.

16 We know the war prepared
  On every peaceful home,
  We know the hells declared
  For such as serve not Rome,
  The terror, threads and dread
  In market, hearth and field:
  We know when all is said
  We perish if we yield.
  1912 'Ulster'.

17 For all we have and are,
  For all our children's fate,
  Stand up and take the war.
  The Hun is at the gate!
  1914 'For All We Have and Are'.

18 There is but one task for all—
  For each one life to give.
  What stands if freedom fall?
  Who dies if England live?
  1914 'For All We Have and Are'.

19 It's north you may run to the rime-ringed sun,
  Or south to the blind Horn's hate;
  Or east all the way into Mississippi Bay,
  Or west to the Golden Gate.
  1918 *Twenty Poems*, 'The Long Trail'.

20 Pull out, pull out on the Long Trail—the trail that
  is always new!
  1918 *Twenty Poems*, 'The Long Trail'.

21 Their Name Liveth for Evermore.
  1919 His suggestion for the text to be carved over the lists of
  the dead in the Commonwealth war cemeteries after World
  War I.
  ▷ See Bible 133:18.

22 If any question why we died,
  Tell them, because our fathers lied.
  1919 *Rudyard Kipling's Verse*, 'Common Form'.

23 The female of the species is more deadly than the
  male.
  1919 *Rudyard Kipling's Verse*, 'The Female of the Species'.

24 Words are, of course, the most powerful drug used
  by mankind.
  1923 Speech, 14 Feb, collected in *A Book of Words*.

25 As it will be in the future, it was at the birth of
  Man—
  There are only four things certain since Social
    Progress began:—
  That the Dog returns to his Vomit and the Sow
    returns to her Mire,
  And the burnt Fool's bandaged finger goes
    wabbling back to the Fire.
  1927 *Rudyard Kipling's Verse*, 'The Gods of the Copybook
  Headings'.

26 England's on the anvil—hear the hammers ring—
  Clanging from the Severn to the Tyne!
  1927 *Rudyard Kipling's Verse*, 'The Anvil'.

Kirkland, (Joseph) Lane 1922–

US labour leader.

27 My pappy told me never to bet my bladder against
  a brewery or get into an argument with people who
  buy ink by the barrel.
  Quoted in David Olive *Business Babble* (1993).

Kirkup, James 1923–

English poet. He held academic posts in Japan from the
early 1960s, and his work has been greatly influenced by
Japanese culture and literature.

28 But the river remains unchanged, sad, refusing
  rehabilitation.
  1962 'No More Hiroshimas'.

Kishen fl.c.1840

Chinese diplomatist.

29 It appears to Your Majesty's slave that we are very
  deficient in means, and have not the shells and
  rockets used by the barbarians. We must, therefore,
  adopt other methods to stop them, which will be
  easy, as they have opened negotiations.
  1841 Report, Mar, to the Chinese Emperor during the 1st
  Opium War, 1839–42.

Kissinger, Henry Alfred 1923–

US academic and statesman. He was the main US figure
in the negotiations to end the Vietnam War (for which he
shared the 1973 Nobel Peace Prize), and Secretary of State
(1973–7). His 'shuttle diplomacy', aimed at improving
Israeli–Egyptian relations, had much success.

30 It is not often that nations learn from the past—
  even rarer that they draw the correct conclusions
  from it. For the lessons of historical experience, as
  of personal experience, are contingent. They teach
  the consequences of certain actions, but they
  cannot force a recognition of comparable
  situations.
  1957 *A World Restored: Castlereagh, Metternich and the
  Restoration of Peace, 1812–22.*

31 We lost sight of one of the cardinal maxims of guerrilla war: the guerrilla wins if he does not lose. The conventional army loses if it does not win.

1969 On the Vietnam War. In *Foreign Affairs*, Jan.

32 Power is the ultimate aphrodisiac.

1969 Comment at the end of his first year as head of the National Security Council. Quoted in Walter Isaacson *Kissinger* (1992).

33 We are all the President's men, and we must behave accordingly.

1970 On the US invasion of Cambodia, alluding to the nursery rhyme *Humpty Dumpty* ('All the king's men…'). The phrase was used in the title of the book by *Washington Post* reporters Bob Woodward and Carl Bernstein on the Watergate scandal.

34 No foreign policy, no matter how ingenious, has any chance of success if it is born in the minds of a few and carried in the heart of none.

1973 Speech to International Platform Association, 2 Aug.

35 Every civilization that has ever existed has ultimately collapsed.

1974 In the *New York Times*, 13 Oct.

36 History is a tale of efforts that failed…aspirations that weren't realized, or wishes that were fulfilled and then turned out to be different from what one expected.

1974 In the *New York Times*, 13 Oct.

37 There can't be any crisis next week. My schedule is already full.

1977 In *Time*, Jan.

38 High office teaches decision-making, not substance. It consumes intellectual capital; it does not create it. Most high officials leave office with the perceptions and insights with which they entered: they learn how to make decisions, but not what decisions to make.

1979 *The White House Years.*

39 The statesman's duty is to bridge the gap between his nation's experience and his vision.

1982 *Years of Upheaval.*

40 The nice thing about being a celebrity is that when you bore people, they think that it's their fault.

Quoted in *Reader's Digest*, Apr 1985.

41 Whatever must happen ultimately should happen immediately.

1986 Of the Iran–Contra scandal. In *Time*, 8 Oct.

42 Any people who have been persecuted for 2,000 years must be doing something wrong.

Of Israel, after its attack on Egypt. Quoted in Walter Isaacson *Kissinger* (1992).

43 I'd do anything for caviar and probably did.

On his visit to Moscow. Quoted in Walter Isaacson *Kissinger* (1992).

Kitchener of Khartoum and Broome, (Horatio) Herbert, 1st Earl 1850–1916

British field marshal. He served in Palestine, Cyprus and the Sudan, which he regained for the British Empire at Omdurman (1898), and was chief-of-staff and commander-in-chief in the Boer War. In World War I he was Secretary of State for War, but was drowned when HMS *Hampshire* struck a mine.

44 You are ordered abroad as a soldier of the King to help our French comrades against the invasion of a common enemy… In this new experience you may find temptations both in wine and women. You must entirely resist both temptations, and while treating all women with perfect courtesy, you should avoid any intimacy. Do your duty bravely. Fear God. Honour the King.

1914 Message to the soldiers of the British Expeditionary Force, reported in *The Times*, 19 Aug.

45 I don't mind your being killed, but I object to your being taken prisoner.

1914 To the Prince of Wales, later Edward VIII, who had asked to be allowed to the Front, 18 Dec.

Klee, Paul 1874–1940

Swiss painter and graphic artist, one of the most influential teachers of the German Bauhaus.

46 I have now reached the point where I can look over the great art of antiquity and its Renaissance. But, for myself, I cannot find any artistic connection with our own times. And to want to create something outside of one's own age strikes me as suspect.

1901–2 *The Diaries of Paul Klee 1898–1918*, entry 294.

47 The worst state of affairs is when science begins to concern itself with art.

1906 Collected in *The Notebooks of Paul Klee* (published 1957).

48 Color possesses me. I don't have to pursue it. It will possess me always, I know it. That is the meaning of this happy hour: Color and I are one. I am a painter.

1914 *The Diairies of Paul Klee 1898–1918*, entry 926.

49 Art is like Creation: it holds good on the last day as on the first.

1916 *The Diaries of Paul Klee 1898–1918*, entry 1008.

50 *Kunst gibt nicht das Sichtbare wieder, sondern macht sichtbar.*

Art does not reproduce the visible; rather it makes visible.

1920 'Creative Credo', in *Inward Vision* (1958).

Klein, Calvin Richard 1942–

US fashion designer.

51 You have to take things to an extreme and then bring them back to reality.

1988 On the fluctuating length of hemlines. In the *New York Times*, 9 Mar.

Kneller, Godfrey 1646–1723

German-born painter who spent most of his working life in England, particularly renowned as a portrait painter.

52 Painters of history make the dead live, and do not begin to live themselves till they are dead. I paint the living, and they make me live!

When asked why he preferred portraits to more prestigious history scenes. Quoted in A Cunningham *The Lives of the Most Eminent Painters, Sculptors and Architects* (1829).

Knight, Frank Hyneman 1885–1972

US economist, Professor at the University of Chicago (1927–58) and an opponent of social planning. His most famous works were *Risk, Uncertainty and Profit* (1921) and *The Ethics of Competition* (1923).

53 Costs merely register competing attractions.

1921 *Risk, Uncertainty and Profit.*

54 I have been increasingly moved to wonder whether my job is a job or a racket, whether economists, and particularly economic theorists, may not be in the position that Cicero, citing Cato, ascribed to the augurs of Rome—that they should cover their faces or burst into laughter when they met on the street.

1950 Collected in *Essays on the History and Method of Economics* (1956).

55 Sociology is the science of talk, and there is only one law in sociology. Bad talk drives out good.

Quoted in Paul A Samuelson *The Samuelson Sampler* (1973).

Knox, John c.1513–72

Scottish Protestant reformer and architect of the Church of Scotland, whose single-minded determination to establish Presbyterianism brought him into conflict with the Catholic Queen Mary.

56 The Monstrous Regiment of Women.

1558 From the title of his pamphlet, *The First Blast of the Trumpet Against the Monstrous Regiment of Women.*

57 To promote a woman to bear rule, superiority, dominion, or empire above any realm, nation, or city, is repugnant to nature, contumely to God, a thing most contrarious to his revealed will and approved ordinance; and, finally, it is the subversion of good order, of all equity and justice.

1558 *First Blast of the Trumpet against the Monstrous Regiment of Women.*

58 If there be not in her, a proud mind, a crafty wit, and an indurate heart against God and his truth, my judgment faileth me.

1561 After his first meeting with Mary, Queen of Scots. *History of the Reformation in Scotland*, vol.2.

59 *Un homme avec Dieu est toujours dans la majorité.*

One man with God is always a majority.

Inscription on the Reformation Monument, Geneva, attributed to Knox.

Knox, Philander Chase 1853–1921

US lawyer and politician. He served as US Attorney General (1901–4) and Secretary of State (1909–13).

60 Oh, Mr President, do not let so great an achievement suffer from any taint of legality.

1903 Quoted in Tom Buckley *Violent Neighbours* (1983), alluding to Theodore Roosevelt's desire to find legal grounds for the seizure of the Panama Canal by the USA.

Knox, Ronald Arbuthnot 1888–1957

English writer and Roman Catholic theologian. He wrote many theological works and Bible translations, and also detective novels.

61 There was once a man who said 'God
Must think it exceedingly odd
If he finds that this tree
Continues to be
When there's no-one about in the Quad.'

Attributed. Quoted in Langford Reed *Complete Limerick Book* (1924).

The limericks summarise Bishop George Berkeley's philosophy that everything is dependent at all times on the will of God.

▷ See Anonymous 25:35.

62 It is stupid of modern civilization to have given up believing in the devil, when he is the only explanation of it.

1939 *Let Dons Delight*, ch.8.

63 A loud noise at one end and no sense of responsibility at the other.

His definition of a baby. Attributed.

Knudsen, Semon Emil 1912–98

US automotive executive.

64 Before you tell someone how good you are, you must tell him how bad you used to be.

1959 In *Time* magazine, 25 May.

Koch, Edward I(rving) 1924–

US lawyer.

65 You're not a nice guy if you have a gun, even if you are a nice guy.

1980 In *Time*, 3 Mar.

66 Each diploma is a lighted match… Each one of you is a fuse.

1983 Addressing students at NY State University. In the *New York Times*, 10 Jun.

Koestler, Arthur 1905–83

Hungarian-born British writer and journalist. He wrote on science and parapsychology, and is best known for his anti-communist novel *Darkness at Noon* (1940). He and his wife committed suicide after he became terminally ill.

67 The definition of an individual was: a multitude of one million divided by one million.
1940 *Darkness at Noon*, 'The Grammatical Fiction', pt.2.

68 A writer's ambition should be...to trade a hundred contemporary readers for ten readers in ten year's time and for one reader in a hundred years.
1951 In the *New York Times Book Review*, 1 Apr.

69 Space-ships and time machines are no escape from the human condition. Let Othello subject Desdemona to a lie-detector test; his jealousy will still blind him to the evidence. Let Oedipus triumph over gravity; he won't triumph over his fate.
1953 'The Boredom of Fantasy', collected in *The Trail of the Dinosaur* (1955), pt.2.

70 Among all forms of mentation, verbal thinking is the most articulate, the most complex, and the most vulnerable to infectious diseases. It is liable to absorb whispered suggestions, and to incorporate them as hidden persuaders into the code.
1964 *The Act of Creation*.

71 Creativity in science could be described as the act of putting two and two together to make five.
1964 *The Act of Creation*.

72 The most persistent sound that reverberates through men's history is the beating of war drums.
1978 *Janus; A Summing Up*, 'Prologue: The New Calendar', sect.1.

Koffler, Murray 1924–

Canadian pharmacist and philanthropist.

73 Dress British, look Irish, think Yiddish.
His formula for success, quoted in Frank Rasky *Just a Simple Pharmacist: The Story of Murray Koffler, Builder of the Shoppers Drug Mart Empire* (1988).

Koh, Harold Hongju

US lawyer, Professor of Law at Yale University.

74 Silence has a sound, and the sound is 'no.'
1991 Testimony to the US Senate Judiciary Committee on the presidential right to enter the Gulf war without congressional approval. Quoted by Senator Joseph R Biden, Jr in NPR broadcast, 10 Jan.

Kohlberg, Jerome 1925–

US investment banker.

75 An ethic is not an ethic, and a value not a value without some sacrifice for it. Something given up, something not gained.
Quoted in Sarah Bartlett *The Money Machine* (1991).

Kollwitz, Käthe 1867–1945

German sculptor and graphic artist. She had two sons, Peter and Hans. Peter was killed at the beginning of World War I, in 1914.

76 As you, the children of my body, have been my tasks, so too are my other works.
1915 Letter to her son Hans, 21 Feb.

77 I have never done any work cold... I have always worked with my blood, so to speak.
1917 Letter to her son Hans, 16 Apr.

Korda, Sir Alexander 1893–1956

Hungarian-born British film producer. He worked in Vienna, Berlin and Hollywood before coming to Britain in the early 1930s where he founded London Film Productions and the Denham Studios.

78 One can be unhappy before eating caviar, even after, but at least not *during*.
1979 In *Newsweek*, 26 Nov.

79 Inside every banker, even the governor of the Bank of England, there lies a gambling streak. In me, they recognise one of their own kind.
Quoted in Michael Wilding and Pamela Wilcox *Apple Sauce* (1982).

80 It's not enough to be Hungarian, you must have talent too.
Attributed. The predominance of Eastern European employees at Denham Studios in the 1930s was a topical joke.

Korn, Arthur 1891–1978

German-born architect, planner and teacher.

81 A new glass age has begun, which is equal in beauty to the old one of Gothic windows.
1926 *Glas im Bau und als Gebrauchsgegenstand* (translated as *Glass in Modern Architecture*, 1967).

Korthals, Robert 1933–

Canadian bank president.

82 The easiest way to steal from a bank is to own one.
Quoted by Diane Francis in *Controlling Interest: Who Owns Canada?* (1986).

Kosinski, Jerzy Nikodem 1933–91

Polish-born US novelist. His best-known books are *The Painted Bird* (1965) and *Being There* (1971).

83 I rent everything, other than the gift of life itself, which was given to me without any predictable lease, a gift that can be withdrawn at any time.

1991 Interview given three days before his suicide, in the *Weekend Guardian*, 25–6 May.

Kramer, Larry (Lawrence) 1935–

US novelist, playwright and screenwriter. He is best known for his controversial gay novel *Faggots* (1978), and his plays dealing with AIDS, notably *The Normal Heart* (1985).

84 We're all going to go crazy, living this epidemic every minute, while the rest of the world goes on out there, all around us, as if nothing is happening, going on with their own lives and not knowing what it's like, what we're going through. We're living through war, but where they're living it's peacetime, and we're all in the same country.

1985 Ned speaking of gay men with AIDS. *The Normal Heart*, act 2, sc.11.

Krasna, Norman 1909–84

US playwright and screenwriter. He won an Academy Award for *Princess O'Rourke* (1943). Other films include *Bachelor Mother* (1939) and *Indiscreet* (1958).

85 How dare he make love to me and not be a married man?

1958 Line delivered by Ingrid Bergman in *Indiscreet*.

Kraus, Karl 1874–1936

Austrian critic and dramatist, publisher and sole writer of the radical satirical magazine *Die Fackel* (The Torch, 1899–1936). He wrote the apocalyptic satirical play *The Last Days of Mankind* (1919), and collections of aphorisms.

86 Today's literature: prescriptions written by patients.

Aphorism collected in Heinrich Fischer (ed) *Beim Wort genommen* (1955). Translated by Harry Zohn in *Half-truths and one-and-a-half truths* (1986).

87 Why didn't Eternity have this deformed age aborted ? Its birthmark is the stamp of a newspaper, its medium is printer's ink, and in its veins flows ink.

Aphorism collected in Heinrich Fischer (ed) *Beim Wort genommen* (1955). Translated by Harry Zohn in *Half-truths and one-and-a-half truths* (1986).

88 The making of a journalist: no ideas and the ability to express them.

Aphorism collected in Heinrich Fischer (ed) *Beim Wort genommen* (1955). Translated by Harry Zohn in *Half-truths and one-and-a-half truths* (1986).

89 A historian is often only a journalist facing backwards.

Aphorism collected in Heinrich Fischer (ed) *Beim Wort genommen* (1955). Translated by Harry Zohn in *Half-truths and one-and-a-half truths* (1986).

90 How is the world ruled and led to war? Diplomats lie to journalists and believe these lies when they see them in print.

Aphorism collected in Heinrich Fischer (ed) *Beim Wort genommen* (1955). Translated by Harry Zohn in *Half-truths and one-and-a-half truths* (1986).

91 One ought to acknowledge the significance for mankind of the simultaneous invention of gunpowder and printer's ink.

Aphorism collected in Heinrich Fischer (ed) *Beim Wort genommen* (1955). Translated by Harry Zohn in *Half-truths and one-and-a-half truths* (1986).

Krishnamurti, Jiddu 1895–1986

Indian-born mystic and spiritual teacher. The theosophist Annie Besant in 1925 proclaimed him Messiah and from then on he travelled the world, teaching a way of life free from the conditioning of culture, race or religion.

92 I maintain that truth is a pathless land, and you cannot approach it by any path whatsoever, by any religion, by any sect.

1929 Speech in Holland. Quoted in Terry Lynn Taylor *Messengers of Light*, ch.32.

93 The authority of a belief imposed by religion surely destroys the discovery of reality. One relies on authority because one is afraid to stand alone.

1970 BBC interview, 7 Dec.

Kristol, Irving 1920–

US economist, Henry Luce Professor of Urban Values at New York University.

94 History does not provide us with any instance of a society that repressed the economic liberties of the individual while being solicitous of his other liberties.

1978 *Two Cheers for Capitalism*, introduction.

95 The fact of affluence is indisputable… Nevertheless, not many of us *feel* that well off. The instinct for contentment seems to have withered even as our economic condition has radically improved.

1978 *Two Cheers for Capitalism*, ch.1.

96 The elitist attitude is basically suspicious of, and hostile to, the market precisely because the market is so vulgarly democratic—one dollar, one vote.

1978 *Two Cheers for Capitalism*, ch.2.

Kroc, Ray(mond) A 1902–84

US entrepreneur, developer of the McDonald's fast-food chain.

97 Luck is a dividend of sweat. The more you sweat, the luckier you get.

1988 Quoted by Penny Moser 'The McDonald's Mystique', in *Fortune*, 4 Jul.

98 If they were drowning to death, I would put a hose in their mouth.

1988 On competitors. In *Fortune*, 4 Jul.

Kronecker, Leopold 1823–91

German mathematician, who worked in algebraic number theory and the foundations of analysis, and lectured widely. He held that mathematics should be based on whole numbers, rejecting the infinite, irrational and imaginary.

99 God made the integers, man made the rest.

Quoted in F Cajori *A History of Mathematics* (1919).

Kronenberger, Louis 1904–80

US writer, lecturer and critic. His books include novels and autobiographical reminiscences as well as critical works on literature and culture, and biographies.

1 Kings and Desperate Men.

1942 Title of book on 18c England.

2 The trouble with our age is that it is all signpost and no destination.

1954 *Company Manners*, 'The Spirit of The Age'.

Kruger, Paulus 1825–1904

South African soldier and statesman, President of the Transvaal (1883–1902) and head of the provisional government in the first Boer War. During the second Boer War he was forced to flee to Europe, and he died in Switzerland.

3 They have asked me for my trousers, and I have given them; for my coat, and I have given that also; now they want my life, and that I cannot give.

1899 Speech in the Raad, 7 Sep, at the beginning of the second Boer War, 1899–1902.

Krugman, Paul R 1953–

US economist, Professor at Stanford University.

4 The trouble with poverty, as an issue, is that it has basically exhausted the patience of the general public.

1992 *The Age of Diminished Expectations*.

5 Given that the deepest problem with the US economy is slow productivity growth, it is difficult to argue for tax increases that might reduce incentives… There seems to be a public consensus that Donald Trump is the price of progress.

1992 *The Age of Diminished Expectations*.

6 The exchange rate is only a statistic, not a symbol of national honor and virility.

1994 Quoted in the *New York Times*, 26 Jun.

Krutch, Joseph Wood 1893–1970

US author, teacher and critic. He is the author of *The Modern Temper* (1929) and *The Measure of Man* (1954).

7 A tragic writer does not have to believe in God, but he must believe in man.

1929 *The Modern Temper*, 'The Tragic Fallacy'.

8 Electronic calculators can solve problems which the man who made them cannot solve; but no government subsidized commission of engineers and physicists could create a worm.

1949 *The Twelve Seasons*, 'February'.

9 The most serious charge which can be brought against New England is not Puritanism but February.

1949 *The Twelve Seasons*, 'February'.

10 Cats seem to go on the principle that it never does any harm to ask for what you want.

1949 *The Twelve Seasons*, 'February'.

Kubrick, Stanley 1928–99

US screenwriter, film producer and director. His films include *Spartacus* (1960), *2001: A Space Odyssey* (1969), the controversial *A Clockwork Orange* (1971) and *Full Metal Jacket* (1987).

11 Gentlemen, you can't fight in here. This is the war room.

1963 *Dr Strangelove: or How I stopped worrying and learned to love the bomb* (with Terry Southern and Peter George).

12 The great nations have always acted like gangsters, and the small nations like prostitutes.

1963 In the *Guardian*.

Kuhn, Maggie 1905–

US writer and social reformer.

13 The ultimate indignity is to be given a bedpan by a stranger who calls you by your first name.

1978 In *The Observer*, 20 Aug.

Kuhn, Thomas S(amuel) 1922–96

US historian and philosopher of science. His major work is *The Structure of Scientific Revolutions* (1962), a cornerstone of modern approaches to the philosophy and history of science.

14 Effective research scarcely begins before a scientific community thinks it has acquired firm answers to questions like the following: What are the fundamental entities of which the universe is composed? How do these interact with each other and with the sense? What questions may legitimately be asked about such entities and what techniques employed in seeking solutions?

1962 *The Structure of Scientific Revolutions*.

Kundera, Milan 1929–

Czech novelist.

15 The Unbearable Lightness of Being.

1984 Title of novel.

Küng, Hans 1928–

Swiss Roman Catholic theologian. His questioning of received doctrine aroused controversy, and the Vatican withdrew his authority to teach as a Catholic theologian in 1979. He defended himself in *Why I Am Still A Christian* (1987).

16 A Church which abandons the truth abandons itself.

Die Kirche (translated by Ray and Rosalee Ockenden as *The Church*, 1967).

Kunitz, Stanley Jasspon 1905–

US poet and editor, whose style is at once intellectual and passionate. His poetry collections include *Intellectual Things* (1930), *Selected Poems, 1928–1958* (1958, Pulitzer Prize winner) and *Next-to-Last Things: New Poems and Essays* (1985).

17 A poem is at once the most primitive and most sophisticated use of language, but my emphasis is on the former.

1985 *Next-to-Last Things*, 'The Wisdom of the Body'.

18 The deepest thing I know is that I am living and dying at once, and my conviction is to report that dialogue.

1987 In the *New York Times*, 11 Mar.

Kuralt, Charles 1934–

US writer and broadcaster.

19 It takes an earthquake to remind us that we walk on the crust of an unfinished earth.

1994 In *Sunday Morning*, CBS TV, 23 Jan.

Kurosawa, Akira 1910–98

Japanese film director and winner of numerous international awards for his films. Best known in the West for his full-blooded adaptations of Shakespeare.

20 Like a steak spread with butter and topped with good, rich, broiled eels.

1965 His concept of a great film. In *Japan Quarterly*, vol.12.

21 The Japanese see self-assertion as immoral and self-sacrifice as the sensible course to take in life.

1982 *Something like an Autobiography*.

Kushner, Tony 1956–

US playwright, whose highly political plays include the two-part *Angels in America* (1991–2, Pulitzer Prize 1993), on the effects of AIDS in New York.

22 I wanted to attempt something of ambition and size even if that meant I might be accused of

straying too close to ambition's ugly twin, pretentiousness.

1993 Of his *Angels in America*, written in two parts. In the *New York Times*, 21 Nov.

Kurz, Mordecai

US economist, Professor at Stanford University.

23 There is only one truth, and many opinions. Therefore, most people are wrong most of the time.

1985 In *Fortune*, 3 Apr.

Kyd, Thomas 1558–94

24 In time the savage bull sustains the yoke;
In time all haggard hawks will stoop to lure;
In time small wedges cleave the hardest oak,
In time the flint is pierced with softest shower,
And she in time will fall from her disdain,
And rue the sufferance of your friendly pain.

c.1589 *The Spanish Tragedy*, act 2, sc.1.

25 Where words prevail not, violence prevails;
But gold doth more than either of them both.

c.1589 *The Spanish Tragedy*, act 2, sc.1.

26 Oh eyes, no eyes, but fountains fraught with tears;
Oh life, no life, but lively form of death;
Oh world, no world, but mass of public wrongs.

c.1589 *The Spanish Tragedy*, act 3, sc.2.

27 I'll trust myself, myself shall be my friend.

c.1589 *The Spanish Tragedy*, act 3, sc.2.

28 Thus must we toil in other men's extremes,
That know not how to remedy our own.

c.1589 *The Spanish Tragedy*, act 3, sc.6.

29 For what's a play without a woman in it?

c.1589 *The Spanish Tragedy*, act 4, sc.1.

Labé, Louise 1526–66

A poet of the Ecole Lyonnaise who wrote sonnets, elegies and a prose work, *Débat d'Amour et de Folie*.

30 *Quelque rigueur qui loge en votre coeur,*
Amour s'en peut un jour rendre vainqueur.

That little harshness which resides in your heart,
Love will vanquish someday.

1555 *Elégies*, no.1.

31 *Où donc es-tu, ô âme bien-aimée?*

Where are you now, oh soul desired?

1555 *Sonnets*, no.6.

32 *Je vis, je meurs; je me brûle et me noie.*

I live, I die; I am on fire and I drown.

1555 *Sonnets*, no.8.

33 *Ne reprenez, dame, si j'ai aimé,*

Si j'ai senti mille torches ardentes,
Mille travaux, mille douleurs mordantes,
Si, en pleurant, j'ai mon temps consumé.

Do not blame me, madam, if I loved,
If I felt one thousand burning torches,
One thousand labors, or one thousand scathing
　pains,
If, in crying, I spent all my time.

1555 *Sonnets*, no.24.

Labouchère, Henry Du Pré　1831–1912

English radical journalist and politician. A Liberal MP
(1865–8, 1880–1906), in 1876 he founded the
investigative journal *Truth*.

34 Nothing has conduced more to shake that decent
respect for the living symbol of the state that goes
by the name of royalty than the ever-recurring
rattle of the money box.

1884 In the *Fortnightly Review*, Feb.

La Bruyère, Jean de　1645–96

French moralist author who tutored Louis de Bourbon,
grandson of the Great Condé. His *Caractères de
Théophraste* (1688) made his reputation but won him
many enemies.

35 *Tout est dit, et l'on vient trop tard depuis plus de sept
mille ans qu'il y a des hommes et qui pensent.*

Everything has been said. After seven thousand
years of human thought, we have come too late.

1688 *Les Caractères ou les mœurs de ce siècle*, 'Des ouvrages de
l'esprit', no.1.

36 *C'est un métier que de faire un livre, comme de faire
une pendule; il faut plus que de l'esprit pour être
auteur.*

It is as much a trade to write a book as it is to make
a watch; it takes more than wit to make an author.

1688 *Les Caractères ou les mœurs de ce siècle*, 'Des ouvrages de
l'esprit', no.3.

37 *Une belle femme qui a les qualités d'un honnête
homme est ce qu'il y a au monde d'un commerce plus
délicieux: l'on trouve en elle tout le mérite des deux
sexes.*

A beautiful woman who has the qualities of a
gentleman is the most pleasing person in all the
world: one finds in her all the merit of both sexes.

1688 *Les Caractères ou les mœurs de ce siècle*, 'Des femmes',
no.13.

38 *Les femmes sont extrêmes: elles sont meilleures ou pires
que les hommes.*

Women are all in extremes: they are either better or
worse than men.

1688 *Les Caractères ou les mœurs de ce siècle*, 'Des femmes',
no.53.

39 *Un homme est plus fidèle au secret d'autrui qu'au sien
propre; une femme au contraire garde mieux son secret
que celui d'autrui.*

A man keeps another person's secret better than his
own; a woman, on the contrary, keeps her own
secrets better than those of others.

1688 *Les Caractères ou les mœurs de ce siècle*, 'Des femmes',
no.58.

40 *Une femme insensible est celle qui n'a pas encore vu
celui qu'elle doit aimer.*

A dispassionate woman is one who has yet to see
the one she should love.

1688 *Les Caractères ou les mœurs de ce siècle*, 'Des femmes',
no.81.

41 *Le temps, qui fortifie les amitiés, affaiblit l'amour.*

Time, which strengthens friendships, weakens love.

1688 *Les Caractères ou les mœurs de ce siècle*, 'Du cœur', no.4.

42 *L'amour et l'amitié s'excluent l'un l'autre.*

Love and friendship exclude one another.

1688 *Les Caractères ou les mœurs de ce siècle*, 'Du cœur', no.7.

43 *L'amour qui naît subitement est le plus long à guérir.*

Love which strikes suddenly takes the longest to
cure.

1688 *Les Caractères ou les mœurs de ce siècle*, 'Du cœur', no.12.

44 *Les amours meurent par le dégoût, et l'oubli les
enterre.*

Loves die from disgust, and forgetting buries them.

1688 *Les Caractères ou les mœurs de ce siècle*, 'Du cœur', no.32.

45 *Qu'il est difficile d'être content de quelqu'un!*

How difficult it is to be happy with someone!

1688 *Les Caractères ou les mœurs de ce siècle*, 'Du cœur', no.65.

46 *L'esclave n'a qu'un maître; l'ambitieux en a autant
qu'il y a des gens utiles à sa fortune.*

A slave has but one master; an ambitious person has
as many as he needs to make his fortune.

1688 *Les Caractères ou les mœurs de ce siècle*, 'Du cœur', no.70.

47 *Il fera demain ce qu'il fait aujourd'hui et ce qu'il fit
hier; et il meurt ainsi après avoir vécu.*

What he does tomorrow will be what he did today
and yesterday; and he shall die after having lived
this way.

1688 *Les Caractères ou les mœurs de ce siècle*, 'De la ville', no.12.

48 *La vie est courte et ennuyeuse: elle se passe toute à
désirer.*

Life is short and bothersome: all we do is desire
what we do not have.

1688 *Les Caractères ou les mœurs de ce siècle*, 'De l'homme',
no.19.

49 *Si la vie est misérable, elle est pénible à supporter; si elle est heureuse, il est horrible de la perdre. L'un revient à l'autre.*

If life is miserable, it is difficult to endure; if it is happy, it is horrible to lose. They come to the same thing.

1688 *Les Caractères ou les mœurs de ce siècle*, 'De l'homme', no.33.

50 *A parler humainement, la mort a un bel endroit, qui est de mettre fin à la vieillesse.*

To speak humanely, death has a useful function: it puts an end to old age.

1688 *Les Caractères ou les mœurs de ce siècle*, 'De l'homme', no.45.

51 *Il n'y a pour l'homme que trois événements: naître, vivre et mourir. Il ne se sent pas naître, il souffre à mourir, et il oublie de vivre.*

There are only three great events for a person: to be born, to live and to die. He does not feel his own birth, he suffers upon death and he forgets to live.

1688 *Les Caractères ou les mœurs de ce siècle*, 'De l'homme', no.48.

52 *Les enfants sont hautains, dédaigneux, colères, envieux, curieux, intéressés, paresseux, volages, timides, intempérants, menteurs, dissimulés…ils ne veulent point souffrir de mal, et aiment à en faire: ils sont déjà des hommes.*

Children are haughty, disdainful, angry, envious, curious, interested, lazy, fickle, shy, self-indulgent, liars, deceivers…they do not wish to suffer evil, but like to do evil: they are already adults.

1688 *Les Caractères ou les mœurs de ce siècle*, 'De l'homme', no.50.

53 *Les enfants n'ont ni passé ni avenir, et, ce qui ne nous arrive guère, ils jouissent du présent.*

Children have neither past nor future. They live in the present, something which rarely happens to us.

1688 *Les Caractères ou les mœurs de ce siècle*, 'De l'homme', no.51.

54 *Il y a une espèce de honte d'être heureux à la vue de certaines misères.*

There is a type of shame which comes from being happy at another's distress.

1688 *Les Caractères ou les mœurs de ce siècle*, 'De l'homme', no.82.

55 *La plupart des hommes emploient la meilleure partie de leur vie à rendre l'autre misérable.*

Most people spend the greater part of their lives making others miserable.

1688 *Les Caractères ou les mœurs de ce siècle*, 'De l'homme', no.102.

56 *Le flatteur n'a pas assez bonne opinion de soi ni des autres.*

The flatterer does not have a good opinion of himself or of others.

1688 *Les Caractères ou les mœurs de ce siècle*, 'Des jugements', no.90.

57 *Ceux qui emploient mal leur temps sont les premiers à se plaindre de sa brièveté.*

Those who make poor use of their time are the first to complain of its brevity.

1688 *Les Caractères ou les mœurs de ce siècle*, 'Des jugements', no.101.

58 *L'impossibilité où je suis de prouver que Dieu n'est pas me découvre son existence.*

The impossibility I find myself in to prove that God does not exist proves to me his existence.

1688 *Les Caractères ou les mœurs de ce siècle*, 'Des esprits forts', no.13.

Laclos, Pierre-Ambroise Choderlos de
1741–1803

French artillery officer, best known for his study of human vices and virtues in *Les Liaisons dangereuses*, as well as his advocacy of women's education in *De l'Education des femmes*.

59 *J'ai bien besoin d'avoir cette femme, pour me sauver du ridicule d'en être amoureux.*

I need to possess this woman in order to save myself from the absurdity of being in love with her.

1782 *Les Liaisons dangereuses*, letter 4.

60 *Nos deux passions favorites, la gloire de la défense et le plaisir de la défaite.*

The glory of the resistance and the pleasure of the defeat are our two favourite passions.

1782 *Les Liaisons dangereuses*, letter 10.

61 *Il ne faut se permettre d'excès qu'avec les gens qu'on veut quitter bientôt.*

We should never permit ourselves to behave in excess except with those whom we will leave soon.

1782 *Les Liaisons dangereuses*, letter 10.

62 *En vérité, plus je vis, et plus je suis tenté de croire qu'il n'y a que vous et moi dans le monde, qui valions quelque chose.*

In truth, the more I live, the more I am tempted to believe that only you and I are of any value at all in the world.

1782 *Les Liaisons dangereuses*, letter 100.

63 *J'avoue bien que l'argent ne fait pas le bonheur; mais il faut avouer aussi qu'il le facilite beaucoup.*

I will admit that money does not bring happiness, but it must also be admitted that it facilitates much.
1782 *Les Liaisons dangereuses*, letter 104.

64 *Ce n'est pas assez pour moi de la posséder, je veux qu'elle se livre.*

It's not enough to possess her. I want her to abandon herself.
1782 *Les Liaisons dangereuses*, letter 110.

65 *La haine est toujours plus clairvoyante et plus ingénieuse que l'amitié.*

Hate is always more clairvoyant and ingenious than friendship.
1782 *Les Liaisons dangereuses*, letter 113.

66 *Pour les hommes, l'infidélité n'est pas l'inconstance.*

For men, infidelity is not inconstancy.
1782 *Les Liaisons dangereuses*, letter 134.

67 *On s'ennuie de tout, mon Ange, c'est une loi de la Nature; ce n'est pas ma faute.*

One gets bored of everything, my Angel, it's a law of nature; it's not my fault.
1782 *Les Liaisons dangereuses*, letter 141.

68 *Quand une femme frappe dans le coeur d'une autre, elle manque rarement de trouver l'endroit sensible, et la blessure est incurable.*

When one woman touches another's heart, she rarely has trouble finding the sensitive spot and the wound is incurable.
1782 *Les Liaisons dangereuses*, letter 145.

69 *Apprenez qu'on ne sort de l'esclavage que par une grande révolution.*

Learn that one never escapes slavery except by a great revolution.
1785 *De l'Education des Femmes*.

Ladd, Alan   1913–64

US film star, best known for *The Blue Dahlia* (1946), *The Great Gatsby* (1949) and *Shane* (1953).

70 A man's gotta do what a man's gotta do.
1953 Line delivered in *Shane* (screenplay by A B Guthrie).

La Fayette, Marie Madeleine Pioche de La Vergne   1634–93

French novelist. Although married to François Motier, she lived with La Rochefoucauld.

71 *L'amour était toujours mêlé aux affaires et les affaires à l'amour.*

Love has always mixed with politics and politics with love.
1678 *La Princesse de Clèves*.

72 *On persuade aisément une vérité agréable.*

It is easy to persuade one with an agreeable truth.
1678 *La Princesse de Clèves*.

73 *Les passions peuvent me conduire; mais elles ne sauraient m'aveugler.*

Passions can lead me on, but never blind me.
1678 *La Princesse de Clèves*.

74 *La honte est la plus violente de toutes les passions.*

Shame is the most violent of all the passions.
1678 *La Princesse de Clèves*.

La Fontaine, Jean de   1621–95

French poet and moralist. His *Contes et nouvelles en vers* (Tales and Novels in Verse, 1665) was followed by *Fables choisies mises en vers* (Selected Fables in Verse, 1668–94).

75 *Je me sers d'animaux pour instruire les hommes.*

I use animals to educate people.
1668 *Fables, à Monseigneur le Dauphin.*

76 *Nous n'écoutons d'instincts que ceux qui sont les nôtres, Et ne croyons le mal que quand il est venu.*

We only trust our own instincts
And only believe the worst when they come true.
1668 *Fables*, pt.1, no.8, 'L'hirondelle et les petits oiseaux'.

77 *La raison du plus fort est toujours la meilleure.*

The reason of the strongest is always the best.
1668 *Fables*, pt.1, no.10, 'Le loup et l'agneau'.

78 *Il accusait toujours les miroirs d'être faux.*

He was always blaming mirrors for being untrue.
1668 *Fables*, pt.1, no.11, 'L'homme et son image'.

79 *Plutôt souffrir que mourir, C'est la devise des hommes.*

It is better to suffer than to die.
That is the motto of mankind.
1668 *Fables*, pt.1, no.16, 'La mort et le bûcheron'.

80 *Je plie, et ne romps pas.*

I bend but do not break.
1668 *Fables*, pt.1, no.22, 'Le chêne et le roseau'. The reed speaks to the oak tree.

81 *Garde-toi, tant que tu vivras, De juger des gens sur la mine.*

Beware as long as you live,
Of judging others according to appearance alone.
1668 *Fables*, pt.6, no.5, 'Le cochet, le chat et la souriceau'.

82 *Sur les ailes du Temps la tristesse s'envole.*

Grief is carried off by the wings of time.
1668 *Fables*, pt.6, no.21, 'La jeune veuve'.

83 *Quand l'eau courbe un bâton, ma raison la redresse.*

When water curves a stick, my reason straightens it out.
1668 *Fables*, pt.7, no.18, 'Un animal dans la lune'.

84 *Fortune aveugle suit aveugle hardiesse.*

Blind fortune follows bold blindness
1668 *Fables*, no.10, pt.13, 'Les deux aventuriers et le talisman'.

85 *Tout est mystère dans l'Amour.*

Everything about love is a mystery.
1668 *Fables*, pt.12, no.14, 'L'Amour et la folie'.

86 *Tous chemins vont à Rome.*

All roads lead to Rome.
1668 *Fables*, pt.12, no.29, 'Le juge arbitre, l'hospitalier, et le solitaire'.

87 *Le mensonge et les vers de tout temps sont amis.*

Lies and literature have always been friends.
1668 *Fables*, pt.2, no.1, 'Contre ceux qui ont le goût difficile'.

88 *Patience et longueur de temps*
Font plus que force ni que rage.

Patience and longevity
Are worth more than force and rage.
1668 *Fables*, pt.2, no.11, 'Le lion et le rat'.

89 *C'est double plaisir de tromper le trompeur.*

It's doubly sweet to deceive the deceiver.
1668 *Fables*, pt.2, no.15, 'Le coq et le renard'.

90 *Tout au monde est mêlé d'amertume et de charmes:*
La guerre a ses douceurs, l'hymen a ses alarmes.

Everything in the world is a mixture of the sweet
  and the sour:
War has its own sweetness and marriage its alarms.
1668 *Fables*, pt.3, no.1, 'Le meunier, son fils et l'âne'.

91 *En toute chose il faut considérer la fin.*

One must consider the end in everything.
1668 *Fables*, pt.3, no.5, 'Le renard et le boue'.

92 *Amour est un étrange maître.*
Heureux qui peut ne le connaître.
Que par récit, lui ne se coups.

Love is a cruel conqueror.
Happy is he who knows him through stories
And not by his blows.
1668 *Fables*, pt.4, no.1, 'Le lion amoureux'.

93 *Le geai paré des plumes du paon.*

A bluejay in peacock feathers.
1668 *Fables*, pt.4, no.9, 'Le geai paré des plumes du paon'.

94 *Chacun se dit ami; mais fol qui s'y repose:*
Rien n'est plus commun que ce nom,
Rien n'est plus rare que la chose.

Everyone calls himself a friend; foolish is he who
  believes it:
Nothing is more common than the name friend,
And nothing is more rare than the real thing.
1668 *Fables*, pt.4, no.17, 'Parole de Socrate'.

95 *Ne possédait pas l'or; mais l'or le possédait.*

He never owned his gold; his gold owned him.
1668 *Fables*, pt.4, no.20, 'L'avare qui a perdu son trésor'.

96 *Une ample comédie à cent actes divers,*
Et dont la scène est l'Univers.

A grand comedy in one hundred different acts,
On the stage of the universe.
1668 *Fables*, pt.5, no.1, 'Le bûcheron et Mercure'.

97 *Un auteur gâte tout quand il veut trop bien faire.*

An author spoils everything when he wants too
much to do good.
1668 *Fables*, pt.5, no.1, 'Le bûcheron et Mercure'.

Lagerfeld, Karl 1938–
German-born French fashion designer.

98 She never wanted to be sexy, but in those days
ambitions were different, and she was the most
ambitious of them all.
1993 Of Wallis Simpson, Duchess of Windsor. In the *New York Times*, 19 Sep.

Lagner, Lawrence
Co-founder, US Theater Guild.

99 I have no interest in anything but *genius*, so please
sit down.
To Tennessee Williams. Recalled in Williams *Memoirs* (1975).

Lamartine, Alphonse Marie Louis de
1790–1869

French poet and revolutionary politician, a minister in the provisional government after 1848. His best-known work is his first volume of lyrical poems, *Méditations poétiques* (1820). His historical works include the *Histoire de la Révolution de 1848* (1849).

1 *Un seul être vous manque, et tout est dépeuplé.*

One being only is wanting, and your whole world
is bereft of people.
1820 *Premières Méditations poétiques*, 'L'Isolement'.

2 France is revolutionary or she is nothing at all. The
revolution of 1789 is her political religion.
1847–8 *Histoire des Girondins*.

3 At its birth, the republic gave voice to three
words—Liberty, Equality, Fraternity! If Europe is
wise and just, each of those words signifies Peace.
1848 *A Manifesto to the Powers*, 4 Mar.

Lamb, Lady Caroline   1785–1828

English novelist and aristocrat, daughter of the Earl of Bessborough and wife of Prime Minister William Lamb, 2nd Viscount Melbourne, notorious for her nine-month devotion (1812–3) to Lord Byron.

4 Mad, bad, and dangerous to know.

1812 Of Byron. Journal entry, Mar, after meeting the poet at a ball. Quoted in Elizabeth Jenkins *Lady Caroline Lamb* (1932), ch.6.

Lamb, Charles   1775–1834

English essayist and critic. Together with his sister Mary, he wrote *Tales from Shakespeare* (1807), and his *Specimens of English Dramatic Poets* (1808) contributed to a revival of interest in Elizabethan plays. As 'Elia', he contributed essays to the *London Magazine* from 1820.

5 I have something more to do than feel.

1796 Letter to Samuel Taylor Coleridge, 27 Sep, on the death of his mother at his sister Mary's hands. Collected in E W Marrs *Letters of Charles and Mary Lamb*, vol.1 (1975).

6 Cultivate simplicity, Coleridge.

1796 Letter to Samuel Taylor Coleridge, 8 Nov. Collected in E W Marrs *Letters of Charles and Mary Lamb*, vol.1 (1975).

7 The man must have a rare recipe for melancholy, who can be dull in Fleet Street.

1802 Letter to Thomas Manning, 15 Feb. Collected in E W Marrs *Letters of Charles and Mary Lamb*, vol.2 (1975).

8 Nursed amid her noise, her crowds, her beloved smoke—what have I been doing all my life, if I have not lent out my heart with usury to such scenes?

1802 Of London. Letter to Thomas Manning, 15 Feb. Collected in E W Marrs *Letters of Charles and Mary Lamb*, vol.2 (1975).

9 Gone before
To that unknown and silent shore.

1803 'Hester', stanza 7.

10 Nothing puzzles me more than time and space; and yet nothing troubles me less, as I never think about them.

1806 Letter to Thomas Manning, 2 Jan. Collected in E W Marrs (ed) *Letters of Charles and Mary Lamb*, vol.3 (1978).

11 A child's a plaything for an hour.

1809 'Parental Recollections'. This is often attributed to his sister Mary.

13 Anything awful makes me laugh.

1815 Letter to Robert Southey, 9 Aug. Collected in E W Marrs (ed) *Letters of Charles and Mary Lamb*, vol.3 (1978).

14 This very night I am going to leave off tobacco! Surely there must be some other world in which this unconquerable purpose shall be realized.

1815 Letter to Thomas Manning, 26 Dec. Collected in E W Marrs (ed) *Letters of Charles and Mary Lamb*, vol.3 (1978).

15 An Archangel a little damaged.

1816 Of Coleridge. Letter to Wordsworth, 26 Apr. Collected in E W Marrs (ed) *Letters of Charles and Mary Lamb*, vol.3 (1978).

16 The rogue gives you Love Powders, and then a strong horse drench to bring 'em off your stomach that they mayn't hurt you.

1816 Of Coleridge. Letter to Wordsworth, 23 Sep. Collected in E W Marrs (ed) *Letters of Charles and Mary Lamb*, vol.3 (1978).

17 Fanny Kelly's divine plain face.

1818 Letter to Mary Wordsworth, 18 Feb. Collected in H H Harpter (ed) *Letters of Charles Lamb*, vol.4 (1905).

18 Newspapers always excite curiosity. No one ever lays one down without a feeling of disappointment.

1822 In the *London Magazine*, May–Jul. Collected *in Essays of Elia*, 'Detached Thoughts of Books and Reading'.

19 Who first invented work—and tied the free
And holy-day rejoicing spirit down
To the ever-haunting importunity
Of business?

1822 Letter to Bernard Barton, 11 Sep. Collected in H H Harpter (ed) *Letters of Charles Lamb*, vol.4 (1905).

20 I hate a man who swallows it, affecting not to know what he is eating. I suspect his taste in higher matters.

1823 *Essays of Elia*, 'Grace Before Meat'.

21 In everything that relates to science, I am a whole Encyclopedia behind the rest of the world.

1823 *Essays of Elia*, 'The Old and the New Schoolmaster'.

22 I know that a sweet child is the sweetest thing in nature…but the prettier the kind of a thing is, the more desirable it is that it should be pretty of its kind.

1823 *Essays of Elia*, 'A Bachelor's Complaint of the Behaviour of Married People'.

23 If the husband be a man with whom you have lived on a friendly footing before marriage,—if you did not come in on the wife's side,—if you did not sneak into the house in her train, but were an old friend in first habits of intimacy before their courtship was so much as thought on,—look about you… Every long friendship, every old authentic intimacy, must be brought into their office to be new stamped with their currency, as a sovereign Prince calls in the good old money that was coined in some reign before he was born or thought of, to be new marked and minted with the stamp of his

authority, before he will let it pass current in the world.

1823 *Essays of Elia*, 'A Bachelor's Complaint of the Behaviour of Married People'.

24 Ceremony is an invention to take off the uneasy feeling which we derive from knowing ourselves to be less the object of love and esteem with a fellow-creature than some other person is. It endeavours to make up, by superior attentions in little points, for that invidious preference which it is forced to deny in the greater.

1823 *Essays of Elia*, 'A Bachelor's Complaint of the Behaviour of Married People'.

25 Sentimentally I am disposed to harmony. But organically I am incapable of a tune.

1823 *Essays of Elia*, 'A Chapter on Ears'.

26 I have no ear.

1823 *Essays of Elia*, 'A Chapter on Ears'.

27 Presents, I often say, endear Absents.

1823 *Essays of Elia*, 'A Dissertation upon Roast Pig'.

28 She unbent her mind afterwards—over a book.

1823 *Essays of Elia*, 'Mrs Battle's Opinions on Whist'.

29 A votary of the desk—a notched and cropt scrivener—one that sucks his substance, as certain sick people are said to do, through a quill.

1823 *Essays of Elia*, 'Oxford in the Vacation'.

30 The uncommunicating muteness of fishes.

1823 *Essays of Elia*, 'A Quakers' Meeting'.

31 The human species, according to the best theory I can form of it, is composed of two distinct races, the men who borrow, and the men who lend.

1823 *Essays of Elia*, 'The Two Races of Men'.

32 Your *borrowers of books*—those mutilators of collections, spoilers of the symmetry of shelves, and creators of odd volumes.

1823 *Essays of Elia*, 'The Two Races of Men'.

33 Not many sounds in life, and I include all urban and rural sounds, exceed in interest a knock at the door.

1823 *Essays of Elia*, 'Valentine's Day'.

34 Credulity is the man's weakness, but the child's strength.

1823 *Essays of Elia*, 'Witches and Other Night-Fears'.

35 How sickness enlarges the dimensions of a man's self to himself.

1823 *Essays of Elia*, 'The Convalescent'.

36 If dirt were trumps, what hands you would hold!

1828 Quoted in Leigh Hunt *Lord Byron and his Contemporaries*, p.299.

37 How sickness enlarges the dimensions of a man's self to himself.

1833 *Last Essays of Elia*, 'The Convalescent'.

38 The drinking man is never less himself than during his sober intervals.

1833 *Last Essays of Elia*, 'Confessions of a Drunkard'.

39 Books think for me.

1833 *Last Essays of Elia*, 'Detached Thoughts on Books and Reading'.

40 Things in book's clothing.

1833 *Last Essays of Elia*, 'Detached Thoughts on Books and Reading'.

41 A poor relation is the most irrelevant thing in nature.

1833 *Last Essays of Elia*, 'Poor Relations'.

42 A pistol let off at the ear; not a feather to tickle the intellect.

1833 Of puns. *Last Essays of Elia*, 'Popular Fallacies', no.9.

43 The greatest pleasure I know, is to do good action by stealth, and to have it found out by accident.

1834 'Table Talk by the late Elia', in *The Athenaeum*, 1834.

44 The last breath I drew in he wished might be through a pipe and exhaled in a pun.

Quoted in W Toynbee *Diaries of William Charles Macready 1833–1851* (1912).

Lamb, Marjorie 1949–

Canadian ecologist.

45 Suppose our ancestors had discovered nuclear power in the middle ages, and had decided to bury their radioactive fuel.

1990 *Two Minutes a Day for a Greener Planet*.

Lambert, Constant 1905–51

English composer, conductor and critic. His first success came with the ballet *Romeo and Juliet*, commissioned by Diaghilev in 1926. Subsequently he worked as conductor for the Camargo Society and for Sadler's Wells Ballet.

46 The Appalling Popularity of Music.

1934 *Music Ho!*, chapter title.

47 There is a definite limit to the length of time a composer can go on writing in one dance rhythm. This limit is obviously reached by Ravel toward the end of *La Valse* and toward the beginning of *Boléro*.

1934 *Music Ho!*

48 To put it vulgarly, the whole trouble with a folk song is that once you have played it through there is nothing much you can do except play it over again and play it rather louder.

1934 *Music Ho!*

Lamming, George Eric 1927–

Barbadian novelist. Winner of the Somerset Maugham Prize for literature for his novel *In the Castle of My Skin* (1953), he has also published *The Emigrants* (1954), *Seasons of Adventure* (1960), and *Natives of My Person* (1972).

49 Histr'y ain't got eyes to see everything.
1953 *In the Castle of My Skin*, ch.6.

50 If you aren't native to a place you have an excellent chance of becoming a gentleman in it.
1953 *In the Castle of My Skin*, ch.14.

Lamport, Allan 1903–

Canadian politician, Mayor of Toronto (1952–42) and a renowned malapropist.

51 If somebody's gonna stab me in the back, I wanna be there.
1990 *Quotations from Chairman Lamport*.

Lancaster, Sir James c.1554–1618

English navigator, soldier and merchant. He visited the East Indies in 1591–4 and in 1595 captured Pernambuco. In 1600–3 he commanded the first fleet of the East India Company to visit the East Indies. He promoted the voyages of Hudson, Baffin and others in search of the Northwest Passage.

52 I cannot tell where you should look for me, if you send out any pinnace to seek me; because I live at the devotion of the wind and seas. And thus fare you well; desiring God to send us a merry meeting in this world, if it be his good will and pleasure.
c.1594 Letter to the East India Company written on the homeward voyage when the two English ships ran into storms off the Cape of Good Hope. Lancaster's ship lost her rudder. Unwilling to risk the other ship, Lancaster ordered her captain to sail straight home, taking the letter with him. *A voyage with three tall ships, the Penelope, admirall, the Marchant Royall, vice-admiral, and the Edward Bonaventure, rear-admiral, to the East Indies … Begun By M. George Raymond, in the yeere 1591, and performed by M. James Lancaster, and written from the mouth of Edmund Barker of Ipswich (his lieutenant in the sayd voyage) by M. Richard Hakluyt.*

Lance, Bert

Former US White House Budget Director.

53 Go out on the front porch of the house, turn the *Washington Post* over with your big toe, and if your name's above the fold, you know you're not going to have a good day.
1993 Of the Bert Lance Toe Test which he devised for his nine months in the Carter administration. In the *Washington Post*, 6 Oct.

Landor, Walter Savage 1775–1864

English writer and poet. His *Imaginary Conversations of Literary Men and Statesmen* (1824–9) was celebrated in its day but has lost popularity. Other works include *Hellenics* (1847) and *Dry Sticks Fagoted* (1858).

54 Ah, what avails the sceptred race!
Ah, what the form divine!
1806 'Rose Aylmer'.

55 Clear writers, like clear fountains, do not seem so deep as they are; the turbid look the most profound.
1824 *Imaginary Conversations of Literary Men and Statesmen*, 'Southey and Porson'.

56 Fleas know not whether they are upon the body of a giant or upon one of ordinary size.
1824 *Imaginary Conversations of Literary Men and Statesmen*, 'Southey and Porson'.

57 Past ruined Ilion Helen lives,
Alcestis rises from the shades;
Verse calls them forth; 'tis verse that gives
Immortal youth to mortal maids.
1831 'To Ianthe'.

58 There is delight in singing, tho' none hear
Beside the singer.
1846 'To Robert Browning'.

59 Thee gentle Spenser fondly led;
But me he mostly sent to bed.
1846 'To Wordsworth: Those Who Have Laid the Harp Aside'.

60 There are no fields of amaranth on this side of the grave.
1846 *Imaginary Conversations of Literary Men and Statesmen*, 'Aesop and Rhodope'.

61 Death stands above me, whispering low
I know not what into my ear;
Of his strange language all I know
Is, there is not a word of fear.
1853 'Death stands above me'.

62 I strove with none; for none was worth my strife;
Nature I loved, and, next to Nature, Art.
1853 'Dying Speech of an Old Philosopher'.

63 Ireland never was contented…
Say you so? You are demented.
Ireland was contented when
All could use the sword and pen,
And when Tara rose so high
That her turrets split the sky,
And about her courts were seen
Liveried Angels robed in green,
Wearing, by St. Patrick's bounty,
Emeralds big as half a county.
1853 'Ireland never was contented'.

64 Prose on certain occasions can bear a great deal of poetry: on the other hand, poetry sinks and swoons under a moderate weight of prose.

1853 *Imaginary Conversations of Greeks and Romans*, 'Archdeacon Hare and Walter Landor'.

Landowska, Wanda 1879–1959

Polish pianist, harpsichordist and musical scholar, who founded the École de Musique Ancienne near Paris in 1927, and stimulated a new interest in the harpsichord. She also composed songs and piano and orchestral pieces and wrote on music.

65 You play Bach your way and I'll play him *his* way.

Refusing to adapt her technique to suit another Bach specialist. Quoted in Clifton Fadiman *The Faber Book of Anecdotes* (1985).

Lang, Andrew 1844–1912

Scottish man of letters. He specialized in mythology, famously arguing against Max Müller that folktale was the foundation of literary mythology. He also wrote history texts, popular fairy books, studies of literary figures and poetry.

66 Politicians use statistics in the same way that a drunk uses lamp-posts—for support rather than illumination.

1910 Speech. Quoted in Alan L Mackay *The Harvest of a Quiet Eye* (1977).

67 If the wild bowler thinks he bowls
Or if the batsman thinks he's bowled,
They know not, poor misguided souls,
They too shall perish unconsoled.
I am the batsman and the bat,
I am the bowler and the ball,
The umpire, the pavilion cat,
The roller, pitch, and stumps and all.

'Brahma'. Quoted by Alan Richardson in a letter to *The Times*, 18 May, 1963.

▷ See Emerson 377:64.

Langbridge, Frederick 1849–1923

English religious writer.

68 Two men look out through the same bars:
One sees the mud, and one the stars.

1896 *A Cluster of Quiet Thoughts*.

Langland, William c.1332–c.1400

English poet. Little is known of his life but he seems to have been in London in 1362 when he began his only known work, the long poem *Vision of William concerning Piers the Plowman*, the greatest poem of the Middle English Alliterative Revival. It deals with the themes of truth, integrity and social justice. Three versions survive in over 60 manuscipts. It was first printed in 1550.

69 In a somer seson, whan softe was the sonne,
I shoop me into shroudes as I a sheep were,
In habite an heremite unholy of werkes,
Went wide in this world wondres to here.

c.1379 *Piers Plowman* (B text), prologue, l.1–4.

(shoop = got, shroudes = garments)

70 A gloten of wordes.

c.1379 *Piers Plowman* (B text), prologue, l.139.

(gloten = glutton)

71 'Though we hadde ykilled the cat, yat sholde there come another
To cracchen us ans al oure kynde, though we cropen under benches.'

c.1379 The wise mouse advises against belling the cat. *Piers Plowman* (B text), prologue, l.185–6.

(cracchen = scratch, cropen = crept)

72 He was bitelbrowed and baberlipped, with two blered eighen,
And as a letheren purs lolled his chekes.

c.1379 A description of the sin of Envy. *Piers Plowman* (B text), 'Passus 5,' l.188–9. (eighen = eyes, letheren = leather)

73 Al the povere peple tho pescoddes fetten;
Benes and baken apples thei broghte in hir lappe,
Chibolles and chervelles and ripe chiries manye,
And profrede Piers this present to plese with Hunger.

c.1379 A description of the sin of Envy. *Piers Plowman* (B text), 'Passus 6,' l.291–4.

(pescoddes = pea-pod, fetten = fetched, chibolles = spring-onions, chervelles = chervil, plese with Hunger = please Hunger with)

74 Ac thorugh his science soothy was nevere no soule ysaved,
Ne broght by hir bokes to blisse ne to joye.

c.1379 *Piers Plowman* (B text), 'Passus 12', l.134–5.

The 'Science' and 'books' are those of pagan scholars who developed natural science from empirical observation only.

75 'Counseilleth me, Kynde,' quod I, 'what craft be best to lerne?'
'Lerne to love,' quod kynde, 'and leef alle othere.'

c.1379 *Piers Plowman* (B text), 'Passus 20', l.207–8.

Lanier, Sidney 1842–81

US poet. He fought in the Civil War for the Confederacy. His critical study *The Science of English Verse* (1880) establishes a musical basis for poetry which he tries to exemplify in his verse.

76 'Music is Love in search of a word.'

1875 *The Symphony*.

Lanyer, Aemilia 1569–1645

English poet. One of the very few professional early female poets, she was unable to secure patronage and published only one work, *Salve Deus Ex Judaeorum* (1611). It has been argued (unconvincingly) that she is the 'dark lady' of Shakespeare's *Sonnets*.

77 Our mother Eve, who tasted of the tree,

Giving to Adam what she held most dear,
Was simply good, and had no power to see.
1611 *Salve Deus Ex Judaeorum*, 'Eve's Apology in Defense of
Women'.

78 But surely Adam cannot be excused;
Her fault though great, yet he was most to blame;
What weakness offered, strength might have
    refused,
Being lord of all, the greater was the shame.
1611 *Salve Deus Ex Judaeorum*, 'Eve's Apology in Defense of
Women'.

79 Not Eve, whose fault was only too much love,
Which made her give this present to her dear,
That what she tasted he likewise might prove,
Whereby his knowledge might become more clear;
He never sought her weakness to reprove
With those sharp words which he of God did hear;
Yet men will boast of knowledge, which he took
From Eve's fair hand, as from a learned book.
1611 *Salve Deus Ex Judaeorum*, 'Eve's Apology in Defense of
Women'.

80 Then let us have our liberty again,
And challenge to yourselves no sovereignty.
You came not in the world without our pain,
Make that a bar against your cruelty;
Your fault being greater, why should you disdain
Our being your equals, free from tyranny?
1611 *Salve Deus Ex Judaeorum*, 'Eve's Apology in Defense of
Women'.

81 Farewell (sweet *Cooke-ham*) where I first obtained
Grace from that grace where perfect grace
    remained;
And where the muses gave their full consent,
I should have power the virtuous to content;
Where princely palace willed me to indite,
The sacred story of the soul's delight.
1611 *Salve Deus Ex Judaeorum*, 'The Description of Cooke-
ham'. Probably the first 'country-house' poem in English, this
work is dedicated to Margaret Russell Clifford, Countess of
Cumberland, and her daughter, Anne Clifford, whose family
home was Cookham.

82 Never shall my sad eyes again behold
Those pleasures which my thoughts did then
    unfold.
1611 *Salve Deus Ex Judaeorum*, 'The Description of Cooke-ham'.

Lao-Tzu 6c BC

Chinese philosopher regarded as the inspiration for
Taoism. Its major work, the *Tao-te-Ching* was compiled
some 300 years after his death but is traditionally ascribed
to him.

83 Free from desire, you realise the mystery.
Caught in desire, you see only the manifestations.
c.250 BC *Tao Te Ching*, no.1 (translated by Stephen Mitchell,
1988).

84 He who defines himself can't know who he really
is.
c.250 BC *Tao Te Ching*, no.24 (translated by Stephen Mitchell,
1988).

85 Even in victory, there is no beauty, and he who calls
it beautiful is one who delights in slaughter.
c.250 BC *Tao Te Ching*, no.31. Collected in Lin Yutang (trans
and ed) *The Wisdom of China and India* (1942).

86 A victory should be celebrated with the funeral rite.
c.250 BC *Tao Te Ching*, no.31. Collected in Lin Yutang (trans
and ed) *The Wisdom of China and India* (1942).

87 When two equally matched armies meet, it is the
man of sorrow who wins.
c.250 BC *Tao Te Ching*, no.69. Collected in Lin Yutang (trans
and ed) *The Wisdom of China and India* (1942).

Lardner, Dionysus 1793–1859

Irish scientific writer, Professor of Natural Philosophy and
Astronomy at University College London (1827). He is
best known as the originator and editor of *Lardner's
Cabinet Cyclopaedia* (133 vols, 1829–49).

88 Men might as well project a voyage to the Moon as
attempt to employ steam navigation against the
stormy North Atlantic Ocean.
1838 Speech to the British Association for the Advancement of
Science, London.

Lardner, James

US journalist, writer for the *New Yorker*.

89 If…Americans do not succeed in engineering an
economic revival, we can look forward to being
remembered as, of all the nations that have
prospered and declined, the one that has done so in
the highest state of self-awareness.
1993 'The Declining Middle', in the *New Yorker*, 3 May.

Lardner, Ring(old Wilmer) 1885–1933

US short story writer, novelist and columnist. He is best
known for his vernacular, comic, satirical and usually
pessimistic short stories.

90 Are you lost daddy I arsked tenderly.
Shut up he explained.
1920 *The Young Immigrunts*, ch.10.

91 I have known what it was like to be hungry, but I
always went right to a restaurant.
1927 *The Lardners: My Family Remembered*, ch.1.

92 'Babe' Ruth and Old Jack Dempsey,
Both Sultans of Swat,
One hits where the other people are,
The other where they're not.
Attributed.

Larionov, Mikhail 1881–1964

93 We declare: the genius of our days to be: trousers,
jackets, shoes, tramways, buses, aeroplanes,
railways, magnificent ships—what an
enchantment—what a great epoch unrivalled in
world history.
1913 'Rayonnist Manifesto', quoted in C Gray *The Russian
Experiment in Art* (revised edn 1986).

Larkin, Philip Arthur 1922–85

94 Always too eager for the future, we
Pick up bad habits of expectancy.
1951 'Next, Please'.

95 What are days for?
Days are where we live.
They come, they wake us
Time and time over.
They are to be happy in:
Where can we live but days?
1953 'Days'.

96 What calls me is that lifted, rough-tongued
bell
(Art, if you like) whose individual sound
Insists I too am an individual.
1953 'Reasons for Attendance'.

97 And the case of butterflies so rich it looks
As if all summer settled there and died.
1953 'Autumn'.

98 Nothing, like something, happens anywhere.
1954 'I Remember, I Remember'.

99 On me your voice falls as they say love should,
Like an enormous yes.
1954 'For Sidney Bechet'.

1 Hatless, I take off
My cycle-clips in awkward reverence.
1954 'Church Going'.

2 A serious house on serious earth it is,
In whose blent air all our compulsions meet,
Are recognised, and robed as destinies.
1954 'Church Going'.

3 Why should I let the toad *work*
Squat on my life?
Can't I use my wit as a pitchfork
And drive the brute off?
Six days of the week it soils

With its sickening poison—
Just for paying a few bills!
That's out of proportion.
1954 'Toads'.

4 Marrying left your maiden name disused.
1955 'Maiden Name'.

5 Time has transfigured them into
Untruth. The stone fidelity
They hardly meant has come to be
Their final blazon, and to prove
Our almost-instinct almost true:
What will survive of us is love.
1956 'An Arundel Tomb'.

6 I thought of London spread out in the sun,
Its postal districts packed like squares of wheat.
1958 'The Whitsun Weddings'.

7 Never such innocence,
Never before or since,
As changed itself to past
Without a word—the men
Leaving the gardens tidy,
The thousands of marriages
Lasting a little while longer:
Never such innocence again.
1960 'MCMXIV'.

8 Get stewed:
Books are a load of crap.
1960 'A Study of Reading Habits'.

9 The widening river's slow presence,
The piled gold clouds, the shining gull-marked
mud,
Gathers to the surprise of a large town:
Here domes and statues, spires and cranes cluster
Beside grain-scattered streets, barge-crowded water,
And residents from raw estates.
1961 Of Hull. 'Here'.

10 Give me your arm, old toad;
Help me down Cemetery Road.
1962 'Toads Revisited'.

11 Life is first boredom, then fear.
1963 'Dockery and Son'.

12 Sexual intercourse began
In nineteen sixty-three
(Which was rather late for me)—
Between the end of the *Chatterly* ban
And the Beatles' first LP.
1967 'Annus Mirabilis'.

13 And beyond it, the deep blue air, that shows
Nothing, and is nowhere, and is endless.
1967 'High Windows'.

14 They fuck you up, your mum and dad.
 They may not mean to, but they do.
 They fill you with the faults they had
 And add some extra, just for you.
 1971 'This Be The Verse'.

15 Man hands on misery to man.
 It deepens like a coastal shelf.
 Get out as early as you can,
 And don't have any kids yourself.
 1971 'This Be The Verse'.

16 I should never call myself a book lover, any more
 than a people lover: it all depends what's inside
 them.
 1972 In the London Antiquarian Book Fair programme.

17 Perhaps being old is having lighted rooms
 Inside your head, and people in them, acting.
 People you know, yet can't quite name.
 1973 'The Old Fools'.

18 You can't put off being young until you retire,
 And however you bank your screw, the money you
 save
 Won't in the end buy you more than a shave.
 1973 'Money'.

19 That sure extinction that we travel to
 And shall be lost in always. Not to be here,
 Not to be anywhere,
 And soon; nothing more terrible, nothing more
 true.
 1977 'Aubade'.

20 That vast moth-eaten musical brocade
 Created to pretend we never die.
 1977 Of religion. 'Aubade'.

21 Far too many relied on the classic formula of a
 beginning, a muddle, and an end.
 1978 On judging the Booker Prize entries for 1977, in *New
 Fiction*, no.15, Jan.

22 Deprivation is for me what daffodils were for
 Wordsworth.
 1983 *Required Writing*.

La Rochefoucauld, François, 6th Duc de
1613–80

French writer. A supporter of the queen, Marie de'
Medici, and an opponent of Richelieu, he was entangled
in a series of amorous adventures and political intrigues.
His *Mémoires*, published secretly in 1662, caused wide
offence and were followed by his *Réflexions, ou sentences et
maximes morales* (1665).

23 The love of justice in most men is simply the fear of
 suffering injustice.
 1665 *Réflexions, ou sentences et maximes morales*, no.78.

24 *Dans l'adversité de nos meilleurs amis, nous trouvons
 toujours quelque chose qui ne nous deplaît pas.*

 In the misfortune of our best friends, we always
 find something which is not displeasing to us.
 1665 *Réflexions, ou sentences et maximes morales*, no.99.

25 *On n'est jamais si malheureux qu'on croit, ni si
 heureux qu'on espère.*

 One is never as unhappy as one thinks, nor as
 happy as one hopes.
 1665 *Réflexions, ou sentences et maximes morales*, no.128.

26 *Nous avons tous assez de force pour supporter les maux
 d'autrui.*

 We are all strong enough to bear the misfortunes of
 others.
 1678 *Maximes*, no.19.

27 *L'hypocrisie est un hommage que le vice rend à la
 vertu.*

 Hypocrisy is a tribute which vice pays to virtue.
 1678 *Maximes*, no.218.

28 *L'absence diminue les médiocres passions, et augmente
 les grandes, comme le vent éteint les bougies, et allume
 le feu.*

 Absence diminishes commonplace passions, and
 increases great ones, as wind extinguishes candles
 and kindles fire.
 1678 *Maximes*, no.276.

29 *L'accent du pays où l'on est né demeure dans l'esprit et
 dans le cœur comme dans le langage.*

 The accent of the place in which one was born
 lingers in the mind and in the heart as it does in
 one's speech.
 1678 *Maximes*, no.342.

Larwood, Harold 1904–95

English cricketer. He became notorious in the 1932–3
tour of Australia, employed by D R Jardine to bowl
'Bodyline', which led to several batsmen being seriously
hurt. He retired from Test cricket as a result of the ensuing
furore and eventually settled in Australia.

30 A cricket tour in Australia would be a most
 delightful period in one's life if one was deaf.
 1933 *Body-line*.

31 Bodyline was devised to stifle Bradman's batting
 genius. They said I was a 'killer with the ball',
 without taking into account that Bradman, with
 the bat, was the greatest killer of all.
 1965 Of the 'Bodyline' controversy. Quoted in Colin Jarman
 The Guinness Dictionary of Sports Quotations (1990).

32 I darned near bowled him that time.

Attributed. Said to an umpire who had disallowed two previous appeals, on clean bowling a batsman, knocking down the entire wicket.

Lasky, Jesse 1880–1958

US film pioneer. He formed his own production company in 1914 and had his first hit with *The Squaw Man*, going on to produce for Paramount, Fox and Warner.

33 I yearned to trespass on Quality Street.

On his desire to produce better films. Quoted in the *New Yorker*, 21 Mar 1994.

Lassels, Richard c.1603–1668

English classical scholar and priest. As tutor to the young English nobility, he travelled widely in Europe. His *Voyage of Italy* was published posthumously in Paris in 1670, and in London in 1698.

34 Pick out of every country what's best in it.

c.1650 *The Voyage of Italy, or a Compleat Journey through Italy* (published 1670).

35 [Travel] preserves my young nobleman from surfeiting of his parents, and weans him from a dangerous fondness of his mother. It teacheth him wholesome hardship… Whereas the country gentleman that never travelled, can scarce go to London without making his will, at least without wetting his handkerchief.

c.1650 *The Voyage of Italy, or a Compleat Journey through Italy* (published 1670).

Latimer, Hugh c.1485–1555

English theologian, Bishop of Worcester and Protestant martyr. After Mary I's accession he was tried for heresy and burned in Oxford.

36 Be of good comfort Master Ridley, and play the man. We shall this day light such a candle by God's grace in England, as (I trust) shall never be put out.

1555 Spoken to Nicholas Ridley, as they waited together to be burned at the stake, 16 Oct. Quoted in Foxe *Acts and Monuments* (1563).

Lauder, Sir Harry (Hugh MacLennan) 1870–1950

Scottish comedian and music-hall entertainer.

37 Will yer stop yer tickling, Jock!
    Oh, stop yer tickling, Jock!
    Dinna mak' me laugh so hearty, or you'll mak' me choke.
    Oh! I wish you'd stop yer nonsense—just look at all the folk.
    Will yer stop yer tickling—tickle-ickle-ickle-ing—
    Stop yer tickling, Jock!

1904 'Stop Yer Tickling, Jock!', chorus.

38 I love a lassie, a bonnie, bonnie lassie,
    She's as pure as the lily in the dell.
    She's as sweet as the heather
    The bonnie bloomin' heather—
    Mary, ma Scotch Bluebell.

1905 'I Love a Lassie', or 'Ma Scotch Bluebell', chorus.

39 Roamin' in the gloamin' on the bonnie banks o' Clyde.
    Roamin' in the gloamin' wae my lassie by my side.
    When the sun has gone to rest,
    That's the time that we love best—
    O, it's lovely roamin' in the gloamin'!

1911 'Roamin' in the Gloamin', chorus.

40 Keep right on to the end of the road,
    Keep right on to the end.
    Tho' the way be long let your heart be strong,
    Keep right on round the bend.
    Tho' you're tired and weary
    Still journey on, till you come to your happy abode,
    Where all you love you've been dreaming of
    Will be there, at the end of the road.

1924 'The End of the Road', chorus.

Laughlin, J Laurence 1850–1933

US economist, Professor at the University of Chicago.

41 Anything from plumbing to philosophy.

His definition of the scope of sociology. Quoted in Joseph Dorfman *Thorstein Veblen and his America* (1934), p.93.

Laughton, Charles 1899–1962

British actor. His many roles include Henry VIII in *The Private Life of Henry VIII* (1933), Captain Bligh in *Mutiny on the Bounty* (1935) and Quasimodo in *The Hunchback of Notre Dame* (1939).

42 But they can't censor the gleam in my eye.

1934 Of his role of Mr Barrett in *The Barretts of Wimpole Street*.

Laurel, Stan pseudonym of *Arthur Stanley Jefferson* 1890–1965

English-born US comedian. He became a teenage member of Fred Karno's touring company and first went to the US in 1910. He appeared in many early silent film comedies before his great partnership with Oliver Hardy began in 1926.

43 Here's another fine mess you've gotten me into.

1930 Of Laurel. Line delivered by Oliver Hardy in *Another Fine Mess* and other films.

Laurence, Margaret 1926–87

Canadian novelist. Her first works were set in Africa, where she lived for seven years. In London she wrote the five Manawaka novels (1964–74). She has received numerous honours, including the Order of Canada.

44 Privacy is a privilege not granted to the aged or the young.
1964 *The Stone Angel*, ch.1.

45 Even if heaven were real, and measured as Revelation says, so many cubits this way and that, how gimcrack a place it would be, crammed with its pavements of gold, its gates of pearl and topaz, like a gigantic chunk of costume jewelry.
1964 *The Stone Angel*, ch.4.

46 In bygone days, Morag had once believed that nothing could be worse than killing a person. Now she perceived river-slaying as something worse.
1974 *The Diviners*, ch.1.

Laurencin, Marie 1885–1956

French artist, best known for her portraits of women in misty pastel colours. She also illustrated many books with water-colours and lithographs. She exhibited at the Salon des Indépendents in 1907.

47 My ambition is that men should have a voluptuous feeling when they look at the portraits I paint of women. Love interests me more than painting. My pictures are the love stories I tell to myself and which I want to tell others.
Quoted in Gabrielle Buffet 'Marie Laurencin', in *The Arts 3* (1903).

Lautréamont, Comte de properly Isidore Lucien Ducasse 1846–70

French writer, hailed by the Surrealists as one of their forerunners for his psychological poetry. His death at the age of twenty-four remains a mystery.

48 *Il n'était pas menteur, il avouait la vérité et disait qu'il était cruel.*

He was not a liar. He admitted the truth and said that he was cruel.
1868 *Les Chants de Maldoror*, pt.1.

49 *Oui, quel est le plus profond, le plus impénétrable des deux: l'océan ou le cœur humain?*

What is deeper, more impenetrable: the ocean or the human heart?
1868 *Les Chants de Maldoror*, pt.1.

50 *Moi, je n'aime pas les femmes! Ni même les hermaphrodites! Il me faut des êtres qui me ressemblent, sur le front desquels la noblesse humaine soit marquée en caractères plus tranchés et ineffaçables!*

Me, I do not like women! Nor even hermaphrodites! I need beings who resemble me, on whose foreheads nobility is engraved in sharp and unerasable characters.
1868 *Les Chants de Maldoror*, pt.5.

51 *Si vous êtes malheureux, il ne faut pas le dire au lecteur. Gardez cela pour vous.*

If you are miserable, you should not say so to the reader. Keep it for yourself.
1870 *Poésies*, pt.1.

52 *Il faut que la critique attaque la forme, jamais le fond de vos idées, de vos phrases. Arrangez-vous.*

A critic must attack the form, never the foundation of your ideas and phrases. See to it.
1870 *Poésies*, pt.1.

53 *Si la morale de Cléopâtre eût été moins courte, la face du monde aurait changé. Son nez n'en serait pas devenu plus long.*

If Cleopatra's morality had been less short, the face of the world would have been altered. Her nose would not thereby have grown longer.
1870 *Poésies*, pt.2.

54 *La poésie doit être faite par tous. Non par un. Pauvre Hugo!*

Poetry should be composed by everyone. Not by one. Poor Hugo!
1870 *Poésies*, pt.2.

55 *On ne peut juger de la beauté de la vie que par celle de la mort.*

One can only judge the beauty of life through death.
1870 *Poésies*, pt.2.

Laver, James 1899–1975

English poet, writer and art critic, and Keeper at the Victoria and Albert Museum (1922–59). He made a substantial contribution to the history of English costume.

56 The same costume will be
Indecent…10 years before its time
Shameless…5 years before its time
Outré (daring)…1 year before its time
Smart
Dowdy…1 year after its time
Hideous…10 years after its time
Ridiculous…20 years after its time
Amusing…30 years after its time
Quaint…50 years after its time
Charming…70 years after its time
Romantic…100 years after its time
Beautiful…150 years after its time.
1937 *Taste and Fashion*, ch.18.

57 A visitor from Mars contemplating a man in a frock coat and top hat and a woman in a crinoline might well have supposed that they belonged to different species.
1969 *The Concise History of Costume and Fashion*, ch.8.

Lavoisier, Antoine Laurent 1743–94

French chemist and physicist, one of the fathers of modern chemistry. He was one of the first to use effective quantitative methods to study chemical reactions.

58 We must trust to nothing but facts. These are presented to us by Nature, and cannot deceive. We ought, in every instance, to submit our reasoning to the test of experiment, and never to search for truth but by the natural road of experiment and observation.

1789 *Traité élémentaire de la chimie* (Elements of Chemistry, translated by Robert Kerr).

Law, (Andrew) Bonar 1858–1923

Canadian-born British Unionist politician. He was Chancellor of the Exchequer (1916–18) and from 1916 Leader of the House of Commons. He retired in 1921, but returned to serve as Prime Minister (1922–3).

59 I can imagine no length of resistance to which Ulster can go in which I should not be prepared to support them, and in which, in my belief, they would not be supported by the overwhelming majority of the British people.

1912 During the Irish Home Rule crisis, 27 Jul.

Law, William 1686–1761

English divine, whose writings expounded the mysticism of Jakob Boehme.

60 I take it for granted that every Christian that is in health is up early in the morning; for it is much more reasonable to suppose a person up early because he is a Christian than because he is a labourer or a tradesman or a servant or has business that wants him.

1728 *A Serious Call to a Devout and Holy Life.*

61 If, therefore, a man will so live as to show that he feels and believes the most fundamental doctrines of Christianity, he must live above the world.

1728 *A Serious Call to a Devout and Holy Life.*

Lawrence, D(avid) H(erbert) 1885–1930

English novelist, poet and essayist. He was the son of a miner, and much of his fiction reflected his upbringing. His candid treatment of emotion and physical love led to prosecution for obscenity with *The Rainbow* in 1915, and *Lady Chatterley's Lover* in 1928 (and 1961). He lived in Italy and Mexico from 1919.

62 'Be a good animal, true to your instincts,' was his motto.

1911 *The White Peacock,* pt.2, ch.2.

63 Curse the blasted, jelly-boned swines, the slimy, the belly-wriggling invertebrates, the miserable sodding rotters, the flaming sods, the snivelling,

dribbling, dithering, palsied, pulse-less lot that make up England today.

1913 Letter to Edward Garnett, 3 Jul, after the rejection of *Sons and Lovers* by Heinemann.

64 I like to write when I feel spiteful; it's like having a good sneeze.

1913 Letter to Lady Cynthia Asquith, Nov.

65 You mustn't look in my novel for the old stable *ego* of the character.

1914 Letter to Edward Garnett, 5 Jun.

66 People are not fallen angels, they are merely people.

1916 Letter to J Middleton Murry and Katherine Mansfield, 17 Feb.

67 I am only half there when I am ill, and so there is only half a man to suffer. To suffer in one's whole self is so great a violation, that it is not to be endured.

1916 Letter to Catherine Carswell, 16 Apr.

68 Not I, not I, but the wind that blows through me! A fine wind is blowing the new direction of Time.

1917 'Song of a Man Who Has Come Through'.

69 The glamour
Of childish days is upon me, my manhood is cast
Down in the flood of remembrance, I weep like a child for the past.

1918 'Piano'.

70 Don't you find it a beautiful clean thought, a world empty of people, just uninterrupted grass, and a hare sitting up?

1920 *Women in Love,* ch.11.

71 In China the bat is a symbol of happiness
Not for me!

1921 'Bat'.

72 I like Australia less and less. The hateful newness, the democratic conceit, every man a little pope of perfection.

1922 Letter, 28 May.

73 Morality which is based on ideas, or on an ideal, is an unmitigated evil.

1922 *Fantasia of the Unconscious,* ch.7.

74 Every race which has become self-conscious and idea-bound in the past has perished.

1922 *Fantasia of the Unconscious,* ch.7.

75 Death is the only pure, beautiful conclusion of a great passion.

1922 *Fantasia of the Unconscious,* ch.15.

76 Better passion and death than any more of these 'isms'. No more of the old purpose done up in aspic. Better passion and death.

1922 *Fantasia of the Unconscious,* ch.15.

77 In the *established* sense it is socially nil. Happy-go-lucky, don't-you-bother, we're-in-Australia. But there also seems to be no inside life of any sort: just a long lapse and drift. A rather fascinating indifference, a *physical* indifference to what we call soul or spirit. It's really a weird show.
1922 Of Australia. Letter, collected in A Huxley (ed) *The Letters of D H Lawrence* (1932).

78 I do not want peace nor beauty nor even freedom from pain. I want to fight and to feel new gods in the flesh.
1922 Letter to E H Brewster, 2 Jan.

79 The wonderful Southern night-sky that makes a man feel so lonely, alien: with Orion standing on his head in the west, and his sword-belt upside down, and his Dog-star prancing in mid-heaven, high above him; and with the Southern Cross insignificantly mixed in with the other stars, democratically inconspicuous.
1923 Of night over Sydney. *Kangaroo*, ch.1.

80 What do the facts we know *about* a man amount to? Only two things we can know of him, and this by pure soul-intuition: we can know if he is true to the flame of life and love which is inside his heart, or if he is false to it.
1923 *Kangaroo*, ch.7.

81 The indifference—the fern-dark indifference of this remote golden Australia. Not to care—from the bottom of one's soul not to care.
1923 *Kangaroo*, ch.10.

82 Life makes no absolute statement. It is all Call and Answer.
1923 *Kangaroo*, ch.10.

83 And so, I missed my chance with one of the lords Of life.
And I have something to expiate;
A pettiness.
1923 'Snake'.

84 Men! The only animal in the world to fear.
1923 'Mountain Lion'.

85 Hanging upside down like rows of disgusting old rags
And grinning in their sleep.
1923 'Bats'.

86 Evil, what is evil?
There is only one evil, to deny life.
1923 'Cypresses'.

87 The dead don't die. They look on and help.
1923 Letter to J Middleton Murry, 2 Feb, on the death of Katherine Mansfield.

88 Never trust the artist. Trust the tale.
1924 *Studies in Classic American Literature*, ch.1.

89 I want to go south, where there is no autumn, where the cold doesn't crouch over one like a snow-leopard waiting to pounce. The heart of the North is dead, and the fingers of cold are corpse fingers.
1924 Letter to J Middleton Murry, 3 Oct.

90 The identifying ourselves with the visual image of ourselves has become an instinct; the habit is already old. The picture of me, the me that is *seen*, is me.
1925 'Art and Morality'.

91 Damn all absolutes. Oh damn, damn, damn all absolutes!
1925 'The Novel'.

92 After the funeral, my father struggled through half a page, and it might as well have been Hottentott.
'And what dun they gi'e thee for that, lad?'
'Fifty pounds, father.'
'Fifty pounds!' He was dumbfounded, and looked at me with shrewd eyes, as if I were a swindler. 'Fifty pounds! An' tha's niver done a day's hard work in thy life.'
1925 Preface to Edward D McDonald (ed) *A Bibliography of D. H. Lawrence*.

93 I'm not sure if a mental relation with a woman doesn't make it impossible to love her. To know the *mind* of a woman is to end in hating her.
1927 Letter to Dr Trigant Burrow, 3 Aug.

94 You have to have something vicious in you to be a creative writer… God save me from being 'nice'.
1927 Book review, re-printed in *Phoenix*.

95 Ours is essentially a tragic age, so we refuse to take it tragically.
1928 *Lady Chatterley's Lover*, ch.1.

96 My God, what a clumsy *olla putrida* James Joyce is! Nothing but old fags and cabbage-stumps of quotations from the Bible and the rest, stewed in the juice of deliberate, journalistic dirty-mindedness.
1928 Letter to Aldous and Maria Huxley, 15 Aug.

97 John Thomas says goodnight to Lady Jane, a little droopingly, but with a hopeful heart.
1928 *Lady Chatterley's Lover*, ch.19.

98 Sentimentalism is the working off on yourself of feelings you haven't really got.
1928 'John Galsworthy'.

99 I am tired of being told there is no such animal by animals who are merely different.
1929 Letter to J Middleton Murry, 20 May.

1 How beastly the bourgeois is
 Especially the male of the species.
 1929 'How Beastly the Bourgeois Is'.

2 I never saw a wild thing
 Sorry for itself.
 1929 'Self-Pity'.

3 When I read Shakespeare I am struck with wonder
 That such trivial people should muse and thunder
 In such lovely language.
 1929 'When I Read Shakespeare'.

4 Pornography is the attempt to insult sex, to do dirt
 on it.
 1929 'Pornography and Obscenity'.

5 Now man cannot live without some vision of
 himself. But still less can he live with a vision that is
 not true to his inner experience and inner feeling.
 1929 'The Risen Lord'.

6 Now it is autumn and the falling fruit
 And the long journey towards oblivion…
 Have you built your ship of death, O have you?
 1932 'The Ship of Death'.

7 To the Puritan all things are impure, as somebody
 says.
 1932 *Etruscan Places*, 'Cerveteri'.

8 And being a novelist, I consider myself superior to
 the saint, the scientist, the philosopher, and the
 poet, who are all great masters of different bits of
 man alive, but never get the whole hog.
 1936 'Why The Novel Matters'.

9 Nothing is more difficult than to determine what a
 child takes in, and does not take in, of its
 environment and its teaching. This fact is brought
 home to me by the hymns which I learned as a
 child, and never forgot. They mean more to me
 almost than the finest poetry, and they have for me
 a more permanent value, somehow or other.
 Collected in *Phoenix II, Uncollected, Unpublished and Other Prose Works* (1968).

10 The sense of wonder
 that is the sixth sense.
 And it is the natural religious sense.
 'Hymns in a Man's Life'.

Lawrence, Gertrude 1898–1952

English actress. A star of revue on both sides of the Atlantic, she was highly popular as the lead in Noël Coward's comedies. She died while appearing in the hit Broadway musical *The King and I.*

11 Pardon my long preamble. It's like a chorus girl's
 tights—it touches everything and covers nothing.
 During an after-dinner speech. Attributed.

Lawrence, T(homas) E(dward) known as 'Lawrence of Arabia' 1888–1935

Anglo-Irish soldier and writer. In World War I he worked for army intelligence in North Africa (1914–16). Espousing the Arab cause, he led the Arabs in their revolt against the Turks.

12 I loved you, so I drew these tides of men into my
 hands
 —and wrote my will across the sky in stars
 To earn you freedom, the seven pillared worthy
 house,
 —that your eyes might be shining for me
 When we came.
 1926 *The Seven Pillars of Wisdom*, dedication.

13 All men dream, but not equally. Those who dream
 by night in the dusty recesses of their minds wake
 in the day to find that it was vanity; but the
 dreamers of the day are dangerous men, for they
 may act their dream with open eyes, to make it
 possible.
 1926 *The Seven Pillars of Wisdom*, ch.1.

14 We were a self-centred army without parade or
 gesture, devoted to freedom, the second of man's
 creeds, a purpose so ravenous that it devoured all
 our strength, a hope so transcendent that our
 earlier ambitions faded in its glare.
 1926 *The Seven Pillars of Wisdom*, ch.1.

15 Many men would take the death sentence without
 a whimper to escape the life-sentence which fate
 carries in her other hand.
 1936 *The Mint*, pt.1, ch.4.

16 A man hates to be moved to folly by a noise.
 1936 Of the emotion aroused by the military trumpets. *The Mint*, pt.3, ch.9.

17 The test of nomadism, that most deeply biting of
 social disciplines.
 Introduction to an edition of Charles Montagu Doughty *Travels in Arabia Deserta*.

Lawson, Henry Hertzberg 1867–1922

Australian writer, son of the writer and feminist Louisa Lawson. His writings for the *Bulletin*, 'The Bushman's Bible', have been collected in *Short Stories in Prose and Verse* (1894) and *While the Billy Boils* (1896).

18 And the sun sank again on the grand Australian
 bush—the nurse and tutor of eccentric minds, the
 home of the weird, and of much that is different
 from things in other lands.
 1892 'The Bush Undertaker', first published in *The Antipodean*.

19 The departed was a 'Roman', and the majority of
 the town were otherwise—but unionism is stronger
 than creed. Drink, however, is stronger than

unionism; and, when the hearse presently arrived, more than two-thirds of the funeral were unable to follow.

1893 'The Union Buries its Dead', first published in *Truth*, Apr.

20 Type of a coming nation,
In the land of cattle and sheep,
Worked on Middleton's station,
'Pound a week and his keep.'

'Middleton's Rouseabout', collected in Colin Roderick (ed) *Henry Lawson: Collected Verse* (3 vols, 1967–9).

21 Have you seen the bush by moonlight, from the train, go running by?
Blackened log and stump and sapling, ghostly trees all dead and dry;
Here a patch of glassy water; there a glimpse of mystic sky?
Have you heard the still voice calling—yet so warm, and yet so cold:
'I'm the Mother-Bush that bore you! Come to me when you are old'?

'On the Night Train', collected in Colin Roderick (ed) *Henry Lawson: Collected Verse* (3 vols, 1967-9).

Layamon fl.c.1190

English author and priest who lived at Arley Regis in Worcestershire. He wrote the *Brut*, the first English version of the story of Arthur, largely based on Wace's French *Roman de Brut*.

22 And I will fare to Avalun, to the fairest of all maidens, to Argante the queen, an elf most fair, and she shall make my wounds all sound.

c. **1190** *Brut* (translated by Eugene Mason, 1912).

Layton, Irving 1912–

Romanian-born Canadian poet, who came to Montreal as an infant. His 35 books of poetry include *The Black Huntsman* (1951), *The Cold Green Element* (1955) and *A Red Carpet for the Sun* (1959).

23 Death is a name for beauty not in use.

1953 'Composition in Late Spring', collected in *The Collected Poems of Irving Layton* (1971).

24 It amazes me that organs that piss
Can give human beings such perfect bliss.

1969 *The Whole Bloody Bird*, 'Aphs'.

25 Only the tiniest fracton of mankind want freedom. All the rest want someone to tell them they are free.

1969 *The Whole Bloody Bird*.

Lazarus, Emma 1849–87

US poet, a champion of oppressed Jewry. Her poems include *Songs of a Semite* (1882) and *By the Waters of*

Babylon (1887). She is best known for her sonnet, 'The New Colossus' which is inscribed on the Statue of Liberty.

26 Give me your tired, your poor,
Your huddled masses yearning to breathe free,
The wretched refuse of your teeming shore,
Send these, the homeless, tempest-tossed, to me:
I lift my lamp beside the golden door.

1883 'The New Colossus', inscribed at the foot of the Statue of Liberty, New York harbour, 1886.

27 Still on Israel's head forlorn
Every nation heaps its scorn.

1886 'The World's Justice'.

Leach, Jim (James Albert Smith) 1942–

US politician.

28 The only thing the Balkans export is history.

1995 WAMU broadcast, Washington, 25 Nov.

Leacock, Stephen Butler 1869–1944

English-born Canadian humorist and economist. Head of Economics at McGill University from 1908, he wrote several books on economics and literary biographies, and is usually remembered for his short stories, essays and parodies, which include *Literary Lapses* (1910), *Nonsense Novels* (1911) and *Winsome Winnie* (1920).

29 There are no handles to a horse, but the 1910 model has a string to each side of its face for turning its head when there is anything you want it to see.

1910 *Literary Lapses*, 'Reflections on Riding'.

30 It takes a good deal of physical courage to ride a horse. This, however, I have. I get it at about forty cents a flask, and take it as required.

1910 *Literary Lapses*, 'Reflections on Riding'.

31 The great man...walks across his century and leaves the marks of his feet all over it, ripping out the dates on his galoshes as he passes.

1910 *Literary Lapses*, 'The Life of John Smith'.

32 I detest life-insurance agents; they always argue that I shall some day die, which is not so.

1910 *Literary Lapses*, 'Insurance Up to Date'.

33 The landlady of a boarding-house is a parallelogram—that is, an oblong angular figure, which cannot be described, but which is equal to anything.

1910 *Literary Lapses*, 'Boarding-House Geometry'.

34 Astronomy teaches the correct use of the sun and the planets.

1910 *Literary Lapses*, 'A Manual of Education'.

35 Electricity is of two kinds, positive and negative. The difference is, I presume, that one comes a little

more expensive, but is more durable; the other is a cheaper thing, but the moths get into it.
1910 *Literary Lapses*, 'A Manual of Education'.

36 Get your room full of good air, then shut up the windows and keep it. It will keep for years. Anyway, don't keep using your lungs all the time. Let them rest.
1910 *Literary Lapses*, 'How to Live to Be 200'.

37 Lord Ronald said nothing; he flung himself from the room, flung himself upon his horse and rode madly off in all directions.
1911 *Nonsense Novels*, 'Gertrude the Governess: or, Simple Seventeen'.

38 When you meet Mr. Smith first you think he looks like an over-dressed pirate. Then you begin to think him a character. You wonder at his enormous bulk. Then the utter hopelessness of knowing what Smith is thinking by merely looking at his features gets on your mind and makes the Mona Lisa seem an open book and the ordinary human countenance as superficial as a puddle in the sunlight.
1912 *Sunshine Sketches of a Little Town*, 'The Hostelry of Mr. Smith'.

39 His life was one round of activity which he himself might deplore but was powerless to prevent.
1912 *Sunshine Sketches of a Little Town*, 'The Ministrations of the Rev. Mr. Drone'.

40 The classics are only primitive literature. They belong to the same class as primitive machinery and primitive music and primitive medicine.
1913 *Behind the Beyond*, 'Homer and Humbug'.

41 The parent who could see his boy as he really is, would shake his head and say: 'Willie is no good; I'll sell him.'
1916 *Further Foolishness*, 'The Lot of the Schoolmaster'.

42 A decision of the courts decided that the game of golf may be played on a Sunday, not being a game within the view of the law, but being a form of moral effort.
1923 *Over the Footlights*, 'Why I Refuse to Play Golf'.

43 Advertising may be described as the science of arresting human intelligence long enough to get money from it.
1924 *The Garden of Folly*, 'The Perfect Salesman'.

44 The general idea, of course, in any first-class laundry, is to see that no shirt or collar ever comes back twice.
1926 *Winnowed Wisdom*, ch.6.

45 I am what is called a *professor emeritus*—from the Latin *e*, 'out', and *meritus*, 'so he ought to be'.
1938 *Here are my Lectures*, ch.14.

46 A sportsman is a man who, every now and then, simply has to go out and kill something. Not that he's cruel. He wouldn't hurt a fly. It's not big enough.
1942 *My Remarkable Uncle*.

47 Presently I shall be introduced as 'this venerable old gentleman' and the axe will fall when they raise me to the degree of 'grand old man'. That means on our continent any one with snow-white hair who has kept out of jail till eighty.
1942 *My Remarkable Uncle*, 'Three Score and Ten'.

48 I have a suspicion it's inevitable, but give me my stick. I'll face it.
1942 On being asked what he thought about death, following a serious throat operation, quoted in John Stevens's introduction to *My Remarkable Uncle* (1965 edn).

Leadbelly pseudonym of *Huddie William Ledbetter* 1889–1949

US blues and folk singer, song-writer and guitarist. He was 'discovered' while serving one of several prison sentences. His recordings include 'Midnight Special' and 'Rock Island Line'.

49 No white man ever had the blues.
1976 Quoted in Joachim Berendt *The Jazz Book* (1984).

Lear, Edward 1812–88

English artist, humorist and traveller, famous for his nonsense verse such as that collected in *A Book of Nonsense* (1846, enlarged 1861, 1863 and 1870), as well as his illustrations and landscapes.

50 There was an Old Man with a beard,
Who said, 'It is just as I feared!—
Two Owls and a Hen,
Four Larks and a Wren,
Have all built their nest in my beard!'
1846 *A Book of Nonsense*.

51 When awful darkness and silence reign
Over the great Gromboolian plain,
Through the long, long wintry nights,
When the angry breakers roar
As they beat on the rocky shore—
When storm-clouds brood on the towering heights
Of the Hills of the Chankly Bore.
1871 *Nonsense Songs, Stories, Botany and Alphabets*, 'The Dong with a Luminous Nose'.

52 And those who watch at that midnight hour
From Hall or Terrace or lofty Tower,
Cry as the wild light passes along,
'The Dong!—the Dong!
The wandering Dong through the forest goes!
The Dong!—the Dong!

The Dong with a Luminous Nose!'
1871 *Nonsense Songs, Stories, Botany and Alphabets*, 'The Dong with a Luminous Nose'.

53 They went to sea in a sieve, they did
In a sieve they went to sea.
1871 *Nonsense Songs, Stories, Botany and Alphabets*, 'The Jumblies'.

54 Far and few, far and few,
Are the lands where the Jumblies live;
Their heads are green, and their hands are blue,
And they went to sea in a Sieve.
1871 *Nonsense Songs, Stories, Botany and Alphabets*, 'The Jumblies'.

55 They called aloud 'Our Sieve ain't big,
But we don't care a button! We don't care a fig!'
1871 *Nonsense Songs, Stories, Botany and Alphabets*, 'The Jumblies'.

56 And they brought an Owl, and a useful Cart,
And a pound of Rice, and a Cranberry Tart,
And a hive of silvery Bees.
And they brought a Pig, and some green Jack-daws,
And a lovely Monkey with lollipop paws, and forty
Bottles of Ring-Bo-Ree,
And no end of Stilton Cheese.
1871 *Nonsense Songs, Stories, Botany and Alphabets*, 'The Jumblies'.

57 Till Mrs Discobbolos said
'Oh! W! X! Y! Z!
It has just come into my head—
Suppose we should happen to fall!!!!
Darling Mr Discobbolos?'
1871 *Nonsense Songs, Stories, Botany and Alphabets*, 'Mr and Mrs Discobbolos'.

58 The Owl and the Pussy-Cat went to sea
In a beautiful pea-green boat.
They took some honey, and plenty of money,
Wrapped up in a five-pound note.
The Owl looked up to the Stars above
And sang to a small guitar,
'Oh lovely Pussy! O Pussy, my love,
What a beautiful Pussy you are'.
1871 *Nonsense Songs, Stories, Botany and Alphabets*, 'The Owl and the Pussy-Cat'.

59 Pussy said to the Owl, 'You elegant Fowl!
How charmingly sweet you sing!
O let us be married! too long we have tarried:
But what shall we do for a ring?'
They sailed away for a year and a day,
To the land where the Bong-tree grows,
And there in a wood a Piggy-wig stood
With a ring at the end of his nose.
1871 *Nonsense Songs, Stories, Botany and Alphabets*, 'The Owl and the Pussy-Cat'.

60 'Dear Pig, are you willing to sell for one shilling
Your ring?' Said the Piggy, 'I will.'
1871 *Nonsense Songs, Stories, Botany and Alphabets*, 'The Owl and the Pussy-Cat'.

61 They dined on mince, and slices of quince,
Which they ate with a runcible spoon;
And hand in hand, on the edge of the sand,
They danced by the light of the moon.
1871 *Nonsense Songs, Stories, Botany and Alphabets*, 'The Owl and the Pussy-Cat'.

62 The Pobble who has no toes
Had once as many as we;
When they said, 'Some day you may lose them all';
He replied—'Fish fiddle de-dee!'
His Aunt Jobiska made him drink
Lavender water tinged with pink,
For she said, 'The world in general knows
There's nothing so good for a Pobble's toes!'
1871 *Nonsense Songs, Stories, Botany and Alphabets*, 'The Pobble Who Has No Toes'.

63 When boats or ships came near him
He tinkledy-binkledy-winkled a bell.
1871 *Nonsense Songs, Stories, Botany and Alphabets*, 'The Pobble Who Has No Toes'.

64 He has gone to fish, for his Aunt Jobiska's
Runcible Cat with crimson whiskers!
1871 *Nonsense Songs, Stories, Botany and Alphabets*, 'The Pobble Who Has No Toes'.

65 'But the longer I live on this Crumpetty Tree
The plainer than ever it seems to me
That very few people come this way
And that life on the whole is far from gay!'
Said the Quangle-Wangle Quee.
1871 *Nonsense Songs, Stories, Botany and Alphabets*, 'The Quangle Wangle's Hat'.

66 And what can we expect if we haven't any dinner,
But to lose our teeth and eyelashes and keep on
growing thinner?
1871 *Nonsense Songs, Stories, Botany and Alphabets*, 'The Two Old Bachelors'.

67 Nasticreechia Krorluppia.
1872 *More Nonsense, Pictures, Rhymes, Botany Etc*, 'Nonsense Botany'.

68 There was an old person of Ware,
Who rode on the back of a bear:
When they asked, 'Does it trot?'
He said, 'Certainly not!
He's a Moppsikon Floppsikon bear.'
1872 *More Nonsense, Pictures, Rhymes, Botany Etc*, 'One Hundred Nonsense Pictures and Rhymes'.

69 There was an old man of Thermopylae,
Who never did anything properly;
But they said, 'If you choose

To boil eggs in your shoes,
You shall never remain in Thermopylae.'
1872 *More Nonsense, Pictures, Rhymes, Botany Etc,* 'One Hundred Nonsense Pictures and Rhymes'.

Leary, Timothy Francis 1920–96

US psychologist, Professor at the Universities of California and Harvard, best known for his advocacy of the drug LSD and his association with the counter-cultural movement of the 1960s and 1970s.

70 My advice to people today is as follows: If you take the game of life seriously, if you take your nervous system seriously, if you take your sense organs seriously, if you take the energy process seriously, you must turn on, tune in, and drop out.
    1966 Lecture, Jun, collected in *The Politics of Ecstasy* (1968), ch.21.

71 Science is all metaphor.
    1980 Interview, 24 Sep, collected in *Contemporary Authors* vol.107.

Lease, Mary Elizabeth Cylens 1853–1933

US reformer, who spoke out for women's suffrage, Irish Home Rule, prohibition and other causes.

72 The farmers of Kansas must raise less corn and more hell.
    1890 Speech, Kansas. This phrase became the slogan of the Populist Party.

Leavis, F(rank) R(aymond) 1895–1978

English critic. He taught at Cambridge University, and was a hugely influential figure, although his ideas have now been superseded by new approaches to textual and cultural criticism.

73 Poetry can communicate the actual quality of experience with a subtlety and precision unapproachable by any other means.
    1932 *New Bearings in English Poetry*, ch.2.

74 The Sitwells belong to the history of publicity rather than of poetry.
    1932 *New Bearings in English Poetry*, ch.2.

75 It is well to start by distinguishing the few really great—the major novelists who count in the same way as the major poets, in the sense that they not only change the possibilities of the art for practitioners and readers, but that they are significant in terms of the human awareness they promote; awareness of the possibilities of life.
    1948 *The Great Tradition*, ch.1.

76 The only way to escape misrepresentation is never to commit oneself to any critical judgement that

makes an impact—that is, never *say anything*.
    1948 *The Great Tradition*, ch.1.

Leavis, Q(ueenie) D(orothy) 1906–81

British literary critic.

77 Really I suppose what I hate myself most on is showing other people where to dig, not having time to do intensive and exclusive digging myself. I am a dowser and not a navvy.
    Quoted in the *Times Literary Supplement*, 8 Sep 1989.

Le Bon, Gustave 1841–1931

French psychologist and sociologist, whose works aim to identify national characteristics and thereby racial superiority.

78 Science has promised us truth—an understanding of such relationships as our minds can grasp; it has never promised us either peace or happiness.
    1895 *Psychologie des foules*, introduction.

Lebowitz, Fran(ces Ann) 1951–

US writer. Her work is marked by an aphoristic sensibility and a caustic, world-weary and rather cynical wit.

79 There is no such thing as inner peace. There is only nervousness or death. Any attempt to prove otherwise constitutes unacceptable behaviour.
    1978 *Metropolitan Life*, 'Manners'.

80 Nothing succeeds like address.
    1978 *Metropolitan Life*, 'The Nail Bank'.

81 Sleep is death without the responsibility.
    1978 *Metropolitan Life*, 'Why I Love Sleep'.

82 It is by this painstaking method of careful examination and eventual rejection that we reach a conclusion: life is something to do when you can't get to sleep.
    1978 *Metropolitan Life*, 'Mars'.

83 Salad is not a meal. It is a style.
    1978 *Metropolitan Life*, 'Food For Thought and Vice Versa'.

84 Perhaps the least cheering statement ever made on the subject of art is that life imitates it.
    1978 *Metropolitan Life*, 'Arts'.

85 Original thought is like original sin: both happened before you were born to people you could not possibly have met.
    1981 *Social Studies*, 'People'.

86 Great people talk about ideas, average people talk about things, and small people talk about wine.
    1981 *Social Studies*, 'People'.

87 The opposite of talking isn't listening. The opposite of talking is waiting.
1981 *Social Studies*, 'People'.

88 There are two modes of transport in Los Angeles: car and ambulance. Visitors who wish to remain inconspicuous are advised to choose the latter.
1981 *Social Studies*, 'Lesson One'.

89 If you're going to America, bring your own food.
1981 *Social Studies*, 'Fran Lebowitz's Travel Hints'.

90 Being offended is the natural consequence of leaving one's home.
1981 *Social Studies*, 'When Smoke Gets In Your Eyes…Shut Them'.

91 War is, undoubtedly, hell, but there is no earthly reason why it has to start so early in the morning.
1981 *Social Studies*, 'War Stories'.

Leboyer, Frédérick 1918–

French gynaecologist and obstetrician, who first drew attention to birth trauma, and has always emphasized the intimate associations between sex, depression and anxiety.

92 Making love is the sovereign remedy for anguish.
1991 *Birth without Violence*.

Le Carré, John pseudonym of *David John Moore Cornwell* 1931–

English novelist. He taught at Eton and entered the Foreign Service, resigning in 1964 to become a full-time writer. His works, many of which have been filmed, are set in the dark underworld of international diplomacy and espionage.

93 The Spy who Came in from the Cold.
1963 Title of novel.

94 A committee is an animal with four back legs.
1974 *Tinker, Tailor, Soldier, Spy*, pt.3, ch.34.

95 Sometimes…we have to do a thing in order to find out the reason for it. Sometimes our actions are questions, not answers.
1986 *A Perfect Spy*, ch.1.

96 The only decent diplomat is a deaf Trappist.
1986 *A Perfect Spy*, ch.3.

97 A society that admires its shock troops had better be bloody careful about where it's going.
1986 *A Perfect Spy*, ch.18.

98 Publishers can get their minds halfway round anything.
1989 *The Russia House*, ch.5.

99 One long act of sadism.
1991 On his boyhood at Sherborne School. In *The Times*, 21 Feb.

Le Corbusier pseudonym of *Charles Édouard Jeanneret* 1887–1965

Swiss architect, co-author of the Purist manifesto. His buildings, which demonstrate the interrelation of machine forms and architectural techniques, include the Cité Universitaire, Paris, and his city planning designs include Buenos Aires (1938). His books have had a worldwide influence.

1 It is a question of building which is at the root of the social unrest of today: architecture or revolution.
1923 *Vers une architecture* (translated as *Towards a New Architecture*, 1927).

2 The day consists of twenty-four hours only. This regulates the size of the house and the rôle it has to fulfil. For the twenty-four hour day is short, and our acts and thoughts are spurred on *by time*. If we were taught to regard the hand of the clock as a beneficent but implacable god, we should order our lives more rationally.
1930 'Twentieth-century living and twentieth-century building'. Collected in Dennis Sharp (ed) *The Rationalists: Theory and Design in the Modern Movement* (1978).

3 Architecture provides the framework for a civilization (housing, work, leisure, circulation); so architecture is also town planning. It is no longer possible to separate architecture and town planning—they are one and the same thing.
1943 'If I had to teach you architecture'. Collected in Dennis Sharp (ed) *The Rationalists: Theory and Design in the Modern Movement* (1978).

Lee, Gypsy Rose stage-name of *Rose Louise Hovick* 1914–70

US actress. Her career as a striptease artist in burlesque on Broadway in the 1930s provided the basis for the film *Gypsy* (1959).

4 I know men aren't attracted to me by my mind. They're attracted by what I don't mind.
Attributed.

5 God is love, but get it in writing.
Attributed.

Lee, (Nelle) Harper 1926–

US writer. She wrote only one novel, *To Kill a Mockingbird*, but it has become a classic of its time.

6 Until I feared I would lose it, I never loved to read. One does not love breathing.
1960 Scout. *To Kill A Mockingbird*, pt.1, ch.2.

7 Shoot all the bluejays you want, if you can hit 'em, but remember it's a sin to kill a mockingbird.
1960 Atticus Finch. *To Kill A Mockingbird*, pt.1, ch.10.

8 The one thing that doesn't abide by majority rule is a person's conscience.

1960 Atticus Finch. *To Kill A Mockingbird*, pt.1, ch.11.

9 Folks don't like to have somebody around knowin' more than they do. It aggravates 'em.

1960 Calpurnia. *To Kill A Mockingbird*, pt.2, ch.12.

10 A court is only as sound as its jury, and a jury is only as sound as the men who make it up.

1960 Atticus Finch. *To Kill A Mockingbird*, pt.2, ch.20.

11 As you grow older, you'll see white men cheat black men every day of your life, but let me tell you something and don't you forget it—whenever a white man does that to a black man, no matter who he is, how rich he is, or how fine a family he comes from, that white man is trash.

1960 Atticus Finch. *To Kill A Mockingbird*, pt.2, ch.23.

Lee, Hsien Loong 1952–

Singaporean politician, son of the former Prime Minister Lee Kuan Yew.

12 In Singapore you don't volunteer to go into politics—you are invited to enter.

1984 Remark. Quoted in Alan Chong *Goh Tok Chong* (1991), ch.4.

Lee, Kuan Yew 1923–

Singaporean politician, the country's first Prime Minister (1959–90), renowned for his authoritarianism and intolerance of political opponents.

13 I have decided that we shall make and build and never give way.

1966 Remark, 27 Dec. Quoted in James Minchin *No Man is an Island* (1986), ch.8.

14 Even from my sick bed, even if you are going to lower me into the grave, and I feel something is wrong, I will get up.

1988 Remark, Aug. Quoted in C M Turnbull *A History of Singapore* (1989).

Lee, Laurie 1914–97

English writer. He fought in the Spanish Civil War, but is best known for *Cider With Rosie*, his evocative account of growing up in an English village between the wars.

15 Such a morning it is when love
  leans through geranium windows
  and calls with a cockerel's tongue.

1947 'Day of these Days'.

16 I was set down from the carrier's cart at the age of three; and there with a sense of bewilderment and terror my life in the village began.

1959 *Cider With Rosie*, 'First Light'.

17 Effie M. was a monster. Six foot high and as strong as a farm horse. No sooner had she decided that she wanted Uncle Tom than she knocked him off his bicycle and told him.

1959 *Cider With Rosie*, 'The Uncles'.

18 As for me—for me, the grass grew longer, and more sorrowful, and the trees were surfaced like flesh, and girls were no longer to be treated lightly but were creatures of commanding sadness, and all journeys through the valley were now made alone, with passion in every bush, and the motions of wind and cloud and stars were suddenly for myself alone, and voices elected me of all men living and called me to deliver the world, and I groaned from solitude, blushed when I stumbled, loved strangers and bread and butter, and made long trips through the rain on my bicycle, stared wretchedly through lighted windows, grinned wryly to think how little I was known, and lived in a state of raging excitement.

1959 *Cider With Rosie*, 'Last Days'.

Lee, Robert E 1807–70

US Confederate General. He fought in the Mexican War and in Texas. During the Civil War, although he defeated McClellan at Richmond, he surrendered to General Grant at Appomatox, Virginia in 1865.

19 It is well that war is so terrible. We should grow too fond of it.

1862 Attributed, after the Battle of Fredericksburg, Dec.

Lees-Smith, Hastings Bernard 1878–1941

British politician. He was associated with Ruskin College, Oxford from its foundation in 1899. He was Liberal MP for Northampton (1910–18), and joined the Labour Party in 1919. He was Labour MP for Keighley (1922–23, 1924–31 and 1935–41).

20 Security can only be obtained by a scheme by which the nations of Europe and outside agree together that all will guarantee each, and each will guarantee all. The purposes of the war will be attained if there is a League of Nations with an absolute and decisive veto upon any mere aggression, and consideration of any legitimate claims that any of the countries engaged in the war may be able to make good.

1916 House of Commons, 21 Oct.

Léger, Fernand 1881–1946

French painter, a major force in the Cubist movement, although his paintings are more 'tubist' than 'cubist'. He executed murals for the UN building in New York (1952).

21 Modern man lives more and more in a preponderantly geometric order. All human creation mechanical or industrial is dependent upon geometric intentions.

1924 'The Aesthetic of the Machine', in *Bulletin de l'Effort Moderne*.

22 The thing depicted is less stationary, even the object in itself is less discernible than it used to be. A landscape broken into and traversed in a car or an express train loses in descriptive value but gains in synthetic value; the window of the railroad carriage or the windshield of the car, combined with the speed at which you are traveling, have changed the familiar look of things. Modern man registers one hundred times more impressions than did an eighteenth century artist.

Quoted in D Cooper *The Cubist Epoch* (1970).

Le Guin, Ursula née *Kroeber* 1929–

US writer. She is best known for her literate, politically aware works of science fiction, and her children's fantasy novels, notably the *Earthsea* trilogy (1968–72) and its overtly feminist sequel, *Tehanu* (1990).

23 It is a terrible thing, this kindness that human beings do not lose. Terrible because when we are finally naked in the dark and cold, it is all we have.

1969 *The Left Hand of Darkness*, ch.13.

24 To be, the will to power must increase with each fulfilment, making the fulfilment only a step to a further one. The vaster the power gained the vaster the appetite for more.

1971 *The Lathe of Heaven*, ch.9.

25 In so far as one denies what is, one is possessed by what is not, the compulsions, the fantasies, the terrors that flock to fill the void.

1971 *The Lathe of Heaven*, ch.10.

26 The years before and after the menstrual years are vestigial: the only meaningful condition left to women is that of fruitfulness.

1976 'The Space Crone', in *The Co-Evolution Quarterly*, Summer.

27 To me the 'female principle' is, or at least historically has been, basically anarchic. It values order without constraint, rule by custom not by force. It has been the male who enforces order, who constructs power structures, who makes, enforces, and breaks laws.

'Is Gender Necessary?', in Anderson and McIntyre (eds) *Aurora* (1976).

28 The preservation of life seems to be rather a slogan than a genuine goal of the anti-abortion forces; what they want is control. Control over behavior: power over women.

1982 Address to the National Abortion Rights Action League, Jan. Collected as 'The Princess' in *Dancing At the Edge of The World* (1989).

29 Success is the American Dream we can keep dreaming because most people in most places, including thirty million of ourselves, live wide awake in the terrible reality of poverty.

1983 Address at Mills College. Collected as 'A Left-Handed Commencement Address' in *Dancing At the Edge of The World* (1989).

30 We are volcanoes. When we women offer our experience as our truth, as human truth, all the maps change. There are new mountains.

1983 Address at Mills College. Collected as 'A Left-Handed Commencement Address' in *Dancing At the Edge of The World* (1989).

31 The children of the revolution are always ungrateful, and the revolution must be grateful that it is so.

1983 Address to Folger Library Poetry Series, Washington. Collected as 'Reciprocity of Prose and Poetry' in *Dancing At the Edge of The World* (1989).

32 When either the political or the scientific discourse announces itself as the voice of reason, it is playing God, and should be spanked and stood in the corner.

1986 Commencement address at Bryn Mawr College. Collected in *Dancing At the Edge of The World* (1989).

33 My imagination makes me human and makes me a fool; it gives me all the world and exiles me from it.

1990 'Winged Creatures On My Mind', in *Harper's*, Aug.

Lehmann-Haupt, Christopher Charles Herbert 1934–

US literary critic, born in Scotland. He has been senior book reviewer on the *New York Times* since 1969.

34 One misses the hiss of acid.

1984 On Gore Vidal's biography *Lincoln* (1984). In the *New York Times*, 30 May.

35 We breathe, we think, we conceive of our lives as narratives.

1984 On Peter Brooks *Reading for the Plot* (1984). In the *New York Times*, 11 Jul.

36 The beginning of a plot…is the prompting of desire.

1984 On Peter Brooks *Reading for the Plot* (1984). In the *New York Times*, 11 Jul.

37 Happiest when he is trying to sculpture fog.

1989 On Robert C Christopher. In the *New York Times*, 29 May.

38 Stevenson's convictions were sometimes too complex for the binary political arena to which he devoted his life.

1989 In the *New York Times*, 31 Jul.

39 The only trouble with this book is that its covers are too close together.
    1992 On Florence King *With Charity Toward None* (1992). In the *New York Times*, 9 Apr.

Lehrer, Tom (Thomas Andrew) 1928–

US teacher and social satirist.

40 In one word he told me the secret of success in mathematics: Plagiarize…only be sure always to call it please research.
    1953 'Lobachevski', satirical song.

41 We're all go together when we go,
    Every Hottentot and every Eskimo,
    When the air becomes uranious,
    We'll all go simultaneous,
    Yes, we'll all go together when we go.
    1953 'We're All Go Together When We Go', satirical song.

Leisen, Mitchell 1898–1972

US film director. His films include *Hold Back the Dawn* (1941), *Frenchman's Creek* (1944) and *Kitty* (1945).

42 He was God out there. He wanted it a certain way, that was the MGM style, and that's what you got.
    On working for Cedric Gibbons on *Young Man with Ideas* (1952), quoted in David Chierichetti *Hollywood Director* (1972).

LeMay, Curtis Emerson 1906–90

US general and air force chief. After commanding in World War II he became air force Chief of Staff (1961–5) and ran unsuccessfully for Vice President as George Wallace's running mate, 1968.

43 My solution to the problem would be to tell them that they've got to draw in their horns, or we're going to bomb them into the Stone Age.
    Of the North Vietnamese. *Mission with LeMay* (1965).

44 A man should have dinner with his friends, and the commanding general has no friends.
    On declining to dine with a group of colonels. Recalled on his death, 1 Oct 1990.

Lemmon, Jack (John Uhler) 1925–

US actor. He made his film début in *It Should Happen to You* (1954), beginning a career as a comic, bittersweet underdog which has won him eight Academy Award nominations and two Oscars.

45 I won't quit until I get run over by a truck, a producer or a critic.
    1986 In *Newsweek*, 5 May.

46 I would rather play Hamlet with no rehearsal than TV golf.
    Quoted in Michael Hobbs *The Golf Quotation Book* (1992).

L'Engle, Madeleine married name *Mrs Hugh Franklin* 1918–

US writer, best known for her children's trilogy *A Wrinkle in Time* (1962), *A Wind in the Door* (1973) and *A Swiftly Tilting Planet* (1978). Her many other works include *Camilla Dickinson* (1951) and the autobiographical *Summer of Great-Grandmother* (1974).

47 Artistic temperament…sometimes seems a battleground for a dark angel of destruction and a bright angel of creativity wrestling.
    1982 *A Severed Wasp*.

Lenin, Vladimir Ilyich originally *Vladimir Ilyich Ulyanov* 1870–1924

Russian Marxist revolutionary and politician. After the Feb 1917 revolution he urged the proletariat to seize power, and in Oct 1917 led the Bolshevik revolution and headed the first Soviet government. After the Civil War (1918–21) he introduced the New Economic Policy, which his critics saw as a retreat from strict socialism.

48 A small, compact core, consisting of reliable, experienced and hardened workers, with responsible agents…connected by all the rules of strict secrecy with the organisations of revolutionists, can, with the wide support of the masses and without an elaborate set of rules, perform all the functions of a trade union.
    1902 *What Is to be Done?*

49 One Step Forward, Two Steps Back
    1904 Title of book.

50 I greet you as the advance guard of the world proletarian army. The hour is not far off when…the German people will turn their weapons against their capitalist exploiters. The sun of the socialist revolution has already risen.
    1917 Speech, Petrograd, 16 Apr.

51 We will now proceed to the building of socialism.
    1917 Speech, Oct. Quoted in A J P Taylor *From the Boer War to the Cold War. Essays on Twentieth-Century Europe* (1995), p.192.

52 A good man fallen among Fabians.
    Of George Bernard Shaw. Quoted in Arthur Ransome *Six Weeks in Russia in 1919* (1919).

53 Chess is the gymnasium of the mind.
    Quoted in Colin Jarman *The Guinness Dictionary of Sports Quotations* (1990).

Lennon, John Winston 1940–80

English rock singer, guitarist and song-writer. A member of The Beatles, he wrote with Paul McCartney many of the hits of the 1960s. He later established himself as a solo artist. He was shot dead by a deranged fan outside his Manhattan apartment.

54 On this next number I want you all to join in.
Would those in the cheap seats clap their hands?
The rest of you can rattle your jewellery.

1963 Addressing the audience during a Royal Command performance. Quoted in Bill Harry *The Ultimate Beatles Encyclopedia* (1992).

55 We're more popular than Jesus Christ now. I don't
know which will go first, rock and roll or
Christianity.

1966 In the *Evening Standard*.

56 All we are saying is give peace a chance.

1969 Song (with his wife, Yoko Ono), used widely in protests against the Vietnam War.

57 Imagine there's no heaven,
It's easy if you try,
No hell below us,
Above us only sky,
Imagine all the people
Living for today.

1971 'Imagine'.

58 Women should be obscene and not heard.

Attributed.

Lennon, John Winston and McCartney, Sir (James) Paul 1940–80; 1942–

English song-writers and composers who formed the Beatles in 1960. They gained international fame with their songs and performances. They disbanded in 1970.

59 For I don't care too much for money,
For money can't buy me love.

1964 'Can't Buy Me Love'.

60 It's been a hard day's night,
And I've been working like a dog.

1964 'A Hard Day's Night'.

61 She's got a ticket to ride, but she don't care.

1965 'Ticket to Ride'.

62 Eleanor Rigby picks up the rice in a church where a
wedding has been,
Lives in a dream.
Waits at the window, wearing the face that she
keeps in a jar by the door,
Who is it for?
All the lonely people, where do they all come from?

1966 'Eleanor Rigby'.

63 Oh I get by with a little help from my friends,
Mm, I get high with a little help from my friends.

1967 'With a Little Help From My Friends'.

64 Will you still need me, will you still feed me,
When I'm sixty four?

1967 'When I'm Sixty Four'.

65 Strawberry fields forever.

1967 Title of song.

66 Back in the USSR.

1968 Title of song.

Lenthall, William 1591–1662

English lawyer and parliamentarian, Speaker of the Long Parliament (1640–53) and Master of the Rolls from 1643. He was again made Speaker in 1654 and 1659, and in 1657 became one of Cromwell's peers.

67 May it please your Majesty, I have neither eye to see
nor tongue to speak in this place, but as this House
is pleased to direct me, whose servant I am.

1642 To Charles I, on his arrival in the Chamber to arrest five Members, House of Commons, 4 Jan.

Leonard, Elmore John 1925–

US novelist and screenwriter. He has written mainly in the field of crime fiction, where he is widely regarded as the foremost practitioner of his era.

68 The Chekhov of the suburbs.

Of John Cheever. Quoted in *The Annual Obituary 1982* (1983).

69 I try to leave out the parts that people skip.

1985 In *Publisher's Weekly*, 8 Mar.

70 If it sounds like writing, I rewrite it.

1985 In *Newsweek*, 22 Apr.

Leonard, Sugar Ray 1956–

US boxer.

71 We're all endowed with certain God-given talents.
Mine happens to be punching people in the head.

Quoted in Colin Jarman *The Guinness Dictionary of Sports Quotations* (1990).

Leonardo da Vinci 1452–1519

Italian painter, sculptor, architect and engineer, the epitome of the 'Renaissance' man. He entered the service of Cesare Borgia in 1500 as architect and engineer, working alongside Michelangelo, and worked for Louis XII of France in 1506.

72 To devise is the work of the master, to execute the
act of the servant.

Treatise on Painting (published 1651, translated by A P McMahon, 1956).

73 I do not find any difference between painting and
sculpture except that the sculptor pursues his work
with greater physical fatigue than the painter and
the painter pursues his with greater mental fatigue.

Treatise on Painting (published 1651, translated by A P McMahon, 1956).

74 Shun those studies in which the work that results
dies with the worker.

The Notebooks of Leonardo da Vinci (translated by Edward MacCurdy, 1938), vol.1, pt.1.

75 Painting is poetry which is seen and not heard, and poetry is a painting which is heard but not seen.

Quoted in J P and Irma A Richter *The Literary Works of Leonardo da Vinci* (2 vols, 1939).

76 Force is the same throughout and the whole is in every part of it. Force is a spiritual power, an invisible energy which is imparted by violence from without to all bodies out of their natural balance.

Quoted in Jean-Paul Richter (ed) *The Literary Works of Leonardo da Vinci* (1939).

77 If a man have a tent made in linen of which the apertures have all been stopped up, and it be twelve *braccia* across and twelve in depth, he will be able to throw himself down from any great height without sustaining injury.

Description of a parachute. *Notebooks.* Quoted in Vincent Cronin *The Flowering of the Renaissance* (1969).

78 The air moves like a river and carries the clouds with it; just as running water carries all the things that float upon it.

Notebooks. Quoted in Vincent Cronin *The Flowering of the Renaissance* (1969).

79 He is a poor disciple who does not excel his master.

Quoted in Irma A Richter (ed) *Selections from the Notebooks of Leonardo da Vinci* (1977).

80 A good painter has two chief objects to paint, man and the intention of his soul; the former is easy, the latter harder, because he has to represent it by the attitudes and movements of the limbs.

Quoted in Irma A Richter (ed) *Selections from the Notebooks of Leonardo da Vinci* (1977).

81 Perspective is the bridle and rudder of painting.

Quoted in Irma A Richter (ed) *Selections from the Notebooks of Leonardo da Vinci* (1977).

82 The span of a man's outspread arms is equal to his height.

Quoted in Irma A Richter (ed) *Selections from the Notebooks of Leonardo da Vinci* (1977).

83 Do not despise my opinion, when I remind you that it should not be hard for you to stop sometimes and look into the stains of walls, or ashes of a fire, or clouds, or mud or like places, in which, if you consider them well, you may find really marvellous ideas.

Quoted in Irma A Richter (ed) *Selections from the Notebooks of Leonardo da Vinci* (1977).

84 Just as a stone flung into the water becomes the centre and cause of many circles, and as sound diffuses itself in circles in the air; so any object, placed in the luminous atmosphere, diffuses itself in circles, and fills the surrounding air with infinite images of itself.

Quoted in Irma A Richter (ed) *Selections from the Notebooks of Leonardo da Vinci* (1977).

85 The painter who draws by practice and judgement of the eye without the use of reason is like a mirror which copies everything placed in front of it without knowledge of the same.

Quoted in Irma A Richter (ed) *Selections from the Notebooks of Leonardo da Vinci* (1977).

Leonidas d.480

King of Sparta, commander of the Greeks when the Persian army of Xerxes invaded mainland Greece. At the narrow pass of Thermopylae he made a heroic stand with 300 Spartans.

86 Come and take them.

Attributed reply when Xerxes summoned him to surrender his weapons at Thermopylae. Quoted in Plutarch, *Apophthegmata Laconica* (225c).

Lerner, Alan Jay 1918–86

US lyricist, screenwriter and producer. He frequently worked in collaboration with Frederick Loewe, and is best known for *Brigadoon* (1955), *Gigi* (1958), *My Fair Lady* (1964) and *Camelot* (1967).

87 Those little eyes so helpless and appealing
    One day will flash and send you crashing through
        the ceiling.

1958 'Thank Heaven for Little Girls', in the musical *Gigi* (music by Frederick Loewe).

88 We met at nine
    —We met at eight
    I was on time
    —No, you were late
    Ah yes! I remember it well.

1958 'I Remember it Well', in the musical *Gigi* (music by Frederick Loewe).

89 I've Grown Accustomed To Her Face.

1964 Title of song, in *My Fair Lady* (music by Marcus Loewe).

90 Oozing charm from every pore
    He oiled his way around the floor.

1964 'You Did It', from *My Fair Lady* (music by Marcus Loewe).

91 Why can't a woman be more like a man?
    Men are so honest, so thoroughly square;
    Eternally noble, historically fair;
    Who, when you win, will always give your back a
        pat.
    Why can't a woman be like that?

1964 'A Hymn to Him', from *My Fair Lady* (music by Frederick Loewe).

92 Because it saves time.

When Andrew Lloyd Webber asked him 'Why do people take an instant dislike to me?' Quoted by Leah Garchik in the *San Francisco Chronicle*, 27 Nov 1990.

Le Sage, Alain René 1668–1747

French novelist and playwright. He is best remembered for his play *Turcaret* (1709), which satirized the financial world, and the picaresque novel *Gil Blas de Santillane* (1715–35).

93 Justice is such a fine thing that we cannot pay too dearly for it.

1707 *Crispin rival de son maître*, pt.9.

Leslie, David 1601–82

Scottish soldier. He fought at Marston Moor (1644), and defeated Montrose at Philiphaugh (1645). Routed by Cromwell at Dunbar in 1650, he was subsequently imprisoned and held in the Tower until the Restoration. He was made Lord Newark in 1651.

94 How glorious it would be in the eyes of God and men, if we managed to hunt the Catholics from England, follow them to France, and, like the bold King of Sweden, rouse the Protestants in France, plant our religion in Paris by agreement or force, and go from there to Rome to chase the Antichrist and burn the town whence superstition comes.

1643 Said to Lord Hume, Council of Scottish Nobles, Aug.

Lessing, Doris May née *Tayler* 1919–

Rhodesian writer, born in Iran. She has lived much of her adult life in England after being exiled for her opposition to the white Southern Rhodesian government. She was a communist for a time, and later an icon of the women's movement. Her best-known works are the novel sequence *Children of Violence* and *The Golden Notebook*.

95 When old settlers say 'One has to understand the country,' what they mean is, 'You have to get used to our ideas about the native.' They are saying, in effect, 'Learn our ideas, or otherwise get out; we don't want you.'

1950 *The Grass Is Singing*, ch.1.

96 When a white man in Africa by accident looks into the eyes of a native and sees the human being (which it is his chief preoccupation to avoid), his sense of guilt, which he denies, fumes up in resentment and he brings down the whip.

1950 *The Grass Is Singing*, ch.8.

97 I had learned that if one cannot call a country to heel like a dog, neither can one dismiss the past with a smile in an easy gush of feeling, saying: I could not help it, I am also a victim.

1951 *This was the Old Chief's Country*, 'The Old Chief Mshlanga'.

98 For she was suffering that misery peculiar to the young, that they are going to be cheated by circumstances out of the full life every nerve and instinct is clamouring for.

1952 *Martha Quest*, pt.1, ch.1.

99 She was thinking—for, since she had been formed by literature, she could think in no other way—that all this had been described in Dickens, Tolstoy, Hugo, Dostoevsky, and a dozen others. All that noble and terrific indignation had done nothing, achieved nothing, the shout of anger from the nineteenth century might as well have been silent—for here came the file of prisoners, handcuffed two by two, and on their faces was that same immemorial look of patient, sardonic understanding.

1952 *Martha Quest*, ch.2.

1 In every city there is a group of middle-aged and elderly women who in fact run it. The extent to which they are formally organised is no gauge of their real power. They way in which they respond to danger is that gauge; and from the frankness with which they express their intentions can be measured the extent of the danger.

1954 *A Proper Marriage*, pt.3, ch.1.

2 Martha and Jasmine smiled at each other…the future they dreamed of seemed just around the corner; they could almost touch it. Each saw an ideal town, clean, noble and beautiful, soaring up over the actual town they saw, which consisted in this area of sordid little shops and third-rate cafés.

1958 *A Ripple from the Storm*, pt.1, ch.1.

3 There is only one real sin, and that is to persuade oneself that the second-best is anything but the second-best.

1962 *The Golden Notebook*, 'The Blue Notebook'.

4 It occurred to her that she was going mad… Yet it did not seem to her that she was even slightly mad; but rather that people who were not as obsessed as she was with the inchoate world mirrored in the newspapers were all out of touch with an awful necessity.

1962 *The Golden Notebook*, 'Free Women 5'.

5 But this novel was not a trumpet for Women's Liberation. It described many female emotions of aggression, hostility, resentment. It put them into print. Apparently what many women were thinking, feeling, experiencing came as a great surprise.

1971 *The Golden Notebook*, preface to new edition.

6 Briefing for a Descent into Hell.

1971 Title of novel.

7 It does no harm to repeat, as often as you can, 'Without me the literary industry would not exist'.

1980 In *The Author*, spring.

8 To be in love with a country or a political regime is
   a tricky business. You get your heart broken even
   more surely than by being in love with a person.
   1992 *African Laughter*, 'Next Time 1988'.

Lessing, Gotthold Ephraim 1729–81

German philosopher and playwright, an important
Enlightenment figure, best known for his essay on
aesthetics, *Laokoon*.

9 *Wie manches würde in der Theorie unwidersprechlich
   scheinen, wenn es dem Genie nicht gelungen wäre, das
   Widerspiel durch die Tat zu erweisen.*

   How many things would have appeared
   incontestable in theory if genius had not proved
   them wrong in practice.
   1766 *Laokoon: an essay upon the limits of painting and poetry*,
   pt.4.

10 *Ein einziger dankbarer Gedanke gen Himmel ist das
    vollkommenste Gebet.*

    One single grateful thought raised to heaven is the
    most perfect prayer.
    1767 *Minna von Barnhelm*, act 2, sc.7.

11 *Wer richtig räsonniert, erfindet auch; und wer
    erfinden will, muß räsonnieren können. Nur die
    glauben, daß sich das eine von dem anderen trennen
    lasse, die zu keinem von beiden aufgelegt sind.*

    The man who can reason properly can invent; and
    anyone who wants to invent must be able to reason.
    The only people who think that the one can be
    separated from the other are those who have no
    inclination for either.
    1769 *Hamburgische Dramaturgie.*

12 *Es ist nich wahr, daß die kürzeste Linie immer die
    Gerade ist.*

    It is not true that the shortest line is always the
    straight one.
    1780 *Die Erziehung des Menschengeschlechts.*
    ▷ See also Brecht 186:27.

L'Estrange, Sir Roger 1616–1704

English journalist and pamphleteer. During the
Restoration he was Licenser of the Press.

13 Supposing the Press in order, the people in their
    right wits, and news or no news to be the question,
    a Public Mercury should not have my Vote, because
    I think it makes the Multitude too familiar with the
    actions and counsels of their superiors, too
    pragmatical and censorious, and gives them not
    only an itch but a kind of colourable right to be
    meddling with the government.
    1663 *The Intelligencer*, 31 Aug.

Leupold, Jakob 1674–1727

German mechanic, machinery constructor and government mining commissioner, who wrote a large and
comprehensive work on the tasks the engineer faced.

14 As in earlier days were our mechanics, such today
    are our engineers, who may be required not only to
    tear down a fortress, and then to build it up again,
    but also to produce all sorts of engines based on
    mechanical principles, and with equal ease to
    defend or to annihilate a fortress.
    1724 *Theatrum machinarum.*

15 The best machines and to be chosen above all
    others are those which consist of the fewest parts or
    which are the simplest, which produce the least
    friction; which are not too heavily loaded, and
    where the power can be conveniently applied
    without any waste.
    1724 *Theatrum machinarum.*

Levant, Oscar 1906–72

US composer, pianist, writer, actor and conductor. He
played Gershwin's 'Rhapsody in Blue' on its first
performance in 1932.

16 It's a right step in the wrong direction.
    1935 Attributed remark at the first performance of George
    Gershwin's *Porgy and Bess*. He in fact had the deepest respect for
    Gershwin's music.

17 Chutzpah—that quality which enables a man who
    has murdered his mother and father to throw
    himself on the mercy of the court as an orphan.
    1968 *The Unimportance of Being Oscar.*

Levenson, Michael

US literary critic, a Professor of English at the University
of Virginia.

18 Although Brooke never succeeded in becoming the
    first modern poet, he may deserve to be called the
    first modern undergraduate, a title of comparable
    significance.
    1987 Of Rupert Brooke. 'Budding Brooke', in the *New
    Republic*, 31 Aug.

Levenstein, Ros

US copywriter.

19 I'm only here for the beer.
    1971 British advertising slogan for Double Diamond beer.

Leverson, Ada 1895–1936

English novelist and journalist, she was friendly with
Beerbohm and Wilde, who called her 'the Sphinx'. She
wrote six novels.

20 You don't know a woman until you have had a
    letter from her.
    1912 *Tenterhooks*, ch.7.

21 He seemed at ease and to have the look of the last
gentleman in Europe.
1930 Of Oscar Wilde. *Letters to the Sphinx.*

Levertov, Denise 1923–97

English-born US poet. She is associated with the Black
Mountain group of poets led by Charles Olsen, but has a
distinctive voice of her own, reflected in numerous
collections.

22 Let's go—much as that dog goes,
intently haphazard.
1958 *Overland to the Islands,* 'Overland to the Islands'.

23 Pergo Park knew me, and Clavering, and Havering-
atte-
Bower,
Stanford Rivers lost me in osier-beds, Stapleford
Abbots
sent me safe home on the dark road after Simeon-
quiet
evensong,
Wanstead drew me over and over into its basic
poetry,
in its serpentine lake I saw bass-viols among the
golden dead
leaves,
through its trees the ghost of a great house.
1961 *The Jacob's Ladder,* 'A Map of the Western Part of the
County of Essex in England'.

24 The world is
not with us enough.
1964 *O Taste and See,* 'O Taste and See'.
▷ See Wordsworth 1096:32.

25 Death and pain dominate this world, for though
many are cured, they leave still weak,

still tremulous, still knowing mortality
has whispered to them; have seen in the folding
of white bedspreads according to rule

the starched pleats of a shroud.
1972 *Footprints,* 'The Malice of Innocence'.

Levi, Primo 1919–87

Italian writer and the author of a series of major works of
remembrance and analysis of his experiences in Nazi
concentration camps in World War II.

26 The future of humanity is uncertain, even in the
most prosperous countries, and the quality of life
deteriorates; and yet I believe that what is being
discovered about the infinitely large and infinitely
small is sufficient to absolve this end of the century
and millennium. What a very few are acquiring in
knowledge of the physical world will perhaps cause
this period not to be judged as a pure return of

barbarism.
1985 *Other People's Trades,* 'News from the Sky' (translated by
Raymond Rosenthal, 1989).

Levin, (Henry) Bernard 1928–

English writer, journalist and critic. In 1985 he crossed
the Alps on foot, following the path of the Carthaginian
general, Hannibal.

27 The musical equivalent of blancmange.
1983 Of the music of Frederick Delius. *Enthusiasms.*

28 I dislike almost all dogs, but Alsatians, I do truly
believe, should be prohibited by law in any civilised
country... The more I see of dogs, the more I
admire men.
1985 *Hannibal's Footsteps.*

29 Baedeker is astonishingly enduring; travellers can
use nineteenth-century editions with confidence,
providing they take some elementary precautions.
Many hotels will long since have disappeared, and
the prices will be somewhat different, but if
Baedeker says 'On leaving the tunnel, the best
view is on the right', it probably still is, unless
somebody has shifted the mountain, and his
descriptions of scenery and where to go to see it at
its best are still valid, as is practically all of his
potted history.
1985 *Hannibal's Footsteps.*

Lévis, Duc de 1764–1830

French soldier and writer.

30 *Noblesse oblige.*

Nobility brings obligations.
1812 *Maximes et Réflexions,* 'Morale: Maximes et Préceptes',
no.73.

Lévi-Strauss, Claude 1908–

French social anthropologist.

31 *La langue est une raison humaine qui a ses raisons, et
que l'homme ne connaît pas.*

Language is a form of human reason, and has its
reasons which are unknown to man.
1962 *La Pensée sauvage,* ch.9.
▷ See Pascal 758:65.

32 The scientific mind does not so much provide the
right answers as ask the right questions.
1964 *The Raw and the Cooked* (translated by John and Doreen
Weightman 1983).

Lewin, Albert 1895–1968

US screenwriter and director. His films include *The Moon
and Sixpence, The Picture of Dorian Gray* and *Pandora and
the Flying Dutchman.*

33 The measure of love is what one is willing to give
up for it.
1950 *Pandora and the Flying Dutchman.*

Lewis, Alun 1915–44

Welsh soldier, poet and short-story writer. His first work
was a collection of short stories on army life, *The Last
Inspection* (1942). He died of gunshot wounds in the
Burma campaign. Other works were published
posthumously.

34 Religion resides in our eyes rather than our minds.
We see, then we love.

Lewis, C(live) S(taples) 1898–1963

English novelist, literary scholar and theological writer.
His most widely read works include the children's series
The Chronicles of Narnia, several allegorical science-fiction
novels, and the Christian apologetics, *The Screwtape
Letters.*

35 Humanity does not pass through phases as a train
passes through stations: being alive, it has the
privilege of always moving yet never leaving
anything behind.
1936 *The Allegory of Love*, ch.1.

36 Out of the Silent Planet.
1938 Title of novel.

37 There is wishful thinking in Hell as well as on
earth.
1942 *The Screwtape Letters*, preface.

38 Gratitude looks to the past and love to the present:
fear, avarice, lust and ambition look ahead.
1942 *The Screwtape Letters*, no.15.

39 He has a vulgar mind.
1942 Of God. *The Screwtape Letters*, no.22.

40 She's the sort of woman who lives for others—you
can always tell the others by their hunted
expression.
1942 *The Screwtape Letters*, no.26.

41 Fatigue makes women talk more and men less.
1942 *The Screwtape Letters*, no.30.

42 Courage is not simply one of the virtues but the
form of every virtue at the testing point.
Quoted in Cyril Connolly *The Unquiet Grave* (1944), ch.3.

43 I remember summing up what I took to be our
destiny, in conversation with my best friend at
Chartres, by the formula, 'Term, holidays, term,
holidays, till we leave school, and then work, work,
work till we die.'
1955 *Surprised by Joy*, ch.4.

44 A sick society must think much about politics, as a
sick man must think much about his digestion.

1980 *The Weight of Glory.*

45 All except the best men would rather be called
wicked than vulgar.
Quoted in *The Guardian*, 21 Aug 1980.

Lewis, Esther married name *Clark* c.1747–89

English poet.

46 Are simple women only fit
To dress, to darn, to flower or knit,
To mind the distaff, or the spit?
Why are the needle and the pen
Thought incompatible by men?
1754 'A Mirror for Detractors', l.146–50.

Lewis, Joe E

US comedian.

47 I distrust camels and anyone else who can go a
week without a drink.
Recalled on his death, 4 Jun 1971.

Lewis, John L(lewellyn) 1880–1969

US labour leader.

48 No tin hat brigade of goose-stepping vigilantes or
bibblebabbling mob of blackguarding and
corporation-paid scoundrels will prevent the
onward march of labor, or divert its purpose to play
its natural and rational part in the development of
the economic, political, and social life of our
nation.
1937 Address, 3 Sep. Recalled on his death 11 Jun 1969.

49 All forms of government fall when it comes up to
the question of bread—bread for the family,
something to eat. Bread to a man with a family
comes first—before his union, before his
citizenship, before his church affiliation. Bread!
1963 In the *Saturday Evening Post*, 12 Oct.

Lewis, (Harry) Sinclair 1885–1951

US novelist. His novels satirized the materialism and
intolerance of US small-town life. He is best known for
his novel *Babbitt* (1922), a study of middle-class
philistinism. In 1930 he became the first American to
receive the Nobel Prize for Literature.

50 He never put on BVDs without thanking the God
of Progress that he didn't wear tight, long, old-
fashioned undergarments.
1922 *Babbitt*, ch.1, section 4. BVD is a trademark for a brand
of US underwear.

51 His name was George F. Babbitt. He was forty-six
years old now, in April, 1920, and he made nothing
in particular, neither butter nor shoes nor poetry,

but he was nimble in the calling of selling houses for more than people could afford to pay.
1922 *Babbitt*, ch.1.

52 To George F. Babbitt, as to most prosperous citizens of Zenith, his motor car was poetry and tragedy, love and heroism. The office was his pirate ship but the car his perilous excursion ashore.
1922 *Babbitt*, ch.3.

53 In other countries, art and literature are left to a lot of shabby bums living in attics and feeding on booze and spaghetti, but in America the successful writer or picture-painter is indistinguishable from any other decent business man.
1922 *Babbitt*, ch.14.

54 Damn the great executives, the men of measured merriment, damn the men with careful smiles, damn the men that run the shops, oh, damn their measured merriment.
1925 *Arrowsmith*, ch.25.

55 Our American professors like their literature clear and cold and pure and very dead.
1930 Nobel Prize address, 12 Dec.

56 Intellectually I know that America is no better than any other country; emotionally I know she is better than every other country.
1930 Interview in Berlin, 29 Dec.

57 It Can't Happen Here.
1935 Title of novel.

58 A man takes a drink, a drink takes another, and the drink takes the man.
Words to his future wife, Dorothy Thompson. Quoted in Vincent Sheean *Dorothy and Red* (1963).

Lewis, (Percy) Wyndham 1882–1957

English novelist, painter and critic. He co-founded the Vorticist movement with Ezra Pound, and remained an important experimental writer and painter between the wars. He became blind in 1951, but continued to write. His works include *The Apes of God* (1930) and the autobiographical *The Self Condemned* (1954).

59 'Dying for an idea,' again, sounds well enough, but why not let the idea die instead of you?
1926 *The Art of Being Ruled*, pt.1, ch.1.

60 When we say 'science' we can either mean any manipulation of the inventive and organizing power of the human intellect: or we can mean such an extremely different thing as the religion of science, the vulgarized derivative from this pure activity manipulated by a sort of priestcraft into a great religious and political weapon.
1926 *The Art of Being Ruled*.

61 The puritanical potentialities of science have never been forecast. If it evolves a body of organized rites, and is established as a religion, hierarchically organized, things more than anything else will be done in the name of 'decency'. The coarse fumes of tobacco and liquors, the consequent tainting of the breath and staining of white fingers and teeth, which is so offensive to many women, will be the first things attended to.
1926 *The Art of Being Ruled*.

62 The revolutionary simpleton is everywhere.
1927 *Time and Western Man*, pt.1, ch.6.

63 Gertrude Stein's prose song is a cold, black suet-pudding…of fabulously reptilian length.
1927 *Time and Western Man*, pt.1, ch.13.

64 If you must go nowhere, step out.
1928 *The Childermass*, final words.

65 It is to what I have called the Apes of God that I am drawing your attention—those prosperous mountebanks who alternately imitate and mock at and traduce those figures they at once admire and hate.
1930 *The Apes of God*, pt.3.

66 The soul started at the knee-cap and ended at the navel.
1930 *The Apes of God*, pt.12.

67 Give me the *outside* of all things, I am a fanatic for the externality of things.
1937 *Blasting and Bombardiering*, ch.1.

68 Then down came the lid—the day was lost, for art, at Sarajevo. World-politics stepped in, and a war was started which has not ended yet: 'a war to end war'. But it merely ended art. It did not end war.
1937 *Blasting and Bombardiering*, pt.5, 'Toward an Art-Less Society'.

69 'The Art of Being Ruled' might be described from some points of view as an infernal Utopia.
1950 *Rude Assignment*, ch.31.

70 An account…of the decadence occupying the trough between the two world wars introduces us to a moronic inferno of insipidity and decay.
1950 *Rude Assignment*, ch.31.

Lewitt, Sol 1928–

US sculptor, one of the developers of the branch of Conceptual art referred to as 'Minimalism'.

71 In Conceptual art the idea or concept is the most important aspect of the work…all planning and decisions are made beforehand and the execution is a perfunctory affair. The idea becomes the machine that makes the art.

1967 'Paragraphs on Conceptual Art', in *Artforum*, summer.

72 One usually understands the art of the past by applying the conventions of the present thus misunderstanding the art of the past.

1969 'Sentences on Conceptual Art', in *Art-Language*, vol.1, no.1, May.

Lewontin, Richard Charles 1929–

US geneticist, Professor of Zoology at Harvard (1973–).

73 It is characteristic of the design of scientific research that exquisite attention is devoted to methodological problems that can be solved, while the pretense is made that the ones that cannot be solved are really nothing to worry about.

1995 'Sex, Lies, and Social Science', in the *New York Review of Books*, 20 Apr.

74 The social scientist is in a difficult, if not impossible position. On the one hand there is the temptation to see all of society as one's autobiography writ large, surely not the path to general truth. On the other hand, there is the attempt to be general and objective by pretending that one knows nothing about the experience of being human, forcing the investigator to pretend that people usually know and tell the truth about important issues, when we all know from our own lives how impossible that is.

1995 'Sex, Lies, and Social Science', in the *New York Review of Books*, 20 Apr.

Leybourne, George pseudonym of *Joseph Saunders* 1842–84

English singer, entertainer and song-writer, a star of the Victorian music-hall.

75 O, he flies through the air with the greatest of ease, This daring young man on the flying trapeze.

1868 'The Daring Young Man on the Flying Trapeze'.

Lezama Lima, José 1910–76

Cuban poet, novelist and essayist. His autobiographical novel *Paradiso* is considered his masterpiece, and he is the key figure of Cuban neo-Baroque literature.

76 *Más que una costumbre, parece como un conjuro para una divinidad que todos desconocemos, que al reunirse varios cubanos…se permanece en un silencio de suspensión, hasta que se oye una voz cualquiera que dice o canta algo, que no tiene relación con la convocatoria para la reunión.*

Rather than custom, it feels more like an invocation to an unknown deity when Cubans get together…they hold a suspenseful silence until any voice is heard saying or singing something that has nothing to do with the purpose of the meeting.

1966 *Paradiso*, ch.3.

Li Po 701–62

Chinese poet, patronized by Emperor Ming Huang until banished from the court. He is said to have drowned after falling intoxicated from a barge, in an attempt to embrace the moon's reflection in the water.

77 Since Life is but a Dream, Why toil to no avail?

c.750 'A Homily on Ideals in Life, Uttered in Springtime on Rising from a Drunken Slumber', collected in *A Golden Treasury of Chinese Poetry* (translated by John Turner, 1967).

Liberace pseudonym of *Wladziu Valentino Liberace* 1919–87

US pianist and entertainer, renowned for his flamboyant lifestyle.

78 What you said hurt me very much. I cried all the way to the bank.

1973 Responding to a hostile critic. *Autobiography*.

Liberman, Alexander 1912–

Russian-born US artist and editor, artistic director of *Vogue* (1943–62). His works include *Olympic Iliad* (1984) and *Faith* (1987). He is the author of *The Artist in his Studio* (1960).

79 All art is solitary and the studio is a torture area.

1979 In the *New York Times*, 13 May.

Lichtenberg, Georg Christoph 1742–99

German scientist and philosopher, a lecturer at the University of Göttingen. His philosophical reputation rests on his aphorisms, collected in notebooks throughout his adult life.

80 Every man also has his moral backside which he refrains from showing unless he has to and keeps covered as long as possible with the trousers of decorum.

c.1770 *Aphorisms*, Notebook B (translated by R J Hollingdale, 1990).

81 If an angel were ever to tell us anything of his philosophy I believe many propositions would sound like 2 times 2 equals 13.

c.1770 *Aphorisms*, Notebook B (translated by R J Hollingdale, 1990).

82 When a book and a head collide and a hollow sound is heard, must it always have come from the book?

c.1773–5 *Aphorisms*, Notebook D (translated by R J Hollingdale, 1990).

83 What they call 'heart' lies much lower than the fourth waistcoat button.

c.1776–9 *Aphorisms*, Notebook F (translated by R J Hollingdale, 1990).

84 It is almost impossible to bear the torch of truth

through a crowd without singeing someone's beard.

c.1779–83 *Aphorisms*, Notebook G (translated by R J Hollingdale, 1990).

85 To *err* is human also in so far as the animals seldom or never err, or at least only the cleverest of them do so.

c.1779–83 *Aphorisms*, Notebook G (translated by R J Hollingdale, 1990).

86 Once he has stolen his 100,100 thalers a rogue can walk through the world an honest man.

c.1784–88 *Aphorisms*, Notebook H (translated by R J Hollingdale, 1990).

87 A golden rule: we must judge men, not by their opinions, but by what their opinions make of them.

c.1791 *Aphorisms*, Notebook J (translated by R J Hollingdale, 1990).

88 Doubt everything at least once, even the proposition that two times two equals four.

c.1796 *Aphorisms*, Notebook K (translated by R J Hollingdale, 1990).

Lichtenstein, Roy 1923–97

US painter, a key figure of Pop Art. He moved from Abstract Expressionism in the 1950s to illustrations from popular magazines and cartoon strips, duplicating the dots of newspaper reproduction in colourful, large-scale works.

89 Paintings are Rorschach ink blots. They are what you want them to be.

1993 In *The Times*, 27 Mar.

Liebermann, Max 1847–1935

German painter and graphic artist. His early works are open-air studies and sentimental scenes of humble life, and he later found a more colourful, romantic style, influenced by Impressionism.

90 The art of drawing is the art of omission.

Quoted in Paul Klee *On Modern Art* (1979).

Liebman, David 1946–

US jazz saxophonist, highly regarded as a performer and teacher.

91 A jazz performance centers upon the process of creation. The final objective is not only the finished product, but the path and process taken towards it.

1988 *Self-Portrait of a Jazz-Artist*, ch.3.

Ligne, Charles Joseph, Prince de 1735–1814

Belgian soldier and man of letters, who served in the Seven Year's War (1756–63) and the Russo-Turkish war (1787–93). A skilful diplomat and royal favourite, he also wrote extensively.

92 *Le congrès ne marche pas, il danse.*

The Congress makes no progress; it dances.

1814 On the Congress of Vienna (1814–15). Quoted in Auguste de la Garde-Chambonas *Souvenirs du Congrès de Vienne, 1814-1815* (1820), ch.1.

93 One could forgive the fiend for becoming a torrent, but to become an earthquake was really too much.

1814 Of Napoleon I. Attributed.

Lillie, Beatrice Gladys stage-name of Constance Sylvia Munston, Lady Peel 1898–1989

Canadian-born actress. A star of light comedy and revue, she married Sir Robert Peel in 1920 and published an autobiography, *Every Other Inch a Lady* (1973).

94 Heard there was a party. Came.

Explaining her presence after staggering to the nearest house, that of film actor John Gilbert, when she was involved in a car accident in Hollywood. Attributed.

Lillo, George 1693–1739

English dramatist and jeweller, of Dutch extraction. His seven plays were among the first to put middle-class rather than royal characters on the English stage.

95 There's sure no passion in the human soul,
But finds its food in music.

1736 *Fatal Curiosity*, act 1, sc.2.

Lin Yutang 1895–1976

Chinese author and philologist. He lived mainly in the US and was Chancellor of Singapore University (1954–5). He is best known for his novels and essays on Chinese culture and wisdom.

96 All women's dresses, in every age and country, are merely variations on the eternal struggle between the admitted desire to dress and the unadmitted desire to undress.

1945 In the *Ladies Home Journal*.

Lincoln, Abraham 1809–65

US Republican statesman, 16th President (1861–5) and opponent of slavery. In the Civil War he defined the issue in terms of national integrity, not anti-slavery, but proclaimed freedom for all slaves in areas of rebellion. He was shot at Ford's Theatre, Washington, by John Wilkes Booth, an actor, and he died next morning.

97 No man is good enough to govern another man without that other's consent.

1854 Speech, Peoria, 16 Oct.

98 'A house divided against itself cannot stand': I believe that this Government cannot endure permanently half-slave and half-free. I do not expect the Union to be dissolved. I do not expect the house to fall—but I do expect it will cease to be divided. It

will become all one thing, or all the other.
1858 Speech, Springfield, 16 Jun.

99 You can fool some of the people some of the time, and some of the people all the time, but you cannot fool all the people all of the time.
1858 Speech, Clinton, 8 Sep.

1 The patent system…added the fuel of *interest* to the *fire* of genius.
1859 Collected in Roy B Basler (ed) *Collected Works* (1953).

2 What is conservatism? Is it not adherence to the old and tried, against the new and untried?
1860 Speech, New York, 27 Feb.

3 Let us have faith that right makes might; and in that faith let us to the end dare to do our duty as we understand it.
1860 Speech, New York, 27 Feb.

4 Four score and seven years ago our fathers brought forth upon this continent a new nation, conceived in liberty and dedicated to the proposition that all men are created equal…we here highly resolve that the dead shall not have died in vain; that this nation, under God, shall have a new birth of freedom; and that government of the people, by the people, and for the people, shall not perish from the earth.
1863 Dedication address, Gettysburg National Cemetery, 19 Nov.

5 The brave men, living and dead, who struggled here, have consecrated [this ground], far above our poor power to add or detract. The world will little note, nor long remember what we say here, but it can never forget what they did here.
1863 Dedication address, Gettysburg National Cemetary, 19 Nov.

6 With malice toward none, with charity for all, with firmness in the right, as God gives us to see the right, let us strive on to finish the work we are in, to bind up the nation's wounds, to care for him who shall have borne the battle, and for his widow and his orphan, to do all which may achieve and cherish a just and and lasting peace among ourselves, and with all nations.
1865 Second inaugural address, 4 Mar, a month before the end of the Civil War.

Lindbergh, Anne Spencer Morrow 1906–

US writer, widow of the aviator Charles Augustus Lindbergh. Her works include *North to the Orient*, an account of flights with her husband (1935), and an essay collection, *Earth Shine* (1970).

7 Thoughts die and are buried in the silences between sentences.
1980 Of the conversational style of US Secretary of State John Foster Dulles. *War Within and Without.*

Lindbergh, Charles A(ugustus) 1902–74

US aviator who made the first solo, non-stop transatlantic flight in *The Spirit of St Louis*, landing in Paris on 21 May 1927. He spoke in favour of isolationism at the beginning of World War II, but subsequently flew in combat missions.

8 I have seen the science I worshipped and the aircraft I loved, destroying the civilization I expected them to serve.
1967 In *Time Magazine*, 26 May.

Lindsay, John Vliet 1921–

US politician, Mayor of New York City (1966–74).

9 You'll make the mummies dance.
To Thomas Hoving, new director of the Metropolitan Museum of Art, who later adopted the phrase as a book title. Quoted in Thomas Hoving *Making the Mummies Dance* (1993).

Lindsay, (Nicholas) Vachel 1879–1931

US poet. He functioned for a time almost as a travelling troubadour across the US, trading his incantatory verses for hospitality. He suffered serious depression in later years, and committed suicide.

10 Booth led boldly with his big brass drum—
(Are you washed in the blood of the Lamb?)
The saints smiled gravely and they said 'He's come.'
1913 *General Booth Enters Into Heaven*, 'General Booth Enters Into Heaven'.

11 Drabs from the alleyways and drug fiends pale—
Minds still passion-ridden, soul-power frail:—
Vermin-eaten saints with moldy breath,
Unwashed legions with the ways of Death—
(Are you washed in the blood of the Lamb?)
1913 *General Booth Enters Into Heaven*, 'General Booth Enters Into Heaven'.

12 Booth died blind and still by faith he trod,
Eyes still dazzled by the ways of God.
1913 *General Booth Enters Into Heaven*, 'General Booth Enters Into Heaven'.

13 Then I saw the Congo, creeping through the black,
Cutting through the forest with a golden track.
1914 *The Congo and Other Poems*, 'The Congo', pt.1.

14 Mumbo-Jumbo is dead in the jungle.
1914 *The Congo and Other Poems*, 'The Congo', pt.3.

15 It is portentous, and a thing of state
That here at midnight, in our little town
A mourning figure walks, and will not rest,
Near the old courthouse pacing up and down.
1914 *The Congo and Other Poems*, 'Abraham Lincoln Walks At Midnight'.

16 And who will bring white peace
That he may sleep upon his hill again?
1914 *The Congo and Other Poems*, 'Abraham Lincoln Walks At Midnight'.

17 The flower-fed buffalos of the spring
In the days of long ago,
Ranged where the locomotives sing
And the prairie flowers lie low.
1926 *Going to the Stars*, 'The Flower-Fed Buffaloes'.

18 They gore no more, they bellow no more,
They trundle around the hills no more:—
With the Blackfeet, lying low,
With the Pawneees, lying low
Lying low.
1926 *Going to the Stars*, 'The Flower-Fed Buffaloes'.

Linklater, Eric Robert 1889–1974

Scottish journalist and writer, born in Wales. While in the
US (1928–30) he wrote *Poet's Pub* (1929), the first of a
series of satirical novels which include *Juan in America*
(1931) and *Private Angelo* (1946). Other works include
books for children, such as *The Wind on the Moon* (1944),
plays and memoirs.

19 All I've got against it is that it takes you so far from
the club house.
1929 Of golf. *Poet's Pub*, ch.3.

20 Authors and uncaptured criminals…are the only
people free from routine.
1929 *Poet's Pub*, ch.23.

21 With a heavy step Sir Matthew left the room and
spent the morning designing mausoleums for his
enemies.
1931 *Juan in America*, prologue.

22 It is notorious that we speak no more than half-
truths in our ordinary conversation, and even a
soliloquy is likely to be affected by the
apprehension that walls have ears.
1931 *Juan in America*, bk.2, pt.4.

23 She looks like a million dollars, but she only knows
a hundred and twenty words and she's only got two
ideas in her head. The other one's hats.
1931 *Juan in America*, bk.2, pt.5.

24 There won't be any revolution in America… The
people are all too clean. They spend all their time
changing their shorts and washing themselves. You
can't feel fierce and revolutionary in a bathroom.
1931 Isadore. *Juan in America*, bk.5, pt.3.

25 I dislike burdens… and at my back I often hear
Time's winged chariot changing gear.
1937 Juan. *Juan in China*, 'End-Piece'.
▷ See Marvell 658:73.

26 Wanting to know an author because you like his
books is like wanting to know a goose because you
like pâté.
Quoted by Kenneth Murphy in the *Washington Post*, 27 Nov
1994.

Linnaeus, Carolus 1707–78

Swedish botanist and taxonomist, the founder of modern
scientific classification of plants and animals.

27 Nature does not make jumps.
1750 *Philosophia Botanica*, no.77.

28 Minerals grow, plants grow and live, animals grow
and live and feel.
'Systema Naturae', collected in E A Hackel *Generelle
Morphologie* (1866).

Lippard, Lucy 1937–

US art critic.

29 The New York Pop artists are often asked whether
or not they like their subjects. This, as Dorothy
Seckler has noted, is as irrelevant as asking whether
Cézanne liked apples, Géricault corpses, or Picasso
guitars.
1966 *Pop Art*.

Lippmann, Walter 1899–1974

US journalist, a columnist with the New York *Herald
Tribune*, awarded a Pulitzer Prize for international
reporting (1962). He also wrote *Public Opinion* (1922)
and *The Cold War* (1947).

30 The present crisis of Western democracy is a crisis
in journalism.
1920 *Liberty and the News*, 'Journalism and the Higher Law'.

31 There can be no higher law in journalism than to
tell the truth and shame the devil.
1920 *Liberty and the News*, 'Journalism and the Higher Law'.
▷ See Shakespeare 876:58.

32 The news of the day as it reaches the newspaper
office is an incredible medley of fact, propaganda,
rumor, suspicion, clues, hopes, and fears, and the
task of selecting and ordering that news is one of
the truly sacred and priestly offices in a democracy.
For the newspaper is in all literalness the bible of
democracy, the book out of which a people
determines its conduct.
1920 *Liberty and the News*, 'What Modern Liberty Means'.

33 Newspapers necessarily and inevitably reflect, and
therefore, in greater or lesser measure, intensify, the
defective organization of public opinion.
1922 *Public Opinion*, ch.1.

34 Usually it is the stereotyped shape assumed by an
event at an obvious place that uncovers the run of
the news.
1922 *Public Opinion*, ch.23.

35 The news is not a mirror of social conditions, but
the report of an aspect that has obtruded itself.
1922 *Public Opinion*, ch.23.

36 The function of news is to signalize an event, the function of truth is to bring to light the hidden facts, to set them into relation with each other, and make a picture of reality on which men can act. Only at those points, where social conditions take recognizable and measurable shape, do the body of truth and the body of news coincide.
    1922 *Public Opinion*, ch.23.

37 Successful politicians…are insecure and intimidated men. They advance politically only as they placate, appease, bribe, seduce, bamboozle, or otherwise manage to manipulate the demanding and threatening elements in their constituencies.
    1955 *The Public Philosophy*, ch.2, sect.4.

38 The public interest may be presumed to be what men would choose if they saw clearly, thought rationally, acted disinterestedly and benevolently.
    1955 *The Public Philosophy*, ch.4.

Lispector, Clarice 1925–77

Brazilian novelist, born in the Ukraine. Her artistic vision transcends time and place, and her characters (often female) are only incidentally modern or Brazilian.

39 *Dessa civilização só pode sair quem tem como função especial a de sair: a um cientista é dada a licença, a um padre é dada a permissão. Mas não a uma mulher que nem sequer tem as garantias de um título.*

    Only he whose special function is departure can depart from that civilization: a scientist is given license, a priest is given permission. But these are not given to a woman who does not even have the guarantee of a title.
    1964 *A Paixão Segundo G.H.* (The Passion According to G.H.).

40 *O bom era ter uma inteligência e não entender. Era uma bênção estranha como a de ter loucura sem ser doida. Era um desinteresse manso em relação às coisaís ditas do intelecto, uma doçura de estupidez.*

    What was good was to have intelligence and yet not understand. It was a strange blessing like experiencing madness without being mad. It was a gentle lack of interest with respect to the so-called things of the intellect, a sweet stupidity.
    1969 *Uma Aprendizagem ou O Livro dos Prazeres*, 'Luminescência' (translated as *An Apprenticeship or The Book of Delights*, 1986).

Liszt, Franz 1811–86

Hungarian composer and pianist. An acclaimed technical and lyrical player, his works include symphonic poems, sacred works, masses and vocal and piano works in which he often experimented with new musical forms.

41 *Ich kann warten.*

I can wait.
When it was suggested to him that his music was being neglected. Quoted in F Lamond *Memoirs* (1949).

Littlewood, John Edensor 1885–1977

English mathematician, whose research included the distribution of prime numbers and ballistics (in World War I). Depite a severe nervous affliction, he continued working into old age. He published the popular *Mathematician's Miscellany* (1953).

42 They are not clever school boys or scholarship candidates, but 'Fellows of another college'.
    1953 Of the ancient Greeks. *A Mathematician's Miscellany.*

Lively, Penelope (Margaret) 1933–

English writer. She is best known as a novelist, and has also written a memoir of her early childhood in Egypt, children's books, and an introduction to landscape history.

43 One never, of course, knows what people in portraits are thinking.
    1982 *Next to Nature, Art*, ch.10.

44 Wars are fought by children—conceived by their mad demonic elders, and fought by boys.
    1987 *Moon Tiger*, ch.8.

45 I believe that the experience of childhood is irretrievable. All that remains, for any of us, is a handful of brilliant frozen moments, already dangerously distorted by the wisdoms of maturity.
    1994 *Oleander, Jacaranda*, preface.

46 All habits are geared towards the linear, the sequential, but memory refuses such orderliness.
    1994 *Oleander, Jacaranda*, ch.3.

Livingstone, Dr David 1813–73

Scottish missionary, doctor and explorer. He devoted his life to fighting the Portuguese slave trade, and to establishing settlements for missions in central Africa. He also explored widely, discovering Lakes Ngami, Shirwa and Nyasa and exploring the course of the Zaire River.

47 The mere animal pleasure of travelling in a wild unexplored country is also great… The effect of travel on a man whose heart is in the right place is that the mind is made more self-reliant: it becomes more confident of its own resources—there is greater presence of mind… The sweat of one's brow is no longer a curse when one works for God: it proves a tonic to the system, and actually a blessing. No one can truly appreciate the charm of repose unles he has undergone severe exertion.
    Collected in H Waller (ed) *The Last Journals of David Livingstone in Central Africa, continued by a narrative of his last moments and sufferings, obtained from his faithful servants, Chuma and Susi* (1874).

Livy full name *Titus Livius* 59 BC–AD 17

Roman historian, admitted to the court of Augustus c.29 BC. His *Ab urbe condita libri* (History of Rome from its Foundations) consisted of 142 books, of which only parts have survived.

48 *Vae victis!*

Down with the defeated!

Attributed to the Gallic King Brennus, who had captured Rome in 390 BC. 5.48.

49 *Dum Romae consulitur, Saguntum expugnatur.*

While they were deliberating in Rome, Saguntum was captured.

Oral tradition deriving from Livy's description of the siege and capture of the Spanish city of Saguntum by the Carthaginians in 219 BC. The Roman senate deliberated endlessly before deciding to take action when it was already too late. Cf. Livy 21.7.1 'Dum ea Romani parant consultantque, iam Saguntum summa vi oppugnabatur'.

Llewellyn, Richard originally *Richard Doyle Vivian Llewellyn Lloyd* 1907–83

Welsh author, who made his name with *How Green was my Valley* (1939), set in a Welsh mining village and later filmed.

50 How Green was my Valley.

1939 Title of book.

Lloyd, Henry Demarest 1847–1903

US journalist, financial writer and editor with the *Chicago Tribune* (1872-85). He crusaded against monopoly, and was a pioneer 'muckraker' journalist.

51 Monopoly is Business at the end of its journey.

1894 *Wealth against Commonwealth*, ch.1.

Lloyd, Marie stage-name of *Matilda Alice Victoria Wood* 1870–1922

English singer. Known simply as 'Our Marie', she became a major star of music hall and pantomime, notorious for her suggestive delivery of such songs as 'A Little of What You Fancy Does You Good'.

52 If we didn't laugh at him, we'd cry our eyes out.

c.1891 Of the singer and comedian Dan Leno, who died insane in 1904. Attributed.

Lloyd George (of Dwyfor), David, 1st Earl 1863–1945

British Liberal Prime Minister. Elected MP for Caernarvon in 1890. President of the Board of Trade 1905-8 and Chancellor of the Exchequer 1905-15. Secretary of War in 1916 and coalition Prime Minister in the same year. After the war, his downfall came when he conceded the Irish Free State in 1921.

53 You cannot feed the hungry on statistics.

1904 Speech advocating tariff reform.

54 This is the trusty mastiff that is to watch over our interests, but which runs away at the first snarl of the trade unions. A mastiff? It is the right honourable gentleman's poodle. It fetches and carries for him. It barks for him. It bites anybody that he sets it on.

1908 Speech to the House of Commons, 21 Dec, referring to the obstructive Conservative majority in the House of Lords exploited by the then Tory leader, A J Balfour.

55 There are no credentials. They do not even need a medical certificate. They need not be sound either in body or mind. They only require a certificate of birth—just to prove that they were the first of the litter. You would not choose a spaniel on those principles.

1909 Referring to the House of Lords, Budget speech, Mar.

56 We are placing the burdens on the broadest shoulders. I made up my mind that, in forming the Budget, no cupboard should be barer, no lot should be harder to bear.

1909 Speech on the People's Budget, London, 30 Jul.

57 Four spectres haunt the poor—old age, accident, sickness, and unemployment. We are going to exorcise them. We are going to drive hunger from the hearth. We mean to banish the workhouse from the horizon of every workman in the land.

1910 Speech, Reading, 1 Jan.

58 We have been too comfortable and too indulgent—many, perhaps, too selfish—and the stern hand of fate has scoured us to an elevation where we can see the great everlasting things that matter for a nation; the great peaks we had forgotten, of honour, duty, patriotism, and, clad in glittering white, the great pinnacle of sacrifice pointing like a rugged finger to Heaven. We shall descend into the valleys again, but as long as men and women of this generation last, they will carry in their hearts the image of those great mountain peaks, whose foundations are not shaken, though Europe rock and sway in the convulsions of a great war.

1914 Speech, London, 19 Sep.

59 By the test of our faith the highest standard of civilization is the readiness to sacrifice for others.

1914 Speech in Queen's Hall, London, 21 Sep.

60 It is a great war for the emancipation of Europe from the thralldom of a military caste which has thrown its shadows upon two generations of men, and is now plunging the world into a welter of bloodshed and death.

1914 Speech in Queen's Hall, London, 21 Sep.

61 At eleven o'clock this morning came to an end the cruellest and most terrible war that has ever scourged mankind. I hope we may say that thus, this fateful morning, came to an end all wars.

1918 Speech in the House of Commons, 11 Nov, announcing the armistice.

62 What is our task? To make Britain a fit country for heroes to live in.

1918 Speech at Wolverhampton, Nov, at the end of World War I.

63 Give it because it is right. Give it because it is just. Give it because it is good for Ireland and good for the United Kingdom. Give it because it brings peace and good will, but do not give it because you are bullied by assassins.

1920 Speech on an Irish settlement, Carnarvon, 9 Oct.

64 Every man has a House of Lords in his own head. Fears, prejudices, misconceptions—those are the peers, and they are hereditary.

1927 Speech, Cambridge

65 It is the old trouble—too late in dealing with Czechoslovakia, too late with Poland, and certainly too late with Finland. It is always too late, or too little, or both. That is the road to disaster.

1940 House of Commons, 13 Mar.

66 A good lord mayor of Birmingham in a lean year.

Of Neville Chamberlain. Quoted in A J P Taylor *From the Boer War to the Cold War. Essays on Twentieth-Century Europe* (1995), p.363

67 A politician is a person with whose politics you don't agree; if you agree with him, he is a statesman.

Attributed.

Locke, John 1632–1704

English philosopher, a formative influence on British Empiricism and on theories of liberal democracy. His most important work is the *Essay Concerning Human Understanding*, published in 1690. His treatises *On Government* (1690) were also influential, inspiring both American and French revolutionaries.

68 Government has no other end but the preservation of property.

1681 *Second Treatise on Civil Government* (published anonymously 1690).

69 Every man has a property in his person. This nobody has any right to but himself. The labour of his body, and the work of his hands, we may say, are properly his.

1681 *Second Treatise on Civil Government* (published anonymously 1690).

70 Freedom of men under government is to have a standing rule to live by, common to every one of that society, and made by the legislative power vested in it; a liberty to follow my own will in all things when the rule prescribes not, and not to be subject to the inconstant, uncertain, unknown, arbitrary rule of another man.

1681 *Second Treatise on Civil Government* (published anonymously 1690).

71 It is ambition enough to be employed as an under-labourer in clearing ground a little, and removing some of the rubbish that lies in the way to knowledge.

1690 *Essay Concerning Human Understanding*, 'Epistle to the Reader'.

72 Let us then suppose the mind to be, as we say, white paper, void of all characters, without any ideas; how comes it to be furnished? Whence comes it by that vast store which the busy and boundless fancy of man has painted on it with an almost endless variety? Whence has it all the materials of reason and knowledge? To this I answer, in one word, from *experience*.

1690 *Essay Concerning Human Understanding*, bk.2, pt.1, section 2.

73 These two, I say, viz. external material things, as the objects of SENSATION, and the operations of our own minds within, as the objects of REFLECTION, are to me the only originals from whence all our ideas take their beginnings.

1690 *Essay Concerning Human Understanding*, bk.2, pt.1, section 4.

74 For should the soul of a prince enter and inform the body of a cobbler, as soon as deserted by his own soul, everyone sees he would be the same *person* with the prince, accountable only for the prince's actions; but who would say it was the same *man*?

1690 *Essay Concerning Human Understanding*, bk.2, pt.27, section 15.

75 A sound mind in a sound body is a short but full description of a happy state in this world. He that has those two, has little more to wish for; and he that wants either of them will be little the better for anything else.

1693 *Some Thoughts Concerning Education*, opening words.

▷ See Juvenal 540:82.

Lodge, David John 1935–

English novelist and critic. His best known novels are set in academic circles, notably *Changing Places* (1975) and *Small World* (1984).

76 Literature is mostly about having sex and not much about having children. Life is the other way round.

1965 *The British Museum is Falling Down*, ch.4.

77 The British, he thought, must be gluttons for satire: even the weather forecast seemed to be some kind of spoof, predicting every possible

combination of weather for the next twenty-four hours without actually committing itself to anything specific.

1975 *Changing Places*, ch.2.

78 He understood…Walt Whitman, who laid end to end words never seen in each other's company before outside of a dictionary, and Herman Melville who split the atom of the traditional novel in the effort to make whaling a universal metaphor.

1975 *Changing Places*, ch.5.

79 Conversation is like playing tennis with a ball made of Krazy Putty that keeps coming back over the net in a different shape.

1984 *Small World*, pt.1, ch.1.

80 The world is a global campus, Hilary, you'd better believe it. The American Express card has replaced the library pass.

1984 *Small World*, pt.1, ch.2.

81 I gave up screwing around a long time ago. I came to the conclusion that sex is a sublimation of the work instinct.

1984 *Small World*, pt.1, ch.2.

82 Another law of academic life: *it is impossible to be excessive in flattery of one's peers.*

1984 *Small World*, pt.3, ch.1.

83 As to our universities, I've come to the conclusion that they are élitist where they should be egalitarian, and egalitarian where they should be élitist.

1988 *Nice Work*, pt.5, ch.4.

Lodge, Henry Cabot 1850–1924

US Republican politician and Senator.

84 The businessman dealing with a large political question is really a painful sight. It does seem to me that businessmen, with a few exceptions, are worse when they come to deal with politics than men of any other class.

1902 Letter to Theodore Roosevelt, 20 Oct.

Loengard, John Borg 1934–

US photographer, picture editor of *Life* (1973–87). His works include *Pictures Under Discussion* (1987) and many essays in *Life*.

85 A bit like God confessing he'd never gotten the hang of the thunderstorms.

1987 On Henri Cartier-Bresson's remark that he was only good at casual photography. In *Life*, Dec.

Lofthouse, Nat 1925–

English footballer. A star centre-forward with Bolton Wanderers in the 1950s, he led the team to victory in the 1958 FA Cup final and also scored 30 goals in 33 internationals for England.

86 There was plenty of fellers who would kick your bollocks off. The difference was that at the end they'd shake your hand and help you look for them.

Comparing football in the 1950s with that of later eras. Quoted in Peter Ball and Phil Shaw *The Book of Football Quotations* (1989).

Logau, Friedrich von 1605–55

German writer, author of epigrams.

87 *Gottesmühlen mahlen langsam, mahlen aber trefflich klein;*
Ob aus Langmut Er sich säumet, bringt mit Schärf'
Er alles ein.

Though the mills of God grind slowly, yet they grind exceeding small;
Though with patience He stands waiting, with exactness grinds He all.

1654 *Sinngedichte*, bk.3, pt.2, no.24 (translated as *Retribution* by Henry Wadsworth Longfellow). Logau used an anonymous classical source for the first line.

Lombardi, Vince(nt Thomas) 1913–70

US American football coach.

88 Winning isn't everything; it's the only thing.

Attributed. His exact words were 'Winning isn't everything, but making the effort is'. Some sources attribute the saying to Red Sanders, coach of the University of California team.

London, Jack (John Griffith) 1876–1916

US writer. His books, such as *The Call of the Wild* (1903) and *White Fang* (1907), reflect his experiences as a sailor, tramp, gold miner in the Klondike and alcoholic. He also wrote a futuristic political novel *The Iron Heel* (1907).

89 The Call of the Wild.

1903 Title of book.

90 In an English ship, they say, it is poor grub, poor pay, and easy work; in an American ship, good grub, good pay, and hard work. And this is applicable to the working populations of both countries.

1903 *The People of the Abyss*, ch.20.

Longden, Robert Paton 1903–40

English classical scholar and historian, writer of limericks on famous figures of Roman history.

91 The Emperor Caligula
's Habits were somewhat irrigula.
When he sat down to lunch
He got drunk at onch.

Quoted and first published in Arnold Silcock *Verse and Worse* (1952), 'Potted Biography'.

92 The Emperor Claudius

Used to keep a baudius.
When he got more criminal
He ran a den on the Viminal.

1952 Quoted and first published in Arnold Silcock, *Verse and Worse* (1952), 'Potted Biography'.

Longfellow, Henry Wadsworth 1807–82

US poet, Professor of Modern Languages and Literature at Harvard for nearly 18 years. His narrative skill made him one of the most popular poets of his day. His best-known poems include *Evangeline* (1847), *Hiawatha* (1855) and *Tales of a Wayside Inn* (1863).

93 Music is the universal language of mankind.

1835 *Outre Mer*. Also attributed to Christopher North (1865–1954).

94 Life is real, life is earnest!
And the grave is not its goal;
Dust thou art, to dust returnest,
Was not spoken of the soul.

1838 'A Psalm of Life'. In *Knickerbocker or New York Monthly Magazine*, Sep. Collected in *Voices of the Night* (1839).

95 Art is long, and time is fleeting,
And our hearts, though stout and brave,
Still, like muffled drums, are beating
Funeral marches to the grave.

1838 'A Psalm of Life', stanza 4. In *Knickerbocker or New York Monthly Magazine*, Sep. Collected in *Voices of the Night* (1839).

96 Lives of great men all remind us
We can make our lives sublime,
And departing, leave behind us
Footprints on the sands of time.

1838 'A Psalm of Life', stanza 7. In *Knickerbocker or New York Monthly Magazine*, Sep. Collected in *Voices of the Night* (1839).

97 Under a spreading chestnut-tree
The village smithy stands;
The smith a mighty man is he,
With large and sinewy hands;
And the muscles of his brawny arms
Are strong as iron bands.

1840 ' The Village Blacksmith', stanza 1. Collected in *Ballads and other Poems* (1841).

98 His brow is wet with honest sweat,
He earns whate'er he can,
And looks the whole world in the face,
For he owes not any man.

1840 'The Village Blacksmith', stanza 2. Collected in *Ballads and other Poems* (1841).

99 Each morning sees some task begin,
Each evening sees it close;
Something attempted, something done,
Has earned a night's repose.

1840 'The Village Blacksmith', stanza 7. Collected in *Ballads and other Poems* (1841).

1 It was the schooner Hesperus,

That sailed the wintry sea.

1841 *Ballads and other Poems*, 'The wreck of the Hesperus'.

2 The shades of night were falling fast,
As through an Alpine village passed
A youth, who bore, 'mid snow and ice,
A banner with a strange device,
Excelsior!

1841 'Excelsior'.

3 I like that ancient Saxon phrase, which calls,
The burial-ground God's-Acre.

1841 'God's-Acre'.

4 And the night shall be filled with music,
And the cares, that infest the day,
Shall fold up their tents like Arabs,
And as silently steal away.

1844 *The Waif*, 'The Day Is Done', stanza 11.
▷ See Kaufman 543:16.

5 I shot an arrow into the air,
It fell to earth, I knew not where.

1845 'The Arrow and the Song'.

6 This is the forest primeval.

1847 *Evangeline*, prologue.

7 Sorrow and silence are strong, and patient
endurance is godlike.

1847 *Evangeline*, pt.2, section 1.

8 Thou, too, sail on, O Ship of State!
Sail on, O UNION, strong and great!
Humanity with all its fears,
With all the hopes of future years,
Is hanging breathless on thy fate!

1849 *The Seaside and Fireside*, 'The Building of the Ship', l.377–81.

9 In the moonlight and the starlight,
Fair Nokomis bore a daughter.
And she called her name Wenonah,
As the first-born of her daughters.

1855 The naming of Hiawatha's mother. *The Song of Hiawatha*, pt.3, 'Hiawatha's Childhood'. The name is now usually spelt Winona.

10 By the shore of Gitche Gumee
By the shining Big-Sea-Water,
Stood the wigwam of Nokomis,
Daughter of the Moon, Nokomis.
Dark behind it rose the forest,
Rose the black and gloomy pine-trees,
Rose the firs with cones upon them;
Bright before it beat the water,
Beat the clear and sunny water,
Beat the shinning Big-Sea-Water.

1855 *The Song of Hiawatha*, pt.3, 'Hiawatha's Childhood'.

11 From the waterfall he named her,

Minnehaha, Laughing Water.

1855 *The Song of Hiawatha*, pt.4, 'Hiawatha and Mudjekeewis'.

12 A boy's will is the wind's will,
And the thoughts of youth are long, long thoughts.

1855 'My Lost Youth', in *Putnam's Monthly Magazine*, vol.6, Aug. Collected in *The Courtship of Miles Standish and Other Poems*, 1858. In his diary Longfellow notes that these lines are from an 'old Lapland song'.

13 But ah! what once has been shall be no more!
The groaning earth in travail and in pain
Brings forth its races, but does not restore,
And the dead nations never rise again.

1855 'The Jewish Cemetery at Newport'.

14 A Lady with a Lamp shall stand
In the great history of the land,
A noble type of good,
Heroic womanhood.

1857 Of Florence Nightingale. 'Santa Filomena'.

15 Between the dark and the daylight,
When the night is beginning to lower,
Comes a pause in the day's occupations,
That is known as the Children's Hour.

1863 'The Children's Hour', stanza 1.

16 Listen, my children, and you shall hear
Of the midnight ride of Paul Revere,
On the eighteenth of April in Seventy-five.

1863 *Tales of a Wayside Inn*, pt.1, 'The Landlord's Tale: Paul Revere's Ride'.

17 Our ingress into the world
Was naked and bare;
Our progress through the world
Is trouble and care.

1872 *Tales of a Wayside Inn*, pt.2, 'The Student's Tale: The Cobbler of Hagenau'.

18 Ships that pass in the night, and speak each other in passing,
Only a signal shown and a distant voice in the darkness;
So on the ocean of life, we pass and speak one another,
Only a look and a voice, then darkness again and a silence.

1873 *Tales of a Wayside Inn*, pt.3. 'The Theologian's Tale: Elizabeth'.

19 If you would hit the mark, you must aim a little above it;
Every arrow that flies feels the attraction of earth.

1881 *Elegaic Verse*, stanza 9.

20 The men that women marry,
And why they marry them, will always be
A marvel and a mystery to the world.

1883 *Michael Angelo*, pt.1, sc.5.

21 There was a little girl
Who had a little curl
Right in the middle of her forehead;
And when she was good
She was very, very good,
But when she was bad, she was horrid.

Attributed to Longfellow by Blanch Roosevelt Tucker Macchetta in *The Home Life of Henry W. Longfellow* (1882).

Longworth, Alice Roosevelt 1884–1980

US political hostess, daughter of Theodore Roosevelt, renowned for her wit.

22 If you can't say something good about someone, sit right here by me.

Motto embroidered on a sofa pillow. Quoted in *Time*, 9 Dec 1966.

Lonsdale, Hugh Cecil Lowther, 5th Earl of
1857–1944

English sportsman. As president of the National Sporting Club, he founded and presented the 'Lonsdale belts' for boxing.

23 I have always considered that boxing really combines all the finest and highest inclinations of a man—activity, endurance, science, temper, and, last, but not least, presence of mind.

1915 Foreword in Eugene Corri *Thirty Years a Boxing Referee*.

Loos, Adolf 1870–1933

Austrian architect and design theorist, a major figure of the 'Modern Movement', whose designs reflect his rejection of ornament and an emphasis on elegant functionalism.

24 I have emerged victorious from my thirty years of struggle. I have freed mankind from superfluous ornament.

1930 *Trotzdem 1900–1930*.

25 The evolution of culture is synonymous with the removal of ornament from utilitarian objects.

1931 *Trotzdem 1900–1930*. Quoted in Franz Glück (ed.) *Adolf Loos, Sämtliche Schriften* (1962), vol. 1.

Loos, Anita c.1893–1981

US writer, best known for her satirical novel *Gentleman Prefer Blondes*. She also wrote plays, screenplays and memoirs.

26 Gentlemen Prefer Blondes.

1925 Title of novel, and subsequently a film starring Marilyn Monroe and Jane Russell (1953).

27 So this gentleman said a girl with brains ought to do something more with them besides think.

1925 *Gentlemen Prefer Blondes*, ch.1.

28 Gentlemen always seem to remember blondes.

1925 *Gentlemen Prefer Blondes*, ch.1.

29 She said she always believed in the old adage, 'Leave them while you're looking good.'

1925 *Gentlemen Prefer Blondes*, ch.1.

30 You have got to be a Queen to get away with a hat like that.

1925 *Gentlemen Prefer Blondes*, ch.4.

31 Any girl who was a lady would not even think of having such a good time that she did not remember to hang on to her jewelry.

1925 *Gentlemen Prefer Blondes*, ch.4.

32 The Eyefull Tower is devine.

1925 *Gentlemen Prefer Blondes*, ch.4.

33 So I really think that American gentlemen are the best after all, because kissing your hand may make you feel very very good but a diamond and safire bracelet lasts forever.

1925 *Gentlemen Prefer Blondes*, ch.4.

34 Fun is fun but no girl wants to laugh all of the time.

1925 *Gentlemen Prefer Blondes*, ch.4

35 So then Dr Froyd said that all I needed was to cultivate a few inhibitions and get some sleep.

1925 *Gentlemen Prefer Blondes*, ch.5.

36 So then he said that he used to be a member of the choir himself, so who was he to cast the first rock at a girl like I.

1925 *Gentlemen Prefer Blondes*, ch.5.

37 Tallulah never bored anyone, and I consider that humanitarianism of a very high order indeed.

1968 Eulogy at Tallulah Bankhead's funeral. Reported in the *New York Times*, 17 Dec.

38 I'm furious about the Woman's Liberationists. They keep getting up on soap-boxes and proclaiming that women are brighter than men. That's true, but it should be kept very quiet or it ruins the whole racket.

Quoted in *The Observer*, 30 Dec 1973.

Lorca, Federico García 1898–1936

Spanish poet and playwright, assassinated on the order of the Nationalist Civil Governor early in the Civil War. He is best known for his Gypsy songs and powerful, elemental tragedies such as *Bodas de Sangre* (1933, translated as *Blood Wedding*, 1947).

39 *Verde que te quiero verde.*
Verde viento. Verdes ramas.
El barco sobre la mar
y el caballo en la montaña.

Green how I love you green.
Green wind. Green boughs.

The ship on the sea
and the horse on the mountain.

1924–7 *Romance sonámbulo.*

40 Spain is the only country where death is the national spectacle.

Quoted in Colin Jarman *The Guinness Dictionary of Sports Quotations* (1990).

Loren, Sophia pseudonym of Sofia Scicolone
1934–

Italian actress. Her films include *El Cid* (1961) and *Two Women* (1961), for which she won an Academy Award.

41 Everything you see I owe to spaghetti.

Attributed.

Lorenz, Konrad 1903–89

Austrian zoologist and ethnologist. Lorenz studied the organization of individual animal and group behaviour patterns. He shared the 1973 Nobel Prize in Physiology or Medicine with Karl von Frisch.

42 *Überhaupt ist es für den Forscher ein guter Morgensport, täglich vor dem Frühstück eine Lieblingshypothese einzustampfen—das erhält jung.*

It is a good morning exercise for a research scientist to discard a pet hypothesis every day before breakfast. It keeps him young.

1963 *Das sogenannte Böse* ('The So-Called Evil', translated by Marjorie Latzke as *On Aggression*, 1966), ch.2.

43 Man appears to be the missing link between anthropoid apes and human beings.

1965 In the *New York Times*, 11 Apr.

Louis IX also called St Louis 1214–70

King of France (1226–70). He led the Seventh Crusade (1248), but was defeated, imprisoned and ransomed. On his return to France (1254) he carried out reforms and encouraged the arts and literature. He began a new Crusade in 1270, but died of plague in Tunis.

44 I would rather have a Scot come from Scotland to govern the people of this kingdom well and justly, than that you should govern them ill in the sight of all the world.

1244 To his son, Louis, at Fontainebleau.

Louis XI 1423–83

King of France (1461–83). By a mixture of force and cunning, he broke the power of the nobility and by 1483 had united most of France under the crown.

45 I have chased the English out of France more easily than my father ever did, for my father drove them out by force of arms, whereas I have driven them out with venison pies and good wine.

1475 Said after the signing of the Treaty of Picquigny, Sep.

Louis XIV known as *the Great* or *le Roi Soleil [the Sun King]* 1638–1715

King of France (1643–1715). His aggressive foreign and commercial policies and his attempt to create a Franco–Spanish Bourbon bloc led to the War of the Spanish Succession (1701–13). Although his old age saw military disaster and its financial toll, he was a model of royal absolutism and courtly brilliance.

46 Everyone knows how much trouble your meetings have caused in my State, and how many dangerous results they have had. I have learnt that you intend to continue them. I have come here expressly to forbid you to do this, which I do absolutely.

1655 Address to the Parlement of Paris, 13 Apr.

47 *L'État, c'est moi.*

I am the State.

1655 Address to the Parlement of Paris, 13 Apr. This is probably apocryphal.

48 Every time that I fill a high office, I make one hundred men discontented and one ungrateful.

c.1669 After the disgrace of the Duke of Lauzun. Quoted in Voltaire *Le Siècle de Louis XIV* (1751), ch.26.

49 How could God do this to me after all I have done for him?

1704 On hearing the news of the French defeat at Blenheim, Aug. Quoted in L Norton *Saint-Simon at Versailles* (1958).

50 The function of kings consists primarily of using good sense, which always comes naturally and easily. Our work is sometimes less difficult than our amusements.

Mémoires for the Instruction of the Dauphin.

Louis XVI 1754–93

King of France (1774–93), deposed during the Revolution. He was tried before the National Convention for conspiracy with foreign powers, and executed in Paris.

51 Louis XVI: Is this a revolt?
Duke of Rochefoucauld-Liancourt: No, sir, it's a revolution.

1789 Exchange after the fall of the Bastille, 14 Jul. Quoted in F Dreyfus *La Rochefoucauld-Liancourt* (1903), ch.2, section 3.

Louis XVIII originally *Stanislaw Xavier* 1755–1824

King of France (from 1795). He fled to Belgium in 1791, proclaiming himself Regent for Louis XVII in 1793 and King in 1795. On the fall of Napoleon, he landed at Calais (1814) and began a severe rule, until Napoleon's return for the Hundred Days (1815). His rule was subsequently more moderate.

52 *L'exactitude est la politesse des rois.*

Punctuality is the politeness of kings.

Quoted in *Souvenirs de J Lafitte* (1844), bk.1, ch.3.

Louis Philippe known as *the Citizen King* 1773–1850

King of France (1830–48). Eldest son of the Duc d'Orléans, he renounced his titles and fought in the wars of the Republic, becoming 'citizen king' after the Revolution of 1830. Demands for electoral reform led to the uprising of 1848 and his forced abdication.

53 Died, has he? Now I wonder what he meant by that.

1838 Said on the death of Talleyrand, his calculating and self-serving adviser, 18 Mar.

54 The entente cordiale.

1843 Speech, 27 Dec. Quoted in Collingham *The July Monarchy* (1988), p.320.

55 What perished in France in 1830 was not respect for a dynasty, but respect for anything.

Of the revolution which brought him to power. Quoted in A J P Taylor *From Napoleon to the Second International* (1993).

Louis, Joe pseudonym of *Joseph Louis Barrow* 1914–81

US boxer. Known as the 'Brown Bomber', he won the world heavyweight title in 1937 and held it for a record 12 years, defending it 25 times. He retired in 1949, attempting two unsuccessful comebacks (1950–1). In all he won 68 of his 71 professional fights.

56 He can run, but he can't hide.

1941 Said during a bout against Billy Conn.

57 Everybody wants to go to heaven, but nobody wants to die.

1965 In *Sports Illustrated*, 'Scorecard', 19 Jul.

58 Every man's got to figure to get beat some time.

Quoted in Colin Jarman *The Guinness Dictionary of Sports Quotations* (1990).

59 I don't like money, actually, but it quiets my nerves.

Quoted in Colin Jarman *The Guinness Dictionary of Sports Quotations* (1990).

60 Why should I? When somebody insulted Caruso, did he sing an aria for him?

When a friend asked why he did not punch a motorist who swore at him following a minor traffic accident. Quoted in Colin Jarman *The Guinness Dictionary of Sports Quotations* (1990).

Love, James pseudonym of *James Dance* 1722–74

English actor and writer.

61 Hail Cricket! glorious, manly, British game!
First of all Sports! be first alike in fame!

1744 'Cricket: An Heroic Poem'.

Lovelace, Richard 1618–58

English Cavalier poet. Twice imprisoned (1642 and 1648–49) by the Puritans for his Royalist sympathies, he spent much of his time behind bars writing poetry, which he published in 1649 as the collection *Lucasta*.

62 When I lie tangled in her hair,
    And fettered to her eye;
    The Gods, that wanton in the air
    Know no such liberty.
    1649 *Lucasta*, 'To Althea, from Prison'.

63 Stone walls do not a prison make,
    Nor iron bars a cage;
    Minds innocent and quiet take
    That for a hermitage;
    If I have freedom in my love,
    And in my soul am free;
    Angels along that soar above,
    Enjoy such liberty.
    1649 *Lucasta*, 'To Althea, from Prison'.

64 If to be absent were to be
    Away from thee;
    Or that when I am gone,
    You or I were alone;
    Then my *Lucasta* might I crave
    Pity from blust'ring wind, or swallowing wave.
    1649 *Lucasta*, 'To Lucasta, Going beyond the Seas'.

65 *Amarantha* sweet and fair,
    Ah braid no more that shining hair!
    As my curious hand or eye,
    Hovering round thee let it fly.
    1649 *Lucasta*, 'To Amarantha, That She Would Dishevel Her Hair'.

66 Tell me not, Sweet, I am unkind,
    That from the nunnery
    Of thy chaste breast, and quiet mind,
    To war and arms I fly.
    1649 *Lucasta*, 'To Lucasta, Going to the Wars'.

67 I could not love thee, Dear, so much,
    Loved I not honour more.
    1649 *Lucasta*, 'To Lucasta, Going to the Wars'.

68 Thus did they live: Thus did they love,
    Repeating only joys above;
    And Angels were, but with clothes on,
    Which they would put off cheerfully,
    To bathe them in the galaxy,
    Then gird them with the Heavenly zone.
    1649 *Lucasta*, 'Love Made in the First Age'.

69 The asp doth on his feeder feed.
    1649 *Lucasta*, 'A Fly Caught in a Cobweb'.

Loveless, George 1805–40

English Methodist preacher, who in 1833 organized the agricultural labourers of Tolpuddle, Dorset, into a trade union. When the men were convicted of taking illegal

oaths and transported, a public outcry ensued and they were eventually pardoned.

70 If we have violated any law, it was not done intentionally. We have injured no man's reputation, character, person, or property. We were meeting together to preserve ourselves, our wives, and our children from utter degradation and starvation.
    1833 Statement to the Dorchester Assizes, Mar, on behalf of the Tolpuddle martyrs.

Lowe, Emily fl.1850s

Englishwoman, who travelled in Norway with her mother.

71 The only use of a gentleman in travelling is to look after the luggage.
    1857 *Unprotected Females in Norway*.

Lowell, Amy 1874–1925

US poet. A descendant of James Russell Lowell, she was associated with the Imagist movement, and wrote free verse in a style she named 'unrhymed cadence'. She also wrote prose and criticism.

72 For books are more than books, they are the life
    The very heart and core of ages past,
    The reason why men lived and worked and died,
    The essence and quintessence of their lives.
    1912 'The Boston Atheneum'.

73 All books are either dreams or swords,
    You can cut, or you can drug, with words.
    1914 'Sword Blades and Poppy Seeds'.

74 And the softness of my body will be guarded by
       embrace
    By each button, hook, and lace.
    For the man who should loose me is dead,
    Fighting with the Duke in Flanders,
    In a pattern called a war.
    Christ! What are patterns for?
    1916 'Patterns'.

75 A man must be sacrificed now and again
    To provide for the next generation of men.
    1922 'A Critical Fable'.

76 I must be mad, or very tired,
    When the curve of a blue bay beyond a railroad track
    Is shrill and sweet to me like the sudden springing
       of a tune,
    And the sight of a white church above thin trees in
       a city square
    Amazes my eyes as though it were the Parthenon.
    1925 'Meeting-House Hill'.

Lowell, James Russell 1819–91

US poet, essayist and diplomat. His popular satiric poems in Yankee dialect were published as *The Biglow Papers*

(1848 and 1867). A lecturer at Harvard, he was also Editor of the *Atlantic Monthly* and US Minister to Spain (1877–80) and Britain (1880–85).

77   It is mediocrity which makes laws and sets
       mantraps and spring-guns in the realm of free song,
       saying thus far shall you go and no further.
       1843 'Elizabethan Dramatists, Omitting Shakespeare: John Webster'.

78   Once to every man and nation comes the moment
           to decide,
       In the strife of Truth with Falsehood, for the good
           or evil side.
       1844 'The Present Crisis', in the *Boston Courier*, 11 Dec. Collected in *Poems: Second Series*, 1848. The poem was written in the midst of the controversy over whether Texas should be annexed and slavery extended.

79   They talk about their Pilgrim blood,
       Their birthright high and holy!
       A mountain-stream that ends in mud
       Methinks is melancholy.
       1846 'An Interview with Miles Standish', stanza 11.

80   Ez fer war, I call it murder,—
       There you hev it plain an' flat;
       I don't want to go no furder
       Than my Testymeny fer that;
       God hez sed so plump an' fairly,
       It's ez long ez it is broad,
       An' you've gut to git up airly
       Ef you want to take in God.
       1846 'A Letter'. In the *Boston Courier*, 17 Jun. Collected in *The Biglow Papers, First Series* (1848), no.1.

81   'Slavery's a thing thet depends on complexion,
       It's God's law thet fetters on black skins don't chafe;
       Ef brains wuz to settle it (horrid reflection!)
       Wich of our onnable body'd be safe?'
       1848 'The Debate in the Sennit', in the Boston *Courier*, 3 May, collected in *The Biglow Papers: First Series* (1848), no. 5.

82   And what is so rare as a day in June?
       Then, if ever come perfect days.
       1848 'The Vision of Sir Launfal', prelude.

83   There comes Poe, with his raven, like Barnaby
           Rudge,
       Three-fifths of him genius and two-fifths sheer
           fudge.
       1848 'A Fable for Critics'.

84   A reading machine, always wound up and going,
       He mastered whatever was not worth knowing.
       1848 Of a scholar. 'A Fable for Critics'.

85   Books are the bees which carry the quickening
       pollen from one to another mind.
       1849 'Nationality in Literature', in the *North American Review*, Jul.

86   Every man feels instinctively that all the beautiful
       sentiments in the world weigh less than a single
       lovely action.
       1867 'Rousseau and the Sentimentalists', in the *North American Review*, Jul.

87   The mind can weave itself warmly in the cocoon of
       its own thoughts, and dwell a hermit anywhere.
       1869 'On a Certain Condescension in Foreigners', in the *Atlantic Monthly*, Jan.

88   Sorrow, the great idealizer.
       1876 *Among My Books*, 'Spenser'.

89   There is no good in arguing with the inevitable.
       The only argument available with an east wind is to
       put on your overcoat.
       1884 'On Democracy', Lowell's inaugural address when he became president of the Birmingham and Midland Institute, 6 Oct.

90   Compromise makes a good umbrella but a poor
       roof.
       1884 'On Democracy', speech in Birmingham, 6 Oct.

91   As life runs on, the road grows strange
       With faces new,—and near the end
       The milestones into headstones change,
       'Neath every one a friend.
       1887 'Sixty-Eighth Birthday'.

Lowell, Robert Traill Spence, Jr 1917–77

US poet. His poems are intensely personal and confessional. His public involvement and outspoken comments, especially during the Vietnam War, have made him one of the best known of all contemporary poets.

92   Let there pass
       A minute, ten, ten trillion; but the blaze
       Is infinite, eternal: this is death.
       To die and know it. This is the Black Widow,
           death.
       1950 'Mr Edwards and the Spider'.

93   They died
       When time was open-eyed,
       Wooden and childish; only bones abide
       There, in the nowhere, where their boats were
           tossed
       Sky-high, where mariners had fabled news
       of IS, the whited monster.
       1950 'The Quaker Graveyard in Nantucket', pt.3.

94   This is the end of the whaleroad and the whale
       Who spewed Nantucket bones on the thrashed
           swell
       And stirred the troubled waters to whirlpools
       To send the Pequod packing off to hell
       1950 'The Quaker Graveyard in Nantucket', pt.4. The Pequod was the ship that sailed after Moby Dick in Melville's novel.

95 The Lord survives the rainbow of his will.
1950 'The Quaker Graveyard in Nantucket', last line.

96 I keep no rank nor station.
Cured, I am frizzled, stale and small.
1956 'Home After Three Months Away'.

97 I myself am hell
1956 'Skunk Hour'.

98 I often sigh still
for the dark downward and vegetating kingdom
of the fish and reptile.
1964 'For the Union Dead'.

99 William James could almost hear the bronze
Negroes breathe.

Their monument sticks like a fishbone
in the city's throat.
1964 'For The Union Dead'.

1 Everywhere,
giant finned cars nose forward like fish;
a savage servility
slides by on grease.
1964 'For the Union Dead'.

2 He is out of bounds now. He rejoices in man's
lovely
peculiar power to choose life and die—
when he leads his black soldiers to death,
he cannot bend his back.
1964 'For The Union Dead'. 'He' refers to Colonel Shaw, the white commander of the black regiment commemorated in the monument.

3 The man is killing time—there's nothing else.
1964 'The Drinker'.

4 But I suppose even God was born
too late to trust the old religion—
all those settings out
that never left the ground,
beginning in wisdom, dying in doubt.
1964 'Tenth Muse'.

5 The elect, the elected…they come here bright as
dimes,
and die dishevelled and soft.
1964 'July in Washington'.

6 Yours the lawlessness
of something simple that has lost its law.
1964 'Caligula'.

7 O that the spirit could remain
tinged but untarnished by its strain!
1967 'Waking Early Sunday Morning'.

8 Pity the planet, all joy gone
from this sweet volcanic cone
1967 'Waking Early Sunday Morning'.

9 Life is too short to silver over this tarnish.
The gods, employed to haunt and punish
husbands,
have no hand for trigger-fine distinctions,
their myopia makes all error mortal.
1968 'New Year's Eve'.

10 My Darling, prickly hedgehog of the heart,
chocolates, cherries, hairshirts, pinks and glass—
when we joined in the sublime blindness of
courtship
loving lost all its vice with half its virtue.
1968 'New Year's Eve'.

11 Age is our reconciliation with dullness.
1973 'Last Summer at Milgate'.

12 We feel the machine slipping from our hands
As if someone else were steering;
If we see the light at the end of the tunnel,
It's the light of the oncoming train.
1977 *Day by Day*, 'Since 1939'.

13 Those blessed structures, plot and rhyme —
why are they no help to me now
I want to make
something imagined, not recalled?
1977 *Day by Day*, 'Epilogue'.

14 Pray for the grace of accuracy
Vermeer gave to the sun's illumination
stealing like the tide across a map
to his girl solid with yearning.
1977 *Day by Day*, 'Epilogue'.

Lowenthal, Leo 1900–
German-born US sociologist.

15 We call the heroes of the past heroes of production.
We feel entitled to call the present day magazine
heroes 'idols of consumption'. Indeed, almost every
one of them is directly, or indirectly, related to the
sphere of leisure time.
1944 'The Triumph of Mass Idols', collected in *Literature and Mass Culture* (1984).

Lowndes, William 1652–1724
English politician.

16 Take care of the pence, and the pounds will take
care of themselves.
Quoted by Lord Chesterfield in a letter to his son, 5 Feb 1750. In an earlier letter, 6 Nov 1747, he refers to the same adage in the form '*for* the pounds'.

Lowry, (Clarence) Malcolm 1909–57
English novelist. He went to sea as a young man and lived in Mexico and Vancouver. He is best known for his novel, *Under the Volcano* (1947), one of the great 20c

explorations of alcoholism. He died after choking in his sleep.

17 Nothing in the world was more terrible than an empty bottle! Unless it was an empty glass.
   1947 *Under the Volcano*, ch.3.

18 Where are the children I might have had?… Drowned to the accompaniment of the rattling of a thousand douche bags.
   1947 *Under the Volcano*, ch.10.

19 How alike are the groans of love to those of the dying.
   1947 *Under the Volcano*, ch.12.

20 Dark as the Grave Wherein my Friend is Laid.
   Title of novel, published posthumously (1968).

Lucan full name *Marcus Annaeus Lucanus*
AD39–65

Latin poet, born in Spain, nephew of the philosopher Seneca. A favourite at the court of Nero, he lost imperial favour and in 65 joined Piso's conspiracy against Nero, but was betrayed and compelled to commit suicide. His epic poem *Bellum Civile* (or *Pharsalia*) deals with the civil war between Caesar and Pompey.

21 *Victrix causa deis placuit, sed victa Catoni.*

   A victorious case pleased the gods, but a lost one Cato.
   Pharsalia, bk.1, 1.126.

22 *Stat magni nominis umbra.*

   There stands the shade of a great name.
   Of Pompey. *Pharsalia*, bk.1, 1.135.

23 *Coniunx est mihi, sunt nati: didimus tot pignora fatis.*

   I have a wife, I have sons: we have given so many hostages to the fates.
   Pharsalia, bk.6, 1.661–2.
   ▷ See Bacon 57:56.

Lucas, E(dward) V(errell) 1868–1938

English essayist and biographer. He was Assistant Editor of *Punch*, and wrote novels and travel books.

24 I have noticed that people who are late are often so much jollier than the people who have to wait for them.
   1926 *365 Days and One More*.

25 Readers of novels are strange folk, upon whose probable or even possible tastes no wise book-maker would ever venture.
   1932 *Reading, Writing and Remembering*, ch.1.

26 There can be no defence like elaborate courtesy.
   1932 *Reading, Writing and Remembering*, ch.8.

Lucas, F(rank) L(awrence) 1894–1967

English teacher, critic and poet.

27 Unintelligible, the borrowings cheap and the notes useless.
   1923 On T S Eliot's *The Waste Land*, in the *New Statesman and Nation*, Nov.

28 The virtues common to good living and good poetry seem to me not so much matters of what used to be called 'virtue' as, above all, of sane vitality.
   1936 *The Decline and Fall of the Romantic Ideal*, ch.1.

29 Human temperaments are too diverse; we can never agree how drunk we like our art to be.
   1951 *Literature and Psychology*, ch.10.

30 Every author's fairy godmother should provide him not only with a pen but also with a blue pencil.
   1955 *Style*, introduction.

Lucas, George 1944–

US director and screenwriter, best known for his trilogy *Star Wars* (1977), *The Empire Strikes Back* (1980) and *Return of the Jedi* (1983), and for *Raiders of the Lost Ark* (1981).

31 May the Force be with you.
   1977 Line delivered by Alec Guinness as Obi-Wan Kenobi in *Star Wars*.

32 Art is the retelling of certain themes in a new light, making them accessible to the public of the moment.
   1988 In the *New York Times*, 9 Jun.

Luce, Clare Booth 1903–87

US writer, socialite and wit, Associate Editor of *Vogue* (1930), US Ambassador to Italy (1953–7) and author of several Broadway successes including *Kiss the Boys Goodbye* (1938).

33 Communism is the opiate of the intellectuals, with no cure except as a guillotine might be called a cure for dandruff.
   1955 In *Newsweek*, 24 Jan.

Lucretius full name *Titus Lucretius Carus*
98–c.55 BC

Roman poet and philosopher, author of *De Rerum Natura*, a hexameter poem in six books expounding the physical system of Epicurus, in which release from fear, and the mortality of the soul, are central concerns.

34 *Nil posse creari*
   De nilo.

   Nothing can be created from nothing.

De Rerum Natura, bk.1, line 155.

35 *Suave, mari magno turbantibus aequora ventis,*
   E terra magnum alterius spectare laborem;
   Non quia vexari quemquamst iucunda voluptas,
   Sed quibus ipse malis careas quia cernere suave est.
   Suave etiam belli certamina magna tueri
   Per campos instructa tua sine parte pericli.
   Sed nil dulcius est, bene quam munita tenere
   Edita doctrina sapientum templa serena,
   Despicere unde queas alios passimque videre
   Errare atque viam palantis quaerere vitae,
   Certare ingenio, contendere nobilitate,
   Noctes atque dies niti praestante labore
   Ad summas emergere opes rerumque potiri.

What joy it is, when out at sea the stormwinds are lashing the waters, to gaze from the shore at the heavy stress some other man is enduring. Not that anyone's afflictions are in themselves a source of delight; but to realize from what troubles you yourself are free is joy indeed. What joy, again, to watch opposing hosts marshalled on the field of battle when you have yourself no part in their peril! But this is the greatest joy of all: to possess a quiet sancturay, stoutly fortified by the teaching of the wise, and to gaze down from that elevation on others wandering aimlessly in search of a way of life, pitting their wits one against another, disputing for precedence, struggling night and day with unstinted effort to scale the pinnacles of wealth and power.
De Rerum Natura, bk.2, lines 1–13 (translated by R. E. Latham).

36 *Vitaque mancipio, nulli datur, omnibus usu.*

To none is life given in freehold; to all on lease.
De Rerum Natura, bk.3, line 971 (translated by R. E. Latham).

37 *Ut quod ali cibus est aliis fuat acre venenum.*

What is food to one may be literally poison to others.
De Rerum Natura, bk.4, line 637 (translated by R. E. Latham).

Lugones, Leopoldo 1874–1938

Argentinian poet and critic. As a socialist journalist, he joined the *Modernista* group, later becoming a conservative nationalist and, in 1929, a Fascist.

38 *Si tengo la fortuna*
   de que con tu alma mi dolor se integre,
   te diré entre melancólico y alegre
   las singulares cosas de la luna.

If I am fortunate enough
for your soul to mix with my sorrow,
I will tell you, half with melancoly, half with
  gladness,
Unique things about the moon.
1909 *Lunario sentimental*, 'Divagación lunar' ('Lunar digression').

Lukács, Georg 1885–1971

Hungarian-born Marxist scholar, philosopher and aesthetician.

39 Nature is a social category.
   1923 *History and Class Consciousness.*

Lumière, Auguste Marie Louis Nicolas 1862–1954

French film pioneer, brother of Louis Lumière. The brothers owned a factory in Lyons where photographic products were made. They invented the first successful cine camera and projector and presented their film of workers leaving the Lumière factory in 1895.

40 *Mon frère, en une nuit, avait inventé le*
   cinématographe.

   My brother, in one night, had invented the cinema.
   Of the night his brother Louis had a flash of inspiration which resulted in the 'Kinetoscope de projection' patented in 1895. Quoted in C W Ceram *Archaeology of the Cinema* (1965).

Lurie, Alison 1926–

US novelist and academic. She has written a number of acutely observed novels, often with academic settings, as well as non-fiction and children's literature.

41 That is the worst thing about being a middle-class woman…you have more knowledge of yourself and the world: you are equipped to make choices, but there are none left to make.
   1974 *The War Between The Tates*, ch.3.

42 Fashion is free speech, and one of the privileges, if not always one of the pleasures, of a free world.
   1981 *The Language of Clothes.*

43 The most desirable mental state for a potential consumer…is a kind of free-floating anxiety and depression, combined with a nice collection of unrealistic goals and desires.
   1983 Of advertising. In the *New York Review of Books*, 2 Jun.

Luther, Martin 1483–1546

German theologian. Originally an Augustinian monk, he became the leader of Protestant Reformation in Europe. When he publicly burned the Papal Bull against him he was summoned before the Diet at Worms and banned. His followers later founded the Lutheran Church.

44 *Hier stehe ich. Ich kann nicht anders. Gott helfe mir.*
   Amen.

   Here I stand; I can do no other; God help me;
   Amen.
   1521 Speech in defence of his doctrines at the Diet of Worms, 18 Apr. The Diet subsequently denounced his ideas as heretical.

45 I cannot and will not recant anything, for to go against conscience is neither right nor safe.
   1521 Speech in defence of his doctrines at the Diet of Worms, 18 Apr.

46 *Esto peccator et pecca fortiter, sed fortius fide et gaude in Christo.*

Be a sinner and sin boldly, but more boldly believe and rejoice in Christ.
1521 Letter to Melanchthon.

47 *Wenn ich gewußt hätte, daß so viel Teufel auf mich gezielet hätten, als Ziegel auf den Dächern waren zu Worms, wäre ich dennoch eingeritten.*

I would have gone into Worms though there were as many devils as tiles on the roof.
1524 Letter to Frederick, Elector of Saxony, 21 Aug.

48 It is better that all of these peasants should be killed rather than that the sovereigns and magistrates should be destroyed, because the peasants take up the sword without God's authority.
1525 Letter to Nicholas von Ansdorf, 30 May.

49 *Ein' feste Burg ist unser Gott,*
Ein' gute Wehr und Waffen.

A safe stronghold our God is still,
A trusty shield and weapon.
1529 *Ein' feste Burg ist unser Gott* (translated by Thomas Carlyle).

50 *Wo rauff du nu…dein Hertz engest und verleßest, das ist eygentlich dein Gott.*

Whatever your heart clings to and confides in, that is really your God.
1529 *Large Catechism*, 'The First Commandment'.

51 Rough, boisterous, stormy and altogether warlike, I am born to fight against innumerable monsters and devils.
Quoted in Vincent Cronin *The Flowering of the Renaissance* (1969).

52 *Wer nicht liebt Wein, Weib und Gesang,*
Der bleibt ein Narr sein Leben lang.

Who loves not woman, wine and song
Remains a fool his whole life long.
Attributed. This was inscribed in the Luther room at Wartburg, but is probably apocryphal.

Lydgate, John c.1370–c.1451

English poet and Benedictine monk, who travelled widely in Europe. In 1423 he became Prior of the monastery of Hatfield Broadoak. His many works include *The Siege of Thebes* and *The Fall of Princes*.

53 Off our language he was the lodesterre.
1431–8 Of Chaucer. *The Fall of Princes*, prologue, l.252.

54 Lat no man booste of conning nor vertu,
Of tresour, richesse, nor of sapience,
Of worldly support, for all cometh of Jesu.

c.1450 'Lat no man booste', l.1–3.

55 Woord is but wynd; leff woord and tak the dede.
Secrets of Old Philosophers, l.224.

Lyly, John c.1554–1606

English writer and dramatist. He published his prose romance *Euphues, or the Anatomy of Wit* in 1578, and wrote eight plays between 1584 and 1590, including *Endymion, or The Man in the Moon* (1588).

56 Be valiant, but not too venturous. Let thy attire be comely, but not costly.
1578 *Euphues, or the Anatomy of Wit.*

57 What bird so sings, yet so does wail?
O 'tis the ravished nightingale.
Jug, jug, jug, jug, tereu, she cries,
And still her woes at midnight rise.
1584 *Campaspe*, act 5, sc.1.

58 How at heaven's gates she claps her wings,
The morn not waking till she sings.
1584 Of the lark. *Campaspe*, act 5, sc.1.

59 A heat full of coldness, a sweet full of bitterness, a pain full of pleasantness, which maketh thoughts have eyes and hearts ears, bred by desire, nursed by delight, weaned by jealousy, killed by dissembling, buried by ingratitude, and this is love. Fair lady, will you any?
1588 *Gallathea*, act 1, sc.2. The passage gently satirizes the conventions of love sonnets, and is characterized by the yoked opposites called Euphuisms, after Lyly's earlier work, a style later used by the metaphysical poets.

60 If love be a god, why should not lovers be virtuous?
1588 *Gallathea*, act 3, sc.1.

61 Yield, ladies, yield to love, ladies, which lurketh under your eyelids whilst you sleep and playeth with your heartstrings whilst you wake, whose sweetness never breedeth satiety, labour weariness, nor grief bitterness.
1588 *Gallathea*, epilogue.

62 Night hath a thousand eyes.
1600 *The Maydes Metamorphosis*, act 3, sc.1.
▷ See Bourdillon, F W 181:48.

Lynd, Robert 1879–1949

Irish essayist and critic, literary editor of the *Daily News* and a contributor to the *New Statesman* (1913–45). His essay collections include *The Art of Letters* (1920), *The Blue Lion* (1923) and *In Defence of Pink* (1939).

63 It may be that all games are silly. But then, so are humans.
Quoted in Colin Jarman *The Guinness Dictionary of Sports Quotations* (1990).

64 It is almost impossible to remember how tragic a place this world is when one is playing golf.
Attributed.

Lyndon, Neil 1946–

British journalist and writer. His critique of feminism, *No More Sex War: The Failures of Feminism*, was published in 1992.

65 The cardinal tenets of feminism divided my generation, effectively disempowering and disenfranchising its members. It does make me bitterly angry that my generation, which prided itself so complacently on its soul, on its powers of intelligence and analysis, should have fallen so cloddishly for totalitarian simplicities which declared a war of eternal opposition between men and women.
1992 *No More Sex War: The Failures of Feminism*.

Lyte, Henry Francis 1793–1847

Scottish hymn writer, curate of Lower Brixham, Devon, from 1823.

66 Praise, my soul, the King of Heaven;
To his feet thy tribute bring.
Ransomed, healed, restored, forgiven,
Who like me his praise should sing?
1834 'Praise, my Soul, the King of Heaven'.

67 Abide with me; fast falls the eventide;
The darkness deepens; Lord, with me abide;
When other helpers fail and comforts flee,
Help of the helpless, O, abide with me.
1847 *Remains*, 'Abide with Me' (published 1850).

Lyttelton, Humphrey Richard Adeane 1921–

English jazz trumpeter and band-leader. An Old Etonian and former Guardsman, he is the *doyen* of the English jazz scene, both as a musician and as a writer and broadcaster.

68 It is this tendency to play with manic enthusiasm on every possible occasion that distinguishes the amateur jazz musician from the professional, often to the public detriment of the latter, who are regarded as snooty and unfriendly.
1984 *Why No Beethoven?*, ch.1.

MacArthur, Douglas 1880–1964

US soldier. He commanded troops in the Far East (1941) in World War II, directed the recapture of the SW Pacific (1942–5), formally accepted Japan's surrender, and commanded its occupation (1945–51). He led the UN forces in the Korean War, but was relieved of command when he tried to continue the war against China.

69 I came through and I shall return.

1942 On reaching Australia, having broken through Japanese lines en route from Corregidor, 20 Mar. Reported in the *New York Times*, 21 Mar.

70 There lies the Holy Grail.
1943 Remark, 6 May, one year after the fall of Corregidor to the Japanese, recalled in *A Soldier Speaks*.

71 A great tragedy has ended. A great victory has been won. A new era is upon us ... We have had our last chance. If we do not devise some greater and more equitable system, Armageddon will be at our door.
1945 National radio broadcast on the surrender of Japan, 2 Sep.

72 An unsinkable air-craft carrier.
1950 Of Taiwan's military significance for the US. Remark, 27 Aug, recalled in *A Soldier Speaks*.

73 In war, indeed, there can be no substitute for victory.
1951 Address to Congress, 19 Apr. In the *Congressional Record*, vol.97, pt.3, p.4125.

74 The world has turned over many times since I took the oath on the plain at West Point…but I still remember the refrain of one of the most popular ballads of that day which proclaimed most proudly that old soldiers never die; they just fade away.
1951 Address to Congress after being relieved of his duty by President Truman.

75 I now close my military career and just fade away, an old soldier who tried to do his duty as God gave him the light to see that duty.
1951 Address to Congress after being relieved of his duty by President Truman, 19 Apr.

76 It isn't just dust that is settling in Korea, Senator, it is American blood.
1951 During the Senate inquiry on MacArthur's dismissal. Reported in the *New York Times*, 2 May.

77 He'll make a fine president. He was the best clerk who ever served under me.
1952 On Dwight D Eisenhower's election as President. In news summaries, 31 Dec.

78 The chickens are coming home to roost, and you happen to have just moved into the chicken house.
Comment to John F Kennedy on the presidential crisis. Kennedy enjoyed the remark and often quoted it. Quoted in Theodore C Sorensen *Kennedy* (1965).

MacArthur, James

Only son of Helen Hayes.

79 What a wonderful sight, a full house—my mother would have loved it!
1993 Speaking at the memorial service at New York's Shubert's Theater for his mother, Helen Hayes. Reported in the *New York Times*, 19 Jun.

Macaulay, Dame (Emilie) Rose   1881–1958

English novelist and travel writer whose book, *The Pleasure of Ruins* (1953), includes an account of her visit to Cambodia and the ruins of Angkor.

80   You should always believe all you read in newspapers, as this makes them more interesting.
     1925   *A Casual Commentary*, 'Problems of a Reader's Life'.

81   My point of view has sadly changed. For now, should all the books in the world be laid before me, my problem would be how many of them I could avoid. Most books are like that.
     1925   *A Casual Commentary*, 'Problems of a Reader's Life'.

82   Here is one of the points about this planet which should be remembered; into every penetrable corner of it, and into most of the impenetrable corners, the English will penetrate.
     1926   *Crewe Train*, pt.1, ch.1.

83   Gentlemen know that fresh air should be kept in its proper place—out of doors—and that, God having given us indoors and out-of-doors, we should not attempt to do away with that distinction.
     1926   *Crewe Train*, pt.1, ch.5.

84   All is now desolate, fantastic, and ambushed with ghosts; the archaeologists twitter among them like bats.
     1953   Of Angkor Thom. *Pleasure of Ruins*.

85   'Take my camel, dear,' said my aunt Dot, as she climbed down from this animal on her return from High Mass.
     1956   *The Towers of Trebizond*, ch.1.

Macaulay (of Rothley), Thomas Babington Macaulay, 1st Baron   1800–59

English essayist and historian, an MP from 1830 and a skilful orator in the Reform Bill debates. He wrote the highly popular *Lays of Ancient Rome* (1842) and contributed to the *Edinburgh Review*, but his major work was the *History of England from the Accession of James II* (1848–61, fifth volume unfinished).

86   Then, beneath the nine-tailed cat
     Shall they who use it writhe, sir;
     And curates lean, and rectors fat,
     Shall dig the ground they tithe, sir.
     Down with your Bayleys, and your Bests,
     Your Giffords, and your Gurneys;
     We'll clear the island of the pests,
     Which mortals name attorneys.
     1820   'A Radical War Song', stanza 8. The names are those of lawyers and judges who figured in the trial of the Cato Street conspirators.

87   Free trade, one of the greatest blessings which a government can confer on a people, is in almost every country unpopular.

     1824   'Essay on Mitford's *History of Greece*', collected in *Works* (published 1906), vol.7, p.688–9.

88   The men of our time are not to be converted or perverted by quartos.
     1825   'Milton', in the *Edinburgh Review*, Aug.

89   Perhaps no person can be a poet, or can even enjoy poetry, without a certain unsoundness of mind.
     1825   'Milton', in the *Edinburgh Review*, Aug.

90   There is only one cure for the evils which newly aquired freedom produces; and that is freedom…The blaze of truth and liberty may at first dazzle and bewilder nations which have become half blind in the house of bondage. But let them gaze on, and they will soon be able to bear it.
     1825   'Milton', in the *Edinburgh Review*, Aug.

91   Many politicians of our time are in the habit of laying it down as a self-evident proposition, that no people ought to be free till they are fit to use their freedom. The maxim is worthy of the fool in the old story, who resolved not to go into the water till he had learnt to swim. If men are to wait for liberty till they become wise and good in slavery, they may indeed wait for ever.
     1825   'Milton', in the *Edinburgh Review*, Aug.

92   Every man who has seen the world knows that nothing is so useless as a general maxim.
     1827   'Machiavelli', in the *Edinburgh Review*, Mar.

93   It has lately been brought to my knowledge
     That the Ministers fully design
     To supress each cathedral and college,
     And eject every learned divine.
     To assist this detestable scheme
     Three nuncios from Rome are come over;
     They left Calais on Monday by steam,
     And landed to dinner at Dover.
     1827   'The Country Clergyman's Trip to Cambridge', stanza 2. A satirical poem against the opposition to Catholic emancipation.

94   Knowledge advances by steps, and not by leaps.
     1828   'History' in the *Edinburgh Review*, May

95   History, at least in its ideal state of perfection, is a compound of poetry and philosophy.
     1828   'Hallam's *Constitutional History*' in the *Edinburgh Review*, Sep.

96   We know of no spectacle so ridiculous as the British public in one of its periodical fits of morality.
     1828   In the *Edinburgh Review*.

97   The gallery in which the reporters sit has become a fourth estate of the realm.
     1828   'Hallam's *Constitutional History*' in the *Edinburgh Review*, Sep.
     ▷ See Hazlitt 463:11.

98 His writing bears the same relation to poetry which a Turkey carpet bears to a picture.

1830 'Robert Montgomery', in the *Edinburgh Review*, Apr.

99 Mr Robert Montgomery's genius [is] far too free and aspiring to be shackled by the rules of syntax...[His] readers must take such grammar as they can get and be thankful.

1830 'Robert Montgomery', in the *Edinburgh Review*, Apr.

2 From the poetry of Lord Byron they drew a system of ethics, compounded of misanthropy and voluptuousness, a system in which the two great commandments were, to hate your neighbour, and to love your neighbour's wife.

1831 Of the young Byron enthusiasts who emulated and hero-worshipped him. 'Moore's *Life of Lord Byron*', in the *Edinburgh Review*, Jun.

3 Many of the greatest men that ever lived have written biography. Boswell was one of the smallest men that ever lived and he has beaten them all.

1831 'Croker's new edition of *The Life of Samuel Johnson*', in the *Edinburgh Review*, Sep.

4 In the foreground is that strange figure which is as familiar to us as the figures of those among whom we have been brought up, the gigantic body, the huge massy face, seamed with the scars of disease, the brown coat, the black worsted stockings, the grey wig with the scorched foretop, the dirty hands, the nails bitten and pared to the quick.

1831 Of Dr Samuel Johnson. 'Croker's new edition of *The Life of Samuel Johnson*', in the *Edinburgh Review*, Sep.

5 Dark and terrible beyond any season within my remembrance of political affairs was the day of their flight. Far darker and more terrible will be the day of their return.

1831 On the defeat of the Tory Government, House of Commons, 20 Sep.

6 He [John Hampden] knew that the essence of war is violence, and that moderation in war is imbecility.

1831 'Lord Nugent's *Memorials of Hampden*', in the *Edinburgh Review*, Dec.

7 It is not easy to make a simile go on all fours.

1831 Of the task of the allegorist. 'Robert Southey's edition of Bunyan's Pilgrims Progress', in the *Edinburgh Review*, Dec.

8 A broken head in Cold Bath Fields produces a greater sensation among us than three pitched battles in India.

1833 House of Commons, 20 Sep.

9 There was a time when the most powerful of human intellects were deluded by the gibberish of the astrologer and the alchemist...But time advances; facts accumulate; doubts arise... The highest intellects, like the tops of mountains, are the first to catch and to reflect the dawn.

1835 'Sir James Mackintosh's *History of the Revolution in England, in 1688*' in the *Edinburgh Review*, Jul.

10 The history of England is emphatically the history of progress.

1835 'Sir James Mackintosh's *History of the Revolution in England, in 1688*' in the *Edinburgh Review*, Jul.

11 But even Archimedes was not free from the prevailing notion that geometry was degraded by being employed to produce anything useful. It was with difficulty that he was induced to stoop from speculation to practice. He was half ashamed of those inventions which were the wonder of hostile nations, and always spoke of them slightingly as mere amusements, as trifles in which a mathematician might be suffered to relax his mind after intense application to the higher parts of his science.

1837 'Basil Montagu's edition of *The Works of Francis Bacon, Lord Chancellor of England*', in the *Edinburgh Review*, Jul.

12 Lars Porsena of Clusium
By the nine gods he swore
That the great house of Tarquin
Should suffer wrong no more.

1842 *Lays of Ancient Rome*, 'Horatius', stanza 1.

13 Then out spake brave Horatius,
The Captain of the Gate:
'To every man upon this earth
Death cometh soon or late.
And how can man die better
Than facing fearful odds,
For the ashes of his fathers
And the temples of his God?'

1842 *Lays of Ancient Rome*, 'Horatius', stanza 27.

14 'Now who will stand on either hand,
And keep the bridge with me?'

1842 *Lays of Ancient Rome*, 'Horatius', stanza 29.

15 Was none who would be foremost
To lead such dire attack;
But those before cried 'Forward!'
And those before cried 'Back!'

1842 *Lays of Ancient Rome*, 'Horatius', stanza 50.

16 Alone stood brave Horatius,
But constant still in mind;
Thrice thirty thousand foes before,
And the broad flood behind.

1842 *Lays of Ancient Rome*, 'Horatius', stanza 57.

17 And even the ranks of Tuscany
Could scarce forbear to cheer.
1842 *Lays of Ancient Rome*, 'Horatius', stanza 60.

18 With weeping and with laughter
Still is the story told,
How well Horatius kept the bridge
In the brave days of old.
1842 *Lays of Ancient Rome*, 'Horatius', stanza 70.

19 The rugged miners poured to war from Medip's
sunless caves.
1842 'The Armada', in the *Quarterly Magazine*.

20 And broader still became the blaze, and louder still
the din,
And fast from every village round the horse came
spurring in.
1842 'The Armada', in the *Quarterly Magazine*.

21 We hardly know any instance of the strength and
weakness of human nature so striking, and so
grotesque, as the character of this haughty, vigilant,
resolute, sagacious blue-stocking—half Mithridates
and half Trissotin, bearing up against a world in
arms, with an ounce of poison in one pocket, and a
quire of bad verses in the other.
1843 Of Frederick the Great. *Historical Essays*. 'Frederic the
Great', in the *Edinburgh Magazine*, April.

22 I hardly know which is the greater pest to society: a
paternal Government; that is to say, a prying
meddlesome Government, which intrudes itself
into every part of human life and which thinks that
it can do everything for everybody better than
anyone can do for himself, or a careless, lounging
Government, which suffers grievances, such as it
could at once remove, to grow and multiply, and
which to all complaint and remonstrance has only
one answer, 'We must let things take their course,
we must let things find their own level.'
1846 House of Commons, 22 May.

23 Persecution produced its natural effect on them. It
found them a sect; it made them a faction.
1846 On the Puritans, House of Commons, 22 May.

24 The history of England is emphatically the history
of progress.
1846 House of Commons, 22 May

25 Forget all feuds, and shed one English tear
O'er English dust. A broken heart lies here.
'A Jacobite's Epitaph', closing lines.

26 Thus our democracy was, from an early period, the
most aristocratic, and our aristocracy the most
democratic in the world.
1848 *History of England*, Vol.1, ch.1.

27 The Puritan hated bear-baiting, not because it gave
pain to the bear, but because it gave pleasure to the
spectators.
1849 *History of England*, vol.1, ch.2.

28 The Mountjoy began to move, and soon passed
safe through the broken stakes and floating spars.
But her brave master was no more. A shot from one
of the batteries had struck him; and he died by the
most enviable of all deaths, in sight of the city
which was his birthplace, which was his home, and
which had just been saved by his courage and
selfdevotion from the most frightful form of
destruction.
1849 *History of England*, on the relief of Londonderry.

McAuliffe, Anthony 1898–1975

US soldier, a general in World War II.

29 Nuts!
1944 Replying to the German demand for surrender at
Bastogne, Belgium, 23 Dec. His response was reported in this
form in the *New York Times*, 28 Dec; the original may have been
more explicit.

MacBeth, George Mann 1932–92

Scottish writer. He is best known as a poet, but also wrote
novels and children's books.

30 To leave great themes unfinished is
Perhaps the most satisfying exercise
Of power.
1963 'The Spider's Nest'.

31 No one can read a poem unless he realises that it is
a physical object as well as an abstract vehicle for
conveying ideas. A poem has a material existence
like a piece of music or sculpture or a plate of meat.
1967 Introduction to *Poetry 1900 to 1965*.

32 Heap high the
groaning platter with pink fillets, sucking pig and
thick gammon, celestial chef. Be generous with the
crackling. Let your hand slip with the gravy trough,
dispensing plenty.
1977 'An Ode to English Food'.

MacCaig, Norman Alexander 1910–96

Scottish poet. He was a school-teacher for much of his
working life. He was one of Scotland's most distinguished
poets.

33 A man's boots with a woman in them
Clatter across the floor.
1960 'Crofter's Kitchen, Evening'.

34 The stone remains, and the cross, to let us know
Their unjust, hard demands, as symbols do.
1960 'Celtic Cross'.

35 A cubic inch of some stars
   weighs a hundred tons—Blue tit,
   who could measure the power
   of your tiny spark of energy?
   1980 'Blue Tit on a String of Peanuts'.

McCann, M J

36 Proudly the note of the trumpet is sounding,
   Loudly the war-cries arise on the gale,
   Fleetly the steed by Loc Suilig is bounding
   To join the thick squadrons in Saimear's green vale.
   On, every mountaineer,
   Strangers to flight and fear:
   Rush to the standard of dauntless Red Hugh!
   Bonnought and gallowglass,
   Throng from each mountain-pass!
   On for old Erin—O'Donnell abu!
   1845 *The Spirit of the Nation*, 'O'Donnell Abu'.

37 Wildly o'er Desmond the war-wolf is howling,
   Fearless the eagle sweeps over the plain,
   The fox in the streets of the city is prowling —
   All, all who would scare them are banished or slain!
   1845 *The Spirit of the Nation*, 'O'Donnell Abu'.

McCarthy, Eugene J(oseph) 1916–

US Democratic politician, Senator from Minnesota
(1958–70). An opponent of the Vietnam War, in 1968 he
challenged President Johnson for nomination but the bid
failed and he left politics to devote himself to teaching
and writing.

38 The war in Vietnam…[is] of questionable loyalty
   and constitutionality…diplomatically
   indefensible…morally wrong.
   1967 Speech to the Conference of Concerned Democrats, 2
   Dec, an address noted for crystallizing dissent against the
   Vietnam War.

39 The message from the administration today is a
   message of fear—even a message of fear of fear.
   1967 Speech to the Conference of Concerned Democrats, 2
   Dec.

40 Let us pick up again these lost strands and weave
   them again into the fabric of America…sort out
   the music from the sounds and again respond to
   the trumpet and the steady drum.
   1967 Speech to Conference of Concerned Democrats, 2 Dec.

41 Being in politics is like being a football coach. You
   have to be smart enough to know the game and
   stupid enough to think it is important.
   1991 In the *Los Angeles Times*, 7 Dec.

McCarthy, Joseph R(aymond) 1909–57

US Republican politician and inquisitor. As Chairman of
the Permanent Subcommittee on Investigations from
1953, he used hectoring cross-examination and innuendo
to arraign many often innocent citizens for communist
sympathies.

42 While I cannot take time off to name all the men in
   the State Department who have been named as
   members of the Communist Party and members of
   a spy ring, I have here in my hand a list of 205 that
   were known to the Secretary of State as being
   members of the Communist Party, and who
   nevertheless are still working and shaping the
   policy of the State Department.
   1950 Speech at Wheeling, West Virginia, 9 Feb, which marked
   the beginning of the McCarthy 'witch hunts' for communists.

43 McCarthyism is Americanism with its sleeves
   rolled.
   1952 Re-election campaign slogan.

McCarthy, Mary Thérèse 1912–89

US writer, critic and social commentator. She is best
known for her novel *The Group* (1963).

44 When an American heiress wants to buy a man, she
   at once crosses the Atlantic. The only really
   materialistic people I have ever met have been
   Europeans.
   1947 'America the Beautiful', in *Commentary*, Sep.

45 The American character looks always as if it just
   had a rather bad haircut, which gives it, in our eyes
   at any rate, a greater humanity than the European,
   which even among its beggars has an all too
   professional air.
   1947 'America the Beautiful', in *Commentary*, Sep.

46 American life, in large cities, is a perpetual assault
   on the senses and the nerves; it is out of asceticism,
   out of unworldliness, precisely, that we bear it.
   1947 'America the Beautiful', in *Commentary*, Sep.

47 The happy ending is our national belief.
   1947 'America the Beautiful', in *Commentary*, Sep.

48 Liberty, as it is conceived by current opinion, has
   nothing inherent about it; it is a sort of gift or trust
   bestowed on the individual by the state pending
   good behavior.
   1952 Speech. Collected as 'The Contagion of Ideas', in *On the
   Contrary* (1961).

49 Every age has a keyhole to which its eye is pasted.
   1953 'My Confession'. Collected in *On the Contrary* (1961).

50 In the unreal realms of the canals, as in a Swiftian
   Lilliput, the real world, with its contrivances,
   appears as a vast folly.
   1956 Of Venice. *Venice Observed*, ch.1.

51 To care for the quarrels of the past, to identify
   oneself passionately with a cause that became,

politically speaking, a losing cause with the birth of the modern world, is to experience a kind of straining against reality, a rebellious nonconformity that, again, is rare in America, where children are instructed in the virtues of the system they live under, as though history had achieved a happy ending in American civics.
1957 Of Catholicism. *Memories of a Catholic Girlhood*, 'To the Reader'.

52 Bureaucracy, the rule of no one, has become the modern form of despotism.
1958 'Vita Activa', in the *New Yorker*, 18 Oct.

53 There are no new truths, but only truths that have not been recognized by those who have perceived them without noticing.
1958 'Vita Activa', in the *New Yorker*, 18 Oct.

54 The labor of keeping house is labor in its most naked state, for labor is toil that never finishes, toil that has to be begun again the moment it is completed, toil that is destroyed and consumed by the life process.
1958 'Vita Activa', in the *New Yorker*, 18 Oct.

55 In violence, we forget who we are.
1961 *On the Contrary*, 'Characters in Fiction'.

56 An interviewer asked me what book I thought best represented the modern American woman. All I could think of to answer was: *Madame Bovary*.
1961 *On the Contrary*, 'Characters in Fiction'.

57 Being abroad makes you conscious of the whole imitative side of human behavior. The ape in man.
1965 *Birds of America*, 'Epistle from Mother Carey's Chicken'.

58 In politics, it seems, retreat is honorable if dictated by military considerations and shameful if even *suggested* for ethical reasons.
1967 *Vietnam*, 'Solutions'.

59 I once said in an interview that every word she writes is a lie, including 'and' and 'the'.
1980 In response to Lillian Hellman's memoir, *Scoundrel Time*, in the *New York Times*, 16 Feb.

McCartney, Sir (James) Paul 1942–

British rock singer, musician and song-writer. With fellow-Beatle John Lennon, he formed the most successful song-writing team of the 1960s.

60 Pop music is the classical music of now.
Quoted in Tony Palmer *All You Need Is Love* (1976).
▷ See also Lennon, John Winston 596:55.

McClellan, George Brinton 1826–85

Union general in the American Civil War, given command of troops in and around Washington after the

Battle of Bull Run in 1861. He ran unsuccessfully for election against Abraham Lincoln and resigned from the army in 1864.

61 All quiet along the Potomac.
1862 Attributed.

MacColl, Ewan James Miller 1915–89

English folksinger, composer, collector, author, playwright and socialist, whose work was an important influence on the Scottish and worldwide folk music revivals of the 1950s and 1960s.

62 The first time ever I saw your face
I thought the sun rose in your eyes,
And the moon and the stars were the gifts you gave
To the dark and the empty skies.
1962 'The First Time Ever I Saw Your Face', stanza 1.

McCoy, John B(onnet) 1943–

US banker. He joined Banc One in 1970, becoming president (1977–83) and chairman from 1987.

63 I was trying to make it as friendly as you can made an unfriendly offer.
1995 On his unsolicited $5-billion bid in unsuccessful attempt to acquire the Bank of Boston. In *Fortune*, 21 Aug.

McCrae, John 1872–1915

Canadian soldier, physician, and poet, First Brigade surgeon in the Canadian Field Artillery. His most famous poem, 'In Flanders Fields', was written during the Second Battle of Ypres, Belgium, 3 May 1915.

64 In Flanders fields the poppies blow
Between the crosses, row on row,
That mark our place; and in the sky
The larks, still bravely singing, fly
Scarce heard amid the guns below.
1915 'In Flanders Fields', stanza 1.

McCullers, (Lula) Carson née Smith 1917–67

US writer. Her novels, tragic and often symbolic, have been labelled Southern Gothic. She also wrote a novella, *The Ballad of the Sad Café* (1951) as well as short stories and plays.

65 The Heart Is A Lonely Hunter.
1940 Title of novel.

66 All men are lonely. But sometimes it seems to me that we Americans are the loneliest of all. Our hunger for foreign places and new ways has been with us almost like a national disease.
1940 'Look Homeward, Americans', in *Vogue*, 1 Dec.

67 There's nothing that makes you so aware of the improvisation of human existence as a song unfinished. Or an old address book.
1951 *The Ballad of the Sad Café*, 'The Sojourner'.

68 Nothing is so musical as the sound of pouring
    bourbon for the first drink on a Sunday morning.
    Not Bach or Schubert or any of those masters.
    1953 *Clock Without Hands.*

McCurry, Michael D

Clinton White House Press Secretary.

69 There are people around here who think Hillary
    Clinton is responsible for the weather.
    1995 In the *New York Times*, 7 Jan. New revelations about the
    First Lady's role in Whitewater land sales and the firing of the
    presidential travel office had coincided with a heavy Washington
    snowfall.

MacDiarmid, Hugh pseudonym of
Christopher Murray Grieve 1892–1978

Scottish poet, nationalist and communist, the driving-
force behind the modern Scottish literary Renaissance.
He used complex forms of both Scots and English in his
lyrical, philosophical and polemical verse.

70 I myself believe that we have lost this war—in
    everything but actuality. When I see scores of sheep
    go to a slaughter-house I do not feel constrained to
    admire their resignation.
    1918 Letter to George Ogilvie, 12 Nov.

71 Earth, thou bonnie broukit bairn!
    1925 *Sangschaw*, 'The Bonnie Broukit Bairn'. Broukit =
    neglected.

72 But greet, an' in your tears ye'll droun
    The haill clanjamfrie.
    1925 *Sangschaw*, 'The Bonnie Broukit Bairn'.

73 An' see the deid come loupin' owre
    The auld grey wa's.
    1925 *Sangschaw*, 'Crowdieknowe', stanza 1.

74 I met ayont the cairney
    A lass wi' tousled hair
    Singin' till a bairnie
    That was nae langer there.
    1926 *Penny Wheep*, 'Empty Vessel', stanza 1.

75 No' wan in fifty kens a wurd Burns wrote
    But misapplied is a'body's property
    1926 *A Drunk Man Looks at the Thistle*, l.41–2.

76 I'll hae nae hauf-way hoose, buy aye be whaur
    Extremes meet—it's the only way I ken
    To dodge the curst conceit o' bein' richt
    That damns the vast majority o' men.
    1926 *A Drunk Man Looks at the Thistle*, l.141–4.

77 The thistle yet'll unite
    Man and the Infinite!
    1926 *A Drunk Man Looks at the Thistle*, l.481–2.

78 To be yersel's—and to mak' that worth bein'.

Nae harder job to mortals has been gi'en.
1926 *A Drunk Man Looks at the Thistle*, l.745–6.

79 A'thing that ony man can be's
    A mockery o' his soul at last.
    1926 *A Drunk Man Looks at the Thistle*, l.1415–7.

80 Be like the thistle, O my soul,
    Heedless o' praise and quick to take affront
    1926 *A Drunk Man Looks at the Thistle*, l.1709–10.

81 'Let there be Licht,' said God, and there was
    A little: but He lacked poo'er
    To licht up mair than pairt o' space at aince,
    And there is lots o' darkness that's the same
    As gin He'd never spoken
    1926 *A Drunk Man Looks at the Thistle*, l.2101–5.

82 And Jesus and a nameless ape
    Collide and share the selfsame shape
    That nocht terrestial can escape?
    1926 *A Drunk Man Looks at the Thistle*, l.2476–8.

83 He canna Scotland see wha yet
    Canna see the Infinite,
    And Scotland in true scale to it.
    1926 *A Drunk Man Looks at the Thistle*, l.2527–9.

84 O wha's the bride that cairries the bunch
    O' thistles blinterin' white?
    Her cuckold bridegroom little dreids
    What he sall ken this nicht.
    1926 *A Drunk Man Looks at the Thistle.*

85 The number of people who can copulate properly
    may be few; the number who can write well are
    infinitely fewer.
    1928 Review of D H Lawrence's *Lady Chatterley's Lover* in *The
    New Age*, 27 Sep. This may very well have been the first
    published review of Lawrence's novel.

86 Lourd on my hert as winter lies
    The state that Scotland's in the day.
    Spring to the North has aye come slow
    But noo dour winter's like to stay
    For guid,
    And no' for guid!
    1930 *To Circumjack Cencrastus, or The Curly Snake.*

87 Better a'e gowden lyric
    Than a social problem solved.
    1930 *To Circumjack Cencrastus, or The Curly Snake.*

88 Are my poems spoken in the factories and fields,
    In the streets o' the toon?
    Gin they're no', then I'm failin' to dae
    What I ocht to ha' dune.
    1932 *Second Hymn to Lenin.*

89 Scotland is not wholly surrounded by the sea—
    unfortunately.
    1934 *Scottish Scene*, 'The Sea'.

90 We must reconcile ourselves to the stones,
Not the stones to us.
1934 'On a Raised Beach'.

91 The rose of all the world is not for me.
I want for my part
Only the little white rose of Scotland
That smells sharp and sweet—and breaks the
heart.
1934 *Stony Limits and other poems*, 'The Little White Rose'.

92 My aim all along has been (in Ezra Pound's term)
the most drastic *desuetization* of Scottish life and
letters, and, in particular, the de-Tibetanization of
the Highlands and Islands, and getting rid of the
whole gang of high mucky-mucks, famous
fatheads, old wives of both sexes, stuffed shirts,
hollow men with headpieces stuffed with straw,
bird-wits, lookers-under-beds, trained seals,
creeping Jesuses, Scots Wha Ha'evers, village idiots,
policemen, leaders of white-mouse factions and
noted connoisseurs of bread and butter, glorified
gangsters, and what 'Billy' Phelps calls Medlar
Novelists (the medlar being a fruit that becomes
rotten before it is ripe), Commercial Calvinists,
makers of 'noises like a turnip', and all the touts
and toadies and lickspittles o the English
Ascendancy, and their infernal women-folk, and all
their skunkoil skulduggery.
1943 *Lucky Poet*, ch.3, 'The Kind of Poetry I Want'.

93 We do not like the confiding, the intimate, the
ingratiating, the hail-fellow-well-met, but prefer
the unapproachable, the hard-bitten, the
recalcitrant, the sinister, the malignant, the
saturnine, the cross-grained and the cankered, and
the howling wilderness to the amenities of
civilization, the irascible to the affable, the prickly
to the smooth. We have no damned fellow-feeling
at all.
1952 'The Dour Drinkers of Glasgow', in *The American Mercury*, Mar.

94 So this is what our lives have been given to find,
A language that can serve our purposes,
A marvellous lucidity, a quality of fiery aery light,
Flowing like clear water, flying like a bird
Burning like a sunlit landscape.
1955 'The Task'.

95 My job, as I see it, has never been to lay a tit's egg,
but to erupt like a volcano emitting not only flame
but a lot of rubbish.
1964 Letter to George Bruce, 1 Jul.

96 Scotland small? Our multiform, infinite Scotland
small?
1974 'Direadh'.

McDonald, Alonzo L

US government official and businessman, Chief
Executive Officer of the Bendix Corporation and a former
staff director at the White House.

97 Very few factors help produce economies of scale.
Technology may be one, but not people. When it
comes to motivating people and using their
brainpower, you hit diseconomies of scale early. At
that point, bigger isn't better.
1986 'Of Floating Factories and Mating Dinosaurs', in the
Harvard Business Review, Nov/Dec.

MacDonald, George 1824–1905

Scottish pastor, poet and novelist who wrote fantastical
and allegorical works for both adults and children.

98 Here lie I, Martin Elginbrodde:
Hae mercy o' my soul, Lord God;
As I wad do, were I Lord God,
And ye were Martin Elginbrodde.
1863 *David Elginbrod*, bk.1, ch.13.

99 The love of our neighbour is the only door out of
the dungeon of self, where we mope and mow,
striking sparks, and rubbing phosphorescence out
of the walls, and blowing our own breath in our
own nostrils, instead of issuing to the fair sunlight
of God, the sweet winds of the universe.
1867 *Unspoken Sermons*.

1 Where did you come from, baby dear?
Out of the everywhere into here.
1871 *At the Back of the North Wind*, ch.33, 'Song'.

2 They all were looking for a king
To slay their foes and lift them high:
Thou cam'st, a little baby thing
That made a woman cry.
1883 'That Holy Thing', stanza 1.

3 There is no strength in unbelief. Even the unbelief
of what is false is no source of might. It is the truth
shining from behind that gives the strength to
disbelieve.
The Marquis of Lossie (published 1906).

4 To be trusted is a greater compliment than to be
loved.
The Marquis of Lossie (published 1906).

Macdonald, (James) Ramsay 1866–1937

Scottish politician, Prime Minister and Foreign Secretary
of the first British Labour government (1924, 1929–31).
He met the financial crisis of 1931 by forming a
'National' coalition government, which he led after a
general election (1931–5).

5 The League of Nations grows in moral courage. Its
frown will soon be more dreaded than a nation's

arms, and when that happens, you and I shall have security and peace.

1929 Speech, London, 9 Nov.

6 We hear war called murder. It is not: it is suicide.

1930 Quoted in the *Observer*, 3 May.

MacDonnell, A(rchibald) G(ordon) 1895–1941

Scottish writer who lived most of his life in England, the subject of his best-known satirical novel.

7 England, their England.

1933 Title of novel.

▷ See Henley 472:59.

MacDougall, Ranald 1915–73

US screenwriter whose credits include *The Hasty Heart* (1949), *The Naked Jungle* (1954), *Queen Bee* (1955) and *The Mountain* (1956).

8 Alligators have the right idea, they eat their young.

1945 *Mildred Pierce* (with Catherine Turney).

McElligott, Tom (Thomas James) 1943–

US advertising executive, chairman of McElligott Wright Morrison White (1991–).

9 You're never too bad to win.

1987 In the *Wall Street Journal*, 26 Mar.

McEnroe, John Patrick 1959–

US tennis player. He won four US Open singles titles and three Wimbledon titles. He was known for temperamental behaviour on court.

10 You cannot be serious!

1981 In protest at an umpire's decision at Wimbledon.

11 Being a celebrity is like being raped, and there's absolutely nothing a player can do about it.

Quoted in Colin Jarman *The Guinness Dictionary of Sports Quotations* (1990).

McEwan, Ian Russell 1948–

English writer. He established his reputation with two volumes of short stories before turning to novels. He has also written screenplays.

12 Her eyes, nose, mouth, skin, all might have been designed in committee to meet the barest requirements of feasibility.

1981 *The Comfort of Strangers*, ch.6.

13 Shall there be womanly times? Or shall we die?

1983 Refrain from *Or Shall We Die*, an oratorio.

14 Looking after children is one of the ways of looking after yourself.

1992 *Black Dogs*, preface.

McFadden, Robert Dennis 1937–

US journalist and writer. He has worked for the *New York Times* as a senior journalist since 1961, and is the author of two journalism-related books. His numerous press awards have included an Excellence in Journalism award (1994).

15 That rarest of political creatures—a Labor leader who could actually win elections

1995 Of Harold Wilson. In the *New York Times*, 25 May.

16 He was rotund, provincial, resolutely middle-class, studiously ambiguous and sometimes wavering in his opinions.

1995 Of Harold Wilson. In the *New York Times*, 25 May.

17 In an era of precipitous decline for Britain and its once-global empire, Harold Wilson was a fixture for 30 years, a solid workingman's socialist in a rumpled ready-to-wear suit and his trademark Gannex mackintosh.

1995 Of Harold Wilson. In the *New York Times*, 25 May.

18 The silver-haired, pipe-smoking northerner was a consummate British politician: tenacious, shrewd, manipulative, a blend of homespun tastes, acid wit and pragmatic, often shifting policies…the symbol of an emerging middle-class Briton.

1995 Of Harold Wilson. In the *New York Times*, 25 May.

McFarlane, J A, and Clements, Warren 1944–, 1952–

Canadian journalists.

19 Say *quotes* from the shortstop or the Prime Minister, but *quotations* from the Bible, Browning or Churchill.

1990 *The Globe and Mail Style Book.*

20 The patron saint of journalists, officially named by the church, is St. Francis de Sales. The traditional patron saint of editors is St. John Bosco. (The protector of computer-age journalists may well be St. Anthony of Padua, patron saint of searchers for lost articles.)

1990 *The Globe and Mail Style Book.*

McFarlane, Robert Carl 1937–

US government official. After serving with the Marines, he became assistant to the President for national security (1983–5) and chair of the McFarlane Association (1986–).

21 He knows so little and accomplishes so much.

Of President Reagan. Quoted in George P Shultz *Turmoil and Triumph* (1993).

MacGill, Patrick 1890–1963

Irish navvy, novelist and poet. Sold into servitude by his farming parents, he escaped to Scotland where he laboured and hawked his verses before coming to literary attention. He emigrated to the US in 1930, where he fell into poverty and developed muscular sclerosis.

22 All the night the frogs go chuckle, all the day the birds are singing
In the pond beside the meadow, by the roadway poplar-lined,
In the field between the trenches are a million blossoms springing
'Twixt the grass of silver bayonets where the lines of battle wind
Where man has manned the trenches for the maiming of his kind.
1917 *Soldier Songs*, 'The Trench'.

McGonagall, William c.1825–1902

Scottish self-styled 'poet and tragedian' from Dundee, most of his work was doggerel. The majority of his poems were originally produced as broadsheets and not collected until after his death.

23 Alas! Lord and Lady Dalhousie are dead, and buried at last,
Which causes many people to feel a little downcast.
1890 *Poetic Gems*, 'The Death of Lord and Lady Dalhousie', stanza 1.

24 Beautiful Railway Bridge of the Silv'ry Tay!
Alas! I am very sorry to say
That ninety lives have been taken away
On the last Sabbath day of 1879,
Which will be remember'd for a very long time.
1890 *Poetic Gems*, 'The Tay Bridge Disaster', stanza 1.

25 Ye lovers of the picturesque, if ye wish to drown your grief,
Take my advice, and visit the ancient town of Crieff;
The climate is bracing, and the walks lovely to see
Besides, ye can ramble over the district, and view the beautiful scenery.
More Poetic Gems (published 1962), 'Beautiful Crieff', stanza 1.

26 The man that gets drunk is little else than a fool,
And is in the habit, no doubt, of advocating for Home Rule;
But the best Home Rule for him, as far as I can understand,
Is the abolition of strong drink from the land.
Last Poetic Gems (published 1968), 'The Demon Drink', stanza 9.

McGough, Roger 1937–

English poet, playwright and performer, associated with the 1960s Liverpool pop scene. His poetry is characterized by a dry, ironic wit and a feeling for the diction and rhythms of the street.

27 Let me die a youngman's death

not a clean and in-between-the-sheets, holy-water death.
1967 'Let Me Die A Youngman's Death'.

28 Discretion is the better part of Valerie (though all of her is nice).
1969 'Discretion'.

29 by thus keeping one pace ahead of myself
I need never catch up with the truth.
1973 'unlikely now'.

30 I could never begin a poem: 'When I am dead'
In case it tempted Fate, and Fate gave way.
1982 'When I Am Dead'.

31 Do people who wave at trains
Wave at the driver, or at the train itself?
Or, do people who wave at trains
Wave at the passengers? Those hurtling strangers,
The unidentifiable flying faces?
1982 'Waving At Trains'.

32 This is the mother
who one day chose
to smother the child
with kisses, and blows and blows and blows.
1982 'Kisses and Blows'.

McGovern, George S(tanley) 1922–

US Democratic politician, Senator for South Dakota (1963–81). He made a bid for the presidential nomination in 1968, and unsuccessfully opposed Nixon in the 1972 presidential election. He tried again for the presidential nomination in 1984, but withdrew.

33 To those who charge that liberalism has been tried and found wanting, I answer that the failure is not in the idea but in the course of recent history. The New Deal was ended by World War II. The New Frontier was closed by Berlin and Cuba even before it was opened. And the Great Society lost its greatness in the jungles of Indochina.
1973 Lecture at Oxford University, 21 Jan.

Machado de Assis, Joaquim Maria 1839–1908

Brazilian poet and novelist, writer of romantic stories and poems. *Memórias Póstumas de Brás Cubas* marks the beginning of his mature style, informed by both pessimism and wit.

34 *Cada estaç—o da vida é uma ediç—o, que corrige a anterior, e que será corrigida também, até a ediç—o definitiva, que o editor dá de graça aos vermes.*

Each stage in life is an edition that supersedes the previous one and will also be superseded until the definitive edition: the one that the editor gives to the worms.

1881 *As Memórias Póstumas de Brás Cubas*, ch.27 (translated as *Epitaph of a Small Winner*, 1952).

35 *A vida é tão bela que a mesma idéia da morte precisa de vir primeiro a ela, antes de se ver cumprida. Já me vás entendendo; lê agora outro capítulo.*

Life is so beautiful that even the idea of death must be born before it can be realized. You must already understand. Now read another chapter.
1899 *Dom Casmurro*, ch.133.

Machiavelli, Niccolò di Bernardo dei
1469–1527

Italian politician and political theorist. Obliged to withdraw from public life after an accusation of conspiracy (1513), he devoted himself to literature. His masterpiece is the pragmatic manual for statesmen, *Il Principe* (The Prince, 1532).

36 *Gli nomini si debbano o vezzeggiate o peguere; perchè si vendiciano delle leggieri offese, delle gravi non possono.*

Men should be either treated generously or destroyed, because they take revenge for slight injuries—for heavy ones they cannot.
1513 *Il Principe*, ch.3 (translated by Alan Gilbert).

37 *Nasce da questo una disputa: s'egli è meglio essere amato che temuto, o è converso. Rispondesi che si voiebbe essere l'uno e l'altro; ma perchè egli è difficile accozzarli insieme, è molto più sicuro essere temuto che amato, quando si abbia a mancare dell'uno de'due.*

This leads to a debate: is it better to be loved than feared, or the reverse? The answer is that it is desirable to be both, but because it is difficult to join them together, it is much safer for a prince to be feared than loved, if he is to fail in one of the two.
1513 *Il Principe*, ch.8 (translated by Alan Gilbert).

38 It never or rarely happens that a republic or monarchy is well constituted, or its old institutions entirely reformed, unless it is only done by one individual.
1513–17 *Discourses on First Ten Books of Livy.*

McIlvanney, William Angus 1936–

Scottish writer. He is best known for his Ayrshire novels *Docherty* and *The Big Man*, and his series of crime novels featuring the Glaswegian detective, Laidlaw. He has also written poetry, essays and short stories.

39 There is a kind of laughter people laugh at public events, as if a joke were a charity auction and they want to be seen to be bidding.
1985 *The Big Man*, ch.1.

40 That would have been a nice place, inside an idea, but it wasn't a place to live. It was necessary to live where the idea and the fact collided.
1985 *The Big Man*, ch.8.

MacInnes, Colin 1914–79

English writer. He gave a voice to sections of society often ignored. He is best known for his novel *Absolute Beginners*.

41 And I thought, 'My lord, one thing is certain, and that's that they'll make musicals one day about the glamour-studded 1950s.' And I thought, my heaven, one thing is certain too, I'm miserable.
1959 *Absolute Beginners.*

42 Tradition, if not constantly recreated, can be as much a millstone as a mill-wheel.
1961 *England, Half English*, 'England, Half English'.

43 In England, pop art and fine art stand resolutely back to back.
1961 *England, Half English*, 'Pop Songs and Teenagers'.

44 A coloured man can tell, in five seconds dead, whether a white man likes him or not. If the white man *says* he does, he is instantly—and usually quite rightly—mistrusted.
1961 *England, Half English*, 'A Short Guide for Jumbles'.

45 The decorations are like those of the embassy of a nation about to go into voluntary liquidation.
1961 *England, Half English*, 'See You At Mabel's'.

MacInnis, Joseph 1937–

Canadian undersea explorer.

46 The larger the island of knowledge, the longer the shoreline of wonder.
Quoted by Donald Grant in *The Globe and Mail*, 8 Nov 1986.

Mackay, Alan Lindsay 1926–

British scientist and Fellow of the Royal Society.

47 How can we have any new ideas or fresh outlooks when 90 per cent of all the scientists who have ever lived have still not died?
1969 In *Scientific World*, vol.13.

McKay, Claude originally *Festus Claudius*
1890–1948

Jamaican born US writer. He wrote poetry, novels, autobiography and a study of life in Harlem, and was a key figure in the Harlem Renaissance of the 1920s.

48 If we must die, let it not be like hogs
Hunted and penned in an inglorious spot
While round us bark the mad and hungry dogs,
Making their mock at our accursed lot.
1922 *Harlem Shadows*, 'If We Must Die'.

49 Like men we'll face the murderous cowardly pack,
Pressed to the wall, dying, but fighting back!

    1922 *Harlem Shadows*, 'If We Must Die'.

Mackaye, Dorothy Disney 1904–92

US journalist and agony aunt, best known for editing the 'Can This Marriage be Saved?' column for the *Ladies Home Journal* for more than 30 years.

50 'He never listens' is universal in the institution of marriage.

    Recalled on her death, 5 Sep 1992.

Macke, August 1887–1914

German painter, one of the founder members of the *Blaue Reiter* group of Expressionist artists.

51 To create forms means: to live. Are not children more creative in drawing directly from the secret of their sensations than the imitator of Greek forms? Are not savages artists who have forms of their own powerful as the form of thunder?

    1912 *The Blaue Reiter Alamanac*

Mackellar, (Isobel Marion) Dorothea

1885–1968

Australian popular poet and novelist. Her works include *The Witch Maid* (1914), *Dreamharbour* (1923) and the novel *The Little Blue Devil* (1912). She wrote little after the mid-1920s, but translated widely from various European poets.

52 The love of field and coppice,
Of green and shaded lanes,
Of ordered woods and gardens
Is running in your veins.
Strong love of grey-blue distance
Brown streams and soft, dim skies—I know
but cannot share it,
My love is otherwise.

I love a sunburnt country,
A land of sweeping plains,
Of ragged mountain ranges,
Of droughts and flooding rains.
I love her far horizons,
I love her jewel-sea,
Her beauty and her terror—
The wide brown land for me!

    1905 'Core of My Heart', first published in the London *Spectator*. Collected as 'My Country' in *The Closed Door, and Other Verses* (1911).

McKellen, Sir Ian Murray 1939–

English stage and film actor and director.

53 I can't be absolutely certain, 30 years ago when I made the decision to become an actor, but certainly one of the reasons was it was the way to meet other queer men.

    Quoted in Blake Green 'A Kingly McKellen as a Fascist in *Richard II*', in the Pink Pages, *San Francisco Chronicle*, 16 Aug 1992.

MacKenzie, Sir (Edward Montague) Compton 1883–1972

English writer and editor. His best-known books are *Sinister Street* (1913–14) and *Whisky Galore* (1947), which became a famous film.

54 Prostitution. Selling one's body to keep one's soul…one might say of most modern marriages that they were selling one's soul to keep one's body.

    1918 *The Adventures of Sylvia Scarlett*, bk.2, ch.5.

55 You are offered a piece of bread and butter that feels like a damp handkerchief and sometimes, when cucumber is added to it, like a wet one.

    1927 *Vestal Fire*, bk.1, ch.3.

56 Women do not find it difficult nowadays to behave like men, but they often find it extremely difficult to behave like gentlemen.

    1933 *Literature in My Time*, ch.22.

MacKenzie, Lewis W 1940–

Major-General, retired, United Nations Chief of Staff for peacekeeping in Sarajevo, Bosnia-Herzegovina.

57 Countries that have soldiers in charge seem, more often than not, to be the ones where democracy is but a flickering candle sitting in an open window with a forecast of rain.

    1993 Letter about his retirement, in *The Globe and Mail*, 21 Jan.

Mackintosh, Sir James 1765–1832

Scottish writer, philosopher and historian. He studied medicine, but settled in London as a journalist. His *Vindiciae Gallicae* (1791) was a defence of the French Revolution (he later recanted his views, 1815). He spent seven years in Bombay, becoming an MP on his return.

58 Men are never so good or so bad as their opinions.

    1830 *Dissertation on the Progress of Ethical Philosophy*, section 6, 'Jeremy Bentham'.

59 Henry VIII perhaps approached as nearly to the ideal standard of perfect wickedness as the infirmities of human nature will allow.

    1831 Of Henry's actions in executing Thomas More and Anne Boleyn. *History of England*, vol.2.

MacLaine, Shirley pseudonym of Shirley MacLean Beatty 1934–

US actress, sister of Warren Beatty. Her films include *Around the World in Eighty Days* (1956), *The Apartment*

(1959), *Irma La Douce* (1963), *Sweet Charity* (1968) and *Terms of Endearment* (1983).

60 I've played so many hookers they don't pay me in the regular way any more. They leave it on the dresser.
1989 In *New Woman*, Jul.

McLean, Don 1945–

US singer and song-writer. He enjoyed a series of hits in the early 1970s, among them the classic singles 'American Pie' (1972) and 'Vincent' (1972). He later concentrated on country music.

61 I can't remember if I cried
When I read about his widowed bride.
Something touched me deep inside
The day the music died.
1972 Of the death of Buddy Holly. 'American Pie'.

62 So bye, bye, Miss American Pie,
Drove my Chevy to the levee
But the levee was dry.
Them good old boys was drinkin' whiskey and rye
Singin' 'This'll be the day that I die.'
1972 'American Pie'.

63 And the three men I admired most,
The Father, Son and Holy Ghost,
They caught the last train for the coast
The day the music died.
1972 'American Pie'.

Maclean, Sir Fitzroy Hew 1911–96

English diplomat, soldier and traveller. Sent at his own request to Moscow, he travelled in Central Asia. During World War II he joined the Special Air Service in North Africa and later he was parachuted into Yugoslavia as Churchill's personal representative to contact Tito, then a guerrilla leader.

64 At first sight, landing by plane had seemed an infinitely more normal and agreeable method of entering the country than what Mr Churchill called 'jumping out of a parachute'.
1949 *Eastern Approaches.*

65 A spirit of contradiction has always, to some extent, guided my behaviour.
1949 *Eastern Approaches.*

66 It was unhealthy and unsafe, and of no interest whatever.
'But what,' I said, 'about the tigers?'
'Tigers, perhaps,' he replied pityingly, 'but no culture.'
1949 Of Lenkoran, Azerbaijan, in discussion with an Armenian official. *Eastern Approaches.*

Maclean, John 1879–1923

Scottish Marxist and revolutionary of almost legendary status in Glasgow, appointed Soviet Consul on the Clyde

after the Russian Revolution. Ill health accentuated by frequent prison sentences led to his early death.

67 No government is going to take from me my right to speak, my right to protest against wrong, my right to do everything that is for the benefit of mankind. I am not here, then, as the accused; I am here as the accuser of capitalism dripping with blood from head to foot.
1918 Speech at his trial at the High Court, Edinburgh, 9 May, quoted in Nan Milton *John Maclean* (1973), ch.3.

MacLean, Sorley Gaelic name *Somhairle MacGill-Eain* 1911–96

Scottish poet. He wrote in Gaelic, in which language he was the most important late 20th century poet, and prepared his own English translations.

68 *Ma thubhairt ar cainnt gu bheil a' chiall
co-ionann ris a' ghaol
chan fhior dhi.*

If our language has said that reason
is identical with love,
it is not speaking the truth.
1943 'A Chiall's a Ghràidh' ('Reason and Love').

69 *Mairg an t-sòil a chì air fairge
ian mór marbh na h-albann.*

Pity the eye that sees on the ocean
the great dead bird of Scotland.
1943 'An t-Eilean', 'The Island'.

70 *Tha tìm, am fiadh, an coille Hallaig.*

Time, the deer, is in the wood of Hallaig.
1970 'Hallaig', epitaph.

71 *Mura tig's ann theànas ni a Hallaig
a dh' ionnsaigh sàbaid nam marbh,
far a bheil an sluagh a' tathaich,
gach aon ghinealach a dh' fhalbh.*

If it does not, I will go down to Hallaig,
to the Sabbath of the dead,
where the people are frequenting,
every single generation gone.
1970 'Hallaig'.

MacLeish, Archibald 1892–1982

US poet, Librarian of Congress (1939–44), Assistant Secretary of State (1944–5) and Professor of Rhetoric at Harvard (1949–62). He won Pulitzer Prizes for *Conquistador* (1932), *Collected Poems 1917–52* (1952) and his verse drama *J.B.* (1958)

72 A Poem should be palpable and mute
As a globed fruit
1926 'Ars Poetica'.

73 A poem should be wordless
As the flight of birds
1926 'Ars Poetica'.

74 A poem should not mean
But be.
1926 'Ars Poetica'.

75 We have learned the answers, all the answers:
It is the question that we do not know.
1928 'The Hamlet of A. MacLeish'.

76 If the poem can be improved by its author's
explanations, it should never have been
published.
1933 Author's note in *Poems*.

77 Keepers of books, keepers of print and paper on the
shelves, librarians are keepers also of the records of
the human spirit—the records of men's watch upon
the world and on themselves.
1941 A Time to Speak, 'Of the Librarian's Profession'.

78 The dissenter is every human being at those
moments in his life when he resigns momentarily
from the herd and thinks for himself.
1956 'In Praise of Dissent', in the *New York Times*, 16 Dec.

79 Anything can make us look, only art can make us
see.
1961 *Poetry and Experience*. 'Riverside'.

80 History, like a badly constructed concert hall, has
occasional dead spots where the music can't be
heard.
1967 In *The Observer*, 12 Feb.

81 Wildness and silence disappeared from the
countryside, sweetness fell from the air, not because
anyone wished them to vanish or fall but because
throughways had to floor the meadows with
cement to carry the automobiles which advancing
technology produced.
1968 'The Great American Frustration', in the *Saturday
Review*, 9 Jul.

82 To see the earth as we now see it, small and
beautiful in that eternal silence where it floats, is to
see ourselves as riders on the earth together,
brothers on that bright loveliness in the unending
night—brothers who *see* now they are truly
brothers.
1968 On the first pictures from the moon. In the *New York
Times*, 25 Dec.

83 The business of the law is to make sense of the
confusion of what we call human life—to reduce it
to order but at the same time to give it possibility,
scope, even dignity.
1972 'Apologia', in the *Harvard Law Review*, Jun.

84 Poets...are literal-minded men who will squeeze a
word till it hurts.
1972 'Apologia', in *Harvard Law Review*, Jun.

85 We are great as our belief in human liberty—no
greater. And our belief in human liberty is only
ours when it is larger than ourselves.
1976 'Now Let Us Address The Main Question: Bicentennial
of What?', in the *New York Times*, 3 Jul.

86 Poetry is the art of understanding what it is to be
alive.
Recalled on his death, 20 Apr 1982.

87 If the art of poetry is...the art of making sense of
the chaos of human experience, it's not a bad thing
to see a lot of chaos.
On his work in government. Quoted in Scott Donaldson
Archibald MacLeish (1992).

88 Mr Morgan struck me as a healthy and childish
Britisher probably inhabiting the early 19th
century.
Of financier J P Morgan. Quoted in Scott Donaldson *Archibald
MacLeish* (1992).

MacLennan, Hugh 1927–90

Canadian novelist and essayist.

89 Boy Meets Girl in Winnipeg and Who Cares?
1960 Title of a magazine article in *Scotchman's Return and
Other Essays*. It refers to the preference of Canadian editors,
publishers, and readers for romance and drama set in foreign
locales.

Macleod, Fiona

▷ See Sharp, William

Macleod, Iain Norman 1913–70

English Conservative politician, Chairman of the
Conservative Party (1961–3). He refused to serve under
Lord Home (having supported R A Butler's leadership
claim), and spent two years editing the *Spectator*. He was
shadow Chancellor under Heath (1965–70), and briefly
Chancellor (1970).

90 The Socialists can scheme their schemes and the
Liberals can dream their dreams, but we, at least,
have work to do.
1960 Speech at the Conservative Party Conference.

91 We now have the worst of both worlds—not just
inflation on the one side or stagnation on the other,
but both of them together. We have a sort of
stagflation situation.
1965 Speech in the House of Commons, Nov.

McLuhan, (Herbert) Marshall 1911–80

Canadian critic and cultural theorist. He claimed that it is
the communication media *per se*, not the information and
ideas which they broadcast, that influence society. His
books include *The Gutenberg Galaxy* (1962) and *The
Medium is the Message* (1969).

92 For tribal man space was the uncontrollable
mystery. For technological man it is time that
occupies the same role.
1951 *The Mechanical Bride*, 'Magic that Changes Mood'.

93 The medium is the message.
1959 Speech at the University of British Columbia, 30 Jun,
following a symposium in Vancouver on the subject of music
and the mass media. The phrase was later used as the title of ch.1
in *Understanding Media* (1964), and as a book title (1969).

94 The new electronic independence recreates the
world in the image of a global village.
1962 *The Gutenberg Galaxy*.

95 The car has become an article of dress without
which we feel uncertain, unclad, and incomplete in
the urban compound.
1964 *Understanding Media*, ch.22.

96 Persons grouped around a fire or candle for warmth
or light are less able to pursue independent
thoughts, or even tasks, than people supplied with
electric light. In the same way, the social and
educational patterns latent in automation are those
of self-employment and artistic autonomy.
1964 *Understanding Media*, ch.33.

97 If the nineteenth century was the age of the
editorial chair, ours is the century of the
psychiatrist's couch.
1964 *Understanding Media*.

98 Canada is the only country in the world that knows
how to live without an identity.
1967 'Canada: A Borderline Case', CBC radio broadcast, 29
May.

99 Life. Consider the alternative.
1968 *War and Peace in the Global Village*.

1 Television brought the brutality of war into the
comfort of the living room. Vietnam was lost in the
living rooms of America, not on the battlefields of
Vietnam.
1975 Quoted in the *Montreal Gazette*, May.

2 Gutenburg made everybody a reader. Xerox makes
everybody a publisher.
1977 In the *Guardian Weekly*, 12 Jun.

Macmillan, Sir (Maurice) Harold, 1st Earl of Stockton 1894–1986

English Conservative politician. He succeeded Eden as
Prime Minister (1957–63), and was re-elected in 1959.
He resigned through ill health in 1963.

3 We have not overthrown the divine right of kings
to fall down for the divine right of experts.
1950 Speech, Strasbourg, 16 Aug.

4 Forever poised between a cliché and an
indiscretion.
1956 On the role of a Foreign Secretary, in *Newsweek*, Apr.

5 I thought that the best thing to do was to settle up
these little local difficulties, and then turn to the
wider vision of the Commonwealth.
1956 On departing for a Commonwealth conference, after
sacking several members of his Cabinet in his Night of the Long
Knives, Jan.

6 Let us be frank about it. Most of our people have
never had it so good. Go around the country, go to
the industrial towns, go to the farms, and you will
see a state of prosperity such as we have never had
in my lifetime—nor indeed ever in the history of
this country.
1957 Speech, Bedford, 20 Jul. This is the original form of the
oft-misquoted 'You never had it so good'.

7 At home, you always have to be a politician. When
you are abroad, you almost feel yourself to be a
statesman.
1958 Speech during the first visit of a British Prime Minister to
Australia, 17 Feb.

8 The most striking of all the impressions that I have
formed since I left London a month ago is of the
strength of African national consciousness. In
different places it may take different forms, but it is
happening everywhere. The wind of change is
blowing through this continent. Whether we like it
or not, the growth of national consciousness is a
political fact.
1960 Speech to the South African Parliament, 3 Feb.

9 Are we so sure that with 15 representatives…in
NATO, acting under the unanimity rule, the
deterrent would continue to deter? There may be
one finger on the trigger, but there will be 15
fingers on the safety catch.
1960 House of Commons, 30 May.

10 I was determined that no British government
should be brought down by the action of two tarts.
1963 On the Profumo scandal, referring specifically to
Christine Keeler and Mandy Rice Davies, Jul.

11 I have never found, in a long experience of politics,
that criticism is ever inhibited by ignorance.
1963 In the *Wall Street Journal*, 13 Aug.

12 A man who trusts nobody is apt to be the kind of
man whom nobody trusts.
1963 In the *New York Herald Tribune*, 17 Dec.

13 Tradition does not mean that the living are dead; it
means that the dead are living.
1963 In the *Manchester Guardian*, 18 Dec.

14 There are three bodies no sensible man directly
challenges: the Roman Catholic Church, the

Brigade of Guards, and the National Union of Mineworkers.

1981 In *The Observer*, 22 Feb.

15 There is a growing division in our comparatively prosperous society between the south and the north and midlands, which are ailing, that cannot be allowed to continue. There is a general sense of tension. The old English way might be to quarrel and have battles, but they were friendly. I can only describe as wicked the hatred that has been introduced, and which is to be found among different types of people today. Not merely an intellectual but a moral effort is required to get rid of it.

1984 Maiden speech as the Earl of Stockton (60 years after first entering the House of Commons), House of Lords, 13 Nov.

16 First of all the Georgian Silver goes, and then all that nice furniture that used to be in the salon. Then the Canalettos go.

1985 Speech to a private dinner of the Tory Reform Group, 8 Nov., in a reference to privatization and the selling of profitable state-owned enterprises.

17 Margaret Thatcher is a brilliant tyrant surrounded by mediocrities.

1986 In *Newsweek*, 12 Oct.

18 A man who was alleged to have the rigidity of a poker without its occasional warmth.

Of Charles de Gaulle, whose nickname was 'Ramrod'. Quoted by Henry Fairlie in the *New Republic*, 20 Mar 1989.

19 If people want a sense of purpose, they should get it from their archbishop, they should certainly not get it from their politicians.

Quoted in *The Life of Politics*.

20 You've reached the stage where you must decide whether you're going to be a good writer or a good public servant. You can't be both.

Attributed comment to Michael O'Donovan (real name of the writer Frank O'Connor).

McMurtry, Larry Jeff 1936–

US novelist. Several of his novels have been filmed successfully, but his most significant work is the epic fusion of generic western and historical novel in *Lonesome Dove*.

21 The Last Picture Show.

1966 Title of novel, subsequently filmed.

22 Terms of Endearment.

1975 Title of novel, subsequently filmed.

23 'We'll be the Indians, if we last another twenty years,' Augustus said. 'The way this place is settling up it'll be nothing but churches and dry-goods stores before you know it. Next thing you know

they'll have to round up us old rowdies and stick us on a reservation to keep us from scaring the ladies.'

1985 *Lonesome Dove*, ch.42

24 The cowboys had lived for months under the great bowl of the sky, and yet the Montana skies seemed deeper than the skies of Texas or Nebraska. Their depth and blueness robbed even the sun of its harsh force—it seemed smaller, in the vastness, and the whole sky no longer turned white at noon as it had in the lower plains. Always, somewhere to the north, there was a swath of blueness, with white cloads floating in it like petals in a pond.

1985 *Lonesome Dove*, ch.93.

25 Self-parody is the first portent of age.

1989 *Some Can Whistle*, pt.1, ch.14.

26 But the sorrowing are nomads, on a plain with few landmarks and no boundaries; sorrow's horizons are vague and its demands are few.

1989 *Some Can Whistle*, pt.4, ch.9.

McNamara, Robert Strange 1916–

US Democratic politician and businessman, Secretary of Defense in the Kennedy administration (1961) during the Vietnam War. He resigned to become President of the World Bank (1968–81), and later emerged as a critic of the nuclear arms race.

27 I don't object to it being called 'McNamara's war'… It is a very important war and I am pleased to be identified with it and do whatever I can to win it.

1964 On the Vietnam War. In the *New York Times*, 25 Apr.

28 A test case of US capacity to help a nation meet a Communist 'war of liberation'.

1964 Of the Vietnam War. Quoted in N Sheehan *The Pentagon Papers*.

29 Neither conscience nor sanity itself suggests that the United States is, or should or could be the global gendarme.

1966 Speech to US newspaper editors. Reported in the *New York Times*, 19 May.

30 I wondered if I'd ever see another Saturday night.

On the threat of nuclear war from Russian warheads in Cuba, Oct 1962. Quoted in Elie Abel *Missile Crisis* (1966).

31 One cannot fashion a credible deterrent out of an incredible action.

1968 On nuclear weapons. *The Essence of Security*.

32 We had a two-track approach, one political and the other military, and the military was designed to move us along the political track.

On the Vietnam War in late 1967. Quoted in Deborah Shapley *Promise and Power* (1993).

33 We tend to justify our actions and in a sense we color history to achieve that objective.

Quoted in Robert Siegel (ed) *The NPR Interviews* (1994).

34 Although we sought to do the right thing—and believed we were doing the right thing—in my judgement, hindsight proves us wrong.
1995 *In Retrospect: The tragedy and lessons of Vietnam* (with Brian Van de Mark).

MacNeice, (Frederick) Louis 1907–63

Irish poet born in Belfast. He was closely associated with the British left-wing poets of the 1930s, especially W H Auden with whom he wrote *Letters from Iceland* (1937). He also wrote radio drama, including *The Dark Tower* (broadcast 1946, published 1947). His *Collected Poems* was published in 1966.

35 Something of glass about her, of dead water, Chills and holds us,
Far more fatal than painted flesh or the lodestone of live hair
This despair of crystal brilliance.
1935 *Poems*, 'Circe'.

36 World is crazier and more of it than we think,
Incorrigibly plural.
1935 *Poems*, 'Snow'.

37 The little sardine men crammed in a monster toy
Who tilt their aggregate beast against our crumbling Troy.
1935 *Poems*, 'Turf-stacks'.

38 It's no go the merrygoround, it's no go the rickshaw,
All we want is a limousine and a ticket for the peepshow.
Their knickers are made of crêpe-de-chine, their shoes are made of python,
Their halls are lined with tiger rugs and their walls with the heads of bison.
1937 'Bagpipe Music', stanza 1.

39 It's no go my honey love, it's no go my poppet;
Work your hands from day to day, the winds will blow the profit.
The glass is falling hour by hour, the glass will fall for ever,
But if you break the bloody glass, you won't hold up the weather.
1937 'Bagpipe Music', stanza 10.

40 And the gods are absent and the men are still—
Noli me tangere, my soul is forfeit.

Some are now happy in the hive of home,
Thigh over thigh and a light in the night nursery,
And some are hungry under the starry dome
And some sit turning handles.
1938 *Autumn Journal*, part 2.

41 Spider, spider, spin

Your register and let me sleep a little,
Not now in order to end but to begin
The task begun so often.
1938 *Autumn Journal*, part 2.

42 All of London littered with remembered kisses.
1938 *Autumn Journal*, part 4.

43 Tonight we sleep
On the banks of Rubicon—the die is cast;
There will be time to audit
The accounts later, there will be sunlight later
And the equation will come out at last.
1938 *Autumn Journal*, part 24.

44 Time was away and somewhere else.
1939 'Meeting Point'. Collected in *Collected Poems 1925–1948*, 1949.

45 In my childhood trees were green
And there was plenty to be seen.

Come back early or never come.
1941 *Plant and Phantom*, 'Autobiography', l.1–3.

46 The dark was talking to the dead;
The lamp was dark beside my bed.
1941 *Plant and Phantom*, 'Autobiography', l.13–14.

47 The best people never land, sir.
1946 Steward to Roland. *The Dark Tower* (published 1947).

48 For the last blossom is the first blossom
And the first blossom is the best blossom
And when from Eden we take our way
The morning after is the first day.
'Apple Blossom', in *Collected Poems*, 1966.

49 His father gave him a box of truisms
Shaped like a coffin, then his father died;
The truisms remained on the mantelpiece.
'The Truisms', in *Collected Poems*, 1966.

MacQueen, Robert, Lord Braxfield
1722–99

Scottish judge who presided over many famous trials in Edinburgh. Notorious for his harsh sentencing and cruel humour, he was known as the 'hanging judge', and was the original for R L Stevenson's Lord Hermiston in *Weir of Hermiston*.

50 Muckle he made o' that; he was hanget.
1794 Riposte at the trial of a political reformer, when the defendant remarked that all great men had been reformers, 'even our Saviour himself'. Quoted in Lord Cockburn *Memorials of his Time* (1856), ch.2.

51 Ye're a verra clever chiel', man, but ye wad be nane the waur o' a hanging.
Quoted in John G Lockhart *Memoirs of the Life of Sir Walter Scott, Bart.* (1837–8), ch.48.

52 Let them bring me prisoners, and I'll find them law.
Quoted in Lord Cockburn *Memorials of his Time* (1856), ch.2.

MacRéamoinn, Sean Seamas Criostoir
1921–

Irish broadcaster and journalist.

53 I am becoming like the Irish Census, broken down by Age, Sex, and Religion.
1991 Chairing a lecture on Parnell, Merriman Summer School.

Madan, Geoffrey 1895–1947

English aphorist.

54 Conservative ideal of freedom and progress: everyone to have an unfettered opportunity of remaining exactly where they are.
Collected in *Geoffrey Madan's Notebooks* (published 1981).

Madison, James 1751–1836

US politician and 4th President (1809–17), co-author of the *Federalist Papers* (1787–8). Originator of the Virginia Plan, his compromise measure on the status of slaves ensured adoption of the Constitution in slave states. He presided over the 1812 war with Britain.

55 The diversity in the faculties of men, from which the rights of property originate, is not less an insuperable obstacle to a uniformity of interests. The protection of those faculties is the first object of government.
1787 *The Federalist*, Nov.

56 What is government itself but the greatest of all reflections on human nature? If men were angels, no government would be necessary. If angels were to govern men, neither external nor internal controls on government would be necessary.
1788 *The Federalist*, Jan.

Maeterlinck, Maurice 1862–1949

Belgian playwright and poet. The success enjoyed by his play *Pelléas et Mélisande* (1892) established him as the leading playwright of the Symbolist movement. He was awarded a Nobel Prize in 1911.

57 *L'Oiseau Bleu.*

The Blue Bird.
1909 Title of play.

Magidson, Herb 1906–

US song-writer.

58 Music, Maestro, Please.
1938 Title of song.

Mahathir, Mohamad 1925–

Malaysian politician and the country's longest serving Prime Minister, holding office since 1981. He won his record ninth term in 1995.

59 I'm brash and abrasive but that's because I've noticed when people are nice and polite they never get anywhere.
c.1990 Quoted in the *Eastern Express*, 24 Apr 1995.

60 If you can't be famous, at least you can be notorious.
c.1994 Quoted in the *Eastern Express*, 24 Apr 1995.

Mahler, Gustav 1860–1911

Austrian composer, conductor and artistic director at the Vienna State Opera (1897). He resigned after 10 years to conduct the New York Philharmonic (1908–11). He is best-known for the song-symphony *Das Lied von der Erde* (The Song of the Earth).

61 A symphony must be like the world, it must embrace everything.
1907 In conversation with Sibelius. Quoted in Ian Crofton and Donald Fraser *A Dictionary of Musical Quotations* (1985).

62 He is young and perhaps he is right. Maybe my ear is not sensitive enough.
Of Schoenberg's music. Quoted in Lebrecht *Discord* (1982).

63 *Endlich fortissimo!*

Fortissimo at last!
1907 On seeing the Niagara Falls. Quoted in Charles Osborne *The Dictionary of Composers* (1977).

Mahony, Francis Sylvester pseudonym
Father Prout 1804–66

Irish priest and humorous writer. He became a Jesuit priest but was expelled after a late-night frolic. After a spell as a priest in Italy, he turned to journalism in London.

64 And cymbals glorious
Swinging uproarious
In the gorgeous turrets
Of Notre Dame.
'The Bells of Shandon'.

65 O the bells of Shandon
Sound far more grand on
The pleasant waters
Of the River Lee.
'The Bells of Shandon'.

Mailer, Norman Kingsley 1923–

US novelist and journalist. An inveterate polemicist and high-profile public figure, he is arguably the most controversial figure in post-war US letters.

66 The Naked and the Dead.
1948 Title of novel.

67 Hip is the sophistication of the wise primitive in a giant jungle.
1957 In *Dissent*, Summer.

68 Each day a few more lies eat into the seed with which we are born, little institutional lies from the print of newspapers, the shock waves of television, and the sentimental cheats of the movie screen.
1959 *Advertisements for Myself*, 'First Advertisement for Myself'.

69 America is a hurricane, and the only people who do not hear the sound are those fortunate if incredibly stupid and smug White Protestants who live in the center, in the serene eye of the big wind.
1959 *Advertisements for Myself*, 'Advertisement for 'Games and Ends''.

70 There is probably no sensitive heterosexual alive who is not preoccupied with his latent homosexuality.
1959 *Advertisements for Myself*, 'The Homosexual Villain'.

71 The final purpose of art is to intensify, even, if necessary, to exacerbate, the moral consciousness of people.
1959 'Hip, Hell, and The Navigator', in *Western Review*, no.23, Winter.

72 Every moment of one's existence one is growing into more or retreating into less. One is always living a little more or dying a little bit.
1959 'Hip, Hell, and The Navigator', in *Western Review*, no. 23, Winter.

73 Once a newspaper touches a story, the facts are lost forever, even to the protagonists.
1960 In *Esquire*, Jun.

74 A modern democracy is a tyranny whose borders are undefined; one discovers how far one can go only by traveling in a straight line until one is stopped.
1963 *The Presidential Papers*, preface.

75 In America few people will trust you unless you are irreverent.
1963 *The Presidential Papers*, preface.

76 In America all too few blows are struck into flesh. We kill the spirit here, we are experts at that. We use psychic bullets and kill each other cell by cell.
1963 *The Presidential Papers*, 'Fourth Presidential Paper'.

77 A high church for the true mediocre.
1963 Of the FBI. *The Presidential Papers*, 'Sixth Presidential Paper'.

78 Writing books is the closest men ever come to childbearing.
1965 'Mr Mailer Interviews Himself', in the *New York Times Book Review*, 17 Sep.

79 The sense of a long last night over civilization is back again.
1966 *Cannibals and Christians*, 'Introducing Our Argument'.

80 Sentimentality is the emotional promiscuity of those who have no sentiment.
1966 *Cannibals and Christians*, 'My Hope For America'.

81 There is one expanding horror in American life. It is that our long odyssey toward liberty, democracy and freedom-for-all may be achieved in such a way that utopia remains forever closed, and we live in freedom and hell, debased of style, not individual from one another, void of courage, our fear rationalized away.
1966 *Cannibals and Christians*, 'My Hope For America'.

82 What characterizes a member of a minority group is that he is forced to see himself as both exceptional and insignificant, marvelous and awful, good and evil.
1966 *Cannibals and Christians*, 'A Speech At Berkeley on Vietnam Day'.

83 The surest way not to be remembered is to talk about the way you want to be.
1968 Interview in *Playboy*, Aug.

84 New York is one of the capitals of the world and Los Angeles is a constellation of plastic. San Francisco is a lady, Boston has become Urban Renewal, Philadelphia and Baltimore and Washington blink like dull diamonds in the smog of Eastern Megalopolis, and New Orleans is unremarkable past the French Quarter. Detroit is a one-trade town, Pittsburgh has lost its golden triangle. St Louis has become the golden arch of the corporation, and nights in Kansas City close early. The oil depletion allowance makes Houston and Dallas naught but checkerboards for this sort of game. But Chicago is a great American city. Perhaps it is the last of the great American cities.
1969 *Miami and the Siege of Chicago*, 'The Siege of Chicago'.

85 The horror of the Twentieth Century was the size of each event, and the paucity of its reverberation.
1970 *Of A Fire On The Moon*, pt.1, ch.2.

86 The difference between writing a book and being on television is the difference between conceiving a child and having a baby made in a test tube.
1971 'The Siege of Mailer: Hero to Historian', in *Village Voice*, 21 Jan.

87 So we think of Marilyn who was every man's love affair with America, Marilyn Monroe who was blonde and beautiful and had a sweet little rinky-dink of a voice and all the cleanliness of all the clean American backyards.
1973 *Marilyn*.

88 No physical activity is so vain as boxing. A man gets into the ring to attract admiration. In no sport, therefore, can you be more humiliated.
1976 *The Fight.*

89 Ultimately a hero is a man who would argue with the gods, and so awakens devils to contest his vision.
1964 *The Presidential Papers*, 'Preface'.

90 The true religion of America has always been America.
1984 Interview in *Time Out*, 27 Sep–3 Oct.

91 When a novel comes, it's a grace. Something in the cosmos has forgiven you long enough so that you can start.
1991 In *The Guardian*, 5 Oct.

Maillart, Ella Kini 1903–97

Swiss explorer, writer, actress and athlete. She captained the Swiss women's hockey team and represented Switzerland in skiing and sailing. In 1932 she travelled alone to Russian Turkestan and in 1934 to northeastern China.

92 No. Cost what it may I am determined to go East. The nomad's life enthralls me. Its restlessness pursues me: it is as much part of me as of the sailor. All parts and none are home to me, and all arriving only a new setting forth.
1934 *Des Monts Célestes aux Sables Rouges* (translated by John Rodder as *Turkestan Solo: One Woman's Expedition from the Tien Shan to the Kizil Kum*).

93 Wherever I go, it is always the secret life of such simple, straightforward races that I seek, people whom a fair face is sufficient to content. Only by returning to their way of life, can we ever hope to find a way out of the bogs in which we vainly stumble.
1934 *Des Monts Célestes aux Sables Rouges* (translated by John Rodder as *Turkestan Solo: One Woman's Expedition from the Tien Shan to the Kizil Kum*).

94 So far I like India.
1935 On crossing the Mintaka Pass at the extreme border of China. Quoted in Peter Fleming *News from Tartary* (1936).

Maimonides properly Moses ben Maimon
1135–1204

Spanish-born Jewish philosopher, rabbi and physician, one of the greatest Hebrew scholars. His philosophical work *Guide to the Perplexed* (1190) attempts to reconcile Greek philosophy and Judaism.

95 There is one [disease] which is widespread, and from which men rarely escape. This disease varies in degree in different men… I refer to this: that every person thinks his mind…more clever and more learned than it is… I have found that this disease has attacked many an intelligent person… They…express themselves [not only] upon the science with which they are familiar, but upon other sciences about which they know nothing… If met with applause…so does the disease itself become aggravated.
Aphorisms. Quoted in *Bulletin of the History of Medicine*, vol.3, p.555 (1935).

Maintenon, Françoise d'Aubigné, Marquise de known as *Madame de Maintenon* 1635–1719

Second wife of Louis XIV of France. Impoverished widow of the crippled poet Paul Scarron, in 1669 she became governess to Louis' sons. After the queen's death (1683) he married her secretly. She retired to her educational foundation at St-Cyr after his death.

96 You must make use of people according to their abilities, and realize that absolutely no one is perfect.
1679 Letter to Count d'Aubigné, 25 Sep.

Major, John 1943–

English Conservative politician and Prime Minister (1990–7). He rose quickly under Margaret Thatcher to become Chancellor of the Exchequer on Lawson's resignation (1989). After Thatcher's downfall he became Prime Minister, and his government was re-elected in 1992.

97 I hope…to build a society of opportunity. By opportunity, I mean an open society—a society in which what people fulfil will depend upon their talent, their application, and their good fortune. What people achieve should depend particularly on those things, and I hope increasingly in the future that that will be the case.
1990 Address on entering No.10 Downing Street for the first time as Prime Minister, 27 Nov.

98 I think that we had better start again, somewhere else.
1991 Attributed remark during a Cabinet meeting when the Cabinet Room was rocked by an IRA mortar attack on No.10 Downing Street, 7 Feb.

99 Only in Britain could it be thought a defect to be 'too clever by half'. The probability is that too many people are too stupid by three-quarters.
1991 Quoted in *The Observer*, 7 Jul.

Makin, Bathsua b. c.1600

English poet and educator. She was appointed tutor to Princess Elizabeth in the 1640s, a post usually held by a man.

1 A Learned Woman is thought to be a Comet, that bodes Mischief, when ever it appears.

1673 *An Essay to Revive the Antient Education of Gentlewomen In Religion, Manners, Art and Tongues, With An Answer to the Objections against this Way of Education.*

Makwetu, Clarence 1931–

South African politician, president of the radical Pan-Africanist Congress (1990–7). Initially opposed to negotiation, he agreed to talks with other parties in the early 1990s.

2 We are determined to confront the oppressor with one voice.
1991 Addressing the first formal joint meeting of the PAC and the rival African National Congress for 30 years, 15 Apr.

Malamud, Bernard 1914–86

US Jewish writer. Novels including *The Assistant* (1957), *The Fixer* (1966), *Dublin's Lives* (1979) and *God's Grace* (1982) established his reputation as one of the finest novelists of the post-war period.

3 Levin wanted friendship and got friendliness; he wanted steak and they offered spam.
1961 *A New Life*, pt.6.

4 'Mourning is a hard business,' Cesare said. 'If people knew there'd be less death.'
1963 *Idiot's First*, 'Life Is Better Than Death'.

5 There comes a time in a man's life when to get where he has to go—if there are no doors or windows he walks through a wall.
1973 *Rembrandt's Hat*, 'The Man in the Drawer'.

6 I think I said 'All men are Jews except they don't know it.' I doubt I expected anyone to take the statement literally. But I think it's an understandable statement and a metaphoric way of indicating how history, sooner or later, treats all men.
'An Interview', in L and J Fields (eds) *Bernard Malamud* (1975).

7 Comedy, I imagine, is harder to do consistently than tragedy, but I like it spiced in the wine of sadness.
1975 Interview in *Paris Review*, Spring.

8 I love metaphor. It provides two loaves where there seems to be one. Sometimes it throws in a load of fish.
1975 Interview in *Paris Review*, Spring.

9 The past exudes legend: one can't make pure clay of time's mud. There is no life that can be recaptured wholly; as it was. Which is to say that all biography is ultimately fiction.
1979 *Dubin's Lives*.

Malcolm X originally Malcolm Little 1925–65

US black nationalist leader. Converted to the Black Muslims while in prison, on his release he assumed a new name and promoted the sect. He later founded his own organization, for Afro-American Unity, and in the resulting factional feuding was assassinated.

10 We didn't land on Plymouth Rock. It landed on us.
1990 Quoted in *Life*, Fall issue.

Malevich, Kasimir 1878–1935

Russian painter and designer. A pioneer of abstract art.

11 Only when the habit of one's consciousness to see in paintings bits of nature, madonnas and shameless nudes has disappeared, shall we see a pure-painting composition.
1915 Manifesto, quoted in C Gray *The Russian Experiment in Art* (rev edn 1986).

Mallarmé, Stéphane 1842–98

French poet, a leading writer in the Symbolist movement.

12 *Il n'y que la Beauté—et elle n'a qu'une expression parfaite, la Poésie.*

There is only beauty—and it has only one perfect expression, poetry.
1867 Letter to Cazalis.

13 *Le vierge, le vivace et le bel aujourd'hui.*

The virgin, the vibrant and the beautiful today.
1881 *Plusieurs Sonnets*, no.1.

14 *La Poésie est l'expression, par le langage humain ramenée à son rythme essentiel, du sens mystérieux des aspects de l'existence; elle doue ainsi d'authenticité notre séjour et constitue la seule tâche spirituelle.*

Poetry is an expression, through human language restored to its essential rhythm, of the mysteriousness of existence; it endows our life with authenticity and constitutes our only spiritual task.
1884 Letter to M. Léo d'Orfer, 27 Jun.

15 *La chair est triste, hélas! et j'ai lu tous les livres.*

The flesh is sad, alas! and I've read all the books.
1887 'Brise marine', in *Poésies, Du Parnasse Contemporain* (1893).

16 *Dire au peintre qu'il faut prendre la nature comme elle est, vaut dire au virtuose qu'il peut s'asseoir sur le piano.*

Telling a painter that he must take nature as it is is like telling a virtuoso that he can sit on the piano.
1888 *Le 'ten o'clock' de M. Whistler*.

17 *Nuit blanche de glaçons et de neige cruelle!*

White night of icicles and bitter snow!
1893 *Poésies, Hérodiade*, 'La Nourrice'.

18 *Donner un sens plus pur aux mots de la tribu.*

Bestow a purer sense on the language of the horde.
1893 *Poésies, Hommages et Tombeaux*, 'Le Tombeau d'Edgar Poe' (translated by Henry Weinfield, 1994).

19 *Tel qu'en Lui-même enfin l'éternité le change.*

As for Himself at last eternity changes him.
1893 *Poésies, Hommages et Tombeaux,* 'Le Tombeau d'Edgar Poe'.

20 *Un coup de dés n'abolira jamais le hasard.*

A throw of the dice will never abolish chance.
1914 Title of poem, in *Cosmopolis,* May.

Mallet-Stevens, Robert 1886–1945

French architect

21 Architecture is an art which is basically geometrical. The cube is the basis of architecture because the right angle is necessary—the steps of a staircase consist of vertical and horizontal planes and the corners of rooms are nearly always right angles. We need right angles.
1924 'Architecture and Geometry', in *Bulletin de la Vie Moderne,* Paris.

Mallory, George Leigh 1886–1924

English mountaineer. He disappeared while attempting to climb Everest.

22 Because it's there.
1923 When asked 'Why do you want to climb Mount Everest?'. Quoted in the *New York Times,* 18 Mar.

Malory, Sir Thomas d.1471

English writer. His masterpiece, the *Morte d'Arthur,* a cycle of Arthurian legends, influenced Tennyson and other. It was completed c.1470 and a version was printed by Caxton in 1485.

23 The third sister, Morgan le Fey, was put to scole in a nonnery, and ther she lerned so moche that she was a grete clerke of nygromancye.
c.1470 *Morte d'Arthur,* bk.1, ch.2.

24 So the child was delyverd unto Merlyn, and so he bare it forth unto syre Ector and made an holy man to crysten hym and named hym Arthur.
c.1470 *Morte d'Arthur,* bk.1, ch.2.

25 'WHOSO PULLETH OUTE THIS SWERD OF THIS STONE AND ANVYLD IS RIGHTWYS KYNGE BORNE OF ALL ENGLOND'
c.1470 *Morte d'Arthur,* bk.1, ch.4. Inscription on the sword. Arthur was able to remove the sword with ease, and thus became king.

26 And there had Arthure the firste syght of queene Gwenyvere, the kyngis doghter of the londe of Camylarde, and ever afftir he loved hir.
c.1470 *Morte d'Arthur,* bk.1, ch.18.

27 'That is the Ladye of the Lake,' seyde Merlion. 'There ys a grete roche, and therein ys as fayre a paleyce as ony on erthe, and rychely besayne. And thys damesel woll come to you anone, and than speke ye fayre to hir, that she may gyff you that swerde.'
c.1470 To Arthur. *Morte d'Arthur,* bk.1, ch.25.

28 And so kyng Lodgreaunce delyverd hys doughtir Gwenyver unto Merlion, and the Table Rounde.
c.1470 *Morte d'Arthur,* bk.3, ch.1.

29 'What tydynges at Camelot?' seyde that on knyght. 'By my hede, there have I been and aspied the courte of kynge Arthure, and there ys such a felyshyp that they may never be brokyn, and well-nyghe all the world holdith with Arthure, for there ys the floure of chevalry.'
c.1470 *Morte d'Arthur,* bk.3, ch.14.

30 And so at that tyme sir Launcelot had the grettyste name of ony knyght of the worlde, and moste he was honoured of hyghe and lowe.
c.1470 *Morte d'Arthur,* bk.6, ch.18.

31 'But one thyng begyled us, that we myght nat se the Holy Grayle hit was so preciously coverde. Wherefore I woll make here a vow that to-morne, withoute longer abydynge, I shall laboure in the queste of the Sankgreall.'
c.1470 Sir Gawain. *Morte d'Arthur,* bk.13, ch.7.

32 And thus hit passes on frome Candylmas untyll Ester, that the moneth of May was com, whan every lusty harte begynnith to blossom and to burgyne. For, lyke as trees and erbys burgenyth and florysshyth in May, lyke wyse every lusty harte that is ony maner of lover spryngith, burgenyth, buddyth, and florysshyth in lusty dedis.
c.1470 *Morte d'Arthur,* bk.18, ch.25.

33 And there he bounde the gyrdyll aboute the hyltis, and threw the swerde as farre into the watir as he myght. And there cam an arme and an honde above the watir, and toke hit and cleyght hit, and shoke hit thryse and braundysshed, and than vanysshed with the swerde into the watir.
c.1470 *Morte d'Arthur,* bk.21, ch.5.

34 Yet som men say in many partys of Inglonde that kynge Arthur ys nat dede...and men say that he shall com agayne, and he shall win the Holy Crosse. Yet I woll nat say that hit shall be so, but rather I wolde sey: here in thys there ys wrytten uppon the tumbe thys: HIC IACET ARTHURUS, REX QUONDAM REXQUE FUTURUS. [Here lies Arthur, the once and future king].
c.1470 *Morte d'Arthur,* bk.21, ch.7.

35 Herein may be seen noble chyvalrye, curtosye, humanyté, frendlynesse, hardynesse, love, frendshyp, cowardyse, murdre, hate, vertue, and synne.
c.1485 *Morte d'Arthur,* Caxton's preface.

Malouf, David 1934–

Australian novelist, of Lebanese and English extraction. His novels include *An Imaginary Life* (1978) and *Remembering Babylon* (1993).

36 'Do not shoot,' it shouted. 'I am a B-b-british object!'
1993 *Remembering Babylon*, ch.1.

Malthus, Thomas Robert 1766–1834

English economist. His anonymous *Essay on the Principle of Population* (1798) argued that population tends to increase faster than the means of subsistence, and that efforts should be made to cut the birth rate. He also wrote *Principles of Political Economy* (1820).

37 Population, when unchecked, increases in geometrical ratio. Subsistence only increases in arithmetical ratio.
1798 *An Essay on the Principle of Population.*

38 All the immediate checks to population—seem to be resolvable into moral restraint, vice and misery.
1798 *An Essay on the Principle of Population.*

39 The perpetual struggle for room and food.
1798 *An Essay on the Principle of Population.*

40 A man who is born into a world already possessed, if he cannot get subsistence from his parents on whom he has a just demand, and if the society do not want his labour, has no claim of *right* to the smallest portion of food, and, in fact, has no business to be where he is.
1803 *An Essay on the Principle of Population* (revised edn).

41 The employment of the poor in roads and public works, and a tendency among landlords and persons of property to build, to improve and beautify their grounds, and to employ workmen and menial servants, are the means most within our power and most directly calculated to remedy the evils arising from disturbance in the balance of produce and consumption.
1820 *Principles of Political Economy.*

Mamet, David Alan 1947–

US dramatist, screenwriter and director. His demotic language and hard-hitting social observation have made him a significant voice in modern US theatre. He made his film directing début with *House of Games* (1987), and published a novel, *The Village* (1994).

42 Sexual Perversity in Chicago.
1976 Title of play.

43 We respond to a drama to that extent to which it corresponds to our dream life.
1986 *Writing in Restaurants*, 'A National Dream-Life'.

44 We live in oppressive times. We have, as a nation,
become our own thought police; but instead of calling the process by which we limit our expression of dissent and wonder 'censorship', we call it 'concern for commercial viability'.
1986 *Writing in Restaurants*, 'Radio Drama'.

45 Policemen so cherish their status as keepers of the peace and protectors of the public that they have occasionally been known to beat to death those citizens or groups who question that status.
1986 *Writing in Restaurants*, 'Some Thoughts On Writing In Restaurants'.

46 In a world we find terrifying, we ratify that which doesn't threaten us.
1986 *Writing in Restaurants*, 'Notes For a Catalogue for Raymond Saunders'.

47 We recipients of the boon of liberty have always been ready, when faced with discomfort, to discard any and all first principles of liberty, and, further, to indict those who do not freely join with us in happily arrogating those principles.
1986 *Writing in Restaurants*, 'First Principles'.

48 The product of the artist has become less important than the *fact* of the artist. We wish to absorb this person. We wish to devour someone who has experienced the tragic. In our society this person is much more important than anything he might create.
1986 *Writing in Restaurants*, 'Exuvial Magic: An Essay Concerning Magic'.

49 The absence of the urge to create is decadence.
1986 *Writing in Restaurants*, 'Decadence'.

50 Our semantic chickens have come home to roost… We have come to accept all sorts of semantic inversions, just as George Orwell told us we would.
1986 *Writing in Restaurants*, 'Semantic Chickens'.

51 We live in a world ruined by Reason.
1986 *Writing in Restaurants*, 'Oscars'.

52 We Americans have always considered Hollywood, at best, a sinkhole of depraved venality. And, of course, it is. It is not a Protective Monastery of Aesthetic Truth.
1986 *Writing in Restaurants*, 'A Playwright in Hollywood'.

53 There is such a thing as luck. There is such a thing as a *run of luck*. This is an instructive insight I have gained from poker—that all things have a rhythm, even the most seemingly inanimate of statistics.
1986 *Writing in Restaurants*, 'Things I Have Learned Playing Poker On The Hill'.

54 The poker player learns that sometimes both science and common sense are wrong; that the bumblebee *can* fly; that, perhaps, one should never trust an expert; that there are more things in heaven and earth than are dreamt of by those with an academic bent.

1986 *Writing in Restaurants*, 'Things I Have Learned Playing Poker On The Hill'.

55 All plays are about decay… That is why the theater has always been essential to human psychic equilibrium.

1986 *Writing in Restaurants*, 'Decay: Some Thoughts for Actors'.

56 The problems of the world, AIDS, cancer, nuclear war, pollution, are, finally, no more solvable than the problems of a tree which has borne fruit: the apples are overripe and they are falling—what can be done?… What can be done about the problems which beset our life? *Nothing* can be done, and nothing needs to be done. Something *is* being done—the organism is preparing to rest.

1986 *Writing in Restaurants*, 'Decay: Some Thoughts for Actors'.

57 The Film Industry is the American Monarchy: it is strict entailed succession and Horatio Alger in one. Except for the money manipulators and speculators on the top, it is a society built on work, achievement, and fealty to those in power.

1986 *Writing in Restaurants*, 'Observations of a Backstage Wife'.

58 Life in the movie business is like the beginning of a new love affair: it's full of surprises and you are constantly getting fucked.

1988 Charlie. *Speed The Plough*, sc.1.

59 A good film script should be able to do completely without dialogue.

1988 In *The Independent*, 11 Nov.

60 Film is the least realistic of art forms.

1989 In *The Guardian*, 16 Feb.

61 All of us write plays in our heads all the time…before we're going to visit our girl friend, before we're going to talk to a boss—we rehearse.

Quoted in Susan Stamberg *Talk* (1993).

Manchester, William Raymond 1922–

US novelist, foreign correspondent and contemporary historian, born in Attleboro, Massachusetts. His chief work is *The Death of a President* (1967), a landmark account written at the behest of the Kennedys.

62 A leader cut from whipcord.

1967 Of Governor John B Connally Jr. *The Death of a President*.

63 Johnson approached a strongly fortified position by outflanking it, or burrowing under it, or surprising the defenders from the rear, or raining down

obstacles upon them from the sky, or starving them into submission… Rarely, and then only reluctantly, would he proceed directly from A to B, to him the shortest distance between two points was a tunnel.

1967 Of Lyndon B Johnson. *The Death of a President*.

64 His critics called him a wheeler-dealer. They overlooked the subtlety of Johnsonian strategy, his use of wheels within wheels.

1967 Of Lyndon B Johnson. *The Death of a President*.

65 Actors who have tried to play Churchill and MacArthur have failed abysmally because each of those men was a great actor playing himself.

1983 In *Book of the Month Club News*, Jun.

66 He resolved to lead Britain and her fading empire in one last great struggle…to arm the nation, not only with weapons but also with the mace of honor, creating in every English breast a soul beneath the ribs of death.

1988 Of Winston Churchill. *The Last Lion*.

67 It would be inaccurate to say that Churchill and I conversed. Like Gladstone speaking to Victoria, he addressed me as though I were a one-man House of Commons.

1988 *The Last Lion*.

Mandela, Nelson Rolihlahla 1918–

African Nationalist leader, sentenced to life imprisonment in 1964. A potent symbol of black resistance, he was released in Feb 1990, and elected President (1991) of the ANC. In 1993 he was jointly awarded the Nobel Peace Prize with F W de Klerk, and in 1994 became South Africa's first black President.

68 During my lifetime I have dedicated my life to this struggle of the African people. I have fought against white domination, and I have fought against black domination. I have cherished the ideals of a democratic and free society in which all persons live together in harmony with equal opportunities. It is an ideal which I hope to live for, and to see realized. But My Lord, if needs be, it is an ideal for which I am prepared to die.

1964 Speech in court, 20 Apr, when charged under the Suppression of Communism Act and facing the death penalty.

69 We are not a political party. We have not changed at all. On the contrary, the ANC is a Government in waiting.

1991 Interviewed for BBC TV, Feb.

Mandela, (Nomzano) Winnie 1934–

South African civil rights activist, who joined her husband Nelson Mandela in his work with the ANC and on release from prison became controversially involved in the militant politics of the townships. She was divorced by her husband in 1996.

70 With that stick of matches, with our necklaces, we
    shall liberate this country.

    1986 Speech in the black townships, reported in the *Guardian*,
    15 Apr. The 'necklaces' were home-made bombs, car tyres filled
    with petrol.

Mandeville, Bernard 1670–1733

Dutch-born English satirist. After obtaining an MD degree
from Leiden in 1691 he practised as a physician in London.
He was widely denounced for encouraging immorality
through his principle 'private vices are public benefits'.

71 The root of Evil, Avarice
    That damn'd ill-natur'd, baneful Vice,
    Was Slave to Prodigality,
    That noble Sin; whilst Luxury
    Employed a Million of the Poor,
    And odious Pride a Million more;
    Envy itself, and Vanity,
    Were Ministers of Industry;
    Their darling Folly, Fickleness,
    In Diet, Furniture and Dress
    That strange ridic'lous Vice, was made
    That very Wheel that turned the Trade.

    1723 *The Fable of the Bees, or, Private Vices, Publick Benefits*
    (2nd edn.).

Mankiewicz, Herman 1897–1953

US journalist, screenwriter and film producer. He initially
worked in newspapers as a foreign correspondent in
Berlin and as a drama editor in New York, moving to
Hollywood in 1926 where he worked on his screenplays.
He is best remembered for his Academy Award-winning
film *Citizen Kane* (1941), although Orson Welles
originally claimed this script as his own work. He is the
elder brother of the film director Joseph L. Mankiewicz.

72 Old age…it's the only disease you don't look
    forward to being cured of.

    1941 *Citizen Kane* (with Orson Welles).

73 Rosebud.

    1941 Kane's last word, the opening word of the film, and
    constantly referred to throughout. *Citizen Kane* (with Orson
    Welles).

74 Don't believe everything you hear on the radio.

    1941 *Citizen Kane* (with Orson Welles).

75 There are millions to be grabbed out here and your
    only competition is idiots. Don't let this get around.

    Cable to Ben Hecht in the early days of Hollywood. Quoted in
    the *New York Times*, 8 Jan 1993.

Mankiewicz, Joseph 1909–93

US director, producer and writer, brother of Herman. He
won an Oscar for the script of *A Letter for Three Wives*
(1949) and an Oscar for the direction and script of *All
About Eve* (1950).

76 Fasten your seat belts, it's going to be a bumpy night!

    1950 by Bette Davis as Margo Channing in *All About Eve*.

77 We are a breed apart from the rest of humanity, we
    theatre folk. We are the original displaced
    personalities, concentrated gatherings of neurotics,
    egomaniacs, emotional misfits and precocious
    children.

    1950 George Sanders as Addison De Witt in *All About Eve*.

Mann, Thomas 1875–1955

German novelist and short story writer who left Germany
during World War II and settled in California. He
received the Nobel Prize for Literature in 1929.

78 *Wahrscheinlich sind sie der interessanteste Reiz und
    Stoff unsers Nachdenkens und unserer Tätigkeit.*

    Probably they are the most interesting stimulus and
    object of our meditation and our activity.

    1924 Of illnesses. *Der Zauberberg* (The Magic Mountain),
    vol.1.

79 *Bier, Tabak und Musik. Da haben wir Ihr Vaterland!*

    Beer, tobacco, and music. There we have the
    Fatherland!

    1924 *Der Zauberberg* (The Magic Mountain), vol.1.

80 *Leben ist, daß im Wechsel der Materie die Form
    erhalten bleibt.*

    Life is that the form is maintained through the
    change of substance.

    1924 *Der Zauberberg* (The Magic Mountain), vol.1.

81 *Daß nicht alles auf einmal da ist, bleibt als Bedingung
    des Lebens und der Erzählung zu achten, und man
    wird sich doch wohl gegen die gottgegebenen Formen
    menschlicher Erkenntnis nich auflehnen wollen.*

    Let us not forget the condition of life as narration:
    that we can never see the whole picture at once—
    unless we propose to throw overboard all the God-
    conditioned forms of human knowledge.

    1924 *Der Zauberberg* (The Magic Mountain), vol.2.

82 *Zum Leben gibt es zwei Wege: Der eine ist der
    gewöhnliche, direkte und brave. Der andere ist
    schlimm, er führt über den Tod, und das ist der
    geniale Weg!*

    There are two paths in life: one is the regular one,
    direct, honest. The other is bad, it leads through
    death—that is the way of genius!

    1924 *Der Zauberberg* (The Magic Mountain), vol.2.

83 *Und wenn man sich für das Leben interessiert, so
    interessiert man sich namentlich für den Tod.*

    If a person concerns himself with life, he also
    concerns himself with death.

    1924 *Der Zauberberg* (The Magic Mountain), vol.2.

84 *Die Zeit hat in Wirklichkeit keine Einschnitte, es gibt
kein Gewitter oder Drommetengetön beim Beginn
eines neuen Monats oder Jahres, und selbst bei dem
eines neuen Säkulums sind es nur wir Menschen, die
schießen und läuten.*

Time has no divisions to mark its passage, there is
never a thunderstorm or blare of trumpets to
announce the beginning of a new month or year.
Even when a new century begins it is only we
mortals who ring bells and fire off pistols.
1924 *Der Zauberberg* (The Magic Mountain), ch.4, sect.4
(translated by H T Lowe-Porter).

85 *Unser Sterben ist mehr eine Angelegenheit der
Weiterlebenden als unserer selbst.*

A man's dying is more the survivors' affair than his
own.
1924 *Der Zauberberg* (The Magic Mountain), ch.6, section 8
(translated by H T Lowe-Porter).

86 *Die Zeit ist das Element der Erzählung, wie sie das
Element des Lebens ist,—unlösbar damit verbunden,
wie mit den Körpern im Raum. Sie ist auch das
Element der Musik, als welche die Zeit mißt und
gliedert, sie kurzweilig und kostbar auf einmal macht.*

For time is the medium of narration, as it is the
medium of life. Both are inextricably bound up
with it, as are bodies in space. Similarly, time is the
medium of music; music divides, measures,
articulates time, and can shorten it, yet enhance its
value, both at once.
1924 *The Magic Mountain*, ch.7, section 1 (translated by H T
Lowe-Porter).

87 *Liebe zu sich selbst ist immer der Anfang eines
romanhaften Lebens.*

Self-love is always the beginning of a novelistic affair.
1933 *Joseph und seine Brüder* (Joseph and his Brothers).

88 *Man kann sehr wohl in einer Geschichte sein, ohne sie
zu verstehen.*

A person can be fully involved in a story without
understanding it.
1933 *Joseph und seine Brüder* (Joseph and his Brothers).

89 *Denn dem Menschen ist am Wiedererkennen gelegen;
er möchte das Alte im Neuen wiederfinden und das
Typische im Individuellen.*

For man always searches for recognition: he would
like to find the old in the new and the ordinary in
the individual.
1936 *Freud und die Zukunft.*

90 *Ist die Liebe das Beste im Leben, so in der Liebe das
Beste der Kuß.*

If love is the best thing in life, then the best part of
love is the kiss.

1939 *Lotte im Weimar.*

91 *Das Seelische [ist] immer das Primäre und eigentlich
Motivierende; die politische Aktion ist zweiter
Ordnung, Reflex, Ausdruck, Instrument.*

The mental state is always the primary and
ultimately the motivating state. Political action is of
second rank, reflex, expression, instrument.
1947 *Doktor Faustus.*

Mann, Thomas Edward 1944–

US political scientist. He is director of Government
Studies at Brookings Institution and is the author and co-
editor of many books on American political science and
congressional election studies, such as *Renewing Congress,
1992.*

92 He's a great ex-president. It's a shame he couldn't
have gone directly to the ex-presidency.
1994 Of Jimmy Carter and his successful visit to Korea. In
Newsweek, 27 Jun.

Mannheim, Karl 1893–1947

Hungarian-born German sociologist, who taught at the
University of Heidelberg until expelled by Hitler and later
at the LSE, known for his contributions to the sociology
of knowledge.

93 Even the categories in which experiences are
subsumed, collected, and ordered vary according to
the social position of the observer.
1936 *Ideology and Utopia.*

Manning, Henry Edward 1808–92

English Roman Catholic prelate. He succeeded as
Archbishop of Westminster in 1865 and became a
cardinal in 1875. Noted for his support for the
temperance and benevolent movements, he was also a
keen cricketer and captained the Harrow Eleven team.

94 That bat that you were kind enough to send,
Seems (for as yet I have not tried it) good:
And if there's anything on earth can mend
My wretched play, it is that piece of wood.
1826 Verse sent to Charles Wordsworth, nephew of the poet
William Wordsworth, after the latter sent him the present of a
cricket bat.

95 To put labour and wages first and human or
domestic life second is to invert the order of God
and of nature.
1889 On the London dock strike.

Mansfield, Katherine pseudonym of Kathleen Mansfield Beauchamp 1881–1923

New Zealand writer. She moved to London to pursue a
literary career and married John Middleton Murry. She
died prematurely of tuberculosis. She is best known for her

finely crafted short stories, in collections such as *Bliss, and Other Stories* (1920). Her *Journal* was published in 1927.

96 Talk of our enlightened days and our emancipated country—pure nonsense! We are firmly held with the self-fashioned chains of slavery. Yes, now I see that they *are* self-fashioned, and must be self-removed.
1908 Journal entry, May.

97 The trouble with women like me is—they can't keep their nerves out of the job in hand... I walk about with a mind full of ghosts of saucepans and primus stoves and 'Will there be enough to go round?' I loathe myself, today. I detest this woman who 'superintends' you and rushes about, slamming doors and slopping water—all untidy with her blouse out and her nails grimed.
1913 Letter to John Middleton Murry, summer.

98 Why haven't I got a real 'home'—a real life—why haven't I got a Chinese nurse with green trousers and two babies who rush at me and clasp my knees? I'm not a girl—I'm a woman. I *want* things...all this love and joy that fights for outlet—and all this life drying up, like milk in an old breast.
1915 Letter to John Middleton Murry, 23 Mar.

99 I want for one moment to make our undiscovered country leap into the eyes of the Old World. It must be mysterious, as though floating. It must take the breath. It must be 'one of those islands...'.
1916 Journal entry, 22 Jan.

1 E M Forster never gets any further than warming the teapot. He's a rare fine hand at that. Feel this teapot. Is it not beautifully warm? Yes, but there ain't going to be no tea. And I can never be perfectly certain whether Helen was got with child by Leonard Bast or by his fatal forgotten umbrella. All things considered, I think it must have been the umbrella.
1917 Journal entry, May.

2 Her underlip protruded a little; she had a way of sucking it in that somebody else had told her was awfully fascinating.
1920 *Bliss and Other Stories*, 'Prelude'.

3 True to oneself! Which self? Which of my many...hundreds of selves?... There are moments when I feel I am nothing but the small clerk of some hotel without a proprietor, who has all his work cut out to enter the names and hand the keys to the wilful guests.
1920 Journal entry, Apr.

4 I believe that people are like portmanteaux—packed with certain things, started going, thrown about, tossed away, dumped down, lost and found,

half emptied suddenly, or squeezed fatter than ever, until finally the Ultimate Porter swings them on to the Ultimate Train and away they rattle.
1920 *Bliss and Other Stories*, 'Je Ne Parle Pas Français'.

5 Is it not possible that the rage for confession, autobiography, especially for memories of earliest childhood, is explained by our persistent yet mysterious belief in a self which is continuous and permanent; which, untouched by all we acquire and all we shed, pushes a green spear through the dead leaves and through the mould, thrusts a scaled bud through years of darkness until, one day, the light discovers it and shakes the flower free and—we are alive—we are flowering for our moment upon the earth? This is the moment which after all, we live for—the moment of direct feeling when we are most ourselves and least personal.
1920 Journal entry, Apr.

6 If there was one thing he hated more than another it was the way she had of waking him in the morning... It was her way of establishing her grievance for the day.
1920 *Bliss and Other Stories*, 'Mr Reginald Peacock's Day'.

7 The aloe seemed to ride...like a ship with the oars lifted. Bright moonlight hung upon the lifted oars like water, and on the green wave glittered the dew.
1920 *Bliss*, 'Prelude'.

8 He stands, smiling encouragement, like a clumsy dentist.
1922 *The Garden Party*, 'Bank Holiday'.

9 She couldn't possibly go back to the gentleman's flat; she had no right to cry in strangers' houses.
1922 *The Garden Party*, 'The Life of Ma Parker'.

10 What would father say when he found out? For he was bound to find out sooner or later. He always did. 'Buried. You two girls had me *buried!*' She heard his stick thumping. Oh, what would they say? What possible excuse could they make? It sounded such an appallingly heartless thing to do. Such a wicked advantage to take of a person because he happened to be helpless at the moment.
1922 *The Garden-Party*, 'The Daughters of the Late Colonel'.

11 Whenever I prepare for a journey I prepare as though for death. Should I never return, all is in order. This is what life has taught me.
1922 Journal entry, 29 Jan.

12 The longer I live the more I turn to New Zealand. I thank God I was born in New Zealand. A young country is a real heritage, though it takes one time to recognize it. But New Zealand is in my very bones. What I wouldn't give to have a look at it!
1922 Letter to her father, Sir Harold Beauchamp, 18 Mar.

13 Looking back, I imagine I was always writing.
   Twaddle it was, too. But better far write twaddle or
   anything, anything, than nothing at all.
   1922 Journal entry.

Mansfield, Michael Joseph 1903–

US former Democratic senator and ambassador. A
professor of history and political science (1933–42), he
became a congressional member (1943–53) and senator
for Montana (1943–53). As US Ambassador to Japan
(1977–89) in Tokyo, he represented the USA on several
trips to China.

14 A half-creature of the Senate and a half-creature of
   the executive.
   1969 On the role of the Vice President as the Senate's presiding
   officer. In *Time*, 14 Nov.

Mansfield, William Murray, 1st Earl
1705–93

English judge and MP. He was chief-justice of the king's
Bench (1756) and a member of the Cabinet. His rulings
developed the law of maritime contracts, insurance and
bills, and influenced international law.

15 We must not regard political consequences,
   however formidable they may be. If rebellion was
   the certain consequence, we are bound to say,
   'Justitia fiat, ruat coelum' (Let Justice be done,
   though the skies may fall).'
   1768 Judgement against the sentence imposed on John Wilkes
   for publishing the anti-ministerial political newspaper *North
   Briton*, 28 Apr.
   ▷ See Ferdinand I 385:13.

16 Every man who comes to England is entitled to the
   protection of the English law, whatever oppression
   he may heretofore have suffered, and whatever may
   be the colour of his skin, whether it is black or
   whether it is white.
   1772 Judgement on the Somersett slavery case, May

Mao Zedong or Mao Tse-tung 1893–1976

Chinese military and political leader who became the first
Chairman (1949) of the People's Republic. After the
failure of the 1958–60 'Great Leap Forward' economic
programme, his hold on power was weakened but he
regained control by launching the 1966–9 'Cultural
Revolution'.

17 But just think how good communism is! The state
   won't bother us anymore.
   1919 Attributed remark. Quoted in Ross Terrill *Mao: A
   Biography* (1980), ch.4.

18 A revolution is not a dinner party.
   1927 *The Little Red Book*, section 2.

19 A single spark can start a forest fire. Our forces,
   although small at present, will grow rapidly.
   1930 Letter, 5 Jan.

20 If you want to know the taste of a pear, you must
   taste the pear by eating it for yourself. If you want
   to know the theory and methods of revolution, you
   must take part in revolution. All genuine
   knowledge originates in direct experience.
   1937 Address to the Anti-Japanese Military and Political
   College, Jul.

21 Politics is war without bloodshed; war is politics
   with bloodshed.
   1938 'On Protracted War', speech, May.

22 Every Communist must grasp the truth that
   political power grows out of the barrel of a gun.
   1938 'Problems of War and Strategy', speech, 6 Nov.

23 China has stood up.
   1949 Proclaiming the establishment of the People's Republic of
   China, 1 Oct.

24 When a man reaches old age, he will die and the
   same is true of a party.
   1950 Collected in *Selected Works* (1975), vol.4.

25 If the worst came to the worst and half of mankind
   died, the other half would remain while
   imperialism would be razed to the ground and the
   whole world could become socialist.
   1954 Quoted in the *Peking Review*, 9 Jun 1963.

26 All the so-called powerful reactionaries are paper
   tigers, for they are cut off from their people. Was
   not Hitler a paper tiger, and was he not overthrown?
   US imperialism has not yet been overthrown, and it
   has atomic bombs—but I believe that it too will be
   overthrown. It, too, is a paper tiger.
   1957 Speech to Communist International Congress, Moscow,
   Nov.

27 Letting a hundred flowers blossom and a hundred
   schools of thought contend is the policy for
   promoting the progress of the arts and the sciences
   and a flourishing culture in our land.
   1957 Speech, Peking, 27 Feb.

28 The east wind prevails over the west wind.
   1957 Spoken at an international conference of Communist
   leaders in Moscow. Quoted in Ross Terrill *Mao: A Biography*
   (1980), ch.14.

29 People of the world, unite and defeat the US
   aggressors and all their running dogs.
   1958 Speech, Jul.

30 I have seen Lenin's manuscripts, which are filled
   with changes. He too made mistakes.
   1959 Quoted in Ross Terrill *Mao: A Biography* (1980), ch.15.

31 Water too pure breeds no fish.
   1974 Quoted in Han Suyin *Wind in the Tower*.

32 The more books one reads, the more stupid one
becomes.
1976 Quoted in Ross Terrill *Mao: A Biography* (1980), ch.22.

Map, Walter c.1140–c.1209

Welsh poet and ecclesiast, author of *De Nugis Curialium* and possibly new versions of the Arthurian Romances.

33 *Dura est manus cirurgi, sed sanam.*

The hand of the surgeon is hard, but healing.
c.1181 *De Nugis Curalium*, Distinction 4, ch.4.

34 *Numquam enim audiendi quod aliquis monachus super puerum incubuisset, quin statim post ipsum surrexisset puer.*

I have heard before of a monk throwing himself on a boy, but the boy always rose again afterwards.
c.1181 On hearing of an unsuccessful attempt by Saint Bernard of Clairvaux to revive a dead boy by throwing himself on the body and praying. *De Nugis Curialium*, Distinction 4, ch.5.

35 *Hoc sulum deliqui, quod uiuo.*

My only fault is that I am alive.
c.1181 On the refusal of many of his contemporaries to believe that his *Dissuasio Valerii ad Rufinum* could have been composed by a modern writer. *De Nugis Curialium*, Distinction 4, ch.5.

Maraniss, David 1949–

US journalist and author. As a journalist for the *Washington Post*, he received the Pulitzer Prize for national reporting in 1993, and has written a biography of President Bill Clinton.

36 It is…classic Bill Clinton, sincere and deceptive at the same time, requiring a careful reading between the lines.
1995 On President Clinton's letter as a graduate student, 3 Dec 1969, to arrange ROTC enlistment to avoid being drafted for the Vietnam War, a position that was to haunt his future campaigning. *First in His Class.*

37 Natural politicians are skilled actors, recreating reality, adjusting and ad-libbing, synthesizing the scenes, saying the same thing over and over again and making it seem that they are saying it for the first time.
1995 Of Bill Clinton. *First in His Class.*

38 At 34, he fit the ironic description of the quintessential Rhodes Scholar: someone with a great future behind him.
1995 Of Bill Clinton, the youngest defeated state governor in US history. *First in His Class.*

39 He is a congenital campaigner.
1995 Predicting that Bill Clinton would always be a candidate for office or an advocate. CNBC broadcast, 7 Mar.

Marc, Franz 1880–1916

German painter, founder member of the Munich-based Blaue Reiter ('Blue Rider') group. Most of his paintings were of animals (eg *Blue Horses*, 1911) portrayed in forceful colours. He was killed at Verdun during World War I.

40 Today art is moving in a direction of which our fathers would never even have dreamed. We stand before the new pictures as in a dream and we hear the apocalyptic horsemen in the air.
1912 Subscription prospectus of the *Blaue Reiter Almanac*, Jan.

41 Art will liberate itself from the needs and desires of men. No longer will we paint a forest or a horse as we like or as they appear to us, but as they really are.
1914–15 *Aphorisms.*

42 Traditions are lovely things—to create traditions, that is, not to live off them.
1914–15 *Aphorisms.*

43 Who is able to paint the existence of a dog as Picasso paints the existence of a cubic shape?
Quoted in *Briefe, Aufzeichnungen und Aphorismen* (2 vols., 1920), translated by Chipp in his *Theories of Modern Art* (1968).

Marceau, Marcel 1923–

French mime artist. Celebrated for his performances in the role of the white-faced Bip, he is the foremost exponent of the mime theatre of Charles Dullin and Jean-Louis Barrault.

44 Life is a cycle, and mime is particularly suitable for showing fluidity, transformation, metamorphosis. Words can keep people apart; mime can be a bridge between them.
Attributed.

Marcos, Ferdinand Edralin 1917–89

Filipino politician, elected President in 1965 and again in 1969. His years of office became increasingly notorious for widespread corruption but US backing helped keep him in power. He declared martial law in 1972 but was overthrown in 1986 by a popular 'People's Power' campaign.

45 It is easier to run a revolution than a government.
1977 In *Time*, 6 Jun.

46 Some people say the president is incapable of enforcing the law. Let them say that once more and I will set the tanks on them.
1986 Quoted in 'The Snap Revolution', in James Fenton *All the Wrong Places.*

47 History isn't through with me yet.
1986 Remark, quoted in Sterling Seagrave *The Marcos Dynasty.*

Marcos, Imelda Romualdez 1927–

Wife of President Ferdinand Marcos of the Philippines, with whom she fled in 1986. She later faced charges of theft and corruption.

48 Some are smarter than others.

c.1985 Her reply to a question about the great wealth she had accumulated. Quoted in Sterling Seagrave *The Marcos Dynasty*.

49 The real index of this country is the smiles of the people, not the economic index.

c.1985 Quoted in Sterling Seagrave *The Marcos Dynasty*.

Marcus Aurelius full name *Marcus Aelius Aurelius Antoninus* AD 121–180

Roman emperor and philosopher. His spiritual reflections, the *Meditations*, are considered a classic work of Stoicism.

50 Nothing is so conducive to greatness of mind as the ability to examine systematically and honestly everything that meets us in life.

Meditations, vol.3, pt.2 (translated by Charles Reginald Haines, 1901).

Marguerite d'Angoulême 1492–1549

Queen of Navarre and sister of François I. She was a patron of the arts, and wrote poetry.

51 *Je n'ai plus ni père, ni mère,*
Ni sœur, ni frère
Sinon Dieu seul auquel j'espère.

I no longer have a father, nor a mother,
Nor a sister, nor a brother.
I only have God to trust in.

1547 *Cantiques spirituels.*

52 *Plus j'ai d'amour plus j'ai de fâcherie.*

The more I love, the more I quarrel.

1547 *Dizains.*

53 *Depuis qu'Eve fit pécher Adam, toutes les femmes ont pris possession de tourmenter, tuer et damner les hommes.*

Ever since Eve made Adam sin, women have taken it upon themselves to torment, kill and damn men.

1558 *Heptaméron*, pt.1.

54 *Seulement les sots sont punis, et non les vicieux.*

Only the foolish are punished, never the truly vicious.

1558 *Heptaméron*, pt.13.

55 *Un malheureux cherche l'autre.*

One unhappy person seeks out another.

1558 *Heptaméron*, pt.21.

56 *Le scandale est souvent pire que le péché.*

The scandal is often worse than the sin itself.

1558 *Heptaméron*, 25.

57 *Votre plaisir gît déshonorer les femmes, et votre honneur tuer les hommes en guerre; qui sont deux points formellement contraires la loi de Dieu.*

Your pleasure lies in dishonouring women and your honour lies in killing men at war; two acts which stand in contradiction to the law of God.

1558 *Heptaméron*, 26.

58 *Mariage est un état de si longue durée qu'il ne doit être commencé légèrement, ni sans l'opinion de nos meilleurs amis et parents.*

Marriage is a state of such long duration that it should not begin lightly, nor without the opinion of our best friends and parents.

1558 *Heptaméron*, 40.

59 *L'amour n'est pas un feu que l'on tient dans la main.*

Love is not a flame that one holds in the hand.

1558 *Heptaméron*, 47.

60 *A force de jurer, on engendre quelque doute à la vérité.*

When forced to swear an oath, one can encounter doubt about the truth.

1558 *Heptaméron*, 61.

Marhabal

Carthaginian soldier, a cavalry commander under Hannibal at the Battle of Cannae (216 BC).

61 You know how to gain a victory, Hannibal: you know not how to use one.

216 BC Comment to Hannibal after victory at Cannae. Quoted in Livy *Ab urbe condita*, bk.22.

Mariátegui, José Carlos 1895–1930

Peruvian political leader and essayist, who applied Marxist principles to Peruvian problems, while acknowledging the value of religion and myth to the indigenous peoples.

62 *Mientras en Norteamérica la colonización depositó los gérmenes de un espíritu y una economía que se plasmaban entonces en Europa y a los cuales pertenecía el porvenir, a la América española trajo los efectos y los métodos de un espíritu y una economía que declinaban ya y a lo cuales no pertenecía sino el pasado.*

Whereas in North America colonization planted the seeds of the spirit and economy then growing in Europe and representing the future, the Spaniard brought to America the effects and methods of an already declining spirit and economy that belonged to the past.

1928 *Siete ensayos de interpretación de la realidad peruana*, 'El problema de la tierra' (translated as *Seven Interpretive Essays on Peruvian Reality*, 1971).

Marie de France fl.1160–70

French poet, author of *Lais* and *Fables*. Born in Normandy, she spent most of her life in England. Her

Lais in particular were of great influence on French literature.

63 *Qui Deus a duné escience*
e de parler bone eloquence,
ne s'en deit taisir ne celer,
ainz se deit voluntiers mustrer.

Whoever God has given knowledge
and eloquence in speaking,
should not be silent or secretive,
but should willingly show it.
c.1170 *Lais*, prologue, l.1–4.

64 *Ki qu'en plurt ne ki qu'en chant,*
le dreit estuet aler avant.

Whether it makes one cry or sing,
justice must be carried out.
c.1170 *Lanval*, l.437–8.

65 *Mult est fole, ki hume creit.*

She is a fool, who trusts a man.
c.1170 *Eliduc*, line 1084.

Marinetti, Emilio Filippo Tomasso
1876–1944

Italian dramatist, novelist and poet. He published his influential manifesto for Futurism in *Figaro* in 1909, and became a Fascist in 1919. His writings glorify war, the machine age and dynamism, disparaging all traditional forms of art.

66 We sing the love of danger. Courage, rashness, and rebellion are the elements of our poetry. Hitherto literature has tended to exalt thoughtful immobility, ecstasy, and sleep, whereas we are for aggressive movement, febrile insomnia, mortal leaps, and blows with the fist. We proclaim that the world is richer for a new beauty of speed, and our praise is for the man at the wheel. There is no beauty now save in struggle, no masterpiece can be anything but aggressive, and hence we glorify war, militarism and patriotism.
1909 *Manifesto of Futurism*. Quoted in Denis Mack Smith *Italy: A Modern History* (1959), p.270.

67 We affirm that the world's magnificence has been enriched by a new beauty: the beauty of speed. A racing car whose hood is adorned with great pipes, like serpents of explosive breath—a roaring car that seems to ride on grapeshot is more beautiful than the *Victory of Samothrace*.
1909 *Manifesto of Futurism*.

68 It is from Italy that we launch through the world this violently upsetting incendiary manifesto of ours. With it, today, we establish *Futurism*, because we want to free this land from its smelly gangrene of professors, archaeologists, *ciceroni* and antiquarians. For too long has Italy been a dealer in second-hand clothes. We mean to free her from the numberless museums that cover her like so many graveyards.
1909 *Manifesto of Futurism*.

Marion, Frances originally *Frances Marion Owens* 1888–1973

US screenwriter and novelist. She wrote prolifically for the silent screen before working as a war correspondent, and subsequently translated her skills to talking pictures. She later turned to novel writing.

69 Gimme visky…ginger ale on the side. And don't be stingy baby.
1931 Opening lines delivered by Greta Garbo in *Anna Christie*.

70 I read somewhere that machinery is going to take the place of every profession.
Oh my dear that's something you'll never have to worry about.
1933 Dialogue between Jean Harlow and Marie Dressler in *Dinner At Eight* (with Herman Mankiewicz).

Maritain, Jacques 1882–1973

French philosopher and critic. He converted from Protestantism to Catholicism (1906) and gained renown for his interpretations of St Thomas Aquinas. He based his own philosophy on Aristotle and Aquinas.

71 Poetry proceeds from the totality of man, sense, imagination, intellect, love, desire, instinct, blood and spirit together.
Quoted in Robert Fitzgerald (ed) *Enlarging the Change* (1985).

72 The poet knows himself only on the condition that things resound in him, and that in him, at a single awakening, they and he come forth together out of sleep.
Quoted in Robert Fitzgerald (ed) *Enlarging the Change* (1985).

Marivaux, Pierre Carlet de Chamblain de
1688–1763

French author best known for his comedies in which language, more than characters, dictates the action.

73 *Un mari porte un masque avec le monde, et une grimace avec sa femme.*

A husband wears a mask in the world and a smirk with his wife.
1730 *Le Jeu de l'amour et du hasard*, act 1, sc.2.

74 *Dans ce monde, il faut être un peu trop bon pour l'être assez.*

In this world, one must be a little too good in order to be good enough.
1730 *Le Jeu de l'amour et du hasard*, act 1, sc.2.

75 *Les bienfaits des hommes sont accompagnés d'une maladresse si humiliante pour les personnes qui les reçoivent!*

The generosity of men is accompanied by such a humiliating embarrassment for those who benefit from it.

1731 *La vie de Marianne*, ch.1.

76 *C'est presque toujours le péché qui prêche la vertu dans nos chaires.*

It's almost always sin which preaches virtue in our pulpits.

1731 *La vie de Marianne*, ch.4.

77 *Qu'est-ce qu'un charité qui n'a point de pudeur avec le misérable, et qui, avant de le soulager, commence par écraser son amour propre.*

What is that charity worth which does not spare the wretched person's feelings, which instead, before providing comfort, begins by wiping out his self-esteem.

1731 *La vie de Marianne*, ch.14.

78 *L'âme se raffine à mesure qu'elle se gâte.*

The soul refines itself in proportion to how it spoils itself.

1741 *Le Paysan parvenu*, ch.4.

Markham, Dewey 'Pigmeat' 1906–81

US songwriter and comedy writer.

79 Here comes the judge.

1968 Song title, cowritten with Dick Alen, Bob Astor and Sarah Harvey. Often quoted as a vaudeville catchphrase, 'Here come de judge'.

Marks, Leo

British writer. He acted as adviser on the film *Carve Her Name With Pride* (1958), partly based on his own wartime work in cryptography. He also wrote the script of *Peeping Tom* (1960).

80 The life that I have is all that I have
and the life that I have is yours
The love that I have of the life that I have
Is yours and yours and yours.

1958 Poem recited by Virginia McKenna as Violette Szabo in *Carve Her Name With Pride*.

Marlborough, John Churchill, 1st Duke of 1650–1722

English general. He helped quell Monmouth's rebellion at Sedgemoor, but deserted to William of Orange in 1688. Under Queen Anne he was appointed supreme commander of British forces in the War of the Spanish Succession, rewarded for his success with a dukedom.

81 I have not time to say any more, but to beg you will give my duty to the Queen, and let her know her

army has had a glorious victory. Monsieur Tallard and two other generals are in my coach, and I am following the rest.

1704 Note written on a tavern bill to his wife, Sarah, 13 Aug, after the Battle of Blenheim.

Marley, Bob (Robert Nesta) 1945–81

Jamaican singer, guitarist, and composer of reggae music. His hits include 'No woman, no cry', 'I Shot the Sheriff', and 'Exodus'. Among his albums were *Catch a Fire* (1972), *Rastaman Vibration* (1976), and *Uprising* (1980).

82 Get up, stand up
Stand up for your rights
Get up, stand up
Don't give up the fight.

1973 'Get Up, Stand Up'.

83 Don't just move to the music, listen to what I'm saying.

Quoted in Johnson and Pines *Reggae* (1982).

Marlowe, Christopher 1564–93

English poet and playwright. It is thought that he was a spy for the English in the Netherlands, and that he was killed in a tavern brawl. His many dramatic works include *Doctor Faustus* (1592), and his poems include the unfinished *Hero and Leander* and lyrics such as 'The Passionate Shepherd to his Love'.

84 From jigging veins of rhyming mother-wits,
And such conceits as clownage keeps in pay,
We'll lead you to the stately tents of war.

1587 *Tamburlaine the Great* (published 1590), pt.1, prologue.

85 Come, lady, let not this appall your thoughts.

1587 *Tamburlaine the Great* (published 1590), pt.1, act 1, sc.2.

86 Tamburlaine!—
A Scythian shepherd so embellishèd
With nature's pride and richest furniture!
His looks do menace heaven and dare the gods.
His fiery eyes are fixed upon the earth.

1587 *Tamburlaine the Great* (published 1590), pt.1, act 1, sc.2.

87 Accurst be he that first invented war.

1587 *Tamburlaine the Great* (published 1590), pt.1, act 2, sc.4.

88 A god is not so glorious as a king.
I think the pleasure they enjoy in Heaven,
Cannot compare with kingly joys in earth.
To wear a crown enchased with pearl and gold,
Whose virtues carry with it life and death;
To ask and have, command and be obeyed;
When looks breed love, with looks to gain the
   prize,
Such power attractive shines in princes' eyes!

1587 *Tamburlaine the Great* (published 1590), pt.1, act 2, sc.5.

89 Nature that framed us of four elements,
Warring within our breasts for regiment,

Doth teach us all to have aspiring minds:
Our souls, whose faculties can comprehend
The wondrous architecture of the world,
And measure every wandering planet's course,
Still climbing after knowledge infinite,
And always moving as the restless spheres,
Wills us to wear ourselves, and never rest,
Until we reach the ripest fruit of all,
That perfect bliss and sole felicity,
The sweet fruition of an earthly crown.

1587 *Tamburlaine the Great* (published 1590), pt.1, act 2, sc.7.

90 Virtue is the fount whence honour springs.

1587 *Tamburlaine the Great* (published 1590), pt.1, act 4, sc.4.

91 What is beauty, saith my sufferings, then?
If all the pens that ever poets held
Had fed the feeling of their masters' thoughts,
And every sweetness that inspired their hearts,
Their minds, and muses on admirèd themes;
If all the heavenly quintessence they still
From their immortal flowers of poesy,
Wherein, as in a mirror, we perceive
The highest reaches of a human wit;
If these had made one poem's period,
And all combined in beauty's worthiness,
Yet should there hover in their restless heads
One thought, one grace, one wonder, at the least,
Which into words no virtue can digest.

1587 *Tamburlaine the Great* (published 1590), pt.1, act 5, sc.1.

92 And every warrior that is rapt with love
Of fame, of valour, and of victory,
Must needs have beauty beat on his conceits:
I thus conceiving and subduing both,
That which hath stopped the tempest of the gods,
Even from the fiery-spangled veil of heaven,
To feel the lovely warmth of shepherds' flames,
And march in cottages of strowèd weeds,
Shall give the world to note, for all my birth,
That virtue solely is the sum of glory,
And fashions men with true nobility.

1587 *Tamburlaine the Great* (published 1590), pt.1, act 5, sc.1.

93 Helen, whose beauty summoned Greece to arms,
And drew a thousand ships to Tenedos.

1587 *Tamburlaine the Great* (published 1590), pt.2, l.3055–6.

94 More childish valorous than manly wise.

1587 *Tamburlaine the Great* (published 1590), pt.2, l.3690.

95 Holla, ye pampered Jades of Asia;
What, can ye draw but twenty miles a day?

1587 *Tamburlaine the Great* (published 1590), pt.2, l.3980–1.

96 I count religion but a childish toy,
And hold there is no sin but ignorance.

c.1589 *The Jew of Malta* (published 1633), 'Prologue to the Stage, At the Cock-pit'.

97 Might first made kings, and laws were then most
sure
When…they were writ in blood.

c.1589 *The Jew of Malta* (published 1633), 'Prologue'.

98 Thus methinks should men of judgement frame
Their means of traffic from the vulgar trade,
And as their wealth increaseth, so enclose
Infinite riches in a little room.

c.1589 *The Jew of Malta* (published 1633), act 1, sc.1.

99 The sad presaging raven, that tolls
The sick man's passport in her hollow beak,
And in the shadow of the silent night
Doth shake contagion from her sable wings.

c.1589 *The Jew of Malta* (published 1633), act 2, sc.1.

1 As for myself, I walk abroad o'nights
And kill sick people groaning under walls:
Sometimes I go about and poison wells.

c.1589 *The Jew of Malta* (published 1633), act 2, sc.3.

2 Barnardine: Thou hast committed—
Barabas: Fornication—but that was in another
country; and besides, the wench is dead.

c.1589 *The Jew of Malta* (published 1633), act 4, sc.1.

3 'My father is deceased. Come, Gaveston,
And share the kingdom with thy dearest friend.'
Ah, words that make me surfeit with delight!
What greater bliss can hap to Gaveston
Than live and be the favourite of a king?
Sweet prince, I come; these, these thy amorous
lines
Might have enforced me to have swum from
France,
And, like Leander, gasped upon the sand,
So thou woulds't smile, and take me in thy arms.

c.1591 Gaveston is reading a letter from King Edward. *Edward II* (published 1594), act 1, sc.1.

4 My men, like satyrs grazing on the lawns,
Shall with their goat feet dance an antic hay.

c.1591 *Edward II* (published 1594), act 1, sc.1.

5 The griefs of private men are soon allayed,
But not of kings.

c.1591 *Edward II* (published 1594), act 5, sc.1.

6 But what are kings, when regiment is gone,
But perfect shadows in a sunshine day?

c.1591 *Edward II* (published 1594), act 5, sc.1.

7 He hath a body able to endure
More than we can inflict: and therefore now
Let us assail his mind another while.

c.1591 *Edward II* (published 1594), act 5, sc.4.

8 Sweet Analytics, 'tis thou has ravished me!

c.1592 *Doctor Faustus* (published 1604), act 1, sc.1.

9 I'll have them fly to India for gold,
   Ransack the ocean for orient pearl.
   c.1592 *Doctor Faustus* (published 1604), act 1, sc.1.

10 Is, to dispute well, logic's chiefest end?
   Affords this art no greater miracle?
   c.1592 *Doctor Faustus* (published 1604), act 1, sc.1.

11 Oh, what a world of profit and delight,
   Of power, of honour, and omnipotence,
   Is promised to the studious artisan!
   c.1592 *Doctor Faustus* (published 1604), act 1, sc.1.

12 All things that move between the quiet poles
   Shall be at my command: emperors and kings
   Are but obeyed in their several provinces,
   Nor can they raise the wind, or rend the clouds;
   But his dominion that exceeds in this
   Stretcheth as far as doth the mind of man;
   A sound magician is a demi-god.
   c.1592 *Doctor Faustus* (published 1604), act 1, sc.1.

13 How am I glutted with conceit of this!
   Shall I make spirits fetch me what I please,
   Resolve me of all ambiguities,
   Perform what desperate enterprise I will?
   I'll have them fly to India for gold,
   Ransack the ocean for orient pearl,
   And search all corners of the new found world
   For pleasant fruits and princely delicates.
   c.1592 *Doctor Faustus* (published 1604), act 1, sc.1.

14 Why, this is hell, nor am I out of it:
   Thinkst thou that I who saw the face of God,
   And tasted the eternal joys of heaven,
   Am not tormented with ten thousand hells
   In being deprived of everlasting bliss!
   c.1592 *Doctor Faustus* (published 1604), act 1, sc.3.

15 Hell hath no limits, nor is circumscribed
   In one self place; but where we are is hell,
   And where hell is, there must we ever be:
   And, to be short, when all the world dissolves,
   And every creature shall be purified,
   All places shall be hell that is not heaven.
   c.1592 *Doctor Faustus* (published 1604), act 2, sc.1.

16 But think'st thou heaven is such a glorious thing?
   I tell thee, Faustus, it is not half so fair
   As thou, or any man that breathes on earth.
   c.1592 *Doctor Faustus*, act 2, sc.2.

17 Have I not made blind Homer sing to me?
   c.1592 *Doctor Faustus* (published 1604), act 2, sc.2.

18 O gentle Faustus, leave this damnèd art,
   This magic, that will charm thy soul to hell.
   c.1592 *Doctor Faustus* (published 1604), act 5, sc.1.

19 Was this the face that launched a thousand ships,

And burnt the topless towers of Ilium?
Sweet Helen, make me immortal with a kiss!
Her lips suck forth my soul: see, where it flies!
Come Helen, come give me my soul again.
Here will I dwell, for heaven be in these lips,
And all is dross that is not Helena.
c.1592 *Doctor Faustus* (published 1604), act 5, sc.1.

20 Now hast thou but one bare hour to live,
   And then thou must be damned perpetually!
   Stand still, you ever-moving spheres of heaven,
   That time may cease, and midnight never come.
   Fair nature's eye, rise, rise, again, and make
   Perpetual day; or let this hour be but
   A year, a month, a week, a natural day,
   That Faustus may repent and save his soul!
   O lente, lente currite, noctis equi:
   The stars move still, time runs, the clock will
      strike,
   The devil will come, and Faustus must be
      damned.
   Oh, I'll leap up to my God!—Who pulls me
      down?—
   See, see, where Christ's blood streams in the
      firmament!
   One drop would save my soul, half a drop, ah,
      my Christ.
   c.1592 *Doctor Faustus* (published 1604), act 5, sc.2.

21 You stars that reigned at my nativity,
   Whose influence hath allotted death and hell,
   Now draw up Faustus like a foggy mist,
   Into the entrails of yon labouring cloud,
   That when you vomit forth into the air,
   My limbs may issue from your smoky mouths,
   So that my soul may but ascend to heaven.
   c.1592 *Doctor Faustus* (published 1604), act 5, sc.2.

22 Ah, Pythagoras' metempsychosis, were that
      time,
   This soul should fly from me, and I be changed
   Unto some brutish beast.
   c.1592 *Doctor Faustus* (published 1604), act 5, sc.2.

23 Cut is the branch that might have grown full
      straight,
   And burnèd is Apollo's laurel bough,
   That somtime grew within this learned man.
   c.1592 *Doctor Faustus* (published 1604), epilogue.

24 Where Venus in her naked glory strove
   To please the careless and disdainful eyes
   Of proud Adonis.
   1593 *Hero and Leander* (published 1598).

25 So lovely fair was Hero, Venus' nun,
   As Nature wept, thinking she was undone.
   1593 *Hero and Leander* (published 1598).

26 His body was as straight as Circe's wand;
Jove might have sipped out nectar from his
hand.
1593 *Hero and Leander* (published 1598), pt.1, l.61–2.

27 It lies not in our power to love, or hate,
For will in us is overruled by fate.
When two are stripped, lo ere the course begin
We wish that one should lose, the other win;
And one especially do we affect
Of two gold ingots, like in each respect.
The reason no man knows, let it suffice,
What we behold is censured by our eyes.
Where both deliberate, the love is slight;
Who ever loved, that loved not at first sight?
1593 *Hero and Leander* (published 1598), pt.1, l.167–76.

28 Virginity, albeit some highly prize it,
Compared with marriage, had you tried them
both,
Differs as much as wine and water doth.
1593 *Hero and Leander* (published 1598).

29 And as she wept, her tears to pearl he turned,
And wound them on his arm, and for her
mourned.
1593 The mourner is Cupid. *Hero and Leander* (published
1598), pt.1, l.375–6.

30 And to this day is every scholar poor;
Gross gold from them runs headlong to the
boor.
1593 *Hero and Leander* (published 1598).

31 Come live with me and be my love,
And we will all the pleasures prove
That valleys, groves, hills, and fields,
Woods, or steepy mountain yields.

And we will sit upon the rocks,
Seeing shepherds feed their flocks,
By shallow rivers to whose falls
Melodious birds sing madrigals.

And I will make thee beds of roses
And a thousand fragrant posies,
A cap of flowers, and a kirtle
Embroidered all with leaves of myrtle.
'The Passionate Shepherd to His Love' (published 1599).
▷ See Raleigh 800:12.

Marples, Morris

English writer and traveller.

32 The soul of a journey is liberty, perfect liberty to
think, feel, do just as one pleases. We go on a
journey chiefly to be free of all impediments and of
all inconveniences; to leave ourselves behind, much
more to get rid of others. It is because I want a little
breathing space to muse on different matters…that
I absent myself from the town for a while.
Quoted in John Hillaby *Journey through Britain* (1968).

Marquand, John P(hillips) 1893–1960

US novelist. He began as a writer of popular stories for
magazines, and later turned to realist novels in the
manner of Sinclair Lewis.

33 His father watched him across the gulf of years and
pathos which always must divide a father from his
son.
1937 *The Late George Apley*, ch.10.

Marqués, René 1919–79

Puerto Rican playwright, short story writer and nationalist.
Most of his plays and essays are concerned with the problem
of national identity in relation to language, literature and
the prevailing social conditions of Puerto Rico.

34 *Hombre, tienes un hijo, un hijo que te hicieron creer
podría inmortalizarte llevando el germen de ti mismo
por siglos de generaciones… Tu carne, Hombre, carne
deleznable, carne podrida que no puede soportar el
peso de tu inmortalidad. No, no hay nada de ti mismo
en esa carne. ¡Tu hijo no te hará inmortal!'*

Man, you have a son, a son who they made you
believe would make you immortal by carrying your
seed through centuries of generations… Your flesh,
O man, your despicable and rotten flesh that
cannot bear the sight of your immortality. No:
there's nothing of yourself in that flesh. Your son
won't make you immortal!'
1948 *El hombre y sus sueños* (Man and his Dreams), act 2.

Marquis, Don(ald Robert Perry)
1878–1937

US novelist, playwright and poet. He worked as a
journalist and wrote serious work, but is remembered for
his comic poems, notably in the *archy and mehitabel*
series, the tales of a cockroach who can't reach the upper-
case keys of the typewriter, and an alley cat.

35 but wotthehell wotthehell
oh i should worry and fret
death and I will coquette
there s a dance in the old dame yet
toujours gai toujours gai.
1927 *archy and mehitabel*, 'the song of mehitabel'.

36 live so that you
can stick out your tongue
at the insurance.
1927 *archy and mehitabel*, 'certain maxims of archy'.

37 procrastination is the
art of keeping
up with yesterday.
1927 *archy and mehitabel*, 'certain maxims of archy'.

38 millionaires and
bums taste
about alike to me.
1927 *archy and mehitabel*, 'certain maxims of archy'.

39 an optimist is a guy
that has never had
much experience.
1927 *archy and mehitabel*, 'certain maxims of archy'.

40 coarse
jocosity
catches the crowd
shakespeare
and i
are often
low browed
1927 *archy and mehitabel*, 'archy confesses'.

41 persian pussy from over the sea
demure and lazy and smug and fat
none of your ribbons and bells for me
ours is the zest of the alley cat
1927 *archy and mehitabel*, 'mehitabels extensive past'.

42 but wotthehell archy wotthehell
jamais triste archy jamais triste
that is my motto.
1927 *archy and mehitabel*, 'mehitabel sees paris'.

43 honesty is a good
thing but
it is not profitable to
its possessor
unless it is
kept under control.
1933 *archys life of mehitabel*, 'archygrams'.

44 did you ever
notice that when
a politician
does get an idea
he usually
gets it all wrong.
1933 *archys life of mehitabel*, 'archygrams'.

45 now and then
there is a person born
who is so unlucky
that he runs into accidents
which started to happen
to somebody else.
1933 *archys life of mehitabel*, 'archy says'.

46 boss there is always
a comforting thought
in time of trouble when
it is not our trouble
1935 *archy does his part*, 'comforting thoughts'.

47 Writing a book of poetry is like dropping a rose
petal down the Grand Canyon and waiting for the
echo.
Quoted in E Anthony *O Rare Don Marquis* (1962), ch.6.

48 The art of newspaper paragraphing is to stroke a
platitude until it purrs like an epigram.
Quoted in E Anthony *O Rare Don Marquis* (1962), ch.11.

49 By the time a bartender knows what drink a man
will have before he orders, there is little else about
him worth knowing.
Quoted in E Anthony *O Rare Don Marquis* (1962), ch.11.

50 Bores bore each other, too; but it never seems to
teach them anything.
Quoted in E Anthony *O Rare Don Marquis* (1962), ch.11.

51 A demagogue is a person with whom we disagree as
to which gang should mismanage the country.
Quoted in E Anthony *O Rare Don Marquis* (1962), ch.11.

52 Fishing is a delusion entirely surrounded by liars in
old clothes.
Attributed.

Marshall, George C(atlett) 1880–1959

US soldier and statesman. He directed the US army
throughout the war as chief of staff (1939–45), and as
Secretary of State (1947–9) he originated the Marshall
Aid plan for the post-war reconstruction of Europe. He
was awarded the Nobel Peace Prize in 1953.

53 Our policy is directed not against any country or
doctrine, but against hunger, poverty, desperation
and chaos. The purpose shall be the revival of a
working economy in the world so as to permit the
emergence of political and social conditions in
which free institutions can exist.
1947 Speech at Harvard, 5 Jun, announcing the European
Recovery Plan (ERA) that became known as the Marshall Plan.

54 We want you to feel unhampered tactically and
strategically to proceed north of the 38th parallel.
1950 Telegram to General Douglas MacArthur during the
Korean War, Sep, later used by MacArthur as justification for
continuing operations after the Chinese had made their
presence known. Quoted in David S McLellan *Dean Acheson:
The State Department Years* (1976).

Marshall, Thurgood 1908–93

US jurist and civil rights advocate. He worked with the
National Association for the Advancement of Colored
People and the Court of Appeals (1961–5). Solicitor-
General (1965–7), he became the first black Justice of the
US Supreme Court (1967–91).

55 If the United States is indeed the great melting pot,
the negro either didn't get in the pot or he didn't get
melted down.
1987 In the *New York Times*, 9 Sep.

Martí, José 1853–95

Cuban national hero. A journalist, editor and poet, he was a key figure in Cuba's struggle for independence. Exiled for his revolutionary activities, he travelled in Europe and the Americas. He died fighting at Boca de Dos Ríos.

56 *¡Robaron los conquistadores una página al Universo!*
    Aquellos eran los pueblos que llamaban a la Vía
    Láctea 'el camino de las almas'; para quienes el
    Universo estaba lleno del Grande Espíritu, en cuyo
    seno se encerraba toda luz.

The conquistadores stole a page from the Universe! Those were the good people who called the Milky Way 'the souls' path'; for them the Universe was full of the Great Spirit, within which all light was contained.

1884 *Obra literaria*, 'El hombre antiguo de América y sus artes primitivas' ('Ancient Man in America and his Primitive Arts').

57 *Yo soy un hombre sincero*
    De donde crece la palma,
    Y antes de morirme quiero
    Echar mis versos del alma.

I am a sincere man
from where the palm tree grows;
and before I die I want
to loose my verses from my heart.

1891 *Versos sencillos* (Simple Verses), no.1.

Martial full name *Marcus Valerius Martialis* c. 40–104 AD

Latin poet, born in Spain. He went to Rome and became an associate of Lucan and the younger Seneca, who were also Spanish. Martial's most important work is the twelve books of *Epigrams*, each a concise expression of one idea or theme.

58 *Non est, crede mihi, sapientis dicere 'Vivam':*
    Sera nimis vita est crastina: vive hodie.

Believe me, wise men do not say 'I shall live on.'
Tomorrow's life's too late; live today.
Epigrams, bk.1, no.15.

59 *Non amo te, Sabidi, nec possum dicere quare:*
    Hoc tantum possum dicere, non amo te.

I do not love you, Sabidius, and I can't tell you why;
all I can say is this, I don't love you.
Epigrams, bk.1, no.32.

60 *Laudant illa sed ista legunt.*

They praise those works, but read these.
Epigrams, bk.4, no.49.

61 *Bonosque*
    Soles effugere atque abire sentit,
    Qui nobis pereunt et imputantur.

Each of us feels the good days speed and depart,
and they're lost to us and counted against us.
Epigrams, bk.5, no.20.

62 *Non est vivere, sed valere vita est.*

Life is not just to be alive, but to be well.
Epigrams, bk.6, no.70.

63 *Difficilis facilis, iucundus acerbus es idem:*
    Nec tecum possum vivere nec sine te.

Difficult or easy, pleasant or bitter, you are the same: I cannot live with you—or without you.
Epigrams, bk.12, no.46.

64 *Rus in urbe.*

Country in the town.
Epigrams, bk.12, no.57.

Marvell, Andrew 1621–78

English poet. Educated at Cambridge, he held various government posts. His poems cover a variety of genres and classical forms, but he also published anonymously political and satirical prose works.

65 The inglorious arts of peace.
    1650 'An Horatian Ode upon Cromwell's Return from Ireland'.

66 He nothing common did or mean
    Upon that memorable scene:
    But with his keener eye
    The axe's edge did try.
    1650 Of Charles I. 'An Horatian Ode upon Cromwell's Return from Ireland'.

67 How fit he is to sway
    That can so well obey.
    1650 'An Horatian Ode upon Cromwell's Return from Ireland'.

68 See how the Orient dew,
    Shed from the bosom of the morn
    Into the blowing roses,
    Yet careless of its mansion new;
    For the clear region where 'twas born
    Round in its self encloses:
    And in its little globes extent,
    Frames as it can its native element.
    c.1650–2 'On a Drop of Dew' (published 1681).

69 There is not such another in
    The world, to offer for their sin.
    c.1650–2 'The Nymph Complaining for the Death of her Fawn' (published 1681).

70 Had it lived long, it would have been
    Lilies without, roses within.
    c.1650–2 'The Nymph Complaining for the Death of her Fawn' (published 1681)

71 I have a garden of my own,
    But so with roses overgrown,
    And lilies, that you would it guess
    To be a little wilderness.
    c.1650–2 'The Nymph Complaining for the Death of her Fawn' (published 1681).

72 Had we but world enough, and time,
This coyness Lady were no crime.
We would sit down, and think which way
To walk, and pass our long love's day.
Thou by the Indian Ganges' side
Shouldst rubies find: I by the tide
Of Humber would complain. I would
Love you ten years before the flood.
c.1650–2 'To His Coy Mistress' (published 1681).

73 My vegetable love should grow
Vaster than empires, and more slow,
An hundred years should go to praise
Thine eyes, and on thy forehead gaze.
Two hundred to adore each breast:
But thirty thousand to the rest.
An age at least to every part,
And the last age should show your heart.
For Lady you deserve this state;
Nor would I love at lower rate.
But at my back I always hear
Time's winged chariot hurrying near:
And yonder all before us lie
Deserts of vast eternity.
c.1650–2 'To His Coy Mistress' (published 1681).

74 Then worms shall try
That long preserved virginity:
And your quaint honour turn to dust;
And into ashes all my lust.
The grave's a fine and private place,
But none I think do there embrace.
c.1650–2 'To His Coy Mistress' (published 1681).

75 Now let us sport us while we may;
And now, like amorous birds of prey,
Rather at once our time devour,
Than languish in his slow-chapped power.
c.1650–2 'To His Coy Mistress' (published 1681).

76 Let us roll all our strength, and all
Our sweetness, up into one ball:
And tear our pleasures with rough strife,
Through the iron gates of life.
Thus, though we cannot make our sun
Stand still, yet we will make him run.
c.1650–2 'To His Coy Mistress' (published 1681), closing lines.

77 My love is of a birth as rare
As 'tis for object strange and high:
It was begotten by Despair
Upon Impossibility.

Magnanimous Despair alone
Could show me so divine a thing,
Where feeble Hope could ne'er have flown
But vainly flapped its tinsel wing.
c.1650–2 'The Definition of Love' (published 1681).

78 As lines so loves oblique may well
Themselves in every angle greet
But ours so truly parallel,
Though infinite can never meet.

Therefore the love which doth us bind,
But fate so enviously debars,
Is the conjunction of the mind,
And opposition of the stars.
c.1650–2 'The Definition of Love' (published 1681).

79 Ye living lamps, by whose dear light
The nightingale does sit so late,
And studying all the summer night,
Her matchless songs does meditate.
c.1650–2 'The Mower to the Glo-Worms' (published 1681).

80 And now, when I have summed up all my store,
Thinking (so I myself deceive)
So rich a chaplet thence to weave
As never yet the King of Glory wore,
Alas! I find the serpent old,
That, twining in his speckled breast,
About the flowers disguised does fold
With wreaths of fame and interest.
c.1650–2 'The Coronet' (published 1681).

81 My mind was once the true survey
Of all these meadows fresh and gay;
And in the greenness of the grass
Did see its hopes as in a glass.
c.1650–2 'The Mower's Song' (published 1681).

82 How vainly men themselves amaze
To win the palm, the oak, or bays;
And their uncessant labours see
Crown'd from some single herb or tree.
Whose short and narrow verged shade
Does prudently their toils upbraid;
While all flow'rs and all trees do close
To weave the garlands of repose.
c.1650–2 'The Garden' (published 1681).

83 Fair quiet, have I found thee here,
And Innocence thy Sister dear!
Mistaken long, I sought you then
In busy companies of men.
c.1650–2 'The Garden' (published 1681).

84 Society is all but rude,
To this delicious solitude.
c.1650–2 'The Garden' (published 1681).

85 What wondrous life is this I lead!
Ripe apples drop about my head;
The luscious clusters of the vine
Upon my mouth do crush their wine;
The nectarine, and curious peach,
Into my hands themselves do reach;
Stumbling on melons, as I pass,

Ensnared with flowers, I fall on grass.
c.1650–2 'The Garden' (published 1681), stanza 5.

86 Annihilating all that's made
To a green thought in a green shade.
c.1650–2 'The Garden' (published 1681), stanza 6.

87 Such was that happy garden-state,
While man there walked without a mate.
c.1650–2 'The Garden' (published 1681), stanza 8.

88 'Twas beyond a mortal's share
To wander solitary there:
Two paradises 'twere in one
To live in paradise alone.
c.1650–2 'The Garden' (published 1681), stanza 8.

89 No creature loves an empty space;
Their bodies measure out their place.
c.1650–2 'Upon Appleton House, to My Lord Fairfax' (published 1681), stanza 2.

90 'Tis not, what once it was, the world;
But a rude heap together hurl'd.
c.1650–2 'Upon Appleton House, to My Lord Fairfax' (published 1681), stanza 96..

91 Oh thou, that dear and happy isle
The garden of the world ere while,
Thou paradise of four seas,
Which heaven planted us to please,
But, to exclude the world, did guard
With watery if not flaming sword;
What luckless apple did we taste,
To make us mortal, and thee waste?
c.1650–2 'Upon Appleton House, to My Lord Fairfax' (published 1681), stanza 41..

92 What should we do but sing the praise
That led us through the watery maze,
Unto an isle so long unknown,
And yet far kinder than our own?
c.1653 'Bermudas' (published 1681).

Marvell, Holt originally *Eric Maschwitz*
1901–69

English songwriter.

93 These Foolish Things Remind Me of You.
1935 Title of song.

Marx, Chico originally *Leonard Marx*
1891–1961

US film comedian, one of the Marx Brothers, best known as the piano player.

94 I wasn't kissing her, I was just whispering in her mouth.
Explanation to his wife, on being discovered in a compromising position with a chorus girl. Quoted in Groucho Marx and Richard J Anobile *Marx Brothers Scrapbook* (1973), ch.24.

Marx, Groucho originally *Julius Henry Marx*
1895–1977

US film comedian, one of the Marx Brothers. He appeared in many films including *Animal Crackers* (1930), *Monkey Business* (1931), *Horse Feathers* (1932) and *Duck Soup* (1933).

95 What's a thousand dollars? Mere chicken feed. A poultry matter.
1929 Line delivered in *The Cocoanuts* (screenplay by George Kaufman and Morrie Ryskind).

96 One morning I shot an elephant in my pyjamas. How he got into my pyjamas I don't know.
1930 Line delivered in *Animal Crackers* (screenplay by George Kaufman and Morrie Ryskind).

97 You go Uruguay and I'll go mine.
1930 Line delivered in *Animal Crackers* (screenplay by George Kaufman and Morrie Ryskind).

98 I could dance with you till the cows come home. On second thoughts I'll dance with the cows and you come home.
1933 Line delivered in *Duck Soup* (screenplay by Bert Kalmar, Harry Ruby and Arthur Sheekman).

99 There ain't no Sanity Claus.
1935 Line delivered in *A Night at the Opera* (screenplay by George Kaufman and Morrie Ryskind).

1 Either he's dead or my watch has stopped.
1937 Line delivered in *A Day at the Races* (screenplay by George Seaton, Robert Pirosh and George Oppenheimer).

2 Marry me and I'll never look at another horse.
1937 Line delivered in *A Day at the Races* (screenplay by George Seaton, Robert Pirosh and George Oppenheimer).

3 Please accept my resignation. I don't want to belong to any club that will accept me as a member.
1959 Recalled in his autobiography, *Groucho and Me* (1959), ch.26.

4 When's the game itself going to begin?
While watching a game of cricket at Lord's. Quoted in Colin Jarman *The Guinness Dictionary of Sports Quotations* (1990).

Marx, Harpo originally *Adolf Marx*
1893–1961

US film comedian, one of the Marx Brothers. His role within the team was that of dumb clown and harp maestro. He published an autobiography in 1961.

5 No worse than a bad cold.
His winning suggestion when a critic set up a competition for readers' reviews of the long-running play *Abie's Irish Rose* by Anne Nichols. Attributed.

Marx, Karl Heinrich 1818–83

German-born political and economic theorist who began his career as a journalist in 1843. With his lifelong literary collaborator Friedrich Engels he wrote *The Communist*

Manifesto (1848), and settled in London the next year, where he began his unfinished *Das Kapital* (vol.1, 1867, the rest posthumously).

6 Religion is the sigh of the oppressed creature, the feelings of a heartless world, and the spirit of conditions that are unspiritual. It is the opium of the people.
  1843–4 *A Contribution to the Critique of Hegel's Philosophy of Right.*

7 The *division of labour* is nothing but the *alienated* establishment of human activity.
  1844 Collected in T B Bottomore (trans and ed) *Early Writings* (1964), p.181.

8 Political economy thus does not recognize the unoccupied worker, the working man so far as he is outside this work relationship. Swindlers, thieves, beggars, the unemployed, the starving, poverty-stricken and criminal working man, are figures which do not exist for political economy, but only for other eyes; for doctors, judges, grave-diggers, beadles, etc. They are ghostly figures outside the domain of political economy.
  1844 Collected in T B Bottomore (trans and ed) *Early Writings* (1964), p.137–9.

9 The philosophers have only interpreted the world in various ways; the point is to change it.
  1845 *Theses on Feuerbach*, no.11.

10 In communist society, where nobody has one exclusive sphere of activity but each can become accomplished in any branch he wishes, society regulates the general production and thus makes it possible for me to do one thing today and another tomorrow, to hunt in the morning, fish in the afternoon, rear cattle in the evening or criticize after dinner, just as I desire, without ever becoming hunter, fisherman, shepherd or critic.
  1845 *The German Ideology* (with Friedrich Engels).

11 Assume a particular state of development in the productive facilities of man and you will get a particular form of commerce and consumption. Assume particular stages of development in production, commerce and consumption and you will have a corresponding social constitution, a corresponding organisation of the family, of orders or of classes, in a word, a corresponding civil society. Assume a particular civil society and you will get particular political conditions which are only the official expression of civil society.
  1846 Letter to P V Annenkov, 26 Dec.

12 The history of all hitherto existing society is the history of class struggles.
  1848 *The Communist Manifesto* (with Friedrich Engels), opening sentence (translated by Samuel Moore, 1888).

13 The theory of the Communists may be summed up in the single sentence: Abolition of private property.
  1848 *The Communist Manifesto* (with Friedrich Engels, translated by Samuel Moore, 1888).

14 A spectre is haunting Europe—the spectre of communism. All the powers of old Europe have entered into a holy alliance to exorcise this spectre; Pope and Tsar, Metternich and Guizot, French Radicals and German police spies.
  1848 *The Communist Manifesto* (with Friedrich Engels).

15 Let the ruling classes tremble at a communist revolution. The proletarians have nothing to lose but their chains. they have a world to win. Working men of all countries, unite!
  1848 *The Communist Manifesto* (with Friedrich Engels), closing words (translated by Samuel Moore, 1888). This translation was approved by Engels, but the phrase is also known as 'Workers of the world, unite'. The literal translation of the German is 'Proletarians of all lands, unite.'

16 If capital is growing rapidly, wages may rise; the profit of capital rises incomparably more rapidly. The material position of the worker has improved, but at the cost of his social position. The social gulf that divides him from the capitalist has widened.
  1849 'Wage Labour and Capital', collected in Robert C Tucker (ed) *The Marx–Engels Reader* (2nd edn, 1972), p.211.

17 Hegel says somewhere that all great events and personalities in the world reappear in one fashion or another. He forgot to add: the first time as tragedy, the second as farce.
  1852 *The Eighteenth Brumaire of Louis Bonaparte*, section 1.

18 All our inventions have endowed material forces with intellectual life and degraded human life into material force.
  1856 Speech, 14 Apr.

19 Society does not consist of individuals; it expresses the sum of connections and relationships in which individuals find themselves.
  1857–8 *The Grundrisse* (translated by David McLellan, 1971), p.77.

20 The product of mental labour—science—always stands far below its value, because the labour-time necessary to reproduce it has no relation at all to the labour-time required for its original production.
  1862 *Theory of Surplus Value.*

21 The production of surplus-value, or the extraction of surplus labour, is the specific end and aim, the sum and substance, of capitalist production.
  1867 *Das Kapital.*

22 The instruments of labour, when they assume the form of machinery, acquire a kind of material existence which involves the replacement of human forces by the forces of Nature, and of rule-of-thumb methods by the purposeful application of natural science.
1867 *Das Kapital.*

23 In manufacture and in handicrafts, the worker uses a tool; in the factory, he serves a machine.
1867 *Das Kapital.*

24 Only in a higher phase of communist society…can the narrow horizon of bourgeois right be crossed in its entirety, and society inscribe on its banners, 'From each according to his ability, to each according to his needs!'
1875 Critique of the Gotha Programme, May.
▷ See Bakunin 63:87.

25 All I know is that I am not a Marxist.
Recalled by Friedrich Engels in letter to Conrad Schmidt, 3 Aug 1890.

26 The worker becomes poorer the more wealth he produces and the more his production increases in power and extent. The worker becomes an ever cheaper commodity the more good he creates. The *devaluation* of the human world increases in direct relation with the *increase in value* of the world of things. Labour does not only create goods; it also produces itself and the worker *as a commodity*, and indeed in the same proportion as it produces goods.
1844 Collected in T B Bottomore (trans and ed*)* *Early Writings* (1964), p.121.

27 What I did that was new was to prove that the existence of classes is only bound up with particular, historical phases in the development of production; that the class struggle necessarily leads to the dictatorship of the proletariat; and that dictatorship itself only constitutes the transition to the abolition of all classes and to a classless society.
In *Correspondence of Marx and Engels.*

Mary of Teck formerly *Princess Victoria Mary Augusta Louise Olga Pauline Claudine Agnes* known as *Princess May* 1867–1953

Queen-Consort of George V of Britain (married 1893). She helped mould her husband into a 'people's king' and throughout her son's reign was involved in women's war work and philanthropy.

28 God grant that we may not have a European war thrust upon us, and for such a stupid reason too, no I don't mean stupid, but to have to go to war on account of tiresome Serbia beggars belief.
1914 Letter to her aunt Princess Augusta, Grand-Duchess of Mecklenburg-Strelitz, 28 Jul.

Mary, Queen of Scots 1542–87

Queen of Scotland, the daughter of James V. A Catholic, she succeeded to the throne at the age of one week but was forced to sign an act of abdication in favour of her son James VI in 1567. She fled to England and was imprisoned by Elizabeth I for 20 years before being executed.

29 *En ma fin git mon commencement.*
In my end is my beginning.
Embroidered motto, quoted in Antonia Fraser *Mary Queen of Scots* (1969), ch.21, 'My Norfolk'.

Mary Tudor also known as *Mary I* 1516–58

Queen of England and Ireland (from 1553). On Edward VI's death she ousted Lady Jane Grey with popular support and repealed anti-Catholic legislation. Public anger at her persecutions of Protestants and unpopular marriage, and the loss of Calais to the French, broke her down.

30 When I am dead and opened, you shall find 'Calais' lying in my heart.
Quoted in Holinshed *Chronicles*, vol.4 (1808).

Masaryk, Tomás Garrigue 1850–1937

Czechoslovak statesman. An ardent Slovak, while in exile during World War I he organized the Czech independence movement. As the first President of Czechoslovakia (1918–35), he was re-elected on three occasions.

31 Our whole history inclines us towards the democratic powers. Our renaissance is a logical link between us and the democracies of the west.
1918 Inaugural address, 23 Dec.

Masefield, John Edward 1878–1967

English poet and novelist. He served his apprenticeship in the merchant navy, before ill-health forced him to concentrate on writing about the sea rather than sailing it. He became Poet Laureate in 1930.

32 I must down to the seas again, to the lonely sea and the sky,
And all I ask is a tall ship and a star to steer her by,
And the wheel's kick and the wind's song and the white sail's shaking,
And a grey mist on the sea's face and a grey dawn breaking.
1902 'Sea Fever'.

33 I must down to the seas again, for the call of the running tide
Is a wild call and a clear call that may not be denied.
1902 'Sea Fever'.

34 I must down to the seas again, to the vagrant gypsy life,

To the gull's way and the whale's way where the
   wind's like a whetted knife;
And all I ask is a merry yarn from a laughing
   fellow-rover,
And quiet sleep and a sweet dream when the long
   trick's over.
1902 'Sea Fever'.

35 It's a warm wind, the west wind, full of bird's cries;
I never hear the west wind but tears are in my eyes.
1902 'West Wind'.

36 It is good to be out on the road, and going one
knows not where.
1902 'Tewkesbury Road'.

37 Quinquireme of Nineveh from distant Ophir
Rowing home to haven in sunny Palestine,
With a cargo of ivory,
And apes and peacocks,
Sandalwood, cedarwood, and sweet white wine.
1903 'Cargoes'.

38 Dirty British coaster with a salt-caked smoke-stack,
Butting through the Channel in the mad March
   days
1903 'Cargoes'.

39 I have seen dawn and sunset on moors and windy
hills
Coming in solemn beauty like slow old tunes of
   Spain.
1903 'Beauty'.

40 Oh some are fond of Spanish wine, and some are
fond of French,
And some'll swallow tay and stuff fit only for a
   wench.
1903 'Captain Stratton's Fancy'.

41 Most roads lead men homewards,
My road leads me forth.
1903 'Roadways'.

42 My road leads me seawards
To the white dipping sails.
1903 'Roadways'.

43 Death opens unknown doors. It is most grand to
die.
1910 *Pompey the Great*, act 2.

44 In the dark room where I began
My mother's life made me a man.
Through all the months of human birth
Her beauty fed my common earth.
I cannot see, nor breathe, nor stir,
But through the death of some of her.
1910 'C.L.M.'.

45 Out into the street I ran uproarious

The devil dancing in me glorious.
1911 'The Everlasting Mercy'.

46 And he who gives a child a treat
Makes joy-bells ring in Heaven's street,
And he who gives a child a home
Builds palaces in Kingdom come,
And she who gives a baby birth
Brings Saviour Christ again to Earth.
1911 'The Everlasting Mercy'.

47 In this life he laughs longest who laughs last.
1912 *The Widow in Bye Street*, ch.4.

48 The days that make us happy make us wise.
1914 'Biography'.

49 Life's battle is a conquest for the strong;
The meaning shows in the defeated thing.
1914 'The Wanderer'.

50 I have seen flowers come in stony places
And kind things done by men with ugly faces,
And the gold cup won by the worst horse at the
   races,
So I trust, too.
1914 'An Epilogue'.

51 And all the way that wild high crying,
To cold his blood with the thought of dying.
1919 *Reynard the Fox*, pt.2, stanza 49.

52 People who leave their own time out of their work
cannot be surprised if their time fails to find them
interesting.
1925 'With the Living Voice'.

Massinger, Philip 1583–1640

English dramatist. He attended Oxford, but left to join
Henslowe's company. He collaborated with Thomas
Dekker, Ben Jonson and George Chapman, and
particularly John Fletcher, with whom he is buried. His
works include *A New Way to Pay Old Debts* (1633).

53 He that would govern others, first should be
The master of himself.
1623 *The Bondman*, act 1, sc.3.

54 Soar not too high to fall; but stoop to rise.
1623 *The Duke of Milan*, act 1, sc.2.

55 Oh that thou hadst like others been all words,
And no performance.
1624 *The Parliament of Love*, act 4, sc.2.

56 Pleasures of worse natures
Are gladly entertained, and they that shun us
Practice in private sports the stews would blush at.
1626 Of the theatre. *The Roman Actor*, act 1, sc.1.

57 Nay, droop not, fellows; innocence should be bold.
1626 *The Roman Actor*, act 1, sc.1.

58 They are only safe
    That know to soothe the prince's appetite
    And serve his lusts.
    1626 *The Roman Actor*, act 1, sc.1.

59 O master doctor, he is past recovery;
    A lethargy hath seized him.
    1626 *The Roman Actor*, act 2, sc.1.

60 How strangely hopes delude men.
    1626 *The Roman Actor*, act 5, sc.2.

61 Greatness, with private men
    Esteem'd a blessing, is to me a curse;
    And we, whom, for our high births, they conclude
    The happy freemen, are the only slaves.
    Happy the golden mean!
    1627 *The Great Duke of Florence*, act 1, sc.1.

62 Virgin me no virgins!
    I must have you lose that name, or you lose me.
    1633 *A New Way to Pay Old Debts*, act 3, sc.2.

Masters, Edgar Lee 1869–1950

US poet. Although he wrote a number of books of both poetry and prose, he is chiefly remembered for the satirical free verse epitaphs on real and imaginary occupants of a midwestern cemetery in *Spoon River Anthology*.

63 Where are Elmer, Herman, Bert, Tom and Charley,
    The weak of will, the strong of arm, the clown, the
        boozer, the fighter?
    All, all, are sleeping on the hill.
    1915 *Spoon River Anthology*, 'The Hill'.

64 Why, a moral truth is a hollow tooth
    Which must be propped with gold.
    1915 *Spoon River Anthology*, 'Sersmith the Dentist'.

65 Your eight-page paper—behind which you huddle,
    Bawling through the megaphone of big type:
    'This is I, the giant.'
    1915 *Spoon River Anthology*, 'Editor Whedon'.

Matak, Sirik c.1930–75

Cambodian politician and business leader who joined with Lol Nol to overthrow Sihanouk in 1970. Prime Minister of the US-backed Khmer Republic (1970–5), he was executed by the Khmer Rouge after refusing to leave with the US Ambassador.

66 But mark it well, if I shall die here on the spot and in my country that I love, it is too bad because we are all born and must die one day. I have only committed this mistake of believing in you, the Americans.
    1975 Letter to John Dean, US Ambassador to Cambodia (1974–5), Apr.

Mathew, Sir James Charles 1830–1908

Irish judge. He was appointed judge (1881–1901) and Lord Justice of Appeal (1901–6).

67 In England, justice is open to all—like the Ritz Hotel.
    Quoted in R E Megarry *Miscellany-at-Law* (1955). Sometimes attributed to Lord Darling.

Mathews, Harry Burchell 1930–

US writer. His fiction is marked by a rich vein of lexical experiment and unconventional fantasy.

68 Translation is the paradigm, the exemplar of all writing… It is translation that demonstrates most vividly the yearning for transformation that underlies every act involving speech, that supremely human gift.
    1980 *Country Cooking and Other Stories*, 'The Dialect of the Tribe'.

69 Syntax and vocabulary are overwhelming constraints—the rules that run us. Language is using *us* to talk—we think we're using the language, but language is doing the thinking, we're its slavish agents.
    1988 Interview in *City Limits*, 26 May.

Mathias, Charles McCurdy, Jr 1922–

US lawyer and Republican politician. He was a Congressman then Senator from Maryland (1969–87).

70 Most of us are honest all the time, and all of us are honest most of the time.
    1967 Of congressional ethics. In *Time*, 31 Mar.

Mathison, Melissa 1949–

US screenwriter, best known for *E.T.—the Extraterrestrial* (1982).

71 E.T. phone home.
    1982 *E.T.—the Extraterrestrial*.

72 How do you explain school to a higher intelligence?
    1982 *E.T.—the Extraterrestrial*.

Matisse, Henri Emile Benoît 1869–1954

French painter, sculptor, designer and graphic artist, from 1904 leader of the Fauves. His paintings typically display bold use of colour organized within a rhythmic two-dimensional design.

73 Expression, for me, does not reside in passions glowing in a human face or manifested by violent movement. The entire arrangement of my picture is expressive: the place occupied by the figures, the empty spaces around them, the proportions, everything has its share.
    1908 'Notes d'un peintre', in *La Grande Revue*.

74 What I dream of is an art of balance, of purity and serenity…a soothing, calming influence on the mind, rather like a good armchair which provides relaxation from physical fatigue.

1908 'Notes d'un peintre', in *La Grande Revue*.

75 If drawing belongs to the realm of the Spirit and colour to that of the Senses, you must draw first, to cultivate the Spirit and to be able to lead colour through the paths of the Spirit.

1948 Letter to Henry Clifford, quoted in Jack D Flam *Matisse on Art* (1973).

Matlovich, Leonard 1943–88

US soldier, the first active-duty soldier to openly acknowledge his homosexuality.

76 A Gay Vietnam Veteran—They gave me a medal for killing two men, and a discharge for loving one.

Tombstone inscription. Quoted in the *Washington Post*, 22 Apr 1988.

Matos, Gregório de c.1623–1696

Brazilian poet and epigrammatist, born into the slave-owning gentry. His scandalous private life brought him into conflict with the clergy, government and respectable society, but his frankness and rebellious spirit made him a cultural hero.

77 *de dous ff composta*
está a nossa Bahia…
o furtar e o foder bem
s—o os ff que tem
Esta cidade a meu ver.

Of two f's,
as I see it,
is this city composed:
one fraud, the other fornication,
those are the two f's

'Define a sua cidade' ('He defines his city'), collected in *Crônica do viver bahiano* (published 1882).

Matthews, Christopher J

78 Hang a lantern on your problem.

1987 Advice to political candidates to expose their personal frailties before they can be discovered by the media. In the *New York Times*, 10 Jul.

79 The key is to be a porcupine—have a reputation for being difficult.

Advice for success in the political world. Quoted in Hedrick Smith *The Power Game* (1988).

Matthews, Sir Stanley 1915–

English footballer. He was acclaimed the finest winger of his generation and won a total of 54 Caps before his eventual retirement in 1955.

80 I played 33 years and never got cautioned. I like that.

1995 Television interview, on his 80th birthday.

Matthiessen, Peter 1927–

US writer, naturalist and explorer. His novels include *Far Tortuga* (1975) and *Killing Mister Watson* (1990). He won a National Book Award in 1978 for his account of a mystical journey through Tibet, *The Snow Leopard*.

81 At Play In The Fields Of The Lord.

1965 Title of novel.

82 For some time I watch the coming of the night… Above is the glistening galaxy of childhood, now hidden in the Western world by air pollution and the glare of artificial light; for my children's children, the power, peace and healing of the night will be obliterated.

1978 Of the night sky in Nepal. *The Snow Leopard*, 'Northward, October 18'.

Mature, Victor 1915–

US actor whose credits include *Samson and Delilah* (1949), *Androcles and the Lion* (1952) and *The Robe* (1953).

83 Actually, I am a golfer. That is my real occupation. I never was an actor; ask anybody, particularly the critics.

Attributed.

Maugham, W(illiam) Somerset 1874–1965

British writer, born in Paris of Irish descent. He served as a secret agent in World War II, and travelled widely in south-east Asia. His works include the autobiographical novel *Of Human Bondage* (1915) and his satirical masterpiece, *Cakes and Ale* (1930).

84 At a dinner party one should eat wisely but not too well, and talk well but not too wisely.

1896 *A Writer's Notebook* (published 1949).

85 Impropriety is the soul of wit.

1919 *The Moon and Sixpence*.

86 I hate people who play bridge as though they were at a funeral and knew their feet were getting wet.

1921 Quoted in Colin Jarman *The Guinness Dictionary of Sports Quotations* (1990).

87 Hypocrisy is the most difficult and nerve-racking vice that any man can pursue; it needs an unceasing vigilance and a rare detachment of spirit. It cannot, like adultery or gluttony, be practised at spare moments; it is a whole-time job.

1930 *Cakes and Ale*, ch.1.

88 There is no silence in the East.

1930 *The Gentleman in the Parlour*.

89 Mandalay has its name; the falling cadence of the lovely word has gathered about itself the chiaroscuro of romance.

1930 *The Gentleman in the Parlour.*

90 The Chinese are the aristocracy of the East.

1930 *The Gentleman in the Parlour.*

91 They are like a face full of character that intrigues and excites you, but that on closer acquaintance you discover is merely the mask of a vulgar soul. Such is Tourane.

1930 Of Tourane, now Da Nang, Vietnam. *The Gentleman in the Parlour.*

92 Observing these people I am no longer surprised that there is such a scarcity of domestic servants at home.

1960 Said in an uncharacteristically loud voice after being refused entry to the premier British expatriate club in Singapore. Quoted in Robert Calder *Willie.*

Maupassant, Guy de 1850–93

French writer best known for his captivating short stories which explored a wide range of characters and, often, the supernatural world.

93 *L'histoire, cette vieille dame exaltée et menteuse.*

History, this old, honoured and lying woman.

1876 *Sur l'eau.*

94 *Le talent provient de l'originalité, qui est une manière spéciale de penser, de voir, de comprendre et de juger.*

Talent comes from originality which is a special manner of thinking, of seeing, of understanding and of judging.

1877 *Pierre et Jean*, préface.

95 *Raconter tout serait impossible.*

To tell all would be impossible.

1877 *Pierre et Jean*, préface.

96 *Les grands artistes sont ceux qui imposent à l'humanité leur illusion particulière.*

Great artists impose their particular illusion on humanity.

1877 *Pierre et Jean*, préface.

97 *La moindre chose contient un peu d'inconnu. Trouvons-le.*

The least thing contains something mysterious. Find it.

1877 *Pierre et Jean*, préface.

98 *On finirait par devenir fou, ou par mourir, si on ne pouvait pas pleurer.*

We would end by becoming crazy or by dying, if we could not cry.

1888 *Fort comme la mort*, bk.2, ch.1.

Maxton, James 1885–1946

Socialist politician, born in Glasgow, elected as a Labour MP in 1922. One of the group of 'Red Clydesiders', he was a brilliant and colourful orator rather than a skilful political tactician.

99 In the interests of economy they condemned hundreds of children to death and I call it murder.

1923 Speech against the withdrawal of child benefits, including the supply of milk, in Scotland. In *Hansard*, 27 Jun.

1 All I say is, if you cannot ride two horses you have no right in the circus.

1931 On the Scottish Independent Labour Party's proposed disaffiliation from the Labour Party. In the *Daily Herald*, 12 Jan.

May, Elaine originally *Elaine Berlin* 1932–

US actress, director and screenwriter. She wrote screenplays for *A New Leaf* (1971) and *Heaven Can Wait* (1978).

2 All I am or was is rich, and that's all I ever wanted to be.

1971 Line delivered by Walter Matthau in *A New Leaf.*

Mayakovsky, Vladimir 1894–1930

Russian Futurist poet, a supporter of the Bolsheviks in the 1917 Revolution. His works include plays, poems and satirical plays. He committed suicide in Moscow.

3 I'll be irreproachably tender;
    not a man, but—a cloud in trousers!

1915 'The Cloud in Trousers' (translated by Samuel Charteris).

4 We do not need art museums to worship dead works, we need living factories of the soul—in the streets, in the trams, in the factories, in studios, and in the workers' houses.

1918 Quoted in *Futurismo e Futurismi* (1986).

5 To us love says humming that the heart's stalled motor has begun working again.

1928 'Letter from Paris to Comrade Kostorov on the Nature of Love' (translated by Samuel Charteris).

Maybeck, Bernard Ralph 1862–1957

US architect, renowned for his eclectic combinations of styles and materials. His works include the Palace of Fine Arts, San Francisco (1915) and Clyde, a town in California (1917).

6 Let the thing fall down in peace.

On the crumbling remains of his Corinthian classic Palace of Fine Arts, designed for San Francisco's 1915 Panama–Pacific Exposition. Recalled in the *New York Times*, 9 May 1965.

Mayer, Louis B(urt) originally *Eliezer Mayer* 1885–1957

Russian-born US film mogul. A co-founder of Metro Films in 1915, he joined with Sam Goldwyn to form

Metro-Goldwyn-Mayer (MGM) in 1924. He received an honorary Academy Award in 1950.

7 We are the only company whose assets all walk out the gates at night.

Quoted in Leslie Halliwell *The Filmgoer's Book of Quotes* (1973).

Mayhew, Alex

Professor of Political Science, Georgetown University.

8 The future of America is based on one generation sacrificing for the next.

Quoted by David Maraniss in CNBC broadcast, 7 Mar 1995. The phrase was popularized by Mayhew's former student, Bill Clinton.

Mayo, Charles Horace   1865–1939

US surgeon. An authority on the treatment of goitre, he cofounded the Mayo Clinic with his brother in 1905 within what is now St Mary's Hospital, Rochester.

9 The definition of a specialist as one who 'knows more and more about less and less' is good and true.

1939 In *Modern Hospital*, Sep.

Mazarin, Jules, Cardinal   1602–61

Neapolitan statesman. He entered Louis XIII's service in 1639, and succeeded Richelieu as Chief Minister (1642), becoming the lover of Anne of Austria. His domestic policy was problematic, but he negotiated the Peace of Westphalia (1648) and the Treaty of the Pyrenees (1659).

10 The French are nice people. I allow them to sing and to write, and they allow me to do whatever I like.

Attributed by the Duchess of Orléans in a letter dated 25 Oct 1715.

Mazzini, Giuseppe   1805–72

Italian patriot, a leader of the Risorgimento and founder of the revolutionary Young Italy Association. His underground journal, *Young Italy*, fomented revolt throughout Europe.

11 Insurrection—by means of guerrilla bands—is the true method of warfare for all nations desirous of emancipating themselves from a foreign yoke.

1833 *General Instructions for the Members of Young Italy*, section 4.

12 I had thought to evoke the soul of Italy but all I find before me is its corpse.

Attributed. Quoted in Denis Mack Smith *Italy: A Modern History* (1959).

13 A nation is the universality of citizens speaking the same tongue.

In *La Giovine Italia* (Young Italy).

Mead, Margaret   1901–78

US anthropologist. After expeditions to Samoa and New Guinea she wrote books on her experiences, arguing that personality characteristics are shaped by conditioning rather than heredity.

14 The greatest invention since the novel.

1974 Of television. Comment, 31 Dec.

Medawar, Sir Peter Brian   1915–87

British zoologist and immunologist, born in Rio de Janeiro. Professor of Anatomy at University College London, he pioneered experiments in immunological toleration and skin and organ grafting, winning a Nobel Prize with Sir Macfarlane Burnet in 1960.

15 I cannot give any scientist of any age better advice than this: the intensity of a conviction that a hypothesis is true has no bearing over whether it is true or not.

1979 Advice to a young scientist, attributed.

Meijer, Frederik   1919–

US retail executive and chief executive of Meijer Inc.

16 I am more poor than you think.

On trying to secure a low profile. Quoted in *Forbes*, 19 Oct 1992.

Meilhac, Henri   1831–97

French playwright. From 1855 he produced a long series of light comedies, often in conjunction with Ludovic Halévy, with whom he also wrote the libretti for Offenbach's operettas and Bizet's *Carmen*.

17 *L'amour est un oiseau rebelle*
Que nul ne peut apprivoiser.
Love's a bird that will live in freedom
That no man ever learned to tame.

1875 The *Habanéra. Carmen*, act 1.

18 *La fleur que tu m'avais jetée*

Here is the flower that you threw me

1875 Don José's (tenor) *Flower Song* from act 2 of *Carmen*.

19 *Toreador, en garde!*

1875 Escamillo's *Couplets, Carmen*, act 2.

Melba, Dame Nellie   real name *Helen Mitchell*
1861–1931

Australian soprano, who took her stage name from her native Melbourne. Notorious for her many 'farewell' performances, her earthy Australian character contrasted oddly with the graces she adopted in her stage persona.

20 What are you going to sing? All I can say is—sing 'em muck! It's all they can understand!

c.1907 Advice to Dame Clara Butt on her first tour of Australia. Quoted in Winifred Ponder *Clara Butt: Her Life-story* (1928).

21 If you wish to understand me at all (and to write an
    autobiography is only to open a window into one's
    heart) you must understand first and foremost, that
    I am an Australian… I shall always come back to
    rest in the shadow of the blue mountains, in the
    heart of this vast, deserted continent which gave me
    birth.
    1925 *Melodies and Memories*, ch.1.

22 The first rule in opera is the first rule in life: see to
    everything yourself.
    1925 *Melodies and Memories*.

23 If I'd been a housemaid I'd have been the best in
    Australia—I couldn't help it. It's got to be
    perfection for me.
    Said to the conductor Fritz Hart. Quoted in John Thompson
    On Lips of Living Men (1962)

Melbourne, William Lamb, 2nd Viscount
1779–1848

English statesman, Chief Secretary for Ireland (1827–8),
Home Secretary (1830–4), and Whig Prime Minister
(1834, 1835–41), a confidante of the young Queen
Victoria. Defeated in the election of 1841, he resigned
and thereafter took little part in public affairs.

24 I wish that I was as cocksure of anything as Tom
    Macaulay is of everything.
    1889 Attributed by Earl Cowper.

Mellor, D H 1938–

British philosopher, Cambridge University. He has
written several books on philosophy.

25 Appeals to rationality are mostly bluff. There is no
    good theory of what it is nor of how to recognize it.
    1983 'Objective Decision Making', in *Social Theory and
    Practice*, Summer–Fall.

Melville, Andrew 1545–c.1622

Scottish religious and educational reformer, consolidating
the Presbyterianism of the reformed Church of Scotland,
and a fierce critic of royal authority where it impinged on
that of the Kirk. In 1596 he headed a deputation to
'remonstrate' with James VI.

26 God's silly vassal.
    1596 Said of (and to) King James VI, as reported in his nephew
    James Melville's *Diary*. 'Mr Andrew bore him down and uttered
    the commission as from the mighty God, calling him but 'God's
    silly vassal'.

Melville, Herman 1819–91

US novelist. Between 1839 and 1844 he spent time at sea,
working as a cabin-boy and on whaling ships. His
experiences gave him material for many of his best known
books, including *Typee* (1846) and his masterpiece, *Moby
Dick* (1851).

27 We may have civilized bodies and yet barbarous
    souls.
    1849 *Redburn*, ch.58.

28 Toil is man's allotment; toil of brain, or toil of
    hands, or a grief that's more than either, the grief
    and sin of idleness.
    1849 *Mardi*, ch.63.

29 Call me Ishmael.
    1851 *Moby Dick*, ch.1, opening words.

30 Better sleep with a sober cannibal than a drunken
    Christian.
    1851 *Moby Dick*, ch.3.

31 Faith, like a jackal, feeds among the tombs, and
    even from these dead doubts she gathers her most
    vital hope.
    1851 *Moby Dick*, ch.7.

32 A whale ship was my Yale College and my Harvard.
    1851 *Moby Dick*, ch.24.

33 Old age is always wakeful; as if, the longer linked
    with life, the less man has to do with aught that
    looks like death.
    1851 *Moby Dick*, ch.29.

34 All visible objects, man, are but as pasteboard
    masks. But in each event—in the living act, the
    undoubted deed—there, some unknown but still
    reasoning thing puts forth the mouldings of its
    features from behind the unreasoning mask. If man
    will strike, strike through the mask!
    1851 Captain Ahab. *Moby Dick*, ch.36.

35 Though in many of its aspects this visible world
    seems formed in love, the invisible spheres were
    formed in fright.
    1851 *Moby Dick*, ch.42.

36 It was the whiteness of the whale that above all
    things appalled me…for all these accumulated
    associations, with whatever is sweet, and
    honourable, and sublime, there yet lurks an elusive
    something in the innermost idea of this hue, which
    strikes more of a panic to the soul than that redness
    which affrights in blood.
    1851 Ishmael. *Moby Dick*, ch.42.

37 It may seem strange that of all men sailors should
    be tinkering at their last wills and testaments, but
    there are no people in the world more fond of that
    diversion.
    1851 *Moby Dick*, ch.49.

38 There is a wisdom that is woe; but there is a woe
    that is madness.
    1851 *Moby Dick*, ch.96.

39 To produce a mighty book, you must choose a mighty theme. No great and enduring volume can ever be written on the flea, though many there be who have tried it.
1851 *Moby Dick*, ch.104.

40 For whatever is truly wonderous and fearful in man, never yet was put into words or books.
1851 *Moby Dick*, ch.110.

41 Come; let us squeeze hands all round; nay, let us all squeeze ourselves into each other; let us squeeze ourselves universally into the very milk and sperm of kindness.
1851 Ishmael. *Moby Dick*, ch.114.

42 Warmest climes but nurse the cruellest fangs: the tiger of Bengal crouches in spiced groves of ceaseless verdure.
1851 *Moby Dick*, ch.119.

43 Oh God! that man should be a thing for immortal souls to sieve through!
1851 Captain Ahab. *Moby Dick*, ch.125.

44 Let me look into a human eye; it is better than to gaze into sea or sky; better than to gaze upon God.
1851 Captain Ahab. *Moby Dick*, ch.132.

45 Guinea-coast slavery of solitary command!
1851 Captain Ahab. *Moby Dick*, ch.132.

46 He says NO! in thunder; but the Devil himself cannot make him say *yes*. For all men who say *yes*, lie; and all men who say *no*,—why, they are in the happy condition of judicious, unencumbered travellers in Europe; they cross the frontiers into Eternity with nothing but a carpet bag.
1851 Of Nathaniel Hawthorne.

47 The calm, the coolness, the silent grass-growing mood in which a man *ought* always to compose,— that, I fear, can seldom be mine. Dollars damn me; and the malicious Devil is forever grinning in upon me, holding the door ajar... What I feel most moved to write, that is banned,—it will not pay. So the product is a final hash, and all my books are botches.
1851 Letter to Nathaniel Hawthorne, Jun.

48 Why, ever since Adam, who has got to the meaning of this great allegory—the world? Then we pygmies must be content to have our paper allegories but ill comprehended.
1851 Letter to Nathaniel Hawthorne, Nov.

49 Nothing so aggravates an earnest person as a passive resistance.
1853 'Bartleby the Scrivener', in *Putnam's Monthly Magazine*, Nov–Dec.

50 If some books are deemed most baneful and their sale forbid, how, then, with deadlier facts, not dreams of doting men? Those whom books will hurt will no be proof against events. Events, not books, should be forbid.
1854 'The Encantadas, Sketch Eighth', in *Putnam's Monthly Magazine*, May.

51 Who in the rainbow can draw the line where the violet tint ends and the orange tint begins? Distinctly we see the difference of the colors, but where exactly does the one first blendingly enter into the other? So with sanity and insanity.
1891 *Billy Budd, Foretopman*, ch.21 (first published 1924).

52 There is nothing nameable but that some men will, or undertake to, do it for pay.
1891 *Billy Budd, Foretopman*, ch.21 (first published 1924).

Menander c.343–291 BC

Greek comic poet, born in Athens. He wrote more than 100 comedies, most of which are lost. Various fragments and one complete play (*Dyscolus*) have been rediscovered in recent times.

53 He whom the gods love dies young.
Dis Exapaton, fragment 4.

54 The man who runs away will fight again.
Fragment quoted in Aulus Gellius *Noctes Atticae*, 17.21.31 (translated by J C Rolfe, 1967).

Mencius properly Meng-tzu c.371–c.289 BC

Chinese philosopher and sage. He helped to develop and popularize Confucian ideas and founded a school to promote their study. His sayings were recorded by his pupils after his death, and included proposals for social and political reform.

55 If the king loves music, there is little wrong in the land.
3c BC *Discourses*.

Mencken, H(enry) L(ouis) 1880–1956

US journalist and critic. He wrote much literary and political criticism as editor of *The Smart Set* (1914–23) and *American Mercury* (1924–33) and various essays were collected in *Prejudices* (6 vols, 1919–27). Other publications included autobiographical writings and *The American Language* (1919).

56 Democracy is the theory that the common people know what they want, and deserve to get it good and hard.
1916 *Little Book in C Major*.

57 Conscience: the inner voice which warns us that someone may be looking.
1916 *Little Book in C Major*.

58 I can't remember a single masculine figure created by a woman who is not, at bottom, a booby.
1918 *In Defence of Women*, ch.1, pt.1.

59 All successful newspapers are ceaselessly querulous and bellicose.
1919 *Prejudices*, 1st series, ch.13.

60 If, after I depart this vale, you ever remember me and have thought to please my ghost, forgive some sinner and wink your eye at some homely girl.
1921 In *The Smart Set*, Dec.

61 Poetry is a comforting piece of fiction set to more or less lascivious music.
1922 *Prejudices*, 3rd series, ch.7.

62 Faith may be defined briefly as an illogical belief in the occurence of the improbable.
1922 *Prejudices*, 3rd series, ch.14.

63 The man who boasts that he habitually tells the truth is simply a man with no respect for it. It is not a thing to be thrown about loosely, like small change; it is something to be cherished and hoarded, and disbursed only when absolutely necessary.
1922 *Prejudices*, 3rd series, ch.14.

64 [Jeremy] Bentham held no post at the mercy of bankers and tripe sellers; he was a man of independent means, a lawyer and politician and a heretic in general practice. It is impossible to imagine such a man occupying a chair at Harvard or Princeton. He had a hand in too many pies; he was too rebellious and contumacious; he had too little respect for authority, either academic or worldly. Moreover, his mind was too wide for a professor; he could never remain safely in a groove; the whole field of social organization invited his inquiries and experiments.
1922 'The Dismal Science', in *The Smart Set*, Jun.

65 Hygiene is the corruption of medicine by morality.
1922 *Prejudices*.

66 The opera…is to music what a bawdy house is to a cathedral.
1925 Letter to Isaac Goldberg.

67 No one in this world, so far as I know—and I have searched the record for years, and employed agents to help me—has ever lost money by underestimating the intelligence of the great masses of the plain people.
1926 'Notes on Journalism' in the *Chicago Sunday Tribune*, 19 Sep. The phrase is commonly quoted as 'No one ever went broke underestimating the intelligence of the American people.'

68 The saddest life is that of a political aspirant under democracy. His failure is ignominious and his success is disgraceful.
1929 In *the Baltimore Evening Sun*, 9 Dec.

69 Here, indeed, was his one peculiar Fach, his one really notable talent. He slept more than any other President, whether by day or night. Nero fiddled, but Coolidge only snored.
1933 Of Calvin Coolidge. In the *American Mercury*, Apr.

70 Roosevelt will probably go down into American history as a great hero. It is one of our Heavenly Father's characteristic jokes upon the American people, and in the usual bad taste.
1944 Journal entry. Collected in *The Diary of H. L. Mencken* (published 1990).

71 I've made it a rule never to drink by daylight and never to refuse a drink after dark.
1945 In the *New York Post*, 18 Sep.

72 When women kiss it always reminds one of prize-fighters shaking hands.
1949 *Chrestomathy*, ch.30.

73 Love is the delusion that one woman differs from another.
1949 *Chrestomathy*, ch.30.

74 Men have a much better time of it than women. For one thing, they marry later. For another thing, they die earlier.
1949 *Chrestomathy*, ch.30

75 Puritanism. The haunting fear that someone, somewhere, may be happy.
1949 *Chrestomathy*, ch.30.

76 He is a man who sits in the outer office of the White House hoping to hear the President sneeze.
Of the Vice President. Recalled on his death, 29 Jan 1956.

77 Science, at bottom, is really anti-intellectual. It always distrusts pure reason, and demands the production of objective fact.
'Minority Report', collected in *Notebooks* (1956).

78 Some people read too much: the bibliobuli…who are constantly drunk on books, as other men are drunk on whiskey or religion. They wander through the most diverting and stimulating of worlds in a haze, seeing nothing and hearing nothing.
'Minority Report'. Collected in *Notebooks* (1956).

79 We must respect the other fellow's religion, but only in the sense and to the extent that we respect his theory that his wife is beautiful and his children smart.
'Minority Report'. Collected in *Notebooks* (1956).

80 Men always try to make virtues of their weaknesses. Fear of death and fear of life become piety.
'Minority Report'. Collected in *Notebooks* (1956).

81 It is now quite lawful for a Catholic woman to avoid pregnancy by a resort to mathematics, though she is still forbidden to resort to physics and chemistry.
'Minority Report'. Collected in *Notebooks* (1956).

82 The capacity of human beings to bore one another seems to be vastly greater than that of any other animals. Some of their most esteemed inventions have no other apparent purpose, for example, the dinner party of more than two, the epic poem, and the science of metaphysics.
'Minority Report'. Collected in *Notebooks* (1956).

83 Men are the only animals who devote themselves assiduously to making one another unhappy. It is, I suppose, one of their godlike qualities.
'Minority Report'. Collected in *Notebooks* (1956).

84 War will never cease until babies begin to come into the world with larger cerebrums and smaller adrenal glands.
'Minority Report'. Collected in *Notebooks* (1956).

85 Whenever one comes to close grips with so-called idealism, as in war time, one is shocked by its rascality.
'Minority Report'. Collected in *Notebooks* (1956).

86 I hate all sports as rabidly as a person who likes sports hates common sense.
Quoted in Fred Metcalfe *The Penguin Dictionary of Modern Humorous Quotations* (1986).

87 The greatest of all the contributions of the American way of life to the salvation of humanity.
Of the cocktail. Quoted by William Grimes in 'The American Cocktail', *Americana*, Dec 1992.

88 The varnishers and veneerers have been busily converting Abe into a plaster saint…to pump all his human weaknesses out of him, and so leave him a mere moral apparition, a sort of amalgam of John Wesley and the Holy Ghost.
Of popular perceptions of Abraham Lincoln. Quoted in Fred Hobson *Mencken: A Life* (1994).

89 His whole carcass seemed to be made of iron. There was no give in him—no bounce, no softness. He sailed through American history like a steel ship loaded with monoliths made of granite.
Of President Grover Cleveland. Quoted in Fred Hobson *Mencken: A Life* (1994).

90 A third-rate political wheel-horse, with the face of a moving-picture actor, the intelligence of a respectable agricultural implement dealer, and the imagination of a lodge joiner…a benign blank—a decent, harmless, laborious, hollow-headed mediocrity.
Of President Warren G Harding. Quoted in Fred Hobson *Mencken: A Life* (1994).

91 His English reminds me of tattered washing on the line…of stale bean-soup, of college yells, of dogs barking idiotically through endless nights. It is so bad that a sort of grandeur creeps into it.
Of President Warren G Harding. Quoted in Fred Hobson *Mencken: A Life* (1994).

92 He was, on his plane, as insufferable as a Methodist on his.
Of Oscar Wilde. Introduction to a new edition of Wilde *A House of Pomegranates*.

Menzies, Sir Robert Gordon 1894–1978

Australian statesman, Prime Minister (1939–41), Leader of the Opposition (1943–9) and thereafter Premier of the coalition government. He headed the Five Nations Committee which sought a settlement with Nasser on the question of Suez (1956).

93 What Great Britain calls the Far East is to us the near north.
1939 Quoted in the *Sydney Morning Herald*, 27 Apr. Menzies was one of the first Australian statesmen to recognise the importance to his country of Asia.

94 If I were the Archangel Gabriel, madam, I'm afraid you would not be in my constituency.
Attributed reply to a woman who had heckled him with the words 'I wouldn't vote for you if you were the Archangel Gabriel.' Quoted in Ray Robinson *The Wit of Robert Menzies* (1966).

Mercer, David 1928–80

English playwright. Such plays as *A Climate of Fear* (1962) and *In Two Minds* (1967) explored his fascination with mental health, psychiatry and his struggle to reconcile a belief in socialism with the repression revealed during his stays in Eastern Europe. Other writings included the films *Morgan* (1965) and *Providence* (1977) and several plays for television.

95 A Suitable Case for Treatment.
1962 Play title.

Mercer, Johnny 1909–76

US songwriter. His songs include 'Accentuate the Positive', 'Black Magic', 'In the Cool Cool of the Evening' and 'Something's Got to Give'.

96 Hooray for Hollywood.
1937 Title of song which first appeared in the film *Hollywood Hotel*, performed by Johnny Davis and Frances Langford.

Meredith, George 1828–1909

English novelist and poet. He married the daughter of Thomas Love Peacock but she left him for the painter

Henry Wallis, for whose *Death of Chatterton* Meredith
was the model. His volumes of poetry include *Modern
Love* (1862) and *Poems and Lyrics of the Joy of the Earth*
(1883). His novels include *The Ordeal of Richard Feverel*
(1859), *Evan Harrington* (1860), and *The Egoist* (1879).

97 Lovely are the curves of the white owl sweeping
   Wavy in the dusk lit by one large star.
   Lone on the fir-branch, his rattle-note unvaried,
   Brooding o'er the gloom, spins the brown eve-jar.
   1851 *Poems*, 'Love in the Valley', stanza 5. The poem was
   revised and re-published in 1878.

98 Happy happy time, when the white star hovers
   Low over dim fields fresh with blooming dew,
   Near the face of dawn, that draws athwart the
     darkness,
   Threading it with colour, like yewberries the yew.
   1851 *Poems*, 'Love in the Valley', stanza 7. The poem was
   revised and re-published in 1878.

99 I expect that Woman will be the last thing civilized
   by Man.
   1859 *The Ordeal of Richard Feverel*, ch.1.

1 Away with systems! Away with a corrupt world! Let
  us breathe the air of the Enchanted island. Golden
  lie the meadows; golden run the streams; red gold is
  on the pine-stems. The sun's coming down to
  earth, and walks the fields and the waters. The sun
  is coming down to earth, and the fields and the
  waters shout to him golden shouts.
  1859 *The Ordeal of Richard Feverel*, ch.19.

2 Kissing don't last: cookery do!
  1859 *The Ordeal of Richard Feverel*, ch.28.

3 Speech is the small change of silence.
  1859 *The Ordeal of Richard Feverel*, ch.34.

4 It became known that death had taken Mr
  Melchisedec Harrington, and struck one off the list
  of living tailors.
  1860 *Evan Harrington*, ch.1.

5 He fainted on his vengefulness, and strove
  To ape the magnanimity of love.
  1862 *Modern Love*, 2.

6 O have a care of natures that are mute!
  1862 *Modern Love*, 35.

7 Much benevolence of the passive order may be traced
  to a disinclination to inflict pain upon oneself.
  1866 *Vittoria*, ch.24.

8 A dainty rogue in porcelain.
  1879 *The Egoist*, ch.5

9 Cynicism is intellectual dandyism.
  1879 *The Egoist*, ch.7.

10 'But do care a bit for flattery, my lady,' said De
   Craye. ''Tis the finest of the Arts; we might call it
   moral sculpture. Adepts in it can cut their friends
   to any shape they like.'
   1879 De Craye to Lady Busshe. *The Egoist*, ch. 36.

11 Enter these enchanted woods,
   You who dare.
   1883 *Poems and Lyrics of the Joy of Earth*, 'The Woods of
   Westermain'.

12 Soaring through wider zones that pricked his scars
   With memory of the old revolt from Awe,
   He reached the middle height, and at the stars,
   Which are the brain of heaven, he looked, and
     sank.
   Around the ancient track marched, rank on rank,
   The army of unalterable law.
   1883 *Poems and Lyrics of the Joy of Earth*, 'Lucifer in Starlight'.

13 For singing till his heaven fills
   'Tis love of earth that he instils,
   And ever winging up and up,
   Our valley is his golden cup,
   And he the wine which overflows.
   1883 *Poems and Lyrics of the Joy of Earth*, 'The Lark Ascending'.

14 'Tis Ireland gives England her soldiers, her generals
   too.
   1885 *Diana of the Crossways*, ch.2.

15 Affairs of the world he could treat competently; he
   had a head for high politics and the management of
   men; the feminine half of the world was a
   confusion and a vexation to his intelligence,
   characterless; and one woman at last appearing
   decipherable, he fancied it must be owing to her
   possession of character, a thing prized the more
   in women because of his latent doubt of its
   existence.
   1885 Percy Dacier's opinion of Diana. *Diana of the Crossways*,
   ch.28.

16 A wind sways in the pines,
   And below
   Not a breath of wild air;
   Still as the mosses that glow
   On the flooring and over the lines
   Of the roots here and there.
   The pine tree drops its dead;
   They are quiet, as under the sea.
   Overhead, overhead
   Rushes life in a race,
   As the clouds the clouds chase;
   And we go,
   And we drop like the fruits of the tree,
   Even we,
   Even so.
   1888 *A Reading of Earth*, 'Dirge in the Woods'.

Mérimée, Prosper 1803–70

French novelist, Inspector-General of Historical Remains in France (1833) and a Senator (1853). He wrote many short stories and novels, including *Columba* and *Carmen*, as well as archaeological and historical dissertations and travel stories.

17 A colossal bore… I feel I could write something like it tomorrow, if my cat inspired me by walking over the piano.
1861 Of Wagner's opera *Tannhäuser*, after the disastrous première of its revised version at the *Opéra*, 13 Mar. Quoted in Joanna Richardson *La Vie Parisienne* (1971), p.262.
▷ See Gounod 437:79.

Merman, Ethel stage-name of *Ethel Agnes Zimmermann* 1909–84

US singer and actress. Nicknamed 'The Golden Foghorn' because of her powerful singing voice, she established her reputation in cabaret and subsequently starred in such musicals as *Annie Get Your Gun* (1946) and *Hello, Dolly!* (1970).

18 She's OK, if you like talent.
1958 Of Mary Martin. In *Theater Arts*, Sep.

19 Can you imagine the name Zimmermann in bright lights? It would burn you to death!
Explaining why she took a stage-name. Attributed.

Merrifield, Dudley Bruce 1921–

US business lecturer and former government official. He was undersecretary for economic affairs (1966-7) and is has been president of the Pinnacle Research Institutional Development Company since 1991.

20 Innovate, automate—or evaporate!
1987 Address at London's Guildhall to Britain's senior industrialists and bankers. Reported in *The Times*, 19 Feb.

Merrill, James Ingram 1926–95

US poet, the 'ouija poet', whose interest in the occult led him to use a ouija board to communicate with the spirit world. The experience is recorded in an epic poem, *The Changing Light at Sandover* (1982, rev 1992). His collections include *Nights and Days* (1966) and *Divine Comedies* (1976, Pulitzer Prize), and he also wrote plays and novels.

21 Here one is in Later Life, and it's perfectly pleasant really, not for a moment that garden of cactus and sour grapes I'd always assumed it *must* be.
1972 Letter to a friend at age 46.

22 What one wants in this world isn't so much to 'live' as to…*be* lived, to be used by life for its own purposes.
Quoted in the *New Yorker*, 27 Mar 1995.

Merrin, Edward H

Antiquities dealer.

23 The price was quite reasonable. It just happened to be a lot of money.
1989 In the *New York Times*, 16 Jul. On paying $2.09 million for a nine-inch, 5,000-year-old Greek head.

Merton, Robert King 1910–

US sociologist, Columbia University.

24 The self-fulfilling prophecy is, in the beginning, a *false* definition of the situation evoking a new behavior which makes the originally false conception come *true*. The specious validity of the self-fulfilling prophecy perpetuates a reign of error.
1948 'The Self-Fulfilling Prophecy', in *Social Theory and Social Structure* (rev. edn, 1968), p.477. This is the first use of the phrase 'self-fulfilling prophecy'.

25 It would be a curious reading of the history of thought to suggest that the absence of disagreement testifies to a developing discipline.
1961 Defending internal disputes among sociologists. 'Now the Case *for* Sociology', in the *New York Times Magazine*, 16 Jul.

26 The sociologists of knowledge have been among those raising high the banner which reads: 'We don't know if what we say is true, but it is at least significant.' The sociologists and psychologists engaged in the study of public opinion and mass communications are most often found in the opposed camp of the empiricists… 'We don't know that what we say is particularly significant, but it is at least true.'
1968 *Social Theory and Social Structure* (rev. edn), pt.3, introduction.

Merwin, W(illiam) S(tanley) 1927–

US poet. His poetry includes *A Mask for Janus* (1952), *The Carrier of Ladders* (1970, Pulitzer Prize), *Opening the Hand* (1983) and *Selected Poems* (1988). He is also a translator, notably of *The Cid* (1959).

27 The thing that makes poetry different from all of the other arts…[is] you're using language, which is what you use for everything else—telling lies and selling socks, advertising, and conducting law. Whereas we don't write little concerts or paint little pictures.
1994 On receiving the $100,000 Tanning Prize for Poetry. In the *Washington Post*, 30 Sep.

Metternich, Prince Clemens Lothar Wenzel 1773–1859

Austrian statesman, Foreign Minister from 1809. He was a powerful influence for conservatism in Europe, contributing to the tension that produced the upheavals of 1848 and popular rebellions in many countries.

28 When Paris sneezes, Europe catches cold.
1830 Letter, 26 Jan.

29 Italy is a geographical expression.
1847 Letter, 6 Aug.

30 I have been a rock of order.
1859 Attributed, shortly before his death. Quoted in Andrew Milne *Metternich* (1975).

31 Error has never approached my spirit.
Said to Guizot on the steps of the British Museum. Quoted in A J P Taylor *From the Boer War to the Cold War: Essays on Twentieth-Century Europe* (1995).

Meyer, Karl Ernest 1928–

US journalist, staff writer for the *New York Times*.

32 Whatever his private behaviour, the man and his work existed in different realms. Mencken's defects were commonplace; his virtues were not. So wonderfully uninhibited was his style that even a single sentence in a routine article proclaimed its begetter.
1994 Of H L Mencken. In the *New York Times Book Review*, 8 May.

Michelangelo full name Michelangelo Buonarroti 1475–1564

Italian painter, sculptor, architect, draughtsman and poet. Born near Florence, he is one of the most important figures of the Italian Renaissance.

33 I've finished that chapel I was painting. The Pope is quite satisfied.
1512 Letter written to his father after 18 months of painting the vault of the Sistine Chapel, quoted in Robert J Clements (ed) *Michelangelo: A Self-Portrait* (1968).

34 Nothing the greatest artist can conceive
That every marble block doth not confine
Within itself; and only its design
The hand that follows intellect can achieve.
c.1538 Quoted in Robert J Clements (ed) *Michelangelo: A Self-Portrait* (1968). Trans by H W Longfellow.

35 Your Lordship sends to tell me that I should paint and have no doubts. I answer that painting is done with the brain, not the hands.
1542 Letter written to a Cardinal, Oct, collected in Creighton Gilbert (ed and trans) *Complete Poems and Selected Letters of Michelangelo* (1963).

36 I have only too much of a wife in this art of mine, who has always kept me in tribulation, and my children shall be the works I leave, which, even if they are naught, will live a while.
In response to a priest and friend who had said it was a pity he had not married and had children to whom he could leave his works. Attributed in Vasari *Lives of the Artists* (1568).

37 They are so beautiful that they would grace the entrance to Paradise.

Of Ghiberti's doors for the Florence Baptistery. Quoted in Giorgio Vasari's *Lives of the Artists* (1568, translated by George Bull).

38 In my opinion painting should be considered excellent in proportion as it approaches the effect of relief, while relief should be considered bad in proportion as it approaches the effect of painting.
Quoted in Robert J Clements (ed) *Michelangelo: A Self-Portrait* (1968).

Middleton, Thomas c. 1570–1627

English dramatist, who collaborated with Dekker, Webster, Rowley, Massinger, Beaumont and Fletcher and probably Shakespeare. His works include *A Mad World, My Masters* (1608), *Women Beware Women* (1620–7) and *A Chaste Maid in Cheapside* (published 1630). He also wrote pageants and masques for the city of London.

39 But you are dull, nothing comes nimbly from you; you dance like a plumber's daughter and deserve two thousand pound in lead to your marriage, and not in goldsmith's ware.
1613 *A Chaste Maid in Cheapside* (published 1630), act 1, sc.1.

40 Lie soft, sleep hard, drink wine, and eat good cheer.
1613 *A Chaste Maid in Cheapside* (published 1630), act 1, sc.1.

41 Nay, good sir, be not so violent; with speed
I cannot render satisfaction
Unto the dear companion of my soul,
Virginity, whom I thus long have lived with,
And part with it so rude and suddenly.
Can such friends divide, never to meet again,
Without a solemn farewell?
1622 *The Changeling* (with William Rowley), act 1, sc.1.

42 Our eyes are sentinels unto our judgements
And should give certain judgement what they see;
But they are rash sometimes and tell us wonders
Of common things, which when our judgements find,
They can then check the eyes and call them blind.
1622 *The Changeling* (with William Rowley), act 1, sc.1.

43 Now I know
She had rather wear my pelt tanned in a pair
Of dancing pumps.
1622 *The Changeling* (with William Rowley), act 1, sc.1.

44 There's scarce a thing but is both loved and loathed.
1622 *The Changeling* (with William Rowley), act 1, sc.1.

45 I shall run mad with joy.
1622 *The Changeling* (with William Rowley), act 2, sc.2.

46 I'm up to the chin in heaven.
1622 *The Changeling* (with William Rowley), act 2, sc.2.

47 Paper blushes not.
1622 *The Changeling* (with William Rowley), act 3, sc.4.

48 Y'are the deed's creature.

    1622 *The Changeling* (with William Rowley), act 3, sc.4.

49 Beneath the stars, upon yon meteor
Ever hung my fate, 'mongst things corruptible;
I ne'er could pluck it from him. My loathing
Was prophet to the rest, but ne'er believed.

    1622 *The Changeling* (with William Rowley), act 5, sc.3.

Midler, Bette 1945–

US comedienne, singer and actress, whose bawdy nightclub act led to a successful career on Broadway and then in films.

50 There comes a time when you have to let your clothes go out in the world and try to make it on their own.

    1987 On relinquishing the mermaid costume she wore in the 1970s film *Clams on the Half Shell.* In *People,* 31 Aug.

Mies van der Rohe, Ludwig 1886–1969

German-born US architect and furniture designer, a pioneer of glass skyscrapers. He was director of the Bauhaus in Dessau (1930–3) and emigrated to the US in 1937.

51 Architecture is the will of the age conceived in spatial terms.

    1922 *De Stijl,* vol.6.

Mikes, George 1912–

Hungarian-born writer who has written humorous books about his experience of being a foreigner in England.

52 On the Continent people have good food; in England people have good table manners.

    1946 *How to Be an Alien.*

53 Many continentals think life is a game, the English think cricket is a game.

    1946 *How to be an Alien.*

Milestone, Lewis pseudonym of *Levis Milstein* 1895–1980

US film director, best known for *All Quiet on the Western Front* (1930), which won an Academy Award.

54 I've got your happy ending. We'll let the Germans win the war.

    c.1929 Response when asked to provide an up-beat ending for *All Quiet on the Western Front.*

Milius, John 1944–

US screenwriter and director. His writing credits include *Evel Knievel* (1972), *The Life and Times of Judge Roy Bean* (1973), *Magnum Force* (1973) and *The Wind and the Lion* (1975) which he also directed.

55 I know the law since I have spent my entire life in its flagrant disregard.

    1972 *The Life and Times of Judge Roy Bean.*

Mill, James 1773–1836

Scottish philosopher, historian and economist. He was a friend of Jeremy Bentham and an enthusiastic proponent of Utilitarianism.

56 The government and the people are under a moral necessity of acting together; a free press compels them to bend to one another.

    1811 In the *Edinburgh Review,* May–Aug.

Mill, John Stuart 1806–73

English empiricist philosopher, MP (1863–8) and reformer, a supporter of women's suffrage (*Subjection of Women,* 1869) and liberalism. His works include *System of Logic* (1843), *Principles of Political Economy* (1848), *On Liberty* (1859) and *Utilitarianism* (1863).

57 Unlike the Laws of Production, those of Distribution are partly of human institution, since the manner in which wealth is distributed in any given society, depends on the statutes or usages therein obtaining.

    1848 *Principles of Political Economy, with Some Applications to Social Philosophy.*

58 A stationary condition of capital and population implies no stationary state of human improvement. There could be as much scope as ever for all kinds of mental culture, and moral and social progress.

    1848 *Principles of Political Economy, with Some Applications to Social Philosophy.*

59 Happily, there is nothing in the laws of value which remains for the present or any future writer to clear up; the theory of the subject is complete.

    1848 *Principles of Political Economy, with Some Applications to Social Philosophy.*

60 I am not charmed with the ideal of life held out by those who think that the normal state of human beings is that of struggling to get on_I know not why it should be a matter of congratulation that persons who are already richer than any one needs to be, should have doubled their means of consuming things which give little or no pleasure except as representative of wealth.

    1848 *Principles of Political Economy, with Some Applications to Social Philosophy.*

61 The average condition of the people improving or deteriorating, depends upon whether population is advancing faster than improvement, or improvement than population.

    1848 *Principles of Political Economy, with Some Applications to Social Philosophy.*

62 That the whole or any part of the education of the people should be in State hands, I go so far as anyone in deprecating… A general State education is a mere contrivance for molding people to be exactly like one another.

1856 *Utilitarianism, Liberty and Representative Government.*

63 The only purpose for which power can be rightfully exercised over any member of a civilized community, against his will, is to prevent harm to others.
1859 *On Liberty.*

64 A party of order or stability, and a party of progress or reform, are both necessary elements of a healthy state of political life.
1859 *On Liberty.*

65 Everyone who receives the protection of society owes a return for the benefit, and the fact of living in a society renders it indispensable that each should be bound to observe a certain line of conduct towards the rest. That conduct consists…in each person bearing his share of the labours and sacrifices incurred for defending the society or its members from injury and molestation.
1859 *On Liberty.*

66 If all mankind minus one were of one opinion, and only one person were of the contrary opinion, mankind would no more be justified in silencing that one person than he, if he had the power, would be justified in silencing mankind.
1859 *On Liberty.*

67 If the roads, the railways, the banks, the insurance offices, the great joint-stock companies, the universities, and the public charities, were all of them branches of government; if, in addition, the municipal corporations and local boards, with all that now devolves on them, became departments of the central administration; if the employes of all these different enterprises were appointed and paid by the government, and looked to the government for every rise in life; not all the freedom of the press and popular constitution of the legislature would make this or any other country free otherwise than in name.
1859 *On Liberty.*

68 The Conservatives, as being by the law of their existence the stupidest party.
1861 *Considerations on Representative Government*, ch.7, note.

69 The worth of the State, in the long run, is the worth of the individuals composing it.
1861 *Considerations on Representative Government.*

70 It is better to be a human being dissatisfied than a pig satisfied; better to be Socrates dissatisfied than a fool satisfied.
1863 *Utilitarianism*, ch.2.

71 The creed which accepts as the foundation of morals, Utility, or the Greatest Happiness Principle, holds that actions are right in proportion as they tend to promote happiness, wrong as they tend to produce the reverse of happiness.
1863 *Utilitarianism*, ch.2.

72 The sole evidence it is possible to produce that anything is desirable, is that people do actually desire it.
1863 *Utilitarianism*, ch.4.

73 If the universe had a beginning, its beginning, by the very condition of the cases, was supernatural; the laws of Nature cannot account for their own origin.
1865 *Auguste Comte and Positivism.*

74 It is always easy to find fault with a classification. There are a hundred ways of arranging any set of objects, and something may almost always be said against the best, and in favor of the worst of them. But the merits of a classification depend on the purposes to which it is instrumental.
1865 *Auguste Comte and Positivism.*

75 I never was a boy, never played at cricket; it is better to let Nature take her course.
1867 *Autobiography.*

76 It may be asserted without scruple, that no other class of dependants have had their character so entirely distorted from its natural proportions by their relations with their masters.
1869 *The Subjection of Women*, ch.1.

77 With equality of experience and of general faculties, a woman usually sees much more than a man of what is immediately before her.
1869 *The Subjection of Women*, ch.3.

78 Women cannot be expected to devote themselves to the emancipation of women, until men in considerable number are prepared to join with them in the undertaking.
1869 *The Subjection of Women*, ch.3.

79 Marriage is the only actual bondage known to our law. There remain no legal slaves, except the mistress of every house.
1869 *The Subjection of Women*, ch.4.

80 The self-worship of the monarch, or of the feudal superior, is matched by the self-worship of the male.
1869 *The Subjection of Women*, ch.4.

Millay, Edna St Vincent 1892–1950

US poet. Despite her contemporary subject matter, she was a formalist and her poems show a strong technical skill. Her collections include *The Harp-Weaver* (1923), which won a Pulitzer Prize.

81 World, world, I cannot get thee close enough!
Long have I known a glory in it all,
But never knew like this;
Here such a pattern is
As stretcheth me apart. Lord, I do fear
Thou'st made the world too beautiful this year:
My soul is all but out of me—let fall
No burning leaf; prithee, let no bird call.
1917 *God's World*.

82 My candle burns at both ends;
It will not last the night;
But ah, my foes, and oh, my friends—
It gives a lovely light.
1920 *A Few Figs From Thistles*, 'First Fig'.

83 Safe upon solid rock the ugly houses stand:
Come and see my shining palace built upon the
sand.
1920 *A Few Figs From Thistles*, 'Second Fig'.

84 Death devours all lovely things;
Lesbia with her sparrow
Shares the darkness—presently
Every bed is narrow.
1921 *Second April*, 'Passer Mortuus Est'.

85 After all, my erstwhile dear,
My no longer cherished,
Need we say it was not love,
Now that love is perished?
1921 *Second April*, 'Passer Mortuus Est'.

86 What lips my lips have kissed, and where, and why,
I have forgotten, and what arms have lain
Under my head till morning; but the rain
Is full of ghosts tonight, that tap and sigh
Upon the glass and listen for reply
1923 *Harp-Weaver and Other Poems*, 'Sonnet 19: What lips my
lips have kissed'.

87 Thus in the winter stands the lonely tree,
Nor knows what birds have vanished one by one,
Yet knows its boughs more silent than before
1923 *Harp-Weaver and Other Poems*, 'Sonnet 19: What lips my
lips have kissed'.

88 I only know that summer sang in me
A little while, that in me sings no more.
1923 *Harp-Weaver and Other Poems*, 'Sonnet 19: What lips my
lips have kissed'.

89 Euclid alone
Has looked on Beauty bare. Fortunate they
Who, though once only and then but far away,
Have heard her massive sandal set on stone.
1923 *Harp-Weaver and Other Poems*, 'Sonnet 22: Euclid alone
has looked on Beauty bare'.

90 Down, down, down into the darkness of the grave
Gently they go, the beautiful, the tender, the kind;

Quietly they go, the intelligent, the witty, the
brave.
I know. But I do not approve. And I am not
resigned.
1928 *The Buck in the Snow*, 'Dirge Without Music'.

91 It's not true that life is one damn thing after
another—it's one damn thing over and over.
1930 Letter to Arthur Davison Ficke, 24 Oct.

92 Love is not all; it is not meat nor drink.
1931 *Fatal Interview*, title of poem.

93 Childhood is not from birth to a certain age and at
a certain age
The child is grown, and puts away childish things.
Childhood is the kingdom where nobody dies.
Nobody that matters, that is.
1934 *Wine From These Grapes*, 'Childhood is the Kingdom
where Nobody dies'.

Miller, Arthur 1915–

US playwright. *Death of a Salesman* (1949) won a Pulitzer
Prize and established him as a leading contemporary
playwright, dealing with the realities of family life.
Subsequent plays have included *After the Fall* (1964),
thought to have been inspired by his unhappy marriage to
Marilyn Monroe.

94 A small man can be just as exhausted as a great
man.
1949 Linda. *Death of a Salesman*, act 1.

95 Willie was a salesman. And for a salesman, there is
no rock bottom to life… He's a man way out there
in the blue, riding on a smile and a shoeshine. And
when they start not smiling back—that's an
earthquake.
1949 Charley. *Death of a Salesman*, 'Requiem'.

96 A salesman is got to dream, boy. It comes with the
territory.
1949 Charley. *Death of a Salesman*, 'Requiem'.

97 They believed, in short, that they held in their
steady hands the candle that would light the world.
We have inherited this belief, and it has helped and
hurt us.
1953 Of the settlers in Salem in 1692. *The Crucible*, act 1.

98 Spare me! You forget nothin' and forgive nothin'.
Learn charity, woman. I have gone tiptoe in this
house all seven month since she is gone. I have not
moved from there to there without I think to please
you, and still an everlasting funeral marches around
your heart.
1953 Proctor to Elizabeth. *The Crucible*, act 2.

99 Theology, sir, is a fortress; no crack in a fortress
may be accounted small.
1953 Hale. *The Crucible*, act 2.

1 Oh, no, the machine, the machine is necessary. A man comes into a great hotel and says, I am a messenger. Who is this man? He disappears walking, there is no noise, nothing. Maybe he will never come back, maybe he will never deliver the message. But a man who rides up on a great machine, this man is responsible, this man exists. He will be given messages.
1955 Rodolpho. *A View From the Bridge*, act 1.

2 A genuine invention in the realm of ideas must first emerge as an abstruse and even partial concept… At first blush a new idea appears to be very close to insanity because to be new it must reverse important basic beliefs and assumptions which, in turn, have been institutionalized and are administered by one or another kind of priesthood with a vested interest in an old idea.
1958 *The Collected Plays*, 'Introduction, II'.

3 A good newspaper, I suppose, is a nation talking to itself.
1961 In the *Observer*, 26 Nov.

4 How few the days are that hold the mind in place; like a tapestry hanging on four or five hooks. Especially the day you stop becoming; the day you merely are. I suppose it's when the principles dissolve, and instead of the general gray of what ought to be you begin to see what is… The word 'Now' is like a bomb through the window, and it ticks.
1964 Quentin. *After The Fall*, act 1.

5 A suicide kills two people, Maggie. That's what it's for.
1964 Quentin. *After The Fall*, act 2.

6 Part of knowing who we are is knowing we are not someone else. And Jew is only the name we give to that stranger, the agony we cannot feel, the death we look at like a cold abstraction. Each man has his Jew; it is the other.
1964 Leduc. *Incident at Vichy*, act 1.

7 The concentration camp is the final expression of human separateness and its ultimate consequence. It is organized abandonment.
1966 Interview in the *Paris Review*, Summer.

8 Success, instead of giving freedom of choice, becomes a way of life.
1966 Interview in the *Paris Review*, Summer.

9 [Plays that would] cut through time like a knife through a layer cake or a road through a mountain revealing its geologic layers.

1987 Describing the plays he always wished to write. *Timebends: A Life*.

10 Without alienation, there can be no politics.
1988 In *Marxism Today*, Jan.

11 I'm the end of the line; absurd and appalling as it may seem, serious New York theater has died in my lifetime.
1989 In *The Times*, 11 Jan.

12 Maybe all one can do is hope to end up with the right regrets.
1991 Tom. *The Ride Down Mount Morgan*, act 1.

Miller, Henry Valentine 1891–1980

US novelist. An exile in Paris in the 1930s he later returned to live in California. His novels, notorious for sexual explicitness, include *Tropic of Cancer* (1934) and *Tropic of Capricorn* (1939), both at one time banned in the US.

14 The wallpaper with which the men of science have covered the world of reality is falling to tatters.
1934 *The Tropic of Cancer*.

15 This is not a book in the ordinary sense of the word. No, this is a prolonged insult, a gob of spit in the face of Art, a kick in the pants to God, Man, Destiny, Time, Love, Beauty…what you will. I am going to sing for you, a little off-key perhaps, but I will sing.
1934 *Tropic of Cancer*.

16 Chaos is the score upon which reality is written.
1934 *Tropic of Cancer*.

17 Every man with a bellyful of the classics is an enemy of the human race.
1934 *Tropic of Cancer*.

18 We live in the mind, in ideas, in fragments.
1936 *Black Spring*, 'The Fourteenth Ward'.

19 There are passages of Ulysses which can be read only in the toilet—if one wants to extract the full flavour of their content.
1936 *Black Spring*, 'A Saturday Afternoon'.

20 The world is the mirror of myself dying.
1936 Black Spring, 'Third or Fourth Day of Spring'.

21 I see America as a black curse upon the world. I see a long night settling in and that mushroom which has poisoned the world withering at the roots.
1936 *Black Spring*, 'Third or Fourth Day of Spring'.

22 What does it matter how one comes by the truth so long as one pounces upon it and lives by it.
1939 *Tropic of Capricorn.*

23 The artist does not tinker with the universe; he recreates it out of his own experience and understanding of life.
1939 *The Cosmological Eye*, 'An Open Letter to Surrealists Everywhere'.

24 Example moves the world more than doctrine.
1939 *The Cosmological Eye*, 'An Open Letter to Surrealists Everywhere'.

25 Life has no other discipline to impose, if we would but realize it, than to accept life unquestioningly... Every moment is a golden one for him who has the vision to recognize it as such.
1940 *The World of Sex.*

26 Morally, spiritually, we are fettered. What have we achieved in mowing down mountain ranges, harnessing the energy of mighty rivers, or moving whole populations about like chess pieces, if we ourselves remain the same restless, miserable, frustrated creatures we were before. To call such activity progress is utter delusion.
1940 *The World of Sex.*

27 Until we do lose ourselves there is no hope of finding ourselves.
1940 *The World of Sex.*

28 All that matters is that the miraculous becomes the norm.
1940 *The World of Sex.*

29 Though I've never read a line of Homer I believe the Greek of today is essentially unchanged. If anything he is more Greek than he ever was.
1941 *The Colossus of Maroussi*, pt.1.

30 If men cease to believe that they will one day become gods then they will surely become worms.
1941 *The Colossus of Maroussi*, pt.3.

31 To live without killing is a thought which could electrify the world, if men were only capable of staying awake long enough to let the idea soak in.
1944 *Sunday After The War*, 'Reunion in Brooklyn'.

32 No man would set a word down on paper if he had the courage to live out what he believed in.
1945 *Sexus*, ch.1.

33 The world has *not* to be put in order: the world *is* order incarnate. It is for us to put ourselves in unison with this order.
1945 *Sexus*, ch.9.

34 The great joy of the artist is to become aware of a higher order of things, to recognize by the

compulsive and spontaneous manipulation of his own impulses the resemblance between human creation and what is called 'divine' creation.
1945 *Sexus*, ch.9.

35 Imagination is the voice of daring. If there is anything Godlike about God it is that. He dared to imagine everything.
1945 *Sexus*, ch.14.

36 Nowhere have I encountered such a dull, monotonous fabric of life as here in America. Here boredom reaches its peak.
1945 *The Air-Conditioned Nightmare*, preface.

37 Man has demonstrated that he is master of everything—except his own nature.
1945 *The Air-Conditioned Nightmare*, 'With Edgar Varese in the Gobi Desert'.

38 The world goes on because a few men in every generation believe in it utterly, accept it unquestioningly, underwrite it with their lives.
1945 *The Air-Conditioned Nightmare*, 'With Edgar Varese in the Gobi Desert'.

39 Back of every creation, supporting it like an arch, is faith. Enthusiasm is nothing: it comes and goes. But if one *believes*, then miracles occur.
1945 *The Air-Conditioned Nightmare*, 'With Edgar Varese in the Gobi Desert'.

40 The study of crime begins with the knowledge of oneself. All that you despise, all that you loathe, all that you reject, all that you condemn and seek to convert by punishment springs from you.
1945 *The Air-Conditioned Nightmare*, 'The Soul of Anaesthesia'.

41 Art is only a means to life, to the life more abundant. It is not in itself the life more abundant... In becoming an end it defeats itself.
1947 *The Wisdom of the Heart*, 'Reflections on Writing'.

42 I have always looked upon decay as being just as wonderful an expression of life as growth.
1947 *The Wisdom of the Heart*, 'Reflections on Writing'.

43 It is the creative nature of man which has refused to let him lapse back into that unconscious unity with life which characterizes the animal world from which he made his escape.
1947 *The Wisdom of the Heart*, 'Creative Death'.

44 The poem is the dream made flesh, in a two-fold sense: as work of art, and as life, which is a work of art.
1947 *The Wisdom of the Heart*, 'Creative Death'.

45 All growth is a leap in the dark, a spontaneous unpremeditated act without benefit of experience.
1947 *The Wisdom of the Heart*, 'The Absolute Collective'.

46 Life, as it is called, is for most of us one long postponement.
1947 *The Wisdom of the Heart*, 'The Enormous Womb'.

47 It is the American vice, the democratic disease which expresses its tyranny by reducing everything unique to the level of the herd.
1947 On democracy. *The Wisdom of the Heart*, 'Raimu'.

48 History is the myth, the true myth, of man's fall made manifest in time.
1949 *Plexus*, ch.12.

49 In this age, which believes that there is a short cut to everything, the greatest lesson to be learned is that the most difficult way is, in the long run, the easiest.
1951 *The Books in My Life*, preface.

50 Every genuine boy is a rebel and an anarch.
1951 *The Books in My Life*, ch.4.

51 Words divested of their magic are but dead hieroglyphs.
1951 *The Books in My Life*, ch.7.

52 If we are always arriving and departing, it is also true that we are eternally anchored. One's destination is never a place but rather a new way of looking at things.
1957 *Big Sur and the Oranges of Hieronymous Bosch*, 'The Oranges of the Millennium'.

53 We resist only what is inevitable.
1957 *Big Sur and the Oranges of Hieronymous Bosch*, 'Paradise Lost'.

54 Obscenity is a cleansing process, whereas pornography only adds to the murk.
1962 Interview in the *Paris Review*, Summer.

55 The word 'civilization' to my mind is coupled with death. When I use the word, I see civilization as a crippling, thwarting thing, a stultifying thing… Civilization is the arteriosclerosis of culture.
1962 Interview in the *Paris Review*, Summer.

56 The moment you praise a book too highly you waken a resistance in your listener.
1957 *The Books in My Life*.

57 One has to be a lowbrow, a bit of a murderer, to be a politician; ready and willing to see people sacrificed, slaughtered, for the sake of an idea— whether a good one or a bad one.
In Malcolm Crowley (ed) *Writers at Work* (1958).

Miller, Jonathan Wolfe 1934–

British stage director and writer, trained as a doctor.

58 The human species is, to some extent, the result of mistakes which arrested our development and prevented us from assuming the somewhat unglamorous form of our primitive ancestors.
1977 *The Body in Question*.

Miller, William 1810–72

Scottish poet, born in Glasgow, known as the 'Laureate of the nursery' for his children's rhymes, of which only 'Willie Winkie' is now remembered.

59 Wee Willie Winkie rins through the toun,
Up stairs and doun stairs in his nicht-gown,
Tirling at the window, crying at the lock,
'Are the weans in their bed, for it's now ten o' clock?'
1841 'Willie Winkie', stanza 1.

Millett, Kate (Katherine) née Murray 1934–

US feminist critic and activist. Her PhD thesis was published as *Sexual Politics* (1970). Other works include *The Prostitution Papers* (1971), the autobiographical *Flying* (1974), and *The Loony Bin Trip* (1991).

60 Patriarchy's chief institution is the family. It is both a mirror of and a connection with the larger society; a patriarchal unit within a patriarchal whole.
1970 *Sexual Politics*, ch.2, 'Theory of Sexual Politics'.

61 Aren't women prudes if they don't and prostitutes if they do?
1975 Speech at the Women Writers' Conference, Los Angeles, 22 Mar.

Millman, Dan 1946–

US writer, who was world trampoline champion before meeting a remarkable gas station attendant called Socrates. He now writes self-help books and runs courses helping athletes and others make the most of their potential.

62 There are no ordinary moments.
1980 *The Way of the Peaceful Warrior*.

Mills, C(harles) Wright 1916–62

US sociologist, a professor at Columbia University.

63 No social study that does not come back to the problems of biography, of history and of their intersections within a society has completed its intellectual journey.
1959 *The Sociological Imagination*, ch.1.

64 In so far as the family as an institution turns women into darling little slaves and men into their chief providers and unweaned dependents, the problem of a satisfactory marriage remains incapable of purely private solution.
1959 *The Sociological Imagination*, ch.1.

65 If everything is caused by innumerable 'factors,' then we had best be very careful in any practical actions we undertake. We must deal with many details, and so it is advisable to proceed to reform this little piece and see what happens, before we reform that little piece too.

1959 *The Sociological Imagination*, ch.4.

Mills, Irving 1884–1985

66 It don't mean a thing
If it ain't got that swing.

1932 Song (music by Duke Ellington).

Mills, Sir John Lewis Ernest Watts 1908–

English actor, known for his stiff-upper-lip heroes in such films as *In Which We Serve* (1942), *Scott of the Antarctic* (1948) and *The Colditz Story* (1954). He won an Academy Award for his role in *Ryan's Daughter* (1970).

67 I played the young Earl of Dudley and was beheaded in the third reel—not, in my opinion, a moment too soon.

1980 Of his role in the 1936 film *Tudor Rose*. *Up in the Clouds, Gentlemen Please*.

Milne, A(lan) A(lexander) 1882–1956

English writer. He was an editor at *Punch* and wrote comedies and light essays. His works for children, which he began writing for his son Christopher Robin, are *When We were Very Young* (1924), *Winnie-the-Pooh* (1926), *Now We Are Six* (1927) and *The House at Pooh Corner* (1928).

68 It is impossible to win gracefully at chess. No man has yet said 'Mate!' in a voice which failed to sound to his opponent bitter, boastful and malicious.

1919 *Not That It Matters*.

69 They're changing guard at Buckingham Palace—
Christopher Robin went down with Alice.
Alice is marrying one of the guard.
'A soldier's life is terribly hard,'
Says Alice.

1924 *When We Were Very Young*, 'Buckingham Palace'.

70 Little Boy kneels at the foot of the bed,
Droops on the little hands, little gold head;
Hush! Hush! Whisper who dares!
Christopher Robin is saying his prayers.

1924 *When We Were Very Young*, 'Vespers'.

71 The King said
'Butter, eh?'
And bounced out of bed.

1924 *When We Were Very Young*, 'The King's Breakfast'.

72 I have just been thinking, and I have come to a very important decision. *These are the wrong sort of bees.*

1926 *Winnie-the-Pooh*, ch.1.

73 Would you read a Sustaining Book, such as would help and comfort a Wedged Bear in Great Tightness?

1926 Pooh, stuck in the entrance to Rabbit's house after eating too much honey. *Winnie-the-Pooh*, ch.2.

74 I am a Bear of Very Little Brain, and long words Bother me.

1926 *Winnie-the-Pooh*, ch.4.

75 'Help, help!' cried Piglet, 'a Heffalump, a Horrible Heffalump!' and he scampered off as hard as he could, still crying out, 'Help, help, a Herrible Hoffalump! Hoff, Hoff, a Hellible Horralump! Holl, Holl, a Hoffable Hellerump!'

1926 *Winnie-the-Pooh*, ch.5.

76 'I ought to say,' explained Pooh as they walked down to the shore of the island, 'that it isn't just an ordinary sort of boat. Sometimes it's a Boat, and sometimes it's more of an Accident. It all depends.'
'Depends on what?'
'On whether I'm on the top of it or underneath it.'

1926 *Winnie-the-Pooh*, ch.9.

77 The more it
SNOWS-tiddely-pom,
The more it
GOES-tiddely-pom
The more it
GOES-tiddely-pom
On
Snowing.

1928 *The House at Pooh Corner*, ch.1.

78 'It's snowing still,' said Eeyore gloomily.
'So it is.'
'*And* freezing.'
'Is it?'
'Yes,' said Eeyore. 'However,' he said, brightening up a little, 'we haven't had an earthquake lately.'

1928 *The House at Pooh Corner*, ch.1.

79 But whatever his weight in pounds, shillings, and ounces,
He always seems bigger because of the bounces.

1928 Pooh's song about Tigger. *The House at Pooh Corner*, ch.2.

80 I could spend a happy morning
Seeing Roo,
I could spend a happy morning
Being Pooh,
For it doesn't seem to matter,
If I don't get any fatter
(And I don't get any fatter),
What I do.

1928 *The House at Pooh Corner*, ch.4.

81 Then he dropped two in at once, and leant over the bridge to see which of them would come out first;

and one of them did; but as they were both the same size, he didn't know if it was the one which he wanted to win, or the other one. So the next time he dropped one big one and one little one, and the big one came out first, which was what he had said it would do, and the little one came out last, which was what he had said it would do, so he had won twice... And that was the beginning of the game called Poohsticks.

1928 *The House at Pooh Corner*, ch.6.

82 But what care I? It's the game that calls me—
Simply to be on the field of play;
How can it matter what fate befalls me,
With ten good fellows and one good day!

Quoted in Helen Exley *Cricket Quotations* (1992).

83 Golf is so popular simply because it is the best game in the world at which to be bad.

Attributed.

Milner, Alfred, 1st Viscount Milner
1854–1925

English statesman. He held a succession of top administrative posts, including High Commissioner for South Africa during the Boer Wars, Secretary for War (1918–19) and Colonial Secretary (1921). He recommended virtual independence for Egypt.

84 If we believe a thing to be bad, and if we have a right to prevent it, it is our duty to try to prevent it and damn the consequences.

1909 On the blocking by the Conservative majority in the House of Lords of the Liberal Government's budget, speech at Glasgow, Nov.

Milton, John 1608–74

English poet and controversial pamphleteerist, official apologist for the Commonwealth. Blind from 1652, he devoted himself to poetry after the Restoration. His best-known work is the religious epic *Paradise Lost* (1667), followed by *Paradise Regained* and *Samson Agonistes* (both 1671).

85 This is the month, and this the happy morn
Wherein the son of Heaven's eternal King,
Of wedded maid and virgin mother born,
Our great redemption from above did bring.

1629 'On the Morning of Christ's Nativity', 'The Hymn', stanza 1.

86 It was the winter wild
While the Heaven born child
All meanly wrapped in the rude manger lies;
Nature in awe to him
Had doffed her gaudy trim
With her great Master so to sympathize;
It was no season then for her
To wanton with the sun, her lusty paramour.

1629 'On the Morning of Christ's Nativity', 'The Hymn', stanza 3.

87 But peaceful was the night
Wherein the Prince of Light
His reign of peace upon the earth began:
The winds, with wonder whist,
Smoothly the waters kissed,
Whispering new joys to the mild oceàn,
Who now hath quite forgot to rave,
While birds of calm sit brooding on the charmèd wave.

1629 'On the Morning of Christ's Nativity', 'The Hymn', stanza 3.

88 The stars with deep amaze
Stand fixed in steadfast gaze.

1629 'On the Morning of Christ's Nativity', 'The Hymn', stanza 6.

89 Nature that heard such sound
Beneath the hollow round
Of Cynthia's seat, the airy region thrilling,
Now was almost won
To think her part was done,
And that her reign had here its last fulfilling;
She knew such harmony alone
Could hold all heaven and earth in happier uniòn.

1629 'On the Morning of Christ's Nativity', 'The Hymn', stanza 10.

90 Ring out, ye crystal spheres,
Once bless our human ears
(If ye have power to touch our senses so),
And let your silver chime
Move in melodious time,
And let the bass of Heaven's deep organ blow;
And with your ninefold harmony
Make up full consort to th'angelic symphony.

1629 'On the Morning of Christ's Nativity', 'The Hymn', stanza 13.

91 For if such holy song
Enwrap our fancy long,
Time will run back, and fetch the age of gold,
And speckled vanity
Will sicken soon and die.

1629 'On the Morning of Christ's Nativity', 'The Hymn', stanza 14.

92 The oracles are dumb;
No voice or hideous hum
Runs through the archèd roof in words deceiving.

1629 'On the Morning of Christ's Nativity', 'The Hymn', stanza 19.

93 But see! the Virgin blessed
Hath laid her Babe to rest.
Time is our tedious song should here have ending.

1629 'On the Morning of Christ's Nativity', 'The Hymn', stanza 27.

94 What needs my Shakespeare for his honoured bones

The labour of an age in pilèd stones,
Or that his hallowed relics should be hid
Under a star-y-pointing pyramid?
Dear son of memory, great heir of fame,
What need'st thou such weak witness of thy name?
Thou in our wonder and astonishment
Hast built thyself a livelong monument.
1630 'On Shakespeare'.

95 And so sepùlchered in such pomp dost lie,
That kings for such a tomb would wish to die.
1630 'On Shakespeare'.

96 Hence loathèd Melancholy,
Of Cerberus and blackest midnight born,
In Stygian cave forlorn
'Mongst horrid shapes, and shrieks, and sights
unholy,
Find out some uncouth cell,
Where brooding Darkness spreads his jealous
wings,
And the night-raven sings.
c.1631 *L'Allegro*, opening lines.

97 The frolic wind that breathes the spring,
Zephyr with Aurora playing,
As he met her once a-Maying,
There on beds of violets blue,
And fresh-blown roses washed in dew,
Filled her with a daughter fair,
So buxom, blithe, and debonair.
c.1631 *L'Allegro*, l.18–24. The 'daughter fair' is Euphrosyne, or
Mirth, one of the Three Graces.

98 Come, and trip it as ye go
On the light fantastic toe.
c.1631 *L'Allegro*, l.33–4.

99 While the cock with lively din
Scatters the rear of darkness thin,
And to the stack or the barn door,
Stoutly struts his dames before.
c.1631 *L'Allegro*, l.49–52.

1 Straight mine eye hath caught new pleasures
Whilst the landscape round it measures,
Russet lawns and fallows grey,
Where the nibbling flocks do stray,
Mountains on whose barren breast
The labouring clouds do often rest;
Meadows trim with daisies pied,
Shallow brooks, and rivers wide.
c.1631 *L'Allegro*, l.69–76.

2 Then to the spicy nut-brown ale.
c.1631 *L'Allegro*, l.100.

3 Towered cities pleased us then,
And the busy hum of men,
Where throngs of knights and barons bold

In weeds of peace high triumphs hold,
With store of ladies, whose bright eyes
Rain influence, and judge the prize
Of wit or arms, while both contend
To win her grace, whom all commend.
c.1631 *L'Allegro*, l.117–24.

4 Such sights as youthful poets dream
On summer eves by haunted stream.
c.1631 *L'Allegro*, l.129–30.

5 Hence vain deluding Joys,
The brood of Folly without father bred,
How little you bestead,
Or fill the fixèd mind with all your toys;
Dwell in some idle brain,
And fancies fond with gaudy shapes possess,
As thick and numberless
As the gay motes that people the sunbeams.
c.1631 *Il Penseroso*, opening lines.

6 But hail thou Goddess sage and holy,
Hail, divinest Melancholy,
Whose saintly visage is too bright
To hit the sense of human sight,
And therefore to our weaker view
O'erlaid with black, staid Wisdom's hue.
c.1631 *Il Penseroso*, l.11–16.

7 There held in holy passion still,
Forget thyself to marble.
c.1631 *Il Penseroso*, l.37–8.

8 Sweet bird that shunn'st the noise of folly,
Most musical, most melancholy!
c.1631 Of the nightingale. *Il Penseroso*, l.61–2.

9 And missing thee, I walk unseen
On the dry smooth-shaven green,
To behold the wandering moon,
Riding near her highest noon,
Like one that had been led astray
Through the heaven's wide pathless way;
And oft as if her head she bowed,
Stooping through a fleecy cloud.
c.1631 *Il Penseroso*, l.65–72.

10 Where glowing embers through the room
Teach light to counterfeit a gloom,
Far from all resort of mirth.
Save the cricket on the hearth.
c.1631 *Il Penseroso*, l.79–82.

11 Or bid the soul of Orpheus sing
Such notes as, warbled to the string,
Drew iron tears down Pluto's cheek,
And made Hell grant what Love did seek.
c.1631 *Il Penseroso*, l.105–8.

12 Where more is meant than meets the ear.

c.1631 *Il Penseroso*, l.120.

13 Till civil-suited Morn appear,
    Not tricked and frounced as she was wont
    With the Attic boy to hunt,
    But kerchiefed in a comely cloud.
    c.1631 *Il Penseroso*, l.122-5.

14 There in close covert by some brook,
    Where no profaner eye may look,
    Hide me from day's garish eye,
    While the bee with honied thigh,
    That at her flowery work doth sing,
    And the waters murmuring
    And such consort as they keep,
    Entice the dewy-feathered Sleep.
    c.1631 *Il Penseroso*, l.139-46.

15 But let my due feet never fail
    To walk the studious cloister's pale,
    And love the high embowèd roof,
    With antic pillars massy proof,
    And storied windows richly dight
    Casting a dim religious light.
    c.1631 *Il Penseroso*, l.155-60.

16 And may at last my weary age
    Find out the peaceful hermitage,
    The hairy gown and mossy cell,
    Where I may sit and rightly spell
    Of every star that heaven doth shew,
    And every herb that sips the dew,
    Till old experience to attain
    To something like prophetic strain.
    c.1631 *Il Penseroso*, l.167–74.

17 Such sweet compulsion doth in music lie.
    1633 *Arcades*.

18 Before the starry threshold of Jove's court
    My mansion is, where those immortal shapes
    Of bright aerial spirits live inspher'd
    In regions mild of calm and serene air,
    Above the smoke and stir of this dim spot,
    Which men call earth.
    1634 *Comus, A Mask*, opening lines.

19 All other parts remaining as they were,
    And they, so perfect in their misery,
    Not once perceive their foul disfigurement,
    But boast themselves more comely than before
    And all their friends, and native home forget
    To roll with pleasure in a sensual sty.
    1634 Of Odysseus's men changed to beasts by Circe. *Comus, A Mask*, l.72-7.

20 The star that bids the shepherd fold,
    Now the top of heav'n doth hold,
    And the gilded car of day,
    His glowing axle doth allay

In the steep Atlantic stream.
1634 *Comus, A Mask*, l.93–7.

21 What hath night to do with sleep?
    1634 *Comus, A Mask*, l.122.

22 Come, knit hands, and beat the ground,
    In a light fantastic round.
    1634 *Comus, A Mask*, l.143–4.

23 Thus I hurl
    My dazzling spells into the spongy air.
    1634 *Comus, A Mask*, l.153-4.

24 A thousand fantasies
    Begin to throng into my memory
    Of calling shapes, and beckoning shadows dire,
    And airy tongues, that syllable men's names
    On sands, and shores, and desert wildernesses.
    1634 *Comus, A Mask*, l.204-8.

25 These thoughts may startle well, but not astound
    The virtuous mind, that ever walks attended
    By a strong siding champion conscience.
    1634 *Comus, A Mask*, l.209-11.

26 Sweet Echo, sweetest nymph, that liv'st unseen
    Within thy airy shell
    By slow meander's margent green,
    And in the violet-embroidered vale.
    1634 *Comus, A Mask*, l.230-3.

27 How sweetly did they float upon the wings
    Of silence, through the empty-vaulted night
    At every fall smoothing the raven down
    Of darkness till it smil'd.
    1634 *Comus, A Mask*, l.248-251.

28 Virtue could see to do what Virtue would
    By her own radiant light, though sun and moon
    Were in the flat sea sunk. And Wisdom's self
    Oft seeks to sweet retired solitude,
    Where with her best nurse contemplation
    She plumes her feathers, and lets grow her wings
    That in the various bustle of resort
    Were all too ruffl'd, and sometimes impair'd.
    He that has light within his own clear breast
    May sit i' the centre, and enjoy bright day,
    But he that hides a dark soul, and foul thoughts
    Benighted walks under the midday sun;
    Himself is his own dungeon.
    1634 *Comus, A Mask*, l.372-383.

29 Yet where an equal poise of hope and fear
    Does arbitrate the event, my nature is
    That I incline to hope, rather than fear,
    And gladly banish squint suspicion.
    1634 *Comus, A Mask*, l.410–13.

30 Of dire chimeras and enchanted isle

And rifted rocks whose entrance leads to Hell,——
For such there be, but unbelief is blind.
1634 *Comus, A Mask*, l.515–7.

31 A pleasing fit of melancholy.
1634 *Comus, A Mask*, l.545.

32 And filled the air with barbarous dissonance.
1634 *Comus, A Mask*, l.550.

33 I was all ear,
And took in strains that might create a soul.
Under the ribs of Death.
1634 *Comus, A Mask*, l.560–2.

34 Thou canst not touch the freedom of my mind
With all thy charms, although this corporal rind
Thou hast immanacl'd, while heav'n sees good.
1634 *Comus, A Mask*, l.663–5.

35 The unexempt condition
By which all mortal frailty must subsist,
Refreshment after toil, ease after pain.
1634 *Comus, A Mask*, l.684–6.

36 But now my task is smoothly done,
I can fly, or I can run
Quickly to the green earth's end,
Where the bow'd welkin slow doth bend,
And from thence can soar as soon
To the corners of the Moon.
1634 *Comus, A Mask*, l.1012–6.

37 Mortals that would follow me,
Love virtue, she alone is free,
She can teach ye how to climb
Higher than the sphery chime;
Or if virtue feeble were,
Heav'n itself would stoop to her.
1634 *Comus, A Mask*, l.1018–23.

38 Yet once more, O ye laurels, and once more
Ye myrtles brown, with ivy never-sere
I come to pluck your berries harsh and crude,
And with forc'd fingers rude,
Shatter your leaves before the mellowing year.
Bitter constraint, and sad occasion dear,
Compels me to disturb your season due
For Lycidas is dead, dead ere his prime
Young Lycidas, and hath not left his peer.
1637 *Lycidas*, opening lines.

39 For we were nursed upon the self-same hill,
Fed the same flock; by fountain, shade, and rill.
1637 *Lycidas*, l.23–4.

40 But O the heavy change, now thou art gone,
Now thou art gone, and never must return!
Thee shepherd, thee the woods, and desert caves,
With wild thyme and the gadding vine o'ergrown,
And all their echoes mourn.

1637 *Lycidas*, l.37–41.

41 Where were ye Nymphs when the remorseless deep
Clos'd o'er the head of your lov'd Lycidas?
1637 *Lycidas*, l.50–1.

42 Alas! What boots it with uncessant care
To tend the homely slighted Shepherd's trade,
And strictly meditate the thankless muse;
Were it not better done as others use,
To sport with Amaryllis in the shade,
Or with the tangles of Neaera's hair?
Fame is the spur that the clear spirit doth raise
(That last infirmity of noble mind)
To scorn delights, and live laborious days;
But the fair guerdon when we hope to find,
And think to burst out into sudden blaze,
Comes the blind Fury with th' abhorred shears,
And slits the thin-spun life.
1637 *Lycidas*, l.64–76.

43 Fame is no plant that grows on mortal soil.
1637 *Lycidas*, l.78.

44 Blind mouths! that scarce themselves know how to
hold
A sheep-hook.
1637 *Lycidas*, l.119–20.

45 They are sped;
And when they list, their lean and flashy songs
Grate on their scrannel Pipes of wretched straw,
The hungry sheep look up, and are not fed,
But swollen with wind, and the rank mist they
   draw,
Rot inwardly, and foul contagion spread,
Besides what the grim wolf with privy paw
Daily devours apace, and nothing said,
But that two-handed engine at the door,
Stands ready to smite once, and smite no more.
1637 *Lycidas*, l.122–31.

46 Ye valleys low where the mild whispers use,
Of shades and wanton winds, and gushing brooks,
On whose fresh lap the swart star sparely looks,
Throw hither all your quaint enameled eyes,
That on the green turf such the honeyed showers,
And purple all the ground with vernal flowers.
1637 *Lycidas*, l.136–41.

47 Bring the rathe primrose that forsaken dies,
The tufted crow-toe, and pale gessamine,
The white pink, and the pansy freaked with jet,
The glowing violet,
The musk-rose, and the well attir'd woodbine,
With cowslips wan that hang the pensive head,
And every flower that sad embroidery wears:
Bid amaranthus all his beauty shed,
And daffadillies fill their cups with tears,

To strew the laureate hearse where Lycid lies.
1637 *Lycidas*, l.142–51. rathe = early.

48 For to interpose a little ease,
Let our frail thoughts dally with false surmise.
Lycidas, l.152-3.

49 Weep no more, woeful shepherds, weep no more,
For Lycidas your sorrow is not dead,
Sunk though he be beneath the watery floor,
So sinks the day-star in the ocean bed,
And yet anon repairs his drooping head,
And tricks his beams, and with new spangled ore,
Flames in the forehead of the morning sky:
So Lycidas sunk low, but mounted high,
Through the dear might of Him that walked the
   waves.
1637 *Lycidas*, l.165–73.

50 Look homeward Angel, now, and melt with ruth.
1637 *Lycidas*, l.163. The phrase was used by Thomas Clayton
Wolfe for his 1929 novel, *Look Homeward Angel.*

51 There entertain him all the saints above,
In solemn troops, and sweet societies
That sing, and singing in their glory move,
And wipe the tears for ever from his eyes.
1637 *Lycidas*, l.178–81.

52 At last he rose, and twitched his mantle blue:
Tomorrow to fresh woods, and pastures new.
1637 *Lycidas*, l.192–3.

53 This manner of writing wherein knowing myself
inferior to myself… I have the use, as I may
account it, but of my left hand.
1642 Of his use of prose. *The Reason of Church Government*,
bk.2, introduction, 'Plans and Projects'.

54 Beholding the bright countenance of truth in the
quiet and still air of delightful studies.
1642 *The Reason of Church Government*, bk.2, introduction,
'Plans and Projects'.

55 As good almost kill a man as kill a good book: who
kills a man kills a reasonable creature, God's image;
but he who destroys a good book, kills reason itself,
kills the image of God, as it were in the eye.
1644 *Areopagitica: a speech for the liberty of unlicensed printing.*

56 Promiscuous reading is necessary to the
constituting of human nature. The attempt to keep
out evil doctrine by licensing is like the exploit of
that gallant man who thought to keep out the
crows by shutting the park gate.
1644 *Areopagatica: a speech for the liberty of unlicensed printing.*

57 A good book is the precious life-blood of a master
spirit, embalmed and treasured up on purpose to a
life beyond life.
1644 *Areopagatica: a speech for the liberty of unlicensed printing.*

58 It was from out the rind of one apple tasted, that
the knowledge of good and evil, as two twins
cleaving together, leaped forth into the world.
1644 *Areopagitica: a speech for the liberty of unlicensed printing.*

59 Where there is much to learn, there of necessity will
be much arguing, much writing, many opinions;
for opinion in good men is but knowledge in the
making.
1644 *Areopagatica: a speech for the liberty of unlicensed printing.*

60 As therefore the state of man now is, what wisdom
can there be to choose, what continence to forbear,
without the knowledge of good and evil?
1644 *Areopagitica: a speech for the liberty of unlicensed printing.*

61 Give me the liberty to know, to utter, and to argue
freely according to conscience, above all liberties.
1644 *Areopagatica: a speech for the liberty of unlicensed printing.*

62 And though all the winds of doctrine were let loose
to play upon the earth, so Truth be in the field, we
do injuriously by licensing and prohibiting to
misdoubt her strength. Let her and Falsehood
grapple; who ever knew Truth put to the worse in a
free and open encounter ?
1644 *Areopagitica: a speech for the liberty of unlicensed printing.*

63 I cannot praise a fugitive and cloistered virtue,
unexercised and unbreathed, that never sallies out
and sees her adversary, but slinks out of the race
where that immortal garland is to be run for, not
without dust and heat. Assuredly we bring not
innocence into the world, we bring impurity much
rather; that which purifies us is trial, and trial is by
what is contrary.
1644 *Areopagitica: a speech for the liberty of unlicensed printing.*

64 For who knows not that Truth is strong next to the
Almighty? She needs no policies, nor stratagems,
nor licensings to make her victorious.
1644 *Areopagatica: a speech for the liberty of unlicensed printing.*

65 That virtue therefore which is but a youngling in
the contemplation of evil, and knows not the
utmost that vice promises to her followers, and
rejects it, is but a blank virtue, not a pure; her
whiteness is but an excremental whiteness.
1644 *Areopagitica: a speech for the liberty of unlicensed printing.*

66 Since therefore the knowledge and survey of vice is
in this world so necessary to the constituting of
human virtue, and the scanning of error to the
confirmation of truth, how can we more safely, and
with less danger, scout into the regions of sin and
falsity than by reading all manner of tractates and
hearing all manner of reason? And this is the benefit
which may be had of books promiscuously read.
1644 *Areopagitica: a speech for the liberty of unlicensed printing.*

67 When God gave [Adam] reason, he gave him
freedom to choose, for reason is but choosing; he
had been else a mere artificial Adam.
1644 Areopagitica: a speech for the liberty of unlicensed printing.

68 Wherefore did he [God] create passions within us,
pleasures round about us, but that these rightly
tempered are the very ingredients of virtue?
1644 Areopagitica: a speech for the liberty of unlicensed printing.

69 They are not skilful considerers of human things,
who imagine to remove sin by removing the matter
of sin.
1644 Areopagitica: a speech for the liberty of unlicensed printing.

70 We ourselves esteem not of that obedience, or love,
or gift, which is of force: God therefore let him free,
set before him a provoking object, ever almost in
his eyes; herein consisted his merit, herein the right
of his reward, the praise of his abstinence.
1644 Areopagitica: a speech for the liberty of unlicensed printing.

71 Though ye take from a covetous man all his
treasure, he has yet one jewel left: ye cannot bereave
him of his covetousness.
1644 Areopagitica: a speech for the liberty of unlicensed printing.

72 Truth indeed came once into the world with her
divine Master, and was a perfect shape most
glorious to look on: but…a wicked race of
deceivers…took the virgin Truth, hewed her lovely
form into a thousand pieces, and scattered them to
the four winds. From that time ever since, the sad
friends of Truth, such as durst appear, imitating the
careful search that Isis made for the mangled body
of Osiris, went up and down gathering up limb by
limb, still as they could find them. We have not yet
found them all…nor ever shall do, till her Master's
second coming; he shall bring together every joint
and member, and shall mould them into an
immortal feature of loveliness and perfection.
1644 Areopagitica: a speech for the liberty of unlicensed printing.

73 Lords and Commons of England, consider what
nation it is whereof ye are, and whereof ye are the
governors: a nation not slow and dull, but of a
quick, ingenious, and piercing spirit, acute to
invent, subtle and sinewy to discourse, not beneath
the reach of any point the highest that human
capacity can soar to.
1644 Areopagitica: a speech for the liberty of unlicensed printing.

74 God is decreeing to begin some new and great
period in his Church, even to the reforming of
Reformation itself. What does he then but reveal
Himself to his servants, and as his manner is, first
to his Englishmen?
1644 Areopagitica: a speech for the liberty of unlicensed printing.

75 Methinks I see in my mind a noble and puissant
nation rousing herself like a strong man after sleep,
and shaking her invincible locks: methinks I see her
as an eagle mewing her mighty youth, and kindling
her undazzled eyes at the full midday beam;
purging and unscaling her long-abused sight at the
fountain itself of heavenly radiance; while the
whole noise of timorous birds, with those also that
love the twilight, flutter about, amazed at what she
means.
1644 Areopagitica: a speech for the liberty of unlicensed printing.

76 I did but prompt the age to quit their clogs
By the known rules of ancient liberty,
When strait a barbarous noise environs me
Of owls and cuckoos, asses, apes and dogs.
c.1646 'On the Detraction Which Follow'd Upon My Writing
Certain Treatises'.

77 None can love freedom heartily, but good men; the
rest love not freedom, but licence.
1648–9 The Tenure of Kings and Magistrates.

78 No man who knows aught, can be so stupid to
deny that all men naturally were born free.
1648–9 The Tenure of Kings and Magistrates.

79 The power of kings and magistrates is nothing else
but what is only derivative; transformed and
committed to them in trust from the people to the
common good of them all, in whom the power yet
remains fundamentally, and cannot be taken from
them without a violation of their natural
birthright.
1648–9 The Tenure of Kings and Magistrates.

80 Yet much remains
To conquer still; peace hath her victories
No less renowned then war, new foes arise
Threatening to bind our souls with secular chains:
Help us to save free conscience from the paw
Of hireling wolves whose gospel is their maw.
1652 'To the Lord General Cromwell'.

81 When I consider how my light is spent,
E're half my days, in this dark world and wide,
And that one talent which is death to hide,
Lodg'd with me useless, though my soul more bent
To serve therewith my Maker, and present
My true account, least he returning chide,
Doth God exact day-labour, light denied,
I fondly ask; But patience to prevent
That murmur, soon replies, God doth not need
Either man's work or his own gifts, who best
Bear his mild yoke, they serve him best, his state
Is kingly. Thousands at his bidding speed
And post o'er land and ocean without rest:
They also serve who only stand and wait.
c.1652 Sonnets, no.16, 'When I Consider'.

82 Methought I saw my late espoused Saint
    Brought to me like Alcestis from the grave,
    c.1658 *Sonnets*, no.19, 'Methought I Saw'.

83 But O as to embrace me she enclin'd
    I wak'd, she fled, and day brought back my night.
    c.1658 *Sonnets*, no.19, 'Methought I Saw'.

84 Of man's first disobedience, and the fruit
    Of that forbidden tree, whose mortal taste
    Brought death into the world, and all our woe,
    With loss of Eden, till one greater Man
    Restore us, and regain the blissful seat.
    1665 *Paradise Lost* (published 1667), bk.1, opening lines.

85 Things unattempted yet in prose or rhyme.
    1665 *Paradise Lost* (published 1667), bk.1, l.15.

86 And chiefly thou O spirit, that does prefer
    Before all temples th'upright heart and pure,
    Instruct me, for thou know'st; thou from the first
    Wast present, and with mighty wings outspread
    Dove-like sat'st brooding on the vast abyss
    And mad'st it pregnant: what in me is dark
    Illumine, what is low raise and support;
    That to the highth of this great argument
    I may assert Eternal Providence,
    And justify the ways of God to men.
    1665 *Paradise Lost* (published 1667), bk.1, l.16–25.

87 Who first seduced them to that foul revolt?
    1665 *Paradise Lost* (published 1667), bk.1, l.33.

88 Him the Almighty Power
    Hurled headlong flaming from th' ethereal sky
    With hideous ruin and combustion down
    To bottomless perdition, there to dwell
    In adamantine chains and penal fire.
    1665 *Paradise Lost* (published 1667), bk.1, l.44–8.

89 Now the thought
    Both of lost happiness and lasting pain
    Torments him.
    1665 Of Satan. *Paradise Lost* (published 1667), bk.1, l.54.

90 A dungeon horrible, on all sides round
    As one great furnace flamed; yet from those flames
    No light, but rather darkness visible
    Served only to discover sights of woe,
    Regions of sorrow, doleful shades, where peace
    And rest can never dwell, hope never comes
    That comes to all.
    1665 Of Hell. *Paradise Lost* (published 1667), bk.1, l.61–7.

91 O how fall'n! how changed
    From him, who in the happy realms of light
    Clothed with transcendent brightness didst
      outshine
    Myriads though bright.
    1665 Of Satan. *Paradise Lost* (published 1667), bk.1, l.84–7.

92 United thoughts and counsels, equal hope
    And hazard in the glorious enterprise.
    1665 *Paradise Lost* (published 1667), bk.1, l.88.

93 What though the field be lost?
    All is not lost; the unconquerable will,
    And study of revenge, immortal hate,
    And courage never to submit or yield.
    1665 Satan addressing the fallen angels. *Paradise Lost*
    (published 1667), bk.1, l.105–8.

94 Vaunting aloud, but racked with deep despair.
    1665 *Paradise Lost* (published 1667), bk.1, l.126.

95 To be weak is miserable
    Doing or suffering, but of this be sure,
    To do aught good never will be our task,
    But ever to do ill our sole delight.
    1665 *Paradise Lost* (published 1667), bk.1, l.157–60.

96 If then his providence
    Out of our evil seek to bring forth good,
    Our labour must be to pervert that end,
    And out of good still to find means of evil.
    1665 *Paradise Lost* (published 1667), bk.1, l.162–5.

97 What reinforcement we may gain from hope;
    If not, what resolution from despair.
    1665 *Paradise Lost* (published 1667), bk.1, l.190–1.

98 Forthwith upright he rears from off the pool
    His mighty stature; on each hand the flames
    Driv'n backward slope their pointing spires, and
      rolled
    In billows, leave i' th' midst a horrid vale.
    1665 Of Satan. *Paradise Lost* (published 1667), bk.1, l.221.

99 The mind is its own place, and in itself
    Can make a heav'n of hell, a hell of heav'n.
    1665 *Paradise Lost* (published 1667), bk.1, l.254.

 1 Better to reign in hell, than serve in heav'n.
    1665 Satan. *Paradise Lost* (published 1667), bk.1, l.263.

 2 For Spirits when they please
    Can either sex assume, or both; so soft
    And uncompounded is their essence pure,
    Not tied or manacled with joint or limb,
    Nor founded on the brittle strength of bones,
    Like cumbrous flesh; but in what shape they choose
    Dilated or condensed, bright or obscure,
    Can execute their airy purposes,
    And works of love or enmity fulfil.
    1665 *Paradise Lost* (published 1667), bk.1, l.423.

 3 And when night
    Darkens the streets, then wander forth the sons
    Of Belial, flown with insolence and wine.
    1665 *Paradise Lost* (published 1667), bk.1, l.501.

 4 With high words, that bore

Semblance of worth, not substance, gently raised
Their fainting courage, and dispelled their fears.
1665 *Paradise Lost* (published 1667), bk.1, l.528–30.

5 A shout that tore hell's concave, and beyond
Frighted the reign of Chaos and old Night.
1665 *Paradise Lost* (published 1667), bk.1, l.542–3.

6 For who can yet believe, though after loss,
That all these puissant legions, whose exile
Hath emptied heav'n, shall fail to reascend
Self-raised, and repossess their native seat?
1665 *Paradise Lost* (published 1667), bk.1, l.631–4.

7 Who overcomes
By force, hath overcome but half his foe.
1665 *Paradise Lost* (published 1667), bk.1, l.647.

8 War then, war
Open or understood must be resolved.
1665 Satan. *Paradise Lost* (published 1667), bk.1, l.661–2.

9 Let none admire
That riches grow in hell; that soil may best
Deserve the precious bane.
1665 *Paradise Lost* (published 1667), bk.1, l.690–2.

10 Pandemonium, the high capital
Of Satan and his peers.
1665 *Paradise Lost* (published 1667), bk.1, l.756–7.

11 Satan exalted sat, by merit raised
To that bad eminence; and from despair
Thus high uplifted beyond hope.
1665 *Paradise Lost* (published 1667), bk.2, l.5–7.

12 Where there is then no good
For which to strive, no strife can grow up there
From faction; for none sure will claim in hell
Precédence, none, whose portion is so small
Of present pain, that with ambitious mind
Will covet more.
1665 Satan. *Paradise Lost* (published 1667), bk.2, l.30–5.

13 His trust was with the eternal to be deemed
Equal in strength, and rather than be less
Cared not to be at all; with that care lost
Went all his fear.
1665 Of Moloch. *Paradise Lost* (published 1667), bk.2, l.46–9.

14 He seemed
For dignity composed and high exploit:
But all was false and hollow; though his tongue
Dropped manna, and could make the worse appear
The better reason.
1665 Of Belial. *Paradise Lost* (published 1667), bk.2, l.110–14.

15 To be no more; sad cure; for who would lose,
Though full of pain, this intellectual being,

Those thoughts that wander through eternity,
To perish rather, swallowed up and lost
In the wide womb of uncreated night,
Devoid of sense and motion?
1665 Belial. *Paradise Lost* (published 1667), bk.2, l.146–51.

16 Thus Belial with words clothed in reason's garb
Counselled ignoble ease, and peaceful sloth,
Not peace.
1665 *Paradise Lost* (published 1667), bk.2, l.226–8.

17 Our torments also may in length of time
Become our elements, these piercing fires
As soft as now severe, our temper changed
Into their temper.
1665 Mammon. *Paradise Lost* (published 1667), bk.2, l.274–7.

18 There is a place
(If ancient and prophetic fame in heav'n
Err not) another world, the happy seat
Of some new race called Man.
1665 Beelzebub. *Paradise Lost* (published 1667), bk.2, l.345–8.

19 This would surpass
Common revenge.
1665 Beelzebub speaking of the plan to tempt Man away from God. *Paradise Lost* (published 1667), bk.2, l.370–1.

20 When his darling sons
Hurled headlong to partake with us, shall curse
Their frail original, and faded bliss,
Faded so soon.
1665 Beelzebub. *Paradise Lost* (published 1667), bk.2, l.373–6.

21 Who shall tempt with wand'ring feet
The dark unbottomed infinite abyss
And through the palpable obscure find out
His uncouth way, or spread his aery flight
Upborne with indefatigable wings
Over the vast abrupt, ere he arrive
The happy isle.
1665 Beelzebub. *Paradise Lost* (published 1667), bk.2, l.404–10.

22 Long is the way
And hard, that out of hell leads up to light.
1665 *Paradise Lost* (published 1667), bk.2, l.432–3.

23 O shame to men! Devil with devil damned
Firm concord holds, men only disagree
Of creatures rational.
1665 *Paradise Lost* (published 1667), bk.2, l.496.

24 Meanwhile the Adversary of God and man,
Satan with thoughts inflamed of highest design,
Puts on swift wings, and towards the gates of hell
Explores his solitary flight.
1665 *Paradise Lost* (published 1667), bk.2, l.629–32.

25 Chaos umpire sits,

And by decision more embroils the fray
By which he reigns; next him high arbiter
Chance governs all.
1665 *Paradise Lost* (published 1667), bk.2, l.681–4.

26 Whence and what art thou, execrable shape?
1665 *Paradise Lost* (published 1667), bk.2, l.681.

27 A race of upstart creatures.
1665 Satan speaks to his daughter, Sin, of Man. *Paradise Lost* (published 1667), bk.2, l.834.

28 And fast by hanging in a golden chain
This pendent world.
1665 *Paradise Lost* (published 1667), bk.2, l.1051–2.

29 Hail holy Light, offspring of Heav'n first-born.
Bright effluence of bright essence increate.
1665 *Paradise Lost* (published 1667), bk.3, l.5–6.

30 Thee I revisit safe,
And feel thy sovran vital lamp; but thou
Revisit'st not these eyes, that roll in vain
To find thy piercing ray, and find no dawn;
So thick a drop serene hath quenched their orbs,
Or dim suffusion veiled.
1665 Of his blindness. *Paradise Lost* (published 1667), bk.3, l.22–7.

31 Thus with the year
Seasons return, but not to me returns
Day, or the sweet approach of ev'n or morn,
Or sight of vernal bloom, or summer's rose,
Or flocks, or herds, of human face divine;
But cloud instead, and ever-during dark
Surrounds me, from the cheerful ways of men
Cut off, and for the book of knowledge fair
Presented with a universal blank
Of nature's works to me expunged and razed,
And wisdom at one entrance quite shut out.
1665 *Paradise Lost* (published 1667), bk.3, l.40–50.

32 Our two first parents, yet the only two
Of mankind, in the happy garden placed,
Reaping immortal fruits of joy and love,
Uninterrupted joy, unrivalled love
In blissful solitude.
1665 *Paradise Lost* (published 1667), bk.3, l.65–9.

33 So bent he seems
On desperate revenge, that shall redound
Upon his own rebellious head.
1665 Of Satan. *Paradise Lost* (published 1667), bk.3, l.84–8.

34 Whose fault?
Whose but his own? Ingrate, he had of me
All he could have; I made him just and right,
Sufficient to have stood, though free to fall.
1665 God speaking of Satan. *Paradise Lost* (published 1667), bk.3, l.96–9.

35 Freely they stood who stood, and fell who fell.
1665 *Paradise Lost* (published 1667), bk.3, l.102.

36 I formed them free, and free they must remain,
Till they enthrall themselves
1665 *Paradise Lost* (published 1667), bk.3, l.124–5.

37 And I will place within them as a guide
My umpire conscience, whom if they will hear
Light after light well used they shall attain,
And to the end persisting, safe arrive.
1665 *Paradise Lost* (published 1667), bk.3, l.194–7.

38 Die he or justice must.
1665 *Paradise Lost* (published 1667), bk.3, l.210.

39 Behold me then, me for him, life for life
I offer, on me let thine anger fall;
Account me man; I for his sake will leave
Thy bosom, and this glory next to thee
Freely put off, and for him lastly die
Well pleased, on me let Death wreck all his rage.
1665 Christ speaking to God. *Paradise Lost* (published 1667), bk.3, l.236–241.

40 O thou
My sole complacence!
1665 God speaking to Christ. *Paradise Lost* (published 1667), bk.3, l.275–6.

41 So on this windy sea of land, the Fiend
Walked up and down alone bent on his prey.
1665 *Paradise Lost* (published 1667), bk.3, l.440–1.

42 Into a limbo large and broad, since called
The Paradise of Fools, to few unknown.
1665 *Paradise Lost* (published 1667), bk.3, l.495–6.

43 The pure marble air.
1665 *Paradise Lost* (published 1667), bk.3, l.564.

44 For neither man nor angel can discern
Hypocrisy, the only evil that walks
Invisible, except to God alone,
By his permissive will, through heav'n and earth.
1665 *Paradise Lost* (published 1667), bk.3, l.681–4.

45 Horror and doubt distract
His troubled thoughts, and from the bottom stir
The hell within him, for within him hell
He brings, and round about him, nor from hell
One step no more than from himself can fly.
1665 Of Satan. *Paradise Lost* (published 1667), bk.4, l.18–22.

46 Now conscience wakes despair
That slumbered, wakes the bitter memory
Of what he was, what is, and what must be
Worse; of worse deeds worse sufferings must ensue.
1665 Of Satan. *Paradise Lost* (published 1667), bk.4, l.23–6.

47 A grateful mind

By owing owes not, but still pays, at once
Indebted and discharged; what burden then?
1665 *Paradise Lost* (published 1667), bk.4, l.55–7.

48 Which way I fly is hell; myself am hell;
And in the lowest deep a lower deep
Still threat'ning to devour me opens wide,
To which the hell I suffer seems a heav'n.
1665 Satan. *Paradise Lost* (published 1667), bk.4, l.75–8.

49 The lower still I fall, only supreme
In misery; such joy ambition finds.
1665 Satan. *Paradise Lost* (published 1667), bk.4, l.91–2.

50 For never can true reconcilement grow
Where wounds of deadly hate have pierced so deep.
1665 Satan. *Paradise Lost* (published 1667), bk.4, l.98–9.

51 So clomb this first grand thief into God's fold:
So since into his church lewd hirelings climb.
Thence up he flew, and on the Tree of Life,
The middle tree and highest there that grew,
Sat like a cormorant.
1665 Of Satan. *Paradise Lost* (published 1667), bk.4, l.192–6.

52 Out of the fertile ground he caused to grow
All trees of noblest kind for sight, smell, taste;
And all amid them stood the Tree of Life,
High eminent, blooming ambrosial fruit
Of vegetable gold; and next to life
Our death the Tree of Knowledge grew fast by,
Knowledge of good bought dear by knowing ill.
1665 *Paradise Lost* (published 1667), bk.4, l.218–24.

53 Flowers of all hue, and without thorn the rose.
1665 *Paradise Lost* (published 1667), bk.4, l.256.

54 Two of far nobler shape erect and tall,
God-like erect, with native honor clad
In naked majesty seemed lords of all.
1665 Of Adam and Eve. *Paradise Lost* (published 1667), bk.4,
l.288–90.

55 Though both
Not equal, as their sex not equal seemed;
For contemplation he and valour formed,
For softness she and sweet attractive grace,
He for God only, she for God in him.
1665 Of Adam and Eve. *Paradise Lost* (published 1667), bk.4,
l.295–9.

56 Yielded with coy submission, modest pride,
And sweet reluctant amorous delay.
1665 Of Eve. *Paradise Lost* (published 1667), bk.4, l.310–11.

57 Ah gentle pair, ye little think how nigh
Your change approaches, when all these delights
Will vanish and deliver ye to woe,
More woe, the more your taste is now of joy.
1665 *Paradise Lost* (published 1667), bk.4, l.366–9.

58 Sole partner and sole part of all these joys.
1665 Adam to Eve. *Paradise Lost* (published 1667), bk.4, l.411.

59 These two
Emparadised in one another's arms
The happier Eden, shall enjoy their fill
Of bliss on bliss.
1665 Of Adam and Eve. *Paradise Lost* (published 1667), bk.4,
l.505–8.

60 Man hath his daily work of body or mind
Appointed, which declares his dignity,
And the regard of Heav'n on all his ways.
1665 Adam to Eve. *Paradise Lost* (published 1667), bk.4,
l.618–20.

61 God is thy law, thou mine: to know no more
Is woman's happiest knowledge and her praise.
With thee conversing I forget all time.
1665 Eve to Adam. *Paradise Lost* (published 1667), bk.4,
l.637–9.

62 Millions of spiritual creatures walk the earth
Unseen, both when we wake, and when we sleep.
1665 *Paradise Lost* (published 1667), bk.4, l.677–8.

63 Iris all hues, roses, and jessamine
Reared high their flourished heads between, and
  wrought
Mosaic; underfoot the violet,
Crocus, and hyacinth with rich inlay
Broidered the ground, more coloured than with
  stone
Of costliest emblem: other creature here
Beast, bird, insect, or worm durst enter none;
Such was their awe of man.
1665 *Paradise Lost* (published 1667), bk.4, l.698–705.

64 Nor turned I ween
Adam from his fair spouse, nor Eve the rites
Mysterious of connubial love refused:
Whatever hypocrites austerely talk
Of purity and place and innocence,
Defaming as impure what God declares
Pure, and commands to some, leaves free to all.
1665 *Paradise Lost* (published 1667), bk.4, l.741–7.

65 Hail, wedded love, mysterious law, true source
Of human offspring, sole propriety
In Paradise of all things common else.
1665 *Paradise Lost* (published 1667), bk.4, l.750–3.

66 Him there they found
Squat like a toad, close at the ear of Eve.
1665 *Paradise Lost* (published 1667), bk.4, l.799.

67 When I am thy captive talk of chains,
Proud limitary cherub.
1665 *Paradise Lost* (published 1667), bk.4, l.970–1.

68 But wherefore thou alone? Wherefore with thee

Came not all hell broke loose?
1665 *Paradise Lost* (published 1667), bk.4, l.917–8.

69 My fairest, my espoused, my latest found,
Heav'n's last best gift, my ever new delight.
1665 Adam to Eve. *Paradise Lost* (published 1667), bk.5,
l.18–19.

70 Best image of myself and dearer half.
1665 Adam to Eve. *Paradise Lost* (published 1667), bk.5, l.95.

71 Nor jealousy
Was understood, the injured lover's hell.
1665 *Paradise Lost* (published 1667), bk.5, l.449–50.

72 In contemplation of created things
By steps we may ascend to God.
1665 Adam to Raphael. *Paradise Lost* (published 1667), bk.5,
l.511–2.

73 God made thee perfect, not immutable.
1665 Raphael to Adam. *Paradise Lost* (published 1667), bk.5,
l.524.

74 Hear all ye angels, progeny of light,
Thrones, dominations, princedoms, virtues,
powers.
1665 *Paradise Lost* (published 1667), bk.5, l.600–1.

75 All seemed well pleased, all seemed, but were not
all.
1665 *Paradise Lost* (published 1667), bk.5, l.616.

76 Servant of God, well done, well hast thou fought
The better fight.
1665 God to his faithful angels. *Paradise Lost* (published 1667),
bk.6, l.29–30.

77 Proud, art thou met?
1665 Abdiel to Satan. *Paradise Lost* (published 1667), bk.6,
l.131.

78 This is servitude,
To serve th' unwise, or him who hath rebelled
Against his worthier, as thine now serve thee,
Thyself not free, but to thyself enthralled.
1665 Abdiel to Satan. *Paradise Lost* (published 1667), bk.6,
l.178–81.

79 But pain is perfect misery, the worst
Of evils, and excessive, overturns
All patience.
1665 *Paradise Lost* (published 1667), bk.6, l.461–3.

80 On war and mutual slaughter bent.
1665 Of Mankind. *Paradise Lost* (published 1667), bk.6, l.506.

81 Headlong themselves they threw
Down from the verge of heaven, eternal wrath
Burnt after them to the bottomless pit.
1665 Pursued to the wall of Heaven by the Messiah, Satan and
his rebelling angels fall to their punishment as the wall opens.
Rebelling Angels. *Paradise Lost* (published 1667), bk.6, l.867–9.

82 Standing on earth, not rapt above the pole,
More safe I sing with mortal voice, unchanged
To hoarse or mute, though fall'n on evil days,
On evil days though fallen, and evil tongues.
1665 *Paradise Lost* (published 1667), bk.7, l.23–6.

83 But knowledge is as food, and needs no less
Her temperance over appetite, to know
In measure what the mind may well contain,
Oppresses else with surfeit, and soon turns
Wisdom to folly, as nourishment to wind.
1665 *Paradise Lost* (published 1667), bk.7, l.126–30.

84 Necessity and chance
Approach not me, and what I will is fate.
1665 God. *Paradise Lost* (published 1667), bk.7, l.172–3.

85 He took the golden compasses, prepared
In God's eternal store, to circumscribe
This universe, and all created things:
One foot he centred, and the other turned
Round through the vast profundity obscure,
And said, 'Thus far extend, thus far thy bounds
This be thy just circumference, O world.'
1665 *Paradise Lost* (published 1667), bk.7, l.225–11.

86 And the earth self-balanced on her centre hung.
1665 *Paradise Lost* (published 1667), bk.7, l.242.

87 The great creator from his work returned
Magnificent, his six days' work, a world.
1665 *Paradise Lost* (published 1667), bk.7, l.563.

88 Witness this new-made world, another heav'n
From heaven gate not far, founded in view
On the clear hyaline, the glassy sea;
Of amplitude almost immense, with stars
Numerous, and every star perhaps a world
Of destined habitation.
1665 *Paradise Lost* (published 1667), bk.7, l.617–22.

89 O when meet now
Such pairs, in love and mutual honour joined?
1665 *Paradise Lost* (published 1667), bk.8, l.57–8.

90 He his fabric of the heavens
Hath left to their disputes, perhaps to move
His laughter at their quaint opinions wide
Hereafter, when they come to model heaven
And calculate the stars, how they will wield
The mighty frame, how build, unbuild, contrive
To save appearances, how gird the sphere
With centric and eccentric scribbled o'er,
Cycle and epicycle, orb in orb.
1665 *Paradise Lost* (published 1667), bk.8, l.76–84.

91 Heaven is for thee too high
To know what passes there; be lowly wise:
Think only what concerns thee and thy being.
Dream not of other worlds, what creatures there

Live, in what state, condition, or degree,
Contented that thus far hath been revealed
Not of earth only but of highest heav'n.
1665 Raphael to Adam. *Paradise Lost* (published 1667), bk.8,
l.172–8.

92 For man to tell how human life began
Is hard; for who himself beginning knew?
1665 Adam to Raphael. *Paradise Lost* (published 1667), bk.8,
l.250–1.

93 In solitude
What happiness, who can enjoy alone,
Or all enjoying, what contentment find?
1665 Adam. *Paradise Lost* (published 1667), bk.8, l.364–6.

94 Among unequals what society
Can sort, what harmony or true delight?
1665 Adam. *Paradise Lost* (published 1667), bk.8, l.383–4.

95 Yet when I approach
Her loveliness, so absolute she seems
And in herself complete, so well to know
Her own, that what she wills to do or say,
Seems wisest, virtuousest, discreetest, best.
1665 Adam speaking of Eve. *Paradise Lost* (published 1667),
bk.8, l.546–50.

96 All higher knowledge in her presence falls
Degraded, wisdom in discourse with her
Loses discount'nanced, and like folly shows.
1665 Adam speaking of Eve. *Paradise Lost* (published 1667),
bk.8, l.557–3.

97 Love refines
The thoughts, and heart enlarges, hath his seat
In reason, and is judicious, is the scale
By which to heav'nly love thou may'st ascend,
Not sunk in carnal pleasure, for which cause
Among the beasts no mate for thee was found.
1665 Raphael to Adam. *Paradise Lost* (published 1667), bk.8,
l.589–94.

98 My celestial patroness, who deigns
Her nightly visitation unimplored,
And dictates to me slumbering, or inspires
Easy my unpremeditated verse:
Since first this subject for heroic song
Pleased me long choosing, and beginning late.
1665 *Paradise Lost* (published 1667), bk.9, l.21–6.

99 And the more I see
Pleasures about me, so much more I feel
Torment within me.
1665 Satan. *Paradise Lost* (published 1667), bk.9, l.119–21.

1 This man of clay, son of despite.
1665 Satan speaking of Adam. *Paradise Lost* (published 1667),
bk.9, l.176.

2 For nothing lovelier can be found

In woman, than to study household good,
And good works in her husband to promote.
1665 Adam to Eve. *Paradise Lost* (published 1667), bk.9,
l.232–4.

3 That space the Evil One abstracted stood
From his own evil, and for the time remained
Stupidly good, of enmity disarmed,
Of guile, of hate, of envy, of revenge.
1665 Satan gazes upon Eve. *Paradise Lost* (published 1667),
bk.9, l.463–6.

4 She fair, divinely fair, fit love for gods.
1665 Satan speaking of Eve. *Paradise Lost* (published 1667),
bk.9, l.489.

5 O fairest of creation, last and best
Of all God's works, creature in whom excelled
Whatever can to sight or thought be formed,
Holy, divine, good, amiable, or sweet!
How art thou lost, how on a sudden lost,
Defaced, deflow'red, and now to death devote?
1665 Adam to Eve. *Paradise Lost* (published 1667), bk.9,
l.896–91.

6 Flesh of flesh,
Bone of my bone thou art, and from thy state
Mine never shall be parted, bliss or woe.
1665 Adam to Eve. *Paradise Lost* (published 1667), bk.9,
l.914–6.

7 What thou art is mine;
Our state cannot be severed, we are one,
One flesh; to lose thee were to lose my self.
1665 Adam to Eve. *Paradise Lost* (published 1667), bk.9,
l.957–9.

8 Linked in love so dear,
To undergo with me one guilt, one crime,
If any be, of tasting this fair fruit.
1665 Eve to Adam. *Paradise Lost* (published 1667), bk.9,
l.970–2.

9 As with new wine intoxicated both
They swim in mirth, and fancy that they feel
Divinity within them breeding wings
Wherewith to scorn the earth.
1665 *Paradise Lost* (published 1667), bk.9, l.1007–10.

10 Thus they in mutual accusation spent
The fruitless hours, but neither self-condemning,
And of their vain contést appeared no end.
1665 *Paradise Lost* (published 1667), bk.9, l.1187–9.

11 For solitude sometimes is best society,
And short retirement urges sweet return.
1665 *Paradise Lost* (published 1667), bk.9, l.249–50.

12 Her rash hand in evil hour
Forth reaching to the fruit, she plucked, she ate:
Earth felt the wound, and nature from her seat

Sighing through all her works gave signs of woe,
That all was lost.

1665 *Paradise Lost* (published 1667), bk.9, l.781–5.

13 Yet I shall temper so
Justice with mercy.

1665 *Paradise Lost* (published 1667), bk.10, l.77–8.

14 Love was not in their looks, either to God
Or to each other.

1665 *Paradise Lost* (published 1667), bk.10, l.111–2.

15 Adorned
She was indeed, and lovely to attract
Thy love, not thy subjection.

1665 Christ speaking to Adam of Eve. *Paradise Lost* (published 1667), bk.10, l.151–2.

16 Now possess,
As lords, a spacious world, to our native heaven
Little inferior, by my adventure hard
With peril great achieved.

1665 Satan, returning triumphantly from Earth to Hell after tempting Eve. *Paradise Lost* (published 1667), bk.10, l.466–9.

17 He hears
On all sides, from innumerable tongues
A dismal universal hiss, the sound
Of public scorn.

1665 Satan and the rebel angels are turned to snakes. *Paradise Lost* (published 1667), bk.10, l.506–9.

18 O fleeting joys
Of Paradise, dear bought with lasting woes!

1665 Adam's lament. *Paradise Lost* (published 1667), bk.10, l.741–2.

19 But say
That death be not one stroke, as I supposed,
Bereaving sense, but endless misery
From this day onward, which I feel begun
Both in me, and without me, and so last
To perpetuity; ay me, that fear
Comes thund'ring back with dreadful revolution
On my defenceless head; both Death and I
Am found eternal, and incorporate both,
Nor I on my part single, in me all
Posterity stands cursed: fair patrimony
That I must leave ye, sons; O were I able
To waste it all myself, and leave ye none!

1665 Adam muses on death. *Paradise Lost* (published 1667), bk.10, l.808–20.

20 O why did God,
Creator wise, that peopled highest heav'n
With Spirits masculine, create at last
This novelty on earth, this fair defect
Of nature, and not fill the world at once
With men as angels without feminine,
Or find some other way to generate

Mankind?

1665 Adam speaking of Eve. *Paradise Lost* (published 1667), bk.10, l.888–95.

21 Let us seek Death, or he not found, supply
With our own hands his office on ourselves;
Why stand we longer shivering under fears,
That show no end but death, and have the power,
Of many ways to die the shortest choosing,
Destruction with destruction to destroy.

1665 Eve. *Paradise Lost* (published 1667), bk.10, l.1001–6.

22 So send them forth, though sorrowing, yet in
peace.

1665 God speaking to Michael of Adam and Eve. *Paradise Lost* (published 1667), bk.11, l.117.

23 Moping melancholy
And moon-struck madness.

Michael shows Adam a vision of what will happen before the Flood. *Paradise Lost* (published 1667), bk.11, l.485–6.

24 So may'st thou live, till like ripe fruit thou drop
Into thy mother's lap, or be with ease
Gathered, not harshly plucked, for death mature:
This is old age; but then thou must outlive
Thy youth, thy strength, thy beauty, which will
change
To withered weak and grey.

1665 Michael to Adam. *Paradise Lost* (published 1667), bk.11, l.535–40.

25 Nor love thy life, nor hate; but what thou liv'st
Live well, how long or short permit to heaven.

1665 *Paradise Lost* (published 1667), bk.11, l.553–4.

26 Now I see
Peace to corrupt no less than war to waste.

1665 *Paradise Lost* (published 1667), bk.11, l.783–4.

27 O goodness infinite, goodness immense!
That all this good of evil shall produce,
And evil turn to good; more wonderful
Than that which by creation first brought forth
Light out of darkness!

1665 Adam to Michael. *Paradise Lost* (published 1667), bk.12, l.470–4.

28 Let us descend now therefore from this top
Of speculation.

1665 *Paradise Lost* (published 1667), bk.12, l.588–9.

29 Some natural tears they dropped, but wiped them
soon;
The world was all before them, where to choose
Their place of rest, and Providence their guide:
They hand in hand with wand'ring steps and slow,
Through Eden took their solitary way.

1665 *Paradise Lost* (published 1667), bk.12, l.645–9.

30 This having learnt, thou hast attained the sum

Of wisdom; hope no higher, though all the stars
Thou knew'st by name, and all th' ethereal powers,
All secrets of the deep, all nature's works,
Or works of God in heav'n, air, earth, or sea,
And all the riches of this world enjoy'dst,
And all the rule, one empire; only add
Deeds to thy knowledge answerable, add faith,
Add virtue, patience, temperance, add love,
By name to come called charity, the soul
Of all the rest: then wilt thou not be loath
To leave this Paradise, but shalt possess
A paradise within thee, happier far.
1665 Michael to Adam. *Paradise Lost* (published 1667), bk.12, l.575–87.

31 For what can I increase
Or multiply, but curses on my head?
1665 Adam's lament. *Paradise Lost* (published 1667), bk.10, l.731.

32 Skill'd to retire, and in retiring draw
Hearts after them tangled in amorous nets
1671 *Paradise Regained*, bk.2, l.161.

33 The childhood shows the man,
As morning shows the day. Be famous then
By wisdom; as thy empire must extend,
So let extend thy mind o'er all the world.
1671 *Paradise Regained*, bk.4, l.220.

34 The first and wisest of them all professed
To know this only, that he nothing knew.
1671 Of Socrates. *Paradise Regained*, bk.4, l.293.

35 Athens, the eye of Greece, mother of arts
And eloquence, native to famous wits
1671 *Paradise Regained*, bk.4, l.240–1.

36 Who reads
Incessantly, and to his reading brings not
A spirit and judgement equal or superior
(And what he brings, what needs he elsewhere
   seek?)
Uncertain and unsettled still remains,
Deep-versed in books and shallow in himself.
1671 *Paradise Regained*, bk.4, l.322.

37 But here I feel amends,
The breath of Heav'n fresh-blowing, pure and
   sweet,
With day-spring born; here leave me to respire.
1671 *Samson Agonistes*, l.9.

38 Ask for this great deliverer now, and find him
Eyeless in Gaza at the mill with slaves.
1671 *Samson Agonistes*, l.40–1.

39 O impotence of mind, in body strong!
But what is strength without a double share
Of wisdom, vast, unwieldy, burdensome,
Proudly secure, yet liable to fall

By weakest subtleties, not made to rule,
But to subserve where wisdom bears command.
1671 *Samson Agonistes*, l.52–7.

40 O loss of sight, of thee I most complain!
Blind among enemies, O worse than chains,
Dungeon, or beggary, or decrepit age!
Light the prime work of God to me is extinct,
And all her various objects of delight
Annull'd, which might in part my grief have
   eas'd,
Inferior to the vilest now become
Of man or worm; the vilest here excel me,
They creep, yet see, I dark in light expos'd
To daily fraud, contempt, abuse and wrong,
Within doors, or without, still as a fool,
In power of others, never in my own;
Scarce half I seem to live, dead more than half.
1671 *Samson Agonistes*, l.67–79.

41 If it be true
That light is in the soul,
She all in every part; why was the sight
To such a tender ball as th' eye confin'd?
1671 *Samson Agonistes*, l.91–4.

42 To live a life half dead, a living death.
1671 *Samson Agonistes*, l.100.

43 Thou art become (O worst imprisonment!)
The Dungeon of thy self.
1671 *Samson Agonistes*, l.155–6.

44 Salve to thy sores, apt words have power to suage
The tumours of a troubl'd mind,
And are as Balm to fester'd wounds.
1671 *Samson Agonistes*, l.184.

45 Just are the ways of God,
And justifiable to men;
Unless there be who think not God at all.
1671 *Samson Agonistes*, l.293–5.

46 So much I feel my genial spirits droop,
My hopes all flat, nature within me seems
In her functions weary of herself.
1671 *Samson Agonistes*, l.594–6.

47 My race of glory run, and race of shame,
And I shall shortly be with them that rest.
1671 *Samson Agonistes*, l.597–8.

48 God of our Fathers, what is man!
That thou towards him with hand so various,
Or might I say contrarious,
Temperst thy providence through his short
   course,
Not evenly, as thou rul'st
The angelic orders and inferior creatures mute,
Irrational and brute.
1671 *Samson Agonistes*, l.667–73.

49 That grounded maxim
So rife and celebrated in the mouths
Of wisest men; that to the public good
Private respects must yield.
1671 *Samson Agonistes*, l.865–8.

50 In argument with men a woman ever
Goes by the worse, whatever be her cause.
1671 *Samson Agonistes*, l.903–4.

51 At distance I forgive thee, go with that.
1671 *Samson Agonistes*, l.954.

52 Yet beauty, though injurious, hath strange
power,
After offence returning, to regain
Love once possessed.
1671 *Samson Agonistes*, l.1003.

53 Love-quarrels oft in pleasing concord end.
1671 *Samson Agonistes*, l.1008.

54 Lords are lordliest in their wine.
1671 *Samson Agonistes*, l.1418.

55 Evil news rides post, while good news baits.
1671 *Samson Agonistes*, l.1538.

56 Death to life is crown or shame.
1671 *Samson Agonistes*, l.1579.

57 Not willingly, but tangl'd in the fold
Of dire necessity.
1671 *Samson Agonistes*, l.1665.

58 Nothing is here for tears, nothing to wail
Or knock the breast, no weakness, no contempt,
Dispraise, or blame, nothing but well and fair,
And what may quiet us in a death so noble.
1671 Of Samson's heroic death. *Samson Agonistes*, l.1721.

59 All is best, though we oft doubt,
What the unsearchable dispose
Of highest wisdom brings about,
And ever best found in the close.
1671 *Samson Agonistes*, l.1745–8.

60 Calm of mind, all passion spent.
1671 *Samson Agonistes*, l.1758.

Min, Anchee 1957–

Chinese writer who left China for America in 1984. Her autobiography *Red Azalea* (1993) is named after Madame Mao's propaganda film in which Min was an actress.

61 My parents lived like—as the neighbours described them—a pair of chopsticks, always in harmony.
1993 *Red Azalea.*

62 The Chairman looked dissatisfied lying on his death bed.
1993 Of Mao Zedong. *Red Azalea.*

Mingus, Charles 1922–79

US composer and bass player. He was one of the great idiosyncratic geniuses of modern jazz, and his musical legacy is only now being fully absorbed.

63 Today musicians listen to see who makes the most money on a style, and then they set to copying him. And they don't copy the ones that are beautiful, creative and good.
1977 Interview in Enstice and Rubin *Jazz Spoken Here* (1992).

Minot, Laurence d. c.1352

English poet.

64 War yit with the Skottes, for thai er ful of gile.
early to mid 14c 'Skottes out of Berwik', l.6.

Minow, Newton Norman 1926–

US lawyer, author and communications executive. Named Chair of the Federal Communications Commission (1961–63) by President Kennedy, he was noted for his controversial criticism of television broadcasting standards in the USA. He has been the director of the Annenberg Washington Program since 1987.

65 When television is good, nothing is better. When it's bad, nothing is worse.
1961 Speech to the National Association of Broadcasters. Reported in the *New York Times*, 10 May.

66 You will observe a vast wasteland.
1961 Speech to the National Association of Broadcasters, inviting them to watch a full day of television. Reported in the *New York Times*, 10 May.

Minsky, Marvin Lee 1927–

US computer scientist and artificial intelligence researcher.

67 Logic doesn't apply to the real world.
1981 In Douglas R Hofstadter and Daniel C Dennett (eds) *The Mind's I: fantasies and reflections on self and soul.*

Mirabeau, Honoré Gabriel Riqueti, Comte de 1749–91

French revolutionary politician. After the publication of his *Essai sur le despotisme*, he was sentenced to death, but only served three years in prison. He espoused the Revolution, and died soon after he was elected President of the Assembly in 1791.

68 War is the national industry of Prussia.
1788 Attributed to Mirabeau by Albert Sorel (1842–1906), suggested by Mirabeau's introduction to *De la monarchie prussienne sous Frederic le Grand.*

69 We will only leave our places by the force of the bayonet!
1789 Speech at the *Séance Royale.* Quoted in Webster *The French Revolution* (1919), p.50.

70 To administer is to govern; to govern is to reign. That is the problem.
1790 Memorandum, 3 Jul.

Miró, Joán 1893–1983
Spanish painter, graphic artist and designer.

71 I will break their guitar.
Of the Cubists and their reliance upon the still-life. Attributed in Saranne Alexandrian *Surrealist Art* (1970).

Mishan, E J
British economist.

72 If frequent teabreaks and other manifestations of disguised leisure are regarded as goods—and economics suggests that they be so regarded—their inclusion in any index of output per capita might go some way to enhance Britain's comparative performance.
Quoted in Alex Rubner *Three Sacred Cows of Economics* (1970), p.47.

Mishima, Yukio pseudonym of *Hiraoka Kimitake* 1925–70
Japanese writer of novels, plays and short stories. Keenly committed to the chivalrous ideals of Imperial Japan, he committed suicide by performing *seppuku* after a token effort at rallying his country to the right-wing nationalist traditions of pre-war Japan.

73 Teachers—a bunch of men all armed with the same information.
1946 *Acts of Memories*, 'Cigarette' (originally published as 'Tabako', translated by John Bester).

74 He'd been mistaken in thinking that if he killed himself the sordid bourgeois world would perish with him.
1948 *Acts of Memories*, 'Raisin Bread' (originally published as 'Junkyo', translated by John Bester).

75 As he saw it, there was only one choice—to be strong and upright, or to commit suicide.
1963 *Acts of Memories*, 'Sword' (originally published as 'Ken', translated by John Bester).

76 Human beings…they go on being born and dying, dying and being born. It's kind of boring, isn't it?
1963 *Acts of Memories*, 'Sword' (originally published as 'Ken', translated by John Bester).

77 Held in the custody of childhood is a locked chest; the adolescent, by one means or another, tries to open it. the chest is opened: inside, there is nothing.
1964 *Acts of Memories*, 'Cigarette' (originally published as 'Tabako', translated by John Bester).

Mitchel, John 1815–75
Irish patriot. Starting the *United Irishman* (1848) he was tried for 'treason-felony' and transported, but in 1853 he escaped from Van Diemen's Land (Tasmania) to the US. He returned to Ireland in 1874, and was elected to parliament but declared ineligible.

78 Surely, it is in youth man is most thoroughly depraved. Hell lies about us in our infancy. The youthful innocency sung by aged poets (who forget their first childhood) is nothing but ignorance of evil. As the child comes to know evil, he loves it.
1849 In the *Jail Journal*, 13 Apr.

Mitchell, Adrian 1932–
English writer. His poetry is populist and political in nature. He has also written novels and plays.

79 Most people ignore most poetry because most poetry ignores most people.
1964 *Poems*, introduction.

80 The man who believes in giraffes would swallow anything.
1971 'Loose Leaf Poem'.

81 Poetry is an extra hand. It can caress or tickle. It can clench and fight.
1972 'Poetry Lives', in the *Sunday Times*, 13 Feb.

Mitchell, Joni (Roberta Joan) née *Anderson* 1943–
Canadian singer and songwriter. Her highly original and personal compositions made her a central figure in the folk movement of the 1960s. Her albums include *Ladies of the Canyon* (1970) and *Blue* (1971).

82 Woke up, it was a Chelsea morning, and the first thing that I knew
There was milk and toast and honey and a bowl of oranges, too.
And the sun poured in like butterscotch and stuck to all my senses.
1967 'Chelsea Morning'.

Mitchell, Margaret 1900–49
US writer. She worked as a journalist with the Atlanta *Constitution*. Her only novel, *Gone with the Wind* (written 1926–36, published 1936, Pulitzer Prize), rapidly became a best-seller and was made into a celebrated film in 1939.

83 I'm tired of everlastingly being unnatural and never doing anything I want to do…and I'm tired of pretending I don't know anything, so men can tell me things and feel important while they're doing it.
1936 Scarlett O'Hara. *Gone With The Wind*, ch.5.

84 Land is the only thing in the world worth working for, worth fighting for, worth dying for, because it's the only thing that lasts. It will come to you, this love of the land.
1939 *Gone With The Wind*.

85 Young misses whut eats heavy mos' gener'ly doan never ketch husbands.
1936 Mammy. *Gone with the Wind*, ch.5.

86 Until you've lost your reputation, you never realize what a burden it was or what freedom really is.
1936 Rhett Butler. *Gone With The Wind*, ch.9.

87 I'm going to live through this, and when it's over, I'm never going to be hungry again. No, nor any of my folks. If I have to steal or kill—as God is my witness, I'm never going to be hungry again.
1936 Scarlett O'Hara. *Gone with the Wind*, ch.25.

88 Fighting is like champagne. It goes to the heads of cowards as quickly as of heroes. Any fool can be brave on a battlefield when it's be brave or else be killed.
1936 Ashley Wilkes. *Gone With The Wind*, ch.31.

89 Southerners can never resist a losing cause.
1936 Rhett Butler. *Gone With The Wind*, ch.34.

90 Death and taxes and childbirth! There's never any convenient time for any of them!
1936 Scarlett O'Hara. *Gone With The Wind*, ch.38.

91 What is broken is broken, and I'd rather remember it as it was at its best than mend it and see broken places as long as I lived… I wish I could care what you do or where you go, but I can't. My dear, I don't give a damn.
1936 Rhett Butler's parting speech to Scarlett O'Hara. *Gone With The Wind*, ch.63; the more famous version of the final line from the film script by Sidney Howard (1939, spoken by Clark Gable) ran 'Frankly, my dear, I don't give a damn'.

92 Tomorrow, I'll think of some other way to get him back. After all, tomorrow is another day.
1936 Scarlett O'Hara's final words. *Gone With The Wind*, ch.63.

Mitford, Mary Russell 1787–1855

English novelist and dramatist, best known for her sketches of country manners, scenery and character that were collected as *Our Village* (1824–32). Other publications include *Recollections of a Literary Life* (1852).

93 To think of playing cricket for hard cash! Money and gentility would ruin any pastime under the sun.
1823 Letter to R B Haydon, 24 Aug.

94 Who would think that a little bit of leather, and two pieces of wood, had such a delightful and delighting power!
1824–32 *Our Village*.

Mitford, Nancy Freeman 1904–73

English writer. A daughter of the aristocracy, she achieved a considerable reputation for her witty novels.

95 Like all the very young we took it for granted that making love is child's play.
1945 *The Pursuit of Love*, ch.3.

96 Aunt Sadie…so much disliked hearing about health that people often took her for a Christian Scientist, which, indeed, she might have become had she not disliked hearing about religion even more.
1945 *The Pursuit of Love*, ch.4.

97 I have only ever read one book in my life, and that is *White Fang*. It's so frightfully good I've never bothered to read another.
1945 *The Pursuit of Love*, ch.9.

98 Abroad is unutterably bloody and foreigners are fiends.
1945 Uncle Matthew speaking. *The Pursuit of Love*, ch.15.

99 'Always be civil to the girls, you never know who they may marry' is an aphorism which has saved many an English spinster from being treated like an Indian widow.
1949 *Love In A Cold Climate*, pt.1, ch.2.

1 'Twenty three and a quarter minutes past,' Uncle Matthew was saying furiously, 'in precisely six and three-quarter minutes the damned fella will be late.'
1949 *Love In A Cold Climate*, pt.1, ch.13.

2 When the loo paper gets thicker and the writing paper thinner, it's always a bad sign, at home.
1949 *Love In A Cold Climate*, pt.2, ch.2.

3 An aristocracy in a republic is like a chicken whose head has been cut off: it may run about in a lively way, but in fact it is dead.
1956 *Noblesse Oblige*.

Mitsuharu, Kaneko 1895–1975

Japanese poet, noted for his unconventionality. He spent a number of years in Belgium and France and wrote a poem, *Awa* (Foam), about Japanese atrocities in China.

4 The sky snivels green snot.
There is war.
c.1938 *Shijin* (Poet), 'Awa' (translated by A R Davies, 1988).

Mizner, Wilson 1876–1933

US dramatist and wit.

5 Be nice to people on your way up because you'll meet them on your way down.
Quoted in A Johnston *The Legendary Mizners* (1953).

6 Working for Warner Brothers was like fucking a porcupine—it's a hundred pricks against one.
Quoted in David Niven *Bring on the Empty Horses* (1975).

7 A trip through a sewer in a glass-bottomed boat.
   1979 Of life in Hollywood. Quoted in Gary Herman *The Book
   of Hollywood Quotes* (1979).

Mo Yan   1956–

Chinese writer and the winner of nearly all the prestigious
literary awards in China. He has written a number of
novels. *Red Sorghum* (1993), his fourth and most popular
novel, is set principally during the 1930s when Japanese
forces occupied the country.

8 Words spoken on the road are heard by snakes in
   the grass.
   1993 *Red Sorghum*, translated by Howard Goldblatt.

Mo, Timothy   1950–

British novelist. He was born in Hong Kong, and
achieved prominence with *Sour Sweet*, set in the Chinese
community in London.

9 The Chens had been living in the UK for four
   years, which was long enough to have lost their
   place in the society from which they had emigrated
   but not long enough to feel comfortable in the new.
   1982 *Sour Sweet*, opening words.

10 It's all honourable enough in its way, but it creates
   societies which simply cannot sustain any kind of
   democratic structure. It always leads to totalitarian
   and corrupt tyrannies... There's no tradition of
   moral individual courage in Chinese culture.
   1982 Of Chinese tradition. In *The Fiction Magazine*, vol.1,
   no.4.

11 The assaying of tea is an art and not a science. It is
   the man, and not his instruments, which is the
   most important. There can be no substitute for my
   experience and intuited knowledge.
   1986 *An Insular Possession*, ch.4.

12 I see you belong to the category, old friend, which
   will have things in the round, which does love an
   end, causes, the balance sheet drawn and equalled.
   But, my dear Gid, the world is not like that—it *is*
   untidy, there are no reasons, the final sum never
   balances.
   1986 *An Insular Possession*, ch.44.

13 There's no such thing as a hero—only ordinary
   people asked extraordinary things in terrible
   circumstances—and delivering.
   1991 *The Redundancy of Courage*, ch.30.

Modersohn-Becker, Paula   née *Becker*
1876–1907

German painter, a member of the Worpswede artists'
colony near Bremen and an early Expressionist. In her
later works naturalism gives way to simple forms and
strong lyrical colour. She died soon after the birth of her
first child.

14 In art one is usually totally alone with oneself.
   1906 Diary entry, Paris, 18 Nov, quoted in Gillian Perry *Paula
   Modersohn-Becker* (1979).

Mola, Emilio   d.1937

Spanish general, a nationalist leader during the Spanish
Civil War.

15 *La quinta columna.*

   The fifth column.
   1936 Speech, Oct. Of the rebel sympathizers within Madrid
   who would help the four columns of nationalist rebels besieging
   it. Quoted in Hugh Thomas *The Spanish Civil War* (1961),
   ch.4, p.317.

Molière, Jean Baptiste Poquelin   1622–73

French actor and playwright who formed a theatrical
company in 1643 and toured the provinces until 1658.
He gained the patronage of the Duc d'Orléans and later
of Louis XIV.

16 *On ne meurt qu'une fois et c'est pour si longtemps!*

   We only die once; and it's for such a long time!
   1656 *Le Dépit amoureux*, act 5, sc.3.

17 *Hors de Paris, il n'y a pas de salut pour honnêtes gens.*

   Outside of Paris, there is no salvation for
   gentlemen.
   1659 *Les Précieuses ridicules*, sc.9.

18 *Les verrous et les grilles
   Ne font pas la vertu des femmes et des filles.*

   Bolts and bars will not keep wives and daughters
   chaste.
   1661 *L'École des maris*, act 1, sc.2.

19 *Le siècle s'encanaille furieusement.*

   Our times have become vulgar.
   1663 *Critique de l'École des femmes*, sc.7.

20 *Je voudrais bien savoir si la grande
   règle de toutes les règles n'est pas de plaire.*

   I shouldn't be surprised if the greatest
   rule of all weren't to give pleasure.
   1663 *Critique de l'École des femmes*, sc.7.

21 *Le ciel défend, de vrai, certains contentements;
   Mais on trouve avec lui des accommodements.*

   True, heaven forbids us certain pleasures;
   But we always find a way to arrange things.
   1664 *Le Tartuffe*, act 4, sc. 5.

22 *Le scandale du monde est ce qui fait l'offense,
   Et ce n'est pas pécher que pécher en silence.*

   A scandal is that which gives offence to the world.
   To sin in private is not to sin at all.
   1664 *Le Tartuffe*, act 4, sc. 5.

23 *Qui vit sans tabac n'est pas digne de vivre.*

Anyone who lives without tobacco is not worthy of living.
1665 *Don Juan*, act 1, sc.1.

24　*La naissance n'est rien où la vertu n'est pas.*

Birth counts for little when virtue is lacking.
1665 *Don Juan*, act 4, sc.4.

25　*L'ami du genre humain n'est pas du tout mon fait.*

I have no use at all for the friend of mankind.
1666 *Le Misanthrope*, act 1, sc.1.

26　*J'aime mieux un vice commode*
Qu'une fatigante vertu.

I prefer easygoing vice to tiresome virtue.
1666 *Amphitryon*, act 1, sc.4.

27　*Quand il y a à manger pour huit, il y en a bien pour dix.*

When there is enough food for eight, there is enough for ten.
1668 *L'Avare*, act 1, sc.1.

28　*Il faut manger pour vivre et non pas vivre pour manger.*

One should eat to live, not live to eat.
1668 *L'Avare*, act 3, sc.5.

29　*Ils commencent ici par pendre un homme et puis ils lui font son procès.*

Here they hang a men first, and try him afterwards.
1669 In Paris. *Monsieur de Pourceaugnac*, act 3, sc.2.

30　*Par ma foi! il y a plus de quarante ans que je dis de la prose sans que j'en susse rien!*

Good heavens! I've been speaking prose for forty years without knowing it!
1670 *Le Bourgeois Gentilhomme*, act 2, sc.4

31　*La grammaire qui sait régenter jusqu'aux rois.*

Even kings must bow to grammar.
1672 *Les Femmes savantes*, act 2, sc.6.

32　*Je vis de bonne soupe et non de beau langage.*

Its good food and not fine words that keeps me alive.
1672 *Les Femmes savantes*, act 2, sc.7.

33　*Un sot savant est sot plus qu'un sot ignorant.*

A learned fool is more foolish than an ignorant fool.
1672 *Les Femmes savantes*, act 4, sc.3.

34　*Presque tous les hommes meurent de leurs remèdes et non de leurs maladies.*

Almost all men die from their medicines and not from their illnesses.
1673 *Le Malade imaginaire*, act 3, sc.3.

35　We reason with one another; he prescribes the remedies; I omit to take them and I recover.
On his relationship with his doctor, Mauvillan, in the presence of Loius XIV. Quoted in Vincent Cronin *Louis XIV* (1964), p.291.

Moltke, Helmuth von, Count 1800–91

Prussian general. Chief of the General Staff of the Prussian army 1858—88. He presided over successful wars with Denmark (1863–4), Austria (1866), and France (1870–1).

36　Everlasting peace is a dream, and not even a pleasant one; and war is a necessary part of God's arrangement with the world… Without war the world would deteriorate into materialism.
1880 Letter to Dr J K Bluntschi, 11 Dec, collected in *Helmuth von Moltke as a Correspondent* (1893).

37　What our sword has won in half a year, our sword must guard for half a century.
1891 *The Franco-Prussian War of 1870-71.*

Mondale, Walter F(rederick) 1928–

US Democratic politician and lawyer. He served under President Carter as Vice-President (1977–81), and was the Democratic nominee for President in 1984, when he lost to Ronald Reagan.

38　I don't want to spend the next two years in Holiday Inns.
1976 On withdrawing from the presidential campaign.

39　In our system, at about 11.30pm on election night, they just push you off the edge of the cliff—and that's it. You might scream on the way down, but you're going to hit the bottom, and you're not going to be in office.
1984 On losing to Ronald Reagan in the presidential elections, in the *New York Times*, 4 Mar.

Mondrian, Piet 1872–1944

Dutch painter. One of the most important artists in the development of abstract painting.

40　I hate everything approaching temperamental inspiration, 'sacred fire' and all those attributes of genius which serve only as cloaks for untidy minds.
Quoted in F Elgar *Mondrian* (1968).

41　Why should art continue to follow nature when every other field has left nature behind?
Quoted in F Elgar *Mondrian* (1968).

42　The unconscious in us warns us that in art we have to follow one particular path. And if we follow it, it is not the sign of an unconscious act. On the contrary, it shows that there is in our ordinary consciousness a greater awareness of our unconsciousness.
Quoted in F Elgar *Mondrian* (1968).

Monet, Claude 1840–1926

French Impressionist painter. One of the creators of
Impressionism, it was his *Impression: soleil levant* that gave
the movement its name. He spent the last years of his life
as a recluse in Giverny.

43 When you go out to paint, try to forget what
objects you have before you—a tree, a house, a
field, or whatever. Merely think, here is a little
square of blue, here an oblong of pink, here a streak
of yellow, and paint it just as it looks to you, the
exact colour and shape, until it gives your own
naive impression of the scene before you.
*Attributed, in reminiscences written in 1927 by the young
American artist Lilla Cabot Perry.*

44 It was as if a veil had been torn suddenly away; I had
understood, I had grasped what painting could be.
*After painting with the artist Boudin in the open air. Quoted in
J Isaacson* Claude Monet *(1978).*

Monod, Jacques 1910–76

French biologist and author. He proposed (1961) the
concepts of messenger RNA. He shared the 1965 Nobel
Prize in Physiology or Medicine.

45 There are living systems; there is no 'living matter'.
1967 Lecture, College of France.

46 The scientific attitude implies…the postulate of
objectivity—that is to say, the fundamental
postulate that there is no plan; that there is no
intention in the universe.
1970 *Le Hasard et la Necéssité.*

Monro, Harold Edward 1879–1932

English poet. He founded the influential *Poetry Review* in
1912. A *Collected Poems* appeared in 1933.

47 When the tea is brought at five o'clock,
And all the neat curtains are drawn with care,
The little black cat with bright green eyes
Is suddenly purring there.
1914 'Milk for the Cat'.

48 The white saucer like some full moon descends
At last from the clouds of the table above.
1914 'Milk for the Cat'.

Monroe, Marilyn pseudonym of *Norma Jean Baker* 1926–62

US film actress. Her sex appeal was exploited in films such
as *How to Marry a Millionaire* and *Gentlemen Prefer
Blondes* (both 1953), but she went on to light comedy (eg
Some Like It Hot, 1959) and more serious roles such as
The Misfits (1961), written by her third husband, Arthur
Miller. Her suicide made her an icon, and a symbol of
Hollywood's ruthlessness.

49 He's not a director, he's a dictator.

c.1959 On Billy Wilder, the director of *Some Like It Hot*,
attributed.

50 He's the only person I know who's in worse shape
than I am.
1961 On Montgomery Clift, her co-star in *The Misfits*.

Montagu, (Alexander) Victor Edward Paulet 1906–95

Conservative politician, private secretary to Stanley
Baldwin (1932–4) and chairman of the Tory Reform
Committee (1943–4). He succeeded as 10th Earl of
Sandwich in 1962 but disclaimed his peerage for life the
next year. His publications include *The Conservative
Dilemma* (1970).

51 Lord Hailsham said the other day that the
machinery of Government was creaking. My
Lords, it is not even moving sufficiently to emit a
noise of any kind.
1963 House of Lords, 20 Apr, shortly before disclaiming his
peerage.

Montagu, Ashley pseudonym of *Montague Francis Ashley Montague* 1905–

English-born US anthropologist, author of a number of
scholarly and popular works. He has been closely
associated with the view that cultural phenomena are not
the result of genetics.

52 As the god of contemporary man's idolatry, science
is a two-handed engine, and as such science is too
important a human activity to leave to the
scientists.
1964 Book review in the *New York Times*, 26 Apr.

Montagu, Lady Mary Wortley née *Pierrepoint* 1689–1762

English writer and socialite. She accompanied her
ambassador husband to Constantinople (1716–18),
writing there her entertaining *Letters*. She introduced
smallpox inoculation into England, and settled in Italy
with her husband in 1739.

53 'Tis certain we have but very imperfect accounts of
the manners and religion of these people; this part
of the world being seldom visited, but by
merchants, who mind little but their own affairs; or
travellers, who make too short a stay to be able to
report anything exactly of their own knowledge.
c.1716 Of Turkey. Collected in Lord Wharncliffe (ed) *The
Letters and Works of Lady Mary Wortley Montagu* (1837).

54 Thus you see, Sir, that these people are not so
unpolished as we represent them. 'Tis true, their
magnificence is of a different taste from ours, and
perhaps of a better. I am almost of opinion, they
have a right notion of life. They consume it in
music, gardens, wine, and delicate eating, while we

are tormenting our brains with some scheme of politics, or studying some science to which we can never attain, or, if we do, cannot persuade other people to set that value upon it we do ourselves… We die or grow old before we can reap the fruit of our labours. Considering what short-lived weak animals men are, is there any study so beneficial as the study of present pleasure?

c.1716 Collected in Lord Wharncliffe (ed) *The Letters and Works of Lady Mary Wortley Montagu* (1837).

55 I was here convinced of the truth of a reflection I had often made, that if it was the fashion to go naked, the face would be hardly observed.

c.1716 In a Turkish bath in Sofia. Collected in Lord Wharncliffe (ed) *The Letters and Works of Lady Mary Wortley Montagu* (1837).

56 If your daughters are inclined to love reading, do not check their inclination by hindering them of the diverting part of it. It is as necessary for the amusement of women as the reputation of men; but teach them not to expect any applause from it… Ignorance is as much the fountain of vice as idleness, and indeed generally produces it. People that do not read or work for a livelihood have many hours they know not how to employ, especially women, who commonly fall into vapours or something worse.

1750 Letter, Jan. Collected in R Halsband (ed) *Selected Letters of Lady Mary Wortley Montagu* (1970).

57 Their whole business abroad (as far as I can perceive) being to buy new clothes, in which they shine in some obscure coffee-house, where they are sure of meeting only one-another… I look upon them as the greatest blockheads.

1763 On those making the Grand Tour. Quoted in Eric Newby (ed) *A Book of Travellers' Tales* (1985).

Montague, C(harles) E(dward) 1867–1928

English novelist and essayist of Irish parentage. He wrote various novels, a collection of essays and many articles for the *Manchester Guardian* (1890–1925).

58 War hath no fury like a non-combatant.

1922 *Disenchantment*, ch.16.

▷ See Congreve 281:22.

59 I was born below par to the extent of two whiskies.

1923 'Fiery Particles'.

60 The Swiss are inspired hotel-keepers. Some centuries since, when the stranger strayed into one of their valleys, their simple forefathers would kill him and share out the little money he might have about him. Now they know better. They keep him alive and writing cheques.

1926 *The Right Place*.

Montaigne, Michel Eyquem de 1533–92

French essayist. He was a city counsellor of Bordeaux and later its Mayor. From 1571 he lived the life of a country gentleman and started composing his *Essais*, a classic of French literature.

61 *Certes, c'est un sujet merveilleusement vain, divers et ondoyant, que l'homme.*

Man (in good earnest) is a marvellous vain, fickle, and unstable subject.

1580 *Essais*, bk.1, ch.1 (translated by Charles Cotton).

62 *Il faut estre tousjours boté et prest à partir.*

We should always be booted and spurred, and ready to go.

1580 *Essais*, bk.1, ch.20 (translated by Charles Cotton).

63 *Que la mort me trouve plantant mes choux, mais nonchalant d'elle, et encore plus de mon jardin imparfait.*

I would like death to come to me while I am planting cabbages, caring little for death and even less for the imperfection of my garden.

1580 *Essais*, bk.1, ch.20 (translated by Charles Cotton).

64 *Si on me presse de dire pourquoy je l'aymois, je sens que cela ne peut s'exprimer, qu'en respondant: 'Parce que c'estoit luy; par ce que c'estoit moy.'*

If a man should importune me to give a reason why I loved him, I find it could no otherwise be expressed, than by making answer: because it was he, because it was I.

1580 *Essais*, bk.1, ch.28 (translated by Charles Cotton).

65 *Or la fin, ce crois-je, en est tout'une, d'en vivre plus à loisir et à son aise.*

Now the end, I take it, is all one, to live at more leisure and at one's ease.

1580 *Essais*, bk.1, ch.34 (translated by Charles Cotton).

66 *Il se faut reserver une arriere boutique toute nostre, toute franche, en laquelle nous establissons nostre vraye liberté et principale retraite et solitude.*

We must reserve a backshop, wholly our own and entirely free, wherein to settle our true liberty, our principle solitude and retreat.

1580 *Essais*, bk.1, ch.34 (translated by Charles Cotton).

67 *La plus grande chose du monde, c'est de sçavoir estre a soy.*

The greatest thing in the world is for a man to know that he is his own.

1580 *Essais*, bk.1, ch.34 (translated by Charles Cotton).

68 *La gloire et le repos sont choses qui ne peuvent loger en même gîte.*

Fame and tranquility are two things that can't live under the same roof.

1580 *Essais*, bk.1, ch.39 (translated by Charles Cotton).

69 *Mon mestier et mon art, c'est vivre.*

My trade and art is to live.
1580 *Essais*, bk.2, ch.6 (translated by Charles Cotton).

70 *Quand je me joüe à ma chatte, qui sçait si elle passe son temps de moy plus que je ne fay d'elle?*

When I play with my cat, who knows whether I do not make her more sport than she makes me?
1580 *Essais*, bk.2, ch.12 (translated by Charles Cotton).

71 *L'homme est bien insensé. Il ne saurait forger un ciron, et forge des Dieux à douzaines.*

Man is quite insane. He wouldn't know how to make a maggot, and he makes Gods by the dozen.
1580 *Essais*, bk.2, ch.12 (translated by Charles Cotton).

72 *Nous veillons dormans, et veillans dormons.*

We wake sleeping, and sleep waking.
1580 *Essais*, bk.2, ch.12 (translated by Charles Cotton).

73 There is no end to our researches; our end is in the other world.
1588 *Essays*, bk.3, ch.13 (translated by Donald M Frame, 1963)

74 *Nostre grand et glorieux chef-d'oeuvre, c'est vivre à propos.*

The great and glorious masterpiece of man is to know how to live to purpose.
1588 *Essais*, bk.3, ch.13 (translated by Charles Cotton).

75 *Nous sommes par tout vent.*

We are all wind throughout.
1588 *Essais*, bk.3, ch.13 (translated by Charles Cotton).

Montcalm, Marquis de 1712–59

French Governor of Quebec, who unsuccessfully defended the city against General Wolfe's English troops in the Battle of the Plains of Abraham, 13 Sep 1759.

76 I am happy that I shall not live to see the surrender of Quebec.
1759 Spoken to his aides, 13 Sep. He died the following day. Quoted in Francis Parkman *Montcalm and Wolfe* (1884).

Monterroso, Augusto 1921–

Uruguayan writer. His works are mainly collections of short stories in which paradox and a whimsical sense of humour are prominent.

77 *La Historia no se detiene nunca. Día y noche su marcha es incesante. Querer detenerla sería como querer detener la Geografía.*

History never stops. It progresses ceaselessly day and night. Trying to stop it is like trying to stop Geography.
1978 *Lo demás es silencio* (The Rest is Silence), 'Aforismos, dichos, etc'.

Montesquieu, Charles Louis de Secondat, Baron de la Brède et de 1689–1755

French philosopher and jurist, who turned from law to scientific research and literary work. His study of legal and social issues *De l'esprit des lois* (The Spirit of Laws, 1748) was very influential in 18c Europe.

78 *Si l'on vient à savoir mon nom, dès ce moment je me tais. Je connais une femme qui marche assez bien, mais qui boite dès qu'on la regarde.*

Once someone wants to know my name, I become quiet. I know a woman who walks rather well, but who limps once she sees someone watching her.
1721 *Lettres Persanes*, introduction.

79 *Il n'y a jamais eu de royaume où il y ait eu tant de guerres civiles que dans celui du Christ.*

No kingdom has ever been so divided by civil wars as that of Christ.
1721 *Lettres Persanes*, no.29.

80 *Il faut pleurer les hommes à leur naissance, et non pas à leur mort.*

A person should be mourned at his birth, not at his death.
1721 *Lettres Persanes*, no.40.

81 *Si les triangles faisaient un dieu, ils lui donneraient trois côtés.*

If triangles had made a god, it would have three sides.
1721 *Lettres Persanes*, no.59.

82 *Le droit des gens est naturellement fondé sur ce principe: que les diverses nations doivent se faire, dans la paix, le plus de bien, et, dans la guerre, le moins de mal qu'il est possible, sans nuire à leurs véritables intérêts.*

Law is naturally founded on this principle: that different nations should do, in peace and as far as best as they can in war, the least harm as possible, without harming their true interests.
1748 *De l'Esprit des lois*, vol.1, ch.3.

83 *Le gouvernement est comme toutes les choses du monde; pour le conserver, il faut l'aimer.*

Government is like everything else in the world; to conserve it, we must love it.
1748 *De l'Esprit des lois*, vol.4, ch.5.

84 *L'amour de la démocratie est celui de l'égalité.*

Love of democracy is love of equality.
1748 *De l'Esprit des lois*, vol.5, ch.3.

85 *Les républiques finissent par le luxe; les monarchies, par la pauvreté.*

Republics end by wealth; monarchies end by poverty.
1748 *De l'Esprit des lois*, vol.7, ch.4.

86 *La liberté est le droit de faire tout ce que les lois
    permettent.*

    Freedom is the right to do anything the laws
    permit.
    1748 *De l'Esprit des lois*, vol.11, ch.3.

87 *Il en est de la luxure comme de l'avarice: elle
    augmente sa soif par l'acquisition des trésors.*

    The same rule applies for lust, as for avarice: it
    increases its thirst by the acquisition of wealth.
    1748 *De l'Esprit des lois*, vol.16, ch.6.

88 *Le divorce a ordinairement une grande utilité
    politique; et quant à l'utilité civile, il est établi pour le
    mari et pour la femme, et n'est pas toujours favorable
    aux enfants.*

    Divorce generally has a great political use; as for its
    civil use, it is established for the husband and wife
    and is never favourable to the children.
    1748 *De l'Esprit des lois*, vol.16, ch.15.

89 *Les lois inutiles affaiblissent les lois nécessaires.*

    Useless laws weaken the necessary ones.
    1748 *De l'Esprit des lois*, vol.29, ch.16.

Montgomery of Alamein, Bernard Law, 1st Viscount 1887–1976

British field marshal. He led the 8th Army in World War
II, defeating Rommel at El Alamein (1942), and was
Commander-in-Chief of Allied ground forces for the
invasion of Normandy (1944), Chief of the Imperial
General Staff (1946–8) and supreme commander of Nato
forces in Europe (1951–8).

90 Rule 1, on page 1 of the book of war is: 'Do not
    march on Moscow'…[Rule 2] is: 'Do not go
    fighting with your land armies in China.'
    1962 Speech in the House of Lords, 30 May.

Montrose, James Graham, 1st Marquis of 1612–50

Scottish soldier and poet, who, after first supporting the
National Covenant in 1638, fought a brilliant campaign
for Charles I during the Civil War from 1644 to 1645.
Captured in 1650 after an abortive attempt to win
Scotland for Charles II, he was hanged in Edinburgh.

91 My dear and only love, I pray
    That little world of thee
    Be governed by no other sway
    Than purest monarchy.
    'My Dear and Only Love', stanza 1.

92 He either fears his fate too much,
    Or his deserts are small,
    That dares not put it to the touch,
    To gain or lose it all.
    'My Dear and Only Love', stanza 2.

93 Let them bestow on every airth a limb,
    Then open all my veins that I may swim
    To thee, my Maker, in that crimson lake;
    Then place my parboiled head upon a stake,
    Scatter my ashes, strew them in the air—
    Lord! since thou knowest where all these atoms are,
    I'm hopeful thou'lt recover once my dust,
    And confident thou'lt raise me with the just.
    1650 'Lines Composed on the Eve of his Execution'.

Moodie, Susanna née *Strickland* 1803–85

English-born Canadian writer of fiction, non-fiction,
poetry and letters. She reluctantly emigrated to Canada
with her husband in 1832 and wrote for many magazines
but is best remembered for *Roughing it in the Bush* (1852)
and *Life in the Clearing, versus the Bush* (1853).

94 Dear husband! I take shame to myself that my
    purpose was less firm, that my heart lingered so far
    behind yours in preparing for this great epoch in
    our lives; that like Lot's wife, I still turned and
    looked back, and clung with all my strength to the
    land I was leaving. It was not the hardships of an
    emigrant's life I dreaded. I could bear mere physical
    privations philosophically enough; it was the loss of
    society in which I had moved, the want of
    congenial minds, of persons engaged in congenial
    pursuits, that made me so reluctant to respond to
    my husband's call.
    1852 *Roughing it in the Bush; or, A Life in Canada*, ch.11, 'The
    Charivari'.

95 If these sketches should prove the means of
    deterring one family from sinking their property,
    and shipwrecking all their hopes, by going to reside
    in the backwoods of Canada, I shall consider
    myself amply repaid for revealing the secrets of the
    prison-house, and feel that I have not toiled and
    suffered in the wilderness in vain.
    1852 *Roughing it in the Bush; or, A Life in Canada*, ch.19 'Adieu
    to the Woods'.

96 Speaking of the coldness of one particular day, a
    genuine brother Jonathan remarked, with
    charming simplicity, that it was thirty degrees
    below zero that morning, and it would have been
    much colder if the thermometer had been longer.
    1852 *Roughing it in the Bush; or, A Life in Canada*. 'Brother
    Jonathan' refers to a typical Yankee.

97 In most instances, emigration is a matter of
    necessity, not of choice.
    1854 *Roughing it in the Bush; or, A Life in Canada*,
    introduction to the 3rd edition.

98 Will they ever forgive me for writing *Roughing It?*
    They know that it was the truth, but have I not
    been a mark for every vulgar editor of a village
    journal, throughout the length and breadth of the

land to hurl a stone at, and point out as the enemy to Canada.

1856 Letter to her publisher, Richard Bentley, 19 Aug.

Moody, William Vaughn 1869–1910

US poet and playwright. He taught at the University of Chicago. His best known prose play, *The Sabine Woman* (1906), was highly successful and focuses on the contrast between a puritanical woman and a free-thinking man. It was retitled *The Great Divide* (1909).

99 A man's a fool to look at things too near:
   They look back, and begin to cut up queer.
   1901 'The Menagerie'.

Moore, Brian 1921–99

Northern-Irish born writer, who emigrated to Canada in 1948, and also lived in California and New York. His first novel, *The Lonely Passion of Judith Hearne* (1955) was filmed in 1989. Later works include *Black Robe* (1985, filmed 1991), *Lies of Silence* (1990) and *The Statement* (1995).

1 He bathes daily in a running tap of words.
   1987 Of a military colonel's desk work. *The Color of Blood.*

Moore, Charles W(illard) 1925–

US architect, Professor of Architecture at UCLA, California (1975–85). His writings include *The Place of Houses* (1974) and *The Poetics of Gardens* (1988).

2 You bind the goods and trappings of your life together with your dreams to make a place that is uniquely your own.
   1994 On building a house. In the *New York Times*, 20 Oct.

Moore, Clement 1779–1863

US writer and poet.

3 'Twas the night before Christmas, when all through the house
   Not a creature was stirring, not even a mouse.
   1822 *The Night Before Christmas.*

4 The stockings were hung by the chimney with care,
   In hopes that St. Nicholas soon would be there;
   The children were nestled all snug in their beds,
   While visions of sugarplums danced in their heads.
   1822 *The Night Before Christmas.*

5 The moon on the breast of the new-fallen snow,
   Gave the lustre of midday to objects below,
   When, what to my wondering eyes should appear,
   But a miniature sleigh, and eight tiny reindeer.
   1822 *The Night Before Christmas.*

6 More rapid than eagles his coursers they came,
   And he whistled, and shouted, and called them by
      name;

'Now, *Dasher!* Now, *Dancer!* Now, *Prancer* and
   Vixen!
On, *Comet!* On, *Cupid!* On, *Donder* and *Blitzen!*
To the top of the porch! To the top of the wall!
Now dash away! Dash away! Dash away all!'
1822 *The Night Before Christmas.*

7 He was dressed all in fur, from his head to his foot,
   And his clothes were all tarnished with ashes and
      soot;
   A bundle of toys he had flung on his back,
   And he looked like a pedlar just opening his pack.
   1822 *The Night Before Christmas.*

8 He sprang to his sleigh, to his team gave a whistle,
   And away they all flew like the down of a thistle.
   But I heard him exclaim, ere he drove out of sight,
   'Happy Christmas to all. And to all a good night.'
   1822 *The Night Before Christmas.*

Moore, G(eorge) E(dward) 1873–1958

English Empiricist philosopher. He studied and taught at Cambridge, where he was Professor of Mental Philosophy and Logic (1925–39). His most famous and influential work was *Principia Ethica* (1903).

9 'Good', then, if we mean by it that quality which we assert to belong to a thing, when we say that the thing is good, is incapable of any definition, in the most important sense of the word.
   1903 *Principia Ethica*, ch.1.

10 By far the most valuable things, which we know or can imagine, are certain states of consciousness, which may be roughly described as the pleasures of human intercourse and the enjoyment of beautiful objects.
   1903 *Principia Ethica*, ch.6.

Moore, George 1852–1933

Irish novelist, poet and playwright. A co-founder of the Irish Literary Theatre with W B Yeats, he collaborated with Yeats on such poetic dramas as *The Bending of the Bough* (1900) and *Diarmuid and Grania* (1901).

11 A year passed; a year of art and dissipation—one part art, two parts dissipation. We mounted and descended at pleasure the rounds of society's ladder.
   1870 *Confessions of a Young Man* (published 1888).

12 Acting is therefore the lowest of the arts, if it be an art at all.
   1891 *Impressions and Opinions*, 'Mummer-Worship'.

Moore, Henry Spencer 1898–1986

English sculptor and graphic artist. He travelled widely in Europe and was an official war artist (1940–2). His sculptures, mainly semi-abstract figures and groups, are influenced by landscape forms and primitive art.

13　Sculpture in stone should look honestly like stone…to make it look like flesh and blood, hair and dimples is coming down to the level of the stage conjuror.

1930 In the *Architectural Association Journal*.

Moore, John 1729–1802

Scottish physician and writer. He travelled with Douglas, Duke of Hamilton (1772–8), writing accounts of these journeys, then settled in London. His novel *Zeluco* (1789) was the inspiration for Byron's *Childe Harold*.

14　There is no manner of doubt that a town surrounded by water is a very fine sight; but a town surrounded by land is much finer. Can there be any comparison in point of beauty, between the dull monotony of a watery surface, and the delightful variety of gardens, meadows, hills and woods ?

c.1780 *A View of Society and Manners in Italy*.

Moore, Lorrie 1957–

American writer. Her writings include collections of short stories and the novel, *Who Will Run the Frog Hospital?* (1994).

15　Literature…is lonely and waited for, brilliant and pure and frightened, a marriage of birds, a conversation of the blind.

1988 In the *New York Times*, 10 Jul.

Moore, Marianne Craig 1887–1972

US poet, whose crisp language, wit and idiosyncratic style established her as a leading literary figure. Her works include *Observations* (1924, rev 1925), *Collected Poems* (1951, Pulitzer Prize) and *Complete Poems* (1967, rev 1981).

16　It comes to this: of whatever sort it is,
　　it must be 'lit with piercing glances into the life of things';
　　it must acknowledge the spiritual forces which have made it.

1921 *Poems*, 'When I Buy Pictures'.

17　I, too, dislike it: there are things that are important beyond all this fiddle.
　　Reading it, however, with a perfect contempt for it, one discovers in
　　it, after all, a place for the genuine.

1921 *Poems*, 'Poetry'.

18　If 'compression is the first grace of style,' you have it.

1924 *Observations*, 'To A Snail'.

19　My father used to say,
　　'Superior people never make long visits, have to be shown Longfellow's grave or the glass flowers at Harvard.'

1924 *Observations*, 'Silence'.

20　Nor was he insincere in saying, 'Make my house your inn.'
　　Inns are not residencies.

1924 *Observations*, 'Silence'.

21　You are menaced by the goodness of your mechanics.

1937 To fellow-poet Elizabeth Bishop. Quoted in David Kalstone *Becoming a Poet* (1989), p.57.

22　A place as kind as it is green,
　　the greenest place I've never seen.
　　Every name is a tune.

1941 *What Are Years*, 'Spencer's Ireland'.

23　I do not write for money or fame… One writes because one has a burning desire to objectify what it is indispensible to one's happiness to express.

1956 Ewing Lecture, University of California, 3 Oct.

24　Omissions are not accidents.

1956 Ewing Lecture, University of California, 3 Oct.

25　O to be a dragon,
　　a symbol of the power of Heaven—of silkworm size or immense; at times invisible.
　　Felicitous phenomenon!

1959 *O To Be A Dragon*, 'O To Be A Dragon'.

26　A connoisseur of tame excitement.

1960 Self-description, in *Vogue*, 1 Aug.

27　Any writer overwhelmingly honest about pleasing himself is almost sure to please others.

1963 In *Vogue*, 15 Aug.

28　I am governed by the pull of the sentence as the pull of a fabric is governed by gravity.

Quoted in Louis Untermeyer 'Five Famous Poetesses', in *Ladies' Home Journal*, May 1964.

29　Subjects choose me… I lie in wait like a leopard on a branch-strained metaphor.

Quoted in Louis Untermeyer 'Five Famous Poetesses', in *Ladies' Home Journal*, May 1964.

30　Omissions are not accidents.

1967 Epigraph to *Complete Poems*.

31　To cite passages is to pull one quill from a porcupine.

Quoted in Patricia C Willis (ed) *The Complete Prose of Marianne Moore* (1986).

Moore, Thomas 1780–1852

Irish poet, songwriter and biographer. He wrote a number of patriotic songs and poems as well as lives of Sheridan, Byron (a close friend) and others. He also wrote satirical pieces and novels, including *The Fudge Family in Paris* (1818). He is remembered for *Lallah Rookh* (1817), a series of oriental tales in verse, and for the popular songs

'The Harp that once through Tara's Halls', 'The Minstrel-boy', and 'Tis the Last Rose of Summer'.

32 There is not in the wide world a valley so sweet
As that vale in whose bosom the bright waters
meet;
Oh! the last rays of feeling and life must depart
Ere the bloom of that valley shall fade from my
heart.
1807 *Irish Melodies*, 'The Meeting of the Waters'.

33 Let Erin remember the days of Old,
Ere her faithless sons betrayed her;
When Malachi wore the collar of gold
Which he won from her proud invader;
When her kings, with standards of green unfurled,
Led the Red-Branch Knights to danger;
Ere the emerald gem of the western world
Was set in the crown of a stranger.
1807 *Irish Melodies*, 'Let Erin Remember'.

34 The Minstrel-boy to the war is gone,
In the ranks of death you'll find him;
His father's sword he has girded on,
And his wild harp slung behind him.
1807 *Irish Melodies*, 'The Minstrel-boy'.

35 'Tis the last rose of summer
Left blooming alone;
All her lovely companions
Are faded and gone.
1807 *Irish Melodies*, ''Tis the last Rose of Summer'.

36 The harp that once through Tara's halls
The soul of music shed,
Now hangs as mute on Tara's walls
As if that soul were fled.
1807 *Irish Melodies*, 'The Harp that once through Tara's Halls'.

37 No, there's nothing half so sweet in life
As love's young dream.
1807 *Irish Melodies*, 'Love's Young Dream'.

38 Oh! ever thus, from childhood's hour,
I've seen my fondest hopes decay;
I never loved a tree or flower,
But 'twas the first to fade away.
I never nursed a dear gazelle,
To glad me with its soft black eye,
But when it came to know me well,
And love me, it was sure to die!
1817 *Lallah Rookh*, 'The Fire Worshippers'.

39 Yet, who can help loving the land that has taught us
Six hundred and eighty-five ways to dress eggs?
1818 *The Fudge Family in Paris*, letter 8.

Moorhouse, Geoffrey 1931–

English writer and traveller. He attempted to cross the Sahara from Mauretania to the Nile, but in March 1973,

having travelled 2,000 miles (3,200 km), 300 miles (480 km) on foot after the last of his camels died, he reached Tamanrasset and gave up.

40 There was nothing but pain in the desert, for
human beings and animals alike. Life was pain.
Only in death was there relief.
1974 *The Fearful Void*.

Moran, Richard John McMoran Wilson, 2nd Baron 1924–

British diplomat and soldier. He filled a succession of diplomatic posts, including High Commissioner in Canada (1981–4). As John Wilson he wrote a Whitbread Award-winning biography of Sir Henry Campbell-Bannerman (1973)

41 Courage is a moral quality; it is not a chance gift of
nature, like an aptitude for games. It is a cold
choice between two alternatives; the fixed resolve
not to quit, an act of renunciation that must be
made not once but many times by the power of the
will.
1945 *The Anatomy of Courage*.

More, Sir Thomas 1478–1534

English statesman, scholar and writer. Educated at Oxford in the new humanism, he was appointed Lord Chancellor by Henry VIII. He refused to take the oath of supremacy and was executed. His most famous work is *Utopia* (1516; translated into English 1556); other works include *History of King Richard III* (1513) and meditations in prison.

42 In the first place, most princes apply themselves to
the arts of war, in which I have neither ability nor
interest, instead of to the good arts of peace. They
are generally more set on acquiring new kingdoms
by hook or by crook than on governing well those
that they already have.
1516 *Utopia* (English translation 1556), bk.1.

43 It is only natural, of course, that each man should
think his own opinions best: the old crow loves his
fledglings, and the ape his cubs.
1516 *Utopia* (English translation 1556), bk.1.

44 Such proud, obstinate, ridiculous judgements I
have encountered many times, and once even in
England.
1516 *Utopia* (English translation 1556), bk.1.

45 Severe and terrible punishments are enacted against
theft, when it would be much better to enable every
man to earn his own living, instead of being driven
to the awful necessity of stealing and then dying for
it.
1516 *Utopia* (English translation 1556), bk.1.

46 The law of Moses is harsh and severe, as for an
enslaved and stubborn people, but it punishes theft

with a fine, not death. Let us not think that in his new law of mercy, where he treats us with the tenderness of a father, God has given us greater license to be cruel to one another.
1516 *Utopia* (English translation 1556), bk.1.

47 A king who wants to maintain an army can never have too much gold.
1516 *Utopia* (English translation 1556), bk.1.

48 A king has no dignity when he exercises authority over beggars, only when he rules over prosperous and happy subjects.
1516 *Utopia* (English translation 1556), bk.1.

49 The only real thing they accomplish that I can see is to make men feel a little more secure in their consciences about doing evil.
1516 Of preachers. *Utopia* (English translation 1556), bk.1.

50 Hardly any of the women, who are a full half of the population, work; or if they do, then as a rule their husbands lie snoring in bed.
1516 *Utopia* (English translation 1556), bk.2.

51 For where money is the standard of everything, many vain, superfluous trades are bound to be carried on simply to satisfy luxury and licentiousness.
1516 *Utopia* (English translation 1556), bk.2.

52 The chief aim of their constitution is that, whenever public needs permit, all citizens should be free, so far as possible, to withdraw their time and energy from the service of the body, and devote themselves to the freedom and culture of the mind. For that, they think, is the real happiness of life.
1516 *Utopia* (English translation 1556), bk.2.

53 They find pearls by the seashore, diamonds and rubies in certain cliffs, but never go out of set purpose to look for them. If they happen to find some, they polish them, and give them to the children who, when they are small, feel proud and pleased with such gaudy decorations. But after, when they grow a bit older, and notice that only babies like such toys, they lay them aside. Their parents don't have to say anything, they simply put these trifles away out of a shamefaced sense that they're no longer suitable, just as our children when they grow up put away their rattles, marbles and dolls.
1516 *Utopia* (English translation 1556), bk.2.

54 Thus they say that nature herself prescribes for us a joyous life, in other words, pleasure, as the goal of our actions; and living according to her prescriptions is to be defined as virtue.
1516 *Utopia* (English translation 1556), bk.2.

55 Two evils—greed and faction—are the destruction of all justice.
1516 *Utopia* (English translation 1556), bk.2.

56 Is not this house as nigh heaven as my own?
c.1534 Of the Tower of London. Attributed in William Roper *Life of Sir Thomas More* (ed E V Hitchcock, 1935).

57 I pray you, master Lieutenant, see me safe up, and my coming down let me shift for myself.
1535 On mounting the scaffold. Attributed in William Roper *Life of Sir Thomas More* (ed E V Hitchcock, 1935).

58 This hath not offended the king.
1535 Said on the scaffold as he drew his beard to one side. Attributed in William Roper *Life of Sir Thomas More* (ed E V Hitchcock, 1935).

Morell, Thomas 1703–84
English poet and librettist.

59 See, the conquering hero comes! Sound the trumpets, beat the drums!
1747 *Judas Maccabeus*, 'A Chorus of Youths'.

Morey, Larry
US lyricist who frequently worked with Frank Churchill. Best known for contributing to *Snow White and the Seven Dwarfs* (1937) and *Bambi* (1941).

60 Heigh ho, heigh ho It's off to work we go.
1937 First lines of the song 'Heigh-Ho' from the film *Snow White and the Seven Dwarfs*. Music by Frank Churchill.

61 Whistle While You Work.
1937 Title of song from the film *Snow White and the Seven Dwarfs*. Music by Frank Churchill.

Morgan, Edwin George 1920–
Scottish poet. He lectured in English at Glasgow University, and wrote criticism. One of the most important Scottish writers, he is a skilled translator as well as an original poet.

62 Many things are unspoken In the life of a man, and with a place there is an unspoken love also in undercurrents, drifting, waiting its time.
1968 'The Second Life'.

63 And later, wondering farmers as they passed would hear beyond the lighted window in the autumn evening two handsome yellow-bosomed basset-hounds howling to a melodious basset-horn.
1968 'An Addition to the Family'.

64 Deplore what is to be deplored, and then find out the rest.
1968 'King Billy'.

65 The man lies late since he has lost his job,
smokes on one elbow, letting his coughs fall
thinly into an air too poor to rob.
1973 'Glasgow Sonnets, I'.

66 No deliverer ever rose
from these stone tombs to get the hell they made
unmade.
1973 'Glasgow Sonnets, II'.

Morgan, Elaine 1920–

British science writer, journalist and playwright. She
worked on the award-winning television screening of Vera
Brittain's *Testament of Youth* (1980). Her controversial
book *The Descent of Woman* (1972), which explores the
origins of mankind, with special reference to women's
evolution, was followed by *The Aquatic Ape* (1982).

67 It takes two to make a woman into a sex object.
1972 *The Descent of Woman*, ch.11.

Moritz, Karl Philipp 1756–93

German writer, an early Romantic. After travelling in
England and Italy he wrote *Reisen eines Deutschen in
England* (1783) and *Reisen eines Deutschen in Italien*
(1792–3). His autobiographical novel *Anton Reise*
(1785–90) influenced Goethe.

68 When you see how in this happy country the
lowest and poorest member of society takes an
interest in all public affairs; when you see how high
and low, rich and poor, are all willing to declare
their feelings and convictions; when you see how a
carter, a common sailor, a beggar is still a man, nay,
even more, an Englishman—then, believe me, you
find yourself very differently affected from the
experience you feel when staring at our soldiers
drilling in Berlin.
1782 Letter to a friend after observing a London by-election.

Morley, Christopher Darlington
1890–1957

US writer and poet, founder and editor (1924–41) of the
Saturday Review. His many novels include *Parnassus on
Wheels* (1917).

69 Life is a foreign language: all men mispronounce it.
1925 *Thunder on the Left*, ch.14.

70 Dancing is a wonderful training for girls, it's the
first way you learn to guess what a man is going to
do before he does it.
1939 *Kitty Foyle*, ch.11.

71 When you sell a man a book, you don't sell him 12
ounces of paper and ink and glue—you sell him a
whole new life.
Recalled on his death, 28 Mar 1957.

Morley, Robert 1908–92

English actor. A popular comic actor, he also made many
film and television appearances, including *Beat the Devil*
(1953), *Oscar Wilde* (1960) and *Who is Killing the Great
Chefs of Europe?* (1978).

72 The French are a logical people, which is one
reason the English dislike them so intensely. The
other is that they own France, a country which we
have always judged to be much too good for them.
1974 *A Musing Morley*, 'France and the French'.

73 It is a great help for a man to be in love with
himself. For an actor, it is absolutely essential.
1979 In *Playboy*.

74 I started off in films as a king—a French king,
admittedly, but nevertheless a king in *Marie
Antoinette*—and stayed in that sort of income
bracket
Quoted in *The Best of Robert Morley* (1981).

75 Anyone who works is a fool. I don't work: I merely
inflict myself on the public.
Attributed.

Morris, Desmond John 1928–

British anthropologist.

76 The Human Zoo.
1969 Title of book.

Morris, Jan formerly James Morris 1926–

English reporter and writer. As James Morris he wrote books
and essays on travel. He accompanied the 1953 first ascent
of Everest, covering it for *The Times*. As Jan Morris she has
written a moving account of her sex change *Conundrum*
(1974), the *Pax Britannica* trilogy and a novel about a
fictional Mediterranean city *Last Letters from Hav* (1985).

77 Venice will linger in your mind…and wherever you
go in life you will feel somewhere over your
shoulder, a pink, castellated, shimmering presence,
the domes and riggings and crooked pinnacles of
the Serenissima. There's romance for you! There's
the lust and dark wine of Venice! No wonder
George Eliot's husband fell into the Grand Canal.
1960 *Venice*.

78 The genius of Canada remains essentially a
deflationary genius.
1976 'On the Confederation Special,' in *Travels*.

Morris, John 1895–1980

English writer, traveller and academic. He travelled in Asia
and Africa, and took part in two Everest expeditions. He
taught at Keio University in Japan (1938–42) and later
became Head of the Far Eastern Service then Controller of
the Third Programme at the BBC (1952–8).

79 The Japanese…have a saying that there are two

kinds of fool: those who have never climbed Mount Fuji, and those who have climbed it more than once.
1943 *Traveller from Tokyo*.

Morris, Sir Lewis

English versifier.

80 We hold a vaster Empire than has been.
'Song of Empire', written to celebrate Queen Victoria's Jubilee, 20 Jun. The words were printed on Canada's first commemorative postage stamp, 1898.

Morris, William 1834–96

English craftsman and poet, associated with the Pre-Raphaelite Brotherhood, a major figure in the Arts and Crafts Movement. He joined the Social Democratic Federation in 1883, and organized the Socialist League. In 1890 he set up the private Kelmscott Press.

81 The Socialist papers…came out full to the throat of well-printed matter…admirable and straightforward expositions of the doctrines and practice of Socialism, free from haste and spite and hard words…with a kind of May-day freshness amidst the worry and terror of the moment.
1890 *News from Nowhere*

82 Between complete socialism and communism there is no difference whatever in my mind.
Communism is in fact the completion of socialism; when that ceases to be militant and becomes triumphant, it will be communism.
1893 Addressing Hammersmith Socialist Society.

Morris, Wright Marion 1910–98

US writer. He wrote novels, short stories, memoirs and critical essays. He was an accomplished photographer, and published several books marrying text with photographs.

83 A Bill of Rites, A Bill of Wrongs, A Bill of Goods.
1968 Title of essay collection.

Morrison, R F

84 Just a wee deoch-an-doris,
Just a wee yin, that's a'.
Just a wee deoch-an-doris,
Afore we gang awa'.
There's a wee wifie waitin'
In a wee but-an-ben;
If ye can say 'It's a braw bricht moonlicht nicht',
Ye're a' richt, ye ken.
1911 'Just a Wee Deoch-an-Doris', chorus. The song was popularized by Sir Harry Lauder.

Morrison, Toni Chloe Anthony *née Wofford* 1931–

Black US novelist. Her novels have reflected black American experience and consciousness through a

sophisticated literary sensibility. She was awarded the Nobel Prize for Literature in 1993.

85 We have to acknowledge that the thing we call 'literature' is more pluralistic now, just as society ought to be. The melting pot never worked.
1981 In *Newsweek*, 30 Mar.

86 How soon country people forget. When they fall in love with a city it is forever, and it is like forever… There, in a city, they are not so much new as themselves: their stronger, riskier selves.
1991 *Jazz*, ch.2.

87 In this country American means white. Everybody else has to hyphenate.
1992 In *The Guardian*, 29 Jan.

88 Slavery broke the world in half, it broke it in every way. It broke Europe. It made them into something else, it made them slave masters, it made them crazy. You can't do that for hundreds of years and it not take a toll. They had to dehumanize, not just the slaves but themselves.
Quoted in Paul Gilroy *Small Acts* (1993), 'Living memory: a meeting with Toni Morrison'.

89 I have always wanted to develop a way of writing that was irrevocably black. I don't have the resources of a musician but I thought that if it was truly black literature, it would not be black because I was, it would not even be black because of its subject matter. It would be something intrinsic, indigenous, something in the way it was put together—the sentences, the structure, texture and tone—so that anyone who read it would realize.
Quoted in Paul Gilroy *Small Acts* (1993), 'Living memory: a meeting with Toni Morrison'.

Morse, Samuel F(inley) B(reese) 1791–1872

US inventor and painter, who demonstrated (1844) the practicability of an electrical telegraph device to Congress. He had earlier trained as an artist.

90 Alas! My dear sir, the very name of *pictures* produces a sadness of heart I cannot describe. Painting has been a smiling mistress to many, but she has been a cruel jilt to me.
1849 Letter to his friend the writer James Fenimore Cooper, 20 Nov.

Mortimer, Sir John Clifford 1923–

English playwright, novelist and barrister. Called to the bar in 1948, he took part in several celebrated civil cases before achieving wider fame as a writer, notably as creator of the fictitious barrister Horace Rumpole. His other publications include the novels *Paradise Postponed* (1985) and *Summer's Lease* (1988) and several plays.

91 No brilliance is needed in the law. Nothing but common sense, and relatively clean finger nails.
1971 *A Voyage Round My Father*, act 1.

92 The law seems like a sort of maze through which a client must be led to safety, a collection of reefs, rocks, and underwater hazards through which he or she must be piloted.
1982 *Clinging to the Wreckage*, ch.7.

93 They do you a decent death in the hunting field.
1985 *Paradise Postponed*, ch.18.

94 The shelf life of the modern hardback writer is somewhere between the milk and the yoghurt.
1987 In *The Observer*, 28 Jun.

95 Life itself is a mystery which defies solution.
1990 In *The Sunday Times*, 1 Apr.

96 But plots come from—God knows where. They can't be summoned at will. They come reluctantly, unexpectedly, stealthily, when you have given up hope of them ever paying you a visit.
1993 'A Plot at Last', in Brown and Munro (eds) *Writers Writing* (1993).

Mortimer, (Charles) Raymond Bell
1895–1980

English literary and art critic.

97 People don't learn to enjoy pictures because they seldom look at them; and they seldom look at pictures because they have never learnt to enjoy them.
1976 *Try Anything Once*.

Morton, Jelly Roll (Ferdinand) 1890–1941

US jazz pianist. He was an important pioneer of the New Orleans jazz style, but was much given to making extravagant claims about his role in it.

98 It is evidently known, beyond contradiction, that New Orleans is the cradle of *jazz*, and I, myself, happened to be the creator in the year 1902… *Jazz* music is a style, not compositions; any kind of music may be played in *jazz*, if one has the knowledge.
1938 In *Downbeat*, Aug.

Morton, J(ohn Cameron Andrieu) B(ingham Michael) pseudonym Beachcomber 1893–1979

English writer. He wrote many books of humour, fantasy, satire and history, but is chiefly remembered for his humorous columns in the *Daily Express*, under the nom de plume 'Beachcomber'.

99 One disadvantage of being a hog is that at any moment some blundering fool may try to make a silk purse out of your wife's ear.
1931 *By the Way*.

1 Hush, hush!
Nobody cares!
Christopher Robin
Has
  Fallen
   Down
    Stairs
1931 *By the Way*.

2 The Doctor is said also to have invented an extraordinary weapon which will make war less brutal. It is described as a very powerful liquid which rots braces at a distance of a mile.
1936 'Bracerot'.

Morton, Rogers Clark Ballard 1914–1979

US former Republican politician. He was president of a flour manufacturing company and representative for Maryland in the 88th–92nd Congresses. He was Secretary of the Interior (1971–5) and a counsellor to the President on economic and domestic matters (1976–7).

3 I have no intention of rearranging the furniture on the deck of the Titanic.
1976 On declining to rescue President Ford's disastrous election campaign.

Morton, Thomas c.1764–1838

English playwright. He is usually remembered for his comedy *Speed the Plough* (1798).

4 What will Mrs Grundy say? What will Mrs Grundy think?
1798 *Speed the Plough*.

Moses, Anna Mary Robertson known as 'Grandma Moses' 1860–1961

US painter. The wife of a farmer in New York state, with no art training, she did not begin painting until in her 70s. Her primitive paintings are colourful, simple scenes of everyday rural life.

5 Paintin's not important. What's important is keepin' busy.
1954 In news summaries, 2 Jan.

Mosk, Stanley 1912–

US lawyer and Justice of State Supreme Court. He practised law in Los Angeles until 1939 and was Attorney General of California 1959–64. Since 1964 he has been a Justice of the Supreme Court of California.

6 Little old ladies in tennis shoes.
Characterizing older, activist women. Quoted in William Safire *Safire's Political Dictionary* (1975).

Moss, Gary

US marketing executive, vice-president of marketing communications, Campbell Soup Co.

7 You can teach an elephant to dance, but the likelihood of its stepping on your toes is very high.

1993 On the decline of the advertising agencies' monopoly in marketing. In *Forbes,* 15 Mar.

Moss, Stirling 1929–

English racing driver. Though he never won the World Championship, he became one of the most celebrated of all drivers, winning numerous Grand Prix races driving for a variety of teams. He retired in 1962 after a serious crash.

8 It is necessary to relax your muscles when you can. Relaxing your brain is fatal.

1955 In *Newsweek,* 16 May.

9 There are two things no man will admit he can't do well—drive and make love.

Quoted in Colin Jarman *The Guinness Dictionary of Sports Quotations* (1990).

Motherwell, Robert 1915–91

US painter and writer, an exponent of Abstract Realism. His works typically consist of large, amorphous blocks of strong colour, such as his most famous series, *Elegies to the Spanish Republic* (1975).

10 One of the most striking of abstract art's appearance is her nakedness, an art stripped bare.

1951 Paper given at a symposium, 5 Feb, at the Museum of Modern Art, New York, published in *What Abstract Art Means to Me: Bulletin of the Museum of Modern Art* (Spring 1951).

11 Every intelligent painter carries the whole culture of modern painting in his head…everything he paints is both an homage and a critique.

1977 In the *Los Angeles Times,* 31 Jul.

12 All my life I've been working on the work—every canvas a sentence or paragraph of it. Each picture is only an approximation of what I want.

Recalled on his death, 16 Jul 1991.

Mountbatten of Burma, Louis Francis Albert Victor Nicholas, 1st Earl 1900–79

English admiral and statesman, chief of Combined Operations Command (1942) in World War II. As Supreme Commander, SE Asia, he received the Japanese surrender at Singapore, and in 1947 became last Viceroy of India. He returned to the Admiralty as First Sea Lord (1954) and Chief of the Defence Staff (1959). He retired in 1965 but was assassinated by Irish Republican terrorists.

13 As a military man who has given half a century of active service, I say in all sincerity that the nuclear arms race has no military purpose. Wars cannot be fought with nuclear weapons; their existence only

adds to our perils because of the illusions that they have generated. The world now stands on the brink of the final abyss. Let us all resolve to take all possible practicable steps to ensure that we do not, through our own folly, go over edge.

1979 Speech at the Council of Europe in Strasbourg, 11 May.

Moynihan, Daniel Patrick 1927–

US sociologist and diplomat, advisor to Presidents Kennedy, Johnson and Nixon. He was Ambassador to India (1973–5), US representative to the UN (1975–6), and subsequently a Senator and chair of the Senate finance committee (1993). His writings include *Beyond the Melting Pot* (with Nathan Glazer, 1963).

14 We've come full circle but the best remains the heart of the city, the greatest center of the greatest city, our Acropolis, where our Christmas tree is lighted.

1991 On New York's Rockefeller Centre. In the *New York Times,* 15 Mar.

15 Things become complicated if there are enough people to complexify them.

1991 Of the 19,000-member congressional back-up staff. In the *New York Times,* 12 Nov.

16 They live off secrecy…[it] keep the mistakes secret.

1993 Of government intelligence agencies. *President Kennedy.*

17 The Lord looks after drunks and Americans.

1995 Of the avoidance of casualties in the Haitian intervention. In the *US News and World Report,* 9 Jan.

Mozart, (Johann Chrysostom) Wolfgang Amadeus 1756–91

Austrian composer. An infant prodigy, who suffered throughout his life from poverty and overwork, his many compositions include symphonies, concertos, string quintets, string quartets, numerous piano and violin sonatas, choral works and operas such as *The Marriage of Figaro* (1786), *Don Giovanni* (1787), *Cosi fan tutte* (1790) and *The Magic Flute* (1791).

18 It is much easier to play a thing quickly than to play it slowly.

1778 Letter.

19 Melody is the very essence of music. When I think of a good melodist I think of a fine race horse. A contrapuntist is only a post-horse.

1786 Letter to Michael Kelly.

Mugabe, Robert Gabriel 1924–

Zimbabwean politician. He co-founded ZANU (Zimbabwe African National Union, 1963), and on Zimbabwe's independence in 1980 became first Prime Minister (1980–7) and subsequenly President (1987–).

20 Cricket? It civilises people and creates good gentlemen. I want everyone to play cricket in

Zimbabwe. I want ours to be a nation of gentlemen.
Quoted in Helen Exley *Cricket Quotations* (1992).

Muggeridge, Malcolm 1903–90

English journalist. He was editor of *Punch* from 1953 to 1957, and appeared frequently on television as reporter and interviewer. In his later years he became a Roman Catholic.

21 The orgasm has replaced the cross as the focus of longing and the image of fulfilment.
1966 Tread Softly.

22 The media have, indeed, provided the Devil with perhaps the greatest opportunity accorded him since Adam and Eve were turned out of the Garden of Eden.
1976 *Christ and the Media*, introduction.

23 Future historians will surely see us as having created in the media a Frankenstein monster whom no one knows how to control or direct, and marvel that we should have so meekly subjected ourselves to its destructive and often malign influence.
1976 *Christ and the Media*, 'Lecture 1'.

24 It's very nearly impossible to tell the truth in television.
1976 *Christ and the Media*, 'Questions following the 3rd lecture'.

Muir, Edwin 1887–1959

Scottish writer and translator. He is best known as a poet, but also wrote literary and cultural criticism, and an autobiography.

25 The curse of Scottish literature is the lack of a whole language, which finally means the lack of a whole mind.
1936 *Scott and Scotland*, introduction.

26 The hills and towers
Stood otherwise than they should stand,
And without fear the lawless roads
Ran wrong throughout the land.
1937 *Journeys and Places*, 'Hölderlin's Journey', stanza 11.

27 There is a road that turning always
Cuts off the country of Again.
Archers stand there on every side
And as it runs time's deer is slain,
And lies where it has lain.
1937 'The Road'.

28 All through that summer at ease we lay,
And daily from the turret wall
We watched the mowers in the hay
And the enemy half a mile away.
They seemed no threat to us at all.
1946 *The Voyage*, 'The Castle', stanza 1.

29 It was not meant for human eyes,
That combat on the shabby patch
Of clods and trampled earth that lies
Somewhere beneath the sodden skies
For eye of toad or adder to catch.
1949 'The Combat'.

30 Oh these deceits are strong almost as life.
Last night I dreamt I was in the labyrinth,
And woke far on. I did not know the place.
1949 *The Labyrinth*, 'The Labyrinth'.

31 We have seen
Good men made evil wrangling with the evil,
Straight minds grown crooked fighting crooked minds.
Our peace betrayed us; we betrayed our peace.
Look at it well. This was the good town once.
1949 *The Labyrinth*, 'The Good Town'.

32 Kindness and courage can repair time's faults,
And serving him breeds patience and courtesy
In us, light sojourners and passing subjects.
1949 *The Labyrinth*, 'The Good Town'.

33 The life of every man is an endlessly repeated performance of the life of man.
1954 *An Autobiography*, ch.1.

34 Since then they have pulled our ploughs and borne our loads.
But that free servitude still can pierce our hearts.
Our life is changed; their coming our beginning.
1956 *One Foot in Eden*, 'The Horses'.

35 Barely a twelvemonth after
The seven days war that put the world to sleep,
Late in the evening the strange horses came.
1956 *One Foot in Eden*, 'The Horses'.

36 One foot in Eden still, I stand
And look across the other land.
The world's great day is growing late,
Yet strange these fields that we have planted
So long with crops of love and hate.
1956 *One Foot in Eden*, 'One Foot in Eden'.

37 Like quicksilver the scales slip down,
Upon the air the spirit flies,
And so I build me Heaven and Hell
To buy my bartered Paradise.
'The Fall'.

Muir, John 1838–1914

Scottish naturalist. He emigrated with his family to America as a boy, and became a champion of wilderness areas and the establishment of National Parks in the US.

He is regarded as the father of the environmental movement.

38 The tendency nowadays to wander in wildernesses is delightful to see. Thousands of tired, nerve-shaken, over-civilized people are beginning to find out that going to the mountains is going home; that wildness is a necessity; and that mountain parks and reservations are useful not only as fountains of timber and irrigating rivers, but as fountains of life.
1901 *Our National Parks*, ch.1, 'The Wild Parks and Forest Reservations of the West'.

39 When we contemplate the whole globe as one great dewdrop, striped and dotted with continents and islands, flying through space with other stars all singing and shining together as one, the whole universe appears as an infinite storm of beauty.
Travels in Alaska, ch.1, 'The Puget Sound and British Columbia' (published 1915).

40 I have precious little sympathy for the selfish propriety of civilized man, and if a war of races should occur between the wild beasts and Lord Man, I would be tempted to sympathise with the bears.
A Thousand-Mile Walk to the Gulf, ch.5, 'Through Florida Swamps and Forests' (published 1916).

Muir, Willa (Wilhelmina) Johnstone née Anderson also known as Agnes Neill Scott 1890–1970

Scottish poet, novelist and translator, wife of the poet Edwin Muir whose unconventional religious beliefs forced her resignation from a teaching position in 1915. Her published works include many translations, several novels and a book of poetry.

41 Apparently the average man sees woman alternately as an inferior being and as an angel.
1925 *Women: An Inquiry*, pt.1, published as Hogarth Essay no.10 in *The Hogarth Essays* (Second Series, 1926).

42 A man can be a parent without knowing it: a woman cannot.
1925 *Women: An Inquiry*, pt.1, published as Hogarth Essay no.10 in *The Hogarth Essays* (Second Series, 1926).

Muller, Herbert Joseph 1905–80

US writer.

43 Few have probably ever heard of Fra Luca Pacioli, the inventor of double-entry bookkeeping; but he has probably had much more influence on human life than has Dante or Michelangelo.
1957 *Uses of the Past*, ch.8.

Mulroney, (Martin) Brian 1939–

Canadian Conservative politician, Prime Minister (1984–93). His radical reforms included the Meech Lake

Accords (reorganizing French-speaking Quebec as a 'distinct society') and a free-trade agreement with the US.

44 In politics, madame, you need two things: friends, but above all an enemy.
1990 Remark made to a journalist following the by-election victory of Liberal leader Jean Chrétien, 10 Dec, quoted two days later by Graham Fraser in *The Globe and Mail.*

Mumford, Lewis 1895–1990

US sociologist and author. A literary critic and journal editor, he began to write on architecture and urbanization in such works as *The Story of Utopias* (1922) and *The City in History* (1961), stressing the dehumanizing effects of technology.

45 Every generation revolts against its fathers and makes friends with its grandfathers.
1931 *The Brown Decades*, p.3.

46 However far modern science and technics have fallen short of their inherent possibilities, they have taught mankind at least one lesson: Nothing is impossible.
1934 *Technics and Civilization.*

47 The Fujiyama of Architecture…at once a lofty mountain and a national shrine.
1953 Of Frank Lloyd Wright. 'A Phoenix Too Infrequent', in the *New Yorker*, 28 Nov.

48 Our national flower is the concrete cloverleaf.
Collected in *Quote Magazine*, 8 Oct 1961.

49 The life-efficiency and adaptability of the computer must be questioned. Its judicious use depends upon the availability of its human employers quite literally to keep their own heads, not merely to scrutinize the programming but to reserve for themselves the right of ultimate decision. No automatic system can be intelligently run by automatons—or by people who dare not assert human intuition, human autonomy, human purpose.
1970 *The Myth of the Machine.*

50 As full of flavor as hickory smoke.
1994 Of geotechnic expert Benton MacKaye. In *Harvard University Magazine*, Jul.

Munch, Edvard 1863–1944

Norwegian painter and graphic artist.

51 One evening, I was walking along a path, the city was on one side and the fjord below. I felt tired and ill. I stopped and looked out over the fjord—the sun was setting, and the clouds turning blood red. I sensed a scream passing through nature; it seemed to me that I heard the scream. I painted this picture, painted the clouds as actual blood. The colour shrieked. This became The Scream.
1889 *Diary.*

Münch, Richard Friedrich 1945–

German sociologist, a professor at Heinrich Heine University, Düsseldorf.

52 Social life is mutual negotiation and society, social order, relies on this mutual negotiation between individuals; this represents both creed and particular reality in American society. In no other society is this creed and the corresponding reality as prominent as the United States.
1986 'The American Creed in Sociological Theory', in *Sociological Theory*, vol.4, issue 43.

Mundy, Peter c.1596–1667

English trader and seafarer. He was sent to France at the age of 12 to learn French. At 15 he went to sea and travelled continually thereafter. His journal was edited by the Hakluyt Society.

53 We all three got up on our elephant which brought us hither. For my own part I found [it] very uneasy riding, being badly seated and not accustomed (he had such a shuffling, jogging justling pace), sitting hindermost on the ridge of his monstrous massy chine bones, and nothing at all under me (nor they neither) that I wished myself on foot and would have let myself fall off but that it was somewhat too high. In fine, we alighted off from his back into the upper galleries of the house and saved the labour going upstairs.
c.1620 On riding on an elephant. *Travels* (pubished c.1650).

54 So that finding myself at present in or about one hundred and twenty degrees off east longitude from England, it bred in me a desire to proceed on the same easterly course till I had ended where I began, and so to have once made one circle round the globe of the earth, which would have been a voyage of voyages.
c.1640 Objections were raised and Mundy was unable to fulfil this aim. *Travels* (published c.1650).

Munro, Alice née Laidlaw 1931–

Canadian short-story writer; her first collection of short stories *Dance of the Happy Shades* (1968) won the Governor-General's Award, as did *Lives of Girls and Women* (1971).

55 Boys' hate was dangerous, it was keen and bright, a miraculous birthright, like Arthur's sword snatched out of the stone.
1971 *Lives of Girls and Women*, 'Changes and Ceremonies'.

56 I thought of my mother, who would publicly campaign for birth control but would never even think she needed to talk to me, so firmly was she convinced that sex was something no woman—no *intelligent* woman—would ever submit to unless she had to.
1971 *Lives of Girls and Women*, 'Baptizing'.

57 She had reached an age where she thought she could not stand to know any more…she pushed any discovery aside with embarassment.
1978 *Lives of Girls and Women*, 'Royal Beatings'.

58 Country manners. Even if somebody phones up to tell you your house is burning down, they ask first how you are.
1987 *The Progress of Love*, 'The Progress of Love'.

59 Hatred is always a sin, my mother told me. Remember that. One drop of hatred in your soul will spread and discolor everything like a drop of black ink in white milk. I was struck by that and meant to try it, but knew I shouldn't waste the milk.
1987 *The Progress of Love*, 'The Progress of Love'.

60 People live within winter in a way outsiders do not understand. They are watchful, provident, fatigued, exhilarated.
1987 *The Progress of Love*, 'Fits'.

61 Do such moments really mean, as they seem to, that we have a life of happiness with which we only occasionally, knowingly, intersect? Do they shed such light before and after that all that has happened in our lives—or that we've made to happen—can be dismissed?
1987 *The Progress of Love*, 'The Moon in the Orange Street Skating Rink'.

Münster, Count Georg 1794–1868

Hanoverian diplomat.

62 An intelligent Russian once remarked to me, 'Every country has its own Constitution. Ours is absolutism moderated by assassination.'
Political Sketches of the State of Europe 1814–1867

Murdoch, Dame (Jean) Iris 1919–99

Irish novelist and philosopher, of Anglo-Irish descent. Her novels, exploring human relationships with subtlety and humour, include *The Sea, The Sea* (1978) and *The Philosopher's Pupil* (1983).

63 All our failures are ultimately failures in love.
1958 *The Bell*.

64 Love is the extremely difficult realisation that something other than oneself is real. Love, and so art and morals, is the discovery of reality.
1959 'The Sublime and the Good'.

65 What can one do with the past?
Forgive it. Let it enter into you in peace.
1968 *The Nice and the Good*.

66 He was a sociologist; he had gotten into an intellectual muddle early on in life and never managed to get out.
1983 *The Philosopher's Pupil*, 'The Events in Our Town'.

Murdoch, (Keith) Rupert 1931–

Australian-born US newspaper publisher. He expanded his publishing empire first in Australia, then in Britain, buying the *News of the World* in 1969, *The Times* and *The Sunday Times* in 1981. He moved into the US market in 1976 and became a US citizen in 1985.

67 I did not come all this way not to interfere.

> **c.1969** Quoted in S Somerfield *Banner headlines* (1979). Somerfield was editor of the *News of the World* and complained that Murdoch, who had recently bought the paper, was interfering with his editorial role.

Murkowski, Frank M 1933–

Vice Chair, US Senate Select Committee on Intelligence.

68 Low morale and high indigestion.

> **1991** Of the mood of the Senate confirming CIA Director Robert M Gates. In the *New York Times*, 12 Nov.

Murphy, Dervla 1931–

Irish writer and traveller. In 1963 she cycled to India, where she worked with Tibetan children.

69 On my tenth birthday a bicycle and an atlas coincided as presents and a few days later I decided to cycle to India.

> **1965** *Full Tilt: Ireland to India with a Bicycle.*

70 It is on occasions such as these that I thank God for my sanguine temperament, which refuses to allow me to believe in disaster until it is finally manifest.

> **1965** *Full Tilt: Ireland to India with a Bicycle.*

71 Each human spirit is immortal—for time cannot destroy whatever element within us reverences the glory of a dawn in the mountains.

> **1968** *In Ethiopia with a Mule.*

72 Never before had I embarked on a journey that required courage.

> **1978** On embarking on travels and research into the problems of Northern Ireland. *A Place Apart.*

Murphy, Ian

Architect, lecturer at University of Westminster

73 The technology of decentralization can be the saviour or assassin of contemporary and future society. The role of architects may be uncertain, but the role of architecture is not. In order to look forward society may sometimes have to look back. This it should do in order to learn from previous mistakes and oversights and to preclude similar eventualities in the future. This does not imply historical dependency, as some would assert. The symbiosis of architecture and technology should prevail, engendered by honesty and integrity. The task will not be easy.

> **1993** 'The impact of the environment: the shock of the new', in Ben Farmer and Hentie Louw (eds.) *Companion to Contemporary Architectural Thought* (1993).

Murphy, Tom (Thomas) S 1925–

US media company executive, president (1964–72) and chair (from 1966) of ABC Inc.

74 If you hire mediocre people, they will hire mediocre people.

> **1991** In *Fortune*, 6 May.

Murray, Les(lie Allan) 1938–

Australian poet and writer whose exuberant verse reflects both his farming background and his preoccupation with language. His collections include *The Ilex Tree* (1965), *The Weatherboard Cathedral* (1969), *The People's Otherworld* (1976) and *Selected Poems* (1986).

75 The houses there wear verandahs out of shyness.

> **1986** *Selected Poems*, 'Driving Through Sawmill Towns'.

76 If the cardinal points of costume
    are Robes, Tato, Rig and Scunge,
    where are shorts in this compass?

They are the never Robes
as other bareleg outfits have been:
the toga, the kilt, the lava-lava,
the Mahatma's cotton dhoti;

archbishops and field marshals
at their ceremonies never wear shorts.
The very word
means underpants in North America.

> **1986** *Selected Poems*, 'The Dream of Wearing Shorts Forever'.

Murray, Michael

Director of Human Resources, Microsoft.

77 If Microsoft were a car it would have a large gas pedal and a small but workable brake. It would not have a rear-view mirror.

> **1994** In *Newsweek*, 11 Jul.

Murrow, Edward (Edgar) R(oscoe)
1908–65

US journalist and broadcaster. As CBS correspondent from Britain from 1937, he conveyed wartime spirit to the US. He became a producer of current affairs television programmes after the war, and his questioning of Joseph McCarthy contributed to the Senator's fall from grace.

78 He mobilized the English language and sent it into battle to steady his fellow countrymen and hearten those Europeans upon whom the long dark night of tyranny had descended.

> **1954** Of Churchill. Broadcast, 30 Nov, quoted in *In Search of Light* (1967).

79 The people you have seen have the strength to harvest your fruit and vegetables. They do not have the strength to influence legislation. Maybe you do.

1960 *Harvest of Shame*, CBS TV documentary on migrant labour, 25 Nov, concluding words.

80 The politician is trained in the art of inexactitude. His words tend to be blunt or rounded, because if they have a cutting edge they may later return to wound him.

Attributed.

Muschamp, Herbert

81 Red-and-gold disease…an itch, the theater a place to scratch it…a yearning for the wider world.

1995 In the *New York Times*, 30 Jul. The phrase 'red-and-gold disease' was coined by Lincoln Kirstein's mother when her son began haunting theatres.

Musgrove, F

Educationist.

82 It is the business of education to eliminate the influence of parents on the life-chances of the young.

1966 *The Family, Education and Society*.

Mussolini, Benito also called *Il Duce [the Leader]* 1883–1945

Italian politician and Prime Minister (1922). By 1925 he had established himself as dictator. His declaration of war on Britain and France exposed Italy's military unpreparedness, and was followed by a series of defeats; his popularity waned, and he was overthrown and arrested (Jul 1943). Rescued by German paratroopers to head the puppet Italian Social Republic, in 1945 he was captured by the Italian Resistance and shot.

83 I could have transformed this grey assembly hall into an armed camp of Blackshirts, a bivouac for corpses. I could have nailed up the doors of Parliament.

1922 Inaugural speech to the Lower House as Prime Minister, 16 Nov.

84 If I advance, follow me. If I retreat, kill me. If I die, avenge me.

1926 Said to senior officials after an attempt on his life, 6 Apr.

85 Better one day as a lion than a hundred years as a sheep.

c.1930 Quoted in Denis Mack-Smith *Mussolini's Roman Empire* (1976), p.47.

86 War alone can carry to the maximum tension all human energies and imprint with the seal of nobility those people who have the courage to confront it; every other test is a mere substitute.

c.1930 Quoted in Denis Mack-Smith *Mussolini's Roman Empire* (1976), p.47.

87 Words are beautiful things, but muskets and machine guns are even more beautiful.

c.1932 Quoted in Denis Mack-Smith *Mussolini's Roman Empire* (1976).

88 A nation, to remain healthy, should make war every twenty-five years.

1934 Quoted in Denis Mack-Smith *Mussolini's Roman Empire* (1976), p.63.

89 War is to man as maternity to women.

1934 Speech, May. Quoted in Denis Mack-Smith *Mussolini's Roman Empire* (1976), p.54.

90 When the war in Spain is over I shall have to find something else: the Italian character has to be formed through fighting.

1936 Quoted in Thomas *The Spanish Civil War*, p.226.

91 Fascism accepts the individual only insofar as his interests coincide with the state's.

Quoted in the *Enciclopedia Italiana*.

Myrdal, (Karl) Gunnar 1898–1987

Swedish economist. Professor of Economics, Stockholm University (1933–9, 1961–5). A prominent member of the 'Stockholm School' of macroeconomics of the 1930s. Swedish Minister for Trade and Commerce (1945–7) and Executive Secretary of the UN Economic Commerce (1947–57). In 1974 he was jointly awarded the Nobel Prize for Economics with Friedrich Hayek. His wife Alva was awarded the Nobel Prize for Peace in 1982 with Alfonso Garcia Robles.

92 Quantities defined in terms of measurements made at the end of the period in question are referred to as *ex post*; quantities defined in terms of action planned at the beginning of the period in question are referred to as *ex ante*.

1939 *Monetary Equilibrium*

Nabokov, Vladimir 1899–1977

Russian-born US writer. He left Russia in 1917 and began writing in English in the 1940s. His most widely known novel is *Lolita* (1955). His work is multi-layered and highly literary.

93 There are aphorisms that, like airplanes, stay up only while they are in motion.

1937 *The Gift*, ch.1.

94 Poor Knight! he really had two periods, the first—a dull man writing broken English, the second—a broken man writing dull English.

1941 *The Real Life of Sebastian Knight*, ch.1.

95 The cradle rocks above an abyss, and common sense tells us that our existence is but a brief crack of light between two eternities of darkness.

1951 *Conclusive Evidence*, ch.1 (revised as *Speak, Memory*, 1966).

96 Lolita, light of my life, fire of my loins. My sin, my soul. Lo-lee-ta: the tip of the tongue taking a trip of three steps down the palate to tap, at three, on the teeth. Lo. Lee. Ta.
1955 Humbert Humbert. *Lolita*, pt.1, ch.1.

97 You can always count on a murderer for a fancy prose style.
1955 Humbert Humbert. *Lolita*, ch.1.

98 The tiny madman in his padded cell.
1955 Humbert Humbert's description of an embryo. *Lolita*, ch.11.

99 Like so many ageing college people, Pnin had long ceased to notice the existence of students on campus.
1957 *Pnin*, ch.3, section 6.

1 As to the rest, I am no more guilty of imitating 'real life' than 'real life' is responsible for plagiarizing me.
1958 *Nabokov's Dozen*, bibliographical note.

2 Life is a great surprise. I do not see why death should not be an even greater one.
1962 *Pale Fire*.

3 Human life is but a series of footnotes to a vast, obscure unfinished masterpiece.
1962 *Pale Fire*, 'Commentary'.

4 Solitude is the playfield of Satan.
1962 *Pale Fire*, 'Commentary'.

5 I know more than I can express in words, and the little I can express would not have been expressed, had I not known more.
1964 Interview in *Playboy*, Jan.

6 A novelist is, like all mortals, more fully at home on the surface of the present than in the ooze of the past.
1964 Interview in *Playboy*, Jan.

7 A work of art has no importance whatever to society. It is only important to the individual, and only the individual reader is important to me.
1964 Interview in *Playboy*, Jan.

8 Style and structure are the essence of a book; great ideas are hogwash.
1967 Interview in the *Paris Review*, Summer.

9 Derivative writers seem versatile because they imitate many others, past and present. Artistic originality has only itself to copy.
1967 Interview in the *Paris Review*, Summer.

10 Satire is a lesson, parody is a game.
1967 Interview in *Wisconsin Studies in Contemporary Literature*, Spring.

11 Those Eggheads are terrible Philistines. A real good head is not oval but round.
1967 Interview in *Wisconsin Studies in Contemporary Literature*, Spring.

12 A good laugh is the best pesticide.
1968 Interview on BBC television. Reported in *The Listener*, 10 Oct.

13 I think like a genius, I write like a distinguished author, and I speak like a child.
1973 *Strong Opinions*, foreword.

14 Her exotic daydreams do not prevent her from being small-town bourgeois at heart, clinging to conventional ideas or committing this or that conventional violation of the conventional, adultery being a most conventional way to rise above the conventional.
'Madame Bovary'. Collected in *Lectures on Literature* (published 1980).

15 My answer to your question 'Does the writer have a social responsibility?' is NO. You owe me ten cents, sir.
Letter to an editor who had offered him $200 for 2,000 words. Quoted by Eleanor Blau in the *New York Times*, 24 Aug 1989.

Naipaul, Sir V(idiadhar) S(urajprasad)
1932–

Trinidadian writer, brother of the late Shiva Naipaul. Knighted in 1990, his works include *The Mystic Masseur* (1957, John Llewelyn Rhys Memorial Prize), *Miguel Street* (1959, Somerset Maugham Award), *A House for Mr. Biswas* (1961), *A Bend in the River* (1979, Booker Prize) and the autobiographical *Finding the Centre* (1984).

16 Worse, to have lived without even attempting to lay claim to one's portion of the earth; to have lived and died as one had been born, unnecessary and unaccommodated.
1961 *A House for Mr. Biswas*, prologue.

17 All that I know of our history and the history of the Indian Ocean I have got from books written by Europeans... Without Europeans, I feel, all our past would have been washed away, like the scuff marks of fishermen on the beach.
1979 *A Bend in the River*, ch.1, 'The Second Rebellion'.

18 I do not regard the knighthood as a social accomplishment.
1993 Quoted in 'Kingdom of Naipaul' by Zoë Heller in the *Independent on Sunday Review*, 28 Mar.

Nairne, Caroline, Lady 1766–1845
Scottish songwriter, who collected traditional airs and wrote lyrics to them, often on Jacobite themes.

19 The laird o' Cockpen, he's proud an' he's great,

His mind is ta'en up wi' things o' the State.
'The Laird o' Cockpen', stanza 1.

20 I'm wearin' awa', John
Like snaw-wreaths in thaw, John,
I'm wearin' awa'
To the land o' the leal.
'The Land o' the Leal', stanza 1.

21 Bonnie Charlie's now awa,
Safely owre the friendly main;
Mony a heart will break in twa,
Should he ne'er come back again.

Will ye no come back again?
Will ye no come back again?
Better lo'ed ye canna be,
Will ye no come back again?
'Will Ye No Come Back Again?', stanza 1 and chorus.

Namath, Joe Willie (Joseph William)
1943–

US football player. Known as 'Broadway Joe', he was an outstanding quarterback with Alabama University and, from 1965, the New York Jets. In 1969 he led the Jets to unexpected victory in the Superbowl.

22 When you win, nothing hurts.
Quoted in Colin Jarman *The Guinness Dictionary of Sports Quotations* (1990).

Napier, Sir Charles James 1782–1853

Scottish soldier, born in London. He served in Ireland, Portugal, against the United States and in 1841 was sent to India, where he broke the power of the amirs at the Battle of Meeanee and became Governor of Sind.

23 *Peccavi.*

I have sinned [Sind].
1843 Attributed encoded message, 24 Mar, sent after the Battle of Hyderabad and the capture of Sind.

Napoleon I 1769–1821

French general and Emperor. Born in Corsica, he rose to prominence during the French Revolution, and was appointed to command the army of Italy in 1769. Campaigns in Egypt and Austria followed, and his successes allowed him to lead a coup against the government and become dictator. Although he was exiled to Elba by the Allies in 1814, he returned in 1815, when he was finally defeated at Waterloo and exiled to St Helena.

24 *Soldats, songez que, du haut de ces pyramides, quarante siècles vous contemplent.*

Soldiers, think that, from the summit of these pyramids, forty centuries look down upon you.
1798 Speech to the Army of Egypt, before the Battle of the Pyramids, 21 Jul. Quoted in Gaspard Gourgaud *Mémoires* (1823), vol. 2, 'Egypte, Bataille des Pyramides'.

25 China? There lies a sleeping giant. Let him sleep! For when he wakes he will move the world.
c.1800 Attributed.

26 Wisdom and policy dictate that we must do as destiny demands and keep peace with the irresistible march of events.
1808 Said to Alexander I of Russia, 2 Feb.

27 In war, three-quarters turns on moral considerations; the balance of actual forces counts only for the remaining quarter.
1808 Comment, 27 Apr. Quoted in *Observations sur les affaires de l'Espagne, Saint Cloud,* in *Correspondance de Napoleon 1er* (1858–69), vol.17.

28 France has more need of me than I have of France.
1813 Speech to Corps Législatif, Paris, 31 Dec.

29 How beautifully the English fight! But they must give way.
1815 Attributed, at the Battle of Waterloo, 18 Jun.

30 The English conquered us; but they are far from being our equals.
1815 Letter to Gaspar Gourgaud from St Helena, after the Battle of Waterloo.

31 An army marches on its stomach.
1816 Attributed. Probably condensed from a long passage dated 14 Nov in E A de Las Cases *Memoriale de Ste-Helene* (1823), vol.4.

32 In war, as in love, we must come into contact before we can triumph.
1842 Quoted in A G De Liancourt (ed) *Maximes de Napoleon.*

33 William behaved like a bashful girl, who is afraid of her lover's bad reputation and therefore avoids being alone with him.
1860 Of William I of Prussia, who invited other German Princes to attend a meeting with Napoleon at Baden-Baden in June originally intended to be a private discussion on the possibility of a joint alliance with Russia. Quoted in A J P Taylor *Struggle for Mastery in Europe 1848-1918* (1954), p.121.

34 England is a nation of shopkeepers.
Attributed while in exile on St Helena.

35 Power is my mistress. I have worked too hard in conquering her to allow anyone to take her from me, or even to covet her.
The Journal of Roederer.

36 Prussia was hatched from a cannon-ball.
Attributed.

Napoleon III until 1852 Louis-Napoleon in full Charles Louis Napoleon Bonaparte 1808–73

President of the Second French Republic (1848–52) and Emperor of the French (1852–70). He encouraged economic expansion and modernization, and presided over the Crimean conflict (1854–6) and the ill-starred intervention in Mexico (1861–7). After defeat by Prussia in 1870, the remainder of his life was spent in exile in England.

37 For too long, society has resembled a pyramid that has been turned upside down and made to rest on its summit. I have replaced it on its base.
1852 Speech to the Legislative Assembly, 29 Mar.

38 We must not seek to fashion events, but let them happen of their own accord.
1865 In conversation with Bismarck, Biarritz, 4 Oct.

39 When a man of my name is in power, he must do great things.
Quoted in A J P Taylor *From Napoleon to the Second International* (1993).

Narogin, Mudrooroo formerly *Colin Jackson*
1938–
Australian writer and poet; he has piloted Aboriginal literature courses at several Australian universities; his works include *Dr. Wooreddy's Prescription for Enduring the Ending of the World* (1983), the song cycle *Dalwurra: The Black Bittern* (1988) describing a fringe-dweller's search for his true identity, and *Writing from the Fringe* (1990).

40 The Aboriginal writer is a Janus-type figure with one face turned to the past and the other to the future while existing in a postmodern, multicultural Australia in which he or she must fight for cultural space.
1990 *Writing from the Fringe*, ch.1, 'Writing from the Fringe'.

Nash, (Frederic) Ogden 1902–71
US light versifier. His popular verse was published frequently in *The New Yorker* and helped establish its sophisticated tone. His collections include *Hard Lines* (1931) and *Boy is a Boy* (1960).

41 The cow is of the bovine ilk;
One end is moo, the other, milk.
1931 *Free Wheeling*, 'The Cow'.

42 The song of canaries
Never varies,
And when they're moulting
They're pretty revolting.
1931 *Free Wheeling*, 'The Canary'.

43 A bit of talcum
Is always walcum.
1931 *Free Wheeling*, 'The Baby'.

44 One would be in less danger
From the wiles of a stranger
If one's own kin and kith
Were more fun to be with.
1931 *Hard Lines*, 'Family Court'.

45 A girl whose cheeks are covered with paint
Has an advantage with me over one whose ain't.

1931 *Hard Lines*, 'Biological Reflection'.

46 Candy
Is dandy
But liquor
Is quicker.
1931 *Hard Lines*, 'Reflections on Ice-Breaking'.

47 The turtle lives 'twixt plated decks
Which practically conceal its sex.
I think it clever of the turtle
In such a fix to be so fertile.
1931 *Hard Lines*, 'Autres Bêtes, Autres Moeurs'.

48 It's better to be dead, or even perfectly well, than to suffer from the wrong affliction. The man who owns up to arthritis in a beri-beri year is as lonely as a woman in a last month's dress.
1933 'How's Your Sacro-iliac?', in the *Saturday Evening Post*, 14 Oct.

49 Any kiddie in school can love like a fool,
But hating, my boy, is an art.
1933 *Happy Days*, 'Plea for Less Malice Toward None'.

50 I think that I shall never see
A billboard lovely as a tree.
Perhaps, unless the billboards fall,
I'll never see a tree at all.
1933 *Happy Days*, 'Song of the Open Road'.
▷ See Kilmer 556:63.

51 Children aren't happy with nothing to ignore
And that's what parents were created for.
1933 *Happy Days*, 'The Parent'.

52 Home is heaven and orgies are vile,
But you *need* an orgy, once in a while.
1935 *The Primrose Path*, 'Home, 9944/100% Sweet Home'.

53 The camel has a single hump;
The dromedary, two;
Or else the other way around,
I'm never sure. Are you?
1936 *The Bad Parents' Garden of Verse*, 'The Camel'.

54 Let us pause to consider the English,
Who when they pause to consider themselves they get all reticently thrilled and tinglish,
Because every Englishman is convinced of one thing, viz.:
That to be an Englishman is to belong to the most exclusive club there is.
1938 *I'm a Stranger Here Myself*, 'England Expects'.

55 There was a young belle of old Natchez
Whose garments were always in patchez.
When comment arose
On the state of her clothes,
She drawled, When Ah itchez, Ah scratchez.
1938 *I'm a Stranger Here Myself*, 'Requiem'.

56 The trouble with a kitten is
THAT
Eventually it becomes a
CAT.
1940 *The Face Is Familiar*, 'The Kitten'.

57 One day he missed his loving bride.
She had, the guide informed him later,
Been eaten by an alligator.
Professor Twist could not but smile.
'You mean,' he said, 'a crocodile.'
1940 *The Face Is Familiar*, 'The Purist'.

58 Oh, what a tangled web do parents weave
When they think that their children are naïve.
1940 *The Face Is Familiar*, 'Baby, What Makes the Sky Blue'.

59 This infant whose middle
Is diapered still
Will want to marry
My daughter Jill.

Oh sweet be his slumber and moist his middle!
My dreams, I fear, are infanticiddle.
1940 *The Face Is Familiar*, 'Song to be Sung by the Father of Infant Female Children'.

60 Sure, deck your lower limbs in pants;
Yours are the limbs, my sweeting.
You look divine as you advance—
Have you seen yourself retreating?
1940 *The Face Is Familiar*, 'What's The Use'.

61 Life is not having been told that the man has just waxed the floor.
1942 *Good Intentions*, 'You and Me and P. B. Shelley'.

62 Beneath this slab
John Brown is stowed.
He watched the ads,
And not the road.
1942 *Good Intentions*, 'Lather As You Go'.

63 I have a bone to pick with Fate.
Come here and tell me, girlie,
Do you think my mind is maturing late,
Or simply rotted early?
1942 *Good Intentions*, 'Lines On Facing Forty'.

64 I test my bath before I sit,
And I'm always moved to wonderment
That what chills the finger not a bit
Is so frigid upon the fundament.
1942 *Good Intentions*, 'Samson Agonistes'.

65 Women would rather be right than be reasonable.
1942 *Good Intentions*, 'Frailty, Thy Name is a Misnomer'.

66 Parsley
Is gharsely.
1942 *Good Intentions*, 'Further Reflections on Parsley'.

67 God in His wisdom made the fly
And then forgot to tell us why.
1942 *Good Intentions*, 'The Fly'.

68 One thing that literature would be greatly the better for
Would be a more restricted employment by authors of simile and metaphor.
1945 *Many Long Years Ago*, 'Very Like A Whale'.

69 He tells you when you've got on too much lipstick,
And helps you with your girdle when your hips stick.
1949 *Versus*, 'The Perfect Husband'.

70 All winter long,
I am one for whom the bell is tolling;
I can arouse no interest in basketball,
Indoor fly casting or bowling;
The sports pages are strictly no soap!
And until the cry Play Ball! I simply mope.
1957 Quoted in Colin Jarman *The Guinness Dictionary of Sports Quotations* (1990).

71 It is a fact that a lady wants to be dressed exactly like everybody else but she gets pretty upset if she sees anybody else dressed exactly like her.
1964 *Marriage Lines*, 'Thoughts Thought on an Avenue'.

72 My verse represents a handle I can grasp in order not to yield to the centrifugal forces which are trying to throw me off the world.
Recalled on his death, 9 May 1971.

73 Basketball, a game which won't be fit for people until they set the basket umbilicus-high and return the giraffes to the zoo.
Quoted in Colin Jarman *The Guinness Dictionary of Sports Quotations* (1990).

74 I eat my peas with honey;
I've done it all my life.
They do taste kinda funny,
but it keeps 'em on the knife.
Attributed.

Nashe, Thomas 1567–1601

English dramatist and satirist. His play *The Isle of Dogs* (1597, now lost) was so scathing on the subject of state abuses that it was suppressed, the theatre closed down and he himself thrown into Fleet prison. *The Unfortunate Traveller* (1594) is a picaresque tale, one of the earliest of its kind.

75 'New herrings, new!' we must cry, every time we make ourselves public, or else we shall be christened with a hundred new titles of idiotism.
1592 *Pierce Penniless, His Supplication to the Devil*, 'An Invective Against Enemies of Poetry'.

76 Poetry is the honey of all flowers, the quintessence of all sciences, the marrow of wit, and the very phrase of angels.
1592 *Pierce Penniless, His Supplication to the Devil*, 'An Invective Against Enemies of Poetry'.

77 If I be evil intreated, or sent away with a flea in mine ear, let him look that I will rail on him soundly; nor for an hour or a day, whiles the injury is fresh in my memory; but in some elaborate polished poem, which I will leave to the world when I am dead, to be a living image to all ages of his beggarly parsimony and ignoble illiberality.
1592 *Pierce Penniless, His Supplication to the Devil*, 'An Invective Against Enemies of Poetry'.

78 I will confer with thee somewhat gravely, although thou beest a goosecap and hast no judgement.
1592 *Strange News of the Intercepting Certain Letters*.

79 Immortal Spenser, no frailty hath thy fame but the imputation of this idiot's friendship!
1592 *Strange News of the Intercepting Certain Letters*.

80 Spring, the sweet spring, is the year's pleasant king,
Then blooms each thing, then maids dance in a ring,
Cold doth not sting, the pretty birds do sing:
Cuckoo, jug-jug, pu-we, to-witta-woo!
1592 *Summer's Last Will and Testament*, 'Song'.

81 Fair summer droops, droop men and beasts therefore:
So fair a summer look for never more.
All good things vanish, less than in a day,
Peace, plenty, pleasure, suddenly decay.
Go not yet away, bright soul of the sad year;
The earth is hell when thou leav'st to appear.
1592 *Summer's Last Will and Testament*, 'Song'.

82 From winter, plague and pestilence, good lord, deliver us!
1592 *Summer's Last Will and Testament*.

83 Beauty is but a flower
Which wrinkles will devour;
Brightness falls from the air;
Queens have died young and fair;
Dust hath closèd Helen's eye.
I am sick, I must die.
Lord, have mercy on us!
1592 'A Litany in Time of Plague'.

84 He that is a traveller must have the back of an ass to bear all, a tongue like the tail of a dog to flatter all, the mouth of a hog to eat all what is set before him, the ear of a merchant to hear all and say nothing; and if this be not the highest step of thraldom, there is no liberty or freedom.
1594 *The Unfortunate Traveller, or the Life of Jack Wilton*.

Nathan, George Jean 1882–1958

US theatre critic. He was co-editor of *The Smart Set* (1914–24) and founded the *American Mercury* with H L Mencken in 1924. Among the emerging playwrights to whom he gave support was Eugene O'Neill.

85 The most loyal and faithful woman indulges her imagination in a hypothetical liaison whenever she dons a new street frock for the first time.
1921 *The Theatre, the Drama, the Girls*, 'Woman'.

86 The test of a real comedian is whether you laugh at him before he opens his mouth.
Quoted in *American Mercury*, Sep 1929.

87 I always said that I'd like Barrymore's acting till the cows came home. Well, ladies and gentlemen, last night the cows came home.
1939 Review of John Barrymore's performance in *My Dear Children*.

88 Impersonal criticism…is like an impersonal fist fight or an impersonal marriage, and as successful.
Quoted in Charles Angoff (ed) *The World of George Jean Nathan* (1952).

89 The dramatic critic who is without prejudice is on the plane with the general who does not believe in taking human life.
Attributed.

Nation, Carry Amelia née *Moore*
1846–1911

US temperance agitator. She went on saloon smashing expeditions with a hatchet and was frequently imprisoned for breach of the peace.

90 A woman is stripped of everything by them [saloons]. Her husband is torn from her; she is robbed of her sons, her home, her food, and her virtue; and then they strip her clothes off and hang her up bare in these dens of robbery and murder. Truly does the saloon make a woman bare of all things!
c.1893 Quoted in Carleton Beals *Cyclone Carry* (1962), ch.14.

Naughton, Bill 1910–92

Irish novelist and screenwriter. His screen credits include *Alfie* (1966), *The Family Way* (1966) and *Spring and Port Wine* (1970).

91 It seems to me if they ain't got you one way they got you another. So what's the answer? That's what I keep asking myself. What's it all about? Know what I mean?
1966 Line delivered by Michael Caine in *Alfie*.

Neale, J(ames) M(ason) 1818–66

English clergyman and hymn writer

92 All glory, laud and honour
　To Thee, Redeemer, King,
　To whom the lips of children
　Made sweet hosannas ring.
　1851 'All Glory, Laud and Honour'.

93 Jerusalem the golden,
　With milk and honey blessed,
　Beneath thy contemplation
　Sink heart and voice oppressed.
　I know not, O I know not
　What joys await us there,
　What radiancy of glory,
　What light beyond compare.
　1858 'Jerusalem the Golden', translated from the original Latin of St Bernard of Cluny.

Nehru, Jawaharlal 1889–1964

Indian statesman, President of the Indian National Congress (1929) and India's first Prime Minister (1947–64). Neutral in the Cold War, he embarked on industrialization, reorganized the states linguistically and ended the dispute with Pakistan over Kashmir peacefully.

94 Stalin…that great lover of peace, a man of giant stature who moulded, as few other men have done, the destinies of his age…The occasion is not merely the passing away of a great figure but perhaps the ending of an historic era.
　1953 Tribute, Indian Parliament, 9 Mar.

Neilson, John Shaw 1872–1942

Australian poet. His first work was published in the *Bulletin* and first collected in *Heart of Spring* (1919), followed by *Ballad and Lyrical Poems* (1923) and *New Poems* (1927). *Collected Poems* (1934) was followed by posthumous collections.

95 The young girl stood beside me. I
　Saw not what her young eyes could see:
　—A light, she said, not of the sky
　Lives somewhere in the Orange Tree.
　1923 *Ballad and Lyrical Poems*, 'The Orange Tree', stanza 1.

96 Here is the ecstacy
　Of sun-fed wine and song:
　Drink! it is melody
　Under a kurrajong.
　'Under a Kurrajong', stanza 1, in R H Croll (ed) *Collected Poems of John Shaw Neilson* (1934).

Nelson, Horatio, Viscount Nelson
1758–1805

English admiral. In 1794 he commanded at Bastia and Calvi, where he lost the sight of his right eye, and at Santa Cruz in 1796, where he lost his right arm. In 1798 he destroyed Napoleon's fleet in Aboukir Bay, and subsequently began an affair with Emma, Lady Hamilton. In 1805 he defeated the combined French and Spanish fleet at Trafalgar, but was mortally wounded.

97 A fleet of British ships of war are the best negotiators in Europe.
　1801 Letter to Lady Hamilton, Mar, before the Battle of Copenhagen.

98 You know, Foley, I have only one eye—I have a right to be blind sometimes… I really do not see the signal.
　1801 Said to Captain Foley during the Battle of Copenhagen, 2 Apr. Nelson disregarded his superior, Admiral Hyde-Parker's order to break off action and went on to win the engagement.

99 I wish to say Nelson confides that every man will do his duty.
　1805 Instructions to the flag officer on HMS *Victory*, 21 Oct. The signal was amended to begin, 'England expects…'.

1 Kiss me, Hardy.
　1805 Attributed, as he lay dying in the cockpit of the *Victory* during the Battle of Trafalgar, 21 Oct.

2 Thank God, I have done my duty.
　1805 Last words at the Battle of Trafalgar, quoted in Robert Southey *Life of Nelson* (1813), ch.9.

Nemerov, Howard 1920–

US poet, novelist and playwright. He is best known for his poetry, and won a National Book Award for his *Collected Poems* in 1977.

3 Children, to be illustrious is sad.
　1958 *Mirrors and Windows*, 'The Statues in the Public Gardens'.

4 Till I, high in the tower of my time
　Among familiar ruins, began to cry
　For accident, sickness, justice, war and crime,
　Because all died, because I had to die.
　The snow fell, the trees stood, the promise kept,
　And a child I slept.
　1960 *New Poems*, 'The View from an Attic Window'.

5 For a Jewish Puritan of the middle class, the novel is serious, the novel is work, the novel is conscientious application—why, the novel is practically the retail business all over again.
　1965 *Journal of the Fictive Life*, 'Reflexions of the Novelist Felix Ledger'.

6 I've never read a political poem that's accomplished anything. Poetry makes things happen, but rarely what the poet wants.
　1988 In the *International Herald Tribune*, 14 Oct.
　▷ See Auden 47:70.

Nero AD 37–68

Roman Emperor AD (54–68). He was adopted by his step-father Claudius and declared Emperor on Claudius's death. Ancient authors depict him as a debauched tyrant, and accuse him of starting the great fire of Rome in AD 64 (he blamed the Christians). A coup in AD 68 brought Galba to the throne, and Nero committed suicide.

7   *Qualis artifex pereo!*

Dead! And so great an artist!
Attributed words on the point of taking his life. Quoted in Suetonius *Nero*, 49.1 (translated by Robert Graves, 1957).

Neruda, Pablo pseudonym of *Neftalí Ricardo Reyes Basoalto* 1904–73

Chilean poet, essayist and diplomat, who travelled widely as a diplomat. His poetic themes range from subjective love to socially committed epic poems influenced by a communist ideology. He was awarded a Nobel Prize in 1971.

8   *Sucede que me canso de mis pies y mis uñas*
    y mi pelo y mi sombra.
    Sucede que me canso de ser hombre.

I happen to be tired of my feet and my nails
and my hair and my shadow.
I happen to be tired of being a man.
1935 *Residencia en la tierra*, 'Walking Around' (translated as *Residence on earth*, 1946).

9   *A nosotros nos enseñaron a respetar la iglesia,*
    a no toser, a no escupir en el atrio,
    a no lavar la ropa en el altar
    y no es así: la vida rompe las religiones.

We were taught respect for the church,
no hawking and spitting on porticos,
don't soak your socks on the altar—
but things are different: life smashes religions.
1973 *La rosa separada*, 'Los hombres' (translated as *The Separate Rose*, 'The Men', 1985).

Nerval, Gérard de pseudonym of *Gérard Labrunie* 1808–55

French poet, novelist and author of critical essays, he was admired later by the Surrealists for his fantastic short tales.

10 *Philosophie! dont la lumière, comme celle des enfers de Milton, ne sert qu'à rendre les ténèbres visibles.*

Philosophy! In whose light, like that in Milton's hell, only serves to make the shadows visible.
1852 *Fragments*, 'Paradox et vérité'.

11 *Il n'y a qu'un seul vice dont on ne voie personne se vanter, c'est l'ingratitude.*

There is only one vice of which no one boasts—ingratitude.
1852 *Fragments*, 'Paradox et vérité'.

12 *La vie d'un poète est celle de tous.*

The life of the poet is the life of everyone.
1855 *Petits Châteaux de Bohême*, 'A un ami'.

Nervo, Amado pseudonym of *Juan Crisóstomo Ruiz de Nervo* 1870–1919

Mexican poet and diplomat. He abandoned the priesthood in 1888 to work as a journalist. He studied Buddhist philosophy in depth, and his introspective poetry is characterized by deep religious feeling and simple form.

13 *No te juzgues incompleto porque no responden a tus ternuras; el amor lleva en sí su propia plenitud.*
    Siempre que haya un hueco en tu vida, llénalo de amor.

Don't judge yourself incomplete when your tenderness gets no response; love carries within itself its own plenitude.
Whenever there is a void in your life, fill it with love.
1918 *Plenitud*, 'Llénalo de amor' (translated as 'Fill it with love', 1928).

Nevelson, Louise 1900–88

Russian-born US sculptor. Her work incorporates pieces of wood, found objects, cast metal, and other materials, creating great mysterious walls or boxes of complex, abstract forms. Her autobiography, *Dawns and Dusks*, was published in 1976.

14 There's no denying that Caruso came with a voice…that Beethoven came with music in his soul, Picasso was drawing like an angel in the crib. You're born with it.
1976 *Dawns and Dusks*.

Neville, Catherine 1945–

US novelist.

15 'In Scotland,' Tavish muttered, picking up my bags, 'the *women* do the hod carrying while we blokes retire to the nearest pub—to deliberate upon the role of labour in society.'
1992 *A Calculated Risk*.

New York Times

First published 1851 as the *New-York Daily Times*.

16 Who owns history? The public servants who make it, or the people who hire them and to whom they are accountable?
1983 'Who Owns History?', editorial, 19 Nov.

17 Armed with a notebook, ingratiating grin and fine intelligence, he grew to be a most discerning witness of America's most distinctive rite, not just the election but the making of our presidents.
1986 Of journalist Theodore H White. 'Teddy White, the Maker of Epics', editorial, 17 May.

18 The best way to read [a poem] is off the top of your head, and out of the corner of your eye.

1987 *Noted With Pleasure*, in the *New York Times*, 16 Mar.

19 For Palestinians, PLO is a homeland of the mind.

1988 Editorial, 20 Mar.

20 Empty luggage may be easier to carry, but it's still empty.

1988 Of Michael S Dukakis's presidential campaign. 'The Painless Platform', editorial, 20 Jul.

21 Millions drew up before the international hearth of television.

1991 'With Our Own Eyes', editorial, 24 Feb, on international media coverage of the Allied deadline for Iraq's withdrawal from Kuwait.

22 Lightning rods have had it better than Nancy Reagan.

1991 On the publication of Kitty Kelley's unauthorized biography *Nancy Reagan*. 'Scratching at the Teflon', editorial, 10 Apr.

23 Who is quickest on the drawl?

1992 On claims to Texas by both George Bush and rival presidential aspirant Ross Perot. Editorial, 9 Jun.

24 When it comes to the final judgements on political conduct, history is not merciful. It is just.

1994 'Justice and Mercy in *Arkansas*', editorial, 17 Dec.

Newman, Arnold 1918–

US photographer.

25 We don't take our pictures with cameras. We take them with our hearts, and we take them with our minds.

1992 In *Sunday Morning*, CBS TV, 2 Aug.

Newman, James R 1907–

Compiler of the magnum opus *The World of Mathematics*.

26 There are two ways to teach mathematics. One is to take real pains toward creating understanding— visual aids, that sort of thing. The other is the old British style of teaching until you're blue in the face.

1956 Quoted in the *New York Times*, 30 Sep.

Newman, John Henry 1801–90

English theologian, active in Oxford in the Tractarian movement of the Church of England. He converted to the Roman Catholic faith in 1845 and was appointed Cardinal by Pope Leo XIII in 1879.

27 It is as absurd to argue men, as to torture them, into believing.

1831 'The Usurpations of Reason', collected in *Oxford University Sermons* (1843).

28 Lead, kindly Light, amid the encircling gloom,

Lead thou me on;
The night is dark, and I am far from home,
Lead thou me on.
Keep Thou my feet; I do not ask to see
The distant scene; one step enough for me.

1833 'Lead, kindly Light'.

29 May He support us all the day long, till the shades lengthen, and the evening comes, and the busy world is hushed, and the fever of life is over, and our work is done! Then in His mercy may He give us a safe lodging, and a holy rest, and peace at the last.

1834 'Wisdom and Innocence', collected in *Sermons Bearing on Subjects of the Day*.

30 *We can believe what we choose.* We are answerable for what we choose to believe.

1848 Letter to Mre Foude, 27 Jun.

31 It is very difficult to get up resentment towards persons whom one has never seen.

1864 *Apologia pro Vita Sua*, 'Mr Kingsley's Method of Disputation'.

32 Praise to the Holiest in the height,
And in the depth be praise;
In all His words most wonderful,
Most sure in all His ways.

1865 *The Dream of Gerontius*. In *The Month* (published in book form in 1866).

Newman, Peter C 1929–

Canadian author and political columnist.

33 And what I've learned is not to believe in magical leaders any more; that character and compassion are more important than ideology; and that even if it's absurd to think you can change things, it's even more absurd to think that it's foolish and unimportant to try.

1973 *Home Country: People, Places, and Power Politics*.

34 The rich don't have children; they have heirs.

1982 *The Establishment Man: A Portrait of Power*.

Newton, Sir Isaac 1642–1727

English mathematician and physicist, considered the greatest scientist of modern time. Newton was Professor of Mathematics (1669-1701) at Cambridge. Between 1664 and 1666 he discovered the law of gravitation, and began to develop differential calculus.

35 *Corpus omne perseverare in statu suo quiescendi vel movendi uniformiter in directum, nisi quatenus illud a viribus impressis cogitur statum suum mutare.*

Every body continues in its state of rest, or of uniform motion in a right line, unless it is compelled to change that state by forces impressed thereon.

1687 First Law of Motion. *Philosophiae Naturalis Principia Mathematica* (translated by Andrew Motte, 1729).

36 *Mutationem motus proportionalem esse vi motrici impressae et fieri secundum lineam rectam qua vis illa imprimitur.*

The alteration of motion is ever proportional to the motive force impressed; and is made in the direction of the right line in which that force is impressed.

1687 Second Law of Motion. *Philosophiae Naturalis Principia Mathematica* (translated by Andrew Motte, 1729).

37 We are to admit no more causes of natural things than such as are both true and sufficient to explain their appearances... Nature is pleased with simplicity, and affects not the pomp of the superfluous causes.

1687 Newton's First Rule of Reasoning in Philosophy. *Philosophiae Naturalis Principia Mathematica* (translated by Andrew Motte, 1729).

38 *Actioni contrarium semper et aequalem esse reactionem: sive corporum duorum actiones in se mutuo semper esse aequales et in partes contrarias dirigi.*

To every action there is always opposed an equal reaction: or, the mutual actions of two bodies upon each other are always equal, and directed to contrary parts.

1687 Third Law of Motion. *Philosophiae Naturalis Principia Mathematica* (translated by Andrew Motte, 1729).

39 Geometry is that part of universal mechanics which accurately proposes and demonstrates the art of measuring.

1687 *Philosophiae Naturalis Principia Mathematica* (translated by Andrew Motte, 1729).

40 I know not what I may appear to the world, but to myself I seem to have been only like a boy playing on the sea shore, and diverting myself in now and then finding a smoother pebble or a prettier shell than ordinary, whilst the great ocean of truth lay all undiscovered before me.

Quoted in D Brewster (ed) *Memoirs of Newton* (1855), vol.2, ch.27.

41 In the absence of any other proof, the thumb alone would convince me of God's existence.

Attributed.

Newton, John 1725–1807

English divine and writer, converted to Christianity in 1748 and became Curate of Olney, Buckinghamshire, in 1764.

42 Amazing grace! How sweet the sound

That saved a wretch like me!
I once was lost, but now am found,
Was blind, but now I see.

1779 *Olney Hymns*, 'Amazing Grace'.

43 Glorious things of thee are spoken,
Zion, city of our God!

1779 *Olney Hymns*, 'Glorious things of thee are spoken'.

44 How sweet the name of Jesus sounds
In a believer's ear!

1779 *Olney Hymns*, 'How sweet the name of Jesus sounds'.

Ngũgĩ wa Thiong'o originally *James Ngũgĩ* 1938–

Kenyan writer; his early works were written in English, but he now chooses to write solely in his own language. Works include *Weep Not Child* (1964), *The River Between* (1965), *A Grain of Wheat* (1967) and *Petals of Blood* (1977).

45 Today, children, I am going to tell you about the history of Mr. Blackman in three sentences. In the beginning he had the land and the mind and the soul together. On the second day, they took the body away to barter it for silver coins. On the third day, seeing that he was still fighting back, they brought priests and educators to bind his mind and soul so that these foreigners could more easily take his land and produce.

1977 *Petals of Blood*, ch.8.

46 He who produces should be able to control that which he produces.

1990 Quoted in Carol Sicherman *Ngũgĩ wa Thiong'o: The Making of a Rebel*, pt.1, ch.2, 'Ngũgĩ on Ngũgĩ' by Ngũgĩ himself.

Nguyen, Xuan Oanh 1921–

Vietnamese economist who rose to become South Vietnam's acting Prime Minister in 1964. After the country was reunited in 1975 he remained in limbo for ten years before his ideas for economic change were accepted. He is now regarded as the unofficial architect of Vietnam's economic reforms.

47 There is no such thing as communism versus capitalism. There are only degrees of communism and degrees of capitalism.

1995 In the *Eastern Express*, 17 May.

48 Patriotism in Vietnam took the communist road because it was the only one available. It had the appeal of a dream, a dream of social justice.

1995 In the *Eastern Express*, 17 May.

Nicholas I 1796–1855

Tsar of Russia (from 1825). During his reign, wars with Persia and Turkey increased Russia's territory. He died during the Crimean War, when Russia's attempts to absorb Turkey were resisted by Britain and France.

49 Russia has two generals in whom she can confide— Janvier and Février.

1855 Referring to the severe Russian winter climate. Quoted in *Punch*, 10 Mar .

Nicholas II 1868–1919

Last Emperor of Russia (1894–1917), whose reign was marked by alliance with France (1894), *entente* with Britain, disastrous war with Japan (1904–5) and the establishment of the Duma (1906). He fought against the Central Powers in 1915. Forced to abdicate at the Revolution, he was shot with his family by the Red Guards.

50 There are senseless dreams of the participation of local government representatives in the affairs of internal administration. I shall maintain the principle of autocracy just as firmly and unflinchingly as it was upheld by my own, ever to be remembered dead father.

1896 Declaration, 17 Jan.

Nichols, Grace 1950–

Guyanese poet, novelist and journalist, married to the poet John Agard; her publications include *Trust You, Wriggly!* (1981) and *Leslyn in London* (1984) for children, and the poetry sequences *i is a long memoried woman* (1983) (Commonwealth Poetry Prize) and *The Fat Black Woman's Poems* (1984).

51 I have crossed an ocean
I have lost my tongue
from the root of the old one
a new one has sprung

1983 *i is a long memoried woman*, epilogue.

52 IT'S BETTER TO DIE IN THE FLESH OF HOPE
THAN TO LIVE IN THE SLIMNESS OF DESPAIR.

1984 *The Fat Black Woman's Poems*, 'The Fat Black Woman's Motto on Her Bedroom Door'.

Nichols, Mike originally Michael Peschowsky 1931–

American stage and film director. He collected Tony Awards for the plays: *Barefoot in the Park* (1963), *The Odd Couple* (1965) and *Plaza Suite* (1968). More recently he directed *Death and the Maiden* (New York, 1992). His many films include *The Graduate* (1967, Academy Award), *Catch-22* (1969), *Silkwood* (1983), *Working Girl* (1988), *Postcards From The Edge* (1990), *Remains of the Day* (1993, as producer) and *The Birdcage* (1995).

53 Style is beginning something in the manner which will make it necessary for things that happen later to happen.

1991 In *Film Comment*, May.

Nicholson, Bill 1919–

English footballer and manager. He played with Tottenham Hotspur, and as manager of the club achieved the double of the FA Cup and the League Championship (1961). He won two more FA Cup titles (1962 and 1967), the European Cup Winners' Cup (1963), two more League Championships (1971 and 1973) and the UEFA Cup (1972).

54 I prefer players not to be too good or clever at other things. It means they concentrate on football.

1973 Quoted in Peter Ball and Phil Shaw *The Book of Football Quotations* (1989).

Nicholson, Jack 1937–

US film actor. An office boy at MGM, he made his film début in *Cry Baby Killer* (1958) and survived a decade of low-budget exploitation films before *Easy Rider* (1969) established his reputation. He has won two Oscars and nine Academy Award nominations.

55 She's like a delicate fawn, crossed with a Buick.

1984 Of actress Jessica Lange. In *Vanity Fair*, Oct.

Nicholson, Vivian 1936–

English housewife. In 1961 her husband Keith won £152,000 on the football pools, but the couple subsequently had difficulty coping with their fortune. Keith died in a car crash and Viv spent the money in just four years and turned to religion after several failed marriages and alcohol and drug abuse.

56 I want to spend, and spend, and spend!

1961 Quoted in the *Daily Herald*, 28 Sep, when asked what her plans were on winning the pools. The words 'Spend, spend, spend!' were later used as the title of her autobiography and for a biographical television play by Jack Rosenthal in 1977.

Nicias c.470–413 BC

Athenian statesman and soldier, who negotiated a short-lived peace with Sparta (421 BC). He was a commander in the disastrous naval expedition against Sicily in 418 BC, during which he was captured and put to death.

57 For it is men that make a city, and not its walls, nor its ships empty of men.

413 BC Speech to the defeated Athenian army. Quoted in Thucydides 7.77.

Nicklaus, Jack William 1940–

US golfer. He won the US Open Championship in 1962, the first of a record 18 major tournaments. He went into semi-retirement in 1986 and is now in demand as a golf course designer.

58 Golf is not and never has been a fair game.

Quoted in Colin Jarman *The Guinness Dictionary of Sports Quotations* (1990).

59 I think I fail a bit less than everyone else.

Quoted in Michael Hobbs *The Golf Quotation Book* (1992).

Nicolle, Charles Jules Henri 1866–1936

French physician and microbiologist, Director of the Pasteur Institute in Tunis, Tunisia and Professor of Bacteriology at the Collège de France. He was awarded a Nobel Prize in 1928 for demonstrating the transmission of typhus by lice.

60 All method is imperfect. Error is all around it, and at the least opportunity invades it... But what can we do? There is no other way.
Biologie de l'Invention.

Nicolson, Sir Harold 1886–1968

English diplomat, author and critic, born in Tehran. A distinguished diplomat (1909–29), he turned to journalism and was a National Liberal MP (1935–45). He wrote works of literary criticism and literary and historical biography.

61 My first impression is of a slightly bearded spinster: my second is of Willie King made up like Philip II: my third of some thin little bird, peeking, crooked, reserved, violent and timid.
1931 On meeting James Joyce. Diary entry, 30 Jul.

62 I feel pretty glum and devote myself to reviewing. There is Joyce's *Finnegans Wake.* I try very hard indeed to understand that book but fail completely. It is almost impossible to decipher, and when one or two lines of understanding emerge like telegraph poles above a flood, they are at once countered by other poles going in the opposite direction.
1939 Diary entry, 29 Apr.

Niebuhr, Reinhold 1892–1971

US theologian, Professor at the Union Theological Seminary, New York.

63 All men who live with any degree of serenity live by some assurance of grace.
1934 *Reflections on the End of Our Era.*

64 Perhaps the most sublime insights of the Jewish prophets and the Christian gospel is the knowledge that since perfection is love, the apprehension of perfection is at once the means of seeing one's imperfections and the consoling assurance of grace which makes this realization bearable. This ultimate paradox of high religion is not an invention of theologians or priests. It is constantly validated by the most searching experiences of life.
1934 *Reflections on the End of an Era.*

65 The pretensions of final truth are always partly an effort to obscure a darkly felt consciousness of the limits of human knowledge.
1941 *The Nature and Destiny of Man,* vol.1.

66 God, give us grace to accept with serenity the things that cannot be changed, courage to change the things that should be changed, and the wisdom to distinguish the one from the other.
In Richard Wightman Fox, *Reinhold Neibuhr* (1985) ch.12. Attributed to Neibuhr, but more probably 18c German.

Nielsen, Carl August 1865–1931

Danish composer, who experimented with polytonality and developed a characteristic contrapuntal style.

67 Music is life, and, like it, inextinguishable.
1916 Symphony No. 4, motto.

Niemöller, Martin 1892–1984

German submarine commander, pastor and theologian, leader of Christian opposition to Nazism.

68 When Hitler attacked the Jews I was not a Jew, therefore, I was not concerned. And when Hitler attacked the Catholics, I was not a Catholic, and therefore, I was not concerned. And when Hitler attacked the unions and the industrialists, I was not a member of the unions and I was not concerned. Then, Hitler attacked me and the Protestant church—and there was nobody left to be concerned.
1944 *Children of Light and Darkness,* foreword.

Nietzsche, Friedrich Wilhelm 1844–1900

German philosopher, scholar and writer. Professor of Classical Philology at the University of Basel (1868–78), he resigned in ill health. From 1872 he produced a stream of brilliant, unclassifiable works, rejecting Christianity for a new, heroic morality. In 1889 he had a complete mental and physical breakdown, from which he never recovered. His reputation suffered when his ideas were adopted in a distorted form by the Nazis, but he is now regarded as a major influence on 20c thought.

69 *Überzeugungen sind gefährlichere Feinde der Wahrheit als Lügen.*

Convictions are more dangerous enemies of truth than lies.
1878 *Menschliches, Allzumenschliches* (*Human, All Too Human*), section 483 (translated by R J Hollingdale).

70 The press, the machine, the railway, the telegraph are premises whose thousand-year conclusion no one has yet dared to draw.
1880 *The Wanderer and His Shadow,* aphorism 278.

71 *Gott ist tot: aber so wie die Art der Menschen ist, wird es vielleicht noch Jahrtausende lang Höhlen geben, in denen man seinen Schatten zeigt.—Und wir—wir müssen auch noch seinen Schatten besiegen!*

God is dead; but given the way of men, there may still be caves for thousands of years in which his shadow will be shown.—And we—we still have to vanquish his shadow, too.
1882 *Die Fröhliche Wissenschaft* (*The Gay Science*), section 108 (translated by W Kaufmann). This is the first occurrence of the famous phrase, which appears elsewhere in Nietzsche's work.

72 *Moralität ist Herden-Instinkt im Einzelnen.*

Morality is herd instinct in the individual.

1882 *Die Fröhliche Wissenschaft* (*The Gay Science*), section 116 (translated by W Kaufmann).

73 *Und, alles in allem und großem: ich will irgendwann einmal nur noch ein Jasagender sein!*

And all in all and on the whole: some day I wish to be only a Yes-sayer.

1882 *Die Fröhliche Wissenschaft* (*The Gay Science*), section 276 (translated by W Kaufmann).

74 *Glaubt es mir!—das Geheimnis, um die größte Fruchtbarkeit und den größten Genuß vom Dasein einzuernten, heißt: gefährlich leben!*

For believe me: the secret for harvesting from existence the greatest fruitfulness and the greatest enjoyment is—to *live dangerously*.

1882 *Die Fröhliche Wissenschaft* (*The Gay Science*), section 283 (translated by W Kaufmann).

75 *Eins ist not.—Seinem Charakter 'Stil geben'.*

One thing is needful.—To 'give style' to one's character.

1882 *Die Fröhliche Wissenschaft* (*The Gay Science*), section 290 (translated by W Kaufmann).

76 *Ich lehre euch den Übermenschen. Der Mensch ist Etwas, das überwunden werden soll.*

I teach you the Superman. Man is something that should be surpassed.

1883–92 *Also sprach Zarathustra* (*Thus Spake Zarathustra*), prologue, section 3 (translated by R J Hollingdale).

77 *Der Mensch ist ein Seil, geknüpft zwischen Tier und Übermensch,—ein Seil über einem Abgrunde.*

Man is a rope, fastened between animal and Superman—a rope over an abyss.

1883–92 *Also sprach Zarathustra* (*Thus Spake Zarathustra*), prologue, section 4 (translated by R J Hollingdale).

78 *Was groß ist am Menschen, das ist, daß er eine Brücke und kein Zweck ist.*

What is great in man is that he is a bridge and not a goal.

1883–92 *Also sprach Zarathustra* (*Thus Spake Zarathustra*), prologue, section 4 (translated by R J Hollingdale).

79 *Ich sage euch: man muß noch Chaos in sich haben, um einem tanzenden Stern gebären zu können.*

I tell you: one must have chaos in one, to give birth to a dancing star.

1883–92 *Also sprach Zarathustra* (*Thus Spake Zarathustra*), prologue, section 5 (translated by R J Hollingdale).

80 *Du gehst zu Frauen? Vergiß die Peitsche nicht!*

You are going to women? Do not forget the whip!

1883–92 *Also sprach Zarathustra* (*Thus Spake Zarathustra*), bk.1 (translated by R J Hollingdale).

81 Distrust all in whom the impulse to punish is powerful.

1883–92 *Also sprach Zarathustra* (*Thus Spake Zarathustra*) (translated by R J Hollingdale).

82 *Gesetzt, wir wollen Wahrheit: warum nicht lieber Unwahrheit? Und Ungewißheit? Selbst Unwissenheit?*

Granted we want truth: *why not rather* untruth? And uncertainty? Even ignorance?

1886 *Jenseits von Gut und Böse* (*Beyond Good and Evil*), section 1 (translated by R J Hollingdale).

83 *Allmählich hat sich mir herausgestellt, was jede große Philosophie bisher war: nämlich das Selbstbekenntnis ihres Urhebers und eine Art ungewollter und unvermerkter mémoires.*

It has gradually become clear to me what every great philosophy has hitherto been: a confession on the part of its author and a kind of involuntary and unconscious memoir.

1886 *Jenseits von Gut und Böse* (*Beyond Good and Evil*), section 6 (translated by R J Hollingdale).

84 *Sie schafft immer die Welt nach ihrem Bilde, sie kann nicht anders; Philosophie ist dieser tyrannische Treib selbst, der geistigste Wille zur Macht, zur 'Schaffung der Welt'.*

It [philosophy] always creates the world in its own image, it cannot do otherwise; philosophy is this tyrannical drive itself, the most spiritual will to power, to 'creation of the world'.

1886 *Jenseits von Gut und Böse* (*Beyond Good and Evil*), section 9 (translated by R J Hollingdale).

85 *Alles, was tief ist, liebt die Maske.*

Everything profound loves the mask.

1886 *Jenseits von Gut und Böse* (*Beyond Good and Evil*), section 40 (translated by R J Hollingdale).

86 *Das moralische Urteilen und Verurteilen ist die Lieblings-Rache der Geistig-Beschränkten an denen, die es weniger sind.*

Moral judgement and condemnation is the favourite form of revenge of the spiritually limited on those who are less so.

1886 *Jenseits von Gut und Böse* (*Beyond Good and Evil*), section 219 (translated by R J Hollingdale).

87 *Herren-Moral und Sklaven-Moral.*

Master morality and slave morality.

1886 *Jenseits von Gut und Böse* (*Beyond Good and Evil*), section 260 (translated by R J Hollingdale).

88 The thought of suicide is a great source of comfort across many a bad night.

1886 *Jenseits von Gut und Böse* (*Beyond Good and Evil*), (translated by R J Hollingdale).

89 Oh, how much is today hidden by science! Oh, how much it is expected to hide!

1887 *The Genealogy of Morals*, essay 3, 'What Do Ascetic Ideals Mean?'

90 *Durch schlechte Köchinnen—durch den vollkommenen Mangel an Vernunft in der Küche ist die Entwicklung des Menschen am längsten aufgehalten, am schlimmsten beeinträchtigt worden.*

Through bad female cooks—through the entire lack of reason in the kitchen—the development of mankind has been longest retarded and most interfered with.

1886 *Jenseits von Gut und Böse* (*Beyond Good and Evil*), 234. (Translated by Helen Zimmern, 1907).

91 *Hat je sich ein Weib, das sich gut bekleidet wußte, erkältet?*

Has a woman who knew she was well dressed ever caught a cold?

1889 *Die Götzen-Dämmerung* (*Twilight of the Idols*), 'Maxims and Arrows', no.25 (translated by R J Hollingdale).

92 Without music, life would be a mistake.

1889 *Die Götzen-Dämmerung* (*Twilight of the Idols*, translated by R J Hollingdale)

93 *Das, worin man die nationalen Unterschiede findet, ist viel mehr, als man bis jetzt eingesehen hat, nur der Unterschied verschiedener Culturestufen und zum geringsten Teile etwas Bleibendes (und auch dies nicht in einem strengen Sinne).*

National differences consist, far more than has hitherto been observed, only in the differences of various grades of culture, and are only to a very small extent permanent (and not even that in a strict sense).

Nachgelassene Fragmente.

Nightingale, Benedict 1939–

British author and theatre critic. He has written for *The Times* since 1990.

94 He handles symbolism rather like an Olympic weight lifter, raising it with agonizing care, brandishing it with a tiny grunt of triumph, then dropping it with a terrible clang.

1984 Of playwright William Inge. In the *New York Times*, 28 Jul.

Nightingale, Florence 1820–1910

English nurse and hospital reformer during the Crimean War. She subsequently formed an institution for the training of nurses in London.

95 Why have women Passion, intellect, moral activity—these three—and a place in society where no one of the three can be exercised?

1852 'Cassandra' pt.1, part of an unpublished work *Suggestions for Thought to Searchers after Religious Truth* (revised and privately printed 1859). Published as an appendix in Ray Strachey *The Cause: A Short History of the Women's Movement in Great Britain* (1928).

96 Give us back our suffering, we cry to Heaven in our hearts—suffering rather than indifferentism; for out of nothing comes nothing… Better have pain than paralysis!

1852 'Cassandra' pt.1, part of an unpublished work *Suggestions for Thought to Searchers after Religious Truth* (revised and privately printed 1859). Published as an appendix in Ray Strachey *The Cause: A Short History of the Women's Movement in Great Britain* (1928).

97 Look at the poor lives we lead. It is a wonder that we are so good as we are, not that we are so bad.

1852 'Cassandra' pt.2, part of an unpublished work *Suggestions for Thought to Searchers after Religious Truth* (revised and privately printed 1859). Published as an appendix in Ray Strachey *The Cause: A Short History of the Women's Movement in Great Britain* (1928).

98 Marriage is the only chance (and it is but a chance) offered to women for escape from this death…and how eagerly and how ignorantly it is embraced.

1852 'Cassandra' pt.3, part of an unpublished work *Suggestions for Thought to Searchers after Religious Truth* (revised and privately printed 1859). Published as an appendix in Ray Strachey *The Cause: A Short History of the Women's Movement in Great Britain* (1928).

99 The next Christ will perhaps be a female Christ.

1852 'Cassandra' pt.4, part of an unpublished work *Suggestions for Thought to Searchers after Religious Truth* (revised and privately printed 1859). Published as an appendix in Ray Strachey *The Cause: A Short History of the Women's Movement in Great Britain* (1928).

1 No *man*, not even a doctor, ever gives any other definition of what a nurse should be than this— 'devoted and obedient'. This definition would do just as well for a porter. It might even do for a horse. It would not do for a policeman.

1859 *Notes on Nursing.*

Nimitz, Admiral Chester (William) 1885–1966

US naval officer. He was commander-in-chief of the Pacific Fleet 1941–45, contributing significantly to the defeat of Japan. As fleet admiral he signed the Japanese surrender documents in Tokyo Bay (1945). He was chief of naval operations 1945–47.

2 A ship is always referred to as 'she' because it costs so much to keep her in paint and powder.

1959 In the *New York Times*, 24 May.

Nin, Anaïs 1903–77

US writer, born in Paris to parents of Spanish–Cuban descent. Her works explored sexuality and feminism with a frankness unusual in her era.

3 I stopped loving my father a long time ago. What remained was the slavery to a pattern.

1944 *Under a Glass Bell*, 'Birth'.

Nisbet, Robert 1913–

US sociologist.

4 Countless works in the social sciences reveal the inability of their authors to bear in mind the crucial difference between what may properly be called the *logic of discovery* and the *logic of demonstration*. The second is properly subject to rules and prescriptions; the first isn't.

1976 *Sociology as an Art Form*, introduction.

5 With all allowance made for Marx's erudition and his historic impact upon the social sciences, especially sociology, it is as an art united with prophecy, virtually religious prophecy, that Marxism survives.

1976 *Sociology as an Art Form*, ch.5.

Niven, David originally James David Graham Nevins 1910–83

English actor. Signed by Samuel Goldwyn, he developed into a polished light comedian in films such as *The Charge of the Light Brigade* (1936), *The Dawn Patrol* (1938) and *Bachelor Mother* (1939). He won an Academy Award for *Separate Tables* (1958).

6 He passed rapidly through his marriages to Virginia Cherrill, Barbara Hutton and Betsy Drake and filled in the lonely gaps between them by falling in and out of love with most of his leading ladies, which, as his output of films was prodigious, underlined the excellence of his physical condition.

1975 Of Cary Grant. *Bring on the Empty Horses*.

Nixon, Pat 1912–93

Wife of President Richard M. Nixon. She financed herself through college and taught typing until she married Nixon in 1940. She bore two daughters and was known for her gracious hospitality during her years in the White House. She was unswervingly loyal to her husband during and after his resignation in 1974.

7 The hearings are just like a snake about to devour people.

1973 On Watergate. Letter to a friend, quoted in Julie Nixon Eisenhower *Pat Nixon* (1986).

8 Dick, I don't know how you get up in the morning!

To her husband, who later wrote that he replied 'I do it to confound my enemies'. Quoted in Julie Nixon Eisenhower *Pat Nixon* (1986).

Nixon, Richard M(ilhous) 1913–94

US Republican politician and 37th President (1969–74). He resigned under threat of impeachment after the implication of leading members of his government in the Watergate affair. As President, he sought to end the Vietnam War and had diplomatic success with China and the USSR.

9 I don't believe that I ought to quit because I am not a quitter.

1952 National TV broadcast after allegations that he was financing his vice-presidential candidacy from a secret fund, Sep.

10 Tonight—to you, the great silent majority of my fellow Americans—I ask for your support.

1969 Appeal to the nation, 3 Nov, for support in the Vietnam War.

11 This is not an invasion of Vietnam.

1970 Television address to the nation announcing the invasion of Cambodia, 30 Apr.

12 I don't give a shit what happens. I want you all to stonewall...plead the Fifth Amendment, cover-up, or anything else. If that will save it, save the plan.

1973 From the White House tapes relating to the Watergate scandal, recorded Mar.

13 There will be no whitewash in the White House.

1973 Statement on the Watergate affair, 17 Apr.

14 In giving you these tapes, blemishes and all, I am placing my trust in the basic fairness of the American people.

1974 National address, 30 May, on relinquishing the Watergate tapes after the House Judiciary Committee warned him that refusal 'might constitute a ground for impeachment'.

15 Well, I screwed it up real good, didn't I?

1974 Comment to Chief of Staff Alexander M Haig and Press Secretary Ronald L Zeigler, 3 Aug, on beginning work on his resignation address. Recalled in *RN: The Memoirs of Richard Nixon* (1978).

16 When the president does it, that means that it is not illegal...But I brought myself down. I gave them a sword and they stuck it in and twisted it with relish. And I guess that if I had been in their position, I'd have done the same thing.

1977 Interviewed by David Frost, May.

17 American people don't believe anything until they see it on television.

1994 In *Newsweek*, 2 May. He estimated that 80% of US citizens get their news from television.

Noble, Richard 1946–

English car racer. He established a new land-speed record of 1,019.467kmph (633.468mph) in 1983 in the specially built *Thrust 2*.

18 We did it for Britain and for the hell of it.

1983 After setting a new world land-speed record. Quoted in *The Sunday Times*, 'The Week in Words', 9 Oct.

Nofzinger, Lynn

White House Political Director.

19 Cashing in. That's what we all do. It's called experience.

1988 In *This Week*, 31 Jul.

Nolan, Sir Sidney Robert 1917–92

Australian painter. He made his name with a series of *Ned Kelly* paintings (begun 1946), followed by an 'explorer' series.

20 I wanted to know the true nature of the 'otherness' I had been born into. It was not a European thing. I wanted to paint the great purity and implacability of the landscape. I wanted a visual form of the 'otherness' of the thing not seen.
1971 Quoted in E Lynn *Sidney Nolan—Australia* (1979).

Noonan, Peggy 1950–

US writer. She worked in insurance until she became a scriptwriter, producer and director of WEEI (CBS) Boston. She was speechwriter for President Reagan 1984-9 and has since been a columnist for *Newsweek*, the *New York Times* and *Time*. She has written three books.

21 The battle for the mind of Ronald Reagan was like the trench warfare of World War I. Never have so many fought so hard for such barren terrain.
1990 *What I Saw at the Revolution*.

22 A speech is poetry: cadence, rhythm, imagery, sweep…and reminds us that words, like children, have the power to make dance the dullest beanbag of a heart.
1990 *What I Saw at the Revolution*.

Noonuccal, Oodgeroo formerly *Kath Walker* née *Kathleen Jean Mary Ruska* 1920–93

Australian poet and Aboriginal rights activist. Her works include *We Are Going* (1964), the first book by an Aboriginal writer to be published in English. She returned an MBE awarded to her in 1970, in protest at planned Australian bicentennial celebrations.

23 Do you know, Mr Menzies, that where I come from you could be gaoled for supplying alcohol to an Aborigine?
1962 Remark to the then Prime Minister of Australia, Robert Menzies, when he offered her and other Aboriginal delegates a drink after a meeting. Quoted in Kathie Cochrane *Oodgeroo* (1994), pt.1, 'Protest'.

24 What can I tell you, son of mine?
I could tell you of heartbreak, hatred blind,
I could tell of crimes that shame mankind,
Of brutal wrong and deeds malign,
Of rape and murder, son of mine;
But I'll tell instead of brave and fine
When lives of black and white entwine,
And men in brotherhood combine—
This would I tell you, son of mine.
1964 *We Are Going*, 'Son of Mine'.

25 No more boomerang
No more spear;
Now all civilized—

Colour-bar and beer.
1970 *My People*, 'No More Boomerang'.

Norden, Denis 1922–

English broadcaster and humorist.

26 It's a funny kind of month, October. For the really keen cricket fan it's when you realise that your wife left you in May.
Quoted in *She* magazine, 1977.

Norman, Mike

Commanding officer of the 68 Royal marines who comprised the Falklands garrison at the time of the Argentinian invasion.

27 We've never surrendered before. It's not part of our training.
1982 Comment, Apr. Quoted in The Sunday Times Insight Team *The Falklands War* (1982), p.7.

Norris, Frank Benjamin Franklin 1870–1902

US novelist. He worked for the San Francisco *Chronicle* and while reporting became involved in the Jameson raid in South Africa. He was influenced by Zola and was one of the first US naturalist writers. His novels include *McTeague* (1899) and *The Pit* (1903).

28 The kind of a man that *men* like—not women—is the kind of man that makes the best husband.
1903 *The Pit*, ch.2.

29 Here, of all her cities, throbbed the true life—the true power and spirit of America; gigantic, crude with the crudity of youth, disdaining rivalry; sane and healthy and vigorous; brutal in its ambition, arrogant in the new-found knowledge of its giant strength, prodigal of its wealth, infinite in its desires.
1903 Of Chicago. *The Pit*, ch.2.

North, Christopher pseudonym of *John Wilson* 1785–1854

Scottish critic and essayist, Professor of Moral Philosophy at Edinburgh University (1820–51), and regular contributor to *Blackwood's Magazine* under the pseudonym 'Christopher North'.

30 His Majesty's dominions, on which the sun never sets.
1829 'Noctes Ambrosianae', no.42, in *Blackwood's Magazine*, Apr.

31 Laws were made to be broken.
1830 'Noctes Ambrosianae', no.49, in *Blackwood's Magazine*, May.

32 It may be divided into three parts; in one you cannot hear, in another you cannot see, and in the

third you can neither see nor hear. I remember once sitting alone in the third division—and never before or since have I had such a profound feeling of the power of solitude.

1832 Of the Theatre Royal, Glasgow. 'Noctes Ambrosianae', no.64, in *Blackwood's Magazine*, Nov.

33 Such accidents will happen in the best-regulated families.

1834 'Noctes Ambrosianae', no.67, in *Blackwood's Magazine*, Aug.

North, Oliver 1943–

US soldier, a National Security official involved in the 1986 Iran–Contra scandal (the supporting of anti-government Contra rebels in Nicaragua with the proceeds of secret arms sales to Iran). Despite appeals to patriotism, he was convicted on three of twelve charges.

34 I don't think there's another person in America that wants to tell this story as much as I do.

1986 Invoking the Fifth Amendment at the House Committee investigating arms sales to Iran, 10 Dec.

35 I thought using the Ayatollah's money to support the Nicaraguan resistance…was a neat idea.

1987 Testimony at the House Committee investigating arms sales to Iran, 8 Jul.

Novak, Michael 1933–

US critic, writer and philosopher.

36 Baseball is a Lockean game, a kind of contract theory in ritual form, a set of atomic individuals who assent to patterns of limited co-operation in their mutual interest.

1976 *The Joys of Sport*, pt.1.

Novalis pseudonym of *Friedrich von Hardenberg* 1772–1801

German poet, a leading early Romantic. The early death of the woman he loved left a lasting impression on him, and he wrote the prose lyrics of *Hymnen an die Nacht* (1800) in her memory. He died of tuberculosis.

37 *Der Tod ist das romantisierende Prinzip unsers Lebens. Der Tod ist—das Leben. Durch den Tod wird das Leben verstärckt.*

Death is the romantic principle of Life. Death is—life. Through death life is intensified.

1802 *Schriften II, Fragmente*.

38 *Ein Karakter ist ein volkommen gebildeter Willen.*

A character is a perfectly cultivated will.

1802 *Schriften, II, Fragmente*.

39 *Jeder Engländer ist eine Insel.*

Every Englishman is an island.

1802 *Schriften, II, Fragmente*.

40 *Mensch werden ist eine Kunst.*

To become human is art.

1802 *Schriften, II, Fragmente*.

Noyes, Alfred 1880–1958

English writer. He was best known for his florid poems, and especially his sea poems, but also wrote literary essays, plays, and memoirs.

41 Go down to Kew in lilac-time (it isn't far from London!)
And you shall wander hand in hand with love in summer's wonderland.

1904 'The Barrel-Organ'.

42 The wind was a torrent of darkness among the gusty trees,
The moon was a ghostly galleon tossed upon cloudy seas,
The road was a ribbon of moonlight over the purple moor,
And the highwayman came riding—
Riding—riding—
The highwayman came riding, up to the old inn-door.

1907 'The Highwayman'.

43 Watch for me by moonlight;
I'll come to thee by moonlight, though hell should bar the way.

1907 'The Highwayman'.

Nozick, Robert 1938–

US philosopher, Professor at Harvard University.

44 The socialist society would have to forbid capitalist acts between consenting adults.

1974 *Anarchy, State, and Utopia*, p.163.

Nugent, Ted 1949–

US rock guitarist. His albums include *Ted Nugent* (1975), *Free For All* (1976) and *Cat Scratch Fever* (1977).

45 If it's too loud, you're too old.

Quoted in David Pickering *Brewer's Twentieth Century Music* (1994).

Nuttgens, Patrick 1930–

British writer and educationalist. Director of Leeds Polytechnic (1969–86), his works include *The Landscape of Ideas* (1972) and *Understanding Modern Architecture* (1988).

46 In the final analysis, all architecture reveals the application of human ingenuity to the satisfaction

of human needs. And among these needs are not only shelter, warmth and accommodation, but also the needs, felt at every moment in every part of the world in endlessly different ways, for something more profound, evocative and universal, for beauty, for permanence, for immortality.

1993 'The Nature of Architecture', in Ben Farmer and Hentie Louw (eds) *Companion to Contemporary Architectural Thought* (1993).

Nye, Joseph S, Jr 1937–

Director of the Harvard Center for International Affairs (1990–) and Deputy to the Under-Secretary of State for Security.

47 Not their style to say no. But when you listen…you don't hear yes.

1994 On asking for Saudi Arabia's help with the $500-million cost of US troop buildup in the Gulf. In the *New York Times*, 4 Nov.

Oakeshott, Michael Joseph 1901–90

English philosopher and political theorist, Professor of Political Science at the London School of Economics (1951–69). His key philosophical work was *Experience and its Modes* (1933), a broadly idealistic view which he developed in economic theory.

48 The politics of our society are a conversation in which past, present and future each has a voice; and though one or other of them may on occasion properly prevail none permanently dominates, and on this account we are free.

1962 *Rationalism in Politics.*

49 We consider ourselves to be free because no one in our society is allowed unlimited power—no leader, faction, party or 'class', no majority, no government, church, corporation, trade, or professional association or trade union. The secret of its freedom is that it is composed of a multitude of organisations in the constitution of the best of which is reproduced that diffusion of power which is characteristic of the whole.

1962 *Rationalism in Politics.*

50 It is difficult to think of any circumstances where learning may be said to be impossible.

Quoted in R S Peters (ed) *The Concept of Education* (1966), ch.10, 'Learning and Teaching'.

51 Every human being is born an heir to an inheritance to which he can succeed only in a process of learning.

Quoted in R S Peters (ed) *The Concept of Education* (1966), ch.10, 'Learning and Teaching'.

Oakley, Charles Edward 1832–65

English clergyman and hymn writer.

52 Hills of the North, rejoice:
   Rivers and mountain-spring,
   Hark to the advent voice!
   Valley and lowland, sing!
   Though absent long, your Lord is nigh,
   He judgement brings, and victory.

1870 Hymn.

Oates, Joyce Carol 1938–

US writer. She is best known as a novelist, but has also published several volumes of poetry, and essays, critical writings and journalism.

53 The worst cynicism: a belief in luck.

1970 *Do What You Will*, pt.2, ch.15.

54 Nothing is accidental in the universe—this is one of my Laws of Physics—except the entire universe itself, which is Pure Accident, pure divinity.

1970 *Do What You Will*, 'The Summing-Up: Meredith Dawe'.

55 Women Whose Lives Are Food, Men Whose Lives Are Money.

1978 Title of poetry collection.

56 I used to think getting old was about vanity—but actually it's about losing people you love.

1989 In *The Guardian*, 18 Aug.

57 Because It Is Bitter, And Because It Is My Heart.

1990 Title of novel.

58 For what *is* passes so swiftly and irrevocably into what *was*, no human claim can be of the least significance.

1994 *What I Lived For*, prologue, pt.1.

59 And Corky'd protested, You mean it isn't enough to be *right?*—they have to *like* me, too?

1994 *What I Lived For*, pt.1.

Oates, Lawrence Edward Grace 1880–1912

English explorer, one of the members of Captain Scott's ill-fated Antarctic expedition that set out for the South Pole in 1910.

60 I am just going outside and may be some time.

1912 Last words, Mar.

▷ See Scott 852:40.

O'Brien, (Donal) Conor (Dermod David Donat) Cruise 1917–

Irish historian, critic and politician. He wrote *To Katanga and Back* (1962), an autobiographical narrative of the Congo crisis. After a career in politics, he became a political journalist.

61 Irishness is not primarily a question of birth or blood or language: it is the condition of being involved in the Irish situation, and usually of being mauled by it. On that definition Swift is more Irish

than Goldsmith or Sheridan, although by the usual tests they are Irish and he is pure English.

1959 Reviewing *The Oxford Book of Irish Verse* in the *New Statesman*, 17 Jan (written under the pseudonym Donat O'Donnell).

62 Of history and its consequences it may be said: 'Those who can, gloat; those who can't, brood.' Englishmen are born gloaters; Irishmen born brooders. There are, it is true, brooders who take to gloating, and they did much to build the Empire. Yet the brooder-gloater, such as the Irishman turned Englishman, is not, as a human type, altogether a success. He is a little too much on his guard, like an excessively assimilated Jew, or a son of Harlem who has decided to 'pass'. The past of the Irishman, the Jew, the Negro, is, psychologically, too explosive to be buried.

1962 *To Katanga and Back: a UN case history.*

63 In any case you Papists have no right to complain! If you won't have contraception how can you control the population without the assistance of Herod? You ought to be grateful.

1970 *King Herod Explains.*

64 We dislike the IRA, most of us, and fear it. We are a peaceful and democratic people. But our history, our idealistic pretensions and our fatal ambivalence have stuck us with an ideology that is warlike and anti-democratic, and calls increasingly for further human sacrifice.

1985 In the *New York Review of Books*, 29 Apr.

65 The United Nations cannot do anything, and never could. It is not an animate entity or agent. It is a place, a stage, a forum and a shrine…a place to which powerful people can repair when they are fearful about the course on which their own rhetoric seems to be propelling them.

1985 In *New Republic*, 4 Nov.

O'Brien, Flann pseudonym of *Brian O'Nolan,* also known as *Myles na Gopaleen* 1911–66

Irish writer who worked in the Irish Civil Service until 1953. In 1940 he began writing for the *Irish Times* under the pseudonym of Myles na Gopaleen and developed a reputation for being an eccentric and idiosyncratic columnist. He is best known for his novel, *At Swim-Two-Birds* (1939).

66 When things go wrong and will not come right, Though you do the best you can, When life looks black as the hour of night— A PINT OF PLAIN IS YOUR ONLY MAN.

1939 *At Swim-Two-Birds*, ch.1, 'The Workman's Friend' (as Flann O'Brien).

67 There was a frightful, appalling row.

As a matter of fact the Pope told us all to go to hell. He threatened to silence Father Fahrt.

1961 *The Hard Life.*

68 And now the curse has come upon us, because I have personally met in the streets of Ireland persons who are clearly out of Synge's plays. They talk and dress like that, and damn the drink they'll swally but the mug of porter in the long nights after Samhain.

1968 *The Best of Myles.*

O'Brien, John J

Washington correspondent, Philadelphia *Inquirer*.

69 The only candidate who can whistle Dixie while humming the *Battle Hymn of the Republic*.

1976 Of President Johnson. Quoted in Harold Brayman (ed) *The President Speaks Off the Record* (1976).

O'Brien, (Angela Maxine) Margaret

1937–

US child actress, best known for her performance in *Meet Me in St Louis* (1944).

70 When I cry, shall I let the tears run all the way down my face or shall I stop them halfway down?

1944 Attributed remark to director Henry Koster when making *Music for Millions* (1944). Quoted by Larry Adler in *It Ain't Necessarily So* (1984).

O'Brien, Virginia

Manhattan office worker.

71 Crouch, swivel, tug, pull and plop.

1987 Advice on how to seat oneself at a picnic while wearing a mini-skirt. In the *New York Times*, 17 Jul.

O'Brien, William 1852–1928

Irish journalist and politician, born a Catholic but educated at a Protestant college. He founded the Land League journal *United Ireland* (1881) and became a Nationalist MP (1883–95, 1900–18).

72 What are we learning French or the piano for, I would like to know, if it is not to be sold to a man some day… We have to cringe, and manoeuvre, and grimace for a husband—a husband who may be deaf or have a hump if he is rich—a husband that may attack you in *delirium tremens* to-day if he makes a devout act of contrition for it to-morrow.

1890 *When We Were Boys.*

Ó Bruadair, Dáibhídh c.1625–98

Irish-Gaelic poet, who recorded the destruction of his culture. His patrons were exiled by wars and proscription, and he became a farm labourer.

73 I will sing no more songs: the pride of my country I sang

Through forty long years of good rhyme, without
   any avail;
And no one cared even as much as the half of a
   hang
For the song or the singer, so here is an end of the
   tale.

Adapted from the Irish by James Stephens.

O'Casey, Sean 1884–1964

Irish playwright. His early plays, including *Juno and the Paycock* (1924), deal with Dublin working class life and were written for the Abbey Theatre. His later, more experimental, plays include *Cockadoodle Dandy* (1949).

74 Th' whole worl's in a state o' chassis!

   1924 Boyle speaking. *Juno and the Paycock*, act 1.

75 JUNO: Sacred Heart o' Jesus, take away our hearts o'
   stone, and give us hearts o' flesh! Take away this
   murdherin' hate, an' give us Thine own eternal
   love!

   1924 *Juno and the Paycock*, act 3.

76 She dhresses herself to keep him with her, but it's
   no use—afther a month or two, th' wondher of a
   woman wears off.

   1926 *The Plough and the Stars*, act 1.

77 There's no reason to bring religion into it. I think
   we ought to have as great a regard for religion as we
   can, so as to keep it out of as many things as
   possible.

   1926 *The Plough and the Stars*, act 1.

78 English literature's performing flea.

   Of P G Wodehouse. In P G Wodehouse *Performing Flea* (1953).

Occam, William of c.1285–c.1349

English philosopher, theologian and political writer. He was perhaps the most influential of later medieval philosophers.

79 *Entia non sunt multiplicanda praeter necessitatem.*

No more things should be presumed than is
necessary.

This principle of intellectual economy, known as Occam's Razor, is not found in this form in his writings. Similar expressions can be found, eg *Pluralitas non est ponenda sine necessitate* ('Plurality should not be posited unnecessarily') in *Scriptum in Librum Primum Sententiarum*.

O'Connell, Daniel known as *the Liberator*
1775–1847

Irish Catholic political leader, able to take his Commons seat only after Catholic Emancipation (1829). He fought against tithes and in 1840 founded the Repeal Association, agitating to end the union with Britain. In 1844 he was imprisoned on a charge of sedition, and his influence subsequently waned.

80 Let us never tolerate the slightest inroad on the
   discipline of our holy Church. Let us never consent
   that she should be made the hireling of the
   Ministry. Our forefathers would have died—nay,
   perished in hopeless slavery—rather than consent
   to such degradation.

   1814 Speech, Dublin, 23 Feb.

81 Not for all the universe contains would I, in the
   struggle for what I conceive to be my country's
   cause, consent to the effusion of a single drop of
   human blood, except my own.

   1843 Speech, 18 Feb.

82 While I have a tongue I'll abuse you, you most
   inimitable periphery. Look at her, boys! there she
   stands—a convicted perpendicular in petticoats!
   There's contamination in her circumference, and
   she trembles with guilt down to the extremities of
   her corollaries. Ah! you're found out, you rectilineal
   antecedent, and equiangular old hag! 'Tis with you
   the devil will fly away, you porter-swiping
   similitude of the bisection of a vortex!

   Winning thrust in a vituperation contest with Dublin's champion virago, Biddy Moriarty, reported by Daniel Owen-Madden in *Revelations of Ireland* (1877).

O'Connor, Edwin 1918–68

US novelist, originally a radio announcer and producer, best known for his novel *The Last Hurrah* (1956). *The Edge of Sadness* (1961) won a Pulitzer Prize.

83 The Last Hurrah.

   1956 Title of novel, based on the career of politician James M Curley.

O'Connor, (Mary) Flannery 1925–64

US novelist and short-story writer. Her fiction, set in the Deep South, reflects a mordant sense of humour. Her works include two novels and two volumes of short stories.

84 I preach there are all kinds of truth, your truth and
   somebody else's. But behind all of them there is
   only one truth and that is that there's no truth.

   1952 Hazel Motes. *Wise Blood*, ch.10.

85 While the South is hardly Christ-centred, it is most
   certainly Christ-haunted.

   1960 'Some Aspects of the Grotesque in Southern Fiction'. Paper read at Wesleyan College, Fall.

86 There was a time when the average reader read a
   novel simply for the moral he could get out of it,
   and however naïve that may have been, it was a
   good deal less naïve than some of the limited
   objectives he has now.

   1960 'Some Aspects of the Grotesque in Southern Fiction'. Paper read at Wesleyan College, Fall.

87 It's like building a nest. First she thinks about it, then she begins to gather the materials, then she begins to put it together.

On her mother's two-month process of making a fruit cake. Quoted in Sally Fitzgerald (ed) *The Habit of Being* (1979).

O'Connor, Frank pseudonym of *Michael O'Donovan* 1903–66

Irish writer, a member of the IRA in his teens and imprisoned after the War of Independence. His ideal medium was the short story, but he also wrote plays and literary criticism.

88 Every time I leave the old man I feel like a thousand dollars.

1948 Of Yeats. Quoted in Richard Ellmann *Yeats: the Man and the Masks* (1948).

O'Connor, Cardinal John Joseph 1920–

Catholic Archbishop of New York.

89 It is increasingly rare for many of us...to believe that people can be poor, but honest, poor but deserving of respect. Poverty is no longer blamed on anyone but the poor themselves. Contempt for the poor has become a virtue.

1994 In *Catholic New York*, quoted in the *New York Times*, 24 Nov.

Odets, Clifford 1906–63

US playwright and actor, an important figure in the US theatre of the 1930s.

90 Go out and fight so life shouldn't be printed on dollar bills.

1935 Jacob. *Awake and Sing*, act 1.

91 Music is the great cheer-up in the language of all countries.

1937 Mr Bonaparte. *Golden Boy*, act 1, sc.2.

O'Donnell, Phillip Kenneth 1924–

US Senator 1957–9, and Special Assistant to the President of the US, 1961– .

92 Mr President, the president is dead.

1963 To Lyndon B Johnson after the assassination of John F Kennedy, 22 Nov.

Oerter, Al(fred) 1936–

US athlete and discus-thrower. He won an unsurpassed four gold medals for the discus, at Melbourne (1956), Rome (1960), Tokyo (1964) and Mexico (1968).

93 I never had technique.

1978 In *the New York Times*, 16 May.

O'Faolain, Sean 1900–91

Irish writer and educator. He began writing in and translating from Gaelic. A successful novel, *A Nest of*

Simple Folk (1933), was followed by biographies of Irish figures.

94 If we turn to early Irish literature, as we naturally may, to see what sort of people the Irish were in the infancy of the race, we find ourselves wandering in delighted bewilderment through a darkness shot with lightning and purple flame.

1947 *The Irish.*

95 He was like a man who takes a machine-gun to a shooting gallery. Everybody falls flat on his face, the proprietor at once takes to the hills, and when you cautiously peep up, you find that he has wrecked the place but got three perfect bull's-eyes.

On Frank O'Connor (ie Michael O'Donovan), attributed.

O'Flaherty, Liam 1897–1984

Irish Republican writer. He went to London in 1922 to become a writer, finding fame with his novel *The Informer* (1926). In addition to other novels, he wrote three volumes of autobiography (1930–4).

96 When the parish priest rebuked him for his celibacy, saying it would lead him into debauchery and sin, he said that a man who had to be muzzled by a wife as a protection against debauchery was not worthy of the joy of innocence. After that people began to treat him with priestly respect.

'The Mermaid'.

Ogden, Frank 1920–

Canadian futurist.

97 Although I am a futurist today, if I don't change tomorrow, I will be a historian.

1994 *Ogdenisms: The Frank Ogden Quote Book.*

98 As the planet globalizes, groups tribalize.

1994 *Ogdenisms: The Frank Ogden Quote Book.*

99 Holidays are the greatest learning experience unknown to man.

1994 *Ogdenisms: The Frank Ogden Quote Book.*

1 Technology breaks the laws and makes the laws.

1994 *Ogdenisms: The Frank Ogden Quote Book.*

2 My idea of long-range planning is lunch.

1994 *Ogdenisms: The Frank Ogden Quote Book.*

Ogilvy, David 1911–

British-born US advertising executive, with Ogilvy and Mather.

3 It is the professional duty of the advertising agent to conceal his artifice. When Aeschines spoke, they said, 'How well he speaks', but when Demosthenes spoke, they said 'Let us march against Philip.'

1963 *Confessions of an Advertising Man*, ch.5.

4 The consumer isn't a moron. She's your wife.
  1963 *Confessions of an Advertising Man*, ch.5.

Ogilvy, James, 1st Earl of Seafield
1644–1730

Scottish advocate, MP and political manager. He was one of the Scottish commissioners appointed to negotiate the Union of Parliaments.

5 There's ane end of ane auld sang.
  1707 On signing the Treaty of Union betwen Scotland and England. Quoted in George Lockhart of Carnwath *Memoir of the Affairs of Scotland* (1714), vol.1.

O'Hagan, John pseudonym *Sliabh Cuilinn*
1822–90

6 My native heath is brown beneath,
  My native waters blue;
  But crimson red o'er both shall spread,
  Ere I am false to you,
  Dear land!
  Ere I am false to you.
  1845 'Dear Land' in *The Spirit of the Nation*.

O'Hanlon, Redmond 1947–

English naturalist, critic and traveller. With James Fenton, he made an expedition into the heart of Borneo in 1983 and wrote entertainingly about the land and its people.

7 The Iban, when they decide that something is really funny, and know that they are going to laugh for a long time, lie down first.
  Dana, Leon and Inghai lay down.
  1984 *Into the Heart of Borneo*.

O'Hara, Frank 1926–66

US poet and art critic. He published several volumes of poetry, which were closely linked to the New York environment in which he moved.

8 and I am sweating a lot by now and thinking of leaning on the john door in the 5 SPOT
  while she whispered a song along the keyboard
  to Mal Waldron and everyone and I stopped breathing
  1964 Of Billie Holiday. *Lunch Poems*, 'The Day Lady Died'.

O'Hara, John Henry 1905–70

US novelist and short story writer. His best known works, several of which were successfully filmed, included *Appointment in Samarra* (1934), *Butterfield 8* (1935) and *Pal Joey* (1940).

9 George Gershwin died last week. I don't have to believe it if I don't want to.

1937 Quoted in Ian Crofton and Donald Fraser *A Dictionary of Musical Quotations* (1985).

10 But whats the use of being old if you cant be dumb?
  1940 *Pal Joey*, ch.1.

11 I am making a little trip to N.Y. in the near future and we will have a little talk and you can explain your positon, altho the way I feel now if I saw you now your positon would be horizontle.
  1940 *Pal Joey*, ch.2.

12 Illinois is a state of suspended animation and the people live in hibernation from Oct. to whenever it ever gets warmer.
  1940 *Pal Joey*, ch.9.

O Henry pseudonym of *William Sydney Porter*
1862–1910

US writer. He is best known for his comic short stories.

13 Life is made up of sobs, sniffles, and smiles, with sniffles predominating.
  1906 *The Four Million*, 'The Gift of the Magi'.

14 If men knew how women pass the time when they are alone, they'd never marry.
  1906 *The Four Million*, 'Memoirs of a Yellow Dog'.

15 It was beautiful and simple as all truly great swindles are.
  1908 *The Gentle Grafter*, 'The Octopus Marooned'.

16 Whenever he saw a dollar in another man's hands he took it as a personal grudge if he couldn't take it any other way.
  1908 *The Gentle Grafter*, 'The Octopus Marooned'.

17 If ever there was an aviary overstocked with jays it is that Yaptown-on-the-Hudson, called New York.
  1908 *The Gentle Grafter*, 'A Tempered Wind'.

18 A story with a moral appended is like the bite of a mosquito. It bores you, and then injects a stinging drop to irritate your conscience.
  1910 *Strictly Business*, 'The Gold That Glittered'.

19 Turn up the lights; I don't want to go home in the dark.
  Last words. Quoted in Charles Alphonso Smith *O. Henry* (1916), ch.9. The words are taken from the popular song by Harry Williams 'I'm afraid to come home in the dark' (1907).

20 A burglar who respects his art always takes his time before taking anything else.
  Sixes and Sevens, 'Makes The Whole World Kin' (published 1911).

O'Keefe, Georgia 1887–1986

US painter, a pioneer of abstract art (eg *Blue and Green Music*, 1919). She later moved towards a more figurative style, painting close-ups of parts of flowers and plants. Her works include *Black Iris* (New York, 1949).

21 Nobody sees a flower—really—it is so small—we haven't time—and to see takes time like to have a friend takes time… So I said to myself—I'll paint what I see—what the flower is to me, but I'll paint it big and they will be surprised into taking time to look at it—I will make even busy New Yorkers take time to see what I see of flowers.
Quoted in Goodrich and Bry *Georgia O'Keefe* (1970).

22 The men liked to put me down as the best woman painter. I think I'm one of the best painters.
Quoted in W Chadwick *Women, Art and Society* (1990).

Okri, Ben 1959–

Nigerian writer; winner of the 1987 Commonwealth Prize for Africa, and the 1991 Booker Prize for *The Famished Road*. Other works include *Flowers and Shadows* (1980), *Incidents at the Shrine* (1986) and *Songs of Enchantment* (1993).

23 We feared the heartlessness of human beings, all of whom are born blind, few of whom ever learn to see.
1991 *The Famished Road*, ch.1.

Oldenburg, Claes Thure 1929–

Swedish-born US sculptor, who moved to the US in 1936 and took citizenship in 1953. From 1958 he was one of the pioneers of Pop Art. His works include giant hamburgers and other foodstuffs, and the *Giant Clothespin* in Philadelphia (1975).

24 I am for an art that helps old ladies across the street… I am for Kool-art, 7-UP art, Pepsi-art, Sunshine art, 39 cents art, 15 cents art, Vatronol art, Dro-bomb art, Vam art, Menthol art, L & M art, Ex-lax art, Venida art, Heaven Hill art, Pamryl art, San-o-med art, Rx art, 9.99 art, Now art, New art, How art, Fire sale art, Last Chance art, Only art, Diamond art, Tomorrow art, Franks art, Ducks art, Meat-o-rama art.
1961 Written for an exhibition in New York, 1961, quoted in Arts Council of Great Britain *Oldenburg* (1970).

Oliphant, Margaret née Wilson 1828–97

Scottish novelist, essayist and critic. Widowed and debt-ridden at an early age with a large extended family dependent upon her, she was a prolific writer and maintained a long association with *Blackwood's Magazine* and *The Cornhill* as well as completing over 100 novels.

25 A woman who cannot be a governess or a novel-writer must fall back on that poor little needle, the primitive and original handicraft of femininity.
1858 'The Condition of Women', in *Blackwood's Magazine*, vol.83, Feb.

Oliver, Mary 1935–

US poet. Her work includes *No Voyage and Other Poems* (1963, enlarged 1965), *American Primitive* (1983,

Pulitzer Prize) and *New and Selected Poems* (1992, National Book Award).

26 Poetry happens because of life. Poetry happens because of language. And poetry happens because of other poets.
1992 In the *New York Times*, 20 Nov.

Olivier, Laurence Kerr, Baron 1907–89

English actor, producer and director. A great Shakespearean actor, he also produced, directed and played in films of *Henry V*, *Hamlet* and *Richard III*. He campaigned for the foundation of the National Theatre.

27 Make up your mind dearheart. Do you want to be a great actor or a household word?
c.1962 Comment to Richard Burton while filming *Cleopatra*. Burton replied 'Both'.

28 Acting is a masochistic form of exhibitionism. It is not quite the occupation of an adult.
1978 Quoted in *Time Magazine*, 3 Jul.

29 I'm not so artistic that I despise profit.
Attributed.

30 It looks like rows and rows of empty seats.
On being shown the view of the jungle enjoyed from Noël Coward's house on a Jamaican hillside. Attributed.

31 Shakespeare—the nearest thing in incarnation to the eye of God.
Quoted in *Kenneth Harris Talking To…*, 'Sir Laurence Olivier'.

32 What is the main problem of the actor? It is to keep the audience awake, and not let them go to sleep, then wake up and go home feeling they've wasted their money.
Attributed.

Ollivier, Émile 1825–1913

French politician, charged by Napoleon III to form a constitutional ministry. He rushed into war with Germany, was overthrown on 9 Aug 1870, and withdrew to Italy. He wrote numerous works, including *L'Empire libéral* (16 vols, 1894–1912), a defence of his policy.

33 One is never weaker than when one appears to have everybody's support.
1870 Letters.

Olsen, Charles 1910–70

US poet and literary theorist. He taught at Black Mountain College, North Carolina, where his ideas were influential on such poets as Robert Creeley and Robert Duncan. As a poet, he is best known for the sequence *The Maximus Poems*.

34 I take SPACE to be the central fact to man born in America… I spell it large because it comes large here. Large and without mercy.
1947 *Call Me Ishmael*, section 1.

35 But that which matters, that which insists, that
which will last,
that! o my people, where shall you find it, how,
where, where shall you
listen
when all is become billboards, when, all, even
silence, is spray-gunned?
1953 *The Maximus Poems*, 'I, Maximus of Gloucester, To You,
3'.

36 one loves only form,
and form only comes
into existence when
the thing is born.
1953 *The Maximus Poems*, 'I, Maximus of Gloucester, To You,
4'.

Olsen, Elder James 1909–

US poet and critic. In both his formal, cerebral poetry and
criticism he adhered to the neo-Aristotelian principles
espoused at the University of Chicago, where he taught.

37 We shall never know all about art or the values of
art until all art is at an end; meanwhile artists will
continue to instruct us.
Quoted in Elmer Borklund (ed) *Contemporary Literary Critics*
(1977).

Olsen, Tillie 1913–

US writer and feminist. She wrote proletarian fiction in
the 1930s. In the 1960s she emerged as an advocate of
feminism, and her work attracted wide attention for the
first time. Her later work includes *Tell Me a Riddle*
(1960).

38 Vinegar he poured on me all his life; I am well
marinated; how can I be honey now?
1960 *Tell Me a Riddle*, section 1.

Onassis, Jacqueline Lee Kennedy née Bouvier 1929–94

Wife of President John F Kennedy. She supervised the
restoration of the White House and wielded a powerful
and widespread influence on fashion. After her husband's
assassination she returned to private life, and in 1968 she
married Aristotle Onassis, the Greek shipping magnate.

39 Put your brilliant mind to work for…dresses for
public appearances…that I would wear if Jack were
President of France.
1960 Letter to Oleg Cassini 13 Dec. Quoted in Oleg Cassini
In My Fashion (1987).

40 I felt like a moth hanging on the window pane.
1961 On her first night in the White House, in *Newsweek*, 1
Jan.

41 Lincoln's bedroom! And you see that great bed, it
looks like a cathedral.
1961 On her first night in the White House, in *Newsweek*, 1 Jan.

42 You worked together for the finest things in the
finest years… Later on when a series of disastrous
Presidents and Prime Ministers…will have botched
up everything—people will say 'Do you remember
those days—how perfect they were?' The days of
you and Jack.
1964 To Harold Macmillan, 31 Jan.

43 I cast only one vote—for Jack. It is a rare thing to
be able to vote for one's husband for President and I
didn't want to dilute it by voting for anyone else.
On the 1960 elections. Quoted in Arthur M Schlesinger Jr *A
Thousand Days* (1965).

44 There'll never be another Camelot again.
On Frederick Lowe's lyrics from Alan Jay Lerner's *Camelot*, a
title that became synonymous with the Kennedy
administration—'Don't let it be forgot, that once there was a
spot, for one brief shining moment that was known as Camelot.'
Quoted in Theodore H White *In Search of History* (1978).

45 Uncle Cornpone and his Little Porkchop.
On the Johnsons. Quoted in *Newsweek*, 30 May 1994.

Ondaatje, (Philip) Michael 1943–

Sri-Lankan-born Canadian poet and novelist. His poetry
includes *Rat Jelly* (1973) and *Secular Love* (1987); other
works include *The Man With Seven Toes* (1969) and
novels such as *The English Patient* (1992, Booker Prize).

46 There was always, he thought, this pleasure ahead
of him, an ace of joy up his sleeve so he could say
you can do anything to me, take everything away,
put me in prison, but I will know [her] when we are
old.
1987 *In The Skin of a Lion*, 'Remorse'.

O'Neill, Eugene Gladstone 1888–1953

US playwright. His play *Beyond the Horizon* (1920) won a
Pulitzer Prize, and he established his reputation with such
serious-minded plays as *Mourning Becomes Electra* (1931),
The Iceman Cometh (1946) and *Long Day's Journey into
Night* (1956). He was awarded a Nobel Prize in 1936.

47 The action of the play takes place on an island in
the West Indies as not yet self-determined by
White Mariners. The form of native government is,
for the time being, an Empire.
1920 *The Emperor Jones*, scene direction.

48 For de little stealin' dey gits you in jail soon or late.
For de big stealin' dey makes you Emperor and puts
you in de Hall o' Fame when you croaks.
1921 Jones. *The Emperor Jones*, sc.1.

49 Life is for each man a solitary cell whose walls are
mirrors.
1927 Lazarus. *Lazarus Laughed*, act 2, sc.1.

50 When men make gods, there is no God!
1927 Lazarus. *Lazarus Laughed*, act 2, sc.2.

51 Man's loneliness is but his fear of life!
1927 Lazarus. *Lazarus Laughed*, act 3, sc.2.

52 The old—like children—talk to themselves, for they have reached that hopeless wisdom of experience which knows that though one were to cry it in the streets to multitudes, or whisper it in the kiss to one's beloved, the only ears that can ever hear one's secrets are one's own!
1927 Tiberius. *Lazarus Laughed*, act 4, sc.1.

53 Life is perhaps most wisely regarded as a bad dream between two awakenings, and every day is a life in miniature.
1928 Chu-Yin. *Marco Millions*, act 2, sc.2.

54 The devil!…what beastly things our memories insist on cherishing!
1928 Marsden. *Strange Interlude*, pt.1, act 2.

55 Strange interlude! Yes, our lives are merely strange dark interludes in the electrical display of God the Father!
1928 Nina. *Strange Interlude*, pt.2, act 9.

56 Mourning Becomes Electra.
1931 Title of play.

57 The sea hates a coward!
1931 Bryant. *Mourning Becomes Electra*, pt.2, act 4.

58 EDMUND: (*sits down opposite his father—contemptuously*). Yes, facts don't mean a thing, do they? What you want to believe, that's the only truth! (*Derisively.*) Shakespeare was an Irish Catholic, for example.
TYRONE: (*stubbornly*). So he was. The proof is in his plays.
1939–41 *Long Day's Journey Into Night*, act 4 (published 1956).

59 Where do you get your taste in authors—That damned library of yours! (*He indicates the small bookcase at rear.*) Voltaire, Rousseau, Schopenhauer, Nietzsche, Ibsen! Atheists, fools, and madmen! And your poets! This Dowson, and this Baudelaire, and Swinburne and Oscar Wilde, and Whitman and Poe! Whoremongers and degenerates! Pah! When I've three good sets of Shakespeare there (*he nods at the large bookcase*) you could read.
1939–41 Tyrone. *Long Day's Journey Into Night*, act 4 (published 1956).

60 A Long Day's Journey Into Night.
1939–41 Title of play (published 1956).

61 The Iceman Cometh.
1946 Title of play.

62 Little subconscious mind, say I each night, bring home the bacon.

Quoted in Kenneth Tynan *Tynan Right and Left* (1988). Tynan added the question, 'But how much of the bacon can we nowadays stomach?'

O'Neill, Molly

63 Out of the kitchen, to stew is to fret, to worry, to agitate. In the kitchen, however, to stew is to have great expectations.
1994 In the *New York Times*, 30 Jan.

O'Neill, Thomas P known as 'Tip' 1912–94

US Congressman and Speaker of the House of Representatives.

64 Take advantage of the good cigars. You don't get much else in that job.
1977 Advice to Vice President Walter P Mondale. Quoted in *Time*, 4 Jun 1984.

65 Ronald Reagan…wasn't without leadership ability, but he lacked most of the management skills that a President needs. But let me give him his due: he would have made a hell of a king.
1987 *Man of the House*.

66 You can teach on old dog new tricks—if the old dog wants to learn.
1989 On working with President Reagan. In NPR broadcast, 2 Jan.

67 Herbert Hoover with a smile, a cheerleader for selfishness.
On President Reagan. Recalled on O'Neill's death in the *New York Times*, 7 Jan 1994.

68 Keep your left hand high.
Recommending the boxer's defensive posture to President Carter. Recalled on O'Neill's death in the *New York Times*, 7 Jan 1994.

69 The Democratic Party has succeeded so well that many of its members are now Republicans.
Quoted in WAMU radio broadcast, Washington, 29 Mar 1995.

Onetti, Juan Carlos 1909–94

Uruguayan novelist. He moved to Buenos Aires in 1943 and later to Madrid, where he spent his final years. In many of his novels he sets the action in the mythical city of Santa María.

70 *Es asombroso ver en qué se puede convertir la revolución rusa a través del cerebro de un comerciante yanqui; basta ver las fotos de las revistas norteamericanas, nada más que las fotos porque no sé leerlas, para comprender que no hay pueblo más imbécil que ése sobre la tierra; no puede haberlo porque también la capacidad de estupidez es limitada en la raza humana..*

It's astonishing to see what the Russian Revolution can become thanks to the brain of a Yankee entrepreneur; you only have to see the photos in North American magazines, only the photos because I can't read them, to realize they're the most stupid people on earth; that's quite possible because even the human race has a limited potential for idiocy.

1939 *El pozo* (translated as *The Pit*, 1991).

Oppenheimer, J(ulius) Robert 1904–67

US physicist, lecturer at the University of California and the California Institute of Technology and from 1947 director of the Institute for Advanced Study at Princeton. He was director (1942–5) of the laboratory at Los Alamos, New Mexico, that designed and built the first atomic bomb.

71 When you see something that is technically sweet, you go ahead and do it and you argue about what to do about it only after you have had your technical success. That is the way it was with the atomic bomb.

1954 'In the Matter of J. Robert Oppenheimer', USAEC transcript of hearing before Personnel Security Board.

72 Science has, as its whole purpose, the rendering of the physical world understandable and beautiful. Without this you have only tables and statistics.

1966 In *Look* magazine.

73 Science is not everything, but science is very beautiful.

1966 In *Look* magazine.

74 No man should escape our universities without knowing how little he knows.

1967 In *Partisan Review*, Summer issue.

75 The theory of our modern technic shows that nothing is as practical as the theory.

1977 In *Reflex*, Jul.

76 Those two scorpions in a bottle.

On the US and USSR in the early 1950s. Quoted in Anthony Cave Brown *Treason in the Blood* (1994).

O'Rahilly, Egan 1690–1726

Gaelic poet. Little is known of his life except that he lived and died in great poverty and was buried at Muckross Abbey. His *Vision* is regarded as one of the finest poems in Irish Gaelic.

77 For the future I cease, Death approaches with little delay,
Since the dragons of Laune and Lane and Lee are destroyed;
I'll follow the heroes far from the light of day,
The princes my ancestors followed before Christ died.

c.1729 Closing lines of his last known poem, translated from the Irish by Owen Dudley Edwards.

78 That my old bitter heart was pierced in this black doom,

That foreign devils have made our land a tomb,
That the sun that was Munster's glory has gone down
Has made me a beggar before you, Valentine Brown.

'Valentine Brown', translated from the Irish by Michael O'Donovan (Frank O'Connor).

O'Rourke, P(atrick) J(ake) 1947–

US writer and editor. He has written books and articles on government, politics, social mores and travel.

79 The best thing about the violence in Northern Ireland is that it's all so ancient and honorable… The Irish are in the same terrific position as the Shiites in Lebanon, the peasants in El Salvador, the blacks in America, the Jews in Palestine, the Palestinians in Israel (and everybody everywhere, if you read your history)—enough barbarism has been visited on the Irish to excuse all barbarities by the Irish barbarians.

1988 *Holidays in Hell.*

80 Communism doesn't really starve or execute that many people. Mostly it just bores them to death.

1988 *Holidays in Hell.*

81 Republicans are the party that says government doesn't work, and then they get elected and prove it.

1991 *Parliament of Whores.*

82 Sometimes it's hard to remember that bourgeois property is the real revolutionary force these days. All over the world we're bringing down dictatorships—or at least forcing them to go condo.

1992 *Give War a Chance.*

Orozco, José Clemente 1883–1949

Mexican painter, one of the three foremost artists in the revival of monumental fresco painting.

83 The highest, the most logical, the purest and strongest form of painting is the mural… It is, too, the most disinterested form, for it cannot be made a matter of private gain; it cannot be hidden away for the benefit of a certain privileged few. It is for the people. It is for ALL.

1929 *Creative Art.*

Ortega y Gasset, José 1883–1955

Spanish essayist and philosopher, Professor of Metaphysics at Madrid. He gained international fame with *The Revolt of the Masses* (1929), which argued in favour of an intellectual governing elite.

84 The man who discovers a new scientific truth has previously had to smash to atoms almost

everything he had learnt, and arrives at the new truth with hands blood stained from the slaughter of a thousand platitudes.

1930 *The Revolt of the Masses.*

Orton, Joe originally *John Kingsley* 1933–67

English dramatist, known for his blackly comic, outrageous farces such as *Entertaining Mr Sloane* (1964). He was murdered by his lover, Kenneth Halliwell, who then committed suicide.

85 I'd the upbringing a nun would envy... Until I was fifteen I was more familiar with Africa than my own body.

1964 *Entertaining Mr Sloane*, act 1.

86 Every luxury was lavished on you — atheism, breast-feeding, circumcision.

1966 *Loot*, act 1.

87 Reading isn't an occupation we encourage among police officers. We try to keep the paperwork down to a minimum.

1966 *Loot*, act 2.

Orwell, George pseudonym of *Eric Arthur Blair* 1903–50

English novelist, essayist and journalist. He fought in the Spanish Civil War and during World War II worked for the BBC. He developed his own brand of socialism in *The Road to Wigan Pier* (1937) and other essays, but is best known for his satire of totalitarian ideology in *Animal Farm* (1945), and the prophetic novel, *Nineteen Eighty-Four* (1949).

88 While the journalist exists merely as the publicity agent of big business, a large circulation, got by fair means or foul, is a newspaper's one and only aim.

1928 In *G.K.'s Weekly*, 29 Dec.

89 He was an embittered atheist (the sort of atheist who does not so much disbelieve in God as personally dislike Him), and took a sort of pleasure in thinking that human affairs would never improve.

1933 *Down and Out in Paris and London*, ch.30.

90 Keep the Aspidistra Flying.

1936 Title of novel.

91 In the early morning the mill girls clumping down the cobbled street, all in clogs, making a curiously formidable sound, like an army hurrying into battle. I suppose this is the typical sound of Lancashire.

1936 Diary entry, 18 Feb. He used this as material for his book *The Road to Wigan Pier* (1937).

92 It is only because miners sweat their guts out that superior persons can remain superior.

1937 *The Road to Wigan Pier*, ch.2.

93 A thousand influences constantly press a working man into a *passive* role. He does not act, he is acted upon.

1937 *The Road to Wigan Pier*, ch.3.

94 A person of bourgeois origin goes through life with some expectation of getting what he wants, within reasonable limits. Hence the fact that in times of stress 'educated' people tend to come to the front.

1937 *The Road to Wigan Pier*, ch.3.

95 I sometimes think the price of liberty is not so much eternal vigilance as eternal dirt.

1937 *The Road to Wigan Pier*, ch.4.

96 In a Lancashire cotton-town you could probably go for months on end without once hearing an 'educated' accent, whereas there can hardly be a town in the South of England where you could throw a brick without hitting the niece of a bishop.

1937 *The Road to Wigan Pier*, ch.7.

97 As with the Christian religion, the worst advertisement for Socialism is its adherents.

1937 *The Road to Wigan Pier*, ch.11.

98 To the ordinary working man, the sort you would meet in any pub on Saturday night, Socialism does not mean much more than better wages and shorter hours and nobody bossing you about.

1937 *The Road to Wigan Pier*, ch.11.

99 The underlying motive of many Socialists is, I believe, a hypertrophied sense of order...what they desire, basically, is to reduce the world to something resembling a chessboard.

1937 *The Road to Wigan Pier*, ch.11.

1 The high-water mark, so to speak, of Socialist literature is W.H. Auden, a sort of gutless Kipling.

1937 *The Road to Wigan Pier*, ch.11.

2 Cease to use your hands, and you have lopped off a huge chunk of your consciousness.

1937 *The Road to Wigan Pier*, ch.12.

3 It is usual to speak of the Fascist objective as the 'beehive state', which does a grave injustice to bees. A world of rabbits ruled by stoats would be nearer the mark.

1937 *The Road to Wigan Pier*, ch.12.

4 We of the sinking middle class...have nothing to lose but our aitches.

1937 *The Road to Wigan Pier*, ch.13.

5 The era of free speech is closing down. The freedom of the press in Britain was always

something of a fake, because in the last resort, money controls opinion; still, so long as the legal right to say what you like exists, there are always loopholes for an unorthodox writer.

1938 In the *New Leader*, 24 Jun.

6 Roughly speaking it was the sensation of being *at the centre* of an explosion… I fancy you would feel much the same if you were struck by lightning. I knew immediately that I was hit, but because of that seeming bang and flash, I thought it was a rifle nearby that had gone off accidentally and shot me.

1938 Of his wounding during the Spanish Civil War. *Homage to Catalonia*, ch.12.

7 When you have had a glimpse of such a disaster as this…the result is not necessarily disillusionment and cynicism. Curiously enough, the whole experience has left me with not less but more belief in the decency of human beings.

1938 *Homage to Catalonia*, ch.14.

8 Down here it was still the England I had known in my childhood:…all sleeping the deep, deep sleep of England, from which I sometimes fear that we shall never wake till we are jerked out of it by the roar of bombs.

1938 *Homage to Catalonia*, ch.14.

9 I'm fat, but I'm thin inside. Has it ever struck you that there's a thin man inside every fat man, just as they say there's a statue inside every block of stone?

1939 *Coming Up For Air*, pt.1, ch.3.

▷ See Connolly 283:75.

10 Before the war, and especially before the Boer War, it was summer all the year round.

1939 *Coming Up For Air*, pt.2, ch.1.

11 If the war didn't happen to kill you it was bound to start you thinking. After that unspeakable idiotic mess you couldn't go on regarding society as something eternal and unquestionable, like a pyramid. You knew it was just a balls-up.

1939 *Coming Up For Air*, pt.2, ch.8.

12 Most revolutionaries are potential Tories, because they imagine that everything can be put right by altering the *shape* of society; once that change is effected, as it sometimes is, they see no need for any other.

1939 'Charles Dickens', collected in *Inside the Whale* (1940).

13 The novel is practically a Protestant form of art; it is the product of the free mind, of the autonomous individual.

1940 *Inside the Whale*, 'Inside The Whale'.

14 Contrary to popular belief, the past was not more eventful than the present. If it seems so it is because

when you look backward things that happened years apart are telescoped together, and because very few of your memories come to you genuinely virgin.

1940 *Inside the Whale*, 'My Country Right or Left'.

15 As I write, highly civilized human beings are flying overhead, trying to kill me.

1941 *The Lion and The Unicorn: Socialism and the English Genius*, pt.1, 'England Your England'.

16 England is not the jewelled isle of Shakespeare's much-quoted passage, nor is it the inferno depicted by Dr Goebbels. More than either it resembles a family, a rather stuffy Victorian family, with not many black sheep in it but with all its cupboards bursting with skeletons.

1941 *The Lion and The Unicorn: Socialism and the English Genius*, pt.3, 'Shopkeeper at War'.

17 A family with the wrong members in control—that, perhaps, is as near as one can come to describing England in a phrase.

1941 *The Lion and The Unicorn: Socialism and the English Genius*, pt.3, 'The English Revolution'.

18 Probably the battle of Waterloo *was* won on the playing-fields of Eton, but the opening battles of all subsequent wars have been lost there. One of the dominant facts in English life during the past three-quarters of a century has been the decay of ability in the ruling class.

1941 *The Lion and The Unicorn: Socialism and the English Genius*, pt.4.

19 The great enemy of clear language is insincerity. When there is a gap between one's real and one's declared aims, one turns instinctively to long words and exhausted idioms—like cuttlefish squirting out ink.

1941 *The Lion and the Unicorn: Socialism and the English Genius*.

20 I believe that the BBC, in spite of the stupidity of its foreign propaganda and the unbearable voices of its announcers, is very truthful. It is generally regarded here as more reliable than the press.

1941 In the *Partisan Review*, 15 Apr. Reprinted in *Collected Essays, Journalism and Letters*, vol.2.

21 All propaganda is lies, even when one is telling the truth.

1942 Diary entry, 14 Mar.

22 Whatever is funny is subversive, every joke is ultimately a custard pie… A dirty joke is not, of course, a serious attack upon morality, but it is a sort of mental rebellion, a momentary wish that things were otherwise.

1942 'The Art of Donald McGill'.

23 On the whole, human beings want to be good, but not too good, and not all the time.
1942 'The Art of Donald McGill'.

24 Reminds me of nothing so much as a recently-dead fish before it has had time to stiffen.
1942 Of Clement Attlee. Diary entry, 19 May.

25 Any daily journalist will tell you that one of the most important secrets of his trade is the trick of making it appear that there is news when there is no news.
1944 In the *Tribune*, 21 Apr.

26 To blame someone like Northcliffe for making money in the quickest way is like blaming a skunk for stinking.
1944 In the *Tribune*, 21 Apr.

27 Cricket is a game full of forlorn hopes and sudden dramatic changes of fortune and its rules are so ill-defined that their interpretation is partly an ethical business.
1944 *Raffles and Miss Blandish*.

28 If liberty means anything at all, it means the right to tell people what they do not want to hear.
1945 Written for a rejected preface to *Animal Farm*.

29 Man is the only creature that consumes without producing.
1945 *Animal Farm*, ch.1.

30 Four legs good, two legs bad.
1945 *Animal Farm*, ch.3.

31 Napoleon had commanded that once a week there should be held something called a Spontaneous Demonstration.
1945 *Animal Farm*, ch.9.

32 All animals are equal but some animals are more equal than others.
1945 *Animal Farm*, ch.10.

33 The creatures outside looked from pig to man, and from man to pig, and from pig to man again; but already it was impossible to say which was which.
1945 *Animal Farm*, ch.10.

34 No modern Irish writer, even of the stature of Yeats or Joyce, is completely free from traces of nationalism.
1945 'Notes on Nationalism'.

35 In broadcasting your audience is conjectural, but it is an audience of *one*.
1945 'Poetry and the Microphone'.

36 Poetry on the air sounds like the Muses in striped trousers.
1945 'Poetry and the Microphone'.

37 To walk through the ruined cities of Germany is to feel actual doubt about the continuity of civilization.
1945 In *The Observer*, 8 Apr.

38 The books one reads in childhood, and perhaps most of all the bad and good bad books, create in one's mind a sort of false map of the world, a series of fabulous countries into which one can retreat at odd moments throughout the rest of life, and which in some cases can even survive a visit to the real countries which they are supposed to represent.
1946 'Riding Down from Bangor'.

39 Prolonged, indiscriminate reviewing of books involves constantly inventing reactions towards books about which one has no spontaneous feelings whatever.
1946 'Confessions of A Book Reviewer'.

40 The atom bombs are piling up in the factories, the police are prowling through the cities, the lies are streaming from the loudspeakers, but the earth is still going round the sun, and neither the dictators nor the bureaucrats, deeply as they disapprove of the process, are able to prevent it.
1946 'Some Thoughts on the Common Toad'.

41 To see what is in front of one's nose needs a constant struggle.
1946 'In Front of Your Nose'.

42 Good prose is like a window pane.
1946 'Why I Write'.

43 All writers are vain, selfish and lazy, and at the very bottom of their motives lies a mystery.
1946 'Why I Write'.

44 In our time, political speech and writing are largely the defence of the indefensible.
1946 'Politics and the English Language', collected in *Shooting an Elephant* (1950).

45 The inflated style is itself a kind of euphemism.
1946 'Politics and the English Language', collected in *Shooting an Elephant* (1950).

46 The great enemy of clear language is insincerity.
1946 'Politics and the English Language', collected in *Shooting an Elephant* (1950).

47 In prose, the worst thing one can do with words is surrender to them.
1946 'Politics and the English Language', collected in *Shooting an Elephant* (1950).

48 Political language...is designed to make lies sound truthful and murder respectable, and to give an appearance of solidity to pure wind.
1946 'Politics and the English Language', collected in *Shooting an Elephant* (1950).

49 The Catholic and the Communist are alike in assuming that an opponent cannot be both honest and intelligent.
    1946 'The Prevention of Literature', in *Polemic*, Jan.

50 The controversy over freedom of speech and of the press is at the bottom a controversy over the desirability, or otherwise, of telling lies. What is really at issue is the right to report events truthfully, or as truthfully as is consistent with the ignorance, bias and self-deception from which every observer necessarily suffers.
    1946 'The Prevention of Literature', in *Polemic*, Jan.

51 The friends of totalitarianism in this country tend to argue that since absolute truth is not attainable, a big lie is no worse than a little lie.
    1946 'The Prevention of Literature', in *Polemic*, Jan.

52 Literature is doomed if liberty of thought perishes.
    1946 'The Prevention of Literature', in *Polemic*, Jan.

53 The quickest way of ending a war is to lose it.
    1946 'Second Thoughts on James Burnham', in *Polemic*, May.

54 It was a bright cold day in April, and the clocks were striking thirteen.
    1949 *Nineteen Eighty-Four*, pt.1, ch.1.

55 On each landing, opposite the lift shaft, the poster with the enormous face gazed from the wall. It was one of those pictures which are so contrived that the eyes follow you about when you move. BIG BROTHER IS WATCHING YOU, the caption beneath it ran.
    1949 *Nineteen Eighty-Four*, pt.1, ch.1.

56 War is peace. Freedom is slavery. Ignorance is strength.
    1949 *Nineteen Eighty-Four*, pt.1, ch.1.

57 'Who controls the past,' ran the Party slogan, 'controls the future: who controls the present controls the past.'
    1949 *Nineteen Eighty-Four*, pt.1, ch.3.

58 Freedom is the freedom to say that two plus two make four. If that is granted, all else follows.
    1949 *Nineteen Eighty-Four*, pt.1, ch.7.

59 *Doublethink* means the power of holding two contradictory beliefs in one's mind simultaneously, and accepting both of them.
    1949 *Nineteen Eighty-Four*, pt.2, ch.9.

60 If you want a picture of the future, imagine a boot stamping on a human face—for ever.
    1949 *Nineteen Eighty-Four*, pt.3, ch.3.

61 Power is not a means, it is an end. One does not establish a dictatorship in order to safeguard a revolution; one makes the revolution in order to establish the dictatorship.
    1949 *Nineteen Eighty-Four*, pt.3, ch.3.

62 Saints should always be judged guilty until they are proved innocent.
    1949 'Reflections on Gandhi', collected in *Shooting an Elephant* (1950).

63 At 50, everyone has the face he deserves.
    1949 Notebook entry, 17 Apr.

64 Serious sport has nothing to do with fair play. It is bound up with hatred, jealousy, boastfulness, disregard of all rules and sadistic pleasure in witnessing violence: in other words it is war minus the shooting…there are quite enough real causes of trouble already, and we need not add to them by encouraging young men to kick each other on the shins amid the roars of infuriated spectators.
    1950 'The Sporting Spirit'.

65 One ought to be able to hold in one's head simultaneously the two facts that Dali is a good draughtsman and a disgusting human being. The one does not invalidate or, in a sense, affect the other.
    Quoted in Michael Shelden *Orwell* (1991).

Osborne, Dorothy 1627–95
Wife of Sir William Temple.

66 All letters, methinks, should be free and easy as one's discourse, not studied as an oration, nor made up of hard words like a charm.
    1653 Letter to William Temple.

Osborne, John 1929–94
English playwright and actor. The success of *Look Back in Anger* (1956), with its anti-hero Jimmy Porter, marked a new departure in postwar English drama and identified the author as the most famous of the 'angry young men' of the 1950s. Later works included *The Entertainer* (1957), *Luther* (1961), *Inadmissible Evidence* (1964) and *A Patriot for Me* (1969).

67 She's so clumsy. I watch for her to do the same things every night. The way she jumps on the bed, as if she were stamping on someone's face, and draws the curtains back with a great clatter, in that casually destructive way of hers. It's like someone launching a battleship. Have you ever noticed how noisy women are? Have you? The way they kick the floor about, simply walking over it? Or have you watched them sitting at their dressing tables, dropping their weapons and banging down their bits of boxes and brushes and lipsticks?
    1956 *Look Back in Anger*.

68 Don't clap too hard—it's a very old building.
    1957 *The Entertainer*, 7.

69 There will be a quick rash of hairy American filth, but it shouldn't threaten the existence of decent, serious British filth.

  1967 In *Time* magazine, commenting on the opening of the US musical *Hair*.

Osler, Sir William 1849–1919

Canadian physician.

70 The greater the ignorance the greater the dogmatism.

  1902 Quoted in *Montreal Medical Journal*, Sep.

71 The desire to take medicine is perhaps the greatest feature which distinguishes man from animals.

  Quoted in H Cushing *Life of Sir William Osler*, vol.1, ch.14 (1925).

72 One of the first duties of the physician is to educate the masses not to take medicine.

  Collected in W B Bean (ed) *Sir William Osler: Aphorisms from His Bedside Teachings and Writings* (1950).

73 Failure to examine the throat is a glaring sin of omission, especially in children. One finger in the throat and one in the rectum makes a good diagnostician.

  Collected in W B Bean (ed) *Sir William Osler: Aphorisms from His Bedside Teachings and Writings* (1950).

74 To talk of diseases is a sort of *Arabian Nights* entertainment.

  Quoted in Oliver Sacks *The Man Who Mistook his Wife for a Hat*, epigraph (1985).

Otis, James 1725–83

American politician and patriot. As Advocate General he refused to assist royal revenue officers to search individual's homes and resigned to fight for popular rights. In 1769 he was beaten by revenue officers and received a head wound from which he never really recovered.

75 Taxation without representation is tyranny.

  c.1761 His defence, which became a rallying call of the American Revolution.

Otway, Thomas 1652–85

English dramatist. Educated at Oxford. His first play was the tragedy *Alcibiades* (1675); in it his alleged lover, Elizabeth Barry, made her début. His most famous play is *Venice Preserved, or a Plot Discovered* (1682).

76 Ere man's corruptions made him wretched, he
  Was born most noble that was born most free;
  Each of himself was lord; and unconfin'd
  Obey'd the dictates of his godlike mind.

  1676 *Don Carlos*, act 2.

77 You wags that judge by rote, and damn by rule.

  1677 *Titus and Berenice*, prologue.

78 And for an apple damn'd mankind.

  1680 *The Orphan*, act 3.

79 I may boldly speak
  In right, though proud oppression will not hear me!

  1682 *Venice Preserved, or a Plot Discovered*, act 1, sc.1.

80 May the hard hand of a vexatious need
  Oppress and grind you; till at last you find
  The curse of disobedience all your portion.

  1682 *Venice Preserved, or a Plot Discovered*, act 1, sc.1.

81 Home I would go
  But that my doors are hateful to my eyes,
  Fill'd and damm'd up with gaping creditors,
  Watchful as fowlers when their game will spring.

  1682 *Venice Preserved, or a Plot Discovered*, act 1, sc.1.

82 I'm thinking…how that damn'd starving quality
  Call'd honesty, got footing in the world.

  1682 *Venice Preserved, or a Plot Discovered*, act 1, sc.1.

83 Honesty was a cheat invented first
  To bind the hands of bold deserving rogues,
  That fools and cowards might sit safe in power,
  And lord it uncontroll'd above their betters.

  1682 *Venice Preserved, or a Plot Discovered*, act 1, sc.1.

84 'Tis a ragged virtue.

  1682 *Venice Preserved, or a Plot Discovered*, act 1, sc.1.

85 If love be treasure, we'll be wondrous rich.

  1682 *Venice Preserved, or a Plot Discovered*, act 1, sc.1.

86 Is the world
  Reform'd since our last meeting?

  1682 *Venice Preserved, or a Plot Discovered*, act 1, sc.1.

87 No praying, it spoils Business,

  1682 *Venice Preserved, or a Plot Discovered*, act 2, sc.1.

88 Give but an Englishman his whore and ease,
  Beef and a sea-coal fire, he's yours forever.

  1682 *Venice Preserved, or a Plot Discovered*, act 2, sc.3.

89 The poor sleep little.

  1682 *Venice Preserved, or a Plot Discovered*, act 2, sc.3.

90 No, this vile world and I have long been jangling,
  And cannot part on better terms than now,
  When only men like thee are fit to live in't.

  1682 *Venice Preserved, or a Plot Discovered*, act 4, sc.2.

Oud, J(acobus) J(ohannes) P(ieter) 1890–1963

Dutch architect, a pioneer of the modern architectural style based on simplified forms and pure planes.

91 If I was not optimistic, I would not be an architect.

  Quoted in the *New York Times*, 4 Dec 1994.

Overbury, Sir Thomas 1581–1613

English poet and courtier.

92 He disdains all things above his reach, and
preferreth all countries before his own.
1632 'An Affected Traveller', collected in *Miscellaneous Works*.

Overton, Robert fl.1642–68

English soldier. He fought for Parliament in the English
Civil War and was made governor of Hull. He was
imprisoned in 1656 for two years after he fought under
Cromwell in Scotland and was suspected of planning an
insurrection against the government. When Cromwell
fell, Overton was released, but the doubts about him
remained and his further support for a republic led to
imprisonment for almost the rest of his life. The date and
place of his death are unknown.

93 Whatever our forefathers were, or whatever they
did or suffered, or were enforced to yield unto, we
are the men of the present age, and ought to be
absolutely free from all kinds of exorbitancies,
molestations, or arbitrary power.
1646 Remonstrance to the House of Commons.

Ovid full name *Publius Ovidius Naso* 43 BC–AD 17

Roman poet, who trained for law but turned to poetry. His
many works include the *Ars Amatoria*, the *Metamorphoses*
and the *Fasti*. He was banished by Augustus in AD 8 to
Tomi on the Black Sea, where he wrote the *Tristia*.

94 *Procul omen abesto!*

Far away be that fate!
Amores, bk.1

95 *Iuppiter ex alto periuria ridet amantum.*

Jupiter from above laughs at lovers' perjuries.
Ars Amatoria, bk.1, l.633.

96 *Iam seges est ubi Troia fuit.*

Now there are cornfields where Troy once was.
Heroides, bk.1, l.42.

97 *Chaos, rudis indigestaque moles.*

Chaos, a rough unordered mass.
Metamorphoses, bk.1, l.7.

98 *Medio tutissimus ibis.*

You will go most safely by the middle way.
Daedalus speaking to his son, Icarus. *Metamorphoses*, bk.2, l.137
(translated by Peter Green).

99 *Inopem me copia fecit.*

Plenty has made me poor.
Metamorphoses, bk.3, l.466.

1 *Video meliora, proboque;*
Deteriora sequor.

I see the better things, and approve; I follow the
worse.

Metamorphoses, bk.7, l.20 (translated by Peter Green).

2 *Tempus edax rerum.*

Time the devourer of everything.
Metamorphoses, bk.15, l.234 (translated by Peter Green).

3 *Nec species sua cuique manet, rerumque novatrix*
ex aliis alias reddit natura figuras.
nec perit in toto quidquam, mihi credite, mundo,
sed variat faciemque novat, nascique vocatur
incipere esse aliud, quam quod fuit ante, morique,
desinere illud idem. cum sint huc forsitan illa,
haec translata illuc, summa tamen omnia constant.

No species remains constant: that great renovator
of matter
Nature, endlessly fashions new forms from old:
there's nothing
in the whole universe that perishes, believe me;
rather
it renews and varies its substance. What we describe
as birth
is no more than incipient change from a prior state,
while dying
is merely to quit it. Though the parts may be
transported
hither and thither, the sum of all matter is constant.
Metamorphoses, bk.15, l.252–8 (translated by Peter Green).

4 *Donec eris felix, multos numerabis amicos*
Tempora si fuerint nubila, solus eris.

So long as you are fortunate, you will count many
friends; if your life should become clouded, you
will be alone.
Tristia, bk.1, pt.9, l.5–6.

Owen, David Anthony Llewellyn Owen, Baron 1938–

English politician, one of the 'Gang of Four' who formed
the Social Democratic Party (SDP) in 1981, becoming its
leader in 1983. He resigned in 1987 rather than merge
with the Liberal party, and led a minority, reconstituted
SDP, dissolved in 1990. In 1991 he was appointed Co-
Chairman of the International Peace Conference on the
former Yugoslavia.

5 We are fed up with fudging and nudging, with
mush and slush.
1980 Speech to Labour's national conference shortly before
leaving the party to found the Social Democratic Party, Oct.

Owen, Robert 1771–1858

Welsh social former and philanthropist.

6 All the world is queer save thee and me, and even
thou art a little queer.
Attributed; said to his partner W Allen when they ended their
business relationship.

Owen, Wilfred 1893–1918

English poet. Injured in the trenches in 1917, he met Siegfried Sassoon while recuperating in Edinburgh. He died in the last week of the war, and most of his poems were published posthumously. Their vivid and unsentimental realism is a powerful indictment of war, and they were memorably used by Benjamin Britten in his *War Requiem*, first performed in Coventry Cathedral (1962).

7 What passing-bells for these who die as cattle?
Only the monstrous anger of the guns.
Only the stuttering rifles' rapid rattle
Can patter out their hasty orisons.
1917 'Anthem for Doomed Youth'.

8 The pallor of girls' brows shall be their pall;
Their flowers the tenderness of patient minds,
And each slow dusk a drawing-down of blinds.
1917 'Anthem for Doomed Youth'.

9 Red lips are not so red
As the stained stones kissed by the English dead.
1917 'Greater Love'.

10 This book is not about heroes. English poetry is not yet fit to speak of them.
1918 *Poems* (published 1920), preface.

11 Above all, this book is not concerned with Poetry. The subject of it is War, and the pity of War. The Poetry is in the pity.
1918 *Poems* (published 1920), preface.

12 All the poet can do today is to warn.
That is why the true Poet must be truthful.
1918 *Poems* (published 1920), preface.

13 If you could hear, at every jolt, the blood
Come gargling from the froth-corrupted lungs,
Bitter as the cud
Of vile, incurable sores on innocent tongues,—
My friend, you would not tell with such high zest
To children ardent for some desperate glory
The old Lie: *Dulce et decorum est*
Pro patria mori.
1918 'Dulce et Decorum Est', collected in *Poems* (published 1920).
▷ See Horace 493:22.

14 It seemed that out of battle I escaped
Down some profound dull tunnel, long since scooped
Through granites which titanic wars had groined.
1918 'Strange Meeting', collected in *Poems* (published 1920).

15 And by his smile, I knew that sullen hall,
By his dead smile I knew we stood in Hell.
1918 'Strange Meeting', collected in *Poems* (published 1920).

16 'Strange friend,' I said, 'here is no cause to mourn.'
'None,' said the other, 'save the undone years,

The hopelessness. Whatever hope is yours
Was my life also; I went hunting wild
After the wildest beauty in the world.'
1918 'Strange Meeting', collected in *Poems* (published 1920).

17 I am the enemy you killed, my friend.
1918 'Strange Meeting', collected in *Poems* (published 1920).

18 Move him into the sun—
Gently its touch awoke him once,
At home, whispering of fields unsown.
1918 'Futility', collected in *Poems* (published 1920).

19 If anything might rouse him now
The kind old sun will know.
1918 'Futility', collected in *Poems* (published 1920).

20 Was it for this the clay grew tall?
—O what made fatuous sunbeams toil
To break earth's sleep at all?
1918 'Futility', collected in *Poems* (published 1920).

21 So secretly, like wrongs hushed-up, they went.
1918 'The Send-Off', collected in *Poems* (published 1920).

22 Whatever mourns when many leave these shores:
Whatever shares
The eternal reciprocity of tears.
1918 'Insensibility', collected in *Poems* (published 1920).

Owens, Jesse James Cleveland 1913–80

US athlete. The greatest sprinter of his generation, he won four gold medals at the Berlin Olympics in 1936, embarrassing the Nazi hosts, who had hoped to demonstrate the supremacy of Aryan athletes.

23 I let my feet spend as little time on the ground as possible. From the air, fast down, and from the ground, fast up.
Quoted in Colin Jarman *The Guinness Dictionary of Sports Quotations* (1990).

Ozick, Cynthia 1928–

US novelist and short-story writer. She claimed to have begun her first novel, *Trust* (1966), an American writer and finished it six and a half years later a Jewish one.

24 Yiddish is a household tongue, and God, like other members of the family, is sweetly informal in it.
1989 *Metaphor and Memory*.

Pacheco, José Emilio 1939–

Mexican poet, novelist, critic and translator. His poetry expresses his metaphysical concerns in brilliant images. The novel *Morirás lejos* documents the purges of Jews throughout history.

25 *Porque todo es irreal en este cuento. Nada sucedió como se indica. Hechos y sitios se deformaron por el empeño de tocar la verdad mediante una ficción, una mentira. Todo irreal, nada sucedió como aquí se*

refiere. Pero fue un pobre intento de contribuir a que el gran crimen nunca se repita.

For everything in this story is unreal. Nothing happened the way it was suggested. Facts and places were distorted by that persistent desire to touch the truth by means of fiction, a lie. All of it is unreal; nothing happened the way it is told here. It was a poor attempt to help ensure that the great crime is never repeated.

1967 *Morirás lejos* (translated as *You Will Die in a Distant Land*, 1991).

Packard, Vance 1914–96

US writer and journalist.

26 The Hidden Persuaders.
1957 *Title of a book on advertising.*

Packer, Herbert Leslie 1925–72

US Professor of Law, Stanford University (1959–72). He was admitted to the New York Bar in 1950, and the Supreme Court. He practised law in Washington before teaching at Stanford.

27 Crime is a socio-political artifact, not a natural phenomenon. We can have as much or as little crime as we please, depending on what we choose to count as criminal.
1968 *The Limits of Criminal Sanction*, p.364.

Packwood, Bob 1932–

US Senator and lawyer. He has served as Senator for Oregon since 1969 and is also involved with commercial finance committees.

28 I am accused of kissing women…perhaps overeagerly kissing women. And that is the charge, not drugging, not robbing, kissing!
1995 Repying to charges of sexual misconduct, lobbying, and editing diaries subpoenaed by Senate Ethics Committee. In the *New York Times*, 7 Sep.

29 More than Francis of Assisi…less than Wilt Chamberlain.
1995 Estimating the amount of controversial activity documented in his diaries. In the *New York Times*, 9 Sep.

Paderewski, Ignace Jan 1860–1941

Polish pianist, composer and statesman, director of the Warsaw Conservatory (from 1909). In 1919 he became premier of Poland. He retired from politics to return to his music, but in 1940 was elected President by Poland's provisional parliament in Paris.

30 If I don't practise for one day, I know it; if I don't practise for two days, the critics know it; if I don't practise for three days, the audience knows it.
Quoted in Nat Shapiro *An Encyclopedia of Quotations about Music* (1978).

Page, Geraldine 1924–87

US actress. She made her name with the lead role in Tennessee Williams's *Summer and Smoke* (1954).

31 Name me one character in literature or drama who can't be described as neurotic… We wouldn't want to know the people we get to see on the stage. How would you like to have Medea for dinner? Or Macbeth slurping your soup? Or Oedipus with his bloody, blinded eyes dripping all over your tablecloth?
Attributed.

Pagels, Heinz R(udolf) 1939–88

US theoretical physicist and social activist, the author of several works describing the complexities of modern physics for the public.

32 A good simulation, be it a religious myth or scientific theory, gives us a sense of mastery over experience. To represent something symbolically, as we do when we speak or write, is somehow to capture it, thus making it one's own. But with this appropriation comes the realization that we have denied the immediacy of reality and that in creating a substitute we have but spun another thread in the web of our grand illusion.
1988 *The Dreams of Reason.*

33 Science provides a vision of reality seen from the perspective of reason, a perspective that sees the vast order of the universe, living and non-living matter, as a material system governed by rules that can be known by the human mind. It is a powerful vision, formal and austere but strangely silent about many of the questions that deeply concern us. Science shows us what exists but not what to do about it.
1988 *The Dreams of Reason.*

Paglia, Camille 1947–

US writer, Professor of Humanities at the University of the Arts, Philadelphia. Her works include *Sexual Personae* (1990) and *Vamps and Tramps* (1994).

34 The historical repugnance to woman has a rational basis: disgust is reason's proper response to the grossness of procreative nature.
1990 *Sexual Personae: Art and Decadence from Nefertiti to Emily Dickinson*, ch.1, 'Sex and Violence, or Nature and Art'.

35 No woman has to prove herself a woman in the grim way a man has to prove himself a man. He must perform, or the show does not go on. Social convention is irrelevant. A flop is a flop.
1990 *Sexual Personae: Art and Decadence from Nefertiti to Emily Dickinson*, ch.1, 'Sex and Violence, or Nature and Art'.

36 Feminism has become a catch-all vegetable drawer

where bunches of clingy sob sisters can store their moldy neuroses.

1992 'The Return of Carry Nation: Catharine Mackinnon and Andrea Dworkin', in *Playboy*, Oct. Collected in *Vamps and Tramps* (1994).

37 I like Hillary because she's kind of a bitch.

1993 In the *Sunday Times* magazine, 18 Apr. Collected as 'Kind of a Bitch: Why I like Hillary Clinton' in *Vamps and Tramps* (1994).

Pagnol, Marcel 1895–1974

French dramatist and film director, best known for his popular trilogy about Marseilles, *Marius* (1929), *Fanny* (1931) and *César* (1936).

38 *Les coupables, il vaut mieux les choisir que les chercher.*

It's better to choose the culprits than to seek them out.

1930 *Topaze*, act 1.

39 *L'honneur, c'est comme les allumettes: ça ne sert qu'une fois.*

Honour is like a match, you can use it only once.

1929 *Marius*, act 4, sc.5.

40 One has to look out for engineers—they begin with sewing machines and end up with the atomic bomb.

1949 *Critique des critiques*, ch.3.

Paige, Satchel (Leroy Robert) 1906–82

US baseball player. One of the first blacks to play in the major leagues, he was a celebrated pitcher with the Cleveland Indians and the St Louis Browns.

41 1. Avoid fried meats which angry up the blood.
2. If your stomach disputes you, lie down and pacify it with cool thoughts.
3. Keep the juices flowing by jangling around gently as you move.
4. Go very light on vices such as carrying on in society. The social ramble ain't restful.
5. Avoid running at all times.
6. Don't look back. Something may be gaining on you.

1976 'Six Rules for a Happy Life', which he had inscribed on business cards, offered to fans seeking his autograph.

Paine, Thomas 1737–1809

English radical political writer. His *Common Sense* (1776) argued for complete American independence, and *The Rights of Man* (1791–2) supported the French Revolution. Arraigned for treason, he fled to Paris, and wrote *The Age of Reason* in favour of deism.

42 These are the times that try men's souls. The summer soldier and the sunshine patriot will, in

this crisis, shrink from the service of his country; but he that stands it *now*, deserves the love and thanks of man and woman.

1776 *The Crisis*, introduction, Dec.

43 Not all the treasures of the world, so far as I believe, could have induced me to support an offensive war, for I think it murder; but if a thief breaks into my house, burns and destroys my property, and kills or threatens to kill me or those that are in it, and to '*bind me in all cases whatsoever*' to his absolute will, am I to suffer it?

1776 *The Crisis*, introduction, Dec.

44 Government, even in its best state, is but a necessary evil; in its worse state, an intolerable one. Government, like dress, is the badge of lost innocence; the palaces of kings are built upon the bowers of paradise.

1776 *Common Sense*, ch.1.

45 As to religion, I hold it to be the indispensable duty of government to protect all conscientious professors thereof, and I know of no other business which government hath to do therewith.

1776 *Common Sense*, ch.4.

46 Man is not the enemy of Man, but through the medium of a false system of government.

1791–2 *The Rights of Man*.

47 To establish any mode to abolish war, however advantageous it might be to nations, would be to take from such Government the most lucrative of its branches.

1791–2 *The Rights of Man*.

48 Persecution is not an original feature of *any* religion; but it is always the strongly marked feature of all law-religions, or religions established by law.

1791–2 *The Rights of Man*.

49 My country is the world, and my religion is to do good.

1791–2 *The Rights of Man*.

50 The final event to himself has been, that as he rose like a rocket, he fell like the stick.

1792 Of Edmund Burke. Letters to the Addressers on the late Proclamation.

51 It is a fraud of the Christian system to call the sciences human invention; it is only the application of them that is human. Every science has for its basis a system of principles as fixed and unalterable as those by which the universe is regulated and governed. Man cannot make principles, he can only discover them.

1794 *The Age of Reason*, pt.1.

52 It is necessary to the happiness of man that he be mentally faithful to himself. Infidelity does not consist in believing, or in disbelieving, it consists in professing to believe what one does not believe.
1794 *The Age of Reason*, pt.1.

53 One step above the sublime, makes the ridiculous; and one step above the ridiculous, makes the sublime again.
1795 *The Age of Reason*, pt.2.

Paisley, Bob 1919–96

English football manager. He succeeded Bill Shankly as manager of Liverpool in 1974 and led the team through a golden era of League success.

54 Yes, we've had bad times at Anfield; one year we came second.
Quoted in Peter Ball and Phil Shaw *The Book of Football Quotations* (1989).

Palacký, Frantisêk 1798–1876

Czech historian and politician in Prague, and the founder of historiography in Bohemia. He served in the first Austrian Reichstag and campaigned for the formation of a separate Czech nation.

55 If the Austrian Empire did not exist, it would have to be created in the interest of Europe and of humanity.
Quoted in A J P Taylor *From Napoleon to the Second International* (1993), p.169.

Palafox, José de c.1776–1847

Spanish general in the Peninsular War, who defended Saragossa with an improvised garrison of civilians. Despite breaching the city wall, the French were unable to capture the city.

56 *Guerra a cuchillo.*

War to the knife.
1808 His reply to the French suggestion that he surrender during the siege of Saragossa, 4 Aug. The phrase was inscribed on survivors' medals.

Paley, Grace née Goodside 1922–

US writer. She is best known as a writer of short stories, often set in a Jewish milieu in New York, but she has also published poetry and collections of essays.

57 The Little Disturbances Of Man.
1959 Title of story collection.

58 Enormous Changes At The Last Minute.
1974 Title of story collection.

59 Literature, fiction, poetry, whatever, makes justice in the world. That's why it almost always has to be on the side of the underdog.
1974 In *Ms* magazine.

60 All that is really necessary for survival of the fittest, it seems, is an interest in life, good, bad, or peculiar.
1976 In D L Fitzpatrick (ed) *Contemporary Novelists.*

61 No metaphor reinvents the job of the nurture of children
except to muddy or mock.
1992 *Begin Again: New and Collected Poems*, 'Stanzas: Old Age and the Conventions of Retirement Have Driven My Friends from the Work They Love'.

62 Poets!
Madness is a gift
god-given
(though not to me).
1992 *Begin Again: New and Collected Poems*, 'on the Bank Street Pier'.

63 It is the responsibility of society to let the poet be a poet
It is the responsibility of the poet to be a woman
1992 *Begin Again: New and Collected Poems*, 'Responsibility'.

64 It is the responsibility of the poet to be lazy to hang out and prophesy
1992 *Begin Again: New and Collected Poems*, 'Responsibility'.

Paley, William 1743–1805

English theologian, Archdeacon of Carlisle (1782) and Sub-Dean of Lincoln (1795). His most popular work was *Natural Theology, or Evidences of the Existence and Attributed of the Deity* (1802).

65 Suppose I had found a *watch* upon the ground, and it should be enquired how the watch happened to be in that place… The inference, we think, is inevitable; that the watch must have had a maker, that there must have existed, at some time and at some place or other, an artificer or artificers, who formed it for the purpose which we find it actually to answer; who comprehended its construction, and designed its use.
1802 *Natural Theology*, ch.1.

Palmer, Arnold 1929–

US golfer. Between 1958 and 1964 he won the US Masters four times, the British Open twice and the US Open once. He was twice captain of the US Ryder Cup team.

66 Winning isn't everything, but wanting to is.
Quoted in Colin Jarman *The Guinness Dictionary of Sports Quotations* (1990).

Palmerston, Henry John Temple, 3rd Viscount 1784–1865

English politician, Foreign Secretary (1830–41, 1846–51) and Prime Minister (1855–8, 1859–65). His abrasive, bullying approach to foreign affairs and propensity for brinkmanship made him unpopular with his colleagues and the public.

67 Half the wrong conclusions at which mankind arrive are reached by the abuse of metaphors, and by mistaking general resemblance of imaginary similarity for real identity.

1839 Letter to Henry Bulwer, 1 Sep.

68 Diplomats and protocols are very good things, but there are no better peace-keepers than well-appointed three-deckers.

c.1840 Quoted in Denis Judd *Palmerston* (1975). A three-decker is a warship.

69 We said to the Chinese, 'You have behaved very ill; we have had to teach you better manners; it has cost us something to do it, but we will send our bill in, and you must pay our charges.' That was done, and they have certainly profited by the lesson. They have become free traders too.

1847 On the Opium Wars of 1839–42. Election speech at Tiverton, Devon.

70 We have no eternal allies, and we have no perpetual enemies. Our interests are eternal, and it is our duty to follow them.

1848 Speech, House of Commons, 1 Mar.

71 Large republics seem to be essentially and inherently aggressive.

1848 Letter to the British Ambassador to Paris, 5 Mar.

72 I therefore fearlessly challenge the verdict which this house…is to give on the question now brought before it…whether, as the Roman, in days of old, held himself free from indignity, when he could say *Civis Romanus sum*; so also a British subject, in whatever land he may be, shall feel confident that the watchful eye and the strong arm of England will protect him against injustice and wrong.

1850 From his four-and-a-half hour Don Pacifico speech, Jun. Don Pacifico was a Portugese Jew resident in Athens, born in Gibraltar and therefore a British subject. In support of his claims for compensation from the Greek government for damage done to his property by a mob, Palmerston sent the British fleet to blockade Piraeus and brought the two countries to the brink of war.

73 You may call it coalition, you may call it the accidental and fortuitous concurrence of atoms…but when gentlemen are in the habit of finding themselves in the same Lobby, it is not unnatural to suppose that they may, under certain circumstances, be ready to unite themselves together for the purpose of forming an Administration and becoming responsible for the opinions that they severally entertain.

1858 Speech on the rumoured Palmerston–Disraeli coalition, 5 Mar.

74 England is one of the greatest powers of the world. No event or series of events bearing on the balance of power, or on probabilities of peace or war, can be matters of indifference to her, and her right to have and to express opinions on matters thus bearing on her interests is unquestionable.

1859 Letter to Queen Victoria, 23 Aug.

Panama, Norman and Melvin Frank

1914– , 1917–88

US screenwriters, who worked together on films such as *The Road to Utopia* (1945), *The Court Jester* (1955) and *Li'l Abner* (1959).

75 The pellet with the poison's in the chalice from the palace
The flagon with the dragon has the brew that is true.

1955 Lines delivered by Danny Kaye in *The Court Jester*.

Pangkor, Treaty of

The British signed a treaty with a claimant to the Perak Sultanate on the island of Pangkor, off the west coast of what is now peninsular Malaysia, and thereby formalised their economic and political interest in the region. It led to British control over the whole of the peninsula for the following 83 years.

76 A British officer to be called Resident who shall be accredited to his Court and whose advice must be asked and acted upon on all questions other than those touching Malay religion and custom.

1874 Treaty, Nov.

Pankhurst, Christabel 1880–1958

English suffragette and religious writer. Co-founder with her mother Emmeline Pankhurst of the Women's Social and Political Union (1903), she studied law (LLB 1906) and applied to join Lincoln's Inn, but was rejected, as a woman.

77 How long you women have been trying for the vote. For my part, I mean to get it.

c.1890 Childhood remark, quoted by her mother, Emmeline Pankhurst, in *My Own Story* (1914), ch.2.

Pankhurst, Emmeline née Goulden

1858–1928

English suffragette, organizer of the Women's Social and Political Union. A militant campaigner, she was frequently imprisoned and undertook hunger strikes. During World War I she turned her attention to the industrial mobilization of women.

78 Women never took a single step forward without being pushed back first of all by their opponents.

1912 Speech, 14 Jan, during a tour of Canada.

79 There is something that Governments care for far more than human life, and that is the security of

property. So it is through property that we shall strike the enemy... Be militant each in your own way... I incite this meeting to rebellion.

1912 Speech, Royal Albert Hall, 17 Oct.

80 Women had always fought for men, and for their children. Now they were ready to fight for their own human rights.

1914 *My Own Story*, ch.3.

81 There are women today who never thought to envy men their manhood, but who would, at least for this purpose, be glad to be men.

1914 Speech appealing for the right to fight, 30 Nov, at a meeting organized by the Women's Social and Political Union, in the Kingsway Hall, London.

82 What is the use of fighting for the vote if we do not have a country to vote in? With that patriotism that has nerved women to endure torture in prison for the national good, we ardently desire that our country shall be victorious.

1914 Declaring a truce on suffragette activities for the duration of World War I, 10 Aug.

Pareto, Vilfredo 1848–1923

French-born Swiss economist and sociologist.

83 All governments use force and all assert that they are founded on reason. In fact, whether universal suffrage prevails or not, it is always an oligarchy that governs, finding ways to give to 'the will of the people' the expression which the few desire.

Quoted in Arthur Livingstone (ed) *The Mind and Society* (1935).

Parfitt, Harold Robert 1921–

US soldier. He served in Vietnam and advanced through the army grades to reach Major-General in 1971. He was decorated many times. He became governor of the Panama Canal Zone in 1975.

84 There will be no more tomorows, only yesterdays, for the Canal Zone.

1979 On relinquishing authority as last governor of Panama Canal Zone. Quoted in *Time Magazine*, 15 Oct.

Park, Mungo 1771–1806

Scottish explorer. He explored the Niger in 1796, then returned to Scotland and worked as a doctor, publishing *Travels in the Interior Districts of Africa* (1799), before leaving in 1805 for Africa again, sending back journals and letters.

85 I think it not unlikely but I shall be in England before you receive this—You may be sure that I feel happy at turning my face towards home. We this morning have done with all intercourse with the natives; and the sails are now hoisting for our departure for the coast.

1805 Last letter to his wife before leaving Sansanding on the River Niger. Collected in *Journal of a Mission to the Interior of Africa in the Year 1805* (published 1815). Park and his party reportedly drowned in the river when they were ambushed and their boat sank.

Parker, Charlie known as 'Bird' 1920–55

US saxophonist, bandleader and composer, architect of the bebop style. Despite addiction to heroin and alcohol and recurring mental illness, he led jazz groups until his death. His works include 'Now's The Time' and 'Ornithology'.

86 It's just music. It's trying to play clean and looking for the pretty notes.

1949 On Bebop. Quoted in Gary Giddins *Celebrating Bird* (1987), ch.1.

87 There is no boundary line to art. Music is your own experience, your thoughts, your wisdom. If you don't live it, it won't come out of your horn.

1950 Quoted in Ross Russell *Bird Lives!* (1972), pt.4, ch.22.

Parker, Dorothy née Rothschild 1893–1967

US writer and humorist, a central figure of the legendary Algonquin Hotel Round Table. She was an influential book and drama critic, contributing incisive and caustic reviews to the *New Yorker*. Her works include *Enough Rope* (1926) and *Here Lies* (1936).

88 Brevity is the soul of lingerie, as the Petticoat said to the Chemise.

1916 Caption for *Vogue*. Quoted in J Keats *You Might as Well Live* (1970).

89 Excuse My Dust.

1925 Suggested epitaph for herself. Quoted in Alexander Woollcott *While Rome Burns* (1934), 'Our Mrs Parker'. She also suggested 'This is on me' for her tombstone.

90 Lady, lady, should you meet
    One whose ways are all discreet,
    One who murmurs that his wife
    Is the lodestar of his life,
    One who keeps assuring you
    That he never was untrue,
    Never loved another one...
    Lady, lady, better run!

1926 *Enough Rope*, 'Social Note'.

91 Where's the man could ease a heart
    Like a satin gown?

1926 *Enough Rope*, 'The Satin Dress', stanza 1.

92 The affair between Margot Asquith and Margot Asquith will live as one of the prettiest love stories in all literature.

1927 Book review in the *New Yorker*, 22 Oct.

93 If, with the literate, I am
    Impelled to try an epigram,
    I never seek to take the credit;

We all assume that Oscar said it.

1928 *Sunset Gun*, 'Oscar Wilde'.

94 And it is that word 'hummy', my darlings, that
marks the first place in 'The House at Pooh
Corner' at which Tonstant Weader fwowed up.

1928 Book review in the *New Yorker*, 20 Oct.

95 More glutton than artist…he commences to chew
up the scenery.

1930 Play review, alluding to an unidentified actor. This is said
to have been the origin of the phrase 'chew up the scenery', used
to describe an actor who is 'hamming it up'.

96 Now that you've got me right down to it, the only
thing I didn't like about *The Barretts of Wimpole
Street* was the play.

1931 Play review in the *New Yorker*.

97 *House Beautiful* is play lousy.

1933 Review in the *New Yorker*. Quoted in P Hartnoll *Plays
and Players* (1984).

98 How did they know?

1933 Attributed response on hearing of the death of President
Calvin Coolidge.

99 Katharine Hepburn runs the gamut of the
emotions from A to B.

1933 Remark during the interval of *The Lake* on its Broadway
première. Quoted in G Carey *Katharine Hepburn* (1983), ch.6.

1 That woman speaks eighteen languages, and can't
say No in any of them.

Quoted in Alexander Woollcott *While Rome Burns* (1934), 'Our
Mrs Parker'.

2 And there was that wholesale libel on a Yale prom.
If all the girls attending it were laid end to end, Mrs
Parker said, she wouldn't be at all surprised.

Quoted in Alexander Woollcott *While Rome Burns* (1934), 'Our
Mrs Parker'.

3 Good work, Mary. We all knew you had it in you.

On the arrival of a baby. Quoted in Alexander Woollcott *While
Rome Burns* (1934), 'Our Mrs Parker'.

4 Whose love is given over-well
Shall look on Helen's face in hell
Whilst they whose love is thin and wise
Shall see John Knox in Paradise.

1937 *Not So Deep As A Well*, 'Partial Comfort'.

5 Why is it no one ever sent me yet
One perfect limousine, do you suppose?
Ah no, it's always just my luck to get
One perfect rose.

1937 *Not So Deep As A Well*, 'One Perfect Rose'.

6 Four be the things I'd been better without:
Love, curiosity, freckles, and doubt.

1937 *Not So Deep As A Well*, 'Inventory'.

7 By the time you say you're his,
Shivering and sighing
And he vows his passion is
Infinite, undying—
Lady, make a note of this:
One of you is lying.

1937 *Not So Deep As A Well*, 'Unfortunate Coincidence'.

8 Oh, life is a glorious cycle of song,
A medley of extemporanea;
And love is a thing that can never go wrong;
And I am Marie of Roumania.

1937 *Not So Deep As A Well*, 'Comment'.

9 Drink and dance and laugh and lie,
Love, the reeling midnight through,
For tomorrow we shall die!
(But, alas, we never do).

1937 *Not So Deep As A Well*, 'The Flaw in Paganism'.
▷ See Bible 151:69.

10 He lies below, correct in cypress wood,
And entertains the most exclusive worms.

1937 *Not So Deep As A Well*, 'Tombstones in the Starlight'.

11 Men seldom make passes
At girls who wear glasses.

1937 *Not So Deep As A Well*, 'News Item'.

12 Scratch a lover, and find a foe.

1937 *Not So Deep As A Well*, 'Ballade of a Great Weariness'.

13 Razors pain you
Rivers are damp;
Acids stain you;
And drugs cause cramp.
Guns aren't lawful;
Nooses give;
Gas smells awful;
You might as well live.

1937 *Not So Deep As A Well*, 'Résumé'.

14 Sorrow is tranquillity remembered in emotion.

1939 *Here Lies*, 'Sentiment'.
▷ See Wordsworth 1096:37.

15 And I'll stay off Verlaine, too; he was always
chasing Rimbauds.

1939 *Here Lies*, 'The Little Hours'.

16 You can always tell that the crash is coming when
I start getting tender about Our Dumb Friends.
Three highballs and I think I'm St Francis of
Assisi.

1939 *Here Lies*, 'Just A Little One'.

17 There's a hell of a distance between wise-cracking
and wit. Wit has truth in it; wise-cracking is simply
callisthenics with words.

1956 In the *Paris Review*, Summer.

18 All those writers who write about their childhood!
    Gentle God, if I wrote about mine you wouldn't sit
    in the same room with me.
    1956 In the *Paris Review*, Summer.

19 It serves me right for putting all my eggs in one
    bastard.
    On her abortion. Quoted in J Keats *You Might as Well Live*
    (1970).

20 You can lead a horticulture, but you can't make her
    think.
    Response to a challenge to use 'horticulture' in a sentence.
    Quoted in J Keats *You Might as Well Live* (1970).

21 One more drink and I'd have been under the host.
    Quoted in H Teichmann *George S Kaufman* (1972).

22 That should assure us of at least forty-five minutes
    of undisturbed privacy.
    Attributed, after pressing the button marked 'nurse' when her
    secretary came to visit her in hospital. Quoted in Clifton
    Fadiman *The Faber Book of Anecdotes* (1985).

23 Three be the things I shall never attain:
    Envy, content, and sufficient champagne.
    Quoted in Marion Meade *Dorothy Parker* (1988).

24 All writers are either 29 or Thomas Hardy.
    On being asked Hemingway's age. Quoted in Marion Meade
    Dorothy Parker (1988).

25 As American as a sawed-off shotgun.
    Of Dashiell Hammett. Quoted in Marion Meade *Dorothy
    Parker* (1988).

26 Upon my honour, I saw a Madonna
    Standing in a niche
    Above the door of the private whore
    Of the world's worst son of a bitch.
    Jotted into the visitor's book of William Randolph Hearst's
    house San Simeon after she had seen a Della Robbia madonna
    over the entrance to Marion Davies's bedroom. Quoted in R
    Hughes *Culture of Complaint* (1994).

Parker, Hubert Lister 1900–72

English judge. He served as Lord Chief Justice of
England.

27 A judge is not supposed to know anything about
    the facts of life until they have been presented in
    evidence and explained to him at least three times.
    1961 Quoted in *The Observer*, 12 Mar.

Parker, John 1729–75

Commander of the Lexington militia company in the
opening engagement of the American Revolution.

28 Stand your ground. Don't fire unless fired upon,
    but if they mean to have a war, let it begin here!
    1775 Attributed command before the Battle of Lexington, 19
    Apr.

Parker, Ross and Charles, Hugh 1914–74, 1907–

British songwriters.

29 There'll always be an England
    While there's a country lane,
    Wherever there's a cottage small
    Beside a field of grain.
    1939 Song.

Parker, Stewart 1941–88

Northern Irish playwright. A lecturer at Cornell
University, he turned to full-time writing for the stage,
TV and radio. His best known plays are *Spokesong* (1976)
and *Pentecost* (1987).

30 The Kamikaze Ground Staff Re-union Dinner.
    1979 Title of play.

Parkes, Sir Henry 1815–96

English-born Australian statesman, who emigrated to New
South Wales in 1839. A member of the colonial parliament
in 1854, he held various offices, from 1872 was repeatedly
Prime Minister, and was identified with free trade.

31 Why should not the name of an Australian be equal
    to that of a Briton…to that of a citizen of the
    proudest country under the sun? Make yourselves a
    united people, appear before the world as one, and
    the dream of going 'home' will die away.
    1880 Speech to the Australian Federation Conference, Feb.

Parkinson, C(yril) Northcote 1909–93

English political scientist and Professor of History, best
remembered for his seriocomic tilt at bureaucratic
malpractices, *Parkinson's Law: the Pursuit of Progress*
(1958).

32 Work expands so as to fill the time available for its
    completion.
    1958 *Parkinson's Law: the Pursuit of Progress*, ch.1.

33 Time spent on any item of the agenda will be in
    inverse proportion to the sum involved.
    1958 *Parkinson's Law: the Pursuit of Progress*, ch.3.

34 Men enter local politics solely as a result of being
    unhappily married.
    1958 *Parkinson's Law: the Pursuit of Progress*, ch.10.

35 Expenditure rises to meet income.
    1960 *The Law and the Profits*, ch.1.

Parkinson, Norman originally Ronald William Parkinson Smith 1913–90

English magazine photographer.

36 A photographer without a magazine behind him is
    like a farmer without fields.
    1984 In the *New Yorker*, 10 Dec.

37 The camera can be the most deadly weapon since the assassin's bullet. Or it can be the lotion of the heart.

1984 In the *New Yorker*, 10 Dec.

Parks, Rosa Lee née McCauley 1913–

US civil rights protester.

38 All I was doing was trying to get home from work.

On refusing to give up her seat to a white man in Montgomery, Alabama, which led to the 1955 Montgomery bus boycott and in turn to a Supreme Court ruling that bus segregation was unconstitutional, and fuelled the civil rights movement. Quoted in *Time*, 15 Dec 1975.

Parnell, Charles Stewart 1846–91

Irish politician, elected President of the Irish National Land League (1878). In 1886 he allied with the Liberals in support of Gladstone's Home Rule bill, but was forced to retire as leader of the Irish Nationalists in 1890 in disgrace when cited as co-respondent in a divorce case.

39 When a man takes a farm from which another has been evicted, you must show him on the roadside when you meet him; you must show him in the streets of the town; you must show him in the fair and the market place; and even in the house of worship, by leaving him severely alone—by putting him into a moral Coventry, by isolating him from his kind as if he were a leper of old. You must show him your detestation of the crimes that he has committed.

1880 Speech that established the practice of boycotting, Ennis, 19 Sep.

40 And it is a good sign that this masquerading knight-errant, this pretended champion of the rights of every other nation except those of the Irish nation, should be obliged to throw off the mask today, and to stand revealed as the man who by his own utterances is prepared to carry fire and sword into your homesteads unless you humbly abase yourselves before him, and before the landlords of the country.

1881 Speech successfully inciting Gladstone to arrest him, 9 Oct.

41 No man has a right to fix the boundary of the march of a nation. No man has a right to say to his country, 'Thus far thou shalt go and no further.'

1885 Speech, Cork, 21 Jan.

Parr-Davies, Harry 1914–55

Welsh songwriter, best known for the songs he wrote for Gracie Fields. His credits include 'Sing As We Go' (1934), 'Queen of Hearts' (1936) and 'Shipyard Sally' (1939).

42 Wish me luck, as you wave me goodbye— Cheerio, here I go, on my way.

1939 Sung by Gracie Fields in *Shipyard Sally*.

Parra, Nicanor 1914–

Chilean poet and lecturer. He addresses common problems in a clear and direct language, with black humour and a highly ironic vision.

43 *Padre nuestro que estás en el cielo*
Lleno de toda clase de problemas
Con el ceño fruncido
Como si fueras un hombre vulgar y corriente
No pienses más en nosotros.

Our Father who art in Heaven
Full of all kinds of problems
Ceaselessly frowning
As if you were a simple man:
Stop thinking about us.

1969 *Obra gruesa*, 'Padre nuestro' ('Our Father').

Parry, Sir Charles Hubert Hastings 1848–1918

English composer. Director of the Royal College of Music from 1895, he composed the oratorios *Judith*, *Job* and *King Saul*; an opera on *Lancelot and Guinevere*, symphonies, quartets and cantatas. He also wrote various books on music.

44 Look out for this man's music; he has something to say and knows how to say it.

1899 After the première of Elgar's *Enigma Variations*. Quoted in Ian Crofton and Donald Fraser *A Dictionary of Musical Quotations* (1985).

Parsons, Talcott 1902–79

US sociologist and social theorist. A member of the faculty of Harvard University (1927–74), his chief works include *The Social System* (1951) and *Sociological Theory and Modern Society* (1967).

45 Science is intimately integrated with the whole social structure and cultural tradition. They mutually support one another—only in certain types of society can science flourish, and conversely without a continuous and healthy development and application of science such a society cannot function properly.

1951 *The Social System*, ch.8.

Parvin, Landon 1948–

US speechwriter. He was formerly speechwriter to the President. He runs his own speechwriting and communications consultancy.

46 What you do is take the truth and just skew it a bit.

1991 On creating political wit for the Washington press's annual Gridiron dinners. In *New York Times*, 29 Mar.

Pascal, Blaise 1623–62

French philosopher, mathematician and physicist, whose inventions included a calculating machine, barometer, hydraulic press and syringe, and who pioneered probability theory. An ascetic Christian and member of the Jansenist movement, he wrote much spiritual literature. Notes found after his death were published as *Pensées* in 1670.

47 *Il y a deux sortes d'esprits fins, l'un géométrique, et l'autre que l'on peut appeler de finesse. Le premier a des vues lentes, dures et inflexibles; mais le dernier a une souplesse de pensée.*

There are two kinds of mind, one mathematical, the other what one might call the intuitive. The first takes a slow, firm, inflexible view, but the latter has flexibility of thought.
c.1653 *Discours sur les passions de l'amour* (*Discourse on the Passions of Love*) (translated by Michel Petheram). This is usually attributed to Pascal.

48 *Dans une grande âme tout est grand.*

In a great soul everything is great.
c.1653 *Discours sur les passions de l'amour* (*Discourse on the Passions of Love*). This is usually attributed to Pascal.

49 *Quelque étendue d'esprit que l'on ait, l'on n'est capable que d'une grande passion.*

However vast a man's spirit, he is only capable of one great passion.
c.1653 *Discours sur les passions de l'amour* (*Discourse on the Passions of Love*). This is usually attributed to Pascal.

50 *La netteté de l'esprit cause aussi la netteté de la passion; c'est pourquoi un esprit grand et net aime avec ardeur, et il voit distinctement ce qu'il aime.*

Clarity of mind results in clarity of passion; that is why a great mind loves ardently and sees distinctly what it loves.
c.1653 *Discours sur les passions de l'amour* (*Discourse on the Passions of Love*). This is usually attributed to Pascal.

51 *L'on a beau se cacher à soi-même, l'on aime toujours.*

We vainly conceal from ourselves the fact that we are always in love.
c.1653 *Discours sur les passions de l'amour* (*Discourse on the Passions of Love*). This is usually attributed to Pascal.

52 *La vraie éloquence se moque de l'éloquence, la vraie morale se moque de la morale.*

True eloquence has no time for eloquence, true morality has no time for morality.
c.1654–62 *Pensées*, no.4 (translated by A Krailsheimer).

53 *La dernière chose qu'on trouve en faisant un ouvrage, est de savoir celle qu'il faut mettre la première.*

The last thing one discovers in composing a work is what to put first.
c.1654–62 *Pensées*, no.19 (translated by A Krailsheimer).

54 *Quand on voit le style naturel, on est tout étonné et ravi, car on s'attendait de voir un auteur, et on trouve un homme.*

When we see a natural style we are quite amazed and delighted, because we expected to see an author and find a man.
c.1654–62 *Pensées*, no.29 (translated by A Krailsheimer).

55 *L'homme n'est qu'un sujet plein d'erreur, naturelle et ineffaçable sans la grâce.*

Man is nothing but a subject full of natural error that cannot be eradicated except through grace.
c.1654–62 *Pensées*, no.83 (translated by A Krailsheimer).

56 *Condition de l'homme: inconstance, ennui, inquiétude.*

Man's condition. Inconstancy, boredom, anxiety.
c.1654–62 *Pensées*, no.127 (translated by A Krailsheimer).

57 *Notre nature est dans le mouvement; le repos entier est la mort.*

Our nature consists in movement; absolute rest is death.
c.1654–62 *Pensées*, no.129 (translated by A Krailsheimer).

58 *Tout le malheur des hommes vient d'une seule chose, qui est de ne savoir pas demeurer en repos, dans une chambre.*

The sole cause of man's unhappiness is that he does not know how to stay quietly in his room.
c.1654–62 *Pensées*, no.139 (translated by A Krailsheimer).

59 *Le nez de Cléopâtre: s'il eût été plus court, toute la face de la terre aurait changé.*

Cleopatra's nose: if it had been shorter the whole face of the earth would have been different.
c.1654—62 *Pensées*, no.162 (translated by A Krailsheimer).

60 *Le silence éternel de ces espaces infinis m'effraie.*

The eternal silence of these infinite spaces fills me with dread.
c.1654–62 *Pensées*, no.206 (translated by A Krailsheimer).

61 *Combien de royaumes nous ignorent!*

How many kingdoms know nothing of us!
c.1654–62 *Pensées*, no.207 (translated by A Krailsheimer).

62 *Le dernier acte est sanglant, quelque belle que soit la comédie en tout le reste; on jette enfin de la terre sur la tête, et en voilà pour jamais.*

The last act is bloody, however fine the rest of the play. They throw earth over your head and it is finished forever.
c.1654–62 *Pensées*, no.210 (translated by A Krailsheimer).

63 *Pesons le gain et la perte, en prenant croix que Dieu est. Estimons ces deux cas: si vous gagnez, vous gagnez tout; si vous perdez, vous ne perdez rien. Gagez donc qu'il est, sans hésiter.*

Let us weigh up the gain and loss involved in calling heads that God exists. Let us assess the two cases: if you win you win everything, if you lose you lose nothing. Do not hesitate then; wager that he does exist.

c.**1654–62** *Pensées*, no 233 (translated by A Krailsheimer).

64 *Tout notre raisonnement se réduit à céder au sentiment.*

All our reasoning comes down to surrendering to feeling.

c.**1654–62** *Pensées*, no.274 (translated by A Krailsheimer).

65 *Le coeur a ses raisons, que la raison ne connaît point.*

The heart has its reasons of which reason knows nothing.

c.**1654–62** *Pensées*, pt.4, no 277 (translated by A Krailsheimer).

66 *L'homme n'est qu'un roseau, le plus faible de la nature; mais c'est un roseau pensant.*

Man is only a reed, the weakest in nature, but he is a thinking reed.

c.**1654–62** *Pensées*, no 347 (translated by A Krailsheimer).

67 *Le moi est haïssable.*

The self is hateful.

c.**1654–62** *Pensées*, no.455 (translated by A Krailsheimer).

68 *A mesure qu'on a plus d'esprit, on trouve qu'il y a plus d'hommes originaux. Les gens du commun ne trouvent pas de différence entre les hommes.*

The more intelligent one is, the greater the differences one finds among men. Ordinary persons do not perceive differences among men.

c.**1654–62** *Pensées*, pt.1, no.7.

69 *Eloquence qui persuade par douceur, non par empire, en tyran, non en roi.*

Eloquence should persuade gently, not by force or like a tyrant or king.

c.**1654–62** *Pensées*, pt.1, no.15.

70 *Qu'est-ce que l'homme dans la nature? Un néant à l'égard de l'infini, un tout à l'égard du néant, un milieu entre rien et tout.*

What is man in nature? Nothing in comparison to the infinite, all in comparison to nothing, a mean between nothing and everything.

c.**1654–62** *Pensées*, pt.2, no.72.

71 *La chose la plus importante à toute la vie est le choix du métier: le hasard en dispose.*

The most important thing in life is to choose a profession: chance arranges for that.

c.**1654–62** *Pensées*, pt.2, no.97.

72 Knowledge of physical science will not console me for ignorance of morality in time of affliction, but knowledge of morality will always console me for ignorance of physical science.

c.**1654–62** *Pensées*, no.23.

73 *L'homme n'est ni ange ni bête, et le malheur veut que qui veut faire l'ange fait la bête.*

Man is neither angel nor beast. Unfortunately, he who wants to act the angel often acts the beast.

c.**1654–62** *Pensées*, pt.6, no.358.

74 *En un mot, l'homme connaît qu'il est misérable: il est donc misérable, puisqu'il l'est; mais il est bien grand, puisqu'il le connaît.*

In one word, man knows that he is miserable and therefore he is miserable because he knows it; but he is also worthy, because he knows his condition.

c.**1654–62** *Pensées*, pt.6, no.416.

75 *Il n'y a que deux sortes d'hommes: les uns justes, qui se croient pécheurs: les autres pécheurs, qui se croient justes.*

There are only two types of people: the virtuous who believe themselves to be sinners and the sinners who believe themselves to be virtuous.

c.**1654–62** *Pensées*, pt.7, no.534.

76 *Il est non seulement impossible, mais inutile de connaître Dieu sans Jésus-Christ.*

It is not only impossible, but also useless to recognize God without Jesus.

c.**1654–62** *Pensées*, pt.7, no.549.

77 *Je ne crois que les histoires dont les témoins se feraient égorger.*

I only believe in histories told by witnesses who have had their throats slit.

c.**1654–62** *Pensées*, pt.9, no.593.

78 *Le silence est la plus grande persécution: jamais les saints ne se sont tus.*

Silence is the greatest of all persecutions: no saint was ever silent.

c.**1654–62** *Pensées*, pt.14, no.920.

79 *Console-toi, tu ne me chercherais pas si tu ne m'avais trouvé.*

Comfort yourself. You would not seek me if you had not found me.

c.**1654–62** *Pensées* (translated by L Braunschvicg, 1909).

80 *Je n'ai fait plus longue que parce que je n'ai pas eu le loisir de la faire plus courte.*

I have made this letter longer than usual, only because I have not had the time to make it shorter.

1657 *Lettres provinciales*, letter 16.

81 *FEU. Dieu d'Abraham, Dieu d'Isaac, Dieu de Jacob, non des philosophes et savants. Certitude. Certitude. Sentiment. Joie. Paix.*

FIRE. God of Abraham, God of Isaac, God of Jacob, not of the philosophers and scholars. Certainty.

Certainty. Feeling. Joy.

c.1662 Note found after his death on a parchment stitched to his coat.

Passell, Peter

US journalist, columnist with the *New York Times*.

82 Six percent unemployment only looks good from the vantage point of the other 94 percent.
1994 In the *New York Times*, 31 Mar.

Pasternak, Boris 1890–1960

Russian poet and novelist. He was awarded a Nobel Prize for Literature in 1958, but refused it.

83 Yet the order of the acts is planned
And the end of the way inescapable.
I am alone; all drowns in the Pharisees' hypocrisy.
1958 *Doctor Zhivago*.

84 The whole wide world is a cathedral;
I stand inside, the air is calm,
And from afar at times there reaches
My ear the echo of a psalm.
1958 *When It Clears Up* (translated by Lydia Pasternak Slater).

Pasteur, Louis 1822–95

French chemist, the father of modern bacteriology. He promoted inoculation as a means of preventing diseases, and in 1888 he founded the Institut Pasteur and served as its first director.

85 *Dans les champs de l'observation le hasard ne favorise que les esprits préparés.*

Where observation is concerned, chance favours only the prepared mind.
1854 Speech at the inauguration of the Faculty of Science, University of Lille, 7 Dec.

86 Science proceeds by successive answers to questions more and more subtle, coming nearer and nearer to the very essence of phenomena.
c.1856 *Études sur la Bière*, ch.6 (translated by René Dubois).

87 *Il n'existe pas de sciences appliquées, mais seulement des applications de la science.*

There are no such things as applied sciences, only applications of science.
1872 Speech, Lyons, 11 Sep.

88 I am imbued with two deep impressions; the first, that science knows no country; the second, which seems to contradict the first, although it is really a direct consequence of it…that science is the highest personification of the nature. Science knows no country because knowledge belongs to humanity, and is the torch which illuminates the world. Science is the highest personification of the nation because

that nation will remain the first which carries the furthest the works of thought and intelligence.
1876 Toast at the banquet of the International Congress of Sericulture (translated by René Dubois).

89 Outside their laboratories, the physician and chemist are soldiers without arms on the field of battle.
Some Reflections on Science in France, pt.1.

Patchen, Kenneth 1911–72

US author, playwright and poet. His many verse collections, illustrated by him, include *Before the Brave* (1936) and *Hallelujah Anyway* (1967), and his novels include *Memoirs of a Shy Pornographer* (1945).

90 For greatness is only the drayhorse that coaxes
The built cart out; and where we go is reason.
But genius is an enormous littleness, a trickling
Of heart that covers alike the hare and the hunter.
1939 *First Will and Testament*, 'The Character of Love Seen as a Search for the Lost'.

91 Dogs with broken legs are shot; men with broken souls write through the night.
1941 *The Journal of Albion Moonlight*.

92 God must have loved the People in Power, for he made them so very like their own image of him.
Quoted by Adrian Mitchell in *The Guardian*, 1 Feb 1972.

Pater, Walter 1839–94

English critic and essayist, whose highly polished prose style was very influential. He wrote many essays on Renaissance art, and won a wider audience with a romance, *Marius the Epicurean* (1885).

93 She is older than the rocks among which she sits;
like the vampire, she has been dead many times,
and learned the secrets of the grave.
1873 Of the *Mona Lisa*. 'Leonardo da Vinci' in *Studies in the History of the Renaissance*.

94 All art constantly aspires towards the condition of music.
1873 'The School of Giorgione' in *Studies in the History of the Renaissance*.

95 Of such wisdom, the poetic passion, the desire of beauty, the love of art for its own sake, has most. For art comes to you proposing frankly to give nothing but the highest quality to your moments as they pass, and simply for those moments' sake.
1873 'Conclusion' in *Studies in the History of the Renaissance*.

Paterson, Banjo (Andrew Barton) 1864–1941

Australian poet and journalist. He worked on a station near Yass and later practised as a solicitor, contributing to the satirical weekly *Bulletin* as 'The Banjo'. His first collection of bush ballads, *The Man from Snowy River* (1895), gained him massive popularity.

96   Oh there once was a swagman camped in the
     billabongs,
     Under the shade of a Coolibah tree;
     And he sang as he looked at the old billy boiling,
     'Who'll come a-waltzing Matilda with me.'

     Who'll come a-waltzing Matilda, my darling,
     Who'll come a-waltzing Matilda with me.
     Waltzing Matilda and leading a water-bag,
     Who'll come a-waltzing Matilda with me.
     1885 'Waltzing Matilda', in the *Bulletin*, Apr.

97   I had written him a letter which I had, for want of
     better
     Knowledge, sent to where I met him, down the
     Lachlan, years ago.
     He was shearing when I knew him, so I sent the
     letter to him,
     Just 'on spec', addressed as follows: 'Clancy, of the
     Overflow'.
     And an answer came directed in a writing
     unexpected,
     (And I think the same was written with a
     thumbnail dipped in tar)
     'Twas his shearing mate who wrote it, and verbatim
     I will quote it:
     'Clancy's gone to Queensland droving, and we
     don't know where he are.'
     1895 'Clancy of the Overflow', first published in the *Bulletin*,
     collected in *The Man from Snowy River and Other Verses* (1895).

98   In all museums throughout the world one may see
     plaster casts of footprints of weird animals,
     footprints preserved for posterity, not because the
     animals were particularly good of their sort, but
     because they had the luck to walk on the lava while
     it was cooling. There is just a faint hope that
     something of the same sort may happen to us.
     Of Henry Lawson and himself writing in a new land. Quoted in
     Rosamund Campbell and Philippa Harvie *Introduction to A
     Literary Heritage:* 'Banjo' Paterson (1988).

Patmore, Coventry Kersey Dighton

1823–96

English poet. He was associated with the Pre-Raphaelite brotherhood. His best work, *The Angel in the House* (4 vols. 1854–63), was a poetic treatment of married love which delighted a generation devoid of cynicism to whom he and his first wife, Emily, epitomised Victorian values.

99   Oh, wasteful woman, she who may
     On her sweet self set her own price,
     Knowing man cannot choose but pay,
     How has she cheapened paradise:
     How given for naught her priceless gift,
     How spoiled the bread and spilled the wine,
     Which, spent with due, respective thrift,

Had made brutes men, and men divine.
1854 *The Angel in the House*, bk.1, *The Betrothal*, canto 3, prelude 3, 'Unthrift'.

1   Love wakes men, once a lifetime each:
     They lift their heavy lids, and look;
     And, lo, what one sweet page can teach,
     They read with joy, then shut the book.
     1854 *The Angel in the House*, bk.1, *The Betrothal*, canto 8, prelude 2, 'The Revelation'.

2   'I saw you take his kiss!' ''Tis true.'
     'O modesty!' ''Twas strictly kept:
     He thought me asleep—at least, I knew
     He thought I thought he thought I slept.'
     1854 *The Angel in the House*, bk.2, *The Espousal*, canto 8, prelude 3, 'The Kiss'.

3   A woman is a foreign land.
     1854 *The Angel in the House*, bk.2, *The Espousal*, canto 9, prelude 2, 'The Foreign Land'.

4   It was not like your great and gracious ways!
     Do you, that have naught other to lament,
     Never, my love, repent.
     1877 *To the Unknown Eros*, bk.1, no.8, 'Departure'.

5   With all my will, but much against my heart,
     We two now part.
     1877 *To the Unknown Eros*, bk.1, no.16, 'A Farewell'.

6   'O say,
     Shall we no voluntary bars
     Set to our drift? I, Sister of the Stars,
     And Thou, my glorious, course-compelling Day!'
     1877 *To the Unknown Eros*, bk.2, no.2, 'The Contract'.

7   No writer, scared or profane, ever uses the words
     'he' or 'him' of the soul. It is always 'she' or 'her';
     so universal is the intuitive knowledge that the
     soul, with regard to God who is her life, is
     feminine.
     1896 *The Rod, the Root, and the Flower*, 'Aurea Dicta', no.21.

8   Those who know God know that it is a quite a
     mistake to suppose that there are only five senses.
     1896 *The Rod, the Root, and the Flower*, 'Aurea Dicta', no.142.

9   May I know by love and speak by silence.
     1896 *The Rod, the Root, and the Flower*, 'Aphorisms and
     Extracts'.

10   Some dish more sharply spiced than this
     Milk-soup men call domestic bliss.
     1906 *Olympus*.

11   He that but once too nearly hears
     The music of forfended spheres
     Is thenceforth lonely, and for all
     His days as one who treads the Wall
     Of China, and, on this hand, sees

Cities and their civilities
And, on the other, lions.
1863 *The Victories of Love*, bk. 1.

Paton, Alan 1903–88

South African writer and educator. President of the South African Liberal Party (1953–60), he is best remembered for his novel *Cry, The Beloved Country* (1948), on racial divisions in South Africa.

12 Cry, the Beloved Country.
  1948 Title of book.

13 No second Johannesburg is needed upon the earth. One is enough.
  1948 *Cry, The Beloved Country*, bk.2, section 6.

Patrick, John pseudonym of *John Patrick Goggan* 1905–

US playwright and screenwriter, best known for *Three Coins in the Fountain* (1954), *Love is a Many Splendoured Thing* (1955) and *The World of Suzie Wong* (1961).

14 Punctuality is the vice of virtuous women.
  1954 Line delivered by Clifton Webb in *Three Coins in the Fountain*.

St Patrick 5c AD

Bishop and Apostle of Ireland.

15 Christ for my guardianship today: against poison, against burning, against drowning, against wounding, that there may come to me a multitude of rewards;
  Christ with me,
  Christ before me,
  Christ behind me,
  Christ in me,
  Christ over me,
  Christ to right of me,
  Christ to left of me,
  Christ in lying down,
  Christ in sitting,
  Christ in rising up,
  Christ in the heart of every person who may think of me,
  Christ in the mouth of every person who may speak of me,
  Christ in every eye, which may look on me!
  Christ in every ear, which may hear me!
  St Patrick's Breastplate, traditionally attributed to the saint.

Patton, George Smith known as *Old Blood and Guts* 1885–1945

US soldier, a daring and flamboyant commander in World War II. He led numerous expeditions, including the 3rd Army invasion of France, and was killed in a road accident in Germany soon after being appointed general.

16 The object of war is not to die for your country. The object of war is to make damn sure the other sonofabitch dies for *his*.
  Attributed.

Paul, Leslie 1905–85

Irish writer and poet.

17 Angry Young Man.
  1951 Title of book. Later associated with John Osborne.

Pauling, Linus Carl 1901–1994

US chemist. He was Professor at the California Institute of Technology and won the Nobel Prize for Chemistry in 1954. He was awarded the Nobel Peace Prize in 1962.

18 Science is a search for truth—it is not a game in which one tries to best his opponent, to do harm to others.
  1958 *No More War*.

Pavlov, I(van) P(etrovich) 1849–1936

Russian physiologist and experimental psychologist, famed for his work on the physiology of the digestive system. He received the 1904 Nobel Prize for Physiology or Medicine.

19 Learn the ABC of science before you try to ascend to its summit.
  1936 *Bequest to the Academic Youth of Soviet Russia*.

Pavlov, Valentin Sergeyevich 1937–

Russian politician. He was Prime Minister Jan-Aug 1991 when he was arrested as an accomplice in the failed coup d'état of that month.

20 Privatization must come after the liberalization of prices…How on earth can you privatize or denationalize anything if you have no means of assessing the value of assets before offering them on the market?
  1991 Interview, *The Independent*, 18 Apr.

21 Civil war is impossible in the Soviet Union.
  1991 Interview, *The Independent*, 18 Apr.

22 It is no use making revolutionary cavalry charges against the problems that we are facing.
  1991 On Boris Yeltsin's proposals for economic republican autonomy, interview, *The Independent*, 18 Apr.

Paz, Octavio 1914–98

Mexican poet, writer and diplomat. He sided with the Republican cause during the Spanish Civil War. In Paris, he was strongly influenced by the surrealist movement. He was awarded a Nobel Prize in 1990.

23 *Amar es combatir, es abrir puertas,*
  dejar de ser fantasma con un número
  a perpetua cadena condenado
  por un amo sin rostro.

  To love is to battle, to open doors,

to cease to be a ghost with a number
forever in chains, forever condemned
by a faceless master.

1949 *Libertad bajo palabra*, 'Piedra de sol' (translated as 'The Sun Stone', 1963).

24 *Sin duda la cercanía de la muerte y la fraternidad de las armas producen, en todos los tiempos y en todos los países, una atmósfera propicia a lo extraordinario, a todo aquello que sobrepasa la condición humana y rompe el círculo de soledad que rodea a cada hombre.*

No doubt the nearness of death and the brotherhood of men-at-wars, at whatever time and in whatever country, always produce an atmosphere favorable to the extraordinary, to all that rises above the human condition and breaks the circle of solitude that surrounds each one of us.

1950 *El laberinto de la soledad*, pt.1 (translated as *The Labyrinth of Solitude*, 1961).

25 Technology is not an image of the world but a way of operating on reality. The nihilism of technology lies not only in the fact that it is the most perfect expression of the will to power…but also in the fact that it lacks meaning.

1967 *Alternating Current*.

Peace Pilgrim d.1981

US writer and mystic, whose real name is not known. From 1952 to 1981 she walked through North America, carrying only the bare minimum of necessities and teaching wherever she went; her intention was to stop walking only when there was total peace in the world.

26 I never give out my zodiac sign. Do you honestly think I can be pushed around by a planet? Good heavens, your divine nature is always free.

Quoted in Susan Hayward and Malcolm Cohen *The Bag of Jewels* (1988).

Peacock, Thomas Love 1785–1866

English novelist. He entered the service of the East India Company (1819–56) after producing three satirical romances, attacking common prejudices and affectations, and produced further works along similar lines.

27 Marriage may often be a stormy lake, but celibacy is almost always a muddy horsepond.

1817 *Melincourt*, ch.7.

28 Laughter is pleasant, but the exertion is too much for me.

1818 *Nightmare Abbey*, ch.5.

29 Sir, I have quarrelled with my wife; and a man who has quarrelled with his wife is absolved from all duty to his country.

1818 *Nightmare Abbey*, ch.11.

30 The mountain sheep are sweeter,

But the valley sheep are fatter;
We therefore deemed it meeter
To carry off the latter.
We made an expedition;
We met a host, and quelled it;
We forced a strong position,
And killed the men who held it.

1829 *The Misfortunes of Elphin*, 'The War-Song of Dinas Vawr'.

31 But though first love's impassioned blindness
Has passed away in colder light,
I still have thought of you with kindness,
And shall do, till our last goodnight.
The ever-rolling silent hours
Will bring a time we shall not know,
When our young days of gathering flowers
Will be an hundred years ago.

1860 'Love and Age'.

Pearson, Karl 1857–1936

English mathematician and Professor of Mathematics and Eugenics at University College London. Pearson is generally considered one of the founders of modern statistical theory.

32 When every fact, every present or past phenomenon of [the] universe, every phase of present or past life therein, has been examined, classified, and coordinated with the rest, then the mission of science will be completed. What is this but saying that the task of science can never end till man ceases to be, till history is no longer made, and development itself ceases?

1892 *The Grammar of Science*, pt.1, ch.5.

Pearson, Lester Bowles 1897–1972

Canadian politician, president of the UN General Assembly (1952–3). He won the Nobel Peace Prize (1957). Opposition leader from 1958, he became Prime Minister 1963–8.

33 The grim fact, however, is that we prepare for war like precocious giants and for peace like retarded pygmies.

1957 Acceptance speech on receiving the Nobel Peace Prize, 11 Dec.

34 Politics is the skilled use of blunt objects.

Quoted in Canadian Broadcasting Corporation tribute on his death, 1972.

Peary, Robert Edwin 1856–1920

US admiral and explorer. He made eight Arctic voyages by the Greenland coast. In 1906 he reached latitude 87 degrees 6 mins North and on 6 April 1909 was the first to reach the North Pole.

35 I have got the North Pole out of my system after twenty-three years of effort, hard work, disappointments, hardships, privations, more or

less suffering, and some risks… The work is the finish, the cap and climax of nearly four hundred years of effort, loss of life, and expenditure of fortunes by the civilized nations of the world, and it has been accomplished in a way that is thoroughly American. I am content.

1909 Diary entry, Apr. Quoted in *The North Pole* (published 1910).

36 In a march of only a few hours, I had passed from the western to the eastern hemisphere and had verified my position at the summit of the world. It was hard to realise that on the first miles of the brief march we had been travelling due north, while on the last few miles of the same march we had been travelling due south, although we had all the time been travelling precisely in the same direction.

1909 Description of crossing and then passing the Pole. *The North Pole* (published 1910).

Peck, M(organ) Scott 1936–

US writer and psychiatrist, author of the seminal self-help work *The Road Less Traveled* (1978). Later works, combining Christian teaching with psychiatric principles, include *The Different Drum* (1987).

37 Once we truly know that life is difficult—once we understand and accept it—then life is no longer difficult. Because once it is accepted, it no longer matters.

1978 *The Road Less Traveled*, ch.1.

38 The evil in this world is committed by the spiritual fat cats who think that they are without sin because they are unwilling to suffer the discomfort of significant self-examination.

1985 *What Return Can I Make?*

39 What being a Christian means, at the very least, is that whenever there is a decision to be made, which may be several times a day, an alternative should not be discarded simply because it is sacrificial.

1985 *What Return Can I Make?*

40 Simply seek happiness, and you are not likely to find it. Seek to create and love without regard to your happiness, and you will likely be happy much of the time.

1987 *A Different Drum.*

41 The healthy life is hardly one marked by an absence of crises. In fact, an individual's psychological health is distinguished by how early he or she can meet crisis.

1987 *A Different Drum.*

Peel, Sir Robert 1788–1850

English Tory statesman, Secretary for Ireland (1812–18), known as 'Orange Peel' for his strong anti-Catholic spirit.

As Home Secretary (1822–7, 1828–30), he carried through the Catholic Emancipation Act (1829) and reorganized the London police force (the 'Peelers' or 'Bobbies'). As Prime Minister (1834–5, 1841–6), his decision to repeal the Corn Laws (1846) split his party, and precipitated his resignation, though he remained in Parliament as leader of the 'Peelites'.

42 If the spirit of the Reform Bill implies merely a careful review of institutions, civil and ecclesiastical, undertaken in a friendly temper, combining with the firm maintenance of established rights the correction of private abuses and the redress of real grievances, I can for myself and my colleagues undertake to act in such a spirit and with such intentions.

1834 *The Tamworth Manifesto.*

43 During my tenure of power, my earnest wish has been to impress the people of this country with a belief that the legislature was animated by a sincere desire to frame its legislation upon the principles of equity and justice… Deprive me of power tomorrow, but you can never deprive me of the consciousness that I have exercised the powers committed to me from no corrupt or interested motives, from no desire to gratify ambition, or to attain any personal object.

1846 On the repeal of the Corn Laws, House of Commons, 15 May.

44 It asks more steadiness, self-control, ay, and manly courage, than any other exercise. You must take as well as give—eye to eye, toe to toe, and arm to arm.

Of boxing. Quoted in John Boyle O'Reilly *Ethics of Boxing and Manly Sport* (1888).

Peele, George c.1556–96

English dramatist and poet.

45 Fair and fair, and twice so fair,
As fair as any may be;
The fairest shepherd on our green,
A love for any lady.

1584 *The Arraignment of Paris*, act1, sc.5.

46 What thing is love for (well I wot) love is a thing.
It is a prick, it is a sting,
It is a pretty, pretty thing;
It is a fire, it is a coal
Whose flame creeps in at every hole.

c.1591 *The Hunting of Cupid.*

Pei, I(eoh) M(ing) 1917–

Chinese-born US architect. He emigrated to the US in 1935 and was naturalized in 1954. A controversial and adventurous designer, his works include Mile High Center, Denver and the glass pyramid at the Louvre, Paris.

47 Let's do it right. This is for the ages.

1978 Quoted by J Carter Brown, Director, National Gallery of Art, Washington, in the *Washington Post*, 27 Aug 1995. On his design for the gallery's East Building which was soaring to an unbudgeted cost of $94.4m.

48 *Comment respecter la tradition, et innover en même temps? Quel pari difficile!*

How to respect tradition and to innovate at the same time? What a difficult challenge!

1989 *Les Grands Desseins du Louvre* (with E J Biasini).

49 *L'architecture est le miroir même de la vie. Il n'est que de jeter les yeux sur des édifices pour sentir la présence du passé, l'esprit d'un lieu; ils sont le reflet de la société.*

Architecture is the very mirror of life. You only have to cast your eyes on buildings to feel the presence of the past, the spirit of a place; they are the reflection of society.

1989 *Les Grands Desseins du Louvre* (with E J Biasini).

Pelé pseudonym of *Edson Arantes do Nascimento* 1940–

Brazilian footballer. He won World Cup medals with Brazil (1958 and 1970) and scored over 1,000 goals in the first-class game. He left Santos to join the New York Cosmos in 1975.

50 A penalty is a cowardly way to score.

Quoted in Peter Ball and Phil Shaw *The Book of Football Quotations* (1989).

51 I was born for soccer, just as Beethoven was born for music.

Quoted in Colin Jarman *The Guinness Dictionary of Sports Quotations* (1990).

52 Football is like a religion to me. I worship the ball, and I treat it like a god. Too many players think of a football as something to kick. They should be taught to caress it and to treat it like a precious gem.

Quoted in David Pickering *The Cassell Soccer Companion* (1994).

Penecuik, Dr Alex 1652–1722

Scottish poet.

53 To curle on the ice, does greatly please,
Being a manly Scottish exercise;
It clears the Brains, stirs up the Native Heat,
And gives a gallant appetite for Meat.

1715 Quoted in Colin Jarman *The Guinness Dictionary of Sports Quotations* (1990).

Penfield, Wilder Graves 1891–1976

US-born Canadian neurosurgeon, who worked mainly at Montreal's Allan Memorial Institute, where he was first director (1934–60). He famously worked on the exposed

brains of living human subjects, and on retirement turned to writing fiction and biography.

54 In all our studies of the brain, no mechanism has been discovered that can force the mind to think, or the individual to believe, anything. The mind continues free. That is a statement I have long considered. I have made every effort to disprove it, without success.

1970 *Second Thoughts: Science, the Arts, and the Spirit.*

Peniakoff, Vladimir 1897–1951

Belgian-born soldier and writer.

55 A message came on the wireless for me. It said: 'SPREAD ALARM AND DESPONDENCY'. So the time had come, I thought, Eighth Army was taking the offensive. The date was, I think, May 18th, 1942.

1950 *Popski's Private Army.*

Penn, William 1644–1718

English Quaker, imprisoned for his beliefs. In 1681, in settlement of Charles II's debt to his father, he was granted land in America, and founded the colony of Pennsylvania as a refuge for persecuted Quakers.

56 This day my country was confirmed to me under the great seal of England, with large powers and privileges, by the name of *Pennsylvania*; a name the king would give it in honor of my father.

1681 Letter to Robert Turner, 14 Mar.

57 Inquire often, but judge rarely, and thou wilt not often be mistaken.

1693 *Some Fruits of Solitude.*

People's Daily

The official daily newspaper of the Communist Party of China speaks for the Chinese government and in 1979 a series of articles denounced the Democracy Wall Movement. Changan Road in Beijing had been a centre for posters and newsheets demanding democratic rights.

58 The imperialists brought the Chinese people cannons rather than flowers, death instead of 'human rights'... How can they be in a position to instruct us on 'civil rights'?

1979 *People's Daily*, 22 Mar.

Pepys, Samuel 1633–1703

English civil servant and diarist. He rose in the naval service to become Secretary to the Admiral, 1672. His diary, covering the years 1660 to 1669, is an important historical and social document.

59 Boys do now cry 'Kiss my Parliament!' instead of 'Kiss my arse!' so great and general a contempt is the Rump come to among all men, good and bad.

1660 Diary entry, 7 Feb. The Rump Parliament was that which persisted after the fall of Richard Cromwell, and before the restoration of Charles II.

60 And so to bed.
1660 Diary entry, 20 Apr and passim.

61 A silk suit, which cost me much money, and I pray God to make me able to pay for it.
1660 Diary entry, 1 Jul.

62 I went out to Charing Cross to see Major-Generall Harrison hanged, drawn and quartered—which was done there—he looking as cheerfully as any man could do in that condition… Thus it was my chance to see the King beheaded at Whitehall and to see the first blood shed in revenge for the blood of the King at Charing Cross.
1660 Diary entry, 13 Oct.

63 A good honest and painful sermon.
1661 Diary entry, 17 Mar.

64 But methought it lessened my esteem of a king, that he should not be able to command the rain.
1662 Diary entry, 19 Jul.

65 I see it is impossible for the King to have things done as cheap as other men.
1662 Diary entry, 21 Jul.

66 To the King's Theatre, where we saw *Midsummer Night's Dream*, which I had never seen before, nor shall ever again, for it is the most insipid, ridiculous play that ever I ever saw in my life.
1662 Diary entry, 29 Sep.

67 But Lord! to see the absurd nature of Englishmen, that cannot forbear laughing and jeering at everything that looks strange.
1662 Diary entry, 27 Nov.

68 Then over the park (where I first in my life, it being a great frost, did see people sliding with their skates, which is a very pretty art).
1662 Diary entry, 1 Dec.

69 My wife, who, poor wretch, is troubled with her lonely life.
1662 Diary entry, 19 Dec.

70 Most of their discourse was about hunting, in a dialect I understand very little.
1663 Diary entry, 22 Nov.

71 After dinner to the Duke's house, and there saw *Twelfth Night* acted well, though it be but a silly play.
1663 Diary entry.

72 To the Tennis Court, and there saw the King play at tennis and others; but to see how the King's play

was extolled, without any cause at all, was a loathsome sight.
1664 Diary entry, 4 Jan.

73 This day, much against my will, I did in Drury Lane see two or three houses marked with a red cross upon the doors, and 'Lord have mercy upon us' writ there—which was a sad sight to me, being the first of that kind that to my remembrance I ever saw.
1665 Diary entry, 7 Jun. The houses were afflicted with bubonic plague, which lasted in London until the summer of 1666.

74 Up, all of us, and to Billiards.
1665 Diary entry, 17 Jul.

75 The people die so, that now it seems they are fain to carry the dead to be buried by daylight, the nights not sufficing to do it in. And my Lord Mayor commands people to be within at 9 at night, all (as they say) that the sick may have liberty to go abroad for ayre.
1665 Diary entry, 12 Aug.

76 And it is a wonder what will be the fashion after the plague is done as to periwigs, for nobody will dare to buy any haire for fear of the infection—that it had been cut off the heads of people dead of the plague.
1665 Diary entry, 3 Sep.

77 Strange to say what delight we married people have to see these poor fools decoyed into our condition.
1665 Diary entry, 25 Dec.

78 Music and women I cannot but give way to, whatever my business is.
1666 Diary entry, 9 Mar.

79 Poor people staying in their houses as long as till the very fire touched them, and then running into boats or clambering from one pair of stair by the waterside to another. And among other things, the poor pigeons I perceive were loath to leave their houses, but hovered about the windows and balconies till they were some of them burned, their wings, and fell down.
1666 Diary entry, 2 Sep. The Great Fire of London continued for four days, destroying four-fifths of the total area of the city.

80 A most horrid malicious bloody flame… It made me weep to see it.
1666 Observing the Great Fire of London. Diary entry, 2 Sep.

81 Hardly one lighter or boat in three that had the goods of a house in, but there was a pair of virginalls in it.
1666 Describing the chaos on the Thames as people attempted to rescue their possessions from the flames. Diary entry, 2 Sep.

82 Up, and by coach to Sir Ph. Warwickes, the street being full of footballs, it being a great frost.

1665 Diary entry, 2 Jan. Frost restricted the amount of horse traffic in the streets of London, making football a possibility.

83 But it is pretty to see what money will do.

1668 Diary entry, 21 Mar.

Percy, Walker 1916–90

US novelist. His best known work of fiction is *The Moviegoer* (1961), but he wrote several novels, and volumes of collected essays and non-fiction.

84 As Einstein once said, ordinary life in an ordinary day in the modern world is a dreary business. I mean *dreary*. People will do anything just to escape this dreariness.

1977 Interview in *Esquire*, Dec.

85 Unlike God the artist does not start with nothing and make something of it. He starts with himself as nothing and makes something of the nothing with the things at hand.

1977 Interview in *Esquire*, Dec.

Perdue, Franklin P

US businessman. Chief executive of Perdue Farms Inc.

86 I hate pudgy poultry.

1987 In the *New Yorker*, 6 Jul.

Perelman, S(ydney) J(oseph) 1904–79

US humorist. He was a scriptwriter, and later one of the circle of wits who wrote for the *New Yorker*. He published a number of books.

87 I have Bright's disease and he has mine, sobbed the panting palooka.

1929 In *Judge*, 16 Nov. A palooka is US slang for a clumsy person, especially in sports.

88 Crazy Like A Fox.

1944 Title of book.

89 A feeling of emulsion swept over me.

1944 *Crazy Like A Fox*, 'The Love Decoy'.

90 He bit his lip in a manner which immediately awakened my maternal sympathy, and I helped him bite it.

1944 *Crazy Like A Fox*, 'The Love Decoy'.

91 I guess I'm just an old mad scientist at bottom. Give me an underground laboratory, half a dozen atomsmashers, and a beautiful girl in a diaphanous veil waiting to be turned into a chimpanzee, and I care not who writes the nation's laws.

1944 *Crazy Like A Fox*, 'Captain Future, Block That Kick'.

92 She had the rippling muscles of a panther, the solidity of a water buffalo, and the lazy insolence of a shoe salesman.

1944 *Crazy Like A Fox*, 'Kitchen Bouquet'.

93 For years I have let dentists ride roughshod over my teeth; I have been sawed, hacked, chopped, whittled, bewitched, bewildered, tattooed, and signed on again; but this is cuspid's last stand.

1944 *Crazy Like A Fox*, 'Nothing But The Tooth'.

94 You've got a sharp tongue in your head, Mr Essick. Look out it doesn't cut your throat.

1961 *The Rising Gorge*, 'All Out…'.

95 English life, while very pleasant, is rather bland. I expected kindness and gentility and I found it, but there is such a thing as too much couth.

1971 In *The Observer*, 24 Sep.

96 The dogs had eaten the upholstery of a Packard convertible that afternoon, and were consequently somewhat subdued.

1981 *The Last Laugh*, 'The Last Laugh'.

Pericles c.490–429 BC

Athenian statesman, who initiated democratic reforms and a great building programme (including the Parthenon). His famous *epitaphios* (funeral oration on the death of the first year of the Peloponnesian War) was reported by Thucydides. He died of the plague which struck Athens in 430 BC.

97 Famous men have the whole earth as their memorial.

Quoted in Thucydides *History of the Peloponnesian War*, 2.43 (translated by R Warner, 1961).

98 Your great glory is not to be inferior to what you have been given by nature, and the greatest glory of a woman is to be least talked about by men, whether they are praising or criticizing you.

Address to women in the Funerary Oration. Quoted in Thucydides *History of the Peloponnesian War*, 2.45.2 (translated by R Warner, 1961).

Perkins, Carl 1932–98

US songwriter and composer. A key figure of early rock 'n' roll, his guitar playing combines blues and country music.

99 Don't you step on my blue suede shoes.

1956 'Blue Suede Shoes'.

Perkins, Frances 1882–1965

American social reformer and politician. Educated at Mount Holyoke College, Massachusetts, she was the first woman to hold Cabinet rank in the USA. She was appointed US Secretary of Labor (1933-45) in President Franklin D Roosevelt's Cabinet.

1 No one had any measure of its progress; no one had any plan for stopping it. Everyone tried to get out of its way.

On the depression of the 1930s which inspired her to set up the Social Security system. Recalled on her death, 14 May 1965.

Persius, Aulus Flaccus Persius AD 34–62

Latin satirist and Stoic. Only one book of satires has survived.

2 *Quis leget haec?*

Who'll read that sort of thing?
Satirae, 1.2 (translated by W S Merwin, 1961).

Perth, James, 4th Earl of 1648–1716

Scottish Justice-General (1682) and Chancellor (1684). He was imprisoned in Stirling Castle (1688–96), after the fall of James II and VII, but then joined the exiled court of the King at St Germain, where he remained for the rest of his life. He was created Duke of Perth and Knight of the Garter.

3 I have been here a fortnight and I think I shall be here fifteen or twenty days longer, although I do not very much like the place, for this puddling in a tub continually is no charm to me.
On Venice. Collected in *Letters to his sister the Countess of Erroll, and other members of his family.*

Pétain, (Henri) Philippe 1856–1951

French soldier and politician. In World War I his defence of Verdun (1916) made him a national hero, and he became Commander-in-Chief (1917) and Marshal of France (1918). When France collapsed in 1940, he negotiated the armistice with Germany and Italy, became chief of state, and collaborated with Germany in an attempt to keep France out of the war. He is regarded by some as a patriot, by others as a traitor.

4 They shall not pass.
This phrase came to symbolize the stubborn defence of Verdun against Ludendorf's siege, which cost 300,000 German and 400,000 French troops.
▷ See Ibarruri Gomez 510:18.

5 I was with you in the days of glory. At the head of the Government, I shall remain with you during the days of darkness. Stay by my side.
1940 Radio broadcast announcing his intention to seek an armistice, 20 Jun.

Peter, Laurence J 1919–90

Canadian academic and writer, professor at the University of South California.

6 In a hierarchy every employee tends to rise to his level of incompetence; the cream rises until it sours.
1969 *The Peter Principle*, ch.1 (with Raymond Hull).

7 Bureaucracy defends the status quo long past the time when the quo has lost its status.
1978 In the *San Francisco Chronicle*, 29 Jan.

Peters, Professor Richard Stanley 1919–

British educationist. He is a Professor of Education and lectured at Harvard in 1961. He has written widely on education.

8 What matters is not what any individual thinks, but what is true. A teacher who does not equip his pupils with the rudimentary tools to discover this is substituting indoctrination for teaching.
1966 *Ethics and Education.*

Petersen, Henry Edward 1921–

US Assistant Attorney General for Prosecutions. He went from clerk to Chief of the organized crime and racketeering section of the FBI, Washington (1948–69).

9 What you have just said, Mr President, speaks very well of you as a man. It does not speak well of you as a president.
1973 On President Nixon's remark that he would need proof of the guilt of aides John Ehrichman and H R Hadelman on the Watergate break-in and cover-up before he could fire them. Quoted in Richard M Nixon *RN: The Memoirs of Richard Nixon* (1978).

Petrarch, Francis 1304–74

Italian poet and classical scholar, responsible for the discovery of several works, including Cicero's letters and two of his orations, and a portion of Quintilian's *De Oratio*. In 1341 he was crowned Poet Laureate in Rome. Most famous for the lyrics of his *Canzionere*, he also composed prose treatises, historical works, and letters.

10 *Continue morimur, ego dum hec scribo, tu dum leges, alii dum audient dumque non audient, ego quoque dum hec leges moriar, tu moreris dum hec scribo, ambo morimur, omnes morimur, semper morimur.*

We are dying continuously: I while I write this, you while you read it, others while they hear or do not hear it. I will be dying as you read this, you will be dying as I write it. We are both dying, we are all dying, we are always dying.
c.1360 Letter to Philippe de Cabassoles.

Petronius Arbiter d. AD 66

Latin satirical writer, usually thought to be the Gaius Petronius whom Tacitus calls the 'arbiter elegantiae' at the court of Nero. His *Satyricon* wittily depicts the licentious life of the moneyed class of freedmen in southern Italy.

11 *Abiit ad plures.*

He has gone to the majority.
(ie He has died.) *Satyricon*, 42.

12 *Qualis dominus talis est servus.*

Like master like man.
Satyricon, 58.

Petty, Sir William 1623–87

English physician and pioneer economist. From humble beginnings he rose to become Professor of Anatomy at Oxford and of Music at Gresham's College, London. As Physician-General to Cromwell's army he acquired an immense fortune, and he was a founder of the Royal Society of London.

13 If a man bring to London an ounce of Silver out of the Earth in Peru in the same time that he can produce a bushel of Corn, then one is the natural price of the other.
   1662 *Treatise of Taxes.*

14 Labour is the Father and active principle of Wealth, as lands are the Mother.
   1662 *Treatise of Taxes.*

15 Instead of using only comparative Words and intellectual Arguments, I have taken the course…to express myself in Terms of Number, Weight, or Measure; to use only Arguments of Sense, and to consider only such Causes, as have visible Foundations in Nature.
   1690 *Political Arithmetick.*

Phelps, Edward John 1822–1900

US lawyer and diplomat.

16 The man who makes us mistakes does not usually make anything.
   1889 In a speech given in London.

Philip II 1527–98

King of Spain (1556–98), Naples and Sicily (1554–98) and Portugal (1580–98). He married Mary I in 1554, becoming joint sovereign of England until her death in 1558. A secular champion of the Counter-Reformation, he had more success against Turks than Protestant Dutch and English.

17 England's chief defence depends upon the navy being always ready to defend the realm against invasion.
   c.1555 Submission to the Privy Council while King-Consort of England.

Philips, Ambrose c.1675–1749

English poet.

18 The flowers anew, returning seasons bring;
   But beauty faded has no second spring.
   1708 *The First Pastoral*, 'Lobbin'.

Philips, Edward 1931–

Canadian novelist.

19 To grow older is to realize the universe is Copernican, not Ptolemaic, and that self and the loved one do not form the epicentre of the solar system.
   1990 *Sunday Best.*

Philips, Katherine née Fowler 1632–64

English poet. Her reputation was greater during her brief life, when she was known as 'the Matchless Orinda', than after her death, but she proved a significant model to later female poets. Her poems were surreptitiously printed in 1664 and issued in 1667.

20 Thus our twin souls in one shall grow,
   And teach the world new love,
   Redeem the age and sex, and show
   A flame fate dares not move:
   And courting death to be our friend,
   Our lives, together too, shall end.
   1664 'To Mrs. M. A. at Parting'.

21 I did but see him, and he disappeared,
   I did but touch the rosebud, and it fell;
   A sorrow unforeseen and scarcely feared,
   So ill can mortals their afflictions spell.
   'On the Death of My First and Dearest Child, Hector Philips'. (Issued 1667).

Phillips, Arthur Angell 1900–85

Australian academic and literary critic. He wrote for the Melbourne literary journal *Meanjin* and much of his critical writing was collected as *Responses* (1971).

22 Cultural Cringe.
   1950 On Australia's reliance on British cultural values. In *Meanjin.*

Phillips, Wendell 1811–84

US abolitionist, born in Boston Massachusetts. Called to the bar in 1834, by 1837, he was chief orator of the anti-slavery party, associated with William Lloyd Garrison.

23 Some doubt the courage of the Negro. Go to Haiti and stand on those fifty thousand graves of the best soldiers France ever had, and ask them what they think of the Negro's sword.
   1861 Address on Toussaint l'Ouverture, referring to the War of Haitian Independence, 1804.

Picasso, Pablo Ruiz y 1881–1973

Spanish painter, graphic artist, sculptor and ceramicist. The melancholy studies of his early 'blue period' (1902–4) gave way to a life-affirming 'pink period' (1904–6). In later works he moved towards Cubism, along with Georges Braque.

24 There is no abstract art. You must always start with something. Afterward you can remove all traces of reality.
   1935 In an interview with Christian Zervos, editor of *Cahiers d'Art*, translated by Alfred H Barr Jr. in his *Picasso: Fifty Years of his Art* (1946).

25 Art is not the application of a canon of beauty but what the instinct and the brain can conceive beyond any canon. When we love a woman we don't start measuring her limbs.
   1935 In an interview with Christian Zervos, editor of *Cahiers d'Art*, translated by Alfred H Barr Jr. in his *Picasso: Fifty Years of his Art* (1946).

26 No, painting is not done to decorate apartments. It is an instrument of war for attack and defense against the enemy.

1945 Responding to claims that his Communism was a mere caprice. Quoted in Alfred H Barr Jr. *Picasso: Fifty Years of his Art* (1946).

27 I paint objects as I think them, not as I see them.

Quoted in John Golding *Cubism* (1959).

28 God is really only another artist. He invented the giraffe, the elephant, and the cat. He has no real style. He just goes on trying other things.

Quoted in F Gilot and C Lake *Life with Picasso* (1964), pt.1.

29 We all know that art is not truth. Art is a lie that makes us realize truth.

Quoted in Dore Ashton *Picasso on Art* (1972).

Pickens, T(homas) Boone, Jr 1928–

US oil company executive, a geologist with Phillips Petroleum Co (1951–5) then founder and chair of Mesa Petroleum Co.

30 Work eight hours and sleep eight hours and make sure they are not the same.

1992 In NPR broadcast, 28 May.

Pickford, Mary originally *Gladys Mary Smith*
1893–1979

US actress, born in Canada. Known as 'America's sweetheart', she played innocent heroines in a series of silent films (1909–29), and made her sound début in 1929.

31 Adding sound to movies would be like putting lipstick on the Venus de Milo.

Recalled on her death, 29 May 1979.

Pierce, C(harles) S(aunders) 1839–1914

US philosopher.

32 It is the man of science, eager to have his every opinion regenerated, his every idea rationalized, by drinking at the fountain of fact, and devoting all the energies of his life to the cult of truth, not as he understands it, but as he does not yet understand it, that ought properly to be called a philosopher.

Selected Writings, 'Lessons on the History of Science'.

Piercy, Marge 1936–

US novelist and poet. Novels including *Small Changes* (1973), *Woman On the Edge of Time* (1975) and *Vida* (1980) trace the emerging feminist consciousness of the post-60s generation.

33 Burning dinner is not incompetence but war.

1983 *Stone, Paper, Knife*, 'What's that smell in the kitchen?'

34 Your anger was a climate I inhabited

like a desert in a dry frigid weather
of high thin air and ivory sun,
sand dunes the wind lifted into stinging
clouds that blinded and choked me
where the only ice was in the blood.

1983 *Stone, Paper, Knife*, 'The Weight'.

35 On this twelfth day of my diet
I would rather die satiated
than slim.

1983 *Stone, Paper, Knife*, 'On Mental Corsets'.

36 Art is a game only if you play at it,
a mirror that reflects from the inside out.

1983 *Stone, Paper, Knife*, 'Stone, Paper, Knife'.

37 Hope sleeps in our bones like a bear
waiting for spring to rise and walk.

1983 *Stone, Paper, Knife*, 'Stone, Paper, Knife'.

Piero della Francesca c.1420–1492

Italian Renaissance painter.

38 Painting is nothing but a representation of surfaces and solids foreshortened or enlarged, and put on the plane of the picture in accordance with the fashion in which the real objects seen by the eye appear on this plane.

c.1480–90 *De Prospectiva Pingendi*.

Piggott, Lester Keith 1935–

English jockey. He became champion jockey 11 times, from 1948, and totalled 29 Classic winners, including 9 Derbies.

39 People ask me why I ride with my bottom in the air. Well, I've got to put it somewhere.

Quoted in Colin Jarman *The Guinness Dictionary of Sports Quotations* (1990).

Piglia, Ricardo 1941–

Argentinian novelist and critic.

40 *Sencillamente se me ocurre que la parodia se ha desplazado y hoy invade los gestos, las acciones. Donde antes había acontecimientos, experiencias, pasiones, hoy quedan sólo parodias. Eso trataba a veces de decirle a Marcelo en mis cartas: que la parodia ha sustitutido por completo a la historia.*

It's simply that I believe that parody has been displaced and that it now invades all gestures and actions. Where there used to be events, experiences, passions, now there are nothing but parodies. This is what I tried to tell Marcelo so many times in my letters: that parody had completely replaced history.

1980 *Respiración artificial*, pt.2, ch.4 (translated as *Artificial Respiration*, 1994).

Pigou, Arthur Cecil 1877–1959

English economist, a professor at Cambridge (1908–43).

41 If a man marries his housekeeper or his cook, the national dividend is diminished.

1920 *Economics of Welfare.*

Pilger, John 1939–

Australian journalist and film-maker highly regarded for his investigative work in Vietnam and Cambodia. *Year Zero – The Silent Death of Cambodia* (1979), made with David Munro, is the most outstanding of his 38 documentary films. The prolific awards for his work include an Emmy (1991) and the Richard Dimbleby Award (BAFTA) 1991. He has written six books.

42 I used to see Vietnam as a war rather than a country.

1978 *Do you remember Vietnam?*

43 What Nixon and Kissinger began, Pol Pot completed.

Collected in *Distant Voices* (1992).

Pindar c.522–440 BC

Greek lyric poet, born near Thebes in Boeotia.

44 Seek not, my soul, immortal life, but make the most of the resources that are within your reach.

Pythia, 3.109.

Pinochet Ugarte, General Augusto 1915–

Chilean soldier and dictator. He led the coup that overthrew the government of Salvador Allende (1973) and in 1980 enacted a constitution giving himself an eight-year presidential term (1981–9), but the plebiscite of 1988 rejected his candidacy as President beyond 1990.

45 I am not a dictator. It's just that I have a grumpy face.

Attributed.

Pinter, Harold 1930–

English playwright and actor. Such early plays as *The Birthday Party* (1958) were dismissed as obscure, but after *The Caretaker* (1960) his work underwent a reappraisal and he was acknowledged as one of the most interesting playwrights of his generation. Subsequent works for the stage have included *The Homecoming* (1965), the double bill *Landscape* and *Silence* (1969), *Old Times* (1971), *A Kind of Alaska* (1982) and *Mountain Language* (1988).

46 If only I could get down to Sidcup! I've been waiting for the weather to break. He's got my papers, this man I left them with, it's got it all down there, I could prove everything.

1960 *The Caretaker*, Act 1.

47 The weasel under the cocktail cabinet.

1962 His reply when asked what his plays were about. Quoted in J Russell Taylor *Anger and After.*

48 I no longer feel banished from myself.

1995 On completing his first full-length play in 17 years. In *Newsweek*, 18 Sep.

Pirandello, Luigi 1867–1936

Italian playwright, novelist and short-story writer. His play *Right You Are (If You Think You Are)* (1917) was followed by such innovative works as *Six Characters in Search of an Author* (1921), *Enrico IV* (1922) and *Tonight We Improvise* (1929). He was awarded a Nobel Prize in 1934.

49 Six Characters in Search of an Author.

1921 Title of play (translated 1922).

50 Drama is action, sir, action and not confounded philosophy.

1921 *Six Characters in Search of an Author* (translated 1922).

Pirsig, Robert M(aynard) 1928–

US writer. His most noted book is *Zen and the Art of Motorcycle Maintenance* (1974), a rumination on life and technology after a cross-country motorcycle trip.

51 The Buddha, the Godhead, resides quite as comfortably in the circuits of a digital computer or the gears of a cycle transmission as he does at the top of a mountain or in the petals of a flower.

1974 *Zen and the Art of Motorcycle Maintenance*, pt.1, ch.1.

52 When people are fanatically dedicated to political or religious faiths or any other kind of dogmas or goals, it's always because these dogmas or goals are in doubt.

1974 *Zen and the Art of Motorcycle Maintenance*, pt.2, ch.3.

53 Mental reflection is so much more interesting than TV it's a shame more people don't switch over to it. They probably think what they hear is unimportant but it never is.

1974 *Zen and the Art of Motorcycle Maintenance*, pt.3, ch.17.

54 One thing about pioneers that you don't hear mentioned is that they are invariably, by their nature, mess-makers.

1974 *Zen and the Art of Motorcycle Maintenance*, pt.3, ch.21.

55 Traditional scientific method has always been at the very *best*, 20-20 hindsight. It's good for seeing where you've been. It's good for testing the truth of what you think you know, but it can't tell you where you *ought* to go.

1974 *Zen and the Art of Motorcycle Maintenance*, pt.3, ch.24.

56 That's the classical mind at work, runs fine inside but looks dingy on the surface.

1974 *Zen and the Art of Motorcycle Maintenance*, pt.3, ch.26.

57 One geometry can not be more than another; it can only be more *convenient*. Geometry is not true, it is advantageous.
    1974 *Zen and the Art of Motorcycle Maintenance*, pt.3, ch.22.

Pissarro, Camille 1830–1903

French Impressionist artist. Most of his works were painted in or around Paris.

58 But as I see it, the most corrupt art is the sentimental—the art of orange blossoms which make pale women swoon.
    1883 Letter to his son Lucien.

59 Watercolour is not especially difficult, but I must warn you to steer clear of those pretty English watercolorists, so skillful and alas so weak, and so often too truthful.
    1883 Letter to his son Lucien, Jul.

60 Draw more and more often—remember Degas.
    1883 Letter to his son Lucien, Oct.

61 Observe that it is a grave error to believe that all mediums of art are not closely tied to their time.
    1898 Letter to his son Lucien.

Pitt, William, 1st Earl of Chatham known as *the Elder* 1708–78

English statesman and orator. In 1756 he became Secretary of State, virtual Prime Minister. Forced to resign in 1757 by George II, he was recalled by public demand but resigned again in 1761 when his Cabinet refused to declare war on Spain. He formed a new ministry in 1766, but resigned in ill health (1768).

62 The atrocious crime of being a young man, which [Walpole] has, with such spirit and decency, charged upon me, I shall neither attempt to palliate nor deny; but content myself with wishing that I may be one of those whose follies cease with their youth, and not of those who continue ignorant in spite of their age and experience.
    1741 Speech to the House of Commons, 6 Mar.

63 It is now apparent that this great, this powerful, this formidable kingdom is considered only as a province of a despicable electorate.
    1742 Speech to the House of Commons, 10 Dec.

64 I know that I can save this country and that no one else can.
    1756 In conversation with one of his private secretaries, Nov.

65 I was called by my sovereign and by the voice of the people to assist the State when others had abdicated the service of it. That being so, no one can be surprised that I will go on no longer, since my advice is not taken. Being responsible, I will

direct—and will be responsible for nothing that I do not direct.
    1761 On informing Cabinet of his resignation, 3 Oct.

66 I rejoice that America has resisted. Three millions of people, so dead to all the feelings of liberty, as voluntarily to submit to be slaves, would have been fit instruments to make slaves of the rest.
    1766 Speech to the House of Commons, 14 Jan.

67 Where laws end, tyranny begins.
    1770 Speech to the House of Lords, 2 Mar.

68 The spirit that now resists your taxation in America is…the same spirit that established the great fundamental, essential maxim of your liberties— that no subject of England shall be taxed but by his own consent. The glorious spirit of Whigism animates three million in America, who prefer poverty with liberty to gilded chains and sordid affluence; and who will die in defence of their rights as men, as free men.
    1775 Speech to the House of Lords, 20 Jan.

69 You cannot conquer America.
    1777 Speech to the House of Lords, 18 Nov.

70 If I were an American, as I am an Englishman, while a foreign troop was landed in my country, I never would lay down my arms—never—never— never!
    1777 Speech to the House of Lords, 18 Nov.

Pitt, William known as *the Younger*
1759–1806

English statesman and Prime Minister (1783–1801, 1804–6), son of William Pitt, the Elder. Elected MP in 1781, he became Chancellor in 1782 and Britain's youngest-ever Prime Minister in 1783. He resigned over the King's opposition to the union with Ireland in 1801 but returned in 1804 to lead a coalition of European powers against Napoleon.

71 I am sure that the immediate abolition of the slave trade is the first, the principal, the most indispensable act of policy, of duty and of justice the legislature of this country has to take, if it is indeed their wish to secure those important objects… For we continue to this hour a barbarous traffic in slaves, we continue it even yet, in spite of all our great and undeniable pretensions as civilisation.
    1792 Speech to the House of Commons, 2 Apr. The House did not abolish slavery until 1806.

72 We must recollect…what it is we have at stake, what it is we have to contend for. It is for our property, it is for our liberty, it is for our independence, nay for our existence as a nation; it

is for our character, it is for our very name as Englishmen, it is for everything dear and valuable to man on this side of the grave.

1803 Speech, 22 Jul, on the breaking of the Peace of Amiens and the resumption of the war with Napoleon. Quoted in *Speeches of the Rt. Hon. William Pitt* (1806), vol.4.

73 Amid the wreck and the misery of nations it is our just exaltation that we have continued superior to all that ambition or despotism could effect; and our still higher exaltation ought to be that we provide not only for our own safety but hold out a prospect for nations now bending under the yoke of tyranny of what the exertions of a free people can effect.

1804 Speech to the House of Commons, 25 Apr.

74 Roll up that map; it will not be wanted these ten years.

1805 Of a map of Europe. Remark on hearing of Napoleon's victory at Austerlitz, Dec. Quoted in Earl Stanhope *Life of the Rt. Hon. William Pitt*, vol.4 (1862), ch.43.

75 England has saved herself by her exertions, and will, as I trust, save Europe by her example.

1805 Replying to a toast in which he had been described as the saviour of his country in the wars with France. Quoted in R Coupland *War Speeches of William Pitt* (1915).

76 I think that I could eat one of Bellamy's veal pies.

1806 Attributed last words, 23 Jan.

Pittacus of Mytilene 650–570 BC

Greek ruler, one of the Seven Wise Men of Greece.

77 Know thine opportunity.

Attributed. Quoted in *Chambers Biographical Dictionary* (5th edn, 1990).

Pius II real name *Enea Silvio de Piccolomini* 1405–64

Pope from 1458. After entering the service of Emperor Frederick II he took orders, becoming Bishop of Trieste and, on returning to Italy (1456), Cardinal then Pope. He tried unsuccessfully to organize a crusade against the Turks.

78 Of the two lights of Christendom, one has been extinguished.

1453 Attributed, on hearing of the fall of Constantinople to the Turks, 29 May.

79 Glorious deeds are not embraced by democracies, least of all by merchants, who, being by their nature intent on profit, loathe those splendid things that cannot be achieved without expense.

1584 *Commentaries.* Quoted in J H Plumb (ed) *The Horizon Book of the Renaissance* (1961, new edn by Penguin, 1982).

80 Nothing gives the Scots more pleasure than to hear the English abused.

1584 *Commentaries.* Quoted in J H Plumb (ed) *The Horizon Book of the Renaissance* (1961, new edn by Penguin, 1982).

Pius XII real name *Eugenio Pacelli* 1876–1958

Italian-born churchman, Pope from 1939.

81 Sport, rightly conceived, is an occupation carried out by the whole man. It renders the body a more perfect instrument of the soul and at the same time makes the soul itself a finer instrument of the whole man in seeking for Truth and in transmitting it to others. In this way it helps a man to reach that End to which all other ends are subordinate, the service and the greater glory of His Creator.

1945 Speech to the Central School of Sports of the USA, 29 Jul.

Pizzaro, Eddie

US stonecarver.

82 We're not all perfect, but we can do something perfect.

1990 On his work at New York's Cathedral of St John the Divine. Quoted in the *New York Times*, 14 Jul.

Planck, Max Karl Ernst 1858–1947

German physicist. He hypothesized that atoms emit and absorb energy only in discrete bundles called quanta and laid the foundations for quantum theory, the basis of contemporary theorizing in physics. He received the 1918 Nobel Prize in Physics for his work on radiation.

83 Scientific discovery and scientific knowledge have been achieved only by those who have gone in pursuit of them without any practical purpose whatsoever in view.

1932 *Where is Science Going?* pt.4 (translated by James Murphy).

84 Science cannot solve the ultimate mystery of nature. And that is because, in the last analysis, we ourselves are part of nature and therefore part of the mystery that we are trying to solve.

1932 *Where is Science Going?* pt.4 (translated by James Murphy).

85 A new scientific truth does not triumph by convincing its opponents and making them see the light, but rather because its opponents eventually die, and a new generation grows up that is familiar with it.

A Scientific Autobiography and Other Papers (translated by Frank Gaynor, published 1949)

86 Science cannot exist without some small portion of metaphysics.

1931 *The Universe in the Light of Modern Physics*, ch.7.

Plante, Jacques 1929–86

Canadian hockey player, a leading goalkeeper.

87 How would you like a job where, every time you
make a mistake, a big red light goes on and 18,000
people boo?

Attributed. Quoted in John Robert Colombo (ed) *Colombo's All-
Time Great Canadian Quotations* (1994).

Plath, Sylvia 1932–63

US poet who settled in England after her marriage to Ted
Hughes. Her poetry and her only novel, *The Bell Jar*
(1963), are deeply introspective. She committed suicide,
and much of her work was published posthumously.

88 I am afraid of getting married. Spare me from
cooking three meals a day—spare me from the
relentless cage of routine and rote.

1949 Diary entry, 13 Nov. Collected in Aurelia Schober Plath
(ed) *Letters Home by Sylvia Plath*, 'Diary Supplement' (1949).

89 I could never be a complete scholar or a complete
housewife or a complete writer: I must combine a
little of all, and thereby be imperfect in all.

1956 Letter to her mother, Aurelia Schober Plath, 25 Feb.
Collected in Aurelia Schober Plath (ed) *Letters Home by Sylvia
Plath* (1949).

90 Apparently, the most difficult feat for a Cambridge
male is to accept a woman not merely as feeling,
not merely as thinking, but as managing a complex,
vital interweaving of both.

1956 Written while a student at Cambridge University, in *Isis*,
6 May.

91 I saw my life branching out before me like the
green fig-tree in the story.
From the tip of every branch, like a fat purple fig, a
wonderful future beckoned and winked. One fig
was a husband and a happy home and children,
and another fig was a famous poet…I saw myself
sitting in the crotch of this fig-tree, starving to
death, just because I couldn't make up my mind
which of the figs I would choose. I wanted each
and every one of them, but choosing one meant
losing all the rest, and, as I sat there, unable to
decide, the figs began to wrinkle and go black,
and, one by one, they plopped to the ground at
my feet.

1963 *The Bell Jar*, ch.7.

92 If neurotic is wanting two mutually exclusive
things at one and the same time, then I'm neurotic
as hell. I'll be flying back and forth between one
mutually exclusive thing and another for the rest of
my days.

1963 *The Bell Jar*, ch.8.

93 A sort of walking miracle, my skin
Bright as a Nazi lampshade.

1963 'Lady Lazarus', in *Encounter*, Oct.

94 Dying,

Is an art, like everything else.
I do it exceptionally well.

1963 'Lady Lazarus', in *Encounter*, Oct.

95 Not God but a swastika
So black no sky could squeak through.
Every woman adores a Fascist,
The boot in the face, the brute
Brute heart of a brute like you.

1963 'Daddy', in *Encounter*, Oct.

96 Daddy, daddy, you bastard, I'm through.

1963 'Daddy', in *Encounter*, Oct.

97 Out of the ash
I rise with my red hair
And I eat men like air.

1965 *Ariel*, 'Lady Lazarus', published posthumously by Ted
Hughes.

98 Love set you going like a fat gold watch.
The midwife slapped your footsoles, and your bald
cry
Took its place among the elements.

1965 *Ariel*, 'Morning Song', published posthumously by Ted
Hughes.

99 Winter is for women—
The woman still at her knitting,
At the cradle of Spanish walnut,
Her body a bulb in the cold and too dumb to
think.

1965 *Ariel*, 'Wintering', published posthumously by Ted
Hughes.

Plato c.428–c.348 BC

Greek philosopher, a pupil of Socrates and the teacher of
Aristotle. He wrote in the form of dialogues, often with
Socrates as a leading character. Some 30 philosophical
dialogues and some letters (not all considered genuine)
have survived.

1 The wisest of you men is he who has realized, like
Socrates, that in respect of wisdom he is really
worthless.

Apology, 23b (translated by H Tredennick).

2 Socrates is guilty of corrupting the minds of the
young, and of believing in deities of his own
invention instead of the gods recognized by the state.

The formal indictment in Socrates' trial, quoted in the *Apology*,
24b (translated by H Tredennick).

3 For I spend all my time going about trying to
persuade you, young and old, to make your first and
chief concern not for your bodies nor for your
possessions, but for the highest welfare of your souls,
proclaiming as I go, Wealth does not bring goodness,
but goodness brings wealth and every other blessing,
both to the individual and to the state.

Apology, 30b (translated by H Tredennick).

4 The unexamined life is not worth living.
Apology, 38a (translated by H Tredennick).

5 Now it is time that we were going, I to die and you to live, but which of us has the happier prospect is unknown to anyone but God.
Apology, 42a (translated by H Tredennick).

6 It is not living, but living well, which we ought to consider most important.
Crito, 48b (translated by H North Fowler, 1923).

7 Your country is more precious and more to be revered and is holier and in higher esteem among the gods and among men of understanding than your mother and your father and all your ancestors.
Crito, 51a-b (translated by H North Fowler, 1923).

8 Men of sound sense have Law for their god, but men without sense Pleasure.
Epistulae, 8. 354e (translated by R G Bury, 1925).

9 To do wrong is the greatest of evils.
Gorgias 469b (translated by W D Woodhead). There is a similar remark in the *Crito*, 49b.

10 Much more wretched than lack of health in the body, it is to dwell with a soul that is not healthy, but corrupt.
Gorgias, 479b (translated by W R M Lamb, 1967).

11 No one can escape his destiny.
Gorgias, 512e (translated by W R M Lamb 1967).

12 All the gold upon the earth and all the gold beneath it, does not compensate for lack of virtue.
Leges, 728a (translated by Trevor J Saunders, 1970).

13 Every unjust man is unjust against his will.
Leges, 731c (translated by Trevor J Saunders, 1970).

14 Is virtue something that can be taught?
Meno, 70a (translated by W K C Guthrie).

15 If we are ever to have pure knowledge of anything, we must get rid of the body and contemplate things by themselves with the soul by itself.
Phaedo 66d (translated by H Tredennick).

16 One should die in silence.
Phaedo, 117e (translated by D Gallop, 1993).

17 Crito, we ought to offer a cock to Asclepius. See to it, and don't forget.
Phaedo, 118a (translated by H Tredennick).

18 For myself I am fairly certain that no wise man believes anyone sins willingly or willingly perpetrates any evil or base act.
Protagoras, 345e (translated by W K C Guthrie).

19 We must now examine whether just people also live better and are happier than unjust ones. I think it's

clear already that this is so, but we must look into it further, since the argument concerns no ordinary topic, but the way we ought to live.
Republic, bk.1, 352d (translated by G M A Grube, revised by C D C Reeve).

20 Justice is doing one's work and not meddling with what isn't one's own,
Republic, bk.4, 433a (translated by G M A Grube, revised by C D C Reeve).

21 Until philosophers rule as kings or those who are now called kings and leading men genuinely and adequately philosophize, that is, until political power and philosophy entirely coincide...cities will have no rest from evils, nor, I think, will the human race.
Republic, bk.5, 473c (translated by G M A Grube, revised by C D C Reeve).

22 Every soul pursues the good and does whatver it does for its sake.
Republic, bk.6, 505e (translated by G M A Grube, revised by C D C Reeve).

23 The power to learn is present in everyone's soul, and the instrument with which each learns is like an eye that cannot be turned around from darkness to light without turning the whole body.
Republic, bk.7, 518c (translated by G M A Grube, revised by C D C Reeve).

24 If the study of all these sciences which we have enumerated, should ever bring us to their mutual association and relationship, and teach us the nature of the ties which bind them together, I believe that the diligent treatment of them will forward the objects which we have in view, and that the labor, which otherwise would be fruitless, will be well bestowed.
Republic, bk.7 (translated by G M A Grube, revised by C D C Reeve).

25 Extreme freedom can't be expected to lead to anything but a change to extreme slavery, whether for a private individual or for a city.
Republic, bk.8, 564a (translated by G M A Grube, revised by C D C Reeve).

26 Justice is superior to injustice.
Republic, 367b (translated by P Shorey, 1953).

27 The most important stage of any enterprise is the beginning.
Republic, 377b (translated by R Waterfield, 1993).

28 Let no one ignorant of mathematics enter here.
c.380 BC Inscription over the door of the Academy at Athens.

29 God is a geometrician.
Quoted in Plutarch *Symposium*.

Plautus, Titus Maccius Plautus

c.250–184 BC

Roman comic poet, who worked as a trader and craftsman before writing plays in middle life. He became the most important Latin adapter of the Greek New Comedy, which dealt with social life to the exclusion of politics. Only 21 of his comedies have survived.

30 *Lupus est homo homini, non homo, quom qualis sit non novit.*

A man is a wolf, and not a man, to another man, for as long as he doesn't know what he is like.
Asinaria, 495. The phrase is often rendered 'Homo homini lupus' ('Man is a wolf to another man').

Pliny full name *Gaius Plinius Secundus* known as *'the Elder'* AD 23–79

Roman statesman, scholar and writer. His only surviving work is his universal encyclopedia, *Historia Naturalis* (37 vols, AD 77). He was killed while observing the eruption of Vesuvius.

31 *Vulgoque veritas iam attributa vino est.*

And truth has come to be proverbially credited to wine.
AD 77 *Historia Naturalis*, bk.14, section 28 (translated by H Rackham). The phrase is often rendered as 'in vino veritas'.

32 *Addito salis grano.*

With the addition of a pinch of salt.
AD 77 *Historia Naturalis*, bk.23, section 8. This is probably a version of a more ancient proverb, commonly rendered 'Cum grano salis.'

Plomer, William 1903–73

South-African-born British writer.

33 Out of that bungled, unwise war
An alp of unforgiveness grew.
1960 'The Boer War'.

34 On a sofa upholstered in panther skin
Mona did researches in original sin.
1960 'Mews Flat Mona'.

Plout, David

35 Deathbed utterances, like suicide notes, are a powerful coinage, stamped by an awareness that words can outlive us.
1990 In the *Wall Street Journal*, 26 Sep, reviewing J M Coetzee *Age of Iron* (1990).

Plutarch c.46–c.120 AD

Greek historian, biographer and philosopher. His extant writings include the essays in *Opera Moralia*, and the biographical *Bioi paralleloi* (Parallel Lives, translated into

English by Thomas North in 1759), a major source for Shakespeare.

36 He who cheats with an oath acknowledges that he is afraid of his enemy, but that he thinks little of God.
Parallel Lives, 'Lysander', ch.8.

37 Though others before him had triumphed three times, Pompeius, by having gained his first triumph over Libya, his second over Europe, and this the last over Asia, seemed in a manner to have brought the whole world into his three triumphs.
Referring to Pompey's victories against the Marian party in Africa, in Spain, and against Mithradates in Asia Minor (c.62 BC). *Parallel Lives*, 'Pompeius', ch.45.

Po Chü-I 772–846

Chinese poet and civil servant who rose to become the Governor of a number of different cities in China.

38 But now that age comes
A moment of joy is harder and harder to get.
812 'The Chrysanthemums in the Eastern Garden' (in *Chinese Poems*, translated by Arthur Waley, 1946).

39 Deeper and deeper, one's love of old friends;
Fewer and fewer, one's dealings with young men.
835 *Old Age*.

Pobedonostsev, Constantin Petrovich

1827–1907

Russian jurist, tutor to Alexander III and Nicholas II. Initially a liberal, he became an uncompromising champion of autocracy and the supremacy of the Russian orthodox church, strongly opposed to westernization.

40 Parliaments are the great lie of our time.
Moskovskii Shornik.

Poe, Edgar Allan 1809–49

US poet and short story writer, a pioneer of the modern detective story, whose poetry emphasizes the beauty of melancholy. He is best known for stories such as 'The Tell-Tale Heart' (1843) and his poem 'The Raven' (1845).

41 I know not how it was—but, with the first glimpse of the building, a sense of insufferable gloom pervaded my spirit… There was an iciness, a sinking, a sickening of the heart—an unredeemed dreariness of thought which no goading of the imagination could torture into aught of the sublime.
1839 'The Fall of the House of Usher', in the *Gentleman's Magazine*, Sep.

42 As the strong man exults in his physical ability, delighting in such exercises as call his muscles into action, so glories the analyst in that moral activity which *disentangles*.
1841 Of detective work. 'The Murders in the Rue Morgue', in the *Gentleman's Magazine*, Apr.

43 It will be found, in fact, that the ingenious are always fanciful, and the *truly* imaginative never otherwise than analytic.
1841 'The Murders in the Rue Morgue', in the *Gentleman's Magazine*, Apr.

44 And now was acknowledged the presence of the Red Death. He had come like a thief in the night. And one by one dropped the revellers in the blood-bedecked halls of their revel, and died each in the despairing posture of his fall.
1842 'The Masque of the Red Death', in the *Gentleman's Magazine*, May.

45 There is something in the unselfish and self-sacrificing love of a brute, which goes directly to the heart of him who has had frequent occasion to test the paltry friendship and gossamer fidelity of mere *Man.*
1843 'The Black Cat', in the *United States Saturday Post*, 19 Aug.

46 I have no faith in human perfectibility… Man is now only more active—not more happy—nor more wise, than he was 6,000 years ago.
1844 Letter to James Russell Lowell, 2 Jul.

47 On desperate seas long wont to roam, Thy hyacinth hair, thy classic face, Thy Naiad airs have brought me home To the glory that was Greece, And the grandeur that was Rome.
1845 'To Helen', stanza 2.

48 Yes, Heaven is thine; but this Is a world of sweets and sours; Our flowers are merely—flowers.
1845 'Israfel', stanza 7.

49 'Take thy beak from out my heart, and take thy form from off my door!' Quoth the raven, 'Nevermore.'
1845 'The Raven', stanza 17. In *American Review*, Feb 1845.

50 The death…of a beautiful woman is, unquestionably, the most poetical topic in the world.
1846 'The Philosophy of Composition', in *Graham's Magazine*, Apr.

51 Mournful and Never-ending Remembrance.
1846 Of the significance of the bird in his poem 'The Raven'. 'The Philosophy of Composition', in *Graham's Magazine*, Apr.

52 To be *thoroughly* conversant with a Man's heart is to take our final lesson in the iron-clasped volume of despair.
1849 'Marginalia', in the *Southern Literary Messenger*, Jun.

53 The nose of a mob is its imagination. By this, at any time, it can be quietly led.
1849 'Marginalia', in the *Southern Literary Messenger*, Jul.

54 To vilify a great man is the readiest way in which a little man can himself attain greatness.
1849 *Marginalia 1844–49.*

55 Thank Heaven! the crisis— The danger is past, And the lingering illness Is over at last— And the fever called 'Living' Is conquered at last.
1850 'For Annie'.

Poelzig, Hans 1869–1936

German Expressionist architect, Professor of Architecture at Breslau Academy of Arts (1900) and later director.

56 We cannot do without the past in solving the architectural problems of our own day.
1906 *Das Deutsche Kunstgewerbe 1906.*

Poincaré, (Jules) Henri 1854–1912

French mathematician and physicist. In his research in the theory of functions he contributed greatly to the field of mathematical physics.

57 If we ought not to fear mortal truth, still less should we dread scientific truth. In the first place it can not conflict with ethics… But if science is feared, it is above all because it can give no happiness… Man, then, can not be happy through science but today he can much less be happy without it.
1904 *The Value of Science.*

58 Science is facts. Just as houses are made of stones, so science is made of facts. But a pile of stones is not a house and a collection of facts is not necessarily a science.
1905 *Science and Hypothesis*, ch.9.

59 The scientist does not study nature because it is useful to do so. He studies it because he takes pleasure in it, and he takes pleasure in it because it is beautiful.
1909 *Science and Method*, vol.1, ch.1 (translated by Francis Maitland).

Poindexter, John Marlan 1936–

US naval officer and statesman, chief of naval operations in the 1970s. In 1981 he joined Reagan's National Security Council, becoming National Security Adviser in 1985. He resigned (Nov 1986) after implication in the Irangate scandal, and was later convicted.

60 I made a very deliberate decision not to ask the President, so that I could insulate him from the decision and provide some future deniability for him if it ever leaked out.
1987 On his action in diverting funds from arms sales at Iran–Contra hearings, 15 Jul.

Pol Pot real name *Saloth Sar* 1925–98

Cambodian political and military leader whose Khmer Rouge army took over Cambodia, 1975. Prime Minister of Kampuchea (1976–8), he presided over the deaths of over a million people, by starvation or murder, before Vietnam liberated the country in Dec 1978.

61 We will burn the old grass and the new will grow.
c.1975 Quoted in John Pilger *Distant Voices* (1992), section 5.

62 If our people can build Angkor Wat they can do anything.
1979 Quoted by Dennis Bloodworth in *The Observer*, 20 Jan 1980.

Pol-Roger, Christian

US vintner.

63 Champagne! In victory, one deserves it; in defeat, one needs it.
1988 'Champagne, A Magnum Opus', in the *New York Times*, 31 Dec.

Pollock, (Paul) Jackson 1912–56

US artist, best known for his technique of pouring or dripping paint on the canvas. A leader of 'action painting' and the Abstract Expressionist movement, his works include the enormous *One* and the monochrome *Echo and Blue Poles*.

64 On the floor I am more at ease, I feel nearer, more a part of the painting, since this way I can walk around it, work from the four sides and literally be 'in' the painting.
1947 Quoted in Italo Tomassoni *Pollock* (1968).

65 Abstract painting is abstract. It confronts you.
Quoted in Francis V O'Connor *Jackson Pollock* (1967).

Polo, Marco c.1254–1324

Venetian trader and traveller. In 1271–5 he accompanied his father and uncle to China and stayed on for 16 years, becoming the envoy of Kublai Khan. He returned to Venice in 1295 and, imprisoned by the Genoese, used his time to dictate his memoirs.

66 Now it came to pass…that the Tartars made them a King whose name was Chinghis Kaan [Genghis Khan]. He was a man of great worth, and of great ability, and valour. And as soon as the news that he had been chosen King was spread abroad through those countries, all the Tartars in the world came to him and owned him for their Lord.
c.1310 Quoted in Col. Henry Yule (ed and trans) *The Book of Ser Marco Polo, the Venetian, Concerning the Kingdoms and Marvels of the East* (1871), 2 vols.

67 I have not told even the half of the things that I have seen.
c.1320 On being accused of exaggeration in his accounts of China. Quoted in R H Poole and P Finch (eds) *Newnes Pictorial Knowledge* (1950), vol.2.

Pomfret, John 1667–1702

English clergyman and poet.

68 We live and learn, but not the wiser grow.
1700 'Reason'.

Pompadour, Madame de full name *Jeanne Antoinette Poisson, Marquise de Pompadour* 1721–64

French mistress of Louis XV. Installed at Versailles (1745), she assumed control of public affairs and swayed State policy, appointing her favourites. She was a lavish patron of arts and literature.

69 The Duke takes a town in the same light-hearted way as he seduces a woman.
1756 Of Cardinal Duc de Richelieu, following his capture of the reputedly impregnable Fort St Phillip, Minorca, by taking his men up a cliff face to surprise the defenders. Quoted in Nancy Mitford *Madame de Pompadour* (1954), p.201.

70 *Après nous le déluge.*
After us the deluge.
1757 Quoted in Madame de Hausset *Mémoires* (1824).

Pompéia, Raul d'Avila 1863–95

Brazilian novelist, best known for *O Ateneu*, the story of life in an oppressive boarding school. Unable to cope any longer with his emotional problems, he committed suicide at the age of 32.

71 *O tédio é a grande enfermidade da escola, o tédio corruptor que tanto se pode gerar da monotonia do trabalho como da ociosidade.*
Tedium is the worst disease in schools, the corrupting tedium that comes equally from monotony, work or leisure.
1888 *O Ateneu* ('The Atheneum'), ch.7.

Pompidou, Georges 1911–74

Second President (1969–74) of the Fifth French Republic. He served in the Resistance during World War II, and was a member of Charles de Gaulle's staff (1944–6) before taking control of the provisional government.

72 There are three roads to ruin—women, gambling and technicians. The most pleasant is women, the quickest is with gambling, but the surest is with technicians.
1968 In the *Sunday Telegraph*.

Pope, Alexander 1688–1744

English poet and essayist, crippled at 12 by a tubercular infection of the spine. His work, distinguished by its technical brilliance and skilful satire, includes *The Rape of the Lock* (1712, enlarged 1714), *The Dunciad* (1728, revised 1742), and *Essay on Man* (1732–4).

73 A man should never be ashamed to own he has
been in the wrong, which is but saying, in other
words, that he is wiser to-day than he was
yesterday.
1706 *Thoughts on Various Subjects.*

74 Where'er you walk, cool gales shall fan the glade,
Trees where you sit, shall crowd into a shade:
Where'er you tread, the blushing flowers shall
rise,
And all things flourish where you turn your eyes.
1709 *Pastorals*, 'Summer', l.73–6.

75 Some are bewildered in the maze of schools,
And some made coxcombs Nature meant but
fools.
1711 *An Essay on Criticism*, l.26–7.

77 Some have at first for wits, then poets passed,
Turned critics next, and proved plain fools at
last.
1711 *An Essay on Criticism*, l.36–7.

78 First follow Nature, and your judgement frame
By her just standard, which is still the same:
Unerring Nature, still divinely bright,
One clear, unchanged, and universal light,
Life, force and beauty must to all impart,
At once the source and end and test of art.
1711 *An Essay on Criticism*, l.68–73.

79 A little learning is a dangerous thing;
Drink deep, or taste not the Pierian spring:
There shallow draughts intoxicate the brain,
And drinking largely sobers us again.
1711 *An Essay on Criticism*, l.215–8.

80 Poets like painters, thus unskilled to trace
The naked nature and the living grace,
With gold and jewels cover ev'ry part,
And hide with ornaments their want of art.
True wit is Nature to advantage dressed,
What oft was thought, but ne'er so well
expressed.
1711 *An Essay on Criticism*, l.293–8.

81 Expression is the dress of thought.
1711 *An Essay on Criticism*, l.318.

82 In Words, as Fashions, the same rule will hold;
Alike Fantastic, if too New, or Old;
Be not the *first* by whom the New are try'd,
Nor the *last* to lay the Old aside.
1711 *An Essay on Criticism*, l.333–6.

83 As some to church repair,
Not for the doctrine, but the music there.
1711 *An Essay on Criticism*, l.342–3.

84 True ease in writing comes from art, not chance,

As those move easiest who have learned to dance.
'Tis not enough no harshness gives offence,
The sound must seem an echo to the sense.
1711 *An Essay on Criticism*, l.362–5.

85 To err is human; to forgive, divine.
1711 *An Essay on Criticism*, l.525.

86 All seems infected that th'infected spy,
As all looks yellow to the jaundiced eye.
1711 *An Essay on Criticism*, l.558–9.

87 The bookful blockhead, ignorantly read,
With loads of learned lumbers in his head.
1711 *An Essay on Criticism*, l.612–3.

88 For fools rush in where angels fear to tread.
1711 *An Essay on Criticism*, l.625.

89 The hungry judges soon the sentence sign,
And wretches hang that jury-men may dine.
1712 *The Rape of the Lock*, canto 3, l.21–2.

90 What dire offence from am'rous causes springs,
What mighty contests rise from trivial things.
1714 *The Rape of the Lock*, canto 1, l.1–2.

91 Now lap-dogs give themselves the rousing shake,
And sleepless lovers, just at twelve, awake.
1714 *The Rape of the Lock*, canto 1, l.15–16.

92 They shift the moving Toyshop of their heart.
1714 *The Rape of the Lock*, canto 1, l.100.

93 Bright as the sun, her eyes the gazers strike,
And, like the sun, they shine on all alike.
1714 *The Rape of the Lock*, canto 2, l.13–14.

94 If to her share some female errors fall,
Look on her face, and you'll forget 'em all.
1714 *The Rape of the Lock*, canto 2, l.17–18.

95 Belinda smiled, and all the world was gay.
1714 *The Rape of the Lock*, canto 2, l.52.

96 Whether the nymph shall break Diana's law,
Or some frail china jar receive a flaw,
Or stain her honour, or her new brocade,
Forget her pray'rs, or miss a masquerade.
1714 *The Rape of the Lock*, canto 2, l.105–8.

97 Here thou, great Anna! whom three realms obey,
Dost sometimes counsel take—and sometimes tea.
1714 *The Rape of the Lock*, canto 3, l.7–8.

98 At ev'ry word a reputation dies.
1714 *The Rape of the Lock*, canto 3, l.16.

99 Let spades be trumps! she said, and trumps they
were.
1714 *The Rape of the Lock*, canto 3, l.46.

1 Not louder shrieks to pitying heav'n are cast,
  When husbands or when lapdogs breathe their last.
  1714 *The Rape of the Lock*, canto 3, l.157–8.

2 *Sir Plume*, of *Amber Snuff-box* justly vain,
  And the nice Conduct of a *clouded Cane*.
  1714 *The Rape of the Lock*, canto 4, l.123–4.

3 Beauties in vain their pretty eyes may roll;
  Charms strike the sight, but merit wins the soul.
  1714 *The Rape of the Lock*, canto 5, l.33-34.

4 Happy the man, whose wish and care
  A few paternal acres bound,
  Content to breathe his native air,
  In his own ground.
  1717 'Ode on Solitude'.

5 Is there no bright reversion in the sky,
  For those who greatly think or bravely die?
  1717 *Elergy to the Memory of an Unfortunate Lady*, l.9–10.

6 On all the line a sudden vengeance waits,
  And frequent hearses shall besige your gates.
  1717 *Elergy to the Memory of an Unfortunate Lady*, l.37–8.

7 By foreign hands thy dying eyes were closed,
  By foreign hands thy decent limbs composed,
  By foreign hands thy humble grave adorned,
  By strangers honoured, and by strangers mourned
  1717 *Elergy to the Memory of an Unfortunate Lady*, l.51–4.

8 Oh happy state! when souls each other draw,
  When love is liberty, and nature, law:
  All then is full, possessing, and possessed,
  No craving void left aching in the breast.
  1717 'Eloisa to Abelard'.

9 No, make me mistress to the man I love;
  If there be yet another name more free,
  More fond than mistress, make me that to thee!
  1717 'Eloisa to Abelard'.

10 Of all affliction taught a lover yet,
   'Tis sure the hardest science to forget!
   How shall I lose the sin, yet keep the sense,
   And love th'offender, yet detest th'offence?
   How the dear object from the crime remove,
   Or how distinguish penitence from love?
   1717 'Eloisa to Abelard'.

11 How happy is the blameless Vestal's lot!
   The world forgetting, by the world forgot.
   1717 'Eloisa to Abelard'.

12 And wine can of their wits the wise beguile,
   Make the sage frolic, and the serious smile.
   1726 *Odyssey*, bk.14, l.520–1.

13 Welcome the coming, speed the parting guest.
   1726 *Odyssey*, bk. 15, l.83.

14 To endeavour to work upon the vulgar with fine
   sense, is like attempting to hew blocks with a razor.
   1727 *Miscellanies*, 'Thoughts on Various Subjects', vol.2.

15 A man should never be ashamed to own he has
   been in the wrong, which is but saying, in other
   words, that he is wiser to-day than he was yesterday.
   1727 *Miscellanies*, 'Thoughts on Various Subjects', vol.2.

16 It is with narrow-souled people as with narrow-
   necked bottles: the less they have in them, the more
   noise they make in pouring it out.
   1727 *Miscellanies*, 'Thoughts on Various Subjects', vol.2.

17 When men grow virtuous in their old age, they
   only make a sacrifice to God of the devil's leavings.
   1727 *Miscellanies*, 'Thoughts on Various Subjects', vol.2.

18 The most primitive men are the most credulous.
   1727 *Miscellanies*, 'Thoughts on Various Subjects', vol.2.

19 Consult the genius of the place in all.
   1731 *Epistles to Several Persons*, 'To Lord Burlington', l.57.

20 Still follow sense, of ev'ry art the soul,
   Parts answering parts shall slide into a whole.
   1731 *Epistles to Several Persons*, 'To Lord Burlington', l.65–6.

21 No pleasing Intricacies intervene,
   No artful wildness to perplex the scene;
   Grove nods at grove, each a mirror of the other.
   The suff'ring eye inverted Nature sees,
   Trees cut to Statues, Statues thick as trees,
   With here a Fountain, never to be play'd,
   And there a Summer-house, that knows no shade;
   Here Amphitrite sails thro' myrtle bow'rs
   There Gladiators fight, or die, in flow'rs
   Un-water'd see the drooping sea-horse mourn,
   And swallows roost in Nilus' dusty Urn.
   1731 *Epistles to Several Persons*, 'To Lord Burlington', l.115–25.

22 To rest, the cushion and soft Dean invite,
   Who never mentions Hell to ears polite.
   1731 *Epistles to Several Persons*, 'To Lord Burlington', l.149–50.

23 Another age shall see the golden ear
   Imbrown the slope, and nod on the parterre,
   Deep harvests bury all his pride has planned,
   And laughing Ceres re-assume the land.
   1731 *Epistles to Several Persons*, 'To Lord Burlington', l.173–6.

24 'Tis use alone that sanctifies expense,
   And splendour borrows all her rays from sense.
   1731 *Epistles to Several Persons*, 'To Lord Burlington', l.179–80.

25 Who shall decide, when doctors disagree,
   And soundest casuists doubt, like you and me?
   1733 *Epistles to Several Persons*, 'To Lord Bathurst', l.1–2.

26 How often are we to die before we go quite off this
stage? In every friend we lose a part of ourselves,
and the best part.
1732 Letter to Swift, 5 Dec.

27 But thousands die, without or this or that,
Die, and endow a college, or a cat.
1733 *Epistles to Several Persons*, 'To Lord Bathurst', l.95–6.

28 The ruling passion be it what it will,
The ruling passion conquers reason still.
1733 *Epistles to Several Persons*, 'To Lord Bathurst', l.155–6.

29 Who sees pale Mammon pine amidst his store,
Sees but a backward steward for the poor;
This year a reservoir, to keep and spare,
The next a fountain, spouting through his heir,
In lavish streams to quench a country's thirst,
And men and dogs shall drink him 'till they burst.
1733 *Epistles to Several Persons*, 'To Lord Bathurst', l.173–8.

30 In the worst inn's worst room, with mat half-hung,
The floors of plaister, and the walls of dung,
On once a flock-bed, but repaired with straw,
With tape-tied curtains, never meant to draw,
The George and Garter dangling from that bed
Where tawdry yellow strove with dirty red,
Great Villiers lies.
1733 *Epistles to Several Persons*, 'To Lord Bathurst', l.229–35.

31 In faith and hope the world will disagree,
But all mankind's concern is charity.
1733 *An Essay on Man*.

32 Awake, my St. John! leave all meaner things
To low ambition, and the pride of kings.
Let us (since Life can little more supply
Than just to look about us and to die)
Expatiate free o'er all this scene of man;
A mighty maze! but not without a plan.
1733 *An Essay on Man*, epistle 1, l.1–6.

33 Eye Nature's walks, shoot Folly as it flies,
And catch the Manners living as they rise.
Laugh where we must, be candid where we can;
But vindicate the ways of God to man.
1733 *An Essay on Man*, epistle 1, l.13–16.
▷ See Milton 687:86.

34 Observe how system into system runs,
What other planets circle other suns.
1733 *An Essay on Man*, epistle 1, l.25–6.

35 Who sees with equal eye, as God of all,
A hero perish, or a sparrow fall,
Atoms or systems into ruin hurled,
And now a bubble burst, and now a world.
1733 *An Essay on Man*, Epistle 1, l.87–90.

36 Hope springs eternal in the human breast:

Man never Is, but always to be blest.
1733 *An Essay on Man*, epistle 1, l.95–6.

37 Lo! the poor Indian, whose untutored mind
Sees God in clouds, or hears him in the wind;
His soul proud Science never taught to stray
Far as the solar walk, or milky way;
Yet simple Nature to his hope has giv'n,
Behind the cloud-topped hill, an humbler heav'n.
1733 *An Essay on Man*, epistle 1, l.99–104.

38 Pride still is aiming at the blest abodes,
Men would be angels, angels would be gods.
1733 *An Essay on Man*, epistle 1, l.125–6.

39 The spider's touch, how exquisitely fine!
Feels at each thread, and lives along the line.
1733 *An Essay on Man*, epistle 1, l.217–8.

40 All are but parts of one stupendous whole,
Whose body, Nature is, and God the soul.
1733 *An Essay on Man*, epistle 1, l.267–8.

41 All nature is but art, unknown to thee;
All chance, direction, which thou canst not see;
All discord, harmony, not understood;
All partial evil, universal good:
And, spite of Pride, in erring Reason's spite,
One truth is clear, 'Whatever Is, is RIGHT.'
1733 *An Essay on Man*, epistle 1, l.289–94.

42 Know then thyself, presume not God to scan;
The proper study of mankind is man.
Placed on this isthmus of a middle state,
A being darkly wise, and rudely great:
With too much knowledge for the sceptic side,
With too much weakness for the stoic's pride,
He hangs between; in doubt to act or rest,
In doubt to deem himself a god, or beast;
In doubt his mind or body to prefer,
Born but to die, and reas'ning but to err;
Alike in ignorance, his reason such,
Whether he thinks too little, or too much.
1733 *An Essay on Man*, epistle 2, l.1–12.

43 Created half to rise, and half to fall;
Great lord of all things, yet a prey to all;
Sole judge of truth, in endless error hurled:
The glory, jest, and riddle of the world!
1733 *An Essay on Man*, epistle 2, l.15–18.

44 Vice is a monster of so frightful mien,
As, to be hated, needs but to be seen;
Yet seen too oft, familiar with her face,
We first endure, then pity, then embrace.
1733 *An Essay on Man*, epistle 2, l.217–19.

45 The learn'd is happy nature to explore,
The fool is happy that he knows no more.
1733 *An Essay on Man*, epistle 2, l.263–4.

46 For forms of government let fools contest;
   Whate'er is best administered is best.
   1733 *An Essay on Man*, epistle 3, l.303–4.

47 Thus God and nature linked the gen'ral
   frame,
   And bade self-love and social be the same.
   1733 *An Essay on Man*, epistle 3, l.317–18.

48 Order is heaven's first law.
   1733 *An Essay on Man*.

49 Oh Happiness! our being's end and aim!
   Good, pleasure, ease, content! whate'er thy
   name:
   That something still which prompts th' ethernal
   sigh,
   For which we bear to live, or dare to die.
   1734 *An Essay on Man*, epistle 4, l.1–4.

50 A wit's a feather, and a chief a rod;
   An honest man's the noblest work of God.
   1734 *An Essay on Man*, epistle 4, l.247–8.

51 If parts allure thee, think how Bacon shined,
   The wisest, brightest, meanest of mankind:
   Or ravished with the whistling of a name,
   See Cromwell, damned to everlasting fame!
   1734 *An Essay on Man*, epistle 4, l.281–4.

52 Slave to no sect, who takes no private road,
   But looks thro' Nature, up to Nature's God.
   1734 *An Essay on Man*, epistle 4, l.331–2.

53 All our knowledge is, ourselves to know.
   1734 *An Essay on Man*, epistle 4, l.398.

54 Alas! in truth the man but changed his mind,
   Perhaps was sick, in love, or had not dined.
   1734 *Epistles to Several Persons*, 'To Lord Cobham', l.127–8.

55 'Tis from high life high characters are drawn;
   A saint in crape is twice a saint in lawn.
   1734 *Epistles to Several Persons*, 'To Lord Cobham', l.134–6.

56 Search then the Ruling Passion: There, alone,
   The wild are constant and the cunning
   known;
   The fool consistent, and the false sincere;
   Priests, princes, women, no dissemblers here.
   This clue once found, unravels all the rest.
   1734 *Epistles to Several Persons*, 'To Lord Cobham', l.174–8.

57 Odious! in woollen! 'twould a saint provoke!
   1734 *Epistles to Several Persons*, 'To Lord Cobham', l.246.

58 Shut, shut the door, good John! fatigued I
   said,
   Tie up the knocker; say I'm sick, I'm dead.
   The Dog-star rages!

1735 'An Epistle to Dr Arbuthnot', l.1–3.

61 You think this cruel? take it for a rule,
   No creature smarts so little as a fool.
   Let peals of laughter, Codrus! round thee
   break,
   Thou unconcerned canst hear the mighty
   crack.
   Pit, box, and gallery in convulsions hurled,
   Thou stand'st unshook amidst a bursting
   world.
   1735 'An Epistle to Dr Arbuthnot', l.83–8.

62 Destroy his fib, or sophistry; in vain,
   The creature's at his dirty work again.
   1735 'An Epistle to Dr Arbuthnot', l.91–2.

63 Pretty! in amber to observe the forms
   Of hairs, or straws, or dirt, or grubs, or
   worms!
   The things, we know are neither rich nor
   rare,
   But wonder how the Devil they got there.
   1735 'An Epistle to Dr Arbuthnot', l.169–72.

64 And he, whose fustian's so sublimely bad,
   It is not poetry, but prose run mad.
   1735 'An Epistle to Dr Arbuthnot', l.187–8.

65 Damn with faint praise, assent with civil leer,
   And without sneering, teach the rest to sneer;
   Willing to wound, and yet afraid to strike,
   Just hint a fault, and hesitate dislike.
   1735 Of Addison. 'An Epistle to Dr Arbuthnot', l.201–4.

66 But still the great have kindness in reserve,
   He helped to bury whom he helped to starve.
   1735 Of a patron. 'An Epistle to Dr Arbuthnot', l.247–8.

67 Let Sporus tremble—'What? that thing of silk,
   Sporus, that mere white curd of ass's milk?
   Satire or sense, alas! can Sporus feel?
   Who breaks a butterfly upon a wheel?
   1735 Of Lord Hervey. 'An Epistle to Dr Arbuthnot', l.305–8.

68 And he himself one vile antithesis.
   1735 Of Lord Hervey. 'An Epistle to Dr Arbuthnot', l.325.

69 Unlearn'd, he knew no schoolman's subtle art,
   No language, but the language of the heart.
   1735 Of Pope's father. 'An Epistle to Dr Arbuthnot', l.398–9.

70 Most women have no characters at all.
   1735 *Epistles to Several Persons*, 'To a Lady', l.2.

71 A very heathen in the carnal part,
   Yet still a sad, good Christian at her heart.
   1735 *Epistles to Several Persons*, 'To a Lady', l.67–8.

72 Chaste to her husband, frank to all beside,

A teeming mistress, but a barren bride.
1735 *Epistles to Several Persons*, 'To a Lady', l.71–2.

73 'With every pleasing, every prudent part,
Say, what can Cloe want?—she wants a heart.
1735 *Epistles to Several Persons*, 'To a Lady', l.159–60.

74 Virtue she finds too painful an endeavour,
Content to dwell in decencies for ever.
1735 *Epistles to Several Persons*, 'To a Lady', l.163–4.

75 In men, we various ruling passions find,
In women, two almost divide the kind;
Those, only fixed, they first or last obey
The love of pleasure, and the love of sway.
1735 *Epistles to Several Persons*, 'To a Lady', l.207–10.

76 Men, some to business, some to pleasure take;
But every woman is at heart a rake:
Men, some to quiet, some to public strife;
But every lady would be Queen for life.
1735 *Epistles to Several Persons*, 'To a Lady', l.215–8.

77 Still round and round the ghosts of Beauty glide,
And haunt the places where their honour died.
See how the world its veterans rewards!
A youth of frolics, an old age of cards.
1735 *Epistles to Several Persons*, 'To a Lady', l.241–4.

78 Woman's at best a contradiction still.
1735 *Epistles to Several Persons*, 'To a Lady', l.270.

79 The more you drink, the more you crave.
1736 *Imitations of Horace*, l.212–15.

80 Who now reads Cowley? if he pleases yet,
His moral pleases, not his pointed wit.
1737 *Imitations of Horace*, bk.2, epistle 1, l.75–6.

81 The people's voice is odd,
It is, and it is not, the voice of God.
1737 *Imitations of Horace*, bk.2, epistle 1, l.89–90.

82 But those who cannot write, and those who can,
All rhyme, and scrawl, and scribble, to a man.
1737 *Imitations of Horace*, bk.2, epistle 1, l.187–8.

83 Ev'n copious Dryden, wanted, or forgot,
The last and greatest art, the art to blot.
1737 *Imitations of Horace*, bk.2, epistle 1, l.280–1.

84 There still remains, to mortify a wit,
The many-headed monster of the pit.
1737 *Imitations of Horace*, bk.2, epistle 1, l.304–5.

85 Not to go back, is somewhat to advance,
And men must walk at least before they dance.
1738 *Imitations of Horace*, bk.1, epistle 1, l.53–4.

86 Not to admire, is all the art I know,
To make men happy, and to keep them so.
1738 *Imitations of Horace*, bk.1, epistle 6, l.1–2.

87 The worst of madmen is a saint run mad.
1738 *Imitations of Horace*, bk.1, epistle 6, l.27.

88 Ask you what provocation I have had?
The strong antipathy of good to bad.
1738 *Imitations of Horace*, epilogue to the satires, dialogue 2, l.197–8.

89 Yes, I am proud; I must be proud to see
Men not afraid of God, afraid of me.
1738 *Imitations of Horace*, epilogue to the satires, dialogue 2, l.208–9.

90 Teach me to feel another's woe;
To hide the fault I see;
That mercy I to others show,
That mercy show to me.
1738 *The Universal Prayer*.

91 Books and the Man I sing, the first who brings
The Smithfield Muses to the Ear of Kings.
Say great Patricians! (since your selves inspire
These wond'rous works; so Jove and Fate require)
Say from what cause, in vain decry'd and curst,
Still Dunce the second reigns like Dunce the first?
1743 *The Dunciad*, bk.1, l.1–6.

92 Poetic Justice, with her lifted scale,
Where, in nice balance, truth with gold she weighs,
And solid pudding against empty praise.
1743 *The Dunciad*, bk.1, l.52–4.

93 Here gay Description Aegypt glads with showers;
Or gives to Zembla fruits, to Barca flowers;
Glitt'ring with ice here hoary hills are seen,
There painted vallies of eternal green.
1743 *The Dunciad*, bk.1, l.71–4.

94 While pensive poets painful vigils keep,
Sleepless themselves, to give their readers sleep.
1743 *The Dunciad*, bk.1, l.93–4.

95 In each she marks her image full exprest,
But chief, in Tibbald's monster-breeding breast;
Sees Gods with Daemons in strange league ingage,
And earth, and heav'n, and hell her battles wage.
1743 *The Dunciad*, bk.1, l.105–8.

96 Or where the pictures for the page atone,
And Quarles is saved by beauties not his own.
1743 *The Dunciad*, bk.1, l.139–40.

97 A brain of feathers, and a heart of lead.
1743 *The Dunciad*, bk.2, l.44.

98 How little, mark! that portion of the ball,
Where, faint at best, the beams of science fall.
1743 *The Dunciad*, bk.3, l.83–4.

99 None need a guide, by sure attraction led,
And strong impulsive gravity of head.
1743 *The Dunciad*, bk.4, l.75–6.

1 A wit with dunces, and a dunce with wits.
   1743 *The Dunciad*, bk.4, l.90.

2 Leave not a foot of verse, a foot of stone,
   A Page, a Grave, that they can call their own;
   But spread, my sons, your glory thin or thick,
   On passive paper, or on solid brick.
   1743 *The Dunciad*, bk.4, l.127–30.

3 Whate'er the talents, or howe'er designed,
   We hang one jingling padlock on the mind.
   1743 *The Dunciad*, bk.4, l.161–2.

4 The Right Divine of Kings to govern wrong.
   1743 *The Dunciad*, bk.4, l.187.

5 How parts relate to parts, or they to whole,
   The body's harmony, the beaming soul.
   1743 *The Dunciad*, bk.4, l.235–6.

6 Isles of fragrance, lily-silver'd values.
   1743 *The Dunciad*, bk.4, l.303.

7 Love-whispering woods, and lute-resounding
   waves.
   1743 *The Dunciad*, bk.4, l.306.

8 —She marked thee there,
   Stretched on the rack of a too easy chair,
   And heard thy everlasting yawn confess
   The pains and penalties of idleness.
   1743 *The Dunciad*, bk.4, l.341–4.

9 O! would the Sons of Men once think their Eyes
   And Reason giv'n them but to study Flies?
   See Nature in some partial narrow shape,
   And let the Author of the Whole escape.
   1743 *The Dunciad* bk.4, l.453–6.

10 Religion blushing veils her sacred fires,
    And unawares Morality expires.
    1743 *The Dunciad*, bk.4, l.649–50.

11 Lo! thy dread empire, Chaos! is restored;
    Light dies before thy uncreating word:
    Thy hand, great Anarch! lets the curtain fall;
    And universal darkness buries all.
    1743 *The Dunciad*, bk.4, l.653–6.

12 I am his Highness' dog at Kew;
    Pray, tell me sir, whose dog are you?
    'Epigram Engraved on the Collar of a Dog which I gave to His
    Royal Highness'.

13 Here am I, dying of a hundred good symptoms.
    1744 His response to reassurance from his doctors that his
    health was showing signs of improvement. Quoted in Joseph
    Spence *Anecdotes by and about Alexander Pope* (1820).

Popova, Lyubov Sergeevna 1889–1924
Russian painter, theatre and textile designer.

14 Texture is the content of painterly surfaces.
    Quoted in W Chadwick *Women, Art and Society* (1990).

Popper, Sir Karl Raimund 1902–94
Anglo-Austrian philosopher, professor (1949–69) at the
London School of Economics. He expounded his political
theory in *The Open Society and its Enemies* (1945), and his
philosophy of science in *The Logic of Scientific Discovery*
(1931).

15 It must be possible for an empirical system to be
    refuted by experience.
    1934 *The Logic of Scientific Discovery*, ch.1.

16 Every scientific statement must remain *tentative for
    ever*.
    1934 *The Logic of Scientific Discovery*, ch.10.

17 We may become the makers of our fate when we
    have ceased to pose as its prophets.
    1945 *The Open Society and its Enemies*, introduction.

18 There is no history of mankind, there are only
    many histories of all kinds of aspects of human life.
    And one of these is the history of political power.
    This is elevated into the history of the world.
    1945 *The Open Society and its Enemies*, vol.2, ch.25.

19 The belief that we can start with pure observations
    alone, without anything in the nature of a theory, is
    absurd.
    1953 *Conjectures and Refutations* (published 1963), ch.1.

20 Observation is always selective. It needs a chosen
    object, a definite task, an interest, a point of view, a
    problem.
    1953 *Conjectures and Refutations* (published 1963), ch.1.

21 There is at least one philosophical problem in
    which all thinking men are interested. It is the
    problem of cosmology: *the problem of
    understanding the world—including ourselves, and
    our knowledge, as part of the world*. All science is
    cosmology, I believe, and for me the interest of
    philosophy, no less than that of science, lies solely
    in the contributions which it has made to it.
    1959 *The Logic of Scientific Discovery*, preface to 1959 edition.

22 In so far as a scientific statement speaks about
    reality, it must be falsifiable: and in so far as it is not
    falsifiable, it does not speak about reality.
    1959 *The Logic of Scientific Discovery*, appendix to 1959
    edition.

23 In order that a new theory should constitute a
    discovery or step forward it should conflict with its
    predecessor...it should contradict its predecessor;
    it should overthrow it. In this sense, progress in
    science—or at least striking progress—is always
    revolutionary.
    1959 *The Logic of Scientific Discovery*.

24 It is not his possession of knowledge, of irrefutable truth, that makes the man of science, but his persistent and recklessly critical quest for truth.
1959 *The Logic of Scientific Discovery.*

25 What we should do, I suggest, is to give up the idea of ultimate sources of knowledge, and admit that all knowledge is human; that it is mixed with our errors, our prejudices, our dreams, and our hopes; that all we can do is to grope for truth even though it be beyond our reach.
1960 *Conjectures and Refutations* (published 1963), introduction.

26 The history of science, like the history of all human ideas, is a history of irresponsible dreams, of obstinacy, and of error. But science is one of the very few human activities—perhaps the only one—in which errors are systematically criticized and fairly often, in time, corrected. This is why we can say that, in science, we often learn from our mistakes, and why we can speak clearly and sensibly about making progress there.
1960 *Conjectures and Refutations* (published 1963), ch.10.

27 Science starts only with problems.
1960 *Conjectures and Refutations* (published 1963), ch.10.

28 For this, indeed, is the true source of our ignorance—the fact that our knowledge can only be finite, while our ignorance must necessarily be infinite.
1960 Lecture to the British Academy, 20 Jan.

29 Science may be described as the art of systematic over-simplification.
1982 Quoted in *The Observer*, 1 Aug.

Porter, Cole 1891–1964

US composer. He studied law at Harvard before turning to music, composing and writing lyrics for a string of successful stage and screen musicals including *Kiss Me Kate* (1948, filmed 1953), *High Society* (1956) and *Can-Can* (1953, filmed 1960).

30 I get no kick from champagne;
Mere alcohol doesn't thrill me at all.
So tell me why should it be true
That I get a kick out of you?
1934 'I Get a Kick Out of You', from the show *Anything Goes.*

31 In olden days a glimpse of stocking
Was looked on as something shocking.
But now, God knows,
Anything goes.
1934 'Anything Goes', from the show *Anything Goes.*

32 I'm a worthless check, a total wreck, a flop
But if baby I'm the bottom, you're the top.
1936 'You're the Top', from the show *Anything Goes.*

33 You're the top
You're the Louvr' Museum
You're a melody from a symphony by Strauss.
1936 'You're the Top', from the show *Anything Goes.*

34 My sole inspiration is a telephone call from a director.
1955 Interview, 8 Feb.

35 Who wants to be a millionaire?
And go to ev'ry swell affair?
1955 'Who wants to be a millionaire', from the show *High Society.*

Porter, Katherine Anne 1890–1980

US novelist and short story writer. Her works include the novella *Pale Horse, Pale Rider* (1939) and the long allegorical novel *The Ship of Fools* (1962).

36 Most people won't realize that writing is a craft. You have to take your apprenticeship in it like anything else.
1962 In the *Saturday Review*, 31 Mar.

37 The real sin against life is to abuse and destroy beauty, even one's own—even more, one's own, for that has been put in our care and we are responsible for its well-being.
1962 *Ship of Fools*, pt.3.

38 The pimple on the face of American literature.
On Truman Capote. Quoted in Gerald Clarke *Capote* (1988).

39 Oh, poor Pearl Buck! She has no more bounce than a boiled potato.
Quoted from the journals of Glenway Westcott, in Robert Phelps and Jerry Rosco (eds) *Continuous Lessons* (1990).

Porteus, Beilby 1731–1808

English prelate and poet.

40 One murder made a villain
Millions a hero.
1759 'Death'.

41 War its thousands slays, Peace its ten thousands.
1759 'Death'.

42 Teach him how to live,
And, oh! still harder lesson! how to die.
1759 'Death'.

Pott, Frances 1832–1909

English cleric and translator.

43 The strife is o'er, the battle done;
Now is the Victor's triumph won;
O let the song of praise be sung;
Alleluia!
1861 Hymn, translated from the original Latin 'Finita iam sunt praelia'.

Potter, Henry Codman 1835–1908

US religious leader. For 15 years he was rector of Grace Church, NYC. He was elected Bishop Co-adjutor of New York in 1883 and Bishop in 1887. He was known for his diplomacy and was outspoken on corruption.

44 If there be no nobility of descent in a nation, it is all the more indispensable that there should be nobility of ascent; a character in them that bear rule, so fine and high and pure, that as men come within the circle of its influence, they involuntarily pay homage to that which is the one pre-eminent distinction—the royalty of virtue.
1889 Washington centennial address, 30 Apr.

Potter, Stephen 1900–69

English humorous writer.

45 How to be one up – how to make the other man feel that something has gone wrong, however slightly.
1950 *Lifemanship*.

46 Each of us can, by ploy or gambit, most naturally gain the advantage.
1950 *Lifemanship*.

Pound, Ezra Loomis 1885–1972

US poet, a key figure in the Modernist movement, whose chief work was the massive poetic cycle *The Cantos* (collected 1970). He spent much of his life in Italy, and was committed to an asylum for a time after World War II, during which he espoused Fascist sympathies.

47 Bah! I have sung women in three cities,
But it is all the same;
And I will sing of the sun.
1908 *Personae*, 'Cino'.

48 No good poetry is written in a manner twenty years old, for to write in such a manner shows conclusively that the writer thinks from books, convention and cliché; and not from life.
1912 'Prolegomena', in *The Poetry Review*, Feb.

49 All great art is born of the metropolis.
1913 Letter to Harriet Monroe, 7 Nov.

50 Poetry must be *as well written as prose.*
1915 Letter to Harriet Monroe, Jan.

51 Winter is icummen in,
Lhude sing Goddamm,
Raineth drop and staineth slop,
And how the wind doth ramm!
Sing: Goddamm.
1916 *Lustra*, 'Ancient Music'.
▷ See Anonymous 22:67.

52 The apparition of these faces in the crowd;

Petals on a wet, black bough.
1916 *Lustra*, 'In a Station of the Metro'.

53 She is dying piece-meal
of a sort of emotional anaemia.
And round about there is a rabble
of the filthy, sturdy, unkillable infants
of the very poor.
1916 *Lustra*, 'The Garden'.

54 I make a pact with you, Walt Whitman—
I have detested you long enough.
I come to you as a grown child
Who has had a pig-headed father
I am old enough now to make friends.
1916 *Lustra*, 'A Pact'.

55 Poetry must be read as music and not as oratory.
1917 'Vers Libre and Arnold Dolmetsch', in *The Egoist*, Jul.

56 A cryselephantine poem of immeasurable length which will occupy me for the next four decades unless it becomes a bore.
1917 On beginning the poetic series *The Cantos*, which remained unfinished on his death.

57 Great poets seldom make bricks without straw. They pile up all the excellences they can beg, borrow, or steal from their predecessors and contemporaries and then set their own inimitable light atop the mountain.
Quoted in Patricia C Willis (ed) *The Complete Poems of Marianne Moore* (1986).

58 A man of genius has a right to any mode of expression.
1918 Letter to J B Yeats, 4 Feb.

59 Of all those young women
Not one has enquired the cause of the world
Nor the modus of lunar eclipses
Nor whether there be any patch left of us
After we cross the infernal ripples.
1919 *Quia Pauper Amavi*, 'Homage to Sextus Propertius'.

60 For three years, out of key with his time,
He strove to resuscitate the dead art
Of poetry; to maintain 'the sublime'
In the old sense. Wrong from the start—

No, hardly, but seeing he had been born
In a half savage country, out of date.
1920 *Hugh Selwyn Mauberley*, pt.1.

61 His true Penelope was Flaubert,
He fished by obstinate isles;
Observed the elegance of Circe's hair
Rather than the mottoes on sundials.
1920 *Hugh Selwyn Mauberley*, pt.1.

62 Better mendacities

Than the classics in paraphrase!
1920 *Hugh Selwyn Mauberley*, pt.2.

63 Christ follows Dionysus
Phallic and ambrosial
Made way for macerations;
Caliban casts out Ariel.
1920 *Hugh Selwyn Mauberley*, pt.3.

64 Died some, *pro patria*,
non 'dulce' non 'et decor'...
walked eye-deep in hell
believing in old men's lies, then unbelieving
came home, home to a lie,
home to many deceits
home to old lies and new infamy;
usury age-old and age-thick
and liars in public places.
1920 *Hugh Selwyn Mauberley*, pt.4.

65 There died a myriad,
And of the best, among them,
For an old bitch gone in the teeth,
For a botched civilization.
1920 *Hugh Selwyn Mauberley*, pt.5.

66 And no one knows, at first sight, a masterpiece.
And give up verse, my boy.
There's nothing in it.
1920 *Hugh Selwyn Mauberley*, 'MR NIXON'.

67 I never mentioned a man but with the view
Of selling my own works.
The tip's a good one, as for literature
It gives no man a sinecure.
1920 *Hugh Selwyn Mauberley*, 'MR NIXON'.

68 The haven from sophistications and contentions
Leaks through its thatch;
He offers succulent cooking;
The door has a creaking latch.
1920 *Hugh Selwyn Mauberley*, pt.10

69 The curse of me and my nation is that we always
think things can be bettered by immediate action
of some sort, *any* sort rather than no sort.
1920 Letter to James Joyce, 7–8 Jun.

70 And then went down to the ship,
Set keel to breakers, forth on the godly sea
1925 *A Draft of XVI Cantos*, no.1.

71 And even I can remember
A day when the historians left blanks in their
   writings,
I mean for things they didn't know.
1930 *Draft of XXX Cantos*, no.13.

72 Great literature is simply language charged with
meaning to the utmost possible degree.

1931 *How To Read*, pt.2.

73 Any general statement is like a cheque drawn on a
bank. Its value depends on what is there to meet it.
1934 *The ABC of Reading*, ch.1, section 2.

74 One of the pleasures of middle age is to *find out*
that one WAS right, and that one was much righter
than one knew at say 17 or 23.
1934 *The ABC of Reading*, ch.1.

75 Literature is news that STAYS news.
1934 *The ABC of Reading*, ch.2.

76 Real education must ultimately be limited to one
who INSISTS on knowing, the rest is mere sheep-
herding.
1934 *The ABC of Reading*, ch.8.

77 The author's conviction on this day of New Year is
that music begins to atrophy when it departs too
far from the dance; that poetry begins to atrophy
when it gets too far from music...
1934 *The ABC of Reading*, 'Warning'.

78 To the beat of the measure
From star-up to the half-dark
From half-dark to half-dark
Unceasing the measure.
1934 *Eleven New Cantos*, no.34.

79 People find ideas a bore because they do not
distinguish between live ones and stuffed ones on a
shelf.
1938 *Guide to Kulcher*, pt.1, sct.1, ch.5.

80 Civilization itself is a certain sane balance of values.
1938 *Guide to Kulcher*, pt.3, sct.5, ch.20.

81 Man is an over-complicated organism. If he is
doomed to extinction he will die out for want of
simplicity.
1938 *Guide to Kulcher*, pt.3, sct.5, ch.19.

82 Adolf Hitler was a Jeanne d'Arc, a saint. He was a
martyr. Like many martyrs, he held extreme views.
1945 In the *Philadelphia Record* and *Chicago Sun*, 9 May.

83 What thou lovest well remains,
The rest is dross
What thou lov'st well shall not be reft from thee
What thou lov'st well is thy true heritage
1948 *The Pisan Cantos*, no.81.

84 The ant's a centaur in his dragon world.
Pull down thy vanity, it is not man
Made courage, or made order, or made grace
1948 *The Pisan Cantos*, no.81.

85 Learn of the green world what can be thy place
In scaled invention or true artistry,

Pull down thy vanity,
Paquin pull down!
The green casque has outdone your elegance.
1948 *The Pisan Cantos*, no.81.

86 Thou art a beaten dog beneath the hail,
A swollen magpie in a fitful sun,
Half black half white
Nor knowst'ou wing from tail
Pull down thy vanity.
1948 *The Pisan Cantos*, no.81.

87 Tching prayed on the mountain and wrote MAKE IT
NEW
on his bath tub.
Day by day make it new
cut underbrush,
pile the logs
keep it growing.
1954 *The Cantos*, no.53.

88 Artists are the antennae of the race, but the bullet-
headed many will never learn to trust their great
artists.
1954 *Literary Essays*, 'Henry James'.

89 How did it go in the madhouse? Rather badly. But
what other place could one live in America?
1958 On his release after 13 years in St Elizabeth's Hospital,
Washington DC. Recalled on his death, 1 Nov 1972.

90 The worst mistake I made was that stupid,
suburban prejudice of anti-Semitism.
1968 Remark to Allen Ginsberg, 7 Jun. Quoted in H
Carpenter *A Serious Character* (1988), pt.5.

91 Art very possibly *ought* to be the supreme
achievement, the 'accomplished', but there is the
other satisfactory effect—that of a man hurling
himself at an indomitable chaos and yanking and
hauling as much of it as possible into some sort of
order (or beauty) aware of it both as chaos and as
potential.
Quoted in H Kenner (ed) *The Pound Era* (1973).

92 A dirty book worth reading.
Of Henry Miller *Tropic of Cancer* (1934). Recalled on Miller's
death, 7 Jun 1980.

93 All America is an insane asylum.
Quoted in Patricia C Willis (ed) *The Complete Poems of
Marianne Moore* (1986).

94 Some poems have form as a tree has form and some
as water poured into a vase.
Quoted in Patricia C Willis (ed) *The Complete Poems of
Marianne Moore* (1986).

95 The great writer is always the plodder.
Quoted in Patricia C Willis (ed) *The Complete Poems of
Marianne Moore* (1986).

96 The true poet is most easily distinguished from the
false when he trusts himself to the simplest
expression and writes without adjectives.
Quoted in Patricia C Willis (ed) *The Complete Poems of
Marianne Moore* (1986).

97 Use no word that under stress of emotion you
could not actually say.
Quoted in Patricia C Willis (ed) *The Complete Poems of
Marianne Moore* (1986).

Pound, (Nathan) Roscoe 1870–1964

US jurist, Professor of Law at Harvard University.

98 Wealth, in a commercial age, is made up largely of
promises.
1922 *An Introduction to the Philosophy of Law*, ch.6.

Poussin, Nicolas 1594–1665

French painter who spent most of his working life in
Rome. The Classical tradition in French painting
developed from his work.

99 The grand manner consists of four elements:
subject or theme, concept, structure, and style. The
first requirement, fundamental to all the others, is
that the subject and the narrative be grandiose,
such as battles, heroic actions, and religious
themes.
Quoted in Giovanni Pietro Bellori *Lives of the Modern Painters*
(1672).

Powell, Anthony Dymoke 1905–

English novelist. His major work is the sequence of twelve
novels chronicling 20c English upper middle-class life,
collectively known as *A Dance to the Music of Time*
(1951–75).

1 All the same, you know parents—especially step-
parents—are sometimes a disappointment to their
children. They don't fulfil the promise of their early
years.
1952 *A Buyer's Market*, ch.2.

2 There is a strong disposition in youth, from which
some individuals never escape, to suppose that
everyone else is having a more enjoyable time than
we are ourselves.
1952 *A Buyer's Market*, ch.4.

3 He fell in love with himself at first sight and it is a
passion to which he has always remained faithful.
Self-love seems so often unrequited.
1955 *The Acceptance World*, ch.1.

4 Dinner at the Huntercombes possessed 'only two
dramatic features—the wine was a farce and the
food a tragedy.'
1955 *The Acceptance World*, ch.4.

5 All men are brothers, but, thank God, they aren't all brothers-in-law.
   1957 *At Lady Molly's*, ch.4.

6 Books Do Furnish a Room.
   1971 Title of novel.

7 Growing old is like being increasingly penalised for a crime you haven't committed.
   1973 *Temporary Kings*, ch.1.

8 People think that because a novel's invented, it isn't true. Exactly the reverse is the case.
   1975 *Hearing Secret Harmonies*, ch.3.

9 One of the worst things about life is not how nasty the nasty people are. You know that already. It is how nasty the nice people can be.
   1975 *Hearing Secret Harmonies*, ch.7.

10 In this country it is rare for anyone, let alone a publisher, to take writers seriously.
   1979 In the *Daily Telegraph*, 8 Feb.

11 If you don't spend every morning of your life writing, it's awfully difficult to know what to do otherwise.
   1984 In the *Observer*, 3 Apr.

Powell, Colin Luther 1937–

US army general. He fought in Vietnam, and became national security adviser to Reagan (1987–9). In 1989 he was appointed chairman of the Joint Chiefs of Staff, and controlled US strategy during the Gulf War.

12 We have decapitated him from the dictatorship.
   1988 On evicting from office Panama's General Manuel Noriega. Quoted in the *Washington Post*, 21 Dec.

13 First we're going to cut it off, and then we're going to kill it.
   1991 On the opposition to Operation Desert Storm. In the *US News and World Report*, 4 Feb.

14 The American people do not want their young dying for $1.50 gallon oil.
   1990 Urging caution against interfering with Iraq's invasion of oil-rich Kuwait in White House meeting 2 Aug. Quoted in the *New York Times*, 23 Oct 1994.

15 I remember the front door. I remember the auditorium. I remember the feeling that you can't make it. But you can.
   1991 On revisiting the South Bronx high school from which he graduated in 1954. In the *New York Times*, 16 Apr.

Powell, (John) Enoch 1912–98

British Conservative and Ulster Unionist politician. Professor of Greek at Sydney University 1937–9, he was elected MP in 1950. Minister of Health (1960–3), he was dismissed from the shadow cabinet in 1968 for his attitude to immigration. He was returned as an Ulster Unionist in 1974, but lost his seat in 1987. His books include *A Nation Not Afraid* (1965).

16 History is littered with the wars which everybody knew would never happen.
   1967 Speech to Conservative party conference, 19 Oct.

17 As I look ahead, I am filled with much foreboding. Like the Roman, I seem to see 'the River Tiber foaming with much blood.'
   1968 Speech at Birmingham on racial tension in Britain, Apr.

18 I was born a Tory, am a Tory, and shall die a Tory. I never yet heard that it was any part of the faith of a Tory to take the institutions and liberties, thelaws and customs that his country has evolved over the centuries, and merge them with those of eight other nations into a new-made artificial state— and what is more, to do so without the willing approbation and consent of the nation.
   1974 Speech against Britain's entry into the Common Market, Shipley, 25 Feb.

19 All political lives, unless they are cut off in mid-stream at a happy juncture, end in failure, because that is the nature of politics and of human affairs.
   1977 *Joseph Chamberlain*.

Powell, Michael 1905–90

British filmmaker. He made various 'quota quickies' in the 1930s and then began a partnership with Emeric Pressburger. Known as 'the Archers', they collaborated on films like *The Life and Death of Colonel Blimp* (1943), *Black Narcissus* (1947) and *The Red Shoes* (1948).

20 What do they know of England, who only the West End know?
   1950 Attributed comment in defence of *Gone to Earth*.
   ▷ See Kipling 561:42.

Powys, John Cowper 1872–1963

English novelist and essayist.

21 It is that cricket field that, in all the sharp and bitter moments of life as they come to me now, gives me a sense of wholesome proportion: 'At least I am not playing cricket!'
   Quoted in Helen Exley *Cricket Quotations* (1992).

Prather, Hugh

22 If the ocean was pure mind and I was a wave, I would be in terror if I tried to distinguish myself from the water that produced me. What is a wave without water, and what is a mind without God?
   1982 *The Quiet Answer*.

23 Forgive and be happy. That is the ancient
secret…the only wisdom ever to be attained.
1982 *The Quiet Answer.*

Pratt, Edwin John 1882–1964

Canadian poet. Born in Newfoundland, he obtained a
Ph.D. in divinity from the University of Toronto and
became Professor of English there in 1919. He is best-
known for his documentary poetry, including *The Titanic*
(1935), *Brébeuf and His Brethren* (1940) and *Towards the
Last Spike* (1952).

24 It was the same world then as now—the same,
Except for little differences of speed
And power, and means to treat myopia
To show an axe-blade infinitely sharp
Splitting things infinitely small.
1952 'Towards the Last Spike'. The poet is speaking of the
building of the Canadian National Railway, from coast to coast.

Presley, Elvis Aaron 1935–77

US singer and actor.

25 I don't know anything about music—in my line I
don't have to.
Quoted in David Pickering *Brewer's Twentieth Century Music*
(1994).

Preston, James 1933–

US businessman. He joined Avon Products in 1964 as a
management trainee, becoming chief executive officer in
1988 and chair of the board the following year.

26 A bad reputation is like a hangover. It takes a while
to get rid of, and it makes everything else hurt.
1992 In *Fortune*, 10 Feb.

Previn, André (George) 1929–

German-born US conductor and composer. A US citizen
from 1943, he conducted major orchestras around the
word from 1967. His own compositions include musicals,
film scores and orchestral works.

27 The basic difference between classical music and
jazz is that in the former music is always greater
than its performance—whereas the way jazz is
performed is always more important than what is
being played.
1967 Quoted in *The Times.*

Prévost, L'Abbé Antoine-François
1697–1763

French novelist, educated in the Jesuit tradition. He
enlisted in the army before eventually deciding on a
religious life after an unhappy love affair.

28 *Il ne reste donc que l'exemple qui puisse servir de règle
à quantité de personnes dans l'exercice de la vertu.*

Most people can learn only by example to be
virtuous.
1731 *Histoire du chevalier Des Grieux et de Manon Lescaut*, Avis
de l'auteur.

29 *Crois-tu qu'on puisse être bien tendre lorsqu'on
manque de pain?*

Do you believe that a person can be truly
affectionate when he is starving?
1731 *Histoire du chevalier Des Grieux et de Manon Lescaut*, ch.1.

30 *Il faut compter ses richesses par les moyens qu'on a de
satisfaire ses désirs.*

We must count our riches by the means we have to
satisfy our desires.
1731 *Histoire du chevalier Des Grieux et de Manon Lescaut*,
ch.2.

Prial, Frank J

US writer for the *New York Times.*

31 Macaulay, Gibbon, Tolstoy, Francis Parkman and
other immortals…never said anything in two pages
that might possibly sound better in 10.
Quoted in the *New York Times*, 31 Mar 1990.

Price, Ray

Nixon White House speechwriter.

32 The response is to the image, not to the man, since
99 percent of the voters have no contact with the
man.
1967 Memo, 28 Nov. Quoted in the *New York Times*, 31 Oct
1993.

33 It's not what's *there* that counts, it's what's
projected—and…it's not what *he* projects but
rather what the voter receives… It's not the man we
have to change, but rather the *received* impression.
1967 Memo, 28 Nov. Quoted in the *New York Times*, 31 Oct
1993.

Prichard, Katharine Susannah married
name *Throssell* 1883–1969

Australian journalist, novelist and political activist.
Western Australia is the background for her later novels
including *Coonardoo* (1929).

34 Coonardoo they called it, the dark well, or the well
in the shadows.
1929 *Coonardoo*, ch.1.

Priestley, J(ohn) B(oynton) 1894–1984

English writer, whose works include the novel *The Good
Companions* (1929) and plays such as *Dangerous Corner*
(1932). He achieved national renown as deliverer of radio
'postscripts' during World War II.

35 To say that these men paid their shillings to watch
twenty-two hirelings kick a ball is merely to say that

a violin is wood and catgut, that *Hamlet* is so much paper and ink. For a shilling the Bruddersford United AFC offered you Conflict and Art.

1929 *The Good Companions*, bk.1, ch.1.

36 The earth is nobler than the world we have put upon it.

1939 *Johnson Over Jordan*, act 3.

37 This little steamer, like all her brave and battered sisters, is immortal. She'll go sailing proudly down the years in the epic of Dunkirk. And our great-great-great-grand-children, when they learn how we began this war by snatching glory out of defeat, and then swept on to victory, may also learn how the little holiday steamers made an excursion to hell and came back glorious.

1940 Radio broadcast, 5 Jun, quoted in *The Listener*, 13 Jun.

38 An Inspector Calls.

1947 Title of play.

39 The trouble is that we drink too much tea. I see in this the slow revenge of the Orient, which has diverted the Yellow River down our throats.

1949 In *The Observer*, 15 May.

40 Sometimes you might think that the machines we worship make all the chief appointments, promoting the human beings who seem closest to them.

1957 *Thoughts in the Wilderness*.

41 *Finnegans Wake* took him seventeen years to write, a length of time that suggests an elaborate hobby rather than a passionate desire to create something.

1960 Of James Joyce. *Literature and Western Man*.

42 He was a black Irish type, with centuries of rebelliousness behind him, and I decided to chance it.

1961 *Saturn Over the Water*.

43 I can't help feeling wary when I hear anything said about the masses. First you take their faces from 'em by calling 'em the masses and then you accuse 'em of not having any faces.

1961 *Saturn Over the Water*, ch.2.

44 It is hard to tell where the MCC ends and the Church of England begins.

1962 In the *New Statesman*, 20 Jul.

45 Some time ago, in an interview that turned towards the Theatre, I suggested that 'Pubic hair is not an adequate substitute for wit'. My point now is that depending upon shock tactics is easy, whereas writing a good play is difficult.

1974 *Outcries and Asides*, 'Danger of Shock Tactics'.

46 England is not ruined because sinewy brown men from a distant colony sometimes hit a ball further and oftener than our men do.

Quoted in Colin Jarman *The Guinness Dictionary of Sports Quotations* (1990).

Prior, Matthew 1664–1721

English poet and diplomat. His verse includes *The Hind and the Panther Transvers'd to the Story of the Country Mouse and the City Mouse* (with Charles Montagu, 1687, a satire on Dryden). He is remembered for his many witty, epigrammatic occasional verses.

48 They never taste who always drink;
They always talk who never think.

1697 'Upon this Passage in Scaligerana'.

49 Nobles and heralds, by your leave,
Here lies what once was Matthew Prior,
The son of Adam and of Eve,
Can Stuart or Nassaw go higher?

1702 'Epitaph'. In a later version 'Stuart' was changed to 'Bourbon'.

50 Be to her virtues very kind;
Be to her faults a little blind;
Let all her ways be unconfined;
And clap your padlock—on her mind.

1705 'An English Padlock'.

51 And of the pangs of absence to remove
By letters, soft interpreters of love.

1708 'Henry and Emma'.

52 But of good household features her person was made,
Nor by faction cry'd up nor of censure afraid,
And her beauty was rather for use than parade.

1708 'Jinny the Just' (first printed 1907). The title was given by A R Waller.

53 Cured yesterday of my disease,
I died last night of my physician.

1714 'The Remedy Worse than the Disease'.

54 Venus, take my votive glass;
Since I am not what I was,
What from this day I shall be
Venus never let me see.

1718 'The Lady who Offered her Looking-Glass to Venus'.

55 No, no; for my virginity,
When I lose that, says Rose, I'll die:
Behind the elms last night, cried Dick,
Rose, were you not extremely sick?

1718 'A True Maid'.

56 They walked and eat, good folks: What then?

Why then they walked and eat again:
They soundly slept the night away:
They did just nothing all the day.
1718 'An Epitaph', l.9–12.

57 Their beer was strong; their wine was port;
Their meal was large; their grace was short.
They gave the poor the remnant meat,
Just when it grew not fit to eat.
1718 'An Epitaph', l.29–32.

58 On his death bed poor Lubin lies:
His spouse is in despair.
With frequent sobs and mutual cries
They both express their care.

A different cause, says parson Sly,
The same effect may give:
Poor Lubin fears, that he shall die:
His wife, that he may live.
1718 'A Reasonable Affliction'.

59 What I speak, my fair Chloe, and what I write
 shows
The difference there is betwixt Nature and Art:
I court others in verse: but I love thee in prose:
And they have my whimsies, but thou hast my heart.
1718 'A Better Answer', stanza 4.

60 So when I am wearied with wandering all day;
To thee my delight in the evening I come:
No matter what beauties I saw in my way:
They were but my visits; but thou art my home.
1718 'A Better Answer', stanza 6.

61 And 'twould be a cruel thing,
When her black eyes have raised desire,
Should she not her bucket bring
And kindly help to quench the fire.
'Chloe Beauty has and Wit'. (Date unknown. *In Matthew Prior: Literary Works*, edited by H B Wright and M K Spears, 2 vols, 1959.)

62 Rise not till noon, if life be but a dream,
As Greek and Roman poets have exprest:
Add good example to so grave a theme,
For he who sleeps the longest lives the best.
'Epigram'. (Date unknown. *In Matthew Prior: Literary Works*, edited by H B Wright and M K Spears, 2 vols, 1959.)

Pritchett, Sir V(ictor) S(awdon) 1900–97

English writer. He wrote novels and works of literary criticism and biography, but is best known for his short stories.

63 The principle of procrastinated rape is said to be the ruling one in all of the great best-sellers.
1946 *The Living Novel*, 'Clarissa'.

64 A touch of science, even bogus science, gives an edge to the superstitious tale.

1946 *The Living Novel*, 'An Irish Ghost'.

65 The detective novel is…the classic example of a specialized form of art removed from contact with the life it pretends to build on.
1951 In the *New Statesman*, 16 Jun.

66 He watched his restless hands, surprised they had remembered to come with him.
1951 *Mr Beluncle*, ch.15.

67 If evil does not exist, what is going to happen to literature?
1951 *Mr Beluncle*, ch.23.

68 Dickens was not the first or the last novelist to find virtue more difficult to portray than the wish for it.
1953 'Oliver Twist', collected in *Books in General* (1981).

69 It is well known that, when two or three authors meet, they at once start talking about money—like everyone else.
1978 In *The Author*, Spring.

70 What Chekhov saw in our failure to communicate was something positive and precious: the private silence in which we live, and which enables us to endure our own solitude.
1979 *The Myth Makers*, 'Chekhov'.

71 It is the role of the poet to look at what is happening in the world and to know that quite other things are happening.
1979 *The Myth Makers*, 'Pasternak'.

72 The poet is a master of the quotidian, of conveying a whole history in two or three lines that point to an exact past drama and intensify a future one.
1979 *The Myth Makers*, 'Borges'.

73 A short story is always a disclosure.
1981 *The Oxford Book of Short Stories* (edited by Pritchett), introduction.

74 'The firm'—a proud Victorian word. It evokes the lost sense of Victorian regard for the pride of people in their daily trade.
'Betjeman', in the *New Yorker*, 24 Jun.

Private Eye

British satirical magazine, founded 1962.

75 Kill An Argie—Win A Metro!
1982 Front page headline during the Falklands War, parodying the jingoism of tabloid coverage of the conflict.

Proctor, Adelaide Ann pseudonym of *Mary Berwick* 1825–64

English poet. She won renown with her *Legends and Lyrics* (1858–60), and her poem 'The Lost Chord' was set to music by Sir Arthur Sullivan.

76 Seated one day at the organ,
    I was weary and ill at ease,
    And my fingers wandered idly
    Over the noisy keys;
    I know not what I was playing,
    Or what I was dreaming then,
    But I struck one chord of music,
    Like the sound of a great Amen.
    1858 'The Lost Chord'.

Profumo, John Dennis 1915–

English Conservative politician, Secretary of State for War
in 1960. He resigned in 1963 during the 'Profumo
Affair', admitting that he had deceived the House over the
nature of his relationship with Christine Keeler, who was
at the time also involved with a Russian diplomat. He
turned to charitable service, and was awarded the CBE in
1975.

77 There was no impropriety whatsoever in my
    acquaintanceship with Miss Keeler… I shall not
    hesitate to issue writs for libel and slander if
    scandalous allegations are made or repeated outside
    the House.
    1963 House of Commons, Mar.

Prokofiev, Sergei Sergeyevich 1891–1953

Russian composer, who live in exile in the West
(1918–36). His works include the *Classical Symphony*
(1917), the opera *The Love for Three Oranges* (1919), the
ballets *The Prodigal Son* (1928) and *Romeo and Juliet*
(1936), *Peter and the Wolf* (1936) and the opera *War and
Peace* (1943).

78 Bach on the wrong notes.
    Of the music of Stravinsky. Quoted in V Seroff *Sergei Prokofiev*
    (1968).

Propertius 1c BC

Roman poet.

79 *Navita de ventis, de tauris narrat orator,*
    Enumerat miles vulnera, pastor oves.

    The sailor tells stories of the winds, the ploughman
    of bulls; the soldier lists his wounds, the shepherd
    his sheep.
    Elegies bk.2, no.1.

80 *Cedite Romani scriptores, cedite Grai!*
    Nescioquid maius nascitur Iliade.

    Make way, Roman writers, make way, Greeks!
    Something greater than the Iliad is born.

    Of Virgil's Aeneid. *Elegies* bk.2, no.34.

Protagoras c.490–c.420 BC

Greek Sophist and teacher, the first and most famous of
the 'Sophists' who, for a fee, offered professional training

in public life and other skills. His works survive only as
fragments in other writers (notably Plato).

81 Man is the measure of all things.
    Quoted in Plato *Theaetetus*, 160d.

82 Man is the measure of all things, of the existence of
    the things that are, and the non-existence of the
    things that are not.
    Fragment quoted in Plato *Theaetetus*, 152a (translated by H
    North Fowler, 1977).

83 He said that there is no art without practice, and no
    practice without art.
    Fragment quoted in H Diels and W Kranz (eds) *Die Fragmente
    der Vorsokratiker*, vol.2 (1952), 268, no.10.

84 Concerning the gods I am not in a position to
    know either that they are or that they are not, or
    what they are like in appearance; for there are many
    things that are preventing knowledge, the obscurity
    of the matter and the brevity of human life.
    Quoted in G B Kerferd *The Sophistic Movement* (1981), ch.13.

Proudhon, Pierre Joseph 1809–65

French socialist and political theorist, the founder of
French radicalism. His works include the great *Système des
contradictions économiques* (System of Economic
Contradictions, 1846). Imprisoned for three years in
1849 and again in 1858, he spent the time writing further
works arguing for liberty, equality and justice.

85 *La propriété c'est le vol.*

    Property is theft.
    1840 *Qu'est-ce que la Propriété.*

86 Universal suffrage is counter-revolution.
    On Europe after the 1848 revolution. Quoted in A J P Taylor
    From Napoleon to the Second International (1993).

Proust, Marcel 1871–1922

French novelist who withdrew (c.1905) from society
because of asthma, the death of his parents and
disillusionment with the world. He introduced
psychological analysis into fiction, notably in his 13-
volume novel sequence *A la recherche du temps perdu*
(1913-27).

87 *Il vaut mieux rêver sa vie que la vivre, encore que la
    vivre ce soit encore la rêver.*

    It's better to dream your life than to live it, and even
    though you live it, you will still dream it.
    1896 *Les Plaisirs et les Jours.*

88 *Le bonheur est dans l'amour un état anormal.*

    In love, happiness is abnormal.
    1918 *A la recherche du temps perdu*, 'A l'ombre des jeunes filles
    en fleur'.

89 *Nous sommes tous obligés pour rendre la réalité
    supportable d'entretenir en nous quelques petites folies.*

We must all indulge in a few follies if we are to make reality bearable.
1918 *A la recherche du temps perdu*, 'A l'ombre des jeunes filles en fleur'.

90 *L'adolescence est le seul temps où l'on ait appris quelque chose.*

Adolescence is the only time when we can learn something.
1918 *A la recherche du temps perdu*, 'A l'ombre des jeunes filles en fleur'.

91 *On devient moral dès qu'on est malheureux.*

We become moral once we are miserable.
1918 *A la recherche du temps perdu*, 'A l'ombre des jeunes filles en fleur'.

92 *On ne reçoit pas la sagesse, il faut la découvrir soi-même, après un trajet que personne ne peut faire pour nous, ne peut nous épargner.*

We do not receive wisdom. We must discover it ourselves after experiences which no one else can have for us and from which no one else can spare us.
1918 *A la recherche du temps perdu*, 'A l'ombre des jeunes filles en fleur'.

93 *Il n'y avait pas d'anormaux quand l'homosexualité était la norme.*

There was nothing abnormal about it when homosexuality was the norm.
1920 *A la recherche du temps perdu*, 'Sodome et Gomorrhe'.

94 *La médecine a fait quelques petits progrès dans ses connaissances depuis Molière, mais aucun dans son vocabulaire.*

The doctor has made a few, little advances in knowledge since Molière, but none in his vocabulary.
1920 *A la recherche du temps perdu*, 'Sodome et Gomorrhe'.

95 Neurosis has an absolute genius for malingering. There is no illness which it cannot counterfeit perfectly.
1922 *Sodom and Gomorrah*.

96 *L'amour, c'est l'espace et le temps rendus sensibles au cœur.*

Love is space and time made tender to the heart.
1923 *A la recherche du temps perdu*, 'La Prisonnière'.

97 *La possession de ce qu'on aime est une joie plus grande encore que l'amour.*

Possessing what one loves is an even greater joy than love itself.
1923 *A la recherche du temps perdu*, 'La Prisonnière'.

98 *On a dit que la beauté est une promesse de bonheur. Inversement, la possibilité du plaisir peut être un commencement de beauté.*

It has been said that beauty is a guarantee of happiness. Conversely, the possibility of pleasure can be the beginning of beauty.
1923 *A la recherche du temps perdu*, 'La Prisonnière'.

99 *L'adultère introduit l'esprit dans la lettre que bien souvent le mariage eût laissée morte.*

Adultery introduces some energy into an otherwise dead marriage.
1923 *A la recherche du temps perdu*, 'La Prisonnière'.

1 *L'idée qu'on mourra est plus cruelle que mourir, mais moins que l'idée qu'un autre est mort.*

The idea of dying is worse than dying itself, but less cruel than the idea that another has died.
1923 *A la recherche du temps perdu*, 'La Prisonnière'.

2 [Music] a pederast might hum when raping a choirboy.
Of Fauré's *Romances sans paroles*. Quoted in *Musical Quarterly*, 1924.

3 *Laissons les jolies femmes aux hommes sans imagination.*

Leave the pretty women for the men without imagination.
1925 *A la recherche du temps perdu*, 'Albertine disparue'.

4 *Le mensonge est essentiel à l'humanité. Il y joue peut-être un aussi grand rôle que la recherche du plaisir, et d'ailleurs est commandé par cette recherche.*

Lies are essential to humanity. They play perhaps as great a role as the pursuit of pleasure, and are indeed controlled by this pursuit.
1925 *A la recherche du temps perdu*, 'Albertine disparue'.

5 *Si notre vie est vagabonde, notre mémoire est sédentaire.*

Even though our lives wander, our memories remain in one place.
1927 *A la recherche du temps perdu*, 'Le Temps retrouvé'.

6 *Le temps qui change les êtres ne modifie pas l'image que nous avons gardée d'eux.*

Although time changes people, it cannot change the image we have already made of them.
1927 *A la recherche du temps perdu*, 'Le Temps retrouvé'.

7 *Le bonheur est salutaire pour les corps, mais c'est le chagrin qui développe les forces de l'esprit.*

Happiness is healthy for the body, but it is sorrow which enhances the forces of the mind.
1927 *A la recherche du temps perdu*, 'Le Temps retrouvé'.

8 *Le style, pour l'écrivain aussi bien que pour le peintre, est une question non de technique mais de vision.*

For the writer as well as for the painter, style is not a question of technique, but of vision.
1927 *A la recherche du temps perdu*, 'Le Temps retrouvé'.

9 *Pour écrire ce livre essentiel, le seul livre vrai, un grand écrivain n'a pas, dans le sens courant, à l'inventer puisqu'il existe déjà en chacun de nous, mais à le traduire.*

To write the essential book, the only true book, a great writer does not need to invent because the book already exists inside each one of us and merely needs translation.

1927 *A la recherche du temps perdu,* 'Le Temps retrouvé'.

10 *En réalité, chaque lecteur est, quand il lit, le propre lecteur de soi-même. L'ouvrage de l'écrivain n'est qu'une espèce d'instrument optique qu'il offre au lecteur afin de lui permettre de discerner ce que, sans ce livre, il n'eût peut-être pas vu en soi-même.*

In reality, each reader reads only what is already within himself. The book is only a kind of optical instrument which the writer offers to the reader to enable him to discover in himself what he could not have found but for the aid of the book.

1927 *A la recherche du temps perdu,* 'Le Temps retrouvé'.

Prout, Father

▷ See Mahony, Francis Sylvester p.638

Prynne, William 1600–69

English puritan. An opponent of the theatre, he was imprisoned for publishing *Histrio Mastix: The Players' Scourge, or Actors' Tragedie* (1633), with its criticism of Charles I's queen Henrietta Maria. His ears were cut off as a punishment in 1634 and he was imprisoned again in 1650 for refusing to pay taxes.

11 Stage-players…are sinfull, heathenish, lewd, ungodly Spectacles and most pernicious Corruptions, condemned in all ages as intolerable Mischiefes to Churches, to Republickes, to the manners, mindes and soules of men. And that the Profession of Play-poets, of Stage-players; together with the penning, acting and frequenting of Stage-players are unlawfull, infamous and misbeseeming Christians.

1633 *Histrio Mastix: The Players' Scourge, or Actors' Tragedie.*

Publilius Syrus 1c.BC

Writer of Latin mimes.

12 *Formosa facies muta commendatio est.*

A beautiful face is a dumb commendation.

13 *Iuopi beneficium bis dat qui dat celeriter.*

He who gives quickly gives the poor man twice as much.

Pu Yi 1906–67

Chinese puppet emperor who was proclaimed Emperor at the age of two until forced to abdicate in 1912. He

continued to live in the imperial palace until forced to flee in 1924. Captured by the Soviet army in 1945 he was returned to China where he was given a job as a gardener.

14 For the past 40 years I had never folded my own quilt, made my own bed, or poured out my own washing. I had never even washed my own feet or tied my shoes.

1964 *From Emperor to Citizen: The Autobiography of Aisin-Gioro Pu Yi* (translated by W J F Jenner).

Puccini, Giacomo Antonio Domenico Michele Secondo Maria 1858–1924

Italian composer, best-known for his operas *La Bohème* (1896), *Tosca* (1900) and *Madame Butterfly* (1900). His last opera, *Turandot*, was unfinished.

15 Who sent you to me—God?

To Caruso, who was auditioning for him. Quoted in Derek Watson *Music Quotations* (1991).

Puckett, B Earl

US businessman. President, Allied Stores Corp.

16 It is our job to make women unhappy with what they have.

Recalled on his death, in *Newsweek*, 23 Feb 1976.

Pudney, John Sleigh 1909–77

British poet, journalist and novelist. Best known for his poem *For Johnny* (1941) and his novel *The Net* (1952).

17 Do not despair
For Johnny Head-in-Air
He sleeps as sound
As Johnny Underground.

1941 'For Johnny', spoken by Sir Michael Redgrave at the end of the film *The Way to the Stars* (1945).

Puig, Manuel 1932–90

Argentinian novelist. He studied cinema in Rome and spent several years in New York. His novels, which often exploit society's popular icons, include *El beso de la mujer araña*, adapted for stage, screen and Broadway musical.

18 *Porque, sí, fuera de la celda están nuestros opresores, pero adentro no. Aquí nadie oprime a nadie. Lo único que hay, de perturbador, para mi mente…cansada, o condicionada o deformada…es que alguien me quiere tratar bien, sin pedir nada a cambio.*

Because, well, outside of this cell we may have our oppressors, yes, but not inside. Here no one oppresses the other. The only thing that seems to disturb me…because I'm exhausted, or conditioned, or perverted…is that someone wants to be nice to me, without asking anything back for it.

1976 *El beso de la mujer araña,* ch.11 (translated as *Kiss of the Spider Woman*, 1978).

Pulitzer, Joseph 1847–1911

Hungarian-born US newspaper proprietor. He emigrated to US in 1864, became a reporter and began to acquire and revitalize old newspapers, notably the New York *World*. He established the annual Pulitzer prizes.

19 I want to talk to a nation, not to a select committee.
1909 In *Pearson's Magazine*, Mar.

20 We are a democracy, and there is only one way to get a democracy on its feet in the matter of its individual, its social, its municipal, its State, its National conduct, and that is by keeping the public informed about what is going on. There is not a crime, there is not a dodge, there is not a trick, there is not a swindle, there is not a vice which does not live by secrecy. Get these things out in the open, describe them, attack them, ridicule them in the press, and sooner or later public opinion will sweep them away.
c.1910 Quoted in Alleyne Ireland *An Adventure with a Genius*, ch.4.

21 What a newspaper needs in its news, in its headlines, and on its editorial page is terseness, humor, descriptive power, satire, originality, good literary style, clever condensation and accuracy, accuracy, accuracy.
c.1910 Quoted in Alleyne Ireland *An Adventure with a Genius*, ch.4.

Punch

British humourous weekly periodical, founded 1841.

22 Advice to persons about to marry — don't.
1845

23 You pays your money and you takes your choice.
1846

24 Let us be a nation of shopkeepers as much as we please, but there is no necessity that we should become a nation of advertisers.
1848 Quoted in David Ogilvy *Confessions of an Advertising Man* (1963), ch.2.
▷ See Smith, Adam 945:84.

25 Never do today what you can put off till tomorrow.
1849

26 Nothink for nothink 'ere, and precious little for sixpence.
1869

27 Sure, the next train has gone ten minutes ago.
1871

28 Go directly—see what she's doing, and tell her she mustn't.
1872

29 There was one poor tiger that hadn't *got* a Christian.
1875

30 I am not hungry; but thank goodness, I am greedy.
1878

31 Nearly all our best men are dead! Carlyle, Tennyson, Browning, George Eliot! — I'm not feeling very well myself.
1891

32 Botticelli isn't a wine, you Juggins! Botticelli's a *cheese!*
1891

33 Sometimes I sits and thinks, and then again I just sits.
1906

Purdy, Al 1918–

Canadian poet. Born in rural Ontario, he settled there again after some years away. He has published nearly 30 volumes of poetry, including *Poems for All the Annettes* (1962), *The Cariboo Horses* (1965) and *The Stone Bird* (1981).

34 Uneasily the leaves fall at this season,
forgetting what to do or where to go;
the red amnesiacs of autumn
drifting thru the graveyard forest.

What they have forgotten they have forgotten:
what they meant to do instead of fall
is not in earth or time recoverable—
the fossils of intention, the shapes of rot.
1962 *Poems for All the Annettes*, 'Pause' (revised 1968).

35 This is the country of defeat.
1965 *The Cariboo Horses*, 'The Country North of Belleville' (revised 1972).

36 They had their being once
and left a place to stand on.
1968 *Poems for All the Annettes*, 'Roblin Mills' (revised 1972).

Pushkin, Aleksandr Sergeyevich

1799–1837

Russian poet and writer. He is best known for the novel in verse *Eugene Onegin* (1833) and the tragic drama *Boris Godunov* (1825). He also wrote ballads and prose pieces. He was killed in a duel with his brother-in-law.

37 Moscow…what surge that sound can start
In every Russian's inmost heart!
1833 *Eugene Onegin*, ch.7, stanza 36 (translated by Adrian Room, 1995).

Putnam, Israel 1718–90

American general in the American Revolution.

38 Men you are all marksmen—don't one of you fire until you see the white of their eyes.

1775 Order before the Battle of Bunker Hill. Quoted in R Frotherington *History of the Siege of Boston* (1873), ch.5.

Puzo, Mario 1920–99

US novelist. His breakthrough as a writer came with his novel about the Mafia, *The Godfather* (1969). It became a bestseller and the basis of a trilogy of films directed by Francis Ford Coppola.

39 I'll make him an offer he can't refuse.

1969 *The Godfather*, bk.1, ch.1.

40 A lawyer with a briefcase can steal more than a hundred men with guns.

1969 *The Godfather*, bk.1, ch.1.

41 Like many businessmen of genius he learned that free competition was wasteful, monopoly efficient. And so he simply set about achieving that efficient monopoly.

1969 *The Godfather*, bk.3, ch.14.

42 Show me a gambler and I'll show you a loser, show me a hero, and I'll show you a corpse.

1978 *Fools Die*, ch.2.

43 Our own death wish is our only real tragedy.

1978 *Fools Die*, ch.55.

44 No, I never heard nothing about it, but when they name any disease after two guys, it's got to be terrible!

On Guillain-Barré syndrome. Quoted in Heller and Vogel *No Laughing Matter* (1986).

Pyrrhus of Epirus 319–272 BC

Greek king, renowned for his wars against the Romans. In 281 BC he fought Rome on behalf of the Tarentines and won the first battle, but with very high casualties (hence the expression a 'Pyrrhic victory'). He was killed in a street fight in Argos during a war with the Macedonians.

45 One more such victory, and we are lost!

279 BC After defeating the Romans at Asculeum. Quoted in Plutarch *Regum et imperatorum apophthegmata*, 184c.

Pythagoras 6c BC

Greek philosopher and mathematician. He founded a school in Crotona but was persecuted there and settled in Lucania. He taught an abstemious way of life and doctrine of transmigration, but is best remembered for his mathematical work.

46 There is geometry in the humming of the strings. There is music in the spacings of the spheres.

Quoted in Aristotle *Metaphysics*.

Qaboos, Sultan, of Oman 1940–

Sultan of Oman. On the deposition of his father in 1970 he became Oman's ruler. He is also Prime Minister, Minister of Foreign Affairs, Defence and Finance.

47 Don't wait for schools to be built. Teach the children under the nearest tree.

1995 Quoted by Rosalind Miles in 'An Oxonian in Oman', in *Oxford Today*, vol.7, no.2, Hilary Issue, 1995.

Qian, Zhang

48 They gave us our rice bowl and we don't want it broken.

1993 On the need to avoid offending the government that permitted broadcasts by Shanghai's Radio Orient. In the *New York Times*, 26 Apr.

Quant, Mary 1934–

English fashion designer. She opened a small boutique, Bazaar, in Chelsea in 1955. In the 1960s she became one of the best known designers of the 'swinging Britain' era when the simplicity of her designs, especially the mini-skirt, and the originality of her colours attracted international attention.

49 A fashionable woman wears clothes; the clothes don't wear her.

1966 *Quant by Quant*.

50 Fashion should be a game.

1966 *Quant by Quant*.

51 A woman is as young as her knee.

Attributed.

Quarles, Francis 1592–1644

English religious poet. His best-known works are *Emblems* (1635), a series of symbolic pictures with verse commentary, and a book of aphorisms *Enchyridion* (1640).

52 My soul; sit thou a patient looker-on;
Judge not the play before the play is done:
Her plot hath many changes, every day
Speaks a new scene; the last act crowns the play.

1630 *Epigram, Respice Finem*.

Quayle, Dan (J Danforth) 1947–

US politician. He became a member of Congress (1977–81) and the Senate (1981–8) and served as vice-president under George Bush (1988–92).

53 It doesn't help…when primetime TV has a character…bearing a child alone …just another lifestyle choice.

1992 Criticism of Murphy Brown, played by Candice Bergen. In the *Washington Post*, 21 May. The comment set off a great controversy about single mothers and freedom of choice.

Quennell, Sir Peter Courtney 1905–93

English biographer, Professor of English at Tokyo (1930). He wrote travel books, verse and novels, but is best known for his biographies of literary figures.

54 Every occupation, unless it employs the whole mind and satisfies the human creative instinct, is to some extent absurd; and about the advertising business what I chiefly disliked was not so much the work I did as its general atmosphere of unreality. We dealt in fairy-gold—in fugitive dreams and illusions.

1977 *The Marble Foot: an Autobiography, 1905–1938* (New York: Viking Press, 1977), p.227.

Quiller-Couch, Sir Arthur Thomas known as 'Q' 1863–1944

English writer and critic. His prominence as a critic dates from 1900, when he edited the *Oxford Book of English Verse*. He also wrote novels, short stories, children's books and poetry.

55 He that loves but half of Earth
Loves but half enough for me.
1896 'The Comrade'.

56 Not as we wanted it,
But as God granted it.
1896 'To Bearers'.

57 O the Harbour of Fowey
Is a beautiful spot,
And it's there I enjowey
To sail in a yot;
Or to race in a yacht
Round a mark or a buoy—
Such a beautiful spacht
Is the Harbour of Fuoy!
1899 *A Fowey Garland*, 'The Harbour of Fowey'.

58 The best is the best, though a hundred judges have declared it so.
1900 *The Oxford Book of English Verse*, preface.

59 Our fathers have, in process of centuries, provided this realm, its colonies and wide dependencies, with a speech as malleable and pliant as Attic, dignified as Latin, masculine, yet free of Teutonic guttural, capable of being precise as French, dulcet as Italian, sonorous as Spanish, and captaining all these excellences to its service.
1900 *The Oxford Book of English Verse*, preface.

60 Literature is not an abstract science, to which exact definitions can be applied. It is an Art rather, the success of which depends on personal persuasiveness, on the author's skill to give as on ours to receive.
1913 Inaugural lecture as Professor of English at Cambridge University.

61 Gilbert had a baddish streak or two in him; and one in particular which was not only baddish but so thoroughly caddish that no critic can ignore or,

in my view, extenuate it. The man, to summarize, was essentially cruel, and delighted in cruelty.
1929 Of W S Gilbert. *Studies in Literature*, 3rd series, 'Lecture on W.S. Gilbert', no.4.

62 There was an old man of St Omer
Who objected, 'This town's a misnomer;
You've no right to translate
And beatificate
A simple digamma in Homer.'
1941 'A Limerick', in *Chanticlere*, Michaelmas Term.

63 Swinburne is just emptiness to me as he gets older, and the more maddening as he goes on exploiting a heavenly gift. I wish he had just shut up, like Coleridge, and left us surmising wonders.
Quoted in A L Rowse *Quiller-Couch: a Portrait of 'Q'* (1988).

Quin, James 1693–1766

English actor. A performer in the tradition of heroic tragedy, whose most acclaimed roles included Falstaff, he outlived the popularity of the bombastic declamatory style of which he was the master but steadfastly refused to change with the times. He was also noted for his fiery temper.

64 If the young fellow is right, I and the rest of the players have been all wrong.
c.1741 Of David Garrick and his revolutionary, more naturalistic acting style. Attributed.

Quindlen, Anna 1953–

US journalist and author. She worked as a reporter for the *New York Times* (1977–81) and is now a syndicated columnist. She won the Pulitzer Prize for Commentary in 1992 and was named Woman of the Year, 1991 by *Glamour* Magazine.

65 The purse is the mirror of the soul.
1987 In the *New York Times*, 16 Dec.

Quine, Willard Van Orman 1908–

US philosopher and logician, Professor of Philosophy at Harvard (1948–78). He wrote many works on logic and language, including *Two Dogmas of Empiricism* (1951) and *Word and Object* (1960).

66 To define an expression is, paradoxically speaking, to explain how to get along without it. To define is to eliminate.
1987 *Quiddities*, 'Definition'.

67 We can applaud the state lottery as a public subsidy of intelligence, for it yields public income that is calculated to lighten the tax burden of us prudent abstainers at the expense of the benighted masses of wishful thinkers.
1987 *Quiddities*, 'Gambling'.

Quinet, Edgar 1803–75

French writer and politician.

68   *La famille des Bourbons est un poignard que l'étranger en 1814 a laissé dans le coeur de la France: changez le manche comme il vous plaira, dorez la lame si vous voulez, le poignard reste poignard.*

The Bourbon family is a dagger which the foreigner left in the heart of France in 1814: change the haft if you please, gild the blade if you will, the dagger remains a dagger.
1877 *Oeuvres,* vol.3, p.267.

Quinn, Jane Bryant   1939–

US journalist and financial pundit. Her works include *Everyone's Money Book* (1979) and *Making the Most of Your Money* (1991).

69   Half of them don't know what's going to happen tomorrow and the other half don't know they don't know.
1994 Of stock market players. On CNN TV, 4 Apr.

Quintilian, Marcus Fabius Quintilianus

c.35—c.100 AD

Roman rhetorician born in Spain. He studied oratory at Rome and settled there as an advocate and teacher of rhetoric. His pupils included Pliny the Younger. His reputation rests on his *Institutio Oratoria* ('Education of an orator').

70   *Mendaces memorem esse oportere.*

Liars need to have good memories.
Institutio Oratoria, 4.2.9.1 (translated by H E Butler, 1968).

71   *Scribitur ad narrandum, non ad probandum.*

It is written for the purpose of narrative, not of proof.
Of history. *Institutio Oratoria,* 10.1.31 (translated by H E Butler, 1968).

Quiroga, Horacio   1878–1938

Uruguayan short-story writer, who spent most of his life in the Argentinian province of Misiones, where most of his stories, generally dealing with morbid themes, are set. He committed suicide in a charity hospital.

72   *Se comprende muy bien que el advenimiento del cinematógrafo haya sido para mí el comienzo de un nueva era, por la cual cuento las noches sucesivas en que he salido mareado y pálido del cine, porque he dejado mi corazón…en la pantalla que impregnó por tres cuartos de hora el encanto de Brownie Vernon.*

It is easy to understand that, for me, cinema was the beginning of a new era which marked my nights, one after the other, as I left the theatre, dizzy and pale after leaving my heart on the screen…on that screen that for forty-five minutes was impregnated by Brownie Vernon's charm.
1921 *Anaconda,* 'Miss Dorothy Phillips, mi esposa' ('Miss Dorothy Phillips, My Wife').

Raban, Jonathan   1942–

English writer. He has written novels and literary criticism, but is best known for his travel books. He now lives in the US.

73   The Falklands held a mirror up to our own islands, and it reflected, in brilliantly sharp focus, all our injured belittlement, our sense of being beleaguered, neglected and misunderstood.
1986 *Coasting,* ch.3.

74   If we live inside a bad joke, it is up to us to learn, at best and worst, to tell it well.
1986 *Coasting,* ch.6.

75   Good travel books are novels at heart.
Recalled by Christopher Lehmann-Haupt in the *New York Times,* 26 Jan 1987, reviewing Raban's novel *Coasting* (1987).

76   The mythical America…—that marvellous, heroic, sentimental land—was an object of faith. It challenged you to make the believer's leap over the rude facts at your feet.
1990 *Hunting Mister Heartbreak,* ch.2.

Rabelais, François   c.1494–c.1553

French humanist and satirist, who began his career as a Franciscan monk. He studied Greek and Latin as well as medicine, law and philology, and wrote two novels under the pseudonym Alcofribas Nasier.

77   *Mieux est de ris que de larmes écrire Pour ce que rire est le propre de l'homme.*

It is better to write of laughter than of tears For laughter is the basis of humankind.
1532 *Gargantua,* Aux lecteurs.

78   *L'odeur du vin, ô combien plus est friande, riante, priante, plus céleste et délicieuse que d'huile!*

The odour of wine, oh how much sweeter, cheerful, pleasing, heavenly and delicious it is than oil!
1532 *Gargantua,* Prologue de l'Auteur.

79   *Rompre l'os et sucer la substantifique mo'lle.*

Break the bone and suck out the very substance.
1532 *Gargantua,* Prologue de l'Auteur.

80   *L'appétit vient en mangeant.*

Appetite comes with eating.
1532 *Gargantua,* bk.1, ch.5.

81   *Du cheval donné toujours regardait en la gueule.*

Always look a gift horse in the mouth.
1532 *Gargantua,* bk.1, ch.11.

82   *Lever matin n'est point bonheur; Boire matin est le meilleur.*

Getting up in the morning does not make you happy;

Drinking in the morning is the best.
1532 *Gargantua*, bk.1, ch.22.

83 *Nature n'endure mutations soudaines sans grande violence.*

Nature does not endure sudden changes without great violence.
1532 *Gargantua*, bk.1, ch.23.

84 *Thésauriser est fait de vilain.*

To hoard is a villainous act.
1532 *Gargantua*, bk.1, ch.33.

85 *Jamais je ne m'assujettis aux heures: les heures sont faites pour l'homme, et non l'homme pour les heures.*

I never subject myself to hours: hours are made for men; men are not made for hours.
1532 *Gargantua*, bk.1, ch.41.

86 *En leur règle n'était que cette clause: FAIS CE QUE VOUDRAS.*

In their laws there was but this one clause: DO WHAT YOU WISH.
1532 *Gargantua*, bk.1, ch.57.

87 Science without conscience is the soul's perdition.
1534 *Pantagruel*, bk.2, ch.8.

88 *Il avait soixante et trois manières d'en trouver toujours à son besoin, dont la plus honorable et la plus commune était par façon de larcin furtivement fait.*

He had sixty-three ways to find the money when he needed it, the most honourable and most ordinary of which was to steal secretively.
1534 *Gargantua*, bk.2, ch.16.

89 *Un fol enseigne bien un sage.*

A fool has a lot to teach a wise man.
1546 *Tiers Livre*, pt.37.

90 *O que trois et quatre fois heureux sont ceux qui plantent choux!*

Oh, those who plant cabbages are three and four times happier than the rest of us!
1548 *Quart Livre*, pt.18.

91 *Pantagruélisme…est certaine gaieté d'esprit confite en mépris des choses fortuites.*

Pantagruelism is a certain liveliness of mind made in contempt of chance happenings.
1552 *Quart Livre*, Prologue de l'auteur.

92 *Ignorance est mère de tous les maux.*

Ignorance is the mother of all evils.
1564 *Cinquième Livre*, pt.7.

93 Abandon yourself to Nature's truths, and let nothing in this world be unknown to you.
Quoted in J H Plumb (ed) *The Horizon Book of the Renaissance* (1961).

Rabi, Isidor Isaac 1898–1988

US physicist, born in Austria. He taught physics at Columbia from 1929 and served as an adviser to the US Atomic Energy Commission. Rabi won the 1944 Nobel Prize in Physics for his discovery and measurement of the radio-frequency spectra of atomic nuclei.

94 It is only in science, I find, that we can get outside ourselves. It's realistic, and to a great degree verifiable, and it has this tremendous stage on which it plays. I have the same feeling—to a certain degree—about some religious expressions…but only to a certain degree. For me, the proper study of mankind is science, which also means that the proper study of mankind is man.
Quoted in Jeremy Bernstein *Experiencing Science* (1978).

Rachmaninov, Sergey Vasilyevich

1873–1943

Russian composer and pianist, who settled in the US in 1918, best known for his piano music. His style epitomizes the lush romanticism of the later 19c, still apparent in his last major composition, *Rhapsody on a Theme of Paganini* (1934).

95 My dear hands. Farewell, my poor hands.
On being told that he was dying of cancer. Quoted in H Schonberg *The Great Pianists* 1964.

Racine, Jean 1639–99

French court dramatist who studied at Port Royal and went on to write many of his dramatic works for performance there.

96 *Ah! je l'ai trop aimé pour ne le point haïr!*

Oh! I loved him too much not to hate him now!
1667 *Andromaque*, act 2, sc.1.

97 *Les témoins sont fort chers, et n'en a pas qui veut.*

Witnesses are expensive and not everyone can afford them.
1668 *Les Plaideurs*, act 3, sc.3.

98 *J'aimais jusqu'à ses pleurs que je faisais couler.*

I loved even the tears which I made her cry.
1669 *Britannicus*, act 2, sc.2.

99 *J'embrasse mon rival, mais c'est pour l'étouffer.*

If I embrace my rival, it is to strangle him.
1669 *Britannicus*, act 4, sc.3.

1 Crime, like virtue, has its degrees.
1677 *Phèdre*, act 4, sc.2.

2 *Pensez-vous être saint et juste impunément?*

You think you can be holy and righteous with impunity?
1691 *Athalie*, act 1, sc.1.

Radisson, Pierre-Esprit 1636–1710

French traveller, explorer of New France.

3 We were Caesars, there being nobody to contradict us.

Attributed boast of the *coureur de bois* in the Canadian North-West. Quoted in Arthur T Adams (ed) *The Explorations of Pierre-Esprit Radisson* (1961).

Rae, John 1931–

English writer.

4 War is, after all, the universal perversion.

1960 *The Custard Boys*, ch.13.

Rahner, Karl 1904–84

German Jesuit priest, who taught at Innsbruck and Munich and who was widely recognized as a leading Roman Catholic theologian.

5 But there is yet another form of this hidden heresy, and, paradoxically, it can affect those who are proudest of their long-standing and unimpeachable orthodoxy; heresy in the form of indifference.

1963 'Natur und Gnade' in *Fragen der Theologie Heute* (translated by Dinah Wharton as *Nature and Grace*, 1963).

Rainborowe, Thomas 1598–1648

English soldier.

6 The poorest He that is in England hath a life to live as well as the greatest He, and therefore, truly Sirs, I think that every man that is to live under a Government ought first, by his own consent, to put himself under that Government.

1647 Said to Cromwell during the Army Debates, Putney, 29 Oct.

Raine, Craig Anthony 1944–

English poet. His collections include *A Martian Sends a Postcard Home* (1979) and *Rich* (1984).

7 We live in the great indoors:
the vacuum cleaner grazes
over the carpet, lowing,
its udder a swollen wobble.

1978 'An Inquiry into Two Inches of Ivory'.
▷ See Austen 52:60.

8 Caxtons are mechanical birds with many wings
and some are treasured for their markings.

1979 'A Martian Sends a Postcard Home'.

9 But time is tied to the wrist
or kept in a box, ticking with impatience.

1979 'A Martian Sends a Postcard Home'.

10 The mind is a museum
to be looted at night.

1984 'The Grey Boy'.

Raine, Kathleen Jessie 1908–

English poet and critic. Her poetry reflects a mystical, visionary appreciation of nature, and she is a sympathetic critic of symbolists such as Blake, Hopkins and Yeats.

11 Nowadays harmony comes almost as a shock.

Letter to Arthur Bliss.

Raleigh, Sir Walter 1552–1618

English courtier, navigator and poet. His writings include lyric poems, *The Discovery of Guyana* (1596) and an unfinished *History of the World* (1614). Implicated in a plot to overthrow Queen Elizabeth, his death sentence was suspended until 1618, when he was beheaded.

12 If all the world and love were young,
And truth in every shepherd's tongue
These pretty pleasures might me move
To live with thee and be thy love.

c.1592 'The Nymph's Reply to the Shepherd', a response to Marlowe's 'The Passionate Shepherd to His Love', attributed to Raleigh.
▷ See Marlowe 655:31.

13 Give me my scallop-shell of quiet,
My staff of faith to walk upon,
My scrip of joy, immortal diet,
My bottle of salvation,
My gown of glory, hope's true gage,
And thus I'll take my pilgrimage.

1604 *The Passionate Man's Pilgrimage*.

14 What is our life? a play of passion;
Our mirth the music of division;
Our mothers' wombs the tiring-houses be
Where we are dressed for this short comedy.
Heaven the judicious sharp spectator is,
That sits and marks still who doth act amiss;
Our graves that hide us from the searching sun
Are like drawn curtains when the play is done.
Thus march we, playing, to our latest rest,
Only we die in earnest—that's no jest.

1612 'On the Life of Man'.

15 I shall never be persuaded that God hath shut up all light of learning within the lantern of Aristotle's brain.

1614 *The History of the World*.

16 Even such is Time, which takes in trust
Our youth, our joys, and all we have,
And pays us but with age and dust,
Who in the dark and silent grave
When we have wandered all our ways
Shuts up the story of our days,
And from which earth, and grave, and dust
The Lord shall raise me up, I trust.

1628 'The Author's Epitaph, Made By Himself'. Poem written the night before his death.

Ramos, Graciliano 1892–1953

Brazilian novelist. In 1936 he was arrested and imprisoned, and on his release settled in Rio de Janeiro. His work explores the lives of characters shaped by the rural misery of northeast Brazil.

17 *Sempre que os homens sabidos lhe diziam palavras difíceis, ele saía logrado. Sobressaltava-se escutando-as. Evidentemente só serviam para encobrir ladroeiras. Mas eram bonitas.*

   Whenever men with book learning used big words in dealing with him, he came out the loser. It startled him just to hear those words. Obviously they were just a cover for robbery. But they sounded nice.
   1938 *Vidas secas* (translated as *Barren Lives*, 1965), 'Contas'.

Ramsey, Sir Alf(red) 1922–99

English footballer and manager. A player with Southampton and Tottenham Hotspur, he managed Ipswich Town in the early 1960s and went on to manage the England side that won the World Cup in 1966.

18 I feel like jumping over the moon.
   1962 Quoted in Nigel Rees *Dictionary of Popular Phrases* (1990). This is one of the earliest records of the phrase 'over the moon' being used in the context of football.

19 Listen to them moan, but those people will be going mad if we beat West Germany by a goal in the World Cup Final.
   1966 Of press criticism after England lost against West Germany in February, several months before England won the World Cup. Quoted in Bryon Butler *The Official History of the Football Association* (1986).

20 You've beaten them once. Now go out and bloody beat them again.
   1966 Addressing his players when the World Cup final went into extra time.

Rand, Ayn 1905–82

Russian-born US novelist, screenwriter and ardent propagandist for her philosophy of self-interest against the altruistic tendencies of the welfare state. Her novels include *The Fountainhead* (1943) and *Atlas Shrugged* (1957).

21 The entire history of science is a progression of exploded fallacies, not of achievements.
   1957 *Atlas Shrugged.*

Randall, Clarence Beldan 1891–1967

US businessman, chief executive officer of Inland Steel. He wrote several books on business.

22 Every man who has lived his life to the full, should, by the time his senior years are reached, have established a reserve inventory of unfinished thinking.
   1963 *Sixty-five Plus.*

23 The leader must know, must know that he knows and must be able to make it abundantly clear to those about him that he knows.
   1964 *Making Good in Management.*

Randall, Dudley 1914–

US poet and librarian. He established the Broadside Press, which prints the work of black US poets, including his own books.

24 Musing on roses and revolutions,
   I saw night close down on the earth like a great dark wing.
   1968 *Cities Burning*, 'Roses and Revolutions'.

25 I saw dawn upon them like the sun a vision
   of a time when all men walk proudly through the earth
   and the bombs and missiles lie at the bottom of the ocean
   like the bones of dinosaurs buried under the shale of eras.
   1968 *Cities Burning*, 'Roses and Revolutions'.

26 Then washed in the brightness of this vision,
   I saw how in its radiance would grow and be nourished and suddenly
   burst into terrible and splendid bloom
   the blood-red flower of revolution.
   1968 *Cities Burning*, 'Roses and Revolutions'.

Ranjitsinhji, Prince 1872–1933

Indian nobleman and England cricketer. A star batsman with Sussex and England, he succeeded as Jam Sahib of Nawanagar in 1906 (Maharaja in 1918), and did much to modernize and improve conditions in his home state.

27 He turned the old one-stringed instrument into a many-chorded lyre… W.G. discovered batting; he turned its many narrow straight channels into one great winding river.
   1897 Of W G Grace. *The Jubilee Book of Cricket.*

28 Find out where the ball is, get there; hit it.
   Explaining his tactics as a batsman. Quoted in Colin Jarman *The Guinness Dictionary of Sports Quotations* (1990).

Rankin, Jeanette 1880–1973

US pacifist and politician, the first woman in Congress. She voted against US entry into both World Wars and demonstrated against the war in Vietnam.

29 As a woman I can't go to war, and I refuse to send anyone else.
   Quoted in Hannah Josephson *Lady in Congress* (1974).

30 You can no more win a war than you can win an earthquake.
   Quoted in Hannah Josephson *Lady in Congress* (1974).

Ransom, John Crowe 1888–1974

US poet and critic. He was an influential figure in the rise of the New Criticism movement in the US, and an important Southern poet.

31 Here lies a lady of beauty and high degree.
Of chills and fever she died, of fever and chills,
The delight of her husband, her aunts, an infant of three,
And of medicos marvelling sweetly on her ills.
1924 *Chills and Fever*, 'Here Lies a Lady'.

32 The little cousin is dead, by foul subtraction,
A green bough from Virginia's aged tree.
1924 *Chills and Fever*, 'Dead Boy'.

33 Tawny are the leaves turned but they still hold,
And it is harvest; what shall this land produce?
A meagre hill of kernels, a runnel of juice;
Declension looks from our land, it is old.
Therefore let us assemble, dry, gray, spare,
And mild as yellow air.
1924 *Chills and Fever*, 'Antique Harvesters'.

34 The curse of hell upon the sleek upstart
That got the Captain finally on his back
And took the red red vitals of his heart
And made the kites to whet their beaks clack clack.
1924 *Chills and Fever*, 'Captain Carpenter'.

35 Two evils, monstrous either one apart,
Possessed me, and were long and loath at going:
A cry of Absence, Absence, in the heart,
And in the wood the furious winter blowing.
1924 *Chills and Fever*, 'Winter Remembered'.

36 And if no Lethe flows beneath your casement,
and when ten years have not brought full effacement,
Philosophy was wrong, and you may meet.
1924 *Grace After Meat*, 'Parting At Dawn'.

37 Old Hodge stays not his hand, but whips to kennel
The renegade. God's peace betide the souls
Of the pure in heart. But in the box that fennel
Grows around, are two red eyes that stare like coals.
1927 *Two Gentlemen in Bonds*, 'Dog'.

38 God have mercy on the sinner
Who must write with no dinner,
No gravy and no grub,
No pewter and no pub,
No belly and no bowels,
Only consonants and vowels.
1955 *Poems and Essays*, 'Survey of Literature'.

Raphael, Frederic 1931–

British novelist and screenwriter.

39 City of perspiring dreams.
1976 Of Cambridge. *The Glittering Prizes*, ch.3.

Rapoport, Anatol 1911–

Canadian social philosopher and peace advocate.

40 Cooperate on move one; thereafter, do whatever the other player did the previous move.
The two commands for his computer program, Tit for Tat, designed at the University of Toronto. It outperformed all other programs at an international computer tournament in 1979, and it continues to excel in tournaments. The program initiates reciprocal cooperation yet responds in kind to provocation.

Rattigan, Terence 1911–77

English playwright.

41 You can be in the Horseguards and still be common, dear.
1954 *Separate Tables*.

Rauschenberg, Robert 1925–

US artist, whose paintings and collages incorporate images and objects from everyday life. *Gloria* (1956) is a typical example of his 'combines', or collages.

42 I don't like masterpieces having one-night stands in collectors' homes between auctions.
1989 On quick-turn over profits on his work. In the *New York Times*, 10 May.

Ravel, (Joseph) Maurice 1875–1937

French composer. A pupil of Fauré, his innovative early compositions include *Schéhérazade* and the *Pavane pour une infante défunte* (both 1899). Other notable works include the ballet *Daphnis et Chloé* (1912), and *Boléro* (1928).

43 I've still so much music in my head. I have said nothing. I have so much more to say.
1937 Spoken on his deathbed. Quoted in Jourdan-Morhange *Ravel et nous* (1945).

44 A piece for orchestra without music.
Of his *Boléro*. Quoted in R Nichols *Ravel* (1977).

Ravitch, Diane Silvers 1938–

US historian, writer and government official. She left Teachers College, Columbia to join the US Department of Education in 1991.

45 The person who knows 'how' will always have a job. The person who knows 'why' will always be his boss.
1985 Speech at Reed College commencement. Reported in *Time*, 17 Jun.

Ray, Dixy Lee 1914–94

US politician and administrator.

46 The general public has long been divided into two parts: those who think that science can do anything, and those who are afraid that it will.
1973 In *New Scientist*, 5 Jul.

Ray, James Earl 1928–98

US assassin of Martin Luther King. He was imprisoned in 1960 for armed robbery but escaped in 1967 and shot King. He was apprehended in London and sentenced in Memphis to 99 years.

47 I was in Tennessee 24 hours and got 99 years.
1988 On beginning the 20th year of his prison sentence for the assassination of Martin Luther King. In *Life*, March.

Rayburn, Sam(uel Taliaferro) 1882–1961

US politician. A Democrat, he represented Texas (1913–61) and was Speaker of the House for a record 17 terms between 1940 and 1961. He was a supporter of Roosevelt's New Deal.

48 I like to make running water walk.
Quoted in Valton J Young *The Speaker's Agent* (1956).

49 These…society women never serve chilli.
His reason for not attending parties. Quoted in David Brinkley *Washington Goes to War* (1988).

50 Go along and get along.
On politics as a process of accommodation, recalled by former Speaker Gerald R Ford in the *Washington Times*, 24 May 1995.

Read, Sir Herbert Edward 1893–1968

English poet and art critic. Editor of the *Burlington Magazine* (1933–9) and a Professor of Fine Art at Edinburgh (1931–3), he wrote works on art criticism and *Naked Warriors* (1919), a poetry collection inspired by his war experiences.

51 I saw him stab
and stab again
A well-killed Boche.
1919 *Naked Warriors*, 'The Scene of War, 4. The Happy Warrior'.

52 This is the happy warrior,
This is he.
1919 *Naked Warriors*, 'The Scene of War, 4. The Happy Warrior'.

53 It is defiant—the desperate act of men too profoundly convinced of the rottenness of our civilization to want to save a shred of its respectability.
1936 Catalogue of the International Surrealist Exhibition, New Burlington Galleries, London, Jun/Jul, introduction.

54 But one thing we learned: there is no glory in the deed
Until the soldier wears a badge of tarnished braid.
1948 'To a Conscript of 1940'.

55 It will be a gay world. There will be lights everywhere except in the minds of men, and the fall of the last civilization will not be heard above the din.
1964 Quoted in Hoggart and Johnston, *An Idea of Europe* (1987), 'Pyramids and Planes'.

Reade, Charles 1814–84

English novelist and playwright.

56 Take courage, my friend, the devil is dead!
1861 *The Cloister and the Hearth*.

Reagan, Nancy 1923–

US actress and First Lady, second wife of US President Ronald Reagan.

57 If the President has a bully pulpit, then the First Lady has a white glove pulpit…more refined, restricted, ceremonial, but it's a pulpit all the same.
1988 In the *New York Times*, 10 Mar.

58 I'm more aware if somebody is trying to end-run him…it just never occurs to him.
1988 On protecting her husband. In *Time*, 28 Nov.

59 For eight years I was sleeping with the President, and if that doesn't give you special access, I don't know what does!
1989 *My Turn* (with William Novack).

Reagan, Ronald Wilson 1911–

US Republican politician, 40th President (1981–9), a radio sports announcer and film star. A Democrat turned Republican, he won nomination in 1980, defeating Carter to become President. He introduced economic reform, took a strong anti-communist stand and introduced the Strategic Defence Initiative ('Star Wars'). In 1981 he was wounded in an assassination attempt. Re-elected in 1984, he achieved a major arms-reduction accord with Gorbachev. His reputation was tarnished by the Iran–Contra affair.

60 To sit back hoping that some day, some way, someone will make things right is to go on feeding the crocodile, hoping that he will eat you last—but eat you he will.
1974 CBS News, 7 Nov.

61 Recession is when your neighbour loses his job. Depression is when you lose yours.
1980 Election campaign speech, Jersey City, 1 Sep.

62 I can tell a lot about a fellow's character by the way that he eats jelly beans.
1981 In the *Daily Mail*, Jan.

63 This is not the end of anything. This is the beginning of everything.
1984 On his re-election. In *Time*, Nov.

64 We are not going to tolerate these attacks from outlaw states, run by the strangest collection of misfits, looney tunes and squalid criminals since the advent of the Third Reich.

1985 Speech after terrorist attacks by Shi'ite Muslims, Jul.

65 We must say something but not much because I'm being held out to dry.

1986 Comment at a meeting with National Security Council advisers, 10 Nov. Quoted by Theodore Draper *A Very Thin Line* (1991).

66 We make history and changing it is within our power.

1987 On welcoming Soviet Premier Mikhail S Gorbachev to the White House, 8 Dec.

67 We don't know where that money came from and we don't know who had it and we don't know where it went.

1988 Of the Iran-Contra funding. In the *New York Times*, 17 Mar.

68 I paid for this microphone.

1988 To a New Hampshire moderator who tried to keep President Reagan from speaking on behalf of other candidates. Reported in *Congressional Quarterly*, 23 May.

69 There is our little bungalow down there.

1989 On viewing the White House from a helicopter the day he left office. Quoted in the *Washington Post*, 22 Apr 1991.

70 Washington is a sieve…it was virtually impossible to find out who was doing the leaking and shut them up.

1990 Deposition on the Iran-Contra arms sales. In the *New York Times*, 23 Feb.

71 Politics is just like show business…a hell of an opening, you coast for a while, you have a hell of a closing.

1995 In the *New York Times*, 23 Apr.

Reardon, Ray 1932–

Welsh snooker player. He was World Champion in 1970, 1973, 1976 and 1978.

72 I cannot remember anyone ever asking 'Who came second?' Can you?

Quoted in Colin Jarman *The Guinness Dictionary of Sports Quotations* (1990).

73 If I had to make the choice between staying married and playing snooker, snooker would win.

Quoted in Colin Jarman *The Guinness Dictionary of Sports Quotations* (1990).

Red Cloud original name *Mahpiua Luta*
1822–1909

Oglala Sioux chief who led the Indian war against the Americans.

74 You have heard the sound of the white soldier's axe on the Little Piney. His presence here is…an insult to the spirits of our ancestors. Are we to give up their sacred graves to be ploughed for corn? Dakotas, I am for war.

1866 Speech before war council at Fort Laramie, Wyoming.

Redmond, John Edward 1856–1918

Irish politician. A champion of Home Rule, he was Chairman of the Nationalist Party in 1900. He declined a seat in Asquith's coalition ministry (1915), but supported World War I, deplored the Irish rebellion, and opposed Sinn Féin.

75 The government may tomorrow withdraw every one of their troops from Ireland. Ireland will be defended by her armed sons from foreign invasion, and for that purpose the armed Catholics in the south will be only too glad to join arms with the armed Protestant Ulsterman. Is it too much to hope that out of this situation a result may spring that will be good not merely for the Empire but for the future welfare and integrity of the Irish nation?

1914 Speech, House of Commons, 3 Aug.

Redon, Odilon 1840–1916

French Symbolist painter and graphic artist, also well-known for his work in pastel.

76 What distinguishes the artist from the dilettante? Only the pain that the artist feels. The dilettante looks only for pleasure in art.

c.1871 Journal entry, quoted in *Portfolio*, no.8, Spring 1964 (translated by Richard Howard).

77 All my originality consists…in giving life in human fashion to beings which are impossible according to the laws of possibility.

Quoted in Edward Lucie-Smith *Symbolist Art* (1972).

78 I am repelled by those who voice the word 'nature', without having any trace of it in their hearts.

Quoted in Edward Lucie-Smith *Symbolist Art* (1972).

Redtenbacher, Ferdinand 1818–83

German engineer, Professor of Mechanical Engineering, and author on the construction of machinery.

79 Thanks to his bodily form and thanks to his mind, [man] is a universal machine, capable of an infinite diversity of movement.

1840 *Resultate für den Maschinenbau* (published 1848).

Reed, Henry 1914–

English poet and dramatist. He is best known for his war poems, and for his radio plays, notably *The Private Life of Hilda Tablet*. 'Chard Whitlow' is a parody of T S Eliot's 'Burnt Norton'.

80 Today we have naming of parts. Yesterday,

We had daily cleaning. And tomorrow morning,
We shall have what to do after firing. But today,
Today we have naming of parts. Japonica
Glistens like coral in all of the neighbouring
  gardens
And to-day we have naming of parts.
1946 *Lessons of the War*, pt.1, 'Naming of Parts'.

81 We can slide it
Rapidly backwards and forwards: we call this
Easing the spring. And rapidly backwards and
  forwards
The early bees are assaulting and fumbling the
  flowers:
They call it easing the Spring.
1946 *Lessons of the War*, pt.1, 'Naming of Parts'.

82 There may be dead ground in between; and I may
    not have got
The knack of judging a distance; I will only venture
A guess that perhaps between me and the apparent
  lovers,
(Who, incidentally, appear by now to have
  finished,)
At seven o'clock from the houses, is roughly a
  distance
Of about one year and a half.
1946 *Lessons of the War*, pt.2, 'Judging Distances'.

83 As we get older we do not get any younger.
Seasons return, and today I am fifty-five,
And this time last year I was fifty-four,
And this time next year I shall be sixty-two.
1946 'Chard Whitlow (Mr Eliot's Sunday Evening Postscript)',
a parody of T S Eliot's style.

84 It is, we believe,
Idle to hope that the simple stirrup-pump
Can extinguish hell.
1946 'Chard Whitlow (Mr Eliot's Sunday Evening Postscript)'.

85 Modest? My word, no… He was an all-the-lights-
on man.
1953 *A Very Great Man Indeed*, radio play.

86 And the sooner the tea's out of the way, the sooner
we can get out the gin, eh?
1954 *The Private Life of Hilda Tablet*, radio play.

87 In a civil war, a general must know—and I'm afraid
it's a thing rather of instinct than of practice—he
must know exactly when to move over to the other
side.
1959 *Not a Drum was Heard: The War Memoirs of General
Gland*, unpublished radio play.

Reed, Ishmael Scott 1938–

US novelist, poet and publisher. He founded the
experimental literary magazine *East Village Other* in New

York. His best-known novel is *Yellow Back Radio Broke
Down*.

88 When State Magic fails unofficial magic becomes
stronger.
1968 *Yellow Back Radio Broke Down*, 'II. The Loop Garou Kid
Comes Back Mad'.

89 Hoo-doo, which in America flowered in New
Orleans, was an unorganized religion without ego-
games or death worship.
1968 *Yellow Back Radio Broke Down*, 'V. A Jigsaw of a Last
Minute Rescue'.

Reed, John 1887–1920

US writer and journalist. He is best known as a war
correspondent in Mexico and Europe, and for his reports
from Russia in the wake of the revolution.

90 Ten Days That Shook The World.
1919 Title of book.

91 In the relations of a weak Government and a
rebellious people there comes a time when every act
of the authorities exasperates the masses, and every
refusal to act excites their contempt.
1919 *Ten Days That Shook The World*, ch.3.

Rees-Mogg, William Rees-Mogg, Baron
1928–

English journalist. He joined the *Financial Times* (1952)
and the *Sunday Times* (1960), becoming Deputy Editor
(1964). In 1967 he assumed editorship of *The Times*,
which he held for 14 years. In 1988 he headed the new
Broadcasting Standards Council.

92 Information, free from interest or prejudice, free
from the vanity of the writer or the influence of a
Government, is as necessary to the human mind as
pure air and water to the human body.
1970 *Christian Science Monitor*, 22 Sep.

Regan, Donald Thomas 1918–

US financier, writer and lecturer. He was chair of Merrill
Lynch & Co. Inc. (1973–81), secretary to the US
Treasury Department (1981–85) and White House Chief
of Staff (1985–87) for President Reagan. Following the
Tower Commission Report on the Iran Arms-for-
Hostages affair, he was forced to resign.

93 The buck doesn't even *pause* here.
1987 Of his job. In the New York *Times*, 31 Jul.
▷ See Truman 1030:33.

94 I thought I was Chief of Staff to the President, not
to his wife.
1988 On submitting his resignation. *For the Record*.

95 Mistaken in its assumptions, defective in its
evidence and wrong in its conclusions.

1988 Of the congressional report faulting him on lack of direction and public disclosure of Iran-Contra arms sales. *For the Record.*

Reger, Max 1873–1916

German composer. He was Director of Music (1907) and professor (1908) at Leipzig University. His work includes organ music, piano concertos, choral works and songs.

96 *Ich sitze in dem kleinsten Zimmer in meinem Hause. Ich habe Ihre Kritik vor mir. Im nächsten Augenblick wird sie hinter mir sein.*

I am sitting in the smallest room of my house. I have your review before me. In a moment it will be behind me.

1906 Written in response to an unfavourable review by Rudolf Louis. Quoted in Nicolas Slonimsky *Lexicon of Musical Invective* (2nd edn, 1969), p.139.

Reid, Alastair 1926–

Scottish-born poet, essayist and translator of Spanish and Latin American literature. After serving in the Navy in World War II, he became a professional itinerant, his only permanent address the *New Yorker*. His witty poetry collections include *Weathering* (1978).

97 The point is the seeing—the grace
   beyond recognition, the ways
   of the bird rising, unnamed, unknown,
   beyond the range of language, beyond its noun.
   Eyes open on growing, flying, happening,
   and go on opening. Manifold, the world
   dawns on unrecognizing, realizing eyes.
   Amazement is the thing.
   Not love, but the astonishment of loving.

1978 *Weathering*, 'Growing, Flying, Happening'.

Reid, Thomas Mayne 1818–83

Irish writer of boys' stories. After work as a journalist and soldier in the Mexican War of 1847, he won a wide readership with a string of adventure tales, which included such titles as *The Rifle Rangers* (1850), *War Trail* (1857) and *Boy Tar* (1859).

98 Praise the sports of the land
   And water, each one—
   The bath by the beach, or the yacht on the sea—
   But of all the sweet pleasures
   Known under the sun;
   A good game of Croquet's the sweetest to me.

1863 Quoted in Colin Jarman *The Guinness Dictionary of Sports Quotations* (1990).

Remarque, Erich Maria 1898–1970

German novelist, who served in World War I. His novels were banned by the Nazis in 1933, and he emigrated to the US in 1939.

99 *Im Westen nichts Neues.*

All Quiet on the Western Front.

1929 Title of novel.

Renan, (Joseph) Ernest 1823–92

French philologist and historian, whose studies led him to abandon traditional faith. His works include *Histoire général des langues sémitiques* (1854), *Études d'histoire religieuse* (1856) and the controversial *Vie de Jésus* (1863), the first of a series on the history of Christianity.

1 War is a condition of progress; the whip-cut that prevents a country from going to sleep and forces satisfied mediocrity to shake off its apathy.

1871 *La Réforme Intellectuelle et Morale.*

Reno, Janet 1938–

US Attorney General. She was assistant state attorney in Florida from 1978 until 1993 when she was appointed US Attorney–General.

2 I'm just an awkward old maid with a very great affection for men.

1993 Denying rumours that she was a lesbian. In the *Washington Times*, 22 Feb.

3 Nothing can make me madder than lawyers who don't care about others.

1993 Address to the American Bar Association. In the *New York Times*, 9 Aug.

4 Vengeance is a personal reaction. But not one that government can indulge in.

1994 Opposing the death penalty. In the *New York Times*, 15 May.

5 I made the decision long ago that to be afraid would be to diminish my life.

1995 Interview in NPR broadcast, 18 Jul.

Renoir, Jean 1894–1979

French film director, son of Pierre Auguste Renoir. His *La Grande Illusion* (1937) and *La Bête Humaine* (1939) are among the masterpieces of the cinema.

6 Goodbye Mr Zanuck. It certainly has been a pleasure working for 16th Century Fox.

On leaving Hollywood. Attributed.

Renoir, Pierre Auguste 1841–1919

French Impressionist painter, born in Limoges. He exhibited with the Impressionists, and his *Moulin de la Galette* (1876) with sunlight filtering through leaves epitomizes his colourful, happy art. His visit to Italy in 1880 was followed by a series of *Bathers* (1884–7) in a more cold and classical style. He then returned to reds, orange, and gold to portray nudes in sunlight, a style which he continued to develop until his death. His works include *The Umbrellas* (c.1883) and *The Judgement of Paris* (c.1914).

7 There is something in painting which cannot be explained, and that something is essential. You come to nature with your theories, and nature knocks them all flat.

c.1915 Quoted in Ambroise Vollard *Renoir, An Intimate Record* (1930).

8 I have a horror of the word 'flesh', which has become so shopworn. Why not 'meat' while they're about it? What I like is skin, a young girl's skin that is pink and shows that she has a good circulation.

Quoted in Jean Renoir *Renoir, My Father* (translated by R and D Weaver, 1962).

9 The only reward one should offer an artist is to buy his work.

From Renoir's notebook quoted in L Nochlin *Impressionism and Post-Impressionism 1874-1904* (1966).

10 It is impossible to repeat in one period what was done in another. The point of view is not the same, any more than are the tools, the ideals, the needs, or the painters' techniques.

From Renoir's notebook quoted in L Nochlin *Impressionism and Post-Impressionism 1874-1904* (1966).

11 They were madmen, but they had in them that little flame which never dies.

On the Communards. Quoted in A J P Taylor *From Napoleon to the Second International* (1993).

12 Why shouldn't art be pretty? There are enough unpleasant things in the world.

Quoted in Ian Chilvers and Harold Osborne (eds) *The Oxford Dictionary of Art* (1994).

Repplier, Agnes 1858–1950

US writer and social critic.

13 Science may carry us to Mars, but it will leave the Earth peopled as ever by the inept.

1936 *In Pursuit of Laughter.*

Reston, James B(arrett) 1909–95

Scottish-born American journalist and author. He enjoyed a distinguished career with the *New York Times* and his national news reporting in World War II was recognized in a Pulitzer Prize (1945) and in his promotion to Chief of the Washington Bureau (1953–1964). He won a second Pulitzer Prize in 1957. He was vice-president of the *New York Times* (1969–74) and internationally respected for his political analysis.

14 Smarter than most of his colleagues in the Truman cabinet, but not smart enough to hide it.

1991 Of Secretary of State Dean Acheson. *Deadline.*

15 A little shorter than the Washington monument, erect, elegant, dogmatic, and ironically witty.

1991 Of Secretary of State Dean Acheson. *Deadline.*

16 He could strut sitting down.

1991 Of Senator Arthur Vandenberg. *Deadline.*

17 They were always…getting more credit than they deserved, more sorrow than they could bear, climbing into jobs before they were ready and failing just when they were succeeding.

1991 Of John F, Robert F and Edward M Kennedy. *Deadline.*

18 He not only knew a lot about foreign affairs, he *was* a foreign affair.

1991 Of former Secretary of State Henry A Kissinger. *Deadline.*

19 The American people…were like him: cheerful, optimistic, patriotic, inconsistent, and casually inattentive.

1991 Of President Ronald Reagan. *Deadline.*

Revlon, Charles Haskell 1906–75

US cosmetics salesman, founder with his brother Joseph and chemist Charles Lachman of Revlon Inc (1932). His success was due to initiatives such as giving exotic names to colours and also to intimidation and attacks on competitors.

20 I don't meet competition. I crush it.

1958 In *Time*, 16 Jun.

21 In the factory, we make cosmetics; in the store we sell hope.

Quoted in Andrew P Tobias *Fire and Ice* (1976), ch.8.

Reyes, Alfonso 1889–1959

Mexican poet, novelist, essayist, critic, educator and diplomat. His classical background and humanistic approach lend his writings a distinctive elegance.

22 *El orbe hispano nunca se vino abajo, ni siquiera a la caída del imperio español, sino que se ha multiplicado en numerosas facetas de ensanches todavía insospechados… No somos pueblos en estado de candor, que se deslumbren fácilmente con los instrumentos externos de que se acompaña la cultura, sino pueblos que heredan una vieja civilización y exigen la excelencia misma de la cultura.*

The Hispanic world never crumbled, not even after the Spanish Empire fell, but instead has multiplied itself in broad ways that are still largely unknown… Our people are not naive and are not blinded by the external tools that go together with culture; we are rather the inheritors of an old civilization, and we demand the excellence proper to culture itself.

1941 *Páginas escogidas*, 'Valor de la literatura hispanoamericana' (Translated as 'The Value of Hispanic American Literature').

Reynolds, Sir Joshua 1723–92

English painter, writer on art and the first President of the Royal Academy. One of the most important figures in the history of English painting.

23 A mere copier of nature never produces anything great.
1770 *Discourses on Art*, no.3, 14 Dec.

Rhodes, Cecil John 1853–1902

South African statesman. He entered the Cape House of Assembly, where he secured the charter for the British South Africa Company (1889), whose territory was later named Rhodesia. Prime Minister of Cape Colony (1890–6), he resigned after the Jameson raid (when the Boers defeated Dr Jameson's attempt to reach Johannesburg). During the Boer War of 1899–1902 he organized the defences of Kimberley.

24 Remember that you are an Englishman, and have consequently won first prize in the lottery of life.
Quoted in Peter Ustinov *Dear Me* (1977). This has also been attributed to Lord Milner.

Rhys, Jean pseudonym of *Ellen Gwendolen Rees Williams* 1894–1979

British novelist, born in the West Indies, of Welsh and Creole descent. Of her novels and short stories *Wide Sargasso Sea* (1966), redefining Charlotte Brontë's first Mrs Rochester, is the best known.

25 The perpetual hunger to be beautiful and that thirst to be loved which is the real curse of Eve.
1927 *The Left Bank*, 'Illusion'.

26 I wanted to be black. I always wanted to be black… Being black is warm and gay, being white is cold and sad.
1934 *Voyage in the Dark*, ch.1.

27 It's funny when you feel as if you don't want anything more in your life except to sleep, or else to lie without moving. That's when you can hear time sliding past you, like water running.
1934 *Voyage in the Dark*, ch.2.

28 Cold—cold as truth, cold as life. No, nothing can be as cold as life.
1934 *Voyage in the Dark*, ch.3.

29 The feeling of Sunday is the same everywhere, heavy, melancholy, standing still. Like when they say 'As it was in the beginning, is now, and ever shall be, world without end'.
1934 *Voyage in the Dark*, ch. 4, pt.1.

30 We will watch the sun set again—many times, and perhaps we'll see the Emerald Drop, the green flash that brings good fortune.
1966 *Wide Sargasso Sea*, pt.2.

31 There is no looking-glass here and I don't know what I am like now. I remember watching myself brush my hair and how my eyes looked back at me. The girl I saw was myself and yet not quite myself. Long ago when I was a child and very lonely I tried

to kiss her. But the glass was between us—hard, cold and misted over with my breath. Now they have taken everything away. What am I doing in this place and who am I?
1966 The consciousness of Antoinette Mason/Bertha Rochester at a point of intersection with the text *of Jane Eyre*. *Wide Sargasso Sea*, pt.3.

Ricardo, David 1772–1823

English political economist. He set up in business as a young man, and in 1817 produced his chief work, *Principles of Political Economy and Taxation*. In 1819 he became an MP, and was influential in the free-trade movement.

32 It is not to be understood that the natural price of labour, estimated even in food and necessaries, is absolutely fixed and constant. It varies at different times in the same country and very materially differs in different countries. It essentially depends on the habits and customs of the people.
1817 *Principles of Political Economy and Taxation*.

33 In every case, agricultural as well as manufacturing profits are lowered by a rise in the price of raw produce, if it be accompanied by a rise of wages_ The natural tendency of profits is to fall; for in the progress of society and wealth, the additional quantity of food required is obtained by the sacrifice of more and more labour.
1817 *Principles of Political Economy and Taxation*.

34 Like all other contracts, wages should be left to the fair and free competition of the market, and should never be controlled by the interference of the legislature.
1817 *Principles of Political Economy and Taxation*.

35 Possessing utility, commodities derive their exchangeable value from two sources: from their scarcity and from the labour required to obtain them. By far the greatest part of those goods which are the objects of desire, are procured by labour.
1817 *Principles of Political Economy and Taxation*.

36 The interest of the landlord is always opposed to the interests of every other class in the community.
1817 *Principles of Political Economy and Taxation*.

37 The natural price of labour is that price which is necessary to enable the labourers, one with another, to subsist and to perpetuate their race, without either increase or diminution.
1817 *Principles of Political Economy and Taxation*.

Rice, Grantland 1880–1954

US sports writer and poet. He is remembered for his colourful reporting style and popular verse.

38 For when the One Great Scorer comes

To write against your name,
He marks—not that you won or lost—
But how you played the game.
1941 *Only the Brave,* 'Alumnus Football'.

39 All wars are planned by old men
In council rooms apart.
1955 *The Final Answer,* 'The Two Sides of War'.

40 Play ball! Means something more than runs
Or pitches thudding into gloves!
Remember through the summer suns
This is the game your country loves.
Quoted in Colin Jarman *The Guinness Dictionary of Sports Quotations* (1990).

Rich, Adrienne Cecile 1929–

US poet. She is one of the most prominent feminist poets of her generation. Her best known work includes *Diving into the Wreck* (1973).

41 Weather abroad
And weather in the heart alike come on
Regardless of prediction.
1951 *A Change of World,* 'Storm Warnings'.

42 Love only what you do,
And not what you have done.
1955 *The Diamond Cutters and Other Poems,* 'The Diamond Cutters'.

43 Your mind now, moldering like wedding-cake,
heavy with useless experience, rich
with suspicion, rumour, fantasy,
crumbling to pieces under the knife-edge
of mere fact. In the prime of your life.
1963 *Snapshots of a Daughter-in-Law,* 'Snapshots of a Daughter-in-Law, 1'.

44 Only
a fact could be so dreamlike.
1966 *Necessities of Life,* 'Like This Together'.

45 Only where there is language is there world.
1969 *Leaflets,* 'The Demon Lover'.

46 All wars are useless to the dead.
1969 *Leaflets,* 'Implosions'.

47 I am an instrument in the shape
of a woman trying to translate pulsations
into images for the relief of the body
and the reconstruction of the mind.
1971 *The Will To Change,* 'Planetarium'.

48 It's exhilarating to be alive in a time of awakening
consciousness; it can also be confusing,
disorienting, and painful.
1971 Talk delivered to Forum on 'The Woman Writer in the Twentieth Century'. Collected as 'When We Dead Awaken: Writing as Re-Vision', in *College English,* Oct 1972.

49 the thing I came for:
the wreck and not the story of the wreck
the thing itself and not the myth.
1973 *Diving Into The Wreck,* 'Diving Into The Wreck'.

50 When did we begin to dress ourselves?
1973 *Diving Into The Wreck* 'Blood-Sister'.

51 Any woman's death diminishes me
1974 *Poems: Selected and New,* 'From An Old House In America, 16'.
▷ See Donne 339:23.

52 Without contemplating last and late
the true nature of poetry. The drive
to connect. The dream of a common language.
1978 *The Dream of a Common Language,* 'Origins and History of Consciousness'.

53 Since we're not young, weeks have to do time for
years of missing each other. Yet only this odd warp
in time tells me we're not young.
1978 *The Dream of a Common Language,* 'Twenty-One Love Poems, III'.

54 Anger and tenderness: my selves.
And now I can believe they breathe in me
as angels, not polarities.
1981 *A Wild Patience Has Taken Me This Far,* 'Integrity'.

55 I refuse to become a seeker for cures.
Everything that has ever
helped me has come through what already
lay stored in me.
1986 *Your Native Land, Your Life,* 'Sources, II'.

56 This is the day of atonement; but do my people
forgive me?
If a cloud knew loneliness and fear, I would be that
cloud.
1986 *Your Native Land, Your Life,* 'Yom Kippur, 1984'.

57 Experience is always larger than language.
1991 Interview in the *American Poetry Review,* Jan–Feb.

Richard of Devizes fl.c.1190

English Benedictine monk and chronicler.

58 *Si nolueris habitare cum turpidus, non habitatis Londonie.*

If you do not want to live among wicked people, do not live in London.
c.1192 *Chronicle of Richard of Devizes of the Time of King Richard I.*

Richard I known as 'the Lionheart' 1157–99

King of England (from 1189). He led the Crusaders in 1190 and after concluding a peace sailed for home (1191), but was captured by Leopold, Duke of Austria and handed over to Emperor Henry VI. Ransomed in

1194, he went to France where he warred against Philip II until he was killed in the siege of Chaluz.

59 *Si inuenissem emptorum, Londoniam uendidissem.*

If I could have found a buyer I would have sold London itself.

1190 Of his fundraising for the Crusade to Palestine. Quoted in Richard of Devizes *Chronicle of the Time of King Richard I* (c.1192).

Richards, Ann 1933–

US Governor. State Treasurer of Texas from 1982–90, she then became governor of Texas.

60 You can put lipstick on a hog, and it's still a pig.

1992 On Republicans' attempts to enhance their candidates. In *Sunday Morning*, CBS TV broadcast, 25 Oct.

Richards, Sir Gordon 1904–86

English jockey. In 34 seasons (1921–54) he was champion jockey 26 times, and rode 4870 winners. In 1953 he won his first Derby, on Pinza, and also received a knighthood.

61 Mother always told me my day was coming, but I never realized I'd end up being the shortest knight of the year.

1953 Quoted in Colin Jarman *The Guinness Dictionary of Sports Quotations* (1990).

Richards, I(vor) A(rmstrong) 1893–1979

English scholar and literary critic. He was the initiator of the influential 'New Criticism' school of textual criticism at Cambridge University in the 1920s.

62 To be forced by desire into any unwarrantable belief is a calamity.

1924 *Principles of Literary Criticism.*

63 Poetry…is capable of saving us; it is a perfectly possible means of overcoming chaos.

1926 *Science and Poetry*, ch. 7.

Richardson, Henry Handel pen-name of Ethel Florence Lindesay 1870–1946

Australian novelist, who settled in England in 1904. Her first novel was *Maurice Guest* (1908) but she made her name with a trilogy set in Australia, *The Fortunes of Richard Mahoney* (1917–29). She was nominated for the Nobel Prize in 1932.

64 You're blessed with a woman's brain: vague, slippery, inexact, interested only in the personal aspect of a thing.

1910 *The Getting of Wisdom*, ch.9.

Richardson, Tony (Cecil Antonio) 1928–91

British film and stage director. He made a number of highly acclaimed films at the beginning of the 1960s including *The Entertainer* (1960), *A Taste of Honey* (1961) and *Tom Jones* (1963) which won an Academy Award.

65 People in this country haven't got the cinema in their blood—the real creative talent has been drained off into theatre.

1961 On Britain. Quoted in the *Monthly Film Bulletin*, Apr 1993.

Richelieu, Armand Jean du Plessis, Cardinal and Duc de 1585–1642

French statesman. A protégé of the Regent Marie de' Medici, he became Minister of State (1624), and as Chief Minister to Louis XIV (1624–42) was effective ruler of France. He succeeded in destroying Huguenot power, securing universal obedience to the Bourbon monarchy, checking Habsburg power and enhancing France's international prestige, but his ruthless severity, his intrigues and his high taxes earned him the hatred of many.

66 Not least among the qualities in a great King is a capacity to permit his Ministers to serve him.

1688 *Testament Politique.*

67 Secrecy is the first essential in the affairs of State.

1688 *Testament Politique.*

68 When people are too comfortable, it is not possible to restrain them within the bounds of their duty… They may be compared to mules who, being accustomed to burdens, are spoilt by rest rather than labour.

1688 *Testament Politique.*

69 Wounds inflicted by the sword heal more easily than those inflicted by the tongue.

1688 *Testament Politique.*

Richler, Mordecai 1931–

Canadian novelist, journalist and essayist. His greatest works, including *The Apprenticeship of Duddy Kravitz* (1959), *St Urbain's Horseman* (1971) and *Joshua Then and Now* (1980), are darkly comic novels about the working-class Jewish community in Montreal in which he grew up.

70 Thousands of miles of wheat, indifference, and self-apology.

1971 Of Canada. *St Urbain's Horseman*, ch.1.

71 Tomorrow country then, tomorrow country now.

1971 Of Canada. *St Urbain's Horseman*, ch.1.

72 Even in Paris, I remained a Canadian. I puffed hashish, but I didn't inhale.

1971 *St Urbain's Horseman*, ch.2. The last phrase was later popularized by Bill Clinton, responding to claims that he had taken drugs as a student.

73 The Canadian kid who wants to grow up to be
    Prime Minister isn't thinking big, he is setting a
    limit to his ambitions rather early.
    Quoted in *Time* (Canadian edition), 31 May 1971.

Rickword, Edgell 1898–1982
English poet and critic. His early work was influenced by
Sassoon. He edited *Left Review* in the 1930s.

74 The oldest griefs of summer seem less sad
    than drone of mowers on suburban lawns
    and girls' thin laughter, to the ears that hear
    the soft rain falling of the failing stars.
    1921 'Regret for the Passing of the Entire Scheme of Things'.

75 My soul's a trampled duelling ground where Sade,
    the gallant marquis, fences for his life
    against the invulnerable retrograde
    Masoch, his shade, more constant than a wife.
    1928 'Chronique Scandaleuse'.

76 Why stir the wasps that rim Fame's luscious pot?
    Love costs us nothing, satire costs a lot!
    1931 'The Contemporary Muse'.

Ridge, W(illiam) Pett 1857–1930
English novelist. He was a prolific writer, publishing over
60 books in total.

77 He took her up in his arms in the way of a bachelor
    who has had amateur experience of the carrying of
    nieces.
    1902 *Lost Property*, pt.1, ch.8.

78 Ballard admitted he was no hand at giving
    descriptions; the man was apparently a gentleman
    and the woman—well, not exactly a lady, although
    she had a very fine flow of language.
    1905 *Mrs Galer's Business*, ch.6.

79 Gertie recommended her to adopt the habit of not
    magnifying grievances; if you wanted to view
    trouble, you could take opera-glasses, but you
    should be careful to hold them the wrong way
    round.
    1912 *Love At Paddington Green*, ch.4.

80 'How did you think I managed at dinner,
    Clarence?'
    'Capitally!'
    'I had a knife and two forks left at the end,' she said
    regretfully.
    1912 *Love At Paddington Green*, ch.6.

Riding, Laura née Reichenthal 1901–91
US poet and fiction writer. She was first published by
Leonard and by Virginia Woolf's Hogarth Press, and is
more admired as a poet than for her polemical prose
writings.

81 Art, whose honesty must work through artifice,
    cannot avoid cheating truth.
    1975 *Selected Poems: In Five Sets*, preface.

Rifkind, Simon Hirsch 1901–95
US former NY judge. He was a partner in his legal firm
and an adviser to General Eisenhower on Jewish matters
in the American occupied zone (1945).

82 Impartiality is an acquired taste, like olives. You
    have to be habituated to it.
    1979 In *Time*, 20 Aug.

Rilke, Rainer Maria 1875–1926
German poet who travelled widely and lived throughout
Europe.

83 *Ach, aber mit Versen ist so wenig getan, wenn man sie*
    früh schreibt. Man sollte warten damit und Sinn und
    Süßigkeit sammeln ein ganzes Leben lang und ein
    langes womöglich, und dann, ganz zum Schluß,
    vielleicht könnte man dann zehn Zeilen schreiben, die
    gut sind.

    Ah, poems amount to so little when you write them
    too early in your life. You ought to wait and gather
    sense and sweetness for a whole lifetime, and a long
    one if possible, and then, at the very end, you
    might perhaps be able to write ten good lines.
    1910 *Die Aufzeichnungen des Malte Laurids Brigge*. (Translated
    by Stephen Mitchell in *The Selected Poetry of Rainer Maria Rilke*,
    1989).

84 *Ich habe um meine Kindheit gebeten, und sie ist*
    wiedergekommen, und ich fühle, daß sie immer noch
    so schwer ist wie damals, und daß es nichts genützt
    hat, älter zu werden.

    I prayed to rediscover my childhood, and it has
    come back, and I feel that it is just as difficult as it
    used to be, and that growing older has served no
    purpose at all.
    1910 *Die Aufzeichnungen des Malte Laurids Brigge*. (Translated
    by Stephen Mitchell in *The Selected Poetry of Rainer Maria Rilke*,
    1989).

85 *Und das Totsein ist mühsam*
    und voller Nachholn, daß man allmählich ein wenig
    Ewigkeit spürt.

    And being dead is hard work
    and full of retrieval before one can gradually feel
    a trace of eternity.
    1923 *Duinieser Elegien*, no.1. (Translated by Stephen Mitchell
    in *The Selected Poetry of Rainer Maria Rilke*, 1989).

86 *Siehe, wir lieben nicht, wie die Blumen, aus einem*
    einzigen Jahr; uns steigt, wo wir lieben,
    unvordenklicher Saft in die Arme.

    No, we don't accomplish our love in a single year

as the flowers do; an immemorial sap
flows up through our arms when we love.
1923 *Duinieser Elegien*, no.3. (Translated by Stephen Mitchell
in *The Selected Poetry of Rainer Maria Rilke*, 1989).

87 *Wer zeigt ein Kind, so wie es steht? Wer stellt
es ins Gestirn und gibt das Maß des Abstands
ihm in die Hand?*

Who shows a child as he really is? Who sets him
in his constellation and puts the measuring-rod
of distance in his hand?
1923 *Duinieser Elegien*, no.4. (Translated by Stephen Mitchell
in *The Selected Poetry of Rainer Maria Rilke*, 1989.

Rimbaud, (Jean Nicolas) Arthur 1854–91

French poet who wrote his entire work before the age of
20. His relationship with poet Paul Verlaine was
notorious. He eventually became an arms trader in
Abyssinia.

88 *Et j'ai vu quelquefois ce que l'homme a cru voir.*

I've sometimes seen what other men have only
dreamed of seeing.
1871 *Poésies*, 'Le Bateau ivre'.

89 *Je regrette l'Europe aux anciens parapets!*

I long for Europe of the ancient parapets!
1871 *Poésies*, 'Le Bateau ivre'.

90 *O mes petites amoureuses,
Que je vous haïs!*

Oh my little mistresses,
How I hate you!
1871 *Poésies*, 'Mes petites amoureuses'.

91 *On n'est pas sérieux, quand on a dix-sept ans.*

When you are seventeen, you are not serious.
1871 *Poésies*, 'Roman', no.1.

92 *Le poète est vraiment voleur de feu.*

The poet is the true fire-stealer.
1871 Letter to Paul Demeny, 15 May.

93 *La Poésie ne rythmera plus l'action; elle sera en avant.*

Poetry will no longer keep step with the action; it
will be *ahead of it*.
1871 Letter to Paul Demeny, 15 May.

94 *Elle est retrouvée.
Quoi?—L'Eternité.
C'est la mer allée
Avec le soleil.*

It has been recovered.
What?—Eternity.
It is the sea escaping
With the sun.
1872 *Derniers vers, Fêtes de la Patience*, 'L'éternité'.

95 *J'ai fait la magique étude*

Du bonheur que nul n'élude.

I studied the magic lore of happiness
Which no one can escape.
1872 *Derniers vers, Fêtes de la faim*, 'O saisons, ô chateaux…'.

96 *Un soir, j'ai assis la beauté sur mes genoux.—Et je l'ai
trouvée amère.—Et je l'ai injuriée.*

One evening, I sat beauty on my knees.—And I
found her bitter.—And I hurt her.
1873 *Une saison en enfer*, 'Jadis, si je me souviens bien'.

97 *Je me crois en enfer, donc j'y suis.*

I believe myself to be in hell; therefore I am.
1873 *Une saison en enfer*, 'Mauvais sang'.

98 *Le bonheur était ma fatalité, mon remords, mon ver:
ma vie serait toujours trop immense pour être dévouée
à la force et à la beauté.*

Happiness was my fate, my remorse, my worm: my
life would always be too large to be dedicated to
force and to beauty.
1873 *Une saison en enfer, Délires*, no.2, 'Alchimie du verbe'.

Rimsky-Korsakov, Nikolai Andreievich
1844–1908

Russian composer. He established his reputation with
three great orchestral masterpieces, *Capriccio Espagnol,
Easter Festival* and *Scheherazade*. He then turned to opera,
producing *The Snow Maiden* (1882), *The Tsar Saltan*
(1900), *The Invisible City of Kitesh* (1906) and *The Golden
Cockerel* (1906).

99 I have already heard it. I had better not go: I will
start to get accustomed to it and finally like it.
Of the music of Debussy, when invited to a concert where it was
to be performed. Quoted in Igor Stravinsky *Chronicles of my Life*
(1936).

Riva, Maria 1924–

Daughter and biographer of Marlene Dietrich.

1 They filled our hall like a monogrammed
Stonehenge.
1992 Of the six closet-size wardrobe trunks used by her
mother. *Marlene Dietrich*.

Rivera, Diego 1886–1957

Mexican painter, one of the three foremost artists in the
revival of monumental fresco painting.

2 The subject is to the painter what the rails are to a
locomotive. He cannot do without it.
1929 *Creative Art*.

Rivera, José Eustasio 1889–1928

Colombian lawyer, poet and novelist. A journey through
the Amazon jungle with a commission to settle the

boundary dispute between Colombia and Venezuela inspired him to write the magnificently descriptive novel *La vorágine.*

3 *Antes que me hubiera apasionado por mujer alguna, jugué mi corazón al azar y me lo ganó la violencia.*

Before I felt passion for any woman, I gambled my heart and lost it to violence.
1924 *La vorágine*, pt.1 (translated as *The Vortex*, 1935).

Rivers, Joan pseudonym of *Joan Alexandra Molinsky* 1933–

US comedienne and writer. An acid-tongued stand-up comedienne in the 1960s, she went on to host television shows, as well as directing and appearing in films, recording an album and publishing books.

4 I'm Jewish. I don't work out. If God had wanted us to bend over he'd've put diamonds on the floor.
Quoted in Colin Jarman *The Guinness Dictionary of Sports Quotations* (1990).

Robb, Charles S(pittal) 1939–

US senator and lawyer. He entered Congress in 1989 as Senator from Virginia.

5 The threat to morale comes not from the orientation of a few, but from the closed minds of the many.
1993 On gays in the military. In the *New York Times*, 5 Feb.

Robbe-Grillet, Alain 1922–

French novelist and cinéast whose repetitive style blurs the standard narrative distinctions in writing.

6 *On n'échappe pas à son sort.*

One cannot escape destiny.
1953 *Les Gommes.*

7 *Deux mètres—ou un peu plus—séparent donc l'homme de la femme.*

Two metres, or a little more, separates a man from a woman.
1955 *Le Voyeur.*

8 *Le lecteur, lui non plus, ne voit pas les choses du dehors. Il est dans le labyrinthe aussi.*

The reader [as well as the main character] does not view the work from outside. He too is in the labyrinth.
1959 *Dans le labyrinthe.*

9 *Et une fois de plus je m'avançais le long de ces mêmes couloirs, marchant depuis des jours, depuis des mois, depuis des années, à votre rencontre.*

And one more time, I advanced along these same hallways, walking for *days*, for *months*, for *years*, to meet you.

1961 *L'Année dernière à Marienbad: ciné roman.*

10 *Car loin de le [le lecteur] négliger, l'auteur aujourd'hui proclame l'absolu besoin qu'il a de son concours actif, conscient, créateur. Ce qu'il lui demande, ce n'est plus de recevoir tout fait un monde achevé, plein, clos sur lui-même, c'est au contraire de participer à une création, d'inventer à son tour l'oeuvre—et le monde—et d'apprendre ainsi à inventer sa propre vie.*

Far from neglecting him [the reader], the author today proclaims the absolute necessity of the reader's active, conscious and creative assistance. What he demands of the reader is to no longer receive a ready-made world, complete, full, closed in upon itself. This is contrary to the reader's participation in the creation, to invent for himself a work—and the world—and to understand thus how to invent his own life.
1963 *Pour un nouveau roman.*

11 *L'amour est un jeu, la poésie est un jeu, la vie doit devenir un jeu (c'est le seul espoir de nos luttes politiques) et 'la révolution elle-même est un jeu', comme disaient les plus conscients des révolutionnaires de mai.*

Love is a game, poetry is a game, life should become a game (it's the only hope for our political struggles) and 'the revolution itself is a game', as the most aware of the May revolutionaries said.
1970 *Projet pour une révolution à New York.*

12 *Première approximation: j'écris pour détruire, en les décrivant avec précision, des monstres nocturnes qui menacent d'envahir ma vie éveillée.*

First general point: I write to destroy, by describing exactly the nocturnal monsters that threaten to invade my waking life.
1984 *Le Miroir qui revient.*

Robbins, Colonel

US Red Cross representative at Petrograd.

13 A four-kind son-of-a-bitch, but the greatest Jew since Jesus Christ.
Of Leon Trotsky. Quoted by A J P Taylor in the *New Statesman and Nation*, 20 Feb 1954.

Robbins, Lionel Charles, Baron Robbins of Clare Market 1898–1984

English economist, Professor at the London School of Economics and later chairman of the *Financial Times.*

14 Economics is the science which studies human behaviour as a relationship between scarce resources and ends which have alternative uses… It does not attempt to pick out certain *kinds* of behaviour, but

focuses attention on a particular *aspect* of behaviour, the form imposed by the influence of scarcity.

1932 *An Essay on the Nature and Significance of Economic Science*, p.16–17.

Robert of Clari   fl.c.1216

Pickard knight.

15   When they were on that sea and had spread their sails and had their banners set high on the poops of the ships and their ensigns, it seemed indeed as if the sea were all a-tremble and all on fire with the ships they were sailing and the great joy they were making.

1203 Describing the Venetian fleet setting out. *The Conquest of Constantinople* (translated by E H McNeal, 1936), p.42–3.

Roberts, Sir Charles George Douglas

1860–1943

Canadian poet, naturalist, novelist, and short-story writer. His first book of poems, *Orion, and Other Poems* (1880), inspired the group later known as 'The Confederation Poets'. In 1892 he published his first animal story, of which there would eventually be about twenty collected volumes. Roberts also translated French-Canadian literature into English.

16   This is the voice of high midsummer's heat.
The rasping vibrant clamour soars and shrills
O'er all the meadowy range of shadeless hills,
As if a host of giant cicadae beat
The cymbals of their wings with tireless feet,
Or brazen grasshoppers with triumphing note
From the long swath proclaimed the fate that
    smote
The clover and timothy-tops and meadowsweet.

1893 'The Mowing'.

17   When Winter scourged the meadow and the hill
And in the withered leafage worked his will,
Then water shrank, and shuddered, and stood
    still,—
Then built himself a magic house of glass,
Irised with memories of flowers and grass,
Wherein to sit and watch the fury pass.

1898 'Ice'.

18   And I turned and fled, like a soul pursued,
From the white, inviolate solitude.

1901 'The Skater'.

Robin, Leo   1899–1985

US lyricist born in Pittsburgh. Best known for his collaboration with composer Ralph Rainger between 1932 and 1942. After Rainger's death he wrote with various other composers.

19   Thanks For The Memory.

1937 Title of song, which became Bob Hope's signature tune. Music by Ralph Rainger.

Robinson, (Edward) Austin George

1897–1993

English economist, Professor at Cambridge University.

20   All industrial efficiency consists in trying to do with eight men what we have hitherto been doing with ten men. It consists in creating unemployment.

1931 *The Structure of Competitive Industry.*

Robinson, Casey   1903–79

US screenwriter. His credits include *Captain Blood* (1935), *Now, Voyager* (1942) and *The Snows of Kilimanjaro* (1952).

21   Don't let's ask for the moon. We have the stars.

1942 Line delivered by Bette Davis to Paul Henreid in *Now, Voyager.*

22   Where's the rest of me?

1942 Line delivered by Ronald Reagan on discovering his legs have been amputated in *King's Row.*

Robinson, Edward G pseudonym of *Emanuel Goldenberg*   1893–1973

Hungarian-born US actor, whose portrayal of a vicious gangster in *Little Caesar* (1930) brought him stardom. Other films include *The Whole Town's Talking* (1935), *Double Indemnity* (1944) and *Key Largo* (1948).

23   Mother of Mercy, is this the end of Rico?

1930 Line delivered by him in *Little Caesar* (screenplay by Francis Faragoh and Robert E Lee).

Robinson, Edwin Arlington   1869–1935

US poet. He created a fictional New England village, Tilbury Town, in which his best poetry is set. He won three Pulitzer Prizes (1922, 1925 and 1928).

24   In fine, we thought that he was everything
To make us wish that we were in his place.

So on we worked, and waited for the light,
And went without meat, and cursed the bread;
And Richard Cory, one calm summer night,
Went home and put a bullet through his head.

1897 *The Children of the Night*, 'Richard Cory'.

25   Friends
To borrow my books and set wet glasses on them.

1902 *Captain Craig*, 'Captain Craig', pt.2.

26   Miniver Cheevy, child of scorn,
Grew lean while he assailed the seasons;
He wept that he was ever born,
And he had reasons.

1910 *The Town Down the River*, 'Miniver Cheevy'.

27   Miniver loved the Medici,

Albeit he had never seen one;
He would have sinned incessantly
Could he have been one.

1910 *The Town Down the River*, 'Miniver Cheevy'.

28 Miniver Cheevy, born too late,
Scratched his head and kept on thinking;
Miniver coughed, and called it fate,
And kept on drinking.

1910 *The Town Down the River*, 'Miniver Cheevy'.

29 The world is…a kind of kindergarten, where
millions of bewildered infants are trying to spell
God with the wrong blocks.

1917 *Literature in the Making*.

30 I shall have more to say when I am dead.

1920 *The Three Taverns*, 'John Brown'.

31 Below him, in the town among the trees,
Where friends of other days had honored him,
A phantom salutation of the dead
Rang thinly till old Eben's eyes were dim.

1921 *Avon's Harvest*, 'Mr Flood's Party'.

32 The Man Who Died Twice.

1924 Title of book.

33 Joy shivers in the corner where she knits
And Conscience always has the rocking-chair,
Cheerful as when she tortured into fits
The first cat that was ever killed by Care.

1925 *Dionysus in Doubt*, 'New England'.

Robinson, Joan Violet née Maurice 1903–83

English economist 1929–71, a leader of the Cambridge school which developed macro-economic theories of growth and distribution based on the work of Keynes. Her works include *The Economics of Imperfect Competition* (1933) and *Economic Heresies* (1971).

34 The typical entrepreneur is no longer the bold and
tireless man of Marshall, or the sly and rapacious
Moneybags of Marx, but a mass of inert
shareholders, indistinguishable from *rentiers*, who
employ salaried managers to run their concerns.

1947 *An Essay on Marxian Economics*.

35 The purpose of studying economics is not to
acquire a set of ready-made answers to economic
questions, but to learn how to avoid being deceived
by economists.

1955 Quoted in *Contributions to Modern Economics* (1978), p.75.

36 It is impossible to understand the economic system
in which we are living if we try to interpret it as a
rational scheme. It has to be understood as an
awkward phase in a continuing process of historical
development.

1966 *Economics: An Awkward Corner*.

37 Hitler had already found out how to cure
unemployment before Keynes had finished
explaining why it occurred.

1971 Collected in *Contributions to Modern Economics* (1978), p.10.

Robinson, John Arthur Thomas 1919–83

English churchman and radical theologian, Bishop of Woolwich, latterly Dean of Clare College, Cambridge.

38 Jesus never claims to be God, personally, yet he
always claims to bring God, completely.

1963 *Honest to God.*

Roche, Sir Boyle 1743–1807

Irish politician. He joined the British army and fought in the war in America. On returning to Ireland he entered Parliament in 1776 and remained an MP until the Act of Union (1800). He opposed Catholic emancipation and supported the Union. He was granted a pension for his constant support of the government.

39 Mr Speaker, I think the noble young man has no
business to make any apology. He is a gentleman,
and none such should be asked to make an *apology*,
because no *gentleman* could *mean* to *give offence*.

c.1796 Debate on motion to expel Lord Edward Fitzgerald from Irish House of Commons, quoted in Sir Jonah Barrington *Personal Sketches and Recollections of his own Times* (1827).

40 Sir, there is no Levitical degrees between nations,
and on this occasion I can see neither sin nor shame
in *marrying our own sister*.

c.1800 Debate on the Act of Union between Great Britain and Ireland, Irish House of Commons, quoted in Sir Jonah Barrington *Personal Sketches and Recollections of his own Times* (1827).

41 What, Mr Speaker! and so we are to beggar
ourselves for fear of vexing posterity! Now, I would
ask the honourable gentleman, and *still more*
honourable House, why should we put ourselves
out of our way to do anything for *posterity*, for what
has *posterity* done for *us*?

Debate in Irish House of Commons, quoted in Sir Jonah Barrington *Personal Sketches and Recollections of his own Times* (1827).

▷ See Addison 8:38.

42 The best way to *avoid* danger is to *meet it plump*.

Quoted in Sir Jonah Barrington *Personal Sketches and Recollections of his own Times* (1827).

Rochester, John Wilmot, 2nd Earl of
1647–80

English courtier and lyric poet. He is noted for his entertaining letters, for satires, including *A Satyr Against Mankind* (1674), and for his verses and songs, many of which are sexually frank or defamatory.

43 I hold you six to four I love you with all my heart, if
I would bet with other people I'm sure I could get
ten to one.

c.1667 Letter from Newmarket to his wife. In *The Letters of John Wilmot, Earl of Rochester*, edited by Jeremy Treglown (1980).

44 Naked she lay, clasped in my longing arms,
I filled with love, and she all over charms,
Both equally inspired with eager fire,
Melting through kindness, flaming in desire;
With arms, legs, lips, close clinging to embrace.

c.1672 'The Imperfect Enjoyment', l.1–6 (published 1680).

45 'Is there no more?'
She cries. 'All this to love, and rapture's due,
Must we not pay a debt to pleasure too?'

c.1672 'The Imperfect Enjoyment', l.22–4 (published 1680).

46 Restless, he rolls about from whore to whore,
A merry Monarch, scandalous and poor.

1673 Of Charles II. 'I' th' Isle of Britain', l.14–15. The poem resulted in a brief period of exile for Rochester.

47 Great Negative, how vainly would the wise
Enquire, define, distinguish, teach, devise,
Didst thou not stand to point their blind
Philosophies.

c.1673 'Upon Nothing', stanza 10 (published 1679).

48 French truth, Dutch prowess, British policy,
Hibernian learning, Scotch civility,
Spaniards' dispatch, Danes' wit, are mainly seen in
thee.

c.1673 'Upon Nothing', stanza 16 (published 1679).

49 Were I (who to my loss already am
One of those strange prodigious creatures, Man)
A spirit, free to choose for my own share
What case of flesh and blood I'd choose to wear,
I'd be a dog, a monkey, or a bear.

1674 'A Satyr Against Mankind', l.1–5 (published 1679).

50 Reason, an ignis fatuus in the mind,
Which leaving light of nature, sense behind,
Pathless and dangerous wandering ways it takes,
Through error's fenny bogs and thorny brakes;
Whilst the misguided follower climbs, with pain,
Mountains of whimsy heaped in his own brain.

1674 'A Satyr Against Mankind', l.12–17 (published 1679).

51 The old age and experience, hand in hand,
Lead him to death, and make him understand,
After a search so painful and so long,
That all his life he has been in the wrong.
Huddled in dirt, the reasoning engine lies,
Who was so proud, so witty, and so wise.

1674 'A Satyr Against Mankind', l.25–30 (published 1679).

52 Birds feed on birds, beasts on each other prey,

But savage man alone does man betray.

1674 'A Satyr Against Mankind', l.129–130 (published 1679).

53 That cordial drop heaven in our cup has thrown
To make the nauseous draught of life go down.

c.1674 Of love. 'A letter from Artemisa in the Town to Chloe in the Country', l.44–5 (published 1679).

54 What vain, unnecessary things are men,
How well we do without 'em!

c.1674–5 'Fragment of a Satire on Men', l.1–2 (published in full 1953).

55 Dear Madam, You are stark mad, and therefore the
fitter for me to love; and that is the reason I think I
can never leave to be Your humble servant.

c.1675 Letter to his mistress, the actress Elizabeth Barry. In *The Letters of John Wilmot, Earl of Rochester*, edited by Jeremy Treglown (1980).

56 To pick out the wildest and most fantastical odd
man alive, and to place your kindness there, is an
act so brave and daring as will show the greatness of
your spirit and distinguish you in love, as you are in
all things else, from womankind.

c.1675 Letter to his mistress, the actress Elizabeth Barry. In *The Letters of John Wilmot, Earl of Rochester*, edited by Jeremy Treglown (1980).

57 They who would be great in our little government
seem as ridiculous to me as schoolboys
who…climb a crab-tree, venturing their necks for
fruit which solid pigs would disdain if they were
not starving.

c.1676 Letter to Henry Savile. In *The Letters of John Wilmot, Earl of Rochester*, edited by Jeremy Treglown (1980).

58 He is a rarity which I cannot but be fond of, as one
would be of a hog that could fiddle, or a singing
owl.

c.1676 Of Dryden. Letter to Henry Savile. In *The Letters of John Wilmot, Earl of Rochester*, edited by Jeremy Treglown (1980).

59 Son of a whore, God damn you! can you tell
A Peerless Peer the readiest way to Hell?

c.1676 'To the Post-Boy', l.1–2. (published 1926). The postboy's answer is 'The readiest way, my lord, is by Rochester'.

60 My most neglected wife, till you are a much
respected widow, I find you will scarce be a
contented woman, and to say no more than the
plain truth, I do endeavour so fairly to do you that
last good service.

c.1677 Letter to his wife, 20 Nov. In *The Letters of John Wilmot, Earl of Rochester*, edited by Jeremy Treglown (1980).

61 There can be no danger in sweetness and youth
Where love is secured by good nature and truth,
On her beauty I'll gaze, and of pleasure complain,
While every kind look adds a link to my chain.

'The Submission', l.13–16 (published 1680).

62 Farewell Woman, I intend,
    Henceforth, every night to sit,
    With my lewd well natured friend,
    Drinking, to engender wit.
    Song: 'Love a Woman!', l.9–12 (published 1680).

63 Since 'tis nature's law to change,
    Constancy alone is strange.
    'A Dialogue between Strephon and Daphne', l.31–2 (published 1691).

64 An age in her embraces passed,
    Would seem a winter's day;
    Where life and light, with envious haste,
    Are torn and snatched away.

    But, oh how slowly minutes roll,
    When absent from her eyes
    That feed my love, which is my soul,
    It languishes and dies.
    'The Mistress', l.1–8 (published 1691).

65 Ancient Person, for whom I
    All the flattering youth defy;
    Long be it ere thou grow old,
    Aching, shaking, crazy, cold;
    But still continue as thou art,
    Ancient person of my heart.
    'A Song of a Young Lady to her Ancient Lover', stanza 1 (published 1691).

66 God bless our good and gracious King
    Whose promise none relies on,
    Who never said a foolish thing
    Nor ever did a wise one
    Of Charles II (published 1707). The verse was later changed to an epitaph ('Here lies a great and mighty king…').

Rockefeller, David 1915–

US banker, born into the wealthy Rockefeller dynasty, director of the Chase Manhattan Bank.

67 One thing this family does not need to do is make itself resented by thousands more people.
    Explaining his reluctance to join management of the Chase Manhattan Bank. Quoted in Peter Collier and David Horowitz *The Rockefellers* (1976).

68 I was born into wealth and there was nothing I could do about it. It was there like food or air.
    1990 In *Merchants and Masterpieces*, WETA TV broadcast, 31 Dec.

Rockefeller, John D(avison) 1839–1937

US industrialist and philanthropist. In 1875 he founded with his brother William the Standard Oil Company, securing control of US oil trade. After 1897 he devoted himself to philanthropy, and in 1913 established the Rockefeller Foundation 'to promote the wellbeing of mankind'.

69 The growth of a large business is merely a survival of the fittest… The American Beauty rose can be produced in the splendor and fragrance which bring cheer to its beholder only by sacrificing the early buds which grow up around it.
    Quoted in W J Ghent *Our Benevolent Feudalism* (1902).

Rockefeller, John D(avison), Jr 1874–1960

US business and oil magnate. He took over his father's business empire in 1911 and continued the Rockefeller philanthropic tradition. He founded the Rockefeller Center, New York (1931, completed 1939).

70 The secretaries here have an advantage I never had. They can prove to themselves their commercial worth.
    1950 Speech to the New York Chamber of Commerce, 6 Apr. Quoted in Peter Collier and David Horowitz *The Rockefellers* (1976).

71 The rendering of useful service is the common duty of mankind, and [that] only in the purifying fire of sacrifice is the dross of selfishness consumed and the greatness of the human soul set free.
    Credo engraved in Rockefeller Centre Plaza, New York.

Rockefeller, John D(avison) III 1906–78

US businessman and art collector, Governor of West Virginia.

72 If my name were John D Smith IV I wouldn't have been elected to anything.
    1970 On becoming West Virginia's Secretary of State before moving on to be Governor. In the *New York Times*, 4 Oct.

73 It's like orchestrating a symphony of unhappiness.
    1971 On the necessity of compromise in health-care financing. In the *Washington Post*, 1 Jul.

Rockefeller, Laurance S 1910–

US businessman, son of John D Rockefeller, Jr. He has been involved with a variety of conservation and environmental organizations.

74 Lyndon gave me that instead of the Hawaii air route.
    Of the Medal of Freedom which he received from President Johnson after Eastern Airlines failed to receive permission to fly a coveted route. Quoted in Peter Collier and David Horowitz *The Rockefellers* (1978).

Rockefeller, Nelson A(ldrich) 1908–79

US Republican politician. Director of the Rockefeller Center (1931–58), he became Governor of New York State (1958–73) and Vice-President (1974–7) under Ford, after failing to win the presidential nomination.

75 If there is anything more satisfying than dedicating a new building, it is dedicating eight new buildings.
    1970 On Albany's Government Mall. In the *New York Times*, 13 Mar.

76 When you think of what I had, what else was there
to aspire to?

Of his lifelong ambition to be US President. Quoted in Michael
Kramer and Sam Roberts *I Never Wanted to be Vice President of
Anything* (1976).

Rockefeller, Winthrop 1912–73

US businessman and politician, son of John D
Rockefeller Jr, who ran a farm in Arkansas on
experimental principles. He served as Republican
Governor of Arkansas (1967–70).

77 In them one can see the spontaneous—and often
aesthetic—expression of a people reflected, not in a
gilt-framed drawing room mirror, but in an honest
glass held up to the face of a nation.

1962 On an exhibition of American folk art at the US
Embassy, London. In news summaries, 31 Jan.

78 In the springtime of America's cultural life, its
itinerant folk artists took to the road to record the
life and times of a people. Perhaps never again will
we have an artistic record created in such direct and
unassuming terms.

1962 On an exhibition of American folk art at the US
Embassy, London. In news summaries, 31 Jan.

Rockne, Knute Kenneth 1888–1931

Norwegian-born US football coach. Coach for the
University of Notre Dame team after World War I, he
dominated US college football until his death in an air
crash.

79 When the going gets tough, the tough get going.

His catchphrase, later adopted by John F Kennedy.

Rockwell, Norman 1894–1978

US popular illustrator, best known for his *Saturday
Evening Post* covers. His style is typically anecdotal,
idealized scenes of everyday American small-town life.

80 If the public dislikes one of my *Post* covers, I can't
help disliking it myself.

Quoted in the *New York Times*, 28 Sep 1986.

Rodchenko, Alexander 1891–1956

Russian artist who was a leader of the Russian
Constructivist painters before he took up photography in
1922 and became active in the field of typography and
photographic journalism.

81 Tell me, frankly, what ought to remain of Lenin :
an art bronze,
oil portraits,
etchings,
watercolours,
his secretary's diary, his friends' memoirs—
or
a file of photographs taken of him at work and rest,
archives of his books, writing pads, notebooks,

shorthand reports, films, phonograph records?
I don't think there's any choice.
Art has no place in modern life… Every cultured
modern
man must wage war against art, as against opium.

Photograph and be photographed!

Quoted in Robert Hughes *The Shock of the New* (1980).

Roddenberry, Gene 1921–91

US scriptwriter, producer and director. A former Air
Force pilot, he made his name as the creator of the
popular *Star Trek* television series.

82 Space—the final frontier.

1966 Introductory voiceover to *Star Trek*.

83 To boldly go where no man has gone before.

1966 The mission of the starship Enterprise. Introductory
voiceover to *Star Trek*.

84 Beam us up, Mr Scott.

1966 Star Trek, 'Gamesters of Triskelion'. The phrase is often
misquoted as 'Beam me up, Scotty'.

Rodgers, Richard and Hart, Lorenz

1902–79; 1896–1943

US composer and song-writer partnership. They wrote a
series of popular musicals including *Pal Joey* (1940).

85 Sigmund Freud has often stated
Dreams and drives are all related.
Zip, I am such a scholar!

1940 'Zip', in *Pal Joey*.

Rodgers, Thomas J

US businessman. He is president and chief executive
officer of Cypress Semiconductor Corporation.

86 Most entrepreneurs who have the guts to take on a
big challenge are a lot like Babe Ruth—they set
records for both home runs and strike outs.

1993 Letter about Steven Jobs of Next in the *San Francisco
Chronicle*, 6 Dec.

Rodó, José Enrique 1871–1917

Uruguayan essayist and philosopher, a leading stylist
and thinker of the modernist group. His most famous
work, *Ariel*, admonishes the youth of South America to
cultivate spiritual (Ariel) rather than material (Caliban)
values.

87 *La visión de una América deslatinizada por propia
voluntad, sin la extorsión de la conquista, y
regenerada luego a imagen y semejanza del arquetipo
del Norte, flota ya sobre los sueños de muchos sinceros
interesados por nuestro porvenir… Tenemos nuestra
nordomanía. Es necesario oponerle los límites que la
razón y el sentimiento señalan.*

The vision of an America de-Latinized of its own will, without threat of conquest, and reconstituted in the image and likeness of the North, now looms in the nightmares of many who are genuinely concerned about our future… We have our *USA-mania*. It must be limited by the boundaries our reason and sentiment jointly dictate.

1900 *Ariel* (translated 1922), pt.5.

Rodriguez, Richard 1944–

US writer and journalist.

88 The genius of American culture and its integrity comes from fidelity to the light. Plain as day, we say. Happy as the day is long. Early to bed, early to rise. American virtues are daylight virtues: honesty, integrity, plain speech. We say yes when we mean yes and no when we mean no, and all else comes from the evil one. America presumes innocence and even the right to happiness.

1990 *Frontiers*, 'Night and Day'.

89 In the modern city, it takes on the status of a cathedral, our Chartres, our Notre Dame, our marble museum of the soul.

1995 On San Francisco's new Museum of Modern Art. In the *MacNeil-Lehrer Report*, 27 Feb.

Rodriguez, Sue 1950–94

Canadian ALS sufferer (amyotrophic lateral sclerosis, or Lou Gehrig's disease, a progressive and terminal illness) and campaigner for euthanasia.

90 I want to ask you gentlemen, if I cannot give consent to my own death, then whose body is this? Who owns my life?

1992 Video-taped presentation to the justice committee of the House of Commons, Ottawa, Nov. Reported by Deborah Wilson in *The Globe and Mail*, 5 Dec. The Supreme Court of Canada denied Rodriguez's request for a physician-assisted death.

Roethke, Theodore 1908–63

US poet. A Professor of English at Harvard from 1948, he won a Pulitzer Prize for his collection *The Waking*.

91 I have known the inexorable sadness of pencils, Neat in their boxes, dolor of pad and paper-weight, All the misery of manila folders and mucilage, Desolation in immaculate public places.

1948 *The Lost Son*, 'Dolor'.

92 And I have seen dust from the walls of institutions, Finer than flour, alive, more dangerous than silica, Sift, almost invisible, through long afternoons of tedium.

1948 *The Lost Son*, 'Dolor'.

93 To know that light falls and fills, often without our knowing,

As an opaque vase fills to the brim from quick pouring
Fills and trembles at the edge yet does not flow over,
Still holding and feeding the stem of the contained flower.

1948 *The Lost Son*, 'The Shape of Fire'.

94 And what a congress of stinks!—
Roots ripe as old bait,
Pulpy stems, rank, silo-rich,
Leaf-mold, manure, lime, piled against slippery planks.
Nothing would give up life:
Even the dirt kept breathing a small breath.

1948 *The Lost Son*, 'Root Cellar'.

95 I wake to sleep, and take my waking slow.
I feel my fate in what I cannot fear.
I learn by going where I have to go.

1953 *The Waking*, 'The Waking'.

96 Over this damp grave I speak the words of my love;
I, with no rights in this matter,
Neither father nor lover.

1953 Poem addressed to a dead student. *The Waking*, 'Elegy for Jane'.

97 Of her choice virtues only gods should speak,
Or English poets who grew up on Greek
(I'd have them sing in chorus, cheek to cheek).

1958 *Words for the Wind*, 'I Knew A Woman'.

98 What's freedom for? To know eternity.
I swear she cast a shadow white as stone.
But who would count eternity in days?
These old bones live to learn her wanton ways:
(I measure time by how a body sways).

1958 *Words for the Wind*, 'I Knew A Woman'.

99 In a dark time the eye begins to see.

1963 *Sequence, Sometimes Metaphysical*, 'In A Dark Time'.

1 The self persists like a dying star,
In sleep, afraid.

1964 *The Far Field*, 'Meditation at Oyster River'.

Rogers, Carl Ransom 1902–87

US psychologist and pioneer of client-centred counselling. His *Client-Centred Therapy* (1951), and *On Becoming a Person* (1961), emphasized the value of genuine empathy with the patient.

2 Unconditional positive regard.

c.1950 The slogan of the Rogerian counselling movement.

Rogers, Richard George Rogers, Baron 1933–

English architect, concerned with advancing technology in architecture and pushing the limits of design. His works include the Beaubourg or Pompidou Centre, Paris

(1971–9, with Renzo Piano) and the building, Lloyds London (1979–85).

3 'Form follows profit' is the aesthetic principle of our times. Thus, design skill is measured today by the architect's ability to build the largest possible enclosure for the smallest investment in the quickest time.

1990 22nd annual Walter Neurath lecture. Collected in *Architecture: A Modern View*.

4 Architects cannot work in a vacuum; unlike other artists they are totally dependent on a site, a brief and finance.

1990 22nd annual Walter Neurath lecture. Collected in *Architecture: A Modern View*.

5 The problem is not style but quality, not aesthetics but ethics.

1990 22nd annual Walter Neurath lecture. Collected in *Architecture: A Modern View*.

Rogers, Will 1879–1935

US actor, rancher and humorist. His ready wisecracks earned him a syndicated column, and a number of books, including a posthumously compiled *Autobiography*.

6 Will you please tell me what you do with all the vice presidents a bank has?… The United States is the biggest business institution in the world and they only have one vice president and nobody has ever found anything for him to do.

1922 Speech, International Bankers' Association.

7 Well, all I know is what I read in the papers.

1923 In the *New York Times*, 30 Sep.

8 You know everybody is ignorant, only on different subjects.

1924 In the *New York Times*, 31 Aug.

9 The more you read and observe about this Politics thing, you got to admit that each party is worse than the other. The one that's out always looks the best.

1924 *The Illiterate Digest*, 'Breaking Into the Writing Game'.

10 Everything is funny as long as it is happening to Somebody Else.

1924 *The Illiterate Digest*, 'Warning to Jokers: lay off the prince'.

11 The Income Tax return has made more Liars out of the American people than Golf has. Even when you make one out on the level, you don't know when it's through if you are a Crook or a Martyr.

1924 *The Illiterate Digest*, 'Helping the Girls With Their Income Taxes'.

12 I bet you if I had met him and had a chat with him, I would have found him a very interesting and

human fellow, for I never yet met a man that I didn't like.

1926 On Trotsky. In the *Saturday Evening Post*, 6 Nov.

13 Communism is like prohibition, it's a good idea but it won't work.

1927 Syndicated column, Nov. Collected in *The Weekly Articles*, vol 3 (1981).

14 You can't say civilization don't advance, however, for in every war they kill you in a new way.

1929 In the *New York Times*, 23 Dec.

15 Half our life is spent trying to find something to do with the time we have rushed through life trying to save.

1930 In the *New York Times*, 29 Apr.

16 The United States is the only country ever to go to the poorhouse in an automobile.

c.1930 Attributed.

17 I was born because it was a habit in those days, people didn't know anything else.

The Autobiography of Will Rogers (published 1949), ch.1.

18 There is only one thing that can kill the Movies, and that is education.

The Autobiography of Will Rogers (published 1949), ch.6.

19 When a man goes in for politics over here, he has no time to labour, and any man that labours has no time to fool with politics. Over there, politics is an obligation; over here it's a business.

On Britain electing a Labour Government. *The Autobiography of Will Rogers* (published 1949), ch.14.

20 It's great to be great but it's greater to be human.

The Autobiography of Will Rogers (published 1949), ch.15.

21 Being a hero is about the shortest-lived profession on earth.

Quoted in 'A Rogers Thesaurus' in *The Saturday Review*, 25 Aug 1962. Another form of the quote appeared in a syndicated newspaper article, 15 Feb 1925: 'Heroing is one of the shortest-lived professions there is'.

22 I don't make jokes—I just watch the government and report the facts.

Quoted in 'A Rogers Thesaurus' in *The Saturday Review*, 25 Aug 1962.

23 I guess there is nothing that will get your mind off everything like golf. I have never been depressed enough to take up the game but they say you get so sore at yourself you forget to hate your enemies.

Quoted in Michael Hobbs *The Golf Quotation Book* (1992).

Rogers, William Pierce 1913–

US government official. As Deputy Attorney General (1953–7) he supported the 1957 Civil Rights Act, becoming Attorney General (1957–61). As Secretary of

State (1969–73) he brought about a Middle East ceasefire.

24 Making foreign policy is like pornographic movies…more fun doing it than watching it.

1982 On becoming Under Secretary of State for Economic Affairs, 7 Jun.

Rolleston, Humphrey 1862–1944

English physician.

25 Medicine is a noble profession but a damn bad business.

1944 Quoted in *Who Said What When* (1988).

Rollins, Sonny (Theodore Walter) 1929–

US jazz saxophonist. He is a leading figure in the development of jazz in the post-bebop era.

26 America is deeply rooted in Negro culture: its colloquialisms, its humour, its music. How ironic that the Negro, who more than any other people can claim America's culture as his own, is being persecuted and repressed, that the Negro, who has exemplified the humanities in his very existence, is being rewarded with inhumanity.

1958 Statement on sleeve of *Freedom Suite*.

Romani, Felice 1788–1865

Italian librettist, poet, essayist and critic, he provided libretti for more than 100 composers, striking a balance between Classicism and Romanticism. He is best known for his collaborations with Donizetti and Bellini.

27 *Casta Diva.*

Chaste goddess.

1831 Norma's aria. *Norma*, act 1 (music by Bellini, published 1832).

28 *Una furtiva Lagrima.*

A furtive tear.

1832 Nemorino's aria. *L'Elisir d'Amore*, act 2 (music by Donizetti).

Romney, George W 1907–

US politician. Fomer Governor of Michigan.

29 I didn't say I didn't say it. I said I didn't say I said it. I want to make that very clear.

1967 Clarifying his policy. In the *National Review*, 12 Dec.

Roosevelt, (Anna) Eleanor 1882–1962

US humanitarian and diplomat, wife and adviser of Franklin D Roosevelt. After his death she was US delegate to the UN (1945–53, 1961), chair of the Human Rights Commission (1946–51) and US representative to the General Assembly (1946–52).

30 You always admire what you don't really understand.

1956 In *Meet the Press*, NBC TV broadcast, 16 Sep.

31 She can talk beautifully about democracy but doesn't know how to live democracy.

Of Madame Chiang Kai-shek. Recalled on Mrs Roosevelt's death, 7 Nov 1962.

32 Where, after all, do human rights begin? They begin in small places, close to home—so close and so small that they cannot be seen on any map of the world.

1965 Quoted in the *New York Times*, 26 Dec.

33 A woman is like a tea bag; when she is in hot water she just gets stronger.

Quoted by Hillary Rodham Clinton in the *Wall Street Journal*, 30 Sep 1994.

Roosevelt, Franklin D(elano) 1882–1945

US Democratic statesman, 32nd President (1933–45) despite being stricken with polio in 1921. He introduced a 'New Deal' for national recovery (1933), and was re-elected three times. He entered World War II after Pearl Harbor (1941), meeting Churchill and Stalin at Teheran (1943) and Yalta (1945), but died just before the German surrender.

34 I pledge you, I pledge myself, to a New Deal for the American people.

1932 Speech accepting the Democratic Convention's presidential nomination, Chicago, 2 Jul.

35 In the field of world policy, I would dedicate this nation to the policy of the good neighbour.

1933 Inaugural address, 4 Mar.

36 Let me assert my belief that the only thing that we have to fear is fear itself—nameless, unreasoning, unjustified terror that paralyses needed efforts to convert retreat into advance.

1933 Inaugural address, 4 Mar.

37 Better the occasional faults of a Government that lives in a spirit of charity than the consistent omissions of a Government frozen in the ice of its own indifference.

1936 Renomination acceptance speech, Philadelphia, 27 Jun.

38 I have seen war… I hate war.

1936 Speech at Chantauqua, New York, 14 Aug.

39 When peace has been broken anywhere, the peace of all countries is in danger.

1939 Radio broadcast, 3 Sep.

40 A conservative is a man with two perfectly good legs who has never learned to walk forwards. A reactionary is a somnambulist walking backwards. A radical is a man with both feet planted firmly in the air.

1939 Radio broadcast, Oct.

41 I have said this before, but I shall say it again and again and again: Your boys are not going to be sent into any foreign wars.

1940 Speech in Boston, 30 Oct.

42 We have the men—the skill—the wealth—and above all, the will… We must be the great arsenal of democracy.

1940 'Fireside chat' radio broadcast, 29 Dec.

43 In the future days, which we seek to make secure, we look forward to a world founded upon four essential freedoms. The first is freedom of speech and expression, everywhere in the world. The second is the freedom of every person to worship God in his own way, everywhere in the world. The third is freedom from want… The fourth is freedom from fear.

1941 Third inaugural address, 6 Jan.

44 Yesterday, December 7, 1941—a date which will live in infamy—the United States of America was suddenly and deliberately attacked by naval and air forces of the Empire of Japan.

1941 Address to Congress, 8 Dec, following the Japanese attack on Pearl Harbor.

Roosevelt, Theodore 1858–1919

US Republican statesman and 26th President (1901–9). Elected Vice-President in 1900, he became President on McKinley's assassination and was re-elected in 1904. His 'expansionist' policies included a strong navy, the regulation of trusts and monopolies, and his 'Square Deal' policy for social reform.

45 There is a homely adage that runs, 'Speak softly and carry a big stick, and you will go far.' If the American nation will speak softly and yet build, and keep at a pitch of the highest training, the Monroe Doctrine will go far.

1901 Vice-presidential speech, Sep.

46 In the western hemisphere, the adherence of the United States to the Monroe Doctrine may force the United States, however reluctantly, in flagrant cases of wrongdoing or impotence, to the exercise of an international police power.

1904 Message to Congress, 6 Dec.

47 The men with the muck-rakes are often indispensable to the well-being of society, but only if they know when to stop raking the muck.

1906 House of Representatives, 14 Apr.

48 I stand for the square deal…not merely for fair play under the present rules of the game, but for having those rules changed, so as to work for a more substantial equality of opportunity and of reward for equally good service.

1910 Speech, Osawatomie, 31 Aug.

49 Do not hit at all if it can be avoided, but never hit softly.

1913 *Theodore Roosevelt: An Autobiography*.

50 Practical efficiency is common, and lofty idealism is not uncommon; it is the combination that is necessary, and that combination is rare.

1913 *Theodore Roosevelt: An Autobiography*.

51 There is no reason why people should not call themselves Cubists, or Octagonists, Parallelopipedonists, or Knights of the Isosceles Triangle, or Brothers of the Cosine, if they so desire; as expressing anything serious and permanent, one term is as fatuous as another.

1913 His opinion on the *International Exhibition of Modern Art* in New York, popularly known as *The Armoury Show*. 'A Layman's Views of an Art Exhibition', in *The Outlook* (Mar 9).

52 We are fighting in the quarrel of civilization against barbarism, of liberty against tyranny. Germany has become a menace to the whole world. She is the most dangerous enemy of liberty now existing.

1917 Speech at Oyster Bay, Long Island, Apr.

53 We have room in this country but for one flag, the Stars and Stripes. We have room for but one loyalty, loyalty to the United States. We have room for but one language, the English language.

1919 Message to the American Defense Society two days before his death, 3 Jan.

Rosebery, Archibald Philip Primrose, 5th Earl of 1847–1929

English statesman, Foreign Secretary (1886, 1892–4) under Gladstone, whom he succeeded as Prime Minister for a brief period in 1894 before the Liberals lost the election of 1895. He was noted for his racehorse stables, and as a biographer of British statesmen.

54 It is beginning to be hinted that we are a nation of amateurs.

1900 Rectorial address, Glasgow University, 16 Nov.

55 For the present at any rate, I must proceed alone. I must plough my own furrow alone—but before I get to the end of that furrow, it is possible that I may not find myself alone.

1901 On breaking from the Liberal Party, Jul.

Rosenberg, Harold 1906–78

US critic of the modern movement in painting and literature.

56 At a certain moment the canvas began to appear to one American painter after another as an arena in which to act—rather than as a space in which to reproduce, re-design, analyze or 'express' an object, actual or imagined. What was to go on the canvas was not a picture but an event.

1952 'The American Action Painters', in *Art News*, no.51, Dec.

57 A painting that is an act is inseparable from the biography of the artist.
1952 'The American Action Painters', in *Art News*, no.51, Dec.

58 Everyone knows that the label Modern Art no longer has any relation to the words that compose it. To be Modern Art a work need not be either modern nor art; it need not even be a work. A three thousand-year-old mask from the South Pacific qualifies as Modern and a piece of wood found on a beach becomes Art.
1952 'The American Action Painters', in *Art News*, no.51, Dec.

59 As we have seen Modern Art does not have to be actually new; it only has to be new to somebody— to the last lady who found out about the driftwood.
1952 'The American Action Painters', in *Art News*, no.51, Dec.

Rosenberg, Isaac 1890–1918

English poet and artist. He published two volumes of poems before being killed in action in France. A third appeared posthumously, and his *Collected Works* (1937, rev edn 1973) revived his reputation.

60 The darkness crumbles away— It is the same old druid Time as ever.
1916 'Break of Day in the Trenches'.

61 Droll rat, they would shoot you if they knew Your cosmopolitan sympathies.
1916 'And God knows what antipathies'.

62 Earth has waited for them, All the time of their growth Fretting for their decay: Now she has them at last.
1917 'Dead Man's Dump'.

63 Death could drop from the dark As easily as song.
1917 'Returning, We Hear the Larks'.

Rosenblum, Robert 1927–

US art historian. His works include *Cubism and Twentieth Century Art* (1960) and *Andy Warhol: Portrait of the 70s* (1981).

64 She transformed junkyards of secular carpentry into almost sacred altarpieces.
1988 On sculptor Louise Nevelson. In *Time*, 26 Dec.

Ross, Edward Alsworth 1866–1951

US sociologist, Professor at the University of Wisconsin.

65 A society...which is riven by a dozen oppositions along lines running in every direction, may actually be in less danger of being torn with violence or falling to pieces than one split along just one line. For each new cleavage contributes to narrow the cross clefts, so that one might say that society is *sewn together* by its internal conflicts.
1920 *The Principles of Sociology*.

Rossetti, Christina Georgina 1830–94

English poet and sister of Dante Gabriel Rossetti. She helped found with her brother the Pre-Raphaelite Brotherhood. A devout Christian, her poetry has a melancholic and religiously intense quality.

66 Because the birthday of my life Is come, my love is come to me.
1862 *Goblin Market and Other Poems*, 'A Birthday'.

67 Come to me in the silence of the night; Come in the speaking silence of a dream; Come with soft rounded cheeks and eyes as bright As sunlight on a stream; Come back in tears, O memory, hope, love of finished years.
1862 *Goblin Market and Other Poems*, 'Echo'.

68 For there is no friend like a sister In calm or stormy weather; To cheer one on the tedious way, To fetch one if one goes astray, To lift one if one totters down, To strengthen whilst one stands.
1862 *Goblin Market and Other Poems*, 'Goblin Market'.

69 The hope I dreamed of was a dream, Was but a dream; and now I wake, Exceeding comfortless, and worn, and old, For a dream's sake.
1862 *Goblin Market and Other Poems*, 'Mirage'.

70 Oh roses for the flush of youth, And laurel for the perfect prime; But pluck an ivy branch for me Grown old before my time.
1862 *Goblin Market and Other Poems*, 'Oh roses for the flush of youth'.

71 Remember me when I am gone away, Gone far away into the silent land.
1862 *Goblin Market and Other Poems*, 'Remember'.

72 Better by far you should forget and smile Than that you should remember and be sad.
1862 *Goblin Market and Other Poems*, 'Remember'.

73 O Earth, lie heavily upon her eyes; Seal her sweet eyes weary of watching, Earth.
1862 *Goblin Market and Other Poems*, 'Rest'.

74 Silence more musical than any song.
1862 *Goblin Market and Other Poems*, 'Rest'.

75 Does the road wind up-hill all the way?
   Yes, to the very end.
   Will the day's journey take the whole long day?
   From morn to night, my friend.
   1862 *Goblin Market and Other Poems*, 'Up-Hill'.

76 When I am dead, my dearest,
   Sing no sad songs for me;
   Plant thou no roses at my head,
   Nor shady cypress tree:
   Be the green grass above me
   With showers and dewdrops wet;
   And if thou wilt, remember,
   And if thou wilt, forget.
   1862 *Goblin Market and Other Poems*, 'When I am dead'.

77 In the bleak mid-winter
   Frosty wind made moan,
   Earth stood hard as iron,
   Water like a stone;
   Snow had fallen, snow on snow,
   Snow on snow,
   In the bleak mid-winter,
   Long ago.
   1875 'Mid-Winter'.

78 Love came down at Christmas,
   Love all lovely, Love Divine;
   Love was born at Christmas,
   Star and angels gave the sign.
   1893 *Verses* 'Love came down at Christmas'.

Rossetti, Dante Gabriel 1828–82

English painter and poet, who with his sister Christina Rossetti, Millais and Holman Hunt, founded the Pre-Raphaelite Brotherhood. His poetic works include *Poems* (1870) and *Ballads and Sonnets* (1881).

79 The blessed damozel leaned out
   From the gold bar of Heaven;
   Her eyes were deeper than the depth
   Of waters stilled at even;
   She had three lilies in her hand,
   And the stars in her hair were seven.
   1870 *Poems*, 'The Blessed Damozel', stanza 1.

80 Her hair that lay along her back
   Was yellow like ripe corn.
   1870 *Poems*, 'The Blessed Damozel', stanza 2.

81 As low as where this earth
   Spins like a fretful midge.
   1870 *Poems*, 'The Blessed Damozel', stanza 6.

82 And the souls mounting up to God
   Went by her like thin flames.
   1870 *Poems*, 'The Blessed Damozel', stanza 7.

83 'We two,' she said, 'will seek the groves

Where the lady Mary is,
With her five handmaidens, whose names
Are five sweet symphonies,
Cecily, Gertrude, Magdalen,
Margaret and Rosalys.'
1870 *Poems*, 'The Blessed Damozel', stanza 18.

84 I have been here before,
   But when or how I cannot tell:
   I know the grass beyond the door,
   The sweet keen smell,
   The sighing sound, the lights around the shore.
   1870 *Poems*, 'Sudden Light'.

85 A sonnet is a moment's monument,—
   Memorial from the Soul's eternity
   To one dead deathless hour.
   1881 *The House of Life*, introduction.

86 'Tis visible silence, still as the hour-glass.
   1881 *The House of Life*, 'Silent Noon', pt.1.

87 Deep in the sun-searched growths the dragon-fly
   Hangs like a blue thread loosened from the sky:—
   So this winged hour is dropt to us from above.
   Oh! clasp we to our hearts, for deathless dower,
   This close-companioned inarticulate hour
   When twofold silence was the song of love.
   1881 *The House of Life*, 'Silent Noon', pt.1.

88 Lo! as that youth's eyes burned at thine, so went
   Thy spell through him, and left his straight neck
      bent
   And round his heart one strangling golden hair.
   1881 *The House of Life*, 'Body's Beauty', pt.2.

89 They die not,—for their life was death,—but cease;
   And round their narrow lips the mould falls close.
   1881 *The House of Life*, 'The Choice', pt.1.

90 I do not see them here; but after death
   God knows I know the faces I shall see,
   Each one a murdered self, with low last breath.
   'I am thyself,—what hast thou done to me?'
   'And I—and I—thyself,' (lo! each one saith,)
   'And thou thyself to all eternity!'
   1881 *The House of Life*, 'Lost Days', pt.2.

91 Give honour unto Luke Evangelist;
   For he it was (the aged legends say)
   Who first taught Art to fold her hands and pray.
   1881 *The House of Life*, 'Old and New Art', pt.2.

92 When vain desire at last and vain regret
   Go hand in hand to death, and all is vain,
   What shall assuage the unforgotten pain
   And teach the unforgetful to forget?
   1881 *The House of Life*, 'The One Hope', pt.2.

93 Look in my face; my name is Might-have-been;

I am also called No-more, Too-late, Farewell.
1881 *The House of Life*, 'A Superscription', pt.2.

94 Sleepless with cold commemorative eyes.
1881 *The House of Life*, 'A Superscription', pt.2.

95 Unto the man of yearning thought
And aspiration, to do nought
Is in itself almost an act.
1881 *Ballads and Sonnets*, 'Soothsay', stanza 10.

Rossini, Gioacchino Antonio 1792–1868

Italian composer. His early operas including *La Scala de seta* (1812) and *L'Italiana in Algeri* (1813) were followed by his masterpiece, *Il Barbiere de Seviglia* (1816). His later works, mostly written in Paris, include *La Gazza Ladra* (*The Thieving Magpie*) (1817), *Semiramide* (1823) and *Guillaume Tell* (1829).

96 I was born for *opera buffa*, as well Thou knowest. Little skill, a little heart, and that is all. So be Thou blessed and admit me to Paradise.
1863 Manuscript inscription on the score of his 'Petite Messe Solennelle'.

97 *Monsieur Wagner a de beaux moments, mais de mauvais quart-d'heures!*

Monsieur Wagner has good moments, but awful quarters of an hour!
1867 Quoted in Emile Naumann *Italienische Tondichter* (1883).

Rosso, Medardo 1858–1928

Italian sculptor. Sometimes known as the 'Impressionist' sculptor, he was a major influence on the Italian Futurists.

98 When I make a portrait, I cannot limit it to the lines of the head, for that head belongs to a body, it exists in a setting which influences it, it is part of a totality that I cannot suppress. The impression you produce upon me is not the same if I catch sight of you alone in a garden or if I see you in the midst of a group of other people, in a living room or on the street.
Quoted in Edmond Claris *De l'impressionisme en sculpture*, 'Medardo Rosso' (1902).

99 One does not walk around a statue any more than one walks around a painting, because one does not walk around a figure to receive an impression from it. Nothing is material in space.
Quoted in Edmond Claris *De l'impressionisme en sculpture*, 'Medardo Rosso' (1902).

Rostand, Jean 1894–1977

French biologist and writer.

1 A body of work such as Pasteur's is inconceivable in our time: no man would be given a chance to create

a whole science. Nowadays a path is scarcely opened up when the crowd begins to pour in.
1939 'Pensées d'un Biologiste' (1939), collected in *The Substance of Man* (translated by Irma Brandeis, 1962).

2 Nothing leads the scientist so astray as a premature truth.
1939 'Pensées d'un Biologiste' (1939), collected in *The Substance of Man* (translated by Irma Brandeis, 1962).

Rosten, Leo Calvin 1908–97

US writer, humorist and anthologist. He is best known for his humorous compendium *The Joys of Yiddish* (1968), but has also written novels and stage plays (some as Leonard Ross).

3 The only thing I can say about W C Fields, whom I have admired since the day he advanced upon Baby LeRoy with an ice pick, is this: any man who hates dogs and babies can't be all bad.
1939 Speech at a Hollywood dinner in honour of W C Fields, 16 Feb.

4 The only reason for being a professional writer is that you just can't help it.
In D L Kirkpatrick (ed) *Contemporary Novelists* (1976).

Roth, Guenther 1931–

German-born US sociologist, Columbia University.

5 My draft-dodging father proved that in the struggle for survival the fittest are most likely to get killed off.
'Partisanship and Scholarship', collected in Bennett Berger (ed) *Authors of their Own Lives* (1990).

Roth, Henry 1906–95

US novelist. His novel of Jewish life in New York *Call It Sleep* (1934), was rediscovered on its paperback publication in 1962. Apart from the shorter writings collected in *Shifting Landscape* (1987), he did not publish another until the first part of a massive six-book project, *Mercy of a Rude Stream* (1994).

6 The mind shuttles and reminds. We go this way only once; and shuttles again and rejoins: once is enough.
1960 'The Dun Dakotas', in *Commentary*, 30 Aug.

7 Detach the writer from the milieu where he has experienced his greatest sense of belonging, and you have created a discontinuity within his personality, a short circuit in his identity. The result is his originality, his creativity comes to an end. He becomes the one-book novelist or the one-trilogy writer.
1987 'The Eternal Plebeian and Other Matters', in *Shifting Landscape*.

Roth, Philip Milton 1933–

US Jewish novelist. His *succès de scandale*, *Portnoy's Complaint*, was followed by a series of highly literary novels featuring his fictional alter ego, Nathan Zuckerman, all dealing with questions of Jewish identity.

8 Since I was a little girl I always wanted to be Very Decent to People. Other little girls wanted to be nurses and pianists. They were less dissembling.
1962 *Letting Go*, pt.1, ch.1.

9 It's the little questions from women about tappets that finally push men over the edge.
1962 *Letting Go*, pt.1, ch.1.

10 It's a family joke that when I was a tiny child I turned from the window out of which I was watching a snowstorm, and hopefully asked, 'Momma, do we believe in winter?'
1969 *Portnoy's Complaint*, 'The Most Unforgettable Character I've Ever Met'.

11 A Jewish man with parents alive is a fifteen-year-old boy, and will remain a fifteen-year-old boy until *they die*!
1969 *Portnoy's Complaint*, 'Cunt Crazy'.

12 Doctor, doctor, what do you say, LET'S PUT THE ID BACK IN YID!
1969 *Portnoy's Complaint*, 'Cunt Crazy'.

13 Know that famous proverb? When the prick stands up, the brains get buried in the ground!
1969 *Portnoy's Complaint*, 'Cunt Crazy'.

14 My Life as a Man.
1974 Title of novel.

15 Satire is moral outrage transformed into comic art.
1975 *Reading Myself and Others*, 'On *Our Gang*'.

16 The road to hell is paved with works-in-progress.
1979 In the *New York Times Book Review*, 15 Jul.

17 In America everything goes and nothing matters, while in Europe nothing goes and everything matters.
1983 Interview in *Time*, Nov.

18 The sooner we get of losing, the happier everyone will be.
1986 *The Great American Novel*.

19 In Israel it's enough to live—you don't have to do anything else and you go to bed exhausted. Have you ever noticed that Jews shout? Even one ear is more than you need.
1987 *The Counterlife*, ch.2.

20 What makes you a normal Jew, Nathan, is how you are riveted by Jewish abnormality.
1987 *The Counterlife*, ch.2.

21 Is an intelligent human being likely to be much more than a large-scale manufacturer of misunderstanding?

1987 *The Counterlife*, ch.5.

22 For me, as for most novelists, every genuine imaginative event begins down there, with the facts, with the specific, and not with the philosophical, the ideological, or the abstract.
1988 *The Facts: A Novelist's Autobiography*, 'Dear Zuckerman'.

23 In our lore, the Jewish family was an inviolate haven against every form of menace, from personal isolation to gentile hostility. Regardless of internal friction and strife, it was assumed to be an indissoluble consolidation… Family indivisibility, the first commandment.
1988 *The Facts: A Novelist's Autobiography*, 'Dear Zuckerman'.

24 I write fiction and I'm told it's autobiography, I write autobiography and I'm told it's fiction, so since I'm so dim and they're so smart, let *them* decide what it is or it isn't.
1990 Of critics. *Deception*, 'Philip'.

Roth, William V, Jr 1921–

US senator. A member of Congress for Delaware (1967–71), he became a Senator (1971–) and a member of the finance government affairs committee.

25 If only trimmed, it inevitably creeps back…thicker and more deeply rooted than before.
1995 Of bureaucracy, compared to crab grass. In the *Washington Times*, 19 May.

Rothko, Mark originally *Marcus Rothkovitch* 1903–70

Latvian-born painter, who emigrated to the US as a child. A largely self-taught artist, he moved from Surrealism to a distinctively meditative form of Abstract Expressionism, filling large canvases with blocks of pure colour.

26 I am not interested in relationships of color or form or anything else… I am interested only in expressing the basic human emotions—tragedy, ecstasy, doom, and so on—and the fact that lots of people break down and cry when confronted with my pictures shows that I *communicate* with those basic human emotions. The people who weep before my pictures are having the same religious experience I had when I painted them. And if you, as you say, are moved only by their color relationships, then you miss the point!
Quoted in R Rosenblum *Modern Painting and the Northern Romantic Tradition* (1975).

Rothwell, Talbot 1916–74

British screenwriter who wrote for film and television, best known for his contribution to many of the *Carry On…* films.

27 Infamy! Infamy! They've all got it in for me!

1964 Line delivered by Kenneth Williams as Julius Caesar in *Carry on Cleo*.

28 The eunuchs are on strike. They are complaining about loss of assets.
1964 *Carry on Cleo*.

Rouault, Georges (Henri) 1871–1958

French painter and engraver. Apprenticed to a stained-glass designer in his youth, he retained the characteristic glowing colour outlined in black in his later work. He joined the Fauves c.1904. His works include the large religious engravings *Miserere* and *Guerre*.

29 Decorative art does not exist—only art, intimate, heroic, or epic.
1937 *La Renaissance*.

Rous, Sir Stanley 1895–1986

English football administrator. A former player and referee, he became Secretary of the Football Association in 1934 and President of FIFA in 1961. His codification of the rules of football into 17 laws is still followed today.

30 If this can be termed the century of the common man, then soccer, of all sports, is surely his game… In a world haunted by the hydrogen and napalm bomb, the football field is a place where sanity and hope are still left unmolested.
1952 Quoted in Bryon Butler *The Official History of the Football Association* (1986).

Rousseau, Jean Jacques 1712–78

French political philosopher, educationist and writer. The father of French Romanticism, he wrote in many different genres. He is best known for his novel *Julie, ou la Nouvelle Héloïse* (1761), his autobiography, his posthumously published *Confessions*, and for *Du contrat social* (*The Social contract*, 1762).

31 *Le premier qui, ayant enclos un terrain, s'avisa de dire: 'Ceci est à moi' et trouva des gens assez simples pour le croire, fut le vrai fondateur de la société civile.*

The first person who fenced in a piece of land, ventured to say: 'This is mine,' and found others simple enough to believe him, was the true founder of civil society.
1755 *Discours sur l'origine et les fondements de l'inégalité parmi les hommes*, ch.1.

32 *L'homme est né libre, et partout il est dans les fers.*

Man is born free, yet everywhere he is in chains.
1762 *Du contrat social*, bk.1, ch.1 (translated by M Cranston).

33 *Si l'on recherche en quoi consiste précisément le plus grand bien de tous, qui doit être le fin de tout système de législation, on trouvera qu'il se réduit à ces deux objets principaux, la liberté et l'égalité.*

If we enquire wherein lies precisely the greatest good of all, which ought to be the goal of every system of law, we shall find that it comes down to two main objects, *freedom* and *equality*.
1762 *Du contrat social* (*The Social Contract*), bk.2, ch.11 (translated by M Cranston).

34 *La force a fait les premiers esclaves, leur lâcheté les a perpétués.*

Force made the first slaves; their cowardice perpetuated slavery.
1762 *Du contrat social*, bk.1, ch.2 (translated by M Cranston).

35 *L'éducation de l'homme commence à sa naissance; avant de parler, avant que d'entendre, il s'instruit déjà.*

A man's education begins when he is born; before speaking, before understanding, he is already teaching himself.
1762 *Emile ou de l'éducation*, pt.1.

36 *J'aime mieux être homme à paradoxes qu'homme à préjugés.*

I would rather be a man of paradoxes than of prejudices.
1762 *Emile ou de l'éducation*, pt.2.

37 *C'est dans le coeur de l'homme qu'est la vie du spectacle de la nature; pour le voir, il faut le sentir.*

The spectacle of nature is in the heart of a man; to see it, he must feel it.
1762 *Emile ou de l'éducation*, pt.3.

38 *L'homme dit ce qu'il sait, la femme dit ce qui plaît.*

A man says what he knows, a woman says what pleases.
1762 *Emile ou de l'éducation*, pt.5.

39 War, then, is not a relationship between man and man, but between State and State, in which private persons are only enemies accidentally.
Quoted in A J P Taylor *From the Boer War to the Cold War. Essays on Twentieth-Century Europe* (1995), 'War and Peace', p.15.

Rowbotham, Sheila 1943–

British social historian and feminist. Together with Segel and Wainwright, she wrote the controversial *Beyond the Fragments: Feminism and the Making of Socialism* (1979). She has also written *Women, Resistance and Revolution* (1972) and *Hidden From History* (1973).

40 There is no 'beginning' of feminism in the sense that there is no beginning to defiance in women.
1972 *Women, Resistance and Revolution*, ch.1.

Roy, Gabrielle 1909–83

Canadian novelist and memoirist.

41 Every writer must eventually write his Ninth Symphony or give in to despair.
1973 Letter, 1 Aug, quoted in Joan Hind-Smith *Three Voices* (1975).

Royden, Agnes Maude 1887–1967

English social worker and preacher who took a religious and moral approach to women's suffrage.

42 The Church of England should no longer be satisfied to represent only the Conservative Party at prayer.
1917 Address to the Life and Liberty Movement, London, 16 Jul.

Rubenstein, Helena 1870–1965

Polish cosmetics businesswoman. She developed and sold the first tinted foundation and face powder when she moved to New York in World War I and pioneered the use of silk in cosmetics. She used methods of mass production and marketing to attract customers who were intimidated by the cosmetics of her biggest rival - Elizabeth Arden.

43 Some women won't buy anything unless they can pay a lot.
1965 In *Time Magazine*, 9 Apr.

Ruckelhaus, William D(oyle) 1932–

US government administrator, lawyer and businessman. He served Indiana in the House of Representatives (1967–69) as majority leader and as administrator of the Environmental Protection Agency, Washington (1970–73) and (1983–85).

44 Everybody wants you to pick it up, and nobody wants you to put it down.
1988 Articulating 'the First Law of Garbage'. In *Fortune*, 21 Nov.

Rudofsky, Bernard 1905–88

Austrian-born architect, engineer and critic. He studied in Vienna, but worked in New York.

45 For it seems that long before the first enterprising man bent some twigs into a leaky roof, many animals were already accomplished builders.
1964 *Architecture without Architects.*

46 There is much to learn from architecture before it became an expert's art.
1964 *Architecture without Architects.*

Ruether, Rosemary Radford 1936–

US theologian, leading Roman Catholic exponent of feminist and liberation theology.

47 Indeed, if one can say that Christ comes to the oppressed and the oppressed especially hear him, then it is women within these marginal groups who are often seen both as the oppressed of the oppressed and also as those particularly receptive to the gospel.
1981 *To Change the World: Christology and Cultural Criticism.*

Ruiz, Juan c.1290–c.1350

Spanish poet, arch-priest of Hita. He was a vagabond for several years before entering the Church. In 1337 he was imprisoned for 13 years by the Archbishop of Toledo, Don Gil de Ardonoz.

48 *El amor siempre fabla mentiroso.*

Love is always a liar.
c.1330 *Libro de Buen Amor*, stanza 161.

49 *Por las verdades se pierden los amigos,*
e per las non dezir se fazen desamigos.

Telling the truth loses you friends;
not telling it gains you enemies.
c.1330 *Libro de Buen Amor*, stanza 165.

Rulfo, Juan 1918–86

Mexican writer. He grew up in the rural countryside that provides the setting for his two masterpieces, the short story collection *El llano en llamas* and the novel *Pedro Páramo*. Although his writing output is slim, it has been enormously influential.

50 *Sólo yo entiendo lo lejos que está el cielo de nosotros; pero conozco cómo acortar las veredas. Todo consiste en morir, Dios mediante, cuando uno quiera y no cuando Él lo disponga. O, si tú quieres, forzarlo a disponer antes de tiempo.*

I know how far away Heaven is, all right, but I know the shortcuts. You just die, God willing, when you want to, not when He arranges it. Or if you want you can make Him arrange it earlier.
1955 *Pedro Páramo* (translated 1959).

Runcie, Robert Alexander Kennedy Runcie, Baron 1921–

English Anglican prelate and Archbishop of Canterbury (1980–91). His career was marked by a papal visit to Canterbury, controversies over homosexuality and women in the Church, the Falklands War, and his envoy Terry Waite's captivity in Beirut (1987–91).

51 Royalty puts a human face on the operations of government.
1980 Sermon at a service to mark the Queen Mother's 80th birthday, St Paul's Cathedral, 15 Jul.

52 Those who dare to interpret God's will must never claim Him as an asset for one nation or group rather than another. War springs from the love and loyalty that should be offered to God being applied to some God substitute—one of the most dangerous being nationalism.
1982 Sermon at Thanksgiving Service after the Falklands War, St Paul's Cathedral, 26 Jul.

Runciman, Sir Steven 1903–

English historian of the Crusades. His works include *The Fall of Constantinople, 1453* (1965) and *Byzantine Style and Civilization* (1975).

53 The triumphs of the Crusades were the triumphs of

faith. But faith without wisdom is a dangerous thing.

1954 *A History of the Crusades*, vol.3.

Runge, Philipp Otto 1777–1810

German painter and draughtsman, a member of the German Romantic movement.

54 Art of all periods teaches us that humanity changes, and that a period, once past, never returns.

1802 Letter, Feb. Quoted in L Eitner *Neoclassicism and Romanticism 1750–1850* (1964).

55 But could we not reach the point of highest perfection in a new kind of art, in this art of landscape, and perhaps reach a higher beauty than existed before?

1802 Letter, quoted in L Eitner *Neoclassicism and Romanticism 1750–1850* (1964).

56 Colour is the ultimate in art. It is still and will always remain a mystery to us, we can only apprehend it intuitively in flowers.

1802 Letter, quoted in L Eitner *Neoclassicism and Romanticism 1750–1850* (1964).

57 We must become children again if we wish to achieve the best.

1802 From a letter quoted in R Rosenblum *Modern Painting and the Northern Romantic Tradition* (1975).

Runyon, (Alfred) Damon 1884–1946

US journalist, sportswriter and humorist. He is remembered for the colourful argot of his New York stories, which have been gathered in several collections, and provided the basis of the musical *Guys and Dolls*.

58 'My boy,' he says, 'always try to rub up against money, for if you rub up against money long enough, some of it may rub off on you.'

1931 *Guys and Dolls*, 'A Very Honourable Guy'.

59 'You are snatching a hard guy when you snatch Bookie Bob. A very hard guy, indeed. In fact,' I say, 'I hear the softest thing about him is his front teeth.'

1933 *Blue Plate Special*, 'Snatching of Bookie Bob'.

60 Any time you see him he is generally by himself because being by himself is not apt to cost him anything.

1933 *Blue Plate Special*, 'Little Miss Marker'.

61 The best thing to do right now is to throw a feed into her as the chances are that her stomach thinks her throat is cut.

1933 *Blue Plate Special*, 'Little Miss Marker'.

62 'In fact,' Sam the Gonoph says, 'I long ago come to the conclusion that all life is 6 to 5 against.'

1935 *Money From Home*, 'A Nice Price'.

63 I do not approve of guys using false pretences on dolls, except, of course, when nothing else will do.

1935 *Money From Home*, 'It Comes Up Mud'.

64 He is without strict doubt a Hoorah Henry, and he is generally figured as nothing but a lob as far as doing anything useful in this world is concerned.

1935 *Money From Home*, 'Tight Shoes'.

65 I always claim the mission workers came out too early to catch any sinners on this part of Broadway. At such an hour the sinners are still in bed resting up from their sinning of the night before, so they will be in good shape for more sinning a little later on.

1944 *Runyon à la Carte*, 'The Idyll of Miss Sarah Brown'.

66 You can keep the things of bronze and stone and give me one man to remember me just once a year.

1946 Last words.

Rushdie, (Ahmed) Salman 1947–

British novelist, born in Bombay. His works include *Midnight's Children* (1981, Booker Prize), *Imaginary Homelands* (1992) and *The Moor's Last Sigh* (1995). His novel *The Satanic Verses* (1988) provoked Iran's Ayatollah Khomeini to issue a fatwa against him (1989), and he has been in hiding since.

67 Most of what matters in your life takes place in your absence.

1981 *Midnight's Children*, 'Alpha and Omega', bk.2.

68 A poet's work… To name the unnamable, to point at frauds, to take sides, start arguments, shape the world and stop it from going to sleep.

1988 *The Satanic Verses*, pt.2.

69 To burn a book is not to destroy it. One minute of darkness will not make us blind.

1989 Book review in the *Weekend Guardian*, 14–15 Oct.

70 Books have to teach their readers how to read them.

1995 Quoted in *The Observer Review*, 16 Apr.

Rushworth, John c.1612–1690

English historian, whose *Historical Collections of Private Passages of State* (8 vols, 1659–1701) cover the period 1618–48. Clerk-assistant to the House of Commons in the Long Parliament (1640), and a parliamentary secretary, in 1684 he was imprisoned for debt.

71 His Majesty entered the House, and as he passed up towards the Chair, he cast his eye on the right hand near the Bar of the House where Mr Pym used to sit; but His Majesty, not seeing him there (knowing him well) went up to the Chair and said, 'By your leave, Mr Speaker, I must borrow your chair a little.'

1642 His account of the attempt made by Charles I to arrest five Members of Parliament on 4 Jan.

Rusk, (David) Dean 1909–94

US politician. As Secretary of State under Kennedy and Johnson (1961–9), he played a major role in the Cuban Missile Crisis of 1962.

72 We were eyeball to eyeball and the other fellow just blinked.

1962 Recalling his words on the retreat of Soviet ships during the Cuban crisis. In the *Saturday Evening Post*, 8 Dec.

73 Communications today puts a special emphasis on what happens next, for an able, sophisticated and competitive press knows that what happens today is no longer news—it is what is going to happen tomorrow that is the object of interest and concern.

1963 At *Time*'s 40th anniversary dinner, 17 May.

74 We looked into the mouth of the cannon, the Russians flinched.

Of the Cuban missile crisis. Quoted in Robert F Kennedy *Thirteen Days* (1969).

Ruskin, John 1819–1900

English author, the major art critic and social philosopher of his day, champion of Turner and the pre-Raphaelites and an opponent of Utilitarianism. His most famous works are *Modern Painters* (1843) and *The Seven Lamps of Architecture* (1848).

75 I believe the right question to ask, respecting all ornament, is simply this: Was it done with enjoyment—was the carver happy while he was about it?

1849 *Seven Lamps of Architecture*, 'The Lamp of Life', sect.24.

76 Better the rudest work that tells a story or records a fact, than the richest without meaning.

1849 *Seven Lamps of Architecture*, 'The Lamp of Memory', sect.7.

77 When we build, let us think that we build for ever.

1849 *Seven Lamps of Architecture*, 'The Lamp of Memory', sect.10.

78 Remember that the most beautiful things in the world are the most useless; peacocks and lilies for instance.

1851–3 *The Stones of Venice*, vol.i, ch.2.

79 But for me, the Alps and their people were alike beautiful in their snow, and their humanity; and I wanted, neither for them nor myself, sight of any thrones in heaven but the rocks, or any of spirits in heaven but the clouds.

1851–3 *The Stones of Venice*, vol.i, ch.2.

80 The purest and most thoughtful minds are those which love colour the most.

1851–3 *The Stones of Venice*, vol.ii, ch.5.

81 All things are literally better, lovelier, more beloved for the imperfections which have been divinely appointed.

1851–3 *The Stones of Venice*, vol.ii, ch.6.

82 No person who is not a great sculptor or painter can be an architect. If he is not a sculptor or painter, he can only be a *builder*.

1854 *Lectures on Architecture and Painting*.

83 What is poetry?… The suggestion, by the imagination, of noble grounds for the noble emotions.

1856 *Modern Painters*, vol.3, pt.4, ch.1.

84 All violent feelings…produce in us a falseness in all our impressions of external things, which I would generally characterize as the 'Pathetic Fallacy'.

1856 *Modern Painters*, vol.3, pt.4, ch.12.

85 Mountains are the beginning and the end of all natural scenery.

1856 *Modern Painters*, vol.4, pt.5, ch.20.

86 Fine art is that in which the hand, the head, and the heart of man go together.

1859 *The Two Paths*, lecture 2.

87 Not only is there but one way of *doing* things rightly, but there is only one way of *seeing* them, and that is, seeing the whole of them.

1859 *The Two Paths*, lecture 2.

88 Nobody cares much at heart about Titian; only there is a strange undercurrent of everlasting murmur about his name, which means the deep consent of all great men that he is greater than they.

1859 *The Two Paths*, lecture 2.

89 It ought to be quite as natural and straightforward a matter for a labourer to take his pension from his parish, because he has deserved well of his parish, as for a man in higher rank to take his pension from his country, because he has deserved well of his country.

1862 *Unto this Last*, preface.

90 The force of the guinea you have in your pocket depends wholly on the default of a guinea in your neighbour's pocket. If he did not want it, it would be of no use to you.

1862 *Unto this Last*, essay 2.

91 Soldiers of the ploughshare as well as soldiers of the sword.

1862 *Unto this Last*, essay 3.

92 Government and co-operation are in all things the laws of life; anarchy and competition the laws of death.

1862 *Unto this Last*, essay 3.

93 Whereas it has long been known and declared that the poor have no right to the property of the rich, I wish it also to be known and declared that the rich have no right to the property of the poor.
1862 *Unto this Last*, essay 3.

94 There is no wealth but life.
1862 *Unto this Last*, essay 4.

95 Political economy (the economy of a State, or of citizens) consists simply in the production, preservation, and distribution, at fittest time and place, of useful or pleasurable things.
1862 *Unto this Last*.

96 All books are divided into two classes, the books of the hour, and the books of all time.
1865 *Sesame and Lilies*, 'Of Kings' Treasures'.

97 Be sure that you go to the author to get at his meaning, not to find yours.
1865 *Sesame and Lilies*, 'Of Kings' Treasures'.

98 Which of us...is to do the hard and dirty work for the rest—and for what pay? Who is to do the pleasant and clean work, and for what pay?
1865 *Sesame and Lilies*, 'Of Kings' Treasures'.

99 You hear of me, among others, as a respectable architectural man-milliner; and you send for me, that I may tell you the leading fashion.
1866 *The Crown of Wild Olive*, 'Traffic', lecture 2.

1 Labour without joy is base. Labour without sorrow is base. Sorrow without labour is base. Joy without labour is base.
1867 *Time and Tide*, letter 5.

2 Your honesty is *not* to be based either on religion or policy. Both your religion and policy must be based on *it*.
1867 *Time and Tide*, letter 8.

3 The first duty of a state is to see that every child born therein shall be well housed, clothed, fed and educated, till it attain years of discretion.
1867 *Time and Tide*, letter 13.

4 Life without industry is guilt, and industry without art is brutality.
1870 *Lectures on Art*, 'The Relation of Art to Morals', lecture 3, section 95.

5 Engraving then, is, in brief terms, the Art of Scratch.
1870–85 *Ariadne Florentina*, lecture 1.

6 Thackeray settled like a meat-fly on whatever one had got for dinner, and made one sick of it.
1873 *Fors Clavigera* (published 1871–84), letter no.31, 1 Jul.

7 English artists are usually entirely ruined by residence in Italy...
1873 *Modern Painters*, vol.1, pt.1 'Of General Principles'.

8 The greatest thing a human soul ever does in this world is to *see* something, and tell what it *saw* in a plain way. Hundreds of people can talk for one who can think, but thousands can think for one who can see. To see clearly is poetry, prophecy, and religion, all in one.
1873 *Modern Painters*, vol.3, pt.4, ch.16.

9 I have seen, and heard, much of Cockney impudence before now; but never expected to hear a coxcomb ask two hundred guineas for flinging a pot of paint in the public's face.
1877 On Whistler's *Nocturne in Black and Gold*. *Fors Clavigera* (published 1871–84), letter no.79, 18 Jun.

10 Men don't and can't live by exchanging articles, but by producing them. They don't live by trade, but by work. Give up that foolish and vain title of Trades Unions; and take that of Labourers' Unions.
1880 Open Letter to English Trades Unions, 29 Sep.

11 Beethoven always sounds to me like the upsetting of a bag of nails, with here and there an also dropped hammer.
1881 Letter.

12 Of all the affected, sapless, soulless, beginningless, endless, topless, bottomless, topsiturviest, scrannel-pipiest, tongs and boniest doggerel of sounds I ever endured the deadliest of, that eternity of nothing was the deadliest.
1882 Of Wagner's *Die Meistersinger*. Letter to Mrs Burne-Jones, 30 Jun.

13 There was a rocky valley between Buxton and Bakewell...divine as the vale of Tempe; you might have seen the gods there morning and evening— Apollo and the sweet Muses of the Light... You enterprised a railroad...you blasted its rocks away... And, now, every fool in Buxton can be at Bakewell in half-an-hour, and every fool in Bakewell at Buxton.
1886–8 *Praeterita*, vol.3, pt.4, 'Joanna's Cave', note.

Russell, Bertrand Arthur William, 3rd Earl 1872–1970

Welsh philosopher and mathematician, a controversial public figure ('an enemy of religion and morality') who produced a stream of popular and provocative works on social, moral and religious issues. After 1949 he championed nuclear disarmament, and engaged in correspondence with several world leaders. He won the Nobel Prize for Literature in 1950.

14 Mathematics possesses not only truth, but supreme

beauty—a beauty cold and austere, like that of sculpture.

1903 *The Principles of Mathematics.*

15 Philosophy, if it cannot *answer* so many questions as we could wish, has at least the power of *asking* questions which increase the interest of the world, and show the strangeness and wonder lying just below the surface even in the commonest things of daily life.

1912 *The Problems of Philosophy,* ch.1.

16 The essential characteristic of philosophy, which makes it a study distinct from science is *criticism*. It examines critically the principles employed in science and in daily life; it searches out any inconsistencies there may be in these principles, and it only accepts them when, as the result of a critical inquiry, there is no reason for rejecting them.

1912 *The Problems of Philosophy,* ch.14.

17 Philosophy is to be studied, not for the sake of any definite answers to its questions, since no definite answers can, as a rule, be known to be true, but rather for the sake of the questions themselves; because these questions enlarge our conception of what is possible, enrich our intellectual imagination, and diminish the dogmatic assurance which closes the mind against speculation; but above all because, through the greatness of the universe which philosophy contemplates, the mind also is rendered great, and becomes capable of that union with the universe which constitutes its highest good.

1912 *The Problems of Philosophy,* ch.14.

18 Every proposition which we can understand must be composed wholly of constituents with which we are acquainted.

1917 *A Free Man's Worship,* 'Knowledge by Acquaintance and Knowledge by Description'.

19 The true spirit of delight, the exaltation, the sense of being more than man, which is the touchstone of the highest excellence, is to be found in mathematics as surely as in poetry.

1917 *Mysticism and Logic.*

20 The typical Westerner wishes to be the cause of as many changes as possible in his environment; the typical Chinese wishes to enjoy as much and as delicately as possible.

1922 *The Problems of China.*

21 In science men have discovered an activity of the very highest value in which they are no longer, as in art, dependent for progress upon the appearance of continually greater genius, for in science the successors stand upon the shoulders of their predecessors; where one man of supreme genius has invented a method, a thousand lesser men can apply it.

1923 *A Free Man's Worship and Other Essays.*

22 Machines are worshipped because they are beautiful, and valued because they confer power; they are hated because they are hideous, and loathed because they impose slavery.

1928 *Sceptical Essays.*

23 The scientific attitude of mind involves a sweeping away of all other desires in the interest of the desire to know.

1930 Interview in the *New Statesman,* 24 May.

24 It is, of course, clear that a country with a large foreign population must endeavour, through its schools, to assimilate the children of immigrants... It is, however, unfortunate that a large part of this process should be effected by means of a somewhat blatant nationalism.

1935 *In Praise of Idleness,* 'Modern homogeneity'.

25 No rules, however wise, are a substitute for affection and tact.

1935 *In Praise of Idleness,* 'Education and Discipline'.

26 I think modern educational theorists are inclined to attach too much importance to the negative virtue of not interfering with children, and too little to the positive merit of enjoying their company.

1935 *In Praise of Idleness,* 'Education and Discipline'.

27 Two men who differ as to the ends of life cannot hope to agree about education.

1935 *In Praise of Idleness,* 'Education and Discipline'.

28 Can a society in which thought and technique are scientific persist for a long period, as, for example, ancient Egypt persisted, or does it necessarily contain within itself forces which must bring either decay or explosion?

1949 'Can a Scientific Community be Stable?', Lloyd Roberts lecture to the Royal Society of Medicine, 29 Nov.

29 There is only one constant preoccupation: I have throughout been anxious to discover how much we can be said to know and with what degree of certainty or doubtfulness.

1959 *My Philosophical Development,* ch.1.

30 I do not think it possible to get anywhere if we start from scepticism. We must start from a broad acceptance of whatever seems to be knowledge and is not rejected for some specific reason.

1959 *My Philosophical Development,* ch.16.

31 Ever since I was engaged on *Principia Mathematica*, I have had a certain method of which at first I was scarcely conscious, but which has gradually become more explicit in my thinking. The method consists in an attempt to build a bridge between the world of sense and the world of science.
1959 *My Philosophical Development*, ch.16.

32 This idea of weapons of mass extermination is utterly horrible, and is something that no one with a spark of humanity can tolerate. I will not pretend to obey a Government that is organizing a mass massacre of mankind.
1961 Speech urging civil disobedience in support of nuclear disarmament, Birmingham, 15 Apr.

33 Obscenity is what happens to shock some elderly and ignorant magistrate.
1961 Quoted in *Look* magazine.

34 I've got a one-dimensional mind.
Quoted in R Crawshay-Williams *Russell Remembered* (1970), ch.2.

Russell, Dora 1894–1986

English feminist and pacifist, second wife of Bertrand Russell. In her many works she advocated sexual freedom and birth control.

35 We want better reasons for having children than not knowing how to prevent them.
1925 *Hypatia: or Women and Knowledge* ch.4

Russell, George William pseudonym Æ

1867–1935

Irish poet, painter, writer and economist. He met Yeats in Dublin and turned from his art studies to theosophy. His first book *Homeward: Songs by the Way* (1894) established his role in the Irish literary renaissance. He edited the *Irish Homestead* (1906–23) and subsequently the *Irish Statesman* (1923–30).

36 As Michael read the Gaelic scroll
It seemed the story of the soul;
And those who wrought, lest there should fail
From earth the legend of the Gael,
Seemed warriors of Eternal Mind
Still holding in a world gone blind,
From which belief and hope had gone,
The lovely magic of its dawn.
1922 *The Interpreters*, 'Michael'.

37 In ancient shadows and twilights
Where childhood had strayed,
The world's great sorrows were born
And its heroes were made.
In the lost boyhood of Judas,
Christ was betrayed.
1930 *Enchantment and Other Poems*, 'Germinal'.

38 No blazoned banner we unfold—
One charge alone we give to youth,
Against the sceptred myth to hold,
The golden heresy of truth.
'On Behalf of Some Irishmen not Followers of Tradition'.

Russell, Lord John 1792–1878

British Whig politician, proposer of the first Reform Bill (1832) and Prime Minister (1846–52, 1865–6).

39 If peace cannot be maintained with honour, it is no longer peace.
1853 Speech, Greenock, 19 Sep.
▷ See Cecil 247:78, Chamberlain 249:19, Disraeli 333:23.

Russell, John 1919–

English-born US art critic. He was a staff member on the London *Sunday Times* (1946–74) and art critic for the *New York Times* (1974–). His many books include *The Meanings of Modern Art* (1981).

40 It was not in Dali's nature to play Gilbert to someone else's Sullivan.
1989 On Salvador Dali's death. In the *New York Times*, 24 Jan.

41 When Dali hallucinated...the whole world hallucinated with him.
1989 On Salvador Dali's death. In the *New York Times*, 24 Jan.

Russell, Mary Annette Russell, Countess

née *Beauchamp* pseudonym *Elizabeth*

1866–1941

New-Zealand born writer, cousin of Katherine Mansfield. She came to Britain in 1871 and in 1891 married Count Von Arnim and moved to Germany, where she wrote her best-known novel *Elizabeth and her German Garden* (1898). After his death in 1910 she married Francis 2nd Earl Russell, brother of Bertrand (1916, separated 1919). Latterly she spent much time in the USA, where she enjoyed considerable popularity.

42 Far from being half a woman, a widow is the only complete example of her sex. In fact, the finished article.
1936 *All the Dogs of My Life*, pt.2, dog 9, 'Coco'.

Russell, Rosalind 1911–76

US actress. A graduate, she started her acting career in summer stock. After a contract with MGM, she formed the production company Independent Artists with her husband (1947–) and appeared in 51 films. She starred in the Broadway shows *Wonderful Town* (1953) and *Auntie Mame* (1956).

43 Flops are a part of life's menu, and I've never been a girl to miss out on any of the courses.
1957 In the *New York Herald Tribune*, 11 Apr.

Russell, Sir William Howard 1820–1907

Irish-born British war correspondent. He joined *The Times* in 1843, and wrote despatches from the Crimean War (1854–5) which swayed British public opinion against the conflict. He subsequently wrote from the Indian Mutiny (1858), the American Civil War (1861) and the Austro-Prussian War (1866).

44 They dashed on towards that thin red line tipped with steel.

1877 Of the Russians charging the British at the Battle of Balaclava, 14 Nov 1854. *The British Expedition to the Crimea.*

Russell, Willy (William) 1947–

British writer, best known for *Educating Rita* (1983) and *Shirley Valentine* (1989).

45 Of course I'm drunk—you don't really expect me to teach this stuff when I'm sober.

1983 *Educating Rita.*

Rutherford, Ernest, Baron Rutherford of Nelson 1871–1937

New Zealand-born English physicist, taught at McGill, Montreal and the University of Manchester (1907–19). In 1919 he became director Cavendish Laboratory, Cambridge. Rutherford researched radiation and received the 1908 Nobel Prize in Chemistry.

46 All science is either physics or stamp collecting.

Quoted in J B Birks *Rutherford at Manchester* (1962).

Ryan, Desmond 1893–1964

Irish journalist. He fought at the GPO in the 1916 Rising and became a journalist on his release from internment. His books include *The Man called Pearse* (1919), *The Phoenix Flame* (1937) and *The Rising* (1946).

47 The triumph of failure.

1949 Of the Irish uprising of 1916. *The Rising*, closing words.

Rybczynski, Witold Marian 1943–

Scottish-born Canadian architect and writer, whose works include *Taming the Tiger: The Struggle to Control Technology* (1983) and *Home: A Short History of an Idea* (1986).

48 The most beautiful house in the world is the one that you build for yourself.

Quoted by Pamela Young in *Maclean's*, 19 Jun 1989.

49 It is truly a place for self-presentation—of oneself, to oneself. A fitting sign of the self-absorbed 1980s.

1992 On the increasing luxuriousness of bathrooms. *Looking Around.*

Ryder, Albert Pinkham 1847–1917

US painter, whose works are characterized by dream-like figures and landscapes, evoking a romantic, lonely mood, such as *Toilers of the Sea*. His experimental technique of loading paint on the canvas caused many works to deteriorate. He became misanthropic in later life.

50 The artist needs but a roof, a crust of bread, and his easel, and all the rest God gives him in abundance. He must live to paint and not paint to live.

Quoted in Sherman *Albert Pinkham Ryder* (1920).

51 The artist should fear to become the slave of detail. He should strive to express his thought and not the surface of it. What avails a storm cloud accurate in form and colour if the storm is not therein?

Quoted in Goodrich *Albert Pinkham Ryder* (1959).

Ryle, Gilbert 1900–76

English philosopher and Professor of Philosophy at Oxford. His most famous work was *The Concept of Mind* (1949) in which he denounced Cartesian ideas of mind.

52 The dogma of the Ghost in the Machine.

1949 *The Concept of Mind.*

53 The sorts of things that I can find out about myself are the same as the sorts of things that I can find out about other people and the methods of finding them out are much the same.

1949 *The Concept of Mind.*

54 As every teacher, like every drill-sergeant or animal trainer knows in his practice, teaching and training have virtually not yet begun, so long as the pupil is too young, too stupid, too scared or too sulky to respond—and to respond is not just to yield. Where there is a modicum of alacrity, interest or anyhow docility in the pupil, where he tries, however faintheartedly, to get things right rather than awkward, where, even, he registers even a slight contempt for the poor performances of others, of chagrin at his own, pleasure at his own successes and envy of those of others, then he is, in however slight a degree, co-operating and so self-moving.

Quoted in R S Peters (ed) *The Concept of Education* (1966), ch.7.

Saarinen, Aline Bernstein née *Loucheim*

US art critic. She married the architect Eero Saarinen in 1955, who was one of the leaders of a trend in experimentation in American architecture in the 1950s.

55 He meant to gather for America an undreamed-of collection of art so great and complete that a trip to Europe would be superfluous.

1991 On the philanthropist and collector John Pierpont Morgan. In *Antiques*, Oct.

Sábato, Ernesto 1911–

Argentinian novelist, journalist and essayist. Trained in physics, he increasingly devoted himself to literature. *El túnel* is a typical existential novel that confronts the problem of the condition of human life.

56 *Había un solo túnel, oscuro y solitario: el mío, el túnel en que había transcurrido mi infancia, mi juventud, toda mi vida… Y entonces, mientras yo avanzaba siempre por mi pasadizo, ella vivía afuera su vida normal, la vida agitada que llevan esas gentes que viven afuera.*

There was only one tunnel, dark and solitary: mine, the tunnel in which I had spent my childhood, my youth, my entire life… And then, while I kept moving through my passageway, she lived her normal life outside, the exciting life of people who live outside.

1948 *El túnel*, ch.36 (translated as *The Outsider*, 1950).

Sachar, Abram Leon 1899–1993

US educator, president of Brandeis University, Massachusetts (1948–68), chancellor there (1968–82, emeritus from 1982). His works include *A History of the Jews* (1929) and *The Redemption of the Unwanted* (1983).

57 A university where, at last, the Jews are hosts, and not guests as we have always been before.

1956 Of Brandeis University, on its 10th anniversary. Speech, 19 Nov.

Sacks, Oliver Wolf 1933–

English-born US neurologist and writer.

58 The Man who Mistook his Wife for a Hat.

1985 Title of book.

Sackville-West, Vita (Victoria Mary) 1892–1962

English novelist. The daughter of the 3rd Baron Sackville, she married the diplomat Harold Nicolson. She wrote novels, poetry and memoirs, and a regular gardening column for *The Observer*.

59 Forget not bees in winter, though they sleep,
For winter's big with summer in her womb.

1926 *The Land*, 'Spring'.

60 All craftsmen share a knowledge.
They have held
Reality down fluttering to a bench.

1926 *The Land*, 'Summer'.

61 The country habit has me by the heart,
For he's bewitched for ever who has seen,
Not with his eyes but with his vision, Spring
Flow down the woods and stipple leaves with sun.

1926 *The Land*, 'Winter'.

62 The greater cats with golden eyes
Stare out between the bars.
Deserts are there, and different skies,
And night with different stars.

1929 'The Greater Cats with Golden Eyes'.

63 I have come to the conclusion, after many years of sometimes sad experience, that you cannot come to any conclusion at all.

1953 'In Your Garden Again'.

Sade, Donatien-Alphonse-François, Marquis de 1740–1814

French libertine who expressed his critique of society and the Enlightenment through his controversial behaviour. He spent most of his adult life in the prisons of Vincennes, was released during the Revolution, and eventually died in confinement.

64 *La cruauté, bien loin d'être un vice, est le premier sentiment qu'imprime en nous la nature; l'enfant brise son hochet, mord le téton de sa nourrice, étrangle son oiseau, bien avant que d'avoir l'âge de raison.*

Far from being a vice, cruelty is the primary feeling that nature imprints in us. The infant breaks its rattle, bites its nurse's nipple, and strangles a bird, well before reaching the age of reason.

1795 *La Philosophie dans le boudoir*.

65 *Quand l'athéisme voudra des martyrs, qu'il le dise et mon sang est tout prêt.*

When atheism wants martyrs, let it say so and my blood will be ready.

1797 *La Nouvelle Justine*.

Safer, Morley 1931–

Canadian-born journalist and broadcaster, he moved to US in 1964. His distinguished career includes work for Reuters, London (1955), the BBC (1961) and CBS, as Vietnam correspondent (1964–71) and as co-host of *60 minutes* news (1971–). He has seven Emmy and several Peabody awards.

66 BBC Radio is a never-never land of broadcasting, a safe haven from commercial considerations, a honey pot for every scholar and every hare-brained nut to stick a finger into.

1985 In *60 Minutes*, CBS TV broadcast, 15 Sep.

Safire, William 1929–

US journalist and author. A correspondent for radio and TV, he ran his own public relations company before President Nixon made him a special assistant (1969–73). A Pulitzer Prize winner for distinguished commentary (1978), he is a columnist for the *New York Times* (1973–).

67 The new, old, and constantly changing language of politics is a lexicon of conflict and drama…ridicule and reproach…pleading and persuasion.

1968 *Safire's Political Dictionary*, introduction.

68 Color and bite permeate a language designed to rally many men, to destroy some, and to change the minds of others.

1968 *Safire's Political Dictionary*, introduction.

69 Cover your ass—the bureaucrat's method of protecting his posterior from posterity.
1968 *Safire's Political Dictionary*, introduction.

70 A man who lies, thinking it is the truth, is an honest man, and a man who tells the truth, believing it to be a lie, is a liar.
1975 *After the Fall*, referring to Watergate and the resignation of Richard M Nixon.

71 President Reagan is a rhetorical roundheels, as befits a politician seeking empathy with his audience.
1990 *Language Maven Strikes Again*.

72 The remarkable legion of the unremarked, whose individual opinions are not as colorful or different enough to make news, but whose collective opinion, when crystallized, can make history.
1993 Of the so-called 'silent majority'. *Safire's New Political Dictionary*.

73 I was egregiously wrong.
1995 Of serving as a speech-writer for President Nixon. In *USA Today*, 30 Aug.

Sagan, Carl Edward 1934–

US astronomer and popularizer of science. He has advised NASA on interplanetary probes and argued for an active search for extraterrestrial life.

74 There is a lurking fear that some things are not meant 'to be known', that some inquiries are too dangerous for human beings to make.
1979 *Broca's Brain*.

75 Sceptical scrutiny is the means, in both science and religion, by which deep thoughts can be winnowed from deep nonsense.
1980 Interview in *The Times*, 20 Oct.

Saifoutdinov, Anvar

76 Life is not easy. I paint the memory of happiness.
Quoted by M S Mason in *Christian Science Monitor*, 19 Nov 1992.

St Laurent, Louis 1882–1973

Prime Minister of Canada, 1948–57. He was fluently bilingual, having a French father and an English mother.

77 I didn't know at first that there were two languages in Canada. I just thought that there was one way to speak to my father and another to talk to my mother.
Attributed. Quoted in Dale C Thomson *Louis St. Laurent* (1967).

78 Socialists are Liberals in a hurry.
Attributed. Quoted in Dale C Thomson *Louis St. Laurent* (1967).

Saint-Exupéry, Antoine de 1900–44

French author and aviator. A commercial and wartime pilot, his works include *Vol de Nuit*, 1931, and the children's fable *Le Petit Prince*, 1943. He was declared missing after a flight to North Africa in 1944.

79 *Il n'y a pas de fatalité extérieure. Mais il y a une fatalité intérieure.*

There is no exterior fatality, only an interior one.
1931 *Vol de Nuit*.

80 *L'expérience nous montre qu'aimer ce n'est point nous regarder l'un l'autre mais regarder ensemble dans la même direction.*

Life has taught us that love does not consist in gazing at each other but in looking together in the same direction.
1939 *Terre des Hommes*.

81 *Quand une femme me paraît belle, je n'ai rien à en dire. Je la vois sourire, tout simplement. Les intellectuels démontent le visage, pour l'expliquer par les morceaux, mais ils ne voient plus le sourire.*

When I find a woman attractive, I have nothing at all to say. I simply watch her smile. Intellectuals take apart her face in order to explain it bit by bit, but they no longer see the smile.
1942 *Pilote de Guerre*.

82 *Je combattrai pour l'Homme. Contre ses ennemis. Mais aussi contre moi-même.*

I shall fight for mankind. Against his enemies. But also against myself.
1942 *Pilote de Guerre*.

83 *Les grandes personnes ne comprennent jamais rien toutes seules, et c'est fatigant, pour les enfants, de toujours et toujours leur donner des explications.*

Adults never understand anything for themselves, and it is tiresome for children to be always and forever explaining things to them.
1943 *Le Petit Prince*.

84 *On est un peu seul dans le désert.*
—On est seul aussi chez les hommes.

One is a little bit alone in the desert.
One is also alone among others.
1943 *Le Petit Prince*.

85 *On ne voit bien qu'avec le coeur. L'essentiel est invisible pour les yeux.*

Only with the heart can a person see rightly; what is essential is invisible to the eye.
1943 *Le Petit Prince*.

86 *Un sourire est souvent l'essentiel. On est payé par un sourire. On est récompensé par un sourire. On est animé par un sourire. Et la qualité d'un sourire peut faire que l'on meure.*

A smile is often the key thing. One is paid with a smile. One is rewarded with a smile. One is brightened by a smile. And the quality of a smile can make one die.

1944 *Lettre à un otage.*

87   *La vie crée l'ordre, mais l'ordre ne crée pas la vie.*

Life creates order, but order does not create life.

1944 *Lettre à un otage.*

88   *Je suis triste pour ma génération qui est vide de toute substance humaine.*

I am sad for my generation which is empty of all human substance.

1944 *Lettre au général*, no.10. Published 10 Apr 1948 in *Le Figaro littéraire.*

89   *J'aime l'homme délivré par sa religion et vivifié par les dieux que je fonde en lui.*

I admire the person freed from his religion and inspired by the gods inside of himself.

Citadelle (published 1948).

90   *L'homme c'est ce qui est, non point ce qui s'exprime.*

Man is who he is, not how he expresses himself.

Citadelle (published 1948).

91   *Car l'homme, je te le dis, cherche sa propre destinée et non pas son bonheur.*

Because man, I tell you, is looking for his own destiny, not his own happiness.

Citadelle (published 1948).

92   *Prendre conscience, disait ailleurs mon père, c'est d'abord acquérir un style.*

To become conscious, as my father said, one must first acquire a style.

Citadelle (published 1948).

93   *Quiconque craint la contradiction et demeure logique tue en lui la vie.*

Whoever fears contradiction and remains logical kills life within himself.

Carnets (published 1953).

94   *La vérité, pour l'homme, c'est ce qui fait de lui un homme.*

Truth, for a human, is what makes him or her a human being.

Un Sens à la vie (unedited texts collected by Claude Reynal, published 1956).

Saint-Saëns, (Charles) Camille   1835–1921

French composer, music critic, pianist and organist. Founder of the Société Nationale de Musique in 1871, he composed widely and prolifically.

95   There are two kinds: one takes the music too fast, and the other too slow. There is no third!

Of conductors. Quoted in Sir Thomas Beecham *A Mingled Chime* (1944).

Saki pseudonym of *Hector Hugh Munro*
1870–1916

British novelist and short story writer. His short stories are humorous, macabre, and filled with eccentric wit. He was a gifted satirist of the Edwardian world. His collections include *Reginald* (1904) and *The Chronicles of Clovis* (1911). He was killed in World War I.

96   I always say beauty is only sin deep.

1904 *Reginald*, 'Reginald's Choir Treat'.

97   People can say what they like about the decay of Christianity; the religious system that produced green Chartreuse can never really die.

1904 *Reginald*, 'Reginald on Christmas Presents'.

98   Her frocks are built in Paris, but she wears them with a strong English accent.

1904 *Reginald*, 'Reginald on Worries'.

99   The young have aspirations that never come to pass, the old have reminiscences of what never happened.

1904 *Reginald*, 'Reginald at the Carlton'.

1   There may have been disillusionments in the lives of the medieval saints, but they would scarcely have been better pleased if they could have foreseen that their names would be associated nowadays chiefly with racehorses and the cheaper clarets.

1904 *Reginald*, 'Reginald at the Carlton'.

2   The cook was a good cook, as cooks go; and as good cooks go, she went.

1904 *Reginald*, 'Reginald on Besetting Sins'.

3   But, good gracious, you've got to educate him first. You can't expect a boy to be vicious till he's been to a good school.

1910 *Reginald in Russia*, 'The Baker's Dozen'.

4   'Is your maid called Florence?' 'Her name is Florinda.' 'What an extraordinary name to give a maid!' 'I did not give it to her; she arrived in my service already christened'. 'What I mean is,' said Mrs Riversedge, 'that when I get maids with unsuitable names I call them Jane; they soon get used to it.' 'An excellent plan,' said the aunt of Clovis coldly; 'unfortunately I have got used to being called Jane myself. It happens to be my name.'

1911 *The Chronicles of Clovis*, 'The Secret Sin of Septimus Brope'.

5   The censorious said that she slept in a hammock and understood Yeats's poems, but her family denied both stories.

1911 *The Chronicles of Clovis*, 'The Jesting of Arlington Stringham'.

6 You needn't tell me that a man who doesn't love oysters and asparagus and good wines has got a soul, or a stomach either. He's simply got the instinct for being unhappy highly developed.
1911 *The Chronicles of Clovis*, 'The Match-Maker'.

7 His socks compelled one's attention without losing one's respect.
1911 *Chronicles of Clovis*, 'Minister's of Grace'.

8 There's nothing in Christianity or Buddhism that quite matches the sympathetic unselfishness of an oyster.
1911 *Chronicles of Clovis*, 'The Match-Maker'.

9 All decent people live beyond their incomes nowadays, and those who aren't respectable live beyond other peoples. A few gifted individuals manage to do both.
1911 *Chronicles of Clovis*, 'The Match-Maker'.

10 The people of Crete unfortunately make more history than they can consume locally.
1911 *Chronicles of Clovis*, 'The Jesting of Arlington Stringham'.

11 One of the great advantages of Ireland as a place of residence is that a large number of excellent people never go there.
1914 Ludovic. *The Watched Pot, or The Mistress of Briony*.

12 'But why should you want to shield him?' cried Egbert; 'the man is a common murderer.'
'A common murderer, possibly, but a very uncommon cook.'
1914 *Beasts and Super-Beasts*, 'The Blind Spot'.

13 'Waldo is one of those people who would be enormously improved by death,' said Clovis.
1914 *Beasts and Super-Beasts*, 'The Feast of Nemesis'.

14 'I believe I take precedence,' he said coldly; 'you are merely the Club Bore: I am the Club Liar.'
1914 *Beasts and Super-Beasts*, 'A Defensive Diamond'.

15 I should be the last person to say anything against temptation, naturally, but we have a proverb down here 'in baiting a mouse-trap with cheese, always leave room for the mouse'.
The Square Egg, 'The Infernal Parliament' (published 1924).

16 A little inaccuracy sometimes saves tons of explanation.
The Square Egg, 'Clovis on the Alleged Romance of Business' (published 1924).

Sala, George Augustus Henry 1828–95

English journalist, book illustrator and novelist, born in London of Italian ancestry. He was in the US during the Civil War, in Italy with Garibaldi, in France in 1870–71, in Russia in 1876 and in Australia in 1885.

17 The foaminess of the Falls, together with the tinge of tawny yellow in the troubled waters, only reminded me of so much unattainable soda and sherry, and made me feel thirstier than ever.
1865 On seeing Niagara Falls for the first time. *My Diary in America in the Midst of War*.

Salinger, J(erome) D(avid) 1919–

US novelist. His novel *The Catcher in the Rye* is one of the most widely read novels of the era. He has published little since, and lives as a recluse in New Hampshire.

18 If you really want to hear about it, the first thing you'll probably want to know is where I was born, and what my lousy childhood was like, and how my parents were occupied and all before they had me, and all that David Copperfield kind of crap, but I don't feel like going into it.
1951 *The Catcher in The Rye*, ch.1.

19 What really knocks me out is a book that, when you're all done reading it, you wish the author that wrote it was a terrific friend of yours and you could call him up on the phone whenever you felt like it.
1951 *The Catcher in The Rye*, ch.3.

20 Sex is something I really don't understand too hot. You never know *where* the hell you are. I keep making up these sex rules for myself, and then I break them right away.
1951 *The Catcher in The Rye*, ch.9.

21 That's the thing about girls. Every time they do something pretty, even if they're not much to look at, or even if they're sort of stupid, you fall half in love with them, and then you never know *where* you are.
1951 *The Catcher in The Rye*, ch.10.

22 He looked like the kind of guy that wouldn't talk to you much unless he wanted something off you. He had a lousy personality.
1951 *The Catcher in The Rye*, ch.11.

23 The thing is it's really hard to be room-mates with people if your suitcases are much better than theirs—if yours are really good and theirs aren't. You think if they're intelligent and all, the other person, and have a good sense of humour, that they don't give a damn whose suitcases are better, but they do.
1951 *The Catcher in The Rye*, ch.15.

24 The trouble with me is, I always have to read that stuff by myself. If an actor reads it out, I hardly listen. I keep worrying about whether he's going to do something phoney every minute.
1951 Of Hamlet. *The Catcher in The Rye*, ch.16.

25 Take most people, they're crazy about cars… I'd rather have a goddam horse. A horse is at least *human*, for God's sake.
   1951 *The Catcher in The Rye*, ch.17.

26 The trouble with girls is, if they like a boy, no matter how big a bastard he is, they'll say he has an inferiority complex, and if they don't like him, no matter how nice a guy he is, or how big an inferiority complex he has, they'll say he's conceited. Even smart girls do it.
   1951 *The Catcher in The Rye*, ch.18.

27 Sally said I was a sacrilegious atheist. I probably am. The thing that Jesus *really* would've liked would be the guy that plays the kettle drums in the orchestra.
   1951 *The Catcher in The Rye*, ch.18.

28 Anyway, I keep picturing all these little kids playing some game in this big field of rye and all. Thousands of little kids, and nobody's around— nobody big, I mean—except me. And I'm standing on the edge of some crazy cliff. What I have to do, I have to catch everybody if they start to go over the cliff—I mean if they're running and they don't look where they're going I have to come out from somewhere and catch them. That's all I'd do all day. I'd just be the catcher in the rye and all. I know it's crazy, but that's the only thing I'd really like to be.
   1951 *The Catcher in The Rye*, ch.22.

29 For Esmé—with Love and Squalor.
   1953 Title of story.

30 Poetry, surely, is a crisis, perhaps the only actionable one we can call our own.
   1959 'Seymour: An Introduction'.

31 A confessional passage has probably never been written that didn't stink a little bit of the writer's pride in having given up his pride.
   1959 'Seymour: An Introduction'.

32 One of the reasons that I quit going to the theatre when I was about twenty was that I resented like hell filing out of the theatre because some playwright was forever slamming down his silly curtain.
   1959 'Seymour: An Introduction'.

Salisbury, Robert Arthur Talbot Gascoyne Cecil, 3rd Marquis of 1830–1903

English Conservative statesman. He succeeded Disraeli as Leader of the Opposition, and was subsequently Prime Minister (1885–6, 1886–92, 1895–1902), as well as holding other posts. He was head of government during the Boer Wars (1889–1902).

33 Horny-handed sons of toil.
   1873 In the *Quarterly Review*, Oct.

34 No lesson seems to be so deeply inculcated by the experience of life as that you should never trust experts. If you believe the doctors, nothing is wholesome: if you believe the theologians, nothing is innocent: if you believe the soldiers, nothing is safe. They all require to have their strong wine diluted by a very large admixture of insipid common sense.
   1877 Letter to Lord Lytton, 15 Jun. Quoted in Lady Gwendolen Cecil *Life of Robert, Marquis of Salisbury* (1921–32), vol.2, ch.4.

35 We are part of the community of Europe and we must do our duty as such.
   1888 Speech at Caernarvon, 10 Apr. In *The Times*, 11 Apr.

36 By office boys for office boys.
   Of the *Daily Mail*. The phrase recalls Thackeray's Pendennis who started a newspaper 'by gentlemen for gentlemen'. Quoted in S J Taylor *The Great Outsiders: Northcliffe, Rothermere and the Daily Mail* (1966), ch.2.

Sallust, Gaius Sallustius Crispus 86–34 BC

Roman historian and politician. As governor of Numidia he enriched himself enormously. He wrote *Bellum Catilinae*, the *Bellum Iugurthinum* and the *Historiarum libri quinque*, of which only fragments survive.

37 *Alieni appetens, sui profusus.*

   Greedy for the belongings of others, extravagant with his own.
   Bellum Catilinae, 5

38 *Esse quam videri bonus malebat.*

   He preferred to be good, rather than seem good.
   Of Cato. *Bellum Catilinae*, 54

39 *Punica fide.*

   With Punic faith.
   Used ironically (meaning treacherously) of the Numidian Bocchus, a double agent between Iugurtha and Sulla. *Bellum Iugurthinum*, 108.3.

Salter, Sir (James) Arthur, 1st Baron Salter 1881–1975

English economist, international civil servant.

40 The normal economic system works itself.
   Quoted in Ronald H Coase *Essays on Economics and Economists* (1994), p.6.

Salvianus c.400–c.470 AD

Christian writer from Gaul. His surviving works include nine epistles, *Ad Ecclesiam* and the unfinished *De Gubernatione Dei*. He urged that all estates be bequeathed to the poor, and denounced inherited wealth.

41 *Quot curiales, tot tyranni.*

   As many councillors, so many tyrants.
   De Gubernatione Dei, 5.18.27.

Sampson, Anthony (*Terrell Seward*)
1926–

English journalist and writer. His most influential book *The Anatomy of Britain* (1962) was followed by new titles on the same theme in 1965, 1971 and 1992. He was a staff member of *The Observer* (1955–66).

42 In America journalism is apt to be regarded as an extension of history: in Britain, as an extension of conversation.
   1965 *The Anatomy of Britain Today*, ch.9.

Samuel, Herbert Louis, 1st Viscount Samuel 1870–1963

English Liberal statesman and philosophical writer, Home Secretary (1916, 1931–2) and High Commissioner for Palestine (1920–5). His philosophical works include *Practical Ethics* (1935), *Belief and Action* (1937) and *In Search of Reality* (1957).

43 The House of Lords must be the only institution in the world that is kept efficient by the persistent absenteeism of its members.
   1948 In *American News Review*, 5 Feb.

44 Hansard is history's ear, already listening.
   1949 House of Lords, Dec.

Samuelson, Paul Anthony 1915–

US economist and journalist, Professor at Massachusetts Institute of Technology (1940–85). His works include *Foundations of Economic Analysis* (1947) and the classic *Economics* (1948). He won the Nobel Prize for Economics in 1970.

45 The consumer, so it is said, is the king…each is a voter who uses his money as votes to get the things done that he wants done.
   1948 *Economics*.

46 Commentators quote economic studies alleging that market downturns predicted four out of the last five recessions. That is an understatement. Wall Street indexes predicted nine out of the last five recessions!
   1966 Quoted in *The Samuelson Sampler* (1973).

Samuelson, Sir Sydney 1925–

British film commissioner. He started in the film industry in 1939 and worked as a cinema projectionist, editor and cameraman. He founded Samuelson Film Service and in 1991 was appointed the first British Film Commissioner.

47 We welcome all enquiries about the UK climate—after all, we have more weather available in this country than anywhere else.
   1994 *Check Book*.

Sand, George pseudonym of *Amandine Aurore Lucile Dupin, Baronne Dudevant* 1804–76

Popular French novelist, the illegitimate daughter of Marshal de Saxe, known for her scandalous bohemian lifestyle and her liaisons with Musset and Chopin, and later with prominent politicians.

48 *L'amour, heurtant son front aveugle à tous les obstacles de la civilisation.*

   Love, knocking its blind forehead against all of civilization's obstacles.
   1832 *Indiana*, preface.

49 *En France particulièrement, les mots ont plus d'empire que les idées.*

   In France particularly, words reign over ideas.
   1832 *Indiana*, pt.1, ch.2.

50 *L'homme qui a un peu usé ses émotions est plus pressé de plaire que d'aimer.*

   The person who has used his emotions even a little is more anxious to please than to love.
   1832 *Indiana*, pt.1, ch.5.

51 *La société ne doit rien exiger de celui qui n'attend rien d'elle.*

   Society should not ask anything of the person who expects nothing from society.
   1832 *Indiana*, conclusion.

52 *Nous ne pouvons arracher une seule page de notre vie, mais nous pouvons jeter le livre au feu.*

   We cannot tear out a single page from our life, but we can throw the entire book in the fire.
   1832 *Mauprat*.

53 *Nulle créature humaine ne peut commander à l'amour.*

   No human being can give orders to love.
   1833 *Jacques*.

54 *Le vrai est trop simple, il faut y arriver toujours par le compliqué.*

   Truth is too simple; it must always be arrived at in a complicated manner.
   1867 Letter to Armand Barbès, May.

55 *L'art pour l'art est un vain mot. L'art pour le vrai, l'art pour le beau et le bon, voilà la religion que je cherche.*

   Art for art's sake is an empty phrase. Art for the sake of the true, art for the sake of the good and the beautiful, that is the faith I search for.
   1872 Letter to Alexandre Saint-Jean.

Sandburg, Carl 1878–1967

US poet, originally a journalist in Chicago. His volumes of poetry, celebrating US life in free verse, include *Chicago*

Poems (1915) and *Good Morning, America* (1928). He also published a collection of folksongs, *The American Songbag* (1927), and a *Life of Abraham Lincoln* (6 vols, 1926–39, Pulitzer Prize). He was awarded another Pulitzer Prize for his *Complete Poems* (1950).

56 The ache to utter and see in word
    The silhouette of a brooding soul.
    1904 Describing the poet's motivation. *In Reckless Ecstasy.*

57 Hog Butcher for the World,
    Tool Maker, Stacker of Wheat,
    Player with Railroads and the Nation's Freight
      Handler;
    Stormy, husky, brawling,
    City of the Big Shoulders.
    1916 *Chicago Poems*, 'Chicago'.

58 The fog comes
    on little cat feet.

    It sits looking
    over harbor and city
    on silent haunches
    and then moves on.
    1916 *Chicago Poems*, 'Fog'.

59 (All the coaches shall be scrap and rust and all the
      men and women
    laughing in the diners and sleepers shall pass to
      ashes.)
    I ask a man in the smoker where he is going and he
      answers: 'Omaha'.
    1916 *Chicago Poems*, 'Limited'.

60 I tell you the past is a bucket of ashes.
    1918 *Cornhuskers*, 'Prairie'.

61 When Abraham Lincoln was shovelled into the
      tombs,
    he forgot the copperheads and the assassin…
    in the dust, in the cool tombs.
    1918 *Cornhuskers*, 'Cool Tombs'.

62 Pile the bodies high at Austerlitz and Waterloo.
    Shovel them under and let me work—
    I am the grass; I cover all.
    1918 *Cornhuskers*, 'Grass'.

63 Why is there always a secret singing
    When a lawyer cashes in?
    Why does a hearse horse snicker
    Hauling a lawyer away?
    1920 *Smoke and Steel*, 'The Lawyers Know Too Much'.

64 Look how you use proud words,
    When you let proud words go, it is not easy to call
      them back,
    They wear long boots, hard boots; they walk off
      proud; they can't hear you calling—
    look out how you use proud words.
    1922 *Slabs of the Sunburnt West*, 'Primer Lesson'.

65 Poetry is the opening and closing of a door, leaving
    those who look through to guess about what is seen
    during a moment.
    1923 'Poetry Considered', in the *Atlantic Monthly*, Mar.

66 Poetry is the achievement of the synthesis of
    hyacinths and biscuits.
    1923 'Poetry Considered', in the *Atlantic Monthly*, Mar.

67 The people will live on.
    The learning and blundering will live on.
    They will be tricked and sold and again sold
    And go back to the nourishing earth for rootholds.
    1936 *The People, Yes.*

68 I never made a mistake in grammar but once
    in my life and as soon as I done it I seen it.
    1936 *The People, Yes.*

69 'Would you just as soon get off the earth?'
    holding ourselves aloof in pride of distinction
    saying to ourselves this costs us nothing
    as though hate has no cost
    as though hate ever grew anything worth growing.
    1936 On 'the red men'. *The People, Yes.*

70 or we may hold them in respect and affection
    as fellow creepers on a commodious planet
    saying, 'Yes you too you too are people'.
    1936 On 'the red men'. *The People, Yes.*

71 Sometime they'll give a war and nobody will come.
    1936 *The People, Yes*

72 The people know what the land knows.
    1936 *The People, Yes.*

73 I am still studying verbs and the mystery of how
    they connect nouns. I am more suspicious of
    adjectives than at any other time in all my born
    days.
    c.1940 On receiving nearly a dozen honorary doctorates for his
    biography of Lincoln. Quoted in *The Complete Poems of Carl
    Sandburg* (1986), 'Notes for a Preface'.

74 A baby is God's opinion that life should go on.
    1948 *Remembrance Rock*, ch.2.

75 Slang is a language that rolls up its sleeves, spits on
    its hands and goes to work.
    1959 In the *New York Times*, 13 Feb.

76 In these times you have to be an optimist to open
    your eyes when you wake in the morning.
    1960 In the *New York Post*, 9 Sep.

77 The simple dignity of a child drinking a bowl of
    milk embodies the fascination of an ancient rite.
    Quoted in *Personalia, The Complete Poems of Carl Sandburg*
    (1970).

78 In the spacious highways of books major or minor,
    each poet is allowed the stride that will get him

where he wants to go if, God help him, he can hit that stride and keep it.

Quoted in *The Complete Poems of Carl Sandburg* (1986), 'Notes for a Preface'.

79 The more rhyme there is in poetry the more danger of its tricking the writer into something other than the urge in the beginning.

Quoted in *The Complete Poems of Carl Sandburg* (1986), 'Notes for a Preface'.

80 There is a formal poetry perfect only in form…the number of syllables, the designated and required stresses of accent, the rhymes if wanted—they come off with the skill of a solved crossword puzzle.

Quoted in *The Complete Poems of Carl Sandburg* (1986), 'Notes for a Preface'.

Sanders, George 1906–72

British actor who became renowned for playing cads and sophisticated villains. Among his many roles, his parts in *Rebecca* (1940*)*, *The Moon and Sixpence* (1942), *The Picture of Dorian Gray* (1944), *All About Eve* (1950) and *A Shot in the Dark* (1964) were particularly notable.

81 Dear World, I am leaving because I am bored. I feel I have lived long enough. I am leaving you with your worries in this sweet cesspool. Good luck.

1972 His suicide note.

Sandys, George 1578–1644

English translator and traveller, youngest son of the Archbishop of York. He published a verse translation of Ovid's *Metamorphoses*, written while treasurer to the colony in Virginia. He also wrote poetic versions of the *Psalms* (1636) and the *Song of Solomon* (1641).

82 Men ignorant of letters, studious for their bellies, and ignominiously lazy.

1610 On the monks of Patmos. *Relation of a Journey Begun An. Dom. 1610.*

Santayana, George originally *Jorge Augustín Nicolás Ruiz de Santayana* 1863–1952

Spanish–US philosopher, poet and novelist, Professor of Philosophy at Harvard (1907–12). His writing career began as a poet with *Sonnets and other Verses* (1894), but he later became known as a philosopher and stylist, in such works as *The Life of Reason* (5 vols, 1905–6), *Realms of Being* (4 vols, 1927–40), and his novel *The Last Puritan* (1935). He moved to Europe in 1912, stayed at Oxford during World War I, then settled in Rome.

83 Fashion is something barbarous, for it produces innovation without reason and imitation without benefit.

1905–6 *The Life of Reason*, 'Reason in Religion'.

84 Those who cannot remember the past are condemned to repeat it.

1905–6 *The Life of Reason.*

85 For an idea ever to be fashionable is ominous, since it must afterwards be always old-fashioned.

1913 *Winds of Doctrine*, 'Modernism and Christianity'.

86 Philosophy to him was rather like a maze in which he happened to find himself wandering, and what he was looking for was the way out.

1920 Of William James. *Character and Opinion in the United States.*

87 The empiricist…thinks he believes only what he sees, but he is much better at believing than at seeing.

1955 *Scepticism and Animal Faith.*

88 Art is dedicated echo.

Quoted in John Gassner and Sidney Thomas (eds) *The Nature of Art* (1964).

89 Nothing is so poor and melancholy as an art that is interested in itself and not in its subject.

Quoted in John Gassner and Sidney Thomas (eds) *The Nature of Art* (1964).

90 A building without ornamentation is like a heaven without stars.

Quoted in the *Christian Science Monitor*, 14 Dec 1990.

91 Pure poetry is pure experiment…memorable nonsense.

Quoted in Helen Gardner (ed) *The New Oxford Book of English Verse* (1991).

Sappho 7c BC

Greek lyric poetess, born on Lesbos. Most of her surviving poems are from papyrus fragments discovered in recent times.

92 He looks to me to be in heaven,
that man who sits across from you
and listens near you to your soft speaking,
your laughing lovely: that, I vow,
makes the heart leap in my breast;
for watching you a moment, speech fails me,
my tongue is paralysed, at once
a light fire runs beneath my skin,
my eyes are blinded, and my ears drumming,
the sweat pours down me, and I shake
all over, sallower than grass:
I feel as if I'm not far off dying.

D. L. Page (ed) *Lyrica Graeca Selecta* (1968), no.199 (translated by M L West).

93 Just as the sweet-apple reddens on the high branch,
high on the highest, and the apple-pickers missed it,
or rather did not miss it out, but could not reach it.

Of a girl before her marriage. D L Page (ed) *Lyrica Graeca Selecta*, (1968) no.224.

Sarduy, Severo 1937–93

Cuban novelist and essayist. He left his country for Paris in 1960. A practitioner and a theoretician of so-called neo-Baroque, he used in his novels a variety of experimental techniques, satire, parody and a carnivalistic approach.

94 *¡Ah sí, ponerse a escribir otra vez, qué vomitivo! ¡Como si todo esto sirviera para algo, como si todo esto fuera a entrar en alguna cabezota, a entretener a alguno de los lectores babosos, ovillados en sus poltronas, frente al sopón soporífero de cada día!*

Ah yes, going back to writing, what an emetic! As if all this had some purpose, as if all this would penetrate some thick skull, occupy some drivelling reader curled up in his armchair before the soporific stew of every living!
1967 *De donde son los cantantes* (translated as *From Cuba with a Song*, 1972), 'La Dolores Rondón'.

Sargent, Sir (Harold) Malcolm Watts 1895–1967

British conductor. Originally trained as an organist, he was conductor of the Royal Choral Society from 1928, was in charge of the Liverpool Philharmonic Orchestra (1942–48) and led the BBC Symphony Orchestra (1950–57).

95 Just a little more reverence, please, and not so much astonishment.
Attributed, admonishing a choir singing Handel's 'For Unto Us a Child is Born'.

Sarnoff, David 1891–1971

Russian-born US radio and television pioneer. He began with the Marconi Wireless Co, covering the Titanic disaster (1912), and became president (1930) and chairman of the board (1947) of the Radio Corporation of America, a key figure in the development of television.

96 Seldom is it given to one generation to have such an opportunity to rise again, but now before you is that opportunity in television—a larger, richer, broader opportunity than ever existed in radio.
c.1948 Speech to NBC station affiliates. Recalled on his death, 12 Dec 1971.

97 Competition brings out the best in products and the worst in people.
Attributed.

Saroyan, William 1908–81

US playwright and novelist. He was awarded the Pulitzer Prize in 1939 for his best-known play, *The Time of Your Life.*

98 The Daring Young Man on the Flying Trapeze.
1934 Title of story collection.

99 The events of life have never fallen into the form of the short story or the form of the poem, or into any

other form. Your own consciousness is the only form you need.
1934 *The Daring Young Man on the Flying Trapeze*, 'A Cold Day'.

1 Now what?
1981 Last words.

Sarraute, Nathalie 1900–

French novelist and literary critic.

2 *Le mot 'psychologie' est un de ceux qu'aucun auteur d'aujourd'hui ne peut entendre prononcer à son sujet sans baisser les yeux et rougir.*

The word 'psychology' is one that no author today can hear said about her work without lowering her eyes and blushing.
1956 *L'Ere du Soupçon.*

3 *Vous savez qu'on doit se sentir heureux. Tous les vrais écrivains ont éprouvé ce sentiment. Quand on ne l'éprouve pas, je suis obligé de vous en avertir, c'est mauvais signe.*

You know that one should feel happy. All the true writers have experienced this feeling. When one does not experience it, I am obliged to tell you that it is a bad sign.
1968 *Entre la Vie et la Mort.*

4 *Chacun peut éprouver en soi ce double mouvement: désir de s'intégrer à la société, besoin de se réaliser par soi-même en dehors d'elle.*

Each of us experience within ourselves this contradictory motion: the desire to integrate in society and the need to fulfil ourselves outside of society.
La Quinzaine littéraire, 50.

Sarton, George A 1884–1956

US academic and historian of science.

5 Definition—Science is systematized positive knowledge, what has been taken as such in different ages and in different places. Theorem— The acquisition and systematization of positive knowledge are the only human activities which are truly cumulative and progressive. Corollary—The history of science is the only history which can illustrate the progress of mankind. In fact, progress has no definite and unquestionable meaning in other fields than the field of science.
1957 *The Study of the History of Science.*

Sarton, May 1912–95

US poet and novelist. Her poetry collections include *Inner Landscape* (1939), *The Land of Silence* (1953) and *The Silence Now* (1988), and she wrote other works such as *Mrs Stevens hears the Mermaids Singing* (1965) and an autobiography, *A World of Light* (1976).

6 The poet must be free to love or hate as the spirit moves him, free to change, free to be a chameleon, free to be an *enfant terrible*. He must above all never worry about his effect on other people. Power requires that one do just that all the time. Power requires that the inner person never be unmasked. No, we poets have to go naked. And since this is so, it is better that we stay private people; a naked public person would be rather ridiculous, what?

1965 Hilary Stevens speaking, in *Mrs Stevens Hears the Mermaids Singing*, pt.2.

7 I write poems, have always written them, to transcend the painfully personal and reach the universal.

Quoted in *Encore: A Journal of the 80th Year* (1993).

8 When you're a poet, you're a poet first. When it comes, it's like an angel.

Quoted by Mel Gussow in her obituary, in the *New York Times*, 18 Jul 1995.

Sartre, Jean-Paul 1905–80

French existentialist philosopher and writer, a prominent intellectual and friend of Simone de Beauvoir. His works include the trilogy *Les Chemins de la liberté* (The Roads to Freedom, 1945–9) and many plays. His philosophy is presented in *L'Être et le néant* (Being and Nothingness, 1943). In 1964 he published his autobiography *Les Mots* (Words), and was awarded (but declined) the Nobel Prize for Literature.

9 *Trois heures, c'est toujours trop tard ou trop tôt pour tout ce qu'on veut faire.*

Three o'clock is always either too late or too early for anything one might want to do.

1938 *La Nausée*, 'Vendredi'.

10 *L'homme est une passion inutile.*

Man is a useless passion.

1943 *L'Être et le néant* (*Being and nothingness*, 1957) pt.4, ch.2, section 3 (translated by Hazel Barnes).

11 *L'Enfer, c'est les Autres.*

Hell is other people.

1945 *Huis Clos.*

12 *Est-ce qu'au fond, ce qui fait peur, dans la doctrine que je vais essayer de vous exposer, ce n'est pas le fait qu'elle laisse une possibilité de choix à l'homme?*

For at bottom, what is alarming in the doctrine that I am about to try to explain to you is—is it not?—that it confronts man with a possibility of choice.

1946 *L'Existentialisme est un humanisme* (*Existentialism and Humanism*, 1948) (translated by Philip Mairet).

13 *Ce qu'ils ont en commun, c'est simplement le fait qu'ils estiment que l'existence précède l'essence, ou, si vous voulez, qu'il faut partir de la subjectivité.*

What [existentialists] have in common is simply the fact that they believe that *existence* comes before *essence*—or, if you will, that we must begin from the subjective.

1946 *L'Existentialisme est un humanisme* (*Existentialism and Humanism*, 1948) (translated by Philip Mairet).

14 *Qu'est-ce que signifie que l'existence précède l'essence? Cela signifie que l'homme existe d'abord, se rencontre, surgit dans le monde, et qu'il se définit après.*

What do we mean by saying that existence precedes essence? We mean that man first of all exists, encounters himself, surges up in the world—and defines himself afterwards.

1946 *L'Existentialisme est un humanisme* (*Existentialism and Humanism*, 1948) (translated by Philip Mairet).

15 *L'homme n'est rien d'autre que ce qu'il se fait. Tel est le premier principe de l'existentialisme.*

Man is nothing else but that which he makes of himself. That is the first principle of existentialism.

1946 *L'Existentialisme est un humanisme* (*Existentialism and Humanism*, 1948) (translated by Philip Mairet).

16 *L'homme est condamné à être libre.*

Man is condemned to be free.

1946 *L'Existentialisme est un humanisme* (*Existentialism and Humanism*, 1948) (translated by Philip Mairet).

17 *Un homme n'est rien d'autre qu'une série d'entreprises.*

Man is no other than a series of undertakings.

1946 *L'Existentialisme est un humanisme* (*Existentialism and Humanism*, 1948) (translated by Philip Mairet).

18 *Il n'y a pas d'autre univers qu'un univers humain, l'univers de la subjectivité humaine.*

There is no other universe except the human universe, the universe of human subjectivity.

1946 *L'Existentialisme est un humanisme* (*Existentialism and Humanism*, 1948) (translated by Philip Mairet).

19 *Vous êtes libre, choisissez, c'est-à-dire, inventez. Aucune morale générale ne peut vous indiquer ce qu'il y a à faire.*

You are free, therefore choose—that is to say, invent. No rule of general morality can show you what you ought to do.

1946 *L'Existentialisme est un humanisme* (*Existentialism and Humanism*, 1948) (translated by Philip Mairet).

20 The status of 'native' is a nervous condition introduced and maintained by the settler among colonized people *with their consent.*

1961 Preface to Franz Fanon *Les damnés de la Terre* (*The Wretched of the Earth*, 1967, translated by Constance Farrington). Tsitsi Dangarembga uses this sentence to supply both epigraph and title of her 1988 novel *Nervous Conditions*.

Sassoon, Siegfried Louvain 1886–1967

English poet and novelist. He established his reputation as a war poet while serving in World War I. He wrote a semi-autobiographical trilogy, *The Memoirs of George Sherston*, and several volumes of actual memoirs.

21 I am making this statement as an act of wilful defiance of military authority, because I believe that the War is being deliberately prolonged by those who have the power to end it.
1917 'A Soldier's Declaration'. Statement sent to his commanding officer which was read out in the House of Commons and printed in *The Times*.

22 I'd like to see a Tank come down the stalls, Lurching to rag-time tunes, or 'Home sweet Home',—
And there'd be no more jokes in Music-halls To mock the riddled corpses round Bapaume.
1917 'Blighters'.

23 How right it seemed that he should reach the span Of comfortable years allowed to man!
Splendid to eat and sleep and choose a wife, Safe with his wound, a citizen of life.
He hobbled blithely through the garden gate, And thought: 'Thank God they had to amputate!'
1917 'The One-Legged Man'.

24 We'd gained our first objective hours before While dawn broke like a face with blinking eyes, Pallid, unshaved and thirsty, blind with smoke.
1918 'Counter-Attack'.

25 Soldiers are citizens of death's grey land,
—Drawing no dividend from time's to-morrows.
In the great hour of destiny they stand,
—Each with his feuds, and jealousies, and sorrows.
Soldiers are sworn to action; they must win
—Some flaming, fatal climax with their lives.
Soldiers are dreamers; when the guns begin
—They think of firelit homes, clean beds and wives.
1918 'Dreamers'.

26 If I were fierce and bald and short of breath I'd live with scarlet Majors at the Base, And speed glum heroes up the line to death.
1918 'Base Details'.

27 And when war is done and youth stone dead I'd toddle safely home and die—in bed.
1918 'Base Details'.

28 'Good-morning; good-morning!' the General said When we met him last week on our way to the line.
Now the soldiers he smiled at are most of 'em dead, And we're cursing his staff for incompetent swine.
'He's a cheery old card,' grunted Harry to Jack As they slogged up to Arras with rifle and pack.

But he did for them both by his plan of attack.
1918 'The General'.

29 Does it matter?—losing your sight?…
There's such splendid work for the blind; And people will always be kind As you sit on the terrace remembering And turning your face to the light.
1918 'Does It Matter'.

30 From you, Beethoven, Bach, Mozart, The substance of my dreams took fire.
You built cathedrals in my heart, And lit my pinnacled desire.
1918 'Dead Musicians'.

31 You have no part with lads who fought And laughed and suffered at my side.
Your fugues and symphonies have brought No memory of my friends who died.
1918 'Dead Musicians'.

32 Why do you lie with your legs ungainly huddled, And one arm bent across your sullen cold Exhausted face?
1918 'The Dug-Out'.

33 You are too young to fall asleep for ever; And when you sleep you remind me of the dead.
1918 'The Dug-Out'.

34 Everyone suddenly burst out singing; And I was filled with such delight As prisoned birds must find in freedom,
1919 'Everyone Sang'.

35 But the past is just the same,—and War's a bloody game
1919 'Aftermath'.

36 When all is said and done, leading a good life is more important than keeping a good diary.
1923 Diary entry, 8 Jul.

37 In me the tiger sniffs the rose.
1928 *The Heart's Journey*, pt.7, 'In me, past, present, future meet'.

38 And what is time but shadows that were cast By these storm-sculptured stones while centuries fled?
The stones remain; their stillness can outlast The skies of history hurrying overhead.
1928 *The Heart's Journey*, pt.9, 'What is Stonehenge? It is the roofless past'.

39 *Alone*… The word is life endured and known.
It is the stillness where our spirits walk And all but inmost faith is overthrown.
1928 *The Heart's Journey*, pt.11, '"When I'm alone—the words tripped off his tongue"'.

40 They have spoken lightly of my deathless friends, (Lamps for my gloom, hands guiding where I stumble,)

Quoting, for shallow conversational ends,
What Shelley shrilled, what Blake once wildly
   muttered...
How can they use such names and be not humble?
1928 *The Heart's Journey*, pt.15, 'Grandeur of Ghosts'.

41 Who will remember, passing through this Gate,
The unheroic Dead who fed the guns?
Who shall absolve the foulness of their fate,—
Those doomed, conscripted, unvictorious ones?
1928 *The Heart's Journey*, pt.21, 'On Passing the New Menin Gate'.

42 Here Vaughan lies dead, whose name flows on for
   ever
Through pastures of the spirit washed with dew
And starlit with eternities unknown.
1928 *The Heart's Journey*, pt.23, 'At The Grave of Henry Vaughan'.

43 The skull that housed white angels and had vision
Of daybreak through the gateways of the mind.
1928 *The Heart's Journey*, pt.23, 'At The Grave of Henry Vaughan'.

44 A man may be born a poet, but he has to make
himself an artist as well.
1939 *On Poetry*.

Satie, Erik Alfred Leslie 1866–1925

French composer. A pupil of Vincent D'Indy and Albert
Roussel, he wrote ballets, lyric dramas and numerous
whimsical pieces in which he rebelled against Wagnerism
and orthodoxy in general. His music had some influence
on Debussy, Ravel and others.

45 Before I compose a piece, I walk round it several
times, accompanied by myself.
Quoted in *Bulletin des éditions musicales* (1913).

46 To be played with both hands in the pocket.
Instruction on one of his piano compositions. Quoted in Oscar
Levant *The Unimportance of Being Oscar* (1968).

47 It is not enough to refuse the Legion d'Honneur.
One should never have deserved it.
Of Maurice Ravel, who had declined the honour. Quoted by
Alister Kershaw in *The Australian*, 1991.

Sayers, Dorothy L(eigh) 1893–1957

English detective-story writer. Her hero, Lord Peter
Wimsey, is one of the most popular of the great detectives,
and her books are distinguished by realistically created
settings as well as stylish wit. She also wrote plays and
poems.

48 I admit it is more fun to punt than to be punted,
and that a desire to have all the fun is nine-tenths of
the law of chivalry.
1935 *Gaudy Night*, ch.14.

49 I can't see that she could have found anything
nastier to say if she'd thought it out with both
hands for a fortnight.
1937 'Prothalamion'.

50 Plain lies are dangerous.
1937 'The Psychology of Advertising', in *The Spectator*, 19 Nov.

51 Those who prefer their English sloppy have only
themselves to thank if the advertisement writer uses
his mastery of vocabulary and syntax to mislead
their weak minds.
1937 'The Psychology of Advertising', in *The Spectator*, 19 Nov.

52 The moral of all this...is that we have the kind of
advertising we deserve.
1937 'The Psychology of Advertising', in *The Spectator*, 19 Nov.

53 As I grow older and older,
And totter towards the tomb,
I find that I care less and less
Who goes to bed with whom.
'That's Why I Never Read Modern Novels', collected in Janet
Hitchman *Such a Strange Lady* (1975), ch.12.

Scargill, Arthur 1938–

English trade union leader, president of the NUM
(1982), and a member of the TUC General Council. A
powerful orator, his strong defence of miners and his
socialist politics have led to conflict with government,
particularly in the miners' strike of 1984–5. He started a
new socialist party in 1995.

54 My father still reads the dictionary every day. He
says that your life depends on your power to master
words.
1982 In *The Sunday Times*, 10 Jan.

55 I speak of that most dangerous duo—President
Ray-Gun and the plutonium blonde, Margaret
Thatcher.
1984 Quoted in *Time*, 3 Dec.

Scève, Maurice c.1510–c.1564

French poet of the École Lyonnaise. His most famous
collection of poems, *Délie, objet de plus haulte vertu*, is a
meditation on love.

56 *Car loi d'Amour est de l'un captiver,*
L'autre donner d'heureuse liberté.

The law of love is to captivate one,
And to give another joyous freedom.
1544 *Délie*, no.40.

57 *En toi je vis, où que tu sois absente;*
En moi je meurs, où que je sois présent.
Tant loin sois-tu, toujours tu es présente;
Pour près que sois, encore suis-je absent.

I live in you when you are absent;
I die in myself when you are present.
No matter how far away you are, you are always
   present;
And when you are near, I am always absent.
1544 *Délie*, no.144.

58   *Tu es le Corps, Dame, et je suis ton ombre.*

You are the body, lady, and I am your shadow.
1544 *Délie*, no.376.

Schacht, Hjalmar Horace Greely

1877–1970

German financier. As president of the Reichsbank (1923)
he ended inflation, and recalled by the Nazis from
resignation in 1933, he restored the German trade
balance by unorthodox methods. Dismissed after
disagreement with Hitler, he was later acquitted at
Nuremberg of crimes against humanity.

59   I wouldn't believe that Hitler was dead, even if he
   told me himself.
   1945 Attributed remark, 8 May.

Scharansky, Natan Anatoly Borisovich

1948–

Ukrainian-born Soviet dissident and human rights
activist. He was imprisoned (1977–86) by the Soviet
government. As a Jew, he applied for emigration rights to
Israel in 1975, but was harassed by the KGB and
discharged from his job. His command of English helped
him become a spokesman for dissidents to the West. He
was arrested in 1977 and accused of treason and
espionage. On his release from prison he was allowed to
go to Israel.

60   All the resources of a superpower cannot isolate a
   man who hears the voice of freedom; a voice that I
   heard from the very chamber of my soul.
   1986 Speech, New York, 11 May, shortly after his release
   following nine years in a Soviet labour colony.

Schaw, Janet   b.c.1730

Scottish traveller. She was distantly related to Sir Walter
Scott and was well educated, but little is known of
her other than what is told in her *Journal of a Lady of
Quality*, an account of her travels in the West Indies in
1774–6.

61   At last America is in my view; a dreary waste of
   white barren sand, and melancholy, nodding pines.
   In the course of many miles, no cheerful cottage
   has blest my eyes. All seems dreary, savage and
   desert; and was it for this such sums of money, such
   streams of British blood have been lavished away ?
   Oh, thou dear land, how dearly hast thou
   purchased this habitation for bears and wolves.
   Dearly has it been purchased, and at a price far

dearer still it will be kept. My heart dies within me,
while I view it.
   c.1776 On her first sight of the country around Cape Fear.
   *Journal of a Lady of Quality; Being the Narrative of a Journey from
   Scotland to the West Indies, North Carolina, and Portugal, in the
   years 1774 to 1776.*

Schiaparelli, Elsa   1890–1973

Italian fashion designer who opened one of the first
couture boutiques in Paris in 1935. She was known for
introducing the colour 'shocking pink' into the fashion
world.

62   So fashion is born by small facts, trends, or even
   politics, never by trying to make little pleats and
   furbelows, by trinkets, by clothes easy to copy, or
   by the shortening or lengthening of a skirt.
   1954 *A Shocking Life*, ch.9.

63   A good cook is like a sorceress who dispenses
   happiness.
   1954 *A Shocking Life*, ch.21.

Schiller, Friedrich   1759–1805

German poet and playwright who was briefly a surgeon
before turning his attention to writing and travelling.

64   *Alle anderen Dinge müssen; der Mensch ist das Wesen,
   welches will.*

   All other things must; man is the being who wills.
   1794 *Über das Erhabene.*

65   *Man kann den Menschen nicht verwehren,
   Zu denken, was sie wollen.*

   One cannot prevent people from thinking what
   they please.
   1800 *Maria Stuart*, act 1, sc.8.

66   *Was man scheint,
   Hat jedermann zum Richter; was man ist, hat keine.*

   What we appear to be is subject to the judgement
   Of all mankind, and what we truly are, of no one.
   1800 *Maria Stuart*, act 2, sc.5.

67   *Was man nicht aufgibt, hat man nie verloren.*

   What is not abandoned is never completely lost.
   1800 *Maria Stuart*, act 2, sc.5.

68   *Das Leben ist
   Nur ein Moment, der Tod ist auch nur einer.*

   Life is but a moment. Death is but a moment, too.
   1800 *Maria Stuart*, act 3, sc.6.

69   *Den stolzen Sieger stürzt sein eignes Glück.*

   The victor is often vanquished by his own success.
   1801 *Die Jungfrau von Orléans*, act 1, sc.5.

70   *Mehr als das Leben lieb' ich meine Freiheit.*

   More than life, I cherish freedom.
   1801 *Die Jungfrau von Orléans*, act 2, sc.2.

71 *Mitt der dummheit kämpfen Götter selbst vergebens.*

Even the gods themselves struggle in vain against stupidity.

1801 *Die Jungfrau von Orléans*, act 3, sc.6.

72 *In seinen Göttern malt sich der Mensch.*

Humankind is reflected in its gods.

1789 *Was heißt und zu welchem Ende studiert man Universalgeschichte?*

Schlesinger, Arthur Meier 1888–1965

US historian. His works include *New Viewpoints in American History* (1922) and a *History of American Life* (13 vols, 1928–43).

73 The military struggle may frankly be regarded for what it actually was, namely a war for independence, an armed attempt to impose the views of the revolutionists on the British government and large sections of the colonial population at whatever cost to freedom of opinion or the sanctity of life and property.

1919 'The American Revolution Reconsidered', in *Political Science Quarterly*, Mar.

Schlesinger, Arthur M(eier), Jr 1917–

US historian and special assistant to President Kennedy (1961–3). His works include the Pulitzer prizewinners *The Age of Jackson* (1945) and *A Thousand Days: John F Kennedy in the White House* (1965). He became president of the American Institute of Arts and Letters (1981).

74 He read partly for information, partly for comparison, partly for insight, partly for the sheer joy of felicitous statement. He delighted particularly in quotations which distilled the essence of an argument.

1965 Of John F Kennedy. *A Thousand Days*.

75 Ceremony, circus, farce, melodrama, tragedy…nothing else offers all at once the whirl, the excitement, the gaiety, the intrigue and the anguish.

1965 On national political conventions. *A Thousand Days*.

76 At the time it is all a confusion; in retrospect…all a blur.

1965 On national political conventions. *A Thousand Days*.

77 The things people had once held against her…unconventional beauty…un-American elegance, the taste for French clothes and French food—were suddenly no longer liabilities but assets.

1965 On Jacqueline Kennedy's post-election image. *A Thousand Days*.

78 Television has spread the habit of instant reaction and has stimulated the hope of instant results.

1970 In *Newsweek*, 6 Jul.

Schlesinger, James 1932–

79 The notion of a defence that will protect American cities is one that will not be achieved, but it is that goal that supplies the political magic in the President's vision.

1987 Senate Foreign Relations Committee, 6 Feb.

Schmitt, Wolfgang Rudolph 1944–

German-born US businessman. He joined houseware manufacturers Rubbermaid Inc in 1966, becoming president in 1991.

80 Innovation most of the time is simply taking A, B, C and D, which already exist, and putting them together in a form called E.

1994 In *Fortune*, 14 Nov.

Schnabel, Artur 1882–1951

Austrian pianist and composer. He studied under Leschetizsky and made his début at the age of eight. Subsequently he toured throughout Europe and America, where he settled in 1939. He was an authoritative player of a small range of German classics—notably Beethoven, Mozart and Schubert.

81 The notes I handle no better than many pianists. But the pauses between the notes—ah, that is where the art resides.

1958 In the *Chicago Daily News*, 11 Jun.

82 Applause is a receipt, not a bill.

Explaining why he did not play encores. Quoted in I Kolodin *The Musical Life* (1958).

83 I know two kinds of audience only—one coughing and one not coughing.

1961 *My Life and Music*.

84 I don't think there was ever a piece of music that changed a man's decision on how to vote.

1961 *My Life and Music*.

85 When a piece gets difficult make faces.

Quoted in Oscar Levant *The Unimportance of Being Oscar* (1968).

86 The sonatas of Mozart are unique; they are too easy for children, and too difficult for artists.

Quoted in Nat Shapiro *An Encyclopedia of Quotations about Music* (1978).

Schoenbaum, Thomas J

Professor of Political Science, University of Georgia.

87 [He] made himself the rock against which crashed the successive waves of dissent.

1988 Of Secretary of State Dean Rusk during the Vietnam War. *Waging Peace and War*.

Schoenberg, Arnold Franz Walter
1874–1951

Austrian composer, conductor and teacher. A self-taught pioneer of atonality, his works include the tone poem *Pelleas und Melisande* (1903), the song cycle *Pierrot Lunaire* (1912), operas, chamber music and other choral and orchestral pieces. He lived in the US from 1933.

88 Harmony! Harmony!
1951 Attributed last words.

89 My music is not modern, it is merely badly played.
Quoted in C Rosen *Schoenberg* (1976).

90 If it is art it is not for all, and if it is for all it is not art.
Quoted in Ian Crofton and Donald Fraser *A Dictionary of Musical Quotations* (1985).

Schopenhauer, Artur 1788–1860

German philosopher, whose work is often characterized as a systematic philosophical pessimism. His major work was *Die Welt als Wille und Vorstellung* (*The World as Will and Representation*), published in 1819. A second enlarged edition followed in 1844.

91 *Alle Befriedigung, oder was man gemeinhin Glück nennt, ist eigentlich und wesentlich immer nur negativ und durchaus nie positiv.*

All satisfaction, or what is commonly called happiness, is really and essentially always *negative* only, and never positive.
1819 *Die Welt als Wille und Vorstellung* (*The World as Will and Representation*), vol.1, bk.4, ch.58 (translated by E F J Payne).

92 *Wir tappen im Labyrinth unsers Lebenswandels und im Dunkel unserer Forschungen umher: helle Augenblicke erleuchten dabei wie Blitze unsern Weg.*

We grope about in the labyrinth of our life and in the obscurity of our investigations; bright moments illuminate our path like flashes of lightning.
1844 *Die Welt als Wille und Vorstellung* (*The World as Will and Representation*), vol.2, ch.15 (translated by E F J Payne).

93 *Das Ganze der Erfahrung gleicht einer Geheimschrift und die Philosophie der Entzifferung derselben.*

The whole of experience is like a cryptograph, and philosophy is like the deciphering of it.
1844 *Die Welt als Wille und Vorstellung* (*The World as Will and Representation*), vol.2, ch.17 (translated by E F J Payne).

94 *Ist es an und für sich absurd, das Nichtsein für ein Übel zu halten; da jedes Übel wie jedes Gut das Dasein zur Voraussetzung hat, ja sogar das Bewußtsein.*

It is in and by itself absurd to regard non-existence as an evil; for every evil, like every good, presupposes existence, indeed even consciousness.
1844 *Die Welt als Wille und Vorstellung* (*The World as Will and Representation*), vol.2, ch.41 (translated by E F J Payne).

95 *Unsterblichkeit der Individualität verlangen heißt eigentlich einen Irrtum ins Unendliche perpetuieren wollen. Denn im Grunde ist doch jede Individualität nur ein spezieller Irrtum, Fehltritt, etwas, das besser nicht wäre, ja wovon uns zurückzubringen der eigentliche Zweck des Lebens ist.*

To desire immortality for the individual is really the same as wanting to perpetuate an error for ever; for at bottom every individuality is really only a special error, a false step, something that it would be better should not be, in fact something from which it is the real purpose of life to bring us back.
1844 *Die Welt als Wille und Vorstellung* (*The World as Will and Representation*), vol.2, ch.41 (translated by E F J Payne).

96 *Alle Verliebtheit wurzelt allein im Geschlechtstriebe.*

All amorousness is rooted in the sexual impulse alone.
1844 *Die Welt als Wille und Vorstellung* (*The World as Will and Representation*), vol.2, ch.44 (translated by E F J Payne).

97 *Was man auch sagen mag, der glücklichste Augenblick des Glücklichen ist doch der seines Einschlafens wie der unglücklichste des Unglücklichen der seines Erwachens.*

Whatever we may say, the happiest moment of the happy man is that of his falling asleep, just as the unhappiest moment of the unhappy man is that of his awakening.
1844 *Die Welt als Wille und Vorstellung* (*The World as Will and Representation*), vol.2, ch.46 (translated by E F J Payne).

98 *Es gibt nur einen Irrtum, und es ist der, daß wir dasind, um glücklich zu sein.*

There is only one inborn error, and that is the notion that we exist in order to be happy.
1844 *Die Welt als Wille und Vorstellung* (*The World as Will and Representation*), vol.2, ch.49 (translated by E F J Payne).

99 *Die Szenen unsers Lebens gleichen den Bildern in großer Mosaik, welche in der Nähe keine Wirkung tun, sondern von denen man fern stehn muß, um sie schön zu finden.*

The scenes of our life resemble pictures in rough mosaic; they are ineffective from close up, and have to be viewed from a distance if they are to seem beautiful.
1851 *Parerga und Paralipomena*, ch.11 (translated by R J Hollingdale).

1 *Jede Trennung gibt einen Vorgeschmack des Todes— und jedes Wiedersehn einen Vorgeschmack der Auferstehung.*

Every parting is a foretaste of death, and every reunion a foretaste of resurrection.
1851 *Parerga und Paralipomena*, ch.26 (translated by R J Hollingdale).

Schreiner, Olive Emily Albertina

pseudonym *Ralph Iron* 1855–1920

South African feminist, novelist and polemicist. Educated at home against a strict religious background, she is best known for her semi-autobiographical novel, *The Story of an African Farm* (1883) which rejects the spiritual aridity of colonial life and loveless marriage.

2 This pretty ring…I will give it to the first man who tells me he would like to be a woman. It is delightful to be a woman; but every man thanks the Lord devoutly that he isn't one.
1883 *The Story of an African Farm*, ch.17, 'Lyndall'.

3 We are cursed, Waldo, born cursed from the time our mothers bring us into the world till the shrouds are put on us.
1883 Lyndall. *The Story of an African Farm*, ch.17, 'Lyndall'.

4 We sit…and look out at the boys in their happy play…we kneel still with one little cheek wistfully pressed against the pane…and we go and stand before the glass. We see the complexion we were not to spoil, and the white frock… Then the curse begins to act upon us. It finishes its work when we are grown women, who no more look out wistfully at a more healthy life; we are contented. We fit our sphere as a Chinese woman's foot fits her shoe, exactly, as though God made both—and yet he knows nothing of either.
1883 Lyndall. *The Story of an African Farm*, ch.17, 'Lyndall'.

5 Men are like the earth and we are the moon; we turn always one side to them, and they think there is no other, because they don't see it—but there is.
1883 Lyndall. *The Story of an African Farm*, ch.17, 'Lyndall'.

6 Give us labour and the training which fits for labour! We demand this, not for ourselves alone, but for the race.
1911 *Women and Labour*, ch.1.

7 With each generation the entire race passes through the body of its womanhood as through a mould, reappearing with the indelible marks of that mould upon it, that as the *os cervix* of woman, through which the head of the human infant passes at birth, forms a ring, determining for ever the size at birth of the human head…so exactly the intellectual capacity, the physical vigour, the emotional depth of woman, forms also an untranscendable circle, circumscribing with each successive generation the limits of expansion of the human race.
1911 *Women and Labour*, ch.3.

Schroeder, Patricia Scott 1940–

US Congresswoman and lawyer. She practised law in Denver and then became a faculty member of the University of Colorado (1969–72). Elected to Congress in 1972, she is co-chair of the Congressional Caucus for Women's Issues.

8 I was cooking breakfast this morning for my kids and I thought, 'He's just like Teflon. Nothing sticks to him.'
1984 Of President Ronald Reagan. In the *Boston Globe*, 24 Oct.

9 Washington is awash in post-war testosterone.
1991 On her decision not to seek presidential nomination in the wake of victory in the Gulf War. In the *New York Times*, 30 Jun.

Schulberg, Budd Wilson 1914–

US novelist and scriptwriter. He is best known for his screenplay for the film *On The Waterfront*.

10 What Makes Sammy Run?
1941 Title of novel.

11 You don't understand. I could have had class. I could have been a contender. I could have been somebody—instead of a bum, which is what I am, let's face it.
1954 Lines spoken by Marlon Brando. *On The Waterfront*.

Schultz, Howard

US businessman.

13 Retail is detail.
1994 On building Starbucks, the largest US coffee-bar chain and mail-order business. In the *New York Times*, 14 Dec.

Schulz, Charles Monroe 1922–

US cartoonist. He created the syndicated comic strip *Peanuts* (1950), internationally loved for its characters of Charlie Brown, Snoopy, Lucy, Linus, Schroeder, Peppermint Patty, Pigpen, Marcie and the bird Woodstock.

12 Jogging is very beneficial. It's very good for your legs and your feet. It's also very good for the ground. It makes it feel needed.
Quoted in Colin Jarman *The Guinness Dictionary of Sports Quotations* (1990).

Schumacher, E(rnst) F(riedrich) 1911–77

British economist and public servant, member of the Control Commission in Germany (1946–50), economist of the National Coal Board (1950-70).

14 Small is Beautiful: a Study of Economics as if People Mattered.
1973 Title of book.

15 I have no doubt that it is possible to give a new direction to technological development, a direction that shall lead it back to the real needs of man, and that also means: to the actual size of man. Man is

small, and, therefore, small is beautiful. To go for giantism is to go for self-destruction.
1973 *Small is Beautiful.*

Schumpeter, Joseph Alois 1883–1950

Austrian-born US economist, who emigrated to the US in 1932 and later became Professor at Harvard. He emphasized the importance of the entrepreneur in the business cycle and traced the economic history of capitalism.

16 When I was a young man, I wanted to be three things: I wanted to be the world's greatest horseman, the world's greatest economist, and the world's greatest lover. Unfortunately I never became the world's greatest horseman.
1940s Attributed, Harvard oral tradition.

17 The cold metal of economic theory is in Marx's pages immersed in such a wealth of steaming phrases as to acquire a temperature not naturally its own.
1942 *Capitalism, Socialism, and Democracy,* p.21.

18 Can capitalism survive? No, I do not think it can.
1942 *Capitalism, Socialism, and Democracy,* p.61.

19 Queen Elizabeth owned silk stockings. The capitalist achievement does not typically consist in providing more silk stockings for queens but in bringing them within the reach of factory girls in return for steadily decreasing amount of effort.
1942 *Capitalism, Socialism, and Democracy,* p.67.

20 The question that is so clearly in many potential parents' minds: 'Why should we stunt our ambitions and impoverish our lives in order to be insulted and looked down upon in our old age?'
1942 *Capitalism, Socialism and Democracy,* ch. 14.

21 Bureaucracy is not an obstacle to democracy but an inevitable complement to it.
1942 *Capitalism, Socialism and Democracy,* ch. 18.

Schwartz, Eugene M 1927–

US art collector, known for amassing one of the nation's leading collections of contemporary art and giving it away with almost as much zeal.

22 Collecting is the only socially commendable form of greed.
1995 In the *New York Times,* 7 Sep.

Schwartz, Sanford

US writer.

23 Dali's importance for the Surrealists at that time, and for art historians now, is that he found a way to put Freud on canvas.
1994 In the *New Republic,* 17 Oct.

Schwarzenegger, Arnold 1947–

Austrian-born US actor. He began as a body builder, winning the Mr Universe title, and became a Hollywood star in adventure films such as *The Terminator* (1984) and *True Lies* (1994).

24 Posing is a performing art.
Quoted in the *Guardian,* 1975.

25 Hasta la vista, baby.
1984 *The Terminator.*

26 I'll be back.
1984 *The Terminator.*

Schwarzkopf, H Norman 1934–

US army general. He served in the Vietnam War and as deputy commander in Grenada (1983), and in 1991 commanded allied troops in the Gulf War. He retired the following year.

27 We are not going after Saddam Hussein. If I can eliminate his ability to communicate with his forces, I would be entirely satisfied with that result.
1991 Press briefing on the start of the Gulf War, 15 Jan.

28 I don't consider myself dovish and I certainly don't consider myself hawkish. Maybe I would describe myself as owlish—that is wise enough to understand that you want to do everything possible to avoid war.
1991 In the *New York Times,* 28 Jan.

29 I asked you to be the thunder and lightning of Desert Storm. You were all of that and more.
1991 Message to US units on the cease-fire that ended the Gulf War.

Schweikart, Russell 1935–

US astronaut.

30 The most beautiful sight in orbit…is a urine dump at sunset, because as the stuff comes out and as it hits the exit nozzle it instantly flashes into ten million little ice crystals which go out almost in a hemisphere… It's really a spectacular sight.
1981 *The Next Whole Earth Catalog.*

Schweitzer, Albert 1875–1965

German medical missionary, theologian, musician and philosopher. In 1896 he vowed to live for science and art until he was 30, and then devote his life to serving humanity. He became principal of a theological college (1903) and wrote *Von Reimarus zu Wrede* (The Quest for the Historical Jesus, 1906) and major works on St Paul. Despite his international reputation in music and theology, he turned to medicine in 1905, and with his wife set up a hospital in French Equatorial Africa. He was awarded the Nobel Peace Prize in 1952.

31 He comes to us as One unknown, without a name,
as of old, by the lakeside, He came to those who
knew Him not. He speaks to us the same word:
'Follow thou me!' and sets us to the tasks which He
has to fulfil for our time. He commands. And to
those who obey Him, whether they be wise or
simple, He will reveal Himself in the toils, the
conflicts, the sufferings which they shall pass
through in His fellowship, and, as an ineffable
mystery, they shall learn in their own experience
who He is.

1906 *Von Reimarus zu Wrede* (translated by W Montgomery as
The Quest for the Historical Jesus, 1910).

32 An optimist is a person who sees a green light
everywhere, while the pessimist sees only the red
stop-light. The truly wise person is colour-blind.

1965 Quoted in CBS News tribute, 14 Jan.

Scott, C(harles) P(restwich) 1846–1932

English newspaper editor and Liberal MP (1895–1906).
At the age of 26 he became editor of the *Manchester
Guardian*, and made it a serious liberal rival of *The Times*
by a highly independent and often controversial editorial
policy and high literary standards.

33 The newspaper is of necessity something of a
monopoly, and its first duty is to shun the
temptations of a monopoly. Its primary office is the
gathering of News. At the peril of its soul it must
see that the supply is not tainted. Neither in what it
gives, nor in what it does not give, nor in the mode
of presentation, must the unclouded face of Truth
suffer wrong. Comment is free, but facts are sacred.

1921 Of the newspaper industry. In the *Manchester Guardian*,
special centenary issue, 6 May.

34 One of the virtues, perhaps almost the chief virtue,
of a newspaper is its independence. Whatever its
position or character, at least it should have a soul
of its own.

1921 In the *Manchester Guardian*, special centenary issue, 6
May.

Scott, Duncan Campell 1862–1947

Canadian poet. One of 'The Confederation Poets', he also
wrote short stories, biographies and a play.

35 How strange the stars have grown;
The presage of extinction glows on their crests
And they are beautied with impermanence.

1916 'The Height of Land'.

Scott, F(rancis) R(eginald) 1899–1985

Canadian poet. A lawyer, professor and politician (a
founder of the Canadian social democratic party, the Co-
operative Commonwealth Federation), he established
several important literary reviews. His collected poems
were published in 1981.

36 I have sat by night beside a cold lake
And touched things smoother than moonlight on
    still water,
But the moon on this cloud sea is not human,
And here is no shore, no intimacy,
Only the start of space, the road to suns.

1945 'Trans Canada'.

37 Hidden in wonder and snow, or sudden with
    summer,
This land stares at the sun in a huge silence
Endlessly repeating something we cannot hear.
Inarticulate, arctic,
Not written on by history, empty as paper,
It leans away from the world with songs in its lakes
Older than love, and lost in the miles.

1954 Of Canada. 'Laurentian Shield'.

38 Newspapers are born free and everywhere are in
chains.

1973 Aphorism, collected in John Robert Colombo (ed)
Colombo's Canadian Quotations (1974).

▷ See Rousseau 827:32.

Scott, Robert Falcon 1868–1912

English Antarctic explorer. In 1900–4 he commanded the
National Antarctic Expedition to the Ross Sea. On his
second expedition he reached the South Pole (Jan 1912),
only to discover that Amundsen had beaten him by a
month. He and his party died on the way back; their
bodies and diaries were found by a search party eight
months later.

39 Great God! This is an awful place and terrible
enough for us to have laboured to it without the
reward of priority.

1912 Journal entry, 18 Jan. *Scott's Last Expedition: The Personal
Journals of Captain R F Scott, CVO, RN, on his Journey to the
South Pole* (published 1923).

40 For God's sake look after our people.

1912 Last entry in journal. In *Scott's Last Expedition: The
Personal Journals of Captain R F Scott, CVO, RN, on his Journey
to the South Pole* (published 1923).

Scott, Rose 1847–1925

Australian feminist.

41 Life is too short to waste on the admiration of one
man.

Her habitual response to offers of marriage. Quoted in Jennifer
Uglow (ed) *The Macmillan Dictionary of Women's Biography*
(2nd edn, 1989).

Scott, Sir Walter 1771–1832

Scottish novelist and poet. He studied law and became an
advocate and later a sheriff, but achieved worldwide fame
as a writer of epic poetry and as the author of the
Waverley Novels, promoting a fundamentally romantic
image of history and in particular of Scotland's past.

42 The way was long, the wind was cold,
    The Minstrel was infirm and old;
    His withered cheek, and tresses grey,
    Seemed to have known a better day;
    The harp, his sole remaining joy,
    Was carried by an orphan boy,
    The last of all the Bards was he,
    Who sung of Border chivalry.
    1805 *The Lay of the Last Minstrel*, introduction.

43 He poured, to lord and lady gay,
    The unpremeditated lay.
    1805 *The Lay of the Last Minstrel*, introduction.

44 And said I that my limbs were old,
    And said I that my blood was cold,
    And that my kindly fire was fled,
    And my poor withered heart was dead,
    And that I might not sing of Love?
    1805 *The Lay of the Last Minstrel*, canto 1, stanza 1.

45 If thou would'st view fair Melrose aright,
    Go visit it by the pale moonlight.
    1805 *The Lay of the Last Minstrel*, canto 2, stanza 1.

46 The woodland brook he bounding crossed,
    And laughed, and shouted, 'Lost! lost! lost!'
    1805 *The Lay of the Last Minstrel*, canto 3, stanza 13.

47 The Harper smiled, well pleased; for ne'er
    Was flattery lost on poet's ear:
    A simple race! they waste their toil
    For the vain tribute of a smile.
    1805 *The Lay of the Last Minstrel*, canto 4, conclusion.

48 Call it not vain:—they do not err
    Who say, that when the Poet dies,
    Mute Nature mourns her worshipper,
    And celebrates his obsequies.
    1805 *The Lay of the Last Minstrel*, canto 5, stanza 1.

49 Breathes there the man, with soul so dead,
    Who never to himself hath said,
    This is my own, my native land!
    Whose heart hath ne'er within him burned,
    As home his footsteps he hath turned
    From wandering on a foreign strand!
    1805 *The Lay of the Last Minstrel*, canto 6, stanza 1.

50 O Caledonia! stern and wild,
    Meet nurse for a poetic child!
    Land of brown heath and shaggy wood,
    Land of the mountain and the flood.
    Land of my sires! what mortal hand
    Can e'er untie the filial band
    That knits me to thy rugged strand!
    1805 *The Lay of the Last Minstrel*, canto 6, stanza 2.

51 November's sky is chill and drear,
    November's leaf is red and sear.
    1808 *Marmion*, canto 1, introduction.

52 And come he slow, or come he fast,
    It is but Death who comes at last.
    1808 *Marmion*, canto 2, stanza 30.

53 Still is thy name in high account,
    And still thy verse has charms,
    Sir David Lindesay of the Mount,
    Lord Lion King-at-arms!
    1808 *Marmion*, canto 4, stanza 7.

54 O, young Lochinvar is come out of the west,
    Through all the wide Border his steed was the best;
    And save his good broadsword he weapon had
       none,
    He rode all unarmed, and he rode all alone.
    So faithful in love, and so dauntless in war,
    There never was knight like the young Lochinvar.
    1808 *Marmion*, canto 5, stanza 12, 'Lochinvar'.

55 Heap on more wood!—the wind is chill;
    But let it whistle as it will,
    We'll keep our Christmas merry still.
    1808 *Marmion*, canto 6, introduction.

56 And dar'st thou then
    To beard the lion in his den,
    The Douglas in his hall?
    1808 *Marmion*, canto 6, stanza 14.

57 Oh what a tangled web we weave,
    When first we practise to deceive!
    1808 *Marmion*, canto 6, stanza 17.

58 O Woman! in our hours of ease,
    Uncertain, coy, and hard to please,
    And variable as the shade
    By the light quivering aspen made;
    When pain and anguish wring the brow,
    A ministering angel thou!
    1808 *Marmion*, canto 6, stanza 30.

59 The stubborn spearmen still made good
    Their dark impenetrable wood,
    Each stepping where his comrade stood
    The instant that he fell.
    1808 *Marmion*, canto 6, stanza 34.

60 Still from the sire the son shall hear
    Of the stern strife, and carnage drear,
    Of Flodden's fatal field,
    Where shivered was fair Scotland's spear,
    And broken was her shield!
    1808 *Marmion*, canto 6, stanza 34.

61 The stag at eve had drunk his fill,
    Where danced the moon on Monan's rill.
    1810 *The Lady of the Lake*, canto 1, stanza 1.

62 Hail to the Chief who in honour advances!

Honoured and bless'd be the evergreen Pine!

1810 *The Lady of the Lake*, canto 2, stanza 19, 'Boat Song'.

63 Time rolls his ceaseless course.

1810 *The Lady of the Lake*, canto 3, stanza 1.

64 He is gone on the mountain,
He is lost to the forest,
Like a summer-dried fountain,
When our need was the sorest.

1810 *The Lady of the Lake*, canto 3, stanza 16, 'Coronach'.

65 Like the dew on the mountain,
Like the foam on the river,
Like the bubble on the fountain,
Thou art gone, and for ever!

1810 *The Lady of the Lake*, canto 3, stanza 16, 'Coronach'.

66 Merry it is in the good greenwood,
When the mavis and merle are singing,
When the deer sweeps by, and the hounds are in
cry,
And the hunter's horn is ringing.

1810 *The Lady of the Lake*, canto 4, stanza 12, 'Alice Brand'.

67 O, Brignal banks are wild and fair,
And Greta woods are green
And you may gather garlands there
Would grace a summer queen.

1813 *Rokeby*, canto 3, stanza 16.

68 A weary lot is thine, fair maid,
A weary lot is thine!
To pull the thorn thy brow to braid,
And press the rue for wine!

1813 *Rokeby*, canto 3, stanza 28, 'Song'.

69 Look back, and smile at perils past!

1813 *The Bridal of Triermain*, introduction.

70 He that steals a cow from a poor widow, or a stirk
from a cottar, is a thief; he that lifts a drove from a
Sassenach laird, is a gentleman-drover. And,
besides, to take a tree from the forest, a salmon
from the river, a deer from the hill, or a cow from a
Lowland strath, is what no Highlander need ever
think shame upon.

1814 Evan Dhu Maccombich to Edward Waverley. *Waverley*,
ch.18.

71 I am heartily glad you continued to like Waverley
to the end—the hero is a sneaking piece of
imbecility and if he had married Flora she would
have set him up upon the chimney-piece as Count
Boralaski's wife used to do with him.

1814 Letter to John Morritt, 28 Jul. Joseph Borowlaski was a
Polish dwarf known as 'The Little Count' who left France at the
Revolution and exhibited himself at fairs throughout Britain.

72 Then strip lads, and to it, though sharp be the
weather,

And if, by mischance you should happen to fall,
There are worse things in life than a tumble on the
heather
And life is itself a game of football.

1815 On a match between the Scottish teams Ettrick and
Selkirk, published in the *Edinburgh Journal*.

73 But ruffian stern, and soldier good,
The noble and the slave,
From various cause the same wild road,
On the same bloody morning, trode,
To that dark inn—the Grave!

1815 *The Lord of the Isles*, canto 6, stanza 26.

74 Pro-di-gi-ous!

1815 Dominie Sampson. *Guy Mannering*, ch.8.

75 'That sounds like nonsense, my dear.'
'Maybe so, my dear; but it may be very good law
for all that.'

1815 Mrs and Mr Bertram in conversation. *Guy Mannering*,
ch.9.

76 Gin by pailfuls, wine in rivers,
Dash the window-glass to shivers!
For three wild lads were we, brave boys,
And three wild lads were we;
Thou on the land, and I on the sand,
And Jack on the gallows-tree!

1815 *Guy Mannering*, ch.34.

77 The frolicsome company had begun to practise the
ancient and now forgotten pastime of *High Jinks*.

1815 *Guy Mannering*, ch.36.

78 'Why weep ye by the tide, ladie?
Why weep ye by the tide?
I'll wed ye to my youngest son,
And ye sall be his bride:
And ye sall be his bride, ladie,
Sae comely to be seen'—
But aye she loot the tears down fa'
For Jock of Hazeldean.

1816 'Jock of Hazeldean', stanza 1.

79 'A chain of gold ye sall not lack,
Nor braid to bind your hair;
Nor mettled hound, nor managed hawk,
Nor palfrey fresh and fair.'

1816 'Jock of Hazeldean', stanza 3.

80 They sought her baith by bower and ha';
The ladie was not seen!
She's o'er the Border and awa'
Wi' Jock of Hazeldean.

1816 'Jock of Hazeldean', stanza 4.

81 Prætorian here, prætorian there, I mind the bigging
o't.

1816 Edie Ochiltree to Jonathan Oldbuck. *The Antiquary*,
ch.4.

82 It's no fish ye're buying—it's men's lives.
1816 Maggie Mucklebackit to Oldbuck. *The Antiquary*, ch11.

83 It's weel wi' you gentles, that can sit in the house wi'
handkerchers at your een when ye lose a friend; but
the like o' us maun to our wark again, if our hearts
were beating as hard as my hammer.
1816 Saunders Mucklebackit to Oldbuck. *The Antiquary*,
ch.34.

84 He that is without name, without friends, without
coin, without country, is still at least a man; and he
that has all these is no more.
1817 Rob Roy to Francis Osbaldistone. *Rob Roy*, ch.21.

85 Come fill up my cup, come fill up my cann,
Come saddle my horses, and call up my man;
Come open your gates, and let me gae free,
I daurna stay langer in Bonny Dundee!
1817 *Rob Roy*, ch.23.

86 If your honour disna ken when ye hae a gude
servant, I ken when I hae a gude master, and the
deil be in my feet gin I leave ye.
1817 Andrew Fairservice to Francis Osbaldistone. *Rob Roy*, ch.
24.

87 It's ill taking the breeks aff a Hielandman.
1817 Andrew Fairservice to Bailie Nicol Jarvie. *Rob Roy*, ch.27.

88 There's a gude time coming.
1817 Rob Roy to the Duke. *Rob Roy*, ch.32.

89 Speak out, sir, and do not Maister or Campbell
me—my foot is on my native heath, and my name
is MacGregor!
1817 Rob Roy to Francis Osbaldistone. *Rob Roy*, ch.34.

90 Ye ken weel eneugh that women and gear are at the
bottom of a' the mischief in this warld.
1817 Rob Roy to Francis Osbaldistone. *Rob Roy*, ch.35.

91 The hour's come, but not the man.
1818 *The Heart of Midlothian*, ch.4, motto.

92 'I dinna ken muckle about the law,' answered Mrs
Howden; 'but I ken, when we had a king, and a
chancellor, and parliament-men o' our ain, we
could aye peeble them wi' stanes when they werena
gude bairns—But naebody's nails can reach the
length o' Lunnon.'
1818 *The Heart of Midlothian*, ch.4.

93 Jock, when ye hae naething else to do, ye may be
aye sticking in a tree; it will be growing, Jock, when
ye're sleeping.
1818 The Laird of Dumbiedikes to his son. *The Heart of
Midlothian*, ch.8.

94 Never mind my grace, lassie; just speak out a plain
tale, and show you have a Scotch tongue in your
head.
1818 The Duke of Argyle to Jeanie Deans. *The Heart of
Midlothian*, ch.35.

95 Dinna be chappit back or cast down wi' the first
rough answer.
1818 Jeanie Deans to the Duke of Argyle. *The Heart of
Midlothian*, ch.35.

96 Proud Maisie is in the wood,
Walking so early;
Sweet Robin sits on the bush,
Singing so rarely.
1818 *The Heart of Midlothian*, ch.40. (Madge Wildfire's
song).

97 Look not thou on beauty's charming,—
Sit thou still when kings are arming.—
Taste not when the wine-cup glistens,—
Speak not when the people listens,—
Stop thine ear against the singer,—
From the red gold keep thy finger,—
Vacant heart, and hand, and eye,—
Easy live and quiet die.
1819 *The Bride of Lammermoor*, ch.3 (Lucy Ashton's song).

98 But no one shall find me rowing against the stream.
I care not who knows it—I write for the general
amusement.
1822 *The Fortunes of Nigel*, introductory epistle.

99 For a con-si-de-ra-tion.
1822 Trapbois. *The Fortunes of Nigel*, ch.22.

1 O Geordie, Jingling Geordie, it was grand to hear
Baby Charles laying down the guilt of
dissimulation and Steemie lecturing on the
turpitude of incontinence.
1822 *The Fortunes of Nigel*, ch.31.

2 Carle, now the King's come!
Carle, now the King's come!
Thou shalt dance, and I will sing,
Carle, now the King's come!
1822 'Carle, now the King's come', written in celebration of
George IV's visit to Edinburgh.

3 Ah! County Guy, the hour is nigh,
The sun has left the lea,
The orange flower perfumes the bower,
The breeze is on the sea.
1823 *Quentin Durward*, ch.4.

4 Fair, fat, and forty.
1823 *St Ronan's Well*, ch.7.

5 It's ill speaking between a fou man and a fasting.
1824 *Redgauntlet*, letter 11, 'Wandering Willie's Tale'.

6 The ae half of the warld thinks the tither daft.
1824 Peter Peebles to Justice Foxley. *Redgauntlet*, ch.7 .

7 'Then, gentlemen,' said Redgauntlet, clasping his hands together as the words burst from him, 'the cause is lost for ever!'
   1824 *Redgauntlet*, ch.23.

8 Widowed wife, and married maid,
   Betrothed, betrayer, and betrayed!
   1825 *The Betrothal*, ch.15.

9 Came through cold roads to as cold news.
   1826 *Journal*, 16 Jan, referring to the financial collapse of his publisher, Constable, which led directly to Scott's own bankruptcy.

10 We had better remain in union with England, even at the risk of becoming a subordinate species of Northumberland, as far as national consequence is concerned, than remedy ourselves by even hinting the possibility of a rupture. But there is no harm in wishing Scotland to have just so much ill-nature, according to her own proverb, as may keep her good-nature from being abused.
    1826 *Letters of Malachi Malagrowther on the Proposed Change of Currency*, letter 1.

11 If I can but get the sulky Scottish spirit set up, the devil won't turn them.
    1826 *Journal*, 25 Feb.

12 The Big Bow-wow strain I can do myself like any now going; but the exquisite touch, which renders ordinary commonplace things and characters interesting, from the truth of description and the sentiment, is denied to me.
    1826 On Jane Austen. *Journal*, 14 Mar.

13 But if you *unscotch* us you will find us damned mischievous Englishmen.
    1826 Letter to J W Croker, 19 Mar.

14 I would like to be there, were it but to see how the cat jumps. One knows nothing of the world, if you are absent from it so long as I have been.
    1826 *Journal*, 7 Oct, expressing frustration and wonder at the machinations of London bureaucracy which prevented him accessing government papers for his *Life of Napoleon*.

15 Long life to thy fame and peace to thy soul, Rob Burns! When I want to express a sentiment which I feel strongly, I find the phrase in Shakespeare—or thee. The blockheads talk of my being like Shakespeare—not fit to tie his brogues.
    1826 *Journal*, 11 Dec.

16 To the Lords of convention 'twas Claver'se who spoke,
    'Ere the King's crown shall fall there are crowns to be broke;
    So let each Cavalier who loves honour and me,
    Come follow the bonnet of Bonny Dundee.'
    1830 *The Doom of Devorgoil*, act 2, sc.2, 'Bonny Dundee', stanza 1.

17 No repose for Sir Walter but in the grave. Friends, don't let me expose myself—get me to bed—that's the only place.
    1832 Quoted in John G Lockhart *Memoirs of the Life of Sir Walter Scott, Bart.* (1837–8). Scott had fallen asleep in his bath-chair while trying to write a few words.

18 Be a good man—be virtuous—be religious—be a good man. Nothing else will give you any comfort when you come to lie here.
    1832 Last words, addressed to Lockhart, quoted in John G Lockhart *Memoirs of the Life of Sir Walter Scott, Bart.* (1837–8). Scott concluded by saying 'God bless you all.'

Scottish Metrical Psalms

19 The Lord's my shepherd, I'll not want.
    He makes me down to lie
    In pastures green: he leadeth me
    the quiet waters by.
    My soul he doth restore again:
    and me to walk doth make
    Within the paths of righteousness,
    ev'n for his own name's sake.

    Yea, though I walk in death's dark vale,
    yet will I fear no ill:
    For thou art with me; and thy rod
    and staff me comfort still.
    1650 Translation of Psalm 23:1–4.

20 God is our refuge and our strength,
    in straits a present aid;
    Therefore, although the earth remove,
    we will not be afraid.
    1650 Psalm 46:1–2.

21 How lovely is thy dwelling-place
    O Lord of hosts, to me!
    The tabernacles of thy grace
    how pleasant, Lord, they be!
    1650 Psalm 84:1

22 All people that on earth do dwell,
    Sing to the Lord with cheerful voice.
    Him serve with mirth, his praise forth tell,
    Come ye before him and rejoice.
    Know that the Lord is God indeed;
    Without our aid he did us make:
    We are his folk, he doth us feed,
    And for his sheep he doth us take.
    1650 Psalm 100:1–3.

23 I to the hills will lift mine eyes,
    from whence doth come mine aid.
    My safety cometh from the Lord,
    Who heav'n and earth hath made.
    1650 Psalm 121:1–2.

Scribner, Charles, Jr 1921–

US publisher, chairman of Charles Scribner's Sons (1977–8) and Scribner Book Cos from 1978. His autobiography is *In the Company of Writers: A Life in Publishing* (1991).

24 Nowadays a sales conference resembles a Passion play: everybody is invited to participate and marvel at the drama.
1991 *In the Company of Writers: A Life in Publishing.*

Seaton, George pseudonym of *George Stenius* 1911–79

US screenwriter and director. He won Academy Awards for both *Miracle on 34th Street* (1947) and *The Country Girl* (1954).

25 For those who believe in God no explanation is necessary. For those who do not believe in God no explanation is possible.
1943 Prologue to *The Song of Bernadette.*

Seeger, Alan 1888–1916

US poet. He settled in Paris, and enlisted in the French Foreign Legion when war broke out. He was killed at the Battle of the Somme.

26 I have a rendezvous with Death
At some disputed barricade,
When Spring comes round with rustling shade
And apple blossoms fill the air.
I have a rendezvous with Death
When Spring brings back blue days and fair.
1916 'I Have a Rendezvous with Death', in the *North American Review*, Oct.

Seeger, Pete 1919–

US folk singer and songwriter.

27 Where have all the flowers gone?
1961 Title of song.

Seeley, Sir John Robert 1834–95

English historian, Professor of Modern History at Cambridge (1869). His *Ecce Homo* (1865), a popular Life of Christ, caused much controversy. Other works include *Natural Religion* (1882), the authoritative *Life and Times of Stein* (1874) and *The Expansion of England* (1883).

28 We [the English] seem to have conquered and peopled half the world in a fit of absence of mind.
1883 *The Expansion of England.*

Segal, Erich 1937–

US novelist. He is known for the popular success of *Love Story*, which was both a best-selling novel and a major film.

29 Love means not ever having to say you're sorry.
1970 *Love Story*, ch.13.

Segovia, Andrés 1894–1987

Spanish guitarist. Influenced by the Spanish nationalist composers, he evolved a revolutionary guitar technique permitting the performance of a wide range of music, and many composers wrote works for him.

31 Electric guitars are an abomination, whoever heard of an electric violin? An electric cello? Or for that matter an electric singer?
Quoted in Rick Friedman *The Beatles: Words without Music* (1968).

Seibel, Cathy

Assistant US Attorney.

32 Just because you're rich doesn't mean you're not cheap.
1989 On the prosecution of hotel owner Leona Helmsley. In the *New York Times*, 24 Aug.

Selden, John 1584–1654

English jurist, historian and antiquary. A member of the Long Parliament in 1640, he withdrew from politics after the execution of Charles I, of which he disapproved. His many writings on constitutional matters included *Titles of Honour* (1614), *Analecton Britannicon* (1615) and *History of Tithes* (1618). The most notable of his many tracts and treatises was the posthumous *Table Talk* (published 1689).

33 Every law is a contract between the king and the people and therefore to be kept.
Table Talk (published 1689).

34 Ignorance of the law excuses no man; not that all men know the law, but because 'tis an excuse every man will plead, and no man can tell how to confute him.
Table Talk (published 1689).

36 Those that govern most make least noise.
Table Talk (published 1689).

Self, Will 1961–

English novelist. He was a cartoonist with the *New Statesman*, but turned to writing fiction. He was awarded the Geoffrey Faber Memorial Award in 1992.

37 No one ever complains if a great artist says that he was driven to create a masterpiece by a hunger for recognition and money. But a scientist? Well, he is meant to be disinterested, pure, his ambition

merely to descry the cement of the universe. He isn't meant to use it to start laying his own patio.

1991 *The Quantity Theory of Insanity and Five Supporting Propositions*, 'The Quantity Theory of Insanity'.

38 I think in retrospect that all those 'alternative' modes of living were little more than exercises in arrested development.

1991 *The Quantity Theory of Insanity and Five Supporting Propositions*, 'The Quantity Theory of Insanity'.

Sellar, W(alter) C(arruthers) and Yeatman R(obert) J(ulian) 1898–1951, 1897–1968

British humorous writers.

39 [Gladstone] spent his declining years trying to guess the answer to the Irish Question. Unfortunately, whenever he was getting warm, the Irish secretly changed the question.

1930 *1066 And All That*.

40 The National Debt is a very Good thing, and it would be dangerous to pay it off for fear of Political economy.

1930 *1066 And All That*.

Selye, Hans 1907–83

Endocrinologist, founder of Montreal's Institute of Experimental Medicine.

41 Stress is the state manifested by a specific syndrome which consists of all the nonspecifically inducted changes within a biologic system.

1956 *The Stress of Life*.

Selznick, David O(liver) 1902–65

US cinema mogul. He founded his own company in 1936, producing the screen adaptation of *Gone With The Wind* in 1939. Other successes include *Rebecca* (1940), *Duel in the Sun* (1946) and *A Farewell to Arms* (1957).

42 This is the story of the unconquerable fortress— the American home.

1944 *Since You Went Away*, opening line.

43 If they will only do their job…that is all that they are being overpaid for.

Of his stars, while filming *The Garden of Allah*. Quoted in Maria Riva *Marlene Dietrich* (1992).

Seneca full name *Lucius Annaeus Seneca* called *The Younger* c.4 BC–c.65 AD

Roman Stoic philosopher, statesman and tragedian, son of the orator Seneca the Elder. He tutored Nero and for a time enjoyed considerable political influence, but he lost favour and was forced to commit suicide. His works include the *Epistulae morales ad Lucilium*, the

Apocolocyntosis divi Claudii (literally 'The pumpkinification of the Divine Claudius'), and several tragedies.

44 *Utrumque enim vitium est, et omnibus credere et nulli.*

It is equally unsound to trust everyone and to trust no one.

Epistulae, 3.4.

45 *Longum iter est per praecepta, breve et efficax per exempla.*

The way is long if one follows precepts, but short and helpful, if one follows patterns.

Epistulae, 6.5 (translated by R M Gummere).

46 *Homines dum docent discunt.*

Men learn while they teach.

Epistulae 7.8 (translated by R M Gummere).

47 *Vitae, non scholae discimus.*

It is for life, not for school that we learn.

Oral tradition based on Seneca's conclusion of a letter to Lucilius which says the opposite: 'Non vitae, sed scholae discimus', *Epistulae*, 106.12.

48 *Qui timide rogat, docet negare.*

Who makes timid requests, invites denial.

Phaedra, 593–4 (translated by F J Miller).

Senghor, Léopold Sédar 1906–

Senegalese poet who explored the theme of black African culture.

49 *J'ai choisi mon peuple noir peinant, mon peuple paysan, toute la race paysanne, par le monde.*

I chose my black people struggling, my country people, all country people, in the world.

1945 *Chants d'ombre*, 'Que m'accompagnent kára et balafong, 3'.

50 *Seul le rythme le provoque le court-circuit poétique et transmue le cuivre en or, la parole en verbe.*

Only rhythm brings about a poetic short-circuit and transforms the copper into gold, the words into life.

1956 *Ethiopiques*, postface.

51 *Au contraire de l'Européen classique, le Négro-Africain ne se distingue pas de l'objet, il ne le tient pas à distance, il ne le regarde pas, il ne l'analyse pas… Il le touche, il le palpe, il le sent.*

Unlike the classical European, the Black-African does not distinguish himself from an object. He does not hold it at a distance, he does not look at it, he does not examine it… He touches it, he fingers it, he *feels* it.

1960 Au Congrès de l'Union nationale de la Jeunesse du Mali, Dakar, 1960.

52 *Danser, c'est découvrir et recréer, surtout lorsque la danse est danse d'amour. C'est, en tout cas, le meilleur mode de connaissance.*

To dance is to discover and to recreate, above all when the dance is the dance of love. It is the best mode of knowledge.

1960 *Au Congrès de l'Union nationale de la Jeunesse du Mali, Dakar, 1960.*

Senior, Nassau William 1790–1864

English economist. He stressed the importance of the last hour's work in the cotton factories and opposed the trade unions. His works include *On the Cost of Obtaining Money* (1830), *An Outline of the Science of Political Economy* (1836) and *Value of Money* (1840).

53 This barbarous feeling of nationality…has become the curse of Europe.

1850 *Diary*, 20 May.

Service, Robert William 1874–1958

English-born poet. He emigrated to Canada, and became famous for his popular ballads of life in the Canadian wilderness, which earned him the nickname 'The Canadian Kipling'. He also wrote several novels.

54 This is the law of the Yukon, that only the Strong shall thrive;
That surely the Weak shall perish, and only the Fit survive.

1907 *Songs of a Sourdough*, 'The Law of the Yukon'.

55 A promise made is a debt unpaid, and the trail has its own stern code.

1907 *Songs of a Sourdough*, 'The Cremation of Sam McGhee'.

56 Back of the bar, in a solo game, sat dangerous Dan McGrew,
And watching his luck was his light-o'-love, the lady that's known as Lou.

1907 *Songs of a Sourdough*, 'The Shooting of Dan McGrew'.

57 Ah! The clock is always slow;
It is later than you think.

1921 *Ballads of a Bohemian*, 'It Is Later Than You Think'.

58 When we, the Workers, all demand: What are WE fighting for?
Then we'll end that stupid crime, that devil's madness—War.

1921 *Ballads of a Bohemian*, 'Michael'.

Sévigné, Marie de Rabutin-Chantal, Marquise de 1626–96

French writer famed for her letters which recounted daily life at court and in her family. They were collected by her daughter and published in 1725.

59 *La grande amitié n'est jamais tranquille.*

Great friendship is never peaceful.

1671 Letter to Mme de Grignan, 16 Sep.

60 *Le temps vole et m'emporte malgré moi; j'ai beau vouloir le retenir, c'est lui qui m'entraîne; et cette pensée me fait grande peur: vous devinez à peu près pourquoi.*

Time flies and takes me with it despite my efforts; I'd like to hold it back, but it keeps dragging me along and this thought frightens me greatly: you can perhaps guess why.

1691 Letter to the Comte de Bussy-Rabutin, 12 Jul.

Sexton, Anne née Harvey 1928–74

US poet, lecturer, and writer of children's books. Her works include *To Bedlam and Part Way Back* (1962), *All My Pretty Ones* (1962), *Live or Die* (1966) for which she won a Pulitzer Prize (1967), and *The Death Notebooks* (1974). She committed suicide.

61 Go child, who is my sin and nothing more.

1962 *To Bedlam and Part Way Back*, 'Unknown Child in the Maternity Ward'.

62 Now I fold you down, my drunkard, my navigator, my first lost keeper, to love or look at later.

1962 On photographs of her dead father. *All My Pretty Ones*, 'All My Pretty Ones'.

63 Whether you are pretty or not, I outlive you, bend down my strange face to yours and forgive you.

1962 *All My Pretty Ones*, 'All My Pretty Ones'.

64 In a dream you are never eighty.

1962 *All My Pretty Ones*, 'Old'.

65 But suicides have a special language.
Like carpenters they want to know *which tools*.
They never ask *why build*.

1964 'Wanting To Die', dated 3 Feb. Collected in *Live Or Die* (1966).

66 I was tired of being a woman,
tired of the spoons and the pots,
tired of my mouth and my breasts
tired of the cosmetics and the silks…
I was tired of the gender of things.

1967 *Live or Die*, 'Consorting with Angels'.

67 The sea is mother-death and she is a mighty female, the one who wins, the one who sucks us all up.

1971 Journal entry, 19 Nov, in *The Poet's Story*, 'A Small Journal'.

68 It doesn't matter who my father was; it matters who I remember he was.

1972 Journal entry, 1 Jan, in *The Poet's Story*, 'A Small Journal'.

69 The Awful Rowing Towards God.
    1975 Title of book.

70 God owns heaven
    but He craves the earth.
    1975 *The Awful Rowing Toward God*, 'The Earth'.

Shakespeare, William 1564–1616

English poet, playwright and actor. He lived in Stratford-
upon-Avon, where his wife and children lived, and in
London, where he worked in the theatre, becoming
England's greatest playwright. His influence on literature
and language throughout the world has been immense.
The dates of composition of many of the plays are
uncertain. Line numbers conform to *The Oxford
Shakespeare* (Oxford University Press, 1988).

71 Home-keeping youth have ever homely wits.
    1590–1 Valentine. *The Two Gentlemen of Verona*, act 1, sc.1,
    l.2.

72 He was more than over-shoes in love.
    1590–1 Proteus, of Lysander. *The Two Gentlemen of Verona*, act
    1, sc.1, l.24.

73 I have no other but a woman's reason:
    I think him so because I think him so.
    1590–1 Lucetta, explaining her preference for Proteus. *The
    Two Gentlemen of Verona*, act 1, sc.2, l.23–4.

74 O, how this spring of love resembleth
    The uncertain glory of an April day,
    Which now shows all the beauty of the sun,
    And by and by a cloud takes all away.
    1590–1 Proteus. *The Two Gentlemen of Verona*, act 1, sc.3,
    l.84–7.

75 I was in love with my bed.
    1590–1 Speed. *The Two Gentlemen of Verona*, act 2, sc.1, l.76.

76 What, gone without a word?
    Ay, so true love should do. It cannot speak,
    For truth hath better deeds than words to grace it.
    1590–1 Proteus. *The Two Gentlemen of Verona*, act 2, sc.2,
    l.16–18.

77 A fine volley of words, gentlemen, and quickly shot
    off.
    1590–1 Silvia to Thario and Valentine. *The Two Gentlemen of
    Verona*, act 2, sc.4, l.32.

78 When I was sick, you gave me bitter pills,
    And I must minister the like to you.
    1590–1 Porteus to Valentine. *The Two Gentlemen of Verona*, act
    2, sc.4, l.147–8.

79 Love, thou know'st, is full of jealousy.
    1590–1 Valentine. *The Two Gentlemen of Verona*, act 2, sc.4,
    l.175.

80 As one nail by strength drives out another,
    So the remembrance of my former love
    Is by a newer object quite forgotten.

    1590–1 Proteus. *The Two Gentlemen of Verona*, act 2, sc.4,
    l.191–3.

81 Didst thou but know the inly touch of love
    Thou wouldst as soon go kindle fire with snow
    As seek to quench the fire of love with words.
    1590–1 Julia to Lucetta. *The Two Gentlemen of Verona*, act 2,
    sc.7, l.18–20.

82 Win her with gifts if she respects not words.
    Dumb jewels often in their silent kind
    More than quick words do move a woman's mind.
    1590–1 Valentine to Duke. *The Two Gentlemen of Verona*, act
    3, sc.1, l.89–91.

83 Love is like a child
    That longs for everything that he can come by.
    1590–1 Duke to Valentine. *The Two Gentlemen of Verona*, act
    3, sc.1, l.124–5.

84 Except I be by Silvia in the night
    There is no music in the nightingale.
    Unless I look on Silvia in the day
    There is no day for me to look upon.
    1590–1 Valentine. *The Two Gentlemen of Verona*, act 3, sc.1,
    l.178–81.

85 Slander Valentine
    With falsehood, cowardice, and poor descent,
    Three things that women highly hold in hate.
    1590–1 Proteus to Duke. *The Two Gentlemen of Verona*, act 3,
    sc.2, l.31–3.

86 You must lay lime to tangle her desires
    By wailful sonnets.
    1590–1 Proteus to Thurio. *The Two Gentlemen of Verona*, act 3,
    sc.2, l.68–9.

87 Who is Silvia? What is she,
    That all our swains commend her?
    1590–1 Song. *The Two Gentlemen of Verona*, act 4, sc.2, l.38–9.

88 How use doth breed a habit in a man!
    1590–1 Valentine. *The Two Gentlemen of Verona*, act 5, sc.4,
    l.1.

89 O heaven, were man
    But constant, he were perfect!
    1590–1 Proteus. *The Two Gentlemen of Verona*, act 5, sc.4,
    l.109–10.

90 My thoughts are whirlèd like a potter's wheel;
    I know not where I am, nor what I do.
    1592 Talbot. *Henry VI Part One*, act 1, sc.7, l.19–20.

91 I have heard it said, 'Unbidden guests
    Are often welcomest when they are gone'.
    1592 Bedford. *Henry VI Part One*, act 2, sc.2, l.55–6.

92 Faith, I have been a truant in the law,
    And never yet could frame my will to it,
    And therefore fame the law unto my will.
    1592 Suffolk. *Henry VI Part One*, act 2, sc.4, l.7–9.

93 We will bestow you in some better place,
Fitter for sickness and for crazy age.
1592 Talbot to Bedford. *Henry VI Part One*, act 3, sc.5, l.47–8.

94 Beauty's princely majesty is such,
Confounds the tongue, and makes the senses
rough.
1592 Suffolk. *Henry VI Part One*, act 5, sc.5, l.26–7.

95 She's beautiful, and therefore to be wooed;
She is a woman, therefore to be won.
1592 Suffolk, of Margaret. *Henry VI Part One*, act 5, sc.5,
l.34–5.

96 To be a queen in bondage is more vile
Than is a slave in base servility,
For princes should be free.
1592 Margaret. *Henry VI Part One*, act 5, sc.5, l.68–70.

97 Marriage is a matter of more worth
Than to be dealt in by attorneyship.
1592 Suffolk. *Henry VI Part One*, act 5, sc.7, l.55–6.

98 All his mind is bent to holiness,
To number Ave-Maries on his beads.
1592 Queen Margaret of Henry. *Henry VI Part Two*, act 1, sc.3,
l.58–9.

99 Could I come near your beauty with my nails,
I'd set my ten commandments in your face.
1592 Duchess to Queen Margaret. *Henry VI Part Two*, act 1,
sc.3, l.144–5.

1 How irksome is this music to my heart!
When such strings jar, what hope of harmony?
1592 Henry. *Henry VI Part Two*, act 2, sc.1, l.59–60.

2 God shall be my hope,
My stay, my guide, and lantern to my feet.
1592 Henry. *Henry VI Part Two*, act 2, sc.3, l.24–5.

3 Smooth runs the water where the brook is deep,
And in his simple show he harbours treason.
1592 Suffolk to Henry. *Henry VI Part Two*, act 3, sc.1, l.53–4.

4 The fox barks not when he would steal the lamb.
1592 Suffolk. *Henry VI Part Two*, act 3, sc.1, l.55.

5 The commons, like an angry hive of bees
That want their leader, scatter up and down
And care not who they sting.
1592 Warwick to Henry. *Henry VI Part Two*, act 3, sc.2,
l.125–7.

6 What stronger breastplate than a heart untainted?
Thrice is he armed that hath his quarrel just;
And he but naked, though locked up in steel,
Whose conscience with injustice is corrupted.
1592 Henry. *Henry VI Part Two*, act 3, sc.2, l.232–5.

7 Forbear to judge, for we are sinners all.
1592 Henry. *Henry VI Part Two*, act 3, sc.3, l.31.

8 The gaudy, babbling, and remorseful day
Is crept into the bosom of the sea.
1592 Captain. *Henry VI Part Two*, act 4, sc.1, l.1–2.

9 I say it was never merry world in England since
gentle-men come up.
1592 Second rebel. *Henry VI Part Two*, act 4, sc.2, l.9–10.

10 There shall be in England seven halfpenny
loaves sold for a penny, the three-hooped pot shall
have
ten hoops, and I will make it felony to drink small
beer.
1592 Cade. *Henry VI Part Two*, act 4, sc.2, l.67–9.

11 The first thing we do let's kill all the lawyers.
1592 The Butcher. *Henry VI Part Two*, act 4, sc.2, l.78.

12 And Adam was a gardener.
1592 Cade. *Henry VI Part Two*, act 4, sc.2, l.133.

13 Ignorance is the curse of God,
Knowledge the wing wherewith we fly to heaven.
1592 Saye. *Henry VI Part Two*, act 4, sc.7, l.72–3.

14 It is great sin to swear unto a sin,
But greater sin to keep a sinful oath.
1592 Salisbury to Henry. *Henry VI Part Two*, act 5, sc.1,
l.180–1.

15 Thou hast most traitorously corrupted the youth of
the realm in erecting a grammar school; and,
whereas before, our forefathers had no other books
but the score and the tally, thou hast caused
printing to be used and, contrary to the King his
crown and dignity, thou hast built a paper-mill. It
will be proved to thy face that thou hast men about
thee that unsually talk of a noun and a verb and
such abominable words as no Christian ear can
endure to hear.
1592 Cade. *Henry VI Part Two*, act 4, sc.7, l.30–8.

16 Farewell, faint-hearted and degenerate king,
In whose cold blood no spark of honour bides.
1592 Westmorland to Henry. *Henry VI Part Three*, act 1, sc.1,
l.184–5.

17 O tiger's heart wrapped in a woman's hide!
1592 York to Margaret. *Henry VI Part Three*, act 1, sc.4, l.138.

18 Women are soft, mild, pitiful and flexible—
Thou stern, obdurate, flinty, rough, remorseless.
1592 York to Margaret. *Henry VI Part Three*, act 1, sc.4,
l.142–3.

19 Many strokes, though with a little axe,
Hews down and fells the hardest-timbered oak.
1592 Messenger to Richard telling of his father York's death.
Henry VI Part Three, act 2, sc.1, l.54–5.

20 To weep is to make less the depth of grief;

Tears, then for babes-blows and revenge for me!
1592 Richard. *Henry VI Part Three*, act 2, sc.1, l.85–6.

21 This battle fares like to the morning's war,
When dying clouds contend with growing light,
What time the shepherd, blowing of his nails,
Can neither call it perfect day nor night.
1592 Henry. *Henry VI Part Three*, act 2, sc.5, l.1–4.

22 O God! Methinks it were a happy life.
To be no better than a homely swain.
To sit upon a hill, as I do now;
To carve out dials quaintly, point by point.
1592 Henry. *Henry VI Part Three*, act 2, sc.5 l.21–4.

23 Thereby to see the minutes how they run:
How many makes the hour full complete,
How many hours brings about the day,
How many days will finish up the year,
How many years a mortal man may live.
1592 Henry. *Henry VI Part Three*, act 2, sc.5, l.25–9.

24 Gives not the hawthorn bush a sweeter shade
To shepherds looking on their seely sheep
Than doth a rich embroidered canopy
To kings that fear their subjects' treachery?
1592 Henry. *Henry VI Part Three*, act 2, sc.5, l.42–5.

25 The common people swarm like summer flies.
1592 Clifford. *Henry VI Part Three*, act 2, sc.6, l.8.

26 I know I am too mean to be your queen,
And yet too good to be your concubine.
1592 Lady Gray to Edward. *Henry VI Part Three*, act 3, sc.2, l.97–8.

27 Hasty marriage seldom proveth well.
1592 Richard of Gloucester. *Henry VI Part Three*, act 4, sc.1, l.18.

28 Fearless minds climb soonest unto crowns.
1592 Richard of Gloucester. *Henry VI Part Three*, act 4, sc.8, l.62.

29 What fates impose, that men must needs abide.
It boots not to resist both wind and tide.
1592 Edward. *Henry VI Part Three*, act 4, sc.4, l.31–2.

30 My pity hath been balm to heal their wounds.
1592 Henry. *Henry VI Part Three*, act 4, sc.10, l.9.

31 Lo now my glory smeared in dust and blood.
My parks, my walks, my manors that I had,
Even now forsake me, and of all my lands
Is nothing left me but my body's length.
1592 Warwick wounded and dying. *Henry VI Part Three*, act 5, sc.2, l.23–6.

32 Why, courage, then—what cannot be avoided
'Twere childish weakness to lament or fear.
1592 Margaret. *Henry VI Part Three*, act 5, sc.4, l.37–8.

33 Down, down to hell; and say I sent thee thither!
1592 Richard of Gloucester to Henry. *Henry VI Part Three*, act 5, sc.6, l.67.

34 Since the heavens have shaped my body so,
Let hell make crooked my mind to answer it.
I had no father, I am like no father;
I have no brother, I am like no brother;
And this word, 'love', which greybeards call divine,
Be resident in men like one another
And not in me—I am myself alone.
1592 Richard of Gloucester. *Henry VI Part Three*, act 5, sc.6, l.78–84.

35 Wilt thou draw near the nature of the gods?
Draw near them then in being merciful.
1592 Tamora to Titus. *Titus Andronicus*, act 1, sc.1, l.117–8.

36 Give me a staff of honour for mine age,
But not a sceptre to control the world.
1592 Titus. *Titus Andronicus*, act 1, sc.1, l.198–9.

37 Vengeance is in my heart, death in my hand,
Blood and revenge are hammering in my head.
1592 Aaron to Tamora. *Titus Andronicus*, act 2, sc.3, l.38–9.

38 Dost thou not perceive
That Rome is but a wilderness of tigers?
1592 Titus to Lucius. *Titus Andronicus*, act 3, sc.1, l.52–3.

39 To weep with them that weep doth ease some deal,
But sorrow flouted at is double death.
1592 Marcus. *Titus Andronicus*, act 3, sc.1, l.243–4.

40 My heart, all mad with misery,
Beats in the hollow prison of my flesh.
1592 Titus. *Titus Andronicus*, act 3, sc.2, l.9–10.

41 I'll to thy closet and go read with thee
Sad stories chancèd in the times of old.
1592 Titus to Lavinia. *Titus Andronicus*, act 3, sc.2, l.81–2.

42 I have heard my grandsire say full oft
Extremity of griefs would make men mad.
1592 Young Lucius. *Titus Andronicus*, act 4, sc.1, l.18–19.

43 The eagle suffers little birds to sing,
And is not careful what they mean thereby,
Knowing that with the shadow of his wings
He can at pleasure stint their melody.
1592 Tamora to Saturninus. *Titus Andronicus*, act 4, sc.4, l.83–6.

44 If one good deed in all my life I did
I do repent it from my very soul.
1592 Aaron. *Titus Andronicus*, act 5, sc.3, l.188–9.

45 Now is the winter of our discontent
Made glorious summer by this son of York.
1592–3 Richard. *Richard III*, act 1, sc.1, l.1–2.

46 Grim-visaged war hath smoothed his wrinkled front,

And now—instead of mounting barbèd steeds
To fright the souls of fearful adversaries—
He capers nimbly in a lady's chamber
To the lascivious pleasing of a lute.
But I, that am not shaped for sportive tricks
Nor made to court an amorous looking-glass.
1592–3 Richard. *Richard III*, act 1, sc.1, l.9–15.

47   Cheated of feature by dissembling nature,
Deformed, unfinished, sent before my time
Into this breathing world scarce half made up.
1592–3 Richard. *Richard III*, act 1, sc.1, l.19–21.

48   I in this weak piping time of peace
Have no delight to pass away the time,
Unless to spy my shadow in the sun
And descant on mine own deformity.
1592–3 Richard. *Richard III*, act 1, sc.1, l.24–7.

49   Teach not thy lip such scorn, for it was made
For kissing, lady, not for such contempt.
1592–3 Richard to Lady Anne. *Richard III*, act 1, sc.2, l.159–60.

50   Was ever woman in this humour wooed?
Was ever woman in this humour won?
1592–3 Richard. *Richard III*, act 1, sc.2, l.215–6.

51   Were you snarling all before I came,
Ready to catch each other by the throat,
And turn you all your hatred now on me?
1592–3 Margaret. *Richard III*, act 1, sc.3, l.185–7.

52   They that stand high have many blasts to shake
them,
And if they fall they dash themselves to pieces.
1592–3 Margaret. *Richard III*, act 1, sc.3, l.257–8.

53   And thus I clothe my naked villainy
With odd old ends, stol'n forth of Holy Writ,
And seem a saint when most I play the devil.
1592–3 Richard. *Richard III*, act 1, sc.3, l.334–6.

54   O Lord! Methought what pain it was to drown,
What dreadful noise of waters in my ears,
What sights of ugly death within my eyes.
Methoughts I saw a thousand fearful wrecks,
Ten thousand men that fishes gnawed upon,
Wedges of gold, great ouches, heaps of pearl,
Inestimable stones, unvalued jewels,
All scattered in the bottom of the sea.
1592–3 Clarence, shortly before he was murdered. *Richard III*, act 1, sc.4, l.21–8.

55   Woe to that land that's governed by a child.
1592–3 Third Citizen. *Richard III*, act 2, sc.3, l.11.

56   So wise so young, they say, do never live long.
1592–3 Richard, aside. *Richard III*, act 3, sc.1, l.79.

57   Talk'st thou to me of 'ifs'? Thou art a traitor.—

Off with his head.
1592–3 Richard. *Richard III*, act 3, sc.4, l.75–6.

58   I am not in the giving vein today.
1592–3 Richard. *Richard III*, act 4, sc.2, l.119.

59   Thou cam'st on earth to make the earth my hell.
1592–3 Duchess of York to Richard. *Richard III*, act 4, sc.4, l.167.

60   True hope is swift, and flies with swallows' wings.
1592–3 Henry, Earl of Richmond. *Richard III*, act 5, sc.2, l.23.

61   The King's name is a tower of strength.
1592–3 Richard. *Richard III*, act 5, sc.3, l.12.

62   Give me another horse! Bind up my wounds!
Have mercy, Jesu!—Soft, I did but dream.
O coward conscience, how dost thou afflict me?
1592–3 Richard. *Richard III*, act 5, sc.5, l.131–3.

63   My conscience hath a thousand several tongues,
And every tongue brings in a several tale,
And every tale condemns me for a villain.
1592–3 Richard. *Richard III*, act 5, sc.5, l.147–9.

64   There is no creature loves me,
And if I die no soul will pity me.
Nay, wherefore should they?—Since that I myself
Find in myself no pity to myself.
1592–3 Richard. *Richard III*, act 5, sc.5, l.154–7.

65   Methought the souls of all that I had murdered
Came to my tent, and every one did threat
Tomorrow's vengeance on the head of Richard.
1592–3 Richard on the eve of the Battle of Bosworth. *Richard III*, act 5, sc.5, l.158–60.

66   Conscience is but a word that cowards use,
Devised at first to keep the strong in awe.
Our strong arms be our conscience; swords, our
law.
March on, join bravely! Let us to't, pell mell—
If not to heaven, then hand in hand to hell.
1592–3 Richard. *Richard III*, act 5, sc.6, l.39–43.

67   A thousand hearts are great within my bosom.
Advance our standards! Set upon the foes!
Our ancient word of courage, fair Saint George,
Inspire us with the spleen of fiery dragons.
Upon them! Victory sits on our helms!
1592–3 Richard. *Richard III*, act 5, sc.6, l.77–81.

68   Slave, I have set my life upon a cast,
And I will stand the hazard of the die.
1592–3 Richard. *Richard III*, act 5, sc.7, l.9–10.

69   A horse! A horse! My kingdom for a horse!
1592–3 Richard. *Richard III*, act 5, sc.7, l.13.

70   Frame your mind to mirth and merriment,

Which bars a thousand harms, and lengthens life.
1593 Messsenger to Sly. *The Taming of the Shrew,* Induction 2, l.131–2.

71 Thinkest thou, Hortensio, though her father be
very rich, any man is so very a fool to be married to
hell?
1593 Gremio. *The Taming of the Shrew,* act 1, sc.1, l.122–4.

72 There's small choice in rotten apples.
1593 Hortensio to Gremio. *The Taming of the Shrew,* act 1, sc.1, l.133–4.

73 I come to wive it wealthily in Padua;
If wealthily, then happily in Padua.
1593 Petruccio to Hortensio. *The Taming of the Shrew,* act 1, sc.2, l.74–5.

74 O this learning, what a thing it is!
1593 Gremio. *The Taming of the Shrew,* act 1, sc.2, l.157.

75 She is your treasure, she must have a husband.
I must dance barefoot on her wedding day,
And for your love to her lead apes in hell.
1593 Katherine. *The Taming of the Shrew,* act 2, sc.1, l.32–4.

76 I am rough, and woo not like a babe.
1593 Petruccio. *The Taming of the Shrew,* act 2, sc.1, l.137.

77 You are called plain Kate,
And bonny Kate, and sometimes Kate the curst,
But Kate, the prettiest Kate in Christendom,
Kate of Kate Hall, my super-dainty Kate–.
1593 Petruccio. *The Taming of the Shrew,* act 2, sc.1, l.185–8.

78 Your father hath consented
That you shall be my wife, your dowry 'greed on,
And will you, nill you, I will marry you.
1593 Petruccio to Kate. *The Taming of the Shrew,* act 2, sc.1, l.263–5.

79 We will have rings, and things, and fine array;
And kiss me, Kate. We will be married o' Sunday.
1593 Petruccio. *The Taming of the Shrew,* act 2, sc.1, l.319–20.

80 Preposterous ass, that never read so far
To know the cause why music was ordain'd!
Was it not to refresh the mind of man
After his studies or his usual pain?
1593 Lucentio to Hortensio. *The Taming of the Shrew,* act 3, sc.1, l.9–12.

81 Old fashions please me best. I am not so nice
To change true rules for odd inventions.
1593 Bianca to Hortensio. *The Taming of the Shrew,* act 3, sc.1, l.78–9.

82 Go, girl. I cannot blame thee now to weep.
For such an injury would vex a very saint.
1593 Baptisa. *The Taming of the Shrew,* act 3, sc.2, l.27–8.

83 He took the bride about the neck

And kissed her lips with such a clamorous smack
That at the parting all the church did echo.
1593 Gremio, of Petruccio. *The Taming of the Shrew,* act 3, sc.3, l.50–2.

84 To me she's married, not unto my clothes.
1593 Petruccio. *The Taming of the Shrew,* act 3, sc.2, l.117.

85 This is a way to kill a wife with kindness.
1593 Petruccio. *The Taming of the Shrew,* act 4, sc.1, l.194.

86 How say you to a fat tripe finely broiled?
1593 Grumio to Katherine. *The Taming of the Shrew,* act 4, sc.3, l.20.

87 What, is the jay more precious than the lark
Because his feathers are more beautiful?
Or is the adder better than the eel
Because his painted skin contents the eye?
1593–4 Petruccio to Kate. *The Taming of the Shrew,* act 4, sc.3, l.173-76.

88 Your plainness and your shortness please me well.
1593 Baptista to Pedant. *The Taming of the Shrew,* act 4, sc.4, l.38.

89 Thy husband is thy lord, thy life, thy keeper,
Thy head, thy sovereign.
1593 Katherine. *The Taming of the Shrew,* act 5, sc.2, l.151–2.

90 I am ashamed that women are so simple
To offer war where they should kneel for peace.
1593 Katherine. *The Taming of the Shrew,* act 5, sc.2, l.166–7.

91 Affection is a coal that must be cooled;
Else, suffered, it will set the heart on fire.
1593 *Venus and Adonis,* stanza 65, l.387–8.

92 Bid me discourse, I will enchant thine ear.
1593 *Venus and Adonis,* stanza 25, l.145.

93 Love comforteth like sunshine after rain.
1593 *Venus and Adonis,* stanza 134, l.799.

94 Love is a spirit all compact of fire,
Not gross to sink, but light, and will aspire.
1593 *Venus and Adonis,* stanza 25, l.149–50.

95 Melodious discord, heavenly tune harsh sounding,
Ear's deep-sweet music, and heart's deep-sore
wounding.
1593 *Venus and Adonis,* stanza 72, l.431–2.

96 Their copious stories, oftentimes begun,
End without audience, and are never done.
1593 *Venus and Adonis,* stanza 141, l.845–6.

97 Make use of time; let not advantage slip.
Beauty within itself should not be wasted.
Fair flowers that are not gathered in their prime
Rot, and consume themselves in little time.
1593 *Venus and Adonis,* stanza 22, l.129–32.

98 Dismiss your vows, your feignèd tears, your flatt'ry;

For where a heart is hard they make no batt'ry.
1593 *Venus and Adonis*, stanza 71, l.425–6.

99 Hunting he loved, but love he laughed to scorn.
1593 *Venus and Adonis*, stanza 1, l.4.

1 They say this town is full of cozenage,
As nimble jugglers that deceive the eye,
Dark-working sorcerers that change the mind,
Soul-killing witches that deform the body.
1594 Antipholus of Syracuse. *The Comedy of Errors*, act 1, sc.2,
l.97–100.

2 Am I so round with you as you with me,
That like a football you do spurn me thus?
You spurn me hence, and he will spurn me hither.
If I last in this service, you must case me in leather.
1594 Dromio of Ephesus. *The Comedy of Errors*, act 2, sc.1,
l.81–4.

3 They brought one Pinch, a hungry lean-faced
villain,
A mere anatomy, a mountebank,
A threadbare juggler, and a fortune-teller,
A needy, hollow-eyed, sharp-looking wretch,
A living dead man.
1594 Antipholus of Ephesus. *The Comedy of Errors*, act 5, sc.1,
l.238–42.

4 Let fame, that all hunt after in their lives,
Live registered upon our brazen tombs,
And then grace us in the disgrace of death
When, spite of cormorant devouring time,
Th' endeavour of this present breath may buy
That honour which shall bate his scythe's keen edge
And make us heirs of all eternity.
1594–5 King. *Love's Labour's Lost*, act 1, sc.1, l.1–7.

5 Study is like the heavens' glorious sun,
That will not be deep searched with saucy looks.
1594–5 Biron. *Love's Labour's Lost*, act 1, sc.1, l.84–5.

6 Small have continual plodders ever won,
Save base authority from others' books.
1594–5 Biron to King. *Love's Labour's Lost*, act 1, sc.1, l.86–7.

7 How well he's read, to reason against reading!
1594–5 King. *Love's Labour's Lost*, act 1, sc.1, l.94.

8 At Christmas I no more desire a rose
Than wish a snow in May's new-fangled shows.
1594–5 Biron. *Love's Labour's Lost*, act 1, sc.1, l.105–6.

9 Necessity will make us all forsworn
1594–5 Biron. *Love's Labour's Lost*, act 1, sc.1, l.147.

10 A man in all the world's new fashion planted,
That hath a mint of phrases in his brain.
One who the music of his own vain tongue
Doth ravish like enchanting harmony.
1594–5 King, of Armado. *Love's Labour's Lost*, act 1, sc.1,
l.162–5.

11 A child of our grandmother Eve, a female, or, for
thy more sweet understanding, a woman.
1594–5 Armado's letter. *Love's Labour's Lost*, act 1, sc.1, l.255.

12 Assist me, some extemporal god of rhyme, for I am
sure I shall turn to sonnet. Devise wit, write pen,
for I am for whole volumes, in folio.
1594–5 Armado. *Love's Labour's Lost*, act 1, sc.2, l.174–6.

13 This wimpled, whining, purblind, wayward boy,
This Signor Junior, giant dwarf, Dan Cupid,
Regent of love-rhymes, lord of folded arms,
Th' anointed sovereign of sighs and groans,
Liege of all loiterers and malcontents,
Dread prince of plackets, king of codpieces,
Sole imperator and great general
Of trotting paritors—O my little heart!
1594–5 Biron. *Love's Labour's Lost*, act 3, sc.1, l.174–81.

14 A giving hand, though foul, shall have fair praise.
1594–5 Princess. *Love's Labour's Lost*, act 4, sc.1, l.23.

15 O thou monster ignorance, how deformed dost
thou look!
1594–5 Holofernes, to Dull. *Love's Labour's Lost*, act 4, sc.2,
l.23.

16 He hath never fed of the dainties that are bred in a
book.
He hath not eat paper, as it were, he hath not drunk
ink.
1594–5 Nathaniel, of Dull. *Love's Labour's Lost*, act 4, sc.2,
l.24–5.

17 The elegancy, facility, and golden cadence of
poesy—
1594–5 Holofernes. *Love's Labour's Lost*, act 4, sc.2, l.123.

18 By heaven, I do love; and it hath taught me to
rhyme, and to be melancholy.
1594–5 Biron. *Love's Labour's Lost*, act 4, sc.3, l.11.

19 What fool is not so wise
To lose an oath to win a paradise?
1594–5 Longueville. *Love's Labour's Lost*, act 4, sc.3, l.69–70.

20 Love's feeling is more soft and sensible
Than are the tender horns of cockled snails.
1594–5 Biron. *Love's Labour's Lost*, act 4, sc.3, l.313–4.

21 Never durst poet touch a pen to write
Until his ink were tempered with love's sighs.
1594–5 Biron. *Love's Labour's Lost*, act 4, sc.3, l.322–3.

22 From women's eyes this doctrine I derive.
They sparkle still the right Promethean fire.
They are the books, the arts, the academes
That show, contain, and nourish all the world,
Else none at all in aught proves excellent.
1594–5 Biron. *Love's Labour's Lost*, act 4, sc.3, l.326–30.

23 He draweth out the thread of his verbosity finer
than the staple of his argument.
1594–5 Holofernes, of Armado. *Love's Labour's Lost*, act 5, sc.1,
l.16.

24 O, they have lived long in the alms-basket of
words. I marvel thy master hath not eaten thee for a
word, for thou art not so long by
the head as honorificabilitudinitatibus. Thou art
easier swallowed than a flapdragon.
1594–5 Costard. *Love's Labour's Lost*, act 5, sc.1, l.38–42.

25 A light heart lives long.
1594–5 Catherine. *Love's Labour's Lost*, act 5, sc.2, l.18.

26 There's no such sport as sport by sport o'erthrown.
1594–5 Princess. *Love's Labour's Lost*, act 5, sc.2, l.152.

27 Taffeta phrases, silken terms precise,
Three-piled hyperboles, spruce affectation,
Figures pedantical——these summer flies
Have blown me full of maggot ostentation.
1594–5 Biron. *Love's Labour's Lost*, act 5, sc.2, l.406–10.

28 Mirth cannot move a soul in agony.
1594–5 Biron. *Love's Labour's Lost*, act 5, sc.2, l.843.

29 A jest's prosperity lies in the ear
Of him that hears it, never in the tongue
Of him that makes it.
1594–5 Rosaline. *Love's Labour's Lost*, act 5, sc.2, l.847–9.

30 When icicles hang by the wall,
And Dick the shepherd blows his nail,
And Tom bears logs into the hall,
And milk comes frozen home in pail;
1594–5 Winter's song. *Love's Labour's Lost*, act 5, sc.2,
l.897–900.

31 When blood is nipped, and ways be foul,
Then nightly sings the staring owl:
Tu-whit, tu-whoo!——a merry note,
While greasy Joan doth keel the pot.

When all aloud the wind doth blow,
And coughing drowns the parson's saw,
And birds sit brooding in the snow,
And Marian's nose looks red and raw;
When roasted crabs hiss in the bowl.
1594–5 Winter's song. *Love's Labour's Lost*, act 5, sc.2, l.901–9.

32 Respect and reason wait on wrinkled age!
1594 *The Rape of Lucrece*, stanza 39, l.275.

33 Thy beauty hath ensnared thee to this night.
1594 *The Rape of Lucrece*, stanza 70, l.485.

34 To show the beldame daughters of her daughter,
To make the child a man, the man a child,
To slay the tiger that doth live by slaughter,
To tame the unicorn and lion wild,
To mock the subtle in themselves beguiled,

To cheer the ploughman with increasing crops,
And waste huge stones with little water drops.
1594 *The Rape of Lucrece*, stanza 137, l.953–9.

35 Like an unpractised swimmer plunging still,
With too much labour drowns for want of skill.
1594 *The Rape of Lucrece*, stanza 157, l.1098–9.

36 It cannot be, I find,
But such a face should bear a wicked mind.
1594 *The Rape of Lucrece*, stanza 220, l.1539–40.

37 Our doctors say this is no time to bleed.
1595 Richard. *Richard II*, act 1, sc.1, l.157.

38 I am disgraced, impeached, and baffled here,
Pierced to the soul with slander's venomed spear.
1595 Mowbray to Richard. *Richard II*, act 1, sc.1, l.170–1.

39 Lions make leopards tame.
1595 Richard. *Richard II*, act 1, sc.1, l.174.

40 The purest treasure mortal times afford
Is spotless reputation; that away,
Men are but gilded loam, or painted clay.
A jewel in a ten-times barred-up chest
Is a bold spirit in a loyal breast.
Mine honour is my life. Both grow in one.
Take honour from me, and my life is done.
1595 Mowbray to Richard. *Richard II*, act 1, sc.1, l.177–83.

41 As gentle and as jocund as to jest
Go I to fight. Truth hath a quiet breast.
1595 Mowbray. *Richard II*, act 1, sc.3, l.95–6.

42 This must my comfort be:
That sun that warms you here shall shine on me.
1595 Bolingbroke to Richard. *Richard II*, act 1, sc.3, l.138–9.

43 How long a time lies in one little word!
Four lagging winters and four wanton springs
End in a word: such is the breath of kings.
1595 Bolingbroke. *Richard II*, act 1, sc.3, l.206–8.

44 Methinks I am a prophet new-inspired,
And thus, expiring, do foretell of him.
His rash, fierce blaze of riot cannot last,
For violent fires soon burn out themselves.
1595 John of Gaunt, to Richard. *Richard II*, act 2, sc.1, l.31–4.

45 Small showers last long, but sudden storms are
short.
1595 John of Gaunt. *Richard II*, act 2, sc.1, l.35.

46 With eager feeding food doth choke the feeder.
1595 John of Gaunt. *Richard II*, act 2, sc.1, l.37.

47 O, who can hold a fire in his hand
By thinking on the frosty Caucasus,
Or cloy the hungry edge of appetite
By bare imagination of a feast,
Or wallow naked in December snow

By thinking on fantastic summer's heat?
1595 Bolingbroke. *Richard II*, act 1, sc.3, l.257–62.

48   This royal throne of kings, this sceptred isle,
This earth of majesty, this seat of Mars,
This other Eden, demi-paradise,
This fortress built by nature for herself
Against infection and the hand of war,
This happy breed of men, this little world,
This precious stone set in the silver sea,
Which serves it in the office of a wall,
Or as a moat defensive to a house
Against the envy of less happier lands;
This blessèd plot, this earth, this realm, this
   England.
1595 John of Gaunt. *Richard II*, act 2, sc.1, l.40–50.

49   England that was wont to conquer others
Hath made a shameful conquest of itself.
1595 John of Gaunt. *Richard II*, act 2, sc.1, l.65–6.

50   Each substance of a grief hath twenty shadows,
Which shows like grief itself.
1595 Bushy. *Richard II*, act 2, sc.2, l.14–15.

51   Comfort's in heaven, and we are on the earth,
Where nothing lives but crosses, cares, and griefs.
1595 York. *Richard II*, act 2, sc.2, l.78–9.

52   Hope to joy is little less in joy
Than hope enjoyed.
1595 Northumberland. *Richard II*, act 2, sc.3, l.15–16.

53   I count myself in nothing else so happy
As in a soul rememb'ring my good friends.
1595 Bolingboke. *Richard II*, act 2, sc.3, l.46–7.

54   Things past redress are now with me past care.
1595 York. *Richard II*, act 2, sc.3, l.170.

55   Not all the water in the rough rude sea
Can wash the balm from an anointed king.
1595 Richard. *Richard II*, act 3, sc.2, l.50–1.

56   O, call back yesterday, bid time return,
And thou shalt have twelve thousand fighting men.
Today, today, unhappy day too late.
1595 Salisbury. *Richard II*, act 3, sc.2, l.65–7.

57   Time hath set a blot upon my pride.
1595 Richard. *Richard II*, act 3, sc.2, l.77.

58   Cry woe, destruction, ruin, loss, decay;
The worst is death, and death will have his day.
1595 Richard. *Richard II*, act 3, sc.2, l.98–9.

59   And nothing can we call our own but death,
And that small model of the barren earth
Which serves as paste and cover to our bones.
1595 Richard. *Richard II*, act 3, sc.2, l.148–50.

60   For God's sake, let us sit upon the ground,

And tell sad stories of the death of kings—
How some have been deposed, some slain in war,
Some haunted by the ghosts they have deposed,
Some poisoned by their wives, some sleeping killed,
All murdered. For within the hollow crown
That rounds the mortal temples of a king
Keeps Death his court; and there the antic sits,
Scoffing his state and grinning at his pomp,
Allowing him a breath, a little scene,
To monarchize, be freared, and kill with looks,
Infusing him with self and vain conceit,
As if this flesh which walls about our life
Were brass impregnable; and humoured thus,
Comes at the last, and with a little pin
Bores through his castle wall; and farewell, king.
1595 Richard. *Richard II*, act 3, sc.2, l.151–166.

61   O, that I were as great
As is my grief, or lesser than my name,
Or that I could forget what I have been,
Or not remember what I must be now!
1595 Richard. *Richard II*, act 3, sc.3, l.135–8.

62   What must the King do now? Must he submit?
The King shall do it. Must he be deposed?
The King shall be contented. Must he lose
The name of King? A God's name, let it go.
I'll give my jewels for a set of beads,
My gorgeous palace for a hermitage,
My gay apparel for an almsman's gown,
My figured goblets for a dish of wood,
My sceptre for a palmer's walking staff,
My subjects for a pair of carvèd saints,
And my large kingdom for a little grave.
1595 Richard. *Richard II*, act 3, sc.3, l.142–52.

63   Alack, why am I sent for to a king
Before I have shook off the regal thoughts
Wherewith I reigned? I hardly yet have learned
To insinuate, flatter, bow, and bend my knee.
Give sorrow leave awhile to tutor me
To this submission. Yet I well remember
The favours of these men. Were they not mine?
Did they not sometime cry, 'All hail!' to me?
So Judas did to Christ. But He in twelve
Found the truth in all but one; I, in twenty
   thousand, none.
God save the King! Will no man say 'Amen'?
Am I both the priest and clerk? Well then, Amen?
1595 Richard. *Richard II*, act 4, sc.1, l.153–164.

64   You may my glories and my state depose,
But not my griefs; still am I king of those.
1595 Richard. *Richard II*, act 4, sc.1, l.182–3.

65   Mine eyes are full of tears; I cannot see.
And yet salt water blinds them not so much
But they can see a sort of traitors here.

Nay, if I turn mine eyes upon myself
I find myself a traitor with the rest.
1595 Richard. *Richard II*, act 4, sc.1, l.234–8.

66 I am sworn brother, sweet,
To grim necessity, and he and I
Will keep a league till death.
1595 Richard. *Richard II*, act 5, sc.1, l.20–1.

67 The love of wicked friends converts to fear;
That fear to hate.
1595 Richard. *Richard II*, act 5, sc.1, l.66–7.

68 Had not God, for some strong purpose steeled
The hearts of men, they must perforce have melted.
1595 York. *Richard II*, act 5, sc.2, l.34–5.

69 Say 'Pardon', king. Let pity teach thee how.
The word is short, but not so short as sweet;
No word like 'Pardon' for kings' mouths so meet.
1595 Duchess of York. *Richard II*, act 5, sc.3, l.115–6.

70 Thoughts tending to ambition, they do plot
Unlikely wonders: how these vain weak nails
May tear a passage through the flinty ribs
Of this hard world.
1595 Richard. *Richard II*, act 5, sc.5, l.18–21.

71 How sour sweet music is
When time is broke and no proportion kept.
So is it in the music of men's lives.
1595 Richard. *Richard II*, act 5, sc.5, l.42–4.

72 Mount, mount, my soul; thy seat is up on high,
Whilst my gross flesh sinks downward, here to die.
1595 Richard. *Richard II*, act 5, sc.5, l.111–12.

73 From forth the fatal loins of these two foes
A pair of star-crossed lovers take their life.
1595 Chorus. *Romeo and Juliet*, Prologue. l.5–6.

74 Alas that love, so gentle in his view,
Should be so tyrannous and rough in proof.
1595 Benvolio to Romeo. *Romeo and Juliet*, act 1, sc.1, l.166–7.

75 'Tis not hard, I think,
For men so old as we to keep the peace.
1595 Capulet. *Romeo and Juliet*, act 1, sc.2, l.2–3.

76 Such comfort as do lusty young men feel
When well-apparell'd April on the heel
Of limping winter treads.
1595 Capulet. *Romeo and Juliet*, act 1, sc.2, l.24–6.

77 Is love a tender thing? It is too rough,
Too rude, too boist'rous, and it pricks like thorn.
1595 Romeo. *Romeo and Juliet*, act 1, sc.4, l.25–6.

78 She is the fairies' midwife, and she comes
In shape no bigger than an agate stone
On the forefinger of an alderman,

Drawn with a team of little atomi
Athwart man's noses as they lie asleep.
1595 Mercutio. *Romeo and Juliet*, act 1, sc.4, l.55–9.

79 Her chariot is an empty hazelnut
Made by the joiner squirrel or old grub,
Time out o' mind the fairies' coachmakers.
And in this state she gallops night by night
Through lovers' brains, and then they dream of
love.
1595 Mercutio. *Romeo and Juliet*, act 1, sc.4, l.68–72.

80 I talk of dreams,
Which are the children of an idle brain,
Begot of nothing but vain fantasy.
1595 Mercutio. *Romeo and Juliet*, act 1, sc.4, l.96–8.

81 You and I are past our dancing days.
1595 Capulet to his cousin. *Romeo and Juliet*, act 1, sc.5, l.31.

82 O, she doth teach the torches to burn bright!
It seems she hangs upon the cheek of night
As a rich jewel in an Ethiope's ear—
Beauty too rich for use, for earth too dear.
1595 Romeo of Juliet. *Romeo and Juliet*, act 1, sc.5, l.43–6.

83 Did my heart love till now? Forswear it, sight,
For I ne'er saw true beauty till this night.
1595 Mercutio. *Romeo and Juliet*, act 1, sc.5, l.51–2.

84 My only love sprung from my only hate!
Too early seen unknown, and known too late!
1595 Juliet. *Romeo and Juliet*, act 1, sc.5, l.137–8.

85 He jests at scars that never felt a wound.
But soft, what light through yonder window
breaks?
It is the east, and Juliet is the sun.
1595 Romeo. *Romeo and Juliet*, act 2, sc.1, l.43–5.

86 O, speak again, bright angel; for thou art
As glorious to this night, being o'er my head,
As is a wingèd messenger of heaven.
1595 Romeo of Juliet. *Romeo and Juliet*, act 2, sc.1, l.68–70.

87 O Romeo, Romeo, wherefore art thou Romeo?
Deny thy father and refuse thy name,
Or if thou will not, be but sworn my love,
And I'll no longer be a Capulet.
1595 Juliet. *Romeo and Juliet*, act 2, sc.1, l.75–8.

88 What's in a name? That which we call a rose
By any other word would smell as sweet.
1595 Juliet. *Romeo and Juliet*, act 2, sc.1, l.85–6.

89 Call me but love and I'll be new baptized.
Henceforth I never will be Romeo.
1595 Romeo. *Romeo and Juliet*, act 2, sc.1, l.93–4.

90 If thou think'st I am too quickly won,
I'll frown and be perverse and say thee nay,
So thou wilt woo.

1595 Juliet to Romeo. *Romeo and Juliet*, act 2, sc.1, l.137–9.

91   O swear not by the moon, th'inconstant moon
That monthly changes in her circled orb,
Lest that thy love prove likewise variable.
1595 Juliet. *Romeo and Juliet*, act 2, sc.1, l.151–3.

92   My bounty is as boundless as the sea,
My love as deep. The more I give to thee
The more I have, for both are infinite.
1595 Juliet. *Romeo and Juliet*, act 2, sc.1, l.175–7.

93   Parting is such sweet sorrow
That I shall say good-night till it be morrow.
1595 Juliet to Romeo. *Romeo and Juliet*, act 2, sc.1, l.229–30.

94   Sleep dwell upon thine eyes, peace in thy breast.
1595 Romeo to Juliet. *Romeo and Juliet*, act 2, sc.1, l.231.

95   O mickle is the powerful grace that lies
In plants, herbs, stones, and their true qualities,
For nought so vile that on the earth doth live
But to the earth some special good doth give.
1595 Friar Laurence. *Romeo and Juliet*, act 2, sc.2, l.15–18.

96   Virtue itself turns vice, being misapplied,
And vice sometime's by action dignified.
1595 Friar Laurence. *Romeo and Juliet*, act 2, sc.2, l.21–2.

97   Care keeps his watch in every old man's eye.
1595 Friar Laurence to Romeo. *Romeo and Juliet*, act 2, sc.2, l.35.

98   Wisely and slow. They stumble that run fast.
1595 Friar Laurence to Romeo. *Romeo and Juliet*, act 2, sc.2, l.94.

99   He fights as you sing pricksong, keeps time,
distance and proportion…the very butcher of a silk
button, a duellist, a duellist.
1595 Mercutio, of Tybalt. *Romeo and Juliet*, act 2, sc.3, l.19–22.

1   A gentleman, Nurse, that loves to hear himself talk,
and will speak more in a minute than he will stand
to in a month.
1595 Romeo. *Romeo and Juliet*, act 2, sc.3, l.138–9.

2   These violent delights have violent ends.
1595 Friar Laurence. *Romeo and Juliet*, act 2, sc.5, l.9.

3   Thy head is as full of quarrels as an egg is full of
meat.
1595 Mercutio to Benvolio. *Romeo and Juliet*, act 3, sc.1, l.20.

4   A plague o' both your houses.
They have made worms' meat of me.
1595 Mercutio, dying stabbed by Tybalt. *Romeo and Juliet*, act 3, sc.1, l.106–7.

5   Come, civil night,
Thou sober-suited matron all in black.
1595 Juliet. *Romeo and Juliet*, act 3, sc.2, l.10–11.

6   So tedious is this day
As is the night before some festival
To an impatient child that hath new robes
And may not wear them.
1595 Juliet. *Romeo and Juliet*, act 3, sc.2, l.28–31.

7   Steal immortal blessing from her lips.
1595 Romeo. *Romeo and Juliet*, act 3, sc.3, l.37.

8   Hang up philosophy!
Unless philosophy can make a Juliet.
1595 Romeo. *Romeo and Juliet*, act 3, sc.3, l.57–8.

9   A joy past joy calls out on me.
1595 Romeo. *Romeo and Juliet*, act 3, sc.3, l.172.

10   It was the nightingale, and not the lark,
That pierced the fear-full hollow of thine ear.
Nightly she sings on yond pom'granate tree.
1595 Juliet to Romeo. *Romeo and Juliet*, act 3, sc.5, l.2–4.

11   Night's candles are burnt out, and jocund day
Stands tiptoe on the misty mountaintops.
I must be gone and live, or stay and die.
1595 Romeo to Juliet. *Romeo and Juliet*, act 3, sc.5, l.9–11.

12   O, fortune, fortune, all men call thee fickle.
1595 Juliet. *Romeo and Juliet*, act 3, sc.5, l.60.

13   Mistress minion, you,
Thank me no thankings, nor proud me no prouds,
But fettle your fine joints 'gainst Thursday next
To go with Paris to Saint Peter's Church,
Or I will drag thee on a hurdle thither.
Out, you green-sickness carrion! Out, you baggage,
You tallow-face!
1595 Capulet, to Juliet, ordering her marriage to Paris. *Romeo and Juliet*, act 3, sc.5, l.151–7.

14   Is there no pity sitting in the clouds,
That sees into the bottom of my grief?
1595 Juliet. *Romeo and Juliet*, act 3, sc.5, l.196–7.

15   I think it best you married with the County.
O, he's a lovely gentleman!
Romeo's a dishclout to him.
1595 Nurse to Juliet. *Romeo and Juliet*, act 3, sc.5, l.217–19.

16   'Tis an ill cook that cannot lick his own fingers.
1595 Servingman to Capulet. *Romeo and Juliet*, act 4, sc.2, l.6.

17   I have a faint cold fear thrills through my viens
That almost freezes up the heat of life.
1595 Juliet. *Romeo and Juliet*, act 4, sc.3, l.15–16.

18   Out, alas, she's cold.
Her blood is settled, and her joints are stiff.
Life and these lips have long been separated.
Death lies on her like an untimely frost
Upon the sweetest flower of all the field.
1595 Capulet, of Juliet, as she feigns death. *Romeo and Juliet*, act 4, sc.4, l.52–6.

19 She's not well married that lives married long,
But she's best married that dies married young.
1595 Friar Laurence. *Romeo and Juliet*, act 4, sc.4, l.104–5.

20 I dreamt my lady came and found me dead—
Strange dream, that gives a dead man the leave to
think!—
And breathed such life with kisses in my lips
That I revived and was an emperor.
1595 Romeo. *Romeo and Juliet*, act 5, sc.1, l.6–9.

21 Art thou so bare and full of wretchedness,
And fear'st to die? Famine is in thy cheeks,
Need and oppression starveth in thy eyes,
Contempt and beggary hangs upon thy back.
The world is not thy friend, nor the world's law.
1595 Romeo to Aphthecary. *Romeo and Juliet*, act 5, sc.1,
l.68–72.

22 Give me thy hand,
One writ with me in sour misfortune's book.
1595 Romeo to Paris, who he has just killed. *Romeo and Juliet*,
act 5, sc.3, l.81–2.

23 Here, here will I remain
With worms that are thy chambermaids. O, here
Will I set up my everlasting rest,
And shake the yoke of inauspicious stars
From this world-wearied flesh.
1595 Romeo. *Romeo and Juliet*, act 5, sc.3, l.108–12.

24 Never was a story of more woe
Than this of Juliet and her Romeo.
1595 Prince. *Romeo and Juliet*, act 5, sc.3, l.308–9.

25 To you your father should be as a god.
1595 Theseus to Hermia. *A Midsummer Night's Dream*, act 1,
sc.1, l.47.

26 Your eyes are lodestars, and your tongue's sweet air
More tuneable than lark to shepherd's ear
When wheat is green, when hawthorn buds appear.
1595 Helena. *A Midsummer Night's Dream*, act 1, sc.1, l.83–5.

27 The course of true love never did run smooth.
1595 Lysander to Hermia. *A Midsummer Night's Dream*, act 1,
sc.1, l.134.

28 Love looks not with the eyes, but with the mind,
And therefore is winged Cupid painted blind.
1595 Helena. *A Midsummer Night's Dream*, act 1, sc.1,
l.234–5.

29 Marry, our play is The Most Lamentable Comedy
and Most Cruel Death of Pyramus and Thisbe.
1595 Quince. *A Midsummer Night's Dream*, act 1, sc.2,
l.11–12.

30 That will ask some tears in the true performing of
it. If I do it, let the audience look to their eyes. I
will move stones.

1595 Bottom. *A Midsummer Night's Dream*, act 1, sc.2, l.21–3.

31 Nay, faith, let not me play a woman. I have a beard
coming.
1595 Flute, on his reluctance to act the role of Thisbe. *A
Midsummer Night's Dream*, act 1, sc.2, l.43–4.

32 SNUG: Have you the lion's part written? Pray you, if
it be, give it me; for I am slow of study.
QUINCE: You may do it extempore, for it is nothing
but roaring.
BOTTOM: Let me play the lion too. I will roar that I
will do any man's heart good to hear me. I will
roar that I will make the Duke say 'Let him roar
again; let him roar again'.
1595 *A Midsummer Night's Dream*, act 1, sc.2, l.62–69.

33 I will roar you as gently as any sucking dove. I will
roar you an 'twere any nightingale.
1595 Bottom. *A Midsummer Night's Dream*, act 1, sc.2, l.77–8.

34 Ill met by moonlight, proud Titania.
1595 Oberon. A Midsummer Night's Dream, act 2, sc.1, l.60.

35 Over hill, over dale,
Thorough bush, thorough brier,
Over park, over pale,
Thorough flood, thorough fire:
I do wander everywhere
Swifter than the moonës sphere,
And I serve the Fairy Queen
To dew her orbs upon the green.
The cowslips tall her pensioners be.
In their gold coats spots you see;
Those be rubies, fairy favours;
In those freckles live their savours.
I must go seek some dewdrops here,
And hang a pearl in every cowslip's ear.
1595 Fairy. *A Midsummer Night's Dream*, act 2, sc.1, l.2–15.

36 Yet marked I where the bolt of Cupid fell.
It fell upon a little western flower—
Before, milk-white; now, purple with love's
wound—
And maidens call it love-in-idleness.
1595 Oberon. *A Midsummer Night's Dream*, act 2, sc.1,
l.165–8.

37 I'll put a girdle round about the earth
In forty minutes.
1595 Puck. *A Midsummer Night's Dream*, act 2, sc.1, l.175–6.

38 We cannot fight for love, as men may do;
We should be woo'd, and were not made to woo.
1595 Helena. *A Midsummer Night's Dream*, act 2, sc.1,
l.241–2.

39 I know a bank where the wild thyme blows,
Where oxlips and the nodding violet grows,
Quite overcanopied with luscious woodbine,
With sweet musk-roses, and with eglantine.

1595 Oberon. *A Midsummer Night's Dream*, act 2, sc.1, l.249–52.

40 You spotted snakes with double tongue,
Thorny hedgehogs, be not seen;
Newts and blindworms, do not wrong;
Come not near our Fairy Queen.
1595 First Fairy. *A Midsummer Night's Dream*, act 2, sc.2, l.9–12.

41 A surfeit of the sweetest things
The deepest loathing to the stomach brings.
1595 Lysander. *A Midsummer Night's Dream*, act 2, sc.2, l.143–4.

42 A lion among ladies is a most dreadful thing.
1595 Bottom. *A Midsummer Night's Dream*, act 3, sc.1, l.28.

43 FLUTE: (as Thisbe)
Most radiant Pyramus, most lily-white of hue,
Of colour like the red rose on triumphant brier;
Most bristly juvenile, and eke most lovely Jew,
As true as truest horse that yet would never tire:
I'll meet thee, Pyramus, at Ninny's tomb.
QUINCE: Ninus' tomb, man!
1595 *A Midsummer Night's Dream*, act 3, sc.1, l.87–92.

44 What angel wakes me from my flow'ry bed?
1595 Titania, of Bottom. *A Midsummer Night's Dream*, act 3, sc.1, l.122.

45 I pray thee, gentle mortal, sing again.
Mine ear is much enamoured of thy note;
So is mine eye enthrallèd to thy shape;
And thy fair virtue's force perforce doth move me
On the first view to say, to swear, I love thee.
1595 Titania. *A Midsummer Night's Dream*, act 3, sc.1, l.130–4.

46 I go, I go—look how I go,
Swifter than arrow from the Tartar's bow.
1595 Puck to Oberon. *A Midsummer Night's Dream*, act 3, sc.2, l.100–1.

47 Sleep, that sometimes shuts up sorrow's eye,
Steal me a while from mine own company.
1595 Helena. *A Midsummer Night's Dream*, act 3, sc.3, l.23–4.

48 Lord, what fools these mortals be!
1595 Puck. *A Midsummer Night's Dream*, act 3, sc.2, l.115.

49 Methinks I have a great desire to a bottle of hay.
Good hay, sweet hay, hath no fellow.
1595 Bottom. *A Midsummer Night's Dream*, act 4, sc.1, l.32–3.

50 I must to the barber's, monsieur, for methinks I am
marvellous hairy about the face; and I am such a
tender ass, if my hair do but tickle me I must
scratch.
1595 Bottom. *A Midsummer Night's Dream*, act 4, sc.1, l.23–6.

51 My Oberon, what visions have I seen!
Methough I was enamoured of an ass.

1595 Titania. *A Midsummer Night's Dream*, act 4, sc.1, l.75–6.

52 I have had a dream past the wit of man to say what
dream it was.
1595 Bottom. *A Midsummer Night's Dream*, act 4, sc.1, l.202–3.

53 Lovers and madmen have such seething brains,
Such shaping fantasies, that apprehend
More than cool reason ever comprehends.
1595 Theseus. *A Midsummer Night's Dream*, act 5, sc.1, l.4–6.

54 [LYSANDER] (reads)
'A tedious 'brief' scene of young Pyramus
And his love Thisbe: very tragical mirth.'
THESEUS:
'Merry' *and* 'tragical'? 'Tedious' *and* 'brief'?—
That is, hot ice and wonderous strange black snow.
1595 *A Midsummer Night's Dream*, act 5, sc.1, l.56–9.

55 The lunatic, the lover, and the poet
Are of imagination all compact.
One sees more devils than vast hell can hold:
That is the madman. The lover, all as frantic,
Sees Helen's beauty in a brow of Egypt.
The poet's eye , in a fine frenzy rolling,
Doth glance from heaven to earth, from earth to
heaven,
And as imagination bodies forth
The forms of things unknown, the poet's pen
Turns them to shapes, and gives to airy nothing
A local habitation and a name.
Such tricks hath strong imagination
That if it would but apprehend some joy
It comprehends some bringer of that joy;
Or in the night, imagining some fear,
How easy is a bush supposed a bear!
1595 Theseus. *A Midsummer Night's Dream*, act 5, sc.1, l.7–22.

56 A play there is, my lord, some ten words long,
Which is as brief as I have known a play;
But by ten words, my lord, it is too long.
1595 [Egeus]. *A Midsummer Night's Dream*, act 5, sc.1, l.61–3.

57 Anon comes Pyramus, sweet youth and tall,
And finds his trusty Thisbe's mantle slain;
Whereat with blade—with bloody, blameful
blade—
He bravely broached his boiling bloody breast;
And Thisbe, tarrying in mulberry shade,
His dagger drew and died.
1595 Quince's prologue to Pyramus and Thisbe. *A Midsummer Night's Dream*, act 5, sc.1, l.143–8.

58 O dainty duck, O dear!
Thy mantle good,
What, stained with blood?
Approach, ye furies fell.
O fates, come, come,
Cut the thread and thrum,

Quail, crush, conclude, and quell.
1595 Bottom (as Pyramus). *A Midsummer Night's Dream*, act 5, sc.1, l.276–82.

59 His eyes were green as leeks
1595 Flute (as Thisbe). *A Midsummer Night's Dream*, act 5, sc.1, l.330.

60 If we shadows have offended,
Think but this, and all is mended:
That you have but slumbered here,
While these visions did appear;
1595 Epilogue. *A Midsummer Night's Dream*, act 5, sc.2, l.1–4.

61 By how much unexpected, by so much
We must awake endeavour for defence,
For courage mounteth with occasion.
1596 Duke of Austria. *King John*, act 2, sc.1, l.80–2.

62 Well, whiles I am a beggar I will rail,
And say there is no sin but to be rich,
And being rich, my virtue then shall be
To say there is no vice but beggary.
Since kings break faith upon commodity,
Gain, be my lord, for I will worship thee.
1596 Bastard. *King John*, act 2, sc.1, l.594–9.

63 I will instruct my sorrows to be proud,
For grief is proud and makes his owner stoop.
1596 Constance. *King John*, act 2, sc.2, l.68–9.

64 My grief's so great
That no supporter but the huge firm earth
Can hold it up. Here I and sorrows sit.
1596 Constance. *King John*, act 2, sc.2, l.71–3.

65 Bell, book, and candle shall not drive me back
When gold and silver becks me to come on.
1596 Bastard. *King John*, act 3, sc.3, l.12–13.

66 Grief fills the room up of my absent child,
Lies in his bed, walks up and down with me.
1596 Constance. *King John*, act 3, sc.4, l.93–4.

67 Life is as tedious as a twice-told tale
Vexing the dull ear of a drowsy man.
1596 Louis the Dauphin. *King John*, act 3, sc.4, l.108–9.

68 When Fortune means to men most good,
She looks upon them with a threat'ning eye.
1596 Pandolf. *King John*, act 3, sc.4, l.119–20.

69 He that stands upon a slipp'ry place
Makes nice of no vile hold to stay him up.
1596 Pandolf. *King John*, act 3, sc.4, l.137–8.

70 Strong reasons make strange actions.
1596 Louis the Dauphin. *King John*, act 3, sc.4, l.182.

71 To gild refinèd gold, to paint the lily,
To throw a perfume on the violet,
To smooth the ice, or add another hue

Unto the rainbow, or with taper-light
To seek the beauteous eye of heaven to garnish,
Is wasteful and ridiculous excess.
1596 Salisbury. *King John*, act 4, sc.2, l.11–16.

72 The rich advantage of good exercise?
1596 Pembroke. *King John*, act 4, sc.2, l.60.

73 Think you I bear the shears of destiny?
Have I commandment on the pulse of life?
1596 John. *King John*, act 4, sc.2, l.91–2.

74 Entreat the north
To make his bleak winds kiss my parchèd lips,
And comfort me with cold. I do not ask you much;
I beg cold comfort.
1596 John to Prince Henry. *King John*, act 5, sc.7, l.39–42.

75 This England never did, nor never shall,
Lie at the proud foot of a conqueror.
1596 Bastard. *King John*, act 5, sc.7, l.112–3.

76 Now, by two-headed Janus,
Nature hath framed strange fellows in her time:
Some that will evermore peep through their eyes
And laugh like parrots at a bagpiper.
1596–7 Solanio. *The Merchant of Venice*, act 1, sc.1, l.50–3.

77 I hold the world but as the world, Graziano;
A stage where every man must play a part,
And mine a sad one.
1596–7 Antonio. *The Merchant of Venice*, act 1, sc.1, l.77–9.

78 Let him look to his bond.
1596–7 Shylock, of Antonio. *The Merchant of Venice*, act 3, sc.1, l.45–6.

79 Let music sound while he doth make his choice.
Then if he lose he makes a swanlike end,
Fading in music.
1596–7 Portia to Bassanio. *The Merchant of Venice*, act 3, sc.2, l.43–5.

80 Hath not a Jew eyes? Hath not a Jew hands, organs,
dimensions, senses, affections, passions; fed with
the same food, hurt with the same weapons, subject
to the same diseases, healed by the same means,
warmed and cooled by the same winter and
summer as a Christian is? If you prick us do we not
bleed? If you tickle us do we not laugh? If you
poison us do we not die? And if you wrong us shall
we not revenge? If we are like you in the rest, we
will resemble you in that.
1596–7 Shylock. *The Merchant of Venice*, act 3, sc.1, l.54–63.

81 There is no vice so simple but assumes
Some mark of virtue on his outward parts.
1596–7 Bassiano, aside. *The Merchant of Venice*, act 3, sc.2, l.81–2.

82 Look on beauty
And you shall see 'tis purchased by the weight,

Which therein works a miracle in nature,
Making them lightest that wear most of it.

1596–7 Bassanio, aside. *The Merchant of Venice*, act 3, sc.2, l.88–91.

83 Thou gaudy gold,
Hard food for Midas, I will none of thee.

1596–7 Bassiano, aloud. *The Merchant of Venice*, act 3, sc.2, l.101–2.

84 An unlessoned girl, unschooled, unpractisèd,
Happy in this, she is not yet so old
But she may learn.

1596–7 Portia, of herself. *The Merchant of Venice*, act 3, sc.2, l.159–61.

85 Madam, you have bereft me of all words.
Only my blood speaks to you in my veins.

1596–7 Bassanio to Portia. *The Merchant of Venice*, act 3, sc.2, l.175–6.

86 Here are a few of the unpleasant'st words
That ever blotted paper.

1596–7 Bassanio, reading of Antonio's misfortunes. *The Merchant of Venice*, act 3, sc.2, l.249–50.

87 Let it serve for table-talk.
Then, howsome'er thou speak'st, 'mong other
things
I shall digest it.

1596–7 Lorenzo. *The Merchant of Venice*, act 3, sc.5, l.83–5.

88 Let me play the fool.
With mirth and laughter let old wrinkles come.

1596–7 Graziano to Antonio. *The Merchant of Venice*, act 1, sc.1, l.79–80.

89 For silence is only commendable
In a neat's tongue dried and a maid not vendible.

1596–7 Graziano. *The Merchant of Venice*, act 1, sc.1, l.111–2.

90 Some men there are love not a gaping pig,
Some that are mad if they behold a cat,
And others when the bagpipe sings i'th' nose
Cannot contain their urine.

1596–7 Shylock. *The Merchant of Venice*, act 4, sc.1, l.46–49.

91 We turned o'er many books together.

1596–7 Bellario's letter of recommendation for Portia (as Balthasar). *The Merchant of Venice*, act 4, sc.1, l.154–5.

92 The quality of mercy is not strained.
It droppeth as the gentle rain from heaven
Upon the place beneath. It is twice blest:
It blesseth him that gives, and him that takes.

1596–7 Portia. *The Merchant of Venice*, act 4, sc.1, l.181–4.

93 It is enthronèd in the hearts of kings;
It is an attribute to God himself,
And earthly power doth then show likest God's
When mercy seasons justice.

1596–7 Portia. *The Merchant of Venice*, act 4, sc.1, l.190–4.

94 A Daniel come to judgement, yea, a Daniel!
O wise young judge, how I do honour thee!

1596–7 Shylock, of the disguised Portia. *The Merchant of Venice*, act 4, sc.1, l.220–1.

95 Antonio, I am married to a wife
Which is as dear to me as life itself,
But life itself, my wife, and all the world
Are not with me esteemed above thy life.
I would lose all, ay, sacrifice them all
Here to this devil, to deliver you.

1596–7 Bassanio. *The Merchant of Venice*, act 4, sc.1, l.279–84.

96 Take thou thy pound of flesh.

1596–7 Portia to Shylock. *The Merchant of Venice*, act 4, sc.1, l.305.

97 Nay, take my life and all, pardon not that.
You take my house when you do take the prop
That doth sustain my house; you take my life
When do you take the means whereby I live.

1596–7 Shylock to the Duke. *The Merchant of Venice*, act 4, sc.1, l.371–4.

98 How sweet the moonlight sleeps upon this bank!
Here will we sit, and let the sounds of music
Creep in our ears.

1596–7 Lorenzo to Jessica. *The Merchant of Venice*, act 5, sc.1, l.54–6.

99 Look how the floor of heaven
Is thick inlaid with patens of bright gold.
There's not the smallest orb which thou behold'st
But in his motion like an angel sings.

1596–7 Lorenzo to Jessica. *The Merchant of Venice*, act 5, sc.1, l.58–61.

1 O my Antonio, I do know of these
That therefore only are reputed wise
For saying nothing.

1596–7 Graziano. *The Merchant of Venice*, act 1, sc.1, l.95–7.

2 I am never merry when I hear sweet music.

1596–7 Jessica. *The Merchant of Venice*, act 5, sc.1, l.69.

3 The man that hath no music in himself,
Nor is not moved with concord of sweet sounds,
Is fit for treasons, stratagems, and spoils.

1596–7 Lorenzo. *The Merchant of Venice*, act 5, sc.1, l.83–5.

4 A substitute shines brightly as a king
Until a king be by.

1596–7 Portia. *The Merchant of Venice*, act 5, sc.1, l.94–5.

5 The crow doth sing as sweetly as the lark
When neither is attended.

1596–7 Portia. *The Merchant of Venice*, act 5, sc.1, l.102–3.

6 A light wife doth make a heavy husband.

1596–7 Portia. *The Merchant of Venice*, act 5, sc.1, l.130.

7 How far that little candle throws his beams—

So shines a good deed in a naughty world.
1596–7 Portia. *The Merchant of Venice*, act 5, sc.1, l.90–1.

8 Fish not with this melancholy bait
For this fool gudgeon, this opinion.
1596–7 Graziano. *The Merchant of Venice*, act 1, sc.1, l.101–2.

9 Graziano speaks an infinite deal of nothing, more
than any man in all Venice. His reasons are as two
grains of wheat hid in two bushels of chaff: you
shall seek all day ere you find them, and when you
have them they are not worth the search.
1596–7 Bassanio to Antonio. *The Merchant of Venice*, act 1, sc.1, l.114–18.

10 They are as sick that surfeit with too much as they
that starve with nothing.
1596–7 Nerissa. *The Merchant of Venice*, act 1, sc.2, l.5–6.

11 I can easier teach twenty what were good to be
done than to be one of the twenty to follow mine
own teaching.
1596–7 Portia. *The Merchant of Venice*, act 1, sc.2, l.15–17.

12 The brain may devise laws for the blood, but a hot
temper leaps o'er a cold decree.
1596–7 Portia. *The Merchant of Venice*, act 1, sc.2, l.17–18.

13 How like a fawning publican he looks.
1596–7 Shylock, of Antonio. *The Merchant of Venice*, act 1, sc.3, l.39.

14 He doth nothing but talk of his horse.
1596–7 Portia. *The Merchant of Venice*, act 1, sc.2, l.39–40.

15 I fear he will prove the weeping philosopher when
he grows old, being so full of unmannerly sadness
in his youth.
1596–7 Portia, of her suitor, the County Palatine. *The Merchant of Venice*, act 1, sc.2, l.47–9.

16 I will do anything, Nerissa, ere I will be married to
a sponge.
1596–7 Portia. *The Merchant of Venice*, act 1, sc.2, l.95–6.

17 God made him, and therefore let him pass for a
man.
1596–7 Portia, of her suitor M. le Bon. *The Merchant of Venice*, act 1, sc.2, l.54–5.

18 Yes, to smell pork, to eat of the habitation which
your prophet the Nazarite conjured the devil into! I
will buy with you, sell with you, talk with you,
walk with you, and so following, but I will not eat
with you, drink with you, nor pray with you.
1596–7 Shylock, invited to dine with Bassanio. *The Merchant of Venice*, act 1, sc.3, l.31–5.

19 There is not one among them but I dote on his very
absence, and I pray God grant them a fair
departure.

20 Signor Antonio, many a time and oft
In the Rialto you have rated me
About my moneys and my usances.
Still have I borne it with a patient shrug,
For suff'rance is the badge of all our tribe.
1596–7 Shylock. *The Merchant of Venice*, act 1, sc.3, l.105–109.

21 The devil can cite Scripture for his purpose.
An evil soul producing holy witness
Is like a villain with a smiling cheek,
A goodly apple rotten at the heart.
O, what a goodly outside falsehood hath!
1596–7 Antonio. *The Merchant of Venice*, act 1, sc.3, l.97–101.

22 If thou wilt lend this money, lend it not
As to thy friends; for when did friendship take
A breed for barren metal of his friend?
1596–7 Antonio to Shylock. *The Merchant of Venice*, act 1, sc.3, l.130–3.

23 I like not fair terms and a villain's mind.
1596–7 Bassanio. *The Merchant of Venice*, act 1, sc.3, l.178.

24 It is a wise father that knows his own child.
1596–7 Lancelot. *The Merchant of Venice*, act 2, sc.2, l.72–3.

25 I'll take my leave of the Jew in the twinkling.
1596–7 Lancelot to Gobbo. *The Merchant of Venice*, act 2, sc.2, l.161–2.

26 Alack, what heinous sin is it in me
To be ashamed to be my father's child!
But though I am a daughter to his blood,
I am not to his manners.
1596–7 Jessica. *The Merchant of Venice*, act 2, sc.3, l.16–19.

27 Then it was not for nothing that my nose fell a-
bleeding on Black Monday.
1596–7 Lancelot. *The Merchant of Venice*, act 2, sc.5, l.23–5.

28 There is some ill a-brewing towards my rest,
For I did dream of money-bags tonight.
1596–7 Shylock. *The Merchant of Venice*, act 2, sc.5, l.17–18.

29 But love is blind, and lovers cannot see
The pretty follies that themselves commit.
1596–7 Jessica. *The Merchant of Venice*, act 2, sc.6, l.36.

30 I will not choose what many men desire,
Because I will not jump with common spirits
And rank me with the barbarous multitudes.
1596–7 Aragon. *The Merchant of Venice*, act 2, sc.9, l.30–2.

31 O, that estates, degrees, and offices
Were not derived corruptly, and that clear
honour
Were purchased by the merit of the wearer!
1596–7 Aragon. *The Merchant of Venice*, act 2, sc.9, l.40–2.

1596–7 Portia, of the suitors. *The Merchant of Venice*, act 1, sc.2, l.106–8.

32 The ancient saying is no heresy;
Hanging and wiving goes by destiny.
1596–7 Nerissa. *The Merchant of Venice*, act 2, sc.9, l.81–2.

33 A day in April never came so sweet,
To show how costly summer was at hand.
1596–7 Messenger, of Bassanio's arrival. *The Merchant of Venice*, act 2, sc.9, l.92.

34 The bird was fledged; and then it is the complexion
of them all to leave the dam.
1596–7 Solanio, of Jessica. *The Merchant of Venice*, act 3, sc.1, l.27.

35 O, that it could be proved
That some night-tripping fairy had exchanged
In cradle clothes our children where they lay.
1596–7 King Henry of his son, Harry, and Northumberland's son, Hotspur. *Henry IV Part One*, act 1, sc.1, l.85–7.

36 What a devil hast thou to do with the time of the day? Unless hours were cups of sack, and minutes capons, and clocks the tongues of bawds, and dials the signs of leaping-houses, and the blessed sun himself a fair hot wench in flame-coloured taffeta, I see no reason why thou shouldst be so superfluous to demand the time of the day.
1596–7 Prince Harry to Falstaff. *Henry IV Part One*, act 1, sc.2, l.6–12.

37 How now, how now, mad wag? What, in thy quips and thy quiddities? What a plague have I to do with a buff jerkin?
1596–7 Falstaff to Prince Harry. *Henry IV Part One*, act 1, sc.2, l.44–6.

38 I would to God thou and I knew where a commodity of good names were to be bought.
1596–7 Falstaff. *Henry IV Part One*, act 1, sc.2, l.82–3.

39 'Tis my vocation, Hal. 'Tis no sin for a man to labour in his vocation.
1596–7 Falstaff, of Stealing. *Henry IV Part One*, act 1, sc.2, l.104–5.

40 What says Monsieur Remorse? What says Sir John, sack-and-sugar Jack? How agrees the devil and thee about thy soul, that thou soldest him on Good Friday last, for a cup of Madeira and a cold capon's leg?
1596–7 Poins to Falstaff. *Henry IV Part One*, act 1, sc.2, l.111–15.

41 He was never yet a breaker of proverbs: he will give the devil his due.
1596–7 Prince Henry. *Henry IV Part One*, act 1, sc.2, l.117–8.

42 He made me mad
To see him shine so brisk, and smell so sweet,
And talk so like a waiting gentlewoman

Of guns, and drums, and wounds, God save the mark!
And telling me the soverign'st thing on earth
Was parmacity for an inward bruise,
And that it was great pity, so it was,
This villainous saltpetre should be digged
Out of the bowels of the harmless earth,
Which many a good tall fellow had destroyed
So cowardly, and but for these vile guns
He would himself have been a soldier.
1596–7 Hotspur. *Henry IV Part One*, act 1, sc.3, l.52–63.

43 To put down Richard, that sweet lovely rose,
And plant this thorn, this canker, Bolingbroke?
1596–7 Hotspur. *Henry IV Part One*, act 1, sc.3, l.173–4.

44 If he fall in, good night, or sink or swim.
1596–7 Hotspur. *Henry IV Part One*, act 1, sc.3, l.192.

45 —O, the blood more stirs
To rouse a lion than to start a hare!
1596–7 Hotspur. *Henry IV Part One*, act 1, sc.3, l.195–6.

46 By heaven, methinks it were an easy leap
To pluck bright honour from the pale-faced moon,
Or dive into the bottom of the deep,
Where fathom-line could never touch the ground,
And pluck up drownèd honour by the locks.
1596–7 Hotspur. *Henry IV Part One*, act 1, sc.3, l.199–203.

47 I am joined with no foot-landrakers, no longstaff sixpenny strikers, none of these mad mustachio purple-hued maltworms, but with nobility and tranquillity, burgomasters and great 'oyez'-ers; such as can hold in, such as will strike sooner than speak, and speak sooner than drink, and drink sooner than pray.
1596–7 Gadshill. *Henry IV Part One*, act 2, sc.1, l.73–8.

48 I am bewitched with the rogue's company. If the rascal have not given me medicines to make me love him, I'll be hanged.
1596–7 Falstaff, of Prince Harry. *Henry IV Part One*, act 2, sc.2, l.17–20.

49 A plague upon't when thieves cannot be true one to another.
1596–7 Falstaff. *Henry IV Part One*, act 2, sc.2, l.27–8.

50 Hang thyself in thine own heir-apparent garters!
1596–7 Falstaff to Prince Harry. *Henry IV Part One*, act 2, sc.2, l.43.

51 Out of this nettle danger we pluck this flower safety.
1596–7 Hotspur. *Henry IV Part One*, act 2, sc.4, l.9–10.

52 Constant you are,

But yet a woman; and for secrecy
No lady closer, for I well believe
Thou wilt not utter what thou dost not know.
1596–7 Hotspur to Kate. *Henry IV Part One*, act 2, sc.4, l.105–8.

53 I am not yet of Percy's mind, the Hotspur of the North – he that kills me some six or seven dozen of Scots at a breakfast, washes his hands, and says to his wife, 'Fie upon this quiet life! I want work.'
1596–7 Prince Harry. *Henry IV Part One*, act 2, sc.5, l.102–6.

54 There lives not three good men unhanged in England, and one of them is fat and grows old.
1596–7 Falstaff, of himself. *Henry IV Part One*, act 2, sc.5, l.130–1.

55 Give you a reason on compulsion? If reasons were as plentiful as blackberries, I would give no man a reason upon compulsion.
1596–7 Falstaff. *Henry IV Part One*, act 2, sc.5, l.242–4.

56 PRINCE HARRY: This sanguine coward, this bed-presser, this horse-backbreaker, this huge hill of flesh—
SIR JOHN: 'Sblood, you starveling, you elf-skin, you dried neat's tongue, you bull's pizzle, you stock-fish—O, for breath to utter what is like thee!—you tailor's yard, you sheath, you bow-case, you vile standing tuck.
1596–7 *Henry IV Part One*, act 2, sc.5, l.245–52.

57 SIR JOHN: Sweet Jack Oldcastle, kind Jack Oldcastle, true Jack Oldcastle, valiant Jack Oldcastle, and therefore more valiant being, as he is, old Jack Oldcastle
Banish not him thy Harry's company,
Banish not him thy Harry's company.
Banish plump Jack, and banish all the world.
PRINCE HARRY: I do; I will.
1596–7 *Henry IV Part One*, act 2, sc.5, l.480–6.

58 I can teach thee, coz, to shame the devil,
By telling truth: 'Tell truth, and shame the devil'.
1596–7 Hotspur to Glyndwr *Henry IV Part One*, act 3, sc.1, l.55–6.

59 Mincing poetry.
'Tis like the forced gait of a shuffling nag.
1596–7 Hotspur. *Henry IV Part One*, act 3, sc.1, l.130–1.

60 I understand thy kisses, and thou mine,
And that's a feeling disputation.
1596–7 Mortimer to his wife. *Henry IV Part One*, act 3, sc.1, l.200–1.

61 Now I perceive the devil understands Welsh;
And 'tis no marvel, he is so humorous.
1596–7 Hotspur. *Henry IV Part One*, act 3, sc.1, l.226–7.

62 Swear me, Kate, like a lady as thou art,

A good mouth-filling oath.
1596–7 Hotspur. *Henry IV Part One*, act 3, sc.1, l.249–50.

63 Do thou amend thy face, and I'll amend my life.
1596–7 Falstaff to Bardolph. *Henry IV Part One*, act 3, sc.3, l.23.

64 Thou knowest in the state of innocency Adam fell, and what should poor Jack Oldcastle do in the days of villainy? Thou seest I have more flesh than another man, and therefore more frailty.
1596–7 Falstaff. *Henry IV Part One*, act 3, sc.3, l.165–7.

65 I am as vigilant as a cat to steal cream.
1596–7 Falstaff. *Henry IV Part One*, act 4, sc.2, l.58–9.

66 Rebellion lay in his way, and he found it.
1596–7 Falstaff, of Worcester. *Henry IV Part One*, act 5, sc.1, l.28.

67 I would 'twere bed-time, Hal, and all well.
1596–7 Falstaff. *Henry IV Part One*, act 5, sc.1, l.125.

68 Honour pricks me on. Yea, but how if honour prick me off when I come on? How then?
1596–7 Falstaff. *Henry IV Part One*, act 5, sc.1, l.129–131.

69 What is honour? A word.
1596–7 Flastaff. *Henry IV Part One*, act 5, sc.1, l.133–4.

70 Who hath it [honour]? He that died o' Wednesday.
1596–7 Falstaff. *Henry IV Part One*, act 5, sc.1, l.135–6.

71 Treason is but trusted like the fox,
Who, ne'er so tame, so cherished and locked up,
Will have a wild trick of his ancestors.
1596–7 Worcester. *Henry IV Part One*, act 5, sc.2, l.9–11.

72 O gentlemen, the time of life is short.
To spend that shortness basely were too long
If life did ride upon a dial's point,
Still ending at the arrival of an hour.
1596–7 Hotspur. *Henry IV Part One*, act 5, sc.2, l.81–4.

73 Sound all the lofty instruments of war,
And by that music let us all embrace,
For, heaven to earth, some of us never shall
A second time do such a courtesy.
1596–7 Hotspur. *Henry IV Part One*, act 5, sc.2, l.97–100.

74 I am as hot as molten lead, and as heavy too.
1596–7 Falstaff. *Henry IV Part One*, act 5, sc.3, l.33–4.

75 Time, that takes survey of all the world,
Must have a stop.
1596–7 Hotspur. *Henry IV Part One*, act 5, sc.4, l.81–2.

76 Fare thee well, great heart.
Ill-weaved ambition, how much art thou shrunk!
When that this body did contain a spirit,
A kingdom for it was too small a bound,
But now two paces of the vilest earth
Is room enough.

1596–7 Prince Harry, of Hotspur. *Henry IV Part One*, act 5, sc.4, l.86–91.

77   The better part of valour is discretion, in the which better part I have saved my life.
1596–7 Falstaff. *Henry IV Part One*, act 5, sc.4, l.118–20.

78   I owe him little duty and less love.
1592 Somerset, of York. *Henry VI Part One*, act 4, sc.4, l.34.

79   In poison there is physic; and these news,
Having been well, that would have made me sick,
Being sick, have in some measure made me well.
1597–8 Northumberland. *Henry IV Part Two*, act 1, sc.1, l.137–9.

80   I am not only witty in myself, but the cause that wit is in other men.
1597–8 Falstaff. *Henry IV Part Two*, act 1, sc.2, l.9–10.

81   Your lordship, though not clean past your youth, hath yet some smack of age in you, some relish of the saltness of time.
1597–8 Falstaff, of the Lord Justice. *Henry IV Part Two*, act 1, sc.2, l.98–9.

82   I am as poor as Job, my lord, but not so patient.
1597–8 Falstaff. *Henry IV Part Two*, act 1, sc.2, l.128.

83   If it be a hot day and I brandish anything but my bottle, would I might never spit white again.
1597–8 Falstaff. *Henry IV Part Two*, act 1, sc.2, l.211–13.

84   It was alway yet the trick of our English nation, if they have a good thing, to make it too common.
1597–8 Falstaff. *Henry IV Part Two*, act 1, sc.2, l.215–17.

85   I can get no remedy against this consumption of the purse. Borrowing only lingers and lingers it out, but the disease is incurable.
1597–8 Falstaff. *Henry IV Part Two*, act 1, sc.2, l.237–9.

86   [He] lined himself with hope,
Eating the air on promise of supply.
1597–8 Lord Bardloph, of Hostpur. *Henry IV Part Two*, act 1, sc.3, l.27–8.

87   Away, you scullion, you rampallion, you fustilarian! I'll tickle your catastrophe!
1597–8 Page to Mistress Quickly. *Henry IV Part Two*, act 2, sc.1, l.61–2.

88   He hath eaten me out of house and home.
1597–8 Mistress Quickly, of Falstaff. *Henry IV Part Two*, act 2, sc.1, l.75–6.

89   Thus we play the fools with the time, and the spirits of the wise sit in the clouds and mock us.
1597–8 Harry. *Henry IV Part Two*, act 2, sc.2, l.133–5.

90   He was indeed the glass
Wherein the noble youth did dress themselves.
1597–8 Lady Percy, of Hotspur. *Henry IV Part Two*, act 2, sc.3, l.21–2.

91   Shall pack-horses
And hollow pampered jades of Asia,
Which cannot go but thirty mile a day,
Compare with Caesars and with cannibals,
And Trojan Greeks?
Nay, rather damn them with King Cerberus,
And let the welkin roar.
1597–8 Pistol. *Henry IV Part Two*, act 2, sc.4, l.160–6.

92   Thou whoreson little tidy Bartholomew boar-pig, when wilt thou leave fighting o'days, and foining o'nights, and begin to patch up thine old body for heaven?
1597–8 Doll Tearsheet, of Falstaff. *Henry IV Part Two*, act 2, sc.4, l.232–5.

93   Is it not strange that desire should so many years outlive performance?
1597–8 Poins. *Henry IV Part Two*, act 2, sc.4, l.262–3.

94   O sleep, O gentle sleep,
Nature's soft nurse, how have I frighted thee,
That thou no more wilt weigh my eyelids down.
1597–8 Henry. *Henry IV Part Two*, act 3, sc.1, l.5–7.

95   Canst thou, O partial sleep, give thy repose
To the wet sea-boy in an hour so rude,
And in the calmest and most stillest night,
With all appliances and means to boot,
Deny it to a king? Then happy low, lie down.
Uneasy lies the head that wears a crown.
1597–8 King Henry. *Henry IV Part Two*, act 3, sc.1, l.25–31.

96   Death, as the Psalmist saith, is certain to all: all shall die.
1597–8 Shallow. *Henry IV Part Two*, act 3, sc.2, l.35–6.

97   We have heard the chimes at midnight, Master Shallow.
1597–8 Falstaff. *Henry IV Part Two*, act 3, sc.2, l.211.

98   A man can die but once. We owe God a death.
1597–8 Feeble. *Henry IV Part Two*, act 3, sc.2, l.233–4.

99   Lord, Lord, how subject we old men are to this vice of lying!
1597–8 Falstaff. *Henry IV Part Two*, act 3, sc.2, l.298–9.

1   When a was naked, he was for all the world like a forked radish, with a head fantastically carved upon it with a knife.
1597–8 Falstaff, of Shallow. *Henry IV Part Two*, act 3, sc.2, l.305–7.

2   An iron man,
Cheering a rout of rebels with your drum,
Turning the word to sword, and life to death.
1597–8 Prince John. *Henry IV Part Two*, act 4, sc.1, l.234–6.

3   Sudden sorrow

Serves to say thus: some good thing comes
tomorrow.
1597–8 Westmorland. *Henry IV Part Two*, act 4, sc.1,
l.309–10.

4 A peace is of the nature of a conquest,
For then both parties nobly are subdued,
And neither party loser.
1597–8 Archbishop of York. *Henry IV Part Two*, act 4, sc.1,
l.315–7.

5 He saw me, and yielded, that I may justly say, with
the hook-nosed fellow of Rome, 'I came, saw, and
overcame'.
1597–8 Falstaff. *Henry IV Part Two*, act 4, sc.2, l.39–41.

6 A man cannot make him laugh. But that's no
marvel; he drinks no wine.
1597–8 Falstaff. *Henry IV Part Two*, act 4, sc.2, l.85–6.

7 Will fortune never come with both hands full,
But write her fair words still in foulest letters?
1597–8 Henry, receiving good news when ill. *Henry IV Part
Two*, act 4, sc.3, l.103–4.

8 How quickly nature falls into revolt
When gold becomes her object!
1597–8 King Henry, of his son Harry. *Henry IV Part Two*, act
4, sc.3, l.195–6.

9 Revel the night, rob, murder, and commit
The oldest sins the newest kind of ways?
1597–8 King Henry to Harry. *Henry IV Part Two*, act 4, sc.3,
l.254–5.

10 I know thee not, old man. Fall to thy prayers.
How ill white hairs becomes a fool and jester!
1597–8 The newly-crowned Harry, rejecting Falstaff. *Henry
IV Part Two*, act 5, sc.5, l.47–8.

11 Here will be an old abusing of God's patience and
the King's English.
1597–8 Mistress Quickly. *The Merry Wives of Windsor*, act 1,
sc.4, l.4–5.

12 His worst fault is that he is given to prayer; he is
something peevish that way.
1597–8 Mistress Quickly. *The Merry Wives of Windsor*, act 1,
sc.4, l.11–12.

13 Why, then the world's mine oyster,
which I with sword will open.
1597–8 Pistol. *The Merry Wives of Windsor*, act 2, sc.2, l.4–5.

14 Thinkst thou I'll endanger my soul gratis?
1597–8 Falstaff. *The Merry Wives of Windsor*, act 2, sc.2,
l.16–17.

15 If money go before, all ways do lie open.
1597–8 Ford (as Brooke). *The Merry Wives of Windsor*, act 2,
sc.2, l.164–5.

16 Money is a good soldier, sir, and will go on.

1597–8 Falstaff. *The Merry Wives of Windsor*, act 2, sc.2, l.166.

17 There is money. Spend it, spend it; spend more.
1597–8 Ford (as Brooke). *The Merry Wives of Windsor*, act 2,
sc.2, l.223–4.

18 I cannot tell what the dickens his name is.
1597–8 Mistress Page. *The Merry Wives of Windsor*, act 3, sc.2,
l.16.

19 He capers, he dances, he has eyes of youth; he
writes verses, he speaks holiday, he smells April and
May. He will carry't, he will carry't; 'tis in his
buttons he will carry't.
1597–8 Host, of Master Feuton. *The Merry Wives of Windsor*,
act 3, sc.2, l.61–4.

20 O, what a world of vile ill-favoured faults
Looks handsome in three hundred pounds a year!
1597–8 Anne. *The Merry Wives of Windsor*, act 3, sc.4, l.31–2.

21 A woman would run through fire and water for
such a kind heart.
1597–8 Mistress Quickly. *The Merry Wives of Windsor*, act 3,
sc.4, l.101–2.

22 Have I lived to be carried in a basket like a barrow
of butcher's offal, and to be thrown in the Thames?
Well, if I be served such another trick, I'll have my
brains ta'en out and buttered, and give them to a
dog for a New Year's gift. 'Sblood, the rogues
slighted me into the river with as little remorse as
they would have drowned a blind bitch's puppies,
fifteen i'th' litter! And you may know by my size
that I have a kind of alacrity in sinking.
1597–8 Falstaff. *The Merry Wives of Windsor*, act 3, sc.5,
l.4–12.

23 They say there is divinity in odd numbers, either in
nativity, chance, or death.
1597–8 Falstaff. *The Merry Wives of Windsor*, act 5, sc.1, l.3–4.

24 Let the sky rain potatoes, let it thunder to the tune
of 'Greensleeves'.
1597–8 Falstaff. *The Merry Wives of Windsor*, act 5, sc.5,
l.17–18.

25 A victory is twice itself when the achiever brings
home full numbers.
1598 Leonato. *Much Ado About Nothing*, act 1, sc.1, l.8–9.

26 How much better is it to weep at joy than to joy at
weeping!
1598 Leonato. *Much Ado About Nothing*, act 1, sc.1, l.27–8.

27 He wears his faith but as the fashion of his hat, it
ever changes with the next block.
1598 Beatrice, of Benedick. *Much Ado About Nothing*, act 1,
sc.1, l.71–3.

28 He is sooner caught than the pestilence.
1598 Beatrice, of Claudio. *Much Ado About Nothing*, act 1,
sc.1, l.82.

29 I wonder that you will still be talking, Signor
Benedick. Nobody marks you.
    1598 Beatrice. *Much Ado About Nothing*, act 1, sc.1, l.110–11.

30 What, my dear Lady Distain! Are you yet living?
    1598 Benedick to Beatrice. *Much Ado About Nothing*, act 1,
    sc.1, l.112–13.

31 I had rather hear my dog bark at a crow than a man
swear he loves me.
    1598 Beatrice. *Much Ado About Nothing*, act 1, sc.1, l.125–6.

32 Were she other than she is she were unhandsome,
and being no other but as she is, I do not like her.
    1598 Benedick, of Hero. *Much Ado About Nothing*, act 1, sc.1,
    l.166–7.

33 If he send me no husband, for the which blessing I
am at him upon my knees every morning and
evening. Lord, I could not endure a husband with a
beard on his face. I had rather lie in the woollen.
    1598 Beatrice. *Much Ado About Nothing*, act 2, sc.1, l.24–7.

34 He shows me where the bachelors sit, and there live
we as merry as the day is long.
    1598 Beatrice, of St Peter. *Much Ado About Nothing*, act 2, sc.1,
    l.42–4.

35 I have a good eye, uncle. I can see a church by
daylight.
    1598 Beatrice to Leonato. *Much Ado About Nothing*, act 2, sc.1,
    l.74–5.

36 Beauty is a witch
Against whose charms faith melteth into blood.
    1598 Claudio. *Much Ado About Nothing*, act 2, sc.1, l.169–70.

37 She speaks poniards, and every word stabs. If her
breath were as terrible as her terminations, there
were no living near her, she would infect to the
North Star.
    1598 Benedick, of Beatrice. *Much Ado About Nothing*, act 2,
    sc.1, l.231–4.

38 Will your grace command me any service to the
world's end? I will go on the slightest errand now to
the Antipodes that you can devise to send me on. I
will fetch you a tooth-picker now from the furthest
inch of Asia, bring you the length of Prester John's
foot, fetch you a hair off the Great Cham's beard,
do you any embassage to the pigmies, rather than
hold three words' conference with this harpy.
    1598 Benedick, of Beatrice. *Much Ado About Nothing*, act 2,
    sc.1, l.246–53.

39 O God, sir, here's a dish I love not. I cannot endure
my Lady Tongue.
    1598 Benedick, of Beatrice. *Much Ado About Nothing*, act 2,
    sc.1, l.256–7.

40 Silence is the perfectest herald of joy. I were but
little happy if I could say how much.

41 Your silence most offends me, and to be merry best
becomes you; for out o' question, you were born in
a merry hour.
    1598 Don Pedro to Beatrice. *Much Ado About Nothing*, act 2,
    sc.1, l.310–12.

42 There's little of the melancholy element in her, my
lord. She is never sad but when she sleeps, and not
ever sad then; for I have heard my daughter say she
hath often dreamt of unhappiness and waked
herself with laughing.
    1598 Leonato, of Beatrice. *Much Ado About Nothing*, act 2,
    sc.1, l.321–5.

43 If they were but a week married they would talk
themselves mad.
    1598 Leonato, of Beatrice and Benedick. *Much Ado About
    Nothing*, act 2, sc.1, l.330–1.

44 Time goes on crutches till love have all his rites.
    1598 Claudio. *Much Ado About Nothing*, act 2, sc.1, l.334–5.

45 Is it not strange that sheep's guts should hale souls
out of men's bodies?
    1598 Benedick. *Much Ado About Nothing*, act 2, sc.3, l.57–9.

46 Sigh no more, ladies, sigh no more.
Men were deceivers ever,
One foot in sea, and one on shore,
To one thing constant never.
    1598 Balthasar's song. *Much Ado About Nothing*, act 2, sc.3,
    l.61–4.

47 He was wont to speak plain and to the purpose, like
an honest man and a soldier, and now is he turned
orthography. His words are a very fantastical
banquet.
    1598 Benedick, of Claudio. *Much Ado About Nothing*, act 2,
    sc.3, l.18–21.

48 He doth indeed show some sparks that are like wit.
    1598 Don Pedro, of Benedick. *Much Ado About Nothing*, act 2,
    sc.3, l.178–9.

49 I will be horribly in love with her.
    1598 Benedick, of Beatrice, having been tricked into thinking
    she secretly loves him. *Much Ado About Nothing*, act 2, sc.3,
    l.222–3.

50 From the crown of his head to the sole of his foot
he is all mirth.
    1598 Don Pedro, of Benedick. *Much Ado About Nothing*, act 3,
    sc.2, l.7–9.

51 Look where Beatrice like a lapwing runs
Close by the ground to hear our conference.
    1598 Hero to Ursula. *Much Ado About Nothing*, act 3, sc.1,
    l.24–5.

52 He hath twice or thrice cut Cupid's bow-string, and
the little hangman dare not shoot at him. He hath a

heart as sound as a bell, and his tongue is the
clapper, for what his heart thinks his tongue speaks.
1598 Don Pedro, of Benedick. *Much Ado About Nothing*, act 3,
sc.2, l.9–13.

53 Everyone can master a grief but he that has it.
1598 Benedick. *Much Ado About Nothing*, act 3, sc.2, l.26–7.

54 The barber's man hath been seen with him, and the
old ornament of his cheek hath already stuffed
tennis balls.
1598 Claudio, of Benedick. *Much Ado About Nothing*, act 3,
sc.2, l.41–3.

55 Seest thou not, I say, what a deformed thief this
fashion is, how giddily a turns about all the hot-
bloods between fourteen and five-and-thirty…?
1598–9 Borachio to Conrad. *Much Ado About Nothing*, act 3,
sc.3, l.126–9.

56 The fashion wears out more apparel than the man.
1598—99 Conrad to Borachio. *Much Ado About Nothing*, act
3, sc.3, l.134–5.

57 Comparisons are odorous.
1598 Dogberry to Verges. *Much Ado About Nothing*, act 3, sc.5,
l.15.

58 As they say, when the age is in, the wit is out.
1598 Dogberry. *Much Ado About Nothing*, act 3, sc.5, l.32–3.

59 Well, God's a good man. An two men ride of a
horse, one must ride behind.
1598 Dogberry to Verges. *Much Ado About Nothing*, act 3, sc.5,
l.35–6.

60 O, what authority and show of truth
Can cunning sin cover itself withal!
1598 Claudio, of Hero. *Much Ado About Nothing*, act 4, sc.1,
l.35–6.

61 'Tis all men's office to speak patience
To those that wring under the load of sorrow.
1598 Leonato. *Much Ado About Nothing*, act 5, sc.1, l.27–8.

62 There was never yet philosopher
That could endure the toothache patiently.
1598 Leonato. *Much Ado About Nothing*, act 5, sc.1, l.35–6.

63 Though care killed a cat, thou hast mettle enough
in thee to kill care.
1598 Claudio, of Benedick. *Much Ado About Nothing*, act 5,
sc.1, l.133–4.

64 Marry, sir, they have committed false report,
moreover they have spoken untruths, secondarily
they are slanders, sixth and lastly they have belied a
lady, thirdly they have verified unjust things, and to
conclude, they are lying knaves!
1598 Dogberry to Don Pedro. *Much Ado About Nothing*, act 5,
sc.1, l.208–12.

65 I can find out no rhyme to 'lady' but 'baby', an
innocent rhyme; for 'scorn' 'horn', a hard rhyme;

for 'school' 'fool', a babbling rhyme. Very ominous
endings. No, I was not born under a rhyming
planet, nor I cannot woo in festival terms.
1598 Benedick. *Much Ado About Nothing*, act 5, sc.2, l.35–9.

66 If a man do not erect in this age his own tomb ere
he dies, he shall live no longer in monument than
the bell rings and the widow weeps.
1598 Benedick. *Much Ado About Nothing*, act 5, sc.2, l.69–72.

67 Good morrow, Benedick. Why, what's the matter
That you have such a February face,
So full of frost, of storm and cloudiness?
1598 Don Pedro. *Much Ado About Nothing*, act 5, sc.4, l.40–2.

68 Let's have a dance ere we are married, that we may
lighten our own hearts and our wives' heels.
1598 Benedick. *Much Ado About Nothing*, act 5, sc.4,
l.116–18.

69 Prince, thou art sad, get thee a wife, get thee a wife.
1598 Benedick to Don Pedro. *Much Ado About Nothing*, act 5,
sc.4, l.121–2.

70 O for a muse of fire, that would ascend
The brightest heaven of invention.
1598–9 Chorus. *Henry V*, prologue to act 1, l.1–2.

71 When we have matched our rackets to these balls,
We will in France, by God's grace, play a set
Shall strike his father's crown into the hazard.
1598–9 King Harry, on the gift of tennis balls from the
Dauphin. *Henry V*, act 1, sc.2, l.261–3.

72 'Tis ever common
That men are merriest when they are from home.
1598–9 King Harry. *Henry V*, act 1, sc.2, l.271–2.

73 Now all the youth of England are on fire,
And silken dalliance in the wardrobe lies.
1598–9 Chorus. *Henry V*, prologue to act 2, l.1–2.

74 O England! model to thy inward greatness,
Like little body with a mighty heart,
What might'st thou do, that honour would thee
    do,
Were all thy children kind and natural.
1598–9 Chorus. *Henry V*, prologue to act 2, l.16–19.

75 Though Patience be a tired mare, yet she will plod.
1598–9 Nim. *Henry V*, act 2, sc.1, l.22–3.

76 Treason and murder ever kept together,
As two yoke-devils sworn to either's purpose.
1598–9 King Harry. *Henry V*, act 2, sc.2, l.102–3.

77 I saw him fumble with the sheets, and play with
flowers, and smile upon his finger's end.
1598–9 Hostess, describing Falstaff's death. *Henry V*, act 2,
sc.3, l.13–15.

78 Look to my chattels and my movables.

Let senses rule. The word is 'Pitch and pay'.
Trust none, for oaths are straws, men's faiths are
  wafer-cakes,
And Holdfast is the only dog, my duck.
1598–9 Pistol to Nim. *Henry V*, act 2, sc.3, l.45–8.

79 Let us do it with no show of fear,
No, with no more than if we heard that England
Were busied with a Whitsun morris dance.
For, my good liege, she is so idly kinged,
Her sceptre so fantastically borne
By a vain, giddy, shallow, humorous youth,
That fear attends her not
1598–9 The Dauphin to King Charles. *Henry V*, act 2, sc.4,
l.23–9.

80 In cases of defence 'tis best to weigh
The enemy more mighty than he seems.
1598–9 Dauphin. *Henry V*, act 2, sc.4, l.43–4.

81 Self-love, my liege, is not so vile a sin
As self-neglecting.
1598–9 Dauphin, to King Charles. *Henry V*, act 2, sc.4,
l.73–4.

82 Once more unto the breach, dear friends, once
  more,
Or close the wall up with our English dead.
1598–9 King Harry rallying his men at the seige of Harfleur.
Henry V, act 3, sc.1, l.1–2.

83 In peace there's nothing so becomes a man
As modest stillness and humility.
1598–9 King Harry rallying his men at the seige of Harfleur.
Henry V, act 3, sc.1, l.3–4.

84 When the blast of war blows in our ears,
Then imitate the action of the tiger.
Stiffen the sinews, conjure up the blood,
Disguise fair nature with hard-favoured rage.
1598–9 King Harry rallying his men at the seige of Harfleur.
Henry V, act 3, sc.1, l.5–8.

85 I see you stand like greyhounds in the slips,
Straining upon the start. The game's afoot.
1598–9 King Harry. *Henry V*, act 3, sc.1, l.31–2.

86 Cry, 'God for Harry! England and Saint George!'
1598–9 King Harry rallying his men at the seige of Harfleur.
Henry V, act 3, sc.1, l.34.

87 FLUELLEN: Captain Macmorris, I think, look you,
under your correction, there is not many of your
nation—
MACMORRIS: Of my nation? What ish my nation?
Ish a villain and a bastard and a knave and a
rascal? What ish my nation? Who talks of my
nation?
1598–9 *Henry V*, act 3, sc.3, l.64–8.

88 From camp to camp through the foul womb of
  night

The hum of either army stilly sounds.
1598–9 Chorus. *Henry V*, prologue to act 4, l.4–5.

89 A little touch of Harry in the night.
1598–9 Chorus. *Henry V*, prologue to act 4, l.47.

90 There is some soul of goodness in things evil,
Would men observingly distil it out.
1598–9 King Harry. *Henry V*, act 4, sc.1, l.4–5.

91 The King's a bawcock and a heart-of-gold,
A lad of life, an imp of fame,
Of parents good, of fist most valiant.
I kiss his dirty shoe, and from my heartstring
I love the lovely bully.
1598–9 Pistol to King Harry, disguised. *Henry V*, act 4, sc.1,
l.45–9.

92 Every subject's duty is the King's, but every
subject's soul is his own.
1598–9 King Harry. *Henry V*, act 4, sc.1, l.175–6.

93 Be friends, you English fools, be friends. We have
French quarrels enough, if you could tell how to
reckon.
1598–9 Bates. *Henry V*, act 4, sc.1, l.220–1.

94 Upon the King.
'Let us, our lives, our souls, our debts, our care-full
  wives,
Our children, and our sins, lay on the King.'
1598–9 King Harry. *Henry V*, act 4, sc.1, l.227–9.

95 O God of battles, steel my soldiers' hearts.
1598–9 King Harry, before Agincourt. *Henry V*, act 4, sc.1,
l.286.

96 O that we now had here
But one ten thousand of those men in England
That do no work today.
1598–9 Warick before Agincourt. *Henry V*, act 4, sc.3,
l.16–18.

97 If it be a sin to covet honour
I am the most offending soul alive.
1598–9 King Harry. *Henry V*, act 4, sc.3, l.28–9.

98 He which hath no stomach to this fight,
Let him depart.
1598–9 King Harry, before Agincourt. *Henry V*, act 4, sc.3,
l.35.

99 He that shall see this day and live t'old age,
Will yearly on the vigil feast his neighbours
And say, 'Tomorrow is Saint Crispian.'
1598–9 King Harry, before Agincourt. *Henry V*, act 4, sc.3,
l.44–6.

1 Then will he strip his sleeve and show his scars
And say, 'These wounds I had on Crispin's day.'
Old men forget; yet all shall be forgot,
But he'll remember.
1598–9 King Harry, before Agincourt. *Henry V*, act 4, sc.3,
l.47–50.

2 Then shall our names,
   Familiar in his mouth as household words…
   Be in their flowing cups freshly remembered.
   1598–9 King Harry, before Agincourt. *Henry V*, act 4, sc.3,
   l.51–5.

3 This story shall the good man teach his son,
   And Crispin Crispian shall ne'er go by
   From this day to the ending of the world
   But we in it shall be rememberèd,
   We few, we happy few, we band of brothers.
   1598–9 King Harry. *Henry V*, act 4, sc.3, l.56–60.

4 He today that sheds his blood with me
   Shall be my brother; be he ne'er so vile.
   1598–9 King Harry, before Agincourt. *Henry V*, act 4, sc.3,
   l.61–2.

5 And gentlemen in England now abed
   Shall think themselves accursed they were not here,
   And hold their manhoods cheap whiles any speaks
   That fought with us upon Saint Crispin's day.
   1598–9 King Harry. *Henry V*, act 4, sc.3, l.64–7.

6 Let life be short, else shame will be too long.
   1598–9 Bourbon, returning to the battle. *Henry V*, act 4, sc.5,
   l.19.

7 There is occasions and causes why and wherefore in
   all things.
   1598–9 Fluellen. *Henry V*, act 5, sc.1, l.3–4.

8 Not for Cadwallader and all his goats.
   1598–9 Pistol, refusing to eat leeks. *Henry V*, act 5, sc.1, l.27.

9 An angel is like you, Kate, and you are like an
   angel.
   1598–9 King Harry, wooing Catherine. *Henry V*, act 5, sc.2,
   l.109–10.

10 Thou wouldst find me such a plain king that thou
   wouldst think I had sold my farm to buy my
   crown.
   1598–9 King Harry, wooing Catherine. *Henry V*, act 5, sc.2,
   l.125–7.

11 You have witchcraft in your lips, Kate. There is
   more eloquence in a sugar touch of them than in
   the tongues of the French Council.
   1598–9 King Harry, wooing Catherine. *Henry V*, act 5, sc.2,
   l.274–6.

12 God, the best maker of all marriages,
   Combine your hearts in one, your realms in one.
   1598–9 Queen Isabel, on the marriage of King Harry and
   Catherine. *Henry V*, act 5, sc.2, l.354–5.

13 NIM: They say he cried out of sack.
   HOSTESS: Ay, that a did.
   BARDOLPH: And of women.
   HOSTESS: Nay, that a did not.

BOY: Yes, that a did, and said they were devils
   incarnate.
   HOSTESS: A could never abide carnation, 'twas a
   colour he never liked.
   1598–9 Of Falstaff's death. *Henry V*, act 2, sc.3, l.26–32.

14 Hence, home, you idle creatures, get you home!
   1599 Flavius. *Julius Caesar*, act 1, sc.1, l.1.

15 You blocks, you stones, you worse than senseless
   things!
   O, you hard hearts, you cruel men of Rome,
   Knew you not Pompey?
   1599 Murellus, to the citizens of Rome. *Julius Caesar*, act 1,
   sc.1, l.34–7.

16 Beware the ides of March.
   1599 Soothsayer to Caesar. *Julius Caesar*, act 1, sc.2, l.19.

17 Poor Brutus, with himself at war,
   Forgets the shows of love to other men.
   1599 Brutus. *Julius Caesar*, act 1, sc.2, l.48–9.

18 Set honour in one eye and death i' the other,
   And I will look on both indifferently.
   1599 Brutus. *Julius Caesar*, act 1, sc.2, l.88–9.

19 I cannot tell what you and other men
   Think of this life; but for my single self,
   I had as lief not be, as live to be
   In awe of such a thing as I myself.
   I was born free as Caesar, so were you.
   1599 Cassius to Brutus. *Julius Caesar*, act 1, sc.2, l.95–9.

20 He doth bestride the narrow world
   Like a Colossus, and we petty men
   Walk under his huge legs, and peep about
   To find ourselves dishonourable graves.
   Men at sometime were masters of their fates.
   The fault, dear Brutus, is not in our stars,
   But in ourselves, that we are underlings.
   1599 Cassius, of Caesar. *Julius Caesar*, act 1, sc.2, l.136–42.

21 Brutus and Caesar: what should be in that 'Caesar'?
   Why should that name be sounded more than
   yours?
   Write them together: yours is as fair a name.
   Sound them: it doth become the mouth as well.
   Weigh them: it is as heavy. Conjure with 'em:
   'Brutus' will start a spirit as soon as 'Caesar'.
   1599 Cassius to Brutus. *Julius Caesar*, act 1, sc.2, l.143–8.

22 Upon what meat doth this our Caesar feed
   That he is grown so great?
   1599 Cassius to Brutus. *Julius Caesar*, act 1, sc.2, l.150–1.

23 Let me have men about me that are fat;
   Sleek-headed men, and such as sleep o' nights;
   Yond Cassius has a lean and hungry look;
   He thinks too much: such men are dangerous.
   1599 Caesar. *Julius Caesar*, act 1, sc.2, l.193–6.

24 Seldom he smiles, and smiles in such a sort
    As if he mocked himself.
    1599 Caesar, of Cassius. *Julius Caesar*, act 1, sc.2, l.206–7.

25 Cassius from bondage will deliver Cassius.
    Therein, ye gods, you make the weak most strong;
    Therein, ye gods, you tyrants do defeat.
    Nor stony tower, nor walls of beaten brass,
    Nor airless dungeon, nor strong links of iron,
    Can be retentive to the strength of spirit;
    But life, being weary of these worldly bars,
    Never lacks power to dismiss itself.
    1599 Cassius. *Julius Caesar*, act 1, sc.3, l.89–96.

26 It is the bright day that brings forth the adder,
    And that craves wary walking.
    1599 Brutus. *Julius Caesar*, act 2, sc.1, l.14–15.

27 Between the acting of a dreadful thing
    And the first motion, all the interim is
    Like a phantasma or a hideous dream.
    1599 Brutus. *Julius Caesar*, act 2, sc.1, l.63–5.

28 Ambition's debt is paid.
    1599 Brutus, after he has killed Caesar. *Julius Caesar*, act 3,
    sc.1, l.82.

29 Let's carve him as a dish fit for the gods,
    Not hew him as a carcass fit for hounds.
    1599 Brutus, of Caesar. *Julius Caesar*, act 2, sc.1, l.173–4.

30 Am I your self
    But as it were in sort or limitation?
    To keep with you at meals, comfort your bed,
    And talk to you sometimes? Dwell I but in the
      suburbs
    Of your good pleasure? If it be no more,
    Portia is Brutus' harlot, not his wife.
    1599 Portia. *Julius Caesar*, act 2, sc.1, l.281–6.

31 You are my true and honourable wife,
    As dear to me as are the ruddy drops
    That visit my sad heart.
    1599 Brutus to Portia. *Julius Caesar*, act 2, sc.1, l.287–9.

32 When beggars die there are no comets seen;
    The heavens themselves blaze forth the death of
      princes.
    1599 Calpurnia. *Julius Caesar*, act 2, sc.2, l.30–1.

33 Cowards die many times before their deaths;
    The valiant never taste of death but once.
    1599 Caesar. *Julius Caesar*, act 2, sc.2, l.32–3.

34 Of all the wonders that I yet have heard,
    It seems to me most strange that men should fear,
    Seeing that death, a necessary end,
    Will come when it will come.
    1599 Caesar. *Julius Caesar*, act 2, sc.2, l.34–7.

35 Danger knows full well

That Caesar is more dangerous than he.
1599 Caesar. *Julius Caesar*, act 2, sc.2, l.44–5.

36 The cause is in my will; I will not come.
    1599 Caesar. *Julius Caesar*, act 2, sc.2, l.71.

37 Ay me! How weak a thing
    The heart of woman is!
    1599 Portia. *Julius Caesar*, act 2, sc.4, l.41–2.

38 I could be well moved if I were as you.
    If I could pray to move, prayers would move me.
    But I am constant as the Northern star,
    Of whose true fixed and resting quality
    There is no fellow in the firmament.
    The skies are painted with unnumbered sparks;
    They are all fire, and every one doth shine;
    But there's but one in all doth hold his place.
    So in the world: 'tis furnished well with men,
    And men are flesh and blood, and apprehensive;
    Yet in the number I do know but one
    That unassailable holds on his rank,
    Unshaked of motion; and that I am he
    Let me a little show it even in this—
    That I was constant Cimber should be banished,
    And constant do remain to keep him so.
    1599 Caesar. *Julius Caesar*, act 3, sc.1, l.58–73.

39 Et tu, Bruté?—Then fall Caesar.
    1599 *Julius Caesar*, act 3, sc.1, l.76.

40 Fates, we will know your pleasures.
    That we shall die, we know; 'tis but the time
    And drawing days out that men stand upon.
    1599 Brutus. *Julius Caesar*, act 3, sc.1, l.99–101.

41 He that cuts off twenty years of life
    Cuts off so many years of fearing death.
    1599 Casca. *Julius Caesar*, act 3, sc.1, l.102–3.

42 How many ages hence
    Shall this our lofty scene be acted over,
    In states unborn and accents yet unknown!
    1599 Cassius of the murder of Caesar. *Julius Caesar*, act 3, sc.1,
    l.112–14.

43 O mighty Caesar! Dost thou lie so low?
    Are all thy conquests, glories, triumphs, spoils,
    Shrunk to this little measure?
    1599 Antony. *Julius Caesar*, act 3, sc.1, l.149–51.

44 O pardon me, thou bleeding piece of earth,
    That I am meek and gentle with these butchers.
    1599 Antony. *Julius Caesar*, act 3, sc.1, l.257–8.

45 Caesar's spirit, ranging for revenge,
    With Ate by his side come hot from hell,
    Shall in these confines with a monarch's voice
    Cry 'havoc!', and let slip the dogs of war,
    That this foul deed shall smell above the earth
    With carrion men, groaning for burial.
    1599 Antony. *Julius Caesar*, act 3, sc.1, l.273–8.

46 This is my answer: not that I loved Caesar less, but that I loved Rome more.
1599 Brutus, explaining his reasons for killing Caesar. *Julius Caesar*, act 3, sc.2, l.20–1.

47 As Caesar loved me, I weep for him. As he was fortunate, I rejoice at it. As he was valiant, I honour him. But as he was ambitious, I slew him.
1599 Brutus. *Julius Caesar*, act 3, sc.2, l.24–7.

48 Friends, Romans, countrymen, lend me your ears.
I come to bury Caesar, not to praise him.
The evil that men do lives after them;
The good is oft interrèd with their bones.
So let it be with Caesar. The noble Brutus
Hath told you Caesar was ambitious.
If it were so, it was a grievous fault,
And grievously hath Caesar answered it.
Here, under leave of Brutus and the rest—
For Brutus is an honourable man,
So are they all, all honourable men—
Come I to speak in Caesar's funeral.
He was my friend, faithful and just to me.
1599 Antony. *Julius Caesar*, act 3, sc.2, l.74–86.

49 When that the poor have cried, Caesar hath wept.
Ambition should be made of sterner stuff.
1599 Antony. *Julius Caesar*, act 3, sc.2, l.92–3.

50 O judgement! thou art fled to brutish beasts,
And men have lost their reason!
1599 Antony. *Julius Caesar*, act 3, sc.2, l.105–6.

51 Bear with me.
My heart is in the coffin there with Caesar,
And I must pause till it come back to me.
1599 Antony. *Julius Caesar*, act 3, sc.2, l.106–8.

52 But yesterday the word of Caesar might
Have stood against the world. Now lies he there,
And none so poor to do him reverence.
1599 Antony. *Julius Caesar*, act 3, sc.2, l.119–21.

53 If you have tears, prepare to shed them now.
1599 Antony. *Julius Caesar*, act 3, sc.2, l.167.

54 This was the most unkindest cut of all.
For when the noble Caesar saw him stab,
Ingratitude, more strong than traitors' arms,
Quite vanquished him.
1599 Antony of Brutus. *Julius Caesar*, act 3, sc.2, l.181–4.

55 O now you weep, and I perceive you feel
The dint of pity. These are gracious drops.
1599 Antony to the crowd. *Julius Caesar*, act 3, sc.2, l.191–2.

56 I am no orator as Brutus is,
But, as you know me all, a plain blunt man.
1599 Antony. *Julius Caesar*, act 3, sc.2, l.212–13.

57 Fortune is merry,
And in this mood will give us anything.
1599 Antony. *Julius Caesar*, act 3, sc.2, l.259–60.

58 Good reasons must of force give place to better.
1599 Brutus. *Julius Caesar*, act 4, sc.2, l.255.

59 We'll along ourselves, and meet them at Philippi.
1599 Cassius. *Julius Caesar*, act 4, sc.2, l.277.

60 There is a tide in the affairs of men
Which, taken at the flood, leads on to fortune;
Omitted, all the voyage of their life
Is bound in shallows and in miseries.
1599 Brutus. *Julius Caesar*, act 4, sc.3, l.270–3.

61 I should not urge thy duty past thy might.
1599 Brutus to Lucius. *Julius Caesar*, act 4, sc.3, l.312.

62 Good words are better than bad strokes.
1599 Brutus to Octavius. *Julius Caesar*, act 5, sc.1, l.29.

63 Blow wind, swell billow, and swim bark.
The storm is up, and all is on the hazard.
1599 Cassius, at Philippi. *Julius Caesar*, act 5, sc.1, l.67–8.

64 Since the affairs of men rest still incertain,
Let's reason with the worst that may befall.
1599 Cassius to Brutus. *Julius Caesar*, act 5, sc.1, l.95–6.

65 O that a man might know
The end of this day's business ere it come!
But it sufficeth that the day will end,
And then the end is known.
1599 Brutus. *Julius Caesar*, act 5, sc.1, l.123–6.

66 I prithee, Strato, stay thou by thy lord.
Thou art a fellow of a good respect.
Thy life hath had some smatch of honour in it.
Hold then my sword, and turn away thy face
While I do run upon it.
1599 Brutus, killing himself. *Julius Caesar*, act 5, sc.5, l.44–8.

67 Caesar, now be still,
I killed not thee with half so good a will.
1599 *Julius Caesar*, act 5, sc. 5, l.50–1.

68 This was the noblest Roman of them all.
All the conspirators save only he
Did that they did in envy of great Caesar.
He only in a general honest thought
And common good to all made one of them.
His life was gentle, and the elements
So mixed in him that nature might stand up
And say to all the world 'This was a man'.
1599 Antony, of Brutus. *Julius Caesar*, act 5, sc.5, l.67–74.

69 Let us sit and mock the good housewife Fortune from her wheel, that her gifts may henceforth be bestowed equally.
1599–1600 Celia to Rosalind. *As You Like It*, act 1, sc.2, l.30–2.

70 Where is this young gallant that is so desirous to lie
with his mother earth?
1599–1600 Charles to Orlando. *As You Like It*, act 1, sc.2,
l.188–9.

71 My pride fell with my fortunes.
1599–1600 Rosalind. *As You Like It*, act 1, sc.2, l.241.

72 Fare you well.
Hereafter, in a better world than this,
I shall desire more love and knowledge of you.
1599–1600 Le Beau to Orlando. *As You Like It*, act 1, sc.2,
l.273–4.

73 Thy words are too precious to be cast away upon
curs. Throw some of them at me.
1599–1600 Celia to Rosalind. *As You Like It*, act 1, sc.3, l.4–6.

74 What danger will it be to us,
Maids as we are, to travel forth so far!
Beauty provoketh thieves sooner than gold.
1599–1600 Rosalind to Celia. *As You Like It*, act 1, sc.3,
l.107–9.

75 Sweet are the uses of adversity
Which, like the toad, ugly and venomous,
Wears yet a precious jewel in his head.
1599–1600 Duke Senior. *As You Like It*, act 2, sc.1, l.12–14.

76 Thou art thy father's daughter–there's enough.
1599–1600 Duke Frederick to Rosalind, explaining why he
does not trust her. *As You Like It*, act 1, sc.3, l.57.

77 And this our life, exempt from public haunt,
Finds tongues in trees, books in the running brooks,
Sermons in stones, and good in everything.
1599–1600 Duke Senior. *As You Like It*, act 2, sc.1, l.15–17.

78 Sweep on, you fat and greasy citizens.
1599–1600 First Lord, quoting Jaques. *As You Like It*, act 2,
sc.1, l.55.

79 I love to cope him in these sullen fits,
For then he's full of matter.
1599–1600 Duke Senior, of Jaques. *As You Like It*, act 2, sc.1,
l.67–8.

80 Unregarded age in corners thrown.
1599–1600 Adam. *As You Like It*, act 2, sc.3, l.43.

81 He that doth the ravens feed,
Yea providently caters for the sparrow,
Be comfort to my age.
1599–1600 Adam to Orlando. *As You Like It*, act 2, sc.3,
l.44–6.

82 Though I look old, yet I am strong and lusty,
For in my youth I never did apply
Hot and rebellious liquors in my blood,
Nor did not with unbashful forehead woo
The means of weakness and debility.
Therefore my age is as a lusty winter.
1599–1600 Adam to Orlando. *As You Like It*, act 2, sc.3,
l.48–53.

83 Thou art not for the fashion of these times,
Where none will sweat but for promotion.
1599–1600 Orlando, of Adam. *As You Like It*, act 2, sc.3, l.60–1.

84 I think you have no money in your purse.
1599–1600 Touchstone to Celia. *As You Like It*, act 2, sc.4, l.12.

85 Now I am in Ardenne; the more fool I. When I was
at home I was in a better place.
1599–1600 Touchstone. *As You Like It*, act 2, sc.4, l.14–15.

86 Under the greenwood tree
Who loves to lie with me,
And turn his merry note
Unto the sweet bird's throat.
1599–1600 Amiens' song. *As You Like It*, act 2, sc.5, l.1–4.

87 I can suck melancholy out of a song as a weasel
sucks eggs.
1599–1600 Jaques. *As You Like It*, act 2, sc.5, l.11–12.

88 I'll go sleep if I can. If I cannot, I'll rail against all
the firstborn of Egypt.
1599–1600 Jaques. *As You Like It*, act 2, sc.5, l.57–8.

89 A fool, a fool, I met a fool i'th' forest,
A motley fool–a miserable world!–
As I do live by food, I met a fool,
Who laid him down and basked him in the sun,
And railed on Lady Fortune in good terms,
In good set terms, and yet a motley fool.
1599–1600 Jaques. *As You Like It*, act 2, sc.7, l.12–17.

90 'Thus we may see', quoth he, 'how the world wags.
'Tis but an hour ago since it was nine,
And after one hour more 'twill be eleven.
And so from hour to hour we ripe and ripe,
And then from hour to hour we rot and rot;
And thereby hangs a tale.'
1599–1600 Jaques, quoting Touchstone. *As You Like It*, act 2,
sc.7, l.23–8.

91 All the world's a stage,
And all the men and women merely players.
They have their exits and their entrances,
And one man in his time plays many parts.
1599–1600 Jaques. *As You Like It*, act 2, sc.7, l.139–42.

92 Jealous in honour, sudden, and quick in quarrel,
Seeking the bubble reputation
Even in the cannon's mouth.
1599–1600 Jaques, of the soldier. *As You Like It*, act 2, sc.7,
l.151–3.

93 The whining schoolboy with his satchel
And shining morning face.
1599–1600 Jaques. *As You Like It*, act 2, sc.7, l.145–6.

94 Blow, blow, thou winter wind,
Thou art not so unkind
As man's ingratitude.
1599–1600 Amiens singing. *As You Like It*, act 2, sc.7, l.175–7.

95 Most friendship is feigning, most loving, mere
folly.
1599–1600 Amiens. *As You Like It*, act 2, sc.7, l.182.

96 Second childishness and mere oblivion,
Sans teeth, sans eyes, sans taste, sans everything.
1599–1600 Jaques, of old age. *As You Like It*, act 2, sc.7,
l.165–6.

97 These trees shall be my books
And in their barks my thoughts I'll character.
1599–1600 Orlando. *As You Like It*, act 3, sc.2, l.5–6.

98 Run, run, Orlando; carve on every tree
The fair, the chaste, and unexpressive she.
1599–1600 Orlando. *As You Like It*, act 3, sc.2, l.9–10.

99 Hast any philosophy in thee, shepherd?
1599–1600 Touchstone to Corin. *As You Like It*, act 3, sc.2,
l.21–2.

1 This is the very false gallop of verses.
1599–1600 Touchstone, of Orlando's poem. *As You Like It*, act
3, sc.2, l.111.

2 I earn that I eat, get that I wear; owe no man hate,
envy no man's happiness.
1599–1600 Corin. *As You Like It*, act 3, sc.2, l.71–2.

3 I was never so berhymed since Pythagoras' time
that I was an Irish rat, which I can hardly
remember.
1599–1600 Rosalind speaking. *As You Like It*, act 3, sc.2,
l.172–4.

4 O wonderful, wonderful, and most wonderful-
wonderful, and yet again wonderful, and after that
out of all whooping!
1599–1600 Celia, on the arrival of Orlando. *As You Like It*, act
3, sc.2, l.187–9.

5 Do you not know that I am a woman? When I
think, I must speak.
1599–1600 Rosalind to Celia. *As You Like It*, act 3, sc.2,
l.244–5.

6 Time travels in divers paces with divers persons.
1599–1600 Rosalind. *As You Like It*, act 3, sc.2, l.301–2.

7 I do desire we may be better strangers.
1599–1600 Orlando to Jaques. *As You Like It*, act 3, sc.2,
l.253.

8 Love is merely a madness, and, I tell you, deserves
as well a dark house and a whip as madmen do.
1599–1600 Rosalind to Orlando. *As You Like It*, act 3, sc.2,
l.386–8.

9 I would the gods had made thee poetical.
1599–1600 Touchstone to Audrey. *As You Like It*, act 3, sc.3,
l.12–13.

10 The truest poetry is the most feigning.

1599–1600 Touchstone to Audrey. *As You Like It*, act 3, sc.3,
l.16–17.

11 Honesty coupled to beauty is to have honey a sauce
to sugar.
1599–1600 Touchstone to Audrey. *As You Like It*, act 3, sc.3,
l.26–7.

12 His kissing is as full of sanctity as the touch of holy
bread.
1599–1600 Rosalind. *As You Like It*, act 3, sc.4, l.12–13.

13 Mistress, know yourself; down on your knees
And thank heaven, fasting, for a good man's love.
1599–1600 Rosalind to Phoebe. *As You Like It*, act 3, sc.5,
l.58–9.

14 I pray you do not fall in love with me,
For I am falser than vows made in wine.
Besides, I like you not.
1599–1600 Rosalind (in disguise) to Phoebe. *As You Like It*,
act 3, sc.5, l.73–5.

15 Dead shepherd, now I find thy saw of might:
'Who ever loved that loved not at first sight?'
1599–1600 Phoebe, in love with Rosalind (disguised as a
young man). *As You Like It*, act 3, sc.5, l.82–3.

16 It is a melancholy of mine own, compounded of
many simples, extracted from many objects, and
indeed the sundry contemplation of my travels.
1599–1600 Jaques. *As You Like It*, act 4, sc.1, l.15–17.

17 A traveller! By my faith, you have great reason to be
sad. I fear you have sold your own lands to see other
men's.
1599–1600 Rosalind to Jaques. *As You Like It*, act 4, sc.1,
l.20–2.

18 I had rather have a fool to make me merry than
experience to make me sad—and to travel for it
too!
1599–1600 Rosalind to Jaques. *As You Like It*, act 4, sc.1,
l.25–7.

19 JAQUES: Nay then, God b'wi'you an you talk in
blank verse.
ROSALIND: Farewell, Monsieur Traveller. Look you
lisp, and wear strange suits; disable all the benefits
of your own country; be out of love with your
nativity, and almost chide God for making you that
countenance you are, or I will scarce think you have
swam in a gondola.
1599–1600 *As You Like It*, act 4, sc.1, l.29–36.

20 Come, woo me, woo me, for now I am in a holiday
humour, and like enough to consent.
1599–1600 Rosalind, in disguise, to Orlando. *As You Like It*,
act 4, sc.1, l.64–5.

21 Men have died from time to time, and worms have
eaten them, but not for love.

Rosalind to Orlando. *As You Like It*, act 4, sc.1, l.99–101.

22 Can one desire too much of a good thing?
1599–1600 Rosalind, in disguise, to Orlando. *As You Like It*, act 4, sc.1, l.115–16.

23 Men are April when they woo, December when they wed. Maids are May when they are maids, but the sky changes when they are wives.
1599–1600 Rosalind, in disguise, to Orlando. *As You Like It*, act 4, sc.1, l.139–41.

24 Make the doors upon a woman's wit, and it will out at the casement. Shut that, and 'twill out at the keyhole. Stop that, 'twill fly with the smoke out at the chimney.
1599–1600 Rosalind, in disguise, to Orlando. *As You Like It*, act 4, sc.1, l.153–4.

25 'Tis no matter how it be in tune, so it make noise enough.
1599–1600 Jaques. *As You Like It*, act 4, sc.2, l.8–9.

26 The horn, the horn, the lusty horn
Is not a thing to laugh to scorn.
1599–1600 Lords, singing. *As You Like It*, act 4, sc.2, l.18–19.

27 I do now remember a saying: 'The fool doth think he is wise, but the wise man knows himself to be a fool.'
1599–1600 Touchstone to William. *As You Like It*, act 5, sc.1, l.29–31.

28 To wit, I kill thee, make thee away, translate thy life into death, thy liberty into bondage. I will deal in poison with thee, or in bastinado, or in steel. I will bandy with thee in faction, I will o'errun thee with policy. I will kill thee a hundred and fifty ways. Therefore tremble, and depart.
1599–1600 Touchstone. *As You Like It*, act 5, sc.1, l.51–6.

29 [They] no sooner looked but they loved; no sooner loved but they sighed; no sooner sighed but they asked one another the reason; no sooner knew the reason but they sought the remedy.
1599–1600 Rosalind, of Celia and Oliver. *As You Like It*, act 5, sc.2, l.32–5.

30 How bitter a thing it is to look into happiness through another man's eyes.
1599–1600 Orlando. *As You Like It*, act 5, sc.2, l.41–2.

31 I can live no longer by thinking.
1599–1600 Orlando. *As You Like It*, act 5, sc.2, l.48.

32 It was a lover and his lass,
With a hey, and a ho, and a hey-nonny-no,
That o'er the green cornfield did pass
In spring-time, the only pretty ring-time,
When birds do sing, hey ding-a-ding ding,
Sweet lovers love the spring.
1599–1600 Pages' song. *As You Like It*, act 5, sc.3, l.15–20

33 A poor virgin, sir, an ill-favoured thing, sir, but mine own.
1599–1600 Touchstone, of Audrey. *As You Like It*, act 5, sc.4, l.57–8.

34 I durst go no further than the Lie Circumstantial, nor he durst not give me the Lie Direct; and so we measured swords, and parted.
1599–1600 Touchstone. *As You Like It*, act 5, sc.4, l.83–5.

35 O sir, we quarrel in print, by the book, as you have books for good manners. I will name you the degrees. The first, the Retort Courteous; the second, the Quip Modest; the third, the Reply Churlish; the fourth, the Reproof Valiant; the fifth, the Countercheck Quarrelsome; the sixth, the Lie with Circumstance; the seventh, the Lie Direct.
1599–1600 Touchstone. *As You Like It*, act 5, sc.4, l.88–94.

36 Your 'if' is the only peacemaker; much virtue in 'if'.
1599–1600 Touchstone. *As You Like It*, act 5, sc.4, l.100–101.

37 He uses his folly like a stalking-horse, and under the presentation of that he shoots his wit.
1599–1600 Duke Senior, of Touchstone. *As You Like It*, act 5, sc.4, l.104–5.

38 If it be true that good wine needs no bush, 'tis true that a good play needs no epilogue.
1599–1600 Rosalind. *As You Like It*, epilogue.

39 She told him stories to delight his ear.
1599 *The Passionate Pilgrim*, stanza 4, l.5.

40 Age, I do abhor thee; youth, I do adore thee.
1599 *The Passionate Pilgrim*, stanza 12, l.9.

41 Beauty is but a vain and doubtful good,
A shining gloss that fadeth suddenly,
A flower that dies when first it 'gins to bud,
A brittle glass that's broken presently.
1599 *The Passionate Pilgrim*, stanza 13, l.1–4.

42 For this relief much thanks. 'Tis bitter cold,
And I am sick at heart.
1600–1 Francisco. *Hamlet*, act 1, sc.1, l.6–7.

43 Thus twice before, and just at this dead hour,
With martial stalk hath he gone by our watch.
1600–1 Marcellus, of the ghost of Hamlet's father. *Hamlet*, act 1, sc.1, l.64–5.

44 And then it started like a guilty thing
Upon a fearful summons.
1600–1 Horatio, of the ghost. *Hamlet*, act 1, sc.1, l.129–30.

45 The head is not more native to the heart,
The hand more instrumental to the mouth,
Than is the throne of Denmark to thy father.
1600–1 Claudius to Laertes. *Hamlet*, act 1, sc.2, l.47–9.

46 A little more than kin and less than kind.
1600–1 Hamlet, of Claudius. *Hamlet*, act 1, sc.2, l.65.

47 I am too much i' th' sun.
1600–1 Hamlet. *Hamlet*, act 1, sc.2, l.67.

48 Good Hamlet, cast thy nightly colour off,
And let thine eye look like a friend on Denmark.
Do not for ever with thy vailèd lids
Seek for thy noble father in the dust.
1600–1 Gertrude. *Hamlet*, act 1, sc.2, l.68–71.

49 Seems, madam? Nay, it *is*. I know not 'seems'.
1600–1 Hamlet to Gertrude.
Hamlet, act1,sc.2, l.76.

50 But I have that within which passeth show—
These but the trappings and the suits of woe.
1600–1 Hamlet to Gertrude. *Hamlet*, act 1, sc.2, l.85–6.

51 O that this too solid flesh would melt,
Thaw, and resolve itself into a dew,
Or that the Everlasting had not fixed
His canon 'gainst self-slaughter!
1600–1 Hamlet. *Hamlet*, act 1, sc.2, l.129–32.

52 How weary, stale, flat, and unprofitable
Seem to me all the uses of this world!
1600–1 Hamlet. *Hamlet*, act 1, sc.2, l.133–4.

53 So loving to my mother
That he might not beteem the winds of heaven
Visit her face too roughly!
1600–1 Hamlet, of his father. *Hamlet*, act 1, sc.2, l.140–3.

54 Frailty, thy name is woman.
1600–1 Hamlet, of Gertrude. *Hamlet*, act 1, sc.2, l.146.

55 We'll teach you to drink deep ere you depart.
1600–1 Hamlet to Horatio. *Hamlet*, act 1, sc.2, l.174.

56 Thrift, thrift, Horatio. The funeral baked meats
Did coldly furnish forth the marriage tables.
1600–1 Hamlet to Horatio, on the reason for his mother's
swift marriage to Claudius. *Hamlet*, act 1, sc.2, l.179–80.

57 A was a man. Take him for all in all,
I shall not look upon his like again.
1600–1 Hamlet, of his father. *Hamlet*, act 1, sc.2, l.186–7.

58 I doubt some foul play. Would the night were
come.
Till then, sit still, my soul. Foul deeds will rise,
Though all the earth o'erwhelm them, to men's
eyes.
1600–1 Hamlet. *Hamlet*, act 1, sc.2, l.255–7.

59 A countenance more
In sorrow than in anger.
1600–1 Horatio, of Hamlet's father's ghost. *Hamlet*, act 1, sc.2,
l.228–9.

60 And keep within the rear of your affection,
Out of the shot and danger of desire.
1600–1 Laertes to Ophelia. *Hamlet*, act 1, sc.3, l.34–5.

61 The chariest maid is prodigal enough
If she unmask her beauty to the moon.
1600–1 Laertes to Ophelia. *Hamlet*, act 1, sc.3, l.36–7.

62 Do not, as some ungracious pastors do,
Show me the steep and thorny way to heaven,
Whilst, like a puffed and reckless libertine
Himself the primrose path of dalliance treads.
1600–1 Ophelia to Laertes. *Hamlet*, act 1, sc.3, l.47–50.

63 The friends thou hast, and their adoption tried,
Grapple them to thy soul with hoops of steel.
1600–1 Polonius to Laertes. *Hamlet*, act 1, sc.3, l.62–3.

64 Beware
Of entrance to a quarrel, but being in,
Bear't that th' opposèd may beware of thee.
1600–1 Polonius to Laertes. *Hamlet*, act 1, sc.3, l.65–7.

65 Give every man thine ear but few thy voice.
Take each man's censure, but reserve thy
judgement.
1600–1 Polonius to Laertes. *Hamlet*, act 1, sc.3, l.68–9.

66 Neither a borrower nor a lender be.
1600–1 Polonius to Laertes. *Hamlet*, act 1, sc.3, l.75.

67 This above all—to thine own self be true,
And it must follow, as the night the day,
Thou canst not then be false to any man.
1600–1 Polonius to Laertes. *Hamlet*, act 1, sc.3, l.78–80.

68 Ay, springes to catch woodcocks. I do know
When the blood burns how prodigal the soul
Lends the tongue vows.
1600–1 Polonius. *Hamlet*, act 1, sc.3, l.115–7.

69 Costly thy habit as thy purse can buy,
But not expressed in fancy; rich not gaudy;
For the apparel oft proclaims the man.
1600–1 Polonius. *Hamlet*, act 1, sc.3, l.70–2.

70 And to my mind, though I am native here
And to the manner born, it is a custom
More honoured in the breach than the observance.
1600–1 Hamlet. *Hamlet*, act 1, sc.4, l.16–18.

71 Be thou a spirit of health or goblin damned,
Bring with thee airs from heaven or blasts from
hell,
Be thy intents wicked or charitable,
Thou com'st in such a questionable shape
That I will speak to thee.
1600–1 Hamlet to the ghost. *Hamlet*, act 1, sc.4, l.21–5.

72 I do not set my life at a pin's fee,

And for my soul, what can it do to that,
Being a thing immortal as itself?
1600–1 Hamlet. *Hamlet*, act 1, sc.4, l.46–8.

73 Something is rotten in the state of Denmark.
1600–1 Marcellus. *Hamlet*, act 1, sc.4, l.67.

74 I could a tale unfold whose lightest word
Would harrow up thy soul, freeze thy young blood,
Make thy two eyes like stars start from their
    spheres,
Thy knotty and combinèd locks to part,
And each particular hair to stand on end
Like quills upon the fretful porcupine.
1600–1 Ghost to Hamlet. *Hamlet*, act 1, sc.5, l.15–20.

75 Murder most foul, as in the best it is,
But this most foul, strange, and unnatural.
1600–1 Ghost to Hamlet. *Hamlet*, act 1, sc.5, l.27–8.

76 O my prophetic soul! Mine uncle?
1600–1 Hamlet, to the ghost. *Hamlet*, act 1, sc.5, l.41.

77 [My] love was of that dignity
That it went hand-in-hand even with the vow
I made to her in marriage.
1600–1 Ghost, of Gertrude. *Hamlet*, act 1, sc.5, l.48–50.

78 In the porches of mine ears.
1600–1 Ghost. *Hamlet*, act 1, sc.5, l.63.

79 Let not the royal bed of Denmark be
A couch for luxury and damnèd incest.
1600–1 Ghost to Hamlet. *Hamlet*, act 1, sc.5, l.82–4.

80 O all you host of heaven! O earth! What else?
And shall I couple hell? O fie! Hold, hold, my
    heart,
And you, my sinews, grow not instant old,
But bear me stiffly up. Remember thee?
Ay, thou poor ghost, while memory holds a seat
In this distracted globe.
1600–1 Hamlet. *Hamlet*, act 1, sc.5, l.92–7.

81 My tables—meet it is I set it down
That one may smile and smile and be a villain.
1600–1 Hamlet. *Hamlet*, act 1, sc.5, l.108–9.

82 There's ne'er a villain dwelling in all Denmark
But he's an arrant knave.
1600–1 Hamlet. *Hamlet*, act 1, sc.5, l.127–8.

83 Well said, old mole. Canst work i'th' earth so fast?
1600–1 Hamlet. *Hamlet*, act 1, sc.5, l.164.

84 There are more things in heaven and earth,
    Horatio,
Than are dreamt of in our philosophy.
1600–1 Hamlet. *Hamlet*, act 1, sc.5, l.168–9.

85 The time is out of joint. O cursèd spite

That ever I was born to set it right!
1600–1 Hamlet. *Hamlet*, act 1, sc.5, l.189–90.

86 Lord Hamlet, with his doublet all unbraced,
No hat upon his head, his stockings fouled,
Ungartered, and down-gyvèd to his ankle.
1600–1 Ophelia. *Hamlet*, act 2, sc.1, l.79–81.

87 This is the very ecstasy of love,
Whose violent property fordoes itself
And leads the will to desperate undertakings.
1600–1 Polonius, of Hamlet. *Hamlet*, act 2, sc.1, l.103–5.

88 Brevity is the soul of wit.
1600–1 Polonius. *Hamlet*, act 2, sc.2, l.91.

89 More matter with less art.
1600–1 Gertrude to Polonius, urging him to speak more plainly. *Hamlet*, act 2, sc.2, l.96.

90 'To the celestial and my soul's idol, the most
beautified Ophelia'–that's an ill phrase, a vile
phrase, 'beautified' is a vile phrase.
1600–1 Polonius to Gertrude, quoting Hamlet's letter to Ophelia. *Hamlet*, act 2, sc.2, l.110–12.

91 Doubt thou the stars are fire,
Doubt that the sun doth move,
Doubt truth to be a liar,
But never doubt I love.
1600–1 Polonius to Gertrude, quoting Hamlet's letter to Ophelia. *Hamlet*, act 2, sc.2, l.116–19.

92 If circumstances lead me I will find
Where truth is hid, though it were hid indeed
Within the centre.
1600–1 Polonius, of Hamlet's madness. *Hamlet*, act 2, sc.2, l.159–61.

93 POLONIUS: What do you read, my lord?
HAMLET: Words, words, words.
1600–1 *Hamlet*, act 2, sc.2, l.193–5.

94 To be honest, as this world goes, is to be one man
picked out of ten thousand.
1600–1 Hamlet to Polonius. *Hamlet*, act 2, sc.2, l.180–1.

95 POLONIUS: My lord, I will take my leave of you.
HAMLET: You cannot, sir, take from me anything
    that I will more willingly part withal—except my
    life, my life, my life.
1600–1 *Hamlet*, act 2, sc.2, l.215–19.

96 Though this be madness, yet there is method in't.
1600–1 Polonius (aside), of Hamlet. *Hamlet*, act 2, sc.2, l.207–8.

97 [We are] happy in that we are not over-happy,
On Fortune's cap we are not the very button.
1600–1 Guildenstern to Hamlet. *Hamlet*, act 2, sc.2, l.230–1.

98 There is nothing either good or bad, but thinking
makes it so.
1600–1 Hamlet. *Hamlet*, act 2, sc.2, l.251–2.

99 I could be bounded in a nutshell and count myself a king of infinite space, were it not that I have bad dreams.

1600–1 Hamlet. *Hamlet*, act 2, sc.2, l.256–8.

1 I hold ambition of so airy and light a quality that it is but a shadow's shadow.

1600–1 Rosencrantz. *Hamlet*, act 2, sc.2, l.263–4.

2 I have of late–but wherefore I know not–lost all my mirth, forgone all custom of exercise; and indeed it goes so heavily with my disposition that this goodly frame, the earth, seems to me a sterile promontory. This most excellent canopy the air, look you, this brave o'erhanging, this majestical roof fretted with golden fire–why, it appears no other thing to me than a foul and pestilent congregation of vapours.

1600–1 Hamlet. *Hamlet*, act 2, sc.2, l.296–304.

3 Man delights not me—no, nor woman neither.

1600–1 Hamlet. *Hamlet*, act 2, sc.2, l.310–11.

4 What a piece of work is a man! How noble in reason, how infinite in faculty, in form and moving how express and admirable, in action how like an angel, in apprehension how like a god—the beauty of the world, the paragon of animals! And yet to me what is this quintessence of dust?

1600–1 Hamlet. *Hamlet*, act 2, sc.2, l.305–10.

5 HAMLET: What's the news?
ROSENCRANTZ: None, my lord, but that the world's grown honest.
HAMLET: Then is doomsday near.

1600–1 *Hamlet*, act 2, sc.2, l.238–41.

6 If you delight not in man what lenten entertainment the players shall receive from you.

1600–1 Rosencrantz. *Hamlet*, act 2, sc.2, l.317–19.

7 There is something in this more than natural, if philosophy could find it out.

1600–1 Hamlet. *Hamlet*, act 2, sc.2, l.367–9.

8 I am but mad north-north-west; when the wind is southerly, I know a hawk from a handsaw.

1600–1 Hamlet to Guildenstern. *Hamlet*, act 2, sc.2, l.380–1.

9 The best actors in the world, either for tragedy, comedy, history, pastoral, pastoral-comical, tragical-historical, tragical-comical-historical-pastoral, or poem unlimited.

1600–1 Polonius. *Hamlet*, act 2, sc.2, l.398–401.

10 Thy face is valanced since I saw thee last. Com'st thou to beard me in Denmark?

1600–1 Hamlet to one of the players. *Hamlet*, act 2, sc.2, l.426–7.

11 The play, I remember, pleased not the million. 'Twas caviare to the general.

1600–1 Hamlet to one of the players. *Hamlet*, act 2, sc.2, l.438–40.

12 Will you see the players well bestowed? Do ye hear?—let them be well used, for they are the abstracts and brief chronicles of the time.

1600–1 Hamlet to Polonius. *Hamlet*, act 2, sc.2, l.524–7.

13 Use every man after his desert, and who should scape whipping?

1600–1 Hamlet to Polonius. *Hamlet*, act 2, sc.2, l.532–3.

14 O, what a rogue and peasant slave am I!
Is it not monstrous that this player here,
But in a fiction, in a dream of passion,
Could force his soul so to his whole conceit
That from her working all his visage wanned,
Tears in his eyes, distraction in 's aspect,
A broken voice, and his whole function suiting
With forms to his conceit? And all for nothing.
For Hecuba!
What's Hecuba to him, or he to Hecuba,
That he should weep for her?

1600–1 Hamlet. *Hamlet*, act 2, sc.2, l.552–62.

15 But I am pigeon-livered and lack gall
To make oppression bitter

1600–1 Hamlet. *Hamlet*, act 2, sc.2, l.579–80.

16 Why, what an ass am I? Ay, sure, this is most brave,
That I, the son of the dear murderèd,
Prompted to my revenge by heaven and hell,
Must, like a whore, unpack my heart with words.

1600–1 Hamlet. *Hamlet*, act 2, sc.2, l.585–8.

17 Murder, though it have no tongue, will speak
With most miraculous organ.

1600–1 Hamlet. *Hamlet*, act 2, sc.2, l.595–6.

18 The spirit I have seen
May be the devil, and the devil hath power
T'assume a pleasing shape.

1600–1 Hamlet. *Hamlet*, act 2, sc.2, l.600–2.

19 The play's the thing
Wherein I'll catch the conscience of the King.

1600–1 Hamlet. *Hamlet*, act 2, sc.2, l.606–7.

20 The harlot's cheek, beautied with plast'ring art,
Is not more ugly to the thing that helps it
Than is my deed to my most painted word.

1600–1 Claudius. *Hamlet*, act 3, sc.1, l.53–5.

21 To be, or not to be; that is the question:
Whether 'tis nobler in the mind to suffer
The slings and arrows of outrageous fortune,
Or to take arms against a sea of troubles,
And, by opposing, end them. To die, to sleep—
No more, and by a sleep to say we end
The heartache and the thousand natural shocks
That flesh is heir to—'tis a consummation

Devoutly to be wished. To die, to sleep.
To sleep, perchance to dream. Ay, there's the rub,
For in that sleep of death what dreams may come
When we have shuffled off this mortal coil
Must give us pause. There's the respect
That makes calamity of so long life,
For who would bear the whips and scorns of
   time,
Th'oppressor's wrong, the proud man's contumely,
The pangs of disprized love, the law's delay,
The insolence of office, and the spurns
That patient merit of th'unworthy takes,
When he himself might his quietus make
With a bare bodkin? Who would these fardels
   bear,
To grunt and sweat under a weary life,
But that the dread of something after death,
The undiscovered country from whose bourn
No traveller returns, puzzles the will,
And makes us rather bear those ills we have
Than fly to others that we know not of?
Thus conscience does make cowards of us all,
And thus the native hue of resolution
Is sicklied o'er with the pale cast of thought,
And enterprises of great pith and moment
With this regard their currents turn awry,
And lose the name of action.
1600–1 Hamlet. *Hamlet*, act 3, sc.1, l.58–90.

22 To the noble mind
   Rich gifts wax poor when givers prove unkind.
   1600–1 Ophelia to Hamlet. *Hamlet*, act 3, sc.1, l.102–4.

23 The power of beauty will sooner transform honesty
   from what it is to a bawd than the force of honesty
   can translate beauty into his likeness.
   1600–1 Hamlet to Ophelia. *Hamlet*, act 3, sc.1, l.113–5.

24 Get thee to a nunnery. Why wouldst thou be a
   breeder of sinners?
   1600–1 Hamlet to Ophelia. *Hamlet*, act 3, sc.1, l.123–4.

25 I am very proud, revengeful, ambitious, with more
   offences at my beck than I have thoughts to put
   them in, imagination to give them shape, or time
   to act them in.
   1600–1 Hamlet. *Hamlet*, act 3, sc.1, l.126–9.

26 What should such fellows as I do crawling between
   heaven and earth?
   1600–1 Hamlet. *Hamlet*, act 3, sc.1, l.129–31.

27 Let the doors be shut upon him, that he may play
   the fool nowhere but in 's own house.
   1600–1 Hamlet, of Polonius. *Hamlet*, act 3, sc.1, l.134–5.

28 God has given you one face, and you make
   yourselves another.
   1600–1 Hamlet, of women. *Hamlet*, act 3, sc.1, l.145–7.

29 I say we will have no more marriages; those that are
   married already—all but one—shall live. The rest
   shall keep as they are.
   1600–1 Hamlet to Ophelia. *Hamlet*, act 3, sc.1, l.150–2.

30 O what a noble mind is here o'erthrown!
   1600–1 Ophelia, of Hamlet. *Hamlet*, act 3, sc.1, l.153.

31 Madness in great ones must not unwatched go.
   1600–1 Claudius, of Hamlet. *Hamlet*, act 3, sc.1, l.191.

32 Speak the speech, I pray you, as I pronounced it to
   you—trippingly on the tongue; but if you mouth
   it, as many of your players do, I had as lief the
   town-crier had spoke my lines.
   1600–1 Hamlet to the players. *Hamlet*, act 3, sc.2, l.1–4.

33 Hold as 'twere the mirror up to nature, to show
   virtue her own feature, scorn her own image.
   1600–1 Hamlet to the players. *Hamlet*, act 3, sc.2, l.22–3.

34 Let those that play your clowns speak no more than
   is set down for them.
   1600–1 Hamlet to the players. *Hamlet*, act 3, sc.2, l.38–9.

35 A man that Fortune's buffets and rewards
   Hath ta'en with equal thanks.
   1600–1 Hamlet, of Horatio. *Hamlet*, act 3, sc.2, l.65–6.

36 OPHELIA: 'Tis brief, my lord.
   HAMLET: As woman's love.
   1600–1 *Hamlet*, act 3, sc.2, l.146–7.

37 Give me that man
   That is not passion's slave, and I will wear him
   In my heart's core.
   1600–1 Hamlet. *Hamlet*, act 3, sc.2, l.69–71.

38 Our wills and fates do so contrary run
   That our devices still are overthrown.
   1600–1 Player king. *Hamlet*, act 3, sc.2, l.202–3.

39 The lady protests too much, methinks.
   1600–1 Gertrude to Hamlet, of the Player Queen. *Hamlet*, act
   3, sc.2, l.219.

40 KING CLAUDIUS: What do you call the play?
   HAMLET: *The Mousetrap.*
   1600–1 *Hamlet*, act 3, sc.2, l.225–6.

41 No, no, they do but jest, poison in jest.
   1600–1 Hamlet, of the play. *Hamlet*, act 3, sc.2, l.224.

42 Let the galled jade wince, our withers are unwrung
   1600–1 Hamlet, of the play. *Hamlet*, act 3, sc.2, l.231.

43 'Sblood, do you think I am easier to be played on
   than a pipe?
   1600–1 Hamlet to Guildenstern. *Hamlet*, act 3, sc.2, l.357–8.

44 'Tis now the very witching time of night,

When churchyards yawn and hell itself breathes
out
Contagion to this world.
1600–1 Hamlet. *Hamlet*, act 3, sc.2, l.377–9.

45 I will speak daggers to her, but use none;
My tongue and soul in this be hypocrites.
1600–1 Hamlet, of Gertrude. *Hamlet*, act 3, sc.2, l.385–6.

46 O, my offence is rank! It smells to heaven.
1600–1 Claudius. *Hamlet*, act 3, sc.3, l.36.

47 Try what repentance can. What can it not?
Yet what can it when one cannot repent?
1600–1 Claudius. *Hamlet*, act 3, sc.3, l.65–6.

48 O limèd soul that, struggling to be free,
Art more engaged! Help, angels! make assay
1600–1 Claudius. *Hamlet*, act 3, sc.3, l.68–9.

49 My words fly up, my thoughts remain below.
Words without thoughts never to heaven go.
1600–1 Claudius. *Hamlet*, act 3, sc.3, l.97–8.

50 You shall not budge.
You go not till I set you up a glass
Where you may see the inmost part of you.
1600–1 Hamlet to Gertrude. *Hamlet*, act 3, sc.4, l.18–20.

51 A bloody deed–almost as bad, good-mother,
As kill a king and marry with his brother.
1600–1 Hamlet. *Hamlet*, act 3, sc.4, l.27–8.

52 How now, a rat? Dead for a ducat, dead.
1600–1 Hamlet, hearing Polonius behind the arras. *Hamlet*,
act 3, sc.4, l.23.

53 Thou wretched, rash, intruding fool, farewell.
I took thee for thy better.
1600–1 Hamlet to Polonius, who Hamlet has just stabbed.
Hamlet, act 3, sc.4, l.29–31.

54 You cannot call it love, for at your age
The heyday in the blood is tame.
1600–1 Hamlet to Gertrude. *Hamlet*, act 3, sc.4, l.67–8.

55 To flaming youth let virtue be as wax
And melt in her own fire.
1600–1 Hamlet to Gertrude. *Hamlet*, act 3, sc.4, l.74–5.

56 Nay, but to live
In the rank sweat of an enseamèd bed,
Stewed in corruption, honeying and making love
Over the nasty sty.
1600–1 Hamlet to Gertrude. *Hamlet*, act 3, sc.4, l.81–4.

57 Confess yourself to heaven;
Repent what's past, avoid what is to come.
1600–1 Hamlet to Gertrude. *Hamlet*, act 3, sc.4, l.140–1.

58 In the fatness of these pursy times
Virtue itself of vice must pardon beg.
1600–1 Hamlet to Gertrude. *Hamlet*, act 3, sc.4, l.144–5.

59 Assume a virtue if you have it not.
1600–1 Hamlet to Gertrude. *Hamlet*, act 3, sc.4, l.151.

60 I'll lug the guts into the neighbour room.
1600–1 Hamlet, of Polonius, who he has killed. *Hamlet*, act 3,
sc.4, l.186.

61 He is dead and gone, lady,
He is dead and gone.
At his head a grass-green turf,
At his heels a stone.
1600–1 Ophelia, singing. *Hamlet*, act 4, sc.5, l.29–32.

62 A man may fish with the worm that hath eat of a
king, and eat of the fish that hath fed of that worm.
1600–1 Hamlet to Claudius. *Hamlet*, act 4, sc.3, l.27–8.

63 We know what we are, but not what we may be.
1600–1 Ophelia. *Hamlet*, act 4, sc.5, l.42–3.

64 Good night, ladies, good night, sweet ladies, good
night, good night.
1600–1 Ophelia. *Hamlet*, act 4, sc.5, l.71–2.

65 When sorrows come they come not single spies,
But in battalions.
1600–1 Claudius to Gertrude. *Hamlet*, act 4, sc.5, l.76–7.

66 The people muddied,
Thick and unwholesome in their thoughts and
whispers.
1600–1 Claudius to Gertrude. *Hamlet*, act 4, sc.5, l.78–9.

67 There's such divinity doth hedge a king
That treason can but peep to what it would.
1600–1 Claudius to Gertrude. *Hamlet*, act 4, sc.5, l.122–3.

68 O, how the wheel becomes it!
1600–1 Ophelia. *Hamlet*, act 4, sc.5, l.172.

69 There's rosemary, that's for remembrance. Pray,
love, remember. And there is pansies; that's for
thoughts.
1600–1 Ophelia. *Hamlet*, act 4, sc.5, l.175–7.

70 Where th'offence is, let the great axe fall.
1600–1 Claudius. *Hamlet*, act 4, sc.5, l.216.

71 There is a willow grows aslant a brook
That shows his hoar leaves in the glassy stream.
Therewith fantastic garlands did she make
Of crow-flowers, nettles, daisies, and long purples,
That liberal shepherds give a grosser name,
But our cold maids do dead men's fingers call them.
1600–1 Gertrude, describing the scene of Ophelia's death.
Hamlet, act 4, sc.7, l.138–42.

72 Her garments, heavy with their drink,
Pulled the poor wretch from her melodious lay
To muddy death.
1600–1 Gertrude, describing how Ophelia drowned. *Hamlet*,
act 4, sc.7, l.153–5.

73 There is no ancient gentlemen but gardeners,
ditchers, and gravemakers; they hold up Adam's
profession.
1600–1 First Clown. *Hamlet*, act 5, sc.1, l.29–31.

74 Too much of water hast thou, poor Ophelia,
And therefore I forbid my tears.
1600–1 Laertes. *Hamlet*, act 4, sc.7, l.158–9.

75 This might be the pate of a politician which this ass
o'er-offices, one that would circumvent God,
might it not?
1600–1 Hamlet to Horatio. *Hamlet*, act 5, sc.1, l.77–9.

76 HAMLET: Ay, marry, why was he [Hamlet] sent into
England?
FIRST CLOWN: Why, because he was mad. A shall
recover his wits there; or if a do not, 'tis no great
matter there.
HAMLET: Why?
FIRST CLOWN: 'Twill not be seen in him there.
There the men are as mad as he.
1600–1 *Hamlet*, act 5, sc.1, l.146–152.

77 Alas, poor Yorick. I knew him, Horatio–a fellow of
infinite jest, of most excellent fancy. He hath borne
me on his back a thousand times; and now, how
abhorred my imagination is! My gorge rises at it.
1600–1 Hamlet, of Yorick's skull. *Hamlet*, act 5, sc.1, l.180–4.

78 HAMLET: Dost thou think Alexander looked o' this
fashion i'th' earth?
HORATIO: E'en so.
HAMLET: And smelt so? Pah!
1600–1 *Hamlet*, act 5, sc.1, l.193–6.

79 Imperial Caesar, dead and turned to clay,
Might stop a hole to keep the wind away.
1600–1 Hamlet. *Hamlet*, act 5, sc.1, l.208–9.

80 Hold off the earth a while,
Till I have caught her once more in mine arms.
1600–1 Laertes, of Ophelia, at her burial. *Hamlet*, act 5, sc.1,
l.245–6.

81 For though I am not splenative and rash,
Yet have I something in me dangerous,
Which let thy wiseness fear.
1600–1 Hamlet to Laertes. *Hamlet*, act 5, sc.1, l.258–9.

82 Let Hercules himself do what he may,
The cat will mew, and dog will have his day.
1600–1 Hamlet to Laertes. *Hamlet*, act 5, sc.1, l.288–9.

83 There's a divinity that shapes our ends,
Rough-hew them how we will.
1600–1 Hamlet to Horatio. *Hamlet*, act 5, sc.2, l.10–11.

84 The bravery of his grief did put me
Into a tow'ring passion.
1600–1 Hamlet, of Laertes. *Hamlet*, act 5, sc.2, l.80–1.

85 A hit, a very palpable hit.
1600–1 Osric. *Hamlet*, act 5, sc.2, l.232.

86 I am more an antique Roman than a Dane.
Here's yet some liquor left.
1600–1 Horatio, intending to drink from the poisoned chalice.
Hamlet, act 5, sc.2, l.294–5.

87 Absent thee from felicity a while,
And in this harsh world draw thy breath in pain
To tell my story.
1600–1 Hamlet to Horatio. *Hamlet*, act 5, sc.2, l.299–301.

88 O, I die, Horatio!
The potent poison quite o'ercrows my spirit.
1600–1 Hamlet. *Hamlet*, act 5, sc.2, l.304–5.

89 The rest is silence.
1600–1 Hamlet's last words. *Hamlet*, act 5, sc.2, l.310.

90 Good night, sweet prince,
And flights of angels sing thee to thy rest.
1600–1 Horatio. *Hamlet*, act 5, sc.2, l.312–313.

91 If music be the food of love, play on,
Give me excess of it that, surfeiting,
The appetite may sicken and so die.
That strain again, it had a dying fall.
O, it came o'er my ear like the sweet sound
That breathes upon a bank of violets,
Stealing and giving odour. Enough, no more,
'Tis not so sweet now as it was before.
1601 Orsino. *Twelfth Night*, act 1, sc.1, l.1–8.

92 O spirit of love, how quick and fresh art thou
That, notwithstanding thy capacity
Receiveth as the sea, naught enters there,
Of what validity and pitch so e'er,
But falls into abatement and low price
Even in a minute! So full of shapes is fancy
That it alone is high fantastical.
1601 Orsino. *Twelfth Night*, act 1, sc.1, l.9–15.

93 O, when mine eyes did see Olivia first
Methought she purged the air of pestilence;
That instant was I turned into a hart,
And my desires, like fell and cruel hounds,
E'er since pursue me.
1601 Orsino. *Twelfth Night*, act 1, sc.1, l.18–22.

94 He plays o'th' viol-de-gamboys, and speak three or
four languages word for word without book, and
hath all the good gifts of nature.
1601 Sir Toby, of Sir Andrew. *Twelfth Night*, act 1, sc.3, l.23–6.

95 He's a great quarreller, and but that he hath the gift
of a coward to allay the gust he hath in quarrelling,
'tis thought among the prudent he would quickly
have the gift of a grave.
1601 Maria, of Sir Andrew. *Twelfth Night*, act 1, sc.3, l.28–31.

96 I'll drink to her as long as there is a passage in my throat and drink in Illyria.
1601 Sir Toby. *Twelfth Night*, act 1, sc.3, l.36–8.

97 I am a great eater of beef, and I believe that does harm to my wit.
1601 Sir Andrew. *Twelfth Night*, act 1, sc.3, l.83–4.

98 I have unclasped
To thee the book even of my secret soul.
1601 Orsino to Viola, disguised as Cesario. *Twelfth Night*, act 1, sc.4, l.13–14.

99 Many a good hanging prevents a bad marriage.
1601 Orsino. *Twelfth Night*, act 1, sc.5, l.18.

1 'Better a witty fool than a foolish wit.'
1601 Feste. *Twelfth Night*, act 1, sc.5, l.32–3.

2 Virtue that transgresses is but patched with sin.
1601 Feste. *Twelfth Night*, act 1, sc.5, l.44–5.

3 (*He belches*) A plague o' these pickle herring!
1601 Sir Toby. *Twelfth Night*, act 1, sc.5, l.116–7.

4 I would be loath to cast away my speech, for besides that it is excellently well penned, I have taken great pains to con it.
1601 Viola, in disguise, to Olivia. *Twelfth Night*, act 1, sc.5, l.165–7.

5 O sir, I will not be so hard-hearted. I will give out divers schedules of my beauty. It shall be inventoried and every particle and utensil labelled to my will, as *item*, two lips, indifferent red; *item*, two grey eyes, with lids to them; *item*, one neck, one chin, and so forth.
Were you sent hither to praise me?
1601 Olivia to Viola (disguised as a young man). *Twelfth Night*, act 1, sc.5, l.233–8.

6 Make me a willow cabin at your gate
And call upon my soul within the house,
Write loyal cantons of contemnèd love,
And sing them loud even in the dead of night;
Halloo your name to the reverberate hills,
And make the babbling gossip of the air
Cry out 'Olivia!' O, you should not rest
Between the elements of air and earth
But you should pity me.
1601 Viola, describing how she would woo Olivia, were she in love with her. *Twelfth Night*, act 1, sc.5, l.258–65.

7 O mistress mine, where are you roaming?
O stay and hear, your true love's coming,
That can sing both high and low.
Trip no furthur, pretty sweeting.
Journeys end in lovers meeting,
Every wise man's son doth know.
1601 Feste's song. *Twelfth Night*, act 2, sc.3, l.38–43.

8 What is love? 'Tis not hereafter,

Present mirth hath present laughter.
What's to come is still unsure.
In delay there lies no plenty,
Then come kiss me, sweet and twenty.
Youth's a stuff will not endure.
1601 Feste's song. *Twelfth Night*, act 2, sc.3, l.46–51.

9 Is there no respect of place, persons, nor time in you?
1601 Malvolio to Feste, Sir Andrew and Sir Toby. *Twelfth Night*, act 2, sc.3, l.88–9.

10 Dost thou think because thou art virtuous there shall be no more cakes and ale?
1601 Sir Toby to Feste. *Twelfth Night*, act 2, sc.3, l.110–11.

11 Let still the woman take
An elder than herself. So wears she to him;
So sways she level in her husband's heart.
1601 Orsino. *Twelfth Night*, act 2, sc.4, l.28–30.

12 Then let thy love be younger than thyself,
Or thy affection cannot hold the bent;
For women are as roses, whose fair flower
Being once displayed, doth fall that very hour.
1601 Orsino. *Twelfth Night*, act 2, sc.4, l.35–8.

13 Now the melancholy god protect thee, and the tailor make thy doublet of changeable taffeta, for thy mind is a very opal.
1601 Feste to Orsino. *Twelfth Night*, act 2, sc.4, l.72–4.

14 My father had a daughter loved a man
As it might be, perhaps, were I a woman
I should your lordship.
1601 Viola, in disguise, to Orsino. *Twelfth Night*, act 2, sc.4, l.107–9.

15 She never told her love,
But let concealment, like a worm i' th' bud,
Feed on her damask cheek.
1601 Viola, in disguise, to Orsino. *Twelfth Night*, act 2, sc.4, l.110–12.

16 With a green and yellow melancholy
She sat like patience on a monument,
Smiling at grief.
1601 Viola, in disguise, to Orsino. *Twelfth Night*, act 2, sc.4, l.113–15.

17 By my life, this is my lady's hand. These be her very c's, her u's, and her t's, and thus makes she her great P's. It is in contempt of question her hand.
1601 Malvolio. *Twelfth Night*, act 2, sc.5, l.84–7.

18 Be not affraid of greatness. Some are born great, some achieve greatness, and some have greatness thrust upon 'em.
1601 Malvolio. *Twelfth Night*, act 2, sc.5, l.139–41.

19 He will come to her in yellow stockings, and 'tis a colour she abhors, and cross-gartered, a fashion she detests.

1601 Maria, of Malvolio. *Twelfth Night*, act 2, sc.5, l.192–4.

20 Fools are as like husbands as pilchards are to herrings—the husband's the bigger.

1601 Feste to Viola. *Twelfth Night*, act 3, sc.1, l.32–4.

21 Now Jove in his next commodity of hair send thee a beard.

1601 Feste to Viola. *Twelfth Night*, act 3, sc.1, l.43–4.

22 Most excellent accom-plished lady, the heavens rain odours on you.

1601 Viola to Olivia. *Twelfth Night*, act 3, sc.1, l.83–4.

23 O world, how apt the poor are to be proud!

1601 Olivia. *Twelfth Night*, act 3, sc.1, l.126.

24 Then westward ho!

1601 Viola. *Twelfth Night*, act 3, sc.1, l.133.

25 O, what a deal of scorn looks beautiful
In the contempt and anger of his lip!

1601 Olivia, of Viola (as Cesario). *Twelfth Night*, act 3, sc.1, l.143–4.

26 Love sought is good, but given unsought, is better.

1601 Olivia. *Twelfth Night*, act 3, sc.1, l.154.

27 You are now sailed into the north of my lady's opinion, where you will hang like an icicle on a Dutchman's beard unless you do redeem it by some laudable attempt either of valour or policy.

1601 Fabian, of Sir Toby. *Twelfth Night*, act 3, sc.2, l.24–8.

28 There is no love-broker in the world can more prevail in man's commendation with woman than report of valour.

1601 Sir Toby to Sir Andrew. *Twelfth Night*, act 3, sc.2, l.34–6.

29 For Andrew, if he were opened and you find so much blood in his liver as will clog the foot of a flea, I'll eat the rest of th'anatomy.

1601 Sir Toby. *Twelfth Night*, act 3, sc.2, l.58–60.

30 Why, this is very midsummer madness.

1601 Olivia, of Malvolio. *Twelfth Night*, act 3, sc.4, l.54.

31 If this were played upon a stage now, I could condemn it as an improbable fiction.

1601 Fabian. *Twelfth Night*, act 3, sc.4, l.125–6.

32 Still you keep o' th' windy side of the law.

1601 Fabian. *Twelfth Night*, act 3, sc.4, l.162.

33 A terrible oath, with a swaggering accent sharply twanged off, gives manhood more approbation than ever proof itself would have earned him.

1601 Sir Toby to Sir Andrew. *Twelfth Night*, act 3, sc.4, l.176–8.

34 I am sure no man hath any quarrel to me. My remembrance is very free and clear from any image of offence done to any man.

1601 Viola (as Cesario) to Sir Toby. *Twelfth Night*, act 3, sc.4, l.221–3.

35 In nature there's no blemish but the mind.
None can be called deformed but the unkind.

1601 Antonio. *Twelfth Night*, act 3, sc.4, l.359–60.

36 There is no darkness but ignorance.

1601 Feste to Malvolio. *Twelfth Night*, act 4, sc.2, l.43–4.

37 Thus the whirligig of time brings in his revenges.

1601 Feste. *Twelfth Night*, act 5, sc.1, l.373.

38 I'll be revenged on the whole pack of you.

1601 Malvolio. *Twelfth Night*, act 5, sc.1, l.374.

39 When that I was and a little tiny boy,
With hey, ho, the wind and the rain,
A foolish thing was but a toy,
For the rain it raineth every day.

1601 Feste. *Twelfth Night*, act 5, sc.1, l.385–8.

40 Then everything includes itself in power,
Power into will, will into appetite;
And appetite, an universal wolf.

1602 Ulysses. *Troilus and Cressida*, act 1, sc.3, l.119–21.

41 The general's disdained
By him one step below; he, by the next;
That next, by him beneath. So every step,
Exampled by the first pace that is sick
Of his superior, grows to an envious fever
Of pale and bloodless emulation.

1602 Ulysses. *Troilus and Cressida*, act 1, sc.3, l.129–134.

42 The nature of the sickness found, Ulysses,
What is the remedy?

1602 Agamemnon. *Troilus and Cressida*, act 1, sc.3, l.140–1.

43 In such indices, although small pricks
To their subsequent volumes, there is seen
The baby figure of the giant mass
Of things to come at large.

1602 Nestor. *Troilus and Cressida*, act 1, sc.3, l.337–40.

44 The common curse of mankind, folly and ignorance, be thine.

1602 Thersites. *Troilus and Cressida*, act 2, sc.3, l.26–7.

45 He that is proud eats up himself. Pride is his own glass, his own trumpet, his own chronicle.

1602 Agamemnon. *Troilus and Cressida*, act 2, sc.3, l.153–5.

46 To make a sweet lady sad is a sour offence.

1602 Helen to Pandarus. *Troilus and Cressida*, act 3, sc.1, l.71.

47 I am giddy. Expectation whirls me round.
Th'imaginary relish is so sweet
That it enchants my sense.

1602 Troilus, on the prospect of an assignation with Cressida. *Troilus and Cressida*, act 3, sc.2, l.16–18.

48 Words pay no debts.

1602 Pandarus to Troilus. *Troilus and Cressida*, act 3, sc.2, l.54.

49 This is the monstruosity in love, lady—that the will is infinite and the execution confined; that the desire is boundless and the act a slave to limit.

1602 Troilus to Cressida. *Troilus and Cressida*, act 3, sc.2, l.77–80.

50 Some men creep in skittish Fortune's hall
Whiles others play the idiots in her eyes.

1602 Ulysses. *Troilus and Cressida*, act 3, sc.3, l.129–30.

51 Time hath, my lord,
A wallet at his back, wherein he puts
Alms for oblivion.

1602 Ulysses to Achilles. *Troilus and Cressida*, act 3, sc.3, l.139–41.

52 Perseverance, dear my lord,
Keeps honour bright. To have done is to hang
Quite out of fashion, like a rusty mail
In monumental mock'ry.

1602 Ulysses. *Troilus and Cressida*, act 3, sc.3, l.144–7.

53 One touch of nature makes the whole world kin.

1602 Ulysses to Achilles. *Troilus and Cressida*, act 3, sc.3, l.169.

54 I see my reputation is at stake.
My fame is shrewdly gored.

1602 Achilles. *Troilus and Cressida*, act 3, sc.3, l.220–1.

55 The busy day,
Waked by the lark, hath roused the ribald crows,
And dreaming night will hide our joys no longer.

1602 Troilus to Cressida. *Troilus and Cressida*, act 4, sc.2, l.10–11.

56 The kiss you take is better than you give.

1602 Cressida to Menelaus. *Troilus and Cressida*, act 4, sc.6, l.39.

57 With too much blood and too little brain these two may run mad.

1602 Thersites, of Achilles and Patroclus. *Troilus and Cressida*, act 5, sc.1, l.45–7.

58 Lechery, lechery, still wars and lechery! Nothing else holds fashion.

1602 Thersites. *Troilus and Cressida*, act 5, sc.2, l.197–8.

59 Words, words, mere words, no matter from the heart.

1602 Troilus, on his letter from Cressida. *Troilus and Cressida*, act 5, sc.3, l.111.

60 Scare Troy out of itself. But march away.

1602 Troilus. *Troilus and Cressida*, act 5, sc.11, l.21.

61 Heaven doth with us as we with torches do,

Not light them for themselves.

1603 Duke. *Measure for Measure*, act 1, sc.1, l.32–3.

62 I had as lief have the foppery of freedom as the morality of imprisonment.

1603 Lucio to Claudio. *Measure for Measure*, act 1, sc.2, l.125–6.

63 Our doubts are traitors,
And makes us lose the good we oft might win,
By fearing to attempt.

1603 Lucio to Isabella. *Measure for Measure*, act 1, sc.4, l.77–9.

64 We must not make a scarecrow of the law,
Setting it up to fear the birds of prey,
And let it keep one shape till custom make it
Their perch, and not their terror.

1603 Angelo. *Measure for Measure*, act 2, sc.1, l.1–4.

65 'Tis one thing to be tempted, Escalus,
Another thing to fall.

1603 Angelo. *Measure for Measure*, act 2, sc.1, l.17–18.

66 I not deny
The jury passing on the prisoner's life
May in the sworn twelve have a thief or two
Guiltier than him they try.

1603 Angelo. *Measure for Measure*, act 2, sc.1, l.18–21.

67 The jewel that we find, we stoop and take't
Because we see it, but what we do not see
We tread upon.

1603 Angelo. *Measure for Measure*, act 2, sc.1, l.24–26.

68 Some rise by sin, and some by virtue fall.

1603 Escalus. *Measure for Measure*, act 2, sc.1, l.38.

69 ISABELLA: Yet show some pity,
ANGELO: I show it most of all when I show justice,
For then I pity those I do not know.

1603 *Measure for Measure*, act 2, sc.2, l.101–3.

70 The law hath not been dead, though it hath slept.

1603 Angelo to Isabella. *Measure for Measure*, act 2, sc.2, l.92.

71 O, it is excellent
To have a giant's strength, but it is tyrannous
To use it like a giant.

1603 Isabella to Angelo. *Measure for Measure*, act 2, sc.2, l.109–11.

72 But man, proud man,
Dressed in a little brief authority,
Most ignorant of what he's most assured,
His glassy essence, like an angry ape
Plays such fantastic tricks before high heaven
As makes the angels weep.

1603 Isabella to Angelo. *Measure for Measure*, act 2, sc.2, l.120–5.

73 Great men may jest with saints; 'tis wit in them,

But in the less, foul profanation.

1603 Isabella to Angelo. *Measure for Measure*, act 2, sc.2, l.130–1.

74 Thieves for their robbery have authority,
When judges steal themselves.

1603 Angelo. *Measure for Measure*, act 2, sc.2, l.181–2.

75 When I would pray and think, I think and pray
To several subjects; heaven hath my empty words,
Whilst my invention, hearing not my tongue,
Anchors on Isabel.

1603 Angelo. *Measure for Measure*, act 2, sc.4, l.1–4.

76 The miserable have no other medicine
But only hope.

1603 Claudio to the Duke. *Measure for Measure*, act 3, sc.1, l.2–3.

77 Reason thus with life
If I do lose thee, I do lose a thing
That none but fools would keep.

1603 Duke to Claudio. *Measure for Measure*, act 3, sc.1, l.6–8.

78 If thou art rich, thou'rt poor,
For like an ass whose back with ingots bows,
Thou bear'st thy heavy riches but a journey,
And death unloads thee.

1603 Duke to Claudio. *Measure for Measure*, act 3, sc.1, l.25–8.

79 The sense of death is most in apprehension,
And the poor beetle that we tread upon
In corporal sufferance finds a pang as great
As when a giant dies.

1603 Isabella to Claudio. *Measure for Measure*, act 3, sc.1, l.76–9.

80 If I must die,
I will encounter darkness as a bride,
And hug it in mine arms.

1603 Claudio to Isabella. *Measure for Measure*, act 3, sc.1, l.81–3.

81 Sure it is no sin,
Or of the deadly seven it is the least.

1603 Claudio to Isabella, of fornication. *Measure for Measure*, act 3, sc.1, l.109–10.

82 Ay, but to die, and go we know not where.

1603 Claudio. *Measure for Measure*, act 3, sc.1, l.118.

83 The weariest and most loathèd wordly life
That age, ache, penury, and imprisonment
Can lay on nature is a paradise
To what we fear of death.

1603 Claudio to Isabella. *Measure for Measure*, act 3, sc.1, l.129–32.

84 Virtue is bold, and goodness never fearful.

1603 Duke to Isabella. *Measure for Measure*, act 3, sc.1, l.210.

85 Take, O take thy lips away

That so sweetly were forsworn.

1603 Boy, singing. *Measure for Measure*, act 4, sc.1, l.1–2.

86 Music oft hath such a charm
To make bad good, and good provoke to harm.

1603 Duke. *Measure for Measure*, act 4, sc.1, l.14–15.

87 You weigh equally; a feather will turn the scale.

1603 Provost to Abhorson. *Measure for Measure*, act 4, sc.2, l.28–29.

88 Every true man's apparel fits your thief.

1603 Abhorson. *Measure for Measure*, act 4, sc.2, l.41.

89 Drunk many times a day, if not many days entirely
drunk.

1603 Provost, of Barnardine. *Measure for Measure*, act 4, sc.2, l.151–2.

90 Death's a great disguiser.

1603 Duke to Provost. *Measure for Measure*, act 4, sc.2, l.175.

91 If she be mad, as I believe no other,
Her madness hath the oddest frame of sense.

1603 Duke to Isabella. *Measure for Measure*, act 5, sc.1, l.60–1.

92 Haste still pays haste, and leisure answers leisure;
Like doth quit like, and measure still for measure.

1603 Duke. *Measure for Measure*, act 5, sc.1, 407–8.

93 They say best men are moulded out of faults,
And, for the most, become much more the better
For being a little bad. So may my husband.

1603 Mariana, of Angelo. *Measure for Measure*, act 5, sc.1, l.436–8.

94 In following him I follow myself.

1603–4 Iago, of Othello. *Othello*, act 1, sc.1, l.58.

95 For when my outward action doth demonstrate
The native act and figure of my heart
In compliment extern, 'tis not long after
But I will wear my heart upon my sleeve
For daws to peck at. I am not what I am.

1603–4 Iago. *Othello*, act 1, sc.1, l.60–5.

96 Though he in a fertile climate dwell,
Plague him with flies.

1603–4 Iago, of Brabanzio. *Othello*, act 1, sc.1, l.70–1.

97 Even now, now, very now, an old black ram
Is tupping your white ewe.

1603–4 Iago to Brabanzio. *Othello*, act 1, sc.1, l.88–89.

98 I am one, sir, that comes to tell you your daughter
and the Moor are now making the beast with the
two backs.

1603–4 Iago to Brabanzio. *Othello*, act 1, sc.1, l.117–9.

99 Though in the trade of war I have slain men,
Yet do I hold it very stuff o'th' conscience
To do no contrived murder. I lack iniquity,
Sometime, to do me service. Nine or ten times

I had thought to've yerked him here, under the ribs.
1603–4 Iago. *Othello*, act 1, sc.2, l.1–5.

1 But that I love the gentle Desdemona
I would not my unhousèd free condition
Put into circumscription and confine
For the seas' worth.
1603–4 Othello. *Othello*, act 1, sc.2, l.25–8.

2 Whether a maid so tender, fair, and happy,
So opposite to marriage that she shunned
The wealthy curlèd darlings of our nation,
Would ever have, t'incur a general mock,
Run from her guardage to the sooty bosom
Of such a thing as thou.
1603–4 Brabanzio to Othello. *Othello*, act 1, sc.2, l.67–72.

3 My particular grief
Is of so floodgate and o'erbearing nature
That it engluts and swallows other sorrows,
And it is still itself.
1603–4 Brabanzio, learning of Desdemona's marriage. *Othello*, act 1, sc.3, l.55–8.

4 For nature so preposterously to err,
Being not deficient, blind, or lame of sense,
Sans witchcraft could not.
1603–4 Brabanzio, of Desdemona's marriage. *Othello*, act 1, sc.3, l.62–4.

5 Rude am I in my speech,
And little blessed with the soft phrase of peace.
1603–4 Othello. *Othello*, act 1, sc.3, l.81–2.

6 A maiden never bold,
Of spirit so still and quiet that her motion
Blushed at herself—and she in spite of nature,
Of years, of country, credit, everything,
To fall in love with what she feared to look on!
It is a judgement maimed and most imperfect
That will confess perfection so could err
Against all rules of nature.
1603–4 Brabanzio of Desdemona. *Othello*, act 1, sc.3, l.94–100.

7 The Anthropophagi, and men whose heads
Do grow beneath their shoulders.
1603–4 Othello. *Othello*, act 1, sc.3, l.143–4.

8 She gave me for my pains a world of kisses.
She wore in faith 'twas strange, 'twas passing strange,
'Twas pitiful, 'twas wonderous pitiful.
She wished she had not heard it, yet she wished
That heaven had made her such a man.
1603–4 Othello, of his courtship of Desdemona. *Othello*, act 1, sc.3, l.158–162.

9 She loved me for the dangers I had passed,

And I loved her that she did pity them.
1603–4 Othello, of Desdemona. *Othello*, act 1, sc.3, l.166–7.

10 My noble father,
I do perceive here a divided duty.
1603–4 Desdemona. *Othello*, act 1, sc.3, l.179–80.

11 For you sake, jewel,
I am glad at soul I have no other child,
For thy escape would teach me tyranny,
To hang clogs on 'em.
1603–4 Brabanzio to Desdemona. *Othello*, act 1, sc.3, l.194–7.

12 When remedies are past, the griefs are ended
By seeing the worst which late on hopes depended.
To mourn a mischief that is past and gone
Is the next way to draw new mischief on.
1603–4 Duke to Brabanzio. *Othello*, act 1, sc.3, l.201–4.

13 The robbed that smiles steals something from the thief;
He robs himself that spends a bootless grief.
1603–4 Duke. *Othello*, act 1, sc.3, l.207–8.

14 But words are words. I never yet did hear
That the bruised heart was piercèd through the ear.
1603–4 Brabanzio. *Othello*, act 1, sc.3, l.217–8.

15 I never found man that knew how to love himself.
Ere I would say I would drown myself for the love
of a guinea-hen, I would change my humanity with
a baboon.
1603–4 Iago to Roderigo. *Othello*, act 1, sc.3, l.313–6.

16 Virtue? A fig! 'Tis in ourselves that we are thus or
thus. Our bodies are our gardens, to the which our
wills are gardeners.
1603–4 Iago to Roderigo. *Othello*, act 1, sc.3, l.319–21.

17 Make all the money thou canst. If sanctimony and
a frail vow betwixt an erring barbarian and a super-
subtle Venetian be not too hard for my wits and all
the tribes of hell, thou shalt enjoy her.
1603–4 Iago to Roderigo. *Othello*, act 1, sc.3, l.352–6.

18 The Moor is of a free and open nature,
That thinks men honest that but seem to be so,
And will as tenderly be led by th' nose
As asses are.
I ha't. It is ingendered. Hell and night
Must bring this monstrous birth to the world's light.
1603–4 Iago. *Othello*, act 1, sc.3, l.391–6.

19 You are pictures out of doors,
Bells in your parlours; wildcats in your kitchens,
Saints in your injuries; devils being offended,
Players in your housewifery, and hussies in your beds.
1603–4 Iago of women. *Othello*, act 2, sc.1, l.112–15.

20 With as little web as this will I ensnare as great a fly
as Cassio.
1603–4 Iago (aside). *Othello*, act 2, sc.1, l.171–2.

21 If it were now to die
'Twere now to be most happy, for I fear
My soul hath her content so absolute
That not another comfort like to this
Succeeds in unknown fate.
1603–4 Othello to Desdemona. *Othello*, act 2, sc.1, l.190–4.

22 The heavens forbid
But that our loves and comforts should increase
Even as our days do grow.
1603–4 Desdemona to Othello. *Othello*, act 2, sc.1, l.194–6.

23 [I'll] make the Moor thank me, love me, and
reward me
For making him egregiously an ass.
1603–4 Iago. *Othello*, act 2, sc.1, l.307–8.

24 Reputation, reputation, reputation! O—I ha' lost
my reputation, I ha' lost the immortal part of
myself, and what remains is bestial.
1603–4 Cassio to Iago. *Othello*, act 2, sc.3, l.256–8.

25 Reputation is an idle and most false imposition, oft
got without merit and lost without deserving.
1603–4 Iago to Cassio. *Othello*, act 2, sc.3, l.262–4.

26 O God, that men should put an enemy in their
mouths to steal away their brains!
1603–4 Cassio, of wine. *Othello*, act 2, sc.3, l.283–5.

27 So will I turn her virtue into pitch,
And out of her own goodness make the net
That shall enmesh them all.
1603–4 Iago. *Othello*, act 2, sc.3, l.351–3.

28 How poor are they that ha' not patience!
What wound did ever heal but by degrees?
1603–4 Iago to Roderigo. *Othello*, act 2, sc.3, l.360–1.

29 Excellent wretch! Perdition catch my soul
But I do love thee, and when I love thee not,
Chaos is come again.
1603–4 Othello, of Desdemona. *Othello*, act 3, sc.3, l.91–3.

30 I know thou'rt full of love and honesty,
And weigh'st thy words before thou giv'st them
breath.
1603–4 Othello to Iago. *Othello*, act 3, sc.3, l.123–4.

31 Good name in man and woman, dear my lord,
Is the immediate jewel of their souls.
Who steal my purse steals trash; 'tis something,
nothing;
'Twas mine, 'tis his, and has been slave to
thousands.
But he that filches from me my good name
Robs me of that which not enriches him

And makes me poor indeed.
1603–4 Iago to Othello. *Othello*, act 3, sc.3, l.160–6.

32 O. beware, my lord, of jealousy,
It is the green-eyed monster which doth mock
The meat it feeds on.
1603–4 Iago to Othello. *Othello*, act 3, sc.3, l.169–71.

33 Poor and content is rich, and rich enough,
But riches fineless is as poor as winter
To him that ever fears he shall be poor.
1603–4 Iago to Othello. *Othello*, act 3, sc.3, l.176–8.

34 I humbly do beseech you of your pardon
For too much loving you.
1603–4 Iago to Othello. *Othello*, act 3, sc.3, l.216–7.

35 If I do prove her haggard,
Though that her jesses were my dear heart-strings
I'd whistle her off and let her down the wind
To prey at fortune.
1603–4 Othello. *Othello*, act 3, sc.3, l.264–7.

36 If she be false, O then heaven mocks itself!
I'll not believe't.
1603–4 Othello, of Desdemona. *Othello*, act 3, sc.3, l.282–3.

37 Trifles light as air
Are to the jealous confirmations strong
As proofs of holy writ.
1603–4 Iago. *Othello*, act 3, sc.3, l.326–8.

38 Not poppy nor mandragora
Nor all the drowsy syrups of the world
Shall ever medicine thee to that sweet sleep
Which thou owedst yesterday.
1603–4 Iago, of Othello. *Othello*, act 3, sc.3, l.334–7.

39 He that is robbed, not wanting what is stol'n,
Let him not know't and he's not robbed at all.
1603–4 Othello to Iago. *Othello*, act 3, sc.3, l.347–8.

40 I had been happy if the general camp,
Pioneers and all, had tasted her sweet body,
So I had nothing known. O, now for ever
Farewell the tranquil mind, farewell content,
Farewell the plumèd troops and the big wars
That makes ambition virtue! O, farewell,
Farewell the neighing steed and the shrill trump,
The spirit-stirring drum, th'ear-piercing fife,
The royal banner, and all quality,
Pride, pomp, and circumstance of glorious war!
And O, you mortal engines whose rude throats
Th'immortal Jove's dread clamours counterfeit,
Farewell! Othello's occupation's gone.
1603–4 Othello. *Othello*, act 3, sc.3, l.350–62.

41 But this denoted a foregone conclusion.
1603–4 Othello. *Othello*, act 3, sc.3, l.433.

42 My bloody thoughts with violent pace

Shall ne'er look back, ne'er ebb to humble love,
Till that a capable and wide revenge
Swallow them up.
1603–4 Othello to Iago. *Othello*, act 3, sc.3, l.460–3.

43 Jealous souls will not be answered so.
They are not ever jealous for the cause,
But jealous for they're jealous. It is a monster
Begot upon itself, born on itself.
1603–4 Emilia to Desdemona. *Othello*, act 3, sc.4, l.156–9.

44 But yet the pity of it, Iago.
O, Iago, the pity if it, Iago!
1603–4 Othello. *Othello*, act 4, sc.1, l.191–2.

45 Do it not with poison. Strangle her in her bed.
1603–4 Iago to Othello. *Othello*, act 4, sc.1, l.202–3.

46 Is this the noble Moor whom our full senate
Call all-in-all sufficient? Is this the nature
Whom passion could not shake, whose solid virtue
The shot of accident nor dart of chance
Could neither graze nor pierce?
1603–4 Lodovico. *Othello*, act 4, sc.1, l.266–70.

47 O thou weed,
Who art so lovely fair, and smell'st so sweet,
That the sense aches at thee—would thou hadst
ne'er been born!
1603–4 Othello, of Desdemona. *Othello*, act 4, sc.2, l.69–72.

48 I cry you mercy then.
I took you for that cunning whore of Venice
That married with Othello.
1603–4 Othello to Desdemona. *Othello*, act 4, sc.2, l.93–4.

49 I will be hanged, if some eternal villain,
Some busy and insinuating rogue,
Some cogging, cozening slave, to get some office,
Have not devised this slander.
1603–4 Emilia. *Othello*, act 4, sc.2, l.134–7.

50 Mine eyes do itch. Doth that bode weeping?
1603–4 Desdemona to Emilia. *Othello*, act 4, sc.3, l.56–7.

51 Let husbands know
Their wives have sense like them. They see, and
smell,
And have their palates both for sweet and sour,
As husbands have.
1603–4 Emilia to Desdemona. *Othello*, act 4, sc.3, l.92–5.

52 It is the cause, it is the cause, my soul.
Let me not name it to you, you chaste stars.
It is the cause. Yet I'll not shed her blood,
Nor scar that whiter skin of hers than snow,
And smooth as monumental alabaster.
Yet she must die, else she'll betray more men.
Put out the light, and then put out the light.
1603–4 Othello. *Othello*, act 5, sc.2, l.1–7.

53 When I have plucked thy rose
I cannot give it vital growth again.
It needs must wither. I'll smell thee on the tree.
1603–4 Othello. *Othello*, act 5, sc.2, l.13–15.

54 Had all his hairs been lives, my great revenge
Had stomach for 'em all.
1603–4 Othello, of Cassio. *Othello*, act 5, sc.2, l.81–2.

55 Kill me tomorrow; let me live tonight.
1603–4 Desdemona to Othello. *Othello*, act 5, sc.2, l.87.

56 It is the very error of the moon,
She comes more nearer earth than she was wont,
And makes men mad.
1603–4 Othello. *Othello*, act 5, sc.2, l.118–20.

57 Not Cassio killed? Then murder's out of tune,
And sweet revenge grows harsh.
1603–4 Othello. *Othello*, act 5, sc.2, l.124–5.

58 She's like a liar gone to burning hell.
'Twas I that killed her.
1603–4 Othello, of Desdemona who said that she had killed
herself. *Othello*, act 5, sc.2, l.138–9.

59 May his pernicious soul
Rot half a grain a day.
1603–4 Emilia, of Iago. *Othello*, act 5, sc.2, l.162–3.

60 Thou hast not half that power to do me harm
As I have to be hurt. O gull, O dolt,
As ignorant as dirt!
1603–4 Emilia to Othello. *Othello*, act 5, sc.2, l.169–71.

61 Here is my journey's end, here is my butt
And very sea-mark of my utmost sail.
1603–4 Othello. *Othello*, act 5, sc.2, l.274–5.

62 O ill-starred wench,
Pale as thy smock! When we shall meet at count
This look of thine will hurl my soul from heaven,
And fiends will snatch at it.
1603–4 Othello, of Desdemona. *Othello*, act 5, sc.2, l.279–2.

63 Demand me nothing. What you know, you know.
From this time forth I never will speak word.
1603–4 Iago to Othello. *Othello*, act 5, sc.2, l.309–10.

64 I pray you, in your letters,
When you shall these unlucky deeds relate,
Speak of me as I am. Nothing extenuate,
Nor set down aught in malice. Then must you
speak
Of one that loved not wisely but too well,
Of one not easily jealous but, being wrought,
Perplexed in the extreme; of one whose hand,
Like the base Indian, threw a pearl away
Richer than all his tribe; of one whose subdued
eyes,
Albeit unusèd to the melting mood,

Drops tears as fast as the Arabian trees
Their medicinable gum. Set you down this,
And say besides that in Aleppo once,
Where a malignant and a turbaned Turk
Beat a Venetian and traduced the state,
I took by th' throat the circumcisèd dog
And smote him thus.

1603–4 Othello's speech as he stabs himself. *Othello*, act 5, sc.2, l.349–65.

65   I kiss thee ere I killed thee. No way but this:
Killing myself, to die upon a kiss.

1603–4 Othello. *Othello*, act 5, sc.2, l.368–9.

66   Be checked for silence,
But never taxed for speech.

1604–5 Countess to Bertram. *All's Well That Ends Well*, act 1, sc.1, l.64–5.

67   'Twere all one
That I should love a bright particular star
And think to wed it, he is so above me.

1604–5 Helen, of Bertram. *All's Well That Ends Well*, act 1, sc.1, l.84–6.

68   The hind that would be mated by the lion
Must die for love.

1604–5 Helen, of Bertram. *All's Well That Ends Well*, act 1, sc.1, l.90–1.

69   Virginity is peevish, proud, idle, made of self-
love—which is the most inhibited sin in the canon.
Keep it not.

1604–5 Paroles to Helen. *All's Well That Ends Well*, act 1, sc.1, l.141–3.

70   Get thee a good husband, and use him as he uses
thee.

1604–5 Paroles to Helen. *All's Well That Ends Well*, act 1, sc.1, l.209–10.

71   Our remedies oft in ourselves do lie
Which we ascribe to heaven.

1604–5 Helen. *All's Well That Ends Well*, act 1, sc.1, l.212.

72   Though honesty be no puritan, yet it will do no
hurt.

1604–5 Lavatch. *All's Well That Ends Well*, act 1, sc.3, l.91–2.

73   He and his physicians
Are of a mind: he, that they cannot help him;
They, that they cannot help.

1604–5 Countess, of the King. *All's Well That Ends Well*, act 1, sc.3, l.235–7.

74   Why, these balls bound, there's noise in it. 'Tis
hard:
A young man married is a man that's marred.

1604–5 Paroles. *All's Well That Ends Well*, act 2, sc.3, l.294–5.

75   The soul of this man is his clothes.

1604–5 Lafeu. *All's Well That Ends Well*, act 2, sc.5, l.434.

76   No legacy is so rich as honesty.

1604–5 Mariana to Diana. *All's Well That Ends Well*, act 3, sc.5, l.12–13.

77   'Tis not the many oaths that make the truth,
But the plain single vow that is vowèd true.

1604–5 Diana. *All's Well That Ends Well*, act 4, sc.2, l.22–3.

78   My chastity's the jewel of our house,
Bequeathèd down from many ancestors,
Which were the greatest obloquy i' th' world
In me to lose.

1604–5 Diana. *All's Well That Ends Well*, act 4, sc.2, l.47–50.

79   A heaven on earth I have won by wooing thee.

1604–5 Bertram to Diana. *All's Well That Ends Well*, act 4, sc.2, l.67.

80   The web of our life is of mingled yarn, good and ill
together.

1604–5 First Lord Dumaine. *All's Well That Ends Well*, act 4, sc.3, l.74–5.

81   Drunkenness is his best virtue, for he will be swine-
drunk, and in his sleep he does little harm, save to
his bedclothes.

1604–5 Paroles, of the Duke. *All's Well That Ends Well*, act 4, sc.3, l.257–9.

82   'Twas a good lady, 'twas a good lady. We may pick a
thousand salads ere we light on such another herb.

1604–5 Lafeu, of Helen. *All's Well That Ends Well*, act 4, sc.5, l.13–15.

83   I am for the house with the narrow gate, which I
take to be too little for pomp to enter. Some that
humble themselves may, but the many will be too
chill and tender, and they'll be for the flow'ry way
that leads to the broad gate and the great fire.

1604–5 Lavatch to Lafeu. *All's Well That Ends Well*, act 4, sc.5, l.50–5.

84   Praising what is lost
Makes the remembrance dear.

1604–5 King. *All's Well That Ends Well*, act 5, sc.3, l.19–20.

85   Th'naudible and noiseless foot of time.

1604–5 King. *All's Well That Ends Well*, act 5, sc.3, l.42.

86   I wonder men dare trust themselves with men.

1605 Apemantus. *Timon of Athens*, act 1, sc.2, l.42.

87   Grant I may never prove so fond
To trust man on his oath or bond.

1605 Apemantus' grace. *Timon of Athens*, act 1, sc.2, l.63–4.

88   Men shut their doors against a setting sun.

1605 Apemantus. *Timon of Athens*, act 1, sc.2, l.141.

89   Every man has his fault, and honesty is his.

1605 Lucullus, of Timon. *Timon of Athens*, act 3, sc.1, l.27–8.

90   Men must learn now with pity to dispense,

For policy sits above conscience.
1605 First Stranger. *Timon of Athens*, act 3, sc.2, l.87–8.

91 Nothing emboldens sin so much as mercy.
1605 First Senator. *Timon of Athens*, act 3, sc.6, l.3.

92 This yellow slave
Will knit and break religions, bless the accursed.
1605 Timon, of gold. *Timon of Athens*, act 4, sc.3, l.34–5.

93 Thanks I must you con
That you are thieves professed, that you work not
In holier shapes; for there is boundless theft
In limited professions.
1605 Timon to thieves. *Timon of Athens*, act 4, sc.3, l.47–30.

94 Trust not the physician;
His antidotes are poison, and he slays
More than you rob.
1605 Timon to thieves. *Timon of Athens*, act 4, sc.3, l.433–5.

95 Rich men deal gifts,
Expecting in return twenty for one?
1605 Timon to Flavius. *Timon of Athens*, act 4, sc.3, l.510–11.

96 I cannot heave
My heart into my mouth. I love your majesty
According to my bond, nor more nor less.
1605–6 Cordelia to Lear. *King Lear*, act 1, sc.1, l.91–3.

97 Thy youngest daughter does not love thee least,
Nor are those empty-hearted whose low sounds
Reverb no hollowness.
1605–6 Kent to Lear. *King Lear*, act 1, sc.1, l.152–4.

98 Time shall unfold what pleated cunning hides.
1605–6 Cordelia. *King Lear*, act 1, sc.1, l.280.

99 If for I want that glib and oily art
To speak and purpose not—since what I well
intend,
I'll do't before I speak—that you make known
It is no vicious blot, murder, or foulness,
No unchaste action or dishonoured step
That hath deprived me of your grace and favour,
But even the want of that for which I am richer—
A still-soliciting eye, and such a tongue
That I am glad I have not, though not to have it
Hath lost me in your liking.
1605–6 Cordelia to Lear. *King Lear*, act 1, sc.1, l.224–33.

1 Fine word, 'legitimate'.
Well, my legitimate, if this letter speed
And my invention thrive, Edmond the base
Shall to th' legitimate. I grow, I prosper.
Now gods, stand up for bastards!
1605–6 Edmond. *King Lear*, act 1, sc.2, l.18–22.

2 We make guilty of our disasters the sun, the moon,
and stars, as if we were villains on necessity, fools by
heavenly compulsion, knaves, thieves, and

treachers by spherical predominance, drunkards,
liars, and adulterers by an enforced obedience of
planetary influence, and all that we are evil in by a
divine thrusting on. An admirable evasion of
whore-master man, to lay his goatish disposition
on the charge of a star!
1605–6 Edmond. *King Lear*, act 1, sc.2, l.118–26.

3 You base football player.
1605–6 Kent to Oswald. *King Lear*, act 1, sc.4, l.84–5.

4 Have more than thou showest,
Speak less than thou knowest,
Lend less than thou owest.
1605–6 Fool to Kent. *King Lear*, act 1, sc.4, l.117–19.

5 The hedge-sparrow fed the cuckoo so long
That it's had it head bit off by it young.
1605–6 Fool, singing to Lear. *King Lear*, act 1, sc.4, l.198–9.

6 As you are old and reverend, should be wise.
1605–6 Goneril to Lear. *King Lear*, act 1, sc.4. l.218.

7 Ingratitude, thou marble-hearted fiend,
More hideous when thou show'st thee in a
child
Than the sea-monster.
1605–6 Lear. *King Lear*, act 1, sc.4, l.237–9.

8 How sharper than a serpent's tooth it is
To have a thankless child.
1605–6 Lear. *King Lear*, act 1, sc.4, l.268–9.

9 O, let me not be mad, not mad, sweet heaven!
Keep me in temper. I would not be mad!
1605–6 Lear. *King Lear*, act 1, sc.5, l.45–6.

10 Thou whoreson Z, thou unnecessary letter.
1605–6 Kent. *King Lear*, act 2, sc.2, l.63.

11 I have seen better faces in my time
Than stands on any shoulder that I see
Before me at this instant.
1605–6 Kent. *King Lear*, act 2, sc.2, l.91–3.

12 A good man's fortune may grow out at heels.
1605–6 Kent. *King Lear*, act 2, sc.2, l.148.

13 All the stored vengeances of heaven fall
On her ingrateful top!
1605–6 Lear to Regan. *King Lear*, act 2, sc.2, l.334–5.

14 Return to her, and fifty men dismissed?
No, rather I abjure all roofs, and choose
To be a comrade with the wolf and owl,
To wage against the enmity o'th' air,
Necessity's sharp pinch!
1605–6 Lear, of Goneril. *King Lear*, act 2, sc.2, l.380–4.

15 Touch me with noble anger,

And let not women's weapons, water-drops,
Stain my man's cheeks. No, you unnatural hags,
I will have such revenges on you both
That all the world shall—I will do such things—
What they are, yet I know not; but they shall be
The terrors of the earth. You think I'll weep.
No, I'll not weep. I have full cause of weeping,
But this heart shall break into a hundred thousand
  flaws
Or ere I'll weep.—O Fool, I shall go mad!
1605–6 Lear. *King Lear*, act 2, sc.2, l.450–9.

16 No, I'll not weep.
    I have full cause of weeping; but this heart
    Shall break into a hundred thousand flaws
    Or ere I'll weep.
    1605–6 Lear to Goneril and Regan. *King Lear*, act 2, sc.2. l.456–9.

17 Blow, winds, and crack your cheeks! Rage, blow,
    You cataracts and hurricanoes, spout
    Till you have drenched our steeples, drowned the
      cocks!
    1605–6 Lear. *King Lear*, act 3, sc.2, l.1–3.

18 Thou all-shaking thunder,
    Strike flat the thick rotundity o' th' world.
    1605–6 Lear. *King Lear*, act 3, sc.2, l.6–7.

19 I am a man
    More sinned against than sinning.
    1605–6 Lear to Kent. *King Lear*, act 3, sc.2, l.59–60.

20 There was never yet fair woman, but she made
    mouths in a glass.
    1605–6 Fool. *King Lear*, act 3, sc.2, l.35–6.

21 How dost, my boy? Art cold?
    I am cold myself.—Where is this straw, my fellow?
    The art of our necessities is strange,
    And can make vile things precious.
    1605–6 Lear to Fool. *King Lear*, act 3, sc.2, l.68–71.

22 He that has and a little tiny wit,
    With heigh-ho, the wind and the rain,
    Must make content with his fortunes fit,
    Though the rain it raineth every day.
    1605–6 Fool. *King Lear*, act 3, sc.2, l.74–7.

23 O, that way madness lies.
    1605–6 Lear. *King Lear*, act 3, sc.4, l.21.

24 Poor naked wretches, wheresoe'er you are,
    That bide the pelting of this pitiless storm,
    How shall your houseless heads and unfed sides,
    Your looped and windowed raggedness, defend you
    From seasons such as these?
    1605–6 Lear. *King Lear*, act 3, sc.4, l.28–32.

25 Child Roland to the dark tower came,

His word was still 'Fie, fo, and fum;
I smell the blood of a British man.'
1605–6 Edgar. *King Lear*, act 3, sc.4, l.170–2.

26 Let them anatomize Regan; see what breeds about
    her heart. Is there any cause in nature that makes
    these hard-hearts?
    1605–6 Lear. *King Lear*, act 3, sc.5, l.34–6.

27 Out, vile jelly!
    Where is thy lustre now?
    1605–6 Cornwall, pulling out Gloucester's other eye. *King Lear*, act 3, sc.7, l.81–2.

28 Turn out that eyeless villain. Throw this slave
    Upon the dunghill.
    1605–6 Cornwall to his servants. *King Lear*, act 3, sc.7, l.94–5.

29 The worst is not
    So long as we can say 'This is the worst'.
    1605–6 Edgar. *King Lear*, act 4, sc.1, 27–8.

30 As flies to wanton boys are we to th' gods;
    They kill us for their sport.
    1605–6 Gloucester. *King Lear*, act 4, sc.1, l.37–8.

31 GONERIL: I have been worth the whistling.
    ALBANY: O Goneril,
    You are not worth the dust which the rude wind
    Blows in your face.
    1605–6 *King Lear*, act 4, sc.2, l.29–32.

32 Alack, 'tis he! Why, he was met even now,
    As mad as the vexed sea, singing aloud,
    Crowned with rank fumitor and furrow-weeds,
    With burdocks, hemlock, nettles, cuckoo-flowers,
    Darnel, and all the idle weeds that grow
    In our sustaining corn.
    1605–6 Cordelia, of Lear. *King Lear*, act 4, sc.3, l.1–6.

33 GLOUCESTER: The trick of that voice I do well
    remember.
    Is't not the King?
    LEAR: Ay, every inch a king.
    1605–6 *King Lear*, act 4, sc.5, l.106–7.

34 When I do stare, see how the subject quakes!
    I pardon that man's life. What was thy cause?
    Adultery? Thou shalt not die. Die for adultery!
    No, the wren goes to't, and the small gilded fly
    Does lecher in my sight. Let copulation thrive.
    1605–6 Lear. *King Lear*, act 4, sc.5, l.108–12.

35 Down from the waist
    They're centaurs, though women all above.
    But to the girdle do the gods inherit;
    Beneath is all the fiend's. There's hell, there's
      darkness,
    there is the sulphurous pit, burning, scalding
    stench, consumption. Fie, fie, fie; pah, pah! Give

me an ounce of civet, good apothecary, sweeten
my imagination.
1605–6 Lear. *King Lear*, act 4, sc.5, l.121–7.

36 O ruined piece of nature! This great world
Shall so wear out to naught. Dost thou know me?
1605–6 Gloucester to Lear. *King Lear*, act 4, sc.5, l.130–1.

37 A dog's obeyed in office.
Thou rascal beadle, hold thy bloody hand.
Why dost thou lash that whore? Strip thy own
   back.
Thou hotly lusts to use her in that kind
For which thou whip'st her.
1605–6 Lear. *King Lear*, act 4, sc.5, l.154–9.

38 Get thee glass eyes,
And, like a scurvy politician, seem
To see the things thou dost not.
1605–6 Lear. *King Lear*, act 4, sc.5, l.166–8.

39 When we are born, we cry that we are come
To this great stage of fools.
1605–6 Lear to Gloucester. *King Lear*, act 4, sc.5, l.178–9.

40 Mine enemy's dog though he had bit me, should
   have stood
That night against my fire.
1605–6 Cordelia. *King Lear*, act 4, sc.6, l.30–1.

41 I know thee well—a serviceable villain.
1605–6 Edgar, of Oswald. *King Lear*, act 4, sc.5, l.250.

42 You do me wrong to take me out o'th' grave.
Thou art a soul in bliss, but I am bound
Upon a wheel of fire, that mine own tears
Do scald like molten lead.
1605–6 Lear to Cordelia. *King Lear*, act 4, sc.6, l.38–41.

43 Pray do not mock.
I am a very foolish, fond old man,
Fourscore and upward,
Not an hour more nor less; and to deal plainly,
I fear I am not in my perfect mind.
1605–6 Lear to Cordelia. *King Lear*, act 4, sc.6, l.52–6.

44 Hark in thine ear. Change places, and handy-
dandy, which is the justice, which is the thief?
1605–6 Lear. *King Lear*, act 4, sc.5, l.148–50.

45 Men must endure
Their going hence even as their coming hither.
Ripeness is all.
1605–6 Edgar. *King Lear*, act 5, sc.2, l.9–11.

46 [We'll] take upon 's the mystery of things
As if we were God's spies.
1605–6 Lear to Cordelia. *King Lear*, act 5, sc.3, l.16–17.

47 The gods are just, and of our pleasant vices

Make instruments to plague us.
1605–6 Edgar, to Edmond. *King Lear*, act 5, sc.3, l.161–2.

48 The wheel is come full circle. I am here.
1605–6 Edmond to Edgar. *King Lear*, act 5, sc.3, l.165.

49 His flawed heart—
Alack, too weak the conflict to support—
'Twixt two extremes of passion, joy and grief,
Burst smilingly.
1605–6 Edgar, of Gloucester. *King Lear*, act 5, sc.3, l.188–91.

50 The weight of this sad time we must obey,
Speak what we feel, not what we ought to say.
The oldest hath borne most. We that are young
Shall never see so much, nor live so long.
1605–6 Edgar. *King Lear*, act 5, sc.3, l.229–302.

51 Howl, howl, howl, howl! O, you are men of stones.
Had I your tongues and eyes, I'd use them so
That heaven's vault should crack.
1605–6 Lear, grief-stricken at the death of Cordelia. *King Lear*,
act 5, sc.3, l.232–4.

52 Her voice was ever soft,
Gentle, and low, an excellent thing in woman.
1605–6 Lear, of Cordelia. *King Lear*, act 5, sc.3, l.247–8.

53 If I lose mine honour,
I lose myself.
1606 Antony to Octavia. *Antony and Cleopatra*, act 3, sc.4,
l.22–3.

54 His captain's heart,
Which in the scuffles of great fights hath burst
The buckles on his breast.
1606 Philo, of Antony. *Antony and Cleopatra*, act 1, sc.1, l.6–8.

55 There's beggary in the love that can be reckoned.
1606 Antony to Cleopatra. *Antony and Cleopatra*, act 1, sc.1,
l.15.

56 The triple pillar of the world transformed
Into a strumpet's fool. Behold and see.
1606 Philo, of Antony. *Antony and Cleopatra*, act 1, sc.1,
l.12–13.

57 In nature's infinite book of secrecy
A little I can read.
1606 Soothsayer. *Antony and Cleopatra*, act 1, sc.2, l.9–10.

58 Let Rome in Tiber melt, and the wide arch
Of the ranged empire fall.
1606 Antony to Cleopatra. *Antony and Cleopatra*, act 1, sc.1,
l.35–6.

59 I love long life better than figs.
1606 Charmian. *Antony and Cleopatra*, act 1, sc.2, l.28.

60 The tears live in an onion that should water this
sorrow.
1606 Enobarbus, of the death of Fulvia. *Antony and Cleopatra*,
act 1, sc.2, l.161–2.

61 In time we hate that which we often fear.
    1606 Charmian. *Antony and Cleopatra*, act 1, sc.3, l.12.

62 Eternity was in our lips and eyes,
    Bliss in our brow's bent; none our parts so poor
    But was a race of heaven
    1606 Cleopatra, to Antony. *Antony and Cleopatra*, act 1, sc.3,
    l.35–7.

63 The strong necessity of time commands
    Our services a while, but my full heart
    Remains in use with you.
    1606 Antony to Cleopatra. *Antony and Cleopatra*, act 1, sc.3,
    l.42–4.

64 Age from folly could not give me freedom.
    1606 Cleopatra. *Antony and Cleopatra*, act 1, sc.3, l.57.

65 Sir, you and I must part; but that's not it.
    Sir, you and I have loved; but there's not it;
    That you know well. Something it is I would—
    O, my oblivion is a very Antony,
    And I am all forgotten.
    1606 Cleopatra, to Antony. *Antony and Cleopatra*, act 1, sc.3,
    l.88–92.

66 Now I feed myself
    With most delicious poison.
    1606 Cleopatra, thinking of Antony. *Antony and Cleopatra*, act
    1, sc.5, l.26–7.

67 My salad days,
    When I was green in judgement.
    1606 Cleopatra. *Antony and Cleopatra*, act 1, sc.5, l.72–3.

68 The barge she sat in, like a burnished throne
    Burned on the water. The poop was beaten gold;
    Purple the sails, and so perfumèd that
    The winds were love-sick with them. The oars were
      silver,
    Which to the tune of flutes kept stroke, and made
    The water which they beat to follow faster,
    As amorous of their strokes. For her own person,
    It beggared all description.
    1606 Enobarbus, of Cleopatra. *Antony and Cleopatra*, act 2,
    sc.2, l.198–205.

69 Antony,
    Enthroned i'th' market-place, did sit alone,
    Whistling to th'air, which but for vacancy
    Had gone to gaze on Cleopatra too,
    And made a gap in nature.
    1606 Enobarbus. *Antony and Cleopatra*, act 2, sc.2, l.221–5.

70 I saw her once
    Hop forty paces through the public street,
    And having lost her breath, she spoke and panted,
    That she did make defect perfection.
    1606 Enobarbus, of Cleopatra. *Antony and Cleopatra*, act 2,
    sc.2, l.235–8.

71 Age cannot wither her, nor custom stale

Her infinite variety.
    1606 Enobarbus, of Cleopatra. *Antony and Cleopatra*, act 2,
    sc.2, l.241–2.

72 If thou dost play with him at any game
    Thou art sure to lose; and of that natural luck
    He beats thee 'gainst the odds.
    1606 Soothsayer. *Antony and Cleopatra*, act 2, sc.3, l.23–5.

73 Give me some music—music, moody food
    Of us that trade in love.
    1606 Cleopatra. *Antony and Cleopatra*, act 2, sc.5, l.1–2.

74 Let it alone, let's to billiards.
    1606 Cleopatra. *Antony and Cleopatra*, act 2, sc.5, l.3.

75 I laughed him out of patience, and that night
    I laughed him into patience, and next morn,
    Ere the ninth hour, I drunk him to his bed.
    1606 Cleopatra of Antony. *Antony and Cleopatra*, act 2, sc.5,
    l.19–21.

76 There is gold, and here
    My bluest veins to kiss—a hand that kings
    Have lipped, and trembled kissing.
    1606 Cleopatra to a messenger bringing news of Antony.
    Antony and Cleopatra, act 2, sc.5, l.28–30.

77 I will praise any man that will praise me.
    1606 Enobarbus. *Antony and Cleopatra*, act 2, sc.6, l.90.

78 We have kissed away
    Kingdoms and provinces.
    1606 Scarus. *Antony and Cleopatra*, act 3, sc.10, l.7–8.

79 I have offended reputation;
    A most unnoble swerving.
    1606 Antony. *Antony and Cleopatra*, act 3, sc.11, l.48–9.

80 Thou knew'st too well
    My heart was to thy rudder tied by th' strings,
    And thou should'st tow me after.
    1606 Antony. *Antony and Cleopatra*, act 3, sc.11, l.56–8.

81 Fortune knows
    We scorn her most when most she offers blows.
    1606 Antony. *Antony and Cleopatra*, act 3, sc.11, l.74–5.

82 He wears the rose
    Of youth upon him.
    1606 Antony, of Caesar. *Antony and Cleopatra*, act 3, sc.13,
    l.19–20.

83 I dare him therefore
    To lay his gay caparisons apart
    And answer me declined, sword against sword,
    Ourselves alone.
    1606 Antony's message to Caesar. *Antony and Cleopatra*, act 3,
    sc.13, l.24–7.

84 Let's have one other gaudy night. Call to me
    All my sad captains. Fill our bowls once more.
    Let's mock the midnight bell.
    1606 Antony. *Antony and Cleopatra*, act 3, sc.13, l.185–7.

85 Never anger
Made good guard for itself.
1606 Maecenas. *Antony and Cleopatra*, act 4, sc.1, l.9–10.

86 To business that we love we rise betime,
And go to't with delight.
1606 Antony. *Antony and Cleopatra*, act 4, sc.4, l.20–1.

87 There is left us
Ourselves to end ourselves.
1606 Antony to Eros. *Antony and Cleopatra*, act 4, sc.15, l.21–2.

88 All strange and terrible events are welcome,
But comforts we despise.
1606 Cleopatra. *Antony and Cleopatra*, act 4, sc.16, l.3–4.

89 Is it sin
To rush into the secret house of death
Ere death dare come to us?
1606 Cleopatra. *Antony and Cleopatra*, act 4, sc.16, l.82–4.

90 O sovereign mistress of true melancholy,
The poisonous damp of night disponge upon me,
That life, a very rebel to my will,
May hang no longer on me.
1606 Enobarbus. *Antony and Cleopatra*, act 4, sc.10, l.11–14.

91 But I will be
A bridegroom in my death, and run into't
As to a lover's bed.
1606 Antony. *Antony and Cleopatra*, act 4, sc.15, l.99–101.

92 Let him that loves me strike me dead.
1606 Antony. *Antony and Cleopatra*, act 4, sc.15, l.108.

93 So it should be,
That none but Antony should conquer Antony.
1606 Cleopatra. *Antony and Cleopatra*, act 4, sc.16, l.16–17.

94 Of many thousand kisses the poor last
I lay upon thy lips.
1606 Antony to Cleopatra. *Antony and Cleopatra*, act 4, sc.16, l.21–2.

95 Shall I abide
In this dull world, which in thy absence is
No better than a sty?
1606 Cleopatra to Antony. *Antony and Cleopatra*, act 4, sc.16, l.62–4.

96 There is nothing left remarkable
Beneath the visiting moon.
1606 Cleopatra, of the death of Antony. *Antony and Cleopatra*, act 4, sc.16, l.69–70.

97 What's brave, what's noble,
Let's do it after the high Roman fashion,
And make death proud to take us.
1606 Cleopatra. *Antony and Cleopatra*, act 4, sc.16, l.88–90.

98 It is great

To do that thing that ends all other deeds.
1606 Cleopatra. *Antony and Cleopatra*, act 5, sc.2, l.4–5.

99 I dreamt there was an Emperor Antony,
O, such another sleep, that I might see
But such another man!
1606 Cleopatra. *Antony and Cleopatra*, act 5, sc.2, l.75–7.

1 His legs bestrid the ocean; his reared arm
Crested the world.
1606 Cleopatra, of Antony. *Antony and Cleopatra*, act 5, sc.2, l.81–2.

2 The bright day is done,
And we are for the dark.
1606 Iras. *Antony and Cleopatra*, act 5, sc.2, l.189–90.

3 Hast thou the pretty worm
Of Nilus there, that kills and pains not?
1606 Cleopatra. *Antony and Cleopatra*, act 5, sc.2, l.238–9.

4 His biting is immortal; those that do die of it do
seldom or ever recover.
1606 Clown. *Antony and Cleopatra*, act 5, sc.2, l.241–3.

5 Give me my robe. Put on my crown. I have
Immortal longings in me.
1606 Cleopatra. *Antony and Cleopatra*, act 5, sc.2, l.275–6.

6 Husband, I come.
Now to that name my courage prove my title.
1606 Cleopatra. *Antony and Cleopatra*, act 5, sc.2, l.282–3.

7 If thou and nature can so gently part,
The stroke of death is as a lover's pinch,
Which hurts and is desired. Dost thou lie still?
If thus thou vanishest, thou tell'st the world
It is not worth leave-taking.
1606 Cleopatra. *Antony and Cleopatra*, act 5, sc.2, l.289–93.

8 A lass unparalleled. Downy windows, close,
And golden Phoebus never be beheld
Of eyes again so royal.
1606 Charmian. *Antony and Cleopatra*, act 5, sc.2, l.310–12.

9 When shall we three meet again?
In thunder, lightning, or in rain?
1606 First Witch. *Macbeth*, act 1, sc.1, l.1–2.

10 Fair is foul, and foul is fair,
Hover through the fog and filthy air.
1606 Witches. *Macbeth*, act 1, sc.1, l.10–11.

11 Fortune on his damnèd quarry smiling
Showed like a rebel's whore.
1606 Captain. *Macbeth*, act 1, sc.2, l.14–15.

12 A sailor's wife had chestnuts in her lap,
And munched, and munched, and munched. 'Give
me,' quoth I.
'Aroint thee, witch,' the rump-fed runnion cries.

Her husband's to Aleppo gone, master o'th' Tiger.
But in a sieve I'll thither sail,
And like a rat without a tail
I'll do, I'll do, and I'll do.
1606 First Witch. *Macbeth*, act 1, sc.3, l.3–9.

13 I'll drain him dry as hay.
Sleep shall neither night nor day
Hang upon his penthouse lid.
He shall live a man forbid.
Weary sennights nine times nine
Shall he dwindle, peak, and pine.
Though his barque cannot be lost,
Yet it shall be tempest-tossed.
1606 First Witch. *Macbeth*, act 1, sc.3, l.17–23.

14 The weird sisters hand in hand,
Posters of the sea and land,
Thus do go about, about.
1606 Witches. *Macbeth*, act 1, sc.3, l.30–2.

15 So foul and fair a day I have not seen.
1606 Macbeth. *Macbeth*, act 1, sc.3, l.36.

16 Live you, or are you aught
That man may question? You seem to understand
  me
By each at once her choppy finger laying
Upon her skinny lips. You should be women,
And yet your beards forbid me to interpret
That you are so.
1606 Banquo. *Macbeth*, act 1, sc.3, l.40–4.

17 If you can look into the seeds of time
And say which grain will grow and which will not,
Speak then to me.
1606 Banquo to the witches. *Macbeth*, act 1, sc.3, l.56–9.

18 To be king
Stands not within the prospect of belief.
1606 Macbeth to the witches. *Macbeth*, act 1, sc.3, l.71–2.

19 The earth hath bubbles, as the water has,
And these are of them.
1606 Banquo, of the witches. *Macbeth*, act 1, sc.3, l.77–8.

20 What, can the devil speak true?
1606 Banquo, hearing that the first of the witches' predictions
has come true. *Macbeth*, act 1, sc.3, l.105.

21 The Thane of Cawdor lives. Why do you dress me
In borrowed robes?
1606 Macbeth. *Macbeth*, act 1, sc.3, l.106–7.

22 Come what come may,
Time and the hour runs through the roughest day.
1606 Macbeth. *Macbeth*, act 1, sc.3, l.145–6.

23 Nothing in his life
Became him like the leaving of it. He died
As one that had been studied in his death

To throw away the dearest thing he owed
As 'twere a careless trifle.
1606 Malcolm, of Cawdor. *Macbeth*, act 1, sc.4, l.7–11.

24 There's no art
To find the mind's construction in the face.
He was a gentleman on whom I built
An absolute trust.
1606 King Duncan, of Cawdor. *Macbeth*, act 1, sc.4, l.11–14.

25 Yet do I fear thy nature;
It is too full o'th' milk of human kindness
To catch the nearest way.
1606 Lady Macbeth, of Macbeth. *Macbeth*, act 1, sc.5,
l.15–17.

26 Thou wouldst be great,
Art not without ambition, but without
The illness should attend it.
1606 Lady Macbeth, of Macbeth. *Macbeth*, act 1, sc.5,
l.17–19.

27 Come, you spirits
That tend on mortal thoughts, unsex me here,
And fill me from the crown to the toe top-full
Of direst cruelty.
1606 Lady Macbeth. *Macbeth*, act 1, sc.5, l.39–42.

28 Your face, my thane, is as a book where men
May read strange matters.
1606 Lady Macbeth to Macbeth. *Macbeth*, act 1, sc.5, l.61–2.

29 Bear welcome in your eye,
Your hand, your tongue; look like the innocent
  flower,
But be the serpent under't.
1606 Lady Macbeth to Macbeth. *Macbeth*, act 1, sc.5, l.63–5.

30 KING DUNCAN: This castle hath a pleasant seat. The
  air
Nimbly and sweetly recommends itself
Unto our gentle senses.
BANQUO: This guest of summer,
The temple-haunting marlet, does approve
By his loved mansionry that the heavens' breath
Smells wooingly here. No jutty, frieze,
Buttress, nor coign of vantage but this bird
Hath made his pedant bed and procreant cradle;
Where they most breed and haunt I have observed
The air is delicate.
1606 *Macbeth*, act 1, sc.6, l.1–10.

31 If it were done when 'tis done, then 'twere well
It were done quickly. If th'assassination
Could trammel up the consequence, and catch
With his surcease success: that but this blow
Might be the be-all and the end-all, here,
But here upon this bank and shoal of time,
We'd jump the life to come. But in these cases
We still have judgement here, that we but teach

Bloody instructions which, being taught, return
To plague th'inventor.
1606 Macbeth, on the prospect of murdering Duncan. *Macbeth*, act 1, sc.7, l.1–10.

32 Besides, this Duncan
Hath borne his faculties so meek, hath been
So clear in his great office, that his virtues
Will plead like angels, trumpet-tongued against
The deep damnation of his taking-off,
And pity, like a naked new-born babe,
Striding the blast, or heaven's cherubin, horsed
Upon the sightless couriers of the air,
Shall blow the horrid deed in every eye
That tears shall drown the wind. I have no spur
To prick the sides of my intent, but only
Vaulting ambition which o'erleaps itself
And falls on th'other.
1606 Macbeth. *Macbeth*, act 1, sc.7, l.16–29.

33 Wouldst thou have that
Which thou esteem'st the ornament of life,
And live a coward in thine own esteem,
Letting 'I dare not' wait upon 'I would',
Like the poor cat i'th' adage?
1606 Lady Macbeth to Macbeth. *Macbeth*, act 1, sc.7, l.41–45.

34 I dare do all that may become a man;
Who dares do more is none.
1606 Macbeth to Lady Macbeth. *Macbeth*, act 1, sc.7, l.46–7.

35 Screw your courage to the sticking-place
And we'll not fail.
1606 Lady Macbeth to Macbeth. *Macbeth*, act 1, sc.7, l.60–1.

36 Bring forth men-children only,
For thy undaunted mettle should compose
Nothing but males.
1606 Macbeth to Lady Macbeth. *Macbeth*, act 1, sc.7, l.72–4.

37 Away, and mock the time with fairest show.
False face must hide what the false heart doth
know.
1606 Macbeth. *Macbeth*, act 1, sc.7, l.81–2.

38 There's husbandry in heaven,
Their candles are all out.
1606 Banquo. *Macbeth*, act 2, sc.1, l.4–5.

39 Is this a dagger which I see before me,
The handle toward my hand? Come, let me clutch
thee.
I have thee not, and yet I see thee still.
1606 Macbeth. *Macbeth*, act 2, sc.1, l.33–5.

40 Mine eyes are made the fool o'th' other senses,
Or else worth all the rest.
1606 Macbeth. *Macbeth*, act 2, sc.1, l.44–5.

41 Whiles I threat, he lives.

Words to the heat of deeds too cold breath gives.
I go, and it is done. The bell invites me.
Hear it not, Duncan; for it is a knell
That summons thee to heaven or to hell.
1606 Macbeth, steeling himself to murder Duncan. *Macbeth*, act 2, sc.1, l.60–4.

42 That which hath made them drunk hath made me
bold.
What hath quenched them hath given me fire.
1606 Lady Macbeth. *Macbeth*, act 2, sc.2, l.1–2.

43 Th'attempt and not the deed
Confounds us.
1606 Lady Macbeth. *Macbeth*, act 2, sc.2, l.10–11.

44 I laid their daggers ready;
He could not miss 'em. Had he not resembled
My father as he slept, I had done't.
1606 Lady Macbeth, of Duncan. *Macbeth*, act 2, sc.2, l.11–13.

45 I had most need of blessing, and 'Amen'?
Stuck in my throat.
1606 Macbeth. *Macbeth*, act 2, sc.2, l.30–1.

46 Methought I heard a voice cry 'Sleep no more,
Macbeth does murder sleep'—the innocent sleep,
Sleep that knits up the ravelled sleave of care.
1606 Macbeth. *Macbeth*, act 2, sc.2, l.33–5.

47 Still it cried 'Sleep no more' to all the house,
'Glamis hath murdered sleep, and therefore
Cawdor
Shall sleep no more, Macbeth shall sleep no more.'
1606 Macbeth. *Macbeth*, act 2, sc.2, l.39–41.

48 Infirm of purpose!
Give me the daggers. The sleeping and the dead
Are but as pictures. 'Tis the eye of childhood
That fears a painted devil.
1606 Lady Macbeth. *Macbeth*, act 2, sc.2, l.50–4.

49 Will all great Neptune's ocean wash this blood
Clean from my hand?
1606 Macbeth. *Macbeth*, act 2, sc.2, l.58–9.

50 A little water clears us of this deed.
1606 Lady Macbeth. *Macbeth*, act 2, sc.2, l.65.

51 But this place is too cold for hell. I'll devil-porter it
no further. I had thought to have let in some of all
professions that go the primrose way to
th'everlasting bonfire.
1606 Porter. *Macbeth*, act 2, sc.3, l.15–18.

52 The labour we delight in physics pain.
1606 Macbeth. *Macbeth*, act 2, sc.3, l.49.

53 Confusion now hath made his masterpiece.
Most sacrilegious murder hath broke ope
The Lord's anointed temple and stole thence
The life o'th' building.

1606 Macduff, announcing Duncan's murder. *Macbeth*, act 2, sc.3, l.65–8.

54 There's daggers in men's smiles.
1606 Donalbain. *Macbeth*, act 2, sc.3, l.139.

55 Go not my horse the better,
I must become a borrower of the night
For dark hour or twain.
1606 Banquo. *Macbeth*, act 3, sc.1, l.26–8.

56 I could
With barefaced power sweep him from my sight.
1606 Macbeth, of Banquo. *Macbeth*, act 3, sc.1, l.119–20.

57 Things without all remedy
Should be without regard. What's done is done.
1606 Lady Macbeth. *Macbeth*, act 3, sc.2, l.13–14.

58 Duncan is in his grave.
After life's fitful fever he sleeps well.
Treason has done his worst.
1606 Macbeth. *Macbeth*, act 3, sc.2, l.24–5.

59 Come, seeling night,
Scarf up the tender eye of pitiful day.
1606 Macbeth. *Macbeth*, act 3, sc.2, l.47–8.

60 Light thickens, and the crow
Makes wing to th' rooky wood.
Good things of day begin to droop and drowse,
Whiles night's black agents to their preys do rouse.
1606 Macbeth. *Macbeth*, act 3, sc.2, l.51–4.

61 Thou canst not say I did it. Never shake
Thy gory locks at me.
1606 Macbeth to Banquo's ghost. *Macbeth*, act 3, sc.4, l.49–50.

62 You make me strange
Even to the disposition that I owe,
When now I think you can behold such sights
And keep the natural ruby of your cheeks,
When mine is blanched with fear.
1606 Macbeth to Lady Macbeth. *Macbeth*, act 3, sc.4, l.111–15.

63 I am in blood
Stepped in so far that, should I wade no more,
Returning were as tedious as go o'er.
1606 Macbeth. *Macbeth*, act 3, sc.4, l.135–7.

64 Double, double, toil and trouble,
Fire burn, and cauldron bubble.
1606 Witches. *Macbeth*, act 4, sc.1, l.20–1.

65 By the pricking of my thumbs,
Something wicked this way comes.
1606 Second witch. *Macbeth*, act 4, sc.1, l.61–2.

66 MACBETH: How now, you secret, black, and
midnight hags,
What is't you do?

WITCHES: A deed without a name.
1606 *Macbeth*, act 4, sc.1, l.63–5.

67 Be bloody, bold, and resolute. Laugh to scorn
The power of man, for none of woman born
Shall harm Macbeth.
1606 Second apparition to Macbeth. *Macbeth*, act 4, sc.1, l.95–7.

68 Macbeth shall never vanquished be until
Great Birnam Wood to high Dunsinane Hill
Shall come against him.
1606 Third Apparition. *Macbeth*, act 4, sc.1, l.108–10.

69 No boasting like a fool;
This deed I'll do before this purpose cool.
1606 Macbeth, intending to murder Macduff's family. *Macbeth*, act 4, sc.1, l.169–70.

70 Our fears do make us traitors.
1606 Lady Macduff. *Macbeth*, act 4, sc.2, l.4.

71 He loves us not,
He wants the natural touch.
1606 Lady Macduff, of Macduff. *Macbeth*, act 4, sc.2, l.8–9.

72 Each new morn
New widows howl, new orphans cry, new sorrows
Strike heaven on the face.
1606 Macduff. *Macbeth*, act 4, sc.3, l.4–6.

73 MACDUFF: Stands Scotland where it did?
ROSS: Alas, poor country,
Almost afraid to know itself.
1606 *Macbeth*, act 4, sc.3, l.165–6.

74 MACDUFF: He has no children. All my pretty ones?
Did you say all? O hell-kite! All?
What, all my pretty chickens and their dam
At one fell swoop?
MALCOLM: Dispute it like a man.
MACDUFF: I shall do so,
But I must also feel it as a man.
I cannot but remember such things were
That were most precious to me. Did heaven look
on
And would not take their part?
1606 Macduff, of his murdered wife and children. *Macbeth*, act 4, sc.3, l.217–26.

75 The night is long that never finds the day.
1606 Malcolm. *Macbeth*, act 4, sc.3, l.242.

76 It is an accustomed action with her, to seem thus
washing her hands. I have known her continue in
this a quarter of an hour.
1606 Gentlewoman, of Lady Macbeth. *Macbeth*, act 5, sc.1, l.27–9.

77 Out, damned spot; out, I say. One, two,—why,
then 'tis time to do't. Hell is murky. Fie, my lord,
fie, a soldier and afeard? What need we fear who

knows it when none can call our power to account?
Yet who would have thought the old man to have
had so much blood in him?
1606 Lady Macbeth, sleepwalking, of the murdered Duncan.
Macbeth, act 5, sc.1, l.33–8.

78 The Thane of Fife had a wife. Where is
she now? What, will these hands ne'er be clean?
1606 Lady Macbeth. *Macbeth*, act 5, sc.1, l.40–1.

79 Now does he feel
His secret murders sticking on his hands.
Now minutely revolts upbraid his faith-breach.
Those he commands move only in command,
Nothing in love. Now does he feel his title
Hang loose about him, like a giant's robe
Upon a dwarfish thief.
1606 Angus, of Macbeth. *Macbeth*, act 5, sc.2, l.16–22.

80 The devil damn thee black, thou cream-faced loon!
1606 Macbeth to his servant. *Macbeth*, act 5, sc.3, l.11.

81 I have lived long enough. My way of life
Is fall'n into the sere, the yellow leaf,
And that which should accompany old age,
As honour, love, obedience, troops of friends,
I must not look to have.
1606 Macbeth. *Macbeth*, act 5, sc.3, l.24–8.

82 Canst thou not minister to a mind diseased,
Pluck from the memory a rooted sorrow,
Raze out the written troubles of the brain,
And with some sweet oblivious antidote
Cleanse the fraught bosom?
1606 Macbeth to the doctor, of Lady Macbeth. *Macbeth*, act 5,
sc.3, l.42–5.

83 Throw physic to the dogs; I'll none of it.
1606 Macbeth. *Macbeth*, act 5, sc.3, l.49.

84 What rhubarb, cyme, or what purgative drug
Would scour these English hence?
1606 Macbeth to the doctor. *Macbeth*, act 5, sc.3, l.57–8.

85 I have supped full with horrors.
Direness, familiar to my slaughterhouse thoughts,
Cannot once start me.
1606 Macbeth. *Macbeth*, act 5, sc.5, l.13–14.

86 She should have died hereafter.
There would have been a time for such a word.
Tomorrow, and tomorrow, and tomorrow
Creeps in this petty pace from day to day
To the last syllable of recorded time,
And all our yesterdays have lighted fools
The way to dusty death. Out, out, brief candle.
Life's but a walking shadow, a poor player
That struts and frets his hour upon the stage,
And then is heard no more. It is a tale
Told by an idiot, full of sound and fury,
Signifying nothing.

1606 Macbeth, hearing of Lady Macbeth's death. *Macbeth*, act
5, sc.5, l.16–27.

87 They have tied me to a stake. I cannot fly,
But bear-like I must fight the course.
1606 Macbeth. *Macbeth*, act 5, sc.7, l.1–2.

88 YOUNG SIWARD: What is thy name?
MACBETH: Thou'lt be afraid to hear it.
YOUNG SIWARD: No, though thou call'st thyself a
  hotter name
Than any in hell.
MACBETH: My name's Macbeth.
1606 *Macbeth*, act 5, sc.7, l.5–8.

89 Macduff was from his mother's womb
Untimely ripped.
1606 Macduff. *Macbeth*, act 5, sc.10, l.15–16.

90 Lay on, Macduff,
And damned be him that first cries 'Hold, enough!'
1606 Macbeth. *Macbeth*, act 5, sc.10, l.33–4.

91 Your cause of sorrow
Must not be measured by his worth, for then
It hath no end.
1606 Ross to Siward. *Macbeth*, act 5, sc.11, l.10–12.

92 Kings are earth's gods; in vice their law's their will,
And if Jove stray, who dares say Jove doth ill?
1607 Pericles. *Pericles*, sc.1, l.146–7.

93 'Tis time to fear when tyrants seems to kiss.
1607 Pericles. *Pericles*, sc.2, l.84.

94 We'll mingle our bloods together in the earth
From whence we had our being and our birth.
1607 Helicanus to Pericles. *Pericles*, sc.2, l.118–9.

95 They do abuse the King that flatter him,
For flatt'ry is the bellows blows up sin.
1607 Helicanus. *Pericles*, sc.2, l.43–4.

96 I'll take thy word for faith, not ask thine oath;
Who shuns not to break one will sure crack both.
1607 Pericles to Helicanus. *Pericles*, sc.2, l.125–6.

97 Shall we rest us here
And, by relating tales of others' griefs,
See if 'twill teach us to forget our own?
1607 Cleon to Dioniza. *Pericles*, sc.4, l.1–3.

98 One sorrow never comes but brings an heir
That may succeed as his inheritor.
1607 Cleon. *Pericles*, sc.4, l.62–3.

99 He's a very dog to the commonalty.
1608 Fourth citizen. *Coriolanus*, act 1, sc.1, l.27.

1 What's the matter, you dissentious rogues,
That, rubbing the poor itch of your opinion,
Make yourselves scabs?
1608 Martius. *Coriolanus*, act 1, sc.1, l.162–4.

2 On both sides more respect.
   1608 Menenius. *Coriolanus*, act 3, sc.1, l.183.

3 They threw their caps
   As they would hang them on the horns o'th' moon.
   1608 Martius. *Coriolanus*, act 1, sc.1, l.210–11.

4 Nature teaches beasts to know their friends.
   1608 Sicinius. *Coriolanus*, act 2, sc.1, l.6.

5 [I am] one that loves a cup of hot wine with not a
   drop of allaying Tiber in't.
   1608 Menenius. *Coriolanus*, act 2, sc.1, l.47–8.

6 What I think, I utter, and spend my malice in my
   breath.
   1608 Menenius. *Coriolanus*, act 2, sc.1, l.52–3.

7 That's a brave fellow, but he's vengeance proud and
   loves not the common people.
   1608 First Officer, of Coriolanus. *Coriolanus*, act 2, sc.2, l.5–6.

8 He seeks their hate with greater devotion than they
   can render it him.
   1608 First Officer, of Coriolanus. *Coriolanus*, act 2, sc.2,
   l.18–19.

9 Ingratitude is monstrous, and for the multitude to
   be ingrateful were to make a monster of the
   multitude.
   1608 Third Citizen. *Coriolanus*, act 2, sc.3, l.9–10.

10 'Shall remain'?
    Hear you this Triton of the minnows? Mark you
    His absolute 'shall'?
    1608 Coriolanus. *Coriolanus*, act 3, sc.1, l.91–3.

11 You common cry of curs, whose breath I hate
    As reek o'th' rotten fens, whose loves I prize
    As the dead carcasses of unburied men
    That do corrupt my air: I banish you.
    1608 Coriolanus to the citizens. *Coriolanus*, act 3, sc.3,
    l.124–7.

12 Now we have shown our power,
    Let us seem humbler after it is done.
    1608 Brutus. *Coriolanus*, act 4, sc.2, l.3–4.

13 Anger's my meat, I sup upon myself,
    And so shall starve with feeding.
    1608 Volumnia. *Coriolanus*, act 4, sc.2, l.53–4.

14 He'll shake your Rome about your ears.
    1608 Cominius. *Coriolanus*, act 4, sc.6, l.103.

15 Like a dull actor now
    I have forgot my part, and I am out
    Even to a full disgrace.
    1608 Coriolanus. *Coriolanus*, act 5, sc.3, l.40–2.

16 O, a kiss
    Long as my exile, sweet as my revenge!

1608 Coriolanus to Virgilia. *Coriolanus*, act 5, sc.3, l.44–5.

17 Cut me to pieces, Volsces. Men and lads,
    Stain all your edges on me. 'Boy'! False hound,
    If you have writ your annals true, 'tis there
    That, like an eagle in a dove-cot, I
    Fluttered your Volscians in Corioles.
    Alone I did it.
    1608 Coriolanus. *Coriolanus*, act 5, sc.6, l.112–7.

18 We were, fair Queen,
    Two lads that thought there was no more behind
    But such a day tomorrow as today,
    And to be boy eternal.
    1609 Polixenes to Hermione. *The Winter's Tale*, act 1, sc.2,
    l.63–6.

19 He makes a July's day as short as December.
    1609 Polixenes, of Mamillius. *The Winter's Tale*, act 1, sc.2,
    l.170.

20 One good deed dying tongueless
    Slaughters a thousand waiting upon that.
    1609 Hermione. *The Winter's Tale*, act 1, sc.2, l.94–5.

21 Should all despair
    That have revolted wives, the tenth of mankind
    Would hang themselves.
    1609 Leontes. *The Winter's Tale*, act 1, sc.2, l.199–201.

22 I saw his heart in's face.
    1609 Polixenes, of Leontes. *The Winter's Tale*, act 1, sc.2, l.447.

23 A sad tale's best for winter.
    1609 Mamillius. *The Winter's Tale*, act 2, sc.1, l.27.

24 It is an heretic that makes the fire,
    Not she which burns in't.
    1609 Paulina. *The Winter's Tale*, act 2, sc.3, l.115–6.

25 *Exit, pursued by a bear.*
    1609 Stage Direction. *The Winter's Tale*, act 3, sc.3, l.57.

26 A snapper-up of unconsidered trifles.
    1609 Autolycus, of himself. *The Winter's Tale*, act 4, sc.3,
    l.25–6.

27 Jog on, jog on, the footpath way,
    And merrily hent the stile-a.
    A merry heart goes all the day,
    Your sad tires in a mile-a.
    1609 Autolycus, singing. *The Winter's Tale*, act 4, sc.3, l.123–6.

28 Let's be red with mirth.
    1609 Florizel. *The Winter's Tale*, act 4, sc.4, l.54.

29 Blasts of January
    Would blow you through and through.
    1609 Perdita, of Camillo. *The Winter's Tale*, act 4, sc.4,
    l.111–12.

30 Daffodils,

That come before the swallow dares, and take
The winds of March with beauty.
1609 Perdita. *The Winter's Tale*, act 4, sc.4, l.118–20.

31 When you speak, sweet,
I'd have you do it ever; when you sing,
I'd have you buy and sell so, so give alms,
Pray so; and for the ord'ring your affairs,
To sing them too. When you do dance, I wish you
A wave o'th' sea, that you might ever do
Nothing but that, move still, still so,
And own no other function. Each your doing,
So singular in each particular,
Crowns what you are doing in the present deeds,
That all your acts are queens.
1609 Florizel to Perdita. *The Winter's Tale*, act 4, sc.4, l.136–46.

32 Good sooth, she is
The queen of curds and cream.
1609 Camillo, of Perdita. *The Winter's Tale*, act 4, sc.4, l.160–1.

33 Garlic to mend her kissing with!
1609 Dorcas, of Mopsa. *The Winter's Tale*, act 4, sc.4, l.162–3.

34 He says he loves my daughter:
I think, so too, for never gazed the moon
Upon the water as he'll stand and read,
As 'twere, my daughter's eyes.
1609 Old Shepherd. *The Winter's Tale*, act 4, sc.4, l.172–5.

35 He has the prettiest love songs for maids, so
without bawdry, which is strange, with such
delicate burdens of dildos and fadings, 'Jump her,
and thump her'; and where some stretch-mouthed
rascal would, as it were, mean mischief and break a
foul gap into the matter, he makes the maid to
answer, 'Whoop, do me no harm, good man!'
1609 Servant. *The Winter's Tale*, act 4, sc.4, l.193–200.

36 Lawn as white as driven snow.
1609 Autolycus. *The Winter's Tale*, act 4, sc.4, l.219.

37 If I were not in love with Mopsa thou shouldst take
no money of me, but being enthralled as I am, it
will also be the bondage of certain ribbons and
gloves.
1609 Clown to Autolycus (in disguise). *The Winter's Tale*, act 4, sc.4, l.231–3.

38 I love a ballad in print, alife, for then we are sure
they are true.
1609 Mopsa to Autolycus (in disguise). *The Winter's Tale*, act 4, sc.4, l.258–9.

39 Though I am not naturally honest, I am so
sometimes by chance.
1609 Autolycus. *The Winter's Tale*, act 4, sc.4, l.712–13.

40 Stars, stars,

And all eyes else, dead coals!
1609 Leontes. *The Winter's Tale*, act 5, sc.1, l.67–8.

41 Women will love her that she is a woman
More worth than any man; men, that she is
The rarest of all women.
1609 Servant, of Perdita. *The Winter's Tale*, act 5, sc.1, l.110–12

42 My lord, your sorrow was too sore laid on,
Which sixteen winters cannot blow away,
So many summers dry. Scarce any joy
Did ever so long live.
1609 Camillo to Leontes. *The Winter's Tale*, act 5, sc.3, l.49–52.

43 O, she's warm!
If this be magic, let it be an art
Lawful as eating.
1609 Leontes, of the now animated statue of Hermione. *The Winter's Tale*, act 5, sc.3, l.109–11.

44 Thou art thy mother's glass, and she in thee
Calls back the lovely April of her prime.
1609 *Sonnets*, sonnet 3.

45 Music to hear, why hear'st thou music sadly?
Sweets with sweets war not, joy delights in joy.
Why lov'st thou that which thou receiv'st not
   gladly.
1609 *Sonnets*, sonnet 8.

46 For thou art so possessed with murd'rous hate
That 'gainst thyself thou stick'st not to conspire.
1609 *Sonnets*, sonnet 10.

47 If I could write the beauty of your eyes
And in fresh numbers number all your graces,
The age to come would say 'This poet lies;
Such heavenly touches ne'er touched earthly faces.'
1609 *Sonnets*, sonnet 17.

48 Shall I compare thee to a summer's day?
Thou art more lovely and more temperate.
Rough winds do shake the darling buds of May,
And summer's lease hath all too short a date.
Sometime too hot the eye of heaven shines,
And often is his gold complexion dimmed,
And every fair from fair sometime declines,
By chance or nature's changing course untrimmed;
But thy eternal summer shall not fade
Nor lose possession of that fair thou ow'st,
Nor shall death brag thou wander'st in his shade
When in eternal lines to time thou grow'st.
So long as men can breathe or eyes can see,
So long lives this, and this gives life to thee.
1609 *Sonnets*, sonnet 18.

49 Yet do thy worst, old time; despite thy wrong
My love shall in my verse ever live young.
1609 *Sonnets*, sonnet 19.

50 A woman's face with nature's own hand painted
    Hast thou, the master-mistress of my passion.
    1609 *Sonnets*, sonnet 20.

51 My glass shall not persuade me I am old
    So long as youth and thou are of one date;
    But when in thee time's furrows I behold,
    Then look I death my days should expiate.
    1609 *Sonnets*, sonnet 22.

52 Presume not on thy heart when mine is slain:
    Thou gav'st me thine not to give back again.
    1609 *Sonnets*, sonnet 22.

53 O let my books be then the eloquence
    And dumb presagers of my speaking breast,
    Who plead for love, and look for recompense
    More than that tongue that more hath more
        expressed.
    O learn to read what silent love hath writ;
    To hear with eyes belongs to love's fine wit.
    1609 *Sonnets*, sonnet 23.

54 Now see what good turns eyes for eyes have done:
    Mine eyes have drawn thy shape, and thine for me
    Are windows to my breast, wherethrough the sun
    Delights to peep, to gaze therein on thee.
    Yet eyes this cunning want to grace their art:
    They draw but what they see, know not the heart.
    1609 *Sonnets*, sonnet 24.

55 The painful warrior famousèd for might,
    After a thousand victories once foiled
    Is from the book of honour razèd quite,
    And all the rest forgot for which he toiled.
    1609 *Sonnets*, sonnet 25.

56 Weary with toil I haste me to my bed,
    The dear repose for limbs with travel tired;
    But then begins a journey in my head
    To work my mind when body's work's expired.
    1609 *Sonnets*, sonnet 27.

57 When, in disgrace with fortune and men's eyes,
    I all alone beweep my outcast state,
    And trouble deaf heaven with my bootless cries,
    And look upon myself and curse my fate,
    Wishing me like to one more rich hope,
    Featured like him, like him with friends possessed,
    Desiring this man's art and that man's scope,
    With what I most enjoy contented least:
    Yet in these thoughts myself almost despising,
    Haply I think on thee, and then my state,
    Like to the lark at break of day arising
    For sullen earth, sings hymns at heaven's gate;
    For thy sweet love remembered such wealth brings
    That then I scorn to change my state with kings'.
    1609 *Sonnets*, sonnet 29.

58 When to the sessions of sweet silent thought

I summon up remembrance of things past,
I sigh the lack of many a thing I sought,
And with old woes new wail my dear time's waste.
Then can I drown an eye unused to flow
For precious friends hid in death's dateless night,
And weep afresh love's long-since-cancelled woe,
And moan th'expense of many a vanished sight.
Then can I grieve at grievances foregone,
And heavily from woe to woe tell o'er
The sad account of fore-bemoanèd moan,
Which I new pay as if not paid before.
But if the while I think on thee, dear friend,
All losses are restored, and sorrows end.
1609 *Sonnets*, sonnet 30.

59 Full many a glorious morning have I seen
    Flatter the mountain tops with sovereign eye,
    Kissing with golden face the meadows green.
    1609 *Sonnets*, sonnet 33.

60 As a decrepit father takes delight
    To see his active child do deeds of youth,
    So I, made lame by fortune's dearest spite,
    Take all my comfort of thy worth and truth.
    1609 *Sonnets*, sonnet 37.

61 All days are nights to see till I see thee,
    And nights bright days when dreams do show thee
        me.
    1609 *Sonnets*, sonnet 43.

62 O how much more doth beauty beauteous seem
    By that sweet ornament which truth doth give!
    1609 *Sonnets*, sonnet 54.

63 The rose looks fair, but fairer we it deem
    For that sweet odour which doth in it live.
    1609 *Sonnets*, sonnet 54.

64 So, till the judgement that yourself arise,
    You live in this, and dwell in lovers' eyes.
    1609 *Sonnets*, sonnet 55.

65 Not marble nor the gilded monuments
    Of princes shall outlive this powerful rhyme,
    But you shall shine more bright in these contents
    Than unswept stone besmeared with sluttish time.
    1609 *Sonnets*, sonnet 55.

66 Being your slave, what should I do but tend
    Upon the hours and times of your desire?
    I have no precious time at all to spend,
    Nor services to do, till you require;
    Nor dare I chide the world-without-end hour
    Whilst I, my sovereign, watch the clock for you,
    Nor think the bitterness of absence sour
    When you have bid your servant once adieu.
    Nor dare I question with my jealous thought
    Where you may be, or your affairs suppose,
    But like a sad slave stay and think of naught

Save, where you are, how happy you make those.
So true a fool is love that in your will,
Though you do anything, he thinks no ill.
1609 *Sonnets,* sonnet 57.

67 Like as the waves make towards the pebbled shore,
So do our minutes hasten to their end.
1609 *Sonnets,* sonnet 60.

68 Since brass, nor stone, nor earth, nor boundless sea,
But sad mortality o'ersways their power,
How with this rage shall beauty hold a plea,
Whose action is no stronger than a flower?
O how shall summer's honey breath hold out
Against the wrackful siege of battering days
When rocks impregnable are not so stout,
Nor gates of steel so strong, but time decays?
O fearful meditation! where, alack,
Shall time's best jewel from time's chest lie hid,
Or what strong hand can hold his swift foot back,
Or who his spoil of beauty can forbid?
O none, unless this miracle have might:
That is black ink my love may still shine bright.
1609 *Sonnets,* sonnet 65.

69 Right perfection wrongfully disgraced.
1609 *Sonnets,* sonnet 66.

70 Simple truth miscalled simplicity.
1609 *Sonnets,* sonnet 66.

71 They look into the beauty of thy mind,
And that in guess they measure by thy deeds.
1609 *Sonnets,* sonnet 69.

72 No longer mourn for me when I am dead
Than you shall hear the surly sullen bell
Give warning to the world that I am fled
From this vile world with vilest worms to dwell.
Nay, if you read this line, remember not
The hand that writ it; for I love you so
That I in your sweet thoughts would be forgot
If thinking on me then should make you woe.
O, if, I say, you look upon this verse
When I perhaps compounded am with clay,
Do not so much as my poor name rehearse,
But let your love even with my life decay,
Lest the wise world should look into your moan
And mock you with me after I am gone.
1609 *Sonnets,* sonnet 71.

73 That time of year thou mayst in me behold
When yellow leaves, or none, or few, do hang
Upon those boughs which shake against the cold,
Bare ruined choirs where late the sweet birds sang.
In me thou seest the twilight of such day
As after sunset fadeth in the west,
Which by and by black night doth take away,
Death's second self. that seals up all in rest.

1609 *Sonnets,* sonnet 73.

74 O know, sweet love, I always write of you,
And you and love are still my argument.
1609 *Sonnets,* sonnet 76.

75 For as the sun is daily new and old,,
So is my love, still telling what is told.
1609 *Sonnets,* sonnet 76.

76 Thy glass will show thee how thy beauties wear,
Thy dial how thy precious minutes waste,
The vacant leaves thy mind's imprint will bear,
And of this book this learning mayst thou taste:
The wrinkles which thy glass will truly show
Of mouthèd graves will give thee memory;
Thou by thy dial's shady stealth mayst know
Time's thievish progress to eternity.
1609 *Sonnets,* sonnet 77.

77 Who is it that says most which can say more
Than this rich praise: that you alone are you.
1609 *Sonnets,* sonnet 84.

78 Farewell—thou art too dear for my possessing,
And like enough thou know'st thy estimate.
The charter of thy worth gives thee releasing;
My bonds in thee are all determinate.
For how do I hold thee but by thy granting,
And for that riches where is my deserving?
The cause of this fair gift in me is wanting,
And so my patent back again is swerving.
Thyself thou gav'st, thy own worth then not
  knowing,
Or me to whom thou gav'st it else mistaking;
So thy great gift, upon misprision growing,
Comes home again, on better judgement making.
Thus have I had thee as a dream doth flatter:
In sleep a king, but waking no such matter.
1609 *Sonnets,* sonnet 87.

79 So shall I live supposing thou art true
Like a deceived husband; so love's face
May still seem love to me, though altered new.
1609 *Sonnets,* sonnet 93.

80 For sweetest things turn sourest by their deeds:
Lilies that fester smell far worse than weeds.
1609 *Sonnets,* sonnet 94.

81 They that have power to hurt and will do none,
That do not do the thing they most do show,
Who moving others are themselves as stone,
Unmovèd, cold, and to temptation slow—
They rightly do inherit heaven's graces,
And husband nature's riches from expense;
They are the lords and owners of their faces.
1609 *Sonnets,* sonnet 94.

82 How like a winter hath my absence been

From thee, the pleasure of the fleeting year!
What freezings have I felt, what dark days seen.
1609 *Sonnets*, sonnet 97.

83 From you have I been absent in the spring
When proud-pied April, dressed in all his trim,
Hath put a spirit of youth in everything.
1609 *Sonnets*, sonnet 98.

84 To me, fair friend, you never can be old;
For as you were when first your eye I eyed,
Such seems your beauty still.
1609 *Sonnets*, sonnet 104.

85 Kind is my love today, tomorrow kind,
Still constant in a wondrous excellence.
1609 *Sonnets*, sonnet 105.

86 Not mine own fears nor the prophetic soul
Of the wide world dreaming on things to come
Can yet the lease of my true love control,
Supposed as forfeit to a confined doom.
1609 *Sonnets*, sonnet 107.

87 What's in the brain that ink may character
Which hath not figured to thee my true spirit?
What's new to speak, what now to register,
That may express my love or thy dear merit?
Nothing, sweet boy; but yet like prayers divine
I must each day say o'er the very same,
Counting no old thing old, thou mine, I thine,
Even as when first I hallowed thy fair name.
1609 *Sonnets*, sonnet 108.

88 O never say that I was false of heart,
Though absence seemed my flame to qualify.
1609 *Sonnets*, sonnet 109.

89 Let me not to the marriage of true minds
Admit impediments. Love is not love
Which alters when it alteration finds,
Or bends with the remover to remove.
O no, it is an ever fixèd mark
That looks on tempests and is never shaken;
It is the star to every wand'ring barque,
Whose worth's unknown although his height be
    taken.
Love's not time's fool, though rosy lips and cheeks
Within his bending sickle's compass come;
Love alters not with his brief hours and weeks,
But bears it out even to the edge of doom.
If this be error and upon me proved,
I never writ, nor no man ever loved.
1609 *Sonnets*, sonnet 116.

90 What potions have I drunk of siren tears
Distilled from limbecks foul as hell within,
Applying fears to hopes and hopes to fears,
Still losing when I saw myself to win!

1609 *Sonnets*, sonnet 119.

91 For if you were by my unkindness shaken,
As I by yours, you've passed a hell of time.
1609 *Sonnets*, sonnet 120.

92 My mistress' eyes are nothing like the sun;
Coral is far more red than her lips' red.
If snow be white, why then her breasts are dun;
If hairs be wires, black wires grow on her head.
I have seen roses damasked, red and white,
But no such roses see I in her cheeks;
And in some perfumes is there more delight
Than the breath that from my mistress reeks.
I love to hear her speak, yet well I know
That music hath a far more pleasing sound.
I grant I never saw a goddess go:
My mistress when she walks treads on the ground.
And yet, by heaven, I think my love as rare
As any she belied with false compare.
1609 *Sonnets*, sonnet 130.

93 So thou, being rich in Will, add to thy Will
One will of mine to make thy large Will more.
Let no unkind no fair beseechers kill;
Think all but one, and me in that one Will.
1609 *Sonnets*, sonnet 135.

94 Whoever hath her wish, thou hast thy Will,
And Will to boot, and Will in overplus.
1609 *Sonnets*, sonnet 135.

95 When my love swears that she is made of truth
I do believe her though I know she lies.
1609 *Sonnets*, sonnet 138.

96 Two loves I have, of comfort and despair,
Which like two spirits do suggest me still.
The better angel is a man right fair,
The worser spirit a woman coloured ill.
1609 *Sonnets*, sonnet 144.

97 My love is as a fever, longing still
For that which longer nurseth the disease,
Feeding on that which doth preserve the ill,
Th'uncertain sickly appetite to please.
My reason, the physician to my love,
Angry that his prescriptions are not kept,
Hath left me, and I desperate now approve
Desire is death, which physic did except.
Past cure I am, now reason is past care,
And frantic mad with evermore unrest.
My thoughts and my discourse as madmen's are,
At random from the truth vainly expressed;
For I have sworn thee fair, and thought thee bright,
Who art as black as hell, as dark as night.
1609 *Sonnets*, sonnet 147.

98 Was there ever man had such luck? When I kissed
the jack upon an upcast to be hit away! I had a

hundred pound on't, and then a whoreson jackanapes must take me up for swearing.
1610 Cloten. *Cymbeline*, act 2, sc.1, l.1–4.

99 When a gentleman is disposed to swear it is not for any standers-by to curtail his oaths.
1610 Cloten. *Cymbeline*, act 2, sc.1, l.10–11.

1 On her left breast
A mole, cinque-spotted, like the crimson drops
I'th' bottom of a cowslip.
1610 Giacomo, of Innogen. *Cymbeline*, act 2, sc.2, l.37–9.

2 I am advised to give her music o' mornings; they say it will penetrate.
1610 Cloten, of Innogen. *Cymbeline*, act 2, sc.3, l.11–12.

3 Hark, hark, the lark at heaven gate sings,
And Phoebus gins arise.
1610 Musician, singing. *Cymbeline*, act 2, sc.3, l.19–20.

4 Is there no way for men to be, but women
Must be half-workers? We are bastards all.
1610 Posthumus. *Cymbeline*, act 2, sc.5, l.1–2.

5 I thought her
As chaste as unsunned snow.
1610 Posthumus, of Innogen. *Cymbeline*, act 2, sc.5, l.12–13.

6 I am stale, a garment out of fashion.
1610 Innogen. *Cymbeline*, act 3, sc.4, l.51.

7 Against self-slaughter
There is a prohibition so divine
That cravens my weak hand.
1610 Innogen. *Cymbeline*, act 3, sc.4, l.76–8.

8 Thus may poor fools
Believe false teachers.
1610 Innogen. *Cymbeline*, act 3, sc.4, l.84–5.

9 Though those that are betrayed
Do feel the treason sharply, yet the traitor
Stands in worse case of woe.
1610 Innogen. *Cymbeline*, act 3, sc.4, l.85–7.

10 Hath Britain all the sun that shines? Day, night,
Are they not but in Britain? I'th' world's volume
Our Britain seems as of it but not in't,
In a great pool a swan's nest.
1610 Innogen to Pisanio. *Cymbeline*, act 3, sc.4, l.137–40.

11 Thou art all the comfort
The gods will diet me with.
1610 Innogen to Pisanio. *Cymbeline*, act 3, sc.4, l.180–1.

12 Weariness
Can snore upon the flint when resty sloth
Finds the down pillow hard.
1610 Belarius. *Cymbeline*, act 3, sc.6, l.33–5.

13 By Jupiter, an angel—or, if not,
An earthly paragon.
1610 Belarius, of Innogen in disguise. *Cymbeline*, act 3, sc.6, l.42–3.

14 All gold and silver rather turn to dirt.
1610 Arviragus. *Cymbeline*, act 3, sc.6, l.52.

15 Society is no comfort
To one not sociable.
1610 Innogen. *Cymbeline*, act 4, sc.2, l.12–13.

16 Fear no more the heat o'th' sun,
Nor the furious winter's rages.
Thou thy worldly task hast done,
Home art gone and ta'en thy wages.
Golden lads and girls all must,
As chimney-sweepers, come to dust.
1610 Guiderius. *Cymbeline*, act 4, sc.2, l.259–64.

17 By medicine life may be prolonged, yet death
Will seize the doctor too.
1610 Cymbeline. *Cymbeline*, act 5, sc.6, l.29–30.

18 The power that I have on you is to spare you.
1610 Posthumus to Giacomo. *Cymbeline*, act 5, sc.6, l.419.

19 What seest thou else
In the dark backward and abyss of time?
1611 Prospero to Miranda. *The Tempest*, act 1, sc.2, l.49–50.

20 I find my zenith doth depend upon
A most auspicious star, whose influence
If now I court not, but omit, my fortunes
Will ever after droop.
1611 Prospero to Miranda. *The Tempest*, act 1, sc.2, l.182–5.

21 Thou art inclined to sleep; 'tis a good dullness,
And give it way. I know thou canst not choose.
1611 Prospero to Miranda. *The Tempest*, act 1, sc.2, l.186–7.

22 You taught me language, and my profit on't
Is I know how to curse.
1611 Caliban to Miranda. *The Tempest*, act 1, sc.2, l.365–6.

23 Come unto these yellow sands,
And then take hands.
1611 Ariel, singing. *The Tempest*, act 1, sc.2, l.377–8.

24 This music crept by me upon the waters,
Allaying both their fury and my passion
With its sweet air.
1611 Ferdinand. *The Tempest*, act 1, sc.2, l.394–6.

25 Full fathom five thy father lies.
Of his bones are coral made.
1611 Ariel. *The Tempest*, act 1, sc.2, l.399–400.

26 Nothing of him that doth fade
But doth suffer a sea-change
Into something rich and strange.
1611 Ariel. *The Tempest*, act 1, sc.2, l.402–4.

27 He receives comfort like cold porridge.
1611 Sebastian of Alonso. *The Tempest*, act 2, sc.1, l.11.

28 Look, he's winding up the watch of his wit.
    By and by it will strike.
    1611 Sebastian, of Gonzalo. *The Tempest*, act 2, sc.1, l.13–14.

29 Misery acquaints a man with strange bedfellows.
    1611 Trinculo, of Caliban. *The Tempest*, act 2, sc.2, l.39.

30 'Ban, 'ban, Cacaliban
    Has a new master.—Get a new man!
    1611 Caliban. *The Tempest*, act 2, sc.2, l.183–4.

31 FERDINAND: I do beseech you,
    Chiefly that I might set it in my prayers,
    What is your name?
    MIRANDA: Miranda. O my father,
    I have broke your hest to say so!
    FERDINAND: Admired Miranda!
    Indeed the top of admiration, Worth what's
    Worth what's dearest to the world.
    1611 *The Tempest*, act 3, sc.1, l.36–9. Shakespeare invented the
    name Miranda, taking it from the Latin word meaning 'worthy
    to be admired'.

32 Remember
    First to possess his books, for without them
    He's but a sot as I am, nor hath not
    One spirit to command–they all do hate him
    As rootedly as I. Burn but his books.
    1611 Caliban of Prospero. *The Tempest*, act 3, sc.2, l.92–6.

33 He that dies pays all debts.
    1611 Stefano. *The Tempest*, act 3, sc.2, l.134.

34 The isle is full of noises,
    Sound, and sweet airs, that give delight and hurt
      not.
    1611 Caliban. *The Tempest*, act 3, sc.2, l.138–9.

35 Thou shalt find that she will outstrip all praise,
    And make it halt behind her.
    1611 Prospero, of Miranda. *The Tempest*, act 4, sc.1, l.10–11.

36 The cloud-capped towers, the gorgeous palaces,
    The solemn temples, the great globe itself,
    Yea, all which it inherit, shall dissolve;
    And, like this insubstantial pageant faded,
    Leave not a rack behind.
    1611 Prospero. *The Tempest*, act 4, sc.1, l.152–6.

37 We are such stuff
    As dreams are made on, and our little life
    Is rounded with a sleep.
    1611 Prospero. *The Tempest*, act 4, sc.1, l.156–8.

38 They were red-hot with drinking;
    So full of valour that they smote the air
    For breathing in their faces.
    1611 Ariel. *The Tempest*, act 4, sc.1, l.171–3.

39 This rough magic
    I here abjure.
    1611 Prospero. *The Tempest*, act 5, sc.1, l.50–1.

40 I'll break my staff,
    Bury it certain fathoms in the earth,
    And deeper than did ever plummet sound
    I'll drown my book.
    1611 Prospero. *The Tempest*, act 5, sc.1, l.54–7.

41 Where the bee sucks, there suck I:
    In a cowslip's bell I lie;
    There I couch when owls do cry.
    On the bat's back I do fly
    After summer merrily.
    Merrily, merrily shall I live now
    Under the blossom that hangs on the bough.
    1611 Ariel's song. *The Tempest*, act 5, sc.1, l.88–94.

42 How beauteous mankind is! O brave new
      world
    That hath such people in't!
    1611 Miranda. *The Tempest*, act 5, sc.1, l.186–7.

43 What a thrice-double ass
    Was I to take this drunkard for a god,
    And worship this dull fool!
    1611 Caliban. *The Tempest*, act 5, sc.1, l.299–301.

44 Now my charms are all o'erthrown,
    And what strength I have's mine own.
    1611 Prospero. *The Tempest*, epilogue, l. 1–2.

45 Heat not a furnace for your foe so hot
    That it do singe yourself.
    1613 Norfolk. *Henry VIII*, act 1, sc.1, l.140–1.

46 Travelled gallants
    That fill the court with quarrels, talk, and tailors.
    1613 Lovell. *Henry VIII*, act 1, sc.3, l.19–20.

47 Good company, good wine, good welcome
    Can make good people.
    1613 Guildford. *Henry VIII*, act 1, sc.4, l.6–7.

48 Two women placed together makes cold weather.
    1613 Lord Chamberlain. *Henry VIII*, act 1, sc.4, l.22.

49 If I chance to talk a little wild, forgive me.
    I had it from my father.
    1613 Sands. *Henry VIII*, act 1, sc.4, l.26–7.

50 Those you make friends
    And give your hearts to, when they once perceive
    The least rub in your fortunes, fall away
    Like water from ye.
    1613 Buckingham. *Henry VIII*, act 2, sc.1, l.128–31.

51 I would not be a queen
    For all the world.
    1613 Anne Boleyn. *Henry VIII*, act 2, sc.3, l.45–6.

52 You have many enemies that know not
    Why they are so, but, like to village curs,
    Bark when their fellows do.
    1613 Henry to Wolsey. *Henry VIII*, act 2, sc.4, l.155–7.

53 Orpheus with his lute made trees,
And the mountain tops that freeze,
Bow themselves when he did sing.
1613 Gentlewoman, singing. *Henry VIII*, act 3, sc.1, l.3–5.

54 Everything that heard him play,
Even the billows of the sea,
Hung their heads, and then lay by.
In sweet music is such art,
Killing care and grief of heart
Fall asleep, or hearing, die.
1613 Gentlewoman, singing. *Henry VIII*, act 3, sc.1, l. 9–14.

55 Methought I stood not in the smile of heaven.
1613 Henry. *Henry VIII*, act 2, sc.4, l.183–4.

56 In sweet music is such art,
Killing care and grief of heart
Fall asleep, or hearing die.
1613 Gentlewoman. *Henry VIII*, act 3, sc.1, l.13–15.

57 Yet I know her for
A spleeny Lutheran, and not wholesome to
Our cause.
1613 Cardinal Wolsey of Anne Boleyn. *Henry VIII*, act 3, sc.2, l.99–101.

58 Nature does require
Her times of preservation.
1613 Wolsey to Henry. *Henry VIII*, act 3, sc.2, l.147–8.

59 I have touched the highest point of all my
greatness,
And from that full meridian of my glory
I haste now to my setting.
1613 Wolsey. *Henry VIII*, act 3, sc.2, l.224–6.

60 I feel within me
A peace above all earthly dignities,
A still and quiet conscience.
1613 Wolsey. *Henry VIII*, act 3, sc.2, l.379–81.

61 This is the state of man. He puts forth
The tender leaves of hopes; tomorrow blossoms,
And bears his blushing honours thick upon
him;
The third day comes a frost, a killing frost,
And when he thinks, good easy man, full surely
His greatness is a-ripening, nips his root,
And then he falls, as I do.
1613 Wolsey. *Henry VIII*, act 3, sc.2, l.353–9.

62 Had I but served my God with half the zeal
I served my King, He would not in mine age
Have left me naked to mine enemies.
1613 Wolsey. *Henry VIII*, act 3, sc.2, l.456–8.

63 Still in thy right hand carry gentle peace

To silence envious tongues.
1613 Wolsey. *Henry VIII*, act 3, sc.2, l.446–7.

64 An old man broken with the storms of state
Is come to lay his weary bones among ye.
Give him a little earth, for charity.
1613 Griffith, recalling Wolsey. *Henry VIII*, act 4, sc.2, l.21–3.

65 Men's evil manners live in brass, their virtues
We write in water.
1613 Griffith. *Henry VIII*, act 4, sc.2, l.45–6.

66 That comfort comes too late,
'Tis like a pardon after execution.
1613 Katherine. *Henry VIII*, act 4, sc.2, l.121–2.

67 Good grows with her.
In her days every man shall eat in safety
Under his own vine what he plants, and sing
The merry songs of peace to all his neighbours.
1613 Cranmer, of Elizabeth. *Henry VIII*, act 5, sc.4, l.32–5.

Shange, Ntozake originally *Paulette Williams* 1948–

Black US writer, who adopted a Zulu name for political reasons. She has written mainly for the stage, often adopting a multi-media approach combining poetry, dance and music.

68 For coloured girls who have considered suicide /
when the rainbow is enuf.
1975 Title of 'choreo-poem'.

Shankly, Bill (William) 1913–81

Scottish footballer and manager. A player with Preston North End and Scotland, he established a reputation as one of the finest managers of his generation through his management of Liverpool in the 1960s and was widely known for his grim determination and biting wit.

69 Some people think football is a matter of life and death. I don't like that attitude. I can assure them it is much more serious than that.
Quoted in the *Sunday Times*, 4 Oct 1981.

71 I don't drop players, I make changes.
Quoted in Peter Ball and Phil Shaw *The Book of Football Quotations* (1989).

72 If Everton were playing down at the bottom of my garden, I'd draw the curtains.
Quoted in Colin Jarman *The Guinness Dictionary of Sports Quotations* (1989).

73 If you're in the penalty area and aren't sure what to do with the ball, just stick it in the net, and we'll discuss your options afterwards.

Quoted in Colin Jarman *The Guinness Dictionary of Sports Quotations* (1989).

74 Of course I didn't take my wife to see Rochdale as an anniversary present. It was her birthday. Would I have got married during the football season? And anyway it wasn't Rochdale, it was Rochdale reserves.

Quoted in Peter Ball and Phil Shaw *The Book of Football Quotations* (1989).

75 This city has two great teams—Liverpool and Liverpool reserves.

Deliberately ignoring rival club Everton. Quoted in Colin Jarman *The Guinness Dictionary of Sports Quotations* (1989).

76 We murdered them 0–0.

Quoted in Colin Jarman *The Guinness Dictionary of Sports Quotations* (1989).

77 Me having no education, I had to use my brains.

Quoted in David Pickering *The Cassell Soccer Companion* (1994).

Shapin, Steven 1955–

US sociologist.

78 The very power of science to hold knowledge as collective property is founded upon a degree and a quality of trust which are arguably unparalleled elsewhere in our culture... Scientists know so much about the natural world by knowing so much about whom they can trust.

1994 *A Social History of Truth.*

Sharp, William pseudonym *Fiona Macleod*
1855–1905

Scottish writer and traveller. He published poetry and literary criticism, but he is best known as the author of a series of neo-Celtic romantic tales written under the pseudonym he systematically refused to acknowledge.

79 My heart is a lonely hunter that hunts on a lonely hill.

1896 'The Lonely Hunter', stanza 6. Carson McCullers adapted the phrase as the title of a 1940 novel, *The Heart is a Lonely Hunter.*

Sharpe, Tom (Thomas Ridley) 1928–

English novelist. His early works were plays written in South Africa. He returned to England in 1961, and became known for the vigorous satire of his comic novels.

80 The South African police would leave no stone unturned to see that nothing disturbed the even terror of their lives.

1973 *Indecent Exposure*, ch.1.

81 Skullion had little use for contraceptives at the best of times. Unnatural, he called them, and placed them in the lower social category of things along

with elastic-sided boots and made-up bow ties. Not the sort of attire for a gentleman.

1974 *Porterhouse Blue*, ch.9.

82 And besides, Mrs Forthby in the flesh was a different kettle of fish to Mrs Forthby in his fantasies. In the latter she had a multitude of perverse inclinations, which corresponded exactly with his own unfortunate requirements, while possessing a discretion that would have done credit to a Trappist nun. In the flesh she was disappointingly different.

1975 *Blott on the Landscape*, ch.3.

83 In the lotus position at her yoga class she managed to exude energy, and her attempts at Transcendental Meditation had been likened to a pressure-cooker on simmer.

1976 *Wilt*, ch.1.

84 God, in his view, had created a perfect world if the book of Genesis was to be believed and it had been going downhill ever since.

1976 *Wilt*, ch.17

85 All you had to do was tell people what they wanted to hear and they would believe you no matter how implausible your story might be.

1976 *Wilt*, ch.18

86 The Rev St John Froude put the phone down thoughtfully. The notion that he was sharing the house with a disembodied and recently murdered woman was not one that he had wanted to put to his caller. His reputation for eccentricity was already sufficiently widespread without adding to it.

1976 *Wilt*, ch.19

87 If any writer thinks the world is full of middle-class people of nice sensibilities, then he is out of his mind.

1985 In *The Observer*, 3 Feb.

Shaw, George Bernard 1856–1950

Anglo-Irish dramatist and socialist. He moved to London in 1876 and in 1882 joined the Fabian Society. He wrote over 40 plays including *Arms and the Man* (1894, published 1898), *Candida* (1895), *Man and Superman* (1903), *Pygmalion* (1913), *Saint Joan* (1923, published 1924) and *The Apple Cart* (1929). He was also a lifelong advocate of vegetarianism, and a passionate supporter of spelling reform. In 1935 he was awarded the Nobel Prize for Literature.

88 Money is indeed the most important thing in the world: and all sound and successful personal and national morality should have this fact for its basis.

1880 *The Irrational Knot*, preface.

89 Reminiscences make one feel so deliciously aged and sad.

1880 *The Irrational Knot*, ch.14.

90 A man who has no office to go to——I don't care who he is——is a trial of which you can have no conception.
1880 *The Irrational Knot*, ch.18.

91 'Do you know what a pessimist is?'
'A man who thinks everybody is as nasty as himself, and hates them for it.'
1887 *An Unsocial Socialist*, ch.5.

92 Don't ask me for promises until I know what I am promising.
1894 Catherine to Raina. *Arms and the Man*, act 1.

93 You can always tell an old soldier by the inside of his holsters and cartridge boxes. The young ones carry pistols and cartridges; the old ones, grub.
1894 The Man to Raina. *Arms and the Man*, act 1.

94 Oh, you are a very poor soldier—a chocolate cream soldier!
1894 Raina to The Man. *Arms and the Man*, act 1.

95 You're not a man, you're a machine.
1894 Sergius to Bluntschli. *Arms and the Man*, act 3.

96 We have no more right to consume happiness without producing it than to consume wealth without producing it.
1895 Morell to Lexy. *Candida*, act 1.

97 Do you think that the things people make fools of themselves about are any less real and true than the things they behave sensibly about? They are more true: they are the only things that are true.
1895 Marchbanks to Morell. *Candida*, act 1.

98 It is easy—terribly easy—to shake a man's faith in himself. To take advantage of that to break a man's spirit is devil's work.
1895 Morell to Marchbanks. *Candida*, act 1.

99 Wicked people means people who have no love: therefore they have no shame. They have the power to ask for love because they don't need it: they have the power to offer it because they have none to give. But we, who have love, and long to mingle it with the love of others: we cannot utter a word. You find that, don't you?
1895 Marchbanks to Proserpine. *Candida*, act 2.

1 I'm only a beer teetotaller, not a champagne teetotaller.
1895 *Candida*, act 3.

2 I no longer desire happiness: life is nobler than that.
1895 Marchbanks. *Candida*, act 3.

3 We're from Madeira, but perfectly respectable, so far.

1896 Philip Clandon to Valentine. *You Never Can Tell*, act 1.

4 We don't bother much about dress and manners in England, because, as a nation, we don't dress well and we've no manners.
1896 Valentine to Dolly and Philip Clandon. *You Never Can Tell*, act 1.

5 Brains are not everything.
1898 Rev Samuel Gardner. *Mrs Warren's Profession*, act 1.

6 If there is anything I hate in a woman, it's want of character.
1898 Mrs Warren. *Mrs Warren's Profession*, act 2.

7 The only way for a woman to provide for herself decently is for her to be good to some man that can afford to be good to her.
1898 Mrs Warren to Vivie Warren. *Mrs Warren's Profession*, act 2.

8 There are no secrets better kept than the secrets everybody guesses.
1898 Sir George Crofts. *Mrs Warren's Profession*, act 3.

9 'Damn you!'
'You need not. I feel among the damned already.'
1898 Sir George Crofts and Vivie Warren. *Mrs Warren's Profession*, act 3.

10 Miss Warren is a great devotee of the Gospel of Getting On.
1898 Praed. *Mrs Warren's Profession*, act 4.

11 There is nothing so bad or so good that you will not find Englishmen doing it; but you will never find an Englishman in the wrong. He does everything on principle. He fights you on patriotic principles; he robs you on business principles; he enslaves you on imperial principles; he bullies you on manly principles; he supports his king on loyal principles and cuts off his head on republican principles.
1897 *The Man of Destiny*, p.201.

12 The great advantage of a hotel is that it's a refuge from home life.
1896 *You Never Can Tell*, act 2.

13 Well, sir, you never can tell. That's a principle in life with me, sir, if you'll excuse my having such a thing, sir.
1896 Waiter to Fergus Crampton. *You Never Can Tell*, act 2.

14 The worst sin towards our fellow creatures is not to hate them, but to be indifferent to them: that's the essence of inhumanity.
1897 Pastor Anderson to Judith Anderson. *The Devil's Disciple*, act 2.

15 Martyrdom…the only way in which a man can become famous without ability.

1897 *The Devil's Disciple*, act 3.

16 I never expect a soldier to think, sir.
    1897 Richard Dudgeon to Major Swindon. *The Devil's Disciple*, act 3.

17 'I can't believe it! What will History say?'
    'History, sir, will tell lies as usual.'
    1897 Major Swindon and Gen Burgoyne. *The Devil's Disciple*, act 3.

18 Your friend the British soldier can stand up to anything except the British War Office.
    1897 Gen Burgoyne to Major Swindon. *The Devil's Disciple*, act 3.

19 He is a barbarian, and thinks that the customs of his tribe and island are the laws of nature.
    1899 Of the Briton. Caesar to Theodotus. *Caesar and Cleopatra*, act 2.

20 When a stupid man is doing something he is ashamed of, he always declares that it is his duty.
    1899 Apollodorus. *Caesar and Cleopatra*, act 3.

21 A man of great common sense and good taste, meaning thereby a man without originality or moral courage.
    1899 Of Caesar. *Caesar and Cleopatra*, notes.

22 But a lifetime of happiness! No man alive could bear it: it would be hell on earth.
    1903 John Tanner. *Man and Superman*, act 1.

23 I am proud of your contempt for my character and opinions, sir.
    1903 Roebuck Ramsden to John Tanner. *Man and Superman*, act 1.

24 The more things a man is ashamed of, the more respectable he is.
    1903 John Tanner. *Man and Superman*, act 1.

25 Vitality in a woman is a blind fury of creation.
    1903 John Tanner to Octavius Robinson. *Man and Superman*, act 1.

26 Of all human struggles there is none so treacherous and remorseless as the struggle between the artist man and the mother woman.
    1903 John Tanner. *Man and Superman*, act 1.

27 A sensitive boy's humiliations may be very good fun for ordinary thickskinned grown-ups; but to the boy himself they are so acute, so ignominious, that he cannot confess them—cannot but deny them passionately.
    1903 Tanner. *Man and Superman*, act 1.

28 There is no love sincerer than the love of food.
    1903 John Tanner to Octavius. *Man and Superman*, act 1.

29 That damnable woman's trick of heaping obligations on a man, of placing yourself so entirely

and helplessly at his mercy that at last he dare not take a step without running to you for leave. I know a poor wretch whose one desire in life is to run away from his wife. She prevents him by threatening to throw herself in front of the engine of the train he leaves her in. That is what all women do. If we try to go where you do not want us to go there is no law to prevent us; but when we take the first step your breasts are under our foot as it descends: your bodies are under our wheels as we start. No woman shall ever enslave me in that way.
    1903 John Tanner to Ann Whitefield. *Man and Superman*, act 1.

30 You think that you are Ann's suitor; that you are the pursuer and she the pursued... Fool: it is you who are pursued, the marked down quarry, the destined prey.
    1903 John Tanner to Octavius Robinson. *Man and Superman*, act 2.

31 'I am a brigand: I live by robbing the rich.'
    'I am a gentleman: I live by robbing the poor.'
    1903 Mendoza and John Tanner. *Man and Superman*, act 3.

32 Hell is full of musical amateurs: music is the brandy of the damned.
    1903 Don Juan to the Devil. *Man and Superman*, act 3.

33 Englishmen never will be slaves: they are free to do whatever the Government and public allow them to do.
    1903 The Devil to Ann Whitefield. *Man and Superman*, act 3.

34 An Englishman thinks he is moral when he is only uncomfortable.
    1903 The Devil. *Man and Superman*, act 3.

35 In the arts of life man invents nothing; but in the arts of death he outdoes Nature herself, and produces by chemistry and machinery all the slaughter of plague, pestilence and famine.
    1903 The Devil to Don Juan. *Man and Superman*, act 3.

36 In the arts of peace Man is a bungler.
    1903 The Devil to Don Juan. *Man and Superman*, act 3.

37 As an old soldier I admit the cowardice: it's as universal as sea sickness, and matters just as little.
    1903 The Statue. *Man and Superman*, act 3

38 Sexually, Woman is Nature's contrivance for perpetuating its highest achievement.
    1903 Don Juan to Ana. *Man and Superman*, act 3.

39 When the military man approaches, the world locks up its spoons and packs off its womankind.
    1903 Don Juan. *Man and Superman*, act 3.

40 What is virtue but the Trade Unionism of the married?
    1903 Don Juan to Ann Whitefield. *Man and Superman*, act 3.

41 Marriage is the most licentious of human institutions.
   1903 Don Juan. *Man and Superman*, act 3.

42 Those who talk most about the blessings of marriage and the constancy of its vows are the very people who declare that if the claim were broken and the prisoners were left free to choose, the whole social fabric would fly asunder. You can't have the argument both ways. If the prisoner is happy, why lock him in? If he is not, why pretend that he is?
   1903 Don Juan to Ann Whitefield. *Man and Superman*, act 3.

43 Beauty is all very well at first sight; but who ever looks at it when it has been in the house three days?
   1903 Ann Whitefield. *Man and Superman*, act 4.

44 Revolutions have never lightened the burden of tyranny: they have only shifted it to another shoulder.
   1903 *Man and Superman*, 'The Revolutionist's Handbook and Pocket Companion, by John Tanner', foreword.

45 The art of government is the organization of idolatry.
   1903 *Man and Superman*, 'Maxims for Revolutionists: Idolatry'.

46 Democracy substitutes election by the incompetent many for appointment by the corrupt few.
   1903 *Man and Superman*, 'Maxims for Revolutionists: Democracy'.

47 Liberty means responsibility. That is why most men dread it.
   1903 *Man and Superman*, 'Maxims for Revolutionists: Liberty and Equality'.

48 He who can, does. He who cannot, teaches.
   1903 *Man and Superman*, 'Maxims for Revolutionists: Education'.

49 Marriage is popular because it combines the maximum of temptation with the maximum of opportunity.
   1903 *Man and Superman*, 'Maxims for Revolutionists: Marriage'.

50 Titles distinguish the mediocre, embarrass the superior, and are disgraced by the inferior.
   1903 *Man and Superman*, 'Maxims for Revolutionists: Titles'.

51 When domestic servants are treated as human beings it is not worth while to keep them.
   1903 *Man and Superman*, 'Maxims for Revolutionists: Servants'.

52 If you strike a child take care that you strike it in anger, even at the risk of maiming it for life. A blow in cold blood neither can nor should be forgiven.
   1903 *Man and Superman*, 'Maxims for Revolutionists: How to Beat Children'.

53 Beware of the man whose God is in the skies.
   1903 *Man and Superman*, 'Maxims for Revolutionists: Religion'.

54 Self-denial is not a virtue: it is only the effect of prudence on rascality.
   1903 *Man and Superman*, 'Maxims for Revolutionists: Virtues and Vices'.

55 A moderately honest man with a moderately faithful wife, moderate drinkers both, in a moderately healthy house: that is the true middle-class unit.
   1903 *Man and Superman*, 'Maxims for Revolutionists: Moderation'.

56 The reasonable man adapts himself to the world: the unreasonable one persists in trying to adapt the world to himself. Therefore all progress depends on the unreasonable man.
   1903 *Man and Superman*, 'Maxims for Revolutionists: Reason'.

57 The man who listens to Reason is lost: Reason enslaves all whose minds are not strong enough to master her.
   1903 *Man and Superman*, 'Maxims for Revolutionists: Reason'.

58 Decency is Indecency's conspiracy of silence.
   1903 *Man and Superman*, 'Maxims for Revolutionists: Decency'.

59 Life levels all men: death reveals the eminent.
   1903 *Man and Superman*, 'Maxims for Revolutionists: Fame'.

60 Home is the girl's prison and the woman's workhouse.
   1903 *Man and Superman*, 'Maxims for Revolutionists: Women in the Home'.

61 Every man over forty is a scoundrel.
   1903 *Man and Superman*, 'Maxims for Revolutionists: Stray Sayings'.

62 Youth, which is forgiven everything, forgives itself nothing: age, which forgives itself everything, is forgiven nothing.
   1903 *Man and Superman*, 'Maxims for Revolutionists: Stray Sayings'.

63 Take care to get what you like or you will be forced to like what you get.
   1903 *Man and Superman*, 'Maxims for Revolutionists: Stray Sayings'.

64 Beware of the man who does not return your blow: he neither forgives you nor allows you to forgive yourself.
   1903 *Man and Superman*, 'Maxims for Revolutionists: Stray Sayings'.

65 Self-sacrifice enables us to sacrifice other people without blushing.

1903 *Man and Superman*, 'Maxims for Revolutionists: Self-Sacrifice'.

66 Do not do unto others as you would they should do to you. Their tastes may not be the same.
1903 *Man and Superman*, 'Maxims for Revolutionists: The Golden Rule'.

67 The golden rule is that there are no golden rules.
1903 *Man and Superman*, 'Maxims for Revolutionists: The Golden Rule'.

68 When a man wants to murder a tiger he calls it sport; when a tiger wants to murder him he calls it ferocity.
1903 *Man and Superman*, 'Maxims for Revolutionists: Crime and Punishment'.

69 An Irishman's imagination never lets him alone, never convinces him, never satisfies him; but it makes him that he can't face reality nor deal with it nor handle it nor conquer it: he can only sneer at them that do, and be 'agreeable to strangers', like a good-for-nothing woman on the streets.
1904 Larry Doyle to Tom Broadbent. *John Bull's Other Island*, act 1.

70 An Irishman's heart is nothing but his imagination.
1904 Larry Doyle to Tom Broadbent. *John Bull's Other Island*, act 1.

71 The poor silly-clever Irishman takes off his hat to God's Englishman.
1904 Larry Doyle. *John Bull's Other Island*, act 1.

72 My way of joking is to tell the truth. It's the funniest joke in the world.
1904 Peter Keegan to Nora Reilly. *John Bull's Other Island*, act 2.

73 I am sincere; and my intentions are perfectly honourable. I think you will accept the fact that I'm an Englishman as a guarantee that I am not a man to act hastily or romantically.
1904 Tom Broadbent to Nora Reilly. *John Bull's Other Island*, act 2.

74 You jast keep your air on and listen to me. You Awrish people are too well off: thet's wots the matter with you.
1904 Hodson to Matthew Haffigan. *John Bull's Other Island*, act 3.

75 There are only two qualities in the world: efficiency and inefficiency, and only two sorts of people: the efficient and the inefficient.
1904 Tom Broadbent. *John Bull's Other Island*, act 4.

76 In my dreams is a country where the State is the Church and the Church the people: three in one and one in three. It is a commonwealth in which work is play and play is life: three in one and one in three. It is a temple in which the priest is the worshipper and the worshipper the worshipped: three in one and one in three. It is a godhead in which all life is human and all humanity divine: three in one and one in three. It is, in short, the dream of a madman.
1904 Of Heaven, Keegan speaking. *John Bull's Other Island*, act 4.

77 The greatest of evils and the worst of crimes is poverty...our first duty—a duty to which every other consideration should be sacrificed—is not to be poor.
1905 *Major Barbara*, preface.

78 Nobody can say a word against Greek: it stamps a man at once as an educated gentleman.
1905 Lady Britomart Undershaft to Stephen. *Major Barbara*, act 1.

79 I am a Millionaire. That is my religion.
1905 Undershaft to Barbara Undershaft. *Major Barbara*, act 2.

80 I can't talk religion to a man with bodily hunger in his eyes.
1905 Barbara Undershaft. *Major Barbara*, act 2.

81 Alcohol is a very necessary article... It makes life bearable to millions of people who could not endure their existence if they were quite sober. It enables Parliament to do things at eleven at night that no sane person would do at eleven in the morning.
1905 Undershaft to Barbara Undershaft. *Major Barbara*, act 2.

82 It's nao good: you cawnt get rahnd me nah. Aw downt blieve in it; and Awve seen tody that Aw was rawt. Sao long, aol soupkitchener! Ta, ta, Mijor Earl's Grendorter! Wot prawce selvytion nah? Snobby Prawce! Ha! ha!
1905 Bill Walker to Barbara Undershaft. *Major Barbara*, act 2.

83 He knows nothing; and he thinks he knows everything. That points clearly to a political career.
1905 Undershaft speaking of Stephen. *Major Barbara*, act 3.

84 Like all young men, you greatly exaggerate the difference between one young woman and another.
1905 Undershaft about Adolphus Cusins. *Major Barbara*, act 3.

85 Fashions, after all, are only induced epidemics.
1906 *The Doctor's Dilemma*, 'Preface on Doctors: Fashions and Epidemics'.

86 Science becomes dangerous only when it imagines that it has reached its goal.
1906 *The Doctor's Dilemma*, preface, 'The Latest Theories'.

87 There is at bottom only one genuinely scientific treatment for all diseases, and that is to stimulate the phagocytes.
1906 BB (Sir Ralph Bloomfield Bonington). *The Doctor's Dilemma*, act 1.

88 All professions are conspiracies against the laity.
1906 Sir Patrick Cullen. *The Doctor's Dilemma*, act 1.

89 A man's behaviour may be quite harmless and even beneficial, when he is morally behaving like a scoundrel. And he may do great harm when he is morally acting on the highest principles.
1906 BB. *The Doctor's Dilemma*, act 3.

90 The criminal law is no use to decent people.
1906 Sir Patrick. *The Doctor's Dilemma*, act 3.

91 There's almost as many different sorts of marriage as there's different sorts of people. There's the young things that marry for love, not knowing what they're doing, and the old things that marry for money and comfort and companionship. There's the people that marry for children. There's the people that don't intend to have children and that aren't fit to have them. There's the people that marry because they're so much run after by the other sex that they have to put a stop to it somehow. There's the people that want to try a new experience, and the people that want to have done with experiences.
1908 Bill Collins. *Getting Married*.

92 Home life as we understand it is no more natural to us than a cage is natural to a cockatoo.
1908 *Getting Married*, preface, 'Hearth and Home'.

93 The one point on which all women are in furious secret rebellion against the existing law is the saddling of the right to a child with the obligation to become the servant of a man.
1908 *Getting Married*, preface, 'The Right to Motherhood'.

94 Physically there is nothing to distinguish human society from the farm-yard except that children are more troublesome and costly than chickens and calves, and that men and women are not so completely enslaved as farm stock.
1908 *Getting Married*, preface, 'The Personal Sentimental Basis of Monogamy'.

95 You see, family life is all the life she knows: she's like a bird born in a cage, that would die if you let it loose in the woods.
1908 Bill Collins about his wife. *Getting Married*.

96 A man is like a phonograph with half-a-dozen records. You soon get tired of them all; and yet you have to sit at table whilst he reels them off to every new visitor. In the end you have to be content with his common humanity.
1908 The Bishop of Chelsea. *Getting Married*.

97 I am a snob, not only in fact, but on principle.
1908 St John Hotchkiss. *Getting Married*.

98 Optimistic lies have such immense therapeutic value that a doctor who cannot tell them convincingly has mistaken his profession.
1910 *Misalliance*, preface.

99 Anybody on for a game of tennis?
1910 *Misalliance*. This may be the origin of 'Anyone for tennis?', as used in archetypal theatrical drawing-room comedies.

1 The English have no respect for their language, and will not teach their children to speak it. They spell it so abominably that no man can teach himself what it sounds like. It is impossible for an Englishman to open his mouth without making some other Englishman hate or despise him.
1913 *Pygmalion*, Preface.

2 He's a gentleman: look at his boots.
1913 *Pygmalion*, act 1.

3 I don't want to talk grammar, I want to talk like a lady.
1913 Eliza Doolittle. *Pygmalion*, act 2.

4 Have you ever met a man of good character where women are concerned?
1913 Higgins to Pickering. *Pygmalion*, act 2.

5 'Have you no morals, man?'
'Can't afford them, Governor.'
1913 Col Pickering and Alfred Doolittle. *Pygmalion*, act 2.

6 I'm one of the undeserving poor...up agen middle-class morality all the time... What is middle-class morality? Just an excuse for never giving me anything.
1913 Alfred Doolittle. *Pygmalion*, act 2.

7 Gin was mother's milk to her.
1913 Eliza speaking of her Aunt. *Pygmalion*, act 3.

8 Walk! Not bloody likely. I am going in a taxi.
1913 Eliza to Freddy. *Pygmalion*, act 3.

9 The secret of being miserable is to have leisure to bother about whether you are happy or not. The cure for it is occupation.
1914 *Parents and Children*.

10 A perpetual holiday is a good working definition of hell.
1914 *Parents and Children*.

11 I am a woman of the world, Hector; and I can assure you that if you will only take the trouble always to do the perfectly correct thing, and to say the perfectly correct thing, you can do just what you like.
1919 Lady Utterword to Hector Hushabye. *Heartbreak House*, act 1.

12 It's prudent to gain the whole world and lose your own soul. But don't forget that your soul sticks to you if you stick to it; but the world has a way of slipping through your fingers.
1919 Captain Shotover. *Heartbreak House*, act 2.

13 There are only two classes in good society in England: the equestrian classes and the neurotic classes.
1919 Lady Utterword. *Heartbreak House*, act 3.

14 Go anywhere in England where there are natural, wholesome, contented, and really nice English people; and what do you always find? That the stables are the real centre of the household.
1919 Lady Utterword. *Heartbreak House*, act 3.

15 This souls' prison we call England.
1919 Hector Hushabye. *Heartbreak House*, act 3.

16 The captain is in his bunk, drinking bottled ditch-water; and the crew is gambling in the forecastle. She will strike and sink and split. Do you think the laws of God will be suspended in favour of England because you were born in it?
1919 Captain Shotover. *Heartbreak House*, act 3.

17 Everyone can see that the people who hunt are the right people and the people who don't are the wrong ones.
1919 Lady Usherword to Mrs Hushabye. *Heartbreak House*, act 3.

18 All great truths begin as blasphemies.
1919 *Annajanska*, p.262.

19 I enjoy convalescence. It is the part that makes illness worth while.
1921 *Back to Methuselah*.

20 Silence is the most perfect expression of scorn.
1921 *Back to Methuselah*.

21 If ever I utter an oath again may my soul be blasted to eternal damnation!
1923 Captain La Hire. *Saint Joan*, sc.2.

22 No Englishman is ever fairly beaten.
1923 The Chaplain. *Saint Joan*, sc.4.

23 How can what an Englishman believes be heresy? It is a contradiction in terms.
1923 The Chaplain to Peter Cauchon. *Saint Joan*, sc.4.

24 Some men are born kings; and some are born statesmen. The two are seldom the same.
1923 Peter Cauchon. *Saint Joan*, sc.4.

25 Must then a Christ perish in torment in every age to save those that have no imagination?
1923 *Saint Joan*, epilogue.

26 Idiots are always in favour of inequality of income (their only chance of eminence), and the really great in favour of equality.
1928 *The Intelligent Woman's Guide to Socialism and Capitalism*.

27 Many men would hardly miss their heads, there is so little in them.
1929 King Magnus. *The Apple Cart*, act 1.

28 One man that has a mind and knows it can always beat ten men who haven't and don't.
1929 Joe Proteus. *The Apple Cart*, act 1.

29 As interesting as a wall can be.
c.1930 Asked what he thought of the Great Wall after his flight over China. Quoted in Hesketh Pearson *Bernard Shaw : His Life and Personality* (1961).

30 The fact is, there are no rules and there never were any rules, and there never will be any rules of musical composition except rules of thumb; and thumbs vary in length, like ears.
1931 *Music in London, 1890–1894*.

31 [The Red Flag] is the funeral march of a fried eel.
Quoted by Winston Churchill in *Great Contemporaries* (1937).

32 A perpendicular expression of a horizontal desire.
1962 Of dancing. Quoted in the *New Statesman*, 23 Mar.

33 That's the difference between us. You talk of art Mr Goldwyn, I think of money.
To Samuel Goldwyn. Quoted in David Niven *Bring on the Empty Horses* (1975).

34 Baseball has the great advantage over cricket of being sooner ended. It combines the best features of that primitive form of cricket known as Tip-and-Run with those of lawn tennis, Puss-in-the-corner and Handel's Messiah.
Quoted in Colin Jarman *The Guinness Dictionary of Sports Quotations* (1990).

35 No sportsman wants to kill a fox or the pheasant as I want to kill him when I see him doing it.
Quoted in Colin Jarman *The Guinness Dictionary of Sports Quotations* (1990).

36 There is no reason why the infield should not try to put the batter off his stride at the critical moment, by neatly-timed disparagements of his wife's fidelity and his mother's respectability.
Alluding to baseball. Quoted in Colin Jarman *The Guinness Dictionary of Sports Quotations* (1990).

37 Who is this 'Babe' Ruth? And what does she do?
Of the legendary baseball star 'Babe' Ruth. Quoted in Colin Jarman *The Guinness Dictionary of Sports Quotations* (1990).

38 The most intolerable pain is produced by

prolonging the keenest pleasure.

1903 *Man and Superman*, 'Maxims for Revolutionists: Beauty and Happiness'.

40 Economy is the art of making the most of life.

1903 *Man and Superman*, 'Maxims for Revolutionists: Virtues and Vices'.

41 England and America are two countries divided by a common language.

Attributed.

42 If all the economists in the world were laid end to end, they would not reach a conclusion.

Attributed.

43 To begin with, I was born with an unreasonably large stock of relations, who have increased and multiplied ever since. My aunts and uncles were legion, and my cousins as the sands of the sea without number. Consequently, even a low deathrate meant, in the course of mere natural decay, a tolerably steady supply of funerals for a by no means affectionate but exceedingly clannish family to go to. Add to this that the town we lived in, being divided in religious opinion, buried its dead in two great cemeteries, each of which was held by the opposite faction to be the ante-chamber of perdition, and by its own patrons to be the gate of paradise.

'Music in London'.

44 You see things, and you say, 'Why?' But I dream things that never were; and I say 'Why not?'

The Serpent

45 [Lord Rosebery] was a man who never missed an occasion to let slip an opportunity.

Quoted by Winston Churchill in *Great Contemporaries* (1937).

Shawcross, Sir Hartley William, Baron Shawcross 1902–

English jurist, Attorney General (1945–51) and President of the Board of Trade (1951). He established his reputation as chief British prosecutor at the Nuremberg Trials (1945–6), and as prosecutor in the Fuchs atom spy case (1950). He was made a life peer in 1959.

46 We are the masters at the moment, and not only at the moment, but for a very long time to come.

1946 Alluding to Labour's victory in the general election, House of Commons, 2 Apr.

47 The so-called new morality is too often the old immorality condoned.

1963 In *The Observer*, 17 Jul.

Shawcross, William 1946–

English journalist whose book *Sideshow* (1979) detailed US involvement in Cambodia up to 1975.

48 Cambodia was not a mistake; it was a crime. The world is diminished by the experience.

1979 *Sideshow*, afterword.

Sheehy-Skeffington, Francis 1878–1916

Irish pacifist and feminist.

49 A crank is a small engine that causes revolutions.

On being described as a crank, quoted by his son Owen.

Sheen, Fulton John 1895–1979

US Roman Catholic prelate, who has argued strenuously against Communism and birth control.

50 Our Lord…said that if men withheld their praise of him, 'the very stones would cry out', which they did as, later, they burst into Gothic cathedrals.

1962 *These Are the Sacraments*.

Shelley, Mary Godwin 1797–1851

English novelist, who married Percy Bysshe Shelley (1816). Her most famous work is *Frankenstein* (1818), written when she was only 19. After her husband's death she wrote *Valperga* (1823), *The Last Man* (1826), *Perkin Warbeck* (1830), *Lodore* (1835) and *Falkner* (1837) and edited her husband's works.

51 You seek for knowledge and wisdom as I once did; and I ardently hope that the gratification of your wishes may not be a serpent to sting you, as mine has been.

1818 *Frankenstein*, letter 4.

52 I was their plaything and their idol, and something better—their child.

1818 Frankenstein speaking of his parents. *Frankenstein*, ch.1.

53 So much has been done, exclaimed the soul of Frankenstein—more, far more, will I achieve; treading the steps already marked, I will pioneer a new way, explore unknown powers, and unfold to the world the deepest mysteries of creation.

1818 *Frankenstein*, ch.3.

54 All men hate the wretched; how, then, must I be hated, who am miserable beyond all living things! Yet you, my creator, detest and spurn me, thy creature, to whom thou art bound by ties only dissoluble by the annihilation of one of us.

1818 Frankenstein's monster. *Frankenstein*, ch.10.

55 Everywhere I see bliss, from which I alone am irrevocably excluded.

1818 Frankenstein's monster. *Frankenstein*, ch.10.

Shelley, Percy Bysshe 1792–1822

English lyric poet, who eloped with and later married Mary Godwin. He was a leading light of the Romantic movement and a lifelong atheist. His early poems include *Queen Mab* (1813). He later wrote tragedies such as *The Cenci* (1818), lyrical poems such as 'Ode to the West Wind' (1819) and lyric dramas such as *Prometheus Unbound* (1820).

56 The discussion of any subject is a right that you have brought into the world with your heart and tongue. Resign your heart's blood before you part with this inestimable privilege of man.
1812 *An Address to the Irish People.*

57 Titles are tinsel, power a corrupter, glory a bubble, and excessive wealth a libel on its possessor.
1812 *Declaration of Rights*, article 27.

58 That sweet bondage which is freedom's self.
1813 *Queen Mab*, canto 9.

59 There is no disease, bodily or mental, which adoption of vegetable diet and pure water has not infallibly mitigated, wherever the experiment has been fairly tried.
1813 'A Vindication of Natural Diet'.

60 Mont Blanc yet gleams on high: the power is there,
The still and solemn power of many sights
And many sounds, and much of life and death.
In the long glare of day, the snows descend
Upon that Mountain; none beholds them there,
Nor when the flakes burn in the sinking sun,
Or the sunbeams dart through them.
1816 'Mont Blanc'.

61 The awful shadow of some unseen Power
Floats though unseen among us,—visiting
This various world with as inconstant wing
As summer winds that creep from flower to flower.
1816 'Hymn to Intellectual Beauty'.

62 While yet a boy I sought for ghosts, and sped
Through many a listening chamber, cave and ruin,
And starlight wood, with fearful steps pursuing
Hopes of high talks with the departed dead.
1816 'Hymn to Intellectual Beauty'.

63 The day becomes more solemn and serene
When noon is past—there is a harmony
In autumn, and a lustre in its sky,
Which through the summer is not heard or seen,
As if it could not be, as if it had not been!
1816 'Hymn to Intellectual Beauty'.

64 Nought may endure but Mutability.
1816 'Mutability'.

65 In honoured poverty thy voice did weave
Songs concentrate to truth and liberty,—
Deserting these, thou leavest me to grieve,

Thus having been, that thou shouldst cease to be.
1816 'To Wordsworth'.

66 I love all waste
And solitary places; where we taste
The pleasure of believing what we see
Is boundless, as we wish our souls to be.
1818 'Julian and Maddalo', l.14–16.

67 Thou Paradise of exiles, Italy!
1818 'Julian and Maddalo', l.57.

68 Me—who am as a nerve o'er which do creep
The else unfelt oppressions of this earth.
1818 'Julian and Maddalo', l.449–50.

69 Most wretched men
Are cradled into poetry by wrong:
They learn in suffering what they teach in song.
1818 'Julian and Maddalo', l.544–7.

70 Beneath is spread like a green sea
The waveless plain of Lombardy,
Bounded by the vaporous air,
Islanded by cities fair;
Underneath Day's azure eyes,
Ocean's nursling, Venice lies,—
A peopled labyrinth of walls,
Amphitrite's destined halls.
1818 'Lines written amongst the Euganean Hills', l.90–7.

71 Sun-girt city, thou hast been
Ocean's child, and then his queen;
Now is come a darker day,
And thou soon must be his prey.
1818 'Lines written amongst the Euganean Hills', l.115–18.

72 The City's voice itself is soft like Solitude's.
1818 'Stanzas Written in Dejection, near Naples'.

73 I see the waves upon the shore,
Like light dissolved in star-showers, thrown.
1818 'Stanzas Written in Dejection, near Naples'.

74 Alas! I have nor hope nor health,
Nor peace within nor calm around,
Nor that content surpassing wealth
The sage in meditation found.
1818 'Stanzas Written in Dejection, near Naples'.

75 With hue like that when some great painter dips
His pencil in the gloom of earthquake and eclipse.
1818 'The Revolt of Islam'.

76 An old, mad, blind, despised, and dying king.
1819 'England in 1819' (published in 1839).

77 His big tears, for he wept well,
Turned to mill-stones as they fell.
And the little children, who
Round his feet played to and fro,
Thinking every tear a gem,

Had their brains knocked out by them.
1819 Of Fraud (ie, Lord Eldon). 'The Mask of Anarchy'.

78 I met Murder on the way—
He had a mask like Castlereagh.
1819 'The Mask of Anarchy', alluding to English foreign secretary Viscount Castlereagh, who was held responsible for the Peterloo Massacre in 1819.

79 On his brow this mark I saw—
'I AM GOD, AND KING, AND LAW!'
1819 'The Mask of Anarchy'.

80 Rise like Lions after slumber
In unvanquishable number—
Shake your chains to earth like dew
Which in sleep has fallen on you—
Ye are many—they are few.
1819 'The Mask of Anarchy'.

81 And singing still dost soar, and soaring ever singest.
1819 'To a Skylark'.

82 I wield the flail of the lashing hail,
And whiten the green plains under,
And then again I dissolve it in rain,
And laugh as I pass in thunder.
1819 'The Cloud'.

83 That orbèd maiden, with white fire laden,
Whom mortals call the Moon.
1819 'The Cloud'.

84 I am the daughter of Earth and Water,
And the nursling of the Sky;
I pass through the pores of the ocean and shores;
I change, but I cannot die,
For after the rain when with never a stain
The pavilion of Heaven is bare,
And the winds and sunbeams with their convex
  gleams
Build up the blue dome of air,
I silently laugh at my own cenotaph,
And out of the caverns of rain,
Like a child from the womb, like a ghost from the
  tomb,
I arise and unbuild it again.
1819 'The Cloud'.

85 The fountains mingle with the river,
And the rivers with the ocean;
The winds of heaven mix for ever
With a sweet emotion;
Nothing in the world is single;
All things, by a law divine,
In one spirit meet and mingle.
Why not I with thine?
1819 'Love and Philosophy'.

86 O wild West Wind, thou breath of Autumn's being,

Thou, from whose unseen presence the leaves dead
Are driven, like ghosts from an enchanter fleeing.
1819 'Ode to the West Wind', l.1–3.

87 Wild Spirit, which art moving everywhere;
Destroyer and preserver; hear, oh, hear!
1819 'Ode to the West Wind', l.13–4.

88 Thou who didst waken from his summer dreams
The blue Mediterranean, where he lay,
Lulled by the coil of his crystalline streams

Beside a pumice isle in Baiae's bay,
And saw in sleep old palaces and towers
Quivering within the wave's intenser day,

All overgrown with azure moss and flowers
So sweet, the sense faints picturing them.
1819 'Ode to the West Wind', l.29–36.

89 Oh, lift me as a wave, a leaf, a cloud!
I fall upon the thorns of life! I bleed!
1819 'Ode to the West Wind', l.53–4.

90 Make me thy lyre, even as the forest is:
What if my leaves are falling like its own!
The tumult of thy mighty harmonies
Will take from both a deep, autumnal tone,
Sweet though in sadness.
1819 'Ode to the West Wind', l.57–61.

91 And, by the incarnation of this verse,
Scatter, as from an unextinguished hearth
Ashes and sparks, my words among mankind!
Be through my lips to unawakened earth

The trumpet of a prophecy! O, Wind,
If Winter comes, can Spring be far behind?
1819 'Ode to the West Wind', l.65–70.

92 I met a traveller from an antique land
Who said: Two vast and trunkless legs of stone
Stand in the desert.
1819 'Ozymandias'.

93 'My name is Ozymandias, king of kings:
Look on my works, ye Mighty, and despair!'
Nothing beside remains. Round the decay
Of that colossal wreck, boundless and bare
The lone and level sands stretch far away.
1819 'Ozymandias'.

94 Hell is a city much like London—
A populous and smoky city.
1819 'Peter Bell the Third' pt.3, stanza 1.

95 But from the first 'twas Peter's drift
To be a kind of moral eunuch,
He touched the hem of Nature's shift,
Felt faint—and never dared uplift
The closest, all-concealing tunic.
1819 'Peter Bell the Third', pt.4, stanza 11.

96 Men of England, wherefore plough
For the lords who lay you low?
1819 'Song to the Men of England'.

97 Hail to thee, blithe Spirit!
Bird thou never wert,
That from Heaven, or near it,
Pourest thy full heart
In profuse strains of unpremeditated art.
1820 'To a Skylark', stanza 1.

98 Higher still and higher
From the earth thou springest
Like a cloud of fire;
The blue deep thou wingest
And singing still dost soar, and soaring ever singest.
1820 'To a Skylark', stanza 2.

99 In the golden lightning
Of the sunken sun
O'er which clouds are brightening,
Thou dost float and run
Like an unbodied joy whose race is just begun.
1820 'To a Skylark', stanza 3.

1 Keen as are the arrows
Of that silver sphere,
Whose intense lamp narrows
In the white dawn clear
Until we hardly see, we feel that it is there.
1820 'To a Skylark', stanza 5.

2 Like a Poet hidden
In the light of thought,
Singing hymns unbidden,
Till the world is wrought
To sympathy with hopes and fears it heeded not.
1820 'To a Skylark', stanza 8.

3 What objects are the fountains
Of thy happy strain?
What fields, or waves, or mountains?
What shapes of sky or plain?
What love of thine own kind? What ignorance of pain?
1820 'To a Skylark', stanza 15.

4 With thy clear keen joyance
Languor cannot be:
Shadow of annoyance
Never came near thee:
Thou lovest—but ne'er knew love's sad satiety.
1820 'To a Skylark', stanza 16.

5 We look before and after,
And pine for what is not:
Our sincerest laughter
With some pain is fraught:
Our sweetest songs are those that tell of saddest thought.
1820 'To a Skylark', stanza 18.

6 Better than all measures
Of delightful sound,
Better than all treasures
That in books are found,
Thy skill lo poet were, scorner of the ground!
1819 'To a Skylark', stanza 21.

7 Teach me half the gladness
That thy brain must know,
Such harmonious madness
From my lips would flow
The world should listen then—as I am listening now.
1820 'To a Skylark', stanza 21.

8 Chameleons feed on light and air:
Poet's food is love and game.
1820 'An Exhortation'.

9 London, that great sea, whose ebb and flow
At once is deaf and loud, and on the shore
Vomits its wrecks, and still howls on for more.
1820 'Letter to Maria Gisborne', l.193–5.

10 You will see Coleridge—he who sits obscure
In the exceeding lustre and the pure
Intense irradiation of a mind,
Which, through its own internal lighting blind,
Flags wearily through darkness and despair—
A cloud-encircled meteor of the air,
A hooded eagle among blinking owls—
You will see Hunt—one of those happy souls
Which are the salt of the earth, and without whom
This world would smell like what it is—a tomb.
1820 'Letter to Maria Gisborne' l.202–11.

11 Have you not heard
When a man marries, dies, or turns Hindoo,
His best friends hear no more of him?
1820 'Letter to Maria Gisborne' l.235–7.

12 His fine wit
Makes such a wound, the knife is lost in it.
1820 Of Thomas Love Peacock. 'Letter to Maria Gisborne', l.240–1.

13 Ere Babylon was dust,
The Magus Zoroaster, my dead child,
Met his own image walking in the garden,
That apparition, sole of men, he saw.
1820 *Prometheus Unbound*, act 1, l.191–4.

14 Cruel he looks, but calm and strong,
Like one who does, not suffers wrong.
1820 *Prometheus Unbound*, act 1, l.238–9.

15 It doth repent me: words are quick and vain:
  Grief for a while is blind, and so was mine.
  I wish no living thing to suffer pain.
  1820 *Prometheus Unbound*, act 1, l.303–5.

16 Kingly conclaves stern and cold,
  Where blood with guilt is bought and sold.
  1820 *Prometheus Unbound* act 1, l.530–1.

17 The good want power, but to weep barren tears.
  The powerful goodness want: worse need for them.
  The wise want love; and those who love want
    wisdom.
  1820 *Prometheus Unbound* act 1, l.625–7.

18 Peace is in the grave.
  The grave hides all things beautiful and good:
  I am a God and cannot find it there.
  1820 *Prometheus Unbound* act 1, l.638–40.

19 The dust of creeds outworn.
  1820 *Prometheus Unbound* act 1, l.697.

20 On a poet's lips I slept
  Dreaming like a love-adept
  In the sound his breathing kept.
  1820 *Prometheus Unbound*, act 1, l.737–9.

21 To be
  Omnipotent but friendless is to reign.
  1820 *Prometheus Unbound*, act 2, sc.4, l.47–8.

22 He gave man speech, and speech created thought,
  Which is the measure of the universe.
  1820 *Prometheus Unbound*, act 2, sc.4, l.72–3.

23 Fate, Time, Occasion, Chance, and Change? To
    these
  All things are subject but eternal love.
  1820 *Prometheus Unbound*, act 2, sc.4, l.119–20.

24 My soul is an enchanted boat,
  Which, like a sleeping swan, doth float
  Upon the silver waves of thy sweet singing.
  1820 *Prometheus Unbound*, act 2, sc.5, l.72–4.

25 The loathsome mask has fallen, the man remains
  Sceptreless, free, uncircumscribed, but man
  Equal, unclassed, tribeless, and nationless,
  Exempt from awe, worship, degree, the king
  Over himself; just, gentle, wise: but man
  Passionless?—no, yet free from guilt or pain,
  Which were, for his will made or suffered them,
  Nor yet exempt, though ruling them like slaves,
  From chance, and death, and mutability,
  The clogs of that which else might oversoar
  The loftiest star of unascended heaven,
  Pinnacled dim in the intense inane.
  1820 *Prometheus Unbound*, act 3, sc.4, l.193–204.

26 A traveller from the cradle to the grave

Through the dim night of this immortal day.
  1820 *Prometheus Unbound*, act 4, l.551–2.

27 To suffer woes which Hope thinks infinite;
  To forgive wrongs darker than death or night;
  To defy Power, which seems omnipotent:
  To love, and bear; to hope till Hope creates
  From its own wreck the thing it contemplates;
  Neither to change, nor falter, nor repent;
  This, like thy glory, Titan, is to be
  Good, great and joyous, beautiful and free;
  This is alone Life, Joy, Empire and Victory.
  1820 *Prometheus Unbound*, act 4, l.570–8.

28 A Sensitive Plant in a garden grew.
  1820 'The Sensitive Plant', pt.1, l.1.

29 And the rose like a nymph to the bath addressed,
  Which unveiled the depth of her glowing breast,
  Till, fold after fold, to the fainting air
  The soul of her beauty and love lay bare.
  1820 'The Sensitive Plant', pt.1, l.29–32.

30 And the jessamine faint, and the sweet tuberose,
  The sweetest flower for scent that blows.
  1820 'The Sensitive Plant', pt.1, l.37–8.

31 A lovely lady, garmented in light
  From her own beauty.
  1820 'The Witch of Atlas', stanza 5.

32 For she was beautiful—her beauty made
  The bright world dim, and everything beside
  Seemed like the fleeting image of a shade.
  1820 'The Witch of Atlas', stanza 12.

33 The cemetery is an open space among the ruins,
  covered in winter with violets and daisies. It might
  make one in love with death, to think that one
  should be buried in so sweet a place.
  1821 *Adonais*, preface.

34 I weep for Adonais—he is dead!
  O, weep for Adonais! though our tears
  Thaw not the frost which binds so dear a head!
  1821 *Adonais*, stanza 1.

35 He died,
  Who was the Sire of an immortal strain,
  Blind, old and lonely.
  1821 *Adonais*, stanza 4.

36 To that high Capital, where kingly Death
  Keeps his pale court in beauty and decay,
  He came.
  1821 *Adonais*, stanza 7.

37 The quick Dreams,
  The passion-winged Ministers of thought.
  1821 *Adonais*, stanza 9.

38 Lost Angel of a ruined Paradise!

She knew not 'twas her own; as with no stain
She faded, like a cloud which had outwept its rain.
1821 *Adonais*, stanza 10.

39 Ah, woe is me! Winter is come and gone,
But grief returns with the revolving year.
1821 *Adonais*, stanza 18.

40 From the great morning of the world when first
God dawned on Chaos.
1821 *Adonais*, stanza 19.

41 Alas! that all we loved of him should be,
But for our grief, as if it had not been,
And grief itself be mortal!
1821 *Adonais*, stanza 21.

42 Whence are we, and why are we? Of what scene
The actors or spectators?
1821 *Adonais*, stanza 21.

43 A pard-like Spirit, beautiful and swift—
A love in desolation masked;—a Power
Girt round with weakness;—it can scarce uplift
The weight of the superincumbent hour;
It is a dying lamp, a falling shower,
A breaking billow;—even whilst we speak
Is it not broken?
1821 *Adonais*, stanza 32.

44 Our Adonais has drunk poison—oh!
What deaf and viperous murderer could crown
Life's early cup with such a draught of woe?
1821 *Adonais*, stanza 36.

45 He wakes or sleeps with the enduring dead;
Thou canst not soar where he is sitting now—
Dust to the dust! but the pure spirit shall flow
Back to the burning fountain whence it came,
A portion of the Eternal.
1821 *Adonais*, stanza 38.

46 He hath awakened from the dream of life—
'Tis we, who lost in stormy visions, keep
With phantoms an unprofitable strife,
And in mad trance, strike with our spirit's knife
Invulnerable nothings.
1821 *Adonais*, stanza 39.

47 He has out-soared the shadow of our night;
Envy and calumny and hate and pain,
And that unrest which men miscall delight,
Can touch him not and torture not again;
From the contagion of the world's slow stain
He is secure, and now can never mourn
A heart grown cold, a head grown grey in vain.
1821 *Adonais*, stanza 40.

48 He lives, he wakes,—'tis Death is dead, not he.
1821 *Adonais*, stanza 41.

49 He is a portion of the loveliness
Which once he made more lovely.
1821 *Adonais*, stanza 43.

50 The One remains, the many change and pass;
Heaven's light forever shines, Earth's shadows fly:
Life, like a dome of many-coloured glass,
Stains the white radiance of Eternity,
Until Death tramples it to fragments.
1821 *Adonais*, stanza 52.

51 I never was attached to that great sect,
Whose doctrine is that each one should select
Out of the crowd a mistress or a friend,
And all the rest, though fair and wise, commend
To cold oblivion.
1821 'Epipsychidion', l.149–53.

52 The beaten road
Which those poor slaves with weary footsteps
    tread,
Who travel to their home among the dead
By the broad highway of the world, and so
With one chained friend, perhaps a jealous foe,
The dreariest and the longest journey go.
1821 'Epipsychidion', l.154–9.

53 True Love in this differs from gold and clay,
That to divide is not to take away.
1821 'Epipsychidion', l.160–1.

54 An isle under Ionian skies
Beautiful as a wreck of Paradise.
1821 'Epipsychidion', l.422–3.

55 I pant, I sink, I tremble, I expire!
1821 'Epipsychidion', l.591.

56 The vanity of translation; it were as wise to cast a
violet into a crucible that you might discover the
formal principle of its colour and odour, as seek to
transfuse from one language to another the
creations of a poet. The plant must spring again
from its seed, or it will bear no flower.
1821 *A Defence of Poetry.*

57 The great instrument of moral good is the
imagination; and poetry administers to the effect
by acting on the cause.
1821 *A Defence of Poetry.*

58 A single word even may be a spark of
inextinguishable thought.
1821 *A Defence of Poetry.*

59 Poetry is a record of the best and happiest moments
of the happiest and best minds.
1821 *A Defence of Poetry.*

60 Poets are the hierophants of an unapprehended
inspiration; the mirrors of the gigantic shadows

which futurity casts upon the present; the words
which express what they understand not; the
trumpets which sing to battle, and feel not what
they inspire; the influence which is moved not, but
moves. Poets are the influence which is moved not,
but moves. Poets are the unacknowledged
legislators of the world.
1821 *A Defence of Poetry.*

61 Death will come when thou art dead,
Soon, too soon—
Sleep will come when thou art fled;
Of neither would I ask the boon
I ask of thee, belovèd Night—
Swift be thine approaching flight,
Come soon, soon!
1821 'To Night'.

62 Life may change, but it may fly not,
Hope may vanish, but can die not;
Truth be veiled, but still it burneth;
Love repulsed,—but it returneth!
1822 'Hellas', l.34–7.

63 Let there be light! Said Liberty,
And like sunrise from the sea,
Athens arose!
1822 'Hellas', l.682–4.

64 The world's great age begins anew,
The golden years return,
The earth doth like a snake renew
Her winter weeds outworn;
Heaven smiles, and faiths and empires gleam,
Like wrecks of a dissolving dream.
1822 'Hellas', l.1060–5.

65 O cease! must hate and death return,
Cease! must men kill and die?
Cease! drain not to its dregs the urn
Of bitter prophecy.
The world is weary of the past,
Oh, might it die or rest at last!
1822 'Hellas', l.1096–101.

66 I dreamed that, as I wandered by the way,
Bare Winter suddenly was changed to Spring,
And gentle odours led my steps astray,
Mixed with a sound of water's murmuring
Along a shelving bank of turf, which lay
Under a copse, and hardly dared to fling
Its green arms round the bosom of the stream,
But kissed it and then fled, as thou mightst in
  dream.
1822 'The Question', stanza 1.

67 Daisies, those pearled Arcturi of the earth,
The constellated flower that never sets.
1822 'The Question', stanza 2.

68 And in the warm hedge grew lush eglantine,
Green cowbind and the moonlight-coloured may.
1822 'The Question', stanza 3.

69 Less oft peace in Shelley's mind,
Than calm in waters seen.
1822 'To Jane: The Recollection'.

70 Music when soft voices die,
Vibrates in the memory—
Odours, when sweet violets sicken,
Live within the sense they quicken.
'To—: Music when soft voices die' (published 1824).

71 I pursued a maiden and clasped a reed:
Gods and men, we are all deluded thus!
It breaks in our bosom and then we bleed.
'Hymn of Pan' (published 1824).

72 Swiftly walk o'er the western wave,
Spirit of Night!
Out of the misty eastern cave,
Where, all the long and lone daylight,
Thou wovest dreams of joy and fear,
Which make thee terrible and dear,
Swift be thy flight!
'To Night' (published 1824).

73 Art thou pale for weariness
Of climbing heaven, and gazing on the earth,
Wandering companionless
Among the stars that have a different birth,—
And ever-changing, like a joyless eye
That finds no object worth its constancy?
'To the Moon' (published 1824).

74 And like a dying lady, lean and pale,
Who totters forth, wrapped in a gauzy veil.
'The Waning Moon' (published 1824).

Sheridan, Philip Henry 1831–88

American Union cavalry commander in the Civil War and
the American-Indian wars.

75 The only good Indian is a dead Indian.
1869 Attributed comment at Fort Cobb, Jan.

76 We took away their country and their means of
support, broke up their mode of living, their habits
of life, introduced disease and decay among them
and it was for this and against this they made war.
Could anyone expect less?
c.1870 Quoted in Thomas C Leonard *Above the Battle* (1978).

Sheridan, Richard Brinsley 1751–1816

Irish dramatist. His major plays, *The Rivals, The Duenna,*
and *The Critic,* were produced between 1775 and 1779.
He became an MP and in 1782 under-secretary for
foreign affairs, a renowned orator. He lost his seat in
1812.

77 Promise to forget this fellow—to illiterate him, I
   say, quite from your memory.
   1775 Mrs Malaprop to Lydia. *The Rivals*, act 1, sc.2.

78 What business have you, miss, with preference and
   aversion?...You ought to know, that as both always
   wear off, 'tis safest in matrimony to begin with a
   little aversion.
   1775 Mrs Malaprop to Lydia. *The Rivals*, act 1, sc.2.

79 Madam, a circulating library in a town is as an
   evergreen tree of diabolical knowledge!...Depend
   upon it, Mrs Malaprop, that they who are so fond
   of handling the leaves, will long for the fruit at last.
   1775 Sir Anthony Absolute. *The Rivals*, act 1, sc.2.

80 I'll make my old clothes know who's master. I shall
   straightaway cashier the hunting-frock, and render
   my leather breeches incapable. My hair has been in
   training some time.
   1775 Bob Acres. *The Rivals*, act 2, sc.1.

81 Though one eye may be very agreeable, yet as the
   prejudice has always run in favour of two, I would
   not wish to affect a singularity in that article.
   1775 Jack Absolute. *The Rivals*, act 3, sc.1.

82 He is the very pine-apple of politeness.
   1775 Mrs Malaprop of Jack Absolute. *The Rivals*, act 3, sc.3.

83 Sure, if I reprehend anything in this world it is the
   use of my oracular tongue, and a nice derangement
   of epitaphs.
   1775 Mrs Malaprop. *The Rivals*, act 3, sc.3.

84 She's as headstrong as an allegory on the banks of
   the Nile.
   1775 Mrs Malaprop of Lydia Languish. *The Rivals*, act 3, sc.3.

85 That's too civil by half.
   1775 Bob Acres to Sir Lucius O' Trigger. *The Rivals*, act 3, sc.4.

86 Pray, sir, be easy; the quarrel is a very pretty quarrel
   as it stands; we should only spoil it by trying to
   explain it.
   1775 Sir Lucius O'Trigger to Jack Absolute. *The Rivals*, act 4,
   sc.3.

87 [To] have an unmannerly fat clerk ask the consent
   of every butcher in the parish to join John Absolute
   and Lydia Languish, spinster. Oh that I should live
   to hear myself called spinster!
   1775 Lydia Languish, who had hoped for a romantic
   elopement. *The Rivals*, act 5, sc.1.

88 Oh, poor Dolly! I never shall see her like again;
   such an arm for a bandage—veins that seemed to
   invite the lancet.
   1775 Dr Rosy. *St Patrick's Day*, act 1, sc.1.

89 A bumper of good liquor,

Will end a contest quicker
Than justice, judge or vicar.
1775 *The Duenna*, act 2, sc.3.

90 Conscience has no more to do with gallantry than
   it has with politics.
   1775 Isaac to Don Antonio. *The Duenna*, act 2, sc.4.

91 BERINTHIA Your lordship, I suppose, is fond of
      music?
   LORD FOP Oh, passionately, on Tuesdays and
      Saturdays.
   1777 *A Trip to Scarborough*, act 2, sc.1.

92 Ah, Amanda, it's a delicious thing to be a young
   widow!
   1777 *A Trip to Scarborough*, act 2, sc.1.

93 Alas! the devil's sooner raised than laid.
   So strong, so swift, the monster there's no gagging:
   Cut Scandal's head off, still the tongue is wagging.
   1777 *The School for Scandal*, prologue.

94 I think you will like them, when you shall see them
   on a beautiful quarto page, where a neat rivulet of
   text shall meander through a meadow of margin.
   1777 Sir Benjamin Backbite, of his love elegies to Maria. *The
   School for Scandal*, act 1, sc.1.

95 I'm called away by particular business. But I leave
   my character behind me.
   1777 Sir Peter Teazle, leaving a gathering of gossips. *The School
   for Scandal*, act 2, sc.2.

96 I hate to see prudence clinging to the green suckers
   of youth; 'tis like ivy round a sapling, and spoils the
   growth of the tree.
   1777 Sir Oliver Surface. *The School for Scandal*, act 2, sc.3.

97 Here's to the maiden of bashful fifteen;
   Here's to the widow of fifty;
   Here's to the flaunting extravagant quean;
   And here's to the housewife that's thrifty.
   Chorus. Let the toast pass,
               Drink to the lass—
   I'll warrant she'll prove an excuse for a glass!
   1777 Song. *The School for Scandal*, act 3, sc.3.

98 Wine does but draw forth a man's natural qualities.
   1777 Charles Surface. *The School for Scandal*, act 3, sc.3.

99 When a scandalous story is believed against one,
   there is certainly no comfort like the conscience of
   having deserved it.
   1777 Joseph Surface. *The School for Scandal*, act 4, sc.3.

1 There needs no small degree of address to gain the
   reputation of benevolence without incurring the
   expense.
   1777 Joseph Surface. *The School for Scandal*, act 5, sc.1.

2 The *newspapers*! Sir, they are the most villainous—licentious—abominable—infernal—Not that I ever read them—No—I make it a rule never to look into a newspaper.
1779 *The Critic*, act 1, sc.1.

3 If there is anything to one's praise, it is a foolish vanity to be gratified at it; and, if it is abuse—why one is always sure to hear of it from one damned good-natured friend or other!
1779 Sir Fretful Plagiary, of newspaper criticism. *The Critic*, act 1, sc.1.

4 Mr Dangle, here are two very civil gentlemen trying to make themselves understood, and I don't know which is the interpreter.
1779 Mrs Dangle. *The Critic*, act 1, sc.2.

5 Puffing is of various sorts; the principal are, the puff direct, the puff preliminary, the puff collateral, the puff collusive, and the puff oblique, or puff by implication.
1779 Mr Puff. *The Critic*, act 1, sc.2.

6 The number of those who undergo the fatigue of judging for themselves is very small indeed.
1779 Mr Puff. *The Critic*, act 1, sc.2.

7 The puff collusive is the newest of any; for it acts in the disguise of determined hostility. It is much used by bold booksellers and enterprising poets.
1779 Mr Puff. *The Critic*, act 1, sc.2.

8 No scandal about Queen Elizabeth, I hope?
1779 Mr Sneer, of Mr Puff's tragedy 'The Spanish Armada'. *The Critic*, act 2, sc.1.

9 I open with a clock striking, to beget an awful attention in the audience: it also marks the time, which is four o'clock in the morning, and saves a description of the rising sun, and a great deal about gilding the eastern hemisphere.
1779 Mr Puff, of his tragedy 'The Spanish Armada'. *The Critic*, act 2, sc.2.

10 BEEFEATER: [a character in Mr Puff's play within a play, 'The Spanish Armanda'] Perdition catch my soul but I do love thee.
SNEER: Haven't I heard that line before?
PUFF: No, I fancy not.—Where pray?
DANGLE: Yes, I think there is something like it in *Othello*.
PUFF: Gad! now you put me in mind on't, I believe there is—but that's of no consequence; all that can be said is, that two people happened to hit upon the same thought—and Shakespeare made use of it first, that's all.
1779 *The Critic*, act 3, sc.1.

11 When a heroine goes mad, she always goes into white satin.
1779 Mr Puff. *The Critic*, act 3, sc.1.

12 An oyster may be crossed in love!
1779 Tilburnia's 'mad' speech from 'The Spanish Armada'. *The Critic*, act 3, sc.1.

13 Give me the liberty of the Press, and I will give the Minister a venal House of Peers, I will give him a corrupt and servile House of Commons…armed with the liberty of the Press, I will go forth to meet him undismayed.
1810 Speech, House of Commons.

Sherman, Richard M and Robert B
1928–, 1925–

US song-writing brothers, who wrote songs for Disney films from 1959 and also complete scores for musicals. Among their best-known films are *Mary Poppins* and *Chitty Chitty Bang Bang* (1968).

14 Supercalifragilisticexpialidocious.
1964 Title of song from *Mary Poppins*.

15 Protocoligorically Correct.
1976 Title of song from *The Slipper and the Rose*.

Sherman, William Tecumseh 1820–91

US general. He was Union commander during the American Civil War, when he captured Atlanta in 1864 and divided Confederate forces by his 'march to the sea', hastening the surrender of the South.

16 There is many a boy here today who looks on war as all glory, but, boys, it is all hell.
1880 Speech at Columbus, Ohio, 11 Aug. Quoted in Lloyd Lewis Sherman *Fighting Prophet* (1932).

Sherriff, R(obert) C(edric) 1896–1975

British playwright, novelist and screenwriter. He achieved an international reputation with his first play *Journey's End* (1929). He also wrote screenplays for films such as *The Invisible Man* (1933), *Goodbye Mr Chips* (1939) and *The Odd Man Out* (1947).

17 Even the moon is frightened of me, frightened to death! The whole world is frightened to death!
1933 Line delivered by Claude Rains in *The Invisible Man* (with Philip Wylie).

Shevardnadze, Eduard Ambrosievich
1928–

Georgian-born Soviet politician. In 1978 he was inducted into the Politburo and was appointed Foreign Minister in 1985. He rapidly overhauled the Soviet foreign policy machine for a new era of détente. From 1992 he was Chairman of the State Council of Georgia.

18 Democrats are fleeing in all directions. Reformers are going into hiding. A dictatorship is beginning, and no one knows what shape it will take or who will come to power.

1990 On the increasing disarray in the USSR caused by failing Soviet reforms, rivalry between the Gorbachev and Yeltsin factions and unrest in the Baltic states, in *The Sunday Times*, 23 Dec.

Shinwell, Emanuel, Baron Shinwell
1884–1986

English Labour politician. A 'street-corner' socialist in Glasgow, he became Secretary of State for War (1947) and Minister of Defence (1950–1). Known for his belligerence, he mellowed into a backbench 'elder statesman'. He wrote several autobiographical works.

19 We know that you, the organized workers of the country, are our friends… As for the rest, they do not matter a tinker's curse.
    1947 Trade union conference, 7 May.

Shipton, Eric Earle 1908–77

British mountaineer, explorer and writer. The foremost mountain explorer of his generation, he facilitated the successful ascent of Everest in 1953. He wrote seven books, including an autobiography, *That Untravelled World* (1969).

20 I have never been able to decide whether, in mountain exploration, it is the prospect of tackling an unsolved problem, or the performance of the task itself, or the retrospective enjoyment of successful effort, which affords the greatest amount of pleasure.
    1936 *Nanda Devi*.

21 Whatever may have been my enthusiasm or impatience to be up and doing on the night before, the hour for getting up always finds me with no other ambition in the world than to be permitted to lie where I am and sleep, sleep, sleep. Not so Tilman. I have never met anyone with such a complete disregard for the sublime comforts of the early morning bed. However monstrously early we might decide, the night before, to get up, he was about at least half an hour before the time. He was generally very good about it, and used to sit placidly smoking his pipe over the fire.
    1936 On climbing with H W (Bill) Tilman. *Nanda Devi*.

22 We were now actually in the inner sanctuary of the Nanda Devi Basin, and at each step I experienced that subtle thrill which anyone of imagination must feel when treading hitherto unexplored country… My most blissful dream as a child was to be in some such valley, free to wander where I liked, and discover for myself some hitherto unrevealed glory of Nature. Now the reality was no less wonderful than that half-forgotten dream; and of how many childish fancies can that be said, in this age of disillusionment?
    1936 *Nanda Devi*.

Shirley, James 1596–1666

English dramatist. Educated at Oxford and Cambridge, he took holy orders but renounced them upon conversion to Catholicism. He died in the Great Fire of London. He wrote plays and masques, including the comedies *Hyde Park* (1634) and *The Lady of Pleasure* (1635), the tragedy *The Cardinal* (1641), and the masque *The Contention of Ajax and Ulysses* (1659).

23 How little room
    Do we take up in death, that, living know
    No bounds?
    1626 *The Wedding*, act 4, sc.4.

24 'Tis no shame for men
    Of his high birth to love a wench; his honour
    May privilege more sins. Next to a woman,
    He loves a running-horse.
    1634 *Hyde Park*, act 1, sc.1.

25 RIDER: … we can be but
    What we are.
    VENTURE: A pair of credulous fools.
    1634 *Hyde Park*, act 1, sc.1.

26 I presume you're mortal, and may err.
    1635 *The Lady of Pleasure*, act 2, sc.2.

27 The glories of our blood and state
    Are shadows, not substantial things;
    There is no armour against fate;
    Death lays his icy hand on kings:
    Scepter and crown
    Must tumble down,
    And in the dust be equal made
    With the poor crooked scythe and spade.
    1659 *The Contention of Ajax and Ulysses*, act 1, sc.3.

Shultz, George P 1920–

US Former Secretary of State. A Professor of Chicago University's graduate business school (1957–68), he was US Secretary of Labor (1969–70), then assistant to President Nixon (1972–4). He was Secretary of State to President Reagan (1982–9). A fellow of the Hoover Institution, Stanford University (1989–) he is a distinguished author and was awarded the Seoul Peace Prize (1992).

28 He made a combative apology.
    1987 On the ability of Elliott Abrams, Assistant Secretary for Inter-American Affairs, to acknowledge a sensitive question without giving a definite reply. In the *New York Times*, 25 Jul.

29 Gardening…is one of the most underrated aspects of diplomacy.
    1993 On the need to meet people 'on their own turf'. *Turmoil and Triumph*.

30 Washington is a resigning town. Nothing else holds the special excitement of a rumored resignation.
    1993 *Turmoil and Triumph*.

31 The way to keep weeds from overwhelming you is to deal with them constantly and in their early stages.
   1993 *Turmoil and Triumph*.

32 The Soviet game is chess…ours is poker. We will have to play a creative mixture of both games.
   1993 Comment to President Reagan. Recalled in *Turmoil and Triumph*.

33 Better to use force when you *should* rather than when you *must*.
   1993 On Soviet alarm at the prospect of US science 'turned on' and venturing into the realm of space defence. *Turmoil and Triumph*.

34 Agreement reached by the negotiators…usually starts to collapse in the hands of those who implement it, no matter how carefully cleared at the top.
   1993 On negotiating the release of Russian political prisoners. *Turmoil and Triumph*.

35 The decision makers face each other. No safety screen stands between the issues and the highest authorities.
   1993 Of summit meetings, particularly that between the US and the Soviets at Reykjavik, Iceland, 9–12 Oct 1986. *Turmoil and Triumph*.

36 A 'staffocracy' has been created.
   1993 On the National Security Council. *Turmoil and Triumph*.

37 You can't figure him out like a fact, because to Reagan the main fact was a vision… He came from the heartland of the country, where people could be down-to-earth yet feel that the sky is the limit— not ashamed of, or cynical about, the American dream.
   1993 Of Ronald Reagan. *Turmoil and Triumph*.

Shute, Nevil originally *Nevil Shute Norway* 1899–1960

English writer. An aeronautical engineer, he began to write novels in 1926 and after World War II emigrated to Australia, the setting for most of his later books, notably *A Town Like Alice* (1949) and *On the Beach* (1957).

38 A Town Like Alice
   1949 Title of book.

Sidgwick, Henry 1838–1900

British economist, Professor at Cambridge.

39 We cannot not say how much wealth there is in a country till we know how it is shared among its inhabitants.
   1883 *Principles of Political Economy*.

Sidmouth, Henry Addington, 1st Viscount 1757–1844

English statesman and Tory Prime Minister (1801–4) after the resignation of William Pitt the Younger. As Home Secretary (1812–21) he had to deal with the Luddite riots and the 'Peterloo Massacre' in Manchester (1819).

40 I hate liberality. Nine times out of ten it is cowardice—and the tenth time, lack of principle.
   Attributed.

Sidney, Algernon 1622–83

English Whig politician. He fought for the Parliamentary army in the English Civil War and in 1645 entered Parliament, but he resented Cromwell's assumption of power, and retired to Penshurst (1653–9). In exile after the Restoration, in 1677 he was pardoned and returned, but was implicated in the Rye House Plot (1683) and beheaded.

41 Liars ought to have good memories.
   Discourses Concerning Government (published 1689).

Sidney, Sir Philip 1554–86

English poet and patron. Educated at Oxford, he travelled widely; in 1585 he was made Governor of Flushing. He died after being wounded in the battle of Zutphen. His sonnet sequence *Astrophel and Stella* (1591) was an early example of the genre in English, as was his prose romance *The Arcadia* (*The Old Arcadia*, as it is called, was not published during Sidney's lifetime; a revised version, *The New Arcadia*, was first published in 1590); his *Defence of Poetry* (published 1595) was the first English essay on literary criticism.

42 I readily admit that I am often more serious than I should be at my age or in my present circumstances, yet I know from experience that I am never less given to melancholy than when I am keenly applying the feeble powers of my mind to some arduous and difficult matter.
   1574 Letter to Hubert Languet, 4 Feb.

43 O wretched state of man in self-division!
   1581 *The Old Arcadia*, 'First Eclogues'.

44 She was stricken with most obstinate love to a young man.
   1581 *The Old Arcadia*, 'First Eclogues'.

45 What allurements she used indifferently were long to tell.
   1581 *The Old Arcadia*, 'Second Eclogues'.

46 What be the fruits of speaking art? What grows by the words?
   1581 *The Old Arcadia*, 'Second Eclogues'.

47 My true love hath my heart and I have his,
   By just exchange one for the other giv'n;
   I hold his dear, and mine he cannot miss,

There never was a better bargain driv'n.
1581 *The Old Arcadia*, 'Third Eclogues'.

48 O sweet, on a wretch wilt thou be revenged?
Shall such high planets tend to the loss of a worm?
1581 *The Old Arcadia*, 'Fourth Eclogues'.

49 A lamentable tune is the sweetest music to a woeful mind.
1590 *Arcadia*, pt.2.

50 Loving in truth, and vain in verse my love to show,
That she (dear she) might take some pleasure of my pain,
Pleasure might cause her read, reading might make her know;
Knowledge might pity win, and pity grace obtain.
1591 *Astrophel and Stella*, sonnet 1.

51 But words came halting forth, wanting Invention's stay;
Invention, Nature's child, fled step-dame Study's blows...
Biting my truant pen, beating myself for spite,
'Fool,' said my muse to me; 'look in thy heart, and write.'
1591 *Astrophel and Stella*, sonnet 1.

52 Your rhubarb words.
1591 *Astrophel and Stella*, sonnet 14.

53 Come sleep, O sleep, the certain knot of peace,
The baiting place of wit, the balm of woe,
The poor man's wealth, the prisoner's release,
The indifferent judge between the high and low.
1591 *Astrophel and Stella*, sonnet 39.

54 That sweet enemy, France.
1591 *Astrophel and Stella*, sonnet 41.

55 Hope, art thou true, or dost thou flatter me?
1591 *Astrophel and Stella*, sonnet 67.

56 Oh heav'nly fool, thy most kiss-worthy face
Anger invests with such a lovely grace
That Anger's self I needs must kiss again.
1591 *Astrophel and Stella*, sonnet 73.

57 I am no pick-purse of another's wit.
1591 *Astrophel and Stella*, sonnet 74.

58 Stella, think not that I by verse seek fame;
Who seek, who hope, who love, who live, but thee:
Thine eyes my pride, thy lips my history;
If thou praise not, all other praise is shame.
1591 *Astrophel and Stella*, sonnet 90.

59 I have just cause to make a pitiful defence of poor poetry, which from almost the highest estimation of learning is fallen to be the laughingstock of children.
1595 *The Defence of Poetry*.

60 And truly, even Plato, whosoever well considereth shall find that in the body of his work, though the inside and strength were philosophy, the skin as it were and beauty depended most on poetry.
1595 *The Defence of Poetry*.

61 [Nature's] world is brazen, the poets only deliver a golden.
1595 *The Defence of Poetry*.

62 Poetry therefore, is an art of imitation... A speaking picture, with this end: to teach and delight.
1595 *The Defence of Poetry*.

63 With a tale forsooth he cometh unto you, with a tale which holdeth children from play, and old men from the chimney corner.
1595 Of the poet. *The Defence of Poetry*.

64 Comedy is an imitation of the common errors of our life, which he representeth in the most ridiculous and scornful sort that may be, so as it is impossible that any beholder can be content to be such a one.
1595 *The Defence of Poetry*.

65 I...am admitted into the company of paper-blurrers.
1595 *The Defence of Poetry*.

66 [This] much curse I must send you, in the behalf of all poets, that while you live, you live in love, and never get favour for lacking skill of a sonnet, and, when you die, your memory die from the earth for want of an epigraph.
1595 *The Defence of Poetry*.

Siegel, Jerome 1917–92

67 I'm lying in bed counting sheep when all of a sudden it hits me...a character like Samson, Hercules and all the strong men I heard tell of rolled into one. Only more so.
Recalling the inspiration behind Superman, created 1938. Quoted in *Time*, 14 Mar 1988.

68 Faster than a speeding bullet! More powerful than a locomotive! Able to leap tall buildings in a single bound!
Introduction for the Superman radio serial. Quoted in *Time*, 14 Mar 1988.

Sièyes, Emmanuel Joseph, Comte also called Abbé Sièyes 1748–1836

French cleric and political theorist. His pamphlet, *Qu'est-ce que le tiers-état?* (What is the Third Estate?, 1789) was very popular with the bourgeoisie. He helped organize the revolution of 18th Brumaire (in which Napoleon overthrew the Directory, 1799). Exiled at the Restoration (1815), he returned after the July Revolution (1830).

69   Who will dare deny that the Third Estate contains within itself all that is needed to constitute a nation?... What would the Third Estate be without the privileged classes? It would be a whole in itself, and a prosperous one. Nothing can be done without it, and everything would be done far better without the others.

   1789   *Qu'est-ce que le tiers-état?*

Sigismund 1368–1437

Holy Roman Emperor from 1433. He became King of Hungary in 1387 and as Emperor presided over the Council of Constance, which ended the Great Schism (1414–18).

70   Only do always in health what you have often promised to do when you are sick.

   His advice for a happy life, quoted in Clifton Fadiman *Faber Book of Anecdotes* (1985).

Sigourney, Lydia Howard née Huntley 1791–1865

American poet. Her pious, sentimental poetry made her the most popular woman poet of her generation. She was an important campaigner in the cause of higher education for women. Her collections include *Moral Pieces in Prose and Verse* (1815)

71   Ye say, they all have passed away,
   That noble race and brave,
   That their light canoes have vanished
   From off the crested wave;
   That 'mid the forests where they roamed
   There rings no hunter's shout;
   But their name is on your waters,
   Ye may not wash it out.

   1848   *Select Poems*, 'Indian Names'.

Sihanouk, Prince Norodom 1922–

Cambodian politician who as Prime Minister tried but failed to keep his country out of the Vietnam War. He was deposed in 1970 by a military coup but returned in 1993 as President of Cambodia after the Paris Peace Accord. He attacked the intensive US bombing of his country.

72   What is the difference between burning and gassing people in ovens and doing it to a whole nation out in the open?

   1973   Of the US bombing of Cambodia. *My War with the CIA* (with W Burchett).

73   The humble people of Cambodia are the most wonderful in the world. Their great misfortune is that they always have terrible leaders who make them suffer. I am not sure I was much better myself, but perhaps I was the least bad.

   1978   In an interview with William Shawcross, author of *Sideshow* (1979).

Sikorski, Gerry 1948–

74   Like a toothless terrier on Valium.

   1987   On the workings of the Office of Government Ethics. In the *New York Times*, 8 Jul.

Sikorsky, Igor Ivan 1889–1972

Russian-born US aeronautical engineer. He built and flew the first four-engined aeroplane (1913), then founded the Sikorsky Aero Engineering Corporation in the USA (1923). He built several flying boats, and in 1939 produced the first successful helicopter.

75   The work of the individual still remains the spark that moves mankind ahead, even more than teamwork.

   Quoted in his *New York Times* obituary, 27 Oct 1972.

Sillitoe, Alan 1928–

English novelist. Several of his novels set in the north of England have been adapted as successful films, notably *Saturday Night and Sunday Morning* (1960).

76   The Loneliness of the Long Distance Runner.

   1962   Title of book.

Silva, José Asunción 1865–96

Colombian poet whose life was marked by financial reverses, the death of loved ones, and the loss of his manuscripts in a shipwreck. His poetry is characteristically melancholy, and after only ten years of writing he committed suicide.

77   *Y si evitas la sífilis, siguiendo
   la sabia profilaxia,
   al llegar los cuarenta irás sintiendo
   un principio de ataxia.*

   And if you manage to avoid syphilis
   by following a wise course of prophylaxis,
   when you turn forty you will feel
   the beginnings of ataxia.

   1908   *Gotas amargas*, 'Filosofías' ('Philosophies').

Silvers, Phil originally Philip Silver 1912–85

US comic actor. His success in films and on Broadway led to the *Phil Silvers Show* (1955–9) on television, where he introduced the character of Sergeant Bilko. He won three Emmy awards during his career, and a Tony Award for his performance in *A Funny Thing Happened on the Way to the Forum* (1972).

78   Be funny on a golf course? Do I kid my best friend's mother about her heart condition?

   Quoted in Michael Hobbs *The Golf Quotation Book* (1992).

Simon, Caroline K d.1993

Judge, NY State Court of Claims.

79   Look like a girl, act like a lady, think like a man and

work like a dog.

Comment the year after her candidacy for Postmaster General was barred by federal officials who claimed the job was unsuited to a woman. Recalled on her death, in the *New York Times*, 30 Jul 1993.

Simon, Herbert A 1916–

US psychologist and economist; awarded a Nobel Prize in Economics (1978).

80 It is a fatal defect of current principles of administration that, like proverbs, they occur in pairs. For almost every principle one can find a equally plausible and acceptable contradictory principle. Although the two principles of the pair will lead to exactly opposite recommendations, there is nothing in the theory to indicate which is the appropriate one to apply.

1945 *Administrative Behavior.*

Simon (of Stackpole Elidor), John Allsebrook Simon, 1st Viscount 1873–1954

English Liberal politician and lawyer. Attorney-General (1913–15) and Home Secretary (1915–16), he resigned from the Cabinet over conscription. Deserting the Liberals to form the Liberal National Party, he supported Ramsay MacDonald's coalition governments and became Foreign Secretary (1931–5), Home Secretary (1935–7), Chancellor of the Exchequer (1937–40) and Lord Chancellor (1940–5).

81 If Joan of Arc had been born in Austria and worn a moustache, she might have conveyed much the same impression.

1935 Letter to George V, referring to his first meeting with Adolf Hitler, 27 Mar.

Simon, (Marvin) Neil 1927–

US playwright. His plays and musicals include *Barefoot in the Park* (1963), *The Odd Couple* (1965) and the semi-autobiographical trilogy *Brighton Beach Memoirs* (1983), *Biloxi Blues* (1984) and *Broadway Bound* (1986).

82 I've already had medical attention—a dog licked me when I was on the ground.

1982 *Only When I Laugh.*

83 I would have been disappointed if I hung up my pen without ever getting one…[and] now I hope to get one every 30 years like clockwork.

1991 On receiving the Pulitzer Prize for *Lost in Yonkers*. In the *Washington Post*, 10 Apr.

Simone, Nina pseudonym of *Eunice Waymon* 1933–

US singer and pianist. She was a gifted classical pianist as a teenager, but her career was blocked by the racial prejudice of the time, and she went on to become a cult figure in jazz, gospel and soul music.

84 It wasn't a matter of becoming interested in music; music is a gift and a burden I've had since I can remember who I was. I was born into music. The decision was how to make the best use of it.

Quoted in Art Taylor *Notes and Tones* (1977), 'Nina Simone'.

Simonides of Ceos c.556–468 BC

Greek lyric poet. His poetry survives only in fragments, but he is known to have written epitaphs for Greeks who fell in the Persian Wars, and in 489 BC he beat Aeschylus in a competition for the best elegy on those who fell at Marathon.

85 Go, stranger, and tell the Spartans that here we lie, obedient to their commands.

c.480 BC Epitaph for the Spartan army dead after the Battle of Thermopylae. Quoted in Herodotus *Histories*, bk.7, ch.228.

86 Man's strength is but little, and futile his concerns.

Lyrica Graeca Selecta, (ed. D L Page), no.354.

Simons, Henry C 1899–1946

US economist, Professor at the University of Chicago.

87 Monopoly power must be abused. It has no use save abuse.

1944 *Economic Policy for a Free Society*, p.129.

Simple, Peter pseudonym of *Michael Wharton* 1913–

88 Rentacrowd Ltd—the enterprising firm that supplies crowds for all occasions, and has done so much to keep progressive causes in the public eye.

1962 In the *Daily Telegraph*.

Simpson, Alan (Kooi) 1931–

US Senator and lawyer. He was a member of Wyoming's House of Representatives (1964–77) and acted as a majority whip (1973–75) and floor leader (1975–77). He became a member of the US Senate for Wyoming in 1978.

89 Like giving dry birth to a porcupine.

1989 On the passage of immigration reform bill. In the *Washingtonian*, Mar.

90 I come from a state where gun control is just how steady you hold your weapon.

1991 In *Fortune*, 30 Dec.

Simpson, Kirke L 1881–1972

US journalist. He was awarded a Pulitzer Prize in 1921 for his article on the Unknown Soldier.

91 Chosen by a group of men in a smoke-filled room.

Of Warren G Harding, presidential candidate. Recalled on Simpson's death in the *New York Times*, 17 Jun 1972. The 'smoke-filled room' became a common phrase in presidential nomination.

Simpson, O J (Orenthal James) 1947–

US former professional football player, actor, sports commentator. He joined the Buffalo Bills professionally in 1969, and retired in 1979 to become an actor and broadcaster. He was charged with the murder of his estranged wife Nicole and Ronald Goodman, but was acquitted in 1995.

92 Absolutely 100 per cent not guilty.

> **1994** Plea on arraignment for the murder of his estranged wife. Reported in the *New York Times*, 23 Jul. Simpson was later found not guilty.

Simpson, Tommy 1938–67

English cyclist. In 1962 he became the first Briton ever to wear the leader's yellow jersey in the Tour de France. He died from heart failure during the Tour de France.

93 Put me back on my bike.

> **1967** Last words.

Sinatra, Frank (Francis Albert) 1915–98

US singer and actor. He began with the Tommy Dorsey orchestra (1940–2), and starred on radio and in films (eg *Anchors Aweigh*, 1945). His recordings (1956–65) include *Songs For Swinging Lovers, Come Fly With Me*, and *That's Life*. His highly publicized and controversial personal life included four marriages (amongst them, to Ava Gardner and Mia Farrow).

94 My greatest teacher was not a vocal coach, not the work of other singers, but the way Tommy Dorsey breathed and phrased on the trombone.

> Foreword to George T Simon *The Big Bands* (1967).

Singer, Isaac Bashevis 1904–91

US Yiddish writer of novels and short stories. Awarded the Nobel Prize for Literature (1978).

95 Children…have no use for psychology.

> **1978** Speech on receiving his Nobel Prize.

Sisco, Joseph John 1919–

US diplomat and businessman. He set up his own management consultancy (1981–), and also acted as a consultant and adviser to the UN.

96 Welcome to shuttle diplomacy!

> **1995** Comment to reporters Marvin Kalb and Ted Koppel on Henry A Kissinger's first trip to the Middle East after the Yom Kippur War. Reported in the *New York Times*, 29 Oct.

Sisson, C(harles) H(erbert) 1914–

English poet and critic. He is one of the leading poets of the period, and has also written novels and an autobiography.

97 Here lies a civil servant. He was civil
  To everyone, and servant to the devil.

> **1961** 'Civil Servant'.

Sitting Bull real name *Tatanka Iyotake* 1834–90

Chief of the Dakota Sioux, who led the defeat of Custer at Little Big Horn, 1876. He later featured in Buffalo Bill Cody's Wild West Show, 1885, but was killed evading arrest during the 'ghost dance' uprising of 1890.

98 When I was a boy the Sioux owned the world; the sun rose and set on their land; they sent ten thousand men to battle. Where are the warriors today? Who slew them? Where are our lands? Who owns them?…What law have I broken? Is it wrong for me to love my own? Is it wicked for me because my skin is red? Because I am a Sioux; because I was born where my father lived; because I would die for my country?

> **c.1866** Quoted in T C McLuhan *Touch the Earth* (1973).

Sitwell, Dame Edith Louisa 1887–1964

English poet and essayist, sister of Osbert and Sacheverell Sitwell. Her poems were designed to shock her audiences and revitalize English poetry. Her numerous prose works reflect her interest in English history. Her books include *Façade* (1923, set to music by Walton), *English Eccentrics* (1933), and *Fanfare of Elizabeth* (1946).

99 Lady Venus on the settee of the horsehair sea!

> **1923** *Façade*, 'Hornpipe'.

1 This minx, of course,
  Is as sharp as any lynx and blacker—deeper than
    the drinks and quite as
  Hot as any hottentot, without remorse!

> **1923** *Façade*, 'Hornpipe'.

2 An admiral red, whose only notion,
  (A butterfly poised on a pigtailed ocean)
  Is of the peruked sea whose swell
  Breaks on the flowerless rocks of Hell.

> **1923** *Façade*, 'En Famille'.

3 The Admiral said, 'You could never call—
  I assure you it would not do at all!
  She gets down from the table without saying
    'please',
  Forgets her prayers and to cross her T's,
  In short, her scandalous reputation
  Has shocked the whole of the Hellish nation'.

> **1923** *Façade*, 'En Famille'.

4 Those trains will run over their tails, if they can,
  Snorting and sporting like porpoises. Flee
  The burly, the whirligig wheels of the train,
  As round as the world and as large again.

> **1923** *Façade*, 'Mariner Man'.

5 The light is braying like an ass.

> **1923** *Façade*, 'Long Steel Grass'.

6 Through gilded trellises

Of the heat, spangles
Pelt down through the tangles
Of bell-flowers.
1923 *Façade*, 'Through Gilded Trellises'.

7 But a word stung him like a mosquito…
For what they hear, they repeat!
1923 *Façade*, 'Tango-Pasodoble'.

8 In a room of the palace
Black Mrs Behemoth
Gave way to wrath
And the wildest malice.
1923 *Façade*, 'Black Mrs Behemoth'.

9 Where the satyrs are chattering, nymphs with their
flattering
Glimpse of the forest enhance
All the beauty of marrow and cucumber narrow
And Ceres will join in the dance.
1923 *Façade*, 'Tarantella'.

10 That hobnailed goblin, the bob-tailed Hob,
said, 'It is time I began to rob'.
1923 *Façade*, 'Country Dance'.

11 And shade is on the brightest wing,
And dust forbids the birds to sing.
1923 *Façade*, 'Popular Song'.

12 Came the great Popinjay
Smelling his nosegay:
In cage like grots
The birds sing gavottes.
1923 *Façade*, 'Came the Great Popinjay'.

13 Jane, Jane,
Tall as a crane,
The morning light creaks down again.
1923 *Façade*, 'Aubade'.

14 The fire was furry as a bear.
1923 *Façade*, 'Dark Song'.

15 Daisy and Lily,
Lazy and silly,
Walk by the shore of the wan grass sea,—
Talking once more 'neath a swan-bosomed tree.
1923 *Façade* 'Valse'.

16 Still falls the Rain—
Dark as the world of man, black as our loss—
Blind as the nineteen hundred and forty nails
Upon the cross.
1942 'The Raids, 1940. Night and Dawn'.

17 The Englishwoman's clothes, too, have improved
out of all knowledge…no longer are our hats, as in
Victorian days, a kind of Pageant of Empire,
whereon the products of all the colonies battle for
precedence.

1942 *English Women*.

18 I have often wished I had time to cultivate
modesty… But I am too busy thinking about
myself.
1950 In *The Observer*, 30 Apr.

19 I enjoyed talking to her, but thought *nothing* of her
writing. I considered her 'a beautiful little knitter'.
1955 Of Virginia Woolf. Letter to Geoffrey Singleton, 11 Jul.

20 Mr Lewis's pictures appeared, as a very great painter
said to me, to have been painted by a mailed fist in
a cotton glove.
1965 On Wyndham Lewis. *Taken Care Of*, ch.11.

21 I wish the Government would put a tax on pianos
for the incompetent.
Collected in *Letters, 1916–1964* (1970).

Sitwell, Sir (Francis) Osbert 1892–1969

English writer. He was the brother of Edith and
Sacheverell Sitwell, and a friend of Eliot, Pound and
Wyndham Lewis, whose radical aesthetic he shared.

22 The British Bourgeosie
Is not born
And does not die,
But, if it is ill,
It has a frightened look in its eyes.
1921 *At the House of Mrs Kinfoot*.

23 But what is Dust,
Save Time's most lethal weapon,
Her faithful ally and our sneaking foe?
1927 'Mrs Southern's Enemy'.

24 *Educated*: during the holidays from Eton.
1929 From his entry in *Who's Who*.

25 Now the nimble fingers are no more nimble,
And the silver thimble lies cold and tarnished
black.
1931 'Mrs Mew's Windowbox'.

26 But he was never, well,
What I call
A Sportsman:
For forty days
He went out into the desert
—And never shot anything.
1931 Of Jesus Christ. 'Old Fashioned Sportsmen'.

27 The artist, like the idiot or clown, sits on the edge
of the world, and a push may send him over it.
1946 *The Scarlet Tree*, bk.4, ch.2.

28 A word is the carving and colouring of a thought,
and gives it permanence.
1949 *Laughter in the Next Room*, ch.7.

29 In reality, killing time

Is only the name for another of the multifarious ways
By which Time kills us.
1958 'Milordo Inglese'.

30 Hunting the author, painter and musician is a
traditional and popular sport. In this country poet-
baiting at an early stage assumed the place of bull-
baiting.
1963 'What It Feels Like to be an Author'.

Sixtus V originally *Felice Peretti* 1521–90

Franciscan preacher and a professor of theology, created
cardinal in 1570. Elected Pope in 1585, because of his
presumed feebleness, he implemented vigorous moral,
legal and financial reforms.

31 Just see how well she governs! She is only a woman,
only the mistress of half an island, and yet she
makes herself feared by Spain, by France, by the
Empire, by all!
1588 Of Elizabeth I. Quoted in L von Pastor *The History of the
Popes* (edited by Kerr R F, 1932), vol.22, p.34.

Skelton, John c.1460–1529

English poet. Educated at Oxford and Cambridge, he was
tutor to Prince Henry (later Henry VIII). He began his
poetic career with translations and elegies, but turned to
writing satirical vernacular poetry, including *Colin Clout*
(1521) and *Why Come Ye Not to Court?* (1521), both of
which were attacks on Cardinal Wolsey.

32 The sovereign'st thing that any man may have
Is little to say, and much to hear and see.
1499 *The Bouge of Court*, l. 211.

33 With Mannerly Margery milk and ale.
1523 'Mannerly Margery Milk and Ale'.

34 Far may be sought
Erst that ye can find
So courteous, so kind,
As Merry Margaret,
This midsummer flower,
Gentle as falcon
Or hawk of the tower.
1523 *The Garland of Laurel*, 'To Mistress Margaret Hussey'.

35 With lullay, lullay, like a child,
Thou sleepest too long, thou art beguiled.
1527 'Lullay, Lullay, Like a Child'.

36 What dreamest thou, drunkard, drowsy pate?
Thy lust and liking is from thee gone.
Thou blinkard blowboll, thou wakest too late.
1527 'Lullay, Lullay, Like a Child'.

Skelton, (Archibald) Noel 1880–1935

Scottish-born politician and lawyer. He was MP for Perth
(1922–3 and 1924–31) and Parliamentary Under-
Secretary in the Scottish Office (1931–5).

37 To state as clearly as may be what means lie ready
to develop a property-owning democracy, to bring
the industrial and economic status of the wage-
earner abreast of his political and educational
status, to make democracy stable and four-
square.
1923 In *The Spectator*, 19 May.

Skelton, Red (Richard) 1910–

US comedian. A star of radio and television, he also made
a few films in the 1940s, among them *Whistling in the
Dark* (1941) and *DuBarry Was a Lady* (1943).

38 Exercise? I get it on the golf course. When I see my
friends collapse, I run for the paramedics.
Attributed.

Skelton, Robin 1925–

Canadian poet and aphorist.

39 When someone says, 'It is good business', you may
be sure it is bad morality.
1991 *A Devious Dictionary.*

40 Some part of us still believes that men should
kill.
1991 *A Devious Dictionary.*

41 Death is the only mystery we all solve.
1991 *A Devious Dictionary.*

42 Never believe what you cannot doubt.
1991 *A Devious Dictionary.*

43 Headlines pass; breadlines continue.
1991 *A Devious Dictionary.*

44 Anything said off the cuff has usually been written
on it first.
1991 *A Devious Dictionary.*

45 It requires less skill to love than to be loved.
1991 *A Devious Dictionary.*

46 When one hears of progress one should ask for
whom.
1991 *A Devious Dictionary.*

47 Procrustes was an editor.
1991 *A Devious Dictionary.*

48 Kneel to nobody; bow to everyone.
1991 *A Devious Dictionary.*

49 Those who have the habit of revelation lose the
habit of thought.
1991 *A Devious Dictionary.*

50 More dreams are destroyed in bed than are ever
found there.
1991 *A Devious Dictionary.*

Skinner, B(urrhus) F(rederic) 1904–90

US psychologist and social philosopher, developer and exponent of behaviourism, which views human behaviour and learning as physiological responses. His works include *Walden Two* (1961) and *The Technology of Teaching* (1968).

51 Education is what survives when what has been learnt has been forgotten.
1964 In *New Scientist*, 21 May.

52 The real problem is not whether machines think but whether men do.
1969 *Contingencies of Reinforcement*, ch.9.

Skinner, Cornelia Otis 1902–79

US actress, singer and writer.

53 It's as though some poor devil were to set out for a large dinner party with the knowledge that the following morning he would be hearing exactly what each of the other guests thought of him.
1959 Of opening night reviews. *The Ape In Me.*

54 There are compensations for growing older. One is the realization that to be sporting isn't at all necessary. It is a great relief to reach this stage of wisdom.
Attributed.

Skinner, John 1721–1807

Jacobite songwriter and Episcopalian minister in Aberdeenshire, whose 'Tullochgorum' was described by Robert Burns as 'the best Scotch song ever Scotland saw'.

55 Come, gie's a sang, Montgomery cry'd,
And lay your disputes a' aside;
What signifies't for folks to chide
For what's been done before them?
Let Whig and Tory a' agree,
Whig and Tory, Whig and Tory,
Whig and Tory a' agree
To drop their whigmigmorum;
Let Whig and Tory a' agree
To spend this night wi' mirth and glee,
And cheerfu' sing, alang wi' me,
The Reel o ' Tullochgorum.
'Tullochgorum', stanza 1.

Skirving, Adam 1719–1803

Scottish composer of Jacobite songs.

56 Hey, Johnnie Cope, are ye wauking yet?
Or are your drums a-beating yet?
If ye were wauking I wad wait
To gang to the coals i' the morning.
1745 'Johnnie Cope', chorus (commemorating the Battle of Prestonpans and General Cope's flight to Newcastle).

Slessor, Kenneth Adolf 1901–71

Australian poet and journalist. In 1924 he published *Thief of the Moon* and in 1926 *Earth-Visitors*. *Darlinghurst Nights and Morning Glories* (1933) celebrates 'The Cross', the bohemian district of Sydney where he lived for most of his life. His verse was collected in *One Hundred Poems: 1919–1939* (1944, reissued as *Poems*, 1957), and his prose in *Bread and Wine* (1970).

57 Time that is moved by little fidget wheels
Is not my Time, the flood that does not flow.
Between the double and the single bell
Of a ship's hour, between a round of bells
From the dark warship riding there below,
I have lived many lives, and this one life
Of Joe, long dead, who lives between five bells.
1939 Five Bells, title poem. The poem was written as an elegy for Joe Lynch, a friend who fell overboard from a Sydney ferry.

Slezak, Leo 1873–1946

Czech tenor. Tall and commanding, he was internationally famous as an interpreter of the heroes of Wagnerian opera.

58 *Wann geht der nächste?*

What time's the next one?
1900 When the swan-boat failed to arrive to take him off in Wagner's *Lohengrin*. Quoted in Hugh Vickers *Great Operatic Disasters* (1979).

Sloan, John French 1871–1951

US painter of the Ashcan school, painting everyday subjects, particularly street life in New York City. His works include *Sunday, Women Drying Their Hair* (1912) and *Backyards, Greenwich Village* (1914).

59 Facility is a dangerous thing. Where there is too much technical ease the brain stops criticising. Don't let the hand fall into a smart way of putting the mind to sleep.
1939 *Gist of Art.*

60 Artists are the only people in the world who really live. The others have to hope for heaven.
Recalled on his death, 7 Sep 1951, and quoted in the *Smithsonian*, Apr 1988.

Small, Albion W 1854–1926

US sociologist; first head of the first department of sociology in the US, at the University of Chicago.

61 The social problem of the twentieth century is whether civilized nations can restore themselves to sanity after their nineteenth-century aberrations of individualism and capitalism.
1914 'A Vision of Social Efficiency', in the *American Journal of Sociology*, Jan.

62 Sociology was born of the modern ardor to improve society.
1894 *An Introduction to the Study of Society* (with George E Vincent, 1894).

Smart, Christopher 1722–71

English poet. He made a precarious living as a writer, helped by Dr Johnson and others, but suffered from bouts of insanity. His poetry includes *The Hilliad* (1753, a satire on doctors modelled on *The Dunciad*) and the structurally complex *A Song To David* (1763). During one of his confinements in a private madhouse he wrote the extraordinary and highly allusive *Jubliate Agno* (1758–63, first published as *Rejoice in the Lamb* 1939, edited by W F Stead).

63 Night, with all her negro train,
    Took possession of the plain;
    In an hearse she rode reclined,
    Drawn by screech-owls slow and blind:
    Close to her, with printless feet,
    Crept Stillness, in a winding sheet.
> **1748** 'A Night-Piece; or, Modern Philosophy', stanza 2. In the *London Magazine*, no.14, Dec. Collected in *Poems on Several Occasions* (1752).

64 Let Eli rejoice with Leucon—he is an honest fellow, which is a rarity.
    For I have seen the White Raven and Thomas Hall of Willingham and am myself a greater curiosity than both.
    Let Jemuel rejoice with Charadrius, who is from the HEIGHT and the sight of him is good for the jaundice.
    For I look up to heaven which is my prospect to escape envy by surmounting it.
> **1758–63** *Jubilate Agno*, fragment B, stanzas 25–6 (first published 1939). Both the white raven and Thomas Hall, a giant of four feet at the age of three, were curiosities exhibited in the 1740s.

65 *For every word has its marrow in the English tongue for order and for delight.*
    For the dissylables such as able table &c are the fiddle rhymes.
    For all dissylables and some trissylables are fiddle rhymes.
    For the relations of words are in pairs first.
    For the relations of words are sometimes in oppositions.
    For the relations of words are according to their distances from the pair.
> **1758–63** *Jubilate Agno*, fragment B, l. 595–600. (First published 1939.)

66 *For I will consider my cat Jeoffry.*
    For he is the servant of the Living God duly and daily serving him.
    For at the first glance of the glory of God in the East he worships in his way.
> **1758–63** Of his cat Jeoffry. *Jubilate Agno*, fragment B, l. 695–7. (First published 1939.)

67 *For he counteracts the powers of darkness by his electrical skin and glaring eyes.*
    For he counteracts the Devil, who is death, by brisking about the life.
    For in his morning orisons he loves the sun and the sun loves him.
    For he is of the tribe of Tiger.
> **1758–63** Of his cat Jeoffry. *Jubilate Agno*, fragment B, l. 719–22. (First published 1939.)

68 For ADORATION seasons change,
    And order, truth, and beauty range,
    Adjust, attract, and fill:
    The grass the polyanthus cheques;
    And polished porphyry reflects,
    By the descending rill.
> **1763** *A Song to David*, stanza 52.

69 Strong is the lion—like a coal
    His eye-ball—like a bastion's mole
    His chest against the foes:
    Strong, the gier-eagle on his sail,
    Strong against tide, th'enormous whale
    Emerges as he goes.
> **1763** *A Song to David*, stanza 76.

70 Beauteous the fleet before the gale;
    Beauteous the multitudes in mail,
    Rank'd arms and crested heads:
    Beauteous the garden's umbrage mild,
    Walk, water, meditated wild,
    And all the bloomy beds.
> **1763** *A Song to David*, stanza 78.

71 Glorious the northern lights astream;
    Glorious the song, when God's the theme;
    Glorious the thunder's roar:
    Glorious hosanna from the den;
    Glorious the catholic amen;
    Glorious the martyr's gore.
> **1763** *A Song to David*, stanza 85.

72 Lo, thro' her works gay nature grieves
    How brief she is and frail,
    As ever o'er the falling leaves
    Autumnal winds prevail.
    Yet still the philosophic mind
    Consolatory food can find,
    And hope her anchorage maintain:
    We never are deserted quite;
    'Tis by succession of delight
    That love supports his reign.
> **1764** *Ode to the Earl of Northumberland, with Some Other Pieces*, 'On a Bed of Guernsey Lilies: written in September 1763', stanza 2.

Smiles, Samuel 1812–1904

Scottish writer and social reformer who settled as a surgeon in Leeds, and published works encouraging self-improvement such as *Self-Help* (1859), *Character* (1871), *Thrift* (1875) and *Duty* (1880).

73 The spirit of self-help is the root of all genuine growth in the individual.
1859 *Self-Help*, ch.1.

74 The shortest way to do many things is to do only one thing at once.
1859 *Self-Help*, ch.9.

75 We often discover what *will* do, by finding out what will not do; and probably he who never made a mistake never made a discovery.
1859 *Self-Help*, ch.11.

76 The healthy spirit of self-help created among working people would, more than any other measure, serve to raise them as a class; and this, not by pulling down others, but by levelling them up to a higher and still advancing standard of religion, intelligence, and virtue.
1859 *Self-Help*.

Smith, A J M 1902–80
Canadian-born US poet and anthologist.

77 McLuhan put a telescope to his ear;
What a lovely smell, he said, we have here.
1967 *Poems*, 'The Taste of Space'. When McLuhan first heard this couplet, his response was 'Synaesthetsia!'

Smith, Adam 1723–90
Scottish economist and philosopher. His *Inquiry into the Nature and Causes of the Wealth of Nations* (1776), the first major work of political economy, examined in detail the consequences of economic freedom—division of labour, the function of markets and the international implications of a *laissez-faire* economy. He was Professor of Moral Philosophy at the University of Glasgow.

78 In ease of body, peace of mind, all the different ranks of life are nearly upon a level and the beggar who suns himself by the side of the highway, possesses that security which kings are fighting for.
1759 *The Theory of Moral Sentiments*.

79 People of the same trade seldom meet together, even for merriment and diversion, but the conversation ends in a conspiracy against the public, or in some contrivance to raise prices.
1776 *An Inquiry into the Nature and Causes of the Wealth of Nations*, bk.1, ch.10, pt.2.

80 The rate of profit does not, like rent and wages, rise with the prosperity, and fall with the declension, of the society. On the contrary, it is naturally low in rich, and high in poor countries, and it is always highest in the countries which are going fastest to ruin.
1776 *An Inquiry into the Nature and Causes of the Wealth of Nations*, bk.1, ch.11, conclusion.

81 Every individual...intends only his own gain, and he is in this as in many other cases led by an invisible hand to promote an end which was no part of his intention... By pursuing his own interest he frequently promotes that of the society more effectually than when he really intends to promote it. I have never known much good done by those who affected to trade for the publick good.
1776 *An Inquiry into the Nature and Causes of the Wealth of Nations*, bk.4, ch.3.

82 Science is the great antidote to the poison of enthusiasm and superstition.
1776 *An Inquiry into the Nature and Causes of the Wealth of Nations*, bk.5, ch.1, pt.3, article 3.

83 There is no art which one government sooner learns of another than that of draining money from the pockets of the people.
1776 *An Inquiry into the Nature and Causes of the Wealth of Nations*, bk.5, ch.2.

84 To found a great Empire for the sole purpose of raising up a people of customers, may at first sight appear a project fit only for a nation of shopkeepers. It is, however, a project altogether unfit for a nation of shopkeepers; but extremely fit for a nation that is governed by shopkeepers.
1776 *An Inquiry into the Nature and Causes of the Wealth of Nations*.
▷ See Napoleon 718:34, Punch 795:24, Stoppard 978:79.

85 Capitals are increased by parsimony, and diminished by prodigality and misconduct. By what a frugal man annually saves he not only affords maintenance to an additional number of productive hands... but...he establishes as it were a perpetual fund for the maintenance of an equal number in all times to come.
1776 *An Inquiry into the Nature and Causes of the Wealth of Nations*.

86 Consumption is the sole end and purpose of all production.
1776 *An Inquiry into the Nature and Causes of the Wealth of Nations*.

87 It is not from the benevolence of the butcher, the brewer, or the baker, that we expect our dinner, but from their regard to their own interest.
1776 *An Inquiry into the Nature and Causes of the Wealth of Nations*.

88 It is the maxim of every prudent master of a family never to attempt to make at home what it will cost him more to make than to buy. The taylor does not attempt to make his own shoe...All of them find it for their interest to employ their whole industry in a way in which they have some advantage over their neighbours and to purchase with a part of its produce... whatever else they have occasion

for…What is prudence in the conduct of every private family, can scarce be folly in that of a great kingdom…Would it be a reasonable law to prohibit the importation of all foreign wines, merely to encourage the making of claret and burgundy in Scotland?

1776 *An Inquiry into the Nature and Causes of the Wealth of Nations.*

89 The common wages of labour depends every where upon the contract usually made between those two parties whose interests are by no means the same— Masters are always and every where in a sort of tacit, but constant and uniform combination, not to raise the wages of labour above their actual rate.

1776 *An Inquiry into the Nature and Causes of the Wealth of Nations.*

90 The greatest improvement in the productive powers of labour, and the greater part of the skill, dexterity and judgement with which it is any where directed, as applied, seem to have been the effects of the division of labour.

1776 *An Inquiry into the Nature and Causes of the Wealth of Nations.*

91 The man whose life is spent in performing a few simple operations of which the effects too are, perhaps, always the same or very nearly the same, has no occasion to exert his understanding, or to exercise his invention. He generally becomes as stupid and ignorant as it is possible for a human creature to become.

1776 *An Inquiry into the Nature and Causes of the Wealth of Nations.*

92 The principle which prompts to save is the desire of bettering our condition—a desire which…comes with us from the womb and never leaves us till we go into the grave.

1776 *An Inquiry into the Nature and Causes of the Wealth of Nations.*

93 The real price of everything, what everything really costs to the man who wants to acquire it, is the toil and trouble of acquiring it. Labour was the first price, the original purchase money that was paid for all things.

1776 *An Inquiry into the Nature and Causes of the Wealth of Nations.*

94 The word VALUE, it is to be observed, has two different meanings, and sometimes the utility of some particular object, and sometimes the power of purchasing other goods which the possession of that object conveys. This one may be called 'value in use'; the other, 'value in exchange'. The things which have the greatest value in use have frequently little or no value in exchange; and on the contrary, those which have the greatest value in exchange

have frequently little or no value in use. Nothing is more useful than water: but it will purchase scarce any thing; scarce any thing can be had in exchange for it. A diamond, on the contrary, has scarce any value in use; but a very great quantity of other goods may frequently be had in exchange for it.

1776 *An Inquiry into the Nature and Causes of the Wealth of Nations.*

95 The difference between the most dissimilar characters, between a philosopher and a common street porter, seems to arise not so much from nature, as from habit, custom and education

1776 *An Inquiry into the Nature and Causes of the Wealth of Nations.*

Smith, Al(fred) Emmanuel 1873–1944

US Democrat politician, who rose from newsboy to be Governor of New York State (1919–20, 1923–8). He was defeated as Democratic candidate for the Presidency in 1928.

96 Nobody shoots Santa Claus.

1936 Denouncing criticisms of the US aid programme.

97 No matter how thin you slice it, it's still baloney.

1936 Election campaign speech, October.

Smith, Sir Cyril 1928–

English Liberal politician, who founded a spring manufacturing company before his election to Parliament in 1972. A popular MP, of unusually large physical dimensions, he was knighted in 1988.

98 If the fence is strong enough, I'll sit on it.

1974 In *The Observer*, 15 Sep.

Smith, Godfrey 1926–

English writer and columnist. He was Associate Editor of the *Sunday Times* from 1972 to 1991 and has written novels and books about English social life and customs. He has also compiled anthologies.

99 A scoop of pure honey set in a green bowl.

1984 Of Bath. *The English Companion.*

1 Try as one may to stress the cultural and historical role of the place…it still conveys one overwhelmingly powerful image to your average Englishman: the dirty weekend.

1984 Of Brighton. *The English Companion.*

Smith, Iain Crichton Gaelic name *Blain Mac A'Ghobhainn* 1928–

Scottish poet and novelist, who writes in both English and his native Gaelic. His novels include *Consider the Lilies* (1968). His *Collected Poems* were published in 1992.

2 Here they have no time for the fine graces

of poetry, unless it freely grows
in deep compulsion, like water in the well,
woven into the texture of the soil
in a strong pattern.
1955 'Poem of Lewis'.

3 And she, being old, fed from a mashed plate
as an old mare might droop across a fence
to the dull pastures of her ignorance.
Her husband held her upright while he prayed

to God who is all-forgiving to send down
some angel somewhere who might land perhaps
in his foreign wings among the gradual crops.
She munched, half dead, blindly searching the
spoon.
1961 *Thistles and Roses*, 'Old Woman', stanzas 1–2.

4 This is the land God gave to Andy Stewart—we
have our inheritance.
There shall be no ardour, there shall be
indifference.
There shall not be excellence, there shall be the
average.
We shall be the intrepid hunters of golf balls.
1969 'The White Air of March'.

5 I tremble in this factory of books.
What love he must have lost to write so much.
1985 After seeing an exhibit of Sir Walter Scott's manuscripts.
'At the Scott Exhibition, Edinburgh Festival', collected in
Selected Poems (1985).

Smith, Ian Douglas 1919–

Zimbabwean (Rhodesian) politician, a founder of the
pro-independence Rhodesian Front. Prime Minister from
1964, he unilaterally declared independence in 1965.
Britain applied sanctions, and in 1979 majority rule was
granted. He was suspended from government (1987) for
South African links.

6 We have the happiest Africans in the world.
1971 In *The Observer*, 28 Nov.

7 Let me say it again, I don't believe in black majority
rule ever in Rhodesia. Not in a thousand years.
1976 Radio broadcast, 20 Mar.

Smith, John 1938–94

Scottish politician. He was called to the Bar in 1967, and
made a QC in 1983. He became MP for Lanarkshire
North in 1970, and for Monklands East in 1983. He
served as a cabinet minister under Harold Wilson and
James Callaghan, and in the shadow cabinet (1972–92).
He succeeded Neil Kinnock as leader of the Labour Party
in 1992.

8 We will do our best to reward your faith in us, but
please give us the opportunity to serve our country,
that is all we ask.

1994 Address to a European Gala Dinner, 11 May. They were
his final public words; he died the next morning of a heart
attack.

Smith, Logan Pearsall 1865–1946

US-born British writer, who took British nationality in
1913. He is best known for his polished essays and
aphorisms, gathered in books such as *Afterthoughts*
(1931); he also wrote criticism and short stories.

9 The denunciation of the young is a necessary part
of the hygiene of older people, and greatly assists
the circulation of their blood.
1931 *Afterthoughts*, 'Age and Death'.

10 There are two things to aim at in life: first, to get
what you want; and, after that, to enjoy it. Only
the wisest of mankind achieve the second.
1931 *Afterthoughts*, 'Life and Human Nature'.

11 How awful to reflect that what people say of us is
true!
1931 *Afterthoughts*, 'Life and Human Nature'.

12 There are few sorrows, however poignant, in which
a good income is of no avail.
1931 *Afterthoughts*, 'Life and Human Nature'.

13 An improper mind is a perpetual feast.
1931 *Afterthoughts*, 'Life and Human Nature'.

14 There is more felicity on the far side of baldness
than young men can possibly imagine.
1931 *Afterthoughts*, 'Age and Death'.

15 What music is more enchanting than the voices of
young people, when you can't hear what they say?
1931 *Afterthoughts*, 'Age and Death'.

16 Most people sell their souls, and live with a good
conscience on the proceeds.
1931 *Afterthoughts*, 'Other People'.

17 A friend who loved perfection would be the perfect
friend, did not that love shut his door on me.
1931 *Afterthoughts*, 'Other People'.

18 All Reformers, however strict their social
conscience, live in houses just as big as they can pay
for.
1931 *Afterthoughts*, 'Other People'.

19 When they come downstairs from their Ivory
Towers, Idealists are very apt to walk straight into
the gutter.
1931 *Afterthoughts*, 'Other People'.

20 Married women are kept women, and they are
beginning to find it out.
1931 *Afterthoughts*, 'Other People'.

21 A best-seller is the gilded tomb of a mediocre talent.
1931 *Afterthoughts*, 'Art and Letters'.

22 People say that life is the thing, but I prefer reading.
1931 *Afterthoughts*, 'Myself'.

23 Thank heavens, the sun has gone in, and I don't
have to go out and enjoy it.
1931 *Afterthoughts*, 'Myself'.

24 What I like in a good author is not what he says,
but what he whispers.
1933 *All Trivia*, 'Afterthoughts'.

Smith, Margaret Chase 1897–1995

US Senator. Elected to the US Senate in 1948, she served
four terms and continued to be politically active
afterwards. She supported the draft for women, was a
teacher and a syndicated columnist. She held 95 honorary
degrees from various universities and colleges.

25 The greatest deliberative body in the world…has
too often been debased to the level of a forum of
hate and character assassination sheltered by the
shield of congressional immunity.
1950 'Declaration of Conscience' address to the Senate, 1 Jun,
denouncing accusations by Senator Joseph R McCarthy.

Smith, Red 1905–82

US sportswriter.

26 It was an ideal day for football—too cold for the
spectators and too cold for the players.
1963 Reporting on a match between the Chicago Bears and the
New York Giants.

Smith, Samuel Francis 1808–95

US clergyman and poet.

27 My country, 'tis of thee,
Sweet land of liberty,
Of thee I sing:
Land where my fathers died,
Land of the pilgrims' pride,
From every mountain-side
Let the freedom ring.
1831 'America'.

Smith, Stevie (Florence Margaret)

1902–71

English poet and novelist. She lived most of her life with
her aunt in a London suburb, and much of her work
reflected that setting. Loneliness is a persistent theme, but
she was also adept at dealing wittily with serious matters.

28 If you cannot have your dear husband for a comfort
and a delight, for a breadwinner and a crosspatch,
for a sofa, chair or a hot-water bottle, one can use
him as a Cross to be Borne.
1936 *Novel On Yellow Paper*.

29 A Good Time was Had By All.
1937 Title of poetry collection.

30 This Englishwoman is so refined
She has no bosom and no behind.
1937 *A Good Time was Had By All*, 'This Englishwoman'.

31 Here is all straight and narrow as a tomb
Oh shut me not within a little room.
1950 *Harold's Leap*, 'The Commuted Sentence'.

32 Let all the little poets be gathered together in classes
And let prizes be given to them by the Prize Asses.
1950 *Harold's Leap*, 'To School!'

33 Oh, no, no, no, it was too cold always
(Still the dead one lay moaning)
I was much too far out all my life
And not waving but drowning.
1957 *Not Waving but Drowning*, 'Not Waving But Drowning'.

34 People who are always praising the past
And especially the times of faith as best
Ought to go and live in the Middle Ages
And be burnt at the stake as witches and sages.
1957 *Not Waving but Drowning*, 'The Past'.

35 Shall I tell you the signs of a New Age coming?
It is a sound of drubbing and sobbing
Of people crying, We are old, we are old
And the sun is going down and becoming cold.
1957 *Not Waving but Drowning*, 'The New Age'.

36 Why does my Muse only speak when she is
unhappy?
She does not, I only listen when I am unhappy
When I am happy I live and despise writing
For my Muse this cannot but be dispiriting.
1962 *Selected Poems*, 'My Muse'.

37 I long for the Person from Porlock
To bring my thoughts to an end.
I am growing impatient to see him
I think of him as a friend.
1962 *Selected Poems*, 'Thoughts About the Person from
Porlock' (a reference to the 'person from Porlock' mentioned in
Coleridge's preliminary note to 'Kubla Khan').

38 Private Means is dead
God rest his soul, officers and fellow-rankers said.
1962 *Selected Poems*, 'Private Means is Dead'.

39 'This night shall thy soul be required of thee.'
My soul is never required of *me*
It always has to be somebody else of course.
Will my soul be required of me tonight perhaps?
1972 *Scorpion*, 'Scorpion'.
▷ See Bible 143:94.

40 Scorpion so wishes to be gone.
1972 *Scorpion*, 'Scorpion'.

41 Oh I am a cat that likes to

Gallop about doing good.

1972 *Scorpion*, 'The Galloping Cat'.

Smith, Rev Sydney 1771–1845

English journalist, clergymen and preacher and lecturer on moral philosophy, also one of the founders of the *Edinburgh Review*. He wrote letters and pamphlets in favour of Catholic emancipation, the ballot, the abolition of prison abuses and other causes, and is best known as a conversationalist and wit.

42 The moment that the very name of Ireland is mentioned, the English seem to bid adieu to common feeling, common prudence, and common sense, and to act with the barbarity of tyrants and the fatuity of idiots.

1807–8 *Peter Plymley's Letters.*

43 I look upon Switzerland as an inferior sort of Scotland.

1815 Letter to Lord Holland, [August]. In *The Letters of Sydney Smith* edited by Nowell C Smith (1953), vol. 1.

44 What two ideas are more inseparable than Beer and Britannia.

1823 In the *Edinburgh Review*, quoted in H Pearson *The Smith of Smiths* (1934), ch.11.

45 Alas, alas, how easily a priest begets children and with what difficulty he provides for them; a priest I mean who is extravagant enough to keep a conscience; a point wherein our profession commits (I must say) little excess.

1825 Letter to Lord Holland, 14 Jul. In *The Letters of Sydney Smith* edited by Nowell C Smith (1953), vol. 1.

46 He who drinks a tumbler of London Water has literally in his stomach more animated beings than there are men, Women and Children on the face of the globe.

1834 Letter to Lady Grey, 19 Nov.

47 No furniture so charming as books.

Quoted in Lady Holland *Memoir* (1855), vol 1, ch. 9.

48 Take short views, hope for the best, and trust in God.

Quoted in Lady Holland *Memoir* (1855), vol 1, ch. 6.

49 That knuckle-end of England—that land of Calvin, oat-cakes and sulphur.

Quoted in Lady Holland *Memoir* (1855), vol 1, ch. 2.

50 I heard him [Jeffrey] speak disrespectfully of the Equator!

Quoted in Lady Holland *Memoir* (1855), vol.1, ch.2.

51 As the French say, there are three sexes—men, women, and clergymen.

Quoted in Lady Holland *Memoir* (1855), vol.1, ch.9.

52 He is like a book in breeches.

Of Lord Macaulay. Quoted in Lady Holland *Memoir* (1855), vol.1, ch.11.

53 He has occasional flashes of silence that make his conversation perfectly delightful.

Of Lord Macaulay. Quoted in Lady Holland *Memoir* (1855), vol.1. ch.11.

54 My definition of marriage…It resembles a pair of shears, so joined that they cannot be separated; often moving in opposite directions, yet always punishing anyone who comes between them.

Quoted in Lady Holland *Memoir* (1855), vol.1, ch.11.

55 Let onion atoms lurk within the bowl, And, half-suspected, animate the whole.

'Receipt for a Salad', quoted in Lady Holland *Memoir* (1855), vol.1, ch.11.

56 Serenely full, the epicure would say, 'Fate cannot harm me, I have dined today.'

'Receipt for a Salad', concluding lines, quoted in Lady Holland *Memoir*, (1855), vol.1, ch.11.

57 My idea of heaven is, eating *paté de foie gras* to the sound of trumpets.

Quoted in H Pearson *The Smith of Smiths*, (1934), ch.10.

58 What a pity it is we have no amusements in England but vice and religion!

Quoted in H Pearson *The Smith of Smiths*, (1934), ch.10.

59 I am just going to pray for you at St Paul's, but with no very lively hope of success.

Quoted in H Pearson *The Smith of Smiths*, (1934), ch.10.

Smith, Sydney Goodsir 1915–75

New Zealand-born Scottish poet and critic, who played an important part in the 20c revival of poetry in the Scots language. His first volume, *Skail Wind* (1941), was followed by several others. He also edited works on Scottish literature.

60 This rortie wretched city
Sair come down frae its auld hiechts
—The hauf o't smug, complacent,
Lost til all pride of race or spirit,
The tither wild and rouch as ever
In its secret hairt
But lost alsweill, the smeddum tane,
The man o'independent mind has cap in hand the day
—Sits on its craggy spine
And drees the wind and rain
That nourished all its genius
—Weary wi centuries
This empty capital snorts like a great beast
Caged in its sleep, dreaming of freedom.

1954 Of Edinburgh. 'Kynd Kittock's Land' (Kynd Kittock is a character in the poetry of the 16th-century Scottish poet William Dunbar.) rortie=splendid, smeddum=spirit, drees=endures.

Smith, Walter Chalmers 1824–1908

Scottish clergyman and poet.

61 Immortal, invisible, God only wise,
In light inaccessible hid from our eyes,
Most blessèd, most glorious, the Ancient of Days,
Almighty, victorious, Thy great name we praise.

1867 'Immortal, Invisible', hymn.

Smollett, Tobias George 1721–71

Scottish novelist. He wrote a history of England and from 1753 edited the *Critical Review*, which led to his being imprisoned for libel in 1760. His unfavourable account of his travels in France and Italy, which he was ordered to visit for the sake of his health, earned him Sterne's designation as 'Smelfungus'. His novel *Humphrey Clinker* (1771) remains popular.

62 I think for my part one half of the nation is mad—and the other not very sound.

1762 *The Adventures of Sir Launcelot Greaves*, ch.6.

63 They have no education, no taste for reading, no housewifery, nor, indeed, any earthly occupation but that of dressing their hair, and adorning their bodies. They hate walking, and would never go abroad, if they were not stimulated by the vanity of being seen... Nothing can be more parsimonious than the economy of these people. They live upon soup and bouille, fish and salad.

1766 Of the nobility of Boulogne. *Travels through France and Italy*.

64 The capital is become an overgrown monster; which, like a dropsical head, will in time leave the body and extremities without nourishment and support.

1771 Of London. Letter from Matthew Bramble, 29 May, *Humphrey Clinker*, vol.1.

65 I am pent up in frowzy lodgings, where there is not room enough to swing a cat.

1771 Letter from Matthew Bramble, 8 Jun, *Humphrey Clinker*, vol.1.

Smuts, Jan Christian 1870–1950

South African general and statesman, Prime Minister (1919–24). A significant figure at Versailles, he was instrumental in the founding of the League of Nations. As Minister of Justice under Hertzog, his coalition with the Nationalists in 1934 produced the United Party, and he became Premier again (1939–48).

66 Perhaps it is God's will to lead the people of South Africa through defeat and humiliation to a better future and a brighter day.

1902 Speech at the Vereeniging peace talks, 31 May.

67 What was everybody's business in the end proved to be nobody's business. Each one looked to the other to take the lead, and the aggressors got away with it.

1943 Explaining the failure of the League of Nations to the Empire Parliamentary Association, London, 25 Nov.

Snagge, John 1904–96

English radio commentator.

68 I can't tell who's leading—it's either Oxford or Cambridge.

1949 Radio commentary on the Boat Race, when the engine of Snagge's launch broke down. Quoted in C Dodd *Oxford and Cambirdge Boat Race* (1983), ch.14.

Snow, Carmel 1887–1961

Irish-born US journalist. She was fashion editor (1932–35) and then editor-in-chief (1935–57) of *Harper's Bazaar*.

69 Elegance is good taste *plus* a dash of daring.

1962 *The World of Carmel Snow*.

Snow, C(harles) P(ercy), 1st Baron 1905–80

English novelist and physicist. His works include a cycle of novels portraying English life from 1920, including *Strangers and Brothers* (1940), *The Masters* (1951), *The New Men* (1954) and *Corridors of Power* (1964). In his controversial *Two Cultures* (Rede lecture, 1959) he discussed the need for closer contact of science and literature.

70 Drinking the best tea in the world in an empty cricket ground—that, I think, is the final pleasure left to man.

1932 Quoted in Colin Jarman *The Guinness Dictionary of Sports Quotations* (1990).

71 The official world, the corridors of power, the dilemmas of conscience and egotism—she disliked them all.

1956 *Homecomings*, ch.22. This phrase was later used as the title of his 1964 novel, *Corridors of Power*.

72 A good many times I have been present at gatherings of people who...are thought highly educated and who have...been expressing their incredulity at the illiteracy of scientists. Once or twice I have been provoked and have asked the company how many of them could describe the Second Law of Thermodynamics. The response was cold: it was also negative.

1959 *The Two Cultures*, Rede Lecture, ch.1.

73 I believe the intellectual life of the whole of western society is increasingly being split into two polar groups... Literary intellectuals at one pole—at the other scientists, and as the most representative, the physical scientists. Between the two a gulf of mutual incomprehension.

1959 *The Two Cultures*, Rede Lecture.

74 'I grant you that he's not two-faced,' I said. 'But what's the use of that when the one face he has got is so peculiarly unpleasant?'
1960 *The Affair*, ch.4.

75 Technology…is a queer thing. It brings you great gifts with one hand, and it stabs you in the back with the other.
1971 In the *New York Times*, 15 Mar.

76 There have been many crimes committed in the name of duty and obedience—many more than in the name of dissent.
1971 'Testimony of Four Peers', in *Esquire*, Dec.

77 Writers are much more esteemed in Russia, they play a much larger part in society than they do in the West. The advantage of not being free is that people listen to you.
1971 Interview on Radio Moscow.

Snow, Clyde Collins

Forensic anthropologist.

78 The ground is like a beautiful woman. If you treat her gently, she'll tell you all her secrets.
1991 On exploring the massacre of thousands of Mayan Indians in Guatemala in the early 1980s. In the *Washington Post*, 18 Dec.

Snowden, Philip Snowden, 1st Viscount

1864–1937

English Labour statesman, crippled in a cycling accident. A socialist MP from 1906, he opposed conscription and as Chancellor of the Exchequer from 1924 aggravated the financial crises. A free trader, he resigned in 1932, and wrote an *Autobiography* (1934).

79 The Labour Party's election programme…is the most fantastic and impracticable programme ever put before the electors. This is not socialism. It is bolshevism run mad.
1931 Radio broadcast, 17 Oct.

Snyder, Gary Sherman   1930–

US poet. The 'Japhy Ryder' of Kerouac's *The Dharma Bums*, his writings reflect an almost sacramental vision of man's relationship to his natural environment.

80 I cannot remember things I once read
A few friends, but they are in cities.
Drinking cold snow-water from a tin cup
Looking down for miles
Through high still air.
1959 *Riprap*, 'Mid-August at Sourdough Mountain Lookout'.

81 A clear, attentive mind

Has no meaning but that
Which sees is truly seen.
1959 *Riprap*, 'Piute Creek'.

82 In ten thousand years the Sierras
Will be dry and dead, home of the scorpion.
Ice-scratched slabs and bent trees.
No paradise, no fall,
Only the weathering land
The wheeling sky,
Man, with his Satan
Scouring the chaos of the mind.
Oh Hell!
1959 *Riprap*, 'Milton By Firelight (Piute Creek, August 1955)'.

83 After weeks of watching the roof leak
I fixed it tonight
by moving a single board.
1968 *The Back Country*, 'Hitch Haiku'.

84 Down for a new radio, to Ross Lake, and back up.
Three
days walking. Strange how unmoved this place
  leaves one;
neither articulate or worshipful; rather the pressing
  need to look
within and adjust the mechanism of perception.
1969 *Earth House Hold*, 'Lookout's Journal, Crater Shan 28 July'.

85 Beware of anything that promises freedom or enlightenment—traps for eager and clever fools—a dog has a keener nose—every creature in a cave can justify himself. Three-fourths of philosophy and literature is the talk of people trying to convince themselves that they really like the cage they were tricked into entering.
1969 *Earth House Hold*, 'Japan First Time Around, 24: X'.

86 I recalled when I worked in the woods
and the bars of Madras, Oregon.
That short-haired joy and roughness—
America—your stupidity.
I could almost love you again.
1974 *Turtle Island*, 'I Went Into The Maverick Bar'.

Socrates   469–399 BC

Greek philosopher. Our knowledge of his life and teaching derives mainly from the work of his pupil Plato, in dialogues including the *Republic*, and the *Apology*, *Crito* and *Phaedo*, which describe Socrates's trial for 'corrupting the young' and his death by drinking hemlock.

87 I am so far like the midwife that I cannot myself give birth to wisdom, and the common reproach is true, that, though I question others, I can myself bring nothing to light because there is no wisdom in me.
Quoted in Plato *Theaetetus*, 150c (translated by F M Cornford).

88 This sense of wonder is the mark of the philosopher. Philosophy indeed has no other origin.
    Quoted in Plato *Theaetetus*, 150c (translated by F M Cornford).

89 How many things I can do without!
    On viewing goods for sale. Quoted in Diogenes Laertius *Vitae Philosophorum*, 2.25 (translated by R D Hicks, 1950).

90 The unexamined life is not worth living.
    Quoted in Plato *Apology*, 38a.

91 There is only one good, knowledge, and only one evil, ignorance.
    Quoted in Diogenes Laertius *Vitae Philosophorum*, 2.31 (translated by R D Hicks, 1950).

Solon   c.640–c.559BC

Athenian lawgiver and poet. Archon in 594 BC (or 591 BC), he reformed the constitution, abolishing debt-slavery and admitting a fourth class to the Assembly. After 10 years of voluntary exile he returned to Athens in 580 BC

92 As I grow older, I constantly learn more.
    Quoted in Bergk (ed) *Poetae Lyrici Graeci*, 'Solon', no.18.

Solow, Robert M   1924–

US economist, winner of the Nobel Prize (1987).

93 Thinking precisely and systematically about something as complex and irregular as a modern economy is very difficult, maybe impossible.
    1984 In the *New York Times Book Review*, 30 Dec.

94 Merely to adopt the more powerful assumption is no more than to assume the more powerful conclusion.
    1994 In the *Journal of Economic Perspectives*, 8:53.

Solzhenitsyn, Aleksandr Isayevich   1918–

Russian writer, a labour camp prisoner (1945–53). His *One Day in the Life of Ivan Denisovich* (1962) was widely acclaimed, but his subsequent denunciation of Soviet censorship led to the banning of his novels *Cancer Ward* (1968) and *The First Circle* (1968). He was awarded the Nobel Prize for Literature in 1970 (received 1974). After *The Gulag Archipelago* (3 vols, 1973–6), an account of the Stalinist terror, he was exiled (1974). His citizenship was restored in 1990, and the treason charges against him dropped in 1991. In 1994 he returned to Russia.

95 You only have power over people so long as you do not take everything away from them. But when you have robbed man of everything, he is no longer in your pocket—he is free.
    1968 *The First Circle*.

96 In our country the lie has become not just a moral category but a pillar of the State.
    1974 Quoted in the *Observer*, 29 Dec.

97 For us in Russia, communism is a dead dog, while, for many people in the West, it is still a living lion.
    1979 In the *Listener*, 15 Feb.

Somerville, Edith (Anna Oenone) and Violet Florence Martin née Ross
pseudonym of *Martin Ross* 1858–1949; 1862–1915

Irish cousins who first met in 1886. They formed a lasting successful literary partnership and are both know for a series of novels that makes fun of the Irish.

98 'May the divil choke ye!' says he, pleasant enough, but I knew by the blush he had he was vexed.
    1898 *Some Experiences of an Irish R.M.*, 'Lisheen Races, Second-Hand'.

99 'I call it a criminal thing in any one's great-great-grandfather to rear up a preposterous troop of sons and plant them all out in his own country', Lady Knox said to me with apparent irrelevance. 'I detest collaterals. Blood may be thicker than water, but it is also a great deal nastier.'
    1898 *Some Experiences of an Irish R.M.*, 'Philippa's Fox-Hunt'.

1 Every known class of refusal was successfully exhibited. One horse endeavoured to climb the rails into the Grand Stand; another, having stopped dead at the critical point, swung round, and returned in consternation to the starting-point, with his rider hanging like a locket around his neck. Another, dowered with a sense of humour unusual among horses, stepped delicately over the furze-bushes, and, amidst rounds of applause, walked through the lime with a stoic calm.
    1908 *Further Experiences of an Irish R.M.*, 'A Royal Command'.

Somoza, (García) Anastasio   1925–80

Nicaraguan dictator, educated in the US. As Chief of the National Guard he established himself in supreme power in the early 1930s, and retained it until assassinated, when the rule passed to his sons.

2 You won the elections. But I won the count.
    1977 In *The Guardian*, 17 Jun.

Sontag, Susan   1933–

US critic and theorist. She began writing experimental fiction, but has established her intellectual reputation as a critic and polymath. Her essays in leading journals were expanded into books including *On Photography* (1976) and *Illness As Metaphor* (1978).

3 Ambition if it feeds at all, does so on the ambition of others.
    1963 *The Benefactor*, ch.1.

4 Interpretation is the revenge of the intellect upon art.

1964 In *The Evergreen Review*, Dec.

5 Perversity is the muse of modern literature.
1966 *Against Interpretation*, 'Camus' Notebooks'.

6 What pornography is really about, ultimately, isn't sex but death.
1967 In *Partisan Review*, Spring.

7 The white race *is* the cancer of human history, it is the white race, and it alone—its ideologies and inventions—which eradicates autonomous civilizations wherever it spreads, which has upset the ecological balance of the planet, which now threatens the very existence of life itself.
1967 In *Partisan Review*, Winter.

8 The camera makes everyone a tourist in other people's reality, and eventually in one's own.
1974 In the *New York Review of Books*, 18 Apr. Later published in book form as *On Photography* (1976).

9 When we're afraid we shoot. But when we're nostalgic we take pictures.
1974 In the *New York Review of Books*, 18 Apr.

10 The most interesting ideas are heresies.
1975 Interview in *Salmagundi*, Fall–Winter.

11 Illness is the night-side of life, a more onerous citizenship. Everyone who is born holds dual citizenship, in the kingdom of the well and in the kingdom of the sick. Although we all prefer to use only the good passport, sooner or later each of us is obliged, at least for a spell, to identify ourselves as citizens of that other place.
1978 In the *New York Review of Books*, 26 Jan.

12 It seems the very model of all the catastrophes privileged populations feel await them.
1989 Of AIDS. *AIDS and Its Metaphors*, ch.8.

13 I envy paranoids; they actually feel people are paying attention to them.
1992 In *Time Out*, 19 Aug.

Sophocles c.496–405 BC

Athenian playwright. He wrote well over 100 plays, of which seven tragedies have servived, including *Oedipus Tyrannus*.

14 Woman, silence makes a woman beautiful.
Ajax, 293 (translated by H Lloyd-Jones, 1994).

15 Hope has often caused the love of gain to ruin men.
Antigone, 222 (translated by H Lloyd-Jones, 1994).

16 Many things are formidable, and none more formidable than man.
Antigone, 332–3 (translated by H Lloyd-Jones, 1994).

17 One must obey the man whom the city sets up in power in small things and in justice and in its opposite.
Creon speaking. *Antigone*, 666–7 (translated by H Lloyd-Jones, 1994).

18 You see how when rivers are swollen in winter those trees that yield to the flood retain their branches, but those that offer resistance perish, trunk and all.
Haemon speaking. *Antigone*, 712–14 (translated by H Lloyd-Jones, 1994).

19 Love invincible in battle.
Antigone, 781–90 (translated by H Lloyd-Jones, 1994).

20 Remember there is no success without hard work.
Electra, 945 (translated by H Lloyd-Jones, 1994).

21 When I do not understand, I like to say nothing.
Oedipus Tyrannus, 569 (translated by H Lloyd-Jones, 1994).

22 It is best to live anyhow, as one may; do not be afraid of marriage with your mother! Many have lain with their mothers in dreams too. It is he to whom such things are nothing who puts up with life best.
Jocasta to Oedipus, her son and husband, before they both discover the truth of the prophecy. *Oedipus Tyrannus*, 979–83 (translated by H Lloyd-Jones, 1994).

Sorley, Charles Hamilton 1895–1915

Scottish poet, killed in action during World War I.

23 When you see millions of the mouthless dead
Across your dreams in pale battalions go,
Say not soft things as other men have said,
That you'll remember. For you need not so.
Give them not praise. For, deaf, how should they know
It is not curses heaped on each gashed head?
Marlborough and Other Poems, 'A Sonnet' (published 1916).

Soule, John Babsone Lane 1815–91

24 Go West, young man, go West!
Terre Haute Express.

Sousa, John Philip 1854–1932

US composer and bandmaster. He became conductor of the United States Marine Band in 1880 and formed his own band, which built up an international reputation, 12 years later. As well as more than a hundred popular marches, he composed 10 comic operas.

25 Jazz will endure just as long as people hear it through their feet instead of their brains.
c.1920 Attributed.

Soutar, William 1898–1943

Scottish poet and diarist, who was confined to bed for the last 13 years of his life with a form of spondylitis. His poems in Scots for adults and children were praised by Hugh MacDiarmid and others.

26 O luely, luely cam she in
And luely she lat doun:
I kent her be her caller lips
And her breists sae sma' an' roun'.

A' thru the nicht we spak nae word
Nor sinder'd bane frae bane:
A' thru the nicht I heard her hert
Gang soundin' wi' my ain.
1932 'The Tryst', stanzas 1–2.

27 Sae luely, luely, cam she in
Sae luely was she gaen
And wi' her a' my simmer days
Like they had never been.
1932 'The Tryst', stanza 4.

Southey, Robert 1774–1843

English poet and writer and friend of Wordsworth. His epics include *Thalaba* (1801) and *Madoc* (1805). His shorter poems are *The Battle of Blenheim* and *The Inchcape Rock*. He also wrote a *Life of Nelson* (1813), and became Poet Laureate in 1813.

28 She has made me in love with a cold climate, and frost and snow, with a northern moonlight.
1797 On Mary Wollstonecraft. Letter to his brother Thomas Southey, 28 Apr.

29 You are old, Father William, the young man cried,
The few locks which are left you are grey;
You are hale, Father William, a hearty old man,
Now tell me the reason, I pray.
1799 'The Old Man's Comforts'.
▷ See Carroll 238:24.

30 In the days of my youth I remembered my God!
And He hath not forgotten my age.
1799 'The Old Man's Comforts'.

31 It was a summer evening,
Old Kasper's work was done,
And he before his cottage door
Was sitting in the sun,
And by him sported on the green
His little grandchild Wilhelmine.
1800 'The Battle of Blenheim'.

32 Now tell us all about the war,
And what they fought each other for.
1800 'The Battle of Blenheim'.

33 'And everybody praised the Duke,
Who this great fight did win.'
'But what good came of it at last?'

Quoth little Peterkin.
'Why that I cannot tell,' said he,
'But 'twas a famous victory.'
1800 'The Battle of Blenheim'.

34 Blue, darkly, deeply, beautifully blue.
1805 *Madoc*, 'Lincoya', pt.1, canto 5, 1.102.

35 We wage no war with women nor with priests.
1805 *Madoc*, 'The Excommunication', pt.1, canto 15, 1.65.

36 Curses are like young chickens, they always come home to roost.
1810 *The Curse of Kehama*, motto.

37 Thou has been called, O Sleep! the friend of Woe,
But 'tis the happy who have called thee so.
1810 *The Curse of Kehama*, canto 15, stanza 12.

38 Your true lover of literature is never fastidious.
1812 *The Doctor*, ch.12.

39 Show me a man who cares no more for one place than another, and I will show you in that same person one who loves nothing but himself. Beware of those who are homeless by choice.
1812 *The Doctor*, ch.34.

40 Live as long as you may, the first twenty years are the longest half of your life.
1812 *The Doctor*, ch.130.

41 The death of Nelson was felt in England as something more than a public calamity; men started at the intelligence, and turned pale, as if they had heard of the loss of a dear friend.
1813 *The Life of Nelson*, ch.9.

42 My name is Death: the last best friend am I.
1816 'The Lay of the Laureate', stanza 87.

43 The arts babblative and scribblative.
1829 *Colloquies on the Progress and Prospects of Society*, no.10, pt.2.

44 The march of intellect.
1829 *Colloquies on the Progress and Prospects of Society*, no.14.

Soyinka, Wole pseudonym of *Akinwande Oluwole Soyinka* 1934–

Nigerian dramatist, poet and novelist; held as a political prisoner for two years (1967–69); awarded the Nobel Prize for Literature (1986); works include the plays *The Inventor* (1957), *The Swamp-Dwellers* (1958), *The Lion and the Jewel* (1959); the novel *The Interpreters* (1970), and poetry *Idanre and Other Poems* (1967).

45 But the skin of progress
Masks, unknown, the spotted wolf of sameness.
1959 *The Lion and the Jewel* (published 1962), 'Night'.

Spark, Dame Muriel Sarah née *Camberg*
1918–

Scottish novelist, poet, playwright and writer of short stories. Her many works include biographical studies on Mary Wollstonecraft Shelley (1951) and Emily Brontë (1953) and her best-known novel, *The Prime of Miss Jean Brodie* (1961). She converted to Catholicism in 1954 and lives in Italy.

46 The one certain way for a woman to hold a man is to leave him for religion.
  1957 *The Comforters*, ch.1.

47 Parents learn a lot from their children about coping with life.
  1957 *The Comforters*, ch.6.

48 Selwyn MacGregor, the nicest boy who ever committed the sin of whisky.
  1958 *The Go-Away Bird*, 'A Sad Tale's Best for Winter'.

49 She doesn't have anything to do with youth clubs. There are classes within classes in Peckham.
  1960 *The Ballad of Peckham Rye*, ch.3.

50 A short neck denotes a good mind... You see, the messages go quicker to the brain because they've shorter to go.
  1960 *The Ballad of Peckham Rye*, ch.7.

51 I am putting old heads on your young shoulders...all my pupils are the crème de la crème.
  1961 *The Prime of Miss Jean Brodie*, ch.1.

52 One's prime is elusive. You little girls, when you grow up, must be on the alert to recognise your prime at whatever time of your life it may occur. You must live it to the full.
  1961 *The Prime of Miss Jean Brodie*, ch.1.

53 'Whoever has opened the window has opened it too wide,' said Miss Brodie. 'Six inches is perfectly adequate. More is vulgar.'
  1961 *The Prime of Miss Jean Brodie*, ch.3.

54 Give me a girl at an impressionable age, and she is mine for life.
  1961 *The Prime of Miss Jean Brodie*, ch.1.

55 All the nice people were poor; at least, that was a general axiom, the best of the rich being poor in spirit.
  1963 *The Girls of Slender Means*, ch.1.

56 A nice girl should only fall in love once in her life.
  1963 *The Girls of Slender Means*, ch.2.

57 Every communist has a fascist frown, every fascist a communist smile.
  1963 *The Girls of Slender Means*.

58 Well, it's about everything in particular, isn't it?
  1988 Of Proust. *A Far Cry from Kensington*, ch.6.

59 Beware of men bearing flowers.
  Her personal motto, quoted by John Cornwell in the *Sunday Times*, 15 May 1994.

Sparshott, Francis 1926–
Canadian philosopher and professor.

60 For every philosopher, in every age, the first question must be: Just what is philosophy?
  1972 *Looking for Philosophy*, 'Speculation and Reflection'.

Speke, John Hanning 1827–64
English explorer. In 1854, with Richard Burton, he searched for the equatorial lakes of Africa. While travelling alone he discovered Victoria Nyanza, source of the Nile, and in 1860 tracked the Nile flowing out of it. His findings were controversial, and on the day he was to meet with Burton to discuss them he was killed by a shot from his own rifle.

61 The expedition had now performed its functions. I saw that old father Nile without any doubt rises in the Victoria Nyanza, and as I had foretold, that lake is the great source of the holy river which cradled the first expounder of our religious belief.
  1863 *Journal of the Discovery of the Source of the Nile*.

62 As fattening is the first duty of fashionable female life, it must be duly enforced by the rod if necessary. I got up a bit of flirtation with missy, and induced her to rise and shake hands with me. Her face was lovely, but her body was as round as a ball.
  1863 In Karagwe, west of Lake Victoria, among the Galla people. *Journal of the Discovery of the Source of the Nile*.

Spencer, Herbert 1820–1903
English philosopher. He expounded his evolutionary theories in *Principles of Psychology* (1855), and was a leading advocate of 'Social Darwinism'. Other works included *Social Statics* (1851), *System of Synthetic Philosophy* (1862–93) and an *Autobiography* (1904).

63 No one can be perfectly free until all are free; no one can be perfectly moral till all are moral; no one can be perfectly happy till all are happy.
  1851 *Social Statics*, pt.4, ch.30, section 16.

64 Science is organized knowledge.
  1861 *Education*, ch. 2.

65 The preservation of health is a *duty*. Few seem conscious that there is such a thing as physical morality.
  1861 *Education*, ch.4.

66 It cannot but happen...that those will survive whose functions happen to be most nearly in equilibrium with the modified aggregate of external forces... This survival of the fittest implies multiplication of the fittest.
  1865 *Principles of Biology*, pt.3, ch.12, sect.164.

67 How often misused words generate misleading thoughts.
   1879 *Principles of Ethics*, bk.1, pt.2, ch.8, sect.152.

68 The liberty that the citizen enjoys is to be measured not by the governmental machinery that he lives under, whether representative or otherwise, but by the paucity of restraints that it imposes upon him.
   1884 *The Man Versus the State.*

69 The Republican form of government is the highest form of government; but because of this, it requires the highest type of human nature—a type nowhere at present existing.
   'The Americans', collected in *Essays* (1891).

70 It was remarked to me by the late Mr Charles Roupell…that to play billiards well was a sign of an ill-spent youth.
   Quoted in Duncan *Life and Letters of Spencer*, ch.20. Robert Louis Stevenson has also been credited with this observation.

Spender, Sir Stephen Harold 1909–95

English poet and critic. A liberal idealist, he served in the Spanish Civil War, and was a fireman in London during the Blitz. He co-edited *Horizon* (with Cyril Connolly) and later *Encounter*, and has published several volumes of poetry and criticism, as well as journals and a volume of memoirs.

71 I think continually of those who were truly great.
   1933 'I Think Continually of Those'.

72 The names of those who in their lives fought for life,
   Who wore at their hearts the fire's centre.
   Born of the sun they travelled a short while towards the sun,
   And left the vivid air signed with their honour.
   1933 'I Think Continually of Those'.

73 What I had not foreseen
   Was the gradual day
   Weakening the will
   Leaking the brightness away
   1933 'What I Expected, Was'.

74 For I had expected always
   Some brightness to hold in trust,
   Some final innocence
   To save from dust
   1933 'What I Expected, Was'.

75 They lounge at corners of the street
   And greet friends with a shrug of shoulder
   And turn their pockets out,
   The cynical gestures of the poor.
   1933 'Moving Through the Silent Crowd'.

76 Never being, but always at the edge of Being.
   1933 'Never Being'.

77 My parents kept me from children who were rough
   Who threw words like stones and who wore torn clothes
   1933 'My Parents Kept Me from Children Who Were Rough'.

78 Who live under the shadow of war,
   What can I do that matters?
   1933 'Who Live Under the Shadow'.

79 After the first powerful plain manifesto
   The black statement of pistons, without more fuss,
   But gliding like a queen, she leaves the station.
   1933 'The Express'.

80 Pylons, those pillars
   Bare like nude, giant girls that have no secret.
   1933 'Pylons'.

81 Different living is not living in different places
   But creating in the mind a map.
   1933 'Different Living'.

82 Consider: only one bullet in ten thousand kills a man.
   Ask: was so much expenditure justified
   On the death of one so young and so silly
   Stretched under the olive trees, Oh, world, Oh, death?
   1939 'Regum Ultimo Ratio'.

83 Their collected
   Hearts wound up with love, like little watch springs.
   1939 'The Past Values'.

84 The light in the window seemed perpetual
   Where you stayed in the high room for me
   1942 'The Room Above The Square'.

85 The poet shares with other artists the faculty of seeing things as though for the first time.
   1942 *Life and the Poet.*

86 Poetry cannot take sides except with life.
   1942 *Life and the Poet.*

87 My uncle was famous for his balanced point of view. At the time of which I am writing (when he was nearly seventy) it had become so balanced, that the act of balancing seemed rather automatic. One had only to offer him an opinion for him to balance it with a counter-opinion of exactly the same weight, as a grocer puts a pound weight against a pound of sugar.
   1951 *World within World*, p.77.

88 My brothers and sister and I were brought up in an atmosphere which I would describe as 'Puritan decadence'. Puritanism names the behaviour which is condemned; Puritan decadence regards the name

itself as indecent, and pretends that the object behind that name does not exist until it is named.
1951 *World within World*, p.314-315.

89 People sometimes divide others into those you laugh at and those you laugh with. The young Auden was someone you could laugh-at-with.
1973 Address at Auden's Memorial Service, Oxford, 27 Oct.

90 But reading is not idleness…it is the passive, receptive side of civilization without which the active and creative world would be meaningless. It is the immortal spirit of the dead realised within the bodies of the living. It is sacramental.
1980 Journal entry, 4 Jan.

91 We were obsessed by the feeling that this was the supreme cause of our time. The cause of poets and of writers. The cause of freedom. And that unless the cause of anti-Fascism was won, unless Fascism was defeated, we would be unable to exist as writers.
1982 Speaking on the ITV series *The Spanish Civil War*, no.3, 'Battleground for idealists'.

Spenser, Edmund c.1552–1599

English poet. Educated at Cambridge, he held positions in government, including secretary to the lord deputy in Ireland during a period of rebellion, for most of his life, although he died in poverty. His epic Protestant romance, *The Faerie Queen*, was published in two instalments, Books I–III (1590) and Books IV–VI (1596). Other works include *The Shepherd's Calendar* (1579), *Colin Clout's Come Home Again* (1595), *Amoretti* and *Epithalamion* (1595), and *Four Hymns* (1596).

92 Go little book, thy self present,
  As child whose parent is unkent:
  To him that is the president
  Of noblesse and of chivalry,
  And if that Envy bark at thee,
  As sure it will, for succour flee.
1579 *The Shepherd's Calendar*, 'To His Book'.

93 Bring hither the pink and purple columbine,
  With gillyflowers:
  Bring coronation, and sops in wine,
  Worn of paramours.
  Strew me the ground with daffadowndillies,
  And cowslips, and kingcups, and loved lilies.
1579 *The Shepherd's Calendar*, 'April', l.136–41.

94 And he that strives to touch the stars,
  Oft stumbles at a straw.
1579 *The Shepherd's Calendar*, 'July', l.99–100.

95 Uncouth unkist, said the old famous poet Chaucer.
1579 *The Shepherd's Calendar*, 'Letter to Gabriel Harvey'.

96 So now they have made our English tongue a gallimaufry or hodgepodge of all other speeches.
1579 *The Shepherd's Calendar*, 'Letter to Gabriel Harvey'.

97 Discord oft in musick makes the sweeter lay.
1589 *The Faerie Queene*, bk.3.

98 A gentle knight was pricking on the plain.
1590 *The Faerie Queen*, bk.1, canto 1, stanza 1.

99 The sailing pine, the cedar proud and tall,
  The vine-prop elm, the poplar never dry,
  The builder oak, sole king of forests all,
  The aspen good for staves, the cypress funeral.

  The laurel, meed of mighty conquerors
  And poets sage, the fir that weepeth still,
  The willow worn of forlorn paramours,
  The ewe obedient to the benders will,
  The birch for shafts, the sallow for the mill,
  The myrrh sweet bleeding in the bitter wound,
  The warlike beech, the ash for nothing ill,
  The fruitful olive, and the platan round,
  The carver holme, the maple seldom inward sound.
1590 *The Faerie Queen*, bk.1, canto 1, stanzas 8–9. plantan=plane tree; holme=holly.

1 Oft fire is without smoke.
1590 *The Faerie Queen*, bk.1, canto 1, stanza 12.

2 A stately palace built of squarèd brick,
  Which cunningly was without mortar laid,
  Whose walls were high, but nothing strong, nor thick,
  And golden foil all over them displayed,
  That purest sky with brightness they dismayed.
1590 Of the palace of pride. *The Faerie Queen*, bk.1, canto 4, stanza 4.

3 And by his side rode loathsome Gluttony,
  Deformèd creature, on a filthy swine.
1590 *The Faerie Queen*, bk.1, canto 4, stanza 21.

4 Fretting grief the enemy of life.
1590 *The Faerie Queen*, bk.1, canto 4, stanza 35.

5 But who can turn the stream of destiny,
  Or break the chain of strong necessity?
1590 Night argues against the necessity of faith. *The Faerie Queen*, bk.1, canto 5, stanza 25.

6 What worlds delight, or joy of living speech
  Can heart, so plunged in sea of sorrows deep,
  And heapèd with so huge misfortunes, reach?
  The careful cold beginneth for to creep,
  And in my heart his iron arrow steep,
  Soon as I think upon my bitter bale.
1590 *The Faerie Queen*, bk.1, canto 7, stanza 39.

7 Still as he fled, his eye was backward cast,
  As if his fear still followed him behind.
1590 *The Faerie Queen*, bk.1, canto 9, stanza 21.

8 Sleep after toil, port after stormy seas,

Ease after war, death after life does greatly please.
1590 *The Faerie Queen*, bk.1, canto 9, stanza 40.

9 Where justice grows, there grows eke greater grace.
1590 *The Faerie Queen*, bk.1, canto 9, stanza 53

10 His iron coat all overgrown with rust,
Was underneath envelopèd with gold,
Whose glistering gloss darkened with filthy dust,
Well yet appearèd, to have been of old
A work of rich entail, and curious mold,
Woven with antics and wild imagery.
1590 Of Mammon. *The Faerie Queen*, bk.2, canto 7, stanza 4.

11 And all for love, and nothing for reward.
1590 *The Faerie Queen*, bk.2, canto 8 stanza 2.

12 Of all God' works, which do this world adorn,
There is no one more fair and excellent,
Then is mans body both for power and form,
Whiles it is kept in sober government.
1590 *The Faerie Queen*, bk.2, canto 9, stanza 1.

13 So passeth, in the passing of a day,
Of mortal life the leaf, the bud, the flower,
No more doth flourish after first decay,
That erst was sought to deck both bed and bower,
Of many a lady, and many a paramour:
Gather therefore the rose, whilst yet is prime,
For soon comes age, that will her pride deflower:
Gather the rose of love, whilst yet is time,
Whilst loving thou mayst lovèd be with equal
  crime.
1590 *The Faerie Queen*, bk.2, canto 12, stanza 75.

14 Nought so of love this looser dame did skill,
But as a coal to kindle fleshly flame,
Giving the bridle to her wanton will,
And treading underfoot her honest name.
1590 Of Malecasta. *The Faerie Queen*, bk.3, canto 1, stanza 50.

15 But as it falleth, in the gentlest hearts
Imperious love hath highest set his throne,
And tyrannizeth in the bitter smarts
Of them, that to him buxom are and prone.
1590 *The Faerie Queen*, bk.3, canto 2, stanza 23. *buxom* =
'yielding'.

16 Most sacred fire, that burnest mightily
In living breasts, ykindled first above,
Amongst th'eternal spheres and lamping sky,
And thence poured into men, which men call Love.
1590 *The Faerie Queen*, bk.3, canto 3, stanza 1.

17 Where is the antique glory now become,
What whilom wont in women to appear?
Where be the brave achievements doen by some?
Where be the battles, where the shield and spear,
And all the conquests, which them high did rear,
That matter made for famous poet's verse,

And boastful men so oft abashed to hear?
Bene they all dead, and laid in doleful hearse?
Or doen they only sleep, and shall again reverse?
1590 *The Faerie Queen*, bk.3, canto 4, stanza 1.

18 But ah, who can deceive his destiny,
Or ween by warning to avoid his fate?
1590 *The Faerie Queen*, bk.3, canto 4, stanza 27.

19 There is continual spring, and harvest there
Continual, both meeting at one time:
For both the boughs do laughing blossoms bear,
And with fresh colours deck the wanton prime,
And eke attonce the heavy trees they climb,
Which seem to labour under their fruits load:
The whiles the joyous birds make their pastime
Amongst the shady leaves, their sweet above,
And their true loves without suspicion tell abroad.
1590 Of the Garden of Adonis. *The Faerie Queen*, bk.3, canto
6, stanza 42.

20 Yet never can he die, but dying lives,
And doth himself with sorrow new sustain,
That death and life attonce unto him gives,
And painful pleasure turns to pleasing pain.
1590 *The Faerie Queen*, bk.3, canto 10, stanza 60.

21 And as she looked about, she did behold,
How over that same door was likewise writ,
Be bold, be bold, and everywhere Be bold…
At last she spied at that room's upper end
Another iron door, on which was writ
Be not too bold.
1590 *The Faerie Queen*, bk.3, canto 11, stanza 54.

22 Yet is that glass so gay, that it can blind
The wisest sight, to think gold that is brass.
1596 Of the mirror of fashion. *The Faerie Queen*, bk.6, proem,
stanza 5.

23 Of such deep learning little had he need,
Ne yet of Latin, ne of Greek that breed
Doubts 'mongst divines, and difference of texts,
From when arise diversity of sects,
And hateful heresies.
1591 *Prosopopoia*, l.385–9.

24 Most glorious Lord of Life! that, on this day,
Didst make Thy triumph over death and sin;
And having harrowed hell, didst bring away
Captivity thence captive, us to win:
1595 *Amoretti*, sonnet 68.

25 But when I plead, she bids me play my part,
And when I weep, she says tears are but water:
And when I sigh, she says I know the art,
And when I wail, she turns herself to laughter.
1595 *Amoretti*, sonnet 18.

26 The merry cuckoo, messenger of Spring,

His trumpet shrill hath thrice already sounded.
1595 *Amoretti*, sonnet 19.

27 Most glorious Lord of Life! that, on this day,
Didst make Thy triumph over death and sin;
And having harrowed hell, didst bring away
Captivity thence captive, us to win:
1595 *Amoretti*, sonnet 68.

28 One day I wrote her name upon the strand,
But came the waves and washèd it away;
Again I wrote it with a second hand,
But came the tide, and made my pains his prey.
'Vain man,' said she, 'that doest in vain assay
A mortal thing so to immortalise,
For I my self shall like to this decay,
And eke my name be wipèd out likewise.'
'Not so,' quod I, 'let baser things devise
To die in dust, but you shall live by fame:
My verse your virtues rare shall eternise,
And in the heavens write your glorious name.
Where when as death shall all the world subdue,
Our love shall live, and later life renew.'
1595 *Amoretti*, sonnet 75.

29 In youth, before I waxèd old,
The blind boy, Venus' baby,
For want of cunning made me bold,
In bitter hive to grope for honey.
1595 *Amoretti*, 'Anacreontics', no.1.

30 Open the temple gates unto my love,
Open them wide that she may enter in.
1595 *Epithalamion*, section 12.

31 Pour out the wine without restraint or stay,
Pour not by cups, but by the belly full,
Pour out to all that will,
And sprinkle all the posts and walls with wine,
That they may sweat, and drunken be withal.
1595 *Epithalamion*, section 14.

32 Ah when will this long weary day have end,
And lend me leave to come unto my love?
How slowly do the hours their numbers spend!
How slowly does sad Time his feathers move!
1595 *Epithalamion*, section 16.

33 Dan Chaucer, well of English undefiled,
On Fame's eternal beadroll worthy to be filed.
1596 *The Faerie Queen*, bk.4, canto 2, stanza 32.

34 O sacred hunger of ambitious minds.
1596 *The Faerie Queen*, bk.5, canto 12, stanza 1.

35 A monster, which the Blatant beast men call,
A dreadful fiend of gods and men ydrad.
1596 *The Faerie Queen*, bk.5, canto 12, stanza 37.

36 Me seems the world is run quite out of square,
And being once amiss grows daily worse and worse.

1596 *The Faerie Queen*, bk.5, proem, stanza 1.

37 For that which all men then did virtue call,
Is now called vice; and that which vice was hight,
Is now hight virtue, and so used of all:
Right now is wrong, and wrong that was is right,
1596 *The Faerie Queen*, bk.5, proem, stanza 4.

38 The gentle mind by gentle deeds is known.
For a man by nothing is so well bewrayed,
As by his manners.
1596 *The Faerie Queen*, bk.6, canto 3, stanza 1.

39 Sweet Thames, run softly, till I end my song.
1596 *Prothalamion*, l.1.

40 What man that sees the ever-whirling wheel
Of Change, the which all mortal things doth sway,
But that thereby doth find, and plainly feel,
How mutability in them doth play
Her cruel sports, to many men's decay?
1609 *The Faerie Queen*, 'Mutability', canto 6, stanza 1.

41 First, sturdy March with brows full sternly bent,
And armèd strongly, rode upon a ram,
The same which over Hellespontus swam:
Yet in his hand a spade he also hent,
And in a bag all sorts of seeds ysame,
Which on the earth he strowèd as he went,
And filled her womb with fruitful hope of
nourishment.
1609 *The Faerie Queen*, 'Mutability', canto 7, stanza 32. hent = grasped; ysame = together.

42 Jolly June, arrayed
All in green leaves, as he a Player were.
1609 *The Faerie Queen*, 'Mutability', canto 7, stanza 35.

43 Next was November, he full gross and fat,
As fed with lard, and that right well might seem;
For, he had been a fatting hogs of late.
1609 *The Faerie Queen*, 'Mutability', canto 7, stanza 40.

44 I was promised on a time,
To have reason for my rhyme;
From that time unto this season,
I received nor rhyme nor reason.
'Lines on his Pension.' Attributed.

Spillane, Mickey properly *Frank Morrison Spillane* 1918–

US popular novelist. He wrote for pulp magazines to pay for his education, and produced his first novel *I, the Jury* in 1947. His private detective character Mike Hammer inspired many films and a television series.

45 There are more salted peanuts consumed than caviar.
Defending his low-brow fiction. Quoted in Neil J Jones (ed) *A Book of Days for the Literary Year* (1984).

Spinoza, Baruch also known as *Benedict de Spinoza* 1632–77

Dutch philosopher, of Jewish descent. The *Tractatus Theologico-Politicus* was published in 1670, and the more famous *Ethics* in 1677. His pantheistic monism led to accusations of atheism but was influential in the development of metaphysics.

46 *Sedulo curavi, humanes actiones non ridere, non lugare, neque detestari, sed intelligere.*

I have striven not to laugh at human actions, not to weep at them, nor to hate them, but to understand them.
1670 *Tractatus Theologico-Politicus,* bk.1, pt.4.

47 *Quicquid est, in Deo est, et nihil sine Deo esse necque concipi potest.*

Whatever is, is in God, and nothing can exist or be conceived without God.
1677 *Ethics,* bk.1, prop.15.

48 *In rerum natura nullum datur contingens; sed omnia ex necessitate divinae naturae determinata sunt ad certo modo existandum et operandum.*

In the nature of things nothing contingent is granted, but all things are determined by the necessity of divine nature for existing and working in a certain way.
1677 *Ethics,* bk.1, prop.29.

49 *Nempe falluntur homines, quod se liberos esse putant; que opinio in hoc solo consistit, quod suarum actionum sint conscii, et ignari causarum, a quibus determinantur. Haec ergo est eorum libertatis idea, quod suarum actionum nullam cognoscant causam.*

Men are mistaken in thinking themselves free; and this opinion consists of this alone, that they are conscious of their actions and ignorant of the causes by which they are determined. This, therefore, is their idea of liberty, that they should know no cause of their actions.
1677 *Ethics,* bk.2, prop.35, note.

50 *Veritas norma sua est.*

Truth is its own standard.
1677 *Ethics,* bk.2, prop.43, note.

51 *De natura Rationis est, res sub quadam aeternitatis specie percipere.*

It is the nature of reason to perceive things under a certain species of eternity.
1677 *Ethics,* bk.2, prop.44, corollary 2.

52 *Unaquaeque res, quantum in se est, in suo esse persevare conatur.*

Everything in so far as it is in itself endeavours to persist in its own being.
1677 *Ethics,* bk.3, prop.6.

53 *Nihil nos conari, velle, appetere, neque cupere, quia id bonum esse judicamus; sed contra, nos propterea aliquid bonum esse judicare, quia id conamur, volumus, appetimus, atque cupimus.*

We endeavour, wish, desire, or long for nothing because we deem it good; but on the other hand, we deem a thing good because we endeavour, wish for, desire, or long for it.
1677 *Ethics,* bk.3, prop.9, note.

54 *Nempe Amor nihil aliud est, quam Laeititia concomitante idea causae externae; et odium nihil aliud est, quam Tristitia concomitante idea causae externae.*

Love is nothing else than pleasure accompanied by the idea of an external cause; and hate pain accompanied by the idea of an external cause.
1677 *Ethics,* bk.3, prop.13, note.

55 *Ex virtute absoluto agere nihil aliud in obis est, quam ex ductu Rationis agere, vivere, suum esse conservare (haec tria idem significant) ex fundamento proprium utile quaerendi.*

To act absolutely according to virtue is nothing else in us than to act under the guidance of reason, to live so, and to preserve one's being (these three have the same meaning) on the basis of seeking what is useful to oneself.
1677 *Ethics,* bk.4, prop.24.

56 *Summum Mentis bonum est Dei cognitio, et summa Mentis virtus Deum cognoscere.*

The greatest good of the mind is the knowledge of God, and the greatest virtue of the mind is to know God.
1677 *Ethics,* bk.4, prop.28.

57 *Homo liber de nulla re minus quam de morte cogitat; et ejus sapienta non mortis, sed viate meditatio est.*

A free man thinks of nothing less than of death, and his wisdom is a meditation not of death but of life.
1677 *Ethics,* bk.4, prop.67.

58 *In vita itaque apprime utile est, intellectum seu Rationem, quantum possumus, perficere, et in hoc uno summa hominis felicitas seu beatitudo consistit; quippe beatitudo nihil aliud est, quam ipsa animi acquiescentia quae ex Dei intuitiva cognitione oritur.*

It is therefore extremmly useful in life to perfect as much as we can the intellect or reason, and of this alone does the happiness or blessedness of man exist: for blessedness is nothing else than satisfaction of mind which arises from the intuitive knowledge of good.
1677 *Ethics,* bk.4, appendix.

59 *Ex tertio cognitionis genere oritur necessario Amor Dei intellectualis.*

From the third kind of knowledge [intuition] arises necessarily the intellectual love of God.
1677 *Ethics*, bk.5, prop32, corollary.

60 *Per deum intelligo eus absolute infinitum, hoc est, substantiam constantem infinitis attributis, quorum unumquodque aeternam et infinitam essentiam exprimit..*

By God I mean a being absolutely infinite—that is, a substance consisting in infinite attributes, of which each expresses eternal and infinite essentiality.
1677 *Ethics*.

Spock, Dr Benjamin McLane 1903–98

US paediatrician. His *Common Sense Book of Baby and Child Care* (1946) sold over 30 million copies, transforming childcare. He gave up psychiatry to devote himself to pacifism, and ran for the presidency in 1972.

61 You know more than you think you do.
1946 *The Common Sense Book of Baby and Child Care*, opening words.

62 To win in Vietnam, we will have to exterminate a nation.
1968 *Dr Spock on Vietnam*, ch.7.

Spring-Rice, Sir Cecil Arthur 1858–1918

English diplomat.

63 I vow to thee, my country—all earthly things above—
Entire and whole and perfect, the service of my love.
1918 *I Vow To Thee, My Country*.

Spurgeon, Charles Haddon 1834–92

English Baptist preacher, famous for his eloquent sermons. A strong Calvinist, he left the Evangelical Alliance (1864) and Baptist Union (1887) over doctrinal differences and a concern for orthodoxy.

64 If you want truth to go round the world you must hire an express train to pull it; but if you want a lie to go round the world, it will fly: it is as light as a feather, and a breath will carry it. It is well said in the old proverb, 'a lie will go round the world while truth is pulling its boots on'.
Collected in *Gems from Spurgeon* (1859).

Squire, Sir J(ohn) C(ollings) 1884–1958

English poet and editor. He was an influential anti-modernist figure in the 1920s, with a gift for amusing parody.

65 It did not last: the Devil howling 'Ho!

Let Einstein be!' restored the status quo.
1926 'In Continuation of Pope on Newton'.

66 But I'm not so think as you drunk I am.
1931 'Ballade of Soporific Absorption'.

Staël, Germaine Necker, Baronne de
1766–1817

French author of important critical, political and philosophical essays as well as novels and plays seen as precursors of Romanticism. She was an opponent of Napoleon.

67 *L'amour est l'histoire de la vie des femmes, c'est un épisode dans celle des hommes.*

Love is the story of a woman's life, but only an episode in the life of a man.
1796 *De l'influence des passions*.

68 *La force de l'esprit ne se développe toute entière qu'en attaquant la puissance.*

The mind fully develops its faculties when it attacks power.
1800 *De la littérature*.

69 *En cherchant la gloire, j'ai toujours espéré qu'elle me ferait aimer.*

I have pursued fame always in the hope of winning her love.
1807 *Corinne ou de l'Italie*.

70 *Quand une fois on a tourné l'enthousiasme en ridicule, on a tout défait, excepté l'argent et le pouvoir.*

Once we have made enthusiasm ridiculous, there is nothing left but money and power.
1807 *Corinne ou de l'Italie*.

71 *Les païens ont divinisé la vie, et les chrétiens ont divinisé la mort.*

Pagans deified life and Christians deified death.
1807 *Corinne ou de l'Italie*.

72 *On dirait que l'âme des justes donne, comme les fleurs, plus de parfums vers le soir.*

It is said that the soul of the just gives off, like flowers, a stronger scent towards evening.
1807 *Corinne ou de l'Italie*.

73 *On cesse de s'aimer si quelqu'un ne nous aime.*

We stop loving ourselves when no one loves us.
1810 *De l'Allemagne*.

74 *La première condition pour écrire, c'est une manière de sentir vive et forte.*

The primary requirement for a writer is to feel keenly and strongly.
1810 *De l'Allemagne*.

75 *En France, on étudie les hommes; en Allemagne, les livres.*

In France, they study men; in Germany, books.
1810 *De l'Allemagne.*

76 *La poésie est le langage naturel de tous les cultes.*

Poetry is the natural language of all religions.
1810 *De l'Allemagne.*

77 *Le sentiment de l'infini est le véritable attribut de l'âme.*

To feel the infinite is the true attribute of the soul.
1810 *De l'Allemagne.*

Stalin, Joseph originally *Iosif Vissarionovich Dzhugashvili* 1879–1953

Soviet leader. Appointed General Secretary to the Communist Party Central Committee (1922), enabling him to take power after Lenin's death in 1924. His collectivization was responsible for millions of deaths, as were his political purges (1934–38). Although he signed a non-aggression pact with Hitler (1939), he declared war, joining the Allies, when Hitler threatened the Soviet Union in 1941.

78 In the name of the Constitution, Cromwell took up arms, executed the king, dissolved Parliament, imprisoned some, and beheaded others.
1934 In conversation with H G Wells, Moscow.

79 To attempt to export revolution is nonsense.
1936 Said to Roy Howard, US newspaper proprietor, 1 Mar.

80 History shows that there are no invincible armies.
1941 Radio broadcast, 3 Jul, announcing the declaration of war against Germany, three weeks before Hitler invaded.

81 Communism fits Germany as a saddle fits a cow.
1944 In conversation with the Polish politician, Stanislaw Mikolajcik, Aug.

Stallone, Sylvester 1946–

US actor and film director, best known for his roles in action films such as *Rocky* (1976) and *Rambo* (1985) and their sequels.

82 Playing polo is like trying to play golf during an earthquake.
1990 Quoted in Colin Jarman *The Guinness Dictionary of Sports Quotations* (1990).

Stamp, Sir Josiah Charles, Baron Stamp of Shortlands 1880–1941

British economist and statistician, who published early estimates of the British national income.

83 The first argument that is brought against every new proposal departing from conventional lines is nearly always that it is impracticable.
1921 *Fundamental Principles of Taxation*, p.95.

Stanley, Sir Henry Morton originally *John Rowlands* 1841–1904

Welsh-born US explorer and journalist. He fought on both sides in the American Civil War and then, as a journalist, was commissioned by the *New York Herald* to lead an expedition in search of Dr David Livingstone, who was rumoured to have died while exploring rivers in Central Africa. On one of the three subsequent expeditions he travelled the length of the Congo.

84 I would have run to him, only I was a coward in the presence of such a mob—would have embraced him, only, he being an Englishman, I did not know how he would receive me; so I did what cowardice and false pride suggested was the best thing—walked deliberately to him, took off my hat, and said:
'Dr Livingstone, I presume ?'
'Yes,' said he, with a kind smile, lifting his cap slightly.
I replace my hat on my head, and he puts on his cap, and we both grasp hands, and I then say aloud:
'I thank God, Doctor, I have been permitted to see you.'
He answered, 'I feel thankful that I am here to welcome you.'
1872 *How I Found Livingstone in Central Africa.*

Stanton, Elizabeth née *Cady* 1815–1902

US reformer and suffragette; organizer of the first Women's Rights Convention, Seneca Falls, US (1848). She is remembered chiefly as co-author of *The History of Woman Suffrage* (1881–6) and she also wrote *The Women's Bible* (1895).

85 We hold these truths to be self-evident: that all men and women are created equal; that they are endowed by their Creator with certain inalienable rights; that among these are life, liberty, and the pursuit of happiness.
1848 'Declaration of Sentiments', Seneca Falls Women's Rights Convention, 19–20 Jul. This is modelled on the American Declaration of Independence of 4 Jul 1776.

86 Quite as many false ideas prevail as to woman's true position in the home as to her status elsewhere. Womanhood is the great fact in her life; wifehood and motherhood are but incidental relations.
1881 *The History of Woman Suffrage 1848–61*, vol.1, introduction.

87 Men are the Brahmin, women the Pariahs, under our existing civilization.
1881 *The History of Woman Suffrage 1848–61*, vol.1, ch.1, 'Preceding Causes'.

88 Although woman has performed much of the labor of the world, her industry and economy have been the very means of increasing her degradation.

1881 *The History of Woman Suffrage 1848–61*, vol.1, ch.1, 'Preceding Causes'.

89 As to woman's subjection…it is important to note that equal dominion is given to woman over every living thing, but not one word is said giving man dominion over woman.
1895 *The Woman's Bible*, pt.1, ch.1, 'Comments on Genesis'.

90 The Old Testament makes woman a mere afterthought in creation; the author of evil; cursed in her maternity; a subject in marriage; and all female life, animal and human, unclean.
1898 *The Woman's Bible*, pt.2, preface.

91 'Self-development is a higher duty than self-sacrifice', should be a woman's motto henceforward.
1898 *The Woman's Bible*, pt.2, 'Comments on Mark'.

Stanwyck, Barbara originally *Ruby Stevens*
1907–90

American film, television and radio actress. She was a dancer in the Ziegfeld Follies at the age of 13 and went on to play gutsy, pioneering women in westerns such as *Annie Oakley* (1935), as well as sultry femmes fatales in films noirs, including *Double Indemnity* (1944). She became a successful radio star in the 1960s.

92 To eat, to survive and to have a good coat.
1987 Her three goals in life, recalled on receiving the American Film Institute Life Achievement Award. Reported in the *New York Times*, 11 Apr.

Stapledon, Olaf 1886–1950

English writer and social philosopher. He used science fiction as a means of embodying his social theories.

93 That strange blend of the commercial traveller, the missionary, and the barbarian conqueror, which was the American abroad.
1930 *Last and First Men*, ch.3.

Stark, Dame Freya Madeleine 1893–1993

English writer and traveller, born in Paris. She studied Arabic and made her first journey to the Middle East in 1928, after which she travelled extensively in Europe, the Middle East and Asia, writing over 30 books.

94 The great and almost only comfort about being a woman is that one can always pretend to be more stupid than one is and no one is surprised.
1934 *The Valley of the Assassins*.

95 I came to the conclusion that some more ascetic reason than mere enjoyment should be found if one wishes to travel in peace: to do things for fun smacks of levity, immorality almost, in our utilitarian world. And though personally I think the world is wrong, and I know in my heart of hearts that it is a most excellent reason to do things

merely because one likes the doing of them, I would advise all those who wish to see unwrinkled brows in passport offices to start out ready labelled as entomologists, anthropologists, or whatever other -ology they think suitable and propitious.
1936 *The Valleys of the Assassins and other Persian Travels*.

96 The true call of the desert, of the mountains, or the sea, is their silence—free of the networks of dead speech.
1948 *Perseus in the Wind*.

97 This is the prospect from the watershed, and when the traveller reaches it, it is a good thing to take an hour's leisure and look out on the visible portions of the journey, since never in one's life can one see the same view twice.
1948 *Perseus in the Wind*.

98 The *inscrutability* of the East is, indeed, I believe a myth… The ordinary inhabitant is incomprehensible merely to people who never trouble to have anything much to do with them.
1963 *The Journey's Echo*.

Stark, John 1728–1822

American revolutionary commander. He saw service in the French and Indian war (1754–9), and at Bunker Hill (1775) and Bennington (1777) during the American Revolution.

99 We beat them today or Molly Stark's a widow.
1777 Speech before the Battle of Bennington, 16 Aug. Quoted in *Cyclopaedia of American Biography*, vol.5.

Starr, Roger

1 A busy man who can keep up a daily journal resembles a person preparing for bed with the shades up… When such a man publishes parts of his journal, the reader must conclude he always knew the lights were on.
1989 On George F Kennan *Sketches From a Life* (1989). In the *Washington Post*, 8 May.

Steacie, E W 1900–62

Canadian government official, President of the National Research Council of Canada (1952).

2 The academic atmosphere, produced mainly by the humanities, is the only atmosphere in which pure science can flourish.
1956 Collected in J D Babbitt (ed) *Science in Canada: Selections from the Speeches of E. W. Steacie* (1965).

3 An efficient organization is one in which the accounting department knows the exact cost of every useless administrative procedure which they themselves have initiated.
Quoted by J D Babbitt in his introduction to Steacie's *Science in Canada* (published posthumously, 1965).

Stead, William Thomas 1849–1912

4 The Press is at once the eye and the ear and the tongue of the people. It is the visible speech, if not the voice, of the democracy. It is the phongraph of the world.

1886 'Government by Journalism', in the *Contemporary Review*, May. Collected in *A Journalist on Journalism* (1892).

5 He may be more potent than any other man. The damnable iteration day after day of earnest conviction wears like the dropping of the water upon the stone.

1886 Of the journalist. 'Government by journalism', in the *Contemporary Review*, May. Collected in *A Journalist on Journalism* (1892).

6 An editor is the uncrowned king of an educated democracy.

1886 'Government by Journalism', in the *Contemporary Review*, May. Collected in *A Journalist on Journalism* (1892).

7 The duty of a journalist is the duty of a watchman.

1886 'Government by Journalism', in the *Contemporary Review*, May. Collected in *A Journalist on Journalism* (1892).

8 It is the great inspector, with a myriad eyes, who never sleeps, and whose daily reports are submitted, not to a functionary or department, but to the whole people.

1886 Of a newspaper. 'Government by Journalism', in the *Contemporary Review*, May. Collected in *A Journalist on Journalism* (1892).

9 What a marvellous opportunity for attacking the devil!

Letter of appointment to the *Northern Echo*, quoted by Harold Evans in his preface to Ray Boston *The Essential Fleet Street*.

Steel, David Martin Scott Steel, Baron 1938–

10 [Margaret Thatcher] has turned the British bulldog into a Reagan poodle.

1986 In *Time*, 28 Apr.

Steele, Sir Richard 1672–1729

11 Dear Prue,
If a servant I sent last night got to Hampton-court, you received 29 walnuts and a letter from me. I inclose the Gazette; and am, with all my soul, Your passionate lover, and faithful husband,
RICH. STEELE

1708 Letter, 20 Sep (published 1787).

12 I am, dear Prue, a little in drink, but at all times your faithful husband,
RICH. STEELE

1708 Letter, 27 Sep (published 1787).

13 It is to be noted that when any part of this paper appears dull there is a design in it.

1709 In the *Tatler*, no.38, 7 Jul.

14 To love her is a liberal education.

1709 Of Lady Elizabeth Hastings *Tatler*, no.49, 2 Aug.

15 Every man is the maker of his own fortune

1709 In the *Tatler*, no.52, 9 Aug.

16 It gave me a great notion of the credit of our present government and administration, to find people press as eagerly to pay money as they would to receive it; and, at the same time, a due respect for that body of men who have found out so pleasing an expedient for carrying on the common cause, that they have turned a tax into a diversion.

1710 On the first state lottery of 1710. In the *Tatler*, no.124, 24 Jan.

17 Reading is to the mind what exercise is to the body.

1710 In the *Tatler*, no.147, 18 Mar. Also attributed to Addison.

18 Let your precept be, Be Easy.

1710 In the *Tatler*, no.196, 11 Jul.

19 I was undone by my Auxiliary; when I had once called him in, I could not subsist without Dependance on him.

1711 Of Addison's contribution to the *Tatler*. Preface to vol.4 of the collected edition.

20 I have heard Will Honeycomb say, A Woman seldom Writes her Mind but in her Postscript.

1711 In the *Spectator*, no.79, 30 May.

21 We were in some little time fixed in our seats, and sat with that dislike which people not too good-natured usually conceive of each other at first sight.

1711 Embarking on a coach journey. In the *Spectator*, no.132, 1 Aug.

22 I am confident that no boy, who will not be allured to letters without blows, will ever be brought to anything with them.

1711 On flogging in schools. In the *Spectator*, no.157, 30 Aug.

23 Those grave fellows are my aversion who sift everything with the utmost nicety, and find the malignity of a lie in a piece of humour, pushed a little beyond exact truth.

1713 In the *Guardian*, no.42, 29 Apr.

Stefansson, Vilhjalmur 1879–1962

Canadian Arctic explorer and author.

24 There are two kinds of Arctic problems, the imaginary and the real. Of the two, the imaginary are the most real.

1945 *The Arctic in Fact and Fable*.

25 What is the difference between unethical and ethical advertising? Unethical advertising uses falsehoods to deceive the public; ethical advertising uses truth to deceive the public.

Discovery (published 1964).

26 A land may be said to be discovered the first time a European, presumably an Englishman, sets foot on it.

Discovery (published 1964).

Steffens, (Joseph) Lincoln 1866–1936

US journalist. While editor of *McClure's Magazine* (1902–6), his revision of an article on city corruption led to a series published as *The Shame of the Cities* (1904), a key work in urban reform. His *Struggle for Self-Government* (1906) analysed corruption and reform at state level.

27 I have seen the future and it works.

1919 On his visit to post-Revolutionary Russia, in *Autobiography* (2 vols, 1931).

▷ See Toynbee 1024:20.

Stegner, Wallace Earle 1909–93

US novelist. Professor of English at Stanford University.

28 A political animal can be defined as a body that will go on circulating a petition even with its heart cut out.

1954 *Beyond the Hundredth Meridian*.

29 If you're going to get old, you might as well get as old as you can get.

1989 On his 80th birthday. Reported in the *San Francisco Chronicle*, 6 Mar.

Steichen, Edward Jean 1879–1973

Belgian-born US photographer, credited with developing photography as an art form. He also pioneered aerial and naval photography during World Wars I and II.

30 Photography was conceived as a mirror of the universal elements and emotions of the everydayness of life—as a mirror of the essential oneness of mankind throughout the world.

Quoted in *Dialogue*, May 1989.

Stein, Gertrude 1874–1946

US writer, influential in the development of Modernism. She settled in Paris in 1903, where with her friend Alice B Toklas she dominated expatriate life. Her less experimental works include *The Autobiography of Alice B. Toklas* and *Everybody's Autobiography*.

31 You are so afraid of losing your moral sense that you are not willing to take it through anything more dangerous than a mud-puddle.

1903 'Q.E.D.', bk.1. Collected in *Fernhurst, Q.E.D., and Other Early Writings* (1971).

32 Rose is a rose is a rose is a rose, is a rose.

1914 *Tender Buttons*, 'Sacred Emily'.

33 You are all a lost generation.

Quoted as epigraph in Ernest Hemingway *The Sun Also Rises* (1926).

34 He had added to his stories a little story of meditations and in these he said that The Enormous Room was the greatest book he had ever read. It was then that Gertrude Stein said, Hemingway, remarks are not literature.

1933 *The Autobiography of Alice B. Toklas*, ch.7.

35 Pigeons on the grass alas.

1934 *Four Saints in Three Acts*, act 3, sc.2.

36 Disillusionment in living is the finding out nobody agrees with you ... Complete disillusionment is when you realise that no one can for they can't change.

1934 *The Making of Americans*, ch.5.

37 In the United States there is more space where nobody is than where anybody is. That is what makes America what it is.

1936 *The Geographical History of America*.

38 Native always means people who belong somewhere else, because they had once belonged somewhere. That shows that the white race does not really think they belong anywhere because they think of everybody else as native.

1937 *Everybody's Autobiography*, ch.1.

39 Anything scares me, anything scares anyone but really after all considering how dangerous everything is nothing is really very frightening.

1937 *Everybody's Autobiography*, ch.2.

40 It takes a lot of time to be a genius, you have to sit around so much doing nothing, really doing nothing.

1937 *Everybody's Autobiography*, ch.2.

41 What was the use of my having come from Oakland it was not natural to have come from there yes write about it if I like or anything if I like but not there, there is no there there.

1937 *Everybody's Autobiography*, ch.4.

42 Two things are always the same the dance and war.
    1937 *Everybody's Autobiography*, ch.5.

43 Everybody gets so much information all day long
    that they lose their common sense.
    1959 'Reflection on the Atomic Bomb', collected in Robert A
    Goodwin (ed) *Readings in World Politics* (1959).

44 Nature is commonplace. Imitation is more
    interesting.
    Quoted in Sir Charles Spencer Chaplin *My Autobiography*
    (1964).

45 You should only read what is truly good or what is
    frankly bad.
    Quoted in Ernest Hemingway *A Moveable Feast* (1964), ch.3.

46 Anyone who marries three girls from St Louis
    hasn't learned much.
    Of Ernest Hemingway. Quoted in R Mellow *Charmed Circle*
    (1974), ch.16.

47 Just before she died she asked, 'What is the
    answer?' No answer came. She laughed and said,
    'In that case what is the question?' Then she died.
    Last words, as quoted in D Sutherland *Gertrude Stein* (1951),
    ch.6.

48 She said he was a village explainer, excellent if you
    were a village, but if you were not, not.
    Of Ezra Pound. Quoted in J Hobhouse *Everyone Who Was
    Anybody* (1975), ch.6.

Stein, Herbert 1916–

US economist, member of the Council of Economic
Advisers under Nixon, Ford and Reagan.

49 *Consumer.* A person who is capable of choosing a
    president but incapable of choosing a bicycle
    without help from a government agency.
    1979 *Washington Bedtime Stories*.

50 Whatever may be the distribution of uncertainty
    among economists, the public only gets to hear
    from those who have certain opinions.
    1979 *Washington Bedtime Stories*.

51 A few weeks ago I had a revelation and told my
    secretary that I could give him a synthesis of forty-
    six years of living with economic policy. It is:
    'Economic policy is random with respect to the
    performance of the American economy, but, thank
    God, there isn't much of it.'
    1979 *Washington Bedtime Stories*.

Steinbeck, John Ernest 1902–68

US novelist. His works include *Of Mice and Men* (1937),
The Grapes of Wrath (1939) and *East of Eden* (1952). He
received the Nobel Prize for Literature in 1962.

52 Man, unlike any other thing organic or inorganic
    in the universe, grows beyond his work, walks up
    the stairs of his concepts, emerges ahead of his
    accomplishments.
    1939 *The Grapes of Wrath*, ch.14.

53 I know this—a man got to do what he got to do.
    1939 *The Grapes of Wrath*, ch.18.

54 Okie use' ta mean you was from Oklahoma. Now it
    means you're a dirty son-of-a-bitch. Okie means
    you're scum. Don' mean nothing itself, it's the way
    they say it.
    1939 *The Grapes of Wrath*, ch.18.

55 Well, maybe like Casy says, a fellow ain't got a soul
    of his own, but on'y a piece of a big one—an
    then—… Then it don' matter. Then I'll be all
    aroun' in the dark. I'll be everywhere—wherever
    you look. Wherever they's a fight so hungry people
    can eat, I'll be there. Wherever they's a cop beatin'
    up a guy, I'll be there. If Casy knowed, why, I'll be
    in the way guys yell when they're mad an'—I'll be
    in the way kids laugh when they're hungry an' they
    know supper's ready. An' when our folks eat the
    stuff they raise an' live in the houses they build—
    why, I'll be there. See?
    1939 *The Grapes of Wrath*, ch.28.

56 All Americans believe that they are born fishermen.
    For a man to admit a distaste for fishing would be
    like denouncing mother-love or hating moonlight.
    1954 Quoted in Colin Jarman *The Guinness Dictionary of
    Sports Quotations* (1990).

57 Unless the bastards have the courage to give you
    unqualified praise, I say ignore them.
    1958 Of critics. Quoted in J K Galbraith *The Affluent Society*
    (1977), introduction.

58 I pulled to the side of the street and got out my
    book of road maps. But to find where you are
    going, you must know where you are, and I didn't.
    1962 *Travels With Charley In Search of America*.

59 A journey is like a marriage. The certain way to be
    wrong is to think you control it.
    1962 *Travels With Charley In Search of America*, pt.1.

60 It is the nature of a man as he grows older, a small
    bridge in time, to protest against change,
    particularly change for the better.
    1962 *Travels With Charley In Search of America*, pt.2.

61 The profession of book writing makes horse racing
    seem like a solid, stable business.
    1962 In *Newsweek*, 24 Dec.

62 A good writer always works at the impossible.
    Recalled on his death, 20 Dec 1968.

Steinem, Gloria 1934–

US feminist and writer. She emerged as a leading figure in the women's movement in the 1960s, and as a campaigner against the Vietnam War and racism. She co-founded the Women's Action Alliance (1970) and *Ms* magazine (1971).

63 A woman needs a man like a fish needs a bicycle.
c.1970 Attributed, in various forms.

64 This is what forty looks like. We've been lying so long who would know?
c.1974 Response when complimented by a reporter on not looking forty years old, quoted by Lisa Jardine in 'Still Angry After All These Years', in the *Sunday Times*, 15 May 1994.

65 What would happen if…men could menstruate and women could not? Clearly, menstruation would become an enviable, boast-worthy, masculine event: Men would brag about how long and how much. Young boys would talk about it as the envied beginning of manhood… Generals, right-wing politicians, and religious fundamentalists would cite …'*mens*-truation' as proof that only men could serve God and country in combat… If men could menstruate, the power justifications would go on and on. If we let them.
1978 'If Men could Menstruate', collected in *Outrageous Acts and Everyday Rebellions* (1983).

66 I've finally figured out why soap operas are, and logically should be, so popular with generations of housebound women. *They are the only place in our culture where grown-up men take seriously all the things that grown-up women have to deal with all day long.*
1980 'Night Thoughts of a Media Watcher', collected in *Outrageous Acts and Everyday Rebellions* (1983).

Steiner, George 1929–

French-born US literary critic and scholar.

67 Where God's presence is no longer a tenable proposition and where his absence is no longer a felt, indeed overwhelming weight, certain dimensions of thought and creativity are no longer attainable.
1989 *Real Presences.*

Steinmetz, Charles Proteus 1865–1923

German-born US electrical engineer and inventor, whose most notable work was the development of alternating current.

68 In the realm of science, all attempts to find any evidence of supernatural beings, of metaphysical concepts, as God, immortality, infinity, etc have thus far failed, and if we are honest, we must confess that in science there exists no God, no immortality, no soul or mind, as distinct from the body.
1941 In the *American Freeman*, Jul.

Steloff, Frances 1887–(?)1982

US bookseller. She worked at Loeser's Department Store, NYC, then at Bretanos where she ran the drama department (1917–19). She founded Gotham Book Mart, NYC, in 1920.

69 Wise men fish here.
Sign for Gotham Book Mart. Quoted in the *New York Times*, 30 Dec 1987.

Stendhal pseudonym of *Henri Beyle* 1783–1842

French writer who lived many years in Italy, he wrote novels and treatises on literature. He held a modernist concept of Romanticism and was opposed to those who sought literary models from the past.

70 *L'esprit et le génie perdent vingt-cinq pour cent de leur valeur, en débarquant en Angleterre.*

The mind and genius lose twenty-five percent of their value on entry into England.
1830 *Le Rouge et le noir*, bk.2, ch.7.

71 *La politique au milieu des intérêts d'imagination, c'est un coup de pistolet au milieu d'un concert.*

Politics mixed with the imagination is like a shot fired in the middle of a concert.
1830 *Le Rouge et le noir*, bk.2, ch.22.

72 *Grand Dieu! Pourquoi suis-je moi?*

Great God! Why am I me?
1830 *Le Rouge et le noir*, bk.2, ch.28.

73 *Le pire des malheurs en prison, pensa-t-il, c'est de ne pouvoir fermer sa porte.*

The worst of prison life, he thought, was not being able to close his door.
1830 *Le Rouge et le noir*, bk.2, ch.44.

74 *Les gens qu'on honore ne sont que des fripons qui ont eu le bonheur de n'être pas pris en flagrant délit.*

Respected people are only rascals who have had the good fortune not to be caught in the act.
1830 *Le Rouge et le noir*, bk.2, ch.44.

Stengel, Casey (Charles Dillon) 1890–1975

US baseball player and manager. An outfielder with the Brooklyn Dodgers and other teams, he became manager of the New York Yankees (1949–62), leading them to seven World Series victories, and of the New York Mets (1962–5).

75 The secret of managing a ball club is to keep the five guys who hate you away from the five who are undecided.

Quoted in Colin Jarman *The Guinness Dictionary of Sports Quotations* (1990).

76 There's three things you can do in a baseball game–you can win, you can lose, or it can rain.

Quoted in Colin Jarman *The Guinness Dictionary of Sports Quotations* (1990).

77 Without losers, where would the winners be?

Quoted in Colin Jarman *The Guinness Dictionary of Sports Quotations* (1990).

78 Not bad. Most people my age are dead. You could look it up.

Attributed, when asked how he was. 'You could look it up' was one of his catchphrases.

Stephen, J(ames) K(enneth) 1859–92

English lawyer and journalist, a cousin of Virginia Woolf. He began a weekly paper, *The Reflector* in 1888 and was a successful parodist and light versifier.

79 Two voices are there: one is of the deep;
It learns the storm-clouds thundrous melody,
Now roars, now murmurs with the changing sea,
Now bird-like pipes, now closes soft in sleep:
And one is of an old half-witted sheep
Which bleats articulate monotony,
And indicates that two and one are three,
That grass is green, lakes damp, and mountains
  steep
And, Wordsworth, both are thine.

1896 *Lapsus Calami*, 'A Sonnet'.

80 Will there never come a season
Which shall rid us of the curse
Of a prose which knows no reason
And an unmelodious verse...
When there stands a muzzled stripling,
Mute, beside a muzzled bore:
When the Rudyards cease from kipling
And the Haggards Ride no more.

'To R K'.

Stephenson, Bette 1924–

Former President of the Canadian Medical Association and Ontario Minister of Health.

81 Men are very fragile creatures. Their psyches are so closely tied to their epididymis.

1975 Interviewed by Christina McCall Newman in *The Globe and Mail*, 12 Jul. The epididymis is the tube carrying sperm out from the testicle.

Sterling, Bruce 1954–

US science fiction writer.

82 Unfortunately, computers are...stupid. Unlike human beings, computers possess the truly profound stupidity of the inanimate.

1992 *The Hacker Crackdown: law and disorder on the electronic frontier.*

83 It's a truism in technological development that no silver lining comes without its cloud.

1993 Opening statement to the House Subcommittee on Telecommunications and Finance, Washington DC, 29 Apr.

84 Cyberspace is the funhouse mirror of our own society.

1993 National Academy of Sciences Convocation on Technology and Education, Washington DC, 10 May.

Sterling, Rod

85 Every writer is a frustrated actor who recites his lines in the hidden auditorium of his skull.

1957 In *Vogue*, 1 Apr.

Stern, Robert A(rthur) M(orton) 1939–

US architect and writer, author of *New Directions in American Architecture* (1969, revised 1977) and *The House that Bob Built* (1991).

86 The dialogue between client and architect is about as intimate as any conversation you can have because, when you're talking about building a house, you're talking about dreams.

1985 'The Trend-Setting Traditionalism of Architecture', in the *New York Times*, 13 Jan.

87 Our greatest responsibility is not to be pencils of the past.

1985 'The Trend-Setting Traditionalism of Architecture', in the *New York Times*, 13 Jan.

Sterne, Laurence 1713–68

Irish novelist. He extended the scope of the novel with his major work *Tristram Shandy* (1759–67). As his health failed, he spent much of his time in France and Italy and published *A Sentimental Journey through France and Italy* in 1768.

88 I wish either my father or my mother, or indeed both of them, as they were in duty both equally bound to it, had minded what they were about when they begot me.

1759–67 *Tristram Shandy*, bk.1, ch.1.

89 'Pray, my dear,' quoth my mother, 'have you not forgot to wind up the clock?'— 'Good G—?' cried my father, making an exclamation, but taking care to moderate his voice at the same time,—'Did ever woman, since the creation of the world, interrupt a man with such a silly question?'

1759—67 *Tristram Shandy*, bk.1, ch.6.

90 As we jog on, either laugh with me, or at me, or in short do anything,—only keep your temper.
1759–67 Tristram to reader. _Tristram Shandy_, bk.1, ch.6.

91 Have not the wisest of men in all ages, not excepting Solomon himself,—have they not had their Hobby-Horses…and so long as a man rides his Hobby-Horse peaceably and quietly along the King's highway, and neither compels you or me to get up behind him,—pray, Sir, what have either you or I to do with it?
1759–67 _Tristram Shandy_, bk.1, ch.7.

92 He was in a few hours of giving his enemies the slip for ever.
1759–67 Of Eugenis. _Tristram Shandy_, bk.1, ch.12.

93 'Tis known by the name of perseverance in a good cause,—and of obstinacy in a bad one.
1759–67 Toby. _Tristram Shandy_, bk.1, ch.17.

94 What is the character of a family to an hypothesis? my father would reply.
1759–67 _Tristram Shandy_, bk.1, ch.21.

95 My uncle Toby would never offer to answer this by any other kind of argument, than that of whistling half a dozen bars of Lillabullero.
1759–67 _Tristram Shandy_, bk.1, ch.21.

96 Digressions, incontestably, are the sunshine;—they are the life, the soul of reading;—take them out of this book for instance,—you might as well take the book along with them.
1759–67 _Tristram Shandy_, bk.1, ch.22.

97 I should have no objection to this method, but that I think it must smell too strong of the lamp.
1759–67 Toby. _Tristram Shandy_, bk.1, ch.23.

98 Writing, when properly managed (as you may be sure I think mine is) is but a different name for conversation.
1759–67 _Tristram Shandy_, bk.2, ch.11.

99 'I'll not hurt thee,' says my uncle Toby, rising from his chair, and going across the room, with the fly in his hand, 'I'll not hurt a hair of thy head:—Go,' says he, lifting up the sash, and opening his hand as he spoke, to let it escape;—'go, poor devil, get thee gone, why should I hurt thee?—This world surely is wide enough to hold both thee and me.'
1759–67 _Tristram Shandy_, bk.2, ch.12.

1 Whenever a man talks loudly against religion,— always suspect that it is not his reason, but his passions which have got the better of his creed.
1759–67 Trim. _Tristram Shandy_, bk.2, ch.17.

2 It is the nature of an hypothesis, when once a man has conceived it, that it assimilates everything to itself, as proper nourishment; and, from the first moment of your begetting it, it generally grows the stronger by every thing you see, hear, read, or understand.
1759–67 _Tristram Shandy_, bk.2, ch.19.

3 'Our armies swore terribly in Flanders,' cried my uncle Toby,—'but nothing to this.'
1759–67 _Tristram Shandy_, bk.3, ch.11.

4 The corregiescity of Corregio.
1759–67 _Tristram Shandy_, bk.3, ch.12.

5 Of all the cants which are canted in this canting world,—though the cant of hypocrites may be the worst,—the cant of criticism is the most tormenting.
1759–67 _Tristram Shandy_, bk.3, ch.12.

6 Is this a fit time, said my father to himself, to talk of Pensions and Grenadiers?
1759–67 _Tristram Shandy_, bk.4, ch.5.

7 True _Shandeism_, think what you will against it, opens the heart and lungs, and like all those affections which partake of its nature, it forces the blood and other vital fluids of the body to run freely through its channels, and makes the wheel of life run long and cheerfully round.
1759–67 _Tristram Shandy_, bk.4, ch.32.

8 'There is no terror, brother Toby, in its looks, but what it borrows from groans and convulsions—and the blowing of noses, and the wiping away of tears with the bottoms of curtains, in a dying man's room—Strip it of these, what is it?'—''Tis better in battle than in bed,' said my uncle Toby.
1759–67 Of death. _Tristram Shandy_, bk.5, ch.3.

9 There is a North-west passage to the intellectual World.
1759–67 _Tristram Shandy_, bk.5, ch.42.

10 To say a man is fallen in love,—or that he is deeply in love,—or up to the ears in love,—and sometimes even over head and ears in it,—carries an idiomatical kind of implication, that love is a thing below a man:—this is recurring again to Plato's opinion, which, with all his divinityship,— I hold to be damnable and heretical:—and so much for that. Let love therefore be what it will,—my uncle Toby fell into it.
1759–67 _Tristram Shandy_, bk.6, ch.37.

11 My brother Toby, quoth she, is going to be married to Mrs Wadman. Then he will never, quoth my father, lie _diagonally_ in his bed again as long as he lives.
1759–67 _Tristram Shandy_, bk.6, ch.39.

12 Now hang it! quoth I, as I look'd towards the French coast—a man should know something of his own country too, before he goes abroad.
  1759–67 Tristram. *Tristram Shandy*, bk.7, ch.2.

13 And who are you? Said he.—Don't puzzle me, said I.
  1759–67 Tristram to the commissary. *Tristram Shandy*, bk.7, ch.33.

14 'A soldier,' cried my Uncle Toby, interrupting the corporal, 'is no more exempt from saying a foolish thing, Trim, than a man of letters.' —'But not so often, an' please your honour,' replied the corporal.
  1759–67 *Tristram Shandy*, bk.8, ch.19.

15 Everything presses on—whilst thou art twisting that lock,—see! It grows grey; and every time I kiss thy hand to bid adieu, and every absence which follows it, are preludes to that eternal separation which we are shortly to make.
  1759–67 Tristram to Jenny. *Tristram Shandy*, bk.9, ch.8.

16 '—d!' said my mother, 'what is all this story about?'—'A Cock and a Bull,' said Yorick.
  1759–67 *Tristram Shandy*, bk.9, ch.33.

17 A man cannot dress, but his ideas get cloath'd at the same time.
  1759–67 *Tristram Shandy*, bk.9, ch.13.

18 This sad vicissitude of things.
  1767 *Sermons*, 'The Character of Shimei', no.16.

19 They order, said I, this matter better in France.
  1768 *A Sentimental Journey*, opening words.

20 As an Englishman does not travel to see Englishmen, I retired to my room.
  1768 *A Sentimental Journey*, 'Preface. In the Desobligeant'.

21 I pity the man who can travel from Dan to Beersheba, and cry, 'tis all barren.
  1768 *A Sentimental Journey*, 'In the Street. Calais'.

22 I had had an affair with the moon, in which there was neither sin nor shame.
  1768 *A Sentimental Journey*, 'The Monk, Calais'.

23 If ever I do a mean action, it must be in some interval betwixt one passion and another.
  1768 *A Sentimental Journey*, 'Montriul'.

24 Vive l'amour! Et vive la bagatelle!
  1768 *A Sentimental Journey*, 'The Latter'.

25 Hail, ye small sweet courtesies of life.
  1768 *A Sentimental Journey*, 'The Pulse, Paris'.

26 There are worse occupations in this world than feeling a woman's pulse.
  1768 *A Sentimental Journey*, 'The Pulse, Paris'.

27 God tempers the wind, said Maria, to the shorn lamb.
  1768 *A Sentimental Journey*, 'Maria'. This is an allusion to an old French proverb.

28 Dear sensibility! Source inexhausted of all that's precious in our joys, or costly in our sorrows!
  1768 *A Sentimental Journey*, 'The Bourbonnois'.

Steuart (later Denham), Sir James
1712–80

Scottish advocate and economist. A fervent Jacobite who was a member of the Council of Prince Charles Edward Stuart in 1745 and subsequently in exile until 1763, travelling extensively on the Continent and studying political economy. His *Principles of Political Oeconomy* (1767) was soon eclipsed by the *Wealth of Nations* of Adam Smith.

29 To preserve a trading state from decline, the greatest care must be taken, to support a perfect balance between the hands employed in work and the demand for their labour.
  1767 *Inquiry into the Principles of Political Oeconomy*.

30 It is the business of a statesman to judge of the expediency of different schemes of economy, and by degrees to model the minds of his subjects so as to induce them from the allurement of private interest to concur in the execution of his plan.
  1767 *Inquiry into the Principles of Political Oeconomy*.

Stevens, Brooks 1911–

US industrial designer.

31 Our whole economy is based on planned obsolescence... We make good products, we induce people to buy them, and then the next year we deliberately introduce something that will make these products old-fashioned, out of date, obsolete.
  Quoted in Vance Packard *The Waste Makers* (1960), ch.6. This is thought to be the first use of the phrase 'planned obsolescence'.

Stevens, Roger Lacey 1910–98

US theatrical producer. He worked as a real estate broker (1934–60) but was increasingly involved as a producer in over 200 theatrical productions. He was Chair of the National Council on the Arts (1965–9), and a member of the President's Committee on Arts and Humanities from 1982.

32 Whenever I think, I make a mistake.
  1955 In 'How Businessmen Make Decisions', *Fortune*, Aug.

Stevens, Wallace 1879–1955

US poet. He began as a journalist and lawyer, then joined an insurance company. *Harmonium*, his first collection of philosophical verse, appeared in 1923. Further works

include *The Man with the Blue Guitar* (1937) and
Collected Poems (1954, winner of a Pulitzer Prize).

33 I placed a jar in Tennessee,
    And round it was, upon a hill.
    It made the slovenly wilderness
    Surround that hill.
    1923 *Harmonium*, 'Anecdote of the Jar'.

34 Poetry is the supreme fiction, madame.
    Take the moral law and make a nave of it
    And from the nave build haunted heaven.
    1923 *Harmonium*, 'A High-Toned Old Christian Woman'.

35 Call the roller of big cigars,
    The muscular one, and bid him whip
    In kitchen cups of concupiscent curds.
    1923 *Harmonium*, 'The Emperor of Ice-Cream'.

36 The only emperor is the emperor of ice-cream.
    1923 *Harmonium*, 'The Emperor of Ice-Cream'.

37 I shall whisper
    Heavenly labials in a world of gutterals.
    It will undo him.
    1923 *Harmonium*, 'The Plot Against the Giant'.

38 Complacencies of the peignoir, and late
    Coffee and oranges in a sunny chair,
    And the green freedom of a cockatoo
    Upon a rug mingle to dissipate
    The holy hush of ancient sacrifice.
    1923 *Harmonium*, 'Sunday Morning', pt.1.

39 What is divinity if it can come
    Only in silent shadows and in dreams?
    1923 *Harmonium*, 'Sunday Morning', pt.2.

40 And, in the isolation of the sky,
    At evening, casual flocks of pigeons make
    Ambiguous undulations as they sink,
    Downward to darkness, on extended wings.
    1923 *Harmonium*, 'Sunday Morning', pt.8.

41 Chieftain Iffucan of Azcan in caftan
    Of tan with henna hackles, halt!
    1923 *Harmonium*, 'Bantams in Pine-Woods'.

42 Just as my fingers on these keys
    Make music, so the self-same sounds
    On my spirit make a music, too.

    Music is feeling, then, not a sound;
    And thus it is that what I feel,
    Here in this room, desiring you,

    Thinking of your blue-shadowed silk,
    Is music.
    1923 *Harmonium*, 'Peter Quince at the Clavier', pt.1.

43 I do not know which to prefer,

The beauty of inflections
Or the beauty of innuendoes,
The blackbird whistling
or just after.
1923 *Harmonium*, 'Thirteen Ways of Looking At A Blackbird',
pt.5.

44 I know noble accents
    And lucid, inescapable rhythms;
    But I know, too,
    That the blackbird is involved
    In what I know.
    1923 *Harmonium*, 'Thirteen Ways of Looking At A Blackbird',
    pt.8.

45 What counted was the mythology of self,
    Blotched out beyond unblotching.
    1923 *Harmonium*, 'The Comedian as the Letter C', pt.1.

46 Like a dull scholar, I behold, in love,
    An ancient aspect touching a new mind.
    It comes, it blooms, it bears its fruit and dies.
    This trivial trope reveals a way of truth.
    Our bloom is gone. We are the fruit thereof.
    1923 *Harmonium*, 'Le Monocle de Mon Oncle', pt.8.

47 Only, here and there, an old sailor,
    Drunk and asleep in his boots,
    Catches tigers
    In red weather.
    1923 *Harmonium*, 'Disillusionment of Ten O'Clock'.

48 It was her voice that made
    The sky acutest at its vanishing.
    She measured to the hour its solitude.
    She was the single artificer of the world
    In which she sang.
    1935 *Ideas of Order*, 'The Idea of Order at Key West'.

49 They said, 'You have a blue guitar,
    You do not play things as they are.'
    The man replied, 'Things as they are
    Are changed upon a blue guitar.'
    1937 *The Man with the Blue Guitar and Other Poems*, title poem.

50 It has to be living, to learn the speech of the place,
    It has to face the man of the time.
    1942 *Parts of a World*, 'Of Modern Poetry'.

51 The first idea was not our own.
    1942 *Notes Toward A Supreme Fiction*, 'It Must Be Abstract'.

52 There was a muddy centre before we breathed
    There was a myth before the myth began,
    Venerable and articulate and complete.
    1942 *Notes Toward A Supreme Fiction*, 'It Must Be Abstract'.

53 They will get it straight one day at the Sorbonne.
    We shall return at twilight from the lecture
    Pleased that the irrational is rational.
    1942 *Notes Toward A Supreme Fiction*, 'It Must Give Pleasure'.

54 Sentimentality is a failure of feeling.
1957 *Opus Posthumous*, Aphorisms, 'Adagia'.

55 Not evocations but last choirs, last sounds,
With nothing else compounded, carried full,
Pure rhetoric of a language without words.
1947 *Transport to Summer*, 'Credences of Summer'.

56 Poetry is a means of redemption.
1957 *Opus Posthumous*, Aphorisms, 'Adagia'.

57 Literature is based not on life but on propositions
about life, of which this is one.
1957 *Opus Posthumous*, Aphorisms, 'Adagia'.

58 Poetry must resist the intelligence almost
successfully.
1957 *Opus Posthumous*, Aphorisms, 'Adagia'.

59 All poetry is experimental poetry.
1957 *Opus Posthumous*, Aphorisms, 'Adagia'.

60 Ethics are no more a part of poetry than they are of
painting.
1957 *Opus Posthumous*, Aphorisms, 'Adagia'.

61 The poet makes silk dresses out of worms.
1957 *Opus Posthumous*, Aphorisms, 'Adagia'.

62 After one has abandoned a belief in God, poetry is
the essence which takes its place as life's
redemption.
1957 *Opus Posthumous*, Aphorisms, 'Adagia'.

63 Authors are actors, books are theatres.
1957 *Opus Posthumous*, Aphorisms, 'Adagia'.

64 The poet represents the mind in the act of
defending us against itself.
1957 *Opus Posthumous*, Aphorisms, 'Adagia'.

65 Poetry is a rich, full-blooded whistle, cracked ice
crunching in pails, the night that numbers the leaf,
the duet of two nightingales, the sweet pea, that has
run wild, Creation's tears in shoulder blades.
Quoted in *Life*, 13 Jun 1960.

66 Money is a kind of poetry.
Quoted in *Harper's*, Oct 1985.

67 Words of the world are the life of the world.
Quoted in Brendan Gill *A New York Life* (1990).

68 Poetry is the supreme fiction, madame.
Quoted in Helen Gardner (ed) *The New Oxford Book of English Verse* (1991).

Stevenson, Adlai E(wing) 1900–65

US Democratic politician, Governor of Illinois (1948).
He helped to found the United Nations (1946), stood
twice against Eisenhower as presidential candidate (1952,
1956), and was the US Delegate to the UN (1961–5).

69 A lie is an abomination unto the Lord, and a very
present help when in trouble.
1951 Speech, Washington, Jan.

70 It is often easier to fight for principles than to live
up to them.
1952 Speech, New York, 27 Aug.

71 If Republicans will stop telling lies about the
United States, we will stop telling the truth about
them.
1952 Speech at Bakersfield, California. Quoted in *Time*, 10 Sep.

72 Looking back, I am content. Win or lose I have
told you the truth as I see it. I have said what I
meant and meant what I said.
1952 Concluding his campaign. Reported in *Time*, 10 Sep.

73 Man has wrested from nature the power to make
the world a desert or to make the deserts bloom.
There is no evil in the atom—only in men's souls.
1952 Speech, Connecticut, 18 Sep.

74 When political ammunition runs low, inevitably
the rusty artillery of abuse is wheeled into action.
1952 Speech, New York, 22 Sep.

75 My definition of a free society is a society in which
it is safe to be unpopular.
1952 Speech, Detroit, Oct.

76 Eggheads of the world unite; you have nothing to
lose but your yolks.
1952 Presidential election campaign speech.

77 Via ovum cranium difficilis est. The way of the
egghead is hard.
1954 Reply to charges that he was too intellectual. Lecture at Harvard, 17 Mar.

78 Shouting is not a substitute for thinking and reason
is not the subversion but the salvation of freedom.
1954 Lecture at Harvard, 17 Mar.

79 Technology, while adding daily to our physical
ease, throws daily another loop of fine wire around
our souls. It contributes hugely to our mobility,
which we must not confuse with freedom. The
extensions of our senses, which we find so
fascinating, are not adding to the discrimination of
our minds, since we need increasingly to take the
reading of a needle on a dial to discover whether we
think something is good or bad, or right or wrong.
1955 'My Faith in Democratic Capitalism', in *Fortune*, Oct.

80 You will find that the truth is often unpopular and
the contest between agreeable fancy and
disagreeable fact is unequal. For, in the vernacular,
we Americans are suckers for good news.
1958 Speech, Michigan, 8 Jun.

81 Freedom is not an ideal; it is not even a protection, if it means nothing more than the freedom to stagnate.
1960 *Putting First Things First.*

82 We have confused the free with the free and easy.
1960 *Putting First Things First.*

83 The Republican Party needs to be dragged kicking and screaming into the 20th century.
Quoted in Kenneth Tynan *Curtains* (1961).

84 It will be helpful in our mutual objective to allow every man in America to look his neighbour in the face and see a man—not a colour.
1964 In the *New York Times*, 22 Jun.

85 He who slings mud generally loses ground.
Recalled on his death, 14 Jul 1965.

86 You can't teach an underdog new tricks.
On presidential hopeful Estes Kefauver's replay of his anti-bossism theme. Quoted in *Newsweek*, 1 Nov 1971.

87 The best politics is good government.
Quoted by New York Governor Mario Cuomo in the *New York Times*, 26 Aug 1990.

88 A politician is a statesman who approaches every question with an open mouth.
Attributed.

89 An independent is a guy who wants to take the politics out of politics.
The Art of Politics.

90 In America, any boy may become president. I suppose that's just one of the risks that he takes.
Attributed.

Stevenson, Robert Louis 1850–94

Scottish author. He wrote travel sketches, essays, short stories, serials and romantic thrillers, including *Treasure Island* (1883) and *Kidnapped* (1886). In his early years he toured Belgium and northern France by canoe and the Cévennes by donkey, described in *Travels with a Donkey in the Cévennes* (1879). He struggled for many years against tuberculosis and spent the last five years of his life living on his estate in Samoa.

91 For will anyone dare to tell me that business is more entertaining than fooling among boats? He must have never seen a boat, or never seen an office, who says so. And for certain the one is a great deal better for the health.
1878 *An Inland Voyage*, 'The Royal Sport Nautique'.

92 Respectability is a very good thing in its way, but it does not rise superior to all considerations. I would not for a moment venture to hint that it was a matter of taste; but I think I will go as far as this:

that if a position is admittedly unkind, uncomfortable, unnecessary, and superfluously useless, although it were as respectable as the Church of England, the sooner a man is out of it, the better for himself, and all concerned.
1878 *An Inland Voyage*, 'At Maubeuge'.

93 The gauger walked with willing foot,
And aye the gauger played the flute;
And what should Master Gauger play
But *Over the hills and far away?*
1878 'A Song of the Road', stanza 1 (dated 'Forest of Montargis, 1878'), collected in *Underwoods* (1887), bk.1, no.2.

94 If a man knows he will sooner or later be robbed upon a journey, he will have a bottle of the best in every inn, and look upon all his extravagances as so much gained upon the thieves.
1878 *An Inland Voyage*, 'The Oise in Flood'.

95 The most patient people grow weary at last with being continually wetted with rain; except, of course, in the Scottish Highlands, where there are not enough fine intervals to point the difference.
1878 *An Inland Voyage*, 'Down the Oise: to Compiègne'.

96 For my part, I travel not to go anywhere, but to go. I travel for travel's sake. The great affair is to move.
1879 *Travels with a Donkey*, 'Cheylard and Luc'.

97 I opened a tin of Bologna sausage and broke a cake of chocolate, and that was all I had to eat. It may sound offensive, but I ate them together, bite by bite, by way of bread and meat. All I had to wash down this revolting mixture was neat brandy; a revolting beverage in itself. But I was rare and hungry; ate well, and smoked one of the best cigarettes in my experience. Then I put a stone in my straw hat, pulled the flap of my fur cap over my neck and eyes, put my revolver ready to hand, and snuggled well down among the sheepskins.
1879 *Travels with a Donkey.*

98 I own I like definite form in what my eyes are to rest upon; and if landscapes were sold, like the sheets of characters of my boyhood, one penny plain and twopence coloured, I should go the length of twopence every day of my life.
1879 *Travels with a Donkey*, 'Father Apollinaris'.

99 To live out of doors with the woman a man loves is of all lives the most complete and free.
1879 *Travels with a Donkey*, 'A Night Among the Pines'.

1 The fact is, we are much more afraid of life than our ancestors, and cannot find it in our hearts either to marry or not to marry. Marriage is terrifying, but so is a cold and forlorn old age.
1881 *Virginibus Puerisque*, 'Virginibus Puerisque', pt.1.

2 In marriage, a man becomes slack and selfish, and undergoes a fatty degeneration of his moral being.
1881 *Virginibus Puerisque*, 'Virginibus Puerisque', pt.1.

3 I see women marry indiscriminately with staring burgesses and ferret-faced, white-eyed boys, and men dwell in contentment with noisy scullions, or taking into their lives acidulous vestals.
1881 *Virginibus Puerisque*, 'Virginibus Puerisque', pt.1.

4 And you have only to look these happy couples in the face, to see they have never been in love, or in hate, or in any other high passion all their days.
1881 *Virginibus Puerisque*, 'Virginibus Puerisque', pt.1.

5 Even if we take marriage at its lowest, even if we regard it as no more than a sort of friendship recognised by the police.
1881 *Virginibus Puerisque*, 'Virginibus Puerisque', pt.1.

6 Lastly (and this is, perhaps, the golden rule) no woman should marry a teetotaller, or a man who does not smoke.
1881 *Virginibus Puerisque*, 'Virginibus Puerisque', pt.1.

7 Marriage is a step so grave and decisive that it attracts light-headed, variable men by its very awfulness.
1881 *Virginibus Puerisque*, 'Virginibus Puerisque', pt.1.

8 Marriage is like life in this—that it is a field of battle, and not a bed of roses.
1881 *Virginibus Puerisque*, 'Virginibus Puerisque', pt.1.

9 Times are changed with him who marries; there are no more by-path meadows, where you may innocently linger, but the road lies long and straight and dusty to the grave. Idleness, which is often becoming and even wise in the bachelor, begins to wear a different aspect when you have a wife to support.
1881 *Virginibus Puerisque*, 'Virginibus Puerisque', pt.2.

10 To marry is to domesticate the Recording Angel. Once you are married, there is nothing left for you, not even suicide, but to be good.
1881 *Virginibus Puerisque*, 'Virginibus Puerisque', pt.2.

11 Man is a creature who lives not upon bread alone, but principally by catchwords.
1881 *Virginibus Puerisque*, 'Virginibus Puerisque', pt.2.

12 The cruellest lies are often told in silence.
1881 *Virginibus Puerisque*, 'Truth of Intercourse'.

13 Most of our pocket wisdom is conceived for the use of mediocre people, to discourage them from ambitious attempts, and generally console them in their mediocrity.
1881 *Virginibus Puerisque*, 'Crabbed Age and Youth'.

14 Old and young, we are all on our last cruise.

15 It is better to be a fool than to be dead.
1881 *Virginibus Puerisque*, 'Crabbed Age and Youth'.

16 For God's sake give me the young man who has brains enough to make a fool of himself!
1881 *Virginibus Puerisque*, 'Crabbed Age and Youth'.

17 To travel hopefully is a better thing than to arrive, and the true success is to labour.
1881 *Virginibus Puerisque*, 'El Dorado'.

18 Books are good enough in their own way, but they are a mighty bloodless substitute for life.
1881 *Virginibus Puerisque*, 'An Apology for Idlers'.

19 Extreme *busyness*, whether at school or college, kirk or market, is a symptom of a deficient vitality; and a faculty for idleness implies a catholic appetite and a strong sense of personal identity.
1881 *Virginibus Puerisque*, 'An Apology for Idlers'.

20 There is no duty we so much underrate as the duty of being happy.
1881 *Virginibus Puerisque*, 'An Apology for Idlers'.

21 We live the time that a match flickers; we pop the cork of a ginger-beer bottle, and the earthquake swallows us on the instant. Is it not odd, is it not incongruous, is it not, in the highest sense of human speech, incredible, that we should think so highly of the ginger-beer, and regard so little the devouring earthquake?
1881 *Virginibus Puerisque*, 'Aes Triplex'.

22 Think of the heroism of Johnson, think of that superb indifference to mortal limitation that set him upon his dictionary, and carried him through triumphantly until the end! Who, if he were wisely considerate of things at large, would ever embark upon any work much more considerable than a halfpenny post-card? Who would project a serial novel, after Thackeray and Dickens had each fallen in mid-course? Who would find heart enough to begin to live, if he dallied with the consideration of death?
1881 *Virginibus Puerisque*, 'Aes Triplex'.

23 Even if the doctor does not give you a year, even if he hesitates about a month, make one brave push and see what can be accomplished in a week.
1881 *Virginibus Puerisque*, 'Aes Triplex'.

24 Though we are mighty fine fellows nowadays, we cannot write like Hazlitt.
1881 *Virginibus Puerisque*, 'Walking Tours'.

25 We are in such haste to be doing, to be writing, to be gathering gear, to make our voice audible a moment in the derisive silence of eternity, that we

forget that one thing, of which these are but the parts—namely, to live.

1881 *Virginibus Puerisque*, 'Walking Tours'.

26 It seems he had no design except to appear respectable, and here he keeps a private book to prove that he was not.

1882 Of Samuel Pepys and his *Diary. Familiar Studies of Men and Books.*

27 Politics is perhaps the only profession for which no preparation is thought necessary.

1882 *Familiar Studies of Men and Books*, 'Yoshida-Torajiro'.

28 Fifteen men on a dead man's chest—
    Yo-ho-ho, and a bottle of rum!
    Drink and the devil had done for the rest—
    Yo-ho-ho, and a bottle of rum!

1883 *Treasure Island*, ch.1, 'The Old Sea-Dog at the 'Admiral Benbow'.

29 Pieces of eight!

1883 *Treasure Island*, ch.10, 'The Voyage'.

30 You mightn't happen to have a piece of cheese about you, now? No? Well, many's the long night I've dreamed of cheese—toasted, mostly—and woke up again, and here I were.

1883 Ben Gunn to Jim Hawkins. *Treasure Island*, ch.15, 'The Man of the Island'.

31 Under the wide and starry sky,
    Dig the grave and let me lie.
    Glad did I live and gladly die,
    And I laid me down with a will.

    This be the verse you grave for me:
    Here he lies where he longed to be,
    Home is the sailor, home from sea,
    And the hunter home from the hill.

1884 'Requiem' (dated 'Hyères, May 1884'), collected in *Underwoods* (1887), bk.1, no.21.

32 In winter I get up at night
    And dress by yellow candle-light.
    In summer, quite the other way,
    I have to go to bed by day.

    I have to go to bed and see
    The birds still hopping on the tree,
    Or hear the grown-up people's feet
    Still going past me in the street.

1885 *A Child's Garden of Verses*, no.1, 'Bed in Summer', stanzas 1–2.

33 A child should always say what's true,
    And speak when he is spoken to,
    And behave mannerly at table:
    At least as far as he is able.

1885 *A Child's Garden of Verses*, no.5, 'Whole Duty of Children'.

34 Whenever the moon and stars are set,
    Whenever the wind is high,
    All night long in the dark and wet,
    A man goes riding by.
    Late in the night when the fires are out,
    Why does he gallop and gallop about?

1885 *A Child's Garden of Verses*, no.9, 'Windy Nights', stanza 1.

35 When I am grown to man's estate
    I shall be very proud and great,
    And tell the other girls and boys
    Not to meddle with my toys.

1885 *A Child's Garden of Verses*, no.12, 'Looking Forward'.

36 Whenever Auntie moves around,
    Her dresses make a curious sound;
    They trail behind her up the floor,
    And trundle after through the door.

1885 *A Child's Garden of Verses*, no.15, 'Auntie's Skirts'.

37 When I was sick and lay a-bed,
    I had two pillows at my head,
    And all my toys beside me lay
    To keep me happy all the day.

1885 *A Child's Garden of Verses*, no.16, 'The Land of Counterpane', stanza 1.

38 I have a little shadow that goes in and out with me,
    And what can be the use of him is more than I can see.

1885 *A Child's Garden of Verses*, no.18, 'My Shadow', stanza 1.

39 The world is so full of a number of things,
    I'm sure we should all be as happy as kings.

1885 *A Child's Garden of Verses*, no.24, 'Happy Thought'.

40 Children, you are very little,
    And your bones are very brittle;
    If you would grow great and stately,
    You must try to walk sedately.

1885 *A Child's Garden of Verses*, no.27, 'Good and Bad Children', stanza 1.

41 My tea is nearly ready and the sun has left the sky;
    It's time to take the window to see Leerie going
        by;
    For every night at tea-time and before you take
        your seat,
    With lantern and with ladder he comes posting up
        the street.

1885 *A Child's Garden of Verses*, no.30, 'The Lamplighter', stanza 1.

42 Must we to bed indeed? Well then,
    Let us arise and go like men,
    And face with an undaunted tread
    The long black passage up to bed.

1885 *A Child's Garden of Verses*, XLI, 'North-West Passage', pt.1, 'Good Night', stanza 3.

43 In the Land of Nod at last.
1885 *A Child's Garden of Verses*, XLI, 'North-West Passage', pt.3, 'In Port', stanza 3.

44 Am I no a bonny fighter?
1886 Alan Breck to David Balfour. *Kidnapped*, ch.10.

45 Even though his tongue acquire the Southern knack, he will still have a strong Scots accent of the mind.
1887 *Memories and Portraits*, ch.1, 'The Foreigner at Home'.

46 I have thus played the sedulous ape to Hazlitt, to Lamb, to Wordsworth, to Sir Thomas Browne, to Defoe, to Hawthorne, to Montaigne, to Baudelaire and to Obermann.
1887 *Memories and Portraits*, ch.4, 'A College Magazine'

47 Every one lives by selling something, whatever be his right to it.
1888 'Beggars', originally published in *Scribner's Magazine*.

48 Here lies one who meant well, tried a little, failed much:—surely that may be his epitaph, of which he need not be ashamed.
1892 *Across the Plains*, 'A Christmas Sermon', pt.4.

49 The bright face of danger.
1892 *Across the Plains*, 'The Lantern-Bearers', pt.4.

50 Life is not all Beer and Skittles. The inherent tragedy of things works itself out from white to black and blacker, and the poor things of a day look ruefully on. Does it shake my cast-iron faith? I cannot say it does. I believe in an ultimate decency of things: ay, and if I woke in hell, should still believe it!
1893 Letter to Sidney Colvin, 23 Aug.

51 Give to me the life I love,
Let the lave go by me,
Give the jolly heaven above
And the byway nigh me.
Bed in the bush with the stars to see,
Bread I dip in the river—
There's the life for a man like me,
There's the life for ever.
1894 *Songs of Travel* (published 1896), no.1, 'The Vagabond', stanza 1.

52 Wealth I ask not, hope nor love,
Nor a friend to know me.
All I ask, the heaven above,
And the road below me.
1894 *Songs of Travel* (published 1896), no.1, 'The Vagabond', stanza 4.

53 I will make you brooches and toys for your delight
Of bird-song at morning and star-shine at night.
I will make a palace fit for you and me
Of green days in forests and blue days at sea.

I will make my kitchen, and you shall keep your room,
Where white flows the river and bright blows the broom,
And you shall wash your linen and keep your body white
In rainfall at morning and dewfall at night.
1894 *Songs of Travel* (published 1896), no.11, stanza 1.

54 In the highlands, in the country places,
Where the old plain men have rosy faces,
And the young fair maidens
Quiet eyes.
1894 *Songs of Travel* (published 1896), no.16.

55 Trusty, dusky, vivid, true,
With eyes of gold and bramble-dew,
Steel-true and blade-straight,
The great artificer
Made my mate.
1894 *Songs of Travel* (published 1896), 'My Wife'.

56 Blows the wind to-day, and the sun and the rain are flying,
Blows the wind on the moors to-day and now,
Where about the graves of the martyrs the whaups are crying,
My heart remembers how!
1894 *Songs of Travel* (published 1896), no.45, 'To S.R. Crockett (in reply to a dedication)', stanza 1.

57 Be it granted to me to behold you again in dying,
Hills of home! and to hear again the call;
Hear about the graves of the martyrs the peeweets crying,
And hear no more at all.
1894 *Songs of Travel* (published 1896), no.45, 'To S.R. Crockett (in reply to a dedication)', stanza 3.

58 And all that I could think of, in the darkness and the cold,
Was just that I was leaving home and my folks were growing old.
1894 'Christmas at Sea', stanza 11.

59 I saw rain falling and the rainbow drawn
On Lammermuir. Hearkening I heard again
In my precipitous city beaten bells
Winnow the keen sea wind. And here afar,
Intent on my own race and place, I wrote.
1894 *Weir of Hermiston* (published 1896), Dedication 'To My Wife'.

60 It seemed unprovoked, a wilful convulsion of brute nature...
1894 *Weir of Hermiston* (published 1896), ch.9, 'At the Weaver's Stone'. These are the last words of the unfinished novel, dictated by Stevenson on the morning of his death from a blood-clot on the brain.

61 The *bourgeoisie's* weapon is starvation. If as a writer or artist you run counter to their narrow notions they simply and silently withdraw your means of subsistence. I sometimes wonder how many people of talent are executed in this way every year.

Quoted by Lloyd Osbourne in 'The Death of Stevenson', preface to Tusitala edition of *Weir of Hermiston* (published 1924).

62 The saddest object in civilization, and to my mind the greatest confession of its failure, is the man who can work, who wants work, and who is not allowed to work.

Quoted by Lloyd Osbourne in 'The Death of Stevenson', preface to Tusitala edition of *Weir of Hermiston* (published 1924).

Stewart, John Innes Mackintosh 1906–94

Scots-born academic, author and critic, Chair of Literature at Adelaide University (1935–45). His sequence of novels on life at Oxford, *A Staircase in Surrey*, began in 1974 with *The Gaudy*. As 'Michael Innes' he wrote erudite detective novels.

63 I am most grateful to the CLF [Commonwealth Literary Fund] for providing the funds to give these lectures in Australian literature, but unfortunately they have neglected to provide any literature. I will lecture therefore on D H Lawrence's 'Kangaroo'.

1940 Quoted in the *London Magazine*, Nov 1985.

64 On the platform stood a policeman of normal proportions, and instead of a revolver and a truncheon he carried a copy of *Ben Hur* translated into Irish, which he was evidently studying for an examination important to his professional advancement. Mr Thewless realised that the imperial might of Great Britain lay behind him and that in front was the philosophic republic of Mr de Valera.

1949 *The Journeying Boy.*

65 'In about half a mile you cross the river by an Irish bridge—'
'Whatever is that?'
'It's just a bridge, but built under the water instead of over it.'
'Extremely sensible.'

1969 *A Family Affair.*

Stigler, George Joseph 1911–91

US economist, University of Chicago; awarded a Nobel Prize (1982).

66 The branch of economics dealing with how to enrich a new nation ('economic development' was the title) was actually forbidden by the courts, on the grounds that no university could pay for the damage its teachers did.

1973 'The History of Truth in Teaching', in *The Intellectual and the Marketplace* (1984).

Still, Bayrd

67 The tombstone of capitalism…with windows.

1956 Of the Rockefeller Center. *Mirror for Gotham.*

Stilwell, General Joseph 1883–1946

US general, commander in the Far East during World War II, who led the successful attack against the Japanese in Myanmar (1943–4). His acerbic manner earned him the nickname of 'Vinegar Joe'.

68 This little book contains none of your damn business.

Note on flyleaf of 1906 diary. Quoted in Barbara Tuchman *General Stilwell and the American Experience in China* (1970).

Stinchcombe, Arthur S 1933–

US sociologist, University of Chicago.

69 The question of how to apply social theory to historical materials, as it is usually posed, is ridiculous. One does not apply theory to history; rather one uses history to develop theory.

1978 *Theoretical Methods in Social History*, p.1.

Stockwood, (Arthur) Mervyn 1913–

English cleric. As Bishop of Southwark (1959–80) he was renowned for his liberal writings on the uniformity of faith and the communality of belief.

70 A psychiatrist is a man who goes to the Folies-Bergère and looks at the audience.

1961 In *The Observer*, 15 Oct.

Stokowski, Leopold pseudonym of *Antoni Stanislaw Boleslawowich* 1882–1977

US conductor of Polish origin. He built up an international reputation as conductor of the Philadelphia Symphony Orchestra (1912–36), the New York Philharmonic (1946–50) and the Houston Symphony Orchestra (1955–60). He also worked in films and founded the American Symphony Orchestra in New York in 1962.

71 Musicians paint their pictures on silence—we provide the music, and you provide the silence.

Addressing an audience at Carnegie Hall. Quoted in Derek Watson *Music Quotations* (1991).

Stone, Robert Anthony 1937–

US novelist and screenwriter. His best known book is the novel *Dog Soldiers* (1974).

72 People are getting to be a disgrace to the planet.

1982 *A Flag for Sunrise*, ch.6.

Stone, Samuel John 1839–1900

English cleric and hymnwriter

73 The Church's one foundation
Is Jesus Christ, her Lord;
She is his new creation
By water and the word;
From heaven he came and sought her
To be his holy bride,
With his own blood he bought her.
And for her life he died.
    1866 *Lyra fidelium.*

Stoppard, Sir Tom originally *Tom Straussler* 1937–

Czech-born British dramatist. After writing for radio, he
made his name with *Rosencrantz and Guildenstern are
Dead* (1967) at the Edinburgh Festival. Other plays
include the philosophical satire *Jumpers* (1972), *Travesties*
(1974) and *The Real Thing* (1981). He has also written a
novel, *Lord Malquist and Mr Moon.*

74 The House of Lords, an illusion to which I have
never been able to subscribe—responsibility
without power, the prerogative of the eunuch
throughout the ages.
    1966 *Lord Malquist and Mr Moon*, pt.6.
    ▷ See Baldwin 64:9.

75 To sum up: your father, whom you love, dies, you
are his heir, you come back to find that hardly was
the corpse cold before his younger brother popped
on to his throne and into his sheets, thereby
offending both legal and natural practice. Now
why exactly are you behaving in this extraordinary
manner.
    1967 To Hamlet. *Rosencrantz and Guildenstern are Dead*, act 1.

76 Sometimes I dream of revolution, a bloody *coup
d'état* by the second rank—troupes of actors
slaughtered by their understudies, magicians sawn
in half by indefatigably smiling glamour girls,
cricket teams wiped out by marauding bands of
twelfth men.
    1968 *The Real Inspector Hound.*

77 It's not the voting that's democracy; it's the
counting.
    1972 *Jumpers.*

78 War is capitalism with the gloves off.
    1974 *Travesties.*

79 Maybe Napoleon was wrong when he said we were
a nation of shopkeepers… Today England looked
like a nation of goalkeepers.
    1977 *Professional Foul.*
    ▷ See Napoleon 718:34.

80 Ambushing the audience is what theatre is all about.
    1984 In *Newsweek*, 16 Jan.

81 I don't think I can be expected to take seriously a
game which takes less than three days to reach its
conclusion.
    1984 Of baseball. In the *Guardian*, 24 Dec.

Storr, Robert 1949–

US art administrator, curator of painting and sculpture at
the Museum of Modern Art. His writings include *Philip
Guston* (1986).

82 It's a letting go of distances.
    1995 On the necessity of establishing an intimacy and trust
between artist and sitter. In the *New York Times*, 1 Jan.

Stowe, Harriet (Elizabeth) née *Beecher* 1811–96

US novelist. Her novel *Uncle Tom's Cabin* (1852) was
written in anger after the passage of the Fugitive Slave
Law. She caused a furore with *Lady Byron Vindicated*
(1870) in which she accused Byron of having an
incestuous relationship with his sister.

83 What makes saintliness in my view, as
distinguished from ordinary goodness, is a certain
quality of magnanimity and greatness of soul that
brings life within the circle of the heroic.
    1846 'The Cathedral', in the *Atlantic Monthly*, Dec.

84 So long as the law considers all these human beings,
with beating hearts and living affections, only as so
many *things* belonging to the master—so long as
the failure, or misfortune, or imprudence, or death
of the kindest owner, may cause them any day to
exchange a life of kind protection and indulgence
for one of hopeless misery and toil—so long is it
impossible to make anything beautiful or desirable
in the best-regulated administration of slavery.
    1852 *Uncle Tom's Cabin*, ch.1.

85 I've got just as much conscience as any man in
business can afford to keep,—just a little, you
know, to swear by, as 't were.
    1852 *Uncle Tom's Cabin*, ch.1.

86 'Do you know who made you?'
'Nobody, as I knows on,' said the child…I 'spect I
grow'd. Don't think nobody never made me.'
    1852 *Uncle Tom's Cabin*, ch.20. The child is Topsy.

87 Whipping and abuse are like laudanum; you have
to double the dose as the sensibilities decline.
    1852 *Uncle Tom's Cabin*, ch.20.

88 The longest day must have its close,—the
gloomiest night will wear on to a morning. An
eternal, inexorable lapse of moments is ever
hurrying the day of the evil to an eternal night, and
the night of the just to an eternal day.
    1852 *Uncle Tom's Cabin*, ch.40.

89 The bitterest tears shed over graves are for words left unsaid and deeds left undone.
1865 *Little Foxes*, ch.3.

90 The obstinancy of cleverness and reason is nothing to the obstinancy of folly and inanity.
1865 *Little Foxes*, ch.4.

Strachey, (Evelyn) John 1901–63

British writer and political leader.

91 If socialists lose sight of the central importance of social ownership of the means of production, they will cease, in a very real sense, to be socialists at all: they will subside into the role of well-intentioned, amiable, rootless, drifting social reformers.
1956 *Contemporary Capitalism*.

Strachey, (Giles) Lytton 1880–1932

English writer. He is best known for his biographies, especially *Eminent Victorians*, which challenged established concepts of the Victorian age.

92 The history of the Victorian age will never be written: we know too much about it. For ignorance is the first requisite of the historian—ignorance, which simplifies and clarifies, which selects and omits, with a placid perfection unattainable by the highest art.
1918 *Eminent Victorians*, preface.

93 The time was out of joint, and he was only too delighted to have been born to set it right.
1918 Of Hurrell Froude. *Eminent Victorians*, 'Cardinal Manning'.

94 'Before she came,' said a soldier, 'there was cussin' and swearin', but after that it was 'oly as a church.' The most cherished privilege of the fighting man was abandoned for the sake of Miss Nightingale.
1918 *Eminent Victorians*, 'Florence Nightingale'.

95 Yet her conception of God was certainly not orthodox. She felt towards Him as she might have felt towards a glorified sanitary engineer; and in some of her speculations she seems hardly to distinguish between the Deity and the Drains.
1918 *Eminent Victorians*, 'Florence Nightingale'.

96 His legs, perhaps, were shorter than they should have been.
1918 *Eminent Victorians*, 'Dr Arnold'.

97 Johnson's aesthetic judgements are almost invariably subtle, or solid, or bold; they have always some good quality to recommend them—except one: they are never right.
1922 On Samuel Johnson. *Books and Characters*, 'Lives of the Poets'.

98 Asked by the chairman the usual question: 'I understand, Mr Strachey, that you have a conscientious objection to war?' he replied (in his curious falsetto voice), 'Oh no, not at all, only to *this* war.' Better than this was his reply to the chairman's other stock question, which had previously never failed to embarrass the claimant. 'Tell me, Mr Strachey, what would you do if you saw a German soldier trying to violate your sister?' With an air of noble virtue: 'I would try to get between them.'
On his appearance before a military tribunal, in Robert Graves *Goodbye To All That* (1929), ch.23.

99 If this is dying, then I don't think much of it.
1932 Last words, attributed.

Strafford, Thomas Wentworth, 1st Earl of 1593–1641

English statesman. As Lord Deputy of Ireland from 1632 he imposed firm rule, and in 1639 became the King's principal adviser. After failing to suppress the rebellion in Scotland (1639–40), he was impeached by the Long Parliament and executed despite a famous defence.

1 Divide not between Protestant and Papist. Divide not nationally, betwixt English and Irish. The King makes no distinction betwixt you.
1634 To the Irish Parliament, 15 Jul.

2 I would desire that every man would lay his hand on his heart, and consider seriously whether the beginnings of the people's happiness should be written in letters of blood.
1641 At his execution on Tower Hill, 12 May.

Stravinsky, Igor Fedorovich 1882–1971

Russian composer, who achieved fame with his ballet *The Firebird* (1910). Other ballets include *Petrushka* (1911) and the innovative *Rite of Spring* (1913). Among his significant later works are *The Soldier's Tale* (1918), *Orpheus* (1948, using the 12-tone system), *Oedipus Rex* (1927) and the opera *The Rake's Progress* (1951). He lived in France from 1934 and finally settled in the US (1945).

3 My music is best understood by children and animals.
1961 In the *Observer*, 8 Oct.

4 The most perfect of Swiss clockmakers.
Of Ravel. Quoted in R Nichols *Ravel* (1977).

Streeton, Sir Arthur Ernest 1867–1943

Australian landscape painter, one of the founders of the influential Heidelberg School and a contributor to the *9x5 Impression Exhibition* (1889), Australia's first Impressionist exhibition. He was official war artist in France in World War I.

5 Nature's scheme of colour in Australia is gold and blue.

Quoted in William Moore *The Story of Australian Art* (1934), vol. 1.

Strong, L(eonard) A(lfred) G(eorge)
1896–1958

English novelist and poet.

6 Have I a wife? Bedam I have! But we was badly mated.
I hit her a great clout one night And now we're separated.
And mornin's going to me work I meets her on the quay:
'Good mornin' to you, ma'am!' says I, 'To hell with ye!' says she.

1921 *Dublin Days*, 'The Brewer's Man'.

Stuart, Francis 1902–

Australian-born Irish novelist and poet. He was interned by the Free State government as an Irish republican (1992–3), and by the Germans during World War II after he taught at Berlin University. He later lived and wrote in Paris, London and Ireland.

7 Those are old patterns, faded and bleached in the glare of the pressing present moments in the story.

'Jacob: An Episode from a Theme Based upon the Biblical Story of Jacob, Laban and Two Daughters'.

Stuart, John McDouall 1815–66

Scottish-born explorer, who emigrated to Australia aged 25. He led six expeditions from Adelaide (1858–62), becoming in 1860 the first European to reach the centre of the continent and in 1862 the first to cross Australia from south to north. His health was wrecked by his adventures.

8 To-day I find from my observations of the sun…that I am now camped in the centre of Australia. I have marked a tree and planted the British flag there. There is a high mount about two miles and a half to the north-north-east. I wish it had been in the centre; but on it to-morrow I will raise a cone of stones, and plant the flag there, and name it 'Central Mount Stuart'.

1860 Journal entry, 22 Apr. On reaching the centre of Australia, at Small Gum Creek. Collected in W. Hardman (ed) *Journals of John McDou'all Stuart during the Years 1858, 1859, 1860, 1861 and 1862*.

9 If this country is settled, it will be one of the finest Colonies under the Crown, suitable for the growth of any and everything.

1862 On reaching the sea at the Gulf of Carpentaria. Journal entry, Jul.

Stuart, Mary known as *Mary, Queen of Scots*
1542–87

Daughter of James V of Scotland, she married the Dauphin of France in 1558. During her stormy rule, she attempted to support Roman Catholicism in Reformation Scotland, was deposed and fled to England, eventually being imprisoned and executed for treason against her cousin, Queen Elizabeth I of England.

10 *O Domine Deus! speravi in te;*
O care mi Jesu! nunc libera me;
In dura catena, in misera poena,
Desidero te,
Languendo, quaerendo, et genuflectendo
Adoro, imploro, ut liberes me!

O Lord my God, I hope in thee;
My dear Lord Jesus, set me free;
In chains, in pains
On bended knee
I adore thee, implore thee
To set me free.

1587 Poem composed just before her execution (translated by E Milner-White and G W Briggs, 1941).

Stubbes, Philip 1543–93

English Puritan pamphleteer. His *Anatomie of Abuses in the Realme of England* (1583) was a vehement denunciation of the luxury of the times.

11 Lord, remove these exercises from the Sabbath. Any exercise which withdraweth from godliness either upon the Sabbath or on any other day, is wicked and to be forbidden.

1583 *Anatomie of Abuses in the Realme of England.*

12 For as concerning football playing, I protest unto you it may be rather called a friendly kind of fight than a play or recreation, a bloody or murmuring practice than a fellowly sport or pastime.

1583 *Anatomie of Abuses in the Realme of England.*

13 Football causeth fighting, brawling, contention, quarrel-picking, murder, homicide, and a great effusion of blood, as daily experiences teaches.

1583 *Anatomie of Abuses in the Realme of England.*

Studdert Kennedy, G A known as 'Woodbine Willie' 1883–1929

Army chaplain, theologian and poet of World War I.

14 Waste of Blood, and waste of Tears,
Waste of youth's most precious years,
Waste of ways the saints have trod,
Waste of Glory, waste of God,
War!

1919 *More Rough Rhymes of a Padre*, 'Waste'.

15 When Jesus came to Birmingham they simply passed Him by,

They never hurt a hair of him, they only let Him
  die.
For men had grown more tender and they would
  not give Him pain,
They only just passed down the street, and left Him
  in the rain.
1921 *Peace Rhymes of a Padre*, 'Indifference'.

Su Wu fl.c.100 BC

Chinese general whose poem *To his Wife* expresses his
dismay at their forced parting when he was called to
battle.

16 With all your might enjoy the spring flowers,
      But do not forget the time of our love and pride
      c.100 BC *To his Wife* (translated by Arthur Waley).

Suckling, Sir John 1609–41

English poet and playwright. His father was Secretary of
State, and he served as ambassador, but upon his
inheritance devoted himself to extravagance and court
life. Works include the plays *Aglaura* (1638) and *The
Goblins* (by 1641), the mock-ballad *The Wits* (1637) and
shorter lyrics. By 1641 he had fled to France, where
Aubrey says he committed suicide.

17 Why so pale and wan, fond lover?
      Prithee, why so pale?
      Will, when looking well can't move her,
      Looking ill prevail?
      1637 *Aglaura*, act 4, sc.1, 'Song'.

18 'Tis love in love that makes the sport.
      c.1638 Sonnet no.2.

19 'Tis not the meat; but 'tis the appetite
      Makes eating a delight.
      c.1638 Sonnet no.2.

20 Women enjoyed (whatsoe'er before they've been)
      Are like romances read, or sights once seen:
      Fruition's dull, and spoils the play much more
      Than if one read or knew the plot before;
      'Tis expectation makes a blessing dear;
      It were not heaven, if we knew what it were.
      1646 'Against Fruition'.

21 The maid (and thereby hangs a tale)
      For such a maid no Whitson-ale
      Could ever yet produce:
      No grape that's kindly ripe, could be
      So round, so plump, so soft as she,
      Nor half so full of juice.
      1646 'Ballad: Upon a Wedding'.

22 Love is the fart
      Of every heart:
      It pains a man when 'tis kept close,
      And others doth offend, when 'tis let loose.
      1646 'Love's Offence'.

23 Out upon it! I have loved
      Three whole days together;
      And am like to love three more,
      If it prove fair weather.
      1656 'Out Upon It!'

Sullivan, Timothy Daniel 1827–1914

24 High upon the gallows tree
      Swung the noble-hearted three
      By the vengeful tyrant stricken in their bloom;
      But they met him face to face
      With the courage of their race,
      And they went with souls undaunted to their
        doom.
      'God save Ireland!' said the heroes;
      'God save Ireland', say they all:
      Whether on the scaffold high
      Or the battlefield we die,
      Oh, what matter when for Erin dear we fall.
      1867 'God Save Ireland'.

Summa, Mary Potter

US politician, Chair of the Republican Subcommittee on
Individual Rights. She is known for her anti-abortion
views.

25 What's in me is a human life that's kicking me and
      sitting on my bladder.
      1992 In the *New York Times*, 11 Aug, while four and a half
      months pregnant.

Sumner, William Graham 1840–1910

US sociologist, formerly an Episcopal rector, Professor of
Political and Social Science at Yale University. He was a
disciple of Herbert Spencer, and a strong believer in
laissez-faire and free economy.

26 It would be hard to find a single instance of a
      direct assault by positive effort upon poverty,
      vice, and misery which has not either failed or,
      if it has not failed directly and entirely, has not
      entailed other evils greater than the one which it
      removed.
      1881 'Sociology', collected in *War and Other Essays* (1911).

27 The law of the survival of the fittest was not made
      by man and cannot be abrogated by man. We can
      only by interfering with it, produce the survival of
      the unfittest.
      1881 'Sociology', collected in *War and Other Essays* (1911).

28 Society needs first of all to be free from meddlers—
      that is, to be let alone.
      Attributed.

The Sun

British tabloid newspaper.

29 GOTCHA!

1982 Headline, 4 May, reporting the sinking of the Argentinian battleship *General Belgrano* by the British nuclear submarine *HMS Conqueror*. It was withdrawn after the first edition.

Sun Tzu c.500–320 BC

Name used by the Chinese authors of the *Art of War*. The core text was probably written by one person, perhaps a feudal warrior, but the exact date is unknown. It includes many commentaries by later Chinese philosophers.

30 The art of war is of vital importance to the state.

c.500–320 BC *The Art of War*, ch.1, 'Laying Plans', section 1 (translated by James Clavell, 1981).

31 All warfare is based on deception.

c.500–320 BC *The Art of War*, ch.1, 'Laying Plans', section 18 (translated by James Clavell, 1981).

32 There is no instance of a country having benefitted from prolonged warfare.

c.500–320 BC *The Art of War*, ch.2, 'Waging War', section 6 (translated by James Clavell, 1981).

33 Know the enemy and know yourself; in a hundred battles, you will never be defeated.

c.500 BC *Art of War*, ch.3 (translated by Yuan Shibang, 1987).

34 A victorious general is able to make his soldiers fight with the effect of pent-up waters which, suddenly released, plunge into a bottomless abyss.

c.500 BC *Art of War*, ch.4 (translated by Yuan Shibang, 1987).

35 The business of a general is to kick away the ladder behind soldiers when they have climbed up a height.

c.500 BC *Art of War*, ch.10 (translated by Yuan Shibang, 1987).

36 The general who advances without coveting fame and retreats without fearing disgrace, whose only thought is is to protect the country and do good service to his sovereign, is the jewel of the kingdom.

c.500–320 BC *The Art of War*, ch.10, 'Terrain', section 24 (translated by James Clavell, 1981).

37 There is no place where espionage is not possible.

c.500 BC *Art of War*, ch.13 (translated by Yuan Shibang, 1987).

Sun Yat-Sen or Sun Yixian 1867–1925

Chinese non-Communist revolutionary, regarded as the father of the Chinese Republic. Founder and early leader of China's Nationalist Party, he founded the Society for the Revival of China, but was kidnapped by the Chinese legation in London. After his release he organized risings in South China. The assassination of his follower, Sung Chiao-Jen, led to civil war (1913), and he set up a separate government at Guangzhou (Canton).

38 Modern European culture is nothing but a culture of natural sciences.

1924 Speech, Nov, calling for a union of Japan and China to liberate Asia from European influence. Quoted in John Wu *Sun Yat-Sen: The Man and His Ideas* (1971).

39 The foundation of the government of a nation must be built upon the rights of the people, but the administration must be entrusted to experts. We must not look upon those experts as stately and grand presidents and ministers, but simply as our chauffeurs, guards at the gate, cooks, physicians, carpenters, or tailors.

1927 *The Three Principles of the People*.

Surrey, Henry Howard, Earl of c.1517–1547

English poet; of royal blood, he served Henry VIII at court and in France. In the turmoil over the succession, he became the target of the rival Seymour family, and was arrested and executed on trumped-up charges. He, with Wyatt, introduced the sonnet to England. *Tottel's Miscellany* (1557) contained forty of his poems.

40 Love, that doth reign and live within my thought,
And built his seat within my captive breast,
Clad in the arms wherein with me he fought,
Oft in my face he doth his banner rest.

1557 'Love, that doth reign'.

41 Alas! so all things now do hold their peace,
Heaven and earth disturbed in no thing…
Calm is the sea, the waves work less and less;
So am not I whom love, alas, doth wring,
Bringing before my face the great increase
Of my desires, whereat I weep and sing,
In joy and woe, as in a doubtful ease.
For my sweet thoughts sometime do pleasure
  bring,
But by and by the cause of my disease
Gives me a pang that inwardly doth sting,
When that I think what grief it is again
To live and lack the thing should rid my pain.

1557 'Alas! so all things now do hold their peace'.

42 Wyatt resteth here, that quick could never rest;
Whose heavenly gifts increased by disdain,
And virtue sank the deeper in his breast;
Such profit he of envy could obtain.

1557 'Wyatt resteth here'.

43 So cruel prison how could betide, alas,
As proud Windsor? Where I in lust and joy
With a king's son my childish years did pass
In greater feast than Priam's sons of Troy.

1557 'So cruel prison'.

44 London, hast thou accused me
Of breach of laws, the root of strife?
Within whose breast did boil to see,
So fervent hot, thy dissolute life,
That even the hate of sins that grow

Within thy wicked walls so rife,
For to break forth did convert so
That terror could it not repress.
1557 'London, hast thou accused me'.

45 O happy dames, that may embrace
The fruit of your delight,
Help to bewail the woeful case
And eke the heavy plight
Of me, that wonted to rejoice
The fortune of my pleasant choice.
Good ladies, help to fill my mourning voice.
1557 'O happy dames'

46 Set me whereas the sun doth parch the green,
Or where his beams may not dissolve the ice,
In temperate heat, where he is felt and seen,
With proud people, in presence sad and wise;
Set me in base, or yet in high degree,
In the long night, or in the shortest day,
In clear weather, or where mists thickest be,
In lusty youth, or when my hairs be grey…
Yours will I be, and with that only thought
Comfort myself when that my hap is nought.
'Set me whereas the sun doth parch the green'.

Surtees, Robert Smith 1803–64

English journalist and novelist. Founder of the *New Sporting Magazine* in 1831, he introduced the popular Cockney character John Jorrocks. Later works include *Jorrocks' Jaunts and Jollities* (1838) and *Hillingdon Hall* (1845).

47 The horse loves the hound, and I loves both.
Quoted in Colin Jarman *The Guinness Dictionary of Sports Quotations* (1990).

48 There is no secret so close as that between a rider and his horse.
Attributed.

Sutherland, Arthur Jr 1902–73.

US lawyer, Professor of Law at Harvard University.

49 One can scarcely imagine a speaker at a meeting of a county medical society discussing the possible elimination of some disease by public health measures, and then qualifying his observations by the statement that many practitioners make a living out of treating the disease in question; and that unless the physicians are vigilant to prevent the adoption of such measures, this source of business will be taken from them. Yet speakers at bar association meetings are frequently heard to make similar observations about the effect of proposed reforms.
1938 'A New Society and an Old Calling,' in the *Cornell Law Quarterly*.

Swanson, Gloria originally *Gloria May Josephine Svensson* 1897–1983

US film actress. She rose from an extra in silent films in 1915 to leading roles as a chic sophisticate in the front line of the battle of the sexes, under the direction of Cecil B de Mille in the 1920s.

50 Arriving Monday… Arrange ovation.
Trans-Atlantic cable to Adolf Zukor. Quoted in the *New Yorker*, 21 Mar 1994.

Sweezy, Paul Malor 1910–

Independent US Marxist economist, editor of the *Monthly Review*.

51 Capitalism only works well when it has a strong opposition, because that forces it to be more egalitarian than it wants to be.
1992 Interview in *The Progressive*, May.

Swettenham, Sir Frank Athelstane 1850–1946

English colonial administrator, serving as the British Resident in Selangor and Perak before being appointed the Resident General in the Federated Malay States (1896-1901)

52 The Malay Peninsula, with the climate of a perpetual Turkish bath.
1906 *British Malaya*.

Swift, Graham 1949–

English writer. He has written several novels and a number of short stories, but is best known for his successful novel *Waterland*.

53 Life is one tenth Here and Now, nine-tenths a history lesson. For most of the time the Here and Now is neither now nor here.
1983 *Waterland*, ch.8.

54 People die when curiosity goes. People have to find out, people have to know. How can there be any true revolution till we know what we're made of?
1983 *Waterland*, ch.27.

Swift, Jonathan 1667–1745

Anglo-Irish poet, novelist, essayist, pamphleteer and letter writer. Born in Ireland, he became a satirist in London but returned to Dublin to become Dean of St. Patrick's. His works, characterized by biting wit, include *Gulliver's Travels* (1726), a satire on religious dissension, *A Tale of a Tub* (1704), *A Modest Proposal* (1729) and *Drapier's Letters*, in which he campaigned for Irish liberty.

55 Th' artillery of words.
1692 'My Lady's Lamentation'.

56 Philosophy! the lumber of the schools.
1692 'Ode to Dr William Sancroft'.

57 Satire is a sort of glass, wherein beholders do generally discover everybody's face but their own.
1704 *The Battle of the Books*, preface.

58 Instead of dirt and poison we have rather chosen to fill our hives with honey and wax; thus furnishing mankind with the two noblest of things, which are sweetness and light.
1704 *The Battle of the Books*.

59 Books, like men their authors, have no more than one way of coming into the world, but there are ten thousand to go out of it, and return no more.
1704 *A Tale of a Tub*, 'Epistle Dedicatory'.

60 Satire, being levelled at all, is never resented for an offence by any.
1704 *A Tale of a Tub*, 'Author's Preface'.

61 What though his head be empty, provided his commonplace book be full.
1704 *A Tale of a Tub*, 'Digression in praise of digression', ch.7.

62 Last week I saw a woman flayed, and you will hardly believe, how much it altered her person for the worse.
1704 *A Tale of a Tub*, ch.9.

63 Laws are like cobwebs, which may catch small flies, but let wasps and hornets break through.
1709 *A Critical Essay upon the Faculties of the Mind*.

64 There is nothing in this world constant, but inconstancy.
1709 *A Critical Essay upon the Faculties of the Mind*.

65 Surely mortal man is a broomstick!
1710 *A Meditation upon a Broomstick*.

66 We are so fond of one another, because our ailments are the same.
1711 *Journal to Stella*, 1 Feb.

67 Will she pass in a crowd? Will she make a figure in a country church?
1711 *Journal to Stella*, 9 Feb.

68 I love good creditable acquaintance; I love to be the worst of the company.
1711 *Journal to Stella*, 17 May.

69 He was a fiddler, and consequently a rogue.
1711 *Journal to Stella*, 25 July.

70 He showed me his bill of fare to tempt me to dine with him; poh, said I, I value not your bill of fare, give me your bill of company.
1711 *Journal to Stella*, 2 Sep.

71 We have just enough religion to make us hate, but not enough to make us love one another.
1711 *Thoughts on Various Subjects*.

72 When a true genius appears in the world, you may know him by this sign, that the dunces are all in confederacy against him.
1711 *Thoughts on Various Subjects*.

73 What they do in heaven we are ignorant of: what they do *not* we are told expressly, that they neither marry, nor are given in marriage.
1711 *Thoughts on Various Subjects*.

74 The stoical scheme of supplying our wants, by lopping off our desires, is like cutting off our feet when we want shoes.
1711 *Thoughts on Various Subjects*.

75 The reason why so few marriages are happy, is, because young ladies spend their time in making nets, not in making cages.
1711 *Thoughts on Various Subjects*.

76 We were to do more business after dinner, but after dinner is after dinner—an old saying and a true, 'much drinking, little thinking'.
1712 *Journal to Stella*, 26 Feb.

77 Proper words in proper places, make the true definition of style.
1720 *Letter to a Young Gentleman lately entered into Holy Orders*.

78 Indeed the arguments on both sides were invincible; for in reason, all government without the consent of the governed is the very definition of slavery; but in fact eleven men well armed will certainly subdue one single man in his shirt.
1724 *Fourth letter to…Ireland*, written under the pseudonym of 'M B Drapier'.

79 I have heard of a man who had a mind to sell his house, and therefore carried a piece of brick in his pocket, which he shewed as a pattern to encourage purchasers.
1724 *Drapier's Letters*, no.2.

80 In Church your grandsire cut his throat;
To do the job too long he tarried,
He should have had my hearty vote,
To cut his throat before he married.
1724 'Verses on the Upright Judge'.

81 'Libertas et natale solum':
Fine words! I wonder where you stole 'em.
1724 'Whitshed's motto on his Coach'.

82 He is taller by almost the breadth of my nail than any of his court, which alone is enough to strike an awe into the beholders.
1726 Of the Emperor. *Gulliver's Travels*, 'A Voyage to Lilliput', ch.2.

83 It is alleged indeed, that the high heels are most agreeable to our ancient constitution: but however

this be, his Majesty hath determined to make use of only low heels in the administration of the government.
1726 *Gulliver's Travels*, 'A Voyage to Lilliput', ch.4.

84 I cannot but conclude the bulk of your natives to be the most pernicious race of little odious vermin that nature ever suffered to crawl upon the surface of the earth.
1726 *Gulliver's Travels*, 'A Voyage to Brobdingnag', ch.6.

85 And he gave it for his opinion, that whoever could make two ears of corn or two blades of grass to grow upon a spot of ground where only one grew before, would deserve better of mankind, and do more essential service to his country than the whole race of politicians put together.
1726 *Gulliver's Travels*, 'A Voyage to Brobdingnag', ch.7.

86 He had been eight years upon a project for extracting sun-beams out of cucumbers, which were to be put into vials hermetically sealed, and let out to warm the air in raw inclement summers.
1726 *Gulliver's Travels*, 'A Voyage to Laputa, etc.' ch.5.

87 These unhappy people were proposing schemes for persuading monarchs to choose favourites upon the score of their wisdom, capacity and virtue; of teaching ministers to consult the public good; of rewarding merit, great abilities and eminent services; of instructing princes to know their true interest by placing it on the same foundation with that of their people: of choosing for employment persons qualified to exercise them; with many other wild impossible chimeras, that never entered before into the heart of man to conceive, and confirmed in me the old observation, that there is nothing so extravagant and irrational which some philosophers have not maintained for truth.
1726 *Gulliver's Travels*, 'A Voyage to Laputa, etc.' ch.6.

88 He replied that I must needs be mistaken, or that I *said the thing which was not.* (For they have no word in their language to express lying or falsehood.)
1726 *Gulliver's Travels*, 'A Voyage to the Houyhnhnms', ch.3.

89 I told him...that we ate when we were not hungry, and drank without the provocation of thirst.
1726 *Gulliver's Travels*, 'A Voyage to the Houyhnhnms', ch.6.

90 Few are qualified to shine in company; but it is in most men's power to be agreeable.
1727 *Thoughts on Various Subjects* (enlarged edn).

91 Every man desires to live long; but no man would be old.
1727 *Thoughts on Various Subjects* (enlarged edn).

92 A nice man is a man of nasty ideas.
1727 *Thoughts on Various Subjects* (enlarged edn).

93 Old men and comets have been reverenced for the same reason; their long beards, and pretences to foretell events.
1727 *Thoughts on Various Subjects* (enlarged edn).

94 How haughtily he lifts his nose,
To tell what every schoolboy knows.
1727 'The Journal', l.81–2.

95 Walls have tongues, and hedges ears.
1727 'A Pastoral Dialogue between Richmond Lodge and Marble Hill', l.8.

96 Hail fellow, well met,
All dirty and wet:
Find out, if you can,
Who's master, who's man.
1728 'My Lady's Lamentation', l.171.

97 These *Mothers*, instead of being able to work for their honest livelihood, are forced to beg Sustenance for their *helpless Infants*; who, as they grow up either turn *Thieves* for want of Work; or leave their dear native country, to fight for the *Pretender* in Spain; or sell themselves to the *Barbadoes.*
1729 *A Modest Proposal for Preventing the Children of Ireland from being a Burden to their Parents or Country.*

98 I have been assured by a very knowing American of my Acquaintance in London; that a young healthy Child, well nursed, is, at a Year old, a most delicious, nourishing, and wholesome Food; whether Stewed, Roasted, Baked, or Boiled; and, I make no doubt, that it will equally serve in a Fricassee, or a Ragout.
1729 *A Modest Proposal for Preventing the Children of Ireland from being a Burden to their Parents or Country.*

99 A Child will make two Dishes at an Entertainment for Friends; and when the Family dines alone, the fore or hind Quarter will make a reasonable Dish; and seasoned with a little Pepper or Salt, will be very good Boiled on the fourth Day, especially in Winter.
1729 *A Modest Proposal for Preventing the Children of Ireland from being a Burden to their Parents or Country.*

1 Say, Britain, could you ever boast,—
Three poets in an age at most?
Our chilling climate hardly bears
A sprig of bays in fifty years.
1733 'On Poetry', l.5–8.

2 Then, rising with Aurora's light,
The Muse invoked, sit down to write;
Blot out, correct, insert, refine,
Enlarge, diminish, interline.
1733 'On Poetry', l.85–8.

3 As learned commentators view

In Homer than Homer knew.
1733 'On Poetry', l.103–4.

4 So geographers, in Afric-maps,
With savage-pictures fill their gaps;
And o'er unhabitable downs
Place elephants for want of towns.
1733 'On Poetry', l.177–80.

5 He gives direction to the town,
To cry it up, or run it down.
1733 'On Poetry', l.269–70.

6 Hobbes clearly proves, that every creature
Lives in a state of war by nature.
1733 'On Poetry', l.319–20.

7 So, naturalists observe, a flea
Hath smaller fleas on him prey;
And these have smaller fleas to bite 'em,
And so proceed *ad infinitum*.
Thus every poet, in his kind,
Is bit by him that comes behind.
1733 'On Poetry', l.337–42.

8 I mean, you lie—under a mistake.
1738 *Polite Conversation*, dialogue 1.

9 I think she was cut out for a Gentlewoman, but she
was spoiled in the making. She wears her clothes as
if they were thrown on with a pitchfork; and, for
the fashion, I believe they were made in the days of
Queen Bess.
1738 *Polite Conversation*, dialogue 1.

10 The more careless, the more modish.
1738 *Polite Conversation*, dialogue 1.

11 I won't quarrel with my Bread and Butter.
1738 *Polite Conversation*, dialogue 1.

12 He was a bold Man that first ate an Oyster.
1738 *Polite Conversation*, dialogue 2.

13 Faith, that's as well said, as if I had said it myself.
1738 *Polite Conversation*, dialogue 2.

14 I always love to begin a journey on Sundays,
because I shall have the prayers of the church, to
preserve all that travel by land, or by water.
1738 *Polite Conversation*, dialogue 2.

15 Lord, I wonder what fool it was that first invented
kissing!
1738 *Polite Conversation*, dialogue 2.

16 Promises and pie-crust are made to be broken.
1738 *Polite Conversation*.

17 Be she barren, be she old,
Be she slut, or be she scold,
Eat my oysters, and lie near her,

She'll be fruitful, never fear her.
1746 'Verses Made for the Women Who Cry Oysters'.

18 I never saw, heard, nor read, that the clergy were
beloved in any nation where Christianity was the
religion of the country. Nothing can render them
popular, but some degree of persecution.
1765 *Thoughts on Religion*.

19 I must complain the cards are ill shuffled till I have
a good hand.
Quoted in Colin Jarman *The Guinness Dictionary of Sports
Quotations* (1990).

Swinburne, Algernon Charles 1837–1909

English playwright and poet. He made his name with
Poems and Ballads (1866). Later works include *A Song of
Italy* (1867), *Erechtus* (1876) and *Tristam of Lyonesse*.

20 Swallow, my sister, O sister swallow,
How can thine heart be full of the spring?
A thousand summers are over and dead.
What hast thou found in the spring to follow?
What hast thou found in thine heart to sing?
What wilt thou do when the summer is shed?
1864 'Itylus'.

21 Till life and death remember,
Till thou remember and I forget.
1864 'Itylus'.

22 Maiden, and mistress of the months and stars
Now folded in the flowerless fields of heaven.
1865 *Atlanta in Calydon*, l.1

23 When the hounds of spring are on winter's traces,
The mother of months in meadow or plain
Fills the shadows and windy places
With lisp of leaves and ripple of rain;
And the brown bright nightingale amorous
Is half assured for Itylus,
For the Thracian ships and the foreign faces,
The tongueless vigil and all the pain.
1865 *Atlanta in Calydon*, chorus, 'When the hounds of spring'.

24 For winter's rains and ruins are over,
And all the season of snows and sins;
The days dividing lover and lover,
The light that loses, the night that wins;
And time remembered is grief forgotten,
And frosts are slain and flowers begotten,
And in green underwood and cover
Blossom by blossom the spring begins.
1865 *Atlanta in Calydon*, chorus, 'When the hounds of spring'.

25 And soft as lips that laugh and hide
The laughing leaves of the tree divide,
And screen from seeing and leave in sight
The god pursuing, the maiden hid.
1865 *Atlanta in Calydon*, chorus 'When the hounds of spring'.

26 Before the beginning of years
    There came to the making of man
    Time with a gift of tears,
    Grief with a glass that ran.
    1865 *Atlanta in Calydon*, chorus, 'Before the beginning of years'.

27 Strength without hands to smite,
    Love that endures for a breath;
    Night, the shadow of light,
    And Life, the shadow of death.
    1865 *Atlanta in Calydon*, chorus, 'Before the beginning of years'.

28 For words divide and rend;
    But silence is most noble till the end.
    1865 *Atlanta in Calydon*, chorus, 'Who hath given man speech'.

29 Ah, yet would God this flesh of mine might be
    Where air might wash and long leaves cover me;
    Where tides of grass break into foam of flowers,
    Or where the wind's feet shine along the sea.
    1866 'Laus Veneris'.

30 Superflux of pain.
    1866 *Poems and Ballads*, 'Anactoria'

31 We shift and bedeck and bedrape us,
    Thou art noble and nude and antique.
    1866 *Poems and Ballads*, 'Dolores', stanza 7.

32 Change in a trice
    The lilies and languors of virtue
    For the raptures and roses of vice.
    1866 *Poems and Ballads*, 'Dolores', stanza 9.

33 O splendid and sterile Dolores,
    Our Lady of Pain.
    1866 *Poems and Ballads*, 'Dolores', stanza 9.

34 Ah beautiful passionate body
    That never has ached with a heart!
    1866 *Poems and Ballads*, 'Dolores', stanza 11.

35 For the crown of our life as it closes
    Is darkness, the fruit thereof dust;
    No thorns go as deep as a rose's,
    And love is more cruel than lust.
    Time turns the old days to derision,
    Our loves into corpses or wives;
    And marriage and death and division
    Make barren our lives.
    1866 *Poems and Ballads*, 'Dolores', stanza 20.

36 I shall remember while the light lives yet
    And in the night time I shall not forget.
    1866 *Poems and Ballads*, 'Erotion'.

37 Pale, beyond porch and portal,
    Crowned with calm leaves, she stands

Who gathers all things mortal
With cold immortal hands.
    1866 *Poems and Ballads*, 'The Garden of Proserpine'.

38 Here, where the world is quiet,
    Here, where all trouble seems
    Dead winds' and spent waves' riot
    In doubtful dreams of dreams.
    1866 *Poems and Ballads*, 'The Garden of Proserpine'.

39 Yea, is not even Apollo, with hair and harpstring of gold,
    A bitter God to follow, a beautiful God to behold?
    1866 *Poems and Ballads*, 'Hymn to Proserpine'.

40 Thou hast conquered, O pale Galilean; the world
    has grown grey from Thy breath;
    We have drunken of things Lethean, and fed on the
    fullness of death.
    1866 *Poems and Ballads*, 'Hymn to Proserpine'.

41 Though these that were Gods are dead, and thou
    being dead art God,
    Though before thee the throned Cytherean be
    fallen, and hidden her head,
    Yet thy kingdom shall pass, Galilean, thy dead shall
    go down to thee dead.
    1866 *Poems and Ballads*, 'Hymn to Proserpine'.

42 I remember the way we parted,
    The day and the way we met;
    You hoped we were both broken-hearted,
    And knew we should both forget.
    1866 *Poems and Ballads*, 'An Interlude'.

43 And the best and the worst of this is
    That neither is most to blame
    If you have forgotten my kisses
    And I have forgotten your name.
    1866 *Poems and Ballads*, 'An Interlude'.

44 If love were what the rose is,
    And I were like the leaf,
    Our lives would grow together
    In sad or singing weather,
    Blown fields or flowered closes,
    Green pleasure or grey grief.
    1866 *Poems and Ballads*, 'A Match'.

45 I will go back to the great sweet mother,
    Mother and lover of men, the sea.
    I will go down to her, I and no other,
    Close with her, kiss her and mix her with me.
    1866 *Poems and Ballads*, 'The Triumph of Time'.

46 I shall sleep, and move with the moving ships,
    Change as the winds change, veer in the tide.
    1866 *Poems and Ballads*, 'The Triumph of Time'.

47 There lived a singer in France of old

By the tideless dolorous midland sea.
In a land of sand and ruin and gold
There shone one woman, and none but she.
1866 *Poems and Ballads*, 'The Triumph of Time'.

48 O slain and spent and sacrificed
People, the grey-grown speechless Christ.
1871 *Songs before Sunrise*, 'Before a Crucifix'.

49 But God, if a God there be, is the substance of men
which is man.
1871 *Songs before Sunrise*, 'Hymn of Man'.

50 Glory to Man in the highest! for Man is the master
of things.
1871 *Songs before Sunrise*, 'Hymn of Man'.

51 There was a poor poet named Clough,
Whom his friends all united to puff,
But the public, though dull,
Had not such a skull
As belonged to believers in Clough.
1875 *Essays and Studies*, 'Matthew Arnold'.

52 For a day and a night Love sang to us, played with
us,
Folded us round from the dark and the light;
And our hearts were fulfilled with the music he
made with us,
Made with our hands and our lips while he stayed
with us,
Stayed in mid passage his pinions from flight
For a day and a night.
1878 *Poems and Ballads* (2nd edn), 'At Parting'.

53 The deep division of prodigious breasts,
The solemn slope of mighty limbs asleep.
1878 *Poems and Ballads* (2nd edn), 'Ave Atque Vale', stanza 6.

54 Sleep; and if life was bitter to thee, pardon,
If sweet, give thanks; thou hast no more to live;
And to give thanks is good, and to forgive.
1878 *Poems and Ballads* (2nd edn), 'Ave Atque Vale', stanza 17.

55 Villon, our sad bad glad mad brother's name.
1878 *Poems and Ballads* (2nd edn), 'Ballad of François Villon'.

56 In a coign of the cliff between lowland and
highland,
At the sea-down's edge between windward and lee,
Walled round with rocks as an inland island,
The ghost of a garden fronts the sea.
1878 *Poems and Ballads* (2nd edn), 'A Forsaken Garden'.

57 As a god self-slain on his own strange altar,
Death lies dead.
1878 *Poems and Ballads* (2nd edn), 'A Forsaken Garden'.

58 Fiddle, we know, is diddle: and diddle, we take it, is
dee.
1880 *The Heptalogia*, 'The Higher Pantheism in a Nutshell'.

Symington, Stuart (1901–88)

US Senator. In 1939 he became President and Chairman of the Emerson Electric Manufacturing Company. He was the first Secretary of the Air Force (1945–48) and was elected Senator for Missouri in 1952

59 I found out that he was a bachelor, as was his father
before him.
1960 On hiring a speechwriter. Address to Washington's Gridiron Club, 12 Mar, quoted in Harold Brayman *The President Speaks-off-the-Record* (1976).

Synge, John Millington 1871–1909

Irish dramatist. On the advice of W. B. Yeats he travelled to the Aran Islands and there found materials for his plays which include *Riders to the Sea* (1904) and his masterpiece, *The Playboy of the Western World* (1907), which caused riots when it was first staged in Dublin.

60 No man at all can be living for ever, and we must be
satisfied.
1904 *Riders to the Sea*.

61 They're all gone now, and there isn't anything more
the sea can do to me.
1904 Maurya speaking. *Riders to the Sea*.

62 Well, if the worst comes in the end of all, it'll be
great game to see if there's none to pity him but a
widow woman, the like of me, has buried her
children and destroyed her man.
1907 Widow Quin. *The Playboy of the Western World*, act 2.

63 Drink a health to the wonders of the western world,
the pirates, preachers, poteen-makers, with the
jobbing jockies; parching peelers, and the juries fill
their stomachs selling judgments of the English law.
1907 *The Playboy of the Western World*, act 2.

64 I'll say, a strange man is a marvel, with his mighty
talk; but what's a squabble in your back-yard, and
the blow of a loy, have taught me that there's a great
gap between a gallous story and a dirty deed.
1907 Pegeen Mike. *The Playboy of the Western World*, act 3.

65 Oh my grief, I've lost him surely. I've lost the only
Playboy of the Western World.
1907 Pegeen Mike. *The Playboy of the Western World*, act 3, closing words.

Szasz, Thomas Stephen 1920–

Hungarian-born US psychiatrist. His books argue that disease is physical, hence mental illness is a myth, that the individual should be allowed complete freedom within the law, and all psychiatric therapy should be contractual.

66 Formerly, when religion was strong and science
weak, men mistook magic for medicine, now, when
science is strong and religion weak, men mistake
medicine for magic.
1974 *The Second Sin*.

67 Men are rewarded and punished not for what they
    do, but rather for how their acts are defined. This is
    why men are more interested in better justifying
    themselves than in better behaving themselves.
    1974 *The Second Sin.*

68 Psychiatrists classify a person as neurotic if he
    suffers from his problems in living, and a psychotic
    if he makes others suffer.
    1974 *The Second Sin.*

Szent-Györgyi, Albert von Nagyrapolt
1893–1986

Hungarian-born US biochemist, authority on the
processes of biological combustion. He was educated at
the universities of Budapest and Cambridge. In 1947, he
migrated to the US to join the Marine Biological
Laboratories, Massachusetts. He was awarded the 1937
Nobel Prize in Physiology or Medicine.

69 Discovery consists of seeing what everybody has
    seen and thinking what nobody has thought.
    Quoted in Irving Good (ed) *The Scientist Speculates* (1962).

70 Knowledge is a sacred cow, and my problem will be
    how we can milk her while keeping clear of her
    horns.
    1964 In *Science*, vol.146.

Szilard, Leo 1898–1964

Hungarian-born US nuclear physicist, who contributed
to the development of controlled nuclear fission. He left
the University of Berlin with the advent of Hitler, jointing
Columbia University in 1938. He urged Albert Einstein
to write to President Roosevelt warning of the possible
military use of atomic energy by the Nazis.

71 We turned the switch, saw the flashes, watched for
    ten minutes, then switched everything off and went
    home. That night I knew the world was headed for
    sorrow.
    1939 After an early experiment at Columbia University which
    proved the possibility of splitting the atom. Quoted in James B
    Simpson *Simpson's Contemporary Quotations* (1988).

72 Don't lie if you don't have to.
    1972 In *Science*, vol.176, p.966.

Taaffe, Eduard Franz Josef, Graf von
1833–95

Austrian statesman, Minister of the Interior (1867) and
Chief Minister (1869–70, 1879–93).

73 As a Minister, it is my policy to keep all the
    nationalities within the Habsburg monarchy
    in a balanced state of well-modulated
    dissatisfaction.
    1881 Letters.

Tacitus, Cornelius full name *Publius or Gaius Cornelius Tacitus* AD 55–c.120

Roman historian and orator, who lived under Domitian,
Nerva, Trajan and Hadrian. He wrote a biography of his
father-in-law Agricola. His major historical works are the
Historiae (Histories), of which only the first four books
survive whole, and the *Annales* (Annals), of which only
eight books survive.

74 *Solitudinem faciunt pacem appellant.*

    They make a wilderness and they call it peace.
    Speech of the British chieftain Calgacus, before the battle of
    Mons Graupius, referring to the Romans. *Agricola*, ch.30.

75 *Proprium humani ingenii est odisse quem laeseris.*

    It is part of human nature to hate a man you have
    hurt.
    Agricola, ch.42.

76 *Perdomita Britannia et statim omissa.*

    Britain was conquered and immediately lost.
    Referring to Agricola's conquest of Britain, and the loss of much
    of it under Domitian. *Histories*, bk.1, ch.2.

77 *Deos fortioribus adesse.*

    The gods support those who are stronger.
    Histories, bk.4, ch.17.

78 *Miseram pacem vel bello bene mutari.*

    Even war is preferable to a shameful peace.
    Annals, bk.3, ch.44.

79 *Auctor nominis eius Christus, Tiberio imperitante,*
    per procuratorem Pontium Pilatum, supplicio affectus
    erat.

    Christ, the leader of the sect, had been put to death
    by the procurator Pontius Pilate in the reign of
    Tiberius.
    Annals, bk.15, ch.44.

80 *Elegantiae arbiter.*

    The arbiter of taste.
    Of Petronius. *Annals*, bk.16, ch.18.

Taft, Robert A(lphonso) 1889–1953

US politician. Son of US President William Howard Taft,
he entered the Senate in 1932 and was a prominent
isolationist. He co-sponsored the Taft-Hartley Act
(1947), which acted against the 'closed shop' power of
trade unions. He failed three times (1940, 1948, 1952) to
gain the Republican nomination for the US presidency.

81 Lending arms is like lending chewing gum. You
    don't get it back.
    On the lend-lease agreement. Quoted in David Brinkley
    Washington Goes to War (1988).

Taft, William Howard 1857–1930

US Republican Politician and 27th US President.
Secretary of War (1904–8) and provisional governor of

Cuba (1906), he became President in 1909 and remained in the post until 1913, when he was defeated by Woodrow Wilson. Subsequently he became US Chief Justice (1921).

82 There are a great many people who are in favor of conservation no matter what it means.
Quoted in J W Milliman *Land Economics* (1962).

83 Golf is in the interest of good health and good manners. It promotes self-restraint and affords a chance to play the man and act the gentleman.
Quoted in Michael Hobbs *The Golf Quotation Book* (1992).

Takuboku, Ishikawa 1886–1902

Japanese poet whose first book of poems, *Akogare* (Longing), was published in 1905. Five years later, a second collection, *Ichiaku no Suna* (A Handful of Dust), broke new ground by writing about aspects of everyday life.

84 There are some lives duller
Than dusty glass
1910 *Ichiaku no Suna* (translated by Sakanishi Shio).

85 Like a stone
That rolls down a hill,
I have come to this day.
1910 *Ichiaku no Suna* (translated by Sakanishi Shio).

Talbot, Godfrey Walker 1908–

English broadcaster and writer. He was the BBC's war correspondent in World War II and their court correspondent from 1948 to 1969. He wrote articles on the Royal Family and an autobiography, *Ten Seconds from Now* (1973).

86 A man who, until he made the journey from London, thought that woad began at Watford.
1973 *Ten Seconds from Now*, ch.3. An early reference to the 'north of Watford' concept, in which Watford is regarded as the limit of 'civilization' northwards from London.

Talese, Gay 1932–

US writer and journalist. His works include *New York: A Serendipiter's Journey* (1961), *Fame and Obscurity* (1970) and *Unto the Sons* (1992).

87 New glass skyscrapers stand shoulder to shoulder, reflecting one another narcissistically.
1965 In the *New York Times*, 23 Jun.

Talleyrand-Périgord, Charles-Maurice de, Prince of Benevento 1754–1838

French statesman, President of the Assembly (1790). He lived in exile until the fall of Robespierre. As Foreign Minister under the Directory (1797–1807) he helped consolidate Napoleon's position, but alarmed by his ambitions resigned in 1807 to become leader of the anti-Napoleonic faction. Foreign Minister under Louis XVIII, he represented France at the Congress of Vienna (1814–15). He was Louis Philippe's chief adviser at the July Revolution, and Ambassador to England (1830–4).

88 *Ils n'ont rien appris, ni rien oublié.*

They have learned nothing, and forgotten nothing.
Attributed.

89 *Voilà le commencement de la fin.*

This is the beginning of the end.
Attributed.

90 The allies are too frightened to fight each other, too stupid too agree.
1814 Congress of Vienna, Nov.

Tally, Ted 1952–

US screenwriter, best known for *The Silence of the Lambs* (1991) for which he won an Academy Award for Best Adapted Screenplay.

91 A census taker once tried to test me, I ate his liver with some fava beans and a nice Chianti.
1991 Anthony Hopkins as Dr Hannibal Lecter ('Hannibal the Cannibal') in *The Silence of the Lambs*.

92 I do wish we could chat longer but I'm having an old friend for dinner.
1991 Anthony Hopkins as Dr Hannibal Lecter ('Hannibal the Cannibal') in *The Silence of the Lambs*.

Talma, François-Joseph 1763–1826

French actor-manager. He established his reputation as a powerful tragedian in the central role of Chénier's *Charles IX* in 1789, which caused a sensation; subsequently he formed his own company and staged admired productions of Corneille, Shakespeare and others. As head of the French national theatre under Napoleon he introduced various important reforms.

93 *Voltaire! Comme Voltaire, toujours comme Voltaire.*

Voltaire! Like Voltaire, always like Voltaire.
1826 Last words.

Tanaka, Kakuei 1918–93

Japanese politician who rose through the ranks of the Liberal Democratic party to become Prime Minister. Arrested in 1976 for bribery, he resigned the premiership, although he remained influential.

94 The politics of numbers.
1983 Describing democracy, in an interview with the *Nihon Keizai Shimbun*, 25 Jan.

95 Why should not a large shareholder sometimes name the president?
1983 Responding to criticism that candidates for the premiership must win his approval. Quoted in the *Financial Times*, 11 Oct.

Tannahill, Robert 1774–1810

Scottish poet and songwriter, born in Paisley, the son of a weaver.

96 The sun has gane down o'er the lofty Benlomond,
And left the red clouds to preside o'er the scene,
While lanely I stray, in the calm simmer gloamin',
To muse on sweet Jessie, the flower o' Dunblane.
How sweet is the brier wi' its saft faulding blossom,
And sweet is the birk, wi' its mantle o' green;
Yet sweeter, and fairer, and dear to this bosom,
Is lovely young Jessie, the flower o' Dunblane.
1807 'Jessie, the Flower o' Dunblane', stanza 1.

T'ao Ch'ien AD 372–427

Chinese poet about whom little is known.

97 I beg you listen to this advice—
When you get wine, be sure to drink it.
c.400 AD Collected in *Substance, Shadow and Spirit*, translated by Arthur Waley.

Tarkington, (Newton) Booth 1869–1946

US novelist, best known for his Penrod books, *Penrod* (1914) and *Seventeen* (1916). His novel *The Magnificent Ambersons* (1918) won the Pulitzer Prize and was made into a successful film by Orson Welles.

98 There are two things that will be believed of any man whatsoever, and one of them is that he has taken to drink.
1914 *Penrod*, ch.10.

99 The Magnificent Ambersons.
1918 Title of novel.

1 An ideal wife is any woman who has an ideal husband.
1924 *Looking Forward And Others*, 'The Hopeful Pessimist'.

Tate, (John Orley) Allen 1899–1979

US poet, critic and biographer. He was the editor of the influential *Sewanee Review* (1944–7). His own poetry was strongly influenced by T S Eliot.

2 Row upon row with strict impunity
The headstones yield their names to the element
1948 *Poems 1922–1947*, 'Ode to the Confederate Dead'.

3 Autumn is desolation in the plot
Of a thousand acres, where these memories grow
From the inexhaustible bodies that are not
Dead, but feed the grass, row after rich row.
1948 *Poems 1922–1947*, 'Ode to the Confederate Dead'.

4 The brute curiosity of an angel's stare
Turn you like them to stone.
1948 *Poems 1922–1947*, 'Ode to the Confederate Dead'.

5 I've heard the wolves scuffle, and said: So this
Is man; so—what better conclusion is there—
The day will not follow night, and the heart

Of man has a little dignity, but less patience
Than a wolf's, and a duller sense that cannot
Smell its own mortality.
1948 *Poems 1922–1947*, 'The Wolves'.

Tate, Greg

US writer.

6 Commodity fetishism is the true God of this nation.
1992 In *Vibe*, reported in *USA Today*, 14 Sep.

Tawney, R(ichard) H(enry) 1880–1962

British economic historian, active in the Workers' Educational Association at Rochdale, Lancashire, and its President (1928–44). He was Professor of Economic History at London (1931–49) and wrote a number of studies in English economic history.

7 The instinct of mankind warns it against accepting at their face value spiritual demands that cannot satisfy themselves by practical achievements. The road along which the organised workers, like any other class, must climb to power starts from the provision of a more effective economic service than their masters, as their grip upon industry becomes increasingly vacillating and uncertain, are able to supply.
1926 *The Acquisitive Society*.

8 As long as men are men, a poor society cannot be too poor to find a right order of life; nor a rich society too rich to have need to seek it.
1926 *The Acquisitive Society*.

Taylor, A(lan) J(ohn) P(ercivale) 1906–90

English historian, whose major work was *The Struggle for Mastery in Europe 1848–1918* (1954). His controversial revisionist *Origins of the Second World War* (1961) argued against a grand design. Other works include *English History 1914–1945* (1965), *The Trouble Makers* (1957), on critics of British foreign policy, and *A Personal History* (1983).

9 Crimea: The War That Would Not Boil.
1952 *Rumours of Wars*, ch.6, chapter title.

10 Human blunders usually do more to shape history than human wickedness.
1961 *The Origins of the Second World War*.

11 The First World War had begun—imposed on the statesmen of Europe by railway timetables. It was an unexpected climax to the railway age.
1963 *The First World War*, ch.1.

12 Like most of those who study history, Napoleon learned from the mistakes of the past how to make new ones.
1963 BBC radio broadcast, 6 Jun.

13 History gets thicker and thicker as it approaches recent times.

1965 *English History 1914–1945.*

Taylor, Dwight

US screenwriter. Best known for his screenplays for two of the Fred Astaire/Ginger Rogers musicals *Top Hat* (1935) and *Follow the Fleet* (1936).

14 Are you sure you didn't forget yourself in the park? Positive. If I ever forget myself with that girl I'd remember it.

1935 Dialogue between Edward Everett Horton and Fred Astaire in *Top Hat* (with Allan Scott).

Taylor, Elizabeth Rosemond 1932–

English-born US film actress. She graduated from child star to screen goddess in films such as *A Place in the Sun* (1951), *Raintree County* (1957), *Butterfield 8* (1960), *Cleopatra* (1962) and *Who's Afraid of Virginia Woolf?* (1966). She has had seven husbands, most famously Richard Burton, whom she married twice.

15 It will be fun to be the first Jewish Queen of Egypt.

c.1962 On taking the title role in *Cleopatra.* Attributed.

16 If someone was stupid enough to offer me a million dollars to make a picture—I was certainly not dumb enough to turn it down.

Quoted in David Niven *The Moon's a Balloon* (1975).

17 Success is a great deodorant.

1977 ABC TV broadcast, 6 Apr.

18 You help them get elected, and then the Senate becomes the wife, the mistress. That was one lady I couldn't begin to fight. She was too tough.

1987 After her marriage to Senator John Warner. In *Cosmopolitan,* Sep.

19 Some of my best leading men have been horses and dogs.

Attributed.

Taylor, Graham 1944–

English football manager. Manager of Aston Villa and other sides, he succeeded Bobby Robson as manager of England in 1990 but resigned three years later after England failed to qualify for the 1994 World Cup.

20 Agents do nothing for the good of football. I'd like to see them lined up against a wall and machine-gunned…some accountants and solicitors with them.

1983 Quoted in Peter Ball and Phil Shaw *The Book of Football Quotations* (1989).

Taylor, Jeremy 1613–67

English divine, whose sermons and devotional writings are masterpieces are considered to be of sacred eloquence.

21 Faith gives new light to the soul, but it does not put our eyes out; and what God hath given us in our nature could never be intended as a snare to Religion, or engage us to believe a lie.

1660 *The Worthy Communicant.*

Taylor, John Vincent

22 The Holy Spirit is the invisible third party who stands between me and the other, making us mutually aware.

1972 *The Go-Between God.*

23 [God's] changelessness means that he cannot cease to be what he is, but it does not preclude his doing some new thing to express what he is.

1992 *The Christlike God.*

Taylor, Maxwell Davenport 1901–87

US soldier, air commander in World War II and superintendent of West Point (1945–9). After commanding in Korea and the Far East, he was appointed army chief of staff (1955–9) but resigned when his proposals for army reorganization were disregarded. He was instrumental in securing US support for the war in Vietnam.

24 They didn't know how it ran, where you put in the gas, where you put in the oil, where you turn the throttle.

On the Kennedy White House and the botched invasion of Cuba's Bay of Pigs. Quoted in Ralph G Martin *A Hero for Our Time* (1983).

Tebbit, Norman (Beresford) Tebbit, Baron 1931–

English Conservative politician, Employment Secretary (1981–3) and Secretary for Trade and Industry (1983–5). In 1984 he and his wife were injured by an IRA bomb in Brighton. In 1985 he became Chairman of the Party, but after 1987 he returned to the backbenches until his retirement in 1992.

25 He didn't riot. He got on his bike and looked for work, and he kept looking till he found it.

1981 Speaking of his father after criticism of high unemployment under the Conservative Government, party conference, 15 Oct.

Teller, Edward 1908–

Hungarian-born US physicist, called the father of the hydrogen bomb. He was born in Budapest, and educated in Germany. In 1941 he became a US citizen and joined the US atomic bomb development project known as the Manhattan Project.

26 If there ever was a misnomer, it is 'exact science'. Science has always been full of mistakes; they require a genius to correct them. Of course, we do not see our own mistakes.

1991 *Conversations on the Dark Secrets of Physics.*

Temple, William 1881–1944

English prelate. Headmaster of Repton School (1910–14), he became a bishop in 1921, Archbishop of York in 1919, and succeeded as Archbishop of Canterbury in 1942. He was an outspoken advocate of social reform.

27   Personally, I have always looked upon cricket as organized loafing.
   c.1914 Address to parents of pupils at Repton School, Derbyshire.

28   Christianity is the most materialist of all great religions.
   1939 *Readings in St John's Gospel*, vol.1.

29   I believe in the Church, one Holy Catholic and Apostolic Church; and nowhere does it exist.
   Attributed.

Templeton, Charles 1915–

Canadian media personality and author.

30   You are born with two things: existence and opportunity, and these are the raw materials out of which you can make a successful life.
   1989 *Succeeding*.

Tennyson, Alfred, 1st Baron also called *Alfred, Lord Tennyson* 1809–92

English lyric poet, a master of rhythm, mood and imagery. He became Poet Laureate in 1850. Among the finest poems are *Morte d'Arthur* (1842), the elegiac *In Memoriam* (1850) and *The Idylls of the King* (1859).

31   Below the thunders of the upper deep;
   Far, far beneath in the abysmal sea,
   His ancient, dreamless, uninvaded sleep
   The Kraken sleepeth.
   1830 *Poems, Chiefly Lyrical*, 'The Kraken', l.1–4.

32   There hath he lain for ages and will lie
   Battening upon huge seaworms in his sleep
   Until the latter fire shall heat the deep.
   1830 *Poems, Chiefly Lyrical*, 'The Kraken', l.11–13.

33   Vex not thou the poet's mind
   With thy shallow wit:
   Vex not thou the poet's mind;
   For thou canst not fathom it.
   1830 *Poems, Chiefly Lyrical*, 'The Poet's Mind', l.1–4.

34   Airy, fairy Lilian.
   1830 *Poems*, 'Lilian', l.1.

35   A daughter of the gods, divinely tall,
   And most divinely fair.
   1832 *Poems*, 'A Dream of Fair Women', l.87–8.

36   O Love, O fire! once he drew
   With one long kiss my whole soul through

My lips, as sunlight drinketh dew.
   1832 *Poems*, 'Fatima', stanza 3.

37   On either side the river lie
   Long fields of barley and of rye,
   That clothe the wold and meet the sky;
   And through the field the road runs by
   To many-towered Camelot.
   1832 *Poems*, 'The Lady of Shalott' (revised 1842), pt.1, l.1–5.

38   Willows whiten, aspens quiver,
   Little breezes dusk and shiver.
   1832 *Poems*, 'The Lady of Shalott' (revised 1842), pt.1, l.10–11.

39   Four grey walls, and four grey towers,
   Overlook a space of flowers,
   And the silent isle imbowers
   The Lady of Shalott.
   1832 *Poems*, 'The Lady of Shalott' (revised 1842), pt.1, l.15–18.

40   Only reapers, reaping early
   In among the bearded barley,
   Hear a song that echoes cheerly
   From the river winding clearly,
   Down to towered Camelot.
   1832 *Poems*, 'The Lady of Shalott' (revised 1842), pt.1, l.28–32.

41   And moving through a mirror clear
   That hangs before her all the year,
   Shadows of the world appear.
   1832 *Poems*, 'The Lady of Shalott' (revised 1842), pt.2, l.46–8.

42   Or when the moon was overhead,
   Came two young lovers lately wed;
   'I am half sick of shadows,' said
   The Lady of Shalott.
   1832 *Poems*, 'The Lady of Shalott' (revised 1842), pt.2, l.69–72.

43   A bow-shot from her bower-eaves,
   He rode between the barley-sheaves,
   The sun came dazzling through the leaves,
   And flamed upon the brazen greaves
   Of bold Sir Lancelot.
   A red-cross knight forever kneeled
   To a lady in his shield,
   That sparkled on the yellow field,
   Beside remote Shalott.
   1832 *Poems*, 'The Lady of Shalott' (revised 1842), pt.3, l.73–81.

44   All in the blue unclouded weather
   Thick-jewelled shone the saddle leather,
   The helmet and the helmet-feather
   Burned like one burning flame together,
   As he rode down to Camelot.
   1832 *Poems*, 'The Lady of Shalott' (revised 1842), pt.3, l.91–5.

45 She left the web, she left the loom,
     She made three paces through the room,
     She saw the water-lily bloom,
     She saw the helmet and the plume,
     She looked down to Camelot.
     Out flew the web and floated wide;
     The mirror cracked from side to side;
     'The curse is come upon me', cried
     The Lady of Shalott.
     1832 *Poems*, 'The Lady of Shalott' (revised 1842), pt.3, l.109–17.

46 Down she came and found a boat
     Beneath a willow left afloat,
     And round about the prow she wrote
     The Lady of Shalott.
     1832 *Poems*, 'The Lady of Shalott' (revised 1842), pt.4, l.123–6.

47 But Lancelot mused a little space;
     He said, 'She has a lovely face;
     God in his mercy lend her grace,
     The Lady of Shalott.'
     1832 *Poems*, 'The Lady of Shalott' (revised 1842), pt.4, l.168–71.

48 'Courage!' he said, and pointed toward the land,
     'This mounting wave will roll us shoreward soon.'
     In the afternoon they came unto a land
     In which it seemèd always afternoon.
     All round the coast the languid air did swoon,
     Breathing like one that hath a weary dream.
     1832 *Poems*, 'The Lotos-Eaters', l.1–6.

49 There is sweet music here that softer falls
     Than petals from blown roses on the grass,
     Or night dews on still waters between walls
     Of shadowy granite, in a gleaming pass;
     Music that gentlier on the spirit lies,
     Than tired eyelids upon tired eyes.
     1832 *Poems*, 'The Lotos-Eaters', Choric Song, stanza 1, l.46–51.

50 There is no joy but calm!
     1832 *Poems*, 'The Lotos-Eaters', Choric Song, stanza 2, l.68.

51 Death is the end of life; ah, why
     Should life all labour be?
     1832 *Poems* 'The Lotos-Eaters', Choric Song, stanza 4, l.86–87.

52 Live and lie reclined
     On the hills like Gods together, careless of
       mankind.
     For they lie beside their nectar, and the bolts are
       hurled
     Far below them in the valleys, and the clouds are
       lightly curled
     Round their golden houses, girdled with the
       gleaming world.

     1832 *Poems*, 'The Lotos-Eaters', Choric Song, stanza 8, l.154–8.

53 Surely, surely, slumber is more sweet than toil, the
      shore
     Than labour in the deep mid-ocean, wind and
      wave and oar;
     Oh rest ye, brother mariners, we will not wander
      more.
     1832 *Poems*, 'The Lotos-Easters', Choric Song, stanza 8, l.171–3.

54 I built my soul a lordly pleasure-house,
     Wherein at ease for aye to dwell.
     1832 *Poems*, 'The Palace of Art', stanza 1, l.1–2.

55 And 'while the world runs round and round,' I
      said,
     'Reign thou apart, a quiet king,
     Still as, while Saturn whirls, his steadfast shade
     Sleeps on his luminous ring.'
     1832 *Poems*, 'The Palace of Art', stanza 4, l.13–16.

56 An English home—grey twilight poured
     On dewy pasture, dewy trees,
     Softer than sleep—all things in order stored,
     A haunt of ancient Peace.
     1832 *Poems*, 'The Palace of Art', stanza 22, l.85–8.

57 It little profits that an idle king
     By this still hearth, among these barren crags,
     Matched with an agèd wife, I mete and dole
     Unequal laws unto a savage race,
     That hoard, and sleep, and feed, and know not me.
     1833 *Poems*, 'Ulysses' (published 1842), l.1–5.

58 I cannot rest from travel: I will drink
     Life to the lees: all times I have enjoyed
     Greatly, have suffered greatly, both with those
     That loved me, and alone; on shore, and when
     Through scudding drifts the rainy Hyades
     Vext the dim sea: I am become a name;
     For always roaming with a hungry heart
     Much have I seen and known; cities of men
     And manners, climates, council, governments,
     Myself not least, but honoured of them all;
     And drunk delight of battle with my peers,
     Far on the ringing plains of windy Troy.
     I am part of all that I have met;
     Yet all experience is an arch wherethrough
     Gleams that untravelled world, whose margin fades
     For ever and for ever when I move.
     How dull it is to pause, to make an end,
     To rust unburnished, not to shine in use!
     As though to breathe were life.
     1833 *Poems*, 'Ulysses' (published 1842), l.6–24.

59 This grey spirit yearning in desire
     To follow knowledge like a sinking star,

Beyond the utmost bound of human thought.
1833 *Poems*, 'Ulysses' (published 1842), l.30–2.

60 This is my son, mine own Telemachus.
1833 *Poems*, 'Ulysses' (published 1842), l.33.

61 There lies the port; the vessel, puffs her sail:
There gloom the dark broad seas. My mariners,
Souls that have toiled, and wrought, and thought
   with me—
That ever with a frolic welcome took
The thunder and the sunshine, and opposed
Free hearts, free foreheads—you and I are old:
Old age hath yet his honour and his toil;
Death closes all: but something ere the end,
Some work of noble note, may yet be done,
Not unbecoming men that strove with gods.
The lights begin to twinkle from the rocks:
The long day wanes: the slow moon climbs: the
   deep
Moans round with many voices. Come, my friends,
'Tis not too late to seek a newer world.
Push off, and sitting well in order smite
The sounding furrows: for my purpose holds
To sail beyond the sunset, and the baths
Of all the western stars, until I die.
It may be that the gulfs will wash us down:
It may be we shall touch the Happy Isles,
And see the great Achilles, whom we knew.
Though much is taken, much abides: and
   though
We are not now that strength which in old days
Moved earth and hearth: that which we are, we
   are:
One equal temper of heroic hearts,
Made weak by time and fate, but strong in will
To strive, to seek, to find, and not to yield.
1833 *Poems*, 'Ulysses' (published 1842), l.44–70.

63 Break, break, break,
On thy cold grey stones, O Sea!
And I would that my tongue could utter
The thoughts that arise in me.
1842 *Poems*, 'Break, Break, Break', stanza 1.

64 And the stately ships go on
To their haven under the hill;
But O for the touch of a vanished hand,
And the sound of a voice that is still!
1842 *Poems*, 'Break, Break, Break', stanza 3.

65 'Tis not your work, but Love's. Love, unperceived,
A more ideal Artist he than all,
Came, drew your pencil from you, made those
   eyes
Darker than the darkest pansies, and that hair
More black than ashbuds in the front of March.
1842 *Poems*, 'The Gardener's Daughter', l.24–8.

66 A sight to make an old man young.
1842 *Poems*, 'The Gardener's Daughter', l.140.

67 Then she rode forth, clothed on with chastity.
1842 *Poems*, 'Godiva', l.53.

68 With twelve great shocks of sound, the shameless
   noon
Was clashed and hammered from a hundred
   towers.
1842 *Poems*, 'Godiva', l.74–5.

69 At me you smiled, but unbeguiled
I saw the snare, and I retired:
The daughter of a hundred Earls,
You are not one to be desired.
1842 *Poems*, 'Lady Clara Vere de Vere', stanza 1, l.5–8.

70 From yon blue heavens above us bent
The gardener Adam and his wife
Smile at the claims of long descent.
Howe'er it be, it seems to me,
'Tis only noble to be good.
Kind hearts are more than coronets,
And simple faith than Norman blood.
1842 *Poems*, 'Lady Clara Vere de Vere', stanza 7, l.50–6.

71 In the Spring a fuller crimson comes upon the
   robin's breast;
In the Spring the wanton lapwing gets himself
   another crest
In the Spring a livelier iris changes on the
   burnished dove;
In the Spring a young man's fancy lightly turns to
   thoughts of love.
1842 *Poems*, 'Locksley Hall', l.17–20.

72 And our spirits rushed together at the touching of
   the lips.
1842 *Poems*, 'Locksley Hall', l.38.

73 He will hold thee, when his passion shall have
   spent its novel force,
Something better than his dog, a little dearer than
   his horse.
1842 *Poems*, 'Locksley Hall', l.49–50.

74 This is truth the poet sings,
That a sorrow's crown of sorrow is remembering
   happier things.
1842 *Poems*, 'Locksley Hall' l.75–6.

75 Like a dog, he hunts in dreams.
1842 *Poems*, 'Locksley Hall', l.79.

76 But the jingling of the guinea helps the hurt that
   Honour feels.
1842 *Poems*, 'Locksley Hall', l.105.

77 Men, my brothers, men the workers, ever reaping
   something new:

That which they have done but earnest of the
things that they shall do:

For I dipped into the future, far as human eye
could see,
Saw the vision of the world, and all the wonder that
would be;

Saw the heaven fill with commerce, argosies of
magic sails,
Pilots of the purple twilight, dropping down with
costly bales;

Heard the heavens fill with shouting, and there
rained a ghastly dew
From the nations' airy navies grappling in the
central blue;

Far along the world-wide whisper of the south-
wind rushing warm,
With the standards of the peoples plunging
through the thunder-storm;

Till the war-drum throbbed no longer, and the
battle-flags were furled
In the Parliament of man, the Federation of the
world.
1842 *Poems*, 'Locksley Hall', l.117–28.

78 Science moves, but slowly slowly, creeping on from
point to point.
1842 *Poems*, 'Locksley Hall', l.134.

79 Yet I doubt not through the ages one increasing
purpose runs,
And the thoughts of men are widened with the
process of the suns.
1842 *Poems*, 'Locksley Hall', l.137–8.

80 Knowledge comes, but wisdom lingers, and I linger
on the shore,
And the individual withers, and the world is more
and more.
1842 *Poems*, 'Locksley Hall', l.141.

81 I will take some savage woman, she shall rear my
dusky race.
1842 *Poems*, 'Locksley Hall', l.168.

82 I the heir of all the ages, in the foremost files of
time.
1842 *Poems*, 'Locksley Hall', l.178.

83 Forward, forward let us range,
Let the great world spin for ever down the ringing
grooves of change.
1842 *Poems*, 'Locksley Hall', l.181–2.

84 Better fifty years of Europe than a cycle of Cathay.
1842 *Poems*,' Locksley Hall', l.184.

85 This truth within thy mind rehearse,

That in a boundless universe
Is boundless better, boundless worse.
1842 *Poems*, 'The Two Voices', stanza 9, l.25–7.

86 No life that breathes with human breath
Has ever truly longed for death.
1842 *Poems*, 'The Two Voices', stanza 132, l.395–6.

87 Fill the cup, and fill the can:
Have a rouse before the morn:
Every moment dies a man,
Every moment one is born.
1842 *Poems*, 'The Vision of Sin', pt.4, stanza 9, l.95–8.

88 I grow in worth, and wit, and sense,
Unboding critic-pen,
Or that eternal want of pence,
Which vexes public men.
1842 *Poems*, 'Will Waterproof's Lyrical Monologue', stanza 6,
l.41–4.

89 A land of settled government,
A land of just and old renown,
Where Freedom slowly broadens down
From precedent to precedent.
1842 *Poems*, 'You ask me, why, though ill at ease', stanza 3,
l.9–12.

90 But we grow old, Ah! when shall all men's good
Be each man's rule, and universal peace
Lie like a shaft of light across the land,
And like a lane of beams athwart the sea,
Through all the circle of the golden year.
1846 'The Golden Year', l.47–51.

91 With prudes for proctors, dowagers for deans,
And sweet girl-graduates in their golden hair.
1847 *The Princess*, 'Prologue', l.141–2.

92 A classic lecture, rich in sentiment,
With scraps of thundrous Epic lilted out
By violet-hooded Doctors, elegies
And quoted odes, and jewels five-words-long,
That on the stretched forefinger of all Time
Sparkle for ever.
1847 *The Princess*, pt.2, l.352–7.

93 Man is the hunter; woman is his game:
The sleek and shining creatures of the chase,
We hunt them for the beauty of their skins;
They love us for it, and we ride them down.
1847 *The Princess*, pt.5, l.147–50.

94 The woman is so hard
Upon the woman.
1847 *The Princess*, pt.6, l.205–6.

95 No little lily-handed baronet he,
A great broad-shouldered genial Englishman,
A lord of fat prize-oxen and of sheep,

A raiser of huge melons and of pine,
A patron of some thirty charities,
A pamphleteer on guano and on grain.
1847 *The Princess*, 'Conclusion', l.84–9.

96 And blessings on the falling out
That all the more endears,
When we fall out with those we love
And kiss again with tears!
1850 *The Princess*, pt.2, added song, l.6–9.

97 Sweet and low, sweet and low,
Wind of the western sea,
Low, low, breathe and blow,
Wind of the western sea!
Over the rolling waters go,
Come from the dying moon, and blow,
Blow him again to me;
While my little one, while my pretty one,
   sleeps.

Sleep and rest, sleep and rest,
Father will come to thee soon;
Rest, rest, on mother's breast,
Father will come to thee soon;
Father will come to his babe in the nest,
Silver sails all out of the west
Under the silver moon:
Sleep, my little one, sleep, my pretty one,
   sleep.
1850 *The Princess*, pt.3, added song, stanzas 1–2.

98 The splendour falls on castle walls
And snowy summits old in story:
The long light shakes across the lakes,
And the wild cataract leaps in glory.
Blow, bugle, blow, set the wild echoes flying,
Blow, bugle; answer, echoes, dying, dying,
   dying.
1850 *The Princess*, pt.4, added song, stanza 1.

99 O hark, O hear! how thin and clear
And thinner, clearer, farther going!
O sweet and far from cliff and scar
The horns of Elfland faintly blowing!
Blow, let us hear the purple glens replying:
Blow, bugle; answer, echoes, dying, dying,
   dying.
1850 *The Princess*, pt.4, added song, stanza 2.

1 O love, they die in yon rich sky,
They faint on hill or field or river:
Our echoes roll from soul to soul,
And grow for ever and for ever.
1850 *The Princess*, pt.4, added song, stanza 3.

2 Tears, idle tears, I know not what they mean,
Tears from the depth of some divine despair
Rise in the heart, and gather to the eyes,

In looking on the happy autumn-fields,
And thinking of the days that are no more.
1850 *The Princess*, pt.4, added song, stanza 1.

3 So sad, so fresh, the days that are no more.
1850 *The Princess*, pt.4, added song, stanza 2.

4 Ah, sad and strange as in dark summer dawns
The earliest pipe of half-awakened birds
To dying ears, when unto dying eyes
The casement slowly grows a glimmering square;
So sad, so strange, the days that are no more.

Dear as remembered kisses after death,
And sweet as those by hopeless fancy feigned
On lips that are for others; deep as love,
Deep as first love, and wild with all regret;
O Death in Life, the days that are no more.
1850 *The Princess*, pt.4, added song, stanzas 3–4.

5 O Swallow, Swallow, flying, flying South,
Fly to her, and fall upon her gilded eaves,
And tell her, tell her, what I tell to thee.
O tell her, Swallow, thou that knowest each,
That bright and fierce and fickle is the South,
And dark and true and tender is the North.
1850 *The Princess*, pt.4, added song, stanzas 1–2.

6 O tell her, Swallow that thy brood is flown:
Say to her, I do but wanton in the South,
But in the North long since my nest is made.
1850 *The Princess*, pt.4, added song, stanza 6.

7 Home they brought her warrior dead.
She nor swooned, nor uttered cry:
All her maidens, watching said,
'She must weep or she will die.'
1850 *The Princess*, pt.6, added song, stanza 1.

8 Rose a nurse of ninety years,
Set his child upon her knee–
Like summer tempest came her tears–
'Sweet my child, I live for thee.'
1850 *The Princess*, pt.6, added song, stanza 4.

9 Ask me no more: what answer should I give?
I love not hollow cheek or faded eye:
Yet, O my friend, I will not have thee die!
Ask me no more, lest I should bid thee live.
1850 *The Princess*, pt.7, added song, stanza 2.

10 Now sleeps the crimson petal, now the whit;
Nor waves the cypress in the palace walk;
Nor winks the gold fin in the porphyry font:
The fire-fly wakens: waken thou, with me.

Now droops the milk-white peacock like a ghost,
And like a ghost she glimmers on to me.
Now lies the Earth all Danaë to the stars,
And all thy heart lies open unto me.

Now slides the silent meteor on, and leaves
A shining furrow, as thy thoughts in me.

Now folds the lily all her sweetness up,
And slips into the bosom of the lake:
So fold thyself, my dearest, thou, and slip
Into my bosom and be lost in me.
1850 *The Princess*, pt.7, added song, complete.

11 Come down, O maid, from yonder mountain height:
What pleasure lives in height?
1850 *The Princess*, pt.7, added song, l.1–2.

12 For love is of the valley, come thou down
And find him; by the happy threshold, he,
Or hand in hand with Plenty in the maize,
Or red with spirited purple of the vats,
Or foxlike in the vine; nor cares to walk
With Death and Morning on the silver horns.
1850 *The Princess*, pt.7, added song, l.184–9.

13 Sweet is every sound,
Sweeter thy voice, but every sound is sweet;
Myriads of rivulets hurrying through the lawn,
The moan of doves in immemorial elms,
With murmuring of innumerable bees.
1850 *The Princess*, pt.7, added song, l.203–7.

14 Come not, when I am dead,
To drop thy foolish tears upon my grave,
To trample round my fallen head,
And vex the unhappy dust thou wouldst not save.
There let the wind sweep and the plover cry;
But thou, go by.

Child, if it were thine error or thy crime
I care no longer, being all unblest;
Wed whom thou wilt, but I am sick of Time,
And I desire to rest.
Pass on, weak heart, and leave me where I lie:
Go by, go by.
1850 'Come not, when I am dead', complete poem.

15 Strong Son of God, immortal Love,
Whom we, that have not seen thy face,
By faith, and faith alone, embrace,
Believing where we cannot prove.
1850 *In Memoriam A.H.H.*, prologue, l.1–4.

16 Thou madest man, he knows not why,
He thinks he was not made to die;
And thou hast made him: thou art just.
1850 *In Memoriam A.H.H.*, prologue, l.10–12.

17 Our little systems have their day;
They have their day and cease to be;
They are but broken lights of thee,
And thou, O Lord, art more than they.
1850 *In Memoriam A.H.H.*, prologue, l.17–20.

18 Let knowledge grow from more to more,

But more of reverence in us dwell;
That mind and soul, according well,
May make one music as before.
1850 *In Memoriam A.H.H.*, prologue, l.25–8.

19 I sometimes hold it half a sin
To put in words the grief I feel;
For words, like Nature, half reveal
And half conceal the Soul within.

But, for the unquiet heart and brain,
A use in measured language lies;
The sad mechanic exercise,
Like dull narcotics, numbing pain.
1850 *In Memoriam A.H.H.*, canto 5, l.1–8.

20 And common is the commonplace,
And vacant chaff well meant for grain.
1850 *In Memoriam A.H.H.*, canto 6, l.3–4.

21 Never morning wore
To evening, but some heart did break.
1850 *In Memoriam A.H.H.*, canto 6, l.7–8.

22 His heavy-shotted hammock-shroud
Drops in his vast and wandering grave.
1850 *In Memoriam A.H.H.*, canto 6, l.15–16.

23 Dark house, by which once more I stand
Here in the long unlovely street,
Doors, where my heart was used to beat
So quickly, waiting for a hand.
1850 *In Memoriam A.H.H.*, canto 7, l.1–4.

24 And ghastly through the drizzling rain
On the bald street breaks the blank day.
1850 *In Memoriam A.H.H.*, canto 7, l.11–12.

25 The last red leaf is whirled away,
The rooks are blown about the skies.
1850 *In Memoriam A.H.H.*, canto 15, l.3–4.

26 There twice a day the Severn fills;
The salt sea-water passes by,
And hushes half the babbling Wye,
And makes a silence in the hills.
1850 *In Memoriam A.H.H.*, canto 19, l.5–8.

27 The Shadow cloaked from head to foot,
Who keeps the keys of all the creeds.
1850 *In Memoriam A.H.H.*, canto 23, l.4–5.

28 And Thought leapt out to wed with Thought
Ere Thought could wed itself with Speech.
1850 *In Memoriam A.H.H.*, canto 23, l.15–16.

29 I envy not in any moods
The captive void of noble rage,
The linnet born within the cage,
That never knew the summer woods.
1850 *In Memoriam A.H.H.*, canto 27, l.1–4.

30 I hold it true, whate'er befall;
    I feel it, when I sorrow most;
    'Tis better to have loved and lost
    Than never to have loved at all.
    1850 *In Memoriam A.H.H.*, canto 27, l.13–16.

31 A solemn gladness even crowned
    The purple brows of Olivet.
    1850 *In Memoriam A.H.H.*, canto 31, l.11–12.

32 Who trusted God was love indeed
    And love Creation's final law—
    Though Nature, red in tooth and claw
    With ravine, shrieked against his creed.
    1850 *In Memoriam A.H.H.*, canto 31.

33 Her eyes are homes of silent prayer.
    1850 *In Memoriam A.H.H.*, canto 32, l.1.

34 Short swallow-flights of song, that dip
    Their wings in tears, and skim away.
    1850 *In Memoriam A.H.H.*, canto 48, l.15–16.

35 Be near me when my light is low,
    When the blood creeps, and the nerves prick
    And tingle; and the heart is sick,
    And all the wheels of Being slow.

    Be near me when the sensuous frame
    Is racked with pains that conquer trust;
    And Time, a maniac scattering dust,
    And Life, a Fury slinging flame.
    1850 *In Memoriam A.H.H.*, canto 50, l.1–8.

36 Oh yet we trust that somehow good
    Will be the final goal of ill.
    1850 *In Memoriam A.H.H.*, canto 54, l.1–2.

37 That nothing walks with aimless feet;
    That not one life shall be destroyed,
    Or cast as rubbish to the void,
    When God hath made the pile complete.
    1850 *In Memoriam A.H.H.*, canto 54, l.5–8.

38 Behold, we know not anything;
    I can but trust that good shall fall
    At last—far off—at last, to all,
    And every winter change to spring.

    So runs my dream: but what am I?
    An infant crying in the night:
    An infant crying for the light:
    And with no language but a cry.
    1850 *In Memoriam A.H.H.*, canto 54, l.13–20.

39 So careful of the type she seems,
    So careless of the single life.
    1850 Of Nature. *In Memoriam A.H.H.*, canto 55, l.7–8.

40 The great world's altar-stairs
    That slope through darkness up to God.
    1850 *In Memoriam A.H.H.*, canto 55, l.15–16.

41 Man, her last work, who seemed so fair,
    Such splendid purpose in his eyes,
    Who rolled the psalm to wintry skies,
    Who built him fanes of fruitless prayer,
    Who trusted God was love indeed
    And love Creation's final law—
    Though Nature, red in tooth and claw
    With ravine, shrieked against his creed.
    1850 *In Memoriam A.H.H.*, canto 56, l.9–16.

42 Peace; come away: the song of woe
    Is after all an earthly song:
    Peace; come away: we do him wrong
    To sing so wildly: let us go.
    1850 *In Memoriam A.H.H.*, canto 57, l.1–4.

43 O Sorrow, wilt thou live with me
    No casual mistress, but a wife.
    1850 *In Memoriam A.H.H.*, canto 59, l.1–2.

44 Dost thou look back on what hath been,
    As some divinely gifted man,
    Whose life in low estate began
    And on a simple village green;

    Who breaks his birth's invidious bar,
    And grasps the skirts of happy chance,
    And breasts the blows of circumstance,
    And grapples with his evil star.
    1850 *In Memoriam A.H.H.*, canto 64, l.1–8.

45 So many worlds, so much to do,
    So little done, such things to be.
    1850 *In Memoriam A.H.H.*, canto 73, l.1–2.

46 Death has made
    His darkness beautiful with thee.
    1850 *In Memoriam A.H.H.*, canto 74, l.11–12.

47 And round thee with the breeze of song
    To stir a little dust of praise.
    1850 *In Memoriam A.H.H.*, canto 75, l.11–12.

48 O last regret, regret can die!
    1850 *In Memoriam A.H.H.*, canto 78, l.17.

49 Laburnums, dropping-wells of fire.
    1850 *In Memoriam A.H.H.*, canto 83, l.12.

50 God's finger touched him, and he slept.
    1850 *In Memoriam A.H.H.*, canto 85, l.20.

51 He brought an eye for all he saw;
    He mixed in all our simple sports;
    They pleased him, fresh from brawling courts
    And dusty purlieus of the law.
    1850 *In Memoriam A.H.H.*, canto 89, l.9–12.

52 You tell me, doubt is Devil-born.
    1850 *In Memoriam A.H.H.*, canto 96, l.4.

53 There lives more faith in honest doubt,

Believe me, than in half the creeds.
1850 *In Memoriam A.H.H.*, canto 96, l.11–12.

54 Their meetings made December June,
Their every parting was to die.
1850 *In Memoriam A.H.H.*, canto 97, l.11–12.

55 He seems so near and yet so far.
1850 *In Memoriam A.H.H.*, canto 97, l.23.

56 Ring out, wild bells, to the wild sky,
The flying cloud, the frosty light:
The year is dying in the night;
Ring out, wild bells, and let him die.

Ring out the old, ring in the new,
Ring, happy bells, across the snow:
The year is going, let him go;
Ring out the false, ring in the true.
1850 *In Memoriam A.H.H.*, canto 106, l.1–8.

57 Ring out the want, the care, the sin,
The faithless coldness of the times;
Ring out, ring out my mournful rhymes,
But ring the fuller minstrel in.

Ring out false pride in place and blood,
The civic slander and the spite;
Ring in the love of truth and right,
Ring in the common love of good.

Ring out old shapes of foul disease;
Ring out the narrowing lust of gold;
Ring out the thousand wars of old,
Ring in the thousand years of peace.

Ring in the valiant man and free,
The larger heart, the kindlier hand;
Ring out the darkness of the land;
Ring in the Christ that is to be.
1850 *In Memoriam A.H.H.*, canto 106, l.17–32.

58 Not the schoolboy heat,
The blind hysterics of the Celt.
1850 *In Memoriam A.H.H.*, canto 109, l.15–16.

59 Now fades the last streak of snow,
Now burgeons every maze of quick
About the flowering squares, and thick
By ashen roots the violets blow.
1850 *In Memoriam A.H.H.*, canto 115, l.1–4.

60 And drowned in yonder living blue
The lark become a sightless song.
1850 *In Memoriam A.H.H.*, canto 115, l.7–8.

61 There, where the long street roars, hath been
The stillness of the central sea.
1850 *In Memoriam A.H.H.*, canto 123, l.3–4.

62 And thou art worthy; full of power;

As gentle; liberal-minded, great,
Consistent; wearing all that weight
Of learning lightly like a flower.
1850 *In Memoriam A.H.H.*, epilogue, l.37–40.

63 One God, one law, one element,
And one far-off divine event,
To which the whole creation moves.
1850 *In Memoriam A.H.H.*, epilogue, l.142–4.

64 He clasps the crag with crooked hands;
Close to the sun in lonely lands,
Ringed with the azure world, he stands.

The wrinkled sea beneath him crawls;
He watches from his mountain walls,
And like a thunderbolt he falls.
1851 'The Eagle', complete poem.

65 Gigantic daughter of the West,
We drink to thee across the flood,
We know thee most, we love thee best,
For art thou not of British blood?
1852 'Hands all Round', stanza 4, l.37–40.

66 The last great Englishman is low.
1852 'Ode on the Death of the Duke of Wellington', stanza 3, l.18.

67 O good grey head which all men knew!
1852 'Ode on the Death of the Duke of Wellington', stanza 4, l.35.

68 O fall'n at length that tower of strength
Which stood four-square to all the winds that blew!
1852 'Ode on the Death of the Duke of Wellington', stanza 4, l.38–9.

69 That world-earthquake, Waterloo!
1852 'Ode on the Death of the Duke of Wellington', stanza 6, l.133.

70 Who never sold the truth to serve the hour,
Nor paltered with Eternal God of power.
1852 'Ode on the Death of the Duke of Wellington', stanza 7, l.179–80.

71 Half a league, half a league,
Half a league onward,
All in the valley of Death
Rode the six hundred.
1854 'The Charge of the Light Brigade', l.1–4.

72 'Forward, the Light Brigade!'
Was there a man dismayed?
Not though the soldier knew
Some one had blundered:
Their's not to make reply,
Their's not to reason why,
Their's but to do and die:
Into the valley of Death
Rode the six hundred.

Cannon to right of them,
Cannon to left of them,
Cannon in front of them
Volleyed and thundered.
1854 'The Charge of the Light Brigade', l.9–21.

73 Into the jaws of Death,
Into the mouth of Hell
Rode the six hundred.
1854 'The Charge of the Light Brigade', l.24–6.

74 Faultily faultless, icily regular, splendidly null,
Dead perfection, no more.
1855 *Maud*, pt.1, sect.2, l.82–3.

75 The passionate heart of the poet is whirled into
folly and vice.
1855 *Maud*, pt.1, sect.4, stanza 7, l.139.

76 And most of all would I flee from the cruel
madness of love,
The honey of poison-flowers and all the
measureless ill.
1855 *Maud*, pt.1, sect.4, stanza 10, l.156–7.

77 That jewelled mass of millinery,
That oiled and curled Assyrian Bull.
1855 *Maud*, pt.1, sect.6, stanza 6, l.232–3.

78 She came to the village church,
And sat by a pillar alone;
An angel watching an urn
Wept over her, carved in stone.
1855 *Maud*, pt.1, sect.8, l.301–4.

79 I heard no longer
The snowy-banded, dilettante,
Delicate-handed priest intone.
1855 *Maud*, pt.1, sect.8, l.309–11.

80 Ah God, for a man with heart, head, hand,
Like some of the simple great ones gone
For ever and ever by,
One still strong man in a blatant land,
Whatever they call him, what care I,
Aristocrat, democrat, autocrat—one
Who can rule and dare not lie.
1855 *Maud*, pt.1, sect.10, stanza 5, l.389–95.

81 And ah for a man to arise in me
That the man I am may cease to be!.
1855 *Maud*, pt.1, sect.10, stanza 6, l.396–7.

82 I kissed her slender hand,
She took the kiss sedately;
Maud is not seventeen,
But she is tall and stately.
1855 *Maud*, pt.1, sect.12, stanza 4, l.424–7.

83 Gorgonised me from head to foot

With a stony British stare.
1855 *Maud*, pt.1, sect.13, stanza 2, l.464–5.

84 A livelier emerald twinkles in the grass,
A purer sapphire melts into the sea.
1855 *Maud*, pt.1, sect.18, stanza 6, l.649–50.

85 Come into the garden, Maud,
For the black bat, night, has flown,
Come into the garden, Maud,
I am here at the gate alone;
And the woodbine spices are wafted abroad,
And the musk of the rose is blown.

For a breeze of morning moves,
And the planet of Love is on high,
Beginning to faint in the light that she loves
On a bed of daffodil sky.
1855 *Maud*, pt.1, sect.22, stanza 1, l.850–9.

86 All night has the casement jessamine stirred
To the dancers dancing in tune;
Till a silence fell with the waking bird,
And a hush with the setting moon.
1855 *Maud*, pt.1, sect.22, stanza 3, l.864–7.

87 Queen rose of the rosebud garden of girls.
1855 *Maud*, pt.1, sect.22, stanza 9, l.902.

88 There has fallen a splendid tear
From the passion-flower at the gate.
She is coming, my dove, my dear;
She is coming, my life, my fate;
The red rose cries, 'She is near, she is near;'
And the white rose weeps, 'She is late;'
The larkspur listens, 'I hear, I hear;'
And the lily whispers, 'I wait.'

She is coming, my own, my sweet;
Were it ever so airy a tread,
My heart would hear her and beat,
Were it earth in an earthy bed;
My dust would hear her and beat,
Had I lain for a century dead;
Would start and tremble under her feet,
And blossom in purple and red.
1855 *Maud*, pt.1, sect.22, stanzas 10–11, l. 908–23.

89 O that 'twere possible
After long grief and pain
To find the arms of my true love
Round me once again!
1855 *Maud*, pt.2, sect.4, stanza 1, l.141–4.

90 Dead, long dead,
Long dead!
And my heart is a handful of dust,
And the wheels go over my head
1855 *Maud*, pt.2, sect.5, stanza 1, l.239–42.

91 But the churchmen fain would kill their church,

As the churches have killed their Christ.
1855 *Maud*, pt.2, sect.5, stanza 2, l.266–7.

92 O me, why have they not buried me deep enough?
Is it kind to have made me a grave so rough,
Me, that was never a quiet sleeper?
1855 *Maud*, pt.2, sect. 5, stanza11, l.334–6.

93 My life has crept so long on a broken wing
Through cells of madness, haunts of horror and
fear,
That I come to be grateful at last for a little thing.
1855 *Maud*, pt.3, sect.6, stanza1, l.1–3.

94 When the face of night is fair on the dewy downs,
And the shining daffodil dies.
1855 *Maud*, pt.3, sect.6, stanza 1, l.5–6.

95 And now by the side of the Black and the Baltic
deep,
And deathful-grinning mouths of the fortress,
flames
The blood-red blossom of war with a heart of fire.
1855 *Maud*, pt.3, sect.6, stanza 4, l.51–3.

96 It is better to fight for the good, than to rail at the
ill;
I have felt with my native land, I am one with my
kind,
I embrace the purpose of God, and the doom
assigned.
1855 *Maud*, pt.3, sect.6, stanza 5, l.57–9.

97 I come from haunts of coot and hern,
I make a sudden sally
And sparkle out among the fern,
To bicker down a valley.
1855 'The Brook', l.23–6.

98 For men may come and men may go,
But I go on for ever.
1855 'The Brook', l.33–4.

99 That a lie which is all a lie may be met and fought
with outright,
But a lie which is part a truth is a harder matter to
fight.
1859 'The Grandmother', stanza 8, l.31–2.

1 Wearing the white flower of a blameless life,
Before a thousand peering littlenesses,
In that fierce light which beats upon a throne,
And blackens every blot.
1859 *Idylls of the King*, dedication, l.24–7.

2 For man is man and master of his fate.
1859 *Idylls of the King*, 'The Marriage of Geraint', l.355.

3 Our hoard is little, but our hearts are great.
1859 *Idylls of the King*, 'The Marriage of Geraint', l.374.

4 They take the rustic murmur of their bourg

For the great wave that echoes round the world.
1859 *Idylls of the King*, 'The Marriage of Geraint', l.419–20.

5 It is little rift within the lute,
That by and by will make the music mute,
And ever widening slowly silence all.
1859 *Idylls of the King*, 'Merlin and Vivien', l.388–90.

6 And trust me not at all or all in all.
1859 *Idylls of the King*, 'Merlin and Vivien', l.396.

7 Man dreams of fame while woman wakes to love.
1859 *Idylls of the King*, 'Merlin and Vivien', l.458.

8 With this for motto, 'Rather use than fame'.
1859 *Idylls of the King*, 'Merlin and Vivien', l.478.

9 Where blind and naked Ignorance
Delivers brawling judgements, unashamed,
On all things all day long.
1859 *Idylls of the King*, 'Merlin and Vivien', l.662–4.

10 But every page having an ample marge,
And every marge enclosing in the midst
A square of text that looks a little blot.
1859 *Idylls of the King*, 'Merlin and Vivien', l.667–9.

11 Elaine the fair, Elaine the loveable,
Elaine the lily maid of Astolat.
1859 *Idylls of the King*, 'Lancelot and Elaine'.

12 He is all fault who hath no fault at all:
For who loves me must have a touch of earth.
1859 *Idylls of the King*, 'Lancelot and Elaine', l.132–3.

13 In me there dwells
No greatness, save it be some far-off touch
Of greatness to know well I am not great.
1859 *Idylls of the King*, 'Lancelot and Elaine', l.447–9.

14 I know not if I know what true love is,
But if I know, then, if I love not him,
I know there is none other I can love.
1859 *Idylls of the King*, 'Lancelot and Elaine', l.672–4.

15 The shackles of an old love straitened him,
His honour rooted in dishonour stood,
And faith unfaithful kept him falsely true.
1859 *Idylls of the King*, 'Lancelot and Elaine', l.870–2.

16 —Never yet
Was noble man but made ignoble talk.
He makes no friend who never made a foe.
1859 *Idylls of the King*, 'Lancelot and Elaine', l.1081–2.

17 To reverence the King, as if he were
Their conscience, and their conscience as their
King,
To break the heathen and uphold the Christ,
To ride abroad redressing human wrongs,
To speak no slander, no, nor listen to it,

To honour his own words as if his God's.
1859 *Idylls of the King*, 'Guinevere', l.465–70.

18 To love one maiden only, cleave to her,
And worship her by years of noble deeds,
Until they won her; for indeed I knew
Of no more subtle master under heaven
Than is the maiden passion for a maid,
Not only to keep down the base in man,
But teach high thought, and aimable words
And courtliness, and the desire of fame,
And love of truth, and all that makes man.
1859 *Idylls of the King*, 'Guinevere', l.472–80.

19 I thought I could not breathe in that fine air
That pure severity of perfect light—
I yearned for warmth and colour which I found
In Lancelot.
1859 *Idylls of the King*, 'Guinevere', l.640–3.

20 It was my duty to have loved the highest;
It surely was my profit had I known:
It would have been my pleasure had I seen.
We needs must love the highest when we see it,
Not Lancelot, nor another.
1859 *Idylls of the King*, 'Guinevere', l.652–6.

21 The woods decay, the woods decay and fall,
The vapours weep their burthen to the ground,
Man comes and tills the field and lies beneath,
And after many a summer dies the swan.
Me only cruel immortality
Consumes: I wither slowly in thine arms,
Here at the quiet limit of the world.
1860 'Tithonus' (revised 1864), 1.1–7.

22 Why wilt thou ever scare me with thy tears,
And make me tremble lest a saying learnt,
In days far-off, on that dark earth, be true?
'The gods themselves cannot recall their gifts.'
1860 'Tithonus' (revised 1864), 1.46–9.

23 Of happy men that have the power to die,
And grassy barrows of the happier dead.
1860 'Tithonus' (revised 1864), 1.70–1.

24 O mighty-mouthed inventor of harmonies,
O skilled to sing of Time or Eternity,
God-gifted organ-voice of England,
Milton, a name to resound for ages.
1863 'Milton: Alcaics', l.1–4.

25 All that bowery loneliness,
The brooks of Eden mazily murmuring.
1863 'Milton: Alcaics', l.9–10.

26 O you chorus of indolent reviewers.
1863 'Milton: Hendecasyllabics', l.1.

27 And when they buried him the little port

Had seldom seen a costlier funeral.
1864 'Enoch Arden', closing words.

28 The voice of the dead was a living voice to me.
1864 'In the Valley of Cauteretz', l.10.

29 I saw the flaring atom-streams
And torrents of her myriad universe,
Ruining along the illimitable inane
Fly on to clash together again, and make
Another and another frame of things
For ever.
1868 'Lucretius', 1.38–40.

30 Nor at all can tell
Whether I mean this day to end myself,
Or lend an ear to Plato where he says,
That men like soldiers may not quit the post
Allotted by the Gods.
1868 'Lucretius', 1.145–9.

31 Passionless bride, divine Tranquillity,
Yearned after by the wisest of the wise,
Who fail to find thee, being as thou art
Without one pleasure and without one pain.
1868 'Lucretius', 1.265–8.

32 Speak to Him thou for He hears, and Spirit with
     Spirit can meet—
Closer is He than breathing, and nearer than hands
     and feet.
1869 'The Higher Pantheism', l.11–12.

33 Man's word is God in man.
1869 *Idylls of the King*, 'The Coming of Arthur', l.132.

34 Clothed in white samite, mystic, wonderful.
1869 *Idylls of the King*, 'The Coming of Arthur', l.284.

35 Rain, rain, and sun! a rainbow in the sky!
A young man will be wiser by and by;
An old man's wit may wander ere he die.
1869 *Idylls of the King*, 'The Coming of Arthur', l.402–4.

36 From the great deep to the great deep he goes.
1869 *Idylls of the King*, 'The Coming of Arthur', l.410.

37 Blow trumpet, for the world is white with May.
1869 *Idylls of the King*, 'The Coming of Arthur', l.481.

38 For good ye are and bad, and like to coins,
Some true, some light, but every one of you
Stamped with the image of the King.
1869 *Idylls of the King*, 'The Holy Grail', l.25–7.

39 I will be deafer than the blue-eyed cat,
And thrice as blind as any noonday owl,
To holy virgins in their ecstasies.
1869 *Idylls of the King*, 'The Holy Grail', l.862–4.

40 I found Him in the shining of the stars,

I marked Him in the flowering of His fields,
But in His ways with men I find Him not.
1869 *Idylls of the King*, 'The Passing of Arthur', l.9–11.

41 So all day long the noise of battle rolled
Among the mountains by the winter sea.
1869 *Idylls of the King*, 'The Passing of Arthur', l.170–1.

42 On one side lay the Ocean, and on one
Lay a great water, and the moon was full.
1869 *Idylls of the King*, 'The Passing of Arthur', l.179–80.

43 Authority forgets a dying king.
1869 *Idylls of the King*, 'The Passing of Arthur', l.289.

44 Clothed with his breath, and looking, as he walked,
Larger than human on the frozen hills.
He heard the deep behind him, and a cry
Before.
1869 *Idylls of the King*, 'The Passing of Arthur', l.350–3.

45 And the days darken round me, and the years,
Among new men, strange faces, other minds.
1869 *Idylls of the King*, 'The Passing of Arthur', l.405–6.

46 The old order changeth, yielding place to new,
And God fulfils himself in many ways,
Lest one good custom should corrupt the world.
1869 *Idylls of the King*, 'The Passing of Arthur', l.408–10.

47 If thou shouldst never see my face again,
Pray for my soul. More things are wrought by
prayer
Than this world dreams of. Wherefore, let thy
voice
Rise like a fountain for me night and day.
For what are men better than sheep or goats
That nourish a blind life within the brain,
If, knowing God, they lift not hands of prayer
Both for themselves and those who call them
friend?
For so the whole round earth is every way
Bound by gold chains about the feet of God.
1869 *Idylls of the King*, 'The Passing of Arthur', l.414–23.

48 I am going a long way
With these thou seëst—if indeed I go
(For all my mind is clouded with a doubt)—
To the island-valley of Avilion;
Where falls not hail, or rain, or any snow,
Nor ever wind blows loudly; but it lies
Deep-meadowed, happy, fair with orchard lawns
And bowery hollows crowed with summer sea,
Where I will heal me of my grievous wound.
1869 *Idylls of the King*, 'The Passing of Arthur', l.424–32.

49 Like some full-breasted swan
That, fluting a wild carol ere her death,
Ruffles her pure cold plume, and takes the flood
With swarthy webs.

1869 *Idylls of the King*, 'The Passing of Arthur', l.434–7.

50 But I knaw'd a Quaäker feller as often 'as towd ma
this:
'Doänt thou marry for munny, but goä wheer
munny is!'
1869 'Northern Farmer. New Style', stanza 5.

51 Taäke my word for it, Sammy, the poor in a loomp
is bad.
1869 'Northern Farmer. New Style', stanza 12.

52 The dirty nurse, Experience, in her kind
Hath fouled me.
1871 *Idylls of the King*, 'The Last Tournment', l.317–8.

53 The greater man, the greater courtesy.
1871 *Idylls of the King*, 'The Last Tournment', l.628.

54 Live pure, speak true, right wrong, follow the
King—
Else, wherefore born?
1872 *Idylls of the King*, 'Gareth and Lynette', l.117–8.

55 The city is built
To music, therefore never built at all,
And therefore built for ever.
1872 *Idylls of the King*, 'Gareth and Lynette', l.272–4.

56 At Flores in the Azores Sir Richard Grenville
lay,
And a pinnace, like a fluttered bird, came flying
from far away:
'Spanish ships of war at sea! We have sighted fifty-
three!'
Then sware Lord Thomas Howard: ''Fore God I
am no coward;
But I cannot meet them here, for my ships are out
of gear,
And the half my men are sick. I must fly, but follow
quick.
We are six ships of the line; can we fight with fifty-
three?'

Then spake Sir Richard Grenville: 'I know you are
no coward;
You fly them for a moment to fight with them
again.
But I've ninety men and more that are lying sick
ashore.
I should count myself the coward if I left them, my
Lord Howard,
To these Inquisition dogs and the devildoms of
Spain.'

So Lord Howard passed away with five ships of war
that day,
Till he melted like a cloud in the silent summer
heaven.
1878 'The Revenge', stanzas 1–3, l.1–14.

57 And Sir Richard said again: 'We be all good English men.
Let us bang these dogs of Seville, the children of the devil,
For I never turned my back upon Don or devil yet.'
1878 'The Revenge', stanza 4, l.29–31.

58 And the sun went down, and the stars came out far over the summer sea,
But never a moment ceased the fight of the one and the fifty-three.
1878 'The Revenge', stanza 9, l.56–7.

59 'Sink me the ship, Master Gunner—sink her, split her in twain!
Fall into the hands of God, not into the hands of Spain!'
And the gunner said 'Ay, ay,' but the seamen made reply:
'We have children we have wives,
And the Lord hath spared our lives.'
1878 'The Revenge', stanzas 11–12, l.89–93.

60 And they praised him to his face with their courtly foreign grace;
But he rose upon their decks, and he cried:
'I have fought for Queen and Faith like a valiant man and true;
I have only done my duty as a man is bound to do:
With a joyful spirit I Sir Richard Grenville die!'
And he fell upon their decks, and he died.
1878 'The Revenge', stanza 13, l.99–104.

61 And little Revenge herself went down by the island crags
To be lost evermore in the main.
1878 'The Revenge', stanza14, l.118–19.

62 That man's the true Conservative
Who lops the mouldered branch away.
1882 'Hands all Round', l.7–8.

63 Pray God our greatness may not fail
Through craven fears of being great.
1882 'Hands all Around', l.31–2.

64 For nothing worthy proving can be proven,
Nor yet disproven: wherefore thou be wise,
Cleave ever to the sunnier side of doubt.
1885 'The Ancient Sage', l.66–8.

65 France had shown a light to all men, preached a Gospel, all men's good;
Celtic Demos rose a Demon, shriek'd and slaked the light with blood.
1886 'Locksley Hall Sixty Years After', l.89–90.

66 Twilight and evening bell,
And after that the dark!
And may there be no sadness of farewell,

When I embark;
For though from out our bourne of Time and Place
The flood may bear me far,
I hope to see my Pilot face to face
When I have crossed the bar.
1889 'Crossing the Bar', l.9–16. This was Tennyson's last poem.

67 The mellow lin-lan-lone of evening bells.
1889 'Far-Far-Away', l.5.

68 Launch your vessel,
And crowd your canvas,
And, ere it vanishes
Over the margin,
After it, follow it,
Follow The Gleam.
1889 'Merlin and The Gleam', stanza 9, l.126–31.

69 What is it all but a trouble of ants in the gleam of a million million of suns?
1889 'Vastness', stanza 2, l.4.

70 A louse in the locks of literature.
Of Churton Collins. Quoted in Evan Charteris *Life and Letters of Sir Edmund Gosse* (1931), ch.14.

Tenzing Norgay known as *Sherpa Tenzing*
1914–86

Nepalese mountaineer. He took part in several Himalayan expeditions before accompanying Edmund Hillary to the summit of Everest in 1953. Subsequently he became head of the Institute of Mountaineering in Darjeeling and President of the Sherpa Association.

71 We done the bugger!
1953 On reaching the summit of Everest, 29 May.

Terence full name *Publius Terentius Afer*
185–159BC

Roman comic dramatist. A freed slave, his first success was *Andria* (The Andrian Girl, 166 BC). His six surviving comedies are Greek in origin and scene, and four are directly based on Menander. Many of his conventions were later used by European dramatists.

72 *Homo sum: nihil humani a me alienum puto.*
I am a man, I regard nothing that is human alien to me.
163 BC *Heauton timorumenos*, 77.

73 *Fortis fortuna adiuvat.*
Fortune favours the brave.
161 BC *Phormio*.

74 *Quot homines tot sententiae: suo quoique mos.*
There are as many opinions as there are people: each has his own view.
161 BC *Phormio*, 454.

76 *Nil est dictu facilius.*

> Nothing is easier to say.
> **161 BC** *Phormio*, 300.

Terentianus Maurus 2/3c BC

Latin grammarian from north Africa. He is remembered for his didactic poem *De litteris syllabis et metris*.

77 *Pro captu lectoris habent sua fata libelli.*

> Depending on the reception of the reader, books have their own fate.
> *De litteris syllabis et metris*, 1286. The phrase is often incorrectly attributed to Horace.

Tertullian full name *Quintus Septimius Florens Tertullianus* c.160–c.220 AD

Christian theologian, a lawyer in Rome until he converted in c.196, an opponent of worldliness in the Church and leader of the Montanist sect (c.207). His most famous work is *Apologeticus* (circa 197), an impassioned defence of Christianity against pagan charges of immorality, economic worthlessness, and political subversion.

78 *Plures efficimus quoties metimur a vobis, semen est sanguis Christianorum.*

> As often as we are mown down by you, the more we grow in numbers; the blood of the Christians is the seed.
> *Apologeticus*, ch.50, section 13. The phrase is often quoted as 'The blood of the martyrs is the seed of the church'.

79 *Certum est quia impossibile est.*

> It is certain because it is impossible.
> *De Carne Christi*, ch.5. The phrase is commonly rendered 'It is so extraordinary that it must be true.'

Tessimond, A(rthur) S(eymour) J(ohn)
1902–62

80 Cats, no less liquid than their shadows,
> Offer no angles to the wind.
> They slip, diminished, neat, through loopholes
> Less than themselves.
> 'Cats', pt.2.

Thackeray, William Makepeace
1811–63

English novelist. He earned his living from journalism, working for *Punch* from 1842–54. He provided a complex view of the changing nature of English society with its mingling of rich parvenus and decadent upper class. His best known novels include *Vanity Fair* (1847–48) and *Henry Esmond* (1852).

81 'A chilli,' said Rebecca, gasping, 'Oh, yes!' She thought a chilli was something cool, as its name imported, and was served with some. 'How fresh and green they look,' she said, and put one into her mouth. It was hotter than the curry; flesh and blood could bear it no longer. She laid down her fork. 'Water, for Heaven's sake, water!' she cried.
> **1847–8** *Vanity Fair*, ch.3

82 A woman with fair opportunities and without a positive hump, may marry whom she likes.
> **1847–8** Rebecca Sharp. *Vanity Fair*, ch.4.

83 Whenever he met a great man he grovelled before him, and my-lorded him as only a free-born Briton can do.
> **1847–8** Of Old Osbourne. *Vanity Fair*, ch.13.

84 If a man's character is to be abused, say what you will, there's nobody like a relation to do the business.
> **1847–8** Miss Crawley. *Vanity Fair*, ch.19.

85 Them's my sentiments!
> **1847–8** Fred Bullock. *Vanity Fair*, ch.21.

86 Darkness came down on the field and city: and Amelia was praying for George, who was lying on his face, dead, with a bullet through his heart.
> **1847–8** *Vanity Fair*, ch.32.

87 Nothing like blood, sir, in hosses, dawgs, and men.
> **1847–8** James Crawley. *Vanity Fair*, ch.35.

88 How to Live Well on Nothing a Year.
> **1847–8** *Vanity Fair*, ch.36, title of chapter.

89 I think I could be a good woman if I had five thousand a year.
> **1847–8** *Vanity Fair*, ch.36.

90 Ah! Vanitas Vanitatum! Which of us is happy in this world? Which of us has his desire? or, having it, is satisfied?—Come, children, let us shut up the box and the puppets, for our play is played out.
> **1847–8** Concluding words. *Vanity Fair*, ch.67.

91 He who meanly admires mean things is a Snob.
> **1848** *The Book of Snobs*, ch.2.

92 Yes, I am a fatal man, Madame Fribsbi. To inspire hopeless passion is my destiny.
> **1848–50** Mirobolant. *Pendennis*, ch.23.

93 Remember, it is as easy to marry a rich woman as a poor woman.
> **1848–50** *Pendennis*, ch.28.

94 The Pall Mall Gazette is written by gentlemen for gentlemen.
> **1848–50** *Pendennis*, ch.32.

95 For a slashing article, sir there's nobody like the Capting.
1848–50 Mr Bungay. *Pendennis*, ch.32.

96 'Tis not the dying for a faith that's so hard, Master Harry—every man of every nation has done that—'tis the living up to it that is difficult.
1852 *The History of Henry Esmond*, bk.1, ch.6.

97 'Tis strange what a man may do, and a woman yet think him an angel.
1852 *The History of Henry Esmond*, bk.1, ch.7.

98 What money is better bestowed than that of a school-boy's tip?
1853–5 *The Newcomes*, vol.1, ch.16.

99 He lifted up his head a little, and quickly said, 'Adsum!' and fell back… He, whose heart was as that of a little child, had answered to his name, and stood in the presence of The Master.
1853–5 *The Newcomes*, vol.1, ch.80.

1 Werther had a love for Charlotte
Such as words could never utter;
Would you know how first he met her?
She was cutting bread and butter.
1855 'Sorrows of Werther'.

2 Business first; pleasure afterwards
1855 *The Rose and the Ring*, ch.1.

Thatcher, Margaret Hilda Thatcher, Baroness 1925–

English Conservative politician and Prime Minister (1979–90). A research chemist, she entered Parliament (1959) and was Minister of Education (1970–4), becoming party leader in 1975. As premier she instituted privatization of nationalized industries and utilities. She resigned (Nov 1990) after a leadership challenge following controversy over economic union with Europe.

3 No woman in my time will be Prime Minister or Chancellor of the Exchequer or Foreign Secretary—not the top jobs. Anyway, I would not want to be Prime Minister; you have to give yourself 100 per cent.
1969 On her appointment as a junior Education Minister, in the *Sunday Telegraph*, 26 October.

4 I owe nothing to Women's Lib.
1974 Quoted in *The Observer*, 1 Dec.

5 In politics, if you want anything said, ask a man. If you want anything done, ask a woman.
1975 *People*, 15 Sep.

6 Let our children grow tall, and some taller than others if they have it in them to do so.
1975 Speech, Oct.

7 I stand before you tonight in my green chiffon evening gown, my face softly made up, my fair hair gently waved…the Iron Lady of the Western World? Me? A Cold War warrior? Well, yes—if that is how they wish to interpret my defence of values and freedoms fundamental to our way of life.
1976 Speech, Dorking, alluding to the title bestowed upon her by the Soviet defence journal, in *Red Star*, 31 Jan.

8 We want a society in which we are free to make choices, to make mistakes, to be generous and compassionate. That is what we mean by a moral society—not a society in which the State is responsible for everything, and no one is responsible for the State.
1977 Speech, Zurich University, 14 Mar.

9 Let us make this country safe to work in. Let us make this a country safe to walk in. Let us make it a country safe to grow up in. Let us make it a country safe to grow old in.
1979 General election party broadcast, 30 Apr.

10 Unless we change our ways and our direction, our greatness as a nation will soon be a footnote in the history books, a distant memory of an offshore island, lost in the mist of time like Camelot, remembered kindly for its noble past.
1979 General election campaign speech, Bolton, 2 May.

11 Where there is discord, may we bring harmony. Where there is error, may we bring truth. Where there is doubt, may we bring faith. Where there is despair, may we bring hope.
1979 Said on entering No.10 Downing Street for the first time as Prime Minister; 4 May; a misquotation of St Francis of Assisi.
▷ See St Francis 401:91.

12 Any woman who understands the problems of running a home will be nearer to understanding the problems of running a country.
1979 Interviewed by *The Observer* four days after becoming Britain's first woman Prime Minister, 8 May.

13 There is no easy popularity, in that I believe that people accept that there is no alternative.
1980 On her Government's stringent economic policies. Speech at the Conservative Women's Conference, 21 May.

14 Pennies do not come from heaven. They have to be earned here on earth.
1980 Quoted in the *Sunday Telegraph*.
▷ See Burke 208:50.

15 To those who wait with bated breath for that favourite media catchphrase, the U-turn, I have only this to say. You turn if you want to. The lady's not for turning.
1980 Address to the Conservative Party Conference.
▷ See Fry 408:14.

16 It is exciting to have a real crisis on your hands, when you have spent half your political life dealing with humdrum issues like the environment.

1982 Of the Falklands conflict. Speech to the Scottish Conservative Party Conference, 14 May.

17 This is the day that I was meant not to see.

1984 On attending church the Sunday after she had narrowly escaped being killed in the IRA bomb explosion at the Grand Hotel, Brighton, Oct.

18 I like Mr Gorbachev. We can do business together.

1984 Said on her first meeting with him, before he became premier, 17 Dec.

19 Democracies must try to find ways to starve the terrorist and the hijackers of the oxygen of publicity on which they depend.

1985 Speech to the American Bar Association meeting in London, referring in particular to increasing British press coverage of IRA terrorist activities, 15 Jul.

20 I always cheer up immensely if an attack is particularly wounding because…it means that they have not a single political argument left.

1986 In the *Daily Telegraph*, 21 Mar.

21 If you want to cut your own throat, don't come to me for a bandage.

1986 Comment to Robert Mugabe, Prime Minister of Zimbabwe, when he pressed for sanctions against South Africa. Quoted in *Time*, 7 Jul.

22 To wear your heart on your sleeve isn't a very good plan. You should wear it inside, where it functions best.

1987 Interview, ABC TV, 18 Mar.

23 There is no such thing as society. There are individual men and women, and there are families.

1987 In *Woman's Own*, 31 Oct.

24 I don't mind how much my Ministers talk—as long as they do what I say.

1987 In *The Times*.

25 If one leads a country such as Britain—a strong country that has taken a lead in world affairs in good times and bad, that is always reliable, then you must have a touch of iron about you.

1987 In *The Times*.

26 We have become a grandmother

1989 *The Times*, 4 Mar.

27 I seem to smell the stench of appeasement in the air.

1990 Describing the western attitude to the Gulf crisis. In the *Independent*, 31 Oct.

28 After three general election victories, leading the only party with clear policies, resolutely carried out, I intend to continue.

1990 On Michael Heseltine's challenge for the leadership of the Conservative Party, the *Sunday Times*, 18 Nov.

29 I shall fight. I will fight on.

1990 To reporters, on learning that she had not won the necessary majority to secure her re-election as party leader, two days before announcing her decision to step down, 21 Nov.

30 There is no way in which one can buck the market.

1990 Speech to the Commons on 10 Mar., before the Budget, complaining about what she called 'excessive' intervention in the exchange markets which would lead to inflation.

31 If you are guided by opinion polls, you are not practising leadership—you are practising followship.

1991 US TV interview, 5 Mar.

32 Is he one of us?

Attributed comment on considering a candidate for office in her new Government.

Theophilus c.10c

Greek writer and courtier. His *Diversarum Artium Schedula* was the most important art book of the Middle Ages, describing the methods of ecclesiastical art of his time.

33 All arts are taught by degrees. The first process in art of the painter is the composition of colours. Let your mind be afterwards applied to the study of the mixtures.

An Essay Upon Various Arts (trans by Robert Hendrie, 1847), bk.1, preface.

Theophrastus c.372–286 BC

Greek philosopher. A student of Aristotle, he succeeded him as head of the Lyceum from 322. Most of his prolific output is lost; among the writings that survive is a volume of *Characters*, containing 30 sketches of different moral types, which has been widely translated and imitated.

34 The sound of the flute will cure epilepsy and sciatic gout.

Quoted in David Pickering *Brewer's Twentieth Century Music* (1994).

Theresa (of Calcutta), Mother originally Agnes Gonxha Bojaxhiu 1910–97

Roman Catholic nun, born in Yugoslavia. She went to India in 1928 and in 1948 left a convent school to work in the slums. She founded the Missionaries of Charity sisterhood (1950) and a House for the Dying (1952), and in 1957 began work with lepers and in disaster areas of the world. She was awarded the Pope John XXIII Peace Prize in 1971, and the Nobel Peace Prize in 1979.

35 The biggest disease today is not leprosy or tuberculosis, but rather the feeling of being unwanted.

Quoted in *The Observer*, 3 Oct 1971.

36 To keep a lamp burning, we have to keep putting oil in it.
1975 In *Time*, 29 Dec.

37 There should be less talk; a preaching point is not a meeting point. What do you do then? Take a broom and clean someone's house. That says enough.
1975 *A Gift for God*, 'Carriers of Christ's Love'.

38 We need to find God, and he cannot be found in noise and restlessness. God is the friend of silence. See how nature—trees, flowers, grass—grows in silence; see the stars, the moon and the sun, how they move in silence… We need silence to be able to touch souls.
1975 *A Gift for God*, 'Willing Slaves to the Will of God'.

Theroux, Paul Edward 1941–

US novelist and travel writer. His best known novel is *The Mosquito Coast* (1982), but he is best known for his travel writings, notably those concerned with epic rail journeys.

39 Extensive travelling induces a feeling of encapsulation, and travel, so broadening at first, contracts the mind.
1975 *The Great Railway Bazaar*, ch.21.

40 The Japanese have perfected good manners and made them indistinguishable from rudeness.
1975 *The Great Railway Bazaar*, ch.28.

41 Nothing happens in Burma, but then nothing is expected to happen.
1975 *The Great Railway Bazaar*, ch.23.

42 I went to Vietnam to take the train: people have done stranger things in that country.
1975 *The Great Railway Bazaar*, ch.24.

43 Like a lower form of life, like the cross-eyed planarian or squashed amoeba, the sort of creature that can't die even when it is cut to pieces.
1975 Of Laos. *The Great Railway Bazaar*.

44 In Turkey it was always 1952, in Malaysia 1937; Afghanistan was 1910 and Bolivia 1949. It is twenty years ago in the Soviet Union, ten in Norway, five in France. It is always last year in Australia and next week in Japan.
1983 *The Kingdom By The Sea*, ch.1.

Thesiger, Sir Wilfred Patrick 1910–

English explorer. He twice crossed the Empty Quarter (Rub'al Khali) between 1946 and 1949 and wrote sensitively about the Bedu and their changing way of life.

45 For me, exploration was a personal venture. I did not go to the Arabian desert to collect plants nor to make a map; such things were incidental. At heart I knew that to write or even to talk of my travels was to tarnish the achievement. I went there to find peace in the hardship of desert travel and the company of desert people. I set myself a goal on these journeys, and, although the goal itself was unimportant, its attainment had to be worth every effort and sacrifice.
1959 *Arabian Sands*.

Thiers, (Louis) Adolphe 1797–1877

French statesman, twice Prime Minister (1836, 1839). He supported Napoleon in 1848, but was banished in the *coup d'état* of 1851 and re-entered the Chamber in 1863 as a critic. After the collapse of the Second Empire he suppressed the Paris Commune and became first President of the Third Republic (1871–3). Defeated by monarchists, he resigned in 1873. He wrote *L'histoire du consulat et de l'empire* (History of the Consulate and the Empire, 20 vols, 1845–62).

46 The Republic will be conservative, or it will be nothing.
1872 Presidential address to the French National Assembly, Nov.

Thomas, (Walter) Brandon 1857–1914

English playwright, actor and songwriter. He is usually remembered for his classic farce, *Charley's Aunt* (1892).

47 Where the nuts come from.
1892 Of Brazil. *Charley's Aunt*.

Thomas, D(onald) M(itchell) 1935–

English writer. He made his initial reputation as a poet, but became better known as the author of the novel *The White Hotel*.

48 Freud becomes one of the dramatis personae, in fact, as discoverer of the great and beautiful modern myth of psychoanalysis. By myth, I mean a poetic, dramatic expression of a hidden truth; and in placing this emphasis, I do not intend to put into question the scientific validity of psychoanalysis.
1981 *The White Hotel*, author's note.

49 She was cut off from the past and therefore did not live in the present. But suddenly, as she stood close against a pine tree and breathed in its sharp, bitter scent, a clear space opened to her childhood, as though a wind had sprung from the sea, clearing a mist. It was not a memory from the past, it was the past itself, as alive, as real; and she knew that she and the child of forty years ago were the same person.
1981 *The White Hotel*, ch.4.

50 The soul of man is a far country, which cannot be approached or explored. Most of the dead were poor and illiterate. But every single one of them had dreamed dreams, seen visions and had amazing experiences, even the babes in arms (perhaps especially the babes in arms).

1981 *The White Hotel*, ch.5.

Thomas, Dylan Marlais 1914–53

Welsh poet. The son of a schoolmaster, he worked as a journalist for a time. He also wrote short stories and novels, and later turned to drama, notably the celebrated radio play *Under Milk Wood* (published 1954). His tempestuous lifestyle culminated in his death from alcohol abuse on a lecture tour of the US.

51 The force that through the green fuse drives the flower
Drives my green age; that blasts the roots of trees
Is my destroyer.
And I am dumb to tell the crooked rose
My youth is bent by the same wintry fever.
1934 'The Force That Through the Green Fuse Drives the Flower'.

52 Light breaks where no sun shines;
Where no sea runs, the waters of the heart
Push in their tides.
1934 'Light Breaks Where No Sun Shines'.

53 Man be my metaphor.
1934 'If I Were Tickled by The Rub of Love'.

54 I am getting more obscure day by day.
1934 Letter to Pamela Hansford Johnson, 9 May.

55 Though they go mad they shall be sane
Though they sink through the sea they shall rise again;
Though lovers be lost love shall not;
And death shall have no dominion.
1936 'And Death Shall Have No Dominion'.

56 The hand that signed the paper felled a city;
Five sovereign fingers taxed the breath,
Doubled the globe of dead and halved a country;
These five kings did a king to death.
1936 'The Hand That Signed the Paper Felled a City'.

57 The hand that signed the treaty bred a fever,
And famine grew, and locusts came;
Great is the hand that holds dominion over
Man by a scribbled name.
1936 'The Hand That Signed the Paper Felled a City'.

58 What is the metre of the dictionary?
1936 'Altarwise by Owl-light'.

59 Shall gods be said to thump the clouds
When clouds are cursed by thunder?
1936 'Shall Gods be Said to Thump the Clouds'.

60 I hold a beast, an angel and a madman within me, and my enquiry is as to their working, and my

problem is their subjugation and victory, downthrow and upheaval, and my effort is their self expression.
1938 Letter to Henry Treece.

61 Her fist of a face died clenched on a round pain;
And sculptured Ann is seventy years of stone.
1939 'After the Funeral'.

62 I don't think it does any harm to the artist to be lonely as an artist.
1939 Letter to Pennar Davies.

63 Portrait of the Artist as a Young Dog.
1940 Title of book.

64 And the wild boys innocent as strawberries.
1946 'The Hunchback in the Park'.

65 Now as I was young and easy under the apple boughs
About the lilting house and happy as the grass was green.
1946 'Fern Hill'.

66 Oh as I was young and easy in the mercy of his means,
Time held me green and dying
Though I sang in my chains like the sea.
1946 'Fern Hill'.

67 After the first death, there is no other.
1946 'A Refusal to Mourn the Death, By Fire, of a Child in London'.

68 It was my thirtieth year to heaven
Woke to my hearing from harbour and neighbour wood
And the mussel pooled and the heron
Priested shore.
1946 'Poem in October'.

69 Pale rain over the dwindling harbour
And over the sea wet church the size of a snail
With its horns through mist and the castle
Brown as owls.
1946 'Poem in October'.

70 And I rose
In rainy autumn
And walked abroad in the shower of all my days.
1946 'Poem in October'.

71 I hear John Arlott's voice every weekend, describing cricket matches. He sounds like Uncle Tom Cobleigh reading Neville Cardus to the Indians.
1947 Letter to Margaret Taylor, 11 Jul.

72 The joy and function of poetry is, and was, the celebration of man, which is also the celebration of God.
1951 Letter to a student.

73 If you want a definition of poetry, say: 'Poetry is what makes me laugh or cry or yawn, what makes my toenails twinkle, what makes me want to do this or that or nothing' and let it go at that.
1951 Letter to a student.

74 I fell in love—that is the only expression I can think of—at once, and am still at the mercy of words, though sometimes now, knowing a little of their behaviour very well, I think I can influence them slightly and have even learned to beat them now and gain, which they appear to enjoy.
1951 Letter to a student.

75 Do not go gentle into that good night,
Old age should burn and rave at close of day;
Rage, rage against the dying of the light.
1952 'Do Not Go Gentle Into That Good Night'.

76 These poems, with all their crudities, doubts, and confusions, are written for the love of Man, and in praise of God, and I'd be a damn' fool if they weren't.
1952 *Collected Poems*, author's note.

77 The land of my fathers. My fathers can have it.
1953 Of Wales. In *Adam*, Dec.

78 I've had eighteen straight whiskies. I think that's the record.
1953 Attributed, supposedly said before lapsing into his final coma.

79 To begin at the beginning: It is spring, moonless night in the small town, starless and bible-black, the cobblestreets silent and the hunched, courters'-and-rabbits' wood limping invisible down to the sloeblack, slow, black, crowblack, fishingboat-bobbing sea.
1954 *Under Milk Wood*, opening words.

80 Oh I'm a martyr to music.
1954 *Under Milk Wood.*

81 The boys are dreaming wicked or of the bucking ranches of the night and the jolly-rogered sea.
1954 *Under Milk Wood.*

82 And before you let the sun in, mind it wipes its shoes.
1954 *Under Milk Wood.*

83 Alone until she dies, Bessie Bighead, hired help, born in the workhouse, smelling of the cowshed, snores bass and gruff on a couch of straw in a loft in Salt Lake Farm and picks a posy of daisies in Sunday Meadow to put on the grave of Gomer Owen who kissed her once by the pig-sty when she wasn't looking and never kissed her again although she was looking all the time.
1954 *Under Milk Wood.*

84 Straightfaced in his cunning sleep he pulls the legs of his dreams.
1954 *Under Milk Wood.*

85 Nothing grows in our garden, only washing. And babies. And where's their fathers live, my love? Over the hills and far away.
1954 *Under Milk Wood.*

86 You're thinking, you're no better than you should be, Polly, and that's good enough for me. Oh, isn't life a terrible thing, thank God?
1954 *Under Milk Wood.*

87 Hullo, Polly, my love, can you hear the dumb goose-hiss of the wives as they huddle and peck or flounce at a waddle away? Who cuddled you when? Which of their gandering hubbies moaned in Milk Wood for your naughty mothering arms and body like a wardrobe, love?
1954 *Under Milk Wood.*

88 The sun hums down through the cotton flowers of her dress into the bell of her heart and buzzes in the honey there and couches and kisses, lazy-loving and boozed, in her red-berried breast.
1954 *Under Milk Wood.*

89 Alone in the hissing laboratory of his wishes, Mr Pugh minces among bad vats and jeroboams, tiptoes through spinneys of murdering herbs, agony dancing in his crucibles, and mixes especially for Mrs Pugh a venomous porridge unknown to toxicologists which will scald and viper through her until her ears fall off like figs, her toes grow big and black as balloons, and steam comes screaming out of her navel.
1954 *Under Milk Wood.*

90 You just wait. I'll sin until I blow up!
1954 *Under Milk Wood.*

91 Too many of the artists of Wales spend too much time talking about the position of the artists of Wales. There is only one position for an artist anywhere: and that is, upright.
1954 *Quite Early One Morning*, 'Wales and the Artist'.

92 The best poem is that whose worked-upon unmagical passages come closest, in texture and intensity, to those moments of magical accident.
1954 *Quite Early One Morning*, 'On Poetry'.

93 A good poem is a contribution to reality. The world is never the same once a good poem has been added to it.
1954 *Quite Early One Morning*, 'On Poetry'.

94 One Christmas was much like another… I can never remember whether it snowed for six days and

six nights when I was twelve or whether it snowed for twelve days and twelve nights when I was six.
1954 *A Child's Christmas in Wales.*

95 Years and years ago, when I was a boy, when there were wolves in Wales, and birds the colour of red-flannel petticoats whisked past the harp-shaped hills, when we sang and wallowed all night and day in caves that smelt like Sunday afternoons in damp front farmhouse parlours, and we chased, with the jawbones of deacons, the English and the bears, before the motor car, before the wheel, before the duchess-faced horse, when we rode the daft and happy hills bareback, it snowed and it snowed.
1954 *A Child's Christmas in Wales.*

Thomas, (Philip) Edward 1878–1917

English nature writer and poet. His poetry was all written during World War I, in which he was killed in action at Arras. Very few poems were published in his lifetime, but posthumous collections established his reputation as a great nature poet.

96 A merely great intellect can produce great prose, but not poetry, not one line.
1908 Letter to Gordon Bottomley, 26 Feb.

97 When Gods were young
This wind was old.
1914 'The Mountain Chapel'.

98 The Past is a strange land, most strange.
1915 'Parting'.

99 Yes; I remember Adlestrop—
The name, because one afternoon
Of heat the express-train drew up there
Unwontedly. It was late June.
1915 'Adlestrop'.

1 And for that minute a blackbird sang
Close by, and round him, mistier,
Farther and farther, all the birds
Of Oxfordshire and Gloucestershire.
1915 'Adlestrop'.

2 The men, the music piercing that solitude
And silence, told me truths I had not dreamed,
And have forgotten since their beauty passed.
1915 'Tears'.

3 The last light has gone out of the world, except
This moonlight lying on the grass like frost
Beyond the brink of the tall elm's shadow.
1915 'Liberty'.

4 This is no case of petty right or wrong
That politicians or philosophers
Can judge. I hate not Germans, nor grow hot
With love of Englishmen, to please newspapers.
1915 'This Is No Case of Petty Right Or Wrong'.

5 The dark-lit stream has drowned the Future and the Past.
1915 'The Bridge'.

6 The new moon hangs like an ivory bugle
In the naked frosty blue.
1915 'The Penny Whistle'.

7 It is a fine world and I wish I knew how to make £200 a year in it.
1915 Letter to Gordon Bottomley, 16 Jun.

8 The past is the only dead thing that smells sweet,
The only sweet thing that is not also fleet.
1916 'Early One Morning'.

9 For the life in them he loved most living things,
But a tree chiefly.
1916 'Bob's Lane'.

10 That girl's clear eyes utterly concealed all
Except that there was something to reveal.
1916 'That Girl's Clear Eyes'.

11 I have come to the borders of sleep,
The unfathomable deep
Forest, where all must lose
Their way, however straight
Or winding, soon or late;
They cannot choose.
1916 'Lights Out'.

12 As well as any bloom upon a flower
I like the dust on the nettles, never lost
Except to prove the sweetness of a shower.
1916 'Tall Nettles'.

13 Now all the roads lead to France
And heavy is the tread
Of the living: but the dead
Returning lightly dance.
1916 'Roads'.

14 Out in the dark over the snow
The fallow fawns invisible go
With the fallow doe;
And the winds blow
Fast as the stars are slow.
1916 'Out in the Dark'.

15 The sorrow of true love is a great sorrow
And true love parting blackens a bright morrow.
1917 'Last Poem'.

Thomas, Sir George 1881–1972

English badminton administrator, founder and first president of the International Badminton Federation.

16 The art of badminton is to deceive.
Quoted in *The Guinness Book of Badminton* (1983).

Thomas, John Parnell 1895–1970

US congressman. He was an insurance broker before
entering Congress (1937–49). He served as Chairman of
the Committee on Un-American Activities.

17 Are you now, or have you ever been, a member of
the Communist Party?

1947–57 Stock question to those called before the House of
Representatives Committee on Un-American Activities.

Thomas, Michael M

US novelist.

18 Bankers' genes were Wall St. genes, especially in the
big cities. If the banks were conservative just now
[1955], it was because bankers still awoke in the
middle of the night, trembling and sweaty with
thoughts of the Crash. But in time a new
generation would take over: ambitious,
overcompetitive young men to whom 1929 would
be merely a date on a page; such men would sever
the roots of memory as if with an ax, not realizing
that those tendrils were also the rudder cables.

1987 *The Ropespinner Conspiracy.*

Thomas, R(onald) S(tuart) 1913–

Welsh poet. He is a priest, and his poetry characteristically
deals with the themes of nature, religion and his love of
Wales.

19 We were a people taut for war; the hills
Were no harder, the thin grass
Clothed them more warmly than the coarse
Shirts our small bones.

1952 'Welsh History'.

20 An impotent people,
Sick with inbreeding.
Worrying the carcase of an old song.

1952 'Welsh Landscape'.

21 We will listen to the wind's text
Blown through the roof, or the thrush's song
In the thick bush that proved him wrong,
Wrong from the start, for nature's truth
Is primary and her changing seasons
Correct out of a vaster reason
The vague errors of the flesh.

1953 'The Minister'.

22 For the first twenty years you are still growing,
Bodily that is; as a poet, of course,
You are not born yet. It's the next ten
You cut your teeth on to emerge smirking
For your brash courtship of the muse.

1963 'To A Young Poet'.

23 Prompt me, God,
But not yet. When I speak

Though it be you who speak
Through me, something is lost.
The meaning is the waiting.

1968 'Kneeling'.

24 The poem in the rock and
The poem in the mind
Are not one.
It was in dying
I tried to make them so.

1972 'The Epitaph'.

25 Among the forests
Of metal the one human
Sound was the lament of
The poets for deciduous language.

1972 'Postscript'.

26 Life is not hurrying
on to a receding future, nor hankering after
an imagined past. It is the turning
aside like Moses to the miracle
of the lit bush, to a brightness
that seemed as transitory as your youth
once, but is the eternity that awaits you.

1976 *Laboratories of the Spirit*, 'The Bright Field'.

27 We are beginning to see
now it is matter is the scaffolding
of spirit; that the poet emerges
from morphemes and phonemes; that
as form in sculpture is the prisoner
of the hard rock, so in everyday life
it is the plain facts and natural happenings
that conceal God and reveal him to us
little by little under the mind's tooling.

1978 *Frequencies*, 'Emerging'.

Thompson, Francis 1859–1907

English poet. His poems, mainly religious in theme and
collected in such publications as *Poems* (1893) and *Sister
Songs* (1895), include the well-known 'Hound of
Heaven'.

28 I fled Him, down the nights and down the days;
I fled Him, down the arches of the years;
I fled Him, down the labyrinthine ways
Of my own mind; and in the midst of tears
I hid from Him, and under running laughter.

1893 *Poems*, 'The Hounds of Heaven'.

29 I said to Dawn: Be sudden—to Eve: Be soon.

1893 *Poems*, 'The Hounds of Heaven'.

30 O world invisible, we view thee,
O world intangible, we touch thee,
O world unknowable, we know thee,
Inapprehensible, we clutch thee!

1897 'In No Strange Land'.

31 The fairest things have fleetest end,
Their scent survives their close:
But the rose's scent is bitterness
To him that loved the rose.
'Daisy' (published 1890).

32 It is little I repair to the matches of the Southron
folk,
Though my own red roses there may blow;
It is little I repair to the matches of the Southron
folk,
Though the red roses crest the caps, I know.
For the field is full of shades as I near the shadowy
coast,
And a ghostly batsman plays to the bowling of a
ghost,
And I look through my tears on a soundless-
clapping host
As the run-stealers flicker to and fro,
To and fro:—
O my Hornby and my Barlow long ago!
1907 'At Lord's', poem dedicated to friends to explain why he
could not attend a match at Lord's at their invitation for fear of
the sadness it would cause him, remembering the long-dead
friends who had played there (for Lancashire) back in 1878.

33 There is no expeditious road
To pack and label men for God,
And save them by the barrel-load,
Some may perchance, with strange surprise,
Have blundered into Paradise.
1913 'A Judgment in Heaven', epilogue.

34 Wake! for the Ruddy Ball has taken flight
That scatters the slow Wicket of the Night;
And the swift Batsman of the Dawn has driven
Against the Star-spiked Rails a fiery smite.
'Wake! for the Ruddy Ball has Taken Flight', parody of Edward
Fitzgerald, quoted in J C Squire *Apes and Parrots* (1929).
▷ See Fitzgerald 390:87.

Thompson, Hunter S(tockton) 1939–

US writer, inventor of a semi-fictionalized participatory
journalism he dubbed 'gonzo'. His work for *Rolling Stone*
magazine made him a cult figure. He sometimes writes as
'Raoul Duke'.

35 Weird heroes and mould-breaking champions exist
as living proof to those who need it that the
tyranny of 'the rat race' is not yet final.
1969 'Those Daring Young Men In Their Flying Machines…
Ain't What They Used To Be!', in *Pageant*, Sep.

36 History is hard to know…but…it seems entirely
reasonable to think that every now and then the
energy of a whole generation comes to a head in a
long fine flash, for reasons that nobody really
understands at the time—and which never explain,
in retrospect, what actually happened.

1971 *Fear and Loathing in Las Vegas*, ch.8.

37 Absolute truth is a very rare and dangerous
commodity in the context of professional journalism.
1973 'Fear and Loathing at the Superbowl', in *Rolling Stone*, 15
Feb.

38 In a nation ruled by swine, all pigs are upwardly-
mobile—and the rest of us are fucked until we can
put our acts together: not necessarily to win, but
mainly to keep from losing completely. We owe
that to ourselves and our crippled self-image as
something better than a nation of panicked sheep.
1979 *The Great Shark Hunt*, 'Jacket Copy for *Fear and
Loathing in Las Vegas*'.

39 Going to trial with a lawyer who considers your
whole life-style a Crime in Progress is not a happy
prospect.
1990 Letter to *The Champion*, a legal journal, Jul.

Thompson, James E

Governor of Illinois.

40 It is not so much who you elect, it's who you throw
out.
1981 On the campaign to clean up government. In the *Chicago
Tribune*, 26 Jul.

Thompson, Robert 1914–

Candian politician, leader of the Social Credit Party of
Canada (1961–7) and renowned malapropist.

41 The Americans are our best friends, whether we
like it or not.
Oft-quoted remark recalled by Peter C Newman in *Home
Country* (1973).

Thompson, Tommy 1906–

Candian public official, Parks Commissioner, Metropolitan Toronto.

42 Please Walk on the Grass
1960 Message on a sign erected in Toronto's Edwards Gardens,
which attracted national and then international attention for its
'hands-on' approach to public parks.

Thomson, David 1914–88

Scottish writer. His books are *Woodbrook* and *Nairn in
Darkness and Light*.

43 The vice of meanness, condemned in every other
country, is in Scotland translated into a virtue
called 'thrift'.
1987 *Nairn in Darkness and Light*.

44 Even stroking a cat may be regarded by strict
Presbyterians as a carnal sin.
1987 *Nairn in Darkness and Light*.

Thompson, E P 1924–93

British historian.

45 This going into Europe will not turn out to be the thrilling mutual exchange supposed. It is more like nine middle-aged couples with failing marriages meeting in a darkened bedroom in a Brussels hotel for a group grope.
1975 On Britain's entry into the EEC, *The Sunday Times*, 27 Apr.

Thomson, James 1700–48

Scottish poet. He studied for the ministry but moved to London to become a writer. His chief works were *The Castle of Indolence* and *The Seasons*, an early nature poem extensively revised 1730–46.

46 When Britain first, at heaven's command,
Arose from out the azure main,
This was the charter of the land,
And guardian angels sung this strain:
'Rule, Britannia, rule the waves;
Britons never will be slaves.'
1740 *Alfred: a Masque*, act 2, sc.5.

47 Delightful task! to rear the tender thought,
To teach the young idea how to shoot.
1746 *The Seasons*, 'Spring', l.1152–3.

48 An elegant sufficiency, content,
Retirement, rural quiet, friendship, books,
Ease and alternate labour, useful life,
Progressive virtue, and approving Heaven!
1746 *The Seasons*, 'Spring', l.1161–4.

49 Or sighed and looked unutterable things.
1746 *The Seasons*, 'Summer', l.188.

50 Poor is the triumph o'er the timid hare!
1746 *The Seasons*, 'Autumn', l.401.

51 Welcome, kindred glooms!
Congenial horrors, hail!
1746 *The Seasons*, 'Winter', l.5–6.

52 There studious let me sit,
And hold high converse with the mighty dead.
1746 *The Seasons*, 'Winter', l.431–2.

53 A little round, fat, oily man of God,
Was one I chiefly marked among the fry:
He had a roguish twinkle in his eye.
1748 *The Castle of Indolence*, canto 1, stanza 69.

Thomson, James pseudonym "BV', Bysshe Vanolis 1834–82

Scottish poet born in Port Glasgow. He trained as an army schoolmaster but was dismissed from army service in 1862 for alcoholism. He worked in London as a poet, journalist and critic, and published his greatest work *The City of Dreadful Night* in 1874.

54 As we rush, as we rush in the train,
The trees and the houses go wheeling back,
But the starry heavens above that plain
Come flying on our track.
1863–5 'Sunday at Hampstead', stanza 10.

55 The City is of Night, but not of Sleep;
There sweet Sleep is not for the weary brain;
The pitiless hours like years and ages creep,
A night seems termless hell.
1874 *The City of Dreadful Night*, pt.1.

56 The City is of Night; perchance of Death,
But certainly of Night.
1874 *The City of Dreadful Night*, pt.1.

57 As I came through the desert thus it was,
As I came through the desert: All was black,
In heaven no single star, on earth no track;
A brooding hush without a stir or note;
The air so thick it clotted in my throat.
1874 *The City of Dreadful Night*, pt.4.

58 Yet I strode on austere;
No hope could have no fear.
1874 *The City of Dreadful Night*, pt.4.

Thomson, Roy Herbert, 1st Baron Thomson of Fleet 1894–1976

Canadian-born British newspaper and television magnate. After setting up his first radio station in 1931 and buying many Canadian and US newspapers, he settled in Edinburgh on acquiring the *Scotsman* (1952), and bought the Kemsley newspapers (1959) and *The Times* (1966).

59 A TV licence is a licence to print money.
1957 On being awarded the licence to operate Scottish Television Ltd, 19 Jun, recalled in his memoirs *After I Was Sixty* (1975).

Thomson, Virgil 1896–1989

US composer and critic. His work, notable for its simplicity of style, includes operas, *Four Saints in Three Acts* (1934) and *The Mother of Us All* (1947), besides symphonies, ballets, choral, chamber and film music. He was music critic of the *New York Herald* (1940–54).

60 A libretto that should never have been accepted on a subject that should never have been chosen by a man who should never have attempted it.
1935 Of Gershwin's *Porgy and Bess*. *Modern Music*.

61 The way to write American music is simple. All you have to do is be an American and then write any kind of music you wish.
Quoted in Machlis *Introduction to Contemporary Music* (1963).

Thoreau, Henry David 1817–62

US essayist and poet, known as 'the hermit of Walden'. In 1839 he began his nature studies, and lived as a hermit (1845–7). His works include *Walden, or Life in the Woods* (1854) and his nature observations, beginning *Early Spring in Massachusetts* (1881). His essay *Civil Disobedience* (1849) was provoked by his opposition to the Mexican war.

62 We seem but to linger in manhood to tell the dreams of our childhood, and they vanish out of memory ere we learn the language.
1841 Journal entry, 19 Feb.

63 Being is the great explainer.
1841 Journal entry, 26 Feb.

64 Men reverence one another, not yet God.
1849 *A Week on the Concord and Merrimack Rivers*, 'Sunday'.

65 Under a government which imprisons any unjustly, the true place for a just man is also a prison.
1849 *Civil Disobedience*.

66 Read the best books first, or you may not have a chance to read them at all.
1849 *A Week on the Concord and Merrimack Rivers*, 'Sunday'.

67 The lawyer's truth is not Truth, but consistency or a consistent expediency.
1849 *Civil Disobedience*.

68 It takes two to speak the truth,—one to speak, and another to hear.
1849 *A Week on the Concord and Merrimack Rivers*, 'Wednesday'.

69 A truly good book is something as wildly natural and primitive, mysterious and marvelous, ambrosial and fertile, as a fungus or a lichen.
1850 Journal entry, 16 Nov. In Bradford Torrey and F H Allen (eds) *The Journals of Henry David Thoreau* (1906).

70 Some circumstantial evidence is very strong, as when you find a trout in the milk.
1850 Journal entry, 11 Nov.

71 How many a man has dated a new era in his life from the reading of a book!... The at present unutterable things we may find somewhere uttered.
1854 *Walden, or Life in the Woods*, 'Reading'.

72 If we knew all the laws of Nature, we should need only one fact, or the description of one actual phenomenon, to infer all the particular results at that point. Now we know only a few laws, and our result is vitiated, not, of course, by any confusion or irregularity in Nature, but by our ignorance of essential elements in the calculation. Our notions of law and harmony are commonly confined to those instances which we detect; but the harmony which results from a far greater number of seemingly conflicting, but really concurring, laws,

which we have not detected, is still more wonderful. The particular laws are as our points of view, as, to the traveler, a mountain outline varies with every step, and it has an infinite number of profiles, though absolutely but one form. Even when cleft or bored through it is not comprehended in its entirety.
1854 *Walden, or Life in the Woods*, 'The Pond in Winter'.

73 Every man is the builder of a temple, called his body, to the god he worships, after a style purely his own, nor can he get off by hammering marble instead. We are all sculptors and painters, and our material is our own flesh and blood and bones.
1854 *Walden, or Life in the Woods*, 'Higher Laws'.

74 It is a part of the destiny of the human race, in its gradual improvement, to leave off eating animals, as surely as the savage tribes have left off eating each other when they come in contact with the more civilized.
1854 *Walden, or Life in the Woods*, 'Higher Laws'.

75 We can never have enough of nature.... We need to witness our own limits transgressed, and some life pasturing freely where we never wander.
1854 *Walden, or Life in the Woods*, 'Spring'.

76 There is no odor so bad as that which arises from goodness tainted.
1854 *Walden, or Life in the Woods*, 'Economy'.

77 The mass of men lead lives of quiet desperation.
1854 *Walden, or Life in the Woods*, 'Economy'.

78 Our inventions are wont to be pretty toys, which distract our attention from serious things. They are but improved means to an unimproved end.
1854 *Walden, or Life in the Woods*, 'Economy'.

79 Men have become the tools of their tools.
1854 *Walden, or Life in the Woods*, 'Economy'.

80 I have yet to hear the first syllable of valuable or even earnest advice from my seniors.
1854 *Walden, or, Life in the Woods*, 'Economy'.

81 As for Doing-good, that is one of the professions which are full.
1854 *Walden, or Life in the Woods*, 'Economy'.

82 I say, beware of all enterprises that require new clothes, and not rather a new wearer of clothes.
1854 *Walden, or Life in the Woods*, 'Economy'.

83 Every generation laughs at the old fashions, but follows religiously the new.
1854 *Walden, or Life in the Woods*, 'Economy'.

84 As long as possible live free and uncommitted. It makes but little difference whether you are committed to a farm or the county jail.

1854 *Walden, or Life in the Woods*, 'Where I Lived, and What I Lived For'.

85 I went to the woods because I wished to live deliberately, to front only the essential facts of life, and see if I could not learn what it had to teach, and not, when I came to die, discover that I had not lived.

1854 *Walden, or Life in the Woods*, 'Where I Lived, and What I Lived For'.

86 Our life is frittered away by detail.

1854 *Walden, or Life in the Woods*, 'Where I Lived, and What I Lived For'.

87 We do not ride on the railroad; it rides upon us.

1854 *Walden, or Life in the Woods*, 'Where I Lived and What I Lived For'.

88 Will you be a reader, a student merely, or a seer? Read your fate, see what is before you, and walk on into futurity.

1854 *Walden, or Life in the Woods*, 'Sounds'.

89 I never found the companion that was so companionable as solitude.

1854 *Walden, or Life in the Woods*, 'Solitude'.

90 I was determined to know beans.

1854 *Walden, or Life in the Woods*, 'The Bean-Field'.

91 If a man does not keep pace with his companions, perhaps it is because he hears a different drummer.

1854 *Walden, or Life in the Woods*, 'Conclusion'.

92 Why level downward to our dullest perception always, and praise that as common sense?

1854 *Walden, or Life in the Woods*, 'Conclusion'

93 As for style of writing—if one has anything to say, it drops from him simply and directly, as a stone falls to the ground.

1857 Letter to Daniel Ricketson, 18 Aug.

94 I fear that I have not got much to say about Canada, not having seen much; what I got by going to Canada was a cold.

1866 *A Yankee in Canada.*

95 A gun gives you the body, not the bird.

Quoted in Colin Jarman *The Guinness Dictionary of Sports Quotations* (1990).

Thorndike, Dame (Agnes) Sybil 1882–1976

English actress. She made her stage début in 1904 and went on to distinguish herself in both modern and classical tragedies. Her most famous roles included Medea, George Bernard Shaw's St Joan and Shakespeare's Volumnia. She was married to the actor and director Sir Lewis Casson.

96 You're never too old to play Saint Joan; you're only too young.

Quoted in *Julie Harris Talks to Young Actors.*

Thorne, James 1815–81

English antiquary. He contributed topographical articles to many publications and spent many years researching material for his *Handbook to the Environs of London* (1876), in which he combines factual knowledge with entertaining passages on places and personalities of local interest.

97 An unenviable reputation for dirt and ill odours.

1876 Of Brentford, Middlesex, now in Greater London. *Handbook to the Environs of London.*

98 A town of narrow streets, old houses, shops curiously low, with little in it to interest any one.

1876 Of Hatfield, Hertfordshire. *Handbook to the Environs of London.*

99 A waste of modern tenements, mean, monotonous, and wearisome.

1876 On Penge, Surrey, now in Greater London. *Handbook to the Environs of London.*

1 A populous railway town of hideous brick shops and habitations.

1876 Of Redhill, Surrey. *Handbook to the Environs of London.*

2 Twickenham is one of those happy places which is not burdened with a history.

1876 *Handbook to the Environs of London.*

Thorneycroft, Lord (George Edward) Peter 1909–94

English politician. He entered the House of Commons in 1938, and was President of the Board of Trade (1951–7). Appointed Chancellor of the Exchequer in 1957, he resigned a year later, in disagreement with the government's financial policy, and lost his seat in 1966. He was created a life peer in 1967, and was Chairman of the Conservative Party (1975–81).

3 The choice in politics isn't usually between black and white. It is between two horrible shades of grey.

1979 *The Sunday Telegraph*, 11 Feb.

4 Some men go through life absolutely miserable because, despite the most enormous achievements, they just didn't do one thing—like the architect who didn't build St Paul's. I didn't quite build St Paul's, but I stood on more mountain tops than possibly I deserved.

1979 *The Sunday Telegraph*, 11 Feb.

Thornton, Sir Henry 1871–1933

Candian pioneer of public broadcasting.

5 It is essential that broadcasting be surrounded with such safeguards as will prevent the air becoming what might be described as an atmospheric billboard.

1926 Address to the Advertising Clubs of the World, Philadelphia, 21 Jun. Quoted in E Austin Weir *The Struggle for National Broadcasting in Canada* (1965).

Thorpe, (John) Jeremy 1929–

English politician. Leader of the Liberal Party from 1967, he resigned in 1976 following allegations concerning a previous homosexual relationship with a Mr Norman Scott and was later acquitted of charges of conspiracy and incitement to murder Mr Scott.

6 Greater love hath no man than this, that he lay down his friends for his life.

1962 On Harold Macmillan's sacking of several Cabinet members, House of Commons.

7 Looking around the House, one realizes that we are all minorities now.

1974 On the absence of a clear party majority, House of Commons, 6 Mar.

▷ See Shawcross 926:46.

Thrasymachus 5c BC

Greek sophist and rhetorician from Chalcedon in Bithynia, he figures in Plato's *Republic* defending the proposition that might is right.

8 Morality is nothing other than the advantage of the stronger party.

Quoted in Plato *Republic*, 338b (translated by Robin Waterfield, 1993).

Thubron, Colin Gerald Dryden 1939–

English writer, film-maker and novelist. He travelled through western Russia alone by car in the early 1980s and a few years later made a difficult trip through China. He also wrote a number of books on the Middle East.

9 Around me, around them [the dissidents], the total, all-eclipsing Soviet world, which renders any other world powerless and far away, had become profoundly, morally hostile.

1983 *Among the Russians* (published in the US as *Where the Nights are Longest*).

Thucydides c.460–c.400 BC

Athenian politician and historian. As a naval commander in the Peloponnesian war he failed to relieve the Amphipolis in 424, and was exiled from Athens. He began a *History of the Peloponnesian War*, but died before its completion.

10 *Ktema es aei.*

A possession intended to last for ever.

Of his *History of the Peloponnesian War*, 1.22.4.

Thurber, James Grover 1894–1961

US humorist and cartoonist. In 1927 he was appointed managing editor of the *New Yorker* where he published many sketches and cartoons. Collections of his work include *Men Women and Dogs* (1943). His best known short story is *The Secret Life of Walter Mitty* which was later filmed (1946).

11 It takes that *je ne sais quoi* which we call sophistication for a woman to be magnificent in a drawing-room when her faculties have departed but she herself has not yet gone home.

1930 In the *New Yorker*, 2 Aug.

12 All right, have it your own way—you heard a seal bark!

1932 Cartoon caption, in the *New Yorker*, 30 Jan.

13 That's my first wife up there and this is the *present* Mrs Harris.

1933 Cartoon caption, in the *New Yorker*, 16 Mar.

14 I myself have accomplished nothing of excellence except a remarkable and, to some of my friends, unaccountable expertness in hitting empty ginger ale bottles with small rocks at a distance of thirty paces.

1933 *My Life and Hard Times*, preface.

15 They lead, as a matter of fact, an existence of jumpiness and apprehension. They sit on the edge of the chair of Literature. In the house of Life they have the feeling that they have never taken off their overcoats.

1933 On humorists. *My Life and Hard Times*, preface.

16 I suppose that the high-water mark of my youth in Colombus, Ohio, was the night the bed fell on my father.

1933 *My Life and Hard Times*, ch.1.

17 It is better to have loafed and lost than never to have loafed at all.

1939 *Fables of Our Time*, 'The Courtship of Arthur and Al'.

18 Her own mother lived the latter years of her life in the horrible suspicion that electricity was dripping invisibly all over the house.

1933 *My Life and Hard Times*, ch.2.

19 The war between men and women.

1934 Title of series of cartoons in the *New Yorker*, 20 Jan–28 Apr.

20 The Middle-Aged Man on the Flying Trapeze.

1935 Title of book.

21 It's a naïve domestic Burgundy without any breeding, but I think you'll be amused by its presumption.

1937 Cartoon caption, in the *New Yorker*, 27 Mar.

22 Well, if I called the wrong number, why did you answer the phone?

1937 Cartoon caption, in the *New Yorker*, 5 Jun.

23 There is no safety in numbers, or in anything else.

1939 'The Fairly Intelligent Fly', in the *New Yorker*, 4 Feb.

24 Early to rise and early to bed makes a male healthy and wealthy and dead.

1939 'The Shrike and the Chipmunks', in *The New Yorker*, 18 Feb.

25 It's our *own* story *exactly*! He bold as a hawk, she soft as the dawn.

1939 Cartoon caption, in the *New Yorker*, 28 Feb.

26 Then, with that faint fleeting smile playing about his lips, he faced the firing squad; erect and motionless, proud and disdainful, Walter Mitty, the undefeated, inscrutable to the last.
1939 'The Secret Life of Walter Mitty', in the *New Yorker*, 18 Mar.

27 You might as well fall flat on your face as lean over too far backward.
1939 'The Bear Who Let It Alone', in the *New Yorker*, 29 Apr.

28 You can fool too many of the people too much of the time.
1939 'The Owl Who Was God', in the *New Yorker*, 29 Apr.
▷ See Lincoln 605:99.

29 Art—the one achievement of Man which has made the long trip from all fours seem well advised.
1939 In *Forum and Century* magazine, Jun.

30 My World—And Welcome To It.
1942 Title of book.

31 If he knew where he was going, it is not apparent from this distance. He fell down a great deal during this period, because of a trick he had of walking into himself.
1945 Of his young self. *The Thurber Carnival*, preface.

32 I suppose that even the most pleasurable of imaginable occupations, that of batting baseballs through the windows of the RCA Building, would pall a little as the days ran on.
1945 *The Thurber Carnival*, 'Memoirs of a Drudge'.

33 He who hesitates is sometimes saved.
1945 *The Thurber Carnival*, 'The Glass in the Field'.

34 She developed a persistent troubled frown which gave her the expression of someone who is trying to repair a watch with his gloves on.
1948 *The Beast In Me and Other Animals*, 'Look Homeward, Jeannie'.

35 'We all have flaws,' he said, 'and mine is being wicked.'
1950 *The 13 Clocks*, ch.8.

36 'For God, for Country and for Yale', the outstanding single anti-climax in the English language.
1951 In *Time*, 11 Jun.

37 The theater is the primary evidence of a nation's culture.
1952 In the *New York Times*, 27 Jul.

38 Try to imagine a famous witty saying that is not immediately clear.
1954 Letter to Malcolm Cowley, 11 Mar.

39 With sixty staring me in the face, I have developed inflammation of the sentence structure and definite hardening of the paragraphs.
1955 In the *New York Post*, 30 Jun.

40 Seeing is deceiving. It's eating that's believing.
1956 *Further Fables for Our Time*.

41 'I think this calls for a drink' has long been one of our national slogans.
1957 *Alarms and Diversions*, 'Merry Christmas'.

42 'Poe,' I said, 'was perhaps the first great nonstop literary drinker of the American nineteenth century. He made the indulgences of Coleridge and De Quincey seem like a bit of mischief in the kitchen with the cooking sherry.
1957 *Alarms and Diversions*, 'The Moribundant Life, or, Grow Old Along with Whom?

43 I was seized by the stern hand of Compulsion, that dark, unseasonable Urge that impels women to clean house in the middle of the night.
1957 *Alarms and Diversions*, 'There's A Time For Flags'.

44 The laughter of man is more terrible than his tears, and takes more forms—hollow, heartless, mirthless, maniacal.
1958 In the *New York Times Magazine*, 7 Dec.

45 The power that created the poodle, the platypus and people has an integrated sense of both comedy and tragedy.
1959 Letter to Frances Glennon, Jun.

46 'Humour,' he said, 'is emotional chaos remembered in tranquillity.'
1960 In the *New York Post*, 29 Feb.
▷ See Wordsworth 1096:37.

47 Ours is a precarious language, as every writer knows, in which the merest shadow line often separates affirmation from negation, sense from nonsense, and one sex from another.
1961 Of English. *Lanterns and Lances*, 'Such a Phrase as Drifts Through Dreams'.

48 Writers of comedy have outlook, whereas writers of tragedy have, according to them, insight.
1961 *Lanterns and Lances*, 'The Case for Comedy'.

49 The only rules comedy can tolerate are those of taste, and the only limitations those of libel.
1961 *Lanterns and Lances*, 'The Duchess and the Bugs'.

50 God bless... God damn!
1961 Last words.

51 I have the reputation of having read all of Henry James, which would argue a misspent youth *and* middle age.
Recalled on his death, 2 Nov 1961.

52 Word has somehow got around that the split infinitive is always wrong. That is of a piece with the outworn notion that it is always wrong to strike a lady.

Recalled on Thurber's death, 2 Nov 1961.

53 Unless [artists] can remember what it was to be a little boy, they are only half complete as artist and as man.

Quoted in Helen Thurber and Edward Weeks (eds) *Selected Letters of James Thurber* (1981).

54 Laughter need not be cut out of anything, since it improves everything.

Quoted in Helen Thurber and Edward Weeks (eds) *Selected Letters of James Thurber* (1981).

55 There is something about a poet which leads us to believe that he died, in many cases, as long as 20 years before his birth.

Quoted in Helen Thurber and Edward Weeks (eds) *Selected Letters of James Thurber* (1981).

56 Some American writers who have known each other for years have never met in the daytime or when both were sober.

Quoted in Neil T Jones (ed) *A Book of Days for the Literary Year* (1984).

57 It had only one fault. It was kind of lousy.

Of a play he had recently seen. Attributed.

58 No oyster ever profited from its pearl.

'The Philosopher and the Oyster'. Collected in *Further Fables* (1956).

Thurow, Lester C 1938–

US economist, Dean of the School of Management at Massachusetts Institute of Technology.

59 America no longer lives behind its great wall. Economically, Genghis Khan has arrived.

1992 *Head to Head.*

Tilden, Bill (William Tatem II) 1893–1953

US tennis player. One of the greatest players of his time, he was Wimbledon singles champion three times (1920, 1921, 1930) and doubles champion (1927). He was also six times US singles champion and four times doubles champion in the 1920s.

60 Never change a winning game: always change a losing one.

Quoted in Colin Jarman *The Guinness Dictionary of Sports Quotations* (1990).

Tillich, Paul Johannes 1886–1965

German pastor, theologian and philosopher. Dismissed from his professorship by Nazis in 1933, he left to teach in the US. His theories blend philosophical and psychoanalytical elements with the theological.

61 Neurosis is the way of avoiding non-being by avoiding being.

1952 *The Courage to Be.*

62 Faith comprises both itself and doubt of itself.

1955 *Biblical Religion and the Search for Ultimate Reality.*

63 Faith is the state of being ultimately concerned.

1957 *Dynamics of Faith.*

64 I had the honor to be the first non-Jewish professor dismissed from a German university.

Recalled on his death, 22 Oct 1965.

Tilman, Bill (Harold William) 1898–?1977

English mountaineer, explorer and sailor. He went to Kenya as a planter and there met Eric Shipton, with whom he made many notable explorations and climbs. After serving in World War II he took up sailing in remote areas such as Patagonia, the Arctic and the Antarctic. He disappeared on a voyage to the South Shetland Islands in 1977.

65 We live and learn, and big mountains are stern teachers.

1949 *Two Mountains and a River.*

Time

US news periodical.

66 The old man puffed into sight like a venerable battlewagon pressing up over the horizon. First a smudge of smoke, then the long cigar, then the familiar, stoop-shouldered hulk that a generation has come to know as the silhouette of greatness.

1952 Of Winston Churchill disembarking from the *Queen Mary.* 14 Jan.

67 The mighty US suddenly seemed as impotent as a beached whale.

1968 On the fall of 28 of South Vietnam's 44 provincial capitals. 15 Feb

68 His career was a text book example of the rise of a patrician in the snug embrace of the American establishment.

1971 Of Dean Acheson. 25 Oct.

69 The rescuers had to rescue themselves.

1980 On the ill-fated helicopter attempt to free the hostages held in Iran. 5 May.

The Times

British newspaper, founded as the *Daily Universal Register* on 1 Jan 1785. It changed its name to *The Times* on 1 Jan 1788.

70 Of all journals, and of all writers, those will obtain the largest measure of public support who have told the truth most constantly and most fearlessly.

1852 Leading article, 6 Feb.

71 The first duty of the press is to obtain the earliest and most correct intelligence of the events of the time, and by disclosing them, to make them the common property of the nation.
1852 Leading article, 6 Feb.

Tintoretto real name *Jacopo Robusti* 1518–94

Venetian painter.

72 In judging paintings, you should consider whether the first impression pleases the eye and whether the artist has followed the rules; as for the rest, everyone makes some mistakes.
Quoted in Carlo Ridolfi *Life of Tintoretto* (1642).

Tobin, James 1918–

US economist, winner of the Nobel Prize in Economics (1981) and a professor at Yale University.

73 Why do so many talented economic theorists believe and teach elegant fantasies so obviously refutable by plainly evident facts?
1992 'An Old Keynesian Counterattacks', in the *Eastern Economic Journal*, Fall issue.

Tocqueville, Alexis Charles Henri Clérel de 1805–59

French historian and politician, Minister of Foreign Affairs for a few months in 1849. His major works are *De la Démocratie en Amérique* (1835, *Democracy in America*) and *L'Ancien Régime et la Révolution* (1856, *The Old Regime and the Revolution*).

74 Why, as civilization spreads, do outstanding men become fewer? Why, when attainments are the lot of all, do great intellectual talents become rarer? Why, when there are no longer lower classes, are there no longer upper classes? Why, when knowledge of how to rule reaches the masses, is there a lack of great abilities in the direction of society? America clearly poses these questions. But who can answer them?
1831 Translated by George Lawrence. Quoted in J P Mayer (ed) *Journey to America* (1960).

75 *En matière de presse, il n'y a donc réellement pas de milieu entre la servitude et la licence. Pour recueillir les biens inestimables qu'assure la liberté de la presse, il faut savoir se soumettre aux maux inévitables qu'elle fait naître.*

As for the press, there is no middle way between servitude and extreme licence. In order to enjoy the invaluable benefits ensured by freedom of the press, it is necessary to submit to the inevitable evils that it engenders.
1835 *De la Démocratie en Amérique* (*Democracy in America*), vol.1, pt.2, ch.3 (translated by Michel Petheram).

76 *C'est un axiome de la science politique aux Etats-Unis, que le seul moyen de neutraliser les effets des journaux est d'en multiplier le nombre.*

It is an axiom of politics in the United States, that the only means of neutralising the effects of newspapers is to increase their number.
1835 *De la Démocratie en Amérique* (*Democracy in America*), vol.1, pt.2, ch.3.

77 *La presse exerce encore un immense pouvoir en Amérique. Elle fait circuler la vie politique dans toutes les portions de ce vaste territoire. C'est elle dont l'œil toujours ouvert met sans cesse à nu les secrets ressorts de la politique, et force les hommes publics à venir tour à tour comparaître devant le tribunal de l'opinion. C'est elle qui rallie les intérêts autour de certaines doctrines et formule le symbole des partis; c'est par elle que ceux-ci se parlent sans se voir, s'entendent sans être mis en contact.*

The press has enormous power in America. It is the press that circulates political life through all parts of this vast territory. Its eye is always open, and making known the secret springs of politics, thus forcing public men to appear before the tribunal of public opinion. It is the press which rallies the interests of the community round certain principles and forms the creed of different parties. Through the press these parties can speak to each other without seeing each other, can listen without meeting.
1835 *De la Démocratie en Amérique* (*Democracy in America*), vol.1, pt.2, ch.3.

78 *Le journal représente l'association; l'on peut dire qu'il parle à chacun de ses lecteurs au nom de tous les autres, et il les entraîne d'autant plus aisément qu'ils sont individuellement plus faibles. L'empire des journaux doit donc croître à mesure que les hommes s'égalisent.*

A newspaper represents an association; one might say that it addresses each of its readers in the name of all the others, and influences them in proportion to their individual weakness. The power of newspapers should therefore increase as men become more equal.
1835 *De la Démocratie en Amérique* (*Democracy in America*), vol.2, pt.2, ch.6.

79 *Il n'y a qu'un journal qui puisse venir déposer au même moment dans mille esprits la même pensée.*

Only a newspaper can place at the same time in a thousand minds the same thought.
1835 *De la Démocratie en Amérique* (*Democracy in America*), vol.2, pt.2, ch.6.

80 *Un journal est un conseiller qu'on n'a pas besoin d'aller chercher, mais qui se présente de lui-même et qui vous parle tous les jours et brièvement de l'affaire* *commune, sans vous déranger de vos affaires particulières.*

A newspaper is an adviser whom one does not need to seek out, but one who comes of his own accord and speaks to you every day, briefly, of public affairs, without disturbing you from your own.

1835 *De la Démocratie en Amérique* (*Democracy in America*), vol.2, pt.2, ch.6.

81 *Ce serait diminuer leur importance que de croire qu'ils ne servent qu'à garantir la liberté; ils maintiennent la civilisation.*

It would diminish the importance [of newspapers] to believe that they only serve to guarantee freedom; they maintain civilization.

1835 *De la Démocratie en Amérique* (*Democracy in America*), vol.2, pt.2, ch.6.

82 From this foul drain the greatest stream of human industry flows out to fertilize the whole world. From this filthy sewer pure gold flows. Here humanity attains its most complete development and its most brutish, here civilization works its miracles and civilized man is turned almost into a savage.

1835 Of Manchester. Journal entry, 2 Jul. *Journeys to England and Ireland* (translated by George Lawrence and K P Mayer, 1958).

Todd, Mike 1907–58

83 No gals, no gags, no chance.

1943 On attending rehearsals for *Oklahoma!* Quoted in the *US News and World Report*, 12 Apr 1993, on the 50th anniversary of the musical that ran six years, won a Pulitzer Prize, and was to have 750 revivals in 1993.

Todd, Ron(ald) 1927–

English trade-union leader, a member of the Transport and General Workers' Union. He became general-secretary in 1985, with strong left-wing support.

84 You don't have power if you surrender all your principles—you have office.

1988 Speech, London, Jun.

Toffler, Alvin 1928–

US writer and journalist, one of the most successful trend-spotters of the age. Toffler coined the phrase *future shock* and convinced a sizable number of the reading public and policy administrators that what ailed them was the fact that everything was changing so fast.

85 'Future shock'…the shattering stress and disorientation that we induce in individuals by subjecting them to too much change in too short a time.

1970 *Future Shock.*

86 That great, growing engine of change—technology.

1970 *Future Shock.*

87 Technology feeds on itself. Technology makes more technology possible.

1970 *Future Shock.*

Tojo, Hideki 1885–1948

Japanese soldier who rose to become Minister of War (1940–1) and from 1941 premier and dictator of Japan. He was sentenced to death in 1948.

88 This is farewell.
I shall wait beneath the moss
Until the flowers are fragrant
In this island country of Japan.

1948 His final statement before execution, 23 Dec. Quoted in R J C Butow *Tojo and the Coming War* (1961).

Tolkien, J(ohn) R(onald) R(euel) 1892–1973

English writer and philologist. He was born in South Africa, educated in England, and taught at Oxford. He wrote scholarly books, but is famous for his hugely popular fantasy novels *The Hobbit* and *The Lord of the Rings* trilogy.

89 In a hole in the ground there lived a hobbit. Not a nasty, dirty, wet hole, filled with the ends of worms and on oozy smell, nor yet a dry, bare, sandy hole with nothing in it to sit down on or to eat: it was a hobbit-hole, and that means comfort.

1937 *The Hobbit*, ch.1.

90 My political opinions lean more and more to anarchy (philosophically understood, meaning abolition of control not whiskered men with bombs)… The most improper job of any man is bossing other men.

1943 Letter to Christopher Tolkien, 29 Apr.

91 There is only one bright spot and that is the growing habit of disgruntled men of dynamiting factories and power stations. I hope that, encouraged now as patriotism, it may remain a habit! But it won't do any good, if it is not universal.

1943 Letter to Christopher Tolkien, 29 Apr.

92 One Ring to rule them all, One Ring to find them
One Ring to bring them all and in the darkness bind them.
In the Land of Mordor where the Shadows lie.

1954 *The Fellowship of the Ring*, epigraph and passim.

93 But I cordially dislike allegory in all its manifestations, and always have done so since I grew old and wary enough to detect its presence. I much prefer history, true or feigned, with its varied applicability to the thought and experience of readers.

1954 *The Fellowship of the Ring*, foreword.

94 Hobbits are an unobtrusive but very ancient
people, more numerous formerly than they are
today; for they love peace and quiet and good tilled
earth: a well-ordered and well-farmed countryside
was their favourite haunt… Even in ancient days
they were, as a rule, shy of 'the Big Folk', as they call
us, and now they avoid us with dismay and are
becoming hard to find.
1954 *The Fellowship of the Ring*, prologue.

Tolstoy, Leo Nikolayevich 1828–1910

Russian social philosopher, social critic and sometime
mystic. He was one of the greatest novelists of all time.

95 Our body is a machine for living. It is organized for
that, it is its nature. Let life go on in it unhindered
and let it defend itself, it will do more than if you
paralyse it by encumbering it with remedies.
1869 *War and Peace*, bk.10, ch.29.

96 All happy families resemble each other; each
unhappy family is unhappy in its own way.
1874 *Anna Karenina*, opening words.

97 I sit on a man's back, choking him and making him
carry me, and yet assure myself and others that I am
very sorry for him and wish to ease his lot by all
possible means—except by getting off his back.
1886 *What Then Must We Do?* ch.16 (translated by Maude).

98 What is called science today consists of a haphazard
heap of information, united by nothing, often
utterly unnecessary, and not only failing to present
one unquestionable truth, but as often as not
containing the grossest errors today put forward as
truths, and tomorrow overthrown.
1898 *What is Art?* (translated by V Tchertkoff).

99 I am convinced that the history of so-called
scientific work in our famous centers of European
civilization will, in a couple of hundred years,
represent an inexhaustible source of laughter and
sorrow for future generations. The learned men of
the small western part of our European continent
lived for several centuries under the illusion that
the eternal blessed life was the West's future. They
were interested in the problem of when and where
this blessed life would come. But they never
thought of how they were going to make their life
better.
1898 *What is Art?* (translated by V Tchertkoff).

Tomé Pires c.1480–1525

Portuguese scholar and diplomat who came to Malacca in
1512, shortly after his country's conquest of the region.
Portuguese control of new sea routes meant that valuable
spices no longer needed to travel via Venice to reach
Europe.

1 Whoever is Lord of Malacca has his hand on the
throat of Venice.
1512–15 *The Suma Oriental of Tomé Pires* (translated by
Armando Cortasao, 1944).

Tomlinson, (Alfred) Charles 1927–

English poet and critic. Emeritus Professor of English,
University of Bristol. His publications include *Poems*
(1964) and *The Flood* (1981).

2 Everything we see
Teaches the time that we are living in.
1984 'Poem for My Father'.

Tomlinson, H(enry) M(ajor) 1873–1958

English writer. He wrote novels, travel books, memoirs
and a biography of Norman Douglas.

3 I will never believe again that the sea was ever loved
by anyone whose life was married to it.
1912 *The Sea and the Jungle*, ch.1.

Toole, John Kennedy 1937–69

US novelist. He published nothing in his lifetime, and
committed suicide. His novel *A Confederacy of Dunces* was
published to great acclaim in 1980, and *The Neon Bible* in
1989.

4 Her logic was a combination of half-truths and
clichés, her worldview a compound of
misconceptions deriving from a history of our
nation as written from the perspective of a subway
tunnel.
A Confederacy of Dunces (published 1980), ch.5, pt.3.

5 The human desire for food and sex is relatively
equal. If there are armed rapes why should there
not be armed hot dog thefts?
A Confederacy of Dunces (published 1980), ch.7, pt.1.

6 You can always tell employees of the government
by the total vacancy which occupies the space
where most other people have faces.
A Confederacy of Dunces (published 1980), ch.9, pt.1.

Toplady, Augustus Montague 1740–78

English clergyman and hymn writer.

7 Rock of Ages, cleft for me,
Let me hide myself in Thee,
Let the water and the blood,
From thy riven side which flowed,
Be of sin the double cure,
Cleanse me from its guilt and power.
1776 Hymn.

Toscanini, Arturo 1867–1957

Italian conductor. He made his début at La Scala in 1898
and remained there until 1908, returning 1920–9. He

conducted many major orchestras, and created the National Broadcasting Orchestra of America (1937–53). He had a reputation as a tyrannical perfectionist.

8 God tells me how he wants this music played—and you get in his way.

1930 Berating players in his orchestra. Quoted in Howard Tubman *Etude*.

9 After I die I am coming back to earth as the doorkeeper of a bordello. And I won't let a one of you in.

To an uncooperative orchestra. Quoted in Lebrecht *Discord* (1982).

Towne, Robert 1936–

US screenwriter. His credits include *The Tomb of Ligeia* (1964), *The Last Detail* (1973), *Chinatown* (1974) and *Greystoke: the Legend of Tarzan* (1984).

10 Why are you doing it? What can you buy that you can't already afford?
The future, Mr Gittes, the future.

1974 *Chinatown*.

11 Forget it, Jake, it's Chinatown.

1974 *Chinatown*, closing line.

Townsend, Sue 1945–

English writer. She has written novels and plays, but is best known for her 'Adrian Mole' books.

12 The Secret Diary of Adrian Mole Aged 13³/₄

1982 Title of book.

13 I have decided to be a poet. My father said there isn't a suitable career structure for poets and no pensions and other boring things, but I am quite decided.

1982 *The Secret Diary of Adrian Mole*, 'Monday, May 25th'.

Townshend, Pete 1945–

British rock musician.

14 Hope I die before I get old.

1966 'My Generation'.

Toynbee, Arnold 1852–83

English economic historian and social reformer, best known as the author of *The Industrial Revolution in England* (1884). Toynbee Hall, Whitechapel was founded in his memory in 1885.

15 The Industrial Revolution.

1880–1 Title of Oxford lectures, published posthumously in 1884. The phrase passed into common usage.

Toynbee, Arnold Joseph 1889–1975

English historian, nephew of Arnold Toynbee. His greatest work is *A Study of History*, published in 10 volumes (1934–54).

16 No annihilation without representation.

1947 Advocating greater British representation at the United Nations.

▷ See Otis 746:75.

17 America is a large, friendly dog in a very small room. Every time it wags its tail, it knocks over a chair.

1949 Letter, 26 Oct.

18 Civilisation is a movement and not a condition; a voyage and not a harbour.

Quoted in *Reader's Digest*, Oct 1958.

19 Angkor is perhaps the greatest of Man's essays in rectangular architecture that has yet been brought to life.

1958 *East to West*.

Toynbee, (Theodore) Philip 1916–81

English novelist and journalist, son of the historian Arnold Joseph Toynbee. An experimental writer, his semi-autobiographical Pantaloon sequence is particularly innovative.

20 I have seen the future and it does not work.

1974 Of the USA. In *The Observer*, 27 Jan.

▷ See Steffens 965:27.

21 He was the type of man who was always trying to live beyond his moral means.

1975 Of J Middleton Murry. In *The Observer*, 12 Jan.

22 The basic command of religion is not 'do this!' or 'do not do that!' but simply 'look!'

1978 Journal entry, 15 Feb. Collected in *Part of a Journey* (1981).

23 The primary duty of a serious biographer is to illuminate his subject's life work, not to play the spy in his bedroom.

1979 Book review in *The Observer*, 18 Mar.

Traherne, Thomas c.1636–74

English poet and mystic. Educated at Oxford, he took holy orders and in 1667 became Chaplain to the Lord Keeper of the Great Seal. He wrote religious prose, including *Roman Forgeries* (1673), *Christian Ethics* (1675) and *Centuries of Religious Meditations* (published 1908); his poetry was not published until 1903, and 1910.

24 In unexperienc'd Infancy
Many a sweet mistake doth lie.

'Shadows in the Water', published 1903.

25 Some unknown joys there be
Laid up in store for me.

'Shadows in the Water', published 1903.

26 Sleep is cousin-german unto death:
Sleep and death differ, no more, than a carcass
And a skeleton.

'A Serious and a Curious Night-Meditation', published 1903.

27 You never enjoy the world aright, till the sea itself floweth in your veins, till you are clothed with the heavens, and crowned with the stars: and perceive yourself to be the sole heir of the whole world.
Centuries of Meditations, 'First Century', section 29 (published 1908).

28 A Stranger here
Strange things doth meet, strange glories see;
Strange Treasures lodg'd in this fair world appear,
Strange all, and New to me,
But that they mine should be, who nothing was,
That Strangest is of all, yet brought to pass.
The Salutation (published 1903).

Travers, Ben 1886–1980

English dramatist and screenwriter.

29 The really great batsmen fall into two categories. One comes to the wicket saying to the bowlers 'I am going to slaughter you'. The other comes to the wicket saying 'You can't get me out'.
1981 *94 Declared Cricket Reminiscences.*

Travers, P(amela) L(yndon) 1906–96

British writer. She worked as a journalist, actress, and dancer and for the British Ministry of Information in the US during World War II. *Mary Poppins* was published in 1934; subsequent titles include *Mary Poppins Comes Back* (1935), *Mary Poppins Opens the Door* (1943) and *Mary Poppins in the Park* (1952).

30 'Now,' she said, 'spit-spot into bed.'
1934 *Mary Poppins*, ch.1.

31 From the [empty] carpet-bag she took out seven flannel night-gowns, four cotton ones, a pair of boots, a set of dominoes, two bathing-caps and a postcard album. Last of all came a folding camp-bedstead with blankets and eiderdown complete.
1934 *Mary Poppins*, ch.1.

32 Mary Poppins looked down at her feet and rubbed the toe of one shoe along the pavement two or three times. Then she smiled at the shoe in such a way that the shoe knew quite well that the smile wasn't meant for it.
1934 *Mary Poppins*, ch.2.

33 'Don't you know,' she said pityingly, 'that everybody's got a Fairyland of their own?'
1934 *Mary Poppins*, ch.2.

34 If I laugh on that particular day I become so filled with Laughing Gas that I simply can't keep on the ground. Even if I smile it happens. The first funny thought, and I'm up like a balloon. And until I can think of something serious I can't get down again.
1934 Mr Wigg, Mary Poppins's uncle. The 'particular day' is when his birthday falls on a Friday. *Mary Poppins*, ch.3.

35 Oh, my Gracious, Glorious, Galumphing Goodness!
1934 Mr Wigg. *Mary Poppins*, ch.3.

36 The Red Cow was very respectable, she always behaved like a perfect lady and she knew What was What. To her a thing was either black or white—there was no question of it being grey or perhaps pink. People were good or they were bad—there was nothing in between. Dandelions were either sweet or sour—there were never any moderately nice ones.
1934 *Mary Poppins*, ch.5.

37 He could smell her crackling white apron and the faint flavour of toast that always hung about her so deliciously.
1934 Michael's impressions of Mary Poppins. *Mary Poppins*, ch.6.

38 Feed the Birds, Tuppence a Bag! Feed the Birds, Tuppence a Bag!
1934 *Mary Poppins*, ch.7.

39 Trouble trouble and it will trouble you!
1934 Mary Poppins. *Mary Poppins*, ch.12.

Tree, Sir Herbert (Draper) Beerbohm 1852–1917

English actor-manager. He played a wide range of roles, of which the most successful included Svengali in George du Maurier's *Trilby*, Higgins in George Bernard Shaw's *Pygmalion* and Charles Dickens' Fagin. He assumed the management of the Comedy Theatre in London in 1887 and then spent a prosperous 10 years as manager of the Haymarket before opening Her Majesty's in 1897. He was also the founder of the Royal Academy of Dramatic Art (1904).

40 Ladies, just a little more virginity, if you don't mind.
To actresses playing the roles of ladies-in-waiting. Quoted in Alexander Woollcott *Shouts and Murmurs* (1923), 'Capsule Criticism'.

41 He is an old bore. Even the grave yawns for him.
Of Israel Zangill. Quoted in Hesketh Pearson *Beerbohm* (1956).

43 It is difficult to live up to one's poster... When I pass my name in large letters I blush, but at the same time instinctively raise my hat.
Quoted in Hesketh Pearson *Beerbohm* (1956).

44 The national sport of England is obstacle-racing. People fill their rooms with useless and

cumbersome furniture, and spend the rest of their lives trying to dodge it.

Quoted in Hesketh Pearson *Beerbohm* (1956).

Treitschke, Georg Friedrich 1776–1842

German librettist and translator best known for revising the libretto for the final version (1814) of Beethoven's opera *Fidelio* from earlier versions by Stefan von Breuning (1806) and Joseph Sonnleithner (1805).

45 *Abscheulicher!*

Perfidious wretch!

1814 Leonora's recitative and aria, *Fidelio*, act 1.

46 *O welche Lust!*

Oh what delight!

1814 The prisoners' chorus, *Fidelio*, act 1.

Trevelyan, George Macaulay 1876–1962

English historian. After serving in World War I, he became Professor of Modern History at Cambridge (1927–40). A pioneer social historian, his *English Social History* (1944) was a companion volume to his *History of England* (1926).

47 Disinterested intellectual curiosity is the life-blood of real civilisation.

1944 *English Social History.*

48 Village cricket spread fast through the land. In those days, before it became scientific, cricket was the best game in the world to watch—each ball a potential crisis.

Quoted in Helen Exley *Cricket Quotations* (1992).

Trevelyan, John 1904–85

British executive. He was secretary of the British Board of Film Censors between 1958 and 1970.

49 Censors are paid to have dirty minds.

1970 Attributed.

Trevino, Lee Buck 1939–

US golfer. He won his first US Open in 1968 and in 1971 established a record by winning three Open titles (the US, Canadian and British) in the same year, retaining his British title the following year.

50 I'm not saying my golf game went bad, but if I grew tomatoes they'd come up sliced.

Quoted in *Scholastic Coach*, 'Coaches' Corner', Dec 1982.

51 If my IQ had been two points lower, I'd have been a plant somewhere.

Quoted in Colin Jarman *The Guinness Dictionary of Sports Quotations* (1990).

52 I'm hitting the driver so good, I gotta dial the operator for long distance after I hit it.

Attributed.

Trevor-Roper, Hugh Redwald, Baron Dacre of Glanton 1914–

English historian, known for his vivid reconstruction of *The Last Days of Hitler* (1947). He was Professor at Oxford (1957–80) and Master of Peterhouse, Cambridge (1980–7).

53 Any society, so long as it is, or feels itself to be, a working society, tends to invest in itself: a military society tends to become more military, a bureaucratic society more bureaucratic, a commercial society more commercial, as the status and profits of war or office or commerce are enhanced by success, and institutions are framed to forward it. Therefore, when such a society is hit by a general crisis, it finds itself partly paralyzed by the structural weight of increased social investment. The dominant military or official or commercial classes cannot easily change their orientation: and their social dominance, and the institutions through which is exercised, prevent other classes from securing power or changing policy.

1965 *The Rise of Christian Europe.*

Trillin, Calvin Marshall 1935–

US journalist and author.

54 A shelf life somewhere between butter and yoghurt.

1987 On the plethora of new book titles. In the *New York Times*, 14 Jun.

55 Math was my worst subject because I could never persuade the teacher that my answers were meant ironically.

1990 In the *New York Times*, 7 Oct.

Trilling, Lionel 1905–75

US literary critic whose works, such as *The Liberal Imagination* (1950) and *Beyond Culture* (1965), gained him a reputation for scholarly and astute social comment. He also wrote a novel, *The Middle of the Journey* (1947).

56 Literature is the human activity that takes the fullest and most precise account of variousness, possibility, complexity, and difficulty.

1950 *The Liberal Imagination*, preface.

57 We are all ill: but even a universal sickness implies an idea of health.

1950 *The Liberal Imagination*, 'Art and Neurosis'.

58 We who are liberal and progressive know that the poor are our equals in every sense except that of being equal to us.

1950 *The Liberal Imagination*, 'Princess Casamassima'.

59 It would seem that Americans have a kind of resistance to looking closely at society.

1950 *The Liberal Imagination*, 'Manners, Morals and the Novel'.

60 The poet…may be used as a barometer, but let us not forget that he is also part of the weather.
1950 *The Liberal Imagination.*

61 The function of literature through all its mutations, has been to make us aware of the particularity of selves, and the high authority of the self in its quarrel with its society and its culture. Literature is in that sense subversive.
1965 *Beyond Culture*, introduction.

Trollope, Anthony 1815–82

English novelist. He is best known for his two novel sequences, the Barchester novels and the 'Palliser' novels, both of which chronicle the life of a region and are distinguished by their slow pace and quiet comedy. His novels include *Barchester Towers* (1857) and *Can You Forgive Her?* (1864).

62 The tenth Muse, who now governs the periodical press.
1855 *The Warden*, ch.14.

63 She was rich in apparel, but not bedizened with finery…She well knew the great architectural secret of decorating her constructions, and never descended to construct a decoration.
1857 Of Mrs Stanhope. *Barchester Towers*, ch.9.

64 There is no road to wealth so easy and respectable as that of matrimony.
1858 *Doctor Thorne*, ch.16.

65 Let no man boast himself that he has got through the perils of winter till at least the seventh of May.
1858 *Doctor Thorne*, ch.47.

66 Those who have courage to love should have courage to suffer.
1859 *The Bertrams*, ch.27.

67 For the most of us, if we do not talk of ourselves, or at any rate of the individual circles of which we are the centres, we can talk of nothing. I cannot hold with those who wish to put down the insignificant chatter of the world.
1861 *Framley Parsonage*, ch.10.

68 We cannot bring ourselves to believe it possible that a foreigner should in any respect be wiser than ourselves. If any such point out to us our follies, we at once claim those follies as the special evidence of our wisdom.
1862 Stavely. *Orley Farm*, ch.18.

69 It is because we put up with bad things that hotel-keepers continue to give them to us.
1862 Stavely. *Orley Farm*, ch.18.

70 As for conceit, what man will do any good who is not conceited? Nobody holds a good opinion of a man who has a low opinion of himself.
1862 *Orley Farm*, ch.22.

71 Mr Palliser was one of those politicians in possessing whom England has perhaps more reason to be proud than of any other of her resources, and who, as a body, give to her that exquisite combination of conservatism and progress which is her present strength and best security for the future.
1864 *Can You Forgive Her?*, ch.24.

72 To think of one's absent love is very sweet; but it becomes monotonous… I doubt whether any girl would be satisfied with her lover's mind if she knew the whole of it.
1864 *The Small House at Allington*, ch.4.

73 Why is it that girls so constantly do this, so frequently ask men who have loved them to be present at their marriages with other men? There is no triumph in it. It is done in sheer kindness and affection. They intend to offer something which shall soften and not aggravate the sorrow that they have caused… I fully appreciate the intention, but in honest truth, I doubt the eligibility of the proffered entertainment.
1864 John Eames. *The Small House at Allington*, ch.9.

74 It may almost be a question whether such wisdom as many of us have in our mature years has not come from the dying out of the power of temptation, rather than as the results of thought and resolution.
1864 *The Small House at Allington*, ch.14.

75 Never think that you're not good enough yourself. A man should never think that. My belief is that in life people will take you much at your own reckoning.
1864 Lord De Guest to Johnny. *The Small House at Allington*, ch.32.

76 With many women I doubt whether there be any more effectual way of touching their hearts than ill-using them and then confessing it. If you wish to get the sweetest fragrance from the herb at your feet, tread on it and bruise it.
1865 *Miss Mackenzie*, ch.10.

77 It was manifest to me that there was something in the Roman Catholic religion which made the priests very dear to the people; for I doubt whether in any village in England, had such an accident happened to the rector, all the people would have roused themselves at midnight to wreak their vengeance on the assailant.
1866 *Argosy*, 'Father Giles of Ballymoy', May.

78 How I did respect you when you dared to speak the truth to me! Men don't know women, or they would be harder to them.
1867 *The Claverings*, ch.15.

79 She understood how much louder a cock can crow in its own farmyard then elsewhere.
1867 *The Last Chronicle of Barset*, ch.17.

80 It's dogged as does it. It ain't thinking about it.
1867 *The Last Chronicle of Barset*, ch.61, 'Giles Hoggett'.

81 They who do not understand that a man may be brought to hope that which of all things is the most grievous to him, have not observed with sufficient closeness the perversity of the human mind.
1869 Of Trevelyan's paranoia about his wife's fidelity. *He Knew He Was Right*, ch.38.

82 A faineant government is not the worst government that England can have. It has been the great fault of our politicians that they have all wanted to do something.
1869 *Phineas Finn*, ch.13.

83 Mr Turnball had predicted evil consequences…and was now doing the best in his power to bring about the verification of his own prophecies.
1869 *Phineas Finn*, ch.25.

84 Perhaps there is no position more perilous to a man's honesty than that…of knowing himself to be quite loved by a girl whom he almost loves himself.
1869 *Phineas Finn*, ch.50.

85 She knew how to allure by denying, and to make the gift rich by delaying it.
1869 *Phineas Finn*, ch.57.

86 We cannot have heroes to dine with us. There are none. And were those heroes to be had, we should not like them…the persons whom you cannot care for in a novel, because they are so bad, are the very same that you so dearly love in your life, because they are so good.
1873 Of Frank Greystock. *The Eustace Diamonds*, ch.35.

87 What man thinks of changing himself so as to suit his wife? And yet men expect that women shall put on altogether new characters when they are married, and girls think that they can do so.
1874 Lady Chiltern to Mr Maule. *Phineas Redux*, ch.3.

88 It is the necessary nature of a political in this country to avoid, as long as it can be avoided, the consideration of any question which involves a great change…The best carriage horses are those which can most steadily hold back against the coach as it trundles down the hill.
1874 *Phineas Redux*, ch.4.

89 Is it not singular how some men continue to obtain the reputation of popular authorship without adding a word to the literature of their country worthy of note?… To puff and to get one's self puffed have become different branches of a new profession.
1875 *The Way We Live Now*, ch.1.

90 Love is like any other luxury. You have no right to it unless you can afford it.
1875 *The Way We Live Now*, ch.84.

91 Equality would be a heaven, if we could attain it.
1876 Prime Minister to Phineas. *The Prime Minister*, ch.68.

92 I hold that gentleman to be the best dressed whose dress no one observes.
1879 *Thackeray*, ch.9

93 A man's mind will very generally refuse to make itself up until it be driven and compelled by emergency.
1881 Houston. *Ayala's Angel*, ch.41.

94 He must have known me had he seen me as he was wont to see me, for he was in the habit of flogging me constantly. Perhaps he did not recognize me by my face.
1883 *Autobiography*, ch.1.

95 She was neither clear-sighted nor accurate; and in her attempts to describe morals, manners, and even facts, was unable to avoid the pitfalls of exaggeration.
1883 Of his mother, Frances Trollope, author of *The Domestic Manners of the Americans. Autobiography*, ch.2.

96 Take away from English authors their copyrights, and you would very soon take away from England her authors.
1883 *Autobiography*, ch.6.

97 It is admitted that a novel can hardly be made interesting or successful without love… It is necessary because the passion is one which interests or has interested all. Everyone feels it, has felt it, or expects to feel it.
1883 *Autobiography*, ch.12.

98 Three hours a day will produce as much as a man ought to write.
1883 *Autobiography*, ch.15.

99 I think that Plantagenet Palliser, Duke of Omnium, is a perfect gentleman. If he be not, then I am unable to describe a gentleman.
1883 *Autobiography*, ch.20.

Trollope, Joanna 1943–

English writer. She is best known for her novels set in rural English communities, but also writes historical fiction and, under the name Caroline Harvey, romances.

1 Contentment and fulfilment don't make for very good fiction.
1994 In *The Times*, 25 Jun.

Trotsky, Leon originally *Lev Davidovich Bronstein* 1879–1940

Russian Jewish revolutionary, born in Ukraine. Already a noted revolutionary, he played a major role in the October Revolution (1917), and created the Red Army. After Lenin's death (1924) his influence began to decline and under Stalin he was expelled from the Soviet Union (1929) and sentenced to death (1937). He was assassinated in Mexico by one of Stalin's agents.

2 You have played out your role. Go where you belong: to the dustheap of history.
1917 To the Mensheviks, at the first Congress of Soviets following the October Revolution. Quoted in A J P Taylor *From the Boer War to the Cold War: Essays on Twentieth-Century Europe* (1995), p.271.

3 A cossack's whip wrapped in the parchment of a constitution.
1905 On the October Manifesto, a package of limited constitutional reforms conceded by the Tzarist government following the strikes and civil unrest of early October 1905. Quoted in Lionel Kochan *Russia in Revolution* (1967).

4 The Soviet Republic needs an army that will be able to fight and conquer.
1918 Speech to the Moscow Soviet of Workers', Soldiers' and Peasants' Deputies, 19 Mar.

5 It was the supreme expression of the mediocrity of the apparatus that Stalin himself rose to his position.
1930 *My Life*, p.501.

6 Civilization has made the peasantry its pack animal. The bourgeoisie in the long run only changed the form of the pack.
1934 *History of the Russian Revolution* (translated by Max Eastman, 1934) vol.3, pt.3.

7 Old age is the most unexpected of all things that happens to a man.
1935 *Diary in Exile*.

8 In a country that is economically backward, the proletariat can take power earlier than in countries where capitalism is advanced.
1931 *The Permanent Revolution*.

9 Marxism is, above all, a method of analysis.
1931 *The Permanent Revolution*.

10 The end may justify the means, as long as there is something that justifies the end.
An Introduction to his Thought.

Trudeau, Pierre Elliott 1919–

Canadian politician. As Minister of Justice and Attorney-General (1967) he opposed the separation of Quebec from Canada. He became Liberal Prime Minister (1968–79, 1980–4), urging independence from US influence and home economic control. He proposed a new constitution for complete Canadian independence, secured Apr 1982.

11 The state has no place in the bedrooms of the nation.
1967 Of the liberalization of the Criminal Code. Interview in Ottawa, 22 Dec. The remark is based on similar words written by the journalist Martin O'Malley in an unsigned editorial in the *Globe and Mail*, 12 Dec 1967.

12 Living next to you is like sleeping with an elephant. No matter how friendly and even-tempered the beast, one is affected by every twitch and grunt.
1969 Of the US. Speech, National Press Club, Washington DC, 25 Mar. Quoted in Lawrence Martin *The Presidents and the Prime Ministers* (1982).

13 Fuddle-duddle.
1971 Neologism coined by Trudeau when accused of uttering a 'four-letter word' in the House of Commons, Ottawa, 16 Feb. 'No, it was fuddle-duddle,' replied Trudeau. The reply led an opposition Member of Parliament to observe, 'Mr. Trudeau wants to be obscene but not heard.'

Trueman, Fred (*Frederick Sewards*) 1931–

English cricketer, a notoriously fast bowler. He played for Yorkshire (1949–68) and made 67 Test appearances for England (1952–65). He took a record 307 Test wickets.

14 If there is any game in the world that attracts the half-baked theorist more than cricket I have yet to hear of it.
1964 *Freddie Trueman's Book of Cricket*.

15 The difference between a fast bowler and a good fast bowler is not extra muscle but extra brains.
1964 *Freddie Trueman's Book of Cricket*.

Truman, Harry S 1884–1972

US Democratic statesman, 33rd President (1945–53), responsible for the first atom bombing on Japan, the postwar loan to Britain, the establishment of NATO (1949) and the sending of US troops to South Korea (1950). He gave military and economic aid to countries threatened by communist interference, and introduced a 'Fair Deal' of economic reform at home.

16 When I first came to Washington, for the first six months I wondered how the hell I ever got here. For the next six months, I wondered how the hell the rest of them ever got here.
1940 Speech, Apr.

17 Every segment of our population, and every individual, has a right to expect from his Government a Fair Deal.
1945 Speech to Congress, 6 Sep.

18 If you think somebody is telling a big lie about you,

the only way to answer is with the whole truth.

1950 On Senator Joseph R McCarthy. Quoted in John Hersey *Aspects of the Presidency* (1980).

19 The only thing you have to worry about is bad luck. I never had bad luck.

1950 After an assassination attempt, 1 Nov.

20 If you can't stand the heat you better get out of the kitchen.

1952 Address to the Aero Club of Washington, 27 Dec, quoting a colleague from his days as a county judge.

21 Why, this fellow doesn't know any more about politics than a pig on Sunday.

1952 Of presidential hopeful Eisenhower. Quoted in Richard M Nixon *RN: Memoirs of Richard Nixon* (1978).

22 In 1945 we did much more than draft an international agreement among 50 nations. We set down on paper the only principles that will enable civilized human life to continue to survive on this globe.

1955 On the 10th anniversary of the United Nations, 24 Jun.

23 Party platforms are contracts with the people.

1956 *Memoirs: Years of Trial and Hope.*

24 I never give them hell. I just tell the truth and they think it is hell.

1956 Interview, *Look*, 3 Apr.

25 A politician is a man who understands government, and it takes a politician to run a Government. A statesman is a politician who has been dead 10 or 15 years.

1958 New York World Telegram, 12 Apr.

26 It's a recession when your neighbour loses his job; it's a depression when you lose yours.

1958 *The Observer*, 13 Apr.

▷ See Reagan 803:61.

27 Too many…pass judgement on wartime decisions in the luxury of a peacetime environment.

1963 Reply to a Boston University official who had criticized Truman's use of the atomic bomb. Truman Library archives, 23 Sep.

28 The President hears a hundred voices telling him that he is the greatest man in the world. He must listen carefully indeed to hear the one voice that tells him he is not.

1964 In *This Week*, 5 Apr.

29 Being criticized…he never did get it through his head that that's what politics is all about.

Of President Eisenhower. Quoted in Merle Miller (ed) *Plain Speaking* (1974).

30 Can't somebody bring me a one-handed economist?

Recalled on the death of his economic adviser Edwin Nourse, 9

Apr 1974. Nourse had been fond of saying 'on one hand…but on the other'.

31 I told him to fire away. He did and it is dynamite.

On asking Joseph Stalin for the Soviet agenda at the Potsdam Conference. Quoted in the *New York Times*, 2 Jun 1980.

32 Being president is like riding a tiger…keep on riding or be swallowed.

Quoted in the *New York Times*, 28 Dec 1984.

33 The buck stops here.

Motto displayed on a sign on his desk. Quoted in William Safire *Safire's New Political Dictionary* (1993).

34 I don't much care for your law, but, by golly, this bourbon is good.

To US Supreme Court Justice William O Douglas. Attributed.

Trump, Donald 1946–

US businessman, renowned for his flamboyant and initially successful dealings in real estate. His best-known developments include Trump Tower, New York City, and Trump Castle, Trump Plaza and the Taj Mahal casino in Atlantic City. When the real estate market slumped, 1990, he was forced to surrender many of his investments.

35 I like thinking big. If you're going to be thinking anyway, you might as well think big.

1989 In *Time*, 16 Jan.

36 A gambler is someone who plays slot machines. I prefer to own slot machines.

1990 On the opening of his Atlanta City Taj Mahal casino. In *Time*, 9 Apr.

37 See that gold Cadillac down the street? That's the color I want those handrails. Gold. Cadillac Gold. Not yellow like a daisy.

Of the handrails in Manhattan's Trump Tower. Quoted by Paul Trachtman in the *Smithsonian*, Mar 1995, reviewing Alexander Theroux *The Primary Colors*.

Truth, Sojourner née *Isabella* c.1797–1883

American abolitionist. Born a slave, she gained her freedom and later became an ardent evangelist. In 1843 she changed her name to Sojourner Truth and campaigned against slavery and for woman suffrage.

38 Well, chilern, whar dar is so much racket dar must be something out o' kilter. I tink dat 'twixt de niggers of de Souf and de women at de Norf all a talkin' 'bout rights, de white men will be in a fix pretty soon.

1851 Women's Rights Convention, Akron, Ohio. Quoted in *Narrative of Sojourner Truth* (1875), pt.2, 'Book of Life'.

39 Look at me! Look at my arm!… I have plowed, and planted, and gathered into barns, and no man could head me—and ar'n't I a woman? I could work as much and eat as much as a man (when I could get it), and bear de lash as well—and ar'n't I a

woman? I have borne thirteen chilern and seen 'em mos' all sold off into slavery, and when I cried out with a mother's grief, none but Jesus heard—and ar'n't I a woman?

1851 Women's Right Convention, Akron, Ohio. Quoted in *Narrative of Sojourner Truth* (1875), pt.2, 'Book of Life'.

Ts'ao Sung c.830–910

Chinese poet from Anhui about whom very little is known. He was in his seventies before finally passing a set of literary examinations.

40 I charge thee, sir, not to talk of high honours,
A single general achieves fame on the rotting bones of ten thousand.

c.879 'Written in the year Chi hai (879)', collected in *A Book of Chinese Verse* (translated by N L Smith and R H Kotewall).

Tsongas, Paul Efthemios 1941–

US politician, Senator from Massachusetts and a candidate for Democratic presidential nomination.

41 We are becoming an economic colony. America is up for sale. One percent of Japan's manufacturing base is foreign-owned; 2 per cent of Germany's is; 3 per cent of France's. Ours is 18 per cent and growing rapidly.

1992 Quoted in the *Los Angeles Times*, 17 Mar.

42 You cannot be pro-jobs and anti-government at the same time. You cannot love employees and despise employers. You cannot redistribute wealth that you never created. No goose, no golden egg.

1992 Quoted in the *Los Angeles Times*, 19 Feb.

Tu Fu 712–70

Chinese poet who never achieved a settled existence and is known to have spent a large part of his life travelling in a state of hardship.

43 Sundered by peaks unscalable,
Tomorrow shall we strangers be.

c.750 'Visiting an Old Friend', collected in *A Golden Treasury of Chinese Poetry* (translated by John Turner, 1967).

Tuchman, Barbara W(ertheim) 1912–89

US historian, best known for The Guns of August (1962, Pulitzer Prize), tracing the origins of World War I, and Stilwell and the American Experience in China (1970, Pulitzer Prize). Other works include A Distant Mirror (1978).

44 Dead battles, like dead generals, hold the military mind in their dead grip.

1962 *The Guns of August*, ch.2.

45 No more distressing moment can ever face a British Government than that which requires it to come to a hard and fast and specific decision.

1962 *The Guns of August*, ch.9.

46 Reasonable orders are easy enough to obey; it is capricious, bureaucratic or plain idiotic demands that form the habit of discipline.

1970 *Stilwell and the American Experience in China*, pt.1, ch.1.

47 Most people are relieved to find a superior on whose judgment they can rest. That, indeed, is the difference between most people and Generals.

1972 Address at US Army War College, Apr. Collected in *Practising History* (1981).

48 To a historian libraries are food, shelter, and even muse.

1981 *Practising History*, 'The Houses of Research'.

Tucker, Sophie pseudonym of *Sophia Abuza* 1884–1966

US jazz singer, born in Russia. A legendary star of cabaret and vaudeville in the 1920s, she included among her biggest hits such songs as 'Some of These Days' (1926) and 'My Yiddische Momma' (1928). She led her own band in the 1930s and made several appearances on Broadway and in musical films.

49 I've been rich and I've been poor. Believe me, honey, rich is better.

1945 *Some of These Days*.

50 The Last of the Red-Hot Mamas.

Title of song, adopted by Tucker as her nickname.

Turner, Bruce 1922–93

British jazz saxophonist. He played in the Humphrey Lyttelton Band for many years, as well as leading his own groups.

51 Jazz musicians are not demigods. They are warm, vulnerable human beings with a desperate need to go on paying the rent.

1984 *Hot Air, Cool Music*, ch.10.

Turner, Joseph Mallard William 1775–1851

English painter, one of Britian's most important 19c artists.

52 This is the end of Art. I am glad I have had my day.

Attributed, on first seeing a daguerrotype. Quoted in J G Links *Canaletto and his Patrons* (1977).

Tutu, Desmond Mpilo 1931–

Black South African prelate, the first black Bishop of Johannesburg (1984) and Archbishop of Cape Town (1986). A fierce critic of apartheid, advocating international sanctions, he also condemned the use of violence, seeking instead a negotiated solution. He was awarded the Nobel Peace Prize in 1984.

53 Be nice to whites. They need you to rediscover their humanity.
1984 In the *New York Times*, 19 Oct.

54 I am not interested in picking up crumbs of compassion thrown from the table of someone who considers himself to be my master. I want the full menu of rights.
1985 NBC News, 9 Jan.

55 We don't want apartheid liberalized. We want it dismantled. You can't improve something that is intrinsically evil.
1985 Speech, Mar.

Twain, Mark pseudonym of *Samuel Langhorne Clemens* 1835–1910

US writer. He worked as a steamboat pilot and took his pen-name from a term used for measuring the depth of the Mississippi. His novel *Huckleberry Finn* (1884) is a classic. His work ranges from the lightly comic *The Innocents Abroad* (1869) to the darkly pessimistic *What is Man* (1906).

56 No woman can look as well out of the fashion as in it.
1867 Letter, 16 Apr, quoted in Franklin Walker and G Ezra Dane (eds) *Mark Twain's Travels with Mr. Brown* (1940), letter 14.

57 I must have a prodigious quantity of mind; it takes me as much as a week to make it up.
1869 *The Innocents Abroad*, ch.7.

58 They spell it Vinci and pronounce it Vinchy; foreigners always spell better than they pronounce.
1869 *The Innocents Abroad*, ch.19.

59 The French are polite, but it is often mere ceremonious politeness. A Russian imbues his polite things with a heartiness that compels belief in their sincerity.
1869 *The Innocents Abroad*.

60 Lump the whole thing! Say that the Creator made Italy from designs by Michael Angelo!
1869 *The Innocents Abroad*.

61 Travel is fatal to prejudice.
1869 *The Innocents Abroad*, conclusion.

62 Soap and education are not as sudden as a massacre, but they are more deadly in the long run.
1872 *A Curious Dream*, 'Facts Concerning the Recent Resignation'.

63 Nothing helps scenery like ham and eggs.
1872 *Roughing It*, ch.17.

64 Well-a-well, man that is born of woman is of few days and full of trouble, as the Scripture says.
1876 Aunt Polly. *The Adventures of Tom Sawyer*, ch.1.

65 I reckon you're a kind of singed cat, as the saying is—better'n you look.
1876 Aunt Polly to Tom. *The Adventures of Tom Sawyer*, ch.1.

66 He was not the Model Boy of the village. He knew the model boy very well though—and loathed him.
1876 *The Adventures of Tom Sawyer*, ch.1.

67 Tom turned in without the added vexation of prayers.
1876 *The Adventures of Tom Sawyer*, ch.3.

68 He held curls to be effeminate, and his own filled his life with bitterness.
1876 *The Adventures of Tom Sawyer*, ch.4.

69 Often, the less there is to justify a traditional custom, the harder it is to get rid of it.
1876 *The Adventures of Tom Sawyer*, ch.5.

70 Church ain't shucks to a circus.
1876 *The Adventures of Tom Sawyer*, ch.7.

71 So they inwardly resolved that so long as they remained in the business, their piracies should not again be sullied with the crime of stealing.
1876 *The Adventures of Tom Sawyer*, ch.13.

72 There comes a time in every rightly constructed boy's life when he has a raging desire to go somewhere and dig for hidden treasure.
1876 *The Adventures of Tom Sawyer*, ch.25.

73 The cross of the Legion of Honour has been conferred upon me. However, few escape that distinction.
1880 *A Tramp Abroad*, ch.8.

74 An Irishman is lined with copper, and the beer corrodes it. But whiskey polishes the copper and is the saving of him.
1883 *Life on the Mississippi*, ch.23.

75 In the South, the war is what AD is elsewhere: they date from it.
1883 Of the American Civil War. *Life on the Mississippi*, ch.45.

76 Persons attempting to find a motive in this narrative will be prosecuted; persons attempting to find a moral in it will be banished; persons attempting to find a plot in it will be shot.
1884 *The Adventures of Huckleberry Finn*, 'Notice'.

77 She allowed she would sivilize me.
1884 *The Adventures of Huckleberry Finn*, ch.1.

78 If you are with the quality, or at a funeral, or trying to go to sleep when you ain't sleepy…why you itch all over in upward of a thousand places.
1884 *The Adventures of Huckleberry Finn*, ch.2.

79 You think you're a good deal of a big-bug, *don't* you.

1884 Huck's Pap to Huck. *The Adventures of Huckleberry Finn*, ch.5.

80 [He] reckoned a body could reform the old man with a shotgun, maybe, but he didn't know no other way.
1884 Judge Thatcher's opinion of Pap. *The Adventures of Huckleberry Finn*, ch.5.

81 Pap warn't in a good humor—so he was his natural self.
1884 *The Adventures of Huckleberry Finn*, ch.6.

82 A body would 'a thought he was Adam—he was just all mud.
1884 *The Adventures of Huckleberry Finn*, ch.6.

83 After supper Pap took the jug, and said he had enough whisky there for two drunks and one delirium tremens.
1884 *The Adventures of Huckleberry Finn*, ch.6.

84 How slow and still the time did drag along.
1884 *The Adventures of Huckleberry Finn*, ch.6.

85 I's rich now, come to look at it. I owns myself, en I's wuth eight hund'd dollars.
1884 Jim. *The Adventures of Huckleberry Finn*, ch.8.

86 But it warn't no time to be sentimentering.
1884 *The Adventures of Huckleberry Finn*, ch.13.

87 It was fifteen minutes before I could work myself up to go and humble myself to a nigger—but I done it, and I warn't ever sorry for it afterwards, neither. I didn't do him no more mean tricks, and I wouldn' done that one if I'd a knowed it would make him feel that way.
1884 Huck, of Jim. *The Adventures of Huckleberry Finn*, ch.15.

88 Jim said it made him all over trembly and feverish to be so close to freedom.
1884 *The Adventures of Huckleberry Finn*, ch.16.

89 To be, or not to be; that is the bare bodkin
That makes calamity of so long life;
For who would fardels bear, till Birnam Wood do come to Dunsinane,
But that the fear of something after death
Murders the innocent sleep,
Great nature's second course,
And makes us rather sling the arrows of outrageous fortune
Than fly to others that we know not of.
There's the respect must give us pause:
Wake Duncan with thy knocking! I would thou couldst;
For who would bear the whips and scorns of time,
The oppressor's wrong, the proud man's contumely,
The law's delay, and the quietus which his pangs might take,

In the dead waste and middle of the night, when Churchyards yawn
In customary suits of solemn black,
But that the undiscovered country from whose bourne no traveler returns,
Breathes forth contagion on the world,
And thus the native hue of resolution, like the poor cat i' the adage,
Is sicklied o'er with care,
And all the clouds that lowered o'er our housetops,
With this regard their currents turn awry,
And lose the name of action.
'Tis a consummation devoutly to be wished.
But soft you, the fair Ophelia:
Ope not thy ponderous and marble jaws,
But get thee to a nunnery—go!
1884 The Duke's version of Hamlet's soliloquy, combining elements of other speeches by Hamlet and pieces of *Macbeth*. *The Adventures of Huckleberry Finn*, ch.21.
▷ See Shakespeare 890:21.

90 All kings is mostly rapscallions.
1884 *The Adventures of Huckleberry Finn*, ch.22.

91 Hain't we got all the fools in town on our side? And ain't that a big enough majority in any town?
1884 *The Adventures of Huckleberry Finn*, ch.26.

92 It don't make no difference whether you do right or wrong, a person's conscience ain't got no sense, and just goes for him *anyway*. If I had a yaller dog that didn't know no more than a person's conscience does I would poison him. It takes up more room than all the rest of a person's insides, and yet ain't no good, nohow. Tom Sawyer he says the same.
1884 *The Adventures of Huckleberry Finn*, ch.33.

93 But that's always the way; it don't make no difference whether you do right or wrong, a person's conscience ain't got no sense, and just goes for him *anyway*.
1884 Huck. *The Adventures of Huckleberry Finn*, ch.33.

94 But I reckon I got to light out for the territory ahead of the rest, because Aunt Sally she's going to adopt me and sivilize me, and I can't stand it. I been there before.
1884 Huck. *The Adventures of Huckleberry Finn*, closing words.

95 The boy's mouth is a trifle more Irishy than is necessary.
1884 Letter to his publishers.

96 An experienced, industrious, ambitious, and often quite picturesque liar.
1885 'The Private History of a Campaign That Failed'.

97 Many a small thing has been made large by the right kind of advertising.
1889 *A Connecticut Yankee in King Arthur's Court*, ch.22.

98 The master minds of all nations, in all ages, have sprung in affluent multitude from the mass of the nation, and from the mass of the nation only—not from its privileged classes.

1889 *A Connecticut Yankee in King Arthur's Court*, ch.25.

99 If you pick up a starving dog and make him prosperous, he will not bite you. This is the principal difference between a dog and a man.

1894 *Pudd'nhead Wilson*, ch.16, 'Pudd'nhead Wilson's Calendar'.

1 Few things are harder to put up with than the annoyance of a good example.

1894 *Pudd'nhead Wilson*, ch.19, 'Pudd'nhead Wilson's Calendar'.

2 Familiarity breeds contempt—and children.

c.1894 Quoted in Albert Bigelow Paine (ed) *Mark Twain's Notebook* (1935).

3 What marriage is to morality, a properly conducted licensed liquor traffic is to sobriety.

1895 Quoted in Albert Bigelow Paine (ed) *Mark Twain's Notebook* (1935), ch.23.

4 When in doubt, tell the truth.

1897 *Following the Equator*, ch.2, 'Pudd'nhead Wilson's New Calendar'.

5 I admire him, I frankly confess it; and when his time is come I shall buy a piece of the rope for a keepsake.

1897 Of Cecil Rhodes. *Following the Equator* (1897), ch.2.

6 Man is the Only Animal that Blushes. Or needs to.

1897 *Following the Equator*, ch.27, 'Pudd'nhead Wilson's New Calendar'.

7 When people do not respect us we are sharply offended; yet deep down in his private heart no man much respects himself.

1897 *Following the Equator*, ch.29, 'Pudd'nhead Wilson's New Calendar'.

8 The man with a new idea is a crank until the idea succeeds.

1897 *Following the Equator*, ch.32, 'Pudd'nhead Wilson's New Calendar'.

9 There are several good protections against temptation but the surest is cowardice.

1897 *Following the Equator*, ch.36, 'Pudd'nhead Wilson's New Calendar'.

10 It takes your enemy and your friend, working together, to hurt you to the heart; the one to slander you and the other to get the news to you.

1897 *Following the Equator*, ch.45, 'Puddnhead Wilson's New Calendar'.

11 Human nature is the same everywhere; it deifies success, it has nothing but scorn for defeat.

1897 *Joan of Arc*, bk.1, ch.8.

12 Education consists mainly in what we have unlearned.

c.1897 Quoted in Albert Bigelow Paine (ed) *Mark Twain's Notebook* (1935).

13 There are many scapegoats for our blunders, but the most popular one is Providence.

c.1897 Quoted in Albert Bigelow Paine (ed) *Mark Twain's Notebook* (1935).

14 The report of my death was an exaggeration.

1897 In the *New York Journal*, 2 Jun. This was the substance of Twain's cable to the Associated Press in response to the news item that he had died.

15 I am a democrat only on principle, not by instinct—nobody is *that*. Doubtless some people *say* they are, but this world is grievously given to lying.

1898 *Notebook*, ch.31, Feb–Mar.

16 A classic…something that everybody wants to have read and nobody wants to read.

1900 Speech on 'The Disappearance of Literature' at the Nineteenth Century Club, 20 Nov. Quoted in Albert Bigelow Paine (ed) *Mark Twain's Speeches* (1910).

17 Always do right. This will gratify some people, and astonish the rest.

1901 Speech, Brooklyn, 16 Feb.

18 The man who is a pessimist before 48 knows too much; if he is an optimist after it, he knows too little.

1902 Notebook, ch.33, Dec.
▷ See also Willkie 1083:8.

19 Of the delights of this world man cares most for sexual intercourse. He will go any length for it—risk fortune, character, reputation, life itself.

c.1906 Quoted in Albert Bigelow Paine (ed) *Mark Twain's Notebook* (1935).

20 Scientists have odious manners, except when you prop up their theory; then you can borrow money off them.

The Bee (published in 1917).

21 I have been told that Wagner's music is better than it sounds.

Autobiography (published in 1924).

22 I have never taken any exercise, except sleeping and resting, and I never intend to take any. Exercise is loathsome.

Quoted in Colin Jarman *The Guinness Dictionary of Sports Quotations* (1990).

23 Golf is a good walk spoiled.

Attributed. Quoted in Michael Hobbs *The Golf Quotations Book* (1992).

24 I don't know anything that mars good literature so
    completely as too much truth.
    'The Savage Club Dinner'. Quoted in Albert Bigelow Paine (ed)
    Mark Twain's Speeches (1923).

Tynan, Kenneth 1927–80

English theatre critic. Writing for the *Observer* and for the
New Yorker, he argued strongly for the foundation of the
National Theatre and lent his support to many talented
radical playwrights. He was also the moving force behind
the stylish erotic revue *Oh, Calcutta!* (1969).

25 There was a heated division of opinion in the
    lobbies during the interval but a small conservative
    majority took the view that it might be as well to
    remain in the theatre.
    1953 Reviewing the play *The Glorious Days*.

26 A good many inconveniences attend play-going in
    any large city, but the greatest of them is usually the
    play itself.
    1957 In the *New York Herald Tribune*.

27 A novel is a static thing that one moves through; a
    play is a dynamic thing that moves past one.
    1961 *Curtains.*

28 Forty years ago he was Slightly in *Peter Pan*, and
    you might say that he has been wholly in *Peter Pan*
    ever since.
    1961 Of Noël Coward. *Curtains.*

29 A critic is a man who knows the way but can't drive
    the car.
    1966 In the *New York Times Magazine*, 9 Jan.

30 A good drama critic is one who perceives what is
    happening in the theatre of his time. A great drama
    critic also perceives what is *not* happening.
    1967 *Tynan Right and Left*, foreword.

Tyson, Don(ald) John 1930–

US businessman, chairman and chief executive officer of
Tyson Foods Inc, Arkansas.

31 If you can take $20,000 in one-hundred-dollar bills
    and walk up on a windy hill and tear them up and
    watch them blow away, and it doesn't bother you,
    then you should go into the commodities market.
    1994 In the *New Yorker*, 30 May.

Tzara, Tristan pseudonym of *Samy Rosenstock* 1896–1963

Romanian-born poet, essayist and editor in Paris, a leader
of the Dadaist movement.

32 *Dada ne signifie rien.*

    Dada means nothing.
    1918 *Sept manifestes Dada*, 'Manifeste Dada 1918'.

33 All pictorial or plastic art is useless; art should be a
    monster which casts servile minds into terror.
    1918 Quoted in Saranne Alexandrian *Surrealist Art* (1970).

34 *Liberté: DADA DADA DADA, hurlement de couleurs
    crispées, entrelacements des contraires et de toutes les
    contradictions, des grotesques, des inconséquences: LA
    VIE.*

    Freedom: DADA DADA DADA, a howl of unnerving
    colours, intertwinings of contrarities and
    contradictions, of the grotesque, of inconsistencies:
    LIFE.
    1918 *Sept manifestes Dada*, 'Manifeste Dada 1918'.

35 *La mort serait un beau long voyage
    et les vacances illimitées de la chair
    des structures et des os.*

    Death should be a long, beautiful voyage
    and limitless vacations of the flesh.
    1923 *De nos oiseaux*, 'La mort de Guillaume Apollinaire'.

36 Dada began not as an art form but as a disgust.
    Quoted in Saranne Alexandrian *Surrealist Art* (1970).

Uccello, Paolo 1397–1475

Florentine painter. One of the first Italian painters of the
Renaissance to explore the use of perspective.

37 O what a lovely thing this perspective is!
    Attributed in Giorgio Vasari *Lives of the Artists* (1568, translated
    by George Bull, 1965).

Umaseo, Tadao c.1950–

Japanese intellectual who has written about and
commented on his country's social and political traditions.

38 In terms of communication, Japan is like the black
    hole of the universe. It receives signals but does not
    emit them.
    1986 Quoted in David Halberstam *The Reckoning.*

Unamuno, Miguel de 1864–1936

Spanish fatalist philosopher and writer. Rector at the
University of Salamanca, he first supported and then
denounced Franco and subsequently died at the hands of
the Fascists.

39 *La vida es duda, y la fe sin la duda es solo muerte.*

    Life is doubt, and faith without doubt is nothing
    but death.
    1907 *Poesias*, 'Salmo II'.

40 It is not usually our ideas that make us optimistic
    or pessimistic, but it is our optimism or pessimism
    of physiological or pathological origin that makes
    our ideas.
    1913 *The Tragic Sense of Life.*

41 Science is a cemetery of dead ideas.
    1913 *The Tragic Sense of Life* (translated by P Smith, 1953).

42 True science teaches, above all, to doubt and to be ignorant.
1913 *The Tragic Sense of Life* (translated by P Smith, 1953).

43 Science robs men of wisdom and usually converts them into phantom beings loaded up with facts.
Collected in *Essays and Soliloquies* (translated by J E Crawford Flitch, 1925).

Unesco Constitution

An organization founded (in 1946) to promote collaboration among nations through education, science and culture.

44 Since wars begin in the minds of men, it is in the minds of men that the defences of peace must be constructed.
1946

United Nations Charter

Drafted during World War II by the US, UK and USSR. Key figures included John Foster Dulles, Ralph Bunche, Field Marshal Jan Smuts and others.

45 We the Peoples of the United Nations, determined to save succeeding generations from the scourge of war, which twice in our lifetime has brought untold sorrow to mankind, and to reaffirm faith in fundamental human rights, in the dignity and worth of the human person, in the equal rights of men and women and of nations large and small, and to establish conditions under which justice and respect for the obligations arising from treaties and other sources of international law can be maintained, and to promote social progress and better standards of life in larger freedom, and for these ends, to practice tolerance and live together in peace with one another as good neighbours, and to unite our strength to maintain international peace and security, and to ensure by the acceptance of principles and the institution of methods, that armed force shall not be used, save in the common interest, and to employ international machinery for the promotion of the economic and social advancement of all peoples, have resolved to combine our efforts to accomplish these aims.
1945 26 Jun.

Unseld, Siegfried 1924–

Head of Suhrkamp Verlag (Frankfurt).

46 One of the signs of Napoleon's greatness— according to a sociologist who recently wrote to our publishing house—is that he once had a publisher shot.
1978 *The Author and his Publisher* (translated by H and H Hannum, 1980), p.1.

Untermeyer, Louis 1885–1977

US writer and editor, best known as the editor of anthologies such as *Modern American Poetry* (1919), which introduced some important new voices, and *Treasury of Great Poems* (1955).

47 Every poet knows the pun is Pierian, that it springs from the same soil as the Muse…a matching and shifting of vowels and consonants, an adroit assonance sometimes derided as jackassonance.
1965 *Bygones.*

Updike, John Hoyer 1932–

US novelist, poet and critic. He is one of the most successful writers of his period. He is best known for his novels, notably the 'Rabbit' tetralogy, but has also written poetry, short stories, criticism and *Self-Consciousness*, a volume of memoirs.

48 Everybody who tells you how to act has whisky on their breath.
1960 *Rabbit, Run.*

49 The difficulty with humorists is that they will mix what they believe with what they don't; whichever seems likelier to win an effect.
1960 *Rabbit, Run.*

50 Many-maned scud-thumper, tub
of male whales, maker of worn wood, shrub-
ruster, sky-mocker, rave!
portly pusher of waves, wind-slave.
1960 *Telephone Poles and Other Poems*, 'Winter Ocean'.

51 School is where you go between when your parents can't take you and industry can't take you.
1963 *The Centaur*, ch.4.

52 One out of three hundred and twelve Americans is a bore, for instance, and a healthy male adult bore consumes each year one and a half times his own weight in other people's patience.
1965 *Assorted Prose*, 'Confessions of a Wild Bore'.

53 The first breath of adultery is the freest; after it, constraints aping marriage develop.
1968 *Couples*, ch.2.

54 Sex is like money; only too much is enough.
1968 *Couples*, ch.5.

55 Facts are generally overesteemed. For most practical purposes, a thing is what men think it is. When they judged the earth flat, it was flat. As long as men thought slavery tolerable, it was tolerable. We live down here among shadows, shadows among shadows.
1974 Buchanan. *Buchanan Dying*, act 1.

56 To be President of the United States, sir, is to act as advocate for the blind, venomous, and ungrateful

client; still, one must make the best of the case, for the purposes of Providence.
1974 Polk. *Buchanan Dying*, act 2.

57 In general the churches…bore for me the same relation to God that billboards did to Coca-Cola: they promoted thirst without quenching it.
1975 *A Month of Sundays*, ch.2.

58 Americans have been conditioned to respect newness, whatever it costs them.
1975 *A Month of Sundays*, ch.18.

59 One of the last…of the great narrating English virgins.
Of Mildred Lathbury, protagonist of Barbara Pym's *Excellent Women* (1978). Attributed.

60 America is a vast conspiracy to make you happy.
1980 *Problems*, 'How to Love America and Leave It at the Same Time'.

61 Writing criticism is to writing fiction and poetry as hugging the shore is to sailing in the open sea.
1984 *Hugging The Shore*, foreword.

62 Why does one never hear of government funding for the preservation and encouragement of comic strips, girlie magazines and TV soap operas? Because these genres still hold the audience they were created to amuse and instruct.
1985 In the *New York Review of Books*, 18 Jul.

63 There's a crystallization that goes on in a poem which the young man can bring off, but which the middle-aged man can't.
1986 In the *New York Times*, 24 Mar.

64 How circumstantial reality is! Facts are like individual letters, with their spikes and loops and thorns, that make up words: eventually they hurt our eyes, and we long to take a bath, to rake the lawn, to look at the sea.
1989 *Self-Consciousness*, I. 'A Soft Spring Night in Shillington'.

65 A writer's self-consciousness, for which he is much scorned, is really a mode of interestedness, that inevitably turns outward.
1989 *Self-Consciousness*, I. 'A Soft Spring Night in Shillington'.

66 The essential self is innocent, and when it tastes its own innocence knows that it lives forever.
1989 *Self-Consciousness*, I. 'A Soft Spring Night in Shillington'.

67 The throat: how strange, that there is not more erotic emphasis upon it. For here, through this compound pulsing pillar, our life makes its leap into spirit, and in the other direction gulps down what it needs of the material world.
1989 *Self-Consciousness*, III. 'Getting The Words Out'.

68 The great temple of fiction has no well-marked front portal; most devotees arrive through a side door, and not dressed for worship.
1989 *Self-Consciousness*, III. 'Getting The Words Out'.

69 In fact we do not try to picture the afterlife, nor is it our selves in our nervous tics and optical flecks that we wish to perpetuate; it is the self as the window on the world that we can't bear to think of shutting.
1989 *Self-Consciousness*, VI. 'On Being A Self Forever'.

70 Not only are selves conditional but they die. Each day, we wake slightly altered, and the person we were yesterday is dead.
1989 *Self-Consciousness*, VI. 'On Being A Self Forever'.

71 So writing is my sole remaining vice. It is an addiction, an illusory release, a presumptuous taming of reality, a way of expressing lightly the unbearable.
1989 *Self-Consciousness*, VI. 'On Being A Self Forever'.

72 Now that I am sixty, I see why the idea of elder wisdom has passed from currency.
1992 In the *New Yorker*, Nov.

73 [There is] an undercurrent of emotion bred of the deep acquaintance that can take a landscape and its inhabitants to be a vocabulary, a set of wordless symbols effortlessly shared.
1995 On the artist Edward Hopper. In the *Washington Post*, 25 Jun.

Urey, Harold Clayton 1893–1981

US chemist and discoverer of deuterium, or heavy hydrogen. He taught at the Universities of Montana, Johns Hopkins, Columbia, Chicago and Oxford, and was awarded the 1934 Nobel Prize in Chemistry.

74 I thought it might have a practical use in something like neon signs.
c.1934 Recalling his 1932 discovery of heavy water which proved critical to the development of the atomic bomb.

Ustinov, Sir Peter Alexander 1921–

English actor, playwright and director, of Russian descent. He has appeared in a wide range of European works, including both comedies and tragedies, and has also enjoyed success in plays of his own, among them *The Love of Four Colonels* (1951), *Romanoff and Juliet* (1956) and *Beethoven's Tenth* (1983). His talent as a witty raconteur and his many film appearances have also contributed to his international reputation.

75 Critics search for ages for the wrong word, which, to give them credit, they eventually find.
1952 BBC radio broadcast, Feb.

76 A diplomat these days is nothing but a head waiter who's allowed to sit down occasionally.
1956 *Romanoff and Juliet*.

77 Would it have helped Ben Hur if Christ had not been crucified?

1962 Comment when the financiers of his *Billy Budd* expressed their preference for a happy ending. Recalled in his autobiography *Dear Me* (1977).

78 Thanks to the movies, gunfire has always sounded unreal to me, even when being fired at.

1977 *Dear Me.*

79 There is always something engagingly lunatic about Ralph, a Quixotic quality, although his windmills are ditches and his faithful nag a powerful motor-cycle.

1977 Of Sir Ralph Richardson. *Dear Me.*

80 Toronto is a kind of New York operated by the Swiss.

Quoted by John Bentley Mays in the *Globe and Mail*, 1 Aug 1987.

81 I was relieved to hear that your welcome was not excessive.

To the audience, opening a one-man show at the Curran Theater. Quoted in the *San Francisco Chronicle*, 25 Apr 1991.

Uttley, Alison 1884–1976

English writer. She is remembered for her books for children, notably the 'Little Grey Rabbit' series (1929 onwards).

82 For a long time we dreamed of a real leather ball, and at last my brother had one for his birthday. The feel of the leather, the stitching round it, the faint gold letters stamped upon it, the touch of the seam, the smell of it, all affected me so deeply that I still have that ache of beauty when I hold a cricket ball.

1948 'Carts and Candlesticks'.

Vachell, Horace Annesley 1861–1955

British writer.

83 In nature there are no rewards or punishments; there are only consequences.

The Face of Clay.

Valenzuela, Luisa 1940–

Argentinian fiction writer, an outstanding author from the post-boom Latin American literature.

84 *Siendo el esperar sentada la forma más muerta de la espera muerta, siendo el esperar la forma menos estimulante de muerte.*

To wait, seated in a chair, is the deadest form of dead anticipation, and waiting the most uninspired form of death.

1982 *Cambio de armas*, 'Ceremonias de rechazo' (translated as *Other Weapons*, 'Rituals of Rejection', 1985).

Valéry, Paul 1871–1945

French poet, writer and critic, considered one of the great modern philosophical writers in French verse. He wrote widely on philosophical issues and on the metaphysics of life.

85 *Un poème n'est jamais achevé—c'est toujours un accident qui le termine, c'est-à-dire qui le donne au public.*

A poem is never finished; it is always an accident that puts a stop to it, that gives it to the public.

1930 *Littérature.*

86 *Il faut n'appeler Science que l'ensemble des recettes qui réussissent toujours.—Tout le reste est littérature.*

Science means simply the aggregate of all the recipes that are always successful. All the rest is literature.

1932 *Moralités.*

87 *Dieu créa l'homme, et ne le trouvant pas assez seul, il lui donne une compagne pour lui faire mieux sentir sa solitude.*

God created man and, finding him not sufficiently alone, gave him a companion to make him feel his solitude more keenly.

1941 *Tel Quel 1*, 'Moralités'.

88 *La politique est l'art d'empêcher les gens de se mêler de ce qui les regarde.*

Politics is the art of preventing people from taking part in affairs which concern them.

1943 *Tel Quel 2*, 'Rhumbs'.

Valle y Caviedes, Juan del c.1652–?1695

Peruvian poet born in a small town in Andalusia, Spain. He lived most of his life in Lima. Little is known of his life. His collection *Diente del Parnaso* is an earthy satire of the medical profession.

89 *Y así, enfermos, ojo alerta,*
y a ningún médico admitan;
mueran de gorra, sin dar
un real a la medicina.

Be careful then, patients,
and don't accept any doctor;
die for free and do not give
a single coin to medicine.

1689 *Diente del Parnaso* ('Parnassus' Tooth'), 'Prólogo al que leyere este tratado'.

Vallejo, César Abraham 1892–1938

Peruvian poet. A first-hand witness to poverty and the injustices done to the indigenous peoples, after the publication of his collection *Trilce*, he left Peru (1923) and spent the rest of his life in France and Spain living in precarious circumstances and without publishing a single poem. He also wrote novels and non-fiction but his reputation rests on his poetry, much of which was published posthumously.

90 *Yo nací un día*
    que Dios estuvo enfermo.

    I was born on a day
    God was sick.
    1918 *Los heraldos negros* (translated as *The Black Heralds*, 1990), 'Espergesia'.

91 *Absurdo, sólo tú eres puro.*
    Absurdo, este exceso sólo ante ti se
    suda de dorado placer.

    Absurdity, only you are pure.
    Absurdity, only before you
    is this excess sweated out of golden pleasure.
    1922 *Trilce* (translated 1973), no.73.

92 *Me moriré en París con aguacero,*
    un día del cual tengo ya el recuerdo.
    Me moriré en París—y no me corro—
    tal vez un jueves, como es hoy, de otoño.

    I will die in Paris with a sudden shower,
    a day I can already remember.
    I will die in Paris—and I don't budge—
    maybe a Thursday, like today is, in autumn.
    1939 *Poemas humanos*, 'Piedra negra sobre una piedra blanca' (translated as 'Black Stone on a White Stone', 1968).

Vance, Paul and Pockriss, Lee

US songwriters who have composed many popular songs, including 'Catch a Falling Star' which was made popular by Perry Como.

93 Itsy Bitsy Teenie Weenie Yellow Polkadot Bikini.
    1960 Title of song.

van den Berghe, Pierre L 1933–

US sociologist, Professor at the University of Washington.

94 I suffer the anthropological malady diagnosed by Lévi-Strauss in *Tristes tropiques*. I find it much more difficult to suspend value judgments about the society in which I normally reside than I do abroad. It takes physical and cultural distance to gain moral detachment and political noncommitment. Relativism implies a solid measure of indifference.
    'From the Popocatepetl to the Limpopo', collected in Bennett Berger (ed) *Authors of their Own Lives* (1990).

95 Sociology seems to have missed every intellectually promising boat in the last half century.
    'From the Popocatepetl to the Limpopo', collected in Bennett Berger (ed) *Authors of their Own Lives* (1990).

Vanderbilt, Amy 1908–74

US hostess and writer, an authority on social etiquette.

96 Breakfast is the one meal at which it is perfectly good manners to read the paper.
    1954 *Amy Vanderbilt's Complete Book of Etiquette.*

van de Wetering, Janwillem 1931–

Dutch murder-mystery writer.

97 The desire to make money is a symptom of all sorts of emotional disturbances—greed is only one of them.
    1988 *The Maine Massacre.*

Van Druten, John William 1901–57

US playwright of Dutch extraction, who was born in London. His mainly light comic plays include *Old Acquaintance* (1940), *Bell, Book and Candle* (1950) and *I Am a Camera* (1951), a stage adaptation of Isherwood's Berlin stories.

98 If I were a woman I'd wear coffee as a perfume.
    Quoted in *Think*, Feb 1963.

van Gogh, Vincent 1853–90

Dutch Post-Impressionist painter. He was an evangelistic preacher in Le Borinage (1878–80) and after studying in Paris he settled in Arles (1888), where the light and colour transformed his art. He became increasingly mentally disturbed, and finally shot himself.

99 There is no blue without yellow and without orange.
    1888 Letter to Emile Bernard, Jun.

1 I have a terrible lucidity at moments when nature is so beautiful. I am not conscious of myself any more, and the pictures come to me as if in a dream.
    1888 Letter to his brother Theo, c.27 Sep.

2 It is no more easy to make a good picture than it is to find a diamond or a pearl. It means trouble and you risk your life for it.
    1888 From a letter to his brother Theo, early Oct.

3 I cannot help it that my paintings do not sell. The time will come when people will see that they are worth more than the price of the paint.
    1888 Letter to his brother Theo, 24 Oct.

Van Horne, Harriet 1920–

US journalist.

4 Cooking is like love. It should be entered into with abandon or not at all.
    1956 *Vogue*, Oct.

5 After nightfall, I wouldn't leave a burning building without an escort.
    1969 On muggings in Manhattan. In the *Washington Post*, 26 Feb.

Varèse, Edgar 1883–1965

US composer of Italo-French parentage. He settled in New York in 1919 and founded the New Symphony Orchestra to further the cause of modern music. In 1921 he founded the international Composers' Guild, which has become the leading organ of progressive musicians. His work is almost entirely orchestral, examples including the largely abstract *Metal, Ionisation* and *Hyperprism.*

6 There is no avant-garde: only some people a bit behind.

Attributed.

Vargas Llosa, Mario 1936–

Peruvian writer, who spent his early life in Bolivia and moved to Paris in 1959, living in several European cities. He was a defeated candidate for the Peruvian presidency (1989), and remains active and often controversial in literary and political matters.

7 *¿Por qué esos personajes que se servían de la literatura como adorno o pretexto iban a ser más escritores que Pedro Camacho, quien sólo vivía para escribir? ¿Porque ellos habían leído (o, al menos, sabían que deberían haber leído) a Proust, a Faulker, a Joyce, y Pedro Camacho era poco más que un analfabeto?*

Why should those persons who used literature as an ornament or pretext have any more right to be considered real writers than Pedro Camacho, who lived *only* to write? Because they had read (or at least knew that they should have read) Proust, Faulkner, Joyce, while Pedro Camacho was very nearly illiterate?

1977 *La tía Julia y el escribidor* (translated as *Aunt Julia and the Scriptwriter,* 1982), ch.11.

Vasari, Giorgio 1511–74

Italian painter, architect and author of the first biography of the Italian Renaissance artists.

8 According to Pliny, painting was brought to Egypt by Gyges of Lydia; for he says that Gyges once saw his own shadow cast by the light of a fire and instantly drew his own outline on the wall with a piece of charcoal.

1568 *Lives of the Artists,* translated by George Bull, 1965.

9 [Michelangelo] Buonarotti commended it [Titian's painting] highly, saying that his colouring and his style pleased him very much but that it was a shame that in Venice they did not learn to draw well from the beginning.

1568 *Lives of the Artists,* translated by George Bull, 1965.

Vasconcelos, José 1882–1959

Mexican educator, politician, essayist and philosopher, Minister of Education (1920–4). His political activism led to exile on several occasions. His works call for the incorporation of native culture into Mexican life to transcend the limitations of Western culture.

10 *La América Latina debe lo que es al europeo blanco y no va a renegar de él…Sin embargo, aceptamos los ideales superiores del blanco, pero no su arrogancia.*

Latin America owes its being to the European, and should not deny it…but, while accepting the white man's superior ideals, we do not accept his arrogance.

1925 *La raza cósmica* (translated as *The Cosmic Race,* 1979), pt.1, ch.2.

Vaughan Williams, Ralph 1872–1958

British composer. He established his reputation with the choral *Sea Symphony* (1910) and promoted the English folksong movement. His works include *Fantasia on a Theme of Tallis* (1909), for strings, the *Pastoral Symphony* (1922), the opera *The Pilgrim's Progress* (1948–9) and many choral works.

11 Misbegotten abortions.

1930 Of critics. Letter to Holst.

12 I don't know whether I like it, but it's what I meant.

Of his Fourth Symphony. Quoted in Ian Crofton and Donald Fraser *A Dictionary of Musical Quotations* (1985).

13 It takes perhaps a thousand poor musicians to produce one virtuoso.

1954 In *The New York Times,* 5 Dec.

Vaughan, Henry 1622–95

Welsh religious poet. Educated at Oxford, he later practised as a physician. His verse publications include *Silex Scintillans* (1650, enlarged 1655) and *Olor Iscansus* (1651); prose meditations include *The Mount of Olives* (1652) and *Flores Solitudinis* (1652).

14 The skin and shell of things
Though fair
are not
Thy wish nor prayer
but got
My meer despair
of wings.

1650 *Silex Scintillans,* part 1, 'The Search', l.81–7.

15 Happy those early days when I
Shined in my Angel-infancy.
Before I understood this place
Appointed for my second race,
Or taught my soul to fancy aught
But a white, celestial thought;
When yet I had not walked above
A mile or two from my first love,
And looking back (at that short space)
Could see a glimpse of His bright face.
When on some gilded cloud or flower
My gazing soul would dwell an hour
And in those weaker glories spy
Some shadows of eternity.

1650 *Silex Scintillans,* part 1, 'The Retreat', l.1–14.

16　Before I taught my tongue to wound
　　My conscience with a sinful sound,
　　Or had the black art to dispense
　　A several sin to every sense,
　　But felt through all this fleshly dress
　　Bright shoots of everlastingness.
　　1650 *Silex Scintillans*, part 1, 'The Retreat', l.15–20.

17　Some men a forward motion love,
　　But I by backward steps would move,
　　And when this dust falls to the urn
　　In that state I came, return.
　　1650 *Silex Scintillans*, part 1, 'The Retreat', l.29–33.

18　My soul, there is a country
　　Far beyond the stars,
　　Where stands a wingèd sentry
　　All skilful in the wars;
　　1650 *Silex Scintillans*, part 1 'Peace', l.1–2.

19　King of comforts, King of life,
　　Thou hast cheered me,
　　And when fears and doubts were rife,
　　Thou hast cleared me.

　　Not a hook in all my breast
　　But thou fill'st it,
　　Not a thought in all my rest
　　But thou kill'st it.

　　Wherefore with my utmost strength
　　I will praise thee,
　　And as thou giv'st line, and length,
　　I will raise thee.
　　1650 *Silex Scintillans*, part 1, 'Praise', stanzas 1–3.

20　I saw Eternity the other night
　　Like a great ring of pure and endless light,
　　All calm, as it was bright,
　　And round beneath it, Time in hours, days, years
　　Driven by the spheres
　　Like a vast shadow moved.
　　1650 *Silex Scintillans*, part 1, 'The World', l.1–6.

21　Man is the shuttle, to whose winding quest
　　And passage through these looms
　　God ordered motion, but ordained no rest.
　　1650 *Silex Scintillans*, part 1, 'Man', l.26–9.

22　They are all gone into the world of light,
　　And I alone sit lingering here;
　　Their very memory is fair and bright,
　　And my sad thoughts doth clear.
　　1650 *Silex Scintillans*, part 2, 'They Are All Gone', l.1–4.

23　I played with fire, did counsel spurn,
　　Made life my common stake;
　　But never thought that fire would burn,
　　O that a soul could ache.
　　1650 *Silex Scintillans*, part 1, 'The Garland', l.13–16.

Vaz de Caminha, Pero　late 15c–early 16c

Portuguese historian, who came to the New World only eight years after Columbus. His account avoids the prevalent hyperbole, striving instead to give a realistic picture of the native peoples.

24　*Esta gente é boa e de boa simplicidade. E imprimir-se-á ligeiramente neles cualquer cunho, que les quiserem dar. E logo lhes, Nosso Senhor, deu bons corpos e bons rostos, como a bons homens, e Ele que nos por aqui trouxe, creio que n—o foi sem causa. E portanto, Vossa Alteza, pois tanto deseja acrescentar na santa fé católica, deve entender em sua salvaç—o.*

　　These people are good and simple. You can stamp on them any design that you wish to give them. And Our Lord gave them good bodies and good faces, and I think that it was his plan that we arrive here. Therefore, Your Majesty, since you wish so much to increase Catholic faith, you must provide for their salvation.
　　Carta (published 1817).

Veblen, Thorstein　1857–1929

US economist and social critic. He attacked commercial values in his best known work, *Theory of the Leisure Class* (1899). He was instrumental in breaking the hold of neo-classical economic theory and became a leader in the institutional school of economics.

25　The corset is…a mutilation, undergone for the purpose of lowering the subject's vitality and rendering her permanently and obviously unfit for work.
　　1899 *Theory of the Leisure Class.*

26　When seen in the perspective of half-a-dozen years or more, the best of our fashions strike us as grotesque, if not unsightly.
　　1899 *Theory of the Leisure Class.*

27　Conspicuous consumption of valuable goods is a means of reputability to the gentleman of leisure.
　　1899 *Theory of the Leisure Class.*

Vega Carpio, Lope Félix de　1562–1635

Spanish playwright and poet. His prolific output included some 1,800 plays, of which around 600 survive. He served with the Spanish Armada in 1588 and was ordained as a priest in 1614, though he continued to enjoy numerous love affairs.

28　All right, then, I'll say it: Dante makes me sick.
　　1635 Last words.

Vegetius　full name *Flavius Vegetius Renatus*
fl.c.385–400 AD

Roman military writer under Theodosius I, the Great. After AD 375 he produced the *Epitoma Rei Militaris*, mainly extracted from other authors, which was a supreme authority on warfare during the Middle Ages.

29 *Qui desiderat pacem, praeparat bellum.*

Let him who desires peace prepare for war.

c.380 AD *Epitoma Rei Miltaris*, no.3, prologue. This became familiar in the Middle Ages as 'Si vis pacem para bellum' ('If you want peace, prepare for war').

Venables, Terry 1943–

English footballer and manager. He was dismissed as manager of Tottenham Hotspur in 1993, but appointed manager of England a year later. He resigned after the 1996 European championships to prepare his defence against fraud allegations brought by Alan Sugar.

30 I had mixed feelings—like watching your mother-in-law drive over a cliff in your car.

1992 Of Paul Gascoigne's move from Tottenham Hotspur to the Italian club Lazio. Quoted in David Pickering *The Cassell Soccer Companion* (1994).

Venturi, Robert Charles 1925–

US architect, renowned for his eclectic and sometimes humorous designs, a key figure of the postmodernist school.

31 [It is] drawing a moustache on a madonna.

1977 On designing an addition to Oberlin College's 1917 Allen Memorial Art Museum. In the *New York Times*, 30 Jan.

Vergniaud, Pierre Victurnien 1753–93

French revolutionary politician, leader of the Girondists. When the Girondists clashed with the Montagnards, who wished to retain dictatorial power, he and his party were arrested and guillotined.

32 *Il a été permis de craindre que la Révolution, comme Saturne, dévorât successivement tous ses enfants.*

There is reason to fear that the Revolution may, like Saturn, devour each of her children one by one.

1793 Spoken at his trial, Oct.

Verlaine, Paul 1844–96

French poet who befriended and promoted the poetry of Arthur Rimbaud with whom he had a volatile relationship.

33 *Les sanglots longs*
Des violons
De l'automne
Blessent mon coeur
D'une langueur
Monotone.

Slow sobs
Of violins
Of autumn
Wound my heart
With a monotonous languor.

1866 *Poèmes saturniens*, *Paysages tristes*, *V*: 'Chansons d'Automne'.

34 *Un vaste et tendre*
Apaisement
Semble descendre
Du firmament . . .
C'est l'heure exquise.

A vast and tender
Calm
Seems to descend
From the heavens . . .
This is the exquisite hour.

1866 *Poèmes saturniens*, 'La Bonne Chanson, no.6'.

35 *Il pleure dans mon cœur*
Comme il pleut sur la ville.

The tears fall in my heart
As the rain over the town.

1874 *Romances sans paroles*, 'Ariettes oubliées, no.3'.

36 *Voici des fruits, des fleurs, des feuilles et des branches*
Et puis voici mon coeur qui ne bat que pour vous.

Here are fruits, flowers, leaves and branches
And here also is my heart which beats only for you.

1874 *Romances sans paroles*, 'Aquarelles, Green'.

37 *Pas la Couleur, rien que la Nuance!*

No colour, only nuance!

1884 *Jadis et naguère*, 'Art poétique'.

38 *Prends l'éloquence et tords-lui son cou!*

Take eloquence and break its neck!

1884 *Jadis et naguère*, 'Art poétique'.

39 *Que ton vers soit la bonne aventure*
Eparse au vent crispé du matin
Qui va fleurant la menthe et le thym.
Et tout le reste est littérature.

May your verse be a glorious adventure
Strewn by the crisp morning air
Which helps the mint and the thyme grow.
Everything else is mere literature.

1884 *Jadis et naguère*, 'Art poétique'.

Vespasian, Titus Flavius Vespasianus

AD 9–79

Roman Emperor, commander of the legions in the East when Nero was deposed. He was proclaimed emperor by his troops in Alexandria and after defeating his rival Vitellius (AD 69) reached Rome and restored order. He began an ambitious building programme, including the Colosseum, and extended and consolidated the Empire.

40 *Pecunia non olet.*

Money does not smell.

Attributed. His son Titus had objected to a tax on the contents of the city's urinals (used by fullers). Vespasian held a coin to

Titus's nose, asking him whether it smelled. When Titus said no he replied 'Atqui e lotio est' ('And yet, it comes from urine'). Quoted in Suetonius *Vespasian*, 23.

41 *Vae, puto deus fio.*

Dear me, I must be turning into a god.
79 Attributed last words. Quoted in Suetonius *Vespasian*, 23 (translated by Robert Graves, 1967).

Vian, Boris 1920–59

French novelist associated with the Surrealist movement.

42 *Les gens ne changent pas. Ce sont les choses qui changent.*

People do not change. Things change.
1947 *L'Ecume des jours.*

43 *Les masses ont tort et les individus toujours raison.*

The masses are wrong; individuals are always right.
1947 *L'Ecume des jours.*

44 *Mais enfin, bande de critiques, les livres que vous ne comprenez pas ne vaudraient-ils pas au moins que vous les signaliez?*

For heaven's sake, gang of critics, don't the books which you do not understand at least deserve recognition?
1948 In *La Seine*, 19 Apr.

45 *Rien n'est plus parfait, plus achevé qu'un cadavre.*

Nothing is more perfect, more complete than a corpse.
1950 *L'Herbe rouge.*

46 *Savoir qu'il existe des passions et ne pas le ressentir, c'est affreux.*

To know that there are passions and to not feel any, that is horrible.
1950 *L'Herbe rouge.*

47 *Les femmes et les hommes ne vivent pas sur le même plan.*

Women and men do not live according to the same design.
1953 *L'Arrache-coeur.*

48 *Un poète*
C'est un être unique
A des tas d'exemplaires
Qui ne pense qu'en vers
Et n'écrit qu'en musique
Sur des sujets divers
Des rouges ou des verts
Mais toujours magnifiques.

A poet
Is a unique being
From an exemplary multitude

Who only thinks in verse
And only writes in music
On diverse subjects
Reds and greens
But always magnificently.
1962 *Je voudrais pas crever.*

Vicious, Sid pseudonym of John Simon Ritchie

1957–79

British rock bassist. He played with the notorious punk rock group The Sex Pistols in the 1970s, and died of a drug overdose while awaiting trial for the murder of his girlfriend, Nancy Spungen, in the US.

49 You just pick a chord, go twang, and you've got music.
1976 In *The Sun*.

Victoria in full Alexandrina Victoria 1819–1901

Queen of Great Britain (1837–1901). She married Prince Albert of Saxe-Coburg and Gotha (1840), and bore him nine children. After his death (1861) she neglected her duties, but her recognition as Empress of India (1876) and the celebratory Golden (1887) and Diamond (1897) Jubilees restored her prestige. She had strong preferences for certain Prime Ministers (eg Melbourne and Disraeli) over others (notably Peel and Gladstone).

50 This mad, wicked folly of 'Women's Rights' with all its attendant horrors, on which her poor sex is bent, forgetting every sense of womanly feeling and propriety. Lady Amberley ought to get a good whipping.
1870 Letter to Sir Theodore Martin, 29 Mar. The feminist Lady Amberley was Bertrand Russell's mother.

51 Oh, if the Queen were a man, she would like to go and give those Russians, whose word one cannot believe, such a beating! We shall never be friends again till we have it out.
1878 Letter to Lord Beaconsfield, 10 Jan.

52 Please understand that there is no one depressed in this house. We are not interested in the possibilities of defeat; they do not exist.
1899 On the 2nd Boer War. Comment to the Prime Minister, Arthur Balfour, Dec. Quoted in Lady Gwendolen Cecil *Life of Robert, Marquis of Salisbury* (1931), vol.3, ch.6.

53 A strange, horrible business, but I suppose good enough for Shakespeare's day.
Attributed comment after watching a performance of *King Lear*.

54 He speaks to Me as if I were a public meeting.
Of Gladstone. Attributed in G W E Russell *Collections and Recollections*.

55 We are not amused.
Attributed.

Vidal, Gore originally *Eugene Luther Vidal, Jr*
1925–

US writer and polemicist. He ran for congress in 1960 and spent some time as a TV commentator. His novels include the satirical comedies *Myra Breckenridge* (1968) and *Duluth* (1983), and the historical trilogy *Burr* (1974), *1876* (1976) and *Lincoln* (1984).

56 A talent for drama is not a talent for writing, but is an ability to articulate human relationships.
1956 In the *New York Times*, 17 Jun.

57 I'm all for bringing back the birch. But only between consenting adults.
1966 Interview on *The Frost Programme*.

58 It is the spirit of the age to believe that any fact, no matter how suspect, is superior to any imaginative exercise, no matter how true.
1967 'French Letters: Theories of the New Novel', in *Encounter*, Dec.

59 Astronauts! Rotarians in space!
1968 *Myra Breckenridge*.

60 There is something about a bureaucrat that does not like a poem.
1968 *Sex, Death and Money*, preface.
▷ See Frost 406:72.

61 People who obtain power do so because it delights them for its own sake and for no other reason.
1970 In *Esquire*, Sep.

62 From primeval ooze to the stars, we killed anything that stood in our way, including each other.
1970 On the human race. In *Esquire*, Sep.

63 Whenever a friend succeeds, a little something in me dies.
1973 In the *Sunday Times Magazine*, 16 Sep.

64 It is not enough to succeed. Others must fail.
Quoted in G Irvine *Antipanegyric for Tom Driberg* (1976).

65 A triumph of the embalmer's art.
1981 Of Ronald Reagan, quoted in *The Observer*, 26 Apr.

66 But to ignore the absence of evidence is the basis of true faith.
1981 'Pink Triangle and Yellow Star', in the *Nation*, 14 Nov.

67 For certain people, after fifty, litigation takes the place of sex.
1981 Quoted in the *Evening Standard*.

68 Democracy is supposed to give you the feeling of choice, like Painkiller X and Painkiller Y. But they're both just aspirin.
1982 Interview in *The Observer*, 7 Feb.

69 It's a country evenly divided between conservatives and reactionaries.
1984 Of the US. In *The Observer*, 16 Sep.

70 American men do not read novels because they feel guilty when they read books which do not have facts in them.
1984 In *Saturday Review*, 18 Jun.

71 The century that began with a golden age in all the arts (or at least the golden twilight of one) is ending not so much without art as without the idea of art.
Introduction to Logan Pearsall Smith *All Trivia* (1984).

72 Fifty per cent of them won't vote and the other half doesn't read newspapers. I hope it's the same.
1991 In *Emmy*, May.

73 When it comes to getting things wrong, the English are born masters.
1991 'Reflections on Glory Reflected and Otherwise', in the *Threepenny Review*, Spring.

Vidor, King Wallis 1894–1982

US film director, born in Galveston, Texas. In Hollywood from 1915, he worked as a writer and extra before moving into directing. His many films include *The Big Parade* (1925), *The Crowd* (1928), *Our Daily Bread* (1934) and *The Fountainhead* (1949).

74 The crowd laughs with you always but it will cry with you for only a day.
1929 *The Crowd* (with John V A Weaver and Harry Behn).

Vieira, Antônio 1608–97

Jesuit missionary, orator, diplomat and writer, condemned by the Inquisition and briefly imprisoned. His sermons, letters and state papers are a valuable index to the climate of opinion in 17c Brazil and Portugal.

75 *Que coisa é a formosura, sen—o uma caveira bem vestida, a que a menor enfermidade tira a cor, e antes de a morte a despir de todo, os anos lhe v—o mortificando a graça daquela exterior e aparente superfície, de tal sorte, que, se os olhos pudessem penetrar o interior dela, o n—o poderiam ver sem horror?*

What is beauty, but a well-dressed skull that loses colour with the slightest illness, and, before death robs it of everything, the grace of its external and apparent surface is mortified by the years in such a way that, if eyes could penetrate within beauty, they could watch it only full of horror?
c.1666 *Sermões*, 'Serm—o do demónio mudo' ('Sermon of the Silent Devil').

Villon, François 1431–c.1484

French poet, member of the criminal organization 'The Brotherhood of the Cocquille'. Several times sentenced to death for various crimes, he was repeatedly pardoned. In 1463 he was finally sentenced to death, but this was commuted to banishment.

76 *Mais où son les neiges d'antan?*

But where are last year's snows?

1461 'Ballade des Dames du Temps Jadis', refrain.

St Vincent of Lérins known as *Vincentius Lerinensis* d.c.450 AD

Monk of the island of Lerna (Lérins).

77 *Quod ubique, quod semper, quod ab omnibus creditum est.*

What is everywhere, what is always, what is by all people believed.

Commonitorium Primum, section 2 (translated by Heurtley, 1895).

Viner, Jacob 1892–1970

US economist, a professor at the University of Chicago and Princeton University.

78 The classical economists were not wholly free from error, for they were only mortals, even if of a superior species.

1930 *The Long View and the Short.*

Virgil full name *Publius Vergilius Maro*
70–19 BC

Roman poet, under the patronage of Maecenas and Augustus. He published the *Eclogae*, a collection of pastorals, in 37 BC, and the *Georgica* (a didactic poem on husbandry in four books) in 30 BC. The *Aeneid*, a national epic based on the legendary founder of the Roman nation, was published posthumously.

79 *Arma virumque cano, Troiae qui primus ab oris Italiam fato profugus Laviniaque venit Litora.*

This is a tale of arms and of a man. Fated to be an exile, he was the first to sail from the land of Troy and reach Italy, at its Lavinian shore.

Aeneid, opening lines (translated by W F Jackson Knight).

80 *Non ignara mali, miseris succurrere disco.*

No stranger to trouble myself, I am learning to help those who are in distress.

Dido, queen of Carthage. *Aeneid*, bk.1, l.630.

81 *Conticuere omnes intentique ora tenebant Inde toro pater Aeneas sic orsus ab alto.*

They fell silent, every one, and each face was turned intently towards him. From high on the dais Aeneas, Troy's Chieftain, began to speak.

Aeneid, bk.2, l.1 (translated by W F Jackson Knight).

82 *Quidquid id est, timeo Danaos et dona ferentes.*

Whatever it may be, I fear the Greeks, even when bearing gifts.

Spoken by Laocoon, a Trojan prince and priest of Apollo, warning the city against the wooden horse left by the Greeks. *Aeneid*, bk.2, l.49.

83 *Una salus victis nullam sperare salutem.*

Nothing can save the conquered but the knowledge that they cannot now be saved.

Aeneid, bk.2, l.354 (translated by W F Jackson Knight).

84 *Dis aliter visum.*

The gods thought otherwise.

Aeneid, bk.2, l.428.

85 *Fama, malum qua non aliud velocius ullum.*

Rumour is of all pests the swiftest.

Aeneid, bk.4, l.174 (translated by W F Jackson Knight).

86 *Quis fallere possit amantem?*

Who can deceive a lover?

Aeneid, bk.4, l.296.

87 *Varium et mutabile semper femina.*

Women were ever things of many changing moods.

Aeneid, bk.4, l.569 (translated by W F Jackson Knight).

88 *Audentis Fortuna iuvat!*

Fortune helps those who dare.

Aeneid, bk.10, l.284. The phrase is often rendered as 'Fortune favours the brave'.

89 *Experto credite.*

Believe one who has experienced it.

Aeneid, bk.11, l.283.

90 *Latet anguis in herba.*

A snake lurks in the grass.

Eclogues, 3.93.

91 *Sicelides Musae, paulo maiora canamus. Non omnis arbusta iuvant humilesque myricae.*

Sicilian Muses, let us sing a somewhat loftier strain. Not all do orchards please and the lowly tamarisks.

Eclogues, 4.1–2 (translated by H Rushton Fairclough).

92 *Non omnia possumus omnes.*

We cannot all do everything.

Eclogues, 8.63 (translated by H Rushton Fairclough).

93 *Omnia vincit amor.*

Love conquers all things.

Eclogues, 10.69.

94 *Labor omnia vicit improbus et duris urgens in rebus egestas.*

Toil conquered the world, unrelenting toil, and want that pinches when life is hard.

Georgics, 1.145–6 (translated by H Rushton Fairclough).

95 *Felix qui potuit rerum cognoscere causas.*

Blessed is he who has been able to win knowledge of the causes of things.
Georgics, 2.490 (translated by H Rushton Fairclough).

96 *Mantua me genuit, Calabri rapuere, tenet nunc Parthenope; cecini pascua rura duces.*

Mantua brought me life, Calabria death; now Naples holds me: I sang of flocks and farms and heroes.
19BC Epitaph on his tomb near Naples, supposedly dictated on his death-bed, quoted in Donatus *Vita Donati*, 'Life of Virgil'.

Vitruvius full name *Marcus Vitruvius Pollio*
c.70BC–25BC

Roman architect and engineer whose ten books on architecture, *De Architectura*, are the oldest surviving work on the subject.

97 Neither talent without instruction, nor instruction without talent can produce the perfect craftsman.
c.25BC *On Architecture.*

Vlaminck, Maurice de 1876–1958
French painter, graphic artist and writer.

98 Good painting is like good cooking: it can be tasted, but not explained.
On Painting.

Voltaire pseudonym of *François Marie Arouet*
1694–1778

French philosopher. He was imprisoned for lampooning the Duc d'Orleans, 1717–18, and later went into exile in England, 1726–9. He returned to France, but moved to Berlin in 1750 to the court of Frederick the Great. His works include *Oedipe* (1718), *Candide* (1759), and the *Dictionnaire philosophique* (1764).

99 *Le superflu, chose très nécessaire.*

The superfluous, a very necessary thing.
1736 *Le Mondain.*

1 *Dans ce pays-ci il est bon de tuer de temps en temps un amiral pour encourager les autres.*

In this country it is considered a good thing to kill an admiral from time to time, to encourage the others.
1759 Of England; referring to the execution of Admiral Byng following his failure to engage the French at Menorca, 1757. *Candide*, ch.23.

2 *Tout est pour le mieux dans le meilleur des mondes possibles.*

All is for the best in the best of all possible worlds.
1759 *Candide*, ch.30.

3 *Cela est bien dit, répondit Candide, mais il faut cultiver notre jardin.*

'Well said', Candide replied, 'but we must cultivate our own garden.'

1759 *Candide*, ch.30.

4 I am the best-tempered man there ever was, yet I have killed three men, and two of them were priests!
1759 *Candide*, ch.15.

5 You know that these two nations have been at war over a few acres of snow near Canada, and that they are spending on this fine struggle more than Canada itself is worth.
1759 Of the French and English struggle in Quebec. *Candide* (translated by Robert A Adams, 1966).

6 Men will always be mad, and those who think they can cure them are the maddest of all.
1762 Letter.

7 *La superstition met le monde entier en flammes; la philosophie les éteint.*

Superstition sets the whole world in flames; philosophy puts out the fire.
1764 *Dictionnaire philosophique*, 'Superstition'.

8 *En effet, l'histoire n'est que le tableau des crimes et des malheurs.*

In fact, history is nothing but a tableau of crimes and misfortunes.
1767 *L'Ingénu*, ch.10.

9 *Ce corps qui s'appelait et qui s'appelle encore le saint empire romain n'était en aucune manière ni saint, ni romain, ni empire.*

This state which was called and is still called the Holy Roman Empire, was not in any way holy, or Roman or an Empire.
1769 *Essai sur Les Moeurs et l'Esprit des Nations.*

10 *La foi consiste à croire ce que la raison ne croit pas...Il ne suffit pas qu'une chose soit possible pour la croire.*

Faith consists in believing what reason cannot...In order to believe something, it is not enough that it should be possible.
1770 *Questions sur l'Encyclopédie.*

11 *Le mieux est l'ennemi du bien.*

The best is the enemy of the good.
1772 *Contes*, 'La Bégueule', l.2. He is quoting an Italian proverb, *Il meglio è l'inimico del bene.*

12 This enormous dunghill.
1776 Of the works of William Shakespeare. Letter to d'Argental, 19 Jul.

13 *On doit des égards aux vivants; on ne doit aux morts que la vérité.*

We should be considerate to the living; to the dead we owe only the truth.
'Première Lettre sur Oedipe'. In *Oeuvres*, vol.1. Published 1785.

14 *Dieu n'est pas pour les gros bataillons, mais pour ceux qui tirent le mieux.*

God is on the side not of the big battalions, but of the best shots.
In *Voltaire's Notebooks*, edited by Th. Besterman (1952).

15 *Il faut, dans le gouvernement, des bergers et des bouchers.*

Governments need both shepherds and butchers
In *Voltaire's Notebooks*, edited by Th. Besterman (1952).

16 One goes to see a tragedy to be moved, to the opera one goes either for want of any other interest or to facilitate digestion.
Quoted in J Wechsberg *The Opera* (1972).

17 *Si Dieu n'existait pas, il faudrait l'inventer.*

If God did not exist, it would be necessary to invent him.
Epîtres, 'A l'Auteur du Livre des Trois Imposteurs'.

18 The art of medicine consists of amusing the patient while Nature cures the disease.
Attributed.

19 I disapprove of what you say, but I will defend to the death your right to say it.
Attributed.

Vorster, John originally *Balthazar Johannes Vorster* 1915–83

South African Nationalist politician, an extreme Afrikaner. As Prime Minister (1966–78) he maintained a policy of apartheid and protected white interests. In 1978 he became President, but resigned over a financial scandal.

20 As far as criticism is concerned, we don't resent that unless it is absolutely biased—as it is in most cases.
1969 In *The Observer*, 9 Nov.

Vreeland, Diana originally *Diana Dalziel* 1906?–1989

US journalist, editor of *Vogue*. Born in Paris, she married Thomas Vreeland in 1924 in New York and joined Vogue as editor-in-chief in 1962. She transformed the high-fashion magazine into a society journal. She also acted as consultant to the costume institute at the Metropolitan Museum of Art.

21 A little bad taste is like a splash of paprika. We all need a splash of bad taste—it's hearty, it's healthy, it's physical.
1984 *D.V.* (her autobiography, edited by George Plimpton and Christopher Hemphill).

22 The biggest thing since the atom bomb.
1990 On the bikini. In her obituary in the *New York Times*, 1 Apr.

23 People who eat white bread have no dreams.
Quoted in Annette Tapert and Diana Edkins *The Power of Style* (1994).

Vukovich, Bill 1918–55

US motor-racing driver. He won the Indianopolis 500 in 1953 and 1954 but was killed in the race while in the lead the following year.

24 There's no secret. You just press the accelerator to the floor and steer left.
1954 Of his tactics in the Indianapolis 500. Quoted in Colin Jarman *The Guinness Dictionary of Sports Quotations* (1990).

Waddington, Miriam 1917–

Canadian poet and critic. Of Russian-Jewish origin, she was a social worker in Montreal and taught at York University, Toronto. Her works include poetry such as *The Glass Trumpet* (1966), *The Price of Gold* (1976) and *The Visitants* (1981), and short stories and essays.

25 Keep bees and
grow asparagus,
watch the tides
and listen to the
wind instead of
the politicians
make up your own
stories and believe
them if you want to
live the good life.
1972 *Driving Home: Poems New and Selected*, 'Advice to the Young'.

Wagner, Otto 1841–1918

Austrian architect and teacher, considered the founder of the modern movement.

26 The whole basis of the views of architecture prevailing today must be displaced by the recognition that the only possible point of departure for our artistic creation is modern life.
1895 *Modern Architecture* (1895), preface.

Wagner, Robert Ferdinand, Jr. 1944–

Former deputy mayor of New York City.

27 When in danger, ponder. When in trouble, delegate. And when in doubt, mumble.
1991 In the *New York Times*, 17 Feb.

Wain, John Barrington 1925–94

English writer. He is known primarily as a critic and novelist, but he also wrote poetry, plays and a biography of Samuel Johnson.

28 Poetry is to prose as dancing is to walking.
1976 BBC radio broadcast, 13 Jan.

Waite, Terry (Terence Hardy) 1939–

English religious adviser, envoy of Archbishop of Canterbury Robert Runcie from 1980. On 20 Jan 1987, while making inquiries in Beirut about European hostages, he was kidnapped. Following worldwide efforts to secure his release and that of his fellow hostages, 1,763 days later he was freed.

29 Politics come from man. Mercy, compassion, and justice come from God.
    1985 In *The Observer*, 13 Jan.

30 Freeing hostages is like putting up a stage set—which you do with the captors, agreeing on each piece as you slowly put it together. Then you leave an exit through which both the captor and the captive can walk with sincerity and dignity.
    1986 Interviewed on ABC news, 3 Nov.

Walcott, Derek Alton 1930–

West Indian poet and dramatist. He founded the Trinidad Theatre Workshop in 1959 and is Visiting Professor of English at Boston University. His poetry includes *In A Green Night* (1962), *Castaway* (1965), *The Gulf* (1969) and *Collected Poems* (1986). He was awarded the Nobel Prize for Literature, 1992.

31 I who have cursed
    The drunken officer of British rule, how choose
    Between this Africa and the English tongue I love?
    Betray them both, or give back what they give?
    How can I face such slaughter and be cool?
    How can I turn from Africa and live?
    1962 *In a Green Night*, 'A Far Cry from Africa'.

32 I'm just a red nigger who love the sea,
    I had a sound colonial education,
    I have Dutch, nigger, and English in me,
    and either I'm nobody or I'm a nation.
    1980 *The Star-Apple Kingdom*, 'The Schooner *Flight*', pt.1.

33 Who knows
    who his grandfather is, much less his name?
    1980 *The Star-Apple Kingdom*, 'The Schooner *Flight*', pt.5.

34 But we live like our names and you would have to be colonial to know the difference,
    to know the pain of history words contain
    1980 *The Star-Apple Kingdom*, 'The Schooner *Flight*', pt.6.

35 I see these islands and I feel to bawl,
    'area of darkness' with V.S. Nightfall.
    1982 *The Fortunate Traveller*, 'The Spoiler's Return'.

36 The English language is nobody's special property. It is the property of the imagination: it is the property of the language itself.
    1992 Interviewed in George Plimpton (ed) *Writers at Work* (8th series, 1988).

37 every 'I'

is a fiction finally.
    1990 *Omeros*, bk.1, ch.5, section 2.

38 Time is the metre, memory the only plot
    1990 *Omeros*, bk.2, ch.24, section 2.

39 'We were the colour of shadows when we came down with tinkling leg-irons to join the chains of the sea, for the silver coins multiplying on the sold horizon'
    1990 *Omeros*, bk.3, ch.28, section 1.

40 The worst crime is to leave a man's hands empty. Men are born makers, with that primal simplicity in every maker since Adam.
    1990 *Omeros*, bk.3, ch.28, section 2.

41 Art is History's nostalgia, it prefers a thatched roof to a concrete factory, and the huge church above a bleached village
    1990 *Omeros*, bk.6, ch.45, section 2.

42 Poetry…is perfection's sweat but most seen as fresh as the raindrops on a statue's brow.
    1992 In the *New York Times*, 8 Dec.

43 The fate of poetry is to fall in love with the world, in spite of History.
    1992 In the *New York Times*, 8 Dec.

44 The process of poetry is one of excavation and of self-discovery.
    1992 In the *New York Times*, 8 Dec.

Wald, George 1906–97

US biochemist and member of the faculty at Harvard University. He shared the 1967 Nobel Prize in Physiology or Medicine and became known widely for his view opposing the War in Vietnam.

45 We are the products of editing, rather than of authorship.
    1975 'The Origin of Optical Activity', in *Annals of the New York Academy of Sciences*, vol.69.

Wald, Jerry 1911–62

US writer and producer. His films include *Mildred Pierce* (1945), *Johnny Belinda* (1948) and *The Glass Menagerie* (1950).

46 He used to be a big shot.
    1939 The words of Panama Smith (Gladys George) as Eddie Bartlett (James Cagney) dies on the steps of the church in *The Roaring Twenties* (with Richard Macauley and Robert Rossen).

Waldron, Hicks

Chair, Boardroom Consultants Inc.

47 People do what you pay them to do, not what you ask them to do.
    1991 In the *Wall Street Journal*, 17 Apr.

Walesa, Lech 1943–

Polish trade unionist, politician and President. A former shipyard worker, he became leader of the independent trade union, Solidarity, which openly challenged the government's policies, and was imprisoned under martial law (1981). Released in 1982, he was awarded the Nobel Peace Prize in 1983. He was elected President in 1990.

48 He who once became aware of the power of Solidarity and who breathed the air of freedom will not be crushed.
1983 Nobel Peace Prize lecture, read on his behalf, 11 Dec.

49 The English are all right. They're quiet, they're slow, they count things carefully, they hesitate— and I'm switching to their track.
1991 In *The Times*, 17 Apr, on the eve of his state visit to London.

50 The Soviet Union remains a superpower in the military and nuclear sense—only its economy is in difficulty. People want me to lead the troops out or to chuck them over the border, but I have neither the strength nor the will to do it.
1991 In *The Times*, 17 Apr.

Waley, Arthur David 1889–1966

English poet and Sinologist. He is a distinguished translator of Chinese and Japanese literature.

51 It is not difficult to censor foreign news.
What is difficult today is to censor one's own thoughts,—
To sit by and see the blind man
On the sightless horse, riding into the bottomless abyss.
1940 'Censorship'.

Walker, Alice Malsenior 1944–

US writer. She has written poetry and non-fiction, and established her reputation with her novels, notably *The Color Purple* (1983, filmed 1985).

52 The gift of loneliness is sometimes a radical vision of society or one's people that has not previously been taken into account.
1973 Interview in J O'Brien (ed) *Interviews with Black Writers*.

53 It is healthier, in any case, to write for the adults one's children will become than for the children one's 'mature' critics often are.
1976 'A Writer Because of, Not in Spite of, Her Children', *Ms.*, Jan.

54 Writing saved me from the sin and inconvenience of violence.
1979 '*One* Child of One's Own', in *Ms.*, Aug.

55 The good news may be that Nature is phasing out the white man, but the bad news is that's who She thinks we all are.

1982 'Nuclear Madness: What You Can Do', in *Black Scholar*, Spring.

56 Anybody can observe the Sabbath, but making it holy surely takes the rest of the week.
1983 *In Search of Our Mothers' Gardens*, 'To the Editors of *Ms.* Magazine'.

57 The trouble with our people is as soon as they got out of slavery they didn't want to give the white man nothing else. But the fact is, you got to give 'em something. Either your money, your land, your woman or your ass.
1985 Pa. *The Color Purple*.

58 She say, Celie, tell the truth, have you ever found God in church? I never did. I just found a bunch of folks hoping for him to show. Any God I ever felt in church I brought in with me. And I think all the other folks did too. They come to church to *share* God, not find God.
1985 Shug. *The Color Purple*.

59 There are those who believe Black people possess the secret of joy and that it is this which will sustain them through any spiritual or moral or physical devastation.
1992 *Possessing the Secret of Joy*, epigraph.

Wall Street Journal

Leading US financial newspaper.

60 God is registered to vote for Hollywood as a Republican. However, Jesus Christ is a Democrat from Santa Monica.
1995 'God Lives in Hollywood', editorial on California's voter registration lists, 12 Jul.

Wall, Mervyn 1908–

Irish writer.

61 The Bishop gave vent to a long-drawn sigh. 'Did it ever occur to you to wonder why God created women?' he asked. 'It's the one thing that tempts me at times to doubt His infinite goodness and wisdom.'
1946 *The Unfortunate Fursey*.

62 The odour of sanctity was clearly discernible from his breath and person.
1946 *The Unfortunate Fursey*.

63 'Did you ever hear the like?' said the Devil, and a hard note crept into his voice. 'If there's one thing I can't stand', he said, 'it's superstition.'
1946 *The Unfortunate Fursey*.

Wallace, George Corley 1919–98

US Democratic lawyer and politician, opponent of the civil rights movement and Governor of Alabama (1963–7, 1971–4, 1975–8 and 1983–7). A presidential bid ended with an assassination attempt, 15 May 1972, which left him paralyzed.

64 Segregation now, segregation tomorrow, and segregation for ever.

1963 Inaugural speech as Governor of Alabama, 19 Feb.

65 I've climbed my last political mountain.

1972 On retiring after being crippled in an assassination attempt. Quoted in the *New York Times*, 3 Apr 1986.

66 A great deal has been lost and a great deal gained…may your message be heard…your lessons never be forgotten.

1995 Reversing the 'segregation for ever' stance of 1963. In news reports, 11 Mar.

Wallace, Henry Agard 1888–1965

US agriculturist and statesman, editor of *Wallace's Farmer* (1933–40) until nominated Vice-President to Roosevelt. Chairman of the Board of Economic Welfare (1941–5) and Secretary of Commerce (1945–6), he stood unsuccessfully as President in 1948.

67 The century on which we are entering, the century that will come out of this war, can be and must be the century of the common man.

1942 Speech, New York, 8 May.

Wallace, William Ross 1819–81

US poet. Only a few of his poems, mostly militant patriotic songs, have survived as anthology works. He practised as a lawyer in New York from 1841 until his death and was a contributor to Harper's magazine. Stimulated by the American Civil War, he wrote *Sword of Bunker Hill* (1861) and *The Liberty Bell* (1862).

68 The hand that rocks the cradle
Is the hand that rules the world.

c.1865 *John o'London's Treasure Trove.*

Wallach, Eli 1915–

US actor. A star of both stage and screen, he appeared in such films as *The Moonspinners* (1964), *The Tiger Makes Out* (1967) and *The Sentinel* (1977). On the stage he has won particular acclaim in plays by Tennessee Williams and others.

69 There's something about a crowd like that that brings a lump to my wallet.

1964 Observing the crowds that were gathering at the box office to see the highly successful Broadway show *Luv.* Attributed.

Waller, Edmund 1606–87

English poet and politician. Educated at Cambridge, he went on to be an MP; his involvement in a plot against Parliament during the Civil War led to his banishment in 1643. His collected poems were published in 1645.

70 Go, lovely rose,

Tell her that wastes her time and me,
That now she knows,
When I resemble her to thee,
How sweet and fair she seems to be.

1645 'Go, lovely rose'.

71 Small is the worth
Of beauty from the light retir'd;
Bid her come forth,
Suffer her self to be desir'd,
And not blush to be admir'd.

1645 'Go, lovely rose'.

72 Phillis, why shou'd we delay
Pleasures shorter than the day?

1645 'To Phillis'.

73 Since thou wouldst needs, bewitched with some ill charms,
Be buried in those monumental arms:
As we can wish, is, may that earth lie light
Upon thy tender limbs, and so good night.

1645 'To One Married to an Old Man'.

74 Poets may boast (as safely-vain)
Their work shall with the world remain:
Both bound together, live, or die,
The verses and the prophecy.

But who can hope his lines shou'd long
Last, in a daily changing tongue?
While they are new, envy prevails,
And as that dies, our language fails.

1645 'Of English Verse'.

75 We write in sand, our language grows,
And like our tide ours overflows.

1645 'Of English Verse'.

76 Verse thus design'd has no ill fate,
If it arrive but at the date
Of fading beauty, if it prove
But as long-liv'd as present love.

1645 'Of English Verse'.

Waller, Fats (Thomas Wright) 1904–43

US jazz pianist, composer and entertainer. A professional musician at 15, he began his recording career in 1922. Among the jazz standards he wrote were 'Ain't Misbehavin'' and 'Honeysuckle Rose'.

77 Madam, if you don't know by now, don't mess with it!

When asked what jazz was. Quoted in Marshall Stearns *The Story of Jazz* (1956).

▷ See Armstrong 35:46.

Wallis, Hal 1898–1986

US producer. He worked in Hollywood for many years and then became an independent producer.

78 Louis, I think this is the beginning of a beautiful friendship.

1942 Closing words of *Casablanca*, one of his contributions to a script largely written by the Epstein twins and Howard Koch.

Walpole, Horace, 4th Earl of Orford

1717–97

English writer and politician. Architectural pursuits, correspondence, writing, visits to Paris, his house, Strawberry Hill, and the establishment of a private press were the main occupations of his life. He exchanged more than 1600 letters with Mme du Deffand between 1769 and 1797 and corresponded also with Sir Horace Mann and the Countess of Upper Ossory.

79 We were eight days in coming hither from Lyons; the four last in crossing the Alps. Such uncouth rocks, and such uncomely inhabitants!

1739 Letter to Richard West. Collected in P Cunningham (ed) *The Letters of Horace Walpole, Fourth Earl of Orford* (1857–9).

80 I am very glad that I see Rome while it yet exists; before a great number of years are elapsed, I question whether it will be worth seeing. Between the ignorance and poverty of the present Romans, every thing is neglected and falling to decay.

1740 Letter. Collected in P Cunningham (ed) *The Letters of Horace Walpole, Fourth Earl of Orford* (1857–9).

81 It is a little plaything-house that I got out of Mrs Chevenix's shop, and it is the prettiest bauble you ever saw. It is set in enamelled meadows with filigree hedges…barges as solemn as Barons of the Exchequer move under my window…Thank God! the Thames is between me and the Duchess of Queensberry.

1747 Of Strawberry Hill, the first 'Gothic' cottage, a showplace in its day. Letter to Henry Seymour Conway, 8 Jun. In *Selected Letters of Horace Walpole* edited by W S Lewis (1973). Mrs Chevenix kept a well-known toy-shop.

82 Every drop of ink in my pen ran cold.

1752 Letter to George Montague, 30 Jul. In *The Correspondence of Horace Walpole* (Yale edition 1937-38).

83 One of the greatest geniuses that ever existed, Shakespeare, undoubtedly wanted taste.

1764 Letter to Christopher Wren, 9 Aug. In *The Correspondence of Horace Walpole* (Yale edition 1937-38).

84 It is charming to totter into vogue.

1765 Letter to George Selwyn, 2 Dec. In *The Correspondence of Horace Walpole* (Yale edition 1937-38).

85 Wondrously clean, but as evidently an actor as Garrick.

1766 Of the Methodist preacher John Wesley. Letter to John Chute, 10 Oct. In *The Letters of Horace Walpole* selected and edited by William Hadley (1926).

86 It was easier to conquer it than to know what to do with it.

1772 Of the Orient. Letter to Sir Horace Mann, 27 Mar. In *The Correspondence of Horace Walpole* (Yale edition 1937-38).

87 The way to ensure summer in England is to have it framed and glazed in a comfortable room.

1774 Letter to William Cole, 28 May. In *The Correspondence of Horace Walpole* (Yale edition 1937-38).

88 By the waters of Babylon we sit down and weep, when we think of thee, O America!

1775 Letter to William Mason, 12 Jun. In *The Correspondence of Horace Walpole* (Yale edition 1937-38).

89 The world is a comedy to those that think, a tragedy to those that feel.

1776 Letter to Lady Ossory, 11 Dec. In *Selected Letters of Horace Walpole* edited by W S Lewis (1973).

90 Your daughters, I hope, will be married to Americans, and not in this dirty, despicable little island.

1777 Letter to Lady Ossory, 11 Dec. In *Selected Letters of Horace Walpole* edited by W S Lewis (1973).

91 When will the world know that peace and propagation are the two most delightful things in it?

1778 Letter to Sir Horace Mann, 7 Jul. In *The Correspondence of Horace Walpole* (Yale edition 1937-38).

92 It is the story of a mountebank and his zany.

1785 Of Boswell's account of his *Tour of the Hebrides* with Dr Johnson. Letter to Henry Conway, 6 Oct. In *The Correspondence of Horace Walpole* (Yale edition 1937-38).

93 All the sensible Tories that I ever knew were either Jacobites or became Whigs; those that remained Tories remained fools.

Memoirs of the Reign of King George III (published 1845).

94 Virtue knows to a farthing what it has lost by not being vice.

Quoted in L Kronenberger *The Extraordinary Mr Wilkes* (1973).

95 A fertile pedant.

Of Margaret Cavendish, Duchess of Newcastle. Quoted in Nicholas T Parsons *The Joy of Bad Verse* (1988).

Walpole, Sir Robert, 1st Earl of Orford

1676–1745

English statesman and leading minister of George I and II. Elected as a Whig MP in 1701, he became Secretary for War (1708), Treasurer of the Navy (1710), and Chancellor of the Exchequer, (1715). He was recognized as England's first Prime Minister from 1721, but resigned in 1742, when a war he had opposed broke out.

96 Madam, there are fifty thousand men slain this year in Europe, and not one an Englishman.

1734 To Queen Caroline, on avoiding British participation in the War of the Polish Succession. Quoted in John Hervey *Memoirs 1734–43* (1848), vol.1.

97 They may ring their bells now; before long they
   will be wringing their hands.
   1739 Remark on hearing church bells celebrating the
   declaration of war against Spain, 19 Oct.

98 I have lived long enough in the world to know that
   the safety of a Minister lies in his having the
   approbation of this House. Former Ministers
   neglected that and therefore they fell; I have always
   made it my first study to obtain it, and therefore I
   hope to stand.
   1739 Speech, House of Commons, 21 Nov.

99 Patriots spring up like mushrooms. I could raise 50
   of them within the four and twenty hours. I have
   raised many of them in one night. It is but refusing
   to gratify an immeasurable or insolent demand,
   and up starts a patriot.
   1741 Speech, House of Commons, 13 Feb.

 1 All those men have their price.
   Memoirs of Sir Robert Walpole.

Walther Von der Vogelweide c.1170–1230

German poet. One of the most celebrated poets of his
time, he found particular favour at the Austrian court,
and was awarded a small estate by Emperor Frederick II.

 2 *Jâ leider desn mac nicht gesin,*
   Das guot und wertlich êre
   Und gotes hulde mêre
   Zesamene in ein herze komen.

   It is sadly impossible
   For wealth and a good name,
   along with God's favour,
   to be united in one heart.
   c.1195 'Ich sass ûf eime steine', l.16–19.

Walton, Izaak 1593–1683

English writer. He is remembered for *The Compleat
Angler* (1653), which discusses the business of fishing and
is interspersed with scraps of dialogue, moral reflections,
quaint old verses, songs and sayings, and idyllic glimpses
of country life.

 3 But God, who is able to prevail, wrestled with him,
   as the Angel did with Jacob, and marked him;
   marked him for his own.
   1653 Of Donne. *Life of John Donne.*

 4 Angling may be said to be so like mathematics, that
   it can never be fully learnt.
   1653 *The Compleat Angler*, 'Epistle to the Reader'.

 5 I shall stay [the reader] no longer than to wish him
   a rainy day to read this...discourse; and that if he be
   an honest angler, the east wind may never blow
   when he goes a-fishing.

1653 *The Compleat Angler*, 'Epistle to the Reader'.

 6 Angling is somewhat like poetry, men are to be
   born so.
   1653 *The Compleat Angler*, part1, ch.1.

 7 Sir Henry Wotton...was also a most dear lover, and
   a frequent practiser of the art of angling; of which
   he would say, 'it was an employment for his idle
   time...a rest to his mind, a cheerer of his spirits, a
   diverter of sadness, a calmer of unquiet thoughts, a
   moderator of passions, a procurer of contentedness;
   and that it begat habits of peace and patience in
   those that professed and practised it.'
   1653 *The Compleat Angler*, part1, ch.1.

 8 An excellent angler, and now with God.
   1653 Of Sir George Hastings, *The Compleat Angler*, part1,
   ch.4.

 9 She and I both love all anglers, they be such honest,
   civil quiet men.
   1653 The milkwoman. *The Compleat Angler*, part1, ch.4.

10 No life, my honest scholar, no life so happy and so
   pleasant as the life of a well-governed angler; for
   when the lawyer is swallowed up with business, and
   the statesman is preventing or contriving plots, then
   we sit on cowslip-banks, hear the birds sing, and
   possess ourselves in as much quietness as these silver
   streams, which we now see glide so quietly by us.
   1653 *The Compleat Angler*, part1, ch.5.

11 He would often say, Religion does not banish
   mirth, but only moderates and sets rules to it.
   1670 Of George Herbert. *Life of George Herbert.*

Walton, Sir William Turner 1902–83

British composer. His works include *Façade* (1923),
designed to accompany verses by Edith Sitwell, the
Sinfonia Concertante (1927), the biblical cantata
Belshazzar's Feast (1931), the opera *Troilus and Cressida*
(1954) and much incidental music for films.

12 I seriously advise all sensitive composers to die at
   the age of thirty-seven. I know I've gone through
   the first halcyon period, and am just about ripe for
   my critical damnation.
   1939 Letter.

Wang Xizhe 1956–

Chinese dissident, released from prison in 1993 after 12
years for his role in the Democracy Wall Movement, but
told he may not leave the city of Guangzhou (Canton)
until 1999.

13 You may keep me under surveillance until the year
   2000, but will you even be able to hold on to power
   until then?
   1995 Quoted in the *Eastern Express*, 10 May.

Ward, Artemus pseudonym of *Charles Farrar Browne* 1834–67

US humorist. In 1857 he began to publish letters from 'Artemus Ward' in the Cleveland *Plain Dealer*. His backwoods humour was an immediate success, and Lincoln interrupted a Cabinet meeting to read from him. In 1866 he moved to England where he worked for *Punch* and became a popular lecturer.

14 Traters…are a unfortunate class of people. If they wasn't they wouldn't be traters. They conspire to bust up a country—they fail, and they're traters. They bust her, and they become statesmen and heroes.
1867 *Artemus Ward in London and Other Papers*, 'The Tower of London'.

15 Let us all be happy, and live within our means, even if we have to borrow the money to do it with.
1867 *Artemus Ward in London, and Other Papers*, 'Science and Natural History'.

16 I am happiest when I am idle.
I could live for months without performing any kind of labour, and at the expiration of that time I should feel fresh and vigorous enough to go right on in the same way for numerous more months.
1867 *Artemus Ward in London, and Other Papers*, 'Pyrotechny', 3.

17 Why care for grammar as long as we are good?
1867 *Artemus Ward in London, and Other Papers*, 'Pyrotechny', 5.

18 He [Brigham Young] is dreadfully married. He's the most married man I ever saw in my life.
1869 *Artemus Ward's Lecture*, 'Brigham Young's Palace'.

19 'Why is this thus? What is the reason of this thusness?'
1869 *Artemus Ward's Lecture*, 'Heber C. Kimball's Harem'

Warhol, Andy 1928–87

US graphic artist, painter and film-maker. One of the most controversial figures in American Pop Art.

20 If you want to know all about Andy Warhol, just look at the surface of my paintings and films and me, there I am. There's nothing behind it!
1967 Quoted in Gretchen Berg 'Andy: My True Story', *LA Free Press*, 17 Mar.

21 In the future everybody will be world famous for fifteen minutes.
Quoted in Andy Warhol, Kasper König, Pontus Hultén and Olle Granath eds., *Andy Warhol* (1968).

22 The Pop artists did images that anybody walking down Broadway could recognize in a split second—comics, picnic tables, men's trousers, celebrities, shower curtains, refrigerators, Coke bottles—all the great modern things that the

Abstract Expressionists tried so hard not to notice at all.
Quoted in Andy Warhol and Pat Hackett *POPism: The Warhol '60s* (1980).

23 When you think about it, department stores are kind of like museums.
1985 *America*.

Warner, Marina Sarah 1946–

British writer and literary and social critic. Her works include *Alone of All Her Sex* (1976) and *From the Beast to the Blonde* (1994), and novels such as *Indigo* (1992).

24 Although Mary cannot be a model for the New Woman, a goddess is better than no goddess at all, for the sombre-suited masculine world of the Protestant religion is altogether too much like a gentlemen's club to which the ladies are only admitted on special days.
1976 *Alone of All Her Sex; the Myth and Cult of the Virgin Mary*, epilogue.

Warner, Sir Pelham Plum 1873–1963

English cricketer, born in Trinidad. He played for Middlesex and captained England on tours of Australia and South Africa. He was secretary (1939–45) and president (1950) of the MCC and was knighted in 1937.

25 Cricket is the greatest game that the wit of man has yet devised.
Quoted in Colin Jarman *The Guinness Dictionary of Sports Quotations* (1990).

Warner, Rex (Ernest) 1905–86

English-born author, he was University Professor at the University of Connecticut from 1964–74. He wrote poems, plays and novels, and also worked on films and in broadcasting.

26 Spain has torn the veil of Europe.

Warren, Earl 1891–1974

US politician and judge. As chief justice of the US Supreme Court (1943–53) he was a liberalizing influence, ending segregation in schools and protecting accused persons from police abuses. He headed the Commission into the assassination of John F Kennedy (1963–4).

27 We conclude that in the field of public education the doctrine of 'separate but equal' has no place.
1954 Ruling to declare segregated schools unconstitutional, 17 May.

28 The freedom to marry has long been recognized as one of the vital personal rights essential to the orderly pursuit of happiness by free men.
1957 2 Jun. Unanimous ruling against a Virginian law forbidding intermarriage of blacks and whites.

29 I always turn to the sports section first. The sports page records people's accomplishments; the front page has nothing but man's failures.

>**1968** In *Sports Illustrated*, 'Scorecard', 22 Jul.

Warren, Harry pseudonym of *Salvatore Guaragno* 1893–1981

US songwriter, born in Brooklyn. During the 1930s, he collaborated with Al Dubin on several Busby Berkeley movies. During the war years he worked with Mark Gordon for Fox and then also for MGM.

30 Walk two Oscars behind me.

>**1975** Comment to Harold Arlen on winning a second Oscar for *On the Atchison, Topeka and the Santa Fe*. Quoted in Tony Thomas *Harry Warren*.

Warren, Robert Penn 1905–89

US writer, Professor of English at Louisiana, Minnesota and Yale. He established an international reputation with his novel *All the King's Men* (1943, filmed 1949), and wrote several other novels, short stories and volumes of poetry.

31 The poem…is a little myth of man's capacity of making life meaningful. And in the end, the poem is not a thing we see—it is, rather, a light by which we may see—and what we see is life.

>**1958** In the *Saturday Review*, 22 Mar.

32 The urge to write poetry is like having an itch. When the itch becomes annoying enough, you scratch it.

>**1969** In the *New York Times*, 16 Dec.

33 How do poems grow? They grow out of your life.

>**1985** In the *New York Times*, 12 May.

34 What is a poem but a hazardous attempt at self-understanding? It is the deepest part of autobiography.

>**1985** In the *New York Times*, 12 May.

35 I don't expect you'll hear me writing any poems to the greater glory of Ronald and Nancy Reagan.

>**1986** On being appointed the first US Poet Laureate. In the *Washington Post*, 27 Feb.

36 He woke me from the torpor of the accustomed.

>On familiar scenes more fully realized through Walker Evans' realistic photographs. Quoted in Belinda Rathbone *Walker Evans* (1995).

Washington, Booker Taliaferro 1856–1915

African-American educationist, born a slave in Virginia. He became principal of the Tuskegee Institute in Alabama in 1881 and was a moderate in the negro movement. His autobiography, *Up from Slavery*, was published in 1901.

37 No race can prosper until it learns that there is as much dignity in tilling a field as in writing a poem.

It is at the bottom of life we must begin, and not at the top.

>**1895** 'The Atlanta Exposition Address', in *Up from Slavery* (1901), ch.14.

38 In all things that are purely social we can be as separate as the fingers, yet one as the hand in all things essential to mutual progress.

>**1895** 'The Atlanta Exposition Address,' in *Up from Slavery* (1901), ch.14.

Washington, George 1732–99

American soldier and statesman, first President. As commander of American forces in the War of Independence he displayed great powers of leadership, suffering defeats at Brandywine and Germantown, but holding his army together through the winter of 1777–8 at Valley Forge. After the alliance with France (1778), he forced the surrender of Cornwallis (1781) then retired to Mount Vernon, and sought strong constitutional government. In 1787 he presided over the Constitutional Convention and became President, eventually joining the Federalist Party, and retired in 1797.

39 Father, I cannot tell a lie. I did it with my little hatchet.

>In childhood, on admitting to vandalizing a cherry tree, attributed by Mason Locke Weems (Parson Weems) in his *Life and Memorable Actions of George Washington* (5th edn, c.1810). Weems claimed to have heard the tale from an elderly lady, a distant relation of Washington's, 20 years earlier.

40 When we assumed the soldier, we did not lay aside the citizen.

>**1775** Address to the New York legislature, 26 Jun.

41 I can answer for but three things: a firm belief in the justice of our cause, close attention in the prosecution of it, and the strictest integrity.

>**1775** On being elected Commander of the Unionist Army, 19 Jun.

42 The time is now near at hand which must probably determine whether Americans are to be freemen or slaves… The fate of unborn millions will now depend, under God, on the courage and conduct of this army. Our cruel and unrelenting enemy leaves us only the choice of brave resistance or abject submission. We have, therefore, to resolve to conquer or die.

>**1776** General orders, 2 Jul. Quoted in J C Fitzpatrick (ed) *Writings of George Washington* (1932), vol.5.

43 An old-fashioned Virginia fox hunt, gentlemen.

>**1777** Comment on the skirmish at Princeton, 3 Jan. Attributed.

44 It is our true policy to steer clear of permanent alliance with any portion of the foreign world.

>**1796** Farewell address to the union, 17 Sep.

Washington Post

US Newspaper.

45 The Closest of Strangers.

> **1994** Headline, 9 Jan, on the sharing of Nobel Peace Prize by South Africa's F W de Klerk and Nelson Mandela.

Washington Times

US Newspaper.

46 Cool is Hot.

> **1988** Headline, 9 May, on Massachusetts Governor Michael Dukakis's low-key campaign for Democratic presidential nomination.

47 There's no crime like the present.

> **1995** In the week in which three persons jumped the White House fence, 25 May.

Waterhouse, Keith Spencer 1929–

English novelist, dramatist, humorist and journalist. His whimsical novel *Billy Liar* (1959) was adapted for the stage the next year and filmed in 1963, and he continued writing mordantly humorous novels, such as *Jubb* (1963) and *Office Life* (1978).

48 Lying in bed, I abandoned the facts again and was back in Ambrosia.

> **1959** *Billy Liar*, opening sentence.

49 I cannot bring myself to vote for a woman who has been voice-trained to speak to me as though my dog has just died.

> **1978** On Margaret Thatcher, attributed.

50 The 50s face was angry, the 60s face was well-fed, the 70s face was foxy. Perhaps it was the right expression: there was a lot to be wary about.

> **1979** In *The Observer Magazine*, 30 Dec.

Watson, James D(ewey) 1928–

US biochemist who with Frances Crick helped to determine the structure of the nucleic acid known as DNA. Crick, Maurice Wilkins and Watson shared the 1962 Nobel Prize in Physiology or Medicine. Watson wrote *The Double Helix* (1968), the story of the discovery of the structure of DNA.

51 [Science] seldom proceeds in the straightforward logical manner imagined by outsiders. Instead, its steps forward…are often very human events in which personalities and cultural traditions play major roles.

> **1968** *The Double Helix*.

Watson, Thomas John 1874–1956

US businessman and computing pioneer, president of IBM.

52 I think there is a world market for about five computers.

> **1943** Quoted in Christopher Cerf and Victor Navasky *The Experts Speak* (1984).

Watson, Thomas John, Jr 1914–

US businessman, president (1952–61), chairman (1961–71) and chairman of the executive board (1972–9) at IBM. He also served as Ambassador to the USSR (1979–81).

53 Solve it quickly, solve it right or wrong.

> **1977** His advice on dealing with problems. In *Fortune*.

Watson, William c.1559–1603

Catholic conspirator and secular priest.

54 *Fiat justitia et ruant coeli.*

Let justice be done, though the heavens may fall.

> **1602** *A Decacordon of Ten Quodlibeticall Questions Concerning Religion and State.* This was an influential reworking of Ferdinand I's motto.
>
> ▷ See Ferdinand I 385:13.

Watt, James 1736–1819

Scottish inventor and mechanical engineer, best remembered for his refinements to the steam engine.

55 That vessel in which the powers of steam are to be employed to work the engine, which is called the Cylinder in common fire engines, and which I call the Steam Vessel, must, during the whole time the engine is at work, be kept as hot as the steam that enters it; first, by enclosing it in a case of wood, or any other materials that transmit heat slowly; secondly, by surrounding it with steam or other heated bodies; and thirdly, by suffering neither water nor any other substance colder than steam to enter and touch it during that time.

> **1769** Specification of patent, 5 Jan, for a new method of lessing the consumption of steam and fuel in fire engines.

Watts, Isaac 1674–1748

English independent preacher and hymn writer.

56 When I survey the wondrous cross
  On which the prince of glory died,
  My richest gain I count but loss,
  And pour contempt on all my pride.

> **1707** *Hymns and Spiritual Songs*, 'Crucifixion to the World, by the Cross of Christ'.

57 Jesus shall reign where'er the sun
  Does his successive journeys run;
  His kingdom stretch from shore to shore,
  Till moons shall wax and wane no more.

> **1719** *The Psalms of David Imitated*, Psalm 72.

58 Our God, our help in ages past
  Our hope for years to come,
  Our shelter from the stormy blast
  And our eternal home.

> **1719** *The Psalms of David Imitated*, Psalm 90 (John Wesley substituted 'O God' for 'Our God' in 1738).

Waugh, Auberon Alexander 1939–

English writer and editor. The eldest son of Evelyn Waugh. He is a journalist and novelist, and is the editor of the *Literary Review*.

59 I will endeavour to put the word sex in capital letters on the cover of every issue of the *Literary Review* under my editorship, regardless of its actual contents… My purpose is simply to embolden booksellers.
   1986 In the *Daily Telegraph*, 9 May.

Waugh, Evelyn Arthur St John 1903–66

English novelist. He enjoyed great success with his first novel, *Decline and Fall*, the first of a series of barbed satirical novels which included *Vile Bodies* (1930) and *Scoop* (1938). Preoccupied with the decline of English civilization, his works include *Brideshead Revisited* (1945) and the *Sword of Honour* trilogy (1952–61). A supreme stylist, and considered one of the great comic novelists, he also wrote travel books and biographies.

60 I expect you'll be becoming a schoolmaster, sir. That's what most of the gentlemen does, sir, that gets sent down for indecent behaviour.
   1928 *Decline and Fall*, Prelude.

61 'We class schools, you see, into four grades: Leading School, First-rate School, Good School, and School. Frankly,' said Mr Levy, 'School is pretty bad.'
   1928 *Decline and Fall*, pt.1, ch.1.

62 That's the public-school system all over. They may kick you out but they never let you down.
   1928 *Decline and Fall*, pt.1, ch.3.

63 You can't get into the soup in Ireland, do what you like.
   1928 *Decline and Fall*, pt.1, ch.3.

64 Meanwhile, you will write an essay on 'self-indulgence'. There will be a prize of half a crown for the longest essay, irrespective of any possible merit.
   1928 *Decline and Fall*, pt.1, ch.5.

65 For generations the British bourgeoisie have spoken of themselves as gentlemen, and by that they have meant, among other things, a self-respecting scorn of irregular perquisites. It is the quality that distinguishes the gentleman from both the artist and the aristocrat.
   1928 *Decline and Fall*, pt.1, ch.6.

66 There aren't many left like him nowadays, what with education and whisky the price it is.
   1928 *Decline and Fall*, pt.1, ch.7.

67 'I often think,' he continued, 'that we can trace

almost all the disasters of English history to the influence of Wales!'
   1928 *Decline and Fall*, pt.1, ch.8.

68 I have noticed again and again since I have been in the Church that lay interest in ecclesiastical matters is often a prelude to insanity.
   1928 *Decline and Fall*, pt.1, ch.8.

69 I have often observed in women of her type a tendency to regard all athletics as inferior forms of fox-hunting.
   1928 *Decline and Fall*, pt.1, ch.10.

70 I'm one of the blind alleys off the main road of procreation.
   1928 *Decline and Fall*, pt.1, ch.12.

71 I haven't been to sleep for over a year. That's why I go to bed early. One needs more rest if one doesn't sleep.
   1928 *Decline and Fall*, pt.2, ch.3.

72 There is a species of person called a 'Modern Churchman' who draws the full salary of a beneficed clergyman and need not commit himself to any religious belief.
   1928 *Decline and Fall*, pt.2, ch.4.

73 Instead of this absurd division into sexes, they ought to class people as static and dynamic.
   1928 *Decline and Fall*, pt.2, ch.7.

74 I came to the conclusion many years ago that almost all crime is due to the repressed desire for aesthetic expression.
   1928 *Decline and Fall*, pt.3, ch.1.

75 Anyone who has been to an English public school will always feel comparatively at home in prison. It is the people brought up in the gay intimacy of the slums, Paul learned, who find prison so soul-destroying.
   1928 *Decline and Fall*, pt.3, ch.4.

76 Creative Endeavour lost her wings, Mrs Ape.
   1930 *Vile Bodies*, ch.1.

77 Particularly against books the Home Secretary is. If we can't stamp out literature in the country, we can at least stop it being brought in from outside.
   1930 *Vile Bodies*, ch.2

78 When the war broke out she took down the signed photograph of the Kaiser and, with some solemnity, hung it in the men-servants' lavatory; it was her one combative action.
   1930 *Vile Bodies*, ch.3.

79 All this fuss about sleeping together. For physical pleasure I'd sooner go to my dentist any day.
   1930 *Vile Bodies*, ch.6.

80 'The Beast stands for strong mutually antagonistic

governments everywhere,' he said. 'Self-sufficiency at home, self-assertion abroad.'
1938 *Scoop*, bk.1, ch.1.

81 Mr Salter's side of the conversation was limited to expressions of assent. When Lord Copper was right, he said, 'Definitely, Lord Copper'; when he was wrong, 'Up to a point.'
1938 *Scoop*, bk.1, ch.1.

82 'He's supposed to have a particularly high-class style: 'Feather footed through the plashy fen passes the questing vole'…would that be it?' 'Yes,' said the Managing Editor. 'That must be good style.'
1938 *Scoop*, bk.1, ch.1.

83 News is what a chap who doesn't care much about anything wants to read. And it's only news until he's read it. After that it's dead.
1938 *Scoop*, bk.1, ch.5.

84 'I will not stand for being called a woman in my own house,' she said.
1938 *Scoop*, bk.2, ch.1.

85 Other nations use 'force'; we Britons alone use 'might'.
1938 *Scoop*, bk.2, ch.5.

86 Lady Peabury was in the morning room reading a novel; early training gave a guilty spice to this recreation, for she had been brought up to believe that to read a novel before luncheon was one of the gravest sins it was possible for a gentlewoman to commit.
1939 'An Englishman's Home'.

87 Like German opera, too long and too loud.
1941 Of warfare. Attributed.

88 I do not think I shall ever forget the sight of Etna at sunset… Nothing I have ever seen in Art or Nature was quite so revolting.
1946 *Labels*.

89 The historic destiny of the Irish is being fulfilled on the other side of the Atlantic, where they have settled in their millions, bringing with them all their ancient grudges and the melancholy of the bogs, but also their hard, ancient wisdom. They alone of the newcomers are never for a moment taken in by the multifarious frauds of modernity. They have been changed from peasants and soldiers into townsmen. They have learned some of the superficial habits of 'good citizenship', but at heart they remain the same adroit and joyless race that broke the hearts of all who ever tried to help them.
1947 'The American Epoch in the Catholic Church'.

90 You never find an Englishman among the under-

dogs—except in England, of course.
1948 *The Loved One*, ch.1.

91 In the dying world I come from, quotation is a national vice. No one would think of making an after-dinner speech without the help of poetry. It used to be classics, now it's lyric verse.
1948 *The Loved One*, ch.9.

92 Words should be an intense pleasure, just as leather should be to a shoemaker.
1950 In the *New York Times*, 19 Nov.

93 Most writers in the course of their careers become thick-skinned and learn to accept vituperation, which in any other profession would be unimaginably offensive, as a healthy counterpoise to unintelligent praise.
1952 In the *New York Times Magazine*, 30 Nov.

94 He sat at the cocktail bar… It wore the air of a fashion magazine, once stiff and shiny, which too many people had handled.
1955 *Officers and Gentlemen*, bk.1, ch.8.

95 Enclosing every thin man, there's a fat man demanding elbow room.
1955 *Officers and Gentlemen*, interlude.
▷ See Connolly 283:75, Orwell 743:9.

96 He did not, even in his extremity, quite abandon his faith in the magic of official forms. In bumf lay salvation.
1955 *Officers and Gentlemen*, bk.2, ch.5.

97 We are all American at puberty; we die French.
1961 Diary note, 18 Jul.

98 Most of the world's troubles seem to come from people who are too busy. If only politicians and scientists were lazier, how much happier we should all be.
1962 *Seven Deadly Sins*.

99 Punctuality is the virtue of the bored.
1962 Diary note, 26 Mar.

1 Manners are especially the need of the plain. The pretty can get away with anything.
1962 In *The Observer*, 15 Apr.

2 One can write, think and pray exclusively of others; dreams are all egocentric.
1962 Diary entry, 5 Oct.

3 One forgets words as one forgets names. One's vocabulary needs constant fertilizing or it will die.
1962 Diary entry, 25 Dec.

4 All fictional characters are flat.
1963 'The Art of Fiction XXX: Evelyn Waugh', in *The Paris Review*, no.8, Summer/Fall.

5 No writer before the middle of the 19th century wrote about the working classes other than as grotesques or as pastoral decorations. Then when they were given the vote certain writers started to suck up to them.

1963 'The Art of Fiction XXX: Evelyn Waugh', in *The Paris Review*, no.8, Summer/Fall.

6 Only when one has lost all curiosity has one reached the age to write an autobiography.

1964 *A Little Learning*, opening words.

7 With a thorough knowledge of the Bible, Shakespeare and Wisden, you cannot go far wrong.

1964 *A Little Learning*.

8 Randolph Churchill went into hospital…to have a lung removed. It was announced that the trouble was not 'malignant'. Seeing Ed Stanley in White's, on my way to Rome, I remarked that it was a typical triumph of modern science to find the only part of Randolph that was not malignant and remove it.

1964 Diary note, Mar.

9 To watch him fumbling with our rich and delicate English language is like seeing a Sèvres vase in the hands of a chimpanzee.

Of Sir Stephen Spender. Quoted by Eric Pace in Spender's obituary in the *New York Times*, 18 Jul 1995.

Wavell, Archibald Percival, 1st Earl

1883–1950

British field-marshal. He held the Middle East Command from 1939 and was Viceroy of India 1943–7. His *Generals and Generalship* (1941) served as a combat handbook to his most formidable opponent, Erwin Rommel.

10 For sheer courage and endurance, physical and mental, the two men stand together as examples of what toughness the body will find, if the spirit within it is tough; and as very worthy representatives of our national capacity for individual enterprise, which it is hoped even the modern craze for regulating every detail of our lives will never stifle.

1948 Of F Spencer Chapman and T E Lawrence. Quoted in foreword to F Spencer Chapman *The Jungle is Neutral* (1950).

11 The story of Colonel Chapman's adventures is typical of the British way of war, and therefore begins with a complete lack of preparation.

1948 Quoted in foreword to F Spencer Chapman *The Jungle is Neutral* (1950).

Waxman, Howard

Editor of the *Ice Cream Reporter*.

12 The relation between the human tongue, the human psyche and butterfat is not very complex. The first two love the third.

1992 In *Newsweek*, 30 Nov.

Weatherill, (Bruce) Bernard Weatherill, Baron 1920–

English politician, chair of the Ways and Means Committee (1979–1983) and Speaker of the House of Commons (1987–1992). He oversaw with enthusiasm the televising of Parliamentary proceedings.

13 Mine is one of the jobs that, if you want it, you will never get it—and if you're seen to want it you will certainly never get it.

1991 In *The House Magazine*, Jan.

Webb, (Martha) Beatrice née Potter

1858–1943

English social reformer, social historian, and economist. She wrote many studies with her husband, Sidney Webb.

14 His sensuality has all drifted into sexual vanity, delight for being the candle to the moths, with a dash of intellectual curiosity to give flavour to his tickled vanity… His incompleteness as a thinker, his shallow and vulgar view of many human relationships—the lack of a sterner kind of humour which would show him the dreariness of his farce and the total absence of proportion and inadequateness in some of his ideas—all these defects came largely from the flippant and worthless self-complacency brought about by the worship of rather second-rate women.

1897 Of George Bernard Shaw. Diary entry, 8 May.

15 All along the line, physically, mentally, morally, alcohol is a weakening and deadening force, and it is worth a great deal to save women and girls from its influence.

1917 *Health of Working Girls*, ch.10.

Webb, Phyllis 1927–

Canadian poet, university teacher and broadcaster. Her poetry includes *The Sea is Also a Garden* (1962), *Naked Poems* (1965) and *Wilson's Bowl* (1980); she has also published a collection of her essays.

16 Some people swim lakes, others climb flagpoles, some join monasteries, but we, my friends, who have considered suicide take our daily walk with death and are not lonely.
In the end it brings more honesty and care than all the democratic parliaments of tricks.

1956 *Even Your Right Eye*, 'To Friends Who Have Also Considered Suicide'.

Webb, Sidney James 1859–1947

English social reformer, historian and economist. A lawyer and Fabian, he wrote many powerful tracts and in 1892 married fellow socialist Beatrice Potter. They wrote a classic *History of Trade Unionism* (1894) and *English Local Government* (1906–29, 9 vols), and began the *New Statesman* (1913). He became President of the Board of

Trade (1924), Dominions and Colonial Secretary (1929–30) and Colonial Secretary (1930–1).

17 No philosopher now looks for anything but the gradual evolution of the new order from the old... History shows us no example of the sudden substitutions of Utopian and revolutionary romance.
Fabian Essays.

18 How anyone can fear that the British electorate, whatever mistakes it can make or may condone, can ever go too far or too fast is incomprehensible... The Labour Party, when in due course it comes to be entrusted with power, will naturally not want to do everything at once. Once we face the necessity of putting our principles into execution from one end of the kingdom to the other, the inevitability of gradualness cannot fail to be appreciated.
1923 Labour Party Conference, 26 Jun.

Weber, Max 1864–1920
German sociologist and economist.

19 In Baxter's view, the care of external goods should only lie on the shoulders of the 'saint like a light cloak, which can be thrown aside at any moment.' But fate decreed that the cloak should become an iron cage.
1904–5 *The Protestant Ethic and the Spirit of Capitalism* (translated by Talcott Parsons, 1930), ch.5. Richard Baxter (1615–91) was an eminent Puritan, chaplain of Cromwell's army.

20 The impulse to acquisition, pursuit of gain, of money, of the greatest possible amount of money, has in itself nothing to do with capitalism. This impulse exists among waiters, physicians, coachmen, artists, prostitutes, dishonest officials, soldiers, nobles, crusaders, gamblers, and beggars. One may say that it has been common to all sorts and conditions of men at all times and in all cultures of the earth, wherever the objective possibility of it is or has been given.
1904–5 *The Protestant Ethic and the Spirit of Capitalism* (translated by Talcott Parsons, 1930).

21 Capital accounting in its formally most rational shape...presupposes *the battle of man with man.*
1922 Collected in Guenther Roth and Claus Wittich (eds) *Economy and Society* (1978), ch.1.

22 However many people may complain about the 'red tape', it would be sheer illusion to think for a moment that continuous administrative work can be carried out in any field except by means of officials working in offices... The choice is only that between bureaucracy and dilettantism in the field of administration.
1922 Collected in Guenther Roth and Claus Wittich (eds) *Economy and Society* (1978), ch.3.

Webster, Daniel 1782–1852
US lawyer and statesman, one of the greatest of US orators. As Secretary of State (1840–3) he negotiated the Webster–Ashburton treaty with Great Britain. A supporter of free trade, nationality and established institutions, he was unwilling to break the Union to abolish slavery.

23 [Alexander Hamilton] smote the rock of the national resources, and abundant streams of revenue gushed forth. He touched the dead corpse of the public credit, and it sprang upon its feet.
1831 Speech, New York, 10

24 There is always room at the top.
On being advised against joining the overcrowded legal profession, attributed.

Webster, John c.1580–c.1625
English dramatist. He collaborated with Dekker, Drayton, Marston and others. He is best known for two great tragedies, *The White Devil* (1612) and *The Duchess of Malfi* (1623).

25 Fortune's right whore:
If she give aught, she deals it in small parcels,
That she may take away all at one swoop.
1612 *The White Devil*, act 1, sc.1.

26 All the damnable degrees
Of drinking have you staggered through.
1612 *The White Devil*, act 1, sc.1.

27 Perfumes, the more they are chafed, the more they render
Their pleasing scents; and so affliction
Expresseth virtue fully.
1612 *The White Devil*, act 1, sc.1.

28 Oh, they are politic: they know our desire is increased by the difficulty of enjoying, whereas satiety is a blunt, weary, and drowsy passion.
1612 Of women. *The White Devil*, act 1, sc.1.

29 See, the curse of children!
In life they keep us frequently in tears,
And in the cold grave leave us in pale fears.
1612 *The White Devil*, act 1, sc.2.

30 'Tis just like a summer birdcage in a garden; the birds that are without despair to get in, and the birds that are within despair, and are in a consumption, for fear they shall never get out.
1612 *The White Devil*, act 1, sc.2.

31 Lust carries her sharp whip
At her own girdle.
1612 *The White Devil*, act 2, sc.1.

32 See, a good habit makes a child a man,
Whereas a bad one makes a man a beast.
1612 *The White Devil*, act 2, sc.1.

33 A mere tale of a tub, my words are idle.
1612 The White Devil, act 2, sc.1.

34 Only the deep sense of some deathless shame.
1612 The White Devil, act 2, sc.1.

35 Find me but guilty, sever head from body,
We'll part good friends.
1612 The White Devil, act 3, sc.2.

36 For your names
Of whores and murderers, they proceed from you,
As if a man should spit against the wind;
The filth returns in's face.
1612 The White Devil, act 3, sc.2.

37 Sum up my faults, I pray, and you shall find,
That beauty, and gay clothes, a merry heart,
And a good stomach to a feast, are all,
All the poor crimes that you can charge me with.
1612 The White Devil, act 3, sc.2.

38 VITTORIA: A rape! a rape!
MONTICELSO: How!
VITTORIA: Yes, you have ravished justice,
Forced her to do your pleasure.
1612 The White Devil, act 3, sc.2.

39 Woman to man
Is either a God or a wolfe.
1612 The White Devil, act 4, sc.2.

40 For your gifts,
I'll return them all; and I do wish
That I could make you full executor
To all my sins.
1612 The White Devil, act 4, sc.2.

41 He could not have invented his own ruin,
Had he despaired, with more propriety.
1612 The White Devil, act 5, sc.1.

42 They that sleep with dogs shall rise with fleas.
1612 The White Devil, act 5, sc.1.

43 O, the rare tricks of a Machiavellian!
He doth not come, like a gross plodding slave,
And buffet you to death; no, my quaint knave,
He tickles you to death, makes you die laughing.
1612 The White Devil, act 5, sc.3.

44 Call for the robin-red-breast and the wren,
Since o'er shady groves they hover,
And with leaves and flowers do cover
The friendless bodies of unburied men.
1612 The White Devil, act 5, sc.4.

45 I have heard grief named the eldest child of sin.
1612 The White Devil, act 5, sc.4.

46 Are you grown an atheist? Will you turn your body,
Which is the goodly palace of the soul,

To the soul's slaughter-house? Oh, the cursèd devil,
Which doth present us will all other sins
Thrice-candied o'er.
1612 The White Devil, act 5, sc.6.

47 Oh, yes, thy sins
Do run before thee to fetch fire from hell,
To light thee thither.
1612 The White Devil, act 5, sc.6.

48 I myself have heard a very good jest, and have
scorned to seem to have so silly a wit as to
understand it.
1623 The Duchess of Malfi, act 1, sc.1.

49 Then the law to him
Is like a foul black cobweb to a spider;
He makes it his dwelling, and a prison
To entangle those shall feed him.
1623 The Duchess of Malfi, act 1, sc.1.

50 DUCHESS: Diamonds are of most precious value
They say, that have passed through most jewellers'
hands.
FERDINAND: Whores, by that rule, are precious.
1623 The Duchess of Malfi, act 1, sc.1.

51 Wisdom begins at the end.
1623 The Duchess of Malfi, act 1, sc.1.

52 DUCHESS: What do you think of marriage?
ANTONIO: I take't, as those that deny purgatory,
It locally contains or heaven, or hell;
There's no third place in't.
1623 The Duchess of Malfi, act 1, sc.2.

53 Ambition, madam, is a great man's madness,
That is not kept in chains, and close-pent rooms,
But in fair lightsome lodgings, and is girt
With the wild noise of prattling visitants,
Which makes it lunatic beyond all cure.
1623 The Duchess of Malfi, act 1, sc.1.

54 I have long served virtue,
And never ta'en wages of her.
1623 The Duchess of Malfi, act 1, sc.1.

55 The misery of us, that are born great,
We are forced to woo because none dare woo us.
1623 The Duchess of Malfi, act 1, sc.1.

56 I hope in time 'twill grow into a custom
That noblemen shall come with cap and knee
To purchase a night's lodging of their wives.
1623 The Duchess of Malfi, act 3, sc.2.

57 I would sooner swim to the Bermudas on
Two politicians' rotten bladders, tied
Together with an intelligencer's heartstring,
Than depend on so changeable a prince's favour.
1623 The Duchess of Malfi, act 3, sc.2.

58 A politician is the devil's quilted anvil,
    He fashions all sins on him, and the blows
    Are never heard.
    1623 *The Duchess of Malfi*, act 3, sc.2.

59 Love mixed with fear is sweetness.
    1623 *The Duchess of Malfi*, act 3, sc.2.

60 That curious engine, your white hand.
    1623 *The Duchess of Malfi*, act 3, sc.2.

61 Why should only I…
    Be cased up, like a holy relic? I have youth
    And a little beauty.
    1623 *The Duchess of Malfi*, act 3, sc.2.

62 You have shook hands with Reputation
    And made him invisible.
    1623 *The Duchess of Malfi*, act 3, sc.2.

63 Her melancholy seems to be fortified
    With a strange disdain.
    1623 *The Duchess of Malfi*, act 4, sc.1.

64 Other sins only speak; murder shrieks out.
    1623 *The Duchess of Malfi*, act 4, sc.2.

65 What's this flesh? A little crudded milk, fantastical
    puff-paste.
    1623 *The Duchess of Malfi*, act 4, sc.2. crudded = curdled.

66 What would it pleasure me, to have my throat
    cut
    With diamonds? Or to be smothered
    With cassia? Or to be shot to death, with pearls?
    1623 *The Duchess of Malfi*, act 4, sc.2.

68 O, that it were possible,
    We might but hold some two days' conference
    With the dead!
    1623 *The Duchess of Malfi*, act 4, sc.2.

69 I am Duchess of Malfi still.
    1623 *The Duchess of Malfi*, act 4, sc.2.

70 I know death hath ten thousand several doors
    For men to take their exits.
    1623 *The Duchess of Malfi*, act 4, sc.2.

71 FERDINAND: Cover her face; mine eyes dazzle: she
    died young.
    BOSOLA: I think not so; her infelicity
    Seemed to have years too many.
    1623 *The Duchess of Malfi*, act 4, sc.2.

72 Physicians are like kings,—they brook no
    contradiction.
    1623 *The Duchess of Malfi*, act 5, sc.2.

73 We are merely the stars' tennis-balls, struck and
    bandied

Which way please them.
1623 *The Duchess of Malfi*, act 5, sc.4.

Webster, Margaret 1905–72
US actress and director.

74 You must not wear your heart on your sleeve for
    daws to pick at.
    c.1940 To Tennessee Williams on the out-of-town closing of
    his first professionally produced play *Battle of Angels*. Recalled by
    Williams in the *New York Times*, 17 Mar 1957.
    ▷ See Shakespeare 897:95.

Wei Jingsheng 1950–
Chinese dissident, considered one of the fathers of the
Chinese dissident movement, released in 1993 after
serving a 14-year jail sentence for his role in the
Democracy Wall Movement. He was arrested again in
April 1994 and was released in 1997.

75 No leader deserves the unconditional confidence of
    his people.
    1979 Part of a statement appearing on Democracy Wall under
    the pseudonym 'Voice of Today'. Quoted in Uli Franz *Deng
    Xiaoping* (1988).

Weighell, Sidney 1922–
British trade union leader. He was General Secretary of
the National Union of Railwaymen (1975–83) and a
member of the Trades Union General Council
(1975–83). He joined the LNER in 1938 and became a
full-time union official in 1954.

76 If you…believe in the philosophy of the pig
    trough—that those with the biggest snouts should
    get the largest share—I reject it.
    1978 Labour Party Conference 10 Apr.

77 I don't see how we can talk with Mrs Thatcher… I
    will say to the lads, 'Come on, get your snouts in
    the trough.'
    1979 Speech, London, 10 Apr.

Weil, Simone 1909–43
French philosophical writer and mystic, who undertook
manual labour to experience working-class life and served
as a Republican in the Spanish Civil War (1936). A mystic
Catholic who distrusted organized religion, she worked
for the Free French in London, and starved herself to
death in sympathy with the victims of war. Her works
include *La Pesanteur et la Grâce* (Gravity and Grace,
1946) and *Attente de Dieu* (Waiting for God, 1950).

78 To us, men of the West, a very strange thing
    happened at the turn of the century; without
    noticing it, we lost science, or at least the thing that
    had been called by that name for the last four
    centuries. What we now have in place of it is
    something different, radically different, and we
    don't know what it is. Nobody knows what it is.
    1941 *On Science, Necessity and the Love of God*, 'Classical
    Science and After' (translated by Richard Rees, 1968).

79 Science is voiceless; it is the scientists who talk.

1941 *On Science, Necessity and the Love of God* (translated by Richard Rees, 1968).

80 The future is made of the same stuff as the present.

1941 *On Science, Necessity, and the Love of God.*

81 *Tous les péchés sont des tentatives pour combler des vides.*

All sins are attempts to fill voids.

La Pesanteur et la Grâce (published 1946).

82 The beauty of the world is almost the only way by which we can allow God to penetrate us…the beauty of the world is the commonest, easiest and most natural way of approach.

Attente de Dieu (translated as *Waiting on God*, 1951).

83 Bourgeois society is infected by monomania: the monomania of accounting. For it, the only thing that has value is what can be counted in francs and centimes. It never hesitates to sacrifice human life to figures which look well on paper, such as national budgets or industrial balance sheets.

La condition ouvrière, 'La rationalisation' (published 1951).

84 One might lay down as a postulate: All conceptions of God which are incompatible with the movement of pure charity are false

Letter to a Priest (translated by A F Wills, published 1954).

85 The word 'revolution' is a word for which you kill, for which you die, for which you send the labouring masses to their deaths; but which does not contain any content.

Oppression and Liberty (translated by A F Wills and J Petrie, published 1958).

Weinberger, Caspar Willard 1917–

American politician. A former lawyer, he was state finance director of California when Ronald Reagan was Governor (1968–9), served in the administrations of Presidents Nixon and Ford, then became Secretary of Defense under President Reagan (1981–87).

86 Wishful thinking is equally as effective for arms control as it is for birth control.

1986 In *USA Today*, 6 Oct.

Weizsäcker, Richard Freiherr, Baron von 1920–

German politician, President of Germany (1990–). A member of the conservative Christian Democratic Union, he served as CDU deputy chairman (1972–9) and Mayor of West Berlin (1981–4) until being elected President of the Federal Republic of Germany (1984, re-elected 1989). In 1990 he signed the treaty that reunited East and West Germany.

87 There were many ways of not burdening one's conscience, of shunning responsibility, looking away, keeping silent. When the unspeakable truth of the Holocaust became known at the end of the war, all too many of us claimed that they had not known anything about it, or even suspected anything… Whoever refuses to remember the inhumanity is prone to new risks of infection… Seeking to forget makes exile all the longer; the secret of redemption lies in remembrance.

1985 On the 40th anniversary of the end of World War II, in the *New York Times*, 12 May.

Weldon, Fay originally Franklin Birkinshaw 1931–

English writer, an advertising copywriter before turning to novels and screenplays. She is best known for her fiction which addresses feminist issues, including *Female Friends* (1974) and *The Life and Loves of a She-Devil* (1983).

88 Go to work on an egg.

1957 Advertising slogan for the British Egg Marketing Board.

89 The Life and Loves of a She-Devil.

1983 Title of novel.

90 It will do us no harm to retool our imaginations. AIDS is a major revolution in how writers write… Our heroes and heroines will have to change. The only thing AIDS is good for is fiction. Writers will have to think differently.

1987 In *The Guardian*, 7 Mar.

91 Pride comes before a fall; a sense of sisterhood with sad experience.

1987 *The Heart of the Country*, 'Chomp, Chomp, Grittle-Grax, Gone!'

92 Christianity is really a man's religion: there's not much in it for women except docility, obedience, who-sweeps-the-room-as-for-thy-cause, downcast eyes and death in childbirth. For the men it's better: all power and money and fine robes, the burning of the heretics—fun, fun, fun!—and the Inquisition fulminating from the pulpit.

1987 *The Heart of the Country*, 'Love Your Enemy'.

93 To journey is better than to arrive—or so say those who have already arrived.

1987 *The Heart of the Country*, 'Doing It All Wrong'.

94 It's full time work being on social security. They really make you earn your living.

1987 *The Heart of the Country*, 'Driven Mad'.

95 Men are so romantic, don't you think? They look for a perfect partner when what they should be looking for is perfect love.

1987 In the *Sunday Times*, 6 Sep.

96 I didn't set out to be a feminist writer. I just look at the sheep out of the window and watch their behaviour.

1989 In *The Observer*, 30 Apr.

97 I think if you had ever written a book you were absolutely pleased with, you'd never write another. The same probably goes for having children.
1991 In the *Guardian*, 28 Nov.

98 Nature's only interest is in having you procreate, then it throws you away.
1992 In the *Guardian*, 15 Jan.

Welland, Colin 1934–

British actor and writer. Best known for his screenplays for *Yanks* (1979, with Walter Bernstein) and *Chariots of Fire* (1981), for the second of which he won an Academy Award.

99 The British are coming.
1982 At the Academy Award ceremony in Los Angeles, 29 Mar.

Welles, (George) Orson 1915–85

US director and actor. He is best known for his radio production of H G Wells's *The War of the Worlds* (1938), and for the films *Citizen Kane* (1941), a masterpiece of cinema technique, and his adaptation of Booth Tarkington's *The Magnificent Ambersons* (1942).

1 In Italy for thirty years under the Borgias they had warfare, terror, murder, bloodshed—they produced Michelangelo, Leonardo da Vinci and the Renaissance. In Switzerland they had brotherly love, five hundred years of democracy and peace, and what did they produce? The cuckoo clock.
1949 Harry Lime's speech to Holly Martins as he leaves the great wheel, *The Third Man*. This phrase was added to the script by Welles who played Harry Lime.

2 A film is never really good unless the camera is an eye in the head of a poet.
1958 'Un ruban de rêves' in *L'Express*, 5 Jun. Reprinted in English in *International Film Annual*, no.2.

3 A typewriter needs only paper; a camera uses film, requires subsidiary equipment by the truckload and several hundreds of technicians. That is always the central fact about the filmmaker as opposed to any other artist: he can never afford his own tools.
1958 Letter in the *New Statesman*.

4 I started at the top and worked down.
Attributed.

5 Every actor in his heart believes everything bad that's printed about him.
Attributed.

Wellington, Arthur Wellesley, 1st Duke of 1769–1852

British soldier and statesman. He was made a Duke after his defeat of French forces in the Peninsular War, and took command of British forces again after Napoleon's escape from Elba in 1815. After victory at Waterloo, he went into politics, becoming Prime Minister in 1828. His dispatches and other papers were published in three series (1834–80).

6 As Lord Chesterfield said of the generals of his day, 'I only hope that when the enemy reads the list of their names, he trembles as I do'.
1810 Letter, 29 Aug, during the Peninsular War. Collected in *Supplementary Despatches* (1860).

7 We have in the service the scum of the earth as common soldiers.
1813 Comment 21 Jun, before the battle of Vitoria. Quoted in Elizabeth Longford *Wellington: The Years of the Sword*, p.321.

8 Hard pounding this, gentlemen, let's see who will pound longest.
1815 At the battle of Waterloo, 18 Jun. Quoted in Sir Walter Scott *Paul's Letters* (1816), letter 8.

9 Up guards and at them!
1815 Attributed shout at the Battle of Waterloo, 18 Jun.

10 It has been a damned serious business—Blucher and I have lost 30,000 men. It has been a damned nice thing—the nearest run thing you ever saw in your life… By God! I don't think it would have done if I had not been there!
1815 Comment to Thomas Creevey at Brussels, 19 Jun, the day after the Battle of Waterloo. Quoted in Sir Thomas Creevey *The Creevey Papers* (edited by Sir H Maxwell, 1904), p.142.

11 Napoleon did not manoeuvre at all. He just moved forward in the old style, in columns, and was driven off in the old style.
1815 Letter to Sir William Beresford, 2 Jul.

12 Next to a battle lost, the greatest misery is a battle gained.
1815 Of the Battle of Waterloo. Comment to Lady Shelley, Jul. Quoted in Richard Edgcumbe (ed) *The Diary of Frances, Lady Shelley* (1912), vol.1, ch.9, p.102.

13 The history of a battle is not unlike the history of a ball. Some individuals may recollect all the little events of which the great result is the battle won or lost; but no individual can recollect the order in which, or the exact moment at which, they occurred, which makes all the difference.
1815 Of the battle of Waterloo. Letter, 8 Aug.

14 Beginning reform is beginning revolution.
1830 Attributed remark, 7 Nov.

15 I used to say of him that his presence on the field made the difference of 40,000 men.
1831 Of Napoleon. Comment, 2 Nov. Quoted in Philip Henry Stanhope *Notes of Conversations with the Duke of Wellington* (1888).

16 Our course in the House of Lords ought to be very firm and uncompromising but moderate…an example of what has since been called the politics of the extreme centre.

1832 Conduct of Opposition speech, Dec.

17 There is no such thing as a little war for a great nation.

1838 House of Lords, 16 Jan.

18 All the business of war, and indeed all the business of life, is to endeavour to find out what you don't know by what you do; that's what I call 'guessing what was at the other side of the hill'.

Quoted in John Wilson Croker *The Croker Papers* (edited by Bernard Pool, 1885), vol.3, ch.28.

19 Don't quote Latin; say what you have to say, and then sit down.

Advice to a new member of Parliament.

20 The battle of Waterloo was won on the playing fields of Eton.

Attributed, and probably apocryphal. Quoted in Count Charles de Montalembert *De l'Avenir politique de l'Angleterre* (1856), ch.10: 'C'est ici qu'a été gagné la bataille de Waterloo'.

21 There is no mistake; there has been no mistake, and there shall be no mistake.

Wellingtoniana.

22 Publish and be damned.

To the publisher of the *Memoirs* of the courtesan Hariette Wilson, attempting blackmail. Attributed.

23 If you believe that, you'll believe anything.

Attributed

Wells, H(erbert) G(eorge) 1866–1946

English writer and Fabian, best known for his scientific fantasies *The Time Machine* (1895) and *The War of the Worlds* (1898). He also wrote popular comic novels, notably *Kipps* (1905) and *The History of Mr Polly* (1910) and socio-political works on science and world peace (*The Outline of History*, 1920 and *The Work, Wealth and Happiness of Mankind*, 1932).

24 He was a practical electrician but fond of whisky, a heavy, red-haired brute with irregular teeth. He doubted the existence of the Deity but accepted Carnot's cycle, and he had read Shakespeare and found him weak in chemistry.

1894 'The Lord of the Dynamos'.

25 Bah! the thing is not a nose at all, but a bit of primordial chaos clapped on to my face.

1895 *Select Conversations with an Uncle*, 'The Man with a Nose'.

26 Yet, across the gulf of space, minds that are to our minds as ours are to the beasts that perish, intellects vast and cool and unsympathetic, regarded this

earth with envious eyes, and slowly and surely drew their plans against us.

1898 *The War of the Worlds*, bk.1, ch.1.

27 At times I suffer from the strangest sense of detachment from myself and the world about me; I seem to watch it all from the outside, from somewhere inconceivably remote, out of time, out of space, out of the stress and tragedy of it all.

1898 *The War of the Worlds*, bk.1, ch.7.

28 The Social Contract is nothing more or less than a vast conspiracy of human beings to lie to and humbug themselves and one another for the general Good. Lies are the mortar that bind the savage individual man into the social masonry.

1900 *Love and Mrs Lewisham*, ch.23.

29 Notice the smug suppressions of his face. In his mouth are Lies in the shape of false teeth.

1900 *Love and Mrs Lewisham*, ch.23.

30 In the country of the blind the one-eyed man is king.

1904 The Country of the Blind, collected in *The Country of the Blind and Other Stories* (1911).

31 Of course we can Learn even from Novels, Nace Novels that is, but it isn't the same thing as serious reading.

1905 *Kipps*, bk.2, ch.2.

32 He found that a fork in his inexperienced hand was an instrument of chase rather than capture.

1905 *Kipps*, bk.2, ch.7.

33 'I expect,' he said, 'I was thinking jest what a Rum Go everything is.'

1905 *Kipps*, bk.3, ch.3.

34 'You're a Christian?' 'Church of England,' said Mr Polly. 'Mm,' said the employer, a little checked. 'For good all round business work, I should have preferred a Baptist.'

1909 *The History of Mr Polly*, ch.3, pt.2.

35 Arson, after all, is an artificial crime… A large number of houses deserve to be burnt.

1909 *The History of Mr Polly*, ch.10, pt.1.

36 Once they heard someone call for 'Snooks'. 'I always thought that name was invented by novelists,' said Miss Winchelsea. 'Fancy! Snooks. I wonder which is Mr. Snooks?' Finally they picked out a stout and resolute little man in a large check suit. 'If he isn't Snooks, he ought to be,' said Miss Winchelsea.

1913 *Tales of Life and Adventure*, 'Miss Winchelsea's Heart'.

37 The War that will End War.

1914 Title of book.

38 Moral indignation is jealousy with a halo.
1914 *The Wife of Sir Isaac Harman*, ch.9.

39 The uglier a man's legs are, the better he plays golf. It's almost a law.
1915 *Bealby*.

40 He had the face of a saint, but he had rendered this generally acceptable by growing side-whiskers.
1915 'The Story of The Last Trump'.

41 Cynicism is humour in ill-health.
1915 'The Story of The Last Trump'.

42 Human history becomes more and more a race between education and catastrophe.
1920 *The Outline of History*, vol.2, ch.41.

43 Now it is on the whole more convenient to keep history and theology apart.
1922 *A Short History of the World*, ch.37.

44 I am reported to be 'pessimistic' about broadcasting... [The] truth is that I have anticipated its complete disappearance—confident that the unfortunate people, who must now subdue themselves to 'listening-in', will soon find a better pastime for their leisure.
1928 *The Way the World is Going*.

45 In England we have come to rely upon a comfortable time-lag of fifty years or a century intervening between the perception that something ought to be done and a serious attempt to do it.
1931 *The Work, Wealth and Happiness of Mankind*, ch.2.

46 The shape of things to come.
1933 Title of book.

47 If his thinking has been sound, then this world is at the end of its tether. The end of everything we call life is close at hand and cannot be evaded.
1945 *Mind at the End of Its Tether*, ch.1.

Welsh, Irvine 1958–

Scottish writer. He scored a major critical success with his first novel, *Trainspotting* (1993, filmed 1995).

48 I grew up in what was not so much a family as a genetic disaster.
1995 *Marabou Stork Nightmares*, ch.2.

Welty, Eudora 1909–

US novelist and short-story writer. She has written five novels, set in her native Mississippi, and several collections of short stories, issued as *Collected Stories* (1981).

49 I have been told, both in approval and accusation, that I seem to love all my characters. What I do in writing of any character is to try to enter into the mind, heart and skin of a human being who is not myself. Whether this happens to be a man or a woman, old or young, with skin black or white, the primary challenge lies in making the jump itself. It is the act of a writer's imagination that I set most high.
1981 *The Collected Stories of Eudora Welty*, preface.

50 It had been startling and disappointing to me to find out that story books had been written by *people*, that books were not natural wonders, coming up themselves like green grass.
1984 *One Writer's Beginnings*, I. 'Listening'.

51 The events in our lives happen in a sequence in time, but in their significance to ourselves they find their own order, a timetable not necessarily— perhaps not possibly—chronological... It is the continuous thread of revelation.
1984 *One Writer's Beginnings*, II. 'Learning To See'.

52 A sheltered life can be a daring life as well. For all serious daring starts from within.
1984 *One Writer's Beginnings*, III. 'Finding A Voice'.

Wentworth, Peter 1530–96

English parliamentarian. He was a prominent Puritan in the reign of Elizabeth I, to whom he presented challenges on the issues of religion and royal succession. He supported the liberties of parliament against encroachments by Elizabeth I. His speech to Parliament in 1576 was examined by the Star Chamber and he was sent to the Tower of London for it. He was imprisoned twice more, and it is thought he never regained his freedom the second time.

53 In this House, which is termed a place of free speech, there is nothing so necessary for the preservation of the Prince and State as free speech; and without it, it is a scorn and a mockery to call it a Parliament House, for in truth it is none but a very school of flattery and dissimulation, and so fit a place to serve the devil and his angels in, and not to glorify God and benefit the Commonwealth.
1576 House of Commons, 8 Feb.

Wentworth, William Charles 1790–1872

Statesman and explorer, born aboard a convict ship on which his mother was being transported for theft. One of the first to successfully explore beyond the Blue Mountains, he established the first Australian newspaper and was one of the founders of Sydney University. His *Australasia* (1823) was the first book of verse by a native-born Australian.

54 Illustrious Cook, Columbus of our shore,
To whom was left this unknown world t'explore,
Its untraced bounds on faithful chart to mark,
And leave a light where all before was dark.
1823 *Australasia*.

Werefkin, Marianne 1860–1938

Russian-born painter who emigrated to Germany just before 1900. She was a founding member of the Blaue Reiter group in Munich.

55 Art is not made only one way, art is a point of view... Rembrandt in our days would be Rembrandt again, because the work of the master is his self. But in order to be Rembrandt in our days he would have used new ways that would give a new culture.
1902 *Lettres à un Inconnu* (1901–05). Translated by Mara R Witzling (ed) in *Voicing Our Visions: Writings by Women Artists* (1992).

56 There is no history of art—there is the history of artists.
1905 *Lettres à un Inconnu* (1901–05). Translated by Mara R Witzling (ed) in *Voicing Our Visions: Writings by Women Artists* (1992).

Wesker, Arnold 1932–

English playwright.

57 And then I saw the menu ... It said 'Chips with everything'. Chips with every damn thing You breed babies and you eat chips with everything.
1962 *Chips with Everything* act 1, sc.2

Wesley, Charles 1707–88

English Methodist hymnwriter and preacher, brother of John Wesley.

58 Long my imprisoned spirit lay
Fast bound in sin and nature's night;
Thine eye diffused a quickening ray—
I woke, the dungeon flamed with light,
My chains fell off, my heart was free,
I rose, went forth, and followed thee.
1738 Hymn. 'And Can it Be'.

59 Hark! how all the welkin rings,
Glory to the King of kings.
Peace on earth and mercy mild,
God and sinners reconciled.
1739 'Hymn for Christmas'. In *Hymns and Sacred Poems*. The first two lines were changed to 'Hark! the herald-angels sing/Glory to the new born king' in Whitfield's *Hymns for Social Worship* (1753).

60 Jesu, lover of my soul,
Let me to thy bosom fly,
While the nearer waters roll,
While the tempest still is high;
Hide me, O my Saviour, hide,
Till the storm of life is past;
Safe into the haven guide,
O receive my soul at last.
1740 'In Temptation', collected in *Hymns and Sacred Poems*.

61 Gentle Jesus, meek and mild,

Look upon a little child;
Pity my simplicity,
Suffer me to come to thee.
1742 'Gentle Jesus', collected in *Hymns and Sacred Poems*.

62 Rejoice, the Lord is King!
Your Lord and King adore;
Mortals, give thanks and sing,
And triumph evermore:
Lift up your heart, lift up your voice;
Rejoice, again, I say rejoice.
1746 'Rejoice, the Lord is King'. In *Hymns for our Lord's Resurrection*.

63 Love divine, all loves excelling,
Joy of heav'n, to earth come down,
Fix in us thy humble dwelling,
All thy faithful mercies crown.
Jesu, thou art all compassion,
Pure unbounded love thou art;
Visit us with thy salvation,
Enter every trembling heart.
1747 'Love Divine', collected in *Hymns for those that seek...Redemption*.

64 Forth in thy name, O Lord, I go,
My daily labour to pursue.
Thee, only thee, resolved to know,
In all I think or speak or do.
1749 'Forth in Thy Name', collected in *Hymns and Sacred Poems*.

65 Lo! He comes with clouds descending,
Once for favoured sinners slain;
Thousand thousand Saints attending
Swell the triumph of His train.
1758 'Lo! He Comes'. In *Hymns of Intercession for all Mankind*.

Wesley, John 1703–91

English evangelist, preacher and writer. Although he himself remained loyal to the Church of England, he is recognized as the principal founder of Methodism. He published his *Rules* in 1743 for the Methodist Societies.

66 I felt my heart strangely warmed. I felt I did trust in Christ, Christ alone for salvation; and an assurance was given me that he had taken away *my* sins, even *mine*, and saved *me* from the law of sin and death.
1738 Journal entry, 24 May.

67 Thou hidden love of God, whose height,
Whose depth unfathomed no man knows,
I see from far thy beauteous light,
Inly I sigh for thy repose.
1738 *A Collection of Psalms and Hymns*, 'Divine Love'.

68 I look upon all the world as my parish.
1739 Journal entry, 11 Jun.

69 Lord, let me not live to be useless!.

1763 Journal entry, 22 Dec.

70 Sure a more consummate coxcomb never saw the sun! How amazingly full of himself! Whatever he speaks, he pronounces as an oracle.
1770 Of Rousseau. Journal entry, 3 Feb.

71 I have none of the infirmities of old age, and have lost several I had in my youth. The grand cause is, the good pleasure of God, who does whatever pleases him. The chief means are: 1. My constantly rising at four, for about fifty years. 2. My generally preaching at five in the morning; one of the most healthy exercises in the world. 3. My never travelling less, by sea or land, than four thousand five hundred miles in a year.
1774 Journal entry, 28 Jun.

72 I spent two hours with that great man, Dr Johnson, who is sinking into the grave by a gentle decay.
1783 Journal entry, 18 Dec.

73 The best of all is, God is with us!
1791 Quoted in *John Wesley's Journal*, edited by Robert Backhouse (1993), p.256.

74 Beware you be not swallowed up in books! An ounce of love is worth a pound of knowledge.
Quoted in R Southey *Life of Wesley* (1820), ch.16.

75 Do all the good you can
By all the means you can
In all the ways you can
In all the places you can
To all the people you can
As long as ever you can.
1743 'Rules of Conduct'.

West, Benjamin 1738–1820

US painter who spent most of his working life in England.

76 Always remember, sir, that light and shadow never stand still.
Advice to the young John Constable, attributed in C R Leslie *Memoirs of the Life of John Constable* (1845).

West, Mae 1893–1980

US vaudeville and film actress born in Brooklyn, New York. She wrote many of the plays she starred in, including *Sex* (1929) and *Diamond Lil* (1928) later filmed as *She Done Him Wrong*. Other films included *I'm No Angel* (1933) and *My Little Chickadee* (1940).

77 'Goodness what beautiful diamonds!'
'Goodness had nothing to do with it.'
1932 *Night After Night* (screenplay by Vincent Lawrence).

78 Why don't you come up sometime, see me?

1933 As Lou in *She Done Him Wrong*. The line is popularly rendered 'Come up and see me sometime.'

79 When I'm good I'm very very good, but when I'm bad I'm better.
1933 *I'm No Angel.*

80 Beulah, peel me a grape.
1933 *I'm No Angel.*

81 A man has one hundred dollars and you leave him with two dollars, that's subtraction.
1940 Line spoken in *My Little Chickadee.*

82 Lieutenant, is that your sword, or are you just glad to see me?
1944 Ad-libbed when her stage lover in *Catherine Was Great* became entangled with his sword scabbard as he attempted to embrace her. Attributed.

83 Catherine had three hundred lovers. I did the best I could do in a couple of hours.
1944 Curtain speech at the end of her play *Catherine Was Great.* Attributed.

84 I've been in Who's Who and I know what's what, but it's the first time I ever made the dictionary.
Reputedly said on learning that a life jacket was to be named after her.

85 It isn't what I do, but how I do it.
It isn't what I say, but how I say it—
And how I look when I do and say it.
Attributed.

West, Nathanael pseudonym of *Nathan Wallenstein Weinstein* 1903–40

US novelist, who lived for two years in Paris. After he wrote his most famous novel *Miss Lonelyhearts*, he spent his last five years writing scripts for a Hollywood film studio, which provided the material for a final masterpiece, *The Day of the Locust* (1939, filmed 1975).

86 Prayers for the condemned man will be offered on an adding machine. Numbers constitute the only universal language.
1933 *Miss Lonelyhearts.*

West, Dame Rebecca formerly *Cecily Isabel Fairfield* 1892–1983

Anglo-Irish novelist, journalist, biographer and critic. She trained for the stage but her involvement with the suffragettes led her into journalism, and her studies arising out of the Nuremberg war trials include *The Meaning of Treason* (1947) and *A Train of Powder* (1955). She bore a son to H G Wells during an affair which lasted 10 years.

87 Women know the damnation of charity because the habit of civilisation has always been to throw them cheap alms rather than give them good wages.
1912 'The Personal Service Association: Work for Idle Hands to Do', in *The Clarion*, 13 Dec.

88 Antifeminists, from Chesterton down to Dr Lionel Tayler, want women to specialise in virtue. While men are rolling round the world having murderous and otherwise sinful adventures of an enjoyable nature, in commerce, exploration or art, women are to stay at home earning the promotion of the human race to a better world.
1912 'The Personal Service Association: Work for Idle Hands to Do', in *The Clarion*, 13 Dec.

89 I saw in my own education some of the things which eat the power out of women.
1913 'Training in Truculence: The Working Women's College', in *The Clarion*, 14 Feb.

90 We have asked men for votes, they have given us advice. At present they are also giving us abuse.
1913 'The Sex War: Disjointed Thoughts on Men', in *The Clarion*, 18 Apr.

91 I have horrible nightmares of Sir Almwroth Wright's limp sentences wandering through the arid desert of his mind looking for dropped punctuation marks.
1913 'Lynch Law: The Tragedy of Ignorance', in *The Clarion*, 17 Oct. Almwroth Wright was one of the most vocal opponents of women's suffrage.

92 Who is there in that lot one would want as a father, except perhaps Mrs Thatcher? That choice would be irregular but safe.
1982 Of British Prime Ministers. *1900*, introduction.

Wharton, Edith Newbold née Jones
1861–1937

US novelist. She wrote more than 50 books in all, but is best known for her sophisticated novels of manners, which include *The House of Mirth* (1905) and *The Age of Innocence* (1920).

93 I despair of the Republic!… What a horror it is for a whole nation to be developing without a sense of beauty, and eating bananas for breakfast.
1904 On the US. Letter to Sara Norton, 19 Aug.

94 She was like a disembodied spirit who took up a great deal of room.
1905 *The House of Mirth*, bk.1, ch.2.

95 Of course, being fatally poor and dingy, it was wise of Gerty to have taken up philanthropy and symphony concerts.
1905 *The House of Mirth*, bk.1, ch.8.

96 Miss Farish, who was accustomed, in the way of happiness, to such scant light as shone through the cracks of other people's lives.
1905 *The House of Mirth*, bk.1, ch.14.

97 If I were shabby no one would have me: a woman is asked out as much for her clothes as for herself.
1905 *The House of Mirth*, ch.1.

98 She keeps on being Queenly in her own room, with the door shut.
1905 *The House of Mirth*, bk.2, ch.1.

99 Paying for what she doesn't get rankles so dreadfully with Louisa; I can't make her see that it's one of the preliminary steps to getting what you haven't paid for.
1905 *The House of Mirth*, bk.2, ch.2.

1 Almost everyone in the neighbourhood had 'troubles', frankly localized and specified; but only the chosen had 'complications'. To have them was in itself as distinction, though it was also, in most cases, a death warrant. People struggled on for years with 'troubles', but they almost always succumbed to 'complications'.
1911 *Ethan Frome*, ch.7.

2 Mrs Ballinger is one of the ladies who pursue Culture in bands, as though it were dangerous to meet it alone.
1916 *Xingu and Other Stories*, 'Xingu'.

3 An unalterable and unquestioned law of the musical world required that the German text of French operas sung by Swedish artists should be translated into Italian for the clearer understanding of English speaking audiences.
1920 *The Age of Innocence*, bk.1, ch.1.

4 What can you expect of a girl who was allowed to wear black satin at her coming-out ball?
1920 *The Age of Innocence*, bk.1, ch.5.

5 Blessed are the pure in heart for they have so much more to talk about.
1932 In *John O'London's Weekly*, 10 Apr.

6 There is no such thing as old age, there is only sorrow.
1934 *A Backward Glance*, 'A First Word'.

Whately, Richard 1787–1863

English scholar and prelate, Archbishop of Dublin (1831), writer of treatises on logic and rhetoric. A founder of the Broad Church party, he supported Catholic emancipation and rejected sectarianism, but his caustic wit and outspokenness made him unpopular.

7 Preach not because you have to say something, but because you have something to say.
Apophthegms.

8 Happiness is no laughing matter.
Apophthegms.

Whistler, James (Abbott) McNeill
1834–1903

US artist, who moved to Paris and later London, where he was controversially received. He is best known for his 'nocturnes', including *Old Battersea Bridge* (c.1872–5, Tate, London), and the portrait of his mother (*The Artist's Mother*, 1871–2, Louvre, Paris).

9 I am not arguing with you—I am telling you.
1890 *The Gentle Art of Making Enemies.*

10 A picture is finished when all trace of the means used to bring about the end has disappeared.
1890 *The Gentle Art of Making Enemies.*

11 A life passed among pictures makes not a painter—else the policeman in the National Gallery might assert himself.
1890 *The Gentle Art of Making Enemies.*

12 To say to the painter, that Nature is to be taken as she is, is to say to the player, that he may sit on the piano.
1890 *The Gentle Art of Making Enemies.*

13 The imitator is a poor kind of creature. If the man who paints only the tree, or a flower, or other surface he sees before him were an artist, the king of artists would be the photographer.
1890 *The Gentle Art of Making Enemies.*

14 Art should be independent of all clap-trap—should stand alone, and appeal to the artistic sense of eye or ear, without confounding this with emotions entirely foreign to it, as devotion, pity, love, patriotism and the like. All these have no kind of concern with it; and that is why I insist on calling my works 'arrangements' and 'harmonies'.
1890 *The Gentle Art of Making Enemies.*

15 Poor lawyers, like poor paintings, are dear at any price.
On the cost and quality of some of the lawyers he had hired. Quoted in Arthur Jerome Eddy *Recollections and Impressions of J.A.M. Whistler* (1903).

Whitbread, Samuel 1758–1815

English radical Whig politician, founder of the famous brewing firm. The intimate friend of Fox, under Pitt he was leader of the Opposition, and in 1805 headed the attack on the treasurer of the navy, Viscount Melville.

16 The nation suspects that the regular ministerial majorities in Parliament are bought, and that the Crown has made a purchase of the House with the money of the people. Hence the ready, tame and servile compliance to every royal verdict issued by Lord North… It is almost universally believed that this debt has been contracted in corrupting the representatives of the people.
1777 House of Commons, 16 Apr.

17 In a political point of view, nothing can possibly afford greater stability to a popular Government than the education of the people.
1807 House of Commons, 19 Feb.

White, Andrew Dickson 1832–1918

US educationalist. President of Cornell University.

18 I will not permit thirty men to travel four hundred miles to agitate a bag of wind.
On refusing permission for a team from Cornell University to visit Michigan to play a game of American football. Quoted in D Wallechinsky *The People's Almanac* (1975).

White, Edmund 1940–

US writer. His sensitive assessments of gay life have appeared in novels including *A Boy's Own Story* (1982) and *The Beautiful Room Is Empty* (1988), as well as in his essays.

19 In fact, they are the classic scapegoats. Our old fears about our sissiness, still with us though masked by the new macho fascism, are now located, isolated, quarantined through our persecution of the transvestite.
1980 *States of Desire: Travels in Gay America*, ch.2.

20 Those who believe machismo reeks of violence alone choose to forget it once stood for honor as well.
1980 *States of Desire: Travels in Gay America*, ch.5.

21 The AIDS epidemic has rolled back a big rotting log and revealed all the squirming life underneath it, since it involves, all at once, the main themes of our existence: sex, death, power, money, love, hate, disease and panic. No American phenomenon has been so compelling since the Vietnam War.
1986 'Afterword—AIDS: An American Epidemic', added to later editions of *States of Desire: Travels in Gay America*.

White, E(lwyn) B(rooks) 1899–1985

US essayist, children's novelist, poet and parodist. He was closely associated with the rise and development of the *New Yorker* magazine.

22 MOTHER: It's broccoli, dear.
CHILD: I say it's spinach, and I say the hell with it.
1928 Cartoon caption, in the *New Yorker*, 8 Dec.

23 All poets who, when reading from their own works, experience a choked feeling, are major. For that matter, all poets who read from their own works are major, whether they choke or not.
1939 *Quo Vadimus?*, 'How To Tell A Major Poet From A Minor Poet'.

24 It is easier for a man to be loyal to his club than to his planet; the by-laws are shorter, and he is personally acquainted with the other members.
1942 *One Man's Meat*, 'One Man's Meat'.

25 The duty of a democracy is to know then what it knows now.
1942 *One Man's Meat*, 'One Man's Meat'.

26 A poet's pleasure is to withhold a little of his meaning, to intensify by mystification. He unzips the veil from beauty, but does not remove it.
1942 *One Man's Meat*, 'Poetry'.

27 Democracy is the recurrent suspicion that more than half the people are right more than half the time.
1944 In the *New Yorker*, 3 Jul.

28 You can see in pantomime the puppets fumbling with their slips of paper…see them pick up their phone…see the noiseless, ceaseless capital of memoranda, in touch with Calcutta, in touch with Reykjavik, and always fooling with something.
1949 On office windows at twilight. *Here Is New York.*

29 I'm less than two months old and I'm tired of living.
1952 Wilbur the pig. *Charlotte's Web*, ch.3.

30 I can surely fool a man. People are not as smart as bugs.
1952 Charlotte. *Charlotte's Web*, ch.10.

31 It was the best place to be, thought Wilbur, this warm delicious cellar, with the garrulous geese, the changing seasons, the heat of the sun, the passage of swallows, the nearness of rats, the sameness of sheep, the love of spiders, the smell of manure, and the glory of everything.
1952 *Charlotte's Web*, ch.22.

32 It is not often that someone comes along who is a true friend and a good writer. Charlotte was both.
1952 *Charlotte's Web*, ch.22.

33 The time not to become a father is eighteen years before a war.
1954 *The Second Tree from the Corner*, 'The Second Tree from the Corner'.

34 Thurber did not write the way a surgeon operates, he wrote the way a child skips rope, the way a mouse waltzes.
1961 In the *New Yorker*, 11 Nov. Tribute to James Thurber.

35 A man who publishes his letters becomes a nudist—nothing shields him from the world's gaze except his bare skin.
1975 Letter to Corona Macheiner, 11 Jun.

36 Commuter—one who spends his life
In riding to and from his wife;
A man who shaves and takes a train,
And then rides back to shave again.
1982 *Poems and Sketches*, 'The Commuter'.

37 She would write 8 or 10 words, then draw her gun and shoot them down.
1979 On his wife and fellow editor Katharine S White. *Onward and Upward in the Garden.*

White, George Malcolm 1920–

US architect, designer of the Capitol, Washington.

38 The fact that you don't buy a teenager new clothes doesn't mean he isn't going to grow.
1987 On the need for a fourth Senate office building. In *Connoisseur*, Apr.

White, Patrick Victor Martindale 1912–90

Australian novelist, born in London, who went to Australia as an infant and settled there after World War II. He received the Nobel Prize for Literature in 1973, and numerous other awards, particularly for *Voss* (1957).

39 She would imprison the child in her house by the force of love.
1955 *The Tree of Man*, ch.7.

40 So that in the end there were the trees. The boy walking through them with his head drooping as he increased in stature. Putting out shoots of green thought. So that, in the end, there was no end.
1955 *The Tree of Man*, ch.26.

41 The mystery of life is not solved by success, which is an end in itself, but in failure, in perpetual struggle, in becoming.
1957 *Voss*, ch.10.

42 Perhaps true knowledge only comes of death by torture in the country of the mind.
1957 *Voss*, ch.16.

43 There is nothing like a rain of bombs to start one trying to assess one's own achievement.
1958 Essay on his literary career, in *Australian Letters*, 'The Prodigal Son', vol.1, no.3, Apr.

44 In all directions stretched the Great Australian Emptiness, in which the mind is the least of possessions…and the march of material ugliness does not raise a quiver from the average nerves. It was the exaltation of the 'average' that made me panic most.
1958 Essay on his literary career, in *Australian Letters*, 'The Prodigal Son', vol.1, no.3, Apr.

45 Above all I was determined to prove that the Australian novel is not necessarily the dreary, dun-coloured offspring of journalistic realism.
1958 Essay on his literary career, in *Australian Letters*, 'The Prodigal Son', vol.1, no.3, Apr.

White, Theodore H(arold) 1926–

US journalist and political commentator. His *The Making of the President, 1960* (1961), with its characteristic reportage style, won a Pulitzer Prize in 1962.

46 Chafing in action when his nature yearned to act, conscious of indignities real and imagined, Johnson went through three years of slow burn.
Of Lyndon B Johnson as John F Kennedy's Vice President. Quoted in Arthur M Schlesinger *Jr A Thousand Days* (1965).

47 The best time to listen to a politician is when he is on a street corner, in the rain, late at night, when he's exhausted. Then he doesn't lie.
1969 In the *New York Times,* 5 Jan.

48 He was almost a force of nature, like a slumbering volcano, wreathed in clouds, occasionally emitting smoke which soothsayers attempted to interpret.
1969 Of Nelson Rockefeller. *The Making of the President 1968.*

49 The epitaph on the Kennedy administration became Camelot—a magic moment in American history, when gallant men danced with beautiful women, when great deeds were done, when artists, writers and poets met at the White House and the barbarians beyond the walls were held back.
1978 *In Search of History.*

50 Eisenhower has…a magic in American politics that is peculiarly his: he makes people happy.
Of Dwight D Eisenhower's appearances during Richard M Nixon's 1960 presidential campaign. Quoted in Michael R Beschloss *Eisenhower* (1990).

White, Thomas 1550–1624
English Puritan.

51 The cause of plagues is sin, if you look to it well; and the cause of sin are plays; therefore the cause of plagues are plays.
Attributed.

Whitehead, Alfred North 1861–1947
English mathematician and philosopher. He taught at Imperial College London and later at Harvard University. With his former pupil Bertrand Russell he wrote *Principia Mathematica* (1910–13).

52 It is a safe rule to apply that, when a mathematical or philosophical author writes with a misty profundity, he is talking nonsense.
1911 *Introduction to Mathematics.*

53 Knowledge does not keep any better than fish.
1916 'The Aims of Education; a plea for reform', address as president of the Mathematical Association.

54 Familiar things happen, and mankind does not bother about them. It requires a very unusual mind to undertake the analysis of the obvious.
1925 *Science and the Modern World.*

55 Religion is something which stands beyond, behind, and within the passing flux of immediate things; something which is real, and yet waiting to be realized; something which is a remote possibility, and yet the greatest of present facts; something that gives meaning to all that passes, and yet eludes apprehension; something whose possession is the final good, and yet is beyond all reach; something which is the ultimate ideal, and the hopeless quest.
1925 *Science and the Modern World.*

56 The worship of God is not a rule of safety—it is an adventure of the spirit, a flight after the unattainable. The death of religion comes with the repression of the high hope of adventure.
1925 *Science and the Modern World.*

57 Religion is what a man does with his solitariness.
1926 *Religion in the Making.*

58 Mathematics is thought moving in the sphere of complete abstraction from any particular instance of what it is talking about.
1926 *Science And the Modern World.*

59 The safest general characterization of the European philosophical tradition is that it consists of a series of footnotes to Plato.
1929 *Process and reality,* pt.2, ch.1, section 1.

60 The power of Christianity lies in its revelation in act, of that which Plato divined in theory.
1938 *Adventures of Ideas.*

61 The essence of Christianity is the appeal to the life of Christ as a revelation of the nature of God and of his agency in the world. The record is fragmentary, inconsistent and uncertain… But there can be no doubt as to the elements in the record that have evoked the best in human nature. The Mother, the Child and the bare manger: the lowly man, homeless and self-forgetful, with his message of peace, love and sympathy: the suffering, the agony, the tender words as life ebbed, the final despair: and the whole with the authority of supreme victory.
1938 *Adventures of Ideas.*

62 What is morality in any given time or place? It is what the majority then and there happen to like, and immorality is what they dislike.
Dialogues.

Whitehorn, Katharine 1926–
English journalist.

63 Hats divide generally into three classes: offensive hats, defensive hats, and shrapnel.
1963 *Shouts and Murmurs.*

Whitelaw, William Stephen Ian, 1st Viscount 1918–99

Scottish Conservative politician, Leader of the House of Commons (1970–2), Secretary of State for Northern Ireland (1972–3) and Employment (1973–4) and Home Secretary (1979–83). Loyal to Heath and then Thatcher, he led the House of Lords until 1988.

64 I do not intend to prejudge the past.

1973 On arriving in Ulster for the first time as Secretary of State for Northern Ireland, 2 Dec.

65 He is going round the country stirring up apathy.

1974 Of Harold Wilson during the general election campaign. Attributed.

66 A short, sharp shock.

1979 At the Conservative Party Conference, 10 Oct, on the need for more effective treatment of young offenders.

▷ See Gilbert 425:88.

Whiteman, Paul 1891–1967

US bandleader. A pioneer of 'sweet style' jazz in the 1920s, he recruited such talents as trumpeter Bix Beiderbecke. He developed Gershwin's 'symphonic jazz' experiments, commissioning *Rhapsody in Blue* in 1924.

67 Jazz came to America three hundred years ago in chains.

1926 *Jazz.*

Whiting, George 1884–1943

US songwriter.

68 When You're All Dressed Up and Have No Place To Go.

1912 Title of song (music by Newton Harding).

Whitlam, (Edward) Gough 1916–

Australian politician, leader of the Labor Party from 1967 and Prime Minister (1972–5). He resigned in 1978 to move into academia. His works include *The Italian Inspiration in English Literature* (1980).

69 The importance of an historical event lies not in what happened but in what later generations believe to have happened.

1973 Speech at Ballarat, Victoria, 3 Dec.

70 I do not mind the Liberals, still less do I mind the Country party, calling me a bastard. In some circumstances, I am only doing my job if they do. But I hope that you will not publicly call me a bastard, as some bastards in the Caucus have.

1974 Speech to the Australian Labor Party, 9 Jun.

71 We may say 'God Save the Queen', because nothing will save the Governor-General... Maintain your rage and your enthusiasm for the election now to be held and until polling day.

1975 On the Governor-General Sir John Kerr's action in dissolving the Australian Parliament, 11 Nov. Whitlam lost the subsequent election.

Whitman, Christine Todd 1947–

US Republican politician, Governor of New Jersey from 1994, she is a former freeholder in Somerset County, New Jersey and a former president of the State Board of Public Utilities.

72 The states are the laboratories of democracy.

1995 In the *New York Times*, 29 Jan.

Whitman, Walt(er) 1819–91

US poet. He was editor of the *Brooklyn Eagle* and worked as a nurse during the Civil War. His poetry reflected his mystical faith in democracy and was attacked for indecency because it addressed many taboo subjects. It is collected in *Leaves of Grass* (1855–92).

73 The Americans of all nations at any time upon the earth have probably the fullest poetical nature. The United States themselves are essentially the greatest poem.

1855 *Leaves of Grass*, preface.

74 As soon as histories are properly told there is no more need of romances.

1855 *Leaves of Grass*, preface.

75 I too am not a bit tamed, I too am untranslatable, I sound my barbaric yawp over the roofs of the world.

1855 *Leaves of Grass*, 'Song of Myself', section 52.

76 I celebrate myself, and sing myself,
And what I assume you shall assume,
For every atom belonging to me as good belongs to you.

1855 *Leaves of Grass*, 'Song of Myself', section 1.

77 How beggarly appear arguments before a defiant deed!

1855 Leaves of Grass, 'Broad-Axe Song', later 'Song of the Broad-Axe' (from 1867).

78 All goes onward and outward, nothing collapses,
And to die is different from what any one supposed, and luckier.

1855 *Leaves of Grass*, 'Song of Myself', section 6.

79 I believe a leaf of grass is no less than the journey-work of the stars.

1855 *Leaves of Grass*, 'Song of Myself', section 31.

80 I think I could turn, and live with animals, they are so placid and self-contain'd.

1855 *Leaves of Grass*, 'Song of Myself', section 32.

81 I have said that the soul is not more than the body,

And I have said that the body is not more than the
soul,
And nothing, not God, is greater to one than one's
self is.
1855 *Leaves of Grass*, 'Song of Myself', section 48.

82 Do I contradict myself?
Very well then I contradict myself,
(I am large, I contain multitudes.)
1855 *Leaves of Grass*, 'Song of Myself', section 51.

83 If anything is sacred the human body is sacred.
1855 *Leaves of Grass*, 'Children of Adam', 'I Sing the Body
Electric', section 8.

84 I do not think seventy years is the time of a man or
woman,
Nor that seventy millions of years is the time of a
man or woman,
Nor that years will ever stop the existence of me, or
any one else.
1855 *Leaves of Grass*, 'Autumn Rivulets', 'Who Learns My
Lesson Complete?'

85 Henceforth I whimper no more, postpone no
more, need nothing,
Done with indoor complaints, libraries, querulous
criticisms,
Strong and content I travel the open road.
1856 *Leaves of Grass*, 'Song of the Open Road', section 1.

86 What can ever be more stately and admirable to me
than mast-hemm'd Manhattan?
1856 *Leaves of Grass*, 'Crossing Brooklyn Ferry', section 8.

87 He or she is greatest who contributes the greatest
original practical example.
1856 *Leaves of Grass*, 'By Blue Ontario's Shores', section 13.

88 And I will show that nothing can happen more
beautiful than death.
1860 *Leaves of Grass*, 'Proto-Leaf', later renamed 'Starting
From Paumanok' (from 1867).

89 I hear it was charged against me that I sought to
destroy institutions,
But really I am neither for nor against institutions.
1860 *Leaves of Grass*, 'Calamus', 'I Hear It Was Charged
Against Me'.

90 Camarado, this is no book,
Who touches this touches a man.
1860 *Leaves of Grass*, 'Songs of Parting', 'So Long!'

91 O Captain! my Captain! our fearful trip is done,
The ship has weather'd every rack, the prize we
sought is won,
The port is near, the bells I hear, the people all
exulting.
1865 *Leaves of Grass*, 'Memories of President Lincoln', 'O
Captain! My Captain!'

92 When lilacs last in the dooryard bloom'd,
And the great star early droop'd in the western sky
in the night,
I mourn'd, and yet shall mourn with ever-returning
spring.
1865–66 *Leaves of Grass*, 'Memories of President Lincoln',
'When Lilacs Last in the Dooryard Bloom'd', section 1.

93 Come lovely and soothing death,
Undulate round the world, serenely arriving,
arriving,
In the day, in the night, to all, to each,
Sooner or later delicate death.
1865–66 *Leaves of Grass*, 'Memories of President Lincoln',
'When Lilacs Last in the Dooryard Bloom'd', section 14.

94 The Past—the dark unfathom'd retrospect!
The teeming gulf—the sleepers and the shadows!
The past! the infinite greatness of the past!
For what is the present after all but a growth out
of the past?
1871 *Passage to India*, opening verse.

95 Political democracy, as it exists and practically
works in America, with all its threatening evils,
supplies a training-school for making first-class
men. It is life's gymnasium, not of good only, but of
all.
1871 *Democratic Vistas*.

96 In this broad earth of ours,
Amid the measureless grossness and the slag,
Enclosed and safe within its central heart,
Nestles the seed perfection.
1874 *Leaves of Grass*, Birds of Passage, 'Song of the Universal',
section 1.

97 After you have exhausted what there is in business,
politics, conviviality, love, and so on—and found
that none of these finally satisfy, or permanently
wear—what remains? Nature remains.
1876–77 *Specimen Days*, 'New Themes Entered Upon'.

98 Youth, large, lusty, loving—youth full of grace,
force, fascination,
Do you know that Old Age may come after you
with equal grace, force, fascination?
1881 *Leaves of Grass*, 'Youth, Day, Old Age and Night', stanza
1.

99 Have you not learn'd great lessons from those who
reject you,
and brace themselves against you? or who treat you
with
contempt, or dispute the passage with you?
1888 Leaves of Grass, 'Sands at Seventy', 'Stronger Lessons'.

1 No one will get at my verses who insists upon
viewing them as a literary performance.
1888 'A Backward Glance O'er Travel'd Roads'.

Whittier, John Greenleaf 1807–92

US poet and abolitionist. A Quaker, he devoted himself to the cause of emancipation. His ballads and sentimental poems, such as 'Barbara Freitchie', which was included in *In War Time* (1864), were extremely popular in their day. His best work is the nostalgic narrative poem, *Snow-Bound* (1866).

2 When the care-wearied man seeks his mother once
    more,
And the worn matron smiles where the girl smiled
    before,
What moistens the lip and what brightens the eye?
What calls back the past, like the rich Pumpkin pie?
1844 'The Pumpkin,' stanza 3.

3 When faith is lost, when honor dies,
The man is dead!
1850 'Ichabod', stanza 8.

4 Beneath her torn hat glowed the wealth
Of simple beauty and rustic health.
1854 'Maud Muller', l.3–4.

5 For of all sad words of tongue or pen,
The saddest are these: 'It might have been!'
1854 'Maud Muller', l.105–6.

6 The age is dull and mean. Men creep,
Not walk.
1855 'Lines, Inscribed to Friends Under Arrest for Treason Against the Slave Power', stanza 1.

7 Up from the meadows rich with corn,
Clear in the cool September morn.
1863 'Barbara Frietchie', opening lines.

8 'Shoot, if you must this old grey head,
But spare your country's flag,' she said.
1863 'Barbara Frietchie', l.35–36.

9 Dear Lord and Father of mankind,
Forgive our foolish ways!
Re-clothe us in our rightful mind,
In purer lives thy service find,
In deeper reverence praise
1872 'The Brewing of Soma'.

Whitton, Charlotte 1896–1975

Canadian politician, Mayor of Ottawa (1951–6, 1960–4), the first woman to serve as mayor of a Canadian city.

10 Whatever women do they must do twice as well as men to be thought half so good…luckily, it's not difficult.
1963 In *Canada Month*, Jun.

Whymper, Edward 1840–1911

English wood-engraver and mountaineer. In 1860–9 he conquered several hitherto unscaled peaks of the Alps, including the Matterhorn. He later published several books based on his travels in the Alps and elsewhere.

11 Do nothing in haste, look well to each step, and from the beginning think what may be the end.
1871 *Scrambles Amongst the Alps*.

Wiener, Norbert 1894–1964

US academic, who studied mathematics with Bertrand Russell and taught at MIT. His work contributed to the development of the understanding of information systems. He coined the word *cybernetics* to describe the science of feedback control in systems.

12 The automatic machine, whatever we think of any feelings it may or may not have, is the precise economic equivalent of the slave.
1949 *The Human Use of Human Beings*.

13 The new industrial revolution is a two-edged sword. It may be used for the benefit of humanity, assuming that humanity survives long enough to reach a period in which such a benefit is possible. If, however, we proceed along the clear and obvious lines of our traditional behavior, and follow our traditional worship of progress and the fifth freedom—the freedom to exploit—it is practically certain that we shall have to face a decade or more of ruin and despair.
1949 *The Human Use of Human Beings*.

14 Scientific discovery consists in the interpretation for our own convenience of a system of existence which has been made with no eye to our convenience at all.
1949 *The Human Use of Human Beings*.

Wilberforce, Samuel 1805–73

English prelate, Canon of Winchester, later Dean of Westminster and Bishop of Oxford.

15 If I were a cassowary
On the plains of Timbuctoo,
I would eat a missionary,
Cassock, band, and hymn-book too.
Attributed.

Wilbur, Richard 1921–

US poet. He taught at Harvard and Wesleyan Universities, and wrote a significant body of poems. He also contributed lyrics to Leonard Bernstein's opera, *Candide*.

16 We milk the cow of the world, and as we do
We whisper in her ear, 'You are not true.'
1950 *Ceremony and Other Poems*, 'Epistemology'.

17 Forgive the hero, you who would have died
Gladly with all you knew; he rode that tide
To Ararat; all men are Noah's sons.
1950 *Ceremony and Other Poems*, 'Still, Citizen Sparrow'.

18 Outside the open window
    The morning air is all awash with angels.
    1956 *Things of This World,* 'Love Calls Us To The Things of
    This World'.

19 The soul shrinks
    From all that it is about to remember,
    From the punctual rape of every blessèd day
    1956 *Things of This World,* 'Love Calls Us To The Things of
    This World'.

20 Columbus and his men, they say,
    Conveyed the virus hither
    Whereby my features rot away
    And vital powers wither;
    Yet had they not traversed the seas
    And come infected back,
    Why, think of all the luxuries
    That modern life would lack.
    1957 'Pangloss's Song', from *Candide.*

21 It is not tricks of sense
    But the time's fright within me which distracts
    Least fancies into violence
    1969 *Walking To Sleep,* 'On The Marginal Way'.

22 All night, this headland
    Lunges into the rumpling
    Capework of the wind.
    1976 *The Mind Reader,* 'Sleepless at Crown Point'.

23 Most women know that sex is good for headaches.
    1987 Quoted in *The Observer,* 1 Nov.

24 Writing is…waiting for the word that may not be
    there until next Tuesday.
    1987 In the *L A Times,* 13 Oct.

Wilcox, Ella Wheeler   1850–1919

US poet who wrote over 30 volumes of sentimental verse.
Her temperance poems were collected in *Drops of Water*
(1872). *Poems of Passion* (1883) was attacked for its
immorality.

25 Laugh, and the world laughs with you:
    Weep, and you weep alone;
    For the sad old earth must borrow its mirth,
    It has trouble enough of its own.
    1883 Poems of Passion, 'Solitude'.

Wilde, Jane Francesca née Elgee   1826–96

Irish Poet and folklorist, mother of Oscar Wilde. She was
an ardent nationalist and contributed verse and prose to
the *Nation* under the pen name 'Speranza'.

26 'Tis midnight, falls the lamp-light dull and sickly
    On a pale and anxious crowd,
    Through the court, and round the judges
       thronging thickly,

    With prayers they dare not speak aloud—
    Two youths, two noble youths, stand prisoners at
       the bar—
    You can see them through the gloom—
    In the pride of life and manhood's beauty, there
       they are
    Awaiting their death-doom.
    'The Brothers'.

27 Weary men, what reap ye?—Golden corn for the
       stranger.
    What sow ye?—Human corses that wait for the
       avenger.
    Fainting forms, hunger stricken, what see ye in the
       offing?
    Stately ships to bear our food away, amid the
       stranger's scoffing.
    There's a proud array of soldiers—what do they
       round your door?
    They guard our master's granaries from the thin
       hands of the poor.
    Pale mothers, wherefore weeping? Would to God
       that we were dead—
    Our children swoon before us, and we cannot give
       them bread.
    'The Famine Year'.

Wilde, Oscar Fingal O'Flahertie Wills
1854–1900

Anglo-Irish poet and dramatist, renowned for his wit and
flamboyant lifestyle. His works include *The Picture of
Dorian Gray* (1891), *Lady Windermere's Fan* (1892), *An
Ideal Husband* (1895), *The Importance of Being Earnest*
(1895) and *The Ballad of Reading Gaol* (1898). He was
ruined by a trial arising from his homosexual
relationships.

28 To make a good salad is to be a brilliant
    diplomatist—the problem is entirely the same in
    both cases. To know exactly how much oil one
    must put with one's vinegar.
    1880 *Vera, or The Nihilists,* act 2.

29 I have nothing to declare except my genius.
    1882 On passing through US customs on a lecture tour.
    Quoted in F Harris, *Oscar Wilde* (1918), p.75.

30 Over the piano was printed a notice: 'Please do not
    shoot the pianist. He is doing his best.'
    1883 *Impressions of America: Leadville.*

31 What captivity was to the Jews, exile has been to
    the Irish: America and American influence have
    educated them. Their first practical leader is an
    Irish-American.
    1889 Of Charles Stewart Parnell. 'The Two Chiefs of Dunboy:
    or, an Irish Romance of the Last Century' in *Pall Mall Gazette,*
    13 Apr.

32 Books of poetry by young writers are usually promissory notes that are never met. Now and then, however, one comes across a volume that is so far above the average that one can hardly resist the fascinating temptation of recklessly prophesying a fine future for its author. Such a book Mr Yeats's *Wanderings of Oisin* certainly is. Here we find nobility of treatment and nobility of subject-matter, delicacy of poetic instinct and richness of imaginative resource.
1889 In the *Pall Mall Gazette*, 12 Jul.

33 Newspapers have degenerated. They may now be absolutely relied upon.
1889 'The Decay of Lying', first published in the *Nineteenth Century Review*.

34 After playing Chopin, I feel as if I had been weeping over sins that I had never committed.
1891 *Intentions*, 'The Critic as Artist'.

35 Art never expresses anything but itself.
1891 'The Decay of Lying', first published in the *Nineteenth Century Review*.

36 Every great man nowadays has his disciples, and it is always Judas who writes the biography.
1891 *Intentions*, 'The Critic as Artist'.

37 Meredith is a prose Browning, and so is Browning.
1891 *Intentions*, 'The Critic as Artist'.

38 The one duty we owe to history is to rewrite it.
1891 *Intentions*, 'The Critic as Artist'.

39 It is through Art, and through Art only, that we can realise our perfection; through Art, and through Art only, that we can shield ourselves from the sordid perils of actual existence.
1891 *Intentions*, 'The Critic as Artist'.

40 All art is immoral.
1891 *Intentions*, 'The Critic as Artist'.

41 A little sincerity is a dangerous thing, and a great deal of it is absolutely fatal.
1891 *Intentions*, 'The Critic as Artist'.

42 Modern journalism justifies its own existence by the great Darwinian principle of the survival of the vulgarest.
1891 *Intentions*, 'The Critic as Artist'.

43 All that I desire to point out is the general principle that Life imitates Art far more than Art imitates Life.
1891 *Intentions*, 'The Decay of Lying'.

44 There is no such thing as a moral or an immoral book. Books are well written, or badly written.
1891 *The Picture of Dorian Gray*, preface.

45 The nineteenth century dislike of Realism is the rage of Caliban seeing his own face in the glass.
1891 *The Picture of Dorian Gray*, preface.

46 The moral life of man forms part of the subject matter of the artist, but the morality of art consists in the perfect use of an imperfect medium.
1891 *The Picture of Dorian Gray*, preface.

47 I like Wagner's music better than anybody's. It is so loud that one can talk the whole time without other people hearing what one says.
1891 *The Picture of Dorian Gray*.

48 If one hears bad music, it is one's duty to drown it by one's conversation.
1891 *The Picture of Dorian Gray*.

49 Murder is always a mistake… One should never do anything that one cannot talk about after dinner.
1891 *The Picture of Dorian Gray*.

50 There is only one thing in the world worse than being talked about, and that is not being talked about.
1891 Lord Henry. *The Picture of Dorian Gray*, ch.1.

51 A man cannot be too careful in the choice of his enemies.
1891 *The Picture of Dorian Gray*, ch.1.

52 A cigarette is the perfect type of a perfect pleasure. It is exquisite, and it leaves one unsatisfied. What more can one want?
1891 *The Picture of Dorian Gray*, ch.6.

53 It is better to be beautiful than to be good. But…it is better to be good than to be ugly.
1891 *The Picture of Dorian Gray*, ch.17.

54 Anybody can be good in the country.
1891 *The Picture of Dorian Gray*, ch.19.

55 As for the virtuous poor, one can pity them, of course, but one cannot possibly admire them.
1891 *Sebastian Melmoth*, 'The Soul of Man under Socialism'.

56 Democracy means simply the bludgeoning of the people by the people for the people.
1891 *Sebastian Melmoth*, 'The Soul of Man under Socialism'.

57 I can resist everything except temptation.
1892 Lord Darlington. *Lady Windermere's Fan*, act 1.

58 Many a woman has a past, but I am told that she has at least a dozen, and that they all fit.
1892 Said by Duchess of Berwick. *Lady Windermere's Fan*, act 1.

59 Do you know, Mr Hopper, dear Agatha and I are so much interested in Australia. It must be so pretty with all the dear little kangaroos flying about.

Agatha has found it on the map. What a curious shape it is! Just like a large packing case.

1892 Duchess of Berwick to Mr Hopper. *Lady Windermere's Fan*, act 2.

60 We are all in the gutter, but some of us are looking at the stars.

1892 Said by Lord Darlington. *Lady Windermere's Fan*, act 3.

61 There is nothing in the whole world so unbecoming to a woman as a Nonconformist conscience.

1892 Cecil Graham. *Lady Windermere's Fan*, act 3.

62 A man who knows the price of everything and the value of nothing.

1892 Lord Darlington's definition of a cynic. *Lady Winderemere's Fan*, act 3.

63 Experience is the name everyone gives to their mistakes.

1892 Dumby. *Lady Windermere's Fan*, act 3.

64 The play was a great success, but the audience was a disaster.

1892 Attributed comment after the poor reception of *Lady Windermere's Fan*.

65 LORD ILLINGWORTH: The Book of Life begins with a man and a woman in a garden.
MRS ALLONBY: It ends with Revelations.

1893 *A Woman of No Importance*, act 1.

66 The English country gentleman galloping after a fox–the unspeakable in full pursuit of the uneatable.

1893 Lord Illingworth. *A Woman of No Importance*, act 1.

67 MRS ALLONBY: They say, Lady Hunstanton, that when good Americans die they go to Paris.
LADY HUNSTANTON: Indeed? And when bad Americans die, where do they go to?
LORD ILLINGWORTH: Oh, they go to America.

1893 *A Woman of No Importance*, act 1.

68 The youth of America is their oldest tradition. It has been going on now for three hundred years.

1893 Lord Illingworth. *A Woman of No Importance*, act 1.

69 One should never trust a woman who tells one her real age. A woman who would tell one that, would tell one anything.

1893 Lord Illingworth. *A Woman of No Importance*, act 1.

70 Children begin by loving their parents; after a time they judge them; rarely, if ever, do they forgive them.

1893 Lord Illingworth. *A Woman of No Importance*, act 2.

71 After a good dinner one can forgive anybody, even one's own relations.

1893 *A Woman of No Importance*, act 2.

72 GERALD: I suppose society is wonderfully delightful!
LORD ILLINGWORTH: To be in it is merely a bore. But to be out of it is simply a tragedy.

1893 *A Woman of No Importance*, act 3.

73 No woman should have a memory. Memory in a woman is the beginning of dowdiness.

1893 *A Woman of No Importance*, act 3.

74 You should study the Peerage, Gerald… It is the best thing in fiction the English have ever done.

1893 Lord Illingworth. *A Woman of No Importance*, act 3.

75 A man who can dominate a London dinner-table can dominate the world.

1893 *A Woman of No Importance*, act 3.

76 I'm afraid I play no outdoor games at all, except dominoes. I have sometimes played dominoes outside a French café.

1895 Quoted by Gelett Burgess in 'A Talk with Mr Oscar Wilde' in *The Sketch*, 9 Jan.

77 JACK: I think Jack, for instance, a charming name.
GWENDOLEN: Jack?… No, there is very little music in the name Jack, if any at all, indeed. It does not thrill. It produces absolutely no vibrations… I have known several Jacks, and they all, without exception, were more than usually plain. Besides, Jack is a notorious domesticity for John! And I pity any woman who is married to a man called John. She would probably never be allowed to know the entrancing pleasure of a single moment's solitude. The only really safe name is Ernest.

1895 *The Importance of Being Earnest*, act 1.

78 Really, if the lower orders don't set us a good example, what on earth is the use of them?

1895 Algernon. *The Importance of Being Earnest*, act 1.

79 It is very vulgar to talk like a dentist when one isn't a dentist. It produces a false impression.

1895 Jack. *The Importance of Being Earnest*, act 1.

80 The truth is rarely pure, and never simple.

1895 Algernon. *The Importance of Being Earnest*, act 1.

81 In married life three is company and two none.

1895 Algernon. *The Importance of Being Earnest*, act 1.

82 Ignorance is like a delicate exotic fruit; touch it and the bloom is gone. The whole theory of modern education is radically unsound. Fortunately, in England, at any rate, education produces no effect whatsoever.

1895 Lady Bracknell. *The Importance of Being Earnest*, act 1.

83 To lose one parent, Mr Worthing, may be regarded as a misfortune; to lose both looks like carelessness.
1895 Lady Bracknell. *The Importance of Being Earnest*, act 1.

84 All women become like their mothers. That is their tragedy. No man does. That's his.
1895 Algernon. *The Importance of Being Earnest*, act 1, also in *A Woman of No Importance* (1893), act 2.

85 The good ended happily, and the bad unhappily. That is what fiction means.
1895 Miss Prism. *The Importance of Being Earnest*, act 2.

86 The chapter on the fall of the Rupee you may omit. It is somewhat too sensational.
1895 Miss Prism. *The Importance of Being Earnest*, act 2.

87 I hope you have not been leading a double life, pretending to be wicked and being really good all the time. That would be hypocrisy.
1895 Said by Cecily. *The Importance of Being Earnest*, act 2.

88 Charity, dear Miss Prism, charity! None of us are perfect. I myself am peculiarly susceptible to draughts.
1895 Dr Chasuble. *The Importance of Being Earnest*, act 2.

89 CECILY: When I see a spade I call it a spade.
GWENDOLEN: I am glad to say that I have never seen a spade.
1895 *The Importance of Being Earnest*, act 3.

90 Thirty-five is a very attractive age. London society is full of women of the very highest birth who have, of their own free choice, remained thirty-five for years.
1895 Lady Bracknell. *The Importance of Being Earnest*, act 3.

91 She wore far too much rouge last night, and not quite enough clothes. That is always a sign of despair in a woman.
1895 *An Ideal Husband*, act 2.

92 Nothing is so dangerous as being too modern. One is apt to grow old-fashioned quite suddenly.
1895 *An Ideal Husband*, act 2.

93 Fashion is what one wears oneself. What is unfashionable is what other people wear.
1895 *An Ideal Husband*, act 3.

94 If one could only teach the English how to talk, and the Irish how to listen, society here would be quite civilised.
1895 Mrs Cheveley speaking. *An Ideal Husband*, act 3.

95 If this is the way Queen Victoria treats her prisoners she doesn't deserve to have any.
1895 On being obliged to stand in the rain as he awaited transport to take him to prison. Attributed.

96 He did not wear his scarlet coat,

For blood and wine are red,
And blood and wine were on his hands
When they found him with the dead.
1898 *The Ballad of Reading Gaol*, pt.1, stanza 1.

97 I never saw a man who looked
With such a wistful eye
Upon that little tent of blue
Which prisoners call the sky.
1898 *The Ballad of Reading Gaol*, pt.1, stanza 3.

98 Yet each man kills the thing he loves,
By each let this be heard,
Some do it with a bitter look,
Some with a flattering word.
The coward does it with a kiss,
The brave man with a sword!
1898 *The Ballad of Reading Gaol*, pt.1, stanza 7.

99 The Governer was strong upon
The Regulation Act:
The Doctor said that Death was but
A scientific fact:
And twice a day the Chaplain called,
And left a little tract.
1898 *The Ballad of Reading Gaol*, pt.3, stanza 3.

1 Something was dead in each of us,
And what was dead was Hope.
1898 *The Ballad of Reading Gaol*, pt.3, stanza 31.

2 And the wild regrets, and the bloody sweats,
None knew so well as I:
For he who lives more lives than one
More deaths than one must die.
1898 *The Ballad of Reading Gaol*, pt.3, stanza 37.

3 I know not whether Laws be right,
Or whether Laws be wrong;
All that we know who lie in gaol
Is that the wall is strong;
And that each day is like a year,
A year whose days are long.
1898 *The Ballad of Reading Gaol*, pt.5, stanza 1.

4 How else but through a broken heart
May Lord Christ enter in?
1898 *The Ballad of Reading Gaol*, pt.5, stanza 14.

5 I am dying, as I have lived, beyond my means.
1900 Accepting a glass of champagne shortly before his death. Attributed.

6 Either that wallpaper goes or I do.
1900 As he lay dying in a Paris hotel bedroom. Attributed.

7 Football is all very well as a game for rough girls, but it is hardly suitable for delicate boys.
Quoted in Alvin Redman *The Epigrams of Oscar Wilde* (1952).

8 The only possible form of exercise is to talk, not to walk.

Quoted in Alvin Redman *The Epigrams of Oscar Wilde* (1952).

9 Mr Bernard Shaw has no enemies, but is intensely disliked by all his friends.

Quoted in W B Yeats *Autobiographies* (1955).

10 It requires one to assume such indecent postures.

His reason for not playing cricket. Quoted in *Bloomsbury Thematic Dictionary of Quotations* (1988)

11 Work is the curse of the drinking classes.

Attributed.

12 Henry James wrote fiction as if it were a painful duty.

Attributed.

13 The three women I have admired most are Queen Victoria, Sarah Bernhardt and Lillie Langtry. I would have married any one of them with pleasure.

Quoted in Vincent O'Sullivan *Letters of Oscar Wilde*.

Wilder, Billy (Samuel) 1906–

Austrian-born writer and director who moved to Hollywood in 1934. He won Academy Awards for *The Lost Weekend* (1945), *Sunset Boulevard* (1950) and *The Apartment* (1960). Other successes include *Double Indemnity* (1944), *The Seven Year Itch* (1955) and *Some Like It Hot* (1959).

14 Johnny, keep it out of focus. I want to win the foreign picture award.

1950 Remark to cameraman John Seitz during the making of *Sunset Boulevard*.

15 Making a picture with Marilyn Monroe was like going to the dentist. It was hell at the time, but after it was all over it was wonderful.

Quoted in Doug McClelland *Star Speak* (1987).

16 No one ever leaves a star.

1950 *Sunset Boulevard*.

17 Fasten your cigarettes.

1972 *Avanti* (with I A L Diamond).

18 I don't object to foreigners speaking a foreign language; I just wish they'd all speak the same foreign language.

1972 *Avanti* (with I A L Diamond).

19 Hindsight is always twenty-twenty.

Attributed.

Wilder, Thornton Niven 1897–1975

US playwright and novelist. His most successful plays included *Our Town* (1938) and *The Skin of Our Teeth* (1942), while his other writings included the novel *The Bridge of San Luis Rey* (1927). His play *The Matchmaker* (1954) provided the basis for the hit musical *Hello, Dolly!*

20 From what human ill does not dawn seem to be an alleviation.

1927 *The Bridge of San Luis Rey*, ch.3.

21 Most everybody in the world climbs into their graves married.

1938 *Our Town*, act 2.

22 Marriage is a bribe to make a housekeeper think she's a householder.

1939 *The Merchant of Yonkers*, act 1.

23 The fights are the best part of married life. The rest is merely so-so.

1939 *The Merchant of Yonkers*, act 2.

24 My advice to you is not to inquire why or whither, but just enjoy your ice-cream while it's on your plate,—that's my philosophy.

1942 *The Skin of Our Teeth*, act 1.

25 When you're at war you think about a better life; when you're at peace you think about a more comfortable one.

1942 *The Skin of Our Teeth*, act 1.

26 We'll trot down to the movies and see how girls with wax faces live.

1942 *The Skin of Our Teeth*, act 3.

27 I've never forgotten for long at a time that living is a struggle. I know that every good and excellent thing in the world stands moment by moment on the razor-edge of danger and must be fought for— whether it's a field, or a home, or a country.

1942 *The Skin of Our Teeth*, act 3.

28 Literature is the orchestration of platitudes.

1953 In *Time*, 12 Jan.

29 A living is made, Mr Kemper, by selling something that everybody needs at least once a year. Yes, sir! And a million is made by producing something that everybody needs every day. You artists produce something that nobody needs at any time.

1954 *The Matchmaker*, act 1.

30 Ninety-nine percent of the people in the world are fools, and the rest of us are in great danger of contagion.

1954 *The Matchmaker*, act 1.

31 Never support two weaknesses at the same time. It's your combination sinners—your lecherous liars and your miserly drunkards—who dishonour the vices and bring them into bad repute.

1954 *The Matchmaker*, act 3.

32 But there comes a time in everybody's life when he must decide whether he'll live among human beings or not—a fool among fools or a fool alone.

1954 *The Matchmaker*, act 4.

33 I am not interested in the ephemeral—such subjects as the adulteries of dentists. I am interested in those things that repeat and repeat in the lives of the millions.
1961 In the *New York Times*, 6 Mar.

34 The less seen, the more heard. The eye is the enemy of the ear in real drama.
1961 In the *New York Times*, 6 Nov.

35 The process of learning is accompanied by alternations of pain and brief quickenings that resemble pain.
1967 *The Eighth Day.*

Wilding, Michael 1912–79

English actor. He is usually remembered for his performances in such films as *Piccadilly Incident* (1946) and *Spring in Park Lane* (1948).

36 You can pick out actors by the glazed look that comes into their eyes when the conversation wanders away from themselves.
Attributed.

Wilhelm II, Kaiser 1859–1941

Kaiser and King of Prussia 1888–1918. Dismissed Bismarck in 1890, beginning a long period of personal rule. Although his bellicosity contributed to the origins of World War I, he became a figurehead during the course of it. He abdicated at the end of the war and settled in the Netherlands.

37 We have…fought for our place in the sun and have won it. It will be my business to see that we retain this place in the sun unchallenged.
1901 Speech in Hamburg, 18 Jun. Quoted in *The Times*, 20 Jun.

38 You will be home before the leaves have fallen from the trees.
1914 Address to German troops leaving for the Front, Aug.

39 We draw the sword with a clean conscience and with clean hands.
1914 Address from the throne, Berlin, 4 Aug.

40 The machine is running away with him as it ran away with me.
1939 Of Adolf Hitler at the start of World War II, said to Sir Robert Bruce-Lockhart, 27 Aug.

Wilkinson, Anne 1910–61

Canadian poet. One of the founders of the important literary magazine, *The Tamarack Review*, she published poetry (*Counterpoint to Sleep*, 1951, and *The Hangman Ties the Holly*, 1955), a family history (*Lions in the Way*, 1956) and a children's book. Her collected poems were published in 1968.

41 Fabulous the insects

Stud the air
Or walk on running water,
Klee-drawn saints
And bright as angels are.
1955 *The Hangman Ties the Holly*, 'In June and Gentle Oven'.

42 Our hearts, unrisen, yield a heavy bread.
1955 *The Hangman Ties the Holly*, 'Topsoil to the Wind'.

Will, George

43 What the federal government does basically is borrow money from people and mail it to people.
1993 Of entitlement programs. ABC TV broadcast, 19 Sep.

William of Poitiers 11c.

French chronicler of the life of William the Conqueror.

44 A strange manner of battle, where one side works by constant motion and ceaseless charges, while the other can but endure passively as it stands fixed to the sod. The Norman arrow and sword worked on: in the English ranks the only movement was the dropping of the dead: the living stood motionless.
c.1071 Of the Battle of Hastings, 14 Oct 1066. *Gesta Guillelmi ducis Normannorum et regis Anglorum* (edited by R Foreville, 1952).

William of Wykeham 1324–1404

Bishop of Winchester and Chancellor of England.

45 Manners makyth man.
Proverb common from the 14th century and said to be Wykeham's motto.

William III also called William of Orange 1650–1702

Dutch-born King of Great Britain (1689–1702), and Stadholder of the United Provinces (1672–1702). Husband of Mary, daughter of James II, he was invited by Protestant elements to assume the throne in the Glorious Revolution of 1688.

46 People in Parliament occupy themselves with private animosities and petty quarrels, and think little of the national interest. It is impossible to credit the serene indifference with which they consider events outside their own country.
1699 Letter, Jan.

47 The eyes of all England are on this Parliament. If you do in good earnest wish to see England hold the balance of Europe and to be indeed at the head of the Protestant interest, it will appear by your right improving the present opportunity.
1701 At the State Opening of Parliament, Dec.

48 Every bullet has its billet.
Quoted by John Wesley, journal entry, 6 Jun 1765.

Williams, (Hiram) Hank 1923–53

US country singer, the 'Father of Country Music'. His hits include 'Lovesick Blues', 'Hey, Good Lookin'', 'Jambalaya' and 'Your Cheatin' Heart'. His death was the result of alcoholism and drug abuse.

49 You got to have smelt a lot of mule manure before you can sing like a hillbilly.

Quoted in *Rolling Stone*, 1969.

Williams, Harry Abbot 1919–

English cleric and scholar, a member of the Anglican Community of the Resurrection. In his theological writings he combines theology with insights from psychology.

50 The prelude to resurrection as we experience it in this life is always powerlessness. We cannot raise ourselves by our own bootstrings.

The True Resurrection.

Williams, Raymond 1921–88

Welsh critic and novelist. He is best known for his works mixing socio-cultural and literary criticism, including *The Long Revolution* (1966) and *The Country and the City* (1973).

51 The human crisis is always a crisis of understanding: what we genuinely understand we can do.

1958 *Culture and Society*, ch.3.

52 When art communicates, a human experience is actively offered and actively received. Below this activity threshold there can be no art.

1966 *The Long Revolution*, pt.1, ch.1.

Williams, Robin 1952–

US comedian and film actor. He starred in the TV series *Mork and Mindy* (1970s) and in such films as *The World According to Garp* (1982), *Good Morning, Vietnam* (1987), *Dead Poets Society* (1989), *The Fisher King* (1991), *Mrs Doubtfire* (1993) and *The Birdcage* (1995).

53 I thought lacrosse was what you find in la church.

1982 Interview in *Playboy*.

54 Cricket is baseball on valium.

Quoted in Colin Jarman *The Guinness Dictionary of Sports Quotations* (1990).

Williams, Shirley Vivien Teresa Brittain Williams, Baroness 1930–

English politician, a Labour MP from 1964. She lost her seat in 1979, co-founded the Social Democratic Party in 1981 and became its first elected MP. She lost her seat in 1983 but remained as SDP President (1982–8), and supported the merger with the Liberal Party in 1988. A professor at Harvard University, she remains active in British politics.

55 The British Civil Service…is a beautifully designed and effective braking mechanism.

1980 Speech at the Royal Institute of Public Administration, 11 Feb.

Williams, Tennessee Thomas Lanier 1911–83

US playwright. He won recognition as a leading contemporary writer with his play *The Glass Menagerie* (1945), which was followed by such intense, atmospheric and often brutal dramas as *A Streetcar Named Desire* (1947), *The Rose Tattoo* (1951), *Cat On A Hot Tin Roof* (1955), *Suddenly Last Summer* (1958) and *The Night of the Iguana* (1962).

56 In memory everything seems to happen to music.

1945 Tom. *The Glass Menagerie*, sc.1.

57 I didn't go to the moon, I went much further—for time is the longest distance between two places.

1945 Tom. *The Glass Menagerie*, sc.7.

58 I can't stand a naked light bulb, any more than I can a rude remark or a vulgar action.

1947 Blanche. *A Streetcar Named Desire*, sc.3

59 I have always depended on the kindness of strangers.

1947 Blanche. *A Streetcar Named Desire*, sc.11.

60 The only thing worse than a liar is a liar that's also a hypocrite!

1951 Rosa. *The Rose Tattoo*, act 3.

61 It is a terrible thing for an old woman to outlive her dogs.

1953 *Camino Real*, prologue.

62 Caged birds accept each other but flight is what they long for.

1953 Marguerite. *Camino Real*, block 7.

63 Bohemia has no banner. It survives by discretion.

1953 Marguerite. *Camino Real*, block 7.

64 We have to distrust each other. It's our only defence against betrayal.

1953 Marguerite. *Camino Real*, block 10.

65 We're all of us guinea pigs in the laboratory of God. Humanity is just a work in progress.

1953 The Gipsy. *Camino Real*, block 12.

66 Some mystery should be left in the revelation of character in a play, just as a great deal of mystery is always left in the revelation of character in life, even in one's own character to himself.

1955 *Cat On A Hot Tin Roof*, stage direction.

67 What is the victory of a cat on a hot tin roof?—I wish I knew… Just staying on it, I guess, for as long as she can.

1955 *Cat On A Hot Tin Roof*, act 1.

68 You can be young without money but you can't be old without it.
1955 Margaret. *Cat On A Hot Tin Roof*, act 1.

69 A drinking man's someone who wants to forget he isn't still young an' believing.
1955 *Cat On A Hot Tin Roof*, act 2.

70 BRICK: Well, they say nature hates a vacuum, Big Daddy.
BIG DADDY: That's what they say, but sometimes I think that a vacuum is a hell of a lot better than some of the stuff that nature replaces it with.
1955 *Cat On A Hot Tin Roof*, act 2.

71 Mendacity is a system that we live in. Liquor is one way out an' death's the other.
1955 Brick. *Cat On A Hot Tin Roof*, act 2.

72 At the age of 14 I discovered writing as an escape from…being called a sissy by the neighborhood kids, and Miss Nancy by my father.
1957 In the *New York Times*, 17 Mar.

73 The world is a funny paper read backwards. And that way it isn't so funny.
1957 In *The Observer*, 7 Apr.

74 Don't look forward to the day you stop suffering, because when it comes you'll *know* you're dead.
1958 In *The Observer*, 26 Jan.

75 We're all of us sentenced to solitary confinement inside our own skins, for life!
1958 Val. *Orpheus Descending*, act 2, sc.1.

76 It haunts me, the passage of time. I think time is a merciless thing. I think life is a process of burning oneself out and time is the fire that burns you. But I think the spirit of man is a good adversary.
1958 In the *New York Post*, 30 Apr.

77 He was meddling too much in my private life.
1961 Explaining why he had dispensed with the services of his psychoanalyst. Attributed.

78 All cruel people describe themselves as paragons of frankness!
1963 Mrs Goforth. *The Milk Train Doesn't Stop Here Anymore*, sc.1.

79 Life is all memory except for the one present moment that goes by you so quick you hardly catch it going.
1963 Mrs Goforth. *The Milk Train Doesn't Stop Here Anymore*, sc.3.

80 We all live in a house on fire, no fire department to call; no way out, just the upstairs window to look out of while the fire burns the house down with us trapped, locked in it.
1963 Chris. *The Milk Train Doesn't Stop Here Anymore*, sc.6.

Williams, William Carlos 1883–1963

US poet, a paediatrician as well as a writer. His poetry and objectivist aesthetic made him a major Modernist figure. He also wrote novels, stories, plays, literary and cultural essays and memoirs.

81 I will teach you my townspeople
how to perform a funeral
for you have it over a troop
of artists—
unless one should scour the world—
you have the ground sense necessary.
1917 *Al Que Quiere!*, 'Tract'.

82 Covertly the hands of a great clock
go round and round! Were they to
move quickly and at once the whole
secret would be out and the shuffling
of all ants be done forever.
1921 *Sour Grapes*, 'Overture to a Dance of Locomotives'.

83 Lifeless in appearance, sluggish
dazed spring approaches—

They enter the new world naked,
cold, uncertain of all
save that they enter.
1923 *Spring and All*, 'Spring and All'.

84 One by one the objects are defined—
It quickens: clarity, outline of leaf

But now the stark dignity of
entrance—Still, the profound change
has come upon them: rooted, they
grip down and begin to awaken
1923 *Spring and All*, 'Spring and All'.

85 so much depends
upon

a red wheel
barrow

glazed with rain
water

beside the white
chickens.
1923 *Spring and All*, 'The Red Wheelbarrow'.

86 —through metaphor to reconcile
the people and the stones.
1944 *The Wedge*, 'A Sort of Song'.

87 Is it any better in Heaven, my friend Ford,
Than you found it in Provence?
1944 *The Wedge*, 'To Ford Madox Ford in Heaven'.

88 To make a start,
out of particulars
and make them general, rolling
up the sum, by defective means—

Sniffing the trees, just another dog
among a lot of dogs. What
else is there? And to do?
1946 *Paterson*, bk.1, preface.

89 For the beginning is assuredly
the end—since we know nothing, pure
and simple, beyond
our own complexities.
1946 *Paterson*, bk.1, preface.

90 Minds like beds always made up
(more stony than a shore)
unwilling or unable.
1946 *Paterson*, bk.1, preface.

91 Say it, no ideas but in things.
1946 *Paterson*, bk.1, 'The Delineaments of the Giants', 1.

92 Divorce is
the sign of knowledge in our time.
1946 *Paterson*, bk.1, 'The Delineaments of the Giants', 2.

93 Without invention nothing is well-spaced.
1948 *Paterson*, bk.2, 'Sunday in the Park', 1.

94 Unless there is
a new mind there cannot be a new
line, the old will go on
repeating itself with recurring
deadliness:
1948 *Paterson*, bk.2, 'Sunday in the Park',1.

95 Beyond the gap where the river
plunges into the narrow gorge, unseen

—and the imagination soars, as a voice
beckons, a thundrous voice, endless
—as sleep: the voice
that has ineluctably called them—
that unmoving roar!
1948 *Paterson*, bk.2, 'Sunday in the Park', 1.

96 For what we cannot accomplish, what
is denied to love,
what we have lost in the anticipation—
a descent follows,
endless and indestructible.
1948 *Paterson*, bk.2, 'Sunday in the Park', 1.

97 For there is a wind or a ghost of wind
in all books echoing the life
there, a high wind that fills the tubes
of the ear until we think we hear a wind,
actual.
1949 *Paterson*, bk.3, 'The Library'.

98 and there grows in the mind
a scent, it may be, of locust blossoms
whose perfume is itself a wind moving
to lead the mind away.

1949 *Paterson*, bk.3, 'The Library'.

99 It isn't what he says that counts as a work of art, it's
what he makes with such intensity of perception
that it lives with an intrinsic movement of its very
own to verify the authenticity.
Of the poet. Quoted by Richard Eberhart in the *New York Times*, 17 Dec 1950.

1 I have never been one to write by rule, not even by
my own rules.
1954 Letter to Richard Eberhart, 23 May.

2 Love is that common tone
shall raise his fiery head
and sound his note.
1954 *The Desert Music*, 'The Orchestra'.

3 All writing is a disease. You can't stop it.
Quoted in *Newsweek*, 7 Jan 1957.

4 Nothing whips my blood like verse.
Quoted in John Thirlwall (ed) *The Selected Letters of William Carlos Williams* (1957).

5 Though he is approaching death he is possessed by
many poems.
1958 *Paterson*, bk.5.

6 Anything is good material for poetry. Anything.
1958 *Paterson*, bk.5.

Williamson, Roy 1937–90

Scottish folksinger and musician, a partner in the Corries with Ronnie Browne from 1961, and composer of 'Flower of Scotland', adopted by many as an unofficial Scottish national anthem.

7 O flower of Scotland, when will we see your like
again,
That fought and died for your wee bit hill and glen
And stood against him, proud Edward's army,
And sent him homeward tae think again.
1968 'Flower of Scotland', stanza 1.

Willkie, Wendell Lewis 1892–1944

US politician, Republican candidate for the Presidency (1940).

8 Any man who is not something of a Socialist before
he is forty has no heart. Any man who is still a
Socialist after he is forty has no head.
Quoted in Richard Norton Smith *Thomas E. Dewey and his Times* (1982), p.294.
▷ See Twain 1034:18.

Wilmer, Val(erie) 1942–

English writer and photographer. Her books on jazz include *Jazz People* (1970), *As Serious As Your Life* (1977) and the autobiographical *Mama Said There'd Be Days Like This* (1989).

9 A rather bitter British musician once remarked sourly to a friend of mine: 'Oh, all *she* knows about music she learned in bed with musicians.' To that, I can only add, what better place to learn?
1989 *Mama Said There'd Be Days Like This*, ch.3.

Wilson, A(ndrew) N(orman) 1950–

English writer. He has written novels, criticism, journalism and biography, including the controversial *Jesus* (1992).

10 It had never occurred to Giles that there was something perfectly sensible about wanting to hold onto innocence. He had always gone in for the idea that since we only pass this way once, *experience* counts for everything.
1982 *Wise Virgins*, ch.6.

11 Religion is the tragedy of mankind… But I do know, from the inside as well as from personal observation, that religion appeals to something deep and irrational and strong within us, and that is what makes it so dangerous.
1991 *Against Religion*, no.19.

Wilson, Sir Angus Frank Johnstone
1931–91

English writer. He wrote literary criticism, short stories and a play, but was best known for his novels including *Anglo-Saxon Attitudes* (1956) and *The Old Men in the Zoo* (1961).

12 'God knows how you Protestants can be expected to have any sense of direction,' she said. 'It's different with us, I haven't been to mass for years, I've got every mortal sin on my conscience, but I know when I'm doing wrong. I'm still a Catholic, it's there, nothing can take it away from me.' 'Of course, duckie,' said Jeremy… 'once a Catholic always a Catholic.'
1949 The Wrong Set, 'Significant Experience'.

13 She was more than ever proud of the position of the bungalow, so almost in the country.
1957 'A Flat Country Christmas'.

14 All fiction is for me a kind of magic and trickery—a confidence trick, trying to make people believe something is true that isn't.
1957 In *The Paris Review*, no.17.

15 The impulse to write a novel comes from a momentary unified vision of life.
1963 *The Wild Garden*.

16 I have no concern for the common man except that he should not be so common.
1967 *No Laughing Matter*.

17 My theme is always *humanistic*. Life today is junglelike…it is complex, it is inhuman in its materialism.

1972 Letter to David Farrer, his publisher, Jul. Quoted in Margaret Drabble *Angus Wilson—A Biography* (1995).

18 All are deceptions, substitutes for the hard job of using reason and industry and intuition and compassion to solve even a little bit of the muddle with humaneness and awe for the natural world and the complexity of human beings.
1972 Letter to David Farrer, his publisher, Jul. Quoted in Margaret Drabble *Angus Wilson—A Biography* (1995).

19 People are able to live with only half a heart, to live without real compassion, because they are able to use words that are only forms.
1972 Interview in *Iowa Review*, no.3, Fall.

20 The novelist must be his own most harsh critic and also his own most loving admirer—and about both he must say nothing.
1976 Author's comment in D L Kirkpatrick (ed) *Contemporary Novelists*.

Wilson, Charles called 'Engine Charlie'
1890–1961

President of General Motors and Secretary of Defense. He was nicknamed 'Engine Charlie' to distinguish him from 'Electric Charlie' Wilson, president of General Electric.

21 For years I thought what was good for our country was good for General Motors, and vice versa. The difference did not exist. Our company is too big. It goes with the welfare of the country.
1953 Statement to US Senate, Committee on Armed Services, Jan.

Wilson, Edmund 1895–1972

US literary critic, social commentator, and novelist. Although his own fiction, plays and poems are now little read, he was an influential critic with a wide-ranging perspective on art, history and society.

22 In a sense, one can never read the book that the author originally wrote, and one can never read the same book twice.
1938 *The Triple Thinkers*, introduction.

23 Of all the great Victorian writers, he was probably the most antagonistic to the Victorian age itself.
1941 Of Dickens. *The Wound and the Bow*, 'Dickens: The Two Scrooges'.

Wilson, Edward O(sborne) 1929–

US biologist, Professor of Entomology at Harvard University. His works include *Insect Societies* (1971), *Sociobiology. The New Synthesis* (1975) and *Biophilia* (1984).

24 It came by a lightning flash like knowledge from the gods.
1975 On the 1953 discovery of the DNA molecule. *Sociobiology*.

25 Important science is not just any similarity glimpsed for the first time. It offers analogies that map the gateways to unexplored terrain.
    1984 *Biophilia.*

26 To a considerable degree science consists in originating the maximum amount of information with the minimum expenditure of energy.
    1984 *Biophilia.*

Wilson of Rievaulx, (James) Harold Wilson, Baron 1916–95

English Labour politician and Prime Minister (1964–70, 1974–6). A renowned debater, his economic plans were hampered by a balance of payments crisis. He faced too the problems of Rhodesian independence, opposition to Britain's proposed entry into the Common Market, and conflict within the Party. After a third general election victory, he resigned in 1976.

27 The school that I went to in the north was a school where more than half the children in my class never had any boots or shoes to their feet. They wore clogs, because they lasted longer than shoes of comparable price.
    1948 Speech, Birmingham, 28 Jul.
    ▷ See Bulmer-Thomas 204:53.

28 All the little gnomes in Zurich and other finance centres.
    1956 Speech, House of Commons, 12 Nov.

29 Every time that Mr Macmillan comes back from abroad, Mr Butler goes to the airport and grips him warmly by the throat.
    1957 Attributed.

30 We are redefining and restating our socialism in terms of the scientific revolution… The Britain that will be forged in the white heat of this revolution will be no place for restrictive practices or outdated methods on either side of industry.
    1963 Labour Party Conference, 1 Oct. His phrase has since been memorably rendered as 'the white heat of the technological revolution'.

31 The Labour Party is a moral crusade, or it is nothing.
    1964 Scottish Labour Party conference, 5 Sep.

32 A week is a long time in politics.
    1964 Comment to lobby correspondents, Oct. As such meetings are off the record, there is no exact source for this famous phrase.

33 Given a fair wind, we will negotiate our way into the Common Market, head held high, not crawl in… Negotiations? Yes. Unconditional acceptance of whatever terms we are offered? No.
    1966 Speech, Bristol, 20 Mar.

34 In a recent interview, I was asked what, above all, I associated with socialism in this modern age. I answered that if there was one word I would use to identify modern socialism, it was 'Science'.
    1967 Speech, 17 Jun.

35 From now on the pound abroad is worth 14 per cent or so less in terms of other currencies. That does not mean, of course, that the pound here in Britain—in your pocket or purse, or in your bank—has been devalued.
    1967 National broadcast, 19 Nov. The speech gave rise to the well-known phrase, 'the pound in your pocket'.

36 We are creating a Britain of which we can be proud, and the world knows it. The world's tourists are coming here in their millions…because the new Britain is exciting. Yes, Britain with a Labour Government is an exciting place.
    1969 Speech, Labour Party Conference, 30 Sep.

37 One man's wage rise is another man's price increase.
    1970 In *The Observer*, 11 Jan.

38 Have you ever noticed how we only win the World Cup under a Labour government?
    1971 Quoted in Peter Ball and Phil Shaw *The Book of Football Quotations* (1989).

39 The greatest asset that a head of state can have is the ability to get a good night's sleep.
    1975 BBC Radio 4 broadcast, 16 Apr.

40 The party must protect itself against the activities of small groups of inflexible political persuasion…having in common only their arrogant dogmatism… I have no wish to lead a party of political zombies.
    1975 Labour Party Conference, 30 Sep.

41 The main essentials of a successful Prime Minister are sleep and a sense of history.
    1976 *The Governance of Britain.*

42 A constant effort to keep a party together, without sacrificing either principle or the essentials of basic strategy, is the very stuff of political leadership. Macmillan was canonized for it.
    1979 *Final Term: The Labour Government 1974–76.*

Wilson, Michael 1937–

Canadian Minister of Finance in the 1980s.

43 No matter how we define the term, Canada has an acute shortage of rich people.
    1985 Giving one reason why taxing the wealthy would not ensure the continuation of Canada's social programs, at the Canadian Economics Association, Montreal, 30 May.

Wilson, (Thomas) Woodrow 1856–1924

US statesman and 28th President (1913–21). He was twice elected Democratic President. His administration was chiefly remembered for Prohibition, woman's suffrage, US entry into World War I, and his championing of the League of Nations. He was awarded the Nobel Peace Prize (1919).

44 The feelings with which we face this new age of right and opportunity sweep across our heartstrings like some air out of God's own presence, where justice and mercy are reconciled, and the judge and the brother are one.
1913 Inaugural address, 4 Mar.

45 Human rights, national integrity, and opportunity as against material interests…are the issues that we now must face. I take this occasion to say that the United States will never again seek one additional foot of territory by conquest.
1913 Speech, Alabama, 27 Oct.

46 The people of the United States are drawn from many nations, and chiefly from the nations now at war. Some will wish one nation, others another, to succeed in this monumental struggle. I venture to speak a solemn word of warning. The United States must be neutral in fact as well as in name during these days that are to try men's souls. We must be impartial in thought as well as in action.
1914 Message to the Senate, 19 Aug.

47 There is such a thing as a man being too proud to fight; there is such a thing as a nation being so right that it does not need to convince others by force that it is right.
1915 Speech in Philadelphia, 10 May.

48 We are constantly thinking of the great war…which saved the Union…but it was a war which did a great deal more than that. It created in this country what had never existed before—a national consciousness.
1915 Memorial Day Address at Arlington National Cemetery, Virginia, 31 May.

49 America cannot be an ostrich, with its head in the sand.
1916 Speech, New Mexico, 1 Feb.

50 Nations should with one accord adopt the doctrine of President Monroe as the doctine of the world; that every people should be left free to determine its own policy, its own way of development, unhindered, unthreatened, unafraid—the little along with the great and powerful. Those are American principles, American policies. We could stand for no others. They are also the principles of mankind, and must prevail.
1917 Speech to the Senate, 22 Jan.

51 Armed neutrality is ineffectual enough at best.

1917 Speech before a joint session of Congress, 2 Apr, to request a declaration that a state of war exists between Germany and the US.

52 The world must be made safe for democracy. Its peace must be planted on the tested foundations of political liberty.
1917 Speech before a joint session of Congress, 2 Apr, to request a declaration that a state of war exists between Germany and the US.

53 It is not an army that we must train for war; it is a nation.
1917 Speech, Washington, 12 May.

54 In this war, we demand nothing that is peculiar to ourselves; only that the world be made fit and safe to live in. The programme of the world's peace, therefore, is our programme.
1918 The 'Fourteen Points' speech to Congress, 8 Jan.

55 People and provinces must not be bartered about from sovereign to sovereign as if they were chattels, or pawns in a game. Self-determination is not a mere phrase. It is an imperative principle, which statesmen will henceforth ignore at their peril.
1918 Address to Congress, 11 Feb.

56 People call me an idealist. That is how I know that I am an American. America is the only idealistic nation in the world.
1919 Speech, Sioux Falls, 8 Sep.

Wimperis, Arthur 1874–1953

British screenwriter. He provided the screenplays for such movies as *The Private Life of Henry VIII* (1932) and *Mrs Miniver* (1942).

57 My dear fellow, a unique evening! I wouldn't have left a turn unstoned.
After watching a vaudeville show. Quoted in E Short *Fifty Years of Vaudeville*.

Winchell, Walter 1897–1972

US theatre critic and actor. His publications included *Broadway Thro' a Keyhole* (1933).

58 A newspaperman, whose sweetheart ran away with an actor.
Defining a drama critic. Attributed.

Winkworth, Catherine 1827–78

English hymn writer and translator.

59 Now thank we all our God,
With heart and hands and voices,
Who wondrous things hath done,
In whom his world rejoices;
Who from our mother's arms
Hath blessed us on our way

With countless gifts of love,
And still is ours to-day.

1858 *Lyra Germanica* (translated from the original German of
Martin Rinkart 'Nun danket alle Gott', c.1636).

Winner, Langdon

US academic and social critic with an interest in issues
relating to technology and society.

60 The map of the world shows no country called
    Technopolis, yet in many ways we are already its
    citizens.

    1986 *The Whale and the Reactor.*

Winner, Michael 1935–

British director. Credits include *Chato's Land* (1972),
Death Wish (1974) and *The Wicked Lady* (1983).

61 Who says that actors are cattle? Show me a cow
    who can earn a million dollars a film.

    Quoted by David Lewin in *Cinema Today*, 1 Jul 1970.

62 Keeping awake for ten weeks at a stretch.

    1970 When asked what is the hardest part of directing. John
    Player Lecture, London, Sep.

63 A writer of talent needs only a typewriter and
    paper, a painter only needs brushes, canvas and
    paint, but I need a million dollars or more to be in
    business. That's a hell of a business to be in.

    1974 In *The Observer Magazine*, 7 Jul.

64 A team effort is a lot of people doing what I say.

    Attributed.

Winterson, Jeanette 1959–

English novelist. Her autobiographical first novel,
Oranges Are Not the Only Fruit (1985), described her
upbringing as an Evangelical Pentecostalist and her
subsequent realization of her homosexuality. Subsequent
novels include *Sexing the Cherry* (1989), *Written on the
Body* (1992) and *Art and Lies* (1994).

65 I asked why he was a priest and he said that if you
    have to work for anybody an absentee boss is best.

    1987 *The Passion*, ch.1.

66 Adults talk about being happy because largely they
    are not.

    1987 *The Passion*, ch.1.

67 I call him Jordan and it will do. He has no other
    name before or after. What was there to call him,
    fished as he was from the stinking Thames? A child
    can't be called Thames, no and not Nile either, for
    all his likeness to Moses. But I wanted to give him a
    river name, a name not bound to anything, just as
    the waters aren't bound to anything.

    1989 *Sexing the Cherry.*

68 I have met a great many people on their way
    towards God and I wonder why they have chosen
    to look for him rather than themselves.

    1989 *Sexing the Cherry.*

69 I don't hate men, I just wish they'd try harder. They
    all want to be heroes and all we want is for them to
    stay at home and help with the housework and the
    kids. That's not the kind of heroism they enjoy.

    1989 *Sexing the Cherry.*

Wisdom, Norman 1915–

English comedian, born in London. He made his stage
début in 1946 and his first film appearance in *Trouble in
Store* (1953). This was followed by a string of successes
including *Man of the Moment* (1955), *Just My Luck*
(1958) and *Follow a Star* (1959).

70 They don't seem to realize that I have grown up and
    can get laughs without falling downstairs.

    1991 Quoted in Richard Dacre *Trouble in Store: Norman
    Wisdom, a Career in Comedy* (1991).

Witte, Sergei Yulevich 1849–1915

Russian politician. As Minister of Finance (1892) he
encouraged capitalism and industrialization, making
Russia a leading industrial power. He became first Prime
Minister (1905–6) in the Revolution of 1905, but was
unable to satisfy either conservatives or liberals.

71 The world is in flames today for a cause that
    interests Russia first and foremost; a cause that is
    essentially the cause of the Slavs, and which is of no
    concern to France or to England.

    1914 Said to the French Ambassador, 10 Sep.

Wittgenstein, Ludwig Josef Johann
1889–1951

Austrian-born British philosopher who became one of the
most influential and charismatic figures in British
philosophy in this century. He was Professor of
Philosophy at Cambridge (1939–47), and published only
one book in his lifetime, the *Tractatus Logico-
Philosophicus* (1921). Of his many posthumous
publications, by far the most important is the
Philosophical Investigations (1953).

72 *Was sich überhaupt sagen lässt, lässt sich klar sagen;
    und wovon man nicht reden kann, darüber muss man
    schweigen.*

    What can be said at all can be said clearly; and
    whereof one cannot speak thereof one must be
    silent.

    1921 *Tractatus Logico-Philosophicus*, preface (translated by
    Frank Ramsey).

73 *Die Welt ist alles, was der Fall ist.*

    The world is all that is the case.

    1921 *Tractatus Logico-Philosophicus*, prop.1 (translated by Pears
    and McGuinness).

74 *Die Welt ist die Gesamtheit der Tatsachen, nicht der Dinge.*

The world is the totality of facts, not of things.

1921 *Tractatus Logico-Philosophicus*, prop.1.1 (translated by Pears and McGuinness).

75 *Der Tod ist kein Ereignis des Lebens. Den Tod erlebt man nicht.*

Death is not an event in life: we do not live to experience death.

1921 *Tractatus Logico-Philosophicus*, prop 6.4311 (translated by Pears and McGuinness).

76 *Die Probleme werden gelöst, nicht durch Zusammenstellung des längst Bekannten. Die Philosophie ist ein Kampf gegen die Verhexung unsres Verstandes durch die Mittel unserer Sprache.*

The problems are solved, not by giving new information, but by arranging what we have always known. Philosophy is a battle against the bewitchment of our intelligence by means of language.

1945 *Philosophische Untersuchungen* (*Philosophical Investigations*), section 109 (translated by G E M Anscombe).

77 *Ein philosophisches Problem hat die Form: 'Ich kenne mich nicht aus'.*

A philosophical problem has the form: 'I don't know my way about'.

1945 *Philosophische Untersuchungen* (*Philosophical Investigations*), section 123 (translated by G E M Anscombe).

78 *Der Philosoph behandelt eine Frage wie eine Krankheit.*

The philosopher's treatment of a question is like the treatment of an illness.

1945 *Philosophische Untersuchungen* (*Philosophical Investigations*), section 255 (translated by G E M Anscombe).

79 *Was ist dein Ziel in der Philosophie?—'Der Fliege den Ausweg aus dem Fliegenglas zeigen'.*

What is your aim in philosophy?—To shew the fly the way out of the fly-bottle.

1945 *Philosophische Untersuchungen* (*Philosophical Investigations*), section 309 (translated by G E M Anscombe).

80 *Ein 'innerer Vorgang' bedarf äusserer Kriterien.*

An 'inner process' stands in need of outward criteria.

1945 *Philosophische Untersuchungen* (*Philosophical Investigations*), section 580 (translated by G E M Anscombe).

81 *Wenn ein Löwe sprechen könnte, wir könnten ihn nicht verstehen.*

If a lion could talk, we could not understand him.

1945 *Philosophische Untersuchungen* (*Philosophical Investigations*), pt.2, section 11 (translated by G E M Anscombe).

Wittig, Monique 1935–

French feminist novelist who questions traditional gender stereotypes in her writing.

82 *L'expérience…d'une femme écrivain est complètement schizophrénique. Il faut toujours faire coupure entre les deux: d'une part, employer un langage qui n'est pas le nôtre…et la lutte qu'on mène sur un autre plan, qui tend à casser tout ça, à essayer de faire à travers et dans le langage autre chose.*

The experience…of the woman writer is completely schizophrenic. One is always torn between two approaches: on the one hand, to use a language that is not ours…and on the other, the battle one fights to break all this up, in order to do something else through and in language.

Quoted in Jean-François Josselin 'Lettre à Sapho' in *Le Nouvel Observateur* (1973).

Wodehouse, Sir P(elham) G(renville) also known as *Plum* 1881–1975

Anglo-American writer, renowned for his humorous stories of the English country aristocracy. He lived in the US after World War II, taking citizenship in 1955, but never shed his quintessential Englishness.

83 An English peer of the right sort can be bored nearer to the point where mortification sets in, without showing it, than anyone else in the world.

1915 *Something Fresh*, ch.3.

84 She fitted into my biggest arm-chair as if it had been built round her by someone who knew they were wearing arm-chairs tight about the hips that season.

1919 *My Man Jeeves*, 'Jeeves and the Unbidden Guest'.

85 What with excellent browsing and sluicing and cheery conversation and what-not, the afternoon passed quite happily.

1919 *My Man Jeeves*, 'Jeeves and the Unbidden Guest'.

86 'What ho!' I said.
'What ho!' said Motty.
'What ho! What ho!'
'What ho! What ho! What ho!'
After that it seemed rather difficult to go on with the conversation.

1919 *My Man Jeeves*, 'Jeeves and the Unbidden Guest'.

87 In this matter of shimmering into rooms the chappie is rummy to a degree… He moves from point to point with as little uproar as a jellyfish.

1919 *My Man Jeeves*, 'Jeeves and the Hard-Boiled Egg'.

88 Chumps always make the best husbands. When you marry, Sally, grab a chump. Tap his forehead first, and if it rings solid, don't hesitate. All the unhappy marriages come from the husbands

having brains. What good are brains to a man? They only unsettle him.
1920 *The Adventures of Sally,* ch.10.

89 I turned to Aunt Agatha, whose demeanour was now rather like that of one who, picking daisies on the railway, has just caught the down express in the small of the back.
1923 *The Inimitable Jeeves,* ch.4.

90 Jeeves coughed one soft, low, gentle cough like a sheep with a blade of grass stuck in its throat.
1923 *The Inimitable Jeeves,* ch.13.

91 As a rule, you see, I'm not lugged into Family Rows. On the occasions when Aunt is calling to Aunt like mastodons bellowing across the primeval swamps…the clan has a tendency to ignore me. It's one of the advantages I get from being a bachelor— and, according to my nearest and dearest, practically a half-witted bachelor at that.
1923 *The Inimitable Jeeves,* ch.16.

92 It was my Uncle George who discovered that alcohol was a food well in advance of medical thought.
1923 *The Inimitable Jeeves,* ch.16.

93 'Alf Todd,' said Ukridge, soaring to an impressive burst of imagery, 'has about as much chance as a one-armed blind man in a dark room trying to shove a pound of melted butter into a wild cat's left ear with a red-hot needle.'
1924 *Ukridge,* ch.5.

94 Honoria…is one of those robust, dynamic girls with the muscles of a welter-weight and a laugh like a squadron of cavalry charging over a tin bridge.
1925 *Carry On, Jeeves,* 'The Rummy Affair of Old Biffy'.

95 He looked haggard and careworn, like a Borgia who has suddenly remembered that he has forgotten to shove the cyanide in the consommé, and the dinner-gong due any moment.
1925 *Carry On, Jeeves,* 'Clustering Around Young Bingo'.

96 To my daughter Leonora without whose never-failing sympathy and encouragement this book would have been finished in half the time.
1926 *The Heart of a Goof,* dedication.

97 The Right Hon was a tubby little chap who looked as if he had been poured into his clothes and had forgotten to say 'When!'
1930 *Very Good, Jeeves,* 'Jeeves and the Impending Doom'.

98 I have at last come to a momentous decision. I am going to give up my press-clippings agency. I find that even a favourable notice makes me feel sick nowadays, while an unfavourable one, even from a small provincial newspaper, puts me off my work for days.
1934 Letter to Denis Mackail, 15 Oct.

99 Into the face of the young man…had crept a look of furtive shame, the shifty, hangdog look which announces that an Englishman is about to talk French.
1935 *The Luck of the Bodkins,* ch.1.

1 It is never difficult to distinguish between a Scotsman with a grievance and a ray of sunshine.
1935 *Blandings Castle and Elsewhere,* 'The Custody of the Pumpkin'.

2 I can't do with any more education. I was full up years ago.
1938 *The Code of the Woosters,* ch.1.

3 He spoke with a certain what-is-it in his voice, and I could see that, if not actually disgruntled, he was far from being gruntled.
1938 *The Code of the Woosters,* ch.1.

4 Slice him where you like, a hellhound is always a hellhound.
1938 *The Code of the Woosters,* ch.1.

5 Roderick Spode? Big chap with a small moustache and the sort of eye that can open an oyster at sixty paces?
1938 *The Code of the Woosters,* ch.2.

6 He felt like a man who, chasing rainbows, has had one of them suddenly turn and bite him in the leg.
1940 *Eggs, Beans and Crumpets,* 'Anselm Gets His Chance'.

7 My war history has been a simple one. I have just sat in my chair and written all the time.
1946 Letter to Ira Gershwin, 24 Jan.

8 Ice formed on the butler's upper slopes.
1952 *Pigs Have Wings,* ch.5.

9 Has anyone ever seen a dramatic critic in the daytime? Of course not. They come out after dark, up to no good.
1955 In the *New York Mirror,* 27 May.

10 There'll always be an England, but who wants an England full of morons reading the *Express*?
1959 Letter to Denis Mackail, 22 Apr.

Wolf, Naomi 1962–

US writer; she was a Rhodes Scholar in 1986. Her books, *The Beauty Myth* (1990) and *Fire with Fire* (1993) examine the relationship between patriarchal power and female beauty.

11 The more legal and material hindrances women have broken through, the more strictly and heavily

and cruelly images of female beauty have come to weigh upon them.

1990 *The Beauty Myth*, ch.1, 'The Beauty Myth'.

12 'Beauty' is a currency like the gold standard. Like any economy it is determined by politics, and in the modern age in the West it is the last, best belief system that keeps male domination intact.

1990 *The Beauty Myth*, ch.1, 'The Beauty Myth'.

13 When women breached the power structure in the 1980s…two economies finally merged. Beauty was no longer just a symbolic form of currency: it literally *became* money.

1990 *The Beauty Myth*, ch.2 'Work'.

Wolfe, James 1727–59

English general. He fought against the Jacobites at Culloden and was sent to Canada in 1756. Promoted to general after his prominence in the capture of Louisberg, he commanded the British force which took Quebec.

14 Gentlemen, I would rather have written those lines than take Quebec tomorrow.

1759 To his troops, 12 Sep, after reciting Thomas Gray's 'Elegy, Written in a Country Churchyard' the evening before storming the ramparts of Quebec and dying a hero's death on the Plains of Abraham the following day. Quoted in Francis Parkman *Montcalm and Wolfe* (1884).

15 Now God be praised, I will die in peace.

1759 Last words, on hearing of the defeat of the French at Quebec. Quoted in J Knox *Historical Journal of the Campaigns in North America* (1909), ch.17.

Wolfe, Thomas Clayton 1900–38

US novelist. Unsuccessful in drama, he wrote a series of sprawling, uneven but often powerful novels, two of which were published posthumously.

16 Most of the time we think we're sick, it's all in the mind.

1929 *Look Homeward, Angel*, pt.1, ch.1.

17 'Where they got you stationed now, Luke?'… 'At the p-p-p-present time in Norfolk at the Navy base,' Luke answered, 'm-m-making the world safe for hypocrisy.'

1929 *Look Homeward, Angel*, pt.3, ch.36.

18 My efforts to cut out 50,000 words may sometimes result in my adding 75,000.

1929 Letter to his editor, Maxwell Perkins.

19 If a man has a talent and cannot use it, he has failed. If he has a talent and uses only half of it, he has partly failed. If he has a talent and learns somehow to use the whole of it, he has gloriously succeeded, and won a satisfaction and a triumph few men ever know.

The Web and the Rock (published 1939), ch.29.

20 It was a cruel city, but it was a lovely one, a savage city, yet it had such tenderness, a bitter, harsh, and violent catacomb of stone and steel and tunnelled rock, slashed savagely with light, and roaring, fighting a constant ceaseless warfare of men and machinery; and yet it was so sweetly and so delicately pulsed, as full of warmth, of passion, and of love, as it was full of hate.

1939 *The Web and the Rock* (published 1939), ch.30.

21 You Can't Go Home Again.

Title of novel (published 1940).

Wolfe, Tom (Thomas Kennerley) 1931–

US journalist and novelist. He was a leading proponent of the New Journalism, with a propensity for a racy style and attention-grabbing titles. His book on the astronauts, *The Right Stuff*, was filmed, as was his novel *The Bonfire of the Vanities*.

22 The Electric Kool-Aid Acid Test

1968 Title of book.

23 Radical chic invariably favors radicals who seem primitive, exotic and romantic.

1970 *Radical Chic*.

24 Not 'Seeing is Believing', you ninny, but 'Believing is Seeing'. For modern art has become completely literary: the paintings and other works exist only to illustrate the text.

1975 *The Painted Word*, ch.1.

25 The idea was to prove at every foot of the way up…that you were one of the elected and anointed ones who had the right stuff and could move higher and higher and even—ultimately, God willing, one day—that you might be able to join that special few at the very top, that elite who had the capacity to bring tears to men's eyes, the very Brotherhood of the Right Stuff itself.

1979 *The Right Stuff*.

26 A cult is a religion with no political power.

1980 *In Our Time*, ch.2.

27 From Bauhaus to Our House.

1981 Title of book.

28 Today educated people look upon traditional religious ties—Catholic, Episcopal, Presbyterian, Methodist, Baptist, Jewish—as matters of social pedigree. It is only art that they look upon religiously.

1984 'The Worship of Art: Notes on the New God', in *Harper's*, Oct.

29 Yes, the labour movement was truly religious, like Judaism itself. It was one of those things you

believed in for all mankind and didn't care about for a second in your own life.
1987 *The Bonfire of the Vanities*, ch.8.

30 A liberal is a conservative who has been arrested.
1987 *The Bonfire of the Vanities*, ch.24.

31 Pornography was the great vice of the Seventies; plutography—the graphic depiction of the acts of the rich—is the great vice of the Eighties.
1988 In the *Sunday Times Magazine*, 10 Jan.

32 The Versailles of American corporate culture.
1992 Of Manhattan's Four Seasons restaurant, in the *New York Times*, 14 Nov.

Wollstonecraft, Mary also known as *Mrs Godwin* 1759–97

Anglo-Irish feminist and writer. Her *Vindication of the Rights of Man* (1790) was followed by *Vindication of the Rights of Woman* (1792), advocating gender equality. After bearing an illegitimate daughter to Captain Gilbert Imlay (1794) she married political writer William Godwin (1797) but died on the birth of their daughter, Mary Wollstonecraft Shelley.

33 I now speak of the sex in general. Many individuals have more sense than their male relatives; and…some women govern their husbands without degrading themselves, because intellect will always govern.
1792 *A Vindication of the Rights of Woman*, introduction.

34 Men, in general, seem to employ their reason to justify prejudices, which they have imbibed, they can scarcely trace how, rather than root them out.
1792 *A Vindication of the Rights of Woman*, pt.1, ch.1.

35 Men, indeed, appear to me to act in a very unphilosophical manner when they try to secure the good conduct of women by attempting to keep them always in a state of childhood.
1792 *A Vindication of the Rights of Woman*, pt.1, ch.2.

36 Strengthen the female mind by enlarging it, and there will be an end to blind obedience; but as blind obedience is ever sought for by power, tyrants and sensualists are in the right when they endeavour to keep women in the dark, because the former only want slaves, and the latter a play-thing.
1792 *A Vindication of the Rights of Woman*, pt.1, ch.2.

37 Gentleness, docility, and a spaniel-like affection are, on this ground, consistently recommended as the cardinal virtues of the sex; and, disregarding the arbitrary economy of nature, one writer has declared that it is masculine for a woman to be melancholy. She was created to be the toy of man, his rattle, and it must jingle in his ears, whenever, dismissing reason, he chooses to be amused.
1792 *A Vindication of the Rights of Woman*, pt.1, ch.2.

38 Liberty is the mother of virtue, and if women be, by their very constitution, slaves, and not allowed to breathe the sharp invigorating air of freedom, they must ever languish like exotics, and be reckoned beautiful flaws in nature.
1792 *A Vindication of the Rights of Woman*, pt.1, ch.2.

39 The *divine right* of husbands, like the divine right of kings, may it is to be hoped, in this enlightened age, be contested without danger.
1792 *A Vindication of the Rights of Woman*, pt.1, ch.3.

40 A king is always a king—and a woman always a woman; his authority and her sex, ever stand between them and rational converse.
1792 *A Vindication of the Rights of Woman*, pt.1, ch.4.

41 I do not wish them to have power over men; but over themselves.
1792 Of women. *A Vindication of the Rights of Woman*, pt.1, ch.4.

42 Necessity never makes prostitution the business of men's lives; though numberless are the women who are thus rendered systematically vicious.
1792 *A Vindication of the Rights of Woman*, pt.1, ch.4.

43 Let woman share the rights and she will emulate the virtues of man, for she must grow more perfect when emancipated.
1792 *A Vindication of the Rights of Woman*, pt.1, ch.13.

Wolstenholme, Kenneth 1920–

English football commentator. He broadcast for the BBC from 1948 to 1971, covering 22 FA Cup finals and five World Cups.

44 There are people on the pitch…they think it's all over…it is now!
1966 Radio commentary on the last goal of the World Cup final, in which England beat West Germany at Wembley.

Wood, Victoria 1953–

English playwright, lyricist and comedienne. Her comic plays include *Talent* (1979) and *Happy Since I Met You* (1981), and her television work is collected in *Mens Sana in Thingummy Doodah* (1991).

45 Jogging is for people who aren't intelligent enough to watch Breakfast TV.
1989 *Victoria Wood*, television series. Published in *Mens Sana in Thingummy Doodah* (1991).

46 LILL: My massage was marvellous. I feel really relaxed. And my masseur, Harold—
VICTORIA: You can't have a masseur called Harold. It's like having a member of the Royal Family called Ena.
1989 *Victoria Wood*, television series. Published in *Mens Sana in Thingummy Doodah* (1991).

Woodcock, George 1912–

Canadian writer, poet, social critic and biographer. He also wrote several travel books. He has been described as a philosophical anarchist.

47 Well-founded fear, which takes one through the valley of the shadow of death without abandoning one there, is what makes the worst of worse journeys; the situation is made all the more intense when the fear is somehow mingled with delight.
'My Worst Journeys', collected in Keath Fraser (ed) *Worst Journeys: The Picador Book of Travel* (1991).

Woodman, Marion 1928–

Canadian therapist and author.

48 To strive for perfection is to kill love because perfection does not recognize humanity.
1982 *Addition to Perfection: The Still Unravished Bride.*

Woodroofe, Lieut. Commander Thomas
1899–1978

49 The whole fleet's lit up. When I say 'lit up', I mean by fairy lamps.
1937 BBC radio commentary of the Spithead review, 20 May, Britain's first live outside broadcast. 'Lit up' was a common euphemism for 'drunk'.

Woods, Donald 1933–

South African editor and Black civil rights campaigner.

50 When I left South Africa, I arrogantly predicted that within seven years, apartheid would be gone. It has taken a bit longer than that.
1991 BBC TV broadcast, Feb.

Woodsworth, James Shaver 1874–1942

Canadian politician, socialist and pacifist. An MP from 1921, in 1932 he founded the Co-operative Commonwealth Federation, serving as its chairman and parliamentary leader.

51 I take my place with the children.
1939 Casting the sole dissenting voice to ratify Canada's entry into World War II, in the House of Commons, Ottawa, 9 Sep.

Wooldridge, Adrian 1959–

English journalist with the *Economist* (London).

52 America has mitigated poverty by massively increasing pauperism.
1995 'Damned Statistics', in the *Wall Street Journal*, 27 Jul.

Woolf, (Adeline) Virginia née Stephen
1882–1941

English novelist, critic and essayist. Daughter of Sir Leslie Stephen and sister of Vanessa Bell, she married Leonard Woolf and in 1917 they formed the Hogarth Press. Her experimental novels include *Mrs. Dalloway* (1925) and *To the Lighthouse* (1927). *A Room of One's Own* (1929) is a feminist classic. She committed suicide by drowning.

53 For the self-centred and self-limited writers have a power denied the more catholic and broad-minded... Nothing issues from their minds which has not been marked with their own impress.
1916 *Jane Eyre* and *Wuthering Heights.*

54 Life...is a luminous halo, a semi-transparent envelope surrounding us from the beginning of consciousness to the end.
1919 'Modern Fiction'.

55 Each had his past shut in him like the leaves of a book known to him by heart; and his friends could only read the title.
1922 *Jacob's Room*, ch.5.

56 It's not catastrophes, murders, deaths, diseases, that age and kill us; it's the way people look and laugh, and run up the steps of omnibuses.
1922 *Jacob's Room*, ch.6.

57 Never did I read such tosh.
1922 On James Joyce's *Ulysses*. Letter to Lytton Strachey, 24 Apr.

58 I believe that all novels...deal with character, and that it is to express character—not to preach doctrines, sing songs, or celebrate the glories of the British Empire, that the form of the novel, so clumsy, verbose, and undramatic, so rich, elastic, and alive, has been evolved.
1924 'Mr Bennett and Mrs Brown'.

59 Life itself, every moment of it, every drop of it, here, this instant, now, in the sun, in Regent's Park, was enough. Too much, indeed.
1925 *Mrs Dalloway.*

60 It is vain and foolish to talk of knowing Greek.
1925 *The Common Reader*, 'On Not Knowing Greek'.

61 The interest in life does not lie in what people do, nor even in their relations to each other, but largely in the power to communicate with a third party, antagonistic, enigmatic, yet perhaps persuadable, which one may call life in general.
1925 *The Common Reader*, 'On Not Knowing Greek'.

62 A good essay must have this permanent quality about it; it must draw its curtain round us, but it must be a curtain that shuts us in not out.
1925 *The Common Reader*, 'The Modern Essay'.

63 We are nauseated by the sight of trivial personalities decomposing in the eternity of print.
1925 *The Common Reader*, 'The Modern Essay'.

64 *Middlemarch*, the magnificent book which with all its imperfections is one of the few English novels for grown up people.
1925 *The Common Reader*, 'George Eliot'.

65 London is enchanting. I step out upon a tawny coloured magic carpet, it seems, and get carried into beauty without raising a finger… People pop in and out, lightly, divertingly like rabbits; and I look down Southampton Row, wet as a seal's back or red and yellow with sunshine, and watch the omnibuses going and coming and hear the old crazy organs. One of these days I will write about London, and how it takes up the private life and carries it on, without any effort.
1926 Diary entry, 26 May.

66 So that is marriage, Lily thought, a man and a woman looking at a girl throwing a ball.
1927 *To the Lighthouse*, pt.1, ch.13.

67 She faded…became more inconspicuous than ever, in her little grey dress.
1927 *To the Lighthouse*, pt.1, ch.17.

68 One cannot think well, love well, sleep well, if one has not dined well.
1929 *A Room of One's Own*, ch.1.

69 A woman must have money and a room of her own if she is to write fiction.
1929 *A Room of One's Own*, ch.1.

70 Women have served all these centuries as looking-glasses possessing the magic and delicious power of reflecting the figure of man at twice its natural size.
1929 *A Room of One's Own*, ch.2.

71 I would venture to guess that Anon, who wrote so many poems without signing them, was often a woman.
1929 *A Room of One's Own*, ch.3.

72 Literature is strewn with the wreckage of men who have minded beyond reason the opinion of others.
1929 *A Room of One's Own*, ch.3.

73 It is obvious that the values of women differ very often from the values which have been made by the other sex… Yet it is the masculine values that prevail.
1929 *A Room of One's Own*, ch.4.

74 We think back through our mothers if we are women.
1929 *A Room of One's Own*, ch.4.

75 For there is a spot the size of a shilling at the back of the head which one can never see for oneself. It is one of the good offices that sex can discharge for sex—to describe that spot.

1929 *A Room of One's Own*, ch.5.

76 For all the dinners are cooked; the plates and cups washed; the children sent to school and gone out into the world. Nothing remains of it all. All has vanished. No biography or history has a word to say about it.
1929 *A Room of One's Own*, ch.5.

77 I am not trying to tell a story. Yet perhaps it might be done in that way. A mind thinking. They might be islands of light—islands in the stream that I am trying to convey; life itself going on.
1929 Diary entry, 28 May.

78 Killing the Angel in the House was part of the occupation of a woman writer.
1931 'Professions for Women', lecture to the National Society for Women's Service, 21 Jan. Woolf's solution was to throw the inkpot at the Angel (the embodiment of stereotyped Victorian femininity) whenever she appeared.

79 Things have dropped from me. I have outlived certain desires; I have lost friends, some by death—Percival—others through sheer inability to cross the street.
1931 *The Waves*.

80 Yes, always keep the Classics at hand to prevent flop.
1937 Diary entry, 23 Jun.

81 Somewhere, everywhere, now hidden, now apparent in whatever is written down, is the form of a human being. If we seek to know him, are we idly occupied?
The Captain's Death Bed, 'Reading' (published 1950).

82 The poet gives us his essence, but prose takes the mould of the body and mind entire.
The Captain's Death Bed, 'Reading' (published 1950).

Woollcott, Alexander Humphreys

1887–1943

US critic, writer, actor and broadcaster. He became theatre critic for the *New York Times* in 1914 and subsequently became one of the celebrated Algonquin Round Table of wits and literary figures. Noted for his biting humour, he was the inspiration for Kaufman and Hart's play *The Man Who Came to Dinner*.

83 She is so odd a blend of Little Nell and Lady Macbeth. It is not so much the familiar phenomenon of a hand of steel in a velvet glove as a lacy sleeve with a bottle of vitriol concealed in its folds.
1934 Of Dorothy Parker. *While Rome Burns*, 'Our Mrs Parker'.

84 I have no need of your God-damned sympathy. I only wish to be entertained by some of your grosser reminiscences.
1942 Letter to Rex O'Malley. Quoted in Samuel Adams *Alexander Woollcott* (1945), ch.34.

85 A broker is a man who takes your fortune and runs it into a shoestring.
Quoted in Samuel Adams Alexander Woollcott *(1945), ch.15.*

86 Harold Ross…had a contempt for anything he didn't understand, which was practically everything.
Quoted in James Thurber The Years With Ross *(1959), ch.15.*

87 All the things I really like to do are either illegal, immoral or fattening.
Quoted in R Drennan Wit's End *(1968).*

88 The play left a taste of lukewarm parsnip juice.
Play review. Quoted in H Techmann Smart Alex *(1976).*

89 My doctor forbids me to play, unless I win.
Of croquet. Quoted in Colin Jarman The Guinness Dictionary of Sports Quotations *(1990).*

90 It is no game for the soft of sinew and the gentle of spirit. The higher and dirtier croquet-player can use the guile of a cobra and the inhumanity of a boa constrictor.
Quoted in Colin Jarman The Guinness Dictionary of Sports Quotations *(1990).*

91 Always a godfather, never a god!
On serving as godfather at a christening celebration for the 19th time. Attributed.

92 Just what God would do if he had the money.
On being shown round Moss Hart's splendid country retreat. Attributed.

93 The scenery was beautiful, but the actors got in front of it.
Play review.

Wordsworth, William 1770–1850

English poet. At first given to agnosticism and a revolutionary passion for social justice, he then turned to exploring the lives of humble people living in contact with nature. He succeeded Robert Southey as Poet Laureate in 1843.

94 Now, in this blank of things, a harmony,
Home-felt, and home-created, comes to heal
That grief for which the senses still supply
Fresh food.
1786 'Calm is all nature as a resting wheel', 1.7–10. Published in the *Morning Post*, 13 Feb. 1802.

95 In this universe,
Where the least things control the greatest, where
The faintest breath that breathes can move a world.
1795–6 Oswald. *The Borderers*, act 3, 1.1562–4 (published 1842).

96 These beauteous forms,
Through a long absence, have not been to me
As is a landscape to a blind man's eye:
But oft, in lonely rooms, and 'mid the din

Of towns and cities, I have owed to them,
In hours of weariness, sensations sweet,
Felt in the blood, and felt along the heart.
1798 'Lines composed a few miles above Tintern Abbey, on revisiting the banks of the Wye', 1.22–8.

97 That best portion of a good man's life,
His little, nameless, unremembered, acts
Of kindness and of love.
1798 'Lines composed a few miles above Tintern Abbey, on revisiting the banks of the Wye', 1.33–5.

98 For I have learned
To look on nature, not as in the hour
Of thoughtless youth; but hearing often-times
The still, sad music of humanity,
Nor harsh nor grating, though of ample power
To chasten and subdue. And I have felt
A presence that disturbs me with the joy
Of elevated thoughts; a sense sublime
Of something far more deeply interfused,
Whose dwelling is the light of setting suns,
And the round ocean and the living air,
And the blue sky, and in the mind of man.
1798 'Lines composed a few miles above Tintern Abbey, on revisiting the banks of the Wye', 1.88–99.

99 Therefore am I still
A lover of the meadows and the woods,
And mountains; and of all that we behold
From this green earth; of all the mighty world
Of eye, and ear,—both what they half create
And what perceive.
1798 'Lines composed a few miles above Tintern Abbey, on revisiting the banks of the Wye', 1.102–6.

1 Away we go—and what care we
For treasons, tumults, and for wars?
We are as calm in our delight
As is the crescent moon so bright
Among the scattered stars.
1798 'Peter Bell', prologue, stanza 5 (published 1819).

2 Books! 'tis a dull and endless strife:
Come, hear the woodland linnet
How sweet his music! on my life
There's more of wisdom in it.
1798 'The Tables Turned', stanza 3.

3 One impulse from a vernal wood
May teach you more of man,
Of moral evil and of good,
Than all the sages can.

Sweet is the lore which Nature brings;
Our meddling intellect
Mis-shapes the beauteous forms of things:—
We murder to dissect.

Enough of science and of art;
Close up those barren leaves;

Come forth and bring with you a heart
That watches and receives
1798 'The Tables Turned', stanzas 6–8.

4   I heard a thousand blended notes,
    While in a grove I sate reclined,
    In that sweet mood when pleasant thoughts
    Bring sad thoughts to the mind.
    1798 'Lines Written in Early Spring', stanza 1.

5   To her fair works did Nature link
    The human soul that through me ran;
    And much it grieved my heart to think
    What man has made of man.
    1798 'Lines Written in Early Spring', stanza 2.

6   Three years she grew in sun and shower,
    The Nature said, 'A lovelier flower
    On earth was never sown;
    This Child I to myself will take;
    She shall be mine, and I will make
    A Lady of my own.'
    1799 'Three Years she grew in sun and shower', stanza 1
    (published 1800).

7   A slumber did my spirit seal;
    I had no human fears:
    She seemed a thing that could not feel
    The touch of earthly years.

    No motion has she now, no force;
    She neither hears nor sees;
    Rolled round in earth's diurnal course
    With rocks, and stones and trees.
    1799 'A slumber did my spirit seal', complete poem (published
    1800).

8   She dwelt among the untrodden ways
    Beside the springs of Dove,
    A maid whom there were none to praise
    And very few to love:

    A violet by a mossy stone
    Half hidden from the eye!
    —Fair as a star, when only one
    Is shining in the sky.

    She lived unknown, and few could know
    When Lucy ceased to be;
    But she is in her grave, and, oh,
    The difference to me!
    1799 'She dwelt among the untrodden ways', complete poem
    (published 1800).

9   Physician art thou?—one, all eyes,
    Philosopher!—a fingering slave,
    One that would peep and botanize
    Upon his mother's grave?
    1799 'A Poet's Epitaph' stanza 5 (published 1800).

10 One to whose smooth-rubbed soul can cling

Nor form, nor feeling, great or small;
A reasoning, self-sufficing thing,
An intellectual All-in-all!
1799 'A Poet's Epitaph' stanza 8 (published 1800).

11 Shut close the door; press down the latch;
    Sleep in thy intellectual crust;
    Nor lose ten tickings of thy watch
    Near this unprofitable dust.
    1799 'A Poet's Epitaph' stanza 9 (published 1800).

12 In common truths that round us lie
    Some random truths he can impart,—
    The harvest of a quiet eye
    That broods and sleeps on his own heart.
    1799 'A Poet's Epitaph' stanza 13 (published 1800).

13 I travelled among unknown men
    In lands beyond the sea;
    Nor England! did I know till then
    What love I bore to thee.
    1799 'I Travelled Among Unknown Men', stanza 1 (published
    1807).

14 Wisdom and Spirit of the universe!
    Thou soul, that art the eternity of thought,
    And giv'st to forms and images a breath
    And everlasting motion.
    1799 'Influence of Natural Objects', l.1–4 (published in *The
    Friend* 28 Dec 1809).

15 Leaving the tumultuous throng,
    To cut across the reflex of a star;
    Image that, flying still before me, gleamed
    Upon the glassy plain.
    1799 'Influence of Natural Objects', l.49–52 (published in *The
    Friend* 28 Dec 1809).

16 When we had given our bodies to the wind,
    And all the shadowy banks on either side
    Came sweeping through the darkness, spinning
      still
    The rapid line of motion, then at once
    Have I, reclining back upon my heels,
    Stopped short; yet still the solitary cliffs
    Wheeled by me—even as if the earth had rolled
    With visible motion her diurnal round!
    1799 'Influence of Natural Objects', l.53–60 (published in *The
    Friend* 28 Dec 1809).

17 Oh there is blessing in this gentle breeze,
    A visitant that while it fans my cheek
    Doth seem half conscious of the joy it brings
    From the green fields, and from yon azure sky.
    Whate'er its mission, the soft breeze can come
    To none more grateful than to me; escaped
    From the vast city, where I long had pined
    A discontented sojourner: now free,
    Free as a bird to settle where I will.
    1799–1805 *The Prelude*, bk.1, l.1–9 (published 1850).

18 I, methought, while the sweet breath of heaven
 Was blowing on my body, felt within
 A correspondent breeze, that gently moved
 With quickening virtue, but is now become
 A tempest, a redundant energy,
 Vexing its own creation.
 1799–1805 *The Prelude*, bk.1, l.33–8 (published 1850).

19 Either still I find
 Some imperfection in the chosen theme,
 Or see of absolute accomplishment
 Much wanting, so much wanting, in myself,
 That I recoil and droop, and seek repose
 In listlessness from vain perplexity,
 Unprofitably travelling towards the grave.
 1799–1805 *The Prelude*, bk.1, l.261–7 (published 1850).

20 Fair seed-time had my soul, and I grew up
 Fostered alike by beauty and by fear.
 1799–1805 *The Prelude*, bk.1, l.301–2 (published 1850).

21 Dust as we are, the immortal spirit grows
 Like harmony in music; there is a dark
 Inscrutable workmanship that reconciles
 Discordant elements, makes them cling together
 In one society.
 1799–1805 *The Prelude*, bk.1, l.340–4 (published 1850).

22 Then, the calm
 And dead still water lay upon my mind
 Even with a weight of pleasure, and the sky,
 Never before so beautiful, sank down
 Into my heart, and held me like a dream.
 1799–1805 *The Prelude*, bk.2, l.70–4 (published 1850).

23 I was taught to feel, perhaps too much,
 The self-sufficing power of Solitude.
 1799–1805 *The Prelude*, bk.2, l.76–7 (published 1850).

24 Science appears but what in truth she is,
 Not as our glory and our absolute boast,
 But as a succedaneum, and a prop
 To our infirmity.
 1799–1805 *The Prelude*, bk.2, l.212–15 (published 1850).

25 That false secondary power
 By which we multiply distinctions, then
 Deem that our puny boundaries are things
 That we perceive, and not that we have made.
 1799–1805 *The Prelude*, bk.2, l.216–19 (published 1850).

26 A babe, by intercourse of touch
 I held mute dialogues with my Mother's heart.
 1799–1805 *The Prelude*, bk.2, l.267–8 (published 1850).

27 From my pillow, looking forth by light
 Of moon or favouring stars, I could behold
 The antechapel where the statue stood
 Of Newton with his prism and silent face,
 The marble index of a mind for ever

Voyaging through strange seas of Thought alone.
 1799–1805 *The Prelude*, bk.3, l.58–63 (published 1850).

28 There's not a man
 That lives who hath not known his god-like hours.
 1799–1805 *The Prelude*, bk.3, l.190–1 (published 1850).

29 Visionary power
 Attends the motions of the viewless winds,
 Embodied in the mystery of words.
 1799–1805 *The Prelude*, bk.5, l.595–7 (published 1850).

30 Even forms and substances are circumfused
 By that transparent veil with light divine,
 And, through the turnings intricate of verse,
 Present themselves as objects recognised,
 In flashes, and with glory not their own.
 1799–1805 *The Prelude*, bk.5, l.601–5 (published 1850).

31 An open place it was, and overlooked,
 From high, the sullen water far beneath,
 On which a dull red image of the moon
 Lay bedded, changing oftentimes its form
 Like an uneasy snake.
 1799–1805 *The Prelude*, bk.6, l.703–7 (published 1850).

32 In the very world, which is the world
 Of all of us,—the place where, in the end,
 We find our happiness, or not at all!
 1799–1805 *The Prelude*, bk.11, l.142–4 (published 1850).

33 I shook the habit off
 Entirely and for ever, and again
 In Nature's presence stood, as now I stand,
 A sensitive being, a *creative* soul.
 1799–1805 *The Prelude*, bk.12, l.204–7 (published 1850).

34 A balance, an ennobling interchange
 Of action from without and from within;
 The excellence, pure function, and best power
 Both of the object seen, and eye that sees.
 1799–1805 *The Prelude*, bk.13, l.375–8 (published 1850).

35 The thought of death sits easy on the man
 Who has been born and dies among the
  mountains.
 c.1800 The Priest. 'The Brothers', l.182–3.

36 The moving accident is not my trade;
 To freeze the blood I have no ready arts:
 'Tis my delight, alone in summer shade,
 To pipe a simple song for thinking hearts.
 1800 'Hart-Leap Well', part 2, l.97–100.

37 Poetry is the spontaneous overflow of powerful
 feelings: it takes its origin from emotion recollected
 in tranquillity.
 1802 Preface to *Lyrical Ballads* (2nd ed. 1802; *Lyrical Ballads*
 first published 1798, preface added 1800, enlarged 1802).

38 Milton! thou shouldst be living at this hour:

England hath need of thee: she is a fen
Of stagnant waters: altar, sword and pen,
Fireside, the heroic wealth of hall and bower,
Have forfeited their ancient English dower
Of inward happiness. We are selfish men;
Oh! raise us up, return to us again;
And give us manners, virtue, freedom, power.
Thy soul was like a star, and dwelt apart;
Thou hadst a voice whose sound was like the sea:
Pure as the naked heavens, majestic, free,
So didst thou travel on life's common way,
In cheerful godliness; and yet thy heart
The lowliest duties on herself did lay.

1802 'Milton! thou shouldst be living at this hour', complete poem (published 1807).

39 Thrice welcome, darling of the Spring
Even yet thou are to me
No bird, but an invisible thing,
A voice, a mystery.

1802 'To the Cuckoo', stanza 4 (published 1807).

40 It is a beauteous evening, calm and free,
The holy time is quiet as a nun
Breathless with adoration; the broad sun
Is sinking down in its tranquillity;
The gentleness of heaven broods o'er the sea:
Listen! the mighty being is awake,
And doth with his eternal motion make
A sound like thunder—everlastingly.

1802 'It is a beauteous evening calm and free', l.1–8 (published 1807).

41 With little here to do or see
Of things that in the great world be,
Sweet Daisy! oft I talk to thee
For thou art worthy,
Thou unassuming commonplace
Of Nature, with that homely face,
And yet with something of a grace
Which love makes for thee!

1802 'To the Daisy', stanza 1 (published 1807).

42 My heart leaps up when I behold
A rainbow in the sky:
So was it when my life began;
So is it now I am a man;
So be it when I shall grow old,
Or let me die!
The Child is father of the Man;
And I could wish my days to be
Bound each to each by natural piety.

1802 'My heart leaps up when I behold', complete poem (published 1807).

43 My whole life have I lived in pleasant thought,
As if life's business were a summer mood;
As if all needful things would come unsought
To genial faith, still rich in genial good.

1802 'Resolution and Independence', stanza 6 (published 1807).

44 I thought of Chatterton, the marvellous boy,
The sleepless soul that perished in his pride.
Of him who walked in glory and in joy
Following his plough along the mountainside:
By our own spirits are we deified.
We poets in our youth begin in gladness;
But thereof comes in the end despondency and
    madness.

1802 Of the poet Thomas Chatterton, who committed suicide at the age of 17. 'Resolution and Independence', stanza 7 (published 1807).

45 The fear that kills;
And hope that is unwilling to be fed.

1802 'Resolution and Independence', stanza 17 (published 1807).

46 Earth hath not anything to show more fair:
Dull would he be of soul who could pass by
A sight so touching in its majesty:
This City now doth like a garment wear
The beauty of the morning; silent, bare,
Ships, towers, domes, theatres, and to the sky;
All bright and glittering in the smokeless air.
Never did sun more beautifully steep
In his first splendour, valley, rock, or hill;
Ne'er saw I, never felt, a calm so deep!
The river glideth at his own sweet will;
Dear God! the very houses seem asleep;
And all that mighty heart is lying still!

1802 Of London. 'Composed upon Westminster Bridge', complete poem. (Published 1807).

47 Once did she hold the gorgeous East in fee,
And was the safeguard of the West: the worth
Of Venice did not fall below her birth,
Venice, the eldest child of Liberty.

1802 Of Venice. 'On the Extinction of the Venetian Republic: Once Did She Hold', l.1–4 (published 1807).

48 There was a time when meadow, grove, and stream,
The earth, and every common sight,
To me did seem
Apparelled in celestial light,
The glory and the freshness of a dream.
It is not now as it hath been of yore;—
Turn whereso'er I may,
By night or day,
The things which I have seen I now can see no
    more.

c.1802–3 'Ode. Intimations of Immortality from Recollections of Early Childhood', stanza 1 (published 1807).

49 Thou Child of Joy,
Shout round me, let me hear thy shouts.

c.1802–3 'Ode. Intimations of Immortality from Recollections of Early Childhood', stanza 3 (published 1807).

50 But there's a tree, of many, one,
   A single field which I have looked upon,
   Both of them speak of something that is gone:
   The pansy at my feet
   Doth the same tale repeat:
   Whither is fled the visionary gleam?
   Where is it now, the glory and the dream?
   c.1802–3 'Ode. Intimations of Immortality from Recollections
   of Early Childhood', stanza 4 (published 1807).

51 Our birth is but a sleep and a forgetting:
   The soul that rises with us, our life's star,
   Hath elsewhere its setting,
   And cometh from afar:
   Not in entire forgetfulness
   And not in utter nakedness,
   But trailing clouds of glory do we come
   From God, who is our home:
   Heaven lies about us in our infancy!
   Shades of the prison-house begin to close
   Upon the growing boy,
   But he beholds the light, and whence it flows,
   He sees it in his joy;
   The youth, who daily farther from the east
   Must travel, still is nature's priest,
   And by the vision splendid
   Is on his way attended;
   At length the man perceives it die away,
   And fade into the light of common day.
   c.1802–3 'Ode. Intimations of Immortality from Recollections
   of Early Childhood', stanza 5 (published 1807).

52 O joy! that in our embers
   Is something that doth live,
   That nature yet remembers
   What was so fugitive!
   c.1802–3 'Ode. Intimations of Immortality from Recollections
   of Early Childhood', stanza 9 (published 1807).

53 Those obstinate questionings
   Of sense and outward things,
   Fallings from us, vanishings;
   Blank misgivings of a creature
   Moving about in worlds not realised,
   High instincts before which our mortal nature
   Did tremble like a guilty thing surprised.
   c.1802–3 'Ode. Intimations of Immortality from Recollections
   of Early Childhood', stanza 9 (published 1807).

54 Our noisy years seem moments in the being
   Of the eternal silence: truths that wake,
   To perish never:
   Whch neither listlessness, nor mad endeavour,
   Nor man nor boy,
   Nor all that is at enmity with joy,
   Can utterly abolish or destroy!
   Hence in a season of calm weather,
   Though inland far we be,
   Our souls have sight of that immortal sea

Which brought us hither,
   Can in a moment travel thither,
   And see the children sport upon the shore,
   And hear the mighty waters rolling evermore.
   c.1802–3 'Ode. Intimations of Immortality from Recollections
   of Early Childhood', stanza 9 (published 1807).

55 Though nothing can bring back the hour
   Of splendour in the grass, of glory in the flower;
   We will grieve not.
   c.1802–3 'Ode. Intimations of Immortality from Recollections
   of Early Childhood', stanza 10 (published 1807).

56 Thanks to the human heart by which we live,
   Thanks to its tenderness, its joys, and fears,
   To me the meanest flower that blows can give
   Thoughts that do often lie too deep for tears.
   c.1802–3 'Ode. Intimations of Immortality from Recollections
   of Early Childhood', stanza 11 (published 1807).

57 Let beeves and home-bred kine partake
   The sweets of Burn-mill meadow;
   The swan on still St Mary's Lake
   Float double, swan and shadow!
   We will not see them; will not go,
   To-day, nor yet to-morrow;
   Enough if in our hearts we know
   There's such a place as Yarrow.

   Be Yarrow stream unseen, unknown;
   It must, or we shall rue it:
   We have a vision of our own,
   Ah! why should we undo it?
   The treasured dreams of times long past,
   We'll keep them, winsome Marrow!
   For when we're there, although 'tis fair,
   'Twill be another Yarrow!
   1803 'Yarrow Unvisited', stanzas 6–7 (published 1807).

58 For thou wert still the poor man's stay,
   The poor man's heart, the poor man's hand;
   And all the oppressed, who wanted strength,
   Had thine at their command.
   1803 'Rob Roy's Grave', l. 109–12 (published 1807).

59 Thy friends are exultations, agonies,
   And love, and man's unconquerable mind.
   1803 'To Toussaint L'Ouverture', l.13–14 (published in the
   Morning Post 2 Feb).

60 What, you are stepping westward?
   1803–5 'Stepping Westward', l.1 (published 1807).

61 Behold her, single in the field,
   Yon solitary Highland Lass!
   Reaping and singing by herself;
   Stop here, or gently pass!
   1803–5 'The Solitary Reaper', l.1–4 (published 1807).

62 She was a Phantom of delight

When first she gleamed upon my sight;
A lovely apparition sent
To be a moment's ornament.
1804 'She was a Phantom of delight', l.1–4 (published 1807).

63   And now I see with eye serene
The very pulse of the machine;
A being breathing thoughtful breath,
A traveller between life and death;
The reason firm, the temperate will,
Endurance, foresight, strength, and skill;
A perfect woman, nobly planned,
To warn, to comfort, and command.
1804 'She was a Phantom of delight', l.21–8 (published 1807).

64   Chains tie us down by land and sea;
And wishes, vain as mine, may be
All that is left to comfort thee.
1804 'The Affliction of Margaret', stanza 8 (published 1807).

65   My apprehensions come in crowds;
I dread the rustling of the grass;
The very shadows of the clouds
Have power to shake me as they pass.
1804 'The Affliction of Margaret', stanza 10 (published 1807).

66   Oh! pleasant exercise of hope and joy!
For mighty were the auxiliars which then stood
Upon our side, we who were strong in love!
Bliss it was in that dawn to be alive,
But to be young was very heaven!
1804 'The French Revolution as it appeared to enthusiasts at its commencement', l.1–5 (published in *The Friend*, 26 Oct. 1809).

67   I wandered lonely as a cloud
That floats on high o'er vales and hills,
When all at once I saw a crowd,
A host, of golden daffodils;
Beside the lake, beneath the trees,
Fluttering and dancing in the breeze.
1804 'I wandered lonely as a cloud', stanza 1 (published 1807).

68   Continuous as the stars that shine
And twinkle on the milky way
They stretched in never-ending line
Along the margin of a bay:
Ten thousand saw I at a glance,
Tossing their heads in sprightly dance.
1804 'I wandered lonely as a cloud', stanza 2 (published 1807).

69   The waves beside them danced; but they
Out-did the sparkling waves in glee:
A poet could not but be gay,
In such a jocund company:
I gazed—and gazed—but little thought
What wealth the show to me had brought.
1804 'I wandered lonely as a cloud', stanza 3 (published 1807).

70   For oft, when on my couch I lie

In vacant or in pensive mood,
They flash upon that inward eye
Which is the bliss of solitude;
And then my heart wih pleasure fills,
And dances with the daffodils.
1804 'I wandered lonely as a cloud', stanza 4 (published 1807).

71   If mine had been the painter's hand,
To express what then I saw; and add the gleam,
The light that never was, on sea or land,
The consecration, and the poet's dream.
1805 'Elegaic Stanzas: suggested by a picture of Steele Castle in a storm', stanza 4 (published 1807).

72   Not for a moment could I now behold
A smiling sea, and be what I have been.
1805 'Elegaic Stanzas: suggested by a picture of Steele Castle in a storm', stanza 10 (published 1807).

73   The world is too much with us; late and soon,
Getting and spending we lay waste our powers:
Little we see in nature that is ours;
We have given our hearts away, a sordid boon!
The sea that bares her bosom to the moon;
The winds that will be howling at all hours,
And are up-gathered now like sleeping flowers;
For this, for everything, we are out of tune;
It moves us not.—Great God! I'd rather be
A pagan suckled in a creed outworn;
So might I, standing on this pleasant lea,
Have glimpses that would make me less forlorn;
Have sight of Proteus rising from the sea;
Or hear old Triton blow his wreathèd horn.
1806 'The world is too much with us; late and soon', complete poem (published 1807).

74   Two voices are there; one is of the sea,
One of the mountains; each a mighty voice:
In both from age to age thou didst rejoice,
They were thy chosen music, Liberty!
1807 'Thought of a Briton on the Subjugation of Switzerland', l.1–4.

75   These people in the senseless hurry of their idle lives do not *read* books, they merely snatch a glance at them that they may talk about them. And even if this were not so, never forget what I believe was observed by Coleridge, that every great and original writer, in proportion as he is great or original, must himself create the taste by which he is to be relished.
1807 Letter to Lady Beaumont 21 May, on his *Poems in Two Volumes* (1807). In *The Letters of William Wordsworth* edited by Alan G Hill (1984).

76   Surprised by joy—impatient as the wind
I turned to share the transport—Oh! with whom
But thee, deep buried in the silent tomb,
That spot which no vicissitude can find?

c.1812 'Surprised by joy—impatient as the wind', l.1–4 (published 1815). The poet's second daughter, Catherine, who died in June 1812, is the 'thee' refered to in the poem.

77 On Man, on Nature, and on Human Life,
Musing in solitude, I oft perceive
Fair trains of images before me rise,
Accompanied by feelings of delight
Pure, or with no unpleasing sadness mixed.
1814 'The Excursion', preface, l.1–5.

78 Not Chaos, not
The darkest pit of lowest Erebus
Nor aught of blinder vacancy, scooped out
By help of dreams—can breed such fear and awe
As fall upon us often when we look
Into our Minds, into the Mind of Man—
My haunt, and the main region of my song.
1814 'The Excursion', preface, l.35–41.

79 What soul was his, when, from the naked top
Of some bold headland, he beheld the sun
Rise up, and bathe the world in light!
He looked—
Ocean and earth, the solid frame of earth
And ocean's liquid mass, in gladness lay
Beneath him:—Far and wide the clouds were
touched,
And in their silent faces he could read
Unutterable love.
1814 'The Excursion', bk.1, l.198–205.

80 This dull product of a scoffer's pen.
1814 Of Voltaire's novel *Candide*. 'The Excursion', bk.2, l.484.

81 Compassed round by pleasure, sighed
For independent happiness; craving peace,
The central feeling of all happiness,
Not as a refuge from distress or pain,
A breathing-time, vacation, or a truce,
But for its absolute self.
1814 'The Excursion', bk.3, l.380–5.

82 Society became my glittering bride,
And airy hopes my children.
1814 'The Excursion', bk.3, l.735–6.

83 'To every Form of being is assigned,'
Thus calmly spake the venerable Sage,
'An *active* Principle:—howe'er removed
From sense and observation, it subsists
In all things, in all natures.'
1814 'The Excursion', bk.9, l.1–5.

84 For all the startled scaly tribes that slink
Into his coverts, and each fearless link
Of dancing insects forged upon his breast.
1820 *The River Duddon*, no.28, 'Journey Renewed', l.6–8.

85 Still glides the stream, and shall for ever glide;

The Form remains, the function never dies;
While we, the brave, the mighty, and the wise,
We Men, who in our morn of youth defied
The elements, must vanish;—be it so!
1820 *The River Duddon*, no.34, 'After-Thought', l.5–9.

86 Enough, if something from our hands have power
To live, and act, and serve the future hour;
And if, as toward the silent tomb we go,
Through love, through hope, and Faith's
transcendent dower,
We feel that we are greater than we know.
1820 *The River Duddon*, no.34, 'After-Thought', l.10–14.

87 Ethereal minstrel! pilgrim of the sky!
Dost thou despise the earth where cares abound?
Or, while the wings aspire, are heart and eye
Both with thy nest upon the dewy ground?
1825 'To a Skylark', l.1–4 (published 1827).

88 Type of the wise who soar, but never roam;
True to the kindred points of Heaven and Home!
1825 'To a Skylark', l.11–12 (published 1827).

89 But who is innocent? By grace divine,
Not otherwise, O Nature! we are thine.
1834 'Evening Voluntaries', no.4, l.16–17 (published 1835).

90 Even so for me a vision sanctified
The sway of death; long ere my eyes had seen
Thy countenance—the still rapture of thy mien—
When thou, dear Sister! wert become death's bride:
No trace of pain or languor could abide
That change—age on thy brow was smoothed—
thy cold
Wan cheek at once was privileged to unfold
A loveliness to living youth denied.
Oh! if within me hope should e'er decline,
The lamp of faith, lost Friend! too faintly burn;
The may that heaven-revealing smile of thine,
The bright assurance, visibly return:
And let my spirit in that power divine
Rejoice, as, through that power, it ceased to mourn.
1836 'November 1836', complete poem (published 1837).

91 The softest breeze to fairest flowers gives birth:
Think not that Prudence dwells in dark abodes,
She scans the future with the eye of gods.
1837 'At Bologna, In Remembrance of the Late Insurrections:
Continued', l.12–14 (published 1842).

92 Before us lay a painful road,
And guidance have I sought in duteous love
From Wisdom's heavenly Father. Hence hath
flowed
Patience, with trust that, whatsoe'er the way
Each takes in this high matter, all may move
Cheered with the prospect of a brighter day.
1839–40 *Sonnets upon the Punishment of Death*, no.14,
'Apology', l.9–14 (published in the *Quarterly Review* 1841).

93 With what nice care equivalents are given,
How just, how bountiful, the hand of Heaven.
1840 'Poor Robin', l.35–6 (published 1842).

94 That to this mountain-daisy's self were known
The beauty of its star-shaped shadow, thrown
On the smooth surface of this naked stone!
1844 'So fair so sweet', stanza 2 (published 1845).

95 21st May—a glorious day for beauty. I wish you
could see how lovely our country is at this fine
season.
1846 Letter to William Boxall, 21 May.

Worley, Helen

96 Dance, little words, on the end of your string. I can
make you do most anything I want to. I can hide
anywhere and watch you say the things I would
never dare.
1982 *The Soul Survivor*, 'Puppetry and Poetry'.

Wotton, Sir Henry 1568–1639

English traveller, diplomat, scholar and poet. A trusted
ambassador of James I and VI, he served in Venice and
Germany. His tracts and letters were collected as *Reliquiae
Wottonianae* (1651).

97 An ambassador is an honest man sent to lie abroad
for the good of his country.
Quoted in Izaak Walton's *Life (1651)*.

Wragg, Ted (Edward) Conrad 1938–

English educator, a Professor of Education at the
University of Exeter.

98 Nobody loves a bad teacher.
1986 *Education: an Action Guide for Parents*.

Wright, Sir Almroth Edward 1861–1947

English bacteriologist and professor of experimental
pathology, known for his work on parasitic diseases. A
vocal opponent of the suffragettes, he wrote *The
Unexpurgated Case against Woman Suffrage* (1913).

99 The recruiting field for the militant suffragists is
the million of our excess female population—that
million which had better long ago have gone out to
mate with its complement of men beyond the sea.
1912 Letter to *The Times*, 28 Mar.

1 The primordial argument against giving woman
the vote is that that vote would not represent
physical force.
1913 *The Unexpurgated Case against Woman Suffrage*, pt.2.

2 The woman voter would be pernicious to the State
not only because she could not back her vote by

physical force, but also by reason of her intellectual
defects.
1913 *The Unexpurgated Case against Woman Suffrage*, pt.2.

3 Practically every man feels that there is in
woman…an element of unreason which, when you
come upon it, summarily puts an end to purely
intellectual intercourse.
1913 *The Unexpurgated Case against Woman Suffrage*, pt.5.

Wright, Betsey

Aide to President Clinton.

4 Bimbo eruptions.
1994 On an explosion of charges of sexual harassment against
President Clinton. In the *Washington Post*, 30 May.

Wright, Frank Lloyd 1867–1959

US architect, known for his original and controversial
designs exploiting modern technology and cubist spatial
concepts. His works include the Imperial Hotel, Tokyo
(1916–20) and the Guggenheim Museum of Art, New
York (1959).

5 The physician can bury his mistakes, but the
architect can only advise his client to plant vines.
1953 In the *New York Times*, 4 Oct.

6 Architecture is man's great sense of himself
embodied in a world of his own making. It may rise
as high in quality only as its source because great art
is great life.
1930 In Frederick Gutheim (ed) *Frank Lloyd Wright on
Architecture: selected writings (1894-1940)*.

7 I know we can't have a great architecture while it is
only for the landlord.
1932 In Frederick Gutheim (ed) *Frank Lloyd Wright on
Architecture: selected writings (1894-1940)*.

Wright, James C, Jr 1922–

US Congressman, former speaker of the US House of
Representatives.

8 The boiling, churning caldron of America.
1987 On the House of Representatives. In *Life*.

9 I know how that pancake feels when you pour the
syrup all over it.
1991 Of his official portrait, unveiled two years after he was
forced to resign. In the *International Herald Tribune*, 12 Jul.

Wright, Judith Arundell also known as *Judith Wright McKinney* 1915–

Australian poet and conservationist, whose awards
include the Robert Frost Memorial Prize (1976). Selected
works have been published in *A Human Pattern* (1990).

10 The easy Eden-dreamtime then

in a country of birds and trees
made me your shadow-sister, child,
dark girl I couldn't play with.
1990 *A Human Pattern*, 'Two Dreamtimes', stanza 14. The poem is dedicated to Kath Walker (now Oodgeroo Noonuccal).

11 I am born of the conquerors,
you of the persecuted.
Raped by rum and an alien law,
progress and economics,

are you and I and a once-loved land
peopled by tribes and trees;
doomed traders and stock-exchanges,
bought by faceless strangers.
1990 *A Human Pattern*, 'Two Dreamtimes', stanzas 17–18. The poem is dedicated to Kath Walker (now Oodgeroo Noonuccal).

Wright, Kenyon 1932–

Scottish Methodist minister, General Secretary of the Scottish Council of Churches since 1981, and Executive of the Scottish Constitutional Convention from 1989.

12 What if that other single voice we know so well responds by saying, 'We say no, and we are the state'? Well, we say yes—and we are the people.
1989 Calling for a Scottish Parliament. Speech at the inaugural meeting of the Scottish Constitutional Convention, 30 Mar. The 'single voice' is that of Prime Minister Margaret Thatcher.

Wright, Orville and Wright, Wilbur
1871–1948, 1867–1912

Born in Dayton, Ohio, early mechanics and tinkerers, and eventually self-taught aviation engineers.

13 SUCCESS FOUR FLIGHTS THURSDAY MORNING ALL AGAINST TWENTY-ONE MILE WIND STARTED FROM LEVEL WITH ENGINE POWER ALONE AVERAGE SPEED THROUGH AIR THIRTY-ONE MILES LONGEST 59 SECONDS INFORM PRESS HOME CHRISTMAS.
1903 Telegram from the brothers at Kitty Hawk, North Carolina to their father, 17 Dec.

Wriston, Walter Bigelow 1919–

US banker. He joined Citibank in 1946 and worked his way up to chairman (1970–84).

14 Our banking system grew by accident; and wherever something happens by accident, it becomes a religion.
1975 In *Business Week*, 20 Jan.

15 When you retire…you go from who's who to who's that.
1985 In the *New York Times*, 21 Apr.

16 If you put a floor under wages and a ceiling over prices, a free man cannot long stand erect.
1986 *Risk and Other Four-Letters Words.*

17 The Doomsayers have always had their uses, since they trigger the coping mechanism that often prevents the events they forecast.
1986 *Risk and Other Four-Letter Words.*

18 Our current tendency to take our economic blood pressure every few minutes…obfuscates thought on many problems.
1986 *Risk and Other Four-Letter Words.*

19 Banking is a branch of the information business.
1986 *Risk and Other Four-Letters Words.*

20 It is a maxim of cryptology that what one man can devise, another can unravel. This principle keeps armies of tax lawyers and accountants employed, but adds nothing to our national productivity.
1986 *Risk and Other Four-Letters Words.*

21 Rising prices or wages do not cause inflation; they only report it. They represent an essential form of economic speech, since money is just another form of information.
1986 *Risk and Other Four-Letter Words.*

22 Every line in the government's budget has its own constituency.
1986 *Risk and Other Four-Letter Words.*

23 It's a Texas wrestling match with a new team against you every night.
1993 On life as a chief executive officer. In the *New York Times*, 25 Apr.

Wu-ti 157–87 BC

Chinese emperor of the Han dynasty who became its sixth ruler at the age of 16. The Han dynasty saw the Chinese expanding their political power westwards into Central Asia.

24 Autumn wind rises; white clouds fly.
Grass and trees wither; geese go south.
c.127 BC 'The Autumn Wind' (translated by Arthur Waley). The poem is a lament on leaving his mistress behind while he travelled on official business.

Wyatt, Sir Thomas (the Elder) 1503–42

English courtier and poet under Henry VIII. Twice imprisoned on capital offences—on charges of adultery with Anne Boleyn and for treason—he was twice released. Many of his poems were published in *Tottel's Miscellany* (1557). He is credited with introducing the sonnet form to English; many of his are translations from Petrarch.

25 In lusty leas at liberty I walk.
1536 'Mine own John Poins'.

26 But here I am in Kent and Christendom,
Among the Muses, where I read and rhyme.
1536 'Mine own John Poins'.

27 Farewell, Love, and all thy laws forever,

Thy baited hooks shall tangle me no more.
1557 'Farewell, Love'.

28 And graven with diamonds in letters plain
    There is written, her fair neck round about:
    Noli me tangere, for Caesar's I am,
    And wild for to hold, though I seem tame.
    1557 'Whoso list to hunt'. The subject of the poem is thought
    to be Anne Boleyn.
    ▷ See Bible 147:75.

29 My lute, awake! Perform the last
    Labour that thou and I shall waste,
    And end that I have now begun;
    For when this song is sung and past,
    My lute, be still, for I have done.
    1557 'My Lute, awake!'

30 They flee from me, that sometime did me seek,
    With naked foot, stalking in my chamber.
    I have seen them gentle, tame, and meek,
    That now are wild, and do not remember
    That sometime they put themselves in danger
    To take bread at my hand; and now they range,
    Busily seeking with a continual change.
    1557 'They flee from me'.

31 But all is turned, through my gentleness,
    Into a strange fashion of forsaking.
    1557 'They flee from me'.

Wycherley, William c.1640–1716

English dramatist. Educated at Oxford and Middle Temple. Although a successful playwright who garnered attention and support from both Charles II and James II, his fortunes were unsteady. Plays include *The Gentleman Dancing-Master* (1672), *Love in a Wood* (1671), *The Country Wife* (1675) and *The Plain Dealer* (1677), the last two of which were based on plays by Molière.

32 Fy! madam, do you think me so ill bred as to love a
    husband?
    1671 *Love in a Wood*, act 3, sc.4.

33 A good name is seldom got by giving it one's self.
    1675 *The Country Wife*, act 1, sc.1, l.40–1.

34 A mistress should be like a little country retreat
    near the town, not to dwell in constantly, but only
    for a night and away.
    1675 *The Country Wife*, act 1, sc.1, l.196–7.

35 Your virtue is your greatest affectation.
    1675 *The Country Wife*, act 1, sc.1.

36 Women serve but to keep men from better
    company.
    1675 *The Country Wife*, act 1, sc.1.

37 Mistresses are like books. If you pore upon them
    too much, they doze you, and make you unfit for

company; but if used discreetly, you are the fitter
for conversation by 'em.
1675 *The Country Wife*, act 1, sc.1.

38 'Tis as hard to be a good fellow, a good friend, and a
    lover of women, as 'tis to be a good fellow, a good
    friend, and a lover of money.
    1675 *The Country Wife*, act 1, sc.1.

39 Wine gives you liberty, love takes it away.
    1675 *The Country Wife*, act 1, sc.1.

40 For my part, I will have only those glorious manly
    pleasures of being very drunk and very slovenly.
    1675 *The Country Wife*, act 1, sc.1.

41 Wit is more necessary than beauty; and I think no
    young woman ugly that has it, and no handsome
    woman agreeable without it.
    1675 *The Country Wife*, act 1, sc.1.

42 He's a fool that marries; but he's a greater that does
    not marry a fool.
    1675 *The Country Wife*, act 1, sc.1.

43 Poetry in love is no more to be avoided than
    jealousy.
    1675 *The Country Wife*, act 3, sc.2.

44 I love to be envied, and would not marry a wife that
    I alone could love; loving alone is as dull as eating
    alone.
    1675 *The Country Wife*, act 3, sc.2.

Wycliffe, John c.1330–1384

English religious reformer. His many popular vernacular tracts attacked Church hierarchy, priestly powers, and the doctrine of transubstantiation, and he issued the first English translation of the Bible. Although condemned, his teaching was influential in its insistence on inward religion instead of formalism. His followers were derisively known as 'Lollards'.

45 Christ during His life upon earth was of all men the
    poorest, casting from Him all worldly authority. I
    deduce from these premises...that the Pope should
    surrender all temporal authority to the civil power
    and advise his clergy to do the same.
    1384 Dismissing an order to appear before the Papal Court.

Wyeth, Andrew Newell 1917–

US painter, known for his meticulous depictions of the Pennsylvanian and Maine countryside. His most famous work is *Christina's World* (1948).

46 I get excited by the shape of a person's nose, the
    tone of their eyes, or the way their back looks when
    they're turned away from me. That's my reason for
    painting.
    1991 In *National Geographic*, Jul.

Wylie, Betty Jane 1931–

Canadian dramatist and writer.

47 First deal with your own tears; tomorrow do something about acid rain.
1986 *Successfully Single.*

48 There are all kinds of ways of being unfaithful, not the worst of them with your body.
1988 *All in the Family: A Survival Guide for Living and Loving in a Changing World.*

49 Listening is one of the lesser-known skills that mistresses offer.
1988 *All in the Family: A Survival Guide for Living and Loving in a Changing World.*

50 There is a line between sexuality and promiscuity, and the line is closer to celibacy than not.
1988 *All in the Family: A Survival Guide for Living and Loving in a Changing World.*

51 Poverty isn't being broke; poverty is never having enough.
1989 *Everywoman's Money Book* (with Lynne MacFarlane).

Wyman, Jane originally *Sarah Jane Fulks* 1914–

First wife of Ronald Reagan and best known as a film actress, she married Reagan (her second husband) in 1940 and divorced in 1948. She won an Academy Award for *Johnny Belinda* (1948).

52 Ask him what time it is and he'll tell you how the watch was made.
Of Ronald Reagan. Quoted in Jack Finney *From Time to Time* (1995).

Xenophon c.482–c.354 BC

Athenian historian and soldier.

53 *Thalatta! Thalatta!*

The sea! The sea!
Anabasis bk. 4, 24. Shouted by the Greek soldiers from the Expedition of Cyrus in 401 BC when they reached the sea after months inland.

Yarborough, Ralph 1903–96

US liberal politician and Governor of Texas (1957–71).

54 It is the only case on record of a man swimming toward a sinking ship.
1973 On former Texas Governor John B Connally's switch from Democratic to the Republican party in his bid for the presidential nomination. Quoted in the *Washington Post*, 18 Jan 1988.

Yeats, Georgie née *Hyde-Lees* 1892–1968

Wife of Irish poet W B Yeats. Her attempts at automatic writing on their honeymoon in 1917 profoundly influenced Yeats' subsequent writing.

55 After your death people will write of your love affairs, but I shall say nothing, because I will remember how proud you were.
Quoted in Richard Ellman *a long the riverrun: Selected Essays* (1988), p.253.

Yeats, W(illiam) B(utler) 1865–1939

Irish poet. He was a prolific writer influenced by Irish mythology and by his close relationships with a number of women, eventually evolving his own system of symbolism which underlies much of his work. He also edited many books, including the controversial *Oxford Book of Modern Verse* (1936), and served as a Senator of the Irish Free State (1922–9).

56 Down by the salley gardens my love and I did meet;
She passed the salley gardens with little snow-white feet.
She bid me take love easy, as the leaves grow on the tree;
But I, being young and foolish, with her would not agree.

In a field by the river my love and I did stand,
And on my leaning shoulder she laid her snow-white hand.
She bid me take life easy, as the grass grows on the weirs;
But I was young and foolish, and now am full of tears.
1888 'Down by the Salley Gardens', complete poem. Collected in *Crossways.*

57 I will arise and go now, and go to Innisfree,
And a small cabin build there, of clay and wattles made:
Nine bean-rows will I have there, a hive for the honey-bee,
And live alone in the bee-loud glade.

And I shall have some peace there, for peace comes dropping slow,
Dropping from the veils of the morning to where the cricket sings;
There midnight's all a-glimmer, and noon a purple glow,
And evening full of the linnet's wings.
1888 'The Lake Isle of Innisfree', stanzas 1–2. Collected in *The Rose* (1893).

58 O Oisin, mount by me and ride
To shores by the wash of the tremulous tide,
Where men have heaped no burial-mounds,
And the days pass by like a wayward tune.
1889 'The Wanderings of Oisin', l.80–3.

59 The brawling of a sparrow in the eaves,

The brilliant moon and all the milky sky,
And all that famous harmony of leaves,
Has blotted out man's image and his cry.
1891 'The Sorrow of Love', stanza 1. Collected in *The Rose* (1893).

60   When you are old and grey and full of sleep,
And nodding by the fire, take down this book,
And slowly read, and dream of the soft look
Your eyes had once, and of their shadows deep;

How many loved your moments of glad grace,
And loved your beauty with love false or true,
But one man loved the pilgrim soul in you,
And loved the sorrows of your changing face;

And bending down beside the glowing bars,
Murmur, a little sadly how Love fled
And paced among the mountains overhead
And hid his face amid a crowd of stars.
1891 'When You Are Old', complete poem. Collected in *The Rose* (1893).

61   Rose of all Roses, Rose of all the World!
The tall thought-woven sails, that flap unfurled
Above the tide of hours, trouble the air,
And God's bell buoyed to be the water's care.
1891 'The Rose of Battle', l.1–4. Collected in *The Rose* (1893).

62   Out-worn heart, in a time out-worn,
Come clear of the nets of wrong and right;
Laugh, heart, again in the grey twilight,
Sigh, heart, again in the dew of the morn.
1893 'Into the Twilight', stanza 1. Collected in *The Wind Among the Reeds* (1899).

63   And walk among long dappled grass,
And pluck till time and times are done
The silver apples of the moon,
The golden apples of the sun.
1897 'The Song of Wandering Aengus', l.21–4. Collected in *The Wind Among the Reeds* (1899).

64   Half close your eyelids, loosen your hair,
And dream about the great and their pride;
They have spoken against you everywhere,
But weigh this song with the great and their pride;
I made it out of a mouthful of air,
Their children's children shall say they have lied.
1898 'He thinks of those who have Spoken Evil of His Beloved', complete poem. Collected in *The Wind Among the Reeds* (1899).

65   Had I the heavens' embroidered cloths,
Enwrought with golden and silver light,
The blue and the dim and the dark cloths
Of night and light and the half-light,
I would spread the cloths under your feet:
But I, being poor, have only my dreams;
I have spread my dreams under your feet;
Tread softly because you tread on my dreams.
1899 'He Wishes for the Cloths of Heaven', complete poem. Collected in *The Wind Among the Reeds* (1899).

66   You have disgraced yourselves again. You are
rocking the cradle of a new masterpiece.
1907 Addressing the rioting audience at Dublin's Abbey Theatre at the première of J M Synge's *The Playboy of the Western World*.

67   What could have made her peaceful with a mind
That nobleness made simple as a fire,
With beauty like a tightened bow, a kind
That is not natural in an age like this,
Being high and solitary and most stern?
Why, what could she have done, being what she is?
Was there another Troy for her to burn?
1908 'A Second Troy', l.6–12. Collected in *The Green Helmet and Other Poems* (1910).

68   You say, as I have often given tongue
In praise of what another's said or sung,
'Twere politic to do the like by these;
But was there ever dog that praised his fleas?
1909 'To a Poet, who would have me Praise certain Bad Poets, Imitators of His and Mine', complete poem. Collected in *The Green Helmet and Other Poems* (1910).

69   I have made my song a coat
Covered with embroideries
Out of old mythologies
From heel to throat;
But the fools caught it,
Wore it in the world's eyes
As though they'd wrought it.
Song, let them take it,
For there's more enterprise
In walking naked.
1912 'A Coat', complete poem. Collected in *Responsibilities* (1914).

70   Romantic Ireland's dead and gone,
It's with O'Leary in the grave.
1913 'September 1913', refrain. Collected in *Responsibilities* (1914).

71   I have met them at close of day
Coming with vivid faces
From counter or desk among grey
Eighteenth-century houses.
1916 'Easter, 1916', l.1–4. Collected in *Michael Robartes and the Dancer* (1921).

72   The horse that comes from the road,
The rider, the birds that range
From cloud to tumbling cloud,
Minute by minute they change;
A shadow of cloud on the stream
Changes minute by minute;
A horse-hoof slides on the brim,
And a horse plashes within it;
The long-legged moor-hens dive,

And hens to moorcocks call;
Minute by minute they live:
The stone's in the midst of all.

1916 'Easter 1916', l.45–56. Collected in *Michael Robartes and the Dancer* (1921).

73 Too long a sacrifice
Can make a stone of the heart.

1916 'Easter 1916', l.57–8. Collected in *Michael Robartes and the Dancer* (1921).

74 There's nothing but our own red blood
Can make a right Rose Tree.

1917 'The Rose Tree', stanza 3. Collected in *Michael Robartes and the Dancer* (1921).

75 I know that I shall meet my fate
Somewhere among the clouds above;
Those that I fight I do not hate,
Those that I guard I do not love.

1918 'An Irish Airman Foresees his Death', l.1.–4. Collected in *The Wild Swans at Coole* (1919).

76 Very nice, but if I had rehearsed you it would have
been much better.

1919 Of Lady Gregory's title-role performance in his *Kathleen Ni Houlihan*. Recorded in Lady Gregory's journal, entry for 19 Mar.

77 Turning and turning in the widening gyre
The falcon cannot hear the falconer;
Things fall apart; the centre cannot hold;
Mere anarchy is loosed upon the world,
The blood-dimmed tide is loosed, and everywhere
The ceremony of innocence is drowned;
The best lack conviction, while the worst
Are full of passionate intensity.

1919 'The Second Coming', l.1–8. Collected in *Michael Robartes and the Dancer* (1921).

▷ See Achebe 2:18.

78 And what rough beast, its hour come round at last,
Slouches towards Bethlehem to be born?

1919 'The Second Coming', l.21–2. Collected in *Michael Robartes and the Dancer* (1921).

79 An aged man is but a paltry thing,
A tattered coat upon a stick, unless
Soul clap its hands and sing, and louder sing
For every tatter in its mortal dress.

1926 'Sailing to Byzantium', stanza 8. Collected in *The Tower* (1928).

80 O chestnut tree, great-rooted blossomer,
Are you the leaf, the blossom, or the bole?
O body swayed to music, O brightening glance,
How can we know the dancer from the dance?

1927 'Among School Children', stanza 8. collected in *The Tower* (1928).

81 Never to have lived is best, ancient writers say;

Never to have drawn the breath of life, never to
have looked into the eye of day;
The second best's a gay goodnight and quickly turn
away.

1927 'From Oedipus at Colonnus', stanza 4. Collected in *The Tower* (1928).

82 The innocent and the beautiful
Have no enemy but time.

1927 'In Memory of Eva Gore-Booth and Con Markiewicz', l.24–5. Collected in *The Winding Stair and Other Poems* (1933).

83 If I make the lashes dark
And the eyes more bright
And the lips more scarlet,
Or ask if all be right
From mirror after mirror,
No Vanity's displayed:
I'm looking for the face I had
Before the world was made.

1928 'A Woman Young and Old', part 2 'Before the World was Made', stanza 1. Collected in *The Winding Stair and Other Poems* (1933).

84 A starlit or a moonlit dome disdains
All that man is,
All mere complexities
The fury and the mire of human veins.

1930 'Byzantium', stanza 1. Collected in *The Winding Stair and Other Poems* (1933).

85 Marbles of the dancing floor
Break bitter furies of complexity,
Those images that yet
Fresh images beget,
That dolphin-torn, that gong-tormented sea.

1930 'Byzantium', stanza 5. Collected in *The Winding Stair and Other Poems* (1933).

86 Only God, my dear,
Could love you for yourself alone
And not your yellow hair

1930 'For Anne Gregory', l.16–18. Collected in *The Winding Stair and Other Poems* (1933).

87 Grant me an old man's frenzy.
Myself I must remake
Till I am Timon and Lear
Or that William Blake
Who beat upon the wall
Till Truth obeyed his call.

1936 'An Acre of Grass', stanza 3. Collected in *New Poems* (1938).

88 John Bull has gone to India
And all must pay him heed
For histories are there to prove
That none of another breed
Has had a like inheritance,
Or sucked such milk as he,
And there's no luck about a house

If it lacks honesty.
The ghost of Roger Casement
Is beating on the door.

1936 'The Ghost of Roger Casement', stanza 3. Collected in *New Poems* (1938).

89 Now that my ladder's gone,
I must lie down where all the ladders start,
In the foul rag-and-bone shop of the heart.

1937–8 'The Circus Animals' Desertion', part 3, l.6–8. Collected in *Last Poems* (1939).

90 Our master Caesar is in the tent
Where the maps are spread,
His eyes fixed upon nothing,
A hand under his head.

Like a long-legged fly upon the stream
His mind moves upon silence.

1938 'Long-Legged Fly', l.5–10. Collected in *Last Poems* (1939).

91 When Pearse summoned Cuchulain to his side,
What stalked through the Post Office? What
   intellect,
What calculation, number, measurement, replied?
We Irish, born into that ancient sect
But thrown upon this filthy modern tide
And by its formless spawning fury wrecked,
Climb to our proper dark, that we may trace
The lineaments of a plummet-measured face.

1938 'The Statues', stanza 4. Collected in *Last Poems* (1939).

92 Swear by what the sages spoke
Round the Mareotic Lake
That the Witch of Atlas knew,
Spoke and set the cocks a-crow.

1938 'Under Ben Bulben', stanza 1. Collected in *Last Poems* (1939).

93 Under bare Ben Bulben's head
In Drumcliffe churchyard Yeats is laid,
An ancestor was rector there
Long years ago; a church stands near,
By the road an ancient Cross.
No marble, no conventional phrase,
On limestone quarried near the spot
By his command these words are cut:
Cast a cold eye
On life, on death.
Horseman, pass by!

1938 'Under Ben Bulben', stanza 6. Collected in *Last Poems* (1939). The last three lines were used as his epitaph.

94 Propinquity had brought
Imagination to that pitch where it casts out
All that is not itself. I had grown wild
And wandered murmuring everywhere, 'My child,
   my child.'

1939 'A Bronze Head', l.18–21. Collected in *Last Poems* (1939).

95 OLD MAN: Do not let him touch you! It is not true
That drunken men cannot beget,
And if he touch he must beget
And you must bear his murderer.
Deaf! Both deaf!

1939 *Purgatory.*

Yellen, Jack 1892–1991

US lyricist.

96 Happy Days are Here Again.

1930 Title of song. It became linked with US Democrat campaigns.

Yeltsin, Boris 1931–

President of Russia. He graduated as a construction engineer in 1955 and entered work for the Communist Party. Called to Moscow in 1985 by Gorbachev, he was sacked in 1987 and against Gorbachev's wishes became chairman of the Russian Parliament. He was elected President in 1991. His programme for a rapid transition to a market economy, support for other republics to be treated equally, and for multiparty democracy, helped him survive the following politicially tumultuous years, but his policies have caused much domestic criticism.

97 The West has not lived through totalitarianism,
   with a single ideology for 70 years. We are escaping
   from the burden of the past, and only after we have
   done that will we be ready to integrate with
   Europe—and Europe needs Russia.

1991 Addressing socialist MPs in Strasbourg, 15 Apr.

Yevtushenko, Yevegeny Aleksandrovich 1933–

Russian poet. He emerged as a poet representing the young post-Stalin generation with such works as *The Third Snow* (1955), *Chausée Eutuziastov* (1956) and *The Promise* (1957). Later works have included *Babi Yar* (1962), concerning anti-Semitism in Russia, *Love Poems* (1977), *Ivan the Terrible and Ivan the Fool* (1979) and the novel *Berries* (1981).

98 I love sport because I love life, and sport is one of
   the basic joys of life.

1966 In *Sports Illustrated*, 19 Dec.

Yokoi, Shoichi c.1920–

Japanese corporal who emerged from the jungles of Guam in 1972 after hiding for 28 years. He was obeying his commanding officer's 1944 order to evade capture by the enemy.

99 I am deeply ashamed at my failure to serve His
   Majesty.

1972 Announcement to journalists at Tokyo airport, 2 Feb. Quoted in Edward Behr *Hirohito*, epilogue.

Yost, Elwy 1925–

Canadian television personality.

1 If you work very hard, and give life everything
you've got, you may not quite make it.
1990 Comment, 17 Jan.

Young, Arthur 1741–1820

British agriculturalist and writer.

2 Give a man the secure possession of a bleak rock,
and he will turn it into a garden; give him a nine
years' lease on a garden, and he will convert it into a
desert… The magic of PROPERTY turns sand to
gold.
1787 Journal entries, 30 Jul and 7 Nov, published in *Travels in
France and Italy* (1794).

Young, Douglas 1913–73

Scottish poet, scholar and nationalist. He was jailed for
refusing to serve in the British Army in 1941. After the
war he taught classics at universities in Scotland, Canada
and the USA.

3 The Minister said it wald dee,
the cypress-buss I plantit.
But the buss grew til a tree,
naething dauntit.

It's growan, stark and heich,
derk and straucht and sinister,
kirkyairdielike and dreich.
But whaur's the Minister?
1943 *Auntran Blads*, 'Last Lauch'.

Young, Edward 1683–1765

English poet, tragedian and cleric, best known for his
satires, *The Love of Fame, the Universal Passion* (1725–8)
and the remarkable *Complaint, or Night Thoughts on Life,
Death and Immortality* (1742–5), written on the death of
his wife.

4 Some, for *renown*, on scraps of learning doat,
And think they grow immortal as they *quote*.
1725 *The Love of Fame, the Universal Passion* 'Satire 1'.

Yourcenar, Marguerite pseudonym of
Marguerite de Crayencour 1903–87

French novelist. Born into aristocracy, she spent her
childhood travelling in Europe and in 1937 left for the
US, taking dual US–French nationality. She is best
known for her historical novel *Mémoires d'Hadrien*
(Memoirs of Hadrian, 1951), and for being the first
woman elected to the Académie Française.

5 *Un homme qui lit, ou qui pense, ou qui calcule,
appartient à l'espèce et non au sexe; dans ses meilleurs
moments, il échappe même à l'humain.*

A person who reads or thinks or calculates, belongs
to a kind and not to a gender; in his or her best
moments, he or she escapes being human.

1958 *Mémoires d'Hadrien.*

6 *Les trois quarts de nos exercices intellectuels ne sont
plus que broderies sur le vide.*

Three quarters of our intellectual performances are
no more than decorations over a void.
1958 *Mémoires d'Hadrien.*

7 *Tout bonheur est un chef-d'oeuvre: la moindre erreur
le fausse, la moindre hésitation l'altère, la moindre
lourdeur le dépare, la moindre sottise l'abêtit.*

Happiness is always a work of art: the least fault
distorts it, the least hesitation changes it, a little
dullness spoils it, the smallest foolish act makes it
idiotic.
1958 *Mémoires d'Hadrien.*

8 *Entre le rôle de sauveur et celui de complice du
bourreau, j'aperçois tout au plus l'incommode emploi
de victime.*

Between the role of saviour and that of butcher's
accomplice, all I see left for you is the unsavoury
role of victim.
1963 *Qui n'a pas son Minotaure?*, pt.3.

9 *Que le Dieu qui nous tue nous vienne en aide!*

God who kills us, come to our rescue!
1963 *Qui n'a pas son Minotaure?*, pt.3.

10 *ARIANE: Tu n'es que la réponse la plus courte qu'on
puisse faire aux questions des hommes.*
DIEU: En sais-tu de meilleur?
*ARIANE: Oui. Le mot rien est aussi court que le mot
Dieu.*

ARIADNE: You are only the shortest possible answer
to all the questions of men.
GOD (BACCHUS): Do you know a better one?
ARIADNE: Yes, the word no is just as short as the
word God.
1963 *Qui n'a pas son Minotaure?*, pt.9.

11 Out of the debris of a statue thoroughly shattered a
new art work is born: a naked foot unforgettably
resting on a stone; a candid hand; a bent knee
which contains all the speed of the foot race; a torso
which has no face to prevent us from loving it.
Quoted in the *New York Times*, 10 May 1992.

Yüan Mei 1716–98

Chinese poet who was a magistrate for six years before
retiring to live off his writings. Unorthodox and
hedonistic, he also championed women poets.

12 If I can rejoice for a moment,
Death at an early age would still be a long life.
c.746 Collected in *A Book of Chinese Verse* (translated by N L
Smith and R H Kotewall).

Zangwill, Israel 1864–1926

English writer and leading Zionist, known for his novels on Jewish themes including *Children of the Ghetto* (1892) and *Ghetto Tragedies* (1894). Other works include the early collections of witty tales *The Bachelors' Club* (1891) and *The Old Maids' Club* (1892), and the plays *The Melting Pot* (1908) and *We Moderns* (1925).

13 America is God's Crucible, the great Melting Pot where all the races of Europe are melting and re-forming… God is making the American.

1908 *The Melting Pot.*

Zatopek, Emil 1922–

Czech athlete and middle-distance runner. He won the gold medal for the 10,000 metres at the 1948 Olympics in London and subsequently broke 13 world records as well as gold medals in the 10,000 metres and 5,000 metres events at the Helsinki Olympics in 1952.

14 An athlete cannot run with money in his pockets. He must run with hope in his heart and dreams in his head.

Quoted by Christopher Brasher in *The Observer*, 12 Sep 1982.

15 You can't climb up to the second floor without a ladder. When you set your aim too high and don't fulfil it, then your enthusiasm turns to bitterness. Try for a goal that's reasonable, and then gradually raise it. That's the only way to get to the top.

Quoted in Colin Jarman *The Guinness Dictionary of Sports Quotations* (1990).

Zeldin, Theodore

Historian and writer

16 Brilliant lecturers shouldn't be wasted in lecture rooms: they should appear on TV. We need black market universities, in which people just help each other, and which don't leave out the poor.

1995 Quoted in Christina Hardyment 'Zeldin and the art of human relationships', in *Oxford Today*, vol.7, no.2, Hilary Issue.

Zel'dovich, Yakov 1914–87

Russian astrophysicist.

17 Without publicity there is no prosperity.

Quoted by Tony Rothman in *Bostonia*, summer 1993, p.58.

Zhang, Jie 1937–

Chinese writer whose first short story appeared in 1978 and whose writing often sets romantic themes in the contemporary Chinese world of rapid modernization.

18 When we reach communism, will there still be cases of marriage without love?

1979 'Love Must Not Be Forgotten', in *Seven Contemporary Women Writers* (1982).

19 To live single is not such a fearful disaster. I believe it may be a sign of a step forward in culture, education and the quality of life.

1979 'Love Must Not Be Forgotten', in *Seven Contemporary Women Writers* (1982).

Zhao, Zhenkai pen name *Beo Dao* 1949–

Chinese writer who has written poetry and fiction and was associated with China's Democracy Movement. He is currently living in Norway. The use of pen names dates back to the Cultural Revolution when secrecy was often essential.

20 They say the ice age ended years ago. Why are there icicles everywhere?

c.1989 'Answer', collected in Donald Finkel *A Splintered Mirror* (1991).

21 Freedom is only the distance between the hunter and his prey.

c.1989 'Answer', collected in Donald Finkel *A Splintered Mirror* (1991).

Zhivkov, Todor 1911–98

Bulgarian statesman, part of the Communist coup d'état of 1944. Prime Minister from 1962 and Chairman of the Council of State from 1971, he was effectively President of the Republic. Conservative and unquestioningly loyal to the USSR, he was ousted in 1989 and expelled from the Party, charged with nepotism, corruption and abuse of power.

22 If I had to do it over again, I would not even be a communist. And if Lenin were alive today, he would say the same thing.

1990 In the *Sunday Times*, 9 Dec.

Zhou Enlai or *Chou En-Lai* 1898–1975

Chinese Communist Party leader, Prime Minister of the People's Republic from its creation in 1949 until his death. Under Mao Zedong he became the Party's chief negotiator and diplomat, and vastly increased China's international influence. In the Cultural Revolution (1966–76), he worked to preserve national unity.

23 For us, it is all right if the talks succeed; and it is all right if they fail.

1971 On President Nixon's visit, 5 Oct.

Zia Ul-Haq, Mohammed 1924–88

Pakistani soldier and politician. He led the military coup against Zulfikar Ali Bhutto (1977), becoming President a year later. He introduced a new policy of Islamization and freer-market economic programme, finally lifting martial law in 1985. He was killed in an aircrash.

24 Cricket can be a bridge and a glue… Cricket for peace is my mission.

Quoted in Helen Exley *Cricket Quotations* (1992).

Zola, Émile 1840–1902

French novelist, a pioneer of naturalism. His novels include *Thérèse Raquin* (1867) and the great series called *Les Rougon-Macquart*, which depicts all aspects of society under the Second Empire. After impeaching the military authorities over the Dreyfus case, Zola was sentenced to imprisonment (1898), but escaped for a year to England, and was welcomed back as a hero. He died in Paris, accidentally suffocated by charcoal fumes.

25 *J'accuse.*

I accuse.

1898 Title of open letter to the President of France regarding the Dreyfus case.

26 A dead reign…a strange epoch of folly and shame.

On the France of the Second Empire. Quoted in Joanna Richardson *La Vie Parisienne* (1971), p.276.

Zolotow, Maurice

27 There is no more offensive act of theatrical rudeness than coming late to a performance.

1958 In *Theater Arts*, Feb.

Zuckerman, Solly Zuckerman, Baron 1904–84

South-African born English scientist, zoologist and educator, the author of several studies of primate behavior.

28 Science creates the future without knowing what the future will be. If scientists knew tomorrow's discovery they would make it.

1964 In the *Daily Mirror*.

Zwerin, Mike 1930–

US writer and musician. He plays trombone, and has written extensively on jazz.

29 Jazz musicians have some outlaw in them somewhere if they are serious about this music… There is no valid motivation for it other than love—outlaw motivation in a profit-motivated society.

1985 *La Tristesse de Saint Louis: Swing Under the Nazis*, ch.4.

Index

Aaron A. shall bear the judgement   BIBLE 107:70
  rod of A.   BIBLE 107:83
abandon a. established stereotypes   GORB 435:59
  A. all hope   DANTE 305:68
  A. yourself to Nature's truths   RABE 799:93
  don't a. it even now   KAFKA 540:85
  want her to a. herself   LACL 574:64
  with a. or not at all   VANH 1039:4
abandoned What God a.   HOUS 496:78
  What is not a.   SCHI 847:67
abandonment organized a.   MILL 677:7
abase humbly a. yourselves   PARN 756:40
Abba A., Father   BIBLE 149:27
ABC Learn the A. of science   PAVL 761:19
abdicate Better to a.   FULL 410:44
abducted A. by a French Marquis!   GRAH 437:89
Abe converting A. into a...saint   MENC 670:88
abecedary characters...form the a.   DOMI 335:56
abed in England now a.   SHAK 882:5
Abednego Meshach, and A.   BIBLE 129:46
Abel Where is A. thy brother?   BIBLE 104:5
Aberdour Half-owre, half-owre to A.   BALL 67:50
Aberfeldey birks o' A.   BURNS 210:90
aberration not a temporary a.   JAMES 516:9
aberrations nineteenth-century a.   SMALL 943:61
abhor Age, I do a. thee   SHAK 887:40
abhorrent The more a. a news item   FOWL 400:69
  war a. to all real women   FOWL 399:66
abhors two things it a. most   HAZL 463:1
abide A. with me   LYTE 621:67
  Shall I a.   SHAK 906:95
abiding there is none a.   BIBLE 112:86
abilities a. of brain surgeon   BRES 187:36
  born with instincts and a.   BALZ 69:83
  people according to their a.   MAIN 640:96
  uncommon a.   BAGE 62:66
ability a. nor interest   MORE 706:42
  a. to examine systematically   MARC 650:50
  a. to express them   KRAUS 569:88
  a. to get a good night's sleep   WILS 1085:39
  a. to get to the verge   DULL 354:25
  a. to think in quotations   DRAB 344:22
  each according to his a.   MARX 661:24
  eliminate his a. to communicate   SCHW 851:27
  exults in his physical a.   POE 775:42
  famous without a.   SHAW 920:15
  lost your a.   GONC 434:52
abjure a. all roofs   SHAK 902:14
ablaze set the world a.   GILB 424:76
able-bodied every a.-b. man   DORA 340:38
abnormal if everybody is a.   HUTC 506:43
  nothing a. about...homosexuality   PROU 793:93
abnormality riveted by Jewish a.   ROTH 826:20
abode come to your happy a.   LAUD 583:40
  Divides a. with me   DICK 328:16
  live in a numble a.   DICK 324:7
abodes aiming at the blest a.   POPE 780:38
  Prudence...in dark a.   WORD 1100:91
abolished state is not 'a.'   ENGE 378:88
abolition a. of all classes   MARX 661:27
  a. of control   TOLK 1022:90
  a. of poverty   HOOV 490:58
  A. of private property   MARX 660:13
  a. of the slave trade   PITT 771:71

abominable a. no-man   ANON 28:98
  are altogether become...a.   BOOK 176:64
abomination Electric guitars...a.   SEGO 857:31
  Great desolation of a.   COBB 271:55
abominations A. Of The Earth   BIBLE 158:28
  commit...all a.   BARN 72:26
Abora Singing of Mount A.   COLE 275:17
aboriginal a. and savage singer   CHOC 260:55
  A. writer is a Janus-type   NARO 719:40
Aborigine alcohol to an A.?   NOON 731:23
abortions Misbegotten a.   VAUG 1040:11
about minded what they were a.   STER 968:88
above either a. or below it   GILL 426:8
  Unless a. himself he can   DANI 304:64
Abraham carried...into A.'s bosom   BIBLE 144:7
  God of A.   PASC 758:81
Abram when A. was ninety years old   BIBLE 104:22
abrasive brash and a.   MAHA 638:59
abreast gaps even two can pass a.   FROST 406:72
a-brewing some ill a.-b.   SHAK 874:28
abroad A. is bloody   GEOR 419:89
  A. is so unutterably bloody   MITF 697:98
  a., you almost feel...a statesman   MACM 635:7
  before he goes a.   STER 970:12
  don't hold with a.   CRISP 297:35
  haven't been a. in so long   BENC 89:50
  honest man sent to lie a.   WOTT 1101:97
  lov'd at home, rever'd a.   BURNS 209:66
  No more I will a.   HERB 475:27
  scattereth a.   BIBLE 137:90
  to go a. for ayre   PEPYS 765:75
  walked a. in the shower   THOM 1010:70
  Weather a.   RICH 809:41
  whole business a.   MONT 701:57
  without suspicion tell a.   SPEN 958:19
  would never go a.   SMOL 950:63
Absalom O my son A.   BIBLE 110:51
absence a. is no longer a felt...weight   STEI 967:67
  A. diminishes...passions   LARO 582:28
  A. is to love what wind is to fire   BUSS 215:93
  a. of the real thing   BERG 95:48
  a. seemed my flame to qualify   SHAK 915:88
  cry of A., A., in the heart   RANS 802:35
  dote on his very a.   SHAK 874:19
  every a. which follows it   STER 970:15
  fit of a. of mind   SEEL 857:28
  like a winter hath my a. been   SHAK 914:82
  marked by an a. of crises   PECK 763:41
  presence of a.   BERG 95:48
  shoot me in my a.   BEHAN 84:51
  taks place in your a.   RUSH 829:67
  Through a long a.   WORD 1094:96
  world, which in thy a.   SHAK 906:95
absent a. are always in the wrong   DEST 318:86
  a. from it so long   SCOTT 856:14
  a. one from another   BIBLE 105:37
  From you have I been a.   SHAK 915:83
  If to be a.   LOVE 615:64
  live in you when you are a.   SCEVE 846:57
  love the a.   BEHN 85:74
  think of one's a. love   TROL 1027:72
absent-minded motive of the a.-m.   BELL 88:40
absentee a. boss is best   WINT 1087:65
absenteeism persistent a.   SAMU 840:43
absentees those cruel a.!   EDGE 361:34

absents often say, endear A.   LAMB 576:27
absolute a. rest is death   PASC 757:57
  content so a.   SHAK 899:21
  If a. sovereignty be not necessary   ASTE 43:91
  Reaching no a.   GUNN 448:86
absolutely A. 100 percent   SIMP 940:92
absolutes damn, damn all a.!   LAWR 586:91
absolutism a. moderated   MUNS 714:62
absolve History will a. me   CAST 244:31
  Who shall a. the foulness   SASS 846:41
abstainers burden of...prudent a.   QUINE 797:67
abstinence almost a sin of a.   DRYD 352:83
  praise of his a.   MILT 686:70
  total a. is easier   AUGU 49:13
abstract A. Expressionists   WARH 1053:22
  A. painting...confronts you   POLL 777:65
  contain any a. reasoning   HUME 504:10
  ideological, or the a.   ROTH 826:22
  is the a. spirit   KAND 541:94
  Literature is not an a. science   QUIL 797:60
  pictures known...as Cubist and A.   DAVIS 309:35
  test of an a. picture   BETJ 100:34
  there exists none which is a.   HEIN 467:76
abstraction Art is an a.   GAUG 416:39
  death...like a cold a.   MILL 677:6
  thought moving in...complete a.   WHIT 1071:58
abstracts a. and brief chronicles   SHAK 890:12
abstruseness a. in their language   GOWE 437:82
absurd a. is born of...confrontation   CAMUS 229:47
  A. in form   GOET 431:69
  a. is the fundamental idea   CAMUS 228:45
  a. to regard non-existence   SCHO 849:94
  attacked as a.   JAMES 517:49
  nothing so a. that has not been said   CICE 266:62
  something rather a. about the past   BEER 83:23
  war abhorrent...and a.   FOWL 399:66
absurdist A. plays...in No Man's Land   ADAM 4:7
absurdity A. of being in love   LACL 573:59
  a., only you are pure   VALL 1039:91
  fear of being an a.   FIND 389:67
abundance shall have a.   BIBLE 140:42
  sound of a. of rain   BIBLE 111:65
abundant life more a.   MILL 678:41
abuse a. of metaphors   PALM 752:67
  a. the King   SHAK 910:95
  a.—I thrive on it   DOUG 342:65
  also giving us a.   WEST 1068:90
  Bad language or a.   GILB 423:55
  contempt, a. and wrong   MILT 694:40
  if it is a.   SHER 934:3
  more dangerous is the a.   BURKE 206:3
  only offer a.   GALL 412:94
  Whipping and a.   STOWE 978:87
abuses correction of private a.   PEEL 763:42
abusing old a. of God's patience   SHAK 878:11
abyss a. of time?   SHAK 916:19
  brink of the final a.   MOUN 711:13
  brooding on the vast a.   MILT 687:86
  cradle rocks above an a.   NABO 716:95
  facing a deep a.   HUSS 505:35
  mother's heart is an a.   BALZ 69:79
  plunge into a bottomless a.   SUN 982:34
  riding into the bottomless a.   WALEY 1049:51
  rope over the a.   NIET 728:77
  secrets of th' a. to spy   GRAY 443:90

action (*contd.*)
months of a. worse than inactivity — BYRON 221:9
moves great masses of men to a. — BOUL 181:42
Neither a. nor style — ACHE 3:37
Never confuse movement with a. — HEMI 471:46
No unchaste a. — SHAK 902:99
parents…snap into a. — ALLEN 14:44
precondition to meaningful a. — BART 74:74
representation of an a. — ARIS 34:29
right a. is freedom — ELIOT 372:63
sworn to a. — SASS 845:25
taking…a. to stop small ones — EDEN 360:22
than a single lovely a. — LOWE 616:86
That a. is best — HUTC 506:42
Thought is the child of A. — DISR 332:71
true men of a. — AUDEN 48:92
truth in a. — DISR 333:97
vice sometimes by a. dignified — SHAK 869:96
victim and slave of his a. — EMER 377:60
wheeled into a. — STEV 972:74
Youth, beauty, graceful a. — DRYD 349:25
actionable only a. one we can call — SALI 839:30
actions a. and counsels — LEST 599:13
a. are questions — LECA 592:95
a. are right in proportion — MILL 675:71
a. of two bodies — NEWT 725:38
A. receive their tincture — DEFOE 312:79
advantage…in practical a. — DRAKE 345:28
conscious of their a. — SPIN 960:49
consequences of certain a. — KISS 565:30
goal of our a. — MORE 707:54
Great a. are not…true sons — BUTL 216:11
honour and good a. — BACON 58:2
important legislative a. — JEVO 521:23
invades all gestures and a. — PIGL 769:40
man's a. critical a. — ELIOT 365:7
Men's a. are too strong — EMER 377:60
my a. are my Ministers' — CHAR 253:86
poor centre of a man's a. — BACON 58:90
practical a. we undertake — MILLS 680:65
Strong reasons make strangè a. — SHAK 872:70
tend to justify our a. — MACN 636:33
active a. and creative world — SPEN 957:90
a. child do deeds of youth — SHAK 913:60
resignation is a. — FITZ 391:22
take an a. part — JOHN 522:31
activities consequences of their a. — HOBS 483:45
human a. which are truly cumulative — SART 843:5
activity a. of soul exhibiting excellence — ARIS 34:26
a. of the very highest — RUSS 832:21
Imagination…into a separate a. — DUDEK 353:18
life was one round of a. — LEAC 589:39
moral a. which disentangles — POE 775:42
No physical a. is so vain — MAIL 640:88
one exclusive sphere of a. — MARX 660:10
untidy a. continues — BISH 164:31
actor a great a. or a household word? — OLIV 738:27
a. everywhere but upon the stage — CHES 257:84
a. has a natural animosity — BROO 193:43
a. in his heart believes — WELL 1063:5
a. is a kind of guy — BRAN 185:10
as evidently an a. — WALP 1051:85
better the a. the more stupid — CAPO 231:90
decent a. waiting for a chance — FLYNN 395:81
decision to become an a. — MACK 632:53
every a. in Hollywood — GIEL 423:49
Every writer is a frustrated a. — STER 968:85
face of a moving-picture a. — MENC 670:90
For an a., it is…essential — MORL 708:73
great a….walking down the street — COPL 288:56
greatest vice in an a. — HAZL 463:96
If an a. reads it out — SALI 838:24
Like a dull a. — SHAK 911:15
main problem of the a. — OLIV 738:32

actor (*contd.*)
never was an a. — MATU 664:83
sweetheart ran away with an a. — WINC 1086:58
actors a. got in front of it — WOOL 1094:93
A. are cattle — HITC 482:27
a. or spectators? — SHEL 931:42
A. who have tried to play Churchill
— MANC 644:65
Authors are a. — STEV 972:63
best a. in the world — SHAK 890:9
come across a lot with a. — GRANT 438:3
Natural politicians are skilled a. — MARA 649:37
pick out a. by — WILD 1080:36
says that a. are cattle? — WINN 1087:61
troups of a. slaughtered — STOP 978:76
actress a. in motion pictures — DAVIS 308:24
aim of any a. — DAVIS 308:25
For an a. to be a success — BARR 73:56
Next worse to an a. — CARY 243:20
schooling any a. needs — GING 427:21
actresses bosoms of your a. — JOHN 525:87
acts all your a. are queens — SHAK 912:31
comedy in one hundred different a. — LAFO 575:96
five a. of Shakespeare's tragedy — FIELD 387:40
how their a. are defined — SZASZ 989:67
little, nameless, unremembered a. — WORD 1094:97
put our a. together — THOM 1014:38
the order of the a. — PAST 759:83
With such a. fill a pen — DRAY 345:36
acute so a., so ignominious — SHAW 921:27
AD what A. is elsewhere — TWAIN 1032:76
adage homely a. that runs — ROOS 822:45
poor cat i'th' a.? — SHAK 908:33
Adam A. and Eve were dispossessed — BOUL 181:45
A. and Eve were turned out — MUGG 712:22
A. and his wife hid themselves — BIBLE 103:95
A. ate the apple — HUGH 500:42
A. cannot be excused — LANY 580:78
A. from his fair spouse — MILT 690:64
A. knew Eve — BIBLE 104:4
A. like the Lord's First Word — FARJ 383:63
A.'s recollection of his fall — BYRON 222:34
A. was a gardener — KIPL 565:15
A. was a gardener — SHAK 861:12
A. was not Adamant! — HOOD 489:44
as in A. all die — BIBLE 151:67
deep sleep to fall on A. — BIBLE 103:92
Eve made A. — MARG 650:53
every maker since A. — WALC 1048:40
father A. sat — KIPL 561:40
Giving A. what she held — LANY 579:77
hold up A.'s profession — SHAK 893:73
old A. in this Child — BOOK 175:34
seeing what A. had seen — HUXL 507:83
son of A. and of Eve — PRIOR 790:49
state of innocency A. fell — SHAK 876:64
the gardener A. — TENN 995:70
thought he was A. — TWAIN 1033:82
When A. delved and Eve span — BALL 65:27
Why, ever since A. — MELV 668:48
adamant Adam was not A.! — HOOD 489:44
adamantine a. chains and penal fire — MILT 687:88
bar thine a. doors — BLAKE 165:60
adaptability life-efficency and a. — MUMF 713:49
add whatever we a. — JUANA 539:65
addage believed in the old a. — LOOS 613:29
adder a. better than the eel — SHAK 864:87
brings forth the a. — SHAK 883:26
deaf a. that stoppeth her ears — BOOK 177:78
toad or a. to catch — MUIR 712:29
addicted most a. to the belief — JAMES 516:12
wholly a. themselves to her — JONS 536:19
addiction a. of political groups — GALB 411:75
It is an a. — UPDI 1037:71

addiction (*contd.*)
prisoners of a. — ILLI 511:34
rape, sodomy and drug a. — COOK 286:27
terminal point of a. — AUDEN 49:1
Addington Pitt is to A. — CANN 230:69
addition any a. to knowledge — DONNE 339:31
address no small degree of a. — SHER 933:1
Nothing suceeds like an a. — LEBO 591:80
Adenauer dear old Konrad A. — JAY 519:72
adequate a. to take care of everybody
— FULL 410:41
Six inches is perfectly a. — SPARK 955:53
adherents worst advertisement…a. — ORWE 742:97
adhesion Out of association grows a. — BRON 191:3
adieu A., a.! my native shore — BYRON 219:69
A., Farewell — JAME 515:2
A. for evermore — BURNS 213:49
A. tristesse — ELUA 376:23
English seem to bid a. — SMITH 949:42
kiss thy hand to bid a. — STER 970:15
adjectives fatigue of a. — BROY 201:5
more suspicious of a. — SAND 841:73
writes without a. — POUND 787:96
adjoining hold down the a. — BELL 88:22
adjudications body of a. — FRYE 408:20
adjusted happier and more well a. — FALU 382:57
so well a. — JARR 518:59
well a. members of society — CALL 226:99
adjustments clear-eyed a. — DAY 310:47
Adlai Madly for A. — ANON 26:57
Adlestrop I remember A. — THOM 1012:99
ad-libbing a.-l.,synthesizing — MARA 649:37
administer a. is to govern — MIRA 696:70
hated by those who a. it — GOLD 432:94
administered Whate'er is best a. — POPE 781:46
administration a. must be entrusted — SUN 982:39
a. of slavery — STOWE 978:84
affairs of internal a. — NICH 726:50
choice…in the field of a. — WEBER 1059:22
criticism of a. — BAGE 61:52
current principles of a. — SIMON 939:80
departments of the central a. — MILL 675:67
government and a. — STEE 964:16
life of this A. — KENN 550:63
low heels in the a. — SWIFT 984:83
purpose of forming an a. — PALM 752:73
administrations differences of a. — BIBLE 150:61
admirable how express and a. — SHAK 890:4
admiral An a. red — SITW 940:2
it is good to kill an a. — VOLT 1046:4
to kill an a. from time to time — VOLT 1046:1
admiralty price of a. — KIPL 562:51
admiration a. of each other's play — BARR 73:52
a. of one man — SCOTT 852:41
ever-increasing a. and awe — KANT 542:7
near to a. — JOHN 531:10
to attract a. — MAIL 640:88
top of a. — SHAK 917:31
admire a….don't…understand — ROOS 821:30
cannot possibly a. them — WILDE 1076:55
I a. him — TWAIN 1034:5
more things to a. in people — CAMUS 229:52
Not to a., is all the art — POPE 782:86
Women…a., …not understand — CONG 280:15
admired a. but never knew — FENT 385:2
a. by an American — HEPB 473:76
a. through being misunderstood — COCT 272:63
admirer own most loving a. — WILS 1084:20
admires a. all kinds of things — BEER 84:43
adolescence A. is the only time — PROU 793:90
petrified a. — BEVAN 101:67
Theory of Permanent A. — CONN 283:67
to be a poet. A. is enough — CIAR 266:52
adolescent a….tries to open it — MISH 696:77

adolescence (contd.)
sensibility of a male a. — AUDEN 49:3
Adonais A.—he is dead! — SHEL 930:34
Adonis eyes Of proud A. — MARL 654:24
adopt a. me and sivilize me — TWAIN 1033:94
adoption and their a. tried — SHAK 888:63
Spirit of a. — BIBLE 149:27
adoration Breathless with a. — WORD 1097:40
For A. seasons change — SMART 944:68
adore youth, I do a. thee — SHAK 887:40
adorings soft a. from their loves — KEATS 546:87
adroit same a. and joyless race — WAUGH 1057:89
Adsum quickly said 'A.!' — THAC 1007:99
adult a. American Negro female — ANGE 19:20
a. slave — GREER 445:41
not quite the occupation of an a. — OLIV 738:28
adulteries all the a. of art — JONS 535:89
adulterous it would be a. — BENC 89:51
adultery A. introduces some energy — PROU 793:99
Do not a. commit — CLOU 271:48
first breath of a. — UPDI 1036:53
have committed a. in my heart — CART 242:3
hazards…alcohol and a. — CRIT 297:43
Liberty, Equality, A. — BELL 88:30
like a. or gluttony — MAUG 664:87
men call gallantry, and gods a. — BYRON 222:28
rather be taken in a. — HUXL 506:47
Sara could commit a. — CARY 243:19
Thou shalt not commit a. — BIBLE 106:68
Thou shalt not commit a. — BIBLE 134:40
What was thy cause? A.? — SHAK 903:34
adulthood If this was a. — ALTH 15:59
adulthoods a. are reaping — ELLI 375:14
adults a. one's children will become — WALK 1049:53
A. never understand anything — SAIN 836:83
A. talk about being happy — WINT 1087:66
between consenting a. — VIDAL 1044:57
Children…are already a. — LABR 573:52
distinction between children and a. — BART 74:70
advance if it does not a. — GIBB 421:25
If I a., follow me — MUSS 716:84
If there is technological a. — HARR 458:25
retreat into a. — ROOS 821:36
somewhat to a. — POPE 782:85
advanced a. in the way — JONS 536:19
advances little a. in knowledge — PROU 793:94
advantage a. of doing one's praising — BUTL 217:36
a. of not being free — SNOW 951:77
a. of time and place — DRAKE 345:22
a. over their neighbours — SMITH 945:88
a. that no one would — KENN 553:5
Baseball has the great a. — SHAW 925:34
essential a. for a poet — ELIOT 370:16
great a. of a hotel — SHAW 920:12
let not a. slip — SHAK 864:97
Many girls have not the a. — FLEM 394:61
Men have every a. — AUST 52:69
most naturally gain the a. — POTT 785:46
rich a. of good exercise? — SHAK 872:72
take a. of that — SHAW 920:98
advantages a. of Ireland — SAKI 838:11
a.…from being a batchelor — WODE 1089:91
Women are…debarred those a. — ASTE 43:89
advent Hark to the A. voice! — OAKL 733:52
adventure a. hard With peril — MILT 693:16
a. is only an inconvenience — CHES 258:11
a. of the spirit — WHIT 1071:56
But the a. — HEDIN 466:61
death…the most beautiful a. — FROH 406:69
pass out into a. — FORS 398:30
To die will be an awfully big a. — BARR 73:45
verse be a glorious a. — VERL 1042:39
adventurer by temperament…an a. — FREUD 404:40
adventurers two kinds of a. — HEAT 465:46

adventures critic…recognizes the a. — FRAN 400:80
large spiritual a. — DAVI 308:17
murderous and otherwise sinful a. — WEST 1068:88
adverbs glad you like a. — JAMES 516:30
adversaries a. claim that — JAMES 517:49
determination to our a. — KENN 551:82
souls of fearful a. — SHAK 862:46
adversary mine a. had written — BIBLE 113:14
sallies out and sees her a. — MILT 685:63
your a. the devil — BIBLE 156:84
adversity a. doth best discover virtue — BACON 56:52
a. is not without comforts — BACON 56:51
A. is sometimes hard — CARL 236:92
a. is the blessing — BACON 56:50
A. stretcheth our days — BROW 196:97
are the uses of a. — SHAK 885:75
brother is born for a. — BIBLE 121:86
faint in the day of a. — BIBLE 121:97
tested by a. — CART 242:4
virtue of a. — BACON 56:49
advertisement a. writer — SAYE 846:51
patent medicine a. — JERO 521:6
worst a. for Socialism — ORWE 742:97
advertisements ideals…by its a. — DOUG 342:62
advertisers become a nation of a. — PUNCH 795:24
advertising a. business — QUEN 797:54
A.…described as a science — LEAC 589:43
a. we deserve — SAYE 846:52
constant flow of fraudulent a. — CHAN 250:42
duty of the a. agent to conceal — OGIL 736:3
right kind of a. — TWAIN 1033:97
unethical and ethical a. — STEF 965:25
advice a. from my seniors — THOR 1016:80
A. is what we ask for — JONG 534:68
a. on the affairs of the world — FLAU 392:41
A. seldom welcome — CHES 257:5
a. to persons about to marry — PUNCH 795:22
a. to you is not to inquire — WILD 1079:24
aid or a. on any matter — DISR 333:11
buying stocks, not selling a. — AUGU 50:19
give young writers a. — HELL 469:97
given us a. — WEST 1068:90
I never give a. — CHES 257:82
Listen kid, take my a. — BERL 95:64
listen to this a. — TAO 991:97
move on—to new a. — KENN 551:74
my a. is not taken — PITT 771:65
rendering public a. — GALB 412:83
Some a. — GAUG 416:39
strongest possible piece of a. — CURR 301:20
woman seldom asks a. — ADDI 7:24
adviser A newspaper is an a. — TOCQ 1021:80
advisers a. may move — KENN 551:74
advocate a. for the blind, venomous — UPDI 1036:56
a. with the Father — BIBLE 156:89
advocates more potent a. of peace — GEOR 418:83
Aeneas A. Troy's Chieftain — VIRG 1045:81
aeroplanes century of a. — DEBU 311:70
Aeschines When A. spoke — OGIL 736:3
Aeschylean in A. phrase — HARDY 456:99
Aeson A. had (as Poets fain) — HERR 477:52
Aesop A. was writing for the tortoise — BROO 193:36
prettily devised of A. — BACON 59:28
aesthetic a. judgements — STRA 979:97
desire for a. expression — WAUGH 1056:74
enough a. excitement here — BART 74:72
pictures known in a. slang as Cubist — DAVIS 309:35
aestheticism first was a. — HUGH 500:34
aesthetics not a. but ethics — ROGE 820:5
Aetolian Europe to the A. shore — ARNO 38:3
afar and from a. — PAST 759:84
Faintly, faintlier a. — FREE 404:36
affable irascible to the a. — MACD 628:93
more a. than rumour would have it — DAVIS 308:24

affair a. between Margot Asquith — PARK 753:92
an a. with the moon — STER 970:22
And go to ev'ry swell a. — PORT 784:35
beginning of a novelistic a. — MANN 646:87
great a. is to move — STEV 973:96
he was a foreign a. — REST 807:18
squalid a. — HAIL 451:13
affairs advice on the a. of the world — FLAU 392:41
a. of men rest still uncertain — SHAK 884:64
a. of others — BEAU 79:61
a. of the nation — AMERY 16:69
a. which concern them — VALE 1038:21
conduct our a. — KENN 551:79
foreign a. — JOHN 524:58
interest in all public a. — MORI 708:68
knew a lot about foreign a. — REST 807:18
mind little their own a. — MONT 700:53
mind their own a. — HOUS 496:73
mischief in…ordinary everyday a. — CHUR 262:7
nature of…human a. — POWE 788:35
remembrance of political a. — MACA 623:5
Secrecy…in the a. of State — RICH 810:67
tide in the a. of men — SHAK 884:60
time in which our a. prosper — BIER 161:84
turned to their a. — FROST 406:20
write of your love a. — YEATS 1104:55
affect having it a. his mind — HOOV 490:68
affectation so used to a. — ETHE 380:19
too much…for ornament is a. — BACON 59:21
virtue is your greatest a. — WYCH 1103:35
affectations a. rise up in his heart — DIDE 330:42
affected a., sapless, soulless — RUSK 831:12
affection A. beaming in one eye — DICK 322:71
A. is a coal — SHAK 864:91
begin our public a. in our families — BURKE 208:40
in respect and a. — SAND 841:70
judgement is…subject to a. — JOHN 531:10
man's a. — GILB 424:61
rear of your a. — SHAK 888:60
Rearrange a 'Wife's' a.! — DICK 328:18
Set your a. on things above — BIBLE 153:20
sheer kindness and a. — TROL 1027:73
spaniel-like a. — WOLL 1091:37
substitute for a. — RUSS 832:25
what unrequited a. is — DICK 323:97
affectionate a person can be truly a. — PREV 789:2
affections history of the a. — IRVI 513:64
insinuate ourselves into men's a. — CAVE 246:73
living a. — STOWE 978:84
not masters of our own a. — ETHE 380:17
strain on the a. — ELIOT 366:43
affirmation a. of…colonial elites — ILLI 511:32
separates a. from negation — THUR 1019:47
affirmations a. of the soul — EMER 377:53
afflict mine own a. me — JONS 535:90
afflicted a. by the thought — GALS 413:4
affliction all a. taught a lover — POPE 779:10
in time of a. — PASC 758:72
Remembering mine a. — BIBLE 128:31
some a. or defect — BEER 83:39
suffer from the wrong a. — NASH 719:48
afflictions mortals their a. spell — PHIL 768:21
affluence fact of a. is indisputable — KRIS 569:95
gilded chains and sordid a. — PITT 771:68
affluent a. country — GALB 412:82
In the a. society — GALB 411:76
afford a. all kinds — GALB 412:82
a. to be good to her — SHAW 920:7
not everyone can a. them — RACI 799:97
that you can't already a.? — TOWNE 1024:10
unless you can a. it — TROL 1028:90
affront quick to take a. — MACD 627:80
Afghanistan A. was 1910 — THER 1009:44
hill villages of A. — GLAD 429:52

Afghanistan (*contd.*)		**age** (*contd.*)	
left on A.'s plains	KIPL 560:*33*	a. has a keyhole	MACC 625:*49*
afloat A. We move: Delicious!	CLOU 270:*33*	A., I do abhor thee	SHAK 887:*40*
afraid a. of getting married	PLATH 773:*88*	a. in her embraces passed	ROCH 817:*64*
a. of losing your moral sense	STEIN 965:*31*	a. is as a lusty winter	SHAK 885:*82*
a. of something	KIPL 562:*69*	A. is deformed	BAST 76:*8*
a. of the present	GREY 446:*58*	a. is dull and mean	WHIT 1074:*6*
a., reading the passage now	FENT 385:*2*	a….is forgiven nothing	SHAW 922:*62*
a. to ask herself the silent question	FRIE 405:*49*	A. is our reconciliation	LOWE 617:*11*
a. to strike	POPE 781:*65*	A. known by marks	DICK 325:*40*
Almost a. to know itself	SHAK 909:*73*	a. of chivalry is past	DISR 332:*74*
be a. and…forget it forever	FAUL 383:*77*	a. of prudence	ELIOT 369:*96*
Be not a. nor dismayed	BIBLE 112:*90*	a. of right and opportunity	WILS 1086:*44*
be not a.	BIBLE 108:*8*	a….seems to have quickened	CHEE 255:*48*
do not be a. of marriage	SOPH 953:*22*	a. shall not weary them	BINY 162:*7*
general public…are a.	RAY 803:*46*	a. strikes me as suspect	KLEE 566:*46*
man…neither tarnished nor a.	CHAN 250:*33*	a., that believes	MILL 679:*49*
never to be a.	KAVA 543:*26*	a. to come would say	SHAK 912:*47*
not a. of God, a. of me	POPE 782:*89*	a. to quit their clogs	MILT 686:*76*
not so much a. of death	BROW 195:*83*	a. to write an autobiography	WAUGH 1058:*7*
See all nor be a.!	BROW 199:*75*	an a. like this	YEATS 1105:*67*
to be a. would be to diminish	RENO 806:*5*	Another a. shall see the golden ear	POPE 779:*23*
When we're a.	SONT 953:*9*	antagonistic to the Victorian a.	WILS 1084:*23*
Who's a. of Virginia Woolf?	ALBEE 11:*85*	Anyone happy in this a.	FULL 410:*44*
will not be a.	SCOT 856:*20*	astonishing any choose old a.	BAIN 62:*75*
Africa A. and the English tongue	WALC 1048:*31*	At the a. of 14	WILL 1082:*72*
Black A. does not distinguish	SENG 858:*51*	at your a., it is right?	CARR 238:*24*
all A. and her prodigies	BROW 195:*76*	Be comfort to my a.	SHAK 885:*81*
map of A. lies in Europe	BISM 164:*43*	before reaching the a. of reason	SADE 835:*64*
more familiar with A.	ORTON 742:*85*	beggary, or decrepit a.!	MILT 694:*40*
sands of A.	JOHN 527:*23*	Brought up in an a. when	HUXL 506:*59*
Till China and A. meet	AUDEN 47:*60*	buried in a good old a.	BIBLE 104:*20*
West A. today	KING 559:*6*	carefulness bringeth a.	BIBLE 132:*10*
What is A. to me	CULL 299:*68*	cart at the a. of three	LEE 593:*16*
What is A. to me?	CULL 299:*69*	characterise this a. of ours	CARL 234:*37*
Where A.'s sunny fountains	HEBER 466:*58*	characterisitics of the present a.	DISR 333:*5*
white man in A.	LESS 598:*96*	common at your a.	BELL 86:*97*
African A. music	GILL 426:*12*	complain of the a. we live in	BURKE 206:*99*
A. national consciousness	MACM 635:*8*	Death at an early a.	YUAN 1108:*12*
As Irish as Black Americans are A.	GELD 417:*66*	dress acording to your a.	DISR 334:*26*
struggle of the A. people	MAND 644:*68*	dresses, in every a. and country	LIN 604:*96*
Africans happiest A. in the world	SMITH 947:*6*	drives my green a.	THOM 1010:*51*
Africas I see several A. and one	CESA 248:*3*	essentially a tragic a.	LAWR 586:*95*
afric-maps So geographers, in A.-m.	SWIFT 986:*4*	Every a. has a…universal genius	DRYD 347:*57*
Afro-American replaced the term A.	FEIF 384:*98*	Every city has a sex and a.	BERG 95:*47*
after not too damn much a.	HEMI 470:*27*	every philosopher, in every a.	SPAR 955:*60*
afterlife picture the a.	UPDI 1037:*69*	fetch the a. of gold	MILT 681:*91*
afternoon a. or evening cup of tea	HOLM 486:*3*	first portent of a.	MACM 636:*25*
a. passed quite happily	WODE 1088:*85*	Fitter…for crazy a.	SHAK 861:*97*
ceremony known as a. tea	JAMES 516:*14*	from a. to a.	WORD 1099:*74*
lose the war in an a.	CHUR 263:*2*	girl at an impressionable a.	SPARK 955:*54*
one a. of heat	THOM 1012:*99*	ignorant in spite of their a.	PITT 771:*62*
seemèd always a.	TENN 994:*48*	in equal proportion to a.	HEMI 471:*47*
Summer a.—summer a.	JAMES 517:*31*	In every a.	GIBB 421:*20*
afternoons long a. of tedium	ROET 819:*92*	Irish Census, broken down by A.	MACR 638:*53*
aftersight urge…to a. and foresight	ELIOT 372:*73*	language of the a.	GRAY 441:*49*
afterthought woman a man is	STAN 963:*90*	last my weary a.	MILT 683:*16*
afterwards man…defines himself a.	SART 844:*14*	leave it to…the next a.	BACON 60:*30*
Afton flow gently, sweet A.	BURNS 211:*99*	Let a. approve of youth	BROW 199:*77*
again Here we are a.!	GRIM 447:*65*	love…at your a.	SHAK 892:*54*
against a. everything all the time	KENN 552:*2*	men of the present a.	OVER 747:*93*
argument is a. it	JOHN 530:*93*	more serious…at my a.	SIDN 936:*42*
held a. her…unconventional beauty	SCHL 848:*77*	Most people my a.	STEN 968:*78*
man…up a. Nature	GABOR 411:*64*	moulded…destinies of his a.	NEHRU 722:*94*
Agamemnon before A.'s time	HORA 493:*25*	never mellows with a.	IRVI 513:*63*
Agatha A. has found it on the map		new glass a. has begun	KORN 568:*81*
	WILDE 1076:*59*	nineteenth century was the a.	MACL 635:*97*
turned to Aunt A.	WODE 1089:*89*	no such thing as old a.	WHAR 1068:*6*
age a., ache, penury	SHAK 897:*83*	not catastrophes…that a.	WOOLF 1092:*56*
a. and at a certain a.	MILL 676:*93*	not forgotten my a.	SOUT 954:*30*
a. at least to every part	MARV 658:*73*	not of an a.	JONS 536:*10*
A. cannot wither her	SHAK 905:*71*	nothing…a little a….will not cure	DURA 356:*65*
a. conceived in spatial terms	MIES 674:*51*	now that a. comes	PO 775:*38*
A. from folly	SHAK 905:*64*	Of no a.	COLE 275:*29*

age (*contd.*)	
Old a. is always wakeful	MELV 667:*33*
Old A. may come after you	WHIT 1073:*98*
old plays…disgust this refined a.	EVEL 381:*42*
one fixed point in a changing a.	DOYLE 344:*18*
our present a.	JOHN 522:*31*
Perfection…and confusion…our a.	EINS 363:*69*
perish in torment in every a.	SHAW 925:*25*
poets in an a.	SWIFT 985:*1*
print a woman's a.	CHRI 261:*64*
reached an a. where	MUNRO 714:*57*
Redeem the a. and sex	PHIL 768:*20*
Refuse his a.	DRYD 349:*14*
severest writers of the severest a.	DRYD 348:*79*
some smack of a. in you	SHAK 877:*81*
soon comes a.	SPEN 958:*13*
Soul of the A.!	JONS 535:*8*
Spirit of the A.	HAZL 464:*15*
staff of honour for mine a.	SHAK 862:*36*
tell a woman's a.	GILB 425:*80*
tells one her real a.	WILDE 1077:*69*
The more of a.	HENR 472:*67*
Thirty-five very attractive a.	WILDE 1078:*90*
this a. of disillusionment?	SHIP 935:*22*
this deformed a.	KRAUS 569:*87*
This is old a.	MILT 693:*24*
This is the editorial a.	BENN 92:*5*
Time…pays us but with a.	RALE 800:*16*
Tis well an old a. is out	DRYD 352:*97*
tragedy of the a.	DUBO 353:*7*
treasures of a.	IRVI 513:*62*
trouble with our a.	KRON 570:*2*
Unregarded a. in corners thrown	SHAK 885:*80*
violence and ferocity of our a.	JAMES 516:*9*
wait on wrinkled a.!	SHAK 866:*32*
what man's a. is like	DENH 315:*56*
when a., Disease, or sorrow strike	CLOU 270:*36*
When you've reached my a.	EPST 379:*6*
woes that wait on a.?	BYRON 219:*78*
world's great a. begins anew	SHEL 932:*64*
age-old a.-o. and age-thick	POUND 786:*64*
aged An a. man	YEATS 1106:*79*
feet of the a.	BIBLE 132:*8*
granted to the a. or the young	LAUR 584:*44*
introduced to the A.	DICK 326:*71*
neither do the a. understand	BIBLE 113:*15*
so deliciously a. and sad	SHAW 919:*89*
ageing A….the only available way	AUBER 45:*31*
agency a. in the world	WHIT 1071:*61*
agenda any item on the a.	PARK 755:*33*
agent a. of the largest	HAIG 450:*9*
agents A. do nothing for	TAYL 992:*20*
detest life-insurance a.	LEAC 588:*32*
employed a. to help me	MENC 669:*67*
language…we're its slavish a.	MATH 663:*69*
night's black a.	SHAK 909:*60*
people…would not need a.	CHAN 250:*45*
salon for his a.	BYRON 224:*72*
workers, with responsible a.	LENIN 595:*48*
ages a. and a. hence	FROST 406:*77*
doubt not through the a.	TENN 996:*79*
How many a. hence	SHAK 883:*42*
This is for the a.	PEI 764:*47*
Three poets, in three distant a.	DRYD 351:*58*
Throughout the a.	ALAN 11:*80*
wisest of men in all a.	STER 969:*91*
aggrandisement imperial a.	CHUR 264:*10*
aggravates It a. 'em	LEE 593:*9*
aggravating an a. child	BELL 87:*11*
aggregate a. of all recipes	VALE 1038:*86*
modified a. of external forces	SPEN 955:*66*
aggression female emotions of a.	LESS 598:*5*
menace of a.	ASQU 42:*77*
aggressive inherently a.	PALM 752:*71*

aggressor ranged against an a. ATTL 44:8
aggressors a. got away with it SMUTS 950:67
agitators cared for, not by the labor a. BAER 61:48
Agnes St. A.' Eve KEATS 546:85
agnostic appropriate title of 'a.' HUXL 508:97
agnosticism that is all that a. means DARR 306:81
agony a. we cannot feel MILL 677:6
  Birth was Hard and bitter a. ELIOT 369:4
  only a., and that has ending BROO 192:24
  soul in a. SHAK 866:28
agree All colours will a. BACON 56:47
  with her would not a. YEATS 1104:56
agreeable a. person...agrees with me DISR 333:15
  a. to strangers SHAW 923:69
  few hours in life more a. JAMES 516:14
  power to be a. SWIFT 985:90
  so charming and a. ETHE 380:16
agreed except they be a. BIBLE 130:57
agreeing A. or disagreeing? AUDEN 49:5
agreement able to reach an a. KENN 552:86
  A. reached by the negotiators SHUL 936:34
  a. signed last night CHAM 249:18
  a. that satisfies us both FRED 403:27
  draft an international a. TRUM 1030:22
  full a. with Government policy HOWE 497:95
  tacit a. to call all...by one name CARL 233:27
  we shall be in full a. DAYAN 310:53
  with hell are we at a. BIBLE 125:76
agreements A. in likes and dislikes CATI 245:51
agrees nobody a. with you STEIN 965:36
agression veto upon any mere a. LEES 593:20
agriculture bullfighting does to a. HUBB 498:7
Ahab ran before A. BIBLE 111:67
ahem poets get a quizzical a. FULL 410:43
Ahithophel A. saw that his counsel BIBLE 110:50
aid a. or advice on any matter DISR 333:11
  Alliteration's artful a. CHUR 262:87
  but for the a. of the book PROU 794:10
  doth come mine a. SCOT 856:23
  in straits a present a. SCOT 856:20
  lend us Thine a.! HEBER 466:56
  Without our a. he did us make SCOT 856:22
Aïda can't judge Egypt by A. FIRB 389:80
AIDS A....a classic own-goal ANNE 20:38
  A., cancer, nuclear war, pollution MAMET 644:56
  A. epidemic WHITE 1069:21
  A. is a major revolution WELD 1062:90
  One has A. GORB 435:60
  stop them catching A. CURR 301:19
ail what can a. thee KEATS 545:72
ailments our a. are the same SWIFT 984:66
aim a. in philosophy WITT 1088:79
  a. of any actress DAVIS 308:25
  a. of every artist FAUL 384:84
  a. of science JAMES 517:39
  a. of the school of business DEMI 315:44
  a....the pursuit of truth DESC 317:77
  grand a. of all science EINS 363:75
  not make thoughts your a. KIPL 564:8
  our being's end and a. POPE 781:49
  rivalry of a. ADAMS 5:78
  set your a. too high ZATO 1109:15
  strikes...as an ultimate a. ENGE 378:89
aiming Pride is still a. POPE 780:38
  two things worth a. for HIND 481:13
aims accomplish these a. UNIT 1036:45
  modern life...divided a. ARNO 37:92
  real and...declared a. ORWE 743:19
air a. a solemn stillness holds GRAY 441:62
  a. all our compulsions meet LARK 581:24
  a. becomes uranious LEHR 595:41
  a., earth, or sea MILT 693:30
  a. is all awash with angels WILB 1075:18
  a. is not so full of motes DONNE 339:25

air (*contd.*)
  a. ...kept in its proper place MACA 622:83
  a. moves like a river LEON 597:78
  a. of a man ADDI 7:12
  a. of delightful studies MILT 685:54
  a. of the Enchantd island MERE 671:1
  a. out of God's own presence WILS 1086:44
  a. pollution and...arificial light MATT 664:82
  a. shall note her soft DONNE 336:70
  a. that inhabits you ATWO 45:27
  a. that kills HOUS 495:57
  a. the spirit flies MUIR 712:37
  a. too poor to rob MORG 708:65
  a. which is now thoroughly small ELIOT 369:9
  a. with barbarous dissonance MILT 684:32
  all the untilled a. AUDEN 48:97
  among the crowded a. DICK 327:94
  apocalyptic horsemen in the a. MARC 649:40
  arrow into the a. LONG 611:5
  ashes, strew them in the a. MONT 703:93
  babbling gossip of the a. SHAK 894:6
  beyond it the deep blue a. LARK 581:13
  blue dome of a. SHEL 928:84
  Bounded by the vaprous a. SHEL 927:70
  breath his native a. POPE 779:4
  breath of wild a. MERE 671:16
  breathe in that fine a. TENN 1003:19
  breathing English a. BROO 192:21
  Brightness falls from the a. NASHE 721:83
  caste up in the a. ANON 21:64
  Castles in the a. IBSEN 510:22
  Clear the a.! ELIOT 370:34
  cloud-encircled meteor of the a. SHEL 929:10
  corrupt my a. SHAK 911:11
  Courage is in the a. FROST 407:4
  crisp morning a. VERL 1042:39
  dove descending breaks the a. ELIOT 373:77
  Dust in the a. ELIOT 372:71
  Eating the a. SHAK 877:86
  enmity o'th' a. SHAK 902:14
  feet...in the a. ROOS 821:40
  fire-folk sitting in the a.! HOPK 491:87
  flies through the a. LEYB 603:75
  fog and filthy a. SHAK 906:10
  foolscaps of a. AVIS 53:76
  fresh a. and royalties ASHF 41:67
  From the a., fast up OWENS 748:23
  glittering in the smokeless a. WORD 1097:46
  Gods, that wanton in the a. LOVE 615:62
  high thin a. PIER 769:34
  his happy good-night a. HARDY 457:7
  I eat men like a. PLATH 773:97
  Inebriate of A. DICK 328:96
  instead of the Hawaii a. route ROCK 817:74
  invigorating a. of freedom WOLL 1091:38
  left the vivid a. SPEN 956:72
  meet the Lord in the a. BIBLE 153:25
  mild as yellow a. RANS 802:37
  mouthful of a. YEATS 1105:64
  music in the a. ELGAR 364:97
  natural as the a. we breathe COLE 273:78
  Now a. is hushed COLL 277:44
  poetry on the a. ORWE 744:36
  prevent the a. THOR 1017:5
  pure a. and water REES 805:92
  purged the a. of pestilence SHAK 893:93
  raptures were All a. and fire DRAY 345:39
  redesigned everything but the a. CALD 225:95
  room full of good a. LEAC 589:36
  sails...trouble the a. YEATS 1105:61
  second place of a. and light FRAME 400:77
  sightless couriers of the a. SHAK 908:32
  smote the a. SHAK 917:38
  soft summer a. FOST 399:61

air (*contd.*)
  sound...circles in the a. LEON 597:84
  spells into the spongy a. MILT 683:23
  Stud the a. WILK 1080:41
  such a conscience-stricken a.? HOUS 496:87
  sweetness fell from the a. MACL 634:81
  the a. is calm PAST 759:84
  The a. Nimbly and sweetly SHAK 907:30
  The a. so thick THOM 1015:57
  The pure marble a. MILT 689:43
  Through high still a. SNYD 951:80
  to go abroad for a. PEPYS 765:75
  to the fainting a. SHEL 930:29
  to warm the a. SWIFT 985:86
  too professional a. MACC 625:45
  Trifles light as a. SHAK 899:37
  unhealthy for want of a. DICK 324:20
  vomit forth into the a. MARL 654:21
  was there like food or a. ROCK 817:67
  web of sunny a. BRON 190:91
  what are names but a.? COLE 274:2
  where a. might wash SWIN 987:29
  Wild a., world-mothering a. HOPK 492:97
  With its sweet a. SHAK 916:24
  with my bottom in the a. PIGG 769:39
  without the help of the a. ETHE 380:19
  yelling through the troublous a. COLL 277:49
aircraft a. I loved LIND 605:8
  Loud fluttering a. slope above FULL 410:42
  unsinkable a.-c. carrier MACA 621:72
air force naval and a. f. ROOS 822:44
airplane artist...flown in an a. DAVIS 309:34
airplanes a....do not make...happier DE 311:61
  aphorisms that, like a. NABO 716:93
airport pretty as an a. ADAMS 5:69
airs a. from heaven SHAK 888:71
  killing a. and gases were bricked in DICK 325:42
  Naiad a. have brought me home POE 776:47
  Sound and sweet a. SHAK 917:34
  whistle all the a. GILB 424:63
airt plaidie to the angry a. BURNS 213:50
airts Of a' the a. BURNS 211:98
airy A., fairy Lilian TENN 993:34
  so a. and light a quality SHAK 890:1
aitches nothing to lose but our a. ORWE 742:4
aits among green a. and meadows DICK 324:18
alack A., 'tis he! SHAK 903:32
alacrity kind of a. in sinking SHAK 878:22
  modicum of a. RYLE 834:54
Alan A. like a flowing on FARJ 383:63
alarm spread a. PENI 764:55
alarming what is a. in the doctrine SART 844:12
alarms confused a. of struggle ARNO 36:65
  dwell in the midst of a. COWP 292:38
  marriage its a. LAFO 575:90
alas A., a., how easily a priest SMITH 949:45
  May say A. but cannot help AUDEN 46:55
albatross I shot the A. COLE 273:85
Albert A. married beneath him COWA 291:2
  Prince A....discovered the impotence CANN 230:66
albinos a., bonded in their flick AVIS 53:76
Alcestis A. from the grave MILT 687:82
  A. rises from the shades LAND 578:57
alchemist astrologer and the a. MACA 623:9
alchemy all wealth a. DONNE 337:78
alcohol a. is a...deadening force WEBB 1058:15
  A. is a very necessary article SHAW 923:81
  A. is the prince of liquids BRIL 188:55
  a. made the present enough GEE 417:65
  a. produces a delightful social BENN 91:95
  a. to an Aborigine? NOON 731:22
  discovered that a. was a food WODE 1089:92
  help of opium or a. HERZ 478:73
  Mere a. doesn't thrill me PORT 784:30

alcoholic about stray a. drinks	HOOV 490:61	
a. has been lightly defined	BARA 70:5	
keys…to a confirmed a.	BALL 65:25	
Alcoran Talmud, and the A.	BACON 57:64	
Aldershot burnish'd by A. sun	BETJ 100:35	
ale a.'s the stuff to drink	HOUS 495:63	
bliss in a.	CRAB 293:65	
drink your a.	HOUS 496:71	
fed purely upon a.	FARQ 383:70	
Loveth well good a.	ANON 23:86	
milk and a.	SKEL 942:33	
no more cakes and a.?	SHAK 894:10	
send thee good a.	ANON 23:84	
spicy nut-brown a.	MILT 682:2	
ale-house A.-h. is healthy	BLAKE 167:97	
alembic From an antique a.	DOYLE 344:21	
Aleppo husband's to A. gone	SHAK 906:12	
alert must be on the a.	SPARK 955:52	
Alexander A.'s Ragtime Band	BERL 95:57	
Dost thou think A.	SHAK 893:78	
if I were not A.	ALEX 13:13	
Quhen A. oure kyng	ANON 22:68	
Alexandrian A. lighthouses	GILL 426:2	
Alger succession and Horatio A.	MAMET 644:57	
alibi always has an a.	ELIOT 371:41	
Alice A Town like A.	SHUTE 936:38	
alien a. people clutching their gods	ELIOT 369:4	
a. planet is Earth	BALL 68:62	
democratic principles as a.	AUNG 50:22	
nothing that is human a.	TERE 1005:72	
thou art an a.	AESC 9:60	
alienated a. establishment of human	MARX 660:7	
alienation Without a.…no politics	MILL 677:10	
alienists few professional a.	DOCT 334:39	
alive a. for evermore	BIBLE 157:1	
born into the world a.	GILB 424:75	
created for people a.	HERN 476:44	
half dead and half a.	BETJ 99:25	
he is no longer a.	BENT 93:23	
in Christ shall all be made a.	BIBLE 151:67	
Is that thing a.	BERR 98:8	
it's exhilarating to be a.	RICH 809:48	
many ways…of being a.	DAWK 310:45	
need'st not strive…to keep a.	CLOU 271:47	
not just being a.	MART 657:62	
not life-like; it is a.	CECIL 246:74	
only fault is that I am a.	MAP 649:35	
only mission…to come down a.	HELL 468:81	
Sex…keeps us all a.	EWART 381:44	
was I dead before I was a.	BROW 195:88	
wish they were the only one a.	AUDEN 48:90	
Words are taken a.	CIXO 267:74	
all a. for love	SPEN 958:11	
A. are needed by each	EMER 376:28	
A. for one	DUMAS 354:27	
a. have to go through it	JERO 521:4	
a. is always now	ELIOT 370:30	
a. of that and more	SCHW 851:29	
a. shall be well	JULI 539:69	
a. shall die	SHAK 877:96	
A. the Way with LBJ	HOLT 487:6	
A. things perish	KEMP 549:42	
a. things to a. men	BIBLE 150:53	
America I've given you a.	GINS 428:27	
Christ is a., and in a.	BIBLE 153:21	
feared…by a.!	SIXT 942:31	
Goodbye to A. That	GRAV 439:18	
If it is for a.	SCHO 849:90	
nothing, and yet possessing a.	BIBLE 151:83	
silent question—'Is this a.?'	FRIE 405:49	
That's a. folks!	ISING 513:78	
would that you were a. to me	BROW 199:65	
all-forgiving God who is a.-f.	SMITH 947:3	
all-in-all intellectual A.-i.-a.!	WORD 1095:10	

all right make it a. r.	HAMM 454:59	
all-round wonderful a.-r. man	BEER 84:44	
All-Souls Christ-Church and A.-S.	JOHN 528:53	
Allah A. is great	CLOU 271:43	
allegations scandalous a.	PROF 792:77	
allegiance a. to one Crown	GEOR 419:88	
flag…has not pledged its a.	BALD 64:2	
To what…should they owe a.	BAIN 62:77	
allegorical all the a. paintings	JOHN 532:39	
allegories a. are so much lettuce	GINS 427:23	
curtains of a.	DONNE 339:24	
allegory cordially dislike a.	TOLK 1022:93	
great a.—the world	MELV 668:48	
alley dropped it into the a.	CHAN 251:50	
alley cat zest of the a. c.	MARQ 656:41	
alleys lowest and vilest a. in London	DOYLE 344:5	
not worry about the blind a.	FEYN 387:33	
one of the blind a.	WAUGH 1056:70	
alleyways a. and drug fiends	LIND 605:11	
alliance A.…union of two thieves	BIER 160:67	
steer clear of permanent a.	WASH 1054:44	
allies a. are too frightened	TALL 990:90	
no eternal a.	PALM 752:70	
alligator Been eaten by an a.	NASH 720:57	
alligators A. have the right idea	MACD 629:8	
alliteration A.'s artful aid	CHUR 262:87	
alliterations drone of a.	BROY 201:5	
Allonby Mrs A.	WILDE 1077:65	
allotment capable of digging an a.	DORA 340:38	
allowance make a. for their doubting	KIPL 564:8	
allure If parts a. thee	POPE 781:51	
to a. by denying	TROL 1028:85	
allurement a. of private interest	STEU 970:30	
allurements What a. she used	SIDN 936:45	
alluring little scorn is a.	CONG 281:39	
nothing is more a.	CONG 282:43	
ally a. of the people	DODD 334:42	
help of any a.	GARI 415:24	
Her faithful a.	SITW 941:23	
infamy of betraying an a.	CECIL 247:79	
treacherous desertion of an a.	CHUR 263:98	
almighty A. has placed your hand	CURZ 302:29	
A. hearkens unto him	FRIE 405:57	
A.'s orders to perform	ADDI 6:2	
A. would answer me	BIBLE 113:14	
find out the A. unto perfection?	BIBLE 113:5	
Truth is strong next to the A.	MILT 685:64	
work of an A. hand	ADDI 7:22	
almond cut an a. rod	BRON 190:91	
almonds rod of Aaron…yielded a.	BIBLE 107:83	
almost-instinct a.-i. almost true	LARK 581:5	
alms A. for oblivion	SHAK 896:51	
so give a.	SHAK 912:31	
throw them cheap a.	WEST 1067:87	
when thou doest thine a.	BIBLE 134:47	
aloe a. seemed to ride	MANS 647:7	
alone all a. went she	KING 558:80	
All we ask is to be let a.	DAVIS 309:29	
A. and palely loitering	KEATS 545:72	
A. I did it	SHAK 911:17	
a. in a way no earthling has ever been	COLL 276:40	
a. in the desert	SAIN 836:84	
a. on earth	BYRON 219:78	
A.—The word is life	SASS 845:39	
a. until she dies	THOM 1011:83	
a. when he falleth	BIBLE 123:23	
a. with his laughter	KAFKA 541:89	
and a.; on shore	TENN 994:58	
and live a.	YEATS 1104:57	
Antony…did sit a.	SHAK 905:49	
been, shalt be, art, a.	ARNO 38:4	
But wherefore thou a.?	MILT 690:68	
find himself a.	JOHN 526:2	
Hell is a.	ELIOT 373:84	

alone (*contd.*)		
I am a.	GOET 431:83	
imagination never lets him a.	SHAW 923:69	
least unpleasant…to live a.	BERN 97:85	
lie down a.	HOUS 496:82	
live for years a.	AUDEN 47:63	
loving a. is dull as eating a.	WYCH 1103:44	
may not find myself a.	ROSE 822:55	
mortal millions live a.	ARNO 37:9	
never to be a.	BALL 65:26	
no one exists a.	AUDEN 47:76	
not good that man should be a.	BIBLE 103:91	
not sufficiently a.	VALE 1038:87	
One man a. ain't got	HEMI 471:32	
or a fool a.	WILD 1079:32	
to be let a.	SUMN 981:28	
totally a. with oneself	MODE 698:14	
travels fastest who travels a.	KIPL 560:20	
want to be a.	GARBO 414:16	
when we are a.	GRIS 447:68	
you a. are you?	SHAK 914:77	
You'll never walk a.	HAMM 454:54	
aloof a. in pride of distinction	SAND 841:69	
alp an a. of unforgiveness	PLOM 775:33	
Alph A., the sacred river	COLE 274:12	
alpha A. and Omega	BIBLE 156:98	
alpine streams along the A. height	BYRON 220:94	
Alps A. and their people	RUSK 830:79	
beneath some snow-deep A.	ELIOT 368:73	
crossing the A.	WALP 1051:79	
Alsatians dislike… all dogs, but A.	LEVIN 600:28	
altar a., sword and pen	WORD 1096:38	
broken A.	HERB 474:8	
Ever at Thy glowing a.	CULL 299:71	
on his strange a.	SWIN 988:57	
socks on the a.	NERU 723:9	
altarpieces almost sacres a.	ROSE 823:64	
altar-stairs great world's a.-s.	TENN 999:40	
altars even thine a., O Lord	BIBLE 117:93	
wings display and a. raise	DRYD 348:84	
alteration alters when it a. finds	SHAK 915:89	
alterations a. on the map of Europe	CHUR 263:96	
alternative accept that there is no a.	THAT 1007:13	
a. modes of living	SELF 858:38	
an a. should not be discarded	PECK 763:39	
Life. Consider the a.	MACL 635:99	
alternatives a. that are not their own	BONH 173:86	
choice between two a.	MORAN 706:41	
ends which a. uses	ROBB 813:14	
exhausted all other a.	EBAN 359:7	
ignorance of a.	ANGE 19:17	
always a. has to be somebody else	SMITH 948:39	
we are a. dying	PETR 767:10	
what is a.	VINC 1045:77	
am I a. that I a.	BIBLE 106:57	
I a. what I a.	BIBLE 151:65	
know not where I a.	SHAK 860:90	
Amalek A. prevailed	BIBLE 106:67	
amalgamation out of adhesion a.	BRON 191:3	
amaranth fields of a.	LAND 578:60	
Amarantha A. sweet and fair	LOVE 615:65	
amaranthus a. all his beauty shed	MILT 684:47	
Amaryllis A. in the shade	MILT 684:42	
kind A., the wanton country maid	CAMP 228:37	
amateur a. status	GRAV 440:29	
sign of an a. is too much detail	BURG 206:85	
amateurs disease that afflicts a.	CHES 258:98	
Hell is full of musical a.	SHAW 921:32	
that we are a nation of a.	ROSE 822:54	
a-Maying met here once a.-M.	MILT 682:97	
amazement A. is the thing	REID 806:97	
often met with a.	ANGE 19:20	
Amazon She was an A.	BLAN 168:22	
ambassador a. is an honest man	WOTT 1101:97	

ambassador (contd.)
a. that beds a queen CLEV 269:13
no a. would ever be relieved HEAN 465:42
ambassadors a. for Christ BIBLE 151:81
Diplomatic problems...discussed by a. ACHE 2:22
amber a. to observe the forms POPE 781:63
of A. Snuff-box POPE 779:2
turn those a. locks to grey DRAY 345:34
unzipped fly caught in forever a. COND 279:84
Amberley Lady A. ought to get VICT 1043:50
Ambersons Magnificent A. TARK 991:99
ambiguities Resolve me of all a. MARL 654:13
ambiguity Seven Types of A. EMPS 378:82
ambiguous a....in his opinions MACF 629:16
ambition all that a. ...could effect PITT 772:73
A.'s debt is paid SHAK 883:28
A....desire to be vilified BIER 160:68
A., Distraction, Uglification CARR 238:36
a. enough to be employed LOCKE 609:71
A....great man's madness WEBS 1060:53
a. has been growing steadily DALI 303:44
A. if it feeds at all SONT 952:3
a. is that men should have LAUR 584:47
a. merely to descry SELF 857:37
a. of an old man CHUR 263:93
a. of so airy and light SHAK 890:1
A. should be made of sterner stuff SHAK 884:49
attempt something of a. KUSH 571:22
avarice, lust and a. LEWIS 601:38
brutal in its a. NORR 731:29
Ill-weaved a. SHAK 876:76
in those days a. LAGE 575:98
Let not A. mock GRAY 442:66
lilies of a. DOUG 341:59
meaner things To low a. POPE 780:32
no desire to gratify a. PEEL 763:43
no other a. in the world SHIP 935:21
not without a. SHAK 907:26
stimulate their a. CHRI 261:65
Thoughts tending to a. SHAK 868:70
Vaulting a. SHAK 908:32
What argufies pride and a.? DIBD 319:7
when a. blinds! DRYD 349:18
writer's a. KOES 568:68
ambitions all a. are lawful CONR 285:9
a. faded in its glare LAWR 587:14
books...contain our a. CONR 285:3
deceives with whispering a. ELIOT 368:70
limit to his a. RICH 811:73
not favourable to such a. DISR 333:20
stunt our a. SCHU 851:20
such joy a. finds MILT 690:49
ambitious a. attempts STEV 974:13
a. ...needs to make his fortune LABR 572:46
a. not content CARL 234:35
a....young men THOM 1013:18
as he was a., I slew him SHAK 884:47
most a. of all of them LAGE 575:98
too late to be a. BROW 196:99
Ambrosia back in A. WATE 1055:48
ambrosial Phallic and a. POUND 786:63
ambulance car and a. LEBO 592:88
ambushing A. the audience STOP 978:80
Amelia A. was praying for George THAC 1006:86
amen all the people shall say, A. BIBLE 108:97
a.? Stuck in my throat SHAK 908:19
God help me; a. LUTH 619:44
sound of a great a. PROC 792:76
the catholic a. SMART 944:71
amend a. thy face...a. my life SHAK 876:63
amended Corrected and a. FRAN 402:99
amenities a. that count COOKE 286:32
wilderness to the a. MACD 628:93
amenity Claud's landscape...all is a. CONS 285:18

America aboriginal...singer of A. CHOC 260:55
A. as a black curse MILL 677:21
A. as the paperback version DELI 314:37
A....barbarism to decadence CLEM 269:6
A., bring your own food LEBO 592:89
A. came up with the idea HUGH 500:34
A. cannot be an ostrich WILS 1086:49
A.'s cultural life ROCK 818:78
A. de-Latinized RODO 818:87
A. gets Hollywood JONG 534:70
A.! God shed His grace BATES 76:10
A. had plenty of money BEHR 85:76
A. has defaulted KING 557:78
A. has just passed through BENT 93:31
A. has mitigated poverty WOOL 1092:52
A. has the best-dressed poverty HARR 458:26
A. I'm putting my queer shoulder GINS 428:28
A. I've given you all GINS 428:27
A. is a country of young men EMER 378:71
A. is a hurricane MAIL 639:69
A. is a vast conspiracy UPDI 1037:60
A. is an insane asylum POUND 787:93
A. is God's Crucible ZANG 1109:13
A. is in my view SCHAW 847:61
A. is just ourselves ARNO 39:24
A. is not like a blanket JACK 514:87
A. is now wholly given HAWT 461:79
A. is...rooted in Negro culture ROLL 821:26
A. is up for sale TSON 1031:41
A....large, friendly dog TOYN 1024:17
A.'s leading socialist ECON 359:14
A. makes prodigious mistakes CUMM 300:85
A.! my new-found-land DONNE 336:72
A. no longer lives behind THUR 1020:59
A....only idealistic nation WILS 1086:56
A.'s present need HARD 455:79
A.—rather, the United States FERB 385:7
A. settles in the mould JEFF 519:77
A. the beautiful HUXT 509:8
A., the people are friendly CRISP 297:41
A., thou half-brother BAIL 62:71
A.—your stupidity SNYD 951:86
ancient Spanish historians of A. ECHE 359:13
another person in A. NORTH 732:34
Black A. reveals JORD 536:28
Britain...Greece to A.'s Rome BRIN 188:57
cannot conquer A. PITT 771:69
cannot sell anything in A. DONA 335:57
churning caldron of A. WRIG 1101:8
declared war on A. and Britain HIRO 481:17
deserts of A. JOHN 527:23
destroy sex in A. DOCT 334:39
drill to the tooth of A. CLIN 269:19
dull...life as here in A. MILL 678:36
economic insecurity in A. ELLW 375:20
energy stored up in A. GERS 420:7
England and A. GREN 446:54
England and A. SHAW 926:41
every family in A. JOHN 524:57
every man in A. STEV 973:84
every man...in A. GOLD 434:36
fabric of A. MACC 625:40
future of A. is based MAYH 666:8
gather for A. SAAR 834:55
God bless A. ANON 25:33
heart and mind of A. BARZ 75:97
history of A. ADAMS 5:82
Hoo-doo, which in A. flowered REED 805:89
horses of A. KIPL 562:63
I rejoice that A. has resisted PITT 771:66
If there is poetry in our A. DARIO 305:75
In A. all too few blows MAIL 639:76
In A., any boy STEV 973:90
In A. everything goes ROTH 826:17

America (contd.)
In A. few people will trust MAIL 639:75
In A. journalism SAMP 840:42
in A. the...writer LEWIS 602:53
In A....two classes of travel BENC 89:48
A. spirit of Christian France BOUR 181:47
Intellectually I know that A. LEWIS 602:56
Jazz came to A....in chains WHIT 1072:67
last true cowboy in A. HEAT 466:49
Let's get A. moving again ANON 27:64
Lost in the living rooms of A. MACL 635:1
man born in A. OLSEN 738:34
Marilyn...man's love affair with A. MAIL 639:87
morning again in A. ANON 28:11
next to...god a. CUMM 299:82
New York...cultural centre of A. BELL 88:32
noises of A. CUMM 299:76
nonconformity...rare in A. MACC 625:51
Nothing less...than the whole A. BURKE 206:7
Only in A. KING 557:72
Patriotism...understand in A. COOL 287:39
power and spirit of A. NORR 731:29
remind A. KING 557:79
resists your taxation in A. PITT 771:68
revolution in A. LINK 606:24
sailed...Atlantic and found A. BEHAN 84:58
symbol for A. ATWO 45:22
the blacks in A. OROU 741:79
The mythical A. RABAN 798:76
The youth of A. WILDE 1077:68
think of thee, O A.! WALP 1051:88
true religion of A. MAIL 640:90
typical of life in A. BALD 64:92
United States of A. ROOS 822:44
What A. does best FUEN 409:27
what makes A. what it is STEIN 965:37
willing to grant A. independence GEOR 418:81
witness of A.'s...rite NEW 723:17
American critics are like A. universities ALBEE 11:89
A. girls turn into A. women HAMP 454:64
A. principles, A. policies WILS 1086:50
adult A. Negro female ANGE 19:20
All modern A. literature HEMI 470:29
A. abroad STAP 963:93
A. art...sexless ADAMS 5:82
A. at puberty WAUGH 1057:97
A. Beauty rose ROCK 817:69
A. can look forward to KENN 550:50
A. Express card LODGE 610:80
A. gentlemen are the best LOOS 613:33
A. heiress MACC 625:44
A. history all about men BRAD 183:77
A. history as a great hero MENC 669:70
A. influence...educated them WILDE 1075:31
A. men do not read VIDAL 1044:70
A. names BENET 90:59
A. nation will speak ROOS 822:45
A. Negro problem BALD 64:91
A. people do not want POWE 788:14
A. people don't NIXON 730:17
A. people have voted CLIN 269:16
A. people were like him REST 807:19
A. people GERG 420:99
A. phenomenon WHITE 1069:21
A. politics WHITE 1071:50
A. professors LEWIS 602:50
A. ship, good grub LOND 610:90
A. system HOOV 490:59
A. vice, the democratic MILL 679:47
appear to one A. painter ROSE 822:56
As A. as a...shotgun PARK 755:25
being an A. JAMES 516:10
building...the A. consciousness BUSH 215:84

American (*contd.*)
business of the A. people is business COOL 286:36
Chicago…last of the great A. cities MAIL 639:84
contributions of the A. way MENC 670:87
country A. means white MORR 709:87
expanding horror in A. life MAIL 639:81
exploited by A. capital INNIS 512:52
face of A. literature PORT 784:38
faces of A. women FITZ 391:16
failed promises of A. life GILL 426:3
fairness of the A. people NIXON 730:14
fortress—the A. home SELZ 858:42
free man, an A. JOHN 523:49
genius of A. culture RODR 819:88
hairy A. filth OSBO 746:69
hardly find a typical A. BARN 71:24
If I were an A. PITT 771:70
Liars out of the A. people ROGE 820:11
magic moment in A. history WHITE 1071:49
minds of A. women FRIE 405:49
Miss A. Pie MACL 633:62
most A. artist of all ADLER 8:46
most beautiful prose by any A. BLOOM 170:38
New Deal for the A. people ROOS 821:34
not ashamed of…the A. Dream SHUL 936:37
old-fashioned A. hypocrisy GALL 412:91
one dirty secret in A. life…racism CISN 266:68
performance of the A. economy STEIN 966:51
photos in North A. magazines ONET 740:70
police dog of A. fiction FADI 382:53
propaganda arm of the A. Dream HASK 460:56
protect A. cities SCHL 848:79
reality in A. society MUNCH 714:52
sailed through A. history MENC 670:89
send A. boys JOHN 523:52
separating an A. JOHN 524:68
Some A. writers THUR 1020:56
success happens to an A. writer AMIS 17:89
Success is the A. Dream LEGU 594:29
That's A. HUGH 499:20
the A. establishment TIME 1020:68
To be an A. FIED 387:38
To be an A. FRIE 405:56
to write A. music THOM 1015:61
Versailles of A. corporate culture WOLFE 1091:42
very knowing A. SWIFT 985:98
way that is thoroughly A. PEARY 762:35
Americanism McCarthyism is A. MACC 625:43
Americans All A. believe STEI 966:56
A. are our best friends THOM 1014:41
A. are…the most self-conscious JAMES 516:12
A.…considered Hollywood MAMET 643:52
A. do not rear children JARR 518:63
A. have a kind of resistance TRIL 1026:66
A. have always paid it KENN 551:73
A. have been conditioned UPDI 1037:58
A. is a bore UPDI 1036:52
A. of all nations WHIT 1072:73
A. polite by telling truth BRAD 183:78
A. want to bomb ANON 30:57
believing in you, the A. MATAK 663:66
brave A. all DICK 329:21
drunks and A. MOYN 711:17
good A. die they go to Paris WILDE 1077:67
Good A., when they die APPL 32:1
If A. do not succeed in engineering LARD 580:89
Irish A. are about as Irish GELD 417:66
majority of my fellow A. NIXON 730:10
married to A. WALP 1051:90
To A., English manners JARR 518:60
What makes war interesting for A. DALL 303:50
whether A. are to be freemen WASH 1054:42
which amazes A. GALL 412:94
amethyst ruby and a. eyes BRAS 185:13

amethyst (*contd.*)
silver cross soft a. KEATS 546:92
amiable good, a., or sweet! MILT 692:5
how a. are thy dwellings BOOK 177:85
In Claud's landscape…all is a. CONS 285:18
amiss little disdain is not a. CONG 281:39
ammunition pass the a. FORGY 397:25
political a. runs low STEV 972:74
amnesiacs red a. of autumn PURDY 795:34
amoeba squashed a. THER 1009:43
amor Salud, Dinero, A.…y Tiempo ANON 30:68
amorous As a. of their strokes SHAK 905:68
be a., but chaste BYRON 219:61
excite my a. propensities JOHN 525:87
amorousness a. is rooted in SCHO 849:96
amour beginning of an A.! BEHN 85:70
amphibious a. ill-born mob DEFOE 312:76
Amphitrite A.'s destined halls SHEL 927:70
A. sails through myrtle POPE 779:21
ample A. make this Bed DICK 328:7
amplitude action…of some a. ARIS 34:29
amputate Thank God they had to a.! SASS 845:23
amuse created to a. UPDI 1037:62
amused a. by its presumption THUR 1018:21
instructed and a. ATLAS 44:7
People muth be a. DICK 325:45
We are not a. VICT 1043:55
amusement for the a. of women MONT 701:56
I write for the general a. SCOTT 855:98
very pleasant a. JOHN 532:43
work is less boring than a. BAUD 78:41
amusements less difficult than our a. LOUI 614:50
we have no a. SMITH 949:58
amuses a. the people of England JOHN 527:27
amusing I am generally rather a. BEER 83:25
previously a. human beings COUP 289:85
torture and death…is a. FROU 408:9
Amynta give A. so much freedom BEHN 85:67
anabaptist a.…I am not a member FLEM 394:65
anachronistic a., feudal institution ACHE 2:23
Everything a. is obscene BART 75:85
anaemia a sort of emotional a. POUND 785:53
anagram mild a. DRYD 348:84
analogies a. that map the gateways WILS 1085:25
analogue no a. in space EDDI 360:17
analysis a., all architecture NUTT 732:46
a. of the obvious WHIT 1071:54
in the last a. PLAN 772:84
intelligence and a. LYND 621:65
method of a. TROT 1029:9
analyst a. in…moral activity POE 775:42
analytic skilled in a. BUTL 216:5
analytics Sweet A., 'tis thou MARL 653:8
analyzer I am an a. BECK 81:5
anapaestic rolling a. Curled BROW 196:12
Anarch Thy hand, great A.! POPE 783:11
anarchic been, basically a. LEGU 594:27
anarchist To a real a. poke in the eye CARY 243:21
anarchy A. and competition RUSK 830:92
call it a. HOBB 483:41
Freedom…cure of a. BURKE 207:10
Mere a. is loosed YEATS 1106:77
more and more to a. TOLK 1022:90
anatomize Let them a. Regan SHAK 903:26
anatomy A. is destiny FREUD 404:44
portions of the human a. HELP 469:9
ANC A. is a Government in waiting MAND 644:69
ancestors a. had…nuclear power LAMB 577:45
Bequeathed down from many a. SHAK 901:78
form of our primitive a. MILL 679:58
more favourable…than your a. ADAMS 4:61
most obscure of all classes, our a. CHES 258:7
never look backward to their a. BURKE 207:27
of life than our a. STEV 973:1

ancestors (*contd.*)
princes my a. followed ORAH 741:77
spirits of our a. RED 804:74
vices of his a. FAUL 383:76
wild trick of his a. SHAK 876:71
ancestral A. voices prophesying war! COLE 275:16
ancestry delusion about its a. INGE 511:40
reminds world of its dark a. BETH 99:24
whole female line of a. EDGE 361:38
anchorage hope her a. maintain SMART 944:72
anchored eternally a. MILL 679:52
anchorite saintship of an a. BYRON 219:68
anchors A. on Isabel SHAK 897:75
ancient an a. aspect STEV 971:46
a. and prophetic fame MILT 688:18
A. of Days GRANT 438:5
A. of Days SMITH 950:61
a. past GARC 414:19
A. Person, for whom I ROCH 817:65
a. saying is no heresy SHAK 875:32
a. Spanish historians of America ECHE 359:13
a. writers YEATS 1106:81
came to the A. of days BIBLE 130:50
Europe of the a. parapets RIMB 812:89
Even in a. days TOLK 1023:94
held sway since a. days AESC 9:55
poetry…in a. items DARIO 305:75
saying of an a. philosopher ADDI 7:13
That is the a. secret PRAT 789:23
What Art was to the A. world DISR 332:84
With the a. is wisdom BIBLE 113:7
Anderson John A. my jo BURNS 211:6
androids Do A. Dream DICK 320:10
anecdotage man fell into his a. DISR 333:12
anemones amethyst eyes of a. BRAS 185:13
Aneurin A. and Taliesin, cruel owls BUNT 204:59
Anfield bad times at A. PAIS 751:54
angel an a.'s stare TATE 991:4
a. and a madman THOM 1010:60
a. came in unto her BIBLE 141:73
a. departed from her BIBLE 141:74
a. is like you, Kate SHAK 882:9
A. of Death has been abroad BRIG 188:47
a. of the Lord appeared BIBLE 106:53
a. of the Lord BIBLE 142:17
a. watching an urn TENN 1001:78
a. will be there GUST 449:93
battleground for a dark a. L 595:47
being and as an a. MUIR 713:41
better a. is a man SHAK 915:96
bored of everything, my A. LACL 574:67
By Jupiter, an a. SHAK 916:13
clip an A.'s wings KEATS 546:80
drawing like an a. NEVE 723:14
Drew one a. BROW 199:73
drive an a. from your door BLAKE 166:70
form, so a. fair BRON 190:86
golden hours, on a. wings BURNS 211:1
If an a. were ever LICH 603:81
in action how like an a. SHAK 890:4
in his motion like an a. SHAK 873:99
ineffectual a. ARNO 40:38
is man an ape or an a.? DISR 333:7
it's like an a. SART 844:8
Killing the A. in the House WOOLF 1093:78
Look homeward A. MILT 685:50
Lost A. of a ruined Paradise! SHEL 930:38
madman bum and a. GINS 427:24
Man is neither a. nor beast PASC 758:73
man nor a. can discern MILT 689:44
may not be an a. DUBIN 353:3
ministering a. thou! SCOTT 853:58
O lyric love half a. BROW 200:88
O, speak again, bright a. SHAK 868:86

answer (*contd.*)
on-the-one-hand…a.	BLIN 169:30
only way to a.	TRUM 1029:18
Pilate…would not stay for an an.	BACON 56:40
Puzzle me the right a.	HEAN 465:37
right a. to the wrong question	CHRI 262:77
shortest possible a.	YOUR 1108:10
silver a. rang	BROW 196:14
So what is the a.?	NAUG 721:91
soft a. turneth away wrath	BIBLE 121:78
Speak now, and I will a.	HOUS 495:56
The a. is…to be both	MACH 631:37
uncle Toby would never offer to a.	STER 969:95
what a. should I give?	TENN 997:9
What is the a.?	STEIN 966:47

answered a. best with silence — JONS 534:81
a. generally thus — JULI 539:67
Tell them I came, and no one a. — DELA 314:26

answering don't even remember a. — HAMM 453:46

answers a. ask the right questions — LEVI 600:32
a. to its questions — RUSS 832:17
a. were meant ironically — TRIL 1026:55
firm a. to questions — KUHN 570:14
give my friends the incorrect, absurd a. — ELLI 375:17
learned all the a. — MACL 634:75
looking to other lives for a. — BRAU 185:16
questions, not a. — LECA 592:95
resist easy and preferred a. — BLOOM 169:34
set of ready-made a. — ROBI 815:35
successive a. to questions — PAST 759:86

ant a.'s a centaur in his…world — POUND 786:84
Go to the a. — BIBLE 120:63
men of experiment are like the a. — BACON 55:29

antagonism a. between Russia — CECIL 247:85

Antarctica inform you proceeding A. — AMUN 17:98

antecedents a. are rum, Romanism — BURC 205:77

antechamber a. of perdition — SHAW 926:43

antechapel a. where the statue — WORD 1096:27

antennae Artists are the a. — POUND 787:88

anthologies a. will…continue — JANE 518:53

anthology well-chosen a. — GRAV 440:35

Anthony St. A. of Padua — MACF 629:20

anthropological a. malady — VAND 1039:94

anthropologists a. or whatever — STARK 963:95

anthropophagi A., and men — SHAK 898:7

anti-Fascism cause of a.-f. — SPEN 957:91

anti-abortion goal of the a.-a. forces — LEGU 594:28

anti-classic A.-c. art — INGR 512:48

anti-climax a.-c. in the English — THUR 1019:36
curious a.-c. — KAZIN 543:29
everything afterward savors of a.-c. — FITZ 390:98

anti-government a.-g. at the same — TSON 1031:42

anti-intellectual Science… — MENC 669:77

anti-Semitism prejudice of a.-S. — POUND 787:90

Antichrist Rome to chase the A. — LESL 598:94

anticipation dead a. — VALE 1038:84
intelligent a. of the facts — CURZ 302:28
lost in the a. — WILL 1083:96

anticipations parts of their a. — BAGE 61:63

antics Woven with a. — SPEN 958:10

antidote a. against the opium of time — BROW 196:1
Science is the great a. — SMITH 945:82
sweet oblivious a. — SHAK 910:82

antidotes a. are poison — SHAK 902:94

antifeminists A., from Chesterton — WEST 1068:88

antipathy a. to the noisy Plebeian — CHES 257:86
strong a. of good to bad — POPE 782:88

antipodes slightest errand to the A. — SHAK 879:38

antiquated as a. as a duel — GOOCH 435:54

antique more an a. Roman — SHAK 893:86
nude and a. — SWIN 987:31
traveller from an a. land — SHEL 928:92

antique (*contd.*)
Where is the a. glory — SPEN 958:17

antiquities A. are history defaced — BACON 55:11
museum of a. — ENGE 378:90

antiquity A.…clichéd and boring — FLAU 393:44
controversy in a. — GERA 419:95
enforced to awake all a. — BACON 55:8
great art of a. — KLEE 566:46
man who goes to a. — BAUD 77:29
rejected all respect for a. — DISR 332:81

antiseptic a. whiff of destiny — DUNN 356:55

antithesis one vile a. — POPE 781:68
true a. to knowledge — DEQU 316:66

Antonio A., I am married — SHAK 873:95
O my A. — SHAK 873:1

Antony A. should conquer A. — SHAK 906:93
A., who lost the world — DRYD 352:91
Emperor A. — SHAK 906:99
oblivion is a very A. — SHAK 905:65

ants a. in the gleam — TENN 1005:69
Call country a. to harvest offices — DONNE 336:77
shuffling of all a. — WILL 1082:82

anvil devil's quilted a. — WEBS 1061:58
England's on the a. — KIPL 565:26

anxiety free-floating a. — LURIE 619:43
Inconstancy, boredom, a. — PASC 757:56
no comfort, only a. — FRIS 406:66
taboo'd by a. — GILB 424:77

anxious more a. to please — SAND 840:50
most a. for its welfare — BURKE 206:98
pleasing a. being — GRAY 442:74
woman who is very a. — FREUD 404:43

anybody A. on for a game — SHAW 924:99

anything A. scares me — STEIN 965:39
ask for a. more — GERS 420:8
did not say a. — HEMI 470:17
nobody tells me a. — GALS 413:1
now, God knows, A. goes — PORT 784:31
our people…can do a. — POL 777:62
People will do a. — PERCY 766:84
think that science can do a. — RAY 803:46

apace ready men who write a. — BROW 199:56

apartheid a. would be gone — WOODS 1092:50
don't want a. liberalized — TUTU 1032:55

apartments painting…to decorate a. — PICA 769:26

apathetic never flustered, never a. — AURE 50:27

apathy a. in education — FORS 398:38
shake of its a. — RENAN 806:1
stirring up a. — WHIT 1072:65

ape achievement for the neotenic a. — ALDI 12:7
a. his cubs — MORE 706:43
a. is man — MACC 626:57
glassy essence, like an angry a. — SHAK 896:72
How like us is…the a.! — ENNI 379:93
is man an a. or an angel? — DISR 333:7
Jesus and the nameless a. — MACD 627:82
played the sedulous a. — STEV 976:46
story of an a. — HARL 458:20

apertures a. have all been stopped up — LEON 597:77

apes anthropoid a. and human beings — LORE 613:43
called the A. of God — LEWIS 602:65
cargo of ivory, And a. — MASE 662:37
scourge those a. — JONS 534:73
Tarzan of the A. — BURR 213:52

aphorism may marry is an a. — MITF 697:99

aphorisms A.…more for your time — DUDEK 353:13
a. that, like airplanes — NABO 716:93
one of his questionable a. — ELIOT 365:23
translate a. into continuous prose — FRYE 408:23

aphrodisiac Fame is a powerful a. — GREE 444:16
Power is the ultimate a. — KISS 566:53
truffle is not a true a. — BRIL 188:54
used for a. purpose — BLISS 169:31

Aphrodite A. rose up excited — AUDEN 48:78

apocalyptic a. horsemen in the air — MARC 649:40

Apollo A. and the sweet Muses — RUSK 831:13
A.'s laurel bough — MARL 654:23
call the A. a fancy piece? — EMER 376:45
Yea, is not even A. — SWIN 987:39
young A., golden-haired — CORN 288:57

Apollos A. watered — BIBLE 150:47

apology a. for the Devil — BUTL 218:43
A. is only egotism — HOLM 486:96
made a combative a. — SHUL 935:28
miles of…self-a. — RICH 810:70
My conduct shrieks aloud for a. — BEER 83:27
Never make…an a. — CHAR 252:81
no business to make any a. — ROCHE 815:39

apostle a. of the Philistine — ARNO 39:13
A.'s advice to use wine — BERN 96:74

apostles a. of equality — ARNO 39:26
A. would have done as they did — BYRON 222:29
Cristes lore, and his a. twelve — CHAU 255:26
least of the a. — BIBLE 151:65

apostolic Holy Catholic and A. — TEMP 993:29
through his a. skin — BYRON 223:67

apparel a. oft proclaims the man — SHAK 888:69
As men their best a. do — BUTL 216:3
fashion wears out more a. — SHAK 880:56
rich in a. — TROL 1027:63

apparent It is now a. — PITT 771:63
me and the a. lovers — REED 805:82

apparition a. of these faces — POUND 785:52
a., sole of men — SHEL 929:13
as if I had seen an a. — DEFOE 312:80
lovely a. — WORD 1098:62
mere moral a. — MENC 670:88

appeal books of…universal a. — FORD 396:3
He has a gay a. — COWA 290:99

appeals system of a. that pervades — CAPO 231:80

appear merely as I a. to myself — KANT 541:99
wish to a. considerable — JOHN 528:59

appearance according to a. alone — LAFO 574:81
an a. of solidity — ORWE 744:48
a. of…greater genius — RUSS 832:21
gods…what they are like in a. — PROT 792:84
images in a. remote from each other — JOHN 525:90
man looketh on the outward a. — BIBLE 110:36
not considered apart from her a. — DE 311:64

appearances contrary to all a. — GOWE 437:81
depends…upon their personal a. — HAGG 450:7
explain their a. — NEWT 725:37
Keep up a. — CHUR 262:84

appears but by what a. — HARDY 456:95
since so plainly it a. — JUANA 539:65

appeasement stench of a. — THAT 1008:27

appeaser a.…feeds a crocodile — CHUR 265:40

appendix a. makes man his a. — FROMM 406:70

appetite A. comes with eating — RABE 798:80
a. is keen — EMER 377:49
a. may sicken — SHAK 893:91
but 'tis the a. — SUCK 981:19
gallant a. for Meat — PENE 764:53
have an a. for submission — ELIOT 366:31
hungry edge of a. — SHAK 886:47
men in a. — BACON 59:18
Nature or unrestrainèd a. — CAREW 232:16
satisfying a voracious a. — FIEL 388:51
sickly a. to please — SHAK 915:97
vaster the a. for more — LEGU 594:24
will into a. — SHAK 895:40

appetites a. as apt to change — DRYD 348:97
more dinners than a. — CHAM 250:25
Subdue your a. — DICK 321:46

applaud A.…the comedy is over — BEET 84:53
come to a. their money — HIRS 482:22
Fish don't a. — HOPE 491:76

applause amidst rounds of a. — SOME 952:1

applause (*contd.*)
a., delight, the wonder — JONS 535:8
A....echo of platitude — BIER 160:69
A. is a receipt — SCHN 848:82
A. is almost a duty — CHAN 251:59
a. which he cannot keep — JOHN 525:91
expect any a. from it — MONT 701:56
food and shelter and a. — JARR 518:63
her own a. — JONS 536:14
If met with a. — MAIM 640:95
purred a. — GRAY 441:51
apple Adam ate the a. — HUGH 500:42
And for an a. damn'd — OTWAY 746:78
a. a day — ANON 30:60
a....better than an insipid peach — HUNT 504:25
a. blossoms fill the air — SEEG 857:26
a. falling towards England — AUDEN 46:49
a. of his eye — BIBLE 108:2
a. of his eye — BIBLE 130:66
a. of the eye — BIBLE 114:41
a. pressed with specious cant — HOOD 489:44
a. that isn't young anymore — GARBO 414:17
easy under the a. boughs — THOM 1010:65
goodly a. rotten at the heart — SHAK 874:21
luckless a. did we taste — MARV 659:91
millionaires love a baked a. — FIRB 389:70
rind of one a. tasted — MILT 685:58
apple-pickers the a.-p. missed it — SAPP 842:93
apple-pie make an a.-p. — FOOTE 396:95
apples a. are overripe — MAMET 644:56
a. began to be golden-skinned — DAVI 307:99
a. drop about my head — MARV 658:85
a. of gold in pictures of silver — BIBLE 121:98
as a tree bears a. — EMER 377:67
Benes and baken a. — LANG 579:73
Cézanne liked a. — LIPP 606:29
small choice in rotten a. — SHAK 864:72
Stolen, stolen, be your a. — HUNT 504:25
The silver a. — YEATS 1105:63
appliances all a. and means to boot — SHAK 877:95
application a. of human ingenuity — NUTT 732:46
a. of science — PARS 756:45
a. of them that is human — PAINE 750:51
Art is not the a. of a canon — PICA 768:25
novel is conscientious a. — NEME 722:5
applications only a. of science — PAST 759:87
appointed a. unto men once to die — BIBLE 154:81
appointment a. by the corrupt few — SHAW 922:46
a. by the corrupt few — SHAW 926:39
we have kept our a. — BECK 81:97
appraisal a. of the drift of public — DAFOE 303:38
rough a., but curiously true — ACHE 3:31
appreciate a. his efforts — KENN 551:81
appreciated more loved and a. — ELLI 375:17
appreciation object of aesthetic a. — BARR 72:29
apprehension a. of perfection — NIEB 727:64
articulate a. — GERH 420:5
in a. how like a god — SHAK 890:4
Religion...eludes a. — WHIT 1071:55
apprehensions a. come in crowds — WORD 1099:65
apprentice time...to become an a. — BEAV 81:86
apprenticeship a. for freedom — BARA 70:8
at the very beginning of the a. — CIXO 267:77
wonderful a. — JAMES 517:34
writing...take your a. in it — PORT 784:36
approach a. and depart — HERA 473:85
a. to the meaning — ELIOT 372:60
two-track a. — MACN 636:32
approbation a. and consent — POWE 788:18
gives manhood more a. — SHAK 895:33
appropriate a. act of creation — FEIN 385:99
a. one to apply — SIMON 939:80
appropriation with this a. comes — PAGE 749:32
approval a. of course already decided — BIER 161:76

approval (*contd.*)
carries no hint of a. — HEND 472:54
people will not buy...without my a. — BERE 94:37
approve I see...and a. — OVID 747:1
approximation picture is only an a. — MOTH 711:12
reasonable a. to it — KEYN 554:33
April A. is the cruellest month — ELIOT 368:81
A., 1920 — LEWIS 601:51
bright cold day in A. — ORWE 745:54
day in A. — SHAK 875:33
flag to A.'s breeze unfurled — EMER 376:26
glory of an A. day — SHAK 860:74
In A. one seldom seems cheerful — COPE 287:50
lovely A. of her prime — SHAK 912:44
Men are A. — SHAK 887:23
Now that A.'s here — BROW 198:36
of A. in Seventy-five — LONG 612:16
Of A., May, of June — HERR 477:51
proud-pied A. — SHAK 915:83
smells A. and May — SHAK 878:19
that A. morn — BRID 187:42
well-apparell'd A. on the heel — SHAK 868:76
Whan that A. with — CHAU 254:16
apron crackling white a. — TRAV 1025:37
aprons made themselves a. — BIBLE 103:95
apt how a. the poor are — SHAK 895:23
Arabia spell of far A. — DELA 314:28
Arabian A. fleet — GIBB 421:23
A. Nights entertainment — OSLER 746:74
to the A. desert to collect — THES 1009:45
Arabs dirty and ragged little street A. — DOYLE 343:93
Jews and A. should settle — AUST 53:75
joined with the A., by cracky! — ACHE 3:48
Like the A. — KAUF 543:16
up their tents like A. — LONG 611:4
Aral stars...shine upon the A. Sea — ARNO 38:98
Ararat rode that tide To A. — WILB 1074:17
arbeit A. macht frei — ANON 26:45
arbiter A. Chance governs all — MILT 688:25
a. of taste — TACI 989:80
arbitrary accusation of being a. — JAMES 516:18
sociology attaches the adjective 'a.' — ARON 40:46
arch all experience in an a. — TENN 994:58
a. Of the ranged empire fall — SHAK 904:58
a. to build on — ADAMS 5:73
forgot the a. — DICK 320:16
like an a., is faith — MILL 678:39
night's black a. — BURNS 211:16
St Louis...golden a. — MAIL 639:84
archaeologists a. twitter — MACA 622:84
gangrene of professors, a. — MARI 651:84
archangel A. a little damaged — LAMB 576:15
A. Gabriel, madam — MENZ 670:94
voice of the a. — BIBLE 153:25
archangels with angels and a. — BOOK 174:28
archbishop a. had come to see me — BURG 206:88
sense of purpose...from their a. — MACM 636:19
archbishops a. and field marshals — MURR 715:76
archer laughs at the a. — BAUD 77:16
Archer, make...Jeffery A. rich — BRAD 183:87
archers A. stand there on — MUIR 712:27
as for you, a., soldiers — JOAN 522:27
arches a. of the years — THOM 1013:28
Underneath the A. — FLAN 391:23
Archimedes A. was not free — MACA 623:11
architect a.'s ability to build — ROGE 820:3
a....advise his client — WRIG 1101:5
a. of his own fate — CLAU 268:93
a. who didn't build St Paul's — THOR 1017:4
Art and Assistance of the A. — ALBE 12:94
dialogue between client and a. — STERN 968:86
I would not be an a. — OUD 746:91
painter can be an a. — RUSK 830:82
position of the modern a. — BETJ 100:43

architects A. cannot work — ROGE 820:4
a., engineers and builders — BIRNS 163:27
a. of our republic — KING 557:78
role of a. — MURP 715:73
architectural great a. secret — TROL 1027:63
respectable a. man-milliner — RUSK 831:99
architecture analysis, all a. — NUTT 732:46
A. cannot be understood — CASS 243:28
A....how to waste space — JOHN 524:70
A. is an art — MALL 642:21
A. is man's great sense of himself — WRIG 1101:3
A. is the...mirror of life — PEI 764:49
a. is the organization — JOHN 524:65
A. is the will of the age — MIES 674:51
a. of the world — MARL 652:89
A. or revolution — LECO 592:1
A. provides the framework — LECO 592:3
art of a. — JOHN 524:64
can't have great a. — WRIG 1101:7
can't learn a. — JOHN 524:66
co-creator of social a. — BEUYS 101:60
cuckoo clock style of a. — HEMI 470:12
Fashion is a. — CHAN 251:57
Fujiyama of A. — MUMF 713:47
good a. if it works — JOHN 524:63
history of City a. — JOHN 524:67
learn from a. — RUDO 828:46
New styles of a. — AUDEN 46:42
phenomenon of a. — ALLS 15:56
rectangular a. — TOYN 1024:19
rise and fall of English a. — BETJ 99:25
role of a. — MURP 715:73
views of a. — WAGN 1047:26
arctic Inarticulate, a. — SCOTT 852:91
seven months of A. weather — ANON 25:18
two kinds of A. problems — STEF 965:24
Arcturi daisies, those pearled A. — SHEL 932:67
Ardenne Now I am in A. — SHAK 885:85
ardent children a. for...glory — OWEN 748:91
ardently great mind loves a. — PASC 757:50
ardour a. to improve society — SMALL 943:62
There shall be no a. — SMITH 947:4
are know what we a. — SHAK 892:63
what we truly a. — SCHI 847:44
where you a. — ELIOT 371:50
area consciousness is a staging a. — BELL 88:42
must not become the new a. — KENN 551:55
studio is a torture a. — LIBE 603:79
arena a. in which to act — ROSE 822:56
binary political a. — LEHM 594:38
Arethusa like the river A. — BROW 195:70
Argante A. the queen, an elf — LAYA 588:22
Argie Kill an A. — PRIV 791:75
argosy a. of crocs and dragons — AMIS 17:87
argue A. for your limitations — BACH 54:98
a. freely according — MILT 685:7
a. from what has been done — ATTL 44:1
can't a. with a river — ACHE 3:42
enemies of freedom do not a. — INGE 511:38
argues a. by increments of noise — BYATT 218:54
arguing In a. too — GOLD 433:13
much a., much writting — MILT 685:7
not a. with you — WHIS 1069:9
argument All a. is against it — JOHN 530:37
an impression, not an a. — HARDY 456:1
any other kind of a. — STER 969:95
a. against giving women the vote — WRIG 1101:1
a. concerns no ordinary topic — PLATO 774:17
a. with men a woman — MILT 695:50
a. with people — KIRK 565:27
can't have the a. both ways — SHAW 922:42
detected...use of an a. — BENN 91:93
essence of a. — SCHL 848:74
first a. that is brought against — STAMP 962:83

argument (*contd.*)

found you an a.	JOHN 532:31
good life is a main a.	JONS 536:18
highth of this great a.	MILT 687:86
metre-making a….makes a poem	EMER 377:48
never without an a.	HALI 452:28
nice knock-down a. for you!	CARR 240:70
not good at precise, coherent a.	BENN 91:83
only a. available	LOWE 616:89
sharpest men in a.	HOLM 486:83
staple of his a.	SHAK 866:23
supporting their guesses by a.	BAGE 61:63
Whigs admit no force but a.	BROW 196:9
you and love are still my a.	SHAK 914:74
arguments a. in favor of it	JAMES 518:51
a. on both sides	SWIFT 984:78
a. which are brought	JOHN 527:33
beggarly appear a.	WHIT 1072:77
intellectual A.	PETTY 768:15
start a.	RUSH 829:68
tolerate unlikely a.	FORD 397:14
aria sing an a. for him?	LOUIS 614:60
Ariadne Since A. was a vintager	KEATS 545:60
arias Clear a. of light	DAYL 310:55
Ariel Caliban casts out A.	POUND 786:63
arise A., shine	BIBLE 127:11
I will a. and go now	YEATS 1104:57
let us a.	STEV 975:42
Napoleons will duly a.	HUXL 507:75
aristocracy a. in a republic	MITF 697:3
a. means government	CHES 260:43
A. of the Moneybag	CARL 235:69
a. preserves us	BAGE 61:55
a. the most democratic	MACA 624:26
Bunyip A.	DENI 316:57
Chinese are the a.	MAUG 665:90
Clover…is A.	DICK 328:15
displeased with a.	HOBB 483:41
Ireland…an absentee a.	DISR 332:87
moneyed a.	BLEST 169:28
possession of a bourgeois a.	ENGE 387:87
relief for the a. of Great Britain	BRIG 188:48
The true a.	BLIX 169:33
aristocrat A., democrat, autocrat	TENN 1001:80
a. is the democrat ripe	EMER 377:61
Aristotle Every Poet, his own A.	BYRON 222:37
follow this counsel of A.	ASCH 40:50
lantern of A.'s brain	RALE 800:15
arithmetic different branches of A.	CARR 238:36
ark like the A. of the Covenant	JEFF 520:96
Noe entered into the a.	BIBLE 140:39
passage in the a.	DOUG 341:51
two and two unto Noah into the a.	BIBLE 104:10
Uzza…put his hand to the a.	BIBLE 112:85
when he made mention of the a.	BIBLE 110:31
won't start with Noah's A.	ECHE 359:13
Arlott hear John A.'s voice	THOM 1010:71
arm a. of the Lord revealed?	BIBLE 127:99
a. the weak	FRAN 401:88
a. to a.	PEEL 763:44
auld moon in her a.	BALL 67:48
cam an a. and an honde	MALO 642:33
gather the lambs with his a.	BIBLE 126:86
his reared a.	SHAK 906:1
Human on my faithless a.	AUDEN 47:74
Look at my a.!	TRUTH 1030:39
made bare his holy a.	BIBLE 127:97
one a. bent	SASS 845:32
strong a. of England	PALM 752:72
such an a. for a bandage	SHER 933:88
take the skin from the a.	ELIOT 370:34
weak of will, the strong of a.	MAST 663:48
wound them on his a.	MARL 655:29
your a., old toad	LARK 581:10

arm-chair fitted into my biggest a.	WODE 1088:84
Armada English against the A.	CUOMO 300:6
Armageddon A. will be at our door	MACA 621:71
armaments piling up national a.	ATTL 44:8
armchair a. theorists	ASHD 41:62
a. which provides relaxation	MATI 664:74
driveling reader curled up in his a.	SARD 843:94
armed a. force shall not be used	UNIT 1036:45
a. attempt to impose the views	SCHL 848:73
a. with the liberty of the Press	SHER 934:13
defended by her a. sons	REDM 804:75
armies a. swore terribly in Flanders	STER 969:3
ignorant a. clash by night	ARNO 36:65
land a. in China	MONT 703:90
no invincible a.	STAL 962:80
plenty of money and large a.	ANOU 31:80
two equally matched a. meet	LAO 580:87
whose fingers are ten a.	GINS 427:25
armistice a. for twenty years	FOCH 395:84
armour a. of light	BOOK 174:3
no a. against fate	SHIR 935:27
Put on the whole a. of God	BIBLE 152:6
armoury castle without an a.	GEOF 418:79
arms a. and the man	ANON 21:49
A., and the man I sing	DRYD 352:76
a. do flourish	BACON 59:29
a. hang down to laugh	ELIOT 367:66
a. of my true love	TENN 1001:89
buried in those monumental a.	WALL 1050:73
chess with a. and legs	BARZ 75:98
clad in the a.	SURR 982:40
clasped in my longing a.	ROCH 816:44
Come to my a., my beamish boy	CARR 239:47
Cromwell took up a.	STAL 962:78
effective for a. control	WEIN 1062:86
Emparadised in one another's a.	MILT 690:59
For the theatre one needs long a.	BERN 97:95
freeing his a.	JOYCE 538:44
from our mother's a.	WINK 1086:59
green a. around the bosom	SHEL 932:66
history of a. control	ADEL 8:43
hug it in mine a.	SHAK 897:80
I never would lay down my a.	PITT 771:70
if my love were in my a.	ANON 23:83
in my a. till break of day	AUDEN 47:75
in the a. of a chambermaid	JOHN 530:1
laid down his a.!	HOOD 488:34
lay down their a.	GOEB 430:65
Lending a.	TAFT 989:81
lord of folded a.	SHAK 865:13
lore of a.	ANON 22:74
more strong than traitors' a.	SHAK 884:54
muscles of his brawny a.	LONG 611:97
Of seeming a….a short essay	DRYD 352:86
once more in mine a.	SHAK 893:80
outspread a. is equal	LEON 597:82
Prize Of wit or a.	MILT 682:3
Rank'd a. and crested heads	SMART 944:70
sap flows up through our a.	RILKE 811:86
soldiers without a.	PAST 759:89
strong a. be our conscience	SHAK 863:66
take a. against a sea of troubles	SHAK 890:21
take me in thy a.	MARL 653:31
To war and a. I fly	LOVE 615:66
took her up in his a.	RIDGE 811:77
took the ball in his a.	ANON 24:10
underneath are the everlasting a.	BIBLE 108:5
very long a.	HALI 452:29
Weep me not dead, in thy a.	DONNE 337:87
what a. have lain	MILL 676:86
why did we take up a.	CROM 298:52
With a., legs, lips	ROCH 816:44
wither slowly in thine a.	TENN 1003:21
world in a.	MACA 624:21

army accompanied by all the a.	GRAY 440:44
affairs of the a.	JAUR 519:71
a. has had…victory	MARL 652:81
a. hurrying into battle	ORWE 742:91
a. marches on its stomach	NAPO 718:31
a. of unalterable law	MERE 671:12
a. that we must train for war	WILS 1086:53
a. that will be able	TROT 1029:4
a. would be a base rabble	BURKE 207:12
backbone of the A.	KIPL 562:59
conduct of this a.	WASH 1054:42
conventional a. loses	KISS 566:31
efficiency of an a.	JAY 519:74
honour of the…British A.	CHUR 264:22
hum of either a.	SHAK 881:88
proud Edward's a.	WILL 1083:7
to maintain an a.	MORE 707:47
were a self-centred a.	LAWR 587:14
world proletarian a.	LENIN 595:50
aroint A. thee, witch	SHAK 906:12
arrange make Him a. it earlier	RULFO 828:50
arrangement a. into three reigns	GUED 448:74
arranging a. what we have always known	WITT 1088:76
arrant he's an a. knave	SHAK 889:82
Arras slogged up to A.	SASS 845:28
arrest neither a. nor movement	ELIOT 370:25
arrested exercises in a. development	SELF 858:38
arrive a. where we started	ELIOT 373:78
persisting, safe a.	MILT 689:37
rather than striving to a.	HILL 480:5
arriving always a. and departing	MILL 679:52
arrogance do not accept his a.	VASC 1040:10
power leads man towards a.	KENN 552:88
arrogant most a. and invincible	JONS 535:95
not often to the a.	JEFF 519:83
arrow a. into the air	LONG 611:5
a. that flies feels	LONG 612:19
a. that flieth by day	BIBLE 117:2
draw an a. arbitrarily	EDDI 360:17
in my heart his iron a.	SPEN 957:6
killed by the a.	KELL 548:30
shot an a.	HAMER 453:36
Swifter than a.	SHAK 871:46
arrows a. of desire!	BLAKE 168:19
a. of outrageous fortune	TWAIN 1033:89
As a. are in the hand	BIBLE 119:42
children as living a. are sent forth	GIBR 422:38
arse Kiss my a.!	PEPYS 764:59
politician is an a.	CUMM 300:91
arson A.…artificial crime	WELLS 1064:35
art a very pretty a.	PEPYS 765:68
a wife in this a. of mine	MICH 673:36
abstract a.'s appearance	MOTH 711:10
adventures of…a.	WEST 1068:88
adventures…in great works of a.	FRAN 400:80
Affords this a.	MARL 654:10
Aims of A.	KIPL 564:5
All a. is immoral	WILDE 1076:40
All a. is solitary	LIBE 603:79
All great a. is born	POUND 785:49
all mediums of a.	PISS 771:61
all the adulteries of a.	JONS 535:89
American a.	ADAMS 5:82
anything other than ideal a.	BAUD 77:29
a.…achievement of stillness	BELL 88:26
A. among a religious race	FUSE 410:60
A. and Assistance of the Architect	ALBE 12:94
a. and literature are left	LEWIS 602:53
a. and morals	MURD 714:64
A. and Religion…two roads	BELL 88:7
A. and Science cannot exist	BLAKE 168:8
a. can make us see	MACL 634:79
A. …cannot avoid cheating	RIDI 811:81

art (*contd.*)

A. cannot be made…to please	DEGAS 312:93
A. cannot hold its breath	ANTH 31:83
A. comes to you proposing	ANON 28:14
A.…communication that insinuates	CALAS 225:94
a. constantly aspires	PATER 759:94
a. continue to follow nature	MOND 699:41
A. derives a considerable part	JAMES 516:17
A. does not expand	DEGAS 312:89
A. does not reproduce	KLEE 566:50
a. doesn't dare	HUST 505:39
A.…excludes all competition	FUSE 410:58
A. for A.'s sake	FORS 399:50
A. for a.'s sake	CONS 286:22
A. for a.'s sake	SAND 840:55
a. for practitioners and readers	LEAV 591:75
A., Glory, Freedom fail	BYRON 219:77
a. has no place in…life	RODC 818:81
A., if you like	LARK 581:96
a., in London	DRYD 347:74
A. is a jealous mistress	EMER 377:66
A. is a point of view	WERE 1066:55
A. is an abstraction	GAUG 416:39
A. is dedicated echo	SANT 842:88
A. is game	PIER 769:36
A. is history's nostalgia	WALC 1048:41
A. is like Creation	KLEE 566:49
a. is long	CARM 236:4
A. is long, and time	LONG 611:95
A. is not a brassière	BARN 72:32
A. is not truth	PICA 769:29
A. is not…a canon of beauty	PICA 768:25
a. is not…merely skill	FRIE 405:60
A. is nothing without form	FLAU 392:32
A. is only a means to life	MILL 678:41
A. is only possible	BEUYS 101:60
A. is significant deformity	FRY 408:19
a. is the child	KAND 541:96
a. is the perfection of nature	BROW 195:78
A. is the retelling	LUCAS 618:32
A. it the only work	GRAY 461:42
a.…life imitates it	LEBO 591:84
A. may make a suit	HUME 503:6
A. most cherishes	BROW 199:71
a. museums to worship dead works	MAYA 665:4
A. never expresses anything	WILDE 1076:35
a., not chance	POPE 778:84
A. of all periods	RUNGE 829:54
a. of angling	WALT 1052:7
a. of architecture	JOHN 524:64
a. of balance, of purity	MATI 664:74
a. of drawing	LIEB 604:90
a. of getting drunk	JOHN 530:2
a. of government	SHAW 922:45
a. of inexactitude	MURR 716:80
a. of losing	BISH 164:35
a. of making the most	SHAW 926:40
a. of newspaper paragraphing	MARQ 656:48
a. of our necessities	SHAK 903:21
a. of…over-simplification	POPP 784:29
a. of painting cannot be…judged	DURER 356:66
a. of perceiving	DICK 325:46
a. of pleasing	HAZL 463:98
a. of poetry	MACL 634:87
A. of Scratch	RUSK 831:5
a. of the masses	HALL 452:34
a. of the past	LEWI 603:72
a. of the writer	APOL 32:91
A. pales when compared	AQUI 33:8
A. produces ugly things	COCT 272:66
a. pursued with view to money	BUTL 217:41
a. reverenced the while	JONS 535:1
a. should be a monster	TZARA 1035:33
A. should be independent	WHIS 1069:14

art (*contd.*)

A.'s subject human clay	AUDEN 46:54
a. that conceals	HARDY 456:92
a. that helps old ladies	OLDE 738:24
a. that is interested in itself	SANT 842:89
a., that monopolizes	DUDEK 353:18
A.—the one achievement	THUR 1019:29
A.…the supreme achievement	POUND 787:91
A. to fold her hands	ROSS 824:91
a. united with prophecy	NISB 730:5
A. was made to disturb	BRAQ 185:11
A.…will have a country	APOL 32:95
A. will liberate itself	MARC 649:41
a. world is a jungle	HAMM 453:49
as in a., dependent	RUSS 832:21
As the a. of reading	JAMES 517:42
assaying of tea is an a.	MO 698:11
attempt to realize A.	HOLM 486:97
Ausonia, skilled in every a.	BYRON 219:63
beauty in a.	DIDE 329:25
became an expert's a.	RUDO 828:46
become a human is a.	NOVA 732:40
beginning and end of a.	HEIN 467:74
better teachers of the A. of Painting	DURER 356:67
betwixt Nature and A.	PRIOR 791:59
black a. to dispense	VAUG 1041:16
boundaries between politics and a.	DANG 304:60
Bullfighting is the only a.	HEMI 470:24
burglar who respects his a.	OHEN 737:20
clever, but is it A.?	KIPL 561:41
conceptual a. the idea	LEWI 602:71
concern itself with a.	KLEE 566:47
condition of a.	CONR 284:87
corner-stones of literary a.	DUDEK 353:13
corrupt a. is the sentimental	PISS 771:58
counts as work of a.	WILL 1083:99
Dali's importance…for a. historians	SCHW 851:23
Decorative a. does not exist	ROUA 827:29
delights of a. satisfy me	FUEN 409:26
demonstrates the a. of measuring	NEWT 725:39
destroy genius and a.	HAZL 464:24
deviating from the rules of a.	ADDI 8:38
difference between…true a.	CAPO 231:85
difficulty of a.	CHAR 252:78
Dress is a form of visual a.	HOLL 485:70
drunk we like our a.	LUCAS 618:29
Dying Is an a.	PLATH 773:94
emotion of a.	ELIOT 368:74
end and test of a.	POPE 778:78
enemy of good a.	CONN 283:62
Europe had plenty of a.	BEHR 85:76
ever seen in A. or Nature	WAUGH 1057:88
Every a.…is thought to aim	ARIS 34:25
Every true work of a.	FRIE 405:62
expressing emotion in the form of a.	ELIOT 368:76
Faustus, leave this damèd a.	MARL 654:18
Film a. has a greater influence	BALA 63:88
final purpose of a.	MAIL 639:71
find in a. and science	HALD 451:18
Fond without a.	DRYD 348:98
for a shilling…conflict and a.	PRIE 789:35
fruits of speaking a.?	SIDN 936:46
future of a.	FLAU 392:32
give their lives to a. and science	EINS 363:63
glory and good of A.	BROW 200:95
goal of a. is almost divine	HUGO 501:59
good is always a product of a.	BAUD 78:34
great a. is great life	WRIG 1101:6
Great a. is the contempt	FITZ 391:20
great a. of antiquity	KLEE 566:46
Happiness is always a work of a.	YOUR 1108:7
hating, my boy, is an a.	NASH 719:49
hide…their want of a.	POPE 778:80

art (*contd.*)

History…is an a.	FRAN 401:87
If a work of a. is to be truly immortal	CHIR 260:53
If a. does not enlarge…sympathies	ELIOT 365:14
If it is a.	SCHO 849:90
if it may even be called a.	INGR 512:48
In a. economy is always beauty	JAMES 516:28
In a. one is	MODE 698:19
in a. the best is good enough.	GOET 431:71
in a. we have to follow	MOND 699:42
In Spenser, and in Jonson, A.	DENH 315:55
In sweet music is such a.	SHAK 918:54
industry without a.	RUSK 831:4
informing them as a.	BLOOM 169:35
iron palaces of A.	HUGH 499:28
Isherwood became…a work of a.	BURU 214:80
Italy…home Of all A.	BYRON 220:93
knows what a work of a. is	FRY 408:18
last and greatest a.	POPE 782:83
least realistic of a. forms	MAMET 644:60
let it be an a.	SHAK 912:43
Life imitates A. far more	WILDE 1076:43
Like a. and politics	DOCT 334:41
Literature is the a. of writing	CONN 283:58
Literature…is an A.	QUIL 797:60
lost, for a., at Sarajevo	LEWIS 602:68
love of a. for its own sake	PATER 759:95
Love…is also an a.	BALZ 69:77
masterpiece of a.…has a fixed place	EMER 376:45
men who have failed in a.	DISR 333:14
Modern a. does not	ROSE 823:59
Modern A. no longer	ROSE 823:60
Modern a. tends towards	BAUD 78:35
modern a.…completely literary	WOLFE 1090:24
morality of a.	WILDE 1076:46
More matter with less a.	SHAK 889:97
more than Wisdom, A., or Nature	HERR 477:57
My religion and my a.	JOHN 523:39
nation's a. is greatest	HOPP 493:13
Nature in him was almost lost in A.	COLL 276:41
nature is the a. of God	BROW 195:79
Nature that is above all a.	DANI 304:65
nature's handmaid is a.	DRYD 346:54
never know all about a.	OLSEN 739:97
new a. to them is natural	DAVI 307:7
new a. work is born	YOUR 1108:11
next to Nature, A.	LAND 578:62
no a. which one government	SMITH 945:83
no a. without practice	PROT 792:83
no boundary line to a.	PARK 753:87
no history of a.	WERE 1066:56
no one will take to a.	BELL 85:83
no such thing as authentic a.	CUMM 299:75
not as an a. form	TZARA 1035:36
not the courtier's a.	DRYD 350:27
Not to admire, is all the a.	POPE 782:81
of ev'ry a. the soul	POPE 779:20
oldest a. in the world	CHAP 251:64
only a. that they look upon	WOLFE 1090:28
perception of works of a.	DEWEY 319:96
perfection in a new kind of a.	RUNGE 829:55
photography…stand in for a.	BAUD 77:8
Poetry is the a. of understanding	MACL 634:86
Poetry…is an a. of imitation	SIDN 937:62
Politics is the a. of	VALE 1038:48
pop a. and fine a.	MACI 631:43
Posing is a performing a.	SCHW 851:24
power of all true a.	EINS 363:67
pretty, but is it A.?	KIPL 561:40
procrastination is the a.	MARQ 655:37
profuse strains of unpremeditated a.	SHEL 929:97
Protestant form of a.	ORWE 743:17
purpose of a.	GOULD 436:75
reactions to a. or to music	COLE 273:79

art (*contd.*)
reading...itself an a.   CARY 243:*15*
Religion and a....from the same root   CATH 244:*49*
revenge of the intellect upon a.   SONT 952:*4*
rid of the element of a. in their being   CHES 258:*98*
says I know the a.   SPEN 958:*25*
schoolman's subtle a.   POPE 781:*69*
seven...exhibitions of modern a.   DUNL 355:*50*
sharp compassion of the healer's a.   ELIOT 371:*51*
shouldn't talk about a.   JOHN 524:*66*
specialized form of a.   PRIT 791:*65*
spit in the f. of A.   MILL 677:*15*
start on all this A.   HERB 474:*94*
subduers of Nature and A.   DICK 326:*55*
sweet music is such a.   SHAK 918:*56*
symbol of Irish a.   JOYCE 538:*46*
Teaching is not a lost a.   BARZ 75:*93*
than when A.   HERR 478:*68*
The a. of war   SUN 982:*30*
the dead a. of poetry   POUND 785:*60*
the end of A.   TURN 1031:*52*
the necessary a.   DULL 354:*25*
There is no abstract a.   PICA 768:*24*
third great form of a.   HUGO 501:*70*
Though a.'s hid causes   JONS 535:*89*
through A....realise our perfection   WILDE 1076:*39*
Today a. is moving   MARC 649:*40*
trade and a. is to live   MONT 702:*69*
transformed into comic a.   ROTH 826:*15*
truth of a. should never be   HUGO 501:*58*
ultimate in a.   RUNGE 829:*56*
unattainable by the highest a.   STRA 979:*92*
undreamed-of collection of a.   SAAR 834:*55*
want that glib and oily a.   SHAK 902:*99*
What a. can wash her guilt   GOLD 432:*5*
What A. was to the ancient world   DISR 332:*84*
What is a. is not likely to be decided   COND 279:*85*
When a. communicates   WILL 1081:*52*
where the a. resides   SCHN 848:*81*
Why shouldn't a. be pretty?   RENO 807:*12*
without the idea of a.   VIDAL 1044:*71*
work of a.   NABO 717:*7*
work of a., and as life   MILL 678:*44*
writer's only resposibility is to his a.   FAUL 383:*82*
year of a. and dissipation   MOORE 704:*11*
You talk of a.   SHAW 925:*33*
art-form a....invented in England   BEER 84:*46*
arterial it is a. blood   KEATS 548:*21*
arteriosclerosis a. of culture   MILL 679:*55*
artful No a. wildness to perplex   POPE 779:*21*
arthritis man who owns up to a.   NASH 719:*48*
Arthur A.'s sword snatched   MUNRO 714:*55*
A. the firste syght of queene   MALO 642:*26*
courte of kynge A.   MALO 642:*29*
kynge A. ys nat dede   MALO 642:*34*
named hym A.   MALO 642:*24*
Speak for England, A.!   AMERY 16:*68*
article affect a singularity in that a.   SHER 933:*81*
Alcohol is a very necessary a.   SHAW 923:*81*
a. which nobody wants   HONE 488:*27*
desireus of being the correct a.   ASHF 41:*68*
For a slashing a.   THAC 1007:*95*
In fact, the finished a.   RUSS 833:*42*
ordinary home-grown a.   DICK 325:*36*
single sentence in a routine a.   MEYER 673:*32*
What's the next a.?   GILB 424:*71*
articles a. published in scientific   FEYN 387:*33*
exchanging a.   RUSK 831:*10*
These a. subscribed   CONG 282:*34*
articulate a. and complete   STEV 971:*52*
neither a. nor worshipful   SNYD 951:*84*
articulation A. is the tongue-tied's fighting
                                                    HARR 459:*36*
artifice Art...through a.   RIDI 811:*81*

artifice (*contd.*)
to conceal his a.   OGIL 736:*3*
without a., I...work   ARET 33:*17*
artificer an a. ...who formed it   PALEY 751:*65*
single a. of the world   STEV 971:*48*
The great a.   STEV 976:*55*
artificial All things are a.   BROW 195:*79*
arrest motion...by a. means   FAUL 384:*84*
artillery Our light a.   GILB 425:*79*
rusty a. of abuse   STEV 972:*74*
Th' a. of words   SWIFT 983:*55*
artisan promised to the studious a.!   MARL 654:*11*
artist aim of every a.   FAUL 384:*84*
A more ideal A.   TENN 995:*65*
And so great an a.   NERO 723:*7*
a. absolute beauty   HALD 451:*18*
a. best serves his nation   KENN 552:*87*
a. does not start with nothing   PERCY 766:*85*
a. does not tinker   MILL 678:*23*
a....driven by demons   FAUL 383:*17*
a.'s first responsibility is to himself   DAVIS 309:*30*
a. has followed the rules   TINT 1021:*72*
a. is a spectator   ERNST 379:*10*
a. is extremely lucky   BERR 99:*18*
a. is in danger of death   HEMI 470:*24*
a. is making something exist   BURR 213:*58*
a. like the idiot   SITW 941:*27*
a. man and the mother woman   SHAW 921:*26*
a. must possess the courageous soul   CHOP 261:*62*
a. needs but a roof   RYDER 834:*50*
A. of the Floating World   ISHI 513:*75*
a. should fear   RYDER 834:*51*
a. should not only paint   FRIE 405:*61*
a. who has travelled on a steam train   DAVIS 309:*34*
a. who seeks dignity   ALBE 11:*92*
a. will be judged only by...solitude   CONN 283:*79*
a. with true feelings   FRIE 405:*57*
biography of the a.   ROSE 823:*57*
critic when he cannot be an a.   FLAU 392:*33*
eighteenth century a.   LEGER 594:*22*
expect the a. to have more to say   CALAS 225:*94*
filmmaker...other a.   WELL 1063:*7*
function of the a.   BETH 99:*24*
God is...another a.   PICA 769:*28*
greatest a. can conceive   MICH 673:*34*
half complete as a.   THUR 1020:*53*
I am an a.   FUEN 409:*26*
if a great a. says   SELF 857:*37*
innovative and important a.   DAVIS 309:*31*
joy of the a.   MILL 678:*34*
king of a....photographer   WHIS 1069:*13*
life of the a. sufficiently miserable   BELL 85:*83*
make himself an a.   SASS 846:*44*
man who never...is no a..   BLAKE 168:*12*
More glutton than a.   PARK 754:*95*
most American a. of all   ADLER 8:*46*
Never trust the a.   LAWR 586:*88*
not up to the a....to find   GENET 418:*74*
only become a good a.   INGR 512:*49*
pain that the a. feels   REDON 804:*76*
Portrait of the A. as   THOM 1010:*63*
product of the a.   MAMET 643:*48*
qualities essential for the a.   DIDE 330:*39*
Remember I'm an a.   CARY 243:*20*
reward one should offer an a.   RENO 807:*9*
special kind of a.   GILL 426:*7*
subject matter of the a.   WILDE 1076:*46*
to be lonely as an a.   THOM 1010:*42*
what an a. does, is fail   BART 74:*76*
what style is to an a.   BUEC 203:*41*
writer or a.   STEV 977:*61*
artiste a. with short arms   BERN 97:*95*
artistic a. sense of eye or ear   WHIS 1069:*14*
A. growth...a refining of the sense   CATH 244:*41*

artistic (*contd.*)
a. temperament is a disease   CHES 258:*98*
departure for our a. creation   WAGN 1047:*26*
slightly a.   KENN 550:*55*
artistry invention or true a.   POUND 786:*85*
artists are not savages a.   MACKE 632:*51*
A. and poets   ANON 29:*41*
A. are the antennae   POUND 787:*88*
A. are the only people   SLOAN 943:*60*
a....at the White House   WHITE 1071:*49*
A....if you copy others   BERN 97:*90*
a. must break a hole   HALE 451:*21*
a. produce something that   WILD 1079:*29*
a. took to the road   ROCK 818:*78*
a. want to become inhuman   APOL 31:*89*
a. will...instruct us   OLSEN 739:*37*
best subjects for a.   HEIN 467:*75*
conceived...by unknown a.   BART 74:*79*
English a. are...ruined   RUSK 831:*7*
Great a. impose their   MAUP 665:*96*
history of a..   WERE 1066:*56*
Horrible as successful a.   JONG 534:*66*
New York Pop a.   LIPP 606:*29*
no one wants Fine A.   FULL 409:*35*
over a troop of a.   WILL 1082:*81*
poet shares with other a.   SPEN 956:*85*
position of the a. of Wales   THOM 1011:*91*
style of most a. and all humbugs   CONN 283:*66*
Summoning a. to participate   FROST 407:*3*
ten great a.   GREE 443:*1*
too difficult for a.   SCHN 848:*86*
What do these so-called a.   INGR 512:*47*
arts are the books, the a.   SHAK 865:*22*
a. are tought by degrees   THEO 1008:*33*
a. babblative and scribblative   SOUT 954:*43*
a. of war   MORE 706:*42*
brought the a. into rustic Latium   HORA 493:*3*
elegant a. unknown here   BROO 192:*16*
finest of the A.   MERE 671:*10*
France, famed in all great a.   ARNO 36:*63*
France, mother of a.   BELL 86:*89*
Greece, mother of a.   MILT 694:*35*
idea of an a. ghetto   HARR 459:*38*
In the a. of life   SHAW 921:*35*
In the a. of peace   SHAW 921:*36*
inglorious a. of peace   MARV 657:*65*
lowest of all the a.   MOORE 704:*12*
mechanical a. and merchandise   BACON 59:*29*
mind with a. improve   DONNE 337:*79*
Murder...One of the Fine A.   DEQU 316:*67*
no A.; no Letters   HOBB 483:*40*
no ready a.   WORD 1096:*36*
progress of the a. and the sciences   MAO 648:*27*
servant of...the a.   BAUD 77:*28*
so far advanced in the A.   HAZL 463:*13*
turn a. education into a system   HUGH 500:*33*
Arvon On dreary A.'s shore   GRAY 443:*82*
ascend a. it then with religion   JONS 535:*91*
Ascendancy o the English A.   MACD 628:*92*
ascent nobility of a.   POTT 785:*44*
asceticism out of a.   MACC 625:*46*
Asclepius offer a cock to A.   PLATO 774:*17*
ash alone as mountain a.   DAYL 310:*57*
a. for nothing ill   SPEN 957:*99*
Oak, and A., and Thorn   KIPL 563:*98*
Out of the a.   PLATH 773:*97*
There grows the wild a.   CALL 226:*4*
ashamed a. at my failure to serve   YOKOI 1107:*99*
a. of one another   CONG 282:*44*
a. to be my father's child!   SHAK 874:*26*
feel a. of home   DICK 326:*69*
more things a man is a. of   SHAW 921:*24*
naked...and not a.   BIBLE 103:*92*
not...afraid of death, a.   BROW 195:*83*

ashamed (*contd.*)
not a. of the gospel of Christ — BIBLE 148:11
not a. of…the American dream — SHUL 936:37
not a. to fail — JOHN 525:75
seldom a.…that he cannot love — ELIOT 366:41
something he is a. of — SHAW 921:20
Ashbourn native of A., Derbyshire — ANON 24:13
ashbuds More black than a. — TENN 995:65
ashes a. all my lust — MARV 658:74
A. and sparks, my words — SHEL 928:91
a. of an oak — DONNE 338:17
a. taken to Australia — ANON 24:13
a. to a. — BOOK 176:58
a. under Uricon — HOUS 495:54
beauty for a. — BIBLE 127:12
burnt to a. — GRAH 437:88
handful of grey a. — CORY 288:64
men and women…shall pass to a. — SAND 841:59
past is a bucket of a. — SAND 841:60
repent in dust and a. — BIBLE 113:27
sat down among the a. — BIBLE 112:97
Scatter my a. — MONT 703:93
sour grapes and a. — ASHF 41:69
splendid in a. — BROW 196:3
tarnished with a. and soot — MOORE 704:7
ashore perilous excursion a. — LEWIS 602:52
water comes a. — FROST 407:89
ashtrays a. will become as obsolete — BLACK 164:45
Asia dusty catastrophe of A. — BROD 189:68
from the furthest inch of A. — SHAK 879:38
in A. as elsewhere — BALD 65:12
pampered Jades of A. — MARL 653:95
seven churches which are in A. — BIBLE 156:96
Sitting as huge as A. — BARK 71:17
stabilisation of East A. — HIRO 481:17
Asian what A. boys ought — JOHN 523:52
aside all gone a. — BIBLE 114:37
ask again we a. aloud — KEATS 546:81
A., and it shall be given you — BIBLE 135:57
a. for my money back — HUXL 507:70
a. less than one? — JONS 536:13
A. me no more — TENN 997:9
a. not what your country — KENN 551:65
a. the hard question — AUDEN 46:45
If you still have to a. — ARMS 35:46
intend to a. of them — KENN 550:61
then you can a. me — KING 557:69
what you a. them to do — WALD 1048:47
askew come in a. — HEAT 465:45
asking a. too much — CANN 230:72
a. 'Who came second?' — REAR 804:72
You a. me the way? — KAFKA 541:89
asleep Fall a., or hearing die — SHAK 918:56
Fall a., or hearing, die — SHAK 918:54
fast a. and weary — BIBLE 109:13
happiest moment…falling a. — SCHO 849:97
Not to fall a. is distinguished — BELL 88:34
thought me a. — PATM 760:2
too young to fall a. — SASS 845:33
we are a. in this world — BORG 179:13
asp a. doth on his feeder feed — LOVE 615:69
child shall play on the hole of the a. — BIBLE 125:68
small whisper of the a. — BYRON 220:97
asparagus a. of the poor — FRAN 401:89
grow a. — WADD 1047:25
mention A. and it appeared — DICK 325:51
oysters and a., and good wines — SAKI 838:6
aspect evident a. of things — HEID 467:66
aspects a. of human life — POPP 783:18
aspen a. good for staves — SPEN 957:99
By the light quivering a. made — SCOTT 853:58
aspens a. quiver — TENN 993:38
Asperges A. me hyssopo — BIBLE 159:42
asphalt only monument the a. road — ELIOT 370:18

aspic old purpose done up in a. — LAWR 585:76
aspidistra Keep the A. Flying — ORWE 742:90
aspiration thought and a. — ROSS 825:95
aspirations a. that weren't realized — KISS 566:36
poetry of our a. — CUOMO 301:7
young have a. — SAKI 837:99
aspire a. to give…a faithful account — ELIOT 365:6
bade me gaze, and there a. — ARNO 38:1
light, and will a. — SHAK 864:94
what else was there to a. to? — ROCK 818:76
aspirin both just a. — VIDAL 1044:68
Asquith affair between Margot A. — PARK 753:92
Herbert A.'s clarity — BALF 65:21
ass am such a tender a. — SHAK 871:50
back of an a. to bear all — NASHE 721:84
braying like an a. — SITW 940:5
broaden your a. if not your mind — HEMI 471:38
Cover your a. — SAFI 836:69
enamoured of an a. — SHAK 871:51
Hood an a. with reverend purple — JONS 534:77
law is a a. — DICK 321:42
law is such an a. — CHAP 252:76
like an a. whose back — SHAK 897:78
look like an a. — CONG 280:96
Lord opened the mouth of the a. — BIBLE 107:85
make him egregiously an a. — SHAK 899:23
part man, part horse's a. — ACHE 3:31
Preposterous a. — SHAK 864:80
scoreboard is an a. — CARD 232:4
this a. o'er-offices — SHAK 893:75
thrice-double a. — SHAK 917:43
what an a. am I? — SHAK 890:16
With the jawbone of an a. — BIBLE 109:20
assailant vengeance on the a. — TROL 1027:7
assailed a. by eyes — JAMES 517:41
assassin a.'s bullet — PARK 756:37
forgot…the a. — SAND 841:61
in harmony with sentiments of a. — BIER 160:64
saviour or a. — MURP 715:73
assassinated until he's a. — KAUF 542:13
assassination A. had never changed — DISR 333:8
moderated by a. — MUNS 714:62
assassins because you are bullied by a. — LLOY 609:63
assault a. on the mountain — CRAN 295:15
instance of a direct a. — SUMN 981:26
assaulting bees are a. …the flowers — REED 805:81
assay Help, angels! make a. — SHAK 892:48
assent ever given his a. — HUXL 506:53
expressions of a. — WAUGH 1057:81
asserted a. itself in her — HARDY 456:93
assertions falsehood of his a. — JOHN 531:10
asses come out A. — BURNS 209:59
given to them by the Prize A. — SMITH 948:32
led by th' nose As a. — SHAK 898:18
asset greatest a.…good night's sleep — WILS 1085:39
greatest a. any country can have — CHUR 265:27
assets assessing the value of a. — PAVL 761:20
complaining about loss of a. — ROTH 827:28
no longer liabilities but a. — SCHL 848:77
assimilation avenue of a. into society — DOCT 334:41
assistance Art and A. of the Architect — ALBE 12:94
conscious and creative a. — ROBB 813:10
association free and equal a. — ENGE 378:90
newspaper represents an a. — TOCQ 1021:78
Out of a. grows adhesion — BRON 191:3
associations all these accumulated a. — MELV 667:36
assonance adroit a. — UNTE 1036:47
assume A. a virtue — SHAK 892:59
what I a. you shall a. — WHIT 1072:76
assumption more powerful a. — SOLOW 952:94
assumptions a. of the ordinary man — ATTL 44:10
basic beliefs and a. — MILL 677:2
Mistaken in its a. — REGAN 805:95

assurance a. was given to me — WESL 1066:66
bright a. — WORD 1100:90
consoling the a. of grace — NIEB 727:64
diminished the dogmatic a. — RUSS 832:17
old house carried an a. — ACHE 2:25
on whom a. sits — ELIOT 369:89
some a. of grace — NIEB 727:63
assurances greatest a. of safety — ACHE 3:51
assure a. the survival — KENN 550:64
assured ignorant of what he's most a. — SHAK 896:72
Assyrian oiled and curled A. Bull — TENN 1001:77
Astolat lily maid of A. — TENN 1002:11
astonish A. me! — DIAG 319:98
astonished As many were a. at thee — BIBLE 127:98
a. at my own moderation! — CLIVE 270:28
beyond measure a. — BIBLE 141:66
suddenly a. — HEYE 479:88
astonishment not so much a. — SARG 843:95
the a. of loving — REID 806:97
truth which still fills me with a. — DAWK 310:43
your a.'s odd — ANON 25:35
astound startle well, but not a. — MILT 683:25
astounding seek for…the a. — BORG 178:10
astray sheep who've gone a. — KIPL 560:22
taking quite a liberty in going a. — ELIOT 365:2
astrologer gibberish of the a. — MACA 623:9
astronauts A.! Rotarians in space! — VIDAL 1044:59
astronomer no a. can find — HUGH 500:47
astronomy A. teaches the correct — LEAC 588:34
asunder let no man put a. — BOOK 176:52
let no man put a. — BIBLE 139:22
asylum America is an insane a. — POUND 787:93
as though I were in a lunatic a. — CONA 279:81
ataxia beginnings of a. — SILVA 938:77
Ate with A. by his side — SHAK 883:45
Athalus craftier to pley…Than A. — CHAU 254:7
Athanasian reciting the A. Creed — AUDEN 49:41
atheism a. against…our reason — BURKE 208:35
every luxury…a., breast-feeding — ORTON 742:86
inclineth Man's mind to a. — BACON 57:65
religion, not a., true remedy — BURKE 207:10
When a. wants martyrs — SADE 835:65
atheist an embittered a. — ORWE 742:89
a.…no invisible means of support — BUCH 202:27
daylight a. — BEHAN 84:61
grown an a.? — WEBS 1060:46
Sally said I was a sacrilegious a. — SALI 839:27
Thanks to God, I am still an a. — BUNU 204:61
atheists A., fools, and madmen! — ONEI 740:59
should make men a. — CAREW 232:17
Athens A. arose! — SHEL 932:63
A., the eye of Greece — MILT 694:35
Burn, with A. — CAMP 227:18
Who brings owls to A.? — ARIS 34:20
Ye men of A. — BIBLE 148:1
athlete a. cannot run with money — ZATO 1109:14
I'm not an a. — BRYA 201:16
athletes All pro a. are bilingual — HOWE 497:96
athletics regard all a. as inferior — WAUGH 1056:69
Athlone Great Gun of A. — ANON 25:21
Atkins Thank you, Mister A. — KIPL 560:30
Atlanta In A., the first question — BERE 94:36
Atlantic A. to the Pacific — CHUR 264:9
crossed the A. — MACC 625:44
Irish…other side of the A. — WAUGH 1057:89
sailed across the A. — BEHAN 84:58
steep A. stream — MILT 683:20
stormy North A. Ocean — LARD 5803:88
this A. generation — KENN 551:69
atlas bicycle and an a. — MURP 715:69
discumbered A. of the state — COWP 292:34
Witch of A. — YEATS 1107:92
atmosphere academic a. — STEA 963:2
a. favorable to the extraordinary — PAZ 762:24

atmosphere (contd.)

brought up in an a.	SPEN 956:88
delightful social a.	BENN 91:95
general a. of unreality	QUEN 797:54
human creatures breathe an a.	DICK 326:54
placed in the luminous a.	LEON 597:84
atmospheric a. billboard	THOR 1017:5
atom a. bombs are piling up	ORWE 744:40
a….breathed before	BRON 190:81
conceal the power of the a.	COLE 273:76
every a. belonging to me	WHIT 1072:76
Herman Melville who split the a.	LODGE 610:78
knowledge of the a.	EDDI 360:18
mystery of the a.	BRAD 184:93
no evil in the a.	STEV 972:73
atom-streams saw the flaring a.-s.	TENN 1003:29
atomic end up with the a. bomb	PAGN 750:40
forces a. energy on us	FROMM 406:70
form of a. blackmail	KENN 551:68
given us the a. bomb	KING 557:83
Hibakusha, a. victims	GEE 417:64
since the a. bomb	VREE 1047:22
US…has a. b.	MAO 648:26
way it was with the a. bomb	OPPE 741:71
atoms air is not so full…of a.	DONNE 339:25
A. or systems into ruin hurled	POPE 780:35
fortuitous concourse of a.	FISKE 390:86
fortuitous concurrence of a.	PALM 752:73
Let onion a. lurk	SMITH 949:55
Nothing exists except a.	DEMO 315:45
smash to a. …everything learnt	ORTE 741:84
atomsmashers half a dozen a.	PERE 766:91
atone pictures for the page a.	POPE 782:96
atonement This is the day of a.	RICH 809:56
atrocious a. crime of being…young	PITT 771:62
A. in content	GOET 431:69
atrocities a. that horrified us	HELL 468:89
atrophy a. of the imagination	GELL 417:69
music begins to a.	POUND 786:77
attach Where people wish to a.	AUST 52:65
attack a….economic legends	GALB 411:77
a. is particularly wounding	THAT 1008:20
French want to a.	ANON 30:57
lead such dire a.	MACA 623:15
plan of a.	SASS 845:28
serious a. upon morality	ORWE 743:22
attacks a. from outlaw states	REAG 804:64
attain cannot here a. unto them	HOOK 489:55
if we could a. it	TROL 1028:91
attained only wisdom ever to be a.	PRAT 789:23
attainments a. are the lot of all	TOCQ 1021:74
attempt a. at deliberate evasion	JONES 533:56
a. to display qualities	JOHN 525:91
die in the a.	HELL 468:81
fearing to a.	SHAK 896:63
vain a. to subdue	GILL 426:5
attend Another to a. him	HERB 475:23
attendant a. and…inmate	CONA 279:81
attended When neither is a.	SHAK 873:5
attention an awful a.	SHER 934:9
a. on a particular aspect	ROBB 813:14
by paying a.	HUXL 507:79
distract our a.	THOR 1016:78
drawing your a.	LEWIS 602:65
enough to get any child's a.	BAIL 62:69
fix our a. out of ourselves	HUME 503:98
husbands…cannot give their entire a.	BENN 91:91
more a. paid to them	JOHN 529:81
paying a. to them	SONT 953:13
socks compelled one's a.	SAKI 838:7
something worthy of a.	DARW 306:82
undivided a….of entire nation	BORAH 178:8
attentions pleasing a.	AUST 51:36
attentions (contd.)	

superior a. in little points	LAMB 576:24
attic A. boy to hunt	MILT 683:13
little brain a.	DOYLE 344:4
mellow glory of the A. stage	ARNO 36:62
O A. shape!	KEATS 547:10
speech as…pliant as A.	QUIL 797:59
attics shabby bums living in a.	LEWIS 602:53
attire a. be comely	LYLY 620:56
a. for a gentleman	SHAR 919:81
rich a. creeps rustling	KEATS 546:93
attitude don't like that a.	SHAN 918:69
elitist a. is basically suspicious	KRIS 569:96
enchantingly wavering a.	FITZ 390:94
end up with the a.	JACK 514:89
Fair a.!	KEATS 547:10
scientific a. of mind	RUSS 832:23
attitudes a. and movements	LEON 597:80
in-office a. and behavior	COUP 289:78
number of conflicting a.	ALTH 15:61
paid to have a. towards things	HEMI 470:14
attorney Even an a. of modest talent	CAPO 231:80
gentleman is an a.	JOHN 528:58
in love with a rich a.'s…daughter	GILB 423:52
office boy to an a.'s firm	GILB 423:58
attorneyship dealt in by a.	SHAK 861:97
attracted a. by God, or by Nature	INGE 511:37
a. by sure a. led	POPE 782:99
attraction A. and repulsion	BLAKE 166:71
attractions register competing a.	KNIG 567:53
attractive a. to the half-baked mind	FORS 398:32
When I find a woman a.	SAIN 836:81
attractiveness peculiar a. of each child	ACHE 2:20
attribute a. to God himself	SHAK 873:3
important a. of a lawyer	KENN 552:1
true a. of the soul	STAEL 962:77
attributes consisting in infinite a.	SPIN 961:60
attribution a. of false motives	BALD 65:14
Auburn Sweet A., loveliest village	GOLD 432:8
auction a joke were a charity a.	MACI 631:39
auctions stands…between a.	RAUS 802:42
audacity punished for their a.	CABE 224:78
tactful in a.	COCT 272:62
Auden A. ran it	BOWL 182:55
I think I'm A.	EWART 381:46
WH A., a…gutless Kipling	ORWE 742:1
audience Ambushing the a.	STOP 978:80
and looks at the a.	STOC 977:70
a. look to their eyes	SHAK 870:30
a.'s power of judgement	HARD 456:80
a….put up its umbrellas	BEER 83:27
a. was a disaster	WILDE 1077:64
a. would immediately be looking	HITC 482:24
a. yelled 'You're sublime'	HARG 457:15
awful attention in the a.	SHER 934:9
best a….a little drunk	BARK 71:20
End without a.	SHAK 864:96
hold the a.	UPDI 1037:62
if I don't practise…the a. knows	PADE 749:30
inviting his a. to discard him	ANNAN 20:35
keep the a. awake	OLIV 738:32
must have a London a.	AUST 51:50
seeking empathy with his a.	SAFI 836:71
spirits of the a.	BIER 131:40
two kinds of a.	SCHN 848:83
your a. is conjectural	ORWE 744:35
audiences a. come to hear	FREE 403:30
auditorium hidden a. of his skull	STER 968:85
I remember the a.	POWE 788:15
august a. occasions of the state	FROST 407:3
August A. for the people	AUDEN 46:53
winter…To recommence in A.	BYRON 223:58
Augusta A….grandma's maiden name	
	BERE 94:36
Augustus A. was a chubby lad	HOFF 484:58

auld a. lang syne!	BURNS 210:94
aunt A. is calling to A.	WODE 1089:91
A. Jane observed	GRAH 437:86
A. Sally she's going to adopt	TWAIN 1033:94
Her A….from her Earliest Youth	BELL 87:10
said my a. Dot	MACA 622:85
Auntie Whenever A. moves around	STEV 975:36
aunts a. and uncles were legion	SHAW 926:43
cousins, and his a.!	GILB 423:56
her husband, her a.	RANS 802:31
play bridge with my old maid a.	FIEL 388:56
aura a. of one who knows	BANKS 70:98
Aurora rising with A.'s light	SWIFT 985:2
See how A. throws her fair	HERR 477:61
Zephyr and A.	MILT 682:97
Ausonia let A., skilled in every art	BYRON 219:63
Austen Jane A….only novelist	BANKS 70:1
austere strode on a.	THOM 1015:58
austerity high a. to delight	FREE 404:35
Austerlitz Pile the bodies…at A.	SAND 841:62
Australia always last year in A.	THER 1009:44
ashes taken to A.	ANON 25:17
Being lost in A.	CHAT 254:99
camped in the centre of A.	STUA 980:8
colour in A. is gold	STRE 980:5
cricket tour in A.	LARW 582:30
Dead Heart of A.	GREG 446:48
housemaid…the best in A.	MELBA 667:23
indifference of…golden A.	LAWR 586:81
like A. less and less	LAWR 585:72
postmodern, muliticultural A.	NARO 719:40
so much interested in A.	WILDE 1076:59
Spirit of A.	FIELD 387:39
the other in A.	GAY 416:46
Australian A. be equal to…a Briton	PARK 755:31
A. literature	STEW 977:63
A. novel is not…dreary	WHITE 1070:45
first and foremost…a A.	MELBA 667:21
proud that I am an A.	FRAN 402:16
spirit of an A.	FRAN 402:15
stretched the Great A. Emptiness	WHITE 1070:44
Austria A. is the little world	HEBB 466:55
born in A.	SIMON 939:81
Austrian A. Empire did not exist	PALA 751:55
authenticity verify the a.	WILL 1083:99
author a. and finisher of our faith	BIBLE 154:54
a. and giver of all good things	BOOK 174:12
a. because you like his books	LINK 606:26
a.'s fairy godmother	LUCAS 618:30
a.'s mind	GAUG 416:40
a. of peace	BOOK 173:96
a. of the play	GILB 426:99
A. of the Whole escape	POPE 783:9
a. spoils everything	LAFO 575:97
a. today proclaims	ROBB 813:10
a. who speaks about his own books	DISR 333:18
a. writes with a misty profundity	WHIT 1071:52
choose an a.	DILL 331:55
confession…of its a.	NIET 728:83
Corrected…By its A.!	FRAN 402:99
every other a. may aspire to praise	JOHN 526:4
expected to see an a.	PASC 757:54
fine future for its a.	WILDE 1076:31
first-rate a. wants an exquisite heroine	FITZ 391:21
from the a.'s soul	HUXL 506:57
go to the a.	RUSK 831:97
Hunting the a., painter and musician	
	SITW 942:30
improved by it's a.'s explanations	MACL 634:76
in Search of an A.	PIRA 770:49
Literature…depends on the a.'s skill	QUIL 797:60
more than wit to make an a.	LA 572:36
no a. today	SARR 843:2
not only as an a.	GRASS 439:12

babes (*contd.*)
B. reduced to misery	BLAKE 167:*89*
even the b. in arms	THOM 1009:*50*
Out of the mouth of b.	BIBLE 114:*34*
Tears, then for b.	SHAK 861:*20*

babies b....come into the world MENC 670:*84*
b. like such toys	MORE 707:*53*
b. who rush at me	MANS 647:*40*
bit the b. in the cradles	BROW 197:*32*
hates dogs and b.	ROST 825:*3*
having b. without chloroform	BARB 71:*13*
long hours spent as b.	BRAD 183:*76*
only washing. And b.	THOM 1011:*85*
Other people's b.	HERB 474:*95*
putting milk into b.	CHUR 265:*27*
You breed b. and you eat chips	WESK 1066:*57*

baboon humanity with a b. SHAK 898:*15*
morals of a b. CAPO 231:*89*

baby B. in an ox's stall BETJ 100:*47*
b. is God's opinion	SAND 841:*74*
b. made in a test tube	MAIL 639:*86*
b., assailed by eyes	JAMES 517:*41*
blind boy, Venus' b.	SPEN 959:*29*
don't be stingy b.	MARI 651:*69*
Every b. born into the world	DICK 322:*53*
Hasta la vista, b.	SCHW 851:*25*
little b. thing	MACD 628:*2*
mother laid her b.	ALEX 13:*19*
no more...than a man can have a b.	DRAP 345:*30*
no rhyme to 'lady' but 'b.'	SHAK 880:*65*
slept like a b.	DOLE 335:*51*
When the first b. laughed	BARR 72:*43*
Where did you come from, b. dear?	MACD 628:*1*
who gives a b. birth	MASE 662:*46*
why...name your b. 'John'	GOLD 434:*40*

Babylon B. be thrown down BIBLE 158:*29*
B. The Great	BIBLE 158:*28*
By the rivers of B.	BIBLE 119:*47*
By the waters of B.	WALP 1051:*88*
Ere B. was dust	SHEL 929:*13*
London is a modern B.	DISR 333:*96*
through the walls of B.	COMN 278:*68*

Baca through the valley of B. BIBLE 117:*94*

Bacall hint of B.'s slinkiness ALLEN 14:*33*

Bacchus B. hath drowned more men FULL 410:*47*

Bach angels play only B. BARTH 74:*69*
B. on the wrong notes	PROK 792:*78*
not B. or Schubert	MACC 627:*68*
play B. your way	LAND 579:*65*

bachelor b., a solicitor, a Freemason DOYLE 344:*12*
b. who has...experience	RIDGE 811:*77*
half-witted b.	WODE 1089:*91*
he was a b.	SYMI 988:*59*
makes Legree a b.	CHES 256:*69*
married or a b.	ADDI 6:*6*
wise in the b.	STEV 974:*7*

bachelors reasons for b. to go out ELIOT 365:*22*
where the b. sit SHAK 879:*34*

back and they stared b. GILL 426:*3*
at my b. in a cold blast	ELIOT 368:*88*
B. and side go bare	ANON 23:*84*
b. the masses	GLAD 429:*54*
b. to nature	GOTT 436:*73*
b. us or sack us	CALL 226:*2*
b. with ingots bows	SHAK 897:*78*
beast on my b.	DOUG 341:*58*
behind his b.	JOHN 528:*58*
coming b. seems possible	DICK 329:*19*
Dost thou look b.	TENN 999:*44*
down express in the small of the b.	WODE 1089:*89*
flying b. and forth	PLATH 773:*92*
good coat upon his b.	JOHN 527:*32*
hangs upon thy b.	SHAK 870:*21*
I'll be b.	SCHW 851:*26*

back (*contd.*)
it will come drifting b.	HAWES 460:*61*
lean'd my b. unto an aik	BALL 67:*57*
my b. I always hear	MARV 658:*74*
never turned his b.	BROW 200:*2*
not easy to call them b.	SAND 841:*64*
see my b. parts	BIBLE 107:*77*
sit on man's b.	TOLS 1023:*97*
stab me in the b.	LAMP 578:*51*
stabs you in the b.	SNOW 951:*75*
thumps upon your b.	COWP 292:*44*
wallet at his b.	SHAK 896:*51*
way their b. looks	WYETH 1103:*46*
Will you no come b. again	NAIR 718:*21*

back-yard squabble in your b.-y. SYNGE 988:*64*

backbone b. of the Army KIPL 562:*59*

backgammon sport I mastered...b. JERR 521:*18*

backhand make her hit b. volleys KING 557:*70*
wonderful b. drive BETJ 99:*32*

backlash b. against women's rights FALU 382:*58*
finding of limited use to b. publicists FALU 382:*57*

backs b. to the wall HAIG 450:*10*
don't ask employers...to like b.	BORO 179:*22*
on the b. of his friends	HUGH 499:*24*
when our b. are turned	CRISP 297:*35*

backshop reserve a b. MONT 701:*66*

backside moral b. LICH 603:*80*
skelp across her b. ANON 27:*59*

backward b. motion FROST 407:*88*
B. ran sentences	GIBBS 422:*37*
dark b. and abyss of time?	SHAK 916:*19*
fell from off the seat b.	BIBLE 110:*31*
too far b.	THUR 1019:*27*
when you look b.	ORWE 743:*14*

backwards life must be understood b.
                                          KIER 556:*57*
memory that only works b.	CARR 240:*60*
rapidly b. and forwards	REED 805:*81*

backwoods b. of Canada MOOD 703:*95*

backyards American b. MAIL 639:*87*

bacon bring home the b. ONEI 740:*62*
man who never ate b. HATT 460:*58*

Bacon dig up B. GILB 426:*99*
their lordships asked B.	BENT 93:*29*
think how B. shined	POPE 781:*51*

bad almost as b., good-mother SHAK 892:*51*
as b. as b. can be	JOHN 531:*27*
b., and like to coins	TENN 1003:*38*
b. book is as much	HUXL 506:*57*
b. die late	DEFOE 312:*74*
B. laws are the worst sort of tyranny	BURKE 207:*22*
b. poets deface	ELIOT 368:*78*
b.'s the best of us	FLET 394:*72*
b. unhappily	WILDE 1078:*85*
because they are so b.	TROL 1028:*86*
believe a thing to be b.	MILN 681:*84*
better than b. strokes	SHAK 884:*62*
bring them in to b. repute	WILD 1079:*31*
but some b. man	HERB 476:*33*
can't be all b.	FIEL 388:*82*
everything b. that's printed	WELL 1063:*5*
good and b. of every land	BAIL 62:*71*
good Compensate b. in man	BROW 200:*92*
good or they were b.	TRAV 1025:*36*
how b. you used to be	KNUD 567:*64*
How sad and b. and mad	BROW 200:*83*
If we live inside a b. joke	RABAN 798:*74*
Mad, b., and dangerous to know	LAMB 576:*4*
make b. good	SHAK 897:*86*
might also be very b.	HOCK 483:*48*
never a b. peace	FRAN 402:*9*
No man...irreclaimably b.	CARL 234:*46*
not really b. at heart	BELL 87:*11*
not that we are so b.	NIGH 729:*97*

bad (*contd.*)
nothing either good or b.	SHAK 889:*98*
nothing so b. or so good	SHAW 920:*11*
obstinacy in a b. one	STER 969:*93*
people...not good or b. enough	COMP 279:*73*
perhaps I was the least b.	SIHA 938:*73*
put up with the b. things	TROL 1027:*69*
strong antipathy of good to b.	POPE 782:*88*
sure it is b. morality	SKEL 942:*39*
that I have b. dreams	SHAK 890:*99*
think something is good or b.	STEV 972:*79*
though it be from b. to worse	IRVI 513:*67*
was b., she was horrid	LONG 612:*21*
we're not doing too b.	DICK 320:*9*
what is frankly b.	STEIN 966:*45*
what you feel b. after	HEMI 470:*23*
When b. men combine	BURKE 206:*1*
when I'm b. I'm better	WEST 1067:*79*
Where everything is b.	BRAD 184:*92*
world is b. enough	CLOU 270:*34*

baddish Gilbert had a b. streak QUIL 797:*61*

badge b. of all our tribe SHAK 874:*20*
b. of authority	HERB 476:*42*
b. of lost innocence	PAINE 750:*44*
Red B. of Courage	CRANE 295:*11*
soldier wears a b.	READ 803:*54*

badgers When b. fight CLARE 267:*79*

badminton art of b. is to deceive THOM 1012:*16*

bads goods...jointly with b. BOUL 181:*44*

Baedeker B. is astonishingly LEVIN 600:*29*
never Mr B. HERB 474:*97*

baffled b. to fight together BROW 200:*2*

bag agitate a b. of wind WHITE 1069:*18*
in a b. all sorts of seeds	SPEN 959:*41*
into a b. with holes	BIBLE 130:*64*
Tuppence a B.!	TRAV 1025:*38*
upsetting a b. of nails	RUSK 831:*11*
with nothing but a carpet b.	MELV 668:*46*

bagatelle vive la b.! STER 970:*24*

bagel after another like a b. IGNA 510:*28*

baggage believe b. loves me CONG 280:*93*

bagpipe Twelve Highlanders and a b. ANON 30:*64*
when he b. sings i'th' nose SHAK 873:*90*

bagpiper laugh like parrots at a b. SHAK 872:*76*

bags picking up my b. NEVI 723:*15*
thousand douche b. LOWRY 618:*18*

Bah B! said Scrooge DICK 323:*85*

Baiae in B.'s bay SHEL 928:*88*

bairn bonnie broukit b.! MACD 627:*71*

bairnie Singin' till a b. MACD 627:*74*

bairnies waefu' wife and b. three BALL 67:*42*

bairns when they werena gude b. SCOTT 855:*92*

bait Roots ripe as old b. ROET 819:*94*

baiting b. a mouse-trap with cheese SAKI 838:*15*
b. place of wit SIDN 937:*53*

baker b. rhymes for his pursuit BROW 200:*98*
B. Street irregulars DOYLE 343:*93*

Bakewell every fool in B. at Buxton RUSK 831:*13*

Balaam ass...said unto B. BIBLE 107:*85*

balance b., an...interchange WORD 1096:*34*
b. between the hands employed	STEU 970:*29*
b. of actual forces	NAPO 718:*27*
bodies out of their natural b.	LEON 597:*76*
causes, the b. sheet	MO 698:*12*
ecological b. of the planet	SONT 953:*7*
false b. is abomination	BIBLE 120:*69*
held in b. only by the miracle	HONE 488:*29*
hold the b. of Europe	WILL 1080:*47*
redress the b. of the Old	CANN 230:*73*
sane b. of values	POUND 786:*80*
scale...in nice b.	POPE 782:*92*
the b. of power	PALM 752:*74*

balances checks and b. ANON 28:*17*
weighed in the b. BIBLE 129:*49*

bargain (*contd.*)
Necessity never made a good b.   FRAN 402:3
never was a better b. driv'n   SIDN 936:47
Will anyone be satisfied with the b.?   COLL 276:39
bargain-basement b.-b. Boadicea   HEAL 464:29
bargains Queens never make b.   CARR 241:81
rule for b.   DICK 322:73
barge The b. she sat in   SHAK 905:68
barges b. as solemn as Barons   WALP 1051:81
bark B. when their fellows do   SHAK 917:52
come out as I do, and b.   JOHN 531:21
heard a seal b.!   THUR 1018:12
swell billow, and swim b.   SHAK 884:63
Barkis B. is willin'   DICK 324:4
barks in their b. my thoughts   SHAK 886:97
barley among the bearded b.   TENN 993:40
b. and of rye   TENN 993:37
Corn rigs, an' b. rigs   BURNS 210:80
fill his barn with wheat or b.   BUNY 205:75
taste the b. bree   BURNS 211:2
barley-sheaves between the b.-s.   TENN 993:43
Barleycorn John B. should d.   BURNS 210:89
Barlow my Hornby and my B.   THOM 1014:32
barn fill his b. with wheat or barley   BUNY 205:75
men from the b. and the forge   HOUS 495:52
stack or the b. door   MILT 682:99
Barnet old B., the minister's man   HOGG 485:66
barns gathered into b.   TRUTH 1030:39
pull down my b.   BIBLE 143:94
barometer poet...used as a b.   TRIL 1027:60
baronet lily-handed b. he   TENN 996:95
barons b. and their supporters   INNO 512:56
knights and b. bold   MILT 682:3
barque Though his b. cannot be lost   SHAK 907:13
barrel buy ink by the b.   KIRK 565:27
dribble...like a leaky b.   ELIOT 365:9
out of the b. of a gun   MAO 648:22
barrel-load save them by the b.-l.   THOM 1014:33
barrel-organ kind of human b.-o.   DICK 323:92
barren a b. bride   POPE 781:72
b. thing this Conservatism   DISR 332:83
Be she b.   SWIFT 986:17
breed for b. metal   SHAK 874:22
from Dan to Beersheba...'tis all b.   STER 970:21
make b. our lives   SWIN 987:35
small model of the b. earth   SHAK 867:59
Speech is often b.   ELIOT 366:27
Barrets didn't like B. of Wimpole   PARK 754:90
barricade some disputed b.   SEEG 857:26
barriers break down b.   GING 427:22
impenetrable b. of our prison   EDGE 361:32
barrows grassy b.   TENN 1003:23
Barrymore B.'s acting till the cows   NATH 721:87
No B. would allow   BARR 73:58
bars b. a thousand harms   SHAK 863:70
b. of Madras, Oregon   SNYD 951:86
Between their silver b.!   FLEC 393:55
Bolts and b. will not   MOLI 698:18
half a dozen b. of Lillabullero   STER 969:95
looked out through the same b.   LANG 579:68
no voluntary b.   PATM 760:6
Nor iron b. a cage   615:63
Stare out between the b.   SACK 835:62
weary of these worldly b.   SHAK 883:25
bartender By the time a b. knows   MARQ 656:49
good drunk...a good b.   BISH 164:36
bartered People...must not be b.   WILS 1086:55
base b. football player   SHAK 902:3
Joy without Labour is b.   RUSK 831:1
Majors at the B.   SASS 845:26
peace, be it never so b.   CROM 298:52
replaced it on its b.   NAPO 719:37
baseball B....collective chess   BARZ 75:98

baseball (*contd.*)
b....free of chivalry   BROUN 194:50
B. has the great advantage   SHAW 925:34
B. is a Lockean game   NOVAK 732:36
better learn b.   BARZ 75:97
Cricket is b. on valium   WILL 1081:54
things you can do in a b. game   STEN 968:76
baseballs batting b.   THUR 1019:32
baseness dignity or b. of a person   CHRI 262:74
basenesses b. are plainer to no eye   CARL 233:31
basest b. of all things   FAUL 383:77
bashfulness in England a particular b.   ADDI 7:21
Basil steal my B.-pot away   KEATS 546:84
sweet B. evermore   KEATS 546:83
basis laughter is the b. of humankind   RABE 798:77
on the b. of our slendid failure   FAUL 384:85
science has for its b.   PAINE 750:51
whole b....of architecture   WAGN 1047:26
basked b. him in the sun   SHAK 885:89
basket egg heads are in one b.   ANON 27:71
like wet crabs in a b.   DURR 357:76
lived to be carried in a b.   SHAK 878:22
set the b. umbilicus-high   NASH 720:73
basketball B., a game   NASH 720:73
interest in b.   NASH 720:70
bass sustained b. part   KIER 556:60
basset-horn melodious b.-h.   MORG 707:63
basset-hounds yellow-bosomed b.   MORG 707:63
Bast got with child by Leonard B.   MANS 647:1
bastard all my eggs in one b.   PARK 755:19
Daddy, daddy, you b.   PLATH 773:96
knocked me b. off!   HILL 481:7
no matter how big a b.   SALI 839:26
publicly call me a b.   WHIT 1072:70
bastards gods, stand up for b.!   SHAK 902:1
unless the b. have the courage   STEI 966:57
We are b. all   SHAK 916:4
bastinado or in b., or in steel   SHAK 887:28
bastion like a b.'s mole   SMART 944:69
bat b. that you were kind   MANN 646:94
b. with tears in your eyes   BRAD 184:95
batsman and the b.   LANG 579:67
black b., night   TENN 1001:85
Bradman, with the b.   LARW 582:31
click of the b.   COOKE 286:32
come to see me b.   GRACE 437:85
Gave up his b. and ball   EGAN 362:55
history of b. and ball   ARLO 34:37
think he's batting b. on   JOHN 532:46
Twinkle, twinkle, little b.!   CARR 238:29
weak-eyed b....flits by   COLL 277:48
bath b. by the beach   REID 806:98
B. twice a day   BURG 205:80
long to take a b.   UPDI 1037:64
nymph to the b. addressed   SHEL 930:29
soaping her breasts in the b.   EWART 381:43
steamed like a b.   JONS 534:84
test my b. before   NASH 720:64
wrote ... on his b. tub   POUND 787:87
bathes b. daily in a running   MOORE 704:1
bathing-caps two b.-c.   TRAV 1025:31
bathroom as he goes to the b.   BLYT 170:51
revolutionary in a b.   LINK 606:24
baths B. that made him young   HERR 477:52
two walking b.   CRAS 296:21
bats archaeologists...like b.   MACA 622:84
b. have been broken   HOWE 497:94
B. have no bankers   BERR 98:15
covered with the skins of b.   DRAY 346:41
sad b. wheel about the steeple   DEBU 311:84
Suspicions...like b.   BACON 59:4
batsman b. thinks he's bowled   LANG 579:67
B. of the Dawn   THOM 1014:34
b.'s Willey   JOHN 532:45

batsman (*contd.*)
Cricket is a b.'s game   BENA 89:47
ghostly b. plays   THOM 1014:32
premium on temperament for b.   BRAD 184:96
batsmen sending your opening b.   HOWE 497:94
The really great b.   TRAV 1025:29
battalions big b.   VOLT 1047:15
dreams in pale b.   SORL 953:23
sorrows come...in b.   SHAK 892:65
batter put the b. off his stride   SHAW 925:36
batteries shot from one of the b.   MACA 624:28
battery make no b.   SHAK 864:98
batting W. G. discovered b.   RANJ 801:27
battle army hurrying into b.   ORWE 742:91
b. against yourself   KILLY 556:62
B. decides everything   CLAU 268:94
b. for precedence   SITW 941:17
b. for the mind   NOON 731:21
b. for your all   AESC 9:56
B. Hymn of the Republic   OBRI 734:69
b. is not yours, but God's   BIBLE 112:90
b. of man with man   WEBER 1059:21
b. of Waterloo was won   ORWE 743:18
b. of Waterloo   WELL 1064:20
b....to break all this up   WITT 1088:82
b. to the strong   BIBLE 123:35
b. to the strong   DAVI 307:97
B....untying with the teeth   BIER 160:70
Ben B. was a soldier bold   HOOD 488:16
better in b. than in bed   STER 969:8
borne the b.   LINC 605:6
brave that die in b.   CLOU 271:45
drunk delight of b.   TENN 994:58
field of b.   STEV 974:8
fights no uphill b.   HAZL 463:9
forefront of the hottest b.   BIBLE 110:46
Goddess of the B.   BARK 71:19
half the b.   GOLD 433:25
history of a b.   WELL 1063:13
invincible in b.   SOPH 953:19
lines of b. wind   MACG 630:22
lit the b.'s wreck   HEMA 469:11
most serious things...in a b.   CARR 240:58
Next to a b. lost   WELL 1063:12
noise of b. rolled   TENN 1004:41
on the field of b.   PAST 759:89
out of b. I escaped   OWEN 748:14
prepared for the b.   HUSS 505:37
See the front o' b. lour   BURNS 212:37
sent it into b.   KENN 551:76
sent it into b.   MURR 715:78
sent ten thousand men to b.   SITT 940:97
smelleth the b. afar off   BIBLE 113:23
strange manner of b.   WILL 1080:44
strife is o'er, the b. done   POTT 784:43
This b. fares like   SHAK 862:21
trumpets which sing to b.   SHEL 931:60
Tweedledum...agreed to have a b.   CARR 239:53
we never won a b.   DAVIS 309:37
who shall prepare himself to the b.?
  BIBLE 151:63
battle-flags b.-f. were furled   TENN 995:77
battlefield b. of Vietnam   MACL 635:1
brave on the b.   MITC 697:88
or the b. we die   SULL 981:24
soldier dying on the b.   BISM 164:40
battleground b. for a dark angel   ENGL 595:47
battlehorse painting...a b.   DENIS 316:58
battles b. and death   GARI 415:25
b., heroic actions   POUS 787:21
b....were but desparate appeals   CHUR 263:6
b. with the immortals   HOMER 487:16
Dead b.   TUCH 1031:44
exercises are unbloody b.   JOSE 537:35

battles (*contd.*)
fought his b. — BUNY 205:74
hell her b. wage — POPE 782:95
in a hundred b. — SUN 982:33
mother of all b. — HUSS 505:36
not called to win b. — JENK 520:1
O God of b. — SHAK 881:95
pitched b. in India — MACA 623:8
quarrel and have b. — MACM 636:15
where be the b. — SPEN 958:17
battleship like…launching a b. — OSBO 745:67
battlewagon like a venerable b. — TIME 1020:66
bauble fool's b. — CROM 298:56
prettiest b. you ever saw — WALP 1051:81
Baudelaire B.…Whoremongers — ONEI 740:59
Like Shelley and like B. — ISHE 513:73
bauhaus From B. to Our House — WOLFE 1090:27
bawcock King's a b. — SHAK 881:91
bawdry so without b. — SHAK 912:35
Baxter In B.'s view — WEBER 1059:19
bay curve of a blue b. — LOWE 615:76
in Baiae's b. — SHEL 928:88
like a green b.-tree — BOOK 176:70
margin of the b. — WORD 1099:68
planted a green B.-tree — BETH 99:21
Somebody bet on de b. — FOST 399:59
Bayleys B., and your Bests — MACA 622:86
bayonet b. is a weapon — ANON 26:43
force of the b.! — MIRA 695:69
bayonets grass of silver b. — MACG 630:22
throne of b. — INGE 511:36
BBC B. Radio is a never-never land — SAFER 835:66
B. set its house in order — CRIT 297:44
the B. …is very truthful — ORWE 743:20
be can b. but What we are — SHIR 935:25
For what shall b.—yes! — HAMM 453:42
How can I b. who I am? — JORD 536:28
Must it b.? It must b.! — BEET 84:51
only thing I'd like to b. — SALI 839:28
only way one can b. — BECK 81:4
or not to b. — TWAIN 1033:89
thou shouldst cease to b. — SHEL 927:65
To b., or not to b. — SHAK 890:21
What is there to b. — EMPS 378:86
What we appear to b. — SCHI 847:66
what we may b. — SHAK 892:63
you should not b.? — GRAV 439:20
beach Along the hidden b. — KIPL 563:91
dry shell on the b. — DU 354:32
marks of fishermen on the b. — NAIP 717:17
On the B. is a story — GARD 414:20
wood found on the b. — ROSE 823:58
beaches fight on the b. — CHUR 264:14
Beachy Birmingham by B. Head — CHES 259:32
beadle b. on boxin' day — DICK 320:26
Thou rascal b. — SHAK 904:37
beadroll Fame's eternal b. — SPEN 959:33
beads jewels for a set of b. — SHAK 867:62
number Ave-Maries on his b. — SHAK 861:49
beak b. of preposterous widthlessness — CUMM 299:73
thy b. from out my heart — POE 776:49
beaker b. full of the warm South — KEATS 547:14
beaks kites to whet their b. — RANS 802:34
beam b. that is in thine own eye? — BIBLE 135:55
B. us up, Mr Scott — RODD 818:84
eyes at the full midday b. — MILT 686:75
beaming b. soul — POPE 783:5
beams b. may not dissolve the ice — SURR 983:46
b. of science fall — POPE 782:98
little candle throws his b. — SHAK 873:7
splendour of his mid-day b. — HERR 477:56
way your smile just b. — GERS 420:11
bean Boston…home of the b. — BOSS 180:28
Nine b.-rows — YEATS 1104:57

bean (*contd.*)
stale b.-soup, of college yells — MENC 670:91
beanbag b. of the heart — NOON 731:22
beanfields smell of the b. — CHAT 253:98
beans b. and peason put within — ANON 21:64
determined to know b. — THOR 1017:90
hill of b. in this crazy world — EPST 379:1
hill of b. — GARN 415:29
bear b. any burden — KENN 550:64
b. fruit—or wither — JAY 519:74
B. of Very Little Brain — MILNE 680:74
bush supposed a b.! — SHAK 871:55
every b. that ever there was — BRAT 185:15
Exit, pursued by a b. — SHAK 911:25
furry as a b. — SITW 941:14
Grizzly b. is huge — HOUS 496:86
hardest thing to b. — JUVE 540:79
If you b. your cross — KEMP 549:45
last b., shot drinking — CRANE 295:99
many things to say…ye cannot b. — BIBLE 146:65
more sorrow than they could b. — REST 807:17
out of the paw of the b. — BIBLE 110:39
Puritan hated b.-baiting — MACA 624:27
rode on the back of a b. — LEAR 590:68
tree could b. no more — FROST 406:80
Wedged B. in a Great Tightness? — MILNE 680:73
Who can b. the Gracchi — JUVE 540:78
bear-like But b.-l. I must fight — SHAK 910:87
beard b. the lion in his den — SCOTT 853:56
By thy long grey b. — COLE 273:83
Com'st thou to b. me — SHAK 890:10
endure a husband with a b. — SHAK 879:33
even Aaron's b. — BIBLE 119:45
hairs in the b. — GOYA 437:83
have a b. coming — SHAK 870:31
Loose his b., and hoary hair — GRAY 442:81
off the Great Cham's b. — SHAK 879:38
Old Man with a b. — LEAR 589:50
send thee a b. — SHAK 895:21
singeing of the King of Spain's b. — DRAKE 345:27
To shave the b. is a sin — IVAN 514:83
without scratching someone's b. — LICH 604:84
bearded b. like a man! — DICK 328:18
beards b. forbid me to interpret — SHAK 907:16
their long b. — SWIFT 985:93
bearing b. what is laid upon us — ELIOT 365:19
bears beat our tunes for b. — FLAU 392:38
habitation for b. and wolves — SCHAW 847:61
sympathise with the b. — MUIR 713:40
the English and the b. — THOM 1012:95
beast And what rough b. — YEATS 1106:78
b. imbued with such immortal fire? — BYRON 219:73
b. on my back — DOUG 341:58
B. ravens in its own avidity? — EBER 359:11
Better B. and know your end — DEVL 318:88
Blatant b. — SPEN 959:35
call this b. to mind — BELL 87:98
chase had a b. in view — DRYD 352:97
Cocoa is a vulgar b. — CHES 259:30
deem himself a god, or b. — POPE 780:42
even-tempered the b. — TRUD 1029:12
huge inarticulate b. — HOFS 484:62
I hold a b. — THOM 1010:60
makes a man a b. — WEBS 1059:32
making the b. with two backs — SHAK 897:98
Man is neither angel nor b. — PASC 758:73
man who lay with a b. — HELL 468:88
marks of the b. — HARDY 456:94
night out for man or b. — FIEL 388:57
number of the b. — BIBLE 158:22
often acts the b. — PASC 758:73
scarlet coloured b. — BIBLE 158:28
snorts like a great b. — SMITH 949:60
Tam mounts his b. — BURNS 211:16

beast (*contd.*)
tilt their aggregate b. — MACN 637:37
Unto some brutish b. — MARL 654:22
who worship the b. — BIBLE 158:23
wild b., or a god — BACON 58:97
beastie Wee, sleeket, cowrin,…b. — BURNS 209:67
beastly b. to the Bank of England — CRIT 297:44
B. to the Germans — COWA 290:6
beasts all manner of fourfooted b. — BIBLE 147:91
Among the b. no mate — MILT 692:97
b. are our masters — FLET 394:73
b. of the intellectual domain — HOLM 486:80
b. on each other prey — ROCH 816:52
brute b. that have no understanding — BOOK 175:43
droop men and b. — NASHE 721:81
fled to brutish b. — SHAK 884:50
keeping b. of burden patient — KING 559:1
man's distinctive mark…not the b. — BROW 200:80
minds…to the b. that perish — WELLS 1064:26
Music might tame…wild b. — GAY 417:60
Nature teaches b. — SHAK 911:4
round about the throne, were four b. — BIBLE 157:3
small and great b. — BIBLE 118:18
wild b. and Lord man — MUIR 713:40
wild b. ate it — BAUD 77:21
beat b. Mr Turgenev — HEMI 471:37
b. my people to pieces — BIBLE 124:58
b. them now and again — THOM 1011:74
b. them today — STARK 963:99
bloody b. them again — RAMS 801:20
Don't b. me, pa! — JOYCE 537:41
figure to get b. some time — LOUIS 614:58
if we b. West Germany — RAMS 801:19
One man…can always b. ten — SHAW 925:28
this is really a b. generation — KERO 553:15
To the b. of the measure — POUND 786:78
beaten No Englishman is…fairly b. — SHAW 925:22
The b. road — SHEL 931:57
You've b. them once — RAMS 801:20
beatificate translate And b. — QUIL 797:62
beating driven by b. — ASCH 41:51
hear b. of his wings — BRIG 188:47
beatings dread of the b.! — BETJ 101:59
Beatles Chatterly ban And the B. — LARK 581:12
Beatrice B. like a lapwing runs — SHAK 879:51
beauteous b. things for which — CORY 288:66
B. the fleet — SMART 944:71
How b. mankind is! — SHAK 917:42
beautied b. with impermanence — SCOTT 852:35
b. with plast'ring art — SHAK 890:20
beauties b. of the fute-ball — ANON 23:88
B. …their pretty eyes may roll — POPE 779:3
concealed b. of a writer — ADDI 7:15
no matter what b. I saw — PRIOR 791:60
pale, unripened b. — ADDI 8:30
saved by b. not his own — POPE 782:96
Thy b., yet could write — JONS 536:15
beautified b. is a vile phrase — SHAK 889:90
beautiful appear b. outward — BIBLE 139:36
art for the sake…of the b. — SAND 840:55
b. and death-struck year — HOUS 495:59
b. and frozen, I preserve you — ATWO 45:25
B. and the Damned — FITZ 390:96
b., and therefore to be wooed — SHAK 861:95
b. as a wreck — SHEL 931:54
B.! B.! — ALDR 13:11
b. countenance — BIBLE 110:37
B. dreamer — FOST 399:62
B. for situation — BIBLE 116:75
b. is always shocking — BAUD 77:31
b. only when she is loved — EPST 379:4
b. passionate body — SWIN 987:34
b. sentiments — GIDE 423:47
b., the tender, the kind — MILL 676:90

beautiful *(contd.)*		**beauty** *(contd.)*		**beauty** *(contd.)*	
b. things made by renunciation?	DEGAS 312:91	B. is the lover's gift	CONG 281:35	most radiant b.	EINS 363:67
b. woman…qualities of a man	LABR 572:37	B. is truth, truth b.	KEATS 547:12	nation…without a sense of b.	WHAR 1068:93
beginning of a b. friendship	WALL 1051:78	b. is vain	BIBLE 122:13	no b. that we should desire him	BIBLE 127:99
better to be b. than to be good	WILDE 1076:53	b. like a tightened bow	YEATS 1105:67	not b. because it is not nature	CONS 285:17
Black is b.	ANON 27:80	B.…like the gold standard	WOLF 1090:12	On her b. I'll gaze	ROCH 816:61
deal of scorn looks b.	SHAK 895:25	B. lives though lilies die	FLEC 393:48	pale court in b. and decay	SHEL 930:36
desires all b. things	CHES 258:14	b. made The bright world dim	SHEL 930:32	peace nor b.	LAWR 586:78
feathers are more b.?	SHAK 864:87	b. of creatures	AQUI 32:4	power of b.	SHAK 891:23
For she was b.	SHEL 930:32	b. of holiness	BIBLE 117:8	saw true b. till this night	SHAK 868:83
Fowey Is a b. spot	QUIL 797:57	b. of inflections	STEV 971:43	She walks in b.	BYRON 221:16
grave hides all things b.	SHEL 930:18	b. of its…shadow	WORD 1101:94	simple b. and rustic health	WHIT 1074:4
ground is like a b. woman	SNOW 951:78	b.…of life	ALLEN 14:34	since their b. passed	THOM 1012:2
House B. is…lousy	PARK 754:97	b. of marrow	SITW 941:9	some sort of order (or b.)	POUND 787:91
How b. the Republic was	DURR 357:75	b. of sense objects	AQUI 33:7	soul of her b.	SHEL 930:29
How b. upon the mountains	BIBLE 127:96	b. of speed	MARI 651:67	Strength and b.	DEMO 315:46
if they are to seem b.	SCHO 849:99	b.…of the buildings we burnt	ELGIN 364:98	Such seems your b. still	SHAK 915:84
Life…is a b. thing	BURT 214:63	b. of the morning	WORD 1097:46	the b. of the thing	GALL 413:97
make anything b. and desireable	STOWE 978:84	b. of the world	SHAK 890:4	There is only b.	MALL 641:12
more b. than death	WHIT 1073:88	b. of the world	WEIL 1062:82	things of b.	JUANA 539:64
most b. sight in orbit	SCHW 851:30	b. of their s.	TENN 996:93	Tisn't b., so to speak	KIPL 563:96
most b. things on earth	ISAA 513:69	b. of thy mind	SHAK 914:71	trouble with b.	BAZE 79:52
most b. works	FLAU 392:35	B. pains	HAAS 450:98	turns all things to b.	JOHN 522:29
never have a mistress as b.	ARLT 35:41	B.'s princely majesty	SHAK 861:94	unmask her b. to the moon	SHAK 888:61
only b. if it has good grass	BUTL 217:28	B. provoketh thieves	SHAK 885:74	unzips the veil from b.	WHITE 1070:26
only hope of creating something b.	FLAU 392:40	b.'s self she is	ANON 23:91	What is b.	MARL 653:91
pard-like Spirit, b. and swift	SHEL 931:43	B.…should not be wasted	SHAK 864:97	What is b.	VIEI 1044:75
perpetual hunger to be b.	RHYS 808:25	b. so old and so new	AUGU 49:10	where all is order and b.	BAUD 77:22
picture that is b.	FRAN 402:97	b. than existed before	RUNGE 829:55	where B. was	GALS 413:4
pleasure…because it is b.	POIN 776:59	b., though injurious	MILT 695:52	whose b. is past change	HOPK 491:85
saddest and most b. sight	DALG 303:43	B. too rich for use	SHAK 868:82	why talk of b.	CUMM 300:84
science is very b.	OPPE 741:73	b. vanishes; b. passes	DELA 314:29	wildest b. in the world	OWEN 748:16
silence makes a woman b.	SOPH 953:14	B., virtue, happiness	BERN 97:87	Wit is more necessary than b.	WYCH 1103:41
Small is B.	SCHU 850:14	b. was rather for use	PRIOR 790:52	world is richer for a new b.	MARI 651:66
small is b.	SCHU 850:15	B. was their answer	BRID 187:44	write the b. of your eyes	SHAK 912:47
The innocent and the b.	YEATS 1106:82	befriended us with b.	CAVE 246:73	youth and a little b.	WEBS 1061:61
things that are b.	DEBU 311:68	behold the b. of the Lord	BIBLE 115:55	Youth, b., graceful action	DRYD 349:25
too b. to live	DICK 321:48	best part of b.	BACON 59:14	**Beaverbrook** B.…like the town tart	BAXT 78:49
travel…to find the b.	EMER 376:44	cannot write of b.	BELL 86:92	papers conducted by…Lord B.	BALD 64:9
two most b. words	JAMES 517:31	carried into b.	WOOLF 1093:65	**because** B. it's there	MALL 642:22
ugly things…frequently become b.	COCT 272:66	day for b.	WORD 1101:95	**Becher's** deeper foreboding than…B.	FRAN 401:93
When a woman isn't b.	CHEK 256:62	Death is a name for b.	LAYT 588:23	**beck** more offences at my b.	SHAK 891:25
worshipped because they are b.	RUSS 832:22	decay…of b.	CONG 281:28	**become** What's b. of me or you?	EMPS 378:86
beauty absolute b.	HALD 451:18	dedicated to force and to b.	RIMB 812:98	**bed** A b., a b.	BALL -101:34
abuse and destroy b.	PORT 784:37	desire of b. …has most	PATER 759:95	Ample make this B.	DICK 328:7
ache of b.	UTTL 1038:82	divers schedules of my b.	SHAK 894:5	And so to b.	PEPYS 765:60
all that b.…e'er gave	GRAY 442:66	doth b. beauteous seem	SHAK 913:62	As to a lover's b.	SHAK 906:91
And order, truth, and b. range	SMART 944:68	equal in b. to	KORN 568:81	b. fell on my father	THUR 1018:16
Art is not…a canon of b.	PICA 768:25	Euclid alone Has looked on B.	MILL 676:89	b. Of crimson joy	BLAKE 167:88
autumnal face, her pieced b.!	JONS 535:88	fading b.	WALL 1050:76	b. of daffodil sky	TENN 1001:85
b., and gay cloths	WEBS 1060:37	fatal gift of b.	BYRON 220:95	b. of death	DRAY 345:40
B. and the lust for learning	BEER 83:33	Fostered…by b.	WORD 1096:20	b.…the cold, cold grave	BALL 101:35
b. beat on his conceits	MARL 653:92	ghosts of B. glide	POPE 782:77	B.…the poor man's opera	HUXL 507:85
B.…became money	WOLF 1090:13	hardships into forms of b.	CAMP 227:20	Best…place bloody b.	BLAIR 165:52
b. can lie…in days	FOWL 400:70	her…unconventional b.	SCHL 848:77	better in battle than in b.	STER 969:8
b.'s charming	SCOTT 855:97	Honesty coupled to b.	SHAK 886:11	bounced right out of b.	MILNE 680:71
b. cold and austere	RUSS 831:14	I sat b. on my knees	RIMB 812:96	can we go to b.?	COPE 287:52
b. depended most on poetry	SIDN 937:60	If you get simple b.	BROW 198:44	Chairman…lying on his death b.	MIN 695:62
b. faded	PHIL 768:18	images of female b.	WOLF 1089:11	comforts of the early morning b.	SHIP 935:21
b. for ashes	BIBLE 127:12	imagination seizes as b.	KEATS 544:45	Creep into thy narrow b.	ARNO 39:22
b., for permanence	NUTT 732:46	In art economy is always b.	JAMES 516:28	cry in my b.	AGUS 10:72
b. from the light retir'd	WALL 1050:71	in victory, there is no b.	LAO 580:85	dark beside b.	MACN 637:46
B. has only one form	HUGO 501:55	Is there in truth no b.?	HERB 475:24	deck both b. and bower	SPEN 958:13
b. hath ensnared thee	SHAK 866:33	judge the b. of life	LAUT 584:55	destroyed in b.	SKEL 942:50
b. in art	DIDE 329:25	June for b.'s heightening	ARNO 39:15	die—in b.	SASS 845:27
b. in the works of a great genius	ADDI 8:38	Kindness is worth more than b.	ARRAS 40:48	early to b.	THUR 1018:24
b. is a guarantee of happiness	PROU 793:98	Knowledge of ideal b.	BLAKE 168:14	Early to b., early to rise	RODR 819:88
b. is a joy for ever	KEATS 545:56	lady of b. and high degree	RANS 802:31	Every b. is narrow	MILL 676:84
B. is a witch	SHAK 879:36	Life, force and b.	POPE 778:78	get me to b.	SCOTT 856:17
B. is all very well	SHAW 922:43	light…From her own b.	SHEL 930:31	go to b. by day	STEV 975:32
B. is as summer-fruits	BACON 59:12	Look on b.	SHAK 872:82	go to b. early	WAUGH 1056:71
B. is but a vain…good	SHAK 887:41	loved your b.	YEATS 1105:60	go to b. exhausted	ROTH 826:19
B. is only sin deep	SAKI 837:96	manhood's b.	WILDE 1075:26	go to b. sober	FLET 394:71
B. is the first test	HARDY 456:82	March with b.	SHAK 911:30	haste me to my b.	SHAK 913:56

bed (*contd.*)

husbands lie snoring in b.	MORE 707:50
ideal companion in b.	DAVI 308:18
in b. with musicians	WILM 1084:9
in love with my b.	SHAK 860:75
in my b. againe	ANON 23:83
lie diagonally in his b.	STER 969:11
lie down on my b.	HILL 481:10
lie o' both sides of the b.	DEKK 313:15
Lies in his b.	SHAK 872:66
lying in b. counting sheep	SIEG 937:67
Lying in b.	CHES 258:13
Lying in b.	WATE 1055:48
lying in b., thinking	GINS 428:34
made his pedant b.	SHAK 907:30
make my b. in hell	BIBLE 120:49
manger for his b.	ALEX 13:19
mind is not a b.	AGATE 10:64
mostly sent to b.	LAND 578:59
mother, mother, mak my b.	BALL -101:28
Must we to b. indeed?	STEV 975:42
never…made my own b.	PU 794:14
not a b. of roses	STEV 974:8
not mount the marriage b.	JONS 535:91
now 'tis your b. time	DONNE 336:71
pillow on a b.	DONNE 337:93
preparing for b. with the shades up	STARR 963:1
rouse from their lowly b.	GRAY 442:64
royal b. of Denmark	SHAK 889:79
sinners are still in b.	RUNY 829:65
sitting at the edge of a hotel b.	CHEE 255:52
spit-spot into b.	TRAV 1025:30
stay in b. all day	BENC 89:52
still keeping open b.	HUXL 506:49
Strangle her in her b.	SHAK 900:45
sweat of an enseamèd b.	SHAK 892:56
take up thy b., and walk	BIBLE 145:30
this b.-presser	SHAK 876:56
under the b. for Communists	FOOT 396:92
wakes me from my flow'ry b.?	SHAK 871:44
Welcome to your gory b.	BURNS 212:37
When Harriet goes to b.	BROY 201:7
Who goes to b. with whom	SAYE 846:53
you see that great b.	ONAS 739:41
would twere b.-time	SHAK 876:67

bedchamber calls on my b. less — HILL 481:10

bedclothes little harm, save to his b. SHAK 901:81

bedeck b. and bedrape us — SWIN 987:31

bedevilment Of man's b. — HOUS 496:74

bedfellows strange b. — SHAK 917:29

bedpan b. by a stranger — KUHN 570:13

bedrape bedeck and b. us — SWIN 987:31

bedroom b. in a Brussels hotel THOM 1015:45

doesn't matter what you do in the b.	CAMP 226:12
Lincoln's b.!	ONAS 739:41
spy in his b.	TOYN 1024:23
trying on ties in his b.	CURT 301:23
what belongs in the b.	GOLD 434:41

bedrooms b. of the nation — TRUD 1029:11

beds all snug in their b. — MOORE 704:4

hussies in your b.	SHAK 898:19
made the b., shoped for groceries	FRIE 405:49
Minds like b.	WILL 1083:90

bedspreads b. according to rule LEVE 600:25

bee as lightly as the B. — JONS 536:13

b. takes a middle course	BACON 55:29
b. with honied thigh	MILT 683:14
Pedigree…Does not concern the B.	DICK 328:15
sting like a b.	ALI 14:28
Where the b. sucks	SHAK 917:41

beech moss-grown b. — GRAY 441:56

warlike b. — SPEN 957:99

Beecham B.'s Pills are just the thing BEEC 82:14

beef B. and a sea-coal fire — OTWAY 746:88

---

beef (*contd.*)

b., pork and mutton	KIPL 564:12
great eater of b.	SHAK 894:97
roast b. of England	FIEL 388:46

beefsteak as English…as a b. HAWT 462:83

beehive Fascist…b. — ORWE 742:3

been For what has b.—thanks! HAMM 453:42

It might have b.!	WHIT 1074:5
might have b.	HARTE 460:53
what hath b.	TENN 999:44
Where I have b.	GURN 449:89

beer b. corrodes it — TWAIN 1032:74

B. and Britannia	SMITH 949:44
B., tobacco, and music	MANN 645:79
b. was strong	PRIOR 791:57
colour-bar and b.	NOON 731:25
embodied spirit of b.	BENN 92:2
ever taste b.?	DICK 322:60
faint stale smells of b.	ELIOT 367:57
felony to drink small b.	SHAK 861:10
Life isn't all b. and skittles	HUGH 500:50
muddy ecstasies of b.	CRAB 293:65
no wine or good b.	GORO 436:69
not all B. and Skittles	STEV 976:50
only a b. teetotaller	SHAW 920:1
only here for the b.	LEVE 599:19
Pints and quarts of Ludlow b.	HOUS 495:64
teach the Irish to drink b.	EDGE 360:30

Beersheba from Dan to B. — STER 970:21

bees a grave injustice to b. ORWE 742:3

angry hive of b.	SHAK 861:5
B. are sometimes drowned	HAWT 461:67
Books are the b.	LOWE 616:85
early b. are assaulting	REED 805:81
Forget not b. in winter	SACK 835:59
hive of silvery B.	LEAR 590:56
innumerable b.	TENN 998:13
Keep b.	WADD 1047:25
these are the wrong sort of b.	MILNE 680:72

bees-winged b.-w. eyes? — BETJ 99:29

Beethoven as B. was born for music PELE 764:51

B. always sounds	RUSK 831:11
B. came with music	NEVE 723:14
B.'s Fifth Symphony	FORS 398:31
difference between B. and Mahler	COPL 288:56
From you, B., Bach, Mozart	SASS 845:30
how much I appreciate B.	HEIF 467:67
Roll over B.	BERRY 98:4

beetle b. wheels his droning flight GRAY 441:62

b. winds His small but sullen horn	COLL 277:48
into a large brown b.	KAIKO 541:9
poor b. that we tread	SHAK 897:79

beeves Let b. and home-bred kine WORD 1098:57

before B. Thee in humility HAMM 453:44

B., behind, between, above, below	DONNE 336:72
beset me behind and b.	BIBLE 119:48
those things which are b.	BIBLE 153:12

beg b. in the streets — FRAN 401:90

should not b. in vain — JONS 536:11

beget if he touch he must b. YEATS 1107:95

Is there no way to b.	HERR 477:52
never to b.	HOPK 492:6

begetter proclaimed its b. MEYER 673:32

beggar a b. before you — ORAH 741:78

b. begrudges b.	HESI 479:81
b. by banqueting upon borrowing	BIBLE 132:4
b. died, and was carried by the angels	BIBLE 144:7
b. is still a man	MORI 708:68
b. who suns himself	SMITH 945:78
black boundin' b.	KIPL 560:34
whiles I am a b.	SHAK 872:62

beggar-woman b.-w. and single ELIZ 373:85

beggared B. by fools — DRYD 349:24

beggars b….too professional air MACC 625:45

---

beggars (*contd.*)

exercises authority over b.	MORE 707:48
pays us poor b. in red	KIPL 561:37
tiresome Servia b. belief	MARY 661:28
When b. die	SHAK 883:32

beggary b. in the love — SHAK 904:55

Contempt and b. hangs — SHAK 870:21

begging nor his seed b. bread BIBLE 115:65

begin b. from the subjective SART 844:13

B. at the beginning	CARR 239:43
b. to dress ourselves	RICH 809:50
But let us b.	KENN 550:63
time to b. a new	DRYD 352:97
To b. at the beginning	THOM 1011:79
worst of all is to b.	BART 74:73

beginingless b., endless, bottomless RUSK 831:12

beginner man ceases to be a b. COLL 276:36

mere b. — HUGH 498:17

beginning as he was at the b. HICKS 480:96

As it was in the b.	BOOK 173:92
As it was in the b.	RHYS 808:29
b., a middle, and an end	ARIS 34:34
b., a muddle, and an end	LARK 582:21
b. and end of art	HEIN 467:74
b. is assuredly the end	WILL 1083:89
b. is often the end	ELIOT 373:79
b. of everything	REAG 803:63
b. of feminism	ROWB 827:40
b. of the end	TALL 990:89
b. of wisdom	BIBLE 118:24
coming our b.	MUIR 712:34
each venture…a new b.	ELIOT 372:53
end of the b.	CHUR 264:24
end precedes the b.	ELIOT 370:30
from the b. think	WHYM 1074:11
In my b. is my end	ELIOT 371:43
In the b. God created	BIBLE 102:82
In the b. was the Word	BIBLE 144:21
In the b. was the Word	ELIOT 367:65
more accurate in the b.	JONS 536:26
most important…is the b.	PLATO 774:27
my end is my b.	MARY 661:29
Never ending, still b.	DRYD 351:72
pleasure can be the b. of beauty	PROU 793:98
sort of a bad b.	DICK 320:9
urge in the b.	SAND 842:79
voted to make a new b.	CLIN 269:16

beginnings b. of ataxia — SILVA 938:77

ends by our b. know	DENH 315:56
mighty things from small b.	DRYD 346:54

begins Fashion constantly b. and ends HAZL 463:1

where…the Church of England b. PRIE 790:44

begot b. in fear — GRAV 439:20

when they b. me — STER 968:88

begotten B., not made — BOOK 174:91

beguiled B. again — HART 459:46

thou art b. — SKEL 942:35

Behan My name is B. — BEHAN 84:58

behave b. in excess except — LACL 573:61

How well I did b.	HOUS 494:45
must b. accordingly	KISS 566:33
things they b. sensibly about?	SHAW 920:97

behaving better b. themselves SZASZ 989:67

expedient in the way of our b. JAMES 518:50

behaviour abdication…Makes the B. DICK 328:13

certain kinds of b.	ROBB 813:14
constitutes unacceptable b.	LEBO 591:79
decency and discretion in their b.	BACON 55:7
evoking a new b.	MERT 672:24
Fearful and hostile b.	FULB 409:30
guided my b.	MACL 633:65
in-office attitudes and b.	COUP 289:78
knowing…their b. very well	THOM 1011:74
man's b. may be quite harmless	SHAW 924:89

behaviour (*contd.*)

my b. full of rigor	BROW 194:64
Puritanism names a b.	SPEN 956:88
quality of moral b.	HUXL 507:77
social b. displays many features	HOMA 487:7
watch their b.	WELD 1062:96
What ever his private b.	MEYER 673:32

behaviourism Of course, B. works — AUDEN 49:2

beheaded imprisoned…b. others — STAL 962:78

one of our kings who was b.	APPL 32:98
to see the King b.	PEPYS 765:62

behemoth Behold now b. — BIBLE 113:24

Black Mrs B. — SITW 941:8

behind b. the scenes — JOHN 525:87

beset me b. and before	BIBLE 119:48
it will be b. me	REGER 806:96
no bosom and no b.	SMITH 948:30
one must ride b.	SHAK 880:59
turn thee b. me	BIBLE 111:78

behold B. and see — SHAK 904:56

beholder cheer to its b. — ROCK 817:69

impossible that any b. — SIDN 937:64

beholders awe into the b. — SWIFT 984:82

beige B.! Just my color — DEWO 319:97

Beijing say here in B. — HILL 270:25

being A b. darkly wise — POPE 780:42

at the edge of B.	SPEN 956:76
b. absolutely infinite	SPIN 961:60
b. always with myself	GIRO 429:47
b. and as an angel	MUIR 713:41
B. and Ideal Grace	BROW 197:19
b. and our birth	SHAK 910:94
B. is the great explainer	THOR 1016:63
b. is to be perceived	BERK 95:51
b. who…need not even exist	BAUD 78:36
breath of Autumn's b.	SHEL 928:86
by avoiding b.	TILL 1020:61
chain of b.	EMER 376:45
concerns thee and thy b.	MILT 691:91
creation, development and b.	HUMB 503:97
how such a b. could exist	ANDR 18:10
intellectual b.	MILT 688:15
live, and move, and have our b.	BIBLE 148:3
man is the b. who wills	SCHI 847:64
mighty b. is awake	WORD 1097:40
most prostituted b.	BAUD 78:44
part of our very b.	GAND 414:14
persist in its own b.	SPIN 960:52
pleasing anxious b.	GRAY 442:74
poem…once it is in b.	FROST 407:94
preserve one's b.	SPIN 960:55
presuppose a Supreme B.	DOUG 342:70
reason for b.	FRAN 401:85
sensitive b., a creative soul	WORD 1096:33
that is the essence of our b.	BUSH 215:91
They had their b. once	PURDY 795:36
Unbearable Lightness of B.	KUND 571:15
very bottom of her b.	ADAMS 5:70
wheels of B. slow	TENN 999:35

beings b. brighter than have been — BYRON 221:18

b. which are impossible	REDON 804:77
evidence of supernatural b.	STEI 967:68
in his stomach more animated b.	SMITH 949:46
other b. in the zoological scale	CARB 231:95
three respectable b.	BAUD 78:43

Beirut If you liked B. — HEMP 471:51

beleaguered sense of being b. — RABAN 798:73

Belgium B.'s capital had gathered — BYRON 219:84

B. recovers in full measure — ASQU 42:77

Belial B. with words clothed — MILT 688:16

forth the sons of B. — MILT 687:3

belief abandoned a b. in God — STEV 972:62

abdication of B. — DICK 328:13

belief (*contd.*)

any unwarrantable b.	RICH 810:62
assert my b. that	ROOS 821:36
authority of a b.	KRIS 569:93
b. and hope had gone	RUSS 833:36
B. consists in affirming	EMER 377:53
b.…founded upon my experience	DOYLE 344:5
b. in luck	OATES 733:53
b. in their sincerity	TWAIN 1032:59
b. in…human beings	ORWE 743:7
b. is for it	JOHN 530:93
b. is made religious	CUPI 301:10
b. of truth	BACON 56:41
b. that we can start	POPP 783:19
b. which may be right	FORS 398:32
commit…to any religious b.	WAUGH 1056:72
decline of religious b.	FREUD 404:46
do not believe in B.	FORS 399:51
epoch of b.	DICK 326:58
Faith…an illogical b.	MENC 669:62
firm b. in the justice of our case	WASH 1054:41
firm b. that everybody could write	BAIN 62:73
first expounder of our religious b.	SPEKE 955:61
impress the people…with a b.	PEEL 763:43
inherited this b.	MILL 676:97
last, best b. system	WOLF 1090:12
leading to the b.	KAUF 543:21
lose b. in this truth	DU 353:10
My b. is that in life	TROL 1027:75
national b.	MACC 625:47
proportions his b. to the evidence	HUME 503:9
prospect of b.	SHAK 907:18
Rome… trades on b.	BURG 205:81
tiresome Servia beggars b.	MARY 661:28

beliefs All known religious b. — DURK 357:71

b., traditions, and aspirations	DURK 357:72
b.…we hold sacred	ARON 40:46
different people, different b.	CART 242:2
discuss your b.	HELL 468:92
Home of…forsaken b.	ARNO 38:10
reverse important basic b.	MILL 677:2
someone's mistaken b.	ELLI 375:17
strong b. wounded	BROO 193:41
two contradictory b.	ORWE 745:59

believe b. also in me — BIBLE 146:60

b. and rejoice in Christ	LUTH 620:46
b., because they so were bred	DRYD 351:55
B. false teachers	SHAK 916:8
b. in ideas and die for them	ANOU 30:74
b. of my own stories	IRVI 513:66
B. on the Lord Jesus Christ	BIBLE 148:96
B. one who has experienced it.	VIRG 1045:89
b. so that I may understand	ANSE 31:81
b. what we choose	NEWM 724:30
cease to b.	HAMM 453:43
devils also do b.	BIBLE 155:64
don't b. in preachers	BENE 89:58
Except I shall see…I will not b.	BIBLE 147:76
few will consent to b.	KENN 550:50
For those who b. in God	SEAT 857:25
fun to b. them	BACH 54:99
If you b. that	WELL 1064:21
If you don't b. it	AUGU 49:17
live by what they b.	HAMP 454:63
mix what they b.	UPDI 1036:49
never b. again	TOML 1023:3
Never b.	SKEL 942:42
Those who b. that they are	HUXL 506:54
those who b.	WALK 1049:59
what we ourselves b.	GRANT 438:2
willing to b. what they wish	CAES 225:84

believer b. will fight another — GREE 445:27

In a b.'s ear!	NEWT 725:44
make the b.'s leap	RABAN 798:76

believers objectional types of b. — BORN 179:18

believes one b., then miracles occur — MILL 678:39

thinks he b. only what he sees	SANT 842:87
what an Englishman b.	SHAW 925:23
What your government b.	KENN 552:93

believing B. is Seeing — WOLFE 1090:24

better at b. than at seeing	SANT 842:87
eating that's b.	THUR 1019:40
pleasure of b. what we see	SHEL 927:66
torture them, into b.	NEWM 724:27
We are born b.	EMER 377:67

Belinda B. smiled, and all the world — POPE 778:95

belittlement all our injured b. — RABAN 798:73

belittling not b. the brave pioneer men — FERB 385:6

bell B., book, and candle — SHAK 872:65

b. rings and the widow weeps	SHAK 880:66
b.-rope that gathers God	CRANE 295:10
binkledy-winkled a b.	LEAR 590:63
double and the single b.	SLES 943:57
for whom the b. is tolling	NASH 720:70
for whom the b. tolls	DONNE 339:23
God's b. buoyed	YEATS 1105:61
hear the surly sullen b.	SHAK 914:72
lifted, rough-tongued b.	LARK 581:96
like b.-bottoms and W. C. Fields	HAWES 460:61
silver-voiced b.-birds	KEND 550:49
Sunset and evening b.	TENN 1005:66
tangles Of b.-flowers	SITW 940:6
The b. invites me	SHAK 908:41
Time and the b.	ELIOT 370:28
tolling b. Measures time	ELIOT 372:59
word is like a b.	KEATS 548:19

Bellamy one of B.'s veal pies — PITT 772:76

belle my time, my b. époque — HOLL 485:71

young b. of old Natchez — NASH 719:55

bellicose querulous and b. — MENC 669:59

bellies evil beasts, slow b. — BIBLE 154:42

studious for their b. — SAND 842:82

belligerent looked so b. — KARSH 542:11

belligerents Police separate the b. — EDEN 360:22

bellman B. would cry: — CARR 241:85

bellows flatt'ry is the b. — SHAK 910:95

bells beaten b. — STEV 976:59

b. I hear	WHIT 1073:91
B. in your parlours	SHAK 898:19
b. of Shandon	MAHO 638:65
b. off San Salvador	CRANE 294:93
B., the poor man's only music	COLE 274:99
b. they sound so clear	HOUS 494:49
church b. hollowing out	BETJ 101:57
floating many b. down	CUMM 300:94
lin-lan-lone of evening b.	TENN 1005:67
mortals who ring b.	MANN 646:84
name like a ring of b.	BETJ 100:42
none of your ribbons and b.	MARQ 656:41
Oh, noisy b., be dumb	HOUS 495:51
passing-s for these who die	OWEN 748:7
Ring out, wild b.	TENN 1000:56
ring the b. of heaven	HODG 484:53
ring their b.	WALP 1052:97
sleigh b. in the snow	BERL 95:62
tall building with a tower and b.	CRAB 294:79

belly b.…send thee good ale — ANON 23:84

b. was bitter	BIBLE 157:19
bitter b.-tension	GIBB 422:36
does not mind his b.	JOHN 528:40
everything, except this perpetual B.	EMER 377:56
filled his b. with the husks	BIBLE 143:99
Gun Fired in the Pope's B.	ANON 25:21
No b. and no bowels	RANS 802:38
pour…by the b. full	SPEN 959:31
substance into that fat b.	SHAK 877:88
upon thy b. thou shalt go	BIBLE 103:98

belly (*contd.*)
whose God is their b.   BIBLE 153:*13*
belong b. to Britain   GERA 419:*95*
Go where you b.   TROT 1029:*2*
really b.   GREE 444:*8*
belonging greatest sense of b.   ROTH 825:*7*
belongings b. of others   SALL 839:*37*
b. on show   JOYCE 538:*56*
beloved b. is mine, and I am his   BIBLE 124:*50*
Cry, the B. Country   PATON 761:*12*
Dearly b., we are gathered together   BOOK 175:*42*
more b. for the imperfections   RUSK 830:*81*
the kiss to one's b.   ONEI 740:*52*
below either above or b. it   GILL 426:*8*
He lies in.   PARK 754:*10*
belt could not see a b.   ASQU 42:*82*
belted Though I've b. you   KIPL 561:*36*
Ben bare B. Bulben's head   YEATS 1107:*93*
B. Hur translated into Irish   STEW 977:*64*
bench designed a b. in a few moments   BELL 86:*95*
fluttering to a b.   SACK 835:*60*
murd'rous hand a drowsy b. protect   CRAB 293:*75*
benches though we cropen under b.?   LANG 579:*71*
bend b. but do not break   LAFO 574:*80*
b. to the wind   BUCK 203:*37*
right on round the b.   LAUD 583:*40*
bending nations b. under...tyranny   PITT 772:*73*
beneath B. is spread like a green sea   SHEL 927:*70*
B. the visiting moon   SHAK 906:*96*
see b. both beauty and ugliness   ELIOT 370:*16*
Benedick B. Nobody marks you   SHAK 879:*29*
benedicte B., omnia opera Domini   BIBLE 159:*52*
benediction clouds in b.   DAYL 310:*53*
beneficial harmless and even b.   SHAW 924:*89*
Jogging is very b.   SCHU 850:*12*
benefit familiar one of social b.   HUGH 500:*34*
owes a return for the b.   MILL 675:*65*
what b. to the soul   HONO 488:*32*
without the b. o' the Clergy   CONG 280:*11*
benefits disable all the b.   SHAK 886:*19*
so many people...for material b.   COLU 278:*63*
Who b.?   CICE 266:*60*
benefitted b. from prolonged warfare   SUN 982:*32*
benevolence b. of the butcher   SMITH 945:*87*
benevolent what is inexhaustible is b.   FRYE 408:*24*
Bengal tiger of B. crouches   MELV 668:*42*
benighted b. masses   QUINE 797:*67*
must be b. and superstitious   JAMES 518:*51*
benign under the b. sky   BRON 192:*15*
benison b. of hot water   BROO 192:*20*
Benlomond o'er the lofty B.   TANN 991:*96*
bent Still b. to make some port   ARNO 37:*78*
those with an academic b.   MAMET 643:*54*
Bentham B. held no post   MENC 669:*64*
benumbed faculties of the mind b.   BROO 192:*16*
bequeathed B. down from many   SHAK 901:*78*
bereft b. me of all words   SHAK 873:*85*
berhymed never so b.   SHAK 886:*3*
Berkeley fell to earth in B. Square   HAMER 453:*36*
Berlin Be off with your Irving B.!   GERS 420:*9*
B. by Christmas   ANON 25:*31*
Isherwood...find himself in B.   BURU 214:*80*
Let them come to B.!   KENN 552:*83*
New Frontier closed by B.   MACG 630:*33*
soldiers drilling in B.   MORI 708:*68*
Berliner Ich bin ein B.   KENN 552:*85*
Berlitz glibness of B. school   FIRB 389:*78*
Bermudas swim to the B.   WEBS 1060:*57*
Bernard B....was rather pious   ASHF 41:*65*
Bernhardt admired most...Sarah B.   WILDE 1079:*13*
berries b. harsh and crude   MILT 684:*38*
berry God made a better b.   BUTL 218:*51*
berserk Sex suppressed will go b.   EWART 381:*44*
beryl colour of a b.   BIBLE 128:*34*

beseech b. thee, shew me thy glory   BIBLE 107:*76*
humbly do b. you   SHAK 899:*34*
beside Paul, thou art b. thyself   BIBLE 148:*9*
besieging who are b. Orleans   JOAN 522:*27*
best All is for the b.   VOLT 1046:*2*
Always to be b.   HOMER 488:*18*
b. actors in the world   SHAK 890:*9*
b. and the worst of this   SWIN 987:*43*
b. cannot be expected   JOHN 532:*33*
b. ends by the b. means   HUTC 506:*41*
b. is like the worst   KIPL 560:*27*
b. is yet to be   BROW 199:*75*
b. lack conviction   YEATS 1106:*77*
b. married that dies married young   SHAK 870:*19*
b. minds in the world   ACHE 3:*52*
b. of all possible worlds   CABE 224:*80*
b. of all things   HUXL 509:*6*
b. of the rich   SPARK 955:*55*
b. that an American   KENN 550:*50*
b. that has been known   ARNO 39:*30*
b. that is known   ARNO 38:*11*
B. thing in eird   HENR 473:*71*
b. thing to be up and go   EMPS 378:*85*
b....to do what the mob do   DICK 320:*21*
B., to forget!   BROW 200:*99*
the b. words in the b. order   COLE 275:*24*
Competition brings out the b.   SARN 843:*97*
do our b. to reward your faith   SMITH 947:*8*
do the b. you can   ONOL 734:*66*
doing our b. to re-establish peace   ELIZ 374:*96*
Drinking the b. tea   SNOW 950:*70*
English are b.!   FLAN 392:*28*
He is doing his b.   WILDE 1075:*30*
hope for the b.   SMITH 949:*48*
It is b. to live   SOPH 953:*22*
last b. friend   SOUT 954:*42*
learn, at b. and worst   RABAN 798:*74*
mediocrity...always at its b.   BEER 84:*45*
most of everything, b. of nothing   CHAN 250:*40*
Mother Knows B.   FERB 385:*5*
My God must have my b.   HERB 476:*36*
Never to have lived is b.   YEATS 1106:*81*
one of the very b. means   HUXL 509:*5*
people are at their b.   GRAY 440:*41*
record of the b....moments   SHEL 931:*59*
said against the b.   MILL 675:*74*
serves his party b.   HAYES 462:*93*
That action is b.   HUTC 506:*42*
The b. is the b.   QUIL 797:*58*
The b....enemy of the good   VOLT 1046:*11*
very b. and the very worst   FORD 396:*3*
What America does b.   FUEN 409:*27*
Why not the b.?   CART 242:*99*
best-sellers in all of the great b.-s.   PRIT 791:*63*
bestial what remains is b.   SHAK 894:*24*
bestride b. the narrow world   SHAK 882:*20*
bestseller b. is the gilded tomb   SMITH 947:*21*
bet b. you, Ziggie, a hundred bucks   DILL 331:*54*
if I would b. with other people   ROCH 816:*43*
beteem b. the winds of heaven   SHAK 888:*53*
Bethel O God of B.!   DODD 335:*45*
Bethlehem But thou, B.   BIBLE 130:*62*
Christ is born in B.   CASW 244:*37*
Let us now go even unto B.   BIBLE 142:*78*
Slouches towards B.   YEATS 1106:*78*
when Jesus was born in B.   BIBLE 133:*23*
betide God's peace b. the souls   RANS 802:*37*
betray b. them both   WALC 1048:*31*
cruel brother will you b.   BALL -101:*37*
find too late that men b.   GOLD 432:*5*
savage man alone does man b.   ROCH 816:*52*
betrayal defence against b.   WILL 1081:*64*
betrayed Betrothed, betrayer, and b.!   SCOTT 856:*8*
but by ourselves, b.   CONG 280:*94*

betrayed (*contd.*)
by luxury b.   GOLD 433:*16*
democratic people b.   ATTL 44:*9*
those that are b.   SHAK 916:*9*
betrayer Betrothed, b., and betrayed!   SCOTT 856:*8*
betraying b. my country my friend   FORS 399:*52*
betrothed B., betrayer, and betrayed!   SCOTT 856:*8*
better b. future and a brighter day   SMUTS 950:*66*
B. a witty fool   SHAK 894:*1*
B. if he had said   HILL 481:*8*
b. man than I am   KIPL 561:*36*
b. than bad strokes   SHAK 884:*62*
b. than light   HASK 460:*57*
b. that some should   JOHN 530:*86*
b. to dwell in a corner   BIBLE 121:*93*
B. to use force   SHUL 936:*33*
b. world than this   SHAK 885:*72*
change for the b.   STEI 966:*60*
don't know any b.   KENN 550:*54*
Every day...I am getting b.   COUE 289:*72*
far b. without the others   SIEY 938:*39*
for b. for worse   BOOK 176:*49*
from worse to b.   JOHN 526:*3*
give place to b.   SHAK 884:*58*
He is no b.   AUST 52:*72*
I see b. things   OVID 747:*1*
kiss you take is b.   SHAK 896:*56*
Love...unsought, is b.   SHAK 895:*26*
no b. than you should be   BEAU 80:*78*
no b. than you should be   THOM 1011:*86*
not sure I was much b.   SIHA 938:*73*
took thee for thy b.   SHAK 892:*53*
way to the B. there be   HARDY 457:*8*
When you meet someone b.   CONF 280:*89*
would be b. than nothing   KEYN 555:*36*
betters lord it...above their b.   OTWAY 746:*83*
between try to get b. them   STRA 979:*98*
Bevan nurses and Nye B.   HALD 451:*19*
beverage revolting b. in itself   STEV 973:*97*
beware all should cry, B.! B.!   COLE 275:*18*
B. of anything that promises   SNYD 951:*85*
B. Of entrance to a quarrel   SHAK 888:*64*
B. of men   SPARK 955:*59*
B. of over-great pleasure   FULL 409:*32*
B. of quotations in Latin   FLAU 393:*46*
B. of the man   SHAW 922:*53*
B. of the man   SHAW 922:*64*
B. of those who are homeless   SOUT 954:*39*
B. the ides of March   SHAK 882:*16*
O. b., my lord   SHAK 899:*32*
bewildered b. like an old lady   ACHE 3:*40*
by the unprincipled to the utterly b.   CAPP 231:*91*
without finally getting b.   HAWT 461:*71*
bewilderment sense of b. and terror   LEE 593:*16*
wandering in delighted b.   OFAO 736:*94*
bewitch Do more b. me   HERR 478:*68*
bewitched b., bothered...am I   HART 459:*46*
b. for ever   SACK 835:*61*
b. with some ill charms   WALL 1050:*73*
b. with the rogue's company   SHAK 875:*48*
bewitching his wine's sae b.!   BURNS 213:*51*
bewitchment battle against b.   WITT 1088:*76*
bewrayed man is so well b.   SPEN 959:*38*
beyond b. the range of language   REID 806:*97*
He hath been b.-sea   JONS 534:*72*
is there anything b.?   BROO 193:*32*
stands b., behind, and within   WHIT 1071:*55*
bias History must not be with b.   BETJ 100:*45*
biases bundle of b.   BALL 68:*66*
Bible B. as...a constable's handbook   KING 559:*1*
B. said that nothing was permanent   FRAME 400:*79*
cursing the bloody b.   HEMI 470:*16*
do you ever read the B.?   CHAN 250:*38*
He knows...his B.   ARNO 39:*29*

bible (*contd.*)

Jacobean…who translated the B.	ACHE 2:24
knowledge of the B., Shakespeare	WAUGH 1058:6
li'ble To read in the B.	HEYW 480:90
quotations from the B.	LAWR 586:96
quotations from the B., Browning	MACF 629:19
that book is the B.	ARNO 38:7
Those who talk of the B.	ELIOT 370:21
bible-black starless and b.-b.	THOM 1011:79
bibliobuli b.…drunk on books	MENC 669:51
bicycle as common use as the b.	ANON 25:25
b. and an atlas	MURP 715:69
fish needs a b.	STEI 967:63
incapable of choosing a b.	STEIN 966:49
knocked him off his b.	LEE 593:17
rain on my b.	LEE 593:18
bid do as you're b.	EDGE 360:31
Bidford Drunken B.	ANON 26:56
bifocals rest of the world wears b.	GOLD 432:93
big b. one holds its tryouts	HEBB 466:55
boxer never sees the b. one	FORE 397:24
Canadian…isn't thinking b.	RICH 811:73
houses just as b.	SMITH 947:18
I like thinking b.	TRUMP 1030:35
Motels can be b.	HEAT 465:48
never use a b., b. D—	GILB 423:55
big-bug good deal of a b.-b.	TWAIN 1032:79
bigger The b. the organization	JAY 519:75
bigging mind the b. o't	SCOTT 854:81
Bighead Bessie B., hired help	THOM 1011:83
bigotry B. may be roughly defined	CHES 258:79
bike back on my b.	SIMP 940:93
got on his b.	TEBB 992:25
On yer b.!	ANON 28:7
bikini Yellow Polkadot B.	VANCE 1039:93
bilbo B.'s the word	CONG 280:95
bile b. was blak	CHAU 255:45
bilingual pro athletes are b.	HOWE 497:96
bilious the ecstatic and the b.	ELIOT 365:3
bilk ought never to b. his part	HAZL 463:96
bill b. of fare	SWIFT 984:70
B. for the future government	CHUR 263:93
b. of rights	JEFF 520:91
B. of Rites, A B. of	MORR 709:83
Death…like gas b.	BURG 206:86
one more to the plaguey b.?	DONNE 337:80
receipt, not a b.	SCHN 848:82
to pay the b.	HARD 455:76
we will send our b. in	PALM 752:69
billabongs swagman…in the b.	PATE 760:96
billboard atmospheric b.	THOR 1017:5
b. lovely as a tree	NASH 719:50
billboards all is become b.	OLSEN 739:35
b. did to Coca-Cola	UPDI 1037:57
billet Every bullet has its b.	WILL 1080:48
billet-doux b.-d.…in cold blood	ETHE 380:14
billiards and to B.	PEPYS 765:74
B.…three balls and no one watches	
	DAVIS 309:33
let's to b.	SHAK 905:74
play b. well	SPEN 956:70
billie rhyming, ranting, raving b.	BURNS 209:71
billies chapman b. leave the street	BURNS 211:8
billion b. here, a b. there	DIRK 331:66
billow A breaking b.	SHEL 931:43
Blow billow, swell b.	SHAK 884:63
haughty b.'s roar	BYRON 222:41
mirth of the b.	CALL 226:4
billows b. are gone over me	BIBLE 116:70
b. smooth and bright	CARR 240:55
Even the b. of the sea	SHAK 918:54
bills account wife and children…as b.	
	BACON 57:57
Just for paying a few b.!	LARK 581:3

bills (*contd.*)

likeness in the red b.	DICK 326:72
one-hundred-dollar b.	TYSON 1035:31
billy looked at the old b. boiling	PATE 760:96
bimbo B. eruptions	WRIG 1101:4
bind b. another to its delight	BLAKE 167:86
b. up the brokenhearted	BIBLE 127:12
in the darkness b. them	TOLK 1022:92
only b. the hands	GRIL 447:62
binding b. on the consciences	JOHN 522:32
more blessed or more b.	HELO 469:6
must be b. on the conscience	JOHN 522:35
binge Life is…the proper b.	CHILD 260:51
Binnorie bonnie mill-dams o' B.	BALL -101:30
biographer duty of a serious b.	TOYN 1024:23
biographies innumerable B.	CARL 235:72
biography all b. is ultimately fiction	MALA 641:9
art of B.	BENT 93:22
B.…branch of psychiatry	ASLET 42:75
b. of the artist	ROSE 823:57
In writing b.	BOWEN 181:49
Judas who writes the b.	WILDE 1076:36
less errors…than a b.	GREE 444:20
men…have written b.	MACA 623:3
no history, only b.	EMER 376:37
not the way to write b.	ACHE 3:46
nothing but b.	DISR 332:75
problems of b., of history	MILLS 679:63
why not escapist b.?	GALB 412:86
write his b.	ALLEN 14:32
biologic changes within a b. system	SELYE 858:41
birch b. for shafts	SPEN 957:99
bringing back the b.	VIDAL 1044:57
climbing a b. tree	FROST 406:80
bird at least some b. would trust	HERB 475:16
awaken like a frightened b.	KIER 556:58
b. born in a cage	SHAW 924:95
b. of the air shall carry the voice	BIBLE 123:39
b. on the branch	KIER 556:56
b. that shunn'st	MILT 682:8
b. that thinks two notes a song	DAVI 308:22
B. thou never wert	SHEL 929:97
b. was fledged	SHAK 875:34
Blue B. of Happiness	MAET 632:57
body not the b.	THOR 1017:95
but one small b. to shoot	DEVL 318:88
cheerful b. of youth	KHAY 555:44
death, immortal B.!	KEATS 548:20
flying like a b.	MACD 628:94
Free as a b.	WORD 1095:17
gave us the b.	ACHE 3:48
Go, go go, said the b.	ELIOT 370:24
great dead b. of Scotland	MACL 633:69
know why the caged b. sings!	DUNB 355:34
let no b. call	MILL 676:81
Like the first b.	FARJ 382:62
Love's a b. that will	MEIL 666:17
Martin like a flying b.	FARJ 383:63
Most musical, most melancholy' b.!	COLE 274:1
No b., but an invisible thing	WORD 1097:39
of b.-song at morning	STEV 976:53
O lyric love…half b.	BROW 200:88
pinnace, like a fluttered b.	TENN 1004:56
shot one b. flying	HEMI 470:22
strangles a b.	SADE 835:64
The b., the beste	JAME 515:99
thin little b., peeking	NICO 727:61
Unto the sweet b.'s throat	SHAK 885:86
ways of the b. rising	REID 806:97
west wind, full of b.'s cries	MASE 662:35
wet b.-haunted English lawn	ARNO 37:75
What b. so sings	LYLY 620:57
with the waking b.	TENN 1001:86
young b.-catcher	GRAV 440:40

birdcage like a summer b.	WEBS 1059:30
birds all day the b. are singing	MACG 630:22
all the b. are flown	CHAR 252:82
all the b.	THOM 1012:1
amorous b. of prey	MARV 658:75
And no b. sing	KEATS 545:72
between fishes and reptiles and b.	BRYAN 201:15
B. build	HOPK 492:9
B. feed on b.	ROCH 816:52
b. got to fly	HAMM 454:51
b. have vanished	MILL 676:87
b. of calm sit brooding	MILT 681:87
b. of Eden sang?	CULL 299:68
b. of the air come and lodge	BIBLE 138:3
b. of the air have nests	BIBLE 136:66
b. sing gavottes	SITW 941:12
b. sing madrigals	MARL 655:31
b. sit brooding in the snow	SHAK 866:31
b. still hopping on the tree	STEV 975:32
b. that range	YEATS 1105:72
b. the colour of	THOM 1012:95
B. warbling all the music	COWP 293:53
b. without despair	WEBS 1059:30
Caged b. accept each other	WILL 1081:62
chant ye little b.	BURNS 212:22
country of b. and trees	WRIG 1101:10
fear the b. of prey	SHAK 896:64
Feed the B.	TRAV 1025:38
flight of b.	MACL 633:73
flighty as b.	DAYL 310:57
forbids the b. to sing	SITW 941:11
half-awakened b.	TENN 997:4
hear the b. sing	WALT 1052:10
joyous b. make their pastime	SPEN 958:19
late the sweet b. sing	SHAK 914:73
like bats amongst b.	BACON 59:4
listen to the b.	GIBS 422:39
marriage of b.	MOORE 705:15
mechanical b. with many wings	RAINE 800:3
nest of singing b.	JOHN 525:72
pretty b. do sing	NASHE 721:80
prisoned b. must find in freedom	SASS 845:34
song of the b.	GURN 449:88
taked the b. on trust	DICK 323:98
What was good for God's b.	HARDY 457:3
When b. do sing	SHAK 887:32
whole noise of timorous b.	MILT 686:75
birk sweet is the b.	TANN 991:96
birks b. of Aberfeldy	BURNS 210:90
Birmingham B. by…Beachy Head	CHES 259:32
lord mayor of B.	LLOY 609:66
no great hopes for B.	AUST 52:58
When Jesus came to B.	STUD 980:15
Birnam Wood B.…to Dunsinane	TWAIN 1033:89
Great B. to high Dunsinane Hill	SHAK 909:68
birth as we lay at b.	ARNO 37:73
At its b., the republic	LAMA 575:3
at the b. of Man	KIPL 565:25
being and our b.	SHAK 910:94
B., and copulation, and death	ELIOT 370:12
b. and growth…are ubiquitous	DILL 330:52
b. and spirit rather took	HERB 475:14
b. astride of a grave	BECK 81:99
B. counts for little	MOLI 699:24
b.'s invidious bar	TENN 999:44
b. is…incipient change	OVID 747:3
b. of the modern world	MACC 625:51
b. Of your brave soul	CRAS 296:23
b. to a dancing star	NIET 728:79
cannot myself give b. to wisdom	SOCR 951:87
died…before his b.	THUR 1020:55
difference of b. or state?	DEKK 313:10
does not feel his own b.	LABR 573:51
happiness…not with b. born	CHAP 252:70

blemish (*contd.*)
no b. but the mind — SHAK 895:35
blemishes tapes, b. and all — NIXON 730:14
blend strange b. of the commercial — STAP 963:93
bless attend and b. — GILB 425:81
b. the accursed — SHAK 902:92
except thou b. me — BIBLE 105:38
Lord b. thee, and keep thee — BIBLE 107:81
blessed b. and admit me to Paradise — ROSS 825:96
B. are the dead — BIBLE 158:24
B. are the pure in heart — WHAR 1068:5
b. be the evergreen Pine! — SCOTT 853:62
b. be the name of the Lord — BIBLE 112:95
B. is he who — VIRG 1045:96
B. is the almost insensitive tree — DARIO 305:77
b. of my Father — BIBLE 140:44
b. them unaware — COLE 274:91
b. with a woman's brain — RICH 810:64
b. with such happy manners — AUST 51:37
b. you out of the house — BIBLE 118:28
does not make a man b. — ARIS 34:26
more b. to give than to receive — BIBLE 148:6
wife seems more b. — HELO 469:6
blessèd Most b., most glorious — SMITH 950:61
blessedness happiness or b. of man — SPIN 960:58
blesses nation b. what undoes it — HUGO 502:77
blessing b., even life for evermore — BIBLE 119:45
b. like experiencing madness — LISP 607:40
b. of God Almighty — BOOK 175:33
continual dew of thy b. — BOOK 173:98
fear the b. of God — ELIOT 372:60
for the which b. — SHAK 879:33
If this is a b. — CHUR 265:29
most need of b. — SHAK 908:45
Oh there is b. — WORD 1095:17
pour you out a b. — BIBLE 130:70
proceedeth b. and cursing — BIBLE 155:68
Prosperity is the b. — BACON 56:50
steal immortal b. from her lips — SHAK 869:7
Sweet was its b. — COCK 272:60
system, and actually a b. — LIVI 607:47
taken away thy b. — BIBLE 105:33
thou shalt be a b. — BIBLE 104:18
to delight...paid thy utmost b. — DELA 314:34
to us a national b. — HAMI 453:39
truly it's a b. — CLOU 270:35
blessings all the b. of this life — BOOK 174:8
b. of a good thick skirt — KING 559:4
b. of marriage — SHAW 922:42
b. of youth — DEMO 315:46
b. on your frosty pow — BURNS 211:6
Free trade, one of the greatest b. — MACA 622:87
from whom all b. flow — KEN 549:48
glass of b. standing by — HERB 476:34
Life is the greatest of b. — HEINE 467:69
blest be for ever b. — HOW 497:90
still be years b. — GOLD 433:19
blew B. hither — HOUS 495:55
blight b. man was born for — HOPK 492:94
Blimber Doctor B.'s assistant — DICK 323:92
blind all...are born b. — OKRI 738:23
birth and growth...ubiquitous and b. — DILL 330:52
b. and naked Ignorance — TENN 1002:9
b. as any noonday owl — TENN 1003:39
B. as the...nails — SITW 941:16
b. boy, Venus' baby — SPEN 959:29
b. dates are a way of life — EPST 379:6
b., despised, and dying king — SHEL 927:76
b. fury of creation — SHAW 921:25
b. hysterics of the Celt. — TENN 1000:58
b. in the end — BERR 98:10
b. lead the b. — BIBLE 138:10
b. life within the brain — TENN 1004:47
B., old and lonely — SHEL 930:35

blind (*contd.*)
b. receive their sight — BIBLE 137:83
b. with smoke — SASS 845:24
brave sun Die b. — JEFF 519:79
but unbelief is b. — MILT 683:30
chance he might go b. — GREG 446:47
check the eyes and call them b. — MIDD 673:42
conversation of the b. — MOORE 705:15
country of the b. — WELLS 1064:30
drawing back the b. — KIPL 564:2
eyes of the b. shall be opened — BIBLE 126:82
Fortune...she be b. — BACON 59:11
glass so gay, that it can b. — SPEN 958:22
Grief for a while is b. — SHEL 930:15
I was b., now I see — BIBLE 146:52
In the country of the b. — ERAS 379:8
it is the b. watchmaker — DAWK 310:44
love is b. — SHAK 874:29
Love, knocking its b. forehead — SAND 840:48
mathematician is a b. man — DARW 306:91
not worry about the b. alleys — FEYN 387:33
one of the b. alleys — WAUGH 1056:70
one-armed b. man — WODE 1089:93
Passions can...never b. me — LAFA 574:73
religion without science is b. — EINS 363:66
right to be b. — NELS 722:98
splendid work for the b. — SASS 845:29
Was b., but now I see — NEWT 725:42
will not make us b. — RUSH 829:69
winged Cupid painted b. — SHAK 870:28
with its own internal lighting b. — SHEL 929:10
Ye b. guides — BIBLE 139:35
blinded b. by the external tools — REYES 807:22
blindness 'eathen in 'is b. — KIPL 562:58
first love's impassioned b. — PEAC 762:31
fortune follows bold b. — LAFO 575:84
blinds a drawing-down of b. — OWEN 748:7
b. let through the day — HOUS 496:75
blindworms Newts and b. — SHAK 871:40
blink at ane b. — DOUG 341:53
blinkard Thou b. blowboll — SKEL 942:36
bliss Almost the highest b. — KEATS 544:37
b. in ale — CRAB 293:65
B. in our brow's bent — SHAK 905:62
B. it was...to be alive — WORD 1099:66
b. of solitude — WORD 1099:70
deprived of everlasting b.! — MARL 654:14
domestic b. — PATM 760:10
Everywhere I see b. — SHEL 926:55
excels all other b. — DYER 358:87
faded b., faded so soon — MILT 688:20
fill Of b. on b. — MILT 690:59
gate of b. — CRAS 296:22
ignorance is b. — GRAY 441:48
never...parted, b. or woe — MILT 692:6
promise of pneumatic b. — ELIOT 367:64
thou hast not thy b. — KEATS 544:7
winged hours of b. — CAMP 227:28
blissful experience is not always b. — HUXL 507:84
blisters shoes...gave her b. — BAIN 62:74
blithe b. wi' Comrades dear — BURNS 210:79
No b. Irish lad was so happy — CAMP 227:24
blitz b. of a boy — CAUS 246:66
block big black b. — GILB 425:88
changes with the next b. — SHAK 878:27
chip off the old b. — BURKE 207:23
the biggest coal b. — HEAN 465:43
blockade Navy will run the b. — ANDE 18:1
blockhead bookful b. — POPE 778:87
No man but a b. — JOHN 530:89
blockheads b. of all ages — CONG 281:27
The b. talk — SCOTT 856:15
the greatest b. — MONT 701:57
blocks hew b. with a razor — POPE 779:14

blocks (*contd.*)
spell God with the wrong b. — ROBI 815:29
You b., you stones — SHAK 882:15
bloke b. fer showin' off — DENN 316:61
blokes b. retire to the...pub — NEVI 723:15
blond like a b. satan — HAMM 454:58
more b. than you — CUMM 300:87
blonde b. to make a bishop kick — CHAN 250:31
in love with a beautiful b. — FIEL 388:61
blondes Gentlemen Prefer B. — LOOS 612:26
Gentlemen...seem to remember b. — LOOS 613:28
blood always worked with my b. — KOLL 568:77
angry up the b. — PAIGE 750:41
billet-doux written in cold b. — ETHE 380:14
b.'s a rover — HOUS 494:42
B., all price excelling — AQUI 32:5
b. and other vital fluids — STER 969:7
B. and revenge...in my head — SHAK 862:37
b. and spirit together — MARI 651:71
b. and water — BIBLE 147:72
b. and wine are red — WILDE 1078:96
b. be on us — BIBLE 140:53
b.-bedecked halls of their revel — POE 748:44
b. Come gargling — OWEN 748:13
b. enough on your penal code — BYRON 221:9
b. from head to foot — MACL 633:67
b. in torrents pour — DAVI 307:98
b. is settled, and her joints — SHAK 869:18
b. is strong — GALT 413:8
B. may be thicker than water — SOME 952:99
b.[may lose] its fire — BYRON 220:98
b. mixed with wasted gold — KING 559:6
b. of all the martyrs — IVAN 514:83
b. of grape — BLAKE 165:59
B. of our Lord Jesus — BOOK 175:32
b. of patriots and tyrants — JEFF 520:90
b. of the Christians — TERT 1006:78
b. of the saints — BIBLE 158:28
b.-red blossom — TENN 1002:95
b.-red flower of revolution — RAND 801:26
b. rolled out — HUGH 499:21
b. speaks to you in my veins — SHAK 873:85
b., toil, tears and sweat — CHUR 264:13
b. was cold — SCOTT 853:44
b. was shed for me — ELLI 374:9
b. was sprinked on the wall — BIBLE 112:82
b. will be ready — SADE 835:65
b. with guilt is brought — SHEL 930:16
b. with the thought of dying — MASE 662:51
blow in cold b. — SHAW 922:52
brand sae drap wi' b. — BALL 67:39
by man shall his b. be shed — BIBLE 104:14
caked in b. — JOHN 523:43
Christ's b. streams in the firmament! — MARL 654:20
cinema in their b. — RICH 810:65
clouds as actual b. — MUNCH 713:51
conjure up the b. — SHAK 881:84
cooling the b. — FLAN 391:25
dark b. dammed within — CULL 299:70
daughter to his b. — SHAK 874:26
Deliver me from b.-guiltiness. — BIBLE 116:79
dogs licked the b. of Naboth — BIBLE 111:71
drink his b. — BOOK 175:30
dripping b. our only drink — ELIOT 371:52
economic b. pressure — WRIS 1102:18
effusion of...human b. — OCON 735:81
Every drop of my b. — GAND 414:11
faints at the sight of b. — BETJ 100:43
faith melteth into b. — SHAK 879:36
find so much b. — SHAK 895:29
Fire, B., and Famine — HENR 472:64
first b. shed in revenge — PEPYS 765:62
flesh and b. — THAC 1006:81
freeze thy young b. — SHAK 889:74

blood (*contd.*)

give me B.!	DICK 324:*13*
glories of our b. and state	SHIR 935:*27*
glory smeared in dust and b.	SHAK 862:*31*
great effusion of b.	STUB 980:*13*
happit flesh and b.	FERG 386:*18*
heart's b. dyed	CONN 282:*54*
heyday in the b.	SHAK 892:*54*
I am in b.	SHAK 909:*63*
ice was in the b.	PIER 769:*34*
If b. be the price	KIPL 562:*55*
in place and b.	TENN 1000:*57*
In whose cold b.	SHAK 861:*16*
iron and b.	BISM 164:*38*
joys are more to flesh and b.	DRYD 351:*54*
know the colour of that b.	KEATS 548:*21*
laws for the b.	SHAK 874:*12*
laws…writ in b.	MARL 653:*97*
liquors in my b.	SHAK 885:*82*
look like flesh and b.	MOORE 705:*13*
looked kneaed with b.	BROW 198:*50*
love respects no b.	DEKK 313:*10*
May their b. cease to flow!	DAVIS 309:*36*
men are flesh and b.	SHAK 883:*38*
Moloch whose b. is running	GINS 427:*25*
More b.! More b.!	CRON 298:*58*
new testament of my b.	BIBLE 164:*38*
not shed her b.	SHAK 900:*52*
not…a question of birth or b.	OBRI 733:*61*
Nothing like b., sir	THAC 1006:*87*
O, the b. more stirs	SHAK 875:*45*
of British b.?	TENN 1000:*65*
one drop of negro b.	HUGH 499:*22*
one of the b.-suckers	FRAN 402:*16*
our own red b.	YEATS 1106:*74*
poet's feverish b.	ARNO 37:*77*
poison the whole b. stream fills	EMPS 378:*83*
Politics is a b. sport	BEVAN 102:*71*
redness which affrights in b.	MELV 667:*36*
Resign your heart's b.	SHEL 927:*56*
Senator, it is American b.	MACA 621:*76*
sensations…Felt in the b.	WORD 1094:*96*
sheds his b. with me	SHAK 882:*4*
show-business with b.	BELA 85:*77*
slaked the light with b.	TENN 1005:*65*
smell the b. of a British man	SHAK 903:*25*
so much b. in him?	SHAK 909:*77*
stained with b.	SHAK 871:*58*
Stir the Vikings' b.	KING 558:*90*
streams of British b.	SCHAW 847:*61*
sweat and b. and souls	FRAN 402:*16*
talk about their Pilgrim b.	LOWE 616:*79*
the circulation of their b.	SMITH 947:*9*
this is my b.	BIBLE 140:*48*
Tiber foaming with much b.	POWE 788:*17*
To freeze the b.	WORD 1096:*36*
tomahawks, wi b. red-rusted	BURNS 211:*18*
too much b.	SHAK 896:*57*
voice of thy brother's b.	BIBLE 104:*5*
wash this b. Clean	SHAK 908:*49*
washed in the b. of the Lamb?	LIND 605:*10*
washed in the b. of the Lamb?	LIND 605:*11*
Waste of B.	STUD 980:*14*
water and the b.	TOPL 1023:*7*
We be one b.	KIPL 561:*50*
welt'ring in his b.	DRYD 351:*70*
What case of flesh and b.	ROCH 816:*49*
When b. is nipped	SHAK 866:*31*
When the b. burns	SHAK 888:*68*
when the b. creeps	TENN 999:*35*
whips my b. like verse	WILL 1083:*94*
win…By b. or ink	BYRON 222:*33*
with hands b. stained	ORTE 741:*84*
with his own b. he bought	STONE 978:*73*

blood (*contd.*)

Without shedding of b.	BIBLE 154:*47*
would draw b.	DUNC 355:*48*
written in letters of b.	STRA 979:*2*
Young b. must have its course	KING 558:*94*
bloodless b. substitute for life	STEV 974:*18*
bloodmoney Dr B.	DICK 320:*8*
bloods mingle our b. together	SHAK 910:*94*
our two b. mingled be	DONNE 337:*88*
bloodshed Politics is war without b.	MAO 648:*21*
bloodthirsty b. and deceitful man	BOOK 176:*60*
bloody battles b. exercises	JOSE 537:*35*
Be b., bold, and resolute	SHAK 909:*67*
b. beat them again	RAMS 801:*20*
B. instructions, which being taught	SHAK 907:*31*
greet you with b. hands	CORW 288:*62*
head is b. but unbowed	HENL 472:*57*
horrid malicious b. flame	PEPYS 765:*80*
My b. thoughts	SHAK 899:*42*
On the same b. morning	SCOTT 854:*73*
Walk! Not b. likely	SHAW 924:*8*
War's a b. game	SASS 845:*35*
bloom As well as any b.	THOM 1012:*12*
b. is shed	BURNS 211:*15*
b. of that valley shall	MOORE 706:*32*
b. sae fresh and fair	BURNS 212:*22*
Charm…a sort of b.	BARR 73:*46*
Each opening sweet of earliest b.	COLL 276:*42*
hung with b. along the bough	HOUS 494:*39*
look at things in b.	HOUS 494:*41*
Our b. is gone	STEV 971:*46*
risk of spoiling its b.	CONR 285:*14*
terrible and splendid b.	RAND 801:*26*
touch it and the b. is gone	WILDE 1077:*82*
vernal b., or summer's rose	MILT 689:*31*
with the b. go I	ARNO 39:*16*
Bloom Leopold B. ate with relish	JOYCE 538:*53*
blooms b. each thing, then maids	NASHE 721:*80*
bloomy all the b. beds	SMART 944:*70*
blossom Are you…the b.	YEATS 1106:*80*
b. by b. the spring begins	SWIN 986:*24*
b. in purple and red	TENN 1001:*88*
b. of war	TENN 1002:*95*
b. of war	TENN 1002:*95*
full spring-tide of b.	BETJ 100:*37*
last b. is the first b.	MACN 637:*48*
saft faulding b.	TANN 991:*96*
there is a b. about me	BOSW 180:*29*
Under the b.	SHAK 917:*41*
blossomed B. Sarah	BERR 98:*8*
blossomer great-rooted b.	YEATS 1106:*80*
blossoms art of orange b.	PISS 771:*58*
boughs do laughing b. bear	SPEN 958:*19*
cherry b. in the spring	ANON 26:*51*
million b. springing	MACG 630:*22*
of locust b.	WILL 1083:*98*
rod of Aaron…bloomed b.	BIBLE 107:*83*
strange odours of b.	CONR 284:*96*
tender leaves…tomorrow b.	SHAK 918:*61*
blot And blackens every b.	TENN 1002:*1*
b. on the fair face of creation	BRON 191:*94*
b. upon my pride	SHAK 867:*57*
It is no vicious b.	SHAK 902:*99*
text that looks a little b.	TENN 1002:*10*
the art to b.	POPE 782:*83*
This world's no b.	BROW 198:*47*
blotched b. out beyond	STEV 971:*45*
blotted man will be b. out	JEFF 519:*79*
never b. out a line	JONS 536:*20*
blouse b. out and her nails grimed	MANS 647:*97*
blow bless the hand that gave the b.	DRYD 350:*38*
B. him again to me	TENN 997:*97*
b. in cold clood	SHAW 922:*52*
b. of a loy	SYNGE 988:*64*

blow (*contd.*)

b. over the face	AUBR 45:*35*
b., thou winter wind	SHAK 885:*94*
B., winds	SHAK 903:*17*
b. you through and through	SHAK 911:*29*
Death unfailing will strike the b.	CURR 301:*18*
first b. is half the battle	GOLD 433:*25*
Liberty's in every b.	BURNS 212:*38*
man who does not return your b.	SHAW 922:*64*
must strike the b.?	BYRON 219:*75*
put your lips together—and b.	FURT 410:*57*
receive a knock-down b.	HUNT 504:*18*
terrible b.	HAMER 453:*37*
that relaxed alluring b.	HEAN 465:*43*
until I b. up!	THOM 1011:*90*
blowboll Thou blinkard b.	SKEL 942:*36*
blowing furious winter b.	RANS 802:*35*
blown to have b. up the King	HOBY 483:*47*
blows allured…without b.	STEE 964:*22*
b. and revenge for me!	SHAK 861:*20*
fled step-dame Study's b.	SIDN 937:*51*
It b. so hard	HOUS 495:*54*
stories And not through his b.	LAFO 575:*92*
when most she offers b.	SHAK 905:*81*
Blucher B. and I have lost	WELL 1063:*10*
bludgeoning b. of the people	WILDE 1076:*56*
blue b.-and-white young man	GILB 424:*69*
B., darkly, deeply	SOUT 954:*34*
b.-gum nigger	BENET 90:*61*
b. is all in a rush	HOPK 491:*86*
b.…Of night	YEATS 1105:*65*
b. ribbon of the turf	DISR 333:*1*
chic old b.-haired ladies	CAPO 231:*88*
in yonder living b.	TENN 1000:*60*
naked frosty b.	THOM 1012:*6*
no b. without yellow	VAN 1039:*99*
ocean b. or smoke b.	GALE 412:*88*
The b. deep	SHEL 929:*98*
The b. Mediterranean	SHEL 928:*88*
those b. remembered hills	HOUS 495:*57*
bluebell Mary, ma Scotch B.	LAUD 583:*38*
bluejay b. in peacock feathers	LAFO 575:*93*
bluejays shoot all the b.	LEE 592:*7*
blues blue-gum nigger to sing me b.	BENET 90:*61*
No white man ever had the b.	LEAD 589:*49*
soul keeps a singin' the b.	BERRY 98:*3*
Sweet b.!	HUGH 499:*16*
bluest b. veins to kiss	SHAK 905:*76*
bluff no matter how charming a b.	FITZ 391:*12*
blunder frae monie a b. free us	BURNS 210:*77*
so grotesque a b.	BENT 93:*28*
Youth is a b.	DISR 332:*82*
blundered Some one had b.	TENN 1000:*72*
blundering b. will live on	SAND 841:*67*
blunders b.…shape history	TAYL 991:*10*
scapegoats for our b.	TWAIN 1034:*13*
woman…Nature's agreeable b.	COWL 291:*20*
blur in retrospect…all a b.	SCHL 848:*76*
blush At first b. a new idea	MILL 677:*2*
b. at your faults	FLET 394:*74*
call a b. into the cheek	DICK 327:*88*
knew by the b.	SOME 952:*98*
not b. to be admir'd	WALL 1050:*71*
pass my name…I b.	TREE 1025:*43*
with a b. retire	DICK 327:*88*
blushes B. Or needs to	TWAIN 1034:*6*
Who b. at the name?	INGR 511:*44*
blushing b.…a sign of guilt	CONG 281:*30*
Religion b. veils	POPE 783:*10*
sacrifice other people without b.	SHAW 922:*65*
without lowering her eyes and b.	SARR 843:*2*
Blyton E. Blyton of economics	HOLME 485:*73*
boa reach for my feather B.	GINS 428:*29*
Boadicea bargain-basement B.	HEAL 464:*29*

boar-pig Bartholomew b.-p.   SHAK 877:92
board bred in a B.-School   KIPL 562:68
ideal b. of directors   DOCH 334:37
moving a single b.   SNYD 951:83
boarding-house landlady of a b.-h.   LEAC 588:33
boarding-school old-fashioned B.-s.   AUST 51:53
boards he who treads the b.   BISH 163:29
boast b. of heraldry   GRAY 442:66
B. not thyself of tomorrow   BIBLE 122:5
Boston…hast naught to b.   ANON 24:6
Britain, could you ever b.   SWIFT 985:1
empty b. of flesh   HABI 450:99
How many people can b. as much   BECK 81:97
Let no man b. himself   TROL 1027:65
our absolute b.   WORD 1096:24
Such is the patriot's b.   GOLD 432:97
boastful b. men so oft abashed   SPEN 958:17
boasting No b. like a fool   SHAK 909:69
boat beautiful pea-green b.   LEAR 590:58
b. …had the goods of a house   PEPYS 765:81
b. wallows in the sea   IGNA 510:29
came and found a b.   TENN 994:46
glass-bottomed b.   MIZN 698:7
intellectually promising b.   VAND 1039:95
soul is an enchanted b.   SHEL 930:24
Speed, bonnie b.   BOUL 181:46
While his b. hastens   KEATS 544:38
boathook diplomatic b.   CECIL 247:81
boating Jolly b. weather   CORY 288:67
boatman B., do not tarry   CAMP 227:29
boatmen puny b. do not know how   HERZ 478:72
boats b. against the current   FITZ 391:7
b. began to near the winning post   COKE 272:74
b. or ships came near   LEAR 590:63
b. were tossed   LOWE 616:93
fooling among b.?   STEV 973:91
messing about in b.   GRAH 438:90
running into b.   PEPYS 765:79
bob b.-tail nag   FOST 399:59
meek with thirty b. a week   DAVI 307:95
bobolink B. for a Chorister   DICK 328:98
bobtailed b. Hob   SITW 941:10
Boche stab…a well-killed B.   READ 803:51
bodies action of two b.   NEWT 725:38
adorning their b.   SMOL 950:63
angles of their b.   ANGE 20:32
b. are buried in peace   BIBLE 133:18
b. are under our wheels   SHAW 921:29
b. in space   MANN 646:86
b. measure out their place   MARV 659:89
b. of the living   SPEN 957:90
b. of those bones   DOMI 335:56
concern not for your b.   PLATO 773:3
embraces of our b. taste   CAREW 232:14
grave keeps b.   DONNE 338:15
house their b.   GIBR 422:38
inexhaustible b.   TATE 991:3
may have civilized b.   MELV 667:27
other heated b.   WATT 1055:55
Pile the b. high   SAND 841:62
preaches virtue in our b.   MARI 652:76
present your b. a living sacrifice   BIBLE 149:33
scent of unwashed b.   ACKR 4:54
scorn their b.   BAST 76:8
souls out of men's b.?   SHAK 879:45
souls…to your scattered b. go   DONNE 338:3
three b. no sensible man   MACM 635:14
well-developed b.   FORS 398:46
women's b. are more delicate   CHRI 262:75
bodily Close your b. eye   FRIE 405:59
Thanks to his b. form   REDT 804:79
bodkin that is the bare b.   TWAIN 1033:89
With a bare b.?   SHAK 890:21
body air and water to the human b.   REES 805:92

body (*contd.*)
as it is for the b.   HUXL 507:62
as well as of the b.   HAZL 464:23
beautiful passionate b.   SWIN 987:34
best marriage…of mind and b.   FOWL 400:70
b. able to endure   MARL 653:7
b. and material substance   CARL 236:90
B. and soul   JORD 536:28
b. and substance of his works   COLE 275:29
b. away to barter   NGU 725:45
b. between your knees   CORY 288:67
b. continues in its state   NEWT 724:35
b. could reform   TWAIN 1033:80
b.'s harmony   POPE 783:5
b. is a machine for living   TOLS 1023:95
b. is the temple   BIBLE 150:49
b. like a wardrobe.   THOM 1011:87
b. like mine!   ATLAS 44:5
b. meet a b.   BURNS 213:45
b. of a weak…woman   ELIZ 373:90
b. of Benjamin Franklin   FRAN 402:99
b. of its womanhood   SCHR 850:7
B. of our Lord Jesus   BOOK 175:31
b. of generalizations   FRIE 405:52
b. of the cobbler   LOCKE 609:74
b. of this death?   BIBLE 149:24
b. of truth and the b.   LIPP 607:36
b. that will go on circulating   STEG 965:28
b. was as round   SPEKE 955:62
b. will be guarded   LOWE 615:74
b.'s work's expired   SHAK 913:56
brief loan of his own b.   CABE 224:76
bury my b. in Sussex grass   BENET 90:62
children of my b.   KOLL 568:76
commit his b. to ground   BOOK 176:58
commit his b. to the deep   BOOK 178:96
damned of b. and soul   KIPL 561:40
dignity or baseness…not in their b.   CHRI 262:74
ease of b.   SMITH 945:78
Fleas…upon the b.   LAND 578:56
for the relief of the b.   RICH 809:47
get rid of the b.   PLATO 774:15
glorify God in your b.   BIBLE 150:49
gun gives you the b.   THOR 1017:95
had tasted her sweet b.   SHAK 899:40
Happiness is healthy for the b.   PROU 793:7
harmonies of b.   BERN 97:86
head belongs to a b.   ROSSO 825:98
Health and an able b.   FLET 394:76
Her b. a bulb   PLATH 773:99
human b. is sacred   WHIT 1073:83
I knew her b. there   CRANE 295:2
in time leave the b.   SMOL 950:64
keep your b. white   STEV 976:53
knit together in one b. politic   HENR 472:65
labour of his b.   LOCKE 609:69
lack of health in the b.   PLATO 774:10
language is the b. of thought   CARL 234:52
liberation of both b. and mind   BANN 70:3
little b. with a mighty heart   SHAK 880:74
live in company with a b.   DELA 314:21
looking for a b. in the coach   HITC 482:24
man's b. both for power   SPEN 958:12
mind or b. grieved   CAMP 228:40
mind or b. to prefer   POPE 780:42
mind, in b. strong!   MILT 694:39
moist, unpleasant b.   DICK 321:52
more…Africa than my own b.   ORTON 742:85
most erotic part of the b.   BART 75:82
mystery…Of the glorious B.   AQUI 32:5
Naught broken save this b.   BROO 192:24
not a single molecule of my b.   DIDE 330:33
not be sound…in b. or mind   LLOY 608:55
not of her flesh and b.   KEYN 554:28

body (*contd.*)
not that thy whole b. be cast   BIBLE 134:41
nothing…but my b.'s length   SHAK 862:31
O b. swayed to music   YEATS 1106:80
one b. and one heart   DOUG 341:57
onnable b.'d be safe?   LOWE 616:81
Over my dead b.   KAUF 543:20
own your own b.   JONG 533:61
patch up thine old b.   SHAK 877:92
prefer shifting my whole b.   HERZ 478:73
prose takes the mould of the b.   WOOLF 1093:82
Prostitution. Selling one's b.   MACK 632:54
Punish a b.   DRYD 349:14
renders the b. …more perfect   PIUS 772:81
resurrection of the b.   BOOK 178:96
see…my b. without disgust   BAUD 77:26
service of the b.   MORE 707:52
sever head from b.   WEBS 1060:35
shaped my b. so   SHAK 862:34
soul is not more than the b.   WHIT 1072:81
sound mind in a sound b.   JUVE 540:82
sound mind in a sound b.   LOCKE 609:75
Take, eat: this is my b.   BIBLE 150:59
temple, called his b.   THOR 1016:73
that b. of men   STEE 964:16
the gigantic b.   MACA 623:4
this b. did contain a spirit   SHAK 876:76
this is my b.   BIBLE 140:48
time by how the b. sways   ROET 819:98
too violent for the b.   JEFF 520:97
toughness the b. will find   WAVE 1058:10
turn your b.   WEBS 1060:46
turning the whole b.   PLATO 774:23
Upon my buried b. lay   BEAU 80:73
use of my b.   BECK 81:1
vital fluids of the b.   STER 969:7
well proportioned b.   AUBR 45:34
what exercise is to the b.   STEE 964:17
Whether I was in my b.   HAND 455:68
whose b. is it?   RODR 819:90
Whose b., Nature is   POPE 780:40
witches that deform the b.   SHAK 865:1
with my b. I thee worship   BOOK 176:51
work of b. or mind   MILT 690:60
yer b. will disappear   KELM 549:34
You are the b.   SCEVE 847:58
Your b. rocking!   CRANE 294:95
bodyguards Bush has 100 b.   GORB 435:60
bodyline B. was devised to stifle   LARW 582:31
B. was not an incident   JAMES 516:9
Boer before the B. War   ORWE 743:10
Bognor Bugger B.   GEOR 419:85
bogs Brown b. with black water   COLUM 278:61
find a way out of the b.   MAIL 640:93
melancholy of the b.   WAUGH 1057:89
bogus science, even b. science   PRIT 791:64
Bohemia B. has no banner   WILL 1081:63
boil b. at different degrees   EMER 377:74
War That Would Not B.   TAYL 991:9
boils satan has not geven me b.   FLEM 394:61
bold be b., it will not burst thee   BIBLE 132:7
Be b., be b.   SPEN 958:21
b. as a hawk   THUR 1018:25
hath made me b.   SHAK 908:42
He was a b. Man   SWIFT 986:12
lover b. and free   CLEV 269:12
solid, or b.   STRA 979:97
Virtue is b.   SHAK 897:84
want of cunning made me b.   SPEN 959:29
boldness B.…always b.!   DANT 305:74
b. is a child of ignorance   BACON 58:76
b. to wealth   HESI 479:83
differ chiefly in the b.   JEVO 521:22
in a young woman, it is b.   HUGO 502:90

bole Are you…the b.? YEATS 1106:*80*
Bolingbroke this canker, B.? SHAK 875:*43*
Bolivia and B. 1949 THER 1009:*44*
bollocks who would kick your b. LOFT 610:*86*
Boloigne hadde been, and at B. CHAU 254:*24*
Bolshevik B. tyranny is the worst CHUR 263:*98*
Bolsheviks B. are sincere DRIB 346:*44*
bolshevism b. run mad SNOW 951:*59*
bolt b. is shot back ARNO 36:*70*
b. of Cupid felt SHAK 870:*36*
bolts and the b. are hurled TENN 994:*52*
B. and bars will not MOLI 698:*18*
Boléro towards the beginning of B. LAMB 577:*47*
bomb Americans want to b. ANON 30:*57*
Ban the B. ANON 26:*58*
B. brought peace CHUR 265:*28*
b. the knot off a tree JENS 520:*2*
end up with the atomic b. PAGN 750:*40*
How We Got Along After The B. DICK 320:*8*
hydrogen and napalm b. ROUS 827:*30*
Long after the b. falls JANO 518:*54*
production of the fission b. FROMM 406:*70*
the way it was with the atomic b. OPPE 741:*71*
word 'Now' is like a b. MILL 677:*4*
bombardment fury of aerial b. EBER 359:*10*
bombast swelling into b. DRYD 347:*59*
bombed glad we've been b. ELIZ 374:*97*
protect him from being b. BALD 65:*10*
bombs atom b. are piling up ORWE 744:*40*
b. and missiles lie…buried RAND 801:*25*
B. away ANON 27:*83*
b. bursting in air KEY 554:*24*
Come, friendly b. BETJ 99:*31*
construction of…powerful b. EINS 363:*65*
Ears like b. CAUS 246:*66*
rain of b. WHITE 1070:*43*
the roar of b. ORWE 743:*8*
whiskered men with b. TOLK 1022:*91*
bonbon pink b. stuffed with snow DEBU 311:*69*
bond According to my b. SHAK 902:*96*
Let him look to his b. SHAK 872:*78*
neither b. nor free BIBLE 152:*89*
trust man on his oath or b. SHAK 901:*87*
bondag Marriage…only actual b. MILL 675:*79*
bondage b. of certain ribbons SHAK 912:*37*
damn'd to the b. be? HABI 450:*1*
hold another in b. FULL 409:*33*
in the house of b. MACA 622:*90*
out of the house of b. BIBLE 106:*68*
queen in b. SHAK 861:*96*
spirit of b. BIBLE 149:*27*
That sweet b. SHEL 927:*58*
bonds draw tight the b. CHAM 249:*12*
garters to be b. and shackles BACON 57:*58*
bondsmen Hereditary b.! BYRON 219:*75*
bone b.-ache disquietude of life ALLEN 14:*34*
b. and muscle of my nation FRAN 402:*16*
B. of my b. thou art MILT 692:*6*
b. of my bones BIBLE 103:*92*
Break the b. RABE 798:*79*
cricket goes to the b. ARLO 35:*39*
dog…with a juicy b. AUDEN 46:*58*
every b. a-stare BROW 198:*50*
take the muscle from the b. ELIOT 370:*34*
touch his b. and his flesh BIBLE 112:*96*
boneless b. wonder CHUR 263:*7*
bones all my b. are out of joint BIBLE 114:*49*
bodies of those b. DOMI 335:*56*
b. are coral made SHAK 916:*25*
b. are dried BIBLE 129:*44*
b. are smitten asunder BOOK 176:*72*
b. live to learn ROET 819:*98*
brittle strength of b. MILT 687:*2*
broken spirit drieth the b. BIBLE 121:*87*

bones (*contd.*)
can these b. live BIBLE 129:*42*
childish; only b. abide LOWE 616:*93*
conjuring trick with b. JENK 520:*99*
full of dead men's b. BIBLE 139:*36*
Hope sleeps in our b. PIER 769:*37*
interrèd with their b. SHAK 884:*48*
lay his weary b. SHAK 918:*64*
like the b. of dinosaurs RAND 801:*25*
maketh the b. fat BIBLE 121:*82*
massy chine b. MUNDY 714:*53*
never mended no broken b. DICK 320:*14*
New Zealand is in my very b. MANS 647:*12*
O ye dry b. BIBLE 129:*43*
O'er his white b. BALL 67:*56*
our small b. THOM 1013:*19*
paste and cover to our b. SHAK 867:*59*
Pickled his b. ELIOT 369:*91*
rattle of the b. ELIOT 368:*88*
Rest of their b. DONNE 338:*4*
rottenness in his b. BIBLE 121:*71*
rotting b. of ten thousand TS 1031:*40*
Smash the scaffold of the b. HUID 503:*95*
spewed Natucket b. LOWE 616:*94*
the tongue breaketh the b. BIBLE 132:*9*
town of monks and b. COLE 275:*26*
until your b. are clean ADCO 6:*96*
valley which was full of b. BIBLE 129:*41*
your b. are very brittle STEV 975:*40*
bonfire th'everlasting b. SHAK 908:*51*
bonhomie overcame his natural b. BENT 93:*26*
bonjour B. tristesse ELUA 376:*25*
bonkers stark, staring b. HAIL 451:*14*
bonnet b. of Bonny Dundee SCOTT 856:*16*
bonnie b. banks o' Loch Lomond ANON 24:*4*
b., b. broom BALL -101:*33*
b. brow was brent BURNS 211:*6*
B. lassie will ye go BURNS 210:*90*
b. mill-dams o' Binnorie BALL -101:*30*
brisk and b. lad ANON 23:*96*
corn rigs are b. BURNS 210:*78*
gin love be b. BALL 67:*57*
service to my b. lassie BURNS 210:*97*
bonny B. Dundee SCOTT 855:*85*
honest men and b. lasses BURNS 211:*10*
no a b. fighter? STEV 976:*44*
bons trucs b. t.…annihilated CUMM 299:*75*
boo 18,000 people b. PLAN 773:*87*
boobs girl with big b. KING 557:*70*
booby who is not, at bottom, a b. MENC 669:*58*
booh Sing B. to you— GILB 424:*67*
book A good b. MILT 685:*57*
as kill a good b. MILT 685:*55*
as much a trade to write a b. LA 572:*36*
bad b. is as much HUXL 506:*57*
Bell, b., and candle SHAK 872:*65*
betray me to a lingering b. HERB 475:*14*
b. …a kind of optical instrument PROU 794:*10*
b. and a head collide LICH 603:*82*
b. and me together BROW 199:*67*
b.…finished in half the time WODE 1089:*96*
b. in the ordinary sense MILL 677:*15*
b. is not harmless ELIOT 370:*20*
b. of knowledge MILT 689:*31*
b. of life BIBLE 158:*33*
b.…of my secret soul SHAK 894:*98*
b. of road maps STEI 966:*59*
b. out of which a people LIPP 606:*32*
b. this learning mayst SHAK 914:*76*
b.…you're all done reading SALI 838:*19*
burn a b. RUSH 829:*69*
by the b. SHAK 887:*35*
called the b. Men Without Women HEMI 470:*16*
commonplace b. be full SWIFT 984:*61*

book (*contd.*)
cover of an old b. FRAN 402:*99*
dainties…bred in a b. SHAK 865:*16*
damned, thick, square b.! GLOU 430:*62*
difference between writing a b. MAIL 639:*86*
dirty b. worth reading POUND 787:*92*
do not throw this b. about BELL 86:*96*
drown my b. SHAK 917:*40*
Each creature…Is as a b. ALAN 11:*77*
essence of a b. NABO 717:*8*
Europe…a hardcover b. DELI 314:*37*
ever written a b. WELD 1063:*99*
Every b. is like a purge DU 354:*2*
face…is as a b. SHAK 907:*28*
find one English b. ARNO 38:*7*
Finishing a b. CAPO 231:*87*
from the b. of honour razèd SHAK 913:*46*
frowst with a b. KIPL 563:*77*
Go little b. SPEN 957:*92*
greatest b. he had ever read STEIN 965:*34*
He is like a b. in breeches SMITH 949:*52*
ideal companion…a good b. DAVI 308:*18*
In the Penguin b. HEAN 465:*39*
in thy b. all my members BIBLE 120:*50*
little b. out of the angel's hand BIBLE 157:*19*
little black b. with two players in CHAR 253:*98*
Louvre is the b. CEZA 248:*5*
make one b. JOHN 529:*72*
man the index of that b. DONNE 339:*33*
May my b. teach GIDE 423:*2*
men with b. learning RAMOS 801:*17*
mind afterwards—over a b. LAMB 576:*28*
mine adversary had written a b. BIBLE 113:*14*
Mona Lisa seem an open b. LEAC 589:*38*
moral or an immoral b. WILDE 1076:*44*
nature's infinite b. of secrecy SHAK 904:*57*
never call myself a b. lover LARK 582:*16*
never read the same b. twice WILS 1084:*31*
nice new little b. CATU 245:*58*
no instruction b. came with it FULL 409:*40*
of the b. of war MONT 703:*90*
old address in the b. MACC 626:*67*
oldest rule in the b. CARR 239:*47*
one-.b. novelist ROTH 825:*7*
only trouble with this b. LEHM 595:*39*
past…like the leaves of a b. WOOLF 1092:*55*
possession of a b. BURG 205:*84*
praise a b. too highly MILL 679:*57*
private b. to prove STEV 975:*26*
profession of b. writing STEI 966:*61*
read one b. in my life MITF 697:*17*
readers who are pleased with a b. CONN 283:*60*
reading of a b.! THOR 1016:*71*
school history b. GLAS 430:*60*
seal the b. BIBLE 130:*51*
seldom peruses a b. ADDI 6:*6*
sell a man a b. MORL 708:*71*
sour misfortune's b. SHAK 870:*22*
take down this b. YEATS 1105:*60*
take them out of this b. STER 969:*95*
tastes no wiser b.-maker LUCAS 618:*25*
The B. of Life WILDE 1077:*65*
then shut the b. PATM 760:*1*
This b. is not about heroes OWEN 748:*10*
this b. is not concerned with Poetry OWEN 748:*11*
this is no b. WHIT 1073:*90*
This little b. contains STIL 977:*68*
throw the entire b. in the fire SAND 840:*52*
To produce a mighty b. MELV 668:*34*
to write a really funny b. HEMI 470:*13*
To write the essential b. PROU 794:*9*
truly good b. THOR 1016:*69*
understand that b. but fail NICO 727:*62*
until he has written a b. JOWE 537:*39*

book (*contd.*)

when you read a b.	GAUG 416:40
Who is worthy to open the b.	BIBLE 157:11
word for word without b.	SHAK 893:94
Would you read a Sustaining B.	MILNE 680:73
Writing a b. of poetry	MARQ 656:47
writing a b.	GERA 419:94
book-case red mahogany b.-c.	BETJ 99:30
book-keeping double-entry b.	MULL 713:43
book-learning b.-l. in monasteries	GALL 413:97
Bookie snatch B. Bob	RUNY 829:59
books All b. are the Book of Job	ELKIN 374:98
all my b. are botches	MELV 668:47
all the b. you can export	CHIS 260:54
archives of his b.	RODC 818:81
are the b., the arts	SHAK 865:22
author because you like his b.	LINK 606:26
author who speaks about his own b.	DISR 333:18
base authority from others' b.	SHAK 865:6
be not swallowed up in b.!	WESL 1067:74
Before high-piled b.	KEATS 544:49
bibliobuli...who are...drunk on b.	MENC 669:78
B. and the man I sing	POPE 782:91
B. are a load of crap	LARK 581:8
B. are cold and certain	HUGO 502:82
b. are divided	RUSK 831:96
b. are either dreams	LOWE 615:73
b. are good enough	STEV 974:18
b. are more than b.	LOWE 615:72
B. are the bees	LOWE 616:85
b....are the nearest to us	CONR 285:3
B. are the opium	FRAN 400:81
b. are theatres	STEV 972:63
b., convention and cliché	POUND 785:48
B. do furnish a room	POWE 788:6
b. echoing the life	WILL 1083:97
B. from Boots	BETJ 100:33
b. have had their day	BENN 92:6
b. have their own fate	TERE 1006:77
B. have to teach	RUSH 829:70
b. ...how many of them I could avoid	MACA 622:81
b. in running brooks	SHAK 885:77
B., like men	SWIFT 984:59
B. make sense of life	BARN 72:33
B. must follow sciences	BACON 60:36
B. of poetry...promissory notes	WILDE 1076:32
b. one reads in childhood	ORWE 744:38
b. promiscuously read	MILT 685:66
B....propose to instruct	DEQU 316:66
b. teach them	GARC 414:19
b. that have a lot of dreck	BART 74:71
b. that influence us	FORS 399:56
b. that wound	KAFKA 540:84
B. think for me	LAMB 577:39
B.! 'tis a dull...strife	WORD 1094:2
b. to blisse ne to joye	LANG 579:74
b. were read	BELL 87:18
b. which do not have facts	VIDAL 1044:70
b. which you do not understand	VIAN 1043:44
B. written by Europeans	NAIP 717:17
B. written by martyr-men	CARL 236:86
borrowers of b.	LAMB 577:32
British...taste for bad b.	BRAD 183:81
cannot learn men from b.	DISR 332:71
Deep-versed in b.	MILT 694:36
everybody could write b.	BAIN 62:73
factory of b.	SMITH 947:5
First to possess his b.	SHAK 917:32
forefathers had no other b.	SHAK 861:15
Forsake thy b., and mateless play	BRON 191:7
Friends To borrow my b.	ROBI 814:25
Give me b., fruit, french wine	KEATS 545:67
God has written all the b.	BUTL 218:43
Good travel b.	RABAN 798:75

books (*contd.*)

haven't read any of your b.	JOYCE 538:62
I've read all the b.	MALL 641:15
If my b. had been any worse	CHAN 250:35
In b. lies the soul of the whole Past	CARL 236:90
in Germany, b.	STAEL 962:75
indiscriminate reviewing of b.	ORWE 744:39
Keepers of b.	MACL 634:77
let my b. be...eloquence	SHAK 913:53
luminous plectrum of b.	BELLI 86:93
Mistresses are like b.	WYCH 1103:37
more b. one reads	MAO 649:32
more b. we read	CONN 283:68
never yet was put into words of b.	MELV 668:40
of making many b. there is no end	BIBLE 124:43
old b.	GOLD 433:20
people...do not read b.	WORD 1099:75
pictures of obscene b.!	ARLT 35:41
Read the best b. first	THOR 1016:66
reading of good b.	DESC 317:75
so charming as b.	SMITH 949:47
Some b. accrete things	HOLM 485:76
some b. are deemed most baneful	MELV 668:50
Some b. are lies	BURNS 209:63
Some b. are to be tasted	BACON 59:23
Some b. are undeservedly forgotten	AUDEN 48:89
spacious highways of b.	SAND 841:78
spectacles of b.	DRYD 347:59
story b....written by people	WELTY 1065:50
study of mankind is b.	HUXL 506:46
Things in b.'s clothing	LAMB 577:40
trees shall be my b.	SHAK 886:97
true University...is a collection of b.	CARL 236:91
turned o'er many b.	SHAK 873:91
two classes of b.	FORD 396:3
who has written fine b.	GARR 415:31
worse crimes than burning b.	BROD 189:73
Writing b. is the closest men	MAIL 639:78
booksellers bold b.	SHER 934:7
embolden b.	WAUGH 1056:59
boomerang b. No more spear	NOON 731:25
boon for heaven's grace and b.	KEATS 546:92
Of neither would I ask the b.	SHEL 932:61
recipients of the b. of liberty	MAMET 643:47
sordid b.!	WORD 1099:73
boot b. in the face, the brute	PLATH 773:95
imagine a b. stamping	ORWE 745:60
Then hey for b. and horse	KING 558:94
booted always be b. and spurred	MONT 701:62
Booth B. died blind	LIND 605:12
B. led boldly	LIND 605:10
bootless spends a b. grief	SHAK 898:13
boots a pair of b.	TRAV 1025:31
asleep in his b.	STEV 971:47
before the truth has got its b. on	CALL 226:1
children...never had any b.	WILS 1085:27
elastic sided b.	SHAR 919:81
It b. not to resist	SHAK 862:29
look at his b.	SHAW 924:2
pantheon of b. and overalls	DUNN 356:51
truth is pulling its b. on	SPUR 961:64
wear long b., hard b.	SAND 841:64
went to school without any b.	BULM 204:53
when I take my b. off	DICK 323:97
bootstrings raise by our own b.	WILL 1081:50
booty none left to play b.	DICK 321:36
booze B., of course, and then curtains	AMIS 17:83
feeding on b. and spaghetti	LEWIS 602:53
man shouldn't fool with b.	FAUL 384:90
boozer clown, the b. the fighter?	MAST 663:63
boozes tell a man who b.	BURT 213:61
bop Playing b. is like playing Scrabble	ELLI 374:3
Boralaski as Count B.'s wife	SCOTT 854:71
bordello doorkeeper of a b.	TOSC 1024:9

border across the b. to get a drink	ANON 25:33
chuck them over the b.	WALE 1049:50
Night Mail crossing the b.	AUDEN 46:47
o'er the B. and awa'	SCOTT 854:80
sung of B. chivalry	SCOTT 853:42
Through all the wide B.	SCOTT 853:54
borders b., beds and shrubberies	KIPL 564:13
invade the b. of my realm	ELIZ 373:90
no walls, no b.	ATWO 44:18
tyranny whose b. are undefined	MAIL 639:74
bore A colossal b.	MERI 672:17
beside a muzzled b.	STEP 968:80
complaints are a b.	ACHE 3:58
Every hero becomes a b.	EMER 377:58
healthy male adult b.	UPDI 1036:52
If your husband is a b.	BELL 88:31
in it is merely a b.	WILDE 1077:72
is an old b.	TREE 1025:41
merely the Club B.	SAKI 838:14
People find ideas a b.	POUND 786:79
unless it becomes a b.	POUND 785:56
bored better that aged diplomats be b.	AUST 53:74
b. nearer to...mortification	WODE 1088:83
I am heavy b.	BERR 98:12
leaving because I am b.	SAND 842:81
nearly b.	GOSSE 436:71
Never to be b.	BALL 65:26
People do not read to be b.	BEAV 81:87
Punctuality...virtue of the b.	WAUGH 1057:99
so b. with it all	CHUR 265:43
boredom b., and the horror	ELIOT 370:16
b. and pain of it	BUEC 203:42
effect of b. on a large scale	INGE 511:39
Here b. reaches its peak	MILL 678:36
Inconstancy, b., anxiety	PASC 757:56
Life is first b.	LARK 581:11
not waiting for them to die of b.	BLAN 169:24
Symmetry is b.	HUGO 502:84
what makes a journey horrible...is b.	GELL 417:71
bores B. and Bored	BYRON 223:59
B. bore each other	MARQ 656:50
B. have succeeded to dragons	DISR 332:74
Borgia B. who has suddenly	WODE 1089:95
Borgias dining with the B. tonight	BEER 83:42
thirty years under the B.	WELL 1063:1
boring Antiquity...clichéd and b.	FLAU 393:44
Life...is b.	BERR 98:11
previously amusing become b.	COUP 289:85
something curiously b.	HUXL 506:45
work is less b. than amusement	BAUD 78:41
born all b. and must die	MATAK 663:66
as a poet...not b. yet	THOM 1013:22
as if I had insisted on being b.	DICK 326:65
as natural...to be b.	BACON 56:45
as soon as we were b.	BIBLE 131:84
because you were b. in it?	SHAW 925:16
bird b. in a cage	SHAW 924:59
blight man was b. for	HOPK 492:94
b. and dying, dying	MISH 696:76
b....among the mountains	WORD 1096:35
b. And he had reasons	ROBI 814:26
b. below par to the extent	MONT 701:59
B. but to die	POPE 780:42
b. free as Caesar	SHAK 882:19
b. in a merry hour	SHAK 879:41
b. in Canada	JOHN 524:60
b. in the minds of a few	KISS 566:34
b. into music	SIMO 939:84
b. into the world alive	GILB 424:75
B. of the sun	SPEN 956:72
b. of woman	TWAIN 1032:64
b. out of due time	BIBLE 151:65
b. to know you	ELUA 376:24
b. to set it right	STRA 979:93

born (*contd.*)
b....when wits were fresh and clear   ARNO 37:92
b. where my father lived   SITT 940:98
b. with an unreasonably large stock   SHAW 926:43
b....with ready-made parents   FRAME 400:78
b. with two things   TEMP 993:30
Bred en b. in a brier-patch   HARR 458:28
British Bourgeosie Is not b.   SITW 941:22
can't be b., unless it's...in   DICK 324:15
Else, wherefore b.?   TENN 1004:54
engaged, married or b.   GALS 413:2
Every moment one is b.   TENN 996:87
Except a man be b. again   BIBLE 145:32
fashion is b. by small facts   SCHI 847:62
I was b. on a day   VALL 1039:97
I've been b., and once   ELIOT 370:12
If b....were being invented   DOYLE 344:21
if he had happened to be b....there   FRIE 405:54
If Joan of Arc had been b.   SIMON 939:81
in dying that we are b.   FRAN 401:91
less than to be b.   BEAU 80:69
misery of us, that are b. great   WEBS 1060:55
must be b. again   BIBLE 145:33
none of woman b.   SHAK 909:67
not a single molecule...when b.   DIDE 330:33
not b. a parasite   FRAN 402:16
not b. under a rhyming planet   SHAK 880:65
Not to be b. is the best   AUDEN 46:56
One is not b. a woman   DE 311:62
powerless to be b.   ARNO 38:2
remember where I was b.   BENET 90:60
Sociology was b.   SMALL 943:62
Some men are b. kings   SHAW 925:24
That ever I was b.   SHAK 889:85
time to be b.   BIBLE 122:19
to be b., to live and to die   LABR 573:51
to the manner b.   SHAK 888:70
We are all b. crazy   BECK 81:98
We are b. believing   EMER 377:67
When we are b.   SHAK 904:39
where I was b.   SALI 838:18
why wasn't I b. old   DICK 322:65
borne hath b. me on his back   SHAK 893:77
borogove All mimsy were the b.   CARR 239:47
boroughs bright b.   HOPK 491:87
borrow know well enough to b. from   BIER 160:65
poets...beg, b., or steal   POUND 785:57
borrowed b. time, b. money   CALL 225:98
B. garments never fit   FULL 410:48
borrower b. of the night   SHAK 909:55
Neither a b. nor a lender be   SHAK 888:66
borrowing banqueting upon b.   BIBLE 132:4
b. foolishly spent   DUNC 355:44
borrowings b. cheap and the notes   LUCAS 618:27
bosom Amputate my freckled B.!   DICK 328:18
borne, see, on my b.!   BROW 199:73
b. is actually a millstone   GREER 445:38
b. of the great English   ARNO 38:9
b. of the lake   TENN 997:10
b. of the sea   SHAK 861:8
b. of the stream   SHEL 932:66
b. the bright waters meet   MOORE 706:32
breaks in our b.   SHEL 932:71
Can a man take fire in his b.   BIBLE 120:65
charge within the b.   DICK 327:93
Cleanse the fraught b.?   SHAK 910:82
Close b.-friend   KEATS 547:4
dear to this b.   TANN 991:96
from the b. of the morn   MARV 657:68
great within my b.   SHAK 863:67
guardage to the sooty b.   SHAK 898:2
Here in my b.   JONS 535:4
in your fragrant b. dies   CAREW 232:19
Let me to thy b. fly   WESL 1066:60

bosom (*contd.*)
no b. and no behind   SMITH 948:30
not a b. to repose upon   DICK 325:49
sea that bares her b.   WORD 1099:73
shall men give into your b.   BIBLE 142:83
tribes...slumber in its b.   BRYA 201:18
will leave Thy b.   MILT 689:39
bosoms b. of your actresses   JOHN 525:87
hang and brush their b.?   BROW 198:48
Quiet to quick b. is a hell   BYRON 220:86
boss absentee b. is best   WINT 1087:65
b....a comforting thought   MARQ 656:46
talk to the b.   MAMET 644:61
will always be his b.   RAVI 802:45
Boston B. Urban Renewal   MAIL 639:84
B....hast naught to boast   ANON 24:6
B....home of bean and cod   BOSS 180:28
B. is a state of mind   APPL 32:2
B. man is the east wind   APPL 32:3
B. State-House is the hub   HOLM 486:88
bottle of B. sea   BENET 90:61
Boswell B. was one of the smallest   MACA 623:3
botanize peep and b.   WORD 1095:9
botched Presidents...have b. up   ONAS 739:42
bother don't b. much about dress   SHAW 920:4
'b. it' I may Occasionally say   GILB 423:55
bothered buzzard...is never b.   FAUL 384:86
bothersome Life is short and b.   LABR 572:48
Botticelli B. isn't a wine   PUNCH 795:32
bottle a little for the b.   DIBD 319:5
b. of Boston sea   BENET 90:61
b. of salvation   RALE 800:13
b. of the best   STEV 973:94
brandish anything but my b.   SHAK 877:83
cantaloupe in a coke b.   JONES 533:59
desire to a b.   SHAK 871:49
fly the way out of the fly-b.   WITT 1088:79
ginger-beer b.   STEV 974:21
leave the b. on the chimley-piece   DICK 322:75
like magic in a pint b.   DICK 325:51
Poetry in a b.   FADI 382:54
scorpions in a b.   OPPE 741:76
terrible than an empty b.   LOWRY 618:17
vintage wine from a musty old b.   BOYLE 183:69
bottles B. of Ring-Bo-Ree   LEAR 590:56
fill old b. with banknotes   KEYN 555:36
new wine into old b.   BIBLE 136:71
bottom at the b. of a' the mischief   SCOTT 855:90
b. of my grief?   SHAK 869:14
b. stir The hell   MILT 689:45
going to hit the b.   MOND 699:39
I'm the b., you're the top   PORT 784:32
old mad scientist at b.   PERE 766:91
They have...mettle at b.   EMER 377:63
very b. of her being   ADAMS 5:70
will reach the b. first   GRAH 437:87
with my b. in the air   PIGG 769:39
bottomless b., topsiturviest   RUSK 831:12
Law is a b. pit   ARBU 33:9
bottoms b. of my trousers rolled   ELIOT 367:53
bough Apollo's laurel b.   MARL 654:23
blossom that hangs on the b.   SHAK 869:1
b. from Virginia's aged tree   RANS 802:32
bread beneath the b.   FITZ 390:88
Petals on a wet, black b.   POUND 785:52
boughs b. do laughing blossoms bear   SPEN 958:19
b. more silent than before   MILL 676:87
b. off many a tree   HERB 474:11
Green b.   LORCA 613:39
lowest b. and the brushwood sheaf   BROW 198:36
those b. which shake   SHAK 914:73
bouillabaisse B. is only good   DOUG 341:60
bouillion good poem is like a b. cube   DOVE 342:76
boulders spills the upper b.   FROST 406:72

bounce no more b. than...potato   PORT 784:39
bounces bigger because of the b.   MILNE 680:79
bound b. for the same bourn   HOUS 495:59
b. to give it honestly   JOHN 529:65
stream confined in narrow b.   CRAB 294:84
tall buildings in a single b.!   SIEG 937:68
too small a b.   SHAK 876:76
tranced woman, b. and stark   FREE 404:34
boundaries b. between politics   DANG 304:60
b. of the soul   HERA 473:87
cannot remain within their b.   DANTE 305:71
Deem that our puny b.   WORD 1096:25
few landmarks and no b.   MACM 636:26
boundary b. of the march   PARN 756:41
no b. line to art   PARK 753:87
bounded b. in a nutshell   SHAK 890:99
boundless b., as we wish our souls   SHEL 927:66
b., endless, and sublime   BYRON 221:8
Is b. better, b. worse   TENN 996:86
there is a b. theft   SHAK 902:93
bounds Eternity as if it had b.   DUNC 355:47
flaming b. of place and time   GRAY 443:90
is out of b. now   LOWE 617:2
living know No b.?   SHIR 935:23
thus far thy b.   MILT 691:85
untraced b.   WENT 1065:54
wider shall thy b. be set   BENS 92:9
bountiful How just, how b.   WORD 1101:93
nature...careless as it is b.   DILL 330:52
bounty b. is as boundless   SHAK 869:92
b. of God   BLAKE 166:78
those his former b. fed   DRYD 351:70
bouquets b. keep pouring in   FREUD 404:41
bourbon sound of pouring b.   MACC 627:68
this b. is good   TRUM 1030:34
Bourbon B. family is a dagger   QUIN 798:64
bourgeois astound the b.   BAUD 78:47
beastly the b. is   LAWR 587:1
b. always bounces up   CONN 282:56
B. society is infected   WEIL 1062:83
English proletariat...more b.   ENGE 378:87
Hatred of the b.   FLAU 393:42
narrow horizon of b.   MARX 661:24
person of b. origin   ORWE 742:94
small-town b. at heart   NABO 717:14
sordid b. world   MISH 696:74
bourgeoisie b. in the long run   TROT 1029:6
b. of all classes, who deny tragedy   BLIX 169:33
Discreet Charm of B.   BUNU 204:62
fine nervous flower of the b.   BOGAN 171:60
For generations the British b.   WAUGH 1056:65
The b.'s weapon   STEV 977:61
The British B.   SITW 941:22
wanted to make the b. a class   HUGO 502:88
bourn bound for the same b.   HOUS 495:59
Bournemouth B. is one of the few   BETJ 100:41
Bovary Madame B.   MACC 626:56
bovine cow is of the b.   NASH 719:41
bow Ane b. that is ay bent   HENR 473:70
arrow from the Tartar's b.   SHAK 871:46
B., b., ye lower middle classes!   GILB 424:72
b. of burning gold!   BLAKE 168:19
B. themselves when he did sing   SHAK 918:53
b. to everyone   SKEL 942:48
b. was made in England   DOYLE 343:94
breaketh the b.   BIBLE 116:74
breaketh the b.   BOOK 177:74
drew a b. at a venture   BIBLE 111:72
made up b. ties   SHAR 919:81
set my b. in the cloud   BIBLE 104:15
Thou shalt not b. down thyself   BIBLE 106:68
tightened b.   YEATS 1105:67
bow-shot A b.-s. from her   TENN 993:43
bow-wow Big B.-w. strain   SCOTT 856:12

bowels b. of Christ CROM 298:*53*
b. of compassion BIBLE 156:*91*
b. were moved for him BIBLE 124:*53*
melted in the midst of my b. BIBLE 114:*49*
molten b. BOTT 180:*37*
No belly and no b. RANS 802:*38*
bower b. quiet for us KEATS 545:*56*
deck both bed and b. SPEN 958:*13*
flower perfumes the b. SCOTT 855:*3*
hall and b. WORD 1096:*38*
sought her baith by b. and ha' SCOTT 854:*80*
twa sisters in a b. BALL -101:*30*
bowers built upon the b. of paradise PAINE 750:*44*
cedar and sycamore b. KEND 550:*49*
bowl b. of night FITZ 390:*87*
child drinking a b. of milk SAND 841:*77*
Come, dear b. BARL 71:*21*
great b. of the sky MACM 636:*24*
honey set in a green b. SMITH 946:*99*
I b. so slow BARR 73:*51*
love in a golden b. BLAKE 166:*61*
lurk within the b. SMITH 949:*55*
softly in the brimming b. JOYCE 538:*43*
bowled darned near b. him LARW 582:*32*
bowler b. thinks he bowls LANG 579:*67*
b.'s Holding JOHN 532:*45*
difference between a fast b. TRUE 997:*99*
bowling b. lobs and slow twisters JOYCE 538:*43*
bowls bowler thinks he b. LANG 579:*67*
B. is a young man's game BRYA 201:*17*
b. of fierce desire CRAS 296:*27*
Fill our b. once more SHAK 905:*84*
playing b. upon a splitting wreck DAVI 307:*96*
bows b. from which your children GIBR 422:*38*
bowstring thrice cut Cupid's b. SHAK 879:*52*
box b. and the puppets THAC 1006:*90*
B. about AUBR 45:*35*
b. that fennel Grows around RANS 802:*37*
father gave him a b. MACN 637:*49*
jack in the b. ELKIN 374:*99*
Pit, b., and gallery POPE 781:*61*
rattle of the money b. LABO 572:*34*
time…kept in a b. RAINE 800:*9*
boxer b. never sees the big one FORE 397:*24*
With a nation, as with a b. ACHE 3:*51*
boxes banging down their bits of b. OSBO 745:*67*
isolated, shut in little b. BAIN 62:*77*
Neat in their b. ROET 819:*91*
boxing activity is so vain as b. MAIL 640:*88*
b. is everything HEMI 471:*50*
B. is show-business with blood BELA 85:*77*
b. really combines LONS 612:*23*
I have covered b. GALL 412:*93*
Squash is b. BARR 73:*54*
boy any b.…become president STEV 973:*90*
As a b. HATT 460:*58*
Attic b. to hunt MILT 683:*13*
blind b., Venus' baby SPEN 959:*29*
blitz of a b. CAUS 246:*66*
b. always rose again MAP 649:*34*
b.'s ideal of a manly career DISR 332:*89*
B. Meets Girl in Winnipeg MACL 634:*89*
b. playing on the sea NEWT 725:*40*
b. stood on the burning deck HEMA 469:*11*
b. walking…head drooping WHITE 1070:*40*
b.'s will is the wind's LONG 612:*12*
b. with his father IHIM 510:*30*
can't expect a b. to be vicious SAKI 837:*3*
Chatterton, the marvellous b. WORD 1097:*44*
curious mixture in the b. DICK 327:*75*
down to talk poetry, my b. DICK 320:*26*
every b. and every gal GILB 424:*75*
genuine b. is a rebel MILL 679:*50*
Give to your b. DRYD 348:*90*

boy (*contd.*)
growing b. WORD 1098:*51*
hating., my b., is an art NASH 719:*49*
Her little b. weeping sought BLAKE 166:*68*
How dost, my b.? SHAK 903:*21*
if they like a b. SALI 839:*26*
imagination of a b. KEATS 545:*55*
Little B. kneels at the foot MILNE 680:*70*
little tiny b. SHAK 895:*39*
Mad about the b. COWA 290:*99*
many a b. here SHER 934:*16*
modest, good-humoured b. BEER 83:*26*
My b., he says RUNY 829:*58*
never was a b. MILL 675:*75*
no b.,…allured to letters STEE 964:*22*
not the Model B. TWAIN 1032:*66*
office b. GILB 423:*58*
parent who could see his b. LEAC 589:*41*
plump and hearty, healthy b. HOFF 484:*58*
purblind, wayward b. SHAK 865:*13*
read to by a b. ELIOT 368:*68*
remain a fifteen-year-old b. ROTH 826:*11*
Robin was a rovin' B. BURNS 210:*88*
salesman got to dream, b. MILL 676:*96*
Selwyn MacGregor, the nicest b. SPARK 955:*48*
sensitive b.'s humiliations SHAW 921:*27*
Speak roughly to your little b. CARR 238:*26*
speak to your little b. BLAKE 166:*67*
Than when I was a b. HOOD 489:*38*
The b.'s mouth TWAIN 1033:*95*
this b. will be surrounded HARD 455:*76*
to be a little b. THUR 1020:*53*
to be b. eternal SHAK 911:*18*
What a wonderful b. he is! HOGG 485:*66*
when I was a b. THOM 1012:*95*
When I was a b. SITT 940:*98*
While yet a b. SHEL 927:*62*
with our precious b. DICK 323:*78*
You're a human b. DICK 325:*29*
boyfriend and have a French b. HEPB 473:*76*
boyhood characters of my b. STEV 973:*98*
lost b. of Judas RUSS 833:*37*
boys As flies to wanton b. SHAK 903:*30*
Beautiful b. with bright red guitars HENRI 472:*60*
B. do now cry PEPYS 764:*59*
B.' hate was dangerous MUNRO 714:*55*
b. in their happy play SCHR 850:*4*
b. late at their play! ARNO 39:*23*
b.…straight as Circe's wand MARL 655:*26*
b. will not be sent ROOS 822:*41*
breaks are beating the b. GIPP 428:*40*
By office b. for office b. SALI 839:*36*
Christian b. I can scarcely hope ARNO 40:*43*
elders, and fought by b. LIVE 607:*44*
English…half-little b. CELI 247:*92*
give the b. a little tea ANDE 18:*8*
Give them the cold steel, b.! ARMI 35:*44*
good old b. was drinkin' MACL 633:*62*
hardly suitable for delicate b. WILDE 1078:*7*
lightfoot b. are laid HOUS 495:*62*
loaded guns with b. CRAB 294:*89*
only know two sorts of b. DICK 321:*40*
other girls and b. STEV 975:*35*
school b. or scholarship LITT 607:*42*
The b. are dreaming wicked THOM 1011:*81*
three wild lads…brave b. SCOTT 854:*76*
Till the b. come Home FORD 397:*20*
what Asian b. ought JOHN 523:*52*
Young b. would talk about it STEI 967:*65*
bra Burn your b.! ANON 27:*94*
braccia twelve b. across LEON 597:*77*
bracelet diamond and safire b. LOOS 613:*33*
braces liquid which rots b. MORT 710:*2*
bracing Skegness is so b. ANON 25:*28*

Bradford silk hat on a B. millionaire ELIOT 369:*89*
Bradman B.'s batting genius LARW 582:*31*
Bradyism B.…multisibling sensibility COUP 289:*83*
brae waly, waly doun the b. BALL 67:*57*
braes among thy green b. BURNS 211:*99*
banks and b. o' bonie Doon BURNS 212:*22*
b. o' Killiecrankie BURNS 211:*7*
by yon bonnie b. ANON 24:*4*
brag Men would b. STEI 967:*65*
Brahmin Men are the B. STAN 962:*87*
braid badge of tarnished b. READ 803:*54*
b. to bind your hair SCOTT 854:*79*
O' gude B. Claith FERG 385:*15*
thy brow to b. SCOTT 854:*68*
brain are the b. of heaven MERE 671:*12*
blessed with a woman's b. RICH 810:*64*
blind life within the b. TENN 1004:*47*
Bracing b. and sinew KING 558:*90*
b. has Corridors DICK 328:*5*
b. may devise laws SHAK 874:*12*
b. of feathers POPE 782:*97*
b. stops criticising SLOAN 943:*59*
B.…wider than the Sky DICK 328:*3*
B.…with which we think BIER 160:*72*
children of an idle b. SHAK 868:*80*
cobweb of the b. BUTL 216:*15*
Dilutes with drivel every drizzly b. BYRON 219:*67*
dislocate my B.! DICK 328:*18*
draughts intoxicate the b. POPE 778:*79*
dry b. in a dry season ELIOT 368:*72*
Dwell in some idle b. MILT 682:*5*
emptying the native's b. FANON 382:*60*
gladness…thy b. must know SHEL 929:*7*
gleaned my teeming b. KEATS 544:*49*
I feared it might injure the b. CARR 238:*24*
in my b. I sing it BROW 199:*73*
lantern of Aristotle's b. RALE 800:*15*
lenses through which the b. explores DOUG 341:*58*
let the b. lie also BROW 199:*67*
little b. attic DOYLE 344:*4*
madness…should possess a poet's b. DRAY 345:*39*
messages go quicker to the b. SPARK 955:*50*
no one's b. rejects it BACON 60:*41*
not for the weary b. THOM 1015:*55*
painting is done with the b. MICH 673:*35*
passion of the b. BURT 214:*77*
petrifactions of a plodding b. BYRON 219:*62*
phonographs of hades in the b. CRANE 295:*9*
phrases in his b. SHAK 865:*10*
Purple haze is in my b. HEND 472:*55*
puzzle their b. GOLD 433:*21*
rafters of the b. HUID 503:*95*
Relaxing your b. is fatal MOSS 711:*8*
shifting my b. HERZ 478:*73*
so small his b. BUTL 216:*2*
studies on the b. PENF 764:*54*
toil of b., or toil of hands MELV 667:*28*
too little b. SHAK 896:*57*
troubles of the b. SHAK 910:*82*
unquiet heart and b. TENN 998:*19*
What's in the b. SHAK 915:*87*
whimsy heaped in his own b. ROCH 816:*50*
work like madness on the b. COLE 274:*10*
brainpower using their b. MACD 628:*97*
brains big feet and no b. HAGEN 450:*3*
blow out your b. KIPL 560:*33*
Blows out his b. upon the flute BROW 200:*98*
B. are not everything SHAW 920:*5*
b. get buried ROTH 826:*13*
b. go to his head ASQU 42:*84*

brains (*contd.*)

b. knocked out by them	SHEL 927:77
b. of Minerva	BARR 73:56
b. wuz to settle	LOWE 616:81
but extra b.	TRUE 1029:15
clears the b.	PENE 764:53
feet instead of their b.	SOUSA 953:25
gentleman said a girl with b.	LOOS 612:27
had to use my b.	SHAN 919:77
have my b. ta'en out and buttered	SHAK 878:22
make a head and b.	DICK 325:50
steal away their b.!	SHAK 899:26
such seething b.	SHAK 871:53
Through lovers' b.	SHAK 868:79
tormenting our b.	MONT 700:54
What good are b. to a man?	WODE 1088:88
with no b. at all	HERB 474:92
young man who has b.	STEV 974:16

brake small but workable b. — MURR 715:77
bramble-dew eyes of gold and b.-d. — STEV 976:55
brambles like the b. in a wild field — DIDE 330:42
bran eat a lot of b. — MILL 677:13
branch accomplished in any b. — MARX 660:10

blaze of b., or brazier	ELIOT 372:68
b. of…antediluvian families	CONG 281:16
B. shall grow out of his roots	BIBLE 125:67
Cut is the b.	MARL 654:23
Lone on the fir-b.	MERE 671:97
lops the mouldered b. away	TENN 1005:62
neither root nor b.	BIBLE 131:72
pluck an ivy b. for me	ROSS 823:70
reddens on the high b.	SAPP 842:94
tip of every b.	PLATH 773:91

branch-strained b.-s. metaphor — MOORE 705:29
branches b. of government — MILL 675:67

climb black b.	FROST 406:80
most lucrative of its b.	PAINE 750:47
poetry does not swing from the b.	CHOC 260:55
retain their b.	SOPH 953:18

brand b. him either a failure — HOLM 485:74
b. sae drap wi' bluid — BALL 67:49
brandy b. of the damned — SHAW 921:32

must drink b.	JOHN 530:3
neat b.	STEV 973:97

brash when it is b. or noisy — AUDEN 49:98
brashness a certain b. — GALB 411:77
brass belly and thighs of b. — BIBLE 129:45

bound him with fetters of b.	BIBLE 109:21
B. Money	ANON 25:21
b., nor stone, nor earth	SHAK 914:40
evil manners live in b.	SHAK 918:65
feet like unto fine b.	BIBLE 156:99
nor walls of beaten b.	SHAK 883:25
serpent of b.	BIBLE 107:84
sounding b.	BIBLE 150:62
think gold that is b.	SPEN 958:22

brass-collar letter'd, braw b.-c. — BURNS 209:70
brassière Art is not a b. — BARN 72:32
brat you horrid b. — BEME 89:46
brattle Wi' bickering b.! — BURNS 209:67
brave act so b. and daring — ROCH 816:56

b. and battered sisters	PRIE 790:37
b. and meek with thirty bob a week	DAVI 307:95
b., generous…warm-hearted race	BUCH 202:25
b. man with a sword	WILDE 1078:98
b. master was no more	MACA 624:28
B. men are a city's strongest tower	ALCA 12:95
b. on the battlefield	MITC 697:88
b. resistance	WASH 1054:42
b. that die in battle	CLOU 271:45
Fortune favours the b.	TERE 1005:74
Fortune favours the b.	TERE 1006:75
home of the b.?	KEY 554:24
How sleep the b.	COLL 276:43

brave (*contd.*)

instead of b. and fine	NOON 731:24
intelligent, the witty, the b.	MILL 676:90
make one b. push	STEV 974:23
makes e'en the valiant more b.	DIBD 319:6
Many b. men lived before	HORA 493:25
more b. than me	CUMM 300:87
Neither a wise man nor a b. man	EISE 364:79
noble race and b.	SIGO 938:71
None but the b. deserves fair	DRYD 351:67
O b. new world	SHAK 917:42
That's a b. fellow	SHAK 911:7
the b., the mighty	WORD 1100:85
this is most b.	SHAK 890:16
To fight aloud, is very b.	DICK 321:39
What's b., what's noble	SHAK 906:97

braver b. in another language — BROO 193:39
bravery b. of his grief — SHAK 893:84
braw that was b. — BURNS 212:39
brawling b. of a sparrow — YEATS 1104:59
braying light is b. — SITW 940:5
brazen [Nature's] world is b. — SIDN 937:61
brazier blaze of branch, or b. — ELIOT 372:68
Brazil Science fiction, like B. — DISCH 331:69
Brazilification B.…widening gulf — COUP 289:77
breach endure not yet A b. — DONNE 337:91
more unto the b. — SHAK 881:82
bread After b. — JOHN 524:57

b. and butter	MACD 628:92
B. and Butter	SWIFT 986:11
b. and games	JUVE 540:81
b. and meat	STEV 973:97
b. and your butter	KIPL 564:12
b. beneath the bough	FITZ 390:88
b. eaten in secret	BIBLE 120:67
b. for the family	LEWIS 601:49
b. I dip in the river	STEV 976:51
b. sauce of the happy ending	JAMES 516:24
b. to the wise	BIBLE 123:35
b. which strengtheneth	BIBLE 118:16
b. with the salt of tears	KAIKO 541:92
cannot give them b.	WILDE 1075:27
cast my b. on the waters	JACK 514:85
Cast thy b. upon the waters	BIBLE 123:40
Cast your b. upon	HAGG 450:4
Content…To eat dusty b.	BOGAN 171:58
crust of b.	RYDER 834:50
cutting b. and butter	THAC 1007:1
did eat of my b.	BIBLE 115:67
earn my b.	FRAN 402:16
eat b. to the full	BIBLE 106:66
eat the b. of sorrows	BIBLE 119:41
eat thy b. with joy	BIBLE 123:33
eat thy b. with quaking	BIBLE 129:37
give him b. to eat	BIBLE 122:1
Give us this day our daily b.	BIBLE 135:49
half a loaf better than no b.	CHES 259:16
having looked to government for b.	BURKE 208:45
I am the b. of life	BIBLE 145:43
I am the living b.	BIBLE 145:45
if his son ask b.	BIBLE 135:58
Jesus took b.	BIBLE 140:48
Jesus…took b.	BIBLE 150:59
lives not upon b. alone	STEV 974:11
man doth not live by b. only	BIBLE 108:92
Man shall not live by b. alone	BIBLE 133:29
meat, and cursed the b.	ROBI 814:24
nor his seed begging b.	BIBLE 115:65
offered a piece of b. and butter	MACK 632:55
People who eat white b.	VREE 1047:23
ravens brought him b.	BIBLE 111:64
science as well as b.	JAMES 517:36
servants…have b. enough	BIBLE 143:99
shalt thou eat b.	BIBLE 103:2

bread (*contd.*)

Some gave them white b.	CARR 240:71
spend money for that which is not b.?	BIBLE 127:3
spoiled b. and spilled wine	PATM 760:99
steal b.	FRAN 401:90
take b. at my hand	WYATT 1103:30
that b. should be so dear	HOOD 489:47
touch of holy b.	SHAK 886:12
Who never ate his b. in sorrow	GOET 431:72
With the b. eaten	CERV 248:97
yield a heavy b.	WILK 1080:42

breadlines b. continue — SKEL 942:43
breadwinner b. and a crosspatch — SMITH 948:28
break bend but do not b. — LAFO 574:80

B., b., b.	TENN 995:63
b. earth's sleep	OWEN 748:20
b. my staff	SHAK 917:40
B. the bone	RABE 798:79
b. them at pleasure	EDGE 360:26
but they never b.	BUCK 203:37
Never Give…an Even B.	FIEL 388:60
sex rules…I b.	SALI 838:20
those that will not b.	HEMI 470:19
Thou thyself must b.	ARNO 39:22
time to b. down	BIBLE 122:19
Words…sometimes b.	ELIOT 370:31

breaker b. of proverbs — SHAK 875:41
breaker-beaten b.-b. coast — BYRON 222:41
breakers angry b. roar — LEAR 589:51

like b. cliffward leaping!	CRANE 295:6
Set keel to the b.	POUND 786:70

breakfast impossible things before b. — CARR 240:62

bananas for b.	WHAR 1068:93
b., dinner, lunch, and tea	BELL 87:7
B. is the one meal	VAND 1039:96
cooking b. this morning	SCHR 850:8
eat Rockefellers for b.	KENN 553:6
Hope is a good b.	BACON 56:39
hypothesis every day before b.	LORE 613:42
Where shall we our b. take	BALL 67:54

breakfast-table well-provisioned b. — HAWT 461:74
breakfast-time critical…is b.-t. — HERB 474:3
breakfasts b. on…frosty mornings — GRAH 438:92
breakneck riding at b. speed — BLAN 168:22
bream Backed lyke a b. — BERN 97:92
breast boiling bloody b. — SHAK 871:57

b. high amid the corn	HOOD 489:39
b. Still tender	HOPE 490:72
broods with warm b.	HOPK 491:83
buckles on his b.	SHAK 904:54
charms to soothe a savage b.	CONG 281:21
craving void…aching in the b.	POPE 779:43
creating in every English b.	MANC 644:66
creep into my b.	BEAU 80:76
crimson…robin's b.	TENN 995:71
deeply implanted in the human b.	DICK 321:38
depth of her glowing b.	SHEL 930:29
forged upon his b.	WORD 1100:84
fresh, green b. of the new world	FITZ 391:6
heart flutter in my b.	SAPP 842:92
heart to adore each b.	MARV 658:73
in her red-berried b.	THOM 1011:88
Leaning on his b.	GIBB 422:32
light within his own clear b.	MILT 683:28
marched b. forward	BROW 200:2
milk in an old b.	MANS 647:98
miss the white b.	JEFF 520:85
moon in the b. of man	BERR 98:3
moon on the b.	MOORE 704:5
my speaking b.	SHAK 913:53
Not a hook in all my b.	VAUG 1041:19
nunnery Of thy chaste b.	LOVE 615:66
On her left b.	SHAK 916:1
on Madeleine's fair b.	KEATS 546:92

breast (*contd.*)

on mother's b.	TENN 997:97
peace in thy b.	SHAK 869:94
pepper-pot b. of thrush?	FRAME 400:76
publican…smote upon his b.	BIBLE 144:11
seat within my captive b.	SURR 982:40
shining b.	GORD 435:62
shot…in our b.	ARNO 36:70
soft as the b. of doves	CORN 288:58
spirit in a loyal b.	SHAK 866:40
sweetness fills the b.	CASW 244:35
Tibbald's monster-breeding b.	POPE 782:95
toss him to My b.	HERB 476:35
Truth has a quiet b.	SHAK 866:41
twining in his speckled b.	MARV 658:80
tyrant of the throbbing b.	GRAY 443:87
wail Or knock the b.	MILT 695:58
what a panic's in thy b.!	BURNS 209:67
whose b. is a cannibal dynamo	GINS 427:25
windows to my b.	SHAK 913:54
Within whose b. did boil	SURR 982:44
wounds are in his b. and face	DAVIS 309:39
breast-feeding atheism, b.	ORTON 742:86
breastbone your white b.	CAUS 246:65
breastplate b. of righteousness	BIBLE 152:6
put in the b. of judgement	BIBLE 107:70
Unpin that spangled b.	DONNE 336:71
What stronger b.	SHAK 861:6
breasts bore within their b. the grief	AYTO 53:87
b. are like two young roes	BIBLE 124:51
b. are under our foot	SHAW 921:29
b., the hallmark of our culture	DONA 335:57
clos'd within each other's b.	DRYD 348:94
could feel my b.	JOYCE 538:57
In living b.	SPEN 958:16
let her b. satisfy thee	BIBLE 120:62
prodigious b.	SWIN 988:53
soaping her b. in the bath	EWART 381:43
then her b. are dun	SHAK 915:92
Warring within our b.	MARL 652:89
breath air my quiet b.	KEATS 548:18
Art cannot hold its b.	ANTH 31:83
before thou giv'st them b.	SHAK 899:30
borne my b. away!	HOOD 489:37
B.'s a ware	HOUS 494:42
b. And everlasting motion	WORD 1095:14
b. can make them	GOLD 433:10
b. goes now	DONNE 337:90
b. of Autumn's being	SHEL 928:86
b. of buffalo in the winter	HAGG 450:5
b. of degradation	BYRON 221:20
b. of Heav'n fresh-blowing	MILT 694:37
b. of kings	BURNS 209:66
b. of life	YEATS 1106:81
b. Of the night-wind	ARNO 36:64
b. that from my mistress reeks	SHAK 915:92
b. were as terrible	SHAK 879:37
b. will carry it	SPUR 961:64
breathed into nostrils b. of life	BIBLE 103:88
breathes with human b.	TENN 996:86
breathing a small b.	ROET 819:94
breathing thoughtful b.	WORD 1099:63
call the fleeting b.?	GRAY 442:67
Clothed with his b.	TENN 1004:44
cry that was no more than a b.	CONR 284:92
discernible from his b.	WALL 1049:62
draw thy b. in pain	SHAK 893:87
endures for a b.	SWIN 987:27
fluttered and failed for b.	ARNO 37:84
give b. to forms	BYRON 221:18
having lost her b.	SHAK 905:70
healthy b. of morn	KEATS 547:99
last b. I drew in	LAMB 577:44
little b.	AURE 50:24

breath (*contd.*)

love thee with the b.	BROW 197:19
love's latest b.	DRAY 345:40
malice in my b.	SHAK 911:6
Meistersinger…set b. in steel	CRANE 295:7
morn and evening b.	BLAKE 165:57
must take the b.	MANS 647:99
O, for b. to utter	SHAK 876:56
own b. in our own nostrils	MACD 628:99
serpents of explosive b.	MARI 651:67
short of b.	SASS 845:26
sweet b. of heaven	WORD 1096:18
tainting of the b.	LEWIS 602:61
taxed the b.	THOM 1010:56
Th' endeavour of this present b.	SHAK 865:4
The faintest b.	WORD 1094:95
use your b.	FLET 394:70
wait with bated b.	THAT 1007:15
while there's b. of life	BISH 164:33
whose b. I hate	SHAK 911:19
with her thick b.	JONS 534:84
with low last b.	ROSS 824:90
breathe as though to b.	TENN 994:58
b. upon these slain	BIBLE 129:43
can't even hear people b.	CRON 298:60
cannot see, nor b.	MASE 662:44
they b. in me as angels	RICH 809:54
thought I could not b.	TENN 1003:19
When…lapdogs b. their last	POPE 779:1
breathes B. there the man	SCOTT 853:49
hell itself b. out	SHAK 891:44
breathing b. in their faces	SHAK 917:38
B. like one that hath	TENN 994:48
Closer is He than b.	TENN 1003:32
does not love b.	LEE 592:6
health, and quiet b.	KEATS 545:56
sound his b. kept	SHEL 930:20
Trick is to Keep B.	GALL 413:95
breathing-space want a little b.-s.	MARP 655:32
breathing-time b.-t.…or a truce	WORD 1100:81
breathless B. and bewildered	ACHE 3:40
B., we flung us	BROO 192:17
bred B. en bawn in a brier-patch	HARR 458:28
Bredon summertime in B.	HOUS 494:49
bree A little aboon her b.	BALL 67:51
breeches He is like a book in b.	SMITH 949:44
render my leather b. incapable	SHER 933:80
breed b. apart from…humanity	MANK 645:77
b. for barren metal	SHAK 874:22
B. never dies	BENN 90:74
dogs I b. and sell	GRAV 440:31
none of another b.	YEATS 1106:88
not b. one work	HOPK 492:9
Where they most b.	SHAK 907:30
breeder b. of sinners	SHAK 891:24
breeding formed by a different b.	DISR 332:90
guilt, or of ill b.	CONG 281:30
true b. of a gentleman	BYRON 223:49
breeds see what b. about her heart	SHAK 903:26
breeks b. aff a Hielandman	SCOTT 855:87
breeze b. of morning moves	TENN 1001:85
b. of song	TENN 999:47
correspondent b.	WORD 1096:19
dancing in the b.	WORD 1099:67
Each b. from foggy mount	BYRON 219:67
flag to April's b. unfurled	EMER 376:26
fragrance was born upon the b.	DICK 323:77
gentle b.	WORD 1095:17
hay-harvest b.	CORY 288:67
planted…by some unnoticed b.	CARL 235:73
softest b.…gave birth	WORD 1100:91
The b. is on the sea	SCOTT 855:3
tossing b.	ARNO 39:16
wings of the b.	BRON 190:87

breezes little b. dusk	TENN 993:38
Brendan St. B.… Irish boats	BEHAN 84:58
brent bonie brow was b.	BURNS 211:6
Brer Fox en B. F., he lay low	HARR 458:27
brethren b. to dwell together	BIBLE 119:45
mother and my b.!	BIBLE 137:96
one of the least of these my b.	BIBLE 140:45
presence of all his b.	BIBLE 104:21
sent his b. away	BIBLE 106:49
Breughel B. of the 20th century	ADLER 8:46
brevity b. of human life	PROT 792:84
B. is the sister of talent	CHEK 256:57
B. is the soul of lingerie	PARK 753:88
B. is the soul	SHAK 889:88
first to complain of its b.	LABR 573:57
its body b.	COLE 274:9
brew b. that is true	PANA 752:75
brewery bladder against a b.	KIRK 565:27
brews peer of England b.	HOUS 495:63
briars blinding my b. with joy	BLAKE 167:91
bribe man who offers a b.	GREE 444:18
Marriage is a b.	WILD 1079:22
Too poor for a b.	GRAY 443:94
bribes by b. to please	DYER 358:90
How many b. he had taken	BENT 93:29
brick carried a b. in his pocket	JOHN 528:45
men…expect b.	ASTE 43:89
on solid b.	POPE 783:2
palace built of squarèd b.	SPEN 957:2
piece of b. in his pocket	SWIFT 984:79
threw it a b. at a time	HARG 457:15
throw a b. …hitting the niece	ORWE 742:96
town of red b.	DICK 325:41
bricks Great poets seldom make b.	POUND 785:57
bridal b. of the earth and sky	HERB 475:32
bride a barren b.	POPE 781:72
as a b. adorned for her husband	BIBLE 158:34
b. and my darling to be?	BALL 67:43
b. of a ducal coronet	DICK 323:84
b. that cairries the bunch	MACD 627:84
death's b.	WORD 1100:90
encounter darkness as a b.	SHAK 897:80
jealousy to the b.	BARR 72:42
missed his loving b.	NASH 720:57
my glittering b.	WORD 1100:82
Passionless b.	TENN 1003:31
read about his widowed b.	MACL 633:61
So though a virgin, yet a b.	CAREW 233:21
to be his holy b.	STONE 978:73
took the b. about the neck	SHAK 864:83
unravished b. of quietness	KEATS 547:6
virgin-widow…mourning b.	DRYD 352:94
ye sall be his b.	SCOTT 854:78
bride-grooms Of b.-g., brides	HERR 477:51
bridegroom b.…out of his chamber	BIBLE 114:44
b. in my death	SHAK 906:91
b. little dreids	MACD 627:84
funeral train which the b. sees	CLOU 271:42
Like a b. from his room	AYTO 53:86
bridge Beautiful Railway B.	MACG 630:24
b. and not a goal	NIET 728:78
b. between the world	RUSS 833:31
brought his b. technique with him	CECIL 246:77
cavalry charging over a tin b.	WODE 1089:94
Cricket can be a b.	ZIA 1109:24
cross the river by an Irish b.	STEW 977:65
Faith…the Pierless B.	DICK 328:9
Horatius kept the b.	MACA 624:18
keep the b. with me?	MACA 623:14
mime can be a b. between	MARC 649:44
play b. with my old maid aunts	FIEL 388:56
promise to build a b.	KHRU 556:48
rude b. that arched the flood	EMER 376:26
small b. in time	STEI 966:60

bridge (*contd.*)

that great B.   CRANE 295:7
Venice, on the B. of Sighs   BYRON 220:92
bridges sleep on b.   FRAN 401:90
bridle b. and rudder of painting   LEON 597:81
b. reins a shake   BURNS 213:49
b. to her wanton will   SPEN 958:14
held in with bit and b.   BIBLE 115:59
Brie-cheese B.-c. poisoning   ADLER 9:47
brief b. as I have known a play   SHAK 871:56
b. quickenings that resemble pain   WILD 1080:35
hold no b. for private enterprise   BURT 214:62
site, a b. and finance   ROGE 820:4
Tis b., my lord   SHAK 891:36
briefcase lawyer with a b. can steal   PUZO 796:40
briefcases in their b. is terrifying   KHRU 556:52
briefing B. for a Descent   LESS 598:6
brier How sweet is the b.   TANN 991:96
instead of the b....the myrtle   BIBLE 127:8
brier-patch Bred en bawn in a b.-p.   HARR 458:28
brigade chiefs of the Irish B.   DAVIS 309:38
Could thy B. With cold cascade   GILB 424:78
No tin hat b.   LEWIS 601:48
Viva la the New B.!   DAVIS 309:40
brigand I am a b.   SHAW 921:31
Briggs Matilda B....was a ship   DOYLE 344:20
bright b. as angels are   WILK 1080:41
b. day that brings forth   SHAK 883:26
forgetting the b. speed   ARNO 38:98
leaden interfolds are b.   FREE 404:35
torches to burn b.!   SHAK 868:82
westward...the land is b.   CLOU 270:32
Bright I have B.'s disease   PERE 766:87
young lady named B.   BULL 203:50
bright-eyed b.-e. Mariner   COLE 273:84
brightened b. by a smile   SAIN 836:86
brighter better future and a b. day   SMUTS 950:66
brightest B. and best of the sons   HEBER 466:56
part with their b. hour   HELL 469:99
wisest, b., meanest of mankind   POPE 781:51
brightness b. of his glory   BIBLE 154:44
b. of this vision   RAND 801:26
b. to hold in trust   SPEN 956:74
Leaking the b. away   SPEN 956:73
long the b. of the west   BRON 191:92
no b. in it?   BIBLE 130:60
provides the moon with its b.   ANAX 18:99
purest sky with b.   SPEN 957:2
transcendent b. didst outshine   MILT 687:91
Brighton Like B. Pier   KINN 559:10
Brignal B. banks are wild and fair   SCOTT 854:67
brilliance b. of a lightning storm   FLAU 392:37
brilliant b. moon   YEATS 1104:59
everything b. and virgin   DAYL 310:57
far less b. pen than mine   BEER 83:24
brillig Twas b., and the slithy toves   CARR 239:47
brim but sparkles near the b.   BYRON 219:81
full to the b.   DICK 325:39
brimstone b. and fire   BIBLE 105:25
tormented with fire and b.   BIBLE 158:23
brink scared to go to the b.   DULL 354:25
brisking counteracts...by b. about   SMART 944:67
Bristol not the Member for B.   BURKE 206:4
Britain Backing B.   ANON 27:86
belong to B.   GERA 419:95
best built city in B.   DEFOE 312:85
B. a fit country   LLOY 609:62
B. and for the hell of it   NOBLE 730:18
B.'s comparative performance   MISH 696:72
B., could you ever boast   SWIFT 985:1
B. had a savage culture   BANDA 69:86
B. has lost an Empire   ACHE 2:29
B. is a Morris Minor country   ANON 28:9
B. may imagine itself new Greece   BRIN 188:57

Britain (*contd.*)

B....on borrowed time   CALL 225:98
B. set the world ablaze   GILB 424:76
B. was conquered   TACI 989:76
B. will not be involved in...war   DAILY 303:40
end of B.   GAIT 411:73
freedom of the press in B.   ORWE 742:5
Graces not natives of Great B.   CHES 257:78
Hath B. all the sun   SHAK 916:10
In B.'s isle   GRAY 441:59
inability in B. to comprehend   HAUG 460:59
journalism...in B.   SAMP 840:42
lead B. and her fading empire   MANC 644:66
leads a country such as B.   THAT 1008:25
most urgent tasks in B.   BEVE 102:74
new B. is exciting   WILS 1085:96
Only in B.   MAJOR 640:99
precipitous decline for B.   MACF 629:17
When B. first   THOM 1015:46
Britannia beer and B.   SMITH 949:44
B., rule the waves   THOM 1015:46
shouted 'Rule B.'   KIPL 562:67
British A B. officer   PANG 752:76
anything except the B. War Office   SHAW 921:18
as...rude as the B.   GALL 412:94
beneath the B. flag   JOHN 524:60
B. are an aggressive nation   ABSE 1:9
B. are coming   WELL 1063:99
B. bulldog into a Reagan poodle   STEEL 964:10
B. Civil Service   WILL 1081:55
B. Empire has advanced   GEOR 419:88
B....gluttons for satire   LODGE 609:77
B. music...perpetual promise   BEEC 82:11
B.-b.-b. object   MALO 643:36
B. public falls for this   HAIL 451:14
B. soldier can stand up to anything   SHAW 921:18
B. Sphere of Influence   ANON 25:19
B. subject, in whatever land   PALM 752:72
B....taste for bad books   BRAD 183:81
B. want...another meeting   ANON 30:57
B. won't fight   GALT 413:9
broke a B. square!   KIPL 560:34
But B., no, the name's not right   HEAN 465:39
Come you back, you B. soldier   KIPL 560:28
Conversation never easy for B.   BRAD 183:84
decent, serious B. filth   OSBO 746:69
Dirty B. coaster   MASE 662:38
Dress B., look Irish   KOFF 568:73
face a B. Government   TUCH 1031:45
fear that the B. electorate   WEBB 1059:18
fleet of B. ships   NELS 722:97
For generations the B. bourgeoisie   WAUGH 1056:65
greatness of the B. Nation   ADDI 7:18
Hitler never understood...the B.   BULL 204:52
impose the views...on the B.   SCHL 848:73
invade B. territory   HUNT 505:32
irritation with the word B.   BUFO 203:44
manly, B. game!   LOVE 614:61
Most B. statesmen ...drunk too much   GEOR 419:92
no B. government   MACM 635:10
of B. blood?   TENN 1000:65
old B. style of teaching   NEWM 724:26
planted the B. flag there   STUA 980:8
rather bitter B. musician   WILM 1084:9
ridiculous as the B. public   MACA 623:1
ridiculous as the B.   MACA 622:96
smell the blood of a B. man   SHAK 903:25
stony B. stare   TENN 1001:83
streams of B. blood   SCHAW 847:61
supported by...the B. people   LAW 585:59
The B. Bourgeosie   SITW 941:22
typical of the B. way of war   WAVE 1058:11
United States and the B.   CHUR 265:31
Well, B. Public   BROW 200:85

Britisher healthy and childish B.   MACL 634:88
Briton Australian be equal to...a B.   PARK 755:31
better class of B.   BRAD 183:85
free-born B.   THAC 1006:41
Britons B. alone use 'might'   WAUGH 1057:85
Brixton shoddy streets of B.   ABSE 1:9
broadcasting essential that b.   THOR 1017:5
In b. your audience is conjectural   ORWE 744:35
never-never land of b.   SAFER 835:66
'pessimistic' about b.   WELLS 1065:44
broaden b. your ass if not your mind   HEMI 471:38
broadsword save his good b.   SCOTT 853:54
Broadway Has had B.   DAVIS 308:24
Lullaby of B.   DUBIN 353:4
music of B.   GERS 420:9
sinners on this part of B.   RUNY 829:65
sunny street as this B.!   DICK 322:56
walking down B.   WARH 1053:22
brocade moth-eaten musical b.   LARK 582:20
stain...her new b.   POPE 778:96
broccoli It's b., dear   WHITE 1069:22
brogues not fit to tie his b.   SCOTT 856:15
broke 'it bow'd, and syne it b.   BALL 67:57
Poverty isn't being b.   WYLIE 1104:51
'Tis true, I'm b.!   JONS 536:17
When time is b.   SHAK 868:71
broken b. for you   BIBLE 150:59
b. to shivers   BIBLE 157:4
b. with the storms of state   SHAK 918:64
Is it not b.?   SHEL 931:43
jungle has b. down   JUMB 539:70
made to be b.   SWIFT 986:16
staff of this b. reed   BIBLE 126:84
we don' t want it b.   QIAN 796:46
What is b. is b.   MITC 697:91
broken-hearted bind up the b.-h.   BIBLE 127:12
both b., B.   SWIN 987:42
ne'er been b.-h.   BURNS 212:25
broker b....takes your fortune   WOOL 1094:85
honest b.   BISM 164:41
bronchitis unless he or she has b.   AGATE 10:65
bronze art b., oil painting   RODC 818:21
B. cloud-waves   FREE 404:36
more lasting than b.   HORA 493:24
things of b. and stone   RUNY 829:66
brooches I will make you b.   STEV 976:53
brood b. over a full nest   ELIOT 366:27
that thy b. is flown   TENN 997:6
brooders Irishmen are born b.   OBRI 734:62
broods with warm breast   HOPK 491:83
brook b. where you had often fished   COWL 291:24
covert by some b.   MILT 683:14
drank of the b.   BIBLE 111:62
five smooth stones out of the b.   BIBLE 110:40
never-failing b.   GOLD 433:9
where the b. is deep   SHAK 861:3
willow grows aslant a b.   SHAK 892:71
woodland b. he bounding crossed   SCOTT 853:46
Brook B. never succeeded   LEVE 599:18
Brooklyn over the B. Bridge   BISH 164:32
brooks books in running b.   SHAK 885:77
b., and rivers wide   MILT 682:1
b. of Eden   TENN 1003:25
b., On whose fresh lap   MILT 684:46
b. too broad for leaping   HOUS 495:62
golden sands, and crystal b.   DONNE 337:89
sing of b.   HERR 477:51
broom bright blows the b.   STEV 976:53
b. of Cowdenknowes   BALL -101:33
pods went pop on the b.   DAVI 307:99
Take a b. and clean   THER 1009:37
Broom Beggarly B.   ANON 26:56
broomstick man is a b.   SWIFT 984:65
broth cooks spoil the b.   ANON 23:95

brothel couldn't score in a b. — DOCH 334:38
brothels b. with bricks of Religion — BLAKE 166:76
Of stews and b. only knew — HERB 476:36
brother Am I my b.'s keeper? — BIBLE 104:5
At the hand of every man's b. — BIBLE 104:14
Be my b., or I kill you — CHAM 250:27
BIG B. IS WATCHING YOU — ORWE 745:55
b. came with subtilty — BIBLE 105:33
B. can you spare a dime? — HARB 455:72
b., in one night — LUMI 619:40
b. in Shropshire — BARR 73:53
b. is born for adversity — BIBLE 121:86
b.'s name — SWIN 988:55
B. thy tail hangs — KIPL 561:51
B. to Death — DANI 304:62
B. to Death — FLET 394:69
b. was dead, and is alive again — BIBLE 143:2
darker b. — HUGH 499:14
Eat-well is drink-well's b. — FULL 410:49
every man against his b. — BIBLE 130:69
friend that sticketh closer than a b. — BIBLE 121:89
genuine b. Jonathan — MOOD 703:96
how oft shall my b. sin — BIBLE 139:21
I am like no b. — SHAK 862:34
I am sworn b. — SHAK 868:66
judge and the b. are one — WILS 1086:44
kynges court, my b. — CHAU 255:27
Life is very sweet, b. — BORR 179:23
lo'ed him like a vera b. — BURNS 211:12
love God, and hateth his b. — BIBLE 156:95
marry with his b. — SHAK 892:51
more close than a b. — KIPL 564:10
mote that is in thy b.'s eye — BIBLE 135:55
my b. had one — UTTL 1038:82
my fellow man, my b. — BAUD 76:14
Nor a sister, nor a b. — MARG 650:51
scan your b. Man — BURNS 210:83
seeth his b. have need — BIBLE 156:91
Shall be my b. — SHAK 882:4
Still to my b. turns — GOLD 432:96
went in unto his b.'s wife — BIBLE 105:42
whosoever is angry with his b. — BIBLE 134:39
younger b. popped on to his throne — STOP 978:75
brotherhood Bawling B. — GRAND 438:98
b. of men-at-wars — PAZ 762:24
B. of the Right Stuff — WOLFE 1090:25
crown thy good with b. — BATES 76:10
Love the b. — BIBLE 156:79
men in b. combine — NOON 731:24
table of b. — KING 557:82
brotherhoods b. of cedars — BROW 197:26
brothers All men are b. — POWE 788:5
b. be, for a' that — BURNS 213:44
B. of the Cosine — ROOS 822:51
b. on that bright loveliness — MACL 634:82
b. won't mind — COLUM 278:60
happy few, we band of b. — SHAK 882:3
So the two b. — KEATS 546:82
Working for Warner B. — MIZN 697:6
brothers-in-law they aren't all b. — POWE 788:5
brow bonie b. was brent — BURNS 211:6
brotherhoods of cedars on its b. — BROW 197:26
B., bay and tray — DAVI 307:1
b. is wet with — LONG 611:98
b. so grim — ELIOT 371:36
Flushing his b. — KEATS 546:89
Ida's shady b. — BLAKE 165:55
lifted…her white b. — FREE 404:36
meet my Maker b. to b. — CORN 288:60
On his b. this mark — SHEL 928:79
pain and anguish wring the b. — SCOTT 853:58
rugged mountain's b. — GRAH 437:87
speech in that victorious b. — ARNO 36:61
sweat of my b. — FRAN 402:16

brow (*contd.*)
sweat of one's b. — LIVI 607:47
thy b. to braid — SCOTT 854:68
thy b. was smoothed — WORD 1100:90
wrinkle deeper on the b.? — BYRON 219:78
brown hard, b., nutlike word — BART 74:72
have baked me too b. — CARR 239:41
sinewy b. men — PRIE 790:46
Browning Meredith is a prose B. — WILDE 1076:37
quotations from the Bible, B. — MACF 629:19
safety catch on my B.! — JOHST 532:47
brows b. full sternly bent — SPEN 959:41
Gathering her b. — BURNS 211:9
not seen in either of our b. — DRAY 345:40
pallor of girls' b. — OWEN 748:8
purple b. of Olivet — TENN 999:31
unwrinkled b. in passport offices — STARK 963:95
browsing b. and sluicing — WODE 1088:85
Bruce Scots, whom B. has often led — BURNS 212:37
bruise parmacity for an inward b. — SHAK 875:42
shalt b. his heel — BIBLE 103:98
tread on it and b. it — TROL 1027:76
bruised b. for our iniquities — BIBLE 127:1
b. in a new place — IRVI 513:67
b. reed shall he not break — BIBLE 126:92
brush b. should not see better — GOYA 437:83
work with so fine a b. — AUST 52:60
brushwood boughs and b. sheaf — BROW 198:36
brutality without art is b. — RUSK 831:4
brute B. heart of a b. like you — PLATH 773:95
Chuck him out, the b.! — KIPL 560:32
creatures…Irrational and b. — MILT 694:48
heavy, red-haired b. — WELLS 1064:24
lord of the fowl and the b. — COWP 292:38
never saw a b. I hated so — BROW 198:51
that ugly b., the ape! — ENNI 379:93
treated as a b. — EDWA 362:49
Whatever b. and blackguard — HOUS 496:71
Brute Et tu, B.? — CAES 225:88
Et tu, B.? — SHAK 883:39
brutes because the b. are dumb? — ELIOT 365:4
Exterminate all the b.! — CONR 284:91
one with the b. — HUXL 508:1
Brutus B. is an honourable man — SHAK 884:48
b. will start a spirit — SHAK 882:21
no orator as B. is — SHAK 884:56
Poor B., with himself at war — SHAK 882:17
You too, B.? — CAES 225:88
Bubber B. was the first man — ELLI 374:5
bubble break, like a b. — HOLM 486:86
b. burst, and now a world — POPE 780:35
b. on the fountain — SCOTT 854:65
glory a b. — SHEL 927:57
Honour but an empty b. — DRYD 351:72
Seeking the b. reputation — SHAK 885:92
world's a b. — BACON 60:35
bubbles bearded b. winking — KEATS 547:14
dramatic criticism…tattoo soap b. — BROWN 194:55
earth has b. — SHAK 907:19
no harm as b. — KEYN 555:35
bubbling with b. groan — BYRON 221:7
buck b. doesn't even pause here — REGAN 805:93
b. starts here — GREE 445:35
The b. stops here — TRUM 1030:33
Buck poor Pearl B.! — PORT 784:39
bucket not her b. bring — PRIOR 791:61
past is a b. of ashes — SAND 841:60
buckets b. into empty wells — COWP 293:57
Buckingham changing…at B. Palace — MILNE 680:69
buckler b. of the people's cause — DRYD 349:16
shield and b. — BIBLE 117:2
buckles b. on his breast — SHAK 904:54
bucks bet you, Ziggie, a hundred b. — DILL 331:54

bud be a b. again — KEATS 546:94
b. of the spring — DONNE 339:26
b. of thought — DARIO 305:76
like a worm i' th' b. — SHAK 894:15
thrusts a scaled b. — MANS 647:5
when first it 'gins to b. — SHAK 887:41
Buddha The B. …resides — PIRS 770:51
Buddhism Christianity or B. — SAKI 838:8
Buddhist Canadian Hinayana B. — GINS 428:31
budge You shall not b. — SHAK 892:50
budget figures…such as national b. — WEIL 1062:83
forming the B. — LLOY 608:56
size of its military b. — BENN 90:67
buds darling b. of May — SHAK 912:48
rod of Aaron…brought forth b. — BIBLE 107:83
sacrificing the early b. — ROCK 817:69
Buffalo Bill B. B.'s defunct — CUMM 299:79
buffalo breath of b. in the winter — HAGG 450:5
solidity of a water b. — PERE 766:92
where the b. roam — HIGL 480:1
buffalos flower-fed b. — LIND 606:17
buffets Fortune's b. and rewards — SHAK 891:35
buffoon chemist fiddler…and b. — DRYD 349:23
bugger We done the b.! — TENZ 1005:71
bughtin-time b.-t. is near — BURNS 212:35
bugle Blow, b., blow — TENN 997:98
Blow, b.; answer — TENN 997:99
like an ivory b. — THOM 1012:6
bugles Blow out, you b. — BROO 192:23
b. of social change — HANDY 455:69
bugs People are not as smart as b. — WHITE 1070:30
Buick fawn, crossed with a B. — NICH 726:55
build b. and never give way — LEE 593:13
b. himself a throne — INGE 511:36
but not I b. — HOPK 492:9
If you b. it, he will come — KINS 559:13
life it pretends to b. on — PRIT 791:65
never ask why b. — SEXT 859:65
No more to b. — FROST 406:81
one that you b. — RYBC 834:48
so easy to b., too — IBSEN 510:22
think that we b. — RUSK 830:77
time to b. up — BIBLE 122:19
builder b. of a temple — THOR 1016:73
can only be a b. — RUSK 830:82
builders b. have laboured in vain — BIBLE 159:48
Now we are the b. — BEVAN 101:62
building b. is good architecture — JOHN 524:63
b. of God — BIBLE 151:78
b.…with tomorrow inside — AKERS 10:74
b. without ornamentation — SANT 842:90
dedicating a new b. — ROCK 817:75
first glimpse of the b. — POE 775:41
ken by the b. o't — ANON 23:97
My name is on the b. — FORD 397:10
opening the door of the b. — AREN 33:16
question of b. — LECO 592:1
tall b., with a tower and bells — CRAB 294:79
very old b. — OSBO 745:68
Victorians expected every b. — CASS 243:29
wouldn't leave a burning b. — VANH 1039:5
buildings Able to leap tall b. — SIEG 937:68
b. of Hong Kong — BOOTH 178:6
cast your eyes on b. — PEI 764:49
magnificence of the b. we burnt — ELGIN 364:98
built And therefore b. for ever — TENN 1004:55
b. immovable cathedrals — GIDE 422:42
b. in such a logical way — HOLM 486:92
b. to envious show — JONS 535:1
not what they b. — FENT 385:1
wait for the schools to be b. — QABO 796:47
bulb Her body a b. — PLATH 773:99
naked light b. — WILL 1081:58
bulk wonder at his enormous b. — LEAC 589:38

bull gone to milk the b. JOHN 527:34
In time the savage b. KYD 571:24
take the b. GOLD 434:39
taking the b. by both horns ASHF 41:70
you b.'s pizzle SHAK 876:56
Bull John B. has gone to India YEATS 1106:88
bull's-eyes three perfect b.-e. OFAO 736:95
bull-baiting place of b.-b. SITW 942:30
bull-rushes Divine...in b.-r. FRIE 405:58
Buller Captain B. broke a window JOYCE 538:55
bullet assassin's b. PARK 756:37
b....done the job five years ago COLL 276:39
b. though his heart THAC 1006:86
b. through his head ROBI 814:24
Each b. has got its commission DIBD 319:7
Every b. has its billet WILL 1080:48
Faster than a speeding b.! SIEG 937:68
one b. in ten thousand SPEN 956:82
bullet-headed the b.-h. many POUND 787:88
bullets Better b. than yours JEFF 520:85
b. made of platinum BELL 87:99
use psychic b. MAIL 639:76
where the b. all go in CAUS 246:65
bullfighting B. is the only art HEMI 470:24
that b. does to agriculture HUBB 498:7
bullfights Spain gets b. JONG 534:70
bullfrog eyes like a b. DAVIS 308:27
bullies b. you on manly principles SHAW 920:11
bulls b. and foxes dine well JUST 540:75
the ploughman of b. PROP 792:79
bully If the President has a b. pulpit REAG 803:57
let a b. come into JOHN 523:51
love the lovely b. SHAK 881:91
most heinous b. HAIG 450:9
bullying 'b.'...not to his taste ANON 24:14
bum madman b. and angel GINS 427:24
somebody—instead of a b. SCHU 850:11
bumblebee b. can fly MAMET 643:64
bumf In b. lay salvation WAUGH 1057:96
bump don't b. into people COWA 290:7
bumper b. of good liquor SHER 933:89
bums millionaires and b. taste MARQ 656:38
shabby b. living in attics LEWIS 602:53
bunches b. of clingy sob sisters PAGL 749:36
Buncombe speaking...to B. CARL 236:98
bundle b. of biases BALL 68:66
bungalow position of the b. WILS 1084:13
There is our little b. REAG 804:69
bungler Man is a b. SHAW 921:36
poor magnificent b.! BAKER 63:84
bunk captain is in his b. SHAW 925:16
Exercise is b. FORD 396:9
History is more or less b. FORD 396:7
bunyip B. Aristocracy DENI 316:57
Buonarotti B. commended it VASA 1040:9
burden bear the b. ARNO 37:74
b. is light BIBLE 137:88
escaping form the b. of the past YELT 1107:97
heavy b. of responsibility EDWA 362:51
lay the b. equally CHUR 263:1
lighten the tax b. QUINE 797:67
music is a gift and a b. SIMO 939:84
not so heavy a b. EISE 364:81
President bears the b. KENN 551:74
realized what a b. MITC 697:86
Revolutions...never lightened the b.
SHAW 922:44
what b. then.? MILT 689:47
White Man's b. KIPL 562:64
womanhood is a heavy b. DANG 304:59
Words strain...under the b. ELIOT 370:31
burdened present is b. too much HAWT 461:80
burdens b....and at my back LINK 606:25
b. on the broadest shoulders LLOY 608:56

burdocks With b., hemlock, nettles SHAK 903:32
bureaucracy B. defends the status PETER 767:7
B. is not an obstacle SCHU 851:21
B. the rule of no one MACC 626:52
choice...b. and dilettantism WEBER 1059:22
bureaucrat b.'s method of protecting SAFI 836:69
something about a b. VIDAL 1044:60
bureaucratic b. or plain idiotic TUCH 1031:46
b. society TREV 1026:53
bureaucrats dictators nor the b. ORWE 744:40
burgeoned b. without...directors GLEI 430:61
Burger King B. K. and Dairy Queen HUXT 509:8
burgesses b. with staring b. STEV 974:2
burglar b. who respects his art OHEN 737:20
burgundy claret and b. in Scotland? SMITH 945:88
naïve domestic B. THUR 1018:21
burial-mounds no b.-m. YEATS 1104:58
buried b. in a good old age BIBLE 104:20
b. in so sweet a place SHEL 930:33
b. under the shale of eras RAND 801:25
b. with me HEWE 479:86
not b. me deep enough? TENN 1002:92
not mind its being b. HOPK 492:6
Upon my b. body lay BEAU 80:73
when they b. him TENN 1003:27
buries universal darkness b. all POPE 783:11
Burma Nothing happens in B. THER 1009:41
There's a B. girl KIPL 560:28
burn better to marry than to b. BIBLE 150:50
b. and rave at the close of day THOM 1011:75
B., baby, b. ANON 27:84
B., with Athens CAMP 227:18
B. your bra! ANON 27:94
but b., b., b. KERO 553:12
three years of slow b. WHITE 1071:46
Burn-mill B.-m. meadow WORD 1098:57
burn-side waly, waly yon b.-s. BALL 67:57
burned bush b. with fire BIBLE 106:53
clothes not be b.? BIBLE 120:65
got myself b. or hanged JERO 521:11
shalt not be b. BIBLE 126:93
burnie whare the b. rowes BURNS 212:41
burning b. a farthing candle JOHN 528:38
b. and gassing people SIHA 938:72
B. dinner PIER 769:33
B. for b. BIBLE 107:69
b. of the leaves BINY 162:8
Castletown's b. HOGG 485:65
guardianship...against b. PATR 761:15
Lady's not for B. FRY 408:13
burnish thoughts began to b. HERB 475:25
burns b. hurlis all their bankis DOUG 341:54
Not she which b. in't SHAK 911:24
Burns ken a wurd B. MACD 627:75
burnt had to be b. down JOHN 524:69
burst b. into...bloom RAND 801:26
B. smilingly SHAK 904:49
burthen their b. to the ground TENN 1003:22
Burton why was B. built on Trent? HOUS 495:63
bury b. for nothing DICK 323:79
b. them at suitable depths KEYN 555:36
b. whom he helped to starve POPE 781:66
We will b. you KHRU 556:47
went to b. her BIBLE 112:83
bus Hitler has missed the b. CHAM 249:22
no bloody b. BLAIR 165:51
tread in the b. on my toes? AUDEN 47:62
tumbled off a b. GRAH 437:86
buses men are like bloody b. COPE 287:53
bush Bed in the b. STEV 976:51
burdened licorice b. BETJ 101:53
b. afire with God BROW 197:23
b. burned with fire BIBLE 106:53
b. supposed a bear! SHAK 871:55

bush (*contd.*)
child of the mighty b. FRAN 402:16
good wine needs no b. SHAK 887:38
miracle of the lit b. THOM 1013:26
Mother-.h that bore you! LAWS 588:21
passion in every b. LEE 593:18
seen the b. by moonlight LAWS 588:21
sun...on the...Australian b. LAWS 587:18
Sweet Robin sits on the b. SCOTT 855:96
thick b. that proved THOM 1013:21
Thorough b., thorough brier SHAK 870:35
Bush B. has 100 bodyguards GORB 435:60
President B. seems to think CUOMO 300:5
The devil B. HUSS 505:36
bushel a b. of Corn PETTY 768:13
put it under a b. BIBLE 134:36
bushels two b. of chaff SHAK 874:9
business advertising b. ...illusions QUEN 797:54
aim of the school of b. DEMI 315:44
an ethical b. ORWE 744:27
anon we shall dote on b. ETHE 380:17
any man in b. can afford STOWE 978:85
any other decent b. man LEWIS 602:53
broker who really intends to do b. BISM 164:25
B. at the end of its journey LLOYD 608:51
B. carried on as usual CHUR 263:96
B. first; pleasure afterwards THAC 1007:2
b. in great waters BIBLE 118:20
b., industrial and commercial CARN 236:6
b. institution in the world ROGE 820:5
b. is to appraise DEWEY 319:96
b. is very simple GATES 416:37
b. meetings...supply people BOYD 182:61
b. of a comic poet CONG 280:4
b. of a statesman STEU 970:30
b. of the American people is b. COOL 286:36
b. of the day DRYD 352:50
b. of war GERB 420:98
b. that we love SHAK 906:86
but a damn bad b. ROLL 821:25
buy b. executives FORB 396:97
called away by particular b. SHER 933:95
Canada was open for b. ATWO 45:29
Corruption...is Chinese b. life ECON 359:15
damned serious b. WELL 1063:91
dare tell me that b. STEV 973:91
do your own b. BIBLE 153:24
end of this day's b. SHAK 884:65
ever-haunting importunity Of b. LAMB 576:11
exhausted what there is in b. WHIT 1073:97
good all round b. work WELLS 1064:34
growth of large b. ROCK 817:69
He which hath b. DONNE 337:86
heat of the b. is over! ETHE 380:14
hell of a b. to be in WINN 1087:63
horse racing...a solid, stable b. STEI 966:61
If everybody minded their own b. CARR 238:25
In civil b.; What first? BACON 58:71
is the world's b. KENN 552:93
It is good b. SKEL 942:39
jungles of b. HAMM 453:49
know...about b. cycles BECK 81:89
lawyer...swallowed up with b. WALT 1052:10
life's b....a summer mood WORD 1097:43
life...is a dreary b. PERCY 766:84
main b. of socialist parties KING 557:31
make b. for itself DICK 325:35
Men of b. BAGE 61:63
minding my own b. COOL 287:38
more b. after dinner SWIFT 984:76
my b. to see that we retain WILH 1080:37
No B. Like Show B. BERL 95:63
no b., no income GALS 413:1
no concern with b. KIPL 560:24

business (*contd.*)
no other b. which government	PAINE 750:45
No praying, it spoils b.	OTWAY 746:87
none of your damn b.	STIL 977:68
Not slothful in b.	BIBLE 149:34
over here it's a b.	ROGE 820:19
paper of b.	HAZL 463:8
people without b.	DEFOE 312:84
Pleasure is a thief to b.	DEFOE 312:86
principal b. of life to enjoy	BUTL 217:35
publicity agent of big b.	ORWE 742:88
remained in b.	TWAIN 1032:71
retail b. all over agin	NEME 722:5
robs you on b. principles	SHAW 920:11
servant or has a b.	LAW 585:60
servants of b.	BACON 57:68
strange, horrible b.	VICT 1043:53
successful in b.	GILL 427:13
The b. of a general	SUN 982:35
The rest is not our b.	ELIOT 372:54
to do the b.	THAC 1006:84
true b. precept	DICK 322:73
We can do b. together	THAT 1008:18
What b. have you, miss	SHER 933:78
What was everybody's b.	SMUTS 950:67
What's your b.	BERE 94:36
whatever my b.	PEPYS 765:78
when B. gets above sellin' tinpinny	DUNNE 356:60

businessman prominent b.   GALB 411:74
businessmen b....take on a science   ASIM 42:74
like many b. of genius	PUZO 796:41
message to the b.	CURR 301:19
more businesslike than b.	FROST 407:82

busk b. my heid   BALL 67:57
buskins With b. shortened to descry

      HERR 477:59
busses trolley b. hissing   BETJ 100:49
bust animated b.   GRAY 442:67
Uncorseted, her friendly b.	ELIOT 367:64

busy and insinuating rogue   SHAK 900:49
b., and the tired	FITZ 390:2
b. man who can keep up	STARR 963:1
important is keepin' b.	MOSES 710:5
Lord! Thou knowest how b.	ASTL 43:95
Nowher so b. a man	CHAU 254:23

busyness Extreme b.   STEV 974:19
but-an-ben wee b.-a-b.   MORR 709:84
butcher benevolence of the b.   SMITH 945:87
b. of a silk button	SHAK 869:99
Hog B. for the World	SAND 841:57
son of a first rate b.	ASHF 41:68
the consent of every b.	SHER 933:87
want to know a b. paints	BROW 200:98
When a b. tells you	JOHN 527:27

butchered B. to make a...holiday   BYRON 220:1
butchers gentle with these b.   SHAK 883:44
sadists...become policemen or b.	CONN 283:59
shepherds and b.	VOLT 1047:16

buter offered a piece of bread and b.   MACK 632:55
butler A 'great' b. can only be   ISHI 513:76
Ice formed on the b.'s upper slopes	WODE 1089:14

Butler Mr B....grips him warmly   WILS 1085:29
butlers vagaries of b.   ACHE 2:26
butter a pound of melted b.   WODE 1089:93
between b. and yoghurt	TRIL 1026:54
bread and b.	MACD 628:92
Bread and B.	SWIFT 986:11
bread and your b.	KIPL 564:12
b. in a lordly dish	BIBLE 109:14
b. nor shoes nor poetry	LEWIS 601:51
crush these men of b.?	ALBA 11:81
cutting bread and b.	THAC 1007:1
King said B., eh?	MILNE 680:71
loved...bread and b.	LEE 593:18

butter (*contd.*)
manage without b.	GOEB 430:64
rather have b. or guns?	GOER 430:67
steak spread with b.	KURO 571:20

buttercup I'm called little B.   GILB 423:54
buttered b. on both sides   JACK 514:85
butterflies case of b. so rich it looks   LARK 581:97
unsympathetic as b.	ELIOT 365:5

butterfly breaks a b. upon a wheel?   POPE 781:67
breathing incense into b.'s wings	BASHO 76:4
b. poised on a pigtailed ocean	SITW 940:2
b. upon the road	KIPL 559:14
Float like a b.	ALI 14:28
guts of a b.	CAPO 231:89
sharp wings of a b.	HARR 459:35

butterscotch sun poured in like b.   MITC 696:82
buttocks Miss Universe's b.   BENE 89:58
button b., hook, and lace   LOWE 615:74
But we don't care a b.!	LEAR 590:55
butcher of a silk b.	SHAK 869:99
fourth waistcoat b.	LICH 603:83
little round b. at top	FOOTE 396:95
wad na gie a b.	BURNS 212:28
we are not the very b.	SHAK 889:97

buttons in his b. he will carry't   SHAK 878:19
taken off his b.	KIPL 560:29

buxom b. are and prone   SPEN 958:15
Buxton every fool in Bakewell at B.   RUSK 831:13
buy b. his work   RENO 807:9
b. it of thee	BIBLE 110:52
can't b. many business executives	FORB 396:97
farm to b. my crown	SHAK 882:10
I will b. with you	SHAK 874:18
more to make than b.	SMITH 945:88
no man might b. or sell	BIBLE 158:22
What can you b.	TOWNE 1024:10

buyer If I...found a b.   RICH 810:59
buzzard come back as a b.   FAUL 384:86
buzzing b. about between right   HUXL 509:6
by-and-by lest we should be b.-a.-b.   ALDR 12:9
by-laws b.-l. are shorter   WHITE 1069:24
by-product something...as a b.-p.   HUXL 506:61
bygone Her b. simplicity   HARDY 456:92
bygones In commerce b. are for ever b.   JEVO 521:21
Byron B. bore with haughty scorn   ARNO 38:3
B. is only great as a poet	GOET 431:80
the poetry of Lord b.	MACA 623:2

bystanders b....hope that he will die   EMER 377:65
byway and the b. nigh me   STEV 976:51
byword Israel...a proverb and a b.   BIBLE 111:56

cabal killed by the usual c.   DAVI 308:16
cabbage c.-stumps of quotations   LAWR 586:96
cabbage-leaf cut a c.-l.   FOOTE 396:95
cabbages like their c. spherical   BOYD 182:65
Of c.—and kings	CARR 240:57
those who plant c.	RABE 799:90
while I am planting c.	MONT 701:63

cabin a small c. build   YEATS 1104:57
sleep...in a log c.	BIRD 163:14
willow c. at your gate	SHAK 894:6

cabinet colleagues in the Truman c.   REST 807:14
Crossed in his C.	DISR 333:3
mislead the C.	ASQU 42:79

cable c. Hitler and ask him   GOLD 434:35
cables also the rudder c.   THOM 1013:18
cabooses c. of collier-brigs   DICK 324:18
Cabots Lowells talk to the C.   BOSS 180:28
Cacaliban 'Ban, 'ban, C.   SHAK 917:30
cackle c. w'en he fine a wum   HARR 458:30
cackling when it takes to c.   ELIOT 366:27
cactus garden of c. and sour grapes   MERR 672:21
This is the c. land	ELIOT 369:99

cad Flopshus C.   KIPL 562:68

cadence c., a quality of voice   CATH 244:50
golden c. of poesy	SHAK 865:17

cadillac See that gold C.   TRUMP 1030:37
Cadogan One-eighty-nine C. Square   BETJ 100:33
cads c. of the most unscrupulous   FRY 408:10
Cadwallader C. and all his goats   SHAK 882:8
Cadwallon Cold is C.'s tongue   GRAY 443:82
Caesar As C. loved me   SHAK 884:47
born free as C.	SHAK 882:19
C.'s I am	WYATT 1103:28
C. is more dangerous	SHAK 883:35
C., now be still	SHAK 884:67
C.'s spirit, ranging	SHAK 883:45
C.'s wife must be above suspicion	CAES 225:85
decree from C. Augustus	BIBLE 142:76
doth this our C. feed	SHAK 882:22
Either C. or nothing	BORG 179:16
from C.'s laurel crown	BLAKE 168:4
envy of great C.	SHAK 884:68
Imperial C.	SHAK 893:79
in the coffin there with C.	SHAK 884:51
noble C. saw him stab	SHAK 884:54
O mighty C.!	SHAK 883:43
Our master C.	YEATS 1107:90
Religion C. never knew	COWP 292:36
Render therefore unto C.	BIBLE 139:32
speak in C.'s funeral	SHAK 884:48
that C. might be great!	CAMP 227:27
that I loved C.	SHAK 884:46
Then fall C.	SHAK 883:39
what should be in that 'C.'	SHAK 882:21
your boy, your C.	DRYD 348:90

Caesars Compare with C.   SHAK 877:91
We were C.	RADI 800:3
worship the C. and Napoleons	HUXL 507:75

caftan Azcan in c.   STEV 971:41
café dominoes outside a French c.   WILDE 1077:76
In the Garden City C.	BETJ 101:54

cafés shops and third-rate c.   LESS 598:2
cage bird born in a c.   SHAW 924:95
born within the c.	TENN 998:29
c. like grots	SITW 941:12
c. they were tricked into entering	SNYD 951:85
no more natural...than a c.	SHAW 924:92
Nor iron bars a c.	615:63
Over the c. floor	HUGH 500:35
put in a c. if...any sign of fierceness	CARB 231:95
relentless c. of routine	PLATH 773:88
robin red breast in a c.	BLAKE 167:2

cages not in making c.   SWIFT 984:75
Cain before she conceived C.   BROW 195:88
C....dwelt in land of Nod	BIBLE 104:8
conceived and bare C.	BIBLE 104:4
first city C.	COWL 291:18
Had C. been Scot	CLEV 269:9
land God gave to C.	CART 242:10
Lord set a mark upon C.	BIBLE 104:7
tragedy and destiny of C.	JOHN 522:35

cairney ayont the c.   MACD 627:74
cajolery No amount of c.   BEVAN 101:64
cake have your c. and eat it   BARN 72:30
icing that detracts from the c.	AUCH 46:40
layer of c. or a road	MILL 677:9
only a certain sized c.	CRIP 296:31

cakes after tea and c. and ices   ELIOT 367:48
c....looked green with worry	FIRB 389:76
no more c. and ale?	SHAK 894:10

Calabria C. death   VIRG 1046:96
Calais c. lying in my heart   MARY 661:30
left C. on Monday	MACA 622:93
shew light at C.	JOHN 528:38

calamites C. of two kinds   BIER 161:73
calamities Among the c. of War   JOHN 527:21
calamity faint flicker of c.   HOLL 485:71

calamity (*contd.*)
forced...into...belief is a c. RICH 810:62
makes c. of so long life TWAIN 1033:89
something more than a public c. SOUT 954:41
calamus C. saevoir ense patet BURT 214:68
calcine C. its clods BROW 198:49
calculated absence of everything c. DICK 327:82
c. to lighten the tax burden QUINE 797:67
calculation c. shining out DICK 322:71
essential elements in the c. THOR 1016:72
What c., number, measurement YEATS 1107:42
when a c. is made JOHN 529:71
calculators Electronic c. can solve KRUT 570:8
sophists, economists, and c. BURKE 207:31
Calcutta in touch with C. WHITE 1070:28
Caledonia O C.! stern and wild SCOTT 853:50
calendar kind of Newgate c. IRVI 513:61
calf bring hither the fatted c. BIBLE 143:1
c. and the young lion BIBLE 125:68
lion and the c. shall lie down ALLEN 14:38
molten c. BIBLE 107:71
second beast like a c. BIBLE 157:8
When he killed a c. AUBR 45:36
Caliban C. casts out Ariel POUND 786:63
California C.'s power to cloud BAKER 63:86
C., the department-store state CHAN 250:40
From C. to the New York Island GUTH 449:94
Caligula Emperor C.'s Habits LONG 610:91
call all C. and Answer LAWR 586:82
c. in the stream of thought JAMES 517:40
c. me Newt GING 427:22
c. the shots IACO 509:17
c. the whole thing off GERS 420:12
dead men's fingers c. them SHAK 892:71
true c. of the desert STARK 963:96
What do you c. the play? SHAK 891:40
Whatever they c. him TENN 1001:80
wild c. and a clear c. MASE 661:33
You could never c. SITW 940:3
called Come when you're c. EDGE 360:31
how things are c. HOBB 482:35
I'm c. little Buttercup GILB 423:54
calling c. him Smith HOLM 486:94
can't hear you c. SAND 841:64
high c. of God BIBLE 153:12
mercenary c. HOUS 496:77
nimble in the c. LEWIS 601:51
callisthenics c. with words PARK 754:17
calm a c. so deep WORD 1097:46
A vast and tender C. VERL 1042:34
c. in our delight WORD 1094:1
c. simmer gloamin' TANN 991:96
Cruel...but c. and strong SHEL 928:11
flat c. with drizzling rain BOWEN 181:50
for a c. unfit DRYD 349:12
I am not c. KENN 550:58
in the c. bent up we grow ANON 23:87
Lush, c. and voluptuous BAUD 77:22
no joy but c.! TENN 994:50
Nor peace within nor c. around SHEL 927:74
opulent c. of anglefish ALLEN 14:30
something...to c. her down JAGG 515:95
there was a great c. BIBLE 136:68
tumult dwindled to a c. BYRON 224:68
with a stoic c. SOME 952:1
Women are supposed to be very c. BRON 191:93
world's best moment is a c. hour ABU 1:11
calmness smallest space of c. BEDE 82:8
calumnies C. are answered best JONS 534:81
calumny loud roar of foaming c. BYRON 220:97
calves c. of the stall BIBLE 131:72
peculiarly susceptible to c. HUXL 506:59
Calvin that land of C. SMITH 949:49
Calvinists Commercial C. MACD 628:92

camaraderie c. does not hold HUGH 500:40
Cambodia C. was not a mistake SHAW 926:48
humble people of C. SIHA 938:73
Cambridge C. has always tried ANON 27:60
C. ladies...furnished souls CUMM 299:78
C. people rarely smile BROO 192:28
difficult feat for a C. male PLATH 773:90
either Oxford or C. SNAG 950:68
Oxford...more attractive than C. BAED 61:47
to C. books he sent BROW 196:9
Ye fields of C. COWL 291:15
came angel c. GUST 449:93
c., saw, and overcame SHAK 878:5
c. to those who knew Him not SCHW 852:31
I c., I saw JOHN 522:30
I c., I saw, God conquered CHAR 253:88
I c., I saw, I conquered CAES 225:87
know not whence you c. FITZ 390:90
where we c. from HORN 494:36
camel c. has a single hump NASH 719:53
C. humphed himself KIPL 563:79
c.'s hump KIPL 563:76
c. is a horse ISSI 514:81
easier for a c. to go BIBLE 139:25
raiment of c.'s hair BIBLE 133:26
swallow a c. BIBLE 139:35
Take my c. dear MACA 622:85
Camelot Kennedy...became C. WHITE 1071:49
looked down to C. TENN 994:45
lost...like C. THAT 1007:10
many-towered C. TENN 993:37
never be another C. ONAS 739:44
rode down to C. TENN 993:44
to towered C. TENN 993:40
camels distrust c. and anyone LEWIS 601:47
camembert c. of time and space DALI 303:47
camera c. can be the...weapon PARK 756:37
c. is an eye in head WELL 1063:2
c. makes everyone a tourist SONT 953:8
c. relieves...burden of memory BERG 94:43
c. uses film WELL 1063:3
got back to my c. KARSH 542:11
I am a c. ISHE 513:72
cameras pictures with c. NEWM 724:25
camp armed c. of Blackshirts MUSS 716:83
From c. to c. SHAK 881:88
happy if the general c. SHAK 899:40
never fortified a c. CHRI 261:72
camp-bedstead folding c.-b. TRAV 1025:31
campaign after a bloody c. HAYD 462:88
c. for birth control MUNRO 714:56
defeat comparable to...military c. EDIN 361:40
defiant c. of civil disobedience CHUR 264:8
prospect of another c. JOHN 523:44
campaigner congenital c. MARA 649:39
Campbell C.'s Hippocrene BYRON 222:38
do not Maister or C. me SCOTT 855:89
Campbell-Bannerman Henry C.-B. BENT 89:30
Campbells C. are comin' ANON 24:1
camps opposed c. of the empiricists MERT 672:26
campus students on c. NABO 717:99
world is a global c. LODGE 610:80
can fill the c. TENN 996:87
H who c., does SHAW 922:48
Pass me the c., lad HOUS 495:68
queerer than we c. suppose HALD 451:17
Canada as the enemy to C. MOOD 703:98
backwoods of C. MOOD 703:95
born in C. JOHN 524:60
C. could have enjoyed COLO 277:52
C....hardly exists BORG 179:14
C. has an acute shortage of rich WILS 1085:43
C. is not really a place DAVI 308:17
C. is paranoid schizophrenia ATWO 45:20

Canada (*contd.*)
C. moved from colony to nation INNIS 512:52
C. only needs to be known HOPK 492:12
C....the only country MACL 635:98
C. was open for business ATWO 45:29
genius of C. MORR 708:78
graduate from C. FULF 409:31
independent Quebec...united C. DESC 318:85
more than C. itself is worth VOLT 1046:5
not got much to say about C. THOR 1017:94
One foot in C. GAY 416:31
symbol for C....Survival ATWO 45:22
two languages in C. SAINT 836:77
Vive le C. français! DE 313:4
Canadian C. kid who wants RICH 811:73
C....make love in a canoe BERT 99:45
I'm a C. CRON 298:59
in Paris, I remained a C. RICH 810:72
Canadians C....held together ACHE 3:44
My generation of C. FULF 409:31
special task as French C. BOUR 181:47
canal fear the push into the c. ELIOT 370:35
fell into the Grand C. MORR 708:77
yesterdays, for the C. Zone PARF 753:92
Canalettos C. go MACM 636:16
canals unreal realms of the c. MACC 625:50
canaries song of c. NASH 719:42
cancer AIDS, c., nuclear war MAMET 644:56
C. can be rather fun HALD 451:19
c....close to the presidency DEAN 311:59
C.'s no metaphor DUNN 356:57
dying of throat c. BECK 81:6
political c. ANON 29:32
white race is the c. SONT 953:9
candid be c. where we can POPE 780:33
save me, from the c. friend CANN 230:71
candidate c. who can whistle Dixie OBRI 734:67
potato c. ANON 29:44
candidates boys or scholarship c. LITT 607:42
checks go to the c. ANON 28:17
locked c. into ridiculous positions DANF 304:50
candied Of c. apple, quince KEATS 546:95
candle Bell, book, and c. SHAK 872:65
burning a farthing c. JOHN 528:38
day light such a c. LATI 583:36
delight for being the c. WEBB 1058:14
democracy is but a flickering c. MACK 632:57
fire or c. for warmth MACL 635:96
light a c., and sweep the house BIBLE 143:97
little c. throws his beams SHAK 873:7
Neither do men light a c. BIBLE 134:36
candle-ends friends called him 'C.-e.' CARR 241:84
candle-flame feel the steady c.-f. BROW 198:39
candle-light dress by yellow c.-l. STEV 975:32
Fire and fleet and c.-l. BALL 67:44
candlelight by the sun and c. BROW 197:19
candles c. are all out SHAK 908:38
c. burn their sockets HOUS 496:75
c. burns at both ends MILL 676:82
extinguishes c. and kindles fire LARO 582:28
Night's c. are burnt out SHAK 869:11
candlestick-maker C. much aquaints BROW 200:98
candlesticks midst of the seven c. BIBLE 156:99
candy C. Is dandy NASH 719:46
cane nice Conduct of a clouded C. POPE 779:2
canem Cave c.! ANON 20:42
cankered cross-gained and the c. MACD 628:93
cankerworm c., and the caterpiller BIBLE 130:54
cann come fill up my c. SCOTT 855:85
Cannan land of C. BIBLE 104:23
canned C. music is like...wallpaper COOKE 286:33
Cannes C....is 10,000 people ANON 28:13
cannibal Better sleep with sober c. MELV 667:29
cannibals c., And Trojan Greeks? SHAK 877:91

cannon C. to right of them — TENN 1000:72
Even in the c.'s mouth — SHAK 885:92
mouth of the c. — RUSK 830:74
cannon-ball hatched from a c.-b. — NAPO 718:36
cannonball c. took off his legs — HOOD 488:34
cannot He who c., teaches — SHAW 922:48
canoe make love in a c. — BERT 99:20
canoes light c. have vanished — SIGO 938:71
canon Art is not…a c. of beauty — PICA 768:25
c. 'gainst self-slaughter! — SHAK 888:51
most inhibited sin in the c. — SHAK 901:69
canonization sort of natural c. — HAZL 463:12
canonized c. on earth — BROW 195:82
Macmillan was c. — WILS 1085:42
canopy most excellent c. the air — SHAK 890:2
rich embroidered c. — SHAK 862:24
cant clear your mind of c. — JOHN 531:26
Cricket…sentimentalism and c. — CARD 232:3
cantaloupe put a c. in a coke bottle — JONES 533:59
Canterbury compass of his C. Tales — DRYD 352:79
cantos c. of unvanquished space — CRANE 295:5
cants c.…canted in this canting world — STER 969:5
canty wad na been sae c. — BURNS 211:7
canvas c. a sentence or paragraph — MOTH 711:12
c. is to the painter — BRIL 188:53
c. was always saying no — BEAR 79:53
certain moment the c. — ROSE 822:56
crowd your c. — TENN 1005:68
put Freud on c. — SCHW 851:23
see and imitate on c. — CUMM 299:75
cap but in a fool's c. — HOPK 491:78
c. in hand the day — SMITH 949:60
flap of my fur c. — STEV 973:97
Green jacket, red c. — ALLI 15:53
On Fortune's c. — SHAK 889:97
capability Negative C. — KEATS 544:47
capable anyone who was c. — KING 559:7
c. of an infinite diversity — REDT 804:79
c. of choosing a president — STEIN 964:9
c. of higher things — FORS 398:48
capacities vulgar sort of c. — BACON 55:7
capacity c. for innocent enjoyment — GILB 424:65
c. for seeing nothing — DUDEK 354:20
c. to do — FAUL 383:80
How large is the c. of man — AUGU 49:15
infinite c. for taking pains — ACHE 3:38
infinite c. for taking things — HUXL 507:81
caparisons lay his gay c. apart — SHAK 905:83
Capernaum heard done in C. — BIBLE 142:81
capers He c., he dances — SHAK 878:19
capework rumpling C. of the wind — WILB 1075:22
capital awoke in the c. — KAIKO 541:93
c. development — KEYN 555:35
c. is become an overgrown monster — SMOL 950:64
c. of memoranda — WHITE 1070:28
conditions of c. and population — MILL 674:58
consumes intellectual c. — KISS 566:38
controversy over c. punishment — FISH 389:81
empty c. snorts — SMITH 949:60
exploited by American c. — INNIS 512:52
fine thing c. punishment is — DICK 321:36
If c. is growing — MARX 660:16
pandemonium, the high c. — MILT 688:10
To that high C. — SHEL 930:36
capitalism aberrations of c. — SMALL 943:61
acceptable face of c. — HEATH 466:53
accuser of c. — MACL 633:67
Can c. survive? — SCHU 851:18
C. only works well — SWEE 983:51
C. requires people to be pious souls — CHER 256:67
c. with the gloves off — STOP 978:78
C. without bankruptcy — BORM 179:17
communism versus c. — NGUY 725:47
definition of c. — HAMP 454:64

capitalism (*contd.*)
evils of c. — KINN 559:8
nothing to do with c. — WEBER 1059:20
old-fashioned free-market c. — GLEI 430:61
The tombstone of c. — STILL 977:67
unacceptable face of c. — HEATH 466:52
where c. is advanced — TROT 1029:8
capitalist against their c. exploiters — LENIN 595:50
any major crisis of the c. system — EAGL 359:4
c. achievement — SCHU 851:19
forbid c. acts — NOZI 732:44
gulf that divides him from the c. — MARX 660:16
patching up the c. system — CONN 284:83
substance, of c. production — MARX 660:21
worker is the slave of c. society — CONN 284:84
capitals C. are increased — SMITH 945:85
New York is a c. city — MAIL 639:84
Capitol ruins of the C. — GIBB 421:29
capitulate will not c. — JOHN 532:35
capon cold c.'s leg? — SHAK 875:40
caprice rule by whim or c. — DOUG 342:69
Capricorn Lady C., he understood — HUXL 506:49
caps always holding their c. — DUNN 356:52
They threw their c. — SHAK 911:3
captain broken…by the team c. — HOWE 497:94
c.'s heart — SHAK 904:54
c. is in his bunk — SHAW 925:16
c. of a mine-sweeper — CATTO 245:57
C. of the Gate — MACA 623:13
c. over his people — BIBLE 110:34
got the C. …on his back — RANS 802:34
O C.! my C.! — WHIT 1073:91
plain, russet-coated C. — CROM 297:50
well-bred C. of the Pinafore! — GILB 423:55
captains All my sad c. — SHAK 905:84
c. and the kings — KIPL 562:61
C. of Industry — CARL 236:95
Star c. glow — FLEC 393:54
captivate law of love is to c. — SCEVE 846:56
captive both the captor and the c. — WAITE 1048:30
c. talk of chains — MILT 690:67
captives proclaim liberty to the c. — BIBLE 127:12
serve your c.' need — KIPL 562:64
captivity c. thence captive, us to win — SPEN 958:24
C. thence captive, us to win — SPEN 959:27
led c. captive — BIBLE 116:87
nothing beyond c. and depression — HARD 455:78
What c. was to the Jews — WILDE 1075:31
captor both the c. and the captive — WAITE 1048:30
captors with the c. — WAITE 1048:30
capture chase rather than c. — WELLS 1064:32
Capulet no longer be a C. — SHAK 868:87
car bend…with thine iron c. — BLAKE 165:60
buy a used c. — ANON 27:67
can't drive the c. — TYNAN 1035:29
c. and ambulance — LEBO 592:88
c. has become an article of dress — MACL 635:95
Carol like a rolling c. — FARJ 383:63
drive his c. at you at 95 mph — BOYC 182:60
gilded c. of day — MILT 683:20
landscape…traversed in a c. — LEGER 594:22
Microsoft were a c. — MURR 715:7
motor c. was poetry — LEWIS 602:52
over a cliff in your c. — VENA 1042:30
step out in front of a moving c. — DICK 320:12
caravan Put up your c. — HODG 483:49
carbuncle monstrous c. on the face — CHAR 253:91
carbuncular young man c. — ELIOT 369:89
carcase c. of an old song — THOM 1013:20
carcass c. and a skeleton — TRAH 1024:26
c. fit for hounds — SHAK 883:29
c. seemed to be made of iron — MENC 670:89
carcasses c. of old policies — CECIL 247:82
dead c. of unburied men — SHAK 911:11

card American Express c. — LODGE 610:80
cheery old c. — SASS 845:28
time c. office hours — BAND 69:87
card-indexes memories are c.-i. — CONN 283:78
cardinal unbecoming for a c. — JOHN 522:34
cards c. are ill shuffled — SWIFT 986:19
c. as a substitute — ALBEE 11:83
Never play c. with…Doc — ALGR 13:24
old age of c. — POPE 782:77
patience, and shuffle the c. — CERV 248:1
tythe o' what ye waste at c. — BURNS 209:62
Cardus reading Neville C. — THOM 1010:71
care agonizing c. — NIGH 729:94
better c. of myself — BLAKE 165:54
boots it with uncessant c. — MILT 684:42
c. and not to c. — ELIOT 369:10
c. beyond to-day — GRAY 441:47
c. for the elderly — FIELD 388:43
c. is like my shadow — ELIZ 373:89
C. keeps his watch — SHAK 869:97
c. killed a cat — SHAK 880:63
c. less and less — SAYE 846:53
c. lost Went all his fear — MILT 688:13
c. of external goods — WEBER 1059:19
c. of this world — BIBLE 137:98
Casting all your c. upon him — BIBLE 156:83
cat that was ever killed by C. — ROBI 815:33
dark forgetting of my c. — DANI 304:62
despair and sceptred c. — GRAY 443:88
entrust the c. of freedom — EISE 364:82
greatest c. must be taken — STEU 970:24
Have little c. that Life is brief — CARM 236:4
Killing c. and grief — SHAK 918:54
Killing c. and grief — SHAK 918:56
lawyers who don't c. — RENO 806:3
life…full of c. — DAVI 308:20
neat, clean…and I didn't c. — CHAN 250:28
neither of them c. for — HALI 452:32
Nor for itself hath any c. — BLAKE 167:85
past redress…past c. — SHAK 867:54
people which ceases to c. — ELIOT 370:14
ravelled sleave of c. — SHAK 908:46
sickled o'er with c. — TWAIN 1033:89
sought it with c. — CARR 241:87
take c. of everybody — FULL 410:41
Take c. to get — SHAW 922:63
the water's c. — YEATS 1105:61
took a certain amount of c. — KING 559:3
weary fu' o' c.! — BURNS 212:22
With what nice c. — WORD 1101:93
career boy's ideal of a manly c. — DISR 332:89
c.…product of simple observation — BEHR 85:76
c. structure for poets — TOWN 1024:13
c. was a text book example — TIME 1020:68
close my military c. — MACA 621:75
design c. is a process of learning — BELL 86:94
details…of man and c. — ELTON 375:22
for c. advancement — GRANT 438:3
my c., my brilliant c.! — FRAN 402:14
Poetry is not a c. — ELIOT 370:15
points to a political c. — SHAW 923:83
satisfying c. choice — COUP 289:74
careerism vulgar c. — GRAV 440:36
careers People don't choose their c. — DOSP 340:41
careful Be c. for nothing — BIBLE 153:1
c. in the choice of his enemies — WILDE 1076:51
c. not to drink too much — HAMM 454:60
So c. of the type — TENN 999:39
carefulness c. bringeth age — BIBLE 132:10
careless c. people — FITZ 390:5
So c. of the single life — TENN 999:39
The more c. — SWIFT 986:10
carelessness back into their…vast c. — FITZ 390:5
looks like c. — WILDE 1078:83

cares all your c. beguile   DRYD 351:62
c. and pleasures   GIBB 421:20
c. no more for one place   SOUT 954:39
c., that infest the day   LONG 611:4
flesh without c.   CIXO 267:75
soil of his shallow c.!   BRON 192:13
where c. abound   WORD 1100:87
caress can c. and tickle   MITC 696:81
curse sound like a c.   FOOT 395:91
careworn haggard and c.   WODE 1089:95
cargo c. of ivory, And apes   MASE 662:37
caricatures c....most penetrating   HUXL 506:60
caring C. is the greatest thing   HUGEL 498:11
Carle C., now the King's come!   SCOTT 855:2
Carlyle C. has led us all out   CLOU 270:31
let C. and Mrs C. marry   BUTL 217:32
our best men are dead! – C.   PUNCH 795:31
carnage c. drear   SCOTT 853:60
carnal heathen in the c. part   POPE 781:71
carnation could never abide c.   SHAK 882:13
carnations musk c. break and swell   ARNO 39:17
carol fluting a wild c.   TENN 1004:49
Carol C. like a rolling car   FARJ 383:63
Carolina ham 'n' eggs in C.   GORD 435:65
carollings So little cause for c.   HARDY 457:7
carpe C. diem   HORA 493:18
carpenter Walrus and the C.   CARR 240:56
carpenters Like c. they want to know   SEXT 859:65
Politicians...are professionals, like c.   EICH 362:59
carpentry junkyards of secular c.   ROSE 823:64
carpet c. on the floor   JOHN 524:57
firmly rooted to the c.   DICK 326:56
grazes over the c., lowing   RAINE 800:7
Neapolitan c. cleaner   CHEE 256:54
tawny coloured magic c.   WOOLF 1093:65
carpet-bag From the c.-p.   TRAV 1025:31
carpets long c. rose along   KEATS 547:97
carriage c. held but just Ourselves   DICK 328:6
sent a c. to bring you back   CH 248:8
window of a railroad c.   LEGER 594:22
carrion c. comfort   HOPK 492:1
green-sickened c.   SHAK 869:13
carrots overdo it with your c..   BECK 81:96
carry c. all he knew   GOLD 433:13
c. the knowledge with him   JOHN 530:96
c. us not up hence   BIBLE 107:75
must c. it with us   EMER 376:44
Science may c. us to Mars   REPP 807:13
cars armoured c. of dreams   BISH 163:30
c. and sleeping pills   HALD 451:19
C....supreme creation of an era   BART 74:79
crazy about c.   SALI 839:25
finned c. nose forward   LOWE 617:1
like armoured c.   JANO 518:54
cart carrier's c. at the age of three   LEE 593:16
c. with the home packed   COLL 276:38
coaxes the built c. out   PATC 759:90
Owl, and a useful C.   LEAR 590:56
Carterhaugh come or gae by C.   BALL 67:51
Carthage C. must be destroyed   CATO 245:55
cartons slag-heap covered in c.   DRAB 345:21
cartridges carry pistols and c.   SHAW 920:93
Caruso C. came with a voice   NEVE 723:14
when somebody insulted C.   LOUIS 614:60
carve c. him as a dish   SHAK 883:29
c. on every tree   SHAK 886:36
carver was the c. happy   RUSK 830:75
carving c. and colouring of a thought   SITW 941:28
C. is interrelated masses   HEPW 473:79
Casbah Come with me to the C.   BOYER 182:67
case c. me in leather   SHAK 865:2
c....not entirely devoid of interest   DOYLE 343:99
c. of butterflies so rich it looks   LARK 581:97
c. of petty right   THOM 1012:4

case (*contd.*)
c. sae hard is   FERG 386:18
doctors know a hopeless c.   CUMM 300:93
enclosing it in a c. of wood   WATT 1055:55
find in fact to be the c.   HOMA 487:8
heart in a c. o' gowd   BALL 68:58
Just like a large packing c.   WILDE 1076:59
make the best of the c.   UPDI 1036:56
making a c.   KESEY 554:22
presentation of your fraudulent c.   ADAMS 6:92
put under a glass c.   KING 559:5
slavery...condemned in one c.   ASTE 43:92
strong c.   BAIL 62:67
Suitable C. for Treatment   MERC 670:95
terrible c. of the Fountainblues   HUXT 509:7
test c. of US capacity   MACN 636:28
victorious c. pleased   LUCAN 618:21
When a lady's in the c.   GAY 416:50
world is all that is the c.   WITT 1087:73
casement All night has the c.   TENN 1001:86
c. high and triple-arched   KEATS 546:91
c. slowly grows   TENN 997:4
Lethe flows beneath your c.   RANS 802:36
on this c. shone   KEATS 546:92
out at the c.   SHAK 887:24
Casement The ghost of Roger C.   YEATS 1106:88
cases assess the two c.   PASC 757:63
only two types of c.   BENN 91:76
Casey Mr C., freeing his arms   JOYCE 538:44
cash c. cows to feed you pigs   ANDE 18:2
C. for trash   CLIN 269:15
c. payment...sole nexus   CARL 236:84
pay you c. to go away   KIPL 564:11
playing cricket for hard c.!   MITF 697:93
sold myself for very little c.   CARL 233:28
cash-value practical c.-v.   JAMES 517:48
cashing C. in That's what   NOFZ 730:19
casino activities of a c.   KEYN 555:35
law courts...as a c.   INGR 511:45
casket C. of My soul   KEATS 545:42
cassia smothered With c.?   WEBS 1061:66
Cassius C. has a lean...look   SHAK 882:23
cassock c., band, and hymn-book   WILB 1074:15
cassowary If I were a c.   WILB 1074:15
cast c. fear out   GRAV 439:20
friends of the c.   HIRS 482:22
in no wise c. out   BIBLE 145:44
pale c. of thought   SHAK 890:21
shadows that were c.   SASS 845:38
shrieks to...heav'n are c.   POPE 779:1
caste chair is not a c.   HUGO 502:88
thralldom of a military c.   LLOY 608:60
castle bataillèd as it were a c. wal   CHAU 255:45
c. brown as owls   THOM 1010:69
c. hath a pleasant seat   SHAK 907:30
c. without an armoury   GEOF 418:79
falls on c. walls   TENN 997:98
Look owre the c. Doune   BALL -1:32
man's house is his c.   COKE 272:73
rich man in his c.   ALEX 13:18
swimming through an aquarian c.   ALLEN 14:30
through the c. wall   SHAK 867:60
Castlereagh mask like C.   SHEL 928:78
castles C. in the air   IBSEN 510:22
neurotic builds c.   ANON 26:44
War to the c.   CHAM 250:24
Castletown C.'s burning   HOGG 485:65
castor-oil c.-o. of the Palestinian   ANON 29:46
castrate delights of the flesh c. me   FUEN 409:26
casts plaster c. of footprints   PATE 760:98
casualty first c. when war comes   JOHN 523:48
casuists soundest c. doubt   POPE 780:25
Casy maybe like C. says   STEI 966:55
cat a wild c.'s left ear   WODE 1089:93

cat (*contd.*)
Aunt Jobiska's Runcible C.   LEAR 590:64
black c. which isn't there   DARW 306:91
care killed a c.   SHAK 880:63
c. in profound meditation   ELIOT 371:40
c. is black or white   DENG 315:49
c. must have Three...Names   ELIOT 371:39
C. of such deceitfulness   ELIOT 371:41
c. on a hot tin roof   WILL 1081:67
c. that was ever killed by Care   ROBI 815:33
c....walking over the piano   MERI 672:17
c. will mew   SHAK 893:82
c. with bright green eyes   MONRO 700:47
consider my c.   SMART 944:66
deafer than the blue-eyed c.   TENN 1003:39
endow a college, or a c.   POPE 780:27
Even stroking a c.   THOM 1014:44
Eventually it becomes a C.   NASH 720:56
fog come on little c. feet   SAND 841:58
Footed lyke a c.   BERN 97:92
God...invented...the c.   PICA 769:28
Had Tiberious been a c.   ARNO 38:99
kind of singed c.   TWAIN 1032:65
Like the poor c. i'th' adage?   SHAK 908:33
Masserman, the c. man   ANON 26:54
nine-tailed c.   MACA 622:86
Oh I am a c.   SMITH 948:41
play with my c.   MONT 702:70
poor c. i'the adage   TWAIN 1033:89
room to swing a c.   DICK 324:16
support my c.   GRAV 440:31
swing a c.   SMOL 950:65
to see how the c. jumps   SCOTT 856:14
umpire, the pavilon c.   LANG 579:67
very unique c.   GINS 428:31
vigilant as a c.   SHAK 876:65
What c.'s averse to fish?   GRAY 441:52
what you did to that poor c.   BEME 89:46
wildest...was the C.   KIPL 563:86
ykilled the c.   LANG 579:71
catacomb c. of stone and steel   WOLFE 1090:20
catalogue dull c. of common things   KEATS 546:80
catalogues looking at flatware c.   COUP 289:85
catalyst occasion, c., or tripwire   ACKE 4:53
catamite in bed with my c.   BURG 206:38
cataract wild c. leaps   TENN 997:98
cataracts You c. and hurricanoes   SHAK 903:17
catastrophe dusty c. of Asia   BROD 189:68
From such a c.   CHUR 263:3
greatest c.   JOHN 524:67
imminent c.   HUSS 505:35
race between education and c.   WELLS 1065:42
tickle your c.!   SHAK 877:87
catastrophes c. may be inevitable   ASIM 42:72
model of all the c.   SONT 953:12
not c....that age and kill us   WOOLF 1092:56
catch c. everybody if they start   SALI 839:28
never can c. myself   HUME 503:1
you hardly c. it going   WILL 1082:79
Catch-22 only one catch...C.-22   HELL 468:82
catch-as-catch-can game of c.   FOOTE 396:95
catcher c. in the rye   SALI 839:28
catching c. every air-borne particle   JAMES 516:19
catchwords principally by c.   STEV 974:11
catechism c. of comfort   BENE 89:58
categorical in order c.   GILB 424:62
categories batsmen fall into two c.   TRAV 1025:29
c. in which experiences   MANN 646:93
category c. of human being   ASIM 42:73
c. of truth and falsehood   AYER 53:80
lower social c.   SHAR 919:01
Nature is a social c.   LUKA 619:39
never fell into the second c.   GEOR 419:92
not just a moral c.   SOLZ 952:96

category (*contd.*)
to the c., old friend — MO 698:*12*
caterpillar cankerworm and the c. — BIBLE 130:*54*
world for a moss or a c. — BARB 71:*11*
cathedral bawdy house is to a c. — MENC 669:*66*
law courts not as a c. — INGR 511:*45*
pass for a c. doctor — JONS 534:*77*
status of a c. — RODR 819:*89*
supress each c. and college — MACA 622:*93*
that great bed…looks like a c. — ONAS 739:*41*
the ... world is a c. — PAST 759:*84*
cathedrals burst into Gothic c. — SHEEN 926:*50*
c. in my heart — SASS 845:*30*
Gothic c.…supreme creation — BART 74:*79*
immovable c. — GIDE 422:*42*
Catherine C. the Great of Finchley — HEAL 464:*30*
catholic c. appetite — STEV 974:*19*
Holy C. and Apostolic — TEMP 993:*29*
power denied the more c. — WOOLF 1092:*53*
the c. amen — SMART 944:*71*
to increase C. faith — VAZD 1041:*24*
Catholic C. and the Communist — ORWE 745:*49*
C. and the Protestant — CONN 284:*83*
church he…did not attend was C. — AMIS 16:*78*
had once been a C. — FITZ 390:*94*
holy C. Church — BOOK 173:*94*
I am a C. — BELL 87:*4*
it is necessary…he hold the C. Faith — BOOK 174:*2*
lawful for a C. woman — MENC 670:*81*
Once a C. always a C. — WILS 1084:*12*
Shakespeare was an Irish C. — ONEI 740:*58*
Catholics armed C. in the south — REDM 804:*75*
C., bad harvests, and…fluctuations — ELIOT 365:*17*
Hitler attacked the C. — NIEM 727:*68*
hunt the C. from England — LESL 598:*94*
no lapsed C. after…Pavarotti — BURKE 208:*54*
Cato Cicero, citing C. — KNIG 567:*54*
gods, but a lost one C. — LUCAN 618:*21*
cats C. and monkeys — JAMES 516:*13*
C., no less liquid — TESS 1006:*80*
C. seem to go on the principle — KRUT 570:*10*
c. with golden eyes — SACK 835:*62*
evil…committed by spiritual fat c. — PECK 763:*38*
killed the c. — BROW 197:*32*
lotta c. copy the Mona Lisa — ARMS 35:*48*
still…mean to c. — CHEE 256:*54*
wailed like melodious c. — HUXL 507:*69*
windows of the eyes of c. — DRAY 346:*41*
Work was like c. — AMIS 16:*75*
cattle Actors are c. — HITC 482:*27*
All hat and no c. — CONN 282:*52*
cursed above all c. — BIBLE 103:*98*
land of c. and sheep — LAWS 588:*20*
rear c. in the evening — MARX 660:*10*
says that actors are c.? — WINN 1087:*61*
these who die as c. — OWEN 748:*7*
cattle-shed Stood a lowly c.-s. — ALEX 13:*19*
Caucasus thinking on the frosty C.? — SHAK 866:*47*
Caucus some b. in the C. have — WHIT 1072:*70*
caught c. up into the world — HAMI 453:*41*
hanging around until you've c. on — FROST 407:*5*
should have c. it — BEAS 79:*54*
sooner c. than the pestilence — SHAK 878:*28*
cauldron c. of our way of life — GOER 430:*66*
churning c. of America — WRIG 1101:*8*
Fire burn, and c. bubble — SHAK 909:*64*
cause acting on the c. — SHEL 931:*57*
buckler of the people's c. — DRYD 349:*16*
c. is in my will — SHAK 883:*36*
c. is just — DICK 329:*22*
c. is lost for ever! — SCOTT 856:*7*
c. is sometimes simpler — HOPE 490:*71*
c. is the consequence — FANON 382:*59*
c. may be inconvenient — BENN 91:*90*

cause (*contd.*)
c. of plagues are plays — WHITE 1071:*51*
c. or cure! — GOLD 432:*99*
c.…or the Emerald Isle — DREN 346:*42*
c. that interests Russia — WITTE 1087:*71*
c. that perishes with them? — CLOU 271:*45*
c. that wit is in other men — SHAK 877:*80*
c. to write about me — GIOV 428:*36*
c. why music was ordain'd! — SHAK 864:*80*
effect, Whose c. is God — COWP 293:*64*
fighting for every c. — COBD 272:*59*
full c. of weeping — SHAK 903:*16*
grand c. — WESL 1067:*71*
I'll try the whole c. — CARR 238:*23*
idea of an external c. — SPIN 960:*54*
if any man can shew just c. — BOOK 175:*46*
important to the c. of science — AGAS 9:*61*
jealous for the c. — SHAK 900:*43*
just c. to make a pitiful defence — SIDN 937:*59*
justice or injustice of the c. — JOHN 529:*65*
never resist a losing c. — MITC 697:*89*
No man can c. more grief — FAUL 383:*76*
not degrade a First C. — HARDY 456:*90*
not wholesome to Our c. — SHAK 918:*57*
notion of c. and effect — HUME 503:*99*
Obstinacy in a bad c. — BROW 195:*80*
perseverance in a good c. — STER 969:*93*
sole c. of…unhappiness — PASC 757:*58*
supreme c. of our time — SPEN 957:*91*
takes up no falling c. — HAZL 463:*9*
the c. of the world — POUND 785:*59*
the common c. — STEE 964:*16*
various c. the same wild road — SCOTT 854:*73*
Your c. of sorrow — SHAK 910:*91*
causes art's hid c. — JONS 535:*89*
c., and secret motions — BACON 56:*37*
C., as have visible Foundations — PETTY 768:*15*
c. that they represent — FORS 399:*55*
c. why the execution — JOHN 526:*1*
desire to know c. — HAZL 464:*18*
hate the idea of c. — FORS 399:*52*
Home of lost c. — ARNO 38:*10*
ignorant of the c. — SPIN 960:*49*
knowledge of the c. of things — VIRG 1045:*95*
Logic-mill to grind out the true c. — CARL 234:*43*
occasions and c. why — SHAK 882:*7*
pomp of the superflous c. — NEWT 725:*37*
progressive c. in the public eye — SIMP 939:*88*
tough on the c. of crime — BLAIR 165:*53*
caution c. of a sword — CLEV 269:*13*
throw c. to the winds — BENN 91:*80*
cautioned 33 years and never got c. — MATT 664:*80*
cautious Be c., careful — ITO 514:*82*
cavalier C. who loves honour — SCOTT 856:*16*
cavaliero he was a perfect c. — BYRON 221:*21*
cavalry c. commander — BRIN 189:*59*
C. of Woe — DICK 327:*93*
laugh like a squadron of c. — WODE 1089:*24*
cave every creature in a c. — SNYD 951:*85*
Medip's sunless c. — MACA 624:*19*
misty eastern c. — SHEL 932:*72*
secret c. in which he can kneel — ACKR 4:*55*
stand at the jaws of c. — AMIS 17:*86*
Stygian c. forlorn — MILT 682:*96*
cavern Happy field or mossy c. — KEATS 544:*48*
caverns c. measureless to man — COLE 274:*12*
out of the c. of rain — SHEL 928:*84*
Sand-strewn c., cool and deep — ARNO 36:*55*
twice ten Thousand C. — KEATS 544:*42*
caves c. for thousands of years — NIET 727:*71*
c. that smelt like — THOM 1012:*95*
convictions…are c. — FITZ 390:*92*
desert c., With wild thyme — MILT 684:*40*
sunny pleasure-dome with c. of ice! — COLE 275:*15*

caviar do anything for c. — KISS 566:*43*
know about champagne and c. — FERB 385:*8*
more…consumed than c. — SPIL 959:*45*
'Twas c. to the general — SHAK 890:*11*
unhappy before eating c. — KORDA 568:*78*
cavity into the c.…cast all weapons — DEKA 313:*8*
Cawdor The Thane of C. lives — SHAK 907:*21*
Caxtons C. are mechanical birds — RAINE 800:*8*
Ceasar word of C. — SHAK 884:*52*
cease cannot c. to be — TAYL 992:*23*
O c.! must hate and death return — SHEL 932:*65*
whose follies c. with their youth — PITT 771:*62*
Cecilia Blessed C., appear in visions — AUDEN 48:*79*
Cecily C., Gertrude, Magdalen — ROSS 824:*83*
cedar breaks in the c. and sycamore — KEND 550:*49*
moonlit c. what a burst — ARNO 37:*82*
cedars brotherhoods of c. — BROW 197:*26*
cedarwood go of …Sandalwood, c. — MASE 662:*37*
ceiling crashing through the c. — LERN 597:*87*
long enough to draw on the c. — CHES 258:*13*
celebrate c. myself — WHIT 1072:*76*
something artists ought to c. — FROST 407:*3*
to c. the event — JERR 521:*17*
celebrated solaced and c. — BACON 60:*40*
That c.…Nobleman — GILB 426:*95*
celebration c. of man — THOM 1010:*72*
celebrations make great c. — COLU 278:*63*
celebrity a c. is like being raped — MCEN 629:*11*
Moriarty of mathematical c. — DOYLE 344:*8*
nice thing about being a c. — KISS 566:*40*
celery thrives in the dark. Like c. — HUXL 506:*50*
celestial c. and my soul's idol — SHAK 889:*90*
do c. chores — CULL 298:*67*
high c. flavour — BYRON 223:*46*
white c. thought — VAUG 1040:*15*
Celia Come, my C. — JONS 534:*85*
celibacy c. has no pleasures — JOHN 527:*24*
c. is…a muddy horsepond — PEAC 762:*27*
closer to c. than not — WYLIE 1104:*50*
rebuked him for his c. — OFLA 736:*96*
cell Each in his narrow c. — GRAY 442:*64*
Find out some uncouth c. — ONEI 739:*49*
for each man a solitary c. — MILT 682:*96*
gown and mossy c. — MILT 683:*16*
kill each other c. by c. — MAIL 639:*76*
madman in his padded c. — NABO 717:*98*
Minister's room is like a padded c. — CROS 298:*64*
outside of this c. — PUIG 794:*18*
tight hot c. of their hearts — BOGAN 171:*58*
cellar born in a c. — CONG 280:*12*
warm delicious c. — WHITE 1070:*31*
cello An electric c.? — SEGO 857:*31*
cells These little grey c. — CHRI 261:*70*
Celt hysterics of the C. — TENN 1000:*58*
celtic C. Demos rose a Demon — TENN 1005:*65*
C. genius of Wales — ARNO 39:*20*
chair of C. — ARNO 39:*21*
Rangers and C. had both lost — DODD 334:*43*
cement c. of the universe — SELF 857:*37*
floor the meadows with c. — MACL 634:*81*
cemented c. with tears — HERB 474:*8*
cemeteries buried two great c. — SHAW 926:*43*
Corde avoided c. — BELL 88:*39*
cemetery allot a portion…as a c. — HAWT 461:*69*
c. is an open space — SHEL 930:*33*
c. of dead ideas — UNAM 1035:*41*
Help me down C. Road — LARK 581:*10*
new plot in the c. — DAY 310:*51*
only place…is a c. — GENET 418:*77*
Running a c. — ANON 29:*6*
cenotaph laugh at my own c. — SHEL 928:*84*
censor ask the writer to c. — KELM 549:*32*
c. foreign news — WALEY 1049:*51*

censor (*contd.*)
c. the gleam in my eye — LAUG 583:42
censorious c. said that she slept — SAKI 837:5
censors C. are paid — TREV 1026:49
censorship instead of…'c.' — MAMET 643:44
censure every trade save c. — BYRON 219:60
exposed to c. — JOHN 526:4
shame or c. free — JOHN 525:79
Take each man's c. — SHAK 888:65
census c. taker — TALLY 990:91
Irish C. — MACR 638:53
centaur ant's a c. in his…world — POUND 786:84
real C. — ACHE 3:31
centaurs They're c., though women — SHAK 903:35
centipede c. was happy quite — CRAS 296:28
Central Mount Stuart name it C. — STUA 980:8
centre at their hearts the fire's c. — SPEN 956:72
c., and enjoy bright day — MILT 683:28
C. and soul of every sphere — HOLM 486:98
c. cannot hold — YEATS 1106:77
c. is giving way — FOCH 395:83
c. of true religiousness — EINS 363:67
From the c.…to the sea — COWP 292:38
hid…Within the c. — SHAK 889:92
muddy c. before we breathed — STEV 971:52
poor c. of man's actions — BACON 58:90
proclaiming himself the c. — ATWO 44:18
real c.of the household — SHAW 925:14
self-balanced on her c. — MILT 691:86
slightly left of c. — FRYE 409:25
system of which they were the c. — DICK 323:90
centrelight see the blue c. pop — KERO 553:12
cents forty c. a flask — LEAC 588:30
owe me ten c., sir — NABO 717:15
Today I feel like thirty c. — ADE 8:42
wouldn't give you two c. — BUCH 202:30
centuary Sociology…in last half c.
— VAND 1039:95
strange thing…turn of the c. — WEIL 1061:78
centuries All c. but this — GILB 425:85
c. of rebelliousness behind him — PRIE 790:42
country 'tis of c. — CUMM 299:33
customs…evolved over the c. — POWE 788:18
forty c. look down — NAPO 718:24
how shall I lie through c. — BROW 198:39
in process of c. — QUIL 797:59
One three c. removed — CULL 299:69
Through what wild c. — DELA 314:24
Weary wi' c. — SMITH 949:60
well-wrought c. — ARLO 34:37
while c. fled? — SASS 845:38
centurion c. answered and said — BIBLE 136:64
c., which stood over against him — BIBLE 141:71
century absolve this end of the c. — LEVI 600:26
American nineteenth c. — THUR 1019:42
anger from the nineteenth c. — LESS 598:99
born in this c. — KENN 550:64
Britisher…early 19th c. — MACL 634:88
c. of active service — MOUN 711:13
c. of the common man — ROUS 827:30
c. on which are entering — WALL 1050:67
c. that began with golden age — VIDAL 1044:71
guard for half a c. — MOLT 699:37
horror of the Twentieth C. — MAIL 639:85
In the later nineteenth c. — GILL 426:2
intellectual life of our c. — ARNO 38:10
into the 20th c. — STEV 973:83
man walks across his c. — LEAC 588:31
new c. begins — MANN 646:84
nineteenth c. is great — HUGO 502:91
nineteenth c. — MACL 635:97
No writer before the…19th c. — WAUGH -101:5
problem of the twentieth c. — DUBO 353:5
social problem of the twentieth c. — SMALL 943:61

century (*contd.*)
twentieth c. had a capacity — DUDEK 354:20
working for 16th C. Fox — RENO 806:6
Cerberus C. and blackest midnight — MILT 682:96
damn them with King C. — SHAK 877:91
cerebrums c. and smaller adrenal — MENC 670:84
ceremonial refined, restricted, c. — REAG 803:57
ceremonious c. politeness — TWAIN 1032:59
ceremony C., circus, farce — SCHL 848:75
c. known as afternoon tea — JAMES 516:14
C. is an invention — LAMB 576:24
c. of innocence drowned — YEATS 1106:77
depending on the c. — JOHN 524:65
that reverend c. — JONS 535:91
Ceres C. will join in the dance — SITW 941:9
laughing C. re-assume the land — POPE 779:23
cermonies c. never wear shorts — MURR 715:76
certain c. because it is impossible — TERT 1006:79
c. leisure of study — GERB 420:98
c.…something to be sincere about — DRIB 346:44
Death…is c. to all — SHAK 877:96
laws of mathematics…are not c. — EINS 363:76
nothing can be said to be c. — FRAN 402:12
nothing is c. — BINY 162:10
certainties man will begin with c. — BACON 54:6
certainty c. of power — DAYL 310:54
C. C. Feeling. Joy — PASC 758:81
no longer wish to have c. — KAFKA 541:88
certificate need a medical c. — LLOY 608:55
Cervantes C.…puts me to sleep — GONZ 434:53
cervix os c. of a woman — SCHR 850:7
cesspool c. deep — CHAP 252:77
leaving you…in this sweet c. — SAND 842:81
London, that great c. — DOYLE 343:83
cetacean Noble and generous c. — KIPL 562:73
Cezanne All C.'s apples I would give
— AUDEN 46:54
chafe c. and toss in the spray — ARNO 36:54
chaff see that the c. is printed — HUBB 498:6
two bushels of c. — SHAK 874:9
ungodly…are like the c. — BIBLE 113:29
chaffinch C. sings on the orchard — BROW 198:36
chagrin of c. at his own — RYLE 834:54
chain adds a link to my c. — ROCH 816:61
c. I forged in life — DICK 323:86
c. of being — EMER 376:45
c. of gold — SCOTT 854:79
c. of strong necessity? — SPEN 957:5
hanging in a golden c. — MILT 689:28
lengthening c. — GOLD 432:96
Such words as 'c.' or 'train' — JAMES 517:40
tuppence for your old watch c. — COLL 276:37
chains bind our souls with secular c. — MILT 686:80
Bound by gold c. — TENN 1004:47
captive with c. — MILT 690:67
C. and Slaverie! — BURNS 212:37
c. fell off — WESL 1066:58
c. of one's own transient desires — EINS 363:63
c. of slavery — GRIL 447:62
c. of the sea — WALC 1048:39
C. tie us down — WORD 1099:64
clock with weights and c. — COLUM 278:62
everywhere he is in c. — ROUS 827:32
forever in c. — PAZ 761:23
gilded c. and sordid affluence — PITT 771:68
in c., in pains — STUA 980:10
Jazz…in c. — WHIT 1072:67
Man…held only by slightest c. — EDGE 360:26
Newspapers…everywhere in c. — SCOTT 852:38
not kept in c. — WEBS 1060:53
not so heavy…as a prisoner's c. — EISE 364:81
nothing to lose but their c. — MARX 660:15
safer to be in c. — KAFKA 541:87
self-fashioned c. of slavery — MANS 647:96

chains (*contd.*)
Shake your c. — SHEL 928:80
woman must wear c. — FARQ 383:72
worse than c., Dungeon — MILT 694:40
chair a too easy c. — POPE 783:8
age of the editorial c. — MACL 635:97
c. is not a caste — HUGO 502:88
c.…judged by one's pants — ANON 27:62
edge of the c. of Literature — THUR 1018:15
Jumping from the c. — HUNT 505:29
knocks over a c. — TOYN 1024:17
passed up towards the C. — RUSH 829:71
sat in my c. and written — WODE 1089:7
seated in a c. — VALE 1038:84
sunny c. — STEV 971:38
tears and a sedan c. — DICK 321:29
The C. she sat in — ELIOT 368:85
chairman Asked by the c. — STRA 979:98
C. looked dissatisfied — MIN 695:62
c. of the Senate Ethics Committee — BRYAN 201:13
chairmen hooligans…92 club c. — CLOU 271:51
chaise-longue hurly-burly of the c. — CAMP 226:11
chalice c. from the palace — PANA 752:75
chalk c. cliffs of Dover — BALD 65:11
challenge guts to take on a big c. — RODG 818:86
What a difficult c.! — PEI 764:2
challenged c. you to …leap — RABAN 798:76
If one is c. — GALB 411:74
challengers C. of oblivion — JEFF 519:80
challenges is a set of c. — KENN 550:61
chamber c. of my soul — SCHA 847:60
in the c. of consciousness — JAMES 516:19
many a listening c. — SHEL 927:62
nimbly in a lady's c. — SHAK 862:46
One need not be a C. — DICK 328:5
retired into a c. — AUBR 45:37
stalking in my c. — WYATT 1103:30
throw myself down in my C. — DONNE 339:28
Chamberlain less than Wilt C. — PACK 749:25
Neville C. had greatness — CANN 230:67
chambermaid in the arms of a c. — JOHN 530:1
chambermaids worms that are thy c. — SHAK 870:24
chambers c. of the East — BLAKE 165:55
whispering c. of Imagination — DICK 323:83
chameleon c. on plaid — HOOV 490:65
free to be a c. — SART 844:6
chameleons C. feed on light — SHEL 929:8
champ C. and chafe — ARNO 36:54
champagne C.! …one deserves it — POL 777:63
c. and the stars — FITZ 390:99
c. that has stood for five days — ATTL 44:15
drink c. all night and not get drunk — BOHL 171:63
Fighting is like c. — MITC 697:88
I get no kick from c. — PORT 784:30
know about c. and caviar — FERB 385:8
like c. or high heels — BENN 91:90
not a c. teetotaller — SHAW 920:14
sufficient c. — PARK 755:23
champion siding c. conscience — MILT 683:25
this pretended c. — PARN 756:40
champions mould-breaking c. — THOM 1014:35
Champmédy bury my tongue at C. — BENET 90:62
chance ain't got…no c. — HEMI 471:32
All c., direction — POPE 780:41
arbiter C. governs all — MILT 688:25
art, not c. — POPE 778:84
c. as a one-armed blind man — WODE 1089:93
c. favours us — PAST 759:85
c. of being drowned — JOHN 527:25
c. to read them at all — THOR 1016:66
decent actor waiting for a c. — FLYNN 395:81
either in nativity, c., or death — SHAK 878:23
element of c.…is expelled — FISKE 390:86
entirely a matter of c. — AUST 51:35

chance (*contd.*)
Fate, Time, Occasion, C. — SHEL 930:23
From c., and death, and mutability — SHEL 930:25
game of c. — CAPO 231:80
had our last c. — MACA 621:71
haven't got a c. — FIEL 388:56
honest...sometimes by c. — SHAK 912:39
I decided to c. it — PRIE 790:42
If I c. to talk — SHAK 917:49
in contempt of c. happenings — RABE 799:91
mixture of c. and choice — FRIE 405:54
my c. to see the King beheaded — PEPYS 765:62
necessity and c. Approach — MILT 691:84
No gifts from c. — ARNO 36:58
No girls, no legs...no c. — ANON 26:50
now to prove our c. — DRAY 345:35
only c. of eminence — SHAW 925:26
skirts of happy c. — TENN 999:44
through change and c. — BRID 187:43
time and c. happeneth — BIBLE 123:35
Under the bludgeonings of c. — HENL 472:57
various turns of c. below — DRYD 351:71
will never abolish c. — MALL 642:20
chancellor C. of the Exchequer — HOWE 497:94
king, and a c., and parliament-men — SCOTT 855:92
Lord High C. in his High Court — DICK 324:18
Chancery C. Lane young man — GILB 424:70
chances take c. for peace — DULL 354:25
chandeliered mute c. isolation — CAPO 231:88
change beyond her c. of life — HOPE 490:72
birth is...incipient c. — OVID 747:3
bugles of social c. — HANDY 455:69
Busily seeking with a continual c. — WYATT 1103:30
can't c. — GUIR 448:80
certain relief in c. — IRVI 513:67
c., but I cannot die — SHEL 928:84
c., continuing c., inevitable c. — ASIM 42:74
C. in a trice — SWIN 987:32
c. is always nice — EURI 380:33
C. is not made without — JOHN 526:3
c. minds — KING 557:71
c. my state with kings' — SHAK 913:57
c. of consciousness — GINS 428:33
C. proves true — I 510:25
continual occupation and c. — AUST 52:68
ever-whirling wheel Of C. — SPEN 959:40
fundamental c. — GORB 435:57
great, growing engine of c. — TOFF 1022:86
how nigh Your c. — MILT 690:57
leave it to a torrent of c. — CHES 258:8
Life may c. — SHEL 932:62
more things c....stay the same — KARR 542:10
nature's law to c. — ROCH 817:63
necessary not to c. — FALK 382:55
Neither to c., nor falter, nor repent — SHEL 930:27
not the man we have to c. — PRICE 789:33
O the heavy c. — MILT 684:40
once that c. is effected — ORWE 743:12
people c. and forget — HELL 468:96
protest against c. — STEI 966:60
realise...they can't c. — STEIN 965:36
religion, knavery and c. — BEHN 85:66
ringing grooves of c. — TENN 996:83
Speech is the small c. — MERE 671:3
state without the means of some c. — BURKE 207:26
the many c. and pass — SHEL 931:50
Things c. — VIAN 1043:42
through c. and chance — BRID 187:43
thrown about loosely like small c. — MENC 669:43
Time, Occasion, Chance, and C.? — SHEL 930:23
too much c. in too short a time — TOFF 1022:85
which involves a great c. — TROL 1028:88
wonderful c. from wives and work — EWART 381:44
changed Are we correct to have c. — ASAHI 40:49

changed (*contd.*)
c. upon the blue guitar — STEV 971:49
not c. overnight — KAIKO 541:93
Nothing has c. since — HUGH 500:37
shall all be c. — BIBLE 151:72
changelessness [God's] c. means — TAYL 992:23
changes cause of as many c. — RUSS 832:20
c. in circumstances — FRIE 405:52
c. we fear — JOHN 526:9
c. we think we see — FROST 406:71
c. with the next block — SHAK 878:27
c. within a biologic system — SELYE 858:41
Do not...make any c. — ANON 27:66
don't drop...make c. — SHAN 918:71
endure sudden c. — RABE 799:83
Enormous c. — PALEY 751:58
Her plot hath many c. — QUAR 796:52
monthly c. in her circled orb — SHAK 869:91
with foreseeing the c. — KEYN 554:34
world's a scene of c. — COWL 291:13
changing constant in a c. world — JOUV 537:37
loved to be c. — DRAY 345:37
Chankly Hills of the C. Bore — LEAR 589:51
channel Butting through the C. — MASE 662:38
going to watch the shopping c. — COUP 289:85
hot slimy c. slowly glide — CRAB 294:83
channels forced into c. of evil — FAUL 383:80
narrow straight c. — RANJ 801:27
run freely through its c. — STER 969:7
chant c., ye little birds — BURNS 212:22
chaos Be no longer a c. — CARL 235:57
begged God to have retained C. — EVANS 381:37
bit of primordial c. — WELLS 1064:25
born to make c. cosmic — BEER 83:28
C., a rough unordered mass. — OVID 747:97
C. is come again — SHAK 899:29
C. is the score — MILL 677:16
c. of human experience — MACL 634:87
c. of the mind — SNYD 951:82
c. of vacancy — DELA 314:32
C. often breeds life — ADAMS 5:76
c. remembered in tranquillity — THUR 1019:46
C. umpire sits — MILT 688:25
God dawned on C. — SHEL 931:40
means of overcoming c. — RICH 810:63
must have c. in one — NIET 728:79
Not C., not The darkest pit — WORD 1100:77
reduce a c. of experience — GREE 444:21
reign of c. and old Night — MILT 688:5
stillness in the midst of c. — BELL 88:26
thy dread empire, C.! — POPE 783:11
wish for nothing but c. — HITL 482:29
chap Big c. with a small moustache — WODE 1089:5
c. seems bent on cheatin' — HALI 452:25
c. who doesn't care much — WAUGH 1057:83
common old working c. — FYFFE 410:63
decent c. never lets his public down — FLYNN 395:80
My dear c.! — GILB 426:1
tubby little c. — WODE 1089:97
chapel c. was built in the midst — BLAKE 167:90
Devil always builds a c. there — DEFOE 312:75
finished that c. I was painting — MICH 673:33
chapels all churches or c. in New York — BENN 92:6
chaperoning implacably c. a ball — GILL 426:4
chaplain twice a day the C. called — WILDE 1078:99
chaplet So rich a c....to weave — MARV 658:80
Chapman Colonel C.'s adventures — WAVE 1058:11
chappie c. is rummy — WODE 1089:87
chappit Dinna be c. back — SCOTT 855:95
chaps biography is about C. — BENT 93:22
chapter approach c. One each year — FRAN 401:93
c. of accidents — CHES 257:81
c. on the fall of the Rupee — WILDE 1078:86
now read another c. — MACH 631:35

chapters Whole c....one paragraph — CHAN 250:38
character man of good c. — SHAW 924:4
all novels...deal with c. — WOOLF 1092:58
American c. — MACC 625:45
As the c. is — AELI 9:51
begin to think him a c. — LEAC 589:38
Being another c. — GIEL 423:50
by the content of their c. — KING 557:76
c. and compassion — NEWM 724:33
c....bearing a child alone — QUAY 796:53
c. in them that bear rule — POTT 785:44
c. is a...cultivated will — NOVA 732:38
c. is destiny — ELIOT 365:23
c. it gives itself — HAZL 463:7
c. like Samson, Hercules — SIEG 937:67
c. of a family — STER 969:94
c. of those who handle it — AUST 52:56
c....sagacious blue-stocking — MACA 624:21
c. so entirely distorted — MILL 675:76
c. undecided — KEATS 545:55
c. who would sell his grandmother — GRANT 438:3
contempt for my c. and opinions — SHAW 921:23
dignity of soul and c. — CARL 234:41
do justice to my c. — EMMET 378:81
effect on the Parisian c. — HAZL 463:10
emerges a formidable c. — ANGE 19:20
even in one's own c. to himself — WILL 1081:66
for our c. — PITT 771:72
hate and c. assassination — SMITH 948:21
hundred pounds...bad for my c. — CONN 283:60
ideas disintegrate, his c. changes — DIDE 330:42
identity with the c. — HAZL 463:96
leave my c. behind me — SHER 933:95
man' c....abused — THAC 1006:84
moral c....was full of promise — DICK 322:70
more c. than the combined heroes — BROY 201:6
more powerful...than the worth of c. — ALCO 12:99
my c. I despare for — FLEM 394:64
my thoughts I'll c. — SHAK 886:97
one c. in literature — PAGE 749:31
perfection of c. — AURE 50:27
problems with your main c. — ANON 28:25
reputation, c., person — LOVE 615:70
simplification of the human c. — FORS 398:45
Sports do not build c. — BROUN 194:51
stable ego of the c. — LAWR 585:65
stamp on c. on the mind — JEFF 520:97
style to one's c. — NIET 728:75
tell a lot about a fellow's c. — REAG 803:62
think ourselves wise about his c. — ELIOT 365:7
to her possession of c. — MERE 671:15
true index of a man's c. — CONN 283:76
Virtue...is a state of c. — ARIS 34:27
want of c. — SHAW 920:6
weak spot or two in a c. — HOLM 486:99
well as the main c. — ROBB 813:8
What is c. — JAMES 516:21
Whatever its position or c. — SCOTT 852:34
when it most reflects the c. — HOPP 493:13
without...stain upon your c. — ADAMS 6:93
women have no c. — POPE 781:70
writing of any c. — WELTY 1065:49
characteristic c. of philosophy — RUSS 832:16
c. of the design — LEWO 603:73
c. of the really great novelist — BENN 91:85
nothing so c. as its hat — HOLM 486:91
one commanding c. — DISR 333:20
one common c. — DURK 357:71
characteristics c. of the present age — DISR 333:5
characterization safest general c. — WHIT 1071:59
characters Absurdist plays...two c. — ADAM 4:60
altogether new c. — TROL 1028:87
C. in Search of an Author — PIRA 770:49
c. of hell to trace — GRAY 443:84

characters (*contd.*)
comedy paints c. HUGO 501:70
consideration of c. JOHN 529:80
egnraved in...unerasable c. LAUT 584:50
four c. wide CHAP 252:77
give a mind to your c. DIDE 329:23
great c. are formed ADAMS 4:62
high c. are drawn POPE 781:55
I describe imperfect c. BRON 191:11
immense number of c. JOHN 530:99
learn from those c. DOMI 335:56
most dissimilar c. SMITH 946:95
Too many c. AUST 51:47
void of all c. LOCKE 609:72
Charadrius Jemuel rejoice with C. SMART 944:64
charcoal drew...with piece of c. VASA 1040:8
Philosophy...kind of c. appetite CLEV 269:11
charge c. that an idea is radical GALB 411:74
meant to c. me GERH 420:3
most serious c. KRUT 570:9
One c. alone we give RUSS 833:34
One thing alone I c. you DU 353:10
that is the c. ...kissing! PACK 749:28
this exorbitant c. KEMB 549:36
charges ceaseless c. WILL 1080:44
revolutionary cavalry c. PAVL 761:22
Charing Cross I went out to C. C. PEPYS 765:62
chariot Bring me my c. of fire! BLAKE 168:19
burneth the c. in the fire BIBLE 116:74
c. is an empty hazelnut SHAK 868:74
c. of fire BIBLE 111:73
first Sunday in a new c. CONG 282:44
gal in a bang-up c. DICK 327:86
Time's winged c. LINK 606:25
Time's winged c. MARV 658:73
Why is his c. so long in coming? BIBLE 109:14
chariot-wheel axletree of the c.-w. BACON 59:28
chariots burneth the c. in the fire BOOK 177:74
Some trust in c. BIBLE 114:46
charisma C. without substance CAMP 226:9
charitable single men...more c. BACON 57:60
charities cold c. of man to man CRAB 293:74
some thirty c. TENN 996:95
charity called c., the soul MILT 693:30
c. for all LINC 605:6
C. is the power of defending CHES 258:96
c. of its silence EMMET 378:81
c. shall cover the multitude of sins BIBLE 156:82
damnation of c. WEST 1067:87
Do not ask me for c. ADCO 6:96
greatest of these is c. BIBLE 150:62
little earth, for c. SHAK 918:64
lives in the spirit of c. ROOS 821:37
mankind's concern is c. POPE 780:31
Miss Prism, c.! WILDE 1078:88
movement of pure c. WEIL 1062:84
What is that c. worth MARI 652:77
who has great c. KEMP 549:38
Charles grand to hear Baby C. SCOTT 855:1
[Prince C.] is entitled to be JAY 519:76
Charlie C. he's my darling BURNS 213:46
Charlotte love for C. THAC 1007:1
charm C....a sort of bloom BARR 73:46
c. from every pore LERN 597:90
c....getting the answer yes CAMUS 229:57
c. he never so wisely BOOK 177:78
C. never made a rooster ACHE 3:49
c. of all power is modesty ALCO 12:97
c. of novelty FLAU 392:39
Completing the c. ELIOT 371:38
Discreet C. of Bourgeoisie BUNU 204:62
impregnated by Brownie Vernon's c. QUIR 798:72
Music oft hath such a c. SHAK 897:86
no c. to me PERTH 767:3

charm (*contd.*)
paused on every c. GOLD 433:9
What c. can soothe GOLD 432:5
woman loses a c. JOYCE 538:54
charmer Were t'other dear c. away! GAY 417:59
charming beauty's c. SCOTT 855:97
c. people have something to conceal CONN 283:63
c. thing to meet JAMES 516:16
c. to totter into vogue WALP 1051:84
no matter how c. a bluff FITZ 391:12
so c. and agreeable ETHE 380:16
so c. as books SMITH 949:47
charms Against whose c. SHAK 879:36
bewitched with some ill c. WALL 1050:73
c. are all o'erthrown SHAK 917:44
C. strike the sight POPE 779:3
Do not all c. fly KEATS 546:80
fields and flocks have c. CRAB 293:71
Music alone with sudden c. CONG 282:47
O Solitude! where are the c. COWP 292:38
still thy verse has c. SCOTT 853:53
With all thy c. MILT 684:34
chart enigma of the fever c. ELIOT 371:51
on faithful c. to mark WENT 1065:54
charter c. of thy worth SHAK 914:78
condemn thee c. INNO 512:56
chartered through each c. street BLAKE 167:92
Chartres best friend at C. LEWIS 601:43
C., our Notre Dame RODR 819:89
Chartreuse produced...green C. SAKI 837:97
chase c. had a beast in view DRYD 352:97
c. rather than capture WELLS 1064:32
creatures of the c. TENN 996:93
chaser c. of white and blue ACHE 3:33
nuance...is a wide c. COND 279:83
save himself from the c. BANN 70:2
chaste be amorous, but c. BYRON 219:61
c., and unexpressive she SHAK 886:98
c. as unsunned snow SHAK 916:5
C. goddess ROMA 821:27
C. to her husband POPE 781:72
English text is c. GIBB 421:30
Never shall be free Nor ever c. DONNE 338:3
what is c. in Constantinople FORD 396:2
chastity c. of honour BURKE 207:32
c.'s the jewel SHAK 901:78
clothed on with c. TENN 995:67
Grant me c. AUGU 49:8
chat had a c. with him ROGE 820:12
wish we could c. longer TALLY 990:92
Chatfield bloody ships today, C. BEAT 79:58
Chattanooga C. Choo-choo GORD 435:64
chattels Look to my c. SHAK 880:78
chatter insignificant c. of the world TROL 1027:67
Women should...avoid idle c. ANON 21:63
chattering Where the satyrs are c. SITW 941:9
Chatterly C. ban And the Beatles LARK 581:12
Chatterton C., the marvellous boy WORD 1097:44
Chaucer C., well of English undefiled
SPEN 959:33
exuberance of C. HAMER 453:38
old famous poet C. SPEN 957:95
chauffeur could have elected my c. KENN 552:97
chauffeurs simply as our c. SUN 982:39
cheap doesn't mean you're not c. SEIB 857:32
flesh and blood so c.! HOOD 489:47
life...so astonishingly c. DILL 330:52
cheat c. at cards genteelly BOSW 180:32
c. you yet BURNS 209:74
fancy cannot c. so well KEATS 548:19
Honesty was a c. OTWAY 746:83
if both sides agree to c. FRY 408:11
it's so lucrative to c. CLOU 271:49
nothing so monosyllabic as to c. FRY 408:16

cheat (*contd.*)
sweet c. gone DELA 314:32
To c. a man is nothing GAY 417:58
cheated pleasure...Of being c. BUTL 217:20
cheating bent on c. himself HALI 452:54
c. their masters KIER 556:54
cheats all c. and liars JONES 533:56
c. of the movie screen MAIL 639:68
checked Be c. for silence SHAK 901:66
checkerboards Dallas naught but c. MAIL 639:84
checks c. and balances in government ANON 28:17
cheek call a blush into the c. DICK 327:21
c. of night SHAK 868:82
c. wistfully pressed against the pane SCHR 850:1
chorus, c. to c. ROET 819:97
Feed on her damask c. SHAK 894:15
gentle breeze...fans my c. WORD 1095:17
harlot's c. SHAK 890:21
hollow c. or faded eye TENN 997:9
slapped us on our c. KHRU 556:51
smite the c. on thy right c. BIBLE 134:42
tears down Pluto's c. MILT 682:11
thy cold Wan c. WORD 1100:90
withered c. SCOTT 853:42
cheeks c. and eyes as bright ROSS 823:67
c. are covered with paint NASH 719:45
compare the c....to a rose DALI 303:46
crack your c.! SHAK 903:17
Famine is in thy c. SHAK 870:21
Fat, ruddy c. Augustus had HOFF 484:57
mask...hides our c. DUNB 354:33
natural ruby of your c. SHAK 909:62
purs lolled his c. LANG 579:72
roses see I in her c. SHAK 915:92
stain my man's c. SHAK 902:15
tears run down her c. ANON 23:86
cheels Facts are c. BURNS 209:75
cheer Be of good c. BIBLE 146:66
c. up immensely THAT 1008:20
C. up—the worst JOHN 524:61
drink wine, and eat good c. MIDD 673:40
Greet the unseen with a c.! BROW 200:3
piped with merry c. BLAKE 166:62
scarce forbear to c. MACA 624:17
cheer-up Music is the great c.-u. ODETS 736:91
cheerful C. as when she tortured ROBI 815:33
far more c. and hopeful HOLM 486:2
God loveth a c. giver BIBLE 151:84
In April one seldom seems c. COPE 287:50
merry heart maketh a c. BIBLE 121:79
cheerfulness c. fixed and permanent ADDI 7:17
c. was always breaking in EDWA 362:53
cheeriness chintzy c. BETJ 99:25
cheerio C., here I go PARR 756:42
cheerleader a c. for selfishness ONEI 740:67
cheerly But c., c. KEATS 545:61
cheers give three c. GILB 423:55
sounds no worse than c. HOUS 494:47
two c. for democracy FORS 399:53
cheese 246 different types of c. DEGA 313:99
apples and c. KIPL 564:12
baiting a mouse-trap with c. SAKI 838:15
Botticelli's a c.! PUNCH 795:32
C. for dessert BRAC 183:70
C., milk's leap toward immortality FADI 382:52
I do not like green c. CHES 260:44
I've dreamed of c. STEV 975:30
maggot...born i' the rotten c. ELIOT 365:8
no end of Stilton C. LEAR 590:56
cheeses ate the c. out of the vats BROW 197:32
Cheevy Miniver C., born too late ROBI 815:28
Miniver C., child of scorn ROBI 814:26
chef celestial c. MACB 624:32
Chekhov C. of the suburbs LEON 596:68

Chekhov (*contd.*)
What C. saw in our failure — PRIT 791:70
Chelsea was a C. morning — MITC 696:82
chemise Petticoat said to the C. — PARK 753:88
chemist c., fiddler, statesman — DRYD 349:23
physician and c. are soldiers — PAST 759:89
sold at ev'ry c. — FORM 397:27
chemistry by c. and machinery — SHAW 921:35
resort to physics and c. — MENC 670:81
Shakespeare…weak in c. — WELLS 1064:24
Chens C. had been living in the UK — MO 698:9
cheque c. and the postal order — AUDEN 46:47
general statement is like a c. — POUND 786:73
cheques alive and writting c. — MONT 701:60
cherish love, c., and obey — BOOK 176:50
to love and to c. — BOOK 176:49
cherished c. and hoarded — MENC 669:63
fox…so c. and locked up — SHAK 876:71
cheroot whackin' white c. — KIPL 561:38
cherries c.…which none may buy — CAMP 228:39
c., hairshirts, pinks — LOWE 617:10
Cherrill marriages to Virginia C. — NIVEN 730:6
cherry c. blossoms in the spring — ANON 26:51
c. now I'm hung — HOUS 494:39
early c. — JONS 535:2
see the c. hung with snow — HOUS 494:41
taste the ripened c. — CAREW 232:15
cherry-stones carve heads upon c.-s. — JOHN 532:29
cherub Proud limitary c. — MILT 690:67
cherubin heaven's c. horsed — SHAK 908:32
cherubs poor black c. — CULL 298:67
Cheshire cosmic C. cat — HUXL 508:94
chess c. tournament disguised — CONN 282:50
C. is the gymnasium — LENIN 595:53
go mad; but c. players do — CHES 258:4
kind of collective c. — BARZ 75:98
Life's too short for c. — BYRON 224:71
populations like c. pieces — MILL 678:26
Soviet game is c. — SHUL 936:32
win gracefully at c. — MILNE 680:68
chess-board call the c.-b. white — BROW 199:55
chessboard world…a c. — ORWE 742:99
chessman way you'd look at a c. — JARR 518:61
chest best jewel from time's c. — SHAK 914:68
childhood is a locked c. — MISH 696:77
dead man's c. — STEV 975:28
His c. against — SMART 944:69
no medals on my c. — EISE 364:89
Chesterton Antifeminists, from C. — WEST 1068:88
chestnut O c. tree — YEATS 1106:80
showers betumble the c. spikes — HARDY 457:13
spreading c.-tree — LONG 611:97
chestnuts c. in her lap — SHAK 906:12
Chevalier Charlie…the young C. — BURNS 213:46
Chevy Drove my C. — MACL 633:62
chewing gum like lending c. g. — TAFT 989:81
Chianti a nice C. — TALLY 990:91
chiaroscuro c. of romance — MAUG 665:89
chic C. is a convent — BROY 201:8
Radical c. — WOLFE 1090:23
Chicago C. is a great American city — MAIL 639:84
now it's on to C. — KENN 552:3
Sexual Perversity in C. — MAMET 643:42
stock-yards at C. — HEMI 470:17
chicken c. whose head has — MITF 697:3
Gin and c. helpless — BARK 71:17
Mere c. feed — MARX 659:95
Some c., some neck! — CHUR 264:20
chickens beside the white c. — WILL 1082:85
c. are coming home — MACA 621:78
Curses are like young c. — SOUT 954:36
more troublesome and costly than a c. — SHAW 924:94
Our semantic c. — MAMET 643:50
chid you'll never be c. — EDGE 360:31

chide almost c. God — SHAK 886:19
channerin' worm doth c. — BALL 68:61
snarling trumpets 'gan to c. — KEATS 546:86
will not always c. — BIBLE 118:12
chief Hail to the C. — SCOTT 853:62
sinners; of whom I am c. — BIBLE 153:28
chiefs c. of the Irish Brigade — DAVIS 309:38
Confederated C. — DEKA 313:8
chieftain c. to the Highlands bound — CAMP 227:29
Great C. o' the Puddin-race! — BURNS 210:84
chiels couthy c. at e'ening meet — FERG 386:17
Chigwell first sense…of God…at C. — AUBR 45:37
child A C. will make two Dishes — SWIFT 985:99
active c. do deeds of youth — SHAK 913:60
am but a little c. — BIBLE 111:55
an aggravating c. — BELL 87:11
as a grown c. — POUND 785:54
ashamed to be my father's c.! — SHAK 874:26
be a very wicked little c. — DICK 322:59
before fact as a little c. — HUXL 508:96
Better is a poor and a wise c. — BIBLE 123:25
Can a woman forget her suckling c. — BIBLE 126:95
care for the c.'s rattle — JOHN 528:50
Cheevy, c. of scorn — ROBI 814:26
c. a mandrake root — DONNE 336:75
c.'s a plaything for an hour — LAMB 576:11
c. cannot possibly go on — KEMB 549:37
c. comes to know evil — MITC 696:78
C.! do not throw this book about — BELL 86:96
c. ephemeral — AUDEN 47:74
c. from the womb — SHEL 928:84
c. has a first claim — JUVE 540:83
C., if it were thine error — TENN 998:14
c. imposes on the man — DRYD 351:55
C. is father of the Man — WORD 1097:42
c. is grown and puts away — MILL 676:93
c. of eight is many-sided — DOUG 342:68
c. of forty years ago — THOM 1009:49
c. of its time — KAND 541:96
c. of our grandmother Eve — SHAK 865:11
c. of the mighty bush — FRAN 402:16
C. on earth for me — BETJ 100:47
c. ought to be of the party — AUST 50:31
C. Roland to the dark tower — SHAK 903:25
c. should always say — STEV 975:33
c. was dear — COLE 273:81
c. was delyverd unto Merlyn — MALO 642:24
c. whose parent is unkent — SPEN 957:92
Come close to me, my darling c. — BRON 191:7
communism is the illegitimate c. — ATTL 44:13
Credulity…the c.'s strength — LAMB 577:34
devoured the infant c. — HOUS 496:86
difference between conceiving a c. — MAIL 639:86
draw nearer to…the mind of a c. — CHIR 260:53
eldest c. of sin — WEBS 1060:45
Elephant's C. — KIPL 563:81
enough to get any c.'s attention — BAIL 62:69
every c. born therein — RUSK 831:3
father of the c. cried out — BIBLE 141:68
fixity of a thoughtful c.'s — HARDY 456:2
Go c. — SEXT 859:61
good habit makes a c. a man — WEBS 1059:32
Half devil and half c. — KIPL 562:31
have a thankless c. — SHAK 902:8
have no other c. — SHAK 898:11
heart…that of a little c. — THAC 1007:99
Heaven born c. — MILT 681:86
Helen was got with c. — MANS 647:1
hideous when…in a c. — SHAK 902:7
I am to have his c. — BURG 205:79
I was a c. and very lonely — RHYS 808:31
If you strike a c. — SHAW 922:52
imprison the c. in her house — WHITE 1070:39
Invention, Nature's c. — SIDN 937:51

child (*contd.*)
is it well with the c.? — BIBLE 111:76
Jesus Christ her little c. — ALEX 13:19
keeps a secret like a c. — HUGO 502:85
knows his own c. — SHAK 874:24
land that's governed by a c. — SHAK 863:55
lay down my life…for a c. — CLOU 271:40
like a c. waking — KIER 556:58
like an old c. — BEET 84:52
Lillian as a c. — FEIB 384:96
listens like a three years' c. — COLE 273:84
little c. shall lead them — BIBLE 125:68
Look upon a little c. — WESL 1066:61
Lord B.…is a c. — GOET 431:80
Love is like a c. — SHAK 860:83
lullay, lullay, like a c. — SKEL 942:35
Magus Zoroaster, my dead c. — SHEL 929:13
make the c. a man — SHAK 866:34
making love is c.'s play — MITF 697:95
mid-May's eldest c. — KEATS 548:17
most blissful dream as a c. — SHIP 935:22
mother…chose to smother the c. — MACG 630:32
murmuring…'My c., my c.' — YEATS 1107:94
naked c. against hungry wolf — DAVI 307:96
nurse for a poetic c.! — SCOTT 853:50
Ocean's c., and then his queen — SHEL 927:71
old Adam in this C. — BOOK 175:34
On a cloud I saw a c. — BLAKE 166:62
one for a c. — BEEC 82:14
perfect for me this c. — HEAN 464:33
presence of the cherished c. — ELIOT 365:13
promise kept, And a c. — NEME 722:4
receive one such little c. — BIBLE 138:18
receive this C. — BOOK 175:35
refuse in respect of our c. — BIBLE 131:78
room of my absent c. — SHAK 872:66
saddling of the right to a c. — SHAW 924:93
saw the young c. — BIBLE 133:24
seem to hear a c. weeping — DYSON 359:2
send the c. a errand — DICK 323:78
Set his c. — TENN 997:8
simpering, whimpering c. again — HART 459:46
simple dignity of a c. — SAND 841:77
solitary c. and solitary man — ACKR 4:56
something better—their c. — SHEL 926:52
spare the rod and spoil the c. — BUTL 216:17
speak like a c. — NABO 717:13
successful parent…raises a c. — EPHR 379:96
sweet c. is the sweetest thing — LAMB 576:22
that every c. may reach — JONS 535:2
There is a man c. conceived — BIBLE 112:98
This C. I to myself will take — WORD 1095:6
Thou C. of Joy — WORD 1097:49
thought as a c. — BIBLE 150:82
took a c. out in the yard — CAPO 231:87
Train up a c. — BIBLE 121:94
unsatisfied c. — GRAV 440:39
unto us a c. is born — BIBLE 125:66
use of a new-born c.? — FRAN 402:13
virgin shall be with c. — BIBLE 133:22
weep like a c. for the past — LAWR 585:69
what a c. takes in — LAWR 587:9
what it is like to be a c. — JARR 518:65
when I was a tiny c. — ROTH 826:10
When Israel was a c. — BIBLE 130:53
White an angel is the English c. — BLAKE 166:34
who gives a c. a treat — MASE 662:46
Who shows a c. — RILKE 812:87
wondering as a c. — BARB 71:10
wretched c. expires — BELL 87:7
wrote the way a c. skips — WHITE 1070:34
young healthy C. — SWIFT 985:98
childbearing closest…to c. — MAIL 639:78
childbirth death in c. — WELD 1062:92

childbirth (*contd.*)

taxes and c.! — MITC 697:90

childhood about my hard c. — GIOV 428:36

books one reads in c. — ORWE 744:38
c....cannnot remain a fairy-land — BOGAN 171:59
C. is measured out — BETJ 101:58
C. is not from birth — MILL 676:93
c., my youth, my entire life — SABA 835:56
c. shows the man — MILT 694:33
c. trees were green — MACN 637:45
clear space opened to her c. — THOM 1009:49
doing things in c. — GONC 434:52
dreams of our c. — THOR 1016:62
England...in my c. — ORWE 743:8
everything is as it was in my c. — EBER 359:9
experiences of c. — LIVE 607:45
From his c. onwards — HARD 455:76
glistening galaxy of c. — MATT 664:82
I in c. sweetly slept — CLARE 267:83
in the custody of c. — MISH 696:77
keep them always in state of c. — WOLL 1091:35
memories of earliest c. — MANS 647:5
Old age is second c. — ARIS 34:21
one moment in c. — GREE 444:5
prayed to rediscover my c. — RILKE 811:84
prefer to return to c.? — DESAI 317:70
privatize the cost of c. — HEWE 479:87
Remember your own c. — CAMP 228:34
secret of his c. — ACKR 4:55
'Tis the eye of c. — SHAK 908:48
what my lousy c. was like — SALI 838:18
where c. had strayed — RUSS 833:37
wove a web in c. — BRON 190:91
write about their c. — PARK 755:18

childhoods c. are sowing the wind — ELLI 375:14

instead of happy c. — HERR 477:48

childish c. weakness to lament — SHAK 862:32

either knavish or c. — JOHN 530:4
It was c. ignorance — HOOD 489:38
my c. years did pass — SURR 982:43
put away c. things — BIBLE 150:62

childishness Second c....oblivion — SHAK 886:96

What c. is it — BISH 164:33

childlike keep that c. creativity — HIRS 482:23

children account...to c....as bills — BACON 57:57

airy hopes my c. — WORD 1100:82
All God's C. got Rhythm — KAHN 541:91
Americans do not rear c. — JARR 518:63
anxious to get c. — FREUD 404:43
Are not c. more creative — MACKE 632:51
asking a man to list his c. — ACHE 2:20
become as little c. — BIBLE 138:17
Being constantly with c. — BAIN 62:74
blood be on us, and on our c. — BIBLE 140:53
borne thirteen c. — TRUTH 1030:39
bourgeois...reappears in your c. — CONN 282:56
breeds contempt—and c. — TWAIN 1034:2
buried her c. — SYNGE 988:62
c. ardent for...glory — OWEN 748:13
c. are a kind of discipline — BACON 57:60
c. are above average — KEIL 548:25
c. are an heritage of the Lord — BIBLE 119:42
C. are dumb to say — GRAV 439:17
C. are haughty, disdainful, angry — LABR 573:52
c. are instructed — MACC 625:51
c. are more troublesome — SHAW 924:94
c. aren't happy — NASH 719:51
C. begin by loving their parents — WILDE 1077:70
C. being now come to the years — BOOK 175:40
c. being taught mathematical — GIBS 422:40
C.'s c. are the crown — BIBLE 121:85
c. fear to go in the dark — BACON 56:43
c. from utter degradation — LOVE 615:70
c....gone out into the world — WOOLF 1093:76

children (*contd.*)

c. have lost their innocence — GREER 445:41
C. have neither past nor future — LABR 573:53
C. have never been very good — BALD 64:95
C....have no use for psychology — SING 940:95
c. I might have had — LOWRY 618:18
c. inter their parents — HERO 477:47
c. kind and natural — SHAK 880:74
c., let us shut — THAC 1006:90
c. like olive plants — BIBLE 119:43
c. love you and are learning — ANON 27:66
c....never had any boots — WILS 1085:27
c....not returnable — CRISP 296:33
c. of an idle brain — SHAK 868:80
c. of God — BIBLE 149:27
c. of immigrants — RUSS 832:24
c. of men put their trust — BIBLE 115:62
c. of my body — KOLL 568:76
c. of the devil — TENN 1005:57
c. of the kingdom — BIBLE 136:65
c. of the poor — DICK 324:24
c. of the revolution — LEGU 594:31
c. of your Father — BIBLE 134:45
c. one's 'mature' critics often are — WALK 1049:32
c. shall be the works — MICH 673:36
C. should acquire their heroes — AUDEN 49:99
c. sport upon the shore — WORD 1098:54
C. sweeten labours — BACON 57:55
C.'s talent to endure — ANGE 19:17
C., to be illustrious — NEME 722:3
c. were nestled all snug — MOORE 704:4
c. will one day live — KING 557:76
C., you are very little — STEV 975:40
Come, dear c., let us away — ARNO 36:53
curse of c.! — WEBS 1059:29
devour each of her c. — VERG 1042:32
disappointment to their c. — POWE 787:1
distinction between c. and adults — BART 74:70
examine the throat...in c. — OSLER 746:73
exercise the rights of c. — COWP 292:50
father pitieth his c. — BIBLE 118:14
first class, and with c. — BENC 89:48
For all our c.'s fate — KIPL 565:17
for my c.'s c., the power — MATT 664:82
for the procreation of c. — BOOK 175:44
give good gifts unto your c. — BIBLE 135:58
give them to the c. — MORE 707:53
God's police—wives and little c. — CHIS 260:54
happy home and c. — PLATH 773:91
hates c. and dogs — FIEL 388:62
having c. — WELD 1063:97
He has no c. — SHAK 909:74
heart of the c. — BIBLE 131:73
how easily a priest begets c. — SMITH 949:45
hundreds of c. to death — MAXT 665:99
impression made upon c. — BRYAN 201:15
In cradle clothes our c. — SHAK 875:35
in sorrow thou shalt bring forth c. — BIBLE 103:99
interfering with c. — RUSS 832:26
justified of her c. — BIBLE 137:87
kill more women and c. — BALD 65:10
known as the C.'s Hour — LONG 612:15
laughingstock of c. — SIDN 937:39
learn a lot from their c. — SPARK 955:47
Let our c. grow tall — THAT 1007:6
like c.—talk to themselves — ONEI 740:52
Literature...about having c. — LODGE 609:76
little c. died — AUDEN 47:67
little c....Round his feet — SHEL 927:77
Looking after c. — MACE 629:14
man shall be known in his c. — BIBLE 132:98
man...successful with his c. — EURI 381:34
marry for c. — SHAW 924:91
Men are as chancy as c. — KIPL 562:71

children (*contd.*)

Men are but c. — DRYD 348:97
misfits and precocious c. — MANK 645:77
mother who talks about her own c. — DISR 333:18
multitude of unprofitable c. — BIBLE 132:3
must become c. again — RUNGE 829:57
never favourable to the c. — MONT 703:88
No c. run to lisp sire's return — GRAY 442:65
nor do his c. prattle about — HOMER 487:16
Novelists...are also c. — DEVO 318:90
Our c. swoon before us — WILDE 1075:27
Our c., and our sins — SHAK 881:94
parents kept me from c. — SPEN 956:77
peacemakers...the c. of God — BIBLE 133:34
poisoning three little c. — DOYLE 343:89
poor get c. — KAHN 541:90
provoke not your c. to wrath — BIBLE 152:4
put to Dickens as c. — BENN 91:78
Rachel weeping for her c. — BIBLE 128:28
reason for having c. — RUSS 833:35
rich don't have c. — NEWM 724:34
secrets...must be kept from c. — DRYD 346:55
send his c. away to school — BRAD 183:85
sins of the fathers upon the c. — BOOK 174:17
spending my c.'s inheritance — ANON 30:52
started life as c. — AMIS 16:79
Strangelove Reproduction: Having c. — COUP 289:84
Suffer little c....to come unto me — BIBLE 139:23
Suffer the little c. to come unto me — BIBLE 141:69
take my place with the c. — WOOD 1092:51
tale which holdeth forth c. — SIDN 937:63
Teach the c. under the...tree — QABO 796:47
teach them diligently unto thy c. — BIBLE 108:90
that their c. are naïve — NASH 720:58
the nurture of c. — PALEY 751:61
their c.'s c. — YEATS 1105:64
They were privileged c. — BROO 193:40
thou shalt have c. — BOOK 177:73
Thoughtful c. — AUDEN 47:74
tiresome for c. — SAIN 836:83
To rescue our c. — JORD 537:30
Today, c., I am — NGU 725:45
too easy for c. — SCHN 848:86
trade union for pensioners and c. — HEATH 466:50
understood by c. and animals — STRA 979:3
unto us and c. forever — BIBLE 108:98
victory of the c. of light — BEND 89:57
Wars are fought by c. — LIVE 607:44
We have c. — TENN 1005:59
Well, c., whar dar is — TRUTH 1030:38
what is he doing with the c. — CAUS 246:67
what will your c. see? — BETJ 100:44
when I look at my c. — CART 242:9
when mum...looks after the c. — FALU 382:57
whom the lips of c. — NEALE 722:92
wife and c. — BACON 57:56
wife is beautiful and his c. — MENC 669:79
will not teach their c. — SHAW 924:1
wiser than the c. of light — BIBLE 143:3
Women's love...not for their c. — EURI 380:26
Women...fought...for their c. — PANK 753:80
words, like c. — NOON 731:22
world in which c. have their existence — DICK 326:67
world...begat more c. — BACON 59:7
Yes, Sir...many c. — JOHN 527:28
Young c. [are] sooner allured — ASCH 41:51
Your c. are not your c. — GIBR 422:38

Chile in C. everything yields — BLEST 169:28

chill bitter c. it was! — KEATS 546:85

c. down the spine — COOKE 286:32
November's sky is c. — SCOTT 853:51
wind is c. — SCOTT 853:55

chilli c. was something cool — THAC 1006:81

society women never serve c. — RAYB 803:49

chills Of c. and fever she died   RANS 802:31
Chilterns C., the North Downs   FORS 398:28
chime began to whirr and c.   AUDEN 47:61
  higher than the sphery c.   MILT 684:37
  let your silver c.   MILT 681:90
  that harmonious c.   DONNE 336:71
chimera Peace without honour…c.   CECIL 247:78
chimeras wild impossible c.   SWIFT 985:87
chimes c. ring out with a carol gay   BOND 172:79
  heard the c. at midnight   SHAK 877:97
chimley bottle on the c.-piece   DICK 322:75
chimney by the c. with care   MOORE 704:4
  oak in the c.   DONNE 338:17
  old men from the c. corner   SIDN 937:63
  smoke out at the c.   SHAK 887:24
chimney-piece upon the c.-p.   SCOTT 854:71
chimney-sweep there was a little c.-s.   KING 558:92
chimney-sweepers c.-s., come to dust
    SHAK 916:16
chimneys Your c. I sweep   BLAKE 166:66
chimpanzee girl…turned into a c.   PERE 766:91
  vase in the hands of the c.   WAUGH 1058:9
chin obliterated the unimportant c.   CUMM 299:73
  one neck, one c.   SHAK 894:5
  up to the c. in heaven   MIDD 673:46
China C. asked for a sword   BRID 188:45
  C. has stood up   MAO 648:23
  C.? There lies a sleeping   NAPO 718:25
  from C. to Peru   JOHN 525:81
  In C. the bat is a symbol   LAWR 585:71
  In C., even one million people   DENG 315:51
  land armies in C.   MONT 703:90
  outer C. 'crost the Bay!   KIPL 560:26
  than eat C.'s all our lives   HO 482:34
  the Wall of C.   PATM 760:11
  Till C. and Africa meet   AUDEN 47:60
  yesterday in C.   GORD 435:66
Chinatown Forget it, Jake, it's C.   TOWNE 1024:11
Chinese as much C. as French   FLAU 392:30
  brought the C. people cannons   PEOP 764:58
  C. are the aristocracy   MAUG 665:90
  C. cheap labour   HARTE 460:51
  C. nurse with green trousers   MANS 647:98
  C. woman fits her shoe   SCHR 850:4
  Corruption…is C. business life   ECON 359:15
  courage in C. culture   MO 698:10
  difficult to trust the C.   DALAI 303:42
  heathen C. is peculiar   HARTE 459:50
  no one can destroy the C. people   BUCK 203:37
  typical C. wishes   RUSS 832:20
  We said to the C.   PALM 752:69
chintzy c. cheeriness   BETJ 99:25
chip c. off the old block   BURKE 207:23
chips C. with everything   WESK 1066:57
chivalrous from all c. actions   ANON 22:74
chivalry age of c. is gone   BURKE 207:31
  age of c. is past   DISR 332:74
  baseball…free of c.   BROUN 194:50
  Belgium's…beauty and her c.   BYRON 219:84
  may be seen noble c.   MALO 642:35
  nine-tenths of the law of c.   SAYE 846:48
  noblesse and of c.   SPEN 957:92
  sung of Border c.   SCOTT 853:42
Chloe speak, my fair C.   PRIOR 791:59
  what can C. want?   POPE 782:73
chloroform having babies without c.   BARB 71:13
chocolate cake of c.   STEV 973:97
  c. cream soldier!   SHAW 920:94
  entire box of c. liqueurs   CAPO 231:79
chocolates c., cherries, hairshirts   LOWE 617:10
choice and you takes your c.   PUNCH 795:23
  any c. in the matter   JOHN 529:80
  character concerned with c.   ARIS 34:27
  c. between staying married   REAR 804:73

choice (contd.)
  c. between two alternatives   MORAN 706:41
  c. does not interfere   KENN 551:79
  c. virtues only gods   ROET 819:97
  c. would be irregular but safe   WEST 1068:92
  Each to his c.   KIPL 563:93
  feeling of c.   VIDAL 1044:68
  freedom of c.   GITL 429:49
  homeless by c.   SOUT 954:39
  if one had no c.   ANGE 19:19
  just another lifestyle c.   QUAY 796:53
  Life's business…the terrible c.   BROW 200:92
  measure and the c.   JOHN 525:85
  mixture of chance and c.   FRIE 405:54
  only one c.—to be strong   MISH 696:75
  small c. in rotten apples   SHAK 864:72
  while he doth make his c.   SHAK 872:79
choices equipped to make c.   LURIE 619:41
  free to make c.   THAT 1007:8
  sum of all the c. gone before?   DIDI 330:44
choir c. of saints   DONNE 338:18
  member of the c.   LOOS 613:36
  sing in the c.   KINN 559:9
choirboy when raping a c.   PROU 793:2
choirs Bare ruined c.   SHAK 914:73
  last c., last sounds   STEV 972:55
choke doth c. the feeder   SHAK 866:46
  poets…whether they c. or not   WHITE 1069:23
choked experience a c. feeling   WHITE 1069:23
choleric mild or c. disposition   ADDI 6:6
choose c. between betraying   FORS 399:52
  c. what many men desire   SHAK 874:30
  C. you…whom ye will serve   BIBLE 109:12
  do not c. our problems   FROMM 406:70
  free, therefore c.   SART 844:19
  not c. not to be   HOPK 492:1
  spirit, free to c.   ROCH 816:49
  They cannot c.   THOM 1012:11
  thou canst not c.   SHAK 916:21
  woman can hardly ever c.   ELIOT 366:28
  would a man c.   JOHN 531:23
choosing just c. so   BROW 200:82
  reason is but c.   MILT 686:67
Chopin After playing C.   WILDE 1076:34
chopped c. up in bits   JAMES 517:40
chopper cheap and chippy c.   GILB 425:88
chopsticks pair of c.…in harmony   MIN 695:61
chord just as they do in a c.   HONO 488:31
  pick a c., go twang   VICI 1043:49
  struck one c. of music   PROC 792:76
chords c. in the human mind   DICK 325:30
  c. of summer   DAYL 310:55
  vasectomy of the vocal c.   ALTH 15:60
chores do celestial c.   CULL 298:67
chorister Bobolink for a C.   DICK 328:98
chorus c. of indolent reviewers   TENN 1003:26
  like a c. girl's tights   LAWR 587:11
chorus-ending c.-e. from Euripides   BROW 198:54
chosen c. and male   KENN 550:55
  doorman, was the one c.   AREN 33:16
  lesser should always be c.   KEMP 549:46
  ye are a c. generation   BIBLE 156:78
Christ all at once what C. is   HOPK 492:7
  ambassadors for C.   BIBLE 151:81
  believe and rejoice in C.   LUTH 620:46
  bowels of C.   CROM 298:53
  certainly have despised C.   GREE 444:23
  C. being raised from the dead   BIBLE 149:21
  C.'s blood streams in the firmament!   MARL 654:20
  C.'s blood was shed for thee   BOOK 175:32
  C., borne in to virgynyte   ANON 22:68
  C. comes to the oppressed   RUET 828:47
  C. died for us   BIBLE 148:18
  C. follows Dionysus   POUND 786:63

Christ (contd.)
  C. had not been crucified?   USTI 1038:77
  C. if my love were in my armes   ANON 23:83
  C. is all, and in all   BIBLE 153:21
  C. is born in Bethlehem   CASW 244:37
  C. laughed or played   FORS 399:57
  C.'s lore, and his apostles twelve   CHAU 255:26
  C. may dwell in your hearts   BIBLE 152:98
  C.…of all men the poorest   WYCL 1103:45
  C. receive thy saule   BALL 67:44
  C. risen from the dead   BIBLE 151:67
  C., the leader of the sect   TACI 989:79
  C.…the self-confession   FEUE 387:30
  C. the tiger   ELIOT 368:69
  C. was betrayed   RUSS 833:37
  C.…we claym of him   CHAU 255:36
  C.! What are patterns for?   LOWE 615:74
  C. will perhaps be a female   NIGH 729:99
  C. with me   PATR 761:15
  churches have killed their C.   TENN 1001:91
  civil wars as that of C.   MONT 702:79
  come, C.   ANON 23:98
  do all things through C.   BIBLE 153:17
  faith of C.   BOOK 175:35
  followed before C. died   ORAH 741:77
  Hold on to C.   BUTT 218:52
  Jesus C. his only Son our Lord   BOOK 173:94
  Jesus C.…Word of God   BARTH 74:65
  Jesus C., her Lord   STONE 978:73
  life of C. as a revelation   WHIT 1071:61
  May Lord C. enter in?   WILDE 1078:4
  Must then a C. perish   SHAW 925:25
  new illnesses brought by C.   GAUT 416:41
  not ashamed of the gospel of C.   BIBLE 148:11
  O C., O God   HOPK 491:81
  Ring in the C.   TENN 1000:57
  Saviour C. again to Earth   MASE 662:46
  Saviour, which is C. the Lord   BIBLE 142:78
  So Judas did to C.   SHAK 867:63
  speechless C.   SWIN 988:48
  the South is hardly C.-centered   OCON 735:85
  Thou art the C.   BIBLE 138:13
  trust in C.   WESL 1066:66
  unsearchable riches of C.   BIBLE 152:97
  uphold the C.   TENN 1002:17
  whole state of C.'s Church   BOOK 174:22
  words our Saviour C. saith   BOOK 174:26
Christ's College lady of C. C.   AUBR 45:34
Christ-Church light in C.-C. hall   ARNO 37:90
  study at C.-C.   JOHN 528:53
Christendom C. ought to feel joyful   COLU 278:63
  in C. where is the Christian?   EMER 376:31
  Kent and C.   WYATT 1102:26
  live in any place in C.   ELIZ 373:86
  prettiest Kate in C.   SHAK 864:77
  two lights of C.   PIUS 772:78
christened arrived…already c.   SAKI 837:4
  c. with a hundred   NASHE 720:75
  Why c. Pleasant   DICK 327:83
christening Like a c., a wedding,   COOKE 286:31
Christian As with the C. religion   ORWE 742:97
  C. gospel is the knowledge   NIEB 727:64
  C. ideal has not been tried   CHES 258:15
  C. on a Pound a Week?   HARD 455:77
  C. that is in health   LAW 585:60
  every C. in Hitler's Europe   FACK 382:49
  forgive them as a C.   AUST 51:42
  form C. men   ARNO 40:43
  fraud of the C. system   PAINE 750:51
  fruits of C. civilisation   BIRD 163:16
  honourable style of a C.   BROW 194:63
  in Christendom where is the C.?   EMER 376:31
  in what peace a C. can die   ADDI 8:40
  lawful for C. men   BOOK 178:1

Christian (*contd.*)

no C. ear can endure	SHAK 861:*15*
persuadest me to be a C.	BIBLE 148:*10*
sad, good C. at her heart	POPE 781:*71*
same…as a C. is?	SHAK 872:*80*
than a drunken C.	MELV 667:*29*
tiger that hasn't got a C.	PUNCH 795:*96*
took her for a C. Scientist	MITF 697:*96*
What being a C. means	PECK 763:*39*
You're a C.?	WELLS 1064:*34*

Christianity C. has taught us

C. is the most materialist	HUGEL 498:*11*
C.…man's religion	TEMP 993:*28*
decay of C.	WELD 1062:*92*
essence of C.	SAKI 837:*97*
fundamental doctrines of C.	WHIT 1071:*61*
gap in C.	LAW 585:*61*
go first, rock and roll or C.	FORS 399:*57*
grave of C.	LENN 596:*55*
He who begins by loving C.	ELIOT 370:*21*
His C. was muscular	COLE 275:*22*
If religion is only a garment of C.	DISR 334:*25*
like C. without hell	BONH 173:*84*
local thing called C.	BORM 179:*17*
nothing in C. or Buddhism	HARDY 457:*10*
power of C.	SAKI 838:*3*
	WHIT 1071:*60*

Christians blood of the C.

C. are frightened	TERT 1006:*78*
C. are not called	BARTH 74:*68*
C. deified death	JENK 520:*1*
C. have burnt each other	STAEL 961:*71*
C. that travel in Turkey	BYRON 222:*29*
C. will have refreshment	BUTL 216:*1*
home to Jews, Muslims and C.	COLU 278:*63*
Jews and Arabs…like good C.	CLIN 269:*18*
misbeseeming C.	AUST 53:*75*
obstructed by the lives of C.	PRYN 794:*11*
profess and call themselves C.	JOHN 527:*23*
	BOOK 174:*7*

Christmas At C. I no more desire

Berlin by C.	SHAK 865:*8*
C. should fall out	ANON 25:*31*
C. tree decorated by a Pre-Raphaelite	ADDI 7:*14*
	BEER 84:*47*
C. tree is lighted	MOYN 711:*14*
C. without any presents	ALCO 12:*96*
dreaming of a White C.	BERL 95:*62*
football is proposed at C.	ANON 24:*14*
Happy C. to all	MOORE 704:*8*
inform press home C.	WRIG 1102:*13*
keep our C. merry still	SCOTT 853:*55*
Love came down at C.	ROSS 824:*78*
night before C.	MOORE 704:*3*
One C. was much like another	THOM 1011:*94*

Christopher Robin C. R. Has Fallen

	MORT 710:*1*
C. R. is saying his prayers	MILNE 680:*70*
C. R. went down with Alice	MILNE 680:*69*

chronicle Pride…his own C.   SHAK 895:*45*

chronicles c. of the time   SHAK 890:*12*

chubby Augustus was a c. lad   HOFF 484:*58*

chuck C. him out, the brute!   KIPL 560:*32*

chuckle c.…from ear to ear   ELIOT 368:*88*

irritating c.	GILB 425:*80*
reading of a white man's c.	ANGE 20:*32*

chum Nationalism, and its c.   DUNN 356:*59*

chumps C.…the best husbands   WODE 1088:*88*

church a c. stands near   YEATS 1107:*93*

all the c. did echo	SHAK 864:*83*
authority in the affairs of the c.	BECK 82:*7*
before his c. affiliation	LEWIS 601:*49*
believe in the C.	TEMP 993:*29*
Broad of C.	BETJ 99:*27*
Brought you to c. well-dressed	HERB 476:*36*
build my c.	BIBLE 138:*13*
came to the village c.	TENN 1001:*78*

church (*contd.*)

C. ain't shucks	TWAIN 1032:*70*
C.…asks only for peace	BONH 172:*81*
C. clock at ten to three?	BROO 193:*30*
c. for his mother	CYPR 302:*32*
c. he…did not attend	AMIS 16:*78*
C. is cold	BLAKE 167:*97*
c. is my text	BROW 195:*66*
c. is of mercies	DONNE 339:*25*
c. must be reminded	KING 558:*84*
C. of England	ROYD 828:*42*
C. of England	WELLS 1064:*34*
c. to God	BYRON 224:*72*
C. which abandons	KUNG 571:*16*
churchyard into the c.	DONNE 338:*17*
Come all to c.	HOUS 495:*51*
decent c.	GOLD 433:*9*
discipline of our holy C.	OCON 735:*80*
excommunicated by the medieval c.	ANON 29:*42*
fain would kill their c.	TENN 1001:*91*
figure in a country c.	SWIFT 984:*67*
found God in c.?	WALK 1049:*58*
goes to c. as he goes to the bathroom	BLYT 170:*51*
great period in his C.	MILT 686:*74*
Here's a c.!	DICK 327:*74*
high c. for the true mediocre	MAIL 639:*77*
holy Catholick C.	BOOK 173:*94*
huge c. above…village	WALC 1048:*41*
In C. your grandsire	SWIFT 984:*80*
into his c. lewd hirelings	MILT 690:*51*
Ireland…an alien C.	DISR 332:*87*
keep the Sabbath going to C.	DICK 328:*98*
MCC ends and the C.	PRIE 790:*47*
nearer the C.	ANDR 19:*14*
neither despair in the c.	FACK 382:*49*
next to the C.	HOOV 490:*67*
no government, c., corporation	OAKE 733:*49*
no salvation outside the c.	CYPR 302:*33*
noticed…since I have been in C.	WAUGH 1056:*68*
officially named by the c.	MACF 629:*20*
'oly as a c.	STRA 979:*94*
one Catholick and Apostolick C.	BOOK 174:*21*
over the sea wet c.	THOM 1010:*69*
Paris to Saint Peter's C.	SHAK 869:*13*
prayers of the c., to preserve	SWIFT 986:*11*
respectable as the C. of England	STEV 973:*92*
rice in a c.	LENN 596:*62*
see a c. by daylight	SHAK 879:*35*
sight of a white c.	LOWE 615:*76*
some to c. repair	POPE 778:*83*
State is the C.	SHAW 923:*76*
suffer nobody to sleep in…[the c.]	ADDI 7:*11*
taught respect for the c.	NERU 723:*9*
The C.'s one foundation	STONE 978:*73*
true C. ….lies in the Editors	CARL 233:*33*
Unto him be glory in the c.	BIBLE 152:*99*
What is a c.?	CRAB 294:*79*
what you find in la c.	WILL 1081:*53*
Where do you go to c.?	BERE 94:*36*
Where Peter is…is the C.	AMBR 15:*64*
whole state of Christ's C.	BOOK 174:*22*

churches all c. or chapels in New York   BENN 92:*6*

all the c. you can build	CHIS 260:*54*
c. and dry-goods stores	MACM 636:*23*
C. built to please the Priest	BURNS 209:*69*
c. have killed their Christ	TENN 1001:*91*
In general the c.	UPDI 1037:*57*
intolerable Mischiefes to C.	PRYN 794:*11*
seven c. which are in Asia	BIBLE 156:*96*

Churchill Actors…tried to play C.   MANC 644:*65*

C. once sponsored the…idea	GALB 411:*74*
C. on top of the wave	BEAV 80:*79*
inaccurate to say that C.	MANC 644:*67*
opinion of Winston C.	ELTON 375:*22*

Churchill (*contd.*)

quotations from…C.	MACF 629:*19*
Randolph C. went into hospital	WAUGH 1058:*8*
trousers of Winston C.	BREZ 187:*39*

churchman As for the British c.   BLYT 170:*51*

'Modern C.'	WAUGH 1056:*72*

churchmen the c. fain would kill   TENN 1001:*91*

churchyard church into the c.   DONNE 338:*17*

c. full of sailor's graves	BETJ 100:*49*
In Drumcliffe c.	YEATS 1107:*93*
nowhere worse taste, than in a c.	JOWE 537:*40*
palsy-stricken, c. thing	KEATS 546:*90*

churchyards when C. yawn   TWAIN 1033:*89*

When c. yawn	SHAK 891:*44*

Chutzpah C.—that quality   LEVA 599:*17*

Chuzzlewit C. suggested 'Swans'   DICK 322:*68*

cicadae host of giant c. beat   ROBE 814:*16*

cicadas c. have been screaming   BOWL 182:*54*

Cicero C., citing Cato   KNIG 567:*54*

cigar C. out of his mouth   KARSH 542:*11*

substitute out of c. stumps	DOUG 341:*60*
then the long c.	TIME 1020:*66*

cigarette c. is perfect…pleasure   WILDE 1076:*52*

crush a c. out	BERR 99:*19*

cigarettes best c. in my experience   STEV 973:*97*

Fasten your c.	WILD 1079:*17*

cigars I'd like…to smoke c.   DIAZ 319:*2*

roller of big c.	STEV 971:*35*

Cimber C. should be banished   SHAK 883:*38*

cinder how dry a c. this world is   DONNE 338:*14*

scorched my intellect into a c.	CARL 233:*29*

Cinderella If I made C.   HITC 482:*24*

wand of C.'s Fairy Godmother	DIOR 331:*63*

cinema c. in their blood   RICH 810:*65*

c. is truth	GODA 430:*63*
c. was…a new era	QUIR 798:*72*
invented the C.	LUMI 619:*40*

cinnamon c. and cloves   ANON 23:*92*

Spicy grove, c. tree	CULL 299:*69*

Circe body…straight as C.'s wand   MARL 655:*26*

elegance of C.'s hair	POUND 785:*61*

circle c. of its influence   POTT 785:*44*

c. of the golden year	TENN 996:*90*
c. of the heroic	STOWE 978:*83*
c. round the globe	MUNDY 714:*54*
come full c.	MOYN 711:*14*
firmness makes my c. just	DONNE 337:*92*
forms…an untranscendable c.	SCHR 850:*7*
narrow c. of strikes	ENGE 378:*89*
Round and round the c.	ELIOT 371:*38*
Sorrow comes as in a c.	CH 248:*9*
square the c.	HEAN 464:*33*
Weave a c. round him thrice	COLE 275:*18*
What other planets c. other suns	POPE 780:*34*
wheel is come full c.	SHAK 904:*48*

circles centre and cause of many c.   LEON 597:*84*

c. of which we are the centres	TROL 1027:*67*
mind skating c.	FROST 407:*6*
sweep in ever-widening c.	HUXL 508:*95*

circling c. in his desire   FLAU 393:*43*

circuit c. unto the ends of it   BIBLE 114:*44*

short c. in his identity	ROTH 825:*7*
Success in c. lies	DICK 328:*11*

circuits c. of a digital computer   PIRS 770:*51*

circulation she has a good c.   RENO 807:*8*

the c. of their blood	SMITH 947:*9*
work, leisure, c.	LECO 592:*3*

circumcised c. people   GIBB 421:*23*

C. the eighth day	BIBLE 153:*10*

circumcision very luxury… c.   ORTON 742:*86*

circumlocution C.…literary trick   BIER 161:*74*

C. Office	DICK 325:*46*

circumference just c., O world   MILT 691:*85*

circumstance blows of c.   TENN 999:*44*

circumstance (*contd.*)
escape from c. to ecstasy — BELL 85:*81*
foresee no c. — HESE 479:*79*
In the fell clutch of c. — HENL 472:*57*
suspect such a c. — AUST 51:*52*
circumstances cheated by c. — LESS 598:*98*
difficult to think of any c. — OAKE 733:*50*
If c. lead me — SHAK 889:*92*
more serious…in my present c. — SIDN 936:*42*
pain of particular c. — CART 242:*94*
things in terrible c. — MO 698:*13*
circumstantial How c. reality is! — UPDI 1037:*64*
no further than the Lie C. — SHAK 887:*34*
circus ain't shucks to a c. — TWAIN 1032:*70*
celebrated Barnum's c. — CHUR 263:*7*
chess tournament disguised as a c. — CONN 282:*50*
c. remains the same — ASHD 41:*61*
gets the c. it deserves — JONG 534:*70*
no right in the c. — MAXT 665:*1*
cirrhosis end up with c. of the liver — EAGL 359:*3*
cistern wheel broken at the c. — BIBLE 123:*42*
cisterns broken c. — BIBLE 128:*18*
citadel Coketown…ugly c. — DICK 325:*42*
Troy's sacred c. — HOMER 488:*24*
cithera universe is arranged like a c. — HONO 488:*31*
cities American life in large c. — MACC 625:*46*
c. and their civilities — PATM 760:*11*
c. of men — TENN 994:*58*
c., throbbed the true life — NORR 731:*29*
c. will have no rest from evils — PLATO 774:*21*
do not look in great c. — AUST 51:*46*
founder of c.! — COLUM 277:*59*
friends…are in c. — SNYD 951:*80*
great kings and fine c. — CATU 245:*63*
hum Of human c. torture — BYRON 220:*87*
impure love for c. — CASAL 243:*24*
In today's c.…on the outskirts — GENET 418:*77*
inquire of all the C. — ALBE 12:*94*
Islanded by c. fair — SHEL 927:*70*
Of towns and c. — WORD 1094:*96*
protect American c. — SCHL 848:*79*
prowling through the c. — ORWE 744:*40*
ruined c. of Germany — ORWE 744:*37*
seek a livelihood…in c. — CANT 230:*74*
Soveraign of c. — DUNB 355:*39*
streets of a hundred c. — HOOV 490:*57*
sung women in three c. — POUND 785:*47*
Towered c. pleased — MILT 682:*3*
whose c. he saw — HOMER 488:*24*
citizen am to become a private c. — EISE 364:*87*
c. of life — SASS 845:*23*
c. of no mean city — BIBLE 148:*7*
c. of the proudest country — PARK 755:*31*
c. of the world — BOSW 180:*31*
I am a Roman c. — CICE 266:*63*
liberty that the c. enjoys — SPEN 956:*68*
No cold relation is a zealous c. — BURKE 208:*40*
not lay aside the c. — WASH 1054:*40*
Sophia Loren is not a c. — GRAMM 438:*96*
transformed…into a perfect c. — DOUG 342:*68*
citizens all c. should be free — MORE 707:*52*
beat to death those c. — MAMET 643:*45*
c. dream of south and west — HARDY 457:*13*
c. of Berlin — KENN 552:*85*
c. of death's grey land — SASS 845:*25*
c. of that other place — SONT 953:*11*
fat and greasy c. — SHAK 885:*78*
Healthy c. are the greatest asset — CHUR 265:*57*
prosperous c. of Zenith — LEWIS 602:*57*
State, or of c. — RUSK 831:*95*
universality of c. speaking — MAZZ 666:*13*
citizenship more onerous c. — SONT 953:*11*
union, before his c. — LEWIS 601:*49*
city amid the c.'s jar — ARNO 36:*72*

city (*contd.*)
balloon, coming out of a keen c. — CUMM 299:*81*
Beautiful c.! — ARNO 38:*10*
belonging to a race, c., a group — DUDEK 353:*16*
Brave men are a c.'s strongest tower — ALCA 12:*95*
citizen of no mean c. — BIBLE 148:*7*
c. has two great teams — SHAN 919:*75*
c. is built to music — TENN 1004:*55*
C. now doth like a garment wear — WORD 1097:*46*
c. of all time — HAWT 462:*82*
C. of London …clearing-house — CHAM 249:*14*
C. of perspiring dreams — RAND 802:*39*
C. of the Big Shoulders — SAND 841:*57*
c.…out of step with the century — CHEE 255:*48*
c. shoulderingly upwards — CUMM 299:*76*
c. that is set on an hill — BIBLE 134:*36*
c. there is a group — LESS 598:*1*
c. was on one side — MUNCH 713:*51*
c. where most people live — GRAY 440:*43*
c. will follow you — CAVA 246:*70*
decline and fall of the C. — GIBB 421:*29*
depart out of that house or c. — BIBLE 136:*75*
died…in sight of the c. — MACA 624:*28*
escaped From the vast c. — WORD 1095:*17*
Every c. has a sex and age — BERG 95:*47*
except the Lord keep the c. — BIBLE 119:*41*
fall in love with a c. — MORR 709:*86*
felled the c. — THOM 1010:*56*
first c. Cain — COWL 291:*18*
fishbone in the c.'s throat — LOWE 617:*99*
forbid…in the c. in future — EDWA 361:*46*
great noise in the c. — EDWA 361:*46*
hard-boiled c. — CHAN 250:*41*
heart of the c. — MOYN 711:*14*
Hell is a c. — SHEL 928:*94*
history of C. architecture — JOHN 524:*67*
How doth the c. sit solitary — BIBLE 128:*29*
if you would know…live in a c. — COLT 277:*57*
in the c. of our God — BIBLE 116:*75*
Like c. lights, receding — GIBS 422:*40*
looking over harbour and c. — SAND 841:*54*
Lord came down to see the c. — BIBLE 104:*17*
make glad the c. of God — BIBLE 116:*73*
man whom the c. sets up — SOPH 953:*17*
men that make a c. — NICI 726:*57*
modern c., it takes on — RODR 819:*89*
New York was no mean c. — DIDI 330:*45*
O c. of God — BIBLE 117:*96*
Of two f's,…is this c. — MATOS 664:*77*
on the field and c. — THAC 1006:*86*
Once in royal David's c. — ALEX 13:*19*
Paris is a beast of a c. — HAZL 463:*10*
play-going in any large c. — TYNAN 1035:*26*
precipitous c. — STEV 976:*59*
prepared for them a c. — BIBLE 154:*52*
private individual or for a c. — PLATO 774:*25*
realm, nation, or c. — KNOX 567:*57*
roofs of this distracted C. — CARL 235:*63*
run about through the c. — BOOK 177:*79*
sacred c. of the mind — CAMP 227:*18*
streets of the c. — MACC 625:*37*
Sun-girt c., thou hast been — SHEL 927:*71*
that sweet C. — ARNO 39:*15*
The C. is of Night — THOM 1015:*55*
The C. is of Night — THOM 1015:*56*
The C.'s voice — SHEL 927:*72*
thin trees in a c. square — LOWE 615:*76*
This rortie wretched c. — SMITH 949:*60*
took the c. — BIBLE 109:*10*
Towery c. — HOPK 491:*90*
Unless the Lord guards the c. — BIBLE 159:*48*
Unreal C. — ELIOT 368:*34*
vastly overrated c. — BURG 205:*81*
very fine c. — DEFOE 312:*85*

city (*contd.*)
Without a c. wall — ALEX 13:*20*
Zion, c. of our God! — NEWT 725:*43*
civet Give me an ounce of c. — SHAK 903:*35*
civil as for its c. use — MONT 703:*88*
British C. Service — WILL 1081:*55*
c. and obliging young woman — AUST 50:*29*
c. servant lyricism — BAND 69:*87*
C. Service is profoundly deferential — CROS 298:*64*
c., political, and religious — JUNI 540:*74*
c. To everyone — SISS 940:*97*
C. war is impossible — PAVL 761:*21*
c. war obstructs the crusade — INNO 512:*56*
horror of c. war — HOMER 488:*21*
In a c. war, a general must know — REED 805:*87*
corresponding c. society — MARX 660:*11*
dire effects from c. discord flow — ADDI 8:*36*
Here lies a c. servant — SISS 940:*97*
He was very c., 'Masa — DAVI 308:*13*
How can I be c. — GERS 420:*9*
In c. business; What first? — BACON 58:*76*
Pray, good people, be c. — GWYN 449:*97*
too c. by half — SHER 933:*85*
civil-suited c.-s. Morn — MILT 683:*13*
civilities bandy c. with my sovereign — JOHN 528:*51*
cities and their c. — PATM 760:*11*
civility Scotch c. — ROCH 816:*48*
see a wild c. — HERR 478:*68*
civilization advance cause of c. — BRIL 188:*56*
all of c.'s obstacles — SAND 840:*48*
amenities of c. — MACD 628:*93*
as c. spreads — TOCQ 1021:*79*
centers of European c. — TOLS 1023:*99*
c. and profits — COOL 286:*34*
c. don't advance — ROGE 820:*14*
C. has made the peasantry — TROT 1029:*6*
C. is a conspiracy — BUCH 202:*23*
C. is a movement — TOYN 1024:*18*
c. is based on the…materialistic — BONA 172:*78*
c.…is coupled with death — MILL 679:*55*
c. is essentially one of property — EMER 377:*62*
C. itself is a…balance — POUND 786:*80*
c. of one epoch — CONN 283:*73*
c. works its miracles — TOCQ 1022:*82*
continuity of c. — ORWE 744:*37*
curriculum vitae of C. — ANDR 18:*11*
depart from a c. — LISP 607:*39*
destroyed the c. — LIND 605:*8*
Every c. that has ever existed — KISS 566:*35*
fall of the last c. — READ 803:*55*
farmyard c. of the Fabians — INGE 511:*39*
For a botched c. — POUND 786:*65*
fruits of Christian c. — BIRD 163:*16*
great movements of…human c. — BENN 92:*6*
green end of c.'s hardest winters — FOWL 399:*67*
habit of c. — WEST 1067:*87*
highest standard of c. — LLOY 608:*59*
incompatible with c. — COOP 287:*42*
inheritors of an old c. — REYES 807:*22*
life-blood of real c. — TREV 1026:*47*
long last night over c. — MAIL 639:*79*
mark of high c. — BERL 96:*67*
passive, receptive side of c. — SPEN 957:*90*
principle task of c. — FREUD 404:*42*
quarrel of c. against — ROOS 822:*52*
rottenness of our c. — READ 803:*53*
saddest object in c. — STEV 977:*62*
stupid of modern c. — KNOX 567:*62*
sweetness of present c. — HUGO 503:*93*
they maintain c. — TOCQ 1022:*81*
to imbue c. — JOHN 522:*31*
uncompleted c. — DICK 327:*75*
undeniable pretensions as c. — PITT 771:*71*
under our existing c. — STAN 962:*87*

civilization (*contd.*)
vulgar sort of c. · BURG 205:82
wall…separates c. from barbarism · BUCH 202:22
What do I think of Western c.? · GAND 414:15
whole history of c. · JAMES 517:43
without usual interval of c. · CLEM 269:6
civilizations autonomous c. · SONT 953:7
civilize adopt me and c. me · TWAIN 1033:94
allowed she would c. me · TWAIN 1032:77
civilized c. human life · TRUM 1030:22
contact with the more c. · THOR 1016:74
highly c. human beings · ORWE 743:15
I have become c. · BIRD 163:14
society here would be quite c. · WILDE 1078:94
the more a people is c. · DIDE 329:29
civilizers two c. of man · DISR 333:16
clack whet thir beaks c. c. · RANS 802:34
claim c. on your respect · JUVE 540:83
c. those f. · TROL 1027:68
if the c. were broken · SHAW 922:42
no human c.…significance · OATES 733:58
on every beauty's c.? · JUANA 539:64
claimant failed to embarrass the c. · STRA 979:98
clairvoyant Hate is always more c. · LACL 574:65
People always claim to be c. · BOWL 182:58
clairvoyantes C. distress me · COPE 287:50
clamorous with such a c. smack · SHAK 864:83
clamours c. soars and shrills · ROBE 814:16
clan Against the c. M'Tavish · AYTO 53:85
c. has a tendency to ignore me · WODE 1089:91
Clancy C. of the Overflow · PATE 760:97
clanjamfrie haill c. · MACD 627:72
clannish exceedingly c. family · SHAW 926:42
clap Don't c. too hard · OSBO 745:68
trees of the field shall c. · BIBLE 127:7
Clapham safe back to C. Junction? · BUTL 217:39
claret and burgundy in Scotland? · SMITH 945:88
C. is the liquor · JOHN 530:3
C. on my Tomb · KEATS 545:66
clarets racehorses and the cheaper c. · SAKI 837:1
clarions Great winds Thy c. · ELLE 374:1
clarity c. was a great liability · BALF 65:20
C. of mind results in · PASC 757:50
universal and unbounded c. · JOHN 525:74
clark c. ther was of Oxenford · CHAU 254:21
clash c. together again · TENN 1003:29
class c. lies late and snores · CULL 298:67
c. of declassed women · DUMAS 354:29
c. struggle…leads to the dictatorship · MARX 661:27
could have had c. · SCHU 850:11
educated c.…hate us · CHEL 256:65
Every known c. of refusal · SOME 952:1
every other c. in the community · RICA 808:36
he gave her c. · HEPB 473:78
history of the c. struggles · MARX 660:12
like any other c. · TAWN 991:7
lowest c. is literary footmen · HAZL 464:20
make the bourgeoisie a c. · HUGO 502:88
men of any other c. · LODGE 610:84
no other c. of dependants · MILL 675:76
one c. is made to feel · DOUG 342:74
prosperity…through every c. · BRYAN 201:14
raise them as a c. · SMIL 945:76
sector of the liberal middle c. · EAGL 359:4
sinking middle c. · ORWE 742:4
spokesman of a c. · CHAM 249:13
very low c. among European states · GEOR 418:81
We are talking c. · KILP 556:64
Yuppies as a c. · ADLER 9:47
classes All c. of society · JEVO 521:22
c. of people · GARL 415:26
c. within c. in Peckham · SPARK 955:49
Comfort came in with the middle c. · BELL 86:84
curse of the drinking c. · WILDE 1079:11

classes (*contd.*)
decay of the ruling c. · ORWE 743:18
disappearance of the middle c. · COUP 289:77
divided into two c. · RUSK 831:96
equally on all c. · CHUR 263:1
gathered together in c. · SMITH 948:32
General Strike taught working c. · BALF 65:18
Let the ruling c. · MARX 660:15
lower c. had such white skins · CURZ 302:30
masses against the c. · GLAD 429:54
patsies for the ruling c. · HELL 469:98
prove that the existence of c. · MARX 661:27
Society is composed of two large c. · CHAM 250:25
sports for the ruling c. · HOBS 483:46
the privileged c.? · SIEY 938:69
To prove the upper c. · COWA 290:3
two c. in good society · SHAW 925:13
two c. of books · FORD 396:3
two c. of travel · BENC 89:48
wrote about working c. · WAUGH -101:5
classic A c. · TWAIN 1034:16
No c. resembles any previous c. · HEMI 471:42
tread on c. ground · ADDI 6:98
classical c. era was epic · HUGO 501:56
c. music and jazz · PREV 789:27
c. music of now · MACC 626:60
c. period was healthy · GOET 431:79
C. quotations is the parole · JOHN 531:17
classics bellyful of the c. · MILL 677:17
c. are only primitive literature · LEAC 589:40
keep the C. at hand · WOOLF 1093:80
the c. in paraphrase! · POUND 785:62
used to be c. · WAUGH 1057:91
classification c. of all things · DURK 357:71
find fault with a c. · MILL 675:74
classless c. society · MARX 661:27
classroom Socrates in every c. · GRIS 447:66
clatter c. of high voices · DOYLE 343:93
draws the curtains…with a great c. · OSBO 745:67
Claudius Emperor C. · LONG 610:92
clause but this one c. · RABE 799:86
Clavell How to frighten Miss C. · BEME 89:45
Claver'se 'twas C. who spoke · SCOTT 856:16
Clavering C., and Havering · LEVE 600:23
claw red in tooth and c. · TENN 999:32
red in tooth and c. · TENN 999:47
claws c. that catch · CARR 239:47
neatly spreads his c. · CARR 238:22
pair of ragged c. · ELIOT 367:50
clay Art's subject human c. · AUDEN 46:54
C. blurs the whitewash · AVIS 53:76
c. grew tall · OWEN 748:20
C. lies still · HOUS 494:42
compounded am with c. · SHAK 914:72
dead and turned to c. · SHAK 893:79
feet…of iron and part of c. · BIBLE 129:45
from gold and c. · SHEL 931:53
Honouring itself the c. rears up · BARK 71:18
loam, or painted c. · SHAK 866:40
made of c. · GERS 420:15
of c. and wattles · YEATS 1104:57
out of the miry c. · BIBLE 115:66
Potter and c. endure · BROW 199:76
power over the c. · BIBLE 149:32
pure c. of time's mud · MALA 641:9
shall the c. say to him · BIBLE 126:94
clean Bath twice…to be really c. · BURG 205:80
C. from my hand? · SHAK 908:49
c. hands · GALS 413:5
grew more c. and white · BROW 197:18
one more thing to keep c. · FRY 408:14
Then I was c. and brave · HOUS 494:45
thugh dirty is c. · FLEM 394:65
trying to play c. · PARK 753:86

clean (*contd.*)
until your bones are c. · ADCO 6:96
upbringings that were so c. · COUP 289:82
vanished c. · GURN 449:48
will these hands ne'er be c.? · SHAK 910:78
Wondrously c. · WALP 1051:85
cleaners father had a chain of dry c. · BENN 91:82
cleanest c. and beautifullest · DEFOE 312:85
cleaning Yesterday, We had daily c. · REED 804:80
cleanliness c. of…backyards · MAIL 639:87
C. is next to Godliness · DICK 326:64
clear c., attentive mind · SNYD 951:81
free and c. of any image · SHAK 895:34
how thin and c. · TENN 997:99
might be too c. · GREE 445:37
not immediately c. · THUR 1019:30
so c. and distinct · HUXL 508:98
unduly c. · GREE 445:34
want to make that very c. · ROMN 821:29
clear-eyed c.-e. adjustments · DAY 310:47
clear-sighted c.-s. nor accurate · TROL 1028:95
not the c.-s. who rule the world · CONR 285:12
cleared no matter how carefully c. · SHUL 936:34
clearer see a little c. · BRAC 183:71
clearing-house c.-h. of the world · CHAM 249:14
clears water c. us of this deed · SHAK 908:50
cleavage c. contributes to narrow · ROSS 823:65
cleft c. for me · TOPL 1023:7
clefts narrow the cross c. · ROSS 823:65
clench can c. and fight · MITC 696:81
clenched held my flower in a c. fist · HOFF 484:55
clenches wit degenerating into c. · DRYD 347:59
Cleopatra C.'s morality · LAUT 584:53
C.'s nose: if it had been shorter · PASC 757:59
down the Nile as C. · BROWN 194:54
gone to gaze on C. · SHAK 905:69
in the bed of C. · BROW 196:8
not…less than C. · DRYD 348:90
clergy all the c. you can despatch · CHIS 260:54
c. were beloved · SWIFT 986:18
without the benefit o' the C. · CONG 280:11
clergyman salary of a beneficed c. · WAUGH 1056:77
clergymen men, women, and c. · SMITH 949:51
clerical features of c. cut · ELIOT 371:36
clerk an unmannerly fat c. · SHER 933:87
both the priest and c.? · SHAK 867:63
grete c. of nygromancye · MALO 642:23
small c. of some hotel · MANS 647:5
small house agent's c. · ELIOT 369:89
was the best c.. · MACA 621:77
clerks c. been noght wisest men · CHAU 255:74
clever c., but is it Art? · KIPL 561:41
c. enough to get money · CHES 259:34
c. to a fault · BROW 199:56
Everything c. has been thought · GOET 431:79
manage a c. man · KIPL 560:16
too c. by half · MAJOR 640:99
cleverness The obstinacy of c. · STOWE 979:90
cliché books, convention and c. · POUND 785:48
c. and an indiscretion · MACM 635:4
c. of whites being ignorant · ANGE 20:31
clichés half-truths and c. · TOOLE 1023:4
click constant c. and kissing · BETJ 100:49
clicking c. with the subject · EISE 364:94
client c. is fain to hire a lawyer · BUTL 216:1
c. must be led to safety · MORT 710:92
dialogue between c. and architect · STERN 968:86
serving the c. · JOHN 524:64
venomous, and ungrateful c. · UPDI 1036:56
cliff drive over a c. · VENA 1042:30
edge of some crazy c. · SALI 839:28
far from c. and scar · TENN 997:99
In a coign of the c. · SWIN 988:56
lawyers going over a c. · HUNT 504:17

cliff (*contd.*)
like jumping off a c. — BRYAN 201:13
off the edge of the c. — MOND 699:39
cliffs chalk c. of D. — BALD 65:11
c. of fall — HOPK 492:4
rubies in certain c. — MORE 707:53
yet still the solitary c. — WORD 1095:16
clift put thee in a c. of the rock — BIBLE 107:77
climate c. allows him no chance — KIPL 560:21
c. is bracing — MACG 630:25
c. of a perpetual Turkish bath — SWET 983:52
c. of Manitoba — ANON 25:18
c. suspends…understanding — BROO 192:16
cloudy c. — BYRON 221:23
common where the c.'s sultry — BYRON 222:28
enquiries about the UK c. — SAMU 840:47
fertile c. dwell — SHAK 897:96
in love with a cold c. — SOUT 954:28
not so much the result of c. — FUSE 410:59
our chilling c. — SWIFT 985:1
spring in their c. — DOUG 341:59
whole c. of opinion — AUDEN 47:68
Your anger was a c. — PIER 769:34
climates and manners, c. councils — TENN 994:58
climax cap and c. of…years — PEARY 762:35
flaming, fatal c. — SASS 845:25
works its way up to a c. — GOLD 434:42
climb teach ye how to c. — MILT 684:37
climbing c. a birch tree — FROST 406:80
c. into jobs — REST 807:17
C. over rocky mountain — GILB 424:59
clime born in the same c. — BYRON 223:46
Love…no season knows nor c. — DONNE 336:77
sweet golden c. — BLAKE 167:87
visit our c. — BLAKE 165:57
climes styles for different c. — BROD 189:65
clinging c. blindly to the vices — FAUL 383:76
clingy bunches of c. sob sisters — PAGL 749:16
Clinton classic C., sincere — MARA 649:36
Hillary C. is responsible — MACC 627:69
President C. returned today — DOWD 342:77
cloak c.…an iron cage — WEBER 1059:19
knyf under the c. — CHAU 255:31
cloaks c. for untidy minds — MOND 699:40
display of their c. — DICK 322:66
clock Church c. at ten to three? — BROO 193:30
c. is always slow — SERV 859:57
c. with weights and chains — COLUM 278:62
hands of a great c. — WILL 1082:82
I open with a c. striking — SHER 934:9
produce? The cuckoo c. — WELL 1063:1
putting the c. on half an hour — KIER 556:59
regard the hand of the c. — LECO 592:2
time runs, the c. will strike — MARL 654:20
watch the c. for you — SHAK 913:66
wind up the c.? — STER 968:89
clockmakers Swiss c. — STRA 979:4
clocks all the c. in the city — AUDEN 47:61
c. the tongues of bawds — SHAK 875:36
c. were striking thirteen — ORWE 745:54
morning c. will ring — HOUS 494:43
Stop all the c. — AUDEN 46:58
clockwork c. orange — BURG 205:78
every 30 years like c. — SIMON 939:83
clod turned her into the c. — ALTH 15:62
clods Calcine its c. — BROW 198:49
c. and trampled earth — MUIR 712:29
clog c. the foot of a flea — SHAK 895:29
clogs age to quit their c. — MILT 686:76
c.…lasted longer than shoes — WILS 1085:27
c.…which else might oversoar — SHEL 930:25
clumping…all in c. — ORWE 742:91
To hang c. on 'em — SHAK 898:11
cloister c. without a library — GEOF 418:79

cloister (*contd.*)
in the court a c. — AELR 9:52
studious c.'s pale — MILT 683:15
cloisters quiet collegiate c. — CLOU 271:44
clones c. have hung — HUGH 500:32
Clootie Satan, Nick, or C. — BURNS 209:73
Cloots auld C., I ken ye're thinkan — BURNS 209:74
close c. of day — YEATS 1105:71
C. the play — KAUF 543:19
day must have its c. — STOWE 978:88
ineffective from c. up — SCHO 849:99
live too c. to each other — GOLD 432:39
still hasten to a c. — COWP 292:31
closed c. Saturday night — KAUF 542:14
closes or flowered c. — SWIN 987:44
closest human beings who seem c. — PRIE 790:47
closet forth the c. brought a heap — KEATS 546:95
I'll to thy c. — SHAK 862:41
put me in the C. — DICK 328:2
when thou prayest, enter into thy c. — BIBLE 135:48
closets Out of the c. — ANON 27:92
closing opening and c. of a door — SAND 841:65
you have a hell of a c. — REAG 804:71
cloth Fine c. is never out of fashion — FULL 410:50
new c. unto an old garment — BIBLE 136:71
On a c. untrue — GILB 425:91
clothe c. my naked villainy — SHAK 863:53
clothed c. with the heavens — TRAH 1025:27
C. with his breath — TENN 1004:44
clothes Angels were, but with c. — LOVE 615:68
as if she were taking off all her c. — COLE 275:31
as much for her c. as for herself — WHAR 1068:97
being to buy new c. — MONT 701:57
brand-new suit of c. — HERB 476:42
buy a teenager new c. — WHITE 1070:38
c. and hair were neat — GUNT 449:87
C. are our weapons — CART 242:92
c. easy to copy — SCHI 847:62
C. make the poor invisible — HARR 458:26
c. off and hang her up — NATI 721:90
c. possess an influence — ALCO 12:99
c. were all tarnished — MOORE 704:7
covered him with c. — BIBLE 110:53
earthly interests…held up, by C. — CARL 234:50
Englishwoman's c. — SITW 941:17
Fine c. are good — JOHN 529:82
Good c. open all doors — FULL 410:52
good smell of old c. — BROO 192:20
Italy…a dealer in second-hand c. — MARI 651:48
Kindles in c. a wantonness — HERR 478:68
liars in old c. — MARQ 656:52
liquefaction of her c. — HERR 478:67
make a suit of c. — HUME 503:6
married, not unto my c. — SHAK 864:84
musty odour of old c. — ACKR 4:54
not quite enough c. — WILDE 1078:91
Old C. are not venerable — CARL 235:58
old c. know who's master — SHER 933:80
On the state of her c. — NASH 719:55
out of these wet c. — ANON 26:38
politics with c. off — BRAD 183:82
poured into his c. — WODE 1089:97
require new c. — THOR 1016:82
soul…is his c. — SHAK 901:75
take the girl's c. off — CHAN 251:46
taste for French c. — SCHL 848:77
the c. don't wear her — QUANT 796:49
time when you have to let your c. — MIDL 674:50
walked away with their c. — DISR 332:93
wears her c. as if — SWIFT 986:9
Who touched my c.? — BIBLE 141:85
witnesses laid down their c. — BIBLE 147:87
wore torn c. — SPEN 956:77
clothing Be courtly ay in c. — DUNB 355:38

clothing (*contd.*)
c. affords a glimpse — BART 75:82
c. for the soul divine — BLAKE 168:3
c. of a manservant — HUGO 502:73
Gave thee c. of delight — BLAKE 166:63
Things in book's c. — LAMB 577:40
cloths embroidered c. — YEATS 1105:65
cloud a fair luminous c. — COLE 274:6
avails a storm c. — RYDER 834:51
black c. carries the sun away — ELIOT 370:28
c. in trousers! — MAYA 665:3
c. instead, and ever-during — MILT 689:31
From c. to tumbling c. — YEATS 1105:72
great c. came over me — FOX 400:74
he melted like a c. — TENN 1004:56
If a c. knew loneliness — RICH 809:56
kerchiefed in a comely c. — MILT 683:13
Like a fiend hid in a c. — BLAKE 167:94
little c. out of the sea — BIBLE 111:46
moon on this c. sea — SCOTT 852:36
motions of the wind and c. — LEE 593:18
no C. nor Sun — DONNE 339:34
no silver lining…without its c. — STER 968:83
On a c. I saw a child — BLAKE 166:62
peaks of c. — CIAR 265:50
pillar of a c. — BIBLE 106:64
set my bow in the c. — BIBLE 104:15
She faded, like a c. — SHEL 930:38
so great a c. of witnesses — BIBLE 154:54
some gilded c. — VAUG 1040:15
Stooping through a fleecy c. — MILT 682:9
The flying c. — TENN 1000:56
wandered lonely as a c. — WORD 1099:67
wild geese lost in c. — BASHO 76:5
yon labouring c. — MARL 654:21
cloud-capped c.-c. towers — SHAK 917:36
cloud-encircled c.-e. meteor — SHEL 929:71
cloud-topped Behind the c.-t. hill — POPE 780:37
cloud-waves Bronze c.-w. — FREE 404:36
clouded if your life should become c. — OVID 747:4
cloudiness full of frost…and c.? — SHAK 880:67
clouds After the greatest c. — ALAN 11:78
all the c. that lowered — TWAIN 1033:89
carries the c. with it — LEON 597:78
caught up…in the c. — BIBLE 153:25
c. are deep — FREE 404:35
c. are lightly curled — TENN 994:52
c. do often rest — MILT 682:1
c. of his own glory — GREE 444:3
c. of the table above — MONRO 700:48
c., or mud, or like places — LEON 597:83
c. takes all away — SHAK 860:74
c. that blinded — PIER 769:34
c. the chase — MERE 671:16
c. turning blood red — MUNCH 713:51
c. were touched — WORD 1100:79
cometh with c. — BIBLE 156:97
dying to contend — SHAK 862:21
gloom of c. — ADDI 7:17
He comes with c. descending — WESL 1066:65
heaven but the c. — RUSK 830:79
Heaven is free From c. — BYRON 220:94
left the red c. — TANN 991:96
let the c. rain down — BIBLE 159:51
Never doubted c. would break — BROW 200:3
no pity sitting in the c. — SHAK 869:14
nor the c. return after the rain — BIBLE 123:42
O c., unfold! — BLAKE 168:19
O'er which c. — SHEL 929:99
piled gold c. — LARK 581:9
prince of the c. — BAUD 77:16
raise…wind, or rent the c. — MARL 654:12
shadows of the c. — WORD 1099:65
sit in the c. — SHAK 877:89

clouds (*contd.*)
slow movement of c. — DAYL 310:55
Somewhere among the c. — YEATS 1106:75
the poor Indian ... Sees God in c. — POPE 780:37
Through the dark c. — FORD 397:20
tossing sea of c. — BENU 94:33
trailing of glory — WORD 1098:51
When c. are cursed by thunder — THOM 1010:59
white c. floating — MACM 636:24
white c. fly — WU 1102:24
White c. on the wing — ALLI 15:54
wreathed in c. — WHITE 1071:48
Clough poet named C. — SWIN 988:51
clout hit her a great c. — STRO 980:6
cloven espied his c. foot — BALL -101:36
clover c. and timothy-tops — ROBE 814:16
C....is Aristocracy — DICK 328:15
cloverleaf flower is the concrete c. — MUMF 713:48
cloves cinnamon and c. — ANON 23:92
Clovis aunt of C. — SAKI 837:4
clown c., the boozer, the fighter? — MAST 663:63
like the idiot or c. — SITW 941:27
clowns those that play your c. — SHAK 891:34
club any c. that will accept me — MARX 659:3
belong to the most exclusive c. — NASH 719:54
best c. in London — DICK 327:84
far from the c. house — LINK 606:19
harte in one hand and a c. in the other — BILL 162:4
I am the C. Liar — SAKI 838:14
man...loyal to his c. — WHITE 1069:24
No c. has been good enough — BUSBY 215:83
savage wields his c. — HUXL 509:4
secret of managing a ball c. — STEN 968:75
clue Singularity...invariably a c. — DOYLE 343:95
Clunton C. and Clunbury — HOUS 495:60
clusters c. and constellations of data — GIBS 422:40
Where we such c. had — HERR 478:69
clutch Come let me c. thee — SHAK 908:39
clutching c. the inviolable shade — ARNO 38:93
Clyde on the bonnie banks o' C. — LAUD 583:39
co-operating c. and so self-moving — RYLE 834:54
c. in all that concerns — GEOR 419:88
co-operation c. in their mutual — NOVAK 732:36
Government and c. — RUSK 830:92
coach generals are in my c. — MARL 652:81
hold back against the c. — TROL 1028:88
looking for a body in the c. — HITC 482:24
politics is like...a football c. — MACC 625:41
rattling of a c. — DONNE 339:28
Up, and by c. — PEPYS 766:82
coaches c. shall be scrap — SAND 841:59
coachmaker o' mind the fairies' c. — SHAK 868:79
coal Affection is a c. — SHAK 864:91
c. to kindle fleshly flame — SPEN 958:14
island is made mainly of c. — BEVAN 101:63
it is a c. — PEELE 763:46
like a c. — SMART 944:69
live c. in his hand — BIBLE 124:61
the biggest c. block — HEAN 465:43
With England's own c. — KIPL 564:12
coalition You may call it c. — PALM 752:73
coalitions England does not love c. — DISR 333:99
coalminers keep c. off streets — BRES 187:36
coalmines in disused c. — KEYN 555:36
coals all eyes else, dead c.! — SHAK 912:40
Can one go upon hot c. — BIBLE 120:65
c. thereof are c. of fire — BIBLE 124:55
eyes that stare like c. — RANS 802:37
gang to the c. i' the morning — SKIR 943:56
heap c. of fire upon his head — BIBLE 122:1
piles of dry wood with red-hot c. — CISN 266:67
coarse c. emotion of mankind — ELIOT 366:38
c. warty hands — DONO 340:36
such a c. pattern — HARDY 456:98

coast c. where souls are lost — ANON 24:6
last train for the c. — MACL 633:63
look'd towards the French c. — STER 970:12
near the shadowy c. — THOM 1014:32
People can't die, along the c. — DICK 324:15
round the c. the languid air — TENN 994:48
scarcely visited any c. — JOHN 527:23
wild and breaker-beaten c. — BYRON 222:41
you c. for a while — REAG 804:71
coaster dirty British c. — MASE 662:38
coat brown c., the...stockings — MACA 623:4
c., and I would have given that — KRUG 570:2
c. Covered with embroideries — YEATS 1105:69
c. of many colours — BIBLE 105:39
did not wear his scarlet c. — WILDE 1078:96
eternal Footman hold my c. — ELIOT 367:51
for a riband to stick in his c. — BROW 198:34
good c. upon his back — JOHN 527:32
Grab your c. — FIEL 388:55
have a good c. — STAN 963:92
iron c. all overgrown — SPEN 958:10
love that loves a scarlet c. — HOOD 488:36
tattered c. — YEATS 1106:79
coats gold c. spots you see — SHAK 870:35
cobble-stones On c.-s. I lay — FLAN 391:23
cobbler body of a c. — LOCKE 609:74
c. stick to his last — APEL 31:87
cobblestreets the c. silent — THOM 1011:79
Cobleigh sounds like Uncle Tom C. — THOM 1010:71
Uncle Tom C. and all — BALL 68:59
cobra guile of a c. — WOOL 1094:90
cobweb c. of the brain — BUTL 216:15
foul black c. — WEBS 1060:49
cobwebs Laws are like c. — SWIFT 984:63
reasoners...make c. — BACON 55:29
weave fine c. — BUTL 216:8
Coca-Cola billboards did to C.-C. — UPDI 1037:57
cocaine C. habit-forming? — BANK 69:89
cock Before the c. crow — BIBLE 144:15
C. and a Bull — STER 970:16
c. doth craw — BALL 68:61
c. may craw — BURNS 211:2
c.'s shrill clarion — GRAY 442:64
c. who thought the sun had risen — ELIOT 365:10
c. with lively din — MILT 682:99
c. won't fight — BEAV 80:81
louder as the c. can crow — TROL 1028:79
Nationalism is a silly c. — ALDI 12:4
offer a c. to Asclepius — PLATO 774:17
this night, before the c. crow — BIBLE 140:49
with my old c. linnet — COLL 276:34
cock-up wash out of a c.-u. — ANON 29:33
cockade lad wi' his white c. — ANON 23:96
cockatoo cage...to a c. — SHAW 924:92
green freedom of a c. — STEV 971:38
cockatrice hand on the c.' den — BIBLE 125:68
cockerel calls with a c.'s tongue — LEE 593:15
cockle like him that soweth c. — BUNY 205:75
Cockney much of C. impudence — RUSK 831:9
cockroaches c. will still be here — JANO 518:54
cocks drowned the c.! — SHAK 903:17
set the c. a-crow — YEATS 1107:92
cocksure c....as Tom Macauley — MELB 667:24
cocktail c. is to...wine — CLAU 268:92
pause...known as c. hour — DEVO 318:91
weasel under the c. cabinet — PINT 770:47
cocoa C. is a cad — CHES 259:30
cocoon c. of its own thoughts — LOWE 616:87
people live wrapped tight in a c. — CARR 237:13
Cocqcigrues coming of the C. — KING 558:99
Cocteau C. thinks I am a poor thief — GENET 418:73
cod Boston...home of the c. — BOSS 180:28
O bely! O stynkyng c. — CHAU 255:41
code c....for those who oppose us — EISE 364:85

code (*contd.*)
rigid c. of immorality — BRAD 183:73
trail has its own stern c. — SERV 859:55
codes rape us with...their c. — FREN 404:39
codfish taste of c. in it — GRIEG 447:59
Codrus peals of laughter, C.! — POPE 781:61
coelacanth like the c. — HOGG 485:68
coffee c. and doughnuts — DAVI 308:15
c. and oranges — STEV 971:38
measured out my life with c. spoons — ELIOT 367:49
morning cup of c. — HOLM 486:15
Rock 'n' roll is instant c. — GELD 417:67
wear c. as a perfume — VAND 1039:98
went on drinking c. — GREE 444:4
coffee-house some obscure c.-h. — MONT 701:57
coffer litel gold in c. — CHAU 254:22
coffin Bring out the c. — AUDEN 46:58
heart is in the c. — SHAK 884:51
Shaped like a c. — MACN 637:49
silver plate on a c. — CURR 301:17
turns in his c. — GILB 426:99
coffins c. were looking up — DICK 321:35
cogent equally c. — GASK 415:33
cogging Some c., cozening slave — SHAK 900:49
cogitations c. still amaze — ELIOT 367:51
cogito c., ergo sum — DESC 317:79
coherence all c. gone — DONNE 338:13
coign In a c. of the cliff — SWIN 988:56
coil shuffled off this mortal c. — SHAK 890:21
coin single c. to medicine — VALLE 1038:89
smallest current c. — BIER 160:66
coinage powerful c. — PLOUT 775:35
coiner c. of sweet words! — ARNO 38:94
coins and like to c. — TENN 1003:38
bater it for silver c. — NGU 725:45
glory in large c. — HUGO 502:78
silver c. multiplying — WALC 1048:39
coition trivial and vulgar way of c. — BROW 195:91
coke Happiness is like c. — HUXL 506:61
Coke cantaloupe in a C. bottle — JONES 533:59
C. bottles...great modern things — WARH 1053:22
Coketown C....ugly citadel — DICK 325:42
cold being white is c. and sad — RHYS 808:26
blood was c. — SCOTT 853:44
blow in c. blood — SHAW 922:52
called a. a c. — BENN 91:89
Came in from the C. — LECA 592:93
careful c. beginneth — SPEN 957:6
c. and certain friends — HUGO 502:82
c. as truth — RHYS 808:28
c. coming they had of it — ANDR 19:13
c. coming we had of it — ELIOT 369:2
c. doesn't crouch over one — LAWR 586:89
C. doth not sting — NASHE 721:80
C. in the earth — BRON 191:9
c. o' the moon — BROW 200:81
c. reaches of the universe — KENN 551:69
c. roads...c. news — SCOTT 856:9
c., uncertain of all — WILL 1082:83
comfort me with c. — SHAK 872:74
dressed ever caught a c.? — NIET 729:91
Europe catches c. — METT 672:28
feel hot and think c. — CARY 243:17
foot and hand go c. — ANON 23:84
Give them the c. steel — ARMI 35:44
glass...hard, c. and misted over — RHYS 808:31
going down and becoming c. — SMITH 948:35
have to do that c. — HEMI 470:30
heart grown c. — SHEL 931:47
hot temper leaps o'er a c. decree — SHAK 874:12
in love with a c. climate — SOUT 954:28
in the c. grave leave — WEBS 1059:29
in the darkness and the c. — STEV 976:58
ink in my pen ran c. — WALP 1051:82

cold (*contd.*)
makes c. weather — SHAK 917:48
my boy? Art c.? — SHAK 903:21
naked in the dark and c. — LEGU 594:23
neither c. nor hot — BIBLE 157:6
No worse than a bad c. — MARX 659:5
silver thimble lies c. — SITW 941:25
'Tis bitter c. — SHAK 887:42
too c. always — SMITH 948:33
too c. for hell — SHAK 908:51
too c. for the spectators — SMITH 948:26
wert thou in the c. blast — BURNS 213:50
what I got…was a c. — THOR 1017:94
wind was c. — SCOTT 853:42
yet so warm and yet so c. — LAWS 588:21
colder even c. war — KENN 551:69
coldness heat full of c. — LYLY 620:59
colds c. a forward spring remove? — DONNE 337:80
Coleridge C.…has lately taken wing — BYRON 221:25
C. lull the babe at nurse — BYRON 219:64
Cultivate simplicity, C. — LAMB 576:6
indulgences of C. — THUR 1019:42
observed by C. — WORD 1099:75
shut up, like C. — QUIL 797:63
You will see C. — SHEL 929:10
Coliseum While stands the C. — BYRON 220:3
collage C. is a supersensitive — ERNST 379:11
collapse Agreement…starts to c. — SHUL 936:34
all his plans c. — JOSE 537:34
When I see my friends c. — SKEL 942:38
collapses nothing c. — WHIT 1072:78
collar Malachi wore the c. — MOORE 706:33
shirt or c. ever comes back — LEAC 589:44
collar-rolls In velvet c.-r. — KIPL 564:5
collarbone silly old c.'s bust — BETJ 101:56
collaterals I detest c. — SOME 952:99
colleagues for myself and my c. — PEEL 763:42
former c. are to be believed — HOWE 497:95
most eminent of his c. — DISR 333:3
Most of my c. were -ists — HUXL 508:97
Smarter than his c. — REST 807:14
collecting what c. is all about — ANNE 20:39
collection c. of unrealistic goals — LURIE 619:43
extraordinary c. of talent — KENN 551:72
collections those mutilators of c. — LAMB 577:32
collective c. opinion…make history — SAFI 836:72
collectors great c. before me — DOUG 341:59
one-night stands in c.' homes — RAUS 802:42
college at school or c. — STEV 974:19
endow a c., or a cat — POPE 780:27
Fellows of another c. — LITT 607:42
Magdalen C. — GIBB 421:26
supress each cathedral and c. — MACA 622:93
This great C. — HOUS 495:67
collie tither was a ploughman's c. — BURNS 209:71
collier-brigs cabooses of c.-b.'s — DICK 324:18
Collins if you do not marry Mr C. — AUST 51:38
colloquial clear it from c. barbarisms — JOHN 525:93
colloquialisms c., its humour — ROLL 821:26
collusive the puff c. — SHER 934:7
Cologne wash your city of C. — COLE 275:26
colonel c. comes from Brian's race — DAVIS 309:39
For the C.'s Lady — KIPL 562:57
colonial have to be c. to know — WALC 1048:34
large sections of the c. population — SCHL 848:73
colonialism C. forces the people — FANON 382:61
C. is not satisfied — FANON 382:60
colonies finest C. under the Crown — STUA 980:9
In the c. the economic substructure — FANON 382:59
products of all the c. — SITW 941:17
this realm, its c. — QUIL 797:59
colonists Roman c. settled in Britain — HYDE 509:12
colonization c. by any European — ADAMS 6:90
c. planted the seeds — MARI 650:62

colonized among c. people — SART 844:20
Colonus Singer of sweet C. — ARNO 36:62
colony an economic c. — TSON 1031:41
brown men from a distant c. — PRIE 790:46
Crown C. system — KING 559:5
founders of a new c. — HAWT 461:69
from c. to nation to c. — INNIS 512:52
Colossus Like a C. — SHAK 882:20
Milton…could cut a C. from a rock — JOHN 532:29
colour abominable c. of his hair — HOUS 496:88
altered the c. of my mind — BRON 191:10
Any c.—so long as its black — FORD 396:8
Beige! Just my c. — DEWO 319:97
between the mind and the c. — HEPW 473:79
burned gold was his c. — CHAU 255:45
cast thy nightly c. off — SHAK 888:48
citizens of c. are concerned — KING 557:78
C. and bite permeate a language — SAFI 835:68
c. I want those handrails — TRUMP 1030:37
c. is a means of exerting — KAND 541:97
c. is the goal — HEIN 467:74
C. is the ultimate — RUNGE 829:56
c. of a beryl — BIBLE 128:34
c. of my soul is iron-grey — DEBU 311:66
c. of one's skin — BALD 64:93
c. of sand — ASHB 41:54
c. of shadows — WALC 1048:39
c. of the sky — CRANE 295:13
c. of their skin — KING 557:76
C. possesses me — KLEE 566:48
c. shrieked — MUNCH 713:51
c. to that of the Senses — MATI 664:75
exact c. and shape — MONET 700:43
for the c. of his hair — HOUS 496:87
formal principle of its c. — SHEL 931:56
heart never knows the c. of the skin — GEOR 419:90
know the c. of that blood — KEATS 548:21
know the c. rose — ABSE 1:6
life is c. and warmth — GREN 446:52
loses c. with the slightest — VIEI 1044:75
Nature's scheme of c. — STRE 980:5
No c., only nuance! — VERL 1042:37
paint the c. of the wind — BODE 171:56
problem of race and c. — DUBO 353:9
problem of the c. line — DUBO 353:5
relationships of c. or form — ROTH 826:26
see a man…not a c. — STEV 973:84
subtle spies Of c. — FREE 404:31
'tis a c. she abhors — SHAK 895:19
'twas a c. he never liked — SHAK 882:13
What c. is your parachute? — BOLL 172:73
yearned for warmth and c. — TENN 1003:19
colour-bar c.-b. and beer — NOON 731:25
colour-blind wise person is c.-b. — SCHW 852:32
coloured For c. girls — SHAN 918:68
makes a man c. — HUGH 499:22
Negroes…replaced c. people — FEIF 384:98
shadow over the c. — BUCK 203:33
colouring c. of a thought — SITW 941:28
colourists Painters who are not c. — DELA 314:23
colours All c. will agree — BACON 56:47
coat of many c. — BIBLE 105:39
c. don't quite match your face — ASHF 41:64
c. laid so thick — DRYD 346:49
composition of c. — THEO 1008:33
flat surface covered with c. — DENIS 316:58
fresh c. deck the wanton prime — SPEN 958:19
Fresh-quilted c. through the air — HERR 477:61
howl of unnerving c. — TZARA 1035:34
I had shown my c. — ACHE 3:33
Lentil-soup c. — HUGH 499:26
more c. in ten minutes — DICK 322:66
Scents, c., and sounds — BAUD 77:17
see the difference of the c. — MELV 668:51

colours (*contd.*)
table of c. — GALE 412:88
troop their c. — BAIN 62:77
colts play left-guard for the C. — BRES 187:36
columbine pink and purple c. — SPEN 957:93
Columbus C. and his men — WILB 1075:20
C. of our shore — WENT 1065:54
first carnival person was C. — COLE 273:75
my youth in C., Ohio — THUR 1018:16
column The fifth c. — MOLA 698:15
thunderhead-like c. — AGAWA 10:67
urn Throws up a steamy c. — COWP 293:60
columns c. of the old rain forest — AMIS 17:87
Greeks were hiding behind their c. — DEKO 313:18
moved…in c. — WELL 1063:11
coma eight-year c. — BENT 93:31
keep the mothers in a state of c. — DAVI 307:4
Comacho C. was very nearly illiterate — VARG 1040:7
comb c. my hair — BALL 67:57
fight between two bald men over c. — BORG 179:15
combat c. the monster — BALZ 68:68
naval c. — GIBB 421:23
set a c. between them — BALL -101:37
combative made a c. apology — SHUL 935:28
combats causes them to hide their c. — BALZ 69:75
comber c. wind-hounded? — KIPL 563:90
combination c. of half-truths — TOOLE 1023:4
c. of outward and inward facts — ELIOT 365:7
c. that is necessary — ROOS 822:50
constant and uniform c. — SMITH 946:89
exquisite c. — TROL 1027:71
unbeatable c. — ANGE 19:18
combinations irregular c. — JOHN 525:93
combine C. your hearts in one — SHAK 882:12
sure to c. — JAMES 517:38
combustion ruin and c. down — MILT 687:88
come Art thou he that should c. — BIBLE 136:82
avoid what is to c. — SHAK 892:57
c. again with rejoicing — BIBLE 119:40
C. and take them — LEON 597:86
C., seeing night — SHAK 909:59
C. what c. may — SHAK 907:22
hands…remembered to c. with him — PRIT 791:60
know not how to… c. in — BIBLE 111:55
let him c. out — JOHN 531:21
One to c. and one to go — CARR 241:74
shape of things to c. — WELLS 1065:46
Surely I c. quickly — BIBLE 159:40
Then c. on, c. on — HERR 478:65
was, and is, and is to c. — BIBLE 157:9
comedian test of a real c. — NATH 721:86
comedians being c. — GREE 444:19
comedies c. are ended — BYRON 223:48
comedy All I need to make a c. — CHAP 252:65
Applaud…the c. is over — BEET 84:53
at a c. we only look — HUXL 507:82
both c. and tragedy — THUR 1019:45
c. in one hundred different acts — LAFO 575:96
C. is a very serious thing — GARR 415:32
C. is an imitation — SIDN 937:64
C.…is harder to do — MALA 641:7
c. paints characters — HUGO 501:70
Farce is nearer tragedy…than c. — COLE 275:28
happier still is that musical c. — AGATE 10:63
make in som c.! — CHAU 254:14
Most Lamentable C. — SHAK 870:29
rules c. can tolerate — THUR 1019:49
Talking of the C. — JOHN 532:30
world is a c. — WALP 1057:9
Writers of c. have outlook — THUR 1019:48
comeliness no form nor c. — BIBLE 127:99
comely boast themselves more c. — MILT 683:19
Sae c. to be seen — SCOTT 854:78
comet come like a daytime c. — BISH 164:32

comet (*contd.*)
Woman is thought to be a C.   MAKIN 640:1
Comet On, C.! On! Cupid!   MOORE 704:6
comets Old men and c.   SWIFT 985:93
there are no c. seen   SHAK 883:32
comfort Be c. to my age   SHAK 885:81
before providing c.   MARI 652:77
beg cold c.   SHAK 872:74
carrion c.   HOPK 492:1
catechism of c.   BENE 89:58
c. across many a...night   NIET 728:88
C. came in with the middle classes   BELL 86:84
c. comes too late   SHAK 918:66
C.'s in heaven   SHAK 867:51
c. myself when   SURR 983:46
c. of thy worth and truth   SHAK 913:60
c. serves in a whirlwind   HOPK 492:5
c. to shift one's position   IRVI 513:67
c. ye my people   BIBLE 126:85
c. your bed   SHAK 883:30
C. yourself   PASC 758:79
dear husband for a c.   SMITH 948:28
hobbit-hole, and that means c.   TOLK 1022:86
in comparative c.   KING 559:4
loves...of c. and despair   SHAK 915:96
Money is a c.   ANON 21:58
mutual society, help, and c.   BOOK 175:45
no c. like...having deserved it   SHER 933:99
no c., only anxiety   FRIS 406:66
not another c. like to this   SHAK 899:21
not ecstasy but it was c.   DICK 325:51
Nothing else will give you any c.   SCOTT 856:18
only c. about being a woman   STARK 963:94
receives c. like cold porridge   SHAK 916:27
seeketh in society c.   BACON 55:23
sees too deep for c.   FADI 382:53
sense of inward c.   AUBR 45:37
Society is no c.   SHAK 916:15
Such c. as do lusty young men   SHAK 868:76
tell you naught for your c.   CHES 259:18
This must my c. be   SHAK 866:42
Thou art all the c.   SHAK 916:11
willing to live in c.   DUBO 353:9
comfortable c. years allowed to man!   SASS 845:23
Exploring...is not c.   BUTL 217:30
palace more c.   HOOV 490:64
something more c.   HARL 458:21
think about a more c. one   WILD 1079:25
When people are too c.   RICH 810:68
comforted Lord hath c. his people   BIBLE 127:97
refused to be c.   BIBLE 105:41
comforter C., where, where   HOPK 492:3
comforters miserable c. are ye all   BIBLE 113:10
comforting c....to be the recipient   FOWL 400:69
comfortless c., and worn, and old   ROSS 823:69
comforts adversity is not without c.   BACON 56:51
c. we despise   SHAK 906:88
disregard for the sublime c.   SHIP 935:21
helpers fail and c.   LYTE 621:67
King of c.   VAUG 1041:19
love and c. should increase   SHAK 899:22
comic encouragement of c. strips   UPDI 1037:62
comical often think it's c.   GILB 424:75
comics c....great modern things   WARH 1053:22
coming cold c. we had of it   ELIOT 369:3
c.! He is c.!   AYTO 53:86
going out and thy c. in   BIBLE 119:36
Welcome the c.   POPE 779:13
command at your c.   GRAV 439:16
basic c. of religion   TOYN 1024:22
c. me any service   SHAK 879:38
c. of that vital sea   CHUR 265:26
c. what you will   AUGU 49:11
Had thine at their c.   WORD 1098:58

command (*contd.*)
singular c., I do not understand   AUDEN 49:5
The c. 'Thou shall not kill'   JOHN 522:35
wide as his c.   DRYD 349:9
wisdom bears c.   MILT 694:39
commanded Have I not c. thee?   BIBLE 108:8
commanders c. of legions   JUVE 540:81
C. ...should die with their troops   CHUR 264:22
commandment c. of the Lord   BIBLE 114:45
c. on the pulse of life?   SHAK 872:73
c. that states, 'Thou shalt fly'   CLEE 268:99
first and great c.   BIBLE 139:34
indivisibility, the first c.   ROTH 826:23
new c. I give unto you   BIBLE 146:59
Science knows only one c.   BREC 186:28
This is my c.   BIBLE 146:64
commandments Christian c.   KIER 556:59
c. in your face   SHAK 861:99
keep his c.   BIBLE 124:44
love me and keep my c.   BIBLE 106:68
love me and keep my c.   BOOK 174:17
so persuading c.   DONNE 339:24
two great c. were   MACA 623:2
write poetical c.   BYRON 222:37
commands obedient to their c.   SIMO 939:85
commemorative cold c. eyes   ROSS 825:94
commendable silence is only c.   SHAK 873:89
commendation greater c.   DRYD 347:59
man's c. with woman   SHAK 895:28
commended highly c. of all   BUNY 205:72
comment C. is free   SCOTT 852:33
commentary c. on that cry   KAZA 543:28
proliferating c.   GRASS 439:13
commentators As learned c. view   SWIFT 985:3
C. economic studies   SAMU 840:46
commerce adventures...in c.   WEST 1068:88
c....enhanced by success   TREV 1026:53
form of c. and consumption   MARX 660:11
heaven fill with c.   TENN 995:77
In c. bygones are for ever bygones   JEVO 521:21
In matters of c.   CANN 230:72
increase of riches and c.   HUME 504:11
obstructed interstate c.   HOOV 490:69
poets of c.   GRAY 440:7
trade and c.   HALL 452:33
commercial among a c. one   FUSE 410:60
blend of the c. traveller   STAP 963:93
c. society   TREV 1026:53
concern for c. viability   MAMET 643:44
phonograph...is not of any c. value   EDIS 361:43
safe haven from c. considerations   SAFER 835:66
commercials 30-second c.   DANF 304:58
commission c. you to carry out   GOER 431:68
Each bullet has got its c.   DIBD 319:7
commitment C. to the poor   JOHN 523:37
with a three-ocean c.   HAYW 463:94
committee c. is an animal   LECA 592:94
horse designed by a c.   ISSI 514:81
written by a c.   GRIS 447:67
commodities c. derive their...value   RICA 808:35
into the c. market   TYSON 1035:31
levied upon c.   JOHN 526:11
commodity c. of good names   SHAK 875:38
C. fetishism   TATE 991:6
infinitely small amount of c.   JEVO 521:20
worker becomes...cheaper c.   MARX 661:26
Commodus accession of C.   GIBB 421:18
common call not thou c.   BIBLE 148:92
concerns the c. weal   GEOR 419:88
c. cry of curs   SHAK 911:17
c. good to all   SHAK 884:68
c. interest always will prevail   DRYD 349:25
c. is the commonplace   TENN 998:20
C. Law of England   HERB 474:2

common (*contd.*)
c. people swarm   SHAK 862:25
c. property of the nation   TIMES 1021:71
c. prudence, c. sense   SMITH 949:42
Crime is c.   DOYLE 344:6
dream of a c. language   RICH 809:52
he should not be so c.   WILS 1084:16
hose of c. sense   GILB 424:78
insipid c. sense   SALI 839:34
leapt straight past the c. cold   AYRES 53:85
lose their c. sense   STEIN 966:43
loves not the c. people   SHAK 911:7
make it too c.   SHAK 877:84
man of c. opinion   BAGE 62:66
man of great c. sense   SHAW 921:21
nor lose the c. touch   KIPL 564:9
praise that as c. sense   THOR 1017:92
speak as the c. people   ASCH 40:50
still be c., dear   RATT 802:41
surpass C. revenge   MILT 688:19
the man is a c. murderer   SAKI 838:12
Tom Paine's c. sense   ADAMS 5:88
trained and organized c. sense   HUXL 509:4
type of the c. man   ELIOT 370:35
way into the C. Market   WILS 1085:33
What [existentialists] have in c.   SART 844:13
commonalty dog to the c.   SHAK 910:99
commonplace c. young man   GILB 424:79
great minds in the c.   HUBB 498:4
Nature is c.   STEIN 966:44
never yawn or say a c. thing   KERO 553:12
Nothing is so c.   HOLM 486:93
nothing so unnatural as the c.   DOYLE 343:98
unassuming c. of Nature   WORD 1097:41
commons c., like an angry hive   SHAK 861:5
Lords and C. of England   MILT 686:71
commonwealth c. in which work   SHAW 923:76
C. is fixed and stable   BURKE 207:20
glorify God and benefit the C.   WENT 1065:53
head of the C.   ACHE 2:29
service and conduct of c.   BURKE 206:2
vision of the C.   MACM 635:3
commonwealths great c. collapse   HOPE 490:71
raise up c.   DRYD 349:10
communal experiment...in c. living   BOWL 182:55
communicate c. with ...emotions   ROTH 826:26
eliminate his ability to c.   SCHW 851:27
Genuine poetry can c.   ELIOT 369:7
power to c. with a third party   WOOLF 1092:61
communication c. Of the dead   ELIOT 372:70
evasion...rather than c.   JONES 533:56
In terms of c.   UMAS 1035:38
public opinion and mass c.   MERT 672:26
Thank you for your c.   ELLI 375:10
communications c. system   HAYEK 462:90
C. today puts a special   RUSK 830:73
divine c.   AUBR 45:37
Evil c. corrupt   BIBLE 151:70
communicator Great C.   ANON 28:8
communion C. of Saints   BOOK 173:94
equall c. and Identity   DONNE 339:34
communism beginning...of c.   HERZ 478:74
C. ...bores them   OROU 741:80
C. fits Germany   STAL 962:81
c. is a dead dog   SOLZ 952:97
C. is like prohibition   ROGE 820:13
C. is the opiate   LUCE 618:33
c. versus capitalism   NGUY 725:47
consistent opponent of C.   CHUR 264:19
how good c. is!   MAO 648:17
Russian c.is the illegitimate child   ATTL 44:11
socialism and c.   MORR 709:82
spectre of c.   MARX 660:14
USSR to reject C.   KHRU 556:46

communism (*contd.*)
When we reach c. — ZHANG 1109:18
communist Catholic and the C. — ORWE 745:49
C. must grasp the truth — MAO 648:22
C. 'war of liberation' — MACN 636:28
Every c. has a fascist — SPARK 955:57
fully-fledged c. — CAST 244:34
government of Vietnam is C. — GELL 417:72
higher phase of c. society — MARX 661:24
In c. society — MARX 660:10
member of the C. Party — THOM 1013:17
non-Communist premier — BOHL 171:62
tremble at a c. revolution — MARX 660:15
Vietnam took the c. road — NGUY 725:48
would not even be c. — ZHIV 1109:22
communists looking...for C. — FOOT 396:92
theory of the C. — MARX 660:13
communities c....slightly removed — COOP 287:42
filthier and filthier c. — GARD 415:23
half-civilized c. — BAGE 62:64
community c. consisting of a master — BIER 161:87
c. is a fictitious body — BENT 92:12
c. lacks goods — CHUR 263:99
c. of Europe — GLAD 429:55
c. of thought — ADAMS 5:78
interests of the c. — TOCQ 1021:77
interests of...the c. — RICA 808:36
involved as a c. — GINS 428:33
member of a civilized c. — MILL 675:63
no finer investment for any c. — CHUR 265:27
Not c.; we're all isolated — BAIN 62:77
not life that is not in c. — ELIOT 370:19
not of war...but of c. — CHILD 260:52
part of the c. of Europe — SALI 839:35
rule of any modern c. — KEYN 555:39
scientific c. thinks — KUHN 570:14
well-conducted c. — CHIS 260:54
commuter C.—spends life — WHITE 1070:36
commuters C. depress me — COPE 287:50
compact c. of fire — SHAK 864:94
companies busy c. of men — MARV 658:83
great joint-stock c. — MILL 675:67
U.S.A. is a group of holding c. — DOSP 340:40
companion dear c. of my souls — MIDD 673:41
found a c. — THOR 1017:89
gave him a c. — VALE 1038:87
happiness of finding a c. — BERN 97:85
ideal c. in bed — DAVI 308:18
silent c., exacting and eternal — DELA 314:21
companionable c. as solitude — THOR 1017:89
companionless Wandering c. — SHEL 932:73
companions All her lovely c. — MOORE 706:35
c. for middle age — BACON 57:61
keep pace with his c. — THOR 1017:91
company Banish not...Harry's c. — SHAK 876:57
because we have c.? — JARRY 518:67
c. breaks up — CERV 248:67
c. of paper-blurrers — SIDN 937:65
c. of the like-minded — DELI 315:41
crowd is not c. — BACON 58:98
enjoying their c. — RUSS 832:26
frolicsome c. had begun — SCOTT 854:77
from mine own c. — SHAK 871:47
Good c., good wine, good welcome — SHAK 917:47
In c. with several other old ladies — DICK 325:48
In such a jocund c. — WORD 1099:69
leave all this constant c. — DONNE 336:64
live in c. with a body — DELA 314:21
man in jail has...better c. — JOHN 527:25
My idea of good c. — AUST 52:67
only c. whose assets all walk — MAYER 666:7
Our c. is too big — WILS 1084:21
provoked and have asked the c. — SNOW 950:72
tell a man who boozes by c. — BURT 213:61

company (*contd.*)
three is c. and two none — WILDE 1077:81
to shine in c. — SWIFT 985:90
Vandyke is of the c. — GAIN 411:70
When c. comes — HUGH 499:14
with all the c. of heaven — BOOK 174:28
worst of the c. — SWIFT 984:68
your bill of c. — SWIFT 984:70
compare c. to a stick and a string — JOHN 532:43
C. with Caesars — SHAK 877:91
Shall I c. thee — SHAK 912:48
comparison c. on point of beauty — MOORE 705:14
experience and c. — JOHN 531:10
in c. to the infinite — PASC 758:70
involuntary c. becomes a bore — HORN 494:37
read...partly for c. — SCHL 848:74
comparisons C. are odorous — SHAK 880:57
compass c. of his Canterbury Tales — DRYD 352:79
in that narrow c. — HUME 503:98
shorts in this c.? — MURR 715:76
compasses took the golden c. — MILT 691:85
compassion bowels of c. — BIBLE 156:91
character and c. — NEWM 724:33
c. and sacrifice — FAUL 383:77
c. may become a justice — JONS 535:97
c. on the son of her womb? — BIBLE 126:95
c. to solve even a little — WILS 1084:18
crumbs of c. — TUTU 1032:54
heavenly c. in your hearts — DICK 325:37
his father saw him, and had c. — BIBLE 143:1
Jesu, thou art all c. — WESL 1066:63
live without real c. — WILS 1084:19
Mercy, c., and justice — WAITE 1048:29
Samaritan...had c. on him — BIBLE 142:90
sharp c. of the healer's art — ELIOT 371:51
compassionate to be generous and c. — THAT 1007:8
compassions c. fail not — BIBLE 128:32
compensations c. for growing older — SKIN 943:54
competition Art...excudes all c. — FUSE 410:58
c. between expert — KEYN 554:34
C. brings out the best — SARN 843:97
c. the Laws of Death — RUSK 830:92
don't meet c. — REVS 807:20
free c. of the market — RICA 808:34
free c. was wasteful — PUZO 796:41
law [of c.] may be sometimes hard — CARN 236:6
tradition...Approves all forms of c. — CLOU 271:50
your only c. is idiots — MANK 645:75
complacence thou My sole c.! — MILT 689:40
complacent hauf o't smug, c. — SMITH 949:60
shake c. pillars — BETH 99:24
complain But do not c. — HAMM 453:47
farmers...flourish and c. — CRAB 294:78
musn't c. too much — GREE 444:19
Never c. and never explain — BALD 65:14
to whom to c. — FIRB 389:69
complainers loudest c. — BURKE 206:98
complains No one ever c. — SELF 857:37
complaint borne...without c. — ACHE 3:36
most fatal c. of all — HILT 481:11
complement inevitable c. — SCHU 851:21
mate with its c. of men — WRIG 1101:99
complete And in herself c. — MILT 692:95
articulate and c. — STEV 971:22
C. disillusionment — STEIN 965:36
c. sentences — GASS 416:36
Experience...is never c. — JAMES 516:19
made the pile c. — TENN 999:37
most c. and free — STEV 973:99
completion c. of socialism — MORR 709:82
time available for its c. — PARK 755:32
complex c. and irregular — SOLOW 952:93
military-industrial c. — EISE 364:88

complex (*contd.*)
religious beliefs...simple or c. — DURK 357:71
complexion bad c. — GILB 424:61
c. of them all — SHAK 875:34
c. we were not to spoil — SCHR 850:4
different c....than ourselves — CONR 284:89
gold c. dimmed — SHAK 912:48
thet depends on c. — LOWE 616:81
complexities All mere c. — YEATS 1106:84
beyond our own c. — WILL 1083:89
complexity didn't grasp his own c. — ELLI 375:19
possibility, c., and difficulty — TRIL 1026:56
reduce c. to simplicity — JAMES 517:39
respect for the c. of learning — JOVA 537:38
Unthinkable c. — GIBS 422:40
compliance by a timely c. — FIEL 388:49
c. with my wishes — CHUR 265:46
tame and servile c. — WHIT 1069:16
complicated any problem, however c. — ANDE 18:7
arrived at in a c. manner — SAND 840:54
pattern more c. — ELIOT 372:55
Things become c. — MOYN 711:15
When a guy gets too c. he's unhappy — CHAN 250:36
complications mysteries and c. — GELL 417:68
one of the worst c. — AGNEW 10:71
piling up of c. of every sort — JAMES 517:33
complicity our tribe's c. — HEAN 465:37
complies He that c. against his will — BUTL 217:25
compliment empty c. — GILB 425:83
greater c. than to be loved — MACD 628:4
take it as a c. — HAIG 450:9
compliments c. reaching the proper — KIPL 559:15
c. to the purist — CHAN 250:37
comply If you don't c. — KELM 549:32
compose Before I c. a piece — SATIE 846:45
feel the urge to c. — BRAH 185:6
Never c. anything — HOLST 487:5
Whether you c. or act — DIDE 329:27
write, c. or paint — GREE 444:25
composed c. as a conference report? — GRIS 447:67
c. too much — DVOR 357:82
c. wholly of constituents — RUSS 832:18
Cruel, but c. and bland — ARNO 38:99
composer demands of a c. — HONE 488:30
limit to the...time a c. — LAMB 577:47
modern c. is a madman — HONE 488:27
writer, the c., the artist — KENN 552:87
composers advise all sensitive c. — WALT 1052:12
Not many c. have ideas — GERS 420:6
works by contemporary c. — HEIF 467:67
composing C. is not a profession — HONE 488:28
in c. a work — PASC 757:67
composition c. more accurate — JONS 536:26
c. of colours — THEO 1008:33
c....of tried medicines — BACON 55:26
estimating my c. — AUST 51:50
One c. is meager — DIDE 330:40
pure-painting c. — MALE 641:11
style, not a c. — MORT 710:98
compositions Read over your c. — JOHN 529:64
compound urban c. — MACL 635:95
comprehensible world...is c. — EINS 363:73
comprehension c. of the layman — GOWE 437:82
devices of mere c. — HOLM 485:76
comprehensions Wider c. — FERG 385:14
compression c. is the first grace — MOORE 705:18
compromise C. makes a good — LOWE 616:90
C. used to mean — CHES 259:16
English love of c. — CARD 232:2
every prudent act...founded on c. — BURKE 207:14
idea of a c. — HUGH 500:51
would not tolerate c. on goals — DULL 354:26
compulsion c. doth in music lie — MILT 683:17
freely grows in deep c. — SMITH 946:2

compulsion (*contd.*)
Give you a reason on c.? — SHAK 876:55
ne'er can be…happy by c. — COLE 274:8
stern hand of C. — THUR 1019:43
compulsions air all our c. meet — LARK 581:2
c., the fantasies — LEGU 594:25
computer banks of every c. — GIBS 422:40
circuits of a digital c. — PIRS 770:51
c. is a fast idiot — AMER 16:65
c. must be questioned — MUMF 713:49
most extraordinary c. of all — KENN 551:78
no c. will ever ask — HOPP 493:16
computer-age c.-a. journalists — MACF 629:20
computers c. are…stupid — STER 968:82
world market for…five c. — WATS 1055:52
comrade c. with the wolf and owl — SHAK 902:14
Never leave a fallen c. — ANON 29:43
stepping where his c. stood — SCOTT 853:59
comrades blythe wi' C. dear — BURNS 210:79
c. apparently find it hard — GORB 435:56
c. chase…the fliers — CLOU 270:32
help our French c. — KITC 566:44
con great pains to c. it — SHAK 894:4
Thanks I must you c. — SHAK 902:93
concave hell's c., and beyond — MILT 688:5
conceal duty…to c. his artifice — OGIL 736:3
Fate tried to c. him — HOLM 486:94
concealed utterly c. all — THOM 1012:10
concealment c., like a worm — SHAK 894:15
conceit all his c. taken out of him — HOLM 486:82
As for c. — TROL 1027:82
c. o'bein' richt — MACD 627:76
C. spoils the finest genius — ALCO 12:97
in his own c. — GREE 445:33
never forgive any c. — DRYD 352:82
only a c. — KAVA 543:25
self and vain c. — SHAK 867:60
so to his whole c. — SHAK 890:14
conceited say he's c. — SALI 839:26
very c. scurvy one — JONS 535:93
who is not c.? — TROL 1027:70
conceits Be not wise in your own c. — BIBLE 149:36
c. as clownage keeps — MARL 652:84
Some people…run to c. — BART 74:72
conceive whatever we c. very clearly — DESC 317:80
conceived nothing… c. without God — SPIN 960:47
There is a man child c. — BIBLE 112:98
would seem to be well c. — GALB 412:83
concentrate c. on life — GIDE 423:46
c. to truth and liberty — SHEL 927:65
concentrated c. and it nourishes you — DOVE 342:76
concentrates c. his mind — JOHN 530:91
concentration c. camp is the final — MILL 677:7
open-ended stay in a c. camp — JOHN 523:44
concept abstruse and even partial c. — MILL 677:2
c. of God — BALD 64:99
c., structure, and style — POUS 787:99
conception false c. come true — MERT 672:24
questions enlarge our c. — RUSS 832:17
sorrow and c. — BIBLE 103:99
Yet her c. of God — STRA 979:95
conceptions All c. of God — WEIL 1062:84
concepts metaphysical c. — STEI 967:68
mythical c., sun-gods and the like — FRYE 408:21
up the stairs of his c. — STEI 966:52
conceptual c. art the idea — LEWI 602:71
concern c. not for your bodies — PLATO 773:3
c. was speech — ELIOT 372:73
life and its largert c. — ARNO 39:3
no c. for the common man — WILS 1084:16
no c. with business — KIPL 560:24
no kind of c. with it — WHIS 1069:14
two things that c. them — JUVE 540:81

concerned being ultimately c. — TILL 1020:63
concerns first step that c. me — KENN 552:4
futile his c. — SIMO 939:86
concert Christmas c. by Pavarotti — BURKE 208:54
c. is dead — GOULD 436:74
shot fired in…a c. — STEN 967:71
concerts don't write little c. — MERW 672:27
concessions c. of the weak — BURKE 206:5
conciet glutted with c. — MARL 654:13
newness, the democratic c. — LAWR 585:72
conclaves Kingly c. stern and cold — SHEL 930:16
conclusion assume…powerful c. — SOLOW 952:94
cannot come to any c. — SACK 835:63
c.: life is something — LEBO 591:82
c. must be very scientific — JAMES 518:51
c. no one has yet dared — NIET 727:70
c. that sex is a sublimation — LODGE 610:81
c. that they are élitist — LODGE 610:83
denoted a foregone c. — SHAK 899:41
economists…would not reach a c. — SHAW 926:42
glorious c. — HUSS 505:37
impelled to the c. — JERO 521:6
laugh together over so odd a c. — EDDI 360:19
Ninety-nine times, the c. is false — EINS 363:64
other is a c. — JOHN 526:1
Reasoning draws c. — BACON 60:43
three days to reach its c. — STOP 978:81
what better c. — TATE 991:5
conclusions draw the correct c. — KISS 565:30
Prime Minister reading out the c. — HESE 479:78
reach their c. about life — KIER 556:54
wrong c. at which mankind arrive — PALM 752:67
wrong in its c. — REGAN 805:95
concoct c. oneself — DOYLE 344:21
concord c. of sweet sounds — SHAK 873:3
lover of c. — BOOK 173:96
oft in pleasing c. end — MILT 695:53
Sinews of c. — FORD 397:12
concrete flower is the c. cloverleaf — MUMF 713:48
prams on c. balconies — BETJ 100:44
concubine c. or whore — HELO 469:6
too good to be your c. — SHAK 862:26
concupiscence wanderings of c. — BIBLE 131:83
concurrence fortuitous c. of atoms — PALM 752:73
condamné c. à être libre — SART 844:16
condemn cannot c. it — DURK 357:70
c. it as an improbable fiction — SHAK 895:31
thoughtless to c. them — BRON 191:93
condemnation c. is the favourite — NIET 728:86
no c. to them which are in Christ — BIBLE 149:25
condemned behaviour which is c. — SPEN 956:88
c. for what we are — FENT 385:3
c. to be free — SART 844:16
c. to repeat it — SANT 842:84
Grudge not…lest ye be c. — BIBLE 155:71
Prayers for c. man — WEST 1067:86
condensation clever c. — PULI 795:21
condescend c. to men of low estate — BIBLE 149:36
condition average c. of the people — MILL 674:61
bettering our c. — SMITH 946:92
c. By which all mortal — MILT 684:35
c. God hath given liberty — CURR 301:16
c. left to women — LEGU 594:26
c. of art — CONR 284:87
c. of being human — ANOU 31:77
c. of capital and population — MILL 674:56
c. of the case, was supernatural — MILL 675:73
c.…of Working Class — CARL 235:79
c. rather than a profession — GRAV 440:26
c. that things resound — MARI 651:7
economic c. has…improved — KRIS 569:95
Equality of c. is incompatible — COOP 287:42
excellence of his physical c. — NIVEN 730:6
fools decoyed into our c. — PEPYS 765:77

condition (*contd.*)
fugitives are of that c. — BACON 57:59
he knows his c. — PASC 758:74
looking cheerfully…in that c. — PEPYS 765:62
Man's c. Inconstancy — PASC 757:56
movement and not a c. — TOYN 1024:18
perfect c. of slavery — ASTE 43:92
rises above the human c. — PAZ 762:24
towards the c. of music — PATER 759:94
War is a c. of progress — RENAN 806:1
whole human c. — HOPP 493:14
conditioned I'm exhausted, or c. — PUIG 794:18
conditions Bad as our urban c. — HALD 451:16
c. that are unspiritual — MARX 660:6
establish c. — UNIT 1036:45
mirror of social c. — LIPP 606:35
play under bad c. — KAUF 542:15
social c. take recognizable — LIPP 607:36
they are only its c. — HEINE 467:71
under c.…unpropitious — ELIOT 372:54
condo forcing them to go c. — OROU 741:82
conduct c. of every private family — SMITH 945:88
C. is…our life — ARNO 39:33
its National c. — PULI 795:20
judgements on political c. — NEW 724:24
My c. shrieks aloud for apology — BEER 83:27
nice c. of a clouded Cane — POPE 779:2
observe a certain line of c. — MILL 675:65
one code of international c. — EISE 364:85
secure the good c. of women — WOLL 1091:35
strange c. — ASTE 43:93
cone country…is an inverted c. — JOHN 530:95
sweet volcanic c. — LOWE 617:8
treat nature by…the c. — CEZA 248:4
Coney Island C. I. of the Mind — FERL 386:19
confection c. of tried medicines — BACON 55:26
confer c. with thee somewhat — NASHE 721:78
conference c. With the dead! — WEBS 1061:68
naked into c. chamber — BEVAN 101:69
No grand idea…born in c. — FITZ 391:18
rather than hold three words c. — SHAK 879:38
sales c. resembles a Passion play — SCRI 857:24
to hear our c. — SHAK 879:51
confess cannot c. them — SHAW 921:27
C. yourself to heaven — SHAK 892:57
If we c. our sins — BIBLE 156:88
truer than tongue c. — HOPK 491:81
wiser world doth greater c. — CAREW 232:8
confessed before the world c. — HOW 497:90
confession c.…of its author — NIET 728:83
greatest c. of its failure — STEV 977:62
making my Easter c. — JOSE 537:33
rage for c., autobiography — MANS 647:5
silence is your c. — EURI 380:30
sweetness of c. — FIRB 389:72
confide c. freely in death — ANOU 30:73
seldom c. in those who are better — CAMUS 229:59
confidence a c. trick — WILS 1084:14
C. in an unfaithful man — BIBLE 121:99
fight with growing c. — CHUR 264:14
in quietness and in c. — BIBLE 126:79
something like c. — GOOCH 435:54
suaveness isn't born of c. — HYDE 509:15
unconditional c. of his people — WEI 1061:75
confident c. I can do well — JOHN 526:1
in this will I be c. — BIBLE 115:56
confiding c., the intimate — MACD 628:93
confinement c.'s lingering hour — BYRON 218:58
sentenced to solitary c. — WILL 1082:75
confirmation c. of truth — MILT 685:66
conflagrations c.…at Rome — AUGU 49:16
conflict brought into c. — BRIG 188:50
c. of its elements — BYRON 221:20
lexicon of c. and drama — SAFI 835:67

conflict (*contd.*)
Never in the field of human c.   CHUR 264:16
too weak the c. to support   SHAK 904:49
We are in armed c.   EDEN 360:23
conflicts internal c.   ROSS 823:65
conformity c. of the image   DIDE 329:25
reward for c.   BROWN 194:60
confounds not the deed C. us   SHAK 908:43
confronts c. man with...choice   SART 844:12
confrontation born of this c.   CAMUS 229:47
confused c. the free   STEV 973:82
confusing c., disorienting   RICH 809:48
confusion all a c.   SCHL 848:76
C. now hath made his masterpiece   SHAK 908:53
c. of goals   EINS 363:69
C. on thy banners wait   GRAY 442:79
except my own c.   KERO 553:13
great blooming, buzzing c.   JAMES 517:41
let me never be put to c.   BIBLE 117:88
levee from a couch in some c.   CONG 282:43
confute how to c. him   SELD 857:34
how to c. him   SELD 857:35
congestion TB...that is the c.   ALLEN 14:37
Congo C., creeping through   LIND 605:13
congratulate sometimes c. ourselves   HAWT 461:65
congratulations C....keep pouring   FREUD 404:41
congregation C. of Christ's flock   BOOK 175:35
Devil...hast the largest c.   DEFOE 312:75
landlord to the whole c.   ADDI 7:11
congress c. of stinks!   ROET 819:94
C. makes no progress   LIGNE 604:92
congressman easier...than...'C.'   GING 427:22
how to act like a C.   KENN 552:99
conjectural your audience is c.   ORWE 744:35
conjoined always c. together   HUME 503:99
conjunction epithalamic c.   ANDR 18:11
conjure c. up the blood   SHAK 881:84
conjuring c. trick with bones   JENK 520:99
conjuror level of the stage c.   MOORE 705:13
connect drive to c.   RICH 809:52
mystery of how they c. nouns   SAND 841:73
Only c.!   FORS 398:36
connection cannot find any artistic c.   KLEE 566:46
no c. worth speaking of   GALS 413:1
connections expresses the sum of c.   MARX 660:19
connoisseur c. of tame excitement   MOORE 705:26
connoisseurs c. of bread and butter   MACD 628:92
conquer able to fight and c.   TROT 1029:4
Antony should c. Antony   SHAK 906:94
cannot c. America   PITT 771:69
die here, and we will c.   BEE 82:9
easier to c. it   WALP 1051:86
England that was wont to c.   SHAK 867:49
In this sign, thou shalt c.   CONS 286:23
resolve to c. or die   WASH 1054:42
conquered c. and peopled   SEEL 857:28
C. people tend to be witty   BELL 88:29
God c.   JOHN 522:30
nation...perpetually to be c.   BURKE 206:6
Nothing can save the c.   VIRG 1045:84
same thing as the c.   ALEX 13:14
Thou hast c.   SWIN 987:40
will be c.   JOHN 532:35
conquering not c. but fighting well   COUB 289:71
worked too hard in c.   NAPO 718:35
conqueror commercial
traveller...missionary...barbarian c.   STAP 963:93
Love is a cruel c.   LAFO 575:92
overcame her ferocious c.   HORA 493:29
proud foot of a c.   SHAK 872:75
conquerors born of the c.   WRIG 1102:11
laurel, meed of mighty c.   SPEN 957:99
conquers Love c. all things   VIRG 1045:93
ruling passion c. reason   POPE 780:28

conquest c. of an unknown country   HEDIN 466:61
c. of the earth   CONR 284:89
end and object of c.   ALEX 13:14
fanned by C.'s crimson wing   GRAY 442:79
nature of a c.   SHAK 878:4
never again seek...territory by c.   WILS 1086:45
shameful c. of itself   SHAK 867:49
without the threat of c.   RODO 818:87
conquests all the c.   SPEN 958:17
all thy c., glories, triumphs, spoils   SHAK 883:43
conquistador by temperament... c.
                                                    FREUD 404:40
conquistadores c. stole a page   MARTI 657:56
conscience binding on the c.   JOHN 522:35
catch the c. of the King   SHAK 890:19
c., above all liberties   MILT 685:61
c....accomplishment of man's rest   BACON 57:73
c. ain't got no sense   TWAIN 1033:93
C. always has   ROBI 815:33
c. clear my chief defense   DYER 358:90
c. doth make cowards   SHAK 890:21
c. fools my wit!   JONS 534:82
C. has no more to do with gallantry   SHER 933:90
C. is a coward   GOLD 432:3
C. is but a word   SHAK 863:66
c. of the state   KING 558:84
C.: the inner voice   MENC 668:57
c. waked despair   MILT 689:46
c. with injustice is corrupted   SHAK 861:6
dilemmas of c.   SNOW 950:71
exact a survey of his c.   DONNE 339:32
free c. from the paw   MILT 686:80
go against it   LUTH 619:45
good digestion depends on a good c.   DISR 332:73
good music and a clean c.   HIND 481:13
however strict their social c.   SMITH 947:18
In my c....the baggage loves me   CONG 280:93
just as much c.   STOWE 978:85
keeper of his c.   DAVI 308:16
live with a good c.   SMITH 947:16
mortal sin on my c.   WILS 1084:12
Neither c. nor sanity   MACN 636:29
Nobody has any c.   HAWT 461:81
not burdening one's c.   WEIZ 1062:87
O coward c.   SHAK 863:62
People talk about the c.   JAMES 516:26
policy sits above c.   SHAK 901:90
priest...who...[keeps] a c.   SMITH 949:45
rule is a person's c.   LEE 593:8
Science without c.   RABE 799:87
siding champion c.   MILT 683:25
still and quiet c.   SHAK 918:60
sword with a clean c.   WILH 1080:39
testimony of a good c.   KEMP 549:43
the republic of c.   HEAN 465:41
their c. as their King   TENN 1002:17
to irritate your c.   OHEN 737:18
torn c. brings about   HUGO 502:83
umpired c., whom if   MILT 689:37
will not cut my c.   HELL 468:94
wound My c.   VAUG 1041:16
consciences c. about doing evil   MORE 707:49
c. of the citizens   JOHN 522:32
conscious always c. of an inferiority   JOHN 530:87
c. of an uncomfortable situation   DICK 324:23
c. of their actions   SPIN 960:49
Doth seem half c.   WORD 1095:17
first I was scarcely c.   RUSS 833:31
To become c.   SAIN 837:92
tyranny of c. thought   BEEC 83:19
consciousness a time of awakening c.   RICH 809:48
African national c.   MACM 635:8
Allow but a little c.   ELIOT 370:26
building...part of the American c.   BUSH 215:84

consciousness (*contd.*)
chamber of c.   JAMES 516:19
change of c.   GINS 428:33
C., her awful Mate   DICK 328:8
c. is a staging area   BELL 88:42
c. is the only form you need   SARO 843:99
c. of myself   KANT 541:99
c. of science   DEWEY 319:95
c. of the limits   NIEB 727:65
c. that I have exercised the powers   PEEL 763:43
C., then, does not appear   JAMES 517:40
Cosmic c.   BUCKE 203:38
created...national c.   WILS 1086:48
divinity...place in the human c.   DURK 357:72
from beginning of c. to end   WOOLF 1092:54
habit of one's c.   MALE 641:11
in our ordinary c.   MOND 699:42
lopped off...your c.   ORWE 742:2
moral c. of people   MAIL 639:71
morning comes to c.   ELIOT 367:57
multiplicity of agreeable c.   JOHN 528:48
one-eighth part c.   GERH 420:5
states of c.   MOORE 704:10
stream of thought, of c.   JAMES 517:40
sublime c. of striving   HUMB 503:97
consecration c., and...dream   WORD 1099:71
consensus C. Terrorism   COUP 289:78
consent approbation and c.   POWE 788:18
colonized people with their c.   SART 844:20
c. of all great men   RUSK 830:88
c. to the separation   GEOR 418:82
c. ...under that Government   RAIN 800:6
engineering of c.   BERN 97:91
like enough to c.   SHAK 886:20
man without that other's c.   LINC 604:97
will ne'er c.   BYRON 222:31
consented Your father hath c.   SHAK 864:78
consenting between c. adults   NOZI 732:44
consequence as far as national c.   SCOTT 856:10
cause is the c.   FANON 382:59
c. of leaving one's home   LEBO 592:90
mistake subsequence for c.   JOHN 525:73
really a direct c.   PAST 759:88
trammel up the c.   SHAK 907:31
ultimate c.   MILL 677:7
consequences c. of changes   FRIE 405:52
damn the c.   MILN 681:84
In nature...only c.   VACH 1038:83
In nature...there are c.   INGE 511:43
knowledge of c.   HOBB 482:37
of history and its c.   OBRI 734:62
social c. of their activities   HOBS 483:45
teach the c.   KISS 565:30
consequent c. to a time of war   HOBB 483:40
conservation C. of one resource   HERF 476:41
in favor of c.   TAFT 990:82
conservatism barren thing this C.   DISR 332:83
c. and progress   TROL 1027:71
C. discards Prescription   DISR 332:81
c. is based on the idea   CHES 258:8
What is c.?   LINC 605:2
conservative banks were c.   THOM 1013:18
called the C. party   CROK 297:46
C. Backbench MPs   BAKER 63:18
C....enamoured of existing evils   BIER 161:75
C. government is...hypocrisy   DISR 332:94
C. ideal of freedom   MADAN 638:54
c. is a man   ROOS 821:40
C. Party at prayer   ROYD 828:42
leader of the C. Party   BEAV 80:80
leadership of the C. Party   HESE 479:79
make me c. when old   FROST 407:93
Metternich...was so c.   EVANS 381:37
most c. man in the world   BEVIN 102:76

Conservative (*contd.*)
Or else a little C.! GILB 424:75
small c. majority TYNAN 1035:25
The Republic will be c. THIE 1009:46
a true C. TENN 1005:62
conservatives c. and reactionaries VIDAL 1044:69
C., as being by the law MILL 675:68
C. do not believe HAIL 451:12
Life's better with the C. ANON 27:61
conserve to c. it, we must love it MONT 702:83
consider c. the end in everything LAFO 575:91
C. anything, only don't cry! CARR 240:61
considerable wish to appear c. JOHN 528:59
considerate if he were wisely c. STEV 974:22
consideration c. of characters JOHN 529:80
others worthy of c. BLOOM 169:34
turns on moral c. NAPO 718:27
con-si-de-ra-tion For a c. SCOTT 855:99
considerations dictated by military c.
MACC 626:58
considering c. how well they sell JOYCE 538:62
consistency foolish c. EMER 376:33
Too much c. is as bad HUXL 507:62
consolatory mind C. food can find SMART 944:72
console be consoled as to c. FRAN 401:91
generally c. them STEV 974:13
Knowledge...will not c. me PASC 758:72
consolidation indissoluble c. ROTH 826:23
consommé cyanide in the c. WODE 1089:95
consonants Only c. and vowels RANS 802:38
shifting of vowels and c. UNTE 1036:47
thud of c. BROY 201:5
consort But I c. with KIPL 564:5
c. as they keep MILT 683:14
conspiracies All professions are c. SHAW 924:88
conspiracy Civilisation is a c. BUCH 202:23
c. against the public SMITH 945:79
c. is everything that ordinary life DELI 315:42
c. of human beings WELLS 1064:28
c. to make you happy UPDI 1037:60
c. to oppress DOUG 342:74
in a c. to under value them JAMES 516:12
Indecency's c. of silence SHAW 922:50
universal c. of silence JAUR 519:71
conspirators All the c. SHAK 884:68
C. have a logic DELI 315:42
conspire stick'st not to c. SHAK 912:46
constable Bible...c.'s handbook KING 559:1
constabulary c. duty's to be done GILB 424:65
constancy but c. in a good [cause] BROW 195:80
C. alone is strange ROCH 817:63
c. lives in realms above COLE 274:10
c. of its vows SHAW 922:42
no object worth its c.? SHEL 932:73
constant c. as the Northern Star SHAK 883:38
c. in a wondrous excellence SHAK 915:85
C. you are SHAK 875:52
more c. than a wife RICK 811:75
No species remains c. OVID 747:3
nothing in this world c. SWIFT 984:64
only thing c. JOUV 537:37
so c. to me KEATS 545:61
To one thing c. never SHAK 879:46
were man But c. SHAK 860:89
Constantine walled by C. the Great BAIL 62:70
Constantinople what is chaste in C. FORD 396:2
constellation Los Angeles is a c. MAIL 639:84
sets him in his c. RILKE 812:87
constellations c. of data GIBS 422:40
c. of feeling DOUG 341:58
consternation returned in c. SOME 952:1
constituencies elements in their c. LIPP 607:37
constituency c. is the desperate JACK 514:86
Every line in...budget has its own c. WRIS 1102:22

constituency (*contd.*)
would not be in my c. MENZ 670:94
constituents composed wholly of c. RUSS 832:18
constitution abusing the best C. FRAN 402:8
chief aim of their c. MORE 707:52
corresponding social c. MARX 660:11
country has its own C. MUNS 714:62
free c. GIBB 421:19
In the name of the C. STAL 962:78
Like the British c. CARD 232:99
pale of the C. GLAD 429:50
parchment of a c. TROT 1029:3
parliamentary C. is not favourable DISR 333:20
part of an Englishman's c. AUST 51:49
The C. has never greatly bothered BIDD 160:63
to our ancient c. SWIFT 984:83
words of the C. KING 557:78
constitutions men look at the C. JEFF 520:96
most unlikely c. DICK 326:54
political C., are not our Life CARL 235:74
constraint c., and sad occasion dear MILT 684:38
constraints c. aping marriage UPDI 1036:53
construct c. a decoration TROL 1027:63
constructed peace must be c. UNES 1036:44
rightly c. boy's life TWAIN 1032:72
construction c. of...bombs EINS 363:65
lifelong c. GOULD 436:75
who comprehended its c. PALEY 751:65
consul born when I was c. CICE 266:66
consult C. the genius POPE 779:19
C....To seek another's approval BIER 161:76
consume Rot, and c. themselves SHAK 864:97
consumed bush was not c. BIBLE 106:53
c. by use GILL 427:13
consumer C.: A person who is capable STEIN 966:49
c. isn't a moron OGIL 737:4
c....is the king SAMU 840:45
state for a potential c. LURIE 619:43
consuming doubled their means of c. MILL 674:60
consummation c....wished TWAIN 1033:89
consumption balance of...c. MALT 643:41
birds...in a c. WEBS 1059:30
c. is polarized ILLI 511:33
C. is the sole end SMITH 945:86
c. of valuable goods VEBL 1041:27
form of commerce and c. MARX 660:11
galloping c. GAND 414:12
no remedy against this c. SHAK 877:85
not increase its c. KEYN 555:39
universal c. ILLI 511:32
contact Fly hence, our c. fear! ARNO 37:92
removed from c. with...life PRIT 791:65
voters have no c. PRICE 789:32
contagion breathes forth c. TWAIN 1033:89
c. from her sable wings MARL 653:99
c. in the tears DRYD 348:88
c. of the world's slow stain SHEL 931:47
C. to this world SHAK 891:44
c., when it has once made head DICK 326:54
great danger of c. WILD 1079:30
Rot inwardly, foul c. MILT 684:45
contain stating what it is to c. JOHN 526:1
contaminated c. by...an identity HAZL 463:96
contaminates lack of love c. GUNN 448:85
contemplating c....poetry RICH 809:52
contemplation action not c. BRON 190:83
Beneath thy c. NEALE 722:93
best nurse c. MILT 683:28
c. he and valour formed MILT 690:55
c....more than his reading AUBR 45:33
c. of created things MILT 691:72
mind...in a rapt c. ELIOT 371:40
sitting apart in silent c. GRAND 438:98
sundry c. of my travels SHAK 886:16

contemplation (*contd.*)
youngling in the c. of evil MILT 685:65
contemporary c. and future society MURP 715:73
my true c. DUNN 356:56
works by c. composers HEIF 467:67
contempt breeds c.—and children TWAIN 1034:2
c. and anger of his lip! SHAK 895:25
C. and beggary hangs SHAK 870:21
c. for an arrant shit JOSE 537:33
c. for anything he didn't understand WOOL 1094:86
c. for my character and opinions SHAW 921:23
c. for the poor performances RYLE 834:54
C. for the poor OCON 736:89
c. of a great man FITZ 391:20
c. of shame JOHN 527:20
excites their c. REED 805:91
for c. too high COWL 291:19
greatest c. for novels FORD 396:6
held in c. by those GOLD 432:94
hold writers in c. BELL 88:27
in c. of chance happenings RABE 799:91
inward and secret c. BACON 56:42
not for such c. SHAK 863:49
Object of C. AUST 50:29
pour c. on all my pride WATTS 1055:56
so great and general a c. PEPYS 764:59
treat you with c. WHIT 1073:99
weakness, no c. MILT 695:58
contend what we have to c. for PITT 771:72
contender could have been a c. SCHU 850:11
content beautiful...have the least c. FLAU 392:35
contain any c. WEIL 1062:85
C.'s a kingdom HEYW 480:91
c. myself with wishing PITT 771:62
c., retirement THOM 1015:49
c. thyself to be...good ADDI 8:34
c. to be such a one SIDN 937:64
c. with his common humanity SHAW 924:96
draw upon c. GOLD 432:2
emptying...of all form and c. FANON 382:60
full flavour of their c. MILL 677:19
land of lost c. HOUS 495:58
learned...to be c. BIBLE 153:16
Looking back, I am c. STEV 972:71
Must make c. with his fortunes SHAK 903:22
Nor that c. surpassing wealth SHEL 927:74
Nothing less will c. me BURKE 206:7
Poor and c. is rich SHAK 899:33
religious, not so much by its c. CUPI 301:10
soul hath her c. SHAK 899:21
Strong and c. I travel WHIT 1073:85
contented c. sort of discontent KEATS 546:79
scarce be a c. woman ROCH 816:60
we are c. SCHR 850:4
contentedness procurer of c. WALT 1052:7
contention brawling, c. STUB 980:13
Let the long c. cease! ARNO 39:22
contentment C. and fulfilment TROL 1029:1
enjoying, what c. find? MILT 692:93
Preaches c. to that toad KIPL 559:14
contents c. worn out FRAN 402:99
contest c. between agreeable fancy STEV 972:80
counted the cost of this c. DICK 329:22
end a c. quicker SHER 933:89
pissing c. with that skunk EISE 364:83
contests What mighty c. rise POPE 778:90
continence perversion known as c. HUXL 506:48
what c. to forbear MILT 685:60
continent blowing through this c. MACM 635:8
c. a new nation LINC 605:4
C., I do not believe...exists COOK 286:25
c. of energetic mongrels FISH 389:83
C. people have good food MIKES 674:52
c.'s violent requiem DUNC 355:46

continent (*contd.*)
C. will not suffer England DISR 332:79
descended across the C. CHUR 265:30
deserted c. which gave me my birth
MELBA 667:21
every man is a piece of the c. DONNE 339:22
in presence of this c. FITZ 391:6
like having a c. disappear JARR 518:56
part of our European c. TOLS 1023:99
That means on our c. LEAC 589:47
U.S.A. is a slice of a c. DOSP 340:40
continentals c. think life is a game MIKES 674:53
continents dotted with c. and islands
MUIR 713:39
less difficult to join both c. BOLI 172:72
contingent c. and the unforeseen FISH 389:81
nothing c. is granted SPIN 960:48
continually c. with thee BIBLE 117:91
continuance felicity and long c. BACON 60:37
continue c. in this a quarter SHAK 909:76
I intend to c. THAT 1008:28
we c. ...a barbarous traffic PITT 771:71
continuity c. of civilization ORWE 744:37
contraception If you won't have c. OBRI 734:63
contraceptive The C. Problem DALY 304:52
contraceptives little use for c. SHAR 919:81
contract c. ...between those two SMITH 946:89
c. theory in ritual form NOVAK 732:36
Every law is a c. SELD 857:33
Social C. is nothing more WELLS 1064:28
Society indeed a c. BURKE 208:36
verbal c. GOLD 434:43
contracted happen to have c. it JONES 533:55
more c. that power is JOHN 530:95
contracts c. with the people TRUM 1030:23
Like all other c. RICA 808:34
write enough to sign c. GING 427:21
contradict c. myself? WHIT 1073:82
nobody to c. us RADI 800:3
contradiction brook no c. WEBS 1061:72
c. in terms SHAW 925:23
c., that New Orleans MORT 710:98
fundamental c. ...between socialism DENG 315:50
locked...in this impossible c. EAGL 359:3
risings...on c. that they grow EMPS 378:85
spirit of c. MACL 633:65
Whoever fears c. SAIN 837:93
Woman's at best a c. POPE 782:78
contradictions c., of the grotesque TZARA 1035:34
reconcile these c. CARL 233:31
contradictory holding two c. beliefs ORWE 745:59
contrapuntist c. is only a post-horse
MOZA 711:19
contraries Without c. BLAKE 166:71
contrary c. to nature, c. to life HUXL 507:62
c. to that order JOHN 522:32
Hail Mary, quite c.! GREE 444:14
not c. to reason HUME 503:4
On the c.! IBSEN 510:23
contribution c. to reality THOM 1011:93
editor...accepts with joy the c. CANN 230:68
Man's c. to human history JIANG 522:25
contrition a devout act of c. OBRI 734:72
contrivance c. enough JOHN 527:25
c. to raise prices SMITH 945:79
Sexually, Woman is Nature's c. SHAW 921:38
control campaign for birth c. MUNRO 714:56
C. over behavior LEGU 594:28
c. that which he produces NGUGI 725:46
c. the meaning of words DICK 320:13
history of arms c. ADEL 8:43
in c. here HAIG 450:8
knows how to c. or direct MUGG 712:23
methods of c. KEYN 554:31

control (*contd.*)
sceptre to c. the world SHAK 862:36
think you c. it STEI 966:59
white people who were in c. DAVIS 309:31
wrong members in c. ORWE 743:17
controversy c. over capital FISH 389:81
c. over freedom of speech ORWE 745:50
great c. in antiquity GERA 419:95
convalescence c. ...makes illness SHAW 925:19
convenience C. ...elbow-chairs COWP 292:51
convent c. for unloved women BROY 201:8
convention beautiful face is dumb c. PUBL 794:12
books, c. and cliché POUND 785:48
Social c. is irrelevant PAGL 749:35
To the Lords of c. SCOTT 856:16
conventional c. and orthodox way KEYN 554:31
c. army loses KISS 566:31
c. way to rise above the c. NABO 717:14
proposal departing from c. lines STAMP 962:83
conventionality C. is not morality BRON 191:97
conventions c. of the present LEWI 603:72
convergence c. of human lots ELIOT 366:35
conversant c. with a Man's heart POE 776:52
conversation a great deal of c. AUST 52:67
Among the Ibo the art of c. ACHE 2:18
cheery c. and what-not WODE 1088:85
c. ends in a conspiracy SMITH 945:79
c. I do acknowledge austere BROW 194:64
c. is like playing tennis LODGE 610:79
C. is more often JONES 533:56
C. never easy for British BRAD 183:84
c. of the blind MOORE 705:15
c. wanders away from themselves WILD 1080:36
c. with my best friend LEWIS 601:43
c. with the best men DESC 317:75
different name for c. STER 969:98
difficult to go on with the c. WODE 1088:86
drown it by one's c. WILDE 1076:48
fitter for c. by 'em WYCH 1103:37
In private c. CURT 301:23
intimate as any c. STERN 968:86
journalism...as an extension of c. SAMP 840:42
make his c. perfectly delightful SMITH 949:53
materials for c. JOHN 527:18
politics...are a c. OAKE 733:44
state...without the means of its c. BURKE 207:26
stick on c.'s burrs HOLM 486:78
support a flagging c. HUNT 505:31
conversational shallow c. ends SASS 845:40
conversations c., and even a soliloquy LINK 606:22
converse hold high c. THOM 1015:52
sweet c. of an innocent KEATS 544:37
them and rational c. WOLL 1091:40
conversion believed in sudden c. FORS 398:32
converted Except ye be c. BIBLE 138:17
sinners shall be c. unto thee BIBLE 116:78
convertible rogue...is still c. EMER 378:78
upholstery of a Packard c. PERE 766:96
convex Self-portrait in a C. Mirror ASHB 41:55
conviction author's c. on this day POUND 786:77
best lack c. YEATS 1106:77
c. is to report that dialogue KUNI 571:18
c. that a hypothesis MEDA 666:71
damnable iteration...of earnest c. STEAD 964:5
every c. begins as whim BROUN 193:49
striking c. of the vanity JOHN 525:89
what is called c. HUNT 504:18
convictions c. are hills FITZ 390:92
C. are more dangerous NIET 727:69
feelings and c. MORI 708:68
Stevenson's c. LEHM 594:38
convenient any c. time for MITC 697:90
convince labouring to c. JOHN 527:33
persuading others, we c. JUNI 540:73

convince (*contd.*)
works harder to c. himself FRAS 403:18
convincing thought of c. GOLD 433:28
conviviality taper of c. DICK 322:57
convulsion wilful c. STEV 976:60
convulsions groans and c. STER 969:8
in c. hurled POPE 781:61
cook C. is a little unnerved BETJ 100:52
c. was a good c. SAKI 837:2
good c. is like a sorceress SCHI 847:63
'Tis an ill c. SHAK 869:16
very uncommon c. SAKI 838:12
wanted to be a c. DALI 303:44
Cook Illustrious C. WENT 1065:54
Cooke-ham Farewell (sweet C.-h.) LANY 580:81
cookery c. do! MERE 671:2
cookie grandmother...like a c. BAIL 62:69
cooking C. is like love VANH 1039:4
Good painting is like good c. VLAM 1046:98
offers succulent c. POUND 786:68
Spare me from c. PLATH 773:68
cooks bad female c. NIET 729:90
c., physicians, carpenters SUN 982:39
devil sends c. FULL 410:51
not the c. HARI 457:16
Skinny c. can't be trusted ANON 28:20
the Devil sends c. GARR 415:31
Too many c. ANON 23:95
Whoso has sixpence...commands c. CARL 234:49
cool chilli was something c. THAC 1006:81
C. is hot WASH 1055:46
c. of the day BIBLE 103:95
c. white dress FIRB 389:72
intellects vast and c. WELLS 1064:26
Keep c. EMER 377:55
More than c. reason SHAK 871:53
cooled coal that must be c. SHAK 864:91
C. a long age KEATS 547:14
Coolibah shade of a C. tree PATE 760:96
Coolidge Nero fiddled, but C. MENC 669:69
coomb stag in the Priory c. DAVI 307:99
Coonardoo C. they called it PRIC 789:34
Cooper make Jilly C. ...rich BRAD 183:87
rooting for Gary C. BALD 64:2
cooperate C. on move one RAPO 802:40
coot haunts of c. and hern TENN 1002:97
cop c. beatin' up a guy STEI 966:55
Cope Hey, Johnnie C. SKIR 943:56
Copernican universe is C. PHIL 768:19
copier mere c. of nature REYN 808:23
copies Make c., young man, many c. INGR 512:49
coping c. with life SPARK 955:47
trigger the c. mechanism WRIS 1102:17
copper c. into gold SENG 858:50
Irishman is lined with c. TWAIN 1032:74
Copper When Lord C. was right WAUGH 1057:81
Copperfield Bewitching Mrs C.'s DICK 323:99
David C. from head to foot! DICK 323:98
that David C. kind of crap SALI 838:1
copperheads forgot the c. SAND 841:61
coppers c. hot ADE 8:42
old time 'c.' COLL 276:38
coppice love of field and c. MACK 632:52
copulate people who can c. MACD 627:85
copulating two skeletons c. BEEC 82:17
copulation Birth, and c., and death ELIOT 370:12
Let c. thrive SHAK 903:34
Wit...is the unexpected c. of ideas JOHN 525:90
copy all very well to c. DEGAS 312:94
if you c. others BERN 97:90
copying c. the answer out KIER 556:54
copyists shortened the labour of c. CARL 234:47
copyrights Take away...their c. TROL 1028:96
coral bones are c. made SHAK 916:25

coral (*contd.*)
India's c. strand   HEBER 466:58
Japonica Glistens like c.   REED 804:80
corbies twa c. making a mane   BALL 67:55
cord threefold c.   BIBLE 123:24
Corde C. avoided cemeteries   BELL 88:39
cordiale entente c.   LOUIS 614:54
cords c. that hold India   CURZ 302:27
core compact c.   LENIN 595:48
heart and c. of ages   LOWE 615:72
In my heart's c.   SHAK 891:37
red ball of fire at its c.   AGAWA 10:67
Corinna Come, my C., come   HERR 477:62
Corinth Not everyone can sail to C.   ANON 20:43
cork pop the c.   STEV 974:21
tossed like a c.   HUGH 501:54
corked c. up for ever   ELIOT 365:9
corkscrew Bring in...a c.   DICK 322:54
corkscrews crooked as c.   AUDEN 46:56
Corky And C.'d protested   OATES 733:59
cormorant c. devouring time   SHAK 865:4
Sat like a c.   MILT 690:51
corn amid the c.   HOOD 489:39
c. rigs are bonie   BURNS 210:78
Golden c. for the stranger   WILDE 1075:27
golden ears of c.   HERR 478:65
graves...ploughed for c.   RED 804:74
In our sustaining c.   SHAK 903:32
meadows rich with c.   WHIT 1074:7
produce a bushel of C.   PETTY 768:13
raise less c. and more hell   LEASE 591:72
there was c.   HERB 475:28
two ears of c.   SWIFT 985:85
yellow like ripe c.   ROSS 824:80
Corneille C. is...a clipped hedge   JOHN 532:40
Cornelius To you C.   CATU 245:58
corner buy one on a c.   DAY 310:51
drives into a c.   JOHN 531:21
future...just around the c.   LESS 598:2
head stone of the c.   BIBLE 118:27
House at Pooh C.   PARK 754:94
into every penetrable c.   MACA 622:82
Joy shivers in the c.   ROBI 815:33
only one c. of the universe   HUXL 507:78
pointed out one c. of a square   CONF 280:90
some c. of a foreign field   BROO 192:21
spanked and stood in the c.   LEGU 594:32
turn a c. jinkan   BURNS 209:74
wake in a c.   KELM 549:34
what lay round the c.   KAVA 543:27
corner-stones c.-s. of literary art   DUDEK 353:13
corners lounge at c. of the street   SPEN 956:75
obscure c. in one's own mind   HUXL 509:5
planes and c. of rooms   MALL 642:21
round earth's imagined c.   DONNE 338:3
Unregarded age in c. thrown   SHAK 885:80
cornfield o'er the green c.   SHAK 887:32
Cornpone C. and...Porkchop   ONAS 739:45
cornucopia brown paper c.   DUNNE 356:60
corollary C.—The history of science   SART 843:5
coronation Bring c., and sops   SPEN 957:93
coroner like a c.'s inquest   CONG 281:24
coronet bride of ducal c.   DICK 323:84
coronets hearts are more than c.   TENN 995:70
corporal although this c. rind   MILT 684:34
Uncle Toby, interrupting the c.   STER 970:14
corporation C....ingenious device   BIER 161:77
St. Louis...arch of the c.   MAIL 639:84
corporations c. and local boards   MILL 675:67
great c.   GLEI 430:61
great modern c.   JAY 519:73
corps effete c. of impudent snobs   AGNEW 10:69
corpse before me is its c.   MAZZ 666:12
c. of the public credit   WEBS 1059:23

corpse (*contd.*)
fingers of cold are c. fingers   LAWR 586:89
good wishes to the c.   BARR 72:42
greeting a c. would give   BALD 64:5
hardly was the c. cold   STOP 978:75
I'll show you a c.   PUZO 796:42
make a lovely c.   DICK 323:80
more complete than a c.   VIAN 1043:45
resuscitated c.   JENK 520:99
surgeon dissects a c.   APOL 31:90
corpses bivouac for c.   MUSS 716:83
c....their unimportant look   DAVI 308:14
mock the riddled c.   SASS 845:22
corpulence burdenous c. my love   DONNE 338:97
correct about to c. themselves   BRADY 184:4
Are we c. to have changed   ASAHI 40:49
blot out, c., insert   SWIFT 985:2
do the perfectly c. thing   SHAW 924:11
moral is always c.   BART 74:78
not a c. deduction   KEYN 554:32
Protocoligorically c.   SHER 934:15
corrected C. and amended   FRAN 402:99
correcteth Lord loveth he c.   BIBLE 120:58
correction c. of private abuses   PEEL 763:42
look you, under your c.   SHAK 881:87
correctitude feather-bed of c.   BENN 91:98
Corregio corregiescity of C.   STER 969:4
correlative objective c.   ELIOT 368:76
correspondence c. like a duet   DONA 335:58
corridors admit princes to the c.   DOUG 341:58
brain has C.   DICK 328:5
c. of power   ALLEN 14:30
History has many...contrived c.   ELIOT 368:70
corrupt a people generally c.   BURKE 207:17
appointment by the c. few   SHAW 922:46
Beauty...easy to c.   BACON 59:12
c. my air   SHAK 911:11
daft or c.   FULL 410:44
should c. the world   TENN 1004:46
corrupted c. by money   GREE 444:7
froth-.d lungs   OWEN 748:13
corrupter power a c.   SHEL 927:57
corruptible 'mongst things c.   MIDD 674:49
corruption c. in any government   BRUN 201:10
C. is more than a poison   ECON 359:15
c. of power   BRON 190:82
C., the most infallible symptom   GIBB 421:21
dong and c.!   CHAU 255:41
gratify avarice, and extend c.   JOHN 527:23
Louisianans don't tolerate c.   ANON 30:53
Stewed in c.   SHAK 892:56
suffer thine Holy One to see c.   BIBLE 114:40
corruptions man's c.   OTWAY 746:76
most pernicious C.   PRYN 794:11
corruptly Were not derived c.   SHAK 874:31
corset c. is...a mutilation   VEBL 1041:25
Cory C., one calm summer   ROBI 814:24
Corydon Time, not C.   ARNO 39:18
cosine Brothers of the C.   ROOS 822:51
cosmetics c. and the silks   SEXT 859:66
factory, we sell c.   REVS 807:21
cosmic bitter c. joke   GELL 417:69
born to make chaos c.   BEER 83:28
C. consciousness   BUCKE 203:38
cosmology problem of c.   POPP 783:21
cosmos c. has forgiven you   MAIL 640:91
push and pressure of the c.   JAMES 517:46
cossack c.'s whip   TROT 1029:3
cost and counteth the c.   BIBLE 143:50
as though hate has no c.   SAND 841:69
c. of freedom   KENN 551:73
c. to freedom of opinion   SCHL 848:73
counted the c. of this contest   DICK 329:22
greatest c., namely time   ANTI 31:86

cost (*contd.*)
not apt to c. him   RUNY 829:60
that which dost c. me nothing   BIBLE 110:52
costly C. thy habit   SHAK 888:66
how c. summer was   SHAK 875:33
costs C. merely register   KNIG 567:53
Love c. us nothing   RICK 811:76
subtract the c.   GATES 416:37
what everything really c.   SMITH 946:93
whatever it c. them   UPDI 1037:58
costume cardinal points of c.   MURR 715:76
c. will be Indecent   LAVER 584:56
national c., architecture   BIRD 163:17
cot paint the c.   CRAB 293:72
sheltered c.   GOLD 433:9
cottage before his c. door   SOUT 954:31
no cheerful c. has blest my eyes   SCHAW 847:61
removed like a c.   BIBLE 125:72
Wherever there's a c. small   PARK 755:29
cottages march in c. of...weeds   MARL 653:92
peace to the c.   CHAM 250:24
cottar stirk from a c.   SCOTT 854:70
cotton c. flowers of her dress   THOM 1011:88
c. is high   HEYW 479:89
four c. ones   TRAV 1025:31
so are banks, so is c.   DICK 322:67
world wrapped up in...jeweller's c.   DICK 324:20
cotton-town Lancashire c.-t.   ORWE 742:96
couch age of the psychiatrist's c.   MACL 635:97
c. for luxury   SHAK 889:79
hidden c.   GORD 435:62
levee from a c.   CONG 282:43
on a c. of straw   THOM 1011:83
There I c. when owls do cry   SHAK 917:41
when on my c. I lie   WORD 1099:70
cough never let them c.   BARR 73:57
soft, low, gentle c.   WODE 1089:90
coughing one c. and one not c.   SCHN 848:83
coughs C. and sneezes   ANON 26:48
letting his c. fall   MORG 708:65
council C. of Europe   BEVIN 102:78
in danger of the c.   BIBLE 134:39
planned...In c. rooms apart   RICE 809:39
Sagest in the c.   DAVIS 309:37
tongues of the French C.   SHAK 882:11
councillors As many c.   SALV 839:41
councils In the c. of government   EISE 364:88
counsel his c. was not followed   BIBLE 110:50
darkeneth c. by words   BIBLE 113:17
did c. spurn   VAUG 1041:23
Dost sometimes c. take   POPE 778:97
follow this c. of Aristotle   ASCH 40:50
guide me with thy c.   BIBLE 117:91
Who cannot give good c.?   BURT 214:71
counsels all good c.   BOOK 173:99
how many c. sweet!   BURNS 211:11
United thoughts and c.   MILT 687:92
count 10 people who really c.   ANON 28:13
all men c. with you   KIPL 564:9
nothing else to c.   EMER 378:76
they c. things carefully   WALE 1049:49
won the c.   SOMO 952:2
you will c. many friends   OVID 747:4
counted refuse to be c.   DAVI 309:42
countenance beautiful c.   BIBLE 110:37
chide God for making you that c.   SHAK 886:19
c. more In sorrow than in anger   SHAK 888:59
c. was as the sun   BIBLE 156:99
did the C. Divine   BLAKE 168:18
dismal grew his c.   BALL -101:36
help of his c.   BIBLE 116:69
Look not on his c.   BIBLE 110:36
Lord lift up his c. upon thee   BIBLE 107:81
merry heart maketh a cheerful c.   BIBLE 121:79

countenance (*contd.*)

ordinary human c.	LEAC 589:38
Thy c....thy mien	WORD 1100:90
counter All things c.	HOPK 491:85
From c. or desk	YEATS 1105:71
counties England has greater c.	CRIP 296:30
English c. like hunting-tunes	BENET 90:60
see the coloured c.	HOUS 495:50
counting C. the slow heart beats	GRAV 440:30
countries c., art and lit.	LEWIS 602:53
c. divided by a...language	SHAW 926:41
c. engaged in the war	LEES 593:20
c. have too much history	KING 558:88
C. that have soldiers in charge	MACK 632:57
differs in different c.	RICA 808:32
He... preferreth all c. before his own	
	OVER 747:92
in c. where capitalism	TROT 1029:8
Ireland is one of the few c.	DANG 304:60
most prosperous c.	LEVI 600:26
Music...language of all c.	ODETS 736:91
peace of all c.	ROOS 821:39
series of fabulous c.	ORWE 744:38
which of the two c.	GERA 419:95
Working men of all c.	MARX 660:15
Working men of all c.	MARX 660:16
working populations of both c.	LOND 610:90
country a political in this c.	TROL 1028:88
against any c. or doctrine	MARS 656:53
agreeable method of entering the c.	MACL 633:64
Alas poor c.	SHAK 909:73
all in the same c.	KRAM 569:84
all their c.'s wishes blest!	COLL 276:43
allow this c. to be brought in	GEOR 419:86
almost every c. unpopular	MACA 622:87
almost in the c.	WILS 1084:13
America is a c. of young men	EMER 378:77
Anyone who loves his c.	GARI 415:25
around the c.	MACM 635:6
Art...will have a c.	APOL 32:95
ask not what your c.	KENN 551:65
betray my c.	FORS 399:52
born in a half savage c.	POUND 785:60
Britain is a Morris Minor c.	ANON 28:9
bust up a c.	WARD 1053:14
call her a young c.	HOPE 490:72
Canada...the only c. in the world	MACL 635:98
cannot flourish in a c.	HUXL 508:87
clein in the c.	FLEM 394:65
conquest of an unknown c.	HEDIN 466:61
c. American means white	MORR 709:87
c. but for one flag	ROOS 822:53
c. called Technopolis	WINN 1087:60
c....disappointingly empty	BARN 72:29
c. evenly divided	VIDAL 1044:69
c. far beyond the stars	VAUG 1041:18
c. free otherwise than in name	MILL 675:67
c. gentleman...has never travelled	LASS 583:35
c. ...going to sleep	RENAN 806:1
c. governed by a despot	JOHN 530:95
c. green	KEATS 547:14
c. habit has me	SACK 835:61
c. has its own Constitution	MUNS 714:62
C. in the town	MART 657:64
c. is the world	PAINE 750:84
c. is too big for anyone	ATWO 45:21
C. manners.	MUNRO 714:58
c. needs to be united	JOHN 523:47
c. of birds and trees	WRIG 1101:10
c. of defeat	PURDY 795:35
c. of the blind	WELLS 1064:30
c. of the mind	WHITE 1070:42
C. party	WHIT 1072:70
c.'s pride	GOLD 433:10

country (*contd.*)

c. saves the difference	BAGE 61:57
c. so far lost to...self-importance	GEOR 418:81
c. so precipitously convoluted	JAMES 515:7
c. takes her place	EMMET 378:81
c. that is economically backward	TROT 1029:8
c. then, tomorrow c. now	RICH 810:71
c. 'tis of centuries	CUMM 299:83
c., 'tis of thee	SMITH 948:27
c. to heel like a dog	LESS 598:97
c. where death is	LORCA 613:40
c. where the State is the Church	SHAW 923:76
C. will be called upon	HARD 455:76
c. with a large foreign	RUSS 832:24
Cry, the Beloved C.	PATON 761:12
customs that his c. has evolved	POWE 788:18
Cuts off the c. Again	MUIR 712:27
dear native c.	SWIFT 985:97
defence of one's c.	HOMER 488:22
depths of his c.'s soul	DICK 326:55
die but once to serve our c.!	ADDI 8:33
die fighting for his c.	HOMER 488:23
die for my c.?	SITT 940:98
die for your c.	GOLD 434:34
die for your c.	PATT 761:16
die...in my c.	MATAK 663:66
died to save their c.	CHES 260:42
different times in the same c.	RICA 808:32
division in a c. so small	DONO 339:35
done stranger things in that c.	THER 1009:42
dresses, in every age of c.	LIN 604:96
duty to his c.	PEAC 762:29
dying c.'s cries	GRAY 443:83
education...of this c.	DISR 333:19
egg. production in this c.	CURR 301:21
England's not a bad c.	DRAB 345:26
England, this c. of ours	AUDEN 46:44
England...My c.!	COWP 293:54
English c. gentleman	WILDE 1077:66
enough room in your c.	CORW 288:62
events outside their own c.	WILL 1080:46
every c. but his own	GILB 425:85
every c. except Germany	GREY 446:58
every c. in the world	KEEN 548:24
every c. ought to have a President	DOLE 335:54
famous in this c. in seven days	HART 459:42
fight for your c.	HOMER 488:20
films of one's c.	ANDE 18:4
first, best c. ever	GOLD 432:97
fit c. for heroes to live in	LLOY 609:62
for C. and for Yale	THUR 1019:36
for my c.	HALE 451:20
foreign troop...in my c.	PITT 771:70
friends and c. are as nothing to that	JAMES 515:4
from the heartland of the c.	SHUL 936:37
From yon far c. blows	HOUS 495:57
game your c. loves	RICE 809:40
gang should mismanage the c.	MARQ 656:51
God made the c.	COWP 292:52
good for our c.	WILS 1084:21
good in the c.	WILDE 1076:54
greatest asset any c. can have	CHUR 265:27
grow up with the c.	GREE 443:98
halved the c.	THOM 1010:56
has to understand the c.	LESS 598:95
heading into nut c.	KENN 552:91
heart bleeds for his c.	JOHN 527:27
history of every c.	CATH 244:38
hitherto unexplored c.	SHIP 935:22
How else can one govern a c.	DEGA 313:99
how lovely our c. is	WORD 1101:95
how much wealth...in a c.	SIDG 936:39
I can save this c.	PITT 771:64
If this c. is settled	STUA 980:9

country (*contd.*)

impossible to live in a c.	KEATS 544:53
impress the people of this c.	PEEL 763:43
In every age and c.	GIBB 421:20
in every other c.	THOM 1014:43
In love with a c.	LESS 599:8
In our c. the lie	SOLZ 952:96
In the c. of the blind	ERAS 379:8
in the c. places	STEV 976:54
In this c. it is considered a good thing	
	VOLT 1046:1
In this c. it is rare	POWE 788:10
In this c., poet-baiting	SITW 942:30
in this happy c.	MORI 708:68
in whatever c.	PAZ 762:24
index of this c.	MARC 650:49
island c. of Japan	TOJO 1022:88
know something of his own c.	STER 970:12
Labour Governments in every c.	GREY 446:56
landlords of the c.	PARN 756:40
lavish streams to quench a c.'s thirst	POPE 780:29
law in any civilized c.	LEVIN 600:28
leads a c. such as Britain	THAT 1008:25
leave his c. as good as he had found it	
	COBB 271:58
legislature of this c.	PITT 771:71
lie abroad for the good of his c.	WOTT 1101:97
life is a foreign c.	KERO 553:11
likes the c.	COWP 292:35
literature of their c.	TROL 1028:89
looking out for your c.	COOL 287:39
love a sunburnt c.	MACK 632:52
make...wreck of his c.	BIER 162:98
may our c. be always successful	ADAMS 6:89
means nothing in this c.	GOLD 432:91
mistress...little c. retreat	WYCH 1103:34
more than one way to conquer a c.	CHAN 250:42
my c. people	SENG 858:49
my c. was confirmed to me	PENN 764:56
My c., right or wrong	CHES 258:91
native c. was full	IRVI 513:62
no better than any other c.	LEWIS 602:56
no choice here in the c.	BRON 190:89
no instance of a c. having	SUN 982:32
not have a c. to vote in	PANK 753:52
now they desire a better c.	BIBLE 154:52
Of years, of c.	SHAK 898:6
One's c. is where one does well	ANON 20:45
only Shake-scene in a c.	GREE 445:33
opportunity to serve our c.	SMITH 947:8
or a home, or a c.	WILD 1079:27
organized workers of the c.	SHIN 935:19
our c. shall be victorious	PANK 753:82
our c., right or wrong	DECA 311:71
our dear c. had been free	DAVIS 309:37
our emancipated c.	MANS 647:96
our undiscovered c.	MANS 647:99
own France, a c.	MORL 708:72
peace of each c.	JOHN 522:33
pension from the c.	RUSK 830:89
People in this c.	RICH 810:65
Pick out of every c.	LASS 583:34
plant them...in his own c.	SOME 952:99
politics of the c.	HAZL 463:11
problems of running a c.	THAT 1007:12
protect his c.	SUN 982:36
proudest c. under the sun	PARK 755:31
rooms of thy native c.	FULL 410:45
round the c. stirring up apathy	WHIT 1072:65
Saviour of 'is c.	KIPL 560:32
say to his c.	PARN 756:41
science knows no c.	PAST 759:88
service to his c.	SWIFT 985:85
shrink from the service of his c.	PAINE 750:42

country (*contd.*)

silence…seeps out over the c.	ACHE 3:30
soon c. people forget	MORR 709:86
soul of man is a far c.	THOM 1009:50
spirit of our c.	CHEE 256:53
stamp out literature in the c.	WAUGH 1056:77
struggle for…my c.'s cause	OCON 735:81
sunlight falls across the c.	IHIM 510:30
the pride of my c. I sang	OBRU 734:73
the religion of the c.	SWIFT 986:18
this c. safe to work in	THAT 1007:9
This was my c.	BLUN 170:46
to all the c. dear	GOLD 433:11
to be had in the c.	HAZL 463:97
to die for one's c.	HORA 493:22
to your own c.	JOAN 522:27
took away their c.	SHER 932:76
totalitarianism in this c.	ORWE 745:51
undiscovered c.	TWAIN 1033:89
United States is the only c.	ROGE 820:16
unmapped c. within us	ELIOT 366:44
unsubduable c.	GILL 426:5
virtues! they've undone his c.	ADDI 8:32
vow to thee, my c.	SPRI 961:63
war rather than a c.	PILG 770:42
we shall liberate this c.	MAND 645:70
when our c. was born	INOU 512:57
Where is the c., my friend?	ARGU 33:18
who serves his c. best	HAYES 462:93
Who slights his c. thus	INGR 511:44
wild unexplored c.	LIVI 607:47
young c. is a real heritage	MANS 647:12
Your c. is more precious	PLATO 774:7
Your c. needs you!	ANON 25:30

countryman c. must have praise — BLYT 170:52

countrymen sacrifices of our fellow c. — EISE 364:93

steady his fellow c.	MURR 715:78

countryside c. the colour of a lion — BOWL 182:54

disappeared from the c.	MACL 634:81
smiling and beautiful c.	DOYLE 344:5
well-farmed c. is their favourite	TOLK 1023:94

counts grooves that c. — ANON 30:62

county Emeralds big as half a c. — LAND 578:63

married with the C.	SHAK 869:15

couple fool…in every married c. — FIEL 388:54

price paid for becoming a c.	COUP 289:85

couples happy c. in the face — STEV 974:4

courage as good a c.…father had — ELIZ 373:86

Be strong and of a good c.	BIBLE 108:3
c. and faith and zest	KENN 551:75
'C!' he said	TENN 994:48
c. holds firm	ANON 21:53
C. in your own	GORD 435:61
C. is a moral quality	MORAN 706:41
C. is in the air	FROST 407:4
C. is not simply one	LEWIS 601:42
C. is the most important	KENN 552:1
c. mounteth with occasion	SHAK 872:61
c. never to submit or yield	MILT 687:93
c. of the Negro	PHIL 768:23
c. prove my title	SHAK 906:6
C., rashness, and rebellion	MARI 651:66
c. the greater	ANON 21:60
c. to change the things	NIEB 727:66
c. to follow the talent	JONG 533:60
c. to give you unqualified praise	STEI 966:57
c. to know	KANT 542:2
c. to live out	MILL 678:32
c. to love	TROL 1027:66
c. to ride a horse	LEAC 588:30
gently raised Their fainting c.	MILT 687:4
give me…the c.	BAUD 77:26
home…saved by his c.	MACA 624:28
it is not man Made c.	POUND 786:84

courage (*contd.*)

journey that required c.	MURP 715:72
Kindness and c.	MUIR 712:32
manly c.	PEEL 763:44
must have the c. to dare	DOST 340:44
my C. and Skill	BUNY 205:74
Nature all c. me denyis	DUNB 355:42
Neither fear nor c. saves	ELIOT 368:71
never to let…your c. be dimmed	CURZ 302:29
on the c. and conduct	WASH 1054:42
people who have the c.	MUSS 716:86
Red Badge of C.	CRANE 295:11
Screw your c.	SHAK 908:35
sheer and endurance	WAVE 1058:10
Take c., my friend	READE 803:56
void of c.	MAIL 639:81
Why, c., thend	SHAK 862:32
With constant c.	JONS 534:73
with the c. of their race	SULL 981:24
without originality or moral c.	SHAW 921:21

courageous C. and loyal to the tips — ACHE 3:39

faith…creative and c.	CUPI 301:11

couriers sightless c. of the air — SHAK 908:32

course c. already decided upon — BIER 161:76

c. of a dishonest life	FRAS 403:18
c. of true love	SHAK 870:27
c. till I had ended	MUNDY 714:54
c. was unjustified	HIRO 481:19
earth's diurnal c.	WORD 1095:7
face forward his c.	ANON 23:98
finish my earthly c.	BEET 84:52
golf c. is the epitome	GIRA 428:43
have finished my c.	BIBLE 154:41
held in true c.	CARL 235:83
played on a five inch c.	JONES 533:51
take the wrong c.	KENN 551:74
Take you a c.	DONNE 337:79
There is no other c.	HUSS 505:37
things take their c.	MACA 624:22
Time rolls his ceaseless c.	SCOTT 854:63

courses in a series of c. — GOLD 432:92

miss out on any of the c.	RUSS 833:43

court air of the c. — ETHE 380:19

c. an amorous looking-glass	SHAK 862:46
c. as an orphan	LEVA 594:?
c. he practised	DRYD 350:28
c. is only as sound	LEE 593:10
c. of kynge Arthure	MALO 642:29
dreary length before the c.	DICK 324:19
fill the c. with quarrels	SHAK 917:46
in the c. a cloister	AELR 9:52
Keeps his pale c.	SHEL 930:36
kynges c., my brother	CHAU 255:27
taller…than any of his c.	SWIFT 984:82
threshold of Jove's c.	MILT 683:18
Through the c.	WILDE 1075:26
To the Tennis C.	PEPYS 765:72
whole c. of Parliament	HENR 472:65

court-huntsmen tell c.-h. — DONNE 336:77

courted c. by an Italian — HEPB 473:76

courteous first, the Retort C. — SHAK 887:35

So c., so kind	SKEL 942:34

courtesan c. is a myth — FLAU 392:36

when the c. farts	ANON 23:93

courtesans crowd of c. — DUMAS 354:29

courtesies c. that raises me — BROW 196:11

small sweet c. of life	STER 970:25

courtesy breeds patience and c. — MUIR 712:32

defense like elaborate c.	LUCAS 618:26
second time do such a c.	SHAK 876:73
the greater c.	TENN 1004:?

courthouse c. pracing up and down — LIND 605:15

courtier c. grave and serious — GILB 426:96

not the c.'s art	DRYD 350:28

courtings rhetorical c. — CLEV 269:10

courtliness c., and…fame — TENN 1003:18

courtly Be c. ay in clething — DUNB 355:38

courtmartialled c. in my absence — BEHAN 84:57

courts about her c. were seen — LAND 578:63

brawling c.	TENN 999:51
C. for Cowards were erected	BURNS 209:69
c. of Europe are a jungle	BOLT 172:77
day in thy c.	BIBLE 117:95
decision of the c.	LEAC 589:42
forbidden by the c.	STIG 977:66
into his c. with praise	BIBLE 118:9
not enough c.	HUMP 504:13

courtship blindness of c. — LOWE 617:10

brash c. of the muse	THOM 1013:22
C. to marriage	CONG 280:3
c. was so much as thought on	LAMB 576:23

cousin little c. is dead — RANS 802:32

cousins c. as the sands of the sea — SHAW 926:43

c., and his aunts!	GILB 423:56

couth such a thing as too much c. — PERE 766:95

couturiers c. the last possessors — DIOR 331:63

covenant c. between me — BIBLE 104:15

c. from the beginning is	BIBLE 132:2
c. of our fathers?	BIBLE 130:69
c. with death	BIBLE 125:76
establish my c.	BIBLE 104:23

Coventry into a moral C. — PARN 756:39

cover c. of an old book — FRAN 402:99

C. your ass	SAFI 836:69
I c. all	SAND 841:62
on the c. of every issue	WAUGH 1056:59
paste and c. to our bones	SHAK 867:59
they were just a c.	RAMOS 801:17
time to run for c.	ASHD 41:62

cover-up c.-u., or anything else — NIXON 730:12

covering hair is given her for a c. — BIBLE 150:58

covers c. are too close together — LEHM 595:39

covert c. from the tempest — BIBLE 126:81

covertousness bereave him of his c. — MILT 686:71

covet sin to c. honour — SHAK 881:97

Thou shalt not c.	BIBLE 106:68
Thou shalt not c.	CLOU 271:50

covetous Every c. and avaricious man — INNO 512:54

cow c. from a Lowland strath — SCOTT 854:70

c. is of the bovine	NASH 719:41
Kiss till the c. comes home	BEAU 80:71
Knowledge is a sacred c.	SZEN 989:70
milk of the c. of the world	WILB 1074:16
saddle fits a c.	STAL 962:81
show me a c. who can earn	WINN 1087:61
steals a c. from a poor widow	SCOTT 854:70
The Red C.	TRAV 1025:36
Truth, Sir, is a c.	JOHN 527:34

cow-woman c.-w. and scum-woman — GRAND 438:98

coward Conscience is a c. — GOLD 432:3

c. does it with a kiss	WILDE 1078:98
c. in the presence of	STAN 962:84
c. in thine own esteem	SHAK 908:33
Fore God I am no c.	TENN 1004:56
gift of a c.	SHAK 893:95
just a c.	HEMI 471:34
The sea hates a c.!	ONEI 740:57
This sanguine c.	SHAK 876:56

Coward I love you—Nöel C. — COWA 290:4

coward-slave c.-s., we pass him by — BURNS 213:42

cowardice admit the c. — SHAW 921:37

C., as distinguished from panic	HEMI 471:35
Nine times out of ten it is c.	SIDM 936:40
surest is c.	TWAIN 1034:9

cowardly c. way to score — PELE 764:50

cowards conscience doth make c. — SHAK 890:21

Courts for C. were erected	BURNS 209:69

cowards (contd.)
C. die many times	SHAK 883:33
fools and c. might sit safe	OTWAY 746:83
goes to the heads of c.	MITC 697:88
learn'd are c.	DRYD 349:2
Tho' c. flinch	CONN 282:54
When c. mock the patriot's fate	INGR 511:44

cowbind Green c. — SHEL 932:68
cowboy last true c. in America — HEAT 466:49
cowboys c. had lived for months — MACM 636:24
Cowdenknowes broom of C. — BALL -101:33
Cowley Who now reads C.? — POPE 782:80
cowpat humble violet under a c. — BARN 72:28
cows Barrymore's acting till the c. — NATH 721:87

cash c. to feed your pigs	ANDE 18:2
C. are my passion	DICK 323:95
dance with you till the c.	MARX 659:98
Dried up the c.	GRAY 441:61
To be contented…that's for the c.	CHAN 251:58

cowshed smelling of the c. — THOM 1011:83
cowslip C.…like tethered foam — CRANE 295:6

I'th' bottom of a c.	SHAK 916:1
In a c.'s bell I lie	SHAK 917:41

cowslip-banks sit on c.-b. — WALT 1052:10
cowslips c., and kingcups — SPEN 957:93
c. wan that hang — MILT 684:47
coxcomb c. ask two hundred guineas — RUSK 831:9
more consummate c. — WESL 1067:70
coxcombs some made c. — POPE 778:75
cozenage town is full of c. — SHAK 865:1
crab-tree schoolboys …climb a c. — ROCH 816:57
Crabbe With C. it may be difficult — BYRON 222:38
crabbedness not the result of mere c. — FADI 382:53
crabs like wet c. in a basket — DURR 357:76
roasted c. hiss in the bowl. — SHAK 866:31

crack c. your cheeks! — SHAK 903:17
hear the mighty c.	POPE 781:61
heaven's vault should c.	SHAK 904:51
no c. in a fortress	MILL 676:99
will sure c. both	SHAK 910:96
would c. in the flame	JEFF 520:85

crackling c. of thorns under a pot — BIBLE 123:27
generous with the c. — MACB 624:32
cracks c. of other people's lives — WHAR 1068:96
cracky joined with the Arabs, by c.! — ACHE 3:48
cradle c. of new masterpiece — YEATS 1105:66
c. of Spanish walnut	PLATH 773:99
c. rocks above an abyss	NABO 716:95
c. to the grave	ANON 29:40
c. to the grave	BREC 186:26
from the c. to the grave	SHEL 930:26
hand that the rocks c.	WALL 1050:68
high mountain c. in Pamere	ARNO 38:98
In c. clothes our children	SHAK 875:35
Out of the c.	GRIF 447:61

cradled c. into poetry — SHEL 927:69
cradles bit the babies in the c. — BROW 197:32
craft Between c. and credulity — BURKE 207:15
cloaked c. their store of skill	DYER 358:89
continued with my c.	JAMES 517:34
c. be best to lerne?	LANG 579:75
C. is the handprint	ANON 30:59
c. so long to lerne	CHAU 254:4
c. so long	HIPP 481:15
mere c. and cozenage	JONS 536:18
writing is a c.	PORT 784:36

crafts C. which require the most Time — CANT 230:75
craftsman produce the perfect c. — VITR 1046:97
craftsmen c. share a knowledge — SACK 835:40
crag clasps the c. — TENN 1000:64
cragged huge hill, C., and steep — DONNE 336:67
crags among these barren c. — TENN 994:57
craigs bizzing c. and mous to weet — FERG 386:17

cramp drugs cause c. — PARK 754:13
cranberries man wrapping c. — DOLE 335:52
cranberries (contd.)
Rice, and a C. Tart — LEAR 590:56
crane protection of the whooping c. — BRIN 189:60
Tall as a c. — SITW 941:13
Cranford here at C. — GASK 415:33
crank c. is a small engine — SHEE 926:49
c. until the idea succeeds	TWAIN 1034:8
serve apprenticeship as c.	BROUN 193:49

crap David Copperfield kind of c. — SALI 838:18
crape saint in c. is twice — POPE 781:55
crash the c. is coming — PARK 754:16
thoughts of the c. — THOM 1013:18
crave mind forbids to c. — DYER 358:87
the more you c. — POPE 782:79
craved c. no crumb — GILB 425:94
craves c. wary walking — SHAK 883:26
craving c. to risk death — FOWL 399:64
full as c. — DRYD 348:97
Crawford best time…with J. C. — DAVIS 308:26
crawling c. between heaven — SHAK 891:26
maybe she will do the c. — FAUL 384:87
crazed c. with the spell — DELA 314:28
crazy all going to go c. — KRAM 569:84
c. about cars	SALI 839:25
c. for love	BART 74:70
C. Like A Fox	PERE 766:88
edge of some c. cliff	SALI 839:28
grow a little c.	GOLD 432:89
I suppose all writers are c.	CHAN 251:49
Orr was c.	HELL 468:82
that's what is c.	JONAS 533:50
unless I'm c.	HEMI 471:37
We are all born c.	BECK 81:90
would end by becoming c.	MAUP 665:98

cream cat to steal c. — SHAK 876:65
c. rises until it sours	PETER 767:6
queen of curds and c.	SHAK 912:32

cream-faced c.-f. loon! — SHAK 910:80
create absence of the urge to c. — MAMET 643:49
anything he might c.	MAMET 643:48
c. and keep quiet	FLAU 392:41
c., if it concerns poetry	HUGO 501:68
c. in our minds the very things	ABER 1:5
desire to c. something	PRIE 790:41
know, to kill and to c.	BAUD 78:43
To c. is…to destroy	CUMM 299:75
to c. jazz	GILL 426:12

created c. the poodle — THUR 1019:45
C. half to rise	POPE 780:43
wealth that you never c.	TSON 1031:42

creating envisioning all without c. — GORO 436:68
let us start c.	ANON 27:87
Shopping is Not C.	COUP 289:80

creation all of your soul in c.! — HUGO 501:68
appropriate act of c.	FEIN 385:99
Art is like C.	KLEE 566:49
artistic c. is modern life	WAGN 1047:26
Back of every c.	MILL 678:39
between human c.	MILL 678:34
bless thee for our c.	BOOK 174:8
blind fury of c.	SHAW 921:25
blot on the fair face of c.	BRON 191:94
c. first brought forth	MILT 693:27
c. of images	HOLL 485:70
C.'s tears in shoulder blades	STEV 972:65
deepest mysteries of c.	SHEL 926:53
Did ever woman, since the c.	STER 968:89
fairest of c.	MILT 692:5
from that equal c.	JEFF 520:87
horror of C.	HUGH 500:45
inexhaustible fullness of c.	HUMB 503:97
jazz…process of c.	LIEB 604:91

creation (contd.)
Love all God's c.	DOST 341:48
love C.'s final law	TENN 999:32
love C.'s final law	TENN 999:41
morning of his c.	HUXL 507:83
participation in the c.	ROBB 813:10
parts of the C.	HALES 451:23
present at the C.	EVANS 381:37
she is his new c.	STONE 978:73
speak before you think c.'s [motto]	FORS 399:54
spelled out the history of c.	FISKE 390:86
spilled… hate into dearest c.	BURG 206:90
supreme c. of an era	BART 74:79
think more of the c.	GAUG 416:39
through a limitless c.	HUXL 508:95
tire of all c.	HOLM 486:88
took the whole of C.	HUGH 500:36
Vexing its own c.	WORD 1096:18
warrants the c.	FIELD 387:39
whole c. groaneth	BIBLE 149:28
whole c. moves	TENN 1000:63
woman a mere afterthought in c.	STAN 963:90
world was before the c.	BROW 195:88

creations c. of a poet — SHEL 931:56
human c. mechanical	LEGER 593:21
like all c. of the human spirit	DYSON 358:1

creative active and c. world — SPEN 957:90
beautiful, c. and good	MING 695:63
C. Endeavour lost	WAUGH 1056:76
c. gift	HOPK 492:10
c. people hate mathematics	ISSI 514:79
c. talent…drained off	RICH 810:65
reading…highly c.	CARY 243:15
satisfies the human c. instinct	QUEN 797:54
victim of c. suffering	KING 557:81

creativity angel of c. wrestling — L 595:47
c. comes to an end	ROTH 825:7
C. in science	KOES 568:71
dimensions of thought and c.	STEI 967:67
keep that childlike c.	HIRS 482:23
sex and c. are often seen	JONG 533:61

creator all-wise C. — HALES 451:23
c. from his work returned	MILT 691:87
c. in the year 1902	MORT 710:98
C.'s power display	ADDI 7:22
endowed by their C.	STAN 962:85
God C., wise	MILT 693:20
greater glory of his C.	PIUS 772:81
my c., detest and spurn me	SHEL 926:54
Remember now thy C.	BIBLE 123:42
served the creature more than the C.	BIBLE 148:12
the C. made Italy	TWAIN 1032:60

creators c. of odd volumes — LAMB 577:32
creature c.'s at his dirty work — POPE 781:62
c. driven by demons	FAUL 383:81
c. here Beast, bird, insect	MILT 690:63
c. of the common streets	DICK 325:36
Dear is the helpless c.	BYRON 222:33
Deformèd c.	SPEN 957:3
Each c. of the world	ALAN 11:77
every c. in a cave	SNYD 951:85
every c. shall be	MARL 654:15
God's first C.	BACON 60:31
imitator is a poor kind of c.	WHIS 1069:13
in Christ, he is a new c.	BIBLE 151:80
kills a reasonable c.	MILT 685:55
Let the living c. lie	AUDEN 47:74
lone lorn c.	DICK 323:2
Lovely c. in scarlet	GEOR 419:93
Man is a c. who	STEV 974:11
Man is a history-making c.	AUDEN 48:93
Man is the only c.	ORWE 744:29
No c. loves an empty space	MARV 659:89
no c. loves me	SHAK 863:64

creature (*contd.*)
No c. smarts so little	POPE 781:61
Not a c. was stirring	MOORE 704:3
proves, that every c.	SWIFT 986:6
ravished this fair c.	FIEL 388:49
served the c. more than the Creator	BIBLE 148:12
sigh of the oppressed c.	MARX 660:6
small c. of the night	AMIS 16:71
so good a c.	GALT 413:7
some new and wondrous c.	DARW 306:82
sort of c. that can't die	THER 1009:43
thy c., to whom thou art bound	SHEL 926:54
Y'are the deed c.	MIDD 674:48

creatures all c. here below
All c. great and small	ALEX 13:17
births of living c.	BACON 58:93
breastless c. under ground	ELIOT 367:63
countless joyful c. sing	KIER 556:60
c. in warmer countries	GUY 449:96
c....looked from pig to man	ORWE 744:33
c. of commanding sadness	LEE 593:18
c. there Live	MILT 691:91
disagree Of c. rational	MILT 688:23
distinguished from all other c.	ADDI 7:26
fair c. of an hour	KEATS 544:50
frustrated c. we were	MILL 678:26
home, you idle c.	SHAK 882:14
human c. breathe an atmosphere	DICK 326:54
lawful lords of earthly c.	DAVI 307:7
meanest of his c.	BROW 199:72
Men are very fragile c.	STEP 968:41
no better than c.	JOHN 529:76
obedience of c.	HOOK 489:54
orders and inferior c.	MILT 694:48
race of upstart c.	MILT 689:27
rarest of political c.	MACF 629:15
shining c. of the chase	TENN 996:93
solidarity with other isolated c.	BELL 88:36
spiritual c. walk the earth	MILT 690:62
These Ibsen c.	ANON 25:22
widows...the most perverse c.	ADDI 7:16
worst sin towards our fellow c.	SHAW 920:14

credentials There are no c. LLOY 608:55

credit corpse of the public c. WEBS 1059:23
c. cards cancelled	ANON 29:42
c. goes to the man	DARW 306:92
c. to a Trappist nun	SHAR 919:82
faces as thin as c. cards	AMIS 17:84
From your fair c.	FLET 394:78
get c. for anything	JOHN 524:58
impossible to c.	WILL 1080:46
I will take the c. for	BEVIN 102:80
more c. than they deserved	REST 807:17
Of c. lost	JONS 536:17
physicians...take the c.	BURG 205:83
seek to take the c.	PARK 753:93
the c. of our...government	STEE 964:16
to give them c.	USTI 1037:75
world will give thee c.	CHUR 262:84

creditors gaping c. OTWAY 746:81
credulities c. of mankind CONR 285:9
credulity Between craft and c. BURKE 207:15
interest dictates and c. encourages	JOHN 527:21
present age is craving c.	DISR 333:5

credulous men are the most c. POPE 779:18
creed c. and particular reality MUNCH 714:52
c. of a second-rate man	BAGE 62:65
c. of different parties	TOCQ 1021:77
c. which accepts	MILL 675:71
establishing your c.	BAGE 61:49
got the better of his c.	STER 969:1
need...shapes a human c.	CULL 299:72
Non-violence...last article of my c.	GAND 414:13
pagan suckled in a c. outworn	WORD 1099:73

creed (*contd.*)
shrieked against his c.	TENN 999:32
shrieked against his c.	TENN 999:41
solemn c. with a solemn sneer	BYRON 220:89
underlies every c.	BLAV 169:26
unionism is stronger than c.	LAWS 587:19

creeds dust of c. outworn SHEL 930:19
keys of all the c.	TENN 998:27
our casual c.	ARNO 37:91
second of man's c.	LAWR 587:14
than in half the c.	TENN 999:53

creek here and there a c. BYRON 222:41
creeks through c. and inlets CLOU 270:32
creep c. into thy narrow bed ARNO 39:22
Here! c.	HOPK 492:5
Men c., Not walk	WHIT 1074:6
wealth will c. out	JOHN 530:97

creeper in Virginia c. drown BETJ 100:40
creepers fellow c. on...planet SAND 841:70
creeping any manner of c. thing BIBLE 107:78
c. police state	GINS 428:33
things c. innumerable	BIBLE 118:18

creeps C. in this petty pace SHAK 910:86
crest glows on their c. SCOTT 852:35
lapwing...another c.	TENN 995:71
red roses c. the caps	THOM 1014:32

Cretan lied like a C. HARDY 456:88
Cretans C. are always liars BIBLE 154:42
Crete people of C. SAKI 838:10
crevasse scream from a c. GREE 444:9
crew c. is gambling in the forecastle SHAW 925:16
We were a ghastly c.	COLE 274:92

crib angel in the c. NEVE 723:14
cricket At least I am not playing c.! POWYS 788:21
c. as organised loafing	TEMP 993:27
C. can be a bridge	ZIA 1109:24
C. full of theorists	BOTH 180:34
c. goes to the bone	ARLO 35:39
C. is a batsman's game	BENA 89:47
C. is a game of...stresses	ARLO 35:40
C. is baseball on valium	WILL 1081:54
c. is just another game	EDIN 361:41
C. is not illegal	ANNE 20:36
C. is the greatest game	WARN 1053:25
C. is...full of forlorn hopes	ORWE 744:27
C.? It civilises people	MUGA 711:20
c.—it's so very English	BERN 97:94
C., like the novel	ARLO 35:38
c.'s manly toil	BYRON 218:52
c. on the hearth	MILT 682:10
C. remains...the game of games	FOWL 400:70
'C.' said Raffles	HORN 494:37
c. teams wiped out	STOP 978:76
c. tour in Australia	LARW 582:30
C.... towards sentimentalism	CARD 232:3
C....was more than play	BLUN 170:50
c. was not made: it has 'grown'	CARD 232:99
C. weather	JOYCE 538:55
describing c. matches	THOM 1010:71
elements are c.'s presiding geniuses	CARD 232:6
empty c. ground	SNOW 950:70
English c....died at the Oval	ANON 25:17
English think c. is a game	MIKES 674:53
expressing itself in c.	JAMES 516:9
far more than a game, this c.	CARD 232:5
great advantage over c.	SHAW 925:34
Hail C.! glorious	LOVE 614:61
If Stalin had learned to play c.	DOWN 343:80
if there be c. in heaven	HOME 487:14
laws of c. tell of the English love	CARD 232:2
May c. continue to flourish	BRAD 184:97
never played at c.	MILL 675:75
play c. in the summer	KINN 559:9
playing c. for hard cash!	MITF 697:93

cricket (*contd.*)
really keen c. fan	NORD 731:26
sound of the c. bats	JOYCE 538:43
Sphere of Influence—the c. ball	ANON 25:19
theorist more than c.	TRUE 1029:14
Village c. spread fast	TREV 1026:48
when I hold a c. ball	UTTL 1038:82
where the c. sings	YEATS 1104:57
youths at c. did play	JOSE 537:32

cricketer c....by name John Small EGAN 362:55
Cricklewood Midland, bound for C. BETJ 100:39
cried say he c. out of sack SHAK 882:13
Still it c. 'Sleep no more'	SHAK 908:47
when he c....children died	AUDEN 47:67

crime a C. in Progress THOM 1014:39
Arson...artificial c.	WELLS 1064:35
Cambodia...was a c.	SHAW 926:48
commit any c. they like	DOST 340:43
conclusion...that almost all c.	WAUGH 1056:74
coyness Lady was no c.	MARV 658:72
c. against humanity	JOHN 522:36
c. ...dodge...by secrecy	PULI 795:20
C. ...has its degrees	RACI 799:1
C. is common	DOYLE 344:6
C. is...socio-political	PACK 749:27
C. lies not in the deed	HELO 469:8
c. novel is not easy	JAMES 517:34
c. of being a young man	PITT 771:62
c. of stealing	TWAIN 1032:71
c. pays	ALLEN 14:35
c. you haven't committed	POWE 788:7
end that stupid c.	SERV 859:58
loved be with equal c.	SPEN 958:13
Murder is a unique c.	JAMES 517:35
Napoleon of c.	DOYLE 344:8
no c. like the present	WASH 1055:47
No c.'s so great	CHUR 262:88
object from the c.	POPE 779:10
one guilt, one c.	MILT 692:8
promote intellectual c.	BIER 161:86
punishment fit the c.	GILB 425:90
right to commit nearly every c.	BENT 92:16
servitude...consequence of his c.	CURR 301:16
study of c.	MILL 678:40
the great c.	PACH 748:25
The more featureless...a c. is	DOYLE 343:95
tough on c.	BLAIR 165:53
tried...for a capital c.	JOHN 529:83
worst c.	WALC 1048:40

Crimea C....Would Not Boil TAYL 991:9
Crimean C. War is one GUED 448:76
crimes All c. are safe JOHN 525:79
All the poor c.	WEBS 1060:21
C....are their own reward	FARQ 383:67
c. committed in the name of duty	SNOW 951:76
c. confined	GRAY 442:71
c. that shame mankind	NOON 731:24
detestation of the c.	PARN 756:39
How many c. are committed	CAMUS 229:61
our impudent c.	ELIOT 368:71
register of the c.	IRVI 513:61
Successful c. alone are justified	DRYD 350:47
virtues made or c.	DEFOE 312:79
worse c. than burning books	BROD 189:73
worst of c.	SHAW 923:77

criminal call it a c. thing SOME 952:99
choose to count as c.	PACK 749:27
c. law is no use	SHAW 924:90
ends I think c.	KEYN 554:25
fixed in favor of the c.	CAPO 231:80
When he got more c.	LONG 610:92

criminals Authors and uncaptured c. LINK 606:20
misfits, looney tunes, and squalid c.	REAG 804:64
These men too were c.	CLAV 268:97

crimson all c. barred — KEATS 545:75

bed Of c. joy — BLAKE 167:88

c. ...robin's breast — TENN 995:71

like the c. drops — SHAK 916:1

red like c. — BIBLE 124:56

cringe Cultural C. — PHIL 768:22

if you c. before her — FAUL 384:87

crinoline woman in a c. — LAVER 584:57

Cripps C. has a brilliant mind — ASQU 42:83

crises marked by an absence of c. — PECK 763:41

crisis any c. next week — KISS 566:37

any major c. of the capitalist system — EAGL 359:4

c. justifies permanent control — HUXL 508:87

c. of her experience — AUST 52:73

c. of understanding — WILL 1081:51

C.? What c.? — CALL 226:3

each ball a potential c. — TREV 1026:48

exiting to have a real c. — THAT 1008:16

force the moment to its c.? — ELIOT 367:48

how early...she can meet c. — PECK 763:41

In times of c. — BALZ 68:72

patriot will, in this c. — PAINE 750:42

Poetry, surely, is a c. — SALI 839:30

settlement of this c. — HUSS 505:35

the c. ...is past — POE 776:55

Crispian fought...upon St. C.'s — SHAK 882:5

Tomorrow is St. C. — SHAK 881:99

Upon St. C.'s day — DRAY 345:36

criteria need of outward c. — WITT 1088:80

criterion c....to test the genuineness — AYER 53:79

infallible c. of wisdom — BURKE 208:42

known by the c. — JEVO 521:20

critic a c. is a man who — TYNAN 1035:29

A good drama c. — TYNAN 1035:30

c. must attack the form — LAUT 584:52

c. spits on what is done — HOOD 489:53

c. when he cannot be an artist — FLAU 392:33

c. who justly admires — BEER 84:45

dramatic c. in the daytime — WODE 1089:9

dramatic c. who is — NATH 721:89

exposing them to the c. — BIER 161:89

function of the c. — BELL 85:82

good art c. — GREE 443:1

good c....recognizes the adventures — FRAN 400:80

good writer is not...a good book c. — BISH 164:36

in logic a great c. — BUTL 216:5

no c. can ignore — QUIL 797:61

novelist...his own most harsh c. — WILS 1084:20

role of the c.? — DIDE 329:32

role of writer and c. divided — BRAD 184:88

severe though not unfriendly c. — BAGE 61:56

To be a c. — BERR 98:17

Too nicely Jonson knew the c.'s part — COLL 276:41

truck, a producer or a c. — LEMM 595:45

true c. ought to dwell — ADDI 7:15

critic-pen Unboading c.-p. — TENN 996:88

critical c. period in matrimony — HERB 474:2

stopped dead at the c. point — SOME 952:1

criticising brain stops c. — SLOAN 943:59

criticism As far as c. is concerned — VORS 1047:20

cant of c. — STER 969:5

contemporary c. reads to me — CHES 260:44

c. is ever inhibited by ignorance — MACM 635:11

c. is not a body — FRYE 408:20

c.'s motto — FORS 399:54

c. of administration — BAGE 61:52

definition of c. — ARNO 38:11

democracy...permits c. — FORS 399:53

dramatic c....attempt to tattoo — BROWN 194:55

father of English c. — JOHN 531:9

from science is c. — RUSS 832:16

function of c. — DEWEY 319:96

I love c. — COWA 291:10

criticism (*contd.*)

Impersonal c....is like — NATH 721:88

Poetry...a c. of life — ARNO 40:41

To avoid c. — ANON 30:55

Writing c. — UPDI 1037:61

criticisms most penetrating of c. — HUXL 506:60

criticize Do not c. your Government — CHUR 265:48

criticized Being c. — TRUM 1030:29

critics American c. ...universities — ALBEE 11:89

ask anybody, particularly the c. — MATU 664:83

c. all are ready made — BYRON 219:60

C. are like eunuchs — BEHAN 84:60

c. called him a wheeler-dealer — MANC 644:64

C. search for ages — USTI 1037:75

gang of c. — VIAN 1043:44

if I don't practise...the c. know — PADE 749:30

In c. hands, beware — BRAD 184:99

know who the c. are? — DISR 333:14

'mature' c. — WALK 1049:53

more than all the writing of c. — DU 353:12

professional c. make me sick — HEMI 470:14

questioning among my c. — ARNO 38:8

Tudor c. who wrote...Prayer Book — ACHE 2:24

Turned c. next — POPE 778:77

what he thinks about c. — HAMP 454:65

critique both an homage and a c. — MOTH 711:11

Crito C., we ought to offer — PLATO 774:17

crocodile appeaser...feeds a c. — CHUR 265:40

go on feeding the c. — REAG 803:60

hen's egg don't turn into a c. — KING 558:99

How doth the little c. — CARR 238:22

'You mean.'...'a c.' — NASH 720:57

crocodiles wisdom of the c. — BACON 58:92

crocs argosy of c. and dragons — AMIS 17:87

crocus c. dress — JOYCE 538:56

c. lustres of the stars — CRANE 294:93

c. on a garbage heap — GARD 415:23

underfoot the violet, C. — MILT 690:63

Cromwell C., damned to...fame! — POPE 781:51

C. said to the Long Parliament — AMERY 16:69

C. took up arms — STAL 962:78

C.; the Philistine of genius — ARNO 40:36

Some C. guiltless — GRAY 442:70

crook are a C. or a Martyr — ROGE 820:11

by hook or by c. — MORE 706:42

crooked c. be made straight — ELIOT 371:38

c. fighting c. minds — MUIR 712:31

c. shall be made straight — BIBLE 126:85

c. timber of humanity — KANT 542:3

c. winding ways — HERB 475:29

shortest line...may be the c. one — BREC 186:27

crop A runnable stag, a kingly c. — DAVI 307:1

crops among the gradual c. — SMITH 947:3

crops c. of love and hate — MUIR 712:30

with increasing c. — SHAK 866:34

croquet good game of C. — REID 806:98

higher and dirtier c.-player — WOOL 1094:90

cross an ancient C. — YEATS 1107:93

bear your c. willingly — KEMP 549:45

cling to the old rugged C. — BENN 90:70

C. alone has flown the wave — CRANE 294:91

c. be uncrossed — ELIOT 371:30

c. is God's truth — BONH 173:82

c. of the Legion of Honour — TWAIN 1032:73

C. to be Borne — SMITH 948:28

endured the c. — BIBLE 154:54

grace without the c. — BONH 173:83

houses marked with a red c. — PEPYS 765:73

In the c. is salvation — KEMP 549:44

let him now come down from the c. — BIBLE 140:54

little marble c. below the town — HAYES 462:92

orgasm has replaced the c. — MUGG 712:21

shouldered high his voluntary C. — CAMP 227:20

sign of the C. — BOOK 175:35

cross (*contd.*)

stone remains, and the c. — MACC 624:34

survey the wondrous c. — WATTS 1055:56

take up his c. daily — BIBLE 142:85

take up his c., and follow me — BIBLE 138:15

taketh not his c. — BIBLE 136:80

Upon the c. — SITW 941:16

win the Holy C. — MALO 642:34

cross-bow With my c.-b. I shot — COLE 273:85

cross-breed unhappy c.-b. — DISR 332:83

cross-gartered c.-g....she detests — SHAK 895:19

crossed c. in love — AUST 51:40

crosses between the c. — MACC 626:64

nothing lives but c., cares, and griefs — SHAK 867:51

crossness make c. and dirt succeed — FORS 398:45

crossroads c. of all the evil — GENET 418:75

mankind faces a c. — ALLEN 14:50

crossword skill of a solved c. puzzle — SAND 842:80

crotch c. of this fig-tree — PLATH 773:91

crouch c., swivel, tug — OBRI 734:71

make c. beneath his foot — BROW 200:91

crow cock doth c. — BALL 68:61

c. doth sing as sweetly — SHAK 873:5

c. loves his fledglings — MORE 706:43

c. Makes wing — SHAK 909:60

dog bark at a c. — SHAK 879:31

louder a cock can c. — TROL 1028:79

milk-white feather in a c. — CAMP 227:19

sun had risen to hear him c. — ELIOT 365:10

upstart c. — GREE 445:33

crow-flowers Of c.-f., nettles, daisies — SHAK 892:71

crow-toe c.-t., and pale gessamine — MILT 684:47

crowbar straightened out for a c. — HOLM 486:88

crowd c. begins to pour in — ROST 825:1

c. flowed over London Bridge — ELIOT 368:83

c. is not company — BACON 58:98

c. laughs with you always — VIDOR 1044:74

c. of courtesans — DUMAS 354:29

c. will always save Barabbas — COCT 272:64

c. without singeing someone's beard — LICH 604:84

faces in the c. — POUND 785:52

Far from madding c. — GRAY 442:72

flock of sheep...can make a c. — BEER 83:36

I saw a c. — WORD 1099:67

jocosity catches the c. — MARQ 656:40

Out of the c. a mistress — SHEL 931:51

pale and anxious c. — WILDE 1075:26

something about a c. — WALL 1050:69

Will she pass in a c. — SWIFT 984:67

crowded marriage...was a bit c. — DIANA 319:1

crowds apprehensions come in c. — WORD 1099:65

c., her beloved smoke — LAMB 576:8

enterprising firm that supplies c. — SIMP 939:88

talk with c. — KIPL 564:9

crown allegiance to one C. — GEOR 419:88

both divide the c. — DRYD 351:74

cause Against the c. — DRYD 349:16

c. encased with pearl — MARL 652:88

c. enough to virtue — JONS 536:14

C. has made a purchase — WHIT 1069:16

c. of a stranger — MOORE 706:33

c. of our life — SWIN 987:35

c. of sorrow — TENN 995:34

c. of twelve stars — BIBLE 157:20

Ere the King's c. shall fall — SCOTT 856:16

exchange in some day for a c. — BENN 90:70

farm to buy my c. — SHAK 882:10

fill me from the c. to the t. — SHAK 907:27

finest Colonies under the C. — STUA 980:9

from Caesar's laurel c. — BLAKE 168:41

From the c. of his head — SHAK 879:50

fruition of an earthly c. — MARL 652:40

give thee a c. of life — BIBLE 157:3

crown (*contd.*)

hairy gold c.	KIPL 561:37
head that wears a c.	SHAK 877:95
impious hand to C. of Thorns	BRON 191:97
influence of the C.	DUNN 356:63
King his c. and dignity	SHAK 861:15
Lion and the Unicorn…for the c.	CARR 240:71
Put on my c.	SHAK 906:5
S. and c.…tumble down	SHIR 935:27
set the c. upon a stock	HOWA 497:92
strike his father's c.	SHAK 880:71
to wear a c.	ELIZ 373:92
undoubted right of the c. of England	COVE 290:90
virtuous woman is a c.	BIBLE 121:71
wear that c.	HEYW 480:91
within the hollow c.	SHAK 867:60
Word climbs upward into Its c.	DUNC 355:47
worn the c.	BIBLE 132:97

crowned c. knot of fire — ELIOT 373:81
C. with rank fumitor — SHAK 903:32
crowning moment of the Queen's c. — DIMB 331:59
crowns Cast their c. before — BIBLE 157:10
climb soonest unto c. — SHAK 862:28
Give c. and pounds and guineas — HOUS 494:44
last act c. the play — QUAR 796:52
crows roused the ribald c. — SHAK 896:55
thought to keep out the c. — MILT 685:56
crucible America is God's C. — ZANG 1109:13
cast a violet into a c. — SHEL 931:56
man in the c. — ELKIN 374:99
crucibles agony dancing in his c. — THOM 1011:89
crucified choose who is to be c. — COCT 272:64
c. Jesus…picture of God — BAKER 63:82
not been c.? — USTI 1038:77
was c., dead, and buried — BOOK 173:94
crucifixion c.…accuses human — BUTT 218:53
get in a whole C. — HUGH 500:31
crucify people would not even c. him — CARL 236:3
crudities c., doubts and confusions — THOM 1011:76
c. of his period — HAMER 453:38
cruel All c. people — WILL 1082:78
bottom of the sea is c. — CRANE 294:92
c. brother will you betray — BALL -101:37
C., but composed and bland — ARNO 38:99
C. he looks — SHEL 929:14
c. men of Rome — SHAK 882:15
For c. 'tis, said she — KEATS 546:34
her c. sports — SPEN 959:40
single men…are more c. — BACON 57:60
The man…was essentially c. — QUIL 797:61
crueller nothing c. or more vain — JONG 534:66
cruellest The c. lies — STEV 974:12
cruelty bar against your c. — LANY 580:80
C. is the law — HARDY 457:5
c. is the primary feeling — SADE 835:64
c. without incentive — JOHN 527:23
Hanging is too good…said Mr C. — BUNY 205:67
neither kindness or c. — ALBEE 11:82
top-full Of direst c. — SHAK 907:27
cruise all on our last c. — STEV 974:14
crumb craved no c. — GILB 425:94
crumble the Rockies may c. — GERS 420:15
when I c., who will remember — DELA 314:29
crumbled Hispanic world never c. — REYES 807:22
crumbs c. of compassion — TUTU 1032:54
c.…from the rich man's table — BIBLE 143:6
dogs eat of the c. — BIBLE 138:11
not worthy…to gather up the c. — BOOK 175:30
crumpet C. Baking…Company — DICK 321:43
crumpets buttered scones and c. — ELIOT 368:73
crusade moral c., or it is nothing — WILS 1085:31
Presidents pretending to run a c. — COOKE 286:29
crusaders C. have multiplied — BERN 96:77
Crusades triumphs of the C. — RUNC 828:53

crush competition…I c. it — REVS 807:20
crust c. of an unfinished earth — KURA 571:19
Sleep in thy intellectual c. — WORD 1095:11
crutches Time goes on c. — SHAK 879:44
cry agonised c. from the depths — DICK 326:55
and a c. before — TENN 1004:44
answer to 'Hi!' or to any loud c. — CARR 241:83
Consider anything, only don't c. — CARR 240:61
c. I can no more — HOPK 492:1
c. in my bed — AGUS 10:72
c. of Absence…in the heart — RANS 802:35
c. or sing, justice must — MARIE 651:64
c. that was no more than a breath — CONR 284:92
c. that we are come — SHAK 904:39
C., the Beloved Country — PATON 761:12
c. with you for only a day — VIDOR 1044:74
dying, if we could not c. — MAUP 665:98
empty compliment to c. — GILB 425:83
entire soul is a c. — KAZA 543:28
great c. in Egypt — BIBLE 106:62
heard my c. — BIBLE 115:66
hounds are in c. — SCOTT 854:66
If something makes you c. — CLIN 269:21
Need a body c.? — BURNS 213:45
new orphans c. — SHAK 909:72
no language but a c. — TENN 999:38
none to hear my c. — GILM 427:19
nor uttered c. — TENN 997:7
not to be obliged to c. — BEAU 79:60
tears which I made her c. — RACI 799:98
to c. it up — SWIFT 986:5
To c. to thee — HERB 475:31
What shall I c.? — BIBLE 126:85
your bald c. — PLATH 773:98
crying all the way that wild high c. — MASE 662:51
then not hear it c.! — HERB 475:31
cryptograph experience is like a c. — SCHO 849:93
cryptology Maxim of c. — WRIS 1102:20
cryselephantine A c. poem — POUND 785:56
crystal as much as a plant or a c. — EMER 376:45
C. sincerity — HOPK 491:78
ego that can crack a c. — CHEE 256:55
glass like unto c. — BIBLE 157:8
hold my lady's head like a c. — HEAN 465:35
crystalline his c. streams — SHEL 928:88
crystallization c.…in a poem — UPDI 1037:63
crystals teeth of splintered c.? — BROW 199:70
ten million little ice c. — SCHW 851:30
crème pupils are the c. de la c. — SPARK 955:51
Cuba C. is always the best — GUIL 448:78
Havana, C.…high society — CABR 224:81
whirlpool of C.'s political crisis — CAST 244:34
Cubans when C. get together — LEZA 603:76
cube c. is the basis of architecture — MALL 642:21
divide a c. into two other c.s — FERM 386:24
cubic Picasso paints…a c. shape? — MARC 649:43
cubist pictures known…as C. — DAVIS 309:35
cubists C., or Octagonists — ROOS 822:51
cubits c. this way and that — LAUR 584:45
cubs ape his c. — MORE 706:43
Cuchulain Pearse summoned C. — YEATS 1107:91
cuckoldom c. be a discredit — CONG 282:41
cuckoo c. clock style — HEMI 470:12
C., jug-jug, pu-we — NASHE 721:80
c.'s parting cry — ARNO 39:16
hear the pleasant c. — DAVI 308:22
hedge-sparrow fed the c. — SHAK 902:5
Lhude sing c.! — ANON 22:67
merry c., messenger of Spring — SPEN 958:26
One flew over the c.'s nest — KESEY 553:18
produce? The c. clock — WELL 1063:1
rainbow and a c.'s song — DAVI 308:21
Responsive to the c.'s note — GRAY 441:55
weather the c. likes — HARDY 457:13

cuckoo-echoing c., bell-swarmèd — HOPK 491:90
cuckoos Of owls and c., asses — MILT 686:76
cucumber c. is added to it — MACK 632:55
c. narrow — SITW 941:9
c. should be well sliced — JOHN 529:68
cucumbers sun-beams out of c. — SWIFT 985:86
cuddled Who c. you when? — THOM 1011:87
cue With a twisted c. — GILB 425:91
cuff Anything said off the c. — SKEL 942:44
Cuinchy C.…was slaughter yard — BLUN 170:45
cuinsque Mens c. is est — CICE 266:65
cully Man was…Woman's c. — CONG 280:94
culpable How c. was he — HEAN 465:37
culprit Stirs the c. — DICK 327:92
culprits better to choose the c. — PAGN 750:38
cult c. is a religion with no — WOLFE 1090:26
c. of truth — PIER 769:32
cultivate C. simplicity, Coleridge — LAMB 576:6
cultivated C. Underrated Nobleman — GILB 426:95
cultivation structure of her c. — AUCH 46:40
cultural c. and historical role — SMITH 946:1
C. Cringe — PHIL 768:22
C. literacy is the oxygen — HIRS 481:20
fight for c. space — NARO 719:40
personalities and c. traditions — WATS 1055:51
physical and c. distance — VAND 1039:94
culture all kinds of mental c. — MILL 674:58
America is…rooted in Negro C. — ROLL 821:26
arteriosclerosis of c. — MILL 679:55
as some immense yeast c. — BOYD 182:63
breasts, the hallmark of our c. — DONA 335:57
Britain had a savage c. — BANDA 69:86
Canada…enjoyed…French c. — COLO 277:52
courage in Chinese c. — MO 698:10
c. and my language — KELM 549:33
C.…acquainting…with the best — ARNO 39:30
C. is dead — ANON 27:87
C. is the passion for sweetness — ARNO 39:31
C. may…be described simply — ELIOT 373:82
c. of modern painting — MOTH 711:11
elaborate defence of c. — ARNO 39:29
evidence of a nation's c. — THUR 1019:37
evolution of c. — LOOS 612:25
excellence proper to c. itself — REYES 807:22
flourishing c. in our land — MAO 648:27
genius of American c. — RODR 819:88
handprint of all c. — ANON 30:59
hear anyone talk of c. — JOHST 532:47
integral part of c. — GOULD 436:78
marketers in our c. — GITL 429:49
men of c. — ARNO 39:26
Modern European c. — SUN 982:38
new ways…give new c. — WERE 1066:55
no c. of the earth — HOBB 483:40
only place in our c. — STEI 967:66
pursue C. in bands — WHAR 1068:2
sacred cow of American c. — HUGH 500:33
salvage Europe's c. — ADEN 8:44
society and its c. — TRIL 1027:61
Speeches in our c. — GALB 412:87
Tigers,…but no c. — MACL 633:66
tools that go together with c. — REYES 807:22
unparalleled elsewhere in our c. — SHAP 919:78
various grades of c. — NIET 729:93
Versailles of American corporate c. — WOLFE 1091:32
cultures all c. of the earth — WEBER 1059:20
curiosity about alien c. — BOWL 182:56
cumbersome c. unwieldiness — DONNE 338:37
cumulative truly c. and progressive — SART 843:5
cunning c. known — POPE 781:56
c. men pass for wise — BACON 58:88
need have much c. — BACON 59:24
want of c. made me bold — SPEN 959:29

cunning (*contd.*)
what pleated c. hides — SHAK 902:*98*
cup Come fill up my c. — SCOTT 855:*85*
c. is the new testament — BIBLE 150:*59*
c. o' kindness — BURNS 210:*95*
c. of bitterness — KING 557:*80*
c. of full wine — FLET 394:*75*
c. of his indignation — BIBLE 158:*23*
c. of hot wine — SHAK 911:*5*
c. runneth over — BIBLE 115:*50*
death in the c. — BURNS 213:*51*
Death's bitter c. — ABU 1:*12*
Fill the c. — TENN 996:*87*
gold c. won by the worst horse — MASE 662:*50*
heaven in our c. has thrown — ROCH 816:*53*
kiss but in the c. — JONS 535:*5*
League and C. double — BUSBY 215:*83*
let this c. pass from me — BIBLE 140:*50*
life's enchanted c. — BYRON 219:*81*
my c. shall be full — BOOK 176:*67*
no more personality than a paper c. — CHAN 250:*41*
Perfect the c. as planned — BROW 199:*77*
remove this c. from me — BIBLE 144:*14*
snow-water from a tin c. — SNYD 951:*80*
Socrates empties the c. of poison — FEUE 387:*30*
still foul the c. — GREY 446:*55*
cupboard no c. should be barer — LLOY 608:*56*
wicked man in the bathroom c. — EWART 381:*43*
cupboards c. bursting with skeletons — ORWE 743:*16*
Cupid bolt of C. fell — SHAK 870:*36*
thrice cut C.'s bow-string — SHAK 879:*52*
winged C. painted blind — SHAK 870:*28*
cups c. make any guilty men — JONS 535:*99*
c. That cheer but not inebriate — COWP 293:*60*
in kitchen c. — STEV 971:*35*
in their flowing c. — SHAK 882:*2*
pour not by c. — SPEN 959:*31*
cur 'bout the ears of the old c. — BUTL 216:*13*
curate average c. at home — FIRB 389:*77*
c. her dreams and gallery — DUNN 356:*56*
shabby c. who has strayed — AUDEN 48:*92*
sit upon the c.'s knee — CHES 259:*38*
curates abundant shower of c. — BRON 191:*98*
c. lean, and rectors fat — MACA 622:*86*
C., long dust, will come — BROO 192:*26*
curb use the snaffle and the c. — CAMP 227:*15*
curd c. of ass's milk — POPE 781:*67*
soother than the creamy c. — KEATS 546:*95*
curds concupiscent c. — STEV 971:*35*
queen of c. and cream — SHAK 912:*32*
cure as much for prevention as c. — GRAV 440:*35*
be no more; sad c. — MILT 688:*15*
cause or c.! — GOLD 432:*99*
c. except as a guillotine — LUCE 618:*33*
c. for it is occupation — SHAW 924:*9*
c. for this ill — KIPL 563:*77*
c. him for you — JUNG 539:*72*
c. of the id — ANON 25:*34*
c. the disease and kill the patient — BACON 58:*1*
labour against our own c. — BROW 196:*92*
love's a malady without a c. — DRYD 352:*89*
Love…the longest to c. — LABR 572:*43*
lunatic beyond all c. — WEBS 1060:*53*
no c. for this disease — BELL 87:*6*
no hope for a c. — AUST 51:*45*
nothing…a little money will not c. — DURA 356:*65*
palliate what we cannot c. — JOHN 526:*9*
sin the double c. — TOPL 1023:*7*
there is no c. — HOME 487:*12*
think they can c. them — VOLT 1046:*6*
will c. epilepsy — THEO 1008:*34*
cures happy…in their c. — BACON 55:*26*
If lot of c. are suggested — CHEK 256:*63*
seeker for c. — RICH 809:*55*

curfew c. tolls the knell — GRAY 441:*62*
curiales Quot c., tot tyranni — SALV 839:*41*
curiosities c. would be quite forgot — AUBR 45:*32*
curiosity c. about alien cultures — BOWL 182:*56*
c. becomes a sin — FRAN 401:*86*
c. is the life-blood — TREV 1026:*47*
c. of an angel's stare — TATE 991:*4*
die when c. goes — SWIFT 983:*54*
hungry c. — GREE 444:*21*
Love, c., freckles — PARK 754:*6*
Newspapers always excite c. — LAMB 576:*18*
'satiable c. — KIPL 563:*81*
when one has lost all c. — WAUGH 1058:*7*
curious c. in unnecessary matters — BIBLE 132:*89*
What a c. shape it is! — WILDE 1076:*59*
curiouser 'C. and c.!' cried Alice — CARR 238:*21*
curl Who had a little c. — LONG 612:*21*
Curle C.…has been writing letters — ARBU 33:*11*
curlew I could hear a c. — HEAN 465:*41*
curls held c. to be effeminate — TWAIN 1032:*68*
curragh got into…a c. — BEHAN 84:*58*
currency Beauty…form of c. — WOLF 1090:*13*
debauch the c. — KEYN 554:*27*
new stamped with their c. — LAMB 576:*23*
passed from c. — UPDI 1037:*72*
current boats against the c. — FITZ 391:*7*
c. to the source — FROST 407:*88*
c. under sea — ELIOT 369:*91*
giving a c. to the whole — HOPK 492:*97*
misleading guide to c. affairs — KEYN 554:*29*
currents their c. turn awry — TWAIN 1033:*89*
curriculum vitae c. v. of Civilization — ANDR 18:*11*
curry hotter than the c. — THAC 1006:*81*
curs cast away upon c. — SHAK 885:*73*
common cry of c. — SHAK 911:*21*
like to village c. — SHAK 917:*52*
curse America as a black c. — MILL 677:*21*
bless them that c. you — BIBLE 134:*44*
blessing, is to me a c. — MASS 663:*61*
common c. of mankind — SHAK 895:*44*
c. be ended — ELIOT 371:*38*
c. begins to act — SCHR 850:*4*
c. God, and die — BIBLE 112:*97*
c. I must send you — SIDN 937:*30*
c. is come upon me — TENN 994:*45*
C. not the king — BIBLE 123:*39*
c. of children! — WEBS 1059:*29*
c. of Europe — SENI 859:*53*
c. of hell upon the sleek — RANS 802:*34*
c. of me and my nation — POUND 786:*69*
c. of Scottish literature — MUIR 712:*25*
C. on his virtues! — ADDI 8:*32*
c. sound like a caress — FOOT 395:*91*
C. the blasted, jelly-boned — LAWR 585:*63*
c. thee to thy face — BIBLE 112:*96*
c. upon your whunstane hearts — BURNS 209:*62*
c. when one works for God — LIVI 607:*47*
Empty C. — FRAN 402:*5*
Ignorance is the c. — SHAK 861:*13*
know how to c. — SHAK 916:*22*
real c. of Eve — RHYS 808:*25*
smite the earth a c. — BIBLE 131:*73*
the c. has come upon us — ONOL 734:*68*
the c. of a prose — STEP 968:*80*
the c. of disobedience — OTWAY 746:*80*
cursed c. above all cattle — BIBLE 103:*98*
c. is the ground for thy sake — BIBLE 103:*1*
I who have c. — WALC 1048:*31*
We are c., Waldo — SCHR 850:*3*
curses c.…on each gashed head — SORL 953:*23*
C. are like young chickens — SOUT 954:*36*
c. on my head? — MILT 694:*31*
cursing began c. the bloody bible — HEMI 470:*16*

cursing (*contd.*)
c. his staff — SASS 845:*28*
I have set…blessing and c. — BIBLE 108:*99*
proceedeth blessing and c. — BIBLE 155:*68*
curtain as if the c. never rose — DIDE 329:*27*
cloud c. of future — CARL 234:*35*
c. call! — BARR 73:*61*
c. was up — KAUF 542:*15*
essay…must draw its c. round us — WOOLF 1092:*62*
prospectors who can't carry a c.? — DOUG 341:*51*
slamming down his silly c. — SALI 839:*32*
Thy hand…lets the c. fall — POPE 783:*11*
curtains Booze, of course, and then c. — AMIS 17:*83*
bottoms of c. — STER 969:*8*
c. are drawn with care — MONRO 700:*47*
c., never meant to draw — POPE 780:*30*
c. of allegories — DONNE 339:*24*
draw the c. — SHAN 918:*72*
graves…drawn like c. — RALE 800:*14*
Let fall the c. — COWP 293:*60*
people…behind those clean lace c. — CHRI 261:*65*
she…draws the c. back — OSBO 745:*67*
shower c.…great modern things — WARH 1053:*26*
Through windows, and through c. — DONNE 336:*77*
curtsey C. while you're thinking — CARR 239:*48*
curve c. of a blue bay — LOWE 615:*76*
curveship of the c. lend a myth — CRANE 294:*97*
Curzon met C. in Downing Street — BALD 64:*5*
cushion c. and soft Dean invite — POPE 779:*22*
cuspid c.'s last stand — PERE 766:*93*
cuss bloody town's a bloody c. — BLAIR 165:*51*
cussing c. and swearin' — STRA 979:*94*
custard every joke is…a c. pie — ORWE 743:*22*
custody in the c. of childhood — MISH 696:*77*
custom c. has rendered necessary — DICK 321:*33*
C. is the most certain — JONS 536:*25*
c. of readers…pleased with a book — CONN 283:*60*
C. reconciles us to everything — BURKE 206:*97*
C. that is before all law — DANI 304:*65*
justify a traditional c. — TWAIN 1032:*69*
lest one good c. — TENN 1004:*46*
Malay religion and c. — PANG 752:*76*
more than c. has pronounced — BRON 191:*93*
nor c. stale — SHAK 905:*71*
Rather than c. — LEZA 603:*76*
Render c.…to whom c. — BIBLE 149:*39*
rule by c. not by force — LEGU 594:*27*
tea and scandal…ancient c. — CONG 280:*5*
till c. make it — SHAK 896:*64*
'twill grow into a c. — WEBS 1060:*56*
customers raising up a people of c. — SMITH 945:*84*
skinning your c. — KHRU 556:*49*
customs c. of his tribe — SHAW 921:*19*
c.…we hold sacred — ARON 40:*46*
habits and c. of the people — RICA 808:*32*
ill c. influence my very senses — ETHE 380:*19*
laws and c. …evolved — POWE 788:*18*
such a part of our c. — ALME 15:*57*
way to keep up old c. — BAGE 61:*49*
cut c. it off, and…kill it — POWE 788:*13*
C. me to pieces — SHAK 911:*17*
c. out of anything — THUR 1020:*54*
efforts to c. 50,000 words — WOLFE 1090:*18*
most unkindest c. of all — SHAK 884:*54*
pay me the c. — GOMEZ 434:*50*
should have been c. — COWA 291:*11*
soon c. off — BIBLE 117:*99*
cuts c. off twenty years of life — SHAK 883:*41*
cuttlefish like c. squirting out ink — ORWE 743:*19*
cutty sarks c. s. run in your mind — BURNS 212:*21*
cyberspace C.…hallucination — GIBS 422:*40*
C. is the funhouse mirror — STER 968:*84*
C. is where you are — GIBS 422:*41*
cycle C. and epicycle, orb in orb — MILT 691:*90*

cycle (*contd.*)
decided to c. to India — MURP 715:69
Life is a c. — MARC 649:44
cycle-clips c.-c. in awkward reverence — LARK 581:1
cycles know enough about business c. — BECK 81:89
cylinder C. in common fire engines — WATT 1055:55
treat nature by the c. — CEZA 248:4
cymbal talk but a tinkling c. — BACON 58:98
tinkling c. — BIBLE 150:62
cymbals c. glorious — MAHO 638:64
Cymbry Mon Mam C. — FULL 410:46
cyme What rhubarb, c. — SHAK 910:84
Cymric Clear C. voices — BUNT 204:59
cynic C….A blackguard — BIER 161:78
cynical c. gestures of the poor — SPEN 956:75
cynicism C. is an unpleasant way — HELL 468:91
C. is humour in ill-health — WELLS 1065:41
C. is intellectual dandyism — MERE 671:9
the worst c. — OATES 733:53
Cynthia round Of C.'s seat — MILT 681:89
cypress correct in c. wood — PARK 754:10
c.-buss I plantit — YOUNG 1108:3
c. funeral — SPEN 957:99
Nor waves the c. — TENN 997:10
Cyprian forsake her C. groves — DRYD 351:61
Cyril Nice one, C. — ANON 28:97
Cytherean throned C. be fallen — SWIN 987:41
Czechoslovakia dealing with C. — LLOY 609:65
Cézanne C. liked apples — LIPP 606:29

da Vinci d. V. and the Renaissance — WELL 1063:1
dad fuck you up, your mum and d. — LARK 582:14
girls in slacks remember d. — BETJ 100:46
that person is d. — FALU 382:57
Dada D. D. D., a howl — TZARA 1035:34
D. began not as — TZARA 1035:36
D. means nothing — TZARA 1035:32
mama of d. — FADI 382:51
daddy Are you lost d. — LARD 580:90
D., d., you bastard — PLATH 773:96
knocked his D. down — HUGH 500:46
daemon divine d. is absolute — BELL 85:83
daffadillies d. fill their cups — MILT 684:47
daffadowndillies Strew me…with d. — SPEN 957:99
daffodil bed of d. sky — TENN 1001:85
shining d. dies — TENN 1002:94
daffodils D….before the swallow — SHAK 911:30
dances with the d. — WORD 1099:70
host of golden d. — WORD 1099:67
what d. were for Wordsworth — LARK 582:22
daft ae…thinks the tither d. — SCOTT 855:6
d. or corrupt — FULL 410:44
dagger d. drew and died — SHAK 871:57
d. …in the heart of France — QUIN 798:68
d. which I see before me — SHAK 908:39
Distress with d. keen — COLL 277:45
daggers d. in men's smiles — SHAK 909:54
Give me the d. — SHAK 908:48
laid their d. ready — SHAK 908:44
speak d. to her — SHAK 892:45
daily cancer…growing d. — DEAN 311:59
Yesterday, We had d. cleaning — REED 804:80
dainties never fed on the d. — SHAK 865:16
spiced d., every one — KEATS 546:95
dais From high on the d. — VIRG 1045:81
daises Meadows trim with d. — MILT 682:1
daisies covered…with violets and d. — SHEL 930:33
d., those pearled Arcturi — SHEL 932:67
picking d. on the railway — WODE 1089:89
picks a posy of d. — THOM 1011:83
daisy D. and Lily — SITW 941:15
Not yellow like a d. — TRUMP 1030:37
Daisy Sweet D.! oft I talk to thee — WORD 1097:41

Dakotas D., I am for war — RED 804:74
last bear, shot drinking in the D. — CRANE 295:99
dale through the lonely d. — BLAKE 166:68
Through wood and d. — COLE 275:16
Dali D. is…disgusting — ORWE 745:65
D.'s importance for the Surrealists — SCHW 851:23
D.'s nature to play Gilbert — RUSS 833:40
When D. hallucinated — RUSS 833:41
dalliance primrose path of d. — SHAK 888:62
silken d. in the wardrobe — SHAK 880:73
dam d. it up — ACHE 3:42
leave the d. — SHAK 875:34
damage pay for the d. — STIG 977:66
Damascus travelled the road to D. — ASHD 41:60
damask Feed on her d. cheek — SHAK 894:15
dame dance in the old d. yet — MARQ 655:35
La belle d. — KEATS 547:96
La belle D. sans merci — KEATS 545:74
sulky, sullen d. — BURNS 211:9
this looser d. did skill — SPEN 958:14
dames Ah! gentle d.! — BURNS 211:11
laughing d. in who he did delight — BYRON 219:68
O happy d. — SURR 983:45
struts his d. before — MILT 682:99
dammed only saved by being d. — HOOD 489:42
damn d. by rule — OTWAY 746:77
D. the torpedoes! — FARR 383:74
D. you! — SHAW 920:9
dear, I don't give a d. — MITC 697:91
devil d. thee black — SHAK 910:80
don't give a d. — SALI 838:23
one d. thing over and over — MILL 676:91
public doesn't give a d. — BEEC 82:16
save those who d. them — HUGO 502:74
damnable d. degrees of drinking — WEBS 1059:26
d. woman's trick — SHAW 921:29
this d. war — ACHE 3:52
damnation blasted to eternal d.! — SHAW 925:21
critical d. — WALT 1052:12
d. of almost everybody — INGE 511:41
deep d. of his taking-off — SHAK 908:32
which road leads to d. — DYSON 358:1
damnations 29 distinct d. — BROW 197:27
damned always those d. dishes — FREN 404:38
among the d. already — SHAW 920:9
And d. be him — SHAK 910:90
Another d., thick, square book! — GLOU 430:62
Beautiful and the D. — FITZ 390:96
brandy of the d. — SHAW 921:32
Cromwell, d. to everlasting fame! — POPE 781:51
D. from here to eternity — KIPL 560:22
d. long, dark…dangerous way — GOLD 433:24
d. nice thing — WELL 1063:10
If I were d. — KIPL 561:43
must be d. perpetually! — MARL 654:20
the desperate, the d. — JACK 514:86
damozel blessed d. leaned out — ROSS 824:79
damp poisonous d. of night — SHAK 906:90
damsel d. with a dulcimer — COLE 275:17
d. woll come to you anone — MALO 642:27
Dan from D. to Beersheba — STER 970:21
dance best d. e'er cam to the Land — BURNS 212:34
Can d. a little — ANON 26:39
Ceres will join in the d. — SITW 941:9
D., and Provençal song — KEATS 547:14
d. and the war — STEIN 966:42
d. has begun — BETJ 100:36
d. in the old dame yet — MARQ 655:35
d. is a measured pace — BACON 55:15
d. is a poem — DIDE 329:26
D., little words — WORL 1101:96
D. on this ball-floor — BLUN 170:44
d. round in a ring — FROST 407:98
d. round to all Eternity — FLET 394:67

dance (*contd.*)
d. the dullest beanbag — NOON 731:22
d. while you can — AUDEN 46:56
daughters of the year shall d.! — BLAKE 165:59
Drink and d. — PARK 754:9
face the music and d. — BERL 95:61
Learn then to d. — DAVI 307:7
Let's have a d. — SHAK 880:68
music…too far from the d. — POUND 786:77
returning lightly d. — THOM 1012:13
spectral d., before the dawn — BROO 192:26
sprightly d. — WORD 1099:68
teach an elephant to d. — MOSS 711:7
the d. was long — DOWS 343:81
the dancer from the d. — YEATS 1106:80
there the d. is — ELIOT 370:25
time to d. — BIBLE 122:19
To d. is to discover — SENG 859:52
walk…before they d. — POPE 782:85
When you do d. — SHAK 912:31
Will you, won't you…join the d.? — CARR 239:39
danced d. down the street — KERO 553:12
d. his did — CUMM 300:94
d. with a man — FARJ 383:64
David d. before the Lord — BIBLE 110:45
ye have not d. — BIBLE 137:86
dancer Curled minion, d. — ARNO 38:94
How can we know the d. — YEATS 1106:80
move…like a d. — ELIOT 372:74
Now, D.! Now, Prancer — MOORE 704:6
dancers d. dancing in tune — TENN 1001:86
d. quicker and quicker flew — BURNS 211:19
Like d. on the ropes — ETHE 380:13
dances doesn't think she d. — GILB 425:85
He capers, he d. — SHAK 878:19
dancing as d. is to walking — WAIN 1047:28
Ask Nureyev to stop d. — KING 557:69
D. is a frenzy and a rage — DAVI 307:9
D. is a wonderful training — MORL 708:70
d. is love's proper exercise — DAVI 307:6
mourning into d. — BIBLE 115:56
pair Of d. pumps — MIDD 673:43
past our d. days — SHAK 868:81
stillness the d. — ELIOT 371:44
the d. floor — YEATS 1106:79
very merry, d., drinking — DRYD 352:95
dancing-master manners of a d.-m. — JOHN 526:95
dandelions D. were either sweet — TRAV 1025:36
Sheaves of drooping d. — BETJ 100:40
smell of the d. — COOKE 286:32
dandruff cure for d. — LUCE 618:33
dandy d. must aspire to be sublime — BAUD 78:39
dandyism Cynicism is intellectual d. — MERE 671:9
Dane never get rid of the D. — KIPL 564:11
Roman than a D. — SHAK 893:86
Dane-geld paying the D.-g. — KIPL 564:11
danger best way to avoid d. — ROCHE 815:42
bright face of d. — STEV 976:49
but what is d.? — HAWT 461:64
buzzard…is never in d. — FAUL 384:86
d. in touching — BURNS 213:51
d. is that gauge — LESS 598:1
D. knows full well — SHAK 883:35
d. of being torn with violence — ROSS 823:65
d. of coming back prodigies — AUST 51:53
d. of desire — SHAK 888:60
d. of its tricking the writer — SAND 842:79
d. that…he will not recognize — AUCH 46:39
D., the spur — CHAP 252:74
d. to all Christendom — INNO 512:56
d. to speak true — JONS 535:1
doctors are the greater d. — JONS 534:79
foresees d. and avoids it — KEYN 554:31
great d. of contagion — WILD 1079:30

danger (*contd.*)
grouse are in no d.	EDIN 361:42
life from grief or d. free	JOHN 525:82
measure of d.	GREE 444:11
never be in d. of Popery	ADDI 7:18
no d. in sweetness and youth	ROCH 816:61
Out of this nettle d.	SHAK 875:51
Pleased with the d.	DRYD 349:12
political d.	GLAD 429:50
razor-edge of d.	WILD 1079:27
rest in d. are	ETHE 380:13
run into any kind of d.	BOOK 173:97
The d. is past	POE 776:55
united under the threat of d.	DEGA 313:99
What d. will it be	SHAK 885:74
When in d., ponder	WAGN 1047:27
would be less in d.	NASH 719:44

dangerous Caesar is more d.
	SHAK 883:35
d. to climb a mountain	HAWT 461:64
d. to meet it alone	WHAR 1068:2
d. to pay it off	SELL 858:40
delays are d.	DRYD 347:67
dirty, d. way	GOLD 433:24
Facility is a d. thing	SLOAN 943:59
generalizations are d.	DUMAS 354:30
have something in me d.	SHAK 893:81
how d. everything is	STEIN 965:39
Mad, bad, and d. to know	LAMB 576:4
mad, then d.	BENN 90:69
makes it so d.	WILS 1084:11
more d. is the abuse	BURKE 206:3
more d. than a mud-puddle	STEIN 965:31
most d. duo	SCAR 846:55
Nothing is more d.	ALAIN 10:76
Nothing is so d.	WILDE 1078:92
potentially d.	JONES 533:55
Science becomes d.	SHAW 923:86
Sentiment was the more d.	GREE 444:7
sincerity is a d. thing	WILDE 1076:41
some inquiries are too d.	SAGAN 836:74
such men are d.	SHAK 882:23
those, who have to hope…d.	BURKE 207:19

dangers appalling d. of family life
	HUXL 507:67
d. thou canst make us scorn!	BURNS 211:17
limit the d. of this age	KENN 552:86
loved me for the d.	SHAK 898:9
perils and d. of this night	BOOK 174:1

Daniel D. come to judgement SHAK 873:94

Dante D. makes me sick
	VEGA 1041:28
D. or Michelangelo	MULL 713:43
D. turned round violently	JOYCE 538:44
D., who loved well	BROW 199:69

dapper d. from your napper COLL 276:37

dappled for d. things
	HOPK 491:84
long d. grass	YEATS 1105:63

dare art doesn't d. you
	HUST 505:39
bear to live, or d. to die	POPE 781:49
d. lift a hand	JOHN 524:60
d. to eat a peach?	ELIOT 367:54
d., to slay Owen Roe O'Neil?	DAVIS 309:36
helps those who d.	VIRG 1045:48
must have the courage to d.	DOST 340:44
Nobody'll d.	HUGH 499:15
They wouldn't d.	BARR 73:57
what others only d. to think	CHAR 252:80

dared never d. be radical FROST 407:93

dares Who d., wins ANON 26:42

daring d. of a moment's surrender
	ELIOT 369:96
D. Young Man	SARO 843:98
dash of d.	SNOW 950:69
serious d. starts from within	WELTY 1065:52

dark all aroun' in the d.
	STEI 966:55
all before was d.	WENT 1065:54
Between the d. and the daylight	LONG 612:15

dark (*contd.*)
blind man in a d. room	DARW 306:91
children fear to go in the d.	BACON 56:43
Children talking…in the d.	DEVO 318:90
Climb to our proper d.	YEATS 1107:91
colours will agree in the d.	BACON 56:47
come out after d.	WODE 1089:9
D. as the Grave	LOWRY 618:20
D. as the world of man	SITW 941:16
d. backward and abyss of time?	SHAK 916:19
d. in light expos'd	MILT 694:40
D. is Light Enough	FRY 408:17
d.…Of night	YEATS 1105:65
d. place where it leads	JONG 533:60
d. time of the year	ELIOT 372:68
d. was talking to the dead	MACN 637:46
d. with something more than night	CHAN 251:52
Death…drop from the d.	ROSE 823:63
don't be afraid of the d.	HAMM 454:54
drawing you fall over in the d.	HIRS 482:21
For d. hour or twain	SHAK 909:55
naked in the d. and cold	LEGU 594:23
never to refuse a drink after d.	MENC 669:71
night…like a great d. wing	RAND 801:24
O d. d. d.	ELIOT 371:49
on that d. earth	TENN 1003:22
one tunnel, d. and solitary	SABA 835:56
Out in the d.	THOM 1012:14
real d. night of the soul	FITZ 391:14
round from the d. to the light	SWIN 988:52
sinks his ship in the d.	CORN 288:61
the d. well	PRIC 789:34
very d., and no brightness	BIBLE 130:60
Walk between d. and d.	GRAV 439:19
ways that are d.	HARTE 459:50
we are for the d.	SHAK 906:2
what d. days seen.	SHAK 914:82
what in me is d. Illumine	MILT 687:86
when it was yet d.	BIBLE 147:73
With d. forgetting	DANI 304:62
work in the d.	JAMES 516:23

darken days d. round me TENN 1004:45

darkies colored people…replaced d. FEIF 384:98

darkling here as on a d. plain ARNO 36:65

darkness called you out of d.
	BIBLE 156:78
cast away the works of d.	BOOK 174:9
cast out into outer d.	BIBLE 136:65
children of d.	BEND 89:57
d. again and a silence	LONG 612:18
d. and silence reign	LEAR 589:51
d. beautiful with thee	TENN 999:46
D. came down	THAC 1006:86
d. comprehended it not	BIBLE 144:25
d. crumbles away	ROSE 823:60
d. falls at Thy behest	ELLE 374:2
D. falls like a wet sponge	ASHB 41:53
d. from light	BROW 200:79
d. he called Night	BIBLE 102:84
d. of the grave	MILL 676:90
d. ridged the riven dark	FREE 404:34
d. shall be the light	ELIOT 371:44
d. shot with lightning	OFAO 736:94
d.…sifts through your hand	ASHB 41:54
D. spreads his…wings	MILT 682:96
d. visable Served only	MILT 687:87
d. was on face of deep	BIBLE 102:82
Dawn on our d.	HEBER 466:56
day of the Lord be d.	BIBLE 130:60
design of d.	FROST 407:92
during the days of d.	PETA 767:5
first place of liquid d.	FRAME 400:77
Flags wearily through d.	SHEL 929:10
Go out into the d.	HASK 460:57
goeth in the d.	BIBLE 131:75

darkness (*contd.*)
he counteracts the powers of d.	SMART 944:67
Hell's d. under his feet	CARL 236:93
him who gropes painfully in d.	CARL 234:55
horror of outer d.	GORD 435:63
In that d. camaraderie	HUGH 500:40
in the d. and the cold	STEV 976:58
in the d. bind them	TOLK 1022:92
Is d., the fruit	SWIN 987:35
Light out of d.!	MILT 693:27
light out of d.	DONNE 339:26
Lighten our d.	BOOK 174:1
lots o' d.	MACD 627:81
make d. more visible	EDGE 361:32
men loved d.	BIBLE 145:35
minute of d.	RUSH 829:69
no d. but ignorance	SHAK 895:36
not d. but shadow	FRYE 408:24
Of d. till it smil'd	MILT 683:27
Of now done d.	HOPK 492:2
people that walked in d.	BIBLE 125:65
people which sat in d.	BIBLE 133:32
profounder the surrounding d.	HUXL 506:51
rear of d. thin	MILT 682:99
Ring out the d.	TENN 1000:57
season of D.	DICK 326:58
seen in the d.	FRIE 405:59
shades of d.	DELA 314:33
Shares the d.	MILL 676:84
Surely the d. shall cover me	BIBLE 120:49
Swaddled with d.	ELIOT 368:69
sweeping through the d.	WORD 1095:16
there's d.	SHAK 903:35
to d., on extended wings	STEV 971:40
torrent of d.	NOYES 732:42
turned around from d. to light	PLATO 774:23
two eternities of d.	NABO 716:95
universal d. buries all	POPE 783:11
Where there is d.	FRAN 401:91

darling bride and my d. to be?
	BALL 67:43
Charlie he's my d.	BURNS 213:46
d. buds of May	SHAK 912:48
getting someone to call you d.	BARN 72:37

darlings d. of daytime! KEND 550:49

darts fiery d. of the wicked BIBLE 152:6

Darwinian D. principle WILDE 1076:42

dash d. away! Dash away!
	MOORE 704:6
d. of daring	SNOW 950:69
d. of waves	ARNO 38:98
d. themselves to pieces	SHAK 863:52

data constellations of d.
	GIBS 422:40
graphical representation of d.	GIBS 422:40

date all too short a d.
	SHAK 912:48
arrive but at the d.	WALL 1050:76
born…out of d.	POUND 785:60
d. that will live in infamy	ROOS 822:44
doubles your chances for a d.	ALLEN 14:40
merely a d. on a page	THOM 1013:18
Name and d.	BUNT 204:57
out of d., obsolete	STEV 970:31
they d. from it	TWAIN 1032:75

dated might become d. for a while HAWES 460:61

dates blind d. are a way of life
	EPST 379:6
ripping out the d.	LEAC 588:31

daughter begins to think of the d.
	EDGE 361:87
dance like a plumber's d.	MIDD 673:39
d. and the Moor	SHAK 897:98
d. loved a man	SHAK 894:14
d. of a hundred Earls	TENN 995:69
d. of Earth and Water	SHEL 928:84
d. of the gods	TENN 993:35
d. of the Southern Cross	FRAN 402:16
d. to his blood	SHAK 874:26
Don't put your d. on the stage	COWA 290:2

daughter (*contd.*)		**day** (*contd.*)		**day** (*contd.*)	
Elderly, ugly d.	GILB 423:*52*	babbling, and remorseful d.	SHAK 861:*8*	eye of d.	YEATS 1106:*81*
Filled her with a d.	MILT 682:*97*	better future and a brighter d.	SMUTS 950:*66*	far from the light of d.	ORAH 741:*77*
Gigantic d. of the West	TENN 1000:*65*	bisy larke, messager of d.	CHAU 255:*29*	first d.	BIBLE 102:*84*
King o' Spain's d.	COLUM 278:*61*	born on a d.	VALL 1039:*90*	For a d. and a night	SWIN 988:*52*
kyngis d. of the londe	MALO 642:*26*	breaks the blank d.	TENN 998:*24*	for a year and a d.	LEAR 590:*59*
lost your d. to…men	FERRE 387:*28*	bright d. is gone	SHAK 906:*2*	glorious d.	WORD 1101:*95*
loves my d.	SHAK 912:*34*	bright d. that brings forth	SHAK 883:*26*	Good morning to the d.	JONS 534:*74*
loveth son or d.	BIBLE 136:*80*	bring to the light of d.	FRIE 405:*59*	Good things of d.	SHAK 909:*60*
marry My d. Jill	NASH 720:*59*	brings about the d.	SHAK 862:*23*	great d. of his wrath is come	BIBLE 157:*13*
Nokomis bore a d.	LONG 611:*9*	buried the d.	ELIOT 370:*28*	grievance for the d.	MANS 647:*5*
Squire's own d.	GRAV 440:*40*	burn and rave at the close of d.	THOM 1011:*75*	Gwine to run all d.	FOST 399:*59*
Thou art thy father's d.	SHAK 885:*76*	But one d., one cold winter's d.	HOFF 484:*58*	Happy as the d. is long	RODR 819:*88*
To my d. Leonora	WODE 1089:*96*	By d. I shall be well	ARNO 36:*71*	have had my d.	TURN 1031:*52*
youngest d. does not love thee	SHAK 902:*97*	by d. in a pillar of a cloud	BIBLE 106:*64*	have their d. and cease	TENN 998:*17*
daughters d. are inclined to love	MONT 701:*56*	By night or d.	WORD 1097:*48*	heaven to gaudy d. denies	BYRON 221:*16*
d. of her daughter	SHAK 866:*34*	cares, that infest the d.	LONG 611:*4*	hour or a d.	NASHE 721:*77*
d. of Jerusalem	BIBLE 124:*48*	centre, and enjoy bright d.	MILT 683:*28*	I have come to this d.	TAKU 990:*85*
d. of musick shall be brought low	BIBLE 123:*42*	close of d.	YEATS 1105:*71*	ideal d. for football	SMITH 948:*26*
d. of the year shall dance!	BLAKE 165:*59*	coldness of one particular d.	MOOD 703:*96*	If it be a hot d.	SHAK 877:*83*
Earth's heedless sons and d.	BLUN 170:*43*	committed unto him against that d.	BIBLE 154:*37*	in my arms till break of d.	AUDEN 47:*74*
love among the d.	BIBLE 124:*46*	compare this to a summer's d.?	SHAK 912:*48*	in respect to this d.	DONNE 339:*27*
outraging their wives and d.	GENG 418:*78*	course-compelling D.	PATM 760:*6*	In the d., in the night	WHIT 1073:*93*
sons and d. of Life's longing	GIBR 422:*38*	damnable iteration d. after d.	STEAD 964:*5*	it sufficeth that the d. will end	SHAK 884:*65*
sons and your d. shall prophesy	BIBLE 130:*55*	dawning of the d.	DONNE 339:*26*	jocund d. Stands tiptoe	SHAK 869:*11*
wives and d. chaste	MOLI 698:*18*	d. and night shall not cease	BIBLE 104:*13*	journey take the whole long d.?	ROSS 824:*75*
Your d.…will be married	WALP 1051:*90*	d. and the way we met	SWIN 987:*42*	Joy ruled the d.	DRYD 352:*96*
Daumier one small Goya or a D.	AUDEN 46:*54*	d. becomes more solemn and serene	SHEL 927:*63*	July's d. as short	SHAK 911:*19*
dauntless d. in war	SCOTT 853:*54*	d. brought back my night	MILT 687:*83*	knell Of a spent d.	CRANE 295:*10*
dauphin Daylight's d.	HOPK 491:*88*	D. by d. make it new	POUND 787:*87*	knell of parting d.	GRAY 441:*62*
David born this day in the city of D.	BIBLE 142:*78*	d. cometh	BIBLE 131:*72*	knowest not what a d. may bring	BIBLE 122:*5*
D. danced before the Lord	BIBLE 110:*45*	d. consists of twenty-four hours	LECO 592:*2*	known a better d.	SCOTT 853:*42*
D. his ten thousands	BIBLE 110:*42*	d. doth daw	BALL 68:*61*	lamp of d.	DOUG 341:*55*
D. was old and stricken in years	BIBLE 110:*53*	d. for each of us	ANOU 31:*77*	last d. as on the first	KLEE 566:*49*
Hosanna to the Son of D.	BIBLE 139:*30*	d.'s hard work in thy life	LAWR 586:*92*	last d. of 1943	HARD 455:*57*
once in royal D.'s city	ALEX 13:*19*	d. he missed his loving bride	NASH 720:*57*	lease…from d. to d.	ANOU 30:*71*
Philistine said unto D.	BIBLE 110:*41*	d. I can already remember	VALL 1039:*92*	left alone with our d.	AUDEN 46:*55*
upon the throne of D.	BIBLE 125:*66*	d. I wish to be a only	NIET 728:*73*	let the d. be time enough	DANI 304:*62*
Davy D. Abominated gravy	BENT 93:*25*	d. in April	SHAK 875:*33*	Let the d. perish	BIBLE 112:*98*
dawn brown fog of a winter d.	ELIOT 368:*83*	D. in Night	CRAS 295:*17*	light of common d.	WORD 1098:*51*
d. broke like a face	SASS 845:*24*	d. in thy courts	BIBLE 117:*95*	live each d. as though one's last	AURE 50:*27*
d. comes up like thunder	KIPL 560:*26*	d. joins the past eternity	BYRON 220:*94*	live murmur of a summer's d.	ARNO 37:*86*
d. in the mountains	MURP 715:*71*	d. light such candle	LATI 583:*36*	long glare of d.	SHEL 927:*60*
d. of intellectual enlightenment	CURZ 302:*29*	d. look ruefully on	STEV 976:*50*	looking the whole d. long	ANON 25:*26*
d. seem to be an alleviation	WILD 1079:*20*	d. may daw	BURNS 211:*2*	make Perpetual d.	MARL 654:*20*
day doth d.	BALL 68:*61*	d.…meant not to see	THAT 1008:*17*	merry as the d. is long	SHAK 879:*34*
fight it at the d.	BALL -101:*37*	D., night…but in Britain?	SHAK 916:*10*	merry heart goes all the d.	SHAK 911:*27*
gathers God at d.	CRANE 295:*10*	d. of his death	AUDEN 47:*69*	midnight, and it is the d.'s	DONNE 337:*81*
grey d. breaking	MASE 661:*32*	d. of the Lord	BIBLE 156:*87*	misery From this d.	MILT 693:*19*
grey d. of the morning after	ADE 8:*42*	d. of their flight	MACA 623:*5*	morning after is the first d.	MACN 637:*48*
I saw d. upon them	RAND 801:*25*	d., Peace, plenty	NASHE 721:*81*	morning shows the d.	MILT 694:*33*
Lasses a-lilting before the d.	ELLI 374:*8*	d. that I die	MACL 633:*62*	my d. was coming	RICH 810:*61*
magic of its d.	RUSS 833:*36*	d. thou gavest, Lord, is ended	ELLE 374:*2*	myrie someris d.	CHAU 254:*87*
Near the face of d.	MERE 671:*98*	D. unto d. uttereth speech	BIBLE 114:*44*	needs every d.	WILD 1079:*29*
No d.—no dusk	HOOD 489:*51*	d. was lost, for art	LEWIS 602:*68*	never finds the d.	SHAK 909:*75*
peep of d.	GRAY 442:*76*	d. we started to fight	ANON 28:*19*	news of the d.	LIPP 606:*32*
prays…that the d. may ripen	CARL 234:*55*	d. when heaven was falling	HOUS 496:*77*	night of this worrisome d.	BERN 97:*89*
ray, and find no d.	MILT 689:*30*	d. which the Lord hath made	BIBLE 118:*27*	night shineth as the d.	BIBLE 120:*49*
redemption's happy d.	CASW 244:*37*	d. will not follow night	TATE 991:*5*	no d. for me to look upon	SHAK 860:*84*
said to the D.	THOM 1013:*29*	d. you stop becoming	MILL 677:*4*	no proper time of d.	HOOD 489:*51*
see by the d.'s early	CUMM 299:*83*	deal with all d. long	STEI 967:*66*	Nor brought too long a d.	HOOD 489:*37*
seen d. and sunset on moors	MASE 662:*39*	death will have his d.	SHAK 867:*58*	not a second on the d.	COOK 286:*24*
soft as the d.	THUR 1018:*25*	did just nothing all d.	PRIOR 790:*56*	not going to have a good d.	LANCE 578:*53*
spectral dance, before the d.	BROO 192:*26*	dim night of this immortal d.	SHEL 930:*26*	not to me returns D.	MILT 689:*31*
the white d.	SHEL 929:*1*	dog will have his d.	SHAK 893:*82*	Now is come a darker d.	SHEL 927:*71*
to reflect the d.	MACA 623:*9*	Drunk many times a d.	SHAK 897:*89*	now is the d. of salvation	BIBLE 151:*82*
trees at d.	ARNO 37:*75*	each d. is like a year	WILDE 1078:*3*	Now's the d.	BURNS 212:*37*
dawning d. of the day	DONNE 339:*26*	end of a perfect d.	BOND 172:*79*	obscure d. by d.	THOM 1010:*54*
daws For d. to peck at	SHAK 897:*95*	every blessèd d.	WILB 1075:*19*	on the d. it is finished	I 510:*25*
day a hard d.'s night	LENN 596:*60*	every d. is a life	ONEI 740:*53*	On the Last D.	EWART 381:*47*
all I'd do all d.	SALI 839:*28*	every d. Speaks a new scene	QUAR 796:*52*	one d. as a lion	MUSS 716:*85*
all things all d. long	TENN 1002:*9*	every d. surmount a fear	EMER 377:*71*	one d.…does not make a man	ARIS 34:*26*
apple a d.	ANON 30:*60*	every d. to be lost	JOHN 532:*34*	One d. telleth another	BOOK 176:*66*
argue that I shall some d. die	LEAC 588:*32*	Every d., in every way	COUE 289:*72*	one d., the light	MANS 647:*5*

day (*contd.*)

One d. will flash	LERN 597:87
or in the shortest d.	SURR 983:46
ordinary d. in the modern world	PERCY 766:84
our long love's d.	MARV 658:72
passing of a d.	SPEN 958:13
pause in the d.'s occupation	DEVO 318:91
pause in the d.'s occupations	LONG 612:15
perfect d. nor night	SHAK 862:21
Pleasures shorter than the d.	WALL 1050:72
present d. magazine	LOWE 617:15
problems of our own d.	POEL 776:56
rain it raineth every d.	SHAK 895:39
rising fogs prevail upon the d.	DRYD 348:83
runs through the roughest d.	SHAK 907:22
said nothing all the d.	DONNE 337:95
second d., they took	NGU 725:45
see this d. and live	SHAK 881:99
seek all d.	SHAK 874:9
seest the twilight of such d.	SHAK 914:73
Seize the d.	HORA 493:18
shadows in a sunshine d.?	MARL 653:6
So foul and fair a d.	SHAK 907:15
So tedious is this d.	SHAK 869:6
speaks to you every d.	TOCQ 1021:80
stand at the latter d.	BIBLE 113:12
such a d. tomorrow as today	SHAK 911:18
sunny d.	GREE 443:2
support us all the d.	NEWM 724:29
Sweet d., so cool	HERB 475:32
tender eye of pitiful d.	SHAK 909:59
The busy d.	SHAK 896:55
the cool of the d.	ELIOT 370:11
the d. you stop suffering	WILL 1082:74
The long d. wanes	TENN 995:61
The longest d.	STOWE 978:88
the wave's intenser d.	SHEL 928:88
There's night and d., brother	BORR 179:23
third d. comes a frost	SHAK 918:61
this d. is holy unto our Lord	BIBLE 112:32
this d.'s life as yours	EURI 380:23
this d. to end myself	TENN 1003:30
this d. to the ending of the world	SHAK 882:3
those who dwell in realms of d.	BLAKE 168:21
thousand years as one d.	BIBLE 156:86
Three hours a d.	TROL 1028:98
till our wedding d.	COLUM 278:60
time to call it a d.	COMD 278:65
to fill our d.	KIPL 564:6
Today's the d. the Teddy Bears	BRAT 185:15
tomorrow is another d.	MITC 697:92
true judgement d.	ANON 23:98
twelfth d. of my diet	PIER 769:35
Underneath D.'s azure eyes	SHEL 927:70
unhappy d. too late	SHAK 867:56
until polling d.	WHIT 1072:71
up by break of d.	HERB 474:11
vehicle for the thought of our d.	FORD 396:5
wake in the d. to find	LAWR 587:13
wandering all d.	PRIOR 791:60
warm precincts of cheerful d.	GRAY 442:74
Was the gradual d.	SPEN 956:73
wealth abides…but for a d.	EURI 381:35
Went the d. well?	ANON 26:49
when our d. was fair	HARDY 457:12
when will this long weary d.	SPEN 959:32
world's great d.	MUIR 712:36

day-labour God exact d.-l. — MILT 686:81
day-spring d.-s. born; here leave — MILT 694:37
day-star d.-s. in the ocean bed — MILT 685:49
daybreak d. through the gateways — SASS 846:43
daydreams d. of melancholy men — DRYD 346:50

exotic d.	NABO 717:14
other d.	HAMM 453:48

daylight Between the…d.

buried by d.	PEPYS 765:75
d. atheist	BEHAN 84:61
d. in the mind	ADDI 7:17
kingdom of D.'s dauphin	HOPK 491:88
let in d. upon magic	BAGE 61:61
long and lone d.	SHEL 932:72
rule never to drink by d.	MENC 669:71
see a church by d.	SHAK 879:35
When d. comes, comes in the light	CLOU 270:32

days All d. are nights

Ancient of D.	SMITH 950:61
as the d. ran on	THUR 1019:32
As thy d., so shall thy strength be	BIBLE 108:4
beauty can lie…in d.	FOWL 400:70
Beauty…in the house three d.	SHAW 922:43
better than length of d.	AESC 9:57
brave d. of old	MACA 624:18
burnt-out ends of smoky d.	ELIOT 367:56
came to the Ancient of d.	BIBLE 130:50
Channel in the mad march d.	MASE 662:38
count eternity in d.?	ROET 819:98
d. are as grass	BIBLE 118:15
d. are evil	BIBLE 152:2
d. are swifter	BIBLE 112:3
d. at the morn	BROW 197:25
d. darken round me	TENN 1004:45
d.'s garish eye	MILT 683:14
d. go by, I remain	APOL 32:93
d. grow short	ANDE 18:6
d….like a wayward tune	YEATS 1104:58
d. of glory	PETA 767:5
d. of long ago	LIND 606:17
d….of my pilgrimage	BIBLE 106:50
d. of my youth	SOUT 954:30
d. short	ANDR 19:13
d. that are no more	TENN 997:2
d. that are no more	TENN 997:3
d. that are no more	TENN 997:4
d. that are to try men's souls	WILS 1086:46
d. that have gone by	FLEC 393:53
d. that make us happy	MASE 662:48
d. were our mechanics	LEUP 599:14
d. when work was scrappy	CHES 260:39
death my d. should expiate	SHAK 913:51
dirk and drublie d.	DUNB 355:42
drawing d. out	SHAK 883:40
E're half my d.	MILT 686:81
Even as our d. do grow	SHAK 899:22
few the d. that hold	MILL 677:4
fifteen or twenty d. longer	PERTH 767:3
For forty d.	SITW 941:26
for the rest of my d.	PLATH 773:92
friends of other d.	ROBI 815:31
full of d., riches, and honour	BIBLE 112:87
genius of our d.	LARI 581:93
glamour Of childish d.	LAWR 585:69
glorious d.	GILB 424:76
good d. speed and depart	MART 657:61
Happy D. are Here Again	YELL 1107:96
high, clear d.	CHAT 253:98
if ever come perfect d.	LOWE 616:82
In bygone d., Morag	LAUR 584:46
In olden d. a glimpse	PORT 784:31
in the d. of villainy?	SHAK 876:64
In the future d.	ROOS 822:43
in these last d.	BIBLE 154:44
in those d. ambition	LAGE 575:98
Length of d. is in her right hand	BIBLE 120:60
live laborious d.	MILT 684:42
Newgate in our schoolboy d.	DICK 320:15
nights and down the d.	THOM 1013:28
number of my d.	BOOK 176:71
one of my well-looking d.	GOLD 433:22

days (*contd.*)

remember the d. of Old	MOORE 706:33
salad d.	SHAK 905:67
seemed unto him but a few d.	BIBLE 105:36
seven d. war	MUIR 712:35
siege of battering d.	SHAK 914:68
Six d. of the week it soils	LARK 581:3
somewhat troublesome d.	FOST 399:58
Talk of our enlightened d.	MANS 647:96
teach us to number our d.	BIBLE 117:1
Ten D. That Shook	REED 805:90
the d. dividing	SWIN 986:24
though fall'n on evil d.	MILT 691:82
three whole d. together	SUCK 981:23
Time in hours, d., years	VAUG 1041:20
walking for d., for months	ROBB 813:9
was a habit in those d.	ROGE 820:17
What are d. for?	LARK 581:95
what dark d. seen.	SHAK 914:82
wi' her a' my simmer d.	SOUT 954:27
young d. of gathering flowers	PEAC 762:31

daytime never met in the d. — THUR 1020:56

De Maupassant beat Mr D. M. — HEMI 471:37
de profundis D. P. clamavi ad te — BIBLE 159:49
De Quincey Coleridge and D. Q. — THUR 1019:42
deacons jawbones of d. — THOM 1012:95

dead Adonais—he is d.! — SHEL 930:34

all d. men	BIBLE 106:63
as good as d.	EINS 363:67
being d. is hard work	RILKE 811:85
Bene they all d.	SPEN 958:17
better to be d.	NASH 719:48
Blessed are the d.	BIBLE 158:24
bring the d. to life	GRAV 439:23
brother was d., and is alive again	BIBLE 143:2
But he's d., but he's d.	DAVIS 309:37
but in fact it is d.	MITF 697:3
By his d. smile	OWEN 748:15
Christ being raised from the d.	BIBLE 149:21
Christ risen from the d.	BIBLE 151:67
Come not, when I am d.	TENN 998:14
Come up and be d.!	DICK 327:85
communication Of the d.	ELIOT 372:70
communism is a d. dog	SOLZ 952:97
concert is d.	GOULD 436:74
conference With the d.!	WEBS 1061:68
converse with the mighty d.	THOM 1015:52
Culture is d.	ANON 27:87
dark was talking to the d.	MACN 637:46
d. and gone	YEATS 1105:70
d. and gone, lady	SHAK 892:61
d. and half alive	BETJ 99:25
D.! and so great	NERO 723:7
d. and turned to clay	SHAK 893:79
d. are living	MACM 635:13
d. are raised up	BIBLE 137:83
d. bury their d.	BIBLE 136:67
d., but in the Elysian fields	DISR 333:21
d. come loupin' owre	MACD 627:73
d. don't die	LAWR 586:87
D. for a ducat, d.	SHAK 892:52
D. Heart of Australia	GREG 446:48
d. in Christ shall rise first	BIBLE 153:25
d. know not any thing	BIBLE 123:32
d. level of provincial existence	ELIOT 365:70
D., long dead	TENN 1001:90
d. man is the best fall guy	CHAN 251:47
d. man without…the panoply	DAVI 308:14
d. many times	PATER 759:93
D. men are serious	FIND 389:66
D. men never repent	DICK 321:36
d. might as well speak to the living	CATH 244:43
d. more than half	MILT 694:40
d. of winter	ELIOT 369:3

dead (*contd.*)

d. one lay moaning	SMITH 948:33
D. perfection, no more	TENN 1001:74
d. reign	ZOLA 1110:26
d. returning lightly	THOM 1012:13
d. shall be raised incorruptible	BIBLE 151:72
d. shall not have died	LINC 605:4
D. shepherd	SHAK 886:15
d. to sin	BIBLE 149:20
d. which he slew at his death	BIBLE 109:22
d., who will not fight	GREN 446:52
D., your Majesty	DICK 325:37
Death will come when thou art d.	SHEL 932:61
deeper insights to the d. belong	FERG 385:14
democracy of the d.	CHES 258:7
distance that the d. have gone	DICK 329:19
dropping of the d.	WILL 1080:44
dry and d.	SNYD 951:82
Either d. or my watch	MARX 659:1
ended and d.	GLAS 430:60
England mourns for her d.	BINY 162:6
enough room…to buy your d. men	CORW 288:62
fain to carry the d.	PEPYS 765:75
fairy…falls down d.	BARR 73:44
Faith without works is d.	BIBLE 155:65
fear of the d.	ACKR 4:56
fell at his feet as d.	BIBLE 156:99
food that d. men eat	DOBS 334:35
fool than to be d.	STEV 974:15
for the d. remeid is none	DUNB 355:41
found him with the d.	WILDE 1078:96
globe of d.	THOM 1010:56
healthy, wealthy and d.	THUR 1018:24
hear the D.-March play	KIPL 560:29
her warrior d.	TENN 997:7
Heraclitus, they told me you were d.	CORY 288:63
Here Vaughan lies d.	SASS 846:42
heroic happy d.	CUMM 300:84
Hitler was d.	SCHA 847:59
home among the d.	SHEL 931:52
house where there was not one d.	BIBLE 106:62
I expect you'd rather be d.	COPE 287:52
if this is pleasure we'd rather be d.	COWA 290:92
imagined for the mighty d.	KEATS 545:57
immortal spirit of the d.	SPEN 957:30
in the den…nine d. men	BALL -101:38
Joe, long d.	SLES 943:57
judge the quick and the d.	BOOK 173:94
just as easy for your d. to visit you	BELL 88:39
just at this d. hour	SHAK 887:43
kissed by the English d.	OWEN 748:9
lain for a century d.	TENN 1001:88
lasting mansions of the d.	CRAB 293:66
law hath not been d.	SHAK 896:70
literature…very d.	LEWIS 602:55
little cousin is d.	RANS 802:32
live a life half d.	MILT 694:42
liveth, and was d.	BIBLE 157:1
living and the d.	CIXO 267:70
Lycidas is d., d. ere	MILT 684:38
main thing…is that he be d.	HONE 488:30
make sure he was d.	GOLD 434:49
make the d. live	KNEL 567:52
marks our English d.	KIPL 561:54
may be d. ground	REED 805:82
might as well be bloody d.	BLAIR 165:52
millions of the mouthless d.	SORL 953:23
Mindful of the unhonoured d.	GRAY 442:75
more to say when I am d.	ROBI 815:30
most of 'em d.	SASS 845:28
most of my friends are d.	FENT 385:2
Most of the d. were poor	THOM 1009:50
Most people my age are d.	STEN 968:78
Most poets are d.	GRAV 440:36

dead (*contd.*)

mother…must be d.	AUST 50:30
Naked and the D.	MAIL 638:66
networks of d. speech	STARK 963:96
not d. but feed the grass	TATE 991:3
not for the d.	HERN 476:44
not the one d.	FROST 406:81
novel is d.	DELI 314:39
Now thou art d.	CAREW 232:9
of the happier d.	TENN 1003:23
only d. thing that	THOM 1012:8
only good Indian is a d. Indian	SHER 932:75
otherwise d. marriage	PROU 793:99
Over my d. body	KAUF 543:20
over the rich D.!	BROO 192:23
pattern…Of d. and living	ELIOT 372:55
praise the d. which are already d.	BIBLE 122:22
Private Means is d.	SMITH 948:38
quite for ever d.!	CONG 281:23
raise the d.	BIBLE 136:74
recently-.d fish	ORWE 744:24
Remember me when I am d.	DOUG 341:56
remind me of the d.	SASS 846:35
rescue the d.	IGNA 510:29
riddles of birth and d.	FRYE 408:24
risen from the d.	BIBLE 141:57
Sabbath of the d.	MACL 633:71
salutation of the d.	ROBI 815:31
savaged by a d. sheep	HEAL 464:28
saw the d., small and great	BIBLE 158:33
Sea shall give up her d.	BOOK 178:96
She munched, half d.	SMITH 947:3
She, she is d.	DONNE 338:14
Shone round him o'er the d.	HEMA 469:11
shrouded oft our martyred d.	CONN 282:54
Some people are better off d.	CHAN 250:43
Something was d. in each of us	WILDE 1078:1
soul so d.	SCOTT 853:49
speak for sixty thousand d.!	HUGH 501:53
still as the d.	BLUN 170:41
stopped d. at the critical point	SOME 952:1
strike me d.	SHAK 906:92
The man is d.!	WHIT 1074:3
the president is d.	ODON 736:92
The sleeping and the d.	SHAK 908:48
they're a' d.	ANON 24:9
This is the d. land	ELIOT 369:99
thou being d. art God	SWIN 987:41
though he were d., yet shall he live	BIBLE 146:55
'tis Death itself	SHEL 931:48
to be said For being d.	BENT 93:23
to the d. we owe…truth	VOLT 1046:13
tombs of the d. illustrious d.	HOWE 497:97
took their wages and are d.	HOUS 496:77
town…buried its d.	SHAW 926:43
two d. and the other dying	DOCH 334:37
two worlds, one d.	ARNO 38:2
unheroic D. who fed the guns?	SASS 846:41
until read…After that it's d.	WAUGH 1057:83
upon the living and the d.	JOYCE 538:42
useless to the d.	RICH 809:46
vastly more ways of being d.	DAWK 310:45
voice of the d.	TENN 1003:28
wakes or sleeps with the enduring d.	SHEL 931:45
walking d. man	ANON 29:49
was I d. before I was alive	BROW 195:88
was living is now d.	ELIOT 369:93
we are all d.	KEYN 554:29
Weep me not d.	DONNE 337:87
what we call d. is only changed	CARL 235:64
When I am d. and opened	MARY 661:30
When I am d.	BELL 87:18
When I am d.	ROSS 824:76
When I do not write…I'm d.	CIXO 267:76

dead (*contd.*)

when she was d.	GOLD 432:95
Why seek ye…among the d.?	BIBLE 144:20
with the departed d.	SHEL 927:62
withered heart was d.	SCOTT 853:44
word is d.	DICK 328:12
world of the d.	FORS 398:49
you'll know you're d.	WILL 1082:74
youth stone d.	SASS 845:27
dead-born fell d.-b. from the press	HUME 504:12
deadliest endured the d.	RUSK 831:12
deadliness d. of…purely scientific	GILL 426:9
recurring d.	WILL 1083:94
deadlock Holy D.	HERB 474:98
deadly more d. in the long run	TWAIN 1032:62
Deadwood D. and Lost Mule Flat	BENET 90:59
deaf At once is d. and loud	SHEL 929:9
d. adder that stoppeth her ears	BOOK 177:78
D.! Both d!	YEATS 1107:95
d. hear	BIBLE 137:83
d., how should they know	SORL 953:23
d. to hear	BIBLE 141:66
delightful period…if one was d.	LARW 582:30
dialogue of the d.	HOWE 497:93
ears of the d. shall be unstopped	BIBLE 126:82
husband who may be d.	OBRI 734:72
What d…murderer	SHEL 931:44
deafanddumb language even d.	CUMM 299:83
deafening silence was d.	KARSH 542:11
deal d. with them constantly	SHUL 936:31
ease some d.	SHAK 862:39
Fair D.	TRUM 1029:17
good d. of a big-bug	TWAIN 1032:79
great d. has been lost	WALL 1050:66
New D. was ended by World War II	MACG 630:33
stand for the square d.	ROOS 822:48
Deal D. is a most villanous place	COBB 271:55
faith-healer of D.	ANON 26:37
dealer agricultural implement d.	MENC 670:90
dealers d. and collectors	HAMM 453:49
dealing d. in facts, not realities	GOLD 434:46
d. with a woman	JACO 515:93
dealings d. with young men	PO 775:39
dean the cushion and soft D. invite	POPE 779:22
deans dowagers for d.	TENN 996:91
dear dangerously d.	BYRON 221:14
d., I don't give a damn	MITC 697:91
D. is the helpless creature	BYRON 222:33
d., My no longer cherished	MILL 676:81
d. to me as are the ruddy drops	SHAK 883:31
d. to me as life	SHAK 873:95
everything d. and valuable	PITT 771:72
for earth too d.!	SHAK 868:82
last I saw of my d.	COLUM 278:60
My d. hands	RACH 799:95
Plato is d. to me	ARIS 34:36
that bread should be so d.	HOOD 489:47
too d. for my possessing	SHAK 914:78
dearer d. was the mother	COLE 273:81
dearest d. thing he owed	SHAK 907:23
d. to the world!	SHAK 917:31
dearheart Make up your mind, d.	OLIV 738:27
dearie kind D., O	BURNS 212:36
o'er me and my D.	BURNS 211:1
thinkin on my D.	BURNS 211:3
death 25 years after his d.	BEAV 81:83
absolute rest is d.	PASC 757:57
after d. God knows	ROSS 824:90
After the first d.	THOM 1010:67
After your d. people will write	YEATS 1104:55
all Life d. does end	HOPK 492:5
all stories…end in d.	HEMI 470:26
allotted d. and hell	MARL 654:21
Angel of D. has been abroad	BRIG 188:47

death (*contd.*)

announcement of my d.	BROD 189:66
Any man's d. diminishes me	DONNE 339:23
Any woman's d.	RICH 809:51
arise From d.	DONNE 338:3
artist is in danger of d.	HEMI 470:24
battles and d.	GARI 415:25
Be thou faithful unto d.	BIBLE 157:3
beauty of life through d.	LAUT 584:55
bed of d.	DRAY 345:40
Better passion and d.	LAWR 585:76
better than the most glorious d.	EURI 380:31
between life and d.	WORD 1099:63
Birth, and copulation, and d.	ELIOT 370:12
blaze forth the d. of princes	SHAK 883:32
bleeding to d. of time	GRAV 440:30
body of this d.?	BIBLE 149:24
bores them to d.	OROU 741:80
bowl'd out by D.'s unerring ball	EGAN 362:55
bridegroom in my d.	SHAK 906:91
Brother to D.	DANI 304:62
buffet you to d.	WEBS 1060:43
built your ship of d.	LAWR 587:6
Calabria d.	VIRG 1046:96
Capital, where kingly D.	SHEL 930:36
ceaseth only in d.	HOBB 483:39
certain as d. and taxes	DEFOE 312:87
Chairman…lying on his d. bed	MIN 695:62
Christians deified d.	STAEL 961:71
'civilization'…is coupled with d.	MILL 679:55
competition the Laws of D.	RUSK 830:92
concerns himself with d.	MANN 645:83
condemn you to d.	CARR 238:23
consent to my own d.	RODR 819:90
consideration of d.?	STEV 974:22
could not stop for D.	DICK 328:5
courting d. to be our friend	PHIL 768:20
covenant with d.	BIBLE 125:76
craving to risk d.	FOWL 399:64
crushed him to d.!	JOYCE 538:44
daily walk with d.	WEBB 1058:16
danger of violent d.	HOBB 483:40
darker than d. or night	SHEL 930:27
day of his d.	AUDEN 47:16
dead, a living d.	MILT 694:42
dead which he slew at his d.	BIBLE 109:22
d. after life	SPEN 957:8
D.…a good for all	BERN 97:89
D.'s a great disguiser	SHAK 897:90
d. and division	SWIN 987:35
D. and I Am found eternal	MILT 693:19
d. and I will coquette	MARQ 655:35
d. and life at tonce	SPEN 958:20
D. and pain dominate	LEVE 600:25
d. and taxes	FRAN 402:12
D. and taxes	MITC 697:90
d. and the sole d.	BROW 200:79
d., a necessary end	SHAK 883:34
D. approaches with little delay	ORAH 741:77
D.'s artifact	ABSE 1:7
D. at an early age	YUAN 1108:12
D. be not one stroke	MILT 693:19
D. be not proud	DONNE 338:4
d. being contrary to their principles	GALS 413:2
D.'s bitter cup	ABU 1:12
d.…can be done as easily	ALLEN 14:45
D. cancels everything but truth	HAZL 463:12
d. closes all	TENN 995:61
D. comes to everyone	BERG 94:46
D. cometh soon	MACA 623:13
D. complete the same!	BROW 199:77
D. could drop	ROSE 823:63
d.'s dark vale	SCOT 856:19
D. destroys a man	FORS 398:37

death (*contd.*)

D. devours all lovely things	MILL 676:84
d.'s grey land	SASS 845:25
d. had undone so many	ELIOT 368:83
d. has a useful function	LABR 573:50
D. has made	TENN 999:46
d. has taken Mr Melchisedec	MERE 671:4
d. hath no more dominion	BIBLE 149:21
d. hath…several doors	WEBS 1061:70
D. his court	SHAK 867:60
d. i' the other	SHAK 882:18
d. in childbirth	WELD 1062:92
d. in my hand	SHAK 862:37
d. in the cup	BURNS 213:51
d. in the hunting	MORT 710:93
d. instead of 'human rights'	PEOP 764:58
d. into the world	BIBLE 131:80
D. is a dialogue	DICK 328:10
d. is a lover's pinch	SHAK 906:7
D. is a name for beauty	LAYT 588:23
D. is an acquired trait	ALLEN 14:42
D. is but a moment	SCHI 847:68
D.…is certain to all	SHAK 877:96
D. is not an event in life	WITT 1088:75
D.…is nothing	DRYD 347:76
D. is nothing at all	HOLL 485:69
D. is only for the mediocre	JARRY 518:68
d. is the cure of all diseases	BROW 196:92
D. is the end of life	TENN 994:51
d. is the national spectacle	LORCA 613:40
D. is the only mystery	SKEL 942:41
D. is the only pure	LAWR 585:75
D. is the remedy	CHAM 250:26
D. is the romantic	NOVA 732:37
D. is the supreme festival	BONH 173:85
d. is to lose belief	DU 353:10
D. is to Poetry	ABSE 1:8
D. is…degrading punishment	BREN 187:34
D. lays his icy hand	SHIR 935:27
D. lies dead	SWIN 988:57
D. lies on her like	SHAK 869:18
d.…like a cold abstraction	MILL 677:6
D.…like gas bill	BURG 206:86
D., like the quintessence	BURG 206:90
d. means little	CELI 247:88
D. my days should expiate	SHAK 913:51
D. never hurts. D. is sweet	ANOU 30:73
d. …of a beautiful woman	POE 776:50
d. of Domitian	GIBB 421:18
d. of his fellow-creatures	FROU 408:9
d. of his saints	BIBLE 118:26
d. of Nelson	SOUT 954:41
d. of one so young	SPEN 956:82
d. of religion	WHIT 1071:56
d. of some of her	MASE 662:44
d. of the kindest owner	STOWE 978:84
D.…openeth the gate	BACON 56:46
D. opens unknown doors	MASE 662:43
d. reveals the eminent	SHAW 922:59
d. robs it of everything	VIEI 1044:75
'd,' said Mark Staithes	HUXL 507:72
D.'s second self	SHAK 914:73
D.'s shadow at the door	BLUN 170:40
D. shall all the world subdue	SPEN 959:28
D. shall be no more	DONNE 338:5
d. shall have no dominion	THOM 1010:55
D. should be a long	TZARA 1035:35
d. stands above me	LAND 578:61
d. the journey's end	DRYD 352:93
d. the worst of evils	HEINE 467:69
D. to life is crown	MILT 695:56
D. tramples it to fragments	SHEL 931:50
d.…tyrant has in common	BROD 189:67
d.…under the power of language	CIXO 266:69

death (*contd.*)

D. unfailing will strike the blow	CURR 301:18
d. unloads me	SHAK 897:78
D. was the only absolute	GREE 444:12
d. was there relief	MOOR 706:40
d., where is thy sting?	BIBLE 151:73
D., where is thy Sting?	BUNY 205:74
D. who comes at last	SCOTT 853:52
d., who had the soldier singled	DOUG 341:57
D. will come when thou art dead	SHEL 932:61
d. will have his d.	SHAK 867:58
d. Will seize the doctor too	SHAK 916:17
d. without the responsibility	LEBO 591:81
defend to the d.	VOLT 1047:19
deflow'red, and now to d.	MILT 692:5
delivered my soul from d.	BIBLE 118:25
Desire is d.	SHAK 915:97
Desire paces Eternity…craving d.	DUNC 355:47
die the d.	BIBLE 132:2
do not see why d.	NABO 717:2
done to d. by Lenin	CHUR 263:98
doomed to d.	DRYD 350:48
draw near unto the gates of d.	BIBLE 118:19
dull cold ear of D.?	GRAY 442:67
either in nativity, chance, or d.	SHAK 878:23
end thereof are the ways of d.	BIBLE 121:75
enormously improved by d.	SAKI 838:13
ere her d., Ruffles her	TENN 1004:49
eternal: this is d.	LOWE 616:92
fail almost to the point of d.	SAPP 842:92
Fear of d. and fear of life	MENC 670:80
fear of d. disturbs me	DUNB 355:40
fear of something after d.	TWAIN 1033:89
fed on the fullness of d.	SWIN 987:40
feet go down to d.	BIBLE 120:61
first day of our Jubilee is d.	BROW 195:84
foretaste of d.	SCHO 849:1
frightened of d.	DONL 336:60
from famine and d.	DARW 306:84
Glad to d.'s mystery	HOOD 489:49
hand in hand to d.	ROSS 824:92
hard at d.'s door	BOOK 177:91
I am become D.	BHAG 102:81
if ought but d. part thee and me	BIBLE 109:25
If people knew there'd be less d.	MALA 641:4
If they were drowning to d.	KROC 570:98
In every parting…an image of d.	ELIOT 365:1
in love with easeful D.	KEATS 548:18
in most cases, a d. warrant	WHAR 1068:1
in that sleep of d.	SHAK 890:21
in the arts of d.	SHAW 921:35
In the ranks of d.	MOORE 706:34
in their d. they were not divided	BIBLE 110:44
into the dust of d.	BIBLE 114:49
Into the jaws of D.	TENN 1001:73
invincible in his d.	GIBB 421:22
is not d. at watch	BLUN 170:43
isn't sex but d.	SONT 953:6
Judge none blessed before his d.	BIBLE 132:98
keep a league till d.	SHAK 868:66
keys of hell and of d.	BIBLE 157:1
kisses after d.	TENN 997:4
land of the shadow of d.	BIBLE 125:65
last enemy…is d.	BIBLE 151:68
law of d.	ANON 24:13
law of sin and d.	WESL 1066:66
Lead him to d.	ROCH 816:51
leads through d.	MANN 645:82
led all that way for Birth or D.?	ELIOT 369:4
legions with the ways of D.	LIND 605:17
let D. wreck all his rage	MILT 689:39
libraries of d.	DOMI 335:56
life to d.	SHAK 877:2
life was d.	ROSS 824:89

death (*contd.*)

life, d., and that vast for-ever	KING 558:91
Life, the shadow of d.	SWIN 987:27
lively form of d.	KYD 571:26
lost friends, some by d.	WOOLF 1093:79
Love is strong as d.	BIBLE 124:55
love…put it to a violent d.	ETHE 380:18
love thee better after d.	BROW 197:19
lovely and soothing d.	WHIT 1073:93
make d. proud	SHAK 906:97
masters the fear of d.	BACON 56:44
matter of life and d.	SHAN 918:69
May they walk in living d.	DAVIS 309:36
Men fear d.	BACON 56:43
men would take the d. sentence	LAWR 587:15
midst of life we are in d.	BOOK 176:57
misery, suffering and d.	HARD 455:78
moment after d.	HAWT 461:65
more beautiful than d.	WHIT 1073:88
more d. in it than Rubens	HUGH 500:31
mortal taste Brought d.	MILT 687:84
most uninspired form of d.	VALE 1038:84
mourned…not at his d.	MONT 702:80
much of life and d.	SHEL 927:60
much possessed by d.	ELIOT 367:63
My name is D.	SOUT 954:42
my sister, D.	FRAN 401:92
mysterious East…silent like d.	CONR 284:97
name that sat on him was D.	BIBLE 157:12
nearness of d.	PAZ 762:24
necessity of d.	HAWT 461:65
neither d., nor life	BIBLE 149:31
new terrors of D.	ARBU 33:11
Night, perchance of D.	THOM 1015:56
no drinking after d.	FLET 394:70
no lonelier man in d.	HEMI 470:25
no more d.	BIBLE 158:35
Nor shall d. brag	SHAK 912:48
not d….which is terrible	FIEL 388:53
not so much afraid of d.	BROW 195:83
nothing but d.	UNAM 1035:39
nothing…our own but d.	SHAK 867:59
obedient unto d.	BIBLE 153:8
obey in life and d.	BARTH 74:65
Oh, world, Oh, d.?	SPEN 956:82
On his d. bed poor Lubin	PRIOR 791:58
one in love with d.	SHEL 930:33
one medicine is D.	ABU 2:13
only d. can stop it	HEMI 471:43
only ending is d.	GRAY 440:41
only nervousness or d.	LEBO 591:79
Our own d. wish	PUZO 796:43
owe God a d.	SHAK 877:98
pale d. your vital twist shall sever	DAVI 307:7
panoply of d.	DAVI 308:14
Photography…flirting with d.	BERG 94:45
plucked, for d. mature	MILT 693:24
Poets after my d.	KEATS 545:54
poor…whose d. interests no-one	CELI 247:91
power in the day of d.	BIBLE 123:30
power of life and d.	BIBLE 131:86
prepare as though for d.	MANS 647:11
presence of the Red D.	POE 776:44
quiet us in a d. so noble	MILT 695:58
reflections on life and d.	HERN 476:44
refusal of language is a d.	BART 75:81
region and shadow of d.	BIBLE 133:32
remedy for everything except d.	CERV 248:98
rendezvous with D.	SEEG 857:26
report of my d.	TWAIN 1034:14
room…we take up in d.	SHIR 935:23
secret house of d.	SHAK 906:89
seek, D., or he not	MILT 693:21
sense of d. is most	SHAK 897:79

death (*contd.*)

sentence of d. with a stay	CARS 241:90
set before you life and d.	BIBLE 108:99
shadow of d.	BROW 196:5
shew the Lord's d. till he come	BIBLE 150:59
shot to d., with pearls?	WEBS 1061:66
since by man came d.	BIBLE 151:67
six months' oblivion…newspaper d.	ADAMS 5:80
sleep and d. differ	TRAH 1024:26
so many years of fearing d.	SHAK 883:41
sorrow flouted at is double d.	SHAK 862:39
soul beneath the ribs of d.	MANC 644:66
spy sent…by forces of d.	BOWL 182:53
starving to d.	PLATH 773:91
stories of the d. of kings	SHAK 867:60
stream He met his d. in	DEVL 318:88
studied in his d.	SHAK 907:23
suffers upon d.	LABR 573:51
swallow up d. in victory	BIBLE 125:73
Swarm over, D.!	BETJ 99:31
sway of d.	WORD 1100:90
talk of the d. of God	FACK 382:49
that stroke of d.	JOHN 531:13
The way to dusty d.	SHAK 910:86
theft with a fine, not d.	MORE 706:46
This is second d.	BIBLE 158:33
this morning I signed my d. warrant	
	COLL 276:39
Though he is approaching d.	WILL 1083:5
thought of d. sits easy	WORD 1096:35
till d. us do part	BOOK 176:49
Till life and d. remember	SWIN 986:21
time and d. pinned human	FRAME 400:76
time come after d.	GINS 427:24
'tis D. is dead	SHEL 931:48
to be carnally minded is d.	BIBLE 149:26
To muddy d.	SHAK 892:72
tragedies are finished by d.	BYRON 223:48
translate thy life into d.	SHAK 887:28
triumph over d. and sin	SPEN 958:24
triumph over d. and sin	SPEN 959:27
true knowledge only comes of d.	WHITE 1070:42
truly longed for d.	TENN 996:86
ugly d. within my eyes	SHAK 863:54
Under the ribs of D.	MILT 684:31
up the line to d.	SASS 845:26
valiant…taste of d. but once	SHAK 883:33
valley of d.	BIBLE 115:50
valley of D.	TENN 1000:71
vasty hall of d.	ARNO 37:84
victory of sterility and d.	BELL 88:21
virtues carry with it life and d.	MARL 652:88
wages of sin is d.	BIBLE 149:22
walk with D.	TENN 998:12
wast not born for d.	KEATS 548:20
watch the night and d.	APOL 31:88
welter of blood shed and d.	LLOY 608:60
what we fear of d.	SHAK 897:83
When d. approached	GIBB 422:32
who is stronger than d.?	HUGH 500:44
Who owns all of space? D.	HUGH 500:43
whole world is frightened to d.!	SHER 934:17
Why fear d.?	FROH 406:69
with the rich in his d.	BIBLE 127:2
women for escape from this d.	NIGH 729:98
worm of d.	GRAV 440:25
worst friend and enemy is but D.	BROO 192:34
would burn you to d.!	MERM 672:19
would like d.	MONT 701:63
death-dance d.-d. of our times	CHES 259:26
death-doom Awaiting their d.-d.	WILDE 1075:26
death-rate d.-r. meant…supply	SHAW 926:43
infantile d.-r.	HALD 451:16
death-warrant blood is my d.-w.	KEATS 548:21

deathbed D. utterances	PLOUT 775:35
deathless d. friends	SASS 845:40
sense of some d. shame	WEBS 1060:34
deaths d. column brought good	HAMER 453:37
feigned to d. die.	DONNE 336:76
labouring masses to their d.	WEIL 1062:85
many times before their d.	SHAK 883:33
more d. than one must die.	WILDE 1078:2
ready for more d.	GREE 444:3
wars and sudden d. do	HUGH 499:23
debasement d. of the human mind	CHAN 250:27
debate This leads to a d.	MACH 631:37
debauch d. friend's wife genteelly	BOSW 180:32
d. the currency	KEYN 554:27
debauchery lead him into d. and sin	OFLA 736:96
debonair buxom, blithe, and d.	MILT 682:97
debris d. of a statue	YOUR 1108:11
debt Ambition's d. is paid	SHAK 883:28
national d.	HAMI 453:29
old d. for a borrowing	DUNC 355:44
pay a d. to pleasure too?	ROCH 816:45
promise made is a d. unpaid	SERV 859:55
debtors D. can't be leaders	IACO 509:17
debts D. are becoming	BALZ 69:85
forgive us our d.	BIBLE 135:49
our d., our care-full wives	SHAK 881:94
pays all d.	SHAK 917:33
unpaid d.	HALD 451:17
Words pay no d.	SHAK 896:48
decade before this d. is out	KENN 551:66
d. or more of ruin	WIEN 1074:13
decadence absence …is d.	MAMET 643:49
barbarism to d.	CLEM 269:6
describe as 'Puritan d.'	SPEN 956:88
decay after first d.	SPEN 958:13
All human things subject to d.	DRYD 348:81
All things are in d.	HERB 475:27
always looked upon d.	MILL 678:42
bring d. or explosion	RUSS 832:28
by a gentle d.	WESL 1067:72
d. of Christianity	SAKI 837:97
d. of parts	CONG 281:28
d. Of that colossal wreck	SHEL 928:93
d. of the ruling classes	ORWE 743:18
D. with imprecision	ELIOT 370:31
falling to d.	WALP 1051:80
found its d.	COCK 272:60
Fretting for their d.	ROSE 823:62
inferno of insipidity and d.	LEWIS 602:70
introduced disease and d.	SHER 932:76
less apt to d.	JOHN 526:5
like to this d.	SPEN 959:28
many men's d.?	SPEN 959:40
men d.	GOLD 433:10
pale court in beauty and d.	SHEL 930:36
The woods d.	TENN 1003:21
decayed d. in his intellects	JOHN 531:24
decaying we are but d.	HERR 477:62
decays d. in the face	BEHN 85:73
deceased name of the late d.	KIPL 561:45
deceit by d. to breed offense	DYER 358:90
kind without d.	DRYD 348:98
neither was any d. in his mouth	BIBLE 127:2
not up to small d.	HARTE 459:49
shocked by honesty…few by d.	COWA 290:5
deceitful blood-thirsty and d. man	BOOK 176:60
heart is d.	BIBLE 128:26
deceitfulness Cat of such d.	ELIOT 371:41
deceits d. are strong	MUIR 712:30
home to many d.	POUND 786:64
deceive d. and delude mankind	EPHO 379:95
practise to d.!	SCOTT 853:57
sweet to d. the deceiver	LAFO 575:89
deceived Like a d. husband	SHAK 914:79

deceiver sweet to deceive the d. LAFO 575:89
thou kind d.! DRYD 349:99
deceivers Men were d. SHAK 879:46
wicked race of d. MILT 686:72
deceiving Seeing is d. THUR 1019:40
December as short as D. SHAK 911:19
D. when they wed SHAK 887:23
From May to D. ANDE 18:6
made D. June TENN 1000:54
decencies content to dwell in d. POPE 782:74
decency d. of human beings ORWE 743:7
D. is indecency's conspiracy SHAW 922:58
done in the name of 'd.' LEWIS 602:61
fail to observe d. and discretion BACON 55:7
ultimate d. of things STEV 976:50
want of d. DILL 331:56
with such spirit and d. PITT 771:62
decent d. godless people ELIOT 370:18
d. people live beyond their incomes SAKI 838:9
most d. nation BUSH 215:86
no use to d. people SHAW 924:90
decentralization technology of d. MURP 715:73
deception warfare is based on d. SUN 982:31
deceptions All are d. WILS 1084:18
decide If I had to d. GRAMM 438:94
You'll have to d. DYLAN 358:92
decided d. by a person's thoughts KIM 557:65
d. never to be afraid KAVA 543:26
deciduous d. language THOM 1013:25
deciphering philosophy is like the d. SCHO 849:93
decision d. to be made PECK 763:39
a very deliberate d. POIN 776:60
by d. more embroils MILT 688:25
come to a very important d. MILNE 680:72
d. makers face each other SHUL 936:35
d. of the courts LEAC 589:42
Drug misuse…is a d. DICK 320:12
I made the d. long ago RENO 806:5
music that changed a man's d. SCHN 848:84
right of the ultimate d. MUMF 713:49
specific d. TUCH 1031:45
wrong d. can make…miserable DENN 316:60
decisions d. are made beforehand LEWI 602:71
d. to become mothers FRIE 405:51
learn how to make d. KISS 566:38
wartime d. TRUM 1030:27
decisive so grave and d. STEV 974:7
deck boy stood on the burning d. HEMA 469:11
d. of the Titanic MORT 710:3
fall…on the d. DAVI 307:96
decks rose upon their d. and cried TENN 1005:60
turtle…'twixt plated d. NASH 719:47
declaration d. will inspire irony GISC 429:48
D. of Independence KING 557:78
declension D. looks from our land RANS 802:33
fall with d. SMITH 945:40
declensions under a lot of d. BURG 205:82
decline preserve…from d. STEU 970:29
went into a bit of a d. ADAMS 5:67
writing the d. and fall GIBB 421:29
declined answer me d. SHAK 905:83
declining d. age of a state BACON 59:29
decompose d. in a barrel of porter DONL 336:61
decorations d.…of the embassy MACI 631:45
d. over a void YOUR 1108:6
such gaudy d. MORE 707:53
decorative be d. and to do right! FIRB 389:75
decorum hunt D. down BYRON 219:63
sacrifices too much d. HAZL 463:90
trousers of d. LICH 603:80
decoy fashion's brightest arts d. GOLD 433:14
decrease I must d. BIBLE 145:36
decree d. from Caesar Augustus BIBLE 142:76
hot temper leaps o'er a cold d. SHAK 874:12

decrees Levitical d. ROCHE 815:40
decrepit d. father takes delight SHAK 913:60
d., without being venerable HAWT 461:75
dedicated fanatically d. to…dogmas PIRS 770:52
deduction as much d. as you please DARW 306:90
logical d. from…hypotheses EINS 363:75
not a correct d. KEYN 554:32
deductions d. for the modern BROW 196:11
dee diddle, we take it, is d. SWIN 988:58
Dee sands of D. KING 558:89
deed A bloody d. SHAK 892:51
blow the horrid d. SHAK 908:32
By thought, word, and d. BOOK 174:25
Crime lies not in the d. HELO 469:8
d. dying tongueless SHAK 911:20
d. I'll do before SHAK 909:69
d. without a name SHAK 909:66
defiant d.! WHIT 1072:77
dirty d. SYNGE 988:64
foul d. shall smell SHAK 883:45
good d. in a naughty world SHAK 873:7
living act, the undoubted d. MELV 667:34
may do the d. KEATS 544:39
my d. to my most painted word SHAK 890:20
one good d. in all my life SHAK 862:44
right d. for the wrong reason ELIOT 371:33
Th'attempt and not the d. SHAK 908:43
there is no glory in the d. READ 803:54
water clears us of this d. SHAK 908:50
whatever time the d. took place ELIOT 371:41
Y'are the d.'s creature MIDD 674:48
deeds better d. than words SHAK 860:76
D. are nothing BALZ 69:80
d. determine us ELIOT 365:7
d. left undone STOWE 979:89
D., not words EDGE 361:35
d. of youth SHAK 913:60
d. Shall be in water writ BEAU 80:70
ends all other d. SHAK 906:98
gentle mind by gentle d. SPEN 959:38
Glorious d. are not embraced PIUS 772:79
good d. are gone JANO 518:54
great d. were done WHITE 1071:49
measure by thy d. SHAK 914:71
nameless in worthy d. BROW 196:2
these unlucky d. relate SHAK 900:64
Words to the heat of d. SHAK 908:41
worse d. worse suffering MILT 689:46
wrong and d. malign NOON 731:24
years of noble d. TENN 1003:18
deedy haven't been at all d. COMP 279:78
deep beauty is only sin d. SAKI 837:96
Black…Baltic d. TENN 1002:95
clouds are d. FREE 404:35
commit his body to the d. BOOK 178:96
d. beyond d. BETJ 107:81
D. calleth unto d. BIBLE 116:70
d., yet clear DENH 315:53
dive into the bottom of the d. SHAK 875:46
eye that sees too d. FADI 382:53
From the great d. TENN 1003:36
heard the d. behind him TENN 1004:44
lowest d. a lower d. MILT 690:48
Not d. the Poet sees ARNO 36:57
remorseless d. Clos'd o'er MILT 684:41
secrets of the d. MILT 693:30
singularly d. young man GILB 424:66
so d. a measure does it have HERA 473:87
thunders of the upper d. TENN 1002:95
too d. for his hearers GOLD 433:28
Two voices… one is of the d. STEP 968:79
unfathomable d. forest THOM 1012:11
where the brook is d. SHAK 861:3
wonders in the d. BIBLE 118:20

deep (*contd.*)
writers…do not seem so d. LAND 578:55
deep-versed D.-v. in books MILT 694:36
deeper d. than did ever plummet SHAK 917:40
deeps d. are cold HUGH 500:40
deer d. from the hill SCOTT 854:70
d., is in the wood of Hallaig MACL 633:70
d. sweeps by SCOTT 854:66
heart…chasing the d. BURNS 211:5
time's d. is slain MUIR 712:27
where the d. and antelope play HIGL 480:1
Deever they're hangin' Danny D. KIPL 560:29
deface d. the image of man IVAN 514:83
defeat Champagne…in d. POL 777:63
country of d. PURDY 795:35
In d.: defiance CHUR 263:97
In d. unbeatable CHUR 265:47
laughing soldiers fought to their d. FENT 385:2
pleasure of the d. LACL 573:60
possibilities of d. VICT 1043:52
scorn for d. TWAIN 1034:11
snatching glory out of d. PRIE 790:37
suffering a national d. EDIN 361:40
through d. and humiliation SMUTS 950:66
victory turns into a d. DE 311:65
we know we should d. you KIPL 564:11
defeated destroyed but not d. HEMI 471:40
Down with the d.! BREN 187:35
Down with the d. LIVY 608:48
History to the d. AUDEN 46:55
meaning shows in the d. MASE 662:49
you will never be d. SUN 982:33
defect chief d. of Henry King BELL 87:5
d. of nature FRAN 401:83
fatal d. of current principles SIMON 939:80
make d. perfection SHAK 905:70
some affliction or d. BEER 83:39
that which depends on d. ARIS 34:27
defective d. in its evidence REGAN 805:95
defects all these d. came WEBB 1058:14
by reason of her intellectual d. WRIG 1101:2
Mencken's d. were commonplace MEYER 673:32
defence awake endeavour for d. SHAK 872:61
cheap d. of nations BURKE 207:32
conscience clear my chief d. DYER 358:90
d. against betrayal WILL 1081:64
d. like elaborate courtesy LUCAS 618:26
d. of one's country HOMER 488:22
d. of the indefensible ORWE 744:44
d. that will protect SCHL 848:79
die in d. of their rights PITT 771:68
England's chief d. PHIL 768:17
greatest D. lay in the Art ALBE 12:94
Immodest words admit of no d. DILL 331:56
In cases of d. SHAK 881:80
in her d. GARI 415:24
intelligent means of d. KENT 553:8
interpret my d. THAT 1007:7
make a pitiful d. SIDN 937:59
my rock…my d. BIBLE 116:82
Never make a d. CHAR 252:81
only d. is in offence BALD 65:10
tower of d. ALCA 12:95
defences and no d. GOLD 432:88
defend d. ourselves with guns GOEB 430:64
d. to the death VOLT 1047:19
d. us against nature FREUD 404:42
let it d. itself TOLS 1023:95
defended d. by her armed sons REDM 804:75
defenders surprising the d. MANC 644:63
defense painting is…for attack and d. PICA 769:26
strategy of d. GALB 411:74
defer D., d. GILB 425:86
defiance act of wilful d. SASS 845:21

defiance (*contd.*)
  bold d. with his prince — DRYD 349:*16*
defiant before a d. deed — WHIT 1072:*77*
  It is d. — READ 803:*53*
deficiencies d. of fortune — GOLD 432:*2*
deficiency d. in the graces — JOHN 530:*88*
deficient very d. in means — KISH 565:*29*
deficit Olympics...d. — DRAP 345:*30*
  Park Avenue...trade d. — BART 75:*87*
defile neither shall ye d. yourselves — BIBLE 107:*78*
  presumed to d. — DREN 346:*42*
define cannot d. the real problem — FEYN 387:*34*
  d. her feelings in language — HARDY 456:*89*
  d. jazz satisfactorily — KING 559:*7*
  ought to d. a man's income — HICKS 480:*96*
  to d. is to eliminate — QUINE 797:*66*
defines he who d. himself — LAO 580:*84*
definite d. maybe — GOLD 434:*44*
  like d. form — STEV 973:*98*
  no d. answers can — RUSS 832:*17*
definition d. of a free society — STEV 972:*75*
  d. of a 'hero' — FIND 389:*65*
  d. of a horse — DICK 325:*40*
  d. of a specialist — MAYO 666:*9*
  d. of happiness — KENN 552:*90*
  d. of utter waste — HUNT 504:*17*
  d. of what a nurse — NIGH 729:*1*
  D.—Science is systematized — SART 843:*5*
  incapable of any d. — MOORE 704:*9*
  ultimate d. of this uniqueness — COUS 290:*87*
  want a d. of poetry — THOM 1011:*73*
definitions exact d. can be applied — QUIL 797:*60*
  which...they call D. — HOBB 482:*36*
deflationary essentially a d. genius — MORR 708:*78*
deflowered At last you are d. — COWA 290:*4*
deformed how d. dost thou look! — SHAK 865:*15*
  None can be called d. — SHAK 895:*35*
  what a d. thief — SHAK 880:*55*
deformity Art is significant d. — FRY 408:*19*
  mine own d. — SHAK 863:*48*
Degas remember D. — PISS 771:*60*
degenerate creative protests to d. — KING 557:*80*
degradation breath of d. — BYRON 221:*20*
  children from utter d. — LOVE 615:*70*
  consent to such d. — OCON 735:*80*
  means of creating her d. — STAN 962:*88*
  sense of intellectual d. — JAMES 515:*6*
degree d. and quality of trust — SHAP 919:*78*
  d. of grand old man — LEAC 589:*47*
  d. of a person's intelligence — ALTH 15:*61*
  d. of certainty — RUSS 832:*29*
  d. of serenity — NIEB 727:*63*
  didn't get a d. — DOWD 342:*77*
  however in a slight d. — RYLE 834:*54*
  lady of beauty and high d. — RANS 802:*31*
  with d. dispense — JONS 535:*3*
degrees 105 d. in Saigon — ANON 30:*61*
  arts are tought by d. — THEO 1008:*33*
  boil at different d. — EMER 377:*74*
  by d. learn to work at all things — CARL 236:*94*
  Crime...has its d. — RACI 799:*1*
  d. m off east longitude — MUNDY 714:*54*
  d. of anger — EVANS 381:*40*
  d. of communism and d. — NGUY 725:*47*
  heal but by d.? — SHAK 899:*28*
  thirty d. below zero — MOOD 703:*96*
  will name you the d. — SHAK 887:*35*
dehumanize d., not just the slaves — MORR 709:*88*
deities d. of his own invention — PLATO 773:*2*
deity believe in a personal d. — HAMM 453:*43*
  D. and the Drains — STRA 979:*95*
  d. when Cubans get together — LEZA 603:*76*
  Half dust, half d. — BYRON 221:*20*
  Prosperity...not a d. — COOL 286:*37*

Deity doubted...the D. — WELLS 1064:*24*
Dekanahwideh D., and...Chiefs — DEKA 313:*8*
delay reluctant amorous d. — MILT 690:*56*
  We safely may d. — BRON 191:*92*
  why shou'd we d.? — WALL 1050:*72*
delayed it has been d. — JOHN 526:*99*
delays d. are dangerous — DRYD 347:*67*
delegate When in trouble, d. — WAGN 1047:*27*
delicate d. death — WHIT 1073:*93*
  rich and d. English language — WAUGH 1058:*9*
  sufficiently d. — KEYN 554:*33*
  The air is d. — SHAK 907:*30*
delicately d. as possible — RUSS 832:*20*
delicates fruits and princely d. — MARL 654:*13*
delicious d. dinner of too much — JOHN 523:*42*
  d., nourishing, and wholesome — SWIFT 985:*98*
  magic and d. power — WOOLF 1093:*70*
  wine...heavenly and d. — RABE 798:*78*
  With most d. poison — SHAK 905:*66*
delight 'another's pain is our d. — LUCR 619:*35*
  bind another to its d. — BLAKE 167:*86*
  blend profit with d. — HORA 494:*33*
  calm in our d. — WORD 1094:*1*
  decrepit father takes d. — SHAK 913:*60*
  d. in simple things — KIPL 564:*4*
  d. is in the law of the Lord — BIBLE 113:*29*
  d. of her husband — RANS 802:*31*
  d. themselves in...peace — BIBLE 115:*64*
  D. thyself also in the Lord — BIBLE 115:*63*
  do ill our sole d. — MILT 687:*95*
  Energy is Eternal D. — BLAKE 166:*72*
  feelings of d. — WORD 1100:*77*
  filled with such d. — SASS 845:*34*
  gift, my ever new d. — MILT 691:*69*
  give d. and hurt not — SHAK 917:*34*
  go to't with d. — SHAK 906:*86*
  harmony or true d.? — MILT 692:*94*
  high austerity to d. — FREE 404:*35*
  If you d. not in man — SHAK 890:*6*
  inordinate sensual d. — BAXT 79:*51*
  leaping light for your d. — AUDEN 46:*51*
  Love and d. are better teachers — DURER 356:*67*
  makes eating a d. — SUCK 981:*19*
  Moved to d. — AUDEN 48:*78*
  nursed by d. — LYLY 620:*59*
  Phantom of d. — WORD 1098:*62*
  simple human d. — BARB 71:*11*
  source of infinite visible d. — BRON 192:*12*
  stories to d. his ear — SHAK 887:*39*
  succession of d. — SMART 944:*72*
  the fruit of your d. — SURR 983:*45*
  'Tis my d. alone in summer shade — WORD 1096:*86*
  to d....paid thy utmost blessing — DELA 314:*34*
  to teach and d. — SIDN 937:*62*
  Too bright for our infirm D. — DICK 328:*11*
  true spirit of d. — RUSS 832:*19*
  unrest which men miscall d. — SHEL 931:*47*
  various objects of d. — MILT 694:*40*
  what d. we...have — PEPYS 765:*77*
  What worlds d. — SPEN 957:*6*
delighted cruel, and d. in cruelty — QUIL 797:*61*
  d. particularly in quotations — SCHL 848:*74*
  only too d. to have been born — STRA 979:*93*
  primary object...to be d. — CECIL 246:*75*
delightful d. to be a woman — SCHR 850:*2*
  make his conversation perfectly d. — SMITH 949:*53*
  society is wonderfully d.! — WILDE 1077:*72*
  two most d. things in it? — WALP 1051:*91*
delights all d. my fortune — JONS 534:*76*
  d. of a pantomime — DICK 327:*89*
  d. of the flesh castrate me — FUEN 409:*26*
  d. Will vanish — MILT 690:*57*
  mind religiously affected d. — HOOK 490:*56*
  O love, for d.! — BIBLE 124:*54*

delights (*contd.*)
  Of the d. of this world — TWAIN 1034:*19*
  permissible d. of the soul — BACH 54:*93*
  To scorn d., and live — MILT 684:*42*
  violent d. have violent ends — SHAK 869:*2*
delineation d. of that which appeals — HUMB 503:*96*
  happiest d. of its varieties — AUST 52:*63*
delinquencies indulge in a few d. — ELIOT 365:*2*
deliquescent d. leaves of paper — ANDR 18:*11*
delirium and one d. tremens — TWAIN 1033:*83*
  in such pleasant d. — ELIOT 365:*5*
  may attack you in d. tremens — OBRI 734:*72*
delitabill Storyss to rede ar d. — BARB 71:*14*
deliver come down to d. them — BIBLE 106:*56*
  let him d. him — BIBLE 114:*48*
  sacrifice them all...to d. you — SHAK 873:*95*
  who shall d. me — BIBLE 149:*21*
deliverance songs of d. — BIBLE 115:*58*
delivered d. me from all my fears — BIBLE 115:*60*
deliverer No d. ever rose — MORG 708:*66*
delivery Punctual D. Company — DICK 321:*43*
dell pure as the lily in the d. — LAUD 583:*38*
delph dresser filled with shining d. — COLUM 278:*62*
deluded Gods and men, we are all d. — SHEL 932:*71*
deluge After us the d. — POMP 777:*70*
delusion d. that macro-economics — HAYEK 462:*91*
  d. that one likes oneself — DIDI 330:*43*
  give up liberties...under some d. — BURKE 207:*24*
  nothing...but that addled d. — ELIOT 366:*57*
  progress is utter d. — MILL 678:*26*
  Trial...will be a d. — DENM 316:*59*
  united by a d. — INGE 511:*40*
delusions mocked by d. — EMER 377:*62*
demagogue d. is a person — MARQ 656:*51*
demand d. disturbs the happy — BRON 191:*1*
  d. for their labour — STEU 970:*29*
  d. the time of day — SHAK 875:*36*
  d. this...for the race — SCHR 850:*6*
  immeasurable or insolent d. — WALP 1052:*99*
  we d. the excellence — REYES 807:*22*
demands d. of a composer — HONE 488:*30*
  d. that form the habit — TUCH 1031:*46*
  spiritual d. — TAWN 991:*7*
demeanour d. nobly bland — GILB 426:*96*
demented d. Ireland was — LAND 578:*63*
demesne private pagus or d. — AUDEN 48:*97*
demi-god magician is a d.-g. — MARL 654:*12*
demi-monde d. does not represent — DUMAS 354:*29*
demigods musicians are not d. — TURN 1031:*51*
democracies d. of the west — MASA 661:*31*
  D. must try to find ways — THAT 1008:*79*
  not embraced by d. — PIUS 772:*79*
  tendency of d....to mediocrity — COOP 287:*41*
democracy crisis of Western d. — LIPP 606:*30*
  d. and peace — WELL 1063:*1*
  D. and proper drains — BETJ 100:*33*
  D.! Bah! — GINS 428:*29*
  d. is but a flickering candle — MACK 632:*57*
  d. is just a slogan — GORB 435:*56*
  D. is not a polite employer — HOOV 490:*63*
  D. is supposed to give — VIDAL 1044:*68*
  D. is the recurrent suspicion — WHITE 1070:*27*
  D. is the theory — MENC 668:*56*
  D. is the worst form of Goverment — CHUR 265:*32*
  d., it's the counting — STOP 978:*77*
  D. means government by discussion — ATTL 44:*14*
  D....by the uneducated — CHES 260:*43*
  D. means simply — WILDE 1076:*56*
  d. must remain at home — BORAH 178:*3*
  d. of the dead — CHES 258:*7*
  D. substitutes election — SHAW 922:*46*
  D. substitutes election — SHAW 926:*39*

democracy (*contd.*)
duty of a d. — WHITE 1070:25
experience of d. is like…life — CART 242:4
full-blooded and unconditional d. — GORB 435:58
great arsenal of d. — ROOS 822:42
grieved under a d. — HOBB 483:41
ideal form of d. — BEUYS 101:60
In a d. — FULB 409:29
laboratories of d. — WHIT 1072:72
little less d. to save — ATKI 44:2
Love of d. is love — MONT 702:84
make d. stable — SKEL 942:37
modern d. is a tyranny — MAIL 639:74
obstacle to d. — SCHU 851:21
odyssey toward liberty, d. — MAIL 639:81
our d. was — MACA 624:26
political aspirant under d. — MENC 669:68
Political d.…in America — WHIT 1073:95
priestly offices in a d. — LIPP 606:32
property-owning d. — SKEL 942:37
talk…about d. — ROOS 821:31
thanks to wine-less and d. — BROW 200:96
trouble in modern d. — BEVE 102:72
two cheers for d. — FORS 399:53
uncrowned king of an educated d. — STEAD 964:6
voice, of the d. — STEAD 964:4
We are a d. — PULI 795:20
Why D. means — HUGH 499:17
world must be safe for d. — WILS 1086:52
worst thing I can say about d. — BEVAN 101:61
democrat Aristocrat, d., autocrat — TENN 1001:80
aristocrat is the d. ripe — EMER 377:61
d. only on principle — TWAIN 1034:15
free man…and a D. — JOHN 523:49
democratic D. idea — BRYAN 201:14
D. Intellect — DAVIE 307:2
d. parliaments of tricks — WEBB 1058:16
denouncing liberal d. principles — AUNG 50:22
Fig leaves of d. procedure — KENN 550:52
ideals of a d.…society — MAND 644:68
market is so vulgarly d. — KRIS 569:96
The D. Party has succeeded — ONEI 740:69
towards d. powers — MASA 661:31
whole new d. world — CARL 234:47
democrats D. are fleeing — SHEV 934:18
demography nothing to do with d. — BERG 95:47
demolished d. or rebuilt — BOOTH 178:6
demolition Slated for d. — ASHB 41:56
demon Celtic Demos rose a D. — TENN 1005:65
demon-lover wailing for her d.-l. — COLE 275:13
demonic tends towards the d. — BAUD 78:35
demons artist…driven by d. — FAUL 383:81
demonstration logic of d. — NISB 730:4
Spontaneous D. — ORWE 744:31
Demosthenes when D. spoke — OGIL 736:3
demur If I d. — HEAN 465:38
demurest D. of the tabby kind — GRAY 441:50
den beard the lion in his d. — SCOTT 853:56
from the d. — SMART 944:71
in the d.…nine dead men — BALL -101:38
Deng revisionist clique of D. — JIANG 522:26
deniability some future d. — POIN 776:60
denial timid requests, invites d. — SENE 858:48
denied but half d. — BUTL 217:23
Denmark beard me in D.? — SHAK 890:10
example of the king of D. — FACK 382:49
look like a friend on D. — SHAK 888:48
rotten in the state of D. — SHAK 889:73
royal bed of D. — SHAK 889:79
storks in the spires of D. — DOYLE 344:21
throne of D. to thy father — SHAK 887:45
villain dwelling in all D. — SHAK 889:82
denominator lowest common d. — JARR 518:64
lowest common d. of human — CART 242:5

denominator (*contd.*)
no common d. — AUDEN 48:95
denote things which they d. — JOHN 526:5
dens d. of robbery and murder — NATI 721:90
dentist dread this like the d. — AUDEN 46:54
like going to the d. — WILD 1079:15
smiling…like a clumsy d. — MANS 647:8
sooner go to my d. — WAUGH 1056:79
talk like a d. when one isn't — WILDE 1077:79
dentists adulteries of d. — WILD 1080:33
d. ride roughshod — PERE 766:93
denunciation d. of the young — SMITH 947:9
deny cannot but d. them — SHAW 921:27
dare d. that the Third Estate — SIEY 938:91
D. it to a king? — SHAK 877:95
d. knowledge — KANT 542:6
d. me thrice — BIBLE 140:49
d. me thrice — BIBLE 144:15
neither…palliate nor d. — PITT 771:62
reason down or d. everything — EMER 377:56
denying to allure by d. — TROL 1028:85
deoch-an-doris Just a wee d.-a.-d. — MORR 709:84
deodar smell of d. wood burning — CHAT 253:98
deodorant Success is a great d. — TAYL 992:17
depart D.,—be off — HOLM 486:95
d. in God's name — JOAN 522:27
D., I say — AMERY 16:69
D., I say, and let us have done — CROM 298:55
Let him d. — SHAK 881:98
departed d. was a 'Roman' — LAWS 587:19
departing always arriving and d. — MILL 679:52
department d. of psychology — AYER 53:81
d. stores…like museums — WARH 1053:23
fair sex is your d. — DOYLE 344:13
material in every d. — BEAV 81:87
not to a functionary or d. — STEAD 964:8
State D. — MACC 625:42
department-store d.-s. state — CHAN 250:40
departments public d. — DICK 325:46
departure d. from this world — EMMET 378:81
function is d. can depart — LISP 607:39
grant them a fair d. — SHAK 874:19
possible point of d. — WAGN 1047:26
dependence d. of one fact — HOBB 482:37
not subsist without D. — STEE 964:19
total d. on the appreciation of others — CONN 283:63
dependencies colonies and wide d. — QUIL 797:59
deplore d. but was powerless — LEAC 589:39
D. what is to be deplored — MORG 707:64
though still I do d.? — DONNE 339:19
depository d. of power — DISR 332:85
depressed no one d. in this house — VICT 1043:52
depression d., combined with — LURIE 619:43
D. is when you lose — REAG 803:61
d. when you lose yours — TRUM 1030:26
deprivation D. is…daffodils — LARK 582:22
surrender required and d. inflicted — ELIOT 370:35
deprived needy, I was d. — FEIF 384:97
violated and the d. — JORD 536:29
depriving chief means of d. them — HALL 452:33
Deptford famous in D. — DAVI 308:13
depth d. of her glowing breast — SHEL 930:29
d. unfathomed no man knows — WESL 1066:67
in the d. be praise — NEWM 724:32
love thee to the d. — BROW 197:19
depths d. of every heart — HAWT 461:77
d. of his country's soul — DICK 326:55
d. where marvels are manifest — GORD 435:62
Out of the d. have I cried — BIBLE 119:44
people…out of their d. — FITZ 391:12
unfathomable d. of his…mind — COLE 275:29
Up from the d. I have cried to thee — BIBLE 159:49
deputy books…may be read by d. — BACON 59:23
if you and your d. will go back — ANDE 18:1

Derby back streets of D. — CHRI 261:66
deride do not d. the fears — JORD 536:29
derision Lord shall have them in d. — BIBLE 114:31
old days to d. — SWIN 987:35
derivative but what is d. — MILT 686:79
d. from this pure activity — LEWIS 602:60
descendants only chance for their d. — DAVI 307:4
descent claims of long d. — TENN 995:70
no nobility of d. — POTT 785:44
describe do not d. it fitly — JAMES 517:40
do nothing but d. — GRAY 441:60
poet's business is not to d. — ABER 1:5
description d. of a happy state — LOCKE 609:75
d. of the…Rhodes Scholar — MARA 649:38
d. of the rising sun — SHER 934:9
gay D. Aegypt glads — POPE 782:93
It beggared all d. — SHAK 905:68
picture that requires any d. — HOMER 488:26
truth of d. and the sentiment — SCOTT 856:12
descriptions d. of scenery — LEVIN 600:23
Desdemona love the gentle D. — SHAK 898:1
Othello subject D. — KOES 568:69
desert alone in the d. — SAIN 836:84
arid d. of his mind — WEST 1068:91
call of the d. — STARK 963:96
came through the d. — THOM 1015:57
Carlyle has led us all out into the d. — CLOU 270:31
company of d. people — THES 1009:45
d. in a dry frigid weather — PIER 769:34
D. Storm — SCHW 851:29
d. were my dwelling-place — BYRON 220:4
Down my d. rhyme — CRAIK 294:90
Even in thy d. — BYRON 220:93
every man after his d. — SHAK 890:13
found him in a d. land — BIBLE 108:2
garden…into a d. — YOUNG 1108:2
gardens of the D. — BRYA 202:19
knowledge …areas of d. — CHAN 250:39
legs of stone…in the d. — SHEL 928:92
Nothing went unrewarded, but d. — DRYD 349:24
pain in the d. — MOOR 706:40
pained d. lion — ARNO 38:95
power to make the world a d. — STEV 972:73
shores, and d. wildernesses — MILT 683:24
streams in the d. — BIBLE 126:82
to say the d. is stingy — HEAT 465:47
waste its sweetness on d. air — GRAY 442:69
went out into the d. — SITW 941:26
Zuleika, on d. island — BEER 83:29
desertion treacherous d. of an ally — CHUR 263:98
deserts d. of America — JOHN 527:23
D. are there — SACK 835:62
d. of the heart — AUDEN 47:73
D. of vast eternity — MARV 658:73
Or his d. are small — MONT 703:92
Story is just just d. — ELKIN 374:99
deserve advertising we d. — SAYE 846:52
Something you…haven't to d. — FROST 406:79
deserved more credit than they d. — REST 807:17
never have d. it — SATIE 846:47
punished himself…if he d. it — ELIOT 365:15
deserving d. to do it — GRAY 440:41
lost without d. — SHAK 899:25
design according to the same d. — VIAN 1043:47
any d. that you wish to give them — VAZD 1041:24
characteristic of the d. — LEWO 603:73
d. career is a process of learning — BELL 86:94
d. of darkness — FROST 407:92
ill d. is most ill — HESI 479:82
only its d. The hand — MICH 673:34
when…dull there is a d. — STEE 964:17
designed deliberately d. — HAYEK 462:90
d. to show those — KEIL 548:28
designing d. for obsolescence — ISSI 514:80

destroyed (*contd.*)

many a good tall fellow had d.	SHAK 875:*42*
More dreams are d.	SKEL 942:*50*
more easily it is d.	JOHN 530:*95*
once d., can never be supplied	GOLD 433:*10*
What's not d. by Time	BRAM 185:*8*
destroyer D. and preserver	SHEL 928:*87*
Is my d.	THOM 1010:*51*
Time the d.	ELIOT 372:*61*
destruction dark angel of d.	L 595:*47*
d. of all justice	MORE 707:*55*
d. of human life	HARDY 456:*83*
d. of the whole world	HUME 503:*4*
d. that wasteth at noonday	BIBLE 117:*2*
D. with d. to destroy	MILT 693:*21*
for d. ice	FROST 407:*85*
going from us to be utter d.	BIBLE 131:*81*
Hell and d. are never full	BIBLE 122:*9*
most frightful form of d.	MACA 624:*28*
on the side of d.	KEYN 554:*27*
Pride goeth before d.	BIBLE 121:*84*
redeemeth thy life from d.	BIBLE 118:*11*
soul…startles at d.	ADDI 8:*35*
way, that leadeth to d.	BIBLE 135:*50*
Whose end is d.	BIBLE 153:*13*
destructive d. and often malign	MUGG 712:*23*
to the d. element submit yourself	CONR 284:*94*
desuetization d. of Scottish life	MACD 628:*92*
detachment strangest sense of d.	WELLS 1064:*27*
detail become the slave of d.	RYDER 834:*51*
emotion, d. and image	BRAU 186:*22*
frittered away by d.	THOR 1017:*86*
Retail is d.	SCHU 850:*13*
details deal with many d.	MILLS 680:*65*
d.…of man and career	ELTON 375:*22*
particular forms or d.	GOYA 437:*83*
detection d. of…human woes	DEWEY 319:*95*
D. is…an exact science	DOYLE 343:*88*
detective d. novel…form of art	PRIT 791:*65*
writing a d. story	JAMES 517:*34*
determination d. of incident?	JAMES 516:*21*
determinism retrospective d.	BEND 89:*57*
deterrent credible d.	MACN 636:*31*
d. would continue to deter	MACM 635:*9*
detest my creator, d. and spurn me	SHEL 926:*54*
detestation show him your d.	PARN 756:*39*
Detroit D. is a one-trade town	MAIL 639:*84*
deuce how the d. they ever could	BYRON 222:*30*
devaluation d. of the human	MARX 661:*26*
devastation d.…at Rome	AUGU 49:*16*
developed all this will have to be d.	ISHE 513:*72*
development arrested our d.	MILL 679:*58*
continuous and healthy d.	PARS 756:*45*
creation, d. and being	HUMB 503:*97*
d. in the productive facilities	MARX 660:*11*
d. itself ceases	PEAR 762:*32*
d. of mankind	NIET 729:*90*
human history and cosmic d.	BELL 88:*34*
if we approve of the d.	BEND 89:*57*
limit of its d.	ANON 25:*29*
own way of d.	WILS 1086:*50*
phases of its d.	ERNST 379:*31*
process of historical d.	ROBI 815:*36*
progressive d.	GORB 435:*57*
syptomatic of…arrested d.	DISCH 331:*68*
truism in technological d.	STER 968:*83*
device miracle of rare d.	COLE 275:*15*
devices d. still are overthrown	SHAK 891:*38*
devil apology for the D.	BUTL 218:*43*
as though some poor d.	SKIN 943:*53*
break a man's spirit is d.'s work	SHAW 920:*98*
But the D. whoops	KIPL 561:*41*
can the d. speak true?	SHAK 907:*20*

devil (*contd.*)

children of the d.	TENN 1005:*57*
cursed d.	WEBS 1060:*46*
deft the D.'s foot	DONNE 336:*75*
D. always builds a chapel	DEFOE 312:*75*
d., as a roaring lion	BIBLE 156:*84*
d.'s away i' th' Exciseman	BURNS 212:*34*
d. be in my feet	SCOTT 855:*86*
d. cam fiddlin thro' the town	BURNS 212:*33*
d. can cite Scripture	SHAK 874:*21*
d. damn thee black	SHAK 910:*80*
d. dancing in me glorious	MASE 662:*45*
d. had done for the rest	STEV 975:*28*
D. himself cannot make	MELV 668:*46*
D. howling Ho!	SQUI 961:*65*
d. is dead!	READE 803:*56*
D. is forever grinning in upon me	MELV 668:*47*
D. is still at hand	DRYD 349:*8*
d. made himself a woman	HUGO 502:*75*
d.…on the side of the learned	FRAN 401:*86*
D. out of hell!	JOYCE 538:*44*
d. sends cooks	FULL 410:*51*
D. sends cooks	GARR 415:*31*
d. should have all the good tunes	HILL 480:*4*
d.'s sooner raised	SHER 933:*93*
d. taketh him up	BIBLE 133:*31*
d. understands Welsh	SHAK 876:*61*
d.'s walking parody	CHES 257:*87*
d. will come, and Faustus	MARL 654:*20*
D. with d. damned	MILT 688:*23*
D. with perhapse	MUGG 712:*22*
d. won't turn them	SCOTT 856:*11*
envy of the d.	BIBLE 131:*80*
face the d.!	BURNS 211:*17*
favourable reference to the D.	CHUR 265:*35*
fears a painted d.	SHAK 908:*48*
fight against the d.	BOOK 175:*35*
give the d. his due	SHAK 875:*41*
given up believing in the d.	KNOX 567:*62*
go, poor d., get thee gone	STER 969:*99*
Half d. and half child	KIPL 562:*65*
he counteracts the D.	SMART 944:*67*
heaviest stone the d. can throw	HAZL 464:*21*
how the D. they got there	POPE 781:*63*
If the d. doesn't exist	DOST 341:*40*
know he is a d.	ETHE 380:*16*
laughing d. in sneer	BYRON 221:*11*
May be the d.	SHAK 890:*18*
Nazarite conjured the d. into!	SHAK 874:*18*
old serpent, called the D.	BIBLE 157:*21*
opportunity for attacking the d.!	STEAD 964:*9*
plain to see, the D. walks	BETJ 100:*51*
politician is the d.'s quilted anvil	WEBS 1061:*58*
poor d. has ended	BROW 198:*53*
Pope Fired in the D.'s belly	ANON 25:*21*
renounce the d. and all his works	BOOK 175:*36*
Resist the d., and he will flee	BIBLE 155:*69*
sacrifice…of the d.'s leavings	POPE 779:*17*
sacrifice them all…to this d.	SHAK 873:*95*
said the D.	WALL 1049:*63*
saint when most I play the d.	SHAK 863:*53*
servant to the d.	SISS 940:*97*
serve the d. and his angels	WENT 1065:*53*
shame the d.	SHAK 876:*58*
Tell us, pray, what d.	FORD 397:*19*
that d.'s madness—War	SERV 859:*58*
The d. Bush	HUSS 505:*36*
The d.!	ONEI 740:*54*
tempted of the d.	BIBLE 133:*29*
Till the D. whispered	KIPL 561:*17*
truth and shame the d.	LIPP 606:*31*
wiles of the d.	BIBLE 152:*6*
with you the d. will fly away	OCON 735:*82*
devil-born doubt is D.-b.	TENN 999:*52*

devil-porter I'll d.-p. it no further	SHAK 908:*51*
devildoms d. of Spain	TENN 1004:*56*
devilish most D. thing	FLEM 393:*60*
devils cast out d.	BIBLE 136:*74*
casteth out d.	BIBLE 136:*72*
d. also believe	BIBLE 155:*64*
d. as tiles	LUTH 620:*47*
d. being offended	SHAK 898:*19*
d. to contest his vision	MAIL 640:*89*
foreign d. have have made	ORAH 741:*78*
innumerable monsters and d.	LUTH 620:*51*
more d. than vast hell	SHAK 871:*55*
said they were d. incarnate	SHAK 882:*13*
devise what one can d.	WRIS 1102:*20*
Devon D., glorious D.!	BOUL 181:*45*
devotee great d. of the Gospel	SHAW 920:*10*
devotees most d. arrive	UPDI 1037:*68*
devotion d. and our prayers	FRIE 405:*60*
d. to the wind and seas	LANC 578:*52*
hate with greater d.	SHAK 911:*8*
intelligence that moves, d. is	DONNE 338:*16*
object of universal d.	IRVI 513:*68*
passion for abstracted d.	JOHN 528:*49*
promote my invisible d.	BROW 194:*64*
with evergreen d.	BIRN 163:*26*
devour seeking whom he may d.	BIBLE 156:*84*
shed tears when they would d.	BACON 58:*92*
devoured could have d. me	KARSH 542:*11*
has d. the infant child	HOUS 496:*86*
devourer Time the d.	OVID 747:*2*
dew as sunlight drinketh d.	TENN 993:*36*
As the d. of Hermon	BIBLE 119:*45*
continual d. of thy blessing	BOOK 173:*98*
Debauchee of D.	DICK 328:*96*
d. her orbs upon the green	SHAK 870:*35*
d. of heaven	FORD 397:*11*
d. on the mountain	SCOTT 854:*65*
Drop down, d.	BIBLE 159:*51*
fades away like morning d.	BALL 67:*57*
fresh with blooming d.	MERE 671:*98*
honey wild, and manna d.	KEATS 545:*73*
in the d. of the morn	YEATS 1105:*62*
meet the morning d.	ARNO 39:*19*
Orient d., Shed from	MARV 657:*68*
pastures…washed with d.	SASS 846:*42*
rained a ghastly d.	TENN 995:*77*
resolve itself into a d.	SHAK 888:*51*
roses washed in d.	MILT 682:*97*
sea of d.	FIELD 387:*41*
speech shall distil as the d.	BIBLE 108:*1*
wave glittered the d.	MANS 647:*7*
wet with the d. of heaven	BIBLE 129:*47*
who hath begotten the drops of d.?	BIBLE 113:*20*
your chains to earth like d.	SHEL 928:*80*
dew-like d.-l. steel	BRAU 186:*22*
dew-pearled hill-side's d.-p.	BROW 197:*25*
dewdrop fragile d.	KEATS 544:*38*
globe as one great d.	MUIR 713:*39*
Starlight and d.	FOST 399:*62*
dewdrops seek some d. here	SHAK 870:*35*
showers and d. wet	ROSS 824:*76*
Dewey D. has no inner reserve	HOOV 490:*68*
dewfall d. at night	STEV 976:*53*
dews drinker of d.	DOYLE 344:*21*
night d. on still waters	TENN 994:*49*
dewy-feathered d.-f. Sleep	MILT 683:*14*
dhoti Mahatma's cotton d.	MURR 715:*76*
diabetes Politics is like having d.	JONES 533:*55*
diagnose able to d.	KEYN 554:*27*
diagnostician One finger…d.	OSLER 746:*73*
dial d.'s shady stealth	SHAK 914:*76*
needle on a d.	STEV 972:*79*
ride upon a d.'s point	SHAK 876:*72*
dialect d. I understand very little	PEPYS 765:*70*

dialect (*contd.*)
purify the d. of the tribe — ELIOT 372:73
use of d. words — HARDY 456:94
dialogue And the d.! — CHAN 250:38
conviction is to report that d. — KUNI 571:18
Death is a d. — DICK 328:10
d. between client and architect — STERN 968:86
film script…without d. — MAMET 644:59
settlement through genuine d. — AUNG 50:23
unending d. between the present — CARR 237:9
dialogues d. with my Mother — WORD 1096:26
dials carve out d. — SHAK 862:22
d. the signs — SHAK 875:36
diamond d. and safire bracelet — LOOS 613:33
d.…has scarce any value in use — SMITH 946:94
find a d. or a pearl — VAN 1039:2
immortal d. — HOPK 492:7
more rough than polished d. — CHES 257:78
soul…like a rough d. — DEFOE 311:73
diamonds d. and rubies — MORE 707:53
D. are of most precious value — WEBS 1060:50
d. in the smog of…Megalopolis — MAIL 639:84
give him d. back — GABOR 411:66
Goodness what beautiful d.! — WEST 1067:77
graven with d. in letters plain — WYATT 1103:28
put d. on the floor — RIVE 813:4
throat cut With d.? — WEBS 1061:66
Diana awf'lly bad luck on D. — BETJ 101:55
break D.'s law — POPE 778:96
legs were such D. shows — HERR 477:59
diaries good girls keep d. — BANK 70:92
wrote in my d. about…meals — BUSH 215:85
diary life of every man is a d. — BARR 72:41
more important than…d. — SASS 845:36
Secret D. of Adrian Mole — TOWN 1024:12
dice A throw of the d. — MALL 642:20
d. of God — EMER 376:36
[God] does not play d. — EINS 363:62
God not only plays d. — HAWK 461:62
heraldic equivalent of…furry d. — ANON 29:36
If the iron d. roll — BETH 99:23
Dick D., I don't know how — NIXON 730:8
D. the shepherd blows — SHAK 866:30
dickens what the d. his name is — SHAK 878:18
Dickens D., Tolstoy, Hugo — LESS 598:99
D.…unremitting humanity — BENN 91:78
D. was not the first — PRIT 791:68
rewritten by D. — COOKE 286:30
Thackeray and D. — STEV 974:22
dictates d. of reason — DICK 326:65
dictation told at d. speed — AMIS 17:82
dictator I am not a d. — PINO 770:45
not a director, he's a d. — MONR 700:49
dictators d. nor the bureaucrats — ORWE 744:40
personal contact with the d. — CHAM 249:20
seen by d. as subversive — JONG 533:61
dictatorship class struggle…d. — MARX 661:27
decapitated him from the d. — POWE 788:12
d. is beginning — SHEV 934:18
establish a d. — ORWE 745:61
nakedness of Stalinist d. — KENN 550:52
dictatorships bringing down d. — OROU 741:82
dictionaries D. are like watches — JOHN 532:33
To make d. is dull work — JOHN 526:10
writer of d. — JOHN 526:4
writer of d. — JOHN 526:12
dictionary d. of popular usage — GREE 444:17
except in the d. — KIMB 557:66
father still reads the d. — SCAR 846:54
first time I ever made the d. — WEST 1067:84
Like's Webster's d. — BURKE 208:51
outside of a d. — LODGE 610:78
sensible as a d.! — CARR 239:49
set him upon his d. — STEV 974:22

dictionary (*contd.*)
the metre of the d.? — THOM 1010:58
diddle d., we take it, is dee — SWIN 988:58
die After I d. — TOSC 1024:9
all shall d. — SHAK 877:96
and let him d. — TENN 1000:56
appetite may sicken and so d. — SHAK 893:91
appointed unto men once to d. — BIBLE 154:48
as in Adam all d. — BIBLE 151:67
as natural to d. — BACON 56:45
asleep, or hearing, d. — SHAK 918:54
bear to live, or dare to d. — POPE 781:49
Beauty lives though lilies d. — FLEC 393:48
believe in ideas and d. for them — ANOU 30:74
blithe earth d. — JEFF 519:79
Born but to d. — POPE 780:42
break it must d. — KIPL 561:52
but nobody wants to d. — LOUIS 614:57
but they d. — UPDI 1037:70
but to d., and go we — SHAK 897:82
but to do and d. — TENN 1000:72
can't d., along the coast — DICK 324:15
change, but I cannot d. — SHEL 928:84
content to d. — BROWN 194:53
Cowards d. many times — SHAK 883:33
Created to pretent we never d. — LARK 582:20
curse God, and d. — BIBLE 112:97
Death, thou halt d.! — DONNE 338:5
defore I d. — MARTI 657:57
d. after having lived his way — LABR 572:47
d. and be a riddance! — DICK 324:3
d. at the age of thirty-seven — WALT 1052:12
d. but once to serve our country — ADDI 8:33
d. dishevelled and soft — LOWE 617:5
d. each time — HEMI 471:33
d. fighting for his country — HOMER 488:23
D. for adultery! — SHAK 903:34
d. for free — VALLE 1038:89
d. for my country? — SITT 940:98
d. happy — FOX 400:73
d. if you let it loose — SHAW 924:95
d. in errancy — ABU 1:10
d. in exile — GREG 446:46
d. in harness — AMIS 16:75
d. in the Lord — BIBLE 158:24
d. is better than length of days — AESC 9:57
d. is cast — CAES 225:86
D.? I should say not — BARR 73:58
d. laughing — WEBS 1060:43
d. on your feet — IBAR 510:18
d. or get kicked out — HOOV 490:63
d. so young — AUDEN 47:63
d. the death — BIBLE 132:2
d. when curiosity goes — SWIFT 983:54
d.…when you are present — SCEVE 846:57
d. without having played — BORO 179:20
do or d.! — BURNS 212:38
do we not d.? — SHAK 872:80
Don't d. of ignorance — ANON 28:22
Easy live and quiet d. — SCOTT 855:97
either love, or I must d. — FORD 397:15
Even if I d. — GAND 414:11
every man…born to d. — DRYD 352:93
Export or d. — ANON 26:46
Fall asleep, or hearing d. — SHAK 918:56
fated not to d. — DRYD 350:48
fears't to d.? — SHAK 870:21
fight and d. for your country — GOLD 434:34
For another thing, they d. earlier — MENC 669:74
For thou must d. — HERB 475:32
for tomorrow we d. — BIBLE 151:69
For tomorrow we shall d.! — PARK 754:9
God does not d. — HAMM 453:43
Good Americans, when they d. — APPL 32:1

die (*contd.*)
good d. early — DEFOE 312:74
have the power to d. — TENN 1003:23
hazard of the d. — SHAK 863:68
Hope I d. before — TOWN 1024:14
hope that he will d. — EMER 377:65
I clasp them…because they d. — CORY 288:66
I must d. — KEATS 548:21
I will d. in Paris — VALL 1039:92
I will d. in peace — WOLFE 1090:15
I will not have thee d.! — TENN 997:9
idea d. instead of you — LEWIS 602:59
If I d., avenge me — MUSS 716:84
if I shall d. here — MATAK 663:66
If I should d. — BROO 192:21
If it were now to d. — SHAK 899:21
in a month you've got to d. — GILB 425:83
in what peace a Christian can d. — ADDI 8:40
Is not born…does not d. — SITW 941:22
John Barleycorn should d. — BURNS 210:89
lerne to d. gladly — ANON 22:75
let it d. with thee — BIBLE 132:7
Let us determine to d. here — BEE 82:9
Live and Let D. — FLEM 393:57
live forever or d. in the attempt — HELL 468:81
live, I d. — LAB 571:32
love one man till I d. — HAMM 454:51
make a malefactor d. sweetly — DRYD 351:64
man can d. but once — SHAK 877:98
memory d. from the earth — SIDN 937:66
men to d. — BARK 71:19
most grand to d. — MASE 662:43
must men kill and d.? — SHEL 932:65
must needs d. — BIBLE 110:49
never can he d. — SPEN 958:20
not d. when the trees were green — CLARE 267:84
not made to d. — TENN 998:16
not so difficult to d. — BYRON 221:24
not that I'm afraid to d. — ALLEN 14:39
O, I d., Horatio! — SHAK 893:88
One should d. — PLATO 774:16
only d. once — MOLI 698:16
opponents eventually d. — PLAN 772:85
Or let me d.! — WORD 1097:42
parting was to d. — TENN 1000:54
people only d. at the last moment — CELI 247:90
pleasant thing to d. like this — BOUC 180:39
rather d. than not do so — BOUL 181:41
regret can d.! — TENN 999:48
religious system…can never really d. — SAKI 837:97
requested…that he might d. — BIBLE 111:68
resolve to conquer or d. — WASH 1054:42
see my funeral before I d. — EDGE 360:29
smile can make one d. — SAIN 836:86
something he will d. for — KING 557:77
teach rustic moralist to d. — GRAY 442:73
that I Must d. — DONNE 336:76
they only let Him d. — STUD 980:15
those that do d. — SHAK 906:4
thou shalt surely d. — BIBLE 103:90
Thus will I d. — DYER 358:40
time to d. — BIBLE 122:19
to choose life and d. — LOWE 617:2
to d. for one's country — HORA 493:22
to d. in dust — SPEN 959:28
to d. is different — WHIT 1072:78
to d. is gain — BIBLE 153:7
To d. is nothing — ANOU 31:78
To d., to sleep — SHAK 890:21
to d. upon a kiss — SHAK 901:52
To d. will be an awfully big adventure — BARR 73:45
to morrow we shall d. — BIBLE 125:71

die (*contd.*)
To triumph, and to d.	GRAY 443:88
To-morrow let us do or d.!	CAMP 227:31
toddle safely home and d.	SASS 845:27
we d. in earnest	RALE 800:14
we shall d....'tis but the time	SHAK 883:40
we who are about to d.	ANON 21:46
weep or she will d.	TENN 997:7
What 'tis to d.	BEAU 80:69
when I came to d.	THOR 1017:85
When I d. people will say	COMP 279:76
When I d.	DONL 336:61
Where thou diest, will I d.	BIBLE 109:25
Whether we live...or d.	BIBLE 150:42
why will ye d.	BIBLE 129:40
wit may wander ere he d.	TENN 1003:35
with us, or we d.	KEATS 545:58
word...for which you d.	WEIL 1062:85
would surely d.	HELL 468:88
Ye shall not surely d.	BIBLE 103:94
You and I ought not to d.	ADAMS 5:87

died all summer settled there and d. | LARK 581:97
d. amidst dying country's cries	GRAY 443:83
d. as he had lived	CLEM 268:2
d. As one that had been studied	SHAK 907:23
d....before his birth	THUR 1020:55
D., has he?	LOUIS 614:53
d. to save us all	ALEX 13:20
friends who have d.	SASS 845:31
Just before she d.	STEIN 966:47
like saying the patient d.	JACO 514:90
Men have d. from time to time	SHAK 886:21
Mithridates, he d. old	HOUS 495:66
mother-in-law d.	JERO 521:7
question why we d.	KIPL 565:22
She should have d. hereafter	SHAK 910:86
sweet dove d.	KEATS 544:43
when a Forsyte d.	GALS 413:2
When I d.	JARR 518:57
would God I had d. for thee	BIBLE 110:51
Would to God we had d.	BIBLE 106:66
Yes. As I d.	HEMI 471:33

dies Breed never d. | BENN 90:74
d. among the mountains	WORD 1096:35
d. married young	SHAK 870:19
each day d. with sleep	HOPK 492:5
erect...his own tomb ere he d.	SHAK 880:66
flower that d.	SHAK 887:41
He that d.	SHAK 917:33
how a man d.	JOHN 528:55
kingdom where nobody d.	MILL 676:93
man marries, d., or turns Hindoo	SHEL 929:11
something in me d.	VIDAL 1044:63
soul...languishes and d.	ROCH 817:64
spectre-thin, and d.	KEATS 547:15
that little flame which never d.	RENO 807:11
then he d.	KIPL 560:21
when the Poet d.	SCOTT 853:48
who d. fighting has increase	GREN 446:52
worm that never d.	BROO 193:34

diet adoption of vegetable d. | SHEL 927:59
d. unparalleled	DICK 321:44
Give it a d.	DONNE 338:97
gods will d. with me	SHAK 916:11
immortal d.	RALE 800:13
In D., Furniture and Dress	MAND 645:71
twelfth day of my d.	PIER 769:35

differ d. chiefly in the boldness | JEVO 521:22
d. from those of common sense	HUXL 509:4

difference biggest d....she was taller | FEIB 384:96
country saves the d.	BAGE 61:57
crucial d. between	NISB 730:4
d. between a dog and a man	TWAIN 1034:99
d. between burning and gassing	SIHA 938:72

difference (*contd.*)
d. between most people	TUCH 1031:47
d. between one young woman	SHAW 923:84
d. between the most dissimilar	SMITH 946:95
d. between unethical and ethical	STEF 965:25
d. is...that of the living and the dead	
	CIXO 267:70
d. of 40,000 men	WELL 1063:15
d. that makes a d.	BATE 76:11
don't make no d.	TWAIN 1033:92
love...Cares not for d.	DEKK 313:10
made all the d.	FROST 406:77
more d. within the sexes	COMP 279:75
only d. between us	BIRK 163:20
shade of d.	GREE 445:27
That's the d. between us	SHAW 925:33
The d. to me!	WORD 1095:8
trust the very d.	JORD 537:30

differences cannot now end our d. | KENN 551:79
d. one finds among men	PASC 758:68
Jews and Arabs...settle their d.	AUST 53:75
little d. of speed	PRATT 789:24
National d. consist	NIET 729:93
open exchange of major d.	AUNG 50:23

different d. kinds of things sound | HONO 488:31
D. living is not living	SPEN 956:81
d. waters flow	HERA 473:85
do not feel greatly d.	BEAV 81:86
How d., how very d.	ANON 25:23
once you're hungry, you're d.	HUNT 504:16
saying something d.	HAVEL 460:60

differently they do things d. there | HART 460:54

difficult childhood...is just as d. | RILKE 811:84
D. do you call it	JOHN 532:37
d. not to write satire	JUVE 540:77
d. we do immediately	CALO 226:5
Endure what is d. to endure	HIRO 481:18
found d. and left untried	CHES 258:15
living up to it that is d.	THAC 1007:96
more d. from its rudeness	JOHN 530:99
others extremely d.	JOHN 531:22
still more d. question	GRAV 440:39
too d. for artists	SCHN 848:86
very d., maybe impossible	SOLOW 952:93
When a piece gets d.	SCHN 848:85
writing a good play is d.	PRIE 790:45

difficulties d. in providing | COMM 278:66
d. which have...amused philosophers	BERK 95:50
political and practical d.	KEYN 555:36

difficulty complexity, and d. | TRIL 1026:56
if it had much d.	JOHN 531:7

diffidence and her name was D. | BUNY 205:68

dig d. and heap | ARNO 37:74
D. for Victory	DORA 340:38
d. with it	HEAN 464:31

digamma simple d. in Homer | QUIL 797:62

digest inwardly d. them | BOOK 174:10
shall d. it	SHAK 873:87

digestion Few radicals have good d. | BUTL 218:45
good eater must have a good d.	DISR 332:73
man...think...about his d.	LEWIS 601:44
to facilitate d.	VOLT 1047:14

diggeth d. a pit | BIBLE 123:37

dignities by indignities...to d. | BACON 57:70
peace above all earthly d.	SHAK 918:60

dignity assumption of d. | GALT 413:10
confers d. on a picture	ALBE 11:92
declares his d.	MILT 690:60
d. and worth	UNIT 1036:45
d. in tilling a field	WASH 1054:37
d. or baseness of a person	CHRI 262:74
imperishable d. of man	CARL 234:44
love was of that d.	SHAK 889:77
Official d. tends to increase	HUXL 507:71

dignity (*contd.*)
penumbra of somber d.	ATLAS 44:6
sense of...moral d.	CURZ 302:29
simple d. of a child	SAND 841:77
stark d. of entrance	WILL 1082:84
to give it possiblity, scope, even d.	MACL 634:83
walk with sincerity and d.	WAITE 1048:30
with silent d.	GROS 447:72

dildos delicate burdens of d. | SHAK 912:35

dilemmas d. of conscience | SNOW 950:71

dilettante d. looks only for pleasure
	REDON 804:76
snowy-banded, d.	TENN 1001:79

dilettantism bureaucracy and d. | WEBER 1059:22

dilly-dally Don't d.-d. on the way | COLL 276:38

dilute d. it by voting for anyone | ONAS 739:43

dim d....Of night | YEATS 1105:65
Pinnacled in d. in the intense inane	SHEL 930:25
so d. and they're so smart	ROTH 826:24

dime can you spare a d.? | HARB 455:72
still don't have a d.	FEIF 384:97

dimension extra d. of feeling | FOWL 399:66

dimensions certain d. of thought | STEI 967:67
d. of a man's self	LAMB 577:35
d. of a man's self	LAMB 577:37
Time has three d.	HOPK 492:97

dimes come here bright as d. | LOWE 617:5

diminished national dividend is d. | PIGOU 770:41
rights of every man are d.	KENN 551:80
what to make of a d. thing	FROST 406:79

diminution increase or d. | RICA 808:37

diminutive man is a d. to nothing | DONNE 339:20

dimples hair and d. is coming | MOORE 705:13

din her feet made no d. | COLUM 278:60
louder still the d.	MACA 624:20
'mid the d. Of towns and cities	WORD 1094:96
music's d.	GILB 424:63
will not be heard above the d.	READ 803:55

dine bulls and foxes d. well | JUST 540:75
d. with some men	BENT 93:24
English would manage to d.	JERR 521:17
heroes to d. with us	TROL 1028:86
tempt me to d. with him	SWIFT 984:70

dined if one has not d. well | WOOLF 1093:68

diner Dinner in the d. | GORD 435:65
philosophic d.-out	BROW 200:84

dinero Salud, D., Amor...y Tiempo | ANON 30:68

diners feeding the p. back to d. | COUP 289:79
laughing in the d.	SAND 841:59
locations such as d.	COUP 289:76

dines say something when he d. | HUNT 505:30

dingy fatally poor and d. | WHAR 1068:95

dining thought of d. | GOLD 433:28

dinner After a good d. | WILDE 1077:71
After d. to the Duke's house	PEPYS 765:71
At a d. party one should	MAUG 664:84
best number for a d. party	GULB 448:82
Burning d.	PIER 769:33
criticize after d.	MARX 660:10
delicious d. of too much	JOHN 523:42
D. in the diner	GORD 435:65
d. of herbs where love is	BIBLE 121:80
D. parties are for eating	FERB 385:12
d. party of more than two	MENC 670:82
D. ...possessed two dramatic features	
	POWE 787:4
expect if we haven't any d.	LEAR 590:66
expect our d.	SMITH 945:87
get it down onto the d. table	BONA 172:78
I managed at d.	RIDGE 811:80
mak our d. sweet	BALL 67:55
man should have d.	LEMAY 595:44
more business after d.	SWIFT 984:76
Music with d. is an insult	CHES 260:48

dinner (*contd.*)
old friend for d. TALLY 990:*92*
one cannot talk about after d. WILDE 1076:*49*
re-union d. PARK 755:*30*
revolution is not a d. party MAO 648:*18*
sinner…with no d. RANS 802:*38*
three hours' march to d. HAZL 463:*6*
too hungry for d. at eight HART 459:*45*
whatever one had got for d. RUSK 831:*6*
dinner-table dominate a…d.-t. WILDE 1077:*75*
dinners all d. are cooked WOOLF 1093:*76*
housewife's badly-cooked d. BEET 84:*55*
more d. than appetites CHAM 250:*25*
dinosaurs like the bones of d. RAND 801:*25*
dint d. of pity SHAK 884:*55*
Diogenes would be D. ALEX 13:*13*
Dionysus Christ follows D. POUND 786:*63*
dip Leaning over…a lucky d. DAYL 310:*57*
diphtheria d. restored the status HAMER 453:*37*
diploma d. is a lighted match KOCH 567:*66*
diplomacy D.…patriotic art of lying BIER 161:*79*
Megaphone d. HOWE 497:*93*
Rolls Royce d. ANON 28:*9*
superstition of an antiquated d. CECIL 247:*85*
underrated aspects of d. SHUL 935:*29*
diplomat A d. these days USTI 1037:*76*
d. is a deaf Trappist LECA 589:*96*
diplomatic D. problems ACHE 2:*22*
putting out a d. boathook CECIL 247:*81*
diplomatist salad…brilliant d. WILDE 1075:*28*
diplomats better that aged d. AUST 53:*74*
D. and protocols are…good PALM 752:*68*
D. lie to journalists KRAUS 569:*90*
direction any sense of d. WILS 1084:*12*
blowing the new d. of Time LAWR 585:*68*
d. of our fears BERR 98:*5*
d. of society TOCQ 1021:*74*
d. of the right line NEWT 725:*36*
d. to point that organ AUDEN 48:*91*
d., which thou canst not see POPE 780:*41*
going in the opposite d. NICO 727:*62*
I have not settled in which d. BEAV 81:*86*
lines running in every d. ROSS 823:*65*
looking together in the same d. SAIN 836:*80*
new d. to technological SCHU 850:*15*
one positive pitch or d. HOPK 492:*97*
our ways and our d. THAT 1007:*10*
precisely in the same d. PEARY 763:*36*
step in the wrong d. LEVA 599:*16*
directions moving in opposite d. SMITH 949:*54*
not equally stupid in all d. BELL 88:*28*
rode madly off in all d. LEAC 589:*37*
director not a d., he's a dictator MONR 700:*49*
telephone call from a d. PORT 784:*34*
directors ideal board of d. DOCH 334:*37*
direful something d. in the sound AUST 52:*58*
dirge knell is rung…their d. is sung COLL 276:*44*
dirt As ignorant as d.! SHAK 900:*60*
d. doesn't get any worse CRISP 297:*37*
d. kept breathing ROET 819:*94*
d., or grubs, or worms POPE 781:*63*
Huddled in d. ROCH 816:*51*
If d. were trumps LAMB 577:*36*
Instead of d. and poison SWIFT 984:*58*
make crossness and d. succeed FORS 398:*45*
mix sentences with d. BRAU 186:*19*
out of the d. ALTH 15:*62*
reputation for d. THOR 1017:*97*
turn to d. SHAK 916:*14*
dirty big words…about d. things DOCT 334:*39*
d. son-of-a-bitch STEI 966:*54*
D.,ugly, disagreeable DICK 325:*36*
d., wet hole TOLK 1022:*89*
the d. weekend SMITH 946:*1*

dirty (*contd.*)
this d., despicable little island WALP 1051:*90*
thugh d. is clein FLEM 394:*65*
dirty-mindedness journalistic d.-m. LAWR 586:*96*
disabled trade union for the d. HEATH 466:*50*
disadvantage d. of being a hog MORT 710:*99*
disagree when doctors d. POPE 780:*25*
disagreeable not d. to him JOHN 531:*15*
such a d. man GILB 425:*80*
when she stoops to be d. AUST 52:*59*
disagreement absence of d. testifies MERT 672:*25*
disagrees can't find anyone who d. BENN 90:*69*
disappear like having a continent d. JARR 518:*56*
want to d. HUGO 502:*71*
disappointed haven't been d. GRAMM 438:*95*
disappointing war is somewhat d. GRIF 447:*60*
disappointment D. all I endeavour HOPK 492:*8*
parents…sometimes a d. POWE 787:*1*
without a feeling of d. LAMB 576:*18*
disappointments hard work, d. PEARY 762:*35*
disapprove d. of what you say VOLT 1047:*19*
something of which you d. FIND 389:*65*
disarm d. the strong FRAN 401:*88*
disaster a glimpse of such a d. ORWE 743:*7*
audience was a d. WILDE 1077:*64*
d. until it is finally manifest MURP 715:*70*
genetic d. WELSH 1065:*48*
loss is no d. BISH 164:*35*
meet with Triumph and D. KIPL 564:*8*
recent d. at Rome AUGU 49:*16*
road to d. LLOY 609:*65*
single…not such a fearful d. ZHANG 1109:*19*
worst d. since my election BROWN 194:*52*
disasters children…notorious d. EURI 381:*34*
day's d. in his morning face GOLD 433:*32*
d. of the world CONN 283:*74*
make guilty of our d. SHAK 902:*2*
disastrous d. and the unpalatable GALB 411:*78*
d. Presidents and Prime Ministers ONAS 739:*42*
to win a war is as d. as to lose CHRI 262:*73*
disbelief willing suspension of d. COLE 275:*20*
discerning Gives genius a better d. GOLD 433:*21*
discharge d. of any profession JOHN 529:*71*
no d. in that war BIBLE 123:*30*
disciple d. is not above his master BIBLE 136:*77*
d. who does not excel LEON 597:*79*
disciples d. came to him BIBLE 136:*68*
d. rebuked them BIBLE 139:*23*
d. saw him walking on the sea BIBLE 138:*7*
followers of Jesus…his d. JOHN 525:*74*
gave it to the d. BIBLE 140:*48*
hand toward his d. BIBLE 137:*96*
know that ye are my d. BIBLE 146:*59*
Likewise also said all the d. BIBLE 140:*49*
nowadays has his d. WILDE 1076:*36*
discipleship grace without d. BONH 173:*83*
discipline d. of a monastery AELR 9:*52*
d. of humanity BACON 57:*60*
d. of our holy Church OCON 735:*80*
habit of d. TUCH 1031:*46*
Life has no other d. MILL 678:*25*
Nature's stern d. DOBZ 334:*36*
scientist may find his d. severe CORN 288:*61*
testifies to a developing d. MERT 672:*25*
disciplines deeply biting of social d. LAWR 587:*17*
disclosure a short story is always a d. PRIT 791:*73*
Discobbolos Till Mrs D. said LEAR 590:*57*
discomfort d. of…self-examination PECK 763:*38*
d., fatigue, strain in large amounts GELL 417:*71*
disconnect d. it from the rest of them FITZ 390:*95*
discontent contented sort of d. KEATS 546:*79*
divine d. KING 559:*2*
fruitful source of family d. BEET 84:*55*

discontent (*contd.*)
winter of our d. SHAK 862:*45*
discontented hundred men d. LOUI 614:*48*
discontinuity d. within ROTH 825:*7*
discord All d., harmony POPE 780:*41*
dire effects from civil d. ADDI 8:*36*
D. oft in musick SPEN 957:*97*
Harmony in d. HORA 493:*28*
Melodious d. SHAK 864:*95*
Where there is d. THAT 1007:*11*
discourage d. the composer HEIF 467:*67*
d. them from…attempts STEV 974:*13*
discouraged do not be d. HEMI 471:*42*
discourse Bid me d. SHAK 864:*92*
d. of the elders BIBLE 132:*93*
d. was about hunting PEPYS 765:*70*
fittest for d. DRYD 350:*41*
political or the scientific d. LEGU 594:*32*
provisions for d. AUST 50:*31*
Read not to…find talk and d. BACON 59:*22*
subtly and sinewy to d. MILT 686:*73*
discourses all d. but mine JONS 535:*90*
discover anxious to d. RUSS 832:*29*
d. what we ourselves believe GRANT 438:*2*
Man…can only d. PAINE 750:*51*
often d. what will do SMIL 945:*75*
should not d. GORD 435:*62*
To dance is to d. SENG 859:*52*
discoverers They are ill d. BACON 55:*14*
discoveries consequence of d. BACON 55:*30*
d. made FRAN 402:*11*
more important than their d. BRON 190:*79*
discovering Writing a poem is d. FROST 407:*99*
discovery d. aside MUNRO 714:*57*
D. consists of seeing SZEN 989:*69*
d. of some occult relation JOHN 525:*90*
If scientists knew tomorrow's d. ZUCK 1110:*28*
logic of d. NISB 730:*4*
make room for d. APOL 32:*97*
medicinal d. AYRES 53:*83*
moral d.…the object of every tale CONR 285:*5*
never made a d. SMIL 945:*75*
new theory…a d. POPP 783:*23*
portals of d. JOYCE 538:*51*
Scientific d. and …knowledge PLAN 772:*83*
discreet whose ways are all d. PARK 753:*90*
discretion attain years of d. RUSK 831:*3*
better part of valour is d. SHAK 877:*77*
D. is a better part of Valerie MACG 630:*28*
d. that would have done credit SHAR 919:*82*
fail to observe decency and d. BACON 55:*7*
now come to the years of d. BOOK 175:*40*
reached the height of d. BENN 91:*98*
survives by d. WILL 1081:*63*
That which love worst endures, d. DONNE 338:*97*
discrimination D. is a hellhound KING 558:*85*
discussion after reasonable d. CHUR 265:*46*
Democracy means government by d. ATTL 44:*14*
d. of any subject SHEL 927:*56*
opportunity cost of economic d. GALB 412:*82*
discussions hate d. of feminism FREN 404:*38*
disdain d. the future now KENN 551:*82*
fall from her d. KYD 571:*24*
fortified with a strange d. WEBS 1061:*63*
gifts increased by d. SURR 982:*42*
little d. is not amiss CONG 281:*39*
love or more d. CAREW 233:*20*
disdainful d. wave of a white ANGE 20:*32*
disease All writing is a d. WILL 1083:*3*
artistic temperament is a d. CHES 258:*98*
biggest d. today THER 1008:*35*
cause of my d. SURR 982:*41*
cure the d. and kill the patient BACON 58:*1*
democratic d. MILL 679:*47*

disease (*contd.*)
desperate d....dangerous remedy	FAWK 384:95
d. is incurable	CHEK 256:63
d. is incurable	SHAK 877:85
d. will spread with...maliginity	DICK 326:54
d. you don't look forward to	MANK 645:72
Drug misuse is not a d.	DICK 320:12
elimination of some d.	SUTH 983:49
free from bad news and d.	BIOY 162:11
Hypochondria is the only d.	ANON 28:2
I have Bright's d.	PERE 766:87
introduced d. and decay	SHER 932:76
Life is a sexually transmitted d.	ANON 29:28
Life is an incurable d.	COWL 291:16
longer nurseth the d.	SHAK 915:97
name any d. after two guys	PUZO 796:44
national d.	MACC 626:66
no cure for this d.	BELL 87:6
no d., bodily or mental	SHEL 927:59
Progress is a comfortable d.	CUMM 300:92
rarer forms of d.	HARV 460:55
Red-and-gold d.	MUSC 716:81
remedy is worse than the d.	BACON 58:82
scars of d.	MACA 623:4
shapes of foul d.	TENN 1000:57
strange d. of modern life	ARNO 37:92
suffering from the particular d.	JERO 521:6
Tedium is the worst d.	POMP 777:71
There is one d. which is widespread	MAIM 640:95
wasting d. of the frontal lobes	ALBEE 11:88
while Nature cures the d.	VOLT 1047:18
worse d., t'escape	JONS 534:79

diseased romantic d.
	GOET 431:79
When love grows d.	ETHE 380:18

diseases death is the cure for all d.
	BROW 196:92
healeth all thy d.	BIBLE 118:11
lists of fatal d.	HELL 468:84
painful, chronic d.	JONES 533:55
remedy to all d.	BURT 214:73
scientific treatment for all d.	SHAW 923:87
sneezes spread d.	ANON 26:48
subject to the same d.	SHAK 872:80
talk of d. is...entertainment	OSLER 746:74
vulnerable to infectious d.	KOES 568:70

diseconomies hit d. of scale early
	MACD 628:97

disembodied d. and...murdered
	SHAR 919:86

disfigurement perceive their foul d.
	MILT 683:19

disgrace d. to the English nation
	INNO 512:56
d. to the planet	STONE 977:72
d. to the playing fields	FRY 408:10
Even to a full d.	SHAK 911:15
Peace without honour not only a d.	CECIL 247:78
retreats without fearing d.	SUN 982:24

disgraced dies rich...dies d.
	CARN 236:5
d., impeached, and baffled	SHAK 866:38
wrongfully d.	SHAK 914:69
You have d. yourselves	YEATS 1105:66

disgressions D....sunshine
	STER 969:96

disgruntled if not actually d.
	WODE 1089:3

disguise better go in d.
	BRAT 185:15
d. of determined hostility	SHER 934:7
naked is the best d.	CONG 280:10

disguised certainly very well d.
	CHUR 265:29
d. as insoluble problems	GARD 415:22

disguiser Death's a great d.
	SHAK 897:90

disgust but as a d.
	TZARA 1035:36
d. is reason's proper response	PAGL 749:34
Loves die from d.	LABR 572:44
Mummy, I'm sick with d.	BETJ 101:57
see...my body without d.	BAUD 77:26
touch a newspaper without d.	BAUD 78:45

dish butter in a lordly d.
	BIBLE 109:14
discovery of a new d.	BRIL 188:52
d. fit for the gods	SHAK 883:29

dish (*contd.*)
here's a d. I love not	SHAK 879:39
some d. more sharply spiced	PATM 760:10

dishclout Romeo's a d. to him
	SHAK 869:15

dishes Are these the choice d.
	GARR 415:31
child will make two D.	SWIFT 985:99
d. were ill-sorted	DRYD 352:82
Home-made d. that drive	HOOD 489:43
who does the d.	FREN 404:38

dishonour d. the vices
	WILD 1079:31
in d. stood	TENN 1002:15

dishonourable indecent and d.
	HELL 468:93

disillusionment D. in living
	STEIN 965:36
this age of d.?	SHIP 935:22

disillusionments d. in the lives
	SAKI 837:1

disinfectant Sunlight is the best d.
	KENN 550:60

disintegrate People who d.
	AUST 52:71

disinterested meant to be d., pure
	SELF 857:37

dislike d. ...at first sight
	STEE 964:21
like or d. them	FORS 398:40

disliked d. by all his friends
	WILDE 1079:9

disloyalty not like subversion or d.
	HELL 468:93

dismal d. grew his countenance
	BALL -101:36

dismay avoid us with d.
	TOLK 1023:94
flies about in d.	KIER 556:58

dismayed Be not afraid or d.
	BIBLE 112:90
neither be thou d.	BIBLE 108:8

dismissed fifty men d.?
	SHAK 902:14

dismount picking the place to d.
	BALL 65:24

Disney D. probably has the right idea
	HITC 482:27

disobedience campaign of civil d.
	CHUR 264:3
curse of d.	OTWAY 746:80

disorder last d. mortal
	GOLD 432:95
sweet d. in the dress	HERR 478:68

disorders common mental d.
	GRAV 440:35

disorientation stress and d.
	TOFF 1022:85

disorienting d., and painful
	RICH 809:48

disparities not for such large d.
	KEYN 555:41

disparity d. between things
	ALBEE 11:84

dispatch Spaniards' d.
	ROCH 816:48

dispensation in the old d.
	ELIOT 369:4

dispiriting cannot but be d.
	SMITH 948:36

displacement d. is the rust
	ANGE 19:16

displeasing which is not d.
	LARO 582:24

dispone for the dede d.
	DUNB 355:41

disposes God d.
	KEMP 549:40

disposition d. of Working Class
	CARL 235:79
d. that I owe	SHAK 909:62
goes so heavily with my d.	SHAK 890:2
his goatish d.	SHAK 902:2
liveliness of my d.	FRED 403:23
mild or choleric d.	ADDI 6:6
strong d. in youth	POWE 787:2

dispositions d. loved in private
	BURKE 206:2
d. of...mankind	BURKE 206:99

disproof d. is turned aimlessly aside
	EDDI 360:19

disproven Nor yet d.
	TENN 1005:54

disputants d. put me in mind
	ADDI 7:25

disputation that's a feeling d.
	SHAK 876:60

disputations d. of Plato
	HONO 488:32
Doubtful d.	BIBLE 150:41

dispute D. it like a man
	SHAK 909:74
Shakespeare-Bacon d.	GILB 426:99

disputes international d.
	EISE 364:86
lay your d. a' aside	SKIN 943:55
left to their d.	MILT 691:90
traditional d. of philosophers	AYER 53:77

disquieted why art thou d. in me?
	BIBLE 116:91

disquietude bone-ache d. of life
	ALLEN 14:34

disregard d. for the sublime comforts
	SHIP 935:21
entire life in its flagrant d.	MILI 674:55

dissatisfaction well-modulated d.
	TAAF 989:73

dissemble If you d. sometimes
	BACON 59:6

dissembling killed by d.
	LYLY 620:59

dissent d. is an act of faith
	FULB 409:29
in the name of d.	SNOW 951:76
limit our expression of d.	MAMET 643:44
Protestantism...is a sort of d.	BURKE 206:8
successive waves of d.	SCHO 848:87

dissenter d. is every human being
	MACL 634:78

dissidence d. of dissent
	BURKE 206:8

dissipated still keep looking so d.
	BENC 89:53

dissipation d. of energy begin?
	KELV 549:35
year of art and d.	MOORE 704:11

dissociation d. of sensibility
	ELIOT 368:79

dissolve I d. it in rain
	SHEL 928:82

dissonance air with barbarous d.
	MILT 684:32

dissonant No sound is d.
	COLE 273:82

distain What, my dear Lady D.!
	SHAK 879:30

distance apparent from this d.
	THUR 1019:31
At d. I forgive thee	MILT 695:51
d. between your ears	JONES 533:51
d. does not matter	DEFF 311:72
d. lends enchantment to the view	CAMP 227:25
d. that the dead have gone	DICK 329:19
does not hold it at a d.	SENG 858:51
emergency happening at d.	BARZ 76:99
for long d. after I hit it	TREV 1026:52
Freedom is only the d.	ZHAO 1109:21
In notes by d. made more sweet	COLL 277:50
knack of judging a d.	REED 805:82
love of grey-blue d.	MACK 632:52
There's a hell of a d.	PARK 754:17
time is the longest d.	WILL 1081:57
Tyranny of D.	BLAI 165:50
viewed from a d.	SCHO 849:99
worth of d. run	KIPL 564:9

distances decussated at equal d.
	JOHN 526:13
letting go of d.	STORR 978:82

distant We were d.
	JOHN 523:46

distaste d. for fishing
	STEI 966:56

distillation final d. of self
	DELI 315:40

distinction d. among her companions
	AUST 51:40
d. between children and adults	BART 74:70
d. between virtue and vice	JOHN 527:31
d. in the intellectual powers	DARW 306:88
few escape that d.	TWAIN 1032:73
great d. between the sexes	FOWL 399:66
no useful d. can be made	GALB 411:76
one pre-eminent d.	POTT 785:44
only real d.	BELL 88:34
pride of d.	SAND 841:68
without reaching such d.	HUME 504:12

distinctions multiply d.
	WORD 1096:25
trigger-fine d.	LOWE 617:9

distinguished be d. above the rest
	HOMER 488:18
d. by your enemies	HOOV 490:70
d. thing!	JAMES 517:32
more d. than generality of mankind	BOSW 180:29

distorted facts and places were d.
	PACH 748:25

distorts d., disfigures and destroys
	FANON 382:60

distraction create some d.
	HERN 476:44

distress Dear d., and joy allied
	CULL 299:70
D. with dagger keen	COLL 277:45
happy at another's d.	LABR 573:54
refuge from d.	WORD 1100:81
those who are in d.	VIRG 1045:80

distresses insurmountable d.
	JOHN 526:9

distressing most d. thing
	HUXL 507:86

distribution arbitrary...d.
	KEYN 555:38
d., at fittest time	RUSK 831:95
d. of uncertainty among economists	STEIN 966:50
Laws...of d.	MILL 674:57

district ye can ramble over the d.
	MACG 630:25

districts d....like squares of wheat
	LARK 581:6

distrust d. a man that says
	HAMM 454:60
d. each other	BRAD 183:79
d. of its own vision	JEFF 520:93

distrust (*contd.*)
have to d. each other — WILL 1081:64
disturbances The Little D. of Man — PALEY 751:57
ditch both shall fall into the d. — BIBLE 138:10
lay distracted in a d. — CRAS 296:28
ditch-water drinking bottled d.-w. — SHAW 925:16
ditches his windmills are d. — USTI 1038:79
ditties Pipe to the spirit d. — KEATS 547:8
ditty played an ancient d. — KEATS 547:96
diversion merriment and d. — SMITH 945:29
more fond of that d. — MELV 667:37
turned a tax into a d. — STEE 964:16
diversity d. in the faculties of men — MADI 638:55
infinite d. of movement — REDT 804:79
reduction of d. — HUXL 508:90
world safe for d. — KENN 551:79
divide d. people into two groups — HAMP 454:63
D. not nationally — STRA 979:1
People sometimes d. others — SPEN 957:89
divided in...death...not d. — BIBLE 110:44
dividend national d. is diminished — PIGOU 770:41
no d. from time's to-morrows — SASS 845:25
dividing line d. the state — GALB 412:79
divine all humanity d. — SHAW 923:76
Could show me so d. — MARV 658:77
d. and human history — GARC 414:19
'd.' creation — MILL 678:34
D. is everywhere — FRIE 405:58
d. mystery in things — DOST 341:48
double sacrilege on things d. — DRYD 350:47
far-off d. event — TENN 1000:63
hand that made us is d. — ADDI 7:23
image of d. beauty — AQUI 32:4
lool d. as you advance — NASH 720:60
lovely, Love D. — ROSS 824:78
necessity of d. nature — SPIN 960:48
political meetings...at a d. level — ACHE 2:22
prohibition so d. — SHAK 916:7
religion would still be holy and d. — BAUD 78:36
Right D. of Kings — POPE 783:4
some are fou o' love d. — BURNS 209:65
soul so near d. — BRON 190:86
to forgive, d. — POPE 778:81
divineness participation of d. — BACON 55:12
voice of the people hath some d. — BACON 56:35
diviner glad d.'s theme — DRYD 349:17
divines doubts 'mongst d. — SPEN 958:23
little statesmen, philosophers and d. — EMER 376:33
divinest two d. things this world has — HUNT 504:21
divinity d. and humanity — BACON 55:8
d. has provided mortals — GERB 419:97
d....in...human consciousness — DURK 357:72
d. in odd numbers — SHAK 878:23
d. or school metaphysics — HUME 504:10
d. that shapes our ends — SHAK 893:83
d. that stirs within us — ADDI 8:35
piece of d. in us — BROW 196:93
Pure Accident, pure d. — OATES 733:54
Seal of D. and Immortality — AUBR 45:37
such d. doth hedge a king — SHAK 892:67
What is d. — STEV 971:39
divinityship Plato...with all his d. — STER 969:10
division absurd d. into sexes — WAUGH 1056:73
alone in the third d. — NORTH 731:32
d. in our...prosperous society — MACM 636:15
d. is a thread — BUCH 202:22
d. of labor...social functions — DURK 357:69
d. of labour is nothing — MARX 660:7
effects of the d. of labour — SMITH 946:90
heated d. of opinion — TYNAN 1035:25
Irish experience...one of d. — DONO 339:35
music of d. — RALE 800:14
The deep d. — SWIN 988:53
divisions d. and precisions — ELIOT 367:58

divorce D. is the sign of knowledge — WILL 1083:92
D....political — MONT 703:88
with success come drugs, d. — HELL 468:86
Dixie whistle D. while humming — OBRI 734:69
dizzy I left the theatre, d. and pale — QUIR 798:72
do as they d. what I say — THAT 1008:24
capacity to d. — FAUL 383:80
d. for your country — KENN 551:65
d. or die! — BURNS 212:38
d. the perfectly correct thing — SHAW 924:11
d. what he got to d. — STEI 966:53
d. what I please — FRED 403:27
Do not as I d. unto others — SHAW 923:66
D. WHAT YOU WISH — RABE 799:86
don't have to d. anything — FURT 410:57
don't know what to d. — ERTZ 380:12
George—don't d. that — GREN 446:50
How Not To D. It — DICK 325:46
if we but know what to d. — EMER 376:27
isn't what I d., but how I d. it — WEST 1067:85
know not...what I d. — SHAK 860:90
Love only what you d. — RICH 809:42
often discover what will d. — SMIL 945:75
That thou doest, d. quickly — BIBLE 146:58
This will never d. — JEFF 520:98
will d. anything, Nerissa — SHAK 874:16
Doasyouwouldbedoneby Mrs D. — KING 558:97
docile warriors...prefer them d. — ANDR 18:11
docility d. in the pupil — RYLE 834:54
d....cardinal virtues — WOLL 1091:37
except d., obedience — WELD 1062:92
dock bringing the judge...into the d. — ALGR 13:26
dull, dark d. — GILB 425:88
put you in the d. — ADAMS 6:92
you may now leave the d. — ADAMS 6:89
docks No one on the d. — AMADO 15:63
doctor death Will seize the d. too — SHAK 916:17
d. advised him not to — GREG 446:47
D., d., what do you say — ROTH 826:12
d. forbids me to play — WOOL 1094:89
d. has made a few...advances — PROU 793:94
d....has mistaken his profession — SHAW 924:98
D. is said also — MORT 710:2
D. said that Death — WILDE 1078:99
don't accept any d. — VALLE 1038:47
drinks more than his own d. — BARA 70:5
Even if the d. — STEV 974:23
fee the d. for a nauseous draught — DRYD 352:87
I am a D. — ALBEE 11:88
interview with a d. — JAMES 515:6
keeps the d. away — ANON 30:60
man, not even a d. — NIGH 729:1
O master d., he is past — MASS 663:59
pass for a cathedral d. — JONS 534:77
take off your clothes for the d. — CAUS 246:65
thank God, D. — STAN 962:24
The d. found — GOLD 432:95
doctors d. considering it doubtful — DICK 321:49
d., judges...beadles — MARX 660:8
d. of profound wisdom — DICK 321:33
d. say this is no time — SHAK 866:37
if you believe the d. — SALI 839:34
Most of your d. — JONS 534:79
We d. know — CUMM 300:93
when d. disagree — POPE 780:25
doctrine against any country or d. — MARS 656:53
d. of President Monroe — WILS 1086:50
d. of those who desire — INGR 512:48
d. of 'separate but equal' — WARR 1053:27
d. shall drop as the rain — BIBLE 108:1
d....that each one should select — SHEL 931:51
keep out evil d. — MILT 685:56
Sa lyis thair ane d. wyse — HENR 473:69
to church...not for the d. — POPE 778:83

doctrine (*contd.*)
United States to the Monroe D. — ROOS 822:46
what is alarming in the d. — SART 844:12
women's eyes this d. — SHAK 865:22
world more than a d. — MILL 678:24
doctrines all d. plain and clear — BUTL 217:22
d. and practice of Socialism — MORR 709:81
d. chiefly vouched for — JAMES 518:51
fundamental d. of Christianity — LAW 585:61
seven great facts and d. — HUGEL 498:10
dodge trying to d. it — TREE 1025:44
Dodhead Jamie Telfer o' the fair D. — BALL 67:42
doe with the fallow d. — THOM 1012:14
doers d....not hearers only — BIBLE 155:51
not of d. — HAZL 463:13
does He who can, d. — SHAW 922:48
look for what she d. — GOET 431:70
dog A d.'s obeyed in office — SHAK 904:37
always be a lost d. somewhere — ANOU 30:72
Am I a d. — BIBLE 110:41
Artist as a Young D. — THOM 1010:63
as though my d. had just died — WATE 1055:49
be a d., a monkey, or a bear — ROCH 816:49
better than his d. — TENN 995:73
Beware of the d.! — ANON 20:42
circumcisèd d. — SHAK 900:64
communism is dead d. — SOLZ 952:97
country to heel like a d. — LESS 598:97
D. eat d. — CUOMO 301:9
d. goes, intently haphazard — LEVE 600:22
d. has a keener nose — SNYD 951:85
d. is full of fleas — ACHE 3:50
d. is turned to his own vomit — BIBLE 156:85
d. licked me — SIMON 939:82
d. returneth to his vomit — BIBLE 122:2
D. returns to his vomit — KIPL 565:25
d. that praised his fleas? — YEATS 1105:68
d. to the commonalty — SHAK 910:99
d. will have his day — SHAK 893:82
every d. his day — KING 558:94
give them to a d. — SHAK 878:22
giving your heart to a d. — KIPL 564:6
grin like a d. — BOOK 177:79
Holdfast is the only d. — SHAK 880:78
hot d. without the mustard — CHAR 253:93
I am his Highness' d. — POPE 783:12
I've been working like a d. — LENN 596:60
if a man bites a d. — BOGAN 171:61
If I had a yaller d. — TWAIN 1033:92
just another d. — WILL 1082:88
large, friendly d. — TOYN 1024:17
like a d. walking — JOHN 528:39
Like a d., he hunts — TENN 995:75
living d. is better than a dead lion — BIBLE 123:32
Love is a D. from Hell — BUKO 203:48
Mine enemy's d. — SHAK 904:40
No d. can go as fast — FLAN 391:24
not the lead d. — ANON 29:48
paint...a d. as Picasso — MARC 649:43
pancreatic ducts of d. — BANT 70:4
pick up a starving d. — TWAIN 1034:99
police d. of American fiction — FADI 382:53
portrait of a d. that I know — JOHN 532:39
Prevent the d. from barking — AUDEN 46:58
rather have a man d. — FLEM 394:63
rather hear my d. bark — SHAK 879:31
tail must wag the d. — KIPL 561:41
Thou art a beaten d. — POUND 787:86
tongue like the tail of a d. — NASHE 721:84
work like a d. — SIMON 938:79
You can teach an old d. — ONEI 740:66
dogged It's d. as it does — TROL 1028:80
dogma d. of the Ghost — RYLE 834:52
dogmatic erect, elegant, d. — REST 807:15

doorstep worry on the d. — FIEL 388:*55*
dooryard in the d. bloom'd — WHIT 1073:*92*
Dorcas D....full of good works — BIBLE 147:*90*
Dorsey Tommy D. breathed — SINA 940:*94*
dose double the d. — STOWE 978:*87*
Dostoevsky D., and a dozen others — LESS 598:*99*
dote d. on his very absence — SHAK 874:*19*
dots hurrying d. which are men — CUMM 299:*76*
those damned d. — CHUR 263:*94*
double D., d., toil and trouble — SHAK 909:*64*
Global d. zero — ANON 28:*21*
leading up a d. life — WILDE 1078:*87*
double-bed deep peace of the d.-b. — CAMP 226:*11*
doubled found myself d. over — IGNA 510:*28*
doublet Lord Hamlet, with his d. — SHAK 889:*86*
doublethink D. means the power — ORWE 745:*59*
doubt clouded with a d. — TENN 1004:*48*
curiosity, freckles and d. — PARK 754:*6*
Decide this d. for me — COWP 291:*26*
d. about...civilization — ORWE 744:*37*
d. and to be ignorant — UNAM 1036:*42*
d....cannot be removed — CARL 234:*55*
D. everything at least once — LICH 604:*88*
d. His infinite goodness — WALL 1049:*61*
D. is a necessary precondition — BART 74:*74*
d. is Devil-born — TENN 999:*52*
d. is our passion — JAMES 516:*23*
d. of future foes — ELIZ 373:*87*
D. thou the stars — SHAK 889:*91*
d. whether one may not — HAWT 461:*78*
for her, d. — BALZ 69:*76*
fouk wou'd hae a d. on — FERG 385:*15*
he was prey to d. — CHAT 254:*2*
Horror and d. distract — MILT 689:*45*
I d. some foul play — SHAK 888:*58*
imagine the least d. — DESC 317:*77*
in d. to act or rest — POPE 780:*42*
itself and d. of itself — TILL 1020:*62*
Life is d. — UNAM 1035:*39*
life of d. — BROW 199:*55*
more faith in honest d. — TENN 999:*53*
new philosophy calls all in d. — DONNE 338:*11*
no d. as to the elements — WHIT 1071:*61*
prolonged neurotic d. — BARZ 76:*99*
science teaches us to d. — BERN 96:*81*
sunnier side of d. — TENN 1005:*64*
though we oft d. — MILT 695:*59*
troubled with religious d. — CHES 259:*38*
what you cannot d. — SKEL 942:*42*
when all men d. you — KIPL 564:*8*
When in D.—Wash — GALL 412:*92*
When in d. — BLASS 169:*25*
when in d. — ITO 514:*82*
when in d., mumble — WAGN 1047:*27*
When in d., shout — HARD 456:*81*
When in d., tell the truth — TWAIN 1034:*4*
When in d., win — HOYLE 498:*1*
Where there is d. — FRAN 401:*91*
Where there is d. — THAT 1007:*11*
Why do you d. — JONS 536:*13*
wisdom, dying in d. — LOWE 617:*4*
doubted cannot be reasonably d. — HUME 503:*7*
that they cannot be d. — HUXL 508:*98*
doubter d. fights only with himself — GREE 445:*27*
doubtful d. dreams of dreams — SWIN 987:*38*
vain and d. good — SHAK 887:*41*
doubts content to begin with d. — BACON 54:*6*
d. 'mongst divines — SPEN 958:*23*
d. are traitors — SHAK 896:*63*
from these dead d. — MELV 667:*31*
my d. are done — DRYD 350:*50*
paint and have no d. — MICH 673:*35*
dough paper which the masses call d. — ANDR 18:*11*
dough-baked d.-b. prose — CAREW 232:*10*

doughnuts coffee and d. — DAVI 308:*15*
Douglas doughty D. — BALL -101:*29*
D. in his hall? — SCOTT 853:*56*
Doune Look owre the castle D. — BALL -101:*32*
dove Beside the springs of D. — WORD 1095:*8*
burnished d. — TENN 995:*71*
d. came to him in the evening — BIBLE 104:*12*
d. complaining — DAYL 310:*56*
d. descending breaks the air — ELIOT 373:*77*
d. found no rest — BIBLE 104:*11*
gently as any sucking d. — SHAK 870:*33*
Oh that I had wings like a d.! — BIBLE 116:*80*
She is coming, my d. — TENN 1001:*88*
silly, harmless, household d. — DRYD 348:*98*
Spirit of God descending like a d. — BIBLE 133:*28*
sweets d. died — KEATS 544:*43*
thou art the d. that flies — DONNE 339:*24*
wings like a d. — BOOK 177:*76*
dove-like wings outspread D.-l. — MILT 687:*86*
Dover candle at D., to shew light — JOHN 528:*38*
chalk cliffs of D. — BALD 65:*11*
dinner at D. — MACA 622:*93*
doves d.' eyes — BIBLE 124:*51*
harmless as d. — BIBLE 136:*76*
seats of them that sold d. — BIBLE 139:*31*
soft as the breast of d. — CORN 288:*58*
The moan of d. — TENN 998:*13*
dovish don't consider myself d. — SCHW 851:*28*
dowagers d. for deans — TENN 996:*91*
dowdiness beginning of d. — WILDE 1077:*73*
dowdy D. one year after — LAVER 584:*56*
dower ancient English d. — WORD 1096:*38*
Faith's transcendental d. — WORD 1100:*86*
for deathless d. — ROSS 824:*37*
dowered d. with a sense of humour — SOME 952:*1*
dowf sae d. and weary — BURNS 212:*35*
dowie d. houms o' Yarrow — BALL -101:*37*
down brought d. — HAIL 451:*13*
death...done as easily lying d. — ALLEN 14:*45*
D., d. to hell — SHAK 862:*33*
D. on your knees — SHAK 886:*13*
D. she came and found a boat — TENN 994:*46*
D. with purists! — BAND 69:*87*
had me d. — GERS 420:*13*
He that is d. needs fear no fall — BUNY 205:*73*
looked d. upon in our old age? — SCHU 851:*20*
never let you d. — WAUGH 1056:*62*
nobody wants you to put it d. — RUCK 828:*44*
set me d. again — FROST 406:*80*
started at the top and worked d. — WELL 1063:*4*
what they knocked d. — FENT 385:*1*
Why art thou cast d. — BIBLE 116:*69*
wish to level d. — JOHN 527:*37*
down-gyved d.-g. to his ankle — SHAK 889:*86*
down-to-earth people could be d. — SHUL 936:*37*
downfall d. of the British Empire — CHUR 263:*3*
downhill going d. ever since — SHAR 919:*84*
Downing from Germany to D. Street — CHAM 249:*19*
met Curzon in D. Street — BALD 64:*5*
downpour d. of apologies — BEER 83:*27*
downs carved upon her d. — HEAN 465:*35*
fair on the dewy d. — TENN 1002:*94*
o'er unhabitable d. — SWIFT 986:*4*
sun behind the D. — BETJ 100:*51*
downsitting knowest my d. — BIBLE 119:*48*
downstairs d. from their Ivory Towers — SMITH 947:*19*
why did you kick me d.? — BICK 160:*62*
downturns market d. predicted — SAMU 840:*46*
downwards look no way but d. — BUNY 205:*79*
dowry your d. 'greed on — SHAK 864:*78*
dowser d. and not a navvy — LEAV 591:*77*
Dowson D.,...degenerates! — ONEI 740:*59*
dozen d. times and he is great — JARR 518:*58*
she has at least a d. — WILDE 1076:*58*

draft d. an international agreement — TRUM 1030:*22*
happy d. surpassed the image — DRYD 350:*46*
drafted didn't get d. — DOWD 342:*77*
draftsman d. of words — CUMM 300:*98*
drag time did d. along — TWAIN 1033:*84*
dragging D. the whole s. — FROST 406:*74*
keeps d. me along — SEVI 859:*60*
dragnet swept like a d. — DRYD 352:*82*
dragon ant...in his d. world — POUND 786:*84*
d., a symbol — MOORE 705:*25*
flagon with the d. — PANA 752:*75*
laid hold on the d. — BIBLE 158:*32*
Michael...fought against the d. — BIBLE 157:*21*
dragonfly d. Hangs — ROSS 824:*87*
dragons argosy of crocs and d. — AMIS 17:*87*
Bores have succeeded to d. — DISR 332:*74*
d. of Laune and Lane — ORAH 741:*77*
habitation of d. — BIBLE 126:*82*
spleen of fairy d. — SHAK 863:*67*
drain d. him dry as hay — SHAK 907:*13*
From this foul d. — TOCQ 1022:*82*
put it down the d. — HERB 474:*96*
drains Deity and the D. — STRA 979:*95*
drake neckyd lyke a d. — BERN 97:*92*
Drake Hutton and Betsy D. — NIVEN 730:*6*
dram Take aff your d.! — BURNS 209:*72*
drama A good d. critic — TYNAN 1035:*30*
D. is action, sir — PIRA 770:*50*
D. is the third great form — HUGO 501:*7*
d.'s patrons give — JOHN 525:*80*
enemy of the ear in real d. — WILD 1080:*34*
episode in a general d. — HARDY 456:*96*
exact past d. — PRIT 791:*72*
lexicon of conflict and d. — SAFI 835:*67*
marvel at the d. — SCRI 857:*24*
Mistaken Identity is to D. — ABSE 1:*8*
mystical d. of animal life — AMIS 17:*85*
nodus of a d. — CARL 235:*63*
one character in literature or d. — PAGE 749:*31*
respond to a d. — MAMET 643:*43*
talent for d. — VIDAL 1044:*56*
Viewed as a d. — GRIF 447:*60*
dramatic d. criticism...tattoo — BROWN 194:*55*
four most d. words — HART 459:*48*
modern era is d. — HUGO 501:*56*
thirty-seventh d. situation — JARRY 519:*70*
drank d. my ale — FARQ 383:*70*
d. without the provocation — SWIFT 985:*89*
drappie d. in our e'e — BURNS 211:*2*
draught for a d. of vintage! — KEATS 547:*14*
nauseous d. of life — ROCH 816:*53*
nauseous d. — DRYD 352:*87*
draughts great d. of time — BERR 98:*10*
peculiarly susceptible to d. — WILDE 1078:*88*
shallow d. intoxicate — POPE 778:*79*
draughtsman Dali is a good d. — ORWE 745:*65*
draw d. first, to cultivate the Spirit — MATI 664:*75*
D. more and more often — PISS 771:*60*
d. something every day — CENN -101:*94*
d. upon content — GOLD 432:*2*
d. what you see only in memory — DEGAS 312:*94*
seemed to d. the same way — HIRS 482:*23*
wish to d. tears — HORA 493:*31*
drawback d. of all sea-side places — DOUG 342:*54*
drawbacks everything has its d. — JERO 521:*7*
drawer Feminism...vegetable d. — PAGL 749:*36*
drawers d....of political cancer — ANON 29:*32*
drawing art of d. — LIEB 604:*90*
D. is not the form — DEGAS 312:*92*
D. is only a necessary evil — HEIN 467:*74*
growing old in d. nothing up! — COWP 293:*57*
three-dimensional d. — HIRS 482:*21*
drawing-down a d. of blinds — OWEN 748:*8*
drawing-room magnificent in a d. — THUR 1018:*11*

drawing-room (*contd.*)
Suez canal…through my d.-. — EDEN 360:24
drawl quickest on the d.? — NEW 724:23
drawling-master D….conger-eel — CARR 239:37
drayhorse greatness is only the d. — PATC 759:90
dread close your eyes with holy d. — COLE 275:18
  d. of something after death — SHAK 890:21
  every reason to d. — JORD 536:29
  greatest d. of all — BETJ 101:59
  secret d., and inward horror — ADDI 8:35
  silence…fills me with d. — PASC 757:60
  walk in fear and d. — COLE 274:93
dreadful Death…called thee d. — DONNE 338:4
  d. to look on — HAGG 450:7
dream And d. about the great — YEATS 1105:64
  as a d. doth flatter — SHAK 914:78
  as thou mightst in a d. — SHEL 932:66
  Because thou must not d. — ARNO 36:68
  behold it was a d. — BUNY 205:70
  behold, it was a d. — BIBLE 105:44
  better to d. …than to live — PROU 792:87
  consecration, and the poet's d. — WORD 1099:71
  corresponds to our d. life — MAMET 643:43
  deep d. of peace — HUNT 505:27
  draw nearer to d. — CHIR 260:53
  d. about the future — HAMM 453:48
  d. comes to an end — GIRO 429:47
  d. freely — GAUG 416:40
  d. my d.s away — FLAN 391:23
  d. of a common language — RICH 809:52
  d. of being dressed in Paris — ANON 26:36
  D. Of Electric Sheep? — DICK 320:10
  d. of Home — FORD 397:20
  d. of independent power — JAY 519:72
  d. of Jeannie — FOST 399:61
  d. of life — JARR 518:57
  d. of life — SHEL 931:40
  d. of money-bags — SHAK 874:28
  d. of revolution — STOP 978:76
  d. of social justice — NGUY 725:48
  d. of the soft look — YEATS 1105:60
  d. that I am home again! — FLEC 393:53
  d. that they clarify — HERN 476:44
  d. things that never were — SHAW 926:44
  dreamed a dolefu' d. — BALL -101:38
  dreamed of was a d. — ROSS 823:69
  Everlasting peace is a d. — MOLT 699:36
  freshness of a d. — WORD 1097:48
  glory and the d. — WORD 1098:50
  golden d. of love and friendship — DRYD 349:1
  have had a d. past — SHAK 871:52
  held me like a d. — WORD 1096:22
  I have a d. — KING 557:76
  I have a d. — KING 557:82
  If you can d. — KIPL 564:8
  in a d. of passion — SHAK 890:14
  In a d. — SEXT 859:64
  Liberals can d. — MACL 634:90
  life be but a d. — PRIOR 791:62
  Life is but a D. — LI 603:77
  Life is…a bad d. — ONEI 740:53
  Lives in a d. — LENN 596:62
  man that is born falls into a d. — CONR 284:94
  men d., but not equally — LAWR 587:13
  most blissful d. as a child — SHIP 935:22
  must we d. our d.s — BISH 164:34
  new pictures as in a d. — MARC 649:40
  old men shall d. d.s — BIBLE 130:55
  old men's d.! — DRYD 349:17
  one that hath a weary d. — TENN 994:48
  Out of a misty d. — DOWS 343:82
  perchance to d. — SHAK 890:21
  phantasma, or a hideous d. — SHAK 883:27
  pictures come to me as if in a d. — VAN 1039:1

dream (*contd.*)
  quiet sleep and a sweet d. — MASE 661:34
  shining and perishable d. — DIDI 330:45
  silence of a d. — ROSS 823:67
  sister to the d. — BAUD 77:25
  So runs my d. — TENN 999:38
  Soft, I did but d. — SHAK 863:62
  something…to d. about — FORD 397:23
  Success is the American D. — LEGU 594:29
  To d. is happiness — HUGO 501:66
  too old to d. — HAMM 454:53
  vanished like a d. — CARL 236:90
  waking from a troubled d. — HAWT 461:65
  We live, as we d. — CONR 284:90
  What happens to a d. deferred? — HUGH 499:18
  wrecks of a dissolving d. — SHEL 932:64
dreamed at night he d. of it — GREE 444:6
dreamer Beautiful d. — FOST 399:62
  Behold, this d. cometh — BIBLE 105:40
  d. of dreams — BIBLE 108:94
  poet and the d. — KEATS 545:70
dreamers d. of the day — LAWR 587:13
  Soldiers are d. — SASS 845:25
  We have been the d. — BEVAN 101:62
dreamest What d. thou, drunkard — SKEL 942:36
dreaming boys are d. wicked — THOM 1011:81
  D. like a love-adept — SHEL 930:20
  d. of a White Christmas — BERL 95:62
  d. spires — ARNO 39:15
  while d. before it — GAUG 416:39
dreamlike a fact…so d. — RICH 809:44
dreams according to his d. — HUGO 502:87
  advertising…dealt in fugutive d. — QUEN 797:54
  armoured cars of d. — BISH 163:30
  awoke…from uneasy d. — KAFKA 541:86
  books are either d. — LOWE 615:73
  City of perspiring d. — RAND 802:31
  Come to me in my d. — ARNO 36:71
  curate her d. and gallery — DUNN 356:56
  different hopes, different d. — CART 242:2
  doubtful d. of d. — SWIN 987:38
  dreamer of d. — BIBLE 108:94
  D. and drives — RODG 818:85
  d., and our hopes — POPP 784:25
  d. are all egocentric — WAUGH 1057:2
  d….are infanticiddle — NASH 720:59
  d. be tossed and blown — HAMM 454:54
  d. do show thee me — SHAK 913:61
  D. have only the pigmentation — BARN 72:27
  d. in pale battalions — SORL 953:23
  d. of a poet — JOHN 526:8
  d. of our childhood — THOR 1016:62
  d. of perfection — FAUL 384:85
  d. of the participation — NICH 726:50
  d. that have stayed with me — BRON 191:10
  Fanatics have their d. — KEATS 545:68
  Full of sweet d. — KEATS 545:56
  had dreamed d. — THOM 1009:50
  have no d. — VREE 1047:23
  have only my d. — YEATS 1105:65
  he hunts in d. — TENN 995:75
  he pulls the legs of his d. — THOM 1011:84
  help of d. — WORD 1100:78
  his summer d. — SHEL 928:88
  history of irresponsible d. — POPP 784:26
  hopes and d. of the Future — FRAME 400:78
  I talk of d. — SHAK 868:80
  if empty d. so please — HERR 477:53
  in d. behold the Hebrides — GALT 413:8
  In my d. there is a country — SHAW 923:76
  in that sleep of death what d. — SHAK 890:21
  interpretation of d. — FREUD 404:41
  life together with your d. — MOORE 704:2
  Made holy by their d. — GIBS 422:39

  More d. are destroyed — SKEL 942:50
dreams (*contd.*)
  never overstepped it save in d. — FROST 407:83
  Out of d., songs — HERZL 478:75
  Real are the d. of Gods — KEATS 546:76
  shadows and in d. — STEV 971:39
  steeple of my d. — DEBU 311:86
  substance of my d. — SASS 845:30
  such stuff As d. are made — SHAK 917:37
  talking about d. — STERN 968:86
  that I have bad d. — SHAK 890:99
  The quick D. — SHEL 930:37
  The way you haunt my d. — GERS 420:11
  treasured d. — WORD 1098:57
  with their mothers in d. — SOPH 953:22
dreamt d. I went to Manderley again — DU 354:31
  d. of in our philosophy — SHAK 889:84
  d. there was an Emperor — SHAK 906:99
  often d. of unhappiness — SHAK 879:42
dreamtime easy Eden-d. — WRIG 1101:70
dreariness just to escape this d. — PERCY 766:84
  unredeemed d. of thought — POE 775:41
dreary All seems d., savage — SCHAW 847:61
dregs drain not to its d. the urn — SHEL 932:65
  of life — DRYD 347:77
dreich kirkyairdielike and d. — YOUNG 1108:7
drenching in for a thorough d. — BEER 83:27
dress begin to d. ourselves — RICH 809:50
  car has become an article of d. — MACL 635:95
  cool white d. — FIRB 389:2
  cotton flowers of her d. — THOM 1011:88
  crocus d. — JOYCE 538:56
  Diet, Furniture and D. — MAND 645:71
  d. according to your age — DISR 334:26
  d. and manners in England — SHAW 920:4
  d. by yellow candle-light — STEV 975:32
  D. is a form of visual art — HOLL 485:70
  d. is very independent — GASK 415:33
  d. me In borrowed robes? — SHAK 907:31
  d. of thought — POPE 778:81
  d. …the badge of lost innocence — PAINE 750:44
  Fond Pride of D. — FRAN 402:5
  fop values himself upon his d. — CHES 257:71
  glory of man is his d. — ANON 21:51
  Heaven…how they d.! — DICK 322:66
  in a last month's d. — NASH 719:48
  its mortal d. — YEATS 1106:79
  make their d. a principal part — HAZL 463:3
  man cannot d. — STER 970:17
  no such thing as a moral d. — CHUR 263:91
  noble youth did d. — SHAK 877:90
  not a woman's d…a man's d. — BOWIE 181:51
  Peace, the human d. — BLAKE 166:69
  sweet disorder in the d. — HERR 478:68
  this fleshly d. — VAUG 1041:16
  To d., to darn, to flower — LEWIS 601:46
  whose d. no one observes — TROL 1028:92
  Women fond of d. — DE 311:63
dressed All D. Up — BURT 213:60
  d. exactly like her — NASH 720:71
  d. for this short comedy — RALE 800:14
  d. in Paris — ANON 26:36
  good spirits…when he's well d. — DICK 322:69
dresser d. filled with shining delph — COLUM 278:62
dresses d. make a curious sound — STEV 975:36
  silk d. out of worms — STEV 972:61
dressmaker ask for…your d. — DACHE 303:37
drift 'twas Peter's d. — SHEL 928:95
driftwood found out about the d.. — ROSE 823:59
drill d. to the tooth of America — CLIN 269:74
drill-sergeant d.-s. or animal trainer — RYLE 834:54
drink abolition of strong d. — MACG 630:26
  any little delicate thing to d. — DICK 325:72
  as oft as ye d. it — BIBLE 150:59

drink (*contd.*)
be sure to d. it	TAO 991:*97*
better to d. than to fight	KING 559:*3*
careful not to d.	HAMM 454:*60*
damn the d. they'll swally	ONOL 734:*68*
D. a health to	SYNGE 988:*63*
d. all the d.	KEEN 548:*24*
D. and dance	PARK 754:*9*
D. deep, or taste not	POPE 778:*79*
d. for a living	KERR 553:*17*
D.!, for you know not	FITZ 390:*90*
D….is stronger than unionism	LAWS 587:*19*
d. life to the lees	TENN 994:*58*
D. not the third glasse	HERB 474:*7*
d. one another's healths	JERO 521:*5*
d. sooner than pray	SHAK 875:*47*
d. takes the man	LEWIS 602:*58*
D. this in remembrance	BOOK 175:*32*
d. thy wine with a merry heart	BIBLE 123:*33*
d. to her as long	SHAK 894:*96*
D. to me, only	JONS 535:*5*
d. to obliviate that decent actor	FLYNN 395:*81*
d. unto one of these little ones	BIBLE 136:*81*
d. when we are not thirsty	BEAU 80:*64*
dripping blood our only d.	ELIOT 371:*52*
drove me to d.	FIEL 388:*61*
Eat, d., and love	BYRON 223:*64*
every creature d. but I	COWL 291:*17*
every man should eat and d.	BIBLE 122:*20*
first d. on a Sunday morning	MACC 627:*68*
follow strong d.	BIBLE 124:*59*
garments, heavy with their d.	SHAK 892:*72*
go a week without a d.	LEWIS 601:*47*
good as d.	CHES 258:*12*
has taken to d.	TARK 991:*98*
I am … a little in d.	STEE 964:*12*
Let others d. thee freely	HERR 477:*58*
let us eat and d.	BIBLE 125:*71*
let us eat and d.	BIBLE 151:*69*
Love…is not meat and d.	MILL 676:*92*
meaning is my meat and d.	BROW 198:*45*
Nor any drop to d.	COLE 273:*88*
not eat with you, d. with you	SHAK 874:*18*
Now is the time to d.	HORA 493:*19*
One more d.	PARK 755:*21*
rule never to d. by daylight	MENC 669:*71*
taste any d. once	CABE 224:*75*
taste who always d.	PRIOR 790:*48*
teach you to d. deep	SHAK 888:*55*
That I might d.	KEATS 547:*14*
The more you d.	POPE 782:*79*
they gave me vinegar to d.	BOOK 177:*83*
they take to it like d.	HAZZ 464:*27*
think that I can d.	ANON 23:*85*
this calls for a d.	THUR 1019:*41*
those who don't d.	KEIL 548:*28*
to eat and d.	GUIL 448:*78*
too early for a d.?	GORD 435:*66*
wants but little d. below	HOLM 486:*77*
We d. to thee	TENN 1000:*65*
we d. too much tea	PRIE 790:*39*
what d. a man will have	MARQ 656:*49*
Whene'er to d. you are inclin'd	BURNS 212:*21*
wittles and d. to me	DICK 324:*9*

drink-well Eat-well is d.-w.'s brother   FULL 410:*49*
drinker first great…literary d.   THUR 1019:*42*
drinkers moderate d. both   SHAW 922:*55*
drinking A d. man's someone   WILL 1082:*69*
curse of the d. classes	WILDE 1079:*11*
damnable degrees of d.	WEBS 1059:*26*
D. in the morning	RABE 798:*82*
D. is the soldier's pleasure	DRYD 351:*69*
d. out of spittoons	HEMI 471:*39*
d. …sobers us again	POPE 778:*79*

drinking (*contd.*)
D. the best tea	SNOW 950:*70*
D., to engender wit	ROCH 817:*62*
from robbing…next to d.	DEQU 316:*68*
hae been merry d.	BURNS 210:*79*
kept on d.	ROBI 815:*28*
much d., little thinking	SWIFT 984:*76*
no d. after death	FLET 394:*70*
red-hot with d.	SHAK 917:*38*
redfaced from eating and d.	ABBO 1:*1*
there's nothing like d.	DIBD 319:*6*
very merry, dancing, d.	DRYD 352:*95*

drinks couple of d. on a Saturday   FYFFE 410:*63*
he d. no wine	SHAK 878:*6*
He that d. fast	FRAN 402:*2*

drive d. and make love   MOSS 711:*9*
d. fast and furious	ABSE 1:*9*
d. one from home	HOOD 489:*43*

drivel Dilutes with d.   BYRON 219:*67*
when hearing this d.?	GERS 420:*9*

driveling occupy some d. reader   SARD 843:*94*
driven writer is d. out far   HEMI 471:*41*
driver Do people…Wave at the d.   MACG 630:*31*
hitting the d. so good	TREV 1026:*52*
in the d.'s seat	BEAV 81:*84*

drivers d. of negroes   JOHN 529:*77*
driving like the d. of Jehu   BIBLE 111:*79*
dromedary d., two; Or else   NASH 719:*53*
drone d. of alliterations   BROY 201:*5*
droop begin to d. and drowse   SHAK 909:*60*
D. in a hundred A. B. C.'s	ELIOT 368:*73*
fortunes Will ever after d.	SHAK 916:*20*

drop don't d. players   SHAN 918:*71*
d. of a bucket	BIBLE 126:*88*
d. of hatred in your soul	MUNRO 714:*59*
d. serene hath quenched	MILT 689:*30*
Every d. of ink	WALP 1051:*82*
last d. into that…glass	FITZ 390:*3*
Nor any d. to drink	COLE 273:*88*
one d. of negro blood	HUGH 499:*22*
One d. would save my soul	MARL 654:*20*
Raineth d. and staineth slop	POUND 785:*51*
That cordial d.	ROCH 816:*53*

droppeth d. as the gentle rain   SHAK 873:*92*
dropping d. in a very rainy day   BIBLE 122:*8*
drops dear to me as are the ruddy d.   SHAK 883:*31*
like d. of water	JOYCE 538:*43*
These are gracious d.	SHAK 884:*55*

dross the rest is d.   POUND 786:*83*
drought Such thirst will argue d.   CAREW 232:*7*
droughts d. and flooding rains   MACK 632:*52*
drove lifts a d. from a Sassenach   SCOTT 854:*70*
drown d. my book   SHAK 917:*40*
drowned d. a blind bitch's puppies   SHAK 878:*22*
d. in the honey	HAWT 461:*67*
lies d. with us	HERR 477:*62*
photograph…after I d.	ATWO 44:*16*
went and d. themselves	ANON 25:*22*

drowning guardianship…against d.   PATR 761:*15*
like death by d.	FERB 385:*11*
not waving but d.	SMITH 948:*33*

drowns With too much labour d.   SHAK 866:*35*
drowsy dull ear of a d. man   SHAK 872:*67*
drudge harmless d.   JOHN 526:*12*
drudgery Makes d. divine   HERB 474:*12*
drug alleyways and d. fiends   LIND 605:*11*
D. misuse is not a disease	DICK 320:*12*
Everything is a dangerous d.	CONN 283:*72*
most powerful d. used	KIPL 565:*24*
Poetry's a mere d.	FARQ 383:*65*
rape, sodomy and d. addiction	COOK 286:*27*
what purgative d.	SHAK 910:*84*

drugging not d., not robbing   PACK 749:*28*
drugs d. cause cramp   PARK 754:*13*

drugs (*contd.*)
d….electrical appliances	AUDEN 49:*2*
Sex 'n' d. 'n' rock 'n' roll	DURY 357:*81*
taken illegal d.	JOHN 523:*41*
with success come d.	HELL 468:*86*

druid same old d. Time   ROSE 823:*60*
drum Dumb as a d.   DICK 320:*24*
trumpet and the steady d.	MACC 625:*40*
with his big bass d.	LIND 605:*10*
with muffled d.	AUDEN 46:*58*

Drumcliffe In D. churchyard   YEATS 1107:*93*
drummer hears a different d.   THOR 1017:*91*
drums are your d. a-beating yet?   SKIR 943:*56*
d. begin to roll	KIPL 560:*31*
Of guns, and d., and wounds	SHAK 875:*42*
Still, like muffled d.	LONG 611:*95*
trumpets, beat the d.!	MORE 707:*59*

drunk art of getting it   JOHN 530:*2*
Be not d. with wine	BIBLE 152:*3*
best audience…a little d.	BARK 71:*20*
d. and asleep	STEV 971:*47*
d. his fill	SCOTT 853:*61*
D. many times a day	SHAK 897:*89*
d. we like our art	LUCAS 618:*29*
d. with sight of power	KIPL 562:*62*
getting over a four-day d.	HELL 469:*3*
good d….a good bartender	BISH 164:*36*
got d. at onch	LONG 610:*91*
hasten to be d.	DRYD 352:*86*
I d. him to his bed	SHAK 905:*75*
Man…must get d.	BYRON 222:*43*
My mother, d. or sober	CHES 258:*91*
not genteel when he gets d.	BOSW 180:*32*
not so think as you d.	SQUI 961:*66*
Of course I'm d.	RUSS 834:*45*
Often d., and seldom sober	FULL 410:*55*
seen Wordsworth d.	HOUS 495:*67*
That hath hath made them d.	SHAK 908:*42*
this meeting is d.	DICK 320:*27*
very d. and very slovenly	WYCH 1103:*40*
way that a d. uses lamp-posts	LANG 579:*66*

drunkard d., my navigator   SEXT 859:*62*
earth shall reel…like a d.	BIBLE 125:*72*
rolling English d.	CHES 259:*31*
take this d. for a god	SHAK 917:*43*
What dreamest thou, d.	SKEL 942:*36*

drunkards as d. sing and vomit   CARRA 237:*16*
have to become d. first	JONES 533:*54*
miserly d.	WILD 1079:*31*

drunken d. officer of British rule   WALC 1048:*31*
not true that d. men cannot beget	YEATS 1107:*95*
stagger like a d. man	BIBLE 118:*21*

drunkenness anything so bad as d.   CHES 258:*12*
d. expands	JAMES 517:*45*
D. is a joy reserved	CABE 224:*74*
D. is his best virtue	SHAK 901:*81*
man that is given to d.	BIBLE 132:*5*
time for d.	BAUD 77:*30*

drunks d. and Americans   MOYN 711:*17*
for two d.	TWAIN 1033:*83*

Drury I did in D. Lane see   PEPYS 765:*73*
dry d. brain in a d. season   ELIOT 368:*72*
hearts very d. and tough	HOOK 490:*56*
held out to d.	REAG 804:*65*
in a d. and thirsty land	BIBLE 116:*83*
into a d. Martini	ANON 26:*38*
let us assemble, d., gray, spare	RANS 802:*33*
Like giving d. birth	SIMP 939:*89*
Sierras Will be d.	SNYD 951:*82*
within the womb is d.	HOPE 490:*72*
Yankees, feeling very d.	ANON 25:*33*

dry-goods churches and d.-g. stores   MACM 636:*23*
Dryad light-winged D. of the trees   KEATS 547:*13*
Dryden D. fails to render him   ARNO 38:*5*

Dryden (*contd.*)

D., Pope and all their school	ARNO 40:40
Ev'n copious D.	POPE 782:83
dual as antiquated as a d.	GOOCH 435:54
Everyone…holds d. citizenship	SONT 953:11
dualism d. which now weighs	DEWEY 319:95
Dublin features of the D. style	KENN 551:81
served in all the pubs in D.	DONL 336:61
ducat Dead for a d., dead	SHAK 892:52
Duchess D. of Malfi still	WEBS 1061:69
in the arms…of a D.	JOHN 530:1
duck forgot to d.	DEMP 315:47
O dainty d.	SHAK 871:58
ducks Four d. on a pond	ALLI 15:54
ducts pancreatic d. of dog	BANT 70:4
due give the devil his d.	SHAK 875:41
to every one his d.	JUST 540:76
duelling My soul's a d. ground	RICK 811:75
duellist d., a d.	SHAK 869:99
dues Render…to all their d.	BIBLE 149:39
duet d. between a tuba and a piccolo	DONA 335:58
d. of two nightingales	STEV 972:65
dugs old man with wrinkled d.	ELIOT 369:89
duke D. of Plaza-Toro!	GILB 426:95
D. takes a town	POMP 777:69
everybody praised the D.	SOUT 954:33
to the D.'s house	PEPYS 765:71
with the D. in Flanders	LOWE 615:74
Duke will make the D. say	SHAK 870:32
dukes drawing room full of d.	AUDEN 48:92
dulce D. et decorum est	HORA 493:22
D. et decorum est	OWEN 748:13
pro patria, non 'd.'	POUND 786:64
dulcimer damsel with a d.	COLE 275:17
dull But you are d.	MIDD 673:39
d. and mean	WHIT 1074:6
d., insipid thing is a billet-doux	ETHE 380:14
first requirement…be d.	ACHE 3:35
found it so intolerably d.	DARW 306:86
I am always deadly d.	BEER 83:25
In this d. world	SHAK 906:95
Like a d. actor	SHAK 911:15
not stupid, but…very d.	BEAV 80:80
recognize when he is d.	AUCH 46:39
To make dictionaries is d. work	JOHN 526:10
dullard d.'s envy of brilliant men	BEER 83:40
dullest d. person in the world	BENS 92:10
dullness cardinal sin is d.	CAPRA 231:92
everyday life, with its…deadly d.	EINS 363:63
invincible d.	JONS 535:95
little d. spoils it	YOUR 1108:7
reconciliation with d.	LOWE 617:11
'tis a good d.	SHAK 916:21
dumb because the brutes are d.?	ELIOT 365:4
cannot be absolutely d.	FORD 396:1
deaf to hear, and the d. to speak	BIBLE 141:66
D. as a drum	DICK 320:24
d., dark, dull, bitter belly-tension	GIBB 422:36
d. enough to turn it down	TAYL 992:16
D., inscrutable and grand	ARNO 38:99
d. to say how hot	GRAV 439:17
Homage to plain d. luck	ACHE 3:47
if you can't be d.	OHARA 737:10
Our D. Friends	PARK 754:1
So d. he can't fart	JOHN 524:55
tongue of the d. sing	BIBLE 126:82
dump What a d.!	COFF 272:67
Dunblane flower o' D.	TANN 991:96
Duncan D. is in his grave	SHAK 909:58
Hear it not, D.	SHAK 908:41
wake D. with thy knocking	TWAIN 1033:89
dunce amiable d.	CLIF 269:14
because…you're a d.	JOHN 531:19
d. that has been sent to roam	COWP 292:47

dunce (*contd.*)

D. the second reigns	POPE 782:91
d. with wits	POPE 783:1
dunces A wit with a d.	POPE 783:1
d. are all…against him	SWIFT 984:72
Dundee bonnet of Bonny D.	SCOTT 856:16
piper o' D.?	ANON 23:99
stay langer in Bonny D.!	SCOTT 855:85
Dunfermline king sits in D.	BALL 67:47
dung better to sniff France's d.	HO 482:34
d. and corrupcioun!	CHAU 255:41
floors of plaister, and the walls of d.	POPE 780:30
more reeking the d.	INNO 512:55
dungeon door out of the d. of self	MACD 628:99
d. flamed with light	WESL 1066:58
d. horrible, on all sides	MILT 687:90
d. of despair	CESA 248:2
d. of the self	CONN 283:77
Himself in his own d.	MILT 683:28
imprisonment! The D. of	MILT 694:43
Nor airless d.	SHAK 883:25
prisoner in his d.	FLAU 393:43
worse than chains, D.	MILT 694:40
dunghill cock crowing on its own d.	ALDI 12:4
This enormous d.	VOLT 1046:12
Upon the d.	SHAK 903:28
Dunkirk from D. to Belgrade	DAVIS 309:38
the epic of D.	PRIE 790:37
Dunsinane do come to D.	TWAIN 1033:89
duo most dangerous d.	SCAR 846:55
duodecimos humbler band of d.	CRAB 293:67
dupes If hopes were d.	CLOU 270:32
dusk each slow d.	OWEN 748:8
for a moment in the d.	BROW 197:26
In the d.	GILB 423:53
dust a handful of d.	TENN 1001:90
But what is D.	SITW 941:23
chimney-sweepers, come to d.	SHAK 916:16
comprehended the d. of the earth	BIBLE 126:87
darkened with filthy d.	SPEN 958:10
dialogue between Spirit and D.	DICK 328:10
D. as we are	WORD 1096:21
d. forbids the birds	SITW 941:11
D. in the air	ELIOT 372:71
d., in the cool tombs	SAND 841:61
d. of creeds outworn	SHEL 930:19
d. of the churchyard	DONNE 338:17
d. on the nettles	THOM 1012:12
d. return to the earth	BIBLE 123:42
d. returneth to d. again	GORD 435:63
d. shall be the serpent's meat	BIBLE 128:16
d. shalt thou eat	BIBLE 103:98
d. thou art, and unto d.	BIBLE 103:2
d. to d.	BOOK 176:58
D. to the d.!	SHEL 931:45
d. would hear her	TENN 1001:88
Ere Babylon was d.	SHEL 929:13
Excuse My D.	PARK 753:89
fear in a handful of d.	ELIOT 368:82
fine d.	KELM 548:31
first raised a d.	BERK 95:50
formed man out of d.	BIBLE 103:88
frame was D.	DICK 328:17
glory smeared in d. and blood	SHAK 862:31
Guilty of d. and sin	HERB 475:17
Half d., half deity	BYRON 221:20
heat of life in the handful of d.	CONR 284:98
In that rich d. a richer d.	BROO 192:21
in the d. be equal made	SHIR 935:27
into the d. of death	BIBLE 114:49
isn't just d.	MACA 621:76
leaves…turning to d.	ANON 21:56
like d. that is blown away	BIBLE 131:84
little d. of praise	TENN 999:47

dust (*contd.*)

noble father in the d.	SHAK 888:48
not without d. and heat	MILT 685:63
O'er English d.	MACA 624:25
pays us but with age and d.	RALE 800:16
piles of dry d.	GLAS 430:60
proud and angry d.	HOUS 496:71
provoke the silent d.	GRAY 442:67
recover once my d.	MONT 703:93
remembereth that we are d.	BIBLE 118:14
repent in d. and ashes	BIBLE 113:27
save from d.	SPEN 956:74
shouldst give d. a tongue	HERB 475:31
this unprofitable d.	WORD 1095:11
Time, a maniac scattering d.	TENN 999:35
To die in d.	SPEN 959:28
vex the unhappy d.	TENN 998:14
we're only made out of d.	DICK 320:9
what a d. do I raise	BACON 59:28
what is this quintessence of d.?	SHAK 890:4
when this d. falls	VAUG 1041:17
You are not worth the d.	SHAK 903:31
dustbin d. upset in a high wind	GOLD 432:86
dustheap d. of history	TROT 1029:2
dusty d. to the grave	STEV 974:9
Dutch D. may have their Holland	JOHN 524:60
fault of the D.	CANN 230:72
flowered once for D. sailor's eyes	FITZ 391:6
Dutchman icicle on a D.'s beard	SHAK 895:27
duties brace ourselves to do our d.	CHUR 264:15
d. as King	EDWA 362:51
d. of the physician	OSLER 746:72
If I had no d.	JOHN 530:2
lowliest d. on herself	WORD 1096:38
No d., only opportunities	ANON 28:26
Property has its d.	DRUM 346:47
duty absolved from all d.	PEAC 762:29
act…of d. and of justice	PITT 771:71
bounds of their d.	RICH 810:68
crimes committed in the name of d.	SNOW 951:76
declares that it is his d.	SHAW 921:20
do our d. as such	GLAD 429:55
Do the D. which lies nearest thee	CARL 234:55
do your d.	BADE 60:44
done my d. as a man	TENN 1005:60
d. as we understand it	LINC 605:3
d. in that state of life	BOOK 175:38
d. laid down upon us by God	CARY 243:16
d. of a democracy	WHITE 1070:25
d. of a journalist	STEAD 964:7
d. of a serious biographer	TOYN 1024:23
d. of an opposition	CHUR 263:95
d. of being happy	STEV 974:20
d. of government	PAINE 750:45
d. of the writer	KENN 552:87
d., patriotism…clad	LLOY 608:58
d. that Mr Bulstrode rarely shrank	ELIOT 366:36
d. to arouse the sleeper	BETH 99:24
d. to have reported it	HELL 468:37
d. to the Queen	MARL 652:81
d. to try and prevent it	MILN 681:84
d.…to wield the sword of France	DEGA 313:98
d., your reward, your destiny	HAMM 453:48
every man will do his d.	NELS 722:99
Every subject's d.	SHAK 881:92
fattening is the first d.	SPEKE 955:62
fiction…painful d.	WILDE 1079:12
first d. of a state	RUSK 831:3
first d. of the press	TIMES 1021:71
first d. to serve society	JOHN 528:49
first d.…is not to be poor	SHAW 923:77
God, I have done my d.	NELS 722:2
health is a d.	SPEN 955:65
in d. both equally bound	STER 968:88

duty (*contd.*)
little d. and less love	SHAK 877:78
must do our d.	CECIL 247:84
my d. to have loved	TENN 1003:20
one d. we owe to history	WILDE 1076:38
one's d. to drown it	WILDE 1076:48
our d. to follow	PALM 752:70
our only d.	GERG 420:2
perceive here a divided d.	SHAK 898:10
professional d. of the…agent	OGIL 736:3
religious sense of d.	DICK 327:79
Self-development is a higher d.	STAN 963:91
service is the common d.	ROCK 817:71
stage of d. run	KEN 549:47
stirring of d.	CURZ 302:29
terrible notions of d.	CLOU 271:41
tried to do his d.	MACA 621:75
urge thy d.	SHAK 884:61
whole d. of man	BIBLE 124:44

dwarf giant d., Dan Cupid — SHAK 865:13
dwarfish Upon a d. thief — SHAK 910:79
dwarfs D. standing on the shoulders — BERN 96:73
dwell at ease for aye to d. — TENN 994:54
D. I but in the suburbs	SHAK 883:30
means to d. therein	HERB 475:21
upon logic…that you should d.	DOYLE 344:6

dwellers d. in different zones — DISR 332:90
dwelling d. place in all generations — BIBLE 117:97
thy humble d.	WESL 1066:63
whimsical d.	CONG 281:38
Whose d. is the light	WORD 1094:98

dwelling-place desert were my d.-p. — BYRON 220:4
How lovely is thy d.-p. — SCOT 856:21
dwellings how amiable are thy d. — BOOK 177:85
dwells In me there d. — TENN 1002:13
dwindle d. into wife — CONG 282:45
Shall he d., peak, and pine — SHAK 907:13
dye behint yon auld fail d. — BALL 67:55
dying act of d. — JOHN 528:55
After d. has stopped	HOUS 494:47
An old, mad…and d. king	SHEL 927:76
behold you again in d.	STEV 976:57
blood with the thought of d.	MASE 662:51
born and d., d.	MISH 696:76
D. Is an art	PLATH 773:94
d., and, behold, we live	BIBLE 151:83
d., bless the hand	DRYD 350:38
d., if we could not cry	MAUP 665:98
d.…is terrible	FIEL 388:53
d. is merely to quit	OVID 741:9
d. man's room	STER 969:8
d. now and done for	BETJ 100:50
d. pray at the last	DILL 331:53
d. tongueless	SHAK 911:20
D., we live	BROW 200:99
habit of living indisposeth us for d.	BROW 196:96
Here am I, d.	POPE 783:13
hold its breath…without d.	ANTH 31:83
I am d.	WILDE 1078:5
idea of d. is worse than d.	PROU 793:1
If this is d.	STRA 979:99
immortality…through not d.	ALLEN 14:43
in d. that we are born	FRAN 401:91
instead of d., he sings	BENC 89:56
It was in d.	THOM 1013:24
living a little more or d.	MAIL 639:72
love to those of the d.	LOWRY 618:19
men than at d.	JEFF 519:83
so many ways of us d.	BAIN 62:75
We are d. continuously	PETR 767:10
worth fighting for, worth d.	MITC 696:84

dynamic a play is a d. thing — TYNAN 1035:27
class people as static and d.	WAUGH 1056:73
strong and d.	GAND 414:11

dynamic (*contd.*)
world is…in d. unbalance	BART 74:77

dynamite did and it is d. — TRUM 1030:31
dynamo cannibal d. — GINS 427:25
dynasty not respect for a d. — LOUIS 614:55

eager less e.…to marry — FALU 382:56
eagle as an e. toward heaven — BIBLE 121:95
E. has landed	ALDR 12:10
e. know what's in the pit	BLAKE 166:61
e. mewing her mighty youth	MILT 686:75
e. or the snake	KIPL 561:47
e. suffers little birds	SHAK 862:43
e. was killed by the arrow	KELL 548:30
famished e. screams	GRAY 443:82
Fearless the	MACC 625:37
fourth beast was like a flying e.	BIBLE 157:8
hooded e. among blinking owls	SHEL 929:10
like an e. in a dove-cot	SHAK 911:17
youth is renewed like the e.'s	BIBLE 118:11

eagles More rapid than e. — MOORE 704:6
mount up with wings as e.	BIBLE 126:91
swifter than e.	BIBLE 110:44
Where are the e.	ELIOT 368:73
Where his e. never flew	COWP 292:36

eaglet space, an e.'s wing — CRANE 295:2
ear age shall see the golden e. — POPE 779:23
artistic sense of eye or e.	WHIS 1069:14
beat upon my whorled e.	HOPK 491:79
by the hearing of the e.	BIBLE 113:27
Christ in every e.	PATR 761:15
chuckle…from e. to e.	ELIOT 368:88
close at the e. of Eve	MILT 690:66
e. becomes more Irish	BYRON 223:52
E. deep-sweet music	SHAK 864:95
e. for her music	DAYL 310:55
e. is much enamoured	SHAK 871:45
e. is not sensitive enough	MAHL 638:62
e. of a merchant	NASHE 721:84
enchant thine e.	SHAK 864:92
enemy of the e.	WILD 1080:34
Even one e. is more	ROTH 826:19
flattery lost on a poet's e.	SCOTT 853:47
flea in mine e.	NASHE 721:77
Give every man thine e.	SHAK 888:65
Good music…penetrates the e.	BEEC 82:13
Hark in thine e.	SHAK 904:44
have no e.	LAMB 576:26
heart was piercèd through the e.	SHAK 898:14
history's e., already listening	SAMU 840:44
hollow of thine e.	SHAK 869:10
horrid stillness first invades the e.	DRYD 346:48
In a believer's e.!	NEWT 725:44
In Reason's e. they all rejoice	ADDI 7:23
in your husband's e.	GROM 447:69
Jacobites, give an e, give an e.	BURNS 212:27
jest's prosperity lies in the e.	SHAK 866:29
know not what into my e.	LAND 578:61
lark to a shepherd's e.	SHAK 870:26
lend an e. to Plato	TENN 1003:30
meant than meets the e.	MILT 682:12
nor e. heard	BIBLE 150:46
Not to the sensual e.	KEATS 547:8
o'er my e. like the sweet sound	SHAK 893:91
Of eye and e.	WORD 1094:99
penetrated into the e. of man	FORS 398:31
pistol let off at the e.	LAMB 577:42
planted the e.	BIBLE 117:5
presented to the eye or e.	CRAB 294:84
purse out of your wife's e.	MORT 710:99
rich jewel in an Ethiope's e.	SHAK 868:82
Stop thine e. against the singer	SCOTT 855:97
stories to delight his e.	SHAK 887:39
telescope to his e.	SMITH 945:77

ear (*contd.*)
there reaches my e.	PAST 759:84
to the E. of Kings	POPE 782:91
tubes of the e.	WILL 1083:97
Vexing the dull e.	SHAK 872:67
was all e.	MILT 684:33
whisper in her e.	WILB 1074:16
whom he whispers in the e.	BROW 199:74
whose e. is a smoking tomb	GINS 427:25
world-deafened e.	ARNO 36:70

earful Stetson and gave him an e. — COPE 287:50
earl As far as the fourteenth e. — HOME 487:9
e. and a knight of the garter	ATTL 44:12
E. of Dudley was beheaded	MILLS 680:67
Oh I see said the E.	ASHF 41:66
slain the E. of Murray	BALL -101:37

Earls daughter of a hundred E. — TENN 995:69
early always either too late or too e. — SART 844:9
e. will I seek thee	BIBLE 116:83
had it been e.	JOHN 526:99
However monstrously e.	SHIP 935:21
too e. for a drink?	GORD 435:66
try to be e.	DAY 310:48
vain for you to rise up e.	BIBLE 119:41
Woe unto them that rise up e.	BIBLE 124:59

earn e. it by enjoying such authority — BERE 94:37
e. that I eat	SHAK 886:2
e. your living	WELD 1062:94

earnest impotence of being e. — CANN 230:66
in good e. wish	WILL 1080:47
valuable or even e.	THOR 1016:80
we die in e.	RALE 800:14

ears and hedges e. — SWIFT 985:95
blast of war…in our e.	SHAK 881:84
bless our human e.	MILT 681:90
Creep in our e.	SHAK 873:98
distance between your e.	JONES 533:51
drumming in my e.	SAPP 842:92
dying has stopped the e.	HOUS 494:47
e. fall off like figs	THOM 1011:89
e. he likes to bathe in sound	BROWN 194:56
E. like bombs	CAUS 246:66
e. like errant wings	CHES 257:87
e. of every one…shall tingle	BIBLE 109:29
e. of jet	GRAY 441:51
e. of the deaf shall be unstopped	BIBLE 126:82
e. that hear the soft rain	RICK 811:74
e. that…hear one's secrets	ONEI 740:17
e. to hear, let him hear	BIBLE 141:62
e. yielding like swinging doors	DOUG 341:58
eyes and hearts e.	LYLY 620:59
fume of space foams in our e.	CRANE 295:4
golden e. of corn	HERR 478:65
Harrovian pricks up his e.	ANON 24:14
He that hath e. to hear	BIBLE 137:85
if men had e.	BYRON 223:84
In the porches of mine e.	SHAK 889:78
lend me your e.	SHAK 884:48
let thine e. be attentive	BIBLE 119:44
make fur Fly bout the e.	BUTL 216:14
never mentions Hell to e. polite	POPE 779:23
noise of waters in my e.	SHAK 863:54
Pour oil into their e.	JONS 534:78
reaching the proper e.	KIPL 559:15
Rome about your e.	SHAK 911:14
seven thin e.	BIBLE 105:44
shout about my e.	CHES 257:88
That man's e. make	HUGH 499:13
thumbs vary…like e.	SHAW 925:30
To dying e.	TENN 997:4
two ambitious e.	JONS 534:77
up to the e. in love	STER 969:10
Walls have e.	ANON 26:47
walls have e.	LINK 606:22

ears (*contd.*)

With ravished e. — DRYD 351:68

earth air, e., of sea — MILT 693:30
alien planet is E. — BALL 68:62
all cultures of the e. — WEBER 1059:20
All people that on e. — SCOT 856:22
all the corners of the e. — BOOK 177:87
all the e. o'erwhelm them — SHAK 888:58
All the gold upon the e. — PLATO 774:12
alone on e. — BYRON 219:78
although the e. remove — SCOT 856:20
any man that breathes on e. — MARL 654:16
anything on e. can mend — MANN 646:94
anywhere else on e. — GURN 449:88
as if the e. had rolled — WORD 1095:10
As if this e.…were breathing — COLE 275:14
at any time upon the e. — WHIT 1072:73
attempt to create heaven on e. — BORO 179:21
back to e. as the doorkeeper — TOSC 1024:9
back to the nourishing e. — SAND 841:67
beauty fed my common e. — MASE 662:44
believe that the e. is flat — DRIB 346:44
belonging as much to sky as e. — CARR 237:11
bleeding piece of e. — SHAK 883:44
blithe e. die — JEFF 519:79
Born for us on e. below — CASW 244:37
bowels of the harmless e. — SHAK 875:42
break e.'s sleep — OWEN 748:2
bridal of the e. and sky — HERB 475:32
brilliant light on e. — HUSS 505:37
call heaven and e. to witness — BIBLE 108:89
Can the e. do to us — BROW 197:16
Canst work i'th' e. so fast? — SHAK 889:83
care for no man on e. — DICK 326:62
certain fathoms in the e. — SHAK 917:40
Child on e. for me — BETJ 100:47
clear, and the e. sure — DONNE 336:77
clods and trampled e. — MUIR 712:29
cloud Enveloping the E. — COLE 274:6
comprehended the dust of the e. — BIBLE 126:87
conquest of the e. — CONR 284:89
cool flowery lap of e. — ARNO 37:73
crawling between heaven and e.? — SHAK 891:26
crust of an unfinished e. — KURA 571:19
daughter of E. and Water — SHEL 928:84
daughters of the e. — JOHN 526:5
did thee feel the e. move? — HEMI 471:33
dominion…over all the e. — BIBLE 102:86
earned here on e. — THAT 1007:14
e. abideth for ever — BIBLE 122:14
e., and heav'n, and hell — POPE 782:95
e. and heaven fled away — BIBLE 158:33
e. …Apparelled in celestial light — WORD 1097:48
e. as we now see it — MACL 634:82
e. beneath her — GORD 435:82
e. but an echo of the spheres — BYRON 223:63
E. cares for her own ruins — BINY 162:10
E.'s crammed with heaven — BROW 197:23
e. doth like a snake renew — SHEL 932:64
E. felt the wound — MILT 692:12
e. has bubbles — SHAK 907:19
E. has waited — ROSE 823:62
e. hath not anything to show — WORD 1097:46
E.'s heedless sons — BLUN 170:43
e. in an earthly bed — TENN 1001:88
e. in travail and in pain — LONG 612:13
e. is full of his glory — BIBLE 124:60
e. is hell when — NASHE 721:81
E. is here so kind — JERR 521:14
e. is nobler than the world — PRIE 790:36
e. is nothing very special — HOYLE 498:2
e. is still going round the sun — ORWE 744:40
e. is the Lord's — BIBLE 115:51
e. is the Lord's — BIBLE 150:57

earth (*contd.*)

e. its dower of river — KEATS 545:59
E., lie heavily — ROSS 823:73
e. must borrow its mirth — WILC 1075:25
e. of majesty — SHAK 867:48
e. peopled as ever by the inept — REPP 807:13
E. receive an honoured guest — AUDEN 47:71
e. savage, e. broken — COLUM 277:59
e. self-balanced — MILT 691:86
E.'s shadows fly — SHEL 931:50
e. shall be full of the knowledge — BIBLE 125:68
e. shall reel to and fro — BIBLE 125:72
E. stood hard as iron — ROSS 824:77
e. the legend of the Gael — RUSS 833:36
E., thou bonnie — MACD 627:71
e. to e. — BOOK 176:58
e. to love — KIPL 563:92
e. was made for Dombey and Son — DICK 323:90
e. where cares abound — WORD 1100:87
every man upon this e. — MACA 623:13
exalted in the e. — BIBLE 116:74
eyes …throughout the whole e. — BIBLE 112:89
feels the attraction of the e. — LONG 612:19
fell to e. — HAMER 453:36
fell to e. — LONG 611:5
fifth part of the E. — FIELD 387:39
first man is of the e. — BIBLE 151:71
fixed upon the e. — MARL 652:86
for e. too dear! — SHAK 868:82
For sullen e. — SHAK 913:57
For, heaven to e. — SHAK 876:73
foundations of the e.? — BIBLE 113:17
From e.'s wide bounds — HOW 497:91
from which e., and grave — RALE 800:16
furniture of the e. — BERK 95:51
gazing on the e. — SHEL 932:73
get off the e.? — SAND 841:69
girdle round about the e. — SHAK 870:37
glance form heaven to e. — SHAK 871:55
globe of the e. — MUNDY 714:54
God created heaven and e. — BIBLE 102:82
God…craves the e. — SEXT 860:24
going to and fro in the e. — BIBLE 112:94
good men…make the e. wholesome — EMER 377:57
hallowed piece of e. — CLIN 269:18
happiest marriages on e. — DEVO 318:89
heav'n and e. hath made — SCOT 856:23
heaven and e. in …uniòn — MILT 681:89
Heaven and e. shall pass away — BIBLE 140:38
Heaven in E. — CRAS 295:18
heaven on e. I have won — SHAK 901:79
heaven on e. — FORD 397:12
Hell as well as on e. — LEWIS 601:37
hell on e. — SHAW 921:22
Hold off the e. — SHAK 893:80
hover over the entire e. — HUGO 501:57
How on e. can you privatize — PAVL 761:20
in the deep-delvèd e. — KEATS 547:14
in the lowest parts of the e. — BIBLE 120:51
inherit the e. — BIBLE 133:34
Johannesburg is needed upon the e. — PATON 761:13
Judge all of the e. — BIBLE 105:24
judged the e. flat — UPDI 1036:55
kingly joys in e. — MARL 652:88
Kings are e.'s gods — SHAK 910:92
lap of e. — GRAY 442:77
last sound on the worthless e. — FAUL 384:89
let the e. be opened — BIBLE 159:51
lie with his mother e.? — SHAK 885:70
Lightly gentle e. — BEAU 80:73
little e., for charity.' — SHAK 918:64
longer than the e. — BIBLE 113:32
loose to play upon the e. — MILT 685:62
love…good tilled e. — TOLK 1023:94

earth (*contd.*)

loves but half the E. — QUIL 797:55
low as where this e. — ROSS 824:81
make the e. my hell — SHAK 863:59
Man marks the e. with ruin — BYRON 221:6
meek shall inherit the e. — BIBLE 115:64
meek shall inherit the E. — BIRK 163:19
meek shall inherit the E. — DUBO 353:8
memory die from the e. — SIDN 937:66
Men are like the e. — SCHR 850:5
men call e. — MILT 683:18
men from the planet E. — ANON 27:93
men walk proudly through the e. — RAND 801:25
mingle our bloods…in the e. — SHAK 910:94
more nearer e. — SHAK 900:56
more things in heaven and e. — MAMET 643:54
more things in heaven and e. — SHAK 889:84
most beautiful things on e. — ISAA 513:69
most decent nation on…e. — BUSH 215:86
moved e. and hearth — TENN 995:61
much less grief on e. — BROD 189:72
must have a touch of e. — TENN 1002:12
new heaven and a new e. — BIBLE 158:34
new heavens and a new e. — BIBLE 128:15
night close down on the e. — RAND 801:24
no culture of the e. — HOBB 483:40
no power on e. — BALD 65:10
no such thing on e. — CHES 258:94
no supporter from the huge firm e. — SHAK 872:64
none upon e. that I desire — BIBLE 117:91
not in e. or time recoverable — PURDY 795:34
nought…on the e. doth live — SHAK 869:95
novelty on e., this fair defect — MILT 693:20
Ocean and e. — WORD 1100:79
old in the e. — BRON 191:9
ominously upon the e. — GRAV 439:21
on e. a vicious weed — DRYD 349:19
on e. do dwell — KETHE 554:23
on e. I wait forlorn — ARNO 38:2
on e. no track — THOM 1015:57
on that dark e. — TENN 1003:22
On the bare e. expos'd — DRYD 351:70
on the e. he strowèd — SPEN 959:41
oppressions of this e. — SHEL 927:68
other nations of the e. — JAMES 516:12
our moment upon the e. — MANS 647:5
our room on this e. — GREN 446:53
paleyce as ony on e. — MALO 642:27
passenger on the spaceship, E. — FULL 409:39
Peace on e. and mercy mild! — BEEC 82:14
peace upon the e. — MILT 681:87
pearled Arcturi of the e. — SHEL 932:67
place among the nations of the e. — EMMET 378:81
portion of the e. — NAIP 717:16
present life of men on e. — BEDE 82:8
rapture the e. and the seas — BRON 190:87
regarded this e. with envious eyes — WELLS 1064:26
returning him safely to e. — KENN 551:66
revealed Not of e. — MILT 691:91
round e.'s imagined corners — DONNE 338:3
salt of the e. — BIBLE 134:35
salt of the e. — SHEL 929:70
Saviour Christ again to E. — MASE 662:46
scatter them abroad…all the e. — BIBLE 104:17
scum of the e.…soldiers — WELL 1063:7
scum of the e. — CHES 259:24
send peace on e. — BIBLE 136:79
serious house on serious e. — LARK 581:2
shall move the e. — ARCH 33:14
shall not perish from the e. — LINC 605:4
short-lived profession on e. — ROGE 820:21
Silver out of the E. in Peru — PETTY 768:13
Sing…all the e. — BIBLE 159:44
Six miles from e. — JARR 518:57

earth (*contd.*)

sleepers in that quiet e.	BRON 192:15
small model of the barren e.	SHAK 867:59
smell above the e.	SHAK 883:45
smite the e. a curse	BIBLE 131:73
Spaceship E.	FULL 409:40
spiritual creatures walk the e.	MILT 690:62
Standing on e., not rapt	MILT 691:82
strangers and pilgrims on the e.	BIBLE 154:51
sun is coming down to e.	MERE 671:1
sun went around the e.	ARNO 40:44
surface of the e.	SWIFT 985:84
temples of the e.	DIDE 330:36
that e. lie light	WALL 1050:73
Things learned on e.	BROW 199:71
this broad e. of ours	WHIT 1073:96
this e. of ours	DEQU 316:64
this green e.	WORD 1094:99
though the e. be removed	BIBLE 116:72
thought about…the whole e.	BYRON 222:30
three nights in the heart of the e.	BIBLE 137:93
through heav'n and e.	MILT 689:44
through my lips to unawakened e.	SHEL 928:91
throw e. over your head	PASC 757:62
Thy will be done in e.	BIBLE 135:49
Till e. and sky	KIPL 560:23
tread on E.	ARNO 36:61
treasures upon e.	BIBLE 135:50
two paces of the vilest e.	SHAK 876:76
uttermost part of the e.	BIBLE 147:79
uttermost parts of the e.	BIBLE 114:32
wall as solid as the e.	BUCH 202:22
way of all the e.	BIBLE 109:11
way of all the e.	BIBLE 110:54
we are on the e.	SHAK 867:51
what on e. is the use of them	WILDE 1077:78
Wherewith to scorn the e.	MILT 692:9
While e.'s foundations stood	HOUS 496:84
whole e. as their memorial	PERI 766:97
whole face of the e.	PASC 757:59
whole rainy, stony e.?	HUGH 500:43
whole round e.	TENN 1004:47
why e. loves e.	ANON 22:77
Yours is the E.	KIPL 564:9

earthling alone in a way no e. — COLL 276:40

earthly all e. things above — SPRI 961:63

an e. song	TENN 999:42
e. immortality	FORD 397:12
e. paragon	SHAK 916:13
ne'er touched e. faces	SHAK 912:47
Off e. thingis nane bettir be	DUNB 355:36
too well for any e. use	FROST 407:83

earthquake e. swallows us — STEV 974:21

e. was really too much	LIGNE 604:93
e. were to engulf England	JERR 521:17
haven't had an e. lately	MILNE 680:78
Lord was not in the e.	BIBLE 111:69
not smiling back—that's an e.	MILL 676:95
shaken with an e.	ADDI 6:5
starts with an e.	GOLD 434:42
takes an e. to remind us	KURA 571:19
the gloom of e.	SHEL 927:75
to play golf during an e.	STAL 962:82
win a war than win an e.	RANK 801:30

earthquakes e.…bright weather — CARL 235:61

famines, and pestilences, and e.	BIBLE 139:37
thought of e., and of wars	BYRON 222:30

ease Are you at e. now? — FLET 394:78

as in doubtful e.	SURR 982:41
done with so much e.	DRYD 349:5
E. after war	SPEN 957:3
e. of body	SMITH 945:74
e. some deal	SHAK 862:39
for another gives its e.	BLAKE 167:85

ease (*contd.*)

health and perfect e.	DYER 358:90
heart's first e.	DAYL 310:56
hours of e.	SCOTT 853:58
ignobled e., and peaceful sloth	MILT 688:16
interpose a little e.	MILT 685:48
Joys in another's loss of e.	BLAKE 167:56
man is most at e.	ALLS 15:55
no longer at e. here	ELIOT 369:4
prodigal of e.?	DRYD 349:14
Studious of laborious e.	COWP 293:59
True e. in writing	POPE 778:84

easel bread, and his e. — RYDER 834:50

easier e. to conquer it — WALP 1051:86

e. with practice	GREE 444:24
how much e.	HALI 452:26
I am e. to be played on	SHAK 891:43
upon e. terms	JOHN 532:28

easing E. the spring — REED 805:81

east aristocracy of the E. — MAUG 665:90

As far as the e. is from the west	BIBLE 118:13
chambers of the E.	BLAKE 165:55
determined to go E.	MAIL 640:92
E. is E	KIPL 560:22
e. wind made flesh	APPL 32:3
e. wind prevails over the west	MAO 648:28
hold the gorgeous E. in fee	WORD 1097:47
Hunter of the E.	FITZ 390:87
inscrutability of the E.	STARK 963:94
lands of the E.	GILL 426:12
look the E. End in the face	ELIZ 374:97
mysterious E., perfumed	CONR 284:97
politics in the E.	DISR 332:76
sigh of the e. on my face	CONR 284:96
There is no silence in the E.	MAUG 664:88
three kings into the e.	BURNS 210:89
tried to hustle the E.	KIPL 561:45
when the wind blew due E.	CARR 241:86
wind's in the e.	DICK 324:23

Easter frome Candylmas untyll E. — MALO 642:32

making my E. confession	JOSE 537:33

eastern Come o'er the e. hills — BLAKE 165:57

Eastern save in E. clime — BURG 206:95

Eastertide Wearing white for E. — HOUS 494:39

Easthampstead on E. Plain — KING 558:96

easy depending upon shock…is e. — PRIE 790:45

Difficult or e.	MART 657:63
e.—terribly e.	SHAW 920:98
Life is not e.	SAIF 836:76
Life is not meant to be e.	FRAS 403:20
take life e.	YEATS 1104:56
too e. for children	SCHN 848:86

eat all I had to e. — STEV 973:97

best place to e.	GUIL 448:78
but I will not e. with you	SHAK 874:18
buzzard…can e. anything	FAUL 384:86
couldn't e.	GREE 444:4
do not e. for the good of living	EMER 377:49
earn that I e.	SHAK 886:2
e. all the food	KEEN 548:24
e. and sleep and choose a wife	SASS 845:23
e. as much as men	TRUTH 1030:39
E., drink, and love	BYRON 223:64
e.…drink, and to be merry	BIBLE 123:31
e. in safety	SHAK 918:67
e. my ale	FARQ 383:70
e. the power out of women	WEST 1068:89
e. this in remembance	BOOK 175:31
e. thy bread with joy	BIBLE 123:33
e. to live	MOLI 699:28
e.…with glum urge	FISH 390:85
every man should e. and drink	BIBLE 122:20
hoping he will e. you last	REAG 803:60
I did e.	BIBLE 103:97

eat (*contd.*)

I e. what I see	CARR 238:28
kill, and e.	BIBLE 147:91
let us e. and drink	BIBLE 125:31
let us e. and drink	BIBLE 151:69
neither should he e.	BIBLE 153:27
Never e. at…Mom's	ALGR 13:24
So I did sit and e.	HERB 475:1
some wad e. that want it	ANON 24:7
Take, e.: this is my body	BIBLE 150:59
Tell me what you e.	BRIL 188:51
than e. China's all our lives	HO 482:34
To e., to survive	STAN 963:92

eat-well E.-w. is drink-well's brother — FULL 410:49

eaten e. me out of house — SHAK 877:88

has been e. by the bear	HOUS 496:86
never e. bread	KAIKO 541:36

eater good e. must be a good man — DISR 332:73

great e. of beef	SHAK 894:97
Out of the e. came forth meat	BIBLE 109:17

eating Appetite comes with e. — RABE 798:30

e. paté	SMITH 949:57
E. people is wrong!	FLAN 392:26
e. that's believing	THUR 1019:40
E. the air	SHAK 877:36
for e., not mating	FERB 385:12
good news is that he's e. less	JACO 514:90
Lawful as e.	SHAK 912:43
loving alone is dull as e. alone	WYCH 1103:44
redfaced from e. and drinking	ABBO 1:1
subject of e.	HUNT 505:31
While someone else is e.	AUDEN 47:59

eats e. up himself — SHAK 895:45

Man is what he e.	FEUE 387:32
way he e. jelly beans	REAG 803:62
Young misses whut e.	MITC 697:85

eaves sparrow in the e. — YEATS 1104:59

upon her gilded e.	TENN 997:25

ebb ne'er e. to humble love — SHAK 899:42

ebony nine e. spikes — KING 559:4

eccentricity reputation for e. — SHAR 919:86

ecclesiastical interest in e. — WAUGH 1056:68

ecclesiologist keen e. — BETJ 99:27

echo all the church did e. — SHAK 864:83

Art is dedicated e.	SANT 842:88
co-opted and obliterated e.	HEAN 465:43
e. began in some indescribable way	FORS 398:43
E., sweetest nymph	MILT 683:26
Scents, colors, and sounds e.	BAUD 77:17
sound must seem an e.	POPE 778:84
there reaches … an e.	PAST 759:84
waiting for the e.	MARQ 656:47

echoes all their e. mourn — MILT 684:40

Dead e.! But I knew her body	CRANE 295:2
e. of fear	EVANS 381:40
e., dying, dying, dying	TENN 997:99
Our e. roll	TENN 997:1
state-controlled manufactory of e.	DOUG 342:66
wild e. flying	TENN 997:98

eclipse earthquake and e. — SHEL 927:75

eclipses modus of lunar e. — POUND 785:59

ecological e. balance of the planet — SONT 953:7

economic accepted e. legends — GALB 411:77

an e. colony	TSON 1031:41
chief source of e. insecurity	ELLW 375:20
cold metal of e. theory	SCHU 851:17
Commentators quote e. studies	SAMU 840:46
e. condition has…improved	KRIS 569:95
e. equivalent of the slave	WIEN 1074:12
e. factors in society	GILM 427:15
e. ones are incomprehensible	HOME 487:10
E. policy is random	STEIN 966:51
e., political, and social life	LEWIS 601:48
e. services that it can render	DURK 357:68

economic (*contd.*)
e. status of women — GILM 427:14
e. substructure — FANON 382:59
e. value of…women — GILM 427:16
engineering an e. revival — LARD 580:89
essential form of e. speech — WRIS 1102:21
forces of e. law — KEYN 554:27
In e. terms — GLEI 430:61
industrial and e. status — SKEL 942:37
more effective e. service — TAWN 991:7
much of e. theory — HICKS 480:98
normal e. system works — SALT 839:40
not the e. index — MARC 650:49
opportunity cost of e. discussion — GALB 412:82
take our e. blood pressure — WRIS 1102:18
talented e. theorists — TOBIN 1021:73
understand the e. system — ROBI 815:36
When I read e. documents — HOME 487:11
economical e. with the truth — ARMS 35:51
economically e. backward — TROT 1029:8
economics basic law of e. — HARR 459:40
branch of e. — STIG 977:66
E. and art are strangers — CATH 244:49
E. as a positive science — FRIE 405:52
E. as if People Mattered — SCHU 850:14
E., if it is to be — JEVO 521:19
E. is all about…choices — DUES 354:22
E. is the science — ROBB 813:14
e. suggests that they — MISH 696:72
Enid Blyton of e. — HOLME 485:73
from the Principles of E. — KEYN 554:32
master of e. — HOLM 487:4
purpose of studying e. — ROBI 815:35
economies few factors help…e. — MACD 628:97
two e. finally merged — WOLF 1090:13
economist a one-handed e. — TRUM 1030:30
death of a political e. — BAGE 61:50
e. is someone who — HELL 468:90
world's greatest e. — SCHU 851:16
economists a very large number of e. — GALB 412:83
among professional e. — HAYEK 462:91
classical e. — VINER 1045:78
deceived by e. — ROBI 815:35
distribution of uncertainty among e. — STEIN 966:50
e., and…economic theorists — KNIG 567:54
e. are…disinclined to publish — CANN 230:68
e. hardly know enough — BECK 81:89
E. have least influence — BLIN 169:29
E. set themselves — KEYN 554:29
ideas of e. — KEYN 555:37
If all the e. in the world — SHAW 926:42
sophists, e., and calculators — BURKE 207:31
economy arbitrary e. of nature — WOLL 1091:37
Beauty…like any e. — WOLF 1090:12
complex…as a modern e. — SOLOW 952:93
different schemes of e. — STEU 970:30
e. is based on planned obsolescence — STEV 970:31
E. is the art — SHAW 926:40
e. of manufacture — BABB 54:88
e. of these people — SMOL 950:63
e., stupid! — ANON 29:37
her industry and e. — STAN 962:88
In art e. is always beauty — JAMES 516:28
in favour of general e. — EDEN 360:21
In the interests of e. — MAXT 665:99
its e. is in difficulty — WALE 1049:50
No e. ever stands still — HARR 459:41
People want e. — IACO 509:16
performance of the American e. — STEIN 966:51
Political e. the e. — RUSK 831:95
Political e. thus does — MARX 660:8
Political e. traces — BAGE 61:62
seeds of the spirit and e. — MARI 650:62
socialism and a market e. — DENG 315:50

economy (*contd.*)
working e. in the world — MARS 656:53
wrote Principles of Political E. — BENT 93:26
ecstasies muddy e. of beer — CRAB 293:65
ecstasy bells of E. — GINS 428:32
e. of love — SHAK 889:87
e. Of sun-fed wine — NEIL 722:96
escape from circumstance to e. — BELL 85:81
immobility, e., and sleep — MARI 651:66
not e. but it was comfort — DICK 325:51
seraph-wings of e. — GRAY 443:90
think thereof without an e.? — BROW 195:75
What wild e.? — KEATS 547:7
ecstatic the e. and the bilious — ELIOT 365:3
ectoplasms Hollywood-movie e. — ELLI 375:16
Ector bare forth unto syre E. — MALO 642:24
eczema Style…too often hides e. — CAMUS 229:56
eddy action's dizzying e. — ARNO 36:59
Eden birds of E. sang? — CULL 299:68
brooks of E. mazily murmuring — TENN 1003:25
east of E. — BIBLE 104:8
easy E.-dreamtime — WRIG 1101:10
E., demi-paradise — SHAK 867:48
E.'s green and gold — KIPL 561:40
E., shall enjoy their fill — MILT 690:59
E. took their solitary way — MILT 693:29
foot in E. — MUIR 712:36
garden eastwards in E. — BIBLE 103:89
out of the Garden of E. — MUGG 712:22
put him into garden of E. — BIBLE 103:90
sent him forth from the garden of E. — BIBLE 103:3
when from E. we take — MACN 637:48
woe, With you of E. — MILT 687:84
edge at the e. of Being — SPEN 956:76
e. of a new frontier — KENN 550:61
e. of some crazy cliff — SALI 839:28
e. of the stage — DIDE 329:27
e. of the world — SITW 941:27
e. to the superstitious tale — PRIT 791:64
Fills and trembles at the e. — ROET 819:93
hand cutting e. of mind — BRON 190:83
if they have a cutting e. — MURR 716:80
own folly, go over e. — MOUN 711:13
push men over the e. — ROTH 826:9
edges octaves of its parallel e. — CUMM 299:76
Stain all your e. — SHAK 911:17
edify all things e. not — BIBLE 150:56
Edina E.! Scotia's darling seat — BURNS 210:86
Edinburgh Ye E. Gentry! — BURNS 209:62
editing final e. down — DELI 315:40
products of e. — WALD 1048:45
edition new e. of human nature — HAZL 463:14
new…more beautiful e. — FRAN 402:99
not the latest e. — GREE 444:17
editor E.: a person employed — HUBB 498:6
e. is the uncrowned king — STEAD 964:6
e. must always be with the people — BENN 92:4
e. of a village journal — MOOD 703:98
e. of an important magazine — CANN 230:68
e. who cannot contemplate it — JOVA 537:38
Procrustes was an e. — SKEL 942:47
Show me a contented newspaper e. — CHRI 261:1
the one the e. gives to the worms — MACH 630:34
Trust your e. — CHEE 256:56
editorial age of the e. chair — MACL 635:97
This is the e. age — BENN 92:5
editors some newspaper e. — CHOP 261:63
true Church of England…in the E. — CARL 233:33
educability His whole e. — JAMES 517:43
educate e. the masses — OSLER 746:72
go to e. him first — SAKI 837:3
educated another sun to the e. — HERA 473:83
clothed, fed and e. — RUSK 831:3
'e.' people…come to the front — ORWE 742:94

educated (*contd.*)
government by the badly e. — CHES 260:43
instructed and amused…is e. — ATLAS 44:7
liberally e. person — BLOOM 169:34
never preach, but to the e. — AUST 51:50
stamps a man…as an e. gentleman — SHAW 923:78
that is e. — HAMI 453:41
thought highly e. — SNOW 950:72
uncrowned king of an e. democracy — STEAD 964:6
education American e. — ADAMS 5:82
apathy in e. — FORS 398:38
best kind of e. — BUCH 202:26
By e. most have been misled — DRYD 351:55
can't do with any more e. — WODE 1089:2
e. and whisky the price it is — WAUGH 1056:66
E. consists mainly — TWAIN 1034:12
E.…discloses to the wise — BIER 161:80
E. in science and technology — HUXL 508:90
E.…in so much higher a degree — AUST 52:69
E. is a little too pedantic — CONG 281:18
E. is about state-controlled — DOUG 342:66
E. is another sun — HERA 473:83
E. is…hanging around — FROST 407:5
E. is impossible without love — DESB 317:71
E. …is mere sheep-herding — POUND 786:9
E. is taming — BLOOM 169:35
E. is what survives — SKIN 943:51
e. of the people — DISR 333:19
e. of the people — MILL 674:62
e. of the people — WHIT 1069:17
e. produces no effect — WILDE 1077:82
e. to eliminate the influence — MUSG 716:82
field of public e. — WARR 1053:27
finished his e. till after — HAYD 462:88
good e.…to sustain a failure — BELL 85:79
Harvard e. consists of what you learn — CONA 279:82
have no e. — SMOL 950:63
having no e. — SHAN 919:77
hope to agree about e. — RUSS 832:27
If you think e. is expensive — BOK 171:66
lacking mathematical e. — HAYEK 462:91
man of any e. — JOHN 530:88
man's e. begins — ROUS 827:35
Movies, and that is e. — ROGE 820:18
only accomplishment my e. — DRAB 344:22
part of every Englishman's e. — HUGH 500:78
race between e. and catastrophe — WELLS 1065:42
same relation to e. — HUBB 498:7
saw in my own e. — WEST 1068:89
scramble themselves into a little e. — AUST 51:53
So long as e. is not provided — DAVI 307:3
Soap and e. — TWAIN 1032:62
test and use of man's e. — BARZ 75:94
unblunted by formal e. — ANGE 19:18
value of a liberal e. — BREW 187:38
educational modern e. theorists — RUSS 832:26
political and e. status — SKEL 942:37
social and e. patterns — MACL 635:96
educators priests and e. — NGU 725:45
Edward Prayer Book of E. VI — ACHE 2:24
proud E.'s army — WILL 1083:7
proud E.'s power — BURNS 212:37
winding-sheet of E.'s race — GRAY 443:84
eel adder better than the e. — SHAK 864:87
funeral march of a fried e. — SHAW 925:31
eels small e. that left the deeper way — CRAB 294:83
topped with good, rich, broiled e. — KURO 571:20
Eeyore snowing still, said E. — MILNE 680:78
effacement brought full e. — RANS 802:36
effanineffable ineffable effable E. — ELIOT 371:40
effect all that…despotism could e. — PITT 772:73
approaches the e. of painting — MICH 673:38
e. on other people — SART 844:6
instrument that has a good moral e. — ARIS 34:34

effect (*contd.*)
Nature…a name for an e. — COWP 293:*64*
notion of cause and e. — HUME 503:*99*
poetry administers to the e. — SHEL 931:*57*
win an e. — UPDI 1036:*49*
effects dire e. from civil discord — ADDI 8:*36*
e. deprave forever — BRON 191:*5*
e. of the division of labour — SMITH 946:*90*
grind out the true causes and e. — CARL 234:*43*
not in its taste, but its e. — FULB 409:*29*
slow preparation of e. — ELIOT 366:*35*
effectual any more e. way — TROL 1027:*76*
effeminate held curls to be e. — TWAIN 1032:*68*
efficiency competitive race for e. — ARNO 40:*45*
e. and inefficiency — SHAW 923:*75*
E.…is measured — JAY 519:*74*
industrial e. consists — ROBI 814:*20*
Practical e. is common — ROOS 822:*50*
efficient e. organization is one — STEA 963:*3*
kept e. by the persistent absenteeism — SAMU 840:*41*
Effie E. M was a monster — LEE 593:*17*
effigies e. of gods and goddesses — GILL 426:*2*
effluence e. of bright essence increate — MILT 689:*29*
effort e. to keep a party together — WILS 1085:*42*
e. very nearly killed her — BELL 87:*10*
enjoyment of successful e. — SHIP 935:*20*
Evil is done without e. — BAUD 78:*34*
feeling that lures us on…to vain e. — CONR 284:*98*
form of moral e. — LEAC 589:*42*
main e.…has been a critical e. — ARNO 38:*6*
not the e. or the failure — EMPS 378:*83*
only e. worth making — BOWL 182:*59*
steadily decreasing amount of e. — SCHU 851:*19*
team e. is a lot of people — WINN 1087:*64*
unusually obstinate e. — JAMES 517:*37*
worth every e. — THES 1009:*45*
years of e., hard work — PEARY 762:*35*
efforts appreciate his e. — KENN 551:*81*
e. to understand …nature — BUSH 215:*90*
excuse to cease all e. — ANGE 19:*27*
field for their e. — BRON 191:*93*
effusion e. of…human blood — OCON 735:*81*
effusions liveliest e. of wit — AUST 52:*63*
egalitarian e.…should be élitist — LODGE 610:*83*
more e. than it wants — SWEE 983:*51*
egg balancing an e. on a spoon — HILL 480:*2*
bald as an e. — CHEE 256:*54*
broody hen sitting on a china e. — FOOT 396:*93*
e. heads are in one basket — ANON 27:*71*
e. is full of meat — SHAK 869:*3*
e. production in this country — CURR 301:*21*
e.'s way of making another e. — BUTL 217:*31*
hen's e. don't turn into a crocodile — KING 558:*99*
It's very provoking…to be called an e. — CARR 240:*63*
Killers from the e. — HUGH 500:*38*
lay a tit's e. — MACD 628:*95*
like eating an e. — KIPL 560:*19*
No goose, no golden e. — TSON 1031:*42*
Remorse, the fatal e. — COWP 292:*45*
See this e. — DIDE 330:*36*
sitting on one addled e. — ELIOT 366:*27*
to work on an e. — WELD 1062:*88*
when one is eating a demnition e. — DICK 321:*50*
egghead way of the e. is hard — STEV 972:*77*
eggheads E. are terrible Philistines — NABO 717:*11*
E. of the world unite — STEV 972:*76*
eggs all my e. in one bastard — PARK 755:*19*
as a weasel sucks e. — SHAK 885:*87*
boil e. in your shoes — LEAR 590:*69*
helps scenery like ham and e. — TWAIN 1032:*63*
roast their e. — BACON 58:*91*
ways to dress e.? — MOORE 706:*39*
eglantine lush e. — SHEL 932:*68*
ego e. that can crack a crystal — CHEE 256:*55*

ego-games religion without e.-g. — REED 805:*89*
egocentric dreams are all e. — WAUGH 1057:*2*
egomaniacs of neurotics, e. — MANK 645:*77*
egos E. …setting themselves apart — BUBER 202:*20*
individual e., crazy for love — BART 74:*70*
egotism Apology is only e. — HOLM 486:*96*
dilemmas of conscience and e. — SNOW 950:*77*
egotist E.…person of low taste — BIER 161:*81*
egregiously make him e. an ass — SHAK 899:*23*
Egypt brought thee out of…E. — BIBLE 117:*92*
against all the firstborn of E. — SHAK 885:*88*
ancient E. persisted — RUSS 832:*28*
beauty in a brow of E. — SHAK 871:*55*
broken reed, on E. — BIBLE 126:*84*
called my son out of E. — BIBLE 130:*53*
can't judge E. by Aïda — FIRB 389:*80*
died…in the land of E. — BIBLE 106:*66*
good of the land of E. — BIBLE 105:*48*
great cry in E. — BIBLE 106:*62*
Jewish Queen of E. — TAYL 992:*15*
not at war with E. — EDEN 360:*23*
painting was brought to E. — VASA 1040:*8*
pass through the land of E. — BIBLE 106:*61*
this bruised reed, even upon E. — BIBLE 112:*84*
Egyptian as thou killedst the E.? — BIBLE 106:*52*
imagined…ancient E. princess — CASS 243:*26*
Egyptians E.…worship an insect — DISR 333:*2*
E. were urgent upon the people — BIBLE 106:*63*
out of the land of the E. — BIBLE 106:*56*
Eiffel stick them up your E. Tower — JAY 519:*72*
eight Pieces of e.! — STEV 975:*29*
eighteen E. is a good time — GOLD 432:*88*
knew almost as much at e. — JOHN 527:*36*
eighteenth E.-century houses — YEATS 1105:*71*
eighties vice of the E. — WOLFE 1091:*31*
eighty you are never e. — SEXT 859:*64*
Eildon down by the E. Tree — BALL 67:*52*
Einstein As E. once said — PERCY 766:*84*
Let E. be! — SQUI 961:*65*
eird Best thing in e. — HENR 473:*71*
Eisenhower E.…magic — WHITE 1071:*50*
El Salvador peasants in E. — OROU 741:*79*
elaborate suggests an e. hobby — PRIE 790:*41*
Elaine Daintily alights E. — BETJ 100:*48*
E. the fair — TENN 1002:*11*
elasticity maximum e. for our minds — BUTT 218:*52*
elbow man demanding e. room — WAUGH 1057:*95*
seated e. to e. — GILL 426:*4*
smokes on one e. — MORG 708:*65*
elbow-chairs Convenience…e.-c. — COWP 292:*51*
elbows Mr E. and Knees — ANON 28:*24*
elder e. man not at all — BACON 57:*62*
elderly care for the e. — FIELD 388:*43*
e. man of 42 — ASHF 41:*63*
nightmare of e. white males — ABBO 1:*1*
elders discourse of the e. — BIBLE 132:*93*
listening to their e. — BALD 64:*95*
Nat of oure e. — CHAU 255:*36*
party taken over by the e. — FITZ 391:*9*
eldritch e. light of sundown — DAYL 310:*56*
elect e., the elected — LOWE 617:*5*
not…who you e. — THOM 1014:*40*
elected could have e. my chauffeur — KENN 552:*97*
e. and anointed ones — WOLFE 1090:*25*
help them get e. — TAYL 992:*18*
plebiscite e. generals — JUVE 540:*81*
election 11.30pm on e. night — MOND 699:*39*
acrimony of the last e. — DICK 322:*67*
Democracy substitutes e. — SHAW 926:*39*
e. but the making of — NEW 723:*17*
e. by the incompetent many — SHAW 922:*46*
e. is coming — ELIOT 366:*26*
enthusiasm for the e. — WHIT 1072:*71*
Labour Party's e. programme — SNOW 951:*79*

election (*contd.*)
worst disaster since my e. — BROWN 194:*52*
elections leader who can…win e. — MACF 629:*15*
won the e. — SOMO 952:*2*
electorate province of a despicable e. — PITT 771:*63*
electors ever put before the e. — SNOW 951:*79*
Electra Mourning becomes E. — ONEI 740:*56*
electric Along the e. wires — AUST 52:*72*
E. guitars are an abomination — SEGO 857:*31*
E. Kool-Aid Acid Test — WOLFE 1090:*22*
married to an e. light — DIMA 331:*58*
electrician practical e. — WELLS 1064:*24*
electricity e. was dripping — THUR 1018:*94*
E. is of two kinds — LEAC 588:*35*
think that science is e. — GOUR 437:*80*
electrons same number of e. — EDDI 360:*20*
elegance e. is a state of mind — CASS 243:*27*
E. is good taste — SNOW 950:*69*
e. of Circe's hair — POUND 785:*61*
her…un-American e. — SCHL 848:*71*
outdone your e. — POUND 786:*85*
elegancy e., facility…of poesy — SHAK 865:*17*
elegant erect, e., dogmatic — REST 807:*15*
Shakesperian Rag…so e. — ELIOT 368:*86*
elegy e. To crown thy hearse? — CAREW 232:*7*
element can its native e. — MARV 657:*68*
e. of fire is quite put out — DONNE 338:*11*
e. within us — MURP 715:*71*
Of all sweet sounds the life and e.! — COLE 274:*6*
random e. in the world — EDDI 360:*17*
to the destructive e. submit yourself — CONR 284:*94*
yield their names to the e. — TATE 991:*2*
elementary 'e.' said he — DOYLE 344:*9*
elements among the e. — PLATH 773:*98*
conflict of its e. — BYRON 221:*20*
discordant e. — WORD 1096:*21*
e. and an angelic sprite — DONNE 338:*9*
e. are cricket's presiding geniuses — CARD 232:*6*
e. in the record…evoked — WHIT 1071:*61*
e. in their costituencies — LIPP 607:*37*
e. of air and earth — SHAK 894:*6*
framed us of four e. — MARL 652:*89*
Men…defied The e. — WORD 1100:*85*
mirror of the universal e. — STEI 965:*30*
our e., these piercing fires — MILT 688:*17*
elephant E.'s Child — KIPL 563:*81*
e. sings deep in the forest-maze — HUGH 500:*47*
e. that brought us hither — MUNDY 714:*53*
God…invented…the e. — PICA 769:*28*
masterpiece, an E. — DONNE 337:*83*
shot an e. in my pyjamas — MARX 659:*96*
sleeping with an e. — TRUD 1029:*12*
teach an e. to dance — MOSS 711:*7*
thought he saw an E. — CARR 241:*88*
elephants e. for want of towns — SWIFT 986:*4*
True philosophers are like e. — FONT 395:*89*
Women are like e. — FIEL 388:*58*
elevation scoured us to an e. — LLOY 608:*58*
eleventh about the e. hour he went — BIBLE 139:*22*
elf deceiving e. — KEATS 548:*19*
queen, an e. most fair — LAYA 588:*22*
Elfland horns of E. — TENN 997:*99*
Elginbrodde Martin E. — MACD 628:*98*
Eli Let E. rejoice — SMART 944:*64*
ran unto E. — BIBLE 109:*27*
Elijah E.…cast his mantle — BIBLE 111:*70*
E.…girded up his loins — BIBLE 111:*67*
E. went up by a whirlwind — BIBLE 111:*73*
send you E. the prophet — BIBLE 131:*73*
spirit of E. doth rest on Elisha — BIBLE 111:*74*
eliminate e. his ability — SCHW 851:*27*
e. the unnecessary — HOFF 484:*51*
To define is to e. — QUINE 797:*66*
elimination e. of some disease — SUTH 983:*49*

Eliot George E.'s husband   MORR 708:77
How unpleasant to meet Mr E.!   ELIOT 371:36
T S E.'s mother-in-law   BENN 91:84
Elisha spirit of Elijah doth rest on E.   BIBLE 111:74
élites right of colonial é.   ILLI 511:32
Eliza so did take E.   JONS 536:11
Elizabeth God save E.   ANON 23:90
   Queen E. owned silk stockings   SCHU 851:19
   saying…ascribed to Queen E.   ADDI 7:13
Ellie So Tom went home with E.   KING 558:99
elliptics glassy pinnacles correct e.   BISH 163:29
elm tall e.'s shadow   THOM 1012:3
   vine-prop e.   SPEN 957:99
elm-tree round the e.-t. bole   BROW 198:36
elm-trees e. in the … meadows   KING 558:99
elms Behind the e.   PRIOR 790:55
   Beneath those rugged e.   GRAY 442:64
   e. Fade into dimness   ARNO 39:23
   immemorial e.   TENN 998:13
elocutions so harmonious e.   DONNE 339:24
elopement as if you worked…an e.   DOYLE 343:88
eloquence e. in speaking   MARIE 651:63
   e., native to famous wits   MILT 694:35
   E. should persuade   PASC 758:69
   more e. in a sugar touch   SHAK 882:11
   splendour of his e.   HUME 503:7
   Take e. and break its neck!   VERL 1042:38
   True e. has no time for e.   PASC 757:52
eloquent not e., but he talks well   BEAV 80:80
else Who E. but Nelse?   ANON 27:89
elsewhere Altogether e.   AUDEN 48:82
Elsinore wild and stormy steep, E.!   CAMP 227:30
elusive Endings are e.   BART 74:73
elves And the e. also   HERR 478:66
   spite of all the criticizing e.   CHUR 262:83
Elysian dead, but in the E. fields   DISR 333:21
emanation genius is a pure e.   HAZL 464:15
emancipated more perfect when e.   WOLL 1091:43
emancipation e. of women   MILL 675:78
   understand by e.   GREER 445:40
   war for the e.   LLOY 608:60
emancipator e.…as crank   BROUN 193:49
embalmer triumph of the e.'s art   VIDAL 1044:65
embarrass failed to e. the claimant   STRA 979:98
   never e. my family   JOHN 523:41
embarrassed e. by the words   HEMI 470:17
embarrassment discovery with e.   MUNRO 714:57
   e. for those who benefit   MARI 652:75
   E. of Riches   ALLA 14:29
embassies e. …were everywhere   HEAN 465:42
embassy e. of a nation about to go
   into…liquidation   MACI 631:45
embers dead man's e.   GRAV 439:23
   e. through the room   MILT 682:10
   O joy.! that in our e.   WORD 1098:52
emblem e. of ignorance   ATAT 43:1
emblems scarves and e.   BAIN 62:77
embodiment Law is the true e.   GILB 424:73
embody e. the Law   GILB 424:73
embrace close clinging to e.   ROCH 816:44
   e. of the Venus de Milo   DARIO 305:76
   e. she enclin'd   MILT 687:83
   endure, then pity, then e.   POPE 780:14
   I e. the purpose of God   TENN 1002:96
   If I e. my rival   RACI 799:99
   none I think do there e.   MARV 658:74
   snug e. of the   TIME 1020:68
   that may e.   SURR 983:45
   time to e.   BIBLE 122:19
   will be guarded by e.   LOWE 615:74
embraced would have e. him   STAN 962:84
embraces age in her e. passed   ROCH 817:64
   sleepy, soft e.   GORD 435:42
embroidered e. cloths   YEATS 1105:65

embroideries Covered with e.   YEATS 1105:69
embroidery flower that sad e. wear   MILT 684:47
emerald defile…the E. Isle   DREN 346:42
   e. eyes   GRAY 441:51
   e. twinkles in the grass   TENN 1001:84
   see the E. Drop   RHYS 808:30
emeralds E. big as half a county   LAND 578:63
emergency compelled by e.   TROL 1028:93
   e. happening at distance   BARZ 76:99
   Microscopes…In an E.   DICK 327:95
   one e. following another   FISH 389:82
   Whatever the e.   GILB 423:55
emetic writing, what an e.!   SARD 843:94
emigration e. is…necessity   MOOD 703:97
eminence higher in whatever   DARW 306:88
   only chance of e.   SHAW 925:26
   raised To that bad e.   MILT 688:11
eminent death reveals the e.   SHAW 922:59
Emmanuel call his name E.   BIBLE 133:22
emotion coarse e. of mankind   ELIOT 366:38
   conveying an e.   HEPW 473:79
   degree of my aesthetic e.   BELL 85:82
   e. of art   ELIOT 366:37
   e. recollected in tranquillity   WORD 1096:37
   expressing e. in the form of art   ELIOT 368:76
   for it is an e.   GOLD 432:90
   language concentrating e.   BRAU 186:22
   less bounding at e. new   ARNO 39:19
   morality touched with e.   ARNO 39:32
   plastic e. requires it   BOCC 171:55
   Poetry.…an escape from e.   ELIOT 368:75
   Science…a source of strong e.   BARZ 75:96
   tranquillity remembered in e.   PARK 754:14
   under stress of e.   POUND 787:97
   undercurrent of e.   UPDI 1037:73
   Undisciplined squads of e.   ELIOT 372:57
emotional e. depth of a woman   SCHR 850:7
   e. withdrawal in…overcrowding   COUP 289:83
   Humour…is e. chaos   THUR 1019:46
   physical and e. sides   BURG 206:90
emotionally e. I know she is better   LEWIS 602:56
emotions basic human e.   ROTH 826:26
   e. as palpable and as true   HOLM 485:72
   e. entirely foreign   WHIS 1069:14
   e. of the everydayness   STEI 965:30
   grounds for the noble e.   RUSK 830:83
   mother of our e.   KAND 541:96
   purgation of such e.   ARIS 34:29
   raised e. both of rage and fear   BYRON 221:11
   see his e. the sport   HARDY 456:86
   used his e. even a little   SAND 840:50
   world of e.   COLE 276:32
emparadised E. in one another's arms MILT 690:59
empathy politician seeking e.   SAFI 836:71
emperor dey makes you E.   ONEI 739:48
   dreamt there was an E.   SHAK 906:99
   e. of ice-cream   STEV 971:36
   revived and was an e.   SHAK 870:20
Emperor E. Caligula's Habits   LONG 610:91
   E. Claudius   LONG 610:92
emperors e. and and kings   MARL 654:12
   Even e. cannot do it all   BREC 186:30
emphasis e. is on the former   KUNI 571:17
   e. on what happens next   RUSK 830:73
   erotic e. upon it   UPDI 1037:67
empire all the rule, one e.   MILT 693:30
   arch Of the ranged e. fall   SHAK 904:58
   bounds of human E.   BACON 56:37
   bounds of human E.   BACON 60:32
   Britain has lost an E.   ACHE 2:29
   British E. and its Commonwealth   CHUR 264:15
   British E.   GEOR 419:88
   brooders…build the E.   OBRI 734:62
   downfall of the British E.   CHUR 263:3

empire (*contd.*)
   e. is…power in trust   DRYD 349:20
   e. must extend, so let extend   MILT 694:33
   e. wilderness of freight and rails   CRANE 295:1
   German E. arose?   HERZL 478:75
   good…for the E.   REDM 804:75
   government is…an E.   ONEI 739:47
   great e. and little minds   BURKE 207:13
   heavily thickening to e.   JEFF 519:77
   hold a vaster E.   MORR 709:80
   honour of the British E.   CHUR 264:22
   How beautiful…under the E.   DURR 357:75
   If the Austrian E. did not exist   PALA 751:55
   lead Britain and her fading e.   MANC 644:66
   liquidation of the British E.   CHUR 264:25
   Lo! thy dread e., Chaos!   POPE 783:11
   loungers and idlers of the E.   DOYLE 343:83
   Mother E. stands splendidly isolated FOST 399:58
   not…Roman or an E.   VOLT 1046:9
   Pageant of E.   SITW 941:17
   play the old Glasgow E.   DODD 334:43
   To found a great E.   SMITH 945:84
   whole Moghul E. is in our power   CLIVE 270:2
   Without the E.   HUGH 501:54
empires day of E. has come   CHAM 249:15
   E. and old women   BACON 55:26
   faiths and e. gleam   SHEL 932:64
   ridiculous e. break like biscuits   FULL 410:42
   Vaster than e.   MARV 658:73
empirical e. system to be refuted   POPP 783:15
   greatest number of e. facts   EINS 363:75
empiricist e.…thinks he believes   SANT 842:87
empiricists opposed camps of the e.   MERT 672:26
employ e. their whole industry   SMITH 945:88
employed mind is actually e.   JOHN 529:71
   so innocently e.   JOHN 529:70
employee In a hierarchy every e.   PETER 767:6
employees e. of the government   TOOLE 1023:6
   love e. and   TSON 1031:42
employer not a polite e.   HOOV 490:63
employers despise e.   TSON 1031:42
   don't ask e.…to *like* blacks   BORO 179:22
   human e. quite literally   MUMF 713:49
   other sides of their e.   DONO 340:36
employment choosing for e.   SWIFT 985:87
   e. by authors of simile   NASH 720:68
   e. for his idle time   WALT 1052:7
   e. of the poor in roads   MALT 643:41
   engaged in his e.   GILB 424:65
   have to seek…gainful e.   ACHE 2:21
   Hunting is not a proper e.   ADDI 8:41
   lower e. of life   JOHN 526:4
   maintain continuous full e.   KEYN 554:31
   provide for full e.   KEYN 555:38
   Wants steady e. in Hollywood   DAVIS 308:24
employs e. the whole mind   QUEN 797:54
emptiness Swinburne is just e. to me QUIL 797:51
empty e. are e. sounds   JOHN 526:6
   Art for art's sake is an e. phrase   SAND 840:55
   carriage…went e., and e. it returned   CH 248:8
   country…disappointingly e.   BARN 72:29
   e. as paper   SCOTT 852:37
   e. of all human substance   SAIN 837:88
   his head be e.   SWIFT 984:61
   if e. dreams so please   HERR 477:53
   philosophy is virtually e.   AYER 53:82
   rich he hath sent e. away   BIBLE 160:54
empty-hearted e. whose low sound   SHAK 902:97
empty-vaulted through the e. night   MILT 683:27
emulation pale and bloodless e.   SHAK 895:41
emulsion feeling of e.   PERE 766:89
enamoured e. of an ass   SHAK 871:51
enchant e. thine ear   SHAK 864:92
enchanted holy and e.   COLE 275:13

enemy (*contd.*)
still the e. — BIBLE 114:34
strike the e. — PANK 752:79
sweet e., France — SIDN 937:54
The eye is the e. — WILD 1080:34
Thinking is the great e. of perfection — CONR 285:11
unrelenting e. — WASH 1054:42
with the wrong e. — BRAD 184:94
worst friend and e. is but Death — BROO 192:24
energies all the e. of his life — PIER 769:32
e. and skills — KEYN 554:34
religious principles and e. — BERD 94:35
energy Adultery introduces some e. — PROU 793:99
convert weaknesses…into burnable e. — BELL 89:43
deprive soul of its e. — BLOOM 169:35
dissipation of e. begin? — KELV 549:35
E. is Eternal Delight — BLAKE 166:72
e. of a whole generation — THOM 1014:36
e. of mighty rivers — MILL 678:26
e. stored up — GERS 420:7
every e. he may put forward — CURZ 302:27
Force is…an invisible e. — LEON 597:76
lakes of mental e. — GREER 445:43
managed to exude e. — SHAR 919:83
minimum expenditure of e. — WILS 1085:26
reason and e.…are necessary — BLAKE 166:71
Science is an all-pervasive e. — BARZ 75:96
tempest, a redundant e. — WORD 1096:18
time and e. from — MORE 707:52
enfant terrible free to be an e. t. — SART 844:6
engaged When a Forsyte was e. — GALS 413:2
engaging Sex is e. — JIANG 522:24
engendered e. by honesty — MURP 715:73
engine curious e. — WEBS 1061:60
great, growing e. of change — TOFF 1022:86
greatest e. of temporary opinion — HAZL 463:7
in dirt, the reasoning e. lies — ROCH 816:51
notes…from her great e. — AUDEN 48:78
science is a two-handed e. — MONT 700:52
small e. that causes revolutions — SHEE 926:49
steam…work the e. — WATT 1055:55
this formidable e. — COOP 287:44
throw herself in front of the e. — SHAW 921:29
two-handed e. at the door — MILT 684:45
engineer glorified sanitary e. — STRA 979:95
engineering e. of consent — BERN 97:91
engineers e. and physicists — KRUT 570:8
look out for e. — PAGN 750:40
today are our e. — LEUP 599:14
engines by our resistless e. — CARL 234:38
e. based on mechanical — LEUP 599:14
e. to play a little on their own — BURKE 207:25
so noiseless when the e. stopped — HEAN 465:41
England a town in the South of E. — ORWE 742:96
amuses the people of E. — JOHN 527:27
any village in E. — TROL 1027:77
apple falling towards E. — AUDEN 46:49
art-form…invented in E. — BEER 84:46
Be E. what she will — CHUR 262:89
between France and E. — JERR 521:16
bow was made in E. — DOYLE 343:94
Church of E. — ROYD 828:42
common law of E. — HERB 474:2
continent will not suffer E. — DISR 332:79
death of Nelson was felt in E. — SOUT 954:41
deep, deep sleep of E. — ORWE 743:8
defence of E. — BALD 65:11
describing E. in a phrase — ORWE 743:17
dress and manners in E. — SHAW 920:4
dull mercantile E. — BUCH 202:25
earthquake were to engulf E. — JERR 521:17
east longitude from E. — MUNDY 714:54
E. and America — GREN 446:54
E. and America — SHAW 926:41

England (*contd.*)
E. and Saint George! — SHAK 881:86
E.'s chief defence — PHIL 768:17
E.…comfortable time-lag — WELLS 1065:45
E. does not love coalitions — DISR 333:39
E.'s foreign policy — GLAD 429:53
E. full of morons — WODE 1089:10
E.'s green and pleasant land — BLAKE 168:20
E. has greater counties — CRIP 296:30
E. has saved herself — PITT 772:75
E.…in my childhood — ORWE 743:8
E. invented the phrase — BAGE 61:52
E.…is a fen — WORD 1096:38
E. is a garden — KIPL 564:13
E. is a great…nation — GARI 415:24
E. is a nation — NAPO 718:34
E. is not ruined — PRIE 790:46
E. is not the jewelled isle — ORWE 743:16
E. is one of the greatest — PALM 752:74
E. is the mother of Parliaments — BRIG 188:49
E. is the paradise of women — FLOR 394:79
E. is unrivalled for two things — DISR 334:33
E.'s mountains green? — BLAKE 168:17
E. mourns for her dead — BINY 162:6
E., my E.? — HENL 472:59
E.'s not a bad country — DRAB 345:26
E.'s on the anvil — KIPL 565:26
E. people have good table manners — MIKES 674:52
E.'s province stands — BURNS 212:31
E. shall bide — KIPL 563:99
E. still stands outside Europe — KEYN 554:28
E. that was wont to conquer — SHAK 867:49
E.'s the one land I know — BROO 192:27
E., the system is benign — CRISP 297:41
E. their E. — MACD 629:7
E. will always be the sister — HUGO 501:63
E. will have her neck wrung — CHUR 264:20
E., with all thy faults I love thee — COWP 293:54
E. would have preferred the risk — CECIL 247:79
every actor in E. — GIEL 423:49
except in E., of course — WAUGH 1057:90
eyes of all E. — WILL 1080:47
fibres of E. — FORS 398:28
for the honour of E. — CONG 281:27
from E. her authors — TROL 1028:96
gentlemen in E. now abed — SHAK 882:5
Go anywhere in E. — SHAW 925:14
God's grace in E. — LATI 583:36
good society in E. — SHAW 925:13
government that E. can have — TROL 1028:82
greatest mere village in E. — DEFOE 312:83
Greece, Italy, and E. did adorn — DRYD 351:58
healthiest situation in E. — KING 558:96
heard that E. Were busied — SHAK 881:79
Heart of E. — DRAY 345:38
high road…to E. — JOHN 527:29
history of E. — MACA 623:10
how can I help E.? — BROW 198:38
hunt the Catholics from E. — LESL 598:94
I am in E., everywhere — BROW 195:89
I shall be in E. — PARK 753:85
in E. a particular bashfulness — ADDI 7:21
In E., even the poorest — HEGEL 466:62
in E. is generally given — JOHN 526:14
In E., justice is open to all — MATH 663:67
in E. nobody goes to the theatre — AGATE 10:65
In E. pop art — MACI 631:43
in E. seven halfpenny loaves — SHAK 861:10
In rural E., people live wrapped tight — CARR 237:13
inhabitant of the North of E. — FORD 396:1
Into E., to drive a prey — BALL -101:29
Ireland gives E. her soldiers — MERE 671:14
kings of E. — GILB 424:62
kynge borne of all E. — MALO 642:25

England (*contd.*)
lie down…and think of E. — HILL 481:10
live half our lives in E. — HYDE 509:12
loans of E. to foreign nations — BAGE 62:64
Lords and Commons of E. — MILT 686:75
man who comes to E. — MANS 648:16
Men of E. — SHEL 929:96
my grave be E. — BROW 195:88
My politics…is E. — DISR 332:88
national sport of E. — TREE 1025:44
naturalist in E. — DARW 306:82
never merry world in E. — SHAK 861:9
no amusements in E. — SMITH 949:58
no nation…less able to do harm to E. — BRIG 188:50
no subject of E. — PITT 771:68
O E.! model to thy…greatness — SHAK 880:74
Oh, to be in E. — BROW 198:36
old E. to adorn — KIPL 563:98
old E.'s roast beef — FIEL 388:46
old E.'s winding sheet — BLAKE 168:5
once even in E. — MORE 706:44
organ-voice of E. — TENN 1003:24
Our E. is a garden — KIPL 564:14
Parliament of E. — BAIL 62:72
poison E. at her roots — BOTT 180:36
poorest he that is in E. — RAIN 800:6
Prime Minister of E. — BUTL 216:97
pulse-less lot that make up E. — LAWR 585:63
remain in union with E. — SCOTT 856:10
respectable as the Church of E. — STEV 973:92
seeing a worse E. — JOHN 530:94
shower of curates…upon north of E. — BRON 191:96
soul's prison we call E. — SHAW 925:15
Speak for E., Arthur! — AMERY 16:68
speech of E. has no name — BRYA 202:19
stately homes of E. — COWA 290:3
stately homes of E. — HEMA 469:4
stately homos of E. — CRISP 297:39
strength and the greatness of E. — CURZ 302:27
strong arm of E. — PALM 752:72
suspended in favour of E. — SHAW 925:16
symbol for E. is the Island — ATWO 45:22
ten thousand…men in E. — SHAK 881:96
that is for ever E. — BROO 192:21
That knuckle-end of E. — SMITH 949:48
the Church of E. begins — PRIE 790:47
There'll always be an E. — PARK 755:29
things I've done for E. — BIRO 163:28
This E., never did — SHAK 872:75
this realm, this E. — SHAK 867:48
under the great seal of E. — PENN 764:56
undoubted right of the crown of E. — COVE 290:90
value on entry into E. — STEN 967:70
way to ensure summer in E. — WALP 1051:91
What do they know of E. — POWE 788:20
What do you think about E.? — AUDEN 46:44
Who dies if E. live? — KIPL 561:18
who only E. know? — KIPL 561:17
You that love E. — DAYL 310:55
youth of E. are on fire — SHAK 880:73
English Africa and the E. tongue — WALC 1048:31
among the E. Poets — KEATS 545:54
An E. home — TENN 994:56
as E.…as a beefsteak — HAWT 462:83
Be friends, you E. fools — SHAK 881:93
beautifully the E. fight! — NAPO 718:29
betwixt E. and Irish — STRA 979:1
bought and sold for E. gold — BURNS 212:32
Canada…E. government — COLO 277:52
chased the E. out of France — LOUI 613:45
creating in every E. breast — MANC 644:66
cricket—it's so very E. — BERN 97:94
dominant facts in E. life — ORWE 743:18
E. and in writing of oure tonge — CHAU 254:15

English (*contd.*)

E. and not E.	HYDE 509:11
E. are all right	WALE 1049:49
E. are best!	FLAN 392:28
E. are born masters	VIDAL 1044:73
E. are funny and peculiar	CELI 247:92
E. artists are…ruined	RUSK 831:7
E. children	GREER 445:41
E….code of immorality	BRAD 183:73
E. conquered us	NAPO 718:30
E. counties like hunting-tunes	BENET 90:60
E. country gentleman	WILDE 1077:66
E. do add here and there	BEAU 80:65
E. don't raise their voices	HELL 469:1
E. have no respect	SHAW 924:1
E. have used to suffrage	CARL 236:85
E. history all about men	BRAD 183:77
E. language readers	GISC 429:48
E. language	ROOS 822:53
E. life…is rather bland	PERE 766:95
E. love of compromise	CARD 232:2
E….maintain grand talent	CARL 236:89
E. manners	JARR 518:60
E. may not always be the best writers	CHAN 250:34
E. may not like music	BEEC 82:11
E. peer of the right sort	WODE 1088:83
E. plays	GOET 431:69
E. poetry is not yet fit	OWEN 748:10
E. poets who grew up	ROET 819:97
E. policy is to float lazily	CECIL 247:81
E. polite by telling lies	BRAD 183:78
E. proletariat…more bourgeois	ENGE 378:87
E. public school	WAUGH 1056:75
E. seem to bid adieu	SMITH 949:42
E. ship, they say	LOND 610:90
E. speaking audiences	WHAR 1068:3
E. subject's sole prerogative	DRYD 350:45
E. talk is a quadrille	JAMES 516:25
E. text is chaste	GIBB 421:30
E. think cricket is a game	MIKES 674:53
E. unofficial rose	BROO 192:25
E. version of the touching melody	CARL 233:25
E. want to be there when she falls	CAMP 226:13
E. winter	BYRON 223:58
E. without an accent	BENC 89:50
European football without the E.	CHAR 253:93
expression in E.	ARNO 38:12
find one E. book	ARNO 38:7
foreigners speak E.	CRISP 297:35
God's patience and the King's E.	SHAK 878:11
His E. reminds me of tattered	MENC 670:91
In an E. lane	BROW 199:62
in plain E.	JONS 535:93
in the E. language	THUR 1019:36
in the E. ranks	WILL 1080:44
judgments of the E. law	SYNGE 988:63
kissed by the E. dead	OWEN 748:9
knowledge of literate E. …desert	CHAN 250:39
lead the E. against the Armada	CUOMO 300:6
made our E. tongue	SPEN 957:96
man writing broken E.	NABO 716:94
marks our E. dead	KIPL 561:54
marrow in the E. tongue	SMART 944:65
mobilized the E. language	MURR 715:78
more martial air than the E.	HAYD 462:88
most beautiful words in E.	JAMES 517:31
muse is…of the E. strain	DRAY 345:32
narrating E. virgins	UPDI 1037:59
never consent…to E. dominion	ANON 22:70
No real E. gentleman	BAGE 61:50
O the E. Ascendancy	MACD 628:92
Of the bold E.	JONS 534:80
old E. way	MACM 636:15
only come from the E.	GORO 436:69

English (*contd.*)

pause to consider the E.	NASH 719:54
prefer their E. sloppy	SAYE 846:51
principle of the E. law	DICK 325:35
really nice E. people	SHAW 925:14
reason the E. dislike them	MORL 708:72
remains of the E. language	COUP 289:81
rolling E. drunkard	CHES 259:31
Roman-Saxon-Danish-Norman E.	DEFOE 312:77
saved many an E. spinster	MITF 697:99
Scots…hear the E. abused	PIUS 772:80
scour these E. hence?	SHAK 910:84
seven feet of E. ground	HARO 458:22
she quite forgot…good E.	CARR 238:21
somethin' he did against the E.	ANON 25:24
speak E. and profanity	HOWE 497:96
success happens to an E. writer	AMIS 17:89
sweet E. tongue	FLEC 393:47
talent of our E. nation	DRYD 350:36
teach the E. how to talk	WILDE 1078:94
the E. and the bears	THOM 1012:95
the E. will penetrate	MACA 622:82
their E. God is not so dominant	CARR 237:14
they are Irish and he is pure E.	OBRI 733:61
thirst, which makes…the E. mad	DANTE 305:71
those pretty E. watercolorists	PISS 771:59
trick of our E. nation	SHAK 877:84
under an E. heaven	BROO 192:22
unlike being E.	FIED 387:38
usual sloppy E.	JOYCE 538:58
wall up with our E. dead	SHAK 881:82
We be all good E. men	TENN 1005:57
well of E. undefiled	SPEN 959:33
when you can't think of the E.	CARR 239:51
White as an angel is the E. child	BLAKE 166:64
wish…so deeply rooted in the E.	BUTL 217:29
with a strong E. accent	SAKI 837:98

Englishman as I am an E.

as thorough an E.	KING 558:95
being an E.	STAN 962:84
E….afraid to feel	FORS 398:47
E. among the under-dogs	WAUGH 1057:90
E. as a guarantee	SHAW 923:73
E. does not travel to see Englishmen	STER 970:20
E….flattered, is a lamb	CHAP 252:75
E.'s heaven-born privilege	ARNO 39:27
E. in the wrong	SHAW 920:11
E. is about to talk French	WODE 1089:99
E. is an island	NOVA 732:39
E. is convinced of one thing	NASH 719:54
E.'s justification in India	CURZ 302:29
E. never enjoys himself	HERB 474:4
E.'s never so natural	JAMES 516:15
E. sets foot on it	STEF 965:26
E….there only a week	FRAS 403:19
E. thinks he is moral	SHAW 921:34
E. was niver improved	DUNNE 356:61
genial E.	TENN 996:95
Give but an E. his whore	OTWAY 746:88
impossible for an E.	SHAW 924:1
in the E. a combination of qualities	DICK 327:82
last great E. is low	TENN 1000:66
man, even more, an E.	MORI 708:68
No E. is ever fairly beaten	SHAW 925:22
not one an E.	WALP 1051:96
one E. could beat three Frenchmen	ADDI 7:18
part of an E.'s constitution	AUST 51:49
part of every E.'s education	HUGH 500:50
powerful image to your average E.	SMITH 946:1
remains an E.!	GILB 423:57
Remember that you are an E.	RHOD 808:1
rights of an E.	JUNI 540:74
takes off his hat to God's E.	SHAW 923:71
the Irishman turned E.	OBRI 734:62

Englishman (*contd.*)

vain, ill-natured thing, an E.	DEFOE 312:76
what an E. believes	SHAW 925:23
Englishmen absurd nature of E.	PEPYS 765:67
damned mischievous E.	SCOTT 856:13
Englishman does not travel to see E.	STER 970:20
E. act better than Frenchmen	BENN 91:87
E. are born gloaters	OBRI 734:62
E. never will be slaves	SHAW 921:33
E….nervously excitable race	DAVI 307:4
find E. doing it	SHAW 920:11
first to his E.?	MILT 686:74
love of E.	THOM 1012:4
Mad dogs and E.	COWA 290:97
our very name as E.	PITT 771:72
When two E. meet	JOHN 527:19
Englishwoman E.'s clothes	SITW 941:17
E. is so refined	SMITH 948:30
Englishwomen better than E.	BENN 91:87
engraving E. then, is, in brief	RUSK 831:5
engulf chasm that threatens to e. him	BANN 70:2
enigma e. of the fever chart	ELIOT 371:51
mystery inside an e.	CHUR 264:11
enjoy did e. the music	JOHN 524:69
do not e. it	JULI 539:68
e. their triumph	HAMM 453:45
here e. the shade	JONS 536:16
highly taught yet not to e.	ELIOT 366:40
impossible to e. idling	JERO 521:3
learnt to e. them	MORT 710:97
liberty, that we'll e.	JONS 535:99
principal business of life to e.	BUTL 217:35
enjoyed e. talking to her	SITW 941:19
enjoying world…worth e.	DRYD 351:72
enjoyment done with e.	RUSK 830:75
essence of Toryism is e.	BAGE 61:49
innocent e.	GILB 424:65
more ascetic reason than mere e.	STARK 963:95
receives as complete e.	HUME 503:7
retrospective e. of successful effort	SHIP 935:20
enjoys Englishman never e. himself	HERB 474:4
enlarge e., diminish, interline	SWIFT 985:2
E. my life	JOHN 525:83
enlargement e. of the language	JOHN 526:7
enlightenment herald of e.	BOOK 178:3
intellectual e.	CURZ 302:29
literature…as transcendent e.	COND 279:85
motto of e.	KANT 542:2
promises freedom or e.	SNYD 951:85
enmities e. between nations	KENN 551:79
enmity at e. with joy	WORD 1098:54
e. between thy seed	BIBLE 103:98
e. o'th' air	SHAK 902:14
enormity e. of the task	ACHE 3:34
enormous Like an e. yes	LARK 581:99
The E. Room was the greatest book	STEIN 965:34
enough e., now, O Lord	BIBLE 111:68
E., if something from our hands	WORD 1100:86
first cries 'Hold, e.!'	SHAK 910:90
if we only get e. of them	JAMES 517:38
not e. jails	HUMP 504:13
poverty is never having e.	WYLIE 1104:51
rainbow is e.	SHAN 918:68
seen e. of one war	JEFF 520:92
Two cheers are quite e.	FORS 399:53
enquire E., define, distinguish	ROCH 816:47
enquiries e. about the UK climate	SAMU 840:47
enrich how to e. a new nation	STIG 977:66
ense calamus saevoir e. patet	BURT 214:68
enshrined e. in 10,000 indexes	ALLEN 14:32
ensigns ships and their e.	ROBE 814:15
enslave No woman shall ever e. me	SHAW 921:29
enslaved either free or e.	GRIL 447:62
e. as farm stock	SHAW 924:94

erotic (*contd.*)
most e. part of the body — BART 75:82
not more e. emphasis — UPDI 1037:67
err fools shall not e. therein — BIBLE 126:83
Kings and Governments may e. — HERB 474:97
Man will e. — GOET 431:73
mortal, and may e. — SHIR 935:26
most may e. — DRYD 350:26
reas'ning but to e. — POPE 780:42
they do not e. — SCOTT 853:48
To e. is human — ANON 28:5
to e. is human — POPE 778:85
errancy die in e. — ABU 1:10
errand in thy joyous e. — FITZ 390:91
send the child a e. — DICK 323:78
slightest e. to the Antipodes — SHAK 879:38
erred have e. exceedingly — BIBLE 110:43
while I e. — GOET 431:83
error commonest e. in politics — CECIL 247:82
discharge from sin and e. — ELIOT 373:77
e.'s fenny bogs — ROCH 816:50
E. is all around it — NICO 727:60
E....never approached — METT 673:31
e. of his way — BIBLE 155:74
e. to imagine the loudest — BURKE 206:98
full of natural e. — PASC 757:55
grave e. to believe — PISS 771:61
judge of truth, in endless e. — POPE 780:43
myopia makes all e. mortal — LOWE 617:9
not a disease but an e. of judgement — DICK 320:12
not wholly free from e. — VINER 1045:78
obstinacy, and e. — POPP 784:26
only one inborn e. — SCHO 849:98
perpetuate an e. for ever — SCHO 849:95
persistent leaning toward e. — CONR 285:3
response to e. that counts — GIOV 428:35
Where there is e. — THAT 1007:11
errors common e. of our life — SIDN 937:64
containing the grossest e. — TOLS 1023:98
e. are volitional — JOYCE 538:51
E., like straws — DRYD 348:85
E. look so very ugly — ELIOT 365:2
e. of the rich — CHES 258:1
knowledge...mixed with our e. — POPP 784:25
less e. of fact — GREE 444:20
multitude of e. — DESC 317:81
point out other people's e. — ELIOT 366:36
reasoned e. — HUXL 509:3
some female e. — POPE 778:94
tares of spiritual e. — HOBB 483:43
erudition e. and his historic impact — NISB 730:5
eruptions Bimbo e. — WRIG 1101:4
Esaias spoken of by the prophet E. — BIBLE 133:25
Esau E. despised his birthright — BIBLE 105:31
E....is a hairy man — BIBLE 105:32
E. sells his birthright — BIBLE 105:29
E. was a cunning hunter — BIBLE 105:30
escalating both sides e. — KENN 552:4
escalator e. from the Social — HUXL 507:66
Escalus thing to be tempted E. — SHAK 896:65
escape Author of the Whole e. — POPE 783:9
from which he made his e. — MILL 678:43
No man should e. — OPPE 741:74
No one can e. — PLATO 774:11
nothing to e. from — ELIOT 373:84
Poetry...an e. from emotion — ELIOT 368:75
poor...can hardly ever e. — FORS 398:34
women cannot e. it — GIBB 422:34
writing as an e. from — WILL 1082:72
escapist e. fiction — GALB 412:86
escarpments screes on her e. — HEAN 465:35
eschew e. the little turf dances — ALLEN 14:31
escort burning building without an e. — VANH 1039:5
Eskimo Hottentot and every E. — LEHR 595:41

Esmé For E. — SALI 839:29
esoteric e. matters — GOWE 437:82
especial Sweet e. rural scene — HOPK 491:67
espionage no place where e. is not — SUN 982:37
espoused fairest, my e. — MILT 691:69
essay e. on 'self-indulgence' — WAUGH 1056:64
good e. ...must draw its curtain — WOOLF 1092:62
Of seeming arms...a short e. — DRYD 352:86
essays greatest of Man's e. — TOYN 1024:19
not much good at e. — BETJ 100:43
essence effluence of bright e. increate — MILT 689:29
e. and quintessence — LOWE 615:72
e. of a book — NABO 717:8
e. of an argument — SCHL 848:74
e. of Christianity — WHIT 1071:61
e. of freedom — ASTE 43:92
e. of inhumanity — SHAW 920:14
e. of music is revelation — HEINE 467:71
e. of real human love — ELIOT 365:13
e. of technology — HEID 467:65
e. of Toryism — BAGE 61:49
e. of war is violence — MACA 623:6
existence comes before e. — SART 844:13
existence precedes e. — SART 844:14
glassy e., like an angry ape — SHAK 896:72
poet gives us his e. — WOOLF 1093:82
poetry is the e. — STEV 972:62
uncompounded is their e. — MILT 687:2
very e. of phenomena — PAST 759:86
with our mixed e. — BYRON 221:20
essential e. oneness of mankind — STEI 965:30
Secrecy is the first e. — RICH 810:67
that something is e. — RENO 807:7
what is e. is invisible — SAIN 836:85
essentiality eternal and infinite e. — SPIN 961:60
essentials e. of a...Prime Minister — WILS 1085:41
Essex fog on the E. marshes — DICK 324:18
In E. seek them all — CRIP 296:30
establishment found a handsome e. — DICK 326:52
the American e. — TIME 1020:68
estate comfortable e. of widowhood — GAY 417:55
e. of the realm — MACA 622:97
Fallen from his high e. — DRYD 351:70
fourth e. in the politics — HAZL 463:11
grown to man's e. — STEV 975:35
in low e. began — TENN 999:44
ordered their e. — ALEX 13:18
out of my e. the sum of £50,000 — CHES 257:83
relieving the human e. — DEWEY 319:95
rescues your e. from your enemies — BROU 193:46
they had his e. — DRYD 349:24
estates live upon their own e. — EDGE 361:33
O, that e., degrees and offices — SHAK 874:31
residents from raw e. — LARK 581:9
esteem come to e. the universe — FONT 395:86
coward in thine own e. — SHAK 908:33
e. not of that obedience — MILT 686:70
expressions of e. for Mr Boss — BAND 69:87
far above him...my e. — DRYD 348:96
higher e. among the gods — PLATO 774:7
lessened my e. of a king — PEPYS 765:64
object of love and e. — LAMB 576:24
esteemed more e. in Russia — SNOW 193:46
not with me e. — SHAK 873:95
shall be lightly e. — BIBLE 109:26
estimate know'st thy e. — SHAK 914:78
estimation highest e. of learning — SIDN 937:59
estranged e. from myself — HUGO 501:64
esurientes E. implevit bonis — BIBLE 160:54
eternal blasted to e. damnation! — SHAW 925:21
Death and I Am found e. — MILT 693:19
e. incognito — BARN 72:26
e., inexorable lapse — STOWE 978:88
e. monotony of passion — FLAU 392:39

eternal (*contd.*)
e. not ourselves — ARNO 40:34
E. Passion! — ARNO 37:83
e. reciprocity of tears — OWEN 748:22
e. want of pence — TENN 996:88
Hope springs e. — POPE 780:36
idea alone is e. — FLAU 392:31
no e. allies — PALM 752:70
not for spreading e. truths — BLISS 169:31
not so much e. vigilance — ORWE 742:95
portion of the E. — SHEL 931:45
Primary word addresses the e. Thou — BUBER 202:21
prompts the e. sigh — POPE 781:49
society as something e. — ORWE 743:11
summer is e. — GUY 449:96
to be boy e. — SHAK 911:18
trust was with the e. — MILT 688:13
variations on the e. struggle — LIN 604:96
eternities starlit with e. unknown — SASS 846:42
eternity are from e. — HOUS 496:71
As doth e. — KEATS 547:11
at last e. changes him — MALL 642:19
certain species of e. — SPIN 960:51
circular e. may seem atrocious — BIOY 162:11
dance round to all E. — FLET 394:67
day joins the past e. — BYRON 220:94
Deserts of vast e. — MARV 658:73
Desire paces E. — DUNC 355:47
e. in an hour — BLAKE 167:1
E. is in love — BLAKE 166:75
'e' is there — DICK 328:16
e....of life — ALLEN 14:34
e. of nothing — RUSK 831:12
E. of pleasures — FORD 397:12
e. of print — WOOLF 1092:63
e. of thought — WORD 1095:14
E. shut in a span — CRAS 295:18
E.! thou pleasing, dreadful thought! — ADDI 8:35
E. was in our lips — SHAK 905:62
E. was in that moment — CONG 280:97
e. without a solecism — BROW 195:75
feel a trace of e. — RILKE 811:85
From Here to E. — JONES 533:53
from here to e. — KIPL 560:22
from the soul's e. — ROSS 824:85
heirs of all e. — SHAK 865:4
image of all e. — BYRON 221:8
in view of God and e. — CAVE 246:71
is the e. that awaits you — THOM 1013:26
Lives in E.'s sunrise — BLAKE 166:82
one equall e. — DONNE 339:34
saw E. the other night — VAUG 1041:20
shadows of e. — VAUG 1040:15
Silence is as deep as E. — CARL 235:78
silence of e. — STEV 974:25
sing of Time or E. — TENN 1003:24
speculation of e. or infinitude — ADDI 7:19
teacher affects e. — ADAMS 5:77
Through all E. to Thee — ADDI 7:20
thyself to all e. — ROSS 824:90
To know e.? — ROET 819:98
wander through e. — MILT 688:15
white radiance of E. — SHEL 931:50
Why didn't E. have this ...age — KRAUS 569:87
ethereal blue e. sky — ADDI 7:22
e. mountain — BENU 94:33
etherized patient e. upon a table — ELIOT 366:46
ethic e. is not an e. — KOHL 568:75
ethical certain e. suspicion — DIDI 330:48
e. reality of the individual — KIER 556:61
unethical and e. advertising — STEF 965:25
ethics aesthetics but not e. — ROGE 820:5
can not conflict with e. — POIN 776:57
drew a system of e. — MACA 623:2

everyone bow to e. SKEL 942:48
  equally faulty to trust e. SENE 858:44
  E. can master a grief SHAK 880:53
  E. feels it TROL 1028:97
  E....holds dual citizenship SONT 953:11
  E. is more or less mad KIPL 560:17
  E. suddenly burst out singing SASS 845:34
  e. will say GILB 424:66
  stop e. from doing it HERB 474:93
everything against e. all the time KENN 552:2
  beginning of e. REAG 803:63
  boxing is e. HEMI 471:68
  Brains are not e. SHAW 920:5
  devourer of e. OVID 747:2
  E. clever has been thought GOET 431:75
  e. could be known and forgiven GEE 417:65
  E....endeavours to persist SPIN 960:52
  e. except space and light HEAT 465:47
  e. had to swing ELLI 374:5
  E. has been discussed ALEM 13:12
  E. has been done INGR 512:47
  E. has been said LABR 572:35
  E. has been written FERN 386:27
  e. I never wanted GARD 414:21
  e. in its place BEET 84:56
  e. includes itself in power SHAK 895:40
  e. is allowed AMIS 17:94
  E. is decided KIM 557:65
  e. is great PASC 757:48
  E. presses on STER 970:15
  e. that he can come by SHAK 860:83
  E. we see TOML 1023:2
  e. would be done far better SIEY 938:69
  good in e. SHAK 885:77
  how dangerous e. is STEIN 965:39
  If you love e. DOST 341:48
  it's about e. in particular SPARK 955:58
  President...has to do e. ASTU 43:99
  real price of e. SMITH 946:93
  Sans teeth, sans eyes...sans e. SHAK 886:96
  Science...knows e. GOUR 437:80
  seeing nothing as the sum of e. DUDEK 354:20
  spirit of youth in e. SHAK 915:83
  sure...that he knows e. CARY 243:23
  take e. away from them SOLZ 952:95
  thanks for e. ATKI 44:3
  there is time for e. BOLD 171:68
  thinks he knows e. SHAW 923:83
  time enough for e. GUNN 448:84
  wanting that have wanted e. HAZL 464:19
  We cannot all do e. VIRG 1045:92
  Where e. is bad BRAD 184:92
  Winning isn't e. PALM 751:66
everywhere E. I see bliss SHEL 926:55
  e.—wherever you look STEI 966:55
  What is e. VINC 1045:77
eves flies in summer e. KEATS 548:17
evidence before one has all the e. DOYLE 343:84
  defective in its e. REGAN 805:95
  e. of our wisdom TROL 1027:68
  e. of supernatural beings STEI 967:68
  e. of things not seen BIBLE 154:50
  false views, if supported by some e. DARW 306:87
  ignore the absence of e. VIDAL 1044:66
  no e. from modern literature BELL 88:27
  presented in e. PARK 755:27
  proportions his belief to the e. HUME 503:9
  Some circumstantial e. THOR 1016:70
  still blind to the e. KOES 568:69
  theater is the primary e. THUR 1019:37
evil accustomed to do e. BIBLE 128:25
  All e. comes from this GIRA 429:46
  all else comes from the e. RODR 819:88
  All partial e. universal good POPE 780:41

evil (*contd.*)
  all that we are e. in SHAK 902:2
  allow its e. effects to go on BUCK 203:33
  an assured e. DOMI 335:56
  an unmitigated e. LAWR 585:73
  being e., speak good things? BIBLE 137:92
  between good and e. HUSS 505:36
  certainty of doing e. BAUD 78:37
  child comes to know e. MITC 696:78
  Children...do not wish to suffer e. LABR 573:52
  clear the land of e. KIPL 561:53
  consciences about doing e. MORE 707:49
  days are e. BIBLE 152:2
  deliver us from e. BIBLE 135:49
  do not easily suspect e. ABEL 1:2
  Drawing is only a necessary e. HEIN 467:74
  Every law is an e. BENT 92:15
  E. be to him that e. thinks EDWA 361:48
  e....face of total need BURR 213:53
  e. in this world PECK 763:38
  e. intreated, or sent NASHE 721:77
  E. is done without effort BAUD 78:34
  e. is wrought by want HOOD 489:50
  E. news rides post MILT 695:55
  e. of...a world wrapped up DICK 324:20
  E. one absbstracted stood MILT 692:3
  E. people...you never forget them DAVIS 308:25
  E. ran like malaria GREE 444:6
  e. seek to bring forth good MILT 687:96
  e. soul producing holy witness SHAK 874:21
  E., what is e.? LAWR 586:86
  e. which I would not, that I do BIBLE 149:23
  e. wrangling with the e. MUIR 712:31
  expose the raw nerves of e. CHUR 262:79
  fear nae e. BURNS 211:17
  fear no e. BIBLE 115:50
  fear of one e. BOIL 171:65
  few and e. have the days...been BIBLE 106:50
  for the good or e. side LOWE 616:78
  forced into channels of e. FAUL 383:80
  free of e. done KIPL 564:4
  good of e. shall produce MILT 693:27
  goodness in things e. SHAK 881:90
  Government...a necessary e. PAINE 750:44
  hurrying the day of e. STOWE 978:88
  Hypocrisy, the only e. MILT 689:44
  If e. does not exist PRIT 791:67
  imagination...is e. from his youth BIBLE 104:13
  intrinsically e. TUTU 1032:55
  Is thine eye e. BIBLE 139:29
  knowing good and e. BIBLE 103:94
  knowledge of good and e. CHEE 255:50
  knowledge of good and e. MILT 685:58
  knowledge of good and e. MILT 685:60
  Man is neither good nor e. BALZ 69:83
  Men's e. manners SHAK 918:65
  mixture of e. in everything COWP 292:50
  no e. in the atom STEV 972:73
  non-existence as an e. SCHO 849:94
  only one e., ignorance SOCR 952:91
  overcome e. with good BIBLE 149:37
  Party is a political e. BOLI 172:71
  passively accepts e. KING 557:73
  perpetrates any e. PLATO 774:18
  places where e. is impossible GENET 418:75
  possible for e. to triumph HAILE 451:11
  practical solutions to...e. GENET 418:74
  predicted e. consequences TROL 1028:83
  preserve thee from all e. BIBLE 119:36
  punishment in itself is e. BENT 92:14
  Recompense to no man e. BIBLE 149:36
  represent poverty as no e. JOHN 527:33
  resist not e. BIBLE 134:42

evil (*contd.*)
  root of all e. BIBLE 154:34
  root of E., Avarice MAND 645:71
  see himself as...good and e. MAIL 639:82
  set in motion the forces of e. CHES 256:70
  Sufficient unto the day is the e. BIBLE 135:53
  sun to rise on the e. BIBLE 134:45
  supernatural source of e. CONR 285:8
  teach...of moral e. WORD 1094:3
  this e. in thy sight BIBLE 116:76
  Those to whom e. is done AUDEN 47:75
  though fallen, and e. tongues MILT 691:87
  vice...lost half its e. BURKE 207:32
  Who knows what e. lurks ATWO 45:30
  woman...author of e. STAN 963:90
  youngling in the contemplation of e. MILT 685:65
evils all its threatening e. WHIT 1073:95
  balls, from which many e. will arise EDWA 361:46
  cure for the e. MACA 622:90
  death the worst of e. HEINE 467:69
  enamoured of existing e. BIER 161:75
  entailed other e. SUMN 981:26
  e. arising from disturbance MALT 643:41
  e. mankind had to fear ELIOT 365:17
  e. of capitalism KINN 559:8
  e. that ye have committed BIBLE 129:31
  e. wrought by...technology GABOR 411:65
  greatest of e. PLATO 774:9
  greatest of e. SHAW 923:77
  mother of all e. RABE 799:92
  must expect new e. BACON 58:94
  necessary e. JOHN 528:47
  no rest from e. PLATO 774:21
  Of two e. the lesser KEMP 549:46
  submit to the inevitable e. TOCQ 1021:75
  Two e.—greed and faction MORE 707:48
  Two e., monstrous either one RANS 802:35
  worst Of e., and excessive MILT 691:79
evocations not e. but last choirs STEV 972:55
evolution birthday present from e. DILL 330:51
  e. of culture LOOS 612:25
  gradual e. of the new order WEBB 1059:17
  method of e. FISKE 390:86
ewe e. obedient to the benders will SPEN 957:97
  one little e. lamb BIBLE 110:47
  tupping your white e. SHAK 897:97
ewe-milking lilting at our e.-m. ELLI 374:2
ewes Ca' the e. to the knowes BURNS 212:41
ex ante referred to as e. a. MYRD 716:92
ex post referred to as e. p. MYRD 716:92
ex-presidency directly to the e.-p. MANN 646:92
ex-president great e.-p. MANN 646:92
exaggerate greatly e. the difference SHAW 923:84
exaggeration my death was an e. TWAIN 1034:14
  pitfalls of e. TROL 1028:95
exaggerations except the e. ADOR 9:50
exalt praise him and e. him BIBLE 159:52
exaltation delight, the e. RUSS 832:19
  e. and horror GRAV 440:27
  e. of the 'average' WHITE 1070:44
  highest pitch of e. BRIL 188:55
  it is our just e. PITT 772:7
  solemn prayers for the great e. COLU 278:63
exalted e. in the earth BIBLE 116:74
  he that humbleth himself shall be e. BIBLE 144:17
  scandal of an e. person's fall CANM 230:31
examination method of careful e. LEBO 591:82
examinations E. are formidable COLT 277:56
example annoyance of a good e. TWAIN 1034:1
  don't set us a good e. WILDE 1077:78
  E. is the school of mankind BURKE 208:48
  E. moves the world MILL 678:24
  e. of the king of Denmark FACK 382:49
  learn by e. PROV 789:28

example (*contd.*)
living e. of natural selection — GOLD 432:87
My great e. — DENH 315:53
practical e. — WHIT 1073:87
exasperate actions continued to e. — BULL 204:52
excavation e. and of self-discovery — WALC 1048:44
excel thou shalt not e. — BIBLE 106:51
excellence acute limited e. — FITZ 390:98
along lines of e. — KENN 552:90
constant in a wondrous e. — SHAK 915:85
e....of the object — WORD 1096:34
e. proper to culture itself — REYES 807:22
ne'er will reach an e. — DRYD 347:66
nothing of e. — THUR 1018:14
of the highest e. — RUSS 832:19
soul exhibiting e. — ARIS 34:26
There shall not be e. — SMITH 947:4
excellencies dwell...upon e. — ADDI 7:15
excellent everything that's e. — GILB 424:73
e. if you were a village — STEIN 966:48
E. wretch! — SHAK 899:29
no one more fair and e. — SPEN 958:12
Excelsior strange device, E.! — LONG 611:2
exceptional e. and insignificant — MAIL 639:82
exceptions I never make e. — DOYLE 343:90
Science does not permit e. — BERN 97:83
excess behave in e. except — LACL 573:61
Give me e. of it — SHAK 893:91
lover...dies from e. — BART 75:83
Nothing in e. — ANON 20:44
road of e. — BLAKE 166:73
that which depends on e. — ARIS 34:27
To some divine e. — COLL 277:47
excesses protection...from...e. — BLACK 164:46
excessive if it is not e. — HAMI 453:39
welcome was not e. — USTI 1038:81
exchange By just e. one for the other — SIDN 936:47
e. rate is only a statistic — KRUG 570:6
open e. of major differences — AUNG 50:23
thrilling mutual e. — THOM 1015:45
value in e.! — SMITH 946:94
exchanged e. in addition — JEVO 521:20
exchequer Barons of the E. — WALP 1051:81
excise E. A hateful tax — JOHN 526:11
Exciseman deil's awa wi' th' E. — BURNS 212:34
excite e. my amorous propensities — JOHN 525:87
others which e. by their vigor — GAUG 416:38
excitement as a source of e. — HORN 494:37
connoisseur of tame e. — MOORE 705:26
enough aesthetic e. here — BART 74:72
e. and gladness — BUEC 203:42
jazz band used for artificial e. — BLISS 169:31
special e. of a rumored resignation — SHUL 935:30
excites e. their contempt — REED 805:91
exciting e. life...outside — SABA 835:56
flute...is too e. — ARIS 34:34
found it less e. — GILB 426:95
look both moral and e. — FERB 385:9
exclude e....the working classes — GLAD 429:50
exclusive One's prime is e. — SPARK 955:52
the most e. worms — PARK 754:10
exclusiveness civilization...of e. — EMER 377:62
excommunicated e. by the medieval — ANON 29:42
excommunication on pain of e. — INNO 512:56
excrement e. is his own — DONNE 336:65
excremental Whiteness is but an e. — MILT 685:65
excrucior sed fieri sentio et e. — CATU 245:64
excursion e. to another planet — BIRD 163:15
excursionist noisy Plebeian e. — CHES 257:86
excuse e. every man will plead — SELD 857:34
e. every man will plead — SELD 857:35
e. for never giving me anything — SHAW 924:6
e. for this war...color and race — DUBO 353:9

excuse (*contd.*)
E. My Dust — PARK 753:89
use the rejection as an e. — ANGE 19:27
excuses Several e....less convincing — HUXL 506:56
execrable E. English Theatre — GOET 431:69
executed e. in this way every year — STEV 977:61
execution e. is a perfunctory affair — LEWI 602:71
e. of his plan — STEU 970:30
pardon after e. — SHAK 918:66
stay of e. for six years — CARS 241:90
stringent e. — GRANT 439:9
why the e. has not been — JOHN 526:1
executioner e.'s repentance — BENE 89:58
Lord High E.! — GILB 425:86
yet I am mine own e. — DONNE 339:21
executive half-creature of the e. — MANS 648:14
nominated by the e. — GIBB 421:19
weakest e. in the world — DISR 332:87
executives Damn the great e. — LEWIS 602:54
executor make you full e. — WEBS 1067:71
exempt no more e. from saying — STER 970:14
exercise accountable for its e. — DISR 332:72
applies himself to labour and e. — CONF 280:91
bodily e. profiteth little — BIBLE 154:30
dancing is love's proper e. — DAVI 307:6
e. for a research scientist — LORE 613:42
E.? I get it on the golf course — SKEL 942:38
E. is bunk — FORD 396:9
e. is invention — SMITH 946:91
e. of his own style — JONS 536:23
forgone all custom of e. — SHAK 890:2
his way of taking e. — DOUG 341:61
imaginative e. — VIDAL 1044:58
manly Scottish e. — PENE 764:53
more...courage, than any other e. — PEEL 763:44
never taken any e. — TWAIN 1034:22
only possible form of e. — WILDE 1079:8
part of its beneficial e. — JAMES 516:17
pleasant e. of hope — WORD 1099:66
rich advantage of good e.? — SHAK 872:72
sad mechanic e. — TENN 998:19
Squash—that's not e. — COWA 291:8
what e. is to the body — STEE 964:17
Whenever I feel like e. — HUTC 506:44
wise, for cure, on e. depend — DRYD 352:87
women...need e. — BRON 191:93
exercises delighting in such e. — POE 775:42
e. are unbloody battles — JOSE 537:35
e. in arrested development — SELF 858:38
preaching...most healthy e. — WESL 1067:71
remove these e. from — STUB 980:11
running around doing e. — ARMS 35:50
exertion e. is too much for me — PEAC 762:28
forced on e. — AUST 52:68
keenest spur to e. — BENT 93:18
undergone severe e. — LIVI 607:47
exertions e. of a free people — PITT 772:73
saved herself by her e. — PITT 772:75
Exhall Dodging E. — ANON 26:56
exhausted e. as a great man — MILL 676:94
I'm e., or conditioned, or perverted — PUIG 794:18
exhibitionism Acting is...e. — OLIV 738:28
exhibitions seven historic e. — DUNL 355:50
exhilarated provident, fatigued, e. — MUNRO 714:60
exhilarating it's e. to be alive — RICH 809:48
exhilaration coffee has an e. about it — HOLM 486:3
feeling of e. — GREE 444:11
exile bind your sons to e. — KIPL 562:64
die in e. — GREG 446:46
e. has been to the Irish — WILDE 1075:31
Fated to be an e. — VIRG 1045:79
forget makes the e. the longer — WEIZ 1062:87
kiss, Long as my e. — SHAK 911:16

exile (*contd.*)
refuge for the e. — GARI 415:24
world is a place of e. — HUGH 498:12
exiles e. and invaders — ATWO 45:21
e. from our fathers' land — GALT 413:8
none save e. feel — AYTO 53:87
Paradise of e. — SHEL 927:67
exist A, B, C and D...already e. — SCHM 848:80
Deeds...do not e. — BALZ 69:80
e., but are identical — FORS 398:43
e. in order to be happy — SCHO 849:98
e. with the nature I actually have — DESC 318:83
Facts do not cease to e. — HUXL 506:52
Facts do not cease to e. — HUXL 506:55
from the people...all must e. — DISR 332:72
he need not e. — DEVR 318:93
If evil does not e. — PRIT 791:67
making something e. by observing — BURR 213:58
nothing can e....without God — SPIN 960:47
nowhere does it e. — TEMP 993:29
right to e. — KELM 549:33
Sir, I e.! — CRANE 295:14
unable to e. as writers — SPEN 957:91
existence Every moment of one's e. — MAIL 639:72
aquire a kind of material e. — MARX 661:22
art, that monopolizes one's whole e. — DUDEK 353:18
certain that e. is meaningful — HAMM 453:46
conceive any kind of e. — HUME 503:98
convince me of God's e. — NEWT 725:41
could not endure their e. — SHAW 923:81
dead level of provincial e. — ELIOT 365:20
diversity of e. — KENN 552:88
every evil...presupposes e. — SCHO 849:94
e. and opportunity — TEMP 993:30
e. as a nation — PITT 771:72
e. comes before essence — SART 844:13
e. in the nature of things — FORD 396:98
e. is but a brief crack — NABO 716:95
e. of decent, serious, British filth — OSBO 746:69
e. of me — WHIT 1073:84
e. of students — NABO 717:99
e. of things that are — PROT 792:82
e. only adds to our peril — MOUN 711:13
e. or...hope is gone — AUST 52:70
e. precedes essence? — SART 844:14
form only comes into e. — OLSEN 739:36
God who would let us prove his e. — BONH 173:87
harvesting from e. — NIET 728:74
historians...He tolerates their e. — BUTL 217:34
humanities in his very e. — ROLL 821:26
impossibility...proves to me his e. — LABR 573:58
Independent e.—so called — HUXL 507:66
justifies its own e. — WILDE 1076:42
law of their e. — MILL 675:68
lead...an e. — THUR 1018:15
Let us contemplate e. — DICK 322:72
main themes of our e. — WHITE 1069:21
matter of fact or e. — HUME 504:10
miracle...of naked e. — HUXL 507:83
mysteriousness of e. — MALL 641:14
necessary to our easy e. — DICK 321:33
paint the e. of a d. — MARC 649:43
prove that the e. of classes — MARX 661:27
put out of e. — DICK 327:81
sordid perils of actual e. — WILDE 1076:39
spheres of e. — ELIOT 372:66
system of e....with no eye — WIEN 1074:14
threatens the very e. of life — SONT 953:7
unmaking so much e. — ANDR 18:10
world in which children have their e. — DICK 326:67
existentialism first principle of e. — SART 844:15
subsequent E. — KERO 557:62
exists man first of all e. — SART 844:14
Nothing e. except atoms — DEMO 315:45

exit E., pursued by a bear — SHAK 911:25
  leave an e. through which — WAITE 1048:30
exits e. and their entrances — SHAK 885:91
exotic Cambridge…less e. — ANON 27:60
  much to be said for e. marriages — BELL 88:31
exotics languish like e. — WOLL 1091:38
expansion e. of the human race — SCHR 850:7
expansionist relax my e. measures — KEYN 554:33
Expatiate E. free o'er all this scene — POPE 780:32
expect a right to e. — TRUM 1029:17
  Could anyone e. less? — SHER 932:76
  e. less of them — JOHN 532:28
  e. the unexpected — HERA 473:87
  takes longer than you e. — HOFS 484:61
expectancy Pick up bad habits of e. — LARK 581:94
expectation e. is equalized — ILLI 511:33
  e. makes a blessing dear — SUCK 981:20
  e. of getting what he wants — ORWE 742:94
  e. of too great a happiness — FONT 395:90
  E. whirls me round — SHAK 895:47
  strain of e. — FIRB 389:76
  trifle short of the wearer's e. — DICK 326:70
expectations to have great e. — ONEI 740:63
expected different from what one e. — KISS 566:36
  e. a man should see — JOHN 530:87
  For I had e. always — SPEN 956:74
  no reasonable man could have e. — HERB 474:99
  nothing is e. to happen — THER 1009:41
expediency consistent e. — THOR 1016:67
  e. of different schemes — STEU 970:41
expedient all things are not e. — BIBLE 150:56
  e. in the way of our thinking — JAMES 518:50
  so pleasing an e. — STEE 964:16
  strikes…not as an e. — ENGE 378:89
expedition abandoning the e. — DOUG 341:59
  e. had now performed — SPEKE 955:61
  We made an e. — PEAC 762:30
expel e. them from here — JOAN 522:27
expenditure annual e. 1996 — DICK 324:6
  e. of fortunes — PEARY 762:35
  E. rises to meet income — PARK 755:35
  general economy and particular e. — EDEN 360:21
  was so much e. justified — SPEN 956:82
expense at the e. of the…masses — QUINE 797:67
  At small e.! — GILB 424:78
  cannot be achieved without e. — PIUS 772:79
  e. damnable — CHES 257:85
  one God…the e. of two? — CLOU 271:46
  repay the trouble and e. — BELL 87:1
  use alone that sanctifies e. — POPE 779:24
  without incurring the e. — SHER 933:1
expenses for the funeral e. — JERO 521:7
expensive comes a little more e. — LEAC 588:35
  e.…to be poor — BALD 64:96
  Witnesses are e. — RACI 799:97
experience a sense of mastery over e. — PAGE 749:32
  according to which we e. them — HEID 467:66
  accumulated and organized the e. — HUXL 508:1
  act without the benefit of e. — MILL 678:45
  actual quality of e. — LEAV 591:73
  all e. is an arch — TENN 994:58
  amateur e. of…nieces — RIDGE 811:77
  belief…founded upon my e. — DOYLE 344:5
  blissful visionary e. — HUXL 507:84
  constantly amalgamating…e. — ELIOT 368:80
  crisis of her e. — AUST 52:73
  different sort of e. — BOWL 182:57
  dirty nurse, E. — TENN 1004:52
  distinctive Irish e. — DONO 339:35
  equality of e. — MILL 675:24
  e. a story within — KAFKA 540:85
  e. and comparison — JOHN 531:10
  E. and history teach — HEGEL 466:63
  e. and intuited knowledge — MO 698:11

experience (*contd.*)
  e. and understanding of life — MILL 678:23
  e. counts for everything — WILS 1084:10
  E. does not show that — KEYN 554:32
  e. has left me with…belief — ORWE 743:7
  E. has taught me — HOUS 496:80
  e. is an arch — ADAMS 5:73
  e. is like a cryptograph — SCHO 849:49
  E. is…larger than language — RICH 809:57
  E. is never limited — JAMES 516:19
  E. is not what happens — HUXL 507:64
  e.…is the bitterest — CONF 279:87
  E. is the child of Thought — DISR 332:71
  E. is the name — WILDE 1077:63
  e. of being human — LEWO 603:74
  e. of life — BEER 83:34
  e. of mixed exaltation and horror — GRAV 440:27
  e. of the ages — CONN 283:81
  e.…of the woman writer — WITT 1088:82
  E. shows…enterprises seldom end — ELIZ 374:96
  e. to make me sad — SHAK 886:18
  e. which led to a former — JEVO 521:23
  e. within…this contradictory motion — SARR 843:4
  feast of e. — GOLD 432:92
  from any human e. — JAMES 515:6
  greatest…e. unknown to man — OGDEN 736:99
  had the e. but missed the meaning — ELIOT 372:60
  heavy with useless e. — RICH 809:43
  I have e.: I have a wife — CONG 281:26
  inner e. and inner feeling — LAWR 587:5
  It's called e. — NOFZ 730:1
  knowledge derived from e. — ELIOT 371:46
  knowledge…by e. — BACON 60:43
  knowledge…recorded e. — CARL 235:71
  learn in their own e. — SCHW 852:31
  lessons of historical e. — KISS 565:30
  light which e. gives — COLE 275:27
  long e. of many generations — GLAD 429:53
  many years of…sad e. — SACK 835:63
  matters outside…everyday e. — CONR 285:10
  Music is your own e. — PARK 753:87
  No matter how vital e. — GLAS 430:60
  old age and e. — ROCH 816:51
  old e. to attain — MILT 683:16
  one word, from e. — LOCKE 609:72
  one year's e. 30 times — CARR 237:12
  optimist…never had much e. — MARQ 656:39
  philosophy teaching by e. — CARL 235:75
  Some by e. find those words — CONG 280:1
  store of e. — FRAME 400:78
  stream of your e. — JAMES 517:48
  substitute for real e. — ALBEE 11:83
  system to be refuted by e. — POPP 783:15
  terminate in sensory e. — ELIOT 368:76
  that hopeless wisdom of e. — ONEI 740:52
  triumph of hope over e. — JOHN 528:57
  try a new e. — SHAW 924:91
  Twenty years e. as an actress — DAVIS 308:24
  very little e. of self-government — EDIN 361:39
  war…we don't have direct e. — DALL 303:50
  When one does not e. it — SARR 843:3
  women offer our e. — LEGU 594:30
  world is diminished by the e. — SHAW 926:48
  world…we don't have to e. — FRIS 406:64
  worth a life's e. — HOLM 486:79
  Your e. will be a lesson — AMIN 16:70
experiences categories in which e. — MANN 646:93
  e. of life — NIEB 727:64
  wisdom…after e. — PROU 793:92
experiment e.…in communal living — BOWL 182:55
  good e. lasts forever — KAPI 542:8
  men of e. — BACON 55:29
  Pure poetry is pure e. — SANT 842:91
  reasoning to the test of e. — LAVO 585:58

experiment (*contd.*)
  wherever the e. has been fairly tried — SHEL 927:59
experimental All poetry is e. — STEV 972:59
  e. reasoning concerning matter — HUME 504:10
experimentation spirit of e. — FRAN 402:11
experiments inquiries and e. — MENC 669:64
  not necessarily…physical e. — CONN 283:80
expert An e. is someone — HEIS 467:79
  became an e.'s art — RUDO 828:46
  never trust an e. — MAMET 643:54
expertness unaccountable e. — THUR 1018:14
experts divine right of e. — MACM 635:3
  e. as stately and grand presidents — SUN 982:39
  stock market e. — AUGU 50:19
  you should never trust e. — SALI 839:34
expiate death my days should e. — SHAK 913:51
  something to e. A pettiness — LAWR 586:83
expiring e. do foretell of him — SHAK 866:44
explain and which never e. — THOM 1014:36
  best way to e. it — CARR 239:46
  e. to Her Majesty — KEMB 549:36
  Never complain and never e. — BALD 65:14
  You e. nothing, O poet — CLAU 268:91
explained painting…cannot be e. — RENO 807:7
  Science has 'e.' nothing — HUXL 506:51
  Shut up he e. — LARD 580:90
explainer Being is the great e. — THOR 1016:63
  said he was a village e. — STEIN 966:48
explanation devil…is the only e. — KNOX 567:62
  explain his e. — BYRON 221:25
  no e. is necessary — SEAT 857:25
  saves tons of e. — SAKI 838:16
  unless there is a verbal e. — COLE 273:79
explanations author's e. — MACL 634:76
explicable all things become e. — CLAU 268:91
explode Or does it e.? — HUGH 499:19
  point where they e. — HENZE 473:75
exploit composed and high e. — MILT 688:14
  e. of the gallant man — MILT 685:56
exploitation e. of their adult slave — GREER 445:41
exploiters against their capitalist e. — LENIN 595:50
exploiting e. a heavenly gift — QUIL 797:63
exploration was a…venture — THES 1009:45
  shall not cease from e. — ELIOT 373:74
explore happy nature to e. — POPE 780:45
  irresistible need to e. — BRON 190:79
  let us e. the stars — KENN 550:62
explorers endeavours are unlucky e. — DOUG 341:59
exploring E. is delightful — BUTL 217:30
explosion at the centre of an e. — ORWE 743:6
  bring decay or e. — RUSS 832:28
  hell of an e. — CATTO 245:57
export attempt to e. revolution — STAL 962:79
  E. or die — ANON 26:46
expose do not let me e. myself — SCOTT 856:17
expositions e. of the doctrines — MORR 709:81
exposure unseemly e. of mind — HAZL 464:23
expounder e. of our religious belief — SPEKE 955:61
express e. in the small of the back — WODE 1089:89
  how e. and admirable — SHAK 890:4
  little I can e. — NABO 717:5
  never keen to e. themselves — BRAD 183:84
  one's happiness to e. — MOORE 705:23
Express morons reading the E. — WODE 1089:10
express-train e.-t. drew up there — THOM 1012:9
expressed could no otherwise be e. — MONT 701:64
  that which cannot be e. otherwise — DELI 315:43
expression define an e. …is to eliminate — QUINE 797:66
  desire for aesthetic e. — WAUGH 1056:74
  E., for me, does not reside — MATI 663:73
  e. for the inner sound — KAND 541:95
  e. in English — ARNO 38:12
  e. in vain — HEMI 470:17

expression (*contd.*)
e. is to the thought — FLAU 392:35
E. is the dress — POPE 778:81
e. may often be called bald — ARNO 40:42
e. of falling gravely downstairs — CUMM 299:73
e. of human separateness — MILL 677:7
e. of life as growth — MILL 678:42
e. of our…state of mind — FEIN 385:99
e. of the will to power — PAZ 762:25
e. which the few desire — PARE 753:83
first man I heard use the e. — ELLI 374:5
gave her the e. — THUR 1019:34
Italy. is a geographical e. — METT 673:29
most perfect e. of scorn — SHAW 925:20
my effort is their self e. — THOM 1010:60
official e. of civil society — MARX 660:11
others by their hunted e. — LEWIS 601:40
Perhaps it was the right e. — WATE 1055:50
perpendicular e. — SHAW 925:32
right to any mode of e. — POUND 785:58
sufficient power of e. — CHES 258:98
supreme e. of the mediocrity — TROT 1029:5
vulgar e. of the passion! — CONG 280:6
expressions e. of a people reflected — ROCK 818:77
e. of esteem for Mr Boss — BAND 69:87
feeling…about some religious e. — RABI 799:94
pure e. of feeling — AYER 53:80
so reserved e. — DONNE 339:24
expressly we are told e. — SWIFT 984:73
exquisite e., and…unsatisfied — WILDE 1076:52
extemporanea medley of e. — PARK 754:8
extensions such e., such spreadings — DONNE 339:24
exterminate e. a nation — SPOCK 961:62
extermination weapons of mass e. — RUSS 833:32
external idea of an e. cause — SPIN 960:54
impression of e. things — RUSK 830:84
extinct labelled 'E.' — KING 559:5
extinction doomed to e. — POUND 786:81
presage of e. — SCOTT 852:35
sure e. that we travel to — LARK 582:19
extinguish e. hell — REED 805:84
e. the light of my mind — JUANA 539:66
extinguished assimilated…never e. — DOUG 342:73
Nature is…seldom e. — BACON 59:9
extra add some e., just for you — LARK 582:14
always pay it e. — CARR 240:67
extra-marital e.-m. relationships — ALLEN 14:49
extraction e. of surplus labour — MARX 660:21
extraordinary E. how potent — COWA 290:95
interested in the e. — HUBB 498:4
work of one e. man — HUBB 498:5
extras No e., no vacations — DICK 321:44
extravagance with e. goes…waste — DILL 330:52
extravagances look upon all his e. — STEV 973:94
extravagant e. and irrational — SWIFT 985:87
e. with his own — SALL 839:37
extreme politics of the e. centre — WELL 1064:16
take things to an e. — KLEIN 567:51
extremes be whaur E. meet — MACD 627:76
E. meet — HOOD 489:41
measured at the e. — JAY 519:74
two e. of passion — SHAK 904:49
woman did not fly to e. — CRISP 296:34
Women are E. in the — LABR 572:38
extremism E. in the defence — GOLD 433:31
extremities e. of her corollaries — OCON 735:82
leave the body and e. — SMOL 950:64
extremity E. of griefs — SHAK 862:42
exuberance e. of his own verbosity — DISR 334:24
exultations friends are e. — WORD 1098:59
eye Affection beaming in one e. — DICK 322:71
an e. simply — DOYLE 344:21
apple of his e. — BIBLE 108:2
apple of his e. — BIBLE 130:66

eye (*contd.*)
artistic sense of e. or ear — WHIS 1069:14
as it were in the e. — MILT 685:55
ball as the e. confin'd? — MILT 694:41
Bear welcome in your e. — SHAK 907:20
brought an e. for all — TENN 999:51
But with his leener e. — MARV 657:66
camera is an e. in head — WELL 1063:2
Care…in every old man's e. — SHAK 869:97
Cast a cold e. — YEATS 1107:93
censor the gleam in my e. — LAUG 583:42
Christ in every e. — PATR 761:15
corner of your e. — NEW 724:18
curious hand or e. — LOVE 615:65
curious hand or e. — LOVE 615:65
dark time the e. — ROET 819:99
drappie in our e. — BURNS 211:2
drown an e. — SHAK 913:58
drumlie grew his e. — BALL -101:36
every e. shall see him — BIBLE 156:97
e. did see Olivia — SHAK 893:93
e. diffused a quickening ray — WESL 1066:58
e…ear…tongue of the people — STEAD 964:4
e. enthrallèd to thy shape — SHAK 871:45
E. for an e. — BIBLE 134:42
E. for e. — BIBLE 107:69
e. has permitted no change — HUGH 500:37
e. hath caught new pleasures — MILT 682:1
E. hath not seen — BIBLE 150:46
e. is the hammer — KAND 541:97
E. Nature's walks — POPE 780:33
e. never sees outlines — GOYA 437:83
e. of Almighty God — GLAD 429:52
e. of American man — BARR 72:3
e. of my vnderstanding — JULI 539:67
e. of the big wind — MAIL 639:69
e. of the gods — WORD 1100:91
e. on the object — ARNO 38:5
e. on the prize — ANON 28:19
e. on the right hand — RUSH 829:71
e. that can open an oyster — WODE 1089:5
e. that cannot be turned around — PLATO 774:23
e. that sees too deep — FADI 382:53
e. to e. — PEEL 763:44
e. to see nor tongue — LENT 596:67
e. was backward cast — SPEN 957:7
e.…with thy nest — WORD 1100:87
Fair nature's e., rise — MARL 654:21
ferlie he spied wi' his e. — BALL 67:52
fettered to her e. — LOVE 615:62
find a friend…close one e. — DOUG 342:67
Foley, I have only one e. — NELS 722:98
formed the e. — BIBLE 117:5
God finally caught his e. — KAUF 543:18
God with his mercyful e. — ANON 22:71
guide them with mine e. — BIBLE 115:59
had but one e. — DICK 321:41
Half hidden from the e.! — WORD 1095:8
harvest of a quiet e. — WORD 1095:12
hath closèd Helen's e. — NASHE 721:83
hollow cheek or faded e. — TENN 997:9
horrid deed in every e. — SHAK 908:32
human e. could see — TENN 995:77
I have a good e., uncle — SHAK 879:35
if thine e. offend thee — BIBLE 138:19
if thy right e. offend thee — BIBLE 134:41
in the twinkling of an e. — BIBLE 151:72
In woman's e. the unanswerable — BYRON 221:14
invisible to the e. — SAIN 836:85
Is thine e. evil — BIBLE 139:21
Its e. is always open — TOCQ 1021:77
its e. is pasted. — MACC 625:49
judgement of the e. — LEON 597:85
less in this than meets the e. — BANK 69:88

eye (*contd.*)
like a joyless e. — SHEL 932:73
long grey beard and glittering e. — COLE 273:83
look into a human e. — MELV 668:44
looked into the e. — YEATS 1106:81
may charm our e. — COLL 277:47
mine e. seeth thee — BIBLE 113:27
Monet is only an e. — CEZA 248:6
more than meets the e. — KIPL 564:13
mote that is in thy brother's e. — BIBLE 135:55
nimble jugglers that deceive the e. — SHAK 865:1
no e. to our convenience — WIEN 1074:14
no profaner e. may look — MILT 683:14
No shape to feed each gazing e. — DYER 358:88
object seen, and e. that sees — WORD 1096:34
objects seen by the e. — PIERO 769:38
Of e., and ear — WORD 1094:99
one e. may be very agreeable — SHER 933:81
One e. was entirely gone — BIRD 162:13
out of the corner of the e. — HOLL 485:71
painted skin contents the e.? — SHAK 864:87
Pity the e. — MACL 633:2
pleases the e. — TINT 1021:72
poke in the e. — CARY 243:21
presented to the e. or ear — CRAB 294:84
roguish twinkle in his e. — THOM 1015:53
Sail and sail, with unshut e. — ARNO 36:56
see e. to e. — BIBLE 127:96
see with the spiritual e. — FRIE 405:59
see with, not thro' the E. — BLAKE 168:6
sees with equal e., as God — POPE 780:35
Set honour in one e. — SHAK 882:18
shuts up sorrow's e. — SHAK 871:47
soft black e. — MOORE 706:38
still-soliciting e. — SHAK 902:99
such a wistful e. — WILDE 1078:97
suff'ring e. inverted Nature sees — POPE 779:21
tender e. of pitiful day — SHAK 909:59
that inward e. — WORD 1099:70
The e. is the enemy — WILD 1080:34
the e. of God — OLIV 738:31
through the e. of a needle — BIBLE 139:25
watchful e. …of England — PALM 752:72
what brightens the e. — WHIT 1074:2
What immortal hand or e. — BLAKE 167:95
when first your e. I eyed — SHAK 915:84
wink your e. at some…girl — MENC 669:60
with a threat'ning e. — SHAK 872:68
with e. serene — WORD 1099:63
with sovereign e. — SHAK 913:59
yellow to the jaundiced e. — POPE 778:86
eye-beams Our e.-b. twisted — DONNE 337:94
eyeball e. to e. — RUSK 830:72
e.—like a bastion's mole — SMART 944:69
eyeballs never to move his e. — AMIS 16:71
eyefull E. Tower is devine — LOOS 613:32
eyelashes lose our teeth and e. — LEAR 590:66
eyeless E. in Gaza at the mill — MILT 694:38
Turn out that e. villain — SHAK 903:28
eyelids close your e. — YEATS 1105:64
tired e. upon tired eyes — TENN 994:49
weigh my e. down — SHAK 877:94
When she raises her e. — COLE 275:31
With e. heavy and red — HOOD 489:45
eyes act their dream with open e. — LAWR 587:13
all tears from their e. — BIBLE 157:15
almost in his e. — MILT 686:70
amazes my e. as though — LOWE 615:76
amethyst of anemones — BRAS 185:13
And all e. else — SHAK 912:40
as frontlets between thine e. — BIBLE 108:90
asked him with my e. — JOYCE 538:57
assailed by e. — JAMES 517:41
audience look to their e. — SHAK 870:30

eyes (*contd.*)

bat with tears in your e.	BRAD 184:95
bees-winged e.?	BETJ 99:29
before the e. of the world	JOHN 523:38
Behind the E. of God	DICK 328:8
bodily hunger in his e.	SHAW 923:80
brightness in their failing e.	BLUN 170:40
cast your e. on buildings	PEI 764:49
cat with bright green e.	MONRO 700:47
cats with golden e.	SACK 835:62
censured by our e.	MARL 655:27
close my e.	HILL 481:10
Closed his e. in endless night	GRAY 443:90
cold commemorative e.	ROSS 825:94
Cortez when with eagle e.	KEATS 544:33
cry our e. out	LLOYD 608:52
dark e. darting light	BYRON 222:44
darkness...no more assail mine e.	DELA 314:33
death, come close mine e.	GIBB 422:32
deign...to turn thine e.	JOHN 525:82
delivered...mine e. from tears	BIBLE 118:25
doors are hateful to my e.	OTWAY 746:81
downcast e.	WELD 1062:92
dwell in lovers' e.	SHAK 913:64
dying e. were closed	POPE 779:7
emerald e.	GRAY 441:51
envious e.	WELLS 1064:26
excited by...tone of their e.	WYETH 1103:46
e., and...forehead gaze	MARV 658:73
e. are blurred	ADE 8:42
e. are lenses	DOUG 341:58
e. are lodestars	SHAK 870:26
e. are made the fool	SHAK 908:40
e. are oddly made	HAMM 454:56
e. are quickened	GRAV 439:15
e. are sentinels unto	MIDD 673:42
e. are to rest upon	STEV 973:98
e. as wide as a football pool	CAUS 246:66
e. at the full midday beam	MILT 686:75
e. can in another's e. read	ARNO 36:70
e. Darker than...pansies	TENN 995:65
e. did see my substance	BIBLE 120:50
e. follow you about	ORWE 745:55
e. have seen the glory	KING 558:86
e. have seen the King	BIBLE 124:61
e. have seen thy salvation	BIBLE 142:79
e. might be shining for me	LAWR 587:12
e. more bright	YEATS 1106:83
e. of all England	WILL 1080:47
e. of all wait upon thee	BIBLE 120:53
e....of an unsuccessful rapist	HEMI 471:44
e. of God and men	LESL 598:94
e. of gold and bramble-dew	STEV 976:55
e. of man are never satisfied	BIBLE 122:9
e. of our mind	GREG 445:45
e. Of proud Adonis	MARL 654:24
e. of the blind shall be opened	BIBLE 126:82
e. of the Lord run to and fro	BIBLE 112:89
e. of the Old World	MANS 647:99
e. of the world are upon you	EISE 363:78
e. of them both were opened	BIBLE 103:95
E. open on growing	REID 806:97
e. shall be opened	BIBLE 103:94
e. so helpless and appealing	LERN 597:87
E. still dazzled	LIND 605:12
e., that roll in vain	MILT 689:30
E. ...to study Flies?	POPE 783:9
e. the gazers strike	POPE 778:93
e., the glow-worm lend thee	HERR 478:66
e. were as a flame of fire	BIBLE 156:99
e. were blind with stars	HODG 484:51
e. were deeper	ROSS 824:79
e. were green as leeks	SHAK 872:59
face with blinking e.	SASS 845:24

eyes (*contd.*)

fiery e. are fixed	MARL 652:86
flourish where you turn your e.	POPE 778:74
fortune and men's e.	SHAK 913:57
frightened look in its e.	SITW 941:22
full of e. within	BIBLE 157:9
gather to the e.	TENN 997:2
Get thee glass e.	SHAK 904:38
glazed e. of a soldier dying	BISM 164:40
glazed look that comes into their e.	WILD 1080:36
Golden slumbers kiss your e.	DEKK 313:11
good turns e. for e. have done	SHAK 913:54
gray hazel e.	GUNT 449:87
great inspector, with a myriad e.	STEAD 964:8
Had I your tongues and e.	SHAK 904:51
happiness through another man's e.	SHAK 887:30
has the e. of youth	SHAK 878:19
Hath not a Jew e.?	SHAK 872:80
have a pair of e.	DICK 320:28
Her e. are homes	TENN 999:33
Her e. nose, mouth, skin	MACE 629:12
hid from our e.	SMITH 950:61
his desperate e.	BERR 98:6
His e. fixed	YEATS 1107:90
His flashing e.	COLE 275:18
Histr'y ain't got e. to see	LAMM 578:49
hit newspaper reader between e.	BRIS 189:61
I have e. like a bullfrog	DAVIS 308:27
I lifted up mine e. again	BIBLE 130:65
I see nothing with my e.	SAPP 842:92
if e. could penetrate	VIEI 1044:75
in our e.	MACC 625:45
in the world's e.	YEATS 1105:69
innocence is closing up his e.	DRAY 345:40
ladies, whose bright e.	MILT 682:3
large blue e., fair locks	BYRON 219:68
Let waking e.	DANI 304:62
lie heavily upon her e.	ROSS 823:73
lift up mine e. unto the hills	BIBLE 119:36
light in a lady's e.	ANON 27:62
long ere my e. had seen	WORD 1100:90
looked at me with shrewd e.	LAWR 586:92
looks into the e. of a native	LESS 598:96
Love looks not with the e.	SHAK 870:28
made one...Stretch one's E.	BELL 87:10
Make thy two e. like stars	SHAK 889:74
mask...shades our e.	DUNB 354:33
Meet in her aspect and her e.	BYRON 221:16
Mine e. are full of tears	SHAK 867:65
mine e. dazzle	WEBS 1061:71
Mine e. doth itch	SHAK 900:50
mine e. had seen it	BIBLE 111:58
Mine e. have seen	HOWE 497:98
mistress' e. are nothing	SHAK 915:92
my daughter's e.	SHAK 912:34
my e. looked back at me	RHYS 808:31
night has a thousand e.	BOUR 181:48
Night hath a thousand e.	LYLY 620:62
no cheerful cottage has blest my e.	SCHAW 847:61
not a friend to close his e.	DRYD 351:70
not meant for human e.	MUIR 712:29
not put our e. out	TAYL 992:21
Not with his e.	SACK 835:61
Oedipus with his bloody, blinded e.	PAGE 749:31
Of e. again so royal	SHAK 906:8
Oh e., no e.	KYD 571:26
old Eben's e. were dim	ROBI 815:31
one whose subdued e.	SHAK 900:64
Only Have E. For You	DUBIN 353:2
only, with thine e.	JONS 535:5
optics of these e. to behold felicity	BROW 195:84
optimist to open your e.	SAND 841:76
Our e., upon one double string	DONNE 337:94
our longing E. are turned	BLAKE 165:57

eyes (*contd.*)

over my neck and e.	STEV 973:97
pair of sparkling e.	GILB 426:97
passion and party blind our e.	COLE 275:27
peep through their e.	SHAK 872:76
Philistines...put out his e.	BIBLE 109:21
pictures in our e. to get	DONNE 337:95
play the idiots in her e.	SHAK 896:50
quaint enamelled e.	MILT 684:46
quiet e.	STEV 976:54
rape us with their e.	FREN 404:39
Religion resides in our e.	LEWIS 601:34
set thine e. upon that which is not?	BIBLE 121:95
shall my sad e. again behold	LANY 580:82
Sleep dwell upon thine e.	SHAK 869:94
Soft e. looked love to e.	BYRON 219:84
Stars scribble on our e.	CRANE 295:5
starveth in thy e.	SHAK 870:21
strike mine e.	JONS 535:1
sun rose in your e.	MACC 626:62
tears are in my e.	MASE 662:35
tears for ever from his e.	MILT 685:51
tempts your wandering e.	GRAY 441:54
That girl's clear e.	THOM 1012:10
that which was right in his own e.	BIBLE 109:23
their pretty e. may roll	POPE 779:3
they hurt our e.	UPDI 1037:64
Thine e. my pride	SIDN 937:58
thou hast doves' e.	BIBLE 124:51
thoughts have e.	LYLY 620:59
To celebrate her e.	GRAY 441:61
to the hills will lift mine e.	SCOT 856:23
to these courteous e.	JONS 534:73
two grey e.	SHAK 894:5
two red e. that stare	RANS 802:37
ugly death within my e.	SHAK 863:54
Underneath Day's azure e.	SHEL 927:70
until you see the white of their e.	PUTN 796:38
unto dying e.	TENN 997:4
When absent from her e.	ROCH 817:64
where you turn your e.	POPE 778:76
wheresoe'er I turn my ravished e.	ADDI 6:98
windows of the e. of cats	DRAY 346:41
with bedroom e.	AUDEN 48:97
With e. up-raised	COLL 277:50
with two blered e.	LANG 579:72
without lowering her e. and blushing	SARR 843:2
wondering e. should appear	MOORE 704:5
write the beauty of your e.	SHAK 912:47
You have lovely e.	CHEK 256:62
young e. could see	NEIL 722:95
your e. had once	YEATS 1105:60
youth's e. burned	ROSS 824:88
eyeservice Not with e.	BIBLE 152:5
eyesight e. has always been weak	GREG 446:47
Eysium E. have ye known	KEATS 544:48
Fabians civilization of the F.	INGE 511:39
man fallen among F.	LENIN 595:52
fable f., song, or fleeting shade	HERR 477:62
nocht but f.	BARB 71:14
vnder ane fenyeit f.	HENR 473:87
fables f. in the legend	BACON 57:64
old wives' f.	BIBLE 154:30
fabric f. of America	MACC 625:40
f. of the heavens	MILT 691:80
monotonous f. of life	MILL 678:36
pull of a f. is governed	MOORE 705:28
face 50s f....60s f....70s f.	WATE 1055:50
a beautiful f. is a dumb convention	PUBL 794:1
acceptable f. of capitalism	HEATH 466:53
Accustomed To Her F.	LERN 597:89
Am I in f. to-day?	GOLD 433:22
at their f. value	TAWN 991:7

face (*contd.*)

autumnal f., her pieced beauty!	JONS 535:*88*
Before I knew thy f.	DONNE 337:*85*
before my f. the great increase	SURR 982:*41*
bend down my strange f.	SEXT 859:*63*
blot on the fair f. of creation	BRON 191:*94*
blow over the f.	AUBR 45:*35*
boot in the f., the brute	PLATH 773:*95*
boot stamping on a human f.	ORWE 745:*60*
born with a different f.?	BLAKE 167:*98*
bright f. of danger	STEV 976:*49*
cannot f. it steadily	ELIOT 372:*62*
canst not see my f.	BIBLE 107:*77*
cause his f. to shine upon us	BIBLE 116:*85*
chaos clapped on to my f.	WELLS 1064:*25*
colors don't quite match your f.	ASHF 41:*64*
commandments in your f.	SHAK 861:*99*
Cover her to	WEBS 1061:*71*
curse thee to thy f.	BIBLE 112:*96*
dar'st not see my f.?	BEAU 80:*76*
decays in the f.	BEHN 85:*73*
Do thou amend thy f.	SHAK 876:*63*
draw a full f.	DRYD 351:*63*
each f. was turned	VIRG 1045:*81*
earn the f. you have at fifty	CHAN 251:*56*
everybody's f. but their own	SWIFT 984:*57*
f. a British Government	TUCH 1031:*45*
f.…in a jar by the door	LENN 596:*62*
f.…is so peculiarly unpleasant	SNOW 951:*74*
f.…like a wedding cake	AUDEN 49:*7*
f. ne'er shows	HERR 477:*54*
f. of a moving-picture actor	MENC 670:*90*
f. of a saint	WELLS 1065:*40*
F. of a traitor!	HUGO 502:*72*
f. of American literature	PORT 784:*38*
f. of night is fair	TENN 1002:*94*
f. of the world	LAUT 584:*53*
f. of Venus	BARR 73:*56*
f. softly made up	THAT 1007:*7*
f. that launched a thousand ships	MARL 654:*19*
f. the man of the time	STEV 971:*50*
f. the music and dance	BERL 95:*61*
F. to f., silent	BROW 197:*16*
f. to the light	SASS 845:*29*
f. turned to the past	NARO 719:*40*
f. wearing the fixity	HARDY 456:*2*
f. with an undaunted tread	STEV 975:*42*
f. with blinking eyes	SASS 845:*24*
f. would be hardly observed	MONT 701:*55*
fall flat on your f.	THUR 1019:*27*
False f. must hide	SHAK 908:*37*
famine in his f.	CHUR 262:*80*
Fanny Kelly's divine plain f.	LAMB 576:*17*
fell on his f.	BIBLE 140:*50*
filth returns in's f.	WEBS 1060:*36*
first time…I saw your f.	MACC 626:*62*
garden in her f.	CAMP 228:*39*
gave his whole f. the expression	CUMM 299:*73*
give me a f.	JONS 535:*89*
glimpse of His bright f.	VAUG 1040:*15*
God has given you one f.	SHAK 891:*28*
golden f. the meadows green	SHAK 913:*59*
good f. is a letter of recommendation	ADDI 7:*13*
hairy about the f.	SHAK 871:*50*
hand…goes over the f.	GARBO 414:*17*
Has he not a rogue's f.?	CONG 280:*11*
heart in's f.	SHAK 911:*22*
Her f. was lovely	SPEKE 955:*62*
Her fist of a f.	THOM 1010:*61*
herds, of human f. divine	MILT 689:*31*
hid the f.	DRYD 346:*49*
hides a smiling f.	COWP 292:*29*
homely f.	GILB 424:*61*
honest, sonsie f.	BURNS 210:*84*

face (*contd.*)

How my f., your flower	BROW 197:*29*
How unlike marble was that f.	KEATS 547:*2*
I have a grumpy f.	PINO 770:*45*
Intellectuals take apart her f.	SAIN 836:*81*
Jezebel…painted her f.	BIBLE 111:*80*
keeping your f. or your figure	CART 242:*11*
King's real. or his stamped f.	DONNE 337:*79*
kissed her…dainty f.	ASHF 41:*70*
like a f. full of character	MAUG 665:*91*
Look into my f.	ROSS 825:*93*
look on Helen's f. in hell	PARK 754:*4*
Look on her f.	POPE 778:*94*
look the East End in the f.	ELIZ 374:*97*
looked him honestly in the f.	DAVI 308:*13*
looking for the f.	YEATS 1106:*83*
Lord spake unto Moses f. to f.	BIBLE 107:*74*
loss made one side of the f. repulsive	BIRD 162:*13*
love's f. May still seem love	SHAK 914:*79*
lying on his f.	THAC 1006:*86*
make his f. shine upon thee	BIBLE 107:*81*
man has a black f.	EDWA 362:*49*
mannish manner of mind and f.	CARY 243:*17*
mark in every f. I meet	BLAKE 167:*92*
met him f. to f.	SULL 981:*24*
mind's construction in the f.	SHAK 907:*24*
mist on the sea's f.	MASE 661:*32*
monstrous carbuncle on the f.	CHAR 253:*91*
morning f.	GOLD 433:*12*
Moses hid his f.	BIBLE 106:*55*
most kiss-worthy f.	SIDN 937:*56*
my pilot f. to f.	TENN 1005:*66*
never see my f. again	TENN 1004:*47*
Newton with…silent f.	WORD 1096:*27*
no f., only two profiles	ASQU 42:*86*
not recognize me by my f.	TROL 1028:*94*
oft in my f.	SURR 982:*40*
oil to make his f. to shine	BIBLE 118:*16*
on the f. of the globe	SMITH 949:*46*
only f. I like to see	CAMP 227:*19*
paint in the public's f.	RUSK 831:*9*
painted f. of a savage	DICK 325:*41*
paradise…in his f.	DRYD 349:*6*
passions glowing in a human f.	MATI 663:*73*
people whom a fair f.	MAIL 640:*93*
Pity a human f.	BLAKE 166:*69*
plummet-measured f.	YEATS 1107:*91*
poster with the enormous f.	ORWE 745:*55*
praised him to his f.	TENN 1005:*60*
prayed for in our f.	BROW 197:*20*
proved to thy f.	SHAK 861:*15*
red in the f.	BENT 93:*29*
Royalty puts a human f.	RUNC 828:*51*
rude wind Blows in your f.	SHAK 903:*31*
sages have seen in thy f.?	COWP 292:*38*
saw the f. of God	MARL 654:*14*
seeing his own f. in the glass	WILDE 1076:*45*
Sex Life in Ancient Rome f.	AMIS 16:*72*
She has a lovely f.	TENN 994:*47*
shining morning f.	SHAK 885:*93*
sigh of the east on my f.	CONR 284:*96*
sing in the robber's f.	JUVE 540:*80*
smug suppressions of his f.	WELLS 1064:*29*
stamping on someone's f.	OSBO 745:*67*
stand f. to f.	KIPL 560:*23*
staring me in the f.	THUR 1019:*39*
straight in the f.	GILL 426:*3*
Strike heaven on the f.	SHAK 909:*72*
string to each side of its f.	LEAC 588:*29*
such a f. should bear	SHAK 866:*36*
such a February f.	SHAK 880:*67*
sullen cold Exhausted f.?	SASS 845:*32*
surgeon…responsible for this f.	CUOMO 300:*4*
tears run…down my f.	OBRI 734:*70*

face (*contd.*)

that homely f.	WORD 1097:*41*
the f. he deserves	ORWE 745:*63*
the huge massy f.	MACA 623:*4*
three have changed the whole f.	BACON 55:*30*
thy classic f.	POE 776:*47*
Thy f. is valanced	SHAK 890:*10*
torso which has no f.	YOUR 1108:*11*
truth has such a f.	DRYD 350:*49*
turn away thy f.	SHAK 884:*66*
turning my f. towards home	PARK 753:*85*
unacceptable f. of capitalism	HEATH 466:*52*
unclouded f. of Truth	SCOTT 852:*33*
until you're blue in the f.	NEWM 724:*26*
up to the f. of a nation	ROCK 818:*77*
upon the night's starred f.	KEATS 544:*50*
Vice…familiar with her f.	POPE 780:*44*
view our inner f.	GREG 445:*45*
Visit her f. too roughly!	SHAK 888:*53*
way plain before my f.	BOOK 176:*61*
wear one f. to himself	HAWT 461:*71*
white f.	GIOV 428:*39*
whole f. of the earth	PASC 757:*59*
whole world in his f.	LONG 611:*98*
woman's f. with nature's own hand	SHAK 913:*50*
wounds are in his breast and f.	DAVIS 309:*39*
your changing f.	YEATS 1105:*60*
Your f., my thane	SHAK 907:*28*

faces almost everywhere two f. | DRYD 347:*73*

among so many millions of f.	BROW 195:*90*
breathing in their f.	SHAK 917:*38*
clouds…silent f.	WORD 1100:*79*
cover their f.	KNIG 567:*54*
f.…a gallery of pictures	BACON 58:*98*
f. as thin as credit cards	AMIS 17:*84*
f. in the crowd	POUND 785:*52*
f. of American women	FITZ 391:*16*
f. was the same immemorial look	LESS 598:*99*
foreign f.	SWIN 986:*23*
God…looks on shock-pried f.	EBER 359:*10*
hid…our f. from him	BIBLE 127:*99*
know the f. I shall see	ROSS 824:*90*
lord and owners of thier f.	SHAK 914:*81*
make f.	JOHN 529:*76*
make f.	SCHN 848:*85*
men with ugly f.	MASE 662:*50*
Mild monastic f.	CLOU 271:*44*
most other people have f.	TOOLE 1023:*6*
ne'er touched earthly f.	SHAK 912:*47*
plain men have rosy f.	STEV 976:*54*
probed their f.	ANGE 20:*32*
seen better f. in my time	SHAK 902:*11*
strange f., other minds	TENN 1004:*45*
take their f. from 'em	PRIE 790:*43*
undentifiable flying f.	MACG 630:*31*
With f. new	LOWE 616:*91*
with vivid f.	YEATS 1105:*71*

facilitates be admitted that it f. much

　　　　　　　　　　　　LACL 573:*63*

facility F. is a dangerous thing | SLOAN 943:*59*

fact a f. …so dreamlike | RICH 809:*44*

apparent statements of f.	AYER 53:*79*
believe that any f.	VIDAL 1044:*58*
by an ugly f.	HUXL 508:*99*
can't figure him out like a f.	SHUL 936:*37*
conceal from ourselves the f.	PASC 757:*51*
concerning matter of f.	HUME 504:*10*
dependence of one f.	HOBB 482:*37*
disagreeable f.	STEV 972:*80*
drinking at the fountain of f.	PIER 769:*32*
every f. …has been examined	PEAR 762:*32*
evil comes from this f.	GIRA 429:*46*
f. and fiction shouldn't be mixed	BOWEN 181:*49*
f. is you got to	WALK 1049:*57*

fairy (contd.)

calls up the realms of f.	BYRON 223:53
Come not near our F. Queen	SHAK 871:40
f. kind of writing	DRYD 351:59
I mean by f. lamps	WOOD 1092:49
moral tests and tasks set in f. tales	ELKIN 374:98
night-tripping f. had exchanged	SHAK 875:35
no one ever marries in a f. tale	KING 558:99
power of f. hands	GRAY 441:59
serve the F. Queen	SHAK 870:35
no one ever marries in a f. tale	KING 558:99
ugliest f. in the world	KING 558:97

fairy-godmother author's f. g.   LUCAS 618:30
fairy-gold We dealt in f.-g.   QUEN 797:54
fairyland childhood...f.   BOGAN 171:39

everybody's got a F.	TRAV 1025:33

faith add f., Add virtue, patience   MILT 693:30

America...was an object of f.	RABAN 798:76
author and finisher of our f.	BIBLE 154:54
basis of true f.	VIDAL 1044:66
By f., and f. alone	TENN 998:15
comes i' f. full sail	CONG 281:34
died in f.	BIBLE 154:51
dissent is an act of f.	FULB 409:24
Draw near with f.	BOOK 174:23
dying for a f.	THAC 1007:96
f., and...fire	ARNO 38:1
F....belief without evidence	BIER 161:82
F. comprises	TILL 1020:62
F. consists in believing	VOLT 1046:10
f. finally free itself	CUPI 301:11
F. gives new light	TAYL 992:21
f., hope, charity	BIBLE 150:62
F., I have been a truant	SHAK 860:92
f. I search for	SAND 840:55
f. in fundamental human rights	UNIT 1036:45
f. in the difficultest points	BROW 195:73
f. in the imperishable dignity of man	CARL 234:44
f. in the magic of official forms	WAUGH 1057:96
f. is a fine invention	DICK 327:95
f. is kneeling by his bed	DRAY 345:40
F. is the state of	TILL 1020:63
f. is the substance of things	BIBLE 154:50
F., like a jackal	MELV 667:31
F. may be defined briefly	MENC 669:62
f. melteth into blood	SHAK 879:36
f. of a Tory	POWE 788:18
f. of Christ	BOOK 175:35
f., so that I could remove mountains	BIBLE 150:62
f. that is the privilege of man	BUSH 215:91
f. that right makes might	LINC 605:3
F., that's as well said	SWIFT 986:13
F....the Pierless Bridge	DICK 328:9
F.'s transcendental dower	WORD 1100:86
f. unfaithful kept	TENN 1002:15
f....we can make it	DICK 320:9
f. without doubt	UNAM 1035:39
F. without works is dead	BIBLE 155:65
For him, f.	BALZ 69:76
fought for Queen and F.	TENN 1005:60
Found f. in me	DRAY 345:37
fright my f.	DRYD 350:50
future states...are left to f.	BYRON 223:48
genial f.	WORD 1097:43
gift of f.	JOHN 522:31
good fight of f.	BIBLE 154:54
have f. as a grain of mustard	BIBLE 138:16
have kept the f.	BIBLE 154:41
heresies...explosions of f.	BREN 187:32
impossibilities...for an active f.	BROW 195:72
In f. and hope	POPE 780:31
increase Catholic f.	VAZD 1041:24
inmost f. is overthrown	SASS 845:39
just shall live by f.	BIBLE 148:11

faith (contd.)

kept f. with me	HARDY 457:14
lamp of f.	WORD 1100:90
life of doubt diversified by f.	BROW 199:55
like an arch, is f.	MILL 678:39
losing or regaining f.	FITZ 390:94
lost f. in individual endeavour	CARL 234:40
make room for f.	KANT 542:6
man's f. in himself	SHAW 920:98
may we bring f.	THAT 1007:11
more f. in honest doubt	TENN 999:53
my cast-iron f.	STEV 976:50
My f. shall wax	DANI 304:61
My staff of f.	RALE 800:13
necessary...he hold the Catholic F.	BOOK 174:2
no f. in human perfectibility	POE 776:46
no f. in physic	JONS 534:79
no need for the f.	HOFF 484:54
Non-violence...first article of my f.	GAND 414:13
not an amiable f.	CARL 235:81
not f., but mere Philosophy	BROW 195:86
not found so great f.	BIBLE 136:64
O thou of little f.	BIBLE 138:8
O ye of little f.?	BIBLE 136:68
reward your f. in us	SMITH 947:8
Science...a f. as fanatical as any	BARZ 75:96
sea of f.	ARNO 36:64
shield of f.	BIBLE 152:8
simple f. than Norman blood	TENN 995:70
stand fast in the f.	BIBLE 151:74
still by f. he trod	LIND 605:12
suspension of disbelief...poetic f.	COLE 275:20
take thy word for f.	SHAK 910:96
test of our f.	LLOY 608:59
there is no f.	KIER 556:55
there is yet f.	ELIOT 371:44
times of f. as best	SMITH 948:34
triumphs of f.	RUNC 828:53
truth of our f.	JOHN 522:36
turning...people to our holy f.	COLU 278:63
unshakeable f. in...enterprise	BURT 214:62
walk by f., not by sight	BIBLE 151:79
was of the f.	AMIS 16:78
wears his f. but as the fashion	SHAK 878:27
When f. is lost	WHIT 1074:3
Where there is doubt, f.	FRAN 401:91
with my childhood's f.	BROW 197:19
With Punic f.	SALL 839:39
with Thee in f.	HAMM 453:44

faith-healer f.-h. of Deal   ANON 26:37
faithful Be thou f. unto death   BIBLE 157:3

called F. and True	BIBLE 158:30
f. friend is the medicine	BIBLE 132:91
f. in that which is least	BIBLE 143:5
f. over a few things	BIBLE 140:41
f. to thee, Cynara!	DOWS 343:81
give...a f. account of men	ELIOT 365:6
moderately f. wife	SHAW 922:55
So f. in love	SCOTT 853:54
Translations...are seldom f.	CAMP 227:22

faithfulness great is thy f.   BIBLE 128:32
faithless Be not f., but believing   BIBLE 147:77
faiths f. and empires gleam   SHEL 932:64

fanatically dedicated to...religious f.	PIRS 770:52
men's f. are wafer-cakes	SHAK 880:78

fake can't f. quality   BURR 213:56

freedom...was...a f.	ORWE 742:5
learned to f. that	GOLD 434:48

fakir posing as a f.   CHUR 264:8
falcon be a f. and go free   DUNC 355:48

dapple-dawn-drawn F.	HOPK 491:88
f. cannot hear the falconer	YEATS 1106:77
Gentle as f.	SKEL 942:34

Falklands F. held a mirror up   RABAN 798:73

Falklands (contd.)

F. thing fight between two bald men	BORG 179:15

fall Another thing to f.   SHAK 896:65

by dividing we f.	DICK 329:21
Created...half to f.	POPE 780:43
dead man is the best f. guy	CHAN 251:47
decline and f.	GIBB 421:29
despairing posture of his f.	POE 776:44
dew shall weep thy f. tonight	HERB 475:32
do not want to f.	HUGO 502:71
f., and not rise again	BIBLE 125:72
f. flat on your face	THUR 1019:27
f. half in love	SALI 838:21
f. of a prince	ANON 21:54
f. of the last civilisation	READ 803:55
f. out with those we love	TENN 997:96
f. through the air	GOLD 432:85
F. to thy prayers	SHAK 878:10
fear no f.	BUNY 205:73
great was the f. of it	BIBLE 135:63
haughty spirit before a f.	BIBLE 121:84
If he f. in	SHAK 875:44
If only we might f.	ANON 26:51
less likely to f.	GAY 416:51
Life is a horizontal f.	COCT 272:65
meditated on the F.	BETJ 101:54
No paradise, no f.	SNYD 951:82
nowhere to f.	ALAN 11:37
pride comes before a f.	WELD 1062:91
Rome alone can make Rome f.	BELL 86:88
should happen to f.	SCOTT 854:72
Soar not too high to f.	MASS 662:54
some by virtue f.	SHAK 896:68
take heed lest he f.	BIBLE 150:55
though free to f.	MILT 689:34
voices dying with a dying f.	ELIOT 367:49
we f. and get crushed	DAY 310:47

fallacies science is...exploded f.   RAND 801:21
fallacy f....about winning   BLAN 169:24

f. of retrospective determinism	BEND 89:57
Pathetic F.	RUSK 830:84
principle...suspect some f.	DARW 306:90

fallen f. from grace   BIBLE 152:90

Greece...though f., great!	BYRON 219:74
How are the mighty f.	BIBLE 110:44
How art thou f.	BIBLE 125:70

falling feeling I'm f.   FERL 386:21

Part of a moon was f.	FROST 406:74
without f. over	FREE 403:30

fallows Russet lawns and f. grey   MILT 682:1
Falls foaminess of the F.   SALA 838:17
false be not f. to others   BACON 58:89

Believe f. teachers	SHAK 916:8
Beware f. prophets	BIBLE 135:60
Ere I am f. to you	OHAG 737:6
every individuality is...a f. step	SCHO 849:95
Everything is f.	BECK 81:2
f. definition of the situation	MERT 672:24
F. face must hide	SHAK 908:37
f. gallop of verses	SHAK 886:1
f. ideas prevail as to woman	STAN 962:86
f. of heart	SHAK 915:88
f. sincere	POPE 781:56
f. to any man	SHAK 888:67
Followed f. lights	DRYD 350:50
idle and most f. imposition	SHAK 899:25
If she be f.	SHAK 899:36
In friendship f.	DRYD 349:15
man who is f. to his friends	BERK 95:56
Ninety-nine times...is f.	EINS 363:48
origin of f. science	HAZL 464:18
prov'd true before, Prove f. again	BUTL 217:22
reject as if absolutely f.	DESC 317:77
reject it as being f.	AYER 53:79

false (*contd.*)

Ring out the f.	TENN 1000:56
they have committed f. report	SHAK 880:64
thoughts dally with f. surmise	MILT 685:48
true poet…from the f.	POUND 787:96
trying to think everything f.	DESC 317:78
with love f.	YEATS 1105:60

falsehood category of truth and f.

	AYER 53:80
cuts f. like a knife	GURN 449:90
distinguishing truth from f.	DESC 317:76
f., cowardice, and poor descent	SHAK 860:85
Let her and F. grapple	MILT 685:62
strife of Truth and F.	LOWE 616:78
to express lying or f.	SWIFT 985:88
unfurnish'd Of f.	DRYD 348:98
what a goodly outside f. hath!	SHAK 874:21

falsehoods f. to deceive the public

	STEF 965:25
f. which interest dictates	JOHN 527:21

falsehood embraced a f.

	ANDE 18:9

falseness f. in all our impressions

	RUSK 830:84
salutary pleasure in proving their f.	DARW 306:87

falser f. than vows made in wine

	SHAK 886:14

falsetto curious f. voice

	STRA 979:98

falsifiable statement…must be f.

	POPP 783:22

falsity regions of sin and f.

	MILT 685:66

Falstaff what should poor Jack F. do

	SHAK 876:64

falter hesitate and f. life away

	ARNO 37:91

fame advances without coveting f.

	SUN 982:36
ancient and prophetic f.	MILT 688:18
by verse seek f.	SIDN 937:58
claim to literary f.	BENN 91:84
Cromwell, damned to everlasting f.!	POPE 781:51
F. and rumour	JONS 534:85
F. and tranquility are two	MONT 701:68
f. can never heal	AYTO 53:87
f. did not delay	DRAY 345:36
F.'s eternal beadroll	SPEN 959:33
F. is a food	DOBS 334:35
F. is a powerful aphrodisiac	GREE 444:16
F. is based on what people say	DUDEK 353:14
f. is in the song	CARM 236:4
F. is no plant	MILT 684:43
f. is shrewdly gored	SHAK 896:54
F. is the spur	MILT 684:42
F.'s luscious pot	RICK 811:76
f., of valour	MARL 653:92
Fareweel to a' our Scottish f.	BURNS 212:30
first alike in f.!	LOVE 614:61
frailty hath thy f.	NASHE 721:79
gate to good f.	BACON 56:46
general achieves f.	TS 1031:40
genius…not to purchase f.	DRYD 348:84
great was his f.	EGAN 362:55
grow great in f.	DIBD 319:4
Let f., that all hunt	SHAK 865:4
live by f.	SPEN 959:28
Long life to thy f.	SCOTT 856:15
love and f. to nothingness sink.	KEATS 544:50
Man dreams of f.	TENN 1002:7
no one shall work for f.	KIPL 562:60
Physicians of the utmost f.	BELL 87:6
pursued f. always in the hope	STAEL 961:69
Rather use than f.	TENN 1002:8
servants of f.	BACON 57:68
that is f.	BERR 98:16
the desire of f.	TENN 1003:18
verse the f. enrols	DONNE 338:15
write for money or for f.	MOORE 705:23

famed As she is f. to do

	KEATS 548:19

familiar Don't let us be f. or fond

	CONG 282:44
F. in his mouth	SHAK 882:2

familiarity F. breeds contempt

	TWAIN 1034:2

families and there are f.

	THAT 1008:23
begin our public affection in our f.	BURKE 208:40

families (*contd.*)

best-regulated f.	DICK 324:14
branch of…antediluvian f.	CONG 281:16
but two f. in the world	CERV 248:99
F.! I hate you!	GIDE 423:45
happy f. resemble each other	TOLS 1023:96
in the best-regulated f.	NORTH 732:33
Mothers of large f.	BELL 87:1
sensibility from…large f.	COUP 289:83
setteth the solitary in f.	BIBLE 116:86

family appalling dangers of f. life

	HUXL 507:67
be so in a f.?	ASTE 43:91
beautiful f. talk	COMP 279:71
bread for the f.	LEWIS 601:49
brought up a large f.	GOLD 432:1
character of a f.	STER 969:94
conduct of every private f.	SMITH 945:88
each member of the f.	FRAME 400:78
every f. in America	JOHN 524:57
exceedingly clannish f.	SHAW 926:43
f. as an institution	MILLS 679:64
f. denied both stories	SAKI 837:5
f. does not need to do	ROCK 817:67
f. from sinking their property	MOOD 703:95
F. indivisibility	ROTH 826:23
f. joke that when	ROTH 826:10
f. life is all the life she knows	SHAW 924:95
f. with the wrong members	ORWE 743:17
fine a f. he comes from	LEE 593:11
fruitful source of f. discontent	BEET 84:55
incest holds the f. together	INNIS 512:53
influence…than that of our own f.	CHUR 262:78
insecurity…in a single-parent f.	ELLW 375:20
member of the f.…is happier	FALU 382:57
not lugged into F. Rows	WODE 1089:91
not of war…but of f.	CHILD 260:52
organization of the f.	MARX 660:11
other members of the f.	OZICK 748:24
Others have their f.	CATH 244:48
patriarchy's…institution is the f.	MILL 679:60
sell members of my f.	ANNE 20:40
study of f. portraits	DOYLE 344:11
stuffy Victorian f.	ORWE 743:16
tense and peculiar f.	BEER 84:48
when a F. dines alone	SWIFT 985:99

famine f. grew, and locusts came

	THOM 1010:57
f. in his face	CHUR 262:80
F. is in thy cheeks	SHAK 870:21
f. was sore in the land	BIBLE 105:47
Fire, Blood, and F.	HENR 472:64
from f. and death	DARW 306:84
Gaunt F. shall never approach	BYRON 223:55
live with f.	JEFF 519:81
not a f. of bread	BIBLE 130:61

famines there shall be f.

	BIBLE 139:37

famous can't be f.…be notorious.

	MAHA 638:60
f. for being f.	ASHB 41:58
f. for fifteen minutes	WARH 1053:21
F. for his laugh	FLAU 393:45
F. without ability	SHAW 920:15
f. witty saying	THUR 1019:38
found myself f.	BYRON 224:70
Let us now praise f. men	BIBLE 133:17
mark of many f. people	HELL 469:99
My uncle was f.	SPEN 956:87
that f. harmony	YEATS 1104:59
'twas a f. victory	SOUT 954:33
You can get awful f.	HART 459:42

fan f. spread and streamers out

	CONG 281:34
with thy mystic f.	HERR 477:57

fanatic f. for the externality

	LEWIS 602:67
f. great leader just entering	BROUN 193:49

fanatics F. have their dreams

	KEATS 545:68

fancies F. fond with gaudy

	MILT 682:5

fancies (*contd.*)

how many childish f.	SHIP 935:22
When you set your f. free	BROW 200:1

fanclub Love is a f.

	HENRI 472:61

fancy agreeable f.

	STEV 972:80
call the Apollo a f. piece?	EMER 376:45
E'er F. you consult	FRAN 402:5
f. cannot cheat so well	KEATS 548:19
f. from a flower-bell	BROW 198:54
f. of the mass of men	BAGE 61:54
hopeless f. feigned	TENN 997:4
keep your f. free	HOUS 494:44
not expressed in f.	SHAK 888:69
now the f. passes by	HOUS 494:46
of most excellent f.	SHAK 893:77
'Orses and dorgs is some men's f.	DICK 324:9
pleasing to the f.	ADDI 7:19
proud f. never taught	CRAB 293:65
unsound f. and self-contradictory	BACON 56:32
young man's f.	TENN 995:71

fangs climes but nurse the cruellest f. MELV 668:42

fans between the F. and me

	KING 559:3
fanclub with only two f.	HENRI 472:61
f. into their hand	BALL 67:49

fantasies compulsions, the f.

	LEGU 594:25
Mrs Forthby in his f.	SHAR 919:82
robbed of his f.	FONT 395:85
Such shaping f.	SHAK 871:53
teach elegant f.	TOBIN 1021:73
thousand f. Begin	MILT 683:24
tree that f. had planted	HERZL 478:75

fantastic light f. round

	MILT 683:22
more f. the world becomes	HUXL 506:51
most f. and impracticable	SNOW 951:79
On the light f.	MILT 682:98

fantasy all f. and veneer

	GALL 413:97
nothing but vain f.	SHAK 868:80
substitute for the f.	ALBEE 11:83
suspicion, rumour, f.	RICH 809:43

far Be it f. from me

	BIBLE 109:26
Britain calls the F. East	MENZ 670:93
F. may be sought	SKEL 942:34
f. side of baldness	SMITH 947:14
how f. one can go too f.	COCT 272:62
No matter how f. away	SCEVE 846:57
so near and yet so f.	TENN 1000:55

farce dreariness of his f.

	WEBB 1058:14
F. is nearer tragedy	COLE 275:28
f., melodrama, tragedy	SCHL 848:75
second time as f.	BARN 72:35
the second as f.	MARX 660:17
wine was a f.	POWE 787:4

farcical marriage is the most f.

	BEAU 79:63

fardels who would f. bear

	TWAIN 1033:89
Who would these f. bear	SHAK 890:21

fare F. thee well, great heart

	SHAK 876:76
F. ye a' weel, ye bitches!	HOME 487:15
F. you well	SHAK 885:72
value not your bill of f.	SWIFT 984:70

farewell Ae f., and then for ever

	BURNS 212:24
F., all joys	GIBB 422:32
F.…degenerate king	SHAK 861:16
F. my friends	DUNC 355:43
F. my poor hands	RACH 799:95
F. sadness	ELUA 376:25
F.…too lately known	DRYD 350:42
F.—thou art too dear	SHAK 914:77
no sadness of f.	TENN 1005:66
This is f.	TOJO 1022:88
Too-late, F.	ROSS 825:93
Without a solemn f.	MIDD 673:41

Farish Miss F.…in the way

	WHAR 1068:96

farm committed to a f.

	THOR 1016:84
cultivated f.	GOLD 433:9

farm (*contd.*)
in a loft in Salt Lake F.	THOM 1011:*83*
language of f., city and love	ENGLE 378:*91*
sold my f.	SHAK 882:*10*
When a man takes a f.	PARN 756:*39*

farmer f. without fields | PARK 755:*36*

farmers embattled f. stood | EMER 376:*26*
f. as they passed	MORG 707:*63*
f....well pleased with constant gain	CRAB 294:*78*
toil of the f.' wives	GARL 415:*27*

farmhouse damp front f. | THOM 1012:*95*

farms fields of millions of f. | HOOV 490:*57*
flocks and f. and heroes	VIRG 1046:*96*
for him that f.	CRAB 293:*19*
what f. are those?	HOUS 495:*57*

farmyard human society from the f. | SHAW 924:*94*
louder...in its own f.	TROL 1028:*79*

farrago f. of superlative nonsense | CHUR 263:*93*

fart can't f. and chew gum | JOHN 524:*55*
F. for the Bishop of Cork!	ANON 25:*21*
f. in a gale of wind	BARN 72:*28*
Love is the f.	SUCK 981:*22*

farthing for a f. less | ADDI 8:*39*
never pay a f.	CROM 298:*54*
threw in two mites, which make a f.	BIBLE 141:*70*
two sparrows sold for a f.?	BIBLE 136:*78*

farts Three f. and a raspberry | BARB 71:*12*
when the courtesan f.	ANON 23:*93*

fascinated f. by the form | JAMES 517:*34*

fascination f. of an ancient rite | SAND 841:*77*
f. of one slowing down	GIBB 421:*31*
f. which draws me	HEDIN 466:*61*
maximum f. can continue	DIOR 331:*62*

fascism F. accepts the individual | MUSS 716:*91*
masked by the new macho f.	WHITE 1069:*19*
unless F. was defeated	SPEN 957:*91*

fascist Every communist has a f. | SPARK 955:*57*
Every woman adores a F.	PLATH 773:*95*
speak of the F. objective	ORWE 742:*3*

Fascists F. are sincere | DRIB 346:*44*

fashion as to its f. and material | HAWT 461:*72*
cannot long one f. entertain	DRAY 345:*32*
dedicated follower of f.	DAVI 308:*11*
deformed thief this f. is	SHAK 880:*55*
faith but as the f.	SHAK 878:*27*
faithful...in my f.	DOWS 343:*81*
F....a despot	BIER 161:*83*
F. anticipates	CASS 243:*27*
f. as in it	TWAIN 1032:*56*
F.—a word which knaves and fools	CHUR 262:*81*
f's brightest arts	GOLD 433:*14*
F. can be bought	CHASE 253:*97*
F. constantly begins and ends	HAZL 463:*1*
F....guide of fools	CRAB 293:*68*
F. is architecture	CHAN 251:*57*
f. is born by small facts	SCHI 847:*62*
F. is free speech	LURIE 619:*42*
F. is made to become unfashionable	CHAN 251:*53*
F. is more tyrannical at Paris	CHES 257:*80*
F. is only the attempt	HOLM 486:*97*
F. is something barbarous	SANT 842:*83*
F. is what one wears oneself	WILDE 1078:*93*
F....produces beautiful things	COCT 272:*66*
f. she detests	SHAK 895:*19*
F. should be a game	QUANT 796:*50*
f. to go naked	MONT 701:*55*
f. wears out more apparel	SHAK 880:*56*
fetch over a f.	JONS 534:*72*
for the f., I believe	SWIFT 986:*9*
garment out of f.	SHAK 916:*6*
high Roman f.	SHAK 906:*91*
highflyer at F.	DICK 327:*76*
independent of f.	GASK 415:*33*
intellectual f.	CONN 283:*80*

fashion (*contd.*)
never out of f.	FULL 410:*50*
not for the f. of these times	SHAK 885:*83*
Nothing else holds f.	SHAK 896:*58*
One had as good be...out of the F.	CIBB 266:*53*
Philosophy...often changes F.	FRAN 402:*6*
present f. is always handsome	FULL 410:*54*
Quite out of f.	SHAK 896:*52*
seek to f. events	NAPO 719:*38*
strange f. of forsaking	WYATT 1103:*31*
tell you the leading f.	RUSK 831:*99*
the f. after the plague	PEPYS 765:*76*
vain to mislike the current f.	FULL 410:*53*
world reappear in one f.	MARX 660:*17*
world's new f.	SHAK 865:*10*
worn-out poetical f.	ELIOT 371:*45*

fashionable f. female life | SPEKE 955:*62*
f. gentleman	ALSOP 15:*58*
f. woman wears clothes	QUANT 796:*49*
For an idea ever to be f.	SANT 842:*85*

fashioned F. so slenderly | HOOD 489:*48*

fashions best of our f. | VEBL 1041:*26*
f. all sins on him	WEBS 1061:*58*
f. of gentlemen	ALSOP 15:*58*
F....are only induced epidemics	SHAW 923:*85*
In Words, as F.	POPE 778:*82*
know his nature and f.	BACON 59:*19*
laughs at the old f.	THOR 1016:*83*
Old f. please me best	SHAK 864:*81*
to fit this year's f.	HELL 468:*94*

fast f. down, and...f. up | OWENS 748:*23*
f., fiery and true	DAVIS 309:*38*
grew f. and furious	BURNS 211:*19*
He that drinks f.	FRAN 402:*2*
More grievous...than a hermit's f.	KEATS 546:*77*
No dog can go as f.	FLAN 391:*24*
one takes the music too f.	SAIN 837:*95*
poor, who will not f. in peace	CRAB 293:*76*
To be human...we must stand f.	BOLT 172:*76*

fasting between a fou man and a f. | SCOTT 855:*5*
f., for a good man's love	SHAK 886:*13*

fasts come in f. divine! | HOPK 491:*80*

fat art waxen f. | BIBLE 108:*3*
Butter merely makes us f.	GOER 430:*67*
eat the f., and drink the sweet	BIBLE 112:*92*
Fair, f. and forty	SCOTT 855:*4*
f. and flourishing	BIBLE 117:*4*
f. and greasy citizens	SHAK 885:*78*
f. and grows old	SHAK 876:*54*
f. man demanding elbow room	WAUGH 1057:*95*
f. of the land	BIBLE 105:*48*
f., oily man of God	THOM 1015:*53*
I'd like to get f.	DIAZ 319:*2*
Imprisoned in every f. man	CONN 283:*75*
maketh the bones f.	BIBLE 121:*82*
men about me that are f.	SHAK 882:*23*
no sex if you're f.	GIOV 428:*37*
November, he full of gross and f.	SPEN 959:*43*
Outside every f. man	AMIS 16:*77*
resolved to grow f.	DRYD 347:*56*
substance into that f. belly	SHAK 877:*88*
trouble is you get f.	BARN 72:*30*
Who's your f. friend	BRUM 201:*9*

fatal f. man | THAC 1006:*92*
f. to good film-making	CHAN 250:*44*
most f. complaint of all	HILT 481:*11*
sincerity...absolutely f.	WILDE 1076:*41*

fatality no exterior f. | SAIN 836:*79*

fate A flame f. dares not move | PHIL 768:*20*
and what I will is f.	MILT 691:*84*
architect of his own f.	CLAU 268:*93*
bone to pick with F.	NASH 720:*63*
books have their own f.	TERE 1006:*77*
breathless on thy f.!	LONG 611:*8*

fate (*contd.*)
build the nation's f.	BLAKE 168:*5*
by warning to avoid his f.?	SPEN 958:*18*
common f. has linked us	BREZ 187:*40*
coughed and called it f.	ROBI 815:*28*
cursed my f.	SHAK 913:*57*
customary f. of new truths	HUXL 508:*2*
Far away be that f.!	OVID 747:*94*
f. as a nation	HOFS 484:*63*
F. cannot harm me	SMITH 949:*56*
f. carries in her other hand	LAWR 587:*15*
f. decreed that the cloak	WEBER 1059:*19*
F....goes as it must	ANON 21:*52*
f. hath held sway	AESC 9:*55*
f. in what I cannot fear	ROET 819:*95*
f. of poetry	WALC 1048:*43*
f. of this country depends	DISR 333:*19*
f. of those who toil	JOHN 526:*4*
f. of unborn millions	WASH 1054:*42*
F. often preserves the undoomed	ANON 21:*53*
f. so enviously debars	MARV 658:*78*
F.'s such a shrewish thing	CHAP 252:*71*
F., Time, Occasion, Chance,	SHEL 930:*23*
F. tried to conceal him	HOLM 486:*94*
F. wrote her a...tragedy	BEER 83:*22*
fears his f. too much	MONT 703:*92*
fits for f.	DRYD 351:*57*
For all our children's f.	KIPL 565:*17*
forced by f.	DRYD 352:*76*
foulness of their f.	SASS 846:*41*
full measure of their f.	CRANE 295:*3*
Happiness was my f.	RIMB 812:*98*
has no ill f.	WALL 1050:*76*
I hold f.	FORD 397:*17*
In case it tempted F.	MACG 630:*30*
It's a complex f.	JAMES 516:*10*
Jove and F. require	POPE 782:*91*
limits of a vulgar f.	GRAY 443:*92*
made weak by time and f.	TENN 995:*61*
makers of their f.	POPP 783:*17*
master of his f.	TENN 1002:*2*
master of my f.	HENL 472:*58*
matter what f. befalls me	MILNE 681:*82*
meet my f.	YEATS 1106:*75*
men cannot suspend their f.	DEFOE 312:*74*
meteor Ever hung my f.	MIDD 674:*49*
mock the patriot's f.	INGR 511:*44*
modern poet's f.	HOOD 489:*53*
my life, my f.	TENN 1001:*88*
no armour against f.	SHIR 935:*27*
no f. that cannot be surmounted	CAMUS 229:*48*
No gifts...have conquered f.	ARNO 36:*58*
our pride, our folly, or our f.	DENH 315:*54*
Politics and the f. of mankind	CAMUS 228:*44*
power above The stars and f.	BUTL 217:*27*
proclaimed the f. that smote	ROBE 814:*16*
Read your f.	THOR 1017:*88*
scorn of f.	DRYD 348:*95*
stern hand of f.	LLOY 608:*58*
torrent of his f.?	JOHN 525:*84*
we know the f. of none	BERR 98:*7*
when f. summons	DRYD 348:*81*
why should they know their f.?	GRAY 441:*48*
will...overruled by f.	MARL 655:*27*
won't triumph over his f.	KOES 568:*69*

fates F., we will know your pleasures | SHAK 883:*40*
hostages to the f.	LUCAN 618:*23*
masters of their f.	SHAK 882:*20*
O f., come, come	SHAK 871:*58*
What f. impose	SHAK 862:*29*
wills and f....contrary run	SHAK 891:*38*

fathead F. poet that nobody reads | CHES 260:*45*

fatheaded f....wash-out of a cock-up | ANON 29:*33*

fatheads famous f., old wives | MACD 628:*92*

father After the funeral, my f. — LAWR 586:92
As my poor f. used to say — HERB 474:94
As the F. knoweth me — BIBLE 146:54
ascend unto my F. — BIBLE 147:75
ashamed to be my f.'s child! — SHAK 874:26
ashes of his f.'s — MACA 623:13
bed fell on my f. — THUR 1018:16
better off dead…your wife and my f. — CHAN 250:43
blessed of my F. — BIBLE 140:44
born where my f. lived — SITT 940:98
boy with his f. — IHIM 510:30
cannot have God for his f. — CYPR 302:32
children of your F. — BIBLE 134:45
Church which prays Our F. — BONH 172:81
decrepit f. takes delight — SHAK 913:60
Deny thy f. — SHAK 868:87
draft-dodging f. — ROTH 825:5
electrical display of God the F. — ONEI 740:55
even as a f. — BIBLE 120:58
f. before him — SYMI 988:59
f.…did not have the time — CIXO 267:71
f. drove them out — LOUI 613:45
F.! f.! where are you going? — BLAKE 166:67
F., forgive them — BIBLE 144:16
f. gave him a box — MACN 637:49
f. had a chain of dry cleaners — BENN 91:82
f. had a daughter — SHAK 894:14
f. hath chastised you with whips — BIBLE 111:60
F. in Heaven — KIER 556:58
F., into thy hands — BIBLE 144:19
F. is rather vulgar — DICK 326:53
f. lived his soul — CUMM 300:90
f. moved through dooms of love — CUMM 300:89
f., nor a mother — MARG 650:51
f. of English criticism — JOHN 531:9
f. of his people — GIBB 421:22
f. of knowledge — HIPP 481:16
F. of lights — BIBLE 155:60
f. of many nations — BIBLE 148:17
F. of our dramatic poets — DRYD 347:65
F. of Peace — DODD 335:47
f. of psychoanalysis — GREER 445:39
f. of the child cried out — BIBLE 141:68
f. of the fatherless — BIBLE 116:86
f. or my mother — STER 968:48
f. should be as a god — SHAK 870:25
f. sold me — BLAKE 166:66
F., Son and Holy Ghost — MACL 633:63
f. still reads the dictionary — SCAR 846:54
f.'s sword he has girded — MOORE 706:34
f., the chariot of Israel — BIBLE 111:73
F.…thou hadst none — BRAD 184:99
f.…throwing rocks at the stork — BREC 186:23
f. used to say — MOORE 705:19
f. watched him across — MARQ 655:33
F. which is in heaven give good things — BIBLE 135:58
F. which is in heaven is perfect — BIBLE 134:46
F. which is in heaven — BIBLE 139:20
F. will come — TENN 997:97
f. worked with a horse-plough — HEAN 464:32
Full fathom five thy f. lies — SHAK 916:25
glorify your F. which is in heaven — BIBLE 134:36
God…an exalted f. — FREUD 404:45
had a pig-headed f. — POUND 785:54
had it from my f. — SHAK 917:49
Hath the rain a f.? — BIBLE 113:20
Have we not all one f. — BIBLE 130:69
heavenly F. feedeth them — BIBLE 135:52
his f. saw him, and had compassion — BIBLE 143:1
Honour thy f. and thy mother — BIBLE 106:68
How like f. — BARR 73:61
I am like no f. — SHAK 862:34

father (contd.)
in the name of the F. — BIBLE 141:58
inherited…melancholy from my f. — JOHN 529:66
it is I, your f. — BELL 85:78
Labour is the F. …of Wealth — PETTY 768:14
Lead us, Heavenly F. — EDME 361:45
Like as a f. pitieth — BIBLE 118:14
Lord and F. of mankind — WHIT 1074:9
loveth f. or mother — BIBLE 136:80
lusts of the f. ye will do — BIBLE 146:51
man leave f. and mother — BIBLE 103:92
man leave f. and mother — BIBLE 139:22
mighty God, The everlasting F. — BIBLE 125:66
murdered his mother and f. — LEVA 599:17
My f. is deceased — MARL 653:3
my f. wept — BLAKE 167:94
My noble f. — SHAK 898:10
Neither f. nor lover — ROET 819:96
no man cometh unto the F. — BIBLE 146:62
O my F., if it be possible — BIBLE 140:50
on the ground without your F. — BIBLE 136:78
one way to speak to my f. — SAINT 836:77
one would want as a f. — WEST 1068:92
Our F. which art in heaven — BIBLE 135:49
Our F. who art — PARRA 756:43
person cannot choose his f. — FRIS 406:67
Praise, Son, and Holy Ghost — KEN 549:48
pray to thy F. — BIBLE 135:48
proceedeth from the F. and the Son — BOOK 174:20
record…of our mother and f. — FRAME 400:78
remembered dead f. — NICH 726:50
resembled My f. — SHAK 908:44
Seek for thy noble f. — SHAK 888:48
Singing to F., Son — HOW 497:91
stopped loving my f. — NIN 729:3
tenderness of a f. — MORE 706:46
Thou art thy f.'s daughter — SHAK 885:76
though her f. be very rich — SHAK 864:71
throne of Denmark to thy f. — SHAK 887:45
Thus his f. wept — BIBLE 105:41
time to become a f. — WHITE 1070:33
To be a successful f. — HEMI 471:48
'twill come to my f. anon — AUBR 45:35
What would f. say — MANS 647:10
where's their f. live — THOM 1011:85
who my f. was — SEXT 859:68
will of my F. which is in heaven — BIBLE 137:96
will of my F. — BIBLE 135:62
Wisdom's heavenly F. — WORD 1100:92
wise f. that knows — SHAK 874:24
wise son heareth his f.'s instruction — BIBLE 121:72
without f. bred — MILT 682:5
You are old. F. William — SOUT 954:29
Your f. hath consented — SHAK 864:78
your f., whom you love, dies — STOP 978:75
fatherland There we have the F.! — MANN 645:79
fatherless fields of the f. — BIBLE 121:96
for the f., and for the widow — BIBLE 108:95
visit the f. and widows — BIBLE 155:63
fathers common revolt against the f. — COWL 291:22
f.…are incurable — DAVI 307:4
f. brought forth upon — LINC 605:4
f. had a Paris — HUGO 501:65
f., provoke not your children — BIBLE 152:4
f. that begat us — BIBLE 133:17
f. would never…have dreamed — MARC 649:40
glory of children are their f. — BIBLE 121:85
God of our F. — MILT 694:48
Hast all our f. led — DODD 335:45
Instead of thy f. — BOOK 177:73
learned of their f. — BIBLE 132:93
men liking their f. — BRAD 183:77
My f. can have it — THOM 1011:77

fathers (contd.)
not better than my f. — BIBLE 111:68
Our f. have…provided — QUIL 797:59
revolts against its f. — MUMF 713:45
scenes his f. loved — CULL 299:69
slept with his f. — BIBLE 111:61
so did their f. to the false prophets — BIBLE 142:3
turn the heart of the f. — BIBLE 131:73
visit the sins of the f. — BOOK 174:17
fathom canst not f. it — TENN 993:33
Full f. five — SHAK 916:25
them that sleep…many a f. deep — CAMP 227:30
fathom-line could never touch — SHAK 875:46
fathoms certain f. in the earth — SHAK 917:40
fifty f. deep — BALL 67:52
fatigue f. of adjectives — BROY 201:5
F. makes women talk — LEWIS 601:41
lover…dies from f. — BART 75:83
physical f. than the painter — LEON 596:73
the f. of judging for themselves — SHER 934:6
fatigued chanced to be f. — FORS 398:43
fatness covered with f. — BIBLE 108:43
f. of these pursy times — SHAK 892:58
let your soul delight itself in f. — BIBLE 127:3
fattening f. is the first duty — SPEKE 955:62
illegal, immoral or f. — WOOL 1094:87
fatter f. man trying to close in — AMIS 16:77
fatuity f. of idiots — SMITH 949:42
fatuous one term is as f. as another — ROOS 822:51
fatuus Better an ignis f. — DICK 328:13
Faulkner read Proust, F., Joyce — VARG 1040:7
fault clever to a f. — BROW 199:56
Every man has his f. — SHAK 901:31
f. being greater — LANY 580:80
f.…is not in our stars — SHAK 882:20
f. of our politicians — TROL 1028:82
f. of the Dutch — CANN 230:72
f. though great, yet he — LANY 580:78
Faultless to a f. — BROW 200:90
He is all f. — TENN 1002:12
hide the f. I see — POPE 782:90
hint at f. — POPE 781:65
His worst f. — SHAK 878:12
least f. distorts it — YOUR 1108:7
never needs to admit a f. — BALZ 68:70
no kind of f. — GILB 424:21
only f. is that I am alive — MAP 649:35
only had one f. — THUR 1020:57
suffer through no f. of their own — ELIZ 374:96
Whose f.? Whose but his — MILT 689:31
faultless Faultily f. — TENN 1001:74
faults America has colossal f. — CUMM 300:85
blush at your f. — FLET 394:74
England, with all thy f. I love thee — COWP 293:54
England…With all her f. — CHUR 262:89
f. it has not strength enough — GOLD 432:3
f. of a Government — ROOS 821:37
f. of the economic society — KEYN 555:38
fill you with the f. they had — LARK 582:14
Jesus! with all thy f. — BUTL 218:49
Neebours' f. and folly — BURNS 210:82
private school has all the f. — CONN 283:65
repair time's f. — MUIR 712:32
Sum up my f., I pray — WEBS 1060:37
to her f. a little blind — PRIOR 790:50
world of vile ill-favoured f. — SHAK 878:20
faun important senior f. — ANON 27:81
Faustus F., it is not half so fair — MARL 654:16
F., leave this damnèd art — MARL 654:18
F. like a foggy mist — MARL 654:21
F. may…save his soul! — MARL 654:20
favour courtesan farts…as a f. — ANON 23:93
depend on…prince's f. — WEBS 1060:57
F. is deceitful — BIBLE 122:13

feel (contd.)

don't know how to f.	KENN 550:58
Englishman…afraid to f.	FORS 398:47
f. good after	HEMI 470:23
f. hot and think cold	CARY 243:17
f. keenly and strongly	STAEL 961:74
f. not what they inspire	SHEL 931:60
f. with them	BENN 92:4
f. you've done something	HEMI 470:15
make him f. that way	TWAIN 1033:87
No comfortable f.	HOOD 489:52
Now does he f.	SHAK 910:79
power…to make you f.	CONR 284:88
something more to do than f.	LAMB 576:5
though you f. nothing	JULI 539:68
thow shalt nat f.	CHAU 254:5
what matters is whether you f. it	COLE 273:79
women f. just as men f.	BRON 191:93

feeling All violent f.

All violent f.	RUSK 830:84
art must express a distinct f.	FRIE 405:62
barbarous f. of nationality	SENI 859:53
Certainty. F. Joy	PASC 758:81
constellations of f.	DOUG 341:58
cruelty is the primary f.	SADE 835:64
extra dimension of f.	FOWL 399:66
failure of f.	STEV 972:54
f.…came as a…surprise	LESS 598:5
f. I'm falling	FERL 386:21
f. of all happiness	WORD 1100:81
f. of emulsion	PERE 766:89
f. of Sunday	RHYS 808:29
f. of vengeance	DREN 346:42
F. teaches much more	DU 353:12
f. that here it is 11 o'clock	BRAN 185:9
f. that lures us on to joys	CONR 284:98
f. that you can't make it	POWE 788:15
f. which we derive from knowing	LAMB 576:24
formal f. comes	DICK 328:99
generous and honest f.	BURKE 206:2
High mountains are a f.	BYRON 220:87
imprecision of f.	ELIOT 372:53
inner experience and inner f.	LAWR 587:5
keen vision and f.	ELIOT 366:37
lie down until the f. passes	HUTC 506:44
lonely f. but euphoric, too	CAMP 228:34
lost pulse of f.	ARNO 36:70
Love is not only a f.	BALZ 69:77
more true f.	JOWE 537:40
must not think that f. is everything	FLAU 392:32
Nor form, nor f.	WORD 1095:10
not merely as f.	PLATH 773:90
obsessed by the f.	SPEN 957:91
profound f. of the power	NORTH 731:32
pure expressions of f.	AYER 53:80
purely personal F.	CUMM 299:75
that's a f. disputation	SHAK 876:60
true writers have experienced this f.	SARR 843:3
without a f. of disappointment	LAMB 576:18

feelings Aren't our best f.

Aren't our best f.	BALZ 69:81
artist with true f.	FRIE 405:57
can't put them out of his f.	CARY 243:18
define her f. in language	HARDY 456:89
f. and convictions	MORI 708:68
f. of awe and respect	DICK 320:15
f. of human beings	JAMES 518:51
f. of liberty	PITT 771:66
f. of Sophia	AUST 50:28
f. on leaving Eton	CONN 283:67
f. prey upon us	AUST 52:68
f. these dull scenes produce	CRAB 294:84
f. you haven't really got	LAWR 586:98
get human f. right	HUTC 506:40
Irish f. and sensitivities	HAUG 460:59
keeping f. at bay	BROO 193:38

feelings (contd.)

language of our f.	FRIE 405:60
no room for new f.	ELIOT 365:18
no spontaneous f.	ORWE 744:39
some of the uneasy f.	HUXL 508:97

feels f. it all as one

f. it all as one	JAMES 517:41

fees answered, as they took their f.

answered, as they took their f.	BELL 87:6
f. are sufficient punishment	BAIL 62:68
very fat f.	BURG 205:83

feet aching hands and bleeding f.

aching hands and bleeding f.	ARNO 37:74
all enemies under his f.	BIBLE 151:68
all things under his f.	BIBLE 114:35
at a funeral and knew their f.	MAUG 664:86
beneath a monarch's f.	BURNS 210:86
black f. of the night	GILM 427:19
blooming round our f.	BETJ 101:53
both f. off the ground	JOHN 523:50
bound…about the f. of God	TENN 1004:47
cloths under your f.	YEATS 1105:65
credit…sprang upon its f.	WEBS 1059:23
crowes f. be grown	CHAU 254:6
cutting of our f.	SWIFT 984:74
dapper from your napper to your f.	COLL 276:37
delivered…my f. from falling	BIBLE 118:25
die on your f.	IBAR 510:18
direct your f.	FIEL 388:55
down at her f.	TRAV 1025:32
due f. never fail	MILT 683:15
exertions of your hands and f.	CONR 284:94
f. began to stutter	BURT 213:61
f. go down to death	BIBLE 120:61
f. in ancient time	BLAKE 168:17
f. like unto fine brass	BIBLE 156:99
f. of him that bringeth good tidings	BIBLE 127:96
f.…of iron and part of clay	BIBLE 129:45
f. of the aged	BIBLE 132:3
f. on the ground	FERL 386:21
f. planted firmly	ROOS 821:40
f. planted on level ground	GOHE 431:84
f. shod with the preparation	BIBLE 152:6
f. thy tribute bring	LYTE 621:66
f. were almost gone	BIBLE 117:89
fog comes on little cat f.	SAND 841:58
get a democracy on its f.	PULI 795:20
goat f. dance an antic hay	MARL 653:4
hear a horse's f.	KIPL 564:2
hear it through their f.	SOUSA 953:25
Hell's darkness under his f.	CARL 236:93
her f. made no din	COLUM 278:60
herb at your f.	TROL 1027:76
I have deserted… sighing at your f.	CONG 282:42
Its f. were tied	KEATS 544:43
Keep Thou my f.	NEWM 724:28
lamp unto my f.	BIBLE 119:33
lantern to my f.	SHAK 861:2
leaves the marks of his f.	LEAC 588:31
let my f. spend…time	OWENS 748:23
like hinds' f.	BIBLE 114:43
little children…Round his f.	SHEL 927:77
little snow-white f.	YEATS 1104:56
meet them dancing f.	DUBIN 352:98
moon under her f.	BIBLE 157:20
nearer than hands to f.	TENN 1003:32
nice f. and plenty of money	ASHF 41:71
not on its f.	HEMP 471:52
of my f. and my nails	NERU 723:8
palms before my f.	CHES 257:88
pansy at my f.	WORD 1098:50
polished with the tread of f.	DICK 322:66
room at your f.?	BALL -101:35
rude facts at your f.	RABAN 798:76
Scots lords at his f.	BALL 67:50
set my f. upon a rock	BIBLE 115:66
shake off the dust of your f.	BIBLE 136:75

feet (contd.)

shoes from off thy f.	BIBLE 106:54
shoes on your f.	BIBLE 106:61
shoes right off its f.	DICK 323:78
skull, and the f.	BIBLE 112:43
slippered f.	GRAH 438:92
swift patterning of naked f.	DOYLE 343:93
tempt with wand'ring f.	MILT 688:21
things before his f.	ENNI 378:92
through the head down to the f.	ANGE 19:23
thy holy f.	BLAKE 165:57
tremble under her f.	TENN 1001:88
walks with aimless f.	TENN 999:37
What stranger's f.	HOUS 496:79
wind's f. shine	SWIN 987:29

feigning Most friendship is f.

Most friendship is f.	SHAK 886:95
truest poetry is the most f.	SHAK 886:10

felicity Absent thee from f.

Absent thee from f.	SHAK 893:87
bliss and sole f.	MARL 652:89
f. in such government a rarer thing	BACON 60:37
more f. on the far side	SMITH 947:14
none can boast sincere f.	DRYD 352:93
optics of these eyes to behold f.	BROW 195:84

fell book be f.

book be f.	SWIFT 984:61
instant that he f.	SCOTT 853:59
stood, and f. who f.	MILT 689:35

fellers f.…kick your bollocks

f.…kick your bollocks	LOFT 610:86

fellow damn f.-feeling

damn f.-feeling	MACD 628:93
f. ain't got a soul	STEI 966:55
f. of a good respect	SHAK 884:66
f. that is neither a wit…nor a fool	CONG 281:17
Hail f., well met	SWIFT 985:96
hard to be a good f.	WYCH 1103:38
hook-nosed f. of Rome	SHAK 878:5
no f. in the firmament	SHAK 883:38
other f. just blinked	RUSK 830:72
perfect citizen may be a fine f.	DOUG 342:68
Promise to forget this f.	SHER 933:77
respect the other f.'s religion	MENC 669:79
sportsman is a f. who	LEAC 589:46
That f. seems…to possess	JOHN 528:56
That's a brave f.	SHAK 911:7
this f. doesn't know	TRUM 1030:21
touchy, testy, pleasant f.	ADDI 7:10

fellow-citizen As f.-c.

As f.-c.	GILB 425:83

fellow-creature esteem with a f.-c.

esteem with a f.-c.	LAMB 576:24

fellow-creatures torture…of his f.-c.

torture…of his f.-c.	FROU 408:9

fellow-men f.-m. can do little

f.-m. can do little	EMER 378:70
one that loves his f.-m.	HUNT 505:28

fellow-rover laughing f.-r.

laughing f.-r.	MASE 661:34

fellowmen majority of their f.

majority of their f.	DUBO 353:9

fellows Bark when their f. do

Bark when their f. do	SHAK 917:52
f. of another college	LITT 607:42
f.…the flood could not wash away	CONG 281:16
f. were practising	JOYCE 538:43
level of his humble f.	HUXL 508:1
mighty fine f. nowadays	STEV 974:24
Nature hath framed strange f.	SHAK 872:76
Nay, droop not, f.	MASS 662:57
some o' them low f.	DICK 320:26
ten good f. and one good day	MILNE 681:82
Those grave f.	STEE 964:23
What should such f. as I do	SHAK 891:26

fellowship f. that they may never

f. that they may never	MALO 642:29
he that hath f.	BIBLE 132:99
no f. with one that is mightier	BIBLE 132:1
pass through in His f.	SCHW 852:31
right hands of f.	BIBLE 152:88

felon When a f.'s not engaged

When a f.'s not engaged	GILB 424:65

felt could not portray all I f.

could not portray all I f.	HOLM 485:72
Genius is f.	DIDE 329:28

female adult American Negro f.

adult American Negro f.	ANGE 19:20
all f. life…unclean	STAN 963:90
bad f. cooks	NIET 729:90

female (*contd.*)
cast on f. wits — BRAD 184:1
child of our grandmother Eve, a f. — SHAK 865:11
chosen and f. shall be homely — KENN 550:55
Christ will perhaps be a f. — NIGH 729:99
fashionable f. life — SPEKE 955:62
f. emotions of aggression — LESS 598:5
f. of the species — KIPL 565:23
f. principle — LEGU 594:27
f. worker is the slave — CONN 284:84
images of f. beauty — WOLF 1089:11
lay down my life for the British f.? — CLOU 271:40
male and f. he created them — BIBLE 102:86
neither male nor f. — BIBLE 152:89
our excess f. population — WRIG 1101:99
sea…is a mighty f. — SEXT 859:67
Strengthen the f. mind — WOLL 1091:36
two and two…male and the f. — BIBLE 104:10
unprotected f. travelling — BUTL 217:39
vindictiveness of the f. — CONN 283:70
What f. heart can gold despise? — GRAY 441:52
whole f. line of ancestry — EDGE 361:38
females imbecility in f. — AUST 52:65
make no fuss about f. — CAMPO 228:42
feminine beautiful f. tissue — HARDY 456:98
distinctively f. — HARDY 456:93
f. half of the world — MERE 671:15
f. in the man — KENT 553:9
Success is f. — FAUL 384:87
tired of being the f. spouse — DIAZ 319:2
who is her life, is f. — PATM 760:7
femininity handicraft of f. — OLIP 738:25
feminism 'beginning' of f. — ROWB 827:40
brief flowerings of f. — FALU 382:58
cardinal tenets of f. — LYND 621:65
F. has become a…vegetable drawer — PAGL 749:36
hate discussions of f. — FREN 404:38
feminist f. writer — WELD 1062:96
I am a f. — JORD 537:31
fen England…is a f. — WORD 1096:34
plashy f. — WAUGH 1057:82
fence Hussein…is the f. — ANON 30:56
If the f. is strong enough — SMITH 946:98
old mare might droop across a f. — SMITH 947:3
fender propped up on the f. — GRAH 438:92
Fenianism guilty authors of F. — ARNO 39:21
fennel box that f. Grows around — RANS 802:37
fens f. of jargon? — BAKER 63:85
reek o' th' rotten f. — SHAK 911:11
ferlie f. he spied wi' his e'e — BALL 67:52
fermentation requires long f. — CAPO 231:86
fern sparkle out among the f. — TENN 1002:97
the f.-dark indifference — LAWR 586:81
ferret-faced f.-f., white-eyed boys — STEV 974:3
ferry row us o'er the f. — CAMP 227:29
fertile ambrosial and f. — THOR 1016:69
f. pedant — WALP 1051:95
such a fix to be f. — NASH 719:47
fertilize f. the whole world — TOCQ 1022:82
fervent f. in spirit — BIBLE 149:34
festal line of f. light — ARNO 37:90
fester Lilies that f. — SHAK 914:80
festina F. lente — AUGU 50:20
festival cannot woo in f. terms — SHAK 880:65
Death is the supreme F. — BONH 173:85
night before some f. — SHAK 869:6
Something like a f. — ANGE 19:24
fetishism Commodity f. — TATE 991:6
fettered so oft has f. me — HERR 478:64
You are f. — DICK 323:86
fetters bound him with f. of brass — BIBLE 109:21
F. of gold are still f. — ASTE 43:90
feud Fhairshon swore a f. — AYTO 53:85
feudal anachronistic, f. institution — ACHE 2:23

feuds f., and jealousies, and sorrows — SASS 845:25
Forget all f. — MACA 624:25
fever bred a f. — THOM 1010:57
enigma of the f. chart — ELIOT 371:51
f. called 'Living' — POE 776:55
life's fitful f. — SHAK 909:58
Of chills and f. she died — RANS 802:31
youth is bent by…wintry f. — THOM 1010:51
fever-trees set about with f.-t. — KIPL 563:82
feverish over trembly and f. — TWAIN 1033:88
Février Janvier and F. — NICH 726:49
few appointment by the corrupt f. — SHAW 926:39
expression which the f. desire — PARE 753:83
f. and evil have the days…been — BIBLE 106:50
Gey f., and they're a' deid — ANON 24:9
grinders cease because they are f. — BIBLE 123:42
hated the ruling f. — BENT 93:19
owed by so many to so f. — CHUR 264:16
There are so f. — JONS 535:6
We f., we happy f. — SHAK 882:3
where f. have been — KENN 550:50
fez necessary to abolish the f. — ATAT 43:1
Fhairshon F. swore a feud — AYTO 53:85
fib Destroy his f. …in vain — POPE 781:62
fibre flesh and bone, f. and liquids — ELLI 375:16
fibres f. of England — FORS 398:28
fickle all men call thee f. — SHAK 869:12
and f. is the South — TENN 997:5
Whatever is f. — HOPK 491:85
Woman is often f. — FRAN 401:95
fiction AIDS is good for is f. — WELD 1062:90
All f. is for me — WILS 1084:14
best thing in f. — WILDE 1077:74
biography is ultimately f. — MALA 641:9
But in a f. — SHAK 890:14
condemn it as an improbable f. — SHAK 895:31
don't make for very good f. — TROL 1029:1
escapist f. — GALB 412:86
every 'I' is a f. — WALC 1048:37
fact and f. shouldn't be mixed — BOWEN 181:49
fascinating f. — BANKS 70:1
f. is a necessity — CHES 257:89
f. …makes justice — PALEY 751:59
F. should render…morals — FORD 396:6
great temple of f. — UPDI 1037:68
heroes and villains from f. — AUDEN 49:99
in f. as in life — AUCH 46:38
Isherwood became a f. — BURU 214:80
money…to write f. — WOOLF 1093:69
more lies than…self-indulgent f. — BYATT 218:55
newspapers…continuous f. — BEVAN 102:70
Poetry is a…piece of f. — MENC 669:61
Poetry is the supreme f. — STEV 971:34
Poetry is the supreme f. — STEV 972:68
police dog of American f. — FADI 382:53
predilection for genre f. — DISCH 331:68
Science f. is like Brazil — DISCH 331:69
Stranger than f. — BYRON 223:60
That is what f. means — WILDE 1078:85
to writing f. — UPDI 1037:61
traditional f. — GALB 412:79
write f. and I'm told — ROTH 826:24
wrote f. as if it were — WILDE 1079:12
fictions Perhaps we are all f. — GREE 444:26
Who says that f. only — HERB 475:24
fiddle F., we know, is diddle — SWIN 988:58
good tune on old f. — BUTL 217:40
hog that could f. — ROCH 816:58
important beyond this f. — MOORE 705:17
Music…plays second f. to none — ELLI 374:7
sell his f. — BURNS 210:92
trissyllables are f. rhymes — SMART 944:65
fiddle-de-dee French for f.-d.-d.? — CARR 241:81
fiddler f., and consequently a rogue — SWIFT 984:69

Fidele fair F.'s grassy tomb — COLL 276:42
fidelity books…our f. to truth — CONR 285:3
disparagements of his wife's f. — SHAW 925:36
gossamer f. of mere Man — POE 776:45
scrupulous f. to the truth — CONR 285:10
stone f. They hardly meant — LARK 581:5
fidget moved by little f. wheels — SLES 943:57
fie F., fo, and fum — SHAK 903:25
field as a flower of the f. — BIBLE 118:15
be on the f. of play — MILNE 681:82
beside a f. of grain — PARK 755:29
big f. of rye — SALI 839:28
death in the hunting f. — MORT 710:93
dignity in tilling a f. — WASH 1054:37
every other f. has left nature — MOND 699:41
f. for their efforts — BRON 191:93
f. is full of shades — THOM 1014:32
f. of social organisation — MENC 669:64
Flodden's fatal f. — SCOTT 853:60
Happy f. or mossy cavern — KEATS 544:48
hill or f. or river — TENN 997:1
In a f. by the river — YEATS 1104:56
In love's f. — CRAS 296:26
It is that cricket f. — POWYS 788:21
leave the whole f. — HELL 468:85
left on the f. not a few — DAVIS 309:38
like the brambles in a wild f. — DIDE 330:42
love of f. and coppice — MACK 632:52
man of the f. — BIBLE 105:30
market, hearth and f. — KIPL 565:16
on the f. and city — THAC 1006:86
on the f. of battle — PAST 759:89
possess the f. — CLOU 270:32
presence on the f. — WELL 1063:15
rushed into the f. — BYRON 220:85
single f. — WORD 1098:50
single in the f. — WORD 1098:61
some corner of a foreign f. — BROO 192:21
tills the f. — TENN 1003:21
What though the f. — MILT 687:93
whether it's a f. — WILD 1079:27
fields At Play In The F. — MATT 664:81
blown f. or — SWIN 987:44
blue f. of heaven — KEATS 544:34
broken head in Cold Bath F. — MACA 623:21
dead, but in the Elysian f. — DISR 333:21
disgrace to the playing f. — FRY 408:10
farmer without f. — PARK 755:36
f. and flocks have charms — CRAB 293:71
f. and the water shout — MERE 671:1
f. of amaranth — LAND 578:60
f. of barley and of rye — TENN 993:37
f. of millions of farms — HOOV 490:57
f. that their fathers have tilled — CHUR 264:14
f. that we have planted — MUIR 712:36
f. where Troy once was — OVID 747:96
fight in the f. — CHUR 264:14
flowering of His f. — TENN 1003:3
flowerless f. of heaven — SWIN 986:22
foreign f., from Dunkirk — DAVIS 309:38
From the green f. — WORD 1095:17
In f. where roses fade — HOUS 495:62
look on the f. — BIBLE 145:31
Low over the dim f. — MERE 671:98
no definite…meaning in other f. — SART 843:5
poems…in the factories or f. — MACD 627:88
Poetic f. encompass me around — ADDI 6:98
rush through the f. in trains — CHES 260:45
sharp light the f. did lie — FREE 404:34
Strawberry f. forever — LENN 596:65
To f. where flies no…hail — HOPK 491:77
unshorn f., boundless and beautiful — BRYA 202:19
walk through the f. — CORN 288:58
What f. — SHEL 929:3

fields (*contd.*)
whispering of f. unsown — OWEN 748:18
Fields like…W C F. movies — HAWES 460:61
say about W C F. — ROST 825:3
fiend Beneath is all the f.'s — SHAK 903:35
dreadful f. of gods — SPEN 959:35
f. for becoming a torrent — LIGNE 604:93
F. walked up and down — MILT 689:41
frightful f.…behind him tread — COLE 274:93
Like a f. hid in a cloud — BLAKE 167:94
marble-hearted f. — SHAK 902:7
fiends alleyways and drug f. — LIND 605:11
f. that plague thee — COLE 273:85
f. will snatch it — SHAK 900:62
fierce f. and bald — SASS 845:26
That bright and f. — TENN 997:5
fierceness cage if…any sign of f. — CARB 231:95
swalloweth the ground with f. — BIBLE 113:23
fiere my trusty f.! — BURNS 210:96
fife Elephant That practised on a f. — CARR 241:88
Fife Thane of F. — SHAK 910:78
fifth And he came f. — JOYCE 538:50
f. of the people — KENN 552:2
f. part of the Earth — FIELD 387:39
plead the F. Amendment — NIXON 730:12
The f. column — MOLA 698:15
fifty At f. you have the choice — CART 242:11
difficult thing is to have it at f. — DEGAS 312:95
Fear of F. — JONG 534:71
won't speak to me for f. minutes — DOYLE 343:1
fig an Olive, and a Turkey F. — BETH 99:21
don't care a f.! — LEAR 590:55
f. for those by law protected — BURNS 209:69
F. leaves of democratic — KENN 550:52
like a fat purple f. — PLATH 773:91
sewed f. leaves together — BIBLE 103:3
fig-tree green f.-t. in the story — PLATH 773:91
Train up a f.-t. — DICK 323:94
fight a harder matter to f. — TENN 1002:99
able to f. and conquer — TROT 1029:4
bear-like I must f. — SHAK 910:87
beautifully the English f.! — NAPO 718:29
believer will f. another — GREE 445:27
better to f. for the good — TENN 1002:96
British won't f. — GALT 413:9
can we f. with fifty-three? — TENN 1004:56
cannot f. against the future — GLAD 429:51
cannot f. for love — SHAK 870:38
clouds of the f. — KEY 554:24
cock won't f. — BEAV 80:81
couldn't begin to f. — TAYL 992:18
day we started to f. — ANON 28:19
don't want to f. — HUNT 504:15
easier to f. for principles — STEV 972:70
f. and die for your country — GOLD 434:34
f. and f. again — GAIT 411:71
f. begins with himself — BROW 199:57
f. between two bald men — BORG 179:15
f. for freedom and truth — IBSEN 510:21
f. for mankind — SAIN 836:82
F. for our National Intelligence — CATT 245:56
f. for the right — CURZ 302:29
f. for your country — HOMER 488:20
f. in defence of one's country — HOMER 488:22
f. it out — GRANT 439:8
f. on the beaches — CHUR 264:14
f. on until the end — HAIG 450:10
F. the good f. — BIBLE 154:35
f. them, and pursue them — JOAN 522:27
fought a good f. — BIBLE 154:41
friendly kind of f. — STUB 980:12
Go I to f. — SHAK 866:41
great f. did win — SOUT 954:33
I shall f. — THAT 1008:29

fight (*contd.*)
life be not a real f. — JAMES 517:44
lost, lost f., for the cause — CLOU 271:45
man…too proud to f. — WILS 1086:47
man who runs away will f. — MENA 668:54
never a moment ceased the f. — TENN 1005:58
Never give up the f. — MARL 652:82
no stomach to this f. — SHAK 881:98
not yet begun to f. — JONES 533:57
only the f. to recover — ELIOT 372:54
recalls…a f. — AMADO 15:63
those that fly, may f. again — BUTL 217:24
Those that I f. — YEATS 1106:75
thou fought the better f. — MILT 691:76
To f. aloud — DICK 327:93
too frightened to f. — TALL 990:90
Ulster will f. — CHUR 263:92
we began this f. — GALS 413:5
when you f. — HEMI 470:30
Wherever they's a f. — STEI 966:55
will not cease from my mental f. — BLAKE 168:20
fighter clown, the boozer, the f.? — MAST 663:63
left to the f.'s honor — HEMI 470:24
no a bonny f.? — STEV 976:44
fighters nightmare f. — JARR 518:57
fighting f. against a superstition — JAMES 516:10
f. amongst one another — CLARK 267:86
f. for one thing—money — DEMP 315:48
F. is like champagne — MITC 697:88
F. still, and still destroying — DRYD 351:72
first twenty days of f. — CHUR 263:6
Football causeth f. — STUB 980:13
foremost f., fell — BYRON 220:85
formed through f. — MUSS 716:90
not conquering but f. well — COUB 289:71
period…between two periods of f. — BIER 161:91
tongue-tied's f. — HARR 459:36
twelve thousand f. men — SHAK 867:56
What are We f. for? — SERV 859:58
What is the use of f. — PANK 753:82
When there was any f. — GILB 426:95
when wilt thou leave f. — SHAK 877:92
who dies f. has increase — GREN 446:52
worth f. for, worth dying — MITC 696:84
fights f. as you sing pricksong — SHAK 869:99
f.…best part of married life — WILD 1079:23
f. historical — GILB 424:62
f. you on patriotic principles — SHAW 920:11
knows what he f. for — CROM 297:50
scuffles of great f. — SHAK 904:54
figs better than f. — SHAK 904:59
ears fall off like f. — THOM 1011:89
figurative f.…metaphorical God — DONNE 339:24
figure baby f. of the giant — SHAK 895:43
built about a mythical f. — HERB 474:2
can't f. him out — SHUL 936:37
f. in a country church — SWIFT 984:67
f. of Juno — BARR 73:56
f. which is familiar to us — MACA 623:4
keeping your face or your f. — CART 242:11
masculine f. created by a woman — MENC 669:58
mourning f. walks — LIND 605:19
not a f. in the landscape — BRON 190:85
oblong angular f. — LEAC 588:33
passing of a great f. — NEHRU 722:94
walk around the f. — ROSSO 825:99
figures f. fail you — ARLO 34:37
f. which do not exist for political — MARX 660:8
mystery is why we collect these f. — BART 75:87
One composition…has many f. — DIDE 330:40
place occupied by the f. — MATI 663:73
prove anything by f. — CARL 235:80
such a height of f. — DONNE 339:24
traduce those f. — LEWIS 602:65

files foremost f. of time — TENN 996:82
filial untie thy f. band — SCOTT 853:50
fill drunk his f. — SCOTT 853:61
much less f. them — ISAA 513:71
fillets pink f. — MACB 624:32
fillip rest's not worth a f. — BYRON 223:64
film average…f. star — HEPB 473:76
earn a million dollars a f. — WINN 1087:61
F. art has a greater influence — BALA 63:88
F. Industry…Monarchy — MAMET 644:57
f. is never really good — WELL 1063:2
F. is the least realistic — MAMET 644:60
A good f. script — MAMET 644:59
only a good f. — BENN 91:79
right place to f. it — GARD 414:20
film-making fatal to good f.-m. — CHAN 250:44
filmmaker central fact about the f. — WELL 1063:3
filmmaking no rules in f. — CAPRA 231:92
films f. of one's country — ANDE 18:4
output of f. was prodigious — NIVEN 730:6
paintings and f. — WARH 1053:20
seldom go to f. — BERR 98:14
started off in f. as a king — MORL 708:74
filth f. and the sordidness — DONO 340:36
f. returns in's face — WEBS 1060:91
hairy American f. — OSBO 746:69
remove f. and foulness — ABEL 1:3
so is f. — FORS 398:43
filthy all together become f. — BIBLE 114:37
f., sturdy, unkillable infants — POUND 785:53
not greedy of f. lucre — BIBLE 154:23
righteousnesses are as f. rags — BIBLE 128:13
fin winks the gold f. — TENN 997:10
final f. pleasure left to man — SNOW 950:70
I must bring out my Late Night F. — BEAV 81:85
My Indecision is F. — EBER 359:12
not f. because we are infallible — JACK 514:88
finality F. is not the language — DISR 333:4
finance functions of national f. — CHUR 263:99
site, a brief and f. — ROGE 820:4
Finchley Catherine the Great of F. — HEAL 464:30
find cannot f. it myself — KAFKA 541:89
ere you f. them — SHAK 874:9
f. information upon it — JOHN 529:74
to f. where you are going — STEI 966:58
with me I f. Him not — TENN 1003:40
finding f. myself everyday — GIRO 429:47
f. of limited use to backlash — FALU 382:57
fine F. art is that which — RUSK 830:86
f. wine leaves you with — AMER 16:66
May will be f. next year — HOUS 496:69
no one wants F. Artists — FULL 409:35
Old Cary Grant f. — GRANT 438:1
pop art and f. art — MACI 631:43
theft with a f., not death — MORE 706:46
think is particularly f. — JOHN 529:64
fineness no f. or accuracy — BELL 88:22
finer nothing could be f. — GORD 435:65
finery not bedizened with f. — TROL 1027:63
finger bandaged f. — KIPL 565:25
Between my f. and my thumb — HEAN 464:31
chills the f. not a bit — NASH 720:64
clean f. nails — MORT 710:91
f. on the trigger — MACM 635:9
From the red gold keep thy f. — SCOTT 855:97
God's f. touched him — TENN 999:50
her choppy f. laying — SHAK 907:16
little f. shall be thicker — BIBLE 111:60
moving f. writes — FITZ 390:89
One f. in the…rectum — OSLER 746:73
pointed to with the f. — CICE 266:65
rugged f. to Heaven — LLOY 608:58
scratching of my f. — HUME 503:4

flavour (*contd.*)
spice…That gives it all its f.	COWP 293:56

flaw china jar receive a f. | POPE 778:96
fault or f. | GILB 424:73

flawed His f. heart | SHAK 904:49
We are the f. ones | DELI 315:42

flaws beautiful f. in nature | WOLL 1091:36
hundred thousand f. | SHAK 903:16
We all have f. | THUR 1019:35

flax smoking f. shall he not quench | BIBLE 126:92
smoking f. shall he not quench | BIBLE 137:89

flayed saw a woman f. | SWIFT 984:62

flaying f. would be fair | HOUS 496:88

flea between a louse and a f. | JOHN 531:25
clog the foot of a f. | SHAK 895:29
English literature's performing f. | OCAS 735:78
f. in mine ear | NASHE 721:77
Mark but this f. | DONNE 337:88
naturalists, observe, a f. | SWIFT 986:7
volume can ever be written on a f. | MELV 668:39

fleas dog is full of f. | ACHE 3:50
f. that tease | BELL 87:17
F.…upon the body | LAND 578:56
praised his f.? | YEATS 1105:60
rise with f. | WEBS 1060:42

fled left his garment…and f. | BIBLE 105:43
lovers f. away | KEATS 547:98

fledglings crow loves his f. | MORE 706:43

flee They f. from me | WYATT 1103:30

fleece f. was white as snow | HALE 451:22
forest f. | HOUS 495:53
won the Golden F. | BELL 86:90

fleet Arabian f. | GIBB 421:23
Beauteous the f. | SMART 944:70
Fire and f. and candle-lighte | BALL 67:44
f. of stars is anchored | FLEC 393:54
that is not also f. | THOM 1012:8
Third F.'s sunken | HALS 452:35
took care of our f. | ADDI 7:18
who can be dull in F. Street | LAMB 576:7
whole f.'s lit up | WOOD 1092:49

fleets Ten thousand f. sweep over | BYRON 221:6

flesh all f. shall see it together | BIBLE 126:85
All f. waxeth old | BIBLE 132:2
bloody f. our only food | ELIOT 371:52
bread and f. in the morning | BIBLE 111:62
bread that I will give is my f. | BIBLE 145:45
caught throughout my f. | SAPP 842:92
delicate white human f. | FIEL 388:51
door of my f. | BRID 187:44
east wind made f. | APPL 32:3
empty boast of f. | HABI 450:99
errors of the f. | THOM 1013:21
feel new gods in the f. | LAWR 586:78
few blows are struck into the f. | MAIL 639:76
f. and blood | THAC 1006:81
f. and blood so cheap! | HOOD 489:47
f.; but in what shape | MILT 687:2
f. and my heart faileth | BIBLE 117:91
f. is as grass | BIBLE 155:76
f. is sad, alas! | MALL 641:15
f. is weak | BIBLE 140:51
f. longeth for thee | BIBLE 116:83
F. of f., Bone | MILT 692:6
f. of her f. | BINY 162:6
F. Of Hope | NICH 726:52
f. of mine might be | SWIN 987:29
f. of my f. | BIBLE 103:92
f. of thy dear Son | BOOK 175:30
f. profiteth nothing | BIBLE 145:46
f. sinks downwards | SHAK 868:72
F. was the reason | DEKO 313:19
f. which walls | SHAK 867:60
f. without cares | CIXO 267:75

flesh (*contd.*)
From this world-wearied f.	SHAK 870:23

give them an heart of f. | BIBLE 129:36
give us hearts o' f.! | OCAS 735:75
happit f. and blude | FERG 386:18
heart and my f. crieth out | BIBLE 117:93
hollow prison of my f. | SHAK 862:40
horror of the word 'f.' | RENO 807:8
huge hill of f. | SHAK 876:56
in my f. shall I see God | BIBLE 113:12
In my somber f. and skin | CULL 299:70
joys are more to f. and blood | DRYD 351:54
Let's press the f. | JOHN 524:56
little f. | AURE 50:24
look like f. and blood | MOORE 705:13
make your f. creep | DICK 320:20
maketh marks in the f. | BIBLE 132:9
marriage makes man and wife one f. | CONG 280:7
material is our own f. | THOR 1016:73
men are f. and blood | SHAK 883:38
more fatal than painted f. | MACN 637:35
Mrs Forthby in the f. | SHAR 919:82
Neither f. nor fleshless | ELIOT 370:25
not of her f. and body | KEYN 554:28
outlive all f. | BYRON 221:18
pleasure of the f. | FUEN 409:26
poem …dream made f. | MILL 678:44
so much f.…so much nimbleness | DEKK 313:14
Take thou thy pound of f. | SHAK 873:96
they shall be one f. | BIBLE 103:92
things of the f. | BIBLE 149:26
this circle of f. | BROW 195:84
thorn in the f. | BIBLE 152:86
too solid f. would melt | SHAK 888:51
touch his bone and his f. | BIBLE 112:96
trees were surfaced like f. | LEE 593:18
twain shall be one f.? | BIBLE 139:22
vacations of the f. | TZARA 1035:35
walk not after the f. | BIBLE 149:25
we are one , One f. | MILT 692:7
What case of f. and blood | ROCH 816:49
What's this f.? | WEBS 1061:65
when we sat by the f. pots | BIBLE 106:66
with the f. the law of sin | BIBLE 149:24
Word made f. | BIBLE 144:27
your despicable and rotten f. | MARQ 655:34

Fletcher gave Shakespeare and F. all | DENH 315:55

fleur f. de France as perdut | ANON 21:61

flew One f. over the cuckoo's nest | KESEY 553:18
something f. between me and sun | BLUN 170:46

flexibility latter has f. of thought | PASC 757:47

flexible f. at all times | DIRK 331:65

flick bonded in their f. and flow | AVIS 53:76

fliers comrades chase…the f. | CLOU 270:32

flies As f. to wanton boys | SHAK 903:30
Dead f. cause the ointment | BIBLE 123:36
eyes and Reason…to study F. | POPE 783:9
f. in summer eves | KEATS 548:11
f. when I pursue it | ELIZ 373:89
may catch small f. | SWIFT 984:63
Plague him with f. | SHAK 897:96
swarm like summer f. | SHAK 862:25
these summer f. | SHAK 866:27
Unfading moths, immortal f. | BROO 193:34

flight alarms of struggle and f. | ARNO 36:65
as immutable as those of f. | HEMI 471:36
day of their f. | MACA 623:74
Explores his solitary f. | MILT 688:24
f. is what they long for | WILL 1081:62
f. of angels sing | SHAK 893:90
spread his airy f. | MILT 688:21
Swift be thine approaching f. | SHEL 932:61
Swift be thy f.! | SHEL 932:72
tiptoe for a f. | KEATS 544:35

flights four f. Thursday morning | WRIG 1102:13

flighty f. as birds | DAYL 310:57

flint snore upon the f. | SHAK 916:12
wait for the great f. | BIRN 163:25

Flintstones like relying on the F. | ARMEY 35:42

flip the rest is not worth a f. | BRON 191:94

flirtation bit of f. with missy | SPEKE 955:62

float English policy is to f. lazily | CECIL 247:81
F. like a butterfly | ALI 14:28

floating Artist of the F. World | ISHI 513:75

floats f. with the tide | HAZL 463:8

flock Christ's f. | BOOK 175:35
Fed the same f. | MILT 684:39
feed his f. like a shepherd | BIBLE 126:86
keeping watch over their f. by night | BIBLE 142:78
silent was the f. | KEATS 546:85
We are his f. | SCOT 856:22

flock-bed once a f.-b., but repaired | POPE 780:30

flocks fields and f. have charms | CRAB 293:71
f., or herds, of human | MILT 689:31
nibbling f. do stray | MILT 682:1
sang of f. and farms | VIRG 1046:96
shepherds feed their f. | MARL 655:31

Flodden F.'s fatal field | SCOT 853:60

flogging f. me constantly | TROL 1028:94

flood across the f. | TENN 1000:65
and takes the f. | TENN 1004:49
broad f. behind | MACA 623:16
days that were before the f. | BIBLE 140:39
f. could not wash away | CONG 281:16
f. may bear me far | TENN 1005:66
f. of remembrance | LAWR 585:69
f. that does not flow | SLES 943:57
not properly born, till f. | DICK 324:15
passage to the fallen f. | CRAB 294:83
rude bridge that arched the f. | EMER 376:26
taken at the f. | SHAK 884:60
telegraph poles above a f. | NICO 727:62
Thorough f., thorough fire | SHAK 870:35
tide…taken at the f. | BYRON 223:54
trees that yield to the f. | SOPH 953:18
years before the f. | MARV 658:72

floods f. of great waters | BIBLE 115:58
rain descended, and the f. came | BIBLE 135:63

floor beneath the watery f. | MILT 685:49
Clatter across the f. | MACC 624:33
f. under wages and a ceiling | WRIS 1102:16
Look how the f. of heaven | SHAK 873:99
man has just waxed the f. | NASH 720:61
oiled his way around the f. | LERN 597:90
On the f. I am…at ease | POLL 777:64
put diamonds on the f. | RIVE 813:4
repeat that on the Golden F.! | HOUS 496:85
rose along the gusty f. | KEATS 547:97
swept the f. | GILB 423:58
three skips on the f. | BALL 67:40
trail…up the f. | STEV 975:36
women…kick the f. | OSBO 745:67

floors f. of memory | ELIOT 367:58
f. of plaister, and the walls of dung | POPE 780:30
f. of silent seas | ELIOT 367:50

flop Classics…prevent f. | WOOLF 1093:80
f. in favour of your husband | DICK 326:61
f. is a f. | PAGL 749:35
total wreck, a f. | PORT 784:32

flops F. are a part of life | RUSS 833:43

Flora if he had married F. | SCOTT 854:71
Tasting of F. | KEATS 547:14

Florence maid called F.? | SAKI 837:4
Rode past fair F. | KEATS 546:82

Flores At F. in the Azores | TENN 1004:56

Florinda Her name is F.' | SAKI 837:4

flotilla old f. lay | KIPL 560:26

flounder f., the air | ATWO 44:17

flour Finer than f., alive — ROET 819:92
flourish f. or may fade — GOLD 433:10
  Human nature will not f. — HAWT 461:68
  No more doth f. — SPEN 958:13
  tidy and satisfactory f. — ELIZ 374:96
flourishing fat and f. — BIBLE 117:4
flow bonded in their flick and f. — AVIS 53:76
flower About the f. disguised — MARV 658:80
  as a f. of the field — BIBLE 118:15
  bar the f. away — ANON 22:66
  bear no f. — SHEL 931:56
  Beauty is but a f. — NASHE 721:83
  blood-red f. of revolution — RAND 801:26
  bloom upon a f. — THOM 1012:12
  blushing f. shall rise — POPE 778:74
  bot ane faiding f. — HENR 473:73
  Buddha...in the petals of a f. — PIRS 770:51
  constelled f. that never sets — SHEL 932:67
  creep from f. to f. — SHEL 927:61
  drives the f. — THOM 1010:51
  fell upon a little western f. — SHAK 870:36
  f. amang the a' — BALL 101:32
  f. born to blush unseen — GRAY 442:69
  f. is the concrete cloverleaf — MUMF 713:48
  f. of France is lost — ANON 21:61
  f. of old age — DEMO 315:46
  f. of Scotland — WILL 1083:7
  f. that dies — SHAK 887:41
  f. that sad embroidery wears — MILT 684:47
  f. thereof falleth away — BIBLE 155:76
  glory in the f. — WORD 1098:55
  grass withereth, the f. fadeth — BIBLE 126:85
  held my f. in a clenched fist — HOFF 484:55
  Here is the f. that you — MEIL 666:18
  How my face, your f. — BROW 197:29
  insect moves toward its f. — BALZ 69:78
  learning lightly like a f. — TENN 1000:62
  look like the innocent f. — SHAK 907:29
  loved a tree or f. — MOORE 706:38
  lovelier f....was never sown — WORD 1095:6
  Man...cometh forth like a f. — BIBLE 113:9
  meanest f. that blows — WORD 1098:56
  mysterious East, perfumed like a f. — CONR 284:97
  nayles whitter than the lylye f. — CHAU 255:45
  Nobody sees a f. — OKEE 738:21
  orange f. perfumes the bower — SCOTT 855:3
  pluck this f. safety — SHAK 875:51
  Poetry...the f. of...experience — HUNT 504:24
  same f. that smiles to day — HERR 477:63
  see...heaven in a wild f. — BLAKE 167:1
  seize the f. — BURNS 211:15
  shakes the f. free — MANS 647:5
  some gilded f. — VAUG 1040:15
  stem of the contained f. — ROET 819:93
  stronger than a f.? — SHAK 914:68
  sweetest f. for scent — SHEL 930:30
  sweetest f. of all the field — SHAK 869:18
  this is the noble f. — DONNE 338:17
  This midsummer f. — SKEL 942:34
  to darn, to f. or knit — LEWIS 601:46
  touch his f. — JONS 536:13
  Wearing the white f. — TENN 1002:1
  white rose and bean f. — FRAME 400:76
  whose fair f. — SHAK 894:12
  ys the f. of chevalry — MALO 642:29
flower-bell fancy from a f.-b. — BROW 198:54
flowering f. of His fields — TENN 1003:10
flowerings brief f. of feminism — FALU 382:58
flowerless f. fields of heaven — SWIN 986:22
  f. rocks of hell — SITW 940:2
flowers And it won't be f. — AUDEN 46:46
  azure moss and f. — SHEL 928:88
  bees are assaulting...the f. — REED 805:81
  better than a bunch of f. — CARY 243:21

flowers (*contd.*)
  blushing f. — POPE 778:76
  brought...cannons instead of f. — PEOP 764:58
  but as a bed of f. — DONNE 339:27
  enjoy the spring f. — SU 981:16
  Fair f. that are not gathered — SHAK 864:97
  fairest f. — WORD 1100:91
  f. begotten — SWIN 986:24
  f. come in stony places — MASE 662:50
  F. of all hue — MILT 690:53
  f. of the forest — COCK 272:61
  F. of the Forest — ELLI 374:8
  f. the tenderness — OWEN 748:8
  f. to strew Thy way — HERB 474:11
  gathers its material from f. — BACON 55:29
  gave her f. to love — BROO 192:21
  glass f. at Harvard — MOORE 705:19
  ground with vernal f. — MILT 684:46
  honey of all f. — NASHE 721:76
  hundred f. blossom — MAO 648:27
  immortal f. of poesy — MARL 653:91
  into a foam of f. — SWIN 987:29
  intuitively in f. — RUNGE 829:56
  leaves and f. do cover — WEBS 1060:44
  like f., a stronger scent — STAEL 961:72
  love to the f. — KEND 550:49
  love...as the f. do — RILKE 811:86
  lusty song of fruits and f. — BLAKE 165:59
  memories of f. and grass — ROBE 814:17
  men bearing f. — SPARK 955:59
  one which gathering f....fears a — DONNE 336:68
  Our f. are merely—f. — POE 776:48
  Overlook a space of f. — TENN 993:39
  play with f. — SHAK 880:71
  prairie f. lie low — LIND 606:17
  sleeping f. — WORD 1099:73
  That f. would bloom — KEATS 545:59
  the f. anew — PHIL 768:18
  thy garden f. — JONS 535:2
  to Barca f. — POPE 782:93
  tomb-stones where f. should be — BLAKE 167:91
  too soon for f. — DELA 314:35
  Until the f. are fragrant — TOJO 1022:88
  Where have all the f. gone? — SEEG 857:27
  With other f. — HERR 478:64
  young days of gathering f. — PEAC 762:31
flowery cool f. lap of earth — ARNO 37:73
  wakes me from my f. bed? — SHAK 871:44
flowing longer f., longer free — HERR 478:64
fluctuations mysterious f. of trade — ELIOT 365:17
fluffy But f., just f. — HERB 474:92
fluidity terrible f. of self-revelation — JAMES 516:29
fluids blood and other vital f. — STER 969:7
flush f. of a new-born sun — KIPL 561:40
flustered never f., never apathetic — AURE 50:27
flute brains upon the f. — BROW 200:98
  f....is too exciting — ARIS 34:34
  gauger played the f. — STEV 973:93
  The sound of the f. will cure — THEO 1008:34
flutes to the tune of f. kept stroke — SHAK 905:68
flutter f. far more, than leaves — CENN 248:95
fluttering f. to a bench — SACK 835:60
flux All is f., nothing is stationary — HERA 473:82
  passing f. of immediate things — WHIT 1071:55
fly as great a f. as Cassio — SHAK 899:20
  cut off, and we f. away — BIBLE 117:99
  f. in his hand — STER 969:99
  f....may sting — JOHN 526:94
  f. sat upon the axletree — BACON 59:28
  I cannot f. — SHAK 910:87
  Indoor f. casting — NASH 720:70
  like a f. crawling — INGR 512:51
  long-legged f. — YEATS 1107:90
  noise of a f. — DONNE 339:28

fly (*contd.*)
  shew the f. way out — WITT 1088:79
  solitary f.! — GRAY 441:59
  those that f., may fight again — BUTL 217:24
  'Thou shalt f.' — CLEE 268:99
  unzipped f. caught in forever amber — COND 279:84
  we cannot f. — EMPS 378:85
  will f. no more — HOLM 486:82
  wisdom made the f. — NASH 720:67
  wouldn't hurt a f. — LEAC 589:46
fly-fishing F.-f. may be...pleasant — JOHN 532:4
flying Armstrongs are f. — HOGG 485:65
  f. in the face of presumptions — JAMES 516:17
  f. through space forever — GAGA 411:68
  growing, f., happening — REID 806:97
  shot one bird f. — HEMI 470:22
foam Cowslip...like tethered f. — CRANE 295:6
  f. on the river — SCOTT 854:65
  into a f. of flowers — SWIN 987:29
  wind...wild and dank with f. — KING 558:89
foaminess f. of the Falls — SALA 838:17
focus Johnny, keep it out of f. — WILD 1079:14
foe angry with my f. — BLAKE 167:83
  Call no man f. — BENS 92:11
  erect and manly f. — CANN 230:71
  everyone's a f. — CLARE 267:79
  find a f. — PARK 754:12
  f. oft-times having the f. in sight — DONNE 336:71
  furnace for your f. — SHAK 917:45
  manxome f. he sought — CARR 239:47
  never made a f. — TENN 1002:16
  our sneaking f.? — SITW 941:23
  overcome but half his f. — MILT 688:7
  perhaps a jealous f. — SHEL 931:52
  wild unsated f.! — COLL 277:45
foes against the f. — SMART 944:69
  doubt of future f. — ELIZ 373:87
  f., and oh, my friends — MILL 676:82
  judge a man by his f. — CONR 284:95
  loins of these two f. — SHAK 868:73
  neither f. nor loving friends — KIPL 564:9
  new f. arise Threatening to — MILT 686:80
  no f. nor friends — DONNE 339:34
  Set upon the f.! — SHAK 863:67
  slay their f. — MACD 628:2
  thirty thousand f. — MACA 623:16
  Words...the great f. of reality — CONR 285:6
fog A f., miss — DICK 324:21
  achievements...in a blessed, warm f. — CONR 285:12
  brown f. of a winter dawn — ELIOT 368:83
  f. comes on little cat f. — SAND 841:58
  F. everywhere — DICK 324:18
  f. is rising — DICK 329:20
  Hover through the f. — SHAK 906:10
  like a cold f. — ACHE 3:30
  natural f. of the good man's mind — BROW 198:42
  trying to sculpture a f. — LEHM 594:37
foggy f. day in London Town — GERS 420:13
fogs rising f. prevail upon the day — DRYD 348:83
foil golden f. all over them — SPEN 957:2
  shining from shook f. — HOPK 491:82
foining f. o'nights — SHAK 877:92
fold f. after f., to the fainting air — SHEL 930:29
  f. my tens — KAUF 543:16
  if your name's above the f. — LANCE 578:53
  Now I f. you down — SEXT 859:62
  one f., and one shepherd — BIBLE 146:54
  tangl'd in the f. — MILT 695:57
folders manila f. and mucilage — ROET 819:91
foliage love for Linton like f. — BRON 192:12
  stillness of the buried f. — HOLM 485:72
Folies-Bergère F.-B. and looks at — STOC 977:70

folio whole volumes, in f.   SHAK 865:12
folios mighty f.…a lordly band   CRAB 293:67
folk All music is f. music   ARMS 35:47
  f. begin to tak the gate   BURNS 211:8
  F. music…fat people   DYLAN 358:98
  f. to goon on pilgrimages   CHAU 254:17
  f. wou'd hae a doubt on   FERG 385:15
  itinerant f. artists   ROCK 818:78
  just look at all the f.   LAUD 583:37
  matches of the Southron f.   THOM 1014:32
  novels are strange f.   LUCAS 618:25
  'the Big F.' as they call us   TOLK 1023:94
  trouble with f. song   LAMB 577:48
  we theatre f.   MANK 645:77
  Wee f., good f.   ALLI 15:53
folks bunch of f. hoping   WALK 1049:58
  Don't let the old f. know   HERB 474:90
  eat, good f.   PRIOR 790:56
  F. don't like to have somebody   LEE 593:9
  f. eat the stuff they raise   STEI 966:55
  hand f. over to God's mercy   ELIOT 365:12
  my f. were growing old   STEV 976:58
  nor any of my f.   MITC 697:87
  That's all f.!   FREL 404:37
  What signifies't for f. to chide   SKIN 943:55
  When f. git ole   HARR 458:32
  where the old f. stay   FOST 399:60
follies charming f.   GILL 426:2
  f. of this dull age   CAREW 232:7
  indulge in a few f.   PROU 792:89
  point out to us our f.   TROL 1027:68
  Pour her exotic f. o'er the town   BYRON 219:63
  pretty f. that themselves commit   SHAK 874:29
  vices and the f. of human kind   CONG 280:4
  whose f. cease with their youth   PITT 771:62
follow f. me   GARI 415:25
  F. thou me!   SCHW 852:31
  he saith unto them, F. me   BIBLE 133:33
  horrid thing to f.   JAMES 516:16
  I f. the worse   OVID 747:1
  In following him I f.   SHAK 897:94
  Jesus said unto him, F. me   BIBLE 136:67
  saith unto him, F. me   BIBLE 136:69
  where few can f.   KENN 550:50
follower misguided f. climbs   ROCH 816:50
followers f. of Jesus   JOHN 525:74
  vice promises to her f.   MILT 685:65
followship practising f.   THAT 1008:31
folls Deal round to happy f.   BYRON 220:97
folly Age from f.   SHAK 905:24
  All my joys to this are f.   BURT 214:64
  brood of F.   MILT 682:5
  curse of mankind, f. and ignorance   SHAK 895:44
  darling F., Fickleness   MAND 645:71
  epoch of f. and shame   ZOLA 1110:26
  Fashion, though F.'s child   CRAB 293:68
  f.…has a certain stamp   GERH 420:4
  f. him that is in reputation   BIBLE 123:36
  f. in that of a great kingdom   SMITH 945:88
  f. is not always f.   AUST 52:56
  f. of 'Women's Rights'   VICT 1043:50
  f. to be wise   GRAY 441:48
  fool returneth to his f.   BIBLE 122:2
  in their f. not less blind   HOPE 490:71
  knavery and f. to excuse   CHUR 262:81
  like f. shows   MILT 692:96
  lovely woman stoops to f.   AUST 52:59
  lovely woman stoops to f.   GOLD 432:5
  make good their own f.   BACON 57:63
  most loving, mere f.   SHAK 886:95
  moved to f. by a noise   LAWR 587:16
  Neebours' fauts and f.   BURNS 210:82
  noise of f.   MILT 682:8
  obstinacy of f.   STOWE 979:90

folly (*contd.*)
  our pride, our f., or our fate   DENH 315:54
  own f., go over edge   MOUN 711:13
  rather of their f.   ELIOT 371:47
  shoot F. as it flies   POPE 780:33
  such gratuitous f.   HUXL 507:65
  too presumptuous f.   HARTE 460:52
  uses his f. like a stalking-horse   SHAK 887:37
  whirled in f. and vice   TENN 1001:75
fond f. thing vainly invented   BOOK 178:98
  F. without art   DRYD 348:98
  never prove so f.   SHAK 901:87
  rarity which I cannot but be f. of   ROCH 816:58
  so f. of one another   SWIFT 984:66
Fonstein F.…advanced category   BELL 89:43
font in the porphyry f.   TENN 997:10
food America, bring your own f.   LEBO 592:89
  and the f. a tragedy   POWE 787:4
  As I do live by f.   SHAK 885:89
  bloody flesh our only f.   ELIOT 371:52
  Continent people have good f.   MIKES 674:52
  desire for f. and sex   TOOLE 1023:5
  discoveres that alcohol was a f.   WODE 1089:92
  enough f. for eight   MOLI 699:27
  estimated even f. and necessaries   RICA 808:32
  every mouthful of f.   FORD 396:98
  Fame is a f.   DOBS 334:35
  fed by a different f.   DISR 332:90
  fed with the same f.   SHAK 872:80
  finds its f. in music   LILLO 604:95
  f. and not fine words   MOLI 699:32
  F. comes first   BREC 186:25
  f. for worms!   FRAN 402:99
  f. is love   SHEL 929:8
  f. of love   SHAK 893:91
  f. out of the earth   BIBLE 118:16
  give them f. and shelter   JARR 518:63
  glum urge for f. to fill us   FISH 390:85
  Hard f. for Midas   SHAK 873:83
  having f. and raiment   BIBLE 154:33
  junk f.   GASS 416:35
  knowledge is as f.   MILT 691:83
  libraries are f.   TUCH 1031:48
  love of f.   SHAW 921:28
  man in jail has…better f.   JOHN 527:25
  more delicate the f.   INNO 512:55
  music, moody f.   SHAK 905:73
  nourishing, and wholesome F.   SWIFT 985:98
  perpetual struggle for room and f.   MALT 643:39
  problem is f.   DONL 336:60
  quantity of f. required   RICA 808:33
  senses…supply Fresh f.   WORD 1094:94
  Sharing f.…an intimate act   FISH 389:84
  ships to bear our f. away   WILDE 1075:27
  taste for…French f.   SCHL 848:77
  think they're still getting real f.   COUP 289:79
  was there like f. or air   ROCK 817:68
  With eager feeding f.   SHAK 866:46
  Women Whose Lives Are F.   OATES 733:55
fool A f., a f., I met a f.   SHAK 885:89
  Any f. can be brave   MITC 697:88
  Any f. may write a…book   GRAY 443:96
  any man is so very a f.   SHAK 864:71
  appear a f., a blockhead,or a knave   DRYD 351:63
  becomes a f. and jester!   SHAK 878:10
  Better a witty f.   SHAK 894:1
  better to be a f.   STEV 974:15
  blundering f. may   MORT 710:99
  Busy old f.   DONNE 336:77
  but in a f.'s cap   HOPK 491:78
  can love like a f.   NASH 719:49
  damn f. if he doesn't   FAUL 384:90
  every f. in Buxton   RUSK 831:13
  f. among fools   WILD 1079:32

fool (*contd.*)
  f. at the other   JOHN 532:43
  f.'s bauble   CROM 298:56
  f. consistent   POPE 781:56
  f. doth think he is wise   SHAK 887:27
  f. has a lot to teach   RABE 799:89
  f. hath said in his heart   BIBLE 114:36
  f. his whole life long   LUTH 620:52
  F. in every man's mouth   BUNY 205:72
  f.…in every married couple   FIEL 388:54
  f., In power of others   MILT 694:40
  f. in the eye of the world   CONG 281:17
  f. is happy   POPE 780:45
  f. is love that in your will   SHAK 913:66
  F.: it is you who are pursued   SHAW 921:30
  f. lies here   KIPL 561:45
  f. o' the other senses   SHAK 908:40
  f. returneth to his folly   BIBLE 122:2
  f. said my muse to me   SIDN 937:51
  f. some of the people   LINC 605:99
  f.…that first invented kissing!   SWIFT 986:15
  f. to make me merry   SHAK 886:18
  f. too large for it   CHES 259:21
  f. too many of the people   THUR 1019:28
  f. uttereth all his mind   BIBLE 122:10
  f., who trusts a man   MARIE 651:65
  greatest f. may ask more   COLT 277:56
  have played the f.   BIBLE 110:43
  He's a f. that marries   WYCH 1103:42
  human and makes me a f.   LEGU 594:33
  I'd be a damn' f.   THOM 1011:76
  idle f.   FORD 397:16
  Into a strumpet's f.   SHAK 904:56
  knaves do work with, called a f.   BUTL 216:2
  laughter of a f.   BIBLE 123:27
  learned f. is more   MOLI 699:33
  Let me play the f.   SHAK 873:88
  like a musical f.   HUGH 499:16
  little else a f.   MACG 630:26
  Love's not time's f.   SHAK 915:89
  make a f. of himself!   STEV 974:16
  man and wife make one f.   JONS 535:94
  manage a f.   KIPL 560:16
  maxim is worthy of the f.   MACA 622:91
  more of the f. than of the wise   BACON 58:77
  Napoleon thinks that I am a f.   ALEX 13:15
  No boasting like a f.   SHAK 909:69
  O heavenly f.   SIDN 937:56
  patriot…a f.   DRYD 350:30
  play the f.…in 's own house   SHAK 891:27
  power to do any damn f. thing   FULB 409:28
  prove one's self a f.   HAWT 461:78
  resolv'd to live a f.   BEAU 80:66
  satisfy anyone but a damned f.   BART 74:72
  'school' 'f.', a babbling rhyme   SHAK 880:65
  smarts so little as a f.   POPE 781:61
  Socates…than a f. satisfied   MILL 675:70
  surely f. a man   WHITE 1070:30
  the more f. I   SHAK 885:85
  time to f. with politics   ROGE 820:19
  To please a f.   CONG 281:37
  What f. is not so wise   SHAK 865:19
  whether he is a wise man or a f.   BLAKE 168:10
  whosoever shall say, Thou f.   BIBLE 134:39
  works is a f.   MORL 708:75
  worship this dull f.   SHAK 917:42
  wretched, rash, intruding f.   SHAK 892:53
foolery most hateful form of f.   BROW 200:84
fooling always f. with something   WHITE 1070:28
foolish Better…than a f. wit   SHAK 894:1
  disguises from the f.   BIER 161:80
  envious at the f.   BIBLE 117:89
  f., fond old man   SHAK 904:43
  F. the man who trusts her   FRAN 401:95

foolish (*contd.*)

f. thing was but a toy	SHAK 895:39
f. thing well done	JOHN 529:63
Forgive our f. ways	WHIT 1074:9
God hath chosen the f. things	BIBLE 150:45
I, being young and f.	YEATS 1104:56
likened unto a f. man	BIBLE 135:63
never said a f. thing	ROCH 817:66
not such a f. thing	ISHI 513:77
old and f. king	BIBLE 123:25
Only the f. are punished	MARG 650:54
saying a f. thing	STER 970:14
smallest f. act makes it idiotic	YOUR 1108:7
These F. Things	MARV 659:93

foolishly don't think f. — JOHN 531:29

foolishness age of f. — DICK 326:58
f. of preaching — BIBLE 150:44

fools all the f. in town — TWAIN 1033:91

Atheists, f. and madmen!	ONEI 740:59
Be friends, you English f.	SHAK 881:93
Beggared by f.	DRYD 349:24
busy f. may be stopped	DONNE 336:71
called the Paradise of F.	MILT 689:42
exportation of f.	CONG 281:27
Fashion…guide of f.	CRAB 293:68
f. and cowards might sit safe	OTWAY 746:83
F. are my theme	BYRON 218:59
F. are as like husbands	SHAK 895:20
F. are in a…majority	IBSEN 510:23
f. by heavenly compulsion	SHAK 902:2
F.! For I also had my hour	CHES 257:88
f. rush in	POPE 778:48
f. shall not err therein	BIBLE 126:83
For…government let f. contest	POPE 781:46
Fortune, that favours f.	JONS 535:92
great stage of f.	SHAK 904:39
I am two f.	DONNE 337:84
If honest Nature made you f.	BURNS 209:58
make f. of themselves about	SHAW 920:97
many f. at a university	GERH 420:4
marriage leaves…still two f.	CONG 280:7
more f. than wise	GIBB 422:32
Nature meant but f.	POPE 778:75
none but f. would keep	SHAK 897:77
pair of credulous f.	SHIR 935:25
people in the world are f.	WILD 1079:30
play the f. with the time	SHAK 877:89
please the f.	DRYD 349:11
poor f. decoyed	PEPYS 765:77
proved plain f.	POPE 778:77
secrets…must be kept…from f.	DRYD 346:55
shoal of f. for tenders	CONG 281:34
soldiers, mostly f.	BIER 161:85
suffer f. gladly	BIBLE 152:85
the f. caught it	YEATS 1105:49
there are two kinds of f.	MORR 708:79
Thus may poor f.	SHAK 916:8
Tories remained f.	WALP 1051:93
traps for eager or clever f.	SNYD 951:85
twenty-seven millions mostly f.	CARL 236:98
vain f. ambitiously contend	LUCR 619:35
virtue of f.	BACON 56:36
What f. middle-class girls are	DRAB 345:24
what f. these mortals be!	SHAK 871:48
wise men follow f.	BACON 58:84
With the flannelled f.	KIPL 563:94
world is made up…of f. and knaves	BUCK 203:40

foolscaps f. of air — AVIS 53:76

foot And the Forty-second F.! — HOOD 488:35

blood from head to f.	MACL 633:67
breasts are under our f.	SHAW 921:29
caught my f.	GROS 447:72
deft the Devil's f.	DONNE 336:75
'eathen idol's f.	KIPL 561:38

foot (*contd.*)

Englishman sets f. on it	STEF 965:26
espied his cloven f.	BALL -101:36
f. and hand go cold	ANON 23:84
f. for f.	BIBLE 107:69
f. in Eden	MUIR 712:36
f. is on my native heath	SCOTT 855:89
f. less prompt	ARNO 39:19
f. out of joint	BIBLE 121:99
f. upon the stirrup	DELA 314:27
from head to f.	TENN 1001:83
from his head to his f.	MOORE 704:7
hand or thy f. offend thee	BIBLE 138:19
his f. is guilty	BECK 81:91
hold Creation in my f.	HUGH 500:36
inaudible and noiseless f.	SHAK 901:85
Leave not a f. of verse	POPE 783:2
length of Prester John's f.	SHAK 879:38
madly squeeze a right-hand f.	CARR 241:78
make crouch beneath his f.	BROW 200:91
never place their second f.	FONT 395:89
no man's f. can pass	BOTT 180:36
no rest for the sole of her f.	BIBLE 104:11
nor can f. feel	HOPK 491:82
One f. he centred	MILT 691:85
One f. in Canada	GAY 416:46
One f. in sea	SHAK 879:46
One square f. less	BENC 89:51
print of a man's naked f.	DEFOE 312:80
proud f. of a conqueror	SHAK 872:75
set her f. upon thy substance	BIBLE 132:95
sole of his f.	SHAK 879:50
speed of the f. race	YOUR 1108:11
stick out a f.	ADLER 8:45
trodden under f. of men	BIBLE 134:35
trode her under f.	BIBLE 112:82
walked with willing f.	STEV 973:93
will not suffer thy f. to be moved	BIBLE 119:36
wished myself on f.	MUNDY 714:53
with shining f. shall pass	FITZ 390:91

foot-in-the-grave F. young man! — GILB 424:71

foot-landrakers joined with no f.-l. — SHAK 875:47

football All …I owe to f. — CAMUS 229:63

base f. player	SHAK 902:3
bewteis of the f.	ANON 23:88
College f. is a sport	HUBB 498:7
College f.	GALL 412:91
concentrate on f.	NICH 726:54
concerning f. playing	STUB 980:12
disregard for the rules of f.	ANON 24:10
European f. without the English	CHAR 253:93
F. causeth fighting	STUB 980:13
f. field is a place	ROUS 827:30
F. hooligans?	CLOU 271:51
F.…is a grand game	BADE 60:45
F. is all very well as a game	WILDE 1078:7
F. is like a religion	PELE 764:52
f. is proposed at Christmas	ANON 24:14
F.…keep coalminers off streets	BRES 187:36
f.—the most exhilarating game	GOOD 435:55
F. then was fighting sorrow	HOUS 494:48
geriatric f. in the winter	KINN 559:9
good of f.	TAYL 992:20
ideal day for f.	SMITH 948:26
In f. it is widely acknowledged	FRY 408:11
kick it about all day like a f.	HOLM 486:86
life is…a game of f.	SCOTT 854:72
like a f. you do spurn me	SHAK 865:2
married during the f. season?	SHAN 919:74
No f. player…within the City	ELIZ 373:88
politics is like…a f. coach	MACC 625:41
Some people think f.	SHAN 918:69
there be used F., Golfe	JAME 515:1

football (*contd.*)

To watch a game of f.	BARZ 76:99
footballer no longer a f.	CRUY 298:66
footballs street being full of f.	PEPYS 766:82
footfalls F. echo in the memory	ELIOT 370:23
foothold f. in a narrow strip of land	BAKER 63:83
footing how…honesty, got f.	OTWAY 746:82
lived on a friendly f.	LAMB 576:23
footman eternal F. hold my coat	ELIOT 367:51
footmen But of all f.	HAZL 464:20
footnote greatness…soon be a f.	THAT 1007:9
footnotes series of f. to Plato	WHIT 1071:59
series of f.	NABO 717:3
serried f. to man	GRASS 439:13
footpath jog on, the f. way	SHAK 911:27
footprint looking for a man's f.	BEER 83:29
footprints f. of a gigantic hound!	DOYLE 344:10
F. on the sand of time	LONG 611:96
plaster casts of f.	PATE 760:98
footsoles midwife slapped your f.	PLATH 773:98
footsteps f. made no noise	DICK 322:61
home his f. …turned	SCOTT 853:49
plants his f. in the sea	COWP 291:27
poors slaves with weary f.	SHEL 931:52
footstool make thine enemies thy f.	BIBLE 118:22
fop f. in my heart	ETHE 380:19
man of sense and a f.	CHES 257:71
foppery f. of freedom	SHAK 896:62
F. often changes Fashion	FRAN 402:6
forbear F. to judge	SHAK 861:7
forbid expressly to f. you	LOUI 614:46
f. the King to keep it	INNO 512:56
therefore I f. my tears	SHAK 893:74
forbidden wicked and to be f.	STUB 980:11
force alcohol is a…deadening f.	WEBB 1058:15
All governments use f.	PARE 753:83
back her vote by physical f.	WRIG 1101:2
Better to use f.	SHUL 936:33
combination of skill and f.	BURKE 207:29
dedicated to f. and to beauty	RIMB 812:98
disputes…settled by using f.	EISE 364:86
envy…is f. t'admire!	DANI 304:63
evil…a f. in he world	CHUR 262:79
F. is the same throughout	LEON 597:76
F. made the first slaves	ROUS 827:34
f. maintaining the world	DOST 340:45
f. of honesty	SHAK 891:23
f. of the bayonet!	MIRA 695:69
f. that propels	KAND 541:94
Life, f. and beauty	POPE 778:74
lost faith…in natural f.	CARL 234:40
May the F.	LUCAS 618:31
motive f. impressed	NEWT 725:36
No f. to win the victory	DYER 358:88
no motion…no f.	WORD 1095:7
not by f. but by understanding	BRON 190:80
not need to convince…by f.	WILS 1086:47
only f. capable	KING 558:37
Other nations use 'f.'	WAUGH 1057:85
out by f. of arms	LOUI 613:45
patience achieve more than f.	BURKE 208:38
persuade gently, not by f.	PASC 758:69
real revolutionary f.	OROU 741:32
spent its novel f.	TENN 995:73
supreme arbitrament of f.	CHUR 263:92
The f. that through	THOM 1010:51
Tonality is a natural f.	HIND 481:12
unofficial f.—the Baker Street	DOYLE 343:93
use of f. alone is temporary	BURKE 206:6
Who overcomes By f.	MILT 688:7
with an irresistible f.	HEDIN 466:61
worth more than f. and rage	LAFO 575:88
forced f.—by what?	FROMM 406:70

forced (contd.)

f. …into any…belief	RICH 810:*62*
f. to like what you get	SHAW 922:*63*

forces acknowledge the spiritual f. MOORE 705:*16*

balance of actual f.	NAPO 718:*27*
centrifugal f. which are	NASH 720:*72*
communicate with his f.	SCHW 851:*21*
enhances the f. of the mind	PROU 793:*7*
f., although small	MAO 648:*19*
f. impressed thereon	NEWT 724:*35*
f. which might bring	RUSS 832:*28*
f. working in inverse order!	CARL 235:*64*
modified aggregate of external f.	SPEN 955:*66*
targeted by powerful f.	BELL 88:*42*

ford bridge the f. KIPL 561:*53*

Ford Jerome to F. Maddox F. COLE 273:*7*

my friend F.	WILL 1082:*87*
Nixon…gave us General F.	ABZUG 2:*15*
Our F.…had been the first	HUXL 507:*67*

Fords swarming in F. FERB 385:*7*

fore at the f. GILB 426:*95*

foreboding I am filled with much f. POWE 788:*17*

with a deeper f.	FRAN 401:*93*

forecast even the weather f. LODGE 609:*7*

prevents the events they f.	WRIS 1102:*17*

forecastle crew is gambling in the f. SHAW 925:*16*

forefathers f. had no other books SHAK 861:*15*

genealogy of his f.	ECHE 359:*13*
Our f. would have died	OCON 735:*80*
recover it from all his f.	BUTL 218:*50*
rude f. of the hamlet	GRAY 442:*64*
simple f. would kill	MONT 701:*60*
Whatever our f. were	OVER 747:*93*

forefinger f. of all Time TENN 996:*92*

f. of an alderman	SHAK 868:*78*

forehead Flames in the f. MILT 685:*49*

He tapped his f.	CHRI 261:*7*
Love, knocking its blind f.	SAND 840:*48*
middle of her f.	LONG 612:*21*
Tap his f. first	WODE 1088:*88*
with unbashful f. woo	SHAK 885:*82*

foreheads f. nobility is engraved LAUT 584:*50*

foreign attacking the F. Secretary BEVAN 101:*68*

courtly f. grace	TENN 1005:*60*
defended…from f. invasion	REDM 804:*75*
do in f. affairs	JOHN 524:*58*
emancipating themselves from a f.	MAZZ 666:*11*
F. Secretary…naked	BEVAN 101:*69*
f. troop…in my country	PITT 771:*70*
in spite of its f. propaganda	ORWE 743:*20*
knew a lot about f. affairs	REST 807:*18*
life is a f. country	KERO 553:*11*
loans…to f. nations	BAGE 62:*64*
No f. policy	KISS 566:*34*
past is a f. country	HART 460:*54*
portion of the f. world	WASH 1054:*44*
sent to any f. wars	ROOS 822:*41*
speaking a f. language	WILD 1079:*18*
win the F. picture award	WILD 1079:*14*
worst of the F.…Office	CRIT 297:*44*

foreigner dagger which the f. left QUIN 798:*68*

f. should in any respect	TROL 1027:*68*

foreigners don't object to f. WILD 1079:*8*

f. always spell better	TWAIN 1032:*58*
f. are fiends	MITF 697:*98*
f. could more easily	NGU 725:*45*
f. speak English	CRISP 297:*35*

forerunner f. of despair KENN 550:*56*

foreseen What I had not f. SPEN 956:*73*

foresight urge…to aftersight and f. ELIOT 372:*73*

forest as a…hedge is to a f. JOHN 532:*40*

behind it rose the f.	LONG 611:*10*
chose the f. path	FAWC 384:*93*
Dong through the f. goes	LEAR 589:*52*

forest (contd.)

even as the f. is	SHEL 928:*90*
flowers of the f.	COCK 272:*61*
Flowers of the F.	ELLI 374:*8*
f. fleece	HOUS 495:*53*
F. where all must lose	THOM 1012:*11*
f. with a golden track	LIND 605:*13*
Glimpse of the f.	SITW 941:*9*
into the f. dim	KEATS 547:*14*
lost to the f.	SCOTT 854:*64*
Marxism…like finding a map in a f.	CAST 244:*34*
met a fool i'th' f.	SHAK 885:*89*
paint a f. or a horse	MARC 649:*41*
redwood f.	GUTH 449:*94*
spark can start a f. fire	MAO 648:*19*
take a tree from the f.	SCOTT 854:*70*
the f.'s ferny floor	DELA 314:*25*
This is the f. primeval	LONG 611:*6*
thru the graveyard f.	PURDY 795:*34*
undulating tropical rain f.	BOYD 182:*62*
whole f. echoes	CARL 235:*73*

forests Among the f. THOM 1013:*25*

F. of middle-aged men	ABBO 1:*1*
f. of the night	BLAKE 167:*96*
f. where they roamed	SIGO 938:*71*
green days in f.	STEV 976:*53*
sole king of f. all	SPEN 957:*99*

foresworn Necessity will make us all f. SHAK 865:*9*

foretaste f. of death SCHO 849:*1*

foretold f. the rest ELIOT 369:*89*

forever experiment lasts f. KAPI 542:*8*

flying through space f.	GAGA 411:*68*
it lives f.	UPDI 1037:*66*
talked f.	HAZL 463:*99*
that vast f.	KING 558:*91*

forfeit f. of their name HABI 450:*1*

forfended music of f. spheres PATM 760:*11*

forget Best, to f.! BROW 200:*99*

cause us to f. their existence	HAWT 461:*77*
either f. right away	BECK 81:*95*
far worse than to f.	BENU 94:*34*
f. because we must	ARNO 36:*69*
F. it, Jake	TOWNE 1024:*11*
f. me not	GINS 428:*26*
f. so much	DAVI 307:*8*
f. that words	JOHN 526:*5*
f. to tell each other	HELL 468:*96*
f. yourself in the park?	TAYL 992:*14*
glad to have humanity f.	HOOV 490:*61*
going to f. the war	HEMI 470:*18*
if thou wilt, f.	ROSS 824:*76*
Lest we f.!	KIPL 562:*61*
Let us not f.	GAIT 411:*72*
lover who does not f.	BART 75:*83*
make one set of people f.	HUXL 508:*92*
never f. that a child	JUVE 540:*83*
Promise to f. this fellow	SHER 933:*77*
quite f.	KEATS 547:*15*
should both f.	SWIN 987:*42*
should f. it	HERR 477:*49*
teach us to f. our own	SHAK 910:*97*
yet will I not f. thee	BIBLE 126:*95*

forgetfulness to dumb F. a prey GRAY 442:*74*

forgetting f. buries them LABR 572:*44*

F. those things which are behind	BIBLE 153:*12*
sleep and f.	WORD 1098:*51*
world f., by the world forgot	POPE 779:*17*

forgive and to f. SWIN 988:*54*

At distance I f. thee	MILT 695:*51*
do my people f. me?	RICH 809:*56*
F. and be happy	PRAT 789:*23*
F. me, sir	KARSH 542:*11*
F., O Lord	FROST 407:*1*
F. the hero	WILB 1074:*17*

forgive (contd.)

f. them; for they know not	BIBLE 144:*16*
f. those sins	DONNE 339:*19*
God will f. me	HEINE 467:*73*
Good, to f.	BROW 200:*99*
one can f. anybody	WILDE 1077:*71*
rarely…do they f. them	WILDE 1077:*70*
sin against me, and I f. him?	BIBLE 139:*21*
to f., divine	POPE 778:*85*

forgiven f. all those who trespass JOSE 537:*33*

healed, restored, f.	LYTE 621:*66*
neither can nor should be f.	SHAW 922:*52*
sins, which are many, are f.	BIBLE 142:*84*

forgiveness After…, what f.? ELIOT 368:*70*

F. free of evil done	KIPL 564:*4*
F. of sins	BOOK 173:*94*
f. to the injured	DRYD 347:*70*
Mutual f. of each vice	BLAKE 166:*81*
there is always f.	BALZ 69:*79*
there is f. with thee	BIBLE 119:*44*

forgives neither f. you nor allows SHAW 922:*64*

forgiving God's slim f. BENE 89:*58*

forgot And she f. the stars KEATS 546:*83*

f. for which he toiled	SHAK 913:*55*
f. to duck	DEMP 315:*47*
f. what things were called	ATWO 45:*28*

forgotten actress—never to be f. DAVIS 308:*25*

always a f. thing	CHES 259:*20*
f. since their beauty	THOM 1012:*2*
f. what it is like	JARR 518:*65*
I am all f.	SHAK 905:*65*
memory of them is f.	BIBLE 123:*32*
present is not f.	GRASS 439:*11*
what has been learnt has been f.	SKIN 943:*51*
what you have f.	FENT 385:*1*

fork f. in his inexperienced hand WELLS 1064:*32*

forks pursued it with f. CARR 241:*87*

forlorn on earth I wait f. ARNO 38:*2*

form All is without f. and void HAZL 464:*25*

All must love the human f.	BLAKE 166:*65*
Art is nothing without f.	FLAU 392:*32*
assume the f. of machinery	MARX 661:*22*
Beauty has only one f.	HUGO 501:*55*
both for power and f.	SPEN 958:*12*
but one f.	THOR 1016:*72*
changing oftentimes its f.	WORD 1096:*31*
critic must attack the f.	LAUT 584:*52*
does a human f. display	BLAKE 168:*21*
Drawing…the way of seeing the f.	DEGAS 312:*92*
emptying…of all f. and content	FANON 382:*60*
Every f. is individual	HEIN 467:*76*
every F. of being	WORD 1100:*83*
experience In a different f.	ELIOT 372:*60*
favourite f. of revenge	NIET 728:*86*
feel the same way about f. and space	DAVIS 309:*34*
f. as a tree has f.	POUND 787:*94*
f., colour, and mood of a picture	FEIN 385:*99*
F. follows profit'	ROGE 820:*3*
f. of moral effort	LEAC 589:*42*
f. of our primitive ancestors	MILL 679:*58*
f. of the short story	SARO 843:*99*
f., so angel fair	BRON 190:*86*
f. that my style cannot discover	DARIO 305:*76*
formal poetry perfect only in f.	SAND 842:*80*
hewed her lovely f.	MILT 686:*72*
highest f. of government	SPEN 956:*69*
Humanity in its basic f.	BARTH 74:*66*
in f. and moving	SHAK 890:*4*
let the f. of an object be what it may	CONS 285:*20*
Life is that the f.	MANN 645:*80*
like definite f.	STEV 973:*98*
Love, the human f. divine	BLAKE 166:*69*
Man found his f.	BERD 94:*35*
never make a god out of f.	KAND 541:*95*

form (*contd.*)

no f. nor comeliness	BIBLE 127:99
Nor f., nor feeling	WORD 1095:10
obituary in serial f.	CRISP 297:40
one loves only f.	OLSEN 739:36
outside to every f.	HEPW 473:80
pretty f. to the lips	DICK 326:53
relationships of color or f.	ROTH 826:26
significant f.	BELL 85:80
take thy f.	POE 776:49
than any other literary f.	DUDEK 353:13
Thanks to his bodily f.	REDT 804:79
The F. remains	WORD 1100:85
theory in ritual f.	NOVAK 732:36
Thou, silent f.	KEATS 547:11
together in a f. called E	SCHM 848:80
visual f. of the 'otherness'	NOLAN 731:20
what the f. divine!	LAND 578:54

formal Wearing underwear is as f. — HEMI 471:49
formality eunuched with f. — CLEV 269:12
former f. are products of fortune — HELO 469:7

f. days were better	BIBLE 123:29
f. things are passed away	BIBLE 158:35

formidable less f. than…Genesis — ACHE 3:34

none more f. than man	SOPH 953:16
this f. kingdom	PITT 771:63

forms disguise…in a thousand f. — BEAU 79:62

Even f. and substances	WORD 1096:30
f. of human knowledge	MANN 645:81
f. of virtue are erect	FUSE 410:61
f. that are lit up	GOYA 437:83
knell is rung By f. unseen	COLL 276:44
magic of official f.	WAUGH 1057:96
may not hope from outward f. to win	COLE 274:5
Mis-shapes the beauteous f.	WORD 1094:3
same f. and the same language	FLAU 392:39
takes more f.	THUR 1019:44
These beauteous f.	WORD 1094:3
To creat f. means: to live	MACKE 632:51

formula f., Term, holidays — LEWIS 601:43

relied on the classic f.	LARK 582:21
use the f. to say something	JAMES 517:34

fornication filthiness of her f. — BIBLE 158:28

F.—but that was in	MARL 653:2
one fraud, the other f.	MATOS 664:77

forsake Even now f. me — SHAK 862:31
will not fail thee, nor f. thee — BIBLE 108:7
forsaken why hast thou f. me? — BIBLE 114:47
why hast thou f. me? — BIBLE 140:55
forsaking strange fashion of f. — WYATT 1103:31
forsook true love has me f. — BALL 67:57
Forster F. never gets any further — MANS 647:1
same gods…and E M F. — DRAB 345:24
forsworn so sweetly were f. — SHAK 897:85
Forsyte When a F. was engaged — GALS 413:2
fort love may win The f. — CRAS 296:25
forth Come f., Lazarus! — JOYCE 538:50
flying back and f. — PLATH 773:92
Forth rather like the F. Bridge — BRIT 189:63
Forthby Mrs F. in the flesh — SHAR 919:82
fortissimo F. at last! — MAHL 638:63
fortitude virtue of adversity, is f. — BACON 56:49
fortnight I have been here a f. — PERTH 767:3
thought it out…for a f. — SAYE 846:49
fortress story of the unconquerable f. — SELZ 858:42

tear down a f.	LEUP 599:14
Theology, sir, is a f.	MILL 676:79

fortresses stone of our f. — FAVRE 384:92
fortunate Ceasar…was f. — SHAK 884:94
So long as you are f. — OVID 747:4
fortune all else as F.'s — EURI 380:23

ambitious…needs to make his f.	LABR 572:46
arrows of outrageous f.	TWAIN 1033:89
broker…takes your f.	WOOL 1094:85

fortune (*contd.*)

deficiencies of f.	GOLD 432:2
dramatic changes of f.	ORWE 744:27
flash that brings good f.	RHYS 808:30
former are products of f.	HELO 469:7
F.'s a right whore	WEBS 1059:25
F.'s buffets and rewards	SHAK 891:35
f. calls me to?	JONS 534:76
f.'s dearest spite	SHAK 913:60
F. favours the brave	TERE 1005:73
F. favours the brave	TERE 1006:75
f. follows bold blindness	LAFO 575:84
F.…has made a mistress	DRYD 348:34
F. helps those who dare	VIRG 1045:88
F. is merry	SHAK 884:57
F. knows We scorn her	SHAK 905:81
f. of my pleasant choice	SURR 983:45
F. on his damnèd quarry	SHAK 906:11
F., that favours fools	JONS 535:92
F. when she comes	HERR 477:54
F. wouldn't exist	ASTU 43:99
good f. of the affluent country	GALB 412:82
good f. to others	BIER 161:73
good man's f.	SHAK 902:12
had not method of making a f.	GRAY 443:94
he shall see F.	BACON 59:11
hostages to f.	BACON 57:56
how does f. banter us	BOLI 172:70
I've seen the smiling of F. beguiling	COCK 272:50
In all adversity of f.	BOET 171:57
leads on to f.	SHAK 884:60
maker of his own f.	STEE 964:15
mock the good housewife F.	SHAK 884:69
mould of a man's f.	BACON 59:10
No…beauty without a f.	FARQ 383:73
not now in f.'s power	BUTL 216:14
not on f. pause	JONS 536:14
O fickle F.	COCK 272:61
O, f., f.	SHAK 869:12
On F.'s cap	SHAK 889:97
people of f. may naturally indulge	ELIOT 365:2
possession of a good f.	AUST 50:33
railed on Lady F.	SHAK 885:89
rascals who have the good f.	STEN 967:74
risk f., character	TWAIN 1034:19
rob a lady of her f.	FIEL 388:52
ruined f. flout	DONNE 337:79
saddest sight f.'s inequality exhibits	CARL 235:82
skittish F.'s hall	SHAK 896:50
slings and arrows of outrageous f.	SHAK 890:21
upon a plentiful f.	JOHN 527:33
When F. means to men most good	SHAK 872:68
Will f. never come	SHAK 878:7
young women of small f.	AUST 51:39
youth to f. unknown	GRAY 442:77

fortune-teller juggler, and a f.-t. — SHAK 865:3
fortunes expenditure of f. — PEARY 762:35

F.…come tumbling	BACON 55:24
f. sharppe adversitee	CHAU 254:10
f. Will ever after droop	SHAK 916:20
least rub in your f.	SHAK 917:50
Men in great f.	BACON 57:72
pride fell with my f.	SHAK 885:71
retrieve his f. by marriage	DICK 326:52
ruined f. are sure to stir	ARIS 34:33

forty Between thirty and f. — BENN 91:98

Between…twenty and f.	AUDEN 48:88
Every man over f.	SHAW 922:61
Fair, fat and f.	SCOTT 855:4
fasted f. days and f. nights	BIBLE 133:29
For f. days	SITW 941:26
to be f. years old	HOLM 486:2
what f. looks like	STEI 967:64
when you turn f.	SILVA 938:77

forty-five f.-f. minutes of…privacy	PARK 755:22
forty-three pass for f.-t.	GILB 423:53
forum f. of hate	SMITH 948:25
United Nations is…a f.	OBRI 734:45
forward f. let us range	TENN 996:83
go f. to nature	GOTT 436:73
forwards F. in reverse	DUNN 356:52
life…must be lived f.	KIER 556:57
rapidly backwards and f.	REED 805:81
fosse sunken f. of her spine	HEAN 465:35
fossils f. of intention	PURDY 795:34
Language does not leave f.	BRAU 186:12
foster-child f.-c. of silence	KEATS 547:6
fou f. for weeks thegither	BURNS 211:12
we're nae that f.	BURNS 211:2
fought f. as they revelled	DAVIS 309:38
f. for our place	WILH 1080:37
f. two draws with Stendhal	HEMI 471:37
f. with us upon Saint Crispin's day	SHAK 882:5
lads who f.	SASS 845:31
met and f. with outright	TENN 1002:99
'Tis better to have f. and lost	CLOU 270:37
That f. and died for	WILL 1083:7
what they f. each other for	SOUT 954:32
foul dead, by f. subtraction	RANS 802:32
doubt some f. play	SHAK 888:58
Fair is f., and f. is fair	SHAK 906:10
f. and pestilent congregation	SHAK 890:2
F. deeds will rise	SHAK 888:58
giving hand, though f.	SHAK 865:14
got by fair means or f.	ORWE 742:88
however f. within	CHUR 262:84
in the less, f. profanation	SHAK 896:73
Murder most f.	SHAK 889:75
nipped, and ways be f.	SHAK 866:31
still f. the cup	GREY 446:55
fouled Hath f. me	TENN 1004:52
foulest fair words…in f. letters?	SHAK 878:7
foulness f. of their fate	SASS 846:41
no vicious blot, murder, or f.	SHAK 902:99
remove filth and f.	ABEL 1:3
found f. and lost again	ELIOT 372:54
f. Him in	TENN 1003:40
f. myself	GRIL 447:64
f. you an argument	JOHN 532:31
Hast thou f. me	BIBLE 111:71
I f. it!	ARCH 33:15
if the ways be f.	JONS 535:96
lost, but now am f.	NEWT 725:42
To f. a great Empire	SMITH 945:84
foundation corner stone, a sure f.	BIBLE 125:7
destroyed the f. of the organization	EISE 364:86
end of our f. is…knowledge	BACON 60:32
f. of all good things	BURKE 208:41
f. of morals, Utility	MILL 675:71
f. of your ideas and phrases	LAUT 584:52
laid the f. of the earth	BIBLE 118:10
on the same f.	SWIFT 985:87
The Church's one f.	STONE 978:73
unassailable f.	ASQU 42:77
foundations again from the very f.	DESC 317:81
firmest f.	GLAD 429:53
f. of political liberty	WILS 1086:52
laid the f. of the earth?	BIBLE 113:17
peaks, whose f.	LLOY 608:58
visible F. in Nature	PETTY 768:15
when earth's f. fled	HOUS 496:77
While earth's f. stood	HOUS 496:94
founder f. of civil society	ROUS 827:31
founders f. of a new colony	HAWT 461:69
fount f. of pride	CULL 299:70
fountain back to the burning f.	SHEL 931:45
broke into a f.	HARR 459:35
bubble on the f.	SCOTT 854:65

fountain (*contd.*)

drinking at the f. of fact	PIER 769:32
F., never to be play'd	POPE 779:21
f. of all goodness	BOOK 176:55
f. of good sense	DRYD 352:80
f. of living waters	BIBLE 128:18
f. of the water of life	BIBLE 159:36
f. of vice as idleness	MONT 701:56
f. sealed	BIBLE 124:52
f. send forth at the same place	BIBLE 155:68
f., shade, and rill	MILT 684:39
f., spouting through his heir	POPE 780:29
Let the healing f. start	AUDEN 47:73
Let thy f. be blessed	BIBLE 120:62
long-abused sight at the f.	MILT 686:75
mighty f. momently was forced	COLE 275:14
pitcher be broken at the f.	BIBLE 123:42
rivulet and f.	GILB 424:59
Sang with a f.'s panache	DAYL 310:57
summer-dried f.	SCOTT 854:64
voice rise like a f.	TENN 1004:47
water in a f.	JOYCE 538:43

Fountainblues terrible case of the F. — HUXT 509:7

fountains Afric's sunny f. — HEBER 466:58

f. are within	COLE 274:5
f. fraught with tears	KYD 571:26
f. mingle with the river	SHEL 928:85
f. of timber	MUIR 713:38
in great f.	GALE 412:88
inscription on public f.	FLAU 393:46
two faithful f.	CRAS 296:21
What objects are the f.?	SHEL 929:3
writers, like a clear f.	LAND 578:55

four F. be things — PARK 754:2

two and two are f.	HOUS 496:76

four-wheeled f.-w. part of him — JOHN 524:68

fourscore F. and upward	SHAK 904:43
if…they be f. years	BIBLE 117:99

fourth f. is like the Son of God — BIBLE 129:46

Fowey O the Harbour of F. — QUIL 797:57

fowl f., blinking at you — ELIOT 366:27

lord of the f.	COWP 292:38
small f. singis on the spray	DOUG 341:55
You elegant F.!	LEAR 590:59

fowler from the snare of the f. — BIBLE 117:2

fowlers Watchful as f. — OTWAY 746:81

fowls f. of the air — BIBLE 135:52

F. are to the kitchen	BRIL 188:53

fox beset the historical f. — HUXL 508:97

Crazy Like A F.	PERE 766:88
f. barks not when he would	SHAK 861:4
f. in the streets	MACC 625:37
galloping after a f.	WILDE 1077:66
kill a f. or the pheasant	SHAW 925:35
trusted like the f.	SHAK 876:71
Virginia f. hunt	WASH 1054:43
working for 16th Century F.	RENO 806:6

fox-hunting inferior forms of f. — WAUGH 1056:69

prefer f.	HAIL 451:12

foxes bulls and f. dine well — JUST 540:75

f. have holes	BIBLE 136:66
f.…prolonging the lives	ELIOT 366:26

foxlike Or f. in the vine — TENN 998:12

foxy 70s face was f. — WATE 1055:50

fraction f. of mankind want freedom — LAYT 588:25

fragile essentially f. — BAIN 62:75

Men are very f.	STEP 968:81

fragments Death tramples it to f. — SHEL 931:50

f. I have shored	ELIOT 369:97
ideas, in f.	MILL 677:18
Live in f. no longer	FORS 398:36

fragrance f. was born upon the breeze — DICK 323:77

Isles of f.	POPE 783:6
splendor and f.	ROCK 817:69

fragrance (*contd.*)

sweetest f. from the herb	TROL 1027:76

frailties as familiar…as my own f. — CONG 281:25

draw his f.	GRAY 442:78

frailty F., thy name is woman — SHAK 888:54

human f. will have it so	ETHE 380:17
human f., folly, also crime	BYRON 223:46
noblest f. of the mind	DRYD 346:51

frame all the human f. requires — BELL 87:7

another f. of things	TENN 1003:29
calm and heav'nly f.	COWP 292:30
f. of mind	FRIE 405:60
f. perish…in conquering pain	BYRON 220:98
f. was Dust	DICK 328:14
in his bodily f.…his lowly origin	DARW 306:89
knoweth our f.	BIBLE 118:14
oddest f. of sense	SHAK 897:91
sensuous f.	TENN 999:35
solid f. of earth	WORD 1100:79
spangled heavens, a shining f.	ADDI 7:22
this goodly f., the earth	SHAK 890:2
universal f. is without a mind	BACON 57:64
an utterly exhausted f.	DOYLE 344:14
Whatever stirs this mortal f.	COLE 274:3
wield The mighty f.	MILT 691:90

framed have it f. and glazed — WALP 1051:87

framework f. for a civilization — LECO 592:3

France always be the sister of F. — HUGO 501:63

best soldiers F. ever had	PHIL 768:23
better to sniff F.'s dung	HO 482:34
between F. and England	JERR 521:16
Cam ye ower frae F.?	ANON 24:2
chased the English out of F.	LOUI 613:45
dagger…in the heart of F.	QUIN 798:68
duty…to wield the sword of F.	DEGA 313:98
fair stood the winds of F.	DRAY 345:35
fight in F.	CHUR 264:14
find your people in F.	JOAN 522:27
five in F.	THER 1009:44
flower of F. is lost	ANON 21:61
follow them to F.	LESL 598:94
F.…a despotism…tempered	CARL 235:48
F., famed in all great arts	ARNO 36:63
F. had shown a light	TENN 1005:65
F. has lost a battle!	DEGA 312:97
F. has more need of me	NAPO 718:28
F. in 1830	LOUIS 614:55
F. is adequately assured	ASQU 42:77
F. is revolutionary	LAMA 575:2
F., mother of arts	BELL 86:89
Here lies F.	BISM 164:43
if Jack were President of F.	ONAS 739:39
in F.…play a set	SHAK 880:71
In F., they study men	STAEL 962:75
In F.…words reign over ideas	SAND 840:49
inadequate for getting to F.	KINN 559:10
insert…spirit of Christian F.	BOUR 181:47
nineteenth-century F.	HELL 469:98
no concern to F.	WITTE 1087:71
order…this matter better in F.	STER 970:19
own F., a country	MORL 708:72
singer in F.	SWIN 987:47
sweet enemy, F.	SIDN 937:54
swum from F.	MARL 653:3
the roads lead to F.	THOM 1012:13
Vive la F.!	DE 313:4
want to know what F. thinks	DEGA 313:5

Francesca F. di Rimini, miminy — GILB 424:69

Francis I think I'm St F. o. Assisi — PARK 754:16

More than F. of Assisi	PACK 749:29
St. F. de Sales	MACF 629:20

frank f. to all beside — POPE 781:72

Frankenstein media a F. monster — MUGG 712:23

soul of F.	SHEL 926:53

frankincense gold, and f. — BIBLE 133:24

hill of f.	BIBLE 124:51

Franklin body of Benjamin F. — FRAN 402:99

frankness paragons of f. — WILL 1082:78

fraternity Liberty, Equality, F! — LAMA 575:3

fraud daily f., contempt — MILT 694:40

f. of the Christian system	PAINE 750:51
one f., the other fornication	MATOS 664:77
Style is a f.	DEKO 313:18

frauds to point at f. — RUSH 829:68

fray Fought was this noble f. — DRAY 345:36

f. By which he reigns	MILT 688:25

freckles love, curiosity, f. — PARK 754:6

Freddy See F. before he sees you! — ANON 28:10

Frederic Stay, F., stay! — GILB 424:64

free A F. Man is he — HOBB 483:42

advantage of not being f.	SNOW 951:77
as a f. man	KENN 552:85
be a falcon and go f.	DUNC 355:48
born f. as Caesar	SHAK 882:19
breed f. men?	HOPE 490:71
cleanly I myself can f.	DRAY 345:40
Comment is f.	SCOTT 852:33
condemned to be f.	SART 844:16
either f. or enslaved	GRIL 447:62
every people should be left f.	WILS 1086:50
exertions of a f. people	PITT 772:73
first people to demand f. speech	BISS 164:41
f. and clear of any image	SHAK 895:34
f. and easy	STEV 973:82
f. and equal association	ENGE 378:90
f., and f. they must remain	MILT 689:37
f. as nature first made man	DRYD 347:69
f. as the road	HERB 475:27
f., but to thyself enthralled	MILT 691:78
f. competition of the market	RICA 808:34
f. constitution	GIBB 421:19
f. from guilt or pain	SHEL 930:25
f. from interest or prejudice	REES 805:92
f. from nationalism	ORWE 744:34
f. man cannot long stand erect	WRIS 1102:16
f. man thinks of nothing less	SPIN 960:57
F. man!	BAUD 77:19
f. of the networks	STARK 963:96
f. their minds of…rubbish	DUDEK 353:17
f., therefore choose	SART 844:19
f. to do whatever the Government	SHAW 921:33
f. to wander where I liked	SHIP 935:22
F. trade…blessings	MACA 622:87
f. world and the Communist	KENN 551:83
give me the f. 'n' easy	GERS 420:9
he is f.	SOLZ 952:95
I am a f. man	ARET 33:17
I was f. born	BIBLE 148:8
If the Son…shall make you f.	BIBLE 146:50
in the cause of the f.	BINY 162:6
keep your fancy f.	HOUS 494:44
know our will is f.	JOHN 528:54
let me gae f.	SCOTT 855:85
live f. and uncommitted	THOR 1016:84
longer f.	HERR 478:64
lover bold and f.	CLEV 269:12
lover…noble and f.?	EMER 376:46
makes the mind very f.	ELIOT 365:19
man is either f.	BARA 70:8
men naturally were born f.	MILT 686:78
mistaken in thinking themselves f.	SPIN 960:49
most complete and f.	STEV 973:99
Mother of the F.	BENS 92:9
music is really a f. thing	COLE 273:78
neither bond nor f.	BIBLE 152:89
never shall be f.	DONNE 338:8
Newspapers are born f.	SCOTT 852:38
No one can be perfectly f.	SPEN 955:63

free (*contd.*)

no such thing as a f. lunch	FRIE 405:53
our dear country had been f.	DAVIS 309:37
people are as f. as they want	BALD 64:97
permanently half-slave and half-f.	LINC 604:98
place of f. speech	WENT 1065:53
poet must be f.	SART 844:6
princes should be f.	SHAK 861:96
prisoners were left f. to choose	SHAW 922:42
product of the f. mind	ORWE 743:13
pursuit…by f. men	WARR 1053:28
safer…than to be f.	KAFKA 541:87
Shall the sex f.	HABI 450:1
So f. we seem	BROW 199:60
So long as man remains f.	DOST 341:47
someone to tell them they are f.	LAYT 588:26
spirit, f. to choose	ROCH 816:49
struggling to be f.	SHAK 892:48
Teach the f. man	AUDEN 47:73
Thou art f.	ARNO 36:60
tied the f. And holy-day…spirit	LAMB 576:19
to set me f.	STUA 980:10
to want to be f.	JONAS 533:50
truth shall make you f.	BIBLE 146:49
uphold me with thy f. spirit	BIBLE 116:78
Was he f.?	AUDEN 47:65
Who would be f.	BYRON 219:75
wholly slaves or wholly f.	DRYD 350:52
Writing f. verse	FROST 407:91
ye shall be f. indeed	BIBLE 146:50
yearning to breathe f.	LAZA 588:26
You who are f.	IGNA 510:29

free-born as only a f.-b. Briton   THAC 1006:83
freed f. from his religion   SAIN 837:89
freedom and that is f.   MACA 622:90

army…devoted to f.	LAWR 587:14
Art, Glory, F. fail	BYRON 219:77
bird that will live in f.	MEIL 666:17
bondage which is f.'s self	SHEL 927:58
breathed the air of f.	WALE 1049:48
cause of f.	SPEN 957:91
cherish f.	SCHI 847:70
conception of autonomy and f.	GEOR 419:88
Conservative ideal of f.	MADAN 638:54
controversy over f. of speech	ORWE 745:50
cost of f. is always	KENN 551:73
cost to f. of opinion	SCHL 848:73
could not give me f.	SHAK 905:64
does not come from f.	GIDE 423:48
dreaming of f.	SMITH 949:60
entrust the care of f.	EISE 364:82
Extreme f. …to extreme slavery	PLATO 774:25
fight for f. and truth	IBSEN 510:21
fit to use their f.	MACA 622:91
foppery of f.	SHAK 896:62
fraction of mankind want f.	LAYT 588:25
f. and culture	MORE 707:52
f. and equality	ROUS 827:33
F. and WHISKEY gang thegither	BURNS 209:72
F.…cure of anarchy	BURKE 207:10
F. doth with degree	JONS 535:3
f. in my love	615:63
F. in no other land	DRYD 350:45
f. is a noble thing!	BARB 71:15
F. is not an ideal	STEV 973:81
f. is only the distance	ZHAO 1109:21
f. is slavery	ORWE 745:56
f. is something people take	BALD 64:97
f. is…supremely valuable	HUXL 508:88
F. is the f. to say	ORWE 745:58
F. is the right	MONT 703:86
f. of choice	GITL 429:49
f. of choice	MILL 677:8
F. of men under government	LOCKE 609:70

freedom (*contd.*)

f. of my mind	MILT 684:34
f. of religion	JEFF 520:94
f. of speech	BLACK 164:47
f. of the press and popular	MILL 675:67
f. of the press in Britain	ORWE 742:5
f. of the press	TOCQ 1021:75
f. of those weakened	CESA 248:2
F. shrieked	CAMP 227:26
f. to exploit	WIEN 1074:13
f. to marry	WARR 1053:28
F., what liberties…in thy name!	GEOR 419:91
gave him f. to choose	MILT 686:67
give another joyous f.	SCEVE 846:56
give you your name F.	ELUA 376:24
greatest f.	BANN 70:3
guarantee f.	TOCQ 1022:81
have a new birth of f.	LINC 605:4
have so much more f.	JOHN 529:81
History may be f.	ELIOT 373:75
honour, f. and curteisie	CHAU 254:18
if f. fall?	KIPL 565:18
illusions that restrict f.	FRYE 408:24
invigorating air of f.	WOLL 1091:38
kept in their full f.	BAIL 62:72
Let the f. ring	SMITH 948:27
live in f. and hell	MAIL 639:81
love of f.	GLAD 429:53
manners, virtue, f., power	WORD 1096:38
must not confuse with f.	STEV 972:79
None can love f. heartily	MILT 686:77
nor even f. from pain	LAWR 586:78
out of servitude into f.	EMER 377:70
particular f. and a general orderliness	CARD 232:2
Perfect f. is reserved for the man	COLL 276:35
perfect f.	HUGEL 498:10
portal of f.	EISE 364:93
power of the hope of f.	BUCK 203:34
prisoned birds must find in f.	SASS 845:34
promises f. or enlightenment	SNYD 951:85
questions of f.	JORD 536:28
right action is f.	ELIOT 372:63
salvation of f.	STEV 972:78
satisfy our thirst for f.	KING 557:80
science…restricting human f.	BOOK 178:3
so close to f.	TWAIN 1033:88
supreme Festival on the road to f.	BONH 173:85
the secret of its f.	OAKE 733:49
there is no liberty or f.	NASHE 721:84
They lyve in f.	JAME 515:99
To earn you f.	LAWR 587:12
unlimited idea of f.	BACH 54:96
voice of f.	SCHA 847:60
what f. really is	MITC 697:86
What's f. for?	ROET 819:90
Where F. slowly broadens	TENN 996:89
whose service is perfect f.	BOOK 173:96
wind of nationalism and f.	BALD 65:12
With a great sum obtained I this f.	BIBLE 148:8
zest for f.	KENN 551:75

freedom-for-all democracy and f.-f.   MAIL 639:81
freedoms F. you'll not to me allow   BEHN 85:67
   upon four essential f.   ROOS 822:43
freeman symbol of f.'s power   BIER 162:98
freemasonry bitter f.   BEER 83:31
freemen happy f., are the only slaves   MASS 663:61
freer I feel strangely f.!   JOHN 523:45
freeze f. thy young blood   SHAK 889:74
freezing Between melting and f.   ELIOT 372:68
freezings What f. have I felt   SHAK 914:82
frei Arbeit macht f.   ANON 26:45
freight Nation's F. Handler   SAND 841:57
   wilderness of f. and rails   CRANE 295:1
French as much Chinese as F.   FLAU 392:30

French (*contd.*)

As the F. say	SMITH 949:51
Englishman is about to talk F.	WODE 1089:99
F. are a logical people	MORL 708:72
F. are nice people	MAZA 666:10
F. are polite	TWAIN 1032:59
F. are wiser than they seem	BACON 58:96
F. Canadian Hinayana Buddhist	GINS 428:31
F. clothes and F. food	SCHL 848:77
F.…differs in nothing from prose	GRAY 441:49
F. had a more martial air	HAYD 462:88
F. is not a static language	HUGO 501:80
F. king, admittedly	MORL 708:74
F. operas sung by Swedish	WHAR 1068:3
F. Radicals…German	MARX 660:14
F. Revolution is merely the herald	BABE 54:91
F. she spak ful faire	CHAU 254:20
F. want to attack	ANON 30:57
F. will only be united	DEGA 313:99
Germans classify…the F. arrange	CATH 244:45
get all the F. fries	GORE 436:67
good because cooked by the F.	DOUG 341:60
help our F. comrades	KITC 566:44
Imagine the Lord talking F.	DAY 310:49
improved her F.	GRAH 437:89
look'd towards the F. coast	STER 970:12
New Orleans…past the F. Quarter	MAIL 639:84
not that the F. are not profound	BROO 193:45
professor of F. letters	JOYCE 538:52
scrofulous F. novel	BROW 197:28
serve the F. in place of a state religion	BIER 161:88
seventeen million F. women	GISC 429:48
Speak in F.	CARR 239:51
special task as F. Canadians	BOUR 181:47
speech…precise as F.	QUIL 797:59
to men [I speak] F.	CHAR 253:90
tongues of the F. Council	SHAK 882:11
we die F.	WAUGH 1057:97
We have F. quarrels	SHAK 881:93
What are we learning F.…for	OBRI 734:72
What's the F. for fiddle-de-dee?	CARR 241:81
wine…some are fond of F.	MASE 662:40

Frenchman to be a F.   FRIE 405:56
Frenchmen act better than F.   BENN 91:87
   one Englishman could beat three F.   ADDI 7:18
Frenchwomen F. better   BENN 91:87
frenzy an old man's f.   YEATS 1106:87
   Dancing is a f. and a rage   DAVI 307:5
frequency tragedy…very fact of f.   ELIOT 366:38
fresh f. air and royalties   ASHF 41:67
   f. and vigorous enough   WARD 1053:16
   F. as the air   JONS 535:2
   f. colours deck the wanton prime   SPEN 958:19
   F. from the Lord!   FARJ 382:62
   how quick and f.   SHAK 893:92
   So sad, so f.   TENN 997:3
freshness f. of a dream   WORD 1097:48
fret Living, we f.   BROW 200:99
fretted so f. fast we are   BROW 199:60
Freud F.…dramatis personae   THOM 1009:48
   F. has often stated   RODG 818:85
   F. is the father   GREER 445:39
   F. shoved that out   BAIN 62:77
   F. would have his revenge   DOCT 334:39
   funny when F. died   JARR 518:56
   If F. had worn a kilt   BURG 206:91
   put F. on canvas   SCHW 851:23
   trouble with F.   DODD 334:43
friars barefooted f.   GIBB 421:29
Fribsbi fatal man, Madame F.   THAC 1006:92
friction f. of the whole machine   CLAU 268:95
   internal f. and strife   ROTH 826:23
   produce the least f.   LEUP 599:15
Friday call this F. good   ELIOT 371:52

Friday (*contd.*)

man F.	DEFOE 312:*81*

friend A woman can become a man's f.   CHEK 256:*61*

angry with my f.	BLAKE 167:*93*
as a f. he drops into poetry	DICK 327:*78*
as you choose a f.	DILL 331:*55*
Best f. and love	DUNN 356:*56*
best f. I could ever have	KARL 542:*9*
choose between…betraying my f.	FORS 399:*52*
confide…in a f.	ANOU 30:*73*
conversation with my best f.	LEWIS 601:*43*
courting death to be our f.	PHIL 768:*20*
enemy and your f.	TWAIN 1034:*10*
enemy into a f.	KING 558:*87*
every f. we lose	POPE 780:*26*
Everybody calls himself a f.	LAFO 575:*94*
fair f., you never can be old	SHAK 915:*84*
Faithful are the wounds of a f.	BIBLE 122:*7*
faithful f. is the medicine	BIBLE 132:*91*
fav'rite has no f.!	GRAY 441:*53*
for the f. of mankind	MOLI 699:*25*
Forsake not an old f.	BIBLE 132:*96*
f. called Piggy	GOLD 432:*85*
f. in first habits of intimacy	LAMB 576:*23*
f. in power is a f. lost	ADAMS 5:*74*
f. loveth at all times	BIBLE 121:*86*
f. of man	COLL 277:*45*
f. of the negro assumes	FULL 409:*33*
f. of the oppressed	GARI 415:*24*
f. that sticketh closer than a brother	BIBLE 121:*89*
f.…the masterpiece of nature	EMER 376:*39*
f. who can talk	ABU 1:*11*
f. who loved perfection	SMITH 947:*17*
God is the f. of silence	THER 1009:*38*
good f. someone who visits you	BRAD 183:*83*
Good wine, a f.	ALDR 12:*9*
hard to be…a good f.	WYCH 1103:*38*
He makes no f.	TENN 1002:*16*
I am the enemy…my f.	OWEN 748:*17*
kingdom with thy dearest f.	MARL 653:*3*
last best f.	SOUT 954:*42*
lewd well natured f.	ROCH 817:*62*
Little F. of all the World	KIPL 562:*70*
look like a f. on Denmark	SHAK 888:*48*
loss of a dear f.	SOUT 954:*41*
lost F.!	WORD 1100:*90*
mine own familiar f.	BIBLE 115:*67*
mistress or a f.	SHEL 931:*51*
morn to night, my f.	ROSS 824:*75*
most reliable f.	GRAMM 438:*97*
myself shall be my f.	KYD 571:*27*
'Neath every one a f.	RODG 818:*85*
no f. like a sister	ROSS 823:*68*
No F.…so persists	DICK 328:*16*
nor a f. to know me	STEV 976:*52*
not a f. to close his eyes	DRYD 351:*70*
O f. unseen, unborn, unknown	FLEC 393:*47*
O f. we have loved	CORN 288:*59*
O Sleep! the f. of Woe	SOUT 954:*37*
old f. for dinner	TALLY 990:*92*
One chained f.	SHEL 931:*52*
one damned good-natured f. or other	SHER 934:*3*
One f. in a lifetime	ADAMS 5:*78*
only way to have f. is to be one	EMER 376:*40*
quarrels…with a tiresome f.	BYRON 222:*33*
save me, from the candid f.	CANN 230:*71*
sincere f. or a sincere enemy	HUGO 501:*52*
Strange f., I said	OWEN 748:*16*
such a f., that one had need	COWP 292:*44*
supreme f. to every individual	BAUD 78:*44*
Take courage, my f.	READE 803:*56*
think of him as a f.	SMITH 948:*37*
those that call them f.	TENN 1004:*47*
to f. and foe alike	KENN 550:*64*

friend (*contd.*)

To find a f.	DOUG 342:*67*
to have a f. takes time	OKEE 738:*21*
to the category, old f.	MO 698:*12*
true f. and a good writer	WHITE 1070:*32*
when ye lose a f.	SCOTT 855:*83*
Whenever a f. succeeds	VIDAL 1044:*63*
Where is the country, my f.?	ARGU 33:*18*
Wherein my F. is Laid	LOWRY 618:*20*
Who's your fat f.	BRUM 201:*9*
wife for his f.	JOYCE 538:*52*
wish the author…was a terrific f.	SALI 838:*19*
world is not thy f.	SHAK 870:*21*
worst f. and enemy is but Death	BROO 192:*24*
Yet, O my f.	TENN 997:*9*
Your f. the British soldier	SHAW 921:*18*

friendless Omnipotent but f.   SHEL 930:*21*

friendliness friendship and got f.   MALA 641:*3*

friendly as f. as you can make   MACC 626:*63*

No matter how f.   TRUD 1029:*12*

friends 50 per cent of his f.   BUSH 215:*88*

All the f. that I loved	BUCH 202:*28*
an Entertainment for F.	SWIFT 985:*99*
Be f., you English fools	SHAK 881:*93*
best f. hear no more of him?	SHEL 929:*11*
better than f.	GERB 419:*97*
cold and certain f.	HUGO 502:*82*
cut their f. to any shape	MERE 671:*10*
dear f. have to part?	BOND 172:*79*
dear f., once more	SHAK 881:*82*
deathless f.	SASS 845:*40*
desires…to be f.	BETH 99:*22*
disliked by all his f.	WILDE 1079:*9*
don't trust him, we are f.	BREC 186:*29*
ensure his making f.	AUST 51:*37*
Farewell, my f.	DUNC 355:*43*
few of his f.' houses	JOHN 531:*23*
foes, and oh, my f.	MILL 676:*82*
For golden f. I had	HOUS 495:*61*
f. all united to puff	SWIN 988:*51*
f., and native home	MILT 683:*19*
f. are beginning to worry	EPST 379:*6*
f.…are in cities	SNYD 951:*80*
f. are true	BIER 161:*84*
f. begin to compliment him	IRVI 513:*65*
f., but above all an enemy	MULR 713:*44*
f. could only read the title	WOOLF 1092:*55*
f. divide, never to meet	MIDD 673:*41*
f. forsake me like memory lost	CLARE 267:*32*
f. love misery	JONG 534:*69*
f. of other days	ROBI 815:*31*
f. of the mammon	BIBLE 143:*4*
f. of totalitarianism	ORWE 745:*51*
f. part forever	BASHO 76:*5*
F., Romans, countrymen	SHAK 884:*48*
f. should drink	KEATS 545:*66*
f. thou hast	SHAK 888:*63*
F. To borrow my books	ROBI 814:*25*
f. who have died	SASS 845:*31*
f. with its grandfathers	MUMF 713:*45*
general has no f.	LEMAY 595:*44*
greet f. with a shrug	SPEN 956:*75*
had been f. in youth	COLE 274:*10*
had many f.	GOET 431:*83*
help from my f.	LENN 596:*63*
honored by your f.	HOOV 490:*70*
judge a man…by his f.	CONR 284:*95*
lay down his f.	THOR 1018:*6*
lay down his life for his f.	BIBLE 146:*64*
leave your f. and go	HOUS 497:*89*
lend it not…to thy f.	SHAK 874:*22*
literature have always been f.	LAFO 575:*87*
lost f., some by death	WOOLF 1093:*79*
love of old f.	PO 775:*39*

friends (*contd.*)

love of wicked f.	SHAK 868:*67*
man that hath f.	BIBLE 121:*89*
man who is false to his f.	BERK 95:*56*
misfortune of our best f.	LARO 582:*24*
most of my f. are dead	FENT 385:*2*
mountains…to him were f.	BYRON 219:*82*
never be f. again	VICT 1043:*51*
old enough not to make f.	POUND 785:*54*
old f.	GOLD 433:*20*
on the backs of his f.	HUGH 499:*24*
one code…for our f.	EISE 364:*85*
organized workers…are our f.	SHIN 935:*19*
our best f.	THOM 1014:*41*
Our Dumb F.	PARK 754:*16*
rich hath many f.	BIBLE 121:*76*
sad f. of Truth	MILT 686:*72*
some of their sad f.	DONNE 337:*90*
soul rememb'ering my good f.	SHAK 867:*53*
tavern for his f.	DOUG 342:*63*
teaches beasts to know their f.	SHAK 911:*4*
tear to pieces,…my f.?	BACON 60:*39*
tears of f.	DRYD 348:*88*
Those you make f.	SHAK 917:*50*
Thy f. are exultations	WORD 1098:*59*
To my f. pictured within	ELGAR 364:*96*
together f. to keep	DRAY 345:*33*
troops of f.	SHAK 910:*81*
truth loses you f.	RUIZ 828:*49*
Unmarried men are best f.	BACON 57:*59*
We'll part good f.	WEBS 1060:*35*
we, my f.	WEBB 1058:*16*
When I see my f. collapse	SKEL 942:*38*
Win F. and Influence People	CARN 237:*7*
with f. possessed	SHAK 913:*57*
without f., without coin	SCOTT 855:*84*
you will count many f.	OVID 747:*4*

friendship Agreements…true f.   CATI 245:*51*

beginning of a beautiful f.	WALL 1051:*78*
certain sort of f.	KING 559:*3*
cultivate your f.	JOHN 531:*20*
dupe of f.	HAZL 464:*16*
Every long f., every old	LAMB 576:*23*
F. and love	GRIL 447:*63*
f., books	THOM 1015:*48*
f. in constant repair	JOHN 526:*2*
F. is a disinterested commerce	GOLD 432:*6*
f. is never peaceful	SEVI 859:*59*
F. needs a certain parallelism	ADAMS 5:*78*
F. of the United States	GEOR 418:*82*
full joys of f.	CATH 244:*48*
golden dream of love and f.	DRYD 349:*1*
imputation of this idiot's f.!	NASHE 721:*79*
In f. false	DRYD 349:*15*
Levin wanted f.	MALA 641:*3*
little f. in the world	BACON 59:*20*
Love and f. exclude one another	LABR 572:*42*
more…ingenious than f.	LACL 574:*65*
Most f. is feigning	SHAK 886:*95*
paltry f. …of mere Man	POE 776:*45*
sort of f. recognised	STEV 974:*5*
Time…strengthens f.	LABR 572:*41*
when did f. take	SHAK 874:*21*
wing of f.	DICK 322:*57*
wing of f.	DICK 322:*58*
woman's f. ever ends in love	GAY 416:*49*

friendships F. begin with liking   ELIOT 366:*45*

f.…invalidated by marriage   BUTL 217:*38*

fright f. my faith   DRYD 350:*50*

in a hell of a f.	CARY 243:*22*
suaveness…it's born of f.	HYDE 509:*15*
time's f. within me	WILB 1075:*21*

frightday f., shatterday   JOYCE 538:*61*

frightened f. look in its eyes   SITW 941:*22*

frightened (*contd.*)
whole world is f. to death! SHER 934:17
frightening manners are far more f. JARR 518:60
nothing is really very f. STEIN 965:39
Friuli blue F.'s mountains BYRON 220:94
frivolity F. is sweet, in season HORA 493:26
how precious is f.! FORS 398:48
frock complexion...and the white f. SCHR 850:4
dons on a new street f. NATH 721:85
f. of frolic green DRAY 345:31
frock-coat man in a f.-c. LAVER 584:57
frocks f. are built in Paris SAKI 837:98
frog f. jumps in BASHO 76:1
frogs All the night the f. go chuckle MACG 630:22
f. are decapitated JAMES 518:51
frolic frock of f. green DRAY 345:31
wine can...Make the sage f. POPE 779:12
with a f. welcome took TENN 995:61
frolicsome f. company had begun SCOTT 854:77
front All Quiet on the Western F. REMA 806:99
f. page has nothing but WARR 1054:29
I remember the f. door POWE 788:15
sit out f. and watch me BARR 73:59
frontier edge of a new f. KENN 550:61
f. from the Atlantic to the Pacific CHUR 264:9
f. of my Person AUDEN 48:97
Rhine...is where our f. lies BALD 65:11
Space—the final F. RODD 818:82
symbol for America is the F. ATWO 45:22
frontiers cross the f. into Eternity MELV 668:46
f. of the impossible KILLY 556:62
frontlets as f. between thine eyes BIBLE 108:90
frost cold climate, and f. and snow SOUT 954:28
early f. to...flowerings of feminism FALU 382:58
it being a great f. PEPYS 765:68
moonlight...like f. THOM 1012:3
So full of f. SHAK 880:67
tears Thaw not the f. SHEL 930:34
The f. performs its secret ministry COLE 274:98
third day comes a f. SHAK 918:61
frosts f. are slain SWIN 986:24
froth Life is mostly f. GORD 435:61
frown communist has a fascist f. SPARK 955:57
f. and be perverse SHAK 868:90
f. of hatred BYRON 221:11
persistent troubled f. THUR 1019:34
frowzy pent up in f. lodgings SMOL 950:65
Froyd So then Dr F. said LOOS 613:35
frozen beautiful and f., I preserve you ATWO 45:25
sends the f.-ground-swell under it FROST 406:72
frugal what a f. man annually saves SMITH 945:85
wit...he was f. of it DRYD 347:62
fruit also beareth f. BIBLE 137:99
And full of f. HENR 473:69
autumn and the falling f. LAWR 587:6
bears its f. and dies STEV 971:46
blooming ambrosial f. MILT 690:52
bringeth forth his f. in season BIBLE 113:29
brought forth f. BIBLE 137:97
brought immortal f. BIBLE 131:76
delicate exotic f. WILDE 1077:82
Forth reaching to the f. MILT 692:12
f. in old age BIBLE 117:4
f. of memory CONR 285:14
f. of our labour MONT 700:54
f. Of that forbidden tree MILT 687:84
f. of the Spirit BIBLE 152:91
globed f. MACL 633:72
green f. would swell KEATS 545:59
Is darkness, the f. SWIN 987:35
like ripe f. thou drop MILT 693:24
long for the f. at last SHER 933:71
medlar being a f. MACD 628:92
O Autumn, laden with f. BLAKE 165:59

fruit (*contd.*)
ripest f. of all MARL 652:89
tasting this fair f. MILT 692:8
the f. of your delight SURR 983:45
To f. or shade HERB 475:16
Too late for f. DELA 314:35
took of the f. BIBLE 103:95
venturing their necks for f. ROCH 816:57
With f. the vines KEATS 547:4
fruitcake it's f. weather! CAPO 231:81
fruitful she'll be f. SWIFT 986:17
fruitfulness f. and...enjoyment NIET 728:74
mellow f. KEATS 547:4
fruition f.'s dull, and spoils SUCK 981:20
fruits bestow all my f. BIBLE 143:94
by their f. ye shall know them BIBLE 135:61
drop like f. of the tree. MERE 671:16
f. and princely delicates MARL 654:13
f. of Christian civilisation BIRD 163:16
f. of knowledge FREUD 404:46
f. of speaking art? SIDN 936:46
gives to Zembla f. POPE 782:93
Here are f., flowers VERL 1042:36
immortal f. of joy and love MILT 689:32
No f., no flowers HOOD 489:52
Of f., and flowers KEATS 546:91
twelve manner of f. BIBLE 159:39
under their f. load SPEN 958:19
frustrated never to be f. BALL 65:26
fry F. me! CARR 241:83
marked among the f. THOM 1015:53
frère mon f.! ELIOT 368:84
fuck Fish f. in it FIEL 388:63
f. you up, your mum and dad LARK 582:14
zipless f. is absolutely pure JONG 533:63
fucked constantly getting f. MAMET 644:58
fudge two-fifths sheer f. LOWE 616:83
fudging f. and nudging OWEN 747:5
fuel bury their radioactive f. LAMB 577:45
fugitive f. and cloistered virtue MILT 685:63
thou art...a f. AESC 9:60
fugitives f. are of that condition BACON 57:59
fugue hum a f. GILB 424:63
fugues f. and symphonies SASS 845:31
fulfil f. ourselves outside of society SARR 843:4
fulfilled f. a long time BIBLE 131:83
till all be f. BIBLE 134:37
fulfilment altered in f. ELIOT 372:69
Before f. is BARK 71:18
Contentment and f. TROL 1029:1
f. only a step LEGU 594:24
full All then is f., possessing POPE 779:8
f. as craving...f. as vain DRYD 348:97
F. many a glorious morning SHAK 913:59
f. of love and honesty SHAK 899:30
f. stop...at the right place BABEL 54:90
f. up years ago WODE 1089:2
live it to the f. SPARK 955:52
lived his life to the f. RAND 801:22
Serenely f., the epicure would say SMITH 949:56
so f. of unmannerly sadness SHAK 874:15
was na f. BURNS 209:64
fuller Money...the true f's earth GAY 416:54
fullers f. and their wailing ANON 21:49
fullness earth...and the f. thereof BIBLE 115:51
filled with all the f. of God BIBLE 152:98
fullstoppers f. and semicolonials JOYCE 538:60
fumble f. with the sheets SHAK 880:77
fumbling f. the flowers REED 805:81
fume captured f. of space CRANE 295:4
fumes f. of tabacco and liquors LEWIS 602:61
fumitor Crowned with rank f. SHAK 903:32
fun Ain't we got f. KAHN 541:90
Cancer can be rather f. HALD 451:19

fun (*contd.*)
do things for f. STARK 963:95
for the f. of the thing DOUG 341:57
f. for...thickskinned grown-ups SHAW 921:27
F. is f. but no girl LOOS 613:34
f. to believe them BACH 54:99
f. where I've found it KIPL 562:56
f. you think they had JONG 534:67
make f. of people GARC 414:18
mirth and f. grew fast BURNS 211:19
more f. to punt SAYE 846:48
most f....without laughing ALLEN 14:47
no reference to f. HERB 474:7
watch a game, it's f. HOPE 491:74
what...was all the f. for BETJ 100:50
function death has a useful f. LABR 573:50
f. is to create...feeling of solidarity DURK 357:68
f. of a writer CONN 283:68
f. of criticism DEWEY 319:96
f. of kings LOUI 614:50
f. of literature TRIL 1027:61
f. of poetry GRAV 440:27
f. of the news LIPP 607:36
happiness is a by-product of f. BURR 213:59
own no other f. SHAK 912:31
proper f. of women ELIOT 365:22
pure f., and best power WORD 1096:34
society cannot f. properly PARS 756:45
special f. is departure LISP 607:39
the f. never dies WORD 1100:85
functionary not to a f. STEAD 964:8
functioning f. out of ignorance DENG 315:51
functions division of labor...social f. DURK 357:69
expedition...performed its f. SPEKE 955:61
f....most nearly in equilibrium SPEN 955:66
In her f. weary MILT 694:46
where it f. best THAT 1008:22
fund f. for the maintenance SMITH 945:85
fundament frigid on the f. NASH 720:64
fundamental f. ...liberties PITT 771:68
f. postulate that there MONOD 700:46
f. question of philosophy CAMUS 228:46
f. things apply HUPF 505:34
funds providing the f. STEW 977:63
funeral After the f., my father LAWR 586:92
at a f. and knew their feet MAUG 664:86
cypress f. SPEN 957:99
for the f. expenses JERO 521:7
f. baked meats SHAK 888:56
f. march of a fried eel SHAW 925:31
f. marches around your heart MILL 676:98
F. marches to the grave LONG 611:95
f. sermon (which was long...) BELL 87:12
f. song GIBB 421:22
f. train which the bridegroom sees CLOU 271:42
how to perform a f. WILL 1082:81
low on his f. couch GRAY 443:85
or at a f. TWAIN 1032:78
present is the f. of the past CLARE 267:81
see my f. before I die EDGE 360:29
seen a costlier f. TENN 1003:27
showed up at his f. GOLD 434:49
two-thirds of the f. LAWS 587:19
victory...celebrated with the f. rite LAO 580:86
funerals go to other men's f. DAY 310:50
steady supply of f. SHAW 926:43
fungus f. or a lichen THOR 1016:69
funhouse Cyberspace is the f. mirror STER 968:84
funny Be f. on a golf course? SILV 938:78
first f. thought TRAV 1025:34
f. as long as it is happening ROGE 820:10
f. is subversive ORWE 743:22
f. paper read backwards WILL 1082:73
F. peculiar, or f. ha-ha? HAY 462:84

funny (*contd.*)
f. when Freud died — JARR 518:56
F. without being vulgar — GILB 426:98
F. you should ask — CECIL 246:76
knowing what's f. is one of them — AMIS 17:81
less f. and lasts longer — ANOU 31:78
Life was a f. thing — CRISP 297:38
to write a really f. book — HEMI 470:13
fur dressed all in f. — MOORE 704:7
I'll make the f. — BUTL 216:13
furbelows little pleats nad f. — SCHI 847:62
furies Break bitter f. — YEATS 1106:85
ye f. fell — SHAK 871:58
furious grew fast and f. — BURNS 211:19
furnace Heat not a f. — SHAK 917:45
one great f. flamed — MILT 687:90
thrown alive into the f. — BELL 88:38
furnaces Your worship is your f. — BOTT 180:37
furnish f. forth the marriage tables — SHAK 888:56
f. the pictures — HEAR 465:44
furnished F. as all Europe is — FRAN 402:11
furnishings f. of each Was-land — FRAME 400:78
furniture brain…with all the f. — DOYLE 344:4
Diet, F. and Dress — MAND 645:71
f. on the deck — MORT 710:3
f. that used to be in the salon — MACM 636:16
nature's pride and richest f.! — MARL 652:86
No f. so charming — SMITH 949:47
useless and cumbersome f. — TREE 1025:44
furrow Between the shaft and the f. — HEAN 464:32
leaves a shining f. — TENN 997:10
plough my own f. — ROSE 822:55
furrows The sounding f. — TENN 995:61
furry fire was f. — SITW 941:14
furtive f. tear — ROMA 821:28
look of f. shame — WODE 1089:99
fury Allaying…their f. — SHAK 916:24
blind f. of creation — SHAW 921:25
formless spawning f. — YEATS 1107:91
full of sound and f. — SHAK 910:86
f., and rage of mortal men — BURT 214:75
f., like a woman scorned — CONG 281:22
f. of a patient man — DRYD 350:32
f. of aerial bombardment — EBER 359:10
f. of the winter — BEDE 82:8
F. with th' abhorred shears — MILT 684:42
Great f., like great whisky — CAPO 231:86
like a f. takest us out — BIBLE 133:20
no f. like an ex-wife — CONN 283:69
sit and watch the f. pass — ROBE 814:17
The f. and the mire — YEATS 1106:84
furze stepped over the f. bushes — SOME 952:1
fuse Each one of you is a f. — KOCH 567:66
through the green f. — THOM 1010:51
fused f. together — GUST 449:92
fuss f. about sleeping together — WAUGH 1056:79
make no f. about females — CAMPO 228:42
without more f. — SPEN 956:79
fustian whose f.'s so sublimely bad — POPE 781:64
futile f. his concerns — SIMO 939:86
future a receding f. — THOM 1013:26
arrow is pointing towards the f. — EDDI 360:17
better f. and a brighter day — SMUTS 950:66
Children have neither past nor f. — LABR 573:53
choose its own f. — KENN 551:79
cloud curtain of f. — CARL 234:35
conceive extravagant hopes for the f. — BURKE 206:19
concerned about our f. — RODO 818:87
controls the f. — ORWE 745:57
dipped into the f. — TENN 995:77
disdain the f. now — KENN 551:82
dream about the f. — HAMM 453:48
drowned the F. — THOM 1012:5
Europe and…the f. — MARI 650:62

future (*contd.*)
eventualities in the f. — MURP 715:73
fight against the f. — GLAD 429:51
For the f. I cease — ORAH 741:77
forbid…in the city i f. — EDWA 361:46
From past and f. — ELIOT 372:63
f. ain't what it used to be — ANON 28:16
f. generations — TOLS 1023:99
f. …has a voice — OAKE 733:48
f. in which our country — KENN 552:89
f. is made of the same stuff — WEIL 1062:80
f. is the man of statistics — HOLM 487:4
f. of art — FLAU 392:35
f. of humanity is uncertain — LEVI 600:26
f. shock…disorientation — TOFF 1022:85
F.…That period of time — BIER 161:84
f. that will live up to my past — BENN 91:81
f. they dreamed of — LESS 598:2
f. was a mystery — CHOP 261:60
f. while existing — NARO 719:40
Germany was afraid of the f. — GREY 446:58
great f. behind him — CART 242:97
great f. behind him — MARA 649:38
great soul in f. — EMER 377:68
happiness that the f. offers — DESB 317:72
have seen the f. — STEF 965:27
hope increasingly in the f. — MAJOR 640:97
hopes and dreams of the F. — FRAME 400:78
hopes of f. years — LONG 611:8
I have seen the f. — TOYN 1024:20
In the f. everybody — WARH 1053:21
in the f. look upon me — KEMB 549:36
lets the f. in — GREE 444:5
liberation From the f. — ELIOT 373:76
nations of the f. — CURZ 302:29
no preparation for the f. — DISR 332:81
one no longer believes in the f. — COUP 289:84
onward into its uncertain f. — HOFS 484:62
orgiastic f. — FITZ 391:7
past and f. were comprehended — GEE 417:65
past and f.…conquered — ELIOT 372:66
people who will run the f. — JONES 533:59
picture of the f. — ORWE 745:60
preparing students for the f. — DEMI 315:44
present or any f. writer — MILL 674:59
present in time f. — ELIOT 370:22
presents, past and f. sees — BLAKE 167:84
prophesying a fine f. — WILDE 1076:32
Prudence…scans the f. — WORD 1100:91
Science creates the f. — ZUCK 1110:28
security for the f. — TROL 1027:71
seen the f. — HALB 451:15
The f., Mr Gittes — TOWNE 1024:10
too eager for the f. — LARK 581:94
train of the f. to run over him — EISE 364:79
will be in the f. — KIPL 565:25
wonderful f. beckoned — PLATH 773:91
futurelessness so free of f. — COUP 289:82
futurism we establish F. — MARI 651:68
futurist I am a f. today — OGDEN 736:97
futurity f. casts upon the present — SHEL 931:60
no reference to f. — JOHN 530:90
walk on into f. — THOR 1017:88
Fuzzy-Wuzzy 'ere's to you, F.-W. — KIPL 560:34

Gael legend of the G. — RUSS 833:36
Gaelic Michael read the G. scroll — RUSS 833:36
gage hope's true g. — RALE 800:13
gags no g., no chance — TODD 1022:83
gaiety eclipsed the g. of nations — JOHN 531:13
g., the intrigue, and the anguish — SCHL 848:51
gain farmers…with constant g. — CRAB 294:78
g. and loss involved — PASC 757:63
g. by marriage — DICK 326:52

gain (*contd.*)
g. I count but loss — WATTS 1055:56
his own g. — SMITH 945:81
loss comes…from his g. — BROW 200:79
love of g. — SOPH 953:15
neither g. nor loss of utility — JEVO 521:20
neither g. nor loss — ELIOT 372:54
no g. — ANON 26:55
no war for…material g. — CHUR 264:10
pursuit of g. — WEBER 1059:20
to g. applause — JOHN 525:91
to speculate is a g. — COUS 290:87
weather that bringeth no g. — DEKK 313:9
what do you g.? — JUANA 539:64
what things were g. to me — BIBLE 153:11
gained something is eternally g. — JAMES 517:44
gains Light g. make heavy purses — BACON 59:26
gait forced g. of a shuffling nag — SHAK 876:59
gaiters All is gas and g. — DICK 322:55
gal every boy and every g. — GILB 424:75
slap-up g. — DICK 327:86
galaxy bathe them in the g. — LOVE 615:68
g. is one billions — BRAUN 186:17
glistening g. of childhood — MATT 664:82
gale before the g. — SMART 944:70
fart in a g. of wind — BARN 72:28
g., it plies the saplings — HOUS 495:54
war-cries…on the g. — MACC 625:36
gales cool g. shall fan the glade — POPE 778:76
g. shall fan the glade — POPE 778:74
Galice G. at Seint-Jame — CHAU 254:24
Galilean Among the G. mountains — CRAS 296:21
G., thy dead shall go down — SWIN 987:41
O pale G. — SWIN 987:40
Galilee before you into G. — BIBLE 141:57
like the Sea of G. — HOPK 492:97
Ye men of G. — BIBLE 147:80
Galileo status of G. — GOULD 436:76
gall pigeon-livered and lack g. — SHAK 890:15
They gave me g. to eat — BOOK 177:83
wormwood and the g. — BIBLE 128:31
gallant g., civilized…people — ATTL 44:9
He was a braw g. — BALL -101:32
Sade, the g. marquis — RICK 811:75
Where is this young g. — SHAK 885:70
gallantry no more to do with g. — SHER 933:90
What men call g. — BYRON 222:28
gallants Travelled g. — SHAK 917:46
galleon g. tossed upon cloudy seas — NOYES 732:42
Stately as a g. — GREN 446:51
galleries g. of the house — MUNDY 714:53
gallery curate her dreams and g. — DUNN 356:56
faces…a g. of pictures — BACON 58:98
g. in which the reporters sit — MACA 622:97
machine-gun to a shooting g. — OFAO 736:95
Pit, box, and g. — POPE 781:61
gallimaufry g. or hodgepodge — SPEN 957:96
gallon dying for $1.50 g. oil — POWE 788:14
gallons imperial g. of facts — DICK 325:39
gallop false g. of verses — SHAK 886:1
G. about doing good — SMITH 948:41
g. and g. about? — STEV 975:34
galloped g., Dirck g. — BROW 198:33
gallowglass Bonnought and g. — MACC 625:36
gallows g. in my garden — CHES 260:40
High upon the g. tree — SULL 981:24
see nothing but the g. — BURKE 207:33
world's going to be…one huge g. — BRAU 186:20
gallows-tree Below the g.-t. — BURNS 210:91
Jack on the g.-t.! — SCOTT 854:76
galoshes on his g. as he passes — LEAC 588:31
gals No g., no gags — TODD 1022:83
galumphing G. Goodness! — TRAV 1025:35
gambit by ploy or g. — POTT 785:46

gambler A g. is someone — TRUMP 1030:36
Show me a g. — PUZO 796:42
Time, that tireless g. — BAUD 77:24
whore and g. — BLAKE 168:5
gambling g. in human lives — DYSON 358:1
Inside every b....a g. streak — KORDA 568:79
women, g. and technicians — POMP 777:72
game any g. in the world — TRUE 1029:14
Anybody on for a g. — SHAW 924:99
Art is g. — PIER 769:36
Athalus, that made the g. — CHAU 254:3
Baseball is a Lockean g. — NOVAK 732:36
best g. in the world to watch — TREV 1026:48
Bowls is a young man's g. — BRYA 201:17
continentals think life is a g. — MIKES 674:53
cricket is just another g. — EDIN 361:41
Cricket is the greatest g. — WARN 1053:25
Cricket...is a manly g. — ANNE 20:36
Cricket...the g. of games — FOWL 400:70
enough to take up the g. — ROGE 820:23
far more than a g., this cricket — CARD 232:5
Fashion should be a g. — QUANT 796:50
food is love and g. — SHEL 929:8
Football...is a grand g. — BADE 60:45
forbid...such a g. — EDWA 361:46
fowlers when their g. — OTWAY 746:81
g. at which to be bad — MILNE 681:83
g. called Poohsticks — MILNE 680:81
g. for rough girls — WILDE 1078:7
g....is never lost till won — CRAB 294:87
g. is so full of plot-interest — FRY 408:12
g. is too hard — JAMES 515:3
g. of catch-as-catch-can — FOOTE 396:95
g. of golf... played on a Sunday — LEAC 589:42
g. of life seriously — LEARY 591:70
g. of no use — BACON 55:22
g. of the most terrifying stresses — ARLO 35:40
g. your country loves — RICE 809:40
giving over of a g. — BEAU 80:69
golf g. went bad — TREV 1026:50
good g. of Croquet — REID 806:98
great g. to see — SYNGE 988:62
how you played the g. — RICE 809:38
If you watch a g. — HOPE 491:74
inside g., cold, sure, undistracted — DELI 315:42
is surely his g. — ROUS 827:30
it is a good g. — HICKS 480:98
It's the g. that calls me — MILNE 681:82
kids playing some g. — SALI 839:28
killing g. with phoney mystique — BRES 187:36
know the g. — MACC 625:41
Love is a g. — ROBB 813:11
manly, British g.! — LOVE 614:61
more than a g. — HUGH 501:52
most exhilarating g. — GOOD 435:55
nature of my g. — JAGG 515:96
Never change a winning g. — TILD 1020:60
no better than a g. — JAMES 517:44
no g. for the soft of sinew — WOOL 1094:90
no hunter's g. — JEFF 520:85
nobly did he play the 'noble g.' — EGAN 362:55
parody is a g. — NABO 717:10
play with him at any g. — SHAK 905:72
poetry pedant's g. — BUNT 204:59
Poetry...a mug's g. — ELIOT 370:15
present rules of the g. — ROOS 822:48
ruin your g. in no time — BOTH 180:34
Science...is not a g. — PAUL 761:18
Soccer is a man's g. — CHAR 253:94
Socratic method is not a g. — BEER 83:37
some g. on these lone heaths — HAZL 463:6
Soviet g. is chess — SHUL 936:32
take seriously a g. — STOP 978:81
The g.'s afoot — SHAK 881:85

game (contd.)
They talk a good g. — BECK 81:89
things you can do in a baseball g. — STEN 968:76
time to win this g. — DRAKE 345:29
Truth is...the g. of the few — BERK 95:55
War's a bloody g. — SASS 845:35
war's a g. — COWP 293:61
What a polite g. tennis is — BARR 73:52
When's the g. itself — MARX 659:4
woman is his g. — TENN 996:93
gameboard steeplechase and g. — ELKIN 374:98
games best and loveliest of g. — CARD 232:4
bread and g. — JUVE 540:81
dread of g.! — BETJ 101:59
G. played with the ball — JEFF 520:97
I play no outdoor g. — WILDE 1077:76
like an aptitude for g. — MORAN 706:41
Most g. are skin-deep — ARLO 35:39
or any sinful g. — HARTE 459:49
playing at children's g. — CHES 258:92
gamester sly g. — BEHN 85:67
gammon sucking pig and thick g. — MACB 624:32
world of g. and spinnage — DICK 324:12
gamut Hepburn runs the g. — PARK 754:99
Gandhi odious to see Mr G. — CHUR 264:3
gang Bush and his treacherous g. — HUSS 505:36
g. should mismanage the country — MARQ 656:51
Ganges by the Indian G. — MARV 658:72
gangrene smelly g. of professors — MARI 651:68
gangsterism g. is a...assimilation — DOCT 334:41
gangsters always acted like g. — KUBR 570:12
glorified g. — MACD 628:92
gaol snail...the world's thy g. — DONNE 338:98
who lie in g. — WILDE 1078:3
gap Beyond the g. where — WILL 1083:95
bridge the g. between the two — CHUR 263:99
duty is to bridge the g. — KISS 566:39
g. between brute power — COMM 278:67
g. in Christianity — FORS 399:57
g. in the hills — ANON 25:26
great g. between — SYNGE 988:64
made a g. in nature — SHAK 905:69
gaps g. even two can pass abreast — FROST 406:72
garb words clothed in reason's g. — MILT 688:16
garbage g. heap — GARD 415:23
G. in, g. out — ANON 27:65
garden alone in a g. — ROSSO 825:98
bleak rock...into a g. — YOUNG 1108:2
Come into the g., Maud — TENN 1001:85
England is a g. — KIPL 564:13
everyone with a g. — DORA 340:38
gallows in my g. — CHES 260:40
g. eastwards in Eden — BIBLE 103:89
g. hard by Heaven — BOUL 181:45
g. in her face — CAMP 228:39
g. inclosed is my sister — BIBLE 124:52
g. of cactus and sour grapes — MERR 672:21
G. of Love — BLAKE 167:90
g. of the world — MARV 659:90
g.'s umbrage mild — SMART 944:70
ghost of a g. — SWIN 988:56
Glory of the G. — KIPL 565:15
God Almighty first planted a g. — BACON 59:16
God the first g. made — COWL 291:18
God walking in the g. — BIBLE 103:95
God's Heart in a g. — GURN 449:88
happy g. placed — MILT 689:32
have a g. of my own — MARV 657:71
I have the whole g. — HAMM 453:50
imperfection of my g. — MONT 701:63
into the g. to cut — FOOTE 396:95
jungles here are a well-kept g. — BOLT 172:77
like a...birdcage in a g. — WEBS 1059:30
man and a woman in a g. — WILDE 1077:65

garden (contd.)
Muses' g. — CAREW 232:12
Newton...in his g. — AUDEN 46:49
Nothing grows in our g. — THOM 1011:85
Our England is a g. — KIPL 564:14
out of the G. of Eden — MUGG 712:22
playing at the bottom of my g. — SHAN 918:72
rosebud g. of girls — TENN 1001:87
Sensitive Plant in a g. grew — SHEL 930:28
we must cultivate our own g. — VOLT 1046:3
garden-state that happy g.-s. — MARV 659:87
gardener Adam was a g. — KIPL 565:15
Adam was a g. — SHAK 861:12
bad for God's g. — HARDY 457:3
supposing him to be the g. — BIBLE 147:75
gardeners g., ditchers, — SHAK 893:73
which our wills are g. — SHAK 898:16
gardening G....most underrated — SHUL 935:29
gardens bodies are our g. — SHAK 898:16
Down by the salley g. — YEATS 1104:56
g. of the Desert — BRYA 202:19
g. of the West — CONN 283:79
g., wine and delicate — MONT 700:54
g. without sorrows — CIXO 267:75
in all of the neighbouring g. — REED 804:80
In his blue g. — FITZ 390:99
men Leaving the g. — LARK 581:7
ordered woods and g. — MACK 632:52
sweetest delight of g. — BROW 196:8
variety of g., meadows — MOORE 705:14
gargling blood come g. — OWEN 748:13
garland immortal g. is to be — MILT 685:63
garlanded g. with carven imag'ries — KEATS 546:91
garlands crowning...with g. — COUB 289:70
Therewith fantastic g. did she make — SHAK 892:71
weave the g. of repose — MARV 658:82
you may gather g. there — SCOTT 854:67
garlic G. to mend her kissing — SHAK 912:31
garment caught him by his g. — BIBLE 105:43
City now doth like a g. wear — WORD 1097:46
every new and eagerly expected g. — DICK 326:70
g. has looked very different — BONH 173:34
g. out of fashion — SHAK 916:6
g. that made skiing — ANON 27:70
Language is called g. of thought — CARL 234:52
new cloth unto an old g. — BIBLE 136:71
Non-violence is not a g. — GAND 414:14
waxeth old as a g. — BIBLE 132:2
garments Borrowed g. never fit — FULL 410:48
g. too good For thee — CRAS 296:20
g. were always in patchez — NASH 719:55
great multitude spread their g. — BIBLE 139:30
Her g., heavy with their drink — SHAK 892:72
keepeth his g. — BIBLE 158:26
Kiss thy perfumed g. — BLAKE 165:57
part my g. among them — BIBLE 114:49
garners Hold like rich g. — KEATS 544:49
garret precious jewels into a g. — BACON 56:38
Garrick as evidently an actor as G. — WALP 1051:85
garter earl and a knight of the g. — ATTL 44:12
George and G. dangling — POPE 780:30
garters girdles and g. to be bonds — BACON 57:58
thine own heir-apparent g.! — SHAK 875:50
gas All is g. and gaiters — DICK 322:55
G. smells awful — PARK 754:13
where you put in the g. — TAYL 992:24
gaseous God...a g. vertebrate — HAEC 450:2
gases killing airs and g. — DICK 325:42
gash g. in its throat — HUGH 500:39
gaslamps light coming from the g. — CASAL 243:24
gasp last g. of love's latest breath — DRAY 345:40
made one G. and Stretch one's Eyes — BELL 87:10
gassing burning and g. people — SIHA 938:72
gate A-sitting on a g. — CARR 241:77

gate (*contd.*)
by shutting the park g. — MILT 685:*56*
Captain of the G. — MACA 623:*13*
Death…openeth the g. — BACON 56:*46*
g. of bliss — CRAS 296:*22*
g. of paradise — SHAW 926:*43*
g. of the year — HASK 460:*57*
gazed upon the g. — BYRON 223:*67*
guards at the g. — SUN 982:*39*
here at the g. alone — TENN 1001:*85*
hobbled…through the garden g. — SASS 845:*23*
house with the narrow g. — SHAK 901:*83*
Hun is at the g. — KIPL 565:*17*
lark at heaven g. — SHAK 916:*3*
matters not how strait the g. — HENL 472:*58*
passing through this G. — SASS 846:*41*
passion-flower at the g. — TENN 1001:*88*
poor man at his g. — ALEX 13:*18*
watchful at his g. — DODD 335:*46*
wide is the g. — BIBLE 135:*59*
gates Come open your g. — SCOTT 855:*85*
Enter into his g. with thanksgiving — BIBLE 118:*9*
g. of pearl and topaz — LAUR 584:*45*
g. of the world — HARDY 456:*97*
g.…shall not be shut — BIBLE 159:*38*
g. to the glorious — FORS 398:*30*
hearses shall besiege your g. — POPE 779:*6*
heaven's g. she claps — LYLY 620:*58*
iron g. of life — MARV 658:*76*
Lift up your heads, O ye g. — BIBLE 115:*52*
Nor g. of steel so strong — SHAK 914:*68*
Open the temple g. — SPEN 959:*30*
shut the g. of mercy — GRAY 442:*71*
Sprouting…at area g. — ELIOT 367:*62*
Such are the G. of Paradise — BLAKE 166:*81*
Through g. of pearl — HOW 497:*91*
towards the g. of hell — MILT 688:*24*
gateways g. of the mind — SASS 846:*43*
g. to unexplored terrain — WILS 1085:*25*
gather g. you out of the countries — BIBLE 129:*39*
G. ye rose-buds — HERR 477:*63*
go and g. them up? — BIBLE 137:*2*
gaucho really a g. — GUIR 448:*80*
gaudy one other g. night — SHAK 905:*84*
rich not g. — SHAK 888:*69*
gauge danger is that g. — LESS 598:*1*
gauger Master G. play — STEV 973:*93*
Gaul G.…is divided into three parts — CAES 224:*83*
Gaullist G. only little by little — DEGA 313:*2*
gauntlet g. with a gift in't — BROW 197:*20*
take up the g. — BROW 195:*68*
gavottes birds sing g. — SITW 941:*12*
gay all the world was g. — POPE 778:*95*
assume everyone is g. — FIER 388:*64*
Being black is warm and g. — RHYS 808:*26*
chimes ring out with a carol g. — BOND 172:*79*
g. Description Aegypt glads — POPE 782:*93*
G. gilded scenes — ADDI 6:*98*
g. nature — SMART 944:*72*
g. goodnight — YEATS 1106:*81*
G. rich and Rich g. — ANON 24:*3*
glass so g. — SPEN 958:*22*
He has a g. appeal — COWA 290:*99*
impiously g. — CRAB 293:*66*
It will be a g. world — READ 803:*55*
lay his g. caparisons apart — SHAK 905:*83*
lord and lady g. — SCOTT 853:*43*
poet could not but be g. — WORD 1099:*69*
verse again shall…make them g. — DRAY 345:*34*
Gaza brought him down to G. — BIBLE 109:*21*
Eyeless in G. at the mill — MILT 694:*38*
gaze fixed in steadfast g. — MILT 681:*68*
g. of dogs — CALV 226:*6*
gone to g. on Cleopatra — SHAK 905:*69*

gaze (*contd.*)
medium's g. is brief — IGNA 510:*27*
seal's wide spindrift g. — CRANE 294:*94*
shields him from the world's g. — WHITE 1070:*35*
star of Truth…bade me g. — ARNO 38:*1*
gazed still they g. — GOLD 433:*13*
gazelle nursed a dear g. — MOORE 706:*38*
gazers eyes the g. strike — POPE 778:*93*
gazes For him that g. — CRAB 293:*71*
Gazette I inclose the G. — STEE 964:*11*
Pall Mall G. is written — THAC 1006:*94*
gazing love does not consist in g. — SAIN 836:*80*
gear goods and her g. — COLUM 278:*60*
Time's…chariot changing g. — LINK 606:*25*
women and g. are at the bottom — SCOTT 855:*90*
geese garrulous g. — WHITE 1070:*31*
G. are swans — ARNO 39:*22*
g. go south — WU 1102:*24*
Like g. about the sky — AUDEN 47:*60*
More g. than swans — GIBB 422:*32*
take their g. for swans — BROO 193:*45*
wild g. lost in cloud — BASHO 76:*5*
Gehenna Down to G. — KIPL 560:*20*
gem every tear a g. — SHEL 927:*77*
Full many a g. — GRAY 442:*69*
g. of the western world — MOORE 706:*33*
treat it like a precious g. — PELE 764:*52*
gendarme United States…global g. — MACN 636:*29*
gender tired of the g. of things — SEXT 859:*66*
to a kind and not to a g. — YOUR 1108:*5*
genealogy g. of his forefathers — ECHE 359:*13*
general business of a g. — SUN 982:*35*
g.'s disdained — SHAK 895:*41*
g. has no friends — LEMAY 595:*44*
g. must know — REED 805:*87*
g. who advances — SUN 982:*36*
g. who does not believe — NATH 721:*89*
good for G. Motors — WILS 1084:*21*
imperator and great g. — SHAK 865:*13*
'Twas caviare to the g. — SHAK 890:*11*
victorious g. — SUN 982:*34*
generalization g. can establish science — BERN 96:*82*
generalizations g. are dangerous — DUMAS 354:*30*
can be no g. — FISH 389:*82*
g. of science sweep — HUXL 508:*95*
tentatively accepted g. — FRIE 405:*52*
generals bite some of my other g. — GEOR 418:*80*
g. are in my coach — MARL 652:*81*
g. of his day — WELL 1063:*6*
G., right-wing politicians — STEI 967:*65*
like dead g. — TUCH 1031:*44*
most people and G. — TUCH 1031:*47*
plebiscite elected g. — JUVE 540:*81*
Russia has two g. — NICH 726:*49*
soldiers, her g. too. — MERE 671:*14*
too serious…to be left to g. — CLEM 268:*1*
Whitehall g. — ASHD 41:*62*
generation all a lost g. — STEIN 965:*33*
energy of a whole g. — THOM 1014:*36*
Every g. laughs — THOR 1016:*83*
Every g. revolts — MUMF 713:*45*
every new idea…takes a g. or two — FEYN 387:*34*
every single g. gone — MACL 633:*71*
evil and adulterous g. — BIBLE 137:*93*
feminism divided my g. — LYND 621:*65*
for the next g. of men — LOWE 615:*75*
g. has come to know — TIME 1020:*66*
G. X — COUP 289:*73*
grieved with this g. — BIBLE 117:*7*
ills of an entire g. — ISHE 513:*73*
in this g. — KENN 552:*92*
is a g. of men — HOMER 487:*17*
meaning of the Lost G. — KERO 553:*15*
men and women of this g. — LLOY 608:*58*

generation (*contd.*)
men in every g. — MILL 678:*38*
My g. of Canadians — FULF 409:*31*
new g. grows up — PLAN 772:*85*
new g. of Americans — KENN 550:*64*
new g. would take over — THOM 1013:*18*
new g.…every 30 years — COWL 291:*22*
O g. of vipers — BIBLE 137:*92*
one g. sacrificing for the next — MAYH 666:*8*
our g., though not indifferent — CECIL 247:*79*
poets of each g. — DAY 310:*46*
refuge from one g. to another — BOOK 177:*86*
remind one g. — JEVO 521:*23*
sad for my g. — SAIN 837:*88*
second g. has no time — BALD 64:*92*
Seldom is it given to one g. — SARN 843:*96*
third and fourth g.…that hate me — BIBLE 106:*68*
This g. shall not pass — BIBLE 140:*38*
To my g. — AUDEN 49:*3*
unto this wicked g. — BIBLE 137:*95*
With each g. — SCHR 850:*7*
ye are a chosen g. — BIBLE 156:*78*
generations dwelling place in all g. — BIBLE 117:*97*
future g. — TOLS 1023:*99*
g. believe to have happened — WHIT 1072:*69*
G. have trod — HOPK 491:*82*
save succeeding g. — UNIT 1036:*45*
shadows upon two g. — LLOY 608:*60*
through centuries of g. — MARQ 655:*34*
generosity luxury of g. — DICK 324:*26*
generous have more g. sentiments — JOHN 527:*35*
to be g. and compassionate — THAT 1007:*4*
genes selfish molecules known as g. — DAWK 310:*43*
Wall St. g. — THOM 1013:*18*
Genesis first chapter of G. — ACHE 3:*34*
G. was to be believed — SHAR 919:*84*
Genet G. had been right — ANGE 20:*32*
Geneva rules…from Rome or G. — BROW 195:*66*
Genghis G. Khan has arrived — THUR 1020:*59*
genitals very different attitude to g. — BURG 206:*91*
genius 25-year old g. — GREE 445:*36*
absolute g. for malingering — PROU 793:*95*
appearance of…greater g. — RUSS 832:*21*
attributes of g. — MOND 699:*40*
Bradman's batting g. — LARW 582:*31*
Celtic g. — ARNO 39:*20*
cocker up my g. — JONS 534:*76*
Conceit spoils the finest g. — ALCO 12:*97*
destroy g. and art — HAZL 464:*24*
dispenses with the need for g. — GALB 412:*80*
each…be considered a g. — BERG 94:*42*
Every age has a …universal g. — DRYD 347:*57*
everything but g. and virtue — HAZL 463:*12*
G. and regularity are utter Enemies — GAIN 411:*69*
g. for painting, poetry, music — EMER 377:*66*
g. found respectable? — BROW 197:*22*
g. is an enormous littleness — PATC 759:*90*
g. is enough — ARET 33:*17*
G. is felt — DIDE 329:*28*
G. is one per cent inspiration — EDIS 361:*44*
g. lies in taking…ordinary people — BANKS 70:*1*
g. makes no mistakes — JOYCE 538:*51*
g.…not to purchase fame — DRYD 348:*84*
g. of Canada — MORR 708:*78*
g. of our days — LARI 581:*93*
g. of the place — POPE 779:*19*
g. that could cut a Colossus — JOHN 532:*29*
g. to correct them — TELL 992:*26*
g. was too sullen — DRYD 347:*63*
g. who invents a noise — DUNN 356:*58*
G. will never mount high — BROO 192:*16*
Gives g. a better discerning — GOLD 433:*21*
In every work of g. — EMER 376:*30*
in theory if g. had not proved — LESS 599:*9*

genius (*contd.*)

interest to the fire of g.	LINC 605:1
like many businessmen of g.	PUZO 796:41
lot of time to be a g.	STEIN 965:40
man of g.	POUND 785:58
men of g.	CONA 279:80
men of g.	DELA 314:20
mind and g.	STEN 967:70
monotony of g.	HAZL 463:95
neither g. nor knowledge	JOHN 527:20
neurotic can…be a literary g.	AUCH 46:39
no interest in anything but g.	LAGN 575:99
no man of g.	BEER 83:39
nothing to declare except my g.	WILDE 1075:29
nourished all its g.	SMITH 949:60
Philistine of g. in religion	ARNO 40:36
Political g.	HEGEL 467:64
some flashes of g.	BYRON 221:15
stereotype of rejected g.	HUGH 499:29
taking pains…said to be g.	ACHE 3:38
talent instantly recognises g.	DOYLE 344:16
that is the way of g.!	MANN 645:82
the g. of the…Press	BENN 92:7
thing demanded of g.	GOET 431:78
think like a g.	NABO 717:13
Though taste, though g. bless	COLL 277:47
Three-fifths of him g.	LOWE 616:83
true g. appears	SWIFT 984:72
true g. is…large general powers	JOHN 531:8
vital g.	GOUR 437:80
works of a great g.	ADDI 8:38

geniuses cricket's presiding g.   CARD 232:6

G. are the luckiest	AUDEN 48:96
One of greatest g.…Shakespeare	WALP 1051:83

genocide g. is being carried out   JOHN 523:38
genres these g. still hold   UPDI 1037:62
gent knight was…a valiant G.   EVEL 381:41
genteel avoid the 'shabby g.'   DISR 334:27

not g. when he gets drunk	BOSW 180:32
truly g.	HARDY 456:94

gentes G. and laitymen   JOYCE 538:60
gentile isolation to g. hostility   ROTH 826:23
Gentiles boasting as the G. use   KIPL 562:62

G.' Lord and King	AQUI 32:5
G., which have not the law	BIBLE 148:13
preach among the G.	BIBLE 152:97

gentility I expected kindness and g.   PERE 766:95

Money and g.	MITF 697:93
Shabby g. has nothing	HOLM 486:91
What's g. worth	GALS 413:5

gentle As g. and as jocund   SHAK 866:41

carry g. peace	SHAK 918:63
Do not go g.	THOM 1011:75
g. and respectful ways	FENW 385:4
G. as falcon	SKEL 942:34
g. mind by g. deeds	SPEN 959:38
g., yet not dull	DENH 315:53
I have seen them g.	WYATT 1103:30
love, so g. in his view	SHAK 868:74

gentleman act the g.   TAFT 990:81

ask the honourable g.	ROCHE 815:41
attire for a g.	SHAR 919:81
back to the g.'s flat	MANS 647:9
chance of becoming a g. in it	LAMM 578:50
fashionable g.	ALSOP 15:58
g. an' scholar	BURNS 209:70
g. is an attorney	JOHN 528:58
g.…loves to hear himself talk	SHAK 869:1
g. on whom I built	SHAK 907:24
g. poet	JOYCE 538:49
g. to be the best dressed	TROL 1028:92
Gladstone…never a g.	DISR 333:20
He's a g.	SHAW 924:2
honourable g. caught the Whigs	DISR 332:93

gentleman (*contd.*)

honourable g.'s poodle	LLOY 608:54
I am a g.	SHAW 921:31
king…cannot make g.	BURKE 208:44
last g. in Europe	LEVE 600:21
legal g. who rescues your estate	BROU 193:46
lovely g.!	SHAK 869:15
man was apparently a g.	RIDGE 811:78
no g. could…give offence	ROCHE 815:39
No real English g.	BAGE 61:50
Once a g.	DICK 326:57
reputability to the g. of leisure	VEBL 1041:27
serving a great g.	ISHI 513:76
So this g. said a girl	LOOS 612:27
stamps a man…as an educated g.	SHAW 923:78
that which you call a G.	CROM 297:50
this venerable old g.	LEAC 589:47
too pedantic for a g.	CONG 281:18
true breeding of a g.	BYRON 223:49
unable to describe a g.	TROL 1028:99
use of a g. in travelling	LOWE 615:71
When a g. is disposed	SHAK 916:99
Who was then a g.	BALL 65:27

gentleman-drover he…is a g.-d.   SCOTT 854:70
gentlemen American g. are the best   LOOS 613:33

ask you g.	RODR 819:90
creates good g.	MUGA 711:20
difficult to behave like g.	MACK 632:56
G. do not take soup	CURZ 302:31
g. in England now abed	SHAK 882:5
g. …in the same Lobby	PALM 752:73
G. know that fresh air	MACA 622:83
g.…possess only strength and valour	BRON 191:94
G. Prefer Blondes	LOOS 612:26
G.-rankers out on the spree	KIPL 560:22
G.…seem to remember blondes	LOOS 613:28
G., you can't fight in here	KUBR 570:11
Hard pounding this, g.	WELL 1063:8
ladies and g., last night	NATH 721:87
male officers are g.	CARD 232:96
most of the g.	WAUGH 1056:60
no ancient g. but gardeners	SHAK 893:73
no salvation for g.	MOLI 698:17
patriots…not forget we are g.	BURKE 206:2
since g. come up.	SHAK 861:9
spoken of themselves as g.	WAUGH 1056:65
Tea…Is a g.	CHES 259:30
Then, g., said Redgauntlet	SCOTT 856:7
two very civil g.	SHER 934:4
When G. can see	DICK 327:95
while the g. go by!	KIPL 564:2
written by g. for g.	THAC 1006:94

gentleness all…through my g.   WYATT 1103:31

Crist…we claym of him oure g.	CHAU 255:36
G.…cardinal virtues	WOLL 1091:37
g. of heaven	WORD 1097:40

gentles It's weel wi' you g.   SCOTT 855:83
gentlest fittest may also be the g.   DOBZ 334:36
gentlewoman cut out for a G.   SWIFT 986:9

talk so like a waiting g.	SHAK 875:42

gently persuade g., not by force   PASC 758:69
gentry Ye Enbrugh G.!   BURNS 209:62
genuine place for the g.   MOORE 705:17
genuineness g. of apparent statements   AYER 53:79

G. only thrives in the dark	HUXL 506:50

geographers So g., in Afric-maps   SWIFT 986:4
geography different from G.   BENT 93:22

g. of one's own nature	BOWL 182:59
like trying to stop G.	MONT 702:77
too much g.	KING 558:88

geology reduced easily to basic g.   HILL 481:6
geometrician God is a g.   PLATO 774:29
geometry does not know his g.   ANON 30:63

g. in the humming of the strings	PYTH 796:46

geometry (*contd.*)

G. is not true	PIRS 771:57
G. is to sculpture	APOL 32:91
G.…the only science	HOBB 482:36
g. was degraded	MACA 623:11
Night G.	KENN 550:53
no 'royal road' to g.	EUCL 380:21

Geometry G. is that part   NEWT 725:39
Geordie Jingling G.   SCOTT 855:1
George Amelia was praying for G.   THAC 1006:86

England and St. G.!	SHAK 881:86
fair St. G.	SHAK 863:67
G. III…consecrated obstruction	BAGE 61:67
G. and Garter dangling	POPE 780:30
G.—don't do that	GREN 446:50
G. the Third	BENT 93:28
G. who discovered that alcohol	WODE 1089:92
great G. weighs twenty stone	BYRON 223:55
King G.'s glorious days	GILB 424:76

Georgian G. Silver goes   MACM 636:16
geranium madman shakes a dead g.   ELIOT 367:59
germ very g. and first upgrowth   KING 559:52
German G. Empire arose?   HERZL 478:75

G. memory was like…tongue	BURU 215:82
G. people will turn	LENIN 595:50
G. police spies	MARX 660:14
G. text of French operas	WHAR 1068:3
like G. opera	WAUGH 1057:87
saw a G. soldier	STRA 979:98
Should the G. people lay down	GOEB 430:65
two literatures [French and G.]	ARNO 38:6
under G. influence	GOER 431:68
wee, wee G. lairdie!	CUNN 300:1

Germans Beastly to the G.   COWA 290:6

G.…are going to pay	GEDD 417:63
G. classify…the French arrange	CATH 244:45
I hate not G.	THOM 1012:4
let the G. win the war	MILE 674:54
problem of the Sudeten G.	HITL 482:32

Germany Communism fits G.   STAL 962:81

country is at war with G.	CHAM 249:21
every country except G.	GREY 446:58
from G. to Downing Street	CHAM 249:19
G. has become a menace	ROOS 822:52
in G., books	STAEL 962:75
ruined cities of G.	ORWE 744:37

germinates g. and gestates by itself   HUST 505:79
germs Trap the g.   ANON 26:48
Gershwin G. keeps pounding on tin   GERS 420:9

G. died last week	OHARA 737:9

Gerty G.…taken up…concerts   WHAR 1068:95
gessamine crow-toe, and pale g.   MILT 684:47
gesture army without parade or g.   LAWR 587:14

never make a fine g.	BERN 97:95

gestures cynical g. of the poor   SPEN 956:75

parody…invades all g.	PIGL 769:40

get g. away inwardly   HERZ 478:73

G. up, g. up for shame	HERR 477:60
time to g.	BIBLE 122:19
will never g. it	WEAT 1058:13

getting g. over a four-day drunk   HELL 469:3

Let's be g. at them	GRACE 437:84
with all thy g. get understanding	BIBLE 120:59

Gettysburg G. address was so short   HEMI 471:35
gewgaw This g. world   DRYD 348:90
ghastly grave is g.   ANON 21:59

more g. a business	HARDY 457:79

ghetto idea of a arts g.   HARR 459:38

radio is a g. of good taste	KEIL 548:27

ghost Ay, thou poor g.   SHAK 889:80

bowling of a g.	THOM 1014:32
cease to be a g.	PAZ 761:23
dogma of the G.	RYLE 834:52
Father, Son and Holy G.	MACL 633:63

ghost (*contd.*)
gave up the g.   BIBLE 144:19
gave up the g.   BIBLE 146:71
g. from the tomb   SHEL 928:84
g. of a garden   SWIN 988:56
g. of a great house   LEVE 600:23
g. of wind   WILL 1083:97
g. stories…for ghosts   ALDI 12:5
g. will walk   BROW 199:62
given up the g.   BIBLE 112:4
mind full of g.   MANS 647:97
peacock like a g.   TENN 997:10
The g. of Roger Casement   YEATS 1106:88
thought to please my g.   MENC 669:60
yielded up the g.   BIBLE 140:56
ghosts ambushed with g.   MACA 622:84
g. of beauty glide   POPE 782:77
haunted by the g.   SHAK 867:60
I sought for g.   SHEL 927:62
like g. from an enchanter fleeing   SHEL 928:86
rain Is full of g.   MILL 676:86
ghoul g. of literature   DELI 314:39
giant As when a g. dies   SHAK 897:79
chalk g.   HEAN 465:35
G's. Causeway worth seeing?   JOHN 530:5
G. Despair had a wife   BUNY 205:68
g. girls that have no secret   SPEN 956:80
g. refreshed with wine   BOOK 177:84
lies the sleeping g.   NAPO 718:25
like a g.'s robe   SHAK 910:79
'This is I , the g.'   MAST 663:65
To have a g.'s strength   SHAK 896:71
upon the body of a g.   LAND 578:56
giantism To go for g.   SCHU 850:15
giants G. in physical power   CARL 234:42
g., the sons of Anak   BIBLE 107:82
like precocious g.   PEAR 762:33
standing on the shoulders of g.   BERN 96:73
Gibraltar G. may tumble   GERS 420:15
giddy g., shallow, humorous youth   SHAK 881:79
Gideon sword of the Lord, and of G.   BIBLE 109:15
gier-eagle Strong, the g.-e.   SMART 944:69
gift horse Always look a g. h.   RABE 798:81
gift Beauty is the lover's g.   CONG 281:35
cause of this fair g.   SHAK 914:78
chance g. of nature   MORAN 706:41
creative g.   HOPK 492:10
destroying her g. by maiming   BACON 60:40
Every good g….is from above   BIBLE 155:60
exploiting a heavenly g.   QUIL 797:63
for a New Year's g.   SHAK 878:22
gauntlet with a g. in't   BROW 197:20
g. half understood   ELIOT 372:65
g. of a coward   SHAK 893:95
g. of God is eternal life   BIBLE 149:22
g. of tears   SWIN 987:26
g. of vanity and pride   GRIL 447:63
g. or trust   MACC 625:48
Heav'n's last best g.   MILT 691:69
love is the g. of oneself!   ANOU 31:79
love, or g., which is   MILT 686:70
Madness is a g.   PALEY 751:62
make the g. rich   TROL 1028:85
music is a g. and a burden   SIMO 939:84
naught a priceless g.   PATM 760:99
only g. is a portion of thyself   EMER 376:29
only g. is a portion of thyself   EMER 377:50
other than the g. of life   KOSI 568:83
problem without a g.   BACH 54:97
speech, that supremely human g.   MATH 663:68
When God hands you a g.   CAPO 231:84
gifted divinely g. man   TENN 999:44
g. individuals manage to do both   SAKI 838:9
young, g. and black   HANS 455:71

gifts cannot recall their g.   TENN 1003:22
countless g. of love   WINK 1086:59
diversities of g.   BIBLE 150:61
even when bearing g.   VIRG 1045:82
For your g.   WEBS 1060:40
g. may henceforth be bestowed   SHAK 884:69
give good g. unto your children   BIBLE 135:58
great g. with one hand   SNOW 951:75
man's work or his own g.   MILT 686:81
No g. from chance   ARNO 36:58
presented unto him g.   BIBLE 133:24
rarer g. than gold   BROO 192:23
received g. for men   BIBLE 116:87
received g. for men   BOOK 177:82
Rich g. wax poor   SHAK 891:22
Rich men deal in G.   SHAK 902:95
Spend not then his g.   JONS 534:85
stars were the g.   MACC 626:62
whose heavenly g.   SURR 982:42
Win her with g.   SHAK 860:82
Gilbert G. had a baddish streak   QUIL 797:61
G. to someone else's Sullivan   RUSS 833:40
laid down by G. and Sullivan   HUTC 506:43
gild g. the blade if you will   QUIN 798:68
verse again shall g.   DRAY 345:34
gilded vegetables too g.   GIRA 429:45
gilding g. of setting sun   GARL 415:27
gile thai er ful of g.   MINOT 695:64
Gilead balm in G.   BIBLE 128:24
gillyflowers With g.   SPEN 957:93
gimble Did gyre and g.   CARR 239:47
gimcrack how g. a placte   LAUR 584:45
gin for a g. and for a snare   BIBLE 125:64
G. and chicken helpless   BARK 71:17
G. by pailfuls   SCOTT 854:76
G. was mother's milk   SHAW 924:7
Of all the g. joints   EPST 379:97
proper union of g. and vermouth   DEVO 318:89
receptacle for Gilbey's g.   CHEE 255:52
sooner we can get out the g.   REED 805:86
ginger empty g. ale bottles   THUR 1018:14
Nutmegs and g.   ANON 23:92
Gipper win…one for the G.   GIPP 428:40
gipsy Time, you old g. man   HODG 483:49
giraffe God…invented the g.   PICA 769:28
Swelling to maculate g.   ELIOT 367:66
giraffes G.!—a People   CAMP 227:21
man who believes in g.   MITC 696:80
return the g. to the zoo   NASH 720:73
gird g. up the loins of your mind   BIBLE 155:75
girders Rumbling under blackened g.   BETJ 100:39
girdle At her own g.   WEBS 1059:31
folds of a bright g.   ARNO 36:64
g. round about the earth   SHAK 870:37
g. when your hips stick   NASH 720:69
leathern g. about his loins   BIBLE 133:26
Off with that g.   DONNE 336:71
the g. do the gods inherit   SHAK 903:35
girdles g. and garters to be bonds   BACON 57:58
girl Boy Meets G. in Winnipeg   MACL 634:89
can't get no g. reaction   JAGG 515:94
dark g. I couldn't play with   WRIG 1101:10
do a g. in   ELIOT 370:10
doubt whether any g.   TROL 1027:72
first rock at a g. like I   LOOS 613:36
forget myself with that g.   TAYL 992:14
Fun is fun but no g.   LOOS 613:34
g. I saw was myself   RHYS 808:31
g. in our town   ANON 24:12
g. likes to be crossed in love   AUST 51:40
g….marries a literary man   CHEE 255:51
g. must marry for love   GABOR 411:67
g. solid with yearning   LOWE 617:14
g. throwing a ball   WOOLF 1093:66

girl (*contd.*)
g. to miss out on any   RUSS 833:43
g. …turned into a chimpanzee   PERE 766:91
g., unschooled, unpractisèd   SHAK 873:84
g., who's danced with the Prince   FARJ 383:64
g. who was a lady   LOOS 613:31
g. whose cheeks   NASH 719:45
g. with big boobs   KING 557:70
Give me a g.   SPARK 955:54
great mountainous sports g.   BETJ 99:32
Home is the g.'s prison   SHAW 922:60
I'm not a g.   MANS 647:98
like a chorus g.'s tights   LAWR 587:11
Look like a g.   SIMON 938:79
maddest, fantasticalest g.   DEKK 313:14
nice g. should only fall   SPARK 955:56
Oh, she's a splendid g.   HUXL 507:68
Poor Little Rich G.   COWA 290:91
pretty g. is like a melody   BERL 95:58
quite loved by a g.   TROL 1028:84
Since I was a little g.   ROTH 826:8
So this gentlman said a g.   LOOS 612:27
There was a little g.   LONG 612:21
There's a Burma g.   KIPL 560:28
What can you expect of a g.   WHAR 1068:4
where the g. smiled before   WHIT 1074:2
wink your eye at some… g.   MENC 669:60
young g. stood beside   NEIL 722:95
young g.'s skin   RENO 807:8
girl-graduates sweet g.-g.   TENN 996:91
girlfriend going to visit our g.   MAMET 644:61
girlie here and tell me, g.   NASH 720:63
girls all the g. …were laid   PARK 754:2
Always be civil to g.   MITF 697:99
Anyone who marries three g.   STEIN 966:46
Dancing…training for g.   MORL 708:70
For coloured g.   SHAN 918:68
game for rough g.   WILDE 1078:7
giant g. that have no secret   SPEN 956:80
G. are so queer   ALCO 12:1
g.'s aren't ignorant   COOP 287:46
G. aren't like that   AMIS 16:73
g. in slacks remember dad   BETJ 100:46
g. so constantly do this   TROL 1027:73
g. suffered this month   BERR 98:17
g.' thin laughter   RICK 811:74
g. think they can do so   TROL 1028:87
g. were no longer to be treated   LEE 593:18
g. with wax faces   WILD 1079:26
Golden lads and g.   SHAK 916:16
good g. keep diaries   BANK 70:92
lads for the g.   HOUS 495:52
lovely, gifted g.   GRAV 440:32
make passes At g.   PARK 754:11
Many g. have not the advantage   FLEM 394:61
men and g. came and went   FITZ 390:99
mill g. clumping   ORWE 742:91
Most plain g. are virtuous   ANGE 19:21
No g.,…no chance   ANON 26:50
other g. and boys   STEV 975:35
pallor of g.' brows   OWEN 748:8
process whereby American g. turn   HAMP 454:64
robust, dynamic g.   WODE 1089:94
rose-lipt g.   HOUS 495:62
save women and g.   WEBB 1058:15
Secrets with g….are never valued   CRAB 294:89
thing about g.   SALI 838:21
to g. and boys   HORA 493:21
Treaties are like g.   DEGA 313:1
trouble with g.   SALI 839:26
twelve little g. in two straight lines   BEME 89:44
two g. had me buried!   MANS 647:10
What do g. do   ALCO 12:2
What fools middle-class g. are   DRAB 345:24

glory (*contd.*)

G. to Man in the highest	SWIN 988:50
going to g.!	DUNC 355:43
good man's g.	KEMP 549:43
gown of g.	RALE 800:13
great and sudden g.	DEVO 318:89
greater g. of His Creator	PIUS 772:81
heaven and earth are full of thy g.	BOOK 174:28
heavens declare the g. of God	BIBLE 114:44
hope of g.	BOOK 174:8
in g. and in joy	WORD 1097:44
In God 'tis g.	DRYD 349:19
joy and their g. must be	ABEL 1:4
King of G. wore	MARV 658:80
King of g., King of peace	HERB 475:20
known a g. in it all	MILL 676:81
Land of Hope and G.	BENS 92:9
like thy g., Titan	SHEL 930:27
Lo, now my g.	SHAK 862:31
looks on war as all g.	SHER 934:16
mellow g. of the Attic stage	ARNO 36:62
Not as our g.	WORD 1096:24
party…may retain its g.	GAIT 411:71
paths of g. lead to grave	GRAY 442:66
power, and the g.	BIBLE 135:49
prince of g. died	WATTS 1055:56
radiancy of g.	NEALE 722:93
sea Of g.	BYRON 220:94
seen the g.	KING 558:86
set thy g. above the heavens	BIBLE 114:34
shew me thy g.	BIBLE 107:76
short of the g. of God	BIBLE 148:15
snatching g. out of defeat	PRIE 790:37
some desperate g.	OWEN 748:13
Son of man shall come in his g.	BIBLE 140:43
spread, my sons, your g.	POPE 783:2
sun that was Munster's g.	ORAH 741:78
there is no g. in the deed	READ 803:54
There's g. for you!	CARR 240:70
this g., this fair luminous mist	COLE 274:7
though not indifferent to g.	CECIL 247:79
Thy g. flames from sun and star	HOLM 486:98
to thy name give g.	BIBLE 159:46
unrevealed g. of Nature	SHIP 935:22
Unto him be g. in the church	BIBLE 152:99
virtue…sum of g.	MARL 653:92
waste of G.	STUD 980:14
What Price G.?	ANDE 18:5
Where is the antique g.	SPEN 958:17
while my g. passeth by	BIBLE 107:77
Who is this King of g.?	BIBLE 115:52
whose g. is in their shame	BIBLE 153:13
Why in the name of G.	KEATS 546:81
Yet I g.	JONS 534:75
Your great g.	PERI 766:98

gloss glittering g. darkened SPEN 958:10
shining g. that fadeth SHAK 887:41

glove hand of steel in a velvet g. WOOL 1093:83
mailed fist in a cotton g. SITW 941:20
play'd at the g. BALL -101:32
white g. pulpit REAG 803:57

gloves capitalism with the g. off STOP 978:78
people in g. and such CHES 260:45
through the fields in g. CORN 288:58
wearing g. more often ANDE 18:3
with his g. on THUR 1019:34

glow a purple g. YEATS 1104:57
g. more…than blaze of branch ELIOT 372:68

glow-worm eyes, the g.-w. lend thee HERR 478:66

glutton g. of wordes LANG 579:70
More g. than artist PARK 754:95

gluttony G. demands a heavy tribute INNO 512:55
like adultery or g. MAUG 664:87
rode loathsome G. SPEN 957:3

glycosuria isolate…to relieve g. BANT 70:4

gnat strain at a g. BIBLE 139:35

gnomes little g. in Zurich WILS 1085:28

go cannot, cannot g. BRON 191:6
G. along and get along RAYB 803:50
G., and the Lord be with thee BIBLE 110:39
G. directly--see what she's doing PUNCH 795:28
G., g., g., said the bird ELIOT 370:24
G., girl SHAK 864:82
g. in there with all they've got GIPP 428:40
g. with so much still to say BART 75:88
I g., I g.; look how I g. SHAK 871:46
know not how to g. out BIBLE 111:55
know not why you g. FITZ 390:90
Led g.! KIPL 563:83
Let my people g. BIBLE 106:59
One to come and one to g. CARR 241:74
When things g. wrong ONOL 734:66
when you have to g. there FROST 406:75
whither thou goest, I will g. BIBLE 109:25
will not let thee g. BIBLE 105:38
Will ye g. wi' me BALL 67:43

goal achieving the g. KENN 551:66
colour is the g. HEIN 467:74
final g. of ill TENN 999:36
g. in the World Cup RAMS 801:19
g. of art is almost divine HUGO 501:59
g. of every system of law ROUS 827:33
g. of our actions MORE 707:54
g. of the anti-abortion forces LEGU 594:28
g. on these journeys THES 1009:45
g. that supplies the political magic SCHL 848:79
grave is not its g. LONG 611:94
imagines that it has reached its g. SHAW 923:86
life…had a g. HAMM 453:46
reach the g. HUXL 508:98
stood to keep the g. HOUS 494:48
Till yon g. be won GORD 435:61
Try for a g. that's reasonable ZATO 1109:15

goalkeepers nation of g. STOP 978:79

goals confusion of g. EINS 363:69
dedicated to…dogmas or g. PIRS 770:52
muddied oafs at the g. KIPL 563:94
'theories' and 'g.' KIPL 564:5
would not tolerate compromise on g. DULL 354:26

goat g. feet dance an antic hay MARL 653:4
g., on which the lot fell BIBLE 107:79

goats better than sheep, or g. TENN 1004:47
g. on the left BIBLE 140:43
hair is as a flock of g. BIBLE 124:51
Not for Cadwallader and all his g. SHAK 882:8

goblets g. for a dish of wood SHAK 867:62

goblin g. Honour CAREW 232:17
spirit of health or g. damned SHAK 888:71
That hobnailed g. SITW 941:10

god Assumes the g. DRYD 351:68
before the g. of science KING 557:83
beneficent but implacable g. LECO 592:2
Cry aloud: for he is a g. BIBLE 111:64
cyclical economic g. CUOMO 300:5
deem himself a g., or beast POPE 780:42
either a g. or a wolf WEBS 1060:39
extemporal g. of rhyme SHAK 865:12
for g. loueth it JULI 539:67
g. going thro' his world BROW 197:26
g. is not so glorious MARL 652:88
g. of contemporary man's MONT 700:52
g. self-slain SWIN 988:57
if g. be pleased EDWA 361:47
immortal g. of harmony BEET 84:49
never a g. WOOL 1094:91
never make a g. out of form KAND 541:95
next to of course g. CUMM 299:83
Now the melancholy g. SHAK 894:13

god (*contd.*)

presents the g. unshorn	HERR 477:60
thank we all our G.	WINK 1086:59
the g. pursuing	SWIN 986:25
to be like a g.	CATU 245:62
to the g. he worships	THOR 1016:73
told me of my g.	BRID 187:44
treat it like a g.	PELE 764:52
triangles had made a g.	MONT 702:81
turning into a g.	VESP 1043:41
wild beast, or a g.	BACON 58:97
Yblessed be g.	CHAU 255:35

God air out of G.'s own presence WILS 1086:44
abandoned a belief in G. STEV 972:62
abide with my Creator G. CLARE 267:33
Adversary of G. and man MILT 688:24
afraid to look upon G. BIBLE 106:55
after death G. knows ROSS 824:90
Ah G., for a man TENN 1001:80
All conceptions of G. WEIL 1062:84
All G.'s Chillum got Rhythm KAHN 541:91
allow G. to penetrate WEIL 1062:82
Almighty G., give us grace BOOK 174:9
Almighty G., the fountain BOOK 176:55
Almighty G., unto whom all hearts BOOK 174:16
America is G.'s Crucible ZANG 1109:13
And G. of Hosts KIPL 562:61
And G.'s bell YEATS 1105:61
as G. granted it QUIL 797:56
as G. is my witness MITC 697:87
As if we were G.'s spies SHAK 904:46
as the angels of G. BIBLE 139:33
as though G. made both SCHR 850:4
asks G. only for peace BONH 172:81
attracted by G. INGE 511:37
Be merciful unto me, O G. BOOK 177:77
Behind the Eyes of G. DICK 328:8
believe in G. the Father Almighty BOOK 173:94
best thing G. invents BROW 198:44
better than to gaze upon G. MELV 668:44
better to have no opinion of G. BACON 58:83
bit like G. confessing LOEN 610:85
bitter G. to follow SWIN 987:39
Blow, thou wind of G.! KING 558:90
bound…about the feet of G. TENN 1004:47
bush afire with G. BROW 197:23
but for the grace of G., goes G. CHUR 265:49
By G. I mean a being SPIN 961:60
'By G.,' quod he CHAU 255:42
by searching find out G.? BIBLE 113:5
By the livin' G. KIPL 561:36
call in, and invite G. DONNE 339:28
calling heads that G. exists PASC 757:63
cannot serve G. and mammon BIBLE 135:51
church to G. BYRON 224:72
closer walk with G. COWP 292:30
community…lived in praise of G. ELIOT 370:19
conceal G. and reveal THOM 1013:27
contumely to G. KNOX 567:57
dazzled by the ways of G. LIND 605:12
dearer…than that son of G.? AIDAN 10:73
depend, under G. WASH 1054:42
desired…even G. CHES 258:14
dice of G. EMER 376:36
die for G.'s eternal truth BROWN 194:53
direct G…a literal G. DONNE 339:24
disbelieve in G. ORWE 742:89
does not have to believe in G. KRUT 570:7
Draw nigh to G. BIBLE 155:69
effect, Whose cause is G. COWP 293:64
embrace the purpose of G. TENN 1002:96
endowed with the idea of G. DESC 318:20
enter into the kingdom of G. BIBLE 139:25
eternal G. is thy refuge BIBLE 108:5

god (*contd.*)

Even if G. did not exist — BAUD 78:36
ever found G. in church? — WALK 1049:58
except G., man is a diminutive — DONNE 339:20
eye of Almighty G. — GLAD 429:52
eye of G. — OLIV 738:31
eyes of G. and men — LESL 598:94
facts and doctrines concerning G. — HUGEL 498:10
fair sunlight of G. — MACD 628:99
Fall into the hands of G. — TENN 1005:59
far more certain than G. — GREE 444:12
Fear G. Honour the King — KITC 566:44
Fear G. — BIBLE 156:79
Fear G. — BORR 179:24
Fear G., and keep his commandments — BIBLE 124:44
fear the blessing of G. — ELIOT 370:35
final proof of G.'s omnipotence — DEVR 318:93
first sense…of G. — AUBR 45:37
fit for the kingdom of G. — BIBLE 142:86
For G. so loved the world — BIBLE 145:34
For G.'s sake — SHAK 867:60
For G.'s sake — STEV 974:16
For G., for Country — THUR 1019:36
For those who believe in G. — SEAT 857:25
Fore G. I am no coward — TENN 1004:56
further from G. — ANDR 19:14
G. appears and G. is light — BLAKE 168:21
G. only, she for G. in him — MILT 690:55
gathered…in the sight of G. — BOOK 175:42
Gentle G., if I wrote — PARK 755:18
glorify G. and benefit — WENT 1065:53
Glory be to G. — HOPK 491:84
glory is to G. — BUEC 203:41
glory of G. is man — ANON 21:51
glory of G. — BLAKE 166:78
go to your G. — KIPL 560:33
G.…a gaseous vertebrate — HAEC 450:2
G.'s a good man — SHAK 880:59
G. Almighty first planted a garden — BACON 59:16
G. and sinners reconciled — WESL 1066:59
G. answers sharp — BROW 197:20
G. be merciful to me a sinner — BIBLE 144:11
G. be merciful unto us — BIBLE 116:85
G. bless America — ANON 25:33
G. bless our good and gracious King — ROCH 817:66
G. bless us every one! — DICK 323:87
G. blessed seventh day — BIBLE 102:87
G. blew — ANON 23:89
G. cannot alter the past — BUTL 217:34
G. cannot grant so much — DRYD 350:31
G. caused deep sleep — BIBLE 103:92
G. comes to thee — DONNE 339:26
G. could have made a better berry — BUTL 218:51
G. created man — VALE 1038:87
G., Creator wise — MILT 693:20
G.…destroys their mind — DRYD 351:57
G. disposes — KEMP 549:40
G. does not die — HAMM 453:43
G. erects a house of prayer — DEFOE 312:75
G.'s eternal store — MILT 691:85
G. exact day-labour — MILT 686:81
G. finally caught his eye — KAUF 543:18
G.'s finger touched him — TENN 999:50
G.'s first Creature — BACON 60:31
G. for Harry! — SHAK 881:86
G. forbid that I should — GOET 431:81
G. forbid — BIBLE 148:14
G. from everlasting — BOOK 177:86
G. fulfils himself — TENN 1004:46
G. gave him the light — MACA 621:75
G. gave the increase — BIBLE 150:47
G. gave [Adam] reason — MILT 686:67
G. gives all men — KIPL 563:92

god (*contd.*)

G. gives him — RYDER 834:50
G. gives us to see…right — LINC 605:6
G. good on the physical — BURG 206:90
G. grant me a failure — GOUN 437:79
G. grant that we may — MARY 661:28
G. ha' mercy — KIPL 560:22
G. had never spoken anything but — DAY 310:31
G. had wanted us to bend over — RIVE 813:4
G. has a few of us — BROW 199:74
G. has given knowledge — MARIE 651:63
G. has given us…license — MORE 706:46
G. has given you one face — SHAK 891:28
G. has instituted in our time — GUIB 448:77
G. has us…on loan — FERRE 387:28
G. has written all the books — BUTL 218:43
G. hath chosen the foolish things — BIBLE 150:45
G. hath given liberty — CURR 301:16
G. hath shut up all light — RALE 800:15
G. have mercy — RANS 802:38
G. having given us indoors — MACA 622:83
G. heard before creating the world — FERN 386:27
G. help me; amen — LUTH 619:44
G. hez sed so plump — LOWE 616:80
G. himself shall be with them — BIBLE 158:35
G.'s in His heaven — BROW 197:25
G. in His wisdom — NASH 720:67
G. in Man — CRAS 295:18
G. in Three Persons — HEBER 466:59
G. is a consuming fire — BIBLE 155:56
G. is a geometrician — PLATO 774:29
G. is…another artist — PICA 769:28
G. is a Spirit — BIBLE 145:37
G.…is a verb — FULL 409:36
G. is beginning to resemble — HUXL 508:94
G. is dead — NIET 727:71
G. is decreeing to begin — MILT 686:74
G. is gone up with a merry noise — BOOK 177:75
G. is good to Israel — BIBLE 117:89
G. is his own interpreter — COWP 291:28
G. is little tribal G. — BURR 213:54
G. is love — BIBLE 156:92
G. is Love — KIER 556:60
G. is love — LEE 592:5
G. is no respecter of persons — BIBLE 148:93
G. is not a man — BIBLE 108:86
G. is not ashamed to be called — BIBLE 154:52
G. is not mocked — BIBLE 152:92
G. is on everyone's side — ANOU 31:80
G. is on the side — VOLT 1047:15
G. is our refuge — SCOT 856:20
G. is our refuge and strength — BIBLE 116:72
G. is present in it — BUEC 203:42
G. is registered to vote — WALL 1049:60
G. is subtle — EINS 363:61
G.…is so great — HOPK 492:98
G. is…sweetly informal — OZICK 748:24
G. is the perfect poet — BROW 197:24
G. is the strength of my heart — BIBLE 117:91
G. is the tangential point — JARRY 518:69
G. is thy law — MILT 690:61
G. is with us! — WESL 1067:73
G. knows where — MORT 710:96
G. loveth a cheerful giver — BIBLE 151:84
G. made and eaten all day — BROW 198:39
G. made him — SHAK 874:17
G. made himself a man — HUGO 502:12
G. made the country — COWP 292:52
G. made the integers — KRON 570:99
G. made thee perfect — MILT 691:73
G. made them, high or lowly — ALEX 13:18
G. …make me able to pay — PEPYS 765:61
G. moves in a mysterious way — COWP 291:27
G. must think — KNOX 567:61

god (*contd.*)

G. never made…for man to mend — DRYD 352:87
G. not only plays dice. — HAWK 461:62
G. of Abraham — PASC 758:81
G. of love! — DODD 335:47
G. of Love…Beteth his wynges — CHAU 255:37
G. of our Fathers — MILT 694:48
G. of things as they are! — KIPL 562:60
G. on his side — DYLAN 358:92
G. ordered motion — VAUG 1041:21
G. owns heaven — SEXT 860:70
G. passes through the thicket — JOHN 522:29
G. planted a garden — BIBLE 103:89
G.'s police — CHIS 260:54
G.'s querulous calling — HUGH 500:42
G. recognizes I will do that — CART 242:3
G. requireth that which is past — BIBLE 122:20
G. rest his soul — SMITH 948:38
G. said…I am that I am — BIBLE 106:57
G. save Elizabeth — ANON 23:90
G. save me from…adventures — BYRON 224:73
G. save me from being 'nice' — LAWR 586:94
G. save the king — BIBLE 110:33
G. save the king — SHAK 867:63
'G. save the Queen' — KIPL 562:67
'G. save the Queen' — WHIT 1072:71
G. save thee, ancient Mariner! — COLE 273:85
G. saw that it was good — BIBLE 102:85
G.; science has got rid of him — BAIN 62:77
G. send thee good ale — ANON 23:84
G. sends meat — FULL 410:51
G. sent not his Son — BIBLE 145:35
G. shall be my hope — SHAK 861:2
G. shall help her — BIBLE 116:73
G. shall supply all your need — BIBLE 153:2
G. shall wipe away all tears — BIBLE 157:15
G. shed His grace — BATES 76:10
G. tells me how — TOSC 1024:8
G. tempers the wind — STER 970:27
G. that made the world — BIBLE 148:2
G. that maketh men to be — BOOK 177:80
G., the best maker — SHAK 882:12
G. the first garden made — COWL 291:18
G. the Omnipotent! — ELLE 374:1
G. the soul — POPE 780:40
G.'s the theme — SMART 944:71
G. their severance ruled — ARNO 37:80
G. therefore let him free — MILT 686:70
G. thi makere — CHAU 254:14
G. to send us a merry meeting — LANC 578:52
G. to trust in — MARG 650:51
G. unmakes but to remake the soul — BROW 200:94
G. was a man — GIRA 429:46
G. was sick — VALL 1039:90
G., who does whatever pleases him — WESL 1067:71
G., who is able to prevail — WALT 1052:3
G. who is all-forgiving — SMITH 947:3
G. who is her life — PATM 760:7
G., who is our home — WORD 1098:51
G. who kills us — YOUR 1108:9
G. who Looks after — KIPL 563:97
G. who made him — KIPL 565:15
G. who made thee mighty — BENS 92:9
G. who would let us prove — BONH 173:87
G. will forgive me — HEINE 467:73
G. will provide himself a lamb — BIBLE 105:28
G. will recognize his own — ARNA 35:52
G. with his mercyful iye — ANON 22:71
G. won't, and we can't mend it — CLOU 270:34
G. would have changed his doom — CLEV 269:9
Great G.! — SCOTT 852:39
Great G.! — STEN 967:72
greatest good… knowledge of G. — SPIN 960:56
ground G.'s-Arce — LONG 611:3

god (*contd.*)

Had I served my G.	SHAK 918:62
hand folks over to G.'s mercy	ELIOT 365:12
hand of G.	BIBLE 131:81
hand of G.	HASK 460:57
hath not one G. created us?	BIBLE 130:69
Have G. to be his guide	BUNY 205:73
heavens declare the glory of G.	BIBLE 114:44
hidden love of G.	WESL 1066:67
holy Lamb of G.	BLAKE 168:17
honest G. is the noblest work	INGE 511:42
honour of G.	BACH 54:93
hope thou in G.	BIBLE 116:69
household of G.	BIBLE 152:96
how can he love G.	BIBLE 156:95
How could I	LOUI 614:49
how dwelleth the love of G. in him?	BIBLE 156:91
How odd Of G.	EWER 381:48
I am a G.	SHEL 930:18
I am G. and King and Law	SHEL 928:79
I came, I saw, G. conquered	JOHN 522:30
I would to G.	SHAK 875:38
if a G. there be	SWIN 988:49
If G. be for us	BIBLE 149:30
if G. chooses	BROW 197:19
If G. did not exist	VOLT 1047:17
If G. had meant us to have group sex	BRAD 183:80
If G....has any validity	BALD 64:99
if this manifest G. enlightens men	CYRA 302:36
If, knowing G.	TENN 1004:47
ignorance G. winked at	BIBLE 148:4
image of man created by G.	IVAN 514:83
imitate G.	FLAU 392:41
immortal, invisible, G.	SMITH 950:61
impulse which G. has	JUANA 539:66
in favour with G. and man	BIBLE 142:80
In G. 'tis glory	DRYD 349:19
in my flesh shall I see G.	BIBLE 113:12
in science there exists no G.	STEI 967:68
in the minds of G.	GREE 444:26
In the name of G., go!	AMERY 16:69
Inclines to think there is a G.	CLOU 270:36
indurate heart against G.	KNOX 567:58
infants are trying to spell G.	ROBI 815:29
intellectual love of G.	SPIN 961:59
interpret G.'s will	RUNC 828:52
Invisible, except to G. alone	MILT 689:44
Is G. by definition indifferent	EBER 359:11
jealous G.	BIBLE 106:68
Jesus never claims to be G.	ROBI 815:38
Just are the ways of G.	MILT 694:45
just die, G. willing	RULFO 828:50
Just what G. would do	WOOL 1094:92
justify G.'s ways to man	HOUS 495:63
justify the ways of G. to men	MILT 687:86
kick in the pants to G.	MILL 677:15
kills the image of G.	MILT 685:55
kingdom of G. is within you	BIBLE 144:9
know that I am G.	BOOK 177:74
know the mind of G.	HAWK 461:63
label men for G.	THOM 1014:33
laboratory of G.	WILL 1081:65
Lamb of G., I come!	ELLI 374:3
lay wrestling with...my G.	HOPK 492:2
leap up to my G.!	MARL 654:20
lend a myth to G.	CRANE 294:97
let me be awake, my G.!	COLE 274:97
light...the shadow of G.	BROW 196:5
like a G. in pain	KEATS 546:88
living G. who made all things	FOX 400:74
Lord G. made them all	ALEX 13:17
Lord G. of Sabaoth	BOOK 173:93
Lord G., we ha' paid	KIPL 562:55
Lord is G. indeed	SCOT 856:22

god (*contd.*)

Lord thy G. am a jealous G.	BOOK 174:17
Lord thy G. is a jealous G.	BIBLE 108:91
love of Man and in praise of G.	THOM 1011:76
love the Lord Thy G.	BIBLE 139:34
man G. hates	DOWL 342:79
man's bedevilment and G.'s	HOUS 496:74
man's distinctive mark...Not G.'s	BROW 200:80
Man's word is G. in man	TENN 1003:33
may G. help us	BETH 99:23
may G. set me there	JOAN 522:28
May G. wither up their hearts!	DAVIS 309:36
men that G. made mad	CHES 259:19
mercy o' my soul, Lord G.	MACD 628:98
more just than G.?	BIBLE 112:1
My G. and King	HERB 474:10
My G. must have my best	HERB 476:36
my G. what an eye!	CEZA 248:6
my G., why hast thou forsaken me?	BIBLE 114:47
my G., why hast thou forsaken me?	BIBLE 140:55
My Lord and my G.	BIBLE 147:77
my spirit hath rejoiced in G.	BIBLE 141:75
nature of G.	WHIT 1071:61
neither doth G. respect any person	BIBLE 110:49
no power but of G.	BIBLE 149:38
noble work of G.	BURNS 209:66
noblest work of G.	POPE 781:50
not afraid of G.	POPE 782:89
not G., is greater	WHIT 1072:81
Not only is there no G.	ALLEN 14:36
not rich toward G.	BIBLE 143:94
not that we loved G.	BIBLE 156:93
not three G.s: but one G.	BOOK 174:3
not yet G.	THOR 1016:64
not...a supremely good G.	DESC 318:82
now with G.	WALT 1052:8
O Christ, O G.	HOPK 491:81
O city of G.	BIBLE 117:96
O G. in Heaven	ANON 22:80
O G. of battles	SHAK 881:95
O G. of Bethel!	DODD 335:45
O G., our help	WATTS 1055:58
O G.! Put back	JONES 533:52
O Lord my G. I hope	STUA 980:10
O my G., Take the gentle path	HERB 476:37
obedience to G.	DAVI 309:42
obey G. rather than men	BIBLE 147:85
observed by Yours faithfully, G.	ANON 25:35
Of all G.'s works	SPEN 958:12
Oh G.! that man	MELV 668:43
Oh, G.! that men would see	BRAC 183:71
oily man of G.	THOM 1015:53
old abusing of G.'s patience	SHAK 878:11
One G., one law	TENN 1000:63
One man with G.	KNOX 567:59
one that would circumvent G.	SHAK 893:75
Only G., my dear	YEATS 1106:86
only make a sacrifice to G.	POPE 779:17
only men could serve G.	STEI 967:65
order of G. and of nature	MANN 646:95
out of the mouth of G.	BIBLE 133:29
owe G. a death	SHAK 877:98
paltered with Eternal G.	TENN 1000:70
person to worship G.	ROOS 822:43
play only Bach in praising G.	BARTH 74:69
pleased G. hitherto to bestow	HOBB 482:37
Praise G., from whom	KEN 549:48
prepare to meet thy G.	BIBLE 130:59
presume not G. to scan	POPE 780:42
prey I G. that non	CHAU 254:15
prime work of G.	MILT 694:47
Prompt me, G.	THOM 1013:23
prove G. statistically	GALL 413:99
prove that G. does not exist	LABR 573:58

god (*contd.*)

pure in heart...shall see G.	BIBLE 133:34
Put your trust in G.	BLAC 165:48
reason and the will of G.	ARNO 39:25
reason, it is playing G.	LEGU 594:32
recognize G. without Jesus	PASC 758:76
remembered my G.!	SOUT 954:30
reserved only for G.	BACON 55:16
riddles of...the purposes of G.	FRYE 408:24
rouse G. to relent	EBER 359:10
Rowing Towards G.	SEXT 860:69
same G. which worketh all in all	BIBLE 150:61
same relation to G.	UPDI 1037:57
saw the face of G.	MARL 654:14
saw the Spirit of G.	BIBLE 133:28
security...in our relationship with G.	EDDI 360:19
sees...as G. of all	POPE 780:35
Servant of G. well done	MILT 691:76
servant of the Living G.	SMART 944:66
shalt not tempt the Lord thy G.	BIBLE 133:30
sinning against G.	BOTHA 180:33
sufficiency is of G.	BIBLE 151:75
suppose even G. was born	LOWE 617:4
Surprising G....in a wink of time	BERR 99:19
sways G. nearby	BERR 98:8
sword without G.'s authority	LUTH 620:48
talk of the death of G.	FACK 382:49
Teach me, my G. and King	HERB 475:13
thank G. for my sanguine	MURP 715:70
thank G. he has spared me	BELL 87:4
thank G., Doctor	STAN 962:84
thank G.?	THOM 1011:86
that is really your G.	LUTH 620:50
their English G. is not so dominant	CARR 237:14
There G. is dwelling too	BLAKE 166:65
there is no G.!	ONEI 739:50
There is no G.	BIBLE 114:36
There is no G.	CLOU 270:35
thinks little of G.	PLUT 775:36
this man was the Son of G.	BIBLE 141:71
Those who know G.	PATM 760:8
Those who marry G.	GREE 444:15
Those whom G. hath joined	BOOK 176:52
thou art G.	BIBLE 117:97
Thou shalt have one G. only	CLOU 271:46
three-personed G.	DONNE 338:7
through darkness up to G.	TENN 999:40
Thus G. and nature linked	POPE 781:47
thy G. my G.	BIBLE 109:25
To G. I speak Spanish	CHAR 253:90
to G. Or to each other	MILT 693:14
To The Unknown G.	BIBLE 148:1
To whom...will ye liken G.?	BIBLE 126:89
trust G.	BROW 199:75
trust in G.	DENN 316:60
trust in G.	SMITH 949:48
unknown to anyone but G.	PLATO 774:1
Unlike G. the artist	PERCY 766:85
unto G. the things that are G.'s	BIBLE 139:32
up to Nature's G.	POPE 781:52
Verb is G.	HUGO 502:79
Very G. of very G.	BOOK 174:19
vindicate the ways of G. to man	POPE 780:33
vision of holiness of G.	BLOOM 170:36
voice of G.	ALCU 12:3
voice of G.	POPE 782:81
wait at G.'s right hand	GURN 449:91
walking...and praising G.	BIBLE 147:83
was G. out there	LEIS 595:42
waste of G.	STUD 980:14
We need to find G.	THER 1009:39
weigh your G. and you	KIPL 562:66
What G. abandoned	HOUS 496:78
What G. hath cleansed	BIBLE 148:92

god (*contd.*)

what G. hath given us	TAYL 992:21
what G. would have done	KAUF 543:17
What hath G. wrought!	BIBLE 108:87
what is a mind without G.?	PRAT 788:22
What therefore G. hath joined	BIBLE 139:22
What was good for G.'s birds	HARDY 457:3
Whatever is, is in G.	SPIN 960:47
When G. at first made man	HERB 476:34
When G. hands you a gift	CAPO 231:84
When G. hath made	TENN 999:37
Where G.'s presence is no longer	STEI 967:67
Where is now thy G.?	BOOK 176:72
White people…deal more with G.	GIOV 428:38
Who trusted G.	TENN 999:32
Who trusted G.	TENN 999:41
whose G. is their belly	BIBLE 153:13
why G. created women?	WALL 1049:61
wild G. of the world	JEFF 519:83
will of G.	JOHN 522:32
wind thrashes G.	HUID 503:95
with G. all things are possible	BIBLE 139:26
with G.'s favour	WALT 1052:2
Word was with G.	BIBLE 144:24
words which he of G.	LANY 580:79
works of G. in heav'n	MILT 693:30
worship of G.	WHIT 1071:56
worship Sunday, not G.	BLYT 170:53
worship the Lord thy G.	BIBLE 133:31
would G. this flesh	SWIN 987:29
Would to G. that we were dead	WILDE 1075:27
ye believe in G.	BIBLE 146:60
Yellow G. forever gazes down	HAYES 462:92
Yet her conception of G.	STRA 979:95
You don't fire G.	KENN 552:95
Zion, city of our G.!	NEWT 725:43

God-conditioned G.-c. forms — MANN 645:81

God-gifted G.-g. organ-voice — TENN 1003:24

god-given g.-g. (though not to me) — PALEY 751:62

god-like G.-l. hours — WORD 1096:28

God-like G.-l. erect, with native — MILT 690:54

goddamn G. is the base — BEAU 80:65

goddess blind g. in the lottery — ASTU 43:99

Chaste g.	ROMA 821:27
g. is better than no g.	WARN 1053:24
G. of the Battle	BARK 71:19
G. sage and holy	MILT 682:6
never saw a g. go	SHAK 915:92

godfather always a g. — WOOL 1094:91

godhead Buddha, the G. — PIRS 770:51

g. in which all life is human — SHAW 923:76

Godhead godless decent g. people — ELIOT 370:18

godlike anything G. about God — MILL 678:35

dictates of his g. mind	OTWAY 746:76
endurance is g.	LONG 611:7
one of their g. qualities	MENC 670:83

godliness Cleanliness is next to G. — DICK 326:64

continual g.	BOOK 174:14
exercise which withdraweth from g.	STUB 980:11
g. is profitable unto all things	BIBLE 154:30
In cheerful g.	WORD 1096:38

godmother Cinderella's Fairy G. — DIOR 331:63

gods against all the g. of Egypt — BIBLE 106:61

alien people clutching their g.	ELIOT 369:4
Allotted by the G.	TENN 1003:30
angels would be g.	POPE 780:38
As flies…are we to the g.	SHAK 903:30
By the nine g. he swore	MACA 623:12
Concerning the g.	PROT 792:84
daughter of the g.	TENN 993:35
dish fit for the g.	SHAK 883:29
do not know much about g.	ELIOT 372:57
dreadful fiend of g.	SPEN 959:35
effigies of g. and goddesses	GILL 426:2

gods (*contd.*)

even the g. themselves struggle	SCHI 848:71
eye of the g.	WORD 1100:91
feel new g. in the flesh	LAWR 586:78
fit love for the g.	MILT 692:4
Give, your g.	DRYD 348:90
G. and men, we are all deluded	SHEL 932:71
g. are absent	MACN 637:40
g. are come down to us	BIBLE 148:94
g. are just	SHAK 904:47
g., employed for	LOWE 617:9
g. had made thee poetical	SHAK 886:9
g. recognized by the state	PLATO 773:2
G., that wanton in the air	LOVE 615:62
g. there morning	RUSK 831:13
g. will diet with me	SHAK 916:11
g.…without their worshippers	DURK 357:72
higher esteem among the g.	PLATO 774:7
In Mexico the g. ruled	COND 279:83
inspired by the g. inside	SAIN 837:89
joy reserved for the G.	CABE 224:78
Kings are earth's g.	SHAK 910:92
knowledge from the g.	WILS 1084:24
Land of lost g.	BYRON 219:76
like G. together	TENN 994:52
looks…dare the g.	MARL 652:86
makes G. by the dozen	MONT 702:71
man who would argue with the g.	MAIL 640:89
masculine invisibility makes g.	DUNN 356:51
men that strove with g.	TENN 995:61
nature of the g.?	SHAK 862:35
no other g. but me	BIBLE 106:68
Now g., stand up for bastards!	SHAK 902:1
on a par with the g.	SAPP 842:92
one day become g.	MILL 678:30
only g. should speak	ROET 819:97
Real are the dreams of G.	KEATS 546:76
reflected in its g.	SCHI 848:72
respect the same g. as themselves	DRAB 345:24
Sees G. with Daemons	POPE 782:95
Shall g. be said to thump	THOM 1010:59
shall not go after other g.	BIBLE 108:91
sinned against my g.	FORD 396:6
superior to the G.	CATU 245:62
tempest of the g.	MARL 653:92
The g. themselves	TENN 1003:22
The g. thought otherwise	VIRG 1045:84
there are innumerable g.	BURR 213:54
These be thy g., O Israel	BIBLE 107:71
these that were G.	SWIN 987:41
utterance of the early G.	KEATS 547:3
What men or G. are these?	KEATS 547:7
what the g. had given him	BEER 83:39
When G. were young	THOM 1012:97
When men make g.	ONEI 739:50
whom the g. love dies young	MENA 668:53
Whom the g. wish to destroy	CONN 283:61
will of the g.	AESC 9:55
ye g., you make the weak	SHAK 883:25
ye shall be as g.	BIBLE 103:94
your g. or your vegetables	GIRA 429:45

Goebbels inferno depicted by Dr G. — ORWE 743:16

going g. out and thy coming in — BIBLE 119:36

lead by g.	KESEY 554:22
long and loath at g.	RANS 802:35

goings established my g. — BIBLE 115:66

gold All the g. upon the earth — PLATO 774:12

apples of g. in pictures of silver	BIBLE 121:98
Beauty… like the g. standard	WOLF 1090:12
blood mixed with wasted g.	KING 559:6
bought and sold for English g.	BURNS 212:37
bow of burning g.!	BLAKE 168:19
burned g. was his colour	CHAU 255:45
but litel g. in cofre	CHAU 254:22

gold (*contd.*)

chain of g.	SCOTT 854:79
colour in Australia is g.	STRE 980:5
copper into g.	SENG 858:50
differs from g.	SHEL 931:53
envelopèd with g.	SPEN 958:10
eyes of g. and bramble-dew	STEV 976:55
Fetters of g.	ASTE 43:90
fly to India for g.	MARL 654:13
fly to India for g.	MARL 654:9
From the red g. keep thy finger	SCOTT 855:97
gild refinèd g.	SHAK 872:1
Glory, the grape, love, g.	BYRON 222:43
g. an' velvet	ANON 24:15
g., and frankincense, and myrrh	BIBLE 133:24
g. and silver becks me	SHAK 872:65
g. and silver	SHAK 916:11
G. Cadillac G.	TRUMP 1030:37
g. doth more than either	KYD 571:25
G. is the gift	GRIL 447:63
g. wes changyd in to lede	ANON 22:68
green tigering the g.	HUGH 500:38
Gross g. from them runs	MARL 655:30
He who hath the g.	ANON 29:34
head was of fine g.	BIBLE 129:45
If g. ruste	CHAU 254:25
Like g. to airy thinness beat	DONNE 337:91
More to be desired are they than g.	BIBLE 114:45
must be propped with g.	MAST 663:54
narrowing lust of g.	TENN 1000:57
never have too much g.	MORE 707:47
never owned his g.	LAFO 575:95
next, my g.!	JONS 534:74
Nor all that glisters g.	GRAY 441:54
patens of bright g.	SHAK 873:99
property turns sand to g.	YOUNG 1108:2
provoketh thieves sooner than g.	SHAK 885:74
pure g. flows	TOCQ 1022:82
rain of g.	DAYL 310:56
rarer gifts than g.	BROO 192:23
religion of g.	BAGE 61:55
sand and ruin and g.	SWIN 987:42
Silver and g. have I none	BIBLE 147:82
street of the city pure g.	BIBLE 159:37
There is g.	SHAK 905:76
think g. that is brass	SPEN 958:22
Thou gaudy g.	SHAK 873:83
tipped with g. for this	JONS 535:87
travell'd in the realms of g.	KEATS 544:32
wear g. on your hair	BALL 67:51
Wedges of g., great ouches	SHAK 863:54
What is bettre than g.?	CHAU 255:43
What use the g. place	FRAME 400:76
what's become of all the g.	BROW 198:48
When g. becomes her object!	SHAK 878:2
With g. …cover ev'ry part	POPE 778:80

golden cats with g. eyes — SACK 835:62

circle of the g. year	TENN 996:90
g. age in all the arts	VIDAL 1044:71
g. and silver	YEATS 1105:65
g. bowl be broken	BIBLE 123:42
g. cadence of poesy	SHAK 865:17
g. ear	POPE 779:23
g. foil all over them	SPEN 957:21
G. lads and girls	SHAK 916:16
g. rules for orchestras	BEEC 82:16
g. years return	SHEL 932:64
In the g. lightning	SHEL 929:91
Kissing the g. face	SHAK 913:59
poets only deliver a g.	SIDN 937:61
west to the G. Gate	KIPL 565:19

golden-calf g.-c. of self-love — CARL 235:70

golden-haired young Apollo, g.-h. — CORN 288:57

Goldengrove Over G. unleaving? — HOPK 492:92

goldsmith not in g.'s ware	MIDD 673:*39*	
Goldsmith G. tells us	AUST 52:*59*	
Here lies Nolly G.	GARR 415:*30*	
Swift is more Irish than G.	OBRI 733:*61*	
Goldwyn You talk of art Mr G.	SHAW 925:*33*	
golf American people than G. has	ROGE 820:*11*	
Be funny on a g. course?	SILV 938:*78*	
better he plays g.	WELLS 1065:*39*	
Fute-ball, G., or uther sik	JAME 515:*1*	
get it on the g. course	SKEL 942:*38*	
g. course is the epitome	GIRA 428:*43*	
g. game went bad	TREV 1026:*50*	
G. is a game	JONES 533:*51*	
G. is a good walk spoiled	TWAIN 1034:*23*	
G. is in the interest	TAFT 990:*83*	
G. is not…a fair game	NICK 726:*58*	
G. is so popular	MILNE 681:*83*	
G.…makes me so damned angry	GEOR 419:*87*	
g. may be played on a Sunday	LEAC 589:*42*	
g.…. way of playing marbles	CHES 260:*49*	
great game of g.	CROS 298:*61*	
intrepid hunters of g. balls	SMITH 947:*4*	
mind off everything like g.	ROGE 820:*23*	
Playing polo is like to play g.	STAL 962:*82*	
thousand lost g. balls	ELIOT 370:*18*	
unforgiving as g. greens	ELKIN 374:*98*	
when one is playing g.	LYND 621:*64*	
work at it, it's g.	HOPE 491:*74*	
golfer Actually, I am a g.	MATU 664:*83*	
gymnast and g., soldered together	BRYA 201:*16*	
make a g. out of him	HAGEN 450:*3*	
Goliath Nobody roots for G.	CHAM 249:*23*	
Gomorah rained upon…G.	BIBLE 105:*25*	
gondola What else is like the g.?	CLOU 270:*33*	
you have swam in a g.	SHAK 886:*19*	
gone all is g.	HOOD 489:*53*	
And they are g.	KEATS 547:*98*	
dead and g.	YEATS 1105:*70*	
dead and g., lady	SHAK 892:*61*	
g., and for ever!	SCOTT 854:*65*	
g. without a word?	SHAK 860:*76*	
Now thou art g.	MILT 684:*40*	
Or that when I am g.	LOVE 615:*64*	
They're all g. now	SYNGE 988:*61*	
gong-tormented g.-t. sea	YEATS 1106:*81*	
gongs struck regularly, like g.	COWA 290:*96*	
good aim at some g.	ARIS 34:*25*	
all men's g.	TENN 996:*90*	
All partial evil, universal g.	POPE 780:*41*	
all things work together for g.	BIBLE 149:*29*	
and when she was g.	LONG 612:*21*	
Any g. thing	GREL 446:*49*	
Anybody can be g. in the country	WILDE 1076:*54*	
art for the sake of the g.	SAND 840:*55*	
Be a g. man	SCOTT 856:*13*	
beautiful, creative and g.	MING 695:*63*	
because they are so g.	TROL 1028:*86*	
because we deem it g.	SPIN 960:*53*	
being really g. all the time	WILDE 1078:*87*	
Beneath the g. how far	GRAY 443:*92*	
better to be g. than to be ugly	WILDE 1076:*53*	
between g. and evil	HUSS 505:*36*	
but to be g.	STEV 974:*17*	
common g. to all	SHAK 884:*68*	
constitutes the highest g.	RUSS 832:*17*	
content…to be obscurely g.	ADDI 8:*34*	
Do all the g. you can	WESL 1067:*75*	
do g. in his life	BIBLE 122:*20*	
do him little g.	JOHN 527:*30*	
does no g.	GILM 427:*20*	
dull prospect of distant g.	DRYD 351:*54*	
enemy of the g.	VOLT 1046:*11*	
every evil, like every g.	SCHO 849:*94*	
every g. and excellent thing	WILD 1079:*27*	

good (*contd.*)		
Every soul pusues the g.	PLATO 774:*22*	
evil seek to bring forth g.	MILT 687:*96*	
evil turn to g.	MILT 693:*27*	
For g. ye are and bad	TENN 1003:*38*	
for the g. or evil side	LOWE 616:*78*	
for the general G.	WELLS 1064:*28*	
Gallop about doing g.	SMITH 948:*41*	
General G. is the plea	BLAKE 168:*8*	
glory and g. of Art	BROW 200:*95*	
God saw that it was g.	BIBLE 102:*85*	
God-willing, I will make g.	HITL 482:*31*	
g. almost kill a man as kill	MILT 685:*55*	
g. and bad of every land	BAIL 62:*71*	
g., and had no power to see	LANY 579:*77*	
g. and ill together	SHAK 901:*31*	
g. both going and coming back	FROST 406:*80*	
G., but not religious-good	HARDY 456:*84*	
G. company, g. wine, g. welcome	SHAK 917:*47*	
g. Compensate bad in man	BROW 200:*90*	
g. die early	DEFOE 312:*74*	
g. ended happily	WILDE 1078:*85*	
g. fast bowler	TRUE 1029:*15*	
g. For which to strive	MILT 688:*12*	
g. for your legs	SCHU 850:*12*	
G., great and joyous	SHEL 930:*27*	
G. grows with her	SHAK 918:*67*	
g., honest and painful	PEPYS 765:*63*	
g. in everything	SHAK 885:*77*	
g. is always a product of art	BAUD 78:*34*	
G. isn't the word	GILB 426:*1*	
g. men starve	DRYD 350:*43*	
g. must associate	BURKE 206:*1*	
g. never will be our task	MILT 687:*95*	
g. news baits	MILT 695:*55*	
g. of the land of Egypt	BIBLE 105:*48*	
g. of the people	CICE 266:*58*	
g. or they were bad	TRAV 1025:*36*	
G., pleasure, ease, content	POPE 781:*49*	
g. that I would I do not	BIBLE 149:*23*	
G. Time was Had By All	SMITH 948:*29*	
G., to forgive	BROW 200:*99*	
g. to know the worst	BRAD 184:*92*	
g. to some man	SHAW 920:*7*	
g. turns out to be	ARIS 34:*26*	
g. we oft might win	SHAK 896:*63*	
great harm and great g.	HESI 479:*83*	
great instrument of moral g.	SHEL 931:*57*	
greatest g. of the mind	SPIN 960:*56*	
He wos wery g. to me	DICK 325:*27*	
hear all g. things said about you	BOUC 180:*39*	
hear more g.	HAZL 463:*4*	
heav'n sees g.	MILT 684:*34*	
hold fast that which is g.	BIBLE 153:*26*	
if we were very g.	FULF 409:*31*	
If ye think g.	BIBLE 130:*68*	
intuitive knowledge of g.	SPIN 960:*58*	
It does g. though	JULI 539:*68*	
It is always g.	BEAU 80:*68*	
it must be g.	HOCK 483:*48*	
it would be a g. idea	GAND 414:*15*	
kills the very g.	HEMI 470:*19*	
knowing g. and evil	BIBLE 103:*91*	
knowing the g.	GRIS 447:*68*	
knowledge of g. and evil	MILT 685:*58*	
knowledge of g. and evil	MILT 685:*58*	
Knowledge of g. bought dear	MILT 690:*52*	
learning things that are g.	HERN 476:*46*	
'Leave…while you're looking g.'	LOOS 613:*29*	
lies precisely the greatest g.	ROUS 827:*33*	
lives not three g. men	SHAK 876:*54*	
make bad g.	SHAK 897:*86*	
Man is neither g. nor evil	BALZ 69:*83*	
men most g.	SHAK 872:*68*	

good (*contd.*)		
never has it so g.	MACM 635:*6*	
never known much g. done	SMITH 945:*81*	
no for ony g. or ill	BURNS 209:*61*	
no g. in arguing	LOWE 616:*89*	
noble type of g.	LONG 612:*14*	
none that doeth g.	BIBLE 114:*37*	
none that doeth g.	BOOK 176:*64*	
not g. enough yourself	TROL 1027:*75*	
not g. enough	GALS 413:*3*	
not necessary…that the world is g.	CONR 285:*2*	
not quite so g.	GALT 413:*7*	
nothing either g. or bad	SHAK 889:*98*	
nothing g. to be had	HAZL 463:*97*	
Nothing is fair or g. alone	EMER 376:*28*	
nothing so bad or so g.	SHAW 920:*11*	
O ye wha are sae g.	BURNS 210:*82*	
only one g., knowledge	SOCR 952:*91*	
only read what is truly g.	STEIN 966:*65*	
only time it isn't g. for you	HEMI 470:*30*	
overcome evil with g.	BIBLE 149:*37*	
preferred to be g.	SALL 839:*38*	
remained stupidly g.	MILT 692:*3*	
rise on the evil and on the g.	BIBLE 134:*45*	
shall he not make it g.?	BIBLE 108:*86*	
shall not want any g. thing	BIBLE 115:*61*	
sick one gets of being 'g.'	JAMES 515:*5*	
single thing that is g.	GALL 412:*93*	
some g. thing comes tomorrow	SHAK 877:*3*	
some special g. doth give	SHAK 869:*95*	
something g. about someone	LONG 612:*22*	
still rich in genial g.	WORD 1097:*43*	
strong antipathy of g. to bad	POPE 782:*88*	
suffer for the G.	KIER 556:*56*	
teach…of g.	WORD 1094:*3*	
tell someone how g.	KNUD 567:*64*	
That is indeed very g.	HOUS 496:*85*	
That was very g. of him	KAUN 543:*23*	
The g. want power	SHEL 930:*17*	
the national g.	PANK 753:*82*	
They love the G.	BROO 192:*29*	
think something is g. or bad	STEV 972:*79*	
To believe in 'the greater g.'	DIDI 330:*48*	
too much of a g. thing?	SHAK 887:*22*	
what g. came of it	SOUT 954:*31*	
what we like is not necessarily g.	BELL 86:*85*	
what were g. to be done	SHAK 874:*11*	
what you feel g. after	HEMI 470:*23*	
What's the g. of a home	GROS 447:*71*	
When I'm g.	WEST 1067:*79*	
When it sounds g., it is g.	ELLI 374:*4*	
where g. men rest	FLEC 393:*48*	
whoso hath this world's g.	BIBLE 156:*91*	
ye're just no a g. man	KELM 549:*34*	
You're g., you're real g.	HUST 505:*38*	
good-for-nothing g.-f.-n. woman	SHAW 923:*69*	
good-looking all the men are g.-l.	KEIL 548:*25*	
good-morning G.-m, g.-m.!	SASS 845:*28*	
good-morrow bade g.-m.	KEATS 545:*61*	
good-mother almost as bad, g.-m.	SHAK 892:*51*	
good-nature keep her g.-n.	SCOTT 856:*10*	
good-tempered g.-t.…young woman	AUST 50:*9*	
Good Friday soldest him on G. F.	SHAK 875:*40*	
goodbye as you wave me g.	PARR 756:*42*	
G. Mr Zanuck	RENO 806:*6*	
G. to All That	GRAV 439:*18*	
goodly g. to look to	BIBLE 110:*37*	
goodman g. of the house	BIBLE 140:*40*	
goodness all my g. pass before thee	BIBLE 107:*77*	
crownest the year with thy g.	BIBLE 116:*84*	
distinguished from ordinary g.	STOWE 978:*83*	
fountain of all g.	BOOK 176:*55*	
Galumphing G.!	TRAV 1025:*35*	
g. and mercy shall follow me	BIBLE 115:*50*	

goodness (*contd.*)
g. in things evil	SHAK 881:90
g. infinite, g. immense!	MILT 693:27
g. never fearful	SHAK 897:84
g. of your mechanics	MOORE 705:21
G. what beautiful diamonds!	WEST 1067:10
If g. lead him not	HERB 476:35
odor…from g. tainted	THOR 1016:76
The powerful g. want	SHEL 930:17
Wealth does not bring g.	PLATO 773:3

goodnight gay g. YEATS 1106:81
G. Ensured release	HOUS 496:84
say g. till it be morrow	SHAK 869:93
till our last g.	PEAC 762:31

goods all my g. to feed the poor BIBLE 150:62
Bill of G.	MORR 709:83
boat…had the g. of a house	PEPYS 765:81
community lacks g.	CHUR 263:99
consumption of valuable g.	VEBL 1041:29
g. and her gear	COLUM 278:60
g. and trappings of your life	MOORE 704:2
g. do not spontaneously present	ECON 360:16
g.…procured by labour	RICA 808:35
g.…produced jointly with bads	BOUL 181:44
Labour does not only create g.	MARX 661:26
power of purchasing other g.	SMITH 946:94
with all my worldly g.	BOOK 176:51

goose every g. a swan KING 558:94
g. because you like pâté	LINK 606:26
No g., no golden egg	TSON 1031:42
on the ground at G. Green	KINN 559:11

goosecap g. and…no judgement NASHE 721:78
goose-hiss dumb g.-h. of the wives THOM 1011:87
goosie Ridin' on a g.? ANON 24:2
Gorbachev G. has 100…advisers GORB 435:60
I like Mr G.	THAT 1008:18

gore g. no more, they bellow LIND 606:18
mayn't be human g.	DICK 322:62
Smeared with g. and ghastly pale	GRAY 443:82

gored fame is shrewdly g. SHAK 896:54
tossed and g. several persons	BOSW 180:30

gorge into the narrow g., unseen WILL 1083:95
My g. rises at it	SHAK 893:77

gorgon taught his g. destinies to sing CAMP 227:20
gorgonised G. me from head TENN 1001:83
gorry by g. by jingo by gee CUMM 299:83
gory Never shake Thy g. locks SHAK 909:61
gospel based on the G. JOHN 523:37
Christian g. is the knowledge	NIEB 727:64
G. of Getting On	SHAW 920:10
light of the g.	JOHN 527:23
not ashamed of the g. of Christ	BIBLE 148:11
preach the g.	BIBLE 141:72
preach'd a G.	TENN 1005:65
receptive to the g.	RUET 828:47
spirit of the g.	JOHN 522:31
wolves whose g.	MILT 686:80

gospels canonical g. do not record FORS 399:57
teachings of the G.	KHRU 556:51

gossip G. is a sort of smoke ELIOT 366:42
G. is the opiate	JONG 534:65
juicy piece of g.	HELL 468:92
pines are g. pines	FLEC 393:52
roving woman gives rise to g.	ANON 21:57

gossiping telling jokes or g. CABR 224:81
gothic burst into G. cathedrals SHEEN 926:50
G. cathedrals…supreme creation	BART 74:79
G. structure, the impenetrable	EDGE 361:32
old one of G. windows	KORN 568:81

gout chide my palsy, or my g. DONNE 337:79
govern administer is to g. MIRA 696:70
have to to g. afterwards	HUGH 499:24
He that would g. others	MASS 662:53
intellect will always g.	WOLL 1091:33

govern (*contd.*)
Right…of Kings to g.	POPE 783:4
Those that g. most	SELD 857:36

governance g. of Ronald Reagan BAKER 63:86
governed g. by no other sway MONT 703:91
g. by the mob	GREN 446:54
g. by the pull	MOORE 705:28
one of the most g. people	EDIN 361:39

governess woman who cannot be a g. OLIP 738:25
governesses If neither g. or mothers DAVI 307:3
government 25 years of Labour g. BEVAN 101:62
administration of the g.	SWIFT 984:83
against every G. on earth	JEFF 520:91
agencies of central g.	HUXL 508:87
All forms of g. fall	LEWIS 601:49
all g.…founded on compromise	BURKE 207:14
all g. without consent	SWIFT 984:78
all of them branches of g.	MILL 675:67
ANC is a G. in waiting	MAND 644:69
art of g.	SHAW 922:45
ask me what a free g. is	BURKE 207:18
At the head of g.	PETA 767:5
attachment to their g.	BURKE 207:12
best politics is good g.	STEV 973:87
British g. and…colonial population	SCHL 848:73
Canada…enjoyed: English g.	COLO 277:52
checks and balances in g.	ANON 28:17
corruption in any g.	BRUN 201:10
Democracy means g. by discussion	ATTL 44:14
Democracy…g. by the uneducated	CHES 260:43
Do not criticize your G.	CHUR 265:48
duty of g.	PAINE 750:45
employees of the g.	TOOLE 1023:6
Every line in the g.'s budget	WRIS 1102:22
every man…under a G.	RAIN 800:6
expect from his G.	TRUM 1029:17
face a British G.	TUCH 1031:45
fainéant g.	TROL 1028:82
false system of g.	PAINE 750:46
faults of a G.	ROOS 821:37
fear that the Russian g.	HERZ 478:74
federal g. does basically	WILL 1080:43
feeble g.	JOHN 525:76
first object of g.	MADI 638:55
form of native g.	ONEI 739:47
Freedom of men under g.	LOCKE 609:70
frightening views of g.	INOU 512:58
giving money to the G.	HERB 474:96
G. …a necessary evil	PAINE 750:44
G. and co-operation	RUSK 830:92
g. and report the facts	ROGE 820:22
g. and the people	MILL 674:56
G. cannot endure…half-slave	LINC 604:98
G. contrivance of human wisdom	BURKE 207:30
g. doesn't work	OROU 741:81
g. funding for…comic strips	UPDI 1037:62
G. has no other end	LOCKE 609:68
g. I despise	KEYN 554:25
g. is far funnier than we are	BUCH 202:31
G. is like everything	MONT 702:83
G. looks with favour	BALF 65:17
g. may…withdraw…troops	REDM 804:75
G.…must fall	DRYD 350:27
g. of a woman	BACON 60:37
g. of laws	ADAMS 5:84
G. of strongest interests	CALH 225:96
g. of the people	LINC 605:4
G. of which Harrow	BALD 65:15
g.…reflections on human nature	MADI 638:56
g. representatives in the affairs	NICH 726:50
g. shall be upon his shoulder	BIBLE 125:66
g. subsidized commission	KRUT 570:2
g. subsidy	ANON 29:40
g. which imprisons any	THOR 1016:65

government (*contd.*)
g. without newspapers	JEFF 520:88
greatest blessings which a g.	MACA 622:87
having looked to g. for bread	BURKE 208:45
help from a g. agency	STEIN 966:49
highest form of g.	SPEN 956:69
husband, like a g.	BALZ 68:70
In the councils of g.	EISE 364:88
influence of a g.	REES 805:92
kept in sober g.	SPEN 958:12
land of settled g.	TENN 996:89
live under one form of g.	JOHN 528:50
machinery of the G.	MONT 700:51
meddling with the g.	LEST 599:13
monarchy…intelligible g.	BAGE 61:59
most important job in G.	GARN 415:28
no art which one g.	SMITH 945:87
no British g. should be brought	MACM 635:10
No G. can be long secure	DISR 332:80
no g., church, corporation	OAKE 733:49
No g. has the right	BROWN 194:58
No g. is going to take from me	MACL 633:67
not one that g. can indulge in	RENO 806:4
only good g.…is a bad one	CARY 243:22
only two kinds of g.	DAFOE 303:39
operations of g.	RUNC 828:51
pretend to obey a G.	RUSS 833:32
prying meddlesome G.	MACA 624:22
relations of a weak G.	REED 805:91
revolution than a g.	MARC 649:45
see the g. get out of the war	HELL 468:85
sister is given to g.	DICK 326:66
so pleased to be in the G.	BAXT 78:49
stability to a popular G.	WHIT 1069:17
studied as a branch of g.	JAY 519:73
take from such G.	PAINE 750:47
The foundation of the g.	SUN 982:39
The object of g.	BEVE 102:73
two ideas of g.	BRYAN 201:14
want of g. is any new kind of g.	HOBB 483:41
What your g. believes	KENN 552:93
whatever the G. and public allow	SHAW 921:59
who understands g.	TRUM 1030:25
wish the G. would put a tax	SITW 941:21
worst form of G.	CHUR 265:32
would be great in our little g.	ROCH 816:57

governmental g. machinery SPEN 956:68
governments All g. use force PARE 753:83
climates, councils, g.	TENN 994:58
G. care for…security of property	PANK 752:79
g. have never learned anything	HEGEL 466:63
G. need…shepherds	VOLT 1047:16
Kings and G. may err	HERB 474:97
most despotic of infidel G.	BYRON 221:9
not to form g.	KING 557:71
nothing new in Third World g.	AUNG 50:22
strong mutually antagonistic g.	WAUGH 1056:80

governor Can't afford them, G. SHAW 924:5
G. of the Bank of England	HOWE 497:94
g. of the Bank of England	KORDA 568:79
G. was strong upon	WILDE 1078:99
I'd be a terrific g.	HILL 270:24

Governor-General save G.-G. WHIT 1072:71
governors whereof ye are the g. MILT 686:73
governs see how well she g. SIXT 942:31
gowd man's the g. BURNS 213:42
gowk be a conceited g. HOGG 485:66
gown dressed in a new g. HUME 503:7
ease a heart Like a satin g.	PARK 753:91
for an almsman's g.	SHAK 867:62
g. and mossy cell	MILT 683:16
g. of glory	RALE 800:13
wrap me in a g.	HERB 475:14

gowns priests in black g. BLAKE 167:91

Goya one small G. AUDEN 46:54
Gracchi Who can bear the G. JUVE 540:78
grace Amazing G.! How sweet NEWT 725:42
  Being and Ideal G. BROW 197:19
  better deeds…to g. it SHAK 860:76
  but for the g. of God, goes God CHUR 265:49
  by g. divine WORD 1100:89
  by the g. of God I am BIBLE 151:65
  Cheap g. is g. without discipleship BONH 173:83
  deprived me of your g. and favour SHAK 902:99
  divine g. cleansed…me ABEL 1:3
  except through g. PASC 757:55
  fallen from g. BIBLE 152:90
  for heaven's g. and boon KEATS 546:92
  full of g. and truth BIBLE 144:27
  glad g. YEATS 1105:60
  God shed his g. BATES 76:10
  G. be unto you BIBLE 156:96
  g. beyond recognition REID 806:97
  g. did much more abound BIBLE 149:19
  G. from that g. LANY 580:81
  G. is given of God CLOU 270:30
  g. is sufficient for thee BIBLE 152:87
  g. of accuracy LOWE 617:14
  g. of its external VIEI 1044:75
  g. of our Lord Jesus Christ BIBLE 159:40
  g. of Terpsichore BARR 73:56
  g. under pressure HEMI 470:20
  g. us in the disgrace SHAK 865:4
  g. was short PRIOR 791:57
  grows eke greater g. SPEN 958:9
  had at least the g. BENT 93:29
  If I am not in g. JOAN 522:28
  into g. againe FLET 394:77
  inward and spiritual g. BOOK 175:39
  it is not man…made g. POUND 786:84
  lend her g. TENN 994:47
  life itself is g. BUEC 203:42
  means of g. BOOK 174:8
  motions all accompanied with g. DRYD 349:6
  nature and the living g. POPE 778:80
  Never mind my g., lassie SCOTT 855:94
  novel…it's a g. MAIL 640:91
  O mickle is the powerful g. SHAK 869:95
  Observe his honour, or his g. DONNE 337:79
  pity g. obtain SIDN 937:50
  something of a g. WORD 1097:41
  such a lovely g. SIDN 937:56
  sweet attractive g. MILT 690:55
  tabernacles of thy g. SCOT 856:21
  To win her g. MILT 682:3
  unbought g. of life BURKE 207:32
  what g. he throws FLEC 393:50
  wordy of a g. BURNS 210:84
graces deficiency in the g. JOHN 530:88
  g. slighted, blossom on the tomb CRAB 294:80
  G.…not natives of Great Britain CHES 257:78
  no time for the fine g. SMITH 946:2
  number all your g. SHAK 912:47
gracious Oh, my G., Glorious TRAV 1025:35
grades various g. of culture NIET 729:93
gradual Was the g. day SPEN 956:73
gradualness inevitability of g. WEBB 1059:18
graduate g. from Canada FULF 409:31
  than to be a g. HARDY 457:4
graft opportunity for g. BIRNS 163:27
Grafton Hungry G. ANON 26:56
grain amber waves of g. BATES 76:10
  beside a field of g. PARK 755:29
  Divine…in a g. of sand FRIE 405:58
  full ripened g. KEATS 544:49
  g. of sense DRYD 350:43
  guano and on g. TENN 996:95
  Rot half a g. a day SHAK 900:59

grain (*contd.*)
  the g. and hammer HEAN 465:43
  well meant for g. TENN 998:20
  which g. will grow SHAK 907:17
grains two g. of wheat SHAK 874:9
grammar don't want to talk g. SHAW 924:3
  down to posterity talking bad g. DISR 334:30
  erecting a g. school SHAK 861:15
  g. is to the art of the writer APOL 32:91
  kings must bow to g. MOLI 699:31
  mystical g. of amorous glances CLEV 269:10
  mystical g. of amorous glances CLEV 269:10
  never made a mistake in g. SAND 841:68
  Once the g. has been learnt BAIN 62:73
  readers must take such g. MACA 623:99
  To be loose with g. EDWA 362:54
  Why care for g. WARD 1053:17
  With g., and nonsense GOLD 433:21
grammars What sairs your G. BURNS 209:58
gramophone puts a record on the g. ELIOT 369:90
granaries guard our master's g. WILDE 1075:27
grand but never g. HEAT 465:48
  g., the barbarous, the savage DIDE 329:30
  petal down the G. Canyon MARQ 656:47
  the g. manner POUS 787:99
grandchild little g. Wilhelmine SOUT 954:31
grandeur baldness full of g. ARNO 40:42
  g. in this view of life DARW 306:84
  g. of the dooms KEATS 545:57
  g. that was Rome POE 776:47
  G.…with disdainful smile GRAY 442:66
  little bit of g. is gone ANON 27:73
  old Scotia's g. BURNS 209:66
  sort of g. creeps into it MENC 670:91
  with the g. of God HOPK 491:82
grandfather who his g. is WALC 1048:33
grandfathers friends with its g. MUMF 713:45
grandma g.'s maiden name BERE 94:36
grandmama dear G. died GEOR 419:84
grandmother child of our g. Eve SHAK 865:11
  day my g. exploded BANKS 70:97
  g. actually smelled like a cookie BAIL 62:69
  have become a g. THAT 1008:26
  look…back to the g. EDGE 361:38
  may not marry his G. BOOK 178:2
  sell his g. GRANT 438:3
grandmothers careful g. DICK 321:33
grandsire heard my g. say SHAK 862:42
  your g. cut his throat SWIFT 984:80
grandstands retire to the g. GERG 420:2
granite monoliths made of g. MENC 670:89
  Of shadowy g. TENN 994:49
Grannie G. remarked FRAN 402:15
Grant Old Cary G. fine GRANT 438:1
granted as God g. it QUIL 797:56
  taking things for g. HUXL 507:81
grape blood of g. BLAKE 165:59
  Glory, the g., love, gold BYRON 222:43
  no g. that's kindly ripe SUCK 981:21
  peel me a g. WEST 1067:80
grapes sour g. and ashes ASHF 41:69
  where the g. of wrath HOWE 497:98
grapeshot car…seems to ride on g. MARI 651:67
  whiff of g. CARL 235:62
graphical g. representation of data GIBS 422:40
grapple G. them to thy soul SHAK 888:63
grasp should exceed his g. BROW 199:61
grass a blade of g. stuck WODE 1089:90
  books…like green g. WELTY 1065:50
  burn the old g. POL 777:61
  causeth the g. to grow BIBLE 118:16
  dappled g. YEATS 1105:63
  days are as g. BIBLE 118:15
  destroy a blade of g. BOTT 180:36

grass (*contd.*)
  eat g. as oxen BIBLE 129:47
  eateth g. as an ox BIBLE 113:24
  emerald twinkles in the g. TENN 1001:84
  fall on g. MARV 658:85
  G. and trees wither WU 1102:24
  g., and a hare sitting up LAWR 585:70
  g. as soft as…doves CORN 288:58
  g. grew longer LEE 593:18
  g. grows on the weirs YEATS 1104:56
  g. is singing ELIOT 369:95
  g., it grew as scant BROW 198:50
  g., so springlike ABSE 1:6
  g. will grow in the streets HOOV 490:57
  g. withereth BIBLE 155:76
  g. withereth, the flower fadeth BIBLE 126:85
  green g. above me ROSS 824:76
  greenness of the g. MARV 658:81
  happy as the g. was green THOM 1010:65
  heard by snakes in the g. MO 698:8
  hearing the g. grow ELIOT 366:37
  I am the g. SAND 841:62
  indicates that… g. is green STEP 968:79
  isn't g. to graze a cow BETJ 99:31
  kissed the lovely g. BROO 192:17
  know the g. beyond ROSS 824:84
  moonlight lying on the g. THOM 1012:3
  not dead but feed the g. TATE 991:7
  only beautiful if it has good g. BUTL 217:28
  paler than g. SAPP 842:92
  Pigeons on the g. STEIN 965:35
  Please Walk on the G. THOM 1014:42
  rustling of the g. WORD 1099:65
  showers upon the g. BIBLE 108:1
  snake lurks in the g. VIRG 1045:90
  soft wind brathing through the g. BRON 192:15
  splendour in the g. WORD 1098:55
  star-scattered on the g. FITZ 390:91
  the g. the polyanthus cheques SMART 944:68
  thin g. clothed them THOM 1013:99
  two blades of g. SWIFT 985:85
  wan g. sea SITW 941:15
grass-growing silent g.-g. mood MELV 668:47
grasshopper afraid as a g.? BIBLE 113:22
  g. shall be a burden BIBLE 123:42
grasshoppers g. with triumphing ROBE 814:16
  in our own sight as g. BIBLE 107:82
grateful g. at last for a little thing TENN 1002:93
  g. to the CLF STEW 977:63
  none more g. WORD 1095:17
  revolution must be g. LEGU 594:31
gratification g. of your wishes SHEL 926:51
gratify g. some people TWAIN 1034:17
gratis endanger my soul g.? SHAK 878:14
gratitude g. is a species JOHN 525:88
  G. looks to the past LEWIS 601:38
  vulgar g. to you DICK 324:26
gratuitous prophecy is the most g. ELIOT 366:33
grave Alcestis from the g. MILT 687:82
  amaranth on this side of the g. LAND 578:60
  A Page, a G. POPE 783:2
  bed…the cold, cold g. BALL -101:35
  birth astride of a g. BECK 81:99
  bring down my gray hairs…to the g. BIBLE 105:46
  broken-hearted woman tends the g. HAYES 462:92
  cold in the dreary g.! BRON 191:9
  cradle to the g. ANON 29:40
  cradle to the g. BREC 186:26
  Dark as the G. LOWRY 618:20
  darkness of the g. MILL 676:90
  dig the g. and let me STEV 975:31
  Duncan is in his g. SHAK 909:58
  dusty to the g. STEV 974:21
  even the g. yawns for him TREE 1025:41

grave (*contd.*)

foolish tears upon my g.	TENN 998:14
from the cradle to the g.	SHEL 930:26
Funeral marches to the g.	LONG 611:95
gift of a g.	SHAK 893:95
go down into the g....mourning	BIBLE 105:41
g.'s a fine and private	MARV 658:74
g. and serious	GILB 426:96
g. is ghastly	ANON 21:59
g. is not its goal	LONG 611:94
g. keeps bodies	DONNE 338:15
g.'s narrowness	GRAV 439:19
g. of Christianity	ELIOT 370:21
G. where is thy Victory?	BUNY 205:74
g., where is thy victory?	BIBLE 151:73
heaped its g.	CRANE 294:91
humours, whether g. or mellow	ADDI 7:10
in the cold g. leave	WEBS 1059:29
in the dark and silent g.	RALE 800:16
jealousy is cruel as the g.	BIBLE 124:55
large kingdom for a little g.	SHAK 867:62
learned the secrets of the g.	PATER 759:93
Longfellow's g. or the glass	MOORE 705:19
lower me into the g.	LEE 593:14
made his g. with the wicked	BIBLE 127:2
made me a g. so rough	TENN 1002:92
Marriage is the g. or tomb of wit	CAVE 246:72
mysterious East...dark like a g.	CONR 284:97
No repose...but in the g.	SCOTT 856:17
no work...in the g.	BIBLE 123:34
now in his colde g.	CHAU 255:32
O'Leary in the g.	YEATS 1105:70
on that g. where English oak	HARTE 460:52
on the way to the g.	CRISP 297:38
Over this damp g.	ROET 819:96
paths of glory lead to g.	GRAY 442:91
Peace is in the g.	SHEL 930:18
pompous in the g.	BROW 196:3
profound as the g.	ADAMS 5:80
put on the g. of Gomer Owen	THOM 1011:83
receive no letters in the g.	JOHN 532:36
she is in her g.	WORD 1095:8
sinking into the g.	WESL 1067:72
So pleasant this side of the g.	DIBD 319:6
sunk into the g.	JOHN 526:6
take me out o'th' g.	SHAK 904:42
that dark inn—the G.!	SCOTT 854:73
this side of the g.	PITT 771:72
thy humble g. adorned	POPE 779:7
till we go to the g.	SMITH 946:92
travelling towards the g.	WORD 1096:19
Upon his mother's g.?	WORD 1095:9
vast and wandering g.	TENN 998:22
Victorious o'er the g.	DODD 335:47
vortex of our g.	CRANE 294:94
within the g.'s brink	ANON 22:77
Without a g., unkindled	BYRON 221:7
gravemakers ditchers, and g.	SHAK 893:73
graves Arise from their g.	BLAKE 167:87
bloody hands and hospitable g.	CORW 288:62
climbs into their g. married	WILD 1079:21
filled with g.	BLAKE 167:91
find ourselves dishonourable g.	SHAK 882:20
g. of the best soldiers	PHIL 768:23
g. of the martyrs	STEV 976:56
g. that hide us	RALE 800:14
g. were opened	BIBLE 140:56
g. will give thee memory	SHAK 914:76
here about the g.	STEV 976:57
never went near the g. of his parents	BELL 88:39
open your g.	BIBLE 129:44
Over the tumbled g.	ELIOT 369:95
sacred g. to be ploughed	RED 804:74
tears shed over g.	STOWE 979:89

gravestones Black village of g.	HUGH 500:48
graveyard thru the g. forest	PURDY 795:34
gravity governed by g.	MOORE 705:28
impulsive g. of head	POPE 782:99
natural force, like g.	HIND 481:12
Playing in musicked g.	AVIS 53:76
gravy No g. and no grub	RANS 802:38
Sir Humphrey Davy Abominated g.	BENT 93:25
slip with the g.	MACB 624:32
graze Could neither g. nor pierce	SHAK 900:46
grazes vacuum cleaner g.	RAINE 800:7
Graziano G. speaks...of nothing	SHAK 874:9
grease slides by on g.	LOWE 617:1
greasy fat and g. citizens	SHAK 885:78
g. Limpopo River	KIPL 563:82
great A being...rudely g.	POPE 780:42
All g. rising	BACON 58:75
All things both g. and small	COLE 274:95
anyone among the g. men	INGR 511:46
dream about the g.	YEATS 1105:64
far above the g.	GRAY 443:92
fears of being g.	TENN 1005:63
g. and almost only comfort	STARK 963:94
g. is thy faithfulness	BIBLE 128:32
G. men are not always wise	BIBLE 113:15
g. men have their poor relations	DICK 325:33
G. men may jest	SHAK 896:73
g. men...in politics	ELTON 375:22
g. minds in the commonplace	HUBB 498:4
g. To do that thing	SHAK 906:98
g. was his fame	EGAN 362:55
he is always g.	DRYD 347:59
He is truly g.	KEMP 549:38
how g. a matter a little fire kindleth	BIBLE 155:66
How indigent the g.!	GRAY 441:57
in order to be g.	HOPK 492:12
leave g. things undone	GLAS 430:58
Madness in g. ones	SHAK 891:31
makes every man feel g.	CHES 258:2
Man is only truly g.	DISR 332:86
Minds that are g.	JONS 536:14
never produces anything g.	REYN 808:23
Nothing g....without enthusiasm	EMER 376:43
Nothing g....without g. men	DEGA 312:96
qualities of a g. King	RICH 810:66
really g. in favour of equality	SHAW 925:26
some g. man	HOOV 490:60
ten g. artists	GREE 443:1
that Caesar might be g.!	CAMP 227:27
the g. crime	PACH 748:25
the g. have kindness	POPE 781:66
this g. ...kingdom	PITT 771:63
those who were truly g.	SPEN 956:71
Thou wouldst be g.	SHAK 907:26
To be g.	EMER 376:34
We live in the g. indoors	RAINE 800:7
when the One G. Scorer comes	RICE 809:38
works of a g. genius	ADDI 8:38
world's g. men	HOLM 486:89
would be g. in our little government	ROCH 816:57
great-grandmothers g.-g. dread	BATT 76:13
great-great-grandchildren our g.-g.-g., when	
they learn	PRIE 790:37
great-great-grandfather in any one's g.-g.-g.	
	SOME 952:99
great-rooted g.-r. blossomer	YEATS 1106:80
Great Britain G. B. calls the Far East	MENZ 670:93
G. B. is going to make war	BETH 99:22
imperial might of G. B.	STEW 977:64
Metropolis of G. B.	BAIL 62:70
Russia and G. B.	CECIL 247:85
greater Four things g. than all	KIPL 561:39
g. cannot be thought	ANSE 31:82
g., broader, and fuller life	DU 353:10

greater (*contd.*)

lesser life shall be the g.	GORD 435:63
Something made g. by ourselves	ANGE 20:29
the g. the differences	PASC 758:68
greatest as well as the g. He	RAIN 800:6
g. thing in the world	FORS 398:39
I am the g.!	ALI 14:27
least...control the g.	WORD 1094:95
nation's art is g.	HOPP 493:13
greatness certain g. in her	ELIOT 366:41
far-off touch of g.	TENN 1002:13
glory and g.	GAIT 411:71
greatest in Europe for Riches and G.	BAIL 62:70
g. is a-ripening	SHAK 918:61
g. of the British Nation	ADDI 7:18
g. thrust upon him	CANN 230:67
highest point of my g.	SHAK 918:59
himself attain g.	POE 776:54
Man's unhappiness...comes of his g.	CARL 235:56
Men who have g. within them	CAMUS 228:44
moment of my g. flicker	ELIOT 367:51
our g. as a nation	THAT 1007:10
some achieve g.	SHAK 894:18
strength and the g. of England	CURZ 302:27
Greece Athens, the eye of G.	MILT 694:35
Britain may magine itself new G.	BRIN 188:57
Fair G.!, sad relic	BYRON 219:74
glory that was G.	POE 776:47
G., Italy, and England did adorn	DRYD 351:58
G. might still be free	BYRON 223:50
summoned G. to arms	MARL 653:93
Vanquished G.	HORA 493:29
greed g. is only one of them	VAND 1039:97
G. begins where poverty ends	BALZ 69:84
politics of g.	ARMEY 35:43
socially commendable form of g.	SCHW 851:22
writer's g. is appalling	BALD 64:94
greedy Be not g. to add money	BIBLE 131:16
G. for the belongings of others	SALL 839:37
not g. of filthy lucre	BIBLE 154:29
thank goodness, I am g.	PUNCH 795:30
Greek By dint o' G.	BURNS 209:59
G. and Roman poets	PRIOR 791:62
G. of today is essentially	MILL 678:29
he could speak G.	BUTL 216:4
imitator of the G. forms	MACKE 632:51
Jew first, and also to the G.	BIBLE 148:11
ne of G.	SPEN 958:23
neither G. nor Jew	BIBLE 153:21
neither Jew nor G.	BIBLE 152:89
poets who grew up in G.	ROET 819:97
questioned him in G.	CARR 241:89
say a word against G.	SHAW 923:78
small Latin, and less G.	JONS 535:9
talk of knowing G.	WOOLF 1092:60
Things in G. are not read	ANON 22:65
Greeks G. Had a Word for It	AKINS 10:75
G....hiding behind their columns	DEKO 313:18
I fear the G.	VIRG 1045:82
make way, G.!	PROP 792:80
superiority of the G.	FUSE 410:59
with cannibals, And Trojan G.?	SHAK 877:91
green believed in the g. light	FITZ 391:18
cakes...looked g. with worry	FIRB 389:76
fairest shepherd on our g.	PEELE 763:45
fresh and g. they look	THAC 1006:81
frock of frolic g.	DRAY 345:31
golden face the meadows g.	SHAK 913:59
g. and yellow melancholy	SHAK 894:16
G. cowbind	SHEL 932:68
g. earth's end	MILT 684:36
g. flash that brings good fortune	RHYS 808:30
G. how I love you g.	LORCA 613:39
g. in judgement	SHAK 905:67

green (*contd.*)

G. only on the banner	BROD 189:68
g. thought in a g. shade	MARV 659:86
honey set in a g. bowl	SMITH 946:99
In pastures g.	SCOT 856:19
In thy g. lap	GRAY 443:89
June…in g. leaves	SPEN 959:42
laid him on the g.	BALL -101:31
leaves are g.	ANON 21:56
leaves are g.	ANON 23:90
Make it a g. peace	DARN 306:80
margent g.	MILT 683:26
passport's g.	HEAN 465:38
sees a g. light everywhere	SCHW 852:32
smooth-shaven g.	MILT 682:9
sported on the g.	SOUT 954:31
What use…the g. river	FRAME 400:76
Where I used to play on the g.	BLAKE 167:90
whiten the g. plains	SHEL 928:82

green-eyed g.-e. monster — SHAK 899:32
greenery-yallery g.-y., Grovesnor — GILB 424:71
greengrocers lying in rain outside g. — BRAD 183:76
Greenland G.'s icy mountains — HEBER 466:58
greens g.…that screeeeeeam — CARRA 237:15
healing g. — ABSE 1:6
Greensleeves to the tune of 'G.' — SHAK 878:24
greenstone lighting up the g. years — IHIM 510:30
greenwood in the good g. — SCOTT 854:66
Under the g. tree — SHAK 885:86
greet it gars me g. — BURNS 211:11
greeted expect to be g. with smiles — BROO 193:40
greeting g. a corpse would give — BALD 64:5
grenadiers Pensions and G. — STER 969:6
Grenville Sir Richard G. lay — TENN 1004:56
Greta G. woods are green — SCOTT 854:67
grey among…houses — YEATS 1105:71

black and g.	GREE 445:29
death's g. land	SASS 845:25
few locks…are g.	SOUT 954:29
g. twilight	YEATS 1105:62
head grown g. in vain	SHEL 931:47
in her little g. dress	WOOLF 1093:67
instead of the general g.	MILL 677:4
Into their g.	FREE 404:35
old and g.	YEATS 1105:60
question of it being g.	TRAV 1025:36
turn those amber locks to g.	DRAY 345:34
two horrible shades of g.	THOR 1017:3
withered weak and g.	MILT 693:24

grey-bearded g.-b. and wrinkled — HAWT 461:75
grey-green great g.-g. greasy — KIPL 563:82
greybeards g. call divine — SHAK 862:34
greyhound g.…heeded lyke a snake — BERN 97:92
greyhounds stand like g. — SHAK 881:85
greyness Bright g. — GUNT 449:87
gridiron act a g. — CLIVE 270:26
grief acquainted with g. — BIBLE 127:99

As is my g.	SHAK 867:61
between g. and nothing	FAUL 383:75
bore within their breasts the g.	AYTO 53:87
bottom of my g.?	SHAK 869:14
bravery of his g.	SHAK 893:24
Each substance of a g.	SHAK 867:50
foundation of g.	HUGO 502:84
Fretting g. the enemy	SPEN 957:4
g. and son of idleness	MELV 667:28
G. fills the room	SHAK 872:66
g. flieth to it	BACON 56:44
G. for a while is blind	SHEL 930:15
g. forgotten	SWIN 986:24
G. is a species of idleness	JOHN 529:62
G. is carried off by the wings	LAFO 574:82
G. is itself a med'cine	COWP 292:41
g. is proud	SHAK 872:63

grief (*contd.*)

g. itself be mortal	SHEL 931:41
G. never mended	DICK 320:14
g. of heart	SHAK 918:56
g. returns with the revolving year	SHEL 931:39
g.…upon the heels of pleasure	CONG 280:99
g. with a glass	SWIN 987:26
heard g. named the eldest	WEBS 1060:45
in much wisdom is much g.	BIBLE 122:17
life from g. or danger free	JOHN 525:82
long g. and pain	TENN 1001:89
make less the depth of g.	SHAK 861:20
master a g.	SHAK 880:53
much less g. on earth	BROD 189:72
My g.'s so great	SHAK 872:64
No man can cause more g.	FAUL 383:76
nor g. bitterness	LYLY 620:61
Oh my g.	SYNGE 988:65
or grey g.	SWIN 987:44
Pale G. and pleasing Pain	GRAY 443:87
part my g. have eas'd	MILT 694:40
particular g. Is of so	SHAK 898:3
pitch of g.	HOPK 492:3
silent manliness of g.	GOLD 433:17
Smiling at g.	SHAK 894:16
so quickened with g.	GRAV 439:15
sounds of g. and mourning	DICK 322:61
spends a bootless g.	SHAK 898:13
That g. for which the senses	WORD 1094:94
the g. I feel	TENN 998:19
The theme…is g., sheer g.	GOLD 432:90
Thine be the g.	AYTO 53:84
Till g. did tell me roundly	HERB 475:15
truth…with its loud g.	DUNN 356:54
wish to drown your g.	MACG 630:21
with a mother's g.	TRUTH 1030:39

griefs Extremity of g. — SHAK 862:42
[Friendship]cutteth g. in half — BACON 58:99
g. are ended — SHAK 898:1
g. which bow — ARNO 36:61
In my old g. — BROW 197:19
oldest g. of summer — RICK 811:74
tales of others' g. — SHAK 910:97
grievance g. for the day — MANS 647:6
grievances not magnifying g. — RIDGE 811:79
redress of real g. — PEEL 763:42
grieve Nor joy nor g. too much — DRYD 352:93
thou leavest me to g. — SHEL 927:65
We will g. not — WORD 1098:55
grieves gay nature g. — SMART 944:72
g. that menial needs — HYDE 509:14
grieving Margaret, are you g. — HOPK 492:92
thought it died of g. — KEATS 544:43
grievous most g. to him — TROL 1028:81
grills As long as mixed g. — JANE 518:53
grim brow so g. — ELIOT 371:36
the g. …to prove himself — PAGL 749:35
grin g. and fine intelligence — NEW 723:17
G. Will Win — ANON 28:99
How cheerfully he seems to g. — CARR 238:22
it vanished…ending with the g. — CARR 238:27
malevolent aged g. — HUGH 500:38
Nature wears universal g. — FIEL 388:47
with a lipless g. — ELIOT 367:63
grind g. in the prison house — BIBLE 109:21
g. the faces of the poor? — BIBLE 124:58
life is one demd horrid g.! — DICK 322:56
grinders forty teeth…twenty-four g. — DICK 325:40
g. cease because they are few — BIBLE 123:42
gringo According to a g. — GUIL 448:73
grip g. down and begin — WILL 1082:84
holding a people in its g. — FANON 382:60
holds us in an iron g. — FRID 404:47
in their dead g. — TUCH 1031:44

groan Condemned alike to g. — GRAY 441:48
hear each other g. — KEATS 547:15
thousands counted every g. — ARNO 38:3
with bubbling g. — BYRON 221:7
groaneth that which g. to be so — HERB 474:9
groans g. and convulsions — STER 969:8
g. of love — LOWRY 618:19
Warring sighs and g. — BURNS 212:24
grocer g. puts a pound weight — SPEN 956:87
Grogan as old mother G. said — JOYCE 538:47
Gromboolian great G. plain — LEAR 589:51
grooves in the g. that those who rob — CONN 283:82
what's in the g. — ANON 30:62
grope g. about in the labyrinth — SCHO 849:92
gross Not g. to sink — SHAK 864:94
November, he full of g. and fat — SPEN 959:43
grossness measureless g. — WHIT 1073:96
vice…losing all its g. — BURKE 207:32
grotesque became a g. — ANDE 18:9
fashions strike us as g. — VEBL 1041:26
from the g. to the horrible — DOYLE 344:19
grots cage like g. — SITW 941:12
ground at length it stands the g. — DRYD 350:32

both feet off the g.	JOHN 523:50
can't keep on the g.	TRAV 1025:34
clearing g. a little	LOCKE 609:71
Close by the g.	SHAK 879:51
commit his body to g.	BOOK 176:58
could never touch the g.	SHAK 875:46
cursed is the g. for thy sake	BIBLE 103:1
dead g. in between	REED 805:82
dewy g.	WORD 1100:87
Exiled to the g.	BAUD 77:16
feet planted on level g.	GOHE 431:84
fertile g. he caused to grow	MILT 690:52
found a watch upon the g.	PALEY 751:65
generally loses g.	STEV 973:85
good for the g.	SCHU 850:12
g. is like a beautiful woman	SNOW 951:54
g. itself is falling	FERL 386:21
g. with vernal flowers	MILT 684:46
grow on a spot of g.	SWIFT 985:85
If that plane leaves the g.	EPST 379:2
In his own g.	POPE 779:4
inlay Broidered the g.	MILT 690:63
kamikaze g. staff	PARK 755:30
knit hands, and beat the g.	MILT 683:22
know you by your g.	BLUN 170:42
leaves…fall to the g.	ANON 21:56
let us sit upon the g.	SHAK 867:60
little time on the g.	OWENS 748:23
lot is fallen to me in fair g.	BOOK 176:65
lying on the g.	ALAN 11:79
Marching o'er the metric g.	CRAIK 294:90
most at ease on the g.	ALLS 15:55
on the g. at Goose Green	KINN 559:11
place…is holy g.	BIBLE 106:54
Resources left in the g. are saved	BRODY 190:5
second foot on the g.	FONT 395:89
seven feet of English g.	HARO 458:22
spilled it on the g.	BIBLE 105:42
Stand your g.	PARK 755:28
stone falls to the g.	THOR 1017:93
swalloweth the g.	BIBLE 113:23
tears have overflowed his g.?	DONNE 337:80
that never left the g.	LOWE 617:4
their burthen to the g.	TENN 1003:21
they plopped to the g.	PLATH 773:91
till the g. from whence he was taken	BIBLE 103:3
till thou return to the g.	BIBLE 103:2
tread on classic g.	ADDI 6:98
unhurried G. swell	ELIOT 372:59
when he has reached g.	JOHN 526:99
when he hit the g.	HUGH 500:46

ground (*contd.*)
when I was on the g. — SIMON 939:82
grounds beautify their g. — MALT 643:41
noble g. for the noble — RUSK 830:83
group characterizes…minority g. — MAIL 639:82
g. of other people — ROSSO 825:98
g. of the unwilling — HARK 457:19
nation or g. — RUNC 828:52
only exploited g. in the world — JONG 533:62
place in any political g. — HELL 468:94
sobs from among the g. — DICK 322:61
groups divide people into two g. — HAMP 454:63
g. of inflexible political persuasion — WILS 1085:40
g. who question that status — MAMET 643:45
marginal g. who — RUET 828:47
split into two polar g. — SNOW 950:73
grouse g. are in no danger — EDIN 361:42
grove deep windings of the g. — BEAT 79:57
G. nods at g., each a mirror — POPE 779:21
meadow, g., and stream — WORD 1097:48
While in a g. I sate — WORD 1095:4
grovelled he g. before him — THAC 1006:83
groves g. of their academy — BURKE 207:33
o'er shady g. they hover — WEBS 1060:44
will seek the g. — ROSS 824:83
Grovesnor G. Gallery — GILB 424:71
grow up country safe to g. u. in — THAT 1007:9
g. u. to be Prime Minister — RICH 811:73
grow For sure then I should g. — HERB 475:16
g. for ever — TENN 997:1
How do poems g.? — WARR 1054:33
isn't going to g. — WHITE 1070:38
its radiance would g. — RAND 801:26
more we g. in numbers — TERT 1006:78
my wrath did g. — BLAKE 167:93
some skin on to g. — KHRU 556:49
which grain will g. — SHAK 907:17
grow'd I 'spect I g. — STOWE 978:86
growing ever grew anything worth g. — SAND 841:69
g., bodily that is — THOM 1013:22
g., flying, happening — REID 806:97
G. old is like being penalised — POWE 788:7
g.…when ye're sleeping — SCOTT 855:93
growl sit and g. — JOHN 531:21
grown now g. up to riper age — BRON 190:91
grown-up g.-u. people's feet — STEV 975:32
g.-u. women take seriously — STEI 967:66
Lillian as a g.-u. — FEIB 384:96
grown-ups obvious facts about g.-u. — JARR 518:65
ordinary thickskinned g.-u. — SHAW 921:27
grows box that fennel G. around — RANS 802:37
g. daily worse and worse — SPEN 959:36
What g. by the words? — SIDN 936:46
growth birth and g.…are ubiquitous — DILL 330:52
children of a larger g. — DRYD 348:97
expression of life as g. — MILL 678:42
for the g. of any and everything — STUA 980:9
g. in the individual — SMIL 945:73
g. is a leap in the dark — MILL 678:45
g. of this nation — GAND 414:11
growths sun-searched g. — ROSS 824:87
grub No gravy and no g. — RANS 802:38
old ones, g. — SHAW 920:93
poor g., poor pay — LOND 610:90
sphere of life…in the g. state — DOUG 341:51
grudge g. against the children — BIBLE 107:80
G. not one against another — BIBLE 155:71
took it as a personal g. — OHEN 737:16
grudges all their ancient g. — WAUGH 1057:89
Grundy What will Mrs G. say? — MORT 710:4
grunt every twitch and g. — TRUD 1029:12
gruntled far from being g. — WODE 1089:3
guarantee beauty is a g. of happiness — PROU 793:98
each will g. all — LEES 593:20

guarantee (*contd.*)
Englishman as a g. — SHAW 923:73
guaranteed G. never to fail — FORM 397:27
guard Alice is marrying one of the g. — MILNE 680:69
g. against…unwarranted influence — EISE 364:88
g. of the world proletarian army — LENIN 595:50
Made good g. for itself — SHAK 906:85
Those that I g. — YEATS 1106:75
guarded G. by timeless principalities — GRAV 440:25
guardian g. angels sung this strain — THOM 1015:46
guardianship Christ for my g. — PATR 761:15
guards Brigade of G. — MACM 635:14
g. at the gate — SUN 982:39
G. die but do not surrender — CAMB 226:7
Up g. and at them — WELL 1063:9
guardsman g.'s cut and thrust differ — HUXL 509:4
guerdon fair g. when we hope — MILT 684:42
guerre mais ce n'est pas la g. — BOSQ 180:27
guerrilla cardinal maxims of g. war — KISS 566:31
Insurrection—by means of g. bands — MAZZ 666:11
guess g. about what is seen — SAND 841:65
venture a g. — REED 805:82
you can perhaps g. why — SEVI 859:60
guesses only hints and g. — ELIOT 372:65
secrets everybody g. — SHAW 920:8
supporting their g. by argument — BAGE 61:63
guest as a g. thanks his host — DILL 331:53
awaited the expected g. — ELIOT 369:89
Earth receive an honoured g. — AUDEN 47:71
g. of one's time — KENN 550:51
remembrance of a g. that tarrieth — BIBLE 131:84
speed the parting g. — POPE 779:13
guests g. should praise it — HARI 457:16
Jews are hosts, and not g. — SACH 835:57
the g. star-scattered — FITZ 390:91
two great classes: hosts and g. — BEER 83:41
Unbidden g. — SHAK 860:91
what…other g. thought of him — SKIN 943:53
guidance act under the g. of reason — SPIN 960:55
g. have I sought — WORD 1100:92
guide be thy g. — ANON 23:81
except some man should g. me? — BIBLE 147:88
g. informed him later — NASH 720:57
g. of life — HUME 505:3
g. thee with mine eye — BIBLE 115:59
Have God to be his g. — BUNY 205:73
infallible critical g. — AUDEN 48:87
None need a g. — POPE 782:99
place within them as a g. — MILT 689:37
probability very g. of life — BUTL 216:95
without a g.…I…work — ARET 33:17
guides Ye blind g. — BIBLE 139:35
Guildford G.…the most agreeable — COBB 271:56
guile g. of a cobra — WOOL 1094:90
Of g., of hate, of envy — MILT 692:3
packed with g. — BROO 192:28
guillotine cure except as a g. — LUCE 618:33
guilt blood with g. is brought — SHEL 930:16
blushing…a sign of g. — CONG 281:30
difference between politics and g. — CLIN 269:21
free from g. or pain — SHEL 930:25
g. and power — TOPL 1023:7
g.; Freud shoved that out — BAIN 62:77
G. in his heart — CHUR 262:80
g. of dissimulation — SCOTT 855:1
g. of flattery — JOHN 531:10
industry is g. — RUSK 831:4
one g., one crime — MILT 692:8
sense of g., which he denies — LESS 598:96
servitude…the punishment of his g. — CURR 301:16
she trembles with g. — OCON 735:82
suspicious of g. in myself — HELL 469:2
What art can wash her g. — GOLD 432:5
guiltier G. than him they try — SHAK 896:66

guiltless Lord will not hold him g. — BIBLE 106:68
guilty 100 per cent not g. — SIMP 940:92
better that ten g. persons escape — BLAC 165:49
cups make any g. men — JONS 535:99
feel somehow g. — GRASS 439:12
Find me but g. — WEBS 1060:35
g. never escape unscathed — BAIL 62:68
g. of corrupting…the young — PLATO 773:2
G. of dust and sin — HERB 475:17
g. spice to this recreation — WAUGH 1057:86
g. when they read — VIDAL 1044:70
his foot is g. — BECK 81:91
innocent while g. — BELL 88:40
like a g. thing surprised — WORD 1098:53
make of our disasters the sun — SHAK 902:2
rich, deep and g. — CHAN 251:61
started like a g. thing — SHAK 887:44
when one loves a g. person? — CYRA 302:34
guinea but the g.'s stamp — BURNS 213:42
force of the g. — RUSK 830:90
g. pigs in the laboratory of God — WILL 1081:65
jingling of the g. — TENN 995:76
guinea-coast G.-c. slavery — MELV 668:45
guineas g. for flinging a pot of paint — RUSK 831:9
twenty g. per annum — DICK 321:44
Guinevere delyverd hys doughtir G. — MALO 642:28
syght of queene G. — MALO 642:26
Guinness G. on a sunny day — GREE 443:2
guise no newe g. that it nas old — CHAU 255:28
guitar sang on a small g. — LEAR 590:58
will break their g. — MIRO 696:71
You have a blue g. — STEV 971:49
guitars boys with bright red g. — HENRI 472:60
corpses, or Picasso g. — LIPP 606:29
gulf across the g. of space — WELLS 1064:26
g. of mutual incomprehension — SNOW 950:37
G. War was like teenage sex — HARK 457:18
peace and civil order in the G. — ELIZ 374:96
social g. that divides him — MARX 660:16
teeming g. — WHIT 1073:94
there is a great g. fixed — BIBLE 144:8
turning of the G. crisis — HUSS 505:35
walking on a string across a g. — DAVI 307:96
widening g. between the rich — COUP 289:77
gulfs g. will wash us down — TENN 995:61
gull g. sees farthest — BACH 54:95
g.'s way and the whale's way — MASE 661:34
image of the Great G. — BACH 54:96
gull-marked shinning g.-m. mud — LARK 581:9
gulls does not even require g. — KEYN 554:34
gum can't fart and chew g. — JOHN 524:55
gun double-barrelled g. and pointers — KING 558:96
draw her g. — WHITE 1070:37
Great G. of Athlone — ANON 25:21
g. gives you the body — THOR 1017:95
Maxim G. — BELL 87:3
nice guy if you have a g. — KOCH 567:65
no g., but I can spit — AUDEN 48:97
out of the barrel of a g. — MAO 648:22
state where g. control — SIMP 939:90
gunfire g.…sounded unreal — USTI 1038:78
Gunga Din than I am, G. D.! — KIPL 561:36
gunner And the g. said — TENN 1005:59
gunpowder g. and printer's ink — KRAUS 569:91
g. ran out of the heels — FOOTE 396:95
printing, g. and the magnet — BACON 55:30
guns but for these vile g. — SHAK 875:42
defend ourselves with g. not butter — GOEB 430:64
G. aren't lawful — PARK 754:13
g. begin to rattle — BARK 71:19
g. begin to shoot — KIPL 560:32
hear amid the g. — MACC 626:64
hundred men with g. — PUZO 796:40
loaded g. with boys — CRAB 294:89

guns (contd.)

monstrous anger of the g.	OWEN 748:7
Of g., and drums, and wounds	SHAK 875:42
rather have butter or g.?	GOER 430:67
slaught'rin g.	BURNS 210:81
spring-.s in the realm	LOWE 616:77
unheroic Dead who fed the g.?	SASS 846:41
when the g. begin	SASS 845:25
gunshot g. is the perfect way	KENN 552:96
gust g. he hath in quarrelling	SHAK 893:95
gusts explanation of our g.	ELIOT 366:44
gut-feel g.-f. of the 55-year old	GREE 445:36
Gutenburg G. made everybody	MACL 635:2
guts g. of a butterfly	CAPO 231:89
I'll lug the g.	SHAK 892:60
gutter born in the g.	KIPL 562:68
I lay down in the g.	BURT 213:61
straight into the g.	SMITH 947:19
We are all in the g.	WILDE 1077:60
gutterals world of g.	STEV 971:37
guy Ah! County G.	SCOTT 855:3
an independent is a g.	STEV 973:89
average g. who could carry a tune	CROS 298:62
cop beatin' up a g.	STEI 966:55
dresses like a g.	GILB 425:85
g. that plays the kettle drums	SALI 839:27
kind of g. that wouldn't talk	SALI 838:22
nice g. if you have a gun	KOCH 567:65
no matter how nice a g.	SALI 839:26
optimist is a g.	MARQ 656:39
snatching a hard g.	RUNY 829:59
guys five g. who hate you	STEN 968:75
g. using false pretences	RUNY 829:63
name any disease after two g.	PUZO 796:44
Nice g. finish last	DURO 357:73
gwine G. to run all night	FOST 399:59
Gyges G. of Lydia	VASA 1040:8
gymnasium g. of the mind	LENIN 595:53
life's g.	WHIT 1073:95
gymnast g. and golfer, soldered	BRYA 201:16
Gyn/Ecologists recommended by G.	DALY 304:52
gypsy Two-wheeled g. queen	DYLAN 358:95
vagrant g. life	MASE 661:34
gyre Did g. and gimble	CARR 239:47
turning in the widening g.	YEATS 1106:74
géométrie Vanité de la g.	FRED 403:26
Géricault G. corpses, or Picasso	LIPP 606:29

ha-ha Funny peculiar, or funny h.-h.?	HAY 462:84
habeas corpus protection of the h. c.	JEFF 520:94
habit because it was a h.	ROGE 820:17
breed a h. in a man!	SHAK 860:88
Costly thy h.	SHAK 888:60
country h. has me	SACK 835:61
gentlemen are in the h.	PALM 752:73
Getting to be a H. with Me	DUBIN 352:99
good h. makes a child a man	WEBS 1059:32
h., custom and education	SMITH 946:95
h. in writing articles	FEYN 387:33
h. of civilisation	WEST 1067:87
h....of correcting things	BRADY 184:4
h. of discipline	TUCH 1031:46
h. of disgruntled men	TOLK 1022:91
h. of profound reflection	CONR 285:11
h. of revelation	SKEL 942:49
H....the test of truth	CRAB 294:82
in the h. of flogging	TROL 1028:94
instinct, the h. is already old	LAWR 586:90
monster that devours everything: h.	BALZ 68:68
order breeds h.	ADAMS 5:76
remnants of such a beautiful h.	ALME 15:57
shook the h. off	WORD 1096:33
taste of lies...a h.	GELL 417:70
Television has spread the h.	SCHL 848:78

habitat

native h. was hot water	ANON 28:18
habitation Deep-founded h.	BLAKE 165:60
God in his holy h.	BIBLE 116:86
h. for bears and wolves	SCHAW 847:61
h. of dragons	BIBLE 126:82
Lord...thy h.	BIBLE 117:3
none doth build a stately h.	HERB 475:21
world Of destined h.	MILT 691:88
habitations brick shops and h.	THOR 1017:1
miles of human h.	CONR 285:13
receive you into everlasting h.	BIBLE 143:4
habitis prelatis in h. clericall	DUNB 355:39
habits each other's h., thoughts	DISR 332:90
first h. of intimacy	LAMB 576:23
h. and customs of the people	RICA 808:32
h. are geared towards	LIVE 607:46
h. of metaphoric thought	FRYE 408:21
h. of peace and patience	WALT 1052:7
Pick up bad h. of expectancy	LARK 581:94
superficial h. of 'good citizenship'	WAUGH 1057:89
habitual that which has become h.	ARIS 34:35
Habsburg H. monarchy	TAAF 989:73
hackles of tan with henna h.	STEV 971:41
hackneyed h. jokes from Miller	BYRON 219:60
hades phonographs of h. in the brain	CRANE 295:9
haemophilia kind of psychological h.	CURR 301:15
haft change the h. if you please	QUIN 798:68
hag h. obscene, and grisly phantom	BEAT 79:57
you equiangular old h.!	OCON 735:82
haggard h. and careworn	WODE 1089:95
h. and lank	GILB 424:71
Haggards the H. Ride no more	STEP 968:80
haggis Gie her a H.!	BURNS 210:85
haggling still h. at the price	GRAV 440:33
hags secret, black, and midnight h.,	SHAK 909:66
hail beaten dog beneath the h.	POUND 787:86
H. Caesar, we...salute you	ANON 21:46
H. fellow, well met	SWIFT 985:96
H. Mary, quite contrary!	GREE 444:14
H. nothing full of nothing	HEMI 470:21
h. shall sweep away the refuge	BIBLE 125:77
H. to the Chief	SCOTT 853:62
lashing h.	SHEL 928:82
say a H. Mary for you	JOYCE 537:41
such a h. of words	JONS 534:84
Where falls not h.	TENN 1004:48
Hailsham Lord H. said	MONT 700:51
hair backward by the h.	BROW 196:14
braid to bind your h.	SCOTT 854:79
braided her yellow h.	BALL 67:51
ceases to alter...her h.	AUST 52:73
dressing their h.	SMOL 950:63
each particular h. stand on end	SHAK 889:74
elegance of Circe's h.	POUND 785:61
fair h. gently waved	THAT 1007:7
fictions only and false h.	HERB 475:24
for the colour of his h.	HOUS 496:87
h. a glory like a saint	KEATS 546:92
h. and dimples is coming	MOORE 705:13
h. and harpstring of gold	SWIN 987:39
h. as white as gin	CAUS 246:67
h. has become very white	CARR 238:24
h. is as a flock of goats	BIBLE 124:51
h. More black than ashbuds	TENN 995:65
h. off the Great Cham's beard	SHAK 879:38
h. that lay along	ROSS 824:87
h. 'twixt south and southwest side	BUTL 216:5
his floating h.!	COLE 275:18
hoary h.	GRAY 442:81
I rise with my red h.	PLATH 773:97
If a man have long h.	BIBLE 150:58
if my h. do but tickle	SHAK 871:50
in politics...with that h.	ASTOR 43:98
in their golden h.	TENN 996:91

hair (contd.)

kame my h.	BALL 67:57
lass wi' tousled h.	MACD 627:74
letters...serve one to pin up one's h.	CONG 281:36
light brown h.	FOST 399:61
lodestone of live h.	MACN 637:35
long h....is a glory to her	BIBLE 150:57
long, limp h.	DAVIS 308:27
loosen your h.	YEATS 1105:64
loses his h.	DIAZ 319:2
man of your head and h.	JONS 535:91
must sugar my h.	CARR 239:41
My h. has been in training	SHER 933:80
never hurt a h. of him	STUD 980:15
no more that shining h.	LOVE 615:65
not hurt a h.	STER 969:45
one strangling golden h.	ROSS 824:88
pin up your h.	CONG 281:33
reft the jewels from her h.	HYDE 509:14
ruddy limbs and flourishing h.	BLAKE 165:64
scant as h. in leprosy	BROW 198:50
smoothes her h.	ELIOT 369:90
snow-white h. who has kept out	LEAC 589:47
space...laid on her h.	CRANE 295:2
stars in her h.	ROSS 824:89
such a head of h.	HOUS 496:88
tangles of Neaera's h.?	MILT 684:42
Thy hyacinth h.	POE 776:47
watching myself brush my h.	RHYS 808:31
wear gowd on your h.	BALL 67:51
weave the sunlight in your h.	ELIOT 367:60
When I lie tangled in her h.	LOVE 615:62
Wi' ribbons in her h.	BALL 67:45
woman, with such h.	BROW 198:48
you have lovely h.	CHEK 256:62
your yellow h.	YEATS 1106:46
haircut rather bad h.	MACC 625:46
hairs bring down my gray h.	BIBLE 105:45
few, sad, last grey h.	KEATS 547:15
five grey h.	DONNE 337:79
Had all his h.	SHAK 900:54
h. of your head are all numbered	BIBLE 136:75
h. were grown like eagles' feathers	BIBLE 129:47
h. were white like wool	BIBLE 156:99
How ill whitе h. becomes	SHAK 878:10
If h. are wires	SHAK 915:37
when my h. be grey	SURR 983:46
hairy Esau...is a h. man	BIBLE 105:32
h. American filth	OSBO 746:69
Haiti Go to H. and stand	PHIL 768:23
hale You are h., Father William	SOUT 954:29
half advantage...is h. the victory	DRAKE 345:28
fall h. in love	SALI 838:21
h. o't smug, complacent	SMITH 949:60
h. of the nation is mad	SMOL 950:62
H. of them don't know	QUINN 798:69
h. the battle	GOLD 433:25
h. the people are right	WHITE 1070:27
h. was not told me	BIBLE 111:14
image of myself and dearer h.	MILT 691:70
live with only h. a heart	WILS 1084:19
longest h. of your life	SOUT 954:40
loves but h. the Earth	QUIL 797:55
No, but h. a one	JONS 535:94
not told even the h.	POLO 777:67
The ae h. of the warld	SCOTT 855:6
to be thought h. so good	WHIT 1074:10
half-baked attractive to the h.-b.	FORS 398:32
half-believers h.-b. in our...creeds	ARNO 37:91
half-brother America, thou h.-b.	BAIL 62:71
half-creature h.-c. of the Senate	MANS 648:14
half-dark From h.-d. to h.-d.	POUND 786:40
half-hour H.-h., h.-h. to Aberdour	BALL 67:50
half-hung with mat h.-h.	POPE 780:30

half-light and the h.-l.   YEATS 1105:65
half-naked striding h.-n. up the steps   CHUR 264:8
half-traitor never be a h.-t   HUGO 501:62
half-truths speak no more than h.-t.   LINK 606:22
half-workers women Must be h.-w.?   SHAK 916:4
hall Douglas in his h.?   SCOTT 853:56
filled our h. like   RIVA 812:1
grey assembly h.   MUSS 716:83
H. or Terrace   LEAR 589:52
hire a h.   BELL 88:39
I knew that sullen h.   OWEN 748:15
kindest in the h.   DAVIS 309:37
logs into the h.   SHAK 866:30
skittish Fortune's h.   SHAK 896:50
sparrow should fly...into the h.   BEDE 82:8
vasty h. of death   ARNO 37:84
waited in our tutor's h.   BYRON 218:58
wealth of h. and bower   WORD 1096:38
Hall I have seen...Thomas H.   SMART 944:64
Halliag will go down to H.   MACL 633:71
hallmark h. of our culture   DONA 335:57
hallowed H. be thy name   BIBLE 135:49
halls Amphitrite's destined h.   SHEL 927:70
blood-bedecked h. of their revel   POE 776:44
h. of the White House   JOHN 523:45
through Tara's h.   MOORE 706:36
hallucinated when Dali h.   RUSS 833:41
hallucination A consensual h.   GIBS 422:40
hallways along these same h.   ROBB 813:9
enclosed h.   GIDE 423:45
halo jealousy with a h.   WELLS 1065:38
Life...is a luminous h.   WOOLF 1092:54
What...Is a h.?   FRY 408:14
halt h. ye between two opinions?   BIBLE 111:63
make it h. behind her   SHAK 917:35
halycon first h. period   WALT 1052:12
ham helps scenery like h. and eggs   TWAIN 1032:63
Hambledonians last of H.   EGAN 362:55
hambre La mejor salsa ...el h.   CERV 248:96
hamburgers future and it is h.   HALB 451:15
Hamelin H. town's in Brunswick   BROW 197:31
Hamilton [H.] smote the rock   WEBS 1059:23
Marie H.'s to the kirk gane   BALL 67:45
Hamlet Could H. have been written   GRIS 447:67
get Tree to recite H.   GILB 426:99
H. is so much paper and ink   PRIE 789:35
H. Prince of Denmark   EVEL 381:42
H. with no rehearsal than TV golf   LEMM 595:46
Lord H., with his doublet   SHAK 889:36
No! I am not Prince H.   ELIOT 367:52
hammer an also dropped h.   RUSK 831:11
beating as hard as my h.   SCOTT 855:83
eye is the h.   KAND 541:97
hit my thumb with a h.   AMIS 16:80
the grain and h.   HEAN 465:43
thunderous h. shall drive thee   BLAKE 168:10
took an h. in her hand   BIBLE 109:13
with the h. she smote Sisera   BIBLE 109:14
hammers hear the h. ring   KIPL 565:26
hammock safety-net, not a h.   ANON 30:54
slept in a h.   SAKI 837:5
slow movement of a tropical h.   CHOC 260:55
hammock-shroud heavy-shotted h.   TENN 998:22
Hampton-court servant... got to H.   STEE 964:11
hand admire his sleight of h.   BUTL 217:20
beloved h. is laid   ARNO 36:70
bishops eat from my h.   DUPL 356:64
bite h. that fed them   BURKE 208:45
bless the h. that gave the blow   DRYD 350:38
bringing me up by h.   DICK 326:68
by whose h....people are still free   DODD 335:45
came forth fingers of a man's h.   BIBLE 129:48
cap in h. the day   SMITH 949:60
Clean from my h.?   SHAK 908:49

hand (*contd.*)
cover thee with my h.   BIBLE 107:77
cravens my weak h.   SHAK 916:7
curious engine, your white h.   WEBS 1061:60
darkness...sifts through your h.   ASHB 41:54
death in my h.   SHAK 862:37
Devil is still at h.   DRYD 349:8
disdainful wave of a white woman's h.   ANGE 20:32
Don't let the h. fall   SLOAN 943:59
end...is close at h.   WELLS 1065:47
Eve's fair h. as from a...book   LANY 580:79
Even there shall thy h. lead me   BIBLE 120:71
eye on the right h.   RUSH 829:71
fans into their h.   BALL 67:49
fate carries in her other h.   LAWR 587:15
fear the h. at the window   ELIOT 370:35
fear thy skinny h.!   COLE 273:89
fearful h. in felling quake   DONNE 336:68
Fed with cold and usurous h.?   BLAKE 167:89
flame...one holds in the h.   MARG 650:59
fly in his h.   STER 969:99
foot and h. go cold   ANON 23:84
fork in his inexperienced h.   WELLS 1064:32
Give me thy h.   SHAK 870:22
giving h., though foul   SHAK 865:14
great gifts with one h.   SNOW 951:75
h. cutting edge of mind   BRON 190:83
h. for h.   BIBLE 107:69
h. from day to day   MACN 637:39
h....goes over the face   GARBO 414:17
h. in all things   WASH 1054:38
h.-in-h. even with the vow   SHAK 889:7
h. in h. to death   ROSS 824:92
h. in h. to hell   SHAK 863:66
h. in h. with Plenty   TENN 998:12
h. in h. with wand'ring   MILT 693:27
h. in h., on the edge   LEAR 590:61
h. in to many pies   MENC 669:64
h. more instrumental to the mouth   SHAK 887:45
h. of God   BIBLE 131:81
h. of Heaven   WORD 1101:93
h. of steel in a velvet glove   WOOL 1093:83
h. on the throat of Venice   TOME 1023:1
h. or foot thy offend thee   BIBLE 138:19
h. so various   MILT 694:48
h. that follows intellect   MICH 673:34
h. that holds dominion   THOM 1010:57
h. that kings Have lipp'd   SHAK 905:76
h. that made us is divine   ADDI 7:23
h. that rocks the cradle   WALL 1050:68
h. that signed the paper   THOM 1010:56
h. that writ it   SHAK 914:72
h., the head   RUSK 830:86
h. under his head   YEATS 1107:90
h. wherewith I write   BROW 197:18
h. will be against every man   BIBLE 104:21
handle raised my h.?   SHAK 908:39
hard h. of...need   OTWAY 746:40
Have still the upper h.   COWA 290:3
have the use...but of me left h.   MILT 685:53
held her in its golden h.   GEE 417:65
hold a fire in his h.   SHAK 866:47
holden me by my right h.   BIBLE 117:91
if they want a h.   GERS 420:9
if thy right h. offend thee   BIBLE 134:41
in his h. a spade   SPEN 959:41
In his h. are all the corners   BOOK 177:87
in the palme of my h.   JULI 539:67
In this close h. of love   BROW 197:17
in thy h. a withered spray   ARNO 37:89
infinity in the palm of your h.   BLAKE 167:1
Into thine h. I commit my spirit   BIBLE 115:57
invisible h. of some...god   CUOMO 300:5
Jesus stretched forth his h.   BIBLE 138:8

hand (*contd.*)
join h. in h.   DICK 329:21
keep Classics at h.   WOOLF 1093:80
Keep your left h. high   ONEI 740:68
kiss thy h. to bid adieu   STER 970:15
kissed her slender h.   TENN 1001:82
kissed the h. and by the h. led   BLAKE 166:68
kissing your h.   LOOS 613:33
laid her snow-white h.   YEATS 1104:56
laid thine h. upon me   BIBLE 119:48
lay his h. on his heart   STRA 979:2
lays his h. on heart   BEER 83:27
lays his icy h. on kings   SHIR 935:27
led by an invisible h.   SMITH 945:81
left h. is my thinking h.   HEPW 473:81
lest he put forth his h.   BIBLE 103:3
let not man have the upper h.   BOOK 176:63
let not thy left h. know   BIBLE 134:47
Let your h. slip   MACB 624:32
lilies in her h.   ROSS 824:79
little cloud...like a man's h.   BIBLE 111:66
made by the h. which feels   HEPW 473:79
magic h. of chance   KEATS 544:50
make your h. so unsteady   CENN 248:95
makes...with the things at h.   PERCY 766:85
man with heart, head, h.   TENN 1001:80
mine...the painter's h.   WORD 1099:71
Moses held up his h.   BIBLE 107:67
murd'rous h. a drowsy bench protect   CRAB 293:75
my h. a needle fits   BRAD 184:1
my hat, and h.   BROW 194:64
My times are in Thy h.!   BROW 199:77
Nature's own h. painted   SHAK 913:50
nectar from his h.   MARL 655:26
of one whose h.   SHAK 900:64
Old Hodge stays not his h.   RANS 802:37
on each h. the flames   MILT 687:94
openest thine h.   BIBLE 120:53
other h. full of seas   HYDE 509:12
other h. held a weapon   BIBLE 112:91
Our times are in His h.   BROW 199:75
Poetry is an extra h.   MITC 696:81
poor man's h.   WORD 1098:58
pure h. can touch a newspaper   BAUD 78:45
put forth thine h. now   BIBLE 112:96
put in his h. by the hole   BIBLE 124:53
put your h. into the h. of God   HASK 460:57
quality made...by the human h.   CATH 244:46
rare fine h. at that   MANS 647:1
rash h. in evil hour   MILT 692:12
regard the h. of the clock   LECO 592:2
right h. of the Majesty   BIBLE 154:44
sandwich in her h.   DICK 320:16
shake your h. and help you   LOFT 610:86
show her the back of your h.   FAUL 384:87
Sit thou at my right h.   BIBLE 118:22
soon as I get hold of a h.   FITZ 390:95
stand on either h.   MACA 623:14
stern h. of Compulsion   THUR 1019:43
stern h. of fate   LLOY 608:58
supplication of a dead man's h.   ELIOT 369:99
tennis-girl's h.!   BETJ 100:36
the kindlier h.   TENN 1000:57
there's a h., my trusty fiere!   BURNS 210:96
this is my lady's h.   SHAK 894:17
this unworthy h.!   CRAN 295:16
thrust my h. into his side   BIBLE 147:16
Thy h., great Anarch!   POPE 783:11
till I have a good h.   SWIFT 986:19
time is now near at h.   WASH 1054:42
tiny h. is frozen   GIAC 421:17
touch of the vanished h.   TENN 995:64
waiting for a h.   TENN 998:23
walking close at h.   CARR 240:56

hand (*contd.*)
wander h. in h.	NOYES 732:41
waters in the hollow of his h.	BIBLE 126:87
What immortal h. or eye	BLAKE 167:95
what mortal h.	SCOTT 853:50
what strong h. can hold	SHAK 914:68
Whatsoever thy h. findeth	BIBLE 123:34
with as delicate a h.	BUTL 216:8
with automatic h.	ELIOT 369:90
Women…tricks by sleight of h.	CONG 280:15
work of an Almighty h.	ADDI 7:22
written…with mine own h.	BIBLE 152:94
wrote it with a second h.	SPEN 959:28
Your h., your tongue	SHAK 907:29
handbag hitting it with her h.	CRIT 297:44
handbook Bible as…a constable's h.	KING 559:1
handclasp h.'s a little stronger	CHAP 252:66
handcuffs with the h. on his wrist?	HOUS 496:87
Handel H. is so great and so simple	BUTL 218:44
wisdom; H. sings it	EMER 377:72
handful fear in a h. of dust	ELIOT 368:82
gave the barest h.	KIPL 562:68
h. of grey ashes	CORY 288:64
handicraft primitive and original h.	OLIP 738:25
handicrafts manufacture and in h.	MARX 661:23
handiwork sheweth his h.	BIBLE 114:44
handkerchief feels like a damp h.	MACK 632:55
germs in your h.	ANON 26:48
without wetting his h.	LASS 583:35
handkerchiefs in the house wi' h.	SCOTT 855:83
waistcoats and moral pocket h.	DICK 320:25
handle h. toward my hand?	SHAK 908:39
h. which fits them all	HOLM 486:87
handles no h. to a horse	LEAC 588:29
handmaid h. of the Lord	BIBLE 141:74
h. to religion	BACON 55:19
nature's h. art	DRYD 346:54
Riches are a good h.	BACON 56:34
handmaiden low estate of his h.	BIBLE 141:75
handmaidens five h., whose names	ROSS 824:83
War has three h.	HENR 472:64
handprint h. of all culture	ANON 30:59
handrails color I want those h.	TRUMP 1030:37
hands aching h. and bleeding feet	ARNO 37:74
additional number of productive h.	SMITH 945:85
And then take h.	SHAK 916:23
and with clean h.	WILH 1080:39
Art to fold her h.	ROSS 824:91
Beneath the bleeding h.	ELIOT 371:51
big h. and big feet	HAGEN 450:3
bind the h. of…rogues	OTWAY 746:83
blood and wine were on his h.	WILDE 1078:96
both grasp h.	STAN 962:84
both h. in the pocket	SATIE 846:46
By fairy h. their knell is rung	COLL 276:44
Cease to use your h.	ORWE 742:2
cheap seats clap their h.	LENN 596:54
clasping his h. together	SCOTT 856:7
clean h.	GALS 413:5
coarse warty h.	DONO 340:36
cold immortal h.	SWIN 987:37
Come; let us squeeze h.	MELV 668:41
dirty h., the nails bitten	MACA 623:4
dollar in another man's h.	OHEN 737:16
done with the brain, not the h.	MICH 673:35
Droops on the little h.	MILNE 680:70
education…should be in State h.	MILL 674:62
engraft our h.	DONNE 337:95
exertions of your h. and feet	CONR 284:94
Farewell my poor h.	RACH 799:95
Father, into thy h.	BIBLE 144:19
flabby h.	GILB 425:84
folding of the h. to sleep	BIBLE 120:64
fortune…with both h. full	SHAK 878:7

hands (*contd.*)
free heart from its own h.!	CRAS 296:24
greet you with bloody h.	CORW 288:62
h. are blue	LEAR 590:54
h. employed in work	STEU 970:29
h. guiding where I stumble	SASS 845:40
h. his office on ourselves	MILT 693:21
h. of the enemy	ANON 29:43
h. of the living God	BIBLE 154:49
H. of the surgeon	MAP 649:33
h. of those who implement	SHUL 936:34
H. that led me to the limelight	HEAN 465:39
h. that would light the world	MILL 676:97
h. themselves do reach	MARV 658:85
h. upon their hearts	HOUS 496:72
hath no h.?	BIBLE 126:94
Hath not a Jew h., organs,	SHAK 872:80
he laid his h. on them	BIBLE 139:23
hearts and h. and voices	WINK 1086:59
heavens are the work of thy h.	BIBLE 118:10
his restless h.	PRIT 791:66
Holding h. at midnight	GERS 420:14
in his h. the print of nails	BIBLE 147:76
Into thy h. I commend	BOOK 176:68
keep my h. from picking	BOOK 175:37
knit h., and beat the ground	MILT 683:22
language that…spits on its h.	SAND 841:75
large and sinewy h.	LONG 611:97
License my roving h.	DONNE 336:72
lift not h. of prayer	TENN 1004:47
made with our h.	SWIN 988:52
man's fortune is in his own h.	BACON 59:10
man's h. empty	WALC 1048:40
murders sticking on his h.	SHAK 910:79
nearer than h. to feet	TENN 1003:32
not into the h. of Spain	TENN 1005:59
only one of the h. tends to get quoted	BLIN 169:30
prize-fighters shaking h.	MENC 669:72
puny h. Of heroes	COWP 293:61
right h. of fellowship	BIBLE 152:88
rise and shake h. with me	SPEKE 955:62
Rose-bloom fell on her h.	KEATS 546:92
seem thus washing her h.	SHAK 909:76
Shake h. forever	DRAY 345:40
shook h. with Reputation	WEBS 1061:42
shook h. with time	FORD 397:13
slipping from our h.	LOWE 617:12
Soon with h., on the sunken fosse	HEAN 465:35
soul clap its h.	YEATS 1106:79
Strength without h.	SWIN 987:27
stretch forth thy h.	BIBLE 147:78
such small h.	CUMM 300:86
Take h. and dance there	BROW 198:54
temples made with h.	BIBLE 148:2
thin h. of the poor	WILDE 1075:27
thought it out with both h.	SAYE 846:49
through most jewellers' h.	WEBS 1060:50
tides of men into my h.	LAWR 587:12
toil of brains, or toil of h.	MELV 667:28
wash your h. and pray	KIPL 565:15
washed his h. before multitude	BIBLE 140:53
washes his h.	SHAK 876:53
what h. you would hold!	LAMB 577:36
will these h. ne'er be clean?	SHAK 910:78
with crooked h.	TENN 1000:64
with h. blood stained	ORTE 741:84
work of his h.	LOCKE 609:69
work with your own h.	BIBLE 153:24
world's great h.	HUNT 504:22
wringing their h.	WALP 1052:97
handsaw know a hawk from a h.	SHAK 890:8
handsome as h. as my sister	KING 558:97
Looks h. in three hundred pounds	SHAK 878:20
once h. and tall as you	ELIOT 369:92

handsome (*contd.*)
present fashion is always h.	FULL 410:54
handy-dandy change…and h.	SHAK 904:44
hang all h. together	FRAN 402:10
as much as the half of a h.	OBRU 734:73
cowslips wan that h.	MILT 684:47
H. my Hat is Home	JERO 521:12
h. no longer on me	SHAK 906:90
H. on thy walls	JONS 535:2
h. them on the horns	SHAK 911:3
H. thyself	SHAK 875:50
let him h. there	EHRL 362:58
to have done is to h.	SHAK 896:52
hangdog shifty, h. look	WODE 1089:99
hanged got myself burned or h.	JERO 521:11
h. for stealing horses	HALI 452:27
h., if some eternal villain	SHAK 900:49
h. in a fortnight	JOHN 530:91
I'll be h.	SHAK 875:48
we shall be h.	CROM 298:52
hanging h. for the colour that it is	HOUS 496:88
H. and marriage…go by destiny	FARQ 383:68
H. and wiving goes by destiny	SHAK 875:32
H. is too good for him	BUNY 205:67
h. on with one hand	HYDE 509:12
nane the waur o' a h.	MACO 637:51
plain piece of work, a bare h.	DRYD 351:64
they're h. Danny Deever	KIPL 560:29
hangman little h. dare not shoot	SHAK 879:52
naked to the h.'s noose	HOUS 494:43
hangover a bad reputation is like a h.	PRES 789:26
what a h. is like	KEIL 548:28
hangs h. before her all the year	TENN 993:50
hangups everybody else's h.	BRAU 186:20
Hannibal how to gain a victory, H.	MARB 650:61
Hanover By famous H. city	BROW 197:31
Hansard H. is history's ear	SAMU 840:44
happen Can't H. Here	LEWIS 602:57
even if it didn't h.	KESEY 553:19
h. later to h.	NICH 726:53
too much seems to h.	COUP 289:75
Whatever must h. ultimately	KISS 566:41
happened fact that it h. elsewhere	FOWL 400:69
reminiscences of what never h.	SAKI 837:99
happenings contempt of chance h.	RABE 799:91
happens not what h. to a man	HUXL 507:64
When something h. to me	KENN 550:58
happier four times h. than the rest	RABE 799:90
h. everybody will be	ROTH 826:18
member of the family…is h.	FALU 382:57
happiest best and h. moments	SHEL 931:59
h. Africans in the world	SMITH 947:6
h. moment of a happy man	SCHO 849:97
H. when he is trying	LEHM 594:37
h. women…have no history	ELIOT 365:21
happiness accustomed, in…h.	WHAR 1068:96
annual expenditure…result h.	DICK 324:6
banquet of h.	HUGO 501:67
bat is a symbol of h.	LAWR 585:71
beauty is a guarantee of h.	PROU 793:98
beginnings of people's h.	STRA 979:2
best recipe for h.	AUST 51:48
Blue Bird of H.	MAET 638:57
consume h. without producing it	SHAW 920:96
definition of h.	KENN 552:90
does more for the h. of mankind	BRIL 188:52
dower Of inward h.	WORD 1096:38
enemy to human h.	JOHN 531:22
envy no man's h.	SHAK 886:2
Greatest H. Principle	MILL 675:71
greatest obstacle to h.	FONT 395:90
H. consists in the multiplicity	JOHN 528:48
H. engulfs our strength	BALZ 68:73
H. in marriage	AUST 51:35

happiness (contd.)

H. is always a work of art	YOUR 1108:7
h. is assured	BIER 161:84
H. is full of strife	ANOU 30:75
H. is healthy for the body	PROU 793:7
H. is like coke	HUXL 506:61
H. is no laughing matter	WHAT 1068:8
H. lies in conquering one's enemies	GENG 418:78
H. Makes up in Height	FROST 407:95
h. mankind can gain	DRYD 346:53
h. of an individual	JOHN 528:60
h. of finding a companion	BERN 97:85
h. of his humble home	GLAD 429:52
h. of knowing	FRAN 402:11
h. of the common man	BEVE 102:73
h. of the greatest number	BENT 92:13
h. of the next w.	BROW 196:95
h. or blessedness of man	SPIN 960:58
h. that the future offers	DESB 317:72
h. through another man's eyes	SHAK 887:30
h. too swiftly flies	GRAY 441:48
H. was my fate	RIMB 812:98
however uncertain of giving h.	AUST 51:39
In love, h. is abnormal	PROU 792:88
independent h.	WORD 1100:81
jealous possessions of h.	GIDE 423:45
lifetime of h.!	SHAW 921:22
lives in sin and looks for h.	BUNY 205:75
longing for h.	CAMUS 229:47
lost h. and lasting pain	MILT 687:89
magic lore of h.	RIMB 812:95
Man's h.	GIDE 423:48
meaning…We can assign to h.	ELIOT 372:60
money does not bring h.	LACL 573:63
nearly like h.	GREE 444:4
no h. within this circle of flesh	BROW 195:84
no longer desire h.	SHAW 920:2
not his own h.	SAIN 837:91
Oh H.! our…end and aim!	POPE 781:49
paint the memory of h.	SAIF 836:74
Perfect h., by princes sought	CHAP 252:70
private h. of the nation	JOHN 528:52
procures the greatest h.	HUTC 506:42
promised…either peace or h.	LEBON 591:78
pursuit of h.	JEFF 520:87
pursuit of h.	STAN 962:85
science…can give no h.	POIN 776:57
seemed to teach that h.	HARDY 456:96
seize more of h.	ANON 22:73
Simply seek h.	PECK 763:40
so much h. is produced	JOHN 529:79
somebody else's h.	HUXL 506:45
sorceress who dispenses h.	SCHI 847:63
sound off about h.	I 510:24
such a short-liv'd h.	BEHN 85:74
To dream is h.	HUGO 501:66
too happy in thine h.	KEATS 547:13
Virtue is simply h.	BURR 213:59
what is commonly called h.	SCHO 849:91
where…We find our h.	WORD 1096:32
white man's h.	DOUG 342:72

happy Adults talk about being h.   WINT 1087:66

all be as h. as kings	STEV 975:39
all the while I was quite h.	GIOV 428:36
all who are h.	JOHN 528:48
Anyone h. in this age	FULL 410:44
bread-sauce of the h. ending	JAMES 516:24
conspiracy to make you h.	UPDI 1037:60
die h.	FOX 400:73
difficult…to be h. with someone!	LABR 572:45
duty of being h.	STEV 974:20
Eisenhower…makes people h.	WHITE 1071:50
exist in order to be h.	SCHO 849:98
Forgive and be h.	PRAT 789:23

happy (contd.)

Getting up…does not make you h.	RABE 798:82
happiest moment of a h. man	SCHO 849:97
h. as the grass was green	THOM 1010:65
H. Days are Here Again	YELL 1107:96
h. families resemble each other	TOLS 1023:96
H., h., h., pair!	DRYD 351:67
h.…is not a characteristic	CHAN 251:58
H. is the country	AGATE 10:63
H. is the man who findeth wisdom	BIBLE 120:60
H. is the man	BIBLE 159:15
h. land	GOLD 433:15
H.…like Ulysses	BELL 86:90
h. man inevitably confines	HAWT 461:76
h. much of the time	PECK 763:40
H. those early days!	VAUG 1040:15
h. through science	POIN 776:57
H. till I woke again	HOUS 495:65
h. time when one is in misery	DANTE 305:69
h.…we are not over-h.	SHAK 889:97
h. who have called thee so	SOUT 954:37
have been very h.	ATTL 44:11
How h. I could be	GAY 417:59
human race was most h.	GIBB 421:18
I were but little h.	SHAK 879:40
I've had a h. life	HAZL 464:26
if life is h.	LABR 573:49
If the prisoner is h.	SHAW 922:42
If you are as h.	BUCH 202:29
in nothing else so h.	SHAK 867:53
keep me h. all the day	STEV 975:37
Let us all be h.	WARD 1053:15
look these h. couples	STEV 974:4
make men h.	POPE 782:86
Marriages would…be as h.	JOHN 529:80
no h. end to it	HEMI 470:25
no one can be perfectly h.	SPEN 955:63
none should be h.	JOHN 530:86
nor as h. as one hopes	LARO 582:25
not a h. one	GILB 424:65
not a h. prospect	THOM 1014:39
now to be most h.	SHAK 899:21
one of those h. places	THOR 1017:2
one of those h. souls	SHEL 929:10
one should feel h.	SARR 843:3
only one thing to make me h.	HAZL 464:19
prevent me from being h.	ANOU 30:72
remote from the h..	AUDEN 48:80
shame…from being h.	LABR 573:47
so few h. marriages	ASTE 43:93
so few marriages are h.	SWIFT 984:75
so h. as to sigh for	BEAU 80:67
So, I'm h. tonight	KING 558:86
someone, somewhere, may be h.	MENC 669:75
strangely h. with myself	IGNA 510:28
think themselves h.	BACON 57:71
This is the h. warrior	READ 803:52
thy h. strain?	SHEL 929:3
too h. in thine happiness	KEATS 547:13
twentieth will be h.	HUGO 502:91
unfurnish'd Of falsehood to be h.	DRYD 348:98
Was he h.?	AUDEN 47:65
When I am h. I live	SMITH 948:36
whether you are h. or not	SHAW 924:9
Which of us is h.	THAC 1006:90
wretched…once to have been h.	BOET 171:57

Happy Isles touch the H. I.   TENN 995:61

harbour a voyage and not a h.   TOYN 1024:18

h. and neighbour wood	THOM 1010:68
h. without ships	DEFOE 312:84
looking over h. and city	SAND 841:58
O the H. of Fowey	QUIL 797:57
rain over the dwindling h.	THOM 1010:69

hard game is too h.   JAMES 515:3

hard (contd.)

gave me the h. shoulder	HENRI 472:62
h. and practical man	HOYLE 498:2
h. on His Majesty's Opposition	HOBH 483:44
h., replied the Dodger	DICK 321:37
h. rhyme	SHAK 880:65
h. to be room-mates	SALI 838:23
h. to be sought out	HERA 473:88
no success without h. work	SOPH 953:20
powerful h. thing	CONN 284:85
read very h.	JOHN 527:26
The woman is so h.	TENN 996:94
when the times were not h.	EMER 377:75
where a heart is h.	SHAK 864:98

hard-hearted more cruel and h.   BACON 57:60

hard-hearts nature…makes these h.   SHAK 903:26

hardcover Europe…a h. book   DELI 314:37

harden H. not your heart   BIBLE 117:7

harder they would be h. to them   TROL 1028:78

hardest h. thing to bear   JUVE 540:79

h. thing to do   HEMI 470:28

hardship experience nothing but h.   BELL 86:92

meet any h.	KENN 550:64
teacheth him wholesome h.	LASS 583:35

hardships disappointments, h.   PEARY 762:35

h. of an emigrant's life	MOOD 703:94
very bottom of h.	DUBO 353:6

Hardy either 29 or Thomas H.   PARK 755:24

Kiss me, H.   NELS 722:1

hare covers…the h. and the hunter   PATC 759:90

grass and a h. sitting up	LAWR 585:70
h. limped trembling	KEATS 546:85
o'er the timid h.!	THOM 1015:50
start a h.!	SHAK 875:45

hare-bells heath and h.-b.   BRON 192:15

hare-brained every h.-b. nut   SAFER 835:66

harem like eunuchs in a h.   BEHAN 84:60

hares h. have no time to read   BROO 193:36

little hunted h.   HODG 484:53

hark H.! ah, the Nightingale!   ARNO 37:82

H., h., the lark	SHAK 916:3
H.! how all the welkin rings	WESL 1066:59
H. in thine ear	SHAK 904:44

Harlem like…a son of H.   OBRI 734:62

harlot h.'s cheek   SHAK 890:20

h.'s cry from street	BLAKE 168:5
he that cleaveth to h.	BIBLE 132:6
Portia is Brutus' h.	SHAK 883:30
prerogative of the h.	BALD 64:9

harlots Mother Of H.   BIBLE 158:28

Harlow 't' is silent, as in H.   ASQU 42:85

harm does h. to my wit   SHAK 894:97

does men great h.	HESI 479:83
does no h.	GILM 427:20
don't think it does any h.	THOM 1010:62
Fate cannot h. me	SMITH 949:56
fear we'll come to h.	BALL 67:48
good provoke to h.	SHAK 897:86
How can it h. you	JUANA 539:64
in his sleep he does little h.	SHAK 901:81
may do great h.	SHAW 924:89
no h. to retool imaginations	WELD 1062:90
Shall h. Macbeth	SHAK 909:67
Whoop, do me no h., good man	SHAK 912:35

harmful may be more h.   HUXL 509:3

who say it is h.   JUANA 539:66

harming perpetual h. of somebody   FORD 396:94

harmless book is not h.   ELIOT 370:20

h. and even beneficial	SHAW 924:89
h. as doves	BIBLE 136:76

harmonies European h.   GILL 426:12

h. are concealed from me	FISH 389:82
h. of body	BERN 97:86
inventor of h.	TENN 1003:24

harmonies (*contd.*)
tranquil h. — GAUG 416:38
tumult of thy mighty h. — SHEL 928:90
harmony ninefold h. — MILT 681:90
All discord, h., not understood — POPE 780:41
body's h. — POPE 783:5
h. comes…as a shock — RAINE 800:11
h.…comes to heal — WORD 1094:94
h. for the honour of God — BACH 54:93
H.!, H.! — SCHO 849:88
h. in autumn — SHEL 927:63
H. in discord — HORA 493:28
h. or true delight? — MILT 692:94
immortal god of h. — BEET 84:49
in h. with sentiments of assassin — BIER 160:64
knew such h. alone — MILT 681:89
Like h. in music — WORD 1096:21
may we bring h. — THAT 1007:11
notions of law and h. — THOR 1016:72
other h. of prose — DRYD 352:77
ravish like enchanting h. — SHAK 865:10
Sentimentally…diposed to h. — LAMB 576:25
that famous h. — YEATS 1104:59
untaught h. of spring — GRAY 441:55
what hope of h.? — SHAK 861:1
harms bars a thousand h. — SHAK 863:70
harness die in h. — AMIS 16:75
joints of the h. — BIBLE 111:72
Harold a masseur called H. — WOOD 1091:46
harp h., his sole remaining joy — SCOTT 853:42
h. that once through — MOORE 706:36
No h.…could so cheerily play — CAMP 227:24
played everything but the h. — BARR 73:62
wild h. slung behind — MOORE 706:34
Harper H. smiled, well pleased — SCOTT 853:47
harps h. upon the willows — BIBLE 119:47
harpstring hair and h. of gold — SWIN 987:39
harpy conference with this h. — SHAK 879:38
harried h. man I think I be! — BALL 67:42
Harris the present Mrs H. — THUR 1018:13
Harrison to see…H. hanged — PEPYS 765:62
if Rex H. doesn't — GRANT 438:99
Harrovian H. pricks up his ears — ANON 24:14
harrow beneath the h. knows — KIPL 559:14
H. the house of the dead — AUDEN 46:42
h. up thy soul — SHAK 889:74
Harrow H. would not be ashamed — BALD 65:15
Harry Banish not…H.'s company — SHAK 876:57
England breed again…a King H.? — DRAY 345:36
grunted H. to Jack — SASS 845:28
Know what I mean, H.? — BRUNO 201:12
little touch of H. — SHAK 881:89
harsh seem h., impertinent — JONS 535:90
harshness h. that resides in your heart — LAB 571:30
no h. gives offence — POPE 778:84
hart As the h. panteth — BIBLE 115:68
Hart one H. that you will not leave — HART 459:43
Harvard chair at H. or Princeton — MENC 669:64
didn't go to H. — JOHN 524:58
glass flowers at H. — MOORE 705:19
graduate of H. or not — JOHN 524:63
H. education consists of what — CONA 279:82
Yale College and my H. — MELV 667:32
harvest And it is h. — RANS 802:33
continual spring, and h. — SPEN 958:19
h. is past — BIBLE 128:23
h. of a quiet eye — WORD 1095:12
laughs with a h. — JERR 521:14
Raymond like the H. Moon — FARJ 383:63
seedtime and h. — BIBLE 104:13
sheaves in h. — DONNE 339:26
When thou cuttest down thine h. — BIBLE 108:95
white already to h. — BIBLE 145:38
harvested heart has been h. — BAUD 77:20

harvesting h. from existence — NIET 728:74
harvests bad h., and…fluctuations — ELIOT 365:17
h. bury all his pride has planned — POPE 779:23
hash product is final h. — MELV 668:47
hashish puffed h. …didn't inhale — RICH 810:72
hasta H. la vista, baby — SCHW 851:25
haste Do nothing in h. — WHYM 1074:11
eat it in h. — BIBLE 106:61
h. now to my setting — SHAK 918:59
life and light, with envious h. — ROCH 817:64
make what h. I can to be gone — CROM 298:57
Married in h. — CONG 280:99
marry in h. — CABE 224:77
Men love in h. — BYRON 223:57
repent in h. — CONG 280:1
send them out of the land in h. — BIBLE 106:63
shall not make h. — BIBLE 125:77
such h. to be doing — STEV 974:25
hasty let not thine heart be h. — BIBLE 123:26
need na start awa sae h. — BURNS 209:67
hastypudding sweets of H. — BARL 71:21
hat All h. and no cattle — CONN 282:52
as is the h. of a soldier — HERB 476:42
Beneath her torn h. — WHIT 1074:4
can't think without his h. — BECK 81:93
coat and top h. — LAVER 584:57
fashion of his h. — SHAK 878:27
from whose h. — KIPL 563:80
get your h. — FIEL 388:55
Hang my H. is Home — JERO 521:12
instinctively raise my h. — TREE 1025:43
Irishman takes off his h. — SHAW 923:71
Mistook his Wife for a H. — SACKS 835:58
Mr Pickwick's h. rolled — DICK 320:19
my knee, my h. — BROW 194:64
No h. upon his head — SHAK 889:86
nothing so characteristic as its h. — HOLM 486:91
puttin' on my top h. — BERL 95:60
Queen to get away with a h. — LOOS 613:30
silk h. on a Bradford millionaire — ELIOT 369:89
still in straw h. and sandals — BASHO 76:3
stone in my straw h. — STEV 973:97
Swept off his tall h. — GRAV 440:40
The way you wear your h. — GERS 420:10
Under the black h. — HEMI 471:44
where he laid his h. — JOHN 531:24
hatches under h.…Rain! — KEATS 544:53
hatchet with my little h. — WASH 1054:39
hate All men h. the wretched — SHEL 926:54
as though h. has no cost — SAND 841:69
Boys' h. was dangerous — MUNRO 714:55
crops of love and h. — MUIR 712:36
deadly h. have pierced so deep — MILT 690:50
do good to them that h. you — BIBLE 134:41
Each sequestered in its h. — AUDEN 47:72
even the h. of sins — SURR 982:44
Families! I h. you! — GIDE 423:45
fear to h. — SHAK 868:67
five guys who h. you — STEN 968:75
free to love or h. — SART 844:6
glance of supernatural h. — BYRON 223:67
God…spilled his own h. — BURG 206:90
h. a fellow whom pride — JOHN 531:21
h. all that don't love me — FARQ 383:66
h. all the people — HAMM 454:56
h. American simplicity — JAMES 517:33
h. and character assassination — SMITH 948:25
h. and death — SHEL 932:65
h. being told How It Is — GALL 413:96
h. discussions of feminism — FREN 404:38
h. Iberian peninsular has inspired — BOLI 172:72
h. in a woman — SHAW 920:6
H. is always more clairvoyant — LACL 574:65
h. is hardly to be hiden — CARL 233:30

hate (*contd.*)
h. (is) pain accompanied by the idea — SPIN 960:54
h. liberality — SIDM 936:40
h. me as much as you love me — BECK 82:7
h. that which we often fear — SHAK 905:61
h. the idea of causes — FORS 399:52
h. the one, and love the other — BIBLE 135:51
h. them if I can — ANON 21:47
h. walking — SMOL 950:63
h. with greater devotion — SHAK 911:8
haughty Juno's unrelenting h. — DRYD 352:76
have I not reason to h. — HAZL 464:16
how I h. you! — RIMB 812:90
I h. and I love. — CATU 245:64
implacable in h. — DRYD 349:15
know enough of h. — FROST 407:85
let him h. you through the glass — BLUN 170:44
Let them h. — ACCI 2:16
love and h.…are necessary — BLAKE 166:71
murd'rous h. — SHAK 912:46
never h. a song — BERL 95:64
not to h. him now — RACI 799:96
not to weep…nor to h. them — SPIN 960:46
Of guile, of h., of envy — MILT 692:3
or in h. — STEV 974:4
owe no man h. — SHAK 886:2
Politicians neither love nor h. — DRYD 349:3
power to love, or h. — MARL 655:27
religion to make us h. — SWIFT 984:71
scarcely h. any one — HAZL 463:5
study of revenge, immortal h. — MILT 687:93
Take away this murdherin' h. — OCAS 735:75
they all do h. him — SHAK 917:32
time to h. — BIBLE 122:19
what I h. myself most — LEAV 591:77
women highly hold in h. — SHAK 860:85
worst sin…is not to h. — SHAW 920:14
hated h. iniquity — GREG 446:46
loved well because he h. — BROW 199:69
never h. a man — GABOR 411:66
never more h. — ELLI 375:17
Or being h. — KIPL 564:8
Vice…to be h. — POPE 780:44
hateful h. heresies — SPEN 958:23
most h. form of foolery — BROW 200:84
my doors are h. — OTWAY 746:81
The self is h. — PASC 758:67
hater join the h. — GORD 435:63
hates h. children and dogs — FIEL 388:62
h. them for it — SHAW 920:91
Nothing h. him or envies him — FAUL 384:86
hating Loving not, h. not — BROW 200:82
hatless H., I take off — LARK 581:1
hatred all your h. now on me? — SHAK 863:51
common h. of its neighbours — INGE 511:40
From envy, h., and malice — BOOK 174:5
frown of h. — BYRON 221:11
h. for the Tory Party — BEVAN 101:64
h. is a tonic — BALZ 68:74
H. is always a sin — MUNRO 714:59
H. is generalized — DUDEK 353:19
h. is not…mere crabbedness — FADI 382:53
h. of progress and civilization — ATAT 43:1
H. of the bourgeois — FLAU 393:42
h.…the longest pleasure — BYRON 223:57
heartbreak, h. blind — NOON 731:24
Ideas are born from h. — GENET 418:76
love to h. turned — CONG 281:22
no h. or bitterness towards anyone — CAVE 246:71
sport is…bound up with h. — ORWE 745:64
stalled ox and h. therewith — BIBLE 121:80
Where there is h. — FRAN 401:91
hatreds systematic organization of h. — ADAMS 5:72
hats h., as in Victorian days — SITW 941:17

heads (*contd.*)

can't mess with people's h.	HEND 472:56
carve h. upon cherry-stones	JOHN 532:29
cut off the h. of people	PEPYS 765:76
egg h. are in one basket	ANON 27:71
goes to the h. of cowards	MITC 697:88
hardly miss their h.	SHAW 925:27
h. are green	LEAR 590:54
h....beneath their shoulders	SHAK 898:7
H., h., take care of your h.	DICK 320:16
h. pass out	BERR 98:10
h. replete with thoughts	COWP 293:62
hover in their restless h.	MARL 653:91
Hung their h.	SHAK 918:54
keep their own h.	MUMF 713:49
lose their h.	FITZ 391:12
old h. on your young shoulders	SPARK 955:51
Reared...their flourished h.	MILT 690:63
sugarplums danced in their h.	MOORE 704:4
tall men had ever very empty h.	BACON 56:38
Tossing their h.	WORD 1099:68
vulgar h. that look asquint	BROW 195:65
with h. on their shoulders	JAMES 518:51
wooden h. may be [inherited]	CONK 282:49
write plays in our h.	MAMET 644:61
headstone h. of the corner	BIBLE 118:27
headstones h. yield their names	TATE 991:2
H. stagger	BERR 98:10
milestones into h.	LOWE 616:91
headstrong h., moody, murmuring	DRYD 349:7
headway women...make some h.	FALU 382:58
heal balm to h. their wounds	SHAK 862:30
fame can never h.	AYTO 53:87
Physician, h. thyself	BIBLE 142:81
time to h.	BIBLE 122:19
What wound did ever h.	SHAK 899:28
healed h. by the same means	SHAK 872:80
with his stripes we are h.	BIBLE 127:1
healer compassion of the h.'s art	ELIOT 371:51
time is no h.	ELIOT 372:62
healing h. in his wings	BIBLE 131:72
leaves of tree for h. of nations	BIBLE 159:39
not heroics but h.	HARD 455:79
of the most High cometh h.	BIBLE 132:15
health Christian that is in h.	LAW 585:60
disliked hearing about h.	MITF 697:96
Drink a h. to	SYNGE 988:63
drink his h. with three cheers	EDGE 360:27
good to preserve the h. of Man	BYRD 218:57
great deal better for the h.	STEV 973:91
H. and an able body	FLET 394:76
h. and plenty cheered	GOLD 432:8
h. of his wife	CONN 283:76
H., Wealth, Love...and Time	ANON 30:68
His h., his honour	BLUN 170:47
hunt in fields, for h.	DRYD 352:87
implies an idea of h.	TRIL 1026:57
in h. wes and gladnes	DUNB 355:40
in sickness and in h.	BOOK 176:49
interest of good h.	TAFT 990:83
lack of h. in the body	PLATO 774:10
no h. in us	BOOK 173:89
nor hope, nor h.	SHEL 927:74
Only do always in h.	SIGI 938:70
people in the soundest h.	DICK 326:54
preservation of h.	SPEN 955:65
psychological h.	PECK 763:41
save men from indifferent h.	DOUG 342:65
saving h. among all nations	BIBLE 116:85
Say that h. and wealth	HUNT 505:29
simple beauty and rustic h.	WHIT 1074:4
spirit of h.	SHAK 888:71
When you have both it's h.	DONL 336:60
healths drink one another's h.	JERO 521:5

healthy classical period was h.	GOET 431:79
Happiness is h. for the body	PROU 793:7
If you are h.	FORD 396:9
makes a male h.	THUR 1018:24
heap all is a knot, a h.	JONS 536:27
dig and h.	ARNO 37:74
garbage h.	GARD 415:23
H. high the ...platter	MACB 624:32
rude h. together hurl'd	MARV 659:90
heaped H. for two days	KHAY 555:42
hear can't h. what they say?	SMITH 947:15
Come on and h.	BERL 95:57
deaf to h.	BIBLE 141:66
Do not let me h.	ELIOT 371:47
ears to h.	BIBLE 137:85
ears to h., let him h.	BIBLE 141:62
h. it through their feet	SOUSA 953:25
H., O Israel	BIBLE 108:90
h. the soft rain	RICK 811:74
I h. you, I will come	HOUS 495:51
I shall h. in heaven	BEET 84:54
If you really want to h.	SALI 838:18
It startled him just to h.	RAMOS 801:17
much to h. and see	SKEL 942:32
neither see nor h.	JOHN 524:69
one you cannot h.	NORTH 731:32
power...to make you h.	CONR 284:88
public only gets to h.	STEIN 966:50
something we cannot h.	SCOTT 852:37
then not h. it crying!	HERB 475:31
unto you that h. shall more be given	BIBLE 141:63
what they h., they repeat!	SITW 941:7
what they wanted to h.	SHAR 919:85
heard Ain't H. Nothin' Yet	JOLS 533:48
every man that h. him	JONS 536:32
fall of...civilisation wiil not be h.	READ 803:55
generally h.	GILB 425:93
have ye not h.?	BIBLE 126:90
I h. no longer	TENN 1001:79
My God, I h. this day	HERB 475:21
never have been h. of	HAZL 464:15
Oon ere it h.	CHAU 254:11
the more h.	WILD 1080:34
We had h. them	HEMI 470:17
hearers Be ye doers...not h. only	BIBLE 155:61
maiming it to suit her h.	BACON 60:40
move his h.	FRAS 403:18
too deep for his h.	GOLD 433:28
hearing Fall asleep, or h. die	SHAK 918:56
mentioned in your h.	AUST 51:42
hearings h. are just like a s.	NIXON 730:7
h. will be remembered	INOU 512:58
hearse h. presently arrived	LAWS 587:19
h. where Lycid lies	MILT 684:47
In an h. she rode	SMART 944:63
laid in doleful h.?	SPEN 958:71
Why does a h. horse snicker	SAND 841:63
heart a trickling of h.	PATC 759:90
abundance of the h.	BIBLE 137:92
actor in his h. believes	WELL 1063:5
adultery with her already in his h.	BIBLE 134:40
affectations rise up in his h.	DIDE 330:42
after Heaven's own h.	DRYD 349:9
after leaving my h. on the screen	QUIR 798:72
age should show your h.	MARV 658:73
always knew in my h.	HOPK 492:11
Ancient person of my h.	ROCH 817:65
and the h. is sick	TENN 999:35
as the h. grows older	HOPK 492:93
As well as want of h.!	HOOD 489:50
At h. I knew	THES 1009:45
Batter my h.	DONNE 338:7
beak from out my h.	POE 776:49
beanbag of the h.	NOON 731:22

heads (*contd.*)

Because it is my H.	OATES 733:57
bind the h. of man!	GILM 427:18
bitter...because it is my h.	CRANE 295:12
Blessed are the pure in h.	WHAR 1068:5
blue and white Wednesday h.	HATT 460:58
books are novels at h.	RABAN 798:75
breaks the h.	MACD 628:91
broken and a contrite h.	BIBLE 116:79
broken h. lies here	MACA 624:25
bullet through his h.	THAC 1006:86
Bury my h. at Wounded Knee	BENET 90:62
'Calais' lying in my h.	MARY 661:30
Calls my h. to be his own	BRID 187:43
calm sunshine of the h.	CONS 285:18
captain's h.	SHAK 904:51
carried out in the h. of none	KISS 566:34
cathedrals in my h.	SASS 845:30
change of h.	AUDEN 46:42
Chloe...wants a h.	POPE 782:73
Christ in the h.	PATR 761:15
commune with your own h.	BIBLE 114:33
conversant with a Man's h.	POE 776:52
corrupt the h.	BYRON 219:63
Create in me a clean h.	BIBLE 116:78
cry of Absence...in the h.	RANS 802:35
dagger...in the h. of France	QUIN 798:68
darkness of man's h.	GOLD 432:85
Dead H. of Australia	GREG 446:48
depths of every h.	HAWT 461:77
deserts of the h.	AUDEN 47:73
desires of the h.	AUDEN 46:56
desperateness of man's h.!	BUNY 204:63
dialogues with my Mother's h.	WORD 1096:26
Did not our h. burn	BIBLE 144:22
directly to the h.	POE 776:45
Don't search...for my h.	BAUD 77:21
dried up your h.	FLAU 392:29
drink thy wine with a merry h.	BIBLE 123:33
ease a h. Like a satin gown	PARK 753:91
Enter every trembling h.	WESL 1066:63
entered into my h.	HOLM 485:72
every Russian's inmost h.	PUSH 795:37
fade from my h.	MOORE 706:32
false h. doth know	SHAK 908:37
Fare thee well, great h.	SHAK 876:76
feed on him in thy h.	BOOK 175:31
felt my h. strangely warmed	WESL 1066:66
figure of my h.	SHAK 897:95
finite number of h.-beats	ARMS 35:50
flesh and my h. faileth	BIBLE 117:81
fop in my h.	ETHE 380:19
for such a kind h.	SHAK 878:21
foul...shop of the h.	YEATS 1107:89
free, the larger h.	TENN 1000:57
from my h. the strings do break	CAMP 228:36
full h. Remains in use	SHAK 905:63
funeral marches around your h.	MILL 676:98
gambled my h. and lost	RIVE 813:3
gay cloths, a merry h.	WEBS 1060:37
give thee the desires of thine h.	BIBLE 115:63
give them an h. of flesh	BIBLE 129:36
give them one h.	BIBLE 129:36
giving your h. to a dog	KIPL 564:6
glad with all my h.	DRAY 345:40
great flint...singing into his h.	BIRN 163:25
grief of h.	SHAK 918:56
Guilt in his h.	CHUR 262:80
Harden not your h.	BIBLE 117:7
harshness which resides in your h.	LAB 571:30
has ached with a h.!	SWIN 987:34
have the h. to stay	BUTL 217:26
haven't the h. to take a minute	CARA 231:94
haven't the h.	GRAH 437:88

heart (*contd.*)

h. aches	KEATS 547:13
h., all mad with misery	SHAK 862:40
h. and core of ages	LOWE 615:72
h. and mind of America	BARZ 75:97
h. and my flesh crieth out	BIBLE 117:93
h. and stomach of a king	ELIZ 373:90
h. as big as Waterloo Station	AGATE 10:66
h. as sound as a bell	SHAK 879:52
h.'s beatin' rhythm	BERRY 98:4
h. be so full of spring?	SWIN 986:20
h. blackening	JEFF 519:79
h. bleeds for his country	JOHN 527:27
h. broken even more surely	LESS 599:8
h. but one	BOUR 181:48
h.'s deep-sore wounding	SHAK 864:2
h. dies within me	SCHAW 847:61
h. distrusting asks	GOLD 433:14
h. either breaks or boldens	BALZ 68:72
h. enough to begin to live	STEV 974:22
h.'s first ease	DAYL 310:56
h. flutter in my breast	SAPP 842:92
h. grown cold	SHEL 931:47
h. has been harvested	BAUD 77:20
h. has its reasons	PASC 758:65
h. hath ne'er within him burned	SCOTT 853:49
h. in a case o' gowd	BALL 68:58
h. in hiding	HOPK 491:89
h. in's face	SHAK 911:22
h.'s in the Highlands	BURNS 211:5
h. into my mouth	SHAK 902:96
H. Is A Lonely Hunter	MACC 626:65
h. is a lonely hunter	SHARP 919:79
h. is deceitful	BIBLE 128:26
h. is Highland	GALT 413:8
h. is in the coffin	SHAK 884:51
h. is in the right place	LIVI 607:47
h. is in their boots	CHES 259:27
h. is like wax	BIBLE 114:49
h. knocked in its cage	GREE 444:22
h. less bounding	ARNO 39:19
h. lies much lower	LICH 603:83
h. lies plain	ARNO 36:70
h. lingered so far	MOOD 703:94
h. love till now?	SHAK 868:83
h. never knows the colour of the skin	GEOR 419:90
h. of a brute like you	PLATH 773:95
h. of a man…lodged in a woman	CONG 281:38
h. of a man	ROUS 827:37
H. of England	DRAY 345:38
h. of fire	TENN 1002:63
h. of lead	POPE 782:97
h. of man go together	RUSK 830:86
h. of man has long been sore	HOUS 496:76
h. of man…dignity	TATE 991:5
h. of our island	FORS 398:28
h. of standing	EMPS 378:85
h. of the city	MOYN 711:14
h. of the North is dead	LAWR 586:89
h. of woman	SHAK 883:37
h. on your sleeve	THAT 1008:22
h. responsive swells	BYRON 221:12
h. Shall break into	SHAK 903:16
h. shall break	SHAK 902:15
h. shall not fear	BIBLE 115:55
h.'s so full of joy	DRYD 348:93
h.'s stalled motor	MAYA 665:5
h.…that of a little child	THAC 1007:99
h. that swells	DRYD 348:95
h. that watches and receives	WORD 1094:3
h. that with every year grows dim	CONR 284:98
h. the keener	ANON 21:60
h. untravelled	GOLD 432:96
h. was free	WESL 1066:58

heart (*contd.*)

h. was glad	FOX 400:74
h. was one of those	BYRON 221:22
h. was to thy rudder	SHAK 905:80
h. was used to beat	TENN 998:23
h. which beats only for you	VERL 1042:36
h. why do you pound	APOL 31:88
h. will break in twa	NAIR 718:21
h. with pleasure fills	WORD 1099:70
h.…with thy nest	WORD 1100:87
h. with usury to such scenes?	LAMB 576:8
heaven-entreated h.	CRAS 296:22
heavenly and hidden h.	BUEC 203:42
hedgehog of the h.	LOWE 617:10
His flawed h.	SHAK 904:49
history…begins in the h.	CATH 244:38
holiness of the h.'s affections	KEATS 544:45
Hope deferred maketh the h. sick	BIBLE 121:73
How irksome…to my h.!	SHAK 861:1
human h. is slightly left of centre	FRYE 409:25
humble and a contrite h.	KIPL 562:61
hurt you to the h.	TWAIN 1034:10
in his painted h.	KEATS 546:89
in his private h.	TWAIN 1034:7
In its secret h.	SMITH 949:60
in my h. his iron arrow	SPEN 957:6
In my h.'s core	SHAK 891:37
in our h. we know	WORD 1098:57
In your h.	GOLD 433:32
index to the h.	DICK 322:76
indurate h. against God	KNOX 567:58
Into my h. an air	HOUS 495:57
into the bell of her h.	THOM 1011:88
into the h. of man	SWIFT 985:87
into the world with your h.	SHEL 927:56
Irishman's h. is nothing	SHAW 923:70
Is your h. at rest?	FLET 394:78
Keep thine h.	CRAS 296:24
kid…about her h. condition?	SILV 938:78
king's h. is in the hand	BIBLE 121:91
know in my h. of h.s	STARK 963:95
know my h.	BIBLE 120:51
know not the h.	SHAK 913:54
knowledge of the h.	JOHN 528:61
land of their h.'s hope	DAVIS 309:38
language of the h.	POPE 781:69
larger was his h.	DRYD 350:28
laughing h.'s long peace	BROO 192:24
lay his hand on his h.	STRA 979:2
lays his hand on h.	BEER 83:27
Left my H. in San Francisco	CROSS 298:63
Let every h. exult with joy	DODD 335:44
let not thine h. be hasty	BIBLE 123:26
Let not your h. be troubled	BIBLE 146:60
Let not your h. be troubled	BIBLE 146:63
Lift up your h.	WESL 1066:62
light h. lives long	SHAK 866:25
like a h. in reserve	CESA 248:3
Like music on my h.	COLE 274:94
listened at his h.	FROST 406:81
little body with a mighty h.	SHAK 880:74
Little skill, little h.	ROSS 825:96
live in my h.	HAMM 454:53
live with only half a h.	WILS 1084:19
long let your h. be strong	LAUD 583:40
look into thy h., and write	SIDN 937:51
loosed our h. in tears	ARNO 37:73
Lord looketh on the h.	BIBLE 110:36
Lord of my h.	MACD 627:86
lotion of the h.	PARK 756:37
love which is inside his h.	LAWR 586:80
love you with all my h.	ROCH 816:43
Mad with much h.	DONNE 336:69
Made of a h.	HERB 474:8

heart (*contd.*)

made tender to the h.	PROU 793:96
make this h. rejoice or ache	COWP 291:26
malpractice of h.	CLOU 271:41
man after his own h.	BIBLE 110:34
man with h., head, hand	TENN 1001:80
man's h. is small	KIPL 563:92
mean to a tired h.	BOND 172:79
mechanical…in h.	CARL 234:40
meek and lowly in h.	BIBLE 137:88
Mercy has a human h.	BLAKE 166:69
merry h. doeth good	BIBLE 121:87
merry h. goes all the day	SHAK 911:27
merry h. maketh a cheerful	BIBLE 121:79
merry h. with small possession	HENR 473:71
mind and in the h.	LARO 582:29
mind, h.…not myself	WELTY 1065:49
more native to the h.	SHAK 887:45
mother's h. is an abyss	BALZ 69:79
much against my h.	PATM 760:5
much it grieved my h.	WORD 1095:5
Must my h. grow sick	CULL 299:71
My h. has made its mind up	COPE 287:54
my h. is a handful of dust	TENN 1001:90
my h. is glad	ANON 23:96
My h. leaps up	WORD 1097:42
my h. remembers how!	STEV 976:56
My h. would hear her	TENN 1001:88
my old bitter h.	ORAH 741:78
nation…had the lion h.	CHUR 265:41
naughtiness of thine h.	BIBLE 110:38
nearly breaks my h.	JERO 521:8
no iron can stab the h.	BABEL 54:90
No nearer the h. than the lip	ANON 23:82
No pitying h.	GRAY 443:85
not in the h. or in the saliva	ARGU 33:18
not my h.	JONS 535:89
not really bad at h.	BELL 87:11
not wear your h. on sleeve	WEBS 1061:74
not your h. away	HOUS 494:44
O my little h.!	SHAK 865:13
O pure of h.	COLE 274:7
O tiger's h.	SHAK 861:17
ocean or the human h.?	LAUT 584:49
oft my h. to ache	BLAKE 168:16
one body and one h.	DOUG 341:57
Only with the h.	SAIN 836:85
open a window into one's h.	MELBA 667:21
Open not thine h.	BIBLE 132:94
Open your h.	BROW 199:63
opens the h. and lungs	STER 969:7
Out-worn h.	YEATS 1105:62
own the h. and stool	COLUM 278:62
pageant of his bleeding h.	ARNO 38:3
Pass on, weak h.	TENN 998:14
passionate h. of the poet	TENN 1001:75
Pitee…in gentil h.	CHAU 255:30
place that's broken my h.	BAUG 78:48
poor man's h.	WORD 1098:58
Pourest thy full h.	SHEL 929:97
Praise…can freeze the h.	BUCK 203:36
Presume not on thy h.	SHAK 913:52
Pride leaves the h.	GAUT 416:43
produces a sadness of h.	MORSE 709:90
quickening of the h.	AUDEN 46:48
red red vitals of his h.	RANS 802:34
rejoicing the h.	BIBLE 114:45
Religion's in the h.	JERR 521:13
removed their h. far from me	BIBLE 125:78
revolting and a rebellious h.	BIBLE 128:20
Rise in the h.	TENN 997:2
road to the h.	BALZ 69:78
roaming with a hungry h.	TENN 994:58
round his h. one…hair	ROSS 824:88

heart (*contd.*)

ruddy drops that warm my h.	GRAY 443:*83*
Sacred H. o' Jesus	OCAS 735:*75*
sad, good Christian at her h.	POPE 781:*71*
safe within its central h.	WHIT 1073:*96*
said to H., How goes it?	BELL 87:*14*
sank down Into my h.	WORD 1096:*22*
sat down…on Henry's h.	BERR 98:*13*
seat…in the h.	GAND 414:*14*
see my h.…without disgust	BAUD 77:*26*
see what breeds about her h.	SHAK 903:*26*
self-destruction enter the h.	CHEE 255:*49*
sensations…felt along the h.	WORD 1094:*96*
set the h. on fire	SHAK 864:*91*
sick at h.	SHAK 887:*42*
sickening of the h.	POE 775:*41*
Sink h. and voice	NEALE 722:*93*
sleeps on his own h.	WORD 1095:*12*
some h. did break	TENN 998:*21*
souls Of the pure in h.	RANS 802:*37*
spring of love gushed from my h.	COLE 274:*91*
stone of the h.	YEATS 1106:*73*
straightest road to a man's h.	FERN 386:*26*
strings…in the human h.	DICK 322:*64*
struggle…fill a human h.	CAMUS 229:*34*
stuffed roast h.	JOYCE 538:*53*
take from them all…hardness of h.	BOOK 174:*11*
take their h. in one hand	BILL 162:*4*
temples th'upright h. and pure	MILT 687:*86*
than a h. untainted?	SHAK 861:*6*
Thanks to the human h.	WORD 1098:*56*
that mighty h. is lying still!	WORD 1097:*46*
That the bruised h.	SHAK 898:*14*
the fart Of every h.	SUCK 981:*22*
The tears fall in my h.	VERL 1042:*35*
the waters of the h.	THOM 1010:*52*
them whose h. is perfect	BIBLE 112:*89*
there will your h. be also	BIBLE 135:*50*
thou hast my h.	PRIOR 791:*59*
thoughts, and h. enlarges	MILT 692:*97*
through a broken h.	WILDE 1078:*4*
Thy rebuke hath broken my h.	BOOK 177:*83*
tiger's h.	GREE 445:*33*
to each loving h. how near!	HOLM 486:*98*
Toyshop of their h.	POPE 778:*92*
tragic h.	BENET 90:*63*
triumph of his h.	ADDI 7:*18*
true love hath my h.	SIDN 936:*47*
trust not the h. of that man	CARL 235:*58*
truths of the h.	FAUL 383:*77*
turn the h. of the fathers	BIBLE 131:*73*
united in one h.	WALT 1052:*2*
United to a h. like thine	BRON 190:*86*
unpack my h. with words	SHAK 890:*16*
unquiet h. and brain	TENN 998:*19*
utmost passion of her h.	HAWT 461:*70*
Vacant h., and hand, and eye	SCOTT 855:*97*
Vengeance is in my h.	SHAK 862:*37*
verses from my h.	MARTI 657:*57*
visit my sad h.	SHAK 883:*31*
walk in the ways of thine h.	BIBLE 123:*41*
weather in the h.	RICH 809:*41*
were my dear h.-strings	SHAK 899:*35*
whan every lusty h.	MALO 642:*32*
What female h. can gold despise?	GRAY 441:*52*
Whatever your h.	LUTH 620:*50*
where a h. is hard	SHAK 864:*98*
where my h. is turning	FOST 399:*60*
Where the h. lies	BROW 199:*67*
wine that maketh glad the h.	BIBLE 118:*16*
with a hopeful h.	LAWR 586:*97*
with its h. cut out	STEG 965:*28*
With rue my h. is laden	HOUS 495:*61*
withered h. was dead	SCOTT 853:*44*

heart (*contd.*)

woman touches another's h.	LACL 574:*68*
word have I hid in mine h.	BIBLE 119:*30*
wound my h.	VERL 1042:*33*
heart-ache h.-a., and the…shocks	SHAK 890:*21*
heart-easing tell the most h. things	KEATS 544:*41*
heart-of-gold bawcock and a h.	SHAK 881:*91*
heartbeats slow h.	GRAV 440:*30*
heartbreak feel the h.	GIBS 422:*39*
h., hatred blind	NOON 731:*24*
in the h. of things?	GIBS 422:*39*
heartening h. and the strong reply	EMPS 378:*85*
hearth as from an unextinguished h.	SHEL 928:*91*
By this still h.	TENN 994:*57*
cricket on the h.	MILT 682:*10*
drive hunger from the h.	LLOY 608:*57*
h. of television	NEW 724:*21*
moved earth and h.	TENN 995:*61*
hearth-fire h.-f. and the home-acre	
heartiness h. that compels belief	TWAIN 1032:*59*
heartland from the h. of the country	SHUL 936:*37*
heartless appallingly h. thing to do	MANS 647:*10*
heartlessness the h. of human beings	OKRI 738:*23*
hearts all that human h. endure	GOLD 432:*99*
any trace of it in their h.	REDON 804:*78*
apply our h. unto wisdom	BIBLE 117:*1*
broke the h.	WAUGH 1057:*89*
cannot find it in our h.	GELL 417:*72*
carry in their h.	LLOY 608:*58*
clasp we to our h.	ROSS 824:*87*
Combine your h. in one	SHAK 882:*12*
Content in the…cell of their h.	BOGAN 171:*58*
curse upon your whunstane h.	BURNS 209:*62*
day with…brave h.	CLIN 269:*16*
dealt in hides, but never in h.	DICK 323:*91*
devices and desires of our own h.	BOOK 173:*89*
enthronèd in the h. of kings	SHAK 873:*93*
evil lurks in the h. of men?	ATWO 45:*30*
eyes and h. ears	LYLY 620:*59*
free h., free foreheads	TENN 995:*61*
given our h. away	WORD 1099:*73*
hands upon their h.	HOUS 496:*72*
harden not your h.	BOOK 177:*88*
H. after them in tangled	MILT 694:*32*
h. all rocky	BYRON 220:*98*
h. and hands and voices	WINK 1086:*59*
H. and minds	ANON 27:*77*
h. are more than coronets	TENN 995:*70*
h. are yearning	FORD 397:*20*
h. be frolic	GREE 445:*32*
h. of men…have melted	SHAK 868:*34*
h., though stout	LONG 611:*95*
h. very dry and tough	HOOK 490:*56*
H. wound up with love	SPEN 956:*83*
Heaven in our h.	NIGH 729:*96*
heavenly compassion in your h.	DICK 325:*37*
if our h. were beating	SCOTT 855:*83*
In h. at peace	BROO 192:*22*
in our h. either to marry	STEV 973:*1*
in the gentlest h.	SPEN 958:*15*
in the imagination of their h.	BIBLE 141:*75*
keep your h. and minds	BIBLE 153:*14*
keep your h. and minds	BOOK 175:*33*
lighten our own h.	SHAK 880:*68*
Lord pondereth the h.	BIBLE 121:*92*
May God wither up their h.!	DAVIS 309:*36*
modern life…palsied h.	ARNO 37:*92*
O, you hard h.	SHAK 882:*15*
Of finite h. that yearn	BROW 199:*66*
our h. are great	TENN 1002:*3*
Our h., unrisen	WILK 1080:*42*
our h. were fulfilled	SWIN 988:*52*
sing to find your h.	FLEC 393:*48*
song for thinking h.	WORD 1096:*36*

hearts (*contd.*)

steel my soldiers' h.	SHAK 881:*95*
still can pierce our h.	MUIR 712:*34*
stout h. and stout swords	BIRK 163:*18*
sweetness…inspired their h.	MARL 653:*91*
take away our h. o' stone	OCAS 735:*75*
take them with our h.	NEWM 724:*25*
tempts your…heedless h.	GRAY 441:*54*
thousand h. are great	SHAK 863:*67*
thousand h. beat happily	BYRON 219:*84*
touching their h.	TROL 1027:*76*
two h. beating each to each!	BROW 198:*40*
undeveloped h.	FORS 398:*46*
unto whom all h. be open	BOOK 174:*16*
Where men with Spendid H.	BROO 192:*27*
with beating h.	STOWE 978:*84*
wore at their h.	SPEN 956:*72*
wot's hidden in each other's h.	DICK 323:*81*
heartstring intelligencer's h.	WEBS 1060:*57*
heartstrings playeth with your h.	LYLY 620:*61*
sweep across our h.	WILS 1086:*44*
hearty h. old man	SOUT 954:*29*
heat ally the h.	BLAKE 165:*58*
bear…the h.	ARNO 37:*74*
but he gat no h.	BIBLE 110:*53*
can't stand the h.	TRUM 1030:*20*
false of h.	SHAK 915:*88*
fantastic summer's h.?	SHAK 866:*47*
h. full of coldness	LYLY 620:*59*
H. not a furnace	SHAK 917:*45*
h. o'th' sun	SHAK 916:*16*
h. of life	CONR 284:*98*
h. of the business is over!	ETHE 380:*14*
In my limbs their former h.?	HERR 477:*52*
in temperate h.	SURR 983:*46*
not without dust and h.	MILT 685:*63*
nothing hid from the h.	BIBLE 114:*44*
of h. or cold	HUME 503:*1*
stirs up the Native H.	PENE 764:*53*
transmit h. slowly	WATT 1055:*55*
trellises Of the h.	SITW 940:*6*
voice of high midsummer's h.	ROBE 814:*16*
white h. of this revolution	WILS 1085:*30*
With h. intense	GILB 424:*78*
heath foot is on my native h.	SCOTT 855:*89*
Land of brown h.	SCOTT 853:*50*
likewise a wind on the h.	BORR 179:*23*
moths fluttering among the h.	BRON 192:*15*
Heathcliff Nelly, I am H.	BRON 192:*12*
heathen break the h.	TENN 1002:*17*
exalted among the h.	BIBLE 116:*74*
h. Chinee is peculiar	HARTE 459:*50*
h. for thine inheritance	BIBLE 114:*32*
h. in 'is blindness	KIPL 562:*58*
h. in the carnal part	POPE 781:*71*
h. so furiously rage	BOOK 176:*59*
In h., Turk or Jew	BLAKE 166:*65*
in soul a h.	DICK 325:*36*
Why do the h. rage	BIBLE 114:*30*
heather pore benighted h.	KIPL 560:*34*
pu'd the h. green	BALL -101:*38*
sweet as the h.	LAUD 583:*38*
tumble on the h.	SCOTT 854:*72*
whare the h. grows	BURNS 212:*41*
heaths some game on these lone h.	HAZL 463:*6*
heats give your h. to	SHAK 917:*50*
h. which my veins fill	DONNE 337:*80*
heaven accusing…h.	CAMUS 229:*58*
after H.'s own heart	DRYD 349:*9*
airs from h.	SHAK 888:*71*
All this, and h. too!	HENRY 472:*46*
all we know of h.	DICK 328:*17*
and approving H.	THOM 1015:*48*
another h. From h. gate	MILT 691:*88*

heaven (*contd.*)

any thing that is in h. above	BIBLE 106:68
are the brains of h.	MERE 671:12
as high as h.	BIBLE 113:5
as near to h.	GILB 423:51
as the h. is high	BIBLE 118:13
at h.'s command	THOM 1015:46
awful rainbow once in h.	KEATS 546:80
beteem the winds of h.	SHAK 888:53
blue fields of h.	KEATS 544:34
breath of H. fresh-blowing	MILT 694:37
brightest h. of invention	SHAK 880:70
build haunted h.	STEV 971:34
build me H. and Hell	MUIR 712:37
But was a race of h.	SHAK 905:62
By h., I do love	SHAK 865:18
By h., methinks it were	SHAK 875:4
call h. and earth to witness	BIBLE 108:89
choir of h.	BERK 95:51
climb…Toward h.	FROST 406:80
Comfort's in h.	SHAK 867:51
Confess yourself to h.	SHAK 892:57
conquer H. also	CARL 234:42
contains or h., or hell	WEBS 1060:52
crawling between h. and earth?	SHAK 891:26
day when h. was falling	HOUS 496:77
descend from h. with a shout	BIBLE 153:25
dew of h.	FORD 397:11
Did h. look on	SHAK 909:74
Down from the verge of h.	MILT 691:81
Down on your knees…thank h.	SHAK 886:13
earth and h. fled away	BIBLE 158:33
Earth's crammed with h.	BROW 197:23
Elijah went up…into h.	BIBLE 111:73
enter into the kingdom of h.	BIBLE 134:38
enter into the kingdom of h.	BIBLE 135:62
Equality would be a h.	TROL 1028:91
eternal joys of h.	MARL 654:14
Even if h. were real	LAUR 584:45
ever-moving spheres of h.	MARL 654:20
every purpose under the h.	BIBLE 122:19
every star that h.	MILT 683:16
exile Hath emptied h.	MILT 688:6
eye of h. shines	SHAK 912:48
eye of h. to garnish	SHAK 872:71
fallen from h.	BIBLE 125:70
fame in h. Err not	MILT 688:18
farther off from h.	HOOD 489:38
Fire…filch'd for us from H.	BYRON 222:34
flowerless fields of h.	SWIN 986:22
for h.'s grace and boon	KEATS 546:92
For, h. to earth	SHAK 876:73
from h. he came	STONE 978:73
From plots and treasons H. preserve	DRYD 350:31
gazing up into h.?	BIBLE 147:80
gentle rain from h.	SHAK 873:92
glance from h. to earth	SHAK 871:55
glorify your Father which is in h.	BIBLE 134:36
God created h. and earth	BIBLE 102:82
God owns h.	SEXT 860:70
going direct to H.	DICK 326:58
going to h.	GAIN 411:70
gold bar of H.	ROSS 824:79
hand of H.	WORD 1101:93
he ascended into h.	BOOK 173:94
h. above her	GORD 435:62
h. admits no jest	FORD 397:14
h. And calculate the stars	MILT 691:90
h. and earth disturbed	SURR 982:41
h. and earth hath made	SCOT 856:23
h. and earth in…union	MILT 681:89
H. and earth shall pass away	BIBLE 140:38
H. and Home	WORD 1100:88
h. be in these lips	MARL 654:19

heaven (*contd.*)

H. born child	MILT 681:86
h.'s cherubin horsed	SHAK 908:32
H.'s deep organ blow	MILT 681:90
H. doth with us	SHAK 896:61
h. endures	HOUS 496:84
h. fill with commerce	TENN 995:77
h. forbids us certain	MOLI 698:21
h.'s gates she claps	LYLY 620:58
H.'s great lamps do dive	CAMP 228:35
h. had made her such	SHAK 898:8
h. hath my empty words	SHAK 897:75
H.…how they dress!	DICK 322:66
H. in Earth	CRAS 295:18
h. in hell's despair	BLAKE 167:85
h. in our cup has thrown	ROCH 816:53
H. in our hearts	NIGH 729:96
H. is for thee	MILT 691:91
H. is free From clouds	BYRON 220:94
h. is like to a grain of mustard	BIBLE 138:3
h. is like unto a merchant	BIBLE 138:4
H. is not a place	BACH 54:94
H. itself would stoop	MILT 684:37
h. keeps souls	DONNE 338:15
H. lies about us	WORD 1098:51
H.'s light forever shines	SHEL 931:50
h. of hell, a hell of h.	MILT 687:99
h. on earth I have won	SHAK 901:79
h. on earth	FORD 397:12
h. planted us to please	MARV 659:92
h.…points out an hereafter	ADDI 8:35
H. sends us fine meat	GARR 415:31
h. sent us Soda Water	CHES 259:26
H. smiles	SHEL 932:64
H.'s splendour over his head	CARL 236:93
H. the judicious…spectator	RALE 800:14
h. to gaudy day denies	BYRON 221:16
h.'s vault should crack	SHAK 904:51
h. we have below	ADDI 6:97
h.'s wide pathless way	MILT 682:9
h. without stars	SANT 842:90
h.'s zone glistering	DONNE 336:71
hell as well as h.	HUXL 507:84
hell I suffer seems a h.	MILT 690:48
hell than serve in h.	MILT 687:1
hell that is not in h.	MARL 654:15
help me h.	FIRB 389:75
Home is h.	NASH 719:52
house as nigh h.	MORE 707:56
how far away H. is	RULFO 828:50
husbandry in h.	SHAK 908:38
I have sinned against h.	BIBLE 143:1
I look up to h.	SMART 944:64
I shall hear in h.	BEET 84:54
If I ascend up into h.	BIBLE 120:49
If not to h., then hand	SHAK 863:60
if there be cricket in h.	HOME 487:14
If there is a h. it's…already filled	DUDEK 353:15
Imagine there's no h.	LENN 596:57
immanacl'd, while h.	MILT 684:34
in at H.'s gate	BLAKE 168:9
In h. no single star	THOM 1015:57
inherit h.'s graces	SHAK 914:81
Is it any better in H.	WILL 1082:87
it were not h., if	SUCK 981:20
jolly h. above	STEV 976:51
keys of the kingdom of h.	BIBLE 138:13
kingdom of h. is at hand	BIBLE 133:25
lark at h. gate	SHAK 916:3
lawyer's dream of h.	BUTL 218:50
lay up for yourselves in h.	BIBLE 135:50
leave to h.	JOHN 525:85
leaving mercy to h.	FIEL 388:50
living bread…from h.	BIBLE 145:45

heaven (*contd.*)

loftiest star of unascended h.	SHEL 930:25
long or short permit to h.	MILT 693:25
Look how the floor of h.	SHAK 873:99
looked up to h.	IHIM 511:31
looks do menace h.	MARL 652:86
mathematics of the city of h.	BROW 196:7
may be h.	BROW 198:41
meted out h. with the span	BIBLE 126:87
mind and thoughts travelled to h.	BLAKE 168:12
more things in h. and earth	MAMET 643:54
more things in h. and earth	SHAK 889:84
My idea of h.	SMITH 949:57
nerar h.'s blis	HENR 472:67
never be Saints in H.	BROW 195:82
never to h. go	SHAK 892:49
new h. and a new earth	BIBLE 158:34
O all you host of h.!	SHAK 889:80
o h. fool	SIDN 937:56
O h., were man	SHAK 860:89
O then h. mocks itself!	SHAK 899:36
offence…smells to h.	SHAK 892:46
offspring of H. first-born	MILT 689:29
Order is h.'s first law	POPE 781:48
others have to hope for h.	SLOAN 943:60
Our Father which art in h.	BIBLE 135:49
patch up thine old body for h.?	SHAK 877:92
pavilion of H. is bare	SHEL 928:84
Pennies do not come from h.	THAT 1007:14
Pennies from H.	BURKE 208:50
peopled highest h.	MILT 693:20
pleasure they enjoy in H.	MARL 652:88
power of H.	MOORE 705:25
Prompted…by h. and hell	SHAK 890:16
Puts all H. in a rage	BLAKE 167:2
regard of H. on all	MILT 690:60
remedies…we ascribe to h.	SHAK 901:71
renounce…attempt to create h.	BORO 179:21
ring in H.'s street	MASE 662:46
ring the bells of h.	HODG 484:53
Road to H.	BALL 67:53
rugged finger to H.	LLOY 608:58
sabill all the h. arrayis	DUNB 355:42
Satan as lightning fall from h.	BIBLE 142:88
Save wings, for h.	KEATS 546:92
saw h. opened	BIBLE 147:91
saw h. opened	BIBLE 158:30
send more souls to H.	BENN 92:6
shall not enter kingdom of h.	BIBLE 138:17
silence in h.	BIBLE 157:16
silent summer h.	TENN 1004:56
sing…of H.	HERR 477:50
singing till h. fills	MERE 671:13
sinned against h.	BIBLE 143:99
slip from h. at night	FROST 407:84
smile of h.	SHAK 918:51
son of H.'s eternal King	MILT 681:85
sons of h.	JOHN 526:5
soul may ascend to h.	MARL 654:21
soul, the King of H.	LYTE 621:90
spark from h.!	ARNO 37:91
spark from h.	ARNO 37:89
star fall from h.	BIBLE 157:17
stored vengeances of h. fall	SHAK 902:13
Strike h. on the face	SHAK 909:72
subtle master under h.	TENN 1003:18
summons thee to h.	SHAK 908:41
sweet breath of h.	WORD 1096:18
Thank H.! the crisis	POE 776:55
the h. above	STEV 976:52
The quincunx of h.	BROW 196:6
theirs is the kingdom of h.	BIBLE 133:34
think'st thou h.	MARL 654:16
thinks that up in h.	CULL 298:67

heaven (*contd.*)

thirtieth year to h.	THOM 1010:68
thorny way to h.	SHAK 888:62
thought raised to h.	LESS 599:10
thrones in h.	RUSK 830:79
through h. and earth	MILT 689:44
to be young was very h.!	WORD 1099:66
top of h. doth hold	MILT 683:20
top of it reached to h.	BIBLE 105:34
treasure in h.	BIBLE 139:24
tricks before high h.	SHAK 896:72
trouble deaf h.	SHAK 913:57
under an English h.	BROO 192:22
up to the chin in h.	MIDD 673:46
wants to go to h.	LOUIS 614:57
war in h.	BIBLE 157:21
watered h. with their tears	BLAKE 167:96
we shall practise in h.	BROW 199:71
weariness of climbing h.	SHEL 932:73
what's a h. for?	BROW 199:61
who art in H.	PARRA 756:43
Whom have I in h.	BIBLE 117:91
will hurl my soul from h.	SHAK 900:62
windows of h.	BIBLE 130:70
winds of h. mix for ever	SHEL 928:85
wing wherewith we fly to h.	SHAK 861:13
winged messenger of h.	SHAK 868:86
with all the company of h.	BOOK 174:28
without a thought of H. or Hell	BROW 195:85
world, to our native h.	MILT 693:16
Yes, H. is thine	POE 776:48

heavenly exploiting a h. gift QUIL 797:63

h. touches ne'er touched	SHAK 912:47
H. weather	JOYCE 538:55

heavens as the h. are higher BIBLE 127:5

chase our imagination to the h.	HUME 503:98
clothed with the h.	TRAH 1025:27
create new h.	BIBLE 128:15
descend from the h.	VERL 1042:34
eternal in the h.	BIBLE 151:78
fabric of the h.	MILT 691:90
From yon blue h.	TENN 995:70
Good h., your divine nature	PEACE 762:26
h. are the work of thy hands	BIBLE 118:10
h. declare glory of God	BOOK 176:66
h. declare the glory of God	BIBLE 114:44
h. free from strife	CORY 288:65
h. rain odours on you	SHAK 895:22
h. themselves blaze forth	SHAK 883:32
h. were opened unto him	BIBLE 133:28
h.' embroidered cloths	YEATS 1105:65
in the h. write	SPEN 959:28
O Thou that in the h. does dwell!	BURNS 209:61
Out-glares the H. Osiris	HERR 477:56
Pure as the naked h.	WORD 1096:38
rideth upon the h.	BIBLE 116:86
Since the h. have shaped	SHAK 862:34
sitteth in the h.	BIBLE 114:31
spangled h., a shining frame	ADDI 7:22
starry h. above me	KANT 542:7
starry h. above	THOM 1015:54
Study is like the h.'	SHAK 865:5
The h. forbid	SHAK 899:22
third h. of hyperboles	DONNE 339:24
though the h. may fall	WATS 1055:54
When I consider thy h.	BIBLE 114:35

heaviness I am full of h. BOOK 177:83

heavy hot as molten lead, and as h. SHAK 876:74

ld man, and h.	BIBLE 110:31
light wife doth make a h. husband	SHAK 873:6
Sob, h. world	AUDEN 48:80
Weigh them: it is as h.	SHAK 882:21

heavy-shotted His h.-s. hammock TENN 998:22

Hebraism H. and Hellenism ARNO 39:28

Hebrew few odd words in H. DAY 310:49

H. of the H.s	BIBLE 153:10

Hebrides behold the H. GALT 413:8

seas colder than the H.	FLEC 393:54

Hector struggles of H. HONO 488:32

Hecuba For H.! What's H. to him SHAK 890:14

hedge in the warm h. SHEL 932:68

whoso breaketh an h.	BIBLE 123:37

hedge-sparrow h.-s. fed the cuckoo SHAK 902:5

hedgehog h. of the heart LOWE 617:10

hedgehogs Thorny h., be not seen SHAK 871:40

hedges and h. ears SWIFT 985:95

heed take h. lest he fall BIBLE 150:55

heel From h. to throat YEATS 1105:69

In the h. of	KIPL 561:47
lifted up his h. against me	BIBLE 115:67
long thrust of his h.	HUGH 500:35
on the boldest h.	CRANE 295:7
shalt bruise his h.	BIBLE 103:98
well-apparell'd April on the h.	SHAK 868:76

heels At his h. a stone SHAK 892:61

double-crossing of a pair of h.	HART 459:44
grief…treads upon the h. of pleasure	CONG 280:99
grow out at h.	SHAK 902:12
gunpowder ran out of the h.	FOOTE 396:75
lighten our wives' h.	SHAK 880:68
like champagne or high h.	BENN 91:90
reclining back upon my h.	WORD 1095:16

Heffalump H., a Horrible H. MILNE 680:75

Hegel H. says somewhere MARX 660:17

heifer plowed with my h. BIBLE 109:18

heigh H. ho, h. ho MOREY 707:60

With h.-ho	SHAK 903:22

height arms is equal to his h. LEON 597:82

climbed up a h.	SUN 982:35
father moved through depths of h.	CUMM 300:89
Happiness Makes up in H.	FROST 407:95
Holiest in the h.	NEWM 724:32
kindred spider to that h.	FROST 407:92
love will be seen at its h.	FORS 398:36
None can usurp this h.	KEATS 545:69
performed…to such an h.	DRYD 347:63
such a h. of figures	DONNE 339:24

heights brood on the towering h. LEAR 589:51

struggle…towards the h.	CAMUS 229:49

heinous what h. sin SHAK 874:26

heir h. of all things BIBLE 154:44

h. to an inheritance	OAKE 733:51
I the h. of all ages	TENN 996:82
never comes but brings an h.	SHAK 910:98
sole h. of the whole world	TRAH 1025:27
son of memory, great h.	MILT 681:94
spouting through his h.	POPE 780:29
you are his h.	STOP 978:75

heiress American h. MACC 625:44

heirs children; they have h. NEWM 724:34

if children, then h.	BIBLE 149:27

held H. we fall to rise BROW 200:2

I'm being h. out to dry	REAG 804:65

Helen hath clos'd H.'s eye NASHE 721:83

H.'s beauty in a brow	SHAK 871:55
H., did Homer never see	JONS 536:15
H., make me immortal	MARL 654:19
H., whose beauty summoned	MARL 653:93
look on H.'s face in hell	PARK 754:4
Past ruined Ilion H. lives	LAND 578:57
where H. lies	BALL 67:41

Helena dross that is not H. MARL 654:18

Helicon watered our houses in H. CHAP 252:72

hell all the tribes of h. SHAK 898:17

all we need of h.	DICK 328:17
allotted death and h.	MARL 654:21
America…may be going to H.	CUMM 300:85
And shall I couple h.?	SHAK 889:80

hell (*contd.*)

ane to heaven, an' ten to h.	BURNS 209:61
art as black as h.	SHAK 915:97
believe myself to be in h.	RIMB 812:97
blasts from h.	SHAK 888:71
build me Heaven and Hell.	MUIR 712:37
Came not all h. broke loose?	MILT 690:68
cannot commit evil in h.	GENET 418:75
carried H. about with him	GREE 444:6
characters of h. to trace	GRAY 443:84
charm thy soul to h.	MARL 654:18
childhood prolonged…h.	BOGAN 171:59
claim in h. Precédence	MILT 688:12
contains or heaven, or h.	WEBS 1060:52
curse of h. upon the sleek	RANS 802:34
deeper than h.	BIBLE 113:5
Descent into H.	LESS 598:6
Devil Fired into H.	ANON 25:21
Down, down to h.	SHAK 862:33
earth is h. when	NASHE 721:81
earth, and heav'n, and h.	POPE 782:95
England…the h. of horses	FLOR 394:79
extinguish h.	REED 805:84
fetch fire from h.	WEBS 1060:47
flowerless rocks of h.	SITW 940:2
focus…on reducing h.	BORO 179:31
foul as h. within	SHAK 915:90
gates of h. shall not prevail	BIBLE 138:13
go to h. like lambs	CHES 259:27
Go to h. Yours sincerely	ELLI 375:10
good…definition of h.	SHAW 924:10
great painter of American h.	ALLEN 14:34
hand in hand to h.	SHAK 863:66
having harrowed h.	SPEN 958:24
having harrowed h.	SPEN 959:27
he descended into h.	BOOK 173:94
heav'n of h., a h. of heav'n	MILT 687:99
heaven in h.'s despair	BLAKE 167:85
H. a fury, like a woman scorned	CONG 281:22
H. and destruction are never full	BIBLE 122:9
H. as well as on earth	LEWIS 601:37
H. at the time	WILD 1079:15
h.'s concave, and beyond	MILT 688:5
H.'s darkness under his feet	CARL 236:93
h. delivered up the dead	BIBLE 158:33
H. followed with him	BIBLE 157:12
H. grant what Love	MILT 682:11
H. hath no limits	MARL 654:15
h. in heaven's despite	BLAKE 167:86
H. is a city	SHEL 928:94
H. is full of musical amateurs	SHAW 921:32
H. is murky	SHAK 909:77
H. is other people	SART 844:11
H.…is to no longer love	BERN 96:72
H. itself breathes out	SHAK 891:44
H. itself cannot encroach	BAUD 77:15
H. lay about him	GREE 444:3
H. lies about us	MITC 696:78
h. make crooked	SHAK 862:34
h., myself am h.	MILT 690:48
h. of a good universe	CUMM 300:93
h. of an explosion	CATTO 245:57
h. of an opening	REAG 804:71
h. on earth	SHAW 921:22
h. should bar the way	NOYES 732:43
h. than serve in heav'n	MILT 687:1
h. they made unmade	MORG 708:66
h. within him, for within him h.	MILT 689:45
her steps take hold on h.	BIBLE 120:61
holiday…excursion to h.	PRIE 790:2
hot from h.	SHAK 883:45
hotter name Than any in h.	SHAK 910:88
how the h. I ever got here	TRUM 1029:16
I myself am h.	LOWE 617:97

hell (*contd.*)

If Hitler invaded H.	CHUR 265:35
I'm neurotic as h.	PLATH 773:92
In h. they'll roast thee	BURNS 211:20
in the interests of H.	FORS 398:45
injured lover's h.	MILT 691:71
Into the mouth of H.	TENN 1001:73
keys of h. and of death	BIBLE 157:1
lead apes in h.	SHAK 864:75
leadest to the gates of h.	BIBLE 131:86
liar gone to burning h.	SHAK 900:58
like Christianity without h.	BORM 179:17
like that in Milton's h.	NERV 723:10
live in freedom and h.	MAIL 639:81
look on Helen's face in h.	PARK 754:4
Love is a Dog from H.	BUKO 203:48
make my bed in h.	BIBLE 120:49
make the earth my h.	SHAK 863:59
married to h.?	SHAK 864:71
more devils than vast h.	SHAK 871:55
never give them h.	TRUM 1030:24
never know where the h. you are	SALI 838:20
never married, and that's his h.	BURT 214:70
never mentions H. to ears polite	POPE 779:22
night seems termless h.	THOM 1015:55
No h. below us	LENN 596:57
Oh H.!	SNYD 951:82
out of h. leads up to light	MILT 688:22
passed a h. of time	SHAK 915:91
paving stones for H.	KING 559:6
Pequod packing off to h.	LOWE 616:94
Pope told us all to go to h.	ONOL 734:67
Prompted...by heaven and h.	SHAK 890:16
Quiet to quick bosoms is a h.	BYRON 220:86
readiest way to H.?	ROCH 816:59
riches grow in h.	MILT 688:9
road to h. is paved	ROTH 826:16
save more souls from H.	BENN 92:6
set on fire of h.	BIBLE 155:67
sounds frae h.	FERG 386:16
There is h. as well	HUXL 507:84
there must be h.	BROW 198:41
There's a h. of a distance	PARK 754:17
There's h.	SHAK 903:35
'To h. with ye!' says she	STRO 980:6
too fond for h.	SHAK 908:51
towards the gates of h.	MILT 688:24
walked eye-deep in h.	POUND 786:64
war...is all h.	SHER 934:16
ways of saying 'To h. with you'	FENW 385:4
we stood in H.	OWEN 748:15
What is h.?	ELIOT 373:84
whole body...cast into h.	BIBLE 134:41
whose entrance leads to H.	MILT 683:30
Why, this is h.	MARL 654:14
wilt not leave my soul in h.	BIBLE 114:40
with h. are we at agreement	BIBLE 125:76
without a thought of Heaven or H.	BROW 195:85
write of H.	HERR 477:50

Hellenism Hebraism and H.   ARNO 39:28

Hellespontus over H. swam   SPEN 959:41

hellfire eyes to be cast into h.   BIBLE 138:19

in danger of h.   BIBLE 134:39

hellhound Discrimination is a h.   KING 558:85

h. is always a h.   WODE 1089:4

hellish whole of the H. nation   SITW 940:3

hello H. sadness   ELUA 376:25

helm at the h. of our country   HOOV 490:50

helmet h. and the h.-feather   TENN 993:44

h. of salvation   BIBLE 152:6

saw the h. and plume   TENN 994:45

help and h. there's none   HODG 484:52

another to h. him up   BIBLE 123:23

best way to h. the poor   HANC 454:66

can't h. people against their will	FREE 404:32
encumbers him with h.?	JOHN 526:99
from whence cometh my h.	BIBLE 119:36
give them h.	GELL 417:72
h. and support of the woman I love	EDWA 362:51
H. angels!	SHAK 892:48
h. from a government agency	STEIN 966:49
h. him to do it	HALI 452:25
h. me heaven	FIRB 389:75
h. of any ally	GARI 415:24
h. of his countenance	BIBLE 116:69
h. our French comrades	KITC 566:44
h. thou my unbelief	FORS 399:51
How shall I h. you	HOUS 495:56
I get by with a little h.	LENN 596:63
look on and h.	LAWR 586:87
make him an h. meet for him	BIBLE 103:91
mutual h....as often as warfare	DOBZ 334:36
mutual society, h., and comfort	BOOK 175:45
no h. for it	AUBER 45:31
seeking h. from none	GORD 435:61
Since there's no h.	DRAY 345:40
there is no h. in them	BOOK 177:95
they cannot h. him	SHAK 901:73
very present h. in trouble	BIBLE 116:72
where no one can h. him	HEMI 471:41
who can h. it?	ETHE 380:17
without the h. of the air	ETHE 380:19

helper mother's little h.   JAGG 515:95

helpers h. fail and comforts   LYTE 621:67

helping h. every feeble neighbour   GORD 435:61

helpless H., naked, piping loud   BLAKE 167:94

Must h. man   JOHN 525:84

hem h. of Nature's shift   SHEL 928:95

Hemingway back to H.'s work   COWL 291:24

H., remarks are not literature   STEIN 965:34

marriage to Ernest H.   BARR 72:40

hemisphere crystals...in a h.   SCHW 851:30

gilding the eastern h.   SHER 934:9

In the western h.   ROOS 822:46

western to the eastern h.   PEARY 763:36

hemlock I had drunk   KEATS 547:13

hen h. only egg's way   BUTL 217:31

nought worth a h.   DUNB 355:38

Royal Commision is a broody h.   FOOT 396:93

Two Owls and a H.   LEAR 589:50

hen-pecked have they not h.-p.   BYRON 222:26

hence going h....coming hither   SHAK 904:45

Henry H VIII.... ideal   MACK 632:59

H. the Eighth Took thucthethtion   BENT 93:27

sat down...on H.'s heart   BERR 98:13

without strict doubt a Hoorah H.   RUNY 829:64

hens h. to moorcocks call   YEATS 1105:72

Hepburn H. runs the gamut   PARK 754:99

Heraclitus H., they told me   CORY 288:63

herald perfectest h. of joy   SHAK 879:40

Revolution is merely the h.   BABE 54:91

heraldic h. equivalent of...furry dice   ANON 29:36

heraldry boast of h.   GRAY 442:66

heralds Nobles and h.   PRIOR 790:49

herb dew-bespangling h. and tree   HERR 477:61

h. for the service of man   BIBLE 118:16

h. that sips the dew   MILT 683:16

light on such another h.   SHAK 907:82

small rain upon the tender h.   BIBLE 108:1

some single h. or tree   MARV 658:82

herbs dinner of h. where love is   BIBLE 121:80

greatest among h.   BIBLE 138:3

In plants, h., stones   SHAK 869:95

spinneys of murdering h.   THOM 1011:89

Hercules character like Samson, H.   SIEG 937:67

Like H. himself   SHAK 893:82

herd h. instinct in the individual   NIET 728:72

more numerous was the h.   DRYD 349:22

resigns momentarily from the h.	MACL 634:78
unique to the level of the h.	MILL 679:47

herds h., of human face divine   MILT 689:31

here From H. To Eternity   JONES 533:53

H. am I   BIBLE 109:27

H. am I; send me   BIBLE 124:61

h. and now cease to matter   ELIOT 372:56

h. and now   HAMM 453:48

h. it is at last   JAMES 517:32

H. we are again!   GRIM 447:65

one tenth H. and Now   SWIFT 983:53

We're h., We're queer   ANON 29:31

Where is h.?   FRYE 408:22

would never happen h.   FOWL 400:69

hereafter heaven...points out an h.   ADDI 8:35

hereditary peers, and they are h.   LLOY 609:64

heresies begin as h.   HUXL 508:2

hateful h.   SPEN 958:23

h....explosions of faith   BREN 187:32

h. perish not with their authors   BROW 195:70

most interesting ideas are h.   SONT 953:10

heresy ancient saying is no h.   SHAK 875:32

this hidden h.   RAHN 800:5

what an Englishman believes be h.?   SHAW 925:23

widespread modern h.   DRIB 346:44

heretic h. that makes the fire   SHAK 911:24

lawyer and a politician and a h.   MENC 669:64

revolutionary ends as...a h.   CAMUS 229:55

heretics burning of h.   WELD 1062:92

heritage children are an h.   BIBLE 119:42

goodly h.   BIBLE 114:39

I have a goodly h.   BOOK 176:65

proud of our ancient h.   KENN 550:64

thy true h.   POUND 786:83

young country is a real h.   MANS 647:12

hermaphrodites Nor even h.   LAUT 584:50

hermit dwell a h. anywhere   LOWE 616:87

In habite an h. unholy   LANG 579:69

hermitage Find out the peaceful h.   MILT 683:16

palace for a h.   SHAK 867:62

That for a h.   615:63

Hermon As the dew of H.   BIBLE 119:45

hern haunts of coot and h.   TENN 1002:97

hero American history as a great h.   MENC 669:70

Being a h. is about   ROGE 820:21

conquering h. comes!   MORE 707:59

definition of a 'h.'   FIND 389:65

Every h. becomes a bore   EMER 377:58

Forgive the h.   WILB 1074:17

h. from his prison   AYTO 53:86

h. is a man that would argue   MAIL 640:89

h. is a sneaking piece   SCOTT 854:71

h. of his own life story   BARTH 74:63

h. perish, or a sparrow fall   POPE 780:35

H., Venus' nun   MARL 654:25

memory of a h.   GIBB 421:22

no such thing as a h.   MO 698:13

one murder...millions a h.   PORT 784:40

Show me a h.   FITZ 391:19

show me a h.   PUZO 796:42

to his very valet seemed a h.   BYRON 221:21

truth about the h.   CHES 258:97

who aspires to be a h.   JOHN 530:3

Herod Oh, for an hour of H.!   HOPE 490:73

heroes become statesmen and h.   WARD 1053:14

cowards as quickly as of h.   MITC 697:88

fit country for h. to live in   LLOY 609:62

h. and heroines will have to change   WELD 1062:90

h. and villains from fiction   AUDEN 49:99

h. of three recent novels   BROY 201:6

h. to dine with us   TROL 1028:86

h. were made   RUSS 833:37

I'll follow the h.   ORAH 741:77

men...want to be h.   WINT 1087:69

Hippocrene blushful H.   KEATS 547:14
H. is somewhat drouthy   BYRON 222:38
hippopotamus shoot the H.   BELL 87:99
hips arm-chairs tight about the h.   WODE 1088:84
girdle when your h. stick   NASH 720:69
hire ask employers to h.   BORO 179:22
hireling h., and not the shepherd   BIBLE 146:54
h. of the Ministry   OCON 735:80
Pay given to state h.   JOHN 526:16
Hispanic H. world never crumbled   REYES 807:22
historian first be an h.   HARR 458:24
first requisite of the h.   STRA 979:92
h. is often only a journalist   KRAUS 569:89
h. must have a third quality   FORS 398:49
I will be a h.   OGDEN 736:97
Only one safe rule for the h.   FISH 389:82
To a h.   TUCH 1031:48
When I meet a h.   ELTON 375:22
historians ancient Spanish h.   ECHE 359:13
Dali's importance…for art h.   SCHW 851:23
Future h. will   MUGG 712:23
God cannot alter the past, h. can   BUTL 217:34
h. left blanks in their writings   POUND 786:71
H. repeat each other   GUED 448:76
H. spend their lives   HOPE 490:71
h. will allocate the responsibility   HIRO 481:19
historical cultural and h. role   SMITH 946:1
fights h.   GILB 424:62
H. Overdosing   COUP 289:75
H. Slumming   COUP 289:76
imply h. dependency   MURP 715:73
importance of an h. event   WHIT 1072:69
It is a h. truth   ANGE 19:22
lessons of h. experience   KISS 565:30
process of h. development   ROBI 815:36
to h. materials   STIN 977:69
histories H. make men wise   BACON 59:25
I only believe in h.   PASC 758:77
soon h. are properly told   WHIT 1072:74
true h. contain instruction   BRON 190:88
history all of his potted h.   LEVIN 600:29
American h. as a great hero   MENC 669:70
Antiquities are h. defaced   BACON 55:11
Art is h.'s nostalgia   WALC 1048:41
bad jokes of h.   GUED 448:76
cancer of human h.   SONT 953:7
collective opinion…can make h.   SAFI 836:72
color h. to achieve that objective   MACN 636:33
contribution to human h.   JIANG 522:25
conveying a whole h.   PRIT 791:72
country which has no h.   AGATE 10:63
dangerous moment in human h.   BELL 88:34
deriving from a h.   TOOLE 1023:4
disasters of English h.   WAUGH 1056:67
discerned in h. a plot   FISH 389:82
distinguishing h. from old movie   BAKER 63:86
divine and human h.   GARC 414:19
do more to shape h.   TAYL 991:10
Does h. repeat itself   BARN 72:35
dustheap of h.   TROT 1029:2
duty we owe to h.   WILDE 1076:38
English h. all about men   BRAD 183:77
entire h. of science   RAND 801:21
epoch unrivalled in world h.   LARI 581:93
exceeds an infamous h.   BROW 196:2
footnote in the h. books   THAT 1007:10
funny pages of the h. books   DEAN 311:58
Hansard is h.'s ear   SAMU 840:44
happiest women…have no h.   ELIOT 365:21
H.…An account, mostly false   BIER 161:85
H., at least   MACA 622:95
H.…badly constructed concert hall   MACL 634:80
H. does not long entrust   EISE 364:82
H. does not provide   KRIS 569:94

history (*contd.*)
H. gets thicker   TAYL 992:13
h. had achieved a happy ending   MACC 625:51
H. has many cunning passages   ELIOT 368:70
H.…is a nightmare   JOYCE 538:48
h. is…a tableau   VOLT 1046:8
H. is a tale of efforts   KISS 566:36
H. is condemned…to lies   FRAN 401:83
H. is hard to know   THOM 1014:36
H. is littered with wars   POWE 788:16
H. is more or less bunk   FORD 396:7
h. is not a science   FRAN 401:87
H. is not merciful   NEW 724:24
H. is on our side   KHRU 556:47
H. is past politics   FREE 404:33
H. is philosophy   CARL 235:75
H. is the endless repetition   DURR 357:79
H. is the essence of…Biographies   CARL 235:72
H. is the myth,   MILL 679:48
H. is written for the victors   DREX 346:43
H. isn't through with me   MARC 649:47
H. may be servitude   ELIOT 373:75
H. must not be written with bias   BETJ 100:45
H. never stops   MONT 702:77
h. of a battle   WELL 1063:13
h. of all hitherto…society   MARX 660:12
h. of America   ADAMS 5:86
h. of bat and ball   ARLO 34:37
h. of City architecture   JOHN 524:67
h. of different intonations   BORG 179:11
h. of England   MACA 623:10
h. of England   MACA 624:24
h. of every country   CATH 244:38
h. of Mr Blackman   NGU 725:45
h. of publicity   LEAV 591:74
h. of science   POPP 784:26
h. of science   SART 843:5
h. of …scientific work   TOLS 1023:99
h. of the affections   IRVI 513:64
h. of the human race   HARL 458:20
h. of the human spirit   ARNO 39:30
h. of the land   LONG 612:14
h. of the Victorian age   STRA 979:92
h. of the world   GIBB 421:18
h. of this country   MACM 635:6
h., real solemn h.   AUST 52:64
H. repeats itself   GUED 448:75
H. shows that   STAL 962:80
H. shows us no example   WEBB 1059:17
H. teaches us   EBAN 359:7
H. teaches us   KENN 551:79
H., this old…lying woman   MAUP 665:93
h.…through the kitchen window   CHILD 260:52
H. to the defeated   AUDEN 46:55
h. whither are you spinning?   GRAY 441:60
H. will absolve me   CAST 244:31
Human h.…a race   WELLS 1065:42
hypochondriacs of h.   AGNEW 10:70
If men could learn from h.   COLE 275:27
if you read your h.   OROU 741:79
in spite of H.   WALC 1048:43
iron laws of h.   EAGL 359:4
journalism…as an extension of h.   SAMP 840:42
just as h. is rushing by   ADLER 8:45
keep h. and theology apart   WELLS 1065:43
know of our h.   NAIP 717:17
knowledge…product of h.   CARL 235:71
large scale in h.   INGE 511:39
lessons of h.   HUXL 508:89
lies down on the tracks of h.   EISE 364:79
life's h.   HOOD 489:49
magic moment in American h.   WHITE 1071:49
make more h. than they can consume   SAKI 838:10
More than at any other time in h.   ALLEN 14:50

history (*contd.*)
much prefer h.   TOLK 1022:93
myth rather than h.   FIED 387:38
never learned anything from h.   HEGEL 466:63
nine-tenths a h. lesson   SWIFT 983:53
no h. of art   WERE 1066:56
no h., only biography   EMER 376:37
not burdened with a h.   THOR 1017:2
Not written on by h.   SCOTT 852:37
novel of mankind, not the h.   GAUT 416:42
Of h. and its consequences   OBRI 734:62
our h., our idealistic pretensions   OBRI 734:64
Our whole h. inclines   MASA 661:31
out of life into h.   CHUR 263:3
pain of h. words contain   WALC 1048:34
Painters of h.   KNEL 567:52
parody had completely replaced h.   PIGL 769:40
people without h.   ELIOT 373:80
political and constitutional h.   JAY 519:73
Political h. is far too criminal   AUDEN 49:99
problems of biography, of h.   MILLS 679:63
Psychology has…a short h.   EBBI 359:8
Read no h.   DISR 332:75
reading of the h. of thought   MERT 672:25
repeat h.   ILLI 511:32
resuscitate, if it concerns h.   HUGO 501:59
reverberates through men's h.   KOES 568:72
sailed through American h.   MENC 670:89
Science…opposed to h.   BORN 179:19
skies of h. hurrying   SASS 845:38
sleep and a sense of h.   WILS 1085:41
so vain that he wants to figure in h.   DISR 333:20
study of military h.   CLAU 268:95
takes a great deal of h.   JAMES 516:11
the h. of the world   POPP 783:18
There is no h. of mankind   POPP 783:18
those who study h.   TAYL 991:12
thousand years of h.   GAIT 411:73
Throughout h.   HAILE 451:11
thy lips my h.   SIDN 937:58
till h. is no longer made   PEAR 762:32
too much h.   KING 558:88
understand a science…know its h.   COMTE 279:79
uses h. to develop theory   STIN 977:69
war h.…simple one   WODE 1089:7
War makes rattling good h.   HARDY 457:11
way of indicating how h.   MALA 641:6
We make h.   REAG 804:66
What is h., in fact   IRVI 513:61
What will H. say?   SHAW 921:17
Who owns h.?   NEW 723:16
You appear before h.   CLEM 269:3
hit A h., a very palpable h.   SHAK 893:85
can't think and h.   BERRA 98:2
get there; h. it   RANJ 801:21
h. a ball further   PRIE 790:46
h. at all if it can be avoided   ROOS 822:49
h. that stride and keep it   SAND 841:78
hither transported h. and thither   OVID 747:3
Hitler cable H. and ask him   GOLD 434:35
destruction of H.   CHUR 265:35
every Christian in H.'s Europe   FACK 382:49
German Chancellor, Herr H.   CHAM 249:18
Herr H. and Signor Mussolini   HALI 452:26
H. attacked the Jews   NIEM 727:68
H. had already found   ROBI 815:37
H. has missed the bus   CHAM 249:22
H. showed surprising loyalty   BULL 204:51
H. was a Jeanne d'Arc   POUND 786:82
H. was dead   SCHA 847:59
Like kissing H.   CURT 302:25
marches with H.   CHUR 264:19
people H. never understood   BULL 204:52
Was not H. a paper tiger   MAO 648:26

Hitler (*contd.*)
When I go to see Herr H.	HEND 472:54
hits go to see h.	JOUR 537:36
hive angry h. of bees	SHAK 861:5
bitter h. to grope for honey	SPEN 959:29
h. for the honey-bee	YEATS 1104:57
in the h. of home	MACN 637:40
hives fill our h. with honey	SWIFT 984:58
hoard Our h. is little	TENN 1002:3
To h. is…villainous	RABE 799:84
Hoare S. H. was the pygmiest	BOOT 178:7
hoary h. hills are seen	POPE 782:93
Hobbes H. clearly proves	SWIFT 986:6
hobbit in the ground there lived a h.	
	TOLK 1022:89
hobbit-hole h.…comfort	TOLK 1022:89
hobbits H. are an unobtrusive	TOLK 1023:94
hobby suggests an elaborate h.	PRIE 790:41
hobby-horse man rides his H.-H.	STER 969:91
hobgoblin h. of little minds	EMER 376:33
hobnailed That h. goblin	SITW 941:10
hobo-trekkers H.-t. that forever	CRANE 295:1
hock sipped at the weak h.	BETJ 99:29
hodgepodge h. of all other speeches	SPEN 957:96
hoe But to take a large h.	KIPL 563:77
tickle her with a h.	JERR 521:14
Hofstadter H.'s Law	HOFS 484:61
hog disadvantage of being a h.	MORT 710:99
H. Butcher for the World	SAND 841:57
h. that could fiddle	ROCH 816:58
mere h. at his trough	HUNT 505:30
put lipstick on a h.	RICH 810:40
talk about h. and hominy	FERB 385:8
hogamus H., higamous	JAMES 518:52
hogs Fattenin' h. ain't in luck	HARR 458:31
fatting h. of late	SPEN 959:43
let it not be like h.	MACK 631:48
Holbein H. of Jell-O ads	ADLER 8:46
hold first cries 'H., enough!'	SHAK 910:90
h. down one thing	BELL 88:22
h. fast that which is good	BIBLE 153:26
H. fast the form of sound words	BIBLE 154:38
H., h., my heart	SHAK 889:80
H. on, h. on!	ANON 28:19
H. them cheap	HOPK 492:4
H. then my sword	SHAK 884:66
like to h. it back	SEVI 859:60
To have and to h.	BOOK 176:49
undermine her h. on life	FORS 398:43
Holding bowler's H.	JOHN 532:45
hole flame creeps in at every h.	PEELE 763:16
decayed h. among the mountains	ELIOT 369:95
drum with a h. in it	DICK 320:24
dry, bare, sandy h.	TOLK 1022:89
h. in the ground	TOLK 1022:89
h. in the subconscious	HALE 451:21
h. that allows the mouse in	JACO 514:91
kick a h. in a stained glass window	CHAN 250:31
Might stop a h.	SHAK 893:79
not enough…to be h.	BRAT 185:14
sphere into an inaccessible h.	CHUR 265:45
holes into a bag with h.	BIBLE 130:64
holiday His first h.	BOUC 181:40
h. steamers made an excursion	PRIE 790:37
in a h. humour	SHAK 886:20
perpetual h. is a good…definition	SHAW 924:10
regular h. to them	DICK 321:31
Roman h.	BYRON 220:1
two years in H. Inns	MOND 699:38
holidays h. from Eton	SITW 941:24
h.…interfere with one's work	EDWA 362:52
H.…learning experience	OGDEN 736:99
Term, h., term, h.	LEWIS 601:43
holier h. lot to be unknown	HOPK 492:95

holier (*contd.*)
h. than thou	BIBLE 128:14
In h. shapes	SHAK 902:93
holiness beauty of h.	BIBLE 117:8
h. of always being the injured party	ANGE 19:27
mind is bent to h.	SHAK 861:98
vision of h. of God	BLOOM 170:36
way of h.	BIBLE 126:83
Holland Dutch may have their H.	JOHN 524:60
H.…lies so low	HOOD 489:42
hollow Down to the h.	FLAN 391:25
h., heartless, mirthless	THUR 1019:44
h. of thine ear	SHAK 869:10
waters in the h. of his hand	BIBLE 126:87
We are the h. men	ELIOT 369:98
hollow-headed h.-h. mediocrity	MENC 670:90
hollowness h. disappoints at the time	
	BRON 191:5
Reverbs no h.	SHAK 902:97
hollows bowery h. crowned	TENN 1004:48
Hollywood America gets H.	JONG 534:70
Americans…considered H.	MAMET 643:52
average H. film star	HEPB 473:76
every actor in H.	GIEL 423:49
Hooray for H.	MERC 670:96
I should not have been invited to H.	CHAN 250:35
Inside this H. playboy	FLYNN 395:81
vote for H. as a Republican	WALL 1049:60
Wants steady employment in H.	DAVIS 308:24
holme carver h.	SPEN 957:99
Holmes J C H.…and I	KERO 553:15
H. remarked, impatiently	DOYLE 344:15
To Sherlock H. she is always	DOYLE 344:2
Holocaust truth of the H.	WEIZ 1062:87
holsters inside of his h.	SHAW 920:93
holy be h. …with impunity?	RACI 799:2
called the H. Roman Empire	VOLT 1046:9
cased up, like a h. relic	WEBS 1061:61
coming to that h. room	DONNE 338:18
discipline of our h. Church	OCON 735:80
give solemn thanks to the H. Trinity	COLU 278:63
great source is the h. river	SPEKE 955:61
h. alliance to exorcise	MARX 660:14
h. and enchanted	COLE 275:13
H. Catholic and Apostolic	TEMP 993:29
H. Deadlock	HERB 474:98
H., divine, good	MILT 692:5
h.; for I am h.	BIBLE 107:78
H., h., h. is the Lord	BIBLE 124:60
H., H., H.! Lord God Almighty!	HEBER 466:59
H., h., h.	BIBLE 157:9
H., h., h.	BOOK 174:28
h. hush	STEV 971:38
h. nation	BIBLE 156:78
h. place of the tabernacles	BIBLE 116:73
h. rest, and peace	NEWM 724:29
h. Satan	DAMI 304:53
h. thing to see	BLAKE 167:89
h. unto the dogs	BIBLE 135:56
Made h. by their dreams	GIBS 422:39
Nothing but h., pure, and clear	HERB 474:9
place…is h. ground	BIBLE 106:54
proofs of h. writ	SHAK 899:37
religion would still be h. and divine	BAUD 78:36
Sabbath…making it h.	WALK 1049:56
Sae pious and sae h.	BURNS 210:82
suffer them H. One	BIBLE 114:40
thy h. feet	BLAKE 165:57
touch of h. bread	SHAK 886:12
holy-day free And h.-d.…spirit	LAMB 576:19
Holy Ghost Because the H. G.	HOPK 491:83
blasphemy against the H. G.	BIBLE 137:91
but by the H. G.	BIBLE 150:60
filled with the H. G.	BIBLE 147:81

Holy Ghost (*contd.*)
Have ye received the H. G.?	BIBLE 148:5
H. G. is come upon you	BIBLE 147:79
I believe in the H. G.	BOOK 174:20
John Wesley and the H. G.	MENC 670:88
pretending to…gifts of the H.G.	BUTL 216:96
temple of the H. G.	BIBLE 150:49
who was conceived by the H. G.	BOOK 173:94
Holy Grail see the H. G.	MALO 642:31
There lies the H. G.	MACA 621:70
Holy See insult to the H. S.	INNO 512:56
Holy Spirit H. S.…invisible	TAYL 992:22
inspiration of thy H. S.	BOOK 174:16
holy-water h.-w. death	MACG 630:27
homage both an h. and a critique	MOTH 711:11
h. of a tear	BYRON 219:71
H. to plain dumb luck	ACHE 3:47
involuntarily pay h.	POTT 785:44
home advocating for H. Rule	MACG 630:26
against books the H. Secretary	WAUGH 1056:7
airs have brought me h.	POE 776:47
ALL parts and none are h.	MAIL 640:92
always a bad sign at h.	MITF 697:2
and I am far from h.	NEWM 724:28
and returning h.	BUCH 202:29
Are they being…too much at h.?	COLE 273:77
At h., whispering	OWEN 748:18
At h., you always have to be	MACM 635:7
best country ever is, at h.	GOLD 432:97
blest by suns of h.	BROO 192:21
both h. runs and strike outs	RODG 818:86
call the cattle h.	KING 558:89
came h., h. to a lie	POUND 786:64
Can't Go H. Again	WOLFE 1090:21
cart with the h. packed	COLL 276:38
chickens come h. to roost	MAMET 643:50
Comes h. again	SHAK 914:78
consequence of leaving one's h.	LEBO 592:90
could have stayed h.	HILL 270:23
domestic servants at h.	MAUG 665:92
dream of going 'h.'	PARK 755:31
dream of H.	FORD 397:20
dream that I am h. again!	FLEC 393:53
drive one from h.	HOOD 489:43
dunce that has been kept at h.	COWP 292:47
E.T. phone h.	MATH 663:71
everything off and went h.	SZIL 989:71
feel ashamed of h.	DICK 326:69
field, or a h.	WILD 1079:27
friends, and native h.	MILT 683:19
gat him h. to his house	BIBLE 110:50
get h. from work	PARKS 756:38
give me a h.	HIGL 480:1
God, who is our h.	WORD 1098:51
Hang my Hat is H.	JERO 521:12
Heaven and H.	WORD 1100:88
hills of h.!	STEV 976:57
'h.'—a real life	MANS 647:98
h. among the dead	SHEL 931:52
h. and put a bullet	ROBI 814:24
h. his footsteps…turned	SCOTT 853:49
H.'s h.	ARBU 33:10
h., in a flood of tears	DICK 321:29
H. is heaven	NASH 719:52
H. is the girl's prison	SHAW 922:60
H. is the place	FROST 406:75
H. is where one starts from	ELIOT 372:15
H. James	HILL 481:9
H. life as we understand it	SHAW 924:92
h. life of our own dear Queen	ANON 25:23
H. of lost causes	ARNO 38:10
h. of the brave?	KEY 554:24
h. of the scorpion	SNYD 951:82
h. of the weird	LAWS 587:18

home (*contd.*)

h....saved by his courage   MACA 624:28
H. they brought   TENN 997:7
h. to...Jews, Muslims and Christians   CLIN 269:18
H. would I go   OTWAY 746:81
h., you idle creature   SHAK 882:14
House is not a H.   ADLER 9:49
humble h.   GLAD 429:52
husbands to stay at h.   ELIOT 365:22
I can get all that at h.   COOK 286:27
if they go h.   GASK 415:33
in my bosom, and at h.   JONS 535:4
in the hive of h.   MACN 637:40
into the h.—where it belongs   HITC 482:25
isn't much to write h. about   HYDE 509:13
it never is at h.   COWP 292:33
keep the Sabbath...staying at H.   DICK 328:98
Kiss till the cow comes h.   BEAU 80:71
last night the cows came h.   NATH 721:87
live at h., quiet, confined   AUST 52:68
lov'd at h., rever'd abroad   BURNS 209:66
luminous h. of waters   ARNO 38:98
Lurching to...'H. sweet H.'   SASS 845:22
man who thinks to found a h.   DOUG 342:63
merely ready to go h.   KAIKO 541:93
merriest when they are from h.   SHAK 880:72
milk comes frozen h.   SHAK 866:30
My h. policy? I wage war   CLEM 269:4
national h. for the Jews   BALF 65:17
never attempt to make at h.   SMITH 945:88
never felt myself from h.   BOSW 180:31
Next to a letter from h.   DOOL 340:37
not a thing remains at h.   BELLI 86:93
not yet gone h.   THUR 1018:11
ocean...was his h.   BYRON 219:82
our eternal h.   WATTS 1055:58
out of house and h.   SHAK 877:88
problems of running a h.   THAT 1007:12
refuge from h. life   SHAW 920:12
Rowing h. to haven   MASE 662:37
small places, close to h.   ROOS 821:32
snail...is at h.   DONNE 338:89
sons, her h., her food   NATI 721:90
stay at h. and help   WINT 1087:69
stay at h., my noble lord   BALL -101:37
Stay h. and cause no trouble   AESC 9:58
thou art my h.   PRIOR 791:60
till the cows come h.   MARX 659:98
to go h. in the dark   OHEN 737:19
to the mountains is going h.   MUIR 713:38
toddle safely h. and die   SASS 845:27
turning my face towards h.   PARK 753:85
unconquerable...the American h.   SELZ 858:42
was just that I was leaving h.   STEV 976:58
welcome to me!   BURNS 210:93
What's the good of a h.   GROS 447:71
When I was at h.   SHAK 885:85
when mum stays at h.   FALU 382:57
who gives a child a h.   MASE 662:46
woman's true position in the h.   STAN 962:86
women are to stay at h.   WEST 1068:88
You will be h. before   WILH 1080:38
home-acre hearth-fire and the h.-a.   KIPL 564:1
home-fires Keep the H.-f. burning   FORD 397:20
home-keeping H.-k. youth   SHAK 860:71
home-made H.-m. dishes   HOOD 489:43
homecoming h. of ...companions   HOMER 488:24
homeland h. is sweet to him   HUGH 498:12
live in his h.   BELL 86:90
PLO is a h.   NEW 724:19
homeless h. and self-forgetful   WHIT 1071:61
h. by choice   SOUT 954:39
h. man in a thousand dollar suit   ANON 29:47
h., tempest-tossed   LAZA 588:26

homely female shall be h.   KENN 550:55
h. slighted Shepherd's trade   MILT 684:42
Homer a simple digamma in H.   QUIL 797:62
blind H. sing to me?   MARL 654:17
Helen, did H. never see   JONS 536:15
H....chronicled the siege of Troy   CUOMO 300:6
H. invariably composes   ARNO 38:5
H. Never existed.   FLAU 393:45
in H. than H. knew   SWIFT 985:3
Mr Gladstone read H.   CHUR 263:4
never read a line of H.   MILL 678:29
Shakespeare was the H.   DRYD 347:65
Virgil and H.   DRYD 348:79
when the worthy H. nods   HORA 494:34
homes firelit h., clean beds and wives   SASS 845:25
h. of silent prayer   TENN 999:33
stately h. of England   COWA 290:3
stately h. of England   HEMA 469:10
homesteads carry fire...into your h.   PARN 756:40
homeward Look h. Angel   MILT 685:50
sent him h. tae think again   WILL 1083:7
homewards Most roads lead men h.   MASE 662:41
homey taste of lies was h.   GELL 417:70
hominy Mrs H....slowly up it   DICK 323:92
talk about hog and h.   FERB 385:8
homme h. n'est rien d'autre   SART 844:17
homo Ecce h.   BIBLE 160:58
H. ludens in his wisdom   DUNN 356:58
h. sapiens a vertebrate mammal   CARB 231:95
neotenic ape, species h. sapiens   ALDI 12:7
homos stately h. of England   CRISP 297:39
homosexuality H. was the badge   EAGL 359:3
preoccupied with his latent h.   MAIL 639:70
honest any h. man's   GILB 424:65
both h. and intelligent   ORWE 745:49
for h. Poverty   BURNS 213:42
good, h. and painful   PEPYS 765:63
hated...when I tried to be h.   ELLI 375:17
h. God   INGE 511:42
h. man's noble work of GOD   BURNS 209:66
h. men and bonny lasses   BURNS 211:10
h. old-fashioned Boarding-school   AUST 51:53
h., sonsie face   BURNS 210:84
hope to remain h.   HOWE 498:99
in a general h. thought   SHAK 884:68
like an h. man   SHAK 879:47
looking for an h. man   DIOG 331:61
man who lies...is an h. man   SAFI 836:70
moderately h. man   SHAW 922:55
most of us are h. all the time   MATH 663:70
not h....but he is most evangelical   BEAV 80:80
not naturally h.   SHAK 912:39
obscure things that are h.   BIBLE 131:83
one of the few h. people   FITZ 390:1
people...are least h.   AUST 51:44
To be h.   SHAK 889:94
whatsoever things are h.   BIBLE 153:15
world's grown h.   SHAK 890:5
write straight h. prose   HEMI 470:28
writer overwhelmingly h.   MOORE 705:27
honestly deal with each other h.   CHAN 250:45
honesty Art, whose h. must work   RIDI 811:81
brings more h. and care   WEBB 1058:16
full of love and h.   SHAK 899:30
h. be no puritan   SHAK 901:72
H. coupled to beauty   SHAK 886:11
h. is a good thing   MARQ 656:43
h. is his   SHAK 901:89
h. is not to be based   RUSK 831:2
H. was a cheat   OTWAY 746:83
it lacks h.   YEATS 1106:88
most important thing... is h.   GOLD 434:48
people are shocked by h.   COWA 290:5
perilous to a man's h.   TROL 1028:84

honesty (*contd.*)

so rich as h.   SHAK 901:76
that damn'd...quality called h.   OTWAY 746:82
transform h. from what it is   SHAK 891:23
Wisdom without h.   JONS 536:18
writers...have a terrible h.   CHAN 251:49
honey Believe me, h.   TUCK 1031:49
bitter hive to grope for h.   SPEN 959:29
buzzes in the h. there   THOM 1011:88
Come Back...Huck H.!   FIED 387:37
drowned in the h.   HAWT 461:67
eat my peas with h.   NASH 720:71
fill our hives with h.   SWIFT 984:58
flowing with milk and h.   BIBLE 106:56
h. a sauce to sugar   SHAK 886:11
h., and plenty of money   LEAR 590:58
h. of all flowers   NASHE 721:76
h. of poison-flowers   TENN 1001:76
h. pot for every scholar   SAFER 835:66
h. wild, and manna dew   KEATS 545:73
how can I be h. now?   OLSEN 739:38
in my mouth sweet as h.   BIBLE 157:19
is there still h. for tea   BROO 193:30
locusts and wild h.   BIBLE 133:26
milk and h. blessed   NEALE 722:91
Money...sweeter than H.   FRAN 402:3
Pedigree of H.   DICK 328:15
Reach me a rose, h.   FITZ 390:3
scoop of pure h.   SMITH 946:99
summer's h. breath   SHAK 914:68
sweeter also than h.   BIBLE 114:45
sweeter than h.   BIBLE 119:32
honey-bee hive for the h.-b.   YEATS 1104:57
honey-dew he on h.-d. hath fed   COLE 275:18
honeycomb gave him ...an h.   BIBLE 144:23
lips...drop as an h.   BIBLE 120:61
honeymoon H.'s over...get married   EPST 379:5
Hong Kong buildings of H. K.   BOOTH 178:6
honour All h.'s mimic   DONNE 337:78
as an h. to Shakespeare   JONS 536:20
Can H.'s voice provoke   GRAY 442:67
Cavalier who loves h.   SCOTT 856:16
chastity of h.   BURKE 207:32
Chief who in h. advances!   SCOTT 853:62
clear h....purchased by the merit   SHAK 874:31
crowned him with glory and h.   BIBLE 114:35
for the h. of England   CONG 281:27
fount whence h. springs   MARL 653:90
from the book of h. razèd   SHAK 913:55
full of days, riches, and h.   BIBLE 112:87
Giving h. unto the wife   BIBLE 156:81
glory, laud and h.   NEALE 722:92
goblin H. which the world adores   CAREW 232:17
had the h. to be   TILL 1020:64
he was valiant, I h. him   SHAK 884:47
his h. and quality taken   BLUN 170:47
His h. rooted   TENN 1002:15
H. all men   BIBLE 156:79
h. and good actions   BACON 58:2
h. aspireth to it   BACON 56:44
H. but an empty bubble   DRYD 351:72
h. cuts falsehood   GURN 449:90
h. did but jest   GREE 445:31
h., duty, patriotism   LLOY 608:58
h., fredom and curteisie   CHAU 254:18
h., her reputation, and her person   GOTT 436:72
h. is a private station   ADDI 8:34
H. is like a match   PAGN 750:39
h. is my life   SHAK 866:40
H. is not the exclusive property   HOOV 490:66
h., it is no longer peace   RUSS 833:39
h. lies in killing men   MARG 650:79
h., love, obedience   SHAK 910:81
h. May privilege more sins   SHIR 935:24

honour: (*cont.*):
h. of God　　BACH 54:*93*
h. of the British Empire　　CHUR 264:*22*
H. pricks me on　　SHAK 876:*68*
h. turn to dust　　MARV 658:*74*
h. unto Luke Evangelist　　ROSS 824:*91*
h. would thee do　　SHAK 880:*74*
h., duty, patriotism　　LLOY 608:*58*
h., fredom and curteisie　　CHAU 254:*18*
h., her reputation, and her person　　GOTT 436:*72*
h., it is no longer peace　　RUSS 833:*39*
h., love, obedience　　SHAK 910:*81*
how I do h. thee!　　SHAK 873:*94*
hurt that H. feels　　TENN 995:*76*
If I lose mine h.　　SHAK 904:*53*
If your h. disna ken　　SCOTT 855:*86*
in her left hand riches and h.　　BIBLE 120:*60*
In search of h.　　LUCR 619:*35*
It is not for me, Your H.　　BIRK 163:*21*
Jealous in h.　　SHAK 885:*92*
Keeps h. bright　　SHAK 896:*52*
leave not a stain in thine h.　　BIBLE 132:*14*
left to the fighter's h.　　HEMI 470:*24*
Legion of H.　　TWAIN 1032:*73*
louder he talked of his h.　　EMER 377:*69*
Loved I not h. more　　LOVE 615:*67*
mace of h.　　MANC 644:*66*
make one vessel unto h.　　BIBLE 149:*32*
no spark of h. bides　　SHAK 861:*16*
Observe his h.　　DONNE 337:*79*
Of power, of h.　　MARL 654:*11*
once stood for h.　　WHITE 1069:*20*
only h. and life…spared　　FRAN 401:*94*
Peace without h.　　CECIL 247:*78*
peace, I hope, with h.　　DISR 333:*23*
pension list…a roll of h.　　CLEV 269:*8*
pluck bright h.　　SHAK 875:*46*
prophet is not without h.　　BIBLE 138:*5*
Render h. to whom h.　　BIBLE 149:*39*
reputation for wisdom and h.　　BIBLE 123:*36*
Set h. in one eye　　SHAK 882:*18*
signed with their h.　　SPEN 956:*72*
sin to covet h.　　SHAK 881:*97*
some smatch of h.　　SHAK 884:*66*
staff of h. for mine age　　SHAK 862:*36*
stain in her h. or…brocade　　POPE 778:*96*
symbol of national h.　　KRUG 570:*6*
them that h. me I will h.　　BIBLE 109:*26*
this journey…and the h. thereof　　EDWA 361:*47*
To h. his own words　　TENN 1002:*17*
Upon my h.　　PARK 755:*26*
when h. dies　　WHIT 1074:*3*
where their h. died　　POPE 782:*77*
with native h. clad　　MILT 690:*54*
with wealth and h. blest　　DRYD 349:*14*
honourable Brutus is an h. man　　SHAK 884:*48*
designs were strictly h.　　FIEL 388:*52*
intentions are perfectly h.　　SHAW 923:*73*
most h. …was to steal　　RABE 799:*88*
surrender…was as h. as resistance　　ANGE 19:*19*
true and h. wife　　SHAK 883:*31*
whatever is sweet, and h.　　MELV 667:*36*
honoured but h. of them all　　TENN 994:*58*
H. and bless'd be　　SCOTT 853:*62*
h. by your friends　　HOOV 490:*70*
More h. in the breach　　SHAK 888:*70*
honouring wirschap and great h.　　DUNB 355:*36*
honours bears his blushing h.　　SHAK 918:*61*
neither h. nor wages　　GARI 415:*25*
talk of high h.　　TS 1031:*40*
Hoo-doo H.-d. …unorganized　　REED 805:*89*
hood him that wears a h.　　ANON 23:*85*
racing car whose h.　　MARI 651:*67*
wear the h.　　DUNC 355:*48*

hoods gaudy h. and linings!　　DICK 322:*66*
hoofs plunging h. were gone　　DELA 314:*27*
hook button, h., and lace　　LOWE 615:*74*
by h. or by crook　　MORE 706:*42*
draw out leviathan with an h.?　　BIBLE 113:*26*
head down on the h.　　JUST 540:*75*
Not a h. in all my breast　　VAUG 1041:*19*
hook-nosed h.-n. fellow of Rome　　SHAK 878:*5*
hookers played so many h.　　MACL 633:*60*
hooks baited h. shall tangle　　WYATT 1102:*27*
With silken lines, and silver h.　　DONNE 337:*89*
hooligans Football h.?　　CLOU 271:*51*
hoops pot shall have ten h.　　SHAK 861:*10*
with h. of steel　　SHAK 888:*63*
hooray Dear Mrs A, H., h.　　COWA 290:*4*
H. for Hollywood　　MERC 670:*96*
hooter because the h. hoots　　CHES 259:*27*
Hoover, H. with a smile　　ONEI 740:*67*
hop H. forty paces　　SHAK 905:*70*
hop-yards for what were h.-y. meant　　HOUS 495:*63*
hope Abandon all h.　　DANTE 305:*68*
against h. believed in h.　　BIBLE 148:*17*
belief and h. had gone　　RUSS 833:*34*
Can something, h.　　HOPK 492:*1*
do not h. to turn　　ELIOT 369:*8*
exercise of h.　　WORD 1099:*66*
fair guerdon when we h.　　MILT 684:*42*
faith, h., charity　　BIBLE 150:*62*
feeble H. could ne'er　　MARV 658:*77*
Flesh Of H..　　NICH 726:*52*
fruitful h. of nourishment　　SPEN 959:*41*
gathers her most vital h.　　MELV 667:*31*
God shall be my h.　　SHAK 861:*2*
high h. of adventure　　WHIT 1071:*56*
high uplifted beyond h.　　MILT 688:*11*
H., art thou true　　SIDN 937:*55*
h. could have no fear　　THOM 1015:*58*
H. deferred maketh the heart sick　　BIBLE 121:*73*
H., for a season　　CAMP 227:*26*
h. for the best　　SMITH 949:*48*
h. full of immortality　　BIBLE 131:*81*
H. guides us by her star　　BRON 191:*2*
H. has often caused　　SOPH 953:*15*
h. in Christ　　BIBLE 151:*66*
H. is a good breakfast　　BACON 56:*39*
H. is the power of being cheerful　　CHES 258:*96*
h. is the thing with feathers　　DICK 328:*97*
h., love of finished years　　ROSS 823:*67*
H. may vanish　　SHEL 932:*62*
h. never comes That comes to all　　MILT 687:*90*
h. of glory　　BOOK 174:*8*
h. of instant results　　SCHL 848:*78*
h. of science　　INGE 511:*41*
h. of winning her love　　STAEL 961:*69*
h. on God is founded　　BRID 187:*43*
h., once crushed　　ARNO 39:*19*
H. sleeps in our bones　　PIER 769:*37*
h. so transcendent　　LAWR 587:*14*
H. springs eternal　　POPE 780:*36*
h. that he will die　　EMER 377:*65*
h. thou in God　　BIBLE 116:*69*
h. to get one every 30 years　　SIMON 939:*83*
H. to joy is little less　　SHAK 867:*52*
h.…unwilling to be fed　　WORD 1097:*45*
H. ushers in a Revolution　　CARL 235:*61*
H. withering fled　　BYRON 221:*11*
h.'s true gage　　RALE 800:*13*
I h. in thee　　STUA 980:*10*
Idle to h.　　REED 805:*84*
if h. should e'er decline　　WORD 1100:*90*
illusions that…limit h.　　FRYE 408:*24*
in the store we sell h.　　REVS 807:*21*
in trembling h. repose　　GRAY 442:*78*
Is it too much to h.　　REDM 804:*75*

hope (*contd.*)
Land of H. and Glory　　BENS 92:*9*
land of their hearts h.　　DAVIS 309:*38*
lined himself with h.　　SHAK 877:*86*
living h. rose in me　　FOX 400:*74*
Love without h.　　GRAV 440:*40*
may be brought to h.　　TROL 1028:*81*
may we bring h.　　THAT 1007:*11*
Maybe all one can do is h.　　MILL 677:*12*
miserable have…only h.　　SHAK 897:*76*
must run with h.　　ZATO 1109:*14*
Nature to his h. has giv'n　　POPE 780:*37*
no h. of finding ourselves　　MILL 678:*27*
no very lively h.　　SMITH 949:*59*
nor h., nor health　　SHEL 927:*74*
one more rich h.　　SHAK 913:*57*
only h. of creating something　　FLAU 392:*40*
others have to h. for heaven　　SLOAN 943:*60*
Our h. for years to come　　WATTS 1055:*58*
place where sanity and h.　　ROUS 827:*30*
poise of h. and fear　　MILT 683:*29*
power of the h. of freedom　　BUCK 203:*34*
Rootless h.　　BINY 162:*9*
Some blessed H.　　HARDY 457:*7*
spring of h.　　DICK 326:*58*
strength and my h. is perished　　BIBLE 128:*31*
this pleasing h.　　ADDI 8:*35*
those, who have to h.　　BURKE 207:*19*
Through love, through h.　　WORD 1100:*86*
triumph of h.　　JOHN 528:*57*
True h. is swift　　SHAK 863:*60*
unconquerable h.　　ARNO 38:*93*
wait without h.　　ELIOT 371:*44*
what h. of harmony?　　SHAK 861:*1*
what was dead was H.　　WILDE 1078:*1*
What…we may gain from h.　　MILT 687:*97*
Whatever h. is yours　　OWEN 748:*16*
Where there is despair, h.　　FRAN 401:*91*
who can h.　　WALL 1050:*74*
wish for what I faintly h.　　DRYD 346:*50*
woes which H. thinks infinite　　SHEL 930:*27*
hopeful To be h. in an artistic sense　　CONR 285:*2*
hopelessness h. of knowing　　LEAC 589:*38*
hopes airy h.　　WORD 1100:*82*
all h. to disappear　　GILB 424:*61*
clues, h., and fears　　LIPP 606:*32*
Cricket is…full of forlorn h.　　ORWE 744:*96*
day with high h.　　CLIN 269:*16*
different yearnings, different h.　　CART 242:*2*
fifty h. and fears　　BROW 198:*54*
fondest h. decay　　MOORE 706:*38*
h. and dreams of the Future　　FRAME 400:*78*
h. and h. to fears　　SHAK 915:*90*
h. and prayers of liberty-loving people　　EISE 363:*78*
h. of future years　　LONG 611:*8*
How strangely h. delude men　　MASS 663:*60*
If h. were dupes　　CLOU 270:*32*
late on h. depended　　SHAK 898:*12*
nor as happy as one h.　　LARO 582:*25*
shipwrecking all their h.　　MOOD 703:*95*
tender leaves of h.　　SHAK 918:*61*
To sympathy with h. and fears　　SHEL 929:*2*
vanity of human h.　　JOHN 525:*89*
hoping go truly h. to find adventure　　HEAT 465:*46*
h. …someone will make things right　　REAG 803:*60*
Hopper Do you know, Mr H.　　WILDE 1076:*59*
H. is the great painter　　ALLEN 14:*34*
hoppy H., Croppy, Droppy　　ELLIS 375:*11*
Horatio more things…H.　　SHAK 889:*84*
O, I die, H.!　　SHAK 893:*88*
Horatius H. kept the bridge　　MACA 624:*18*
out spoke brave H.　　MACA 623:*21*
stood brave H.　　MACA 623:*21*
horde language of the h.　　MALL 641:*18*

horde (*contd.*)
Society is now one polished h. — BYRON 223:59
horizon always somebody else's h.! — GRAH 438:91
h. of daily environment — EINS 363:63
multiplying on the sold h. — WALC 1048:39
narrow h. of bourgeois — MARX 661:24
neither h., cloud, nor sound — CARR 237:11
pressing up over the h. — TIME 1020:66
workhouse from the h. — LLOY 608:57
horizons h. come — HUGH 500:35
sorrow's h. are vague — MACM 636:26
horizontal h. desire — SHAW 925:32
your position would be h. — OHARA 737:11
horn blind H.'s hate — KIPL 565:19
h., the h. the lusty h. — SHAK 887:26
hunter's h. is ringing — SCOTT 854:66
if we can pick up a h. — FREE 403:30
it won't come out of your h. — PARK 753:87
keys of the postboy's h. — BENET 90:60
Poured thro' the mellow h. — COLL 277:50
'scorn' 'h.', a hard rhyme — SHAK 880:65
small but sullen h. — COLL 277:48
wreathèd h. — WORD 1099:73
Hornby my H. and my Barlow — THOM 1014:32
hornets wasps and h. break through — SWIFT 984:63
Hornie Auld H., Satan, Nick — BURNS 209:73
hornpipes h. and strathspeys — BURNS 212:34
horns got to draw in their h. — LEMAY 595:43
h. of cockled snails — SHAK 865:20
h. of Elfland — TENN 997:99
keeping clear of her h. — SZEN 989:70
Morning on the silver h. — TENN 998:12
on the h. o'th' moon — SHAK 911:3
pulled in their h. — JUVE 540:81
taking the bull by both h. — ASHF 41:70
With its h. through mist — THOM 1010:69
horny-handed H.-h. sons of toil — SALI 839:33
horrible grotesque to the h. — DOYLE 344:19
It is h., yet fascinating — DOYLE 344:14
not to feel any, that is h. — VIAN 1043:46
people were so h. — AMIS 16:79
horribly h. in love with her — SHAK 879:49
horrid h. malicious bloody flame — PEPYS 765:80
h. thing to follow — JAMES 516:16
h. thing, a very h. thing — BUTL 216:96
was bad, she was h. — LONG 612:21
horror beauty…watch it only full of h. — VIEI 1044:75
boredom, and the h., and the glory — ELIOT 370:16
define your own h. journey — GELL 417:71
haunts of h. and fear — TENN 1002:93
H. and doubt distract — MILT 689:45
h.…for whole nation — WHAR 1068:93
h. of civil war — HOMER 488:21
h. of Creation — HUGH 500:45
h. of outer darkness — GORD 435:63
h. of the Twentieth Century — MAIL 639:85
H., tyrant of the throbbing breast — GRAY 443:87
I have a h. of the word — RENO 807:8
no imagination…no h. — DOYLE 343:85
one expanding h. in American life — MAIL 639:81
secret dread, and inward h. — ADDI 8:35
The h.! The h.! — CONR 284:92
horrors Congenial h., hail! — THOM 1015:51
I have supped full with h. — SHAK 910:85
horse Always look a gift h. — RABE 798:81
Be ye not as the h. — BIBLE 115:59
behold a pale h. — BIBLE 157:12
behold a white h. — BIBLE 158:30
between a rider and his h. — SURT 983:48
camel is a h. — ISSI 514:81
courage to ride a h. — LEAC 588:30
cup won by the worst h. — MASE 662:50
dearer than his h. — TENN 995:73

horse (*contd.*)
definition of a h. — DICK 325:40
duchess-faced h. — THOM 1012:95
even do for a h. — NIGH 729:1
flung himself upon his h. — LEAC 589:37
fond of a h. — HALI 452:24
for want of a h. — FRAN 402:7
Give me another h.! — SHAK 863:62
given the h. his strength? — BIBLE 113:22
Go not my h. the better — SHAK 909:55
hear a h.'s feet — KIPL 564:2
h. came spurring in — MACA 624:20
h. drench to bring' em off — LAMB 576:16
h. in the silence champed the grasses — DELA 314:25
h. is drawn by the cart — KIPL 561:41
h. on the mountain — LORCA 613:39
kingdom for a h.! — SHAK 863:69
leene was his h. as is a rake — CHAU 254:21
never heard no h. sing — ARMS 35:47
never look at another h. — MARX 659:2
No h.'s cry was that — ARNO 38:95
no handles to a h. — LEAC 588:29
nothing but talk of his h. — SHAK 874:14
One h. endeavoured to climb — SOME 952:1
One stiff blind h. — BROW 198:50
paint a forest or a h. — MARC 649:41
part man, part h.'s ass — ACHE 3:31
rather have a goddam h. — SALI 839:25
ridden the passions…magnificent h. — BROY 200:4
sightless h. — WALEY 1049:51
sting a stately h. — JOHN 526:94
strong as a farm h. — LEE 593:17
The h. loves the hound — SURT 983:47
The h. that comes — YEATS 1105:72
Then hey for boot and h. — KING 558:94
thrown from his h. — ANON 23:98
to my h. [I speak]—German — CHAR 253:90
true as truest h. — SHAK 871:43
two men ride of a h. — SHAK 880:59
where's the bloody h.? — CAMP 227:15
Why does a hearse h. snicker — SAND 841:63
horse-backbreaker this h.-b. — SHAK 876:56
horse-hoof A h.-h. slides — YEATS 1105:72
horse-plough worked with a h.-p. — HEAN 464:32
horse-racing makes h.-r.…stable — STEI 966:61
horseback as long as I live on h. — BIRD 163:14
horseguards can be in the H. — RATT 802:41
horsehair settee of the h. sea! — SITW 940:99
horseless-carriage h.…a luxury — ANON 25:25
horseman H., pass by! — YEATS 1107:93
world's greatest h. — SCHU 851:16
horsemen apocalyptic h. in the air — MARC 649:40
chariot of Israel, and the h. thereof — BIBLE 111:73
horsepond celibacy is…a muddy h. — PEAC 762:27
horses as fed h. in the morning — BIBLE 128:19
best carriage h. — TROL 1028:88
Bring on the empty h.! — CURT 302:26
But so are h. — GILM 427:15
cannot ride two h. — MAXT 665:1
Come saddle my h. — SCOTT 855:85
Don't Spare the H. — HILL 481:9
England…the hell of h. — FLOR 394:79
evening the strange h. — MUIR 712:35
frighten the h. — CAMP 226:12
generally given to h. — JOHN 526:14
hanged for stealing h. — HALI 452:27
heaven…filled—with h. — DUDEK 353:15
h. and dorgs is some men's fancy — DICK 324:9
h. o' Kansas — KIPL 562:63
h. of instruction — BLAKE 166:77
h. who had never seen a man — BRIN 189:59
hurdling meter like tired h. — BROY 201:5
in h., dawgs, and men — THAC 1006:87
love of h. — FIND 389:67

horses (*contd.*)
never know what Trojan h. — BEVIN 102:77
what they value in their h. — EMER 377:63
wild white h. play — ARNO 36:54
Women and H. — KIPL 561:39
horticulture You can lead a h. — PARK 755:20
hosanna Glorious the h. — SMART 944:71
H. in the highest — BIBLE 139:50
hosannas Made sweet h. ring — NEALE 722:92
hose h. of common sense — GILB 424:78
put a h. in their mouth — KROC 570:98
hospital I was in h. once — BECK 81:6
Randolf Churchill went into h. — WAUGH 1058:8
hospitality old Irish h. — EDGE 360:28
host a h. of golden daffodils — WORD 1099:67
as a guest thanks his h. — DILL 331:52
Guarded…as by an h. — BYRON 222:41
met a h. and quelled it — PEAC 762:30
O all you h. of heaven! — SHAK 889:80
soundless-clapping h. — THOM 1014:32
streams in the countless h. — HOW 497:91
tattered h. of eucalypt — ADAMS 4:63
Though an h. should encamp — BIBLE 115:55
under the h. — PARK 755:21
hostage h. to hostage-takers — INOU 512:59
other guy is called a h. — IACO 509:17
hostages Freeing h. is like — WAITE 1048:30
h. to fortune — BACON 57:56
h. to the fates — LUCAN 618:23
hostile Fearful and h. behavior — FULB 409:30
morally h. — THUB 1018:9
hostilities prevent a resumption of h. — EDEN 360:22
hostility the disguise of determined h. — SHER 934:7
hosts God of H., be with us — KIPL 562:61
Lord of h., to me! — SCOT 856:21
two great classes: h. and guests — BEER 83:41
university where…the Jews are h. — SACH 835:57
armed h. dog thefts — TOOLE 1023:5
hot beat the iron while it is h. — DRYD 352:75
Can one go upon h. coals — BIBLE 120:65
Cool is h. — WASH 1055:46
don't understand too h. — SALI 838:20
feel h. and think cold — CARY 243:17
for your foe so h. — SHAK 917:45
H. and rebellious liquors — SHAK 885:82
H. as any hottentot — SITW 940:1
h. as molten lead — SHAK 876:74
h. as the steam — WATT 1055:55
h. from hell — SHAK 883:45
h. temper leaps o'er a cold decree — SHAK 874:12
how h. the day is — GRAV 439:17
If it be a h. day — SHAK 877:83
while the strike is h. — ANON 29:30
hot-bloods h.-b between fourteen — SHAK 880:55
hotel great advantage of a h. — SHAW 920:12
man comes into a great h. — MILL 677:1
open to all—like the Ritz H. — MATH 663:67
small clerk of some h. — MANS 647:3
hotel-keepers Swiss are inspired h.-k. — MONT 701:60
that h.-k. continue — TROL 1027:69
hotels all stuck over with large brown h. — HEMI 470:12
h. will…have disappeared — LEVIN 600:29
Hotspur H. of the North — SHAK 876:53
hottentot Hot as any h. — SITW 940:1
Hottentot H. and every Eskimo — LEHR 595:41
might as well have been H. — LAWR 586:92
hotter call'st thyself a h. name — SHAK 910:88
houms dowie h. o' Yarrow — BALL -101:37
hound footprints of a gigantic h.! — DOYLE 344:10
hawk, his h., and his lady fair — BALL 67:55
mettled h. — SCOTT 854:79
slepyng h. to wake — CHAU 254:7

hound (*contd.*)

The horse loves the h.	SURT 983:47

hounding World, in h. me — JUANA 539:64

hounds carcass fit for h. — SHAK 883:29

h. are in cry	SCOTT 854:66
keep...any racehorse or pack of h.	CHES 257:83
like fell and cruel h.	SHAK 893:93
When the h. of spring	SWIN 986:23

hour arrival of an h. — SHAK 876:72

At such an h. the sinners	RUNY 829:65
Awaits the inevitable h.	GRAY 442:66
awful quarters of an h.!	ROSS 825:97
books of the h.	RUSK 831:96
but one bare h. to live	MARL 654:20
child's a plaything for an h.	LAMB 576:11
companioned inarticulate h.	ROSS 824:87
dead deathless h.	ROSS 824:85
Do not expect again a phoenix h.	DAYL 310:56
during that h....I forgot	ATWO 45:28
eternity in an h.	BLAKE 167:1
falling h. by h.	MACN 637:39
For dark h. or twain	SHAK 909:55
from childhood's h.	MOORE 706:38
great h. of destiny	SASS 845:25
h. ago since it was nine	SHAK 885:90
h. approaches Tam maun ride	BURNS 211:16
h. be but A year	MARL 654:20
h.'s come, but not the man	SCOTT 855:91
h. for getting up	SHIP 935:21
h. is not that far off	LENIN 595:50
h. is upon her again	GIBB 422:34
h. of my death	KEATS 545:28
h. Of thoughtless youth	WORD 1094:98
h. or a day	NASHE 721:77
h. when earth's foundations fled	HOUS 496:77
How many makes the h.	SHAK 862:23
humblest h. is when he compares	BARR 72:41
I also had my h.	CHES 257:88
I Have known the lightning's h.	DAYL 310:54
its h. come round	YEATS 1106:78
just at this dead h.	SHAK 887:43
known as the Children's H.	LONG 612:15
meaning of this happy h.	KLEE 566:48
mine h. is not yet come	BIBLE 145:30
Not an h. more nor less	SHAK 904:43
nothing can bring back the h.	WORD 1098:55
now's the h.	BURNS 212:37
Of a ship's h.	SLES 943:57
Of thee one h.	DONNE 338:96
Oh, for an h. of Herod!	HOPE 490:73
pause...known as cocktail h.	DEVO 318:91
rash hand in evil h.	MILT 692:12
ring out the h.	APOL 32:93
serve the future h.	WORD 1100:86
Some luckless h.	BURNS 209:74
take an h.'s leisure	STARK 963:97
the h. is nigh	SCOTT 855:3
their finest h.	CHUR 264:15
This is the exquisite h.	VERL 1042:34
Time and h. runs	SHAK 907:22
to serve the h.	TENN 1000:70
to the h. its solitude	STEV 971:48
uncertain h. before the morning	ELIOT 372:72
watch at the midnight h.	LEAR 589:52
weight of the superincumbent h.	SHEL 931:43
world's best moment is a calm h.	ABU 1:11
world-without-end h.	SHAK 913:66

hour-glass still as the h.-g. — ROSS 824:86

hours best in a couple of h. — WEST 1067:83

crime...The h. are good	ALLEN 14:35
ever-rolling silent h.	PEAC 762:31
few h. in life more agreeable	JAMES 516:14
few h. of giving his enemies	STER 969:92
fruitless h., but neither	MILT 692:10

hours (*contd.*)

glare Of the interminable h.	ARNO 36:70
golden H., on angel wings	BURNS 211:1
hath not known his god-like h.	WORD 1096:28
h. are made for men	RABE 799:85
h., days, months...rags of time	DONNE 336:77
h. of weariness	WORD 1094:96
h. they know how to employ	MONT 701:56
h. were cups of sack	SHAK 875:36
h. will take care of themselves	CHES 257:77
How slowly do the h.	SPEN 959:32
I was in Tennessee 24 h.	RAY 803:47
march of only a few h.	PEARY 763:36
sweetest h. that e'er I spend	BURNS 209:56
talk its pensive h. away	BRON 191:7
the darksome h.	GOET 431:72
The pitiless h.	THOM 1015:55
three and a half h. long	CHAP 252:77
Three h. a day	TROL 1028:98
tide of h.	YEATS 1105:61
time card office h.	BAND 69:87
Time in h., days, years	VAUG 1041:20
Upon the h. and times	SHAK 913:66
Work eight h.	PICK 769:30

house About the lilting h. — THOM 1010:65

allegations...repeated outside the H. — PROF 792:77

All my h.	JONS 534:84
approbation of this H.	WALP 1052:98
as for me and my h.	BIBLE 109:12
bawdy h. is to a cathedral	MENC 669:66
boat...had the goods of a h.	PEPYS 765:81
brawling woman in a wide h.	BIBLE 121:93
built his h. upon a rock	BIBLE 135:63
called woman in own h.	WAUGH 1057:84
Calls a h. a rookery	DICK 323:98
clean someone's h.	THER 1009:37
corrupt and servile H. of Commons	SHER 934:13
dark h. and a whip	SHAK 886:8
Dark h., by which	TENN 998:23
depart out of that h. or city	BIBLE 136:75
doll in the doll's h.	DICK 327:87
dwell in the h. of the Lord	BIBLE 115:50
dwell in the h. of the Lord	BIBLE 115:55
even in the h. of worship	PARN 756:39
Except the Lord build the h.	BIBLE 119:41
far from the club h.	LINK 606:19
From Bauhaus to Our H.	WOLFE 1090:27
full h.	MACA 621:79
galleries of the h.	MUNDY 714:53
gat him home to his h.	BIBLE 110:50
ghost of a great h.	LEVE 600:23
go into the h. of the Lord	BIBLE 119:37
gone tiptoe in this h.	MILL 676:98
great h. of our humanity	DUNC 355:49
great h. of Tarquin	MACA 623:12
Harrow the h. of the dead	AUDEN 46:42
hauf-way h.	MACD 627:76
H....a place of free speech	WENT 1065:53
h. as nigh heaven	MORE 707:56
H. at Pooh Corner	PARK 754:94
H. Beautiful is...lousy	PARK 754:97
h....become a den of robbers	BIBLE 128:22
h. divided against itself	LINC 604:98
h. fell upon the lords	BIBLE 109:22
h. in the world	RYBC 834:48
H. is not a Home	ADLER 9:49
H. is pleased to direct me	LENT 596:67
h. not made with hands	WELL 1064:16
H. of Lords	STOP 978:74
H. of Lords an illusion	LLOY 609:64
H. of Lords in his own head	FIELD 388:43
H. of Lords is a model	ATTL 44:15
H. of Lords is like a glass	

house (*contd.*)

H. of Lords must be the only institution	SAMU 840:43
H. of peers	GILB 424:76
h. rose like magic	HARG 457:15
h. that has got over	JERO 521:10
h. they shall dwell	DONNE 339:34
h. to be broken up	BIBLE 140:40
h. was filled with smoke	BIBLE 124:60
h. where I was born	HOOD 489:37
h. where there was not one dead	BIBLE 106:62
h. wherein our Life is led	CARL 235:74
h., which I have hallowed	BIBLE 111:56
h. with the narrow gate	SHAK 901:83
imprison the child in her h.	WHITE 1070:39
In my Father's h. are many mansions	BIBLE 146:61
in the h. of bondage	MACA 622:90
In the h. of Life	THUR 1018:15
invisibly all over the h.	THUR 1018:18
jewel of our h.	SHAK 901:78
just moved into chicken h.	MACA 621:78
Killing the Angel in the H.	WOOLF 1093:78
labour of keeping a h.	MACC 626:54
Leader of the H. of Commons	DISR 333:2
live in a h. on fire	WILL 1082:80
Looking around the H.	THOR 1018:79
love the H. of Commons so passionately	CHAN 251:62
luck about a h.	YEATS 1106:88
magic h. of glass	ROBE 814:17
Majesty entered the H.	RUSH 829:71
'Make my h. your inn.'	MOORE 705:20
man...in the way in the h.	GASK 415:34
man's h. is his castle	COKE 272:73
Marriage is not a h.	ATWO 45:19
meanest member of the H.	HENR 472:65
Members of this H.	BAXT 78:50
mind to sell his h.	SWIFT 984:79
mistress of every h.	MILL 675:79
moat defensive to a h.	SHAK 867:48
moderately healthy h.	SHAW 922:55
neighbour's h. is on fire	BURKE 207:25
no one depressed in this h.	VICT 1043:52
offered his h. to sale	JOHN 528:45
office of the White H.	MENC 669:76
Oh, to have a little h.!	COLUM 278:62
old h. carried an assurance	ACHE 2:25
on the front porch of the h.	LANCE 578:53
one-man H. of Commons	MANC 644:67
One need not be a H.	DICK 328:5
out of h. and home	SHAK 877:88
out of the h. of the Lord	BIBLE 118:28
Peace be to this h.	BIBLE 142:87
Peace be to this h.	BOOK 176:54
play the fool...in 's own h.	SHAK 891:27
regulates the size of the h.	LECO 592:2
return into my h.	BIBLE 137:95
secret h. of death	SHAK 906:89
serious h. on serious earth	LARK 581:2
set a h. on fire	BACON 58:91
seven pillared worthy h.	LAWR 587:12
sharing the h. with a disembodied	SHAR 919:86
sit in the h. wi' handkerchers	SCOTT 855:83
snail...Carrying his h.	DONNE 338:98
sneak into the h. in her train	LAMB 576:22
sparrow hath found an h.	BIBLE 117:93
Speaker of the H.	GARN 415:28
spoil his h.	BIBLE 141:61
still more the honourable H.	ROCHE 815:41
talking about building a h.	STERN 968:86
tell you your h. is burning	MUNRO 714:58
Tenants of the h.	ELIOT 368:92
the h. of tomorrow	GIBR 422:38
thief breaks into my h.	PAINE 750:43

house (*contd.*)
this is no my ain h.	ANON 23:97
to clean h.	THUR 1019:43
to the Duke's h.	PEPYS 765:71
Unless the Lord has built the h.	BIBLE 159:48
upon the posts of thy h.	BIBLE 108:90
venal H. of Peers	SHER 934:13
What h. more stately	HERB 475:21
when all through the h.	MOORE 704:3
Wisdom hath builded her h.	BIBLE 120:66
women in the h.	GILM 427:15
You take my h.	SHAK 873:97
young and inexperienced h.	JERO 521:10

housed h., clothed, fed — RUSK 831:3

household a great actor or a h. word? — OLIV 738:27
Her h. to me	HERB 475:16
h. features her person	PRIOR 790:52
h. of God	BIBLE 152:96
keep thy h. the Church	BOOK 174:14
My name…a h. word	ASHB 41:58
not a member of the h.	KENN 550:51
our names…as h. words	SHAK 882:2
put his h. in order	BIBLE 110:50
real centre of the h.	SHAW 925:14
women, than to study h.	MILT 692:2
Yiddish is a h. tongue	OZICK 748:24

housekeeper a man marries his h. — PIGOU 770:41
h. think she's a householder	WILD 1079:22

housekeeping H. ain't no joke — ALCO 12:98

housemaid If I'd been a h. — MELBA 667:23
nice to the second h.	JAMES 516:26

housemaids damp souls of h. — ELIOT 367:62

houses big h. sat in…propinquity — GILL 426:4
calling of selling h.	LEWIS 601:51
cry in strangers' h.	MANS 647:9
Eighteenth-century h.	YEATS 1105:71
few of his friends' h.	JOHN 531:23
going on inside their h.	ALME 15:57
h. are made of stones	POIN 776:58
h. deserve to be burnt	WELLS 1064:35
h. just as big	SMITH 947:18
h. marked with a red cross	PEPYS 765:73
h. there wear verandahs	MURR 715:75
live in the h. they build	STEI 966:55
narrow streets, old h.	THOR 1017:98
not the h.	FENT 385:1
pigeons…loath to leave their h.	PEPYS 765:79
plague o' both your h.	SHAK 869:4
round their golden h.	TENN 994:52
sandstone apartment h.	CHEE 255:48
sensible to build h.	KEYN 555:36
seven o'clock from the h.	REED 805:82
staying in their h.	PEPYS 765:79
studios, and in the workers' h.	MAYA 665:4
The trees and the h.	THOM 1015:54
the very h. seem asleep	WORD 1097:46
towns or h. raised by poetry	COWL 291:14
ugly h. stands	MILL 676:83
unessential h. began to melt	FITZ 391:6

housetops lowered o'er our h. — TWAIN 1033:89

housewife busy h. ply her care — GRAY 442:65
h.'s badly-cooked dinners	BEET 84:55
Many a h.	GREER 445:42
mock the good h. Fortune	SHAK 884:69
scholar or a complete h.	PLATH 773:89
the h. that's thrifty	SHER 933:97

housework help with the h. — WINT 1087:69
no need to do any h.	CRISP 297:37

Houston oil depletion…makes H. — MAIL 639:84

how H. you? — GRANT 438:1
person who knows 'h.'	RAVI 802:45

how-de-do Here's a h.-d.-d.! — GILB 425:89

Howard Then sware Lord Thomas H. — TENN 1004:56

Howell H. & James young man — GILB 424:71

howl hear a famisht h. — BERR 98:8
H., h., h., h.!	SHAK 904:51
New widows h.	SHAK 909:72

howling h. commercial success — GREE 444:23

howls h. on for more — SHEL 929:9

hub h. of the solar system — HOLM 486:88

hubris H. clobbered by Nemesis — ALDI 12:8

Hudson Close by the H. — HUGH 499:28

hue innermost idea of this h. — MELV 667:36
most lily-white of h.	SHAK 871:43
native h. of resolution	SHAK 890:21
of dazzling h.	KEATS 545:75

hues all one's favourite h. — DOYLE 344:21
Rainbow…left thee all her lovely h.	DAVI 308:19

huffing h. of hyphenated words — BROY 201:5

huffy Not h., or stuffy — HERB 474:92

hugged h. the offender and forgave — DRYD 352:85

hulk stoop-shouldered h. — TIME 1020:66

hum h. a fugue — GILB 424:63
h. of either army	SHAK 881:88
h. Of human cities	BYRON 220:87
mist and h.	ARNO 38:97
pilgrim borne in heedless h.	COLL 277:48
propels the h. s.	KAND 541:94

human accusing…the h. race — CAMUS 229:58
all female life, animal and h.	STAN 963:90
All h. things subject to decay	DRYD 348:81
All must love the h. form	BLAKE 166:65
all that h. hearts endure	GOLD 432:99
All that is h.	GIBB 421:25
all the months of h. birth	MASE 662:44
animals could be made h.	HEINE 467:70
application of h. ingenuity	NUTT 732:46
articulate h. relationships	VIDAL 1044:56
as h. eye could see	TENN 995:77
awing the h. mind	JEFF 520:93
basic h. emotions	ROTH 826:26
become a h. is art	NOVA 732:40
Being h., she must	KIPL 562:69
belief in h. liberty	MACL 634:85
believe in taking h. life	NATH 721:8
between h. creation	MILL 678:34
bless our h. ears	MILT 681:90
boot stamping on a h. face	ORWE 745:60
bounds of h. Empire	BACON 56:37
breathes with h. breath	TENN 996:86
But h. creatures' lives!	HOOD 489:46
but it's greater to be h.	ROGE 820:20
call the sciences h. invention	PAINE 750:51
can no longer bear to be h.	BECK 81:90
cancer of h. history	SONT 953:7
care for far more than h. life	PANK 752:79
chaos of h. experience	MACL 634:87
chords in the h. mind	DICK 325:30
civilized h. life	TRUM 1030:22
collection…of h. knowledge	KENN 551:72
condition of being h.	ANOU 31:77
condition of the h. race	GIBB 421:18
considerers of h. things	MILT 686:69
constituting of h. virtue	MILT 685:66
contribution to h. history	JIANG 522:25
could be the whole h. condition	HOPP 493:14
death instead of 'h. rights'	PEOP 764:58
degraded h. life	MARX 660:18
destiny of the h. race	THOR 1016:74
destruction of h. life	HARDY 456:83
devaluation of the h. world	MARX 661:26
development of h. destinies	FISH 389:82
do h. rights begin	ROOS 821:32
does a h. form display	BLAKE 168:21
enemy of the h. race	MILL 677:17
escapes being h.	YOUR 1108:5
essence of real h. love	ELIOT 365:13

human (*contd.*)
establishment of h.activity	MARX 660:7
every h. has a finite number	ARMS 35:50
experience of being h.	LEWO 603:74
fight for their own h. rights	PANK 753:80
For insight into h. affairs	DYSON 358:99
forget the h. race	BYRON 220:4
form of h. reason	LEVI 600:31
forms of h. knowledge	MANN 645:81
frightened by h. impossibility	ANDR 18:10
from any h. experience	JAMES 515:6
From what h. ill	WILD 1079:20
get h. feelings right	HUTC 506:40
giving life in h. fashion	REDON 804:77
godhead in which all life is h.	SHAW 923:76
greatest thing a h. soul	RUSK 831:3
greatness of the h. soul	ROCK 817:71
herds, of h. face divine	MILT 689:31
histories…of h. life	POPP 783:18
history of the h. race	HARL 458:20
Hope…in the h. breast	POPE 780:36
horse is at least h.	SALI 839:25
h. activity that takes	TRIL 1026:56
h. affairs would never improve	ORWE 742:89
h. body is sacred	WHIT 1073:83
h. creation mechanical	LEGER 593:21
h. desire for food	TOOLE 1023:5
h. employers quite literally	MUMF 713:49
h. enterprise	GOULD 436:77
h. experience is actively offered	WILL 1081:52
H. history…a race	WELLS 1065:42
h. history	GARC 414:19
h. intellectual tradition	GOULD 436:78
h. kind Cannot bear…reality	ELIOT 370:24
H. life is but a series	NABO 717:3
h. life that's kicking me	SUMMA 981:25
h. offspring	MILT 690:65
h. or domestic life second	MANN 646:95
h. plane	GILL 426:8
h. progress	GARI 415:24
h. psychic equilibrium	MAMET 644:55
h. race commit suicide	ADAMS 5:71
h. race has…potential for idiocy	ONET 740:70
h. race…playing at children's games	CHES 258:92
h. species is	MILL 679:58
h. species, according to…theory	LAMB 577:31
h. spirit is immortal	MURP 715:71
H. temperaments	LUCAS 618:29
Humane, but not h.	CUMM 300:97
If h. souls did never	KEATS 545:59
imagination makes me h.	LEGU 594:33
imitative side of h. behavior	MACC 626:57
immeasurable h. misery	HARD 455:78
important a h. activity	MONT 700:52
improvisations of h. existence	MACC 626:67
increase in h. misery	HARR 458:25
influence on h. life	MULL 713:43
inherent in the h. situation	GREE 444:25
interesting and h. fellow	ROGE 820:12
key to h. warmth	ISHI 513:77
known by the h. mind	PAGE 749:33
Larger than h.	TENN 1004:44
laugh at h. actions	SPIN 960:46
limits of h. knowledge	NIEB 727:65
look into a h. eye	MELV 668:44
man to tell how h.	MILT 692:92
many h. relationships	WEBB 1058:14
mayn't be h. gore	DICK 322:62
Mercy has a h. heart	BLAKE 166:69
moon…is not h.	SCOTT 852:36
necessary to h. existence	BLAKE 166:71
necessary to the h. mind	REES 805:92
no h. claim can be of…significance	OATES 733:58

human (*contd.*)

No perfect solution…in h. affairs	BERL 96:69
nor…will the h. race	PLATO 774:21
not meant for h. eyes	MUIR 712:29
not, as a h. type,…a success	OBRI 734:62
nothing that is h. alien	TERE 1005:72
nothing to distinguish h. society	SHAW 924:94
objects of h. reason	HUME 503:8
ocean or the h. heart?	LAUT 584:49
Of all h. struggles	SHAW 921:26
one h. sound	THOM 1013:25
ordinary h. countenance	LEAC 589:38
other sets of people are h.	HUXL 508:92
own-goal scored by the h. race	ANNE 20:38
partly in h. institution	MILL 674:57
passion in the h. soul	LILLO 604:95
passions glowing in a h. face	MATI 663:73
paucity of h. pleasures	JOHN 532:41
people are only h.	COMP 278:69
people being more than h.	AMIS 17:96
perversity of the h. mind	TROL 1028:81
pleasures of h. intercourse	MOORE 704:10
Poetry…through h. language	MALL 641:14
point the highest that h.	MILT 686:73
portions of the h. anatomy	HELP 469:9
possible for a h. creature	SMITH 946:91
power of the h. intellect	LEWIS 602:60
propels the h. spirit	KAND 541:94
promotion of the h. race	WEST 1068:88
pump all his h. weaknesses	MENC 670:88
reaches of h. wit	MARL 653:91
records of the h. spirit	MACL 634:77
redressing h. wrongs	TENN 1002:17
relation between the h. tongue	WAXM 1058:12
replacement of h. forces	MARX 661:22
Royalty puts a h. face	RUNC 828:51
sacrifice h. life to figures	WEIL 1062:83
satisfies the h. creative instinct	QUEN 797:54
science of arresting h. intelligence	LEAC 589:43
sense of h. sight	MILT 682:6
skins fewer than any other h.	CURR 301:15
Socialism…is only H.	CONN 284:83
Somewhere…form of a h. being	WOOLF 1093:81
speech, that supremely h. gift	MATH 663:68
springs of h. character	HAMI 453:40
state of h. improvement	MILL 674:58
strange mutability of h. affairs	DICK 320:17
stream of h. industry	TOCQ 1022:82
studies h. behavior	ROBB 813:14
tension all h. energies	MUSS 716:86
terms of the h. awareness	LEAV 591:75
The h. crisis	WILL 1081:51
The H. Zoo	MORR 708:76
ticking…of the h. timepiece	ASLET 42:76
To be h.…we must stand fast	BOLT 172:76
To err is h.	LICH 604:85
to err is h.	POPE 778:85
To step aside is h.	BURNS 210:83
too impersonally h.	HARDY 456:93
triumph of h. reason	HAWK 461:63
truth, as h. truth	LEGU 594:30
turf dances of h. encounter	ALLEN 14:31
universe of h. subjectivity	SART 844:18
utmost bound of h. thought	TENN 994:59
Utopia of h. virtue	HAWT 461:69
vanity of h. hopes	JOHN 525:89
very h. events	WATS 1055:91
vices and the follies of h. kind	CONG 280:4
Whites…are only h.	BIKO 162:1

human being category of h. b.   ASIM 42:73

disgusting h. b.	ORWE 745:65
dissenter is every h. b.	MACL 634:78
every h. b. has	CARL 236:86
Every h. b. is born	OAKE 733:51

human being (*contd.*)

h. b. dissatisfied	MILL 675:70
h. b. who is not myself	WELTY 1065:49
intelligent h. b.	ROTH 826:21
native and sees the h. b.	LESS 598:96
No h. b. can give orders	SAND 840:53
no sane h. b.	HUXL 506:53
tourist is an ugly h. b.	KINC 557:68
Truth…makes him or her a h.b.	SAIN 837:94

human beings apes and h. b.   LORE 613:43

capacity of h. b. to bore	MENC 670:82
civilised h. b. are flying	ORWE 743:15
complexity of h. beings	WILS 1084:18
considers all these h. b.	STOWE 978:84
decency of h. b.	ORWE 743:7
feelings of h. b.	JAMES 518:51
heartlessness of h. b.	OKRI 738:23
h. b. and animals	MOOR 706:40
h. b. cannot become fully human	HUXL 508:88
H. b.…go on being	MISH 696:76
H. b.…have always hesitated	HARDY 456:90
h. b. have an infinite capacity	HUXL 507:81
h. b. such perfect bliss	LAYT 588:24
h. b. they ought to leave	HEIN 467:75
h. b. want to be good	ORWE 744:23
h. b. will live and progress	DU 353:10
kindness that h. b. do not lose	LEGU 594:23
last sound…will be two h. beings	FAUL 384:89
live among h. beings or not	WILD 1079:32
machines…promoting the h. b.	PRIE 790:40
man who does not believe in h. b.	CAST 244:33
normal state of h. b.	MILL 674:60
number of h. b. involved	HUXL 507:77
previously amusing h. b.	COUP 289:85
straight honest prose on h. b.	HEMI 470:28
to dangerous for h. b.	SAGAN 836:74
treated as h. b.	SHAW 922:51
Unlike h. b., computers possess	STER 968:82
vulnerable h. b.	TURN 1031:51

human nature best in h. n.   WHIT 1071:61

conquered h. n.	DICK 321:46
constituting h. n.	MILT 685:56
crucifixion…accuses h. n.	BUTT 218:53
disappointed in h. n.	DONL 336:62
government…reflections on h. n.	MADI 638:56
great ignorance of h. n.	JOHN 531:10
highest type of h. n.	SPEN 956:69
h. n. is finer	KEATS 544:52
H. n. is the same	TWAIN 1034:11
H. n. will not flourish	HAWT 461:68
infirmities of h. n. will allow	MACK 632:59
new edition of h. n.	HAZL 463:14
noblest production of h. n.	ADDI 7:9
observer of h. n.	DICK 320:17
part of h. n. to hate a man	TACI 989:75
salty quality of h. n.	ARLO 35:38
shame to h. n.	HOUS 496:88
sovereign good of h. n.	BACON 56:41
There is in h. n.	BACON 58:77
thorough knowledge of h. n.	AUST 52:63
Treatise of H. N.	HUME 504:12
weakness of h. n.	MACA 624:21

human rights fundamental h. r.   UNIT 1036:45

separate from h. r.	HILL 270:25
undoing of those h. r.	KENN 550:64

humane H., but not human   CUMM 300:97
| h.…are not the leaders | CONR 285:7 |

humaneness h. and awe   WILS 1084:18

humanistic My theme is always h.   WILS 1084:17

humanitarian man…not first a h.   FAUL 384:88

humanitarianism h. of…high order   LOOS 613:37

humanities exemplified the h.   ROLL 821:26
| produced…by the h. | STEA 963:2 |

humanity all h. divine   SHAW 923:76

humanity (*contd.*)

always treat h.…as an end	KANT 542:5
breed apart from the rest of h.	MANK 645:77
conscience of h.	JOHN 522:35
content with his common h.	SHAW 924:96
crooked timber of h.	KANT 542:3
discipline of h.	BACON 57:60
distresses of h.?	JOHN 526:9
divinity and h.	BACON 55:8
dualism…weighs h. down	DEWEY 319:95
future of h. is uncertain	LEVI 600:26
glad to have h. forget	HOOV 490:61
great house of our h.	DUNC 355:49
H.…a superhuman undertaking	GIRA 428:42
h. attains…complete development	TOCQ 1022:82
H. does not pass through phases	LEWIS 601:35
h., frendlyness	MALO 642:35
H. i love you	CUMM 299:80
H. in its basic form	BARTH 74:66
H. is just a work in progress	WILL 1081:65
H. with all its fears	LONG 611:8
I hate 'H.'	CAMP 227:23
knowledge belongs to h.	PAST 759:88
Lies are essential to h.	PROU 793:4
music of h.	WORD 1094:98
out of h.'s reach	COWP 292:39
particular illusion on h.	MAUP 665:96
Passion is all of h.	BALZ 69:82
perfection does not recognize h.	WOOD 1092:48
popular h. is treason	ADDI 8:32
raw nerve ends of h.	ANON 29:41
rediscover their h.	TUTU 1032:53
salvation of h.	MENC 670:87
save h. from lapsing back	HUGH 499:25
snow, and their h.	RUSK 830:79
spark of h. can tolerate	RUSS 833:32
teaches us that h.	RUNGE 829:54
through the latter, to serving h.	ISHI 513:76
truth of our h.	JOHN 522:36
unremitting h.	BENN 91:78
used for the benefit of h.	WIEN 1074:13
what h., reason, and justice, tells me	BURKE 207:9

humankind look below on h.   LUCR 619:35

highest bliss of h.	KEATS 544:37
H. is reflected	SCHI 848:87
laughter is the basis of h.	RABE 798:77

humans But then, so are h.   LYND 620:63

cats and h.…symptotic?	ANON 26:54
h.…categorized as vermin	CAREY 233:22
Slough…isn't fit for h.	BETJ 99:31

Humber Of H. would complain   MARV 658:72

humble He that is ever h.   BUNY 205:73

h. and aloof	BETJ 99:26
h. people of Cambodia	SIHA 938:73
mother is…a very h. person	DICK 324:7
ne'r ebb to h. love	SHAK 899:42
no normal h. man can help	HERB 476:42
thy h. dwelling	WESL 1066:46
use such names and be not h.?	SASS 845:40
we are so very h.	DICK 324:8
Wisdom is h.	COWP 293:63

humbler has gi'vn…an h. heav'n   POPE 780:37
| h. after it is done | SHAK 911:10 |

humbly h. do beseech you   SHAK 899:34

humbug lie to and h. themselves   WELLS 1064:28

humbugs most artists and all h.   CONN 283:66

humdrum dealing with h. issues   THAT 1008:7
| just as h. a marriage | GREE 444:15 |

humiliation except the course of h.   HUSS 505:37

sense by…shades of h.	EVANS 381:40
through defeat and h.	SMUTS 950:66
valley of H.	BUNY 205:65
With publicity comes h.	JANO 518:55

humiliations sensitive boy's h.   SHAW 921:27

humility Before Thee in h.   HAMM 453:44
haven't the h.   BAIN 62:76
wisdom of h.   ELIOT 371:48
humorist know I was a h.   JERO 521:11
humorists difficulty with h.   UPDI 1036:49
H. are not happy men   CONN 283:64
not an easy time for h.   BUCH 202:31
humorous 'tis no marvel, he is so h.   SHAK 876:61
humour dowered with a sense of h.   SOME 952:1
effusions of wit and h.   AUST 52:63
have a good sense of h.   SALI 838:23
h. in ill-health   WELLS 1065:41
H.…is emotional chaos   THUR 1019:46
h., its music   ROLL 821:26
h. of a scholar   BACON 59:21
in a holiday h.   SHAK 886:20
lack of a sterner kind of h.   WEBB 1058:14
malignity…in a piece of h.   STEE 964:23
no h. to marry   DEKK 313:15
no sense of h.   ALBEE 11:86
sufficient sense of h.   HALD 451:19
warn't in a good h.   TWAIN 1033:81
woman in this h. wooed?   SHAK 863:50
humours h. of the whole English   DRYD 352:79
h., whether grave or mellow   ADDI 7:10
in all h. sportively I range   DRAY 345:32
hump camel has a single h.   NASH 719:53
camel's h.   KIPL 563:76
husband who may…have a h.   OBRI 734:72
without a positive h.   THAC 1006:82
humph H. yourself!   KIPL 563:79
Hun H. is at the gate   KIPL 565:17
hundred all be one a h. years hence   EMER 377:55
As long as one h.…remain   ANON 22:70
dying of a h. good symptoms   POPE 783:13
h. judges have declared   QUIL 797:58
h. pound on't   SHAK 915:98
h. years later   FAUL 384:84
Rode the six h.   TENN 1001:73
steal more than a h. men   PUZO 796:40
trade a h. contemporary readers   KOES 568:68
hundredth h. time I am right   EINS 363:64
hung who ne'er h. there   HOPK 492:4
Hungarian not enough to be H.   KORDA 568:80
Hungary sons of H.   GILB 425:81
hunger against h., poverty   MARS 656:53
bodily h. in his eyes   SHAW 923:80
drive h. from the hearth   LLOY 608:57
Fainting forms, with h. stricken   WILDE 1075:27
fed your h. like an endless task   CRANE 294:98
he that cometh to me shall never h.   BIBLE 145:43
H. allows no choice   AUDEN 47:76
H. and love   FRAN 401:82
h. for recognition and money   SELF 857:37
H. is the best sauce   CERV 248:96
h. no more   BIBLE 157:15
h., thirst…and death   GARI 415:25
idle if h. didn't pinch him   ELIOT 366:29
kill this whole assembly with h.   BIBLE 106:66
O sacred h.   SPEN 959:34
perish with h.!   BIBLE 143:99
perpetual h. to be beautiful   RHYS 808:25
present to plese with H.   LANG 579:73
suffered thee to h.   BIBLE 108:92
hungred h., and ye gave me meat   BIBLE 140:44
hungry ate when we were not h.   SWIFT 985:89
feed the h. on statistics   LLOY 608:52
fight so h. people can eat   STEI 966:55
filled the h. with good things   BIBLE 141:75
filled the h. with good things   BIBLE 160:54
I am not h.   PUNCH 795:98
if ever thou art h.   KIPL 561:50
If thine enemy be h.   BIBLE 122:1
known what it is like to be h.   LARD 580:91

hungry (*contd.*)
lean and h. look   SHAK 882:23
never going to be h. again   MITC 697:87
once you're h., your different   HUNT 504:16
rare and h.   STEV 973:97
small h. shivering self   ELIOT 366:40
Huns H.…chanted a funeral song   GIBB 421:22
hunt h., and vote, and raise the price   BYRON 224:69
h. in fields, for health   DRYD 352:87
H., shoot, and fight   BRON 191:94
people who h.   SHAW 925:17
To H. an assault   CRAN 295:15
You will see H.   SHEL 929:10
hunter between the h. and his prey   ZHAO 1109:21
covers…the hare and h.   PATC 759:90
Esau was a cunning h.   BIBLE 105:30
heart is a lonely h.   SHARP 919:79
Heart Is A Lonely H.   MACC 626:65
h. home from the hill   STEV 975:31
h.'s horn is ringing   SCOTT 854:66
h.'s javelin in his side   ARNO 38:95
H. of the East   FITZ 390:87
Man is the h.   TENN 996:93
mighty h. before the Lord   BIBLE 104:16
Miss Joan H. Dunn   BETJ 100:35
no h.'s game   JEFF 520:85
rings no h.'s shout   SIGO 938:71
without ever becoming h.   MARX 660:10
hunters intrepid h. of golf balls   SMITH 947:4
hunting call h. one of them   JOHN 532:41
discourse was about h.   PEPYS 765:70
English counties like h.-tunes   BENET 90:60
hound is to the h. gane   BALL 67:55
h. he loved   SHAK 865:99
H. is not a proper employment   ADDI 8:41
H. the author, painter and musician   SITW 942:30
I went h. wild   OWEN 748:16
passion for h.   DICK 321:38
tuckt up she a h. goes   HERR 477:59
hunting-frock cashier the h.-f.   SHER 933:80
hunting-grounds h. for the poetic   ELIOT 366:32
Huntlie lay on H. bank   BALL 67:52
hunts he h. in dreams   TENN 995:75
hurled Atoms or systems into ruin h.   POPE 780:35
Swift to be h.   HOOD 489:49
hurly-burly h.-b. of the chaise   CAMP 226:11
hurrah The Last H.   OCON 735:83
hurricane America is a h.   MAIL 639:69
crazy-eyed H. blowing   KIPL 563:90
Irish h., a flat calm   BOWEN 181:50
Let the h. drag the pieces   HUID 503:95
hurricanoes You cataracts and h.   SHAK 903:17
hurroosh h. that follows   CRIT 297:43
hurry h. slowly   AUGU 50:20
Liberals in a h.   SAINT 836:78
modern life…sick h.   ARNO 37:92
senseless h.   WORD 1099:75
So who's in a h.?   BENC 89:54
there will be no special h.   HEMI 470:19
hurt done the lover mortal h.   DOUG 341:57
give delight and h. not   SHAK 917:34
helped and h. us   MILL 676:97
h. one till one sweats   HALD 451:19
h. that Honour feels   TENN 995:76
I h. her   RIMB 812:96
it will do no h.   SHAK 901:72
never h. a hair of him   STUD 981:15
Nothing doth more h.   BACON 58:88
shall not h. nor destroy   BIBLE 125:68
stomach that they mayn't h.   LAMB 576:16
they had never h. us   GELL 417:72
what you said h. me   LIBE 603:78
Wrath brings…gravest h.   EURI 380:32
hurting instead of h.   HUME 504:11

hurting (*contd.*)
You are h. be!   KIPL 563:83
husband at all times your faithful h.   STEE 964:12
attempting to cuckold a h.   JONG 533:63
back of her h.'s newspaper   GREER 445:42
Chaste to her h.   POPE 781:72
dear h. for a comfort   SMITH 948:28
Dear h.! I take shame   MOOD 703:94
delight of her h.   RANS 802:31
established for the h. and wife   MONT 703:88
finding a h. for one's mistress   COOP 287:47
flop in favour of your h.   DICK 326:61
Get thee a good h.   SHAK 901:70
good works in her h.   MILT 692:2
hands of the h.   ADAMS 4:61
has an ideal h.   TARK 991:1
h. and a happy home   PLATH 773:91
h. be a man   LAMB 576:23
h. frae the wife despises!   BURNS 211:11
h. held her upright   SMITH 947:3
H., I come   SHAK 906:6
h. is a whole-time job   BENN 91:91
h. is thy lord   SHAK 864:89
h. is torn from her   NATI 721:90
h., like a government   BALZ 68:70
h. pays for all   DUNB 355:38
h.…shall rule over thee   BIBLE 103:99
h. wears a mask   MARI 651:73
if she loses her h.   EURI 380:25
If your h. is a bore   BELL 88:31
in her h.'s heart   SHAK 894:11
in your h.'s ear   GROM 447:69
is it well with thy h.?   BIBLE 111:76
life her h. makes for her   ELIOT 366:39
light wife doth make a heavy h.   SHAK 873:6
Like a deceivèd h.   SHAK 914:79
makes a bad h.   EMER 377:66
man…makes the best h.   NORR 731:28
most indulgent h.   DICK 325:51
must have a h.   SHAK 864:75
My H. and I   ELIZ 374:95
nothing but his being my h.   CONG 281:19
send me no h.   SHAK 879:33
so ill bred as to love a h.   WYCH 1103:32
So may my h.   SHAK 897:93
to vote for one's h.   ONAS 739:43
to yourself, that h.   JAMES 515:4
unbelieving h. is sanctified   BIBLE 150:51
We have to grimace for a h.   OBRI 734:72
husbandry h. in heaven   SHAK 908:38
husbands bad h.…good wives   BACON 57:63
Chumps…make the best h.   WODE 1088:88
divine right of h.   WOLL 1091:39
doan never ketch h.   MITC 697:85
Fools are as like h.   SHAK 895:20
h. lie snoring in bed   MORE 707:50
H., love your wives   BIBLE 153:22
h. to stay at home   ELIOT 365:22
Let h. know Their wives   SHAK 900:51
reformed rakes make the best h.   BRON 190:89
some women govern their h.   WOLL 1091:33
When h.…breathe their last   POPE 779:1
hush A brooding h.   THOM 1015:57
h. with the setting moon   TENN 1001:86
somebody ought to have said 'h.'   CAMP 226:10
hushed h. and anxious hours   HOOV 490:60
hushed-up like wrongs h.-u.   OWEN 748:21
husk h. of meaning   ELIOT 372:69
Hussein H. isn't just sitting   ANON 30:56
not going after Saddam H.   SCHW 851:27
hussies h. in your beds   SHAK 898:19
hustle tried to h. the East   KIPL 561:45
hut Love in a h.   KEATS 546:77
hyacinth h. with rich inlay   MILT 690:63

hyacinth (*contd.*)
Thy h. hair | POE 776:47
hyacinths h. and biscuits | SAND 841:66
Hyades rainy H. vext the dim sea | TENN 994:58
hybreds h. and lubberds! | JOYCE 538:60
hydrogen h. bomb | FROMM 406:70
hyena wolf, the h., and the skunk? | BRYAN 201:15
hygiene H. is the corruption | MENC 669:65
h. of older people | SMITH 947:9
hymns brought home to me by the h. | LAWR 587:9
Sing on, with h. uproarious | BETJ 99:26
Singing h. unbidden | SHEL 929:2
sings h. at heaven's gate | SHAK 913:57
hyperbole encourage unedifying h. | DUNN 356:59
scarcely h. to say | CLIVE 270:27
speaking in perpetual h. | BACON 57:66
hyperboles third heavens of h. | DONNE 339:24
Three-piled h. | SHAK 866:27
hyphenate Everybody else has to h. | MORR 709:87
hypochondria H. is the only disease | ANON 28:2
hypochondriacs h. of history | AGNEW 10:70
hypocrisy H. is a tribute | LARO 582:27
H. is the most difficult…vice | MAUG 664:87
H., the only evil | MILT 689:44
making world safe for h. | WOLFE 1090:17
old-fashioned American h. | GALL 412:91
organized h. | DISR 332:94
That would be h. | WILDE 1078:87
the Pharisees' h. | PAST 759:83
hypocrite first bolt-hole of h. | BRAGG 185:5
h. lecteur! | ELIOT 368:84
H. reader | BAUD 76:14
liar that's also a h. | WILL 1081:60
No man is a h. | JOHN 532:32
hypocrites h.…in the synagogues | BIBLE 134:47
cant of h. | STER 969:5
h. austerely talk | MILT 690:64
scribes and Pharisees, h.! | BIBLE 139:36
tongue and soul…be h. | SHAK 892:45
ye h., ye can discern | BIBLE 138:12
hypotheses smallest number of h. | EINS 363:75
hypothesis character…to an h.? | STER 969:44
conviction that a h. | MEDA 666:15
discard a pet h. | LORE 613:42
endeavour to construct a h. | HARDY 456:90
nature of an h. | STER 969:2
slaying of a beautiful h. | HUXL 508:99
hyssop Purge me with h. | BIBLE 116:77
sprinkle me with h. | BIBLE 159:42
Hyssopps H. of the Glen | ASHF 41:68
hysteria therapy of h. | FREUD 404:41
hysterics blind h. of the Celt | TENN 1000:58

iacta I. est alea | CAES 225:86
Iago I.'s soliloquy | COLE 275:30
yet the pity of it, I. | SHAK 900:44
iambics In keen i. | DRYD 348:84
Iban The I., when they decide | OHAN 737:7
Ibo Among the…I. conversation | ACHE 2:87
Ibsen Nietzsche, I.… madmen! | ONEI 740:59
These I. creatures | ANON 25:22
ice Baby LeRoy with an i. p. | ROST 825:3
bloody i. on bloody head | BLAIR 165:52
cracked i. crunching | STEV 972:65
Glitt'ring with i. | POPE 782:93
good to break the i. | BACON 58:87
hot i. and wondrous…snow | SHAK 871:54
i. age ended years ago | ZHAO 1109:20
I. formed on the butler | WODE 1089:8
i. of its own indifference | ROOS 821:37
i. on a hot stove | FROST 407:94
i. was in the blood | PIER 769:34
may not dissolve the i. | SURR 983:46
'mid snow and i. | LONG 611:2

ice (*contd.*)
skating on very thin i. | CAMP 226:13
skating over thin i. | EMER 376:41
sunny pleasure-dome with caves of i.! | COLE 275:15
talent, a glass, and some cracked i. | BARR 73:60
To curle on the i. | PENE 764:53
To smooth i. | SHAK 872:71
world will end…in i. | FROST 407:85
ice-cream emperor of i.-c. | STEV 971:36
enjoy your i.-c. | WILD 1079:24
ice-scratched I.-s. slabs | SNYD 951:82
iceberg portent of an i. | BROW 199:70
The i. rises | BISH 163:29
icebergs like i. in the ocean | GERH 420:5
icecaps blue i. on the mountains | CHAT 253:98
Iceman The I. Cometh | ONEI 740:61
ices after tea and cakes and i. | ELIOT 367:48
ichor perspiration was but i. | BYRON 223:67
icicle hang like an i. | SHAK 895:27
icicles When i. hang by the wall | SHAK 866:30
White night of i. | MALL 641:17
Why are there i. everywhere? | ZHAO 1109:20
iciness an i., a sinking | POE 775:41
icing i. that detracts from the cake | AUCH 46:40
id cure of the i. | ANON 25:34
Ida I.'s shady brow | BLAKE 165:55
idea absurd is the fundamental i. | CAMUS 228:45
Alligators have the right i. | MACD 629:8
always gone in for the i. that | WILS 1084:10
Between the i. And the reality | ELIOT 369:1
charge that an i. is radical | GALB 411:74
controlling i. that holds us | FRID 404:47
Dying for an i. | LEWIS 602:59
endowed with the i. of God | DESC 318:83
entertain an i. | JARR 518:62
every new i.…takes a generation | FEYN 387:34
failure not in the i. | MACG 630:33
first i. was not our own | STEV 971:51
For an i. ever to be fashionable | SANT 842:85
general i., of course | LEAC 589:44
good i. but it won't work | ROGE 820:17
had the wrong i. first | FEYN 387:33
Hang your i. on a peg | BRIS 189:62
hate the i. of causes | FORS 399:52
his every i. rationalized | PIER 769:32
i. alone is eternal | FLAU 392:31
i.-bound in the past | LAWR 585:74
i. for which I can live | KIER 556:53
i.…has still not been said enough | DELA 314:20
i. of a system | GEOR 419:88
i. of an external cause | SPIN 960:54
i. of death saves him | FORS 398:37
i. of dying is worse | PROU 793:1
i. of elder wisdom | UPDI 1037:72
i. of liberty | SPIN 960:49
i. of weapons | RUSS 833:32
i. or concept | LEWI 602:71
i. that they are going to live | DAVIS 308:23
innermost i. of this hue | MELV 667:36
it would be a good i. | GAND 414:15
let the i. soak in | MILL 678:31
new i.…close to insanity | MILL 677:2
nice place, inside an i. | MACI 631:40
No grand i. was ever born | FITZ 391:18
Nothing is more dangerous than an i. | ALAIN 10:76
possess but one i. | JOHN 528:56
sacrificed…for…an i. | MILL 679:57
shoot his like in name of i. | BROD 189:72
slightest i. what they should be doing | FULL 409:35
teach the young i. | THOM 1015:47
the i. of death must be born | MACH 631:35
The man with a new i. | TWAIN 1034:3
to whom the i. first occurs | DARW 306:92
What redeems it is an i. only | CONR 284:89

idea (*contd.*)
Whatever is…perceived is an i. | BERK 95:52
when a politician does get an i. | MARQ 656:44
ideal American is an i. | FRIE 405:56
An i. wife | TARK 991:1
boy's i. of a manly career | DISR 332:89
Christian i. has not been tried | CHES 258:15
Conservative i. of freedom | MADAN 638:54
Freedom is not an i. | STEV 973:81
i. day for football | SMITH 948:26
i. that I hope to live for | MAND 644:68
i. would be to belong to none | DUDEK 353:16
ideas, or on an i. | LAWR 585:73
my song has an i. | CHOC 260:55
nearer today the i. | HOOV 490:58
not charmed with the i. of life | MILL 674:60
Religion…ultimate i. | WHIT 1071:55
softly sleep the calm I. | DICK 323:83
idealism grips with so-called i. | MENC 670:85
i. is not uncommon | ROOS 822:50
I. is the noble toga | HUXL 508:91
idealistic America…only i. nation | WILS 1086:56
our i. pretensions | OBRI 734:64
idealists I. are very apt to walk | SMITH 947:19
idealized i. into powerlessness | JONG 533:62
idealizer Sorrow, the great i. | LOWE 616:88
ideals forever hallowed by the i. | EISE 364:93
i. and visions to the past | KENN 551:82
i. of a democratic…society | MAND 644:68
i. …painter's techniques | RENO 807:10
men without i. | CAMUS 228:44
tell the i. of a nation | DOUG 342:62
white man's superior i. | VASC 1040:10
ideas addiction…to the i. | GALB 411:75
alter and exchange our i. | BERN 96:79
believe in i. and die for them | ANOU 30:74
borrowed i. | CALL 225:98
cemetery of dead i. | UNAM 1035:41
dreams that have…changed my i. | BRON 191:10
false i. prevail as to woman's | STAN 962:86
find really marvellous i. | LEON 597:83
foundation of your i. and phrases | LAUT 584:52
founded not upon visionary i. | GLAD 429:53
great i. are hogwash | NABO 717:8
Great people talk about i. | LEBO 591:86
i. about the native | LESS 598:95
I. are born from hatred | GENET 418:76
i. begin to destroy sex in America | DOCT 334:39
i. get cloath'd | STER 970:17
i. must be as broad as Nature | DOYLE 343:87
i. of economists | KEYN 555:37
i., or on an ideal | LAWR 585:73
i. take their beginnings | LOCKE 609:73
Innate i. in every man | BLAKE 168:14
isolate him, and his i. disintegrate | DIDE 330:42
live in the mind, in i. | MILL 677:18
machine for transmission of i. | BOWL 182:53
most interesting i. | SONT 953:10
new i. or fresh outlooks | MACK 631:47
no i. and the ability | KRAUS 569:88
no i. but in things | WILL 1083:91
Not many composers have i. | GERS 420:6
of nasty i. | SWIFT 985:92
our i. that make us | UNAM 1035:40
People find i. a bore | POUND 786:79
publishing of his i. | KAZIN 543:29
realm of i. | MILL 677:22
Relations of I. | HUME 503:8
signs of i. | JOHN 526:5
subsist on i. | BALZ 69:80
two i. in her head | LINK 606:23
two i. more inseparable | SMITH 949:44
two i. of government | BRYAN 201:14
two opposed i. in the mind | FITZ 391:13

ideas (*contd.*)
 unexpected copulation of i. — JOHN 525:90
 vehicle for conveying i. — MACB 624:31
 without any i. — LOCKE 609:72
 words reign over i. — SAND 840:49
identical exist, but are i. — FORS 398:43
identity live without an i. — MACL 635:98
 mistaking…similarity for real i. — PALM 752:67
 questions of freedom and i. — JORD 536:28
 sense of personal i. — STEV 974:19
 short circuit in his i. — ROTH 825:7
ideological i., or the abstract — ROTH 826:22
ideologies i. and inventions — SONT 953:7
 not to have i. — HOFS 484:63
ideology an i. that is warlike — OBRI 734:64
 more important than i. — NEWM 724:33
 single i. for 70 years — YELT 1107:97
ides Beware the i. of March — SHAK 882:16
idiocy facilitate the infection of i. — BIER 161:86
 human…potential for i. — ONET 740:70
idioms licentious i. — JOHN 525:93
 long words and exhausted i. — ORWE 743:19
idiot artist like the i. — SITW 941:27
 computer is a fast i. — AMER 16:65
 good loser…an i. — DURO 357:74
 i. who praises — GILB 425:85
 law is…a i. — DICK 321:42
 possibly an i. — DALI 303:46
 tale Told by an i. — SHAK 910:86
idiotism hundred new titles of i. — NASHE 720:75
idiots village i., policemen — MACD 628:92
 fatuity of i. — SMITH 949:42
 I. are always in favour — SHAW 925:26
 play the i. in her eyes — SHAK 896:50
 your only competition is i. — MANK 645:75
idle all be i. if we could — JOHN 530:84
 all the day i.? — BIBLE 139:28
 As i. as a painted ship — COLE 273:87
 be not i. — BURT 214:79
 happiest when I am i. — WARD 1053:16
 I. to hope — REED 805:84
 If you are i. — JOHN 530:6
 many a one who would be i. — ELIOT 366:29
 merely the art of the i. — INGR 512:48
 Most 'scruciating i. — KIPL 563:78
 most i. and unprofitable — GIBB 421:26
 Reputation is an i.…imposition — SHAK 899:25
 such i. fellows as I — AUBR 45:32
idleness faculty for i. — STEV 974:19
 grief and sin of i. — MELV 667:28
 Grief is a species of i. — JOHN 529:62
 pains and penalties of i. — POPE 783:8
 reading is not i. — SPEN 957:90
 I., which is often becoming — STEV 974:9
idlers loungers and i. of the Empire — DOYLE 343:83
idling enjoy i. thoroughly — JERO 521:3
idol ancient i., on his base again — BROW 198:54
 celestial and my soul's i. — SHAK 889:90
 'eathen i.'s foot — KIPL 561:38
 God…would be an i. — BONH 173:87
 i. to offend the national religion — BENT 92:16
 natural i. of the Anglo-Saxon — BAGE 61:55
 one-eyed yellow i. — HAYES 462:92
 play thing and their i. — SHEL 926:52
idolatry contemporary man's i. — MONT 700:52
 on this side i. — JONS 536:20
 organization of i. — SHAW 922:45
 stubbornness is as iniquity and i. — BIBLE 110:35
idols i. of consumption' — LOWE 617:15
 like old i. — BOTT 180:37
if i. is the only peacemaker — SHAK 887:36
Iffucan Chieftain I. of Azcan — STEV 971:41
ignis fatuus Reason, an i. f. — ROCH 816:50
ignoble made i. talk — TENN 1002:16

ignominious so acute, so i. — SHAW 921:27
ignorance acknowledge our own i. — HAZL 464:18
 Alike in i. — POPE 780:42
 between the i. and poverty — WALP 1051:80
 blind and naked I. — TENN 1002:9
 but i. of evil — MITC 696:78
 child of i. — BACON 58:76
 consistent with the i. — ORWE 745:50
 criticism is ever inhibited by i. — MACM 635:11
 curse of mankind, folly and i. — SHAK 895:44
 Don't die of i. — ANON 28:22
 dull pastures of her i. — SMITH 947:3
 education…expensive—try i. — BOK 171:66
 from knowledge i. — BROW 200:79
 functioning out of i. — DENG 315:51
 great i. of human nature — JOHN 531:10
 I. is as much the fountain — MONT 701:56
 i. is bliss — GRAY 441:48
 I. is like a delicate exotic fruit — WILDE 1077:82
 i. is never better than knowledge — FERMI 386:25
 i. is not innocence — BROW 200:97
 i. is strength — ORWE 745:56
 I. is the curse — SHAK 861:13
 i. is the first requisite — STRA 979:92
 I. is the mother of all evils — RABE 799:92
 I., madam, pure i. — JOHN 526:97
 i. of alternatives — ANGE 19:17
 i. of morality — PASC 758:72
 i. of our own i. — BUTL 218:46
 I. of the law — SELD 857:34
 I. of the law — SELD 857:35
 in i. sedate — JOHN 525:84
 in i., to refrain — BERN 96:81
 It was childish i. — HOOD 489:38
 make us wish for i.? — DENH 315:52
 night of our natural i. — HOBB 483:43
 no darkness but i. — SHAK 895:36
 no sin but i. — MARL 653:96
 only one evil, i. — SOCR 952:91
 opinion breeds i. — HIPP 481:16
 O thou monster i. — SHAK 865:15
 our i. must…be infinite — POPP 784:28
 take from them all i. — BOOK 174:11
 The greater the i. — OSLER 746:70
 times of this i. God winked at — BIBLE 148:4
 true source of our i. — POPP 784:28
 uncertainty? Even i. — NIET 728:82
 Until you understand a writer's i. — COLE 275:19
 wake from i. — JOHN 525:77
 where i. prevails — DOUG 342:74
ignorant Be not i. of any thing — BIBLE 132:90
 doubt and to be i. — UNAM 1036:42
 foolish than an i. fool — MOLI 699:33
 girls aren't i. — COOP 287:46
 i. and unpolished people — DICK 327:79
 i. in spite of their age — PITT 771:62
 i. of all the rules of art — ADDI 8:38
 i. of each other's habits — DISR 332:90
 i. of the causes — SPIN 960:49
 i. of what he's most assured — SHAK 896:72
 i., only on different subjects — ROGE 820:8
 many i. men are sure — DARR 306:81
 Men i. of letters — SAND 842:82
 right of the i. man — CARL 235:83
 stupid and i. — SMITH 946:91
 Then I should be i. — GREG 446:47
 we are i. of — SWIFT 984:73
 we are utterly i. — BEDE 82:8
 We live i. — ABU 1:10
ignore First they i. you — BENN 90:69
ignored because they are i. — HUXL 506:55
Ike I like I. — ANON 26:52
Iliad as in the I. itself — ARNO 38:7
 something greater than the I. — PROP 792:90

Ilion Past ruined I. Helen lives — LAND 578:57
Ilium topless towers of I.? — MARL 654:19
ill all the measureless i. — TENN 1001:76
 ash for nothing i. — SPEN 957:99
 British Bourgeosie…if it is i. — SITW 941:22
 cure for this i. — KIPL 563:77
 do i. our sole delight — MILT 687:95
 fear no i. — SCOT 856:19
 good and i. together — SHAK 901:80
 How i. white hairs becomes — SHAK 878:10
 i. and old and terrified — BETJ 100:50
 i. design is most i. — HESI 479:82
 I. fares the land — GOLD 433:10
 I. is the weather — DEKK 313:9
 looking i. prevail? — SUCK 981:17
 Love worketh no i. — BIBLE 150:40
 no for ony gude or i. — BURNS 209:61
 only half there when I am i. — LAWR 585:67
 so i. bred as to love a husband — WYCH 1103:32
 some desperate i. — JONS 536:17
 some i. a-brewing — SHAK 874:28
 speak i. of any man — JOHN 528:58
 speak i. of it — HAZL 464:22
 though she's not really i. — JAGG 515:95
 'Tis an i. cook — SHAK 869:16
 to rail at the i. — TENN 1002:96
 warn you not to fall i. — KINN 559:12
 We are all i. — TRIL 1026:57
 We fell morally i. — HAVEL 460:10
 woman colour'd i. — SHAK 915:96
ill-born amphibious i.-b. mob — DEFOE 312:76
ill-dresssed ill-kept, and i.-d. — JOHN 531:27
ill-fame clearer of i. — AUST 52:59
ill-favoured poor virgin…an i. thing — SHAK 887:33
ill-fed it is i.-f., ill-killed — JOHN 531:27
ill-health humour in i.-h. — WELLS 1065:41
ill-nature just so much i.-n. — SCOTT 856:10
ill-natured vain, i.-n. thing — DEFOE 312:76
ill-shapen creatures at first are i. — BACON 58:93
ill-spent sign of an i.-s. youth — SPEN 956:70
illegal Cricket is not i. — ANNE 20:36
 i., immoral or fattening — WOOL 1094:87
 means that it is not i. — NIXON 730:16
 taken i. drugs — JOHN 523:41
illiberality ignoble i. — NASHE 721:77
illimitable i. inane — TENN 1003:29
Illingworth Lord I. — WILDE 1077:65
Illinois I.…in hibernation — OHARA 737:12
illiterate i. know how to count — BACON 60:41
 to i. him, I say — SHER 933:77
illness i. should attend it — SHAK 907:26
 I. is the night-side — SONT 953:11
 I.…tyrant has in common — BROD 189:67
 like the treatment of i. — WITT 1088:77
 lingering i. Is over — POE 776:55
 Living is an i. — CHAM 250:26
 makes i. worth while — SHAW 925:19
 mental i. of the United States — ATWO 45:20
 no i.…it cannot counterfeit — PROU 793:95
illnesses not from their i. — MOLI 699:34
 three new i. brought by Christ — GAUT 416:41
ills All the i. of mankind — DUDEK 353:16
 i. of an entire generation — ISHE 513:73
 marvelling sweetly on her i. — RANS 802:31
 no sense of i. to come — GRAY 441:47
 O'er a' the i. o' life — BURNS 211:14
 quack, long versed in human i. — CRAB 293:75
 what i. the scholar's life assail — JOHN 525:52
illume Better…Than no i. at all — DICK 328:13
illuminate i. his subject's life work — TOYN 1024:23
illuminated not enough to be i. — JOHN 522:31
illumination Painters…produce i. — DELA 314:23
 support rather than i. — LANG 579:66
illumine what in me is dark I. — MILT 687:86

illumined i. by the steady radiance HAMM 453:43
illusion an i. to which STOP 978:74
consecrated…to i. BYRON 224:72
great poetry gives the i. ELIOT 369:5
i. that eternal blessed life TOLS 1023:99
not to foster the i. GOWE 437:81
nothing but sophistry and i. HUME 504:10
particular i. on humanity MAUP 665:96
sheer i. to think WEBER 1059:22
web of our grand i. PAGE 749:32
illusions books…contain our i. CONR 285:3
discard i. GORB 435:59
friend of flattering i. CONR 284:99
i. that restrict freedom FRYE 408:24
i. that they have generated MOUN 711:13
lost all his i. HOLM 486:82
illustrate i. and simplify HOME 487:11
illustration i. of character? JAMES 516:21
illustrious Children, to be i. NEME 722:3
Illyria drink in I. SHAK 894:96
Ilsley looks on I. downs ARNO 39:14
image any graven i. BIBLE 106:68
conformity of the i. with the thing DIDE 329:25
created him in his own i. DOST 341:46
cried in a whisper at some i. CONR 284:92
dull red i. of the moon WORD 1096:31
emotion, detail and i. BRAU 186:22
Every painted i. BERG 95:48
express i. of his person BIBLE 154:44
fleeting i. of a shade SHEL 930:32
i. in her mind DRYD 350:46
i. of divine beauty AQUI 32:4
i. of life ANOU 30:71
i. of myself and dearer half MILT 691:70
i. of myself AUDEN 48:94
i. of offence SHAK 895:34
i. of the King TENN 1003:38
i. of those…mountain peaks LLOY 608:58
I. that…gleamed WORD 1095:15
i. we have already made PROU 793:6
In every parting…an i. of death ELIOT 365:1
in the i. of God made he man BIBLE 104:14
living i. to all ages NASHE 721:77
made them…like their own i. PATC 759:92
man's i. YEATS 1104:59
Met his own i. SHEL 929:13
powerful i. to…Englishman SMITH 946:1
reconstituted in the i. RODO 818:87
Scattered his Maker's i. DRYD 349:4
scorn her own i. SHAK 891:33
she marks her i. POPE 782:95
Technology is not an i. PAZ 762:25
to the i., not to the man PRICE 789:32
visual i. of ourselves LAWR 586:90
world in its own i. NIET 728:84
imagery antics and wild i. SPEN 958:10
rhythm, i., sweep NOON 731:22
images Fair trains of i. WORD 1100:77
Here the stone i. ELIOT 369:99
i. of Nature were…present to him DRYD 347:59
i.…remote from each other JOHN 525:90
infinite i. of itself LEON 597:84
novel is…philosophy put into i. CAMUS 229:64
Those i. that yet…beget YEATS 1106:85
traditional stories and i. FRYE 408:21
translate pulsations into i. RICH 809:47
imaginary the i. and the real STEF 965:24
imagination act of a writer's i. WELTY 1065:49
An Irishman's i. SHAW 923:69
anyone of i. must feel SHIP 935:22
appeals most strongly to the i. HUMB 503:85
atrophy of the i. GELL 417:69
by reason of corrupt i. BURT 214:77
chase our i. to the heavens HUME 503:98

imagination (*contd.*)
computer…has no i. AMER 16:65
depends only upon force of i. DRYD 351:59
enrich our intellectual i. RUSS 832:17
For those who have no i. CELI 247:88
goading of the i. POE 775:41
great instrument…is the i. SHEL 931:57
help of a powerful i. HERZ 478:73
History…succeed in it through the i. FRAN 401:87
how abhorred my i. is! SHAK 893:77
hunting-grounds for the poetic i. ELIOT 366:32
i. created the world BAUD 77:33
I. is the queen BAUD 77:32
I. is the voice MILL 678:35
i. makes me human LEGU 594:33
i. of a boy KEATS 545:55
i. of man is evil from his youth BIBLE 104:13
i. soars, as a voice WILL 1083:95
I. should be integrated with life DUDEK 353:18
i. the rudder KEATS 544:44
Liberty of the i. CONR 285:1
men without i. PROU 793:3
mysterious power of i. HOLM 485:76
no i.…no horror DOYLE 343:85
nothing but his i. SHAW 923:70
Politics mixed with the i. STEN 967:71
power of i. FEUE 387:31
property of the i. WALC 1048:36
Propinquity had brought I. YEATS 1107:94
protein of our cultural i. HUGH 499:27
save those that have no i.? SHAW 925:25
schools for the i. GIRA 429:44
see only…figments of their i. ELLI 375:16
suspend the functioning of the i. HEMI 471:35
sweeten my i. SHAK 903:35
travel…engages the i. CELI 247:87
truth of the i. KEATS 544:45
Were it not for i. JOHN 530:1
whispering chambers of I. DICK 323:83
woman indulges her i. NATH 721:85
imaginations jumbled…in our i. AUST 51:41
perish through their own i. BOOK 176:62
imaginative genuine i. event ROTH 826:22
richness of i. resource WILDE 1076:32
the truly i. analytic POE 776:41
imagine i. a boot stamping ORWE 745:60
i. a destiny FIED 387:38
Try to i. THUR 1019:38
young men can possibly i. SMITH 947:14
imagined i., not recalled? LOWE 617:13
imbecility i. in females AUST 52:65
i., extravagance and politial hysteria CHUR 263:93
reduce women of certain age to i. BROO 193:42
sneaking piece of i. SCOTT 854:71
imbrown golden ear I. the slope POPE 779:23
imitate i. the action of the tiger SHAK 881:84
never failed to i. them BALD 64:95
imitated Genius…is not i. DIDE 329:28
who has not i.? INGR 511:46
imitation Comedy is an i. SIDN 937:64
I. is more interesting STEIN 966:44
i.…is the easiest CONF 279:87
I. is the sincerest form of flattery COLT 277:55
Poetry…is an art of i. SIDN 937:62
servile i. thrown away CAREW 232:12
What is a beautiful i.? DIDE 329:25
imitator i. is a poor kind of creature WHIS 1069:13
Immanuel call his name I. BIBLE 125:63
immensity I. cloistered DONNE 338:2
in that enormous i. BRAUN 186:17
immigrants all i. to this place ATWO 45:21
children of i. RUSS 832:24
immoral All art is i. WILDE 1076:40
illegal, i. or fattening WOOL 1094:87

immoral (*contd.*)
i. is what you feel bad after HEMI 470:23
moral or an i. book WILDE 1076:44
not considered i., or even bad form CECIL 246:77
people looked on it as i. GALS 413:4
self-assertion as i. KURO 571:21
immorality i. is what they dislike WHIT 1071:62
old i. condoned SHAW 926:47
rigid code of i. BRAD 183:73
smacks of levity, i. almost STARK 963:99
immortal Being a thing i. SHAK 888:72
cold i. hands SWIN 987:37
dim night of this i. day SHEL 930:26
grow i. as they quote YOUNG 1108:4
His biting is i. SHAK 906:4
human spirit is i. MURP 715:71
i.…because he has a soul FAUL 383:78
i. diamond HOPK 492:7
i. diet RALE 800:13
i. god of harmony BEET 84:49
I., invisible, God SMITH 950:61
I. longings in me SHAK 906:5
i. part of myself SHAK 899:24
i. spirit of the dead SPEN 957:90
I. youth to mortal maids LAND 578:57
lifting…into i. sunlight CUMM 299:76
long i. dream KEATS 546:76
Sire of an i. strain SHEL 930:35
son who…would make you i. MARQ 655:34
taken an i. wound FROST 408:7
This little steamer…is i. PRIE 790:37
What i. hand or eye BLAKE 167:35
immortality angling for i. HUXL 507:76
belief in i. DOST 340:45
cannot bear the sight of your i. MARQ 655:34
earthly i. FORD 397:12
hope full of i. BIBLE 131:81
i.…through not dying ALLEN 14:43
I.…to such as are fit for it EMER 377:68
just Ourselves and I. DICK 328:6
longing after i.? ADDI 8:35
milk's leap toward i. FADI 382:52
millions long for i. ERTZ 380:12
no i., n soul or mind STEI 967:64
only cruel i. TENN 1003:21
permanence, for i. NUTT 732:46
Seal of Divinity and I. AUBR 45:37
To desire i. SCHO 849:95
immortals battles with the i. HOMER 487:16
Francis Parkman and other i. PRIAL 789:31
President of the I. HARDY 456:99
verbal portraits…of the i. CHUR 262:78
immunity shield of congressional i. SMITH 948:25
Sleep demands…guilty i. BARN 72:26
immutable Few things are as i. GALB 411:75
laws of prose writing are as i. HEMI 471:36
perfect, not i. MILT 691:73
imp i. of fame SHAK 881:91
wicked i. they call a poet GRAY 441:61
impact historic i. upon the social NISB 730:5
judgement that makes an i. LEAV 591:76
impartial i. in thought as well WILS 1086:46
impartiality I. is an acquired taste RIFK 811:82
Protestations of i. I shall make none COBB 271:53
impassioned i., at the birth ERNST 379:10
impatience time…ticking with i. RAINE 800:9
Whatever…my enthusiasm or i. SHIP 935:21
impatient i. as the wind WORD 1099:76
i. to see him SMITH 948:37
so i. of inferiority JOHN 525:80
impediment know cause or just i. BOOK 175:41
impediments free of all i. MARP 655:32
impenetrable what is i.…really exists EINS 363:67
imperfect abhor the i. CURZ 302:29

imperfect (*contd.*)
I describe i. characters   BRON 191:99
i. is all our knowledge!   DONNE 339:29
perfect use of an i. medium   WILDE 1076:46
thereby be i. in all   PLATH 773:89
imperfection hold on to my i.   FRAN 401:85
still I find Some i.   WORD 1096:19
imperfections dwell rather upon…i.   ADDI 7:15
means of seeing one's i.   NIEB 727:64
more beloved for the i.   RUSK 830:81
imperial enslaves you on i. principles
  SHAW 920:11
imperialism i. would be razed   MAO 648:25
US i.   MAO 648:26
imperialists i. brought…cannons   PEOP 764:58
impermanence beautied with i.   SCOTT 852:35
impersonation i. of desire   BROO 193:42
impertinent Ask an i. question   BRON 190:84
impinged desire not to be i. upon   BERL 96:67
impious i. men bear sway   ADDI 8:34
implacable i. in hate   DRYD 349:15
implanted God has i. in me   JUANA 539:66
implausible no matter how i.   SHAR 919:85
implication idiomatical kind of i.   STER 969:17
implore I adore thee, i. thee   STUA 980:10
importance attach too much i.   RUSS 832:26
diminish the i. (of newspapers)   TOCQ 1022:81
inverse ratio to the i.   HUXL 507:71
little of his own i.   GREE 444:18
important i. while they're doing it   MITC 696:83
little things are infinitely the most i.   DOYLE 343:97
living well…most i.   PLATO 774:6
look i. and to say   KIPL 564:11
more i. than keeping a good diary   SASS 845:36
most i. of all the lessons   HUXL 508:89
most i. single thing   JOVA 537:38
most i. thing in acting   GOLD 434:48
most i. thing in life   PASC 758:71
most i. thing in the world   SHAW 919:88
Paintin's not i.   MOSES 710:5
Personal relations are the i. thing   FORS 398:35
seen to be so i.   JAMES 517:49
think that's pretty i.   KING 557:74
importation i. of all foreign wines   SMITH 945:88
importune too proud to i.   GRAY 443:94
imposition idle and most false i.   SHAK 899:25
impossibility frightened by human i.   ANDR 18:10
i.…to prove that God does not exist   LABR 573:58
Upon I.   MARV 658:77
impossible beings which are i.   REDON 804:77
certain because it is i.   TERT 1006:79
frontiers of the i.   KILLY 556:62
i. that any beholder   SIDN 937:64
i. to find out who was…leaking   REAG 804:71
i.…to open his mouth   SHAW 924:1
i. to repeat in one period   RENO 807:10
i.…will be done   CALO 226:5
Love your neighbour…bloody i.   CLEE 268:99
nothing shall be i. unto you   BIBLE 138:16
one can't believe i. things   CARR 240:62
peaceful revolution i.   KENN 551:71
scientist…states that something is i.   CLAR 268:90
splendid failure to do the i.   FAUL 384:85
think on things i.   DRYD 346:50
very difficult, maybe i.   SOLOW 952:93
when you have eliminated the i.   DOYLE 343:91
wish it were i.   JOHN 532:37
works at the i.   STEI 966:62
imposters treat those two i.   KIPL 564:8
impotence case of wrongdoing or i.   ROOS 822:46
i. of being earnest   CANN 230:66
impotent An i. people   THOM 1013:20
i. as a beached whale   TIME 1020:67
impoverishment increase…in i.   HARR 458:25

imprecision Decay with i.   ELIOT 370:31
i. of feeling   ELIOT 372:53
impress marked with their own i.   WOOLF 1092:51
impression change…the received i.   PRICE 789:33
conveyed much the same i.   SIMON 939:81
figure to recieve an i.   ROSSO 825:99
first i. pleases   TINT 1021:72
i. is of a slightly   NICO 727:61
i. you produce   ROSSO 825:98
naïve i. of the scene   MONET 700:43
novel is an i.   HARDY 456:1
produce an i. on the reader   BENN 92:1
produces a false i.   WILDE 1077:79
impressionable girl at an i. age   SPARK 955:54
impressions falseness in all our i.   RUSK 830:84
few true i.   BELL 88:37
imbued with two deep i.   PAST 759:88
most striking of all the i.   MACM 635:8
occupation and change…weaken i.   AUST 52:68
one hundred times more i.   LEGER 594:22
weaving and unweaving of false i.   ELIOT 365:99
imprison i. the child in her house   WHITE 1070:39
Take me to You, i. me   DONNE 338:8
imprisoned i. some, and beheaded   STAL 962:78
imprisonment i.! The Dungeon of   MILT 694:43
morality of i.   SHAK 896:62
on pain of i.   EDWA 361:46
upon pain of i.   ELIZ 373:88
improbabilities adding to the i.   HAWT 461:81
improbable occurence of the i.   MENC 669:62
improbity guards against i.   BENT 93:18
impromptu preparing his i. speeches   BIRK 163:24
improper conceal something i.   FLAU 393:46
impropriety I. is the soul of wit   MAUG 664:85
no i. …with Miss Keeler   PROF 792:77
without i.   GILB 424:77
improve can't i. something   TUTU 1032:55
done to i. it   KEIL 548:26
i. the means for achieving   HUXL 507:74
improved Englishman was niver i.   DUNNE 356:61
enormously i. by death   SAKI 838:13
i. her French   GRAH 437:89
i. out of all knowledge   SITW 941:17
improvement i. in the productive   SMITH 946:90
in its gradual i.   THOR 1016:74
only i. she could detect   ALTH 15:59
or i. than population   MILL 674:61
improvements no i.…introduced   ANON 25:29
improving an i., an advancing   DONNE 339:31
certain of i.   HUXL 507:78
improvisation i. of human existence   MACC 626:67
impudence much of Cockney i.   RUSK 831:9
starve for want of i.   DRYD 350:43
impudent i. mountebank who sold pills   ADDI 6:5
silly things…in an i. way   AUST 52:56
impulse i. from a vernal wood   WORD 1094:3
i. of the moment   AUST 51:36
i. to acquisition   WEBER 1059:20
i. to punish is powerful   NIET 728:81
i. to write a novel   WILS 1084:15
i. without purpose   BIER 162:97
natural i. which God   JUANA 539:6
owes all its onward i.   HAWT 461:76
rooted in the sexual i.   SCHO 849:96
their wonted i. give   COLE 274:4
impulses manipulation of his own i.   MILL 678:34
impunity cannot trespass with i.   AUDEN 48:48
holy…with i.?   RACI 799:2
with strict i.   TATE 991:2
impure To the Puritan all things are i.   LAWR 587:7
impurity bring i. much rather   MILT 685:63
imputation i. of this idiot   NASHE 721:79
inability historic i. in Britain   HAUG 460:59

inability (*contd.*)
i. to cross the street   WOOLF 1093:79
i. to put on your socks   GONC 434:52
inaccuracy little i. sometimes saves   SAKI 838:16
inaction i. of those who could   HAILE 451:11
inadequate i. for getting to France   KINN 559:10
inane Pinnacled dim in the intense i.   SHEL 930:25
inanimate stupidity of the i.   STER 968:82
inanity folly and i.   STOWE 979:90
inapprehensible I., we clutch thee!   THOM 1013:30
inarticulate I., arctic   SCOTT 852:37
raid on the i.   ELIOT 372:53
inattention same i. is discovered   JOHN 531:24
inbreeding sick with i.   THOM 1013:20
Inca sensuous and elegant I.   DARIO 305:75
Who was our first I.?   GARC 414:19
incantation overlay of priestly i.   GALB 412:84
incantations Whispering lunar i.   ELIOT 367:58
incapacitated man who is not i.   GLAD 429:50
incapacity i. is worse   JEFF 519:82
incarnate Jesus Christ, living and i.   BONH 173:83
world is order i.   MILL 678:33
incarnation gift…is I.   ELIOT 372:65
i. of this verse   SHEL 928:91
nearest thing in i. to…God   OLIV 738:31
incense morning i.   BARL 71:21
Orchid—breathing i.   BASHO 76:4
stupefying i.-smoke   BROW 198:39
incentive cruelty without i.   JOHN 527:23
incentives might reduce i.   KRUG 570:5
inceptions mutiplying of former i.   DONNE 339:31
incest i. holds the family together   INNIS 512:53
luxury and damnèd i.   SHAK 889:79
inch cubic i. of some stars   MACC 625:35
every i. a king   SHAK 903:33
no painful i. to gain   CLOU 270:32
Not an i. of our territory   FAVRE 384:92
inch-rule his own i.-r. of taste   ADAMS 5:75
incident Body-line was not an i.   JAMES 516:9
determination of i.?   JAMES 516:21
incidental wifehood…but i.   STAN 962:86
incidents i. well linked   COWP 292:31
incisions Underneath their fine i.   DICK 327:92
incite do not rear children, you i.   JARR 518:63
incivility sabbath-breaking…to i.   DEQU 316:68
inclination as the i. leads him   JOHN 527:30
do not check their i.   MONT 701:56
door of i.   DEFOE 312:82
general i. of all mankind   HOBB 483:39
i. of my reason   ELIZ 373:85
who have no i. for either   LESS 599:11
wicked i. in most people   JOHN 531:24
inclinations highest i. of a man   LONS 612:23
multitude of perverse i.   SHAR 919:82
our i. daily alter   ETHE 380:11
include I. me out   GOLD 434:45
incognito eternal i.   BARN 72:26
income Annual i. twenty pounds   DICK 324:6
as a source of i.   KEMB 549:36
define a man's i.   HICKS 480:96
good i. is of no avail   SMITH 947:12
in favour of inequality of i.   SHAW 925:26
I. Tax return has made   ROGE 820:11
large i. is the best recipe   AUST 51:42
lottery…yields public i.   QUINE 797:67
real i. is increased   KEYN 555:39
real i. of the community   KEYN 555:36
rises to meet i.   PARK 755:35
that sort of i. bracket   MORL 708:74
incomes inequalities of i. and wealth   KEYN 555:41
live beyond their i.   SAKI 838:9
incompetence not i. but war   PIER 769:33
rise to his level of i.   PETER 767:6
incompetent election by the i. many   SHAW 922:46

incompetent (*contd.*)
election by the i. many — SHAW 926:39
i. as the average male — CUNN 300:2
i. swine — SASS 845:28
tax on pianos for the i. — SITW 941:21
incomplete i. self — GASS 416:36
judge yourself i. — NERVO 723:13
incomprehension gulf of mutual i. — SNOW 950:73
inconsistencies searches out any i. — RUSS 832:16
inconstancy I., boredom, anxiety — PASC 757:56
infidelity is not i. — LACL 574:66
Man with that i. was born — BEHN 85:74
nothing…constant, but i. — SWIFT 984:64
inconstant i., uncertain, unknown — LOCKE 609:70
incontinence turpitude of i. — SCOTT 855:1
inconvenience adventure is…i. — CHES 258:11
i. is often considerable — AUST 52:57
not made without i. — JOHN 526:3
inconveniences free…of all i. — MARP 655:32
i. attend play-going — TYNAN 1035:26
inconvenient cause may be i. — BENN 91:90
i. to be poor — COWP 292:42
incorruptible sea-green I. — CARL 235:66
increase another man's price i. — WILS 1085:37
From…snapped i. — DUNN 356:57
God gave the i. — BIBLE 150:47
He must i. — BIBLE 145:36
i. in inverse ratio — HUXL 507:71
i. of riches and commerce — HUME 504:11
not i. its consumption — KEYN 555:39
without either i. or diminution — RICA 808:37
increases What judgement I had i. — DRYD 352:77
incredulity epoch of i. — DICK 326:58
increments i. of noise — BYATT 218:56
incumbrance Mrs Copperfield's i. — DICK 323:99
indebted I. and discharged — MILT 689:47
thing I'm i. to her for — FIEL 388:61
indecency I.'s conspiracy of silence — SHAW 922:58
indecent i. behaviour — WAUGH 1056:60
I. 10 years before — LAVER 584:56
inhuman and i. and dishonorable — HELL 468:93
name itself as i. — SPEN 956:88
to assume such i. postures — WILDE 1079:10
indecision My I. is Final — EBER 359:12
indefensible defence of the i. — ORWE 744:44
defending…i. — CHES 258:96
indemnity Double I. — CAIN 225:93
independence chief virtue…is its i. — SCOTT 852:34
for our i. — PITT 771:72
new electronic i. — MACL 635:94
war for i. — SCHL 848:73
willing to grant America i. — GEOR 418:81
independent An i. is a guy — STEV 973:89
Britain as an i. European state — GAIT 411:73
free and i. condition — ADAMS 6:90
I. existence—so called — HUXL 507:16
i. of the vagaries — ACHE 2:26
indestructible endless and i. — WILL 1083:96
We, i.! — GRASS 439:13
indeterminate Science rejects the i. — BERN 96:80
index i. of a feeling mind — CRAB 294:88
i. of output per capita — MISH 696:72
i. of this country — MARC 650:49
i. to the heart — DICK 322:76
man the i. of that book — DONNE 339:33
marble i. of a mind — WORD 1096:27
true i. of a man's character — CONN 283:76
indexes enshrined in 10,000 i. — ALLEN 14:32
Wall Street i. predicted — SAMU 840:46
India decided to cycle to I. — MURP 715:69
Englishman's justification in I. — CURZ 302:29
fly to I. for gold — MARL 654:9
From I.'s coral strand — HEBER 466:58
gone to I. — YEATS 1106:88

India (*contd.*)
in twentieth century I. — FRIE 405:54
loss of I. — CHUR 263:3
money in I. — KIPL 562:72
Nothing in I. is identifiable — FORS 398:42
pitched battles in I. — MACA 623:8
realise what I. is — CURZ 302:27
So far I like I. — MAIL 640:94
Indian history of the I. Ocean — NAIP 717:17
Like the base I. — SHAK 900:64
likely to be an I. — HEAT 466:49
Lo! the poor I. — POPE 780:37
only good I. — SHER 932:75
poetry…in the legendary I. — DARIO 305:75
Shadow…an old I. name — AMIS 17:85
treated like an I. widow — MITF 697:99
Indians I. are you — BALD 64:2
I., if we last another twenty years — MACM 636:23
I. of Surinam represented — BEHN 85:71
I. singing the…requiem — SASS 845:46
reading Neville Cardus to the I. — THOM 1010:71
Indies carry the wealth of the I. — JOHN 530:96
indifference heresy in the form of i. — RAHN 800:5
i., a physical i. — LAWR 586:77
i. of those — HAILE 451:11
i.—the fern-dark i. — LAWR 586:81
pass over youth in dull i. — CONG 281:31
serene i. — WILL 1080:46
superb i. to mortal — STEV 974:22
there shall be i. — SMITH 947:4
indifferent delayed till I am i. — JOHN 526:99
i.…at the birth of his work — ERNST 379:10
i. judge — SIDN 937:53
Is God by definition i. — EBER 359:11
worst sin…to be i. — SHAW 920:14
indifferentism rather than i. — NIGH 729:96
indifferently look on both i. — SHAK 882:18
indigenous intrinsic, i., something — MORR 709:89
indigent How i. the great! — GRAY 441:57
indigestion moral and high i. — MURK 715:68
indignation cup of his i. — BIBLE 158:23
Moral i. — WELLS 1065:38
noble and terrific i. — LESS 598:99
wrath and i. against us — BOOK 174:25
indignations books…contain our i. — CONR 285:3
indignities i. real and imagined — WHITE 1071:46
by i.…to dignities — BACON 57:70
indignity God…spared me i. — BELL 87:4
held himself free from i. — PALM 752:72
ultimate i. is to be given — KUHN 570:13
indirection sense by i. — EVANS 381:40
indiscretion cliché and an i. — MACM 635:4
i. without temptation — BIER 162:97
individual and every i. — TRUM 1029:17
And the i. withers — TENN 996:80
bestowed on the i. — MACC 625:84
capacity for i. enterprise — WAVE 1058:10
debased of style, not i. — MAIL 639:81
definition of an i. — KOES 568:67
difficult…for the i. — HAYEK 462:89
economic liberties of the i. — KRIS 569:94
ethical reality of the i. — KIER 556:61
Every form is i. — HEIN 467:76
Every i.…intends only — SMITH 945:81
faith in i. enterprise — BURT 214:62
feeling i. appeared weak — BELL 88:36
for a private i. or for a city — PLATO 774:25
force…the i. to believe — PENF 764:54
growth in the i. — SMIL 945:73
happiness of an i. — JOHN 528:60
herd instinct in the i. — NIET 728:72
idea…extinguished in i. minds — DURK 357:72
immortality for the i. — SCHO 849:95
i., and only the i. — NABO 717:7

individual (*contd.*)
i. features are portrayed — HUMB 503:96
i. is a minority — ELLI 375:18
i. is no longer to be sovereign — DOUG 342:71
i. men and women — THAT 1008:23
i. opinions are not as colorful — SAFI 836:72
i. profit without i. responsibility — BIER 161:77
Insists I too am an i. — LARK 581:96
law [of competition]…hard for the i. — CARN 236:6
moral i. courage in Chinese — MO 698:10
no i. can recollect the order — WELL 1063:13
of the ignorant i. — KEYN 554:34
only done by one i. — MACH 631:38
oppressed or obscure i. — HAZL 463:9
ordinary in the i. — MANN 646:89
the autonomous i. — ORWE 743:13
the i. and…the state — PLATO 773:3
wanted to be an i. — GULL 448:83
what any i. thinks — PETE 767:8
work of the i. — SIKO 938:75
individualism aberrations of i. — SMALL 943:61
American system of rugged i. — HOOV 490:59
individuality i. is…special error — SCHO 849:95
I.…the aim of political liberty — COOP 287:43
i.…the weakness of our race — DELA 314:21
men without i. have no taste — BENN 91:99
individuals gifted i. manage — SAKI 838:9
hostile behavior…to i. — FULB 409:30
i. are always right — VIAN 1043:43
I. pass like shadows — BURKE 207:20
i. when they make up — KEYN 554:32
negotiation between i. — MUNCH 714:52
not consist of i. — MARX 660:19
satisfactory to i. inside — BIOY 162:11
set of atomic i. — NOVAK 732:36
worth of the i. composing — MILL 675:69
Indochina jungles of I. — MACG 630:33
passed in I. — GREE 444:10
indoctrination substituting i. — PETE 767:9
indoor Done with i. complaints — WHIT 1073:85
indoors We live in the great i. — RAINE 800:7
indubitable absolutely i. — DESC 317:77
inducement if…i. were offered — KING 559:3
indulge i. in a few follies — PROU 792:89
naturally i. in a few delinquencies — ELIOT 365:2
not one that government can i. in — RENO 806:4
indulgence i. encourages us — COWP 292:50
i. to sit in a room — HELL 468:92
kind protection and i. — STOWE 978:84
indulgences i.…never change — BEAU 79:62
industrial advanced i. society — HAYEK 462:90
i. and economic status — SKEL 942:37
i. balance sheets — WEIL 1062:83
i. worker would sooner have £5 — BLYT 170:52
new i. revolution — WIEN 1074:13
The I. Revolution — TOYN 1024:15
industrially they who rule i. — CONN 283:81
industrious man who…is i. — DICK 324:17
industry British i. — HEATH 466:52
Captains of I. — CARL 236:95
employ their whole i. — SMITH 945:88
grip upon i. — TAWN 991:7
her i. and economy — STAN 962:88
I am an i. — CRUY 298:66
I. and all the virtues — HUXL 506:58
i. and intuition — WILS 1084:18
i. can't take you — UPDI 1036:51
i. that…needs better people — DRUC 346:46
Life without i. — RUSK 831:4
literary i. would not exist — LESS 598:7
Ministers of I. — MAND 645:71
re-equipping of British i. — BEVE 102:74
stream of human i. — TOCQ 1022:82
subsidy to high technology i. — CHOM 261:58

industry (*contd.*)
there is no place for i. — HOBB 483:*40*
War is the national i. — MIRA 695:*68*
whole field to private i. — HELL 468:*85*
inedible i. raised to the unspeakable — BASK 76:*7*
ineffable as an i. mystery — SCHW 852:*31*
i. effable — ELIOT 371:*40*
ineffective i. from close up — SCHO 849:*99*
inefficiency efficiency and i. — SHAW 923:*75*
inept earth peopled as ever by the i. — REPP 807:*13*
inequalities significant i. of incomes — KEYN 555:*41*
inequality great i. of environment — CARN 236:*6*
in favour of i. of income — SHAW 925:*26*
saddest sight fortune's i. exhibits — CARL 235:*82*
inevitable arguing the i. — LOWE 616:*89*
foresee the i. — ASIM 42:*72*
have a suspicion it's i. — LEAC 589:*48*
violent revolution i. — KENN 551:*71*
inexhaustible what is i. is benevolent — FRYE 408:*24*
inexpressible expressing the i. — HUXL 507:*63*
infallible i. criterion of wisdom — BURKE 208:*42*
i. symptom — GIBB 421:*21*
not final because we are i. — JACK 514:*88*
infamous acting...unlawfull, i. — PRYN 794:*11*
infamy I.! I! — ROTH 826:*27*
old lies and new i. — POUND 786:*64*
infancy about him in his i. — GREE 444:*3*
dug a spring in i. — BRON 190:*91*
Heaven...in our i. — WORD 1098:*51*
In unexperienc'd i. — TRAH 1024:*24*
i. of our poetry — DRYD 352:*78*
Irish...in the i. of the race — OFAO 736:*94*
lies about us in i. — MITC 696:*78*
Women are from their very I. — ASTE 43:*89*
infant an i. of three — RANS 802:*31*
describe the i. phenomenon — DICK 321:*51*
head of the human i. — SCHR 850:*7*
i. breaks its rattle — SADE 835:*64*
i. crying for the light — TENN 999:*38*
i. whose middle — NASH 720:*59*
Sooner murder an i. — BLAKE 166:*79*
to a little i. — BACON 56:*45*
infantile i. death-rate — HALD 451:*14*
infants filthy, sturdy, unkillable i. — POUND 785:*53*
i. are trying to spell God — ROBI 815:*29*
Sustenance for their helpless I. — SWIFT 985:*97*
infect she would i. to the North Star — SHAK 879:*37*
infected come i. back — WILB 1075:*20*
infection difficult to stay a moral i. — DICK 326:*54*
facilitate the i. of idiocy — BIER 161:*86*
for feare of the i. — PEPYS 765:*76*
i. and the hand of war — SHAK 867:*48*
i. of politics — BRON 190:*82*
i. of the common sky — GRAV 439:*21*
new risks of i. — WEIZ 1062:*87*
infelicity her i....years too many — WEBS 1061:*71*
inference i....watch...had a maker — PALEY 751:*65*
inferior becomes the i. — GREE 444:*18*
i. to most civilised ages — CARL 234:*41*
not to be i. to...nature — PERI 766:*98*
Switzerland as an i. — SMITH 949:*43*
Titles...are disgraced by the i. — SHAW 922:*50*
inferiority always conscious of an i. — JOHN 530:*87*
lie of their i. — KING 558:*85*
preserved from a state of i. — GEOR 418:*81*
say he has an i. complex — SALI 839:*26*
inferno i. depicted by Dr Goebbels — ORWE 743:*16*
moronic i. — BELL 88:*33*
moronic i. of insipidity — LEWIS 602:*70*
infidelity I. does not consist — PAINE 751:*52*
i. is not inconstancy — LACL 574:*66*
infield No reason why the i. — SHAW 925:*36*
infinite being absolutely i. — SPIN 961:*60*
Canna see the I. — MACD 627:*83*

infinite (*contd.*)
everything would appear... i. — BLAKE 166:*80*
for both are i. — SHAK 869:*92*
Her i. variety — SHAK 905:*71*
his passion is I. — PARK 754:*7*
how i. in faculty — SHAK 890:*4*
in comparison to the i. — PASC 758:*70*
i. can never meet — MARV 658:*78*
i. choice — GITL 429:*49*
i. diversity of movement — REDT 804:*79*
i. number of possibilities — GREE 444:*22*
man and the i.! — MACD 627:*77*
striving toward the i. — HUMB 503:*97*
there is an I. in him — CARL 235:*56*
To feel the i. — STAEL 962:*77*
zero and the i. — JARRY 518:*69*
infinitely i. large and the i. small — LEVI 600:*26*
i. small amount of commodity — JEVO 521:*20*
infinities arise...you numberless i. — DONNE 338:*3*
infinitive split an i....stay split — CHAN 250:*37*
split i. is always wrong — THUR 1020:*52*
infinitude speculation of eternity or i. — ADDI 7:*19*
infinity i. in the palm of your hand — BLAKE 167:*1*
infirm I. of purpose! — SHAK 908:*48*
Minstrel was i. and old — SCOTT 853:*42*
infirmities glory in my i. — BIBLE 152:*87*
i. of old age — WESL 1067:*71*
infirmity feblit with i. — DUNB 355:*40*
i. of the noble mind — MILT 684:*42*
prop To our i. — WORD 1096:*24*
inflammation i. of the sentence — THUR 1019:*39*
inflation Having a little i. — HEND 471:*53*
not just i....or stagnation — MACL 634:*91*
Rising prices...do not cause i. — WRIS 1102:*21*
Steel prices cause i. — BLOU 170:*39*
inflexible i. political persuasion — WILS 1085:*40*
inflict i. myself on the public — MORL 708:*75*
influence auspicious star, whose i. — SHAK 916:*20*
books that i. us — FORS 399:*56*
bright eyes Rain i. — MILT 682:*3*
British Sphere of I. — ANON 25:*19*
clothes possess an i. — ALCO 12:*99*
direct i. upon the soul — KAND 541:*97*
Film art has a greater i. — BALA 63:*88*
guard against...unwarranted i. — EISE 364:*88*
i. of a government — REES 805:*92*
i. of a nation — BENN 90:*67*
i. of...Milton and Dryden — ELIOT 368:*79*
i....of our own family — CHUR 262:*78*
i. of the Crown — DUNN 356:*63*
i. them from within — JOHN 522:*31*
i. which is moved not — SHEL 931:*60*
no i. on the future value — JEVO 521:*21*
often malign i. — MUGG 712:*23*
save from its i. — WEBB 1058:*15*
think I can i. them slightly — THOM 1011:*74*
two points of i. — ARNO 39:*28*
where his i. stops — ADAMS 5:*77*
influences i. them in proportion — TOCQ 1021:*78*
intellectual i. — KEYN 555:*37*
thousand i. constantly press — ORWE 742:*93*
influenza call it i. if ye like — BENN 91:*89*
information armed with the same i. — MISH 696:*73*
branch of the i. business — WRIS 1102:*19*
dispersed i. — HAYEK 462:*90*
Everybody gets so much i. — STEIN 966:*43*
find i. upon it — JOHN 529:*74*
haphazard heap of i. — TOLS 1023:*98*
I. is any difference — BATE 76:*11*
I. ...necessary to the human mind — REES 805:*92*
i. vegetable, animal and mineral — GILB 424:*62*
knowledge...lost in i.? — ELIOT 370:*17*
maximum amount of i. — WILS 1085:*26*
money is just another form of i. — WRIS 1102:*21*

information (*contd.*)
not by giving new i. — WITT 1088:*76*
only ask for i. — DICK 324:*10*
pure i. — GOULD 436:*77*
read partly for i. — SCHL 848:*74*
woman of...little i. — AUST 50:*34*
informed but far better i. — BIRK 163:*22*
desire to be i. — BROW 195:*67*
informer i....cannot be a soldier — FLAU 392:*33*
informing i. them narrowly — GALB 412:*80*
ingenious no matter how i. — KISS 566:*34*
i. are always fanciful — POE 776:*43*
ingots back with i. bows — SHAK 897:*78*
i., like in each respect — MARL 655:*27*
ingrateful for the multitude to be i. — SHAK 911:*9*
On her i.top! — SHAK 902:*13*
ingratitude As man's i. — SHAK 885:*94*
buried by i. — LYLY 620:*59*
I. is monstrous — SHAK 911:*9*
I., more strong than traitors' arms — SHAK 884:*54*
I., thou marble-hearted fiend — SHAK 902:*7*
ingredients the very i. of virtue — MILT 686:*68*
ingress i. into the world — LONG 612:*17*
inhabitant i. of the North of England — FORD 396:*1*
ordinary i. is incomprehensible — STARK 963:*98*
inhabitants i. not...grow old — CONN 283:*74*
i. of different planets — DISR 332:*90*
i. of myth — FIED 387:*38*
landscape and its i. — UPDI 1037:*73*
shared among its i. — SIDG 936:*39*
such uncomely i. — WALP 1051:*79*
inhale as if she would i. them — FIRB 389:*79*
but I didn't i. — RICH 810:*72*
didn't i. — DOWD 342:*77*
To i. Paris — HUGO 502:*86*
inherent i. in the human situation — GREE 444:*25*
inherit all which it i. — SHAK 917:*36*
inheritance care for its literary i. — ELIOT 370:*14*
Has had a like i. — YEATS 1106:*88*
have our i. — SMITH 947:*4*
heathen for thine i. — BIBLE 114:*32*
heir to an i. — OAKE 733:*51*
how my i. was proceeding — HAMER 453:*27*
spending my children's i. — ANON 30:*52*
inheritor succeed as his i. — SHAK 910:*98*
inheritors i. of an old civilisation — REYES 807:*22*
inhibition I. is no good provider — HESI 479:*83*
inhibitions cultivate a few i. — LOOS 613:*35*
inhuman artists...want to become i. — APOL 31:*89*
i. and indecent and dishonorable — HELL 468:*93*
i. in its materialism — WILS 1084:*71*
inhumanity essence of i. — SHAW 920:*14*
i. of a boa-constrictor — WOOL 1094:*90*
Man's i. to Man — BURNS 209:*76*
refuses to remember the i. — WEIZ 1062:*87*
rewarded with i. — ROLL 821:*26*
iniquities bruised for our i. — BIBLE 127:*1*
forgiveth all thine i. — BIBLE 118:*11*
If thou, Lord, shouldest mark i. — BIBLE 119:*44*
rewarded us according to our i. — BIBLE 118:*12*
iniquity hated i. — GREG 446:*46*
infamous seminary of i. — CHES 257:*83*
i. is taken away — BIBLE 124:*61*
shapen in i. — BIBLE 116:*76*
stubbornness is as i. — BIBLE 110:*35*
tongue...is a world of i. — BIBLE 155:*67*
visiting the i. of the fathers — BIBLE 106:*68*
initiation i. into a new state — ELIOT 365:*11*
injured always being the i. party — ANGE 19:*27*
injures forgiveness to the i. — DRYD 347:*70*
injuries i. sustained in his native town — ANON 24:*13*
poisons and awkward i. — ANOU 30:*73*
take revenge for slight i. — MACH 631:*36*
injurious highly i. to the poor — HALL 452:*33*

injury height without sustaining i.	LEON 597:77
i. is much sooner forgotten	CHES 257:73
i. would vex a very saint	SHAK 864:82
members from i. and molestation	MILL 675:65
result of a critical i.	RUSS 832:16
Where there is i.	FRAN 401:91
injustice cruel i. if you deny it	CARL 236:86
fear of suffering i.	LARO 582:23
grave i. to bees	ORWE 742:3
I. anywhere is a threat	KING 557:75
i. of taking a speck for the whole	EDGE 361:36
I....prevents my doing it	BUTL 218:42
nothing so finely perceiveds i.	DICK 326:67
protect him against i.	PALM 752:72
superior to i.	PLATO 774:26
Who fear the i. of men	ELIOT 370:35
injustices i. are sanctioned	FRAN 401:88
ink 12 ounces of paper and i.	MORL 708:71
black i. in white milk	MUNRO 714:59
brain that i. may character	SHAK 915:87
buy i. by the barrel	KIRK 565:27
cuttlefish squirting out i.	ORWE 743:19
Every drop of i.	WALP 1051:82
gunpowder and printer's i.	KRAUS 569:91
Hamlet is as much paper and i.	PRIE 789:35
hath not drunk i.	SHAK 865:16
I....A villainous compound	BIER 161:86
i....tempered with love's sighs	SHAK 865:21
medium is printer's i.	KRAUS 569:87
mix...water with their i.	GOET 431:77
Rorschach i. blots	LICH 604:89
spend time and i.	GALS 413:3
win...By blood or i.	BYRON 222:33
inlets through creeks and i.	CLOU 270:32
inmate who is...the i.	CONA 279:81
inn best in every i.	STEV 973:94
brought him to an i.	BIBLE 142:90
Do you remember an I.	BELL 87:17
In the worst i.'s worst room	POPE 780:30
no room for them in the i.	BIBLE 142:77
that dark i.—the Grave!	SCOTT 854:31
world's an i.	DRYD 352:93
inn-door up to the old i.-d.	NOYES 732:42
inner i. process	WITT 1088:80
strengthened...in the i. man	BIBLE 152:98
innings life was like his i.	EGAN 362:55
Innisfree go to I.	YEATS 1104:57
innocence ceremony of i. is drowned	
	YEATS 1106:77
end of i.	GOLD 432:85
first state of i.	BEHN 85:71
Ignorance is not i.	BROW 200:97
i. and even the right	RODR 819:88
I. ends when one is stripped	DIDI 330:43
I. is a science of the sublime	CIXO 267:77
i. is closing up his eyes	DRAY 345:40
i. should be bold	MASS 662:57
I. thy Sister dear!	MARV 658:83
lost her i.	GREER 445:41
Never such i.	LARK 581:7
purity and place and i.	MILT 690:64
Some final i.	SPEN 956:74
spurious i.	BELL 88:40
though conscious of your i.	JOHN 529:83
wanting to hold on to i.	WILS 1084:10
worthy of the joy of i.	OFLA 736:96
innocency state of i. Adam fell	SHAK 876:64
innocent 'baby', an i. rhyme	SHAK 880:65
But who is i.?	WORD 1100:89
Can one be i.	CYRA 302:34
essential self is i.	UPDI 1037:66
guilty then...proved i.	ORWE 745:62
i. as strawberries	THOM 1010:64
look like the i. flower	SHAK 907:29

innocent (*contd.*)	
one i. suffer	BLAC 165:49
sleep—the i. sleep	SHAK 908:46
sores on i. tongues	OWEN 748:13
The i. and the beautiful	YEATS 1106:82
to hurt i. people	HELL 468:93
innocents We are...the i.	DELI 315:42
innovate I....or evaporate!	MERR 672:20
To i. is not to reform	BURKE 208:46
innovation Fashion...produces i.	SANT 842:83
I. most of the time	SCHM 848:80
innovations ill-shapen, so are all i.	BACON 58:93
innovator time is the greatest i.	BACON 58:94
inns i. of Molten Blue	DICK 328:96
two years in Holiday I.	MOND 699:38
innuendoes beauty of i.	STEV 971:43
in-office i.-o. attitudes and behaviour	COUP 289:78
inquest like a coroner's i.	CONG 281:24
inquire i. in his temple	BIBLE 115:55
I. often	PENN 764:57
not to i. why or whither	WILD 1079:24
inquiries invited his i.	MENC 669:64
religious i.	GIBB 421:27
some i. are too dangerous	SAGAN 836:74
inquiry every i....is thought to aim	ARIS 34:25
i. of truth	BACON 56:41
inquisition I....from the pulpit	WELD 1062:92
To these I. dogs	TENN 1004:56
inquisitiveness tribalism and i.	ALDI 12:7
inquisitors severe i.	BACON 57:60
inroad i. on the discipline	OCON 735:80
insane among the i.	DE 311:63
Man is quite i.	MONT 702:71
insanity new idea...close to i.	MILL 677:2
prelude to i.	WAUGH 1056:68
So with sanity and i.	MELV 668:51
inscription i. on public fountains	FLAU 393:46
inscriptions In lapidary i.	JOHN 529:78
inscrutability i. of the East	STARK 963:98
inscrutable i. singular name	ELIOT 371:40
i. to the last	THUR 1019:26
insect Egyptians came to worship an i.	DISR 333:2
i. moves toward its flower	BALZ 69:78
i. youth on the wing	GRAY 441:58
into a gigantic i.	KAFKA 541:86
one is but an i.	JOHN 526:94
insects dancing i.	WORD 1100:84
Fabulous the i.	WILK 1080:41
I. are what neurosis	AMIS 17:95
keep down microscopic i.	DOUG 341:51
insecurity source of economic i.	ELLW 375:20
inseparable found i.	HUME 503:99
i. part	GAND 414:14
inside i. and an outside	HEPW 473:30
i. and strength were philosophy	SIDN 937:60
i. the tent pissing out	JOHN 523:53
insides rest of a person's i.	TWAIN 1033:92
insight For i. into human affairs	DYSON 358:99
if it only added judgement to i.	FORS 398:39
i. I have gained from poker	MAMET 643:53
moment's i.	HOLM 486:79
most revolutionary i. of all	JONG 533:91
read...partly for i.	SCHL 848:74
insights deeper i. to the dead belong	FERG 385:14
i. of the Jewish prophets	NIEB 727:64
perceptions and i.	KISS 566:38
insignificance Men thin away to i.	HARDY 456:87
without losing their i.	BAXT 78:50
insignificant as i. as possible	GALT 413:10
obvious and i.	JAMES 517:49
see himself as both exceptional and i.	MAIL 639:82
insincerity clear language is i.	ORWE 744:46
enemy of...language is i.	ORWE 743:19
insipid He is many times flat, i.	DRYD 347:59

insipid (*contd.*)	
i. thing is a billet-doux	ETHE 380:14
Simplicity...is wholly i.	HOGA 485:64
insipidity inferno of i. and decay	LEWIS 602:70
insolence i. is not invective	DISR 333:98
i. of wealth	JOHN 530:97
lazy i. of a shoe salesman	PERE 766:92
supports with i.	JOHN 526:15
insolencies i. of other Turks	BUTL 216:1
insoluble political ones are i.	HOME 487:10
science leads only to the i.	DISR 333:10
insomnia febrile i., moral leaps	MARI 651:66
ideal i.	JOYCE 538:59
inspector An I. Calls	PRIE 790:38
great i., with a myriad eyes	STEAD 964:8
inspiration Genius is one per cent i.	EDIS 361:44
hierophants of an unapprehended i.	SHEL 931:60
My sole i.	PORT 784:34
scripture is given by i.	BIBLE 154:38
temperamental i.	MOND 699:40
inspire feel not what they i.	SHEL 931:60
i. free hearts	KENN 551:75
i. hopeless passion	THAC 1006:92
your selves i. These...works	POPE 782:91
inspired i. by the gods inside	SAIN 837:89
inspirer poet is more the i.	ELUA 376:23
instalment last i. missing	CRISP 297:40
instant at that i.	KARSH 542:11
be i. in season	BIBLE 154:40
Before me at this i.	SHAK 902:11
Every i. of our lives	GIDE 423:46
i. that he fell	SCOTT 853:59
perish in the very i.	GRAY 440:44
instinct delicacy of poetic i.	WILDE 1076:32
i. for being unhappy	SAKI 838:6
i. for contentment	KRIS 569:95
i. for not ruining...vision	BLUN 170:48
i. of mankind	TAWN 991:7
i. the habit is already old	LAWR 586:90
i. told him that the best liar	BUTL 217:37
intimate with him by i.	AUST 51:49
Love has its own i.	BALZ 69:78
maternal i.	FRID 404:47
natural i. to abjure man	HARDY 456:91
nerve and i. is clamouring	LESS 598:90
rather of i. than of practice	REED 805:87
satisfies the human creative i.	QUEN 797:54
sublimation of the work i.	LODGE 610:81
what the i. ...can conceive	PICA 768:25
what we believe upon i.	BRAD 184:91
womanly i. that clothes possess	ALCO 12:99
instinctively what you know i.	BELL 86:94
instincts atheism against...our i.	BURKE 208:35
born with i. and abilities	BALZ 69:83
High i.	WORD 1098:53
i. already catered for	BENN 90:72
only trust our own i.	LAFO 574:76
true to your i., was his motto	LAWR 585:62
institution cannot see an i.	CRIT 297:44
deep stake...in such a glorious i.	BURKE 207:12
family as an i.	MILLS 679:64
feature of this i.	DICK 322:67
i. of the throne	ACHE 2:23
Is an i. always	JARR 518:64
It's an i.	HUGH 501:52
no major i. in the US	FRIE 405:55
only i. in the world	SAMU 840:43
partly of human i.	MILL 674:57
such as are in the i.	EMER 377:54
institutions destroy i.	WHIT 1073:89
free i. can exist	MARS 656:52
i. are framed	TREV 1026:53
i., civil and ecclesiastical	PEEL 763:42
i. presuppose a Supreme Being	DOUG 342:70

institutions (*contd.*)
most licentious of human i. — SHAW 922:*41*
old i. entirely reformed — MACH 631:*38*
take the i. and liberties — POWE 788:*18*
walls of i. — ROET 819:*92*
instruct amuse and i. — UPDI 1037:*62*
i. thee and teach thee — BIBLE 115:*59*
instructed i. and amused — ATLAS 44:*7*
instruction all the i. and knowledge — JAY 519:*74*
All true histories contain i. — BRON 190:*88*
horses of i. — BLAKE 166:*77*
i. in righteousness — BIBLE 154:*39*
i. without talent — VITR 1046:*97*
no i. book came with it — FULL 409:*40*
instructions Bloody i. — SHAK 907:*31*
instructive something i. — KHOM 555:*45*
instrument great i. of moral good — SHEL 931:*57*
I am an i. — RICH 809:*47*
i. might be less — JOHN 526:*5*
i. of chase — WELLS 1064:*32*
i. of Your peace — FRAN 401:*91*
i. plays itself — BACH 54:*92*
i. that has a good moral effect — ARIS 34:*34*
i. with which each learns — PLATO 774:*23*
more perfect i. of the soul — PIUS 772:*81*
most sensitive i. known to man — BEEC 83:*20*
old one-stringed i. — RANJ 801:*27*
painting…an i. of war — PICA 769:*26*
Polling is merely an i. — GALL 413:*98*
Prosperity is only an i. — COOL 286:*37*
supersensitive i. — ERNST 379:*11*
The book…a kind of optical i. — PROU 794:*10*
tune the i. here at the door — DONNE 338:*17*
instruments all the i. agree — AUDEN 47:*69*
fit i. to make slaves — PITT 771:*66*
Furnished…with nice i. — FRAN 402:*11*
i. ill-adapted for the purpose — CHUR 265:*45*
i. of labour — MARX 661:*22*
i. of vengeance — DONO 340:*36*
I. of War — ALBE 12:*94*
i., strung to a vast precision — CRANE 295:*99*
i. to plague us — SHAK 904:*47*
lofty i. of war — SHAK 876:*73*
man, not his i. — MO 698:*11*
insufferable Oxford…has made me i. — BEER 83:*26*
insufferables sovereign of i. — BIER 162:*99*
insult His presence here…an i. — RED 804:*74*
i. of each other's presence — ISHE 513:*74*
i. of each shabby skirt — DONO 340:*36*
i. to the cook — CHES 260:*40*
i. to the Holy See — INNO 512:*56*
much sooner forgotten than an i. — CHES 257:*73*
prolonged i. — MILL 677:*15*
ring of a really original i. — CARR 237:*18*
standing i. to sportsmen — FRY 408:*10*
who do not understand studied i. — GALL 412:*94*
insulted i.…in our old age? — SCHU 851:*20*
possible for me to get i. — DAVIS 309:*32*
when somebody i. Caruso — LOUIS 614:*60*
insults Clothes are our…visible i. — CART 242:*92*
insurance for their i. money — DOYLE 343:*89*
tongue at the i. — MARQ 655:*36*
insurrection I.…guerrilla bands — MAZZ 666:*11*
intangible O world i. — THOM 1013:*30*
integrate desire to i. in society — SARR 843:*4*
integrity i. of her honour — GOTT 436:*72*
i. of the Irish nation — REDM 804:*75*
national i. — WILS 1086:*45*
still retain thine i.? — BIBLE 112:*97*
strictest i. — WASH 1054:*41*
intellect Democratic I. — DAVIE 307:*2*
feather to tickle the i. — LAMB 577:*42*
i. of Europe — ARNO 38:*6*
i. will always govern — WOLL 1091:*33*

intellect (*contd.*)
march of i. — SOUT 954:*44*
merely great i. — THOM 1012:*96*
Our meddling i. — WORD 1094:*3*
power of the human i. — LEWIS 602:*60*
put on i. — BLAKE 168:*10*
revenge of the i. upon art — SONT 952:*4*
scorched my i. into a cinder — CARL 233:*29*
so-called things of i. — LISP 607:*40*
sob in the i. — DUNN 356:*54*
to perfect…the i. or reason — SPIN 960:*58*
What i., what calculation — YEATS 1107:*91*
intellects decayed in his i. — JOHN 531:*24*
i. vast and cool — WELLS 1064:*26*
powerful of human i. — MACA 623:*9*
intellectual beasts of the i. domain — HOLM 486:*80*
by reason of her i. defects — WRIG 1101:*2*
chief distinction in the i. powers — DARW 306:*88*
dash of i. curiosity — WEBB 1058:*14*
Disinterested i. — TREV 1026:*47*
end to purely i. intercourse — WRIG 1101:*3*
great i. talents — TOCQ 1021:*74*
i. attraction — HICKS 480:*98*
i. capacity — SCHR 850:*7*
i. fashion — CONN 283:*80*
i. life of our century — ARNO 38:*10*
i. life of …western society — SNOW 950:*73*
i. love of God — SPIN 961:*59*
I.: someone whose mind watches — CAMUS 228:*43*
most i. of all ages — BENN 92:*5*
passage to the i. World — STER 969:*9*
promote i. crime — BIER 161:*86*
Tears may be i. — BELL 88:*38*
The i.…flower of the bourgeoisie — BOGAN 171:*60*
then an i. — HOOK 489:*55*
word I. suggests — AUDEN 48:*77*
ye lords of ladies i. — BYRON 222:*26*
intellectually I.…America — LEWIS 602:*56*
I.…people never wash — DUDEK 353:*17*
intellectuals characterize…as i. — AGNEW 10:*69*
I. can tell themselves anything — HELL 469:*98*
I.…no longer see the smile — SAIN 836:*81*
opiate of the i. — LUCE 618:*33*
intelligence bewitchment of our i. — WITT 1088:*76*
degree of a person's i. — ALTH 15:*61*
elaborate waste of human i. — CHAN 251:*51*
explain school to a higher i.? — MATH 663:*72*
Fight for our National I. — CATT 245:*56*
grin and fine i. — NEW 723:*17*
have i. and yet not understand — LISP 607:*40*
i. and necessity — ANGE 19:*18*
i. in the winds — HOLM 485:*72*
i. of a respectable agricultural — MENC 670:*90*
i. that moves — DONNE 338:*16*
men started at the i. — SOUT 954:*47*
morning and evening with i. — JOHN 527:*18*
most correct i. — TIMES 1021:*71*
Oh i., flaming solitude — GORO 436:*68*
Poetry must resist the i. — STEV 972:*58*
powers of i. — LYND 621:*65*
public subsidy of i. — QUINE 797:*67*
science of arresting human i. — LEAC 589:*43*
test of a first-rate i. — FITZ 391:*13*
Truths discovered by i. — FRAN 401:*84*
works of thought and i. — PAST 759:*88*
intelligent attacked many an i. — MAIM 640:*95*
best audience is i. — BARK 71:*20*
both honest and i. — ORWE 745:*49*
first rule of i. tinkering — EHRL 362:*56*
i. are not the leaders — CONR 285:*7*
i. Mr Toad — GRAH 438:*93*
no i. woman — MUNRO 714:*56*
not a very i. means — KENT 553:*8*
not…quite i. enough — HUXL 507:*65*

intelligent (*contd.*)
room-mates…if they're i. — SALI 838:*23*
Shakesperian Rag…So i. — ELIOT 368:*86*
The more i. one is — PASC 758:*68*
too old and i. — BRAD 183:*85*
intend i. to prejudice the past — WHIT 1072:*64*
since what I well i. — SHAK 902:*99*
intensions geometric i. — LEGER 593:*21*
intensity i. of perception — WILL 1083:*99*
passionate i. — YEATS 1106:*77*
texture and i. — THOM 1011:*92*
intensiveness i. as stricture — BURKE 208:*53*
intent prick the sides of my i. — SHAK 908:*32*
intention appreciate the i. — TROL 1027:*73*
fossils of i. — PURDY 795:*34*
in the doer's i. — HELO 469:*8*
no i. of rearranging — MORT 710:*3*
no part of his i. — SMITH 945:*81*
plain i. — HERB 475:*25*
intentions act…with such i. — PEEL 763:*42*
express their i. — LESS 598:*1*
i. are perfectly honourable — SHAW 923:*73*
prince whose i. were pure — JOSE 537:*34*
intents i. wicked or charitable — SHAK 888:*71*
interchange ennobling i. — WORD 1096:*34*
intercourse i. of touch — WORD 1096:*26*
i. with foreign nations — DECA 311:*71*
i. with the natives — PARK 753:*85*
living forms and social i. — HOLM 486:*97*
nations; between whom there is no i. — DISR 332:*90*
oxygen of social i. — HIRS 481:*20*
pleasures of human i. — MOORE 704:*10*
purely intellectual i. — WRIG 1101:*3*
Sexual i. began — LARK 581:*12*
synonym for i. — DWOR 358:*86*
interest ability nor i. — MORE 706:*42*
allurement of private i. — STEU 970:*30*
an i., a point of view — POPP 783:*20*
an i. in life — PALEY 751:*60*
By pursuing his own i. — SMITH 945:*81*
case…not entirely devoid of i. — DOYLE 343:*99*
common i. always will prevail — DRYD 349:*25*
derives its collective i. — HUMB 503:*50*
falsehoods which i. dictates — JOHN 527:*21*
free from i. or prejudice — REES 805:*92*
fuel of i. to the fire — LINC 605:*1*
gentle lack of i. — LISP 607:*40*
i. in life does not lie — WOOLF 1092:*61*
i. of the community — BENT 92:*12*
little in it to i. — THOR 1017:*98*
no i. in anthing but genius — LAGN 575:*99*
no i. whatever — MACL 633:*66*
operates in the public i. — KEYN 554:*32*
public i. may — LIPP 607:*38*
regard to their own i. — SMITH 945:*87*
sustain a uniform degree of i. — BOWL 182:*58*
want of any other i. — VOLT 1047:*14*
what sustains i. — JIANG 522:*24*
interested i. in music — SIMO 939:*84*
more i. in himself than me — BIER 161:*81*
more i. in yourself — GIDE 423:*43*
interesting hardly be made i. — TROL 1028:*97*
Imitation is more i. — STEIN 966:*44*
i. as a wall can be — SHAW 925:*29*
law of the newspaper is to be i. — DANA 304:*57*
more i. than being yourself — GIEL 423:*50*
most i. ideas — SONT 953:*10*
that it be i. — JAMES 516:*18*
time fails to find them i. — MASE 662:*52*
interests harming their true i. — MONT 702:*82*
in the i. of Hell — FORS 398:*45*
i. are by no means the same — SMITH 946:*89*
i. coincide with the state's — MUSS 716:*91*
i. of…the community — RICA 808:*36*

interests (contd.)
Man's earthly i....held up — CARL 234:50
matters thus bearing on her i. — PALM 752:74
opportunity as against material i. — WILS 1086:45
Our i. are eternal — PALM 752:70
power of vested i. — KEYN 555:37
pursue their respective i. — JEVO 521:22
uniformity of i. — MADI 638:55
watch over our i. — LLOY 608:54
interference trophy to magisterial i. — ANON 24:13
interfolds leaden i. are bright — FREE 404:35
interim i. is Like a phantasma — SHAK 883:27
interjection life is but an i. — BYRON 223:61
interline enlarge, diminish, i. — SWIFT 985:2
interlude Strange i.! — ONEI 740:55
interludes our lives are...dark i. — ONEI 740:55
Internet I. has taken shape — GLEI 430:61
interpretation i. for...convenience — WIEN 1074:14
I. is the revenge of the intellect — SONT 952:4
i. of dreams — FREUD 404:41
other i. is nonsense — GALL 413:98
their i. is...ethical — ORWE 744:27
what is lost in i. — FROST 408:8
interpreter God is his own i. — COWP 291:28
I don't know which is the i. — SHER 934:4
soul...has an i. — BRON 191:95
interrupted when I was i. — CONN 284:85
intersection old lady at a busy i. — ACHE 3:40
intersections i. within a society — MILLS 679:63
intersices between the i. — JOHN 526:13
interstellar vacant i. spaces — ELIOT 371:49
interval during the i. — TYNAN 1035:2
i. betwixt one passion and another — STER 970:23
make a lucid i. — DRYD 348:83
intervals during his sober i. — LAMB 577:38
enough fine i. — STEV 973:95
interview after an i. with a doctor — JAMES 515:6
I once said in an i. — MACC 626:59
interviewer i. asked me — MACC 626:56
interweaving complex, vital i. — PLATH 773:90
intestine dark i. — HUGH 500:42
tapeworm in the i. — GOLD 432:87
intimacy avoid any i. — KITC 566:44
cases of oral-genital i. — HOOV 490:69
determine i. — AUST 50:32
i. of a surgeon's scalpel — ANGE 20:31
no shore, no i. — SCOTT 852:36
intimate art, i., heroic — ROUA 827:29
confiding, the i. — MACD 628:93
i. as any conversation — STERN 968:86
Sharing food...an i. act — FISH 389:84
intonations history of different i. — BORG 179:11
intoxicated exposes himself when i. — JOHN 530:2
intoxication best of Life is but i. — BYRON 222:43
not in the delicious i. — HUXL 507:74
intricacies No pleasing I. intervene — POPE 779:21
intrigue clannishness, routine and i. — JAUR 519:71
Everything is done by i. — HUGO 502:76
intrigues I. half-gathered — CRAB 294:81
introduce allow me to i. myself — JAGG 515:96
introduced i. to the Aged — DICK 326:71
introduction one is an i. — JOHN 526:1
intuition by pure soul-i. — LAWR 586:80
human i., human autonomy — MUMF 713:49
i. and compassion — WILS 1084:18
invade dare to i....my realm — ELIZ 373:90
very uncivilised to i. — HUNT 505:32
invader won from her proud i. — MOORE 706:33
invaders exiles and i. — ATWO 45:21
invasion defend the realm against i. — PHIL 768:17
defended...from foreign i. — REDM 804:75
i. of a common enemy — KITC 566:44
not an i. of Vietnam — NIXON 730:11
invective insolence is not i. — DISR 333:98

invent choose—that is to say, i. — SART 844:19
God...necessary to i. him — VOLT 1047:17
I just i. — FULL 409:37
reason properly can i. — LESS 599:11
writer does not need to i. — PROU 794:9
invented Everything...has been i. — DUELL 354:21
fond thing vainly i. — BOOK 178:98
If born...were being i. — DOYLE 344:21
i. to make fun — GARC 414:18
i. what I conceived — HUXL 508:97
invention brightest heaven of i. — SHAK 880:7
call the sciences human i. — PAINE 750:51
Ceremony is an i. — LAMB 576:24
deities of his own i. — PLATO 773:2
exercise his i. — SMITH 946:91
'Faith' is a fine i. — DICK 327:95
fresh i. planted — CAREW 232:12
genuine i. in the realm — MILL 677:2
greatest i. since the novel — MEAD 666:14
i., hearing not my tongue — SHAK 897:75
I., Nature's child — SIDN 937:51
i. of a mouse! — DISN 331:70
i. of gunpowder — KRAUS 569:91
i. of the landscape painter — FUSE 410:62
i. or true artistry — POUND 786:85
no i. as to stories — BYRON 221:15
poem is a test of i. — KEATS 544:44
their own i. shall furnish — HOBB 483:40
trim i. — HERB 475:25
Without i. — WILL 1083:93
inventions half ashamed of those i. — MACA 623:11
ideologies and i. — SONT 951:7
i. have endowed material forces — MARX 660:18
i. have no other apparent purpose — MENC 670:82
Our i. are wont — THOR 1016:78
rules for odd i. — SHAK 864:81
What excellent i. — AUGU 49:15
inventive manipulation of the i. — LEWIS 602:60
inventor i. of harmonies — TENN 1003:24
inventory i. of unfinished thinking — RAND 801:22
inversions all sorts of semantic i. — MAMET 643:50
invertebrates belly-wriggling i. — LAWR 585:63
investigation careful i. of cases — HARV 460:55
sphere of natural i. — HUMB 503:96
sufficiently careful i. — GALB 411:74
investigations obscurity of our i. — SCHO 849:92
investigator i. to pretend — LEWO 603:74
investment i. in the quickest time — ROGE 820:3
i. over its whole life — KEYN 554:34
no finer i. for any community — CHUR 265:27
investor average private i. — KEYN 554:34
invicility sabbath-breaking...to i. — DEQU 316:68
invidiousness in sheer i. — ACHE 2:20
invincible both sides were i. — SWIFT 984:78
i. dullness — JONS 535:91
Love i. in battle — SOPH 953:19
no i. armies — STAL 962:80
inviolable clutching the i. shade — ARNO 38:93
i. in the eye of Almighty God — GLAD 429:52
invisibility This masculine i. — DUNN 356:51
invisible Clothes make the poor i. — HARR 458:26
Fortune...she is not i. — BACON 59:11
I am an i. man — ELLI 375:16
immense; at times i. — MOORE 705:25
i. man was...i. to himself — ELLI 375:19
led by an i. hand — SMITH 945:81
limping i. down to — THOM 1011:79
no i. means of support — BUCH 202:27
Reputation...made him i. — WEBS 1061:62
skuttle fish...becomes i. — ADDI 7:25
things visible and i. — BOOK 174:18
what is essential is i. — SAIN 836:35
Women...are i. people — FRIE 405:50
invocation i. of the Muse — GRAV 440:27

invocation (contd.)
more like an i. — LEZA 603:76
invulnerable I. nothings — SHEL 931:46
inwards from the outside i. — FRIE 405:59
Ionian under I. skies — SHEL 931:54
IOUs guy holding the I. — IACO 509:17
IQ I. had been two points lower — TREV 1026:51
IRA We dislike the I. — OBRI 734:64
Iraqi I. is really not whacky — ACHE 3:48
ire 'shinning' arouses his i. — ANON 24:14
Ireland advantages of I. — SAKI 838:11
Consider I. — DISR 332:87
do nothing...for I. — FREE 404:32
enemies to I. — EDGE 361:34
future government of I. — CHUR 263:93
'God save I.' — SULL 981:24
great Gaels of I. — CHES 259:19
I. and...for the United Kingdom — LLOY 609:63
I.'s dead — YEATS 1105:70
I. gives England her soldiers — MERE 671:14
I. is one of the few countries — DANG 304:60
I. never was contented — LAND 578:63
I. still continues poor ? — BERK 95:54
mad I. hurt you — AUDEN 47:70
message of peace to I. — ARNO 39:21
met in the streets of I. — ONOL 734:68
name of I. is mentioned — SMITH 949:42
never met anyone in I. — FRAS 403:79
soup in I. — WAUGH 1056:63
Think what have I got for I. — COLL 276:39
Though I. starve — BYRON 223:55
violence in Northern I. — OROU 741:79
west of I., the Romans — CHRI 261:72
withdraw...troops from I. — REDM 804:75
iris I. all hues, roses — MILT 690:63
I. of the West — BYRON 220:94
livelier I. — TENN 995:71
irises better than I. — HAMM 453:50
Irish becoming like the I. Census — MACR 638:53
answer to the I. Question — SELL 858:39
as I. as Black Americans are African — GELD 417:66
Ben Hur translated into I. — STEW 977:64
betwixt English and I. — STRA 979:1
chiefs of the I. Brigade — DAVIS 309:38
cross the river by an I. bridge — STEW 977:65
distinctive I. experience — DONO 339:35
Dress British, look I. — KOFF 568:73
ear becomes more I. — BYRON 223:52
exile has been to the I. — WILDE 1075:31
He was a black I. type — PRIE 790:42
helpless in her I. hand — BARK 71:17
historic destiny of the I. — WAUGH 1057:89
integrity of the I. nation — REDM 804:75
involved in the I. situation — OBRI 733:61
I. are in the same...position — OROU 741:79
I. feelings and sensitivities — HAUG 460:59
I. hurricane, a flat calm — BOWEN 181:50
I. melts into the tune — CARL 233:25
I. people are too well off — SHAW 923:74
I. question — FRAS 403:19
Let the I. vessel lie — AUDEN 47:71
Look at the I.! — BUCH 202:25
No blithe I. lad was so happy — CAMP 227:24
No modern I. writer — ORWE 744:34
old I. hospitality — EDGE 360:28
one of our little I. boats — BEHAN 84:58
President of I. descent — KENN 551:81
Shakespeare was an I. Catholic — ONEI 740:58
symbol of I. art — JOYCE 538:46
teach the I. to drink beer — EDGE 360:30
teach...the I. how to listen — WILDE 1078:94
The I. and the Jews have a psychosis — BEHAN 84:62
those of the I. nation — PARN 756:40
To marry the I. — DONL 335:59

Irish (*contd.*)
turn to early I. literature — OFAO 736:94
Upon the I. shore — BURNS 213:49
was an I. rat — SHAK 886:3
We I....that ancient sect — YEATS 1107:91
Irish-American leader is an I. — WILDE 1075:31
Irishman I.'s heart is nothing — SHAW 923:70
I.'s imagination — SHAW 923:69
I. is lined with copper — TWAIN 1032:74
I. turned Englishman — OBRI 734:62
I. would kill a negro — FREE 404:31
poor silly-clever I. — SHAW 923:71
Irishmen I. are born brooders — OBRI 734:62
Irishness I. is not...question of birth — OBRI 733:61
Irishy more I. than is necessary — TWAIN 1033:95
irksome harsh, impertinent and i. — JONS 535:90
How i. is this music — SHAK 861:1
iron An i. man — SHAK 877:2
another i. door — SPEN 958:21
Any old i. — COLL 276:37
beat the i. while it is hot — DRYD 352:75
bend thy pillars with thine i. car — BLAKE 165:60
break them with a rod of i. — BIBLE 114:32
but he has i. teeth — GROM 447:70
carcass seemed to be made of i. — MENC 670:89
cloak should become an i. cage — WEBER 1059:19
Don't i. — ANON 29:30
hard as i. bloody bars — GALL 413:97
If the i. dice roll — BETH 99:23
in my heart his i. arrow — SPEN 957:6
i. and blood — BISM 164:38
i. coat all overgrown — SPEN 958:10
i. curtain has descended — CHUR 265:30
i. curtain would at once descend — GOEB 430:65
i. entered into his soul — BOOK 177:90
I. Lady of the Western World? — THAT 1007:7
legs of i. — BIBLE 129:45
meddles with cold i.! — BUTL 216:12
men of i. — ALBA 11:81
no i. can stab the heart — BABEL 54:90
Nor i. bars a cage — 615:63
nor strong links of i. — SHAK 883:25
rule them with a rod of i. — BIBLE 157:4
shod with i. — DICK 325:40
sound of i. on stone — DELA 314:27
touch of i. about you — THAT 1008:25
what shall i. do? — CHAU 254:25
iron-grey colour of my soul is i.-g. — DEBU 311:66
ironically answers were meant i. — TRIL 1026:55
dogmatic, and i. witty — REST 817:15
ironmongery warlike i. — GILB 425:81
irons two i. in the fire — BEAU 80:68
irony calculated i. — ELIOT 366:35
inspire i. — GISC 429:48
irradiation Intense i. of a mind — SHEL 929:10
irrational i. is rational — STEV 971:53
something deep and i. — WILS 1084:11
irrecoverable advantage...lost is i. — DRAKE 345:28
irregularity i. in Nature — THOR 1016:72
natural world full of i. — BOYD 182:65
irrelevance said...with apparent i. — SOME 952:99
irreplaceable essentially i. — GIDE 423:46
irresistible changes...be thus i. — JOHN 526:9
theatre is i. — ARNO 40:37
irresponsible better to be i. — CHUR 265:36
irreverence New York, thy name is i. — HUXT 509:9
irreverent unless you are i. — MAIL 639:75
irritates Perfection is i. — AUCH 46:38
is Whatever i., i. in God — SPIN 960:47
Isaac God of I. — PASC 758:81
I., whom thou lovest — BIBLE 105:27
Isabel Anchors on I. — SHAK 897:75
Isabella I. forbid me to — FLEM 394:66
Isaiah consults the prophet I. — CROM 297:47

Isherwood I....not...in Berlin — BURU 214:80
Ishmael Call me I. — MELV 667:30
shalt call his name I. — BIBLE 104:21
Isis careful search that I. — MILT 686:72
island air of the Enchanted i. — MERE 671:1
an i. in the West Indies — ONEI 739:47
as an inland i. — SWIN 988:56
cast my lot in an i.? — DICK 326:60
defend our i. — CHUR 264:14
down by the i. crags — TENN 1005:61
Englishman is an i. — NOVA 732:39
heart of our i. — FORS 398:28
furnishings of each I. — FRAME 400:78
i. of the pests — MACA 622:86
i. rock in space — CIAR 265:50
larger the i. of knowlege — MACI 631:46
lone shieling of the misty i. — GALT 413:8
Look, stranger, at this i. — AUDEN 46:51
memory of an offshore i. — THAT 1007:10
mistress of half an i. — SIXT 942:31
No man is an i. — DONNE 339:22
old i. here that flowered — FITZ 391:6
symbol for England is the I. — ATWO 45:22
this dirty, despicable little i. — WALP 1051:90
whole i. was shaken — ADDI 6:5
Zuleika, on desert i. — BEER 83:29
island-valley i.-v. of Avilion — TENN 1004:48
islands Among the smaller i. — GERA 419:95
dotted with continents and i. — MUIR 713:39
Highlands and the I. — MACD 628:92
i. of light — WOOLF 1093:77
mirror...to our own i. — RABAN 798:73
one of those i. — MANS 647:99
people and their favourite i. — AUDEN 46:53
see these i. — WALC 1048:35
isle a pumice i. — SHEL 928:88
an i. so long unknown — MARV 659:92
An i. under Ionian skies — SHEL 931:54
called the I. of Man — GERA 419:95
chimeras and enchanted i. — MILT 683:30
dear and happy i. — MARV 659:91
England is not the jewelled i. — ORWE 743:16
ere he arrive The happy i. — MILT 688:21
Fairest I. — DRYD 351:61
i. is full of noises — SHAK 917:34
ship, an i., a sickle moon — FLEC 393:55
shores of this happy i. — GLAD 429:53
silent i. imbowers — TENN 993:39
this sceptres i. — SHAK 867:48
isles fished by obstinate i. — POUND 785:61
I. of fragrance — POPE 783:6
taketh up the i. — BIBLE 126:88
Venice...thron'd on her hundred i.! — BYRON 220:92
islets acini degenerate leaving I. — BANT 70:4
Islington from I. to Marybone — BLAKE 168:7
isolated i., shut in little boxes — BAIN 62:77
splendidly i. in Europe — FOST 399:58
isolation mute chandeliered i. — CAPO 231:88
personal i. to gentile — ROTH 826:23
Israel bring you into the land of I. — BIBLE 129:39
chariot of I. — BIBLE 111:73
glory of thy people I. — BIBLE 142:79
God is good to I. — BIBLE 117:89
Hear, O I. — BIBLE 108:90
If he be the King of I. — BIBLE 140:54
In I. it's enough — ROTH 826:19
I.'s head forlorn — LAZA 588:27
I. loved Joseph — BIBLE 105:39
I.'s monarch — DRYD 349:9
I. shall be a proverb — BIBLE 111:56
judgement of the children of I. — BIBLE 107:70
lost sheep of the house of I. — BIBLE 136:73
no king in I. — BIBLE 109:23
no, not in I. — BIBLE 136:64

Israel (*contd.*)
of the stock of I. — BIBLE 153:10
Palestinians in I. — OROU 741:79
ruler in I. — BIBLE 130:62
smote the king of I. — BIBLE 111:72
there is a prophet in I. — BIBLE 111:77
These be thy gods, O I. — BIBLE 107:71
When I. was a child — BIBLE 130:53
issue great i. between the free world — KENN 551:83
i. of that darling Plea — FLET 394:67
poverty, as an i. — KRUG 570:4
issues i. and the highest authorities — SHUL 936:35
truth about important i. — LEWO 603:74
isthmus this i. of a middle state — POPE 780:42
Italia I.! oh I. — BYRON 220:95
Italian cursed be the I. — GARI 415:24
expensive i. pictures — BERE 94:37
I. character has to — MUSS 716:90
speech...dulcet as I. — QUIL 797:59
to women [I speak] I. — CHAR 253:90
Italy evoke the soul of I. — MAZZ 666:12
from I. that we launch — MARI 651:68
graved inside of it, 'I.' — BROW 199:63
Greece, I., and England did adorn — DRYD 351:58
I....garden of the world — BYRON 220:93
I. is a geographical expression — METT 673:29
made I. from designs — TWAIN 1032:60
not been in I. — JOHN 530:87
opera houses in I. — JOHN 524:69
Paradise of exiles, I.! — SHEL 927:67
ruined by residence in I. — RUSK 831:7
Troy and reach I. — VIRG 1045:79
itch disease...an i. — MUSC 716:81
i. all over — TWAIN 1032:76
i. but a kind of colourable right — LEST 599:13
i. of praise? — CAREW 232:7
Mine eyes doth i. — SHAK 900:50
poetry is like having an i. — WARR 1054:32
poor i. of your opinion — SHAK 910:1
item any i. on the agenda — PARK 755:33
iteration damnable i. day after day — STEAD 964:5
i. of nuptials — CONG 282:46
Ithaka I. always in your mind — CAVA 246:74
itself Forever be I. again — GINS 428:32
i. and doubt of i. — TILL 1020:62
itsy I. bitsy...Bikini — VANCE 1039:93
Itylus half assured for I. — SWIN 986:23
ivory cargo of i., And apes — MASE 662:37
downstairs from their I. Towers — SMITH 947:19
i. on which I work — AUST 52:60
i. sun — PIER 769:34
ivy creeping i. clings to wood — COWP 292:46
dead walls...Their i. mantles — BYRON 220:99
like i. round a sapling — SHER 933:96
myrtle and i. of sweet — BYRON 223:65
myrtles, brown i. — MILT 684:38
pluck an i. branch for me — ROSS 823:70
ivy-mantled yonder i.-m. tower — GRAY 442:63

Jabberwock Beware the J., my son! — CARR 239:47
jack j. in the box — ELKIN 374:99
When I kissed the j. — SHAK 915:98
Jack grunted Harry to J. — SASS 845:28
if J. were President — ONAS 739:39
J....a charming name — WILDE 1077:77
J.—I'm all right! — BONE 172:80
J. on the gallows-tree! — SCOTT 854:76
one vote—for J. — ONAS 739:43
sack-and-sugar J.? — SHAK 875:40
The days of you and J. — ONAS 739:42
This J., joke — HOPK 492:7
jack-in-a-box bounced up like a j. — HUGH 500:46
jack-knife Just a j.-k. has Macheath — BREC 186:24
jackal Faith, like a j. — MELV 667:31

Jesus (*contd.*)

Sacred Heart o' J. — OCAS 735:75
Stand Up For J.! — DUFF 354:23
sweet reasonableness of J. — ARNO 40:35
sweet the name of J. — NEWT 725:44
thing that J. really would've liked — SALI 839:27
When J. came to Birmingham — STUD 980:15
When J. heard it, he marvelled — BIBLE 136:64
when J. was born in Bethlehem — BIBLE 133:23
wrong to…blame J. — BENN 90:66

Jesuses trained seals, creeping J. — MACD 628:92

Jew eke most lovely J. — SHAK 901:78
greatest J. since Jesus Christ — ROBB 813:13
Hath not a J. eyes? — SHAK 872:80
In heathen, Turk or J. — BLAKE 166:65
J. is only the name — MILL 677:6
J. of Tarsus — BIBLE 148:7
like an…assimilated J. — OBRI 734:62
makes you a normal J. — ROTH 826:20
neither Greek nor J. — BIBLE 153:21
neither J. nor Greek — BIBLE 152:80
States…the J. among the nations — FERB 385:7
take my leave of the J. — SHAK 874:25
to the J. first — BIBLE 148:11

jewel chastity's the j. — SHAK 901:78
For your sake j. — SHAK 898:11
has one j. left — MILT 686:71
j. in a…chest. — SHAK 866:40
j.…judged by the light — ANON 27:62
j. of the kingdom — SUN 982:36
j. that we find — SHAK 896:67
precious j. in his head — SHAK 885:75
rich j. in an Ethiope's ear — SHAK 868:82
time's best j. — SHAK 914:68

jewel-sea love her j.-s. — MACK 632:52

jewelled j. mass of millinery — TENN 1001:77

jewellers through most j.' hands — WEBS 1060:50

jewelry Don't ever wear artistic j. — COLE 276:33
gigantic chunks of costume j. — LAUR 584:45
hang on to her j. — LOOS 613:31
rest…can rattle your j. — LENN 596:54

jewels capital bosom to hang j. upon — DICK 325:49
Dumb j.…move a woman's mind — SHAK 860:82
Health and…body are two j. — FLET 394:76
j. five-words long — TENN 996:92
j. for a set of beads — SHAK 867:62
precious j. into a garret — BACON 56:38
reft the j. from her hair — HYDE 509:14
unvalued j. — SHAK 863:54
With gold and j. cover — POPE 778:80

Jewish insight of the J. prophets — NIEB 727:64
J. family was an inviolate — ROTH 826:23
J. I don't work out — RIVE 813:4
J. Puritan of the middle — NEME 722:5
J. Queen of Egypt — TAYL 992:15
solution of the J. problem — GOER 431:68

Jews All men are J. — MALA 641:6
don't ask employers…to like J. — BORO 179:22
Have mercy upon all J. — BOOK 174:11
Hitler attacked the J. — NIEM 727:68
J., a headstrong…race — DRYD 349:7
J. and Arabs should settle — AUST 53:75
J. in Palestine — OROU 741:79
J. which believeth not — BIBLE 148:97
King of the J. — BIBLE 146:69
national home for the J. — BALF 65:17
noticed that J. shout? — ROTH 826:19
The Irish and the J. have a psychosis — BEHAN 84:62
To choose The J. — EWER 381:48
university where…the J. are hosts — SACH 835:57
What captivity was to the J. — WILDE 1075:31

Jezebel J.…painted her face — BIBLE 111:80

jib cut of his j. — DOUG 342:71

jilt cruel j. to me — MORSE 709:90

jingle must j. in his ears — WOLL 1091:37

jingles trifles and j. — BACON 59:8

jingling one j. padlock — POPE 783:3

Jingo by J. if we do — HUNT 504:15

jo For auld lang syne, my j. — BURNS 210:95
John Anderson, my j. — BURNS 211:6

Joan If J. of Arc had been born — SIMON 939:81
play St. J. — THOR 1017:96

job $60 GI j. — EISE 364:89
difficultest j. a man can do — DAVI 307:95
finish the j. — CHUR 264:18
hard j. of using reason — WILS 1084:18
How would you like a j. — PLAN 773:87
husband is a whole-time j. — BENN 91:91
If they will only do their j. — SELZ 858:43
In this j., to tell — MILL 677:13
It's a man's j. — AESC 9:58
j., as I see it — MACD 628:95
j. is likely to be ill-done — KEYN 555:35
j. of the nurture of children — PALEY 751:61
Keeping up…a full-time j. — CRISP 296:32
loneliest j. in the world — BALD 64:8
loses his j. — TRUM 1030:26
lost the j. — JOYCE 538:50
man who wants to do a good j. — ELIOT 371:42
most improper j. — TOLK 1022:90
Nae harder j. to mortals — MACD 627:78
neighbour loses his j. — REAG 803:61
only doing my j. if they do — WHIT 1072:70
our j. to make women unhappy — PUCK 794:16
second most important j. — GARN 415:28
since he lost his j. — MORG 708:65
social order…my j. to preserve — FRAN 401:88
to do the j. too long — SWIFT 984:80
whether my j. is a j. — KNIG 567:54
will always have a j. — RAVI 802:45

Job All books are the Book of J. — ELKIN 374:98
blessed the latter end of J. — BIBLE 113:28
J. open his mouth in vain — BIBLE 113:16
poor as J. — SHAK 877:82

Jobiska Aunt J. made him drink — LEAR 590:62
Aunt J.'s Runcible Cat — LEAR 590:64

jobs climbing into j. — REST 807:17
fewer the j. worth doing — JAY 519:75
Mine is one of the j. — WEAT 1058:13
woman…not the top j. — THAT 1007:3

Jock J., when ye hae naething — SCOTT 855:93
stop yer tickling, J.! — LAUD 583:37
tears…For J. of Hazeldean — SCOTT 854:78
Wi' J. of Hazeldean — SCOTT 854:80

jocosity j. catches the crowd — MARQ 656:40

jocund As gentle and as j. — SHAK 866:41
j. day Stands tiptoe — SHAK 869:11

Joe J., long dead — SLES 943:57
Say it ain't so, J. — ANON 25:32

jog As we j. on — STER 969:90
J. on, j. on — SHAK 911:27

jogging J. is for people — WOOD 1091:45
J. is very beneficial — SCHU 850:12

Johannesburg No second J. — PATON 761:13

john leaning on the j. door — OHARA 737:8

John I J. saw the holy city — BIBLE 158:34
J. Brown is stowed — NASH 720:62
J., like J. — FARJ 383:63
J. had his raiment of camel's hair — BIBLE 133:26
J. seeth Jesus — BIBLE 145:28
J. to the seven churches — BIBLE 156:96
notorious domesticity for J. — WILDE 1077:77
shew J. again those things — BIBLE 137:83
unto the multitudes concerning J. — BIBLE 137:84
why…name your baby 'J.' — GOLD 434:40

Johnny Little J. Head-in-Air — HOFF 484:59
not despair For J. Head-in-Air — PUDN 794:17
sleeps as sound As J. Underground — PUDN 794:17

Johnson heroism of J. — STEV 974:22
J. approached a…position — MANC 644:63
J.'s morality — HAWT 462:83
J. went through three years — WHITE 1071:46
that great man, Dr J. — WESL 1067:72
You are a philosopher, Dr J. — EDWA 362:53

Johnsonian subtlety of J. strategy — MANC 644:64

joined j. with no foot-landrakers — SHAK 875:47

joiner imagination of a lodge j. — MENC 670:90
j. with j. — HESI 479:81

joint manacled with j. or limb — MILT 687:25
The time was out of j. — STRA 979:93
together every j. and member — MILT 686:72

jointed It is nothing j.; it flows — JAMES 517:40

joints between the j. of the harness — BIBLE 111:72
fettle your fine j. — SHAK 869:13
j. are stiff — SHAK 869:14

joke bitter cosmic j. — GELL 417:69
every j. is…a custard pie — ORWE 743:22
family j. that when — ROTH 826:10
funniest j. in the world — SHAW 923:72
Housekeeping ain't no j. — ALCO 12:98
if a j. were a charity auction — MACI 631:39
If we live inside a bad j. — RABAN 798:74
j.'s a very serious thing — CHUR 262:36
many a j. had he — GOLD 433:12
our only j. — BARR 73:49

jokes bad j. of history — GUED 448:76
difference of taste in j. — ELIOT 366:43
don't forget j. — ROGE 820:22
hackneyed j. from Miller — BYRON 219:60
Krishna's j. may be vapid — FORS 399:57
my little j. on Thee — FROST 407:1
no j.,…no chance — ANON 26:50
no more j. in Music-halls — SASS 845:22
shouldn't make j. — CARR 239:52
telling j. back there — KAUF 543:21
telling j. or gossiping — CABR 224:81

joking My way of j. — SHAW 923:72

jollier j. than the people — LUCAS 618:24

jolly If I was very ragged and j. — DICK 322:69

jolly-rogered and the j.-r. sea — THOM 1011:81

Jonas sign of the prophet J. — BIBLE 137:93

Jonathan distressed for…J. — BIBLE 110:44

Joneses Keeping up with the J. — CRISP 296:32

jonquils land-locked pools of j. — BETJ 100:37

Jonson Ben J. his best piece of poetry — JONS 535:7
In Spenser, and in J., Art — DENH 315:55
J. was the Virgil — DRYD 347:65
O rare Ben J. — JONS 536:12
Too nicely J. knew the critic's part — COLL 276:41

Jordan draw up J. into his mouth — BIBLE 113:25
I call him J. — WINT 1087:67
J. running through it — HOPK 492:97

jostle rough sense of the daily j. — DELI 315:42

jot j. of former love retain — DRAY 345:40

jouissance naught but j. — GREE 445:32

journal editor of a village j. — MOOD 703:98
keep up a daily j. — STARR 963:1
leading j. of Europe — HAZL 463:7

journalism context of… j. — THOM 1014:37
crisis in j. — LIPP 606:30
higher law in j. — LIPP 606:31
j.…as an extension of history — SAMP 840:42
j. largely consists in saying' — CHES 259:35
j.…read once — CONN 283:58
Modern j. — WILDE 1076:42

journalist Any daily j. will tell you — ORWE 744:25
duty of a j. — STEAD 964:7
functions of the modern j. — CURZ 302:28
historian is often only a j. — KRAUS 569:89
j. exists…as the publicity agent — ORWE 742:88
j. is hardly an authority — DAFOE 303:38
life of the j. — GIBB 422:33

journalist (*contd.*)
making of a j. — KRAUS 569:88
journalists Diplomats lie to j. — KRAUS 569:90
J. say a thing — BENN 91:92
J....require some protection — BLACK 164:46
journals articles...in scientific j. — FEYN 387:33
Of all j. — TIMES 1020:70
journey A Long Day's J. — ONEI 740:60
begin a j. on Sundays — SWIFT 986:14
Business at the end of its j. — LLOYD 608:51
day's j. into the wilderness — BIBLE 111:68
death the j.'s end — DRYD 352:93
define your own horror j. — GELL 417:71
dreariest and longest j. — SHEL 931:52
he who...has taken a wondrous j. — BELL 86:90
heavy riches but a j. — SHAK 897:78
intellectual j. — MILLS 679:63
j.'s end, here is my butt — SHAK 900:61
j. from London — TALB 990:86
j. in my head — SHAK 913:56
j. is like a marriage — STEI 966:59
j. of life — DICK 327:79
j. of our life — DANTE 305:67
j. on, till you come — LAUD 583:40
j. ov life — BILL 162:4
j. take the whole long day? — ROSS 824:75
j. that required courage — MURP 715:72
j. towards oblivion — LAWR 587:6
Nothing for my J. Now — ANGE 20:34
pursuing, or he is in a j. — BIBLE 111:64
robbed upon a j. — STEV 973:94
soul of a j. is liberty — MARP 655:32
such a long j. — ELIOT 369:3
To j. is better than to arrive — WELD 1062:93
visible portions of the j. — STARK 963:97
well this j. be his — EDWA 361:47
when the j.'s over — HOUS 494:42
Whenever I prepare for a j. — MANS 647:11
worst time...to take a j. — ANDR 19:13
journey-work j.-w. of the stars — WHIT 1072:79
journeys Do not plan long j. — AUGU 50:18
j. through the valley — LEE 593:18
successive j. run — WATTS 1055:57
who was driven far j. — HOMER 488:24
worst of worse j. — WOOD 1092:47
Jove if J. stray — SHAK 910:92
J. and Fate require — POPE 782:91
J.'s dread clamours — SHAK 899:40
J. might have sipped — MARL 655:26
Now J. in his next commodity — SHAK 895:21
threshold of J.'s court — MILT 683:18
jow j. or ring — FERG 386:16
joy amidst that j. and uproar — CAMP 227:30
an ace of j. up his sleeve — ONDA 739:46
at enmity with j. — WORD 1098:54
at the expense of j. — FORS 398:33
bed Of crimson j. — BLAKE 167:88
better...to weep at j. — SHAK 878:26
binds to himself a j. — BLAKE 166:82
Break forth into j. — BIBLE 127:97
Certainty. Feeling. J. — PASC 758:81
Dear distress, and j. allied — CULL 299:70
doubt...exiles my present j. — ELIZ 373:87
eat thy bread with j. — BIBLE 123:33
enter thou into the j. of thy lord — BIBLE 140:41
go out with j. — BIBLE 127:7
good tidings of great j. — BIBLE 142:78
greater j. than love itself — PROU 793:97
harp, his sole remaining j. — SCOTT 853:42
heart's so full of j. — DRYD 348:93
Hope to j. is little less — SHAK 867:52
if this be j. — GOLD 433:14
in glory and in j. — WORD 1097:44
in j. and woe — SURR 982:41

joy (*contd.*)
is no j. but calm! — TENN 994:50
it is a j. to enjoy what is good — GOET 431:71
J. always came after pain — APOL 32:92
J. and function of poetry — THOM 1010:72
j. and their glory must be — ABEL 1:4
j. at last — GUY 449:96
j. delights in j. — SHAK 912:45
j....From the green fields — WORD 1095:17
j. he gave me — AUDEN 49:3
J., I did lock thee up — HERB 476:33
j. in the presence of the angels — BIBLE 143:97
J. is fleeting — KENN 550:56
j. of elevated thoughts — WORD 1094:98
J. of heav'n...come down — WESL 1066:63
j. of living speech — SPEN 957:6
j. of the artist — MILL 678:34
j. of the Lord is your strength — BIBLE 112:92
j. of the whole earth — BIBLE 116:75
j. of thy salvation — BIBLE 116:78
j. of working — KIPL 562:60
j. past j. calls out — SHAK 869:9
J. ruled the day — DRYD 352:96
J. shivers in the corner — ROBI 815:33
j. that the day has brought — BOND 172:79
j. they were making — ROBE 814:15
j. to his mighty heart — KIPL 561:40
know of no j. — FIRB 389:72
Labour without j. — RUSK 831:1
Let every heart exult with j. — DODD 335:44
Like an unbodied j. — SHEL 929:99
love and j. that fights — MANS 647:98
Man was made for J. and Woe — BLAKE 168:3
moment of j. is...harder to get — PO 775:38
My scrip of j. — RALE 800:13
no j. in poring out one's sins — FIRB 389:73
Nor j. nor grieve too much — DRYD 352:93
not an obligation but a j. — KILLY 556:62
now 'tis little j. — HOOD 489:38
O j.! that in our embers — WORD 1098:52
oil of j. for mourning — BIBLE 127:12
passages of j. — JOHN 525:83
perfect j. therein I find — DYER 358:87
planet, all j. gone — LOWE 617:8
prefectest herald of j. — SHAK 879:40
promise of untrammeled j. — HOLM 485:75
reap in j. — BIBLE 119:40
running stream of sparkling j. — DICK 325:29
Scarce any j. — SHAK 912:42
secret of j. — WALK 1049:59
shall run mad with j. — MIDD 673:45
sheer j. of felicitous statement — SCHL 848:74
short-haired j. and roughness — SNYD 951:86
snatch a fearful j. — GRAY 441:46
sons of God shouted for j. — BIBLE 113:18
taste is now of j. — MILT 690:57
There's not a j. — BYRON 221:17
Thine be ilka j. and treasure — BURNS 212:26
Thou Child of J. — WORD 1097:14
Uninterrupted j., unrivalled love — MILT 689:32
vehicle of j. — HOOV 490:61
Where I in lust and j. — SURR 982:43
Where there is sadness, j. — FRAN 401:91
joy-bells Makes j.-b. ring — MASE 662:46
joyance With thy keen clear j. — SHEL 929:4
Joyce clumsy olla putirida J. — LAWR 586:96
J. was a synthesizer — BECK 81:5
J.'s Finnegans Wake — NICO 727:62
read Proust, Faulkner, J. — VARG 1040:7
joyful a j. Song I'll raise — ADDI 7:20
All Christendom ought to feel j. — COLU 278:63
be j. in the Lord — BOOK 177:89
j. with swift movement — ANON 21:55
make a j. noise — BIBLE 117:6

joys all that's precious in our j. — STER 970:28
All my j. to this are folly — BURT 214:64
blinding with brairs my j. — BLAKE 167:91
buy the j. o'er dear — BURNS 212:21
feeling that lures us on to j. — CONR 284:98
fleeting j. Of Paradise — MILT 693:18
[Friendship] redoubleth j. — BACON 58:99
hide our j. no longer — SHAK 896:55
homely j. — GRAY 442:66
its j., and fears — WORD 1098:56
j. await us there — NEALE 722:93
J. in another's loss of ease — BLAKE 167:86
j. of marriage — FORD 397:12
j. of parents — BACON 57:54
present j....to flesh and blood — DRYD 351:54
profanation of our j. — DONNE 337:90
Repeating only j. above — LOVE 615:68
rich man's j. increase — GOLD 433:15
should we defer our j.? — JONS 534:85
sole part of all these j. — MILT 690:58
Some unknown j. there be — TRAH 1024:25
Time, which takes...our j. — RALE 800:16
vain deluding J. — MILT 682:5
voice less loud, through its j. — BROW 198:40
jubilate J. Deo, omnis terra — BIBLE 159:44
jubilation extraordinary sense of j. — GREE 444:22
Jubilee first day of our J. is death — BROW 195:84
Jubjub Beware the J. bird — CARR 239:47
Judas Damned below J. — COWP 291:25
J. Iscariot, went unto the chief priests — BIBLE 140:47
J. who writes the biography — WILDE 1076:36
So J. did to Christ — SHAK 867:63
Whether J. I. Had God on his side — DYLAN 358:92
judge after a time they j. them — WILDE 1077:70
bringing the j....into the dock — ALGR 13:26
decided by the j. — JOHN 529:65
Forbear to j. — SHAK 861:7
Here comes the j. — MARK 652:79
I'll be j., I'll be jury — CARR 238:23
in righteousness he doth j. — BIBLE 158:30
indifferent j. — SIDN 937:53
j. a man by his foes — CONR 284:95
j. a man more certainly — HUGO 502:87
j. and the brother are one — WILS 1086:44
j. how wide the limits stand — GOLD 433:15
j. I carried within me — CARP 237:8
j. in the legal and moral sense — DEWEY 319:96
j. is not supposed to know — PARK 755:27
j. less harshly — BRAC 183:71
J. not the play — QUAR 796:52
J. not, that ye be not judged — BIBLE 135:54
J. of all the earth — BIBLE 105:24
j. of the widows — BIBLE 116:86
j. of truth, in endless error — POPE 780:43
j. rarely — PENN 764:57
j. standeth before the door — BIBLE 155:71
Let India be my j. — CURZ 302:29
make us a king to j. us — BIBLE 110:32
O wise young j. — SHAK 873:94
sober as a J. — FIEL 388:48
Who made thee a prince and a j. — BIBLE 106:52
You wags that j. — OTWAY 746:77
judged j. by our peers — BALZ 68:71
j. by the color — KING 557:76
j....through her toilette — DE 311:64
that you are j. — HARDY 456:95
judgement Aaron shall bear the j. — BIBLE 107:70
after this the j. — BIBLE 154:48
better j. growing — SHAK 914:78
biases the j. — DOYLE 343:84
conformity of our j. — DIDE 329:25
criterion of wisdom to vulgar j. — BURKE 208:42
Daniel come to j. — SHAK 873:94
Do not wait for the last j. — CAMUS 229:60

judgement (*contd.*)

expect a j.	DICK 324:22
God will bring thee into j.	BIBLE 123:41
goosecap and hast no j.	NASHE 721:78
great J. seat	KIPL 560:23
greater j. shewn in deviating	ADDI 8:38
green in j.	SHAK 905:67
He j. brings	OAKL 733:52
if it only added j. to insight	FORS 398:39
in danger of the j.	BIBLE 134:39
j. faileth me	KNOX 567:58
j. fouk wou'd hae a dubt on	FERG 385:15
j. frame By her...standard	POPE 778:78
j. is a mere lottery	DRYD 347:61
j. is...subject to affection	JOHN 531:10
j. Of all mankind	SCHI 847:66
j. of the great whore	BIBLE 158:27
j. that makes an impact	LEAV 591:76
j. that yourself arise	SHAK 913:64
j. what they see	MIDD 673:42
j. with this generation	BIBLE 137:94
Last J.'s fire must cure this place	BROW 198:49
last j. of mankind	FRYE 408:20
Men of business have a solid j.	BAGE 61:63
men of j. frame	MARL 653:98
Moral j.	NIET 728:86
neither do the aged understand j.	BIBLE 113:15
not a disease but an error of j.	DICK 320:12
notoriously unsound in j.	HOLM 486:83
O j.! thou art fled	SHAK 884:50
on whose j. they	TUCH 1031:47
people's j. always true	DRYD 350:26
possessing j.	KEYN 554:34
power of j.	HARD 456:80
put in the breastplate of j.	BIBLE 107:70
reserve thy j.	SHAK 888:65
spirit and j. equal	MILT 694:36
still have j. here	SHAK 907:31
till J. Tide	KIPL 563:99
Too many pass j.	TRUM 1030:27
true j. day	ANON 23:98
vulgar...capacities do make a j.	BACON 55:7
wait till J. break	DICK 328:7
What j. I had increases	DRYD 352:77
would not give his j. rashly	ADDI 7:12

judgements Delivers brawling j.

	TENN 1002:9
j. below our own	BROW 195:67
j. of the English law	SYNGE 988:63
j. of the Lord are true	BIBLE 114:45
j. on political conduct	NEW 724:24
moral j. do not say anything	AYER 53:80
obstinate, ridiculous j.	MORE 706:44
sentinels unto our j.	MIDD 673:42

judges doctors, j....beadles

	MARX 660:8
hundred j. have declared	QUIL 797:58
hungry j.	POPE 778:89
j. thronging thickly	WILDE 1075:26
threw me in front of the J.	BETJ 101:56
When j. steal themselves	SHAK 897:74

judging j. others according to

	LAFO 574:81
j. the values of things	JEVO 521:21
knack of j. a distance	REED 805:82
the fatigue of j. for themselves	SHER 934:6
happy condition of j.	MELV 668:46
Heaven the j. ...spectator	RALE 800:14

jug j., j., j., tereu

	LYLY 620:57
Pap took the j.	TWAIN 1033:83
w'en it git loose fum de j.	HARR 458:29

Juggins you J.! — PUNCH 795:32

juggler perceive a j.'s sleight — BUTL 217:20

jugglers nimble j. that deceive the eye — SHAK 865:1

juice j. of deliberate, journalistic — LAWR 586:96

lukewarm parsnip j.	WOOL 1094:88
nor half so full of j.	SUCK 981:21

juice (*contd.*)

runnel of j.	RANS 802:33
whether there is enough j.	GEDD 417:63

juices Keep the j. flowing

	PAIGE 750:41
sexual j. flow toward a painting	FUEN 409:26

juke j. box's blowin' a fuse — BERRY 98:4

Julia in silks my J. goes — HERR 478:67

thought of Donna J.'s eyes — BYRON 222:30

Julian remembered poor J. — HEMI 471:31

Juliet east, and J. is the sun

	SHAK 868:85
J. and her Romeo	SHAK 870:24
Unless philosophy can make a J.	SHAK 869:8

July born on the fourth of J.

	COHAN 272:69
J.'s day as short	SHAK 911:19
second day of J. 1776	ADAMS 5:86
winter—ending in J.	BYRON 223:58

Jumblies land where the J. live — LEAR 590:54

jump decide which way to j.

	BOYC 182:60
J. her, and thump her	SHAK 912:35
the life to come	SHAK 907:31
j. with common spirits	SHAK 874:30

jumping j. over the moon — RAMS 801:18

June It was late J.

	THOM 1012:99
Jolly J., arrayed	SPEN 959:42
J. for beauty's heightening	ARNO 39:15
made December J.	TENN 1000:54
newly sprung in J.	BURNS 212:40
rare as a day in J.	LOWE 616:82

jungle art world is a j.

	HAMM 453:49
courts of Europe are a j.	BOLT 172:77
dangerous to explore a j.	HAWT 461:64
J. star or j. track	CULL 299:68
law of the j.	JUMB 539:70
Law of the J.	KIPL 561:52
Mumbo-Jumbo is dead in the j.	LIND 605:14
New York is a j.	AMIS 17:87
wise primitive in a giant j.	MAIL 639:67

jungles lost...in the j. of Indochina — MACG 630:33

juniper sat down under a j. tree

	BIBLE 111:68
white leopards sat under a j.-tree	ELIOT 370:11

junk j. food — GASS 416:35

junkyards j. of secular carpentry — ROSE 823:64

Juno figure of J.

	BARR 73:56
haughty J.'s unrelenting hate	DRYD 352:76

Jupiter By J., an angel

	SHAK 916:13
J. from above	OVID 747:95
temple of J.	GIBB 421:29

juries j. fill their stomachs — SYNGE 988:63

jurisprudence American j. — CAPO 231:80

jury acquitted by a Limerick j.

	ADAMS 6:93
I'll be judge, I'll be j.	CARR 238:23
j. is only as sound	LEE 593:10
j. passing on the prisoner's life	SHAK 896:66
lawyer trying to pick a smart j.	BAIL 62:67
Press is the living J.	BENN 92:3
Trial by j.	DENM 316:59
tried before a j.	JOHN 529:83

jury-men that j.-m. may dine — POPE 778:89

just and I should be j.

	HERB 475:16
Be j., my lovely swain	BEHN 85:67
cause is j.	DICK 329:22
Give it because it is j.	LLOY 609:63
gods are j.	SHAK 904:47
How j., how bountiful	WORD 1101:93
it is our j. exaltation	PITT 772:73
j....are not the leaders	CONR 285:7
j., gentle, wise	SHEL 930:25
j. people...are happier than unjust	PLATO 774:19
j. shall live by faith	BIBLE 148:11
sendeth rain on the j.	BIBLE 134:45
Shall mortal man be more j.	BIBLE 112:1
soul of the j.	STAEL 961:72
Thou art indeed j., Lord	HOPK 492:8
thou art j.	TENN 998:16

just (*contd.*)

whatsoever things are j.	BIBLE 153:15

justice act...of duty and of j.

	PITT 771:71
ain't the shop for j.	DICK 321:71
destruction of all j.	MORE 707:55
Die he or j. must	MILT 689:38
do j. to my character	EMMET 378:81
dream of social j.	NGUY 725:48
Equal and exact j.	JEFF 520:94
fear...the j. of God	ELIOT 370:35
firm belief in the j. of our case	WASH 1054:41
have ravished j.	WEBS 1060:1
Injustice anywhere is a threat to j.	KING 557:75
j. and mercy are reconciled	WILS 1086:44
J. being allowed to do	BUTL 218:42
J. is doing one's work	PLATO 774:20
J. is such a fine thing	LESA 598:1
J. is superior	PLATO 774:26
J. is the constant	JUST 540:76
J. is the means	FRAN 401:88
J. is truth	DISR 333:97
j. must be carried out	MARIE 651:64
j., or happiness or prosperity	CURZ 302:29
j. should consider	HELO 469:8
J. should not only be done	HEWA 479:85
j. was done	HARDY 456:7
Let j. be done	FERD 385:13
Let J. be done	MANS 648:15
Let j. be done	WATS 1055:54
Literature...makes j.	PALEY 751:59
love of j. in most men	LARO 582:23
may become a j.	JONS 535:97
Mercy...and j. come from God	WAITE 1048:9
no business with j.	JOHN 529:65
of all equity and j.	KNOX 567:57
Poetic j., with her lifted scale	POPE 782:92
Posterity will do j. to...Gladstone	DISR 333:20
price of j. is eternal publicity	BENN 91:87
principles of equity and j.	PEEL 763:43
Publicity is the very soul of j.	BENT 93:18
pursuit of j.	GOLD 433:31
quicker Than j., judge or vicar	SHER 933:89
Revenge is a kind of wild j.	BACON 56:7
rule of distributive j.	HOMA 487:8
seldom has j. enough to accuse	GOLD 432:3
small things and j.	SOPH 953:17
temper so J. with mercy	MILT 693:42
Thwackum was for doing j.	FIEL 388:50
treat the films...with less than j.	ANDE 18:4
under which j.	UNIT 1036:45
what humanity, reason, j., tells me	BURKE 207:9
when I show j.	SHAK 896:69
When mercy seasons j.	SHAK 873:93
Where j. grows	SPEN 958:9
Where j. is denied	DOUG 342:74
which is the j.	SHAK 904:44

justification Englishman's j. in India — CURZ 302:29

j. in every line	CONR 284:87
social and psychological j.	KEYN 555:41

justifications power j. would go on — STEI 967:65

justified half as good as j. — BUTL 217:23

justifies that j. the end — TROT 1029:10

justify end cannot j. the means — HUXL 507:73

the less there is to j.	TWAIN 1032:10
j. and affirm...beliefs	ELLI 375:17

justifying better j. themselves — SZASZ 989:67

justitia Fiat j. — FERD 385:13

Fiat j.	WATS 1055:54
Fiat j., pereat coelum	ADAMS 6:3

jutty No j., frieze — SHAK 907:30

juvescence j. of the year — ELIOT 368:69

juxtaposition Allah...and J. — CLOU 271:43

Kaa thou art hungry, O K. — KIPL 561:50

kaleidoscope it's like a beautiful k. — COLE 273:80
kamikaze the k. ground staff — PARK 755:30
kangaroo K., K.! — FIELD 387:39
Tie Me K. Down, Sport — HARR 458:34
kangaroos little k. flying about — WILDE 1076:59
Kansas famers of K. — LEASE 591:72
horses o' K. think — KIPL 562:63
nights in K. City close early — MAIL 639:84
Kasper Old K.'s work was done — SOUT 954:31
Kate angel is like you, K. — SHAK 882:9
kiss me, K. — SHAK 864:79
sometimes K. the curst — SHAK 864:77
Swear me, K. — SHAK 876:62
witchcraft in your lips, K. — SHAK 882:11
Kathmandu to the north of K. — HAYES 462:92
Kean K. is original — COLE 275:21
There is in K. — HAZL 463:95
keel Set k. to the breakers — POUND 786:70
keener grows k. with constant use — IRVI 513:63
keep k., and pass, and turn again — EMER 377:64
k. our people in — KENN 552:84
k. the salary — GOMEZ 434:50
k. things like this — HUGH 500:37
love to k. it by me — JERO 521:8
may God k. me there — JOAN 522:28
time to k. — BIBLE 122:19
To k. him...two — DOUG 342:67
you can k. the lot — JAY 519:72
keeper Am I my brother's k.? — BIBLE 104:5
first lost k. — SEXT 859:62
k. of his conscience...k. of the stone — DAVI 308:16
Lord is thy k. — BIBLE 119:36
keepers k. of the house shall tremble — BIBLE 123:42
keeps gave it us for k. — AYRES 53:83
keepsake rope for a k. — TWAIN 1034:5
Kelly Fanny K.'s divine plain face — LAMB 576:17
Kemble Mr K. sacrifices too much — HAZL 463:96
Kennedy epitaph on the K. — WHITE 1071:49
Mrs K. is going to marry — JOHN 523:45
you're no Jack K. — BENT 93:32
Kennedys we K., we eat Rockerfellers — KENN 553:6
Who killed the K.? — JAGG 515:97
kennel whips to k. The renegade — RANS 802:37
Kensal Paradise by way of K. — CHES 259:33
Kent everyone knows K. — DICK 320:18
K. and Christendom — WYATT 1102:26
Kentish courts of K. Town — BETJ 100:40
fog on the K. heights — DICK 324:18
kept Married women are k. women — SMITH 947:20
kerchiefed k. in a comely cloud — MILT 683:13
Kern to K. or Cole Porter — GERS 420:9
kernel Haldis the k., sueit — HENR 473:69
k. is boredom — GELL 417:71
k. scarcely compensates...cracking — BRON 190:88
kernels meagre hill of k. — RANS 802:33
Kerouac not even Mr K. — CAPO 230:78
Ketch as Jack K.'s wife said — DRYD 351:64
kettle different k. of fish — SHAR 919:82
guy that plays the k. drums — SALI 839:27
how agree the k. — BIBLE 132:1
Polly put the k. on — DICK 322:63
speech is like a cracked k. — FLAU 392:38
Kew his Highness' dog at K. — POPE 783:12
K. in lilac-time — NOYES 732:41
key easy k. Dost open life — DRYD 349:99
Getting into the k. of C sharp — BUTL 217:39
k. is Russian national interest — CHUR 264:11
k. of knowledge — BIBLE 143:93
k. of the bottomless pit — BIBLE 157:17
k. to human warmth — ISHI 513:77
looking for the k. — BENN 90:71
out of k. with his time — POUND 785:60
smile is often the k. — SAIN 836:86
the k., the minor k., to existence — BLIX 169:33

key (contd.)
Turn the k. deftly — KEATS 545:63
keyboard Color is the k. — KAND 541:97
song along the k. — OHARA 737:8
keyhole age has a k. — MACC 625:49
out at the k — SHAK 887:24
Keynes cure...before K. — ROBI 815:37
keys enter the names and hand the k. — MANS 647:3
fingers on these k. — STEV 971:42
k. of all the creeds — TENN 998:27
k. of hell and of death — BIBLE 157:1
k. of Paradise — DEQU 316:65
k. of the kingdom of heaven — BIBLE 138:13
k. of the...liquor store — BALL 65:25
Over the noisy k. — PROC 792:76
keystone night's black arch the k. — BURNS 211:16
khaki gentleman in K. — KIPL 562:67
zephyr and k. shorts — BETJ 99:32
Khan In Xanadu did K. Kubla — COLE 274:12
kick I get no k. from champagne — PORT 784:30
If I can k. them for four years — CHAR 253:95
k. against the pricks — BIBLE 147:89
k. it about all day — HOLM 486:86
k. you out — WAUGH 1056:92
sold...for 'one and a k.' — FORM 397:27
watch...hirelings k. a ball — PRIE 789:35
kicked die or get k. out — HOOV 490:63
get his head k. off — KHRU 556:51
kicking k. and screaming — STEV 973:83
kid Here's looking at you, k. — EPST 379:99
leopard shall lie down with the k. — BIBLE 125:68
when you have a k. — HEMI 471:48
When you're a k. — ALBEE 11:83
kiddies You k. have crumpled — BETJ 100:52
kidnapped realize that I'm k. — ALLEN 14:44
kidney most unscrupulous k. — FRY 408:10
kidneys liked grilled mutton k. — JOYCE 538:53
kids cooking breakfast...for my k. — SCHR 850:8
don't have any k. yourself — LARK 582:15
help with the housework and the k. — WINT 1087:69
How many k. did you kill — ANON 27:79
k. playing some game — SALI 839:28
way k. laugh when they're hungry — STEI 966:55
Kildare broke a window in K. — JOYCE 538:55
kill almost k. a man as k. — MILT 685:55
As k. a king — SHAK 892:51
canst thou k. me — DONNE 338:4
cure the disease and k. the patient — BACON 58:1
How many kids did you kill — ANON 27:79
intendest thou to k. me — BIBLE 106:52
k. a man that a hawk — JEFF 520:84
k. a wife with kindness — SHAK 864:85
k. all the lawyers — SHAK 861:11
k., and eat — BIBLE 147:91
k. my mother — BOYD 182:64
k. sick people — MARL 653:1
K. them all — ARNA 35:52
k. us for their sport — SHAK 903:30
know, to k. and to create — BAUD 78:43
men should k. — SKEL 942:40
mettle enough...to k. care — SHAK 880:63
must men k. and die? — SHEL 932:65
My k. shall by thy k. — KIPL 561:50
never k. for sport — FROU 408:9
no approaches, but to k. — JONS 536:17
No sportsman wants to k. a fox — SHAW 925:35
not catastrophes...k. us — WOOLF 1092:56
simply has to go out and k. — LEAC 589:46
The command 'Thou shall not k.' — JOHN 522:35
Thou shalt not k. — BIBLE 106:68
Thou shalt not k. — CLOU 271:47
time to k. — BIBLE 122:19
To wit, I k. thee — SHAK 887:28
will not actually k. him — BERR 99:18

kill (contd.)
word for which you k. — WEIL 1062:85
killed don't mind your being k. — KITC 566:45
effort very nearly k. her — BELL 87:10
k. all the day long — BIBLE 116:71
k. in no time — DICK 321:33
k. not thee — SHAK 884:67
kiss thee ere I k. thee — SHAK 901:65
Who k. the Kennedys? — JAGG 515:97
would have k. each other — KING 559:3
killer k. with a ball — LARW 582:31
lover and k. are mingled — DOUG 341:57
killers K. from the egg — HUGH 500:38
Killiecrankie braes o' K. — BURNS 211:7
killing if war did not include k. — ANGE 19:24
K. care and grief — SHAK 918:54
K. care and grief — SHAK 918:56
kills cancer often k. — HALD 451:19
it k. me — HOPK 492:6
k. life within himself — SAIN 837:93
k. me some six of seven dozen — SHAK 876:53
k. the very good — HEMI 470:19
that k. and pains not? — SHAK 906:3
Time k. us — SITW 941:29
time quietly k. them — BOUC 180:38
waste remains and k. — EMPS 378:83
kilt k., the lava-lava — MURR 715:76
kin and kith own k. and k. — NASH 719:44
kin little more than k. — SHAK 888:46
makes the whole world k. — SHAK 896:53
Religon and art...close k. — CATH 244:49
kind children k. and natural — SHAK 880:74
Earth is here so k. — JERR 521:14
euerich in his k. — JAME 515:99
finish...among k. people — BEET 84:52
for such a k. heart — SHAK 878:21
for the maiming of his k. — MACG 630:22
I am one with my k. — TENN 1002:96
isolating him from his k. — PARN 756:39
K. is my love today — SHAK 915:85
k. its caressing — COCK 272:60
k. without deceit — DRYD 348:98
more than kin and less than k. — SHAK 888:46
one of their own k. — KORDA 568:79
people will always be k. — SASS 845:29
romantic poet...no other k. — FROST 407:90
should be pretty of its k. — LAMB 576:22
so constant...so k. — KEATS 545:61
So courteous, so k. — SKEL 942:34
to a k. and not to a gender — YOUR 1108:5
woman who is really k. to dogs — BEER 83:32
your lack of k. — COLUM 278:60
kinder k. to the brutes — ELIOT 365:4
kindergarten kind of spiritual k. — ROBI 815:29
kindness acts of k. — WORD 1094:97
cup o' k. — BURNS 210:95
husband's k. when it comes — BACON 57:63
I expected k. and gentility — PERE 766:95
kill a wife with k. — SHAK 864:85
K. and courage — MUIR 712:32
K. in another's trouble — GORD 435:61
K. is worth more than beauty — ARRAS 40:48
k. of strangers — WILL 1081:59
k. that human beings do not lose — LEGU 594:23
k. that I can show — GREL 446:49
little bit of plain, ordinary k. — BUCH 202:30
Melting through k. — ROCH 816:44
milk of human k. — SHAK 907:25
neither k. or cruelty — ALBEE 11:82
place your k. there — ROCH 816:56
sheer k. and affection — TROL 1027:71
the great have k. — POPE 781:66
thought of you with k. — PEAC 762:31
value on spontaneous k. — JOHN 531:20

kindred k. spider — FROST 407:92
kindreds all nations, and k. — BIBLE 157:14
all k. of the earth shall wail — BIBLE 156:97
kinds divided into two k. — HUME 503:8
Knowledge is of two k. — JOHN 529:74
There are two k. — SAIN 837:95
two k. of audience — SCHN 848:83
two k. of Methodists — ELIOT 365:3
two k. of minds — PASC 757:47
kine home-bred k. — WORD 1098:57
king a' or our rightfu' k. — BURNS 213:47
abuse the K. — SHAK 910:95
abusing...the best k. — FRAN 402:8
am I sent for to a k. — SHAK 867:63
Authority forgets a dying k. — TENN 1004:43
balm from an anointed k. — SHAK 867:55
be the favourite of a k.? — MARL 653:3
beat the K. ninety-nine times — CROM 298:52
between the k. and the people — SELD 857:33
blind, despised, and dying k. — SHEL 927:76
bold K. of Sweden — LESL 598:94
born K. of the Jews? — BIBLE 133:23
Carle, now the K.'s come! — SCOTT 855:2
catch the conscience of the K. — SHAK 890:19
consumer...is the k. — SAMU 840:45
contrary to the k. — SHAK 861:15
Creston Clarke played K. Lear — FIELD 387:40
Curse not the k. — BIBLE 123:39
Deny it to a k.? — SHAK 877:95
did a k. to death — THOM 1010:56
editor is the uncrowned k. — STEAD 964:6
England breed again...a K. Harry? — DRAY 345:36
every inch a k. — SHAK 903:33
example of the k. of Denmark — FACK 382:49
executed the k. — STAL 962:78
Exempt from awe...the k. — SHEL 930:25
faint-hearted and degenerate k. — SHAK 861:16
follow the K. — TENN 1004:44
forbid on behalf of the K. — EDWA 361:46
forced from the K. — INNO 512:56
found in the k. a monk — AELR 9:52
Gentiles' Lord and K. — AQUI 32:5
Glory to the K. of k.s — WESL 1066:59
go in unto the k. — BIBLE 112:93
God bless our good and gracious K. — ROCH 817:66
God save the K. — ANON 25:33
God save the k. — BIBLE 110:33
God's patience and the K.'s English — SHAK 878:11
hath not offended the k. — MORE 707:58
heart and stomach of a k. — ELIZ 373:90
Here lies a k. — CAREW 232:13
Honour the k. — BIBLE 156:79
If he be the K. of Israel — BIBLE 140:54
If the k. loves music — MENC 668:55
image of the K. — TENN 1003:78
impossible for the K. — PEPYS 765:65
In sleep a k. — SHAK 914:78
is the year's pleasant k. — NASHE 721:80
kill a k. and marry — SHAK 892:51
K.'s a bawock — SHAK 881:91
k. borne of all Englond — MALO 642:25
K. George's glorious days — GILB 424:76
k. has no dignity — MORE 707:48
k.'s heart is in the hand — BIBLE 121:91
k. is always a k. — WOLL 1091:40
k. is strongest — BIBLE 131:74
k. Londgreaunce delyverd — MALO 642:28
k. may make nobleman — BURKE 208:44
K.'s name is a tower — SHAK 863:61
k. of codpieces — SHAK 865:13
K. of comforts, K. of life — VAUG 1041:19
K. of Glory wore — MARV 658:80
K. of glory, K. of peace — HERB 475:20
k. of infinite space — SHAK 890:99

king (contd.)
K. of K.s — BIBLE 158:31
K. o' Spain's daughter — COLUM 278:61
K. of the Jews — BIBLE 146:69
K. of the world shall raise us — BIBLE 133:20
K.'s real, or his stamped face — DONNE 337:79
K. said 'Butter, eh?' — MILNE 680:7
K. shall answer and say unto them — BIBLE 140:45
k. sits in Dunfermline — BALL 67:47
k. thought mair o' Marie — BALL 67:45
k.'s torch throws its light — CYRA 302:36
k. was much moved — BIBLE 110:51
K., who ordainest Great winds — ELLE 374:1
k. who wants to maintain — MORE 707:47
lad that was born to be k. — BOUL 181:46
lessened my esteem of a k. — PEPYS 765:64
Let a k. recall — ERAS 379:9
like a tyrant or k. — PASC 758:69
looking for a k. — MACD 628:2
Lord Lion K.-at-arms! — SCOTT 853:53
make us a k. to judge us — BIBLE 110:32
Man who Would be K. — KIPL 560:18
mortal temples of a k. — SHAK 867:60
my crowned K. — HOWA 497:92
My dead k.! — JOYCE 538:44
My God and K.! — HERB 474:10
name the k. would give it — PENN 764:56
no k. in Israel — BIBLE 109:23
not so glorious as a k. — MARL 652:88
O worship the K. — GRANT 438:5
old and foolish k. — BIBLE 123:25
once and future k. — MALO 642:34
one-eyed man is k. — ERAS 379:8
one-eyed man is k. — WELLS 1064:30
Ozymandias, k. of k.s — SHEL 928:93
passions of a k. — HUGO 502:73
priests ruled, the k. interpreted — COND 279:83
profits that an idle k. — TENN 994:57
qualities of a great K. — RICH 810:66
Quhen Alysaunder oure k. — ANON 22:68
quietly along the K.'s highway — STER 969:91
Reagan...hell of a k. — ONEI 740:65
receive honour of the k. — BIBLE 132:15
Rejoice, the Lord is K.! — WESL 1066:62
ruthless K.! — GRAY 442:79
saw the K. play tennis — PEPYS 765:95
Say 'Pardon' k. — SHAK 868:69
served my K. — SHAK 918:62
singeing of the K. of Spain's beard — DRAKE 345:27
smote the K. of Israel — BIBLE 111:72
soldier of the K. — KITC 566:44
sole k. of forests all — SPEN 957:99
son of Heavens eternal K. — MILT 681:85
soul, the K. of Heaven — LYTE 621:66
started off in films as k. — MORL 708:74
still am I K. of those — SHAK 867:64
subject's duty is the K.'s — SHAK 881:92
substitute shines brightly as a k. — SHAK 873:4
such a plain k. — SHAK 882:10
such divinity doth hedge a k. — SHAK 892:67
supports his k. on loyal principles — SHAW 920:11
Tartars made them a K. — POLO 777:66
Teach me, my God and K. — HERB 475:13
The K. dropp'd a tear — BLAKE 168:15
The K. makes no distinction — STRA 979:1
The K. to Oxford sent a troop — BROW 196:9
the K. will ride — DONNE 336:77
Thee, Redeemer, K. — NEALE 722:92
To be a K. — ELIZ 373:92
To be a Pirate K. — GILB 424:60
To be k. — SHAK 907:18
to have blown up the K. — HOBY 483:47
To reverence the K. — TENN 1002:17
to see the K. beheaded — PEPYS 765:62

king (contd.)
To the K. Theatre — PEPYS 765:66
Upon the K. — SHAK 881:94
Wha...hae we got for a K. — CUNN 300:1
What must the K. do now? — SHAK 867:62
when we had a k. — SCOTT 855:92
Who is this K. of glory? — BIBLE 115:52
Who...is a k. indeed — CHAP 252:60
with a k.'s son my childish — SURR 982:43
worm that hath eat of a k. — SHAK 892:62
King chief defect of Henry K. — BELL 87:5
could a Don K. happen — KING 557:72
Willie K. made up like Philip — NICO 727:61
kingdom best walls of this k. — COVE 290:90
Childhood is the k. — MILL 676:93
children of the k. — BIBLE 136:65
Content's a k. — HEYW 480:95
folly in that of a great k. — SMITH 945:88
God hath numbered thy k. — BIBLE 129:49
His k. stretch — WATTS 1055:57
if a k. be divided against itself — BIBLE 141:61
inherit the k. prepared for you — BIBLE 140:44
jewel of the k. — SUN 982:36
k. against k. — BIBLE 139:37
k. for a horse! — SHAK 863:69
k. for it was too small — SHAK 876:76
k. has ever been so — MONT 702:79
k. is as wide as the universe — FLAU 392:34
k. of God is within you — BIBLE 144:3
k. of the well — SONT 953:11
k. shall not continue — BIBLE 110:34
large k. for a little grave — SHAK 867:62
mind to me a k. is — DYER 358:87
My k., safeliest when one man — DONNE 336:72
one end of the k. to the other — WEBB 1059:18
palaces in K. come — MASE 662:46
people of this k. — LOUI 613:44
re-establishment of laws of k. — BLOOM 170:37
share the k. with — MARL 653:3
this formidable k. — PITT 771:63
Thy k. come — BIBLE 135:49
vegetating k. — LOWE 617:90
when thou comest into thy k. — BIBLE 144:17
yet thy k. shall pass — SWIN 987:41
kingdoms acquiring new k. — MORE 706:42
children of former k. — BACON 59:7
How many k. — PASC 757:61
kissed away K. — SHAK 905:78
returned to...these K. — ELIOT 369:4
sheweth him all the k. of the world — BIBLE 133:31
kinged England...is so idly k. — SHAK 881:94
kingfisher After the k.'s wing — ELIOT 370:29
kings accounted poet k. — KEATS 544:41
all be as happy as k. — STEV 975:39
axe to fell k. — BUNT 204:60
breath of k. — BURNS 209:66
But not of k. — MARL 653:15
captains and the k. depart — KIPL 562:61
change my state with k.' — SHAK 913:57
divine right of k. — MACM 635:3
enthronèd in the hearts of k. — SHAK 873:93
functions of k. — LOUI 614:50
great k. and fine cities — CATU 245:63
hand that k. have lipp'd — SHAK 905:76
K. and Desperate Men — KRON 570:1
K. and Governments may err — HERB 474:97
K. are earth's gods — SHAK 910:92
K....began their reigns — GARC 414:19
k. break faith — SHAK 872:62
k. can cause or cure — GOLD 432:99
k. for such a tomb — MILT 682:95
k. is mostly rapscallions — TWAIN 1033:90
K. may be blest — BURNS 211:14
k. must bow to grammar — MOLI 699:31

kings (contd.)
k. of the earth stand up	BOOK 176:59
k. shall shut their mouths	BIBLE 127:98
K. should not p.	COWP 293:61
k. that fear their subjects' treachery?	SHAK 862:24
k. to mount guard	CARL 234:49
K. will be tyrants from policy	BURKE 207:34
k., with standards	MOORE 706:33
know the k. of England	GILB 424:62
lays his icy hand on k.	SHIR 935:27
Many k. have sat down	BIBLE 132:97
Might first made k.	MARL 653:97
palaces of k. are built	PAINE 750:44
pale k., and princes	KEATS 545:74
Physicians are like k.	WEBS 1061:72
power of k. and magistrates	MILT 686:79
powerful K. and…Queens	DONNE 339:27
pride of k.	POPE 780:32
punctuality of k.	LOUI 614:52
raise up commonwealths and ruin k.	DRYD 349:10
security which k. are fighting for	SMITH 945:78
Some men are born k.	SHAW 925:24
statue of one of our k.	APPL 32:98
stories of the death of k.	SHAK 867:60
such is the breath of k.	SHAK 866:43
than that of most k.	HOOV 490:64
three k. into the east	BURNS 210:89
throne of k.	SHAK 867:48
to the Ear of K.	POPE 782:91
Until philosophers rule as k.	PLATO 774:21
Walk with K.	KIPL 564:9
War is the trade of k.	DRYD 351:60
what are k.	MARL 653:6

Kinnock K. has travelled the road   ASHD 41:60
Kipling a sort of gutless K.   ORWE 742:1
| the boys, principally K. | HEMI 470:16 |
kirk k. or market   STEV 974:19
| Marie Hamilton's to the k. gane | BALL 67:45 |
Kirkaldy Prisbeterien at K.   FLEM 394:65
Kirkconnell On fair K. lea!   BALL 67:41
kirtle kilted her green k.   BALL 67:51
kiss about to k. your hand   GILB 426:96
Ae fond k.	BURNS 212:24
Anger's self I needs must k.	SIDN 937:56
best part of love is the k.	MANN 646:90
bluest veins to k.	SHAK 905:76
body k. a body	BURNS 213:45
can no more keep…a k. there	DEVO 318:92
clung to a k.	BYRON 222:44
cup…leaped to k. me	FLET 394:75
did never k. and greet?	KEATS 545:59
drew with one long k.	TENN 993:36
envied k. to share	GRAY 442:65
first k. is magic	CHAN 251:46
glowing k. had won	HOOD 489:39
heralded by a k.	DARIO 305:76
I tried to k. her	RHYS 808:31
k. again with tears!	TENN 997:96
k. but in the cup	JONS 535:5
k. her and mix her with me	SWIN 987:45
k. his dirty shoe	SHAK 881:91
k. is still a k.	HUPF 505:34
k., Long as my exile	SHAK 911:16
K. me as if you made	BROW 197:29
k. me once again	JONS 536:13
K. me, Hardy	NELS 722:1
k. my ass in Macy's window	JOHN 523:54
k. my parched lips	SHAK 872:74
k. thee ere I killed thee	SHAK 901:65
k. thy hand to bid adieu	STER 970:15
K. till the cow comes home	BEAU 80:71
k. you take is better	SHAK 896:56
let us k. and part	DRAY 345:40
make me immortal with a k.!	MARL 654:19

kiss (contd.)
rough male k. of blankets	BROO 192:19
Salute…with an holy k.	BIBLE 150:43
saw you take his k.	PATM 760:2
took the k. sedately	TENN 1001:82
visit with a wandering k.	CAREW 232:15
when tyrants seems to k.	SHAK 910:93
When women k.	MENC 669:72
whisper it in the k.	ONEI 740:52
With this k. I wed thee	HEYW 480:93

kiss-worthy most k.-w. face   SIDN 937:56
kissed had I wist, before I k.   BALL 68:58
how he k. me	JOYCE 538:57
Jenny k. me	HUNT 505:29
k. away Kingdoms and provinces	SHAK 905:78
k. by a man	KIPL 560:19
k. by the English dead	OWEN 748:9
k. her once by the pig-sty	THOM 1011:83
k. her violently	ASHF 41:70
k. it and then fled	SHEL 932:66
When first we k.	BRID 187:42
When I k. the jack	SHAK 915:98

kisses a-wastin' Christian k.   KIPL 561:38
Are not your k.…filthy	DONNE 336:68
couches and k.	THOM 1011:88
forgotten my k.	SWIN 987:43
how many k.	CATU 245:60
k. of an enemy are deceitful	BIBLE 122:7
littered with remembered k.	MACN 637:42
More than k.	DONNE 338:99
numbering of k.	CLEV 269:10
Of many thousand k.	SHAK 906:94
remembered k.	TENN 997:4
Stolen k. much completer	HUNT 504:23
understand thy k.	SHAK 876:60

kissing constant click and k.   BETJ 100:49
fool…that first invented k.!	SWIFT 986:15
Garlic to mend her k.	SHAK 912:33
I wasn't k. her	MARX 659:94
K. don't last	MERE 671:2
k. had to stop?	BROW 198:47
k. is as full of sanctity	SHAK 886:12
K. the golden face	SHAK 913:59
Like k. Hitler	CURT 302:25
lip…it was For k.	SHAK 863:49
lipped and trembled k.	SHAK 905:76
overeagerly k. women	PACK 749:28

Kissinger if Mr K. is a great writer   ANON 29:45
| Nixon and K. began | PILG 770:43 |
kitchen better get out of the k.   TRUM 1030:20
Eat in the k.	HUGH 499:15
Fowls are to the k.	BRIL 188:53
history…through the k. window	CHILD 260:52
in k. cups	STEV 971:35
k. in the right place	JOHN 524:63
lack of reason in the k.	NIET 729:90
make my k.	STEV 976:53
mischief in the k.	THUR 1019:42
Out of the k., to stew	ONEI 740:63
perpetually clean k.	BUKO 203:45
send me to eat in the k.	HUGH 499:14

Kitchener K.…a great poster.   ASQU 42:80
kitchens talked of warm k.   GRAH 438:92
kites k. to whet their beaks   RANS 802:34
kitten trouble with a k.   NASH 720:56
kittle place Ca'd the K. Housie?   ANON 24:2
knack k. of judging a distance   REED 805:82
| Technology…the k. of so arranging | FRIS 406:64 |
knave all a k. or half a slave   INGR 511:44
he's an arrant k.	SHAK 889:82
K. of Hearts	CARR 239:42
my quaint k.	WEBS 1060:43
knavery k. and folly to excuse   CHUR 262:81
| religion, k., and change | BEHN 85:66 |

knaves Bold k. thrive   DRYD 350:43
K. and Knavery	ANON 25:21
rulers, mostly k.	BIER 161:85
to conclude, they are lying k.!	SHAK 880:64
world is made up…of fools and k.	BUCK 203:40
knavish either k. or childish   JOHN 530:4
knee A little aboon her k.   BALL 67:51
and bend my k.	SHAK 867:63
child upon her k.	TENN 997:8
civility of my k.	BROW 194:64
every k. should bow	BIBLE 153:3
k. which contains all speed	YOUR 1108:11
noblemen…cap and k.	WEBS 1060:56
on bended k.	STUA 980:10
sit upon the curate's k.	CHES 259:38
Sitting on a wise man's k.	HUXL 507:30
woman is as young as her k.	QUANT 796:51
knee-cap soul started at the k.-c.   LEWIS 602:66
kneel k. still with one little cheek   SCHR 850:4
| K. to nobody | SKEL 942:48 |
knees body between your k.   CORY 288:67
climb upon his k.	GRAY 442:65
creeps rustling to her k.	KEATS 546:93
Down on your k.	SHAK 886:13
just on its k.	HEMP 471:52
live on your k.	IBAR 510:18
Mr Elbows and K.	ANON 28:24
not in the k.	JERR 521:13
Sweeney spreads his k.	ELIOT 367:66
upon my k. every morning	SHAK 879:33
work is done upon his k.	KIPL 565:15
knell for it is a k.   SHAK 908:41
k. Of a spent day	CRANE 295:10
k. of parting day	GRAY 441:62
sound strikes like a rising k.!	BYRON 219:84
knew Adam k. Eve   BIBLE 104:4
I k. him, Horatio	SHAK 893:71
k. a lot about foreign affairs	REST 807:18
k. almost as much at eighteen	JOHN 527:36
k. too well	FROST 407:83
that he nothing k.	MILT 694:34
those who k. Him not	SCHW 852:31
knickers k.…of crêpe-de-chine   MACN 637:38
| wearing calico k. | JAMES 516:8 |
knife carved upon it with a k.   SHAK 877:1
crumbling…under the k.-edge	RICH 809:43
cuts as keen as a k.	BAUG 78:48
gave her a dull paring k.	BRID 188:45
I had a k. and two forks	RIDGE 811:80
keeps 'em on the k.	NASH 720:74
k. is lost in it	SHEL 929:74
k. through a layer of cake	MILL 677:9
sharpness like a clasping k.	BROW 197:17
smylere with the k.	CHAU 255:31
strike with our spirit's k.	SHEL 931:46
Surgeons…take the k.!	DICK 327:92
War to the k.	PALA 751:56
wind's like a whetted k.	MASE 661:34
knight gentle k. was pricking   SPEN 957:98
k. at arms	KEATS 545:72
K. had made a sudden pause	CARR 241:76
K. in the triumph	ADDI 7:18
k. of the garter	ATTL 44:12
k. to be their wooer	BALL -101:30
k. was…a valiant Gent	EVEL 381:41
name of ony k.	MALO 642:30
never was k. like…Lochinvar	SCOTT 853:54
new-slain k.	BALL 67:55
parfit gentil k.	CHAU 254:19
Poor K.!	NABO 716:94
red-cross k.	TENN 993:43
seyde that on k.	MALO 642:30
shortest k. of the year	RICH 810:61
knight-errant masquerading k.-e.   PARN 756:40

knighthood k. as...accomplishment NAIP 717:18
knights k. and barons bold MILT 682:3
K. of Isosceles Triangles ROOS 822:51
order of k. GUIB 448:77
Red-Branch K. to danger MOORE 706:33
knit to darn, to flower or k. LEWIS 601:46
knits k. me to thy rugged strand! SCOTT 853:50
knitter beautiful little k. SITW 941:39
knitting as if it were k. GLAS 430:59
woman still at her k. PLATH 773:99
knob brains out of a brass k. DICK 325:50
knock k., and it shall be opened BIBLE 135:57
k., breathe, shine and...mend DONNE 338:7
k. over the first one EISE 364:84
none will hear the postman's k. AUDEN 46:48
right to k. him down JOHN 531:14
stand at the door, and k. BIBLE 157:7
knocked k. the bastard off! HILL 481:7
knocker Tie up the k. POPE 781:58
knocks nature k. them all flat RENO 807:7
What really k. me out SALI 838:31
knot bomb the k. off a tree JENS 520:2
certain k. of peace SIDN 937:53
crowned by k. of fire ELIOT 373:81
k. be unknotted ELIOT 371:38
political k. that would not yield BIER 160:70
then all is a k. JONS 536:27
know all we need to k. KEATS 547:12
already k. the answer JONG 534:68
As I k. more of mankind JOHN 532:28
Be still, and k. BIBLE 116:74
by their fruits ye shall k. them BIBLE 135:61
can be said to k. RUSS 832:21
courage to k. KANT 542:2
don't k. where you are GROS 447:73
Dost thou k. me? SHAK 904:36
full up with the things they k. HERN 476:46
general must k. REED 805:87
greatest virtue...is to k. God SPIN 960:56
hate any one that we k. HAZL 463:5
How did they k.? PARK 754:98
I do not k. myself GOET 431:81
I k. it well, your mishap HEINE 467:72
I k. not HAND 455:68
I k. thee well SHAK 904:41
K. all there is to be knowed GRAH 438:93
k. I'm right GOLD 433:32
k. more than you think SPOCK 961:61
K. most of the rooms FULL 410:45
k. nothing whatever about you DOYLE 344:12
k. thee not, old man SHAK 878:10
k. this in order to concentrate GIDE 423:46
k., to kill and to create BAUD 78:43
k. what to do with it WALP 1051:86
k. what we are SHAK 892:63
k. without learning INGR 512:48
leader...must k. that he knows RAND 801:23
Let him not k.'t SHAK 899:39
let's learn not to k. JUANA 539:65
Mistress, k. yourself SHAK 886:13
must k. where you are STEI 966:58
never k. what's hit you KENN 552:96
no one knows what he doesn't k. CARY 243:23
not stand to k. anymore MUNRO 714:57
O that a man might k. SHAK 884:65
other half k. they don't k. QUINN 798:69
people k. what the land k.s SAND 841:72
pity those I do not k. SHAK 896:69
place thereof shall k. it no more BIBLE 118:15
reading might make her k. SIDN 937:50
report on what I k. FRIS 406:63
Scientists k. so much SHAP 919:78
something that you k. HEMI 470:27
the more we k. HUXL 506:51

know (contd.)
thought to k. this BIBLE 117:90
We don't k. where that money REAG 804:67
what I do k. I k. better AGATE 10:64
what should they k. of England KIPL 561:42
what thou dost not k. SHAK 875:52
what you do not k. ELIOT 371:50
When will the world k. WALP 1051:91
Yet I k. her for SHAK 918:57
You k. I k. you k. GUNN 448:85
know-how American k.-h. COLO 277:52
knowes Ca' the yowes to the k. BURNS 212:41
knoweth be as one that k. BIBLE 132:13
knowing art of k. what to overlook JAMES 517:42
k. there was no corner KAVA 543:27
k. what will be known FRAN 402:11
k. who we are is k. MILL 677:6
lust of k. FLEC 393:49
precisely in k. its limits KANT 541:1
knowledge a pound of k. WESL 1067:74
After such k., what forgiveness? ELIOT 368:70
all branches of k. ARNO 38:6
all k. and wonder BACON 54:4
all k. is human POPP 784:25
all k....my province BACON 54:1
any addition to k. DONNE 339:31
because they lead to k. JONG 533:61
best made of k. SENG 859:52
Bitter is the k. BAUD 77:27
blocked up the way to k. BERK 95:50
by words without k.? BIBLE 113:17
Can k. have no bound DENH 315:52
carry the k. with him JOHN 530:96
chapter of k. is very short CHES 257:81
climbing after k. MARL 652:89
collection...of human k. KENN 551:72
craftsmen share a k. SACK 835:60
deny k. KANT 542:1
dissemble sometimes your k. BACON 59:6
enlightenment in all spheres of k. BOOK 178:3
ethics, as a branch of k. AYER 53:81
evergreen tree of diabolical k. SHER 933:79
ever to have pure k. PLATO 774:15
exactly of their own k. MONT 700:53
experience and intuited k. MO 698:11
father of k. HIPP 481:16
for want of better K. PATE 760:97
forms of human k. MANN 645:81
from k. ignorance BROW 200:79
fruits of k. FREUD 404:46
genius of k. GOUR 437:80
God has given k. MARIE 651:63
greatest good...is the k. of God SPIN 960:56
ignorance is never better than k. FERMI 386:25
imperfect is all our k.! DONNE 339:29
impersonation...of secret k. BROO 193:42
improved out of all k. SITW 941:17
inner reserve of k. HOOV 490:68
intuitive k. of good SPIN 960:58
jazz, if one has the k. MORT 710:98
key of k. BIBLE 143:93
K. advances by steps MACA 622:94
k. and is not rejected RUSS 832:30
k. and love of God BOOK 175:33
K. and survey of vice MILT 685:66
K. and timber shouldn't HOLM 486:90
k. as a collective property SHAP 919:70
k....at the centre of true religiousness EINS 363:67
k. belongs to humanity PAST 759:88
k. can only be finite POPP 784:28
k. combined with that of other GALB 412:80
K. comes, but wisdom TENN 980:80
k. derived from experience ELIOT 371:46
k....did ne'er unroll GRAY 442:68

knowledge (contd.)
K. dwells In heads COWP 293:62
k. for the sake of understanding BUSH 215:91
k. from the gods WILS 1084:24
k. in her presence MILT 692:96
k. increaseth sorrow BIBLE 122:17
K. is a polite word CUMM 300:95
k. is a sacred cow SZEN 989:70
k. is as food MILT 691:83
k. is bought in the market CLOU 270:30
K. is of two kinds JOHN 529:74
K. is power BACON 54:2
k. is proud COWP 293:63
k. is, ourselves to know POPE 781:53
K....keep any better than fish. WHIT 1071:53
k....lost in information? ELIOT 370:17
k. might become more clear LANY 580:71
K. might pity win SIDN 937:50
k. of causes BACON 60:32
k. of good and evil MILT 685:60
k. of its giant strength NORR 731:29
k. of literate English...desert CHAN 250:39
k. of man is as the waters BACON 55:13
k. of oneself MILL 678:40
k. of the Bible, Shakespeare WAUGH 1058:6
k. of the boundless skies BYRON 222:30
k. of the heart JOHN 528:61
k. of the stars EDDI 360:18
k. originates in...experience MAO 648:20
k....recorded experience CARL 235:71
k. shall be increased BIBLE 130:51
k....shall vanish away BIBLE 150:62
k. that he lived in vain BYRON 219:83
k. that since perfection NIEB 727:64
k. that the soul PATM 760:7
k. that you can have is inexhaustible FRYE 408:24
k. that you'll grow out of it DAY 310:52
K. the wing SHAK 861:31
K. ...will not console me PASC 758:72
larger the island of k. MACI 631:46
Let k. grow TENN 998:18
lies in the way to k. LOCKE 609:71
limits of human k. NIEB 727:65
little advances in k. PROU 793:94
love of Christ, which passeth k. BIBLE 152:98
materials of reason and k. LOCKE 609:72
men naturally desire k. ARIS 34:23
more love and k. of you SHAK 885:72
multiplieth words without k. BIBLE 113:16
no k. of myself KANT 541:99
no k. when the day was done KEATS 546:83
nor k....in the grave BIBLE 123:34
not be lessened by the k. HUXL 508:1
Of k. there is no satiety BACON 55:20
one who speaks, without k. BIER 161:82
only one good, k. SOCR 952:91
opinion...is but k. MILT 685:59
ourselves, and our k. POPP 783:21
Out-topping k. ARNO 36:60
possession of k. POPP 784:24
presupposition of the k. HEID 467:66
progress of human k. FRAN 402:11
province of k. to speak HOLM 486:1
Science is k. arranged BURB 205:76
Science is organized k. SPEN 955:64
Science is systematized positive k. SART 843:5
scientific k. have been achieved PLAN 772:83
seek for k. and wisdom SHEL 926:61
sign of k. in our times WILL 1083:92
sociologists of k. MERT 672:26
Sorrow is k. BYRON 221:19
Such k. is too wonderful BIBLE 119:48
Such k. is too wonderful BOOK 177:93
things that are preventing k. PROT 792:84

knowledge (*contd.*)

third kind of k.	SPIN 961:59
thorough k. of human nature	AUST 52:63
through their union can k. arise	KANT 541:98
time to close the five parts of k.	BROW 196:6
to follow k.	TENN 994:59
too much k.	POPE 780:42
Tree of K. grew fast	MILT 690:52
tree of k.	BYRON 222:34
true antithesis to k.	DEQU 316:66
true k. only comes of death	WHITE 1070:42
two modes of acquiring k.	BACON 60:43
Why seek for k.	EDGE 361:32
win k. of the causes	VIRG 1045:99
without k. of the same	LEON 597:85
known be k., and not know	COLT 277:57
Canada only needs to be k.	HOPK 492:12
Have ye not k.?	BIBLE 126:90
k. them all already, k. them all	ELIOT 367:49
must have k. me	TROL 1028:94
not meant 'to be k.'	SAGAN 836:74
than to be k.	HOPK 492:95
till I am k.	JOHN 526:99
knows going one k. not where	MASE 662:36
He k. nothing	SHAW 923:83
person who k. 'how'	RAVI 802:45
Knox Lady K....irrelevance	SOME 952:99
see John K. in Paradise	PARK 754:4
knuckle-end That k.-e. of England	SMITH 949:49
Ko-Ko If K.-K. tells us true	GILB 425:83
Koran interpretation of the K.	GIBB 421:23
Korea dust that is settling in K.	MACA 621:76
shall go to K.	EISE 364:80
Kosciusko as K. fell!	CAMP 227:26
Kraken the K. sleepeth	TENN 993:31
Krazy ball made of K. Putty	LODGE 610:79
Krieg K. findet immer einen Ausweg	BREC 186:31
Krishna K.'s jokes may be vapid	FORS 399:57
Kruger finished killing K.	KIPL 562:67
kurrajong Under a k.	NEIL 722:96
Kurtz Mistah K.— he dead	CONR 284:93
kuwaiting We're k.	ANON 29:29
Kyle lad was born in K.	BURNS 210:87
Kyrie K. eleison	ANON 22:80
Köhln K., a town of monks	COLE 275:26
label l. our toys good and bad	DYSON 358:1
rag of a l. to cover himself	HUXL 508:97
labials heavenly l.	STEV 971:37
labor onward march of l.	LEWIS 601:48
laboratories Outside their l.	PAST 759:89
states are the l. of democracy	WHIT 1072:72
laboratory Give me an...l.	PERE 766:91
hissing l. of his wishes	THOM 1011:89
l. of God	WILL 1081:65
laborious rising unto place is l.	BACON 57:70
Studious of l. ease	COWP 293:59
labour 25 years of L. Government	BEVAN 101:62
all ye that l.	BIBLE 137:88
applies himself to l. and exercise	CONF 280:91
as much of a l. to write	HUXL 506:57
Britain with a L. Government	WILS 1085:36
British L. movement...strikes	ENGE 378:84
calamity of a L. Government	HESE 479:80
Chinese cheap l.	HARTE 460:51
common wages of l.	SMITH 946:89
daily l. to pursue	WESL 1066:64
demand for their l.	STEU 970:29
dignify the l.	CRANE 294:98
division of l.	BABB 54:88
division of l. is nothing	MARX 660:7
division of l....social functions	DURK 357:69
do ye not l. and toil	BIBLE 131:75
don't let L. ruin it	ANON 27:61

labour (*contd.*)

Ease and alternate l.	THOM 1015:48
enjoy the good of all his l.	BIBLE 122:20
example of unproductive l.	GRAY 440:44
extraction of surplus l.	MARX 660:21
fruit of our l.	MONT 700:54
Give us l.	SCHR 850:9
good reward for their l.	BIBLE 123:23
I in l. lie	DONNE 336:71
In all l. there is profit	BIBLE 121:77
In l. and trouble...more dignified	CHES 257:86
instruments of l.	MARX 661:22
intellectual l. (of science)	HUMB 503:97
l. and wages first	MANN 646:95
L. does not only create goods	MARX 661:26
l. going upstairs	MUNDY 714:53
L. government	GEOR 419:84
L. Governments in every country	GREY 446:56
l. in his vocation	SHAK 875:39
l. in the deep mid-ocean	TENN 994:53
l. in vain	BIBLE 119:41
L. is the Father...of Wealth	PETTY 768:14
L. is the Party of law and order	BLAIR 165:53
L. isn't working	ANON 28:6
L. leader	MACF 629:15
l. movement was truly religious	WOLFE 1090:29
L. of an age in piled stones	MILT 681:94
l. of his body	LOCKE 609:69
l. of keeping a house	MACC 626:54
l. of women	GILM 427:15
l. once spent	JEVO 521:21
L. Party's election programme	SNOW 951:79
L. Party is a moral crusade	WILS 1085:31
L. Party when...entrusted with power	WEBB 1059:18
l. required to obtain...goods	RICA 808:35
l.-time necessary to reproduce	MARX 660:20
l....to pervert that end	MILT 687:96
l. until the evening	BIBLE 118:17
L. was the first p.	SMITH 946:93
l. we delight in	SHAK 908:52
l. weariness	LYLY 620:61
l. which he taketh under the sun?	BIBLE 122:14
L. without joy	RUSK 831:1
last l. that thou and I shall waste	WYATT 1103:20
little effect after much l.?	AUST 52:60
many still must l. for one	BYRON 221:10
more l. in hewing	JOHN 530:99
mountains will fall into l.	HORA 493:32
natural price of l.	RICA 808:37
no time to l.	ROGE 820:19
performed much of the l.	STAN 962:88
performing any kind of l.	WARD 1053:16
product of mental l.	MARX 660:20
productive powers of l.	SMITH 946:90
rest rather than l.	RICH 810:68
role of l. in society	NEVI 723:15
sacrifice of more and more l.	RICA 808:33
shortened the l. of copyists	CARL 234:47
Six days shalt thou l.	BIBLE 106:68
society do not want his l.	MALT 643:40
they that live l.	BIBLE 131:76
this waye to l.	ANON 21:64
To learn and l.	BOOK 175:38
true success is to l.	STEV 974:17
understood the natural price of l.	RICA 808:32
With too much l. drowns	SHAK 866:35
yet is their strength l.	BIBLE 117:99
laboured l. to it without the reward	SCOTT 852:39
labourer employed as an under-l.	LOCKE 609:71
king's torch throws its light upon a l.	CYRA 302:36
l. is worthy of his hire	BIBLE 142:87
l. or a tradesman	LAW 585:60

labourer (*contd.*)

l. to take his pension	RUSK 830:89
labourers enable the l....to subsist	RICA 808:37
take that of L.' Unions	RUSK 831:10
too many L. to cultivate the Lands	CANT 230:74
labouring A l. man that is given	BIBLE 132:5
l. swain	GOLD 432:8
Sleep sweet to l. man	BUNY 205:69
labours Children sweeten l.	BACON 57:55
from their l. rest	HOW 497:90
notice...of my l.	JOHN 526:99
One thousand l.	LAB 571:33
share of l. and sacrifices	MILL 675:65
uncessant l. see	MARV 658:82
laburnums L., dropping-wells	TENN 999:49
labyrinth dreamt I was in the l.	MUIR 712:30
is in the l.	ROBB 813:8
l. of our life	SCHO 849:92
peopled l. of walls	SHEL 927:70
labyrinthine down the l. ways	THOM 1013:28
lace button, hook, and l.	LOWE 615:74
Lachlan I met him, down the L.	PATE 760:97
lack l. of many a thing	SHAK 913:58
l. their sacred poet	HORA 493:25
lacked If I l. any thing	HERB 475:17
lacrosse I thought l. was	WILL 1081:53
lad brisk and a bonnie l.	ANON 23:96
l. does not care for	JOHN 528:50
l. of life	SHAK 881:91
l. that was born to be king	BOUL 181:46
l. was born in Kyle	BURNS 210:87
many a lightfoot l.	HOUS 495:61
myself a sterling l.	HOUS 495:65
Up, l.	HOUS 494:42
When I was a l.	GILB 423:58
ladder can't climb...without a l.	ZATO 1109:15
kick away the l.	SUN 982:35
l. set up on the earth	BIBLE 105:34
Now that my l.'s gone	YEATS 1107:89
raise a l. without a wall	HONE 488:29
rounds of society's l.	MOORE 704:11
with lantern and with l.	STEV 975:41
laden heart is l.	HOUS 495:61
ladies art that helps old l.	OLDE 738:24
by act of God, we are l.	CARD 232:96
Cambridge l....furnished souls	CUMM 299:78
chic old blue-haired l.	CAPO 231:88
delectable lusty l.	DUNB 355:39
Good l., help to fill	SURR 983:45
good night, sweet l.	SHAK 892:64
keep us from scaring the l.	MACM 636:23
l....admitted on special days	WARN 1053:24
l. and gentlemen, last night	NATH 721:87
l. apparently rolled along	HUXL 506:59
l. in very high positions	AMIN 16:70
L., just a little more virginity	TREE 1025:40
l. that must be wooed	CAMP 228:37
l., whose bright eyes	MILT 682:3
l., yield to love	LYLY 620:61
lang may the l. sit	BALL 67:49
lion among l.	SHAK 871:42
old l. in tennis shoes	MOSK 710:6
old l. of both sexes	DICK 325:48
remember the l.	ADAMS 4:61
Sigh no more, l.	SHAK 879:46
worth any number of old l.	FAUL 383:38
ye lords of l. intellectual	BYRON 222:26
young l. spend their time	SWIFT 984:75
lads Golden l. and girls	SHAK 916:16
l. are far away	FORD 397:20
l. in their hundreds	HOUS 495:52
l. who fought	SASS 845:31
Then strip l.	SCOTT 854:72
three wild l. were we	SCOTT 854:76

lads (contd.)
Two l. that thought — SHAK 911:18
lady accomplished l. — SHAK 895:22
act like a l. — SIMON 938:79
behaved like a perfect l. — TRAV 1025:36
cannot endure my L. Tongue — SHAK 879:39
certain little l. comes by — GAY 417:62
Come, l., let not this — MARL 652:85
coyness L. was no crime — MARV 658:72
dreamt my l. came — SHAK 870:20
Fair l., will you any? — LYLY 620:59
for the love of a l.! — GILB 425:94
girl who was a l. — LOOS 613:31
hawk, his hound, and his l. fair — BALL 67:55
Here lies a l. of beauty — RANS 802:31
hold my l.'s head — HEAN 465:35
l. as thou art — SHAK 876:62
l. from the provinces — GILB 425:85
l. in the wig — DICK 323:83
L., l., should you meet — PARK 753:90
L.'s not for Burning — FRY 408:13
l. novelist — GILB 425:85
l. of Christ's College — AUBR 45:34
L. of my own — WORD 1095:6
L. of Shalott — TENN 993:39
l. of the Lake — MALO 642:27
l. of the West Country? — DELA 314:29
l. protests too much — SHAK 891:39
l. rose and with a grace — GRAY 441:61
l. that's known as Lou — SERV 859:56
l. wants to be dressed — NASH 720:71
l. was not seen! — SCOTT 854:80
l. who found out — ROSE 823:59
L. with a Lamp — LONG 612:14
l. would be a queen — POPE 782:76
L. you deserve this state — MARV 658:73
like a dying l. — SHEL 932:74
lord and l. gay — SCOTT 853:43
lovely l., garmented in light — SHEL 930:31
Lydia The Tattooed L. — HARB 455:74
make a sweet l. sad — SHAK 895:46
manners of a l. — FRAN 402:15
No l. closer — SHAK 875:52
no rhyme to 'l.' — SHAK 880:65
not exactly a l. — RIDGE 811:78
O lang will his l. — BALL -101:32
Of many a l. — SPEN 958:13
old l. at a busy intersection — ACHE 3:40
quarrel for a l. — HALI 452:32
San Francisco is a l. — MAIL 639:84
saw a l. bright — BALL 67:52
talk like a l. — SHAW 924:3
the l. is a tramp — HART 459:45
'Twas a good l. — SHAK 901:82
When a l.'s in the case — GAY 416:50
wrong to strike a l. — THUR 1020:52
You are the body, l. — SCEVE 847:58
lag with some l. — HOMA 487:1
lain l. for ages and will lie — TENN 993:32
l. with their mothers — SOPH 953:22
lair silence round about his l. — KEATS 547:99
laird l. o' Cockpen — NAIR 717:19
lifts a drove from a Sassenach l. — SCOTT 854:70
laity conspiracies against the l. — SHAW 924:88
tell the l. of our love — DONNE 337:90
laitymen Gentes and l. — JOYCE 538:60
lake beside a cold l. — SCOTT 852:36
bosom of the l. — TENN 997:10
daffodils…beside the l. — WORD 1099:67
glitter like a l. — BYRON 222:41
I am in the l. — ATWO 44:16
l. I saw bass-viols — LEVE 600:23
l. is the great source — SPEKE 955:61
l. of fire — BIBLE 158:33

lake (contd.)
Maker, in that crimson l. — MONT 703:93
Marriage may…be a stormy l. — PEAC 762:27
middle of a stormy l. — EISE 364:91
real pitch l. — HUXL 507:70
Round the Mareotic l. — YEATS 1107:92
swan…moves over the l. — COLUM 278:60
lakes grass is green, l. damp — STEP 968:79
L., mountains, and rivers — AUST 51:41
shakes across the l. — TENN 997:98
Some people swim l. — WEBB 1058:16
songs in its l. — SCOTT 852:37
lakeside by the l. — SCHW 852:31
lamb ape to Hazlitt, to L. — STEV 976:46
Behold the L. of God — BIBLE 145:28
brought as a l. to the slaughter — BIBLE 127:1
Did he who made the L. make thee? — BLAKE 167:96
Englishman…flattered, is a l. — CHAP 252:75
God will provide himself a l. — BIBLE 105:28
holy L. of God — BLAKE 168:17
L. of God — CASW 244:37
L. of God, I come! — ELLI 374:9
l. shall be without blemish — BIBLE 106:60
leads me to the L.! — COWP 292:30
Little l., who made thee? — BLAKE 166:63
Maria, to the shorn l. — STER 970:27
Mary had a little l. — HALE 451:22
one little ewe l. — BIBLE 110:47
Pipe a song about a l.! — BLAKE 166:62
washed in the blood of the L.? — LIND 605:11
when he would steal the l. — SHAK 861:4
wolf also shall dwell with the l. — BIBLE 125:68
wolf and l. shall feed together — BIBLE 128:16
wolf and the l.…united — ARIS 34:22
lambs gather the l. with his arm — BIBLE 126:86
go to hell like l. — CHES 259:27
l. end up head down — JUST 540:75
poor little l. — KIPL 560:22
lame l. man leap as an hart — BIBLE 126:82
l. man who keeps the right road — BACON 56:33
l. walk — BIBLE 137:83
made l. by…spite — SHAK 913:60
Science without religion is l. — EINS 363:66
lament childish weakness to l. — SHAK 862:32
l. of the poets — THOM 1013:25
l. the past — BURKE 206:99
naught other to l. — PATM 760:4
lamentation l., and bitter weeping — BIBLE 128:28
lamented ye have not l. — BIBLE 137:86
Lammas It fell about the L. tide — BALL -101:24
It was upon a L. night — BURNS 210:78
lamp dying l., a falling shower — SHEL 931:43
Eternal l. of love! — HERR 477:56
Lady with a L. — LONG 612:14
l. beside the golden door — LAZA 588:26
l. of day — DOUG 341:55
l. of faith — WORD 1100:90
l. unto my feet — BIBLE 119:33
l. was dark — MACN 637:46
smell of the l. — HERR 477:58
smell too strong of the l. — STER 969:97
sovran vital l. — MILT 689:30
To keep a l. burning — THER 1009:36
lamplight l. dull and sickly — WILDE 1075:26
lamppost asking a l. how it feels — HAMP 454:65
leaning on a l. — GAY 417:62
lampposts way that a drunk uses l. — LANG 579:66
lamps I mean by fairy l. — WOOD 1092:49
l. are going out — GREY 446:57
l. are guttering low — HOUS 497:89
l., by whose dear light — MARV 658:79
L. for my gloom — SASS 845:40
l. that shone o'er fair women — BYRON 219:84
lampshade a Nazi l. — PLATH 773:93

Lancashire In a L. cotton-town — ORWE 742:96
typical sound of L. — ORWE 742:91
Lancelot at that tyme sir L. — MALO 642:30
bold Sir L. — TENN 993:43
L. mused a little space — TENN 994:47
Not L., nor another — TENN 1003:20
which I found in L. — TENN 1003:19
lances Shall be our l. — GILB 425:79
lancet veins…to invite the l. — SHER 933:88
land across the other l. — MUIR 712:36
all that travel by l. — SWIFT 986:14
America…heroic, sentimental l. — RABAN 798:76
away into the silent l. — ROSS 823:71
best dance e'er cam to the L. — BURNS 212:34
best people never l. — MACN 637:47
brought me in to possess this l. — BIBLE 108:93
by l. and sea — WORD 1099:64
by sea as by l. — GILB 423:51
clear the l. of evil — KIPL 561:53
clung to…the l. — MOOD 703:94
cut off Israel out of the l. — BIBLE 111:56
darkness of the l. — TENN 1000:57
death's grey l. — SASS 845:25
doghter of the l. of Camylarde — MALO 642:24
England's green and pleasant l. — BLAKE 168:20
exact survey of the l. — DONNE 339:32
exiles from our fathers' l. — GALT 413:3
famine was sore in the l. — BIBLE 105:47
fat of the l. — BIBLE 105:48
flourishing culture in our l. — MAO 648:27
glorious l. above the sky — HILL 480:3
glorious l. of ours — FERB 385:6
good and bad of every l. — BAIL 62:71
happy l. — GOLD 433:15
harsh l.'s red and green — HYDE 509:14
his hands prepared dry l. — BOOK 177:87
history of the l. — LONG 612:14
Ill fares the l. — GOLD 433:10
in a blatant l. — TENN 1001:80
in a dry and thirsty l. — BIBLE 116:83
in a strange l.? — BIBLE 119:47
in the l. of the living — BIBLE 118:25
l. and ocean without rest — MILT 686:81
l. and the mind — NGU 725:45
l. flowing with milk and honey — BIBLE 106:56
l. God gave to Andy Stewart — SMITH 947:4
l. God gave to Cain — CART 242:10
L. is the only thing — MITC 696:84
l. lies desolate and stripped — ADAMS 4:63
l. may be said to be discovered — STEF 965:24
l. may vary more — FROST 407:89
l. o' the leal — NAIR 718:20
L. of brown heath — SCOTT 853:50
l. of Calvin — SMITH 949:44
l. of cattle and sheep — LAWS 588:20
L. of hope and glory — BENS 92:9
L. of hope and glory — CLIN 269:18
L. of light and revelation — HOUS 495:58
l. of lost content — BYRON 219:10
L. of lost gods — STEV 976:43
l. of Nod at last — BIBLE 104:8
L. of Nod — KIPL 564:37
L. of our birth — SWIN 987:47
l. of sand and ruin — TENN 996:89
l. of settled government — DICK 326:55
l. of Shakespeare, Milton, Bacon — KEY 554:24
l. of the free — CUMM 299:83
l. of the pilgrims' — DAVIS 309:38
l. of their heart's hope — SCOTT 852:37
l. stares at the sun — BIBLE 107:82
l. that eateth up the inhabitants — HARB 455:78
l. that I heard of — SMITH 948:27
L. where my father died — LEAR 590:59
l. where the Bong-tree — BIBLE 104:23
l. wherein thou art a stranger

land (*contd.*)

laughing Ceres re-assume the l.	POPE 779:23
length and breadth of the l.	MOOD 703:98
light across the l.?	TENN 996:90
Lilacs out of the dead l.	ELIOT 368:81
little wrong in the l.	MENC 668:55
love-sick l. that mourns for thee	BLAKE 165:57
loving the l.	MOORE 706:39
made our l. a tomb	ORAH 741:78
Maker's image through the l.	DRYD 349:9
Marched into their l.	AYTO 53:85
mist and hum of that low l.	ARNO 38:97
my own, my native l.!	SCOTT 853:49
nakedness of the l..	BIBLE 105:45
narrow strip of l.	BAKER 63:83
Oh, thou dear l.	SCHAW 847:61
once-loved l.	WRIG 1102:11
Only the weathering l.	SNYD 951:82
Past is a strange l.	THOM 1012:98
people know what the l. knows	SAND 841:72
pocket of my l.	FRAME 400:76
pointed toward the l.	TENN 994:48
poor race in a l. of dollars	DUBO 353:6
Praise the sports of the l.	REID 806:98
publishes to every l.	ADDI 7:22
rich and fruitful l.	BLAKE 167:89
rural virtues leave the l.	GOLD 433:18
security of the l.	COVE 290:90
She was our l.	FROST 407:96
Silence ruled this l.	DARK 305:78
sun rose and set on their l.	SITT 940:98
than ever before in any l.	HOOV 490:58
The l. of my fathers	THOM 1011:77
there was no l. left	IHIM 511:31
think of my own native l.	COWP 292:40
This is the dead l.	ELIOT 369:99
This l. is your l.	GUTH 449:94
Thou on the l.	SCOTT 854:76
Thus fares the l.	GOLD 433:16
town. surrounded by l.	MOORE 705:14
traveller from an antique l.	SHEL 928:92
truth is a pathless l.	KRIS 569:92
unto a l. that I will shew thee	BIBLE 104:18
want to build a better l.	CHRI 261:51
want to free this l.	MARI 651:68
westward...the l. is bright	CLOU 270:32
what shall this l. produce?	RANS 802:33
wide brown l. for me	MACK 632:52
windy strip of l.	MILT 689:41
with my native l.	TENN 1002:96
Woe to that l.	SHAK 863:55
woman is a foreign l.	PATM 760:3
workman in the l.	LLOY 608:57
would be a grand l.	FREE 404:31
wrong throughout the l.	MUIR 712:26
Your l., your wealth	JAY 519:72

landing l. a man on the moon — KENN 551:66

landlady l. of a boarding-house — LEAC 588:33

landlord architecture...for the l. — WRIG 1101:7

interests of the l.	RICA 808:36
l. does not intend to repair	ADAMS 6:91
l. to the whole congregation	ADDI 7:11

landlords before the l. of the country — PARN 756:40

l. and persons of property	MALT 643:41

landmark Remove not the old l. — BIBLE 121:96

removeth his neighbour's l.	BIBLE 108:97

landmarks l. that are scarcely more — HUBB 498:9

nomads,on a plain with few l.	MACM 636:26

landmined l. and unforgiving — ELKIN 374:98

lands By foreign l. thy dying eyes — POPE 779:7

different from things in other l.	LAWS 587:18
envy of less happier l.	SHAK 867:48
forsake me and of all my l.	SHAK 862:31
l. are the mother	PETTY 768:14

lands (*contd.*)

l. beyond the sea	WORD 1095:13
l. where the Jumblies live	LEAR 590:54
satisfies the poor in other l.	HEGEL 466:62
sold your own l.	SHAK 886:17
songs of other l.	EVANS 381:39
Where are our l.?	SITT 940:98

landscape art of l. — RUNGE 829:55

beauty of the l.	HILL 481:6
Burning like a sunlit l.	MACD 628:94
half the l. is unavailable	DOUG 342:64
implacability of the l.	NOLAN 731:20
invention of the l. painter	FUSE 410:62
l. and its inhabitants	UPDI 1037:73
l. broken into	LEGER 594:22
L. is to American painting	HUGH 500:30
l. round it measures	MILT 682:1
l. to a blind man's eye	WORD 1094:96
shaper of the l.	BRON 190:85

landscapes fades the glimmering l. — GRAY 441:62

if l. were sold	STEV 973:98
l. of seas full of fish	CIXO 267:75
Someone said of his l.	HAZL 464:25

landslide Republican l. on Nov 8 — CUOMO 301:8

lane country l. — PARK 755:29

dragons of Laune and L.	ORAH 741:77
In an English l.	BROW 199:62
l. was made	DICK 323:82
walk down the l.	FREED 403:28

lanes green and shaded l. — MACK 632:52

language abstruseness in their l. — GOWE 437:82

American l.	ADAMS 5:82
any l. you choose	GILB 424:77
Bad l. or abuse	GILB 423:55
base of their l.	BEAU 80:65
beyond the l. of the living	ELIOT 372:70
beyond the range of l.	REID 806:97
braver in another l.	BROO 193:39
certain mistress of l.	JONS 536:25
Color and bite permeate a l.	SAFI 835:68
confound the l. of all the earth	BIBLE 104:17
constantly changing l. of politics	SAFI 835:67
conveyed...in the best chosen l.	AUST 52:63
countries divided by a common l.	SHAW 926:41
deciduous l.	THOM 1013:25
define her feelings in l.	HARDY 456:89
don't use whatever l.	KELM 549:32
dramatic words in the English l.	HART 459:48
dream of a common l.	RICH 809:52
enemy of clear l.	ORWE 743:19
enemy of clear l.	ORWE 744:46
English l. is nobody's...property	WALC 1048:36
English l. readers	GISC 429:48
enlargement of the l.	JOHN 526:7
ere we learn the l.	THOR 1016:62
every l. even deafanddumb	CUMM 299:83
Experience is...larger than l.	RICH 809:57
Finality is not the l. of politics	DISR 333:4
fine flow of l.	RIDGE 811:78
French is not a static l.	HUGO 501:61
from one l. to another	SHEL 931:56
fumbling with...English l.	WAUGH 1058:9
gifted glassblower of l.	HERS 478:71
Great literature is simply l.	POUND 786:72
greed wrapped in the l. of love	ARMEY 35:43
in a room with the English l.	HUTC 506:40
in the English l.	THUR 1019:36
inaccessible...except...their l.	FRAME 400:78
lack of a whole l.	MUIR 712:25
l. all nations understand	BEHN 85:65
l. an opera is sung in	APPL 32:99
l. can serve our purposes	MACD 628:94
l. concentrating emotion	BRAU 186:22
L. does not leave fossils	BRAU 186:18

language (*contd.*)

l. has said that reason	MACL 633:68
l. have the right	KELM 549:33
l. he was the lodesterre	LYDG 620:53
L. is a form	LEVI 600:31
L. is a skin	BART 75:84
L. is only an instrument	JOHN 526:5
L. is the flesh-garment	CARL 234:52
L. is using us to talk	MATH 663:69
l. of our feelings	FRIE 405:60
l. of the age	GRAY 441:49
l. of the heart	POPE 781:69
l. of the horde	MALL 641:18
l. that is not ours	WITT 1088:92
L. was not powerful enough	DICK 321:51
l., which is what you use	MERW 672:27
learned l.	GIBB 421:30
life...under the power of l.	CIXO 266:69
Life is a foreign l.	MORL 708:69
Man's natural l.	FLAU 393:46
mobilized the English l.	MURR 715:78
mobilized the English l.	KENN 551:76
more learning in their l.	JOHN 530:99
most beautiful words in the...l.	JAMES 517:31
Music is the universal l.	LONG 611:93
must re-invent l.	IRIG 512:60
My l. fails!	BELL 87:3
my l. is plain	HARTE 459:50
natural l. of all religions	STAEL 962:76
neither speech nor l.	BOOK 176:66
no l. but a cry	TENN 999:38
No respect for their l.	SHAW 924:1
no word in their l.	SWIFT 985:88
not a question of...blood or l.	OBRI 733:61
Numbers...universal l.	WEST 1067:86
obligated to its l.	BROD 190:74
Only where there is l.	RICH 809:45
our l. fails	WALL 1050:74
our l. grows	WALL 1050:75
Ours is a precarious l.	THUR 1019:47
people...of an hard l.	BIBLE 128:35
Poetry happens because of l.	OLIV 738:26
Poetry...through human l.	MALL 641:14
Political l.	ORWE 744:48
pure rhetoric of l.	STEV 972:55
refine our l.	JOHN 525:93
refusal of l. is a death	BART 75:81
remains of the English l.	COUP 289:81
room for but one l.	ROOS 822:53
same forms and the same l.	FLAU 392:39
Slang is a l.	SAND 841:75
sociologists...I do not speak their l.	DYSON 358:99
sophisticated use of l.	KUNI 571:17
sorry when any l. is lost	JOHN 529:67
speak the same foreign l.	WILD 1079:18
strange l. all I know	LAND 578:61
suicides have a special l.	SEXT 859:65
sure in l. strange she said	KEATS 545:73
taught me l.	SHAK 916:22
The l. plain	COWP 292:31
They are, after all, a l.	BANKS 70:94
unvisionary l. of farm, city and love	ENGLE 378:91
use in measured l.	TENN 998:19
Words are...from a defunct l.	CIXO 267:74
world understands my l.	HAYDN 462:87
writers...make their l. convey more	CONN 283:66

languages dictate the l. in which — BALL 68:64

Do you know L.	CARR 241:81
exchanged...in our respective l.	COOK 286:28
Fluent in all the l.	CURN 301:13
instructed in all l. living and dead	DICK 321:44
three or four l.	SHAK 893:94
thunder In such lovely l.	LAWR 587:3
two l. in Canada	SAINT 836:77

languages (*contd.*)
wit in all l. — DRYD 347:58
woman speaks eighteen l. — PARK 754:1
langue au pouvoir de la l. — CIXO 266:69
languish l. like exotics — WOLL 1091:38
Relieve my l. — DANI 304:62
languor L. cannot be — SHEL 929:4
pain or l. — WORD 1100:90
languors lilies and l. of virtue — SWIN 987:32
lank haggard and l. young man — GILB 424:71
lanky that l. Yankee finger — CONN 282:53
lantern Hang a l. on your problem — MATT 664:78
hast no l. — JONS 535:1
l. of Aristotle's brain — RALE 800:15
l. on the stern — COLE 275:27
with l. and with ladder — STEV 975:41
lanterns jaunty gilded l. — GILL 426:2
Laocoön L….made different? — EMER 376:45
lap brooks, On whose fresh l. — MILT 684:46
cool flowery l. of earth — ARNO 37:73
drop Into thy mother's l. — MILT 693:24
In thy green l. — GRAY 443:89
lap-dogs l.-d. …shake — POPE 778:91
lapidary In l. inscriptions — JOHN 529:78
laps tumbling into some men's l. — BACON 55:24
lapse l. of moments is ever — STOWE 978:88
l. of one lesser — CANM 230:65
lapwing Beatrice like a l. runs — SHAK 879:51
wanton l. — TENN 995:71
lard as fed with l. — SPEN 959:43
large l. as life — CARR 241:75
small thing…made l. — TWAIN 1033:97
Lariston Lock the door, L. — HOGG 485:65
lark bisy l., messager of day — CHAU 255:29
jay more precious than the l. — SHAK 864:87
l. at break of day arising — SHAK 913:57
l. at heaven gate — SHAK 916:3
l.'s on the wing — BROW 197:25
l.…sightless song — TENN 1000:60
More tuneable than l. — SHAK 870:26
nightingale, and not the l. — SHAK 869:10
sing as sweetly as the l. — SHAK 873:5
Waked by the l. — SHAK 896:55
larks Four L. and a Wren — LEAR 589:50
hear the l. so high — HOUS 495:50
imprisoned l. — GRAV 440:40
l.…singing the same five notes — CATH 244:39
larkspur The l. listens — TENN 1001:88
lash bear de l. as well — TRUTH 1030:97
Why dost thou l. that whore? — SHAK 904:37
lashes make the l. dark — YEATS 1106:83
lass A l. unparalleled — SHAK 906:8
Drink to the l. — SHER 933:91
every l. a queen — KING 558:94
it came with a l. — JAME 515:2
l. wi' tousled hair — MACD 627:74
lover and his l. — SHAK 887:32
my bonie l. — BURNS 212:40
solitary Highland L. — WORD 1098:61
lasses honest men and bonny l. — BURNS 211:10
L. a-lilting before the dawn — ELLI 374:8
lassie Bony l. will ye go — BURNS 210:90
love a l., a bonnie — LAUD 583:38
love she's but a l. — BURNS 211:4
Never mind my grace, l. — SCOTT 855:94
service to my bonie l. — BURNS 210:97
wae my l. by my side — LAUD 583:39
last cobbler stick to his l. — APEL 31:87
great thing is to l. — HEMI 470:27
here it is at l. — JAMES 517:32
l. best friend — SOUT 954:42
l. of all he was seen of me — BIBLE 151:65
l. of all the Bards — SCOTT 853:42
l. one is as good — HEMI 470:22

last (*contd.*)
l. person to say anything — SAKI 838:15
l. shall be first — BIBLE 139:27
l. to lay the Old aside — POPE 778:82
l.…will go over very quickly — EISE 364:84
l. word on nothing — HUGO 503:94
One of the l. — UPDI 1037:59
She is the l. of lands — HOPE 490:72
sung her first and l. — GIBB 422:32
the l. act crowns the play — QUAR 796:52
lasting more l. than bronze — HORA 493:24
lasts It l. and ever shall — JULI 539:67
latch door has a creaking l. — POUND 786:68
press down the l. — WORD 1095:11
late always either too l. or too early — SART 844:9
comfort comes too l. — SHAK 918:66
coming l. to a performance — ZOLO 1110:27
Dread of being l.! — BETJ 101:59
five minutes too l. — COWL 291:21
L. have I loved you — AUGU 49:10
long choosing, and beginning l. — MILT 692:98
make sure of not being l. — KIER 556:59
people who are l. — LUCAS 618:24
sit up l. — BIBLE 119:41
soon or l. — THOM 1012:11
unhappy day too l. — SHAK 867:56
wakest too l. — SKEL 942:36
we have come too l. — LABR 572:35
later l. than you think — SERV 859:57
Latin Don't quote L. — WELL 1064:19
from the L. e, out — LEAC 589:45
L. America owes its being — VASC 1040:10
L. Man's natural language — FLAU 393:46
more fanatical official than a L. — HAZZ 464:27
ne yet of L. — SPEN 958:23
small L., and less Greek — JONS 535:9
speech as…dignified as L. — QUIL 797:59
latitude wishes to claim a certain l. — HAWT 461:72
Latium arts into rustic L. — HORA 493:29
latrine mouth…used as a l. — AMIS 16:71
latter l. stems from virtue — HELO 469:7
lattice cried through the l. — BIBLE 109:14
laudanum abuse…like l. — STOWE 978:87
laudate L. Dominum, omnes gentes — BIBLE 159:47
laugh And l. as I pass — SHEL 928:82
Anything awful makes me l. — LAMB 576:13
arms hang down to l. — ELIOT 367:66
But I l. — HUGH 499:14
Dinna mak' me l. — LAUD 583:37
do we not l.? — SHAK 872:80
Famous for his l. — FLAU 393:45
heard…a meaning l. — EWART 381:43
if I l. at any mortal thing — BYRON 223:51
If we didn't. — LLOYD 608:52
l. a like squadron of cavalry — WODE 1089:94
l. all of the time — LOOS 613:34
l. and lie — PARK 754:9
L. at all you trembled at — COWP 292:48
l. at him before — NATH 721:86
l. at human actions — SPIN 960:46
l. at…l. with — SPEN 957:89
l. broke into a thousand pieces — BARR 72:43
L., heart — YEATS 1105:62
l. is the best pesticide — NABO 717:12
l. like parrots — SHAK 872:76
l. me to scorn — BIBLE 114:48
L. no man to scorn — BIBLE 132:97
l. of superiority — GREE 445:28
l. on that particular day — TRAV 1025:34
L. to scorn — SHAK 909:67
l. uproariously in youth — BROO 192:29
L. where we must — POPE 780:33
l. with me, or at me — STER 969:90
lips that l. and hide — SWIN 986:25

laugh (*contd.*)
man cannot make him l. — SHAK 878:6
more ridiculous than a ridiculous l. — CATU 245:61
not a thing to l. to scorn — SHAK 887:26
nothing more unbecoming…to l. — CONG 280:6
Poetry is what makes me l. — THOM 1011:73
quick to l. at everything — BEAU 79:60
sitteth in the heavens shall l. — BIBLE 114:31
those whom I love…make me l. — AUDEN 48:95
way people look and l. — WOOLF 1092:56
laughed Full well they l. — GOLD 433:12
I l. him out of patience — SHAK 905:75
l. and suffered at my side — SASS 845:31
speck ter be l. at — HARR 458:32
When he l. — AUDEN 47:67
laughing boughs do l. blossoms bear — SPEN 958:69
cannot forebear l. — PEPYS 765:67
l. in the diners — SAND 841:59
L., quaffing, and unthinking — DRYD 352:95
most fun…without l. — ALLEN 14:47
so filled with L. Gas — TRAV 1025:99
waked herself with l. — SHAK 879:42
when I am l. at anyone — BEER 83:25
laughing-stock l.-s. of children — SIDN 937:59
laughs crowd l. with you always — VIDOR 1044:74
get l. without falling — WISD 1087:70
he l. longest who l. last — MASE 662:47
he who l. last — ALEX 13:15
irritating l. — GILB 425:84
l. with a harvest — JERR 521:14
world l. with you — WILC 1075:25
laughter alone with his l. — KAFKA 541:89
better to write of l. — RABE 798:7
bitterness in our l. — EMER 377:62
faculty of l. — ADDI 7:26
feast is made for l. — BIBLE 123:38
girls' thin l. — RICK 811:74
'Homeric l.' — FLAU 393:45
illiberal and ill-bred, as audible l. — CHES 257:77
inexhaustible source of l. — TOLS 1023:99
kind of l. people laugh at — MACI 631:39
l. at their quaint opinions — MILT 691:90
L. is a reward — CHAN 251:59
l., It is mad — BIBLE 122:18
L. need not be cut out — THUR 1020:54
l. of a fool — BIBLE 123:27
L. pleasant — PEAC 762:28
Let us have…mirth and l. — BYRON 222:42
listens to your sweet l. — CATU 245:62
love and l. — GORD 435:63
no time for mirth and l. — ADE 8:42
Our sincerest l. — SHEL 929:5
peals of l. …round thee — POPE 781:61
produce l. — JOHN 529:79
scattered l. in the rear — KAUF 543:21
seismic with l. — BARK 71:17
senators burst with l. — AUDEN 47:67
The l. of man — THUR 1019:44
turns herself to l. — SPEN 958:25
under running l. — THOM 1013:28
weeping and with l. — MACA 624:18
With mirth and l. — SHAK 873:88
laundries Land of l. — BETJ 100:39
laundry any first-class l. — LEAC 589:44
goes into the l. — KIPL 563:95
Laune dragons of L. and Lane — ORAH 741:77
Laura if L. had been Petrach's wife — BYRON 223:47
Rose-cheeked L. — CAMP 228:38
laurel l. for the perfect prime — ROSS 823:70
l., meed of mighty conquerors — SPEN 957:99
laurels 'Tis sweet to win…ones l. — BYRON 222:33
worth all your l. — BYRON 223:65
ye l., and once more — MILT 684:38

lava walk on the l. …while cooling   PATE 760:*98*
lavatory men-servants' l.   WAUGH 1056:*78*
lavender L. water tinged with pink   LEAR 590:*62*
Lavinian Italy, at its L. shore   VIRG 1045:*79*
law All things, by a l. divine   SHEL 928:*85*
almost a l.   WELLS 1065:*39*
Angel, it's a l. of nature   LACL 574:*67*
basic l. of economics   HARR 459:*40*
bondage known to our l.   MILL 675:*79*
both the l. and the gospel   JONS 536:*19*
break Diana's l.   POPE 778:*96*
breeds without the L.   KIPL 562:*62*
brilliance is needed in the l.   MORT 710:*91*
business of l.   MACL 634:*83*
care for your l.   TRUM 1030:*34*
come to destroy the l.   BIBLE 134:*37*
Conservatives, as being by the l.   MILL 675:*68*
Creation's final l.   TENN 999:*32*
Creation's final l.   TENN 999:*41*
criminal l. is no use   SHAW 924:*90*
Custom that is before all l.   DANI 304:*65*
dinna ken muckle about the l.   SCOTT 855:*92*
Every l. is a contract   SELD 857:*33*
Every l. is an evil   BENT 92:*15*
first is l.   DRYD 350:*51*
fulfilled the l.   BIBLE 149:*39*
game within the view of the l.   LEAC 589:*42*
goal of every system of l.   ROUS 827:*33*
God is thy l.   MILT 690:*61*
God's l. thet fetters   LOWE 616:*81*
good of the people is the chief l.   CICE 266:*58*
hang all the l. and the prophets   BIBLE 139:*34*
he whom l. calls yours   DRYD 348:*96*
higher l. in journalism   LIPP 606:*31*
Hofstader's L.   HOFS 484:*61*
Ignorance of the l.   SELD 857:*34*
Ignorance of the l.   SELD 857:*35*
in his l. doth he meditate   BIBLE 113:*29*
internal equivalent of…rule of l.   EDEN 360:*22*
invariable l. of the newspaper   DANA 304:*57*
it is of no force in l.   COKE 272:*71*
judgments of the English l.   SYNGE 988:*63*
Keep ye the l.   KIPL 561:*53*
keepeth the l., happy is he   BIBLE 122:*11*
know the l. since I have spent   MILI 674:*55*
l. cannot make a man love   KING 557:*74*
l. has very wisely given   JOHN 528:*42*
l. hath not been dead   SHAK 896:*70*
l. is a ass   DICK 321:*42*
L. is a bottomless pit   ARBU 33:*9*
L. is naturally founded   MONT 702:*82*
l. is such an ass   CHAP 252:*76*
l. is the most powerful   GIRA 429:*44*
L. is the true embodiment   GILB 424:*73*
l. like…black cobweb   WEBS 1060:*49*
l. not supported by the people   HUMP 504:*13*
l. of academic life   LODGE 610:*82*
l. of death   ANON 24:*13*
l. of God   MARG 650:*57*
l. of love   SCEVE 846:*56*
l. of Moses is harsh   MORE 706:*46*
l. of nature   HOOK 489:*54*
l. of the jungle   JUMB 539:*70*
L. of the Jungle   KIPL 561:*49*
l. of the Lord is perfect   BIBLE 114:*45*
l. of the musical world   WHAR 1068:*3*
l. of the Yukon   SERV 859:*54*
l. pervading all nature   HARDY 457:*5*
l. seems like a sort of maze   MORT 710:*92*
l.'s their will   SHAK 910:*92*
l. to weed it out   BACON 56:*48*
l. unto themselves   BIBLE 148:*13*
l. [of competition]…hard   CARN 236:*6*
love is liberty, and nature, l.   POPE 779:*8*

law (*contd.*)
love is the fulfilling of the l.   BIBLE 150:*40*
love thy l.   BIBLE 119:*35*
Men…have L. for their god   PLATO 774:*8*
moral l. within me   KANT 542:*7*
mysterious l., true source   MILT 690:*65*
nine points of the l.   ANON 23:*94*
nine-tenths of the l. of chivalry   SAYE 846:*48*
no l. if we were to invoke one code   EISE 364:*85*
no l. to prevent us   SHAW 921:*29*
No man may point to any l.   DOUG 342:*75*
no right to transgress the l.   DOST 340:*43*
nor the world's l.   SHAK 870:*21*
not according to the l.   BIBLE 112:*93*
one l., one element   TENN 1000:*63*
Order is heaven's first l.   POPE 781:*48*
Party of l. and order   BLAIR 165:*53*
People crushed by l.   BURKE 207:*19*
prayers for the observers of his l.   BACON 58:*78*
president…incapable of enforcing l.   MARC 649:*46*
principle of the English l.   DICK 325:*35*
prisoners…I'll find them l.   MACQ 638:*52*
Prisons are built with stones of L.   BLAKE 166:*76*
prohibited by l.   LEVIN 600:*28*
protection of the English l.   MANS 648:*16*
purlieus of the l.   TENN 999:*51*
Raped by…alien l.   WRIG 1102:*11*
rational study of the l.   HOLM 487:*4*
rebellion against the existing l.   SHAW 924:*93*
religions established by l.   PAINE 750:*48*
rigid l. pursues   JOHN 525:*79*
rule by l. and rule by whim   DOUG 342:*69*
saved me from the l. of sin   WESL 1066:*66*
scarecrow of the l.   SHAK 896:*64*
serve the l. of God   BIBLE 149:*24*
shatterday till the fear of the L.   JOYCE 538:*61*
should become a universal l.   KANT 542:*4*
simple that has lost its l.   LOWE 617:*6*
So long as the l. considers   STOWE 978:*84*
sources of international l.   UNIT 1036:*45*
sufficient to keep His L.   JUANA 539:*66*
suppressed by federal l.   HOOV 490:*61*
Take the moral l.   STEV 971:*34*
that is the l.   BAUD 77:*24*
The l. of the survival   SUMN 981:*27*
The l.'s delay   TWAIN 1033:*89*
those by l. protected   BURNS 209:*69*
truant in the l.   SHAK 860:*92*
usual l. of nature   HARV 460:*55*
very good l. for all that   SCOTT 854:*75*
violated any l.   LOVE 615:*70*
we're l. reformers   HUMP 504:*14*
What l. have I broken?   SITT 940:*98*
where no l.…no transgression   BIBLE 148:*16*
Who to himself is l.   CHAP 252:*69*
whole of the L.   CROW 298:*65*
windward of the l.   CHUR 262:*85*
windy side of the l.   SHAK 895:*32*
Would it be a reasonable l.   SMITH 945:*88*
law-courts regard the l.-c.   INGR 511:*45*
law-religions feature of all l.-r.   PAINE 750:*48*
lawbreakers We're not l.   HUMP 504:*14*
lawful All things are l. for me   BIBLE 150:*56*
L. as eating   SHAK 912:*43*
not l. for me to do   BIBLE 139:*29*
lawless Tribeless, l., homeless   HOMER 488:*21*
lawlessness l. of something simple   LOWE 617:*6*
lawn l. about the shoulders   HERR 478:*68*
L. as white as driven snow   SHAK 912:*36*
l. tennis…and Handel's Messiah   SHAW 925:*34*
L. Tennyson   JOYCE 538:*49*
Out on the l. I lie   AUDEN 46:*50*
rivulets…through the l.   TENN 998:*13*
to rake the l.   UPDI 1037:*64*

lawn (*contd.*)
twice a saint in l.   POPE 781:*55*
vomit on somebody's …l.   BOYD 182:*62*
wet bird-haunted English l.   ARNO 37:*75*
lawns fair with orchard l.   TENN 1004:*48*
l. and avenues   KIPL 564:*13*
level green l.   GILL 426:*4*
mowers on suburban l.   RICK 811:*74*
Russet l. and fallows grey   MILT 682:*1*
satyrs grazing on the l.   MARL 653:*4*
Lawrence D H L. was right   GIBB 422:*36*
D H L.'s 'Kangaroo'   STEW 977:*63*
keep D H L. poor   BRAD 183:*87*
laws all the l. of Nature   THOR 1016:*72*
as for Thy l.   HERB 474:*12*
bad and obnoxious l.   GRANT 439:*9*
Bad l. are the worst sort of tyranny   BURKE 207:*22*
base l. of servitude   DRYD 347:*69*
brain may devise l.   SHAK 874:*12*
customs…are the l. of nature   SHAW 921:*19*
do anything the l. permit   MONT 703:*86*
dole unequal l.   TENN 994:*57*
drama's l.   JOHN 525:*80*
eluded L.   JOHN 525:*76*
enforces, and breaks l.   LEGU 594:*27*
except general l. of nature   HUGO 501:*57*
explained by a few simple l.   BROWN 194:*57*
Farewell, Love, and all thy l.   WYATT 1102:*27*
good l. should make   JONS 535:*98*
government of l.   ADAMS 5:*84*
If there are…iron l. of history   EAGL 359:*4*
In their l. …one clause   RABE 799:*86*
l. and customs…evolved   POWE 788:*18*
l. and sets mantraps   LOWE 616:*77*
L. are like cobwebs   SWIFT 984:*63*
L.…are not our Life   CARL 235:*74*
l. bound in calf   DOSP 340:*40*
L. grind the poor   GOLD 432:*98*
l. of fallen world   BLOOM 170:*37*
l. of God will be suspended   SHAW 925:*70*
l. of God, the l. of man   HOUS 496:*73*
L. of Nature cannot account   MILL 675:*73*
l. of possibility   REDON 804:*77*
L. of Production   MILL 674:*57*
l. of prose writing   HEMI 471:*36*
l. of space and time   CORY 288:*66*
l. or kings can cause   GOLD 432:*99*
l.…silent in time of war   CICE 266:*59*
l. were made to be   NORTH 731:*31*
l. were then most sure   MARL 653:*97*
majestic equality of l.   FRAN 401:*90*
makers, and their l. approve   DRYD 351:*56*
more we know of the l.   HARDY 457:*9*
neither the l. made   JOHN 522:*32*
new code of l.   ADAMS 4:*61*
No doubt there are l.   HEINE 467:*71*
not governed by the same l.   DISR 332:*30*
nothing in the l. of value   MILL 674:*59*
nothing to do with the l.   HORS 494:*38*
of breach of l.   SURR 982:*44*
offended…thy holy l.   BOOK 173:*89*
one of my L. of Physics   OATES 733:*54*
rape us with…their l.   FREN 404:*39*
skulked behind the l.   DRYD 349:*16*
Technology breaks the l.   OGDEN 736:*1*
things the l. of life   RUSK 830:*92*
Useless l. weaken   MONT 703:*89*
Where l. end   PITT 771:*67*
whether L. be right   WILDE 1078:*3*
who writes the nation's l.   PERE 766:*91*
women themselves help to make l.   ANTH 31:*85*
lawsuits L. make poverty   ANON 22:*79*
lawyer client is fain to hire a l.   BUTL 216:*1*
I am only a l.   BIRK 163:*23*

lawyer (*contd.*)
important attribute of a l.	KENN 552:1
l. and politician and a heretic	MENC 669:64
l. could not have been heard	JONS 534:84
l.'s dream of heaven	BUTL 218:50
l. has no business	JOHN 529:65
l. interprets the truth	GIRA 429:44
l....swallowed up with business	WALT 1052:10
l.'s truth is not Truth	THOR 1016:67
l. trying to pick a smart jury	BAIL 62:67
l. with a briefcase can steal	PUZO 796:40
not, what a l. tells me I may do	BURKE 207:9
seditious Middle Temple l.	CHUR 264:8
trial with a l.	THOM 1014:39
When a l. cashes in?	SAND 841:63

lawyers coachload of l.
kill all the l.	SHAK 861:11
l. find out...Litigous men	DONNE 337:80
l. who don't care	RENO 806:3
Poor l....dear	WHIS 1069:15
Woe unto you, l.!	BIBLE 143:93

lay Discord...makes the sweeter l.
from her melodious l.	SHAK 892:72
l. it on so thick	BUTL 217:36
L. on, Macduff	SHAK 910:90
unpremeditated l.	SCOTT 853:43

layman comprehension of the l. — GOWE 437:82

lays constructing tribal l. — KIPL 561:48

Lazarus certain beggar named L. — BIBLE 143:6
Come forth, L.!	JOYCE 538:50
L. in his bosom	BIBLE 144:7

lazy ignominiously l. — SAND 842:82
L. and silly	SITW 941:15
l., long, lascivious reign	DEFOE 312:78
responsibility...to be l.	PALEY 751:64

LBJ All the Way with L. — HOLT 487:6
Hey, hey, L.!	ANON 27:79

lea On fair Kirkconnell l.! — BALL 67:41
On yonder l.	BURNS 213:50
The sun has left the l.	SCOTT 855:3
this pleasant l.	WORD 1099:73

lea-rig meet thee on the l.-r. — BURNS 212:36

lead don't l. by pointing — KESEY 554:22
Go down like lumps of l.	HODG 484:52
gold wes changyd in to l.	ANON 22:68
heart of l.	POPE 782:97
hot as molten l.	SHAK 876:74
L. us, Heavenly Father	EDME 361:45
looked to the other to take the l.	SMUTS 950:67
not the l. dog	ANON 29:48
pound in l. to your marriage	MIDD 673:39
scald like molten l.	SHAK 904:42

leaden if I use the l. ones — BELL 87:99

leader commons...want their l. — SHAK 861:5
fanatic great l. just entering	BROUN 193:49
first practical l.	WILDE 1075:31
l. cut from whipcord	MANC 644:62
l. of the Conservative Party	BEAV 80:80
L. of the Opposition	DISR 333:20
No l. deserves	WEI 1061:75
no l., faction, party or class	OAKE 733:49
One realm, one people, one l.	ANON 26:40
rarest...—a Labour l.	MACF 629:15
such a man were L. of the House	DISR 333:2
The l. must know	RAND 801:23

leaders believe in magical l. — NEWM 724:33
choose l. on basis of reading	BROD 189:72
continue being l. of the world	IACO 509:17
l. of white-mouse faction	MACD 628:92
l. who make them suffer	SIHA 938:73
L....do the right things	BENN 92:8
scrupulous ...are not the l.	CONR 285:7

leadership men do not approach to l. — BEVE 102:72
not practising l.	THAT 1008:31

leadership (*contd.*)
put forward for the l.	HESE 479:79
Reagan...wasn't without l. ability	ONEI 740:65
stuff of political l.	WILS 1085:42

leading can't tell who's l. — SNAG 950:68
L. School, First-rate School	WAUGH 1056:61
l. the Conservatives	HESE 479:80
with most of his l. ladies	NIVEN 730:6

leads dark place where it l. — JONG 533:60

leaf Are you the l. — YEATS 1106:80
aspes l. she gan to quake	CHAU 254:7
burning l.; prithee,	MILL 676:81
I were like the l.	SWIN 987:44
last red l.	TENN 998:25
l. also shall not wither	BIBLE 113:29
l. of grass is no less than	WHIT 1072:79
l. still in October	FLET 394:71
l. that lies rotting	CARL 235:64
l., the bud, the flower	SPEN 958:13
Love every l.	DOST 341:48
night that numbers the l.	STEV 972:65
November's l. is red	SCOTT 853:51
olive l. pluckt off	BIBLE 104:12
outline of l.	WILL 1082:81
the sere, the yellow l.	SHAK 910:81
Where the dead l. fell	KEATS 547:1

league believe in a L. system — ATTL 44:8
devotion to this great L. of Nations	CHAM 249:12
hadna sailed a l., a l.	BALL -101:36
Half a l. onward	TENN 1000:71
keep a l. till death	SHAK 868:66
L. and Cup double	BUSBY 215:83
L. of Nations	MACD 628:5
L. of Nations with an absolute	LEES 593:20
smaller but older l.	CHAM 249:12

leaking who was doing the l. — REAG 804:70

leal land o' the l. — NAIR 718:20

lean dying lady, l. and pale — SHEL 932:74
l. and hungry look	SHAK 882:23
l. over too far	THUR 1019:27

leap giant l. forward — ARMS 35:49
it were an easy l.	SHAK 875:46
l. over the rude facts	RABAN 798:76

leaping l., and praising God — BIBLE 147:83

leaps moves in mighty l. — AYRES 53:83

Lear King L....closest you can get — BUEC 203:41

learn can't l. architecture — JOHN 524:66
constantly l. more	SOLO 952:92
enough...know how to l.	ADAMS 5:79
for life...that we l.	SENE 858:47
From all I can l.	GALS 413:1
it is up to us to l.	RABAN 798:74
l. all the Law	KIPL 561:47
L. even from Novels	WELLS 1064:31
l. how we began this war	PRIE 790:37
l. in suffering	SHEL 927:69
l. so little	DAVI 307:8
l. to love by loving	HUXL 507:79
l. to pray	HERB 476:41
l. what not to play	GILL 426:10
l. while they teach	SENE 858:46
l....who He is	SCHW 852:31
let's l. not to know	JUANA 539:65
men do not l. very much	HUXL 508:89
Parents l. a lot	SPARK 955:47
she may l.	SHAK 873:84
To l. and labour	BOOK 175:38
We live and l.	POMF 777:68
We live and l.	TILM 1020:65
what you l. while...not studying	CONA 279:82
Where there is much to l.	MILT 685:59
you shall l. nothing	HUXL 508:96

learned devil...on the side of the l. — FRAN 401:86
Entrepreneurship can be l.	DRUC 346:45

learned (*contd.*)
For I have l.	WORD 1094:98
l. are cowards	DRYD 349:2
L. men...do many times fail	BACON 55:7
l....to be content	BIBLE 153:16
marries...hasn't l. much	STEIN 966:46
of the opinion with the l.	CONG 280:92
one thing we l.	READ 803:54
who has l. to obey	KEMP 549:41

learning a' the l. I desire — BURNS 209:60
accuse him to have wanted l.	DRYD 347:59
attain good l.	ASCH 41:51
Beauty and the lust for l.	BEER 83:33
better than l. a lot of things	HERN 476:46
can't be alwayth a l.	DICK 325:45
complexity of l.	JOVA 537:38
design career is a process of l.	BELL 86:94
Hibernian l.	ROCH 816:48
highest estimation of l.	SIDN 937:59
just enough l. to misquote	BYRON 219:50
know without l.	INGR 512:48
l. and blundering will live on	SAND 841:67
L., cobweb of the brain	BUTL 216:18
l. is...dangerous	POPE 778:79
l. what not to say	BAIN 62:73
let all l. in	ANON 23:82
light of l.	RALE 800:15
lost in their collected l.	HAWT 461:67
men with book l.	RAMOS 801:17
more l. in their language	JOHN 530:99
much l. doth make thee mad	BIBLE 148:9
O this l.!	SHAK 864:74
Of such deep l.	SPEN 958:23
on scraps of l. doat	YOUNG 1108:4
process of l. is accompanied	WILD 1080:35
the magazines of l.	LUCR 619:35
tough time l. how	KENN 552:99
Wear your l. like your watch	CHES 257:76
where l. may be...impossible	OAKE 733:50

learnt smash...everything l. — ORTE 741:84
what has been l. has been forgotten	SKIN 943:51

leas In lust l. at liberty — WYATT 1102:25

lease l. for a year — ANOU 30:71
summer's l.	SHAK 912:48
without any predictable l.	KOSI 568:3

leash Mankind Under The L. — DISCH 331:67

least l. of all the saints — BIBLE 152:97
Where the l....control	WORD 1094:95

leather case me in l. — SHAK 865:2
Gave up...his l. wax and all	EGAN 362:55
l....to a shoemaker	WAUGH 1057:92
little bit of l.	MITF 697:94
real l. ball	UTTL 1038:82

leave For who would l. — JOHN 525:78
l. her far away	KEATS 545:61
l. out of the definition	KING 559:7
l. some skin on	KHRU 556:49
not l. in San Francisco	HART 459:43
shall be happy to l.	BAUD 77:25
take my l. of the Jew	SHAK 874:25
will take my l. of you	SHAK 889:95
will ye l. me thus?	HERB 476:36

leave-taking It is not worth l.-t. — SHAK 906:7

leaves amongst the shady l. — SPEN 958:19
Autumn fills thy lap with l.	COLL 277:49
before the l. have fallen	WILH 1080:38
between The sleeping l.	COWP 293:53
burning of the l.	BINY 162:2
covered up in l.	KEATS 548:17
crowned with calm l.	SWIN 987:37
dazzling through the l.	TENN 993:43
deliquescent l. of paper	ANDR 18:11
Falls like the l. in October	FULL 410:55
famous harmony of l.	YEATS 1104:59

leaves (*contd.*)

flutter far more, than l. do	CENN 248:95
fond of handling the l.	SHER 933:79
golden dead l.	LEVE 600:23
June…in green l.	SPEN 959:42
laughing l. of the tree	SWIN 986:25
l. and flowers do cover	WEBS 1060:44
l. are green	ANON 21:56
l. are green	ANON 23:90
l. dead Are driven	SHEL 928:86
l. grow on the tree	YEATS 1104:56
l. of myrtle	MARL 655:31
l. of tree for healing of nations	BIBLE 159:39
l. to a tree	KEATS 544:51
Like that of l.	HOMER 487:17
lisp of l.	SWIN 986:23
long l. cover me	SWIN 987:29
noise among the l.	KEATS 544:34
on Severn snow the l.	HOUS 495:53
only l. me fifty more	HOUS 494:40
past…like the l. of a book	WOOLF 1092:55
sewed fig l. together	BIBLE 103:95
Shatter your l.	MILT 684:38
shows his hoar l.	SHAK 892:71
spear through the dead l.	MANS 647:5
Tawny are the l.	RANS 802:33
tender l. of hopes	SHAK 918:61
the falling l.	SMART 944:72
The riverbed… half full of l.	HEAN 465:40
those barren l.	WORD 1094:3
thou among the l.	KEATS 547:15
to some, l. free to all	MILT 690:64
Uneasily the l. fall	PURDY 795:34
What if my l. are falling	SHEL 928:90
yellow drifts Of withered l.	ARNO 39:23
yellow l., or none	SHAK 914:73

leaving Dear World, I am l.

his life…the l. of it	SHAK 907:23
L. reminds us	FORD 397:23
prevent them from l.	KENN 552:84

leavings sacrifice…of the devil's l. | POPE 779:17

Lebanon cedared L. | KEATS 546:95
Irish…as the Shiites in L. | OROU 741:79

Leben L. ist Nur ein Moment | SCHI 847:68
Mehr als das L. | SCHI 847:70

lechery L., l., still | SHAK 896:58

lecteur hypocrite l.! | ELIOT 368:84

lecture classic l. | TENN 996:92
twilight from the l. | STEV 971:53

lecturers l. shouldn't be wasted | ZELD 1109:16

lectures comes to hear your l. | BRAD 183:83
l. & my poetry | BERR 98:17

lecturing experience of popular l. | HUXL 509:5

lederhosen Metaphysical l. | ENRI 379:94

lee between windward and l. | SWIN 988:56
dragons of Laune…and L. | ORAH 741:77

leek l. is the asparagus | FRAN 401:89

leeks eyes were green as l. | SHAK 872:59

leer assent with civil l. | POPE 781:65
fascinating l. | GILB 425:80

lees l. left by Bismarck | GREY 446:55

le Fey third sister, Morgan l. F. | MALO 642:23

left better to be l. than never…loved | CONG 281:32
Keep your l. hand high | ONEI 740:68
l. hand is my thinking hand | HEPW 473:81
l. the room | GROS 447:72
Let them be l. | HOPK 492:96
liberal middle class will shift to the l. | EAGL 359:4
not allowing his l. wing to see | ASQU 42:87
slightly l. of centre | FRYE 409:25

left-guard play l.-g. for the Colts | BRES 187:36

leg here I leave my second l. | HOOD 488:35
literary man—with a wooden l. | DICK 327:77
sell his wooden l. | DICK 323:78

leg (*contd.*)

which l. went after which	CRAS 296:28

leg-irons with tinkliing l.-i. | WALC 1048:39

legacy No l. is so rich | SHAK 901:76

legal hasn't exactly got a l. mind | BETJ 100:43
judge in the l. and moral sense | DEWEY 319:96
l. and material hindrances | WOLF 1089:11
l. gentleman who rescues your estate | BROU 193:46
l. or moral responsibility | HAYD 462:88
l. requirements | BIRNS 163:27

legality taint of l. | KNOX 567:60

legend bloody tough being a l. | ATKI 44:4
fables in the l. | BACON 57:64
l. of the Gael | RUSS 833:36
past exudes l. | MALA 641:9

legends accepted economic l. | GALB 411:77
aged l. say | ROSS 824:91

legion aunts and uncles were l. | SHAW 926:43
L. of Honour | TWAIN 1032:73
l. of the unremarked | SAFI 836:72
L.: for we are many | BIBLE 141:64
refuse the L. d'Honneur | SATIE 846:47

legions give me back my l. | AUGU 50:19
l. with the ways of Death | LIND 605:11
puissant l., whose exile | MILT 688:6
the moving l. mingled | LUCR 619:35

legislate If civil authorities l. | JOHN 522:32
l. to make the well-to-do | BRYAN 201:14

legislation foundation of…l. | BENT 92:13
frame its l. upon…justice | PEEL 763:43
L.'s sov'reign pow'rs | BURNS 210:86
strength to influence l. | MURR 716:79

legislative important l. actions | JEVO 521:23
l. power | GIBB 421:19

legislators unacknowledged l. | SHEL 931:60

legislature constitution of the l. | MILL 675:67
interference of the l. | RICA 808:34
l. of this country | PITT 771:71
l. was animated by a sincere desire | PEEL 763:43

Legree makes L. a bachelor | CHES 256:69

legs animal with four back l. | LECA 592:94
asure were his l. | CHAU 255:45
chess with arms and l. | BARZ 75:98
could never have stood upon his l. | DICK 323:89
Dogs with broken l. | PATC 759:91
Four l. good | ORWE 744:30
good for your l. | SCHU 850:12
he pulls the l. of his dreams | THOM 1011:84
His l. bestrid the ocean | SHAK 906:1
His l., perhaps, were shorter | STRA 979:96
l. go first | FRAY 403:21
l. ungainly huddled | SASS 845:32
l. were such Diana shows | HERR 477:59
more to marriage than four bare l. | DAVI 308:12
no l.,…no chance | ANON 26:50
not for your bad l. | ELIZ 373:91
open my l. | HILL 481:11
recuvver the use o' his l. | DICK 321:49
same old l. | GIRO 429:47
see my l. when I take my boots off | DICK 323:97
slimy things did crawl with l. | COLE 273:88
strongest l. in Pontefract | BETJ 101:53
two perfectly good l. | ROOS 821:40
Two vast and trunkless l. | SHEL 928:92
uglier a man's l. are | WELLS 1065:34
under his huge l. | SHAK 882:20
walking on its hinder l. | JOHN 528:39
walls of spiders' l. | DRAY 346:41
Wooden l. are not inherited | CONK 282:49
you have between your l. | BEEC 83:20

Leibniz L. never married | FONT 395:88

leisure At l. married | CONG 280:1
better pastime for l. | WELLS 1065:44
disguised l. are regarded | MISH 696:72

leisure (*contd.*)

Increased means and increased l.	DISR 333:16
iron…polish it at l.	DRYD 352:75
l. answers l.	SHAK 897:92
l. of study	GERB 420:98
l. ruined great kings	CATU 245:63
l. to bother about	SHAW 924:9
live at more l.	MONT 701:65
Men…detest at l.	BYRON 223:57
monotony, work or l.	POMP 777:71
repeat at l.	CABE 224:77
repent at l.	CONG 280:99
reputability to the gentleman of l.	VEBL 1041:27
take an hour's l.	STARK 963:97
wisdom…by opportunity of l.	BIBLE 132:16

LeMay Bombs away with Curtis L. | ANON 27:83

lemon in a squeezing of a l. | GOLD 433:23
squeezed as a l. is squeezed | GEDD 417:63
with a slice of l. | FLEM 393:59

lend If thou wilt l. this money | SHAK 874:22
L. less than thou owest | SHAK 902:4

lender Neither a borrower nor a l. be | SHAK 888:66

lendeth l. unto the Lord | BIBLE 121:90

length drags its dreary l. | DICK 324:19
nothing…but my body's l. | SHAK 862:31
of fabulously reptilian l. | LEWIS 602:63
poem of immeasurable l. | POUND 785:56
thou giv'st line, and l. | VAUG 1041:19
thumbs vary in l. | SHAW 925:30
What it Lacks in L. | FROST 407:95

Lenin done to death by L. | CHUR 263:98
L. was right | KEYN 554:27
L.…would say the same | ZHIV 1109:93
ought to remain of L. | RODC 818:81

lenses eyes are l. | DOUG 341:58

lenten what l. entertainment | SHAK 890:6
L. is come with love | ANON 22:69

lentil-soup L.-s. colors | HUGH 499:26

lentils pottage of l. | BIBLE 105:31

Leonora L., L., How the word rolls | CRAIK 294:90
To my daughter L. | WODE 1089:96

leopard l. his spots? | BIBLE 128:25
l. on a branch-strained | MOORE 705:29
l. shall lie down with the kid | BIBLE 125:68
whiff of a snow l. | CHAT 253:98

leopards Lions make l. tame | SHAK 866:34
three white l. | ELIOT 370:11

leper if he were a l. of old | PARN 756:39

lepers cleanse the l. | BIBLE 136:74
l. are cleansed | BIBLE 137:83

leprosy not l. or tuberculosis | THER 1008:35
scant as hair in l. | BROW 198:50

LeRoy Baby L. with an ice pick | ROST 825:3

Lesbia L. with her sparrows | MILL 676:84
My sweetest L. | CAMP 228:35

less do more with l. | FULL 410:41
expect l. of them | JOHN 532:28
in the l., foul profanation | SHAK 896:36
l. a man knows, the more sure he is | CARY 243:23
l. in this than meets the eye | BANK 69:88
l. than 'arf o' that | KIPL 561:35
L. than themselves | TESS 1006:80
Not a Penny l. | ARCH 33:12
The l. seen | WILD 1080:34
You mean you can't take l. | CARR 238:30

lesser l. life shall be the greater | GORD 435:63
Of two evils the l. should | KEMP 549:46

lesson final l. in…despair | POE 776:52
l. of life | EMER 377:71
l. to all of us men | AMIN 16:70
l. to be learned | MILL 679:49
l. we learn from life | FORD 396:94
mankind at least one l. | MUMF 713:46
No l. seems to be so deeply inculcated | SALI 839:34

lesson (*contd.*)

paradoxical l.	GLEI 430:61
profited by the l.	PALM 752:69
Satire is a l.!	NABO 717:10
still harder l.!	PORT 784:42
lessons first l.	GREER 445:41
give l. to the public	DIDE 329:32
history, what l. it might teach us!	COLE 275:27
learn'd great l. from	WHIT 1073:99
l....lessen from day to day	CARR 238:35
l. of historical experience	KISS 565:30
l. they might have drawn	HEGEL 466:63
most important of all the l.	HUXL 508:89
your l. never forgotten	WALL 1050:66
lethargy l. hath seized him	MASS 663:59
Lethe if no L. flows beneath	RANS 802:36
L.-wards had sunk	KEATS 547:13
Lethean drunken of things L.	SWIN 987:40
letter deal by speech than by l.	BACON 59:17
good face is a l. of recommendation	ADDI 7:13
had a l. from her	LEVE 599:20
I had written him a l.	PATE 760:97
if this l. speed	SHAK 902:1
l. from his wife	CARR 241:88
l. killeth, but the spirit giveth life	BIBLE 151:75
lone l. from a young man	BERR 98:16
made this l. longer	PASC 758:80
Next to a l. from home	DOOL 340:37
See what a large l.	BIBLE 152:3
thou unnecessary l.	SHAK 902:10
uncertain process of l.-writing	ELIOT 365:99
you received ... a l. from me	STEE 964:11
lettering stripped of its l.	FRAN 402:99
letters all l....should be free and easy	OSBO 745:66
allured to l.	STEE 964:22
answer 20,000 l. a year	CART 243:12
faint gold l.	UTTL 1038:82
fair words...in foulest l.?	SHAK 878:7
graven with diamonds in l. plain	WYATT 1103:28
l. at the end of an address	DOSP 340:40
l. mingle souls	DONNE 338:99
l., of soft interpreters	PRIOR 790:51
like individual l.	UPDI 1037:64
like to write l.?	HEMI 470:15
Men ignorant of l.	SAND 842:82
nat the l. space	254:13
no more exempt...than a man of l.	STER 970:14
Nobody knows how to write l.	CONG 281:36
Pause awhile from l.	JOHN 525:82
pin up your hair with... l.?	CONG 281:33
pray you, in your l.	SHAK 900:64
publishes his l.	WHITE 1070:35
sayings are generally like women's l.	HAZL 464:17
Scottish life and l.	MACD 628:92
shall receive no l.	JOHN 532:36
writing l. to every body	ARBU 33:11
lettuce allegories are so much l.	GINS 427:23
Leucon Let Eli rejoice with L.	SMART 944:64
levee Chevy to the l.	MACL 633:62
l. from a couch	CONG 282:43
level dead l. of provincial existence	ELIOT 365:20
l. of the light	FORD 396:6
l. to which it belongs	HAMM 453:45
meetings...held at a divine l.	ACHE 2:22
ranks of life...upon a l.	SMITH 945:78
Those who attempt to l.	BURKE 207:28
wish to l. down	JOHN 527:37
levellers l. wish to level	JOHN 527:37
Lévi-Strauss diagnosed by L.-S.	VAND 1039:94
leviathan draw out l. with an hook?	BIBLE 113:26
there is that l.	BIBLE 118:14
levitate People always claim...to l.	BOWL 182:58
levity smacks of l., immorality almost	STARK 963:95

lewd l. fellows of the baser sort	BIBLE 148:97
l. well natured friend	ROCH 817:62
lewdness aspect of l. in Liverpool	FORD 396:2
Lewis Daniel Day L. has what	GIEL 423:49
Mr L.'s pictures	SITW 941:20
lexicographer l. can only hope	JOHN 526:4
L. A writer of dictionaries	JOHN 526:12
wake a l.	JOHN 526:8
lexicography lost in l.	JOHN 526:5
lexicon international l.	GORB 435:57
l. of conflict and drama	SAFI 835:61
liabilities no longer l. but assets	SCHL 848:77
liability clarity was a great l.	BALF 65:20
liable l. To read in the Bible	HEYW 480:90
liaison hypothetical l.	NATH 721:85
l. is almost always pardonable	GRAV 440:28
liar best l. he who makes	BUTL 217:37
every man a l.	BIBLE 148:14
exceptionally good l.	JERO 521:9
He was not a l.	LAUT 584:48
I am the Club L.	SAKI 838:14
l. gone to burning hell	SHAK 900:58
Love is always a l.	RUIZ 828:48
man who tells the truth...is a l.	SAFI 836:70
only thing worse than a l.	WILL 1081:60
picturesque l.	TWAIN 1033:96
proved l.	HAIL 451:13
liars all cheats and l.	JONES 533:56
All men are l.	BIBLE 118:25
Cretans are always l.	BIBLE 154:42
fears may be l.	CLOU 270:32
lecherous l.	WILD 1079:31
l. in old clothes	MARQ 656:52
l. in public places	POUND 786:64
L. need to have good memories	QUIN 798:70
L. ought to have good memories	SIDN 936:41
L. out of the American people	ROGE 820:11
libel excessive wealth a l.	SHEL 927:57
limitations those of l.	THUR 1019:49
that wholesale l.	PARK 754:2
writs for l. and slander	PROF 792:77
liberal either a little L.	GILB 424:75
l....conservative...arrested	WOLFE 1091:30
l. democratic principles	AUNG 50:22
l....tells other people	BARA 70:7
L....wishes to replace them	BIER 161:75
sector of the l. middle class	EAGL 359:4
value of a l. education	BREW 187:38
We who are l.	TRIL 1026:58
liberal-minded gentle; l.-m., great	TENN 1000:62
liberalism l. has been tried	MACG 630:33
liberality hate l.	SIDM 936:40
liberalization l. of prices	PAVL 761:20
Liberals L. can dream	MACL 634:90
L. in a hurry	SAINT 836:78
not mind the L.	WHIT 1072:70
liberate we shall l. this country	MAND 645:70
liberated l. from a small...self	ELIOT 366:40
liberation between further l.	GINS 428:33
Communist 'war of l.'	MACN 636:28
For l.—not less of love	ELIOT 373:76
l. of both body and mind	BANN 70:3
trumpet for Women's L.	LESS 598:5
Women's l. is the l.	KENT 553:9
liberationists Woman's L.	LOOS 613:38
libertas L. et natale solum	SWIFT 984:81
liberté Pour te nommer L.	ELUA 376:24
liberties conscience, above all l.	MILT 685:61
essential maxim of your l.	PITT 771:68
Freedom, what l....in thy name!	GEOR 419:91
people never give up l.	BURKE 207:24
repressed the economic l.	KRIS 569:94
take the institutions and l.	POWE 788:18
libertine puffed and reckless l.	SHAK 888:62

liberty belief in human l.	MACL 634:85
blaze of truth and l.	MACA 622:90
can be no effective l.	BELL 86:85
cause of a single life is l.	BACON 57:58
certainly destroys l.	JOHN 531:22
conceived in l. ·	LINC 605:2
concentrate to truth and l.	SHEL 927:65
condition...God hath given l.	CURR 301:16
constitutional l.	GIBB 421:21
contend for their l.	HALI 452:31
defence of l.	GOLD 433:31
desire...to lose l.	BACON 57:69
desiren l.	CHAU 255:38
Enjoy such l.	LOVE 615:63
every law is an infraction of l.	BENT 92:15
feelings of l.	PITT 771:66
for our l.	PITT 771:72
foundations of political l.	WILS 1086:52
Give me the l. to know	MILT 685:61
greater license...to obtain l.	COOP 287:44
idea of l.	SPIN 960:49
If l. means anything	ORWE 744:28
if l. of thought perishes	ORWE 745:52
Individuality...the aim of political l.	COOP 287:43
Know no such l.	LOVE 615:62
lakkith l.!	JAME 515:99
let us have our l. again	LANY 580:80
l. against tyranny	ROOS 822:52
L.'s a glorious feast!	BURNS 209:69
l., and the pursuit of happiness	JEFF 520:87
l....cannot flourish	HUXL 508:87
l. cannot long exist	BURKE 207:17
L....conceived by current opinion	MACC 625:48
L., Equality, Adultery	BELL 88:30
L., Equality, Faternity!	LAMA 575:3
L.'s exquisite pain	BROW 196:13
L.'s in every blow	BURNS 212:38
L. is l.	BERL 95:66
L. is...working or starving	JOHN 527:26
L. lends us her wings	BRON 191:2
L. means responsibility	SHAW 922:47
L....mother of virtue	WOLL 1091:38
L....must be limited	BURKE 207:16
l. of the press	JOHN 528:52
l. of the press	JUNI 540:74
l. of the Press	SHER 934:13
l. that the citizen enjoys	SPEN 956:68
l., that we'll enjoy	JONS 535:99
l. to follow my own will	LOCKE 609:70
l. to go abroad for ayre	PEPYS 765:75
life, l., and the pursuit of happiness	STAN 962:85
light, of l. and of learning	DISR 333:17
long odyssey toward l.	MAIL 639:81
love of l.	HAZL 463:2
lusty leas at l.	WYATT 1102:25
men are to wait for l.	MACA 622:91
notion of l.	JOHN 527:27
prefer poverty with l.	PITT 771:68
price of l. is...dirt	ORWE 742:95
proclaim l. to the captives	BIBLE 127:12
recipients of the boon of l.	MAMET 643:47
recovering l.	GALT 413:10
rules of ancient l.	MILT 686:76
settle our true l.	MONT 701:66
so easy as l.	ASTE 43:90
soul of a journey is l.	MARP 655:32
spirit of l.	HAND 455:67
survival and success of l.	KENN 550:64
Sweet land of l.	SMITH 948:27
taking quite a l. in going astray	ELIOT 365:2
there is no l. or freedom	NASHE 721:84
thy chosen music, L.!	WORD 1099:74
thy l. into bondage	SHAK 887:28
tree of l. must be refreshed	JEFF 520:90

liberty (contd.)
voices of l. be mute? — CUMM 300:84
walking…with the Statue of L. — CONR 285:16
When love is l. — POPE 779:8
Wine gives you l. — WYCH 1103:39
yelps for l. — JOHN 529:77
liberty-loving prayers of l.-l. people — EISE 363:78
librarians l. are keepers — MACL 634:77
libraries l. are food — TUCH 1031:48
L. are reservoirs of strength — GREER 445:43
l. of death — DOMI 335:56
l., querulous criticisms — WHIT 1073:85
When we run over l. — HUME 504:10
library a circulating l. in a town — SHER 933:79
cloister without a l. — GEOF 418:79
damned l. of yours! — ONEI 740:59
lumber room of his l. — DOYLE 344:4
public l. full of old newspapers — DOSP 340:40
replaced the l. pass — LODGE 610:80
smell of the l. — ACKR 4:54
than a public l. — JOHN 525:89
turn over half a l. — JOHN 529:72
libre condamné à être l. — SART 844:16
No vers is l. — ELIOT 371:42
Vive le Québec l.! — DE 313:4
libretto l. that should never — THOM 1015:60
Libya first triumph over L. — PLUT 775:37
licence love not freedom, but l. — MILT 686:77
scientist is given l. — LISP 607:39
servitude and extreme l. — TOCQ 1021:75
TV l. — THOM 1015:59
license accord greater l. — COOP 287:44
licensing l. and prohibiting — MILT 685:62
licentious l. passages — GIBB 421:30
Marriage is the most l. — SHAW 922:41
licentiousness satify luxury and l. — MORE 707:51
lichen fungus or a l. — THOR 1016:69
licker L. talks mighty loud — HARR 458:29
licorice l. fields at Pontefract — BETJ 101:53
lid down came the l. — LEWIS 602:68
I dips me l. — DENN 316:61
lids lift their heavy l. — PATM 760:1
with thy vailèd l. — SHAK 888:48
lie Art is a l. — PICA 769:29
believe a l. — TAYL 992:21
big l. is no worse — ORWE 745:51
cannot tell a l. — WASH 1054:39
Don't l. — SZIL 989:72
Dost thou l. so low? — SHAK 883:43
every word she writes is a l. — MACC 626:59
fall victim to a big l. — HITL 482:28
honest man sent to l. abroad — WOTT 1101:97
I mean, you l. — SWIFT 986:8
isn't told a l. — KIPL 564:2
know to be a l. — HAMP 454:63
led to believe a l. — BLAKE 168:6
l. can travel halfway round the world — CALL 226:1
L. Circumstantial — SHAK 887:34
l. down alone — HOUS 496:82
l. down until the feeling passes — HUTC 506:44
L. follows by post — BERE 94:38
l. has become…a pillar — SOLZ 952:96
l.…is a beautiful twilight — CAMUS 229:62
l. is an abomination — STEV 972:69
l. is the handle — HOLM 486:87
L. not one to another — BIBLE 153:21
l. of their inferiority — KING 558:85
L. soft, sleep hard — MIDD 673:40
l. to and humbug themselves — WELLS 1064:28
l. where I am and sleep — SHIP 935:21
l. which is all a l. — TENN 1002:99
l. will go round the world — SPUR 961:64
l. with his mother earth? — SHAK 885:70
L. with me — BIBLE 105:43

lie (contd.)
l. with your legs ungainly — SASS 845:32
l. without moving — RHYS 808:27
loves to l. with me — SHAK 885:86
makes me down to l. — SCOT 856:19
misleading impression, not a l. — ARMS 35:51
Nature admits no l. — CARL 236:97
not a man, that he should l. — BIBLE 108:86
old L.: Dulce et decorum est — OWEN 748:13
Parliaments are the great l. — POBE 775:40
rather l. in the woollen — SHAK 879:33
remedies oft in ourselves do l. — SHAK 901:71
rule and dare not l. — TENN 1001:80
Science…is the great l. — GOUR 437:80
sixth, the L. with Circumstance — SHAK 887:35
Soul of my l. — HERR 477:56
telling a big l. about you — TRUM 1029:18
truth of God into a l. — BIBLE 148:12
Violence is a l. — JOHN 522:36
what is a l.? — BYRON 223:56
What's the good of a l. — GREE 445:30
When he speaketh a l. — BIBLE 146:51
when you come to l. here — SCOTT 856:18
lied to women l. like a Cretan — HARDY 456:88
lies all propaganda is l. — ORWE 743:21
Autobiographies tell more l. — BYATT 218:55
dashed and brewed with l. — DRYD 349:11
desirability…of telling l. — ORWE 745:50
don't deal in l. — KIPL 564:8
English polite by telling l. — BRAD 183:78
few more l. eat into the seed — MAIL 639:68
here he l. — STEV 975:31
Here l. Nolly Goldsmith — GARR 415:30
History is condemned…to l. — FRAN 401:83
History, sir, will tell l. — SHAW 921:17
how do passions resist l.? — DIDE 329:24
L. and literature — LAFO 575:87
l. are essential to humanity — PROU 793:4
l. are invented — BRAQ 185:12
l., damned l. and statistics — DISR 334:31
l.…from the loudspeakers — ORWE 744:40
l. one who meant well — STEV 976:48
L. That Are My Life — ELLI 375:15
l., thinking it is the truth — SAFI 836:70
make l. sound truthful — ORWE 744:48
Matilda told such Dreadful L. — BELL 87:10
more readily swallow l. than truth — GELL 417:70
old men's l. — POUND 786:64
one of the social l. — IBSEN 510:20
Plain l. are dangerous — SAYE 846:50
Some books are l. — BURNS 209:63
sweep away the refuge of l. — BIBLE 125:77
tell me no more unnecessary l. — ADAMS 6:92
telling l. and selling socks — MERW 672:27
The cruellest l. — STEV 974:12
truth to cover l. — CONG 280:10
lieutenant died…like a second l. — CLEM 268:2
life A missed l. — HEINE 467:72
access to a better l.…denied — ANGE 19:27
advances through l. — JOHN 526:2
afraid of l. — STEV 973:1
Alcohol…makes l. bearable — SHAW 923:81
all female l.…unclean — STAN 963:90
all his l.…in the wrong — ROCH 816:51
all human l. is there! — JAMES 516:31
all L. death does end — HOPK 492:5
all my l. — JOHN 523:39
all the blessings of this l. — BOOK 174:8
all the emergencies of l. — FORS 398:33
all the energies of his l. — PIER 769:32
amend my l. — SHAK 876:63
America's cultural l. — ROCK 818:78
American l. — MACC 625:46
American way of l. — MENC 670:87

life (contd.)
American writer…acquires a new l. — AMIS 17:89
and for her l. he died — STONE 978:73
And the l. everlasting — BOOK 173:94
And this our l. — SHAK 885:77
animal thirst for l. — BANKS 70:99
Anythin' for a quiet l. — DICK 321:32
appeal to the l. of Christ — WHIT 1071:61
Architecture is the…mirror of l. — PEI 764:49
arena to which he devoted his l. — LEHM 594:38
Art is only a means to l. — MILL 678:41
as though my very l. — JORD 537:31
At fifteen l. had taught me — ANGE 19:17
Bankrupt of l. — DRYD 349:14
be a queen for l. — POPE 782:76
beauty of l. through death — LAUT 584:55
believe in l.! — DU 353:10
believe in taking human l. — NATH 721:89
best of L. is but intoxication — BYRON 222:43
best part of married l. — WILD 1079:23
better standards of l. — UNIT 1036:45
better to dream your l. — PROU 792:87
better to enjoy l. — JOHN 527:17
between l. and death — WORD 1099:63
Bewilder'd in the maze of l. — LUCR 619:35
birthday of my l. — ROSS 823:66
bitter moments of l. — POWYS 788:21
bitterness of l.! — CARR 241:88
blind dates are a way of l. — EPST 379:6
blood-thirsty clinging to l. — ARNO 38:9
bone-ache disquietude of l. — ALLEN 14:34
Book of L. — WILDE 1077:65
books echoing the l. — WILL 1083:97
Books make sense of l. — BARN 72:33
books, they are l. — LOWE 615:72
born to eternal l. — FRAN 401:91
bottom of l. — WASH 1054:37
breath of l. — YEATS 1106:81
breathed into nostrils breath of l. — BIBLE 103:88
brevity of human l. — PROT 792:4
bring the dead to l. — GRAV 439:23
brings about a disconnected l. — HUGO 502:83
brisking about the l. — SMART 944:67
broke up their…habits of l. — SHER 932:76
business of l. — WELL 1064:18
but one in my l. — SAND 841:68
By my l. — SHAK 894:17
calamity of so long l. — TWAIN 1033:89
care for far more than human l. — PANK 752:79
careless of the single l. — TENN 999:39
cause of a single l. is liberty — BACON 57:34
cessation of individual l. — HUXL 508:1
chain I forged in l. — DICK 323:86
changes…we see in l. — FROST 406:71
Chaos often breeds l. — ADAMS 5:76
choice, becomes a way of l. — MILL 677:8
choose l. — BIBLE 108:99
cities, throbbed the true l. — NORR 731:9
citizen of l. — SASS 845:23
civilized human l. — TRUM 1030:22
cold as l. — RHYS 808:28
comes late in l. — JERR 521:15
common errors of our l. — SIDN 937:64
compensate for too little l. — BURG 206:85
concentrate on l. — GIDE 423:46
conclusions about l. — KIER 556:54
consumed by l. process — MACC 626:54
continentals think l. is a game — MIKES 674:53
contrary to l. — HUXL 507:62
cool sequestered vale of l. — GRAY 442:72
coping with l. — SPARK 955:47
corresponds to our dream l. — MAMET 643:43
course of a dishonest l. — FRAS 403:18
course to take in l. — KURO 571:21

life (*contd.*)

think about a better l.	WILD 1079:25
think it that 'New L.!'	DICK 327:94
Think of this l.	SHAK 882:19
this day's l. as yours	EURI 380:23
This was l.—my l.	FRAN 402:14
thorns of l.	SHEL 928:89
those with an irrational fear of l.	CONN 283:59
thread from l.'s frayed mantle	ABU 2:14
threaten to invade my waking l.	ROBB 813:12
threatened its l. with a railway-share	CARR 241:87
threatens the very existence of l.	SONT 953:7
three-fourths of our l.	ARNO 39:33
throughout the rest of l.	ORWE 744:38
thy dissolute l.	SURR 982:44
Till l. and death remember	SWIN 986:21
time in a man's l.	MALA 641:5
time in everybody's l.	WILD 1079:32
time is eating away my l.	BAUD 77:18
time of l. is short	SHAK 876:72
time of this mortal l.	BOOK 174:9
time…medium of l.	MANN 646:86
'Tis from high l.	POPE 781:55
to be spiritually minded is l.	BIBLE 149:26
to breathe were l.	TENN 994:58
to choose l. and d.	LOWE 617:2
too far back…in anybody's l.	AMIS 17:94
too far out all my l.	SMITH 948:33
tragedy of l. is not that man loses	BROUN 193:48
translate thy l. into death	SHAK 887:28
tree of knowledge is not that of L.	BYRON 221:19
tried to live his l. by it	ANDE 18:9
troubled with her lonely l.	PEPYS 765:69
turn to poetry to interpret l.	ARNO 40:39
two paths in l.	MANN 645:82
two things to aim at in l.	SMITH 947:10
unbought grace of l.	BURKE 207:32
unconscious unity of l.	MILL 678:43
undermine her hold on l.	FORS 398:43
unexamined l.	PLATO 774:4
unexamined l. is not worth living	SOCR 952:90
unified vision of l.	WILS 1084:15
Unless you stake your l.	HEIS 467:78
used by l. for its own purposes	MERR 672:22
Variety's the spice of l.	COWP 293:56
virtues carry with it l. and death	MARL 652:88
vision…of all ordinary human l.	ELIOT 366:37
voyage of their l.	SHAK 884:60
walls about our l.	SHAK 867:60
wastes part of his l.	JOHN 525:91
way of l.	GOER 430:34
way, which leadeth unto l.	BIBLE 135:59
we are all selling l.	CHER 256:66
Wealth cannot make a l.	HERR 477:55
web of our l.	SHAK 901:80
well-written l. almost as rare	CARL 235:76
what have I been doing all my l.	LAMB 576:8
What is L.?	HAGG 450:5
What is our l.?	RALE 800:14
What is this l.	DAVI 308:20
What is your l.?	BIBLE 155:70
what l. has taught me	MANS 647:11
what l. honestly and deeply means	JAMES 517:46
What l.…if…not l. together?	ELIOT 370:70
what matters in your l.	RUSH 829:67
What signifies the l. o' man	BURNS 209:57
What wonderous l.	MARV 658:85
whatever time of your l.	SPARK 955:52
wheel of l.	STER 969:7
when l. is hard	VIRG 1045:94
When l. looks black	ONOL 734:66
wherever you go in l.	MORR 708:77
whether l. is or is not worth living	CAMUS 228:46
while his l. lingered on	HOOV 490:60

life (*contd.*)

whole l. was spent riding	BLAN 168:22
whose l. in low estate	TENN 999:44
Wine is as good as l.	BIBLE 132:12
Without music, l.	NIET 729:92
without…any practical part of l.	ADDI 6:7
woman's whole l.	IRVI 513:64
words into l.	SENG 858:50
world of material l.	ARNO 39:20
worrisome day one calls l.	BERN 97:89
worst of prison l.	STEN 967:73
worth a l.'s experience	HOLM 486:79
yet been brought to l.	TOYN 1024:19
you risk your l. for it	VAN 1039:2
life-blood l.-b. of a master spirit	MILT 685:57
life-chances l.-c. of the young	MUSG 716:82
life-efficiency l.-e. and adaptability	MUMF 713:49
life-insurance detest l.-i. agents	LEAC 588:32
life-jacket French for l.	BARN 72:32
life-like not l.-l.; it is alive	CECIL 246:74
life-long l.-l. lock	GILB 425:88
life-sentence escape the l.-s.	LAWR 587:15
l.-s. in the dungeon of the self	CONN 283:77
life-style considers your whole l.-s.	THOM 1014:39
life-support kept on a l.-s. system	HARR 459:38
lifeless l. as the piles of dry dust	GLAS 430:60
L. in appearance	WILL 1082:83
lifetime During my l.	MAND 644:68
gather sense…for a whole l.	RILKE 811:83
in our l.	GREY 446:57
In the l. of one person	HORN 494:36
lifetime's happiness!	SHAW 921:22
l. of standing out	JARR 518:58
l. on this planet	KENN 550:63
locked for a l. in this impossible contradiction	
	EAGL 359:3
Love…once a l.	PATM 760:1
Once in a l.	ELIOT 370:13
prosperity…never had in my l.	MACM 635:6
theatre has died in my l.	MILL 677:11
too late all my l.!	COWL 291:21
twice in our l.	UNIT 1036:45
lift L. her with care	HOOD 489:48
opposite the l. shaft	ORWE 745:55
lifting inside work with no heavy l.	DOLE 335:50
ligate L. pancreatic ducts of dogs	BANT 70:4
light a l. to all men	TENN 1005:65
against the dying of the l.	THOM 1011:75
air pollution and …artificial l.	MATT 664:42
all the l. they wish	COWP 293:53
angels, progeny of l.	MILT 691:74
answered l. to l.	ELIOT 370:29
as l. fell short	HODG 483:50
bathe the world in l.	WORD 1100:79
beauty from the l. retir'd	WALL 1050:71
believed in the green l.	FITZ 391:7
Beneath thy lingering l.	COLL 277:49
big red l. goes on	PLAN 773:87
birth to the world's l.	SHAK 898:18
blasted with excess of l.	GRAY 443:90
bring nothing to l.	SOCR 951:87
bring to the l. of day	FRIE 405:59
burning and a shining l.	BIBLE 145:40
But soft, what l.	SHAK 868:85
by l. Of moon	WORD 1096:27
candle for warmth or l.	MACL 635:96
Casting a dim religious l.	MILT 683:15
celestial l.	WORD 1097:48
circumfused…with l. divine	WORD 1096:30
Clear arias of l.	DAYL 310:55
contend with growing l.	SHAK 862:21
correct incidence of l.	ALBE 11:93
crack of l. between	NABO 716:95
Cry as the wild l. passes	LEAR 589:52

light (*contd.*)

danced by the l. of the moon	LEAR 590:61
dark in l. expos'd	MILT 694:40
Dark is L. Enough	FRY 408:17
Darkness from l.	BROW 200:79
darkness shall be the l.	ELIOT 371:44
dawn's early l.	KEY 554:24
Dear as the l.	GRAY 443:83
dear to me as l. and life	BURNS 211:1
deriving l. from each other	BERL 96:70
dungeon flamed with l.	WESL 1066:58
eldritch l. of sundown	DAYL 310:56
entrance of thy words giveth l.	BIBLE 119:34
every ray of God's l.	DOST 341:48
everything except space and l.	HEAT 465:47
face to the l.	SASS 845:29
far from the l. of day	ORAH 741:77
fierce l. which beats	TENN 1002:1
'Forward, the L. Brigade!'	TENN 1000:72
from far thy beauteous l.	WESL 1066:67
from fidelity to the l.	RODR 819:88
from those flames No l.	MILT 687:90
Give me a l.	HASK 460:57
gives a lovely l.	MILL 676:82
God called the l. Day	BIBLE 102:84
golden and silver l.	YEATS 1105:65
Hail holy L.	MILT 689:29
hands that would l. the world	MILL 676:97
happy realms of l.	MILT 687:91
Heaven's l. forever shines	SHEL 931:50
hours of l. return	ARNO 37:74
how my l. is spent	MILT 686:81
I am black…bereaved of l.	BLAKE 166:64
I am the l. of the world	BIBLE 145:48
In l. inaccessible	SMITH 950:61
infant crying for the l.	TENN 999:38
into his marvellous l.	BIBLE 156:78
jewel…judged by the l.	ANON 27:62
lamps, by whose dear l.	MARV 658:79
land of l.	CLIN 269:18
last l. has gone	THOM 1012:3
laws…of l. and shade	CAPO 231:83
Lead, kindly L.	NEWM 724:28
leaping l. for your delight	AUDEN 46:51
leave a l.…before was dark	WENT 1065:54
Let there be l.!	SHEL 932:63
Let there be l.	BIBLE 102:83
Let there be L.	MACD 627:81
level of the l.	FORD 396:6
life and l., with envious haste	ROCH 817:64
l., and will aspire	SHAK 864:94
l. after l. well used	MILT 689:37
l. and shadow never stand still	WEST 1067:76
l. at the end	LOWE 617:12
l. beyond compare	NEALE 722:93
L. breaks where	THOM 1010:52
L. dies before thy…word	POPE 783:11
l. dissolved in star-showers	SHEL 927:73
l. falls and fills	ROET 819:93
l. fantastic round	MILT 683:22
l. gleams an instant	BECK 81:99
l. heart lives long	SHAK 866:25
l. in manners	ASCH 41:52
l. in the white mackerel sky	BISH 164:32
l. in the window	SPEN 956:84
l. is braying	SITW 940:5
l. is in the soul	MILT 694:41
l. is still	ELIOT 370:29
l. of learning	RALE 800:15
l. of my mind	JUANA 539:66
l. of setting suns	WORD 1094:98
l. of Terewth	DICK 325:31
l. of the bright world dies	BOUR 181:48
l. of the gospel	JOHN 527:23

light (*contd.*)

l. of the world	BIBLE 134:36
l. of thought	SHEL 929:2
l. out for the territory	TWAIN 1033:94
L. out of darkness!	MILT 693:27
l. out of darkness	DONNE 339:26
l. ranged in non-space	GIBS 422:40
l., shade and perspective	CONS 285:20
l., she said, not of the sky	NEIL 722:95
l. shineth in darkness	BIBLE 144:25
l. that is love	KEND 550:49
l. that she loves	TENN 1001:85
L. thickens	SHAK 909:60
l. to counterfeit a gloom	MILT 682:10
l. to lighten the Gentiles	BIBLE 142:79
l. to see that duty	MACA 621:75
l. to shine upon the road	COWP 292:30
l. unto my path	BIBLE 119:33
l. which experience gives	COLE 275:27
l. wife doth make a heavy husband	SHAK 873:6
l. within his own clear breast	MILT 683:28
L. wrestling…incessantly with l.	CRANE 294:95
like a shaft of l.	TENN 996:90
line of festal l.	ARNO 37:90
lived l. in the spring	ARNO 36:67
long l. shakes	TENN 997:98
Lord is my l.	BIBLE 115:54
lord of l.	DOUG 341:55
lost to l. for evermore	BYRON 221:12
lovely lady, garmented in l.	SHEL 930:31
making them see the l.	PLAN 772:85
married to an electric l.	DIMA 331:58
mellowed to that tender l.	BYRON 221:16
men loved darkness rather than l.	BIBLE 145:35
More l.!	GOET 431:82
morning l. creaks down again	SITW 941:13
mosquitoey summer night l.	ASHB 41:57
naked l. bulb	WILL 1081:58
night, the shadow of l.	SWIN 987:27
noose of l.	FITZ 390:87
Not l. for themselves	SHAK 896:41
Of night and l.	YEATS 1105:65
On the l. fantastic	MILT 682:98
one day, the l.	MANS 647:5
one equall l.	DONNE 339:34
out of hell leads up to l.	MILT 688:22
passed away in colder l.	PEAC 762:31
passion for sweetness and l.	ARNO 39:31
poem is…a l. by which	WARR 1054:31
poets…set their own inimitable l.	POUND 785:57
Prince of L.	MILT 681:87
pure and endless l.	VAUG 1041:20
put out the l.	SHAK 900:52
quality of fiery aery l.	MACD 628:94
radiant l., though sun	MILT 683:28
realms of l.	GURN 449:91
reft the sonne his l.	CHAU 255:39
remember while the l.	SWIN 987:36
restore the l.	DANI 304:62
river of crystal l.	FIELD 387:41
round from the dark to the l.	SWIN 988:52
saw great l.	BIBLE 133:32
season of L.	DICK 326:58
second place of air and l.	FRAME 400:77
seen a great l.	BIBLE 125:65
sees a green l. everywhere	SCHW 852:32
severity of perfect l.	TENN 1003:19
sharp l. the fields did lie	FREE 404:34
shed such l. before	MUNRO 714:61
shew l. at Calais	JOHN 528:38
slaked the l. with blood	TENN 1005:65
so airy and l. a quality	SHAK 890:1
Some true, some l.	TENN 1003:46
such scant l.	WHAR 1068:96

light (*contd.*)

sun and moon to give them l.	DICK 323:90
sweetness and l.	ARNO 39:25
sweetness and l.	SWIFT 984:58
that earth lie l.	WALL 1050:73
That was the true L.	BIBLE 144:26
the frosty l.	TENN 1000:56
the l. that loses	SWIN 986:24
The l. that never was	WORD 1099:71
the way, the truth, and the l.	BIBLE 146:62
themes in a new l.	LUCAS 618:32
This l., this glory	COLE 274:7
To l. thee thither	WEBS 1060:47
turned around from darkness to l.	PLATO 774:23
unchanged, and universal l.	POPE 778:78
University should be a place of l.	DISR 333:17
waited for the l.	ROBI 814:24
when my l. is low	TENN 999:35
where sweetness and l. failed	FORS 398:45
Where there is darkness, l.	FRAN 401:91
with a l. behind her!	GILB 423:53
within…all l. was contained	MARTI 657:56
world of l.	VAUG 1041:22
light-headed l.-h. variable men	STEV 974:7
light-hearted l.-h. way…he seduces	POMP 777:69
light-o'-love his l.-o'-l.	SERV 859:56
lighten l. our own hearts	SHAK 880:68
l. the tax burden	QUINE 797:67
lightest l. that wear most of it	SHAK 872:82
lighthouse Keeping a l. with his eyes	CAMP 227:21
sitivation at the l.	DICK 321:32
lighting Bring in the bottled l.	DICK 322:54
with its own internal l. blind	SHEL 929:10
lightning beheld Satan as l.	BIBLE 142:88
brilliance of a l. storm	FLAU 392:37
came by a l. flash	WILS 1084:24
different as moonbeam from l.	BRON 192:11
I Have known the l.'s hour	DAYL 310:54
In the golden l.	SHEL 929:99
In thunder, l., or in rain?	SHAK 906:9
L. rod have had it better	NEW 724:22
like flashes of l.	SCHO 849:92
loosed the fatal l.	HOWE 497:98
Mirth is like a flash of l.	ADDI 7:17
O at l. and lashed rod	HOPK 491:81
rather be a l. rod	KESEY 553:20
reading Shakespeare by flashes of l.	COLE 275:21
struck by l. five or six times	JARR 518:58
struck by l.	ORWE 743:6
thunder and l. of Desert Storm	SCHW 851:29
tree On fire by l.	BYRON 220:88
lights always knew the l. were on	STARR 963:1
an all-the-l.-on man	REED 805:85
broken l. of thee	TENN 998:17
carnival l.	GREE 444:22
Father of l.	BIBLE 155:60
Followed false l.	DRYD 350:50
l. around the shore	ROSS 824:84
l. begin to twinkle	TENN 995:61
name Zimmermann in bright l.?	MERM 672:19
spent l. quiver and gleam	ARNO 36:55
There will be l. everywhere	READ 803:55
though the l.	HAWT 461:77
turn on the l.	GUIM 448:79
Turn up the l.	OHEN 737:19
two l. of Christendom	PIUS 772:78
like as she is, I do not l. her	SHAK 879:32
Besides, I l. you not	SHAK 886:14
does not mean you l. him	CHUR 265:37
don't l. something	GREE 443:99
get what you l.	SHAW 922:63
If we are l. you	SHAK 872:80
l. enough to consent	SHAK 886:20
l. it or not	THOM 1014:41

like (*contd.*)

l. or dislike them	FORS 398:40
more l. my own	HOPK 492:11
nothing…made me l. him less	CONG 281:19
shall not look upon his l. again	SHAK 888:57
What I l. about Clive	BENT 93:23
what is l. to thee?	BYRON 220:93
whether I l. it	VAUG 1040:12
Whether you l. it not	KHRU 556:47
woman you do not l.	ANOU 30:69
like-minded company of the l.-m.	DELI 315:41
liked l. by only four people	HOCK 483:48
likeness any l. of any thing	BIBLE 106:68
l. and correct incidence of light	ALBE 11:93
translate beauty into his l.	SHAK 891:23
likes Agreements in l. and dislikes	CATI 245:51
everyone l. you except yourself	BROWN 194:60
liking Friendships begin with l.	ELIOT 366:45
Thy lust and l.	SKEL 942:36
lilac-time Kew in l.-t.	NOYES 732:41
lilacs l. last…bloom'd	WHIT 1073:92
L. out of the dead land	ELIOT 368:81
Lilian Airy, fairy L.	TENN 993:34
lilies And a few l. blow	HOPK 491:77
Beauty lives though l. die	FLEC 393:48
Consider the l. of the field	BIBLE 135:52
feedeth among the l.	BIBLE 124:50
l. and languors of virtue	SWIN 987:32
l. in her hand	ROSS 824:79
l. of ambition	DOUG 341:59
L. that fester	SHAK 914:80
L. without, roses	MARV 657:70
peacocks and l.	RUSK 830:78
put thy pale, lost l. out of mind	DOWS 343:81
roses overgrown, And l.	MARV 657:71
Ye L. male!	CRAB 294:81
Lillabullero half a dozen bars of L.	STER 969:95
Lillian L. as a grown-up	FEIB 384:96
L., you should have stayed a virgin	CART 242:9
Lilliput Swiftian L.	MACC 625:50
lilting l. at our yowe-milking	ELLI 374:8
lily Daisy and L.	SITW 941:19
How sweet the l. grows	HEBER 466:57
l. all her sweetness	TENN 997:10
l. of the valleys	BIBLE 124:46
pure as the l. in the dell	LAUD 583:38
splendid…glows the l.	FLEC 393:50
The l. whispers	TENN 1001:88
to paint the l.	SHAK 872:71
lily-handed l.-h. baronet he	TENN 996:95
lily-silvered l.-s. values	POPE 783:6
lily-white l.-w. reserve	HOLM 485:75
limb bestow on every airth a l.	MONT 703:93
gathering up l. by l.	MILT 686:72
manacled with joint or l.	MILT 687:2
one l. to another	HERB 475:22
limbo l. large and broad	MILT 689:42
limbs decent l. composed	POPE 779:7
don't start measuring her l.	PICA 768:25
ere their l. grew stiff	CONN 282:54
In my l. their former heat?	HERR 477:52
l. may issue	MARL 654:21
l. that fester	ABSE 1:6
l. were old	SCOTT 853:44
lower l. in pants	NASH 720:60
mighty l. asleep	SWIN 988:53
movements of the l.	LEON 597:80
repose for l.	SHAK 913:56
ruddy l. and flourishing hair	BLAKE 165:58
upon thy tender l.	WALL 1050:73
lime lay l. to tangle her desires	SHAK 860:86
walked through the l.	SOME 952:1
limèd O l. soul	SHAK 892:48
limelight led me to the l.	HEAN 465:39

Limerick acquitted by a L. jury — ADAMS 6:*93*
limestone On l. quarried near — YEATS 1107:*93*
limit l. of its development — ANON 25:*29*
  l. the dangers — KENN 552:*86*
  l. to his ambitions — RICH 811:*73*
  l. to the…time a composer — LAMB 577:*47*
  sky is the l. — SHUL 936:*37*
limitations Argue for your l. — BACH 54:*98*
  l. of our nature — AUDEN 48:*88*
  only l. those of libel — THUR 1019:*49*
  poetry reminds him of his l. — KENN 552:*88*
limited Experience is never l. — JAMES 516:*19*
  In l. professions — SHAK 902:*93*
  Liberty must be l. — BURKE 207:*16*
limits in knowing its l. — KANT 541:*1*
  l. of all possible sense-experience — AYER 53:*78*
  l. of expansion — SCHR 850:*7*
  small imperfect l. — HEAN 464:*33*
  wants have no l. — FLAU 392:*34*
  within ancient l. — HAWT 461:*76*
  witness our own l. — THOR 1016:*75*
limner-laureate l.-l. of the beauty — ALLEN 14:*34*
limousine All we want is a l. — MACN 637:*38*
  One perfect l. — PARK 754:*5*
Limpopo greasy L. River — KIPL 563:*82*
  L. of swamped Ninth Avenue — AMIS 17:*87*
limps l. once she sees someone — MONT 702:*78*
Lin young Tam L. is there — BALL 67:*51*
Lincoln L.'s bedroom! — ONAS 739:*41*
  reservoir from which L. also drew — ACHE 2:*24*
  When Abraham L. was shovelled — SAND 841:*61*
Lindsay gang wi' me, Lizzy L — BALL 67:*43*
line all along the l. — WEBB 1058:*15*
  cancel half a l. — FITZ 390:*89*
  cannot be a new l. — WILL 1083:*94*
  Choose thou whatever suits the l. — COLE 274:*2*
  direction of the right l. — NEWT 725:*36*
  end of the l. — MILL 677:*11*
  fight it out on this l. — GRANT 439:*8*
  Haven't I heard that l. before? — SHER 934:*10*
  justification in every l. — CONR 284:*87*
  l. dividing the state — GALB 412:*79*
  l. of least resistance — AMERY 16:*67*
  l. where man leaves off — FROST 407:*83*
  measuring l. in his hand — BIBLE 130:*65*
  motion in a right l. — NEWT 724:*35*
lion L. and the Unicorn…fighting — CARR 240:*71*
  l. hath roared — BIBLE 130:*58*
  l. in the way — BIBLE 122:*3*
  L. looked at Alice — CARR 241:*73*
  l. shall eat straw like the ox — BIBLE 125:*68*
  l. shall eat straw — BIBLE 128:*16*
  living dog is better than a dead l. — BIBLE 123:*32*
  looketh upon a l. — BIBLE 131:*75*
  nation…had the l. heart — CHUR 265:*41*
  one day as a l. — MUSS 716:*85*
  out of the paw of the l. — BIBLE 110:*39*
  pained desert l. — ARNO 38:*95*
  still a living l. — SOLZ 952:*97*
  Strong is the l. — SMART 944:*69*
  To rouse a l. — SHAK 875:*45*
  unicorn and l. wild — SHAK 866:*34*
  winged L.'s marble piles — BYRON 220:*92*
  would be mated to a l. — SHAK 901:*68*
  wrath of the l. — BLAKE 166:*78*
lion-like L.-l., in full-mouthed — CRAIK 294:*90*
lions like l. to the roaring slaughter — CUMM 300:*84*
  L. make leopards tame — SHAK 866:*39*
  Rise like L. — SHEL 928:*80*
  stronger than l. — BIBLE 110:*44*
  throne was supported by l. — BACON 57:*53*
  young l. do lack — BIBLE 115:*61*
lip contempt and anger of his l.! — SHAK 895:*25*
  He bit his l. — PERE 766:*90*

lip (*contd.*)
  l. Of his world — DAYL 310:*57*
  No nearer the heart than the l. — ANON 23:*82*
  shoot out the l. — BIBLE 114:*48*
  Teach not thy l. — SHAK 863:*49*
  what moistens the l. — WHIT 1074:*2*
lipped l., and trembled kissing — SHAK 905:*76*
lips And soft as l. — SWIN 986:*25*
  at the touching of the l. — TENN 995:*72*
  coming from the l. of another — CARP 237:*8*
  Eternity was in our l. — SHAK 905:*62*
  far more red than her l. — SHAK 915:*92*
  From thy l. would flow — SHEL 929:*7*
  hands and our l. — SWIN 988:*52*
  k. that is placed on my l. — DARIO 305:*76*
  keep the door of my l. — BIBLE 120:*52*
  kent her be her caller l. — SOUT 954:*26*
  kiss my parched l. — SHAK 872:*74*
  kissed her l. with such a…smack — SHAK 864:*83*
  lay upon thy l. — SHAK 906:*94*
  let me put my l. to it — DICK 322:*75*
  Life and these l. — SHAK 869:*18*
  life with kisses in my l. — SHAK 870:*20*
  l. are like a thread of scarlet — BIBLE 124:*51*
  l. are not yet unsealed — BALD 65:*13*
  l., as sunlight drinketh dew — TENN 993:*36*
  l. espous'd — HERR 477:*58*
  l. more scarlet — YEATS 1106:*83*
  l. of a strange woman — BIBLE 120:*61*
  l. suck forth my soul — MARL 654:*19*
  l. that are for others — TENN 997:*4*
  man of unclean l. — BIBLE 124:*61*
  never come out of a ladys l. — FLEM 394:*62*
  On a poet's l. — SHEL 930:*20*
  open thou my l. — BIBLE 116:*79*
  playing about his l. — THUR 1019:*26*
  pretty form the l. — DICK 326:*53*
  put your l. together—and blow — FURT 410:*57*
  Read my l. — BUSH 215:*87*
  Red l. are not so red — OWEN 748:*9*
  rosy l. and cheeks — SHAK 915:*89*
  round their narrow l. — ROSS 824:*89*
  steal immortal blessing from her l. — SHAK 869:*7*
  sulky l. were shaped for sin — BETJ 101:*53*
  take thy l. away — SHAK 897:*85*
  through my l. to unawakened earth — SHEL 928:*91*
  thy l. my history — SIDN 937:*58*
  Truth sits upon the l. — ARNO 38:*96*
  two l., indifferent red — SHAK 894:*5*
  Upon her skinny l. — SHAK 907:*16*
  What l. my l. have kissed — MILL 676:*86*
  witchcraft in your l. — SHAK 882:*11*
  with stammering l. — BIBLE 125:*75*
  with l. to dishonour me — BIBLE 125:*78*
lipstick got on too much l. — NASH 720:*69*
  put l. on a hog — RICH 810:*60*
  putting l. on the Venus de Milo — PICK 769:*31*
liquefaction That l. of her clothes — HERR 478:*67*
liquid Cats, no less l. — TESS 1006:*80*
  first place of l. darkness — FRAME 400:*77*
  let their l. siftings fall — ELIOT 368:*67*
  l. Euclids in foolscaps of air — AVIS 53:*76*
  L. had no time — GREE 444:*4*
  l. which rots braces — MORT 710:*2*
liquidation l. of the British Empire — CHUR 264:*25*
  nation about to go into voluntary l. — MACI 631:*45*
liquids l., all one's favourite hues — DOYLE 344:*21*
liquor bring it home in l. — DICK 323:*78*
  bumper of good l. — SHER 933:*89*
  Good l., I stoutly maintain — GOLD 433:*21*
  Here's yet some l. left — SHAK 893:*80*
  lads for the l. are there — HOUS 495:*52*
  licensed l. traffic — TWAIN 1034:*3*
  l. for boys — JOHN 530:*3*

liquor (*contd.*)
  L. is one way out — WILL 1082:*71*
  l. is quicker — NASH 719:*46*
  l. is the only mechanical relief — HEMI 470:*30*
  L. …sidestepping necessity — FADI 382:*50*
  Livelier l. than the Muse — HOUS 495:*63*
  some such…spiritual l. — BYRON 223:*67*
  world's largest l. store — BALL 65:*25*
liquors fumes of tabacco and l. — LEWIS 602:*61*
  Hot and rebellious l. — SHAK 885:*82*
lisp Look you l. — SHAK 886:*19*
list enemy reads the l. — WELL 1063:*6*
  got a little l. — GILB 425:*84*
  l. of subscribers — JOHN 531:*18*
listen don't l. to writers talking — HELL 469:*97*
  If an actor reads…I hardly l. — SALI 838:*24*
  l. carefully indeed — TRUM 1030:*28*
  l. to others — GRANT 438:*3*
  L. to them moan — RAMS 801:*19*
  l. to what I'm saying — MARL 652:*83*
  l. to what others say — HOLM 486:*90*
  l. when I am unhappy — SMITH 948:*36*
  l. without meeting — TOCQ 1021:*77*
  l. …you don't hear — NYE 733:*47*
  people l. to you — SNOW 951:*77*
  privilege of wisdom to l. — HOLM 486:*7*
  rather l. than work — BOYD 182:*61*
  teach me now to l. — HEAN 465:*43*
  wonderful to l. to — HARDY 456:*85*
listener give a picture to the l. — COLT 277:*58*
  modern l. is…overloaded — BELL 88:*42*
  resistance in your l. — MILL 679:*56*
listening Children never…good at l. — BALD 64:*95*
  L. …that mistresses offer — WYLIE 1104:*49*
  nobody's l. — ANON 29:*50*
  subdue themselves to 'l.-in' — WELLS 1065:*44*
listlessness l., nor mad endeavour — WORD 1098:*54*
  seek repose In l. — WORD 1096:*19*
lists collected l. of fatal diseases — HELL 468:*84*
lit not see them l. again — GREY 446:*57*
  whole fleet's l. up — WOOD 1092:*40*
literacy Cultural l. is the oxygen — HIRS 481:*20*
literal money stays l. — DWOR 358:*84*
literary care for its l. inheritance — ELIOT 370:*14*
  claim to l. fame — BENN 91:*84*
  fully mature l. tradition — FRYE 408:*21*
  l. education did not fit — BURG 206:*94*
  l. industry would not exist — LESS 598:*7*
  L. intellectuals at one pole — SNOW 950:*73*
  l. man—with a wooden leg — DICK 327:*77*
  L. Review under my editorship — WAUGH 1056:*59*
  l. work — JOHN 526:*1*
  lowest class is l. footmen — HAZL 464:*20*
  more…than any other l. form — DUDEK 353:*13*
  neurotic can…be a l. genius — AUCH 46:*39*
  Never l. attempt was more — HUME 504:*12*
  parole of l. men — JOHN 531:*17*
  too much affected by l. refinements — CHES 258:*95*
  viewing them as a l. performance — WHIT 1073:*1*
  when she marries a l. man — CHEE 255:*51*
literate with the l., I am Impelled — PARK 753:*93*
literature All modern American l. — HEMI 470:*29*
  All the rest is l. — VALE 1038:*86*
  art and l. are left — LEWIS 602:*53*
  Bad l. — GIDE 423:*47*
  base of all l. — GIRA 428:*41*
  camp-following eunuchs of l. — HEMI 470:*14*
  classics are only primitive l. — LEAC 589:*40*
  curse of Scottish l. — MUIR 712:*25*
  edge of the chair of L. — THUR 1018:*15*
  English l.'s performing flea — OCAS 735:*78*
  English poetic l. — GRAV 440:*36*
  every other branch of classical l. — DICK 321:*44*

live (*contd.*)
Whether we l. …or die	BIBLE 150:*42*
Who can l. under the shadow	SPEN 956:*78*
would you l. for ever?	FRED 403:*24*
Yif thou wolte l. frely	ANON 22:*75*
You might as well l.	PARK 754:*13*

lived died as he had l. — CLEM 268:*2*
discover I had not l.	THOR 1017:*85*
Had he l., Had he l.	DAVIS 309:*37*
Had it l. long	MARV 657:*70*
I have l., beyond my means	WILDE 1078:*5*
l. before Agamemnon's time	HORA 493:*25*
l. long enough	SAND 842:*81*
l. more than people who cannot	HAYA 462:*85*
l. to be carried in a basket	SHAK 878:*22*
Mary l. by wondering	KAVA 543:*27*
must be l. forwards	KIER 556:*57*
tell me roundly, that I l.	HERB 475:*15*
while you l. it	GLAS 430:*60*

livelihood read or work for a l. — MONT 701:*56*
seek a l. elsewhere	CANT 230:*74*
work for their honest l.	SWIFT 985:*97*

liveliness a certain l. of mind — RABE 799:*91*
l. of my disposition	FRED 403:*23*

liver blood in his l. — SHAK 895:*24*
end up with cirrhosis of the l.	EAGL 359:*3*
I ate his l.	TALLY 990:*91*
Life loves the l.	ANGE 20:*28*
l. slices fried	JOYCE 538:*53*

Liverpool aspect of lewdness in L. — FORD 396:*2*
folk that live in L.	CHES 259:*27*
L. and L. reserves	SHAN 919:*75*
young men from L.	BAIN 62:*77*

livery part-coloured l. — CONG 280:*96*

lives all their l. …they'll have to rush — DUNN 356:*52*
but dying l.	SPEN 958:*20*
But human creatures' l.!	HOOD 489:*46*
conceive of our l. as narratives	LEHM 594:*35*
cracks of other people's l.	WHAR 1068:*96*
door to their own l.	AREN 33:*16*
even terror of their l.	SHAR 919:*80*
Even though our l. wander	PROU 793:*5*
events in our l.	WELTY 1065:*51*
every detail of our l.	WAVE 1058:*10*
Every instant of our l.	GIDE 423:*46*
fatal climax with their l.	SASS 845:*25*
gambling in human l.	DYSON 358:*1*
going on in their own l.	KRAM 569:*84*
has happened in our l.	MUNRO 714:*61*
He l., he wakes	SHEL 931:*48*
he who lives more l.	WILDE 1078:*2*
how he l.	JOHN 528:*55*
idle l.	WORD 1099:*75*
impoverish our l.	SCHU 851:*20*
in their l. fought for life	SPEN 956:*72*
lead people to give their l.	EINS 363:*63*
light heart l. long	SHAK 866:*25*
lived many l.	SLES 943:*57*
L. and Loves of a She-Devil	WELD 1062:*89*
l. cease to be illumined	HAMM 453:*43*
l. have been given to find	MACD 628:*94*
l. not three good men	SHAK 876:*54*
L. of great men	LONG 611:*96*
l. of men and women	HOOV 490:*58*
l. of quiet desperation	THOR 1016:*77*
l. of the medieval saints	SAKI 837:*1*
looking to other l. for answers	BRAU 185:*16*
Man l. by science	JAMES 517:*36*
man l. well	KIPL 560:*21*
Most people spend…their l.	LABR 573:*55*
music of men's l.	SHAK 868:*71*
ninety l. have been taken away	MACG 630:*24*
no fish ye're buying—it's men's l.	SCOTT 855:*82*
Not a moment of your l.	BLUN 170:*42*

lives (*contd.*)
obstructed but the l. of Christians	JOHN 527:*23*
of all l.	STEV 973:*99*
other Annapurnas in the l. of men	HERZ 479:*77*
Our l. …shall end	PHIL 768:*20*
our l. are…dark interludes	ONEI 740:*55*
our l. would grow together	SWIN 987:*44*
political l. …end in failure	POWE 788:*19*
poor l. we lead	NIGH 729:*97*
pounces upon it and l.	MILL 678:*22*
quintessence of their l.	LOWE 615:*72*
repeat in the l. of millions	WILD 1080:*33*
rest of their l.	TREE 1025:*44*
some l. duller	TAKU 990:*84*
statements about world and our l.	BOYD 182:*66*
their jumpsome l.	KIPL 563:*58*
Upon the K. …our l.	SHAK 881:*94*
waking moment of their l.	KING 558:*85*
Where nothing l. but crosses	SHAK 867:*51*
Women Whose L. Are Food	OATES 733:*55*
writers' l.	GIBB 421:*31*

liveth l., and was dead — BIBLE 157:*1*

living act of l. had been enjoyable — BOWL 182:*57*
'alternative' modes of l.	SELF 858:*38*
Are you yet l.?	SHAK 879:*30*
be considerate to the l.	VOLT 1046:*13*
Begin by l.	ANOU 31:*78*
better than l. badly?	CRIT 297:*45*
beyond the language of the l.	ELIOT 372:*7*
bodies of the l.	SPEN 957:*90*
by l. well	JONS 536:*18*
catch the Manners l.	POPE 780:*33*
cut off out of the land of the l.	BIBLE 127:*2*
dead might as well speak to the l.	CATH 244:*43*
difference is…that of the l.	CIXO 267:*70*
Different l. is not l.	SPEN 956:*81*
Disillusionment in l.	STEIN 965:*36*
do not eat for the good of l.	EMER 377:*49*
drink for a l.	KERR 553:*17*
equal dominion…over every l. thing	STAN 963:*89*
fever called 'L.'	POE 776:*55*
get mine own l.	BOOK 175:*30*
good l. and good poetry	LUCAS 618:*28*
in the land of the l.	BIBLE 118:*25*
l. a little more or dying	MAIL 639:*72*
l. and dying at once	KUNI 571:*18*
L. and partly l.	ELIOT 370:*32*
l. are dead	MACM 635:*13*
l. dead man	SHAK 865:*3*
l. dog is better than a dead lion	BIBLE 123:*32*
l. in sin	HERB 474:*90*
L. is an illness	CHAM 250:*26*
l. is made…by selling	WILD 1079:*29*
l. know No bounds?	SHIR 935:*23*
l. next to you	TRUD 1029:*12*
l. stood motionless	WILL 1080:*44*
L., we fret	BROW 200:*99*
l. well…most important	PLATO 774:*6*
l. which are yet alive	BIBLE 122:*21*
long habit of l.	BROW 196:*96*
man to earn his own l.	MORE 706:*45*
miserable beyond all l. things	SHEL 926:*54*
New York…'l.' there	DIDI 330:*45*
no l. with thee	ADDI 7:*10*
no pleasure i' l.	ELIOT 365:*9*
partnership not only between l.	BURKE 208:*36*
pattern…Of dead and l.	ELIOT 372:*55*
prospect of l. in it	JAY 519:*76*
realize Art in l. forms	HOLM 486:*97*
repetition of the wrong way of l.	DURR 357:*79*
scale of l. must be reduced	CHUR 263:*7*
soporific stew of every l.!	SARD 843:*94*
still a l. lion	SOLZ 952:*97*
sure of l. forever	HAWT 461:*66*

living (*contd.*)
tired of l.	WHITE 1070:*29*
upon the l. and the dead	JOYCE 538:*42*
was l. is now dead	ELIOT 369:*93*
wasted his substance with riotous l.	BIBLE 143:*98*
who l. had no note	GIBB 422:*32*
Why seek ye the l. among the dead?	BIBLE 144:*20*
world…does not owe us a l.	EDIN 361:*40*

living-room comfort of the l.-r. — MACL 635:*1*

Livingstone 'Dr. L., I presume?' — STAN 962:*84*

Lloyd L. George could not see a belt — ASQU 42:*82*
L. George spoke	BENN 91:*93*

lo L., through her works — SMART 944:*72*

load for her the heavier l. — BALZ 69:*76*
how to l. and bless	KEATS 547:*4*
like a heavy l.	HUGH 499:*19*
l. of sorrow	SHAK 880:*61*
taking home my l.	BURT 213:*61*
under their fruits l.	SPEN 958:*19*

loaded dice of God are always l. — EMER 376:*36*

loads ploughs and borne our l. — MUIR 712:*34*

loaf half a l. better than no bread — CHES 259:*16*

loafed to have l. and lost — THUR 1018:*17*

loafing cricket as organised l. — TEMP 993:*27*

loam Men are but gilded l. — SHAK 866:*40*
rife as the l. Of prairies	CRANE 295:*6*

loan brief l. of his own body — CABE 224:*76*
God has us…on l.	FERRE 387:*20*
memories on l.	FRAME 400:*78*

loaning moaning on ilka green l. — ELLI 374:*8*

loans effect of new l. of England — BAGE 62:*64*
l. to cast away my speech	SHAK 894:*4*

loath long and l. at going — RANS 802:*35*
shall l. yourselves	BIBLE 129:*39*

loathe l. to rin an' chase thee — BURNS 209:*67*

loathed and l. him — TWAIN 1032:*66*
both loved and l.	MIDD 673:*44*

loathèd most l. worldly life — SHAK 897:*83*

loathing deepest l. to the stomach — SHAK 871:*41*

loathsome Exercise is l. — TWAIN 1034:*22*
l. mask has fallen	SHEL 930:*25*

loaves five barley l. — BIBLE 145:*42*
five l., and two fishes	BIBLE 138:*6*
l. sold for a penny	SHAK 861:*50*
metaphor…provides two l.	MALA 641:*25*

lob nothing but a l. — RUNY 829:*64*

lobbies l. during the interval. — TYNAN 1035:*25*

lobby gentlemen…in the same L. — PALM 752:*73*
go into the l. against us	BALD 65:*13*

lobes disease of the frontal l. — ALBEE 11:*88*

lobster 'Tis the voice of the l. — CARR 239:*41*

Loc Suilig steed by L. S. — MACC 625:*36*

local little l. difficulties — MACM 635:*5*
l. thing called Christianity	HARDY 457:*10*

location worst possible l. in the world — ACHE 3:*52*

locations visiting l. such as diners — COUP 289:*76*

loch bonnie banks o' L. Lomond — ANON 24:*4*

Lochinvar O, young L. — SCOTT 853:*54*

lock crying at the l. — MILL 679:*59*
Joy, I did l. thee up	HERB 476:*33*
life-long l.	GILB 425:*88*
L. the door, Lariston	HOGG 485:*65*
twisting that l.	STER 970:*15*
why l. him in?	SHAW 922:*42*

lockèd l., letter'd, braw brass-collar — BURNS 209:*70*

locket l. around his neck — SOME 952:*1*

locks drownèd honour by the l. — SHAK 875:*46*
few l. which are left	SOUT 954:*29*
knotty and combinèd l.	SHAK 889:*74*
l. were like a raven	BURNS 211:*6*
Never shake Thy gory l.	SHAK 909:*61*
shaking her invincible l.	MILT 686:*75*
turn those amber l. to grey	DRAY 345:*34*

locomotion purposes of human l. — DOUG 342:*64*

lost all a l. generation	STEIN 965:33
every day to be l.	JOHN 532:34
go after that which is l.	BIBLE 143:96
Hath l. me in your liking	SHAK 902:99
I shall be l.	BLAKE 166:67
If we l. them	HAGG 450:7
lambs who've l. our way	KIPL 560:22
l. all his illusions	HOLM 486:82
l. all my mirth	SHAK 890:2
l. beyond the hills	HYDE 509:10
l., but now am found	NEWT 725:42
l. by not being vice	WALP 1051:94
l. happiness and lasting pain	MILT 687:89
l. him surely	SYNGE 988:65
l. in the miles	SCOTT 852:37
l. in their collected learning	HAWT 461:67
l. indeed	GREER 445:40
L., l.! l.!	SCOTT 853:46
l. my reputation	SHAK 899:24
l. the job	JOYCE 538:50
L. 'til all pride	SMITH 949:60
l. without deserving	SHAK 899:25
l. your ability	GONC 434:52
never completely l.	SCHI 847:67
no love l. between us	GOLD 433:26
none of them is l.	BIBLE 146:67
not that you won or l.	RICE 809:38
on whom nothing is l.!	JAMES 516:20
Poetry is what is l.	FROST 408:8
Praising what is l.	SHAK 901:84
principles…are irrevocably l.	GIBB 421:19
recover what has been l.	ELIOT 372:54
something is l.	THOM 1013:23
'Tis better to have fought and l.	CLOU 270:37
to have loafed and l.	THUR 1018:17
to have loved and l.	TENN 999:30
to ourselves were l.	DRYD 348:94
we are l.!	PYRR 796:45
What one gives…is forever l.	DESB 317:71
woman that deliberates is l.	ADDI 8:31
lot got a l. of what it takes	DUBIN 353:1
l. is fallen to me	BOOK 176:65
Not milder is the general l.	ARNO 36:59
policeman's l.	GILB 424:65
uneasy l. at best	ELIOT 366:40
weary l. is thine	SCOTT 854:68
wish to ease his l.	TOLS 1023:97
Lot like l.'s wife	MOOD 703:94
Remember L.'s wife	BIBLE 144:10
lotion l. of the heart	PARK 756:37
lots cast l. upon my vesture	BIBLE 114:49
stealthy convergence of human l.	ELIOT 366:35
lottery blind goddess in the l.	ASTU 43:99
first prize in the l. of life	RHOD 808:24
judgement is a mere l.	DRYD 347:61
state l. as a public subsidy	QUINE 797:67
lotus l. position of her yoga class	SHAR 919:83
Lou lady that's known as L.	SERV 859:56
loud l., you're too old	NUGE 732:45
too long and too l.	WAUGH 1057:87
louder l. he talked of his honour	EMER 377:69
music like Wagner, only l.	GOLD 434:38
loudspeakers lies are… from the l.	ORWE 744:40
Louis L., I think	WALL 1051:78
St L. …golden arch	MAIL 639:84
Louisianans L. don't tolerate	ANON 30:53
loungers l. and idlers of the Empire	
	DOYLE 343:83
louse between a l. and a flea	JOHN 531:25
l. in the locks of literature	TENN 1005:70
lousy had a l. personality	SALI 838:22
it was kind of l.	THUR 1020:57
what my l. childhood was like	SALI 838:18
louts oafish l. remember Mum	BETJ 100:46

Louvre L. is the book	CEZA 248:5
love a missed l.!	HEINE 467:72
Absence is to l. what wind is to fire	BUSS 215:93
absurdity of being in l.	LACL 573:59
acts…of l.	WORD 1094:97
admire and l. thee	HERR 477:58
Alcohol is like l.	CHAN 251:46
all for l.	DIBD 319:5
all for l.	SPEN 958:11
All l., all liking	HERR 477:62
All must l. the human form	BLAKE 166:65
All this to l.	ROCH 816:45
almost l. you again	SNYD 951:86
almost l. you	HEAN 464:34
am like to l. three more	SUCK 981:23
an old l. straitened him	TENN 1002:15
an ounce of l.	WESL 1067:74
An oyster may be crossed in l.!	SHER 934:12
ape the magnanimity of l.	MERE 671:5
arms of my true l.	TENN 1001:89
as though you l. him	BLUN 170:44
As woman's l.	SHAK 891:36
attract Thy l., not thy subjection	MILT 693:15
banner over me was l.	BIBLE 124:47
beauty and l. lay bare	SHEL 930:29
before we can l. it much	HOLM 486:99
beggary in the l.	SHAK 904:55
Best friend and l.	DUNN 356:56
better to l. a woman	HARDY 457:4
bind my l.	HERR 478:64
Black l.	GIOV 428:36
bring back the things we l.	CHAT 253:98
bringeth it to his l.	BIBLE 131:75
brotherly l.	WELL 1063:1
burdenous…my l. had grown	DONNE 338:97
business that we l.	SHAK 906:86
but not for l.	SHAK 886:21
but sworn to my l.	SHAK 868:87
By heaven, I do l.	SHAK 865:18
by the force of l.	WHITE 1070:39
Call me but l.	SHAK 868:89
cannot fight for l.	SHAK 870:38
cannot l. a woman so well	ELIOT 366:41
cannot l. any of them	BEER 84:43
cannot make a life, but L.	HERR 477:55
cannot make a man l.	KING 557:74
cannot think well, l. well	WOOLF 1093:68
cannot write of l.	BELL 86:92
cantons of contemnèd l.	SHAK 894:6
cocktail is to…wine as rape is to l.	CLAU 268:92
come unto my l.?	SPEN 959:32
Come…and be my l.	DONNE 337:89
comely in nothing but l.	BACON 57:66
connubial l. refused	MILT 690:64
Cooking is like l.	VANH 1039:4
could not l.	LOVE 615:67
countless gifts of l.	WINK 1086:59
courage to l.	TROL 1027:66
course of true l.	SHAK 870:27
crazy for l.	BART 74:70
crops of l. and hate	MUIR 712:36
crossed in l.	AUST 51:40
cruel madness of l.	TENN 1001:76
daily possibility of l. dying	GREE 444:12
dance of l.	SENG 859:52
dark secret l.	BLAKE 167:88
dear and only l.	MONT 703:91
dearly l. in your life	TROL 1028:86
deep as first l.	TENN 997:4
deep l. for women	HAGG 450:7
dinner of herbs where l. is	BIBLE 121:80
distinguish you in l.	ROCH 816:56
do not fall in l. with me	SHAK 886:14
does not l. thee least	SHAK 902:97

love (*contd.*)	
dooms of l.	CUMM 300:89
dream of l. survives…houses	CHEE 255:48
drive and make l.	MOSS 711:9
duteous l.	WORD 1100:92
Eat, drink and l.	BYRON 223:64
ecstasy of l.	SHAK 889:87
Education is impossible without l.	DESB 317:71
either l., or I must die	FORD 397:15
essence of real human l.	ELIOT 365:13
Eternal lamp of l.!	HERR 477:56
Eternity is in l.	BLAKE 166:75
every morning is the l.	KEBLE 548:23
evil of those whom we l.	ABEL 1:2
exponent of free l.	DOCT 334:39
express my l.	SHAK 915:87
eyes That feed my l.	ROCH 817:64
fail at mother l.	FRID 404:47
failures in l.	MURD 714:63
fall half in l.	SALI 838:21
fall in l. as quickly as possible	ACHE 3:32
fall in l. once	SPARK 955:56
fall in l. with a city	MORR 709:86
fall in l. with the world	WALC 1048:43
fall out with those we l.	TENN 997:96
falling in and out of l.	NIVEN 730:6
Farewell, L., and all thy laws	WYATT 1102:27
fasting, for a good man's l.	SHAK 886:13
fault was only too much l.	LANY 580:79
favor mother l.	BRIN 189:60
fear the l. of God	ELIOT 370:35
feeling that lures us on…to l.	CONR 284:98
fell in l. with himself	POWE 787:3
Filled with her l.	DONNE 336:69
filled with l.	ROCH 816:44
first l.'s impassioned blindness	PEAC 762:31
first two l. the third	WAXM 1058:12
fit l. for the gods	MILT 692:4
fitter for me to l.	ROCH 816:55
flame of life and l.	LAWR 586:80
food is l.	SHEL 929:8
food of l.	SHAK 893:91
fool of l.	HAZL 464:16
for L. thou wakest not	FERG 385:14
For L.'s sake	JONS 536:13
For liberation—not less of l.	ELIOT 373:76
for the l. he had to her	BIBLE 105:36
for the l. of a ladye!	GILB 425:94
For thy sweet l. remembered	SHAK 913:57
for your l. to her	SHAK 864:75
free to l. or hate	SART 844:6
freedom in my l.	615:63
Friendship and l.	GRIL 447:63
From Russia with L.	FLEM 393:58
fruit of the Spirit is l.	BIBLE 152:91
full of l. and honesty	SHAK 899:30
Garden of L.	BLAKE 167:90
Give me more l.	CAREW 233:20
give orders to l.	SAND 840:53
give them your l.	GIBR 422:38
give us thine own eternal l.!	OCAS 735:75
Glory, the grape, l., gold	BYRON 222:43
God is l.	BIBLE 156:92
God is L.	KIER 556:60
God is l.	LEE 592:5
God of l.!	DODD 335:47
God of L. …Beteth his wynges	CHAU 255:37
golden dream of l. and friendship	DRYD 349:1
got to l. one man	HAMM 454:51
grace Which l. makes	WORD 1097:41
great, powerful souls l. life	HEINE 467:68
Greater l. hath no man	BIBLE 146:64
Greater l. hath	THOR 1018:6
Greater l. than this	JOYCE 538:52

love (*contd.*)

greed wrapped in the language of l.	ARMEY 35:43
groans of l.	LOWRY 618:19
hate all that don't l. me	FARQ 383:66
hate me as much as you l. me	BECK 82:7
hate the one, and l. the other	BIBLE 135:51
hath business, and makes l.	DONNE 337:86
Have I forgot, my only L.	BRON 191:9
have you left the ancient l.	BLAKE 165:56
Health, Wealth, L. …and Time	ANON 30:68
Hearts wound up with l.	SPEN 956:83
Hell grant what L.	MILT 682:11
Hell…is to no longer to l.	BERN 96:72
help and support of the woman I l.	EDWA 362:51
Herein is l.	BIBLE 156:93
hidden l. of God	WESL 1066:67
his l. made mine	DRYD 348:96
His strange l. admire	DONNE 338:6
honeying and making l.	SHAK 892:56
hope nor l.	STEV 976:52
hope of winning her l.	STAEL 961:69
horribly in l. with her	SHAK 879:49
How dare he make l. to me	KRAS 569:85
How do I l. thee?	BROW 197:19
how dwelleth the l. of God in him?	BIBLE 156:91
how to l. himself	SHAK 898:15
Humanity i l. you	CUMM 299:80
Hunger and l.	FRAN 401:92
I behold, in l.	STEV 971:46
I do not l. thee, Dr Fell	BROWN 194:61
I don't l. you, Sabidius	MART 657:59
I fell in l. …at once	THOM 1011:74
I had definitely fallen in l.	BENU 94:33
I l. all waste	SHEL 927:66
I l. metaphor	GASS 416:35
I l. not hollow cheek	TENN 997:9
I wish I were in l. again	HART 459:44
If l. be a god	LYLY 620:60
If l. be treasure	OTWAY 746:85
If l. remains	BROW 199:62
if l. were all	COWA 290:93
If l. were what the rose is	SWIN 987:44
if my l. were in my armes	ANON 23:83
If thou beest l., begone	BEAU 80:76
If thou must l. me	BROW 197:15
If two people l. each other	HEMI 470:25
If you don't l. life	CLARK 267:85
immortal L.	TENN 998:15
Imperious l. hath highest	SPEN 958:15
impure l. for cities	CASAL 243:24
in business, politics, l.!	WHIT 1073:97
in l. as in sport	GRAV 440:29
In l.'s field	CRAS 296:26
In l., happiness is abnormal	PROU 792:88
in l. with a beautiful blonde	FIEL 388:61
in l. with a cold climate	SOUT 954:28
in l. with a country	LESS 599:8
in l. with American names	BENET 90:59
in l. with easeful Death	KEATS 548:18
in l. with my bed	SHAK 860:75
in l. with seventeen million	GISC 429:48
In this close hand of l.	BROW 197:17
intellectual l. of God	SPIN 961:59
Is first and passionate l.	BYRON 222:34
Is l. a tender thing?	SHAK 868:77
jot of former l. retain	DRAY 345:40
Kind is my l. today	SHAK 915:85
know by l.	PATM 760:9
knowledge and l. of God	BOOK 175:33
lack of l. contaminates	GUNN 448:85
lack of l. from l.	BROW 200:79
Lassie I l. best	BURNS 211:98
late remorse of l.	BYRON 220:98
law of l.	SCEVE 846:56

love (*contd.*)

learn to l. by loving	HUXL 507:79
left thy first l.	BIBLE 157:2
Lenten is come with l.	ANON 22:69
Lerne to l.,	LANG 579:75
less skill to l.	SKEL 942:45
let me l.	DONNE 337:79
let me sow l.	FRAN 401:91
let us l.!	CATU 245:59
let us live and l.	CAMP 228:35
Linked in l. so dear	MILT 692:8
little duty and less l.	SHAK 877:78
live in l.	SIDN 937:66
live with me and be my l.	MARL 655:31
lived to l.	DESB 317:74
long-liv'd as present l.	WALL 1050:76
looking for is perfect l.	WELD 1062:95
looks breed l.	MARL 652:88
lost the world for l.	DRYD 352:91
L.'s a bird that will	MEIL 666:17
l. a bright particular star	SHAK 901:67
l.'s a malady without a cure	DRYD 352:89
l.'s a noble madness	DRYD 348:89
l. a quarrel	ETHE 380:15
l. a wench	SHIR 935:24
l. a womman that she woot it nought	CHAU 254:5
L., all alike, no season knows	DONNE 336:77
L. all God's creation	DOST 341:48
l. all my characters	WELTY 1065:49
l. among the daughters	BIBLE 124:46
l., an abject intercourse	GOLD 432:6
L. and delight are better teachers	DURER 356:67
L., and do what you like	AUGU 49:14
l. and friendship exclude	LABR 572:42
l. and hate…are necessary	BLAKE 166:71
l. and honour and pity	FAUL 383:7
l. and joy that fights	MANS 647:98
l. and laughter	GORD 435:63
l. and marriage rarely combine	BYRON 223:46
l. and murder will out	CONG 280:9
l. and mutual honour	MILT 691:89
l. and no sex if you're fat	GIOV 428:37
L. and scandal	FIEL 388:44
l., and she be fair!	KEATS 547:9
l. and toil	KIPL 564:3
l. as deep	SHAK 869:92
L. bade me welcome	HERB 475:17
l. be younger than thyself	SHAK 894:12
l. betwixt us two?	COWL 291:15
l. but only her!	BYRON 220:2
L.'s but the frailty of the mind	CONG 282:40
L. came down at Christmas	ROSS 824:78
l. can claim no place	ANDR 19:12
l. can do with a twined thread	BURT 214:75
l. …can never go wrong	PARK 754:8
l. carries within itself	NERVO 723:13
L. ceases to be a pleasure	BEHN 85:69
l., cherish, and obey	BOOK 176:50
l. colour the most	RUSK 830:80
l. comes to me	ROSS 823:66
L. comforteth like sunshine	SHAK 864:93
L. conquers all things	VIRG 1045:93
L. costs us nothing	RICK 811:76
L. Creation's final law	TENN 999:32
L., curiosity, freckles	PARK 754:6
l. divine…excelling	WESL 1066:63
l. does not consist in gazing	SAIN 836:80
l. endures no tie	DRYD 352:90
l. everything that's old	GOLD 433:20
l., excludes all competition	FUSE 410:58
l.'s face May still seem love	SHAK 914:79
L.'s feeling is more	SHAK 865:20
l. for Linton like foliage	BRON 192:12
l., frendship, cowardyse	MALO 642:35

love (*contd.*)

L. give me more such nights	HERR 477:53
L. has always mixed	LAFA 574:71
L. has its own instinct	BALZ 69:78
l. he laughed to scorn	SHAK 865:99
l. in a golden bowl	BLAKE 166:61
L. in a hut	KEATS 546:77
l. in desolation masked	SHEL 931:43
l. in public	DRYD 348:93
l. in shadow best is made	JONS 536:16
l. in summer's wonderland	NOYES 732:41
L. interests me more	LAUR 584:47
L. invincible in battle	SOPH 953:19
L. is a boy	BUTL 216:17
L. is a cruel conqueror	LAFO 575:92
L. is a Dog from Hell	BUKO 203:48
L. is a fanclub	HENRI 472:61
L. is a game	ROBB 813:11
l. is a mystery	LAFO 575:85
L. is a payment	DUNC 355:54
L. is a spirit	SHAK 864:94
L. is a universal migraine	GRAV 440:34
L. is a very papithatick thing	FLEM 394:66
l. is always a liar	RUIZ 828:48
l. is as a fever	SHAK 915:74
l. is blind	SHAK 874:29
L. is ever rewarded	BACON 56:42
L. is for the particular	DUDEK 353:19
L. …is full of jealousy	SHAK 860:79
L. is here to stay	GERS 420:15
L. is just a system	BARN 72:37
L. is like a child	SHAK 860:83
L. is like any other luxury	TROL 1028:90
L. is like the measles	JERO 521:4
L. is merely a madness	SHAK 886:8
l. is more cruel than lust	SWIN 987:35
L. is most nearly itself	ELIOT 372:56
L. is not a flame	MARG 650:59
L. is not l.	SHAK 915:89
L. …is not meat and drink	MILL 676:92
L. is not only a feeling	BALZ 69:77
l. is not secure	CHES 259:20
l. is nothing else than	SPIN 960:54
l. is of a birth	MARV 658:77
l. is of the valley	TENN 998:12
L. is off sae mekill mycht	BARB 71:16
L. is only one of many	JOHN 528:46
l. is secured by good nature	ROCH 816:61
L. is space and time	PROU 793:96
l. is strong as death	BIBLE 124:55
l. is that common tone	WILL 1083:2
l. is the best thing in life	MANN 646:90
L. is the delusion	MENC 669:73
L. is the extremely	MURD 714:64
l. is the fart	SUCK 981:22
l. is the fulfilling of the law	BIBLE 150:40
L. is the gift of oneself!	ANOU 31:79
L. is the only force	KING 558:87
l. is the story	STAEL 961:67
l. is the whole	CUMM 300:90
L. knocking its blind forehead	SAND 840:48
L. leans through geranium windows	LEE 593:15
L.'s like the measles	JERR 521:15
l. long life	SHAK 904:59
L. looks not with the eyes	SHAK 870:28
l. [looks] to the present	LEWIS 601:38
L. means never	SEGAL 857:30
l. means not ever	SEGAL 857:29
l. men too little	BURKE 208:39
L. mixed with fear	WEBS 1061:59
l. not a gaping pig	SHAK 873:90
l. not in their looks	MILT 693:14
l. not man less	BYRON 220:5
l. of art for its own sake	PATER 759:95

love (*contd.*)

l. of Christ, which passeth	BIBLE 152:98
l. of country	HOWE 497:97
l. of earth	MERE 671:13
l. of Englishmen	THOM 1012:4
l. of finished years	ROSS 823:67
l. of food	SHAW 921:28
l. of freedom	GLAD 429:53
l. of horses	FIND 389:67
l. of justice in most men	LARO 582:23
l. of liberty	HAZL 463:2
l. of life is necessary	JOHN 525:92
l. of man	JEFF 519:78
l. ...of man and woman	PAINE 750:42
l. of money is the root	BIBLE 154:34
l. of old friends	PO 775:39
l. of our neighbour	MACD 628:99
L. of Peace, and lonely musing	COLL 277:51
l. of pleasure	POPE 782:75
l. of posterity	HAWT 461:66
l. of spiders	WHITE 1070:31
l. of the people	BURKE 207:12
l. of truth and right	TENN 1000:57
l. of truth	GOET 431:78
l. of wicked friends	SHAK 868:67
l. one another or die	AUDEN 47:76
l. one another	BIBLE 146:59
l. one another	BIBLE 149:39
l. one maiden only	TENN 1003:18
l. only means one thing	BENN 91:86
L. only what you do	RICH 809:42
l., or gift, which is	MILT 686:70
l. or look at later	SEXT 859:62
l., patriotism and the like	WHIS 1069:14
l. prove likewise variable	SHAK 869:91
L. refines The thoughts	MILT 692:97
L. repulsed	SHEL 932:62
L. respects no blood	DEKK 313:10
L. [ruled] the night	DRYD 352:96
l. ...sae ill to win	BALL 68:58
l.'s sad satiety	SHEL 929:4
L. sang to us	SWIN 988:52
l. says humming	MAYA 665:5
L. seeketh not itself to please	BLAKE 167:85
L. seeketh only to please	BLAKE 167:86
L. set you going	PLATH 773:98
l. Shakespeare	DRYD 347:65
l. shall come	GRAV 439:16
l. shall in my verse	SHAK 912:49
l. shall live	SPEN 959:28
l. she's but a lassie	BURNS 211:4
l. should appear instantaneously	FLAU 392:37
l. shut his door on me	SMITH 947:17
l. slights	BACON 56:44
l., so gentle in his view	SHAK 868:74
L. sought is good	SHAK 895:26
l. sprung from my...hate!	SHAK 868:84
l. supports his reign	SMART 944:72
l. takes [liberty] away	WYCH 1103:39
L. taught me	GREE 445:31
L. that dare not speak	DOUG 341:49
L. that doth reign and live	SURR 982:40
l. that endures	SWIN 987:27
l. that I have	MARKS 652:80
l. that loves a scarlet coat	HOOD 488:36
l. that moves the sun	DANTE 305:73
L. the Beloved Republic	FORS 399:53
L., the human form divine	BLAKE 166:69
l. the Lord thy God	BIBLE 108:90
l. the Lord Thy God	BIBLE 139:34
l. the lovely bully	SHAK 881:91
l.'s the noblest frailty	DRYD 346:51
l. the noise it makes	BEEC 82:11
l. the things we l.	FROST 406:78

love (*contd.*)

L., the reeling midnight through	PARK 754:9
l. thee in prose	PRIOR 791:59
l. them—against my will	ANON 21:47
l. to all men 'neath the sun!	KIPL 564:4
l. to cope him in these sullen fits	SHAK 885:79
l. to hatred turned	CONG 281:22
l. to lie o' both sides	DEKK 313:15
l. to me was wonderful	BIBLE 110:44
l. to the flowers	KEND 550:49
l. to wander in that golden maze	DRYD 346:50
L., unperceived	TENN 995:65
l. upon the honest square	BEHN 85:67
L. wakes men, once	PATM 760:1
l. was of that dignity	SHAK 889:77
l. was passion's essence	BYRON 220:88
l. which doth us bind	MARV 658:78
l. which strikes suddenly	LABR 572:43
l. will be seen at its height	FORS 398:36
l. will change in growing old	BRID 187:42
L. will live in my heart	HAMM 454:53
L. will vanquish someday	LAB 571:30
L. without hope	GRAV 440:40
L. wol nat been constreyned	CHAU 255:71
l. ...would at once be dried up	DOST 340:45
l. you more than one	JOHN 531:20
L. you shall perfect for me	HEAN 464:33
l. you till the ocean	AUDEN 47:60
l. you with all my heart	ROCH 816:43
l. you've been dreaming of	LAUD 583:40
l.'s young dream	MOORE 706:37
l. your majesty	SHAK 902:96
L. your neighbour as...yourself	CLEE 268:99
loved as to l.	FRAN 401:91
L. of democracy is l.	MONT 702:84
loyal sport of l.	ANON 22:74
make l. at any time	BEAU 80:64
make l. in a canoe	BERT 99:20
make l. to every woman	KEEN 548:24
make l. with a woman	ANOU 30:69
Make l., not war	ANON 27:74
make us l. one another	SWIFT 984:71
making l. is child's play	MITF 697:95
Making l. is the sovereign	LEBO 592:92
man is fallen in l.	STER 969:10
man to be in l.	MORL 708:73
man who any woman might l.	BIRD 162:12
Man's l. is of man's life	AMIS 16:73
Man's l. is of man's life	BYRON 222:36
Marilyn...every man's l. affair	MAIL 639:87
marriages without l.	ZHANG 1109:18
marry for l.	GABOR 411:67
me and my true l.	ANON 24:4
measure of l.	LEWIN 601:33
medicines to make me l. him	SHAK 875:48
Men l. in haste	BYRON 223:57
message of peace, l. and sympathy	WHIT 1071:61
might not sing of L.?	SCOTT 853:44
mile or two from my first l.	VAUG 1040:15
ministers of L.	COLE 274:3
Moderate sorrow Fits vulgar l.	DRYD 348:91
money can't buy me l.	LENN 596:59
monstruosity in l.	SHAK 896:49
more anxious to please than to l.	SAND 840:50
more l. and knowledge of you	SHAK 885:72
more of l. than of matrimony	GOLD 432:4
Music is L. in search	LANI 579:76
must undertake to l. myself	JORD 537:31
my l. and I did meet	BETJ 101:53
my l. and I did meet	YEATS 1104:56
My l. and I would lie	HOUS 495:50
My l. has died	BALL -101:28
My L. in her attire	ANON 23:91
my L.'s like a red, red rose	BURNS 212:40

love (*contd.*)

ne'er ebb to humble l.	SHAK 899:42
necessity of l.	ANGE 19:26
Need we say it was not l.	MILL 676:85
needs must l. the highest	TENN 1003:20
never been in l.	STEV 974:4
never doubt I l.	SHAK 889:91
Never pain to tell thy l.	BLAKE 167:83
never told her l.	SHAK 894:15
never with the women we l.	DIDE 330:37
Never, my l., repent.	PATM 760:4
nexus of all l. and money and power	DIDI 330:45
no go my honey l.	MACN 637:39
no l. lost between us	GOLD 433:26
no more bear to lose sight...than l.	ELIOT 365:16
none other I can l.	TENN 1002:14
Not Death, but L.	BROW 196:14
not from reason but from l.	GIDE 423:44
not in l. with Mopsa	SHAK 912:37
Not l., but the astonishn	REID 806:97
not to travel but to l.	AUGU 50:18
Nothing in l.	SHAK 910:79
Nought so of l.	SPEN 958:14
Now with his l.	CHAU 255:32
O L., O fire!	TENN 993:36
O lyric l.	BROW 200:88
O mighty l.!	HERB 475:23
O spirit of l.	SHAK 893:92
object of l. and esteem	LAMB 576:24
objects of reverence and l.	CARL 233:31
Older than l.	SCOTT 852:37
one in l. with death	SHEL 930:33
One wakes only to the touch of l.	CIXO 267:75
one who gives me her l.	CAMPO 228:42
only queer people...don't l.	BROWN 194:58
or successful without l.	TROL 1028:97
over-shoes in l.	SHAK 860:72
Ovid, the soft philosopher of l.	DRYD 351:65
Pains of l.	DRYD 347:68
party we l.	GAIT 411:71
passing the l. of women	BIBLE 110:44
penitence form l.?	POPE 779:10
people who have no l.	SHAW 920:99
perfect l. casteth out fear	BIBLE 156:94
physic of l.	CLEV 269:10
planet of L. is on high	TENN 1001:85
Poetry in l. is no more to be	WYCH 1103:43
Politicians neither l. nor hate	DRYD 349:3
power above...to manage l.	BUTL 217:27
power and his l.	GRANT 438:5
power Of unreflecting l.	KEATS 544:15
power to hurt us that we l.	BEAU 80:74
power to l., or hate	MARL 655:27
Pride leaves...the moment l. enters	GAUT 416:43
purple, with l.'s wound	SHAK 870:86
Quhome that ye l.	HENR 473:72
reason is identical with l.	MACL 633:68
rebuke is better than secret l.	BIBLE 122:7
regain L. once possessed	MILT 695:52
remembrance of my former l.	SHAK 860:80
reservoir of l.	BAUD 78:44
rogue gives you L. Powders	LAMB 576:16
rooted and grounded in l.	BIBLE 152:98
rose of l.	SPEN 958:13
sacrifice L. to pity	GRAV 440:33
said, I l. thee true.	KEATS 545:73
seem to disregard l.	HUNT 504:20
seldom find him making l.	DRYD 347:63
separate us from the l. of God	BIBLE 149:31
service of my l.	SPRI 961:63
sex with someone I l.	ALLEN 14:48
shalt l. thy neighbour	BIBLE 134:44
shows of l. to other men	SHAK 882:17
silence was the song of l.	ROSS 824:87

love (*contd.*)

since perfection is l.	NIEB 727:64
sing the l. of danger	MARI 651:66
so charming…I must l. him	ETHE 380:16
So faithful in l.	SCOTT 853:54
So is my l.	SHAK 914:75
so true l. should do	SHAK 860:76
soft interpreters of l.	PRIOR 790:51
some are fou o' l. divine	BURNS 209:65
Something…that doesn't l. a wall	FROST 406:72
sonnets and courtly l.	GALL 413:97
sooner allured by l.	ASCH 41:51
sorrow of true l.	THOM 1012:15
spirit…of power, and of l.	BIBLE 154:36
sports of l.	JONS 534:85
spring of l.	COLE 274:91
stricken with most obstinate l.	SIDN 936:44
strive for perfection is to kill l.	WOOD 1092:48
strong l. shielding	GORD 435:62
subject but eternal l.	SHEL 930:23
supreme pleasure of l.	BAUD 78:37
Sweet lovers l. the spring	SHAK 887:32
Sweetest l. I do not go	DONNE 336:76
symptom of true l.	HUGO 502:90
Take them, L.	BROW 199:67
teach the world new l.	PHIL 768:20
tell me the truth about l.	AUDEN 47:62
tell the laity of our l.	DONNE 337:90
temper'd with l.'s sighs	SHAK 865:21
temple gates unto my l.	SPEN 959:30
that l. may never cease	HERB 475:20
that we may perfectly l. thee	BOOK 174:16
the life I l.	STEV 976:51
The more I l. …I quarrel	MARG 650:52
The wise want l.	SHEL 930:17
then they dream of l.	SHAK 868:79
There is no l.	AUDEN 48:43
They l. us for it	TENN 996:93
thine inestimable l.	BOOK 174:8
think of one's absent l.	TROL 1027:72
this l. of ours is immoderate	BURT 214:74
this l. of the land	MITC 696:84
this spring of l.	SHAK 860:74
this word 'l.'	SHAK 862:34
those whom they want to l.	FORS 398:34
thoughts of l.	TENN 995:71
thousands…that l. me	BOOK 174:17
Through l., through hope	WORD 1100:86
Thus did they l.	LOVE 615:68
till l. has all his rites	SHAK 879:44
time of our l. and pride	SU 981:16
time to l.	BIBLE 122:19
Time…weakens l.	LABR 572:41
'Tis l. in l.	SUCK 981:18
to be wroth with one we l.	COLE 274:10
to conserve it we must l. it	MONT 702:83
to dissemble your l.	BICK 160:62
to l. and to be wise	BACON 55:21
to l. and to cherish	BOOK 176:49
To l. is to be a fish	IGNA 510:29
To l., and bear	SHEL 930:27
To live is like to l.	BUTL 218:47
touch of l.	SHAK 860:81
tragedy, l. and heroism	LEWIS 602:52
true l. hath my heart	SIDN 936:47
two Milwaukeeans in l.	HECHT 466:60
Type of true l. kept under!	GILB 424:78
Uninterrupted joy, unrivalled l.	MILT 689:32
unselfish and self-sacrificing l.	POE 776:45
unspoken l.	MORG 707:62
Unutterable l.	WORD 1100:79
us that trade in l.	SHAK 905:73
vain in verse my l. to show	SIDN 937:50
vanity, sets l. a task	HUNT 504:26

love (*contd.*)

vegetable l. should grow	MARV 658:73
visible world seems formed in l.	MELV 667:35
voice falls as they say l.	LARK 581:99
wait without l.	ELIOT 371:44
War springs from the l.	RUNC 828:52
war, as in l.	NAPO 718:32
warrior that is rapt with l.	MARL 653:92
was sick, in l.	POPE 781:54
we are always in l.	PASC 757:51
we don't accomplish our l.	RILKE 811:86
we l. thee best	TENN 1000:65
we who were strong in l.	WORD 1099:66
What is commonly called l.	FIEL 388:51
what is denied to l.	WILL 1083:96
What is l.	SHAK 894:8
What l. he must have lost	SMITH 947:5
What l. I bore to thee	WORD 1095:13
What l.?	SHEL 929:3
what manner of l.	BIBLE 156:90
What one gives in l.	DESB 317:73
What thing is l.	PEELE 763:46
What will survive of us is l.	LARK 581:5
when I l. thee not	SHAK 899:29
when I was in l. with you	HOUS 494:45
When l. grows diseased	ETHE 380:18
When l. is done	BOUR 181:48
When l. is liberty	POPE 779:8
Where I and my l. wont to gae	BALL 67:57
Where mercy, L. and Pity dwell	BLAKE 166:65
where there is no l.	BACON 58:98
which men call L.	SPEN 958:16
who's injured by my l.?	DONNE 337:80
Whose l. is given	PARK 754:4
wilder shores of l.	BLAN 168:22
will not be long, l.	COLUM 278:60
with an everlasting l.	BIBLE 128:27
with L. and Squalor	SALI 839:29
with l. false	YEATS 1105:60
woman wakes to l.	TENN 1002:7
woman's friendship ever ends in l.	GAY 416:49
Women will l. her	SHAK 912:41
Women's l. is for their men	EURI 380:26
wondrous miracle did L. devise	DAVI 307:6
write of your l. affairs	YEATS 1104:55
written for the l. of Man	THOM 1011:76
wrong for me to l. my own?	SITT 940:98
yet His l. observes	AUDEN 48:81
yet to see the one she should l.	LABR 572:40
yield to l., ladies	LYLY 620:61
yield, that l. may win	CRAS 296:25
you and I are still my argument	SHAK 914:74
you'll l. Mogadishu	HEMP 471:51
'You must sit down,' says L.	HERB 475:18
young things that marry for l.	SHAW 924:91
Youth means l.	BROW 200:87
love-adept Dreaming like a l.-a.	SHEL 930:20
love-broker no l.-b. in the world	SHAK 895:28
love-in-idleness maidens call it l.-i.-i.	SHAK 870:36
love-lorn By a l.-l. loon	GILB 425:94
love-making l.-m., or wooing of it	BACON 56:41
love-quarrels L.-q. oft in pleasing	MILT 695:53
love-sick l.-s. land that mourns	BLAKE 165:57
love-story as if you worked a l.-s.	DOYLE 343:88
love-whispering L.-w. woods	POPE 783:7
loved Alas! that all we l. of him	SHEL 931:41
As Caesar l. me	SHAK 884:47
Be l. like Nature!	COLE 274:1
beautiful only when she is l.	EPST 379:4
both l. and loathed	MIDD 673:44
Dante, who l. well	BROW 199:69
daughter l. a man	SHAK 894:14
didn't come…to be l.	GRAMM 438:95
each l. one blotted	BYRON 219:78

loved (*contd.*)

for she l. much	BIBLE 142:84
greater compliment than to be l.	MACD 628:4
Had he never l. sae kindly	BURNS 212:25
Hail, wedded l.	MILT 690:65
I have l.	SUCK 981:23
I l. even the tears	RACI 799:98
I l. him too much	RACI 799:96
is it better to be l. than feared	MACH 631:37
Late have I l. you	AUGU 49:10
l. her against reason	DICK 327:73
l. me for the dangers	SHAK 898:9
l. most living things	THOM 1012:9
l. not at first sight?	MARL 655:27
l. not at first sight?	SHAK 886:15
l. righteousness	GREG 446:46
l. the man	JONS 536:20
l. thee once	AYTO 53:84
l. to be changing	DRAY 345:37
many l. your moments	YEATS 1105:60
never been more l.	ELLI 375:17
no sooner looked but they l.	SHAK 887:29
Now thou has l. me	DONNE 336:74
self and the l. one	PHIL 768:19
Sir, you and I have l.	SHAK 905:65
skill…to be l.	SKEL 942:45
thirst to be l.	RHYS 808:25
to be l. needs only to be seen	DRYD 350:49
to have l. and lost	TENN 999:30
To have l., to have thought	ARNO 36:67
Twice or thrice had I l. thee	DONNE 337:85
We l., sir	BROW 200:83
what thou and I Did, till we l.?	DONNE 336:73
loveliness Its l. increases	KEATS 545:56
l. to living youth denied	WORD 1100:90
portion of the l.	SHEL 931:49
lovely Her face was l.	SPEKE 955:62
How l. is thy dwelling-place	SCOT 856:21
In Claud's landscape all is l.	CONS 285:3
Look thy last on all things l.	DELA 314:34
more l. and more temperate	SHAK 912:48
once he made more l.	SHEL 931:49
whatsoever things are l.	BIBLE 153:15
woods are l., dark, and deep	FROST 407:86
lover all affliction taught a l.	POPE 779:10
As to a l.'s bed	SHAK 906:91
Beauty is the l.'s gift	CONG 281:35
death is a l.'s pinch	SHAK 906:7
dividing l. and l.	SWIN 986:24
ex-wife looking for a new l.	CONN 283:69
fause L. staw my rose	BURNS 212:23
fond l.?	SUCK 981:31
Give me a l. bold and free	CLEV 269:12
hard to be…a l. of women	WYCH 1103:38
Have I a l.	EMER 376:46
Having a l. isn't much	HYDE 509:13
injured l.'s hell	MILT 691:71
l. and his lass	SHAK 887:32
l. and killer are mingled	DOUG 341:57
l., and the poet	SHAK 871:55
l.'s bad reputation	NAPO 718:33
l. chosen	GRAV 440:28
l., of angling	WALT 1052:7
l. of life	GORD 435:63
l. of men, the sea	SWIN 987:45
l. of the meadows	WORD 1094:99
l.'s quarrel with the world	FROST 407:97
l. who does not forget	BART 75:83
mankind love a l.	EMER 376:30
namer of l. spryngith	MALO 642:32
Neither father nor l.	ROET 819:96
place her l. as high as she	BALZ 68:67
Scratch a l.	PARK 754:12
sighed as a l.	GIBB 421:28

lover (*contd.*)
sweeter…will be the word l.   HELO 469:6
true l. of literature   SOUT 954:38
weary l.   GORD 435:62
Who can deceive a l.?   VIRG 1045:86
woman loves her l.   BYRON 223:45
world's greatest l.   SCHU 851:16
Your passionate l.   STEE 964:11
lovers Catherine had…l.   WEST 1067:83
Journeys end in l.   SHAK 894:7
L. and madmen   SHAK 871:53
l. be virtuous   LYLY 620:16
L. be war and tak gude heid   HENR 473:72
l. cannot see   SHAK 874:29
l. fled away   KEATS 547:98
l. lately wed   TENN 993:42
l. of the picturesque,   MACG 630:25
l. old are I and she   BROW 199:63
l.' perjury   DRYD 352:90
l. were all untrue   DRYD 352:97
me and the apparent l.   REED 805:82
Mirrors are the perfect l.   ATWO 45:24
Mitterrand has 100 l.   GORB 435:60
sleepless l. …awake   POPE 778:91
star-crossed l.   SHAK 868:73
Though l. be lost   THOM 1010:55
time becometh l. best   DRAY 345:33
to thy motions l.' seasons run?   DONNE 336:77
track for l. on the printed snow   CAREW 232:15
loves Anyone who l. his country   GARI 415:25
for god l. it   JULI 539:67
For who l. me must   TENN 1002:12
from their l. receive   KEATS 546:87
game your country l.   RICE 809:40
He l. us not   SHAK 909:71
kills the thing he l.   WILDE 1078:98
Let him that l. me   SHAK 906:92
Lives and L. of a She-Devil   WELD 1062:89
l. and comforts should increase   SHAK 899:22
l. but half the Earth   QUIL 797:55
L. die from disgust   LABR 572:44
l. me dearly   KEATS 545:41
l., must I remember them?   APOL 32:92
l. my daughter   SHAK 912:34
l. nothing but himself   SOUT 954:39
l. the horror   HOMER 488:21
l. to lie with me   SHAK 885:86
man swear he l. me   SHAK 879:31
one that l. his fellow-men   HUNT 505:28
pettiness ruins the greatest l.   ANOU 30:70
Seat of pleasures, and of l.   DRYD 351:61
true l. without suspicion   SPEN 958:19
Two l. I have   SHAK 915:96
when no one l. us   STAEL 961:73
whose l. I prize   SHAK 911:11
lovest What thou l. well   POUND 786:83
loveth He prayeth well, who l. well   COLE 274:95
Lord l. he chasteneth   BIBLE 155:55
l. father or mother   BIBLE 136:80
loving but the astonishment of l.   REID 806:97
discharge for l. one   MATL 664:76
For l., and for saying so   DONNE 337:84
Hated wickedness that hinders l.   BROW 199:69
l. alone is dull as eating alone   WYCH 1103:44
L. in truth   SIDN 937:50
L. not, hating not   BROW 200:82
most l., mere folly   SHAK 886:95
privilege…of l. longest   AUST 52:70
So l. to my mother   SHAK 888:53
stop l. ourselves   STAEL 961:73
too much l. you   SHAK 899:34
loving-kindness crowneth…l.-k.   BIBLE 118:11
with l.-k. have I drawn thee   BIBLE 128:27
low between the high and l.   SIDN 937:53

low (*contd.*)
Dost thou lie so l.?   SHAK 883:43
en Brer Fox, he lay l.   HARR 458:27
had me l.   GERS 420:13
He that is l.   BUNY 205:73
Holland…lies so l.   HOOD 489:42
l. in rich…countries   SMITH 945:80
Sweet and l.   TENN 997:97
Too l. for envy   COWL 291:19
low-pay l.-p., low-prestige   COUP 289:74
lowbrow l., a bit of a murderer   MILL 679:57
lowcut l., belongings on show   JOYCE 538:56
Lowells L. talk to the Cabots   BOSS 180:28
lower gittin a little l. ever since   BILL 162:2
if the l. orders don't   WILDE 1077:78
l. middle classes!   GILB 424:72
no longer l. classes   TOCQ 1021:74
lowing grazes over the carpet, l.   RAINE 800:7
lowland between l. and highland   SWIN 988:56
Ye Highlands and ye L.   BALL -101:31
loy blow of a l.   SYNGE 988:64
loyal l. sport of love   ANON 22:74
l. to the tips of his stubby fingers   ACHE 3:39
supports his king on l. principles   SHAW 920:11
loyalties above all other l.   JAMES 515:4
Home of…impossible l.   ARNO 38:10
loyalty applauded…his l.   HATT 460:58
done by intrigue, not by l.   HUGO 502:76
I want l.   JOHN 523:54
love and l.   RUNC 828:52
l. and order   GLAD 429:53
l. to the United States   ROOS 822:53
l. to the world organisation?   CHUR 265:31
l. we all feel   GREE 444:8
lucasta L. might I crave   LOVE 615:64
lucid l., inescapable rhythms   STEV 971:44
make a l. interval   DRYD 348:83
lucidity I have a terrible l.   VAN 1039:1
Lucifer L., son of the morning!   BIBLE 125:70
luck always just my l.   PARK 754:5
belief in l.   OATES 733:53
Fattenin' hogs ain't in l.   HARR 458:31
Homage to plain dumb l.   ACHE 3:47
I never had bad l.   TRUM 1030:19
L. is a dividend of sweat   KROC 569:97
l. o' the prize   BURNS 212:33
l. to be called upon   CHUR 265:41
man…down on his l.   DAVI 308:15
more l. …than any other game   ARLO 35:40
no l. about a house   YEATS 1106:88
Oedipus he had the l.   HUGH 500:46
of that natural l.   SHAK 905:72
such a thing as l.   MAMET 643:53
Was there ever man had such l.?   SHAK 915:98
watching his l.   SERV 859:56
when he's unhappy—his l. runs out   CHAN 250:36
Wish me l., as you wave   PARR 756:42
worst l. any man could have   HEMI 471:34
your faltering l.   CIAR 265:50
luckier to die is different…and l.   WHIT 1072:78
luckiest l. of mortals   AUDEN 48:96
luckless poor and l. …as a nuisance   CARL 235:81
lucky Do I feel l.   EAST 359:5
if we are too l.   JONG 534:69
L. is the man   EURI 381:34
My L. Star   FREED 403:29
lucrative most l. of its branches   PAINE 750:47
lucre not greedy of filthy l.   BIBLE 154:29
Lucy When L. ceased to be   WORD 1095:8
ludicrous dignity becomes l.   GALT 413:10
rogue alive to the l.   EMER 378:78
Ludlow L. fair   HOUS 495:64
to L. come   HOUS 495:52
luely O l., l. cam she in   SOUT 954:26

luely (*contd.*)
Sae l., l., cam she in   SOUT 954:27
lug I'll l. the guts   SHAK 892:60
luggage Empty l. may be easier   NEW 724:20
look after the l.   LOWE 615:71
luggies jaups in l.   BURNS 210:85
lukewarm thou art l.   BIBLE 157:6
lullaby dreamy l.!   GILB 425:82
L. of Broadway   DUBIN 353:4
Once in a l.   HARB 455:75
Rock them, rock them, l.   DEKK 313:11
lullay l., l., like a child   SKEL 942:35
lullings l. and the relishes of it   HERB 475:19
lumber l. of the schools   SWIFT 983:56
l. room of his library   DOYLE 344:4
luminous l. home of waters   ARNO 38:98
lump l. of clotted nonsense   DRYD 347:75
L. the whole thing!   TWAIN 1032:60
ugly l.   KIPL 563:76
lumps Go down like l. of lead   HODG 484:52
lunar Held in l. synthesis   ELIOT 367:58
lunatic all in l. asylums   CHES 258:5
as though I were in a l. asylum   CONA 279:81
certified a l.   CROS 298:64
engagingly l. about Ralph   USTI 1038:79
l., the lover   SHAK 871:55
lunatics if any l. were at large   ELIOT 366:30
L. are sincere   DRIB 346:44
lunch long-range planning is l.   OGDEN 736:2
naked l. is natural   GINS 427:23
no such thing as a free l.   FRIE 405:53
When he sat down to l.   LONG 610:91
wish the meeting…as the l.   CHRI 262:76
lunch-time Every l.-t.   HAMER 453:37
luncheon do not take soup at l.   CURZ 302:31
l. with a city friend   BELL 87:19
lung have a l. removed   WAUGH 1058:8
our left l.   GAND 414:12
lungs air ungainly in our new l.   ATWO 44:17
opens the heart and l.   STER 969:7
using your l. all the time   LEAC 589:36
lure swimming towards the l.   HEAN 465:36
wherever you may l. it   KAFKA 540:85
luscious Fame's l. pot   RICK 811:76
lush L., calm and voluptuous   BAUD 77:22
lust avarice, l. and ambition   LEWIS 601:38
Beauty and the l. for learning   BEER 83:33
hutch of tasty l.   HOPK 491:80
looked on a lot of women with l.   CART 242:3
looketh on a woman to l. after her   BIBLE 134:40
love is more cruel than l.   SWIN 987:35
L. carries her sharp whip   WEBS 1059:31
l. of knowing   FLEC 393:49
l. of the goat   BLAKE 166:78
same rule applies for l.   MONT 703:87
Thy l. and liking   SKEL 942:36
weigh their pleasure by their l.   DYER 358:89
women's unnatural, unsatiable l.   BURT 214:76
lustre exceeding l. and the pure   SHEL 929:10
l. in its sky   SHEL 927:63
l. of it will never appear   DEFOE 311:73
l. of midday to objects   MOORE 704:5
Where is thy l. now?   SHAK 903:27
lusts l. of the father ye will do   BIBLE 146:51
prince's appetite And serve his l.   MASS 663:58
Thou hotly l.   SHAK 904:37
to satisfy men's carnal l.   BOOK 175:43
lusty and strong and l.   SHAK 885:82
In l. leas at liberty   WYATT 1102:25
l. song of fruits   BLAKE 165:59
l. young men   SHAK 868:76
lute As her l. doth live   CAMP 228:36
little rift within the l.   TENN 1002:5
l. its tones   KEATS 545:59

lute (*contd.*)
My l., awake! WYATT 1103:29
pleasing of a l. SHAK 862:46
with his l. made trees SHAK 918:53
lute-resounding l.-r. waves POPE 783:7
Luther L.; the Philistine of genius ARNO 40:36
Lutheran spleeny L. SHAK 918:57
luxuries distinction…between l. GALB 411:76
l. That modern life WILB 1075:20
l. to brood over in my walks KEATS 545:65
luxury by l. betrayed GOLD 433:16
couch for l. SHAK 889:79
every l. was lavished on you ORTON 742:86
horseless-carriage is at present a l. ANON 25:25
Love is like any other l. TROL 1028:90
l. of a peacetime environment TRUM 1030:27
l. of doing good CRAB 294:86
l. the accomplished sofa COWP 292:51
satisfy l. and licentiousness MORE 707:51
whilst L. Employed MAND 645:71
Lycid hearse where L. lies MILT 684:47
Lycidas head of your lov'd L. MILT 684:41
L. is dead, dead ere MILT 684:38
L. your sorrow MILT 685:49
Lydia L. The Tattooed Lady HARB 455:74
lying l. for one's country BIER 161:79
One of you is l. PARK 754:7
putting away l. BIBLE 152:1
smallest amount of l. BUTL 217:37
subject…to this vice of l.! SHAK 877:99
We've been l. so long STEI 967:64
you can tell when a man is l. BOHL 171:63
lynching keep him from l. me KING 557:74
Lyndon L. gave me that instead ROCK 817:74
lynx sharp as any l. SITW 940:1
Lyons coming hither from L. WALP 1051:79
lyre Make me thy l. SHEL 928:90
many-chorded l. RANJ 801:27
my l. has a soul CHOC 260:55
remembered tone of mute l. BYRON 220:98
lyric a'e gowden l. MACD 627:87
O l. love BROW 200:88
lyrical primitive e. was l. HUGO 501:56
lyricism sick of cautious l. BAND 69:87

ma Look M.! CAGN 225:91
M.'s out, Pa's out FLAN 392:27
Mabel Nay, M., nay! GILB 424:64
macadam made of melting m. AMIS 17:87
Macaulay cocksure…as Tom M. MELB 667:24
M., Gibbon, Tolstoy PRIAL 789:31
memory of M. BARR 73:56
Philistine, Lord M. ARNO 39:13
young M. or Ruskin BARB 71:10
Macavity M., M. …no one like M. ELIOT 371:41
Macbeth Little Nell and Lady M. WOOL 1093:83
M. does murder sleep SHAK 908:46
M. shall sleep no more SHAK 908:47
M. slurping your soup? PAGE 749:31
My name's M. SHAK 910:88
Shall harm M. SHAK 909:67
Macduff Lay on, M. SHAK 910:90
M. was from his mother's womb SHAK 910:89
mace fool's bauble—the M. CROM 298:56
m. of honor MANC 644:66
m. to knock down the passengers BENT 92:16
macerations Made way for m. POUND 786:63
MacGregor name is M.! SCOTT 855:89
Selwyn M., the nicest boy SPARK 955:48
Macheath Just a jack-knife has M. BREC 186:24
Machiavellian rare tricks of a M. WEBS 1060:43
machine A reading m. LOWE 616:84
automatic m. WIEN 1074:12
body is a m. for living TOLS 1023:95

machine (*contd.*)
depressing the keys of the m. BIER 161:93
friction of the whole m. CLAU 268:95
Ghost in the M. RYLE 834:52
m. for transmission of ideas BOWL 182:53
m.-gun to a shooting gallery OFAO 736:95
m. is running away with him WILH 1080:40
m. slipping from LOWE 617:12
m. that makes the art LEWI 602:71
m., the m. is necessary MILL 677:1
m., the railway NIET 727:70
man…a minutely set, ingenious m. REDT 804:79
[man] is a universal m. REDT 804:79
muskets and m. guns MUSS 716:87
not a man you're a m. SHAW 920:95
One m. can do the work HUBB 498:5
Prayers…on the adding m. WEST 1067:86
pulse of the m. WORD 1099:63
pulverizing m. BACON 60:38
machine-gunned wall and m.-g. TAYL 992:20
machinery Age of M. CARL 234:37
assume the forms of m. MARX 661:22
by chemistry and m. SHAW 921:35
governmental m. he lives under SPEN 956:68
m. of the Government MONT 700:51
mind is pure m. GINS 427:25
primitive m. and primitive music LEAC 589:40
read somewhere that m. MARI 651:70
warfare of men and m. WOLFE 1090:20
whole m. of the state ENGE 378:90
machines begin with sewing m. PAGN 750:40
m. and to be chosen LEUP 599:15
M. are worshipped RUSS 832:22
m. devised by mankind BORE 178:9
m. …do not make men…happier DE 311:61
m. for making more m. BOTT 180:37
m. we worship PRIE 790:40
problem is not whether m. think SKIN 943:52
We are survival m. DAWK 310:43
machismo m. reeks of violence WHITE 1069:20
macho the new m. fascism WHITE 1069:19
mackerel light in the white m. sky BISH 164:32
mackintosh trademark Gannex m. MACF 629:17
Macmillan M. comes back WILS 1085:29
M. held his party together ASQU 42:87
M. was canonized WILS 1085:42
Macmorris Captain M., I think SHAK 881:87
Macon In M. …Where do you go BERE 94:36
macro-economics delusion that m.-e. HAYEK 462:91
maculate Swelling to m. giraffe ELIOT 367:66
mad All poets are m. BURT 214:66
As m. as the vexed sea SHAK 903:32
bolshevism run m. SNOW 951:79
but m. north-north-west SHAK 890:8
Dear Madam, You are stark m. ROCH 816:55
Don't get m. KENN 552:98
for me are the m. ones KERO 553:12
grave of M. Carew HAYES 462:92
grief would make men m. SHAK 862:42
half of the nation is m. SMOL 950:62
he is m. is he? GEOR 418:80
He made me m. SHAK 875:42
heart, all m. with misery SHAK 862:42
heroically m. DRYD 350:34
How sad and bad and m. BROW 200:83
If she be m. SHAK 897:91
If you fear making anyone m. CART 242:5
laughter, It is m. BIBLE 122:18
let me not be m. SHAK 902:9
M. about the boy COWA 290:99
m. all my life JOHN 529:66
m. and hungry dogs MACK 631:48
m. as a hatter ELIOT 371:39
M., bad, and dangerous to know LAMB 576:4

mad (*contd.*)
M. from life's history HOOD 489:49
m. if they behold a cat SHAK 873:90
m., or very tired LOWE 615:76
M. with much heart DONNE 336:69
madness without being m. LISP 607:40
Mahdi pretends to be half m. CECIL 247:83
men that God made m. CHES 259:19
Men will always be m. VOLT 1046:6
more or less m. KIPL 560:17
much learning doth make thee m. BIBLE 148:9
not poetry, but prose run m. POPE 781:64
now run m. JONS 536:17
O Fool, I shall go m.! SHAK 902:15
pleasure…In being m. DRYD 350:37
saint run m. POPE 782:87
shall run m. with joy MIDD 673:45
some believed him m. BEAT 79:56
talk themselves m. SHAK 879:43
that she was going m. LESS 598:4
there the men are as m. SHAK 893:76
these people will be going m. RAMS 801:19
these two may run m. SHAK 896:57
they say you are m. BENN 90:69
Though they go m. THOM 1010:55
way guys yell when they're m. STEI 966:50
will think me m. DRYD 348:93
madam Dear Sir or M. ELLI 375:10
Do not blame me, m. LAB 571:33
M., if you don't WALL 1050:77
M., there are fifty thousand men WALP 1051:96
M., you have bereft me SHAK 873:85
Seems, m.? Nay, it is SHAK 888:49
madame M. Bovary MACC 626:56
maddening more m. as he goes on QUIL 797:63
madder Nothing can make me m. RENO 806:3
maddest of all VOLT 1046:6
made All things were m. by him BIBLE 144:24
Do you know who m. you? STOWE 978:86
everything has been m. FERN 386:27
fearfully and wonderfully m. BIBLE 120:50
land was m. for you and me GUTH 449:94
m. at one stroke FRAN 402:97
m. by the Lord Chancellor JOHN 529:80
no straight thing was ever m. KANT 542:3
when you or I are m. HERR 477:62
Madeira cup of M. SHAK 875:40
We're from M. SHAW 920:3
madhouse How…in the m.? POUND 787:89
Madison M. Square Garden AUCH 46:41
madman angel and a m. THOM 1010:60
dream of a m. SHAW 923:76
either a failure or m. HOLM 485:74
m. bum and angel GINS 427:24
m. in his padded cell NABO 717:98
m. shakes a dead geranium ELIOT 367:59
modern composer is a m. HONE 488:27
That is the m. SHAK 871:55
madmen as m. do SHAK 886:8
Atheists, fools, and m.! ONEI 740:59
discourse as m.'s are SHAK 915:97
Lovers and m. SHAK 871:53
M. in authority KEYN 555:37
none but m. know! DRYD 350:37
They were m. RENO 807:11
worst of m. POPE 782:44
madness Ambition…man's m. WEBS 1060:53
blesing like experiencing m. LISP 607:40
cells of m. TENN 1002:93
close to m. ALCU 12:3
cruel m. of love TENN 1001:76
Don't hide the m. GINS 427:23
escape the m. GREE 444:25
fine m. still he did retain DRAY 345:39

making (*contd.*)

somebody who is obsessed by M.	CUMM 299:82

mal Honi soit qui m. y pense — EDWA 361:48
Malacca Whoever is Lord of M. — TOME 1023:1
maladies all the m. of stinking states — JOHN 525:76
call all sorts of m. ...by one name — CARL 233:27
malady Life is a m. — ABU 2:13
love's a m. without a cure — DRYD 352:89
malaria like m. in his veins — GREE 444:6
Malay M. Peninsula...climate — SWET 983:52
M. religion and custom — PANG 752:76
Malaysia in M. 1937 — THER 1009:44
male chosen and m. shall go forth — KENN 550:55
Especially the m. of the species — LAWR 587:1
incompetent as the average m. — CUNN 300:2
keeps m. domination intact — WOLF 1090:12
makes a m. healthy — THUR 1018:24
m. and female he created them — BIBLE 102:86
m. officers are gentlemen — CARD 232:96
m. quality — HOPK 492:10
m. who enforces order — LEGU 594:27
more deadly than the m. — KIPL 565:23
neither m. nor female — BIBLE 152:89
rough m. kiss of blankets — BROO 192:10
self-worship of the m. — MILL 675:80
weapon of the m. — CONN 283:70
Ye Lilies m.! — CRAB 294:81
malefactor make a m. die sweetly — DRYD 351:64
males Nothing but m. — SHAK 908:36
six left...all m. — BENN 90:75
malevolent something m. — CATH 244:44
thought a m. speech — JONS 536:20
Malfi Duchess of M. still — WEBS 1061:69
malice crabbed m. — DISR 333:3
From envy, hatred, and m. — BOOK 174:5
m. in my breath — SHAK 911:6
M. is of a low stature — HALI 452:29
m. mingled with a little wit — DRYD 351:53
m. toward none — LINC 605:6
the wildest m. — SITW 941:8
worst your m. can — DRYD 348:96
malicious God is...not m. — EINS 363:61
horrid m. bloody flame — PEPYS 765:80
malignity m. and rapidity — DICK 326:54
motiveless m. — COLE 275:30
the m. of a lie — STEE 964:23
malingering absolute genius for m. — PROU 793:95
malleable speech as m. and pliant — QUIL 797:59
malpractice m. of heart — CLOU 271:41
malt m. does more than Milton — HOUS 495:63
maltworms purple-hued m. — SHAK 875:47
Malvernian That old M. brother — BETJ 99:32
mama m. of dada — FADI 382:51
mamas Red-Hot M. — TUCK 1031:50
mamby-pambies outing for m.-p. — CHAR 253:94
mammal You are...a vertebrate m. — CARB 231:95
mammon cannot serve God and m. — BIBLE 135:51
friends of the m. — BIBLE 143:4
pale M. pine amidst his store — POPE 780:29
man A was a m. — SHAK 888:57
Account me m. — MILT 689:39
affairs of m. rest still uncertain — SHAK 884:64
all animals, except m., know — BUTL 217:35
all that may become a m. — SHAK 908:34
All visible objects, m. — MELV 667:34
almost kill a m. as kill — MILT 685:55
always in m.'s shadow — JARR 518:64
an all-the-lights-on m. — REED 805:85
an educated m. — HEAN 465:37
An iron m. — SHAK 877:2
an old m. young — TENN 995:66
And ah for a m. — TENN 1001:81
and all that makes m. — TENN 1003:18
Angry Young M. — PAUL 761:17

man (*contd.*)

Any m.'s death diminishes me — DONNE 339:23
any m. is so very a fool — SHAK 864:71
any m. that breathes on earth — MARL 654:16
any m. whatsoever — TARK 991:98
anything said, ask a m. — THAT 1007:5
ape is m. — MACC 626:57
apparel oft proclaims the m. — SHAK 888:69
architectural m.-milliner — RUSK 831:99
arms and the m. — ANON 21:49
Arms, and the m. I sing — DRYD 352:76
Art...absorbs the m. — FUSE 410:58
artist m. and the mother woman — SHAW 921:26
as artist and as m. — THUR 1020:53
as good as life to a m. — BIBLE 132:12
as if you were a simple m. — PARRA 756:43
As m.'s ingratitiude — SHAK 885:94
as much as a m. — TROL 1028:98
Athwart m.'s noses — SHAK 868:78
average m. sees woman — MUIR 713:41
battle of m. with m. — WEBER 1059:21
Be a good m. — SCOTT 856:18
beautiful woman...qualities of a m. — LABR 572:37
before m. knew how to sin — BEHN 85:71
Behold the m. — BIBLE 160:58
being more than a m. — RUSS 832:19
better angel is a m. — SHAK 915:96
better m. than I am — KIPL 561:36
between a m. and a woman — GIBB 422:36
between m. and wife — ANDR 19:12
bind the heart of m.! — GILM 427:18
Books and the m. I sing — POPE 782:91
Both m. and bird and beast — COLE 274:95
bread to a m. — LEWIS 601:49
breed a habit in a m.! — SHAK 860:88
bring a m. peace — BOOK 176:70
busy m. who can keep up — STARR 963:1
call m. a little world — DONNE 339:20
call up my m. — SCOTT 855:85
Can a M. be a Christian — HARD 455:77
can throw at a m. — HAZL 464:21
cannot be abrogated by m. — SUMN 981:27
cannot make a m. love — KING 557:74
care for no m. on earth — DICK 326:62
care-wearied m. — WHIT 1074:2
Care...in every old m.'s eye — SHAK 869:97
celebration of m. — THOM 1010:72
century of the common m. — ROUS 827:30
century of the common m. — WALL 1050:96
Chancery Lane young m. — GILB 424:70
Child is father of the M. — WORD 1097:42
child...in the debased, degraded m. — ELIOT 365:13
civilized m. ...into a savage — TOCQ 1022:82
clever chiel', m. — MACQ 637:51
cold charities of m. to m. — CRAB 293:74
coloured m. — MACI 631:44
comfort to each m. — ANON 21:58
comfortable years allowed to m.! — SASS 845:23
commonplace young m. — GILB 424:68
confronts m. with...choice — SART 844:12
conservative is a m. — ROOS 821:40
contemporary m.'s idolatry — MONT 700:52
conversant with a M.'s heart — POE 776:52
covetous m. all his treasure — MILT 686:71
create m. in our image — BIBLE 102:86
creative nature with m. — MILL 678:43
crime of being a young m. — PITT 771:72
cultured modern m. — RODC 818:81
Dark as the world of m. — SITW 941:16
darkness of m.'s heart — GOLD 432:85
dat m. of mine — HAMM 454:51
dead m. the leave to think! — SHAK 870:20
dead m.'s embers — GRAV 439:23
Dealing with a m. — JACO 515:93

man (*contd.*)

dear and valuable to m. — PITT 771:72
Death destroys a m. — FORS 398:37
deface the image of m. — IVAN 514:83
degree of grand old m. — LEAC 589:47
Desiring this m.'s art — SHAK 913:57
desperateness of m.'s heart! — BUNY 204:63
dimensions of a m.'s self — LAMB 577:35
dimensions of a m.'s self — LAMB 577:37
Dispute it like a m. — SHAK 909:74
distinguishes m. from animals — OSLER 746:71
divinely gifted m. — TENN 999:44
double minded m. is unstable — BIBLE 155:59
dream past the wit of m. — SHAK 871:52
drinking m. is never less — LAMB 577:38
drive a m. out of his wits — ALCO 12:1
dull ear of a drowsy m. — SHAK 872:67
dying m.'s room — STER 969:8
Each m. has his Jew — MILL 677:6
each m. is alone — BERG 94:41
Each m. is the architect — CLAU 268:93
Ech m. for hymself — CHAU 255:27
effect of travel on a m. — LIVI 607:47
elderly m. of 42 — ASHF 41:63
employment for a thinking m. — ADDI 8:41
Enclosing every thin m. — WAUGH 1057:95
end of m.'s motion — BACON 57:73
episode in the life of a m. — STAEL 961:67
ever tasted M.? — KIPL 562:73
every great m. nowadays — WILDE 1076:36
every m. a liar — BIBLE 148:14
every m. against his brother — BIBLE 130:69
every m. and nation — LOWE 616:78
Every m. at every moment — BAUD 78:42
every m. ...born to die — DRYD 352:93
Every m. has a right — JOHN 531:14
Every m. has his fault — SHAK 901:89
every m. is enemy to every m. — HOBB 483:40
Every m. is not a proper champion — BROW 195:68
Every m. is the maker — STEE 964:15
every m. is two men — BORG 179:13
Every m. is wanted — EMER 377:51
every m. must play a part — SHAK 872:77
Every m. of every nation — THAC 1007:96
Every m. over forty — SHAW 922:61
Every m.'s own reason — BROW 195:69
every m. reclaimed his own property — BUTL 218:50
every m. shall eat — SHAK 918:67
every m. straight before him — BIBLE 109:10
every m. ...under a Government — RAIN 800:6
Every m. ...who is high up — BARR 73:49
every m. will do his duty — NELS 722:99
every m., woman and child — GOLD 434:36
every m. would lay his hand — STRA 979:2
Every moment dies a m. — TENN 996:87
Every time I leave the old m. — OCON 736:88
Every true m.'s apparel — SHAK 897:88
Every unjust m. — PLATO 774:13
Every wise m.'s son — SHAK 894:7
everyone has sat except a m. — CUMM 300:91
exploit of the gallant m. — MILT 685:56
eye of American m. — BARR 72:39
facts we know about a m. — LAWR 586:80
faith that is the privilege of m. — BUSH 215:91
false to any m. — SHAK 888:67
fancy of a m. has painted — LOCKE 609:72
fasting, for a good m.'s love — SHAK 886:13
Fathers, what is m.! — MILT 694:48
fear of every m. — JONS 536:22
feminine in the m. — KENT 553:9
final pleasure left to m. — SNOW 950:70
find a m. — PASC 757:54
fine m. who...knows nothing — EISE 364:91
first enterprising m. — RUDO 828:45

man (*contd.*)

first m. I heard use the expression	ELLI 374:5
first m. is of the earth	BIBLE 151:71
first-class fightin' m.	KIPL 560:34
fog of the good m.'s mind	BROW 198:42
fool, who trusts a m.	MARIE 651:65
Foolish the m. who trusts her	FRAN 401:95
foolish, fond old m.	SHAK 904:43
For a m. to admit a distaste	STEI 966:56
For he owes not any m.	LONG 611:98
For m. will be blotted out	JEFF 519:79
For tribal m. space	MACL 635:92
formed m. out of dust	BIBLE 103:88
free m. thinks of nothing less	SPIN 960:57
Free m.!	BAUD 77:19
free m.	JOHN 523:49
friend of m.	COLL 277:45
fury of a patient m.	DRYD 350:32
gave m. speech	SHEL 930:22
Get a new m.!	SHAK 917:30
ghastly to every m.	ANON 21:59
Give a m. the secure possession	YOUNG 1108:2
Give every m. thine ear	SHAK 888:65
give it to the first m.	SCHR 850:2
Give me a m.	HAGEN 450:3
Give me that m.	SHAK 891:37
give the white m. nothing else	WALK 1049:57
giving m. dominion over woman	STAN 963:89
glory of God is m.	ANON 21:51
Go West, young m.	SOULE 953:24
God created m.	VALE 1038:87
God hath given liberty to m.	CURR 301:16
God in M.	CRAS 295:18
God is not a m.	BIBLE 108:86
God made himself a m.	HUGO 502:75
God never made…for m. to mend	DRYD 352:87
God was a m.	GIRA 429:46
God, M., Destiny	MILL 677:15
good eater must be a good m.	DISR 332:73
good habit makes a child a m.	WEBS 1059:32
good m.'s glory	KEMP 549:43
good to preserve the health of M.	BYRD 218:57
good to some m.	SHAW 920:7
gossamer fidelity of mere M.	POE 776:45
great m. walking down the street	COPL 288:56
Greater love hath no m.	BIBLE 146:64
greatest m. in the world	TRUM 1030:28
guess what a m.	MORL 708:70
had made her such a m.	SHAK 898:8
haggard and lank young m.	GILB 424:71
half a m. to suffer	LAWR 585:67
hang a m. first	MOLI 699:29
happiness of m.	PAINE 751:52
happiness or blessedness of m.	SPIN 960:58
happiness through another m.'s eyes	SHAK 887:30
Happy is the m.	BIBLE 159:45
harried m. I think I be!	BALL 67:42
hate a m. who swallows it	LAMB 576:20
hate a m. you have hurt	TACI 989:75
heaping obligations on a m.	SHAW 921:29
heart of a m. lodged in a woman	CONG 281:38
heart of a m.	ROUS 827:37
heart of m. go together	RUSK 830:86
hearty old m.	SOUT 954:29
hero is a m.	MAIL 640:89
holy m. to crysten hym	MALO 642:24
honest m.'s	GILB 424:65
honest m. who married	GOLD 432:1
honest m.'s the noble work	BURNS 209:66
honest m.'s the noblest	POPE 781:50
hour's come, but not the m.	SCOTT 855:91
how a m. dies	JOHN 528:55
how hard it is to become a m.	CARP 237:8
How many roads must a m. walk	DYLAN 358:91

man (*contd.*)

However vast a m.'s spirit	PASC 757:49
husband be a m.	LAMB 576:23
hyest thynge that m. may kepe	CHAU 255:40
I am a free m.	ARET 33:17
I am a m.	SHAK 903:19
I am a m.	TERE 1005:72
I am a sincere m.	MARTI 657:57
I got my m.	GERS 420:8
I saw an aged, aged m.	CARR 241:77
if a m. bites a dog	BOGAN 171:61
If a m. do not erect	SHAK 880:66
If a m. does not make	JOHN 526:2
If a m. have a tent	LEON 597:77
If a m. have long hair	BIBLE 150:58
If a m. look sharply	BACON 59:1
if a m. should spit	WEBS 1060:36
If a m. were called	GIBB 421:18
If a m. were sure of living	HAWT 461:66
If a m. write faith	BACON 59:24
if any m. be in Christ	BIBLE 151:80
If any m. will come after me	BIBLE 138:15
If any m. will come after me	BIBLE 142:85
If m. were anything	DONNE 338:12
If m. were robbed	FONT 395:46
if the Queen were a m.	VICT 1043:51
If this young m.	GILB 424:66
If you delight not in m.	SHAK 890:6
If you hate a m.	CARL 233:30
If you would work any m.	BACON 59:19
Ignorance…excuses no m.	SELD 857:34
Ignorance…excuses no m.	SELD 857:35
immense new powers on m.	CHUR 265:33
imperishable dignity of m.	CARL 234:44
Imprisoned in every fat m.	CONN 283:75
in a young m. is timidity	HUGO 502:90
in favour with God and m.	BIBLE 142:80
in spirit she is a m.	GOTT 436:72
in the image of God made he m.	BIBLE 104:14
in truth the m.	POPE 781:54
in youth m. is…depraved	MITC 696:78
inclinations of a m.	LONS 612:23
inestimable privilege of m.	SHEL 927:56
injured no m.'s reputation	LOVE 615:70
Innate ideas are in every m.	BLAKE 168:14
interrupt a m.	STER 968:89
is m. an ape or an angel?	DISR 333:7
It profits a m. nothing	BOLT 172:75
It's a m.'s job	AESC 9:58
Japanese young m.	GILB 424:72
Jewish m. with parents	ROTH 826:11
join together this m.	BOOK 175:42
justify God's ways to m.	HOUS 495:63
kill a m. than a hawk	JEFF 520:84
know thee not, old m.	SHAK 878:17
labouring m. that is given	BIBLE 132:5
large-hearted m.	BROW 196:10
last strands of m.	HOPK 492:1
laws of m.	HOUS 496:73
less m. has to do with…death	MELV 667:33
let him pass for a m.	SHAK 874:17
let not m. have the upper hand	BOOK 176:63
Life as a M.	ROTH 826:14
life of every m.	MUIR 712:33
life of m. …heroic poem	CARL 235:77
life of m.	BACON 60:35
like a m. …chasing rainbows	WODE 1089:6
like an honest m.	SHAK 879:47
Like master like m.	PETR 767:12
like unto the Son of m.	BIBLE 156:99
line where m. leaves off	FROST 407:83
Little m., little m.!	ELIZ 373:93
lonely m. is a lonesome thing	CHEE 255:52
Look out for this m.'s music	PARRY 756:44

man (*contd.*)

looked from pig to m.	ORWE 744:33
looking for an honest m.	DIOG 331:61
love freedom…but good m.	MILT 686:77
love is a thing below a m.	STER 969:10
love not m. less	BYRON 220:5
love of m.	JEFF 519:78
lowly m.	WHIT 1071:61
make a deal with one m.	DWOR 358:85
make a m. appear a fool	DRYD 351:63
make a m. by standing a sheep	BEER 83:36
make a m. happy and blessed	ARIS 34:26
make a monkey of a m.	BENC 89:49
make me bearded like a m.!	DICK 328:18
make me mistress to the m.	POPE 779:9
makes a m. stand straight	HELL 468:95
making of m.	SWIN 987:26
m. a child	SHAK 866:34
m.'s a fool to look	MOODY 704:99
m. a little pope of perfection	LAWR 585:72
m., a madyn, and a tre	ANON 22:78
m.'s a m.	BURNS 213:43
m. about whom all is forgotten	BENT 93:30
m.'s affection	GILB 424:61
m. after his own heart	BIBLE 110:34
m. alone can keep that peace	CHUR 265:24
m. alone does m. betray	ROCH 816:52
m. alone in a room	HUTC 506:40
m. also has his moral	LICH 603:80
M. always desires…happiness	ANON 22:73
M. …always to be blest	POPE 780:36
m. and a woman in a garden	WILDE 1077:65
m. and a woman looking at a girl	WOOLF 1093:66
m. and his wine's sae bewitching!	BURNS 213:51
m. and his work existed	MEYER 673:32
m. and the infinite!	MACD 627:77
m. and the intention	LEON 597:80
m. and wife make one fool	JONS 535:94
M. appears to be the missing link	LORE 613:43
m. at the wheel	MARI 651:66
M. be my metaphor	THOM 1010:53
m. bears beliefs	EMER 377:67
m.'s behaviour…harmless	SHAW 924:89
M., being reasonable	BYRON 222:43
m.'s body both for power	SPEN 958:12
m. booste of conning	LYDG 620:54
m.'s boots	MACC 624:33
m. born in America	OLSEN 738:34
m. by nothing is so well bewrayed	SPEN 959:38
m. can be a parent	MUIR 713:42
m. can be destroyed	HEMI 471:40
m. can be so innocently employed	JOHN 529:70
m. can become famous	SHAW 920:15
m. can die but once	SHAK 877:98
m. can never elevate his mistress	BALZ 68:67
M. …can not be happy	POIN 776:57
m. cannot be too careful	WILDE 1076:51
m. cannot choose but pay	PATM 760:99
m. cannot dress	STER 970:17
m. cannot…hold another	FULL 409:33
M. cannot live	GILL 426:8
M. cannot live without seeking	BERL 96:68
m. cannot make him laugh	SHAK 878:84
M. cannot make principles	PAINE 750:51
m. ceases to be a beginner	COLL 276:36
M. comes and tills	TENN 1003:21
m. comes around to needing	FULL 409:37
m. comes into a great hotel	MILL 677:1
m.'s commendation with woman	SHAK 895:28
M.'s condition. Inconstancy	PASC 757:56
M.'s contribution to human history	JIANG 522:19
m.'s corruptions	OTWAY 746:76
m. couldn't wear a moustache	HOOV 490:68
m.'s critical actions	ELIOT 365:7

man (*contd.*)

m.'s decision on how to vote — SCHN 848:*84*
M. delights not me — SHAK 890:*3*
m.'s desire is for the woman — COLE 275:*25*
m. desires to live long — SWIFT 985:*91*
m. die better — MACA 623:*13*
m. does not attain — GOULD 436:*76*
m. does not keep pace — THOR 1017:*91*
M. does not live by bread alone — GILL 426:*9*
M. does what he likes — GILL 426:*6*
m. doth not live by bread only — BIBLE 108:*92*
M. doth seek a triple perfection — HOOK 489:*55*
m. ...down on his luck — DAVI 308:*15*
M. dreams of fame — TENN 1002:*7*
m.'s dying — MANN 646:*85*
m.'s education begins — ROUS 827:*35*
m. enough for a woman — DEKK 313:*16*
m., even more, an Englishman — MORI 708:*68*
m.'s failures — WARR 1054:*29*
m.'s fall made manifest — MILL 679:*48*
m. fallen among Fabians — LENIN 595:*52*
m. feels instinctively — LOWE 616:*86*
m. feels so lonely, alien — LAWR 586:*79*
m. feels there is in woman — WRIG 1101:*3*
m.'s first disobedience — MILT 687:*84*
m. first of all exists — SART 844:*14*
M. for all seasons — BOLT 172:*74*
M. found his form — BERD 94:*35*
m. Friday — DEFOE 312:*81*
m. gets into a ring — MAIL 640:*88*
m. God hates — DOWL 342:*79*
m. goes for politics — ROGE 820:*19*
M. goeth forth unto his work — BIBLE 118:*17*
m. goeth to his long home — BIBLE 123:*42*
m. got to do — STEI 966:*53*
m.'s got to figure — LOUIS 614:*58*
m.'s gotta do what a m.'s — LADD 574:*70*
m. had one hundred dollars — WEST 1067:*81*
M. hands on misery to m. — LARK 582:*15*
M.'s happiness — GIDE 423:*48*
m. has a House of Lords — LLOY 609:*64*
m. has a property — LOCKE 609:*69*
m. has created him — DOST 341:*46*
m. has just waxed the floor — NASH 720:*61*
m. has to prove himself — PAGL 749:*35*
m. has two irons — BEAU 80:*68*
m. hasn't discovered — KING 557:*77*
m. hates to be moved — LAWR 587:*16*
M. hath his daily work — MILT 690:*60*
M. ...held only by the slightest — EDGE 360:*26*
m. he was to all the country — GOLD 433:*11*
m.'s heart good to hear — SHAK 870:*32*
M., her last work — TENN 999:*41*
m. hurling himself at...chaos — POUND 787:*91*
m.'s image — YEATS 1104:*59*
M.'s inhumanity to M. — BURNS 209:*76*
m. in a frock coat — LAVER 584:*57*
m. in a large check suit — WELLS 1064:*36*
m. in all the world's — SHAK 865:*10*
M. (in good earnest) — MONT 701:*61*
m. in higher rank — RUSK 830:*89*
m. in his entirety — BECK 81:*91*
m. in London — GALT 413:*7*
m. in the crucible — ELKIN 374:*99*
M. in the highest — SWIN 988:*50*
m. in the smoker — SAND 841:*59*
m. in the street — BALD 65:*10*
m....in the way in the house — GASK 415:*34*
M.'s loneliness is but his fear — ONEI 740:*51*
m. invents nothing — SHAW 921:*35*
M. is a bungler — SHAW 921:*34*
m. is a common murderer — SAKI 838:*12*
m. is a creature who — STEV 974:*11*
M. is a history-making creature — AUDEN 48:*93*

man (*contd.*)

M. is a noble animal — BROW 196:*3*
M. is a rope, fastened — NIET 728:*77*
M. is a singular creature — BRON 190:*85*
M. is a tool-using animal — CARL 234:*48*
M. is a torch borne in the wind — CHAP 252:*68*
M. is a useless passion — SART 844:*10*
m. is a wolf — PLAU 775:*30*
M. is all symmetry — HERB 475:*22*
m. is become as one of us — BIBLE 103:*3*
M. is born free — ROUS 827:*32*
M. is born to live in society — DIDE 330:*42*
m. is born unto trouble — BIBLE 112:*2*
m. is bound to rebel against — IBSEN 510:*20*
M. is by his constitution — BURKE 208:*35*
M. is condemned — SART 844:*16*
m. is distinguished — ADDI 7:*26*
m. is either free — BARA 70:*8*
M. is essentially the imitative — JAMES 517:*43*
m. is in substance — HUXL 508:*1*
m. is killing time — LOWE 617:*3*
m. is like a phonograph — SHAW 924:*96*
m. is m. and master — TENN 1002:*2*
m. is most at ease — ALLS 15:*55*
M. is neither angel nor beast — PASC 758:*73*
M. is neither good nor evil — BALZ 69:*83*
M. is no other — SART 844:*17*
M. is...not more happy — POE 776:*46*
m. is not 'taking' — JONG 533:*63*
M. is not the enemy of M. — PAINE 750:*46*
m. is nothing but a subject — PASC 757:*55*
M. ...is of few days — BIBLE 113:*9*
M. is one world — HERB 475:*23*
M. is only a reed — PASC 758:*66*
M. is only truly great — DISR 332:*86*
M. is...over-complicated — POUND 786:*81*
M. is polygamous — JAMES 518:*52*
M. is quite insane — MONT 702:*71*
M. is something that — NIET 728:*76*
M. is still — KENN 551:*78*
m. is strong before he is moral — FAUL 383:*80*
M. is the being who wills — SCHI 847:*64*
M. is the hunter — TENN 996:*93*
M. is the measure of all things — PROT 792:*81*
M. is the measure of all things — PROT 792:*82*
M. is the Only Animal — TWAIN 1034:*6*
M. is the only creature — ORWE 744:*29*
M. is the only one — FROU 408:*9*
M. is the shuttle — VAUG 1041:*21*
M. is what he eats — FEUE 387:*32*
m. is who he is — SAIN 837:*90*
m. keep another person's secret — LABR 572:*39*
m. knows he is to be hanged — JOHN 530:*91*
m. knows that he is miserable — PASC 758:*74*
m. lay down his wife — JOYCE 538:*52*
m. lies late — MORG 708:*65*
M. ...little lower than angells — BILL 162:*2*
M. lives by science as well — JAMES 517:*36*
M. lives well — KIPL 560:*21*
m. looketh on the outward — BIBLE 110:*36*
M.'s love is of m.'s life — AMIS 16:*73*
M.'s love is...a thing apart — BYRON 222:*36*
m.'s lovely...power — LOWE 617:*2*
M. ...loyal to his club — WHITE 1069:*24*
m. made the rest — KRON 570:*99*
m. made the town — COWP 292:*52*
M. ...makes of himself — SART 844:*15*
m. marks the earth with ruin — BYRON 221:*6*
m. married is...marred — SHAK 901:*74*
m. marries his housekeeper — PIGOU 770:*41*
m. may be born a poet — SASS 846:*44*
m. may be brought to hope — TROL 1028:*81*
m. may fish with the worm — SHAK 892:*62*
M. may not marry his Grandmother — BOOK 178:*2*

man (*contd.*)

m. may write — JOHN 525:*86*
m. ...mere complexities — YEATS 1106:*84*
m. must be sacrificed — LOWE 615:*75*
m. must have a rare recipe — LAMB 576:*7*
M.'s natural language — FLAU 393:*46*
m.'s natural qualities — SHER 933:*98*
m. ...never have attempted — THOM 1015:*60*
m. nor angel can discern — MILT 689:*44*
m., not even a doctor — NIGH 729:*1*
m., not his instruments — MO 698:*11*
m. o' independent mind — SMITH 949:*60*
m. of clay, son — MILT 692:*1*
m. of...comprehensive nature — DRYD 352:*79*
m. of genius — BEER 83:*39*
m. of genius — POUND 785:*50*
m. of giant stature — NEHRU 722:*94*
m. of good character — SHAW 924:*4*
m. of great common sense — SHAW 921:*21*
m. of great worth — POLO 777:*66*
m. of independent means — MENC 669:*64*
m. of many ways — HOMER 488:*24*
m. of my name — NAPO 719:*39*
m. of paradoxes — ROUS 827:*36*
m. of science — PIER 769:*32*
m. of sense and a fop — CHES 257:*71*
m. of sorrow who wins — LAO 580:*87*
m. of substance, of flesh and bone — ELLI 375:*16*
m. of the present — HOLM 487:*4*
m. of wealth and taste — JAGG 515:*96*
m. of yearning thought — ROSS 825:*95*
m. on the flying trapeze — LEYB 603:*75*
m. on the Flying Trapeze — SARO 843:*98*
M. on the moon — BAKER 63:*84*
m. or a woman — WELTY 1065:*49*
M. ...political animal — ARIS 34:*31*
m. possesses nothing certainly — CABE 224:*76*
m.'s power of selection — DARW 306:*83*
M. proposes — KEMP 549:*40*
m., proud m. — SHAK 896:*72*
m. ...proud and yet a wretched thing — DAVI 307:*9*
m.'s reach should exceed — BROW 199:*61*
m. reaches old age — MAO 648:*24*
m. says he likes a woman — HEPB 473:*77*
m. says what he knows — ROUS 827:*38*
m. ...searches for recognition — MANN 646:*89*
m. shall be as an hiding place — BIBLE 126:*81*
m. shall be known in his children — BIBLE 132:*98*
M. shall not live by bread alone — BIBLE 133:*29*
m. should have dinner — LEMAY 595:*14*
m. should importune me — MONT 701:*64*
m. should know something — STER 970:*12*
m. should never be ashamed — POPE 778:*73*
m. should never think that — TROL 1027:*75*
m. should rejoice in his own works — BIBLE 122:*21*
m. should think — MORE 706:*43*
m. shouldn't fool with booze — FAUL 384:*90*
m. so various — DRYD 349:*23*
M. stands face to face — CAMUS 229:*47*
m.'s strength is but little — SIMO 939:*86*
m. ...successful with his children — EURI 381:*34*
m. swear he loves me — SHAK 879:*31*
m. takes a drink — LEWIS 602:*58*
m. taketh his sword — BIBLE 131:*75*
m. talks loudly about religion — STER 969:*1*
m. telling the truth — JONES 533:*58*
m. that could look no way — BUNY 205:*71*
m. that Fortune's buffets — SHAK 891:*35*
m. that gets drunk — MACG 630:*26*
m. that hails you Tom or Jack — COWP 292:*44*
m. that hath friends — BIBLE 121:*89*
m. that hath no music — SHAK 873:*45*
m. that is born falls into a dream — CONR 284:*94*
m. that is born — TWAIN 1032:*64*

man (*contd.*)

Nowher so bisy a m.	CHAU 254:23
O wretched state of m.	SIDN 936:43
o'er all this scene of m.	POPE 780:32
obstinate love to a young m.	SIDN 936:44
of all 'rights of m.'	CARL 235:83
Of m. or worm	MILT 694:40
Of m.'s bedevilment	HOUS 496:74
Of some new race called M.	MILT 688:18
Oh God! that m.	MELV 668:43
Ol' M. River	HAMM 454:52
old m. broken	SHAK 918:64
Old m.!...difficult to die	BYRON 221:24
old m. ...had so much blood	SHAK 909:77
old m. in a hurry	CHUR 263:79
old m. of Thermopylae	LEAR 590:69
old m. puffed into sight	TIME 1020:66
old m. with a shotgun	TWAIN 1033:80
On M., on Nature	WORD 1100:77
once as m. has conceived it	STER 969:2
one bullet...kills a m.	SPEN 956:82
one m. for every seven women	BERN 96:77
One m. in a thousand	KIPL 564:10
one m. in his time	SHAK 885:91
One m. is as good	JOWE 537:39
one m. picked out of ten thousand	SHAK 889:94
One m. shall have one vote	CART 243:13
One m. that has a mind	SHAW 925:28
one m. to remember	RUNY 829:66
One m. with God	KNOX 567:59
one-eyed m.	WELLS 1064:30
Only m. behaves with such	HUXL 507:65
Only m. delights	AQUI 33:7
only m. I knew	FOOT 395:91
only repelled by m.	INGE 511:37
ony m. can be's	MACD 627:79
Or can he, than is M.?	HERB 475:21
ordinary working m.	ORWE 742:98
Our m. in Havana	GREE 444:13
out of the mouth...defileth a m.	BIBLE 138:9
Outside every fat m.	AMIS 16:77
owe no m. hate	SHAK 886:2
Parliament of m.	TENN 995:77
part m., part horse's ass	ACHE 3:31
penetrated into the ear of m.	FORS 398:31
people arose as one m.	BIBLE 109:24
Peter chose from m. to hide	CRAB 294:83
phasing out the white m.	WALK 1049:55
phenomenon of m.	ALLS 15:56
philosophy inclineth M.'s mind	BACON 57:65
plain blunt m.	SHAK 884:56
play the m.	TAFT 990:83
poor a thing is m.!	DANI 304:64
poor m.'s Parnassus	EMER 378:79
poor m.'s wealth	SIDN 937:53
power of m.	SHAK 909:67
power of m.'s concentrated efforts	BUSH 215:90
praise any m.	SHAK 905:77
privilege of the fighting m.	STRA 979:94
problems which the m.	KRUT 570:8
productive facilities of m.	MARX 660:11
proper study of mankind is m.	RABI 799:94
proper study of mankind is m.	POPE 780:42
propriety of civilized m.	MUIR 713:40
put off the old m.	BIBLE 153:21
rather have a m. dog	FLEM 394:63
real needs of m.	SCHU 850:15
reason no m. knows	MARL 655:27
reasonable m. adapts himself	SHAW 922:56
reasons...unknown to m.	LEVI 600:31
reflecting the figure of m.	WOOLF 1093:70
refresh the mind of m.	SHAK 864:80
rejoiceth as a strong m.	BIBLE 114:44
relationship between m. and m.	ROUS 827:39

man (*contd.*)

remember one m. saw	BROW 199:64
revealed as the m.	PARN 756:40
revive the stature of m.	CHUR 264:10
rich m. in his castle	ALEX 13:18
Ridley, and play the m.	LATI 583:36
rights of one m.	KENN 551:80
Ring in the valiant m.	TENN 1000:57
robbed m. of everything	SOLZ 952:95
rule of another m.	LOCKE 609:70
sabbath was made for m.	BIBLE 141:60
sadder and wiser m.	COLE 274:96
savage individual m.	WELLS 1064:28
saving one m. at a time	BUKO 203:46
say it was the same m.?	LOCKE 609:74
scan your brother M.	BURNS 210:83
scenes where m. hath never trod	CLARE 267:83
scribble, to a m.	POPE 782:82
second of m.'s creeds	LAWR 587:14
see a m. ...not a colour	STEV 973:84
sell a m. a book	MORL 708:71
separates a m. from a woman	ROBB 813:7
serried footnotes to m.	GRASS 439:13
servant of a m.	SHAW 924:93
shake a m.'s faith	SHAW 920:98
Shall mortal m. be more just	BIBLE 112:1
shew thyself a m.	BIBLE 110:54
sick m. must think	LEWIS 601:44
sick m.'s passport	MARL 653:99
since by m. came death	BIBLE 151:67
sit by and see the blind m.	WALEY 1049:51
sit on a m.'s back	TOLS 1023:97
slave themselves to m.'s desire	HABI 450:1
small m. can be	MILL 676:94
smith a mighty m.	LONG 611:97
so becomes a m.	SHAK 881:83
So long as m. remains free	DOST 341:47
So this is m.	TATE 991:5
Soccer is a m.'s game	CHAR 253:94
solace to m. giffis	BARB 71:15
sole nexus of m. to m.	CARL 236:84
solitary child and solitary m.	ACKR 4:56
some great m.	HOOV 490:60
Son of m. shall come in his glory	BIBLE 140:43
sorrow...for a vulgar m.	DRYD 348:91
soul of m.	AUBR 45:37
soul of this m.	SHAK 901:75
sovereign'st thing that any m.	SKEL 942:32
spake on that ancient m.	COLE 273:84
span of m.'s...arms	LEON 597:82
special kind of m.	GILL 426:7
spirit of m. is a good adversary	WILL 1082:76
stamps a m. at once	SHAW 923:78
state of m.	SHAK 918:61
still at least a m.	SCOTT 855:84
straightest road to a m.'s heart	FERN 386:26
strange prodigious creatures, M.	ROCH 816:49
strange what a m. may do	THAC 1007:97
strengthened...in the inner m.	BIBLE 152:98
strips a m. of everything	HAZL 463:12
strong m. after sleep	MILT 686:75
strong m. exults in his...ability	POE 775:42
stupid m. is doing something	SHAW 921:20
such a degradation of m.?	BRYAN 201:15
such a disagreeable m.	GILB 425:80
such another m.?	SHAK 906:99
Such was their awe of m.	MILT 690:63
superiority of one m.'s opinion	JAMES 516:22
surely fool a m.	WHITE 1070:30
system...makes m. its appendix	FROMM 406:70
Take up the White M.'s burden	KIPL 562:64
teach a wise m.	RABE 799:89
Teach the free m.	AUDEN 47:73
thanks of m. and woman	PAINE 750:42

man (*contd.*)

That m. seems...par with the gods	SAPP 842:92
That m.'s silence	HARDY 456:85
That which once united m.	BOLD 171:68
The greater m.	TENN 1004:53
The Little Disturbances of M.	PALEY 751:57
The m. is dead!	WHIT 1074:3
The Reasonable M.	HERB 474:2
their murdered m.	KEATS 546:82
There is a m. child conceived	BIBLE 112:98
there the m. are as mad	SHAK 893:76
There was an old m.	QUIL 797:62
There was once a m.	KNOX 567:61
There's not a m. That lives	WORD 1096:28
therefore the state of m.	MILT 685:60
thin m. inside every fat m.	ORWE 743:9
thing civilized by M.	MERE 671:99
think like a m.	SIMON 938:79
thinking m.'s television	HAMP 454:62
third beast had a face as a m.	BIBLE 157:8
This m., Comrades	GROM 447:70
This was a m.	SHAK 884:68
Thou art the m.	BIBLE 110:48
Thou madest m.	TENN 998:16
till m. ceases to be	PEAR 762:1
time in a m.'s life	MALA 641:7
time of a m. or woman	WHIT 1073:84
tired of being a m.	NERU 723:8
tireless m. of Marshall	ROBI 815:34
'Tis no sin for a m.	SHAK 875:39
To be a poor m.	DUBO 353:6
To cheat a m. is nothing	GAY 417:58
to the image, not to the m.	PRICE 789:32
to the last m.	HAIG 450:10
Toil is m.'s allotment	MELV 667:28
totality of m., sense	MARI 651:71
touches this touches a m.	WHIT 1073:90
truth in no m.	BEAU 80:7
two civilizers of m.	DISR 333:16
two things no m.	MOSS 711:9
type of m.	TOYN 1024:21
understand a m. better	HUGO 502:81
Use every m.	SHAK 890:13
used car from this m.?	ANON 27:67
'Vain m.,' said she	SPEN 959:28
value of m.	ANON 28:1
value, or worth of a m.	HOBB 483:38
Victory switches from m. to m.	HOMER 488:19
vilify a great m.	POE 776:54
vindicate the ways of God to m.	POPE 780:33
walking dead m.	ANON 29:49
want to buy a m.	MACC 625:44
War to a m.	MUSS 716:89
was a self-made m.	HELL 468:80
was a spare m.	AUBR 45:34
Was m. made stupid	EBER 359:11
Was there a m. dismayed?	TENN 1000:72
Was there ever m. had such luck?	SHAK 915:98
Wash That M.	HAMM 454:54
wasn't the m. who could do it	JOHN 523:47
watching m.	BYATT 218:54
way to meet other queer m.	MACK 632:53
wears m.'s smudge	HOPK 491:82
wed a fair young m.	CAMP 228:40
what a frugal m. annually saves	SMITH 945:85
what a m. does with his solitariness	WHIT 1071:67
what a m. would like to be true	BACON 55:28
What a piece of work is a m.!	SHAK 890:4
what drink a m. will have	MARQ 656:49
What is great in m.	NIET 728:78
What is m. in nature?	PASC 758:70
What is m.	BLIX 169:3
What is m., that thou art mindful	BIBLE 114:35
What m. has made of m.	WORD 1095:5

man (*contd.*)
what m. is there of you — BIBLE 135:58
What m. that sees — SPEN 959:40
middle-management of M. — AMIS 17:84
statistics for M. Island — BART 75:87
manhood envied beginning of m. — STEI 967:65
envy men their m. — PANK 753:81
gives m. more approbation — SHAK 895:33
linger in m. — THOR 1016:62
M. a struggle — DISR 332:82
m.'s beauty — WILDE 1075:26
m. is cast Down — LAWR 585:69
m., long misled — DRYD 350:50
nobility of m. — HUXL 508:1
manhoods hold their m. cheap — SHAK 882:5
mania Composing…is a m. — HONE 488:28
m. for sentences — FLAU 392:29
maniacal mirthless, m. — THUR 1019:44
manifest disaster until it is finally m. — MURP 715:70
It was m. to me — TROL 1027:77
manifestation teabreaks and…m. — MISH 696:72
manifestations see only the m. — LAO 580:83
manifesto first powerful plain m. — SPEN 956:79
rely on some political m. — JOHN 523:37
upsetting incendiary m. — MARI 651:68
manipulation m. of…impulses — MILL 678:34
m. of the inventive — LEWIS 602:60
science…system of m. — BOOK 178:3
Manitoba climate of M. — ANON 25:18
mankind All the ills of m. — DUDEK 353:16
an apple damn'd m. — OTWAY 746:78
As I know more of m. — JOHN 532:28
benefit of m. — MACL 633:67
bestow on m. — HOBB 482:36
careless of m. — TENN 994:52
coarse emotion of m. — ELIOT 366:38
common curse of m. — SHAK 895:44
common duty of m. — ROCK 817:71
conclusions at which m. arrive — PALM 752:67
crimes that shame m. — NOON 731:24
deceive and delude m. — EPHO 379:95
deserve better of m. — SWIFT 985:85
destroy in m. the belief — DOST 340:45
development of m. — NIET 729:90
drug used by m. — KIPL 565:24
essential oneness of m. — STEI 965:30
evils m. had to fear — ELIOT 365:17
Example is the school of m. — BURKE 208:48
existence of m. in its power — ADAMS 5:71
Father of m. — WHIT 1074:9
fight for m. — SAIN 836:82
for the friend of m. — MOLI 699:25
fraction of m. want freedom — LAYT 588:25
furnishing m. with the two — SWIFT 984:58
general inclination of all m. — HOBB 483:39
generality of m. — BOSW 180:29
giant leap forward for m. — ARMS 35:49
great mass of m. — HALL 452:33
greatest of m. — DRYD 348:96
half of m. died — MAO 648:25
happiness m. can gain — DRYD 346:53
How beauteous m. is! — SHAK 917:42
I am involved in m. — DONNE 339:23
instinct of m. — TAWN 991:7
judgment Of all m. — SCHI 847:66
last judgement of m. — FRYE 408:20
machines devised by m. — BORE 178:9
m. at least one lesson — MUMF 713:46
m.'s concern is charity — POPE 780:31
m. does not bother — WHIT 1071:54
m. faces a crossroads — ALLEN 14:50
m. from superfluous ornament — LOOS 612:24
m. is divisible into two great classes — BEER 83:41
M. is resilient — HELL 468:89
m. love a lover — EMER 376:38

Manhattan in M.'s Town — HUGH 499:28
mast-hemm'd M. — WHIT 1073:86

mankind (*contd.*)
m. minus one — MILL 675:66
M. must put an end to war — KENN 551:70
m. rules its women — CATO 245:52
M. Under The Leash — DISCH 331:67
M. won — KHRU 556:50
mass massacre of m. — RUSS 833:32
mass of m. understand it — BAGE 61:59
miseries or credulities of m. — CONR 285:9
motto of m. — LAFO 574:79
my words among m. — SHEL 928:91
Nature has in store for m. — FERMI 386:25
novel of m. — GAUT 416:42
only the wisest of m. — SMITH 947:10
only two Of m. — MILT 689:32
peace for all m. — ANON 27:93
principles of m. — WILS 1086:50
progress of m. — SART 843:5
proper study of m. is man — POPE 780:42
proper study of m. is science — RABI 799:94
ride m. — EMER 377:52
shut the gates of mercy on m. — GRAY 442:71
significance for m. — KRAUS 569:91
small step for m. — BROD 189:71
spark that moves m. — SIKO 938:75
Spectator of m. — ADDI 6:7
study of m. is books — HUXL 506:46
Survey m. — JOHN 525:31
tenth of m. — SHAK 911:21
There is no history of m. — POPP 783:18
Three quarters of m. — COTM 289:69
tragedy of m. — WILS 1084:11
universal language of m. — LONG 611:93
untold sorrow to m. — UNIT 1036:45
war that has ever scourged m. — LLOY 608:61
wisest, brightest, meanest of m. — POPE 781:51
manliness sense of m. — CURZ 302:29
silent m. of grief — GOLD 433:17
manly boy's ideal of a m. career — DISR 332:89
bullies you on m. principles — SHAW 920:11
glorious m. pleasures — WYCH 1103:41
manna fathers did eat m. — BIBLE 145:45
M. and dates — KEATS 546:95
m., which thou knewest not — BIBLE 108:92
tongue Dropped m. — MILT 688:14
We loathe our m. — DRYD 350:39
manner extraordinary m. — STOP 978:75
m. rude and wild — BELL 86:97
m. which will make — NICH 726:53
poetry is written in a m. — POUND 785:48
to the m. born — SHAK 888:70
treated in…unemotional m. — DOYLE 343:88
urbanity of m. — CHES 259:25
mannerly M. Margery — SKEL 942:33
manners bewrayed…by his m. — SPEN 959:38
blessed with such happy m. — AUST 51:37
catch the M. living — POPE 780:33
cities of men and m. — TENN 994:58
corrupt good m. — BIBLE 151:70
Country m. — MUNRO 714:58
describe morals, m. — TROL 1028:95
dress and m. in England — SHAW 920:4
have b. for good m. — SHAK 887:35
health and good m. — TAFT 990:83
in divers m. — BIBLE 154:44
Japanese have perfected good m. — THER 1009:40
Leave off first for m.' sake — BIBLE 132:11
light in m. — ASCH 41:52
magic of m. — ALCO 12:99
m. and religion of — MONT 700:53
m. are far more frightening — JARR 518:60
M. makyth man — WILL 1080:45
m. of a dancing master — JOHN 526:95
m. of a lady — FRAN 402:15

what one m. can devise — WRIS 1102:20
Whatever each m. can do — BURKE 207:29
whatsoever a m. soweth — BIBLE 152:92
When a m. marries — SHEL 929:11
when a m. should marry? — BACON 57:62
When a m. takes a farm — PARN 756:39
When God at first made m. — HERB 476:34
When I was a young m. — SCHU 851:16
When the military m. approaches — SHAW 921:39
Where m. has manned the trenches — MACG 630:22
where no m. has gone before — RODD 818:83
Where's the m. could ease — PARK 753:91
whether m. is good or evil — BLAKE 168:10
white m. in Africa — LESS 598:96
Who's master, who's m. — SWIFT 985:96
whole duty of m. — BIBLE 124:44
whore-master m. — SHAK 902:2
Whoso must be a m. — EMER 376:32
wicked m. in the bathroom — EWART 381:43
wife full of words to a quiet m. — BIBLE 132:8
wise m. knows himself to be a fool — SHAK 887:27
wit of m. — WARN 1053:25
within this learned m. — MARL 654:23
woman a m. loves — STEV 973:99
woman more like a m.? — LERN 597:91
woman needs a m. — STEI 967:63
woman…to be the toy of m. — WOLL 1091:37
woman to hold a m. — SPARK 955:46
Woman to m. — WEBS 1060:39
women…sees much more than a m. — MILL 675:77
wonderous and fearful in m. — MELV 668:40
work of one extraordinary m. — HUBB 498:5
working m. into a passive role — ORWE 742:93
world as an honest m. — LICH 604:86
worm, and no m. — BIBLE 114:48
worst luck any m. could have — HEMI 471:34
Would this m. …ask w.? — AUDEN 48:84
wrong m. the woman — HARDY 456:98
Yet each m. kills — WILDE 1078:98
You'll be a M., my son! — KIPL 564:9
young m. at the age of twenty-three — DAMR 304:54
young m. cleanse his way? — BIBLE 118:29
young m. will be wiser — TENN 1003:35
man-cub m.-c. is a m.-c. — KIPL 561:49
man-in-the-street To the m.-i.-t.-s. — AUDEN 48:77
manage by those who m. it — JOHN 531:7
m. a clever man — KIPL 560:16
m. without butter — GOEB 430:64
managed world is disgracefully m. — FIRB 389:69
management m. can only be properly — JAY 519:73
m. of external things — CARL 234:41
Reagan…lacked m. skills — ONEI 740:65
manager Want To See The M. — BURR 213:55
managers M. …do things right — BENN 92:8
m. to run their concerns — ROBI 815:34
Manchester M. …mere village — DEFOE 312:83
Mandalay come you back to M.! — KIPL 560:28
Come you back to M. — KIPL 560:26
M. has its name — MAUG 665:89
Mandarin great yellow M. — CHES 259:25
M. style — CONN 283:66
Manderley went to M. again — DU 354:31
mandrake child a m. root — DONNE 336:75
manger laid him in a m. — BIBLE 142:77
m. for his bed — ALEX 13:19
Mother, Child bare m. — WHIT 1071:61
wrapped in the rude m. — MILT 681:86
mangle immense pecuniary M. — DICK 326:59

marriage (*contd.*)

m. of birds	MOORE 705:15
m. …of mind and body	FOWL 400:70
m. of true minds	SHAK 915:89
m. on the part of a man	DICK 326:52
M. …only actual bondage	MILL 675:79
m. …prostitution to one man	CART 242:95
M. should always combat	BALZ 68:68
m. to Ernest Hemingway	BARR 72:40
m. with your mother!	SOPH 953:22
marrying and giving in m.	BIBLE 140:39
merry as a m. bell	BYRON 219:84
monotony of m.	GIBB 422:36
more to m. than four bare legs	DAVI 308:12
nor are given in m.	SWIFT 984:73
not fit for m.	BERG 95:49
not mount the m. bed	JONS 535:91
opposite to m.	SHAK 898:2
otherwise dead m.	PROU 793:99
pound in lead to your m.	MIDD 673:39
prevents a bad m.	SHAK 894:99
problem of a satisfactory m.	MILLS 679:64
rob…by way of m.	FIEL 388:52
So that is m.	WOOLF 1093:66
take m. at its lowest	STEV 974:5
three of us in this m.	DIANA 319:1
universal in the insitition of m.	MACK 632:50
Virginity…Compared with m.	MARL 655:28
vow…made to her in m.	SHAK 889:77
was m. ever out of fashion?	BUTL 217:21
What do you think of m.?	WEBS 1060:52
will not contain itself within m.	BURT 214:74
woman…a subject in m.	STAN 963:90
woman dictates before m.	ELIOT 366:31

marriages best maker of all m.   SHAK 882:12

m. Lasting a little while longer	LARK 581:7
m. with other men	TROL 1027:73
m. without love	ZHANG 1109:18
M. would in general	JOHN 529:80
much to be said for exotic m.	BELL 88:31
no more m.	SHAK 891:29
one might say of most modern m.	MACK 632:54
one of the happiest m.	DEVO 318:89
so few m. are happy	SWIFT 984:75
unhappy m. …brains	WODE 1088:88

married all right when he's m.   BRON 190:89

anes we m. be!	BALL -101:34
as if we had been m.	CONG 282:44
At leisure m.	CONG 280:1
best part of m. life	WILD 1079:23
but a week m.	SHAK 879:43
characters when they are m.	TROL 1028:87
climbs into their graves m.	WILD 1079:21
cut his throat before he m.	SWIFT 984:80
dance ere we are m.	SHAK 880:68
fool…in every m. couple	FIEL 388:54
he that is m. careth	BIBLE 150:52
honest man who m.	GOLD 432:1
if ever we had been m.?	GAY 416:53
if he had m. Flora	SCOTT 854:71
imprudently m. the barber	FOOTE 396:95
in m. life	WILDE 1077:81
Leibnitz never m.	FONT 395:88
life was m. to it	TOML 1023:3
man m. is…marred	SHAK 901:74
m. and endowed the public	BACON 57:56
m. any one of them	WILDE 1079:13
m. beneath me	ASTOR 43:97
M.,…chaste and twenty-three	BYRON 222:27
m. during the football season?	SHAN 919:74
M. impossible men?	GRAV 440:32
M. in haste	CONG 280:99
M. life requires shared mystery	FORD 397:22
m. or a batchelor	ADDI 6:1

married (*contd.*)

m. past redemption	DRYD 347:72
m. people live longer?	FIEL 388:59
m. to a single life	CRAS 296:19
m. to a sponge	SHAK 874:16
m. to a sort	SHAK 873:95
m. to Americans	WALP 1051:90
m. to an electric light	DIMA 331:58
m. to an Englishman	HEPB 473:76
m. to hell?	SHAK 864:71
m. to Mrs Wadman	STER 969:11
m. woman is a slave	BALZ 68:69
M. women are kept women	SMITH 947:20
most m. man	WARD 1053:18
Next to being m.	AUST 51:40
not well m. that lives m. long	SHAK 870:19
One was never m.	BURT 214:70
rather than queen and m.!	ELIZ 373:85
Reader, I m. him	BRON 191:96
result of being unhappily m.	PARK 755:34
staying m. and playing snooker	REAR 804:73
those that are m. already	SHAK 891:29
time to get m.	EPST 379:5
To me she's m.	SHAK 864:84
Trade Unionism of the m.?	SHAW 921:40
we m. people	PEPYS 765:77
when a m. man doth woo	DONNE 337:86

marries Anyone who m. three girls   STEIN 966:46

man m. his housekeeper	PIGOU 770:41
When a man m.	SHEL 929:11
with him who m.	STEV 974:9

marrow beauty of m.   SITW 941:9

stay at hame, my m.	BALL -101:37
winsome M.!	WORD 1098:57

marry advice…about to m.   PUNCH 795:22

better to m. than to burn	BIBLE 150:50
careful not to m. ladies	AMIN 16:70
Doant thou m. for munny	TENN 1004:50
easy to m. a rich woman	THAC 1006:93
For one thing, they m. later	MENC 669:74
freedom to m.	WARR 1053:24
I will m. you	SHAK 864:78
if you do not m. Mr Collins	AUST 51:38
in the resurrection they neither m.	BIBLE 139:33
less eager…to m.	FALU 382:56
m. for love	GABOR 411:67
m. for purely selfish reasons	BROO 193:35
m. his wife's mother	EDGE 361:38
m. in haste	CABE 224:77
M. me and I'll never	MARX 659:2
m. thee…to be rid of thee	CONG 280:2
m. whom she likes	THAC 1006:82
m. with his brother	SHAK 892:51
may not m. his Grandmother	BOOK 178:2
Mrs Kennedy is going to m.	JOHN 523:45
no humour to m.	DEKK 313:15
no sane woman would m.	BIRD 162:12
no woman should m. a teetotaller	STEV 974:6
taken in when they m.	AUST 51:44
they neither m.	SWIFT 984:73
Those who m. God	GREE 444:15
To m. is to domesticate	STEV 974:10
to m. or not to m.	STEV 973:1
when a man should m.?	BACON 57:62
When you m. …grab a chump	WODE 1088:88
why young women should m.	JOHN 529:81
women m. indiscriminately	STEV 974:3
young things that m. for love	SHAW 924:91

Mars Science may carry us to M.   REPP 807:13

this seat of M.	SHAK 867:48
visitor from M. contemplating	LAVER 584:57

Marshall tireless man of M.   ROBI 815:34

marshes fog on the Essex m.   DICK 324:18

Marston Dancing M.   ANON 26:56

Martha M. and Jasmine smiled   LESS 598:2

M. was cumbered about much	BIBLE 143:92

martial enterprise of m. kind   GILB 426:95

more m. air than the English	HAYD 462:88
valiant and m.	BACON 59:3

martian M. met me   ANDR 18:10

Martin M. like a flying bird   FARJ 383:63

Mr Raymond M., beyond question	KIPL 562:68

martini into a dry M.   ANON 26:38

keep a m. in the refrigerator	DEVO 318:92

martinis dry M. did the work   ADE 8:42

martyr Crook or a M.   ROGE 820:11

Hitler…was a m.	POUND 786:82
I'm a m. to music	THOM 1011:80
m. of the people	CHAR 252:83
the m.'s gore	SMART 944:71

martyr-men Books written by m.-m.   CARL 236:86

martyrdom m. to live   BROW 196:95

M. is the test	JOHN 531:14
M. …is the only way	SHAW 920:15

martyrs blood of all the m.   IVAN 514:83

blood of the m.	BIBLE 158:28
m. or reformers—or both	CHAR 252:80
the graves of the m.	STEV 976:57
When atheism wants m.	SADE 835:65

marvel a strange man is a m.   SYNGE 988:64

m. and a mystery	LONG 612:20
m. at the drama	SCRI 857:24
m. more and more	BELL 87:98
Match me such m.	BURG 206:95
that's no m.	SHAK 878:6
'tis no m.	SHAK 876:61

marvelling m. sweetly on her ills   RANS 802:31

marvellous America…m. …land   RABAN 798:76

repositories of the m.	DIOR 331:63

Marx cold metal…in M.'s pages   SCHU 851:17

illegitimate child of Karl M.	ATTL 44:13
M.'s erudition	NISB 730:5
M. is a case in point	GALB 412:85
Moneybags of M.	ROBI 815:34
wrong to blame M.	BENN 90:66
you have Dr M	HESS 479:84

Marxism cowardly M.   GOER 430:66

Discovering M. …finding a map	CAST 244:34
M. is, above all	TROT 1029:9
prophecy, that M. survives	NISB 730:5

Marxist I am not a M.   MARX 661:25

Marxists sociologists are akin to M.   ARON 40:47

Mary born of the Virgin M.   BOOK 173:94

cometh M. Magdalene early	BIBLE 147:73
Good work, M.	PARK 754:3
Hail M., quite contrary!	GREE 444:14
Jesus saith unto her, M.	BIBLE 147:75
M. …call the cattle home	KING 558:90
M. had a little lamb	HALE 451:22
M. hath chosen that good part	BIBLE 143:92
M. said, Behold the handmaid	BIBLE 141:74
M. said, My soul doth magnify	BIBLE 141:75
M. was that mother mild	ALEX 13:19
passion for the name 'M.'	BYRON 223:53
sweet Highland M.	BURNS 211:1
Where the lady M. is	ROSS 824:83
young child with M. his mother	BIBLE 133:24

Marybone from Islington to M.   BLAKE 168:7

masculine adoption of the m.   GREER 445:40

dignified as Latin, m.	QUIL 797:59
enviable, boast-worthy, m. event	STEI 967:65
feminine spouse to the m. animal	DIAZ 319:2
m. for a woman to be melancholy	WOLL 1091:37
m. in the woman	KENT 553:9
m. values that prevail	WOOLF 1093:73
say she has a m. mind	FULL 409:34
sombre-suited m. world	WARN 1053:24
This m. invisibility	DUNN 356:51

mask husband wears a m. — MARI 651:73
loathsome m. has fallen — SHEL 930:25
m. like Castlereagh — SHEL 928:78
m. of a vulgar soul — MAUG 665:91
m. of prevailing morals — BEAU 79:62
monkey's m. reveals the monkey — BASHO 76:2
No m. like open truth — CONG 280:10
obliged to throw off the m. — PARN 756:40
pluck m. from face of Pharisee — BRON 191:97
profound loves the m. — NIET 728:85
thousand-year-old m. — ROSE 823:58
We wear the m. that grins — DUNB 354:33
masked love in desolation m. — SHEL 931:43
masks are but as pasteboard m. — MELV 667:34
trying on gas m. — CHAM 249:17
masochism spirit of national m. — AGNEW 10:69
masonry bind…into the social m. — WELLS 1064:28
masons professionals, like…m. — EICH 362:59
masquerade miss a m. — POPE 778:96
truth in m. — BYRON 223:56
masquerading m. knight-errant — PARN 756:40
mass blessed mutter of the m. — BROW 198:39
broad m. of a nation — HITL 482:28
Chaos, a rough unordered m. — OVID 747:97
from its m. Walls — BYRON 220:2
go to M. every day — BELL 87:4
haven't been to m. for years — WILS 1084:12
malicious…crapulous m. — ADAMS 5:88
m. of the nation — TWAIN 1034:98
ocean's liquid m. — WORD 1100:79
opium for every conceivable m. — KENN 550:57
The m. of men — THOR 1016:77
We were one m. — DRYD 348:94
massacre mass m. of mankind — RUSS 833:32
not as sudden as m. — TWAIN 1032:62
Masserman M. the cat man — ANON 26:54
masses anything said about the m. — PRIE 790:43
art of the m. — HALL 452:34
back the m. — GLAD 429:54
benighted m. of wishful thinkers — QUINE 797:67
bow ye m.! — GILB 424:72
Carving is interrelated m. — HEPW 473:79
educate the m. — OSLER 746:72
gathered itself…into m. — CARL 234:39
Government…exasperates the m. — REED 805:91
intelligence of the great m. — MENC 669:67
make the m. prosperous — BRYAN 201:14
m. yearning to breathe — LAZA 588:26
paper which the m. call dough — ANDR 18:11
philosopher should judge the m. — CYRA 302:35
The m. are wrong — VIAN 1043:43
tumult of the m. — ALCU 12:3
wide support of the m. — LENIN 595:48
masseur m. called Harold — WOOD 1091:46
Massey M. won't be satisfied — KAUF 542:13
mast bends the gallant m. — CUNN 300:99
mast-hemm'd m.-h. Manhattan — WHIT 1073:86
master belonging to the m. — STOWE 978:84
brave m. was no more — MACA 624:28
condemned by a faceless m. — PAZ 761:23
disciple is not above his m. — BIBLE 136:77
do not M. or Campbell me — SCOTT 855:89
does not excel his m. — LEON 597:94
great M. so to sympathize — MILT 681:86
Has a new m. — SHAK 917:30
himself to be my m. — TUTU 1032:54
In order to become the m. — DEGA 313:6
insufferable m. — JEFF 519:78
Like m. like man — PETR 767:12
man…becomes a m. in that science — COLL 276:36
Man…is m. of everything — MILL 678:37
Man is the m. of things — SWIN 988:50
marvel thy m. hath not — SHAK 866:24
m. a grief — SHAK 880:53

master (contd.)
m., a mistress and two slaves — BIER 161:87
m. minds of all nations — TWAIN 1034:98
m.-mistress of my passion — SHAK 913:50
M. morality — NIET 728:87
m. of himself — MASS 662:53
m. of his fate — TENN 1002:2
m. of his trade — DRAY 346:41
m. or servant of the state — KING 558:84
M.: records prove the title — ARLO 34:37
maxim of every prudent m. — SMITH 945:88
no more subtle m. — TENN 1003:18
not make dreams your m. — KIPL 564:8
O divine M. — FRAN 401:91
O m. doctor, he is past — MASS 663:59
Oh my divine m.! — HUGO 501:69
old clothes know who's m. — SHER 933:80
only the m. shall praise — KIPL 562:60
Our m. Caesar — YEATS 1107:90
poet is a m. of the quotidian — PRIT 791:72
press…a terrible m. — COOP 287:44
Rabboni; which is to say, M. — BIBLE 147:75
slave has but one m. — LABR 572:46
village m. taught his little school — GOLD 433:12
when I hae a gude m. — SCOTT 855:86
which is to be m. — CARR 240:66
Who's m., who's man — SWIFT 985:96
Without a m. …I…work — ARET 33:17
work of the m. — LEON 596:72
world with her divine M. — MILT 686:72
mastered m. what ever was — LOWE 616:84
only athletic sport I m. — JERR 521:18
masterpiece cradle of new m. — YEATS 1105:66
driven to create a m. — SELF 857:37
friend…the m. of nature — EMER 376:39
function…is to produce a m. — CONN 283:68
great and glorious m. — MONT 702:74
knows, at first sight, a m. — POUND 786:66
m. of art has…a fixed place — EMER 376:45
Nature's great m. — DONNE 337:83
no m. can be anything — MARI 651:66
now hath made his m. — SHAK 908:53
obscure unfinished m. — NABO 717:3
masterpieces creation of genuine m. — DALI 303:48
m. having one-night stands — RAUS 802:42
masters any of those m. — MACC 627:68
beasts are our m. — FLET 394:73
copying the m. — INGR 512:49
fall from their m.' table — BIBLE 138:11
made them slave m. — MORR 709:88
m. at the moment — SHAW 926:46
m. of different bits of man — LAWR 587:8
m. of their fates — SHAK 882:20
m.' thoughts — MARL 653:91
new m. — HALI 452:31
not m. of our own affections — ETHE 380:17
Old M.: how well they understood — AUDEN 47:59
people are the m. — BURKE 207:21
Power of new M. — ALBE 12:94
relations with their m. — MILL 675:76
serve two m. — BIBLE 135:51
Unmarried men…best m. — BACON 57:59
mastery Love…constreyned by m. — CHAU 255:37
m. of the thing! — HOPK 491:89
m. of vocabulary and syntax — SAYE 846:51
mastiff trusty m. that is to watch — LLOY 608:54
mastodons calling to Aunt like m. — WODE 1089:91
masturbation Don't knock m. — ALLEN 14:48
M. is the thinking man's television — HAMP 454:62
mat foot in the m. — GROS 447:72
worst room, with m. half-hung — POPE 780:30
match burnt m. skating in a urinal — CRANE 295:9
diploma is a lighted m. — KOCH 567:66
Honour is like a m. — PAGN 750:39

match (contd.)
m. flickers — STEV 974:21
m. its military strength — KENN 552:89
strike a m. — AMIS 17:86
matchboxes substitute…empty m. — DOUG 341:60
matches as m. in the rough — DICK 323:78
extravagant m. — GILB 425:91
have to have a box of m. — HOME 487:11
little I repair to the m. — THOM 1014:32
playing with a box of m. — HARL 458:20
With that stick of m. — MAND 645:70
mate Among beasts no m. — MILT 692:97
Consciousness, her awful M. — DICK 328:8
lady's ta'en another m. — BALL 67:55
man there walked without a m. — MARV 659:87
m. with its complement of men — WRIG 1101:99
Not…one solitary m. — EGAN 362:55
people should m. for life — ALLEN 14:49
shearing m. who wrote it — PATE 760:97
mated But we was badly m. — STRO 980:6
material basic m. a writer works with — CATH 244:47
body and m. substance — CARL 236:90
Corridors—surpassing M. Place — DICK 328:5
endowed M. forces with — MARX 660:18
external m. things — LOCKE 609:73
From a m. and spiritual terrain — FULL 410:94
gathers its m. from flowers — BACON 55:29
good m. for poetry — WILL 1083:6
good m. …to build a life from — CAREY 233:23
make its m. …interesting — BEAV 81:87
march of m. ugliness — WHITE 1070:44
m. …and the moral — DEWEY 319:95
m. is our own flesh — THOR 1016:73
m. position of the worker — MARX 660:16
moral or a m. one — ARNO 38:5
Nothing is m. in space — ROSSO 825:99
only objects in the m. world — FORS 399:50
so many people…for m. benefits — COLU 278:63
universe…as a m. system — PAGE 749:33
world of m. life — ARNO 39:20
materialism deteriorate into m. — MOLT 699:36
inhuman in its m. — WILS 1084:17
materialist m. of all great religions — TEMP 993:28
materials action…essential m.? — CARL 235:71
m. for conversation — JOHN 527:18
m. of reason and knowledge — LOCKE 609:72
raw m. out of which — TEMP 993:30
sculptor can use twenty different m. — BOCC 171:55
she begins to gather the m. — OCON 736:87
maternity m. to women — MUSS 716:89
woman…cursed in her m. — STAN 963:90
mates thuctheththion of m. — BENT 93:27
very popular among his m. — EWART 381:46
math m. is quite straightforward — GATES 416:37
M. was my worst subject — TRIL 1026:55
Mathematica Principia M. — RUSS 833:31
mathematical m. concepts — GIBS 422:40
m. elegance — GREE 445:36
m. or philosophical author — WHIT 1071:52
Moriarty of m. celebrity — DOYLE 344:8
must be a m. science — JEVO 521:19
one m., the other…intuitive — PASC 757:47
The m. is that evident aspect — HEID 467:66
mathematician m. is a blind man — DARW 306:91
trifles in which a m. — MACA 623:11
mathematicians m. …cabbages — BOYD 182:65
mathematics All science requires m. — BACON 60:41
Angling…like m. — WALT 1052:4
Between the penis and m. — CELI 247:86
creative people hate m. — ISSI 514:79
extensive use of m. — HAYEK 462:91
laws of m. …are not certain — EINS 363:76
m. as surely as in poetry — RUSS 832:19
M. is the door — BACON 60:42

mathematics (*contd.*)
M. is thought moving — WHIT 1071:58
m., orthography, geometry, — DICK 321:44
M. possesses not only truth — RUSS 831:14
no one ignorant of m. — PLATO 774:28
of flight, of m., of physics — HEMI 471:36
order and mystical m. — BROW 196:7
secret of success in m. — LEHR 595:40
ugly m. — HARDY 456:82
Vanity of m.! — FRED 403:26
ways to teach m. — NEWM 724:26
Matilda a-waltzing M. with me — PATE 760:96
M. told such Dreadful Lies — BELL 87:10
mating for eating, not m. — FERB 385:12
matrimony argument in favour of m. — AUST 52:61
critical period in m. — HERB 474:3
holy estate of M. — BOOK 176:47
holy estate of M. — BOOK 176:48
in holy M. — BOOK 175:42
more of love than of m. — GOLD 432:4
not be joined together in holy M. — BOOK 175:41
respectable as that of m. — TROL 1027:64
safest in m. …a little aversion — SHER 933:78
Without thinking…of men or m. — AUST 51:39
matron sober-suited m. — SHAK 869:5
worn m. smiles — WHIT 1074:2
matrons stout m. — GILL 426:4
matter Does it m.? — SASS 845:29
doesn't so much m. what you do — JAMES 516:27
few things m. at all — BALF 65:21
here and now cease to m. — ELIOT 372:56
here's no great m. — ELIOT 367:51
if it is it doesn't m.! — GILB 425:93
is no 'living m.' — MONOD 700:45
least m. dear to Him — AUDEN 48:81
living and non-living m. — PAGE 749:33
Marriage is a m. — SHAK 861:97
m. is the scaffolding — THOM 1013:27
m. of life and death — SHAN 918:69
More m. with less art — SHAK 889:89
no rights in the m. — ROET 819:96
no subject m. — DAVIS 309:35
not the m. of the work — GLAS 430:58
obscurity of the m. — PROT 792:84
order…this m. better — STER 970:19
removing the m. of sin — MILT 686:69
some arduous and difficult m. — SIDN 936:42
straightforward a m. — RUSK 830:89
subsists on m. he destroys — BELL 89:43
that great renovator of m. — OVID 747:3
then he's full of m. — SHAK 885:79
thet's wots the m. with you — SHAW 923:74
this high m. — WORD 1100:92
throat of well-printed m. — MORR 709:81
Vain m. is worse — BACON 55:9
when all the m.'s spent — DANI 304:61
Why, what's the m. — SHAK 880:67
matter-of-fact m.-o.-f. young man — GILB 424:68
matters m. just as little — SHAW 921:37
m. not how a man dies — JOHN 528:55
m. outside…everyday experience — CONR 285:10
questions about the great m. — ARIS 34:24
read strange m. — SHAK 907:28
suspect his taste in higher m. — LAMB 576:20
What can I do that m.? — SPEN 956:78
what m. in your life — RUSH 829:67
Matthew saw a man, named M. — BIBLE 136:69
Sir M. left the room — LINK 606:21
mattress cold porridge on a damp m. — BRID 188:46
gasping on a little flock m. — DICK 321:33
snug as a feather m. — ANGE 19:25
mature have in our m. years — TROL 1027:74
m. imagination of a man — KEATS 545:55
m. poets steal — ELIOT 368:78

maturity wisdoms of m. — LIVE 607:45
Maud M. is not seventeen — TENN 1001:82
maul not afraid…of a 'm.' — ANON 24:14
maunder Let her m. and mumble — CARL 235:60
mausoleum mouth…as its m. — AMIS 16:71
mausoleums m. for his enemies — LINK 606:21
mavis m. and merle are singing — SCOTT 854:66
mawkishness thence proceeds m. — KEATS 545:55
maws feed the m. — KEYN 554:34
maxim essential m. of your liberties — PITT 771:68
grounded m. So rife — MILT 695:49
M. Gun — BELL 87:3
m. is worthy of the fool — MACA 622:91
m. of every prudent master — SMITH 945:88
so useless as a general m. — MACA 622:92
will that my m. — KANT 542:4
maxims cardinal m. of guerrilla war — KISS 566:31
m., of self-justification — EDGE 360:25
maximum m. of temptation — SHAW 922:49
May 21st M.—a glorious day — WORD 1101:95
airiest M.? — GRAV 439:21
at least the seventh of M. — TROL 1027:65
darling buds of M. — SHAK 912:48
end of M. — HOUS 495:68
From M. to December — ANDE 18:6
Maids are M. — SHAK 887:23
M.'s new-fangled shows — SHAK 865:8
M. will be fine next year — HOUS 496:69
mid-m.'s eldest child — KEATS 548:17
moonlight-coloured m. — SHEL 932:68
nightingale when M. is past — CAREW 232:18
that the moneth of M. — MALO 642:32
wife left you in M. — NORD 731:26
world is white with M. — TENN 1003:37
May-day M.-d. freshness amidst — MORR 709:81
May-poles sing of M.-p. — HERR 477:51
maybe definite m. — GOLD 434:44
Maying let's go a M. — HERR 477:62
mayonnaise M. …One of the sauces — BIER 161:88
mayor lord m. of Birmingham — LLOY 609:66
my Lord M. commands — PEPYS 765:75
tart who has…married me. — BAXT 78:49
maypole where's the M. in the Strand — BRAM 185:8
maze A mighty m.! — POPE 780:32
Bewilder'd in the m. of life — LUCR 619:35
every m. of quick — TENN 1000:59
law seems like a sort of m. — MORT 710:92
Life is a m. — CONN 283:71
Philosophy for him was…a m. — SANT 842:86
the m. of schools — POPE 778:75
through the watery m. — MARV 659:92
wander in that golden m. — DRYD 346:50
MCC where the M. ends — PRIE 790:44
McCarthyism M. is Americanism — MACC 625:43
McGrew dangerous Dan M. — SERV 859:56
Mcjob M. …no-future job — COUP 289:74
McLuhan M. put a telescope — SMITH 945:77
McNamara M.'s war — MACN 636:27
McTavish Against the clan M. — AYTO 53:85
me gone up and met m. — HOFF 484:56
I most delight in M. — CAMP 227:16
M., evidently — HUGH 500:44
not with m. is against m. — BIBLE 137:90
soul is not required of m. — SMITH 948:39
trouble with m. — SALI 838:24
mea see m. bat — GRACE 437:85
mead By the stream and o'er the m. — BLAKE 166:63
meadow a m. of margin — SHER 933:94
Burn-mill m. — WORD 1098:57
in m. or plain — SWIN 986:23
m., grove, and stream — WORD 1097:48
painted m., or a purling stream — ADDI 6:99
Winter scouraged the m. — ROBE 814:17
meadows among green aits and m. — DICK 324:18

meadows (*contd.*)
by-path m. — STEV 974:9
enamelled m. with filigree hedges — WALP 1051:81
Fair these broad m. — GALT 413:8
floor the m. with cement — MACL 634:81
golden face the m. green — SHAK 913:59
Golden lie the m. — MERE 671:1
lover of the m. — WORD 1094:99
m. fresh and gay — MARV 658:81
m. runnels — KEATS 545:59
M. trim with daisies — MILT 682:1
undulating green m. — HUXL 507:70
Up from the m. — WHIT 1074:7
variety of gardens, m. — MOORE 705:14
meadowsweet timothy-tops and m. — ROBE 814:16
meagre m. hill of kernels — RANS 802:33
One composition is m. — DIDE 330:40
meal Breakfast is the one m. — VAND 1039:96
can't fake…a good m. — BURR 213:56
evening m. — BARL 71:21
m. was large — PRIOR 791:57
Salad is not a m. — LEBO 591:83
meals cooking three m. a day — PLATH 773:88
good m. I…am wearing — BUSH 215:85
keep with you at m. — SHAK 883:30
lessen thy M. — FRAN 402:1
mealy M. boys, and beef-faced boys — DICK 321:40
mean abhor…the m. — CURZ 302:29
dull and m. — WHIT 1074:6
family talk, m. and worried — COMP 279:71
Happy the golden m.! — MASS 663:61
I m. what I say — CARR 238:28
improved m. — THOR 1016:78
m. between nothing and everything — PASC 758:70
m. between two vices — ARIS 34:27
meanly admires m. things — THAC 1006:91
no m. city — BIBLE 148:7
too m. to be your queen — SHAK 862:26
woman of m. understanding — AUST 50:34
meaner m. things To low ambition — POPE 780:32
She must take m. things — ELIOT 366:28
meanest wisest, brightest, m. — POPE 781:51
meaning control the m. of words — DICK 320:13
experience but missed the m. — ELIOT 372:60
Free from all m. — DRYD 350:34
Has no m. — SNYD 951:81
husk of m. — ELIOT 372:69
Is there a m. to music? — COPL 288:55
it lacks m. — PAZ 762:25
language charged with m. — POUND 786:72
m. is my meat and drink — BROW 198:45
m., not find yours — RUSK 831:97
m. of the Lost Generation — KERO 553:15
no definite and unquestionable m. — SART 843:5
precise m. of a word — BAND 69:87
Religion…gives m. to all — WHIT 1071:55
richest without m. — RUSK 830:76
to some faint m. make pretence — DRYD 348:83
true m. of religion — ARNO 39:32
meaningless creative world…m. — SPEN 957:90
half of what she wrote would be m. — CHAN 250:39
meanings let my m. show — CAMP 227:19
Minding our m. — AUDEN 48:81
two m. packed up into one word — CARR 240:68
VALUE…has two different m. — SMITH 946:94
war…an openness about the m. — DALL 303:50
wrestle…words and m. — ELIOT 371:45
meanness land of m. — BYRON 219:66
vice of m. — THOM 1014:43
meannesses assorted m. — GILL 426:3
means best ends by the best m. — HUTC 506:41
by defective m. — WILL 1082:41
doubled their m. of consuming — MILL 674:60
end may justify the m. — TROT 1029:10

men (*contd.*)

But while m. slept	BIBLE 137:*1*
by pains m. come to greater pains	BACON 57:*70*
By this shall all m. know	BIBLE 146:*59*
called the book M. Without Women	HEMI 470:*16*
cannot fight…as m. may do	SHAK 870:*38*
cannot learn m. from books	DISR 332:*71*
cause that wit is in other m.	SHAK 877:*80*
challenge all the m. alive	ANON 24:*8*
cheerful ways of m.	MILT 689:*31*
chiefly made by m.	HARDY 456:*89*
clerkes been noght the wisest m.	CHAU 255:*34*
clever m. at Oxford	GRAH 438:*93*
closest m. ever come to childbearing	MAIL 639:*78*
Columbus and his m.	WILB 1075:*20*
common to all…conditoins of m.	WEBER 1059:*20*
common wonder of all m.	BROW 195:*90*
consent of all great m.	RUSK 830:*88*
cunning m. pass for wise	BACON 58:*88*
Dead m. are serious	FIND 389:*66*
dealings with young m.	PO 775:*39*
depends upon that of m.	GILM 427:*14*
difference of 40,000 m.	WELL 1063:*15*
diversity in the faculties of m.	MADI 638:*55*
Do other m., for they would do you	DICK 322:*73*
domination by fat-minded m.	ARNO 40:*45*
doon m., if I sooth	CHAU 255:*38*
dreadful fiend of gods and m.	SPEN 959:*35*
droop m. and beasts	NASHE 721:*81*
drowned more m. than Neptune	FULL 410:*47*
enables m. to produce more	GILM 427:*15*
Eve upon the first of M.	HOOD 489:*44*
evil lurks in the hearts of m.	ATWO 45:*30*
except in the minds of m.	READ 803:*55*
eyes of God and m.	LESL 598:*94*
failed to inspire sympathy in m.	BEER 83:*32*
faithful account of m. and things	ELIOT 365:*6*
Famous m. have the whole earth	PERI 766:*97*
fancy of the mass of m.	BAGE 61:*54*
fashions m. with true nobility	MARL 653:*92*
favours of these m.	SHAK 867:*63*
fear of little m.	ALLI 15:*53*
fifty m. and women	BROW 199:*67*
fifty thousand m. slain	WALP 1051:*96*
find too late that m. betray	GOLD 432:*5*
first-class m.	WHIT 1073:*95*
fisher of m., and of women	DOUG 341:*61*
For the m. it's better	WELD 1062:*92*
for the next generation of m.	LOWE 615:*75*
for us m. and for our salvation	BOOK 174:*19*
Forests of middle-aged m.	ABBO 1:*1*
form Christian m.	ARNO 40:*43*
Freedom of m. under government	LOCKE 609:*70*
fruits…accessible to m.	FREUD 404:*46*
furnished well with m.	SHAK 883:*38*
fury, and rage of mortal m.	BURT 214:*75*
gallant m. danced	WHITE 1071:*49*
generation of m.	HOMER 487:*17*
generosity of m.	MARI 652:*75*
God, justifiable to m.	MILT 694:*45*
Gods and m., we are all deluded	SHEL 932:*71*
Good m. made evil	MUIR 712:*31*
government…not of m.	ADAMS 5:*84*
Great m. are almost always bad m.	ACTON 4:*59*
great m. …in politics	ELTON 375:*22*
Great m. may jest	SHAK 896:*73*
great m. of the past	DESB 317:*71*
greatest m. that ever lived	MACA 623:*3*
grief would make m. mad	SHAK 862:*42*
griefs of private m.	MARL 653:*5*
half my m. are sick	TENN 1004:*56*
happy m. that have the power	TENN 1003:*23*
hearts of m. …have melted	SHAK 868:*68*
honest m. and bonny lasses	BURNS 211:*10*

men (*contd.*)

honour lies in killing m.	MARG 650:*57*
hosses, dawgs, and m.	THAC 1006:*87*
How can m. bear…to live	CORN 288:*59*
how imprudently m. engage	ASTE 43:*93*
How strangely hopes delude m.	MASS 663:*60*
how subject we old m.	SHAK 877:*99*
How vainly m. themselves	MARV 658:*82*
Humorists are not happy m.	CONN 283:*64*
hundred m. discontented	LOUI 614:*48*
hurrying dots which are m.	CUMM 299:*76*
I don't hate m.	WINT 1087:*69*
I eat m. like air	PLATH 773:*97*
If all m. are born free	ASTE 43:*92*
If m. cease to believe	MILL 678:*30*
If m. could learn from history	COLE 275:*27*
If m. knew how women	OHEN 737:*14*
If m. were angels	MADI 638:*56*
if m. withheld their praise	SHEEN 926:*50*
In France, they study m.	STAEL 962:*75*
In the hands of m.	DWOR 358:*84*
in the likeness of m.	BIBLE 148:*94*
incompatible by m.?	LEWIS 601:*46*
insecure and intimidated m.	LIPP 607:*37*
insinuate…into m.'s affections	CAVE 246:*73*
Is there no way for m. to be	SHAK 916:*4*
justice to all m.	JEFF 520:*94*
justify the ways of God to m.	MILT 687:*86*
killed the m. who held it	PEAC 762:*30*
Kings and Desperate M.	KRON 570:*1*
Land of…godlike m.!	BYRON 219:*76*
Learned m. …do many times fail	BACON 55:*7*
lesson to all of us m.	AMIN 16:*70*
Let m. tremble	HAWT 461:*70*
Let us now praise famous m.	BIBLE 133:*17*
Liberty…most m. dread it	SHAW 922:*47*
Life levels all m.	SHAW 922:*59*
life of m. is painful	EURI 380:*28*
Like all young m.	SHAW 923:*84*
Like m. we'll face the…pack	MACK 632:*49*
lips of dying m.	ARNO 38:*96*
Lives of great m.	LONG 611:*96*
lost 30,000 m.	WELL 1063:*10*
lot of hard-faced m.	BALD 64:*4*
love m. too little	BURKE 208:*39*
love of gain to ruin m.	SOPH 953:*15*
love of justice in most m.	LARO 582:*23*
Love wakes m., once	PATM 760:*1*
lusty young m.	SHAK 868:*76*
make m. happy	POPE 782:*86*
make you fishers of m.	BIBLE 133:*33*
makes m. look ridiculous	JUVE 540:*79*
maketh m. to be of one mind	BOOK 177:*80*
man that m. like	NORR 731:*28*
management of m.	MERE 671:*15*
Many m. have pride	BALZ 69:*75*
Many m. would hardly miss	SHAW 925:*27*
Married incompatible m.?	GRAV 440:*32*
medal for killing two m.	MATL 664:*76*
m. about me that are fat	SHAK 882:*23*
m. agree to be of one mind	BACON 56:*35*
m. all so good for nothing	AUST 52:*64*
m. always try…virtues	MENC 670:*80*
m. and dogs shall drink him	POPE 780:*29*
m. and girls came and went	FITZ 390:*99*
m. and nations behave wisely	EBAN 359:*7*
m. and women are created equal	STAN 962:*85*
m. and women are not so…enslaved	SHAW 924:*94*
m. and women laughing	SAND 841:*59*
m. and women merely players	SHAK 885:*91*
m. and women of this generation	LLOY 608:*59*
M. are April	SHAK 887:*23*
M. are as chancy as children	KIPL 562:*71*
M. are born makers	WALC 1048:*40*

men (*contd.*)

M. are but children	DRYD 348:*97*
M. are but gilded loam	SHAK 866:*40*
m. are equal before a fish	HOOV 490:*62*
m. are good-looking	KEIL 548:*25*
M. are like the earth	SCHR 850:*5*
M. are lived over again	BROW 195:*71*
M. are merriest	SHAK 880:*72*
M. are mistaken	SPIN 960:*49*
M. are nearly always willing	CAES 225:*84*
M. are never so good	MACK 632:*58*
M. are not hanged	HALI 452:*27*
m. are not made for hours	RABE 799:*85*
M. are rewarded	SZASZ 989:*67*
M. are so romantic	WELD 1062:*95*
m. are still	MACN 637:*40*
M. are the Brahmin	STAN 962:*87*
M. are the only animals	MENC 670:*83*
m. are to wait for liberty	MACA 622:*91*
M. are very fragile	STEP 968:*81*
m. aren't attracted to me	LEE 592:*4*
m. as angels without feminine	MILT 693:*20*
M. at sometime were masters	SHAK 882:*20*
m. at whiles are sober	HOUS 496:*72*
m. call earth	MILT 683:*18*
m. can tell me things	MITC 696:*83*
m. cannot suspend their fate	DEFOE 312:*74*
m. …capable of every wickedness	CONR 285:*8*
m. creep, Not walk	WHIT 1074:*6*
m. dare trust themselves	SHAK 901:*86*
m. decay	GOLD 433:*10*
m. do not learn very much	HUXL 508:*89*
M., don't and can't	RUSK 831:*10*
M. don't know women	TROL 1028:*78*
m. dream, but not equally	LAWR 587:*13*
M. …employ their reason	WOLL 1091:*34*
M. enter local politics	PARK 755:*34*
M.'s evil manners	SHAK 918:*65*
m. …expect brick	ASTE 43:*89*
M. fear death	BACON 56:*43*
m. feel a little more secure	MORE 707:*49*
m. first make slaves	DOUG 342:*75*
M. from the planet Earth	ANON 27:*93*
M. from whom my ways begin	BLUN 170:*42*
M. grown mechanical in head	CARL 234:*40*
m. have a much better time	MENC 669:*74*
M. have died from time to time	SHAK 886:*21*
M. have every advantage	AUST 52:*69*
M. have lost their reason!	SHAK 884:*50*
m. have their price	WALP 1052:*1*
M. ignorant of letters	SAND 842:*82*
m. ill at ease	HAWT 461:*76*
m. in a smoke-filled room	SIMP 939:*91*
m. in appetite	BACON 59:*18*
m. in brotherhood	NOON 731:*24*
m. in considerable number	MILL 675:*78*
m. in every generation	MILL 678:*38*
M. in great fortunes	BACON 57:*72*
M. in great place	BACON 57:*68*
m. in the habits of women	CHAR 253:*84*
m. …in their old age	POPE 779:*17*
m. into their chief providers	MILLS 679:*64*
m. it hurt when it fell	DONNE 338:*17*
m. kill the fat swine	ANON 21:*64*
m. know so little of m.	DUBO 353:*7*
M. learn while they teach	SENE 858:*46*
m. Leaving the gardens	LARK 581:*7*
m., like satyrs grazing	MARL 653:*4*
m. liked to put me down	OKEE 738:*22*
m. liking their fathers	BRAD 183:*75*
M. love in haste	BYRON 223:*57*
m. loved darkness	BIBLE 145:*31*
M.'s manners	JONS 535:*98*
m. may come	TENN 1002:*98*

men (contd.)

M. might as well project	LARD 580:88
m. mispronounce it	MORL 708:69
m. most good	SHAK 872:68
M. multiply like Mice	CANT 230:76
M. must endure	SHAK 904:45
M. must learn now	SHAK 901:90
m. must needs abide	SHAK 862:29
m. must walk	POPE 782:85
M., my brothers	TENN 995:77
m. naturally desire knowledge	ARIS 34:23
M. not afraid of God	POPE 782:89
m. of a great stature	BIBLE 107:82
m. of any other class	LODGE 610:84
M. of business	BAGE 61:63
m. of culture	ARNO 39:26
m. of England	SHEL 929:96
m. of experiment	BACON 55:29
m. of genius	DELA 314:20
m. of iron	ALBA 11:81
m. of judgement frame	MARL 653:98
m. of like passions	BIBLE 148:95
m. of measured merriment	LEWIS 602:54
m. of our time	MACA 622:88
M. of power	FOOT 396:94
m. of science	MILL 677:14
M. of sound sense	PLATO 774:8
m. of the hour	HAMM 453:45
m. of the present age	OVER 747:93
m. of the West	WEIL 1061:78
m. of the world	DICK 321:30
m. only become great	DEGA 312:96
m. out of servitude	EMER 377:70
M. reverence one another	THOR 1016:64
M. see objects	FOWL 399:66
M. seldom make passes	PARK 754:11
M. should be either treated	MACH 631:36
m. should have a…feeling	LAUR 584:47
m. should kill	SKEL 942:40
m. should put an enemy	SHAK 899:26
M. shut their doors	SHAK 901:88
m. sit and hear	KEATS 547:15
m. so old as we	SHAK 868:75
M., some to business	POPE 782:76
m. started at the intelligence	SOUT 954:41
m. strive for Right	BROW 197:19
M. talk of killing time	BOUC 180:38
m. that are dying	JEFF 519:83
m. that God made mad	CHES 259:19
m. that make a city	NICI 726:57
m. that strove with gods	TENN 995:61
m. that women marry	LONG 612:20
M.! The only animal	LAWR 586:84
m., their rights and nothing more	ANTH 31:84
m. there are love not a gaping pig	SHAK 873:90
M. thin away to insignificance	HARDY 456:87
m. to take their exits	WEBS 1061:70
m. too profoundly convinced	READ 803:53
m. trying to be writers	JONES 533:54
m. walk proudly through the earth	RAND 801:25
m.'s watch upon the world	MACL 634:77
M. were deceivers	SHAK 879:46
m. were only capable	MILL 678:31
m. were the answer	BARN 72:34
m. who are as various as the sands	FORS 398:46
m. who are not historians	FORS 398:49
m. who argue by increments	BYATT 218:56
m. who borrow	LAMB 577:31
m. who had never seen a horse	BRIN 189:59
m. who have minded	WOOLF 1093:72
m. who live with	NIEB 727:63
m. who really believe in themselves	CHES 258:5
m. who say yes, lie	MELV 668:46
m. who want to become inhuman	APOL 31:89

men (contd.)

M. Whose Lives Are Money	OATES 733:55
m. will boast of knowledge	LANY 580:79
m. will…do it for pay	MELV 668:52
m. wish to hear no stories	BERN 97:84
m. with book learning	RAMOS 801:17
m. with broken souls	PATC 759:91
M. with secrets	DELI 315:41
m. with sisters dear	HOOD 489:46
m. with the muck-rakes	ROOS 822:47
m. with ugly faces	MASE 662:50
m. without ideals	CAMUS 228:44
m. without imagination	PROU 793:3
m., women, and clergymen	SMITH 949:51
M. would be angels	POPE 780:38
m. would take the death sentence	LAWR 587:15
m. write in place lite	254:13
M. you are all marksmen	PUTN 796:38
more animated beings than…m.	SMITH 949:46
more I admire m.	LEVIN 600:28
Most wretched m.	SHEL 927:69
music marreth m. manners	GALE 412:89
must m. kill and die?	SHEL 932:65
must not judge m.	LICH 604:87
name all the m.	MACC 625:42
Nearly all our best m. are dead!	PUNCH 795:31
No m. who knows aught	MILT 686:78
Noble m. in the quiet of morning	DUNC 355:46
not dreams of doting m.?	MELV 668:50
not into the hands of m.	BIBLE 131:88
not permit thirty m.	WHITE 1069:18
nothing noble-minded m.	KINC 557:67
O shame to m.!	MILT 688:23
obey God rather than m.	BIBLE 147:85
of all m. most miserable	BIBLE 151:66
of war I have slain m.	SHAK 897:99
Old m. and comets	SWIFT 985:93
Old m. forget	SHAK 881:1
only m. like thee are fit	OTWAY 746:90
other m. are tempted	BUTL 217:19
pacific—and all his m.	KEATS 544:33
port, for m.	JOHN 530:3
powerful m. in our society	BELL 88:27
present life of m. on earth	BEDE 82:8
presumed to be what m.	LIPP 607:38
primitive m. are…credulous	POPE 779:18
problem is…whether m. do	SKIN 943:52
the purgatory of all m.	FLOR 394:79
pursuit…by free m.	WARR 1053:28
push m. over the edge	ROTH 824:49
quit you like m.	BIBLE 151:74
quit yourselves like m.	BIBLE 109:30
rank of devoutly religious m.	EINS 363:67
reality on which m. can act	LIPP 607:36
reason m. are greater than animals	ELLI 375:13
reason why m. lived	LOWE 615:72
reputation of m.	MONT 701:56
resident in m.	SHAK 862:34
reverberates through m.'s history	KOES 568:72
Rich m. deal gifts	SHAK 902:95
rich m. rule the law	GOLD 432:98
rights as m., free m.	PITT 771:68
robot mice and robot m.	BRAD 184:90
sardine m. crammed in	MACN 637:37
say best m. are moulded	SHAK 897:93
see m. as trees, walking	BIBLE 141:67
Sensible m. are all the same religion	DISR 334:27
sent ten thousand m. to battle	SITT 940:98
short-lived weak animals m.	MONT 700:54
should make m. atheists	CAREW 232:17
show m. energetically	GRAY 440:41
shows of love to other m.	SHAK 882:17
sinewy brown m.	PRIE 790:46
single m.,…more charitable	BACON 57:60

men (contd.)

So long as m. can breathe	SHAK 912:48
So long as m. worship	HUXL 507:75
so many kinds of awful m.	COPE 287:51
som m. say in many partys	MALO 642:34
Some m. are born kings	SHAW 925:24
Some m. creep in	SHAK 896:50
some m. who have their heads	HERN 476:46
something true about m.	JAMES 517:34
sound as the m. who make it	LEE 593:10
Strong bronzed m.	CULL 299:68
stuffed shirts, hollow m.	MACD 628:92
substance of m.	SWIN 988:49
take a minute from the m.	CARA 231:94
taking ordinary m.	GALB 412:80
tale which holdeth forth old m.	SIDN 937:63
talked about by m.	PERI 766:98
tall m. had ever very empty heads	BACON 56:38
ten thousand of those m.	SHAK 881:96
these m. paid their shillings	PRIE 789:35
think as wise m.	ASCH 40:50
thou hast m.	SHAK 861:15
thousand m. that fishes gnawed	SHAK 863:54
three m. I admire most	MACL 633:63
tide in the affairs of m.	SHAK 884:60
tides of m. into my hands	LAWR 587:12
'Tis all m.'s office	SHAK 880:61
'Tis no shame for m.	SHIR 935:24
to m. [I speak] French	CHAR 253:90
toil in other m.'s extremes	KYD 571:28
torment, kill and damn m.	MARG 650:53
transform M. into Monsters	FORD 397:19
travelled among unknown m.	WORD 1095:12
truthful towards m.	HARDY 456:88
trying to do with eight m.	ROBI 814:20
twelve thousand fighting m.	SHAK 867:56
twice as well as m.	WHIT 1074:11
two m. looked out	LANG 579:68
two m. stand together	WAVE 1058:10
Two m. who differ	RUSS 832:27
two strong m.	KIPL 560:23
understanding better than other m.	DRYD 348:78
Unmarried m. are best friends	BACON 57:59
unmarried or childless m.	BACON 57:56
upon two generations of m.	LLOY 608:60
vain, unnecessary things are m.	ROCH 816:54
vast majority o' m.	MACD 627:76
vexes public m.	TENN 996:88
voices elected me of all m.	LEE 593:18
war between m. and women	THUR 1018:19
war… between m. and women	LYND 621:65
war is obsolete or m. are	FULL 409:38
wasteful of promising young m.	HUGH 499:23
We are hollow m.	ELIOT 369:98
We are selfish m.	WORD 1096:38
we've got the m.	HUNT 504:15
weak and miserable m.	CHOM 261:56
Weary m., what reap ye?	WILDE 1075:27
What all m. should avoid	DISR 334:27
What are m. to rocks	AUST 51:41
What m. or Gods are these?	KEATS 547:7
what many m. desire	SHAK 874:30
when all m. shall speak well	BIBLE 142:82
When m. make gods	ONEI 739:50
when shall English m.	DRAY 345:36
where good m. rest	FLEC 393:48
where m. May read	SHAK 907:28
which all m. knew!	TENN 1000:67
which m. call Love	SPEN 958:16
While m. are rolling round	WEST 1068:88
white m. cheat black m.	LEE 593:11
Who fear the injustice of m.	ELIOT 370:35
Who, of m., can tell	KEATS 545:59
Wine and women will make m.	BIBLE 132:6

men (*contd.*)
wise m. don't say	MART 657:58
Wise m. fish here	STEL 967:69
wisest of all you m.	PLATO 773:1
wisest of m. in all ages	STER 969:91
With four-and-twenty m.	AYTO 53:85
With m. this is impossible	BIBLE 139:26
with m.'s blood	KING 559:6
Without thinking highly…of m.	AUST 51:39
Women…behave like m.	MACK 632:56
women…envy m.	PANK 753:81
Working m. of all countries	MARX 660:15
Working m. of all countries	MARX 660:16
Would m. …distil it out	SHAK 881:90
Wrath brings mortal m. …hurt	EURI 380:32
Yes, Sir, many m.	JOHN 527:28
Yesterday's m.	ANON 27:95
you are m. of stones	SHAK 904:51
Young m. mend not their sight	DONNE 339:30
young m. think it is	HOUS 496:83
young m.'s vision	DRYD 349:17

men-children Bring forth m.-c.   SHAK 908:36
menace against every form of m.   ROTH 826:23
| m. of aggression | ASQU 42:77 |
| public m. | BURG 205:80 |

Mencken M.'s defects   MEYER 673:32
mend Garlic to m. her kissing   SHAK 912:33
| God won't, and we can't m. it | CLOU 270:34 |

mendacities Better m.   POUND 785:62
mendacity M. is a system   WILL 1082:71
mene M., M., Tekel, Upharsin   BIBLE 129:49
menpleasers with eyeservice, as m.   BIBLE 152:5
Mensch M. ist das Wesen   SCHI 847:64
| M. ist, was er ißt | FEUE 387:32 |

menstrual m. years are vestigial   LEGU 594:26
menstruation m. …enviable   STEI 967:65
mental sort of m. rebellion   ORWE 743:22
mentally m. …deadening force   WEBB 1058:15
mentation forms of m.   KOES 568:70
mention recourse to the m. of it   JOHN 531:15
menu and then I saw the m.   WESK 1066:57
| full m. of rights | TUTU 1032:54 |
| part of life's m. | RUSS 833:43 |

Menuhin first choice…M.   ADLER 9:48
mercantile dull m. England   BUCH 202:25
Mercaptan M. went on to preach   HUXL 506:48
Mercator M.'s North Poles   CARR 241:85
merchandise mechanical arts and m.
| | BACON 59:29 |

merchant ear of a m.   NASHE 721:84
| heaven is like unto a m. | BIBLE 138:4 |
| What m.'s ships have my sighs | DONNE 337:80 |

merchants m. …intent on profit   PIUS 772:79
| m. full of sybstaunce and myght | DUNB 355:39 |
| m., who mind little | MONT 700:53 |

mercies All occasions invite his m.   DONNE 339:26
church is of m.	DONNE 339:25
tender m.	BIBLE 118:11
thy faithful m. crown	WESL 1066:63

merciful Blessed are the m.   BIBLE 133:34
| Draw near…in being m. | SHAK 862:35 |
| God be m. unto us | BIBLE 116:85 |

merciless sunlight streaming m.   ATWO 44:17
| time is a m. thing | WILL 1082:76 |

mercury M. with a Pitchfork   BRAU 186:21
mercy Abraham, have m. on me   BIBLE 144:7
at the m. of the reflexes	BALD 64:93
easy in the m. of his means	THOM 1010:66
entirely and helplessly at his m.	SHAW 921:29
God ha' m.	KIPL 560:22
God have m.	RANS 802:38
goodness and m. shall follow me	BIBLE 110:59
hand folks over to God's m.	ELIOT 365:12
have m., and not sacrifice	BIBLE 136:70

mercy (*contd.*)
Have m. upon all Jews	BOOK 174:11
have m. upon us	BOOK 174:4
in wrath remember m.	BIBLE 130:63
justice and m. are reconciled	WILS 1086:44
La belle dame sans m.	KEATS 547:96
Large and without m.	OLSEN 738:34
leaving m. to heaven	FIEL 388:50
'Lord have m. upon us'	PEPYS 765:73
M., compassion, and justice	WAITE 1048:29
m. endureth for ever	BIBLE 119:46
M. has a human heart	BLAKE 166:69
m. is everlasting	BIBLE 118:9
m. is on them that fear him	BIBLE 141:75
m. show to me	POPE 782:90
M. sighed farewell!	BYRON 221:11
m. to forgive	DRYD 350:51
merciful…shall obtain m.	BIBLE 133:34
most tender m. is neglect	CRAB 293:75
Mother of M.	ROBI 814:23
new law of m.	MORE 706:46
Nothing emboldens sin…as m.	SHAK 902:91
Peace on earth and m. mild!	BEEC 82:14
Peace on earth and m. mild	WESL 1066:26
plenteous in m.	BIBLE 118:12
property is always to have m.	BOOK 175:30
quality of m. is not strained	SHAK 873:92
shew m. unto thousands in them	BOOK 174:17
shewed m. on him	BIBLE 143:91
shewing m. unto thousands	BIBLE 106:68
shut the gates of m.	GRAY 442:71
so great is his m.	BIBLE 118:13
so is his m.	BIBLE 131:88
still at the m. of words	THOM 1011:74
temper so Justice with m.	MILT 693:13
When m. seasons justice	SHAK 873:93
Where m., Love and Pity dwell	BLAKE 166:65

Meredith M. is a prose Browning   WILDE 1076:37
mergers m.-and-acquisitions   GLEI 430:61
meridian full m. of my glory   SHAK 918:59
merit greatest m. for the public   BACON 57:56
herein consisted his m.	MILT 686:70
How he esteems your m.	COWP 292:44
irrespective of any possible m.	WAUGH 1056:64
M. and good works	BACON 57:73
m. of both sexes	LABR 572:37
m. of the wearer!	SHAK 874:31
m. wins the soul	POPE 779:3
modernness is the measure of m.	EMER 377:59
of rewarding m.	SWIFT 985:87
oft got without m.	SHAK 899:25
positive m. of enjoying	RUSS 832:26

merits m. of a classification   MILL 675:74
| seek his m. to disclose | GRAY 442:78 |

meritus m., so he ought to be   LEAC 589:45
merle mavis and m. are singing   SCOTT 854:66
Merlin child was delyverd unto M.   MALO 642:24
| unto M., and the Table Rounde | MALO 642:28 |

mermaid Choicer…M. Tavern?   KEATS 544:48
| Done at the M.! | BEAU 80:66 |
| m. …tolled my son to shipwreck | DEKK 313:13 |

mermaids heard the m. singing   ELIOT 367:55
merriest men are m.   SHAK 880:72
merrily M., m. shall I live now   SHAK 917:41
merriment damn…measured m.   LEWIS 602:54
| even for m. and diversion | SMITH 945:79 |
| Frame your mind…to m. | SHAK 863:70 |

merry As M. Margaret   SKEL 942:34
began to be m.	BIBLE 143:1
eat…drink, and to be m.	BIBLE 123:31
fool to make me m.	SHAK 886:18
Fortune is m.	SHAK 884:57
keep our Christmas m. still	SCOTT 853:55
Let us be m.	CURR 301:18

merry (*contd.*)
meet that we should make m.	BIBLE 143:2
m. as a marriage bell	BYRON 219:84
m. as the day is long	SHAK 879:34
m. cuckoo, messenger of Spring	SPEN 958:26
m. heart goes all the day	SHAK 911:27
m. heart maketh a cheerful	BIBLE 121:79
M. it is in the good greenwood	SCOTT 854:66
m. songs of peace	SHAK 918:67
never m. when I hear	SHAK 873:2
to be m. best becomes you	SHAK 879:41
very m., dancing, drinking	DRYD 352:95
wine maketh m.	BIBLE 123:38

Meshach Shadrach, M.   BIBLE 129:46
mess don't m. with it   WALL 1050:77
general m. of…feeling	ELIOT 372:53
God has made an awful m.	BURR 213:54
Here's another fine m.	LAUR 583:43
let other people clean up the m.	FITZ 390:5
m. of pottage	BIBLE 105:29
unspeakable idiotic m.	ORWE 743:11
what we can make of the m.	ELIOT 371:37

mess-makers pioneers…m.-m.   PIRS 770:54
message may your m. be heard   WALL 1050:66
medium is the m.	MACL 635:93
m. came… for me	PENI 764:55
m. of fear	MACC 625:39
m. of peace to Ireland	ARNO 39:21
m. to the businessmen	CURR 301:19
Send them a m.	ANON 28:96
the m. came	AUST 52:72
will never deliver the m.	MILL 677:1

messages m. go quicker to the brain
| | SPARK 955:50 |

messenger Anglo-Saxon M.   CARR 240:72
m. of Satan	BIBLE 152:86
m. of Spring	SPEN 958:26
says, I am a m.	MILL 677:1
send my m. before thy face	BIBLE 137:84
wingèd m. of heaven	SHAK 868:86

messing m. about in boats   GRAH 438:90
| m. with people's heads | HEND 472:56 |

met way we m.   SWIN 987:42
| when We innocently m. | JONS 535:99 |

metal breed for barren m.   SHAK 874:22
| cold m. of economic theory | SCHU 851:17 |
| forests of m. | THOM 1013:25 |

metaphor All slang is m.   CHES 257:90
authors of simile and m.	NASH 720:68
branch-strained m.	MOORE 705:29
Cancer's no m.	DUNN 356:57
Cricket…the great m.	FOWL 400:70
I love m.	GASS 416:35
I love m.	MALA 641:8
Man be my m.	THOM 1010:53
No m. reinvents…nurture	PALEY 751:61
Science is all m.	LEARY 591:71
through m. to reconcile	WILL 1082:86
whaling a universal m.	LODGE 610:78

metaphoric habits of m. thought   FRYE 408:21
metaphorical deeper than m. sense   CARL 234:42
metaphors abuse of m.   PALM 752:67
Curling with m.	HERB 475:25
handful of m.	BORG 179:11
m. by which it is most naturally	JAMES 517:40
remote and precious m.	DONNE 339:24
sweet phrases, lovely m.	HERB 476:36

metaphysic high As m. wit can fly   BUTL 216:7
metaphysical M. lederhosen   ENRI 379:94
| M. questions and reflections | HERN 476:44 |

metaphysics divinity or school m.   HUME 504:10
Explaining m. to the nation	BYRON 221:10
m. is a branch of fantastic literature	BORG 178:10
M. is the finding of bad reasons	BRAD 184:91

metaphysics (*contd.*)

M. means nothing but	JAMES 517:37
science of m.	MENC 670:82
small portion of m.	PLAN 772:86

meteor cloud-encircled m. of the air SHEL 929:10

m. Ever hung my fate	MIDD 674:49
slides the silent m.	TENN 997:10
Streamed, like a m.	GRAY 442:81

methinks lady protests too much, m. SHAK 891:39

method All m. is imperfect NICO 727:60

anything other than…general m.!	BAUD 77:29
genius has invented a m.	RUSS 832:21
has a certain m.	RUSS 833:31
M. acting?	BARR 73:60
m. and secret…of Jesus	ARNO 40:35
m. of assisting…pure science	CONA 279:80
no objection to this m.	STER 969:97
our m. of questioning	HEIS 467:77
people and the m.	RYLE 834:53
scientific m. has always been	PIRS 770:55
there is m. in't	SHAK 889:96
true m. of warfare	MAZZ 666:11
You know my m.	DOYLE 343:96

Methodist insufferable as a M. MENC 670:92

Methodists two kinds of M. ELIOT 365:3

methods institution of m. UNIT 1036:45

m. are outdated and incorrect	ANON 27:66
m. differ from those	HUXL 509:4
m. of control	KEYN 554:33
other m. to stop them	KISH 565:29
rule-of-thumb m.	MARX 661:22
theory and m. of revolution	MAO 648:20
You know my m.	DOYLE 343:92

Methuselah days of M. BIBLE 104:9

metre hurdling m. like tired horses BROY 201:5

m. of the dictionary?	THOM 1010:58
Time is the m.	WALC 1048:38

metres not m., but…argument EMER 377:48

Two m., or a little more ROBB 813:7

Metro Win a M.! PRIV 791:75

metropolis art is born of the m. POUND 785:40

M. of Great-Britain BAIL 62:70

Metternich M. …so conservative EVANS 381:37

mettle m. enough in thee SHAK 880:63

undaunted m. should compose SHAK 908:36

mettlesome m. women ANDR 18:11

mew cat will m. SHAK 893:82

Mexican If I were a M. CORW 288:62

Mexico In M. the gods ruled COND 279:83

Poor M., so far from God DIAZ 319:3

Micawber never desert Mr M. DICK 324:5

mice as long as it catches m. DENG 315:49

best-laid schemes o' M. an' Men	BURNS 209:68
Men multiply like M.	CANT 230:76
robot m. and robot men	BRAD 184:90

Michael M. …against the dragon BIBLE 157:21

M. read the Gaelic scroll RUSS 833:36

Michelangelo Dante or M. MULL 713:43

If M. were heterosexual BROWN 194:59

women…Talking of M. ELIOT 367:47

mickle O m. is the powerful grace SHAK 869:95

microbe M. is so very small BELL 87:2

microcosm m. of little world BROW 196:93

microphone paid for this m. REAG 804:68

microscopes magnifyin' gas m. DICK 320:28

M. are prudent DICK 327:95

Microsoft M. were a car MURR 715:77

mid-heaven prancing in m.-h. LAWR 586:79

Midas Hard food for M. SHAK 873:83

midday walks under the m. sun MILT 683:28

middle honeyed m. of the night KEATS 546:87

In the m.-ages	JERO 521:11
live in the M. Ages	SMITH 948:34
m. management of Manhattan	AMIS 17:84

middle (*contd.*)

m. of the journey of our life	DANTE 305:67
moist his m.!	NASH 720:59
nuclear power in the m.-ages	LAMB 577:45
politics the m. way	ADAMS 5:85
royal family in the m. ages	HALD 451:16
reconnected with the angry m.?	ANON 29:51
safely by the m. way	OVID 747:98
Secret sits in the m.	FROST 407:98

middle-age companions for m.-a. BACON 57:61

frightening thing about m. a.	DAY 310:52
mere m. snuffs out	HUGH 499:23
m.-a. of a state	BACON 59:29
misspent youth and m.-a.	THUR 1019:51
pleasure of m. a.	POUND 786:74

middle-aged m.-a. man can't UPDI 1037:63

nine m.-a. couples	THOM 1015:45
The M.-A. Man	THUR 1018:20

middle class great English m. c. ARNO 38:9

M. C. was quite prepared	BELL 87:9
m. c. women	LURIE 619:41
provincial, resolutely m. c.	MACF 629:16
Puritan of the m. c.	NEME 722:5
symbol of an emerging m. c. Britain	MACF 629:18
true m. c. unit	SHAW 922:55
up agen m. c. morality	SHAW 924:6
We of the sinking m. c.	ORWE 742:4
What fools m. c. girls are	DRAB 345:24
world is full of m. c. people	SHAR 919:87

middle classes lower m. c. GILB 424:72

Middlemarch M. …grown up WOOLF 1093:64

middles m. are nowhere to be found BART 74:73

Middlesex All M. is ugly COBB 271:54

midge lightly skims the m. BETJ 100:38

like a fretful m. ROSS 824:81

Midland M., bound for Cricklewood BETJ 100:39

midlands living in the M. BELL 87:15

south…north and m. MACM 636:15

midnight Cerberus and blackest m. MILT 682:96

gathered at m.	KEATS 545:62
heard the chimes at m.	SHAK 877:97
Holding hands at m.	GERS 420:14
If you wake at m.	KIPL 564:2
Love the reeling m. through	PARK 754:9
m.'s all a-glimmer	YEATS 1104:57
m., in our little town	LIND 605:15
m. in the silence	BROW 200:1
m. never come	MARL 654:20
M. shakes the memory	ELIOT 367:59
m. with no pain	KEATS 548:18
mock the m. bell	SHAK 905:84
roused themselves at m.	TROL 1027:77
shadow of the m. hour	BYRON 220:99
stroke of m. ceases	HOUS 496:82
'Tis m., falls lamp-light	WILDE 1075:26
troubled m. and the noon's repose	ELIOT 367:61

midst there am I in the m. of them BIBLE 139:20

through the m. JONS 536:26

midstream has to stop in m. BAND 69:87

midsummer high M. pomps ARNO 39:17

saw M. Night's Dream	PEPYS 765:66
This m. flower	SKEL 942:34
very m. madness	SHAK 895:30

midwife fairies' m. SHAK 868:78

m. slapped your footsoles	PLATH 773:98
revolution was our m.	INOU 512:57
so far like the m.	SOCR 951:87

midwinter M. Spring ELIOT 372:67

mien monster of so frightful m. POPE 780:44

rapture of thy m. WORD 1100:90

might as our m. lessens ANON 21:60

danced…with all his m.	BIBLE 110:45
do it with thy m.	BIBLE 123:34
duty past thy m.	SHAK 884:61

might (*contd.*)

faith that right makes m.	LINC 605:3
famousèd for m.	SHAK 913:55
M. first made kings	MARL 653:97
Not by m., nor by power	BIBLE 130:67
O tell of his m.	GRANT 439:6
sovereign sway…dissolved by m.?	DRYD 350:26
unbelief…no source of m.	MACD 628:3

mightier m. and richer than thyself BIBLE 132:1

mightily levis mirry…levis m. DUNB 355:37

mighty God who made thee m. BENS 92:9

How are the m. fallen	BIBLE 110:44
little body with a m. heart	SHAK 880:74
Look on my works, ye M.	SHEL 928:93
m. things from small beginnings	DRYD 346:54
more m. than he seems	SHAK 881:80
some have called thee M.	DONNE 338:4
the brave, the m.	WORD 1100:85
with his m. talk	SYNGE 988:64

migraine Love is a universal m. GRAV 440:34

Major Earl M. E.'s Grendorter! SHAW 923:82

mild m. or choleric disposition ADDI 6:6

weakens and turns m. DIDE 329:29

milder Not m. is the general lot ARNO 36:59

mile braces at a distance of a m. MORT 710:2

compel thee to go a m.	BIBLE 134:43
enemy half a m. away	MUIR 712:28

mile-a sad tires in a m.-a SHAK 911:27

miles end of evening smiles M. BROW 198:43

first m. of the brief march	PEARY 763:36
had gone m. away	HEAN 465:36
Looking down for m.	SNYD 951:80
lost in the m.	SCOTT 852:37
m. of human habitations	CONR 285:13
m. to go before I sleep	FROST 407:86
Six m. from earth	JARR 518:57
Thousands of m. of wheat	RICH 810:70
twenty m. a day?	MARL 653:95
two m. more and then we rest!	BRON 191:92

milestones m. into headstones LOWE 616:91

milieu writer from the m. ROTH 825:7

militant ceases to be m. MORR 709:82

military among a m. one, trophies FUSE 410:60

close my m. career	MACA 621:75
defeat… lost m. campaign	EDIN 361:40
defiance of m. authority	SASS 845:21
hold the m. mind	TUCH 1031:44
m. and nuclear sense	WALE 1049:50
m. society	TREV 1026:53
m. struggle may frankly be regarded	SCHL 848:73
m. success will have achieved	ELIZ 374:90
m. system…subsidy	CHOM 261:58
m. take positions	KENN 553:5
M. Two-Step	GREN 446:51
political and the other m.	MACN 636:32
race has no m. purpose	MOUN 711:13
species of m. instinct	HAYD 462:94
study of m. history	CLAU 268:95
thralldom of a m. caste	LLOY 608:60
When the m. man approaches	SHAW 921:39

military-industrial m.-i. complex EISE 364:88

milk black ink in white m. MUNRO 714:59

child drinking a bowl of m.	SAND 841:77
crudded m.	WEBS 1061:65
curd of ass's m.	POPE 781:67
drunk the m. of Paradise	COLE 275:18
end is moo, the other, m.	NASH 719:41
find a trout in the m.	THOR 1016:70
flowing with m. and honey	BIBLE 106:56
for water…brought him m.	BIBLE 109:14
Gin was mother's m.	SHAW 924:7
gone to the bull	JOHN 527:34
how we can m. her	SZEN 989:70
hubbies moaned in M. Wood	THOM 1011:87

milk (*contd.*)
m. and ale — SKEL 942:33
m. and honey blessed — NEALE 722:93
m., and not of strong meat — BIBLE 154:46
m. and sperm of kindness — MELV 668:41
m. and the yoghurt — MORT 710:94
m. and toast and honey — MITC 696:82
m. comes frozen home — SHAK 866:30
m. in an old breast — MANS 647:98
m.'s leap toward immortality — FADI 382:52
m. of human kindness — SHAK 907:25
m. the cow of the world — WILB 1074:16
putting m. into babies — CHUR 265:27
sincere m. of the word — BIBLE 155:77
sinews even in thy m. — DONNE 339:24
sucked such m. — YEATS 1106:88
this m.-soup men call domestic bliss — PATM 760:10
milk-white m.-w.; now, purple — SHAK 870:36
milky called the M. Way — MARTI 657:56
Far as the solar walk, or m. way — POPE 780:37
m. sky — YEATS 1104:59
stars…on the m. way — WORD 1099:68
mill busy m. — GOLD 433:9
Gaza at the m. with slaves — MILT 694:38
God's m. grinds slow — HERB 476:40
sallow for the m. — SPEN 957:99
stomach is a m. — HUNT 505:33
Mill J S M. …effort of will — BENT 93:26
mill-dams bonnie m.-d. o' Binnorie — BALL -101:30
mill-wheel millstone as a m.-w. — MACI 631:42
millennium century and m. — LEVI 600:26
millinery jewelled mass of m. — TENN 1001:77
million a m. is made by producing — WILD 1079:29
looked like a m. dollars — CART 242:98
make a m. — HUBB 498:8
m. dollars to make a picture — TAYL 992:16
multitude of one m. — KOES 568:67
patent double m. — DICK 320:28
turn-up in a m. — BEVIN 102:79
millionaire I am a m. — SHAW 923:79
poor devil of a m. — BAGE 61:55
Who wants to be a m.? — PORT 784:35
millionaires m. and bums taste — MARQ 656:38
m. love a baked apple — FIRB 389:70
millions 'as m. at 'ome — KIPL 561:37
M. drew up before — NEW 724:21
m. long for immortality — ERTZ 380:12
m. of the mouthless dead — SORL 953:23
m. which it is…sucking up — COBB 271:54
probably been m. of earths — HOYLE 498:2
repeat in the lives of m. — WILD 1080:33
There are m. to be grabbed — MANK 645:75
Three m. of people — PITT 771:66
What m. died — CAMP 227:27
mills dark Satanic m.? — BLAKE 168:18
m. of God grind slowly — LOGAU 610:87
millstone bosom is actually a m. — GREER 445:38
m. were hanged about his neck — BIBLE 138:18
m. …into the sea — BIBLE 158:29
Tradition…can be as much a m. — MACI 631:42
millstones M. around our neck — DISR 334:32
m. …about your neck — DAVI 307:96
tears…Turned to m. — SHEL 927:77
Milton like that in M.'s hell — NERV 723:10
malt does more than M. — HOUS 495:63
M., a name to resound — TENN 1003:24
M.! thou shouldst be living — WORD 1096:38
M. …was a genius — JOHN 532:29
Some mute inglorious M. — GRAY 442:70
Thou shall believe in M. — BYRON 222:38
Milwaukeeans two M. in love — HECHT 466:60
mime m. can be a bridge between — MARC 649:44
mimic All honour's m. — DONNE 337:78
mimsy All m. were the borogoves — CARR 239:47

mince m., and slices of quince — LEAR 590:61
mincing M. poetry — SHAK 876:59
mind A m. thinking — WOOLF 1093:77
A man's m. — TROL 1028:93
A Woman seldom Writes her M. — STEE 964:20
agree to be of one m. — BACON 56:35
all in the m. — WOLFE 1090:16
altered the colour f my m. — BRON 191:10
ambitious m. Will covert more — MILT 688:12
And to my m. — SHAK 888:70
angling…rest to his m. — WALT 1052:9
arid desert of his m. — WEST 1068:91
assail his m. another while — MARL 653:7
attracted to me by my m. — LEE 592:4
attractive to the half-baked m. — FORS 398:32
author's m. — GAUG 416:40
awing the human m. — JEFF 520:93
beauty of thy m. — SHAK 914:71
best marriage…of m. and body — FOWL 400:70
blessedness is…satisfaction of m. — SPIN 960:58
Boston is a state of m. — APPL 32:2
breast, and quiet m. — LOVE 615:66
brilliant m. — ASQU 42:83
broad of M. — BETJ 99:27
Calm of m., all passion — MILT 695:60
calm the troubled m. — CONG 282:47
calming influence on the m. — MATI 664:74
certain liveliness of m. — RABE 799:91
certain unsoundness of m. — MACA 622:89
chaos of the m. — SNYD 951:82
chords in the human m. — DICK 325:30
Clarity of m. results in — PASC 757:50
classical m. at work — PIRS 770:56
clear your m. of cant — JOHN 531:26
clear, attentive m. — SNYD 951:81
concentrates his m. wonderfully — JOHN 530:91
Coney Island of the M. — FERL 386:19
conjunction of the m. — MARV 658:78
consistency is as bad for the m. — HUXL 507:62
constant still in m. — MACA 623:16
contracts the m. — THER 1009:39
contradictory beliefs in one's m. — ORWE 745:59
converse of an innocent m. — KEATS 544:37
corners in one's own m. — HUXL 509:5
corridors into the m. — DOUG 341:58
corrupt and befool the m. — BAXT 79:51
couldn't make up my m. — PLATH 773:91
country of m. — WHITE 1070:42
creating in the m. a map — SPEN 956:81
crooked my m. to answer — SHAK 862:34
culture of the m. — MORE 707:52
cutty sarks run in your m. — BURNS 212:21
debasement of the human m. — CHAN 250:42
depths of his own oceanic m. — COLE 275:29
dictates of his godlike m. — OTWAY 746:76
does not m. his belly — JOHN 528:40
don't m. not being President — KENN 550:59
dribble your m. out — ELIOT 365:9
elegance is a state of m. — CASS 243:27
employs the whole m. — QUEN 797:54
enter into the m. …not myself — WELTY 1065:49
exist out of the m. — BERK 95:52
extreme thoughts…in his m. — DIDE 330:42
face should bear a wicked m. — SHAK 866:36
facility for m. games — COUP 289:83
fair terms and a villain's m. — SHAK 874:23
Farewell the tranquil m. — SHAK 899:47
favours the prepared m. — PAST 759:85
features gets on your m. — LEAC 589:38
feeble powers of my m. — SIDN 936:42
fit of absence of m. — SEEL 857:28
fog of the good man's m. — BROW 198:42
frailty of the m. — CONG 282:40
frame of m. — FRIE 405:60

mind (*contd.*)
Frame your m. to mirth — SHAK 863:70
freedom of my m. — MILT 684:34
gateways of the m. — SASS 846:43
gentle m. by gentle deeds — SPEN 959:38
gird up the loins of your m. — BIBLE 155:75
give a m. to your characters — DIDE 329:23
God…destroys their m. — DRYD 351:57
greatest good of the m. — SPIN 960:56
greatness of m. — MARC 650:50
green sickness of the m. — CLEV 269:11
gymnasium of the m. — LENIN 595:53
hand cutting edge of m. — BRON 190:83
has a vulgar m. — LEWIS 601:39
having it affect his m. — HOOV 490:68
heart and m. of America — BARZ 75:97
His m. moves — YEATS 1107:90
hold the m. in place — MILL 677:4
hold the military m. — TUCH 1031:44
homeland of the m. — NEW 724:19
If I am out of my m. — BELL 88:24
If the ocean was pure m. — PRAT 788:22
ignis fatuus in the m. — ROCH 816:50
image in her m. — DRYD 350:46
impotence of m. — MILT 694:42
improper m. is a perpetual feast — SMITH 947:13
Indian, whose untutored m. — POPE 780:37
in one's m. a…map — ORWE 744:38
In youth open your m. — ANON 23:82
index of a feeling m. — CRAB 294:88
infirmity of the noble m. — MILT 684:42
Intense irradiation of a m. — SHEL 929:10
interwoven with the highest m. — AGAS 9:62
Ithaka always in your m. — CAVA 246:69
Jealousy…tyrant of the m.! — DRYD 351:66
Keep violence in the m. — ALDI 12:6
know the m. of a woman — LAWR 586:93
know the m. of God — HAWK 461:57
known by the human m. — PAGE 749:33
lack of a whole m. — MUIR 712:25
land and the m. — NGU 725:45
leaves thy m.'s imprint — SHAK 914:76
Let this m. be in you — BIBLE 153:8
liberation of both body and m. — BANN 70:3
light of my m. — JUANA 539:66
lingers in the m. — LARO 582:29
Little subconscious m. — ONEI 740:62
live in the m., in ideas — MILL 677:18
long in your m. — HOLM 486:90
Love looks…with the m. — SHAK 870:28
made up my m. — LLOY 608:56
maintain a quiet m. — DYER 358:89
Make up your m. dearheart — OLIV 738:27
makes the m. very free — ELIOT 365:19
man but changed his m. — POPE 781:54
man o'independent m. — SMITH 949:60
man's unconquerable m. — WORD 1098:59
mannish manner of m. — CARY 243:17
masterpiece of art…in the m. — EMER 376:45
measure what the m. — MILT 691:22
might…be said to possess a m. — ELLI 375:16
m. against speculation — RUSS 832:17
m. and genius — STEN 967:70
m. be afterwards applied — THEO 1008:33
m. By owing owes not — MILT 689:47
m. can make Substance — BYRON 221:18
m. can weave clear — LOWE 616:87
m. charged with an eager purpose — ELIOT 365:18
m.'s construction in the face — SHAK 907:24
m. doth serve for all — DYER 358:88
m. …fixed on the horizon — EINS 363:63
m. for ever Voyaging — WORD 1096:27
m. full of ghosts — MANS 647:97
m. fully develops its faculties — STAEL 961:68

mind (*contd.*)

m. has a thousand eyes — BOUR 181:48
m. …in a rapt contemplation — ELIOT 371:40
m. is a museum — RAINE 800:10
m. is actually employed — JOHN 529:71
m. is bent to holiness — SHAK 861:98
m. is clouded — TENN 1004:48
m. is its own place — MILT 687:99
m. is maturing late — NASH 720:63
m. is…more self-reliant — LIVI 607:47
m. is not a bed — AGATE 10:64
m. is pure machinery — GINS 427:25
m. is ta'en up wi' — NAIR 717:19
m. is the least of possessions — WHITE 1070:44
m. is the true self — CICE 266:65
m. makes us — GRIL 447:62
m. may lose its force — BYRON 220:98
m. may rest on intuition — BACON 60:43
m. o'er all the world — MILT 694:33
m. of large general powers — JOHN 531:8
m. of man — MARL 654:12
m. of man — WORD 1094:98
M. of Man — WORD 1100:78
m. of Ronald Reagan — NOON 731:21
m. off everything like golf — ROGE 820:23
m. or body grieved — CAMP 228:40
m. or body to prefer — POPE 780:42
'm. over matter', said the lady — DICK 323:83
m. religiously affected — HOOK 490:56
m. shuttles and reminds — ROTH 825:6
m. skating circles — FROST 407:6
m. sliding against events — DUNN 356:55
m. that has seen, and suffered — CARL 233:32
m. that went into it — GLAS 430:58
m. to me a kingdom is — DYER 358:87
m. to prance — JOHN 528:53
m. too wide for a professor — MENC 669:64
m. was less difficult to develop — AUST 50:34
m. was once the true — MARV 658:81
m. watches itself — CAMUS 228:43
m. with all your toys — MILT 682:5
m. with arts improve — DONNE 337:79
minister to a m. diseased — SHAK 910:82
mirrored themselves in my m. — ELIOT 365:6
miserable state of m. — BACON 58:86
most personal state of m. — FEIN 385:99
move a woman's m. — SHAK 860:82
Music affects the human m. — KHOM 555:45
necessary to the human m. — REES 805:92
never brought to it? — BURNS 210:94
no blemish but the m. — SHAK 895:35
no grayness in the m. — GUNT 449:87
no passion in the m. of man — BACON 56:44
noble m. is here o'erthrown! — SHAK 891:30
noblest frailty of the m. — DRYD 346:51
non-space of the m. — GIBS 422:40
not astound The virtuous m. — MILT 683:25
not be sound…in body or m. — LLOY 608:55
not in my perfect m. — SHAK 904:43
not m. its being buried — HOPK 492:6
not yet of Percy's m. — SHAK 876:53
nothing unbends the m. like them — GAY 417:57
O the m., m. has mountains — HOPK 492:4
of a m. …that they cannot help — SHAK 901:73
Of any good m. — JONS 535:6
Of my own m. — THOM 1013:28
One man that has a m. — SHAW 925:28
one-dimensional m. — RUSS 833:34
our better m. — ARNO 39:21
our rightful m. — WHIT 1074:9
out of his m. — SHAR 919:87
padlock—on her m. — PRIOR 790:50
peace of m. — SMITH 945:78
pendulum of the m. — JUNG 539:71

mind (*contd.*)

perversity of the human m. — TROL 1028:81
philosophy inclineth Man's m. — BACON 57:65
plastic state of m. — CARRA 237:16
pleasure in the exercise of the m. — BARZ 75:94
poet represents the m. — STEV 972:64
poet's m. is perfectly equipped — ELIOT 368:80
pollen from one to another m. — LOWE 616:85
pray to have a sound m. — JUVE 540:82
presence of m. — LONS 612:23
prodigious quantity of m. — TWAIN 1032:57
product of the free m. — ORWE 743:13
proud m., a crafty wit — KNOX 567:58
Put your brilliant m. to work — ONAS 739:39
putting the m. to sleep — SLOAN 943:59
raise and erect the m. — BACON 55:12
Reading is to the m. — STEE 964:17
reconstruction of the m. — RICH 809:47
refresh the m. of man — SHAK 864:80
relationship between the m. — HEPW 473:79
renewing of your m. — BIBLE 149:33
robs the m. of all its powers — BURKE 206:96
Sa dois the m. that is ay diligent — HENR 473:70
sacred city of the m. — CAMP 227:18
same m. animating them all — BROWN 194:57
satisfied with her lover's m. — TROL 1027:72
say she has a masculine m. — FULL 409:34
scientific attitude of m. — RUSS 832:23
scientific m. does not — LEVI 600:32
scorn…our m. — BAST 76:8
Scots accent of the m. — STEV 976:45
see in my m. a noble — MILT 686:75
shackled the enquiring m. — HOPE 490:71
short neck denotes a good m. — SPARK 955:50
sorcerers that change the m. — SHAK 865:1
sorrow which enhances…the m. — PROU 793:7
sound m. in a sound body — LOCKE 609:75
spirit…of a sound m. — BIBLE 154:36
stamp no character on the m. — JEFF 520:97
state of m. from which it springs — DURK 357:70
steal Fire from the m. — BYRON 219:81
stock my m. — JUANA 539:64
suffered to relax his m. — MACA 623:11
suppose the m. to be — LOCKE 609:72
sweetest music to a woeful m. — SIDN 937:49
thanks to his m. — REDT 804:79
That m. and soul — TENN 998:18
The m. continues free — PENF 764:54
The poem in the m. — THOM 1013:24
the poet's m. — TENN 993:33
there grows in the m. — WILL 1083:98
thinks his m. …more clever — MAIM 640:95
To the noble m. — SHAK 891:22
touching a new m. — STEV 971:46
tumours of a troubl'd m. — MILT 694:44
two kinds of m. — PASC 757:47
Two things fill the m. — KANT 542:7
unbent her m. afterwards — LAMB 576:28
undermine the simple m. — BIBLE 131:83
universal frame is without a m. — BACON 57:64
Unless…new m. — WILL 1083:94
unseemly exposure of m. — HAZL 464:23
until reeled the m. — GIBBS 422:37
urge the m. to aftersight — ELIOT 372:73
Venice will linger in your m. — MORR 708:77
very unusual m. — WHIT 1071:54
warriors of Eternal M. — RUSS 833:36
whatever in my m. — MORR 709:82
white m. — GIOV 428:39
Whitman's m. to be more like — HOPK 492:11
whose m. is stayed on thee — BIBLE 125:74
with a quiet m. — BOOK 174:13
With equal m. — DRYD 352:93
with the m. …serve the law of God — BIBLE 149:24

within they m. rehearse — TENN 996:85
words echo…in your m. — ELIOT 370:23
work my m. — SHAK 913:56
work of body or m. — MILT 690:60
you put me in m. on't — SHER 934:10
Your m. now, moldering — RICH 809:43
minded m. what they were about — STER 968:88
minds add to our m. — JUANA 539:65
begins in the m. of men — UNES 1036:44
best m. in the world — ACHE 3:52
born in the m. of a few — KISS 566:34
Cambridge…comfortable m. — CUMM 299:78
change m. — KING 557:71
change the m. of others — SAFI 835:68
cloaks for untidy m. — MOND 699:40
corrupting the m. of the young — PLATO 773:2
Danger, the spur of all great m. — CHAP 252:74
discrimination of our m. — STEV 972:79
dusty recesses of their m. — LAWR 587:13
except in the m. of men — READ 803:55
extinguished in individual m. — DURK 357:72
eyes rather than our m. — LEWIS 601:34
fairly developed m. — FORS 398:46
far from their nasty little m. — DEBU 311:68
Fearless m. climb — SHAK 862:28
free their m. of…rubbish — DUDEK 353:17
from the closed m. of many — ROBB 813:5
great empire and little m. — BURKE 207:13
great m. in the commonplace — HUBB 498:4
happiest and best m. — SHEL 931:59
have aspiring m. — MARL 652:89
Hearts and m. — ANON 27:77
hobgoblin of little m. — EMER 376:33
hunger of ambitious m. — SPEN 959:34
image…in the m. of others — AUDEN 48:94
in the m. of God — GREE 444:26
infirm and baby m. — COWP 293:61
keep your hearts and m. — BIBLE 153:14
keep your hearts and m. — BOOK 175:33
Little things affect little m. — DISR 332:91
live…close to great m. — BUCH 202:26
marriage of true m. — SHAK 915:89
maximum elasticity for our m. — BUTT 218:52
m., and muses on — MARL 653:91
m. and soules of men — PRYN 794:11
m. grown crooked — MUIR 712:31
m. innocent and quiet — LOVE 615:63
M. like beds — WILL 1083:90
m. of American women — FRIE 405:49
m. so impatient — JOHN 525:88
M. still passion-ridden — LIND 605:11
M. that are great — JONS 536:14
m. that are to our m. — WELLS 1064:26
mislead their weak m. — SAYE 846:51
model the m. of his subjects — STEU 970:30
most thoughtful m. — RUSK 830:80
Nothing issues from their m. — WOOLF 1092:53
nurse and tutor of eccentric m. — LAWS 587:18
one thing on their m. — EVANS 381:40
operations of our own m. — LOCKE 609:73
payed to have dirty m. — TREV 1026:49
power to cloud men's m. — BAKER 63:86
praise effect in mighty m. — DRYD 349:11
Publishers can get their m. — LECA 592:98
question…potential parents' m. — SCHU 851:20
Reason enslaves all those m. — SHAW 922:57
reflection of your own m. — ASTE 42:88
Regimented m. cannot grasp — AUNG 50:23
self-pleasing and humorous m. — BACON 57:58
strange faces, other m. — TENN 1004:45
such relationships as our m. — LEBON 591:78
Superstition religion of feeble m. — BURKE 208:37
take them with our m. — NEWM 724:25
tenderness of patient m. — OWEN 748:8

minds (*contd.*)
thousand m. in the same thought — TOCQ 1021:79
virtue of weak m. — DRYD 346:52
want of congenial m. — MOOD 703:94
whose m. he learned of — HOMER 488:24
Women never have young m. — DELA 314:36
writers could live in own m. — BRAD 183:86
mine You go Uruguay...I'll go m. — MARX 659:97
mine-sweeper captain of a m.-s — CATTO 245:57
mineral vegetable, animal and m. — GILB 424:62
minerals M. grow, plants grow — LINN 606:28
miners m. poured to war — MACA 624:19
m. sweat their guts out — ORWE 742:92
Minerva brains of M. — BARR 73:56
mineworkers Union of M. — MACM 635:14
mingle m. it with the love of others — SHAW 920:99
m. our bloods together — SHAK 910:94
miniature life in m. — ONEI 740:53
mining snakeskin-titles of m.-claims — BENET 90:59
minion Curled m. — ARNO 38:94
Mistress m., you — SHAK 869:13
morning's m. — HOPK 491:88
minister As a M. — TAAF 989:73
fair spirit for my m. — BYRON 220:4
first M. in history — HOWE 497:95
give the M. a venal House of Peers — SHER 934:13
King's First M. — CHUR 264:25
M. said it wald dee — YOUNG 1108:3
m. the like to you — SHAK 860:78
m. to a mind diseased — SHAK 910:82
old Barnet, the m.'s man — HOGG 485:66
quotes from the...Prime M. — MACF 629:19
safety of a M. — WALP 1052:98
Yes, M.! No, M.! — CROS 298:64
ministerial regular m. majorities — WHIT 1069:16
ministering m. angel thou! — SCOTT 853:58
ministers changed my M. — ANNE 20:37
confirmed by the Council of M. — FREUD 404:41
Foreign M. were called — ACHE 2:22
hard on His Majesty's M. — HOBH 483:44
how much my M. talk — THAT 1008:24
M. fully design — MACA 622:93
M. of Industry — MAND 645:71
m. of Love — COLE 274:3
m. of the new testament — BIBLE 151:75
M. of thought — SHEL 930:37
m. to consult the public good — SWIFT 985:87
my actions are my M. — CHAR 253:86
permit his M. to serve him — RICH 810:66
ministration gentle m. of science — ARNO 39:21
ministries *Times* has made many m. — BAGE 61:53
ministry hireling of the M. — OCON 735:80
Miniver M. loved the Medici — ROBI 814:27
minnows this Triton of the m.? — SHAK 911:10
minor books major or m. — SAND 841:78
minorities m. who...suffer — ELIZ 374:96
we are all m. now — THOR 1018:7
minority individual is a m. — ELLI 375:18
member of a m. group — MAIL 639:82
minstrel Ethereal m.! — WORD 1100:87
fuller m. in — TENN 1000:57
M. was infirm and old — SCOTT 853:42
wandering m. — GILB 425:82
minstrel-boy M.-b. to the war — MOORE 706:34
mint helps the m. and the thyme — VERL 1042:39
mark of the m. — CHES 260:39
minute both in the same m. — KEATS 545:65
Changes at the Last M. — PALEY 751:58
do something phoney every m. — SALI 838:24
Even in a m.! — SHAK 893:92
fill the unforgiving m. — KIPL 564:9
Let there pass A m. — LOWE 616:92
m. bit of...Feeling — CUMM 299:75
M. by m. they change — YEATS 1105:72

minute (*contd.*)
m. of darkness — RUSH 829:69
speak more in a m. — SHAK 869:1
sucker born every m. — BARN 72:38
take a m. from the men — CARA 231:94
minutes and m. capons — SHAK 875:36
forty-five m. of...privacy — PARK 755:22
how slowly m. roll — ROCH 817:64
m. hasten to their end — SHAK 914:67
m. how they run — SHAK 862:23
precious m. waste — SHAK 914:76
seem to do it every 10 m. — FULB 409:28
take care of the m. — CHES 257:74
Twenty three and a quarter m. — MITF 697:1
was fifteen m. before — TWAIN 1033:87
watched for ten m. — SZIL 989:71
minx This m., of course — SITW 940:1
Mirabeau Under M. Bridge — APOL 32:92
miracle m. in me — DANI 304:61
m., moment by moment — HUXL 507:83
m. not breaking of laws — BLOOM 170:37
m. of a kind of internal logic — HONE 488:29
m. of rare device — COLE 275:15
m. of the lit bush — THOM 1013:26
no greater m.? — MARL 654:10
power of m. — FEUE 387:31
sort of walking m. — PLATH 773:93
therein works a m. in nature — SHAK 872:82
to be rich...it's a m. — CONN 282:51
unless this m. have might — SHAK 914:68
wondrous m. did Love devise — DAVI 307:6
miracles civilization works its m. — TOCQ 1022:82
m. are ceased — COWL 291:14
one believes, then m. occurs — MILL 678:39
miraculous m. becomes the norm — MILL 678:28
reduce the m. to the mundane — DIDI 330:45
Miranda Admired M.! — SHAK 917:31
mire Sow returns to her M. — KIPL 565:25
The fury and the m. — YEATS 1106:84
wallowing in the m. — BIBLE 156:85
mirror Art is...a m. — PIER 769:36
as in a m., we perceive — MARL 653:91
bevelled edge of a sunlit m. — ABSE 1:7
Cyberspace is the funhouse m. — STER 968:84
each a m. of the other — POPE 779:21
Each creature...a m. — ALAN 11:77
Falklands held a m. up. — RABAN 798:73
From m. after m. — YEATS 1106:83
gilt-framed drawing room m. — ROCK 818:77
Hold...the m. up to nature — SHAK 891:33
like a m. which copies — LEON 597:85
live and sleep in front of a m. — BAUD 78:39
m. cracked from side — TENN 994:45
m. of and a connection — MILL 679:60
m. of the soul — QUIN 797:65
moving through a m. clear — TENN 993:41
news is not a m. — LIPP 606:35
not have a rear-view m. — MURR 715:77
oppose a m. — JONS 534:73
Photography was conceived as a m. — STEI 965:30
prince is like a m. — CHAR 253:89
scripture...like a m. — GREG 445:45
Self-portrait in a Convex M. — ASHB 41:55
world is the m. — MILL 677:20
mirrored m. themselves in my mind — ELIOT 365:6
mirrors Better m. than yours — JEFF 520:85
blaming m. for being untrue — LAFO 574:78
cell whose walls are m. — ONEI 740:89
live without m. — ATWO 45:26
M. are the perfect lovers — ATWO 45:24
m. of the gigantic shadows — SHEL 931:60
m. of the sea — FLEC 393:55
sexual pull towards m. — COND 279:86
women have walked past m. — ALLEN 14:33

mirth all resort of m. — MILT 682:10
commended m. — BIBLE 123:31
earth must borrow its m. — WILC 1075:25
Frame your mind to m. — SHAK 863:70
he is all m. — SHAK 879:50
Him serve with m. — SCOT 856:22
lost all my m. — SHAK 890:2
m. and fun grew fast — BURNS 211:19
M. cannot move — SHAK 866:28
m. hath present l. — SHAK 894:8
M. is short and transient — ADDI 7:17
m. of the billow — CALL 226:4
m. that has no bitter springs — KIPL 564:4
m., What doeth it? — BIBLE 122:18
no time for m. and laughter — ADE 8:42
Our m. the music — RALE 800:14
red with m. — SHAK 911:28
Religion does not banish m. — WALT 1052:11
so much wit, and m. — ADDI 7:10
sunburnt m.! — KEATS 547:14
swim in m. and fancy — MILT 692:9
this night wi' m. and glee — SKIN 943:55
With m. and laughter — SHAK 873:88
mirthless heartless, m., maniacal — THUR 1019:44
misanthropy compounded of m. — MACA 623:2
Racism...a form of m.? — BROD 189:24
misbehave Even if I m. — ANON 29:40
miscarriage disgraced by m. — JOHN 526:4
success and m. — JOHN 526:6
mischief All punishment is m. — BENT 92:14
at the bottom of a' the m. — SCOTT 855:90
Comet, that bodes M. — MAKIN 640:1
evil...working visible m. — CHUR 262:79
if any m. follow — BIBLE 107:69
if m. befall him — BIBLE 105:46
mean m. and break a foul gap — SHAK 912:35
minds...gratified with m. — COWP 293:61
mourn a m. that is past — SHAK 898:12
seem like a bit of m. — THUR 1019:42
mischiefs intolerable M. — PRYN 794:11
misconception prejudices, m. — LLOY 609:64
misconduct prodigality and m. — SMITH 945:85
misdeed planning any m. — JUVE 540:83
miserable arise and make them m. — HUXL 507:75
If life is m. — LABR 573:99
If you are m. — LAUT 584:51
Life becomes m. — BAUD 77:20
life of the artist sufficiently m. — BELL 85:83
live a m. life — BEET 84:50
making others m. — LABR 573:55
man knows that he is m. — PASC 758:74
m. beyond all living things — SHEL 926:54
m. have no other medicine — SHAK 897:76
m. people on earth — CELI 247:90
m. sinners — BOOK 174:4
m. state of mind — BACON 58:86
moral once we are m. — PROU 793:91
of all men most m. — BIBLE 151:66
one thing is certain too, I'm m. — MACI 631:41
secret of being m. — SHAW 924:9
through life absolutely m. — THOR 1017:4
wrong decision can make me very m. — DENN 316:60
miseries ambitions...on the m. — CONR 285:9
bound in shallows and in m. — SHAK 884:60
m. of the world — KEATS 545:69
misery affluent m. — GARD 415:23
Amid...the m. of nations — PITT 772:73
annual expenditure...result m. — DICK 324:6
can only mean common m. — COOP 287:42
departure is taken for m. — BIBLE 131:81
Friends are m. — JONG 534:69
greatest m. is a battle — WELL 1063:12
heart, all mad with m. — SHAK 862:40

model (*contd.*)
very m.	GILB 424:62
without a m. ...I...work	ARET 33:17

modelling go after m. like a fly — INGR 512:51
models Children...have no other m. — BALD 64:95
| m. destroy genius | HAZL 464:24 |
| writers...find their own m. | COWL 291:22 |

moderate be in nothing so m.
	JEFF 519:78
uncompromising but m.	WELL 1064:16
under a m. weight of prose	LAND 578:64

moderation astonished...own m.!
	CLIVE 270:28
easier than perfect m.	AUGU 49:13
I am still for m.	ANNE 20:37
Let your m. be known	BIBLE 153:14
m. in the pursuit of justice	GOLD 433:31
m. in war is imbecility	MACA 623:6
playful m. in politics	HUNT 504:19

modern being too m. — WILDE 1078:92
cultured m. man	RODC 818:81
m. art tends towards	BAUD 78:35
m. Churchman	WAUGH 1056:72
m. craze for regulating	WAVE 1058:10
m. democracy is a tyranny	MAIL 639:74
m. era is dramatic	HUGO 501:56
M. European culture	SUN 982:38
m. hardback writer	MORT 710:94
m. life would lack	WILB 1075:20
m. Major-General	GILB 424:62
M. poets mix	GOET 431:77
m. science and technology	GALB 412:80
muse of m. literature	SONT 953:5
My music is not m.	SCHO 849:89
not be either m. or art	ROSE 823:58
our m. technic shows	OPPE 741:75
point of departure...is m. life	WAGN 1047:26
Science is to the m.	DISR 332:84
this filthy m. tide	YEATS 1107:91
triumph of m.. science	WAUGH 1058:8
waste of m. tenements	THOR 1017:99

modernity frauds of m. — WAUGH 1057:89
modernness Perpetual m. — EMER 377:59
modes m. of thinking are different — JOHN 531:16
modest M.? My word, no — REED 805:85
modesty charm of all power is m. — ALCO 12:97
maintain a becoming m.	BOUL 181:42
m., an independence, a responsibility	DICK 327:82
time to cultivate m.	SITW 941:18

modicum m. of alacrity — RYLE 834:54
modish the more m. — SWIFT 986:10
modus m. of lunar eclipses — POUND 785:59
Mogadishu you'll love M. — HEMP 471:51
Moghul M. Empire is in our power — CLIVE 270:27
mold work of...curious m. — SPEN 958:10
mole like a bastion's m. — SMART 944:69
On her left breast A m.	SHAK 916:1
Well said, old m.	SHAK 889:83
wilt thou go ask the m.?	BLAKE 166:61

Mole Diary of Adrian M. — TOWN 1024:12
molecule not a single m. of my body — DIDE 330:33
molecules preserve the selfish m. — DAWK 310:43
molestation injury and m. — MILL 675:65
Molière advances ...since M. — PROU 793:94
Moloch M. ...is pure machinery — GINS 427:25
mome m. raths outgrabe — CARR 239:47
moment at the last m. — GUIM 448:79
awful daring of a m.'s surrender	ELIOT 369:96
carefully choose one's m.	BECK 81:4
Consider every m. past	ABU 2:14
dangerous m. in human history	BELL 88:34
Eternity was in that m.	CONG 280:97
Every great mistake has a halfway m.	BUCK 203:35
Every m. dies a man	TENN 996:87
Every m. is a golden one	MILL 678:25
exact m. at which	WELL 1063:13

moment (*contd.*)
force the m. to its crisis?	ELIOT 367:48
happiest m. of a happy man	SCHO 849:97
Life is but a m.	SCHI 847:68
masters at the m.	SHAW 926:46
m. after death	HAWT 461:65
m.'s insight	HOLM 486:79
m. of joy is...harder to get	PO 775:38
m. of my greatness flicker	ELIOT 367:51
m.'s ornament	WORD 1098:62
m. when curiosity becomes a sin	FRAN 401:86
m. white	BURNS 211:15
naked m. in politics	GERG 420:1
No more distressing m.	TUCH 1031:45
Not for a m.	WORD 1099:72
of no m. to the happiness	JOHN 528:60
one m. in childhood	GREE 444:5
people only die at the last m.	CELI 247:90
present m. that goes by	WILL 1082:79
public of the m.	LUCAS 618:32
rejoice for a m.	YUAN 1108:12
see you even for a m.	SAPP 842:92
stands m. by m.	WILD 1079:27
state of mind at that particular m.	FEIN 385:99
suspension of disbelief for the m.	COLE 275:20
there is only the unattended M.	ELIOT 372:64
what is seen during a m.	SAND 841:65
world's best m. is a calm hour	ABU 1:11
worry and terror of the m.	MORR 709:81

momentariness delight in m. — GRAV 439:19
moments all m. are key m. — BUEC 203:42
best and happiest m.	SHEL 931:59
bitter m. of life	POWYS 788:21
bright m. illuminate our path	SCHO 849:92
brilliant frozen m.	LIVE 607:45
designed a bench in a few m.	BELL 86:95
highest quality to your m.	ANON 28:14
m. of vision	BLUN 170:48
pattern Of timeless m.	ELIOT 373:80
pressing present m.	STUA 980:7
quality to your m.	PATER 759:95
such m. really mean	MUNRO 714:61
There are no ordinary m.	MILL 679:62
Wagner had his good m.	ROSS 825:97
worst m. into money	DONL 336:63

Mona Lisa lotta cats copy the M. L. — ARMS 35:48
M. L. of the vegetable world	HUGH 500:32
M. L. painted by a club?	GRIS 447:67
M. L. seem an open book	LEAC 589:38

Monan danced the...on M.'s rill — SCOTT 853:61
monarch beneath a m.'s feet — BURNS 210:86
invades authors like a m.	DRYD 347:60
Israel's m.	DRYD 349:9
merry M., scandalous and poor	ROCH 816:46
m. of all I survey	COWP 292:38
m. of the sea	GILB 423:56
self-worship of the m.	MILL 675:80
With a m.'s voice	SHAK 883:45
With ravished ears The m. hears	DRYD 351:68

monarchies All the four M. — DONNE 339:27
| m. end by poverty | MONT 702:85 |

monarchs m. to choose favourites — SWIFT 985:87
| when fate summons, m. must obey | DRYD 348:81 |

monarchy discontented under m. — HOBB 483:41
Film Industry is the American M.	MAMET 644:57
Habsburg m.	TAAF 989:73
m. ...intelligible government	BAGE 61:59
Than purest m.	MONT 703:91

monasteries some join m. — WEBB 1058:16
monastery discipline of a m. — AELR 9:52
| Protective M. of Aesthetic Truth | MAMET 644:57 |

Monday Arriving M. — SWAN 983:50
| fell a-bleeding on Black M. | SHAK 874:27 |
| left Calais on M. | MACA 622:93 |

Monday (*contd.*)
worked M. ...fired Wednesday	ALGR 13:25

Monet M. is only an eye — CEZA 248:6
money America had plenty of m. — BEHR 85:76
Aphorisms...more for your...m.	DUDEK 353:13
art pursued with view to m.	BUTL 217:41
ask for my m. back	HUXL 507:70
athlete cannot run with m.	ZATO 1109:14
authors...talking about m.	PRIT 791:69
Ayatollah's m. to support	NORTH 732:35
Beauty...became m.	WOLF 1090:13
blame someone...for making m.	ORWE 744:26
borrow m. from people	WILL 1080:43
borrow m. off them	TWAIN 1034:20
borrow the m.	WARD 1053:15
borrowed time, borrowed m.	CALL 225:98
Brass M.	ANON 25:21
can be young without m.	WILL 1082:68
clever enough to get all that m.	CHES 259:34
come to applaud their m.	HIRS 482:22
corrupted by m.	GREE 444:7
cost me much m.	PEPYS 765:61
desire to make m.	VAND 1039:97
divided from courtesans...by m.	DUMAS 354:29
don't like m., actually	LOUIS 614:59
Either your m.	WALK 1049:56
enough to get m. from it	LEAC 589:43
except for m.	JOHN 530:39
feeling they've wasted their m.	OLIV 738:32
for such sums of m.	SCHAW 847:61
give thee my m.	CONG 280:96
giving m. to the Government	HERB 474:96
goa wheer m. is	TENN 1004:50
God would do if he had the m.	WOOL 1094:92
greatest possible amount of m.	WEBER 1059:20
greedy to add m. to m.	BIBLE 131:17
happened to be a lot of m.	MERR 672:23
hard to be...a lover of m.	WYCH 1103:38
hath no m.	BIBLE 127:3
his private parts, his m.	BUTL 218:48
honey, and plenty of m.	LEAR 590:58
hunger for recognition and m.	SELF 857:37
if he'd had the m.	KAUF 543:17
If m. goes before	SHAK 878:15
If thou wilt lend this m.	SHAK 874:22
In the absence of m.	BALC 64:89
innocently employed...in getting m.	JOHN 529:70
leg for any m.	DICK 323:78
licence to print m.	THOM 1015:99
little m., but not much	BEAV 80:80
lost m. by underestimating	MENC 669:67
love of m. is the root	BIBLE 154:34
Make all the m.	SHAK 898:17
make the white people...some m.	DAVIS 309:31
makes the current m.	JONS 536:25
making m. at the same time	BENN 92:6
man's reputashun outlasts his m.	BILL 162:3
marry for m. and comfort	SHAW 924:91
Men Whose Lives Are M.	OATES 733:55
M.'s a horrid thing	JAMES 516:16
m. and a room of her own	WOOLF 1093:69
M. and gentility	MITF 697:93
m. answereth all things	BIBLE 123:38
m. appears to vary	HUXL 508:93
m. can't buy me love	LENN 596:59
m. controls opinion	ORWE 742:5
m. does not bring happiness	LACL 573:50
M. does not smell	VESP 1042:40
m. from the pockets of the people	SMITH 945:83
m. has a power above	BUTL 217:27
m. has dissolved more worries	BLEST 169:28
M. is a comfort	ANON 21:58
M. is a good soldier	SHAK 878:16
M. is a kind of poetry	STEV 972:66

money (*contd.*)

M. is better than poverty	ALLEN 14:46
M. is how we keep the score	CHAP 252:67
m. is just…information	WRIS 1102:21
M. is like muck	BACON 58:81
m. is the standard	MORE 707:51
M. ∴.is the true fuller's earth	GAY 416:54
m. manipulators and speculators	MAMET 644:57
m. on de bob-tail nag	FOST 399:59
m. pur et simple	BAGE 61:55
M. speaks sense	BEHN 85:65
m. Spend it, spend it	SHAK 878:17
M. …sweeter than Honey	FRAN 402:3
m. …that purchased the manor?	DONNE 339:32
M. …the most important thing	SHAW 919:88
M. …was exactly like sex	BALD 64:98
m. was not scarce?	EMER 377:75
m. you bet on him	FLAN 391:24
m. you save	LARK 582:18
most m. on a style	MING 695:63
Much discussion of m.	GALB 412:84
nexus of all love and m. and power	DIDI 330:45
nice feet and plenty of m.	ASHF 41:71
no m. in poetry	GRAV 440:37
no m. in your purse	SHAK 885:84
no one shall work for m.	KIPL 562:60
nothing left but m. and power	STAEL 961:70
nothing…a little m. will not cure	DURA 356:65
original purchase m.	SMITH 946:93
poet can earn much more m.	AUDEN 48:86
poisoning…for their insurance m.	DOYLE 343:89
possession of m.	KIPL 562:72
power and m. and fine robes	WELD 1062:92
power of m. is…male power	DWOR 358:84
press…eagerly to pay m.	STEE 964:16
Prince calls in the good old m.	LAMB 576:23
put your m. in trust	HOLM 486:84
rattle of the m. box	LABO 572:34
ready m.	GRAMM 438:97
religion of m.	GAUT 416:44
retreated back into their m.	FITZ 390:5
rub up against m.	RUNY 829:58
runs into real m.	DIRK 331:66
Sex is like m.	UPDI 1036:54
share out the little m.	MONT 701:60
side with plenty of m.	ANOU 31:80
sixty-three ways to find the m.	RABE 799:88
spent all the m.	JOHN 531:18
spent some of my own m.	KENN 552:99
state…master of m.	BEVE 102:75
take no m. of me	SHAK 912:37
tells you it is not a m. problem	CLIN 269:17
Time is m.	FRAN 402:4
unlimited m.	CICE 266:61
voice is full of m.	FITZ 390:4
voter who uses his m.	SAMU 840:45
We're in the m.	DUBIN 353:1
we've got the m. too!	HUNT 504:15
What m. is better bestowed	THAC 1007:98
what m. will do	PEPYS 766:83
what to do with their m.	BARA 70:7
when m. rolled in	HUGH 499:21
when you don't have any m.	DONL 336:60
where that m. came from	REAG 804:67
With the m. I spent	KENN 552:97
with the m. of the people	WHIT 1069:16
women who have the most m.	GILM 427:16
worst moments into m.	DONL 336:63
write for m. or fame	MOORE 705:23
Yes, they have more m.	HEMI 471:31
You pays your m.	PUNCH 795:23
You talk of art…I think of m.	SHAW 925:33
money-bags dream of m.-b.	SHAK 874:28
money-changers tales of the m.-c.	BIBLE 139:31

moneybag Aristocracy of the M.	CARL 235:69
moneys my m. and my usances	SHAK 874:20
Mongolia British Outer M.	BENN 90:65
mongrels continent of energetic m.	FISH 389:83
monitor sad m. scorning	CALL 226:4
monk found in the king a m.	AELR 9:52
m. throwing himself	MAP 649:34
monkey make a m. of a man	BENC 89:49
M. with lollipop paws	LEAR 590:56
m.'s mask reveals the m.	BASHO 76:2
never look long upon a M.	CONG 281:20
no reason to attack the m.	BEVAN 101:68
monkeys Cats and m.	JAMES 516:13
monks m. …lathy lot of thkunkth	BENT 93:27
m. …naturally have a weak stomach	BERN 96:74
town of m. and bones	COLE 275:26
monogamous Woman m.	JAMES 518:52
monoliths m. made of granite	MENC 670:89
monomania m. of accounting	WEIL 1062:83
monopoly best of all m. profits	HICKS 480:95
M. is Business	LLOYD 608:51
M. power must be abused	SIMO 939:87
newspaper is…a m.	SCOTT 852:33
that efficient m.	PUZO 796:41
monosyllabic nothing so m.	FRY 408:16
monotonous becomes m.	TROL 1027:72
m., and wearisome	THOR 1017:99
monotony articulate m.	STEP 968:79
certain m. of genius	HAZL 463:95
eternal m. of passion	FLAU 392:39
m. of a watery surface	MOORE 705:14
m. of marriage	GIBB 422:36
m., work or leisure	POMP 777:71
Monroe doctrine of President M.	WILS 1086:50
making a picture with M.	WILD 1079:15
Marilyn M. who was blonde	MAIL 639:87
Unites States to the M. Doctrine	ROOS 822:46
monsieur m., for methinks	SHAK 871:50
monster art should be a m.	TZARA 1035:33
capital is become an overgrown m.	SMOL 950:64
Effie M. was a m.	LEE 593:17
Frankenstein m.	MUGG 712:23
IS, the whited m.	LOWE 616:93
jealousy…the green-eyed m.	SHAK 899:32
make a m. of the multitude	SHAK 911:9
many-headed m. of the pit	POPE 782:84
m. that devours everything	BALZ 68:68
m. was indeed the best	KARL 542:9
m., which the Blatant beast men call	SPEN 959:35
O thou m. ignorance	SHAK 865:15
the m. there's no gagging	SHER 933:93
this busy m., manunkind	CUMM 300:92
Vice is a m.	POPE 780:44
monster-breeding m.-b. breast	POPE 782:95
monsters m. and devils	LUTH 620:51
nocturnal m. that threaten	ROBB 813:12
stay out of politics or become m.	GINS 428:30
transform Men into M.	FORD 397:19
vile unloveable, morbid m.	ANON 25:42
monstrous all that is m.	GOLD 432:89
Ingratitude is m.	SHAK 911:9
m. with politics	GINS 428:30
seem a m. thing	FORD 396:2
Two evils, m. either one	RANS 802:35
Mont Blanc M. B. yet gleams	SHEL 927:60
Montana M. skies seemed deeper	MACM 636:24
Monte Testaceo its own M. T.	CLOU 270:38
Montgomery gie's a sang, M. cried	SKIN 943:55
Montgomery Robert M.'s genius	MACA 623:99
month April is the cruellest m.	ELIOT 368:81
beginning of a new m. or year	MANN 646:84
hesitates about a m.	STEV 974:23
m. God designed	KEIL 548:22
old man in a dry m.	ELIOT 368:68

month (*contd.*)

one m. you have to live	GILB 425:83
stand to in a m.	SHAK 869:1
this is the m.	MILT 681:85
months all the m. of human birth	MASE 662:44
few m. obliterate	BUNT 204:57
first six m.	TRUM 1029:16
for m., for years	ROBB 813:9
go for m. on end	ORWE 742:96
of the m. and stars	SWIN 986:22
seven m. since she is gone	MILL 676:98
think for m.	EINS 363:64
Monticelso M.: How!	WEBS 1060:38
Montmorenci steep Of M.	KEATS 544:38
Montparnasse not rest quiet in M.	BENET 90:62
Montreal M. Olympics	DRAP 345:30
monument Builds his m. mockingly	JEFF 519:79
built thyself a livelong m.	MILT 681:94
like patience on a m.	SHAK 894:16
live no longer in m.	SHAK 880:66
m. of English prose	ELIOT 370:21
m. of old Irish hospitality	EDGE 360:28
m. sticks like a fishbone	LOWE 617:99
m. to the man who did it	APPL 32:98
not trying to make a m.	HARR 459:39
only m. left of R.	BELL 86:87
only m. the asphalt road	ELIOT 370:18
sonnet is a moment's m.	ROSS 824:85
monumental buried in m. arms	WALL 1050:73
monuments nor the gilded m.	SHAK 913:65
mood In vacant or in pensive m.	WORD 1099:70
life's business…a summer m.	WORD 1097:43
m. will give us anything	SHAK 884:57
silent grass-growing m.	MELV 668:47
that sweet m.	WORD 1095:4
moods envy not in any m.	TENN 998:29
ever…changing m.	VIRG 1045:87
moon an affair with the m.	STER 970:22
and the m. was full	TENN 1004:42
apples of the m.	YEATS 1105:63
ask for the m.	ROBI 814:21
beneath a waning m.	COLE 275:24
Beneath the visiting m.	SHAK 906:96
brilliant m.	YEATS 1104:59
broad m. rose circling into sight	BYRON 222:44
calm…As is the crescent m.	WORD 1094:1
carry the m. in my pocket?	BROW 198:53
cold o' the m.	BROW 200:81
corners of the M.	MILT 684:36
course of one revolving m.	DRYD 349:23
danced by the light of the m.	LEAR 590:64
danced the m.	SCOTT 853:61
Daughter of the M.	LONG 611:10
dull red image of the m.	WORD 1096:31
empty when the m. is full	BUTL 216:8
even the m. is frightened	SHER 934:17
from the dying m.	TENN 997:97
honour from the pale-faced m.	SHAK 875:46
How many miles the m. might	BYRON 222:30
hush with the setting m.	TENN 1001:86
I didn't go to the m.	WILL 1081:57
if the m.'s a balloon	CUMM 299:81
jumping over the m.	RAMS 801:18
landing a man on the m.	KENN 551:66
lovely m.—she lifted	FREE 404:36
Man on the m.	BAKER 63:84
melodious cats under the m.	HUXL 507:69
m. and stars are set	STEV 975:34
m. and the stars	MACC 626:62
m. …in her silver shoon	DELA 314:31
m. in the breast of man	BERR 98:7
m. is up	BYRON 220:94
m. of moons	DICK 325:31
m. on the breast	MOORE 704:5

moon (*contd.*)

m. on this cloud sea	SCOTT 852:36
m. or favouring stars	WORD 1096:27
m.'s unclouded light	BURNS 210:78
m. under her feet	BIBLE 157:20
m. was a ghostly	NOYES 732:42
m. was overhead	TENN 993:42
m. …which thou hast ordained	BIBLE 114:35
mortals call the M.	SHEL 928:83
never gazed the m.	SHAK 912:34
new m. hangs	THOM 1012:6
nor the m. by night	BIBLE 119:36
O more than m.	DONNE 337:87
O swear not by the m.	SHAK 869:47
on the horns o'th' m.	SHAK 911:3
only a paper m.	HARB 455:73
Part of a m.	FROST 406:74
project a voyage to the m.	LARD 580:88
Raymond like the Harvest M.	FARJ 383:63
saucer like some full m.	MONRO 700:48
saw the new m.	BALL 67:48
Scotland kens beneath the m.	FERG 386:17
set foot upon the m.	ANON 27:93
shone the wintery m.	KEATS 546:92
slow m. climbs	TENN 995:61
sun and m. to give them light	DICK 323:90
sun and m. Were in	MILT 683:28
sun provides the m.	ANAX 18:99
sun, m., and stars, brother	BORR 179:23
sung to the m.	GILB 425:94
the m. and the sun…in silence	THER 1009:38
under the sun and m.	GOLD 432:89
Unique things about the m.	LUGO 619:38
unmask her beauty to the m.	SHAK 888:61
wandering m., Riding	MILT 682:9
we are the m.	SCHR 850:5
wind up the sun and m.	BYRON 223:66

moon-struck m.-s. madness — MILT 693:23

moonbeam different as m. — BRON 192:11

m. …all the light they wish — COWP 293:53

moonbeams Carry m. home — BURKE 208:52

moonlight braw bricht m. nicht — MORR 709:84

except this m.	THOM 1012:3
hating m.	STEI 966:56
How sweet the m.	SHAK 873:98
Ill met by m.	SHAK 870:34
In the faint m.	ELIOT 369:95
m. and the starlight	LONG 611:9
m. hung upon the lifted oars	MANS 647:7
m. over the purple moor	NOYES 732:42
seen the bush by m.	LAWS 588:21
slow tyranny of m.	CRANE 294:96
the m.-coloured may	SHEL 932:68
things smoother than m.	SCOTT 852:36
visit it by the pale m.	SCOTT 853:45
Watch for me by m.	NOYES 732:43
while there's m. and music	BERL 95:61
with a northern m.	SOUT 954:28

moonlit m. cedar what a burst — ARNO 37:82

m. dome — YEATS 1106:84

moons Till m. shall wax — WATTS 1055:57

moonshine m. that are gilded — DRAY 346:41

Transcendental m. — CARL 236:99

moor moonlight over the purple m. NOYES 732:42

Moor daughter and the M. — SHAK 897:98

make the M. thank me	SHAK 899:23
M. is of a free…nature	SHAK 898:18
noble M. whom our	SHAK 900:46

moor-hens long-legged m.-h. — YEATS 1105:72

moorcocks hens to m. call — YEATS 1105:72

Moore muse of M. — BYRON 222:38

trouble with M. — FRY 408:18

Moorish under the M. wall — JOYCE 538:57

moors blows the wind on the m. — STEV 976:56

moors (*contd.*)

sunset on m. and windy hills	MASE 662:39
moping merryman m. mum	GILB 425:94
Moppsikon M. Foppsikon bear	LEAR 590:68
Mopsa not in love with M.	SHAK 912:37
moral afraid of losing your m. sense	STEIN 965:31
All reform except m. one	CARL 236:2
building…to point to a m.	CASS 243:29
contaminated m. environment	HAVEL 460:60
degeneration of his m. being	STEV 974:2
difficult to stay a m. infection	DICK 326:54
don't have a m. plan	CRON 298:59
Englishman thinks he is m.	SHAW 921:34
Everything's got a m.	CARR 238:32
febrile insomnia, m. leaps	MARI 651:66
gain m. detachment	VAND 1039:94
great instrument of m. good	SHEL 931:57
high m. tests and tasks	ELKIN 374:98
His m. pleases	POPE 782:80
instrument that has a good m. effect	ARIS 34:34
intellect, m. activity	NIGH 729:95
into a m. Coventry	PARN 756:39
judge in the legal and m. sense	DEWEY 319:96
kind of m. eunuch	SHEL 928:95
League…grows in m. courage	MACD 628:5
legal or m. responsibility	HAYD 462:88
Let us be m.	DICK 322:72
live beyond his m. means	TOYN 1024:21
look both m. and exciting	FERB 385:9
lower m. quality	HARDY 456:90
man is strong before he is m.	FAUL 383:80
mean by a m. society	THAT 1007:8
m. activity which disentangles	POE 775:42
m. and social progress	MILL 674:58
m. character…was full of promise	DICK 322:70
m. consciousness of people	MAIL 639:71
m. crusade, or it is nothing	WILS 1085:31
m. discovery…the object of every tale	CONR 285:5
m. effort is required to get rid of it	MACM 636:15
m. in it will be banished	TWAIN 1032:76
M. indignation	WELLS 1065:38
m. is always correct	BART 74:78
m. is what you feel good after	HEMI 470:23
m. judgements do not say anything	AYER 53:80
m. law within	KANT 542:7
m. life of man	WILDE 1076:46
m. necessity of acting together	MILL 674:56
m. of all this	SAYE 846:52
m. once we are miserable	PROU 793:91
m. or a material one	ARNO 38:5
m. or an immoral book	WILDE 1076:44
m. or physical devastation	WALK 1049:59
m. restraint, vice and misery	MALT 643:38
no one can be perfectly m.	SPEN 955:63
no such thing as a m. dress	CHUR 263:91
not just a m. category	SOLZ 952:96
physics, chemistry…become m.	DEWEY 319:96
picayune compared to the m. effect	DURK 357:68
quality of m. behaviour	HUXL 507:77
read a novel…for the m.	OCON 735:86
shelf life of the m. causes	IGNA 510:27
story with a m.	OHEN 737:18
threat to m.	ROBB 813:5
without originality or m. courage	SHAW 921:21

morale greatest m. builder — DOOL 340:37

Low m. and high — MURK 715:68

moralist Poor m.! — GRAY 441:59

teach rustic m. to die — GRAY 442:73

morality All…about m. — CAMUS 229:63

British public…fits of m.	MACA 622:96
cities for our best m.	AUST 51:46
Cleopatra's m.	LAUT 584:53
Conventionality is not m.	BRON 191:97
corruption of medicine by m.	MENC 669:65

morality (*contd.*)

Dr Johnson's m.	HAWT 462:83
Goodbye, m.!	HERB 474:94
ignorance of m.	PASC 758:72
marriage is to m.	TWAIN 1034:3
m. and slave m.	NIET 728:87
M. is herd instinct	NIET 728:72
M. is nothing other	THRA 1018:8
m. of imprisonment	SHAK 896:62
m. touched with emotion	ARNO 39:32
M. Weighs heavily	KEATS 544:36
No rule of general m.	SART 844:19
periodical fits of m.	MACA 623:1
personal and national m.	SHAW 919:88
qualities essential for the artist: m.	DIDE 330:39
serious attack upon m.	ORWE 743:22
so-called new m.	SHAW 926:47
such a thing as physical m.	SPEN 955:65
sure it is bad m.	SKEL 942:39
true m. has no time for m.	PASC 757:52
unawares M. expires	POPE 783:10
up agen middle-class m.	SHAW 924:6
What is m.	WHIT 1071:62

moralizing aestheticizing or m. — CABR 224:81

morally M., spiritually — MILL 678:26

morals also true in m. — FONT 395:87

art and m.	MURD 714:64
attempts to describe m.	TROL 1028:95
food first, then m.	BREC 186:25
foundation of m.	BENT 92:13
foundation of m., Utility	MILL 675:71
greatest teacher of m.	HOOV 490:67
Have you no m., man?	SHAW 924:5
mask of prevailing m.	BEAU 79:62
m. of a baboon	CAPO 231:89
teach the m. of a whore	JOHN 526:95
the less his m. are poetic	DIDE 329:29
what m.!	CICE 266:57

Mordor In the Land of M. — TOLK 1022:92

more do m. with less — FULL 410:41

Is there no m.?	ROCH 816:45
It's very easy to take m. than nothing	CARR 238:30
M. is vulgar	SPARK 955:53
M. will mean worse	AMIS 16:76
Not a Penny m.	ARCH 33:12
Please, sir, I want some m.	DICK 321:34
the m. heard	WILD 1080:34

mores O m. — CICE 266:57

Morgan M. liked to imagine — BOYD 182:63

morganatic m. alliance — HARD 455:76

Moriarty Ex-Professor M. — DOYLE 344:8

Morison Ye are na Mary M. — BURNS 212:39

morn approach of ev'n or m. — MILT 689:31

civil-suited M.	MILT 683:13
days at the m.	BROW 197:25
dew of the m.	YEATS 1105:62
Each new m.	SHAK 909:72
ever-blessèd m.	CASW 244:37
Fair laughs the m.	GRAY 443:86
golden light of m.	HOOD 489:39
He rose the morrow m.	COLE 274:96
healthy breath of m.	KEATS 547:99
incense-breathing M.	GRAY 442:64
long before the m.	DICK 327:94
m. not waking	LYLY 620:58
m. of youth	WORD 1100:85
new m. she saw not	KEATS 546:83
No m.—no noon	HOOD 489:51
old Autumn in the misty m.	HOOD 488:33
peeping in at m.	HOOD 489:37
rouse before the m.	TENN 996:87
When the bedabbled m.	HERR 478:65

morning all in one m. — DONNE 339:27

always three o'clock in the m. — FITZ 391:14

m....shall break forth	BIBLE 127:7
m....to him were friends	BYRON 219:82
m. were there	HERZ 478:76
m. will fall into labour	HORA 493:32
remove m., and makes seas	CARL 234:38
said to the m....Fall on us	BIBLE 157:13
shadow of the blue m.	MELBA 667:21
skill to move m.	HOFF 484:54
There are new m.	LEGU 594:30
to the m. is going home	MUIR 713:38
true call...of the m.	STARK 963:96
voices...One of the m.	WORD 1099:74
weighed the m. in scales	BIBLE 126:87
What are men to rocks and m.?	AUST 51:41
Woods, or steepy m.	MARL 655:31
mountainside along the m.	WORD 1097:44
every m.	SMITH 948:27
mountebank impudent m. who sold pills	ADDI 6:5
mere anatomy, a m.	SHAK 865:3
story of a m. and his zany	WALP 1051:92
mountebanks m. ...imitate	LEWIS 602:65
mounted always well m.	HALI 452:24
Mountjoy M. began to move	MACA 624:28
mourn Blessed are they that m.	BIBLE 133:34
countless thousands m.!	BURNS 209:76
Margaret you m. for	HOPK 492:94
m. a mischief that is past	SHAK 898:12
m. with ever-returning spring	WHIT 1073:92
secure, and now can never m.	SHEL 931:47
time enough to m.	DANI 304:62
time to m.	BIBLE 122:19
mourned m. unto you	BIBLE 137:86
mourners let the m. come	AUDEN 46:58
m. go about the streets	BIBLE 123:42
mournful M. and Never-ending	POE 776:51
mourning in such very deep m.	AUST 50:30
M. becomes Electra	ONEI 740:56
m. for my life	CHEK 256:58
m. into dancing	BIBLE 115:56
M. is a hard business	MALA 641:4
mourns m. when many leave	OWEN 748:22
one m. alone	BERG 94:46
mouse absurd little m.	HORA 493:32
catch a m. or two (for form's sake)	GRAY 443:93
invention of a m.!	DISN 331:70
leave room for the m.	SAKI 838:15
m. in a mousehole	EISE 364:95
m. sticks in his sharp paw	ANON 21:55
not even a m.	MOORE 704:3
not the m. who is the thief	JACO 514:91
way a m. watzes	WHITE 1070:34
mouse-trap baiting a m.-t.	SAKI 838:15
The M.	SHAK 891:40
moustache Big chap with a small m.	WODE 1089:5
couldn't wear a m. like that	HOOV 490:68
didn't wax his m.	KIPL 560:19
drawing a m. on a madonna	VENT 1042:31
worn a m.	SIMON 939:81
moustaches Nothing...except m.	BROD 189:68
mouth Christ in the m.	PATR 761:15
doth become the m. as well	SHAK 882:21
draw near me with their m.	BIBLE 125:78
Even in the cannon's m.	SHAK 885:92
Familiar in his m.	SHAK 882:2
for an Englishman to open his m.	SHAW 924:1
gift horse in the m.	RABE 798:81
hand more instrumental to the m.	SHAK 887:45
have not found the m.	ACHE 2:19
heart into my m.	SHAK 902:96
In his m. are Lies	WELLS 1064:29
in my m. sweet as honey	BIBLE 157:19
Into the m. of Hell	TENN 1001:73
just whispering in her m.	MARX 659:94
keep your m. shut	ITO 514:82

mouth (*contd.*)

laugh...before he opens his m.	NATH 721:86
m. and my breasts	SEXT 859:66
m. do crush their wine	MARV 658:85
m. is smoother than oil	BIBLE 120:61
m. it, as many of your players do	SHAK 891:32
m. must be held in	BIBLE 115:59
m. of a hog to eat	NASHE 721:84
m. of the cannon	RUSK 830:74
m. shall shew forth thy praise	BIBLE 116:79
m. so prim	ELIOT 371:36
m....used as a latrine	AMIS 16:71
No M. And I Must Scream	ELLI 375:12
no m. to put it in	DICK 320:16
open thy m. wide	BIBLE 117:92
opened not his m.	BIBLE 127:1
out of his m. went a...sword	BIBLE 156:99
Out of same m. proceedeth	BIBLE 155:68
purple-stained m.	KEATS 547:14
put a hose in their m.	KROC 570:98
put my words in thy m.	BIBLE 128:17
put one into her m.	THAC 1006:81
rash with thy m.	BIBLE 123:26
satisfieth thy m. with good things	BIBLE 118:11
Set a watch...before my m.	BIBLE 120:52
slap-dash down in the m.	CONG 280:98
strawberries at the m. of their pot	ELIZ 374:94
tail in its m.	FERL 386:23
that which goeth into the m.	BIBLE 138:9
The boy's m.	TWAIN 1033:95
When the m. says yes	HUGO 502:72
wine will burn our m.	EMER 377:62
with an open m.	STEV 973:88
with its tail in its m.	HOOD 489:41
z is keeping your m. shut	EINS 363:72
mouth-organ Menuhin on the m.-o.	ADLER 9:48
mouthful every m. of food	FORD 396:98
m. of air	YEATS 1105:64
mouthless millions of the m. dead	SORL 953:23
mouths bizzing craigs and m. to weet	FERG 386:17
Blind m.! that scarce	MILT 684:44
from your smoky m.	MARL 654:21
made m. in a glass	SHAK 903:20
m. Of wisest men	MILT 695:49
'Pardon' for kings' m.	SHAK 868:69
put an enemy in their m.	SHAK 899:26
speaking truth, to m. like mine	BROW 200:95
move America is always on the m.	CUMM 300:85
feel the earth m.?	HEMI 471:33
if it made its own m.	JARR 518:61
in him we live, and m.	BIBLE 148:3
m. his hearers	FRAS 403:18
Sometimes you m. publicly	BAKER 63:81
moveables to my chattels and my m.	SHAK 880:78
moved Being m. is what collecting	ANNE 20:39
do not like being m.	CLOU 271:41
m. by what is not unusual	ELIOT 366:38
m., not only as an author	GRASS 439:12
not m. with concord	SHAK 873:3
shall not be m.	BIBLE 116:73
movement aggressive m.	MARI 651:66
infinite diversity of m.	REDT 804:79
joyful with swift m.	ANON 21:55
neither arrest nor m.	ELIOT 370:25
Never confuse m. with action	HEMI 471:46
only m....dropping of the dead	WILL 1080:44
Our m. took a grip	GOER 430:66
Our nature consists in m.	PASC 757:57
slow m. of clouds	DAYL 310:55
ticking m. of the human timepiece	ASLET 42:76
movements m. of human thought	BENN 92:6
m. of the limbs	LEON 597:80
natural and ordinary m.	FONT 395:87
physical m.	GALS 413:3

mover Fear is the great m.	BART 74:74
moves it m. again since it is life	FAUL 384:84
Nevertheless, it m.	GALI 412:90
movie cheats of the m. screen	MAIL 639:68
Life in the m. business	MAMET 644:58
m.-makers...put more reality	HECHT 466:60
old m. plots	BAKER 63:86
only a m. of the past	KESEY 553:21
movies Adding sound to m.	PICK 769:31
lesson in how not to write for the m.	CHAN 250:38
like making pornographic m.	ROGE 821:23
Thanks to the m.	USTI 1038:74
thing that can kill the M.	ROGE 820:18
trot down to the m.	WILD 1079:26
W C Fields on	HAWES 460:61
moving always already m.	HEID 467:66
face of a m.-picture actor	MENC 670:90
in form and m.	SHAK 890:4
lie without m.	RHYS 808:27
privilege of always m.	LEWIS 601:35
mowers m. in the hay	MUIR 712:28
Mowgli M. answered	KIPL 561:50
mown often as we are m. down	TERT 1006:78
Mozart en famille they play M.	BARTH 74:69
sonatas of M.	SCHN 848:86
MP goings-on of an unlucky M.	CRIT 297:43
much how m. unexpected, by so m.	SHAK 872:61
m. I want which most men have	DYER 358:87
m. to hear and see	SKEL 942:32
no man is wanted m.	EMER 377:51
muck in lovely m. I've lain	HOUS 495:65
Money is like m.	BACON 58:81
sing 'em m.	MELBA 666:20
when to stop raking the m.	ROOS 822:47
muckle M. he made o' that	MACQ 637:50
muckrake with a m. in his hand	BUNY 205:71
mud blades pricked the m.	BROW 198:50
clouds, or m., or like places	LEON 597:83
cover the universe with m.	FORS 398:45
gaping mussels, left upon the m.	CRAB 294:83
he was just all m.	TWAIN 1033:82
He who slings m.	STEV 973:85
made up of marble and m.	HAWT 461:73
more dangerous than a m.-puddle	STEIN 965:31
M.! M.! Glorious m.!	FLAN 391:25
pure clay of time's m.	MALA 641:4
Science is angling in the m.	HUXL 507:76
sees the m., and one sees the stars	LANG 579:68
shining gull-marked m.	LARK 581:9
stream that ends in m.	LOWE 616:79
muddied The people m.	SHAK 892:66
muddle Ah, Rachel, aw a m.!	DICK 325:44
beginning, a m., and an end	LARK 582:21
intellectual m. early	MURD 714:60
meddle and m.	DERBY 316:69
solve...the m. with humaneness	WILS 1084:18
muddy to m. or mock	PALEY 751:61
muffin Hot M. ...Company	DICK 321:43
mug Poetry...a m.'s game	ELIOT 370:15
muir-men m.-m. win their hay	BALL -101:29
mulberry tarrying in m. shade	SHAK 871:57
mule m. of politics	DISR 332:83
not as the horse, or as the m.	BIBLE 115:59
Sicilian m. was to me	GLAD 429:56
smelt a lot of m. manure	WILL 1081:49
mules m. ...accustomed to burdens	RICH 810:68
multifarious another of the m. ways	SITW 941:29
multiplication m. of the fittest	SPEN 955:66
multiplied m. itself in broad ways	REYES 807:22
multiply be fruitful and m.	BIBLE 102:86
multitude another to the m.	HAWT 461:71
by reason of this great m.	BIBLE 112:90
cover the m. of sins	BIBLE 156:82
for the m. to be ingrateful	SHAK 911:9

multitude (*contd.*)

From an exemplary m.	VIAN 1043:48
great m. spread their garments	BIBLE 139:30
hide a m. of sins	BIBLE 155:74
m. of one million	KOES 568:67
m. of perverse inclinations	SHAR 919:82
M. too familiar	LEST 599:13
m., which no man could number	BIBLE 157:14
sprung in affluent m.	TWAIN 1034:98
stupidity of the m.	BAUD 77:28
washed his hands before the m.	BIBLE 140:53

multitudes I contain m.

rank me with barbarous m.	SHAK 874:30
seeing the m., he went up	BIBLE 133:34
Weeping, weeping m.	ELIOT 368:73

mum fuck you up, your m.

merryman moping m.	GILB 425:94
M., the Persil-user	BETJ 100:51
oafish louts remember M.	BETJ 100:46
when m. stays at home	FALU 382:57

mumble Let her maunder and m.

m. with great coherence	GREE 445:34
when in doubt, m.	WAGN 1047:27

mummies make the m. dance

	LIND 605:9

mummy had his M.'s leave

	KIPL 562:75
M., I'm sick with disgust	BETJ 101:56

munched And m., and m., and m.

	SHAK 906:12

mundane miraculous to the m.

	DIDI 330:45

mundus pereat m.

	FERD 385:13

Munster sun that was M.'s glory

	ORAH 741:78

mural purest…is the m.

	OROZ 741:83

murals m. on the wall

	BETJ 101:54

murder anyone meditating m.

	FISH 389:81
brought back m. into the home	HITC 482:25
call it m.	MAXT 665:99
commit rape, m.	BARN 72:26
dens of robbery and m.	NATI 721:90
hard to tell it fr'm m.	DUNNE 356:60
in five years…ready to commit m.	DAMR 304:54
love and m. will out	CONG 280:9
Macbeth does m. sleep	SHAK 908:46
man indulges himself in m.	DEQU 316:68
man wants to m. a tiger	SHAW 923:68
met M. on the way	SHEL 928:78
Most sacreligious m.	SHAK 908:52
m. and to ravish	AYTO 53:85
M. doesn't round out	HAMM 454:61
m., hate, vertue	MALO 642:35
m., homicide	STUB 980:13
M. is a unique crime	JAMES 517:35
M. is always a mistake	WILDE 1076:49
M. most foul	SHAK 889:75
M….One of the Fine Arts	DEQU 316:67
m. shrieks out	WEBS 1061:64
M., though it have no tongue	SHAK 890:17
m. to dissect	WORD 1094:3
M. wol out	CHAU 255:46
no vicious blot, m.	SHAK 902:99
one m. made a villain	PORT 784:40
rape and m.	NOON 731:24
scymitars wi' m. crusted	BURNS 211:18
Sooner m. an infant	BLAKE 166:7
took m. out of the Venetian vase	CHAN 251:50
Treason and m.	SHAK 880:76
war, I call it m.	LOWE 616:80
war…I think it m.	PAINE 750:43
warfare, terror, m.	WELL 1063:1

murdered all that I had m.

	SHAK 863:65
except the m.'s	HAMM 454:61
Glamis hath m. sleep	SHAK 908:47
m. them 0–0	SHAN 919:76
one a m. self	ROSS 824:90
recently m. woman	SHAR 919:86
their m. man	KEATS 546:82

murderèd son of the dear m.

	SHAK 890:16

murderer m. for a fancy prose

	NABO 717:97
m. from the beginning	BIBLE 146:51
m., to be a politician	MILL 679:57
sometimes the m.'s	HAMM 454:61
the man is a common m.	SAKI 838:12
you must bear his m.	YEATS 1107:95

murderers of whores and m.

	WEBS 1060:36

murderous m. hate

	SHAK 912:46

murders m. sticking on his hands

	SHAK 910:79

murk only adds to the m.

	MILL 679:54

murmur live m. of a summer's day

	ARNO 37:86
m. about the name	RUSK 830:88
m. among the zealots	HUME 504:12
m., soon replies	MILT 686:81

murmurings noise of m.

	BIBLE 131:79

murmurs In hollow m. died away

	COLL 277:51

muscle m. of my nation

	FRAN 402:16
not the extra m.	TRUE 1029:15
take the m. from the bone	ELIOT 370:34

muscles call his m. into action

	POE 775:42
girls with the m. of a welter-weight	WODE 1089:94
m. of his brawny arms	LONG 611:97
relax your m.	MOSS 711:8
She had the rippling m.	PERE 766:92

muscular His Christianity was m.

	DISR 334:25

muse brash courtship of the m.

	THOM 1013:22
'Fool,' said my M. to me	SIDN 937:51
invocation of the M.	GRAV 440:27
Let my M.	HERR 477:58
Livelier liquor than the M.	HOUS 495:63
loving foreign a m.	BENET 90:61
meditate the thankless m.	MILT 684:42
M. invoked	SWIFT 985:2
m. is…of the English strain	DRAY 345:32
m. of Moore	BYRON 222:38
M. shall sit, and think	GRAY 441:56
O for a m. of fire	SHAK 880:70
Perversity is the m.	SONT 953:5
provokes the snarling m.	JOHN 525:79
same soil as the M.	UNTE 1036:47
shelter, and even m.	TUCH 1031:48
spelt by the unlettered m.	GRAY 442:73
Tell me, M.	HOMER 488:24
The tenth M.	TROL 1027:62
trivial people should m. and thunder	LAWR 587:3
Who loves not…the heavenly m.	DOWL 342:79
Why does my M. only speak	SMITH 948:36

muses Among the M.

	WYATT 1102:26
M.' garden	CAREW 232:12
m. gave their full consent	LANY 580:81
M. in striped trousers	ORWE 744:36
M. sing of happy swains	CRAB 293:70
priest of the M.	HORA 493:21
sweet M. of Light	RUSK 831:13
who brings the Smithfield M.	POPE 782:91

museum in the South Kensington M.

	KING 559:5
marbled m. of the soul	RODR 819:89
mind is a m.	RAINE 800:10
m. of antiquities	ENGE 378:90
You're the Louvr' M.	PORT 784:33

museums art m. to worship dead works

	MAYA 665:4
department stores…like m.	WARH 1053:23
free her from the numberless m.	MARI 651:68
In all m. throughout the world	PATE 760:98

mush m. and slush

	OWEN 747:5

mushroom I am…a m.

	FORD 397:11
Life…too short to stuff a m.	CONR 285:15
m. which has poisoned	MILL 677:21

mushrooms Patriots…like m.

	WALP 1052:99

music advised to give her m.

	SHAK 916:2
after the m. had finished	HELP 469:9
All m. is folk m.	ARMS 35:47

music (*contd.*)

Appalling Popularity of M.	LAMB 577:46
as Beethoven was born for m.	PELE 764:51
Beer, tobacco, and m.	MANN 645:79
Bells, the poor man's only m.	COLE 274:99
Birds warbling all the m.	COWP 293:53
British m….perpetual promise	BEEC 82:18
by that m….embrace	SHAK 876:73
Canned m. …audible wallpaper	COOKE 286:33
century…deserves its own m.	DEBU 311:70
city is built to m.	TENN 1004:55
compulsion doth in m. lie	MILT 683:17
cosume it in m.	MONT 700:54
creation of m. is…natural	COLE 273:78
daughters of m. shall be brought low	BIBLE 123:42
day the m. died	MACL 633:61
day the m. died	MACL 633:63
did enjoy the m.	JOHN 524:69
Discord oft in m.	SPEN 957:97
Do not take up m.	BOUL 181:41
doesn't want new m.	HONE 488:30
Don't just move to the m.	MARL 652:83
don't know anything about m.	BEER 83:35
ear for her m.	DAYL 310:55
Ear's deep-sweet m.	SHAK 864:95
English may not like m.	BEEC 82:11
essence of m.	MOZA 711:19
ethereal m.	GALL 413:97
everything seems to happen to m.	WILL 1081:56
existence like a piece of m.	MACB 624:31
face the m. and dance	BERL 95:61
finds its food in m.	LILLO 604:95
function of m. is to release us	BEEC 83:19
go twang, and you've got m.	VICI 1043:49
good m. and a clean conscience	HIND 481:13
Good m….penetrates the ear	BEEC 82:13
good old m.	HAWES 460:61
heard the m.'s din	GILB 424:63
how he wants this m. played	TOSC 1024:8
How irksome is this m.	SHAK 861:1
how our m. should be played	GILL 426:11
How potent cheap m. is	COWA 290:95
How sour sweet m. is	SHAK 868:71
How sweet his m.!	WORD 1094:2
humour, its m.	ROLL 821:26
I don't know anything about m.	PRES 789:25
I got m.	GERS 420:8
I'm a martyr to m.	THOM 1011:80
If m. be the food of love	SHAK 893:91
If one hears bad m.	WILDE 1076:48
If that was m.	FAURE 384:91
If the king loves m.	MENC 668:55
In sweet m. is such art	SHAK 918:54
inexpressible is m.	HUXL 507:63
Is there a meaning to m.?	COPL 288:55
It isn't just m.	PARK 753:86
jazz m. is a style	MORT 710:98
learn a sense of m.	JOHN 524:66
Let m. sound	SHAK 872:79
let the sound of m.	SHAK 873:98
lights, the m., and revelry	HAWT 461:77
Like harmony in m.	WORD 1096:21
Like m. on my heart	COLE 274:94
like Wagner's m. better	WILDE 1076:47
little m. in the name Jack	WILDE 1077:77
little m. out of doors	KEATS 545:67
live entirely in my m.	BEET 84:50
Look out for this man's m.	PARRY 756:44
make the m. mute	TENN 1002:5
man that hath no m.	SHAK 873:98
man who can read m.	BEEC 82:10
May make one m.	TENN 998:18
M. …all your cares beguile	DRYD 351:62
M. alone with sudden charms	CONG 282:47

music (*contd.*)

M. and women I…give way to	PEPYS 765:78
m. begins to atrophy	POUND 786:77
m. can't be heard	MACL 634:80
m. crept by me	SHAK 916:24
m. feedeth that disposition	BACON 60:34
m. from a farther room	ELIOT 367:49
m. from the sounds	MACC 625:40
m. …greater than its performance	PREV 789:27
m. has a taste	GRIEG 447:59
M. has charms to soothe	CONG 281:21
m. hath a far more pleasing sound	SHAK 915:92
M. helps not the toothache	HERB 476:39
m. in its roar	BYRON 220:5
m. in the air	ELGAR 364:97
m. in the sighing of a reed	BYRON 223:63
m. in the spacings of the spheres	PYTH 796:46
m. is a gift and a burden	SIMO 939:84
M. is feeling	STEV 971:42
M. is life	NIEL 727:67
M. is Love in search	LANI 579:76
M. is my mistress	ELLI 374:7
M. is no different from opium	KHOM 555:45
M. is the art of sounds	BUSO 215:92
M. is the best means	AUDEN 49:4
m. is the brandy	SHAW 921:32
M. is the great cheer-up language	ODETS 736:91
m. is the least disagreeable	JOHN 532:42
M. is the poor man's Parnassus	EMER 378:79
M. is the universal language	LONG 611:93
m. is universal	GILL 426:12
M. is your own experience	PARK 753:87
M., Maestro, Please	MAGI 638:58
m. marreth men's manners	GALE 412:89
M. might tame and civilize	GAY 417:60
m.—m., moody food	SHAK 905:73
m. of Broadway	GERS 420:9
m. of forfended spheres	PATM 760:11
m. of his own vain tongue	SHAK 865:10
m. of its trees	ARNO 37:75
M. oft hath such a charm	SHAK 897:86
m. on diverse subjects	VIAN 1043:48
m. piercing that solitude	THOM 1012:2
M. says nothing to the reason	BURG 206:93
m. she learned in bed	WILM 1084:9
m. soars within the…lark	BROW 197:21
m. that changed a man's decision	SCHN 848:84
m. that expresses…nothing	BART 75:89
M. that gentlier	TENN 994:49
m. that I care to hear	HOPK 491:79
M., the greatest good	ADDI 6:97
M. to hear	SHAK 912:45
M. was invented to deceive	EPHO 379:95
M. when soft voices	SHEL 932:70
M. with dinner is an insult	CHES 260:48
m.…with its voluptuous swell	BYRON 219:84
m., yearning like a God	KEATS 546:88
My m. is best understood	STRA 979:3
My m. is not modern	SCHO 849:89
New m.?	ELLI 374:6
night…filled with m.	LONG 611:4
no m. in the nightingale	SHAK 860:84
not for the doctrine, but the m.	POPE 778:83
one takes the m. too fast	SAIN 837:95
opera…is to m.	MENC 669:66
Our mirth the m.	RALE 800:14
piece for orchestra without m.	RAVEL 802:44
Poetry is m.	ANGE 20:33
Poetry must be read as m.	POUND 785:55
Pop m. is the classical m.of now	MACC 626:60
primitive m. and primitive medicine	LEAC 589:40
reactions to art or to m.	COLE 273:79
serious about this m.	ZWER 1110:29

music (*contd.*)

set to more or less lascivious m.	MENC 669:61
shall be made Thy M.	DONNE 338:18
so much m. in my head	RAVEL 802:43
soul of m. shed	MOORE 706:36
sound of m.	HAMM 454:57
still, sad m.	WORD 1094:98
stop when there's no more m.	ARMS 35:45
strong m. in my soul	COLE 274:7
struck one chord of m.	PROC 792:76
sweet m. is such art	SHAK 918:56
sweetest m. to a woeful mind	SIDN 937:49
taught me…to face the m.	HEAN 465:43
that's what m.'s all about	HEND 472:56
theorizing about m.	HEINE 467:13
thou hast thy m. too	KEATS 547:5
thy beauty's Silent m.	CAMP 228:38
thy chosen m.	WORD 1099:74
time is the medium of m.	MANN 646:86
to write American m.	THOM 1015:61
To write m. is to raise a ladder	HONE 488:29
Wagner's m. is better	TWAIN 1034:21
we provide the m.	STOK 977:71
well set to m.	ADDI 7:8
What m. is more enchanting	SMITH 947:15
when I hear sweet m.	SHAK 873:2
when you listen to m.	GAUG 416:40
Who loves not m.	DOWL 342:79
Why is Schoenberg's M. so Hard	BERG 94:39
why m. was ordain'd!	SHAK 864:80
Without m., life	NIET 729:92
worth expressing in m.	DELI 315:43
write m. like Wagner	GOLD 434:38
Your lordship…is fond of m.	SHER 933:91
music-halls no more jokes in M.-h.	SASS 845:22
musical happier still is that m.	AGATE 10:63
Hell is full of m. amateurs	SHAW 921:32
no rules…of m. composition	SHAW 925:30
Which is more m.	CAGE 225:89
musicals m.…about…1950's	MACI 631:41
musician amateur jazz m.	LYTT 621:68
main thing a m. would like to do	COLT 277:58
no one but a professional m.	BUTL 218:44
rather bitter British m.	WILM 1084:9
resources of a m.	MORR 709:89
You could be a great m.	DAVIS 309:31
musicians appear…To all m.	AUDEN 48:79
Jazz m. are	TURN 1031:51
M. don't retire	ARMS 35:45
m. listen to see who	MING 695:63
M. paint their pictures	STOK 977:71
M. wrestle everywhere	DICK 327:94
older m. like me	FREE 403:30
thousand poor m.	VAUG 1040:13
'tis we m. know	BROW 199:74
musicked Playing in m. gravity	AVIS 53:76
musicologist m.…can read music	BEEC 82:10
musing Love of Peace, and lonely m.	COLL 277:51
M. on roses	RAND 801:24
musk m. of the rose is blown	TENN 1001:85
musk-rose m.-r., full	KEATS 548:17
violet, The m.-r.	MILT 684:47
musk-roses sweet m.-r.	SHAK 870:39
muskets m. and machine guns	MUSS 716:87
Muslims home to…Jews, M.	CLIN 269:18
mussel And the m. pooled	THOM 1010:68
mussels gaping m.	CRAB 294:43
Mussolini Hitler…loyalty to M.	BULL 204:51
M. had been at Oxford	HALI 452:26
must All other things m.	SCHI 847:64
'M.' is not to be used to princes!	ELIZ 373:93
rather than when you m.	SHUL 936:33
mustard have faith as a grain of m.	BIBLE 138:16
heaven is like to a grain of m.	BIBLE 138:3

mustard (*contd.*)

hot dog without the m.	CHAR 253:93
sowed in youth a m. seed	BRON 190:91
mutability m. in them doth play	SPEN 959:40
Nought may endure but M.	SHEL 927:64
strange m. of human affairs	DICK 320:17
mutations through all its m.	TRIL 1027:61
mute long since m.	KEATS 547:96
make the music m.	TENN 1002:5
M. and magnificent	DRYD 350:44
m. on Tara's walls	MOORE 706:36
use those languages, or we remain m.	BALL 68:64
voices of liberty be m.?	CUMM 300:84
mutilation corset is…a m.	VEBL 1041:25
mutton kill their own m.	EDGE 361:33
mutual gulf of m. incomprehension	SNOW 950:73
m. objective to allow	STEV 973:84
muzzle m. of the revolver	GREE 444:22
shalt not m. the ox	BIBLE 108:96
my-lorded and m.-l. him	THAC 1006:83
myopia means to treat m.	PRATT 789:24
m. makes all error mortal	LOWE 617:9
myriad inspector, with a m. eyes	STEAD 964:8
There died a m.	POUND 786:66
myriads outshine M. though bright	MILT 687:91
myrrh get me to the mountain of m.	BIBLE 124:51
gold, and frankincense, and m.	BIBLE 133:24
m. sweet bleeding	SPEN 957:99
myrtle instead of the brier…the m.	BIBLE 127:8
leaves of m.	MARL 655:31
m. and ivy	BYRON 223:65
sails through m. bow'rs	POPE 779:21
secure all the m. and turkey	AUST 51:48
myrtles m. brown, with ivy	MILT 684:38
myself being always with m.	GIRO 429:47
can't even tell it m.	GREE 445:30
consciousness of m.	KANT 541:99
cry for m.…cry for all	AGUS 10:72
estranged from m.	HUGO 501:64
girl I saw was m.	RHYS 808:31
In awe…of m.	SHAK 882:19
in order to save m.	HELL 468:93
into what I call m.	HUME 503:1
lose mine honour I lose m.	SHAK 904:53
quite m. again	HOUS 494:46
searched for m. across time	CIXO 267:73
too busy thinking about m.	SITW 941:18
mysteries childlike m.	JAUR 519:71
deepest m. of creation	SHEL 926:53
display her secret m.	HARV 460:55
m. and complications	GELL 417:68
understand all m.	BIBLE 150:62
mysterious m. and marvelous	THOR 1016:69
something m. Find it.	MAUP 665:97
mystery as an ineffable m.	SCHW 852:31
at the…bottom…lies a m.	ORWE 744:43
confound strangeness with m.	DOYLE 343:86
Death is the only m.	SKEL 942:41
death's m.	HOOD 489:49
divine m. in things	DOST 341:48
do not have to solve all the m.	HERN 476:44
fathomless m.	BUEC 203:42
lose myself in a m.	BROW 195:74
love is a m.	LAFO 575:85
Married life requires shared m.	FORD 397:22
M., Babylon The Great	BIBLE 158:28
m. behind knowledge	FRYE 408:24
m. is its life	BAGE 61:61
m. is why we collect these figures	BART 75:87
m. of life	WHITE 1070:41
m.…Of the glorious Body	AQUI 32:5
m. of things	SHAK 904:26
m. of words	WORD 1096:29
m. to the world	LONG 612:20

mystery (contd.)

m. which defies solution	MORT 710:95
Out of silence m. comes	DARK 305:78
realise the m.	LAO 580:83
remain a m. to us	RUNGE 829:56
riddle wrapped inside a m.	CHUR 264:11
separates us from the m.	HUGO 502:80
shew you a m.	BIBLE 151:72
Some m. should be left	WILL 1081:66
space was the uncontrollable m.	MACL 635:92
ultimate m. of nature	PLAN 772:84
verbs and the m.	SAND 841:73
voice., a m.	WORD 1097:39

mystic how a m. shape did move — BROW 196:14

m. way	GILB 424:66
white samite, m., wonderful	TENN 1003:34
with thy m. fan	HERR 477:57

mystical most beautiful...the m. — EINS 363:67

m. drama of the animal life — AMIS 17:85

mysticism m., melancholy! — GAUT 416:41

mystification intensity by m. — WHITE 1070:26

statue of m. — DICK 326:56

mystique phoney m. — BRES 187:36

myth courtesan is a m. — FLAU 392:36

History is the m., the true m.	MILL 679:48
inscrutability of the East is...a m.	STARK 963:98
lend a m. to G.	CRANE 294:97
modern of psychoanalysis	THOM 1009:48
m. before the m. began	STEV 971:52
M. deals in false universals	CART 242:94
m. rather than history	FIED 387:38
m. that if you're liked	HOCK 483:48
M., whereof I sing	CRANE 295:7
poem...is a little m.	WARR 1054:31
sceptred m. to hold	RUSS 833:38
starting point is m.	FRAME 400:77
thing itself and not the m.	RICH 809:49

mythical built about a m. figure — HERB 474:2

The m. America — RABAN 798:76

mythologies old m. — YEATS 1105:49

mythology Literature is conscious m. — FRYE 408:21

m. of self — STEV 971:45

nabobs nattering n. — AGNEW 10:70

Naboth dogs licked the blood of N. — BIBLE 111:71

nace N. Novels that is — WELLS 1064:31

nag bob-tail n. — FOST 399:59

forced gait of a shuffling n. — SHAK 876:59

Nagasaki even in the ruins of N. — BRON 190:78

Naiad N. airs have brought me home — POE 776:47

nail breadth of my n. — SWIFT 984:82

Dick...blows his n.	SHAK 866:30
for want of a n.	FRAN 402:7
n. by strength	SHAK 860:80
put her hand to the n.	BIBLE 109:14
smote the n. into his temples	BIBLE 109:13

nails 'As n.,' added Charley — DICK 321:37

beauty with my n.	SHAK 861:99
blouse out and her n. grimed	MANS 647:97
blowing of his n.	SHAK 862:21
half a dozen pounds of n.	CONR 285:13
in his hands the print of n.	BIBLE 147:76
naebody's n. can reach	SCOTT 855:92
n. bitten and pared	MACA 623:4
n. like birds' claws	BIBLE 129:47
n. whitter than the lylye flour	CHAU 255:45
nineteen hundred and forty n.	SITW 941:16
of my feet and my n.	NERU 723:8
sellin' tinpinny n.	DUNNE 356:60
these vain weak n.	SHAK 868:30
upsetting of a bag of n.	RUSK 831:11

naïve Our people are not n. — REYES 807:22

naked blind and n. Ignorance — TENN 1002:9

clothe my n. villainy — SHAK 863:53

naked (contd.)

enterprise in walking n.	YEATS 1105:69
Helpless, n., piping loud	BLAKE 167:94
knew that they were n.	BIBLE 103:95
lest he walk n.	BIBLE 158:26
n....and not ashamed	BIBLE 103:92
N. and stone-like	FREE 404:34
N. and the Dead	MAIL 638:66
N., and ye clothed me	BIBLE 140:44
N. came I out of my mother's womb	BIBLE 112:95
n. in the dark and cold	LEGU 594:23
n. into conference chamber	BEVAN 101:69
n. is the best disguise	CONG 280:10
n. lunch a tune	GINS 427:23
n. moment in politics	GERG 420:1
N. she lay	ROCH 816:44
n. shingles of the world	ARNO 36:64
n. to mine enemies	SHAK 918:62
n. to the hangman's noose	HOUS 494:43
poets have to go n.	SART 844:6
Poor n. wretches	SHAK 903:24
Th' have left thee n., Lord	CRAS 296:20
wallow in n. in December snow	SHAK 866:47
When a was n.	SHAK 877:1
Who told thee thou wast n.?	BIBLE 103:96
whore may be n.	KILP 556:64
With n. foot, stalking	WYATT 1103:30

nakedness n., an art stripped — MOTH 711:10

n. of Stalinist dictatorship	KENN 550:52
n. of the land	BIBLE 105:45
n. of woman	BLAKE 166:78
not in utter n.	WORD 1098:51

name another n. more free — POPE 779:9

answered to his n.	THAC 1007:99
as its n. imported	THAC 1006:81
as my poor n. rehearse	SHAK 914:72
bless his holy n.	BIBLE 118:11
brother's n.	SWIN 988:55
called thee by thy n.	BIBLE 126:93
called them by n.	MOORE 704:6
ches, so was the n.	CHAU 254:3
cometh in the n. of the Lord	BIBLE 118:28
dare not speak its n.	DOUG 341:49
Death is a n. for beauty	LAYT 588:23
deed without a n.	SHAK 909:66
different n. for conversation	STER 969:98
done in the n. of 'decency'	LEWIS 602:61
ease, content, whate'er thy n.	POPE 781:49
Every n. is a tune	MOORE 705:22
extraordinary n. to give a maid!	SAKI 837:4
followed in its n.	CRANE 294:91
for his own n.'s sake	SCOT 856:19
For my n. and memory	BACON 60:30
forfeit of their n.	HABI 450:1
forgotten your n.	SWIN 987:43
Forth in thy n.	WESL 1066:64
Freedom, what liberties...in thy n.	GEOR 419:91
give you your n.	ELUA 376:24
good n. it is	DICK 320:22
good n.'s seldom got	WYCH 1103:33
great N. we praise	SMITH 950:61
Guess her n.	ANON 24:12
Halloo your n.	SHAK 894:6
hallowed thy fair n.	SHAK 915:87
hast not denied my n.	BIBLE 157:5
have you lose that n.	MASS 663:62
He has no other n.	WINT 1087:67
He that is without n.	SCOTT 855:84
hope you guess my n.	JAGG 515:96
hotter n. Than any in hell	SHAK 910:88
house...hallowed for my n.	BIBLE 111:56
how excellent is thy n.	BIBLE 114:34
I am become a n.	TENN 994:58
if your n.'s above the fold	LANCE 578:53

name (contd.)

in the n. of duty and obedience	SNOW 951:76
In the n. of the Constitution	STAL 962:78
inscrutable singular n.	ELIOT 371:40
Jack...a charming n.	WILDE 1077:77
Jew is only the n.	MILL 677:6
kept them in thy n.	BIBLE 146:67
killing time Is only the n.	SITW 941:29
known by the n. of perseverance	STER 969:93
laud and magnify thy glorious N.	BOOK 174:28
lesser than my n.	SHAK 867:61
Let me not n.	SHAK 900:52
liberal shepherds give a grosser n.	SHAK 892:71
local habitation and a n.	SHAK 871:55
lose the n. of action	TWAIN 1033:89
lose The n. of King	SHAK 867:62
magnify thy holy N.	BOOK 174:16
Man by a scribbled n.	THOM 1010:57
man of my n.	NAPO 719:39
Marrying left your maiden n.	LARK 581:4
mentioned your n.	DOYLE 344:12
more common than the n. friend	LAFO 575:94
much less his n.?	WALC 1048:33
murmur about the n.	RUSK 830:88
My n. ...a household word	ASHB 41:58
My n. is Death	SOUT 954:42
My n. is on the building	FORD 397:10
My n. is Ozymandias	SHEL 928:93
n. all the men	MACC 625:42
N. and date	BUNT 204:57
n. any disease after two guys	PUZO 796:44
n. everyone gives	WILDE 1077:63
n. flows on forever	SASS 846:42
n. for problems...headaches	ACHE 3:41
n. ...in honor of my father	PENN 764:56
n. in man and woman	SHAK 899:31
n. is MacGregor!	SCOTT 855:89
n. is Might-have-been	ROSS 825:93
n. is on your waters	SIGO 938:71
n. is Truthful James	HARTE 459:49
n. not bound to anything	WINT 1087:67
n. of an Australian be equal	PARK 755:31
n. of Ireland is mentioned	SMITH 949:42
n. of pictures produces	MORSE 709:90
n. of royalty	LABO 572:34
n. of the beast	BIBLE 158:22
n. of the late deceased	KIPL 561:45
n. of the Lord thy God in vain	BIBLE 106:68
n. of wife seems more blessed	HELO 469:41
n. shall be called Wonderful	BIBLE 125:66
n. to be put forward	HESE 479:79
n. upon the strand	SPEN 959:28
n. was invented by novelists	WELLS 1064:36
n. was small	EGAN 362:55
n. were John D Smith IV	ROCK 817:72
n. which is above every n.	BIBLE 153:8
Nature is but a n.	COWP 293:64
New York, thy n. is irreverence	HUXT 509:9
No one...has just one n.	AMADO 15:63
none other n. under heaven	BIBLE 147:84
object behind that n.	SPEN 956:88
one whose n. was writ in water	KEATS 548:22
only a woman in n.	GOTT 436:72
our very n. as Englishmen	PITT 771:72
pass my n. in large letters	TREE 1025:43
People you know, yet can't quite n.	LARK 582:17
Puritan decadence regards the n.	SPEN 956:88
ravished with the whistling of a n.	POPE 781:51
refuse thy n.	SHAK 868:87
remember the n. of the Lord	BIBLE 114:41
sacred n. of Smith	CHES 258:95
shade of a great n.	LUCAN 618:22
someone wants to know my n.	MONT 702:78
sons acclaim you glorious n.	CUMM 299:83

name (*contd.*)

spell my n. right	COHAN 272:70
stranger…calls you by your first n.	KUHN 570:13
strong n. of the Trinity	ALEX 13:21
sweet the n. of Jesus	NEWT 725:44
terror of his n.	BEAU 80:75
that n. for the last four centuries	WEIL 1061:78
their n. liveth for evermore	BIBLE 133:18
Their N. Liveth	KIPL 565:21
thought of his n.	ELIOT 371:40
thy n. in high account	SCOTT 853:53
thy n. is woman	SHAK 888:54
Thy N., O Jesu	HOW 497:90
To n. the unnamable	RUSH 829:68
to that n. my courage	SHAK 906:6
to thy n. give glory	BIBLE 159:46
under any other n.	DOYLE 344:2
underfoot her honest n.	SPEN 958:14
weak witness of thy n.	MILT 681:94
wealth and a good n.	WALT 1052:2
What is thy n.?	BIBLE 141:64
What is your n.?	SHAK 917:31
what the dickens his n. is	SHAK 878:18
what was done in his n.	BENN 90:66
What's in a n.?	SHAK 868:88
Why should that n. be sounded	SHAK 882:21
With a n. like yours	CARR 240:64
without a n.	SCHW 852:31
write against your n.	RICE 809:38
write your glorious n.	SPEN 959:28
Yossarian? Is that his n.?	HELL 468:83
your n. moves, Leonora	CRAIK 294:90
nameless n. in worthy deeds	BROW 196:2
names American n.	BENET 90:59
Called him soft n.	KEATS 548:18
called them by wrong n.	BROW 199:58
calleth them all by their n.	BIBLE 120:54
cat must have Three Different N.	ELIOT 371:39
commodity of good n.	SHAK 875:38
enter the n. and hand the keys	MANS 647:3
five handmaidens, whose n.	ROSS 824:83
For your n.	WEBS 1060:36
forgets words as one forgets n.	WAUGH 1057:3
given their n. up to her	JONS 536:19
Home of…unpopular n.	ARNO 38:10
How can they use such n.	SASS 845:40
live like our n.	WALC 1048:34
live so long in our n.	BROW 196:98
lost all the n.	JOHN 531:18
men whose n. you never knew	ARLO 34:37
men's n. On sand	MILT 683:24
n.…associated…with racehorses	SAKI 837:1
n. in print	CHES 260:39
n. of blasphemy	BIBLE 158:28
n. of dogs	AMIS 17:85
n. of those who in their lives	SPEN 956:72
n. to be mentioned	AUST 51:42
our n.…as household words	SHAK 882:2
spare the grossness of the n.	DRYD 351:63
what are n. but air?	COLE 274:2
naming n. of parts	REED 804:80
Nanda N. Devi Basin	SHIP 935:22
Nanki-Poo Long life to N.-P.	GILB 425:83
nanny n. seemed to be extinct	HOGG 485:68
Nantucket spewed N. bones	LOWE 616:94
nap short n. at sermon	ADDI 7:11
Naples now N. holds me	VIRG 1046:96
Napoleon Maybe N. was wrong	STOP 978:79
N. did not manoeuvre	WELL 1063:11
N. had commanded	ORWE 744:31
N. learned from mistakes	TAYL 991:12
N. of crime	DOYLE 344:8
N. thinks that I am a fool	ALEX 13:15
signs of N.'s greatness	UNSE 1036:46

Napoleon (*contd.*)

wanted to be N.	DALI 303:44
Napoleons Caesars and N.	HUXL 507:75
napper from your n. to your feet	COLL 276:37
narcissistically reflecting…n.	TALE 990:87
narcotics Like dull n.	TENN 998:19
narration life as n.	MANN 645:81
time is the medium of n.	MANN 646:86
narrative construct a n. for ourselves	AUST 52:71
motive in this n.	TWAIN 1032:76
n. impulse is always with us	COOV 287:48
no longer…fiction…only n.	DOCT 334:40
narratives conceive of our lives as n.	LEHM 594:35
narrow bestride the n. world	SHAK 882:20
cucumber is	SITW 941:9
margin is too n.	FERM 386:24
n. straight channels	RANJ 801:27
path…sometimes is too n.	DRYD 348:87
straight and n. as a tomb	SMITH 948:31
narrow-necked as with n.-n. bottles	POPE 779:16
narrow-souled It is with n.-s. people	POPE 779:16
Nasticreechia N. Krorluppia	LEAR 590:67
nastier anything n. to say	SAYE 846:49
Blood…a great deal n.	SOME 952:99
nasty everybody is as n. as himself	SHAW 920:91
far from their n. little minds	DEBU 311:68
how n. the n. people are	POWE 788:9
of n. ideas	SWIFT 985:92
Something n. in the woodshed	GIBB 422:35
Zip that turns n.	CHRI 261:71
nation affairs of the n.	AMERY 16:69
America…only idealistic n.	WILS 1086:56
American n. will speak	ROOS 822:45
any n. where Christianity	SWIFT 986:18
any other n. may be its workshop	CHAM 249:14
arm the n.	MANC 644:80
as a n. taste-blind	FISH 390:85
as a n., we don't dress well	SHAW 920:4
asset for one n.	RUNC 828:52
be a n. of shopkeepers	PUNCH 795:24
bedrooms of the n.	TRUD 1029:11
best serves his n.	KENN 552:87
Better one suffer, than a n. grieve	DRYD 349:21
bind up the n.'s wounds	LINC 605:6
British are an aggressive n.	ABSE 1:9
broad mass of a n.	HITL 482:28
build the n.'s fate	BLAKE 168:5
common property of the n.	TIMES 1021:71
continent a new n.	LINC 605:4
credit of the n.	CONG 281:27
curse of me and my n.	POUND 786:69
darlings of our n.	SHAK 898:2
doing it to a whole n.	SIHA 938:72
every man and n.	LOWE 616:78
every man of every n.	THAC 1007:96
existence as a n.	PITT 771:72
Explaining metaphysics to the n.	BYRON 221:25
exterminate a n.	SPOCK 961:62
fate as a n.	HOFS 484:63
fetishism…God of this n.	TATE 991:6
fourth-class n.	JAY 519:76
general synod of the n.	BAIL 62:72
government of a n.	SUN 982:39
great and powerful n.	GARI 415:24
great n. betrayed	INOU 512:59
half of the n. is mad	SMOL 950:62
happiness of the n.	JOHN 528:52
history of our n.	TOOLE 1023:4
holy n.	BIBLE 156:78
I want to talk to a n.	PULI 795:19
in any one n.	HUME 504:11
influence of a n.	BENN 90:62
inspired the n.	CHUR 265:41
integrity of the Irish n.	REDM 804:75

nation (*contd.*)

little war for a great n.	WELL 1064:17
living Jury of the N.	BENN 92:3
lowest rank of every n.	JOHN 527:26
make war on a kindred n.	BETH 99:22
most decent n.	BUSH 215:86
muscle of my n.	FRAN 402:2
n. about to go into…liquidation	MACI 631:45
n. …against n.	BIBLE 124:57
n. being so right	WILS 1086:47
n. blesses what undoes it	HUGO 502:77
n.'s experience and his vision	KISS 566:39
N.'s Freight Handler	SAND 841:57
n. has always been committed	KENN 550:64
n. heaps its scorn	LAZA 588:27
n. is a rainbow	JACK 514:87
n. is a society united	INGE 511:40
n. is not governed	BURKE 206:6
n. is the universality	MAZZ 666:13
n. not slow and dull	MILT 686:73
n. of gentlemen	MUGA 711:20
n. of shopkeepers	NAPO 718:34
n. of shopkeepers	SMITH 945:92
n. of shopkeepers	STOP 978:79
n. of violence	JORD 536:92
n. ruled by swine	THOM 1014:74
n.…run by old man	BROD 189:67
n. seems to slouch onward	HOFS 484:62
n. shall rise against n.	BIBLE 139:37
n. should commit itself	KENN 551:66
n. suspects…regular ministerial	WHIT 1069:16
n. talking to itself	MILL 677:21
n., to remain healthy	MUSS 716:88
n. to the policy	ROOS 821:35
n. was ever blessed with	FRAN 402:8
n.'s whole scale of living	CHUR 263:17
n.…without a sense of beauty	WHAR 1068:93
needed to constitute a n.?	SIEY 938:69
nobility of descent in a n.	POTT 785:44
nobody…or I'm a n.	WALC 1048:32
our greatness as a n.	THAT 1007:10
parcel of rogues in a n.!	BURNS 212:31
personification of the n.	PAST 759:88
puissant n. rousing herself	MILT 686:75
realm, n., or city	KNOX 567:57
reform a n.	CARL 234:45
rich and lazy n.	KIPL 564:21
service of this n.	GAND 414:11
social life of our n.	LEWIS 601:48
tell the ideals of a n.	DOUG 342:62
that we are a n. of amateurs	ROSE 822:54
things that matter for a n.	LLOY 608:52
thinking in terms of n. states	ADEN 8:44
to enrich a new n.	STIG 977:66
trade union for the n.	HEATH 466:53
train for war…a n.	WILS 1086:50
Type of a coming n.	LAWS 588:20
up to the face of a n.	ROCK 818:77
We have, as a n.	MAMET 643:44
What ish my n.?	SHAK 881:42
what our N. stands for	BETJ 100:33
what stupid age or n.	BUTL 217:21
who writes the n.'s laws	PERE 766:91
whole of the Hellish n.	SITW 940:3
will make of thee a great n.	BIBLE 104:18
wise n. preserves its records	HOWE 497:97
With a n., as with a boxer	ACHE 3:51
Youth of a N.	DISR 332:92
national African n. consciousness	MACM 635:8
German N. Socialism	GOER 430:66
n. capacity for individual enterprise	WAVE 1058:10
n. costume…architecture or art	BIRD 163:17
N. Debt is a very Good thing	SELL 858:40
n. dividend is diminished	PIGOU 770:41

national (*contd.*)

our n. slogans	THUR 1019:41
policeman in the N. Gallery	WHIS 1069:11
rock of the n. resources	WEBS 1059:23
suffering a n. defeat	EDIN 361:40
think little of the n. interest	WILL 1080:46

nationalism also took…their n. GOER 430:66

Canadian n. was systematically	INNIS 512:52
Current n. is merely	ILLI 511:32
dangerous being n.	RUNC 828:52
free from n.	ORWE 744:34
N., and its chum, patriotism	DUNN 356:59
N. is a silly cock	ALDI 12:4
somewhat blatant n.	RUSS 832:24
wind of n. and freedom	BALD 65:12

nationalities smaller n. ASQU 42:77

nationality barbarous feeling of n. SENI 859:53

Other people have a n. BEHAN 84:62

nations advantageous…to n. PAINE 750:47

all n., and kindreds	BIBLE 157:14
Amid…the misery of n.	PITT 772:73
among 50 n.	TRUM 1030:22
before him shall be gathered all n.	BIBLE 140:43
both rich and poor n.	ILLI 511:33
cheap defence of n.	BURKE 207:32
civilized n. of the world	PEARY 762:35
day of small n. has passed away	CHAM 249:15
dazzle and bewilder n.	MACA 622:90
dead n. never rise again	LONG 612:13
deceive the n. no more	BIBLE 158:32
different n. should do	MONT 702:82
enmities between n.	KENN 551:79
fierce contending n.	ADDI 8:36
great n. have always acted	KUBR 570:12
happiest n., have no history	ELIOT 365:21
hostile behavior…to n.	FULB 409:30
intercourse wih foreign n.	DECA 311:71
Jew among the n.	FERB 385:7
king to judge us like all the n.	BIBLE 110:32
language all n. understand	BEHN 85:65
League of n.	MACD 628:5
leave it to…foreign n.	BACON 60:30
leaves of tree for healing of n.	BIBLE 159:39
Levitical decrees between n.	ROCHE 815:40
living n. wait	AUDEN 47:72
loans…to foreign n.	BAGE 62:64
master minds of all n.	TWAIN 1034:98
men and n. behave wisely	EBAN 359:7
most bourgeois of all n.	ENGE 378:87
n. and governments have never	HEGEL 466:63
n. are as a drop	BIBLE 126:88
n.; between whom…no intercourse	DISR 332:90
n. desirous of emancipating	MAZZ 666:11
n. into a new-made artificial state	POWE 788:18
n. large and small	UNIT 1036:45
n. of Europe and outside	LEES 593:20
n. of the future	CURZ 302:29
n. that have prospered and declined	LARD 580:89
N. touch at their summits	BAGE 61:58
n. which spoiled you	BIBLE 130:66
N. would do well	COWP 293:61
no very good symptom…of n.	CARL 233:34
not living n. but dead states	CHAM 249:12
often that n. learn	KISS 565:30
other n. of the earth	JAMES 516:12
Other n. use 'force'	WAUGH 1057:85
peace…with all n.	LINC 605:6
place among the n. of the earth	EMMET 378:81
Praise the Lord, all n.	BIBLE 159:47
seek in vain among the N.	DICK 327:82
Spaniards and other n.	GARC 414:19
system of British n.	GEOR 419:88
teach all n.	BIBLE 141:58
the pedigrees of n.	JOHN 529:67

nations (*contd.*)

To belong to other n.	GILB 423:57
two n. have been at war	VOLT 1046:5
war between civilised n.	GOOCH 435:54
whether civilized n. can restore	SMALL 943:61
wickedness of these n.	BIBLE 108:93
wonder of hostile n.	MACA 623:11

native aren't n. to a place LAMM 578:50

can its n. element	MARV 657:68
considerable in his n. place	JOHN 528:59
dear n. country	SWIFT 985:97
emptying the n.'s brain	FANON 382:60
foot is on my n. heath	SCOTT 855:89
form of n. government	ONEI 739:47
ideas about the n.	LESS 598:95
looks into the eyes of a n.	LESS 598:96
My n. heath	OHAG 737:6
N. always means people	STEIN 965:38
n. of Ashbourn, Derbyshire	ANON 24:13
status of 'n.'	SART 844:20
though I am n. here	SHAK 888:70

natives bulk of your n. SWIFT 985:84

intercourse with the n. PARK 753:85

nativity in n., chance, or death SHAK 878:23

out of love with your n. SHAK 886:19

NATO 15 representatives…in N. MACM 635:9

natural causes of n. things NEWT 725:37

culture of n. sciences	SUN 982:38
double action, n. and supernatural	HUGEL 498:10
Home life…is no more n.	SHAW 924:92
in the n. way	KIPL 564:6
know so much about the n. world	SHAP 919:78
large as l. and twice as n.!	CARR 241:75
living example of n. selection	GOLD 432:87
lost faith…in n. force	CARL 234:40
most n. way of approach	WEIL 1062:82
naked lunch is n.	GINS 427:23
n. and ordinary movements	FONT 395:87
n. language of all religions	STAEL 962:76
N. rights is simple nonsense	BENT 93:17
n. science accumulates new riches	ALEM 13:12
n., simple, affecting	GOLD 433:29
n. to please	DRYD 349:5
n., wholesome…English people	SHAW 925:14
never so n.	JAMES 516:15
new art to them is n.	DAVI 307:7
not n. in an age	YEATS 1105:67
not n. to have come from there	STEIN 965:41
of that n. luck	SHAK 905:72
said something n.	HILL 481:8
something…more than n.	SHAK 890:7
wants the n. touch	SHAK 909:71
was his n. self	TWAIN 1033:81
what is n. cannot touch me	ETHE 380:19
When we see a n. style	PASC 757:54
wildly n. and primative	THOR 1016:69
Woman is n.	BAUD 78:33

naturalist n. in England DARW 306:82

naturalists n. observe, a flea SWIFT 986:7

nature Abandon yourself to N. RABE 799:93

absurd n. of Englishmen	PEPYS 765:67
All n. is but art	POPE 780:41
All N. was degraded	BLAKE 168:15
all the laws of N.	THOR 1016:72
almost a force of n.	WHITE 1071:48
Angel, it's a law of n.	LACL 574:67
arbitrary economy of n.	WOLL 1091:37
art continue to follow n.	MOND 699:41
art is the perfection of n.	BROW 195:78
as broad as N.…to interpret N.	DOYLE 343:87
at once as N.'s self	BROW 198:54
attracted by God, or by N.	INGE 511:37
back to n.	GOTT 436:73
beautiful flaws in n.	WOLL 1091:38

nature (*contd.*)

betwixt N. and Art	PRIOR 791:59
blank Of n.'s work	MILT 689:31
bold and adventurous piece of n.	BROW 195:77
by their n. intent on profit	PIUS 772:79
by their n., mess-makers	PIRS 770:54
cannot command N.	BACON 56:31
chance gift of n.	MORAN 706:41
chance of n.'s changing	SHAK 912:48
child…sweetest thing in n.	LAMB 576:22
come to n. with your theories	RENO 807:7
commonplace of N.	WORD 1097:41
Consistency is contrary to n.	HUXL 507:62
Constant, in N. were inconstancy	COWL 291:13
control the forces of n.	BUSH 215:90
convulsion of brute n.	STEV 976:60
creative n. with man	MILL 678:43
customs…are the laws of n.	SHAW 921:19
defect of n.	FRAN 401:83
defend us against n.	FREUD 404:42
describe and explain n.	HEIS 467:77
despite her n.	GOTT 436:72
determine the n. of the ends	HUXL 507:73
Disguise fair n.	SHAK 881:84
do by n. the things…in the law	BIBLE 148:13
ever seen in Art or N.	WAUGH 1057:87
except his own n.	MILL 678:37
exist with the n. I actually have	DESC 318:83
existence in the n. of things	FORD 396:98
Eye N.'s walks	POPE 780:33
fair defect Of n.	MILT 693:20
Fair n.'s eye, rise	MARL 654:24
fear thy n.	SHAK 907:25
First follow n.	POPE 778:78
floodgate and o'erbearing n.	SHAK 898:3
For n., heartless, witless n.	HOUS 496:79
forces of N.	MARX 661:22
fortress built by n.	SHAK 867:48
free as n. first made man	DRYD 347:69
friend…the masterpiece of n.	EMER 376:39
gay n. grieves	SMART 944:72
general laws of n.	BURB 205:76
general laws of n.	HUGO 501:57
geography of one's own n.	BOWL 182:59
good gift of n.	SHAK 893:94
Great n.'s second course	TWAIN 1033:89
grossness of procreative n.	PAGL 749:34
hand of N.	GIBB 422:34
happy n. to explore	POPE 780:45
hem of N.'s shift	SHEL 928:95
Hold…the mirror up to n.	SHAK 891:33
How quickly N. falls	SHAK 878:8
husband n.'s riches	SHAK 914:81
If honest N. made you fools	BURNS 209:58
If N. had not befriended us	CAVE 246:73
images of N. were…present to him	DRYD 347:59
In n…no rewards	VACH 1038:83
In N.'s presence stood	WORD 1096:33
in n. the only ending	GRAY 440:41
In n. there are no rewards	INGE 511:43
In n. there's no blemish	SHAK 895:35
In the n. of things	SPIN 960:48
inclination of my n.	ELIZ 373:85
informed by light of n.	BACON 55:13
insight into the n.	HALES 451:23
interpreted in. as freely	GIRA 429:34
Invention, N.'s child	SIDN 937:51
irrelevant thing in n.	LAMB 577:41
Is there any cause in n.	SHAK 903:26
It can't be N.	CHUR 262:30
it is its n.	TOLS 1023:95
know his n. and fashions	BACON 59:19
law of n.	HOOK 489:54
law pervading all n.	HARDY 457:5

nature (*contd.*)

Laws of N. cannot account	MILL 675:73
lay on n.	SHAK 897:83
leaving light of n.	ROCH 816:50
let N. take her course	MILL 675:75
like N., half reveal	TENN 998:19
limitations of our n.	AUDEN 48:88
lines in n.	GOYA 437:83
Little we see in n.	WORD 1099:73
lore which N. brings	WORD 1094:3
love is liberty, and n., law	POPE 779:8
made a gap in n.	SHAK 905:69
Man has wrested from n.	STEV 972:73
Man masters n.	BRON 190:80
man's n. runs to	BACON 56:48
man of...comprehensive n.	DRYD 352:79
man...outdoes N. herself	SHAW 921:35
man...up against N.	GABOR 411:64
Man was by N. woman's cully	CONG 280:94
may delight N.	CAREW 232:16
mere copier of n.	REYN 808:23
more than Wisdom, Art, or N.	HERR 477:57
Mute N. mourns her worshipper	SCOTT 853:48
N. admits no lie	CARL 236:97
N. all curage me denyis	DUNB 355:42
N. always does contrive	GILB 424:75
N. can decree	BYRON 220:93
n. cannot be fooled	FEYN 387:36
n....careless as it is bountiful	DILL 330:52
n. could never be intended	TAYL 992:21
N. could no farther go	DRYD 351:58
N.'s darling	GRAY 443:89
N. does not endure	RABE 799:83
N. does not makes jumps	LINN 606:27
N. does require	SHAK 918:58
n. from her seat Sighing	MILT 692:12
N. gives you the face	CHAN 251:56
N.'s great masterpiece	DONNE 337:83
n.'s handmaid art	DRYD 346:54
N. has given women	JOHN 528:42
N. hates a vacuum	WILL 1082:70
N. hath framed strange fellows	SHAK 872:76
n. having intended greatness	ELIOT 366:41
n. herself prescribes	MORE 707:54
N. I loved...next to N.	LAND 578:62
N. in him was almost lost in Art	COLL 276:41
n. in hir corages	CHAU 254:17
N. in some partial...shape	POPE 783:9
n.'s infinite book of secrecy	SHAK 904:17
N. is a social category	LUKA 619:39
N. is as wasteful	HUGH 499:23
N. is but a name	COWP 293:64
N. is commonplace	STEIN 966:44
N. is nowhere accustomed	HARV 460:55
N. is often hidden	BACON 59:9
n. is That I incline	MILT 683:29
n. is the art of God	BROW 195:79
N. is to be taken as she is	WHIS 1069:12
n.'s law to change	ROCH 817:63
N. made him	ARIO 34:19
N. meant but fools	POPE 778:75
N. meant me A wife	DRYD 348:94
n. might stand up	SHAK 884:68
n. must produce a man	HUME 503:6
N....nothing without...purpose	ARIS 34:32
n. of a conquest	SHAK 878:4
n. of a man	STEI 966:60
n. of a river	BACON 55:10
n. of a theory	POPP 783:19
n. of an hypothesis	STER 969:2
n. of God	WHIT 1071:61
n. of my game	JAGG 515:90
n. of politics	POWE 788:19
n. of reason to perceive things	SPIN 960:51

nature (*contd.*)

n. of the gods?	SHAK 862:35
n. of the sickness	SHAK 895:42
n. of the Universe	HARDY 457:9
N.'s only interest	WELD 1063:98
n.'s own hand painted	SHAK 913:50
N., red in tooth and claw	TENN 999:32
N. remains	WHIT 1073:97
N. repents she made her	DEKK 313:13
N.'s scheme of colour	STRE 980:5
n. so preposterously to err	SHAK 898:4
n.'s state, where all have right	DRYD 350:27
N.'s stern discipline	DOBZ 334:36
N. still is fair	BYRON 219:77
N. teaches beasts	SHAK 911:4
N. that framed us	MARL 652:89
N. that heard that sound	MILT 681:89
N. that is above all art	DANI 304:65
n.'s truth is primary	THOM 1013:21
N. was as strongly bricked out	DICK 325:42
N.'s way of telling you	ANON 27:63
N. wears universal grin	FIEL 388:47
N. wept, thinking she	MARL 654:25
n. within me seems	MILT 694:46
n. yearned to a.	WHITE 1071:46
n. yet remembers	WORD 1098:52
necessary n. of a political	TROL 1028:88
Never...did N. say one thing	BURKE 208:49
never have enough of n.	THOR 1016:75
never trifle with n.	AGAS 9:62
noble n....treats with simplicity	ARNO 38:8
not beauty because it is not n.	CONS 285:17
O N.! we are thine	WORD 1100:89
O ruined piece of n.	SHAK 904:36
odious vermin that n.	SWIFT 985:84
Old Mother Wit, and N.	DENH 315:55
On Man, on N.	WORD 1100:77
One of n.'s Balkans	CURR 301:14
order of God and of n.	MANN 646:95
order of n.	FONT 395:86
our mortal n.	WORD 1098:53
Our n. consists	PASC 757:57
painter...must take n.	MALL 641:16
physicians...leave it to N.	BURG 205:83
poetical n.	WHIT 1072:73
presented to us by N.	LAVO 585:54
primary feeling n. imprints on us	SADE 835:64
pure mortal n.	CARL 234:41
renovator of matter N.	OVID 747:3
representations of general n.	JOHN 528:44
repugnant to n.	KNOX 567:57
rich in n.'s store	FORD 397:18
scientist does not study n.	POIN 776:59
scream passing through n.	MUNCH 713:51
secured by good n. and truth	ROCH 816:61
See how n....grows in silence	THER 1009:38
Sexually, Woman is N.'s contrivance	SHAW 921:38
she in spite of n.	SHAK 884:68
Simple N. is the most harmless	BEHN 85:72
simple N. to his hope has giv'n	POPE 780:37
singing is delightful to n.	BYRD 218:57
sketch from n.	CONS 285:19
spark o' N.'s fire	BURNS 209:60
spectacle of n.	ROUS 827:37
state of war by n.	SWIFT 986:6
struggles and strives against n.	INNO 512:54
subduers of N. and Art	DICK 326:55
subtlety of n.	BACON 55:27
suff'ring eye inverted N. sees	POPE 779:21
teach us the n. of the ties	PLATO 774:24
therein works a miracle in n.	SHAK 872:82
thou and n. can so gently part	SHAK 906:7
thro' N., up to N.'s God	POPE 781:52
Thus God and n. linked	POPE 781:47

nature (*contd.*)

To look on n.	WORD 1094:98
to see in paintings bits of n.	MALE 641:11
to sin our biased n. leans	DRYD 349:8
too much after n.	GAUG 416:39
touch of n.	SHAK 896:53
trace The naked N.	POPE 778:80
travellers and wanderers by n.	FERB 385:7
treat n. by the cylinder	CEZA 248:4
true n. of poetry	RICH 809:52
true n. of the 'otherness'	NOLAN 731:20
ultimate mystery of n.	PLAN 772:84
Unerring n., still divinely bright	POPE 778:1
unrevealed glory of N.	SHIP 935:22
Verse hath a middle n.	DONNE 338:15
violates the order of n.	HERO 477:47
visible Foundations in N.	PETTY 768:75
voice the word 'n.'	REDON 804:7
Vows can't change n.	BROW 200:87
war of n.	DARW 306:84
war with rude N.	CARL 234:38
weakest in n.	PASC 758:66
What is man in n.?	PASC 758:70
what n. itselfe cant endure	FLEM 393:60
what you have been given by n.	PERI 766:98
Whatever N. has in store	FERMI 386:25
whatsoever abysses N. leads	HUXL 508:96
when n. is so beautiful	VAN 1039:1
where man leaves off and n. starts	FROST 407:83
while N. cures the disease	VOLT 1047:18
Whose body, N. is	POPE 780:40
Wise n. did never put her...jewels	BACON 56:38
wished to copy n.	CEZA 248:7
woman...N.'s agreeable blunders	COWL 291:20
workings of n.	AQUI 33:8
works of N. are...simple	BORE 178:9
writer...an outcast by n.	BARN 72:31
your divine n. is always free	PEACE 762:26
youth...is n.'s priest	WORD 1098:51
natures alien to their n.	HAZZ 464:27
n. that are mute!	MERE 671:6
Pleasure of worse n.	MASS 662:56
subsists...in all n.	WORD 1100:83
naught falling into n.?	ADDI 8:35
haif n. quhen he wald	HENR 473:68
n. but jouissance	GREE 445:32
wear out to n.	SHAK 904:36
naughtiness n. of thine heart	BIBLE 110:38
bewitching of n.	BIBLE 131:83
naval n. and air force	ROOS 822:44
n. combat	GIBB 421:23
nave make a n. of it	STEV 971:34
walk down the n. of his abbey	HOME 487:13
navel soul...ended at the n.	LEWIS 602:66
steam comes...her n.	THOM 1011:89
navies nations airy n.	TENN 995:77
navigation employ steam n.	LARD 580:88
navigator drunkard, my n.	SEXT 859:62
navvy dowser and not a n.	LEAV 591:77
navy England's chief defence...the n.	PHIL 768:17
n. nothing but rotten timber	BURKE 207:12
N. will run the blockade	ANDE 18:1
one-and-a-half ocean n.	HAYW 463:44
put at the head of the n.	CARS 242:91
Queen's N.	GILB 423:56
Queen's N.	GILB 423:58
nay N., Mabel, n.!	GILB 424:64
yea be yea; and your n., n.	BIBLE 155:12
Nazareth any good...out of N.?	BIBLE 145:29
Nazarite your prophet the N.	SHAK 874:18
Nazi a N. lampshade	PLATH 773:93
give him the N. salute	HEND 472:54
Nazidom fights on against N.	CHUR 264:19
Neaera tangles of N.'s hair?	MILT 684:42

near as n. to heaven	GILB 423:51	
come not n. to me	BIBLE 128:14	
so n. and yet so far	TENN 1000:55	
when you are n.	SCEVE 846:57	
nearer draw a little n.	BRAC 183:71	
n. by not keeping still	GUNN 448:86	
nearness n. of death	PAZ 762:24	
neat n., clean, shaved and sober	CHAN 250:28	
n. as a furled umbrella	EMERY 378:80	
Still to be n.	JONS 535:89	
You look n.	COLL 276:37	
Nebraska skies of Texas or N.	MACM 636:24	
Nebuchadnezzar N....was driven	BIBLE 129:47	
necessaries required three n.	JONS 536:23	
necessary absolutely n.	JOHN 527:20	
love of life is n.	JOHN 525:92	
n. for mortals to be worn	EURI 380:29	
n. not to change	FALK 382:55	
n. to the human mind	REES 805:92	
no explanation is n.	SEAT 857:25	
no more things...than n.	OCCAM 735:79	
Notes are often n.	JOHN 528:47	
slavery...is n.	ASTE 43:92	
so that the n. may speak	HOFF 484:57	
that unnoticed and that n.	ATWO 45:27	
The superfluous, a very n. thing	VOLT 1046:99	
whatever language is n.	KELM 549:32	
necessities art of our n.	SHAK 903:21	
distinction...luxuries and n.	GALB 411:76	
earliest practical n.	HAWT 461:69	
n. call out...virtues	ADAMS 4:62	
simple n. of human life	COMM 278:66	
necessity chain of strong n.?	SPEN 957:5	
door of n.	DEFOE 312:82	
fold Of dire n.	MILT 695:57	
hard n. of bringing the judge	ALGR 13:26	
intelligence and n.	ANGE 19:18	
Liquor...sidestepping n.	FADI 382:50	
N. and chance Approach	MILT 691:84	
n. has induced...greater license	COOP 287:44	
n. invented stools	COWP 292:51	
N. never made a good bargain	FRAN 402:3	
N. never makes prostitution	WOLL 1091:42	
n. of divine nature	SPIN 960:48	
n. of doing so	GERH 420:3	
n. of making things plain	HUXL 509:5	
n. of stealing	MORE 706:45	
N.'s sharp pinch!	SHAK 902:14	
N. will make us forsworn	SHAK 865:9	
nothing stronger than N.	EURI 380:24	
strong n. of time	SHAK 905:63	
sworn...To grim N.	SHAK 868:66	
neck clothed his n. with thunder?	BIBLE 113:22	
eloquence and break its n.!	VERL 1042:38	
had but one n.!	CALI 225:97	
his n. brake, and he died	BIBLE 110:31	
left his straight n.	ROSS 824:88	
locket around his n.	SOME 952:1	
millstone around a woman's n.	GREER 445:38	
millstone were hanged about his n.	BIBLE 138:18	
Millstones around our n.	DISR 334:32	
millstones...about your n.	DAVI 307:96	
n. God made for other use	HOUS 494:43	
n. is like the tower	BIBLE 124:51	
n. like an ostrich	DAVIS 308:27	
one n., one chin	SHAK 894:5	
one washes one's n.	BARN 72:25	
over my n. and eyes	STEV 973:97	
rain on the n.	COOKE 286:32	
short n. denotes a good mind	SPARK 955:50	
Some chicken, some n.!	CHUR 264:20	
sticks its n. out	ANON 29:39	
took the bride about the n.	SHAK 864:83	
necklaces with our n.	MAND 645:70	

necks venturing their n. for fruit	ROCH 816:57	
necktie left my n. God knows where	HOUS 495:64	
necromancy grete clerke of n.	MALO 642:23	
nectar as butterflies sipping n.	ELIOT 365:5	
lie beside their n.	TENN 994:52	
n. from his hand	MARL 655:26	
nectarine n., and curious peach	MARV 658:85	
need Deserted at his utmost n.	DRYD 351:70	
evil...face of total n.	BURR 213:53	
God shall supply all your n.	BIBLE 153:18	
hand of a vexatious n.	OTWAY 746:80	
human n. and...silence	CAMUS 229:47	
human n. continues to grow	COMM 278:67	
In thy most n.	ANON 23:81	
Lord, forgive me if my n.	CULL 299:72	
most n. of blessing	SHAK 908:45	
N. and oppression starveth	SHAK 870:21	
n. for a well-defined personal space	COUP 289:83	
n. to look within	SNYD 951:84	
n. was the sorest	SCOTT 854:64	
no n. for the faith	HOFF 484:54	
seeth his brother have n.	BIBLE 156:91	
Will you still n. me	LENN 596:64	
worse n. for them	SHEL 930:17	
needed makes it feel n.	SCHU 850:12	
needing n. what I've invented	FULL 409:37	
needle my hand a n. fits	BRAD 184:1	
n. and the pen	LEWIS 601:46	
n. is not worth the search	JACK 514:89	
phonograph n.	GOLD 433:33	
Plying her n. and thread	HOOD 489:45	
reading of a n.	STEV 972:79	
shove...with a red-hot n.	WODE 1089:93	
that poor little n....of femininity	OLIP 738:25	
through the eye of a n.	BIBLE 139:25	
needs according to his n.	BAKU 63:87	
each according to his n.!	MARX 661:24	
menial n. and base	HYDE 509:14	
must n. die	BIBLE 110:49	
primary n.	GABOR 411:65	
real n. of man	SCHU 850:15	
tools, the ideals, the n.	RENO 807:10	
needy provider for a n. man	HESI 479:83	
wasn't poor, I was n.	FEIF 384:97	
negation affirmation from n.	THUR 1019:47	
negative All satisfaction...always n.	SCHO 849:91	
Electricity...positive and n.	LEAC 588:35	
Great N.	ROCH 816:47	
it was also n.	SNOW 950:72	
N. Capability	KEATS 544:47	
negativism nattering nabobs of n.	AGNEW 10:70	
neglect easy to n. the truth	CORN 288:61	
most tender mercy is n.	CRAB 293:75	
n. God and his Angels	DONNE 339:28	
punished for n.	JOHN 526:4	
sweet n. more taketh me	JONS 535:89	
neglected n. and misunderstood	RABAN 798:73	
negotiate If we are to n.	BISM 164:41	
n. ...into the Common Market	WILS 1085:33	
never n. out of fear	KENN 550:62	
negotiation n. and society	MUNCH 714:52	
negotiations opened n.	KISH 565:29	
negotiators Agreement...by the n.	SHUL 936:34	
best n. in Europe	NELS 722:97	
negro all her n. train	SMART 944:63	
America is...rooted in N. culture	ROLL 821:26	
American N. female	ANGE 19:20	
American N. problem	BALD 64:91	
average N. could never hope to go	DAVIS 309:32	
courage of the N.	PHIL 768:23	
every Irishman would kill a n.	FREE 404:31	
friend of the n. assumes	FULL 409:33	
n. either didn't get in the pot	MARS 656:55	
N. or saint	HOLM 485:74	

negro (*contd.*)		
N....was never looked at	BALD 64:93	
One drop—you are a N.!	HUGH 499:22	
The past of...the N.	OBRI 734:62	
negroes Afro-American...replaced N.	FEIF 384:98	
bronze N. breathing	LOWE 617:99	
drivers of n.	JOHN 529:77	
gnaws at n.	KING 558:85	
infant n. in the West Indies	DICK 320:25	
neighbour covet thy n.'s wife	BIBLE 106:68	
false witness against thy n.	BIBLE 106:68	
guinea in your n.'s pocket	RUSK 830:90	
into the n. room	SHAK 892:60	
look his n. in the face	STEV 973:84	
love thy n. as thyself	BIBLE 107:80	
love thy n.	BIBLE 134:44	
love thy n.	BIBLE 139:34	
Love your n. as much as yourself	CLEE 268:99	
n. loses his job	REAG 803:61	
n. loses his job	TRUM 1030:26	
policy of the good n.	ROOS 821:35	
removeth his n.'s landmark	BIBLE 108:97	
stare...at our unintroduced n.	ELIOT 366:35	
to hate your n.	MACA 623:2	
wrest the ball from your n.	ANON 25:16	
neighbourhood everyone in the n.	WHAR 1068:1	
n. kids	WILL 1082:72	
neighbourly like to be n.	HALI 452:25	
neighbours advantage over their n.	SMITH 945:88	
as the n. described them	MIN 695:61	
commerce of all its n.	HUME 504:11	
common hatred of its n.	INGE 511:40	
drouthy n....meet	BURNS 211:8	
feast his n.	SHAK 881:99	
merry songs...to all his n.	SHAK 918:67	
Sane people did what their n. did	ELIOT 366:30	
sport for our n.	AUST 51:43	
Whenever our n.'s house is on fire	BURKE 207:25	
neighed n. after his neighbour's wife	BIBLE 128:19	
Nell Little N. and Lady Macbeth	WOOL 1093:83	
Nelly Let not poor N. starve	CHAR 253:87	
Nelson death of N.	SOUT 954:41	
N. confides that every man	NELS 722:99	
nemesis Hubris clobbered by N.	ALDI 12:8	
neon something like n. signs	UREY 1037:74	
neotenic achievement for the n. ape	ALDI 12:7	
nephew n....propounded 'Oysters'	DICK 322:68	
Neptune more men than N.	FULL 410:47	
Nerissa will do anything, N.	SHAK 874:16	
Nero N., fiddled, but Coolidge	MENC 669:69	
nerve Anatomised in every n.	JONS 534:73	
every n. a man may strain	CURZ 302:27	
n. and instinct is clamouring	LESS 598:34	
n. o'er which do creep	SHEL 927:68	
raw n. ends of humanity	ANON 29:41	
nerve-shaken n.-s., over-civilized	MUIR 713:38	
nerves but it quiets my n.	LOUIS 614:59	
n. out of the job in hand	MANS 647:97	
n. prick and tingle	TENN 999:35	
N. sit ceremonious	DICK 328:99	
quiver from the average n.	WHITE 1070:44	
nervos N. belli	CICE 266:61	
nervous n. tics	UPDI 1037:69	
'native' is a n. condition	SART 844:20	
take your n. system seriously	LEARY 591:70	
nest brood over a full n.	ELIOT 366:27	
It's like building a n.	OCON 736:87	
long since my n. is made	TENN 997:6	
n. of singing birds	JOHN 525:72	
n. upon the dewy ground	WORD 1100:87	
One flew over the cuckoo's n.	KESEY 553:18	
swallow a n. for herself	BIBLE 117:93	
nestling N. me everywhere	HOPK 492:99	
nests because he see's the n.!	DICK 323:98	

net admiration…crosses the n.	BARR 73:*52*	
bring her to the n.	KING 557:*70*	
goodness make the n.	SHAK 899:*27*	
just get rid of the n.	HUGH 500:*33*	
N. Anything reticulated	JOHN 526:*13*	
over the n. in a different shape	LODGE 610:*79*	
stick it in the n.	SHAN 918:*73*	
tennis with the n. down	FROST 407:*91*	
Whizzing them over the n.	BETJ 99:*32*	
nets fishery without n.	DEFOE 312:*84*	
n. of wrong	YEATS 1105:*62*	
tangled in amorous n.	MILT 694:*32*	
time in making n.	SWIFT 984:*75*	
nettle Out of this n. danger	SHAK 875:*51*	
nettles dust on the n.	THOM 1012:*12*	
network indispensable n.	GLEI 430:*61*	
networks n. of dead speech	STARK 963:*96*	
neuroses store their mouldy n.	PAGL 749:*36*	
neurosis N. has…genius	PROU 793:*95*	
N. is the way of	TILL 1020:*61*	
what n. would sound like	AMIS 17:*95*	
neurotic character…described as n.	PAGE 749:*31*	
I'm n. as hell	PLATH 773:*92*	
Makes cats n.	ANON 26:*54*	
n. builds castles	ANON 26:*44*	
n. can…be a literary genius	AUCH 46:*39*	
person as n.	SZASZ 989:*68*	
prolonged n. doubt	BARZ 76:*99*	
the n. classes	SHAW 925:*13*	
neurotics gathering of n.,	MANK 645:*77*	
neutral United States must be n.	WILS 1086:*46*	
neutrality Armed n. is ineffectual	WILS 1086:*51*	
overwhelmingly for policy of n.	BORAH 178:*8*	
neutralizing n. …newspapers	TOCQ 1021:*76*	
never could n. tell why	GILB 423:*54*	
everything I n. wanted	GARD 414:*21*	
N. again	ANON 27:*69*	
n., n. use	GILB 423:*55*	
N. to have lived	YEATS 1106:*81*	
This will n. do	JEFF 520:*98*	
never-ending n.-e. Remembrance	POE 776:*51*	
never-never in the N.-N.	GUNN 448:*84*	
Radio is a n.-n. land	SAFER 835:*66*	
never-sere ivy n.-s.	MILT 684:*38*	
nevermore Quoth the raven, 'N.'	POE 776:*49*	
new against the n. and untried	LINC 605:*2*	
all things are become n.	BIBLE 151:*80*	
brook the n.	FERG 386:*18*	
discovery of the 'n.'?	INGR 512:*47*	
draw n. mischief on	SHAK 898:*12*	
feel comfortable in the n.	MO 698:*9*	
find the old in the n.	MANN 646:*89*	
I make all things n.	BIBLE 158:*35*	
making something n.	GILL 426:*11*	
n. and original plan	GILB 424:*74*	
N. Deal for the American people	ROOS 821:*34*	
N. Deal was ended by World War II	MACG 630:*33*	
n. every morning	BIBLE 128:*32*	
n. heaven and a n. earth	BIBLE 158:*34*	
N. to me	TRAH 1025:*28*	
not make a n. acquaintance	JOHN 532:*34*	
Nothing…Which is not n.	FLET 394:*77*	
put on the n. man	BIBLE 153:*21*	
ring in the n.	TENN 1000:*56*	
Shock of the N.	DUNL 355:*50*	
something n. to look forward to	FORD 397:*23*	
the n. will grow	POL 777:*61*	
things n. and curious	CUMM 299:*76*	
New Age signs of a N. A. coming?	SMITH 948:*35*	
new born pity, like a n. b.	SHAK 908:*32*	
use of a n.-b. child?	FRAN 402:*13*	
New England brought against N. E.	KRUT 570:*9*	
Newgate gaze on the exterior of N.	DICK 320:*15*	
kind of N. calendar	IRVI 513:*61*	

New Jersey learned in N. J.	BALD 64:*93*	
Newman new-manned By N.	BROW 200:*86*	
Newmarket N., that infamous	CHES 257:*83*	
New Orleans Hoo-doo…in N. O.	REED 805:*89*	
N. O. is unremarkable	MAIL 639:*84*	
New South Wales govern N. S. W.!	BELL 87:*9*	
New Testament blessing of the N.	BACON 56:*50*	
blood of the n. t.	BIBLE 140:*48*	
Could the N. T. have	GRIS 447:*67*	
ministers of the n. t.	BIBLE 151:*75*	
N. T. had not proved in time	GREE 444:*23*	
n. t. in my blood	BIBLE 150:*59*	
New Year on this day of N. Y.	POUND 786:*77*	
New York a kind of N. Y.	USTI 1038:*81*	
all churches or chapels in N. Y.	BENN 92:*6*	
an aviary…called N.Y.	OHEN 737:*17*	
In N. Y. people don't	JOUR 537:*36*	
little trip to N.Y.	OHARA 737:*11*	
N. Y. is a jungle	AMIS 17:*87*	
N.Y. is not the cultural centre	BELL 88:*32*	
N.Y. is one of the capitals	MAIL 639:*84*	
N.Y. is the meeting place	BARN 71:*24*	
N. Y. Island	GUTH 449:*94*	
N. Y. Pop artists	LIPP 606:*29*	
N. Y. State will decertify him	CUOMO 300:*4*	
N. Y. theatre has died	MILL 677:*11*	
N. Y., thy name is irreverence	HUXT 509:*9*	
N. Y. was no mean city	DIDI 330:*45*	
New Yorkers busy N. Y. take time	OKEE 738:*21*	
New Zealand I was born in N. Z.	MANS 647:*12*	
newness conditioned to respect n.	UPDI 1037:*58*	
n., the democratic conceit	LAWR 585:*72*	
news a newspaper needs in its n.	PULI 795:*21*	
always n. to somebody	KAVA 543:*26*	
brought bitter n. to hear	CORY 288:*63*	
cold roads…cold n.	SCOTT 856:*9*	
dog bites a man, that is not n.	BOGAN 171:*61*	
Evil n. rides post	MILT 695:*55*	
free from bad n. and disease	BIOY 162:*11*	
function of the n.	LIPP 607:*36*	
good n. is that he's eating less	JACO 514:*90*	
good n. yet to hear	CHES 259:*33*	
literature is n.	POUND 786:*75*	
mariners had fabled n.	LOWE 616:*93*	
master passion is the love of n.	CRAB 294:*77*	
media for the dissemination of n.	CHRI 261:*68*	
n.…and nothing but the n.	DANA 304:*56*	
n. is not a mirror	LIPP 606:*35*	
n. of the day	LIPP 606:*32*	
N., Opinion and Advertisement	BEAV 81:*87*	
n. or no n. to be	LEST 599:*13*	
n. when there is no n.	ORWE 744:*25*	
n.…would have made me sick	SHAK 877:*79*	
not…different enough to make n.	SAFI 836:*72*	
only n. until he's read it	WAUGH 1057:*83*	
primary office is the gathering of N.	SCOTT 852:*33*	
suckers for good n.	STEV 972:*80*	
Tell Tchaikovsky the n.	BERRY 98:*4*	
The more abhorrent a n. item	FOWL 400:*69*	
to get the n. to you	TWAIN 1034:*10*	
today is no longer the n.	RUSK 830:*73*	
uncovers the run of the n.	LIPP 606:*34*	
What's the n.?	SHAK 890:*5*	
when I see the evening n.	CLIN 269:*22*	
newspaper art of n. paragraphing	MARQ 656:*48*	
daily n.…greatest organ	BENN 92:*6*	
even a from small provincial n.	WODE 1089:*98*	
every word in…my n. must be clear	CHRI 261:*65*	
good n., I suppose	MILL 677:*3*	
hit n. reader between eyes	BRIS 189:*61*	
I will show you a bad n.	CHRI 261:*67*	
invariable law of the n.	DANA 304:*57*	
n. is…a monopoly	SCOTT 852:*33*	
n. is an adviser	TOCQ 1021:*80*	

newspaper (*contd.*)		
n.'s one and only aim	ORWE 742:*88*	
n. represents an association	TOCQ 1021:*78*	
oblivion amounts to n. death	ADAMS 5:*80*	
Once a n. touches a story	MAIL 639:*73*	
One of the virtues…of a n.	SCOTT 852:*34*	
Only a n. can place	TOCQ 1021:*79*	
person employed by a n.	HUBB 498:*6*	
reaches the n. office	LIPP 606:*32*	
Reading someone else's n.	BRAD 183:*74*	
stamp of a n.	KRAUS 569:*87*	
subsist without a n.	JOHN 527:*11*	
touch a n. without disgust	BAUD 78:*45*	
What a n. needs	PULI 795:*21*	
newspapers believe all you read in n.	MACA 622:*80*	
I read the n. avidly	BEVAN 102:*70*	
importance (of n.)	TOCQ 1022:*19*	
lies from the print of the n.	MAIL 639:*68*	
My approach to n.	CHRI 261:*69*	
neutralising the effects of n.	TOCQ 1021:*76*	
N. always excite curiosity	LAMB 576:*18*	
n. and dogeared history-books	DOSP 340:*40*	
N. are born free	SCOTT 852:*38*	
n.…are the most villainous	SHER 934:*2*	
N. have degenerated	WILDE 1076:*89*	
N.…inevitably reflect	LIPP 606:*32*	
n.…querulous and bellicose	MENC 669:*59*	
n. without government	JEFF 520:*88*	
not n. in the ordinary acceptance	BALD 64:*9*	
other half doesn't read n.	VIDAL 1044:*71*	
Rage…writing columns for n.	BRES 187:*37*	
to please n.	THOM 1012:*4*	
world mirrored in the n.	LESS 598:*4*	
Newton make us as N. was	AUDEN 46:*49*	
N. with his prism	WORD 1096:*27*	
Shakespeare or Sir Isaac N.	FERG 385:*15*	
newts N. and blindworms	SHAK 871:*94*	
next What time's the n. one?	SLEZ 943:*58*	
nexus n. of all love and money	DIDI 330:*45*	
sole n. of man to man	CARL 236:*84*	
NHS N. is quite like heaven	HALD 451:*19*	
Nicaraguan N. resistance	NORTH 732:*35*	
nice All the n. people	SPARK 955:*55*	
But they sounded n.	RAMOS 801:*17*	
change is always n.	EURI 380:*33*	
don't try to make things n.!	IVES 514:*94*	
e sae n. wi' Robin	BURNS 210:*87*	
how nasty the n. people	POWE 788:*9*	
Makes n. of no vile hold	SHAK 872:*69*	
n. girl should only fall	SPARK 955:*58*	
N. guys finish last	DURO 357:*73*	
n. man	SWIFT 985:*92*	
n. to the second housemaid	JAMES 516:*26*	
someone wants to be n. to me	PUIG 794:*11*	
Too n. for a statesman	GOLD 433:*28*	
nicety sift…with the utmost n.	STEE 964:*23*	
niche Madonna Standing in a n.	PARK 755:*26*	
Nicholas St N. would soon be there	MOORE 704:*4*	
Nick Satan, N. or Clootie	BURNS 209:*73*	
nickel if it doesn't make a n.	GOLD 434:*7*	
nickname Everybody has a n.	AMADO 15:*63*	
n. is the heaviest stone	HAZL 464:*21*	
only one…that ain't got a n.	DICK 320:*22*	
niece hitting the n. of a bishop	ORWE 742:*96*	
nieces carrying of n.	RIDGE 811:*77*	
Nietzsche N.…fools, and madmen!	ONEI 740:*59*	
Nigel dogs called N.	AMIS 17:*85*	
nigger blue-gum n. to sing me blues	BENET 90:*61*	
humble myself to a n.	TWAIN 1033:*87*	
just a 'red n.	WALC 1048:*32*	
niggers 'twixt de n. of de Souf	TRUTH 1030:*38*	
nigh Draw n. to God	BIBLE 155:*50*	
night 11.30pm on election n.	MOND 699:*39*	
ability to get a good n.'s sleep	WILS 1085:*39*	

nights All days are n. — SHAK 913:61
dogs barking…through endless n. — MENC 670:91
fled Him, down the n. — THOM 1013:28
long n. after Samhain — ONOL 734:68
long, long wintery n. — LEAR 589:51
Love give me more such n. — HERR 477:53
n. in Kansas City — MAIL 639:84
n. not sufficing to do it in — PEPYS 765:75
nihilism n. of technology — PAZ 762:25
Nile banks of the N. — SHER 933:84
down the N. as Cleopatra — BROWN 194:54
more impassable than the N. — GIBB 421:23
old father N. — SPEKE 955:61
sources of the N. — ELIOT 366:32
waters of the N. — CARR 238:22
Nilus pretty worm Of N. — SHAK 906:3
nimble n. fingers are no more n. — SITW 941:25
nimbleness so much n. — DEKK 313:14
Nimrod N. the mighty hunter — BIBLE 104:16
nine hour ago since it was n. — SHAK 885:90
n. points of the law — ANON 23:94
nineteen doesn't mean n. — BENN 91:86
n. hundred and forty nails — SITW 941:16
nineteenth n. century is great — HUGO 502:91
Nineveh Quinquireme of N. — MASE 662:37
ninth about the n. hour Jesus cried — BIBLE 140:55
Limpopo of swamped N. Avenue — AMIS 17:87
nipple bites its nurse's n. — SADE 835:64
Nixon N.'s motto — COUS 290:88
If Richard N. is second-rate — HELL 468:87
Richard N. self-impeached — ABZUG 2:15
What N. …began — PILG 770:43
Nkongsamba N. was built — BOYD 182:62
no land of omnipotent N. — BOLD 171:67
n. is just as short as…God — YOUR 1108:10
n. one else can — PITT 771:64
n. one ever sent me — PARK 754:5
N. sun—n. moon! — HOOD 489:51
N. warmth, n. cheerfulness — HOOD 489:52
Oh, n., n., n. — SMITH 948:33
rebel…says n. — CAMUS 229:53
say n. when they mean yes — ALCO 12:1
sound is 'n.' — KOH 568:74
That woman…can't say n. — PARK 754:1
The everlasting N. — CARL 234:54
We say n., and we are the state — WRIG 1102:12
Noah all men are N.'s sons — WILB 1074:17
fellow think…of Old N. — DOUG 341:51
N. entered into the ark — BIBLE 140:39
N. he often said to his wife — CHES 259:23
two and two unto N. — BIBLE 104:10
won't start with N.'s Ark — ECHE 359:13
Nobel worth the N. Prize — FEYN 387:35
nobility destroy the pretended n. — BOCC 171:55
fashions men with true n. — MARL 653:92
New n. is but the act of power — BACON 58:79
no n. of descent — POTT 785:44
N. brings obligations — LEVIS 600:30
n. is of great use — BAGE 61:55
pain is the one n. — BAUD 77:15
seal of n. those people — MUSS 716:86
with n. and tranquillity — SHAK 875:47
noble all were n., save Nobility — BYRON 219:70
fredome is a n. thing! — BARB 71:15
How n. in reason — SHAK 890:4
I know n. accents — STEV 971:44
My n. father — SHAK 898:10
no good at being n. — EPST 379:1
n. and the slave — SCOTT 854:73
n.…are not the leaders — CONR 285:7
n. grounds for the n. — RUSK 830:83
n., historically fair — LERN 597:91
N. men in the quiet of morning — DUNC 355:46
n. mind is here o'erthrown! — SHAK 891:30

noble (contd.)
n. race and brave — SIGO 938:71
n. to be good — TENN 995:70
position where they may be n. — KAZIN 543:30
silence is most n. — SWIN 987:28
thou art n. and nude — SWIN 987:31
To the n. mind — SHAK 891:22
Was n. man — TENN 1002:16
What's brave, what's n. — SHAK 906:97
noble-hearted swung the n.-h. three — SULL 981:24
nobleman Cultivated Underrated N. — GILB 426:95
king may make n. — BURKE 208:44
n. from surfeiting of his parents — LASS 583:35
noblemen n.…cap and knee — WEBS 1060:56
nobleness allied with perfect n. — ARNO 38:7
That n. made simple — YEATS 1105:67
nobler earth is n. than the world — PRIE 790:36
life is n. — SHAW 920:2
nobles luxurious N. — JOHN 525:76
N. and heralds — PRIOR 790:49
noblesse n. and of chivalry — SPEN 957:92
nobody either I'm n. — WALC 1048:32
I care for n., not I — BICK 160:60
Kneel to n. — SKEL 942:48
more space where n. is — STEIN 965:37
n. agrees with you — STEIN 965:36
n.'s around—n. big — SALI 839:28
N., as I knows on — STOWE 978:86
N. can be exactly like me — BANK 70:93
N. can say a word against Greek — SHAW 923:78
n. comes, n. goes — BECK 81:92
N. has any conscience — HAWT 461:81
N. holds a good opinion — TROL 1027:70
n. is anybody — HUTC 506:43
N. rules safely — KEMP 549:41
N. shoots Santa Claus — SMITH 946:96
n. tells me anything — GALS 413:1
n. wants to read — TWAIN 1034:16
proved to be n.'s business — SMUTS 950:67
someone gave a war & N. came? — GINS 428:32
where n. knows us? — GASK 415:33
nod Affects to n. — DRYD 351:68
dwelt in the land of N. — BIBLE 104:8
Land of N. at last — STEV 976:43
n. on the parterre — POPE 779:23
nods Grove n. at grove — POPE 779:21
when the worthy Homer n. — HORA 494:34
nodus n. of a drama — CARL 235:39
noise argues by increments of n. — BYATT 218:56
barbarous n. environs me — MILT 686:76
cannot be found in n. — THER 1009:38
emit a n. of any kind — MONT 700:51
genius who invents a n. — DUNN 356:58
great n. in the city — EDWA 361:46
happy n. to hear — HOUS 494:49
if neurosis could make a n. — AMIS 17:95
is no n., nothing — MILL 677:1
let us melt, and make no n. — DONNE 337:90
little noiseless n. — KEATS 544:34
loud n. at one end — KNOX 567:63
love the n. it makes — BEEC 82:11
make a joyful n. — BIBLE 117:6
Make a joyful n. — BIBLE 118:9
make least n. — SELD 857:36
make n. enough — SHAK 887:25
more n. they make pouring — POPE 779:16
most sublime n. — FORS 398:31
moved to folly by a n. — LAWR 587:16
never valued till they make a n. — CRAB 294:89
n. machines — AMIS 17:87
n. of a fly — DONNE 339:28
n. of battle rolled — TENN 1004:41
Nursed amid her n. — LAMB 576:8
that kind of background n.? — HOWE 497:94

noise (contd.)
wild n. of prattling visitants — WEBS 1060:53
noiseless inaudible and n. foot — SHAK 901:85
noises isle is full of n. — SHAK 917:34
n. of America — CUMM 299:76
Of all n. — JOHN 532:42
painting of sounds, n. and smells — CARRA 237:15
noisy when it is brash or n. — AUDEN 49:98
Nokomis N. bore a daughter — LONG 611:9
Noll for shortness called N. — GARR 415:30
nomad n.'s life enthralls — MAIL 640:92
nomadism test of n. — LAWR 587:17
nomads sorrowing are n. — MACM 636:26
nomination decide the n. — DAUG 306:93
non N. nobis, Domine — BIBLE 159:46
non-being avoiding n.-b. — TILL 1020:61
non-combatant no fury like a n.-c. — MONT 701:58
non-existence n.-e. as an evil — SCHO 849:94
n.-e. of things that are not — PROT 792:82
non-necessity n.-n. of it — HARDY 457:9
non-space n.-s. of the mind — GIBS 422:40
non-violence N.-v. is not a garment — GAND 414:14
N.-v.…first article of my faith — GAND 414:13
nonconformist man must be a n. — EMER 376:32
N. conscience — WILDE 1077:61
nonconformity n.…in America — MACC 625:15
none better than n. — JOHN 532:33
n. but Anthony — SHAK 906:93
n. should be happy — JOHN 530:86
nonsense author…talking n. — WHIT 1071:52
between sense and n. — JUNG 539:71
export revolution is n. — STAL 962:79
farrago of superlative n. — CHUR 263:93
grammar, and n., and learning — GOLD 433:21
infernal n. — GILB 424:63
lump of clotted n. — DRYD 347:75
may call it 'n.' — CARR 239:49
memorable n. — SANT 842:91
music that is not n. — ADDI 7:8
Music…closely structured n. — BURG 206:93
n. upon stilts — BENT 93:17
other interpretation is n. — GALL 413:98
perfect republics are a perfect n. — FOWL 399:64
Protestations…perfect n. — COBB 271:53
secondary showbiz n. — AMIS 17:88
sense from n. — THUR 1019:47
sounds like n., my dear — SCOTT 854:75
say nothing, or talk n. — HUXL 507:80
winnowed from deep n. — SAGAN 836:75
wish you'd stop yer n. — LAUD 583:37
noon as the sun at n. — DONNE 339:26
from the fiery n. — KEATS 547:99
liquid n. — GRAY 441:58
midnight and the n.'s repose — ELIOT 367:61
near her highest n. — MILT 682:91
n. a purple glow — YEATS 1104:57
Rise not till n. — PRIOR 791:67
the shameless n. — TENN 995:68
turned white at n. — MACM 636:22
When n. is past — SHEL 927:63
noonday wasteth at n. — BIBLE 117:2
noose naked to the hangman's n. — HOUS 494:43
n. of light — FITZ 390:87
nooses N. give — PARK 754:13
Norfolk bear him up the N. sky — BETJ 99:30
Very flat, N. — COWA 290:94
norm miraculous becomes the n. — MILL 678:28
when homosexuality was the n. — PROU 793:93
normal n. economic system works — SALT 839:40
that is the n. thing — HEND 472:54
normalcy not nostrums but n. — HARD 455:79
Norman N. arrow and sword — WILL 1080:44
N. blood — TENN 995:70
north Entreat the n. — SHAK 872:74

north (*contd.*)
Far East is to us the near n.   MENZ 670:93
heart of the N. is dead   LAWR 586:89
Hills of the N., rejoice   OAKL 733:52
in the N. long since   TENN 997:6
likeness of the N.   RODO 818:87
proceed n. of the 38th parallel   MARS 656:54
sailed into the n.   SHAK 895:27
school I went to in the n.   WILS 1085:27
Spring to the N.   MACD 627:86
talk slid n.   KIPL 561:39
tender is the N.   TENN 997:5
travelling due n.   PEARY 763:36
unripened beauties of the n.   ADDI 8:30
women at de N.   TRUTH 1030:38
north-north-west but mad n.-n.-w.   SHAK 890:8
north-west N.-w. passage   STER 969:9
North America N. A. colonization   MARI 650:62
underpants in N. A.   MURR 715:76
Northcliffe blame someone like N.   ORWE 744:26
North Pole N. P. out of my system   PEARY 762:35
North Sea oil rig in the N. S.   HEATH 466:53
North Star infect to the N. S.   SHAK 879:37
northern constant as the N. Star   SHAK 883:38
Glorious the n. lights   SMART 944:71
with a n. moonlight   SOUT 954:28
Northern Ireland violence in N. I.   OROU 741:79
Northumberland species of N.   SCOTT 856:10
Norway ten in N.   THER 1009:44
nose assiduously picking his n.   FIRB 389:73
Cleopatra's n.: if it had been shorter   PASC 757:59
dog has a keener n.   SNYD 951:85
Dong with a Luminous N.!   LEAR 589:52
Entuned in her n.   CHAU 254:20
haughtily he lifts his n.   SWIFT 985:94
He had no n.   CUMM 299:73
Marian's n. looks red   SHAK 866:31
noise with its n.   AMIS 17:95
n. fell a-bleeding on Black Monday   SHAK 874:27
N., n., jolly red n.   ANON 23:92
n. of a mob is…imagination   POE 776:53
n. would not…have grown   LAUT 584:53
not a n. at all   WELLS 1064:25
picking my n.   AUDEN 47:62
ring at the end of his n.   LEAR 590:59
same old n.   GIRO 429:47
thirty inches from my n.   AUDEN 48:97
To see…in front of one's n.   ORWE 744:41
what lies under one's n.   AUDEN 48:91
nosegay smelling his n.   SITW 941:71
noselessness N. of Man   CHES 259:29
noses blowing of n.   STER 969:8
haven't got no n.   CHES 259:28
slightly flatter n. than ourselves   CONR 284:89
nostalgia N. IS A Weapon   COUP 290:86
nostalgic n. about old fears?   ACKR 4:57
when we're n.   SONT 953:9
nostrils breathed into his n.   BIBLE 103:88
flames from their large n.!   BLAKE 165:58
glory of his n. is terrible   BIBLE 113:22
own breath in our own n.   MACD 628:99
nostrum never-failing n.   BYRON 221:9
note and sound his n.   WILL 1083:2
keeps warm her n.   CAREW 232:18
Lady, make a n.   PARK 754:7
Tu-whit, tu-whoo!—a merry n.   SHAK 866:31
turn his merry n.   SHAK 885:86
Twenty Volume Suicide N.   BARA 70:6
without a stir or n.   THOM 1015:57
Wrapped up in a five-pound n.   LEAR 590:58
notebook Armed with a n.   NEW 723:17
notes Bach on the wrong n.   PROK 792:78
cheap and the n.   LUCAS 618:27
dark n. rose everywhere   HARR 459:35

notes (*contd.*)
In n. by distance made more sweet   COLL 277:50
larks…singing the same five n.   CATH 244:39
looking for the pretty n.   PARK 753:86
million dollars…in well-used n.   CART 242:98
n. are few!   BLAKE 165:56
N. are often necessary   JOHN 528:47
n. I handle no better   SCHN 848:81
n. of the bell-birds   KEND 550:49
n. tremendous   AUDEN 48:78
right n. at the right t.   BACH 54:92
sing Such n.   MILT 682:11
suicide n.   PLOUT 775:35
tearing up £5 n.   HEATH 466:54
There are only twelve n.   HIND 481:14
thousand blended n.   WORD 1095:4
two n. a song   DAVI 308:22
wrong n. are right   IVES 514:84
nothing Ain't Heard N. Yet   JOLS 533:48
artist…makes something of the n.   PERCY 766:85
Between grief and n.   FAUL 383:75
Between the penis…there's n.   CELI 247:86
brought n. into this world   BIBLE 154:33
cannot get something for n.   HARR 459:40
do n.…for Ireland   FREE 404:32
don't know n.   DICK 325:28
doth n. but talk of his horse   SHAK 874:14
Either Caesar or n.   BORG 179:16
elsewhere they say n.   HUXL 507:80
expects n. from society   SAND 840:51
Hail n. full of n.   HEMI 470:21
having n., and yet possessing all   BIBLE 151:83
He knows n.   SHAW 923:83
He's done n.   HOPE 491:75
I have said n.   RAVEL 802:43
I know n.   GALS 413:1
I never heard n. about it   PUZO 796:44
I shall say n.   YEATS 1104:55
infinite deal of n.   SHAK 874:9
Is it n. to you   BIBLE 128:30
know n. of us!   PASC 757:61
like to say n.   SOPH 953:21
Live Well on N.   THAC 1006:88
long for n.   SPIN 960:53
lose n. again for ever   GREE 444:12
man invents n.   SHAW 921:35
Man is n. but a subject   PASC 757:55
means n. in this country   GOLD 432:91
moral crusade, or it is n.   WILS 1085:31
not be responsible for n.   PITT 771:65
n. at all to say   SAIN 836:81
n. but his imagination   SHAW 923:70
N. but males   SHAK 908:36
n.…but my body's length   SHAK 862:31
n. but our own red blood   YEATS 1106:74
n. but the highest quality   PATER 759:95
n.…by which so much happiness   JOHN 529:79
N. can be created from n.   LUCR 618:34
N. can be done without n.   SIEY 938:69
n. can be put to it   BIBLE 122:20
n. can be said to be certain   FRAN 402:12
N. can please many   JOHN 528:44
n. either good or bad   SHAK 889:98
N. for my Journey Now   ANGE 20:34
n. for n. 'ere   PUNCH 795:26
n. for reward   SPEN 958:11
n. good to be had   HAZL 463:97
N. happens, nobody comes   BECK 81:92
N. has changed since   HUGH 500:37
N. has raised more questioning   ARNO 38:8
n. he cannot do   KIM 557:65
N. in comparison to the infinite   PASC 758:70
N. in excess   ANON 20:44
N. in his life   SHAK 907:23

nothing (*contd.*)
n. in particular   GILB 424:76
N. in the world is single   SHEL 928:85
n. in thy purse   BIBLE 132:4
N. is easier to say   TERE 1006:76
N. is made with n.   INGR 511:46
N. is really very frightening   STEIN 965:39
N. is wasted, n. is in vain   HERB 474:6
n. left remarkable   SHAK 906:96
N., like something   LARK 581:98
n. mattered, n. was lost   GEE 417:65
n. matters   AMIS 17:94
N. matters very much   BALF 65:21
n. much to lose   HOUS 496:83
n. much to worry about   HERR 478:70
N. of him doth fade   SHAK 916:26
N. really wrong with him   HILT 481:11
N. remains of it all   WOOLF 1093:76
n. to do with the laws   HORS 494:38
n. to offer anybody   KERO 553:13
n. to say…that is poetry   CAGE 225:90
n. to say, say n.   COLT 277:54
n. will remain   HOUS 494:46
now I'm n.   GINS 428:27
Now we know n.   CORN 288:59
on whom n. is lost!   JAMES 516:20
pictures of n.   HAZL 464:25
reason knows n.   PASC 758:65
say n., do n., be n.   ANON 30:55
Science…knows n.   GOUR 437:80
seeing n. as the sum of everything   DUDEK 354:20
sees n. within him   FRIE 405:61
sit around so much doing n.   STEIN 965:40
that which dost cost me n.   BIBLE 110:52
them for whom n. is prepared   BIBLE 112:92
thenceforth good for n.   BIBLE 134:35
There is n. to it   BACH 54:92
there is n.—absolutely n.   GRAH 438:50
there is n.   BECK 81:2
there was n. before   HEMI 470:29
There's n. behind it!   WARH 1053:20
they that starve with n.   SHAK 874:10
those who do n.…make no mistakes   CONR 284:86
those who had n.   BEER 83:38
though you feel n.   JULI 539:68
thought to n. of her writing   SITW 941:19
To do n. and get something   DISR 332:89
To say n. is out here   HEAT 465:47
to whom such things are n.   SOPH 953:22
we can talk of n.   TROL 1027:67
wise For saying n.   SHAK 873:1
writing is n.   HEMI 471:50
you shall learn n.   HUXL 508:96
Youth…forgives itself n.   SHAW 922:62
nothingness never Pass into n.   KEATS 545:56
old, split N.   FERN 386:27
nothings Invulnerable n.   SHEL 931:46
notice n. makes me sick   WODE 1089:98
n. which you have been pleased   JOHN 526:99
Over the piano was printed a n.   WILDE 1075:30
without my n.   HOMER 488:25
noticed hardly n. how it came   KHAY 555:44
notion a great n.   STEE 964:16
foolish n.   BURNS 210:77
give up every preconceived n.   HUXL 508:96
n. of cause and effect   HUME 503:99
n. that geometry was degraded   MACA 623:11
outworn n.   THUR 1020:74
what a silly n.!   KING 558:99
notions counter to their narrow n.   STEV 977:61
notorious can't be famous…be n.   MAHA 638:60
Notre Dame turrets of N. D.   MAHO 638:64
Nottingham N. lace of the curtains   BETJ 99:29
nought n. so vile   SHAK 869:95

nought (*contd.*)	
N. may endure but Mutability	SHEL 927:64
when that my hap is n.	SURR 983:46
noun beyond its n.	REID 806:97
God...is a verb, not a n.	FULL 409:36
n. and a verb	SHAK 861:15
nouns how they connect n.	SAND 841:73
nourish n. a blind life	TENN 1004:47
nourished grow and be n.	RAND 801:26
nourishing back to the n. earth	SAND 841:67
nourishment as n. to wind	MILT 691:83
fruitful hope of n.	SPEN 959:41
proper n.	STER 969:2
without n. and support	SMOL 950:64
Novalis 'Character' says N.	ELIOT 365:23
novel admitted that a n.	TROL 1028:97
aesthetic debate about n.	BRAD 184:88
American n.	HUGH 500:30
atom of the traditional n.	LODGE 610:78
Australian n. is not...dreary	WHITE 1070:45
because a n.'s invented	POWE 788:8
cannot care for in a n.	TROL 1028:86
Cricket, like the n.	ARLO 35:38
crime n. is not easy	JAMES 517:34
given away by a n.	KEATS 545:64
greatest invention since the n.	MEAD 666:14
had he professed to be writing a N.	HAWT 461:72
impulse to write a n.	WILS 1084:15
in morning room reading a n.	WAUGH 1057:86
modern n. has been many things	BRAD 183:87
notion of a British n.	BUFO 203:44
n. ...a Protestant form of art	ORWE 743:13
n. and art would be useless	BALZ 69:82
n. for the age old...ego	LAWR 585:65
n. is absolutely the only vehicle	FORD 396:5
n. is a static thing	TYNAN 1035:27
n. is an impression	HARDY 456:1
n. is balanced between...impressions	BELL 88:37
n. is dead	DELI 314:39
n. is serious, the n.	NEME 722:5
n. of mankind	GAUT 416:42
n. ...philosophy put into images	CAMUS 229:64
n. tells a story	FORS 398:44
n. was not a trumpet	LESS 598:5
obligation to which...hold a n.	JAMES 516:18
Oh! it is only a n.!	AUST 52:63
project a serial n.	STEV 974:22
read a n....for the moral	OCON 735:86
scrofulous French n.	BROW 197:28
When a n. comes	MAIL 640:91
Writing a n.	GREE 444:24
novel-writer woman...n.-w.	OLIP 738:25
novelist admire you more as a n.	COOP 287:45
being a n., I consider	LAWR 587:8
characteristic of the really great n.	BENN 91:85
Jane Austen...only n. I know	BANKS 70:1
lady n.	GILB 425:85
made me a n.	GREE 444:21
most precious possession of a n.	CONR 285:1
No poet or n. wishes	AUDEN 48:90
n....does not have the right	FLAU 392:41
n....his own most harsh critic	WILS 1084:20
n. is, like all mortals	NABO 717:6
popular n.'s trade	BURG 206:94
novelistic beginning of a n. affair	MANN 646:87
novelists as for most n.	ROTH 826:22
major n. who count	LEAV 591:75
N....are also children	DEVO 318:90
Phelps calls Medlar N.	MACD 627:58
novels all n....deal with character	WOOLF 1092:58
books are n. at heart	RABAN 798:75
cultivation sits on her n.	AUCH 46:40
do not read n.	VIDAL 1044:70
few English n. for grown up	WOOLF 1093:4

novels (*contd.*)	
heroes of three recent n.	BROY 201:6
Learn even from N.	WELLS 1064:31
n. are about certain minorities	ELLI 375:18
n. written with a purpose	FORD 396:6
Readers of n.	LUCAS 618:25
reading all the n. you can	HUGH 499:25
which among my n. is my favourite	ACHE 2:20
novelty charm of n.	FLAU 392:39
Japan offers as much n.	BIRD 163:15
November N., he full of gross	SPEN 959:43
N.'s sky is chill	SCOTT 853:51
On the 5th of N.	HOBY 483:47
those N. skies	FREE 404:35
now all is always n.	ELIOT 370:30
fierce urgency of n.	KING 557:79
here and n. cease to matter	ELIOT 372:30
Live always in this paradisal n.	KHAY 555:43
must be a great soul n.	EMER 377:68
n. is the day of salvation	BIBLE 151:82
N. is the time to drink	HORA 493:19
N. what?	SARO 843:1
nowadays many left like him n.	WAUGH 1056:66
nowhere From n. we came	HAGG 450:5
in other words, n.	JARRY 518:66
n. to fall	ALAN 11:79
you're n.	GROS 447:73
nowt Say n.	CLOU 271:52
nozzle hits the exit n.	SCHW 851:30
nuance No colour, only n.!	VERL 1042:37
n. in an ideological difference	COND 279:83
nubbly Nice but n.	KIPL 562:73
nuclear AIDS, cancer, n. war	MAMET 644:56
ancestors had discovered n. power	LAMB 577:45
military and n. sense	WALE 1049:50
n. arms race	MOUN 711:13
n. reaction in uranium	EINS 363:65
n. war survivors	COUP 289:81
so-called independent n. weapons	BENN 90:68
nude Bare like n.	SPEN 956:80
mistress is n.	KILP 556:64
n. and antique	SWIN 987:31
nudes madonnas and shameless n.	MALE 641:11
nudging fudging and n.	OWEN 747:5
nudism lyrical bit about n.	JOYCE 538:58
nudist becomes a n.	WHITE 1070:35
nugget n. of the human condition	ACKE 4:53
nuisance n. for a few people	CHES 258:92
pleasant n. in not being able to walk	DARW 306:82
poor and luckless...as a n.	CARL 235:81
positive n. to you	HOLST 487:5
nuisances pestilential n.	GILB 425:84
null splendidly n.	TENN 1001:74
number best n. for a dinner party	GULB 448:82
big positive n.	GATES 416:37
called the wrong n.	THUR 1018:22
cousins...without a n.	SHAW 926:43
express myself in Terms of N.	PETTY 768:15
finite n. of heart-beats	ARMS 35:50
ghost with a n.	PAZ 761:23
increase their n.	TOCQ 1021:76
n. all your graces	SHAK 912:47
n. of syllables	SAND 842:80
n. of the beast	BIBLE 158:22
n. of the stars	BIBLE 120:54
n., weigh and measure	HALES 451:23
n. who can write	MACD 627:85
On this next n.	LENN 596:54
teach us to n. our days	BIBLE 117:1
numbers better than n.	CROM 297:49
brings home full n.	SHAK 878:25
By n. here from shame	JOHN 525:79
divinity in odd n.	SHAK 878:23
greatest happiness for the greatest n.	HUTC 506:47

numbers (*contd.*)	
hours their n. spend!	SPEN 959:32
more we grow in n.	TERT 1006:78
no safety in n.	THUR 1018:23
N....universal language	WEST 1067:86
n. which could call	COWL 291:14
politics of n.	TANA 990:94
write the beauty...in fresh n.	SHAK 912:47
numbness drowsy n. pains	KEATS 547:13
numerous more n. formerly	TOLK 1023:94
nun credit to a Trappist n.	SHAR 919:82
Hero, Venus' n.	MARL 654:25
quiet as a n.	WORD 1097:40
nunc N. dimittis	BIBLE 160:55
N. est bibendum	HORA 493:19
nunnery get thee to a n.	TWAIN 1033:89
Get thee to a n.	SHAK 891:24
n. Of thy chaste breast	LOVE 615:66
put to scole in a n.	MALO 642:23
nuptials iteration of n.	CONG 282:46
Nureyev Ask N. to stop dancing	KING 557:69
nurse best n. contemplation	MILT 683:28
Chinese n. with green trousers	MANS 647:46
definition of what a n.	NIGH 729:1
dirty n., Experience	TENN 1004:21
keep a hold of N.	BELL 87:8
Nature's soft n.	SHAK 877:94
n. and tutor of eccentric minds	LAWS 587:18
n. for a poetic child!	SCOTT 853:50
n. of manly sentiment	BURKE 207:32
n. of ninety years	TENN 997:8
priest continues what the n. began	DRYD 351:55
nursery light in the night n.	MACN 637:40
nurses old men's n.	BACON 57:61
to be n. and pianists	ROTH 826:8
nursing n. the unconquerable hope	ARNO 38:93
nursling n. of the sky	SHEL 928:84
Ocean's n., Venice	SHEL 927:70
nurture job of the n. of children	PALEY 751:61
nut cracking the n.	BRON 190:88
every hare-brained n.	SAFER 835:66
heading into n. country	KENN 552:70
n.'s schell, thocht it be hard	HENR 473:69
nut-brown spicy n.-b. ale	MILT 682:2
nutlike hard, brown, n. word	BART 74:72
nutmegs N. and ginger	ANON 23:92
nutrition People in n.	DAVIS 308:23
nuts fearful...would go n.	CUMM 299:74
where the n. come from	DISCH 331:69
Where the n. come from	THOM 1009:47
nutshell bounded in a n.	SHAK 890:99
Nyasaland bring Stonehenge to N.	BANDA 69:86
nymph Echo, sweetest n.	MILT 683:21
n. shall break Diana's law	POPE 778:96
rose like a n.	SHEL 930:29
nymphs n. with their flattering	SITW 941:9
Where were ye N.	MILT 684:1
Ye N. that reign o'er sewers and sinks	COLE 275:40
O altitudo reason to an O. a.!	BROW 195:74
oak ashes of an o.	DONNE 338:17
builder o., sole king	SPEN 957:99
charms...to bend a knotted o.	CONG 281:21
English o. and holly	HARTE 460:52
fell the hardest-timbered o.	SHAK 861:19
O., and Ash, and Thorn	KIPL 563:70
o.'s thick branches	GRAY 441:56
plant an o. in a flower-pot	BRON 192:13
wedges cleave the hardest o.	KYD 571:24
win the palm, the o.	MARV 658:82
oak-tree When the o.-t. is fallen	CARL 235:73
Oakland having come from O.	STEIN 965:41
oaks Beneath our o. has slept	BLAKE 165:58
oar wind and wave and o.	TENN 994:53

oars like a ship with the o. lifted	MANS 647:7
The o. were silver	SHAK 905:68
oat-cakes o.-c. and sulphur	SMITH 949:49
oath A terrible o.	SHAK 895:33
forced to swear an o.	MARG 650:60
good mouth-filling o.	SHAK 876:62
He who cheats with an o.	PLUT 775:36
If I ever utter an o. again	SHAW 925:21
lose an o.	SHAK 865:19
man is not upon o.	JOHN 529:78
neither by any other o.	BIBLE 155:72
not ask thine o.	SHAK 910:96
sin to keep a sinful o.	SHAK 861:14
since I took the o.	MACA 621:74
sworn a solemn o.	BURNS 210:89
trust man on his o.	SHAK 901:87
oaths for o. are straws	SHAK 880:78
o. are but words	BUTL 217:18
standers-by to curtail his o.	SHAK 916:99
'Tis not the many o.	SHAK 901:77
oats O. A grain…given to horses	JOHN 526:14
obedience end to blind o.	WOLL 1091:36
except docility, o.	WELD 1062:92
in the name of duty and o.	SNOW 951:76
infuses…that liberal o.	BURKE 207:12
life of strict o.	DOST 340:43
O.…is Good Luck's mother	AESC 9:59
o. of creatures	HOOK 489:54
o. to God	DAVI 309:42
swift in all o.	KIPL 561:53
truth in no man, nor o.	BEAU 80:77
obedient o. to their commands	SIMO 939:85
o. unto death	BIBLE 153:8
obey easy enough to o.	TUCH 1031:46
love, cherish, and o.	BOOK 176:50
o. God rather than men	BIBLE 147:85
One must o. the man	SOPH 953:17
That can so well o.	MARV 657:67
to o. is better than sacrifice	BIBLE 110:35
to those who o. Him	SCHW 852:31
who has learned to o.	KEMP 549:41
wise ridicule and o.	BIER 161:83
obeyed G. has more right to be o.	JOHN 522:32
o. as a son	GIBB 421:28
She who must be o.	HAGG 450:6
when to be o.	HAWT 461:78
obituary autobiography is an o.	CRISP 297:40
object America…an o. of faith	RABAN 798:76
B-b-british o.	MALO 643:36
chosen o., a definite task	POPP 783:20
desperately insignificant o.	DAVI 308:14
distinguish himself from an o.	SENG 858:51
end and o. of conquest	ALEX 13:14
'express' an o.	ROSE 822:56
eye on the o.	ARNO 38:5
let the form of an o. be what it may	CONS 285:20
most exalted o.	DARW 306:84
no o. worth its constancy?	SHEL 932:73
o. all sublime	GILB 425:90
o. behind that name	SPEN 956:88
o. from the crime	POPE 779:10
o.…is less than discernible	LEGER 594:22
o. of aesthetic appreciation	BARR 72:39
O. of C.	AUST 50:29
o. of interest	RUSK 830:73
o. of love and esteem	LAMB 576:24
o. of universal devotion	IRVI 513:68
o. of war is not to die	PATT 761:16
o. quite forgotten	SHAK 860:80
o. seen, and eye that sees	WORD 1096:34
o. strange and high	MARV 658:77
o. to seeing on the screen	GOLD 434:41
Picasso studies an o.	APOL 31:90
poem…is a physical o.	MACB 624:31

object (*contd.*)	
saddest o. in civilisation	STEV 977:62
see the o. as in itself	ARNO 38:6
set before him a provoking o.	MILT 686:70
sex o.	GIOV 428:37
stimulus and o. of our meditation	MANN 645:78
utility of some particular o.	SMITH 946:94
When gold becomes her o.!	SHAK 878:8
why should…your team o.?	HEND 472:54
women into a sex o.	MORG 708:67
objection no o. to this method	STER 969:97
objectionable O. in action	GOET 431:69
objections o. to this proposition	HOBH 483:44
objective achieve that o.	MACN 636:33
final o. is not	LIEB 604:91
gained our first o.	SASS 845:24
o. by pretending	LEWO 603:74
o. correlative	ELIOT 368:76
o. was the world	DULL 354:26
production of fact	MENC 669:77
speak of the Fascist o.	ORWE 742:3
objectives limited o. he has now	OCON 735:86
objectivity slivers and shreds of o.	CUPI 301:11
objects All visible o., man	MELV 667:34
arranging any set of o.	MILL 675:74
bad poet dwells…in a world of o.	ELIOT 368:77
credit ordinary and visible o.	BROW 195:73
enjoyment of beautiful o.	MOORE 704:10
extracted from many o.	SHAK 886:16
forward the o. which we have	PLATO 774:24
lose sight of their o.	ELIOT 365:16
lustre of midday to o.	MOORE 704:5
Men see o.	FOWL 399:66
o. as I think them	PICA 769:27
o. of desire	RICA 808:35
o. of human reason	HUME 503:8
o. of Sensation	LOCKE 609:73
o. recognised In flashes	WORD 1096:30
o. seen by the eye	PIERO 769:38
One by one the o.	WILL 1082:84
only o. in the material world	FORS 399:50
ornament from utilitarian o.	LOOS 612:25
secure those important o.	PITT 771:71
too visible as sex o.	FRIE 405:50
try to forget what o.	MONET 700:43
obligated o. to Russia	BROD 190:74
obligation acknowledge no o.	GIBB 421:26
because o. is a pain	JOHN 525:88
not an o. but a joy	KILLY 556:62
o. of a more scrupulous fidelity	CONR 285:10
o. to become a servant	SHAW 924:93
o. to which…we may hold a n.	JAMES 516:18
pile o. on o.	CHAM 249:12
politics is an o.	ROGE 820:19
sense of o.	CRANE 295:14
obligations honourable o.	CHUR 264:9
Nobility brings o.	LEVIS 600:30
o. arising	UNIT 1036:45
o. of man	CAMUS 229:63
trick of heaping o.	SHAW 921:29
obliging civil and o. young woman	AUST 50:29
obliviate drink to o.	FLYNN 395:81
oblivion Alms for o.	SHAK 896:51
Challengers of o.	JEFF 519:80
cold o.	SHEL 931:51
memory be left in o.	EMMET 378:81
o. amounts to newspaper death	ADAMS 5:80
O, my o. is a very Antony	SHAK 905:65
Second childishness and mere o.	SHAK 886:96
oblong o. of pink	MONET 700:43
obloquy greatest o. i' th' world	SHAK 901:78
speechless o.	BYRON 220:97
obnoxious o. to each carping tongue	BRAD 184:1
obscene anachronistic is o.	BART 75:85

obscene (*contd.*)	
pictures of o. books!	ARLT 35:41
obscenity o., a depraved act	CHOM 261:56
o. is what happens	RUSS 833:33
O. is a cleansing process	MILL 679:54
Sex and o. not synonymous	BREN 187:33
obscure getting more o.	THOM 1010:54
he who sits o.	SHEL 929:10
succeed in being o.	HORA 493:30
through the palpable o.	MILT 688:21
obscurity afraid of losing my o.	HUXL 506:50
o. of a learned language	GIBB 421:30
o. of our investigations	SCHO 849:92
o. of the matter	PROT 792:84
rest in o. and peace!	EMMET 378:81
obsequies celebrates his o.	SCOTT 853:48
tear to grace his o.	GRAY 443:85
obsequiousness O. is glorified	CHAO 251:63
observance breach than the o.	SHAK 888:70
o. of trifles	DOYLE 343:96
observation from personal o.	WILS 1084:11
Let o. with extensive	JOHN 525:81
O. is always selective	POPP 783:20
product of that simple o.	BEHR 85:76
road of experiment and o.	LAVO 585:58
Scientific o. is always a viewing	HUXL 508:90
sense and o.	WORD 1100:83
things…worth their o.	ADDI 7:15
Where o. is concerned	PAST 759:85
observations pure o. alone	POPP 783:19
what o. would lead him	AYER 53:79
observe never can o. anything	HUME 503:7
O. how system into system runs	POPE 780:34
o.…just by watching	BERRA 98:1
o. the best speakers	JONS 536:23
You see, but you do not o.	DOYLE 344:3
observed exists until it is o.	BURR 213:58
o. by Yours faithfully, God	ANON 25:35
o. with sufficient closeness	TROL 1028:81
observer every o. necessarily suffers	ORWE 745:50
keen o. of life	AUDEN 48:77
o. of human nature	DICK 320:17
social position of the o.	MANN 646:93
obsessed o. by the feeling	SPEN 957:91
obsolescence designing for o.	ISSI 514:80
obsolete Either war is o.	FULL 409:38
out of date, o.	STEV 970:31
obstacle Bureaucracy is not an o.	SCHU 851:21
gameboard and o. course	ELKIN 374:98
greatest o. to being heroic	HAWT 461:78
greatest o. to happiness	FONT 395:90
obstacle-racing sport…is o.-r.	TREE 1025:44
obstacles all of civilization's o.	SAND 840:48
If there are o.	BREC 186:27
raining down o.	MANC 644:63
obstinacy o., and error	POPP 784:26
o. in a bad one	STER 969:93
O. in a bad cause	BROW 195:80
o. of cleverness and reason	STOWE 979:90
obstinate not because he is o.	BLOOM 169:34
stricken with most o. love	SIDN 936:44
obstructed o. interstate commerce	HOOV 490:69
obstruction consecrated o.	BAGE 61:60
obtain o. the largest measure	TIMES 1020:70
o. the reputation	TROL 1028:89
obviating o. of all future wars	FORD 396:6
obvious afraid of the deafeningly o.	KAVA 543:26
analysis of the o.	WHIT 1071:54
occasion constraint, and sad o. dear	MILT 684:38
courage mounteth with o.	SHAK 872:61
every possible o.	LYTT 621:68
had frequent o. to test…friendship	POE 776:45
man who never missed an o.	SHAW 926:45
nations, and on this o.	ROCHE 815:40

occasion (*contd.*)
no o. to exert his understanding — SMITH 946:91
o., catalyst, or tripwire — ACKE 4:53
O., Chance, and Change? — SHEL 930:23
o. is not merely — NEHRU 722:94
occasions All o. invite his mercies — DONNE 339:26
august o. of the state — FROST 407:3
crowds for all o. — SIMP 939:88
feeling…on rare o. — FERL 386:21
o. and causes why — SHAK 882:7
o. such as these — MURP 715:70
Prose on certain o. — LAND 578:64
occult some o. relation — JOHN 525:90
occupation continual o. and change — AUST 52:68
cure for it is o. — SHAW 924:9
Every o. …is…absurd — QUEN 797:54
golfer…my real o. — MATU 664:83
no housewifery, nor…earthly o. — SMOL 950:63
not quite the o. of an adult — OLIV 738:28
pause in the day's o. — DEVO 318:91
pause in the day's o. — LONG 612:15
Sport…is an o. — PIUS 772:81
occupations imaginable o. — THUR 1019:32
worse o. in this world — STER 970:26
occurred never o. to him — GARC 414:18
ocean at the bottom of the o. — RAND 801:25
butterfly poised on a pigtailed o. — SITW 940:2
crossed an o. — NICH 726:51
dark unfathomed caves of o. — GRAY 442:69
day-star in the o. bed — MILT 685:49
eye that sees on the o. — MACL 633:69
from o.'s farthest coast — HOW 497:91
His legs bestrid the o. — SHAK 906:1
icebergs in the o. — GERH 420:5
If the o. was pure mind — PRAT 788:22
land and o. without rest — MILT 686:81
lavished the o. on you in vain — BORG 179:12
life at the o. bottom — HECHT 466:60
Neptune's o. wash this blood — SHAK 908:49
new joys to the mild o. — MILT 681:87
O. and earth — WORD 1100:79
O.'s child, and then his queen — SHEL 927:71
o. for orient pearl — MARL 654:9
o. for orient pearl — MARL 654:13
o. is flat again — KEYN 554:29
O.'s nursling, Venice — SHEL 927:70
o. of truth lay all — NEWT 725:40
o. or the human heart? — LAUT 584:49
o. protesting against separation — GRAT 439:14
O. racing is like standing — HEATH 466:54
o.…was his home — BYRON 219:82
On one side lay the O. — TENN 1004:42
one-and-a-half o. navy — HAYW 463:94
outstretch'd o. glitter — BYRON 222:41
painted ship Upon a painted o. — COLE 273:87
pores of the o. and shores — SHEL 928:84
rivers with the o. — SHEL 928:85
round o. — WORD 1094:98
sky…Spread like a rosy o. — BYRON 222:44
So on the o. life — LONG 612:18
till the o. Is folded — AUDEN 47:60
Tweed rins into the o. — BURNS 212:31
ocean-roll deep and dark blue O.-r. — BYRON 221:6
oceans Portable and compendious o. — CRAS 296:21
octaves o. of its parallel edges — CUMM 299:76
octavos o. fill a spacious plain — CRAB 293:67
October Falls like the leaves in O. — FULL 410:55
fifteenth of O. 1764 — GIBB 421:29
funny…month, O. — NORD 731:26
leaf still in O. — FLET 394:71
O.'s strife — GURN 449:90
octopus o. is soft — ARNO 40:45
odd cure of the id by the o. — ANON 25:34
divinity in o. numbers — SHAK 878:23

odd (*contd.*)
o. old ends stol'n — SHAK 863:53
people's voice is o. — POPE 782:81
something o. about women — BENN 91:77
odds beats thee 'gainst the o. — SHAK 905:72
face the o. — HOUS 496:74
ode O. on a Grecian Urn — FAUL 383:83
odes quoted o. — TENN 996:92
odi O. et amo — CATU 245:64
odium He lived in the o. — BENT 93:25
odorous Comparisons are o. — SHAK 880:57
odour no o. so bad — THOR 1016:76
o. of sanctity — WALL 1049:62
o. of wine — RABE 798:78
principle of its colour and o. — SHEL 931:56
Stealing and giving o. — SHAK 893:91
sweet o.…doth in it live — SHAK 913:63
odours dirt and ill o. — THOR 1017:97
gentle o. led my steps — SHEL 932:66
phoenix…Exhales her o. — BYRON 219:65
probed…their o. — ANGE 20:32
puff of wind…laden with strange o. — CONR 284:96
Odysseus Like O., the President — KEYN 554:26
odyssey long o. toward liberty — MAIL 639:81
Oedipus O. …dripping — PAGE 749:31
O. he had the luck — HUGH 500:46
O. triumph over gravity — KOES 568:69
reason is his best O. — BROW 195:69
Oedipuses peculiar family, the O. — BEER 84:48
off if honour prick me o. — SHAK 876:68
Want To Get O. — ANON 27:68
off-key sing o.-k. — GERS 420:11
sing…off-key o.-k. — MILL 677:15
offal barrow of butcher's o. — SHAK 878:22
offence After o. returning — MILT 695:52
by deceit to breed o. — DYER 358:90
forgave the o. — DRYD 352:85
greatest o. against virtue — HAZL 464:22
image of o. — SHAK 895:34
like to give o. — FROST 406:73
means to give o. — ROCHE 815:39
never resented for an o. — SWIFT 984:60
no harshness give o. — POPE 778:84
O, my o. is rank! — SHAK 892:46
only defence is in o. — BALD 65:10
Shipton assault…a criminal o. — CRAN 295:15
sour o. — SHAK 895:46
What dire o. …springs — POPE 778:90
whatsoever o. or injury — HENR 472:65
offences more o. at my beck — SHAK 891:25
offend nothing shall o. them — BIBLE 119:35
o., when 'tis let loose — SUCK 981:22
offended I have o. reputation — SHAK 905:79
no one is consciously o. — ELIOT 370:20
This hath o.! — CRAN 295:16
we are sharply o. — TWAIN 1034:7
offender hugged the o. — DRYD 352:85
offenders society o. — GILB 425:84
offensive It may sound o. — STEV 973:97
someone else is being o. — BROO 193:37
taking the o. — PENI 764:55
offer intend to o. — KENN 550:61
nothing to o. anybody — KERO 553:13
o. he can't refuse — PUZO 796:39
o. so willingly after this sort? — BIBLE 112:86
power to o. love — SHAW 920:99
offering delightest not in burnt o. — BIBLE 116:79
lamb for a burnt o. — BIBLE 105:28
o. too little — CANN 230:72
offerings burnt o. — BIBLE 110:52
delight in burnt o. — BIBLE 110:35
offers when most she o. blows — SHAK 905:81
office A dog's obeyed in o. — SHAK 904:37
By o. boys for o. boys — SALI 839:36

office (*contd.*)
don't have power…have o. — TODD 1022:84
Each in his o. wait — DODD 335:46
eternal villain…to get some o. — SHAK 900:44
fill a high o. — LOUI 614:48
gainful employment…not public o. — ACHE 2:21
high officials leave o. — KISS 566:38
in which the o. is held — HUXL 507:71
man who has no o. — SHAW 920:90
never pretend to any other o. — HUME 503:3
never seen an o. — STEV 973:91
not going to be in o. — MOND 699:39
o. boy — GILB 423:58
o. of respiration — DICK 321:33
o. of the White House — MENC 669:76
o. sanctifies the holder — ACTON 4:59
o. to be new stamped — LAMB 576:23
o. was his pirate ship — LEWIS 602:52
primary o. is the gathering of News — SCOTT 852:33
raised taxes before he took o. — DOLE 335:53
reaches the newpaper o. — LIPP 606:32
seven years in o. — GISC 429:34
So clear in his great o. — SHAK 908:32
they have once won o. — GALB 411:75
'Tis all men's o. — SHAK 880:61
vote somebody into o. — GERG 420:2
way out of elective o. — HOOV 490:63
officer British o. — PANG 752:76
officers o. and fellow-rankers said — SMITH 948:38
offices ants to harvest o. — DONNE 336:77
go back to your o. — ANDE 18:1
good o. that sex can discharge — WOOLF 1093:75
great o.…give social prestige — BAGE 61:57
official more fanatical o. — HAZZ 464:27
The o. world — SNOW 950:71
officials high o. leave office — KISS 566:38
o. are the servants — GOWE 437:81
o. working in offices — WEBER 1059:22
set of bigmouthed o. — DOSP 340:40
offspring human o. — MILT 690:65
o. of Heav'n first-born — MILT 689:29
o. of journalistic realism — WHITE 1070:45
would not care about his o. — HAWT 461:66
often written it so o. — GERG 420:99
OG O. = PLR × AEB — BIRNS 163:27
oil anointest my head with o. — BIBLE 115:50
go out to an o. rig — HEATH 466:53
how much o.…with one's vinegar — WILDE 1075:28
in him we see O. — GOLD 433:27
keep putting o. in it — THER 1009:36
mix like O. and Vinegar — GAIN 411:69
mouth is smoother than o. — BIBLE 120:61
o. can is mightier than the sword — DIRK 331:64
o. depletion…makes Houston — MAIL 639:84
o. to make his face to shine — BIBLE 118:16
Pour o. into their ears — JONS 534:78
Some people find o. — GETTY 421:16
thou hast anointed my head with o. — BOOK 176:67
Warren's blackin' or Rowland's o. — DICK 320:26
where you put in the o. — TAYL 992:24
why o. painting was invented — DEKO 313:19
wine…sweeter…than o. — RABE 798:78
oily o. man of God — THOM 1015:53
ointment Dead flies cause the o. — BIBLE 123:36
like the precious o. — BIBLE 119:45
Oisin O O. — YEATS 1104:58
Wanderings of O. — WILDE 1076:32
okie O. use' ta mean — STEI 966:54
Oklahoma Okie…from O. — STEI 966:54
old adherence to the o. and tried — LINC 605:2
And she, being o. — SMITH 947:3
appeared in o. unto me — BIBLE 128:27
appearèd, to have been of o. — SPEN 958:10
As an o. soldier — SHAW 921:37

old (*contd.*)

As you are o. and reverend	SHAK 902:6
be she o.	SWIFT 986:17
beauty so o. and so new	AUGU 49:10
Behold, thou art o.	BIBLE 110:32
Being an o. maid	FERB 385:11
being o. is having lighted rooms	LARK 582:17
born o. and ugly?	DICK 322:65
brook the o.	FERG 386:18
buried in a good o. age	BIBLE 104:20
can't be o. without it	WILL 1082:68
chancèd in the times of o.	SHAK 862:41
chilly and grown o.	BROW 198:48
country safe to grow o. in	THAT 1007:9
crown of o. men	BIBLE 121:85
die before I get o.	TOWN 1024:14
die of grow o.	MONT 700:54
fat and grows o.	SHAK 876:54
find the o. in the new	MANN 646:89
folks git o. en strucken	HARR 458:32
foolish, fond o. man	SHAK 904:43
Grow o. along with me	BROW 199:75
growing o. in drawing nothing up!	COWP 293:57
how subject we o. men	SHAK 877:99
I grow o....I grow o.	ELIOT 367:53
I'm just an awkward o. maid	RENO 806:2
If you're going to get o.	STEG 965:29
ill and o. and terrified	BETJ 100:50
insecurity in America...growing o.	ELLW 375:20
know thee not, o. man	SHAK 878:10
Long be it ere thou grow o.	ROCH 817:65
love everything that's o.	GOLD 433:20
make me conservative when o.	FROST 407:93
more virtue than o. men	JOHN 527:35
never can be o.	SHAK 915:84
never too o.	THOR 1017:96
no fashion for the o.	CHAN 251:55
no man would be o.	SWIFT 985:91
now am not too o.	BLUN 170:47
now am o.	BIBLE 115:65
o. and stricken in years	BIBLE 110:53
O. and young	STEV 974:14
o. fashioned	ALLEN 14:49
o., For a dream's sake	ROSS 823:69
o. have reminiscences	SAKI 837:99
o. heads on your young shoulders	SPARK 955:51
o. immorality condoned	SHAW 926:47
o., mad...dying king	SHEL 927:76
o. man, and heavy	BIBLE 110:31
o. man broken	SHAK 918:64
o. man does not care for	JOHN 528:50
o. man in a dry month	ELIOT 368:68
O. Man with a beard	LEAR 589:50
o. man with wrinkled dugs	ELIOT 369:89
o. man young	TENN 995:66
o. men shall dream	BIBLE 130:55
o.[might as well speak] to the young	CATH 244:43
o. people make so many journeys	BLYT 171:54
o. ways are the safest	COKE 272:72
our land, it is o.	RANS 802:33
persuade you, young and o.	PLATO 773:3
put off the o. man	BIBLE 153:21
redress the balance of the O.	CANN 230:73
remember the days of O.	MOORE 706:33
Ring out the o.	TENN 1000:56
same o. nose	GIRO 429:47
Say I'm growing o.	HUNT 505:29
she is not yet so o.	SHAK 873:84
socialize the cost of growing o.	HEWE 479:87
Some day before I'm o.!	KIPL 563:84
suppose an o. man decayed	JOHN 531:24
Tell me the o., o. story	HANK 455:70
tell when one is getting o.	EDWA 362:52
the o. will go on	WILL 1083:94

old (*contd.*)

The o....talk to themselves	ONEI 740:52
think he is growing o.	IRVI 513:65
Though I look o.	SHAK 885:82
times begin to wax o.	BIBLE 131:77
'Tis well an o. age is out	DRYD 352:97
to be forty years o.	HOLM 486:2
too o. and intelligent	BRAD 183:85
too o. to dream	HAMM 454:53
warn you not to get o.	KINN 559:12
We are o., we are o.	SMITH 948:35
we grow o.	TENN 996:90
what's the use of being o.	OHARA 737:10
when he is o., he will not depart	BIBLE 121:94
when they get to feeling o.	BROO 192:29
when thou shalt be o.	BIBLE 147:78
when you are o. sit	DICK 323:94
When you are o.	YEATS 1105:60
you and I are o.	TENN 995:61
youth, before I waxèd o.	SPEN 959:29
old-fashioned be always o.-f.	SANT 842:85
apt to grow o.-f.	WILDE 1078:92
make these products o.-f.	STEV 970:31
o.-f. Boarding-school	AUST 51:53
o.-f. Virginia fox hunt	WASH 1054:43
old age cold and forlorn o. a.	STEV 973:1
death...puts an end to o. a.	LABR 573:50
died in a good o. a.	BIBLE 112:87
first sign of o. a.	HICKS 480:94
flower of o. a.	DEMO 315:46
fruit in o. a.	BIBLE 117:4
infirmities of o. a.	WESL 1067:71
looked down upon in our o. a.?	SCHU 851:20
man reaches o. a.	MAO 648:24
men...in their o. a.	POPE 779:17
O. A. a regret	DISR 332:82
o. a., accident, sickness	LLOY 608:57
o. a. and experience	ROCH 816:51
o. a. hath his yet honour	TENN 995:61
o. a. is always fifteen years older	BARU 75:92
O. a. is second childhood	ARIS 34:21
O. A. may come after you	WHIT 1073:98
o. a. of cards	POPE 782:77
O. a. should burn and rave	THOM 1011:75
O. a....it's the only disease	MANK 645:72
should accompany o. a.	SHAK 910:81
son of his o. a.	BIBLE 105:39
Oldcastle Sweet Jack O.	SHAK 876:57
Old Testament O. T. makes	STAN 963:90
Prosperity...blessing of the O. T.	BACON 56:50
Old World eyes of the O. W.	MANS 647:99
older As I get o.	FERL 386:23
As I grow o.	SOLO 952:92
As we get o.	REED 805:83
As we grow o.	ELIOT 372:55
grow o. and o.	SAYE 846:53
growing o. has served no purpose	RILKE 811:84
man as he grows o.	STEI 966:60
O. than love	SCOTT 852:37
O. than the time of chronometers	ELIOT 372:59
The o. I get	FRID 405:48
was so much o. then	DYLAN 358:93
oldest o. hath borne most	SHAK 904:50
O'Leary with O. in the grave	YEATS 1105:70
oligarchy always an o. that governs	PARE 753:83
call it o.	HOBB 483:41
olive an O., and a Turkey Fig	BETH 99:21
children like o. plants	BIBLE 119:43
fruitful o.	SPEN 957:99
o. leaf pluckt off	BIBLE 104:12
Stretched under the o. trees	SPEN 956:82
Oliver difficulty in inducing O.	DICK 321:33
olives acquired taste, like o.	RIFK 811:82
Olivet brows of O.	TENN 999:31

Olympic O. games	COUB 289:71
O. weight-lifter	NIGH 729:94
Olympics Montreal O.	DRAP 345:30
omega Alpha and O.	BIBLE 156:98
omen One o. is best of all	HOMER 488:20
ominous fashionable is o.	SANT 842:85
omission art of o.	LIEB 604:90
glaring sin of o.	OSLER 746:73
omissions o. of a Government	ROOS 821:37
O. are not accidents	MOORE 705:24
O. are not accidents	MOORE 705:30
omit o. to paint that which he sees	FRIE 405:61
omnibuses run up the steps of o.	WOOLF 1092:56
omnipotence final proof of God's o.	DEVR 318:93
honour, and o.	MARL 654:11
omnipotent God the O.	ELLE 374:1
O. but friendless	SHEL 930:21
Power, which seems o.	SHEL 930:27
omniscience his specialism is o.	DOYLE 344:17
Omnium Duke of O.	TROL 1028:99
Onan O....spilled it on the ground	BIBLE 105:42
Onassis going to marry...O.!	JOHN 523:45
once O. upon a time	KING 558:92
once-bitten happily for the o.-b.	HOME 487:12
ondulous lifting with great o. stride	CUMM 299:76
one all but o.—shall live	SHAK 891:29
all o. in Christ Jesus	BIBLE 152:89
At o. with the O.	GREE 443:2
being o. and not two	FLET 394:67
forgive Thy great big o.	FROST 407:1
hearts in o., realms in o.	SHAK 882:12
how to be o. up	POTT 785:45
If ever two were o.	BRAD 184:2
it ought to be Number O.	CARR 239:44
it will be all be o.	EMER 377:55
not o. among them	SHAK 874:19
o. bullet in ten thousand	SPEN 956:82
o. for all	DUMAS 354:27
o. in three	SHAW 923:76
o. of the twenty	SHAK 874:11
only o. to make a quarrel	INGE 511:35
people arose as o. man	BIBLE 109:24
souls in o. shall grow	PHIL 768:20
The O. remains	SHEL 931:50
Three in O.	ALEX 13:21
Two are better than o.	BIBLE 123:23
one-and-twenty When I was o.-a.-t.	HOUS 494:44
one-armed o.-a. man	DOLE 335:52
one-dimensional o.-d. mind	RUSS 833:34
one-eyed o.-e. man is king	ERAS 379:8
o.-e. man is king	WELLS 1064:30
one-handed a o.-h. economist	TRUM 1030:30
one-man o.-m. House of Commons	MANC 644:67
one-night o.-n. stands in collectors'	RAUS 802:42
one-stringed old o.-s. instrument	RANJ 801:27
one-trade Detroit is a o.-t. town	MAIL 639:84
one-way o.-w. property of time	EDDI 360:17
O'Neil slay Owen Roe O.?	DAVIS 309:36
oneness essential o. of mankind	STEI 965:30
onerous more o. citizenship	SONT 953:11
ones weaken the necessary o.	MONT 703:89
oneself delusion that one likes o.	DIDI 330:43
Hell is o.	ELIOT 373:24
left to o.	BERL 96:67
love is the gift of o.!	ANOU 31:79
what is useful to o.	SPIN 960:55
onion Let o. atoms lurk	SMITH 949:55
tears live in an o.	SHAK 904:60
only o. things that are true	SHAW 920:97
O. in America	KING 557:72
onward o. and outward	WHIT 1072:78
ooze present than in the o.	NABO 717:6
opal mind is a very o.	SHAK 894:13
open get these things out in the o.	PULI 795:20

open (*contd.*)
getting out into the o.   KELM 548:31
keep the store o. nights   KAUF 543:19
Never lay yourself o.   HUNT 504:18
o. door, and no man can shut it   BIBLE 157:5
o. thy mouth wide   BIBLE 117:92
whole nation out in the o.?   SIHA 938:72
opening Eyes…go on o.   REID 806:97
hell of an o.   REAG 804:71
No better o. anywhere   DICK 324:17
o. and closing of a door   SAND 841:65
opening-night o.-n. audience   HIRS 482:22
opera born for o. buffs   ROSS 825:96
first rule in o.   MELBA 667:22
language an o. is sung in   APPL 32:99
like German o.   WAUGH 1057:87
No good o. plot   AUDEN 48:85
o.…composed by God   CARD 232:1
o.…is to music   MENC 669:66
O. is where the guy gets stabbed   BENC 89:56
o. isn't what it used to be   COWA 290:1
poor man's o.   HUXL 507:85
Some of the o. houses   JOHN 524:69
to the o. one goes either   VOLT 1047:14
opera-glasses to view…take o.-g.   RIDGE 811:79
operas French o. sung by Swedish   WHAR 1068:3
operation military-style o.   CRAN 295:15
o. of separating   JOHN 524:68
refused an o.   GREG 446:47
operations diversities of o.   BIBLE 150:61
field of o.   BELL 88:42
o. of government   RUNC 828:51
o. of our own minds   LOCKE 609:73
performing a few simple o.   SMITH 946:91
operator dial the o.   TREV 1026:52
operators billions of legitimate o.   GIBS 422:40
Ophelia most beautified O.   SHAK 889:90
much of water hast thou, poor O.   SHAK 893:74
soft you, the fair O.   TWAIN 1033:89
Ophir Nineveh from distant O.   MASE 662:37
opiate Communism is the o.   LUCE 618:33
emptied some dull o.   KEATS 547:13
o. of the oppressed   JONG 534:65
opinion almost of the o.   MONT 700:54
better to have no o. of God   BACON 58:83
Busy o.   FORD 397:16
client asks his o.   JOHN 529:65
collective o.…can make history   SAFI 836:72
combat…with particular o.   DRYD 348:78
cost to freedom of o.   SCHL 848:73
current o.   MACC 625:48
Do not despise my o.   LEON 597:83
drift of public o.   DAFOE 303:38
engine of temporary o.   HAZL 463:7
everything else is o.   DEMO 315:45
flatterer does not have a good o.   LABR 573:56
fool gudgeon, this o.   SHAK 874:8
form a clear o.   BONH 173:86
gave it for his o.   SWIFT 985:85
give him my o.   DICK 325:32
God's o. that life should go on   SAND 841:74
guided by o. polls   THAT 1008:31
have his o. regenerated   PIER 769:32
heated division of o.   TYNAN 1035:25
high in Mr Podsnap's o.   DICK 327:80
instrument for gauging public o.   GALL 413:98
laughter at their quaint o.   MILT 691:90
low o. of himself   TROL 1027:70
man of common o.   BAGE 62:66
mankind…of one o.   MILL 675:66
money controls o.   ORWE 742:5
north of my lady's o.   SHAK 895:27
of his own o. still   BUTL 217:25
of the o. with the learned   CONG 280:92

opinion (*contd.*)
offer him an o.   SPEN 956:87
o. breeds ignorance   HIPP 481:16
o. in good men   MILT 685:59
o. is about a woman   JAMES 516:22
o. of himself, having once risen   BENN 91:88
o. of our best friends   MARG 650:58
o. of Winston Churchill   ELTON 375:22
organization of public o.   LIPP 606:33
Party is organized o.   DISR 333:6
poor itch of your o.   SHAK 910:1
Prejudice…vagrant o.   BIER 161:95
public o. will sweep them away   PULI 795:20
reason the o. of others   WOOLF 1093:72
recurring again to Plato's o.   STER 969:10
scorching world's o.   FLET 394:78
was ever of the o.   GOLD 432:1
whole climate of o.   AUDEN 47:68
wolf remains of a different o.   INGE 511:35
opinions As many o. as…people   TERE 1005:74
borrow other men's o.   BACON 57:71
confirm and establish our o.   BROW 195:67
contempt for my character and o.   SHAW 921:23
don't care to give o.   HERN 476:45
How long halt ye between two o.?   BIBLE 111:63
Men…bad as their o.   MACK 632:58
men who have no o.   CHES 258:99
one truth, and many o.   KURZ 571:23
o. for the time of year   AUDEN 47:64
o. that they…entertain   PALM 752:73
o. were not acted on   ELIOT 366:30
private parts…and religious o.   BUTL 218:48
Stiff in o.   DRYD 349:23
takes no notice of their o.   CROM 298:51
think his own o.   MORE 706:43
those who have certain o.   STEIN 966:50
what their o. make of them   LICH 604:87
wish to spread those o.   BUTL 217:29
Women are expected to have weak o.   ELIOT 366:30
opium against art, as against o.   RODC 818:81
antidote against the o. of time   BROW 196:1
help of o. or alcohol   HERZ 478:73
It is the o. of the people   MARX 660:4
just, subtle, and mighty o.!   DEQU 316:65
Music is no different from o.   KHOM 555:45
o. for every conceivable mass   KENN 550:57
o. has left the happiest memory   GREE 444:10
o. of the West   FRAN 400:81
opium-dose Bible as…an o.-d.   KING 559:1
opponent an o. cannot be…honest   ORWE 745:49
sound to his o. bitter   MILNE 680:68
tries to best his o.   PAUL 761:18
opponents pushed back…by their o.   PANK 752:78
trip, push and hack their o.   FRY 408:10
truth…convincing its o.   PLAN 772:85
opportunist rather be an o. and float   BALF 65:22
opportunities equal o.   MAND 644:68
No duties, only o.   ANON 28:26
o.…thicker than anywhere else   BALD 64:92
series of great o.   GARD 415:22
wise man will make more o.   BACON 59:27
woman with fair o.   THAC 1006:82
opportunity age of right and o.   WILS 1086:44
build a society of o.   MAJOR 640:97
Equality of o.   KENN 551:77
existence and o.   TEMP 993:30
giving you the o.   DICK 324:26
improving the present o.   WILL 1080:47
Know thine o.   PITT 772:77
least o. invades it   NICO 727:60
let slip an o.   SHAW 926:45
maximum of o.   SHAW 922:49
not time or o.   AUST 50:32
o. accorded him since Adam   MUGG 712:22

opportunity (*contd.*)
o. as against material interests   WILS 1086:45
o. cost of economic discussion   GALB 412:82
o. for attacking the devil!   STEAD 964:9
o. for graft   BIRNS 163:27
O. makes a thief   BACON 54:3
o. to rise again   SARN 843:96
o. to serve our country   SMITH 947:8
scarcity of o.   ANGE 19:21
strong seducer, o.!   DRYD 347:71
substantial equality of o.   ROOS 822:48
unfettered o.   MADAN 638:54
opposed o. may beware of thee   SHAK 888:64
opposite in justice and in its o.   SOPH 953:17
o. of talking   LEBO 592:87
opposition duty of an O.   CHUR 263:95
formidable O.   DISR 332:80
Her Majesty's O.   BAGE 61:52
His Majesty's O.   HOBH 483:44
Prime Minister or Leader of the O.   DISR 333:20
war of eternal o.   LYND 621:65
when it has a strong o.   SWEE 983:51
oppositions riven by a dozen o.   ROSS 823:65
oppress o., rob and degrade them   DOUG 342:74
oppressed Christ comes to the o.   RUET 828:47
friend of the o.   GARI 415:24
opiate of the o.   JONG 534:65
o. can find…safety   ANGE 19:27
o., who wanted strength   WORD 1098:58
past of the o. people   FANON 382:60
oppression Need and o. starveth   SHAK 870:21
often a mechanical o.   HEMI 470:30
o. he may heretofore have suffered   MANS 648:16
proud o. will not hear me   OTWAY 746:79
To make o. bitter   SHAK 890:15
oppressions o. of this earth   SHEL 927:68
oppressor confront the o.   MAKW 641:2
day o' the O. is ended   KIPL 562:63
revolutionary ends as an o.   CAMUS 229:55
The o.'s wrong   TWAIN 1033:89
oppressors we may have our o.   PUIG 794:18
optical o. flecks   UPDI 1037:69
o. form of thought   HUGO 501:60
optimism as agreeable as o.   BENN 91:96
optimist have to be an o.   SAND 841:76
o. after it, he knows too little   TWAIN 1034:18
o. is a guy   MARQ 656:39
o. proclaims that we live in the best   CABE 224:38
o.…sees a green light everywhere   SCHW 852:32
optimistic If I was not o.   OUD 746:91
make us o. or   UNAM 1035:40
O. lies have…therapeutic value   SHAW 924:98
options discuss your o. afterwards   SHAN 918:73
opulent o. calm of angelfish   ALLEN 14:30
oracle pronounces as an o.   WESL 1067:70
oracles o. are dumb   MILT 681:92
o. of God   BIBLE 154:46
orange clockwork o.   BURG 205:78
Orangeman Pocket of a Stout O.   ANON 25:21
oranges bowl of o., too   MITC 696:82
coffee and o.   STEV 971:38
orator An o. is a good man   CATO 245:53
greatest o., who triumphs   HUME 503:7
no o. as Brutus is   SHAK 884:56
oratory Poetry…not as o.   POUND 785:55
orb Cycle and epicycle, o. in o.   MILT 691:90
monthly changes in her circled o.   SHAK 869:91
There's not the smallest o.   SHAK 873:99
orbit most beautiful sight in o.   SCHW 851:92
orbits circled in their o.   DICK 323:90
orbs dew her o. upon the green   SHAK 870:35
o. Or dim suffusion veiled   MILT 689:30
orchard fair with o. lawns   TENN 1004:48
hath thy o. fruit   JONS 535:2

orchard (*contd.*)
O., for a Domee — DICK 328:98
orchards Not all do o. please — VIRG 1045:91
orchestra for o. without music — RAVEL 802:44
plays the kettle drums in the o. — SALI 839:27
separates you from the o. — DIDE 329:27
orchestras golden rules for o. — BEEC 82:16
orchestrated Three farts…o. — BARB 71:12
orchestration o. of platitudes — WILD 1079:28
orchid O.—breathing incense — BASHO 76:4
White as an o. — AUDEN 48:78
ordeal o. of meeting me — CHUR 265:34
worst possible o. — BERR 99:18
order all in o. stand — CRAB 293:67
And o., truth, and beauty range — SMART 944:68
arranged them in alphabetical o. — HELL 468:84
been a rock of o. — METT 673:30
benevolence of the passive o. — MERE 671:7
change the social o. — FRAN 401:88
colours assembled in a certain o. — DENIS 316:58
decently and in o. — BIBLE 151:64
establishing a world o. — EISE 364:86
explain our sense of o. — HARDY 456:98
fairest o. in the world — HERA 474:89
forces working in inverse o.! — CARL 235:64
Good o. is the foundation — BURKE 208:41
loyalty and o. — GLAD 429:53
new o. from the old — WEBB 1059:17
old o. changeth — TENN 1004:46
ordainer of o. — BROW 196:7
o. breeds habit — ADAMS 5:76
o. does not create life — SAIN 837:87
O. is heaven's first law — POPE 781:48
o. of Melchizedek — BIBLE 118:23
o. of nature — FONT 395:86
o. of the acts — PAST 759:83
o. our lives more rationally — LECO 592:2
possess internal o. — FORS 399:50
precise idea of o. — BERN 97:87
preponderantly geometric o. — LEGER 593:21
re-establish peace and civil o. — ELIZ 374:96
recollect the o. in which — WELL 1063:13
reminders of o. — GREER 445:43
sense of o. — ORWE 742:99
significance to ourselves…find o. — WELTY 1065:51
society, and social o. — MUNCH 714:52
some sort of o. (or beauty) — POUND 787:91
some sort of o. — GREE 444:21
subversion of good o. — KNOX 567:57
sudden light that shows new o. — CORN 288:61
values o. without constraint — LEGU 594:27
vast o. of the universe — PAGE 749:33
where all is o. and beauty — BAUD 77:22
words in their best o. — COLE 275:24
world has not be put in o. — MILL 678:33
ordered You o. I obeyed — BERN 96:77
orderliness freedom and a general o. — CARD 232:2
orders Almighty's o. to perform — ADDI 6:2
'E don't obey no o. — KIPL 562:58
give o. to love — SAND 840:53
Gordon should be under my o. — CROM 297:47
in all his tinted o. — FIRB 389:74
lower o. are seen unfavourably — CHES 257:86
o. and inferior creatures — MILT 694:48
organisation…of o. — MARX 660:11
Reasonable o. are — TUCH 1031:46
willing to follow his o. — BIBLE 159:45
ordinary all o. people — CHEK 256:60
divided into 'o.' and 'extraordinary' — DOST 340:43
o. affairs of o. people — GOWE 437:82
o. in the individual — MANN 646:89
o. man and woman — ATTL 44:11
o. people through o. situations — BANKS 70:1
o. wine just leaves — AMER 16:66

ordinary (*contd.*)
taking o. men — GALB 412:80
There are no o. moments — MILL 679:62
warn you not to be o. — KINN 559:12
work of fifty o. men — HUBB 498:5
ore slaves that dig the golden o. — CRAB 293:73
organ direction to point that o. — AUDEN 48:91
Heavens deep o. blow — MILT 681:90
o. to enlarge her prayer — AUDEN 48:78
Seated one day at the o. — PROC 792:76
With most miraculous o. — SHAK 890:17
organ-grinder o.-g. is present — BEVAN 101:68
organism o. is preparing to rest — MAMET 644:56
over-complicated o. — POUND 786:81
organization appropriate o. — GALB 412:80
bigger the o. — JAY 519:75
destroyed the foundation of the o. — EISE 364:86
efficient o. is one in which — STEA 963:3
o. for pleasure — JOHN 524:65
O. is alien to their natures — HAZZ 464:27
o. is the greatest morale builder — DOOL 340:37
o. of idolatry — SHAW 922:45
o. of public opinion — LIPP 606:33
systematic o. of hatreds — ADAMS 5:72
organizations part in the various o. — JOHN 522:31
organized highly o. part of it — GALB 412:79
o. for that — TOLS 1023:95
organs given us all more o. — BRAD 183:80
inner o. of beasts — JOYCE 538:53
take your sense o. seriously — LEARY 591:70
that o. that piss — LAYT 588:24
orgasm o. has replaced the cross — MUGG 712:21
orgy need an o., once — NASH 719:52
Orient O. dew, Shed from — MARV 657:68
slow revenge of the O. — PRIE 790:39
oriental Tea, although an O. — CHES 259:30
you are an O. — FORS 398:40
orientation from the o. of a few — ROBB 813:5
origin account for their o. — MILL 675:73
indelible stamp of his lowly o. — DARW 306:89
Philosophy…has no other o. — SOCR 952:88
takes its o. from emotion — WORD 1096:37
original curse Their frail o. — MILT 688:20
great O. proclaim — ADDI 7:22
greatest o. practical example — WHIT 1073:87
in order to imitate the o. — BERN 97:96
line up to see the o. — ARMS 35:48
new and o. plan — GILB 424:74
She's the o. good time — DAVIS 308:28
things counter, o., spare — HOPK 491:85
thought is like o. sin — LEBO 591:85
thought is often o. — HOLM 486:81
originality All my o. consists — REDON 804:77
Artistic o. has only — NABO 717:9
o.…manner of thinking — MAUP 665:94
result is his o. — ROTH 825:7
without o. or moral courage — SHAW 921:21
originals o. from whence all — LOCKE 609:73
Orion loose the bands of O.? — BIBLE 113:21
O. standing on his head — LAWR 586:79
orisons his morning o. — SMART 944:67
their hasty o. — OWEN 748:7
Orkney In bloody O. — BLAIR 165:51
Orlando Run, run, O. — SHAK 886:98
Orleans who are besieging O. — JOAN 522:27
ornament esteem'st the o. of life — SHAK 908:33
mankind from superfluous o. — LOOS 612:24
moment's o. — WORD 1098:62
old o. of his cheek — SHAK 880:54
o. from utilitarian objects — LOOS 612:25
o. which truth doth give — SHAK 913:62
respecting all o. — RUSK 830:75
used literature as an o. — VARG 1040:7
ornamentation building without o. — SANT 842:90

ornaments hide with o. their…art — POPE 778:80
orphan carried by an o. boy — SCOTT 853:42
court as an o. — LEVA 599:17
widow and his o. — LINC 605:6
orphans new o. cry — SHAK 909:72
Orpheus O. with his lute made trees — SHAK 918:53
soul of O. sing — MILT 682:11
orthodox certainly not o. — STRA 979:95
orthodoxy o. no longer means — CHES 258:93
O. or My-doxy — CARL 235:65
unimpeachable o. — RAHN 800:5
orthography now is he turned o. — SHAK 879:47
Orwell episode out of George O. — COOKE 286:30
O. told us we would — MAMET 643:50
Oscar assume that O. said it — PARK 753:93
Oscars Walk two O. behind — WARR 1054:30
Osiris mangled body of O. — MILT 686:72
Out-glares the Heav'ns O. — HERR 477:56
ostrich America cannot be an o. — WILS 1086:49
neck like an o. — DAVIS 308:27
Othello O. subject Desdemona — KOES 568:69
something like it in O. — SHER 934:10
other think there is no o. — SCHR 850:5
Were she o. than she is — SHAK 879:32
otherness quintessence of o. — BURG 206:92
visual form of the 'o.' — NOLAN 731:20
others alone among o. — SAIN 836:84
Do not do unto o. — SHAW 923:66
liberty is the love of o. — HAZL 463:2
love of o. — SHAW 920:99
more pleasing to o. — JOHN 530:98
o. were only my wives — GUIT 448:81
pity o. had to leave — KINN 559:11
ought It is, but hadn't o. to be — HARTE 460:53
o. to flow through — KIPL 560:25
what o. to be — HOMA 487:8
what you o. to do — SART 844:19
ounce o. of Silver out of the Earth — PETTY 768:13
ourselves advance a step beyond o. — HUME 503:98
do not talk of o. — TROL 1027:67
how to get rid of o. — HORN 494:36
interplay between nature and o. — HEIS 467:77
no hope of finding o. — MILL 678:27
O. to end o. — SHAK 906:87
power is the love of o. — HAZL 463:2
stop loving o. — STAEL 961:73
vainly conceal from o. — PASC 757:51
out fall not o. by the way — BIBLE 106:49
I don't have to go o. — SMITH 948:23
Let me o.! — ATWO 44:18
O., damned spot — SHAK 909:77
O., vile jelly! — SHAK 903:27
relevance…for what it leaves o. — FERL 386:22
wit is o. — SHAK 880:58
out-worn o.-w. heart — YEATS 1105:62
outcast writer…an o. by nature — BARN 72:31
outcome o. of the struggle — ANGE 19:20
outdated methods are o. — ANON 27:66
outdoor I play no o. games — WILDE 1077:76
outfits bareleg o. — MURR 715:76
outlaw attacks from o. states — REAG 804:64
Jazz musicians have some o. — ZWER 1110:29
wandering o. of his…mind — BYRON 219:80
outline drew his own o. — VASA 1040:8
mountain o. varies — THOR 1016:72
outlines eye never sees o. — GOYA 437:83
outlive o. this powerful rhyme — SEXT 859:63
many years o. performance? — SHAK 877:93
outlook Writers of comedy have o. — THUR 1019:48
outrage do o. to its…unity — HOMA 487:7
Satire is moral o. — ROTH 826:15
outside England…Europe — KEYN 554:28
from the o. inwards — FRIE 405:59
Give me the o. of things — LEWIS 602:67

outside (contd.)
I am just going o. — OATES 733:60
o. pissing in — JOHN 523:53
o. to every form — HEPW 473:80
people who live o. — SABA 835:56
watch…from the o. — WELLS 1064:27
we can get o. ourselves — RABI 799:94
outsider can an o. understand — KAFKA 540:85
outsiders imagined by o. — WATS 1055:51
o. do not understand — MUNRO 714:60
war against the o. — GARI 415:25
outstanding o. men become fewer — TOCQ 1021:74
outstrip o. all praise — SHAK 917:35
outward inevitably turns o. — UPDI 1037:65
man looketh on the o. appearance — BIBLE 110:36
need of o. criteria — WITT 1088:80
onward and o. — WHIT 1072:78
virtue on his o. parts — SHAK 872:81
outworn free itself from all that is o. — CUPI 301:11
Oval English cricket…died at the O. — ANON 25:17
ovation Arrange o. — SWAN 983:50
oven burn as an o. — BIBLE 131:72
ovens gassing people in o. — SIHA 938:72
over It ain't o. 'til it's o. — BERRA 98:3
never get o. it — FROST 408:7
O. after o. — JOYCE 538:55
O. my dead body — KAUF 543:20
they think it's all o. — WOLS 1091:44
over-shoes o.-s. in love — SHAK 860:72
over-simplification systematic o. — POPP 784:29
over-well love is given o.-w. — PARK 754:4
overalls pantheon of boots and o. — DUNN 356:51
overboard propose to throw o. — MANN 645:81
throw the occasional man o. — GILM 427:20
overcoat meaning…only its o. — CAREY 233:24
put on your o. — LOWE 616:89
overcoats never taken off their o. — THUR 1018:15
overcrowding situations of o. — COUP 289:83
overesteemed Facts are generally o. — UPDI 1036:55
overflow 'Clancy, of the O.' — PATE 760:97
spontaneous o. — WORD 1096:37
overlook knowing what to o. — JAMES 517:42
overpaid all that they are being o. for — SELZ 858:43
overpower She can o., astonish — HUNT 504:20
overrated three most o. things — KENN 552:94
override she will o. you — FAUL 384:87
oversights mistakes and o. — MURP 715:73
oversimplification O. is now — BERG 94:40
overstepped never o. it — FROST 407:83
overstocked aviary o. with jays — OHEN 737:17
overthrow think'st, thou dost o. — DONNE 338:4
Ovid O., the soft philosopher — DRYD 351:65
ovum Via o. cranium — STEV 972:77
owe O. no man anything — BIBLE 149:39
o. no man hate — SHAK 886:20
o. nothing to Women's Lib — THAT 1007:4
Owen grave of Gomer O. — THOM 1011:83
owl blind as any noonday o. — TENN 1003:39
comrade with the wolf and o. — SHAK 902:14
moping o. — GRAY 442:63
of the white o. sweeping — MERE 671:97
O., and a useful Cart — LEAR 590:56
O. and the Pussy-Cat — LEAR 590:58
o., for all his feathers — KEATS 546:85
singing o. — ROCH 816:58
sings the staring o. — SHAK 866:31
white o.'s feather — ALLI 15:53
owlish describe myself as o. — SCHW 851:28
owls castle brown as o. — THOM 1010:69
hooded eagle among blinking o. — SHEL 929:10
Of o. and cuckoos, asses — MILT 686:76
Two O. and a Hen — LEAR 589:50
Who brings o. to Athens? — ARIS 34:20
own AIDS…a classic o. goal — ANNE 20:38

own (contd.)
call my o. — DRYD 350:42
crisis…we can call our o. — SALI 839:30
of thine o. have we given thee — BIBLE 112:86
prefer to o. slot machines — TRUMP 1030:36
what isn't one's o. — PLATO 774:20
what you o. — ELIOT 371:50
wouldn't want to o. one — FIEL 388:58
own-alone All by my o.-a. self — HARR 458:33
owner rather o. be — DONNE 338:96
owners sons of former slave o. — KING 557:82
ownership importance of social o. — STRA 979:91
source of its power: o. — KINN 559:8
owns Who o. all of space? — HUGH 500:43
ox Baby in an o.'s stall? — BETJ 100:47
eateth grass as an o. — BIBLE 113:24
shalt not muzzle the o. — BIBLE 108:96
stalled o. and hatred therewith — BIBLE 121:80
oxen eat grass as o. — BIBLE 129:47
o. frae the furrowed field — BURNS 212:35
Oxenford clark ther was of O. — CHAU 254:21
Oxford clever men a O. — GRAH 438:93
either O. or Cambridge — SNAG 950:68
Mussolini had been at O. — HALI 452:26
O.…has made me insufferable — BEER 83:26
O.…more attractive than Cambridge — BAED 61:47
poetry, which is in O. made — DRYD 347:74
schools of O. — GIBB 421:23
stagecoach from London to O. — HAZL 463:4
The King to O. sent a troop of horse — BROW 196:9
to found at O. a chair — ARNO 39:21
University of O. — GIBB 421:26
Oxfordshire all the b. of O. — THOM 1012:1
oxlips o. and the nodding violet — SHAK 870:39
Oxtail university of O. — JOYCE 538:52
Oxus O., forgetting the bright speed — ARNO 38:98
oxygen of publicity — THAT 1008:19
o. of social intercourse — HIRS 481:20
oyster An o. may be crossed in love! — SHER 934:12
bold Man that first ate an O. — SWIFT 986:12
eye that can open o. — WODE 1089:5
No o. ever profited — THUR 1020:58
o. of the old school — DICK 324:25
o. shell on top of the sea — AUDEN 48:78
sympathetic unselfishness of an o. — SAKI 838:8
world's mine o. — SHAK 878:13
you can't enjoy an o. — CLARK 267:85
oyster-knife sneer…like an o.-k. — ANNAN 20:35
oysters But by no means unlike o. — DICK 322:68
eat my o. — SWIFT 986:17
man who doesn't love o. — SAKI 838:6
Poverty and o.…seem to go — DICK 320:23
Ozymandias My name is O. — SHEL 928:93

pa Don't beat me, p.! — JOYCE 537:41
Ma's out, P.'s out — FLAN 392:27
pace bloody thoughts with violent p. — SHAK 899:42
dance is a measured p. — BACON 55:15
jogging justling p. — MUNDY 714:53
know how to p. themselves — DIOR 331:62
not keep p. — THOR 1017:91
one p. ahead of myself — MACG 630:29
p. of science — FROMM 406:70
paces Hop forty p. — SHAK 905:70
three p. through the room — TENN 994:45
Time travels in divers p. — SHAK 886:6
paciencia p. y barajar — CERV 248:1
Pacific Atlantic to the P. — CHUR 264:9
star'd at the p. — KEATS 544:33
Pacioli heard of Fra Luca P. — MULL 713:43
pack changed the form of the p. — TROT 1029:6
face the murderous cowardly p. — MACK 632:49
God! I will p., and take a train — BROO 192:27
revenged on the whole p. — SHAK 895:38

pack (contd.)
soldier's p. is not so heavy — EISE 364:81
with rifle and p. — SASS 845:28
pack-horses Shall p.-h. — SHAK 877:91
packages internationally marketed p. — ILLI 511:32
Packard upholstery of a P. — PERE 766:96
pact I make a p. with you — POUND 785:54
pad dolor of p. — ROET 819:91
Paddington As London is to P. — CANN 230:69
paddle leave to p. — KIPL 562:75
paddles 'ear their p. chunkin' — KIPL 560:26
padlock clap your p. — PRIOR 790:50
one jingling p. on the mind — POPE 783:3
pads writing p., notebooks — RODC 818:81
Padua wive it wealthily in P. — SHAK 864:73
paeans laurels to p. — CICE 266:64
paga Non si p., non si p. — FO 395:82
pagan animals (p., I regret to say) — DICK 322:68
p. suckled in a creed — WORD 1099:73
pagans example of the ancient p. — GUIB 448:71
P. deified life — STAEL 961:71
wild p. at the cash register — CHER 256:67
page A P., a Grave — POPE 783:2
blotted from life's p. — BYRON 219:78
cannot tear out a single p. — SAND 840:52
father struggled through half a p. — LAWR 586:92
looks well enough on the p. — BUNT 204:58
on a beautiful quarto p. — SHER 933:94
one sweet p. — PATM 760:1
p. having an ample marge — TENN 1002:10
pictures for the p. atone — POPE 782:96
Rule 1, on p. 1 — MONT 703:90
sports p. records — WARR 1054:27
stole a p. from the Universe! — MARTI 657:56
when you looked at the front p. — CHRI 261:69
pageant like this insubstantial p. — SHAK 917:36
P. of Empire — SITW 941:17
p. of his bleeding heart — ARNO 38:3
pages funny p. of the history books — DEAN 311:58
read the first two p. — JOYCE 538:58
pagoda old Moulmein P. — KIPL 560:28
pagus private p. or demesne — AUDEN 48:17
paid Ambition's debt is p. — SHAK 883:28
being p. in or p. out — HUXL 508:93
getting what you haven't p. for — WHAR 1068:99
more women are p. — FALU 382:56
p. for a woman — GREE 444:18
p. for this microphone — REAG 804:68
p. the prices of life — GURN 449:90
p. with a smile — SAIN 836:86
p. with flattery — JOHN 526:15
these men p. their shillings — PRIE 789:35
you p. us more — HAMM 454:59
pail milk comes frozen home in p. — SHAK 866:30
pails ice crunching in p. — STEV 972:64
pain After great p. — DICK 328:99
alternations of p. — WILD 1080:35
always in p. — BELL 86:92
and all the p. — SWIN 986:23
boredom and p. of it — BUEC 203:42
cause of all this p. — JULI 539:69
clenched on a round p. — THOM 1010:61
delight in physics p. — SHAK 908:52
drama of p. — HARDY 456:96
draw thy breath in p. — SHAK 893:87
earth in travail and in p. — LONG 612:13
ease after p. — MILT 684:35
equal ease unto my p. — CAREW 233:20
Eternal P.! — ARNO 37:83
first feel p. yourself — HORA 493:31
for quhome ye suffer p. — HENR 473:72
forget the wandering and the p. — FLEC 393:53
forgets the p. — JEFF 520:86
frame perish…in conquering p. — BYRON 220:98

palate (*contd.*)
Glide o'er my p.	BARL 71:21
man's heart is through his p.	FERN 386:26
P., the hutch of tasty lust	HOPK 491:80
steps down the p.	NABO 717:96

palates p. both for sweet and sour — SHAK 900:51

pale Art thou p. for weariness — SHEL 932:73
I left the theatre, dizzy and p.	QUIR 798:72
In p. contented sort	KEATS 546:79
in sorrow p.	BLAKE 166:68
P., beyond porch	SWIN 987:37
p. of the Constitution	GLAD 429:50
p., unripened beauties	ADDI 8:30
started…and turned p.	SOUT 954:41
Why so p. and wan	SUCK 981:17

Palenke poetry in P. and Uatlán — DARIO 305:75
Palestine establishment in P. — BALF 65:17
| haven in sunny P. | MASE 662:37 |
| Jews in P. | OROU 741:79 |

Palestinian P. peace movement — ANON 29:46
Palestinians P. in Israel — OROU 741:79
| P., PLO is a homeland | NEW 724:19 |

palfrey p. fresh and fair — SCOTT 854:79
pall pallor…shall be their p. — OWEN 748:8
| would be a little | THUR 1019:32 |

Pall Mall P. M. Gazette is written — THAC 1006:94
Palladium P. of all the civil — JUNI 540:74
palliate p. what we cannot cure — JOHN 526:9
palliative sleep…a p. — CHAM 250:26
pallid p. and thin young man — GILB 424:70
| P., unshaved and thirsty | SASS 845:24 |

Palliser Mr P. was one of those — TROL 1027:71
| P., Duke of Omnium | TROL 1028:99 |

pallor p. of girls' brows — OWEN 748:8
palm where the p. tree grows — MARTI 657:57
| win the p., the oak | MARV 658:82 |
| wind is in the p. tree | KIPL 560:28 |

palm-oil proverbs are the p.-o. — ACHE 2:18
palms p. in their hands — BIBLE 157:14
| the p. of her hands | BIBLE 112:83 |

palooka sobbed the panting p. — PERE 766:87
palpable very p. hit — SHAK 893:85
palsy chide my p., or my gout — DONNE 337:79
| p. shakes a few | KEATS 547:15 |
| strucken wid de p. | HARR 458:32 |

paltry man is but a p. thing — YEATS 1106:79
Pam P., I adore you, P. — BETJ 99:32
Pamere high mountain cradle in P. — ARNO 38:98
pan fish that talks In the frying p. — DELA 314:30
panacea suffrage is their p. — CARL 236:85
panache Sang with a fountain's p. — DAYL 310:57
Panama Vietnam…near P. — ANON 27:88
pancake know how that p. feels — WRIG 1101:9
pancreatic p. ducts of dog — BANT 70:4
pandemic AIDS p. …own-goal — ANNE 20:38
pandemonium p., the high capital — MILT 688:10
pandering p. to the public taste — BEAV 81:88
Pandora If you open that P.'s box — BEVIN 102:77
pane cheek…against the p. — SCHR 850:4
| tap at the p. | BROW 198:40 |

panegyrics Coarse p. — GRAY 441:61
panes diamonded with p. — KEATS 546:91
pangs More p. will — HOPK 492:3
| quietus which his p. might take | TWAIN 1033:89 |

panic Don't P. — ADAMS 4:65
made me p. most	WHITE 1070:44
p. in which the passenger is kept	HAZL 463:10
What a p.'s in thy breastie!	BURNS 209:61

Panjandrum Grand P. himself — FOOTE 396:95
panoply p. of death — DAVI 308:14
pansies p.; that's for thoughts — SHAK 892:69
pansy p. at my feet — WORD 1098:50
| pink, and the p. | MILT 684:47 |

pant I p., I sink — SHEL 931:55

Pantagruelism P. is…liveliness — RABE 799:91
pantheon dome of the P. — BRAM 185:7
| p. of boots and overalls | DUNN 356:37 |

panther muscles of a p. — PERE 766:92
| sofa upholstered in p. skin | PLOM 775:34 |

pantomime delights of a p. — DICK 327:89
| in p. the puppets fumbling | WHITE 1070:28 |

pantry stow'd his p. — BURNS 209:62
pants chair…judged by one's p. — ANON 27:62
in fast thick p. were breathing	COLE 275:14
kick in the p. to God	MILL 677:15
lower limbs in p.	NASH 720:60
secret of life in your p.	CUMM 299:80
Stretch p.	ANON 27:70

Pap P. warn't in a good humor — TWAIN 1033:81
papa P.…gives a pretty form — DICK 326:53
paper 12 ounces of p. and ink — MORL 708:71
crawling over a piece of p.	INGR 512:51
deliquescent leaves of p.	ANDR 18:11
empty as p.	SCOTT 852:37
few sheets of p.	ARET 33:17
figures which look well on p.	WEIL 1062:83
good manners to read the p.	VAND 1039:96
grey p. with blunt type!	BROW 197:28
Hamlet is so much p. and ink	PRIE 789:35
hand that signed the p.	THOM 1010:56
hath not eat p.	SHAK 865:16
here is the p. that bears his name	CHAM 249:18
I had the p.	HEMI 470:18
It is a commercial p.	HAZL 463:8
just for a scrap of p.	BETH 99:22
keepers of print and p.	MACL 634:77
loo p. gets thicker	MITF 697:2
on passive p.	POPE 783:2
only a p. moon	HARB 455:73
only needs a typewriter and p.	WINN 1087:63
p. allegories but ill comprehended	MELV 668:48
P. blushes not	MIDD 673:47
p. it's written on	GOLD 434:43
puppets…with their slips of p.	WHITE 1070:28
reactionaries are p. tigers	MAO 648:26
run the p.	BEAV 80:82
sheet of green p.	ATWO 44:18
talking on p.	BAIN 62:73
unpleasant'st words…blotted p.	SHAK 873:86
We set down on p.	TRUM 1030:22
when…this p. appears dull	STEE 964:13
white p., void of all	LOCKE 609:72
word down on p.	MILL 678:32
Your eight-page p.	MAST 663:65

paper-blurrers company of p.-b. — SIDN 937:65
paper-mill thou hast built a p.-m. — SHAK 861:15
paper-weight pad and p.-w. — ROET 819:91
paperback America as the p. version — DELI 314:37
papers He's got my p. — PINT 770:46
| what I read in the p. | ROGE 820:7 |

paperwork keep p. down — ORTON 742:87
papist between Protestant and P. — STRA 979:1
| P. have no right to complain! | OBRI 734:63 |

paprika splash of p. — VREE 1047:21
parables end up writing p. — BERG 94:44
| many things unto them in p. | BIBLE 137:97 |

parachute jumping out of a p. — MACL 633:64
| What color is your p.? | BOLL 172:73 |

parade army without p. or gesture — LAWR 587:14
| solemnised with pomp and p. | ADAMS 5:86 |

paradise be with me in p. — BIBLE 144:17
blessed and admit me to P.	ROSS 825:96
blundered into P.	THOM 1014:33
built upon the bowers of p.	PAINE 750:44
buy my bartered P.	MUIR 712:37
called the P. of Fools	MILT 685:22
cheapened p.	PATM 760:99
Cheese for dessert…like P. Lost	BRAC 183:70

---

paradise (*contd.*)
closest you can get this side of P.	BUEC 203:41
drunk the milk of P.	COLE 275:18
England is the p. of women	FLOR 394:79
fleeting joys Of P.	MILT 693:18
gate of p.	SHAW 926:43
grace the entrance to P.	MICH 673:37
heavenly p. is that place	CAMP 228:39
In P. of all things	MILT 690:65
keys of P.	DEQU 316:65
lay on nature is a p.	SHAK 897:83
Life's p.	FORD 397:12
Lost Angel of a ruined P.!	SHEL 930:38
my dying place was P.	BROW 195:88
No p., no fall	SNYD 951:82
P. by way of Kensal Green	CHES 293:87
p. for a sect	KEATS 545:68
p.…in his face	DRYD 349:6
P. of exiles	SHEL 927:67
p. of four seas	MARV 659:85
possess A p. within	MILT 693:30
see John Knox in P.	PARK 754:4
serpent…in P.	HUGH 500:42
spindrift gaze toward p.	CRANE 294:94
Such are the Gates of P.	BLAKE 166:81
wilderness is p.	FITZ 390:88
win a p.?	SHAK 865:19
wreck of P.	SHEL 931:54

paradises Two p. 'twere in one — MARV 659:88
paradox p. of high religion — NIEB 727:64
paradoxes man of p. — ROUS 827:36
paragon earthly p. — SHAK 916:13
| p. of animals! | SHAK 890:4 |

paragons p. of frankness — WILL 1082:78
paragraph canvas a sentence or p. — MOTH 711:12
| most beautiful prose p. | BLOOM 170:38 |

paragraphing art of newspaper p. — MARQ 656:48
paragraphs hardening of the p. — THUR 1019:39
parallel north of the 38th p. — MARS 656:54
| speaks…of things without p. | BIER 161:82 |
| there is no p. term | BERG 94:40 |

parallelism Friendship needs…p. — ADAMS 5:78
parallelogram landlady…is a p. — LEAC 588:33
paralyse p. it by encumbering — TOLS 1023:95
paralysis pain than p.! — NIGH 729:96
paramedics run for the p. — SKEL 942:38
paramour her lusty p. — MILT 681:86
| many a p. | SPEN 958:13 |

paramours willow worn of forlorn p. — SPEN 957:99
| Worn of p. | SPEN 957:93 |

paraphrase soul in p. — HERB 475:30
| the classics in p.! | POUND 785:62 |

parasite not born a p. — FRAN 402:16
parasols What various p.! — DICK 322:66
parcel p. of rogues — BURNS 212:31
parcels deals it in small p. — WEBS 1059:25
parched p. ground…a pool — BIBLE 126:82
parchment p. of a constitution — TROT 1029:3
pard freckled like a p. — KEATS 545:75
pard-like p.-l. Spirit, beautiful — SHEL 931:43
pardon beseech you of your p. — SHAK 899:34
bitter to thee, p.	SWIN 988:54
cannot help nor p.	AUDEN 46:55
I p. that man's life	SHAK 903:34
ne'er p., who have done wrong	DRYD 347:70
O p. me	SHAK 883:44
p. after execution	SHAK 918:66
P. me boy	GORD 435:64
p. not that	SHAK 873:97
Say 'P.' king	SHAK 868:69
Where there is injury, p.	FRAN 401:91

pardonable almost always p. — GRAV 440:28
pardoning in p. that we are — FRAN 401:91
parent child whose p. is unkent — SPEN 957:92

parent (*contd.*)

man can be a p.	MUIR 713:42
p. who could see his boy	LEAC 589:41
successful p....raises a child	EPHR 379:96
To lose one p.	WILDE 1078:83

parents avoid having p. — CRISP 297:36

best friends and p.	MARG 650:58
born...with ready-made p.	FRAME 400:78
cannot get subsistence from his p.	MALT 643:40
children inter their p.	HERO 477:47
how my p. were occupied	SALI 838:18
influence of p.	MUSG 716:82
Jewish man with p.	ROTH 826:11
joys of p.	BACON 57:54
loving their p.	WILDE 1077:70
No person...understands his p.	FRIS 406:65
noblemen from surfeiting of his p.	LASS 583:35
Of p. good	SHAK 881:91
p. can't take you	UPDI 1036:51
p. don't have to say	MORE 707:53
p. kept me from children	SPEN 956:77
P. learn a lot	SPARK 955:47
p. lived like	MIN 695:61
p....realize that I'm kidnapped	ALLEN 14:41
p....sometimes a disappointment	POWE 787:1
p. were created for	NASH 719:51
p. won't slight you	COLUM 278:60
question...in many potential p.	SCHU 851:20
stranger to one of your p.	AUST 51:38
two first p.	MILT 689:32
web do p. weave	NASH 720:58

Pariahs women the P. — STAN 962:87

Paris As far as P. — JONS 534:72

dressed in P.	ANON 26:36
Fashion is more tyrannical at P.	CHES 257:80
frocks are built in P.	SAKI 837:98
good Americans die they go to P.	WILDE 1077:67
I will die in P.	VALL 1039:92
in P. I remained a Canadian	RICH 810:72
Nothing can compare to P.	DESC 318:84
old house in P.	BEME 89:44
Outside of P.	MOLI 698:17
P. is a beast of a city	HAZL 463:10
P. made of stone	HUGO 501:65
P. preserves the soul	HUGO 502:86
plant our religion in P.	LESL 598:94
When P. sneezes	METT 672:28
when they die, go to P.	APPL 32:1

parish all the world as my p. — WESL 1066:68

consent of every butcher in the p.	SHER 933:87
p. of rich women	AUDEN 47:70
pension from the p.	RUSK 830:89

park All I need...is a p. — CHAP 252:65

don't want to come out to the p.	BERRA 98:98
gentleman's p. is my aversion	CONS 285:17
Over p., over pale	SHAK 870:35
P. Avenue ...trade deficit	BART 75:87
Then over the p.	PEPYS 765:68

Park as Mungo P. once had to do — GALT 413:10

Parker Charlie P. ...always filled — KAVA 543:24

When I first heard Charlie P. — GILL 426:11

parks mountain p. and reservations — MUIR 713:38

p., my walks, my manors — SHAK 862:31

parliament are on this P. — WILL 1080:47

as in the time of P.	HENR 472:65
began our P.	HOBY 483:47
Cromwell said to the Long P.	AMERY 16:69
dissolved P.	STAL 962:78
enables P. to do things	SHAW 923:81
Kiss my P.!	PEPYS 764:59
majorities in P.	WHIT 1069:16
mockery to call it a P. House	WENT 1065:54
nailed...the doors of P.	MUSS 716:83
P. is a deliberative assembly	BURKE 206:4

parliament (*contd.*)

P. must lay the burden equally	CHUR 263:1
P. of England	BAIL 62:72
P. of man	TENN 995:77
P. speaking through reporters	CARL 236:98
People in P.	WILL 1080:46
two-thirds majority in P.	FREUD 404:41

parliamentarian pleasure for a p. — CRIT 297:43

parliaments democratic p. of tricks — WEBB 1058:16

England is the mother of P. — BRIG 188:49

P. are the great lie — POBE 775:40

Parlock a person on business from P. — COLE 274:11

parlour perfumed p. snake — DUNNE 356:62

parlours farmhouse p. — THOM 1012:95

Parma P....should dare to invade — ELIZ 373:90

parmacity P. for an inward bruise — SHAK 875:42

Parnassus climb to P. — BURNS 209:59

poor man's P. — EMER 378:79

Parnell Poor P.! — JOYCE 538:44

parodies P. and caricatures — HUXL 506:60

parody between an epitome and a p. — ISAA 513:70

p. is a game	NABO 717:10
p. ...replaced history	PIGL 769:40

parole p. of literary men — JOHN 531:17

parrot Sick as a p. — ANON 28:4

with a p. and five companions — HEYE 479:88

parrots keep p. or puppy dogs — CAMP 227:23

laugh like p. — SHAK 872:76

Parsee There lived a P. — KIPL 563:80

parsimonious Nothing...more p. — SMOL 950:63

parsimony beggarly p. and ignoble — NASHE 721:77

Capitals are increased by p. — SMITH 945:85

parsley P. Is gharsely — NASH 720:66

parsnip lukewarm p. juice — WOOL 1094:88

parson different cause, says p. Sly — PRIOR 791:58

drowns the p.'s saw	SHAK 866:31
If P. lost his senses	HODG 484:53
p. owned his skill	GOLD 433:13

part bids me play my p. — SPEN 958:25

every man must play a p.	SHAK 872:77
every prudent p.	POPE 782:73
fifth p. of the Earth	FIELD 387:39
forgot my p.	SHAK 911:15
however and whenever we p.	DICK 323:88
know in p....prophesy in p.	BIBLE 150:52
let us kiss and p.	DRAY 345:40
lose a p. of ourselves	POPE 780:26
no p. of his intention	SMITH 945:81
no p. with the lads	SASS 845:31
Not a tolerable woman's p.	AUST 51:47
P. of a moon	FROST 406:74
p. of all that I have met	TENN 994:58
p. on better terms	OTWAY 746:90
p. with their brightest hour	HELL 469:99
play its...rational p.	LEWIS 601:48
principal p. of themselves	HAZL 463:3
see the inmost p.of you	SHAK 892:50
Sir, you and I must p.	SHAK 905:65
Some p. of us	SKEL 942:47
take your own p.	BORR 179:24
thou and nature can so gently p.	SHAK 906:7
we are p. of nature	PLAN 772:84
what we can p. with	FORD 397:23
white yet a p. of me	HUGH 499:20
will more willingly p. withal	SHAK 889:95

parted measured swords, and p. — SHAK 887:34

the way we p. — SWIN 987:42

parterre nod on the p. — POPE 779:23

Parthenon though it were the P. — LOWE 615:76

Parthenons miniature P. — GILL 426:2

particel every p. and utensil — SHAK 894:5

participant point of view of p. — GALL 412:93

participate everybody is invited to p. — SCRI 857:24

p. in a tragedy — HUXL 507:82

participation dreams of the p. — NICH 726:50

particle catching every air-borne p. — JAMES 516:19

pushing young p. — GILB 424:71

particular Every p. Thou — BUBER 202:21

it's about everything in p.	SPARK 955:58
p. and universal	BERG 94:44
p. expenditure	EDEN 360:21
So singular in each p.	SHAK 912:31

particulars must do it in Minute P. — BLAKE 168:8

out of p. — WILL 1082:88

parties both p. nobly are subdued — SHAK 878:4

contract...between those two p.	SMITH 946:89
cowardly, middle-class p.	GOER 430:66
creed of different p.	TOCQ 1021:77
Dinner p. are for eating	FERB 385:12
Things must be done by p.	DISR 333:20
without the p.	JOHN 529:80

parting at our p. — JONS 535:99

Every p. is a foretaste	SCHO 849:1
In every p....an image of death	ELIOT 365:1
P. is all we know	DICK 328:17
P. is such sweet sorrow	SHAK 869:93
true love p.	THOM 1012:15

partitions thin p. do their bounds — DRYD 349:12

partner look for a perfect p. — WELD 1062:95

Sole p. and sole part — MILT 690:58

partnership p. between living — BURKE 208:36

parts All p. and none are home — MAIL 640:92

better p. must dance...forever	DAVI 307:7
consist of the fewest p.	LEUP 599:15
decay of p.	CONG 281:28
directed to contrary p.	NEWT 725:38
divided into three p.	NORTH 731:32
first rule...is to save all the p.	EHRL 362:56
Gaul...is divided into three p.	CAES 224:83
How p. relate to p.	POPE 783:5
in his time plays many p.	SHAK 885:91
p. answering p.	POPE 779:20
p. may be transported	OVID 747:3
p. of one stupendous whole	POPE 780:40
p. remaining as they were	MILT 683:19
p. that people skip	LEON 596:69
three p. iced over	ARNO 37:81
woman must have fine p.	GAY 417:58

party advantage of a stronger p. — THRA 1018:8

At a dinner p. one should	MAUG 664:84
blame it on the other p.	ANON 28:5
child ought to be of the p.	AUST 50:31
children's p. taken over by the elders	FITZ 391:9
communist p.	MACC 625:42
Conservatives...the stupidest p.	MILL 675:68
each p. is worse	ROGE 820:9
effort to keep a p. together	WILS 1085:42
expression of the p. line	GINS 428:34
great p. ought not to	HAIL 451:13
Heard there was a p.	LILL 604:94
holiness of always being the injured p.	ANGE 19:27
If I'd seen me at a p.	HOFF 484:56
Labour is the P. of law and order	BLAIR 165:53
Macmillan held his p. together	ASQU 42:87
neither p. loser	SHAK 878:4
only p. with clear policies	THAT 1008:28
P. is a political evil	BOLI 172:71
p. is organized opinion	DISR 333:6
p. of order or stability	MILL 675:64
p. of political zombies	WILS 1085:40
P. platforms are contracts	TRUM 1030:23
P. slogan	ORWE 745:57
p. we love	GAIT 411:71
passion and p. blind our eyes	COLE 275:27
property of any political p.	HOOV 490:66
same is true of a p.	MAO 648:24
serves his p. best	HAYES 462:93
The p.'s over	COMD 278:65

party (*contd.*)

The sooner every p. breaks up	AUST 51:55
third p. who stands	TAYL 992:22
pasarán No p.!	IBAR 510:18
pass all ye that p. by?	BIBLE 128:30
aspirations that never come to p.	SAKI 837:99
in a gleaming p.	TENN 994:49
it will p. with a lass	JAME 515:2
neither can they p. to us	BIBLE 144:8
p. for a cathedral doctor	JONS 534:77
p. for forty-three	GILB 423:53
p. through this world	GREL 446:49
replaced the library p.	LODGE 610:80
They shall not p.	PETA 767:4
passage afraid reading the p. now	FENT 385:2
confessional p....that didn't stink	SALI 839:31
dispute the p. with you	WHIT 1073:99
long black p. up to bed	STEV 975:42
meet with a p.	JOHN 529:64
p. in my throat	SHAK 894:96
p. of good style	FORD 396:4
p. through these looms	VAUG 1041:21
p. to the intellectual world	STER 969:9
p. which we did not take	ELIOT 370:23
slow p. to the fallen flood	CRAB 294:83
Your last high p.	CIAR 265:50
passages cite p. is to pull	MOORE 705:31
History has many cunning p.	ELIOT 368:70
p. of Ulysses	MILL 677:19
shall not lose our p.	DONNE 336:70
shuts up all the p.	JOHN 525:83
unmagical p. come closest	THOM 1011:92
passageway moving through my p.	SABA 835:56
passageways smell of steaks in p.	ELIOT 367:56
passed all have p. away	SIGO 938:71
passenger p. on the spaceship, Earth	FULL 409:39
passengers Wave at the p.	MACG 630:31
passes hands...move towards the p.	HEAN 465:35
Men seldom make p.	PARK 754:11
passing-bells p.-b. for these who die	OWEN 748:7
passion Better p. and death	LAWR 585:76
betwixt one p. and another	STER 970:23
Calm of mind all p.	MILT 695:60
capable of one great p.	PASC 757:49
clarity of p.	PASC 757:50
conference resembles a P. play	SCRI 857:24
connect the prose and the p.	FORS 398:36
Cows are my p.	DICK 323:95
Death...conclusion of a great p.	LAWR 585:75
desolate and sick of an old p.	DOWS 343:81
destructive p.	BURT 214:74
eternal monotony of p.	FLAU 392:39
Eternal P.!	ARNO 37:83
extremes of p., joy and grief	SHAK 904:49
he vows his p.	PARK 754:7
held in holy p.	MILT 682:7
In a tow'ring p.	SHAK 893:84
In her first p.	BYRON 223:45
in love with himself...a p.	POWE 787:3
Infinite p., and the pain	BROW 199:66
inspire hopeless p.	THAC 1006:92
led by her p.	CAMP 228:36
life? a play of p.	RALE 800:14
lingering and consumptive p.	ETHE 380:18
lov'd with such transcendent p.	DRYD 348:91
love thee with the p.	BROW 197:19
love was p.'s essence	BYRON 220:88
Man is a useless p.	SART 844:10
man...not p.'s slave	SHAK 891:37
master p. is the love of news	CRAB 294:77
master-mistress of my p.	SHAK 913:50
Minds still p.-ridden	LIND 605:11
no p. in the mind of man	BACON 56:44
No p. so effectively robs the mind	BURKE 206:96

passion (*contd.*)

one p. of my life	GOOD 435:55
or in any other high p.	STEV 974:4
p. and party blind our eyes	COLE 275:27
p. and the life	COLE 274:5
P. and the power to roam	BYRON 219:82
p. could not shake	SHAK 900:46
p. for abstracted devotion	JOHN 528:49
p. for any woman	RIVE 813:3
p. for hunting	DICK 321:38
p. for sweetness and light	ARNO 39:31
p. for the name 'Mary'	BYRON 223:53
p. in the human soul	LILLO 604:95
P., intellect, moral activity	NIGH 729:95
P. is all of humanity	BALZ 69:82
p. is one which interests	TROL 1028:97
p. is our task	JAMES 516:23
p. of the brain	BURT 214:77
p. speechless lies	DRAY 345:40
poetic p. ...has most	PATER 759:95
ruling p. conquers reason	POPE 780:28
Search then the Ruling P.	POPE 781:56
their fury and my p.	SHAK 916:24
utmost p. of her heart	HAWT 461:70
vulgar expression of the p.!	CONG 280:6
weary, and drowsy p.	WEBS 1059:28
when his p. shall have spent	TENN 995:73
passion-flower p.-f. at the gate	TENN 1001:88
passion-winged p.-w. Ministers	SHEL 930:47
passionate beautiful p. body	SWIN 987:34
p. desire to create	PRIE 790:41
p. heart of the poet	TENN 1001:75
passionless but man P.?	SHEL 930:25
P. bride	TENN 1003:31
passions governs the p.	HUME 503:7
Man...when he acts from the p.	DISR 332:86
men of like p.	BIBLE 148:95
moderator of all p.	WALT 1052:7
most violent of all p.	LAFA 574:74
not his reason, but his p.	STER 969:1
only one of many p.	JOHN 528:46
P. can lead me on	LAFA 574:7
P. destroy more prejudices	DIDE 329:24
p. of a king	HUGO 502:73
ridden the p. as if...horse	BROY 200:4
slave of the p.	HUME 503:3
taming of soul's raw p.	BLOOM 169:35
To know that their are p.	VIAN 1043:46
to move the p.	DRYD 347:63
tragedy paints the p.	HUGO 501:70
two favourite p.	LACL 573:60
various ruling p.	POPE 782:75
passive p., receptive side	SPEN 957:90
Patience is p.	FITZ 391:22
passivity people are reduced to p.	GITL 429:49
Passover it is the Lord's p.	BIBLE 106:61
passport man's p. in her...beak	MARL 653:99
p.'s green	HEAN 465:38
p. sometimes asked for	BAED 61:46
unwrinkled brows in p. offices	STARK 963:95
use only the good p.	SONT 953:11
warmonger put on my p.	BYRON 224:74
past always praising the p.	SMITH 948:34
an imagined p.	THOM 1013:26
ancient p.?	GARC 414:19
arrow points towards the p.	EDDI 360:17
art of the p.	LEWI 603:72
atone for the p.	CHEK 256:64
back ceaselessly into the p.	FITZ 391:7
burthened too much with the p.	HAWT 461:80
cannot do without the p.	POEL 776:56
changed...to p. Without a word	LARK 581:7
Children have neither p. nor future	LABR 573:53
cut off from the p.	THOM 1009:49

past (*contd.*)

dismiss the p. with a smile	LESS 598:97
drowned...the P.	THOM 1012:5
economy that belonged to the p.	MARI 650:62
escaping from the burden of the p.	YELT 1107:97
face turned to the p.	NARO 719:40
feel the presence of the p.	PEI 764:49
From p. and future	ELIOT 372:63
future as well as the p.	ELIOT 373:76
future contained in time p.	ELIOT 370:22
future that will live up to my p.	BENN 91:81
give you back the p.	HAMM 453:48
glories of the p.	HOWE 497:97
God cannot alter the p.	BUTL 217:34
God requireth that which is p.	BIBLE 122:20
Gratitude looks to the p.	LEWIS 601:38
great men of the p.	DESB 317:71
greatest secrets of the p.	FAWC 384:93
History is p. politics	FREE 404:33
inherited the p.	ACKR 4:58
intend to prejudge the p.	WHIT 1072:64
journeys into p.	BLYT 171:54
learn from the p.	KISS 565:30
Leave thy low-vaulted p.	HOLM 486:85
Many a woman has a p.	WILDE 1076:58
mistakes of the p.	TAYL 991:12
never pity the p.	FOWL 399:65
one do with the p.?	MURD 714:65
only a movie of the p.	KESEY 553:21
ooze of the p.	NABO 717:6
others, p. and present	NABO 717:9
p. and future...conquered	ELIOT 372:66
p. and future were comprehended	GEE 417:65
p. exudes legend	MALA 641:9
p. ...has a voice	OAKE 733:48
p. is a bucket of ashes	SAND 841:60
p. is a foreign country	HART 460:54
P. is a strange land	THOM 1012:98
p. is just the same	SASS 845:35
p. is the only dead	THOM 1012:8
p....is...too explosive	OBRI 734:62
p.... like the leaves of a book	WOOLF 1092:55
p. of the oppressed people	FANON 382:60
p. redress...p. care	SHAK 867:54
p. was not more eventful	ORWE 743:14
p. was nothing to her	CHOP 261:60
p., with its crimes	CHUR 264:19
p. would have been washed away	NAIP 717:17
pencils of the p.	STERN 968:87
present is the funeral of the p.	CLARE 267:81
presents, p. and future sees	BLAKE 167:84
Psychology has a long p.	EBBI 359:8
quarrels of the p.	MACC 625:51
remember what is p.	HALI 452:30
Repent what's p.	SHAK 892:57
scraps of the p.	GREE 444:21
something rather absurd about the p.	BEER 83:23
such great writers in the p.	HEMI 471:41
Those who cannot remember the p.	SANT 842:84
visions to the p.	KENN 551:82
weary of the p.	SHEL 932:65
weep like a child for the p.	LAWR 585:69
What calls back the p.	WHIT 1074:2
When remedies are p.	SHAK 898:12
Who controls the p.	ORWE 745:57
paste p. and cover to our bones	SHAK 867:59
Pasteur work such as P.'s	ROST 825:1
pastime ancient...forgotten p.	SCOTT 854:77
better p. for leisure	WELLS 1065:44
fellowly sport or p.	STUB 980:12
joyous birds make their p.	SPEN 958:19
ruin any p. under the sun	MITF 697:93
pastimes Proust of p.	FOWL 400:70
pastoral Cold P.!	KEATS 547:11

peace (*contd.*)

all her paths are p.	BIBLE 120:60
as we to keep p.	SHAK 868:75
asks God only for p.	BONH 172:81
at p. you think about	WILD 1079:25
author of p.	BOOK 173:96
bodies are buried in p.	BIBLE 133:18
Bomb brought p.	CHUR 265:28
bring a man p.	BOOK 176:70
bring the white p.	LIND 605:16
brings p. and good will	LLOY 609:63
but in p. Hung over	KEATS 546:83
carry gentle p.	SHAK 918:63
certain knot of p.	SIDN 937:53
chastisement of our p.	BIBLE 127:1
craving p.	WORD 1100:81
Cricket for p.	ZIA 1109:24
deathless and painless p.	HUGH 500:47
deep p. of the double-bed	CAMP 226:11
defences of p.	UNES 1036:44
demands and keep p.	NAPO 718:26
democracy and p.	WELL 1063:1
each of those words signifies p.	LAMA 575:3
enter into you in p.	MURD 714:29
Everlasting p. is a dream	MOLT 699:36
Father of P.	DODD 335:47
find p. in…desert travel	THES 1009:45
for ever hold his p.	BOOK 175:46
give p. a chance	LENN 596:56
Give p. in our time	BOOK 173:95
give thee p.	BIBLE 107:81
God's p. betide the souls	RANS 802:37
good arts of p.	MORE 706:42
good p. would never have won	CHUR 263:5
good war makes a good p.	HERB 476:38
government in p. and in war	BEVE 102:73
habits of p. and patience	WALT 1052:7
hard and bitter p.	KENN 550:64
haunt of ancient P.	TENN 994:56
hold their p.	BIBLE 144:12
holy rest, and p.	NEWM 724:29
honey p. in old poems	JEFF 519:79
if one wishes to travel in p.	STARK 963:95
Imperishable p.	HOUS 496:84
In hearts at p.	BROO 192:22
In His will is our p.	DANTE 305:72
in p. and…in war	MONT 702:82
In p., children inter their parents	HERO 477:47
In p.: goodwill	CHUR 263:97
In the arts of p.	SHAW 921:36
in Thee in p.	HAMM 453:44
in what p. a Christian can die	ADDI 8:40
inglorious arts of p.	MARV 657:65
instrument of Your p.	FRAN 401:91
just and lasting p.	LINC 605:6
keep him in perfect p.	BIBLE 125:74
King of glory, King of p.	HERB 475:20
led forth with p.	BIBLE 127:7
Let him who desires p.	VEGE 1042:29
let us make p.	CROM 298:52
lettest thou thy servant depart in p.	BIBLE 160:55
live together in p.	UNIT 1036:45
Love of P., and lonely musing	COLL 277:51
made a desolation they called it a p.	BURG 205:82
made a separate p.	HEMI 470:18
Make it a green p.	DARN 306:80
merry songs of p.	SHAK 918:67
message of p., love	WHIT 1071:61
more p. and it is the holier	HOPK 492:95
more potent advocates of p.	GEOR 418:83
never a bad p.	FRAN 402:9
no better p.-keepers	PALM 752:68
no p.…to the wicked	BIBLE 127:10
no such thing as inner p.	LEBO 591:79

peace (*contd.*)

Nor for my p.	JONS 535:4
Nor p. within nor calm around	SHEL 927:74
not a p. treaty	FOCH 395:84
Nothing can bring you p.	EMER 376:35
now do hold their p.	SURR 982:41
Now we have to win the p.	CLEM 269:7
Palestinian p. movement	ANON 29:46
P.…a period of cheating	BIER 161:91
p. above all earthly dignities	SHAK 918:60
p. among our peoples	KIPL 561:53
p. and propagation	WALP 1051:91
p. and rest can never dwell	MILT 687:90
P. be to this house	BIBLE 142:87
P. be to this house	BOOK 176:54
P. be unto you	BIBLE 160:56
p. betrayed us	MUIR 712:31
p. cannot be maintained	RUSS 833:39
p. comes dropping slow	YEATS 1104:57
P.; come away	TENN 999:42
P., Enjoyment, Love and Pleasure!	BURNS 212:26
p. for our time	CHAM 249:19
p. has been broken	ROOS 821:39
p. hath her victories	MILT 686:80
p. have they which love thy law	BIBLE 119:35
p., I hope, with honour	DISR 333:23
P. I leave with you	BIBLE 146:63
p. in Shelley's mind	SHEL 932:69
p. in thy breast	SHAK 869:94
P. is in the grave	SHEL 930:18
p. is of the nature	SHAK 878:4
P. is poor reading	HARDY 457:11
P. its ten thousands	PORT 784:41
P. makes plenty	ANON 22:79
p. nor beauty	LAWR 586:78
p. of each country	JOHN 522:33
p. of God, which passeth	BIBLE 153:14
p. of God, which passeth	BOOK 175:33
p. of mind	SMITH 945:78
P. on earth and mercy mild	BEEC 82:14
P. on earth and mercy mild	WESL 1066:59
p.…on the tested foundations	WILS 1086:52
P., p.; when there is no p.	BIBLE 128:21
P., the human dress	BLAKE 166:69
p. there's nothing	SHAK 881:83
P. to corrupt no less	MILT 693:26
p. to hers is small	CRIP 296:30
p. to him that is far off	BIBLE 127:9
p. to Ireland	ARNO 39:21
p. to the cottages	CHAM 250:24
p. to thy soul	SCOTT 856:15
p. to you which were afar off	BIBLE 152:95
p. which world cannot give	BOOK 173:99
P. without honour	CECIL 247:78
peaceful sloth Not p.	MILT 688:16
piping time of p.	SHAK 863:48
Policemen…keepers of the p.	MAMET 643:45
poor, who will not fast in p.	CRAB 293:76
power, p. and the healing	MATT 664:82
Pray for the p. of Jerusalem	BIBLE 119:38
Prince of P.	BIBLE 125:66
probabilities of p. or war	PALM 752:74
programme of the world's p.	WILS 1086:54
promised…either p. or happiness	LEBON 591:78
publisheth p.	BIBLE 127:96
re-establish p. and civil order	ELIZ 374:96
rest in obscurity and p.!	EMMET 378:81
Rest in soft p.	JONS 535:7
send p. on earth	BIBLE 136:79
shall the Great P. be established	DEKA 313:8
should kneel for p.	SHAK 864:90
soft phrase of p.	SHAK 898:5
Stalin…lover of p.	NEHRU 722:94
take chances for p.	DULL 354:25

peace (*contd.*)

there abides a p. of thine	ARNO 36:72
they are in p.	BIBLE 131:81
they love p. and quiet	TOLK 1023:94
thing fall down in p.	MAYB 665:6
though not its p.	GRAV 439:19
thousand years of p.	TENN 1000:67
through sorrowing, yet in p.	MILT 693:22
time of p.	BIBLE 122:19
Universal p. is declared	ELIOT 366:26
universal p. lie	TENN 996:90
War is p.	ORWE 745:56
war preferable to a shameful p.	TACI 989:78
war yield to p.	CICE 266:64
We came in p.	ANON 27:93
we prepare…for p.	PEAR 762:33
weeds of p.…triumphs	MILT 682:3
What hast thou to do with p.?	BIBLE 111:78
When there was p.	AUDEN 47:64
whisper 'P.'	GROM 447:69
wilderness and call it p.	TACI 989:74
workshop for world p.	HARR 459:39
peace-keepers no better p.-k.	PALM 752:68
peaceful friendship is never p.	SEVI 859:59
On every p. home	KIPL 565:16
p. revolution impossible	KENN 551:71
What…made her p.	YEATS 1105:67
peacemaker 'if' is the only p.	SHAK 887:36
peacemakers Blessed are the p.	BIBLE 133:34
peacetime p. environment	TRUM 1030:27
where they're living it's p.	KRAM 569:84
peach better than an insipid p.	HUNT 504:25
dare to eat a p.?	ELIOT 367:54
nectarine, and curious p.	MARV 658:85
peacock bluejay in p. feathers	LAFO 575:93
droops the milk-white p.	TENN 997:10
Eyed like a p.	KEATS 545:75
pride of the p.	BLAKE 166:78
peacocks p. and lilies	RUSK 830:78
p. strutting by	KIPL 564:13
peak 17,000-foot p.	BENU 94:33
upon a p. in Darien	KEATS 544:33
peaks great p. we had forgotten	LLOY 608:58
Sundered by p.	TU 1031:43
peal widest p. for years	HODG 484:53
peals p. of laughter…round thee	POPE 781:61
peanut P. butter has survived	KEIL 548:26
peanuts more salted p. consumed	SPIL 959:45
pear know the taste of a p.	MAO 648:20
p. on top of two toothpicks	ACHE 2:28
pear-tree glassy p.-t.	HOPK 491:86
pearl crown encased with p.	MARL 652:88
find a diamond or a p.	VAN 1039:2
gates of p. and topaz	LAUR 584:45
great ouches, heaps of p.	SHAK 863:54
ocean for orient p.	MARL 654:13
ocean for orient p.	MARL 654:9
p. in every cowslip's ear	SHAK 870:35
profited from its p.	THUR 1020:58
tears to p. he turned	MARL 655:29
threw a p. away	SHAK 900:64
pearls Give p. away	HOUS 494:44
p. by the seashore	MORE 707:53
Scatter thy p.	BLAKE 165:57
search for p.	DRYD 348:85
seeking goodly p.	BIBLE 138:4
shot to death, with p.?	WEBS 1061:66
Pearse P. summoned Cuchulain	YEATS 1107:91
peas eat my p. with honey	NASH 720:74
Here are the sweet p.	KEATS 544:35
peasant p. and a philosopher	JOHN 528:48
thankful I am a p.	FRAN 402:16
peasantry bold p.	GOLD 433:10
p. its pack animal	TROT 1029:6

peasants changed from p. — WAUGH 1057:89
p. in El Salvador — OROU 741:79
p. now Resign their pipes — CRAB 293:70
p. should be killed — LUTH 620:48
peason beans and p. put within — ANON 21:64
pebble p. or a prettier shell — NEWT 725:40
p. Ruttled in dry ground — JEFF 520:86
Pebworth Piping P. — ANON 26:56
pecker p. in my pocket — JOHN 523:54
Peckham classes within classes in P. — SPARK 955:49
peculiar Funny p., or funny ha-ha? — HAY 462:84
p. people — BIBLE 156:78
pecuniam p. infinitem — CICE 266:61
pecuniary immense p. Mangle — DICK 326:59
pedagogic for p. and other purposes — GALB 412:83
pedal large gas p. — MURR 715:77
pedant fertile p. — WALP 1051:95
like the p. in Hierocles — JOHN 528:45
poetry p.'s game — BUNT 204:59
pedantic too p. for a gentleman — CONG 281:18
pedants P. may cry out loud — GONZ 434:53
pederast [Music] a p. might hum — PROU 793:2
pedestalled p. in triumph? — BROW 200:91
pedigree P. of Honey — DICK 328:15
religious ties...social p. — WOLFE 1090:28
pedigrees p. of nations — JOHN 529:67
pedlar looked like a p. — MOORE 704:7
pee P., po, belly, bum, drawers — FLAN 392:2
peel p. me a grape — WEST 1067:80
peep p. and botanize — WORD 1095:9
p. through their eyes — SHAK 872:76
treason can but p. — SHAK 892:67
peeping p. Tom of the sciences — BISH 164:37
peepshow ticket for the p. — MACN 637:38
peer English p. of the right sort — WODE 1088:83
Lycidas...not left his p. — MILT 684:38
Peerless P. — ROCH 816:59
peerage were I to be offered a p. — CHAN 251:62
You should study the P. — WILDE 1077:74
peers flattery of one's p. — LODGE 610:82
House of P. — GILB 424:76
judged by our p. — BALZ 68:71
Of Satan and his p. — MILT 688:10
p., and they are hereditary — LLOY 609:64
peevish something p. that way — SHAK 878:12
temper...has become licentiously p. — DISR 333:3
Virginity is p., proud, idle — SHAK 901:69
peeweets the p. crying — STEV 976:57
peg Hang your idea on a p. — BRIS 189:62
Pegasus thought it P. — KEATS 544:40
peignoir Complancies of the p. — STEV 971:38
pellet p. with the poison — PANA 752:75
pelt wear my p. tanned — MIDD 673:43
pelting p. of this pitiless storm — SHAK 903:24
pen altar, sword and p. — WORD 1096:38
Before my p. has gleaned — KEATS 544:49
Biting my truant p. — SIDN 937:51
could use the sword and p. — LAND 578:63
Devise wit, write p. — SHAK 865:12
drop of ink in my p. — WALP 1051:82
far less brilliant p. than mine — BEER 83:24
garden with your p. — CAMP 227:17
hung up my p. — SIMON 939:83
needle and the p. — LEWIS 601:46
Never durst poet touch a p. — SHAK 865:21
p. but also with a blue pencil — LUCAS 618:30
p. has been in their hands — AUST 52:69
p. is worse than the sword — BURT 214:68
p. mightier than sword — BULW 204:55
p. refusing to draw anything — BRON 191:99
poet's p. all scorn — BRAD 184:1
poet's p. Turns them to shapes — SHAK 871:55
prevents his holding a p. — DICK 321:49
sad words of tongue or p. — WHIT 1074:5

pen (contd.)
squat p. rests — HEAN 464:31
This p.'s all I have — HARR 459:37
With such acts fill a p. — DRAY 345:36
words of tongue and p. — HARTE 460:53
penal blood...on your p. code — BYRON 221:9
penalties pains and p. of idleness — POPE 783:8
penalty in the p. area — SHAN 918:73
lines marking a p. area — FRY 408:10
p. is...cowardly — PELE 764:50
pence Take care of the p. — LOWN 617:16
pencil coloured p. long enough — CHES 258:13
dips His p. — SHEL 927:75
drew your p. from you — TENN 995:75
pen but also a blue p. — LUCAS 618:30
p. drew whate'er her soul designed — DRYD 350:46
pencils inexorable sadness of p. — ROET 819:91
p. of the past — STERN 968:87
pendulum p. of the mind — JUNG 539:71
p. swinging back and forth — COLUM 278:62
Penelope His true P. — POUND 785:61
penetrate music...will p. — SHAK 916:2
p. some thick skull — SARD 843:94
penguin In the P. book — HEAN 465:39
young p. lies screaming? — EWART 381:45
penis p. and mathematics — CELI 247:86
pennies P. do not come from heaven — THAT 1007:14
P. from Heaven — BURKE 208:50
Pennsylvania by the name of P. — PENN 764:56
penny Germans...pay every p. — GEDD 417:63
loaves sold for a p. — SHAK 861:10
Not a p. off the pay — COOK 286:24
not give one p. — CATU 245:59
one p. plain — STEV 973:98
pens p. that ever poets held — MARL 653:91
Penshurst Thou art not, P. — JONS 535:1
pension labourer to take his p. — RUSK 830:89
p. list...a roll of honour — CLEV 269:8
P. Pay given — JOHN 526:16
pensioners cowslips tall her p. be — SHAK 870:35
trade union for p. and children — HEATH 466:50
pensions p. and other boring — TOWN 1024:13
P. and Grenadiers — STER 969:6
Pentecost day of P. was fully come — BIBLE 147:81
pentecostal no wind, but p. fire — ELIOT 372:50
penthouse Hang upon his p. lid — SHAK 907:13
penumbra p. of somber dignity — ATLAS 44:6
penuries sheave...to fill all p. — DONNE 339:26
penury Chill P. — GRAY 442:68
ragged p. of shade — ADAMS 4:63
talk...tendeth only to p. — BIBLE 121:77
people 10,000 p. looking for 10 p. — ANON 28:13
18,000 p. boo — PLAN 773:87
advice to p. today — LEARY 591:70
after p. who interest me — KERO 553:12
ageing college p. — NABO 717:99
ain't twelve hundred p. — KIPL 561:44
all country p., in the world — SENG 858:49
All cruel p. — WILL 1082:78
All nations...and p. — BIBLE 157:14
All p. that on earth — SCOT 856:22
All the nice p. — SPARK 955:55
Alps and their p. — RUSK 830:79
American p. were like him — REST 807:19
American p. — GERG 420:99
Among a p. generally corrupt — BURKE 207:17
Artists are the only p. — SLOAN 943:60
as long as p. hear it — SOUSA 953:25
August for the p. — AUDEN 46:53
average condition of the p. — MILL 674:61
balance to the p. — ANON 28:7
Be nice to p. on your — MIZN 697:5
bearable to millions of p. — SHAW 923:81
beat my p. to pieces — BIBLE 124:58

people (contd.)
Before we were her p. — FROST 407:96
before you were born to p. — LEBO 591:85
believe that p. accept — THAT 1007:13
best p. never land — MACN 637:47
between the king and the p. — SELD 857:33
Black p. possess the secret of joy — WALK 1049:59
black p. with Jesus — GIOV 428:38
brings out the worst...in p. — SARN 843:97
buckler of the p.'s cause — DRYD 349:16
burning and gassing p. — SIHA 938:72
but ye are the p. — BIBLE 113:6
by all p. believed — VINC 1045:77
by the p., and for the p. — LINC 605:4
Can make good p. — SHAK 917:47
can't help p. against their will — FREE 404:32
cannot prevent p. from thinking — SCHI 847:65
causes many p. to be downcast — MACG 630:23
certain sick p. are said to do — LAMB 576:29
character of its p. — HOPP 493:13
Church (is) the p. — SHAW 923:76
circumcised p. — GIBB 421:23
city where most p. live — GRAY 440:32
civilized and democratic p. — ATTL 44:9
class of p. — WARD 1053:14
classes of p. — GARL 415:26
clever, well-informed p. — AUST 52:67
colonialism forces the p. — FANON 382:61
common p. know what they — MENC 668:56
common p. swarm — SHAK 862:25
confident that the unfortunate p. — WELLS 1065:44
Conquered p. tend to be witty — BELL 88:29
contracts with the p. — TRUM 1030:23
control the p. — DICK 320:13
country p. forget — MORR 709:86
Cricket? It civilises p. — MUGA 711:20
Cultured p. practice self-examination — I 510:26
DEAL...full of filthy-looking p. — COBB 271:55
decent godless p. — ELIOT 370:18
decent p. live beyond their incomes — SAKI 838:9
desire of our two p. — CHAM 249:18
different p., different beliefs — CART 242:2
different sorts of p. — SHAW 924:91
do my p. forgive me? — RICH 809:56
don't think I understand p. — FORS 398:40
drawn between him and the p. — HARD 455:76
Eating p. is wrong! — FLAN 392:26
economy of these p. — SMOL 950:63
education of the p. — DISR 333:39
education of the p. — MILL 674:62
effect on other p. — SART 844:6
enslaved and stubborn p. — MORE 706:46
every p. should be left free — WILS 1086:50
excellent p. never go there — SAKI 838:11
exertions of a free p. — PITT 772:73
express purpose of letting p. in — DICK 320:15
eye...ear...tongue of the p. — STEAD 964:4
far into other p. — AMIS 17:86
father of his p. — GIBB 421:22
fight so hungry p. can eat — STEI 966:55
folk music...fat p. — DYLAN 358:98
fool some of the p. — LINC 605:39
for many p. in the West — SOLZ 952:97
French are a logical p. — MORL 708:72
from the p. to the common good — MILT 686:79
from the p., and for the p. — DISR 332:72
get p. into a position — KAZIN 543:30
get p. to call me Newt — GING 427:22
good of the p. — CICE 266:58
good...To all the p. — WESL 1067:99
govern by p. — LOUI 613:44
government and the p. — MILL 674:56
government can confer on a p. — MACA 622:87
great many p. — TAFT 990:82

people (*contd.*)

great masses of the plain p.	MENC 669:67
Great p. talk about ideas	LEBO 591:86
habits and customs of the p.	RICA 808:32
half the p. are right	WHITE 1070:27
hate p. and children	CAMP 227:23
hate p. who play bridge	MAUG 664:86
hath such p. in't!	SHAK 917:42
Hell is other p.	SART 844:11
hire mediocre p.	MURP 715:74
hits where the other p. are	LARD 580:92
holding a p. in its grip	FANON 382:60
humble p. of Cambodia	SIHA 938:73
Hundreds of p. can talk	RUSK 831:8
If by the p. …multitude	DRYD 347:61
If p. could deal… honestly	CHAN 250:45
If p. knew there'd be less death	MALA 641:4
Imagine all the p.	LENN 596:57
In America few p. will trust	MAIL 639:75
induce p. to buy them	STEV 970:31
industry that…needs better p.	DRUC 346:46
investigator to pretend that p.	LEWO 603:74
It is for the p.	OROZ 741:83
jokes upon the American p.	MENC 669:70
keen city…filled with pretty p.	CUMM 299:81
Let my p. go	BIBLE 106:59
Let the p. praise thee	BIBLE 116:85
Liars out of the American p.	ROGE 820:11
life and times of a p.	ROCK 818:78
live among wicked p.	RICH 809:58
look after our p.	SCOTT 852:40
losing p. you love	OATES 733:56
lot of p. doing what I say	WINN 1087:64
lot of p. under you	ANON 29:50
love of the p.	BURKE 207:12
make fun of p.	GARC 414:18
make one set of p. forget	HUXL 508:92
make p. believe	WILS 1084:14
makes p. happy	WHITE 1071:50
many p. in the world	KENN 551:83
mark of many famous p.	HELL 469:99
married p. live longer?	FIEL 388:59
martyr of the p.	CHAR 252:83
materialistic p.	MACC 625:44
money from the pockets of the p.	SMITH 945:83
moral consciousness of p.	MAIL 639:71
more a p. lover	LARK 582:16
more than p. could afford	LEWIS 601:51
Most p. are relieved	TUCH 1031:47
most p. are wrong	KURZ 571:23
most p. in most places	LEGU 594:29
Most p. my age	STEN 968:78
Most p. sell their souls	SMITH 947:16
Most p. spend…their lives	LABR 573:55
motivating p.	MACD 628:97
mouths of fallible p.	BENN 91:83
New Deal for the American p.	ROOS 821:34
nice to meet serious p.	COPE 287:52
no use to decent p.	SHAW 924:90
no vision, the p. perish	BIBLE 122:11
number of p. have tried	KERR 553:17
o my p.	OLSEN 739:35
Observing these p.	MAUG 665:92
Of all the clever p. round me	CAMP 227:16
of the p. by the p. for the p.	WILDE 1076:56
one million p.…a small sum	DENG 315:51
one of the few honest p.	FITZ 390:1
one of the p. took one	ANDE 18:9
One realm, one p., one leader	ANON 26:40
only ordinary p. asked	MO 698:13
Only the little p. pay taxes	HELM 469:5
opium of the p.	MARX 660:6
Other p.'s babies	HERB 474:95
ought to class p. as static	WAUGH 1056:73

people (*contd.*)

Our p. are not naive	REYES 807:22
our p. can build Angkor Wat	POL 777:62
over-civilized p.	MUIR 713:38
parts that p. skip	LEON 596:69
peculiar p.	BIBLE 156:78
p.…abusing the best Constitution	FRAN 402:8
p. according to their abilities	MAIN 640:96
p. all exulting	WHIT 1073:91
p., after fifty	VIDAL 1044:67
p. always say	GOTT 436:73
p. and I have come to an agreement	FRED 403:27
p. and the method	RYLE 834:53
p., and the sheep of his pasture	BIBLE 118:9
p. and the stones	WILL 1082:86
p. answered him not a word	BIBLE 111:63
p. are all too clean	LINK 606:24
p. are entitled to	JEFF 520:91
p. are fanatically dedicated	PIRS 770:52
p. are frequenting	MACL 633:71
p. are hostile	CRISP 297:41
p. are like portmanteaux	MANS 647:4
p. are nice and polite	MAHA 638:59
P. are not as smart as bugs	WHITE 1070:38
P. are not fallen angels	LAWR 585:66
p. are not so unpolished	MONT 700:54
p. are only human	COMP 278:69
p. are paying attention	SONT 953:13
p. are reduced to passivity	GITL 429:41
p. are shocked by honesty	COWA 290:5
p. are the masters	BURKE 207:21
p. are too stupid by three-quarters	MAJOR 640:99
p. are travellers	FERB 385:7
p. arose as one man	BIBLE 109:24
p. believe that they have rights	HEGEL 466:62
p. between…of twenty and forty	FAUL 383:80
p. brought up in…slums	WAUGH 1056:75
p. came to theirs	HODG 484:53
p. can be poor	OCON 736:89
p. can claim America	ROLL 821:26
p. change and forget	HELL 468:96
p. contemplate writing	GERA 419:94
p. contend for their liberty	HALI 452:31
p. could be down-to-earth	SHUL 936:37
p. could neither see	JOHN 524:69
p. do actually desire it	MILL 675:72
P. do not change	VIAN 1043:42
P. do what you pay	WALD 1048:47
P. don't choose their careers	DOSP 340:41
p. don't go to the theater	JOUR 537:36
P. don't…like …beautiful	DEBU 311:68
p. don't resent having nothing	COMP 279:70
p.…don't trust their reactions	COLE 273:79
P. find ideas a bore	POUND 786:79
p.'s flag is deepest red	CONN 282:54
p. free from routine	LINK 606:20
p. getting into a state	GALS 413:3
p. I hate	HART 459:45
P. in nutrition	DAVIS 308:23
p. in portraits are thinking	LIVE 607:43
P. in Power	PATC 759:92
p. in the back streets of Derby	CHRI 261:66
p. in the world are fools	WILD 1079:30
P. in this country	RICH 810:65
p. know what the land knows	SAND 841:72
p. listen to you	SNOW 951:77
P. live within winter	MUNRO 714:60
p. look at the sea	FROST 407:89
p. love junk food	GASS 416:35
p. may be made to follow	CONF 279:88
p. may complain	WEBER 1059:22
P.…must not be bartered	WILS 1086:55
P. must not do things for fun	HERB 474:1
P. mutht be amuthed	DICK 325:45

people (*contd.*)

p. never give up liberties	BURKE 207:24
p. not spoken about	GEE 417:64
p. of a strange speech	BIBLE 128:35
p. of all sorts	APOL 32:94
p. of Crete	SAKI 838:10
p. of his pasture	BOOK 177:87
p. of South Africa	SMUTS 950:40
P. of the same trade	SMITH 945:79
P. of the world, unite	MAO 648:29
p. of this country	PEEL 763:43
p. of whom we know nothing	CHAM 249:17
p. on their way towards God	WINT 1087:90
p. on whom nothing is lost!	JAMES 516:20
p. ought to be free	MACA 622:91
P. out of work	EVANS 381:40
p. overlaid with taxes	BACON 59:3
p. say the president	MARC 649:46
p. seem to be divided	DOST 340:43
p. should mate for life	ALLEN 14:49
p. show that I communicate	ROTH 826:26
p. sinned against	COMP 279:77
p. sliding with their skates	PEPYS 765:68
P. sometimes divide others	SPEN 957:89
p. starved for self-definition	BURNS 208:55
P. struggled on for years	WHAR 1068:1
p. supplied with electric light	MACL 635:96
p. taut for war	THOM 1013:19
p. that do err in their heart	BIBLE 117:7
p. that on earth	KETHE 554:23
p. that walked in darkness	BIBLE 125:65
p. that want to try a new experience	SHAW 924:91
p. to complexify them	MOYN 711:15
p. trying to convince themselves	SNYD 951:85
p. until they set the basket	NASH 720:73
p.'s voice is odd	POPE 782:81
p. want a sense of purpose	MACM 636:19
P. want economy	IACO 509:16
p. were a kind of solution	CAVA 246:68
p. were so horrible	AMIS 16:79
p.'s wery scarce	DICK 320:14
p. which ceases to care	ELIOT 370:14
P. who are always praising	SMITH 948:34
p. who are late	LUCAS 618:24
p. who are moral or immoral	CHUR 263:91
p. who are paid to have attitudes	HEMI 470:14
p. who are too busy	WAUGH 1057:98
p. who belong somewhere else	STEIN 965:38
p. who called the Milky Way	MARTI 657:56
p. who can copulate	MACD 627:85
p. who can't get along	GRAY 440:14
p. who dare not assert	MUMF 713:49
p. who do not hear the sound	MAIL 639:69
p. who have been persecuted	KISS 566:42
p. who have flabby hands	GILB 425:84
p. who have no love	SHAW 920:99
p. who have read	HAYA 462:85
p. who have the courage	MUSS 716:86
p. who hire them	NEW 723:16
p. who hunt	SHAW 925:17
P. who leave their own time	MASE 662:52
p. who live outside	SABA 835:56
P. who never get carried away	FORB 396:96
p. who never trouble	STARK 963:98
P. who obtain power	VIDAL 1044:61
p. who shoot grouse	EDIN 361:42
p. who want to do nothing	DODD 334:42
p. who wave at trains	MACG 630:31
p. who were not as obsessed	LESS 598:4
p. who will run the future	JONES 533:59
p. whom a fair face	MAIL 640:93
p. will always be kind	SASS 845:24
P. will do anything	PERCY 766:84
p. will live on	SAND 841:67

people (*contd.*)
p. will more readily swallow lies	GELL 417:70
P. wish to be settled	EMER 376:42
p. without business	DEFOE 312:84
p. without history	ELIOT 373:80
P. would rather sleep	ALBEE 11:90
p.'s wrongs his own	DRYD 349:25
p. you have seen	MURR 716:79
P. you know	LARK 582:17
persuade…half the p.	GAIT 411:72
photographing p.	EISE 364:94
platypus and p.	THUR 1019:45
please all of the p.	CONN 284:85
pleasure of pleasing inferior p.	CLOU 270:39
poetry ignores most p.	MITC 696:79
poor little street-bred p.	KIPL 561:42
Poor p. staying	PEPYS 765:79
power over p.	SOLZ 952:95
Power to the p.	ANON 27:91
Pray, good p., be civil	GWYN 449:97
prayers of liberty-loving p.	EISE 363:78
present at gathering of p.	SNOW 950:72
problems of three little p.	EPST 379:1
proud conceited ignorant p.	ANON 24:6
punching p. in the head	LEON 596:71
Quiet p. avoid the question	DICK 322:67
raising up a p. of customers	SMITH 945:84
really nice English p.	SHAW 925:14
rebellious p.	REED 805:91
religion of these p.	MONT 700:53
representatives of the p.	WHIT 1069:16
resented by thousands more p.	ROCK 817:67
Respected p. are only rascals	STEN 967:74
sacrifice other p. without blushing	SHAW 922:65
self-help created among working p.	SMIL 945:76
shame more p. don't switch	PIRS 770:53
showing other p. where to dig	LEAV 591:77
slam at the p.	FITZ 391:17
smiles of the p.	MARC 650:49
snake about to devour p.	NIXON 730:7
so long as the right p. get shot	EAST 359:6
so many p.	GALS 413:4
so many p. showed up	GOLD 434:49
society in which what p. fulfil	MAJOR 640:97
some p. a bit behind	VARE 1040:6
Some p. find oil	GETTY 421:16
Some p. read too much	MENC 669:78
Some p. swim lakes	WEBB 1058:16
Some p. think football	SHAN 918:69
Soviet p.	GORB 435:58
speak as the common p.	ASCH 40:50
stiffnecked p.	BIBLE 107:72
struggle of the African p.	MAND 644:68
submitted… to a whole p.	STEAD 964:8
suicide kills two p.	MILL 677:5
Superior p. never make	MOORE 705:19
supported by…the British p.	LAW 585:59
Take most p.	SALI 839:25
tell p. what they do not want	ORWE 744:28
TELL THE P.!	CHRI 261:68
tells other p. what to do	BARA 70:7
The p. die so	PEPYS 765:75
The p. muddied	SHAK 892:66
These p. are good	VAZD 1041:24
These p….do not *read* books	WORD 1099:75
they shall be his p.	BIBLE 158:35
things p. had once held against her	SCHL 848:77
thy p. shall be my p.	BIBLE 109:25
till p. behave themselves	KING 558:97
time changes p.	PROU 793:6
too many of the p.	THUR 1019:28
trivial p. should muse and thunder	LAWR 587:3
two p. miserable instead of four	BUTL 217:32
two sorts of p.	SHAW 923:75

people (*contd.*)
two types of p.	PASC 758:75
unconditional confidence of his p.	WEI 1061:75
united p.	PARK 755:31
very ancient p.	TOLK 1023:94
Very Decent to P.	ROTH 826:8
very few p. come this way	LEAR 590:65
views of the p.	GALL 413:98
voice of the p.	ALCU 12:3
voice of the p.	BACON 56:35
voice of the p.	PITT 771:65
voices of young p.	SMITH 947:15
Waldo is one of those p.	SAKI 838:13
way p. look and laugh	WOOLF 1092:56
We are a religious p.	DOUG 342:70
we are the p.	WRIG 1102:12
What kind of p.	CHUR 264:21
what other p. wear	WILDE 1078:93
what p. have got against	HOPE 491:75
what p. say of us	SMITH 947:11
what the p. think it so	BURKE 207:18
When p. are too comfortable	RICH 810:68
When p. do not respect us	TWAIN 1034:7
when you bore p.	KISS 566:40
wherever I find your p.	JOAN 522:27
whether just p. …are happier	PLATO 774:19
whole world is bereft of p.	LAMA 575:1
will of the p.	PARE 753:83
willing to see p. sacrificed	MILL 679:57
Win Friends and Influence P.	CARN 237:7
without other p. hearing	WILDE 1076:47
Women…are invisible p.	FRIE 405:50
Words can keep p. apart	MARC 649:44
world empty of p.	LAWR 585:70
world is full of middle-class p.	SHAR 919:87
you too are p.	SAND 841:70
peopled earth p. as ever by the inept	REPP 807:13
p. half the world	SEEL 857:28
peoples meeting place of the p.	BARN 71:24
new-caught, sullen p.	KIPL 562:65
other p.' Kings	GARC 414:19
peace among our p.	KIPL 561:53
silent sullen p.	KIPL 562:66
We the P.	UNIT 1036:45
pepper a little P. or Salt	SWIFT 985:99
cucumber…dressed with p.	JOHN 529:68
pepper-pot p.-p. breast of thrush?	FRAME 400:76
Pequod P. packing off to hell	LOWE 616:94
perceive nature of reason to p. things	SPIN 960:51
p. their foul disfigurement	MILT 683:19
perceived being is to be p.	BERK 95:51
percent Six p. unemployment	PASS 759:82
perception doors of p.	BLAKE 166:80
dullest p. always	THOR 1017:92
intensity of p.	WILL 1083:99
Japanese…destitute of p.	BIRD 163:17
mechanism of p.	SNYD 951:84
outside a central p.	DELI 314:39
p. that something ought to be done	WELLS 1065:45
reeducation of p.	DEWEY 319:96
some particular p. or other	HUME 503:1
perceptions but those p.	HUME 503:98
perch p., and not their terror	SHAK 896:64
percussion Like a P. Instrument	BUKO 203:49
Percy not yet of P.'s mind	SHAK 876:53
perdition antechamber of p.	SHAW 926:43
P. catch my soul	SHAK 899:29
P. catch my soul	SHER 934:10
Science…is the soul's p.	RABE 799:87
son of p.	BIBLE 146:67
To bottomless p.	MILT 687:88
peregrinations p. to fetch remote	DONNE 339:24
perestroika Russian word 'p.'	GORB 435:57
perfect be thou p.	BIBLE 104:22

perfect (*contd.*)
Be ye therefore p.	BIBLE 134:46
Can a man be p.	FORS 399:57
constant, he were p.!	SHAK 860:89
end of a p. day	BOND 172:79
formal poetry p. only in form	SAND 842:80
God…had created a p. world	SHAR 919:84
grow more p. when emancipated	WOLL 1091:43
gunshot is the p. way	KENN 552:96
Heaven is being p.	BACH 54:94
If thou wilt be p.	BIBLE 139:24
most p. expression of scorn	SHAW 925:20
most p. of Swiss clockmakers	STRA 979:4
no knowledge comes to be p.	DONNE 339:31
no one is p.	MAIN 640:96
None of us are p.	WILDE 1078:88
not in my p. mind	SHAK 904:43
Nothing is more p.	VIAN 1043:45
One p. limousine	PARK 754:5
p. as much as we can	SPIN 960:58
p. condition of slavery	ASTE 43:92
p. in a short time	BIBLE 131:83
p. republics are a p. nonsense	FOWL 399:64
P. the cup as planned	BROW 199:77
p. use of an imperfect medium	WILDE 1076:84
strength is made p. in weakness	BIBLE 152:87
them whose heart is p.	BIBLE 112:89
thought p. by every body	AUST 51:52
three inches long, p.	HUGH 500:38
union is p.	DICK 329:22
We're not all p.	PIZZ 772:82
when that which is p. is come	BIBLE 150:62
would be the p. friend	SMITH 947:17
perfectability no faith in human p.	POE 776:45
perfection a placid p. unattainable	STRA 979:92
achieved p.	HUGH 498:12
achieved some sort of p.	HOYLE 498:2
Almighty unto p.?	BIBLE 113:5
confess p. so could err	SHAK 898:6
Dead p., no more	TENN 1001:74
dreams of p.	FAUL 384:85
friend who loved p.	SMITH 947:17
got to be p. for me	MELBA 667:23
make defect p.	SHAK 905:70
man a little pope of p.	LAWR 585:72
Nestles the seed of p.	WHIT 1073:96
p. does not recognize humanity	WOOD 1092:48
p. in a new kind of art	RUNGE 829:55
P. irritates	AUCH 46:38
P., of a kind	AUDEN 47:66
p. of behaviour	CHRI 262:74
p. of character	AURE 50:27
p. of the human race	INGE 511:41
Pictures of p.	AUST 52:62
pursuit of p.	ARNO 39:25
Right p.	SHAK 914:69
seek a triple p.	HOOK 489:55
since p. is love	NIEB 727:64
Thinking is the great enemy of p.	CONR 285:17
through Art…realise our p.	WILDE 1076:39
What's come to p. perishes	BROW 199:71
perfidious P. wretch!	TREI 1026:45
perfidy petty p.	BYRON 220:97
performance any p. is discussable	BURKE 208:53
been all words, And no p.	MASS 662:55
brilliance of the p.	HEMI 470:24
Britain's comparative p.	MISH 696:72
coming late to a p.	ZOLO 1110:27
full of promise but of no p.	DICK 322:70
instant of their p.	GRAY 440:44
jazz p. centers	LIEB 604:21
literary p.	WHIT 1073:1
many years outlive p.?	SHAK 877:93
music…greater than its p.	PREV 789:27

performance (*contd.*)
p. is everything HUNT 504:25
p. of the American economy STEIN 966:51
p. of the life of man MUIR 712:33
p. of the task itself SHIP 935:20
resulting p. GALB 412:80
so poor a record of p. FRIE 405:55
performances intellectual p. YOUR 1108:6
p. of the others RYLE 834:54
performed be p. with tact JOHN 524:68
perfume all p. yes JOYCE 538:57
p. is itself a wind WILL 1083:90
p. of a thousand roses BERN 97:88
wear coffee as a p. VAND 1039:98
perfumes p....are chafed WEBS 1059:27
p. is there more delight SHAK 915:92
Pergo P. Park knew me LEVE 600:23
peril at his p. further go HERB 474:9
At the p. of its soul SCOTT 852:33
perilous no position more p. TROL 1028:84
perils feeling that lures us on...to p. CONR 284:98
p. and dangers of this night BOOK 174:1
p. do environ BUTL 216:12
smile at p. past! SCOTT 854:69
sordid p. of actual existence WILDE 1076:34
through the p. of winter TROL 1027:65
period during this p. THUR 1019:31
from an early p. MACA 624:26
lived in any other p. HAZL 464:15
p. in one's life LARW 582:30
p. in question MYRD 716:92
p. not to be judged LEVI 600:26
p. of cheating BIER 161:91
p., once past RUNGE 829:54
persist for a long p. RUSS 832:28
repeat in one p. RENO 807:10
periodical governs the p. press TROL 1027:62
periods for all of p. RUNGE 829:54
really had two p. NABO 716:94
periphery you most inimitable p. OCON 735:82
periphrastic p. study ELIOT 371:45
perish All things p. KEMP 549:42
hero p., or a sparrow fall POPE 780:35
If I had to p. twice FROST 407:85
if I p., I p. BIBLE 112:93
p. in the very instant GRAY 440:44
shall p. unconsoled LANG 579:67
those that offer resistance p. SOPH 953:18
perishing p. never entered my head DOUG 341:52
periwigs fashion...as to p. PEPYS 765:76
perjuries Jupiter...laughs at lovers' p. OVID 747:95
perjury lovers' p. DRYD 352:90
permanent cheerfulness fixed and p. ADDI 7:17
less p. than thought BUNT 204:56
P. crisis justifies p. control HUXL 508:87
p., like the things JOHN 526:5
The word p. FRAME 400:79
very small extent p. NIET 729:93
pernicious most p. race SWIFT 985:84
perpendicular p. expression SHAW 925:32
perpetual light...seemed p. SPEN 956:84
no p. enemies PALM 752:70
p. holiday is a good...definition SHAW 924:10
p. hunger to be beautiful RHYS 808:25
steady and p. serenity ADDI 7:17
'Tis with us p. night JONS 534:85
perpetuate helps to p. it KING 557:73
p. an error for ever SCHO 849:95
perpetuated So they are p. GALB 411:77
perpetuating contrivance for p. SHAW 921:38
perplex wildness to p. the scene POPE 779:21
perplexed p., but not in despair BIBLE 151:77
perplexities obvious p. ARIS 34:24
perplexity listlessness from vain p. WORD 1096:19

perquisites scorn of irregular p. WAUGH 1056:65
persecute Why p. we him BIBLE 113:13
persecuted because he is p. GOULD 436:76
born...of the p. WRIG 1102:11
p. for righteousness' sake BIBLE 133:34
persecution p. of the transvestite WHITE 1069:19
P. is a bad...way to plant religion BROW 195:81
P. is not an original feature PAINE 750:48
P. produced its natural effect MACA 624:23
some degree of p. SWIFT 986:18
persecutions greatest of all p. PASC 758:78
perseverance by the name of p. STER 969:93
P., dear my lord SHAK 896:52
Persian p. pussy from over the sea MARQ 656:41
Persians Truth-loving P. GRAV 440:24
Persil Mum, the P.-user BETJ 100:51
persist p. in its own being SPIN 960:52
person advantage to take of a p. MANS 647:10
aggravates an earnest p. MELV 668:49
altered her p. SWIFT 984:62
Ancient P., for whom I ROCH 817:65
another p. in America NORTH 732:34
being in love with a p. LESS 599:8
but as a p. GRASS 439:12
can a p. see rightly SAIN 836:85
classify a p. SZASZ 989:68
demagogue is a p. MARQ 656:51
dullest p. in the world BENS 92:10
explain it to the average p. FEYN 387:35
For her own p. SHAK 905:68
his breath and p. WALL 1049:62
household features her p. PRIOR 790:52
judged as done against our p. HENR 472:65
last p. to say anything SAKI 838:15
lifetime of one p. HORN 494:36
most pleasing p. in all the world LABR 572:37
My idea of an agreeable p. DISR 333:15
never met a steadily logical p. GELL 417:68
no more a p. AUDEN 47:68
no p. can be a poet MACA 622:89
No p....understands his parents FRIS 406:65
no sane p. would do SHAW 923:81
not a political p. HELL 468:94
not a well-rounded p. BELL 88:28
not at all the sort of p. CARL 233:26
one p. of contrary opinion MILL 675:66
old p. of Ware LEAR 590:68
only in memory...same p. DIDE 330:33
only thing...is an uninterested p. CHES 258:94
p. bearing his share of labours MILL 675:65
p. born who is so unlucky MARQ 656:45
p. can be fully involved MANN 646:88
p. can be truly affectionate PREV 789:29
p. cannot choose his father FRIS 406:67
p. concerns himself with life MANN 645:83
p. freed from his religion SAIN 837:89
P. from Porlock SMITH 948:37
p. seldom falls sick EMER 377:65
p. should be mourned MONT 702:80
p. to worship God ROOS 822:43
p. up early...is a Christian LAW 585:60
p. we were yesterday UPDI 1037:70
p. who expects nothing from society SAND 840:51
p. who has used his emotions SAND 840:50
p. who is capable of choosing STEIN 966:49
p. who is not RUSK 830:82
p. who knows 'how' RAVI 802:45
p. who lives for today MENC 670:86
p. who lives for today BELL 86:91
p. who reads or thinks YOUR 1108:5
poet is a p. FROST 407:90
politician is a p. LLOY 609:67
species of p. WAUGH 1056:72
the only p. I know MONR 700:50

person (*contd.*)
three great events for a p. LABR 573:51
Time, the world and the p. CIXO 267:72
'umblest p. going DICK 324:7
unhappy p. seeks out another MARG 650:55
unmusical p. HENZE 473:74
when you live with a p. FORD 396:1
wish to absorb this p. MAMET 643:48
worse than killing a p. LAUR 584:46
wretched p.'s feelings MARI 652:77
personal ourselves and least p. MANS 647:5
p. and national morality SHAW 919:88
p. aspect of a thing RICH 810:64
P. relations are the important thing FORS 398:35
transcend the painfully p. SART 844:7
Vengeance is a p. reaction RENO 806:4
personalities all great events and p. MARX 660:17
original displaced p. MANK 645:77
People who disintegrate as p. AUST 52:71
p. and cultural traditions WATS 1055:51
trivial p. decomposing WOOLF 1092:63
personality discontinuity in his p. ROTH 825:7
had a lousy p. SALI 838:22
no more p. than a paper cup CHAN 250:41
P. is an unbroken series FITZ 390:97
P. Tithe: A price paid COUP 289:85
Poetry...an escape from p. ELIOT 368:75
persons civilized p. are willing DUBO 353:9
congratulation that p. MILL 674:60
divers paces with divers p. SHAK 886:6
God is no respecter of p. BIBLE 148:93
great p....borrow BACON 57:71
interested in things, not in p. CURIE 301:12
neither p. nor property will be safe DOUG 342:74
Ordinary p. do not perceive PASC 758:68
P....entering into relations BUBER 202:20
p. of small means ELIOT 365:2
p. using parties as tools DISR 333:20
p. who are accused DENM 316:59
p. who are considered...its members BENT 92:12
p. who fenced in...land ROUS 827:31
p. whom you cannot care for TROL 1028:86
resentment towards p. NEWM 724:31
some have done in their p. BROW 196:98
which private p. ROUS 827:39
perspective everything in p. CEZA 248:4
light, shade and p. CONS 285:20
lovely thing this p. UCCE 1035:37
P. is the bridle LEON 597:81
p. of a subway tunnel TOOLE 1023:4
reality seen from the p. of reason PAGE 749:33
scenic p. suits it HUGO 501:60
Writing has laws of p. CAPO 231:83
perspiration Genius is...p. EDIS 361:44
p. was but ichor BYRON 223:67
persuade p. gently, not by force PASC 758:62
p....half the people GAIT 411:72
trying to p. you PLATO 773:3
persuaded p. that God hath shut RALE 800:15
persuaders hidden p. into the code KOES 568:70
the hidden p. PACK 749:26
persuading By p. others JUNI 540:73
persuasion lexicon of...p. SAFI 835:67
not faith but p. BROW 195:73
P. is the resource of the feeble GIBB 421:24
persuasions so commanding p. DONNE 339:24
persuasiveness personal p. QUIL 797:60
Peru Silver out of the Earth in P. PETTY 768:13
peruked p. sea whose swell SITW 940:2
perverse frown and be p. SHAK 868:90
multitude of p. inclinations SHAR 919:82
widows...the most p. creatures ADDI 7:16
perversion last great p. FOWL 399:64
melancholy sexual p. HUXL 506:48

perversion (*contd.*)
War…the universal p. — ROE 800:4
perversity p. of the human mind — TROL 1028:81
P. is the muse — SONT 953:5
Sexual P. in Chicago — MAMET 643:42
perverted I'm exhausted…or p. — PUIG 794:18
pessimism P.…as agreeable — BENN 91:96
pessimist p. before 48 — TWAIN 1034:18
p. fears that this is true — CABE 224:80
p. sees only the red — SCHW 852:32
what a p. is? — SHAW 920:91
pessimistic optimistic or p. — UNAM 1035:40
'p.' about broadcasting — WELLS 1065:44
pesticide laugh is the best p. — NABO 717:12
pestilence noisome p. — BIBLE 117:2
purged the air of p. — SHAK 893:93
sooner caught than the p. — SHAK 878:51
who desires…breeds p. — BLAKE 166:74
winter, plague and p. — NASHE 721:82
pestilences famines, and p. — BIBLE 139:37
pests Rumour is of all p. the swiftest — VIRG 1045:85
petal dropping a rose p. — MARQ 656:47
sleeps the crimson p. — TENN 997:10
petals Buddha…in the p. of a flower — PIRS 770:51
clouds floating…like p. in a pond — MACM 636:24
P. on a wet, black bough — POUND 785:52
pursed Its p. up — BROW 197:29
softer falls Than a p. — TENN 994:49
Peter other disciple did outrun P. — BIBLE 147:74
P., and upon this rock — BIBLE 138:13
P. chose from man to hide — CRAB 294:83
P.'s drift — SHEL 928:95
P. like a piper's tune — FARJ 383:63
P. remembered the word of the Lord — BIBLE 144:15
P. said unto him — BIBLE 140:49
P. took him, and began to rebuke — BIBLE 138:14
St. P.…pattered with his keys — BYRON 223:67
Where P. is…is the Church — AMBR 15:64
wholly in P. Pan ever since — TYNAN 1035:28
Peterkin Quoth little P. — SOUT 954:33
petition circulating a p. — STEG 965:28
petitioners save me…from my p. — DRYD 350:31
Petrarch I do not…copy P. — ARET 33:17
if Laura had been P.'s wife — BYRON 223:47
petrifactions p. of a plodding brain — BYRON 219:62
petrol matches on a p. dump — HARL 458:20
petticoat P. said to the Chemise — PARK 753:88
turned out of the realm in my p. — ELIZ 373:86
petticoats perpendicular in p.! — OCON 735:82
red-flannel p. — THOM 1012:95
pettiness p. ruins the greatest loves — ANOU 30:70
something to expiate; A p. — LAWR 586:83
petulance p. is not sarcasm — DISR 333:98
pewter No p. and no pub — RANS 802:38
phagocytes stimulate the p. — SHAW 923:87
phallic P. and ambrosial — POUND 786:63
phantasma Like a p. — SHAK 883:27
phantom hag obscene, and grisly p. — BEAT 79:57
p. beings loaded up with facts — UNAM 1036:43
P. of delight — WORD 1098:62
phantoms p. an unprofitable strife — SHEL 931:46
Pharaoh P. awoke — BIBLE 105:44
P. rose up in the night — BIBLE 106:62
Pharisee P. stood and prayed — BIBLE 144:11
pluck mask from face of P. — BRON 191:97
Pharisees P. said, He casteth out — BIBLE 136:72
righteousness of the scribes and P. — BIBLE 134:38
the P. hypocrisy — PAST 759:83
when he saw many of the P. — BIBLE 133:27
Woe unto you, scribes and P. — BIBLE 139:36
phase p. in a continuing process — ROBI 815:36
p. of…life — PEAR 762:32
phases Humanity does not pass through p. — LEWIS 601:35

phases (*contd.*)
p. of its development — ERNST 379:10
p. in the development — MARX 661:27
Phelps P. calls Medlar Novelists — MACD 628:92
phenomena economic p. — FRIE 405:52
very essence of p. — PAST 759:86
phenomenon Crime…not a natural p. — PACK 749:27
describe the infant p. — DICK 321:51
describe the opposite p. — BERG 94:40
Felicitous p.! — MOORE 705:25
one actual p. — THOR 1016:72
p. has been so compelling — WHITE 1069:21
present or past p. — PEAR 762:32
recurring p. — FALU 382:58
phial take the p. cleanly — DOYLE 344:21
Philadelphia P.…like dull diamonds — MAIL 639:84
P. in the development — MARX 661:27
philanthropy p. and symphony — WHAR 1068:95
Philip Let us march against P. — OGIL 736:3
Willie King made up like P. — NICO 727:61
Philippi meet them at P. — SHAK 884:59
Philippines In the P. there are — COWA 290:98
Philistine apostle of the P. — ARNO 39:13
P. of genius in religion — ARNO 40:36
P. said unto David — BIBLE 110:41
Philistines angelic revenges on P. — ARNO 39:21
Barbarians, P., and Populace — ARNO 39:24
Eggheads are terrible P. — NABO 717:11
Let me die with the P. — BIBLE 109:22
P. be upon thee — BIBLE 109:21
P. took him, and put out his eyes — BIBLE 109:21
Philistinism P.!…we have not — ARNO 38:12
Phillipines In the P. there are — COWA 290:98
Phillis P., why shou'd — WALL 1050:72
philosopher For every p. — SPAR 955:60
he was a p. — CHAU 254:22
man of science is a poor p. — EINS 363:70
mark of the p. — SOCR 952:88
No p. now looks — WEBB 1059:17
nothing so absurd…said by some p. — CICE 266:62
Ovid, the soft p. of love — DRYD 351:65
peasant and a p. — JOHN 528:48
P.!—a fingering slave — WORD 1095:9
p. and a common street porter — SMITH 946:95
p., and the poet — LAWR 587:8
p. should judge the masses — CYRA 302:35
p.'s treatment of a question — WITT 1088:78
properly to be called a p. — PIER 769:32
prove the weeping p. — SHAK 874:15
saying of an ancient p. — ADDI 7:13
There was never yet p. — SHAK 880:62
You are a p., Dr Johnson — EDWA 362:53
philosophers amused p. — BERK 95:50
economists and political p. — KEYN 555:37
God of Jacob, not of the p. — PASC 758:81
little statesmen, p. and divines — EMER 376:33
or p. can judge — THOM 1012:4
p. have not maintained — SWIFT 985:87
p.…interpreted the world — MARX 660:9
P.…stand among us — CARL 234:43
p. to teach him — CARL 234:49
traditional disputes of p. — AYER 53:77
True p. are like elephants — FONT 395:89
Until p. rule as kings — PLATO 774:21
philosophic p. diner-out — BROW 200:84
p. republic of Mr de Valera — STEW 977:64
the p. mind — SMART 944:72
philosophical European p. — WHIT 1071:59
mathematical or p. author — WHIT 1071:52
one p. problem — POPP 783:21
one truly serious p. problem — CAMUS 228:46
p. problem has the form — WITT 1088:77
p., the ideological — ROTH 826:22
philosophies all p. shall fail — CHES 259:21
point their blind P. — ROCH 816:47
philosophizing p. or aestheticizing — CABR 224:81

philosophy aim in p. — WITT 1088:79
angel…tell…his p. — LICH 603:81
any p. in thee, shepherd? — SHAK 886:99
characteristic of p. — RUSS 832:16
compound of poetry and p. — MACA 622:95
destroy more prejudices than p. — DIDE 329:24
dreamt of in our p. — SHAK 889:84
from plumbing to p. — LAUG 583:41
Hang up p.! — SHAK 869:8
Histories make…natural p., deep — BACON 59:25
History is p. — CARL 235:75
if p. could find it out — SHAK 890:7
in knowing its limits that p. consists — KANT 541:1
inside and strength were p. — SIDN 937:60
interest of p. — POPP 783:21
mere touch of cold p.? — KEATS 546:80
moral p.…handmaid to religion — BACON 55:19
new p. calls all in doubt — DONNE 338:11
Nice p. — FORD 397:14
not confounded p. — PIRA 770:50
not faith, but mere P. — BROW 195:86
Not p., after all — BEER 83:40
p. has hitherto been — NIET 728:83
P.…has no other origin — SOCR 952:88
P., if it cannot — RUSS 832:15
P.! In whose light — NERV 723:10
p. inclineth Man's mind — BACON 57:65
P. is a battle against bewitchment — WITT 1088:76
p. is like the deciphering — SCHO 849:93
p. is this tyrannical — NIET 728:84
p. is to be studied — RUSS 832:17
P.…kind of charcoal appetite — CLEV 269:11
p. of the pig trough — WEIG 1061:76
P.…often changes Fashion — FRAN 402:6
p. puts out the fire — VOLT 1046:7
P.…route of many roads — BIER 161:92
P.! the lumber of — SWIFT 983:56
P. to him was…a maze — SANT 842:86
P. was wrong — RANS 802:36
p. which is so important — JAMES 517:46
p. will be replaced by poetry — ARNO 40:39
Plain women…to be faced with p. — ELIOT 366:34
political power and p. — PLATO 774:21
science…blind without p. — AYER 53:82
spoil you through p. — BIBLE 153:19
that's my p. — WILD 1079:24
Three-fourths of p. — SNYD 951:85
true business of p. — BACON 55:29
truth in p. — DIDE 329:25
universe which p. contemplates — RUSS 832:17
what is p.? — SPAR 955:60
years of analytical p. — HARDY 456:98
Phlebas Consider P. — ELIOT 369:92
Phoebus golden P. never be beheld — SHAK 906:8
P. gins arise — SHAK 916:3
phoenix Do not expect…p. hour — DAYL 310:56
P. builds her spicy nest — CAREW 232:19
p. midst her fires — BYRON 219:65
phone answer the p. — THUR 1018:22
call him up on the p. — SALI 838:19
P. for the fish knives — BETJ 100:52
pick up their p. — WHITE 1070:28
put the p. down thoughtfully — SHAR 919:86
phonemes morphemes and p. — THOM 1013:27
phoney going to do something p. — SALI 838:24
phonograph man is like a p. — SHAW 924:96
p.…is not of any commercial value — EDIS 361:43
p. of the world — STEAD 964:4
vaccinated with a p. needle — GOLD 433:33
phonographs p. of hades — CRANE 295:9
phosphorescence rubbing p. — MACD 628:99
photograph like flames around a p. — HOLL 485:71
p.…after I drowned — ATWO 44:16
p. and be photographed! — RODC 818:81

photograph (*contd.*)
p. of the Pope	ANON 29:38
signed p. of the Kaiser	WAUGH 1056:78
took the p.	KARSH 542:11

photographer p. without a magazine PARK 755:36

photographing p. people EISE 364:94

photographs p., of the immortals CHUR 262:78
p. taken of him at work	RODC 818:81
use p....literally	BACON 60:38

photography If p. is allowed BAUD 77:28
P. is truth	GODA 430:63
P....stops the flow of life	BERG 94:45
P. was conceived as a mirror	STEI 965:30

phrase beauty...in a tiny p. FOWL 400:70
empty p.	SAND 840:55
I find the p. in Shakespeare	SCOTT 856:15
that's an ill p.	SHAK 889:90

phrases Farewell, sweet p. HERB 476:36
foundation of your ideas and p.	LAUT 584:52
p. in his brain	SHAK 865:10
ready-wrapped p.	HILL 481:6
Taffeta p., silken terms	SHAK 866:27
wealth of steaming p.	SCHU 851:17

physic In poison there is p. SHAK 877:79
no faith in p.	JONS 534:79
Throw p. to the dogs	SHAK 910:83

physical adding daily to our p. ease STEV 972:79
affliction...either p. or spiritual	BEER 83:39
emotions that are so lightly called p.	COLE 276:32
endurance, p. and mental	WAVE 1058:10
Knowledge of p. science	PASC 758:72
most representative, p. scientists	SNOW 950:73
p. and cultural distance	VAND 1039:94
p. and emotional sides	BURG 206:90
p. pleasure	WAUGH 1056:79
p. vigour	SCHR 850:7
relaxation from p. fatigue	MATI 664:74
rendering of the p. world	OPPE 741:72
such a thing as p. morality	SPEN 955:65
takes the p. out on whores	FROST 407:90

physically developing a lad p. BADE 60:45
p....deadening force	WEBB 1058:15

physician As if you would call a p. BACON 58:1
died last night of my p.	PRIOR 790:53
duties of the p.	OSLER 746:72
Honour a p.	BIBLE 132:15
is there no p. there?	BIBLE 128:24
no need of the p.	BIBLE 141:59
p. and chemist are soldiers	PAST 759:89
P. art thou?	WORD 1095:9
p. can bury his mistakes	WRIG 1101:5
P., heal thyself	BIBLE 142:81
p. to my love	SHAK 915:97
They that be whole need not a p.	BIBLE 136:70
Time is a great p.	DISR 332:77
Trust not the p.	SHAK 902:94

physicians He and his p. SHAK 901:73
It is incident to p.	JOHN 525:73
Keep away from p.	BURG 205:83
more happy...than learned p.	BACON 55:26
P. are like kings	WEBS 1061:72
P. of the utmost fame	BELL 87:6
unless the p. are vigilant	SUTH 983:49

physicists p. could create a worm KRUT 570:8

physics delight in p. pain SHAK 908:52
resort to p. and chemistry	MENC 670:81
science is either p.	RUTH 834:46
Theoretical p. forces atomic	FROMM 406:70
When p., chemistry, biology	DEWEY 319:95

physiological p. or pathological UNAM 1035:40

physiologists Some p. will have it HUNT 505:33

pianist do not shoot the p. WILDE 1075:30

pianists no better than many p. SCHN 848:81
to be nurses and p.	ROTH 826:8

piano cat...walking over the p. MERI 672:17
he may sit on p.	WHIS 1069:12
Over the p. was printed a notice	WILDE 1075:30
P....a parlour utensil	BIER 161:93
Play the P. drunk	BUKO 203:49
soul is the p.	KAND 541:97
virtuoso...can sit on a p.	MALL 641:16
What are we learning...the p. for	OBRI 734:72

pianos put a tax on p. SITW 941:21
Silence the p.	AUDEN 46:58

Picasso corpses, or P. guitars LIPP 606:29
paint...a dog as P.	MARC 649:43
P. studies an object	APOL 31:90
P. was drawing	NEVE 723:14

picayune economic services...are p. DURK 357:68

piccolo duet between a tuba and a p. DONA 335:58

pick Everybody wants you to p. RUCK 828:44
p., pack, pock, puck	JOYCE 538:43

pick-axes take up p.-a. and sticks HO 482:33

pick-purse no p.-p. of another's wit SIDN 937:51

picked p. out of ten thousand SHAK 889:94

pickle Don't p. me away as done CARR 237:10

picnic morning-mist p. FRAME 400:76
p. tables...great modern things	WARH 1053:22
Teddy Bears have their p.	BRAT 185:15

Picninnies P....the Joblillies FOOTE 396:95

picture arrangement of my p. is MATI 663:73
best p. that was ever painted	HEMI 471:45
confers dignity on a p.	ALBE 11:92
Each creature...a p.	ALAN 11:77
forget that I have ever seen a p.	CONS 285:19
give a p. to the listener	COLT 277:58
Last P. Show	MACM 636:21
make a p. of reality	LIPP 607:36
making a p. with Marilyn	WILD 1079:15
million dollars to make a p.	TAYL 992:16
never see the whole p.	MANN 645:81
not a p. but an event	ROSE 822:56
One p. is worth	BARN 71:22
only accurate p. of God	BAKER 63:82
paint my p. truly like me	CROM 298:54
p. about the terrors of life	HECHT 466:60
p. cannot express	BACON 59:14
p. is finished when	WHIS 1069:10
p. is only an approximation	MOTH 711:12
p. of me, the me that is seen	LAWR 586:90
p. of the future	ORWE 745:60
p. on the wall	JOHN 524:57
p. that is beautiful	FRAN 402:97
p. that requires any description	HOMER 488:26
p. the afterlife	UPDI 1037:69
plane of the p.	PIERO 769:38
rhythm, form...mood of a p.	FEIN 385:99
speaking p., with this end	SIDN 937:62
the more successful the p.	HITC 482:26
to make a good p.	VAN 1039:2
Turkey carpet bears to a p.	MACA 623:98
win the foreign p. award	WILD 1079:14

pictures actress in motion p. DAVIS 308:24
all his p. faded	BLAKE 168:15
apples of gold in p. of silver	BIBLE 121:98
Are but as p.	SHAK 908:48
book...without p.	CARR 238:19
cutting all the p. out!	BELL 86:96
enjoy p. because	MORT 710:97
expensive Italian p.	BERE 94:37
faces...a gallery of p.	BACON 58:98
fighting tooth and nail for p.	HAMM 453:49
furnish the p.	HEAR 465:44
life passed among p.	WHIS 1069:11
looking at p.	HAZL 464:19
Mr Lewis's p.	SITW 941:20
name of p. produces	MORSE 709:90
or paint little p.	MERW 672:27

pictures (*contd.*)
paint their p. on silence	STOK 977:71
people...who understand p.	KIPL 561:44
p. are the love stories	LAUR 584:47
p. come to me as if in a dream	VAN 1039:1
p. for the page atone	POPE 782:96
p. in a rough mosaic	SCHO 849:99
p. in our eyes to get	DONNE 337:95
p. of nothing	HAZL 464:25
p. of obscene books!	ARLT 35:41
P. of perfection	AUST 52:62
p. which are so contrived	ORWE 745:55
p. with cameras	NEWM 724:25
stand before the new p.	MARC 649:40
weep before my p.	ROTH 826:26
when we're nostalgic we take p.	SONT 953:9

pie every joke is...a custard p. ORWE 743:22
If they see p. in the sky	BONA 172:78
p. in the sky when you die	HILL 480:3

pie-crust promises and p.-c. SWIFT 986:16

piece Before I compose a p. SATIE 846:45
p. of a big one	STEI 966:55
reform that little p. too	MILLS 680:65
When a p. gets difficult	SCHN 848:85

piece-meal She is dying p.-m. POUND 785:53

pieces dash themselves to p. SHAK 863:52
laugh broke into a thousand p.	BARR 72:43
p., and scattered them	MILT 686:72
P. of eight!	STEV 975:29
'Tis all in p.	DONNE 338:13
took her to p.	CONG 281:25
Who can I tear to p.	BACON 60:39

pier effusive welcome of the p. AUDEN 46:53

pierced P. to the soul SHAK 866:38

Pierian pun is P. UNTE 1036:47
taste not the P. spring	POPE 778:79

pies Bellamy's veal p. PITT 772:76
hand in to many p.	MENC 669:64
venison p. and good wine	LOUI 613:45

piety Bound...by natural p. WORD 1097:42
fear of life becomes p.	MENC 670:80
p. nor wit	FITZ 390:87
weaker sex, to p. more prone	ALEX 13:22

piffle p. before the wind ASHF 41:66

pig Dear P., are you willing LEAR 590:60
it's such a p.	RICH 810:60
looked from a p. to man	ORWE 744:33
love not a gaping p.	SHAK 873:90
philosophy of the p. trough	WEIG 1061:76
P., and some green Jack-daws	LEAR 590:56
p. got up and slowly walked away	BURT 213:61
p. on Sunday	TRUM 1030:21
p. satisfied	MILL 675:70
sucking p. and thick gammon	MACB 624:32

pig-headed had a p.-h. father POUND 785:54

pig-sty kissed her once by the p.-s. THOM 1011:83

pigeon-livered But I am p.-l. SHAK 890:15

pigeons break one two...p. CUMM 299:79
casual flocks of p.	STEV 971:40
mate for life, like p.	ALLEN 14:39
p. ...hovered about the windows	PEPYS 765:79
P. on the grass	STEIN 965:35

piglet cried P., a Heffalump MILNE 680:75

pigmentation only the p. BARN 72:27

pigmies embassage to the p. SHAK 879:38

pigs as much right...as p. have to fly CARR 238:34
as naturally as p. squeak	BUTL 216:4
cash cows to feed your p.	ANDE 18:2
p. are upwardly-mobile	THOM 1014:38
solid p. would disdain	ROCH 816:57
whether p. have wings	CARR 240:57

pigtailed butterfly...on a p. ocean SITW 940:2

pike P., three inches long HUGH 500:38
The great p. lies	BLUN 170:41

Pilate jesting P. — BACON 56:40
Made damn sure that P. — JAGG 515:96
P. saith...What is truth? — BIBLE 146:68
suffered under Pontius P. — BOOK 173:94
the good thief than P.? — BROW 196:2
When P. saw that — BIBLE 140:53
pilchards as p. are to herrings — SHAK 895:20
pile standst an ancient p. — JONS 535:1
pilgrim p. borne in heedless hum — COLL 277:48
p. of the sky! — WORD 1100:87
p. soul in you — YEATS 1105:60
talk about their P. blood — LOWE 616:79
pilgrimage I'll take my p. — RALE 800:13
shall succeed me in my P. — BUNY 205:74
songs beguile your p. — FLEC 393:48
through this weary p. — DODD 335:45
years of my p. — BIBLE 106:50
pilgrimages folk to goon on p. — CHAU 254:17
pilgrims land of the p. — CUMM 299:83
Land of the p.' pride — SMITH 948:27
Like p. to th' appointed place — DRYD 352:93
p., passynge to and fro — CHAU 255:33
strangers and p. on the earth — BIBLE 154:51
pill little yellow p. — JAGG 515:95
pillar compound pulsing p. — UPDI 1037:67
p. of a cloud — BIBLE 106:64
p. of salt — BIBLE 105:26
p. of the State — SOLZ 952:96
sat by a p. alone — TENN 1001:78
triple p. of the world — SHAK 904:56
pillars antic p. massy proof — MILT 683:15
bend thy p. wth thine iron car — BLAKE 165:60
builded over with p. of gold — BLAKE 168:7
hewn out her seven p. — BIBLE 120:66
Of polished p. — JONS 535:1
Pylons like p. — SPEN 956:80
shake complacent p. — BETH 99:24
strong p. and pregnant supporters — BAIL 62:72
pillow finds the down p. hard — SHAK 916:12
From my p., looking forth — WORD 1096:27
p. on a bed — DONNE 337:93
pillows two p. at my head — STEV 975:37
pills Beecham's P. are just the thing — BEEC 82:14
gave me bitter p. — SHAK 860:78
mountebank who sold p. — ADDI 6:5
pilot my p. face to face — TENN 1005:70
pimple p. ...of literature — PORT 784:38
pimps p. for ill desires — DRYD 349:8
pin every p. she takes out — JOYCE 538:54
p....punctures my skin — ANON 26:37
set my life at a p.'s fee — SHAK 888:72
stand as straight as a p. — CAUS 246:65
wi' a siller p. — BALL 68:58
with a little p. — SHAK 867:60
Pinafore that infernal nonsense P. — GILB 424:63
well-bred Captain of the P. — GILB 423:55
pinch death is a lover's p. — SHAK 906:7
Necessity's sharp p.! — SHAK 902:14
With a p. of salt — PLIN 775:32
pine black and gloomy p.-trees — LONG 611:10
bless'd be the evergreen P.! — SCOTT 853:62
Learn about a p. tree — BASHO 76:6
pale Mammon p. amidst his store — POPE 780:29
p. for what is not — SHEL 929:5
raiser...of p. — TENN 996:95
sailing p., the cedar proud — SPEN 957:99
spray of Western p.! — HARTE 460:52
stood close against a p. trees — THOM 1009:49
uproot the tallest p. — DEKA 313:3
pineapple the very p. of politeness — SHER 933:82
pines melancholy nodding p. — SCHAW 847:61
p. are gossip p. — FLEC 393:42
pinions p. from flight — SWIN 988:52
pink girl's skin that is p. — RENO 807:8

pink (*contd.*)
grey or perhaps p. — TRAV 1025:36
p. and purple columbine — SPEN 957:93
p., and the pansy — MILT 684:47
pinko-grey white...really p.-g. — FORS 398:41
pinnace p., like a fluttered bird — TENN 1004:56
send out any p. to seek me — LANC 578:52
pinnacle p. of sacrifice — LLOY 608:58
pinnacled lit my p. desire — SASS 845:30
pinnacles glassy p. correct elliptics — BISH 163:29
p. of the Serenissima — MORR 708:77
pint fetch to me a p. o' wine — BURNS 210:97
p. of plain — ONOL 734:66
pints P. and quarts of Ludlow beer — HOUS 495:64
pioneer not belittling...p. men — FERB 385:6
p. a new way — SHEL 926:53
pioneering P. is not feeling well — BERR 98:3
pioneers One thing about p. — PIRS 770:54
P. and all — SHAK 899:40
pious In p. times — DRYD 349:4
p. man prays without speaking — FRIE 405:57
Sae p. and sae holy — BURNS 210:82
pipe easier to be played on than a p.? — SHAK 891:43
his p. and my yowes — BALL -101:33
P. a song about a lamb! — BLAKE 166:62
p. with solemn interposing puff — COWP 292:32
puff of the p. — COOKE 286:32
sit placidly smoking his p. — SHIP 935:21
The earliest p. — TENN 997:4
through a p. and exhaled in a pun — LAMB 577:44
tune thy jolly voice to my fresh p. — BLAKE 165:59
pipe-smoking p.-s. northerner — MACF 629:18
piped p. unto you — BIBLE 137:86
piper Peter like a p.'s tune — FARJ 383:63
p. louder and louder blew — BURNS 211:19
p. o' Dundee? — ANON 23:99
pipers five-and-thirty p. — AYTO 53:85
pipes bird-like p. — STEP 968:79
boast their peasants' p. — CRAB 293:70
P. of wretched straw — MILT 684:45
What p. and timbrels? — KEATS 547:7
ye soft p., play on — KEATS 547:4
piping Helpless, naked, p. loud — BLAKE 167:94
pips squeezed—until the p. squeak — GEDD 417:63
piqued always p. myself — HALI 452:24
piracies P. should not again — TWAIN 1032:71
pirate Smith...an over-dressed p. — LEAC 589:38
To be a P. King — GILB 424:60
pirates p., preachers — SYNGE 988:63
piss pitcher of warm p. — GARN 415:29
pissing inside the tent p. out — JOHN 523:53
p. contest with that skunk — EISE 364:83
pistol p. let off at the ear — LAMB 577:42
pistols carry p. and cartridges — SHAW 920:93
mortals who...fire off p. — MANN 646:84
pistons black statement of p. — SPEN 956:79
pit after them to the bottomless p. — MILT 691:81
cast him into the bottomless p. — BIBLE 158:32
diggeth a p. — BIBLE 123:37
eagle know what's in the p. — BLAKE 166:61
key of the bottomless p. — BIBLE 157:17
Law is a bottomless p. — ARBU 33:9
many-headed monster of the p. — POPE 782:84
out of an horrible p. — BIBLE 115:66
P., box, and gallery — POPE 781:61
The darkest p. — WORD 1100:78
there is the sulphurous p. — SHAK 903:35
To your black p. — BURNS 200:74
pit-ponies wretched, blind, p.-p. — HODG 484:53
pitch drove him into such a p. — CRAS 296:28
He that toucheth p. — BIBLE 132:99
Imagination to that p. — YEATS 1107:94
one positive p. or direction — HOPK 492:97
people on the p. — WOLS 1091:44

pitch (*contd.*)
p. that is near madness — EBER 359:9
Pitched past p. of grief — HOPK 492:3
roller, p., and stumps — LANG 579:67
turn her virtue into p. — SHAK 899:27
word is 'P. and pay' — SHAK 880:78
pitcher P. be broken at the fountain — BIBLE 123:42
p. of warm piss — GARN 415:29
pitches p. thudding into gloves — RICE 809:40
pitchfork Mercury with a P. — BRAU 186:21
thrown on with a p. — SWIFT 986:9
use my wit as a p. — LARK 581:3
pitfalls p. of exaggeration — TROL 1028:95
pith all the p. is in the postscript — HAZL 464:17
pities what a thousand p. then — HOOD 489:44
Pitt P. is to Addington — CANN 230:69
Pittsburgh P. has lost...triangle — MAIL 639:84
pity avoid the feeling of p. — COMP 279:76
by means of p. and fear — ARIS 34:29
childish wave of p. — BETJ 100:40
dint of p. — SHAK 884:55
endure, then p., then embrace — POPE 780:44
Kind p. chokes my spleen — DONNE 336:66
Knowledge might p. win — SIDN 937:50
Let p. teach thee — SHAK 868:69
looked for some to have p. — BOOK 177:34
loved her that she did p. them — SHAK 898:9
move the stars to p. — FLAU 392:38
never p. the past — FOWL 399:65
no p. sitting in the clouds — SHAK 869:14
none to p. him — SYNGE 988:62
one can p. them — WILDE 1076:55
P. a human face — BLAKE 166:69
p. hath been balm — SHAK 862:30
P....in gentil herte — CHAU 255:30
p., like a new-born — SHAK 908:32
P. lost in rage — CARL 235:67
p., love, patriotism — WHIS 1069:14
P. my simplicity — WESL 1066:61
p. never ceases to be shown — DRYD 349:25
p. to ill-humour — GRAV 440:33
p. upon the poor — BIBLE 121:90
p....weakens our weaknesses — BALZ 68:74
The Poetry is in the p. — OWEN 748:11
Then cherish p. — BLAKE 166:70
'tis p. she's a whore — FORD 397:18
What a p. is it — ADDI 8:33
What a p. — SMITH 949:58
Where mercy, Love and P. dwell — BLAKE 166:65
with p. to dispense — SHAK 901:90
Yet show some p. — SHAK 896:89
pitying shrieks to p. heav'n — POPE 779:1
pix Sticks nix hick p. — ANON 26:41
placate p., appease, bribe — LIPP 607:37
place accent of the p. — LARO 582:29
advantage of time and p. — DRAKE 345:28
all other things give p. — GAY 416:50
All rising to a great p. — BACON 57:67
an awful p. — SCOTT 852:39
An open p. it was — WORD 1096:31
any given time or p. — WHIT 1071:62
aren't native to a p. — LAMM 578:50
at some p. or other — PALEY 751:65
bestow you in some better p. — SHAK 861:93
bodies measure out their p. — MARV 659:84
bourne of time and p. — TENN 1005:66
bruised in a new p. — IRVI 513:67
buried in so sweet a p. — SHEL 930:33
cares no more or one p. — SOUT 954:39
choose Their p. of rest — MILT 693:29
citizens of that other p. — SONT 953:11
colours...thick on every p. — DRYD 346:49
cultural and historical role of the p. — SMITH 946:1
destination is never a p. — MILL 679:52

platitudes orchestration of p. — WILD 1079:28
slaughter of a thousand p. — ORTE 741:84
Plato disputations of P. — HONO 488:32
lend an ear to P. — TENN 1003:30
P. divined in theory — WHIT 1071:60
P....in the body of his work — SIDN 937:60
P. is dear to me — ARIS 34:36
P., thou reason'st well! — ADDI 8:35
recurring again to P.'s opinion — STER 969:10
series of footnotes to P. — WHIT 1071:59
platypus poodle, the p. and people — THUR 1019:45
play admiration of each other's p. — BARR 73:52
author of the p. — GILB 426:99
band begins to p. — KIPL 560:30
Better than a p. — CHAR 253:85
boys in their happy p. — SCHR 850:4
boys late at their p.! — ARNO 39:23
Close the p. — KAUF 543:19
do not p. things as they are — STEV 971:49
done your work and may go p. — ASTL 43:96
Everything that heard him p. — SHAK 918:54
for fair p. — ROOS 822:48
Forsake thy books, and mateless p. — BRON 191:7
good p. needs no epilogue — SHAK 887:38
holdeth forth children from p. — SIDN 937:63
Judge not the p. — QUAR 796:52
learn what not to p. — GILL 426:10
life? a p. of passion — RALE 800:14
loved your p. — ANON 28:25
made to p. therein — BIBLE 118:18
Marry, our p. is — SHAK 870:29
mend My wretched p. — MANN 646:94
most insipid, ridiculous p. — PEPYS 765:66
Mr Puff's p. within a p. — SHER 934:10
Not only will I not p. — GRANT 438:99
nothing to do with fair p. — ORWE 745:64
our p. is played out — THAC 1006:90
perfectly dreadful p. — BANK 70:91
p. a creative mixture — SHUL 936:32
p. a thing quickly — MOZA 711:18
P. ball! — RICE 809:40
p., I remember, pleased not — SHAK 890:19
p. is a dynamic thing — TYNAN 1035:27
p. is life — SHAW 923:76
p. it over again and p. — LAMB 577:48
P. it! — EPST 379:98
p. left a taste of...parsnip — WOOL 1094:88
p. lousy — PARK 754:97
p....never really takes on — HART 459:47
p....some ten words long — SHAK 871:56
p. that after you've been — KEIL 548:29
p. the fools with the time — SHAK 877:89
p.'s the thing — SHAK 890:19
p. under bad conditions — KAUF 542:15
p. well and lose — FULL 410:56
p. with him at any game — SHAK 905:72
p. without a woman — KYD 571:29
rest of the p. — PASC 757:62
Shakespeare set his p. writing aside — CUOMO 300:6
spoils the p. much more — SUCK 981:20
The action of the p. — ONEI 739:47
The p. is over — AUGU 50:21
The p. was a great success — WILDE 1077:64
thing I didn't like about...the p. — PARK 754:96
unless the p. is stopped — KEMB 549:37
usually the p. itself — TYNAN 1035:26
What do you call the p.? — SHAK 891:40
what's the p.? — BOOTH 178:5
will not let my p. run — DENN 316:62
witty prologue to a very dull p. — CONG 280:3
woman's part in the p. — AUST 51:47
writing a good p. is difficult — PRIE 790:45
y is p. — EINS 363:72
youths at cricks did p. — JOSE 537:32

play-going p.-g. in any large city — TYNAN 1035:26
play-poets Profession of P.-p. — PRYN 794:11
playboy expected me to be a p. — FLYNN 395:80
Inside this Hollywood p. — FLYNN 395:81
P. of the Western World — SYNGE 988:65
played easier to be p. on — SHAK 891:43
how you p. the game — RICE 809:38
My music...is merely badly p. — SCHO 849:89
p. an ancient ditty — KEATS 547:96
p. on a five inch course — JONES 533:51
p. the way I would — KAVA 543:24
p. with both hands — SATIE 846:46
player as he a P. were — SPEN 959:42
not monstrous that this p. here — SHAK 890:14
raped...nothing a p. — MCEN 629:11
say to the p. — WHIS 1069:21
walking shadow, a poor p. — SHAK 910:86
whatever the other p. did — RAPO 802:40
wrapped in a p.'s hide — GREE 445:33
players don't drop p. — SHAN 918:71
entertainment the p. shall receive — SHAK 890:6
I and the rest of the p. — QUIN 797:64
little black book with two p. in — CHAR 253:95
men and women merely p. — SHAK 885:91
mouth it, as many of your p. do — SHAK 891:32
p. have often mentioned — JONS 536:20
p. not to be to good — NICH 726:54
P., Sir! — JOHN 529:76
p. think of a football — PELE 764:52
too cold for the p. — SMITH 948:26
Will you see the p. — SHAK 890:12
playfield p. of Satan — NABO 717:4
playing ask me to stop p. — KING 557:69
staying married and p. snooker — REAR 804:73
playing-fields p.-f. of Eton — ORWE 743:18
plays Absurdist p....in No Man's Land — ADAM 4:60
All p. are about decay — MAMET 644:55
cause of is sin p. — WHITE 1071:51
don't want to see p. about rape — COOK 286:27
English p. — GOET 431:69
Leave writing p. — DRYD 348:84
old p....disguise this refined age — EVEL 381:42
p. are suited to incoherent argument — BENN 91:83
The proof is in his p. — ONEI 740:58
tremendous stage on which it p. — RABI 799:94
women's parts in p. — CHAR 253:84
write p. in our heads — MAMET 644:61
plaything literature was the best p. — GARC 414:18
p. and their idol — SHEL 926:52
sensualists...want...a p. — WOLL 1091:36
plaything-house little p.-h. — WALP 1051:81
playthings choice of p. — KIPL 562:71
playwright some p. was forever — SALI 839:32
Plaza-Toro Duke of P.-T.! — GILB 426:95
plea beauty hold a p. — SHAK 914:68
issue of that darling P. — FLET 394:67
without one p. — ELLI 374:9
plead But when I p. — SPEN 958:25
so what I p. it just — HOPK 492:8
pleasant fallen unto me in p. places — BIBLE 114:39
How fair and how p. — BIBLE 124:54
how p., Lord, they be! — SCOT 856:21
Laughter is p. — PEAC 762:28
make myself as p. as I can — GILB 425:80
more glorious...than it is p. — ELIZ 373:92
of our p. vices — SHAK 904:47
p. and clean work — RUSK 831:98
p. or bitter — MART 657:63
p. situation, and yet nothing p. — DEFOE 312:84
Why christened P. — DICK 327:83
wine leaves you with something p. — AMER 16:66
pleasantness pain full of p. — LYLY 620:59
please Art cannot be made...to p. — DEGAS 312:93
can p. many, and p. long — JOHN 528:44

please (*contd.*)
hard thing to p. all of the people — CONN 284:85
more anxious to p. — SAND 840:50
must p. to live — JOHN 525:80
natural to p. — DRYD 349:5
not p. but thank you — DILL 331:53
say what they p. — FRED 403:27
thinking what they p. — SCHI 847:65
those whom I wished to p. — JOHN 526:6
who would not wish to p. her! — GRAY 441:61
without saying 'p.' — SITW 940:3
pleased All seemed well p. — MILT 691:75
makes a man better p. — JOHN 530:98
p. not the million — SHAK 890:11
P. to meet you — JAGG 515:96
pleasing art of p. — HAZL 463:98
p. fit of melancholy — MILT 684:31
p. himself is almost sure — MOORE 705:27
pleasurable even the most p. — THUR 1019:32
pleasure antithesis...is not p. — DEQU 316:66
at p. stint their melody — SHAK 862:43
be his good will and p. — LANC 578:52
Beware of over-great p. — FULL 409:32
Business first; p. afterwards — THAC 1007:2
cannot write of p. — BELL 86:92
Compassed round by p. — WORD 1100:4
descended at p. — MOORE 704:11
dilettante only looks for p. — REDON 804:76
entrancing p. of — WILDE 1077:77
Excess of p. — BAXT 79:51
fatal egg by p. laid — COWP 292:45
final p. left to man — SNOW 950:70
fine p. is not to do — HOPK 492:6
for thy p. they...were created — BIBLE 157:10
forced...your p. — WEBS 1060:38
forms of p. undulate — FUSE 410:61
good p. of God — WESL 1067:71
Good, p., ease, content — POPE 781:49
greatest amount of p. — SHIP 935:20
greatest p. I know — LAMB 577:43
green p. — SWIN 987:44
grief...treads upon the heels of p. — CONG 280:99
hatred...the longest p. — BYRON 223:57
heart with p. fills — WORD 1099:70
if this is p. we'd rather be dead — COWA 290:92
impression of p. — BACON 54:4
invented any new sensual p. — FLAU 392:36
know the ways of P. — HERB 475:19
leave...an intangible residuum of p. — CATH 244:50
lonely p. — KENN 550:50
Love ceases to be a p. — BEHN 85:69
major vice and greatest p. — HEMI 471:43
married any one of them with p. — WILDE 1079:13
Much p., then from thee — DONNE 338:4
must give you p. — KILLY 556:62
no p. i' living — ELIOT 365:9
no p. in the death of the wicked — BIBLE 129:40
not in p. — DRYD 346:53
Not sunk in carnal p. — MILT 692:97
now we love p. — ETHE 380:17
of p. complain — ROCH 816:61
only safe p. for a parliamentarian — CRIT 297:43
only sensual p. without vice — JOHN 532:38
organization for p. — JOHN 524:65
other words, p. — MORE 707:54
owes it's p. to another's pain — COWP 293:58
painful p. turns — SPEN 958:20
pay a debt to p. too? — ROCH 816:45
physical p. — WAUGH 1056:79
P.'s a sin — BYRON 222:35
p. accompanied by the idea — SPIN 960:54
p. and pain — GORD 435:63
p. at his own successes — RYLE 834:54
P. at the helm — GRAY 443:86

pleasure (*contd.*)
p. can be the beginning of beauty	PROU 793:98
p. in a sensual sty	MILT 683:19
p....In being mad	DRYD 350:37
p. in poetic pains	COWP 293:55
p. in the exercise of the mind	BARZ 75:94
p. in the pathless woods	BYRON 220:5
p. in what yet remain	DRYD 347:77
P. is a thief to business	DEFOE 312:86
p. is momentary	CHES 257:85
p. is not enhanced	AUST 52:57
P. is...the least fallible	AUDEN 48:87
p. of believing what we see	SHEL 927:66
p. of hearing them rattle a little	FARQ 383:72
p. of my pain	SIDN 937:50
p. of not being surpassed	HALI 452:24
p. of pleasing inferior people	CLOU 270:39
p. of the defeat	LACL 573:60
p. of the fleeting year!	SHAK 914:82
p. of the flesh	FUEN 409:26
p. ...to hear the English abused	PIUS 772:80
poet's p. is to withhold...meaning	WHITE 1070:26
prolonging the keenest p.	SHAW 925:38
pursuit of p.	PROU 793:4
rare and simple p.	DRAB 345:23
recompense is a p.	JOHN 525:88
Refrain from the unholy p.	BELL 86:96
rule...to give p.	MOLI 698:20
sadistic p. in...violence	ORWE 745:64
salutary p. in proving their falseness	DARW 306:87
seldom peruses a book with p.	ADDI 6:6
some to p. take	POPE 782:76
Some weigh their p.	DYER 358:89
sometime do p. bring	SURR 982:41
sort of p. in thinking	ORWE 742:89
stock of harmless p.	JOHN 531:13
study of present p.?	MONT 700:54
suburbs Of your good p.?	SHAK 883:30
supreme p. of love	BAUD 78:37
sweated out of golden p.	VALL 1039:91
Sweet is p. after pain	DRYD 351:69
takes p. in it	POIN 776:59
try a little p.	BAGE 61:49
Unlawful p....is delusive	BRON 191:5
Variety is the soul of p.	BEHN 85:63
weight of p.	WORD 1096:22
Were it but to p. you	HERR 477:52
What p. lives in height?	TENN 998:11
what p. would be left him?	FONT 395:85
when of p. she doth sing	CAMP 228:36
which give little or no p.	MILL 674:60
without one p.	TENN 1003:31
Words...intense p.	WAUGH 1057:92
would have been my p.	TENN 1003:20
would it p. me	WEBS 1061:66

pleasure-dome stately p.-d.   COLE 274:12
pleasure-house lordly p.-h.   TENN 994:54
pleasures cares and p.   GIBB 421:20
celibacy has no p.	JOHN 527:24
Eternity of p.	FORD 397:12
eye hath caught new p.	MILT 682:1
Fates, we will know your p.	SHAK 883:40
forbids us certain p.	MOLI 698:21
glorious manly p.	WYCH 1103:40
hypocrite in his p.	JOHN 532:32
more I see P. about	MILT 692:99
not with their p.	HUXL 506:45
of all the sweet p. Known	REID 806:98
paucity of human p.	JOHN 532:41
p. are like poppies spread	BURNS 211:15
p. in a long immortal dream	KEATS 546:76
p. in the world	CORY 289:68
p., of a free world	LURIE 619:42

pleasures (*contd.*)
p. of middle age	POUND 786:74
p. of the other	AUST 51:54
P. of worse natures	MASS 662:56
p. round about us	MILT 686:68
P. shorter than	WALL 1050:72
p. which my thoughts	LANY 580:82
purest of human p.	BACON 59:16
Seat of p.	DRYD 351:61
sucked on country p., childishly?	DONNE 336:73
sweeter...Than all other p.	DRYD 347:68
tear our p.	MARV 658:76
These pretty p.	RALE 800:12
we will some new p. prove	DONNE 337:89
will all the p. prove	MARL 655:31

pleats little p. and furbelows   SCHI 847:62
plebeian this the P. bran   DONNE 338:17
plebiscite p. elected generals   JUVE 540:81
plectrum luminous p. of books   BELLI 86:93
pledge p. to thee   KIPL 564:3
p. with mine	JONS 535:5

Pleiades sweet influences of P.   BIBLE 113:21
plenitude carries itself its own p.   NERVO 723:13
plenty health and p. cheered   GOLD 432:8
here is God's p.	DRYD 352:81
just had p.	BURNS 209:64
p. has made me poor	OVID 747:99
P. makes pride	ANON 22:79
Where P. smiles	CRAB 293:73

pleonasm fashion...is a p.   CHAN 251:55
plethora p. of legal requirements   BIRNS 163:27
plight eke the heavy p.   SURR 983:45
Pliny According to P.   VASA 1040:8
plodder always the p.   POUND 787:95
plodders Small have continual p.   SHAK 865:6
plop tug, pull and p.   OBRI 734:71
plot beginning of a p.   LEHM 594:36
discerned in history a p.	FISH 389:82
Her p. hath many changes	QUAR 796:52
In some melodious p.	KEATS 547:13
knew the p. before	SUCK 981:20
new p. in the cemetery	DAY 310:51
No good opera p.	AUDEN 48:85
p. and rhyme	LOWE 617:13
p. in it will be shot	TWAIN 1032:76
p. thickens	BUCK 203:39
p. was to have blown up	HOBY 483:47
p....where these memories grow	TATE 991:3

plot-interest game is so full of p.-i.   FRY 408:12
plots From p. and treasons   DRYD 350:31
P....are necessary things	DRYD 349:10
p. come from	MORT 710:96
p. from old novels	BYRON 221:15
preventing or contriving p.	WALT 1052:10
Real time seems to have no p.	COMP 279:72
spoil her simple p.	HOLME 485:73

plotting p. some new reformation   DRYD 350:36
plough p. ...doth rent?   DONNE 336:68
Following his p.	WORD 1097:44
plod behind the p.	CRAB 293:70
P....twin to the Sword	COLUM 277:59
put his hand to the p.	BIBLE 142:86
wherefore p.	SHEL 929:96

ploughman cheer the p.   SHAK 866:34
p. homeward plods	GRAY 441:62
the p. of bulls	PROP 792:79
tither was a p.'s collie	BURNS 209:71

ploughs greatest of his p.   CURZ 302:29
p. and borne our loads	MUIR 712:34

ploughshare Soldiers of the p.   RUSK 830:91
ploughshares p. into swords   BIBLE 130:56
swords into p.	BIBLE 124:57

plover wind sweep and the p. cry   TENN 998:14
plowed p., and planted   TRUTH 1030:39

ploy by p. or gambit   POTT 785:46
pluck And p....The...apples   YEATS 1105:63
p. it out, and cast it from thee	BIBLE 134:41
p. it out, and cast it from thee	BIBLE 138:19

plucked p. the cigar out   KARSH 542:11
plum with the later p.   JONS 535:2
plum-cake Some gave them p.-c.   CARR 240:71
plumber dance like a p.'s daughter   MIDD 673:39
p. on weekends	ALLEN 14:36

plumbing from p. to philosophy   LAUG 583:41
plume blast-beruffled p.   HARDY 457:7
danced on a p. of words	DAYL 310:57
Ruffles her pure cold p.	TENN 1004:49
Sir P., of Amber Snuff-box	POPE 779:2

plummet deeper than did ever p.   SHAK 917:40
plump danger is to meet it p.   ROCHE 815:42
p. Venetian, fat, and lusty	FLET 394:75
so round, so p., so soft	SUCK 981:21

plunder cannot separately p. a third   BIER 160:67
plundering p....at Rome   AUGU 49:16
plural Incorrigibly p.   MACN 637:36
pluralism P.—that is the conception   BERL 96:70
plures Abiit ad p.   PETR 767:11
plutography p....vice   WOLFE 1091:31
plutonium p. blonde   SCAR 846:55
Plymouth land on P. Rock   MALC 641:10
pneumatic Wonderfully p.   HUXL 507:68
Pobble P. who has no toes   LEAR 590:62
pocket both hands in the p.   SATIE 846:46
carry the moon in my p.?	BROW 198:53
guinea...in your p.	RUSK 830:90
hands...in each other's p.	BIER 160:67
no longer in your p.	SOLZ 952:95
pecker in my p.	JOHN 523:94
piece of brick in his p.	SWIFT 984:79
p. of my land	FRAME 400:76
poison in one p.	MACA 624:21
pound...in your p.	WILS 1085:35
smile I could feel in my hip p.	CHAN 250:32
would not scruple to pick a p.	DENN 316:63

pocketbook not their p.   KENN 550:61
pocketmoney furnished with p.   DICK 321:44
pockets fill my p. with change   DICK 321:52
money from the p. of the people	SMITH 945:83
rare in our p.	CHES 260:39
turn their p. out	SPEN 956:75
young man feels his p.	HOUS 496:75

pods p. went pop on the broom   DAVI 307:99
Podsnap Mr P. settled that   DICK 327:81
Mr P. was well to do	DICK 327:80

Poe P.! ...and degenerates!   ONEI 740:59
P....nonstop literary drinker	THUR 1019:42
P., with his raven	LOWE 616:83
those who haunted P.	ELLI 375:16

poem best way to read [a p.]   NEW 724:18
cryselephantine p.	POUND 785:56
dance is a p.	DIDE 329:26
does not like a p.	VIDAL 1044:60
elaborate polished p.	NASHE 721:77
epic p.and the science	MENC 670:82
form of the p.	SARO 843:99
goes on in a p.	UPDI 1037:63
good p. is a contribution	THOM 1011:93
good p. is like a bouillion cube	DOVE 342:76
haven't written the p. yet	BORG 179:12
I could never begin a p.	MACG 630:30
life of man...is a heroic p.	CARL 235:77
made one of p.'s period	MARL 653:91
married to a p.	KEATS 545:64
metre-making...makes a p.	EMER 377:48
never started a p.	FROST 407:99
only the p. comes near	DUDEK 353:52
p. can be improved	MACL 634:76
p....dream made flesh	MILL 678:44

poem (*contd.*)
p. full of space and reverie — BAUD 78:46
p. has a material existence — MACB 624:31
p....is a little myth — WARR 1054:31
p. is a test of invention — KEATS 544:44
p. is never finished — VALE 1038:85
p. is...the most primitive — KUNI 571:17
p. must ride — FROST 407:94
P. should be palpable — MACL 633:72
p. should be wordless — MACL 633:73
p. should not mean — MACL 634:74
read a political p. — NEME 722:6
right reader of a good p. — FROST 408:7
The best p. is that — THOM 1011:92
The p. in the rock — THOM 1013:24
United States...greatest p. — WHIT 1072:74
vices nor...virtues further the p. — DUNC 355:45
What is a p. — WARR 1054:34
writing a p. — WASH 1054:37
poems Anon...wrote so many p. — WOOLF 1093:71
any to the greater glory — WARR 1054:35
he is possessed by many p. — WILL 1083:5
honey peace in old p. — JEFF 519:79
How do p. grow? — WARR 1054:32
I write p. — SART 844:7
Naming me the fifty p. — BROW 199:67
p. amount to so little — RILKE 811:83
p. spoken in the factories — MACD 627:88
Some p. have form — POUND 787:94
These p. with all their crudities — THOM 1011:76
turn to p. and stories — DYSON 358:99
understood Yeats's p. — SAKI 837:5
We all write p. — FOWL 400:68
poesy call p. *vinum daemonum* — BACON 55:18
elegancy, facility...of p. — SHAK 865:17
Myself in p. — KEATS 544:39
poet accounted p. kings — KEATS 544:41
another fig was a famous p. — PLATH 773:91
as a p....not born yet — THOM 1013:22
bad p. dwells...in a world of objects — ELIOT 368:77
because I was a p. — BROW 196:11
becoming the first modern p. — LEVE 599:18
better p. than Porson — HOUS 495:67
business of a comic p. — CONG 280:4
Byron is only great as a p. — GOET 431:80
consecration, and the p.'s dream — WORD 1099:71
creations of a p. — SHEL 931:56
decided to be a p. — TOWN 1024:13
don't have to suffer to be a p. — CIAR 266:52
dreams of a p. — JOHN 526:2
each p. took the color he needed — GALE 412:88
essential advantage for a p. — ELIOT 370:16
Every P. his own Aristotle — BYRON 222:37
Every p. knows — UNTE 1036:47
every p., in his kind — SWIFT 986:7
eye in the head of a p. — WELL 1063:2
Fat-head p. that nobody reads — CHES 260:45
flattery lost on a p.'s ear — SCOTT 853:47
gentleman p. — JOYCE 538:49
God is the perfect p. — BROW 197:24
good p. is someone — JARR 518:58
I was a p. — FLEC 393:47
If a p. is anybody — CUMM 299:82
Is this the great p. — GARR 415:31
let the p. be a p. — PALEY 751:63
Like a P. hidden — SHEL 929:2
madness...should possess a p.'s brain — DRAY 345:39
man may be born a p. — SASS 846:44
matter made for famous p.'s verse — SPEN 958:17
more correct p. — DRYD 347:64
Never durst p. touch a pen — SHAK 865:21
no other English p. seemed — AUDEN 49:3
no p. ever interpreted nature — GIRA 429:44
No p. is ever competely lost — ACKR 4:55

poet (*contd.*)
No p. or novelist wishes — MACA 622:89
no person can be a p. — ARNO 36:57
Not deep the P. sees — DALI 303:46
obviously a p. — HUGO 501:69
Oh Virgil! Oh p.! — SHEL 930:20
On a p.'s face — GRAV 440:25
once more a p. — TENN 1001:75
passionate heart of the p. — KEATS 545:70
p. and the dreamer — ABER 1:5
p.'s business is not to describe — AUDEN 48:86
p. can earn much more money — OWEN 748:12
p. ...can warn — WORD 1099:69
p. could not but be gay — THOM 1013:27
p. emerges from morphemes — ARNO 37:77
P.'s food — SHEL 929:8
p. gives us his essence — WOOLF 1093:82
p.'s inward pride — DAYL 310:54
p. is a master of the quotidian — PRIT 791:72
p. is a person — FROST 407:90
p. is a unique being — VIAN 1043:48
p. is allowed the stride — SAND 841:78
P. is like that prince — BAUD 77:16
p. is more the inspirer — ELUA 376:23
p. is the life of everyone — NERV 723:12
p. is the true fire-stealer — RIMB 812:92
p. is the unsatisfied child — GRAV 440:39
p. knows himself — MARI 651:72
p. like an acrobat — FERL 386:20
p. lives as long as his lines — BOLD 172:69
p. makes silk dresses — STEV 972:61
p.'s mind is perfectly equipped — ELIOT 368:80
p. must be free — SART 844:6
p. named Clough — SWIN 988:51
p.'s pen all scorn — BRAD 184:1
p.'s pleasure is to withhold — WHITE 1070:26
p. reminds men of their uniqueness — COUS 290:87
p. represents the mind — STEV 972:64
p. shares with other artists — SPEN 956:85
p....spewed up — DRYD 347:75
p....used as a barometer — TRIL 1027:60
p.'s work...To name — RUSH 829:68
priest, warrior, p. — BAUD 78:43
rank of every p. is well known — AUDEN 47:63
rarely what the p. wants — NEME 722:4
responsibility of the p. — PALEY 751:64
role of the p. to look — PRIT 791:71
something about a p. — THUR 1020:55
Spare the p. — COWP 292:43
The p. as well — JEFF 519:79
their sacred p. — HORA 493:25
This is truth the p. sings — TENN 995:74
This p. lies — SHAK 912:47
Thy skill lo p. — SHEL 929:6
To be a p. — GRAV 440:26
true p. that you are! — BROW 199:64
true p....trusts himself — POUND 787:96
war p. — GURN 449:90
What is a modern p.'s fate? — HOOD 489:53
what the p. does — GINS 428:34
when the P. dies — SCOTT 853:48
When you're a p. — SART 844:8
wicked imp they call a p. — GRAY 441:61
worst tragedy for a p. — COCT 272:63
You explain nothing, O p. — CLAU 268:91
poet-baiting In this country, p.-b. — SITW 942:30
poetic delicacy of p. instinct — WILDE 1076:32
English p. literature — GRAV 440:36
nurse for a p. child! — SCOTT 853:50
P. fields encompass me around — ADDI 6:98
P. justice, with her lifted scale — POPE 782:92
short-circuit — SENG 858:50
subtlest and most p. — FOWL 400:70

poetic (*contd.*)
suspension of disbelief...p. faith — COLE 275:20
the less his morals are p. — DIDE 329:29
poetical fullest p. nature — WHIT 1072:73
gods had made thee p. — SHAK 886:9
Smith, the name is so p. — CHES 258:95
worn-out p. fashion — ELIOT 371:45
poetry all metaphor is p. — CHES 257:90
All p. is experimental — STEV 972:59
almost than the finest p. — LAWR 587:9
Angling is somewhat like p. — WALT 1052:6
art of p. — MACL 634:87
Ben Jonson his best piece of p. — JONS 535:7
butter nor shoes nor p. — LEWIS 601:51
compound of p. and philosophy — MACA 622:95
cradled into p. — SHEL 927:69
create, if it concerns p. — HUGO 501:59
Death is to P. — ABSE 1:8
drops into p. — DICK 327:78
elements of our p. — MARI 651:66
Emptied of its p. — AUDEN 47:71
English p. is not yet fit — OWEN 748:10
even bad p. has relevance — FERL 386:22
fate of p. — WALC 1048:43
fine graces of p. — SMITH 946:2
force from widowed p. — CAREW 232:5
formal p. perfect only in form — SAND 842:80
function of p. — GRAV 440:27
Genuine p. can communicate — ELIOT 369:7
glamor of p. — GARL 415:27
good living and good p. — LUCAS 618:28
good material for p. — WILL 1083:6
good p. is forged slowly — DOUG 341:50
grand style arises in p. — ARNO 38:8
great p. gives the illusion — ELIOT 369:5
If there is p. in our America — DARIO 305:75
In whining p. — DONNE 337:84
infancy of our p. — DRYD 352:78
joy and function of p. — THOM 1010:72
lectures & my p. — BERR 98:17
made p. pedant's game — BUNT 204:59
made p. seen word-bound — KAVA 543:24
mathematics as surely as in p. — RUSS 832:19
Mincing p. — SHAK 876:59
Money is a kind of p. — STEV 972:66
more rhyme there is in p. — SAND 842:79
never the language of p. — GRAY 441:49
No good p. is written — POUND 785:48
no money in p. — GRAV 440:37
no more a part of p. — STEV 972:60
not p., but prose run mad — POPE 781:64
nothing to say...that is p. — CAGE 225:90
one perfect expression of p. — MALL 641:12
or can enjoy p. — MACA 622:89
over into its basic p. — LEVE 600:23
Painting is p. which is seen — LEON 597:75
people ignore most p. — MITC 696:79
pitiful defence of poor p. — SIDN 937:59
P....a criticism of life — ARNO 40:41
P.'s a mere drug — FARQ 383:65
p. administers to the effect — SHEL 931:57
P....an escape from emotion — ELIOT 368:75
p. and tragedy, love — LEWIS 602:52
p....as you please — BAUD 77:30
p. begins to atrophy — POUND 786:77
p. by young writers — WILDE 1076:32
P. can communicate — LEAV 591:73
P. cannot take sides — SPEN 956:86
p. comes not as naturally — KEATS 544:51
p. conceived in the soul — ARNO 40:40
p. consists largely in instinct — BLUN 170:48
p. different from all...arts — MERW 672:27
p. does not swing from the branches — CHOC 260:55
p. equals the best words — COLE 275:24

police (*contd.*)

God's p.	CHIS 260:54
international p. power	ROOS 822:46
P. action must be to separate	EDEN 360:22
p. are prowling	ORWE 744:40
p. can pick him up	DOUG 342:71
p. dog of American fiction	FADI 382:53
p. state	GINS 428:33
Reading…among p. officers	ORTON 742:87
recognised by the p.	STEV 974:5
South African p. would leave	SHAR 919:80

policeman p. in the National

	WHIS 1069:11
p.'s lot is not a happy one	GILB 424:65
p. of normal proportions	STEW 977:64
terrorist and p. from the same basket	CONR 285:4
would not do for a p.	NIGH 729:1

policemen how young the p. look

	HICKS 480:94
not enough p.	HUMP 504:13
P. so cherish their status	MAMET 643:45
repressed sadists…become p.	CONN 283:59
village idiots, p.	MACD 628:92

policies carcasses of old p.

	CECIL 247:82
only party with clear p.	THAT 1008:28
p., nor stratagems	MILT 685:64

policy active p. is best advanced

	BAKER 63:81
agreement with Government p.	HOWE 497:95
best p. to speak	JERO 521:9
British p.	ROCH 816:48
conforms to the party p.	BEAV 80:80
Economic p. is random	STEIN 966:51
either on religion or p.	RUSK 831:2
England's foreign p.	GLAD 429:53
English p. is to float lazily	CECIL 247:81
field of world p.	ROOS 821:35
foreign p. of the noble Earl	DERBY 316:69
From great defects of p.	HOPE 490:71
indispensable act of p.	PITT 771:71
least influence on p.	BLIN 169:29
Making foreign p.	ROGE 821:24
No foreign p.	KISS 566:34
our true p.	WASH 1054:44
p.? I wage war	CLEM 269:4
p. sits above conscience	SHAK 901:90
p. to keep all nationalities	TAAF 989:73
tyrants from p.	BURKE 207:34
Wisdom and p. dictates	NAPO 718:26

polished p. up the handle

	GILB 423:58
p. with the tread of feet	DICK 322:66
soul…must be p.	DEFOE 311:73

polite English p. by telling lies

	BRAD 183:78
imbues his p. things	TWAIN 1032:59
never mentions Hell to ears p.	POPE 779:22
not a p. employer	HOOV 490:63
The French are p.	TWAIN 1032:59
What a p. game tennis is	BARR 73:52

politeness ceremonious p.

	TWAIN 1032:59
Punctuality is the p.	LOUI 614:52

politic they are p.

	WEBS 1059:28
'Twere p. to do the like	YEATS 1105:68

political addiction of p. groups

	GALB 411:75
binary p. arena	LEHM 594:38
circulates p. life	TOCQ 1021:77
climbed my last p. mountain	WALL 1050:65
Divorce…has a great p.	MONT 703:88
fear of P. economy	SELL 858:40
foundations of p. liberty	WILS 1086:52
frightened by p. sermons	BARTH 74:68
goal that supplies the p. magic	SCHL 848:79
half your p. life	THAT 1008:16
lucky…discovered a p. theory	CAST 244:34
making man a p. animal	ARIS 34:32
model our p. systems	HAMI 453:40
My p. opinions	TOLK 1022:90
national consciousness is a p. fact	MACM 635:8

political (*contd.*)

not a p. person	HELL 468:94
particular p. conditions	MARX 660:11
points to a p. career	SHAW 923:83
P. action is of second rank	MANN 646:91
P. ammunition runs low	STEV 972:74
p. and constitutional history	JAY 519:73
p. and educational status	SKEL 942:37
p. and practical difficulties	KEYN 555:36
p. and social conditions	MARS 656:53
p. and the other military	MACN 636:32
p. animal can be defined	STEG 965:28
p. aspirant under democracy	MENC 669:68
p. cancer	ANON 29:32
p. consequences	MANS 648:15
p. danger	GLAD 429:50
P. democracy…in America	WHIT 1073:95
P. economy thus does	MARX 660:8
P. economy traces	BAGE 61:62
P. genius	HEGEL 467:64
p. gentlemen drape over	HUXL 508:91
p. in this country	TROL 1028:88
p. meetings…at a divine level	ACHE 2:22
p. noncommitment	VAND 1039:94
p. ones are insoluble	HOME 487:10
p. or religious faiths	PIRS 770:52
p. point of view	WHIT 1069:17
p. power grows out of the barrel	MAO 648:22
p. question is…a painful sight	LODGE 610:84
p. struggle	HAIL 451:12
p. zombies	WILS 1085:40
single p. argument left	THAT 1008:20
stuff of p. leadership	WILS 1085:42
Tears…can never be p.	BELL 88:38
third-rate p. wheel-horse	MENC 670:90
We are not a p. p.	MAND 644:69

politically rule industrially…rule p. CONN 283:81

politician At home, you always have to be a p.

	MACM 635:7
consummate British p.	MACF 629:18
lawyer and a p. and a heretic	MENC 669:64
like a scurvy p.	SHAK 904:38
more of a missionary than a p.	CART 242:8
murderer, to be a p.	MILL 679:57
No man can be a p.	HARR 458:24
pate of a p.	SHAK 893:75
p. is a man	TRUM 1030:25
p. is a person	LLOY 609:67
p. is a statesman who	STEV 973:88
p. is an arse	CUMM 300:91
p. is the devil's quilted anvil	WEBS 1061:58
p. is trained	MURR 716:80
p.…on a street corner	WHITE 1071:47
p. poses as the servant	DEGA 313:6
p. rises on the backs	HUGH 499:24
p. seeking empathy	SAFI 836:71
when a p. does get an idea	MARQ 656:44

politicians always impress p.

	HAYEK 462:91
fault of our p.	TROL 1028:82
Natural p. are skilled actors	MARA 649:37
one of those p.	TROL 1027:71
Outer Mongolia for retired p.	BENN 90:65
p. and scientists were lazier	WAUGH 1057:98
P. are neither bad nor good	EICH 362:59
P. are the same all over	KHRU 556:48
p.…enormous sexual pull	COND 279:86
p.…hold writers in contempt	BELL 88:27
P. neither love nor hate	DRYD 349:17
p. of our time	MACA 622:91
p. or philosophers	THOM 1012:4
P. use statistics	LANG 579:66
race of p. put together	SWIFT 985:85
revolution to get the p. out	CAST 244:32
sense of purpose…not from their p.	MACM 636:19

politicians (*contd.*)

Successful p.	LIPP 607:37
too important to be left to the p.	DEGA 313:7
Two p.' rotten bladders	WEBS 1060:57
wind instead of the p.	WADD 1047:25

politics American p.

	GRAMM 438:97
American p.	WHITE 1071:50
any more about p.	TRUM 1030:21
axiom of p.	TOCQ 1021:76
Beauty…determined by p.	WOLF 1090:12
best p. is good government	STEV 973:87
boundaries between p. and art	DANG 304:40
choice in p.	THOR 1017:3
commonest error in p.	CECIL 247:82
constantly changing language of p.	SAFI 835:67
contact I have had with p.	HEMI 471:39
cross current of world p.	HUGH 501:54
difference between p. and guilt	CLIN 269:21
Don't be 'practical' in p.	CONN 283:82
England is unrivalled for…p.	DISR 334:33
Finality is not the language of p.	DISR 333:4
get on in p.	BAKER 63:83
great men…in p.	ELTON 375:22
History is past p.	FREE 404:33
In p.…anything said	THAT 1007:5
In p., madame	MULR 713:44
In p.…retreat is honorable	MACC 626:58
infection of p.	BRON 190:82
Like art and p.	DOCT 334:41
long experience of p.	MACM 635:11
making p. a spectator sport	GERG 420:2
man goes for p.	ROGE 820:19
matter of modern p.	ARNO 39:20
Men enter local p.	PARK 755:34
mistaken zeal in p.	JUNI 540:73
mixed with p. and p.	LAFA 574:71
mule of p.	DISR 332:83
My p.…is England	DISR 332:88
naked moment in p.	GERG 420:1
nature of p.	POWE 788:19
never get on in p.	ASTOR 43:98
observe about this p. thing	ROGE 820:9
Philistine ogenius in p.	ARNO 40:36
playful moderation in p.	HUNT 504:19
poets should stay out of p.	GINS 428:30
P. and the fate of mankind	CAMUS 228:44
P. are much discussed	DICK 322:67
P. are now nothing more	JOHN 529:75
P., as a practice	ADAMS 5:72
p. as a profession	HOWE 498:99
P. come from man	WAITE 1048:29
p. in the East	DISR 332:76
P. is a blood sport	BEVAN 102:71
P. is a thing	AMIS 16:74
P. is just like show business	REAG 804:71
p. is like…a football coach	MACC 625:41
P. is like having diabetes	JONES 533:55
P. is not an exact science	BISM 164:39
P. is not the art of the possible	GALB 411:78
P. is perhaps the only profession	STEV 975:27
P. is the art of preventing	VALE 1038:88
P. is the art of the possible	BUTL 216:98
P. is the skilled use	PEAR 762:34
P. is too important	DEGA 313:7
P. is war	MAO 648:21
P. mixed with the imagination	STEN 967:71
p. of greed	ARMEY 35:43
p. of numbers	TANA 990:94
p. of the country	HAZL 463:11
p. of the extreme centre	WELL 1064:16
p. than men of any other class	LODGE 610:84
p. the middle way	ADAMS 5:85
Practical p. consists in	ADAMS 5:81
secret springs of p.	TOCQ 1021:77

population (*contd.*)

control the p. without…Herod?	OBRI 734:63
foreign p. must endeavour	RUSS 832:24
full half of the p.	MORE 707:50
immediate checks to p.	MALT 643:38
Ireland…a starving p.	DISR 332:87
only talked of p.	GOLD 432:1
P. EXPLOSION	BRUN 201:11
P.…increases in geometrical ratio	MALT 643:37
p. provides subsidy	CHOM 261:58
segment of our p.	TRUM 1029:17
populations moving whole p.	MILL 678:26
privileged p.	SONT 953:12
working p. of both countries	LOND 610:90
populous p. and smoky city	SHEL 928:94
p. railway town	THOR 1017:1
porcelain rogue in p.	MERE 671:4
porch beyond p. and portal	SWIN 987:37
he'll be on your p.	JOHN 523:51
on the front p. of the house	LANCE 578:53
To the top of the p.!	MOORE 704:6
porches In the p. of mine ears	SHAK 889:78
porcupine dry birth to a p.	SIMP 939:89
key is to be a p.	MATT 664:79
like fucking a p.	MIZN 697:6
quill from a p.	MOORE 705:31
quills upon a fretful p.	SHAK 889:74
pore charm from every p.	LERN 597:90
pores came through the p.	GREE 444:4
p. of the ocean and shores	SHEL 928:84
pork Yes, to smell p.	SHAK 874:18
porkchop Uncle…and his Little P.	ONAS 739:45
Porlock Person from P.	SMITH 948:37
pornography give p. a bad name	BARN 71:23
P.…attempt to insult sex	LAWR 587:4
p. is really about	SONT 953:6
p. only adds to the murk	MILL 679:54
P.…vice of the Seventies	WOLFE 1091:31
porphyry and polished p.	SMART 944:68
porpoise living p. in a strong tide	DICK 320:19
p.…treading on my tail	CARR 239:38
porpoises sporting like p.	SITW 940:4
porridge lines falling like cold p.	BRID 188:46
receives comfort like cold p.	SHAK 916:27
sand in the p.	COWA 290:92
venomous p.	THOM 1011:89
Porson better poet than P.	HOUS 495:67
port brother…who drinks p.	BARR 73:53
p. after stormy seas	SPEN 957:8
p., for men	JOHN 530:3
p. is near	WHIT 1073:91
p. without trade	DEFOE 312:84
ship in p. is safe	HOPP 493:17
Still bent to make some p.	ARNO 37:78
the little p.	TENN 1003:27
There lies the p.	TENN 995:61
portal beyond porch and p.	SWIN 987:37
p. of freedom	EISE 364:93
well-marked front p.	UPDI 1037:68
portals p. of discovery	JOYCE 538:51
portent p. of an iceberg	BROW 199:70
Self-parody is the first p.	MACM 636:25
This is the best p.	HOMER 488:22
porter all p. and skittles	DICK 321:31
decompose in a barrel of p.	DONL 336:61
definition…for a p.	NIGH 729:1
mug of p. in the long nights	ONOL 734:68
philosopher and…p.	SMITH 946:95
Ultimate P.	MANS 647:4
Porter to Kern or Cole P.	GERS 420:9
Portia P. is Brutus' harlot	SHAK 883:30
porticos spitting on p.	NERU 723:9
portion no claim…to the smallest p.	MALT 643:40
only gift is a p. of thyself	EMER 376:29

portion (*contd.*)

only gift is a p. of thyself	BIBLE 117:91
p. for ever	MILT 688:12
p. is so small Of…pain	NAIP 717:16
p. of the earth	SHEL 931:45
p. of the Eternal	SHEL 931:49
p. of the loveliness	BURKE 207:29
right to a fair p.	WORD 1094:97
That best p. of…life	BIBLE 122:21
that is his p.	POPE 782:98
that p. of the ball	OTWAY 746:80
the curse…all your p.	CARR 240:68
portmanteau p.…two meanings	MANS 647:4
portmanteaux people are like p.	DALI 303:45
portrait do not paint a p.	ROSSO 825:98
make a p.	BERN 97:96
p. in marble	JOHN 532:39
p. of a dog that I know	HUGH 500:31
p. of a trout	THOM 1010:63
P. of the Artist	DICK 321:47
two styles of p. painting	CHUR 262:78
portraits accept the verbal p.	LIVE 607:43
people in p. are thinking	LAUR 584:47
p. I paint of women	DOYLE 344:11
study of family p.	HOLM 485:72
portray could not p. all I felt	ACHE 2:25
Portuguese assurance, typically P.	GILB 426:96
pose combine a p. imperious	MARL 655:31
posies thousand fragrant p.	SCHW 851:24
posing P. is a performing art	MARX 660:16
position at the cost of social p.	HAIG 450:10
Every p. must be held	OHARA 737:11
explain your p.	KAZIN 543:30
get people into a p.	BERN 96:75
high p., but not a safe one	LEWO 603:74
if not impossible p.	PEOP 764:58
in a p. to instruct us	AMERY 16:67
lucidly justifying his p.	HEID 467:66
mathematical is the fundamental p.	TROL 1028:84
no p. more perilous	THOM 1011:91
only one p. for an artist	PEARY 763:36
p. at the summit of the world	NIXON 730:16
p., I'd have done the same	THOM 1011:91
p. of the artists of Wales	CHES 257:85
p. ridiculous	ECON 359:14
p.…epitomized marginality	TROT 1029:5
rose to his p.	SCOTT 852:34
Whatever its p. or character	KENN 553:5
positions military take p.	DANF 304:58
ridiculous p.	SCHO 849:91
positive All satisfaction…never p.	BIER 161:94
P.…Mistaken at top of voice	PRIT 791:70
something p. and precious	LACL 574:64
possess not enough to p. her	BURKE 207:16
possessed limited in order to be p.	LEGU 594:25
p. by what is not	SHAK 912:46
p. with murd'rous hate	PROU 793:97
possessing P. what one loves	SHAK 914:78
too dear for my p.	BIBLE 104:23
possession everlasting p.	JONS 534:75
in the glad p.	HENR 473:71
merry hart with small p.	DONNE 339:34
one equall p.	THUC 1018:10
p. intended to last	WHIT 1071:55
p. is final good	ANON 23:94
P. is nine points	ENGE 378:87
p. of a bourgeois aristocracy	SMITH 946:94
p. of that object conveys	YOUNG 1108:2
secure p. of a bleak rock	PLATO 773:3
possessions concern not for…p.	BIBLE 139:24
for he had great p.	GIDE 423:45
jealous p.	WHITE 1070:44
mind is the least of p.	SHEL 927:57
possessor libel on its p.	

possessor (*contd.*)

not profitable to its p.	MARQ 656:43
possibilities p. of life	LEAV 591:75
short of their inherent p.	MUMF 713:46
To believe only in p.	BROW 195:86
possibility How great a P.	CARL 235:59
laws of p.	REDON 804:77
life…to give it p.	MACL 634:83
objective p.	WEBER 1059:20
p. of anybody getting me out	BRAD 184:98
p. of human happiness	ERNST 379:11
Religion…a remote p.	WHIT 1071:55
Violent, vivid and of infinite p.	EBER 359:9
possible art of the p.	GALB 411:78
if a thing is p.	CALO 226:5
no explanation is p.	SEAT 857:25
Politics is the art of the p.	BUTL 216:98
p. one of the provinces	BAUD 77:32
scientist states that something is p.	CLAR 268:90
thank all those who made this p.	ANDR 19:15
wasn't p. for me or anyone	KAVA 543:24
possum Honourable P.	BERR 98:14
post boats near the winning p.	COKE 272:74
Lie follows by p.	BERE 94:38
may not quit the p.	TENN 1003:29
p. of honour	ADDI 8:37
stalked through the P. Office	YEATS 1107:91
post-chaise driving briskly in a p.-c.	JOHN 530:90
post-horse contrapuntist…p.-h.	MOZA 711:19
post-war awash in p.-w. testosterone	SCHR 850:9
postal cheque and the p. order	AUDEN 46:47
desire to take p. courses	BRAD 183:72
postboy keys of the p.'s horn	BENET 90:60
postcard and a p. album	TRAV 1025:31
postcards have a set of p. printed	ELLI 375:10
poster Kitchener…a great p.	ASQU 42:80
live up to one's p.	TREE 1025:43
p. with the enormous face	ORWE 745:55
posterior protecting his p.	SAFI 836:69
posterity fear of vexing p.!	ROCHE 815:41
footprints preserved for p.	PATE 760:98
love of p.	HAWT 461:66
People will not look forward to p.	BURKE 207:27
p. be after him	CROM 298:52
P. do something for us	ADDI 8:37
p. talking bad grammar	DISR 334:30
P. will do justice to…Gladstone	DISR 333:20
protecting his posterior from p.	SAFI 836:69
Thy p. shall sway	COWP 292:36
To evoke p.	GRAV 439:22
To invoke one's p.	CELI 247:89
trustees of P.	DISR 332:92
posters P. of the sea and land	SHAK 907:14
postman hear the p.'s knock	AUDEN 46:48
The P. Always Rings Twice	CAIN 225:92
postmodern p.…Australia	NARO 719:40
postpone p. no more	WHIT 1073:85
postponement Life…one long p.	MILL 679:46
posts sprinkle all the p.	SPEN 959:31
upon the p. of thy house	BIBLE 108:90
postscript pith is in the p.	HAZL 464:17
seldom Writes…but in her P.	STEE 964:20
postulate lay down as a p.	WEIL 1062:84
p. of objectivity	MONOD 700:46
Postumus Oh, my P., P.	HORA 493:20
posture died each in the despairing p.	POE 776:44
postures indecent p.	WILDE 1079:10
posy picks a p. of daisies	THOM 1011:83
pot don't make them in the one p.	JOYCE 538:47
Fame's luscious p.	RICK 811:76
great Melting P.	ZANG 1109:13
Joan doth keep the p.	SHAK 866:31
melting p. never worked	MORR 709:85
not a melting p.	CART 242:2

power (*contd.*)
p. of purchasing other goods　SMITH 946:94
p. of reasoned speech　ARIS 34:32
p. of science　SHAP 919:78
p. of Solidarity　WALE 1049:48
p. of solitude　NORTH 731:32
p. of steady misrepresentation　DARW 306:85
p. of temptation　TROL 1027:74
p. of the hope of freedom　BUCK 203:34
p. of the human intellect　LEWIS 602:60
p. of the will　MORAN 706:41
p. of the written word　CONR 284:88
p. or respect in the world　BAGE 61:62
p. over people　SOLZ 952:95
p. over women　LEGU 594:28
p., peace and the healing　MATT 664:82
P. requires that one do　SART 844:6
P. tends to corrupt　ACTON 4:59
p. that can make us truthful　BONH 173:82
p. that created　THUR 1019:45
p. that I have on you　SHAK 916:18
p. to add or detract　LINC 605:5
p. to ask for love　SHAW 920:99
p. To chasten and subdue　WORD 1094:98
p. to cloud men's minds　BAKER 63:86
p. to communicate　WOOLF 1092:61
p. to do any damn fool thing　FULB 409:28
p. to do me harm　SHAK 900:49
p. to end it　SASS 845:21
P.…to him who dares　DOST 340:44
p. to hurt and will　SHAK 914:81
p. to learn　PLATO 774:23
p. To live, and act　WORD 1100:86
p. to love, or hate　MARL 655:27
p. to make dance　NOON 731:22
p. to make the world a desert　STEV 972:73
p. to master words　SCAR 846:54
p. to shake me　WORD 1099:65
P. to the people　ANON 27:91
p. to touch our senses　MILT 681:90
p. we embody　JORD 537:30
p. with our purpose　KENN 552:89
p. without responsibility　BALD 64:9
present possessors of p.　BURKE 206:99
proletariat can take p.　TROT 1029:8
proud Edward's p.　BURNS 212:37
pure function, and best p.　WORD 1096:34
Repentance…want of p. to sin　DRYD 352:92
responsibility without p.　STOP 978:74
satisfying exercise Of p.　MACB 624:30
self-limited writers have a p.　WOOLF 1092:53
self-sufficing p. of Solitude　WORD 1096:23
sheer joyous p. of song　BEER 83:40
slow-chapped p.　MARV 658:75
some P. the giftie gie us　BURNS 210:77
source of its p.　KINN 559:8
spirit…of p., and of love　BIBLE 154:36
spiritual will to p.　NIET 728:84
still and solemn p.　SHEL 927:60
such unlimited p.　ADAMS 4:61
that diffusion of p.　OAKE 733:49
That false secondary p.　WORD 1096:25
the balance of p.　PALM 752:74
The good want p.　SHEL 930:17
The greater the p.　BURKE 206:3
The press has enormous p.　TOCQ 1021:77
This beautiful and beauty-making p.　COLE 274:7
Thy p. to save　DODD 335:47
ungodly in great p.　BOOK 176:70
United States as an independent p.　GEOR 418:82
use of his p.　HOBB 483:38
vast amounts of p. could be released　EINS 363:65
Visionary p.　WORD 1096:29
weakening of the royal p.　INNO 512:56

power (*contd.*)
welcome, thou dread p.!　BYRON 220:99
what sustains interest…is p.　JIANG 522:24
When p. corrupts　KENN 552:88
When p. leads man　KENN 552:88
who will come to p.　SHEV 934:18
will to p. must increase　LEGU 594:24
With barefaced p.　SHAK 909:56
women breached the p. structure　WOLF 1090:13
ye shall receive p.　BIBLE 147:79
You don't have p. if　TODD 1022:84
powerful evil spirit…supremely p.　DESC 318:82
'It's p.,' he said　HUGH 499:22
more p. conclusion　SOLOW 952:94
More p. than a locomotive!　SIEG 937:68
p. hard thing　CONN 284:85
p. men in our society　BELL 88:27
preparedness makes us p.　GOER 430:67
republic has been much more p.　ADDI 6:4
this p.…kingdom　PITT 771:63
two most p. poets　ELIOT 368:79
wealthier or more p.　HELO 469:7
powerless any other world p.　THUB 1018:9
FBI are p. to act　HOOV 490:69
p. to be born　ARNO 38:2
powerlessness idealized into p.　JONG 533:62
resurrection…is always p.　WILL 1081:50
powers all rest my p. defy　DONNE 336:71
all th' ethereal p.　MILT 693:30
distinction in the intellectual p.　DARW 306:88
exercised the p. committed to me　PEEL 763:43
explore unknown p.　SHEL 926:53
feeble p. of my mind　SIDN 936:42
full use of your p.　KENN 552:90
greatest p. in the world　PALM 752:74
immense new p. on man　CHUR 265:33
Legislation's sov'reign p.　BURNS 210:86
mind of large general p.　JOHN 531:8
p. of intelligence　LYND 621:65
p. of old Europe　MARX 660:14
p. of the state　GIBB 421:20
p. that be are ordained　BIBLE 149:38
productive p. of labour　SMITH 946:90
prostitute all their p.!　FORS 398:48
rise of misplaced p.　EISE 364:88
towards democratic p.　MASA 661:31
vital p. wither　WILB 1075:20
we lay waste our p.　WORD 1099:73
with large p. and privileges　PENN 764:56
ye heavenly p.　GOET 431:72
pox p. of her autumnal face　JONS 535:88
practical as p. as the theory　OPPE 741:75
by p. achievements　TAWN 991:7
Don't be 'p.' in politics　CONN 283:82
For most p. purposes　UPDI 1036:55
hard and p. man　HOYLE 498:2
might have a p. use　UREY 1037:74
original p. example　WHIT 1073:87
seeks after immediate p. utility　HELM 469:4
practice bloody or murmuring p.　STUB 980:12
doctrines and p. of Socialism　MORR 709:81
easier with p.　GREE 444:24
no p. without art　PROT 792:83
offending both legal and natural p.　STOP 978:75
Politics, as a p.　ADAMS 5:72
p.…be greatly simplified　CARL 233:27
proved them wrong in p.　LESS 599:9
rather of instinct than of p.　REED 805:87
respiration—a troublesome p.　DICK 321:33
something which works in p.　HELL 468:90
stoop from speculation to p.　MACA 623:17
trainer knows in his p.　RYLE 834:54
practices consists of p. of this kind　HEATH 466:52
no place for restrictive p.　WILS 1085:30

practise p. to deceive!　SCOTT 853:57
practiser frequent p. of…angling　WALT 1052:7
practising p. long shies　JOYCE 538:43
practitioners art for p. and readers　LEAV 591:75
many p. make a living　SUTH 983:49
pretorian P. here, p. there　SCOTT 854:81
prairie p. flowers lie low　LIND 606:17
prairies rife as the loam Of p.　CRANE 295:6
speech of England…The P.　BRYA 202:19
praise all other p. is shame　SIDN 937:58
as they turn from P.　BROW 197:19
community…lived in p. of God　ELIOT 370:19
counterpoise to unintelligent p.　WAUGH 1057:93
countryman must have p.　BLYT 170:52
courage to give you unqualified p.　STEI 966:57
Damn with faint p.　POPE 781:65
garment of p.　BIBLE 127:12
girded with p.　GRANT 438:5
Give them not p.　SORL 953:23
giving hand…shall have fair p.　SHAK 865:11
guests should p. it　HARI 457:16
Heedless o' p.　MACD 627:80
His p. forth tell　KETHE 554:23
his p. forth tell　SCOT 856:22
if men withheld their p.　SHEEN 926:19
In deeper reverence p.　WHIT 1074:95
In p. of what another's said　YEATS 1105:68
into his courts with p.　BIBLE 118:9
itch of p.?　CAREW 232:7
knowledge and her p.　MILT 690:61
let all the people p. thee　BIBLE 116:85
let the song of p. be sung　POTT 784:44
little dust of p.　TENN 999:47
mouth shall shew forth thy p.　BIBLE 116:79
Never p. a sister　KIPL 559:15
only the master shall p.　KIPL 562:60
outstrip all p.　SHAK 917:35
paint 'em truest p. 'em most　ADDI 6:3
p. any man　SHAK 905:77
P.…can freeze the heart　BUCK 203:36
p. effect in mighty minds　DRYD 349:18
P. for them singing!　FARJ 382:62
P. God, from whom　KEN 549:48
p. him and exalt him　BIBLE 159:52
P. him　HOPK 491:85
P. life, it deserves p.　JEFF 520:86
p. should sing　LYTE 621:66
P. the Lord　FORGY 397:25
P. the sports of the land　REID 806:98
P. to the Holiest　NEWM 724:32
pudding against empty p.　POPE 782:92
sing the p.　MARV 659:92
so long as it's unqualified p.　COWA 291:10
song in thy p.　BURNS 211:99
Teach the free man how to p.　AUDEN 47:73
the p. of his holy Name　BOOK 175:44
this rich p.　SHAK 914:77
unmerited p.　JOHN 531:10
utter all thy P.　ADDI 7:20
wins everyone's p.　HORA 494:33
without hope of p.　JOHN 526:4
praised more in him to be p.　JONS 536:21
p. him to his face　TENN 1005:60
p. the living God　FOX 400:74
praises high p. of God　BIBLE 120:55
sing p. lustily　BOOK 176:39
praising doing one's p. for oneself　BUTL 217:36
P. all alike, is p. none　GAY 416:47
P. what is lost　SHAK 901:84
walking, and leaping, and p. God　BIBLE 147:83
when I am p. anyone　BEER 83:25
pram enemy of good art…the p.　CONN 283:24
prams p. on concrete balconies　BETJ 100:44
prance mind to p.　JOHN 528:53

prater pert, prim P. — CHUR 262:80
pray drink sooner than p. — SHAK 875:47
dying p. at the last — DILL 331:53
fold her hands and p. — ROSS 824:91
learn to p. — HERB 476:41
nor p. with you — SHAK 874:18
P. do not mock — SHAK 904:43
p. exclusively of others — WAUGH 1057:2
p. for my soul — TENN 1004:47
p. for you — SMITH 949:59
P. God our greatness — TENN 1005:63
p. inwardly — JULI 539:68
P., love, remember — SHAK 892:69
'p. my dear' — STER 968:89
p. thee then — HUNT 505:28
p. to have a sound mind — JUVE 540:82
p. to thy Father — BIBLE 135:48
p. we have the wisdom — ALLEN 14:50
p. you do not fall in love — SHAK 886:14
wash your hands and p. — KIPL 565:15
Watch and p. — BIBLE 140:51
When I would p. and think — SHAK 897:75
prayer Conservative Party at p. — ROYD 828:42
fruitless p. — TENN 999:41
given to p. — SHAK 878:12
God erects a house of p. — DEFOE 312:75
homes of silent p. — TENN 999:33
house of p. — BIBLE 139:31
More things are wrought by p. — TENN 1004:47
most perfect p. — LESS 599:10
organ to enlarge her p. — AUDEN 48:78
people's p. — DRYD 349:17
P. Book of Edward VI — ACHE 2:24
p., observance, discipline — ELIOT 372:65
p. of a righteous man — BIBLE 155:73
Shakespeare and p. book — BAIN 63:78
Thy wish not p. — VAUG 1040:14
wing and a p. — ADAM 6:95
wish for p. — BERN 96:71
wish her gratefu' p. — BURNS 210:85
prayers added vexation of p. — TWAIN 1032:67
Christopher Robin is saying his p. — MILNE 680:70
devotion and our p. — FRIE 405:60
Fall to thy p. — SHAK 878:10
Forgets her p. — SITW 940:3
Knelt down in angry p. — HODG 484:53
know whose p. — KIPL 561:43
not very addicted to p. — ASHF 41:65
P. for the condemned man — WEST 1067:86
p. for the observers of his law — BACON 58:78
p. of liberty-loving people — EISE 363:78
p. of the church, to preserve — SWIFT 986:14
p. they dare not speak aloud — WILDE 1075:26
set in my p. — SHAK 917:31
solemn p. for the great exaltation — COLU 278:63
sudden on some p. — BROW 197:20
yet like p. divine — SHAK 915:87
prayeth He p. well — COLE 274:95
praying No p., it spoils business — OTWAY 746:87
pre-eminence keep...the p.-e. — BIBLE 132:14
Pre-Raphaelite decorated by P.-R. — BEER 84:47
preach could never p. — AUST 51:50
p. among the Gentiles — BIBLE 152:97
p. good tidings unto the meek — BIBLE 127:12
P. not because you have to say — WHAT 1068:7
p. the discovery of the 'new'? — INGR 512:47
P. the word — BIBLE 154:40
preacher as the P. saith — HARDY 457:9
village p.'s modest mansion — GOLD 433:11
preachers don't believe in p. — BENE 89:58
pirates, p. — SYNGE 988:63
preaching Christian p. — BARTH 74:68
foolishness of p. — BIBLE 150:44
gone about p. — JERO 521:11

preaching (*contd.*)
p....one of the most healthy exercises — WESL 1067:71
p. point is not a meeting point — THER 1009:37
whether p., praying, speechifying — DISR 333:20
woman's p. is like a dog — JOHN 528:39
preamble Pardon my long p. — LAWR 587:11
precautions take some elementary p. — LEVIN 600:29
take the necessary p. — CRISP 297:36
took p. against it — GALS 413:2
precedence battle for p. — SITW 941:17
believe I take p. — SAKI 838:14
claim in hell P. — MILT 688:12
precedency p. between a louse — JOHN 531:25
precedent From p. to p. — TENN 996:89
precedents there are no p. — DEBU 311:70
precept carry p. to the highest — BYRON 222:37
Let your p. be, Be Easy — STEE 964:18
p. must be upon p. — BIBLE 125:75
true business p. — DICK 322:73
very little p. and practice — EDGE 360:25
preceptions p. and insights — KISS 566:38
preceptor artist p. of his time — BETH 99:24
precepts if one follows p. — SENE 858:45
precincts warm p. of cheerful day — GRAY 442:74
precious all p. in God's sight — JACK 514:87
all that's p. in our joys — STER 970:28
how p. is frivolity! — FORS 398:48
Life is too p. — ELIOT 365:99
make vile things p. — SHAK 903:21
most p. to me — SHAK 909:74
P. in the sight of the Lord — BIBLE 118:26
something positive and p. — PRIT 791:70
Thy words are too p. — SHAK 885:73
precipice On the summit of the p. — HOLM 485:72
precise too p. in every part — HERR 478:68
precisely Thinking p. — SOLOW 952:93
precision p. unapproachable — LEAV 591:73
strung to a vast p. — CRANE 295:99
precisions divisions and p. — ELIOT 367:58
precondition p. to meaningful action — BART 74:74
predecessors shoulders of their p. — RUSS 832:21
steal from their p. — POUND 785:57
predestination Social P. Room — HUXL 507:66
prediction regardless of p. — RICH 809:41
predilection p. for genre fiction — DISCH 331:68
p....is with us — AUDEN 48:81
preface P. to a...Suicide Note — BARA 70:6
prefer Did not p. You — DRAY 345:37
p. the destruction — HUME 503:4
preference p. which it is forced — LAMB 576:24
P. and prejudice creep in — HILL 481:6
with p. and aversion — SHER 933:78
work: if not by p. — BAUD 78:41
preferment knocking at P.'s door — ARNO 37:87
pregnancy avoid p. ...mathematics — MENC 670:81
pregnant finish...without getting p. — ANON 28:23
like being a little p. — HEND 471:53
Like finding oneself p. — ACHE 3:32
mad'st it p. — MILT 687:86
strong pillars and p. supporters — BAIL 62:72
trying to stay half p. — BOHL 171:62
prejudice critic...without p. — NATH 721:89
free from interest or p. — REES 805:92
let no p....asperse them — EMMET 378:81
Preference and p. creep in — HILL 481:6
p. runs in favour of two — DICK 321:45
P....vagrant opinion — BIER 161:95
Race p....a shadow — BUCK 203:33
suburban p. of anti-Semitism — POUND 787:90
the p....run in favour of two — SHER 933:81
To everybody's p. — GILB 425:80
Travel is fatal to p. — TWAIN 1032:61
prejudices Drive out p. — FRED 403:25

prejudices (*contd.*)
employ their reason to justify p. — WOLL 1091:34
honest p. of a true Englishman — ADDI 7:18
our errors, our p., our dreams — POPP 784:25
paradoxes not of p. — ROUS 827:36
Passions destroy more p. — DIDE 329:24
p., misconceptions — LLOY 609:64
prelates p. in habitis clericall — DUNB 355:39
prelude p. to insanity — WAUGH 1056:68
p. to resurrection — WILL 1081:50
preludes p. to that eternal separation — STER 970:15
premium greater p. on temperament — BRAD 184:96
prentices schoolboys and sour p. — DONNE 336:77
preoccupation chief p. to avoid — LESS 598:96
one constant p. — RUSS 832:29
preparation complete lack of p. — WAVE 1058:11
no p. for the future — DISR 332:81
no p. is thought necessary — STEV 975:27
preparations all the p. with regard to — GOER 431:68
prepare p. to meet thy God — BIBLE 130:59
p. to shed them now — SHAK 884:53
prepared Be P. — BADE 60:44
preparedness p. makes us powerful — GOER 430:67
preposterous p. troop of sons — SOME 952:99
prerogative first is law, the last p. — DRYD 350:51
p. of the eunuch — STOP 978:74
presage p. of extinction — SCOTT 852:35
presagers dumb p. — SHAK 913:53
Presbyterian P. at Kercaldy — FLEM 394:63
Presbyterians regarded by strict P. — THOM 1014:44
prescription discards P. — DISR 332:81
prescriptions according to her p. — MORE 707:54
p. are not kept — SHAK 915:97
p. written by patients — KRAUS 569:86
rules and p. — NISB 730:4
presence Cast me not...from thy p. — BIBLE 116:78
castellated, shimmering p. — MORR 708:77
come before his p. with song — BOOK 177:89
come before his p. with thanksgiving — BIBLE 117:5
feel the p. of the past — PEI 764:49
from whose unseen p. — SHEL 928:86
His p. here is...an insult — RED 804:74
horror that her p. excites — GRAV 440:27
If thy p. go not with me — BIBLE 107:75
insult of each other's p. — ISHE 513:74
majestic p. — HUNT 504:20
not often let their p. be known — DUBO 353:8
p. of a bad historian — ELTON 375:22
p. of absence — BERG 95:48
p. of the cherished child — ELIOT 365:13
p. of the Red Death — POE 776:44
Where God's p. is no longer — STEI 967:67
whither shall I flee from thy p.? — BIBLE 120:49
present afraid of the p. — GREY 446:58
alcohol made the p. enough — GEE 417:65
bitter birthday p. — DILL 330:51
Children...live in the p. — LABR 573:53
conventions of the p. — LEWI 603:72
dialogue between the p. and the past — CARR 237:9
die...when you are p. — SCEVE 846:57
except for the one p. moment — WILL 1082:79
finding myself at p. — MUNDY 714:54
For the p. at any rate — ROSE 822:55
Forsytes were p. — GALS 413:2
future...same stuff as the p. — WEIL 1062:80
futurity casts on the p. — SHEL 931:60
gave it me...for an un-birthday p. — CARR 240:65
give this p. to her dear — LANY 580:79
It is the p. that counts — CELI 247:89
love [looks] to the p. — LEWIS 601:38
man of the p. — HOLM 487:4
men of the p. age — OVER 747:93
more eventful than the p. — ORWE 743:14
no crime like the p. — WASH 1055:47

present (*contd.*)
no redress for the p. — DISR 332:81
not live well in the p. — THOM 1009:49
others, past and p. — NABO 717:9
Piers this p. to plese — LANG 579:73
politics is p. history — FREE 404:33
p. alone was significant — CHOP 261:60
p. at the Creation — EVANS 381:37
p. at their marriages — TROL 1027:73
p....growth out of the past — WHIT 1073:94
p. ...has a voice — OAKE 733:48
p. in time future — ELIOT 370:22
p. is an age of talkers — HAZL 463:13
p. is an important time — CARL 234:36
p. is burthened too much — HAWT 461:80
p. is not forgotten — GRASS 439:11
p. is the funeral of the past — CLARE 267:81
p. or any future writer — MILL 674:59
p. than in the ooze — NABO 717:6
p. things as they are — FRED 403:22
shows world its p. — BETH 99:24
think we're in the p. — KESEY 553:21
this p. were the world's last night? — DONNE 338:10
who controls the p. — ORWE 745:57
presentation mode of p. — SCOTT 852:33
under the p. of that — SHAK 887:37
presents Christmas without any p. — ALCO 12:96
coincided as p. — MURP 715:69
P., I often say — LAMB 576:27
p., past and future sees — BLAKE 167:84
preservation p., and distribution — RUSK 831:95
p. of health — SPEN 955:65
p. of property — LOCKE 609:68
times of p. — SHAK 918:58
preservative pleasantest p. from want — AUST 51:39
preserve frozen, I p. you — ATWO 45:25
p. it from putrefaction — JOHN 532:30
p. thy body and soul — BOOK 175:32
p. thy soul — BIBLE 119:36
preserver Destroyer and p. — SHEL 928:87
time the p. — ELIOT 372:61
presidence making of our p. — NEW 723:17
presidency cancer...close to the p. — DEAN 311:59
P. provides some happiness — KENN 552:90
question of the P. — DICK 322:67
what does he think the P. is? — EISE 364:92
president all the P.'s men — KISS 566:33
another Democratic P. — CART 242:6
any boy may become p. — STEV 973:90
any P. of Irish descent — KENN 551:81
bank p. finish the script — EPST 379:7
Being p. is like — TRUM 1030:32
capable of choosing a p. — STEIN 966:49
does not speak well of you as a p. — PETE 767:9
don't mind not being P. — KENN 550:59
elected Vice P. — GARN 415:28
every country ought to have a P. — DOLE 335:54
George Meany could run for P. — DOLE 335:49
him that is the p. — SPEN 957:92
hoping to hear the P. sneeze — MENC 669:76
I can't stop being P. — CLIN 269:20
I was sleeping with the P. — REAG 803:59
if Jack were P. of France — ONAS 739:39
If the P. has a bully pulpit — REAG 803:57
If you want to be vice p. — BRADY 184:3
make a fine p. — MACA 621:77
Mr P., I speak for sixty thousand — HUGH 501:53
Mr P., the p. is dead — ODON 736:92
never...bothered any wartime P. — BIDD 160:63
not to ask the P. — POIN 776:91
Oh, Mr P., do not let — KNOX 567:60
one thing to be said about being P. — EISE 364:90
one's husband for P. — ONAS 739:43
only have one vice p. — ROGE 820:6

president (*contd.*)
P. bears the burden — KENN 551:74
P. can't get to — GORE 436:67
P. Clinton returned today — DOWD 342:77
P....has to do everything — ASTU 43:99
p....incapable of enforcing law — MARC 649:46
P. is a walking dead man — ANON 29:49
P. looked wiser — KEYN 554:26
P. of the Immortals — HARDY 456:99
P. of the United States — UPDI 1036:56
P. Robbins was so well — JARR 518:59
P.'s vision — SCHL 848:79
P. will go down in history — DOLE 335:53
Running a cemetery...like being a P. — ANON 29:50
skills that a P. needs — ONEI 740:65
slept more than any other P. — MENC 669:69
sometimes name the p.? — TANA 990:95
terrific p. — HILL 270:24
The P. hears a hundred — TRUM 1030:28
to the P., not to his wife — REGAN 805:94
When a p....pays attention — GALL 413:98
when the p. does it — NIXON 730:16
presidents disastrous P. — ONAS 739:42
do with all the vice p. — ROGE 820:6
p. and ministers — SUN 982:39
P....pretending to run a crusade — COOKE 286:29
press As for the p. — TOCQ 1021:75
competitive p. knows — RUSK 830:73
controversy over freedom...of the p. — ORWE 745:50
fell dead-born from the p. — HUME 504:12
first duty of the p. — TIMES 1021:71
free p. compels them to bend — MILL 674:56
freedom of the p. in Britain — ORWE 742:5
freedom of the p. — JEFF 520:94
give up p.-clippings agency — WODE 1089:98
governs the periodical p. — TROL 1027:62
inform p. home Christmas — WRIG 1102:13
Let's p. the flesh — JOHN 524:56
liberty of the p. — JOHN 528:52
liberty of the p. — JUNI 540:74
liberty of the P. — SHER 934:13
more reliable than the p. — ORWE 743:20
p....an excellent servant — COOP 287:44
P. is at once the eye — STEAD 964:4
P. is the living Jury — BENN 92:3
P. was squared — BELL 87:9
ridicule them in the p. — PULI 795:20
Supposing the P. — LEST 599:13
The p. has enormous power — TOCQ 1021:77
The p., the machine — NIET 727:70
pressure economic blood p. — WRIS 1102:18
grace under p. — HEMI 470:20
pressure-cooker p.-c. on simmer — SHAR 919:83
prestige authority and p. — BERE 94:37
great offices...give social p. — BAGE 61:57
presume p. not God to scan — POPE 780:42
p. you're mortal — SHIR 935:26
presumed no more things...be p. — OCCAM 735:79
presumption amused by its p. — THUR 1018:21
height of p. — BRAUN 186:17
presumptions in the face of p. — JAMES 516:17
presupposition fundamental p. — HEID 467:66
pretences false p. on dolls — RUNY 829:63
pretend others p. and don't care — KIPL 561:44
p. to be more stupid — STARK 963:94
why p. that he is? — SHAW 922:42
pretender fight for the P. — SWIFT 985:97
Old P. — GUED 448:74
pretending what you're p. to be — BARN 72:36
pretension p. is nothing — HUNT 504:25
pretensions p. of final truth — NIEB 727:65
undeniable p. as civilization — PITT 771:71
pretentiousness ugly twin, p. — KUSH 571:22
pretext the rest is only a p. — ELTIT 375:21

pretexts Tyrants seldom want p. — BURKE 208:43
pretty All my p. ones? — SHAK 909:74
Every time they do something p. — SALI 838:21
Leave the p. women — PROU 793:3
p. and picturesque use — HARDY 456:94
p. as an airport — ADAMS 5:69
p., but is it Art? — KIPL 561:40
p. can get away with anything — WAUGH 1057:1
p. follies that themselves commit — SHAK 874:29
p. to see what money — PEPYS 766:83
sex object if you're p. — GIOV 428:37
These p. pleasures — RALE 800:12
too successful or too p. — JONG 534:69
Whether you're p. or not — SEXT 859:63
Why shouldn't art be p.? — RENO 807:12
prevenience adorableness and his p. — HUGEL 498:10
prevent knowing how to p. them — RUSS 833:35
p. them from leaving — KENN 552:84
prevention as much for p. as cure — GRAV 440:35
prey alone bent on his p. — MILT 689:41
between the hunter and his p. — ZHAO 1109:21
destined — SHAW 921:30
expects his evening p. — GRAY 443:86
fear the birds of p. — SHAK 896:64
fleas on him p. — SWIFT 986:7
Into England, to drive a p. — BALL -101:21
lord...and yet a p. to all — POPE 780:43
made my pains his p. — SPEN 959:28
soon must be his p. — SHEL 927:71
preys to their p. do rouse — SHAK 909:60
Priam P.'s sons of Troy — SURR 982:43
price another man's p. increase — WILS 1085:37
at a p. far dearer — SCHAW 847:61
Blood, all p. excelling — AQUI 32:5
bought with a p. — BIBLE 150:49
buy it of thee at a p. — BIBLE 110:52
couldn't name its p. — GREE 444:7
dear at any p. — WHIS 1069:15
give me my p. — BIBLE 130:68
haggling at the p. — GRAV 440:33
If blood be the p. — KIPL 562:55
men have their p. — WALP 1052:1
natural p. of labour — RICA 808:37
pay any p. to get it — IACO 509:16
p. he has to pay — HUXL 507:65
p. is far above rubies — BIBLE 122:12
p....is poverty, ignorance and disease — DUBO 353:9
p. of everything...value of nothing — WILDE 1077:62
p. of liberty is...dirt — ORWE 742:95
p. of raw produce — RICA 808:33
p. on the Washington Monument? — KENN 553:7
p. paid for becoming a couple — COUP 289:85
p. that the market sets — FRIE 405:54
p. was quite reasonable — MERR 672:23
p. will probably fall — ANON 25:25
real p. of everything — SMITH 946:93
sold at a reasonable p. — AUST 51:53
the natural p. of the other — PETTY 768:13
What P. Glory? — ANDE 18:5
worth more than the p. of paint — VAN 1039:3
worth of a man is...his p. — HOBB 483:38
prices ceiling over p. — WRIS 1102:16
contrivance to raise p. — SMITH 945:79
liberalization of p. — PAVL 761:20
p. will be...different — LEVIN 600:29
reduce the rise in p. — HEATH 466:51
Rising p....do not cause inflation — WRIS 1102:21
prick If you p. us — SHAK 872:80
it is a p. — PEELE 763:46
pain...after the p. — BERN 97:88
p. the sides of my intent — SHAK 908:32
When the p. stands up — ROTH 826:13
pricking By the p. of my thumbs — SHAK 909:65
p. on the plain — SPEN 957:98

prickly p. to the smooth	MACD 628:93	**priests** invention of theologians or p.	NIEB 727:64	**princes** (*contd.*)	
pricks Honour p. me on	SHAK 876:68	p. and educators	NGU 725:45	make p. in all lands	BOOK 177:73
hundered p. against one	MIZN 697:6	p. are only men	BROW 200:87	'must' is not to be used to p.!	ELIZ 373:93
kick against the p.	BIBLE 147:89	p. in black gowns	BLAKE 167:91	Of p. shall outlive	SHAK 913:65
p. like thorn	SHAK 868:77	p. interpreted and interposed	COND 279:83	pale kings, and p.	KEATS 545:74
pricksong fights as you sing p.	SHAK 869:99	P., princes, women	POPE 781:56	Perfect happiness, by p. sought	CHAP 252:70
pride appeals to their p.	KENN 550:61	p. very dear to the people	TROL 1027:77	power shines in p.' eyes!	MARL 652:88
As a matter of racial p.	FEIF 384:98	p. were infinitely more attentive	FITZ 390:94	P. and lords may flourish	GOLD 433:10
blot upon my p.	SHAK 867:57	seize our p.	ANON 22:80	P. and lords…the breath of kings	BURNS 209:66
breath of degradation and of p.	BYRON 221:20	women nor with p.	SOUT 954:35	p. apply themselves	MORE 706:42
bursting with p.	JOSE 537:33	**primary** cruelty is the p. feeling	SADE 835:64	p. my ancestors followed	ORAH 741:77
country's p.	GOLD 433:10	p. requirement of a writer	STAEL 961:74	p. should be free	SHAK 861:96
cowardice and false p.	STAN 962:84	p. word addresses the eternal Thou	BUBER 202:21	p. to know their true interest	SWIFT 985:87
coy submission, modest p.	MILT 690:56	**primative** wildly natural and p.	THOR 1016:69	put not your trust in p.	BOOK 177:95
Fond P. of Dress	FRAN 402:5	**prime** dead ere his p.	MILT 684:38	She's all states, and all p.	DONNE 337:78
fosters national p.	HOWE 497:97	fresh colours do deck the wanton p.	SPEN 958:19	though p. rage	ANON 23:87
fount of p.	CULL 299:70	gathered in their p.	SHAK 864:97	you that are p. born	DAVI 307:7
harvests bury all his p. has planned	POPE 779:23	In the p. of your life	RICH 809:43	**princess** ancient Egyptian p.	CASS 243:26
He that is low no p.	BUNY 205:73	lovely April of her p.	SHAK 912:44	great p.	FORD 397:12
In the p. of life	WILDE 1075:26	One's p. is exclusive	SPARK 955:52	p. among the provinces	BIBLE 128:29
know thy p.	BIBLE 110:38	**Prime Minister** best P. M. we've got	BUTL 216:99	**Princeton** chair at Harvard or P.	MENC 669:64
Many men have p.	BALZ 69:75	essentials of a successful P. M.	WILS 1085:41	**principalities** timeless p.	GRAV 440:25
nature's p. and richest furniture!	MARL 652:86	grow up to be P. M.	RICH 811:73	**principle** active p. of Wealth	PETTY 768:14
odious P.	MAND 645:71	man who nearly becomes P. M.	BUTL 216:97	advocates no great p.	HAZL 463:9
poet's inward p.	DAYL 310:54	next P. M. but three	BELL 87:9	aesthetic p. of our times	ROGE 820:3
p. come before a fall	WELD 1062:91	P. M. is the loneliest job	BALD 64:8	an active P.	WORD 1100:83
p. fell with my fortunes	SHAK 885:71	P. M. or Leader of the Opposition	DISR 333:20	called this p.…Natural Selection	DARW 306:83
P. goeth before destruction	BIBLE 121:84	P. M. reading out the conclusions	HESE 479:78	Cats seem to go on the p.	KRUT 570:10
p. in having given up his p.	SALI 839:31	unknown P. M.	ASQU 42:78	Conservatism…shrinks from P.	DISR 332:81
P. is his own glass	SHAK 895:45	would not want to be P. M.	THAT 1007:3	does everything on p.	SHAW 920:11
P. is still aiming	POPE 780:38	**prime ministers** disastrous…P.M.	ONAS 739:42	facts and not…a p.	DARW 306:90
P. leaves the heart	GAUT 416:43	**primetime** doesn't help when p. TV	QUAY 796:53	female p.	LEGU 594:27
P. makes lawsuits	ANON 22:79	**primeval** p. ooze to the stars	VIDAL 1044:62	first p. of existentialism	SART 844:15
p. of distinction	SAND 841:69	This the forest p.	LONG 611:6	formal p. of its colour	SHEL 931:56
p. of kings	POPE 780:32	**primitive** comprehend…p. forms	EINS 363:67	Greatest Happiness P.	MILL 675:71
p. of people in their…trade	PRIT 791:74	most p. and most sophisticated	KUNI 571:17	identifying oneself with a p.	HEGEL 467:64
p. of race or spirit	SMITH 949:60	p. era was lyrical	HUGO 501:56	It has no other p.	HAZL 463:8
p. of the peacock	BLAKE 166:78	p. form of cricket…Tip-and-Run	SHAW 925:34	on p., not by instinct	TWAIN 1034:15
p., or cowardice	JOHN 531:21	p. men are…credulous	POPE 779:18	p. laid down by Gilbert	HUTC 506:43
p. struck out new sparkles	DRYD 350:50	p. music and p. medicine	LEAC 589:40	p. of life with me	SHAW 920:13
p. which causes thirst	DANTE 305:71	radicals who seem p.	WOLFE 1090:23	p. of the English law	DICK 325:35
rank p., and haughtiness of soul	ADDI 8:29	wise p. in a giant jungle	MAIL 639:67	p. that gives us a firm Rock	BUTT 218:52
Ring out false p.	TENN 1000:57	**primrose** p. path of dalliance	SHAK 888:62	p. which prompts to save	SMITH 946:92
soul that perished in his p.	WORD 1097:44	P. Hill and Saint John's Wood	BLAKE 168:7	rebels from p.	BURKE 207:34
spite of P.	POPE 780:41	p. that forsaken dies	MILT 684:47	romantic p. of life	NOVA 732:37
Such is our p.	DENH 315:54	p. way	SHAK 908:51	self-determination…imperative p.	WILS 1086:55
take p. in the words	KENN 552:85	**primroses** Wan as p.	KEATS 545:62	sensibility of p.	BURKE 207:32
the great and their p.	YEATS 1105:64	**prince** Advise the p.	ELIOT 367:52	snob…on p.	SHAW 924:97
the p. of my country I sang	OBRU 734:73	bold defiance with his p.	DRYD 349:16	tenth time, lack of p.	SIDM 936:40
Thine eyes my p.	SIDN 937:58	danced with the P. of Wales	FARJ 383:54	**principles** acceptance of p.	UNIT 1036:45
time of our love and p.	SU 981:16	Dread p. of plackets	SHAK 865:13	action of religious p.	BERD 94:35
too much weakness for the stoic's p.	POPE 780:42	fall of a p.	ANON 21:54	based on mechanical p.	LEUP 599:14
What argufies p. and ambition?	DIBD 319:7	Good night, sweet p.	SHAK 893:90	betrayed by its p.	INOU 512:59
will her p. deflower	SPEN 958:17	Here lies a p.	JOSE 537:34	civilization with sound p.	JOHN 522:31
priest both the p. and clerk?	SHAK 867:63	His Weariness the P.	FIRB 389:74	contrary to their p.	GALS 413:2
came down a certain p.	BIBLE 142:89	preservation of the P. and State	WENT 1065:53	current p. of administration	SIMON 939:80
Churches built to please the P.	BURNS 209:69	P. calls in the good old money	LAMB 576:23	denouncing liberal democratic p.	AUNG 50:22
Delicate-handed p. intone	TENN 1001:79	p. is like a mirror	CHAR 253:89	easier to fight for p.	STEV 972:70
parish p. rebuked him	OFLA 736:96	P. of Europe, should dare to invade	ELIZ 373:90	fights you on patriotic p.	SHAW 920:11
p. begets children	SMITH 949:45	p. of glory died	WATTS 1055:56	happily arrogating those p.	MAMET 643:47
p. continues what the nurse began	DRYD 351:55	P. of Light	MILT 681:87	if you surrender all your p.	TODD 1022:84
p. is given permission	LISP 607:39	p. of the clouds	BAUD 77:16	man of fixed and unbending p.	DIRK 331:65
p. is the worshipper	SHAW 923:76	p. of the devils	BIBLE 136:72	man without p.	FORD 396:99
p. of the Muses	HORA 493:21	P., thou art sad	SHAK 880:69	morally acting on the highest p.	SHAW 924:89
p., warrior, poet	BAUD 78:43	safer for a p. to be feared	MACH 631:37	mythical stories become structural p.	FRYE 408:21
rid me of this turbulent p.?	HENR 472:63	soothe the p.'s appetite	MASS 663:58	p. are the same	JOHN 531:16
Thou art a p. for ever	BIBLE 118:23	soul of a p.	LOCKE 609:74	p. employed in science	RUSS 832:16
why he was a p.	WINT 1087:65	Sweet p., I come	MARL 653:3	p. form the bright constellation	JEFF 520:94
youth…is nature's p.	WORD 1098:51	under the rank of a p.	KING 558:99	p. of a free constitution	GIBB 421:19
priestcraft ere p. did begin	DRYD 349:4	Were you with these, my p.	ADDI 8:30	p. of equity and justice	PEEL 763:43
p. into a great religious	LEWIS 602:60	Who made thee a p.	BIBLE 106:52	p. of mankind	WILS 1086:50
priesthood arcane p.	GOULD 436:78	**princedoms** p., virtues, powers	MILT 691:74	p. round my neck	BALF 65:22
one or other kind of p.	MILL 677:2	**princes** admit p. to the corridors	DOUG 341:58	p. which at first lead to scepticism	BERK 95:53
royal p.	BIBLE 156:78	blaze forth the death of p.	SHAK 883:32	putting our p. into execution	WEBB 1059:18

principles (*contd.*)

round certain p.	TOCQ 1021:77
when the p. dissolve	MILL 677:4
wrote P. of Political Economy	BENT 93:26
print definite…in p.	COMP 279:73
eternity of p.	WOOLF 1092:63
keepers of p. and paper	MACL 634:77
love a ballad in p.	SHAK 912:38
names in p.	CHES 260:39
p. of a man's naked foot	DEFOE 312:80
put them into p.	LESS 598:5
we quarrel in p.	SHAK 887:35
when they see them in p.	KRAUS 569:90
printed chaff is p.	HUBB 498:6
developed, carefully p., fixed	ISHE 513:72
printing invented the art of p.	CARL 234:47
p., gunpowder and the magnet	BACON 55:30
restrained from p.	JOHN 528:52
Prior once was Matthew P.	PRIOR 790:49
priority without the reward of p.	SCOTT 852:39
priory stag in the P. coomb	DAVI 307:99
prism Newton with his p.	WORD 1096:27
Prism Charity, dear Miss P.	WILDE 1078:86
prison endure torture in p.	PANK 753:82
good friend visits you…in p.	BRAD 183:83
hero from his p.	AYTO 53:86
his dwelling, and a p.	WEBS 1060:49
hollow of my flesh	SHAK 862:40
Home is the girl's p.	SHAW 922:60
impenetrable barriers of our p.	EDGE 361:32
in p., and ye came unto me	BIBLE 140:44
opening of the p.	BIBLE 127:12
palace and a p. on each hand	BYRON 220:92
pestilential p.	GILB 425:88
portion as the site of a p.	HAWT 461:69
P., dungeons, blessed places	GENET 418:75
p. is to live without mirrors	ATWO 45:26
p. of his days	AUDEN 47:73
public school…at home in p.	WAUGH 1056:75
put me in p.	ONDA 739:46
So cruel! how could	SURR 982:43
soul's p. we call England	SHAW 925:15
Stone walls do not a p. make	LOVE 615:63
taking him to p.	HOUS 496:87
true place…also a p.	THOR 1016:65
What is ship but p.	BURT 214:72
worst of p. life	STEN 967:73
prison-house grind in the p.-h.	BIBLE 109:21
secrets of the p.-h.	MOOD 703:95
Shades of the p.-h.	WORD 1098:51
prisoned p. birds must find	SASS 845:34
prisoner passing on the p.'s life	SHAK 896:66
p. in his dungeon	FLAU 393:43
p.'s release	SIDN 937:53
sculpture is the p.	THOM 1013:27
your being taken p.	KITC 566:45
prisoners p., be not despairit	ANON 23:87
p., handcuffed two	LESS 598:99
p.…I'll find them law	MACQ 638:52
p. of addiction	ILLI 511:34
p. out of captivity	BOOK 177:80
p. were left free to choose	SHAW 922:42
p. whom they hide	HAWT 461:77
Queen Victoria treats her p.	WILDE 1078:95
stand p. at the bar	WILDE 1075:26
which p. call the sky	WILDE 1078:97
prisons P. are built with stones	BLAKE 166:76
privacy P. is a privilege not granted	LAUR 584:44
undisturbed p.	PARK 755:22
private allurement of p. interest	STEU 970:30
am to become a p. citizen	EISE 364:37
better that we stay p. people	SART 844:6
his p. parts, his money	BUTL 218:48
hold no brief for p. enterprise	BURT 214:62

private (*contd.*)

in his p. heart	TWAIN 1034:7
making the p. world public	GINS 428:34
matter of p. gain	OROZ 741:83
meddling too much in my p. life	WILL 1082:71
p. animosities	WILL 1080:46
p. enterprise	GALB 412:79
P. faces in public places	AUDEN 46:43
p. life…by…public life	ELIOT 366:25
P. Means is dead	SMITH 948:38
p. silence in which we live	PRIT 791:70
p. sports the stews would blush	MASS 662:56
public good P. respects	MILT 695:49
She's p. to herself	BEAU 80:67
takes no p. road	POPE 781:52
privations hardships, p.	PEARY 762:35
physical p. philosophically	MOOD 703:94
privatization P. must come after	PAVL 761:20
privatize p. the cost of childhood	HEWE 479:87
privilege heaven-born p.	ARNO 39:27
inestimable p. of man	SHEL 927:56
most cherished p.	STRA 979:94
p. I claim for my own sex	AUST 52:70
p. of always moving	LEWIS 601:35
p. of wisdom to listen	HOLM 486:1
to maintain this p.	DUBO 353:9
privileged certain p. few	OROZ 741:83
not from its p. classes	TWAIN 1034:98
They were p. children	BROO 193:40
Third Estate…without the p. classes?	SIEY 938:69
privileges one of the p.	LURIE 619:42
p. of misery	DONO 340:36
p. on basis of physical characteristic	BOTHA 180:33
with large powers and p.	PENN 764:56
prize eye on the p.	ANON 28:19
lawful p.	GRAY 441:54
Let old Timotheus yield the p.	DRYD 351:74
looks to gain the p.	MARL 652:88
luck o' the p.	BURNS 212:33
one receiveth the p.?	BIBLE 150:54
p. of half a crown	WAUGH 1056:64
p. of the high calling	BIBLE 153:12
p. Of wit or arms	MILT 682:3
p. we sought is won	WHIT 1073:91
prize-fighters p. shaking hands	MENC 669:72
prizes p. be given to them	SMITH 948:32
world continues to offer glittering p.	BIRK 163:18
probability p. very guide of life	BUTL 216:95
problem A point of view, a p.	POPP 783:20
American Negro p.	BALD 64:91
dearly loved difficult p.	ANON 21:55
Hang a lantern on your p.	MATT 664:78
have yet to see any p.	ANDE 18:7
it is not a money p.	CLIN 269:17
main p. of the actor?	OLIV 738:32
obvious that there's no real p.	FEYN 387:34
one philosophical p.	POPP 783:21
one truly serious philosophical p.	CAMUS 228:46
only concrete p. I know	CAMUS 229:51
philosophical p. has the form	WITT 1088:77
p. for the invisible man	ELLI 375:19
p. in making our power	KENN 551:67
p. is food	DONL 336:60
p. is not style but quality	ROGE 820:5
p. is not whether machines think	SKIN 943:52
p. is their subjugation	THOM 1010:60
p. lay buried	FRIE 405:49
p. of race and color	DUBO 353:9
p. of the Sudeten Germans	HITL 482:32
p. of the twentieth century	DUBO 353:5
p. of when and where	TOLS 1023:99
p. was to make unfamiliar	CONR 285:10
p. within the US economy	KRUG 570:5
p. without a gift	BACH 54:97

problem (*contd.*)

prospect of tackling an unsolved p.	SHIP 935:20
social p. of the twentieth century	SMALL 943:61
social p. solved	MACD 627:87
solution to the p.	LEMAY 595:43
they can't see the p.	CHES 260:46
three-pipe p.	DOYLE 343:1
you're part of the p.	CLEA 268:98
problems all kinds of p.	PARRA 756:43
architectural p. of our own day	POEL 776:56
Diplomatic p. used to be discussed	ACHE 2:22
do not choose our p.	FROMM 406:70
his p. in living	SZASZ 989:68
insoluble p.	GARD 415:22
methodological p.	LEWO 603:73
No p. can be solved	BURR 213:57
p. are solved…by arranging	WITT 1088:76
p.…may be inevitable	ASIM 42:72
p. of biography, of history	MILLS 679:63
p. of three little people	EPST 379:1
p. that we are facing	PAVL 761:22
p. which the man	KRUT 570:8
p. with your main character	ANON 28:25
Science…with p.	POPP 784:27
so many couples are having p.	CART 243:12
two kinds of Arctic p.	STEF 965:24
two p. in my life	HOME 487:10
procedure p. that spells much	DOUG 342:69
procedures set p. and expressions	BAND 69:87
proceeds p. of human sweat	FRAN 402:16
with a good conscience on the p.	SMITH 947:16
process inner p.	WITT 1088:80
malpractice…and illegitimate p.	CLOU 271:41
Obscenity is a cleansing p.	MILL 679:54
painful p. of Unthinking	CUMM 299:75
path and p. taken	LIEB 604:91
phase in a continuing p.	ROBI 815:36
p. of learning	WILD 1080:35
p. should be effected	RUSS 832:24
take the energy p. seriously	LEARY 591:70
The first p. in art	THEO 1008:33
too considered a p.	BARN 72:35
uncertain p. of letter-writing	ELIOT 365:99
procession p. of one	DICK 323:82
proclaiming p. as I go	PLATO 773:3
proclamations p. …slapped up	HEMI 470:17
procrastination invicility and p.	DEQU 316:68
p. is the art	MARQ 655:37
procreation main road of p.	WAUGH 1056:70
Procrustes P. was an editor	SKEL 942:47
proctors prudes for p.	TENN 996:91
procurator p. Pontius Pilate	TACI 989:79
prodigal chariest maid is p. enough	SHAK 888:61
how p. the soul	SHAK 888:68
p. of ease?	DRYD 349:14
prodigality diminished by p.	SMITH 945:85
prodigies danger of coming back p.	AUST 51:53
thousand horrid P.	JOHN 525:76
prodigy normal child and not as a p.	BARB 71:10
produce price of raw p.	RICA 808:33
p. and consumption	MALT 643:41
p. something cheap	GILL 427:13
p. without working	INGR 512:48
what shall this land p.?	RANS 802:33
producer truck, a p. or a critic	LEMM 595:45
producers association of the p.	ENGE 378:90
produces never p. anything great	REYN 808:23
product artist p.…of his time	BETH 99:24
infinitesimal fraction of a p.	CARL 235:57
p. of a scoffer's pen	WORD 1100:80
p. of mental labour	MARX 660:20
p. of the untalented	CAPP 231:91
production development in p.	MARX 660:11
development of p.	MARX 661:27

production (*contd.*)
end and purpose of all p. — SMITH 945:86
labour-time…for its original p. — MARX 660:20
Laws of P. — MILL 674:57
noblest p. of human nature — ADDI 7:9
past heroes of p. — LOWE 617:15
p. of objective fact — MENC 669:77
p. of surplus-value — MARX 660:21
p. of the higher animals — DARW 306:84
simply in the p. — RUSK 831:95
society that will organize p. — ENGE 378:90
the means of p. — STRA 979:91
productivity increase p. — HEATH 466:51
national p. — WRIS 1102:20
products brings out the best in p. — SARN 843:97
do not choose our p. — FROMM 406:70
make good p. — STEV 970:31
p. of all the colonies — SITW 941:17
p. of editing — WALD 1048:45
profanation in the less, foul p. — SHAK 896:73
p. of our joys — DONNE 337:90
profane as all p. authors seem — DONNE 339:24
Coldly p. — CRAB 293:69
profaneness Avoid, P.; come not here — HERB 474:9
profanity speak English and p. — HOWE 497:96
through the vast p. — MILT 691:85
utter a p. to see how exciting it was — CHRI 261:69
profession adopt politics as a p. — HOWE 498:19
branches of a new p. — TROL 1028:89
choose a p. — PASC 758:71
Composing is not a p. — HONE 488:28
cowards by p. — DRYD 349:2
discharge of any p. — JOHN 529:71
doctor who…has mistaken his p. — SHAW 924:98
general scandal of my p. — BROW 194:63
hold up Adam's p. — SHAK 893:73
honourable p. — GREE 444:19
in any other p.…offensive — WAUGH 1057:93
Medicine is a noble p. — ROLL 821:25
only p. for which no — STEV 975:27
practice of his own p. — JOHN 522:31
p.…consists of bringing truths — HENZE 473:75
p. of book writing — STEI 966:61
P. of Play-poets…unlawfull — PRYN 794:11
put into a 'p.' — BETJ 100:43
rather than a p. — GRAV 440:26
short-lived p. on earth — ROGE 820:21
take the place of every p. — MARI 651:70
You have always a p. — AUST 52:68
professional being a p. writer — ROST 825:4
distinguishes… from the p. — LYTT 621:68
maws of the p. — KEYN 554:34
p. duty of the advertising agent — OGIL 736:3
p. players are soccer slaves — CHAR 253:92
professionals between expert p. — KEYN 554:34
Politicians…are p. — EICH 362:59
professions All p. are conspiracies — SHAW 924:88
go forth unto p. — KENN 550:55
In limited p. — SHAK 902:93
let in some of all p. — SHAK 908:51
Politics…whatever its p. — ADAMS 5:72
p. which are are full — THOR 1016:81
way of their own p. — JONS 536:19
professor called a p. emeritus — LEAC 589:45
mind to wide for a p. — MENC 669:64
non-Jewish p. — TILL 1020:64
P. Twist could not — NASH 720:57
Zarathustra, sometime regius p. — JOYCE 538:52
professors American p. — LEWIS 602:55
conscientious p. thereof — PAINE 750:45
Respectable P. of the Dismal Science — CARL 236:96
smelly gangrene of p. — MARI 651:68
profiles infinite number of p. — THOR 1016:72
two p. clapped together — ASQU 42:86

profit blend p. with delight — HORA 494:33
I despise p. — OLIV 738:29
In all labour there is p. — BIBLE 121:77
merchants…intent on p. — PIUS 772:79
my p. had I known — TENN 1003:20
my p. on't — SHAK 916:22
p. of capital rises — MARX 660:16
p. without individual responsibility — BIER 161:77
rate of p. — SMITH 945:80
refreshment and p. — COLU 278:63
such p. he of envy — SURR 982:42
Thieves out, p. in! — ANON 21:48
What p. hath a man — BIBLE 122:14
profits best of all monopoly p. — HICKS 480:95
civilization and p. — COOL 286:34
natural tendency of p. — RICA 808:33
status and p. of war — TREV 1026:53
profound French are not p. — BROO 193:45
p., evocative and universal — NUTT 732:46
p. loves the mask — NIET 728:85
turbid look and most p. — LAND 578:55
profundity misty p. — WHIT 1071:52
programme Labour …election p. — SNOW 951:79
p. of the world's peace — WILS 1086:54
terrorist's p. — JONAS 533:49
programming scrutinize the p. — MUMF 713:49
progress any measure of its p. — PERK 766:1
Congress makes no p. — LIGNE 604:92
conservatism and p. — TROL 1027:71
Conservatism…disavows P. — DISR 332:81
Conservative ideal of…p. — MADAN 638:54
dependent for p. — RUSS 832:21
Donald Trump is the price of p. — KRUG 570:5
encouraging the p. of science — JEFF 520:93
essential to mutual p. — WASH 1054:38
essential to the future p. of the race — CARN 236:6
great p. in the world — HALI 452:24
history of p. — MACA 623:10
history of p. — MACA 624:24
human beings will live and p. — DU 353:10
human p. — GARI 415:24
injurious to the p. of science — DARW 306:87
its p. cannot but be slow — JOHN 527:23
moral and social p. — MILL 674:58
party of p. or reform — MILL 675:64
present stage of human p. — HOOV 490:61
p. depends on the unreasonable — SHAW 922:56
p. has no definite…meaning — SART 843:5
P. is a comfortable disease — CUMM 300:92
p. … is always revolutionary — POPP 783:23
p. is utter delusion — MILL 678:26
P., man's distinctive mark — BROW 200:80
p. of human knowledge — FRAN 402:11
p. of society and wealth — RICA 808:33
p. through the world — LONG 612:17
promote social p. — UNIT 1036:45
same each time with p. — BENN 90:69
scientific and technical p. — JOHN 522:31
since Social P. began — KIPL 565:25
sing the p. — DONNE 337:82
skin of p. — SOYI 954:45
social p. — JOHN 522:31
speak…about making p. — POPP 784:26
swell a p. — ELIOT 367:52
thanking the God of P. — LEWIS 601:50
turtle…makes p. — ANON 29:39
War is a condition of p. — RENAN 806:1
When one hears of p. — SKEL 942:46
progression by gradual p. — ARIS 34:24
p. of exploded fallacies — RAND 801:21
Without contraries is no p. — BLAKE 166:71
progressive liberal and p. — TRIL 1026:58
p. who is prudent — JOHN 523:50
truly cumulative and p. — SART 843:5

prohibiting licensing and p. — MILT 685:62
prohibition Communism is like p. — ROGE 820:13
p. so divine — SHAK 916:7
project p. for…shopkeepers — SMITH 945:84
p. for extracting sun-beams — SWIFT 985:86
projected it's what's p. — PRICE 789:33
projections other figures…p. — ELIOT 373:84
pro-jobs cannot be p.-j. — TSON 1031:42
proletarians p. have nothing to lose — MARX 660:15
proletariat dicatorship of the p. — MARX 661:27
English p.…more bourgeois — ENGE 378:87
p. can take power — TROT 1029:8
the true p. — BLIX 169:33
prologue foolish thing…long p. — BIBLE 133:19
witty P. to a very dull play — CONG 280:3
prolonged War is being deliberately p. — SASS 845:21
prom libel on a Yale p. — PARK 754:2
Prometheus Fire which P. filch'd — BYRON 222:34
promiscuity emotional p. — MAIL 639:80
sexuality and p. — WYLIE 1104:50
promise against reason, against p. — DICK 327:73
appalling p. — AUDEN 48:81
black p. of untrammeled joy — HOLM 485:75
Eating the air on p. — SHAK 877:86
full of p. but of no performance — DICK 322:70
full of youthful p. — IRVI 513:62
gaudy p. of what life ought to be — COOKE 286:31
p. kept, And a child — NEME 722:4
p. made is a debt unpaid — SERV 859:55
p. none relies on — ROCH 817:66
p. of fair weather — DICK 323:70
p. of pneumatic bliss — ELIOT 367:64
p. of their early years — POWE 787:1
p. to build a bridge — KHRU 556:48
state of perpetual p. — BEEC 82:18
promised p. to do when you are sick — SIGI 938:70
seen the p. land — KING 558:86
promises Don't ask me for p. — SHAW 920:92
failed p. of American life — GILL 426:3
not a set of p. — KENN 550:61
not having received the p. — BIBLE 154:51
P. and pie-crust — SWIFT 986:16
p. to keep — FROST 407:86
Wealth…made up largely of p. — POUND 787:90
young man of p. — BALF 65:19
promissory one long p. note — BEEC 82:18
signing a p. note — KING 557:78
promontory See one p. — BURT 214:69
seems to me a sterile p. — SHAK 890:2
promote he will p. himself — DUGO 354:24
promotion p. of the human race — WEST 1068:88
sweat but for p. — SHAK 885:83
prompt I meant to be p. — DAY 310:40
pronounce frame to p. it right — BIBLE 109:16
p. it Vinchy — TWAIN 1032:58
proof absence of any other p. — NEWT 725:41
admirable p. of this — FERM 386:24
exist as living p. — THOM 1014:35
final p. of God's omnipotence — DEVR 318:93
flawless p. of the existence of God — EDDI 360:19
no need of formal p. — BOYD 182:46
p. that only men — STEI 967:65
p. through the night — KEY 554:24
The p. is in his plays — ONEI 740:58
tyrannous and rough in p. — SHAK 868:74
written for…narrative, not p. — QUIN 798:71
proofs purist who reads your p. — CHAN 250:37
prop Science…a p. — WORD 1096:24
you do take the p. — SHAK 873:97
propaganda all p. is lies — ORWE 743:21
engines of p. — BALD 64:9
full of p. — ACHE 3:50
in spite of its foreign p. — ORWE 743:20

propaganda (*contd.*)
piece of p. in favour — JOYCE 538:58
p. arm of the American Dream — HASK 460:56
p., rumor, suspicion — LIPP 606:32
strikes…not as a means of p. — ENGE 378:89
propagandist p.'s purpose — HUXL 508:92
propagandists cleverest p. extant — BUCH 202:25
propagation peace and p. — WALP 1051:91
Was all our p. — DONNE 337:95
propensities excite my amorous p. — JOHN 525:37
side of their natural p. — BURKE 208:47
propensity hereditary p. — EDGE 360:25
p. for being p. — AUST 52:61
property Abolition of private p. — MARX 660:13
any object of p. — BENT 92:16
bourgeois p. is…revolutionary — OROU 741:82
character, person, p. — LOVE 615:70
civilization…of p., of fences — EMER 377:62
common p. of the nation — TIMES 1021:71
consider himself as public p. — JEFF 520:95
destroys my p. — PAINE 750:43
every man reclaimed his own p. — BUTL 218:50
families from sinking their p. — MOOD 703:95
for our p. — PITT 771:72
Happiness…in taking their p. — GENG 418:78
knowledge as a collective p. — SHAP 919:78
landlords and persons of p. — MALT 643:41
life is… given… to none for p. — LUCR 619:36
magic of P. — YOUNG 1108:2
misapplied is a 'body's p. — MACD 627:75
neither persons nor p. will be safe — DOUG 342:74
on their p. — GALS 413:2
one-way p. of time — EDDI 360:17
preservation of p. — LOCKE 609:68
P. has its duties — DRUM 346:47
p. in his person — LOCKE 609:69
P. is theft — PROU 792:85
P. like incest — INNIS 512:53
p. of any political party — HOOV 490:66
p. of the rich — RUSK 831:93
rights of p. originate — MADI 638:55
sanctity of life and p. — SCHL 848:73
security of p. — PANK 752:79
Thieves respect p. — CHES 258:10
violent P. fordoes itself — SHAK 889:87
property-owning p.-o. democracy — SKEL 942:37
prophecies verification of…p. — TROL 1028:83
prophecy art united with p. — NISB 730:5
p., and religion, all in one — RUSK 831:8
p. is the most gratuitous — ELIOT 366:33
self-fulfilling p. is — MERT 672:24
though I have the gift of p. — BIBLE 150:62
trumpet of a p.! — SHEL 928:91
urn Of bitter p. — SHEL 932:65
verses and the p. — WALL 1050:74
prophesy hang out and p. — PALEY 751:64
P. upon these bones — BIBLE 129:43
who can but p.? — BIBLE 130:58
prophet banner of the P. — BROD 189:68
happen to a p. — HUXL 507:86
I am no p. — ELIOT 367:51
If there arise among you a p. — BIBLE 108:94
Juxtaposition his p. — CLOU 271:43
loathing Was p. to the rest — MIDD 674:49
Methinks I am a p. — SHAK 866:44
more than a p. — BIBLE 137:84
p. is not without honour — BIBLE 138:5
there is a p. in Israel — BIBLE 111:77
What-you-may-call-it is his p. — DICK 323:96
your p. the Nazarite — SHAK 874:18
prophetic like p. strain — MILT 683:11
O my p. soul! — SHAK 889:76
prophets Beware of false p. — BIBLE 135:60
destroy the law, or the p. — BIBLE 134:37

prophets (*contd.*)
films of one's country like the p. — ANDE 18:4
hang all the law and the p. — BIBLE 139:34
persecuted they the p. — BIBLE 133:34
so did their fathers to the false p. — BIBLE 142:82
spake by the P. — BOOK 174:20
prophilaxis wise course of p. — SILVA 938:77
propinquity P. had brought — YEATS 1107:94
self-congratulatory p. — GILL 426:4
proportion bills! That's out of p. — LARK 581:3
in equal p. to age — HEMI 471:47
in inverse p. to the sum — PARK 755:33
innate sense of p. — HONE 488:29
no p. kept — SHAK 868:71
sense of wholesome p. — POWYS 788:21
soul refines…in p. — MARI 652:78
strangeness in the p. — BACON 59:15
proportions distorted…p. — MILL 675:76
exact p. — HALES 451:23
Fashion…is a matter of p. — CHAN 251:57
Full of p., one limb to another — HERB 475:22
p. are easily determined — HEIN 467:74
p., everything has its share — MATI 663:73
proposal every new p. — STAMP 962:83
propose We p. it, we massage it — CUOMO 300:3
proposes Man p., but God disposes — KEMP 549:40
proposition no longer a tenable p. — STEI 967:67
p. that all men are created — LINC 605:4
p. that two times two — LICH 604:88
p. which it purports to express — AYER 53:79
p. which we can understand — RUSS 832:18
self-evident p. — MACA 622:91
thinks over that p. — KIER 556:57
propositions central p….are these — HUXL 508:98
p. would sound like — LICH 603:81
truth of P. — HOBB 482:35
proprietor hotel without a p. — MANS 647:3
propriety despaired, with more p. — WEBS 1060:41
p. of thoughts and words — DRYD 348:80
prosaic name of 'Smith' p. — CHES 258:95
proscription punished-by p. — CHES 257:80
prose condescend to p. — BYRON 222:37
connect the p. and the passion — FORS 398:36
dough-baked p. — CAREW 232:10
fancy p. style — NABO 717:97
for discourse and nearest p. — DRYD 350:41
Gertrude Stein's p. song — LEWIS 602:63
Good p. is like a window — ORWE 744:42
In p., the worst thing — ORWE 744:47
laws of p. writing — HEMI 471:36
love thee in p. — PRIOR 791:59
'monument of English p.' — ELIOT 370:21
most beautiful p. paragraph — BLOOM 170:38
never pin up my hair with p. — CONG 281:33
not poetry, but p. run mad — POPE 781:64
other harmony of p. — DRYD 352:77
Poetry is to p. — WAIN 1047:28
produce great p. — THOM 1012:96
P. books are the show dogs — GRAV 440:31
P. equals words in their best order — COLE 275:24
P. is when all the lines — BENT 93:20
p. of the realities — CUOMO 301:7
P. on certain occasions — LAND 578:64
p. takes the mould of the body — WOOLF 1093:82
shut me up in P. — DICK 323:2
speaking p. for forty years — MOLI 699:30
straight honest p. — HEMI 470:28
translate aphorisms into…p. — FRYE 408:23
unattempted yet in p. or rhyme — MILT 687:85
well written as p. — POUND 785:50
prosecution attention in the p. — WASH 1054:41
p. of any undertaking — JOHN 525:92
prospect dull p. of distant good — DRYD 351:54
hold out a p. for the nations — PITT 772:73

prospect (*contd.*)
noblest p. — JOHN 527:29
p. from the watershed — STARK 963:97
p. of a brighter day — WORD 1100:92
p. of another campaign — JOHN 523:44
p. of belief — SHAK 907:18
p. of reigning — JAY 519:76
p. of tackling an unsolved problem — SHIP 935:20
which…has the happier p. — PLATO 774:5
prospectors unoffending p. — DOUG 341:51
prospects few pleasanter p. — HAWT 461:74
gilded scenes and shining p. rise — ADDI 6:98
Wide and undetermined p. — ADDI 7:19
prosper keep it may p. — KIPL 561:52
p. that love thee — BIBLE 119:38
Treason doth never p. — HARI 457:17
prosperity Grit riches and p. — BROWN 194:62
jest's p. lies in the ear — SHAK 866:29
man to han ben in p. — CHAU 254:10
man who can stand p. — CARL 236:92
No, for p. — BERL 95:65
P. is not without many fears — BACON 56:51
P. is only an instrument — COOL 286:31
P. is the blessing — BACON 56:50
p. of the wicked — BIBLE 117:89
P. stands cursed — MILT 693:19
p. will leak through — BRYAN 201:14
rise with p. — SMITH 945:80
state of p. — MACM 635:6
virtue of p. — BACON 56:49
Without publicity…no p. — ZELD 1109:17
prostitute p. all their powers! — FORS 398:48
prostituted most p. being — BAUD 78:44
prostitutes p. if they do — MILL 679:61
small nations like p. — KUBR 570:12
thoughts are my p. — DIDE 330:34
prostitution marriage and p. — DWOR 358:85
Necessity never makes p. — WOLL 1091:42
P. Selling one's body — MACK 632:54
rent it (p.) — DWOR 357:83
protagonists lost…even to the p. — MAIL 639:73
protect only thought is to p. — SUN 982:36
protection it is not even a p. — STEV 973:81
Journalists…require some p. — BLACK 164:46
life of kind p. — STOWE 978:84
receives the p. of society — MILL 675:65
protections p. against temptation — TWAIN 1034:9
protein p. of…imagination — HUGH 499:27
proteins not getting the right p. — CART 243:12
protest First I p. — DOUG 341:53
men p. and disapprove — CATU 245:59
strongest p. against selfishness — GOOD 435:55
protestant armed P. Ulsterman — REDM 804:75
attacked…P. church — NIEM 727:68
between P. and Papist — STRA 979:1
care at one time for the p. interest — BRIG 188:48
free p. assemblies — BAIL 62:72
head of the P. interest — WILL 1080:47
P.…can only go to his solicitor — DISR 333:11
P. form of art — ORWE 743:13
P. religion…like a gentlemen's club — WARN 1053:24
P. whore — GWYN 449:97
Protestantism P.…is…dissent — BURKE 206:8
Protestants P. can be expected — WILS 1084:12
rouse the P. in France — LESL 598:94
White P. who live in the center — MAIL 639:69
protestations P. of impartiality — COBB 271:53
protests creative p. to degenerate — KING 557:80
The lady p. too much — SHAK 891:19
Proteus P. rising from the sea — WORD 1099:73
protocoligorically P. correct — SHER 934:15
protocols p. are very good things — PALM 752:68
protons p. in the universe — EDDI 360:20
prototypes Spanish….our p. — ECHE 359:13

protracted life p. is p. woe JOHN 525:83
p. my work JOHN 526:6
proud all the p. BIBLE 131:72
better than the p. in spirit BIBLE 123:28
but he's vengeance p. SHAK 911:7
Death be not p. DONNE 338:4
He that is p. SHAK 895:45
how little are the p. GRAY 441:57
how you use p. words SAND 841:64
I have no p. looks BOOK 177:92
instruct my sorrows to be p. SHAK 872:63
make death p. SHAK 906:97
man…a p. and yet a wretched thing DAVI 307:9
man, p. man SHAK 896:72
man…too p. to fight WILS 1086:47
poor are to be p.! SHAK 895:23
p. an' he's great NAIR 717:19
p. and disdainful THUR 1019:26
P., art thou met? MILT 691:77
p. conceited ignorant people ANON 24:6
p. foot of a conqueror SHAK 872:75
p. of one another CONG 282:44
p. of the position of the bungalow WILS 1084:13
p. of your contempt SHAW 921:23
p., revengeful, ambitious SHAK 891:25
p. that I am an Australian FRAN 402:16
p. to tell their sons ARLO 34:37
remember how p. you were YEATS 1104:55
so p., so witty, and so wise ROCH 816:51
too p. for a wit GOLD 433:28
too p. to importune GRAY 443:94
very p. and great STEV 975:35
Why were they p.? KEATS 546:81
with p. people SURR 983:46
Yes, I am p. POPE 782:89
proud-pied p.-p. April SHAK 915:83
Proust P. of pastimes FOWL 400:70
read P., Faulkner, Joyce VARG 1040:7
prove determined to p. WHITE 1070:45
P. all things BIBLE 153:26
p. God statistically GALL 413:99
p. him with hard questions BIBLE 111:57
p. one's self a fool HAWT 461:78
p. the weeping philosopher SHAK 874:15
wakening and uprising p. KEBLE 548:23
proved O, that it could be p. SHAK 875:35
That which was to be p. EUCL 380:20
Provence In P. called KEATS 547:96
Than you found it in P.? WILL 1082:87
proverb according to her own p. SCOTT 856:10
have a p. down here SAKI 838:15
Israel shall be a p. and a byword BIBLE 111:56
Italian p. succinctly puts it HUXL 507:85
Know that famous p.? ROTH 826:13
Spanish p. says JOHN 530:96
proverbs breaker of p. SHAK 875:41
like p., they occur in pairs SIMON 939:80
p. are the palm-oil ACHE 2:18
providence assert Eternal P. MILT 687:86
Behind a frowning p. COWP 292:29
fathom the inscrutable workings of P. BIRK 163:21
go the way that P. HITL 482:30
popular one is P. TWAIN 1034:13
P. Out of our evil MILT 687:96
P. their guide MILT 693:29
P. would have cast my lot DICK 326:60
purposes of P. UPDI 1036:56
Temperst thy p. MILT 694:48
whatever Divine P. permitted DANA 304:55
provident watchful, p., fatigued MUNRO 714:60
Women…are p. instead BOGAN 171:58
provider bad husband and ill p. EMER 377:66
good p. for a needy man HESI 479:83
providers men into their chief p. MILLS 679:64

province all knowledge…my p. BACON 54:1
p. of a despicable electorate PITT 771:63
provinces lady from the p. GILB 425:85
obeyed in their several p. MARL 654:12
princess among the p. BIBLE 128:29
p. must not be bartered WILS 1086:55
p. of the truth BAUD 77:32
provincialism taken in…p. HUXL 506:47
proving nothing worthy p. TENN 1005:64
provision p. for…young women AUST 51:39
provisions p. for discourse AUST 50:31
provocation as in the p. BIBLE 117:7
what p. I have had? POPE 782:88
prow round about the p. she wrote TENN 994:46
their head the p. DRYD 346:54
prowess Dutch p. ROCH 816:48
prowl spirits…began to p. around ADAMS 5:70
prudence age of p. ELIOT 369:96
effect of p. on rascality SHAW 922:54
I hate to see p. clinging SHER 933:96
p. in the conduct SMITH 945:88
Prudence P. dwells in dark abodes WORD 1100:91
prudent progressive who is p. JOHN 523:50
p. to gain the whole world SHAW 925:12
prudes p. for proctors TENN 996:91
women p. if they don't MILL 679:61
pruning-hooks spears into p.-h. BIBLE 124:57
p.-h. into spears BIBLE 130:56
Prussia military domination of P. ASQU 42:77
national industry of P. MIRA 695:68
P. was hatched from NAPO 718:36
psalm practising the hundredth p. BYRON 224:52
rolled the p. TENN 999:41
the echo of a p. PAST 759:84
psalmist Death, as the P. saith SHAK 877:96
psalms melody of the p. HOOK 490:56
shew ourselves glad with p. BOOK 177:87
psyche human p. and butterfat WAXM 1058:12
psyches p.…tied to their epididymis STEP 968:81
psychiatrist man who goes to a p. GOLD 434:37
p. is a man who goes STOC 977:70
psychiatrists P. classify a person SZASZ 989:68
psychiatry branch of p. ASLET 42:75
psychic human p. equilibrium MAMET 644:55
use p. bullets MAIL 639:76
psychoanalysis father of p. GREER 445:39
In p. nothing is true ADOR 9:50
modern myth of p. THOM 1009:48
pay for their own p. EPHR 379:96
P. is a permanent fad DEVR 318:94
what sex and p. are HUGH 500:30
psychoanalytic p. therapy FREUD 404:41
psychologists p.…in the study MERT 672:26
psychology department of p. and sociology AYER 53:81
no use for p. SING 940:95
P. has a long past EBBI 359:8
The word 'p.' SARR 843:2
When my daughter needs p. ANON 27:59
psychosis The Irish…have a p. BEHAN 84:62
psychotic castles…a p. lives in them ANON 26:44
p. if he makes others SZASZ 989:68
Ptolemaic Copernican, not P. PHIL 768:19
pub No pewter and no p. RANS 802:38
puberty American at p. WAUGH 1057:97
pubic P. hair…substitute for wit PRIE 790:45
public as if I were a p. meeting VICT 1043:54
because the p. praised BROW 196:11
British p. MACA 622:96
conspiracy against the p. SMITH 945:79
consult the p. good SWIFT 985:87
contented section of the p. HUGO 502:88
corpse of the p. credit WEBS 1059:23
decent chap never lets his p. down FLYNN 395:80

public (*contd.*)
dresses for p. appearances ONAS 739:39
falsehoods to deceive the p. STEF 965:25
field of p. education WARR 1053:27
give lessons to the p. DIDE 329:32
gulls amongst the p. KEYN 554:34
I and the p. know AUDEN 47:75
inflict myself on the p. MORL 708:75
keeping the p. informed PULI 795:20
liars in p. places POUND 786:64
loudest complainers for the p. BURKE 206:98
love in p. DRYD 348:93
make ourselves p. NASHE 720:75
making the private world p. GINS 428:34
man assumes a p. trust JEFF 520:95
married and endowed the p. BACON 57:56
mass of p. wrongs KYD 571:26
measure of p. support TIMES 1020:70
minds of the general p. BALA 63:81
mislead the p. ASQU 42:79
more than a p. calamity SOUT 954:41
naked p. person…ridiculous SART 844:6
paint in the p.'s face RUSK 831:9
patience of the general p. KRUG 570:4
Policemen…protectors of the p. MAMET 643:45
private life…by a wider p. life ELIOT 366:25
progressive causes in the p. eye SIMP 939:88
p. consensus that Donald Trump KRUG 570:5
p. detriment of the latter LYTT 621:68
p. dislikes one of my…covers ROCK 818:80
p. …divided into two parts RAY 803:46
p. does not always know DIDE 329:31
p. doesn't give a damn BEEC 82:16
p. doesn't want new music HONE 488:30
p. faces in private places AUDEN 46:43
p. falls for this HAIL 451:14
p. good Private respects MILT 695:49
p. health measures SUTH 983:49
p. interest may LIPP 607:38
p. is an old woman CARL 235:60
p. man lays his hand BEER 83:27
P. Mercury should have my Veto LEST 599:13
p. needs permit MORE 707:52
p. of the moment LUCAS 618:32
p. only gets to hear STEIN 966:50
p. subsidy of intelligence QUINE 797:67
p. …thinks there may be something in it CANN 230:68
p., though dull SWIN 988:51
reality…over p. relations FEYN 387:36
roads and p. works MALT 643:41
servants of the p. GOWE 437:81
sound of p. scorn MILT 693:17
speaks to you…of p. affairs TOCQ 1021:80
spotlight of p. life FOST 399:63
strike against p. safety COOL 286:35
that gives it to the p. VALE 1038:85
that incredible thing, a p. CRAW 296:29
trade for the p. good SMITH 945:81
tribunal of p. opinion TOCQ 1021:77
true to the p. BERK 95:56
vexes p. men TENN 996:88
Well, British P. BROW 200:85
whatever the…p. allow SHAW 921:33
Whatever they may be in p. life FREN 404:39
write for yourself and have no p. CONN 282:55
public-address station p.-a. system JAMES 516:8
public-school English p.-s. WAUGH 1056:75
p.-s. system all over WAUGH 1056:62
publican How like a fawning p. SHAK 874:13
p., standing afar off, would not lift BIBLE 144:11
publicists use to backlash p. FALU 382:57
publicity history of p. LEAV 591:74
oxygen of p. THAT 1008:19

publicity (*contd.*)
price of justice is eternal p.   BENN 91:97
p. agent of big business   ORWE 742:88
P. is the very soul of justice   BENT 93:18
With p. comes humiliation   JANO 518:55
Without p....no prosperity   ZELD 1109:17
publicly Sometimes you move p.   BAKER 63:81
publish ask a superior to p.   HOPK 492:95
I'll p., right or wrong   BYRON 218:59
P. and be damned.   WELL 1064:22
p. what you actually did   FEYN 387:33
published never have been p.   MACL 634:76
publisher Barabbas was a p.   CAMP 227:33
had a p.   UNSE 1036:46
p. to take writers seriously   POWE 788:10
Xerox makes everybody a p.   MACL 635:2
publishers fear...become p.   CONN 283:59
P. can get their minds   LECA 592:98
publishing important...in p.   JOVA 537:38
p. of his ideas   KAZIN 543:29
pubs served in all the p. in Dublin   DONL 336:61
Puddin-race Chieftain o' the P.-r.!   BURNS 210:84
pudding cold, black suet-p.   LEWIS 602:63
p. against empty praise   POPE 782:92
puddle p. wonderful   CUMM 299:77
superficial as a p. in the sunlight   LEAC 588:38
puddling p. in a tub continually   PERTH 767:3
pudenda vile members...called 'p.'   ABEL 1:3
puff friends all united to p.   SWIN 988:51
pipe with solemn interposing p.   COWP 292:32
the p. oblique, or p. by implication   SHER 934:5
puff-paste fantastical p.-p.   WEBS 1061:65
puffed get one's self p.   TROL 1028:89
puffing P. is of various sorts   SHER 934:5
puffs p. from the hookah-mouth   KIPL 561:39
Pugh Mr P. minces among bad vats   THOM 1011:89
pull tug, p. and plop   OBRI 734:71
pulp become so much p.   CAMP 226:8
If P. Fiction had been set   GRANT 438:4
pulpit If the President has a bully p.   REAG 803:57
Inquisition fulminating from the p.   WELD 1062:92
pulsations translate p. into images   RICH 809:47
pulse feeling a woman's p.   STER 970:26
his p. failing   DRAY 345:40
lost p. of feeling   ARNO 36:70
p. of life?   SHAK 872:73
p. of the machine   WORD 1099:63
scene before him beat like a p.   AMIS 16:71
pulse-less p. lot...England   LAWR 585:63
pulses feeling of p. the physic of love   CLEV 269:10
pumice Beside a p. isle   SHEL 928:88
polished with dry p.?   CATU 245:58
pumpkin like the rich P. pie   WHIT 1074:2
pun p. is Pierian   UNTE 1036:47
so vile a p.   DENN 316:63
through a pipe and exhaled in a p.   LAMB 577:44
punctual p. rape of every...day   WILB 1075:19
punctuality Painting and P.   GAIN 411:69
P. is the politeness   LOUI 614:52
P. is the vice   PATR 761:14
P....virtue of the bored   WAUGH 1057:99
punctuation dropped p. marks   WEST 1068:91
mix...the sun with p.   BRAU 186:19
Punic With P. faith   SALL 839:39
punish impulse to p. is powerful   NIET 728:81
P. a body   DRYD 349:14
p. everyone who would deserve it   ELIOT 365:15
punished p. not for what they do   SZASZ 989:67
punishment All p. is mischief   BENT 92:14
Death is...degrading p.   BREN 187:34
fees are sufficient p.   BAIL 62:68
marked out for p.   BUCH 202:28
p. fit the crime   GILB 425:90
p. is greater than I can bear   BIBLE 104:6

punishment (*contd.*)
seek to convert by p.   MILL 678:40
servitude...the p. of his guilt   CURR 301:16
Some p. seems preparing   FRAN 402:8
take a lot of p. to write   HEMI 470:13
punishments charged with p.   HENL 472:58
no rewards nor p.   INGE 511:43
Severe and terrible p.   MORE 706:45
punk Well do you p.?   EAST 359:5
punt more fun to p.   SAYE 846:48
slow p. swings round   ARNO 37:88
punters p. don't want to sleep   CURT 302:24
pupil p. is too young   RYLE 834:54
pupils P. are crème de la crème   SPARK 955:51
p. might demonstrate   GIBB 421:23
teacher who does not equip his p.   PETE 767:8
puppets box and the p.   THAC 1006:90
p....with their slips of paper   WHITE 1070:28
puppies drowned a blind bitch's p.   SHAK 878:22
puppy p.'s insolent yelp   ANON 23:82
purchase More in the cunning p.   JONS 534:75
water...will p. scarce any thing   SMITH 946:94
purchased see 'tis p. by weight   SHAK 872:82
purchasers to encourage p.   SWIFT 984:79
pure Be warm, but p.   BYRON 219:61
blank virtue, not a p.   MILT 685:65
Blessed are the p. in heart   BIBLE 133:34
ever to have p. knowledge   PLATO 774:15
in gudis be p.   DUNB 355:37
know nothing, p. and simple   WILL 1083:89
Live p., speak true   TENN 1004:54
meant to be disinterested, p.   SELF 857:37
more p. than his maker?   BIBLE 112:1
Nothing but holy, p., and clear   HERB 474:9
O p. of heart   COLE 274:7
only you are p.   VALL 1039:91
prince whose intentions were p.   JOSE 537:34
p. air and water   REES 805:92
p. as the driven slush   BANK 70:90
p. science can flourish   STEA 963:2
souls Of the p. in heart   RANS 802:37
temples th'upright heart and p.   MILT 687:86
truth is rarely p.   WILDE 1077:80
Unto the p. all things are p.   BIBLE 154:43
whatsoever things are p.   BIBLE 153:15
zipless fuck is absolutely p.   JONG 533:63
purest p. and most thoughtful   RUSK 830:80
purgation p. of such emotions   ARIS 34:29
purgatory England...p. of all men   FLOR 394:79
no other p. but a woman   BEAU 80:72
those that deny p.   WEBS 1060:52
purge Every book is like a p.   DU 354:32
P. me with hyssop   BIBLE 116:77
purify p. the dialect of the tribe   ELIOT 372:73
purists Down with p.!   BAND 69:87
puritan describe as 'P. decadence'   SPEN 956:65
honesty be no p.   SHAK 901:72
P. hated bear-baiting   MACA 624:27
P. of the middle class   NEME 722:5
To the P. all things are impure   LAWR 587:7
puritanism not P. but February   KRUT 570:9
P. names a behaviour   SPEN 956:88
P. The haunting fear   MENC 669:75
purity preserve unblemished p.   ABEL 1:3
P. of race does not exist   FISH 389:80
purling p. stream   ADDI 6:99
purple Before milk-white; now, p.   SHAK 870:36
pink and p. columbine   SPEN 957:93
P. haze is in my brain   HEND 472:55
p. wardrobe of thy side   CRAS 296:20
So cool a p.   KEATS 545:60
with reverend p.   JONS 534:77
purpose art achieves a p.   CONS 286:22
As if all this had some p.   SARD 843:94

purpose (*contd.*)
before this p. cool   SHAK 909:69
called according to his p.   BIBLE 149:29
can cite Scripture for his p.   SHAK 874:21
devoted to a nobler p.   CURZ 302:27
end and p. of all production   SMITH 945:86
except for a noble p.   HERB 474:4
God, for some strong p.   SHAK 868:68
human autonomy, human p.   MUMF 713:49
impulse without p.   BIER 162:97
know how to live to p.   MONT 702:74
mind charged with an eager p.   ELIOT 365:18
Nature...nothing without some p.   ARIS 34:32
novels written with a p.   FORD 396:6
old p. done up in aspic   LAWR 585:76
one increasing p. runs   TENN 996:79
power with our p.   KENN 552:89
p. and determination   KENN 551:82
p. breaks...when it is fulfilled   ELIOT 372:69
p. of art   GOULD 436:75
p. so ravenous   LAWR 587:14
p. was less firm   MOOD 703:94
real p. of life   SCHO 849:95
set p. and...exhausted frame   DOYLE 344:14
speak plain and to the p.   SHAK 879:47
system which has no p.   FROMM 406:70
unconquerable p. shall be realized   LAMB 576:19
without any practical p.   PLAN 772:83
yoke-devils sworn to either's p.   SHAK 880:76
purposes Can execute their airy p.   MILT 687:2
p. to which it is instrumental   MILL 675:74
put it to useful p.   ACHE 3:42
riddles of...the p. of God   FRYE 408:24
purring p. of contented cats   GRAH 438:92
purse as thy p. can buy   SHAK 888:69
carrying a very heavy p.   ASCH 41:52
consult your P.   FRAN 402:5
consumption of the p.   SHAK 877:85
no money in your p.   SHAK 885:84
nothing in thy p.   BIBLE 132:4
p. is the mirror   QUIN 797:65
silk p. out of your wife's   MORT 710:99
steals my p. steals trash   SHAK 899:31
purses Light gains make heavy p.   BACON 59:26
pursue fight them, and p. them   JOAN 522:27
pursued only the p., the pursuing   FITZ 390:2
want to be p. by it   KAFKA 540:85
you who are p.   SHAW 921:30
pursuer you are the p.   SHAW 921:30
pursuit every action and p.   ARIS 34:25
p. of happiness   WARR 1053:28
p. of pleasure   PROU 793:4
p. of sanity   BELL 88:23
p. of truth   DESC 317:77
p. ...without any practical purpose   PLAN 772:83
spare no p.   DICK 326:54
What mad p.?   KEATS 547:7
pursuits dress according to...your p.   DISR 334:26
engaged in congenial p.   MOOD 703:94
pursy fatness of these p. times   SHAK 892:58
push fear...the p. into the canal   ELIOT 370:35
p. may send him over it   SITW 941:27
total p. and pressure   JAMES 517:46
pussy Owl and the P.-Cat   LEAR 590:58
persian p. from over the sea   MARQ 656:41
P. said to the Owl   LEAR 590:59
putrefaction preserve it from p.   JOHN 532:30
puzzle Don't p. me   STER 970:13
p. all the wise   DRYD 349:11
puzzling But what's p. you   JAGG 515:96
pygmies like retarded p.   PEAR 762:33
Of all the p.   BOOT 178:7
p....content to have our paper   MELV 668:48
pyjamas shot an elephant in my p.   MARX 659:96

pylons P. like pillars — SPEN 956:*80*
Pym Mr. P. used to sit — RUSH 829:*71*
pyramid society has resembled a p. — NAPO 719:*37*
  stary-pointing p.? — MILT 681:*94*
  unquestionable, like a p. — ORWE 743:*11*
pyramids p. of sweetmeats — DRYD 352:*82*
  summit of these p. — NAPO 718:*24*
Pyramus Death of P. and Thisbe — SHAK 870:*29*
  Most radiant P. — SHAK 871:*43*
  scene of young P. — SHAK 871:*54*
Pyrenees tease in the High P. — BELL 87:*17*
Pythagoras never…since P.' time — SHAK 886:*3*
  P.' metempsychosis — MARL 654:*22*
python shoes are made of p. — MACN 637:*38*

quack potent q., long versed — CRAB 293:*75*
quad always about in the Q. — ANON 25:*35*
  no-one about in the Q. — KNOX 567:*61*
quadrille q. in a sentry box — JAMES 516:*25*
quaffing q., and unthinking — DRYD 352:*95*
quails we long for q. — DRYD 350:*39*
quaint Q. 50 years after — LAVER 584:*56*
Quaker But I knaw'd a Q. feller — TENN 1004:*50*
quaking eat thy bread with q. — BIBLE 129:*37*
qualifications only q. I…respect — JAMES 516:*30*
qualities a man's natural q. — SHER 933:*98*
  combination of q. — DICK 327:*82*
  endued with such q. — ELIZ 373:*86*
  herbs…and their true q. — SHAK 869:*95*
  man with all his noble q. — DARW 306:*89*
  one of their godlike q. — MENC 670:*83*
  q. essential for the artist — DIDE 330:*39*
  q. of a great King — RICH 810:*66*
  q.…of the leader — BEAV 80:*80*
  q. which he does not possess — JOHN 525:*91*
  two q. in the world — SHAW 923:*75*
quality can't fake q. — BURR 213:*56*
  certain q. of magnanimity — STOWE 978:*83*
  Courage is a moral q. — MORAN 706:*41*
  degree and q. of trust — SHAP 919:*78*
  highest q. to your moments — PATER 759:*95*
  his honour and q. taken — BLUN 170:*47*
  historian must have a third q. — FORS 398:*49*
  male q. — HOPK 492:*10*
  q. of a smile — SAIN 836:*86*
  q. of his despair — CONN 283:*79*
  q. of mercy is not strained — SHAK 873:*92*
  q. of things made…by the human — CATH 244:*46*
  q. which we assert — MOORE 704:*9*
  Rage is only q. — BRES 187:*37*
  salty q. of human nature — ARLO 35:*38*
  so airy and light a q. — SHAK 890:*1*
  some good q. to recommend — STRA 979:*97*
  some other means of reckoning q. — CARD 232:*4*
  trespass on Q. Street — LASKY 583:*33*
  true fixed and resting q. — SHAK 883:*38*
  unbecoming of a man of q. — CONG 280:*6*
  with the q. — TWAIN 1032:*78*
Quangle Q.-Wangle Quee — LEAR 590:*65*
quantitative triumph of q. method — BELL 88:*21*
quantities Q. defined in terms — MYRD 716:*92*
quantity prodigious q. of mind — TWAIN 1032:*57*
  q. of delicate…flesh — FIEL 388:*51*
  reasoning concerning q. — HUME 504:*10*
  treasure…so trivial in q. — BRON 190:*88*
Quarles Mr Q. …susceptible — HUXL 506:*59*
  Q. is saved by beauties — POPE 782:*96*
quarrel entrance to a q. — SHAK 888:*64*
  hath his q. just — SHAK 861:*6*
  I won't q. with my Bread — SWIFT 986:*11*
  love a q. — ETHE 380:*15*
  lover's q. with the world — FROST 407:*97*
  no man hath any q. — SHAK 895:*34*

quarrel (*contd.*)
  only one to make a q. — INGE 511:*35*
  q. for a lady — HALI 452:*32*
  q. in a far away country — CHAM 249:*17*
  q. with society — TRIL 1027:*61*
  sudden, and quick in q. — SHAK 885:*92*
  The more I love…I q. — MARG 650:*52*
  the q. is a very pretty q. — SHER 933:*86*
  we q. in print — SHAK 887:*35*
quarreling q. about…going — FAUL 384:*89*
quarreller He's a great q. — SHAK 893:*95*
quarrels head is as full of q. — SHAK 869:*3*
  Litigous men, which q. move — DONNE 337:*80*
  petty q. — WILL 1080:*46*
  q., talk, and tailors — SHAK 917:*46*
  sometimes sweet to have our q. — BYRON 222:*33*
  We have French q. — SHAK 881:*93*
quarry Fortune on his damnèd q. — SHAK 906:*11*
  just a q. of paving stones — KING 559:*6*
  marked down q. — SHAW 921:*30*
quarter fore or hind Q. — SWIFT 985:*99*
  only for the remaining q. — NAPO 718:*27*
quartos perverted by q. — MACA 622:*88*
  q. their well-ordered ranks maintain — CRAB 293:*67*
quay meets her on the q. — STRO 980:*6*
quean flaunting extravagant q. — SHER 933:*97*
Quebec independent Q. — DESC 318:*85*
  see the surrender of Q. — MONT 702:*76*
  written those lines than take Q. — WOLFE 1090:*14*
  Vive le Q.! — DE 313:*4*
queen ambassador that beds a q. — CLEV 269:*13*
  be a q. for life — POPE 782:*76*
  dropp'd a tear in the Q.'s ear — BLAKE 168:*15*
  duty to the Q. — MARL 652:*81*
  Elizabeth, our noble q. — ANON 23:*90*
  every lass a q. — KING 558:*94*
  flame-sceptred Irish q. — HYDE 509:*14*
  fought for Q. and Faith — TENN 1005:*60*
  gliding like a q. — SPEN 956:*79*
  'God save the Q.' — WHIT 1072:*71*
  grace a summer q. — SCOTT 854:*67*
  Great Q. in her regalia — GAY 416:*46*
  home life of our own dear Q. — ANON 25:*23*
  I am your anointed q. — ELIZ 373:*90*
  I have been to the Q. — GLAD 429:*56*
  if the Q. were a man — VICT 1043:*51*
  Jewish Q. of Egypt — TAYL 992:*15*
  laughing q. — HUNT 504:*22*
  made in the days of Q. Bess — SWIFT 986:*9*
  moment of the Q.'s crowning — DIMB 331:*59*
  No scandal about Q.Elizabeth — SHER 934:*8*
  Ocean's child, and then his q. — SHEL 927:*71*
  q., an elf most fair — LAYA 588:*22*
  q. had four Maries — BALL 67:*46*
  q. in bondage — SHAK 861:*96*
  q. of curds and cream — SHAK 912:*32*
  Q. of Hearts — CARR 239:*42*
  q. of the south — BIBLE 137:*94*
  q. of the truth — BAUD 77:*32*
  Q. rose of the rosebud — TENN 1001:*87*
  Q. to get away with a hat — LOOS 613:*30*
  rather than q. and married! — ELIZ 373:*85*
  ruler of the Q.'s Navee — GILB 423:*58*
  Solomon gave to the q. of Sheba — BIBLE 112:*88*
  sung 'God save the Q.' — KIPL 562:*67*
  To toast The Q. — HEAN 465:*38*
  too mean to be your q. — SHAK 862:*26*
  Two-wheeled gypsy q. — DYLAN 358:*95*
  was the Q.'s luve — BALL -101:*32*
  would not be a q. — SHAK 917:*51*
queenly being Q. in her own room — WHAR 1068:*98*
queens all the beautiful Q. — DONNE 339:*27*
  all you acts are q. — SHAK 912:*31*
  Q. have died young — NASHE 721:*83*

Queensland gone to Q. droving — PATE 760:*97*
queer all the world is q. — OWEN 747:*6*
  begin to cut up q. — MOODY 704:*99*
  q. shoulder — GINS 428:*28*
  Scotland q. country — BORR 180:*26*
  Technology…is a q. thing — SNOW 951:*75*
  The only q. people…don't love — BROWN 194:*58*
  We're here, We're q. — ANON 29:*31*
queerer q. than we suppose — HALD 451:*17*
quench q. the fire of love — SHAK 860:*81*
  Q. my great love — GILB 424:*78*
quenched What hath q. them — SHAK 908:*42*
quest bless the q. — CRANE 294:*98*
  persistent and…critical q. for truth — POPP 784:*24*
  q. of the Sankgreall — MALO 642:*31*
  Religion…hopeless q. — WHIT 1071:*55*
  winding q. — VAUG 1041:*21*
question almost be a q. — TROL 1027:*74*
  approaches every q. — STEV 973:*84*
  Ask an impertinent q. — BRON 190:*84*
  ask the hard q. — AUDEN 46:*45*
  ask themselves the q. constantly — FANON 382:*61*
  ask yourself a q. — EAST 359:*5*
  avoid the q. of the Presidency — DICK 322:*67*
  consideration of any q. — TROL 1028:*88*
  contempt of q. her hand — SHAK 894:*17*
  difficult q. — GRAV 440:*39*
  first q. is What's your business? — BERE 94:*36*
  first q. must be — SPAR 955:*60*
  Great Q. Of…Life — ADAMS 5:*66*
  interrupt…with such a silly q.? — STER 968:*89*
  Irish q. — FRAS 403:*19*
  Irish secretly changed the q. — SELL 858:*39*
  mere asking of a q. — FORS 398:*42*
  no q. of it being grey — TRAV 1025:*36*
  not…consulted on the q. — DICK 327:*83*
  other stock q. — STRA 979:*98*
  Others abide our q. — ARNO 36:*60*
  philosopher's treatment of a q. — WITT 1088:*78*
  political q. is…a painful sight — LODGE 610:*84*
  q.…in…parents' minds — SCHU 851:*20*
  q. is absurd — AUDEN 47:*65*
  Q. not, but live — GORD 435:*61*
  q. that he frames — FROST 406:*79*
  q. whether…worth seeing — WALP 1051:*80*
  right answer to the wrong q. — CHRI 262:*77*
  right q. to ask — RUSK 830:*75*
  silent q.—'Is this all?' — FRIE 405:*49*
  still the q. of what — JENK 520:*99*
  style is not a q. of technique — PROU 793:*8*
  That is the Irish Q. — DISR 332:*87*
  That man may q.? — SHAK 907:*16*
  thinking about any significant q. — BELL 88:*27*
  though I q. others — SOCR 951:*87*
  up to the q. of bread — LEWIS 601:*49*
  what is the q.? — STEIN 966:*47*
  Who—or what—put the q. — HAMM 453:*46*
  will ever ask a new q. — HOPP 493:*16*
  without having asked any clear q. — CAMUS 229:*57*
question-mark gigantic q.-m. — AGAWA 10:*67*
questioning sweetly q. — HERB 475:*17*
questionings Those obstinate q. — WORD 1098:*53*
questions advice…on all q. — PANG 752:*76*
  all q. are open — BELL 86:*85*
  answer so many q. — RUSS 832:*15*
  answer to all the q. of men — YOUR 1108:*70*
  answers ask the right q. — LEVI 600:*32*
  answers to economic q. — ROBI 815:*35*
  answers to its q. — RUSS 832:*17*
  ask me the most ridiculous q. — EVANS 381:*38*
  bring out crucial q. — BONH 173:*86*
  ever so many q. — KIPL 563:*81*
  firm answers to q. — KUHN 570:*14*
  great q. of our day — BISM 164:*38*

questions (*contd.*)
little q. from women — ROTH 826:9
men…weren't even one of the q. — BARN 72:34
prove him with hard q. — BIBLE 111:57
q. about the great matters — ARIS 34:24
q. and reflections on life — HERN 476:44
q., not answers — LECA 592:95
q. of contemporary life — JORD 536:28
q. that deeply concern us — PAGE 749:33
q. that we do not know — MACL 634:75
q. the distempered part — ELIOT 371:51
q. which some newspaper editors — CHOP 261:63
settler of all great q. — DISR 333:20
substituting unimportant q. — BOUL 181:43
successive answers to q. — PAST 759:86
Them that asks no q. — KIPL 564:2
three most important q. — BRAH 185:6
quick judge the q. and the dead — BOOK 173:94
q. in wit — ASCH 41:52
sudden, and q. in quarrel — SHAK 885:92
words are q. and vain — SHEL 930:15
quickening q. of the heart — AUDEN 46:48
quickly play a thing q. — MOZA 711:18
quickness sickness…cured by q. — CAMP 228:40
quicksilver q. the scales slip — MUIR 712:37
quiddities in thy quips and thy q.? — SHAK 875:37
quiet All Q. on the Western Front — REMA 806:99
choose one's moment and keep q. — BECK 81:4
create and keep q. — FLAU 392:41
Fie upon this q. life! — SHAK 876:53
q. life — HICKS 480:95
q. moments in q. places — GRIS 447:68
q. of morning — DUNC 355:46
scallop-shell of q. — RALE 800:13
still and q. conscience — SHAK 918:24
Study to be q. — BIBLE 153:24
where the world is q. — SWIN 987:38
quiet-coloured q.-c. end of evening — BROW 198:43
quietest q. places Under the sun — HOUS 495:60
quietness in q. and in confidence — BIBLE 126:79
possess ourselves in…much q. — WALT 1052:10
unravished bride of q. — KEATS 547:6
quill q. from a porcupine — MOORE 705:31
sucks its substance…through a q. — LAMB 576:29
With a goose q. — ARET 33:17
quills q. upon a fretful porcupine — SHAK 889:74
quilt America is more like a q. — JACK 514:87
never folded my own q. — PU 794:1
quince mince, and slices of q. — LEAR 590:61
quincunx The q. of heaven runs low — BROW 196:6
Quinquireme Q. of Nineveh — MASE 662:37
quintessence heavenly q. — MARL 653:91
q. of all sciences — NASHE 721:76
q. of their lives — LOWE 615:72
what is this q. of dust? — SHAK 890:4
quip second, the Q. Modest — SHAK 887:35
quips What, in thy q. — SHAK 875:37
quit q. because I am not a quitter — NIXON 730:9
q. until I get run over — LEMM 595:45
q. yourselves like men — BIBLE 109:30
quitter I am not a q. — NIXON 730:9
quiver man that hath his q. full — BIBLE 119:42
raise a q. — WHITE 1070:44
spent lights q. and gleam — ARNO 36:55
Quixotes Don Q. of Europe — COBD 272:59
quixotic Q. quality — USTI 1038:79
quo Q. vadis — BIBLE 160:57
quotation Every q. contributes — JOHN 526:7
q. is a national vice — WAUGH 1057:91
quotations ability to think in q. — DRAB 344:22
Classical q. is the parole — JOHN 531:17
delighted particularly in q. — SCHL 848:74
q. from the Bible — LAWR 586:96
q. from the Bible, Browning — MACF 629:19

quotations (*contd.*)
q. in Latin — FLAU 393:46
recommend him by select q. — JOHN 528:45
quote grow immortal as they q. — YOUNG 1108:4
q. the fights historical — GILB 424:62
quotes q. from the shortstop — MACF 629:19
quotidian poet is a master of the q. — PRIT 791:72

rabbits r. ruled by stoats — ORWE 742:3
rabble r. of the filthy…infants — POUND 785:53
Rabboni R.; which is to say, Master — BIBLE 147:75
Raca say to his brother, R. — BIBLE 134:39
race horse think of a fine r. h. — MOZA 711:19
race adroit and joyless r. — WAUGH 1057:89
antennae of the r. — POUND 787:88
Art among a religious r. — FUSE 410:60
avoid a competitive r. — ARNO 40:45
brave, generous, humorous, talented, warm-
hearted r. — BUCH 202:25
But was a r. of heaven — SHAK 905:62
colonel comes from Brian's r. — DAVIS 309:39
courage of their r. — SULL 981:24
demand this…for the r. — SCHR 850:6
destiny of the human r. — THOR 1016:74
Englishmen…nervously excitable r. — DAVI 307:4
entire r. passes through — SCHR 850:7
ills…spring from belonging to a r. — DUDEK 353:16
intent on my own r. — STEV 976:59
Irish…in the infancy of the r. — OFAO 736:94
Jews…murmuring r. — DRYD 349:7
law [of competition]…for the r. — CARN 236:6
like the rest of my r.? — BLAKE 167:98
men and women with our r. — KIPL 564:3
my second r. — VAUG 1040:15
No r. can prosper — WASH 1054:37
noble r. and brave — SIGO 938:71
northern r. — CHUR 262:80
nuclear arms r. — MOUN 711:13
Of some new r. called Man — MILT 688:18
perpetuate their r. — RICA 808:37
poor r. in a land of dollars — DUBO 353:6
pride of r. or spirit — SMITH 949:60
problem of r. and color — DUBO 353:9
Purity of r. does not exist — FISH 389:83
quiet, pilfering, unprotected r. — CLARE 267:80
r. between education — WELLS 1065:42
r. is not to the swift — BIBLE 123:35
r. is to the swift — DAVI 307:97
r. of glory run — MILT 694:47
r. of upstart creatures — MILT 689:27
R. prejudice…a shadow — BUCK 203:33
r. that is set before us — BIBLE 154:54
r. which has become self-conscious — LAWR 585:77
rear my dusky r. — TENN 996:81
simple r.! — SCOTT 853:47
slinks out of the r. — MILT 685:93
Swift was the r. — DRYD 350:29
they which run in a r. — BIBLE 150:54
unbodied joy whose r. — SHEL 929:99
unto a savage r. — TENN 994:57
what avails the sceptred r.! — LAND 578:54
white r. does not really think — STEIN 965:38
white r. is the cancer — SONT 953:7
racehorse keep…any r. — CHES 257:83
racehorses associated…with r. — SAKI 837:1
races after they have won a few r. — DIOR 331:62
Bring forth its r. — LONG 612:13
composed of two distinct r. — LAMB 577:31
glory of r. or of rulers — BEVE 102:73
so-called white r. — FORS 398:41
war of the r. — MUIR 713:40
worst horse at the r. — MASE 662:50
Rachel R. weeping for her children — BIBLE 128:28
seven years for R. — BIBLE 105:36

racial As a matter of r. pride — FEIF 384:98
r. antipathies…of Old World — BORAH 178:8
racing Ocean r. is like standing — HEATH 466:54
r. car whose hood — MARI 651:67
rack Leave not a r. behind — SHAK 917:36
stretched on the r. — POPE 783:8
racket job or a r. — KNIG 567:54
ruins the whole r. — LOOS 613:38
whar dar is so much r. — TRUTH 1030:38
rackets matched our r. to these balls — SHAK 880:71
Rackrent Sir Patrick R. lived — EDGE 360:28
racquets boxing with r. — BARR 73:54
radiance fountain itself of heavenly r. — MILT 686:75
its r. would grow — RAND 801:26
white r. of Eternity — SHEL 931:50
radiant cherry blossoms…r. — ANON 26:51
radical charge that an idea is r. — GALB 411:74
never dared be r. — FROST 407:93
R. chic — WOLFE 1090:23
r. is a man — ROOS 821:40
radicalism feeling…R. cannot allow — CHES 257:86
radicals Few r. have good digestion — BUTL 218:45
French R. and German — MARX 660:14
radio BBC R. is a never-never land — SAFER 835:84
Down for a new r. — SNYD 951:84
everything you hear on the r. — MANK 645:74
Public r. is a ghetto — KEIL 548:27
than ever existed in r. — SARN 843:96
U.S.A. is…a r. network — DOSP 340:40
radioactive bury their r. fuel — LAMB 577:45
radish like a forked r. — SHAK 877:1
Raffles 'Cricket,' said R. — HORN 494:37
raft Come Back To The R. — FIED 387:37
put to sea on a wooden r. — HEYE 479:88
rag that Shakespeherian r. — ELIOT 368:86
That Shakespearian r. — BUCK 202:32
rag-time Lurching to r.-t. tunes — SASS 845:22
rage Dancing is a frenzy and a r. — DAVI 307:99
fury, and r. of mortal men — BURT 214:75
let Death wreck all his r. — MILT 689:39
Maintain your r. — WHIT 1072:71
no r., like love to hatred turned — CONG 281:22
Pity lost in r. and fear — CARL 235:67
R. is only quality — BRES 187:37
r. of Caliban — WILDE 1076:45
r. of will — DYER 358:89
R., r. against the dying — THOM 1011:75
repressed their noble r. — GRAY 442:68
Strong without r. — DENH 315:53
such an immodest r. — CAREW 232:7
void of noble r. — TENN 998:29
Why do the heathen r. — BIBLE 114:30
with hard-favoured r. — SHAK 881:84
worth more than force and r. — LAFO 575:88
ragged a virtue — OTWAY 746:84
If I was very r. and jolly — DICK 322:69
raggedness looped and windowed r. — SHAK 903:24
rags no scandal like r. — FARQ 383:71
r., hags, and hideous wenches — COLE 275:26
r. of time — DONNE 336:77
righteousnesses are as filthy r. — BIBLE 128:13
row of disgusting old r. — LAWR 586:85
You had better be in r. — DISR 334:27
raid r. on the inarticulate — ELIOT 372:53
rail never…any body else to r. me — CONG 280:93
r. against all the firstborn — SHAK 885:88
r. at the ill — TENN 1002:96
railed r. on Lady Fortune — SHAK 885:89
railroad r.…you blasted its rocks — RUSK 831:13
ride on the r. — THOR 1017:87
railroads country of r. — CHEE 256:53
Player with R. — SAND 841:57
rails r. are to a locomotive — RIVE 812:2

realization (*contd.*)
r. that we have denied…reality — PAGE 749:32
With this r. we turn — HERZ 479:77
realize dare you to r. it — HUST 505:39
realm better to improve his r. — ERAS 379:9
corrupted the youth of the r. — SHAK 861:15
estate of the r. — MACA 622:97
in na place of the R. — JAME 515:1
In the r. of science — STEI 967:68
invade the borders of my r. — ELIZ 373:90
One r., one people, one leader — ANON 26:40
provided this r. — QUIL 797:59
ready to defend the r. — PHIL 768:17
r., nation, or city — KNOX 567:57
r. of free song — LOWE 616:77
r. of ideas — MILL 677:2
r. of the Spirit — MATI 664:75
this r., this England — SHAK 867:48
turned out of the r. in my petticoat — ELIZ 373:86
realms constancy lives in r. above — COLE 274:10
existed in different r. — MEYER 673:32
great Anna, whom three r. obey — POPE 778:97
happy r. of light — MILT 687:91
hearts in one, r. in one — SHAK 882:12
travell'd in the r. of gold — KEATS 544:32
unreal r. of the canals — MACC 625:50
whatever r. to see — GOLD 432:96
reap r. where he hath sown — KIPL 561:52
that shall he also r. — BIBLE 152:92
reapers r., reaping early — TENN 993:40
reaping r. something new — TENN 995:77
rear Americans do not r. children — JARR 518:63
r. of your affection — SHAK 888:60
surprising the defenders from the r. — MANC 644:63
reascend fail to r. Self-raised — MILT 688:6
reason act under the guidance of r. — SPIN 960:55
asked one another the r. — SHAK 887:29
atheism against…or r. — BURKE 208:35
before reaching the age of r. — SADE 835:64
believing what r. cannot — VOLT 1046:10
beyond all r. — HAMM 453:43
Blotting out r. — GRAV 440:34
boundaries of our r. — RODO 818:87
but a woman's r. — SHAK 860:73
cleverness and r. — STOWE 979:90
dark of r. grows — BETJ 101:58
dictates of r., religion, and morality — DICK 326:65
disgust is r.'s proper response — PAGL 749:34
Eyes And R. …to study Flies — POPE 783:9
find out the r. for it — LECA 592:95
for some specific r. — RUSS 832:30
form of human r. — LEVI 600:31
Give you a r. on compulsion? — SHAK 876:55
God gave [Adam] r. — MILT 686:67
governments…founded on r. — PARE 753:83
great r. to be sad — SHAK 886:17
hearing all manner of r.? — MILT 685:66
How noble in r. — SHAK 890:4
Human r. won — KHRU 556:50
if it be against r. — COKE 272:71
ignorance, his r. such — POPE 780:42
in erring R.'s spite — POPE 780:41
In R.'s they all rejoice — ADDI 7:23
It is not, therefore, r. — HUME 503:5
kills r. itself — MILT 685:55
lack of r. in the kitchen — NIET 729:90
let us r. together — BIBLE 124:56
Let's r. with the worst — SHAK 884:64
live in a world ruined by R. — MAMET 643:51
longing…for r. — CAMUS 229:14
lost everything except his r. — CHES 258:3
loved her against r. — DICK 327:73
man who can r. — LESS 599:11
man who listens to R. — SHAW 922:57

reason (*contd.*)
materials of r. and knowledge — LOCKE 609:72
men have lost their r.! — SHAK 884:50
more ascetic r. than…enjoyment — STARK 963:95
More than cool r. — SHAK 871:53
Music says nothing to the r. — BURG 206:93
nature of r. to perceive things — SPIN 960:51
not contrary to r. — HUME 503:4
not from r. but from love — GIDE 423:44
not his r. but his passions — STER 969:1
not to r. why — TENN 1000:72
Now tell me the r. — SOUT 954:29
objects of human r. — HUME 503:8
Only r. can convince us — BELL 86:85
produces innovation without r. — SANT 842:83
prose which knows no r. — STEP 968:80
pursue my r. to an O altitudo! — BROW 195:74
reality…from the perspective of r. — PAGE 749:33
r. against reading! — SHAK 865:7
R., an ignis fatuus — ROCH 816:50
r. and energy…are necessary — BLAKE 166:71
r. and the will of God — ARNO 39:25
r. doth buckle and bow — BACON 55:12
r. down or deny everything — EMER 377:56
r. for being — FRAN 401:85
r. for being a professional — ROST 825:4
r. for having children — RUSS 833:35
r. for my rhyme — SPEN 959:44
r. for rejecting them — RUSS 832:16
r. I escaped — DOUG 341:52
r. I should be the same? — AYTO 53:84
r. is best and pleasantest — ARIS 34:28
r. is equally cogent — GASK 415:33
r. is identical with love — MACL 633:68
r., is naturally equal in all men — DESC 317:76
r. is not the subversion — STEV 972:78
R. is…the slave of the passions — HUME 503:3
r. knows nothing — PASC 758:65
r. of the strongest — LAFO 574:77
r. so many people — GOLD 434:49
r. straightens it out — LAFO 574:83
R. thus with life — SHAK 897:77
R. to rule all — AURE 50:24
R. to rule — DRYD 350:51
r. why I loved him — MONT 701:54
r. why [war] has to start — LEBO 592:91
r. with one another — MOLI 699:35
Respect and r. — SHAK 866:32
rest may r. and welcome — BROW 199:74
right deed for the wrong r. — ELIOT 370:33
ruling passion conquers r. — POPE 780:28
Science…distrusts pure r. — MENC 669:77
there is r. to hope — JOHN 527:23
There's r. good — JONS 535:98
to perfect…the intellect or r. — SPIN 960:58
triumph of human r. — HAWK 461:63
vaster r. — THOM 1013:21
voice of r. is stifled — BURKE 207:15
war…for such a stupid r. — MARY 661:28
what humanity, r.…tells me — BURKE 207:9
what's the r.? — HARI 457:17
where we go is r. — PATC 759:90
with how little r. — JOHN 525:74
without the use of r. — LEON 597:85
words clothed in r.'s garb — MILT 688:16
worse appear The better r. — MILT 688:14
reasonable Man, being r. — BYRON 222:43
no r. man could have expected — HERB 474:99
r. man adapts himself — SHAW 922:56
right than be r. — NASH 720:65
The R. Man — HERB 474:2
reasonableness sweet r. of Jesus — ARNO 40:35
reasoning contain any abstract r. — HUME 504:10
knowledge…by r. — BACON 60:43

reasoning (*contd.*)
r. and belief…essential materials? — CARL 235:71
r. comes down to…feeling — PASC 758:64
r. to the test of experiment — LAVO 585:58
What has R. to do with…Painting — BLAKE 168:13
reasons bad r. for what we believe — BRAD 184:91
born And he had r. — ROBI 814:26
five r. why men drink — ALDR 12:9
function…to make r. for husbands — ELIOT 365:22
Good r. must…give place — SHAK 884:58
heart has its r. — PASC 758:65
r. are as two grains of wheat — SHAK 874:9
r. for making war — FRED 403:23
r. I quit going to the theatre — SALI 839:32
Strong r. make strange actions — SHAK 872:70
there are no r. — MO 698:12
two very cogent r. — JOHN 531:18
rebel bound to r. against — IBSEN 510:20
boy is a r. and an anarch — MILL 679:50
r.…turning into an autocrat — DURR 357:77
Showed like a r.'s whore — SHAK 906:11
very r. to my will — SHAK 906:90
What is a r.? — CAMUS 229:53
rebelled or him who hath r. — MILT 691:78
rebellion a sort of mental r. — ORWE 743:22
between sycophancy and r. — BAKER 63:83
Courage, rashness and r. — MARI 651:66
I incite this meeting to r. — PANK 752:79
If r. was the certain consequence — MANS 648:15
little r. now and then — JEFF 520:89
r. against being what he is — CABE 224:79
R. against tyrants — DAVI 309:42
r. is as the sin of witchcraft — BIBLE 110:35
R. lay in his way — SHAK 876:66
Twelve Highlanders…make a r. — ANON 30:64
woman are in furious secret r. — SHAW 924:74
rebellious for the r. also — BIBLE 116:87
Hot and r. liquors — SHAK 885:82
r. dwell in a dry land — BIBLE 116:86
r. people — REED 805:91
revolting and a r. heart — BIBLE 128:20
rebelliousness centuries of r. — PRIE 790:42
rebels Cheering a rout of r. — SHAK 877:2
r. from principle — BURKE 207:34
rebuke Open r. is better — BIBLE 122:7
r. of his people shall he take away — BIBLE 125:73
scorner heareth not r. — BIBLE 121:72
Thy r. hath broken my heart — BOOK 177:83
recant will not r. anything — LUTH 619:45
receipt Applause is a r. — SCHN 848:82
receive in giving that we r. — FRAN 401:91
more blessed to give than r. — BIBLE 148:6
r. no letters in the grave — JOHN 532:36
skill to give as…to r. — QUIL 797:60
those who r. it — GOLD 432:94
whosoever shall not r. you — BIBLE 136:75
reception meets with a better r. — JOHN 527:32
r. of the reader — TERE 1006:71
recesses dusty r. of their minds — LAWR 587:13
recession r. when your neighbour — TRUM 1030:26
R. is when your neighbour — REAG 803:61
recessions four out of the last five r. — SAMU 840:46
recipe best r. for happiness — AUST 51:48
man must have a rare r. — LAMB 576:7
recipes r. that are always successful — VALE 1038:86
recipient comforting to be…the r. — FOWL 400:69
reciprocity eternal r. of tears — OWEN 748:22
reciproque rewarded…with the r. — BACON 56:42
reckon if you could tell how to r. — SHAK 881:93
reckoning much at your own r. — TROL 1027:75
recognition books…deserve r. — VIAN 1043:44
cannot force a r. — KISS 565:30
displaced by the r. — WAGN 1047:26
grace beyond r. — REID 806:97

recognition (*contd.*)
hunger for r. and money — SELF 857:37
recognize as if I should r. it — DOYLE 344:12
not r. me by my face — TROL 1028:94
r. the honourable Member — CHUR 265:37
r. your prime — SPARK 955:52
recollect does not r. where — JOHN 531:24
r. all the little events — WELL 1063:13
We must r. — PITT 771:72
recollection alas!, r. at hand — COWP 292:40
recommendation letter of r. — ADDI 7:13
recommendations opposite r. — SIMON 939:80
recompense r. is a pleasure — JOHN 525:88
reconcilement never can true r. — MILT 690:50
reconciliation r. with dullness — LOWE 617:11
record artistic r. created — ROCK 818:78
dreadful r. of sin — DOYLE 344:5
I think that's a r. — THOM 1011:78
Poetry is a r. — SHEL 931:59
puts a r. on the gramophone — ELIOT 369:90
r. is fragmentary — WHIT 1071:61
r. of his triumphant passage — KENN 551:75
r....of our mother and father — FRAME 400:78
searched her. for years — MENC 669:67
set down the following r. — FRAME 400:77
recording r., not thinking — ISHE 513:72
records half-a-dozen r. — SHAW 924:96
r. for both home runs — RODG 818:86
r. of human spirit — MACL 634:77
r. prove the title good — ARLO 34:37
wise nation preserves its r. — HOWE 497:97
recover r. what has been lost — ELIOT 372:54
seldom or ever r. — SHAK 906:4
recreation guilty spice to this r. — WAUGH 1057:86
play or r. — STUB 980:12
recruiting r. field for the militant — WRIG 1101:99
rector accident happened to the r. — TROL 1027:77
An ancestor was r. — YEATS 1107:93
rectors curates lean and r. fat — MACA 622:86
rectum portion of the r. — BELLI 86:93
red An Admiral r. — SITW 940:2
crimson r., blood r., wine r. — GALE 412:88
fiction...printed in r. ink — BOWEN 181:49
keep the r. flag flying. — CONN 282:54
November's leaf is r. — SCOTT 853:51
pessimist sees only the r. — SCHW 852:32
R. F. is the funeral march — SHAW 925:31
r. in the face — BENT 93:29
r. like crimson — BIBLE 124:56
R. lips are not so r. — OWEN 748:9
r. r. vitals of his heart — RANS 802:34
r. wheel barrow — WILL 1082:85
r. with mirth — SHAK 911:28
rose is r. — ANON 23:90
tawdry yellow strove with dirty r. — POPE 780:30
The r. rose cries — TENN 1001:88
took the r. straight — ACHE 3:33
two r. eyes that stare — RANS 802:37
unnatural r. and black — DICK 325:41
When in doubt wear r. — BLASS 169:25
red-branch R.-B. Knights — MOORE 706:33
red-haired R.-H. Man's Wife — CARL 233:25
red-hot Last of the R.-H. — TUCK 1031:50
r.-h. with drinking — SHAK 917:38
redeemed Fear not: for I have r. thee — BIBLE 126:93
not r. from time — ELIOT 373:80
redeemer know that my r. liveth — BIBLE 113:12
redemption life's r. — STEV 972:62
married past r. — DRYD 347:72
Our great r. — MILT 681:80
Poetry is a means of r. — STEV 972:56
secret of r. — WEIZ 1062:87
redfaced r. from eating and drinking — ABBO 1:1
Redgauntlet 'Then...' said R. — SCOTT 856:7

rediscover r. their humanity — TUTU 1032:53
redress no r. for the present — DISR 332:81
r. of real grievances — PEEL 763:42
Things past r. — SHAK 867:54
reds R....that shouuuuuuut — CARRA 237:15
reed And night this toppling r. — BLUN 170:41
bruised r. shall he not break — BIBLE 126:92
bruised r. shall he not break — BIBLE 137:89
clasped a r. — SHEL 932:71
Man is only a r. — PASC 758:66
r. shaken with the wind — BIBLE 137:84
sighing of a r. — BYRON 223:63
staff of this broken r. — BIBLE 126:84
staff of this bruised r. — BIBLE 112:84
reeducation r. of perception — DEWEY 319:96
reefs collection of r., rocks — MORT 710:92
Reekie Auld R.! — FERG 386:17
reel beheaded in the third r. — MILLS 680:67
earth shall r. to and fro — BIBLE 125:72
R. o' Tullochgorum — SKIN 943:55
r. to and fro — BIBLE 118:21
world must r. — BERR 98:10
reeling Love, the r. midnight through — PARK 754:9
reels threesome r....foursome r. — BURNS 212:34
refer r. to Rule 1 — ITO 514:82
reference favourable r. to the Devil — CHUR 265:35
no r. to fun in any Act — HERB 474:1
references R. upon request — DAVIS 308:24
refine correct, insert, r. — SWIFT 985:2
r. our language — JOHN 525:93
refined Englishwoman is so r. — SMITH 948:30
more r., restricted, ceremonial — REAG 803:57
R. himself to soul — DRYD 352:83
refinement r. on the principle — BURKE 206:8
reflect gave Leibniz time to r. — FONT 395:88
r. what people say — SMITH 947:11
reflection after long r. — GALL 412:93
buildings...the r. of society — PEI 764:49
habit of profound r. — CONR 285:11
humiliating r. — FERN 386:26
Mental r. is...more interesting — PIRS 770:53
objects of R. — LOCKE 609:73
probably a r. — HOPP 493:14
r. of your own minds — ASTE 42:88
truth of a r. — MONT 701:55
reflections Mortifying R. — CONG 281:20
reflex r. of a star — WORD 1095:15
reflexes r....caused in other people — BALD 64:93
reform All r. except moral one — CARL 236:2
Beginning r. — WELL 1063:14
party of progress or r. — MILL 675:64
r. a world — CARL 234:45
r. the old man — TWAIN 1033:91
r. this little piece — MILLS 680:65
spirit of the R. Bill — PEEL 763:42
To innovate is not to r. — BURKE 208:46
reformation plotting some new r. — DRYD 350:36
reforming of R. itself — MILT 686:74
reformers All R., however strict — SMITH 947:18
drifting social r. — STRA 979:91
martyrs or r.—or both — CHAR 252:80
R. are going into hiding — SHEV 934:18
we're law r. — HUMP 504:14
refrain still remember the r. — MACA 621:74
with a happy r. — FREED 403:28
refreshment R. after toil — MILT 684:35
refrigerator keep a martini in the r. — DEVO 318:92
refrigerators r....great modern — WARH 1053:22
refuge eternal God is thy r. — BIBLE 108:5
God is our r. and strength — BIBLE 116:72
God is our r. — SCOT 856:20
last r. of a scoundrel — JOHN 529:73
Lord, which is my r. — BIBLE 117:3
r. from distress — WORD 1100:81

refuge (*contd.*)
r. from home life — SHAW 920:12
r. open to every man — BABE 54:91
safe r. for the exile — GARI 415:24
so easy to take r. in — IBSEN 510:22
thou hast been our r. — BOOK 177:86
thy wings shall be my r. — BOOK 177:77
refusal every r. to act — REED 805:91
Every known class of r. — SOME 952:1
r. of language is a death — BART 75:81
refuse an offer he can't r. — PUZO 796:39
I r. to become a seeker — RICH 809:55
I r. to send anyone else — RANK 801:29
large r. bin — BAIN 63:78
mind will generally r. — TROL 1028:93
no just government should r. — JEFF 520:91
people r. to see me — ELLI 375:16
r. in respect of our child — BIBLE 131:78
refute r. it thus — JOHN 528:41
regalia Great Queen in her r. — GAY 416:46
regard has great a r. for religion — OCAS 735:77
r. the law courts — INGR 511:45
r. to their own interest — SMITH 945:87
Should be without r. — SHAK 909:57
Unconditional positive r. — ROGE 819:2
Victorian r. for the pride of people — PRIT 791:74
without r. to your happiness — PECK 763:40
regeneration r....into a new state — ELIOT 365:11
Regent's Park in the sun, in R. P. — WOOLF 1092:59
regime in love...a political r. — LESS 599:8
we enter a new r. — DOUG 342:71
regiment breasts for r. — MARL 652:89
kings, when r. is gone — MARL 653:6
led his r. from behind — GILB 426:95
Monstrous R. of Women — KNOX 567:56
r.'s in 'ollow square — KIPL 560:29
region airy r. thrilling — MILT 681:89
r. is facing a deep abyss — HUSS 505:35
r. where 'twas born — MARV 657:68
regions r. mild of calm and...air — MILT 683:18
r. of sin and falsity — MILT 685:66
r. of sorrow, doleful shades — MILT 687:90
unknown r. preserved — ELIOT 366:32
views...the r. of the sky — ENNI 378:92
register r. of the crimes and miseries — IRVI 513:61
regress r. is...downfall — BACON 57:70
regret at last and vain r. — ROSS 824:92
If that plane leaves...you'll r. it — EPST 379:2
Old Age a r. — DISR 332:82
one r. in life — ALLEN 14:41
only possible r. I have — BORO 179:20
only r. in the theatre — BARR 73:59
r. can die! — TENN 999:48
r. that I have but one — HALE 451:20
r. very much that — HOMER 488:26
said goodbye to without r. — HARD 455:78
seldom spoken with greater r. — BALD 65:13
wild with r. — TENN 997:2
regrets end up with the right r. — MILL 677:12
regular icily r. — TENN 1001:74
regularity Genius and r. — GAIN 411:69
regulation The R. Act — WILDE 1078:99
regulations cannot frame r. — HAWT 461:64
rehabilitation sad, refusing r. — KIRK 565:28
rehearsal Comedy of 'The R.' — JOHN 532:37
rehearsed if I had r. you — YEATS 1106:76
Reich greater part of the R. — GOEB 430:65
reign called upon some day to r. — HARD 455:76
coined in some r. — LAMB 576:23
dead r. — ZOLA 1110:70
govern is to r. — MIRA 696:70
lazy, long, lascivious r. — DEFOE 312:78
Omnipotent but friendless is to r. — SHEL 930:21
r. had here its last — MILT 681:89

reign (*contd.*)

r. in this horrible place	COWP 292:38
r. of chaos and old Night	MILT 688:5
reigning r. over a fourth-class nation	JAY 519:76
reigns arrangement into three r.	GUED 448:74
Dunce the second r.	POPE 782:91
reincarnated If I were r.	FAUL 384:86
reindeer Herds of r. move across	AUDEN 48:82
sleigh, and eight tiny r.	MOORE 704:5
reinforcement r. of the State	CAMUS 229:54
reins try the r.	BIBLE 128:26
reinvent r. himself	BURU 214:80
reject those who r. you	WHIT 1073:99
rejected despised and r. of men	BIBLE 127:99
rejection eventual r.	LEBO 591:82
use the r. as an excuse	ANGE 19:27
rejoice before him and r.	SCOT 856:22
before Him, and r.	KETHE 554:23
fortunate, I r. at it	SHAK 884:47
I r. that America has resisted	PITT 771:66
r. and be glad	BIBLE 118:27
R., and be exceeding glad	BIBLE 133:34
r., and to do good	BIBLE 122:20
r. for a moment	YUAN 1108:12
R. in the Lord alway	BIBLE 153:14
R., O young man	BIBLE 123:41
R., the Lord is King!	WESL 1066:62
R. with them that do r.	BIBLE 149:35
that wonted to r.	SURR 983:45
rejoicing come again with r.	BIBLE 119:40
related men to whom they are r.	GILM 427:14
relation mental r. with a woman	LAWR 586:93
No cold r. is a zealous citizen	BURKE 208:40
nobody like a r.	THAC 1006:84
poor r. is the most irrelevant	LAMB 577:41
some occult r.	JOHN 525:90
relations altering the old r.	CARL 234:39
even one's own r.	WILDE 1077:71
great men have their poor r.	DICK 325:33
memory…all its clear r.	ELIOT 367:58
r. of…Government and…people	REED 805:91
unreasonably large stock of r.	SHAW 926:43
whatever their r. with men	FREN 404:39
relationship if we have that r.	EDDI 360:19
outside this work r.	MARX 660:8
r. between man and man	ROUS 827:39
remains of the 'special r.'	BENN 90:68
special r.	CHUR 265:31
special r. with the United States	ACHE 2:29
their mutual association and r.	PLATO 774:24
women see the r. between objects	FOWL 399:66
relationships don't spend…in r.	BRAD 183:76
extra-marital r.	ALLEN 14:49
r. of colour or form	ROTH 826:26
such r. as our minds	LEBON 591:78
sum of connections and r.	MARX 660:19
relative set out…In a r. way	BULL 203:50
Success is r.	ELIOT 371:37
relatives people your r. hate	HAMM 454:56
relativism R. implies…indifference	VAND 1039:94
relaxation form of r. to me	HAMM 453:49
release illusory r.	UPDI 1037:71
inescapable, imperative need for r.	FEIN 385:99
prisoner's r.	SIDN 937:53
relic cased up, like a holy r.	WEBS 1061:61
rob the r.	DRYD 350:47
sad r. of departed worth!	BYRON 219:74
relics hallowed r.	MILT 681:94
R. from the past	CHEE 255:48
relief approaches the effect of r.	MICH 673:38
certain r. in change	IRVI 513:67
experience r. when one returns	COUP 289:76
for the r. of the body	RICH 809:47
For this r. much thanks	SHAK 887:42

relief (*contd.*)

great r. to reach this	SKIN 943:54
liquor is the only mechanical r.	HEMI 470:30
r. and depth	GOYA 437:83
sleep provides r.	CHAM 250:26
religion all the r. I want	HALD 451:18
anger about r.	HALI 452:32
any r., by any sect	KRIS 569:92
Art and R.…two roads	BELL 85:81
As to r.	PAINE 750:45
as well as in r.	JUNI 540:73
As with the Christian r.	ORWE 742:97
basic command of r.	TOYN 1024:22
belief imposed by r.	KRIS 569:93
black face and a different r.	EDWA 362:49
broken down by Age, Sex, and R.	MACR 638:53
brothels with bricks of R.	BLAKE 166:76
can't talk r. to a man	SHAW 923:80
Christianity was the r.	SWIFT 986:18
Christianity…man's r.	WELD 1062:92
cult is a r. with no…power	WOLFE 1090:26
do the same by their r.	DICK 326:64
drunk on whiskey or r.	MENC 669:78
each r. only one of the seven colours	BLAV 169:27
either on r. or policy	RUSK 831:2
established as a r.	LEWIS 602:61
Football is like a r.	PELE 764:52
For my r.	BROW 194:63
freed from his r.	SAIN 837:89
freedom of r.	JEFF 520:94
handmaid to r.	BACON 55:19
happens by accident…becomes a r.	WRIS 1102:14
hearing about r. even more	MITF 697:96
Hoo-doo…was an unorganized r.	REED 805:89
If r. is only a garment	BONH 173:84
if R. were intended	BUTL 216:9
in both science and r.	SAGAN 836:75
In matters of r.…I never give advice	CHES 257:82
in the Roman Catholic r.	TROL 1027:77
indirect way to plant r.	BROW 195:81
late to trust the old r.	LOWE 617:4
leave him for r.	SPARK 955:46
life smashes r.	NERU 723:9
literature is a substitute for r.	ELIOT 369:6
Malay r. and custom	PANG 752:76
man talks loudly about r.	STER 969:1
man's r. is the chief fact	CARL 236:87
manners and r.	MONT 700:53
Men will wrangle for r.	COLT 277:53
My r. and my art	JOHN 523:39
no reason to bring r. into it	OCAS 735:77
not impossibilities enough in r.	BROW 195:72
of any r., or party or profession	COLE 275:29
One r. is as true as another	BURT 214:78
original feature of any r.	PAINE 750:48
paradox of high r.	NIEB 727:64
Philistine of genius in r.	ARNO 40:36
philosophy bringeth…to r.	BACON 57:65
plant our r. in Paris	LESL 598:94
prophecy, and r., all in one	RUSK 831:8
Pure r. and undefiled	BIBLE 155:63
reject me on account of my r.	BELL 87:4
R. and art…from the same root	CATH 244:49
R. blushing veils	POPE 783:10
r. but a childish toy	MARL 653:96
R. Caesar never knew	COWP 292:36
R. does not banish mirth	WALT 1052:11
r. has had its day	BENN 92:6
r., history…would be useless	BALZ 69:82
R. is far more acute than science	FORS 398:39
R.'s in the heart	JERR 521:13
R. is something which stands	WHIT 1071:55
R. is the sigh	MARX 660:6
r. is to do good.	PAINE 750:49

religion (*contd.*)

R. is what a man does	WHIT 1071:57
r., knavery, and change	BEHN 85:66
r. most prevalent in our northern	BURKE 206:8
r.…not simply morality	ARNO 39:32
r. of gold	BAGE 61:55
r. of money	GAUT 416:44
r. of science	LEWIS 602:60
R. resides in our eyes	LEWIS 601:34
r. to make us hate	SWIFT 984:71
R.…tragedy of mankind	WILS 1084:11
r.…true remedy for superstition	BURKE 207:10
r. whatevermost interested in	BARR 73:10
r.…will be replaced by poetry	ARNO 40:39
r. without science is blind	EINS 363:66
r. would still be holy and divine	BAUD 78:36
respect the other fellow's r.	MENC 669:79
revolution of 1789 is her political r.	LAMA 575:2
rules of my r. from Rome	BROW 195:66
rum and true r.	BYRON 222:91
Self-righteousness is not r.	BRON 191:97
Sensible men are all the same r.	DISR 334:28
serve the French in place of a state r.	BIER 161:88
snare to R.	TAYL 992:21
standard of r., intelligence, and virtue	SMIL 945:34
start your own r.	HUBB 498:8
Superstition r. of feeble minds	BURKE 208:37
That is my r.	SHAW 923:79
Theosophy is the essence of all r.	BLAV 169:26
this man's r. is vain	BIBLE 155:62
true r. of America	MAIL 640:90
when r. was strong	SZASZ 988:66
wisest of r.	HAIL 451:12
with r. and fear	JONS 535:91
religions knit and break r.	SHAK 902:92
natural language of all r.	STAEL 962:76
of all great r.	TEMP 993:28
R. kept alive by heresies	BREN 187:32
religious All known r. beliefs	DURK 357:71
Art among a r. race	FUSE 410:60
be virtuous—be r.	SCOTT 856:18
belief is made r.	CUPI 301:10
Casting a dim r. light	MILT 683:15
commit…to any r. belief	WAUGH 1056:72
decline of r. belief	FREUD 404:41
feeling…about some r. expressions	RABI 799:94
first expounder of our r. belief	SPEKE 955:61
hope I will be r. again	FLEM 394:64
labour movement was truly r.	WOLFE 1090:29
Man…a r. animal	BURKE 208:35
natural r. sense	LAWR 587:10
private parts…and r. opinions	BUTL 218:48
r. inquiries	GIBB 421:27
r. system…green Chartreuse	SAKI 837:9
r. ties…social pedigree	WOLFE 1090:28
same r. experience	ROTH 826:26
seem to be r.	BIBLE 155:62
take an almost r. view	HOYLE 498:2
troubled with r. doubt	CHES 259:38
virtually r. prophecy	NISB 730:5
We are a r. people	DOUG 342:70
religious-good Good, but not r.-g.	HARDY 456:84
religiously follows r. the new	THOR 1016:83
religiousness centre of true r.	EINS 363:67
reliques religious race produces r.	FUSE 410:60
relish some r. of the saltness	SHAK 877:81
relishes lullings and the r. of it	HERB 475:19
reluctantly r., unexpectedly	MORT 710:96
remain but the rocks r.	HERB 474:6
days go by, I r.	APOL 32:93
nothing will r.	HOUS 494:46
'Shall r.'?	SHAK 911:10
so r. ignorant	GREG 446:47
south of us r.	JOHN 524:60

remains cut up what r. — KIPL 560:*33*
r. an Englishman! — GILB 423:*57*
remake Myself I must r. — YEATS 1106:*87*
remark can't stand…rude r. — WILL 1081:*58*
fowl, blinking at you without r. — ELIOT 366:*27*
Which I wish to r. — HARTE 459:*50*
remarkable nothing left r. — SHAK 906:*96*
r. thing about Shakespeare — GRAV 440:*38*
to wish to be r. — HOLM 486:*93*
remarks r. are not literature — STEIN 965:*34*
remedies encumbering it with r. — TOLS 1023:*95*
not apply new r. — BACON 58:*94*
prescribes the r. — MOLI 699:*35*
r. oft in ourselves — SHAK 901:*71*
When r. are past — SHAK 898:*12*
remedy Auntie Maggie's…r. — FORM 397:*27*
Death is the r. — CHAM 250:*26*
desperate…dangerous r. — FAWK 384:*95*
for the deid r. is none — DUNB 355:*41*
know not how to r. — KYD 571:*28*
no r. against this consumption — SHAK 877:*85*
r. for everything except death — CERV 248:*98*
r. is worse than the disease — BACON 58:*82*
sought the r. — SHAK 887:*29*
Things without all r. — SHAK 909:*57*
What is the r.? — SHAK 895:*42*
remember Ah yes! I r. well — LERN 597:*88*
cannot but r. such things — SHAK 909:*74*
cannot r. anyone ever asking — REAR 804:*72*
day I can already r. — VALL 1039:*92*
I r. watching myself — RHYS 808:*31*
I r., I r., The fir trees — HOOD 489:*38*
I r., I r., The house — HOOD 489:*37*
if thou wilt, r. — ROSS 824:*76*
must r. this — HUPF 505:*34*
never r. whether it snowed — THOM 1011:*94*
r. Degas — PISS 771:*60*
R. First to possess his books — SHAK 917:*32*
R. me when I go — ROSS 823:*71*
R. that you are an Englishman — RHOD 808:*24*
R. the rights — GLAD 429:*52*
R. thee? — SHAK 889:*80*
r. what is past — HALI 452:*30*
thou r. and I forget — SWIN 986:*21*
To r. is far worse — BENU 94:*34*
who I r. he was — SEXT 859:*68*
Who will r. — SASS 846:*41*
wrong people r. Vietnam — HERR 477:*49*
ye want to r. — KELM 549:*34*
remembered But we in it shall be r. — SHAK 882:*3*
Campbell-Bannerman is r. chiefly — BENT 93:*30*
names…freshly r. — SHAK 882:*2*
r.…for the invention of a mouse! — DISN 331:*70*
r. poor Julian — HEMI 471:*31*
surest way not to be r. — MAIL 639:*83*
tranquillity r. in emotion — PARK 754:*14*
remembrance book of r. was written — BIBLE 131:*71*
first…to my I ever saw — PEPYS 765:*73*
flood of r. — LAWR 585:*69*
Makes the r. dear — SHAK 901:*84*
Mournful and never-ending R. — POE 776:*51*
My r. is very free — SHAK 895:*34*
r. of things past — SHAK 913:*58*
rosemary, that's for r. — SHAK 892:*69*
this do in r. of me — BIBLE 150:*59*
reminiscences old have r. — SAKI 837:*99*
R. make one feel — SHAW 919:*89*
some of your grosser r. — WOOL 1093:*84*
remission Without…no r. — BIBLE 154:*47*
remnants r. of such a beautiful habit — ALME 15:*57*
remodified We can be r., changed — DOUG 342:*73*
remonstrance all complaint and r. — MACA 624:*22*
remorse hottentot, without r.! — SITW 940:*1*
r., my worm — RIMB 812:*98*

remorse (*contd.*)
R., the fatal egg — COWP 292:*45*
What says Monsieur R.? — SHAK 875:*40*
with as little r. — SHAK 878:*22*
remorseless treacherous and r. — SHAW 921:*26*
remote inconceivably r. — WELLS 1064:*27*
removed cannot be r., but abideth — BIBLE 119:*39*
It ought to be r. — BEEC 82:*12*
r. from contact with…life — PRIT 791:*65*
r. from the sphere — KING 559:*5*
remuneration r. for…footballer — ANON 25:*20*
renaissance antiquity and its R. — KLEE 566:*46*
Leonardo da Vinci and the R. — WELL 1063:*1*
r. is a logical fact — MASA 661:*31*
R. was simply the green end — FOWL 399:*67*
rend time to r. — BIBLE 122:*19*
render perfumes…more they r. — WEBS 1059:*27*
r. to every one his due — JUST 540:*76*
rendezvous r. with Death — SEEG 857:*26*
renegade whips to kennel The r. — RANS 802:*37*
renewal Boston…Urban R. — MAIL 639:*84*
renovator that great r. of matter — OVID 747:*3*
renown high r., riches, and royaltie — DUNB 355:*39*
Some, for r., on scraps — YOUNG 1108:*4*
rent like r. and wages — SMITH 945:*80*
r. everything — KOSI 568:*83*
r. out my room — ALLEN 14:*44*
r. we pay — GREN 446:*53*
to go on paying the r. — TURN 1031:*51*
rent-day awesome reality to R.-D. — ANGE 20:*30*
Rentacrowd R. Ltd. — SIMP 939:*88*
rentiers indistinguishable from r. — ROBI 815:*34*
renunciation act of r. — MORAN 706:*41*
beautiful things made by r. — DEGAS 312:*91*
repair friendship in constant r. — JOHN 526:*2*
reparation never make r. — JAMES 517:*35*
repartee majority…the best r. — DISR 332:*95*
repeal method to secure the r. — GRANT 439:*9*
repeat condemned to r. it — SANT 842:*84*
does no harm to r. — LESS 598:*7*
r. in one period — RENO 807:*10*
shall have to r. that — HOUS 496:*85*
those things that r. and r. — WILD 1080:*33*
what they hear, they r.! — SITW 941:*7*
repel retard what we cannot r. — JOHN 526:*9*
repelled I am r. by those — REDON 804:*78*
only r. by man — INGE 511:*37*
repent all men every where to r. — BIBLE 148:*4*
Dead men never r. — DICK 321:*36*
It doth r. me — SHEL 930:*15*
r. at leisure — CONG 280:*99*
r. in dust and ashes — BIBLE 113:*27*
r. in haste — CONG 280:*1*
r. it from my very soul — SHAK 862:*44*
R. what's past — SHAK 892:*57*
R. ye: for the kingdom of heaven — BIBLE 133:*25*
when one cannot r.? — SHAK 892:*47*
repentance R. is the virtue of weak — DRYD 346:*52*
R.…want of power to sin — DRYD 352:*92*
sinners to r. — BIBLE 136:*70*
sinners to r. — BIBLE 141:*59*
Try what r. can — SHAK 892:*47*
repetition r. of the wrong way — DURR 357:*79*
repetitions use not vain r. — BIBLE 135:*48*
reply heartening and the strong r. — EMPS 378:*85*
not to make r. — TENN 1000:*72*
sportive kind r. — GRAY 441:*59*
third, the R. Churlish — SHAK 887:*35*
report composed as a conference r.? — GRIS 447:*67*
good r. maketh the bones fat — BIBLE 121:*82*
not too proud to r. — DANA 304:*55*
r. of an aspect — LIPP 606:*35*
r. of my death — TWAIN 1034:*14*
r. of valour — SHAK 895:*28*

report (*contd.*)
r. on what I know — FRIS 406:*63*
r. what he means — ANON 27:*76*
the right to r. events — ORWE 745:*50*
they have committed false r. — SHAK 880:*64*
Who hath believed our r.? — BIBLE 127:*99*
reporters gallery in which the r. sit — MACA 622:*97*
reports daily r. are submitted — STEAD 964:*8*
r., films, phonograph records? — RODC 818:*81*
r. that I took the loss badly — DOLE 335:*51*
repose appreciate the charm of r. — LIVI 607:*47*
give thy r. To the wet sea-boy — SHAK 877:*95*
hushed in grim r. — GRAY 443:*86*
In Claud's landscape…all is r. — CONS 285:*18*
No r. for Sir Walter — SCOTT 856:*17*
r. implicitly on — JEFF 520:*93*
r. is taboo'd — GILB 424:*77*
r. of a pacific station — ADAMS 4:*62*
seek r. In listlessness — WORD 1096:*19*
sigh for thy r. — WESL 1066:*67*
repositories r. of the marvellous — DIOR 331:*63*
representation Taxation without r. — OTIS 746:*75*
Tragedy is…a r. — ARIS 34:*29*
without r. — TOYN 1024:*16*
representations just r. of general — JOHN 528:*44*
representative being your r. — BELL 87:*4*
most r., physical scientists — SNOW 950:*73*
r. of wealth — MILL 674:*60*
representatives r. of the people — WHIT 1069:*16*
repressed being persecuted and r. — ROLL 821:*26*
repression r. of the high hope — WHIT 1071:*56*
reproach common r. is true — SOCR 951:*87*
common term of r. — BERG 94:*40*
escape r. — JOHN 526:*4*
lexicon of…ridicule and r. — SAFI 835:*67*
reproduce cannot be expected to r. — HOLM 486:*5*
reproduction Strangelove R. — COUP 289:*84*
reptile of the fish and r. — LOWE 617:*98*
reptiles fishes and r. — BRYAN 201:*15*
poisonous r. — GERA 419:*35*
republic architects of our r. — KING 557:*78*
At its birth, the r. — LAMA 575:*3*
despair of the R.! — WHAR 1068:*93*
How beautiful the R. was — DURR 357:*75*
Love the Beloved R. — FORS 399:*53*
rarely happends that a r. — MACH 631:*38*
r. has been much more powerful — ADDI 6:*4*
R. has no need for scientists — COFF 272:*68*
r. of conscience — HEAN 465:*41*
R. of equals — BABE 54:*91*
The R. will be conservative — THIE 1009:*46*
true R. — ANTH 31:*84*
republican on r. principles — SHAW 920:*11*
R. form of government — SPEN 956:*69*
R. landslide on Nov 8 — CUOMO 301:*8*
The R. Party — STEV 973:*83*
vote for Hollywood as a R. — WALL 1049:*60*
Republicans If R. will stop — STEV 972:*71*
its members are now R. — ONEI 740:*69*
R. …get elected — OROU 741:*81*
republics Large r. seem — PALM 752:*71*
Mischiefes to Churches and R. — PRYN 794:*11*
perfect r. are a perfect nonsense — FOWL 399:*64*
R. end by wealth — MONT 702:*85*
repugnance historical r. to woman — PAGL 749:*34*
repulsion Attraction and r. — BLAKE 166:*71*
reputation At ev'ry word a r. dies — POPE 778:*98*
bad r. is like a hangover — PRES 789:*26*
better for the r. — KEYN 555:*40*
dignity has descended over his r. — ATLAS 44:*6*
her scandalous r. — SITW 940:*3*
I have offended r. — SHAK 905:*79*
injured no man's r. — LOVE 615:*70*
lover's bad r. — NAPO 718:*33*

restless his r. hands　　PRIT 791:66
its people…moving, shifting, r.　　FERB 385:7
R., he rolls　　ROCH 816:46
restoration not revolution but r.　　HARD 455:79
worst of a revolution is r.　　FOX 400:72
restoratives No r.　　FORD 397:12
restrain it is not possible to r. them　　RICH 810:68
restraint free from this r.　　CONG 282:48
praise the firm r.　　CAMP 227:15
suffer from too rigid a r.　　BRON 191:93
with our moral r.　　KENN 552:89
would that r. upon us　　JOHN 528:52
restraints paucity of r.　　SPEN 956:68
restrictions r. on woman　　FULL 409:33
restructuring whole world needs r.　　GORB 435:57
result accomplished the r.　　ACHE 3:37
how small a realized R.　　CARL 235:59
our r. is vitiated　　THOR 1016:72
r. is the battle won or lost　　WELL 1063:13
r. looked rather like the Forth Bridge　　BRIT 189:33
r. of my upbringing　　DYSON 358:99
r. of the energy stored　　GERS 420:7
satisfied with that r.　　SCHW 851:27
secure and lasting r.　　DESC 317:81
results hope of instant r.　　SCHL 848:78
how many dangerous r.　　LOUI 614:46
poll r.　　GALL 413:98
r. dies with the worker　　LEON 596:74
r. of thought and resolution　　TROL 1027:74
resurrection by man came also the r.　　BIBLE 151:67
foretaste of r.　　SCHO 849:1
I am the r., and the life　　BIBLE 146:55
in the r. they neither marry　　BIBLE 139:33
prelude to r.　　WILL 1081:50
reclaimed…property at the r.　　BUTL 218:50
r. is rare　　ADAMS 5:80
R. of the body　　BOOK 173:94
r. of the body　　BOOK 178:96
R. to eternal life　　BOOK 176:58
resuscitate r., if it concerns history　　HUGO 501:59
retail R. is detail　　SCHU 850:13
retard r. what we cannot repel　　JOHN 526:9
reticence R., in three volumes　　GLAD 430:57
retire being young until you r.　　LARK 582:18
r., and in retiring draw　　MILT 694:32
r.…from who's who to who's that　　WRIS 1102:19
r. to the grandstands　　GERG 420:2
sign for him to r.　　DISR 333:12
want to r. at 50　　KINN 559:9
retirement must be no r.　　HAIG 450:10
short r. urges sweet return　　MILT 692:11
retiring r. at high speed　　HALS 452:35
retort first, the R. Courteous　　SHAK 887:35
retreat If I r., kill me　　MUSS 716:84
into which one can r.　　ORWE 744:38
mistress…little country r.　　WYCH 1103:34
principle solitude and r.　　MONT 701:66
r.…in his own soul　　AURE 50:25
r. into advance　　ROOS 821:36
retrograde r. if it does not advance　　GIBB 421:25
retrospect dark unfathom'd r.　　WHIT 1073:94
in r.…all a blur　　SCHL 848:76
we live in r.　　HAZL 463:13
return alas! we r.　　FORS 398:30
came through and…shall r.　　MACA 621:69
day of their r.　　MACA 623:5
r. no more　　SWIFT 984:59
shall not r. unto me void　　BIBLE 127:6
returnable children…are not r.　　CRISP 296:33
returned r. from battle　　HOMER 487:16
returning In r.…shall ye be saved　　BIBLE 126:79
r. him safely to earth　　KENN 551:66
R. were as tedious　　SHAK 909:63
returns gives the basest r.　　INNO 512:55

reunion every r. is a foretaste　　SCHO 849:1
reveal r. the appalling dangers　　HUXL 507:67
something to r.　　THOM 1012:10
revealed those things which are r.　　BIBLE 108:98
revel blood-bedecked halls of their r.　　POE 776:44
R. the night　　SHAK 878:9
revelation continuous thread of r.　　WELTY 1065:51
essence of music is r.　　HEINE 467:71
few weeks ago I had a r.　　STEIN 966:51
habit of r.　　SKEL 942:49
inspired by divine r.　　BACON 55:13
land of light and r.　　CLIN 269:18
lies in its r. in act　　WHIT 1071:60
man's r. to man　　FRYE 408:20
r. of character in a play　　WILL 1081:66
r. of Jesus Christ　　BIBLE 155:75
r. of Mahomet　　GIBB 421:23
r. of the nature of God　　WHIT 1071:61
r. of the sexual goings-on　　CRIT 297:43
r. of Thought　　EMER 377:70
revelations extraordinary r.　　BUTL 216:96
heaven…measured as R. says　　LAUR 584:45
It ends with R.　　WILDE 1077:65
sounded like the book of R.　　JAMES 516:8
revelled fought as they r.　　DAVIS 309:38
revellers one by one dropped the r.　　POE 776:44
revelry sound of r. by night　　BYRON 219:84
revenge Blood and r.…in my head　　SHAK 862:37
blows and r. for me!　　SHAK 861:20
Caesar's spirit, ranging for r.　　SHAK 883:45
capable and wide r.　　SHAK 899:42
favourite form of r.　　NIET 728:86
first blood shed in r.　　PEPYS 765:62
Freud would have his r.　　DOCT 334:39
General Ford as his r.　　ABZUG 2:15
harbour any thoughts of r.　　JOSE 537:33
in r. I took her to pieces　　CONG 281:25
kiss…sweet as my r.!　　SHAK 911:16
little R. herself　　TENN 1005:61
On desperate r.　　MILT 689:33
permanent…had its own kind of r.　　FRAME 400:79
Prompted to my r.　　SHAK 890:16
R. is a kind of wild justice　　BACON 56:48
r. of the intellect upon art　　SONT 952:4
R. triumphs over death　　BACON 56:44
shall we not r.?　　SHAK 872:80
slow r. of the Orient　　PRIE 790:39
species of r.　　JOHN 525:88
study of r., immortal hate　　MILT 687:93
surpass Common r.　　MILT 688:19
Sweet is r.　　BYRON 222:32
revenged on a wretch wilt thou be r.?　　SIDN 937:48
r. on the whole pack　　SHAK 895:38
revenges angelic r. on Philistines　　ARNO 39:21
time brings in his r.　　SHAK 895:37
will have such r. on both of you　　SHAK 902:15
revenue abundant streams of r.　　WEBS 1059:23
reverberation paucity of its r.　　MAIL 639:85
Revere ride of Paul R.　　LONG 612:16
reverence cycle-clips in awkward r.　　LARK 581:1
In deeper r. praise　　WHIT 1074:9
little more r., please　　SARG 843:95
objects of r. and love　　CARL 233:31
poor to do him r.　　SHAK 884:52
r. in us dwell　　TENN 998:18
with sanctimonious r.　　JEFF 520:96
reverend As you are old and r.　　SHAK 902:6
reverends Right R. and Wrong R.　　DICK 325:37
reverie poem full of space and r.　　BAUD 78:46
reveries r. so airy　　COWP 293:57
reverse Forwards in r.　　DUNN 356:52
produce the r. of happiness　　MILL 675:71
sleep, and shall again r.　　SPEN 958:17
review I have your r. before me　　REGER 806:96

review (*contd.*)
r. of institutions　　PEEL 763:42
reviewers chorus of indolent r.　　TENN 1003:26
metropolitan r.　　BEER 83:38
reviewing devote myself to r.　　NICO 727:62
revisionist r. clique of Deng　　JIANG 522:26
revival engineering an economic r.　　LARD 580:89
revive r. thy work　　BIBLE 130:63
revolt Is this a r.?　　LOUI 614:51
nature falls into r.　　SHAK 878:8
of the old r. from Awe　　MERE 671:1
seduced them to that foul r.?　　MILT 687:87
sign of a r.　　EAGL 359:3
writers…join in a common r.　　COWL 291:22
revolting r. and a rebellious heart　　BIBLE 128:20
revolution any true r.　　SWIFT 983:54
attempt to export r.　　STAL 962:79
beginning r.　　WELL 1063:14
blood-red flower of r.　　RAND 801:26
children of the r.　　LEGU 594:31
dream of r.　　STOP 978:76
Gracchi deploring r.?　　JUVE 540:78
Hope ushers in a R.　　CARL 235:61
new industrial r.　　WIEN 1074:13
No, sir, it's a r.　　LOUI 614:51
not the leaders of a r.　　CONR 285:7
r. has been stolen　　JIANG 522:26
r. in America　　LINK 606:24
r. in how writers write　　WELD 1062:90
r. is not a dinner party　　MAO 648:18
r. itself is a game　　ROBB 813:11
r. of 1789 is her political religion　　LAMA 575:2
r. than a government　　MARC 649:45
r. to get the politicians out　　CAST 244:32
r. was our midwife　　INOU 512:57
r. where love is not allowed　　ANGE 19:26
safeguard a r.　　ORWE 745:61
some kind of cultural r.　　GINS 428:33
sun of the socialist r.　　LENIN 595:50
The Industrial R.　　TOYN 1024:15
the R. may…devour　　VERG 1042:32
theory and methods of r.　　MAO 648:20
tremble at a communist r.　　MARX 660:15
Universal suffrage is counter-r.　　PROU 792:86
violent r. inevitable　　KENN 551:71
what the Russian R. can become　　ONET 740:70
white heat of this r.　　WILS 1085:30
worst of a r.　　FOX 400:72
revolutionaries May r. said　　ROBB 813:11
Most r. are…Tories　　ORWE 743:12
revolutionary not believe…not a r.　　CAST 244:33
most r. insight　　JONG 533:61
r. ends as an oppressor　　CAMUS 229:55
revolutionists organisations of r.　　LENIN 595:48
views of the r.　　SCHL 848:73
revolutions main cause of r.　　INGE 511:39
modern r. have ended　　CAMUS 229:54
R. have never lightened the burden　　SHAW 922:44
roses and r.　　RAND 801:24
small engine that causes r.　　SHEE 926:49
sure to stir up r.　　ARIS 34:33
revolver instead of a r.　　STEW 957:64
r. into my right ear　　GREE 444:22
r. ready to hand　　STEV 973:97
reward Crimes…are their own r.　　FARQ 383:67
fruit of the womb is his r.　　BIBLE 119:42
good r. for their labour　　BIBLE 123:23
in no wise lose his r.　　BIBLE 136:81
nothing for r.　　SPEN 958:11
only r. of virtue is virtue　　EMER 376:40
only r. one should offer　　RENO 807:9
r. for conformity　　BROWN 194:60
r. of a thing well done　　EMER 376:47
R. that young man　　DUGO 354:24

reward (*contd.*)
r. your faith in us — SMITH 947:8
right of his r. — MILT 686:70
without the r. of priority — SCOTT 852:39
rewarded r. and punished — SZASZ 989:67
r. with a smile — SAIN 836:86
rewarder who now will be my R. — BUNY 205:74
rewards Fortune's buffets and r. — SHAK 891:35
multitude of r. — PATR 761:15
no r. nor punishments — INGE 511:43
r. for being sane — AMIS 17:81
world its veterans r. — POPE 782:77
rewrite owe to history is to r. it — WILDE 1076:38
Reykjavik in touch with R. — WHITE 1070:28
rhetoric fearful...about their own r. — OBRI 734:65
logic and r. — BACON 59:25
r. passed for reality — BENT 93:31
rhetorical artlessly r. — BISH 163:29
rhetorician sophistical r. — DISR 334:24
Rhine R....Doth wash your city — COLE 275:26
R....is where our frontier lies — BALD 65:11
The R. is not more impassable — GIBB 421:23
rhino like the White R. — BENN 90:75
rhinoceros hide of a r. — BARR 73:56
Rhodesia black...rule ever in R. — SMITH 947:7
rhubarb r. words — SIDN 937:52
What r., cyme — SHAK 910:84
rhyme All r., and scrawl — POPE 782:82
Down my desert r. — CRAIK 294:90
forty long years of good r. — OBRU 734:73
love...hath taught me to r. — SHAK 865:18
more r. there is in poetry — SAND 842:79
names in many a musèd r. — KEATS 548:18
no r. to 'lady' — SHAK 880:65
outlive this powerful r. — SHAK 913:65
plot and r. — LOWE 617:13
poet...climbs on r. — FERL 386:20
reason for my r. — SPEN 959:44
R. is the rock — DRYD 350:35
r. rudder is of verses — BUTL 216:10
unattempted yet in prose or r. — MILT 687:85
where I read and r. — WYATT 1102:26
rhymes Different r. — BROD 189:65
ring out my mournful r. — TENN 1000:57
rhyming drasty r. is nat worth — CHAU 255:42
not born under a r. planet — SHAK 880:65
r., ranting, raving b. — BURNS 209:71
rhythm all things have a r. — MAMET 643:53
All God's Chillum got R. — KAHN 541:91
I got r. — GERS 420:8
language restored to its essential r. — MALL 641:14
r. brings about a poetic short-circuit — SENG 858:50
r. ...of a picture — FEIN 385:99
rhythms lucid, inescapable r. — STEV 971:44
Rialto In the R. you have rated me — SHAK 874:20
ribald roused the r. crows — SHAK 896:55
riband for a r. to stick in his coat — BROW 198:34
ribbon blue r. of the turf — DISR 333:1
like a soldier's r. — ABSE 1:7
ribbons bondage of certain r. — SHAK 912:37
fluttering of r. — DICK 322:66
none of your r. and bells — MARQ 656:41
Wi' r. in her hair — BALL 67:45
ribs soul beneath the r. of death — MANC 644:66
through the flinty r. — SHAK 868:70
took one of his r. — BIBLE 103:92
yerked him here, under the r. — SHAK 897:99
Ribstone Pippin Right as a R. P.! — BELL 87:14
rice R., and a Cranberry Tart — LEAR 590:56
r. in a church — LENN 596:62
They gave us our r. bowl — QIAN 796:48
rich acute shortage of r. people — WILS 1085:43
All I am or was is r. — MAY 665:2
Be r. in patience — DUNB 355:37

rich (*contd.*)
Beauty too r. for use — SHAK 868:82
best of the r. — SPARK 955:55
both r. and poor nations — ILLI 511:33
consumed almost wholly by...the r. — HALL 452:33
curse not the r. — BIBLE 123:39
demand disturbs...the r. — BRON 191:1
desire to be r. — BAGE 61:62
distance between r. and poor — CARL 234:39
equality of laws forbids the r. — FRAN 401:90
errors of the r. — CHES 258:1
Gay r. and R. gay — ANON 24:3
gift r. by delaying it — TROL 1028:85
graphic description...of the r. — WOLFE 1091:31
high and low, r. and poor — MORI 708:68
I's r. now — TWAIN 1033:85
If thou art r. — SHAK 897:78
Into something r. and strange — SHAK 916:26
Just because you're r. — SEIB 857:32
Let him be r. and weary — HERB 476:35
low in r....countries — SMITH 945:80
making Gay r. — JOHN 531:11
man who dies r. — CARN 236:5
marry a r. woman — THAC 1006:93
No legacy is so r. — SHAK 901:76
not a sin to be r. — CONN 282:51
One composition...is r. — DIDE 330:40
Poor and content is r. — SHAK 899:33
Poor Little R. Girl — COWA 290:91
poor, yet making many r. — BIBLE 151:83
property of the r. — RUSK 831:93
r. and delicate English language — WAUGH 1058:9
R. And The Poor — DISR 332:90
r....are different from you and me — FITZ 391:8
r. are the scum — CHES 259:24
r. because you are white — FANON 382:59
r. don't have children — NEWM 724:34
r. get r. — KAHN 541:90
R. gifts wax poor — SHAK 891:22
r. hath many friends — BIBLE 121:76
r. he hath sent empty away — BIBLE 141:75
r. in apparel — TROL 1027:63
r. in nature's store — FORD 397:18
r. is better — TUCK 1031:49
r. man in his castle — ALEX 13:18
r. man to enter into the kingdom — BIBLE 139:25
r. man told me recently — BARA 70:7
r. man's joys increase — GOLD 433:15
r. man's wealth is his strong city — BIBLE 120:68
R. men deal gifts — SHAK 902:95
r. men rule the law — GOLD 432:98
r. not gaudy — SHAK 888:69
r. should become poor — ARIS 34:33
r. society too r. — TAWN 991:8
r. with forty pounds a year — GOLD 433:11
R. with spoils of time — GRAY 442:68
r. with suspicion — RICH 809:43
robbing the r. — SHAW 921:31
shall not be r. — BIBLE 132:5
the r. he hath sent empty away — BIBLE 160:54
The very r. are different — HEMI 471:31
There was a certain r. man — BIBLE 143:6
this r. praise — SHAK 914:77
though her father be very r. — SHAK 864:71
to strike it r. — HEAN 465:43
we'll be wondrous r. — OTWAY 746:85
widening gulf between the r. — COUP 289:77
with the r. in his death — BIBLE 127:2
Richard on the head of R. — SHAK 863:65
To put down R. — SHAK 875:43
Richardson one letter of R.'s — JOHN 528:61
Richelieu Gladstone, like R. — DISR 333:22
richer for r. for poorer — BOOK 176:49
for which I am r. — SHAK 902:99

richer (*contd.*)
get r. and r. — GARD 415:23
mightier and r. thah thyself — BIBLE 132:1
riches according to his r. in glory — BIBLE 153:18
bear'st thy heavy r. — SHAK 897:78
count our r. — PREV 789:30
deceitfulness of r. — BIBLE 137:98
Embarrassment of R. — ALLA 14:29
full of days, r., and honour — BIBLE 112:87
greatest in Europe for R. — BAIL 62:70
Grit r. and prosperitie — BROWN 194:36
hire old r. — CHAU 255:36
in her left hand r. — BIBLE 120:60
increase of r. and commerce — HUME 504:11
infinite r. in a little room — MARL 653:98
natural science accumulates new r. — ALEM 13:12
R. are a good handmaid — BACON 56:34
R. are for spending — BACON 58:2
r. certainly make themselves wings — BIBLE 121:95
r. fineless is as poor — SHAK 899:33
r. grow in hell — MILT 688:9
r. to men of understanding — BIBLE 123:35
r. where is my deserving? — SHAK 914:71
r. will leave us sick — EMER 377:62
unsearchable r. of Christ — BIBLE 152:97
world's r., which dispersèd lie — HERB 476:34
richness all in a rush With r. — HOPK 491:86
r.; his double action — HUGEL 498:10
r....of existence — KENN 552:88
rickshaw no go the r. — MACN 637:38
Rico is this the end of R. — ROBI 814:23
rid harder it is to get r. — TWAIN 1032:69
how to get r. of ourselves — HORN 494:36
idea of getting r. of it — JERO 521:8
r. of Paul Revere — LONG 612:71
time we got r. of Him — BALD 64:99
riddance die and be a r.! — DICK 324:3
riddle could not...expound the r. — BIBLE 109:17
dish-cover the r. — CARR 241:71
glory, jest, and r. — POPE 780:43
had not found out my r. — BIBLE 109:18
How still the R. lies! — DICK 327:91
r. wrapped inside a mystery — CHUR 264:11
riddles r. of birth and dead — FRYE 408:27
riddling Not all their r. can forestall — BERR 98:9
ride being taken for a r. — JOSE 537:33
mount by me and r. — YEATS 1104:58
ticket to r. — LENN 596:61
two men r. of a horse — SHAK 880:59
we r. them down — TENN 996:93
rider between a r. and his horse — SURT 983:48
good r. may often be thrown — ANON 23:98
r. hanging with a locket — SOME 952:1
steed That knows his r. — BYRON 219:79
The r., the birds — YEATS 1105:72
the r. was lost — FRAN 402:7
riders r. on the earth together — MACL 634:53
ridge r. of monstrous massy — MUNDY 714:53
ridicule wise r. and obey — BIER 161:83
ridiculous fine sense of the r. — ALBEE 11:86
made r. by friends — BIER 160:68
makes men look r. — JUVE 540:79
most r. and scornful sort — SIDN 937:64
R. 20 years after — LAVER 584:56
step above the r. — PAINE 751:36
To the R. — GRAH 437:86
we have made enthusiasm r. — STAEL 961:70
riding keep on r. — TRUM 1030:32
Ridley good comfort Master R. — LATI 583:36
rife r. as the loam Of prairies — CRANE 295:3
rifle a r. ...had gone off — ORWE 743:6
Let him who has a r. — HO 482:33
r. all the breathing spring — COLL 276:42
roll to your r. — KIPL 560:33

rifle (*contd.*)
with r. and pack   SASS 845:28
rifles stuttering r.' rapid rattle   OWEN 748:7
rift little r. within the lute   TENN 1002:5
rig Tato, R. and Scrunge   MURR 715:76
Rigby Eleanor R. picks up the rice   LENN 596:62
right absolute and unlimited r.   BENT 92:16
age of r. and opportunity   WILS 1086:44
All's r. with the world   BROW 197:25
Always do r.   TWAIN 1034:17
as much r....as pigs have to fly   CARR 238:34
be decorative and to do r.!   FIRB 389:75
belief which may be r.   FORS 398:32
better to be approximately r.   BUFF 203:43
boldly speak in r.   OTWAY 746:79
born to set it r.!   SHAK 889:85
Brotherhood of the R. Stuff   WOLFE 1090:25
D H Lawrence was r.   GIBB 422:36
desire to do r.   DICK 327:79
discussion of any subject is a r.   SHEL 927:56
divine r. of husbands   WOLL 1091:39
editor...will always be r.   BENN 92:4
every man did that which was r.   BIBLE 109:23
exclusively in the r.   HUXL 506:54
fight for the r.   CURZ 302:29
Give it because it is r.   LLOY 609:63
great r. of an excessive wrong   BROW 200:89
have the r. to exist   KELM 549:33
her r. to...opinions   PALM 752:74
hundredth time I am r.   EINS 363:64
If the young fellow is r.   QUIN 797:64
if two wrongs don't make a r.   COUS 290:88
irresponsible and r.   CHUR 265:36
it isn't enough to be r.?   OATES 733:34
itch but a kind of colourable r.   LEST 599:13
Judge of all the earth do r.   BIBLE 105:24
know I'm r.   GOLD 433:32
legal r. to say what you like   ORWE 742:5
Lenin was r.   KEYN 554:27
Let's do it r.   PEI 764:47
majority never has r.   IBSEN 510:20
may she always be in the r.   DECA 311:71
meet and r. so to do   BOOK 174:27
men strive for R.   BROW 197:19
must also be r.   GOULD 436:76
My country, r. or wrong   CHES 258:91
nation being so r.   WILS 1086:47
nature's state, where all have r.   DRYD 350:27
neither r. nor safe   LUTH 619:45
Next to being r.   HUXL 506:6
no claim of r.   MALT 643:40
No government has the r.   BROWN 194:58
no more r. to...happiness   SHAW 920:96
no r. to strike   COOL 286:35
no r. to transgress the law   DOST 340:43
not between r. and wrong   JUNG 539:71
novelist...does not have the r.   FLAU 392:41
on the r. side   GALB 412:81
one thing we did r.   ANON 28:19
people who hunt are the r. people   SHAW 925:17
petty r. or wrong   THOM 1012:4
quite r. too   GREY 446:56
r. action is freedom   ELIOT 372:63
r. angle is necessary   MALL 642:21
R. as a Ribstone Pippin!   BELL 87:14
R. Divine of Kings   POPE 783:4
r. in his own eyes   BIBLE 121:92
r. is not what someone gives you   CLARK 268:87
r. is only a motor hand   HEPW 473:81
r. is retreating   FOCH 395:83
r. not to understand   CALV 226:6
r. now is wrong   SPEN 959:37
r. out of wrong   JONS 535:96
R. perfection   SHAK 914:69

right (*contd.*)
r. place to film it   GARD 414:20
r. to a fair portion   BURKE 207:29
r. to hear what other...human   CARL 236:86
r. to the property   RUSK 831:93
r. to utter what he thinks   JOHN 531:14
saddling of the r. to a child   SHAW 924:93
secure of private r.   DRYD 350:26
settle what's r. and fair   HUGH 500:51
Sit thou at my r. hand   BIBLE 118:22
solve it r. or wrong   WATS 1055:53
someone will make things r.   REAG 803:60
sometimes in the r.   DRYD 347:61
Still in thy r. hand   SHAK 918:63
successful or otherwise, always r.   ADAMS 6:89
sure that it is r.   HAND 455:67
take from me the r. to speak   MACL 633:67
'the r.' is only the expedient   JAMES 518:50
the r. to report events   ORWE 745:50
the r. to tell people   ORWE 744:28
They can't all be r.   DRIB 346:44
things...will not come r.   ONOL 734:66
though r. were worsted   BROW 200:2
to be proved r.   HUXL 507:86
to get things r.   RYLE 834:54
turned him r. and round about   BURNS 213:49
Ulster will be r.   CHUR 263:92
undoubted r. of the crown   COVE 290:90
way which seemeth r.   BIBLE 121:75
what his r. wing was doing   ASQU 42:87
whatever be his r. to it   STEV 976:47
when ye turn to the r. hand   BIBLE 126:70
whether you do r.   TWAIN 1033:92
whether you do r.   TWAIN 1033:93
wrong and r.   YEATS 1105:62
wrong because not all was r.   CRAB 294:85
wrong notes are r.   IVES 514:84
young and perhaps he is r.   MAHL 638:62
righted none that could be r.   JONAS 533:49
righteous came not to call the r.   BIBLE 141:59
I have seen r. forsaken   BLUN 170:47
not come to call the r.   BIBLE 136:70
not seen the r. forsaken   BIBLE 115:65
r. runneth into it   BIBLE 121:88
r. with impunity?   RACI 799:2
souls of the r.   BIBLE 131:81
righteousness breastplate of r.   BIBLE 152:6
eternal...makes for r.   ARNO 40:34
feareth him, and worketh r.   BIBLE 148:93
For my r. the Lord hath brought   BIBLE 108:93
hunger and thirst after r.   BIBLE 133:34
kingdom of God, and his r.   BIBLE 135:53
let the clouds rain down r.   BIBLE 159:51
loved r.   GREG 446:46
paths of r.   BIBLE 115:50
paths of r.   SCOT 856:19
r. shall exceed the r. of the scribes   BIBLE 134:38
Sun of r. arise   BIBLE 131:72
things that we think are our r.   BUTT 218:53
what r. really is   ARNO 40:35
worketh r.   BIBLE 114:38
righteousnesses r. are as filthy rags   BIBLE 128:13
rights all a talkin' 'bout r.   TRUTH 1030:38
backlash against women's r.   FALU 382:58
believe that they have r.   HEGEL 466:62
bill of r.   JEFF 520:91
certain inalienable r.   STAN 962:85
death instead of 'human r.'   PEOP 764:58
die in defence of their r.   PITT 771:68
discuss women's r.   HILL 270:25
exercise the r. of children   COWP 292:50
fight for their own human r.   PANK 753:80
full menu of r.   TUTU 1032:54
Human r., national integrity   WILS 1086:45

rights (*contd.*)
Let woman share the r.   WOLL 1091:43
maintenance of established r.   PEEL 763:42
men, their r. and nothing more   ANTH 31:84
Natural r. is simple nonsense   BENT 93:17
of all 'r. of man'   CARL 235:83
Property has...its r.   DRUM 346:47
r. inherent and inalienable   JEFF 520:87
r. of an Englishman   JUNI 540:74
r. of every man   KENN 551:80
r. of every other nation   PARN 756:40
r. of the individual   CHUR 264:10
r....of the laboring man   BAER 61:48
r. of the savage   GLAD 429:52
r. of the smaller nationalities   ASQU 42:77
r. of women   COPE 287:52
r....on basis of physical   BOTHA 180:33
Stand up for your r.   MARL 652:82
the r. of the people   SUN 982:39
trenching on another's r.   BRON 191:5
vital personal r.   WARR 1053:28
rill By cool Siloam's shady r.   HEBER 466:57
danced the moon on Monan's r.   SCOTT 853:61
gushing of a r.   BYRON 223:63
the descending r.   SMART 944:68
Rimbauds always chasing R.   PARK 754:15
ring clear, clean r. of...insult   CARR 237:18
dance round in a r.   FROST 407:98
fantastic r., Round   BROW 198:54
form a r.   SCHR 850:7
four walls and a r.   HEAN 464:33
get me in any r. with Mr Tolstoy   HEMI 471:37
great r. of...light   VAUG 1041:39
his luminous r.'   TENN 994:55
jow or r.   FERG 386:16
man gets into a r.   MAIL 640:86
One R. to rule them all   TOLK 1022:92
R. out the want   TENN 1000:57
R. out, wild bells   TENN 1000:56
This pretty r.   SCHR 850:2
unconquered in a r.   CHES 259:37
what shall we do for a r.?   LEAR 590:59
willing to sell...Your r.?   LEAR 590:60
with this r. I thee wed   BOOK 176:51
ringmaster r. has altered   ASHD 41:61
rings r., and things   SHAK 864:79
their r. or green mantles   BALL 67:51
Rio roll to R.   KIPL 563:84
riot blaze of r. cannot last   SHAK 866:44
He didn't r.   TEBB 992:25
ripe we r. and r.   SHAK 885:90
ripeness R. is all   EMPS 378:84
R. is all   SHAK 904:45
ripped Untimely r.   SHAK 910:89
ripples the infernal r.   POUND 785:59
rise but stoop to r.   MASS 662:54
Created half to r.   POPE 780:43
Early to r.   THUR 1018:24
One man's wage r.   WILS 1085:37
opportunity to r. again   SARN 843:96
R., take up thy bed   BIBLE 145:39
R. up, my love   BIBLE 124:49
Some r. by sin   SHAK 896:68
risen He is not here, but is r.   BIBLE 144:20
rising All great r.   BACON 58:75
constantly r. at four   WESL 1067:71
means of r. in the world   JOHN 529:70
ways of the bird r.   REID 806:97
risings r....on contradiction   EMPS 378:85
risk England...preferred the r.   CECIL 247:79
increases in relation to r.   HEMI 471:47
r. of becoming a subordinate species   SCOTT 856:10
r. of being heroes   BOLT 172:76
r. of maiming it for life   SHAW 922:52

Rochdale take my wife to see R.   SHAN 919:74
Rochefoucauld Duke of R.-Liancourt   LOUI 614:51
rock been a r. of order   METT 673:30
blue-black tooth of sheer r.   BENU 94:33
cut a Colossus from a r.   JOHN 532:29
first r. at a girl like I   LOOS 613:36
go first, r. and roll or Christianity   LENN 596:55
It's Only R. and Roll   JAGG 515:98
made himself the r.   SCHO 848:87
my r. and my salvation   BIBLE 116:82
principle that gives us a firm R.   BUTT 218:52
prisoner of the hard r.   THOM 1013:24
put thee in a clift of the r.   BIBLE 107:77
Rhyme is the r.   DRYD 350:35
r. a quarter of a million miles up   BAKER 63:84
R. of Ages   TOPL 1023:7
r. of offence   BIBLE 125:64
r. of the national resources   WEBS 1059:23
r. that is higher than I   BIBLE 116:81
Safe upon solid r.   MILL 676:83
secure possession of a bleak r.   YOUNG 1108:2
set my feet upon a r.   BIBLE 115:66
Sex 'n' drugs 'n' r. 'n' roll   DURY 357:81
shadow of a great r.   BIBLE 126:81
The poem in the r.   THOM 1013:24
truth is the uncharted r.   CORN 288:61
rock-n-roll R.-n-r. is instant coffee   GELD 417:67
Rockefellers eat R. for breakfast   KENN 553:6
rocket he rose like a r.   PAINE 750:50
r.'s red glare   KEY 554:24
rockets r. used by the barbarians   KISH 565:29
Rockies the R. may crumble   GERS 420:15
rocking-chair always has the r.-c.   ROBI 815:33
rocking-horse about upon a r.-h.   KEATS 544:40
rocks begin to twinkle from the r.   TENN 995:61
but the r. remain   HERB 474:6
change the r. of Scotland   JOHN 525:78
charms...To soften r.   CONG 281:21
father...throwing r. at the stork   BREC 186:23
flowerless r. of hell   SITW 940:2
Guarded by shoals and r.   BYRON 222:41
heaven but the r.   RUSK 830:79
hitting...bottles with small r.   THUR 1018:14
love resembles eternal r.   BRON 192:12
miraculously glide past the r.   CUOMO 300:5
older than the r.   PATER 759:93
railroad...you blasted its r.   RUSK 831:13
rifted r. whose entrance leads   MILT 683:30
r. melt wi' the sun   BURNS 212:40
steering...for the r.   GILM 427:20
Such uncouth r.   WALP 1051:79
walled round with r.   SWIN 988:56
What are men to r.   AUST 51:41
will sit upon the r.   MARL 655:31
With r., and stones and trees   WORD 1095:7
Rockwell Norman R., the Brueghel   ADLER 8:46
rod chief a r.   POPE 781:50
enforced by the r.   SPEKE 955:62
r. and staff me comfort still   SCOT 856:19
r. and thy staff   BIBLE 115:50
r. out of the stem of Jesse   BIBLE 125:67
rule them with a r. of iron   BIBLE 157:4
spare the r., and spoil the child   BUTL 216:17
spareth his r.   BIBLE 121:74
steel r. runs right through   ANGE 19:23
The r. of Aaron   BIBLE 107:83
Throw away thy r.   HERB 476:37
wisdom be put in a silver r.   BLAKE 166:61
rode Then she r. forth   TENN 995:67
roe following the r.   BURNS 211:5
loving hind and pleasant r.   BIBLE 120:62
roes breasts are like two young r.   BIBLE 124:51
Roger Sir R. is landlord   ADDI 7:11
steal from Samuel R.   BYRON 222:38

rogue 100,000 thalers a r.   LICH 604:86
bewitched with the r.'s company   SHAK 875:48
busy and insinuating r.   SHAK 900:49
easy it is to call r.   DRYD 351:63
fiddler, and consequently a r.   SWIFT 984:69
Has he not a r.'s face?   CONG 280:11
O, what a r. and peasant slave   SHAK 890:14
r. alive to the ludicrous   EMER 378:78
r. gives you Love Powders   LAMB 576:16
r. in porcelain   MERE 671:8
r. is outlining a treacherous plan   FRAS 403:18
wasna he a r.   ANON 23:99
rogues bold, deserving r.   OTWAY 746:83
parcel of r.   BURNS 212:31
r. slighted me into the river   SHAK 878:22
you dissentious r.   SHAK 910:1
Roland Child R. to the dark tower   SHAK 903:25
role How do you approach a r.?   EVANS 381:38
masculine r.   GREER 445:40
play the r. of watchmaker   DAWK 310:44
r. is...filling vacuums   CART 242:7
r. of the poet to look   PRIT 791:71
subside into the r.   STRA 979:91
time that occupies the same r.   MACL 635:92
You have played your r.   TROT 1029:2
roll r. us shoreward soon   TENN 994:48
R. darkling down   JOHN 525:84
roller basic white and with a r.   BROWN 194:59
rolling r. down the street   IGNA 510:28
Rolls Royce R. R. diplomacy   ANON 28:9
roman Before the R. came to Rye   CHES 259:31
challenges the R. Catholic   MACM 635:14
departed as a 'R.'   LAWS 587:19
fabulous yellow r. candles   KERO 553:12
Greek and R. poets   PRIOR 791:62
heard the snobbish R. say   BEER 83:42
high R. fashion   SHAK 906:97
I am a R. citizen   CICE 266:63
in the R. Catholic religion   TROL 1027:77
Like the R., I seem to see   POWE 788:17
Make way, R. writers   PROP 792:80
more an antique R.   SHAK 893:86
noblest R. of them all   SHAK 884:68
not...holy, or R.   VOLT 1046:9
R. holiday   BYRON 220:1
since the R. colonists   HYDE 509:12
the R. in days of old   PALM 752:72
Thundered out on the R. air   AUDEN 48:78
To-day the R. and his trouble   HOUS 495:54
Would that the R. people   CALI 225:97
romance calls his work a R.   HAWT 461:72
chiaroscuro of r.   MAUG 665:89
cloudy symbols of a high r.   KEATS 544:50
fine r.   FIEL 388:56
not a little given to r.   EVEL 381:41
There's r. for you!   MORR 708:77
Utopian and revolutionary r.   WEBB 1059:17
while there's...love and r.   BERL 95:61
romances are like r. read   SUCK 981:20
no more need of r.   WHIT 1072:74
Romans Friends, R., countrymen   SHAK 884:48
poverty of the present R.   WALP 1051:80
R. call it stoicism   ADDI 8:29
west of Ireland, the R. had never   CHRI 261:72
romantic defining a r. poet   FROST 407:90
Men are so r.   WELD 1062:95
New York...an infinitely r. notion   DIDI 330:45
R. 100 years after   LAVER 584:56
r. awe of them   HEMI 471:31
r. diseased   GOET 431:79
r. interest in our own sex   CONN 283:80
R. Ireland's dead   YEATS 1105:70
romanticism all else is grandiose r.   BUKO 203:46
tinge it with r.   DOYLE 343:88

Rome All roads lead to R.   LAFO 575:86
ascribed to the augurs of R.   KNIG 567:54
At R. she hadde been   CHAU 254:24
Bishop of R. hath no jurisdiction   BOOK 178:99
Britain...Greece to America's R.   BRIN 188:57
Burn, with Athens and with R.   CAMP 227:18
cruel men of R.   SHAK 882:15
deliberating in R.   LIVY 608:49
founded before the City of R.   BAIL 62:70
grandeur that was R.   POE 776:47
hook-nosed fellow of R.   SHAK 878:5
Humorists...burn while R. fiddles   CONN 283:64
irreverential word of R.?   HAWT 462:82
It was at R.   GIBB 421:29
Let R. in Tiber melt   SHAK 904:58
Like R., Nkongsamba was built   BOYD 182:62
O lucky R.   CICE 266:66
on my way to R.   WAUGH 1058:8
Only R. can resemble R.   BELL 86:88
out of R.   GARI 415:25
recent disaster at R.   AUGU 49:16
R.!...city of the soul   BYRON 220:96
R. immortal   GURN 449:90
R. is but a wilderness   SHAK 862:38
R. is like its own Monte Testaceo   CLOU 270:38
R.'s just a city   BURG 205:81
R....only monument left of R.   BELL 86:87
R. shall perish   COWP 292:37
R. shall stand   BYRON 220:3
R. to chase the Antichrist   LESL 598:94
rules of my religion from R.   BROW 195:66
see R. while it yet exists   WALP 1051:80
serve not R.   KIPL 565:16
Sex Life in Ancient R. face   AMIS 16:72
shake your R.   SHAK 911:14
that I loved R. more   SHAK 884:46
thousand roads lead to R.   ALAN 11:80
Three nucios from R.   MACA 622:93
Romeo Juliet and her R.   SHAK 870:24
never will be R.   SHAK 868:89
O R., R.   SHAK 868:87
roof artist needs but a r.   RYDER 834:50
Beneath my shady r.   BLAKE 165:59
Blown through the r.   THOM 1013:21
can't live under the same r.   MONT 701:68
cat on a hot tin r.   WILL 1081:67
corrugated tin r.   BEEC 82:17
good umbrella but a poor r.   LOWE 616:90
He has restored the r.!   BETJ 99:26
high embowèd r.   MILT 683:15
majestical r.   SHAK 890:2
prefers a thatched r.   WALC 1048:41
r. in the words deceiving   MILT 681:92
r., instead of slats   DRAY 346:41
r. of gold   JONS 535:1
tiles on the r.   LUTH 620:47
twigs into a leaky r.   RUDO 828:45
weeks of watching the r. leak   SNYD 951:83
roofs abjure all r.   SHAK 902:14
over the r. of the world   WHIT 1072:75
r. of this distracted City   CARL 235:63
Shake not thy r.   BLAKE 165:60
slate in sun   DAYL 310:57
rook not a r. near it   DICK 323:98
rookery Calls a house a r.   DICK 323:98
rooks r. came home   HODG 483:50
The r. are blown about   TENN 998:25
rooky Makes ring to th' r. wood   SHAK 909:60
room although the r. grows chilly   GRAH 437:88
always r. at the top   WEBS 1059:24
being Queenly in her own r.   WHAR 1068:98
Books do furnish a r.   POWE 788:6
coming to that holy r.   DONNE 338:18
dark r. where I began   MASE 662:44

room (*contd.*)
dog in a very small r.	TOYN 1024:*17*
dying man's r.	STER 969:*8*
embers through the r.	MILT 682:*10*
enough r. in your country	CORW 288:*62*
flung himself from the r.	LEAC 589:*37*
framed …in a comfortable r.	WALP 1051:*87*
Grief fills the r.	SHAK 872:*66*
Here in this r.	STEV 971:*42*
How little r.	SHIR 935:*23*
in morning r. reading	WAUGH 1057:*86*
infinite riches in a little r.	MARL 653:*98*
into the neighbour r.	SHAK 892:*60*
leave r. for the mouse	SAKI 838:*15*
left the r.	GROS 447:*72*
lights in the r.	GUIM 448:*79*
make r. for discovery	APOL 32:*97*
make r. for faith	KANT 542:*6*
man in jail has more r.	JOHN 527:*25*
men in a smoke-filled r.	SIMP 939:*91*
Minister's r. is like a padded cell	CROS 298:*64*
music from a farther r.	ELIOT 367:*49*
no r. for new feelings	ELIOT 365:*18*
no r. in his workshop	FAUL 383:*77*
not r.…to swing a cat	SMOL 950:*65*
only slipped away into the next r.	HOLL 485:*69*
our r. on this earth	GREN 446:*53*
Paces about her r. again	ELIOT 369:*90*
parents…rent out my r.	ALLEN 14:*41*
perpetual struggle for r. and food	MALT 643:*39*
retired to my r.	STER 970:*20*
r. at your head	BALL 101:*35*
r. full of good air	LEAC 589:*36*
r. in the west for wolves	BABB 54:*31*
r. in this country	ROOS 822:*53*
r. of her own	WOOLF 1093:*69*
r. of the palace	SITW 941:*8*
r. or on the street	ROSSO 825:*98*
r. to recognize him	BUEC 203:*42*
r. to swing a cat	DICK 324:*16*
R. with a View	FORS 398:*29*
silence in the r.	KINS 559:*13*
Sir Matthew left the r.	LINK 606:*21*
sit in the same. r. with me	PARK 755:*18*
Social Predestination R.	HUXL 507:*66*
stay quietly in his r.	PASC 757:*58*
stayed in the high r.	SPEN 956:*84*
that r.'s upper end	SPEN 958:*21*
took up a great deal of r.	WHAR 1068:*94*
vilest earth Is r. enough	SHAK 876:*76*
within a little r.	SMITH 948:*31*
you shall keep your r.	STEV 976:*53*

room-mates hard to be r.-m. — SALI 838:*23*

rooms close-pent r. — WEBS 1060:*53*
Know more of the r.	FULL 410:*45*
lighted r. Inside your head	LARK 582:*17*
Other Voices, Other R.	CAPO 230:*77*
People fill their r.	TREE 1025:*44*
planes and corners of r.	MALL 642:*21*
shimmering into r.	WODE 1088:*87*

Roosevelt answer I will give…R. — CHUR 264:*18*
R.'s spare tire	GARN 415:*28*
R. will…go down in American	MENC 669:*70*

roost come home to r. — SOUT 954:*36*

rooster Charm never made a r. — ACHE 3:*49*
Hungry r. don't cackle	HARR 458:*30*

root March hath perced to the r. — CHAU 254:*16*
neither r. nor branch	BIBLE 131:*72*
nips his r.	SHAK 918:*61*
r. of all evil	BIBLE 154:*34*
r. of all genuine growth	SMIL 945:*73*
r. of the matter is found in me?	BIBLE 113:*13*
r. of the old one	NICH 726:*51*
r. of the social unrest	LECO 592:*1*

root (*contd.*)
r. out of a dry ground	BIBLE 127:*99*
rooted thicker and more deeply r.	ROTH 826:*25*
rootholds nourishing earth for r.	SAND 841:*67*
roots blasts the r. of trees	THOM 1010:*51*
Dull r. with spring rain	ELIOT 368:*81*
r. here and there	MERE 671:*16*
r. of relish sweet	KEATS 545:*73*
R. ripe as old bait	ROET 819:*94*
r. that can be pulled up	ELIOT 366:*45*
send my r. rain	HOPK 492:*9*
world withering at the r.	MILL 677:*21*
rope buy a piece of the r.	TWAIN 1034:*5*
child skips r.	WHITE 1070:*34*
Man is a r., fastened	NIET 728:*77*
suspicious then…piece of r.	DALAI 303:*42*
ropes Like dancers on the r.	ETHE 380:*13*
Rorschach R. ink blots	LICH 604:*89*
rortie This r. wretched city	SMITH 949:*60*
rose Al night by the r.	ANON 22:*66*
all-willowed and white r.	FRAME 400:*76*
American Beauty r.	ROCK 817:*69*
colour like the red r.	SHAK 871:*43*
compare the cheeks…to a r.	DALI 303:*46*
dropping a r. petal down	MARQ 656:*47*
dumb to tell the crooked r.	THOM 1010:*51*
English unofficial r.	BROO 192:*25*
fause Lover stole my r.	BURNS 212:*23*
fire and the r. are one	ELIOT 373:*81*
go as deep as a r.'s	SWIN 987:*35*
Go happy r.	HERR 478:*64*
Go, lovely r.	WALL 1050:*70*
have plucked thy r.	SHAK 900:*53*
know the colour r.	ABSE 1:*6*
last r. of summer	MOORE 706:*35*
like a full-blown r.	KEATS 546:*89*
make a right R. Tree	YEATS 1106:*74*
musk of the r. is blown	TENN 1001:*85*
no more desire a r.	SHAK 865:*8*
O r., thou art sick!	BLAKE 167:*88*
One perfect r.	PARK 754:*5*
Queen r. of the rosebud	TENN 1001:*87*
raise up the ghost of a r.	BROW 196:*8*
Reach me a r., honey	FITZ 390:*3*
red, red r.	BURNS 212:*40*
R. is a r. is a r.	STEIN 965:*32*
r. is red	ANON 23:*90*
r. like a nymph	SHEL 930:*29*
R. of all R.s	YEATS 1105:*61*
r. of all the world	MACD 628:*91*
r. of love	SPEN 958:*13*
r. of Sharon	BIBLE 124:*46*
r. Of youth	SHAK 905:*82*
r.'s scent is bitterness	THOM 1014:*31*
Roves back the r.	DELA 314:*24*
summer r.	GRAV 439:*17*
supplication to the r.	FLEC 393:*50*
That r. looks fair	SHAK 913:*63*
that sweet lovely r.	SHAK 875:*43*
That which we call a r.	SHAK 868:*88*
The red r. cries	TENN 1001:*88*
though a r. should shut	KEATS 546:*94*
thought that wants to be a r.	DARIO 305:*76*
tiger sniffs the r.	SASS 845:*37*
vernal bloom, or summer's r.	MILT 689:*31*
Viva la, the R. shall fade	DAVIS 309:*40*
what the r. is	SWIN 987:*44*
without thorn the r.	MILT 690:*53*
rose-bloom R.-b. fell on her hands	KEATS 546:*92*
rose-buds Gather ye r.-b.	HERR 477:*63*
rose-garden door…into the r.-g.	ELIOT 370:*23*
rose-red r.-r. city	BURG 206:*95*
Rosebery [Lord R.]…never missed an occasion

SHAW 926:*45*

rosebud r. garden of girls — TENN 1001:*87*
touch the r., and it fell	PHIL 768:*21*
rosebuds r. in their perfumed bed	CAREW 232:*15*
rosemary r., that's for remembrance	SHAK 892:*69*
roses days of wine and r.	DOWS 343:*82*
field where r. fade	HOUS 495:*62*
flung r.	DOWS 343:*81*
For women are a r.	SHAK 894:*12*
garden…with r.	MARV 657:*71*
Into the blowing r.	MARV 657:*68*
Lilies without, r.	MARV 657:*70*
make thee beds of r.	MARL 655:*31*
not a bed of r.	STEV 974:*8*
perfume of a thousand r.	BERN 97:*88*
petals from blown r.	TENN 994:*49*
raptures and r. of vice	SWIN 987:*32*
red r. there may blow	THOM 1014:*32*
r. and revolutions	RAND 801:*24*
r. at my head	ROSS 824:*76*
r. for the flush of youth	ROSS 823:*70*
r., r., all the way	BROW 198:*52*
r. washed in dew	MILT 682:*97*
seen r. damasked	SHAK 915:*92*
Ross Down…to R. Lake	SNYD 951:*84*
Rosseau mock on, Voltaire R.	BLAKE 167:*99*
Rossetti R. …without principles	FORD 396:*99*
rot R., and consume themselves	SHAK 864:*97*
R. inwardly, foul contagion	MILT 684:*45*
shapes of r.	PURDY 795:*34*
we r. and r.	SHAK 885:*90*
rotarians R. in space!	VIDAL 1044:*59*
rote cage of routine and r.	PLATH 773:*88*
judge by r.	OTWAY 746:*77*
Rothermere papers…by Lord R.	BALD 64:*9*
rotten goodly apple r. at the heart	SHAK 874:*21*
r. in the state of Denmark	SHAK 889:*73*
small choice in r. apples	SHAK 864:*72*
rottenness r. in his bones	BIBLE 121:*71*
r. of our civilisation	READ 803:*53*
rotters miserable sodding r.	LAWR 585:*63*
rotundity thick r. o' th' world	SHAK 903:*18*
rouge wore far too much r.	WILDE 1078:*91*
rough And what r. beast	YEATS 1106:*78*
children who were r.	SPEN 956:*77*
I am r.	SHAK 864:*76*
love…so tyrannous and r.	SHAK 868:*74*
real world…is r.	DAY 310:*47*
r. and ready man	BROW 199:*56*
R. winds do shake	SHAK 912:*48*
Too r., Too rude, too boist'rous	SHAK 868:*77*
rough-hew R.-h. them how we will	SHAK 893:*83*
rough-tongued lifted, r.-t. bell	LARK 581:*96*
Roughing It writing R. I.	MOOD 703:*98*
roughness short-haired joy and r.	SNYD 951:*86*
roughnesses remark all these r.	CROM 298:*54*
round act of walking r. him	BEER 84:*44*
Am I so r. with you	SHAK 865:*2*
As r. as the world	SITW 940:*4*
body was as r.	SPEKE 955:*62*
Cricket…presents men in the r.	ARLO 35:*38*
Glasgow…going r. and r.	FYFFE 410:*63*
other way r.	GOWE 437:*81*
r. and full at evening	HOLM 486:*86*
r. it was, upon a hill	STEV 971:*33*
r. of bells	SLES 943:*57*
teach it r. or flat	JOHN 524:*59*
unto Merlion, and the Table R.	MALO 642:*28*
With visible motion her diurnal r.!	WORD 1095:*16*
roundabouts What's lost upon the r.	CHAL 248:*11*
roundheels Reagan is a rhetorical r.	SAFI 836:*71*
rounds priests…walking their r.	BLAKE 167:*91*
Roupell by the late Mr C R.	SPEN 956:*70*
rouse If anything might r. him	OWEN 748:*19*
r. before the morn	TENN 996:*87*

Rousseau Imagine R., Voltaire — HESS 479:84
R. said…he was only trying — HAZL 463:10
Voltaire, R.…fools, and madmen! — ONEI 740:59
rout feasts where meet a public r. — DAVI 307:10
route r. towards the unknown — HUGO 502:92
routine people free from r. — LINK 606:20
relentless cage of r. — PLATH 773:88
rove she may r. as well — BEHN 85:67
roving r. woman gives rise to gossip — ANON 21:57
row canst boast a r. — JONS 535:1
frightful, apalling r. — ONOL 734:67
r. of dominoes set up — EISE 364:84
R. upon r. — TATE 991:2
sitting in the last r. — KAUF 542:12
rowdies round up us old r. — MACM 636:23
rowing R. Towards God — SEXT 860:69
rows not lugged into Family R. — WODE 1089:91
ranged in more frequented r. — CRAB 293:67
r. and r. of empty seats — OLIV 738:30
royal every r. verdict — WHIT 1069:16
member of R. Family called Ena — WOOD 1091:46
no 'r. road' to geometry — EUCL 380:21
Of eyes again so r. — SHAK 906:8
r. bed of Denmark — SHAK 889:79
R. Commission is a broody hen — FOOT 396:93
r. corpses — GILL 426:2
r. family in the middle ages — HALD 451:16
r. priesthood — BIBLE 156:78
stand so highly in our estate r. — HENR 472:65
royalties fresh air and r. — ASHF 41:67
royalty r. is to be reverenced — BAGE 61:61
R. puts a human face — RUNC 828:51
the r. of virtue — POTT 785:44
rub Ay, there's the r. — SHAK 890:21
least r. in your fortunes — SHAK 917:50
r. my language against another — BART 75:84
rubbish cast as r. to the void — TENN 999:37
flames but a lot of r. — MACD 628:95
r. of centuries — DUDEK 353:17
r. that lies in the way — LOCKE 609:71
r. was sent to Stockport — ANON 30:66
somewhere among the r. — JERR 521:17
Rubens more death in it than R. — HUGH 500:31
rubies diamonds and r. — MORE 707:53
price is far above r. — BIBLE 122:12
Shouldst r. find — MARV 658:72
Those be r., fairy favours — SHAK 870:35
wisdom…more precious than r. — BIBLE 120:60
ruby natural r. of your cheeks — SHAK 909:62
r. and amethyst eyes — BRAS 185:13
rudder bridle and r. of painting — LEON 597:81
heart was to thy r. — SHAK 905:80
rhyme r. is of verses — BUTL 216:10
Their tail the r. — DRYD 346:54
ruddy r.…and goodly to look to — BIBLE 110:37
r. limbs and flourishing hair — BLAKE 165:58
rude first r. sketch — KIPL 561:40
let's talk r. — FLAN 392:27
manner r. and wild — BELL 86:97
rather r. and wild — BELL 87:11
r. facts at your feet — RABAN 798:76
when people are r. — FITZ 391:17
rudeness difficult from its r. — JOHN 530:99
indistinguishable from r. — THER 1009:40
offensive act of theatrical r. — ZOLO 1110:27
Rudge raven, like Barnaby R. — LOWE 616:83
rudiments after the r. of the world — BIBLE 153:19
Rudyards R. cease from kipling — STEP 968:80
rue press the r. for wine! — SCOTT 854:68
ruffian r. stern, and soldier good — SCOTT 854:73
rug upon a r. mingle — STEV 971:38
Rugby feature of the R. game — ANON 24:10
turns up his nose at R. — ANON 24:14
rugs lined with tiger r. — MACN 637:38

ruin Atoms or systems into r. hurled — POPE 780:35
countries…going fastest to r. — SMITH 945:80
don't let Labour r. it — ANON 27:61
God to r. has designed — DRYD 351:57
hideous r. and combustion down — MILT 687:88
hides the r. that it feeds upon — COWP 292:46
invented his own r. — WEBS 1060:41
love of gain to r. men — SOPH 953:15
Man marks the earth with r. — BYRON 221:6
r. and despair — WIEN 1074:13
r. or rule the state — DRYD 349:15
R. seize thee — GRAY 442:79
r.—yet what r.! — BYRON 220:2
three roads to r. — POMP 777:72
ruined England is not r. — PRIE 790:46
O r. piece of nature — SHAK 904:36
r. by Chinese cheap labour — HARTE 460:51
r. in a conventional…way — KEYN 554:31
r. the whole estate and kingdom — HOBY 483:47
r. your perfectly dreadful play — BANK 70:91
ruins familiar r., began to cry — NEME 722:4
fragments…shored against my r. — ELIOT 369:97
mortality, the r. of forgotten times — BROW 196:94
open space among the r. — SHEL 930:33
r. of the Capitol — GIBB 421:29
Ruislip Gaily into R. Gardens — BETJ 100:48
rule abide by majority r. — LEE 593:8
acting under the unanimity r. — MACM 635:9
be each man's r. — TENN 996:90
bedspreads according to r. — LEVE 600:25
been one to write by r. — WILL 1083:1
best fitted to r. — GILM 427:17
damn by r. — OTWAY 746:77
exceptions disproves the r. — DOYLE 343:90
first r. of intelligent tinkering — EHRL 362:56
fundamental psychological r. — KEYN 555:39
gold maketh the r. — ANON 29:34
gold r. — LICH 604:87
golden r. — MOLI 698:20
greatest r. of all — TOCQ 1021:74
knowledge of how to r. — SART 844:19
No r. of general morality — HEMI 471:48
one absolute r. — HUXL 508:98
one guiding r. — CHRI 261:68
One Ring to r. them all — TOLK 1022:92
one who can r. — TENN 1001:80
perpetuate authoritarian r. — AUNG 50:22
Reason to r. — DRYD 350:51
rich men r. the law — GOLD 432:98
ruin or r. the state — DRYD 349:15
R. 1: Be cautious — ITO 514:82
R. 1, on page 1 — MONT 703:90
r.…assumes players intend to trip — FRY 408:10
r. by custom not by force — LEGU 594:27
r. by law and r. by whim — DOUG 342:69
r. for bargains — DICK 322:73
r. is Do anything you can — BROUN 194:50
r. is, jam to-morrow — CARR 240:59
r. never to drink by daylight — MENC 669:71
r. never to look into a newspaper — SHER 934:2
r. of another man — LOCKE 609:70
r. of distributive justice — HOMA 487:8
r. of safety — WHIT 1071:56
r. of wealth — BAGE 61:55
R. that Love is ever rewarded — BACON 56:42
r. that may serve for a statesman — CHAR 252:81
safe r. to apply — WHIT 1071:56
same r. applies for lust — MONT 703:87
same r. will hold — POPE 778:82
standing r. to live by — ASTE 43:92
standing r. to live by — LOCKE 609:70
take it as a general r. — DESC 317:80
that's not a regular r. — CARR 239:44
they who r. industrially — CONN 283:81

rule (contd.)
we r. all mankind — CATO 245:52
rule-of-thumb r.-o.-t. methods — MARX 661:22
ruled Art of Being R. — LEWIS 602:69
world is r. by little else — KEYN 555:37
ruler make thee r. over many things — BIBLE 140:41
resemble not a r. — HUXL 508:94
r. in Israel — BIBLE 130:62
R. of the Queen's Navee — GILB 423:56
rulers events…brought about by r. — BIER 161:85
government…not the glory of r. — BEVE 102:73
r. take counsel…against the Lord — BOOK 176:59
rules depending not on r. — JOHN 531:10
deviating from the r. of art — ADDI 8:38
disregard of all r. — ORWE 745:64
follow the r. until I go against them — FRAN 402:98
golden r. for orchestras — BEEC 82:16
No r., however wise — RUSS 832:25
no r. in filmmaking — CAPRA 231:92
no r.…of musical composition — SHAW 925:30
not even by my own r. — WILL 1083:1
present r. of the game — ROOS 822:48
rearrange r. to suit yourself — CAPO 231:83
R. and models destroy genius — HAZL 464:24
r. and prescriptions — NISB 730:4
r. are so ill-defined — ORWE 744:27
r. comedy can tolerate — THUR 1019:49
r. for odd inventions — SHAK 864:81
r. made poetry pedant's game — BUNT 204:59
r. of ancient liberty — MILT 686:76
r. of strict secrecy — LENIN 595:48
sex r. for myself — SALI 838:20
the universe…governed by r. — PAGE 749:33
there are no golden r. — SHAW 923:67
There are no r. or models — HUGO 501:57
two cents for your fancy r. — BUCH 202:30
ruling decay of the r. classes — ORWE 743:18
r. passion conquers reason — POPE 780:28
sports for the r. classes — HOBS 483:46
rum bottle of r.! — STEV 975:28
Raped for r. — WRIG 1102:11
r. and true religion — BYRON 222:81
r., Romanism, and rebellion — BURC 205:77
what a R. Go everything is — WELLS 1064:33
rummy chappie is r. — WODE 1088:87
rumour Fame and r. — JONS 534:85
R. is of all pests the swiftest — VIRG 1045:85
suspicion, r., fantasy — RICH 809:43
rump contempt is the R. come to — PEPYS 764:59
run many shall r. to and fro — BIBLE 130:51
minutes how they r. — SHAK 862:23
or r. it down — SWIFT 986:5
r. after it and bring it back — BARR 73:51
r., and not be weary — BIBLE 126:91
r. before it — KAFKA 540:85
r., but he can't hide — LOUIS 614:56
R., r., Orlando — SHAK 886:98
r., that ye may obtain — BIBLE 150:54
r. with patience the race — BIBLE 154:54
Still as they r. — GRAY 441:46
stumble that r. fast — SHAK 869:98
What Makes Sammy R.? — SCHU 850:10
While I do r. upon it — SHAK 884:66
would have r. to him — STAN 962:84
would r. — GRAMM 438:94
run-stealers r.-s. flicker to and fro — THOM 1014:32
runagates letteth the r. continue — BOOK 177:80
runic full of r. tales — FLEC 393:52
runner lame man…outstrips the r. — BACON 56:33
Loneliness of the Long Distance R. — SILL 938:76
running Avoid r. at all times — PAIGE 750:41
first sprightly r. could not give — DRYD 347:77
it takes all the r. you can do — CARR 239:50
r. people down is considered sport — FOST 399:63

sand (*contd.*):
Divine…in a grain of s.	FRIE 405:58
edge of the s.	LEAR 590:61
every grain of s.	DOST 341:48
gasped upon the s.	MARL 653:3
I on the s.	SCOTT 854:76
no bigger than a grain of s.	CHEE 255:49
ostrich, with its head in the s.	WILS 1086:49
palace built upon the s.	MILL 676:83
print…plain to be seen in the s.	DEFOE 312:80
property turns s. to gold	YOUNG 1108:2
s. and ruin and gold	SWIN 987:47
s. dunes the wind lifted	PIER 769:34
s. in the porridge	COWA 290:92
see a world in a grain of s.	BLAKE 167:1
Such quantities of s.	CARR 240:56
throw the s. against the wind	BLAKE 167:99
waste of white barren s.	SCHAW 847:61
write in s.	WALL 1050:75

sand-strewn S.-s. caverns — ARNO 36:55
sandal massive s. set on stone — MILL 676:89
sandals still in straw hat and s. — BASHO 76:3
Sanders a bed, Clerk S. said — BALL -101:34
sandfly mosquito and s. — DOUG 341:51
sands Come unto these yellow s. — SHAK 916:23

cousins as the s. of the sea	SHAW 926:43
Footprints on the s. of time	LONG 611:96
golden s., and crystal brooks	DONNE 337:89
lone and level s.	SHEL 928:93
men who are as various as the s.	FORS 398:46
men's names On s.	MILT 683:24
s. o' life shall run	BURNS 212:40
s. of Africa	JOHN 527:23
s. of Dee	KING 558:89
smoothed down like silly s.	BUNT 204:56
steer too near the s.	DRYD 349:12
vision of the crowded, howling s.	CHES 257:86

sandwich raw-onion s. — BARN 72:35
sandwiches mother…eating s. — DICK 320:16
| we eat reality s. | GINS 427:23 |

sane above all, of s. vitality — LUCAS 618:28
Mahdi…is very s.	CECIL 247:83
no s. person would do	SHAW 923:81
rewards for being s.	AMIS 17:81
s. balance of values	POUND 786:80
S.…did what their neighbours	ELIOT 366:30
Show me a s. man	JUNG 539:72
they shall be s.	THOM 1010:55

sang s. and wallowed — THOM 1012:95
| s. his didn't | CUMM 300:94 |
| s. themselves to sleep | HODG 483:50 |

sanitary glorified s. engineer — STRA 979:95
sanity fight…to bring back s. — GAIT 411:71
Neither conscience nor s.	MACN 636:29
place where s. and hope	ROUS 827:30
pursuit of s.	BELL 88:23
restore themselves to s.	SMALL 943:61
So with s. and insanity	MELV 668:51
There ain't no S. Claus	MARX 659:99

sans S. teeth, s. eyes, s. taste — SHAK 886:41
sanspareil Cricket…the s. — FOWL 400:70
Santa Claus Nobody shoots S. C. — SMITH 946:96
sap s. flows up through our arms — RILKE 811:86
| soul's s. quivers | ELIOT 362:68 |

sapient s. sutlers of the Lord — ELIOT 367:65
saplings gale, it plies the s. — HOUS 495:54
sapphire s. melts into the sea — TENN 1001:84
sapphire-blaze throne, the s.-b. — GRAY 443:90
Sappho Call me S., Call me Chloris — COLE 274:2
| Dark S.! | BYRON 219:73 |

Sara S. could commit adultery — CARY 243:19
Sarajevo lost, for art, at S. — LEWIS 602:68
sarcasm petulance is not s. — DISR 333:98
sardines Life…like a tin of s. — BENN 90:71

---

sark S. rins o'er the Solway sands — BURNS 212:31
sashes nice new s. — GRAH 437:88
Sassenach drove from a S. laird — SCOTT 854:70
sat s. down on the right hand — BIBLE 154:44
| you have s. too long here | CROM 298:55 |

Satan beheld S. as lightning — BIBLE 142:88
called the Devil, and S.	BIBLE 157:21
diligence of S.	BUNY 204:60
Get thee behind me, S.	BIBLE 138:14
Get thee hence, S.	BIBLE 133:31
holy S.	DAMI 304:53
if S. rise up against himself	BIBLE 141:41
like a blond S.	HAMM 454:58
Lord said unto S.	BIBLE 112:94
Man, with his S.	SNYD 951:82
messenger of S.	BIBLE 152:86
Of S. and his peers	MILT 688:10
other toward S.	BAUD 78:42
playfield of S.	NABO 717:4
S. exalted sat	MILT 688:11
s. has not geven me boils	FLEM 394:61
S., Nick or Clootie	BURNS 209:73
S. with thoughts inflamed	MILT 688:24

satchel schoolboy with his s. — SHAK 885:93
satiated rather die s. than slim — PIER 769:35
satiety love's sad s. — SHEL 929:4
| Of knowledge there is no s. | BACON 55:20 |
| s. is a blunt,…passion | WEBS 1059:28 |

satin allowed to wear black s. — WHAR 1068:4
ease a heart Like a s. gown	PARK 753:91
heroine… goes into white s.	SHER 934:11
loll on velvet and s.	FRAN 402:16
Silk an' s.	ANON 24:12

satire British…gluttons for s. — LODGE 609:77
difficult not to write s.	JUVE 540:77
let s. be my song	BYRON 218:59
s., being levelled at all	SWIFT 984:60
s. costs a lot!	RICK 811:76
S. is a lesson	NABO 717:10
S. is a sort of glass	SWIFT 984:57
S. is dependent on strong beliefs	BROO 193:41
S. is moral outrage	ROTH 826:15
S. is what closed	KAUF 542:14
S. or sense, alas!	POPE 781:67

satiric have the s. temperament — BEER 83:25
satisfaction All s.…never positive — SCHO 849:91
can't get no s.	JAGG 515:94
cannot render s.	MIDD 673:41
s. of human needs	NUTT 732:46
s.…too much to expect	BART 74:71
What's the s.	HORN 494:37
won a s. and triumph	WOLFE 1090:19

satisfied and we must be s. — SYNGE 988:60
eyes of man are never s.	BIBLE 122:9
forces s. mediocrity	RENAN 806:1
having it, is s.?	THAC 1006:90
kisses…to make me fully s.?	CATU 245:60
Massey won't be s.	KAUF 542:13
may be equally s.	JOHN 528:48
s. with her lover's mind	TROL 1027:72
s. with that result	SCHW 851:27
way to be s.	BAGE 61:49

satisfy delights of art s. me — FUEN 409:26
none of these finally s.	WHIT 1073:97
s. our thirst for freedom	KING 557:80
those who are hardest to s.	DESC 317:76

saturated too s. with it — DURK 357:70
Saturday closed S. night — KAUF 542:14
couple of drinks on a S.	FYFFE 410:63
date on S. night	ALLEN 14:40
Glasgow Empire on a S. night	DODD 334:43
see another S. night	MACN 636:30

Saturdays passionately, on…S. — SHER 933:91
saturn Sat grey-haired S. — KEATS 547:99

---

saturn (*contd.*):
while S. whirls	TENN 994:55

Saturn the Revolution may, like S. — VERG 1042:32
saturnie s., the cross-gained — MACD 628:93
satyrs men, like s. grazing — MARL 653:4
| Where the s. are chattering | SITW 941:9 |

sauce honey a s. to sugar — SHAK 886:11
| Hunger…best s. in the world | CERV 248:96 |

saucepans ghosts of s. — MANS 647:97
saucer s. like some full moon — MONRO 700:48
saucy no be half so s. — BURNS 211:5
Saul S. and Jonathan were lovely — BIBLE 110:44
S. hath slain his thousands	BIBLE 110:42
S., S., why persecutest thou me?	BIBLE 147:87
whose name was S.	BIBLE 147:87

sausage tin of Bologna s. — STEV 973:97
savage civilized man…into a s. — TOCQ 1022:82
manner in which a s. wields	HUXL 509:4
not a genuine foreign-grown s.	DICK 325:37
painted face of a s.	DICK 325:41
removed from the s. state	COOP 287:42
rights of the s.	GLAD 429:52
s. individual man	WELLS 1064:28
s. man…does man betray	ROCH 816:52
s. place!	COLE 275:13
s. servility slides by	LOWE 617:1
subtle, but s.	CAPO 231:85
take some s. woman	TENN 996:81
unto a s. race	TENN 994:57
wild…the noble s. ran	DRYD 347:69

savage-pictures s.-p. fill their gaps — SWIFT 986:1
savaged s. by a dead sheep — HEAL 464:28
| We s. them | GELL 417:72 |

savagery uncompleted s. — DICK 327:75
savages plant where s. are — BACON 59:8
Savannah In S.…drink? — BERE 94:36
savannahs s. grew lonely as the sea — HARR 459:35
savant Buddhist Beat Catholic s. — GINS 428:31
save bit to s. humanity — HUGH 499:25
destroy the town to s. it	ANON 27:85
himself he cannot s.	BIBLE 140:54
I can s. this country	PITT 771:64
need not exist in order to s. us	DEVR 318:93
nothing will s. the Governor	WHIT 1072:71
principle which prompts to s.	SMITH 946:92
s. a shred of its respectability	READ 803:53
s. everything that everyone else	DOWD 342:78
S. something	ANON 28:15
s. those that have no imagination?	SHAW 925:25
s. those who damn them	HUGO 502:74
s. us from the power	JORD 537:30

saved is sometimes s. — THUR 1019:33
name…whereby we must be s.	BIBLE 147:84
only s. by being dammed	HOOD 489:42
s. the sum of things	HOUS 496:78
we are not s.	BIBLE 128:23
what must I do to be s.?	BIBLE 148:96
Who then can be s.?	BIBLE 139:26
Whosoever will be s.	BOOK 174:2

saviour a s. spring to life — BIBLE 159:51
Between the role of s.	YOUR 1108:8
God my S.	BIBLE 160:53
Hark…The S. comes	DODD 335:44
Hide me, O my S.	WESL 1066:60
in the city of David a S.	BIBLE 142:78
S. of 'is country	KIPL 560:32
s. or assassin	MURP 715:73
words our S. Christ saith	BOOK 174:26

savour if the salt have lost his s. — BIBLE 134:35
s. like unto a blessed field	HERR 478:65
stinking s.	BIBLE 123:36
very homely household s.	BYRON 223:46
with your sweet s.	BIBLE 129:39

savoury meat is s. — EMER 377:49

saw find thy s. of might — SHAK 886:15
sawdust S. and spangles — CARD 232:98
sawed-off as a s.-o. shotgun — PARK 755:25
Sawyer Tom S. he says the same — TWAIN 1033:92
saxophone s. is the embodied spirit — BENN 92:2
s. was…his key to the world — HOLM 485:74
say can s. only one thing at a time — HOMA 487:7
don't have to s. anything — FURT 410:57
have something to s. — WHAT 1068:7
I have so much more to s. — RAVEL 802:43
isn't what I s., but how I s. it — WEST 1067:85
like to s. nothing — SOPH 953:21
little to s. — SKEL 942:32
may things to s. unto you — BIBLE 146:65
must s. something but not much — REAG 804:65
not moved to s. something — HUNT 505:30
nothing at all to s. — SAIN 836:81
Nothing is easier to s. — TERE 1006:76
nothing to s. — BALF 65:20
nothing to s., s. nothing — COLT 277:54
O s., can you see — KEY 554:24
relevance for what it does not s. — FERL 386:22
S. not soft things — SORL 953:23
s. nothing, do nothing, be nothing — ANON 30:55
s. the perfectly correct thing — SHAW 924:11
s. what they please — FRED 403:27
s. what you have to s. — WELL 1064:19
so much still to s. — BART 75:88
that's what I shall s.! — GILB 424:67
you should s. what you mean — CARR 238:28
saying ancient s. is no heresy — SHAK 875:32
do now remember a s. — SHAK 887:27
famous witty s. — THUR 1019:38
lest a s. learnt — TENN 1003:22
s. of an ancient philosopher — ADDI 7:13
This is a faithful s. — BIBLE 153:28
used to s. something different — HAVEL 460:60
sayings heareth these s. of mine — BIBLE 135:63
s. are generally like women's letters — HAZL 464:17
says Don't report what he s. — ANON 27:76
Who is it that s. most — SHAK 914:77
scabs Make yourselves s.? — SHAK 910:1
scaffold content to die on s. — BROWN 194:53
s. and the doom — AYTO 53:86
whether on the s. high — SULL 981:24
scaffolding s. of spirit — THOM 1013:27
There is no s. — HONE 488:29
scald s. and viper through her — THOM 1011:89
tears Do s. like molten lead — SHAK 904:42
scale judicious, is the s. — MILT 692:97
On every golden s.! — CARR 238:22
Poetic justice, with her lifted s. — POPE 782:92
s. doesn't matter — DONO 339:35
Scotland the true s. — MACD 627:83
something on the s. of the grand — DIDE 329:30
scales cannot balance tragedy in s. — BENET 90:63
quicksilver the s. slip — MUIR 712:37
weighed the mountains in s. — BIBLE 126:87
scallop-shell s.-s. of delight — RALE 800:13
scalpel intimacy of a surgeon's s. — ANGE 20:31
scan presume not God to s. — POPE 780:42
scandal Cut S.'s head off — SHER 933:93
divided…by public s. — DUMAS 354:29
Love and s. — FIEL 388:44
No s. about Queen Elizabeth — SHER 934:8
no s. like rags — FARQ 383:71
Retired to their tea and s. — CONG 280:5
s.…gives offence — MOLI 698:22
s. is…worse than the sin — MARG 650:56
s. of…exalted person's fall — CANM 230:65
scandalous Monarch, s. and poor — ROCH 816:46
scapegoat let him go for a s. — BIBLE 107:79
poor s. — HEAN 464:34
scapegoats s. for our blunders — TWAIN 1034:13

scapegoats (*contd.*):
they are classic s. — WHITE 1069:19
scar far from cliff and s. — TENN 997:90
scarce money was not s.? — EMER 377:75
s. a thing but is — MIDD 673:44
scarcity by the influence of s. — ROBB 813:14
from their s. and from…labour — RICA 808:35
s. of opportunity — ANGE 19:21
scarecrow s. of the law — SHAK 896:64
scared s. or too sulky — RYLE 834:54
scarf S. up the tender eye — SHAK 909:59
scarlet bind this line of s. thread — BIBLE 109:9
lips more s. — YEATS 1106:83
live with s. Majors — SASS 845:26
Lovely creature in s. — GEOR 419:93
raise the s. standard — CONN 282:54
s. coat — WILDE 1078:96
sins were s. — BELL 87:18
though your sins be as s. — BIBLE 124:56
scars My Marks and S. I carry — BUNY 205:74
scarred who carry our s. — GEE 417:64
s. that never felt a wound — SHAK 868:85
sleeve and show his s. — SHAK 881:1
scarves present them with s. — BAIN 62:77
scatter s. and gather — HERA 473:85
s. up and down — SHAK 861:5
scattered God blew and they were s. — ANON 23:89
scene Act One, S. One — HART 459:48
ask to see The distant s. — NEWM 724:28
breath, a little s. — SHAK 867:60
every day Speaks a new s. — QUAR 796:52
lofty s. be acted over — SHAK 883:42
naive impression of the s. — MONET 700:43
Of what s. — SHEL 931:42
preside o'er the s. — TANN 991:96
start a s. or two — ELIOT 367:52
Supporting…Unto the S. — DICK 328:9
Sweet especial rural s. — HOPK 491:91
this s. of man — POPE 780:32
Upon that memorable s. — MARV 657:66
waste his destined s. — COLL 277:45
wildness to perplex the s. — POPE 779:21
scenery chew up the s. — PARK 754:95
end of all natural s. — RUSK 830:85
helps s. like ham and eggs — TWAIN 1032:63
lovely descriptions of s. — BELL 86:86
S. is fine — KEATS 544:52
s. was beautiful — WOOL 1094:93
scenes behind the s. — JOHN 525:87
feelings these dull s. produce — CRAB 294:84
From s. like these — BURNS 209:66
heart with usury to such s. — LAMB 576:8
s. his fathers loved — CULL 299:69
s. of our life — SCHO 849:99
s. where man hath never trod — CLARE 267:83
seldom…making love in any of his s. — DRYD 347:63
synthesizing the s. — MARA 649:37
scent first s. you pour — HORA 493:27
How hot the s. is — GRAV 439:17
s.…locust blossoms — WILL 1083:97
s. of unwashed bodies — ACKR 4:54
s. survives their close — THOM 1014:31
stronger s. towards evening — STAEL 961:72
sweetest flower for s. — SHEL 930:30
scents render Their pleasing s. — WEBS 1059:27
S., colours, and sounds echo — BAUD 77:17
sceptic knowledge for the s. side — POPE 780:42
scepticism if we start from s. — RUSS 832:30
preserve our s. — HUME 503:2
principles which at first lead to s. — BERK 95:53
sceptre s. as an emblem of royalty — BENT 92:16
S. and crown…tumble down — SHIR 935:27
s. for a palmer's…staff — SHAK 867:62
s. so fantastically borne — SHAK 881:79

sceptre (*contd.*):
s. to control the world — SHAK 862:36
sceptreless S., free…but man — SHEL 930:25
schedule s. is already full — KISS 566:37
Scheherazadesworth S. of stories — BARTH 74:64
Scheisskopf S. has the facts — HELL 468:83
scheme assist this detestable s. — MACA 622:93
interpret it as a rational s. — ROBI 815:36
s. by which the nations — LEES 593:20
s. of merriment — JOHN 527:22
Socialists can s. — MACL 634:90
stoical s. of supplying — SWIFT 984:74
schemes best-laid s. o' Mice — BURNS 209:68
expediency of different s. — STEU 970:30
s. for persuading monarchs — SWIFT 985:87
schizophrenia Canada is paranoid s. — ATWO 45:20
schizophrenic experience…is s. — WITT 1088:82
Schoenberg Why is S.'s Music — BERG 94:39
scholar better s. than Wordsworth — HOUS 495:67
gentleman an' s. — BURNS 209:70
humour of a s. — BACON 59:21
Like a dull s. — STEV 971:46
my honest s. — WALT 1052:10
never be a complete s. — PLATH 773:89
s. of the world — JOHN 525:82
to this day is every s. poor — MARL 655:30
Zip, I am such a s.! — RODG 818:85
scholars nor its great s. great men — HOLM 486:89
philosophers and s. — PASC 758:81
scholarship boys or s. candidates — LITT 607:42
school aim of the s. of business — DEMI 315:44
at s. or college — STEV 974:19
Example is the s. of mankind — BURKE 208:48
explain s. to a higher intelligence? — MATH 663:72
for life, not for s. — SENE 858:47
get the feeling…you're not in s. — BRAN 185:9
growth of the Skyscraper S. — JOHN 524:62
kiddie in s. — NASH 719:49
no rhyme…for 's.' — SHAK 880:65
oyster of the old s. — DICK 324:25
playing fields of a public s. — FRY 408:10
private s. has all the faults — CONN 283:65
s. boys or scholarship — LITT 607:42
s. I went to in the north — WILS 1085:27
S. is where you go — UPDI 1036:51
s. of flattery and dissimulation — WENT 1065:53
s.…with tomorrow inside — AKERS 10:74
taught his little s. — GOLD 433:12
Three little maids from s. — GILB 425:87
till he's been to a good s. — SAKI 837:3
till we leave s. — LEWIS 601:43
truck passing by a music s.? — CAGE 225:89
went to s. without any boots — BULM 204:53
school-inspector s.-i. of average — KING 558:98
schoolboy Not the s. heat — TENN 1000:58
what every s. knows — SWIFT 985:94
whining s., with his satchel — SHAK 885:93
schoolboys go chide Late s. — DONNE 336:77
like s. — KIER 556:54
s. who…climb a crab-tree — ROCH 816:57
schoolchildren What all s. learn — AUDEN 47:75
schoolgirl Pert as a s. — GILB 425:87
schooling finish my s. without — ANON 28:23
s. any actress needs — GING 427:21
schoolman s.'s subtle art — POPE 781:21
schoolmaster s.'s answer — GRAV 440:39
you'll be becoming a s. — WAUGH 1056:60
schoolmasters all the s. you can — CHIS 260:54
Let s. puzzle their brain — GOLD 433:21
schools class s.…in four grades — WAUGH 1056:61
endeavour through its s. — RUSS 832:24
hundred s. of thought — MAO 648:27
in the maze of s. — POPE 778:75
lumber of the s. — SWIFT 983:56

scientific (*contd.*):
S. discovery consists — WIEN 1074:*14*
s. mind does not — LEVI 600:*32*
s. revolution — WILS 1085:*30*
s. statement speaks — POPP 783:*15*
s. treatment for all diseases — SHAW 923:*87*
s. validity of psychoanalysis — THOM 1009:*48*
technique are s. — RUSS 832:*28*
scientist But a s.? — SELF 857:*37*
Dissent...native activity of s. — BRON 190:*77*
exercise for a research s. — LORE 613:*42*
give any s....better advice — MEDA 666:*15*
I'm an old mad s. — PERE 766:*91*
Nothing leads the s. — ROST 825:*2*
s. does not study nature — POIN 776:*59*
s. is given license — LISP 607:*39*
s. is trying to expand — HALD 451:*18*
s. may find his discipline severe — CORN 288:*61*
s. states something is possible — CLAR 268:*90*
social s. is in a difficult — LEWO 603:*74*
took them for a Christian S. — MITF 697:*96*
scientists 90 per cent of all the s — MACK 631:*47*
Curse the s. — COOK 286:*26*
incredulity at the illiteracy of s. — SNOW 950:*72*
no more written for s. — ALDI 12:*5*
politicians and s. were lazier — WAUGH 1057:*98*
Republic has no need for s. — COFF 272:*68*
s. have in their briefcases — KHRU 556:*52*
S. have odious manners — TWAIN 1034:*20*
s....hold writers in contempt — BELL 88:*27*
S. know so much — SHAP 919:*78*
S. should be on tap — CHUR 265:*42*
s. who talk — WEIL 1062:*79*
socially responsible s. — HOBS 483:*45*
society of s. is more important — BRON 190:*79*
scimitars s., wi' murder crusted — BURNS 211:*18*
scissor-man red-legged s.-m. — HOFF 484:*60*
scoffer product of a s.'s pen — WORD 1100:*80*
scold or be she s. — SWIFT 986:*17*
scones buttered s. and crumpets — ELIOT 368:*73*
scoop s. of pure honey — SMITH 946:*99*
score Chaos is the s. — MILL 677:*16*
Money is how we keep the s. — CHAP 252:*67*
scoreboard s. is an ass — CARD 232:*4*
scorer when the One Great S. comes — RICE 809:*38*
scorn Fortune knows We s. her — SHAK 905:*81*
laugh me to s. — BIBLE 114:*48*
Laugh no man to s. — BIBLE 132:*92*
Laugh to s. — SHAK 909:*67*
little s. is alluring — CONG 281:*39*
love...the present s. — BEHN 85:*74*
nation heaps its s. — LAZA 588:*27*
not a thing to laugh to s. — SHAK 887:*26*
O, what a deal of s. — SHAK 895:*25*
s. and a mockery to call it — WENT 1065:*53*
s. for defeat — TWAIN 1034:*11*
s. her own image — SHAK 891:*33*
's.' 'horn', a hard rhyme — SHAK 880:*65*
s. of fate — DRYD 348:*95*
s. to change my state — SHAK 913:*57*
self-respecting s. — WAUGH 1056:*65*
suffice to wail their s. — DANI 304:*62*
surmounted by s. — CAMUS 229:*48*
take no s. — DAVI 307:*7*
Teach not thy lip such s. — SHAK 863:*49*
think foul s. — ELIZ 373:*90*
thou canst make us s.! — BURNS 211:*17*
With haughty s. — ARNO 38:*3*
scorner s. heareth not rebuke — BIBLE 121:*72*
s. of the ground! — SHEL 929:*6*
scornful most ridiculous and s. sort — SIDN 937:*64*
sitteth in the seat of the s. — BIBLE 113:*29*
scorpion home of the s. — SNYD 951:*82*
S. so wishes — SMITH 948:*40*

scorpions chastise you with s. — BIBLE 111:*60*
Those two s. — OPPE 741:*76*
Scot Had Cain been S. — CLEV 269:*9*
S. come from Scotland — LOUI 613:*44*
Scotch queerer set of people than S. — BORR 180:*26*
show you have a S. tongue — SCOTT 855:*94*
Scotia old S.'s grandeur — BURNS 209:*66*
S.'s darling seat — BURNS 210:*86*
Scotland canna S. see wha yet — MACD 627:*83*
claret and burgundy in S.? — SMITH 945:*88*
dead bird of s. — MACL 633:*69*
fair S.'s spear — SCOTT 853:*60*
flower of S. — WILL 1083:*7*
in S. afore ye — ANON 24:*4*
in S. supports the people — JOHN 526:*14*
in S. translated into virtue — THOM 1014:*43*
inferior sort of S. — SMITH 949:*43*
left fair S.'s strand — BURNS 213:*47*
multiform, infinite S. small? — MACD 628:*96*
no harm in wishing S. — SCOTT 856:*10*
Scot come from S. — LOUI 613:*44*
S. for the Strand? — JOHN 525:*78*
S. is not wholly surrounded by sea — MACD 627:*89*
S. kens beneath the moon — FERG 386:*17*
S., land of omnipotent No — BOLD 171:*67*
S. queer country — BORR 180:*26*
'S.,' Tavish muttered — NEVI 723:*15*
S. wants nae skinking ware — BURNS 210:*85*
Seeing S. — JOHN 530:*94*
Stands S. where it did? — SHAK 909:*73*
state that S.'s in — MACD 627:*86*
Succour S., and remede — ANON 22:*68*
white rose of S. — MACD 628:*91*
Scots S. accent of the mind — STEV 976:*45*
S. ...hear the English abused — PIUS 772:*80*
S. lords at his feet — BALL 67:*50*
S. Wha Ha'evers — MACD 628:*92*
S., wha hae — BURNS 212:*37*
six or seven dozen of S. — SHAK 876:*53*
upon the S. with a Vengeance — FLET 394:*67*
Scotsman S. on the make — BARR 73:*47*
S. with a grievance — WODE 1089:*1*
Scottish Fareweel to a' our S. fame — BURNS 212:*30*
S. life and letters — MACD 628:*92*
sulky S. spirit — SCOTT 856:*11*
scoundrel Every man...is a s. — SHAW 922:*61*
last refuge of a s. — JOHN 529:*73*
last refuge of s. — BRAGG 185:*5*
morally behaving like a s. — SHAW 924:*89*
plea of the s., hypocrite, and flatterer — BLAKE 168:*8*
scoundrels corporation-paid s. — LEWIS 601:*48*
scour s. these English hence? — SHAK 910:*84*
Scrabble Playing bop is like playing S. — ELLI 374:*3*
scramble days...into a wild s. — ANGE 20:*30*
scrap coaches shall be s. — SAND 841:*59*
just for a s. of paper — BETH 99:*22*
scratch all you can do is s. it — BEEC 83:*20*
Art of S. — RUSK 831:*5*
quick sharp s. — BROW 198:*40*
scrawl s. and scribble — POPE 782:*82*
scream I'll s. and s. and s. — CROM 297:*48*
No Mouth And I Must S. — ELLI 375:*12*
s. from a crevasse — GREE 444:*9*
sensed a s. passing — MUNCH 713:*51*
to get wounded one needs the s. — ELTIT 375:*37*
screams I could hear his s. continually — BECK 81:*6*
screech-owls Drawn by s.-o. — SMART 944:*63*
screen leaving my heart on the s. — QUIR 797:*35*
Life is a s. — HUGO 502:*80*
No safety s. stands between — SHUL 936:*35*
seeing on the s. — GOLD 434:*41*
screens Phillipines...lovely s. — COWA 290:*98*
with its s. and nodules — CESA 248:*3*
screes s. on her escarpments — HEAN 465:*35*

screw Don't s. around — CURR 301:*20*
S. your courage — SHAK 908:*35*
screwed s. it up real good — NIXON 730:*15*
screwing gave up s. around — LODGE 610:*81*
screwy s. visions — BELL 88:*30*
scribblative arts babblative and s. — SOUT 954:*43*
scribble Always s., s., s.! — GLOU 430:*62*
scrawl and s. — POPE 782:*82*
scribblement all his s. — DISR 333:*22*
scribes righteousness of the s. — BIBLE 134:*38*
Woe unto you, s. and Pharisees — BIBLE 139:*36*
scrimmage 'maul' or 's.' — ANON 24:*14*
scrip My s. of joy — RALE 800:*13*
script bank president finish the s. — EPST 379:*7*
no such thing as a good s. — BENN 91:*79*
Whatever your s. is like — CURT 302:*24*
scripture as the S. says — TWAIN 1032:*64*
devil can cite S. — SHAK 874:*21*
Holy S. containeth — BOOK 178:*97*
s. is given by inspiration — BIBLE 154:*39*
s. is placed before the eyes — GREG 445:*45*
S. is silent — BROW 195:*66*
S. moveth us — BOOK 173:*88*
scriptures Search the s. — BIBLE 145:*41*
while he opened to us the s.? — BIBLE 144:*22*
scrivener notched and cropt s. — LAMB 577:*29*
scroll Michael read the Gaelic s. — RUSS 833:*36*
scrotumtightening s. sea — JOYCE 538:*45*
scruple not s. to pick a pocket — DENN 316:*63*
scrupulous s.... are not the leaders — CONR 285:*7*
scrutiny Sceptical s. is the means — SAGAN 836:*75*
scud-thumper Many-maned s.-t. — UPDI 1036:*50*
scuffles s. of great fights — SHAK 904:*54*
scullion Away, you s. — SHAK 877:*87*
scullions contentment with noisy s. — STEV 974:*3*
sculptor I was a s. — HIRS 482:*21*
not a great s. or a painter — RUSK 830:*82*
s. can use twenty different materials — BOCC 171:*55*
s. pursues his work — LEON 596:*73*
sculptors We are all s. — THOR 1016:*73*
sculpture difference between...s. — CELL 247:*93*
difference between painting and s. — LEON 596:*73*
Geometry is to s. — APOL 32:*91*
In s., did ever anybody call — EMER 376:*45*
like that of a s. — RUSS 831:*14*
mediocre s. — ALBE 11:*93*
might call it moral s. — MERE 671:*10*
music or s. — MACB 624:*31*
S. in stone — MOORE 705:*13*
s. is the prisoner — THOM 1013:*27*
sculptured s. Ann is seventy — THOM 1010:*61*
sculptures accept paintings and s. — CHUR 262:*78*
scum Okie means you're s. — STEI 966:*54*
rich are the s. — CHES 259:*24*
s. of the earth...as soldiers — WELL 1063:*7*
scurvy like a s. politician — SHAK 904:*38*
very conceited s. one — JONS 535:*93*
scythe poor crooked s. and spade — SHIR 935:*27*
s.'s keen edge — SHAK 865:*4*
Scythian S. shepherd — MARL 652:*86*
sea all men at s. — GOLD 432:*89*
All the rivers run into the s. — BIBLE 122:*15*
always ourselves we find in the s. — CUMM 300:*96*
am wholly at s. — CARS 242:*91*
anything more the s. can do — SYNGE 988:*61*
As mad as the vexed s. — SHAK 903:*32*
as the waters cover the s. — BIBLE 125:*68*
Beneath is spread like a green s. — SHEL 927:*70*
beyond it the s. — ANON 25:*29*
blue days at s. — STEV 976:*53*
bosom of the s. — SHAK 861:*8*
bottom of the s. — SHAK 863:*54*
bottom of the s. is cruel — CRANE 294:*92*
boundless as the s. — SHAK 869:*92*

sea (*contd.*):

broader than the s.	BIBLE 113:5
by land and s.	WORD 1099:64
by s. as by land	GILB 423:51
Calm is the s.	SURR 982:41
changing s.	STEP 968:79
cherish the s.	BAUD 77:19
Copper sun or scarlet s.	CULL 299:68
crowned with summer s.	TENN 1004:48
current under s.	ELIOT 369:91
dark...serpent-haunted s.	FLEC 393:51
disciples saw him walking on the s.	BIBLE 138:7
dolorous midland s.	SWIN 987:47
dominion of the s.	COVE 290:90
Down to a sunless s.	COLE 274:12
drowned in the depth of the s.	BIBLE 138:18
eastward to the s.	KIPL 560:28
far over the summer s.	TENN 1005:58
fed our s.	KIPL 561:54
fishingboat-bobbing s.	THOM 1011:79
flat s. sunk	MILT 683:28
forth on the godly s.	POUND 786:70
France and England is—the s.	JERR 521:16
From s. to shining s.	BATES 76:10
From s. to shining s.	HUXT 509:8
From the centre...to the s.	COWP 292:38
garden fronts the s.	SWIN 988:56
gaze in the s. or sky	MELV 668:44
gazed upon the glittering s.	BYRON 222:44
go down to the s. in ships	BIBLE 118:20
gong-tormented s.	YEATS 1106:85
great and wide s.	BIBLE 118:18
grey stones, O S.!	TENN 995:63
hate...broader than s.	BOLI 172:72
home from s.	STEV 975:31
hyline, the glassy s.	MILT 691:88
if we gang to s.	BALL 67:48
in the abysmal s.	TENN 993:31
Into that silent s.	COLE 273:86
jolly-rogered s.	THOM 1011:81
keen s. wind	STEV 976:59
let him go to s.	HERB 476:41
like any river or any s.	HOPK 492:97
like sunrise from the s.	SHEL 932:63
London, that great s.	SHEL 929:9
lonely as the s.	HARR 459:35
lonely s. and the sky	MASE 661:32
love the s.	WALC 1048:32
lover of men, the s.	SWIN 987:45
man that is born...falls into the s.	CONR 284:94
Marathon looks on the s.	BYRON 223:50
Mediterranean...that vital s.	CHUR 265:26
mirrors of the s.	FLEC 393:55
monarch of the s.	GILB 423:56
moon on this cloud s.	SCOTT 852:36
More hideous...Than the s. monster	SHAK 902:7
more steady than an ebbing s.	FORD 397:17
mountains by the winter s.	TENN 1004:41
not wholly surrounded by s.	MACD 627:84
One foot in s.	SHAK 879:46
out of the swing of the s.	HOPK 491:77
over a cardboard s.	HARB 455:73
oyster shell on top of the s.	AUDEN 48:78
people look at the s.	FROST 407:89
persian pussy from over the s.	MARQ 656:41
peruked s. whose swell	SITW 940:2
plants his footsteps in the s.	COWP 291:27
Posters of the s. and land	SHAK 907:14
Pussy-Cat went to s.	LEAR 590:58
put to s. on a wooden raft	HEYE 479:88
quiet, as under the s.	MERE 671:16
rebuked the winds and the s.	BIBLE 136:68
Receiveth as the s.	SHAK 893:92
rough rude s.	SHAK 867:55

sea (*contd.*):

sail upon the s.	BIBLE 131:75
sailed the wintery s.	LONG 611:1
sailing in the open s.	UPDI 1037:61
sang in my chains like the s.	THOM 1010:66
sapphire melts into the s.	TENN 1001:84
s. escaping With the sun	RIMB 812:94
s. gave up the dead	BIBLE 158:33
s. is a teacher	BELL 87:16
s. is all about us	ELIOT 372:58
s. is his, and he made it	BOOK 177:87
s. is mother-death	SEXT 859:67
s. is the universal sewer	COUS 290:89
s. itself floweth in your	TRAH 1025:27
s. of dew	FIELD 387:41
s. of faith	ARNO 36:64
s. of glass	BIBLE 157:8
s. of glass mingled with fire	BIBLE 158:25
s. of life	ARNO 37:79
s. of sorrows deep	SPEN 957:6
s. protesting against union	GRAT 439:14
s. rises higher	CHES 259:18
S. shall give up her dead	BOOK 178:96
s. that bares her bosom	WORD 1099:73
s. was ever loved	TOML 1023:3
s. would fold me	GORD 435:62
see nothing but s.	BACON 55:14
sent them o'er the s.	BALL 68:60
settee of the horsehair s.!	SITW 940:99
shine along the s.	SWIN 987:29
shining Big-S.-Water	LONG 611:10
ship on the s.	LORCA 613:39
sink through the s.	THOM 1010:55
smiling s.	WORD 1099:72
snotgreen s.	JOYCE 538:45
squires ride slowly towards the s.	CHES 259:36
stillness of the central s.	TENN 1000:61
stone set in the silver s.	SHAK 867:48
sun was shining on the s.	CARR 240:55
Sussex by the s.!	KIPL 563:93
that immortal s.	WORD 1098:54
The breeze is on the s.	SCOTT 855:3
The s. hates a coward!	ONEI 740:57
The s.! The s.!	XENO 1104:53
there was no more s.	BIBLE 158:34
they to s. in a Sieve	LEAR 590:54
they were on the s.	ROBE 814:15
to look at the s.	UPDI 1037:64
tossing s. of clouds	BENU 94:33
true call...of the s.	STARK 963:96
universal as s. sickness	SHAW 921:37
unplumbed, salt, estranging s.	ARNO 37:80
Upon the slimy s.	COLE 273:88
uttermost parts of the s.	BIBLE 120:49
Vaulting the dim s.	CRANE 294:97
vext the dim s.	TENN 994:58
voice...like the s.	WORD 1096:38
voice of the s.	CHOP 261:59
voices...one of the s.	WORD 1099:74
wan grass s.	SITW 941:15
wander from s. to s.	BIBLE 130:61
went to s. in a sieve	LEAR 590:53
wet sheet and a flowing s.	CUNN 300:99
Where no s. runs	THOM 1010:52
Who hath desired the S.?	KIPL 563:90
why the s. is boiling hot	CARR 240:57
will not find another s.	CAVA 246:70
wind had sprung from the s.	THOM 1009:49
Wind of western s.	TENN 997:97
windy s. of land	MILT 689:41
world's tempestuous s.	EDME 361:45
wrecks will surface over the s.	EWART 381:47
wrinkled s. beneath him	TENN 1000:64
yacht on the s.	REID 806:98

sea-boy repose To the wet s.-b.	SHAK 877:95
sea-change But doth suffer a s.-c.	SHAK 916:26
sea-down at the s.-d.'s edge	SWIN 988:56
sea-fogs s.-f. lap and cling	KIPL 563:91
sea-green s.-g. Incorruptible	CARL 235:66
sea-sand ribbed s.-s.	COLE 273:89
sea-side drawback of all s.-s. places	DOUG 342:64
sea-water salt s.-w. passes by	TENN 998:26
seagull s. is...unlimited...freedom	BACH 54:96
seal heard a s. bark!	THUR 1018:12
opened the seventh s.	BIBLE 157:16
s. is set	BYRON 220:99
S. of Divinity and Immortality	AUBR 45:37
s. of nobility those people	MUSS 716:86
s. of the weakness of our race	DELA 314:21
s.'s wide spindrift gaze	CRANE 294:94
under the great s. of England	PENN 764:56
sealing-wax like sticks of s.-w.	DICK 323:89
seals faint aroma of performing s.	HART 459:44
loose the s. thereof?	BIBLE 157:11
trained s., creeping Jesuses	MACD 628:92
seam touch of the s.	UTTL 1038:82
seamen s. made reply	TENN 1005:59
Seamus Yours truly, S.	HEAN 465:39
search needle is not worth the s.	JACK 514:89
not worth the s.	SHAK 874:9
Science is a s. for truth	PAUL 761:18
S. me, O God	BIBLE 120:51
s. so painful and so long	ROCH 816:51
S. the scriptures	BIBLE 145:41
seas dark broad s.	TENN 995:61
devotion to the wind and s.	LANC 578:52
down the salt s.	KIPL 564:12
Draw not up s.	DONNE 337:87
fight on the s. and oceans	CHUR 264:14
floors of silent s.	ELIOT 367:50
For the s.' worth	SHAK 898:1
landscapes of s. full of fish	CIXO 267:75
make s. our smooth highway	CARL 234:38
must go down to the s.	MASE 661:32
On desperate s.	POE 776:47
other hand full of s.	HYDE 509:12
paradise of four s.	MARV 659:91
port after stormy s.	SPEN 957:8
rapture the earth and the s.	BRON 190:87
Rivers and s....to float their ships	DICK 323:90
s. colder than the Hebrides	FLEC 393:54
s. roll over	HERB 474:6
strange s. of Thought	WORD 1096:27
Till a' the s. gang dry	BURNS 212:40
tossed upon cloudy s.	NOYES 732:42
traversed the s.	WILB 1075:20
waste of s.	GALT 413:8
seashore pearls by the s.	MORE 707:53
playing on the s.	NEWT 725:40
season be instant in s.	BIBLE 154:40
buy himself a s. ticket	ASHD 41:60
disturb your s. due	MILT 684:38
dry brain in a dry s.	ELIOT 368:72
every s. she hath dressings	ANON 23:91
for a s., Let us be merry	CURR 301:18
Frivolity is sweet, in s.	HORA 493:26
from that time unto this s.	SPEN 959:44
In a somer s.	LANG 579:69
in due s. we shall reap	BIBLE 152:93
loosed a little s.	BIBLE 158:32
meat in due s.	BIBLE 118:18
Midwinter Spring is its own s.	ELIOT 372:60
nice sickly s.	DICK 321:35
Praise out of s.	BUCK 203:36
s. of calm weather	WORD 1098:54
s. of love and laughter	GORD 435:63
S. of mists	KEATS 547:4
s. of snows and sins	SWIN 986:24

season (*contd.*):

s. ticket on the line	AMERY 16:*67*
s. was the airiest May?	GRAV 439:*21*
stay the due s.	JONS 535:*91*
terrible beyond any s.	MACA 623:*5*
this fine s.	WORD 1101:*95*
To every thing there is a s.	BIBLE 122:*19*
was no s. then for her	MILT 681:*86*
Will there never come a s.	STEP 968:*80*
willing for a s.	BIBLE 145:*40*
word spoken in due s.	BIBLE 121:*81*
worse this s. than ever	DOUG 341:*51*

seasoned till they are s. — HOLM 486:*90*

seasons All times are his s. — DONNE 339:*26*

As the swift s. roll	HOLM 486:*85*
assailed the s.	ROBI 814:*26*
changing s.	WHITE 1070:*31*
her changing s.	THOM 1013:*21*
Man for all s.	BOLT 172:*74*
not for you to know…the s.	BIBLE 147:*79*
returning s. bring	PHIL 768:*18*
s. never change	GUY 449:*96*
S. return	REED 805:*83*
s. such as these?	SHAK 903:*24*
to thy motions lovers' s. run?	DONNE 336:*77*

seat and built his s. — SURR 982:*40*

another world, the happy s.	MILT 688:*18*
before you take your s.	STEV 975:*41*
castle hath a pleasant s.	SHAK 907:*30*
Fasten your s. belts	MANK 645:*76*
fell from off the s. backward	BIBLE 110:*31*
from her wild sequestered s.	COLL 277:*50*
got to save your s.	ANON 29:*27*
providing he was in the driver's s.	BEAV 81:*84*
regain the blissful s.	MILT 687:*84*
repossess their native s.	MILT 688:*6*
round of Cynthia's s.	MILT 681:*89*
Scotia's darling s.	BURNS 210:*86*
s. of this sensation	HOUS 496:*81*

seated looked wiser when he was s. — KEYN 554:*26*

Seaton Marie S., and Mari Beaton — BALL 67:*46*

seats cheap s. clap their hands — LENN 596:*54*

fixed in our s.	STEE 964:*21*
rows of empty s.	OLIV 738:*30*
with three empty s.	HUNT 504:*17*

seawards road leads me s. — MASE 662:*42*

seaworms huge s. in his sleep — TENN 993:*32*

Seckler Dorothy S. has noted — LIPP 606:*29*

second asking 'Who came s.?' — REAR 804:*72*

blinding split s.	FOWL 400:*70*
here I leave my s. leg	HOOD 488:*35*
not a s. on the day	COOK 286:*24*
one year we came s.	PAIS 751:*54*
S. childishness and mere oblivion	SHAK 886:*96*
s. guessing	PHIL 768:*18*
split s. when it can be recalled	BUCK 203:*35*
The s. best's	YEATS 1106:*81*
travel any road a s. time	IBN 510:*19*
wrote it with a s. hand	SPEN 959:*28*

second-best s.-b. is anything but — LESS 598:*3*

second-rate creed of a s.-r. man — BAGE 62:*65*

If Richard Nixon is s.-r. — HELL 468:*87*

secrecy crime…vice…by s. — PULI 795:*20*

for s. No lady closer	SHAK 875:*52*
live of s.	MOYN 711:*16*
nature's infinite book of s.	SHAK 904:*57*
S. is the first essential	RICH 810:*67*
s. with which they pursue	JEVO 521:*22*

secret alms may be in s. — BIBLE 134:*47*

always a s. singing	SAND 841:*63*
book…of my s. soul	SHAK 894:*98*
bread eaten in s.	BIBLE 120:*67*
ceases to be a s.	BEHN 85:*69*
Father which is in s.	BIBLE 135:*48*

secret (*contd.*):

giant girls that have no s.	SPEN 956:*80*
in my soul that tender s. dwells	BYRON 221:*12*
in s. sin	CHUR 262:*84*
joys of parents are s.	BACON 57:*54*
keep a s. like a child	HUGO 502:*85*
keep the mistakes s.	MOYN 711:*16*
know that's a s.	CONG 280:*13*
man keeps another person's s.	LABR 572:*39*
members of our s. service	FOOT 396:*92*
method and s.…of Jesus	ARNO 40:*35*
no s. better kept	SHAW 920:*8*
no s. so close	SURT 983:*48*
one dirty s. in American life…racism	CISN 266:*68*
s. for harvesting	NIET 728:*74*
s. house of death	SHAK 906:*89*
s. of being miserable	SHAW 924:*9*
s. of decorating	TROL 1027:*63*
s. of life	CUMM 299:*80*
s. of managing a ball club	STEN 968:*75*
s. of redemption	WEIZ 1062:*87*
s. of success in mathematics	LEHR 595:*40*
S. sits in the middle	FROST 407:*98*
s. things belong unto the Lord	BIBLE 108:*90*
That is the ancient s.	PRAT 789:*23*
The S. Diary of Adrian	TOWN 1024:*12*
There's no s.	VUKO 1047:*24*
when I was made in s.	BIBLE 120:*50*
whole s. would be out	WILL 1082:*82*

secretaries s.…have an advantage — ROCK 817:*70*

secretary s.'s diary — RODC 818:*81*

revelation and told my s.	STEIN 966:*51*
S. of State	MACC 625:*42*

secretion isolate the internal s. — BANT 70:*4*

secretly go s. hoping they won't — HEAT 465:*46*

So s. …they went — OWEN 748:*21*

secrets ears that…hear one's s. — ONEI 740:*52*

from whom no s. are hid	BOOK 174:*16*
greatest s. of the past	FAWC 384:*93*
guilty s. of Europe	DUNN 356:*53*
learned the s. of the grave	PATER 759:*93*
Men with s.	DELI 315:*41*
s. are edged tools	DRYD 346:*55*
S.…Are never valued	CRAB 294:*89*
s. of his trade	ORWE 744:*25*
s. of the prison-house	MOOD 703:*95*
tell you all her s.	SNOW 951:*78*
walls…sharers of s.	AMMI 17:*97*

sect any religion, by any s. — KRIS 569:*92*

attached to that great s.	SHEL 931:*51*
Christ…leader of the s.	TACI 989:*79*
found them a s.	MACA 624:*23*
Irish…that ancient s.	YEATS 1107:*91*
loving his own s. better	COLE 275:*22*
paradise for a s.	KEATS 545:*68*
sad-coloured s.	HOOD 489:*40*

sects diversity of s. — SPEN 958:*23*

secure No Government can be long s. — DISR 332:*80*

s., and now can never mourn — SHEL 931:*47*

security beggar…possesses that s. — SMITH 945:*78*

being on social s.	WELD 1062:*94*
from s. into something malevolent	CATH 244:*44*
live without other s.	HOBB 483:*40*
lost…a lovely feeling of s.	CHAT 254:*99*
peace and s.	UNIT 1036:*45*
sacrifice instead of more s.	KENN 550:*61*
s. and peace	MACD 628:*5*
S. can only be obtained	LEES 593:*20*
s. for the future	TROL 1027:*71*
s.…in our relationship with God	EDDI 360:*19*
s. of property	PANK 752:*79*
s. of the land	COVE 290:*90*
s. to persons who are accused	DENM 316:*59*

sedate s., sober, silent	HOOD 489:*40*
sedately took the kiss s.	TENN 1001:*82*
try to walk s.	STEV 975:*40*
sedge s. is wither'd	KEATS 545:*72*
seditions surest way to prevent s.	BACON 58:*80*
seduce s., bamboozle	LIPP 607:*37*
seducer Thou strong s.	DRYD 347:*71*
seduction ethical or social s.	BEVAN 101:*64*
persuade her to give it away (s.)	DWOR 357:*83*
see cannot s., and in the third	NORTH 731:*32*
complain we cannot s.	BERK 95:*50*
day…meant not to s.	THAT 1008:*17*
few…learn to s.	OKRI 738:*23*
Helen, did Homer never s.	JONS 536:*15*
I s. what I eat	CARR 238:*28*
I was blind, now I s.	BIBLE 146:*52*
In all things Thee to s.	HERB 475:*13*
lovers cannot s.	SHAK 874:*29*
much to hear and s.	SKEL 942:*32*
neither s. nor hear	JOHN 524:*69*
not that I did not s.	HOLM 485:*72*
pleasure of believing what we s.	SHEL 927:*66*
power…to make you s.	CONR 284:*88*
s. and hear and understand	HEMI 470:*27*
s. better than I do	GOYA 437:*83*
S. one…s. all	BURT 214:*69*
s. them as they are	JOHN 532:*44*
s. things, and you say, 'Why?'	SHAW 926:*44*
s. this day and live	SHAK 881:*99*
still can't s.	HUGH 499:*17*
stream…we s. ourselves in	FROST 407:*88*
what we do not s.	SHAK 896:*67*
what we s. is life	WARR 1054:*31*
won't even go to s. it	GRANT 438:*99*
yet I s. thee still	SHAK 908:*39*
You s., but you do not observe	DOYLE 344:*3*
seed bearing precious s.	BIBLE 119:*40*
blood…is the s.	TERT 1006:*78*
carrying your s.	MARQ 655:*34*
democrat…gone to s.	EMER 377:*61*
enmity between thy s. and her s.	BIBLE 103:*98*
few more lies eat into the s.	MAIL 639:*68*
Nestles the s. of perfection	WHIT 1073:*96*
nor his s. begging bread	BIBLE 115:*65*
received s. among the thorns	BIBLE 137:*98*
received s. into the good ground	BIBLE 137:*99*
s. its harvest	KEATS 545:*59*
s. of knowledge	BACON 54:*4*
s. of the serpent	DONNE 339:*24*
s. should not be his	BIBLE 105:*42*
sowed in youth a mustard s.	BRON 190:*91*
spring again from its s.	SHEL 931:*56*
thy s. may live	BIBLE 108:*99*
weed…of celestial s.	DRYD 349:*19*
seed-time Fair s.-t.	WORD 1096:*20*
s.-t. and harvest	BIBLE 104:*13*
seeds colonization planted the s.	MARI 650:*62*
in a bag all sorts of s.	SPEN 959:*41*
s. of time	SHAK 907:*17*
some s. fell by the wayside	BIBLE 137:*97*
seeing better at believing than at s.	SANT 842:*87*
faculty of s. things	SPEN 956:*85*
gave up s. years ago	JOHN 524:*69*
Not S. is Believing	WOLFE 1090:*24*
point is the s.	REID 806:*97*
S. is deceiving	THUR 1019:*40*
s. on the screen	GOLD 434:*41*
s. what Adam had seen	HUXL 507:*83*
s. what everybody has seen	SZEN 989:*69*
way of s. is also a way of not s.	BURKE 208:*53*
way of s. them	RUSK 830:*87*
Worth s.?	JOHN 530:*5*
seek do not s. to understand	ANSE 31:*81*
may not so much s.	FRAN 401:*91*

seek (*contd.*):
not need to s. out   TOCQ 1021:80
not s. to make them like you   GIBR 422:38
s. all day   SHAK 874:9
s., and ye shall find   BIBLE 135:57
S. ye the Lord   BIBLE 127:4
To strive, to s.   TENN 995:62
Who s., who hope, who love   SIDN 937:58
seeker s. for cures   RICH 809:55
seemed s. well pleased, all s.   MILT 691:75
seems know not 's.'   SHAK 888:49
seen as I done it I s. it   SAND 841:68
cannot be s. and sung   ISAA 513:69
God whom he hath not s.?   BIBLE 156:95
I have sometimes s.   RIMB 812:88
if it's. through   GREE 445:30
much have I s.   TENN 994:58
not having s.   JOHN 530:87
s. enough of one war   JEFF 520:92
s. for what one is   DRAB 345:23
s. to be done   HEWA 479:85
s. to want...certainly never get   WEAT 1058:13
The less s.   WILD 1080:34
Things that are s.   JOHNS 523:40
things that I have s.   POLO 777:67
to be loved needs only to be s.   DRYD 350:49
vanity of being s.   SMOL 950:63
what is s. during a moment   SAND 841:65
where they cannot be s.   HAWK 461:62
sees s. is truly seen   SNYD 951:81
thinks he believes only what he s.   SANT 842:87
segment s. of our population   TRUM 1029:17
segregation S. now, s. tomorrow   WALL 1050:64
Seine flows the S.   APOL 32:92
seismograph Collage...a s.   ERNST 379:11
lightning rod than a s.   KESEY 553:20
seize S. the day   HORA 493:18
seldom s. look at them   MORT 710:97
select not to a s. committee   PULI 795:19
selection called this...Natural S.   DARW 306:83
S. is the invention   FUSE 410:62
selective even more s.   GREE 444:20
Observation is always s.   POPP 783:20
selects s. and omits   STRA 979:97
self All by my own-along s.   HARR 458:33
Am I your s.   SHAK 883:30
Anger's s. I needs must kiss   SIDN 937:56
at once as Nature's s.   BROW 198:54
Dearer than s.   BYRON 219:71
door out of the dungeon of s.   MACD 628:99
dungeon of the s.   CONN 283:77
fictitious s.   CHOP 261:61
final distillation of s.   DELI 315:40
for its absolute s.   WORD 1100:81
greater to one than one's s.   WHIT 1072:81
high authority of the s.   TRIL 1027:61
incomplete s.   GASS 416:36
knowledge of the s.   KANT 541:99
live without the s.   ATWO 45:26
look within and examine your own s.
   CONF 280:89
mysterious belief in a s.   MANS 647:5
s. as the window   UPDI 1037:69
s. cannot be escaped   BART 74:75
s. ...epicentre of the solar system   PHIL 768:19
s. is now the sacred cow   HUGH 500:33
s. persists like a dying star   ROET 819:1
small hungry shivering s.   ELIOT 366:40
that's your own s.   HUXL 507:78
The essential s.   UPDI 1037:66
The s. is hateful   PASC 758:67
thy s. present   SPEN 957:92
to thine own s. be true   SHAK 888:67
was his natural s.   TWAIN 1033:81

self (*contd.*):
weave my s. into the sense   HERB 475:26
Wisdom's s. Oft seeks   MILT 683:28
write for the public and have no s.   CONN 282:55
self-absorbed sign of the s.-a.   RYBC 834:49
self-assertion Japanese see s.-a.   KURO 571:21
self-assured s.-a. who strut   HAMM 453:45
self-awareness highest state of s.-a.   LARD 580:89
self-complacency s.-c. brought   WEBB 1058:14
self-condeming neither s.-c.   MILT 692:10
self-confession Christ...the s.-c.   FEUE 387:30
self-conscious most s.-c. people   JAMES 516:12
race which has become s.-c.   LAWR 585:74
self-consciousness writer's s.-c.   UPDI 1037:65
self-consumer s.-c. of my woes   CLARE 267:82
self-contain'd placid and s.-c.   WHIT 1072:81
self-contradiction poet is a s.-c.   FROST 407:90
self-control s.-c....courage   PEEL 763:44
self-definition starved for s.-d.   BURNS 208:55
self-denial S.-d. is not a virtue   SHAW 922:54
self-destruction beginnings of s.-d.   CHEE 255:49
self-determination s.-d. is not   WILS 1086:55
self-development S.-d. is...duty   STAN 963:91
self-devotion saved by his...s.-d.   MACA 624:28
self-discovery of s.-d.   WALC 1048:44
self-division man in s.-d.!   SIDN 936:43
self-esteem s.-e. is sacrosanct   HUGH 500:33
wiping out his s.-e.   MARI 652:77
self-examination practice s.-e.   I 510:20
significant s.-e.   PECK 763:38
self-fashioned s.-f. chains of slavery   MANS 647:96
self-flagellation for s.-f. solely   CAPO 231:84
self-fulfilling s.-f. prophecy   MERT 672:24
self-government experience of s.-g.   EDIN 361:39
self-help healthy spirit of s.-h.   SMIL 945:76
spirit of s.-h.   SMIL 945:73
self-image crippled s.-i.   THOM 1014:38
self-indulgence essay on s.-i   WAUGH 1056:64
self-interest enlightened s.-i.   KEYN 554:32
self-justification habit...of s.-j.   EDGE 360:25
self-love golden-calf of s.-l.   CARL 235:70
life depends upon s.-l.   JORD 537:31
s.-l. and social be the same   POPE 781:47
s.-l. is always the beginning   MANN 646:87
S.-l. is so natural   FONT 395:87
S.-l., my liege   SHAK 881:81
S.-l. ...often unrequited   POWE 787:3
self-lovers nature of extreme s.-l.   BACON 58:91
self-made was a s.-m. man   HELL 468:80
self-neglecting vile a sin As s.-n.   SHAK 881:81
self-parody S.-p. is the first portent   MACM 636:25
self-pity S.-p....is as snug   ANGE 19:25
self-portrait S.-p. in a Convex Mirror   ASHB 41:55
self-presentation place for s.-p.   RYBC 834:49
self-preservation ensure Japan's s.-p.   HIRO 481:17
self-raised fail to reascend S.-r.   MILT 688:6
self-removed must be s.-r.   MANS 647:96
self-respect self-love and s.-r.   JORD 537:31
S.-r....comes to us   GRIS 447:68
self-restraint promotes s.-r.   TAFT 990:83
self-revelation fluidity of s.-r.   JAMES 516:29
self-righteousnes S.-r. is not religion
   BRON 191:97
self-sacrifice higher duty than s.-s.   STAN 963:91
s.-s. as the sensible course   KURO 571:21
S.-s. enables us to sacrifice   SHAW 922:65
self-schooled s.-s., self-scanned   ARNO 36:61
self-seeking in a less s.-s. age   CECIL 254:50
self-slain god s. us.   SWIN 988:57
self-slaughter Against s.-s.   SHAK 916:7
canon 'gainst s.-s.!   SHAK 888:51
self-sufficing reasoning, s.-s. thing   WORD 1095:10
self-worship s.-w. of the monarch   MILL 675:80
selfish s. molecules known as genes   DAWK 310:43

selfish (*contd.*):
s. propriety of civilized man   MUIR 713:40
slack and s.   STEV 974:2
selfishness a cheerleader for s.   ONEI 740:67
dross of s.   ROCK 817:71
S. must always be forgiven   AUST 51:45
strongest protest against s.   GOOD 435:55
sell as if it were to s.   HERB 475:25
buy with you, s. with you   SHAK 874:18
how well they s.   JOYCE 538:62
no man might buy or s.   BIBLE 158:22
s. his grandmother   GRANT 438:3
selling lives by s. something   STEV 976:47
selves Anger and tenderness: my s.   RICH 809:54
many...hundreds of s.?   MANS 647:3
nor is it our s.   UPDI 1037:69
s. conditional   UPDI 1037:70
stronger, riskier s.   MORR 709:86
the particularity of s.   TRIL 1027:61
semantic s. inversions   MAMET 643:50
semblable mon s.   ELIOT 368:84
semblance bore S. of worth   MILT 687:4
semicolon not enough...to be s.   BRAT 185:14
semicolony to be s.   BRAT 185:14
seminars girls suffered...so did my s.   BERR 98:17
sempiternal S. though sodden   ELIOT 372:67
Sempronius we'll do more, S.   ADDI 8:28
senate half-creature of the S.   MANS 648:14
S. becomes the wife   TAYL 992:18
tuned in the US S.   BRIN 189:58
senator Korea, S....American blood
   MACA 621:76
Time is the 101st S.   DODD 334:42
United States S.   JOHN 523:49
senators group of s.   DAUG 306:93
s. burst with laughter   AUDEN 47:67
send I refuse to s. anyone else   RANK 801:29
not about to s. American boys   JOHN 523:52
time for you to s. it back   JACK 514:85
Whom shall I s.   BIBLE 124:61
senior s. years are reached   RAND 801:22
sennights Weary s. nine times nine   SHAK 907:13
sensation delightful s.   FERB 385:11
objects of S.   LOCKE 609:73
seat of this s.   HOUS 496:81
s. is the same   HEMI 470:22
s. of a short, sharp shock   GILB 425:88
sensational somewhat too s.   WILDE 1078:86
sensations life of s.   KEATS 544:46
penultimate s.   GALS 413:3
secret of their own s.   MACKE 632:51
s. sweet   WORD 1094:96
truth of my s.   CONR 285:10
sense afraid of losing your moral s.   STEIN 965:31
any s. of direction   WILS 1084:12
art of making s.   MACL 634:37
beauty to my s. shall run   DONNE 336:70
Bereaving s., but endless   MILT 693:19
Bestow a purer s.   MALL 641:18
between s. and nonsense   JUNG 539:71
bring men back to common s.   BERK 95:53
common s. tells us   NABO 716:95
common s., and relatively   MORT 710:91
creeps after s.   DRYD 347:66
Decking the s.   HERB 475:25
deep s. of...shame   WEBS 1060:34
Devoid of s. and motion   MILT 688:15
don't need so much s.   HERN 476:46
each other and with the s.   KUHN 570:14
echo to the s.   POPE 778:84
established s. it is socially nil   LAWR 586:77
fine s. of the ridiculous   ALBEE 11:86
fountain of good s.   DRYD 352:80
free of s. and restriction   HEAT 465:45

sense (*contd.*):
glorious s. of words — ACHE 2:24
Good s. is the most fairly — DESC 317:76
If that s. is lost — EMER 378:78
in a two-fold s. — MILL 678:44
integrated s. — THUR 1019:45
it is not s. — CHUR 262:90
It is not tricks of s. — WILB 1075:21
lose the sin, yet keep the s. — POPE 779:10
lost s. of Victorian regard — PRIT 791:74
man of s. and a fop — CHES 257:71
Men of sound s. — PLATO 774:8
more or less dumb s. — JAMES 517:46
Much S.—the starkest Madness — DICK 328:1
none in her s. — BEHN 85:73
oddest frame of s. — SHAK 897:91
one…of s. forlorn — COLE 274:96
poor toper whose untutored s. — CRAB 293:65
religious s. of duty — DICK 327:79
rough s. of the daily jostle — DELI 315:42
Seal thy s. in deathly slumber — DELA 314:34
s. and observation — WORD 1100:83
s. and outward things — WORD 1098:53
s. by indirection, degrees of anger — EVANS 381:40
s. from nonsense — THUR 1019:47
s. is mocked in every thing — DAVI 307:9
s. of a long last night — MAIL 639:79
s. of being more — RUSS 832:19
s. of intellectual degradation — JAMES 515:6
s. of taste — BALL 68:66
s. of what is going on — BART 74:71
s. of wonder — SOCR 952:88
s. sublime — WORD 1094:97
Shadwell never deviates into s. — DRYD 348:83
shamefaced s. — MORE 707:53
sing good s. — LOUI 614:50
splendid borrows…from s. — POPE 779:24
Still follow s. — POPE 779:20
Take care of the s. — CARR 238:33
That it enchants my s. — SHAK 895:47
That the s. aches — SHAK 900:47
the ground s. necessary — WILL 1082:81
the s. faints — SHEL 928:88
Through s. and nonsense — DRYD 350:34
to curb the s. — DRYD 352:83
Touch…most demystifying of all s. — BART 75:80
use only Arguments of S. — PETTY 768:15
want of s. — DILL 331:56
weave my self into the s. — HERB 475:26
without any sign of common s. — CHIR 260:53
without one grain of s. — DRYD 350:43
work upon the vulgar with fine s. — POPE 779:14
world of s. and the world — RUSS 833:31
sense-experience limits of…s.-e. — AYER 53:78
senseless worse than s. things! — SHAK 882:15
senses the s. still supply — WORD 1094:94
assault on the s. — MACC 625:46
colour to that of the S. — MATI 664:75
come to my s. — GRAMM 438:94
disagreeable to the s. — DICK 325:36
extensions of our s. — STEV 972:79
five s. within whose pentagon — BERG 94:41
fool o' the other s. — SHAK 908:40
ill customs influence my very s. — ETHE 380:19
Let s. rule — SHAK 880:78
makes the s. rough — SHAK 861:94
Parson lost his s. — HODG 484:53
power to touch our s. — MILT 681:90
s. can think nothing — KANT 541:98
stuck to all my s. — MITC 696:82
subtlety of the s. — BACON 55:27
there are only five s. — PATM 760:8
Unto our gentle s. — SHAK 907:30
use of the s. and hands — DARW 306:88

sensibilities as the s. decline — STOWE 978:87
middle-class people of nice s. — SHAR 919:87
one's own fine s. — HELL 469:2
sensibility Dear s.! — STER 970:28
dissociation of s. — ELIOT 368:79
Experience…an immense s. — JAMES 516:19
multisibling s. — COUP 289:83
self-confession of human s. — FEUE 387:30
s. of a male adolescent — AUDEN 49:3
s. of principle — BURKE 207:32
s. transformed into intelligence — GOUR 437:80
sensible Extremely s. — STEW 977:65
no s. man directly challenges — MACM 635:14
s. as a dictionary — CARR 239:49
S.…beyond understanding — DUNN 356:54
S. men are all the same religion — DISR 334:28
silly things…done by s. people — AUST 52:56
sing when they are feeling s. — AUDEN 48:85
sensitive s. boy's humiliations — SHAW 921:27
s. man understands — FRIE 405:57
S. Plant in a garden grew — SHEL 930:28
sensitivities Irish feelings and s. — HAUG 460:59
sensual first a s. — HOOK 489:55
inordinate s. delight — BAXT 79:51
music and s. matters — KHOM 555:45
only s. pleasure without vice — JOHN 532:38
sensualists tyrants and s. — WOLL 1091:36
sensuality s.…into sexual vanity — WEBB 1058:14
sent Who s. you to me—God? — PUCC 794:15
sentence canvas a s. or paragraph — MOTH 711:72
declared meaning of a spoken s. — CAREY 233:24
hit reader…with first s. — BRIS 189:61
if this is slavery, give me a life s. — CHAR 253:92
judges…the s. sign — POPE 778:89
most important…the English s. — JOVA 537:38
pronounced a more rounded s. — JOHN 532:30
pull of the s. — MOORE 705:28
S. first—verdict afterwards — CARR 239:45
s. is a sound — FROST 406:76
s. is factually significant — AYER 53:79
s. structure — THUR 1019:39
single s. in a routine article — MEYER 673:32
sentences Backward ran s. — GIBBS 422:37
complete s. — GASS 416:36
mania for s. — FLAU 392:29
mix s. with dirt — BRAU 186:19
Mr Blackman in three s. — NGU 725:45
s., the structure — MORR 709:89
S. which simply express moral — AYER 53:80
silences between the s. — LIND 605:7
sentiment corrupted by s. — GREE 444:7
nurse of manly s. — BURKE 207:32
rich in s. — TENN 996:92
s. jointly dictate — RODO 818:87
s. which I feel strongly — SCOTT 856:15
those who have no s. — MAIL 639:48
truth of description and the s. — SCOTT 856:12
sentimental America…s. land — RABAN 798:76
corrupt art is the s. — PISS 771:58
getting more s. as I get older — CART 242:96
sentimentalism S. is the working off — LAWR 586:98
inclined towards s. — CARD 232:3
sentimentality S. is a failure — STEV 972:54
S. is the emotional promiscuity — MAIL 639:47
Sledgehammer s. — KENT 553:10
sentimentering no time to be be s. — TWAIN 1033:86
sentiments beautiful s. — GIDE 423:47
s. in the world — LOWE 616:86
Them's my s.! — THAC 1006:85
sentry quadrille in a s. box — JAMES 516:25
stands a wingèd s. — VAUG 1041:18
separated now we're s. — STRO 980:6
separately all hang s. — FRAN 402:10
separateness his weakness and his s. — BELL 88:36

separation consent to the s. — GEOR 418:82
preludes to that eternal s. — STER 970:15
protesting against s. — GRAT 439:14
s. breeds…regrets — CH 248:10
sepòlchered s. in such pomp — MILT 682:95
September cool S. morn — WHIT 1074:7
sing in S. — KEND 550:49
When you reach S. — ANDE 18:6
sepulchre came first to the s. — BIBLE 147:74
man the living s. — CLARE 267:81
no man knoweth of his s. — BIBLE 108:6
stone taken away from the s. — BIBLE 147:73
sepulchres like unto whited s. — BIBLE 139:36
sequence events…happen in a s. — WELTY 1065:51
sequential s., but memory — LIVE 607:46
sequestered Each s. in its hate — AUDEN 47:72
one of those s. spots — HARDY 456:97
sere fall'n into the s. — SHAK 910:81
serene more solemn and s. — SHEL 927:63
Serengeti six left in the S. — BENN 90:75
Serenissima pinnacles of the S. — MORR 708:77
serenity complaints…undermine the s. — ACHE 3:36
steady and perpetual s. — ADDI 7:17
serf hands of a s. — HYDE 509:14
serfdom abolish s. from above — ALEX 13:16
serial obituary in s. form — CRISP 297:40
series in a s. of courses — GOLD 432:92
s. of great opportunities — GARD 415:22
s. of undertakings — SART 844:17
serious Comedy is a very s. thing — GARR 415:32
Dead men are s. — FIND 389:66
from s. things — THOR 1016:78
Make…the s. smile — POPE 779:12
more s. than I should be — SIDN 936:42
much more s. than that — SHAN 918:69
Of all s. things — BEAU 79:63
position is s. — KEYN 555:35
s. attempt to do it — WELLS 1065:45
s. reading — WELLS 1064:31
tell when one is getting old and s. — EDWA 362:52
the s. and the smirk — DICK 321:47
think of something s. — TRAV 1025:34
you are not s. — RIMB 812:91
You cannot be s.! — MCEN 629:10
seriousness wallowing in low s. — BELL 88:35
sermon funeral s. — BELL 87:12
painful s. — PEPYS 765:63
preach a brilliant s. — HUXL 506:48
rejected the S. on the Mount — BRAD 184:93
short nap at s. — ADDI 7:11
whole of her s. — FORS 398:36
sermons frightened by political s. — BARTH 74:68
S. and soda water the day after — BYRON 222:42
S. in stones — SHAK 885:77
serpent dust shall be the s.'s meat — BIBLE 128:16
find the s. old — MARV 658:80
old s., called the Devil — BIBLE 157:21
seed of the s. that creeps — DONNE 339:24
s. beguiled me — BIBLE 103:97
s. did not seduce Eve — HUGH 500:42
s. of brass — BIBLE 107:84
s. shall bite him — BIBLE 123:37
s. to sting you — SHEL 926:51
s. under't — SHAK 907:29
s. was more subtil — BIBLE 103:93
sharper than a s.'s tooth — SHAK 902:8
Time like a s. — CRANE 295:2
venomous as poison of s. — BOOK 177:78
will he give him a s.? — BIBLE 135:58
serpent-haunted s.-h. sea — FLEC 393:51
serpents s. of explosive breath — MARI 651:67
wise as s. — BIBLE 136:76
servant act of the s. — LEON 596:72
bid your s. once adieu — SHAK 913:66

servant (*contd.*):
cast ye the unprofitable s. — BIBLE 140:42
clever s. — JEFF 519:78
good and faithful s. — BIBLE 140:41
he is the s. of the Living God — SMART 944:66
lookingglass of a s. — JOYCE 538:46
Lord, thy s. rears — HERB 474:8
never leave to be Your humble s. — ROCH 816:55
nor the s. above his lord — BIBLE 136:77
now lettest thou thy s. — BIBLE 160:55
obligation to become a s. — SHAW 924:93
politician poses as the s. — DEGA 313:6
press…is an excellent s. — COOP 287:44
public s. who makes it — NEW 723:16
S. of God, well done — MILT 691:76
s. of the sciences — BAUD 77:28
s. or has a business — LAW 585:60
s. shall be healed — BIBLE 136:64
s. to be bred at University — CONG 281:18
s. to the devil — SISS 940:97
s. with this clause — HERB 474:12
services of a menial s. — GRAY 440:44
Speak, Lord; for thy s. heareth — BIBLE 109:28
took upon him the form of a s. — BIBLE 153:8
wakes them himself, or sends his s. — ADDI 7:11
when ye had a gude s. — SCOTT 855:86
whose s. I am — LENT 596:67
writer or good public s. — MACM 636:20
servants as one of thy hired s. — BIBLE 143:9
domestic s. at home — MAUG 665:92
Give unto thy s. that peace — BOOK 173:99
reveal Himself to his s. — MILT 686:74
S. accumulate the privileges — DONO 340:36
s. of the public — GOWE 437:81
s. of the sovereign — BACON 57:68
Unmarried men…best s. — BACON 57:59
When domestic s. are treated — SHAW 922:51
workmen and menial s. — MALT 643:41
Ye s. of the Lord — DODD 335:46
serve Choose you…whom ye will s. — BIBLE 109:12
Him s. with fear — KETHE 554:23
s. and obey them — HUME 503:3
serves S. to say thus — SHAK 877:3
service abdicated the s. of it — PITT 771:65
any s. to the world's end? — SHAK 879:38
arrived in my s. already christened — SAKI 837:4
century of active s. — MOUN 711:13
did more s. than he — GOLD 432:1
do you…much s. — ASTE 42:88
do you that last good s. — ROCH 816:60
essential s. to his country — SWIFT 985:85
If I last in this s. — SHAK 865:2
in purer lives thy s. find — WHIT 1074:9
in the s. the scum — WELL 1063:7
no-future job in the s. sector — COUP 289:74
point to his years of s. — ISHI 513:76
rewarded for good s. — ROOS 822:48
s. and greater glory — PIUS 772:81
s., as to the Lord — BIBLE 152:5
s. is the common duty — ROCK 817:71
s. of my love — SPRI 961:63
s. of this nation — GAND 414:11
s. to my bonie lassie — BURNS 210:97
s. we render to others — GREN 446:53
shrink from the s. of his country — PAINE 750:42
soong the s. dyvgne — CHAU 254:20
whose s. is perfect freedom — BOOK 173:96
serviceable s. villain — SHAK 904:41
serviceman do not call a s. — BRIN 189:58
services commands Our s. a while — SHAK 905:63
if his s. are not recognised — DUGO 354:24
Nor s. to do — SHAK 913:66
price…on the s. — FRIE 405:54
s. of a menial servant — GRAY 440:44

serviettes crumpled the s. — BETJ 100:52
servile s. minds into terror — TZARA 1035:33
servility slave in base s. — SHAK 861:96
serving s. the client — JOHN 524:64
servitude base laws of s. — DRYD 347:69
History may be s. — ELIOT 373:75
out of s. into freedom — EMER 377:70
s. and extreme licence — TOCQ 1021:75
s. still can pierce — MUIR 712:34
s.…the consequence of his crime — CURR 301:16
s. To serve th' unwise — MILT 691:78
sesquipedalian S. blackguard — CLOU 270:29
sessions s. of sweet silent thought — SHAK 913:58
set by God's grace, play a s. — SHAK 880:71
s. down This — ELIOT 369:4
turn on your s. — BRIN 189:58
Virtue is…best plain s. — BACON 59:13
Setebos S., S., and S.! — BROW 200:81
settee Lady Venus on the s. — SITW 940:99
setting haste now to my s. — SHAK 918:59
Hath elsewhere its s. — WORD 1098:51
s. which influences it — ROSSO 825:98
settle helped s. this glorious land — FERB 385:6
less will you s. for one — KIPL 562:56
settlement political s. of this crisis — HUSS 505:35
s. through genuine dialogue — AUNG 50:23
settler maintained by the s. — SART 844:20
settlers When old s. say — LESS 598:95
seven hewn out her s. pillars — BIBLE 120:66
Jacob served s. years — BIBLE 105:36
s. great facts and doctrines — HUGEL 498:10
seventy times s. — BIBLE 139:21
seventh God blessed s. day — BIBLE 102:87
opened the s. seal — BIBLE 157:16
seventies vice of the S. — WOLFE 1091:31
seventy To be s. years young — HOLM 486:2
seventy-seven At s.-s. it is time — JOHN 529:69
severance God their s. ruled — ARNO 37:80
severe intentionally a little too s. — KIER 556:59
s. he was and stern to view — GOLD 433:12
severest s. writers of the s. age — DRYD 348:79
severity pure s. of perfect light — TENN 1003:19
simplicity or with s. — ARNO 38:8
Summer…with its usual s. — COLE 275:23
Severn from the S. to the Tyne! — KIPL 565:26
on S. snow the leaves — HOUS 495:53
the S. fills — TENN 998:26
Seville dogs of S. — TENN 1005:57
sew time to s. — BIBLE 122:19
Sewell S. & Cross young man — GILB 424:71
sewer filthy s. pure gold flows — TOCQ 1022:82
sea is the universal s. — COUS 290:89
trip through a s. — MIZN 698:7
sewers Ye Nymphs that reign o'er s. — COLE 275:26
sex accident of s. — GILM 427:17
broken down by Age, S. — MACR 638:53
call you darling after s. — BARN 72:37
can either s. assume — MILT 687:2
cardinal virtues of the s. — WOLL 1091:37
complete example of her s. — RUSS 833:42
desire for food and s. — TOOLE 1023:5
destroy s. in America — DOCT 334:39
difference is not that of s. or age — CIXO 267:70
eclipses and predominates…her s. — DOYLE 344:2
equal, as their s. not equal — MILT 690:55
Every city has a s. and age — BERG 95:47
fair s. is your department — DOYLE 344:13
Gulf War was like teenage s. — HARK 457:18
his authority and her s. — WOLL 1091:40
If God had meant…group s. — BRAD 183:80
In the s. war — CONN 283:70
isn't s. but death — SONT 953:6
Literature is…about having s. — LODGE 609:76
litigation takes the place of s. — VIDAL 1044:67

sex (*contd.*):
money buys women, s., status — DWOR 358:84
Money…was exactly like s. — BALD 64:98
offices s. can discharge for s. — WOOLF 1093:75
one s. from another — THUR 1019:47
Pornography…attempt to insult s. — LAWR 587:4
practically conceal its s. — NASH 719:47
privilege…for my own s. — AUST 52:70
Redeem the age and s. — PHIL 768:20
riding high on s. and self-esteem — HOLL 485:71
romantic interest in our own s. — CONN 283:80
run after by the other s. — SHAW 924:91
s. and creativity are often — JONG 533:61
S. and obscenity not synonymous — BREN 187:33
S. had never before asserted — HARDY 456:93
S.…I really don't understand — SALI 838:20
S. is engaging — JIANG 522:24
s. is good for headaches — WILB 1075:23
S. is like money — UPDI 1036:54
s. just politics — BRAD 183:82
S. Life in Ancient Rome face — AMIS 16:72
s. object — GIOV 428:37
s. rears its ugly 'ead — ALLI 15:52
S.…single-crop farming — BELL 88:41
S. suppressed will go berserk — EWART 381:44
s. was something no woman — MUNRO 714:56
S.! What is that but life — CHER 256:66
s. with someone I love — ALLEN 14:48
Shall the s. free — HABI 450:1
She gave him s. — HEPB 473:78
soft, unhappy s. — BEHN 85:75
talk on 'S. and Civics' — BETJ 101:54
too visible as s. objects — FRIE 405:50
weaker s., to piety more prone — ALEX 13:22
what s. and psychoanalysis are — HUGH 500:30
When you have money, it's s. — DONL 336:60
women into a s. object — MORG 708:67
word s. in capital letters — WAUGH 1056:59
sexes absurd division into s. — WAUGH 1056:73
great distinction between the s. — FOWL 399:66
intellectual powers of the two s. — DARW 306:88
merit of both s. — LABR 572:37
more difference within the s. — COMP 279:75
old ladies of both s. — DICK 325:48
there are three s. — SMITH 949:51
wiser…of the two s. — GIBB 421:20
wives of both s. — MACD 628:92
sexologist kind of German s. — DOCT 334:39
sexophones s. wailed like…cats — HUXL 507:69
sexual felt s. urgings — COND 279:86
man cares most for s.intercourse — TWAIN 1034:19
rooted in the s. impulse — SCHO 849:96
s. juices flow toward a painting — FUEN 409:26
sublimated…into s. activity — BRAD 183:72
sexuality s. and promiscuity — WYLIE 1104:50
s.…suddenly recognized — FREUD 404:41
shabby If I were s. — WHAR 1068:97
S. gentility has nothing — HOLM 486:91
shackles garters to be bonds and s. — BACON 57:58
Memories are not s. — BENN 90:73
s. of an old love — TENN 1002:15
shad-blow s.-b., flaked — CRANE 295:6
shade alone in summer s. — WORD 1096:36
Amaryllis in the s. — MILT 684:42
broader browner s. — GRAY 441:56
clutching the inviolable s. — ARNO 38:93
enjoy the s. — JONS 536:16
fleeting image of a s. — SHEL 930:32
fountain, s., and rill — MILT 684:39
his steadfast s. — TENN 994:55
laws…of light and s. — CAPO 231:83
light, s. and perspective — CONS 285:20
Lord is thy s. upon thy right hand — BIBLE 119:36

shade (*contd.*):
No s., no shine — HOOD 489:52
ragged penury of s. — ADAMS 4:63
returned the s. — KEATS 545:69
s. is on the brightest wing — SITW 941:11
s. of a great name — LUCAN 618:22
S. off the trees — CORY 288:67
shall crowd into a s. — POPE 778:74
sit under the s. of it — DICK 323:94
sitting in the s. — KIPL 564:14
Spring...with rustling s. — SEEG 857:26
Summer-house, that knows no s. — POPE 779:21
throw no one into the s. — BULOW 204:54
Under the s. of a Coolibah — PATE 760:96
variable as the s. — SCOTT 853:58
Within its s. we'll live — CONN 282:54
shades Alcestis rises from the s. — LAND 578:57
luminous s. — GORD 435:62
preparing for bed with the s. up — STARR 963:1
regions of sorrow, doleful s. — MILT 687:90
s. and wanton winds — MILT 684:46
s. of darkness — DELA 314:33
s. of humiliation — EVANS 381:40
shadow ancient s. and twilights — RUSS 833:37
awful s. of some unseen Power — SHEL 927:61
but a s.'s s. — SHAK 890:1
care is like my s. — ELIZ 373:89
days on the earth are as a s. — BIBLE 112:86
dream...of a s. — CHAP 252:68
Falls the s. — ELIOT 369:1
hair and my s. — NERU 723:8
have to vanquish his s. — NIET 727:71
I am your s. — SCEVE 847:58
I have a little s. — STEV 975:38
land of the s. of death — BIBLE 125:65
Life's but a walking s. — SHAK 910:86
light and s. never stand still — WEST 1067:76
love in s. best is made — JONS 536:16
Man...fleeth also as a s. — BIBLE 113:9
merest s. line — THUR 1019:47
neither s. of turning — BIBLE 155:60
No s. walks behind me — JOHN 523:45
not darkness but s. — FRYE 408:24
out-soared the s. of our night — SHEL 931:47
s. at morning striding behind — ELIOT 368:2
s. cast by the light of a fire — VASA 1040:8
s. of a great rock. — BIBLE 126:81
S. of annoyance — SHEL 929:4
s. of cloud — YEATS 1105:72
s. of the midnight hour — BYRON 220:99
s. of the silent night — MARL 653:99
s. over the coloured — BUCK 203:33
s. shortened in the sun — JARR 518:64
S. That Comes in Sight — AMIS 17:85
s. that runs across the grass — HAGG 450:5
s. white as a stone — ROET 819:98
spy my s. — SHAK 863:48
star-shaped s. — WORD 1101:94
swan and s. — WORD 1098:57
tall elm's s. — THOM 1012:3
The S. cloaked — TENN 998:27
Time...a vast s. — VAUG 1041:20
under the s. of thy wings — BIBLE 114:41
under the s. of thy wings — BIBLE 115:62
under the s. of war — SPEN 956:78
with the s. of his wings — SHAK 862:43
you have got a s. — FLET 394:78
shadow-sister your s.-s. — WRIG 1101:10
shadowless Stand s. like Silence — HOOD 488:33
shadows Cats...than their s. — TESS 1006:80
colour of s. — WALC 1048:39
Each substance...hath twenty s. — SHAK 867:55
Earth's s. fly — SHEL 931:50
fills the s. — SWIN 986:23

shadows (*contd.*):
half sick of s. — TENN 993:42
illustrate all s. — DONNE 339:26
individuals pass like s. — BURKE 207:20
live to trace Their s. — KEATS 544:50
make the s. visable — NERV 723:10
measure s. — HUBB 498:9
mirrors of the gigantic s. — SHEL 931:60
s. among s. — UPDI 1036:55
s. have offended — SHAK 872:60
s. in a sunshine day? — MARL 653:6
s., not substantial things — SHIR 935:27
s. of eternity — VAUG 1040:15
S. of the world appear — TENN 993:41
s. upon two generations — LLOY 608:60
shapes, and beckoning s. — MILT 683:24
silent s. and in dreams? — STEV 971:39
sleepers and the s. — WHIT 1073:94
the well in the s. — PRIC 789:34
their s. deep — YEATS 1105:60
Types and s. have their ending — AQUI 32:6
very s. of the clouds — WORD 1099:65
what is time but s. — SASS 845:38
where the S. lie — TOLK 1022:92
Shadrach S., Meshach — BIBLE 129:46
Shadwell S. never deviates — DRYD 348:83
S....of all my sons — DRYD 348:2
shafts Between the s. and the furrow — HEAN 464:32
birch for s. — SPEN 957:99
shake seems to s. the spheres — DRYD 351:68
s. a man's faith — SHAW 920:98
s. off its apathy — RENAN 806:1
s. your Rome — SHAK 911:14
the rousing s. — POPE 778:91
shaken S. and not stirred — FLEM 393:59
Shakespeare as wise...As S. — FERG 385:15
closest you can get to S. — BUEC 203:41
compare [Jonson] with S. — DRYD 347:64
complete S. and prayer book — BAIN 63:78
dig up S. and dig up Bacon — GILB 426:99
five acts of S.'s tragedy — FIELD 387:40
gave S. and Fletcher all — DENH 315:55
good enough for S.'s day — VICT 1043:53
honour to S. — JONS 536:20
I find the phrase in S. — SCOTT 856:15
knowledge of the Bible, S. and Wisden — WAUGH 1058:6
land of S., Milton, Bacon, Newton — DICK 326:55
read S. I am struck — LAWR 587:3
remarkable thing about S. — GRAV 440:38
s. and i are often low browed — MARQ 656:40
S. by flashes of lightning — COLE 275:21
S....eye of God — OLIV 738:31
S. for his honoured bones — MILT 681:94
S....had the largest and most comprehensive soul — DRYD 347:59
S. is...a forest — JOHN 532:40
S. is the great genius of drama — BENN 92:7
S. made use of it first — SHER 934:10
S.'s much-quoted passage — ORWE 743:16
S.'s name...stands absurdly too high — BYRON 221:15
S. one gets acquainted with — AUST 51:49
S. set his play writing aside — CUOMO 300:6
S.,...wanted taste — WALP 1051:83
S. was an Irish Catholic — ONEI 740:40
S. was the Homer — DRYD 347:65
S....weak in chemistry — WELLS 1064:24
souls most fed with S.'s flame — CHES 259:37
special reservoir...fed by S. — ACHE 2:24
Stratford trades on S. — BURG 205:81
three good sets of S. — ONEI 740:59
tried...to read S. — DARW 306:86
Whaur's yer Wullie S. noo? — ANON 24:5

Shakespearian that S. rag — ELIOT 368:86
That S. rag — BUCK 202:32
shall His absolute 's.'? — SHAK 911:10
shallow s. conversational ends — SASS 845:40
shallows bound in s. and in miseries — SHAK 884:60
small eels...within the s. play — CRAB 294:83
Shalott beside remote S. — TENN 993:43
Lady of S. — TENN 993:39
shame all other praise is s. — SIDN 937:58
contempt of s. — JOHN 527:20
epoch of folly and s. — ZOLA 1110:26
greater was the s. — LANY 580:78
hangs his head for s.? — INGR 511:44
look of furtive s. — WODE 1089:99
neither sin nor s. — ROCHE 815:40
neither sin nor s. — STER 970:22
no love...no s. — SHAW 920:99
no s. for a man to die — HOMER 488:23
noble s. — KING 559:2
race of s. — MILT 694:47
sense of...deathless s. — WEBS 1060:34
s....from being happy at another's distress — LABR 573:54
S. is the most violent — LAFA 574:74
S. of the versifying tribe! — GRAY 441:60
s. on you — ARMS 35:46
s. or censure free — JOHN 525:79
s. the devil — SHAK 876:58
s. will be too long — SHAK 882:6
'Tis no s. for men — SHIR 935:24
whose glory is in their s. — BIBLE 153:13
shameful s. conquest of itself — SHAK 867:49
vile members...called 'pudenda' ['s.'] — ABEL 1:3
shameless S. 5 years before — LAVER 584:56
shamrock S. shine for ever new! — DAVIS 309:40
shandeism True S....opens the heart — STER 969:7
Shandon bells of S. — MAHO 638:65
Shannon green banks of S. — CAMP 227:24
shape art thou, execrable s.? — MILT 689:26
assume a pleasing s. — SHAK 890:18
com'st in such a questionable s. — SHAK 888:71
exact colour and s. — MONET 700:43
eyes have drawn a s. — SHAK 913:54
flesh; but in what s. they — MILT 687:2
good s. for more sinning — RUNY 829:65
gordian s. of dazzling hue — KEATS 545:75
in the s. of a woman — RICH 809:47
let it keep one s. — SHAK 896:64
might be any s. — CARR 240:64
most rational s. — WEBER 1059:21
No s. to feed each gazing eye — DYER 358:88
nobler s.erect and tall — MILT 690:54
O Attic s.! — KEATS 547:10
over the net in a different s. — LODGE 610:79
s. of things to come — WELLS 1065:46
share the selfsame s. — MACD 627:82
some partial narrow s. — POPE 783:9
stereotyped s. assumed — LIPP 606:34
what s. it will take — SHEV 934:18
who's in worse s. than — MONR 700:50
shaper s. of the landscape — BRON 190:85
shapes full of s. is fancy — SHAK 893:92
horrid s., and shrieks — MILT 682:96
immortal s. Of bright — MILT 683:18
In holier s. — SHAK 902:93
s., and beckoning shadows — MILT 683:24
s. of rot — PURDY 795:34
Turns them to s. — SHAK 871:55
share biggest snouts...largest s. — WEIG 1061:76
s. the insult — ISHE 513:74
to her s. ...errors fall — POPE 778:94
shareholder large s. — TANA 990:95
shareholders mass of inert s. — ROBI 815:34
shares sell its s. — DRUC 346:46

sharing not of war…but of s. — CHILD 260:52
shark oppose the man-eating s. — BRIN 189:60
s. has pretty teeth dear — BREC 186:24
Sharon rose of S. — BIBLE 124:46
sharp s. as any lynx — SITW 940:1
s. be the weather — SCOTT 854:72
short, s. shock — WHIT 1072:66
so s. the conquerynge — CHAU 254:4
sharper s. than a serpent's tooth — SHAK 902:8
s. than any twoedged sword — BIBLE 154:45
sharpest s. men in argument — HOLM 486:83
shatterday frightday, s. — JOYCE 538:61
shatterer s. of worlds — BHAG 102:81
shave buy you more than a s. — LARK 582:18
rides back to s. again — WHITE 1070:36
To s. the beard is a sin — IVAN 514:83
shaving when am I s. of a morning — HOUS 496:80
Shaw S. has no enemies — WILDE 1079:9
shay wonderful one-hoss s. — HOLM 486:92
she great S.-who-must-be-obeyed — HEAL 464:30
S. who must be obeyed — HAGG 450:6
she-bear s.-b. coming up the street — FOOTE 396:95
She-Devil Loves of a S.-D — WELD 1062:89
she-elephant great S.-e. — HEAL 464:30
sheaf forgot a s. in the field — BIBLE 108:95
shears Fury with th' abhorred s. — MILT 684:42
resembles a pair of s. — SMITH 949:54
s. of destiny? — SHAK 872:73
sheath never s. the sword — ASQU 42:77
you s. — SHAK 876:56
sheaves bringing his s. — BIBLE 119:40
s. in harvest — DONNE 339:26
Sheba queen of S. — BIBLE 111:57
Solomon gave to the queen of S. — BIBLE 112:88
shedding Without s. of blood — BIBLE 154:47
sheep All we like s. have gone astray — BIBLE 127:1
an old half-witted s. — STEP 968:79
as a s. before her shearers — BIBLE 127:1
as s. going astray — BIBLE 156:80
come to you in s.'s clothing — BIBLE 135:60
counted as s. for the slaughter — BIBLE 116:71
Dream Of Electric S.? — DICK 320:10
erred and strayed…like lost s. — BOOK 173:89
giveth his life for the s. — BIBLE 146:54
go rather to the lost s. — BIBLE 136:73
having an hundred s. — BIBLE 143:96
hundred years as a s. — MUSS 716:85
hungry s. look up — MILT 684:45
land of cattle and s. — LAWS 588:20
like a s. with a blade of grass — WODE 1089:90
little black s. — KIPL 560:22
lying in bed counting s. — SIEG 937:67
men better than s. — TENN 1004:47
mountain s. are sweeter — PEAC 762:30
mountain which is no use for s. — BUTL 217:28
nation of panicked s. — THOM 1014:38
prize-oxen and of s. — TENN 996:95
sameness of s. — WHITE 1070:31
savaged by a dead s. — HEAL 464:28
s. go to the slaughter-house — MACD 627:70
s. he doth us take — SCOT 856:22
s. in s.'s clothing — GOSSE 436:70
s. in the midst of wolves — BIBLE 136:76
s. of his hand — BOOK 177:87
s. on his right hand — BIBLE 140:43
s. out of the window — WELD 1062:96
shepherds looking on their seely s. — SHAK 862:24
shroudes as I a s. were — LANG 579:69
standing a s. on its hind-legs — BEER 83:36
strange that s.'s guts — SHAK 879:45
teeth are like a flock of s. — BIBLE 124:51
the shepherd his s. — PROP 792:79
useless for the s. to pass — INGE 511:35
with not many black s. — ORWE 743:16

sheep-bells s.-b. and the ship-bells — KIPL 563:91
sheep-herding mere s.-h. — POUND 786:76
sheep-hook how to hold A s.-h. — MILT 684:44
sheepfold let the wolf into the s.! — INGR 512:50
sheepskins well down among the s. — STEV 973:97
sheet causes, the balance s. — MO 698:12
great s. knit at the four corners — BIBLE 147:91
old England's winding s. — BLAKE 168:5
wet s. and a flowing sea — CUNN 300:99
sheets brother popped…into his s. — STOP 978:75
fumble with the s. — SHAK 880:77
Sheffield 'Brooks of S.' — DICK 323:1
reminded him of S. United — HATT 460:58
shelf deepens like a coastal s. — LARK 582:15
Life…Behind the S. — DICK 328:4
stuffed ones on a s. — POUND 786:79
take the phial cleanly from its s. — DOYLE 344:21
shelf-life s.-l. of the moral causes — IGNA 510:27
s. l. somewhere between — TRIL 1026:54
shell dry s. on the beach — DU 354:32
pebble or a prettier s. — NEWT 725:40
s. of his victim — ANNAN 20:35
s.…of meaning — ELIOT 372:69
skin and s. of things — VAUG 1040:14
Within thy airy s. — MILT 683:26
Shelley did you once see S. plain — BROW 199:59
Like S. and like Baudelaire — ISHE 513:73
peace in S.'s mind — SHEL 932:69
What S. shrilled — SASS 845:40
shells not the s. and rockets — KISH 565:29
shelter no s. but in a fool's cap — HOPK 491:78
Our s. from the stormy blast — WATTS 1055:58
running to the s. — JAGG 515:95
s., and even muse — TUCH 1031:48
s. thee, I'd s. thee — BURNS 213:50
s., warmth and accommodation — NUTT 732:46
shelves symmetry of s. — LAMB 577:32
shepherd any philosophy in thee, s.? — SHAK 886:99
as a s. divideth his sheep — BIBLE 140:43
Dead s. — SHAK 886:15
Dick the s. blows — SHAK 866:30
feed his flock like a s. — BIBLE 126:86
finding herself at S.'s Bush — BUTL 217:39
homely slighted S.'s trade — MILT 684:42
I am the good s. — BIBLE 146:54
Lord is my s. — BIBLE 115:50
Lord's my s. — SCOT 856:19
power by which our S. rose — DODD 335:47
Scythian s. — MARL 652:86
S. and Bishop of your souls — BIBLE 156:80
S., from the hill — ARNO 37:85
s., thee the woods — MILT 684:40
star that bids the s. — MILT 683:20
the fairest s. — PEELE 763:45
the s. his sheep — PROP 792:79
truth in every s.'s tongue — RALE 800:12
shepherds liberal s. — SHAK 892:71
s. abiding in the field — BIBLE 142:78
s. and butchers — VOLT 1047:16
s. feed their flocks — MARL 655:31
s. looking on their seely sheep — SHAK 862:24
s., weep no more — MILT 685:49
warmth of the s.' flames — MARL 653:92
What time the s. — SHAK 862:21
sherry have a sweet s. — BENN 91:80
mischief…with the cooking s. — THUR 1019:42
unattainable soda and s. — SALA 838:17
very fond of brown s. — CHES 260:44
Shibboleth Say now S. — BIBLE 109:16
shield broken was her s. — SCOTT 853:60
lady in his s. — TENN 993:43
Our S. and Defender — GRANT 438:5
our sword and our s. — HUGH 501:54
s. me with shining breast — GORD 435:62

shield (*contd.*):
s. of congressional immunity — SMITH 948:25
s. of faith — BIBLE 152:6
s. ourselves from sordid perils — WILDE 1076:39
trusty s. and weapon — LUTH 620:49
truth shall be thy s. — BIBLE 117:2
where the s. and spear — SPEN 958:17
why should you want to s. him? — SAKI 838:12
shift let me s. for myself — MORE 707:57
shifty s., hangdog look — WODE 1089:99
Shiites Irish…as the S. in Lebanon — OROU 741:79
shilling kindly drop a s. — KIPL 562:67
s. life will give you — AUDEN 46:52
willing to sell for one s. — LEAR 590:60
shillings these men paid their s. — PRIE 789:35
weight in pounds, s. — MILNE 680:79
shimmering s. into rooms — WODE 1088:87
shine Arise, s. — BIBLE 127:11
can give me a s. — GORD 435:64
every one doth s. — SHAK 883:38
No one could s. his shoes — ISAA 513:71
not to s. in use! — TENN 994:58
see it s. plain — HOUS 495:58
sun…shall s. on me — SHAK 866:42
To see him s. so brisk — SHAK 875:42
shingles naked s. of the world — ARNO 36:64
shinning those who do not allow 's.' — ANON 24:14
shins not afraid of his s. — ANON 24:14
ship aloe…like a s. — MANS 647:7
As idle as a painted s. — COLE 273:87
being in a s. — JOHN 527:25
built your s. of death — LAWR 587:6
English s., they say — LOND 610:90
Matilda Briggs…was a s. — DOYLE 344:20
mildest…That ever scuttled s. — BYRON 223:49
O S. of State — LONG 611:8
Of a s.'s hour — SLES 943:67
office was his pirate s. — LEWIS 602:52
sail this new s. of mine? — BALL 67:47
s., an isle, a sickle moon — FLEC 393:55
s. has weather'd every rack — WHIT 1073:91
s. in port is safe — HOPP 493:71
s. is always referred — NIMI 729:2
S. me somewhere — KIPL 560:27
s. [of state] will be saved — CUOMO 300:5
s. on the sea — LORCA 613:39
s.'s upon the sea — KIPL 561:47
s. would not travel due West! — CARR 241:86
Sink me the s. — TENN 1005:59
steel s. loaded with monoliths — MENC 670:89
Swimming full upon the s. — BROW 199:70
swimming toward a sinking s. — YARB 1104:54
tall s. and a star to steer — MASE 661:32
the rolling s. — LUCR 619:35
The s.'s ignored — BISH 163:29
truth…sinks his s. — CORN 288:61
went down to the s. — POUND 786:70
whale s. was my Yale College — MELV 667:32
What is s. but prison — BURT 214:72
ship-bells sheep-bells and the s.-b. — KIPL 563:91
shipping fishes first to s. did impart — DRYD 346:54
tiers of s. — DICK 324:18
ships as s. on the foam — KIPL 561:37
boats or a s. came near — LEAR 590:63
down to the sea in s. — BIBLE 118:20
drew a thousand s. — MARL 653:93
face that launched a thousand s. — MARL 654:19
fleet of British s. — NELS 722:97
harbour without s. — DEFOE 312:84
My experience of s. — BRAD 183:75
my s. are out of gear — TENN 1004:56
my thoughts on white s. — COLUM 278:61
nor its s. empty of men — NICI 726:57
old s. sail like swans — FLEC 393:56

sights (*contd.*):

few more impressive s.	BARR 73:47
most poignant s.	JOHN 523:43
power of many s.	SHEL 927:60
seen some strange s.	HOUS 495:67
s. as youthful poets	MILT 682:4
sounds and smells And s.	BETJ 101:58

sign And it is a good s.   PARN 756:40

In this s. thou shalt conquer	CONS 286:23
In this s....victorious	EUSE 381:36
it is a bad s.	SARR 843:3
know him by this s.	SWIFT 984:72
might be the s. of something	JENK 520:99
never give out my zodiac s.	PEACE 762:26
outward and visible s.	BOOK 175:39
s. for him to retire	DISR 333:12
s. of an ill-spent youth	SPEN 956:71
s. of an unconscious act	MOND 699:42
s. of the Cross	BOOK 175:35
s. of the self-absorbed	RYBC 834:49
s. or a wonder	BIBLE 108:94
s. that silence heaves.	KEATS 544:34
s. upon thine hand	BIBLE 108:90

signal Only a s. shown   LONG 612:18

really do not see the s.	NELS 722:98

signal-elm s.-e., that looks on   ARNO 39:14

signals receives s.   UMAS 1035:38

significance literal s.   AYER 53:78

significations s. of their words   HOBB 482:36

signify What does it s.   GASK 415:33

signifying S. nothing   SHAK 910:86

signpost all s. and no destination   KRON 570:2

signs merely conventional s.!   CARR 241:85

S. are taken for wonders	ELIOT 368:69
s. might be permanent	JOHN 526:5
s. of a New Age coming?	SMITH 948:35
s. of our own time	CARL 234:36
something like neon s.	UREY 1037:74

silence After s.   HUXL 507:63

all in s....stand	CRAB 293:67
answered best with s.	JONS 534:81
Be checked for s.	SHAK 901:66
charity of its s.	EMMET 378:81
conspiracy of s.	JAUR 519:71
darkness again and a s.	LONG 612:18
darkness and s. reign	LEAR 589:51
die in s.	PLATO 774:16
earth...in that eternal s.	MACL 634:82
Elected S., sing to me	HOPK 491:79
eternal s. of these...spaces	PASC 757:60
eternal s.	WORD 1098:54
even s., is spray-gunned?	OLSEN 739:35
foster-child of s.	KEATS 547:6
God is the friend of s.	THER 1009:38
grand talent pour le s.	CARL 236:89
great beauty of s.	CHAP 251:64
heart...trembles into s.	BYRON 221:12
in that s. we the tempest fear	DRYD 346:48
Indecency's conspiracy of s.	SHAW 922:58
land stares...in a huge s.	SCOTT 852:37
Learning to lie with s.	BYRON 220:97
midnight in the s.	BROW 200:1
most magical moment...is a s.	CRON 298:60
moves upon the s.	YEATS 1107:90
no noyse nor s.	DONNE 339:34
No voice, but oh! the s. sank	COLE 274:94
occasional flashes of s.	SMITH 949:53
often told in s.	STEV 974:12
pink, spread s.	CARR 237:11
private s. in which we live	PRIT 791:70
roar...on the other side of s.	ELIOT 366:37
sign that s. heaves.	KEATS 544:34
s....does not necessarily brood	ELIOT 366:27
s. envious tongues	SHAK 918:63

silence (*contd.*):

S. has a sound	KOH 568:74
s. in heaven	BIBLE 157:16
s. in the hills	TENN 998:26
s. in the room	KINS 559:13
s. in the White House	ACHE 3:30
S. is become his mother tongue	GOLD 432:7
S. is more musical	ROSS 823:74
s. is most noble till the end	SWIN 987:28
S. is only commendable	SHAK 873:89
S. is the greatest of all persecutions	PASC 758:78
S. is the most perfect expression	SHAW 925:20
S. is the perfectest herald	SHAK 879:40
S. is the virtue of fools	BACON 56:36
s. is your confession	EURI 380:30
s. makes a woman beautiful	SOPH 953:14
s. most offends me	SHAK 879:41
s. of eternity	STEV 974:25
s. of the night	ROSS 823:67
s. of the voice of justice	HAILE 451:11
s. round about his lair	KEATS 547:99
S. ruled this land	DARK 305:78
s. sounds no worse	HOUS 494:47
s. surged softly backward	DELA 314:27
s., told me truths	THOM 1012:2
s. until any voice is heard	LEZA 603:76
s. was deafening	KARSH 542:11
small change of s.	MERE 671:3
soft grey s.	JOYCE 538:43
solemn s.	GILB 425:88
Sorrow and s. are strong	LONG 611:7
speak by s.	PATM 760:9
Stand shadowless like S.	HOOD 488:33
stones of s.	HEAN 464:34
Sunset and s.!	COLUM 277:59
That man's s.	HARDY 456:85
The rest is s.	SHAK 893:89
There is no s. in the East	MAUG 664:88
There is s.	BLUN 170:42
threatened to s. Father Fahrt	ONOL 734:67
Till a s. fell	TENN 1001:86
time to keep s.	BIBLE 122:19
'Tis visable s.	ROSS 824:86
true call...is their s.	STARK 963:96
Under all speech there lies a s.	CARL 235:78
upon wings Of s.	MILT 683:27
widening slowly s. all	TENN 1002:5
Wildness and s. disappeared	MACL 634:81
you provide the s.	STOK 977:71

silencer rattlesnake with a s.   ACHE 3:45

silences s. between the sentences   LIND 605:7

silencing no more be justified in s.   MILL 675:66

silent in the dark and s. grave   RALE 800:16

infinite spaces Are still s.	EBER 359:10
kingfisher's wing...is s.	ELIOT 370:29
not enough...to be s.	BRAT 185:14
Out of the S. Planet	LEWIS 601:36
should not be s.	MARIE 651:63
S.;—hardly a shout	ARNO 39:23
s. majority of my fellow Americans	NIXON 730:10
s. manliness of grief	GOLD 433:17
s. sullen peoples	KIPL 562:66
s. was the flock	KEATS 546:85
t is s., as in Harlow	ASQU 42:85
thereof one must be s.	WITT 1087:72
They fell s.	VIRG 1045:81
Thou, s. form	KEATS 547:11
ways of...keeping s.	WEIZ 1062:87

silhouette s. of a brooding soul   SAND 841:56

the s. of greatness	TIME 1020:66

silica more dangerous than s.   ROET 819:92

silk blue-shadowed s.   STEV 971:42

S. an' satin	ANON 24:12

silk (*contd.*):

s. dresses out of worms	STEV 972:61
s. stockings...within the reach	SCHU 851:19
s. suit	PEPYS 765:61
s., too often hides eczema	CAMUS 229:56
skein of s.	JONS 536:27
that thing of s.	POPE 781:67

silks rainbow s. and satins!   DICK 322:66

Whenas in s. my Julia goes	HERR 478:67

silkworm Heaven—of s.   MOORE 705:25

silly Lazy and s.   SITW 941:15

s. things do cease to be s.	AUST 52:56
so young and so s.	SPEN 956:82
You were s. like us	AUDEN 47:70

silly-clever poor s.-c. Irishman   SHAW 923:71

Siloam By cool S.'s shady rill   HEBER 466:57

silver apples of gold in pictures of s.   BIBLE 121:98

better than the merchandise of s.	BIBLE 120:60
Between their s. bars!	FLEC 393:55
breast and his arms of s.	BIBLE 129:45
fill it in a s. tassie	BURNS 210:97
Georgian S. goes	MACM 636:16
give thee a s. pound	CAMP 227:29
gold and s.	SHAK 916:14
gold and s. becks me	SHAK 872:65
golden and s.	YEATS 1105:65
Just for a handful of s.	BROW 198:34
no s. lining...without its cloud	STER 968:83
S. and gold have I none	BIBLE 147:82
s. cord be loosed	BIBLE 123:42
S. out of the Earth in Peru	PETTY 768:13
S. sails all out of the west	TENN 997:97
s. thimble lies cold	SITW 941:25
s. waves of thy sweet singing	SHEL 930:24
that s. sphere	SHEL 929:1
There's a s. lining	FORD 397:20
thirty pieces of s.	BIBLE 130:68
thirty pieces of s.	BIBLE 140:47
what woman having ten pieces of s.	BIBLE 143:97

Silvia S. in the night   SHAK 860:84

Who is S.?	SHAK 860:87

Simeon S.-quiet evensong   LEVE 600:23

similar s. to independent...states   JAY 519:73

similarity science is not just any s.   WILS 1085:25

simile authors of s. and metaphor   NASH 720:68

Simon Blessed art thou, S.   BIBLE 138:13

simple as s. as possible   EINS 363:77

beliefs...whether s. or complex	DURK 357:71
business is very s.	GATES 416:37
good and s.	VAZD 1041:24
Life was s.	HOPP 493:15
making wise the s.	BIBLE 114:45
nature...runs on s. things	FONT 395:86
no vice so s.	SHAK 872:81
pure and s. beyond	WILL 1083:89
s. great ones gone	TENN 1001:80
s. question	GRAV 440:39
S. truth	SHAK 914:70
spoil her s. plots	HOLME 485:73
Truth is too s.	SAND 840:54
truth...never s.	WILDE 1077:80
understanding unto the s.	BIBLE 119:34
whether they be wise or s.	SCHW 852:31

simples compounded of many s.   SHAK 886:16

simpleton revolutionary s.   LEWIS 602:50

simplicities totalitarian s.   LYND 621:65

simplicity Cultivate s., Coleridge   LAMB 576:6

die out for want of s.	POUND 786:81
hate American s.	JAMES 517:33
Her bygone s.	HARDY 456:92
makes s. a grace	JONS 535:89
miscalled s.	SHAK 914:70
reduce complexity to s.	JAMES 517:39
s. cannot endure for long	DELA 314:22

sink (*contd.*):
s. her, split her in twain! TENN 1005:59
sinkhole Hollywood...a s. MAMET 643:52
sinking kind of alacrity in s. SHAK 878:22
s., a sickening of the heart POE 775:41
s. middle class ORWE 742:4
swimming toward a s. ship YARB 1104:54
sinned all have s. BIBLE 148:15
have s. [Sind] NAPI 718:23
More s. against SHAK 903:19
people s. against COMP 279:77
s. against my gods FORD 396:6
would have s. incessantly ROBI 814:27
sinner converteth the s. BIBLE 155:74
dead s. revised and edited BIER 162:96
God be merciful to me a s. BIBLE 144:11
make of...her a s. CONG 282:48
please my ghost, forgive some s. MENC 669:60
s. and sin boldly LUTH 620:46
s. ...with no dinner RANS 802:38
who is that young s. HOUS 496:87
sinners believe themselves to be s. PASC 758:75
combination s. WILD 1079:31
for favoured s. slain WESL 1066:65
for we are s. all SHAK 861:7
God and s. reconciled WESL 1066:59
miserable s. BOOK 174:4
s. before the Lord BIBLE 104:19
s.; of whom I am chief BIBLE 153:28
s. on this part of Broadway RUNY 829:65
s. shall be converted unto thee BIBLE 116:78
s. to repentance BIBLE 136:70
s. to repentance BIBLE 141:59
standeth in the way of s. BIBLE 113:29
While we were yet s. BIBLE 148:18
Why do s.' ways prosper? HOPK 492:8
wouldst thou be a breeder of s.? SHAK 891:24
sins believes anyone s. willingly PLATO 774:18
confess our manifold s. BOOK 173:88
cover the multitude of s. BIBLE 156:82
executor To my s. WEBS 1060:40
fashions all s. on him WEBS 1061:58
Forgiveness of s. BOOK 173:94
hate of s. that grow SURR 982:44
hath not dealt with us after our s. BIBLE 118:12
hide a multitude of s. BIBLE 155:74
manifold s. and wickedness BOOK 174:25
no rules...Only s. CAPRA 231:92
not constant thought of s. BLOOM 170:36
oldest s. the newest kind of ways? SHAK 878:9
Other s. only speak WEBS 1061:64
Other s. only speak WEBS 1061:67
pouring out one's s. FIRB 389:73
present us with all other s. WEBS 1060:46
privilege more s. SHIR 935:24
propitiation for our s. BIBLE 156:93
save his people from their s. BIBLE 133:21
season of snows and s. SWIN 986:24
shed...for the remission of s. BIBLE 140:48
s. are attempts to fill voids WEIL 1062:81
s. I had never committed WILDE 1076:34
s. of my youth BIBLE 115:53
s. of the whole world BOOK 175:29
s. were scarlet BELL 87:18
s., which are many BIBLE 142:84
taken away my s. WESL 1066:66
though your s. be as scarlet BIBLE 124:56
thy s. Do run WEBS 1060:47
visit the s. of the fathers BOOK 174:17
weep for her s. CARY 243:19
ye that...repent of your s. BOOK 174:24
Sioux S. owned the world SITT 940:98
sip can't be tasted in a s.! DICK 322:60
sipped s. no sup GILB 425:94

sir Dear S. or Madam ELLI 375:10
sire from the s. the son shall hear SCOTT 853:60
S. of an immortal strain SHEL 930:35
siren potions have I drunk of s. tears SHAK 915:90
sirens S.! Dear me! s. DICK 322:68
sires Land of my s.! SCOTT 853:50
Sisera mother of S. looked out BIBLE 109:14
sissiness old fears about our s. WHITE 1069:19
sissy called a s. by neighbourhood kids WILL 1082:72
sister always be the s. of France HUGO 501:63
as handsome as my s. KING 558:97
Bless you, S. BEHAN 84:59
dear S.!...death's bride WORD 1100:90
garden inclosed is my s. BIBLE 124:52
gentler s. BURNS 210:83
Innocence thy S.dear! MARV 658:83
marrying our own s. ROCHE 815:40
my s., Death FRAN 401:92
no friend like a s. ROSS 823:68
Nor a s., nor a brother MARG 650:51
O s. swallow SWIN 986:20
praise a s. to a s. KIPL 559:15
s. hath left me to serve alone? BIBLE 143:92
s. is given to government DICK 326:66
S. of the Stars PATM 760:6
s. to the dream BAUD 77:25
third s., Morgan le Fey MALO 642:23
trying to violate your s. STRA 979:98
your shadow-s. WRIG 1101:10
sisterhood sense of s. WELD 1062:91
sisters brave and battered s. PRIE 790:37
bunches of clingy sob s. PAGL 749:36
men with s. dear HOOD 489:46
s., and his cousins GILB 423:56
s. under their skins! KIPL 562:57
twa s. in a bower BALL -101:30
weird s. hand in hand SHAK 907:14
Sistine S....painted basic white BROWN 194:59
Sisyphus imagine that S. is happy CAMUS 229:49
sit cannot s. on it INGE 511:36
has the time to s. down HUGO 502:88
nobody can tell you when to s. down EISE 364:90
s. around so much doing nothing STEIN 965:40
s. back hoping that some day REAG 803:60
S. down before fact HUXL 508:96
s. down with trouble GLAS 430:59
s. right here by me LONG 612:22
s. thou a patient looker-on QUAR 796:52
s. up and take notice BENN 91:82
Teach us to s. still ELIOT 369:10
Though I s. down now DISR 332:78
we s. down and weep WALP 1051:88
You must s. down HERB 475:18
sitting s. in the last row KAUF 542:12
strut s. down REST 807:16
situation Beautiful for s. BIBLE 116:75
conscious of an uncomfortable s. DICK 324:23
faith that even in this lousy s. DICK 320:9
false definition of the s. MERT 672:24
find yourself in an odd s. HEYE 479:88
only improvement...in her s. ALTH 15:59
pleasant s. of having no fear CUMM 299:74
quarrelling about its relative s. AUST 51:41
s. at the lighthouse DICK 321:32
s. excellent, I am attacking FOCH 395:83
The healthiest s. in England KING 558:96
thirty-seventh dramatic s. JARRY 519:70
vanity of person and of s. AUST 52:66
situations comparable s. KISS 565:30
s. which will give it to them DIDE 329:23
Sitwells S. belong to the history LEAV 591:74
six hold you s. to four ROCH 816:43
Rode the s. hundred TENN 1001:73

six (*contd.*):
s. hundred threescore and s. BIBLE 158:22
S. inches is perfectly adequate SPARK 955:53
S. percent unemployment PASS 759:82
twelve nights when I was s. THOM 1011:94
sixpence precious little for s. PUNCH 795:26
shot at for s. DIBD 319:4
Whoso has s. is sovereign CARL 234:49
sixth don't go to the s. KENN 552:4
wonder that is the s. sense LAWR 587:10
sixty Now that I am s. UPDI 1037:72
s. staring me in the face THUR 1019:39
When I'm s. four LENN 596:64
size actual s. of man SCHU 850:15
s. of sums of money HUXL 508:93
s. ...of the human head SCHR 850:7
upon one of ordinary s. LAND 578:56
skates climbing...wearing roller s. DEAN 311:60
skating mind s. circles FROST 407:6
s. over thin ice EMER 376:41
Skegness S. is so bracing ANON 25:28
skein s. of silk JONS 536:27
skeleton carcus and a s. TRAH 1024:26
skeletons bursting with s. ORWE 743:16
two s. copulating BEEC 82:17
skelp s. across her backside ANON 27:59
sketch first rude s. KIPL 561:40
s. from nature CONS 285:19
sketches s. should prove MOOD 703:95
strong, manly, spirited s. AUST 52:60
skew take the truth and s. it PARV 756:46
ski cardinal to s. badly JOHN 522:34
skies beautiful for spacious s. BATES 76:10
beneath the sodden s. MUIR 712:29
blown about the s. TENN 998:25
Can I expound the s.? DICK 327:91
cloudless climes and starry s. BYRON 221:16
dark and empty s. MACC 626:62
Deserts...and different s. SACK 835:32
God is in the s. SHAW 922:53
knowledge of the boundless s. BYRON 222:30
look, look up at the s.! HOPK 491:87
love of...dim s. MACK 632:52
raised a mortal to the s. DRYD 351:74
s. are not cloudy HIGL 480:1
s. are painted with unnumbered SHAK 883:38
s. of history hurrying SASS 845:34
s. of Texas or Nebraska MACM 636:24
those November s. FREE 404:35
though the s. may fall MANS 648:15
under Ionian s. SHEL 931:54
watcher of the s. KEATS 544:33
When morning gilds the s. CASW 244:36
skiing garment that made s. ANON 27:70
S. is a battle KILLY 556:62
skill art is not...merely s. FRIE 405:60
combination of s. and force BURKE 207:29
depends on the author's s. QUIL 797:60
drowns for want of s. SHAK 866:35
favour to men of s. BIBLE 123:35
greater part of s., dexterity SMITH 946:90
lacking s. of a sonnet SIDN 937:66
less s. to love SKEL 942:45
Little s., little heart ROSS 825:96
men—the s. ROOS 822:42
my Courage and S. BUNY 205:74
no s. involved DIMA 331:57
S. comes so slow DAVI 307:8
s. of a solved crossword puzzle SAND 842:80
s. that is measured today ROGE 820:3
s. to move mountains HOFF 484:54
store of s. DYER 358:89
Thy s. lo poet SHEL 929:6
use all your s. CROM 298:54

slave (*contd.*):

permanently half-s. and half-free	LINC 604:98
Philosopher!—a fingering s.	WORD 1095:9
s. has but one master	LABR 572:46
S., I have set my life	SHAK 863:68
s. in base servility	SHAK 861:96
s. morality	NIET 728:87
s. of some defunct economist	KEYN 555:37
s. of the author's mind	GAUG 416:40
s. of the passions	HUME 503:3
S. to no sect	POPE 781:52
S. to Prodigality	MAND 645:71
Some cogging, cozening s.	SHAK 900:49
This yellow s.	SHAK 902:92
Throw this s.	SHAK 903:28
victim and s. of his action	EMER 377:60
worker is the s. of capitalist society	CONN 284:84
Your Majesty's s.	KISH 565:29

slavery administration of s.

	STOWE 978:84
because they impose s.	RUSS 832:22
Chains and S.!	BURNS 212:37
chains of s.	GRIL 447:62
cowardice perpetuated s.	ROUS 827:34
definition of s.	SWIFT 984:78
escapes s. except by a…revolution	LACL 574:69
Extreme freedom…to extreme s.	PLATO 774:25
freedom is s.	ORWE 745:56
nothing so dreadful as voluntary s.	DICK 329:22
perfect condition of s.	ASTE 43:92
perished in hopeless s.	OCON 735:80
S.'s a thing thet depends	LOWE 616:81
S. broke the world	MORR 709:88
s. to a pattern	NIN 729:3
s. was originally established	DOUG 342:75
S….weed that grows	BURKE 207:11
sold off into s.	TRUTH 1030:39
soon as they got out of s.	WALK 1049:57
state of S.	GILL 426:6
thought s. tolerable	UPDI 1036:55
worst possible kind of s.	BARA 70:9

slaves all women are born s.

	ASTE 43:92
asking s. what was going on	ALME 15:57
barbarous traffic in s.	PITT 771:71
Britons never will be s.	THOM 1015:46
Englishmen never will be s.	SHAW 921:33
Force made the first s.	ROUS 827:34
freemen or s.	WASH 1054:42
Gaza at the mill with s.	MILT 694:38
happy freemen, are the only s.	MASS 663:61
impart to wives and s.	DRYD 349:9
intercourse between tyrants and s.	GOLD 432:6
martyred s. of Time	BAUD 77:30
only fit for the s.	FLET 394:68
our posterity made s.	CROM 298:52
poor s. with weary footsteps	SHEL 931:52
professional players are soccer s.	CHAR 253:92
remain no legal s.	MILL 675:79
ruling them like s.	SHEL 930:25
S. and Slavery	ANON 25:21
s. that dig the golden ore	CRAB 293:73
s. we'll ever be	DAVIS 309:37
sons of former s.	KING 557:82
soul of the s.	GILL 426:12
two kinds of s.	ILLI 511:34
tyrants…only want s.	WOLL 1091:36
voluntarily submit to be s.	PITT 771:66
wholly s. or wholly free	DRYD 350:52
women into darling little s.	MILLS 679:64

Slavs cause of the S.   WITTE 1087:71
slay Though he s. me, yet will I trust   BIBLE 113:8
slayer red s. thinks he slays   EMER 377:64
slaying s. of a beautiful hypothesis   HUXL 508:99
slays s. More than you rob   SHAK 902:94
sleave ravelled s. of care   SHAK 908:46

sledgehammer S. sentimentality   KENT 553:10
sleek curse…upon the s. upstart   RANS 802:34
sleek-headed S.-h. men   SHAK 882:23
sleeket Wee, s., cowrin, tim'rous   BURNS 209:67
sleep ability to get a good night's s.

	WILS 1085:39
afford much comfort in s.	BROW 196:8
awaked out of his s.	BIBLE 105:35
azure-lidded s.	KEATS 546:95
battening…in his s.	TENN 993:32
bleary eyed for lack of s.	DAUG 306:93
borders of s.	THOM 1012:11
break earth's s.	OWEN 748:20
Caged in its s.	SMITH 949:60
calf won't get much s.	ALLEN 14:38
Care-charming S.	FLET 394:69
Cervantes usually puts me to s.	GONZ 434:53
closes soft in s.	STEP 968:79
Come s., O s.	SIDN 937:53
country…going to s.	RENAN 806:1
deep House of Commons s.	CHAN 251:61
deep, deep s. of England	ORWE 745:2
dewy-feathered S.	MILT 683:14
doen they only s.	SPEN 958:17
dreamless, uninvaded s.	TENN 993:31
each day dies with s.	HOPK 492:5
endless—as s.	WILL 1083:95
full of s.	YEATS 1105:60
get a good night's s.	KEEN 548:24
giveth his beloved s.	BIBLE 119:41
go to s. if I can	SHAK 885:88
grinning in their s.	LAWR 586:85
have a nice, quiet s.	CHAM 249:19
haven't been to s. for	WAUGH 1056:71
I shall s.	SWIN 987:46
immobility, ecstacy, and s.	MARI 651:66
in his cunning s.	THOM 1011:84
in his s. he does little harm	SHAK 901:81
in s. old palaces	SHEL 928:88
In s., afraid	ROET 819:1
inhibitions and get some s.	LOOS 613:35
lack of s.	GOLD 432:89
lasting s.	BEAU 80:69
let me s. a little	MACN 637:41
let me s. alway	COLE 274:97
Lie soft, s. hard	MIDD 673:40
lie where I am and s., s., s.	SHIP 935:21
like unwilling s.	KEATS 544:36
miles to go before I s.	FROST 407:86
more in your life except to s.	RHYS 808:27
Murders the innocent s.	TWAIN 1033:89
never s. with aanyone	ALGR 13:24
night doth summon all to s.?	DRAY 345:33
night to do with s.?	MILT 683:21
O partial s.	SHAK 877:95
O s., O gentle s.	SHAK 877:94
O S.! the friend of Woe	SOUT 954:37
O, such another s.	SHAK 906:99
of Night, but not of S.	THOM 1015:55
One short s. past	DONNE 338:5
poets…give their readers s.	POPE 782:94
poor Indian's s.	KEATS 544:38
putting the mind to s.	SLOAN 943:59
quiet s. and a sweet dream	MASE 661:34
rounded with a s.	SHAK 917:37
sang themselves to s.	HODG 483:50
shall not all s.	BIBLE 151:72
S. after toil	SPEN 957:8
s. and a forgetting	WORD 1098:51
s. and a sense of history	WILS 1085:41
s. and death differ	TRAH 1024:26
S. and rest	TENN 997:97
S. demands…guilty immunity	BARN 72:26
S. dwell upon thine eyes	SHAK 869:94
s. Full of sweet dreams	KEATS 545:56

sleep (*contd.*):

S. I can get nane	BURNS 211:3
S. is death without	LEBO 591:81
S. is when all the unsorted stuff	GOLD 432:86
S. no more	SHAK 908:46
s. on bridges	FRAN 401:90
S. out-of-doors	BIRD 163:14
s. provides relief	CHAM 250:26
S. shall neither night nor day	SHAK 907:13
S., son of the sable Night	DANI 304:62
S. sweet to labouring man	BUNY 205:69
S., that sometimes shuts	SHAK 871:47
s….through life	ALBEE 11:90
S. to wake	BROW 200:2
s. upon ale	FARQ 383:70
s. when you ain't sleepy	TWAIN 1032:78
S. will come when thou art fled	SHEL 932:61
s. with dogs	WEBS 1060:42
s. with women we do not love	DIDE 330:37
softer than s.	TENN 994:56
Still it cried 'S. no more'	SHAK 908:47
stop it from going to s.	RUSH 829:68
such as s. o'nights	SHAK 882:23
The poor s. little	OTWAY 746:89
think of them that s.	CAMP 227:30
Thou art inclined to s.	SHAK 916:21
time enough to s.	HOUS 494:42
To die, to s.	SHAK 890:21
together out of s.	MARI 651:72
wake to s.	ROET 819:95
waking from its s.	KIER 556:58
when you s. you remind me	SASS 845:33
Where fain, fain I would s.?	BALL -101:35
Yet a little s.	BIBLE 120:64

sleep-time silence of the s.-t.   BROW 200:1
sleeper duty to arouse s.   BETH 99:24
  never a quiet s.?   TENN 1002:92
sleepers in the diners and s.   SAND 841:59
  s. in that quiet earth   BRON 192:15
sleepest Thou s. too long   SKEL 942:35
sleepeth s., and must be wakened   BIBLE 111:64
sleeping except s. and resting   TWAIN 1034:22
  growing…when ye're s.   SCOTT 855:93
  I was s. with the President   REAG 803:3
  The s. and the dead   SHAK 908:48
  wake s., and sleep   MONT 702:72
sleepless S. as the river   CRANE 294:97
  s., in all them time   BERR 98:13
  S. with cold   ROSS 825:94
sleeps never sad but when she s.   SHAK 879:42
sleepwalker assurance of s.   HITL 482:30
sleepy not s. and…no place   DYLAN 358:97
sleeve ace of joy up his s.   ONDA 739:46
  heart on your s.   THAT 1008:22
  heart upon my s.   SHAK 897:95
  lacy s. with a bottle of vitriol   WOOL 1093:83
  not wear your heart on your s.   WEBS 1061:74
  strip his s.   SHAK 881:5
sleeves language that rolls up its s.   SAND 841:75
  s. rolled   MACC 625:43
sleigh s., and eight tiny reindeer   MOORE 704:5
  sprang to his s.   MOORE 704:8
sleight admire his s. of hand   BUTL 217:20
slender kissed her s. hand   TENN 1001:82
slept and he s.   TENN 999:50
  But while men s.   BIBLE 137:1
  s. with his fathers   BIBLE 111:61
slew as he was ambitious, I s. him   SHAK 884:47
  dead which he s. at his death   BIBLE 109:22
  Who s. them?   SITT 940:98
slice people want a larger s.   CRIP 296:31
sliced they'd come up s.   TREV 1026:50
slide We can s. it   REED 805:81
sliding hear time s. past you   RHYS 808:27

society (*contd.*):

loss of s. in which	MOOD 703:*94*
Man is born to live in s.	DIDE 330:*42*
Man seeketh in s.	BACON 55:*23*
member of s.	MORI 708:*68*
mirror of our own s.	STER 968:*84*
modern ardor to improve s.	SMALL 943:*62*
mutual s., help, and comfort	BOOK 175:*45*
negotiation and s.	MUNCH 714:*52*
no Arts; no Letters, no S.	HOBB 483:*40*
no importance…to s.	NABO 717:*7*
no one in our s. is allowed	OAKE 733:*49*
no such thing as s.	THAT 1008:*23*
noble s. for providing	DICK 320:*25*
nothing to distinguish human s.	SHAW 924:*94*
pervading all nature and s.	HARDY 457:*5*
place in s.	NIGH 729:*95*
play a larger part in s.	SNOW 951:*77*
poor s.	TAWN 991:*8*
powerful men in our s.	BELL 88:*27*
progress of s. and wealth	RICA 808:*33*
promotes that of the s.	SMITH 945:*81*
quarrel with s.	TRIL 1027:*61*
radical vision of s.	WALK 1049:*52*
receives the protection of s.	MILL 675:*65*
responsibility of s.	PALEY 751:*63*
role of labour in s.	NEVI 723:*15*
rounds of s.'s ladder	MOORE 704:*11*
sick s. must think	LEWIS 601:*44*
socialist s.	NOZI 732:*44*
s. as something eternal	ORWE 743:*11*
S. became my…bride	WORD 1100:*82*
s. distributes itself	ARNO 39:*24*
s. do not want his labour	MALT 643:*40*
s. has resembled a pyramid	NAPO 719:*37*
s. here would be quite civilised	WILDE 1078:*94*
s. in which they live	JAMES 517:*34*
s. in which thought	RUSS 832:*28*
S. indeed a contract	BURKE 208:*36*
S. is all but rude	MARV 658:*84*
S. is an organized conspiracy	DOUG 342:*74*
S. is composed of two large classes	CHAM 250:*25*
S. is full of women	WILDE 1078:*90*
S. is no comfort	SHAK 916:*15*
S. is now one polished horde	BYRON 223:*59*
S. needs first of all	SUMN 981:*28*
s. offenders	GILB 425:*84*
S. requires…retrieve his fortunes	DICK 326:*52*
S. should not ask anything	SAND 840:*51*
s. that admires	LECA 592:*97*
s. that repressed	KRIS 569:*94*
s. that will organize production	ENGE 378:*90*
s.…they had emigrated	MO 698:*9*
s., where none intrudes	BYRON 220:*5*
s.…which is riven	ROSS 823:*65*
s., with all its…skill and force	BURKE 207:*29*
s. women never serve chilli	RAYB 803:*49*
solitude sometimes is best s.	MILT 692:*11*
suppose s. is wonderfully	WILDE 1077:*72*
temptation to see all of s.	LEWO 603:*74*
the politics of our s.	OAKE 733:*48*
truth in the s.	KING 558:*85*
two classes in good s.	SHAW 925:*13*
unequals what s.	MILT 692:*94*
value judgements about the s.	VAND 1039:*94*
very fabric of s.	JOHN 522:*36*
We want a s. in which	THAT 1007:*8*
well adjusted members of s.	CALL 226:*99*
well-being of s.	ROOS 822:*47*
working s.	TREV 1026:*53*

sociologist according to a s. | UNSE 1036:*46*
| was a s. | MURD 714:*66* |

sociologists s. are akin to Marxists | ARON 40:*47*
| s. of knowledge | MERT 672:*26* |

sociology department of…s. | AYER 53:*81*

s. attaches the adjective 'arbitrary'	ARON 40:*46*
S. is a new science	GOWE 437:*82*
S. is…about why they don't have	DUES 354:*22*
S. is the science of talk	KNIG 567:*55*
S. seems to have missed	VAND 1039:*95*
s., it is as an art	NISB 730:*5*
S. was born	SMALL 943:*62*
What is it about s.	BAKER 63:*85*

sockets candles burn their s. | HOUS 496:*75*

socks inability to put on your s. | GONC 434:*62*
s. compelled one's attention	SAKI 838:*7*
s. on the altar	NERU 723:*9*
telling lies and selling s.	MERW 672:*27*
women who wear ankle s.	BENN 91:*77*

Socrates be S. dissatisfied | MILL 675:*70*
realized, like S.	PLATO 773:*1*
S. empties the cup of poison	FEUE 387:*30*
S. in every classroom	GRIS 447:*66*
S. is guilty	PLATO 773:*2*

Socratic S. method is not game | BEER 83:*37*

sod prairies' dreaming s. | CRANE 294:*97*
| stands fixed to the s. | WILL 1080:*44* |
| withered in the s.? | BRON 190:*91* |

soda heaven sent us S. Water | CHES 259:*26*
| Sermons and s. water | BYRON 222:*42* |
| unattainable s. and sherry | SALA 838:*17* |

sodden s. towards sundown | ELIOT 372:*67*

sodium having discovered s. | BENT 93:*25*

Sodom men of S. were wicked | BIBLE 104:*19*
| rained upon S. and upon Gomorrah | BIBLE 105:*25* |

sodomy rape, s. and drug addiction | COOK 286:*27*

sods flaming s., the sinivelling | LAWR 585:*63*
| heaped-up s. upon the fire | COLUM 278:*62* |

sofa fainted alternately on the s. | AUST 50:*28*
luxury the accomplished s.	COWP 292:*51*
s., chair or a hot-water bottle	SMITH 948:*28*
s. upholstered in panther skin	PLOM 775:*34*
wheel the s. round	COWP 293:*60*

soft cushion and s. Dean invite | POPE 779:*22*
Her voice was ever s.	SHAK 904:*52*
meets me s. and supple	FLET 394:*75*
Say not s. things	SORL 953:*23*
wanted your s. verges	HENRI 472:*62*

softly but never hit s. | ROOS 822:*49*

Soho Perambulate in glamorous S. | HUGH 499:*22*

soil don't fight war on our s. | DALL 303:*50*
Foul as their s.	BYRON 219:*67*
grows on mortal s.	MILT 684:*43*
portion of this virgin s.	HAWT 461:*69*
same s. as the Muse	UNTE 1036:*47*
same worn-out s.	HAWT 461:*68*
s. Is bare now	HOPK 491:*82*
s. may best Deserve	MILT 688:*9*
s. of his shallow cares!	BRON 192:*13*
texture of the s.	SMITH 946:*2*

soils Six days of the week it s. | LARK 581:*3*

sojourner discontented s. | WORD 1095:*17*

sojourners strangers…and s. | BIBLE 112:*86*
| s. and passing subjects | MUIR 712:*32* |

solace s. to man giffis | BARB 71:*15*

solar hub of the s. system | HOLM 486:*88*
| self…epicentre of the s. system | PHIL 768:*19* |

sold and s. again | SAND 841:*67*
s. my farm	SHAK 882:*10*
s. your own lands	SHAK 886:*17*
think I've s. myself	CARL 233:*28*
would have s. London	RICH 810:*59*

soldier always tell an old s. | SHAW 920:*93*
'A s.,' cried my Uncle Toby	STER 970:*14*
As an old s.	SHAW 921:*37*
as is the hat of a s.	HERB 476:*42*
assumed the s.	WASH 1054:*40*
Ben Battle was a s. bold	HOOD 488:*34*

soldier (*contd.*):

British s. can stand up to anything	SHAW 921:*18*
Christ's faithful s.	BOOK 175:*35*
Come you back, you British s.	KIPL 560:*59*
death who had the s. singled	DOUG 341:*57*
Drinking is the s.'s pleasure	DRYD 351:*69*
Every British and French s. killed	CHUR 263:*98*
For a s. I listed	DIBD 319:*4*
German s. trying to violate	STRA 979:*98*
glazed eyes of a s. dying	BISM 164:*40*
go to your Gawd like a s.	KIPL 560:*33*
honest man and a s.	SHAK 879:*47*
informer when he cannot be a s.	FLAU 392:*33*
like a s.'s ribbon	ABSE 1:*7*
Money is a good s.	SHAK 878:*16*
never expect a s. to think	SHAW 921:*16*
Not though the s. knew	TENN 1000:*72*
ruffian stern, and s. good	SCOTT 854:*73*
s.'s life is terribly hard	MILNE 680:*69*
s. of the King	KITC 566:*44*
s.'s pack is not so heavy	EISE 364:*81*
s. wears a badge	READ 803:*54*
sound of the white s.'s axe	RED 804:*74*
summer s. and the sunshine patriot	PAINE 750:*42*
the s. lists his wounds	PROP 792:*79*
Unknown S.	ASQU 42:*78*
very poor s.	SHAW 920:*94*
would himself have been a s.	SHAK 875:*42*

soldiers best s. France ever had | PHIL 768:*23*
black s. to death	LOWE 617:*2*
changed from peasants and s.	WAUGH 1057:*89*
common s.	WELL 1063:*7*
Countries that have s. in charge	MACK 632:*57*
if you believe the s.	SALI 839:*34*
ladder behind the s.	SUN 982:*35*
laughing s. fought to their defeat	FENT 385:*2*
make his s. fight	SUN 982:*34*
men like s. may not quit	TENN 1003:*79*
old s. never die	MACA 621:*74*
physician and chemist are s.	PAST 759:*89*
proud array of s.	WILDE 1075:*27*
S. are citizens	SASS 845:*45*
s. drilling in Berlin	MORI 708:*68*
S. find wars	DONNE 337:*80*
s. he smiled at	SASS 845:*28*
S., I'm getting out	GARI 415:*25*
s., mostly fools	BIER 161:*85*
s.…of the Irish Brigade	DAVIS 309:*38*
s. of the ploughshare	RUSK 830:*91*
S., think that	NAPO 718:*24*
steel my s.' hearts	SHAK 881:*95*

sole no rest for the s. of her foot | BIBLE 104:*11*
s. cause of…unhappiness	PASC 757:*58*
s. evidence…possible	MILL 675:*72*
s. of his foot	SHAK 879:*67*

solecism eternity without a s. | BROW 195:*75*
| Japanese…rarely commit a s. | BIRD 163:*17* |

solemn more s. and serene | SHEL 927:*63*
s. creed with a s. sneer	BYRON 220:*89*
s. gladness even crowned	TENN 999:*31*
s. slope of mighty limbs	SWIN 988:*53*

solicitor can only go to his s. | DISR 333:*11*

solicitors accountants and s. | TAYL 992:*20*

solid not s. at all, but liquid | CAREY 233:*23*
only s.…reformation	CARL 234:*45*
s. pudding against empty praise	POPE 782:*92*
something s. and concrete	KELM 548:*31*

solidarity create…a feeling of s. | DURK 357:*48*
| power of S. | WALE 1049:*48* |
| s. with other isolated creatures | BELL 88:*36* |

solidity an appearance of s. | ORWE 744:*48*
| s. of a water buffalo | PERE 766:*92* |

solids surfaces and s. | PIERO 769:*38*

soliloquy conversation, and even a s. | LINK 606:*22*

soliloquy (*contd.*):
Iago's s.	COLE 275:30

solitariness man does with his s.   WHIT 1071:57

solitary be not s.   JOHN 530:6
Be not s.	BURT 214:79
for each man a s. cell	ONEI 739:49
high and s.	YEATS 1105:67
How doth the city sit s.	BIBLE 128:29
one tunnel, dark and s.	SABA 835:56
Only s. men know the full joys	CATH 244:48
sentenced to s. confinement	WILL 1082:75
setteth the s. in families	BIBLE 116:86
s. child and s. man	ACKR 4:56
s. laugh	GREE 445:28
the life of man, s.	HOBB 483:40
till I am s.	JOHN 526:99
To wander s. there	MARV 659:88

solitude bliss of s.   WORD 1099:70
companionable as s.	THOR 1017:89
endure our own s.	PRIT 791:70
feel his s. more keenly	VALE 1038:87
flaming s.	GORO 436:68
groaned from s.	LEE 593:18
In blissful s.	MILT 689:32
inviolate s.	ROBE 814:18
music piercing that s.	THOM 1012:2
Musing in s.	WORD 1100:77
O S.! where are the charms	COWP 292:38
one to s.	ARNO 37:77
power of s.	NORTH 731:32
principle s. and retreat	MONT 701:66
resonance of his s.	CONN 283:79
self-sufficing power of S.	WORD 1096:23
single moment's s.	WILDE 1077:77
soft like S.'s	SHEL 927:72
S. is the playfield	NABO 717:4
S. is un-American	JONG 534:64
S. restores the harmonies	BERN 97:86
s. sometimes is best society	MILT 692:11
s. What happiness	MILT 692:93
sweet retired s.	MILT 683:28
to the hour its s.	STEV 971:48
To this delicious s.	MARV 658:84
total is the s.	BRON 191:92
Whosoever is delighted in s.	BACON 58:97

solo in a s. game   SERV 859:56
Solomon even S. in all his glory   BIBLE 135:52
fame of S.	BIBLE 111:57
greater than S. is here	BIBLE 137:94
S. gave to the queen of Sheba	BIBLE 112:88
S. his son reigned in his stead	BIBLE 112:87
S. loved many strange women	BIBLE 111:59
S. of saloons	BROW 200:84
S. says	KIPL 564:10
S.'s throne was supported by lions	BACON 57:53
song of songs, which is S.'s	BIBLE 124:45
wisest of men…not excepting S.	STER 969:91

solution crowding towards s.   CARL 235:63
incapable of purely private s.	MILLS 679:64
It isn't that they can't see the s.	CHES 260:46
mystery which defies s.	MORT 710:95
No perfect s.…possible	BERL 96:69
people were a kind of s.	CAVA 246:68
s. for…habitual accidents	BENC 89:52
s. to the problem	LEMAY 595:43
total s. of the Jewish problem	GOER 431:68
You're either part of the s.	CLEA 268:99

solutions employed in seeking s.   KUHN 570:14
inevitable, s. are not	ASIM 42:72
practical s. to the problems of evil	GENET 418:74
slogans…confused with s.	BENT 93:31
s. lead to more p.	BURR 213:57

solve mystery we all s.   SKEL 942:41
| S. it quickly | WATS 1055:53 |

Solway Sark rins o'er the S. sands   BURNS 212:31
Somalia years to get S. not on its feet   HEMP 471:52
sombre penumbra of s. dignity   ATLAS 44:6
sombrero sunbonnet as well as the s.   FERB 385:6
some S. people find oil   GETTY 421:16
| s. should be unhappy | JOHN 530:86 |

somebody could have been s.   SCHU 850:11
| s. was telling jokes | KAUF 543:21 |

someone mind that s. else is   KENN 550:59
| S.—or Something | HAMM 453:46 |

somersault one complete s.   IGNA 510:28
Somerset in the records of S. House   BIRK 163:19
| S. House young man | GILB 424:70 |

something always start with s.   PICA 768:24
artist…make s. of the nothing	PERCY 766:85
cannot get s. for nothing	HARR 459:40
feel you've done s.	HEMI 470:15
I,…thinking this, was s.	DESC 317:78
say s. about me	COHAN 272:70
s. flew between me and sun	BLUN 170:46
S. is rotten	SHAK 889:73
s. more comfortable	HARL 458:21
S. nasty in the woodshed	GIBB 422:35
s. ought to be said	CARL 235:79
S. there had been	HYDE 509:10
To do nothing and get s.	DISR 332:89

sometime come up s.   WEST 1067:78
sometimes S. I sits and thinks   PUNCH 795:33
somewhere once belonged s.   STEIN 965:38
somnambulist reactionary is a s.   ROOS 821:40
son bring forth a s.   BIBLE 133:21
bring forth a s.	BIBLE 133:22
brought forth her firstborn s.	BIBLE 142:77
by this s. of York	SHAK 862:45
dirty s. of a bitch	STEI 966:54
divide a father from his s.	MARQ 655:33
Father, and Holy Ghost	MACL 633:63
from the Father and the S.	BOOK 174:20
from the sire the s. shall hear	SCOTT 853:60
gave his only begotten S.	BIBLE 145:34
God sent not his S.	BIBLE 145:35
hateth his s.	BIBLE 121:74
if his s. ask bread	BIBLE 135:58
if the s. of peace be there	BIBLE 142:87
If the S.…shall make you free	BIBLE 146:50
if thou be the S. of God	BIBLE 133:29
into the grave unto my s.	BIBLE 105:41
loveth s. or daughter	BIBLE 136:80
man of clay, s.	MILT 692:1
Man, you have a s.	MARQ 655:34
no more worthy to be called thy s.	BIBLE 143:99
O my s. Absalom	BIBLE 110:51
obeyed as a s.	GIBB 421:28
one like the S. of man	BIBLE 130:50
only s. Isaac	BIBLE 105:27
preserve thy s.	BIBLE 119:36
renounce me as a s.	GIBB 421:26
s. in whom he delighteth	BIBLE 120:58
s. of a carpenter	GREE 444:23
S. of a mare	AIDAN 10:73
S. of a whore	ROCH 816:59
s. of Heaven's eternal King	MILT 681:85
s. of his old age	BIBLE 105:39
S. of man be three days	BIBLE 137:93
S. of man hath not where	BIBLE 136:66
S. of man is Lord	BIBLE 141:60
S. of man shall come in his glory	BIBLE 140:43
s. of memory, great heir	MILT 681:94
s. of the dear murderèd	SHAK 890:16
s. shall not go down	BIBLE 105:46
Strong S. of God	TENN 998:10
tell you, s. of mine	NOON 731:24
This is my beloved S.	BIBLE 133:28
This is my s.	TENN 995:60

son (*contd.*):
this man was the S. of God	BIBLE 141:71
Thou art my S.	BIBLE 114:32
unfeathered two-legged thing, a s.	DRYD 349:14
unto us a s. is given	BIBLE 125:66
virgin shall conceive, and bear a s.	BIBLE 125:63
wed ye to my youngest s.	SCOTT 854:78
wise s. heareth his father	BIBLE 121:72
Woman, behold thy s.!	BIBLE 146:70
younger s. gathered all together	BIBLE 143:98
worst s. of a bitch	PARK 755:26

sonatas s. of Mozart   SCHN 848:86
song aquaints His soul with s.   BROW 200:98
As easily as a s.	ROSE 823:63
Assist our s.	GURN 449:91
awake for sake of S.!	FERG 385:14
breeze of s.	TENN 999:47
carcase of an old s.	THOM 1013:20
come before his presence with s.	BOOK 177:89
Come, gie's a s.	SKIN 943:55
Dance, and Provençal s.	KEATS 547:14
every voice be s.!	DODD 335:44
fame is in the s.	CARM 236:4
followed by a sacred s.	BELL 87:12
For I have a s. to sing	GILB 425:94
For if such a holy s.	MILT 681:91
funeral s.	GIBB 421:22
Glorious the s.	SMART 944:71
How shall we sing the Lord's s.	BIBLE 119:47
human existence as a s. unfinished	MACC 626:67
I have made my s.	YEATS 1105:69
joyful S. I'll raise	ADDI 7:20
lark…sightless s.	TENN 1000:10
let satire be my s.	BYRON 218:59
let the s. of praise be sung	POTT 784:43
life is a…cycle of s.	PARK 754:8
more musical than any s.	ROSS 823:74
my s. has an ideal	CHOC 260:55
new unhallowed s.	DAVI 307:97
no horse sing a s.	ARMS 35:47
One grand, sweet s.	KING 558:91
our s. shall rise to Thee	HEBER 466:59
picnic of s.	FRAME 400:76
play a s. for me	DYLAN 358:97
poets…seldom sing a new s.	DAY 310:46
rainbow and a cuckoo's s.	DAVI 308:21
realm of free s.	LOWE 616:77
region of my s.	WORD 1100:78
run softly till I end my s.	ELIOT 368:88
sang the 'S. of the Shirt'	HOOD 489:45
she whispered a s.	OHARA 737:8
sheer joyous power of s.	BEER 83:40
silence was the s. of love	ROSS 824:87
Sing to the Lord a new s.	BIBLE 159:43
Sing unto Lord a new s.	BOOK 176:69
s. about a whore-house	GUTH 449:95
s. for thinking hearts	WORD 1096:36
s. in thy praise	BURNS 211:99
s. is ended	BERL 95:59
s. of canaries	NASH 719:42
s. of songs	BIBLE 124:45
s. Should make all Nature lovelier	COLE 274:1
s. that echoes cheerly	TENN 993:40
s. that has sold half a million	BERL 95:58
subject for this heroic s.	MILT 692:98
suck melancholy out of a s.	SHAK 885:71
swallow-flights of s.	TENN 999:34
sweet silver s.	HAMM 454:54
teach in s.	SHEL 927:69
that's my kind of s.	HERN 476:45
the burthen of his s.	BICK 160:42
the s. of woe	TENN 999:42
thow be, or elles s.	CHAU 254:15
thrush…sings each s. twice over	BROW 198:37

soul (*contd.*):

dear companion of my s.	MIDD 673:41
depths of his country's s.	DICK 326:55
devil and thee about thy s.	SHAK 875:40
dignity of s. and character	CARL 234:41
dividing asunder of s. and spirit	BIBLE 154:45
drop of hatred in your s.	MUNRO 714:59
Dull would he be of s.	WORD 1097:46
endanger my s. gratis?	SHAK 878:14
entire s. is a cry	KAZA 543:28
Every s. pursues the good	PLATO 774:22
everything I have in my s.	BROD 190:74
evoke the s. of Italy	MAZZ 666:12
Fair seed-time had my s.	WORD 1096:20
father lived his s.	CUMM 300:90
Faustus may...save his s.!	MARL 654:20
fellow ain't got a s.	STEI 966:55
fire of the s.	DICK 322:57
for my s., what can it do	SHAK 888:72
force his s.	SHAK 890:14
freed my s.	BERN 96:78
from the author's s.	HUXL 506:57
from the s. must issue forth	COLE 274:6
genial current of the s.	GRAY 442:68
Give not thy s. unto a woman	BIBLE 132:95
glad at s.	SHAK 898:11
God rest his s.	SMITH 948:38
God the s.	POPE 780:40
Grapple them to thy s.	SHAK 888:63
greatest thing a human s.	RUSK 831:8
greatness of s.	STOWE 978:83
greatness of the human s.	ROCK 817:71
half conceal the S. within	TENN 998:19
harmonical and ingenious s.	AUBR 45:34
harmonies...of s.	BERN 97:86
harrow up thy s.	SHAK 889:74
haughtiness of s.	ADDI 8:29
'he' or 'him' of the s.	PATM 760:7
he who would be a great s.	EMER 377:68
height My s. can reach	BROW 197:19
His s. proud Science never taught	POPE 780:37
Hope...perches in the s.	DICK 328:97
how prodigal the s.	SHAK 888:68
I am black...my s. is white	BLAKE 166:64
I...am, with all my s.	STEE 964:11
immortal...because he has a s.	FAUL 383:78
Impropriety is the s. of wit	MAUG 664:85
In a great s.	PASC 757:48
in exchange for his s.?	BIBLE 138:15
in my s. am free	615:63
in my s. that tender secret dwells	BYRON 221:12
in s. a heathen	DICK 325:36
influence upon the s.	KAND 541:97
inspire my s.	BARL 71:21
intention of his s.	LEON 597:80
Involve all of your s.	HUGO 501:68
iron entered into his s.	BOOK 177:90
Is my s.'s pleasure	KEATS 544:37
Is the eternal truth man's fighting s.	EBER 359:11
it is the cause, my s.	SHAK 900:52
Jesu, lover of my s.	WESL 1066:60
largest and most comprehensive s.	DRYD 347:59
Let man's s. be a sphere	DONNE 338:16
light is in the s.	MILT 694:41
like a s. pursued	ROBE 814:18
lips suck forth my s.	MARL 654:19
living factories of the s.	MAYA 665:4
lose your own s.	SHAW 925:12
love...with all thy s.	BIBLE 108:90
magic, that will charm thy s.	MARL 654:18
man who doesn't love...has got a s.	SAKI 838:6
man with an immortal s.	BRYAN 201:15
marbled museum of the s.	RODR 819:89
Marlbro's mighty s.	ADDI 6:1

soul (*contd.*):

mask of a vulgar s.	MAUG 665:91
May his pernicious s.	SHAK 900:59
may my s. be blasted	SHAW 925:21
Memorial from the s.'s	ROSS 824:85
mercy o'my s.	MACD 628:98
merit wins the s.	POPE 779:3
might create a s.	MILT 684:33
mind and the s. together	NGU 725:45
mirror of the s.	QUIN 797:65
mockery o' his s.	MACD 627:79
most offending s. alive	SHAK 881:97
Mount, mount, my s.	SHAK 868:72
must return to the s.	ISAA 513:69
my gazing s.	VAUG 1040:15
my lyre has a s.	CHOC 260:55
My s.'s a duelling ground	RICK 811:75
My s. doth magnify the Lord	BIBLE 160:53
My s.; sit thou	QUAR 796:52
My s., there is a country	VAUG 1041:18
my s. trusteth in thee	BOOK 177:77
my whole s. through	TENN 993:36
narrow For his vast s.	DRYD 348:47
never thought...a s. could ache	VAUG 1041:23
nevere no s. ysaved	LANG 579:74
new light to the s.	TAYL 992:21
No coward s.	BRON 191:8
No...gentleman, in his secret s.	BAGE 61:50
no s. will pity me	SHAK 863:64
nor the prophetic s.	SHAK 915:86
not spoken of the s..	LONG 611:94
O limèd s.	SHAK 892:48
O my prophetic s.!	SHAK 889:76
of ev'ry art the s.	POPE 779:20
oh s. desired?	LAB 571:31
only thou can'st raise the meeting s.!	COLL 277:47
Oppressed the s.!	CRAB 294:84
pain in the s.	HAMM 453:48
palace of the s.	WEBS 1060:46
Paris preserves the s.	HUGO 502:86
passion in the human s.	LILLO 604:95
Perdition catch my s.	SHAK 899:29
Perdition catch my s.	SHER 934:10
permissible delights of the s.	BACH 54:93
Pierced to the s.	SHAK 866:38
pilgrim s. in you	YEATS 1105:60
poetry...composed in the s.	ARNO 40:40
Poured thro'...her pensive s.	COLL 277:50
pouring forth thy s.	KEATS 548:18
Praise, my s.	LYTE 621:66
pray for my s.	TENN 1004:47
prepare thy s. for temptation	BIBLE 131:87
present in everyone's s.	PLATO 774:23
prided itself... on its s.	LYND 621:65
profits a man nothing to give his s.	BOLT 172:75
progress of a deathless s.	DONNE 337:82
rap and knock and enter our s.	BROW 198:54
real dark night of the s.	FITZ 391:14
Refined himself to s.	DRYD 352:83
remake the s.	BROW 200:94
repent it from my very s.	SHAK 862:44
restoreth my s.	BIBLE 115:56
retreat...in his own s.	AURE 50:25
Revolving in his altered s.	DRYD 351:71
roll from s. to s.	TENN 997:1
Rome...city of the s.	BYRON 220:96
sacred story of the s.'s delight	LANY 580:81
said to my s., be still	ELIOT 371:44
save a s. from death	BIBLE 155:74
save thy secret s.	GRAY 442:80
Science...is the s.'s perdition	RABE 799:87
sea speaks to the s.	CHOP 261:59
Seek not, my s.	PIND 770:44
Selling one's body to keep one's s.	MACK 632:54

soul (*contd.*):

sent my s. abroad	COLE 274:4
silhouette of a brooding s.	SAND 841:56
sleepless s. that perished	WORD 1097:44
smooth-rubbed s.	WORD 1095:10
so panteth my s. after thee	BIBLE 115:68
some s. of goodness	SHAK 881:90
Sorrow was all my s.	HERB 475:15
s. abhorreth all manner of meat	BIBLE 118:19
s. abhorred all...meat	BOOK 177:91
s. and God laugh together	EDDI 360:19
s. beneath the ribs of death	MANC 644:66
s. by itself	PLATO 774:15
s. doth magnify the Lord	BIBLE 141:51
s. exhibiting excellence	ARIS 34:26
s....has an interpreter	BRON 191:95
s. has to itself decreed	KEATS 544:39
s. has wings	DELA 314:21
s. hath her content	SHAK 899:21
s. he doth restore again	SCOT 856:19
s. in agony	SHAK 866:28
s. in paraphrase	HERB 475:30
S. is all but out of me	MILL 676:81
s. is an enchanted boat	SHEL 930:24
s. is awakened	BRON 190:87
s. is forfeit	MACN 637:40
s. is in a ferment	KEATS 545:55
s. is not more than the body	WHIT 1072:81
s. keeps a singin' the blues	BERRY 98:4
s....languishes and dies	ROCH 817:64
s. leading the way	GUIR 448:80
s., like lightning	HERR 477:57
s....like a rough diamond	DEFOE 311:73
s. longeth, yea, even fainteth	BIBLE 117:93
s. may ascend to heaven	MARL 654:21
s. more bent To serve	MILT 686:81
s. moves in his fee	JONS 534:86
s. of a journey is liberty	MARP 655:32
s. of a prince	LOCKE 609:74
s. Of all the rest	MILT 693:30
s. of Frankenstein	SHEL 926:53
s. of her beauty	SHEL 930:29
s. of its own	SCOTT 852:34
s. of man	AUBR 45:37
s. of man is a far country	THOM 1009:50
s. of music shed	MOORE 706:36
S. of my lie	HERR 477:56
s. of Orpheus sing	MILT 682:11
s. of reading	STER 969:96
S. of the Age!	JONS 535:8
s. of the just	STAEL 961:72
s. of the slaves	GILL 426:12
s. of the whole Past Time	CARL 236:90
s. of this man	SHAK 901:75
s. of wit	SHAK 889:88
s.-power frail	LIND 605:11
s.'s prison we call England	SHAW 925:15
s.'s quiet	FORD 397:12
s. refines itself	MARI 652:78
s. rememb'ring my good friends	SHAK 867:53
s.'s sap quivers	ELIOT 372:68
s. should fly from me	MARL 654:22
s. so dead	SCOTT 853:49
s. so near divine	BRON 190:86
s. started at the knee-cap	LEWIS 602:66
s. swooned slowly	JOYCE 538:42
s. that is not healthy	PLATO 774:10
s. that rises with us	WORD 1098:51
s. that through me ran	WORD 1095:5
s....the eternity of thought	WORD 1095:14
s. thirsteth for God	BIBLE 115:68
s. thirsteth for thee	BIBLE 116:31
S., thou hast much goods	BIBLE 143:94
s. waiteth upon God	BIBLE 116:82

soul (contd.):

s. was forwarded	BERR 99:19
s. was like a star	WORD 1096:38
s. within the house	SHAK 894:6
Stole many a man's s. and faith	JAGG 515:96
story of the s.	RUSS 833:36
strikes more of a panic to the s.	MELV 667:36
strong music in my s.	COLE 274:7
subject's s. is his own	SHAK 881:92
taming of s.'s raw passions	BLOOM 169:35
taught my s. to fancy aught	VAUG 1040:15
That mind and s.	TENN 998:18
that my s. knoweth right well	BOOK 177:94
The s. shrinks	WILB 1075:19
This night shall thy s.	SMITH 948:39
this night thy s. shall be required	BIBLE 143:94
thistle, O my s.	MACD 627:80
Thou art a s. in bliss	SHAK 904:42
Till then, sit still, my s.	SHAK 888:58
Tommy 'ow's yer s.?	KIPL 560:31
tongue and s....be hypocrites	SHAK 892:45
true attribute of the s.	STAEL 962:77
unless S. clap	YEATS 1106:79
Variety is the s. of pleasure	BEHN 85:63
what benefit to the s.	HONO 488:32
What of s. was left	BROW 198:47
What s. was his	WORD 1100:79
whate'er her s. designed	DRYD 350:46
Whose s. was sad	GILB 425:94
Why shrinks the s.	ADDI 8:35
will hurl my s. form heaven	SHAK 900:62
With consistency a great s.	EMER 376:33
with unshaken s.	FEUE 387:30
yet my s. drew back	HERB 475:17
young man's s.	HOUS 494:48
your s. ... my sorrow	LUGO 619:38
soul-destroying prison so s.-d.	WAUGH 1056:75
soul-making vale of s.-m.	KEATS 545:71
soul-sides boasts two s.-s.	BROW 199:72
soulless sapless, s., beginningless	RUSK 831:12
souls About their blessed s.	KIPL 564:5
All great, powerful s. love life	HEINE 467:68
bind our s. with secular chains	MILT 686:80
boundless, as we wish our s. to be	SHEL 927:66
coast where s. are lost	ANON 24:6
contented your s.	KIPL 563:94
damp s. of housemaids	ELIOT 367:62
days that are to try men's s.	WILS 1086:46
find rest unto your s.	BIBLE 137:88
fine wire around our s.	STEV 972:79
fright the s.	SHAK 862:46
God's peace betide the s.	RANS 802:37
hale s. out of men's bodies?	SHAK 879:45
heaven keeps s.	DONNE 338:15
highest welfare of your s.	PLATO 773:3
human s. did never kiss	KEATS 545:59
immortal s. to sieve through!	MELV 668:43
Jealous s. will not be answered	SHAK 900:43
jewel of their s.	SHAK 899:31
join both countries' s.	BOLI 172:72
letters mingle s.	DONNE 338:99
live in furnished s.	CUMM 299:78
men with broken s.	PATC 759:91
mindes and s. of men	PRYN 794:11
Most people sell their s.	SMITH 947:16
numberless infinities Of s.	DONNE 338:3
one of those happy s.	SHEL 929:10
only in men's s.	STEV 972:73
our s. that cannot be embraced	CAREW 232:14
our twin s. in one	PHIL 768:20
pious s. in the workplace	CHER 256:67
poor misguided s.	LANG 579:67
poor s. who dwell in night	BLAKE 168:21
possess ye your s.	BIBLE 144:13

souls (contd.):

salvation of our own s.	JOHN 528:49
send more s. to Heaven	BENN 92:6
Shepherd and Bishop of your s.	BIBLE 156:80
s. departed but the shadows	BROW 196:5
s. most fed with Shakespeare	CHES 259:37
s. mounting up to God	ROSS 824:30
s. negotiate there	DONNE 337:95
s. of all that I had murdered	SHAK 863:65
S. of Poets dead	KEATS 544:48
s. of the brave	CLOU 271:45
s. of the righteous	BIBLE 131:81
s.' path	MARTI 657:56
s. that have toiled	TENN 995:61
s. undaunted to their doom	SULL 981:24
s. washed	BOOK 175:30
s., whose faculties	MARL 652:89
sweat and blood and s.	FRAN 402:16
their s. dwell in the house	GIBR 422:38
times that try men's s.	PAINE 750:42
to be able to touch s.	THER 1009:38
two s....are one	DONNE 337:91
two s. stand up erect	BROW 197:16
Upon the King...our s.	SHAK 881:94
when s. each other draw	POPE 779:8
whisper to their s.	DONNE 337:90
yet barbarous s.	MELV 667:27
Young s....as unsympathetic	ELIOT 365:5
sound Adding s. to movies	PICK 769:31
all is not s.	JONS 535:89
all s. and successful...morality	SHAW 919:88
deeper than did ever plummet s.	SHAK 917:40
delightful s.	SHEL 929:6
dull, unvaried, sad'ning s.	CRAB 294:84
ears he likes to bathe in s.	BROWN 194:56
empty-hearted whose low s.	SHAK 902:97
expression for the inner s.	KAND 541:95
full of s. and fury	SHAK 910:86
Hark, the glad s.!	DODD 335:44
hollow s. is heard	LICH 603:82
individual s. Insists	LARK 581:96
last s. on the worthless earth	FAUL 384:89
let the s. of music	SHAK 873:98
Lion-like, in full-mouthed s.	CRAIK 294:90
maple seldom inward s.	SPEN 957:99
most persistent s.	KOES 568:72
No s. is dissonant	COLE 273:82
not very s.	SMOL 950:62
sentence is a s.	FROST 406:76
sighing s., the lights	ROSS 824:4
Silence has a s.	KOH 568:74
S. and sweet airs	SHAK 917:34
's.' banker, alas!	KEYN 554:31
s. diffuses itself in circles	LEON 597:84
s. his breathing kept	SHEL 930:20
s. is forced	BLAKE 165:56
s. is gone out into all lands	BOOK 176:66
s. mind in a body	JUVE 540:82
s. must seem an echo	POPE 778:84
s. of a great amen	PROC 792:76
s. of abundance of rain	BIBLE 111:65
s. of drubbing and sobbing	SMITH 948:35
S. of Surprise	BALL 68:65
s. of the cricket bats	JOYCE 538:43
s. of the white soldier's axe	RED 804:74
s. of water's murmuring	SHEL 932:66
s. strikes like a rising knell!	BYRON 219:84
s., substantial flesh and blood	ELIOT 371:52
s. That saved a wretch	NEWT 725:42
s. together harmoniously	HONO 488:31
Sweet is every s.	TENN 995:67
sweet s....upon a bank of violets	SHAK 893:91
thinking has been s.	WELLS 1065:47
thund'ring s.	GOLD 433:13

sound (contd.):

twelve great shocks of s.	TENN 995:68
typical s. of Lancashire	ORWE 742:91
what surge that s. can start	PUSH 795:37
wound...with a sinful s.	VAUG 1041:16
sounded But they s. nice	RAMOS 801:17
s. like the book of Revelations	JAMES 516:8
sounds better than it s.	TWAIN 1034:21
concord of sweet s.	SHAK 873:3
doggerel of s.	RUSK 831:12
empty s.	JOHN 526:6
measured out by s.	BETJ 101:58
Music is the art of s.	BUSO 215:92
Not many s. in life	LAMB 577:33
Of all sweet s. the life and element!	COLE 274:6
painting of s., noises and smells	CARRA 237:15
power of...many s.	SHEL 927:66
Scents, colors, and s.	BAUD 77:17
self-same s.	STEV 971:42
s. frae hell	FERG 386:76
s. of their voices	ANGE 20:32
s. which oft have raised me	COLE 274:4
s. will take care of themselves	CARR 238:33
When it s. good	ELLI 374:4
soup Beautiful S.	CARR 239:40
Gentlemen do not take s.	CURZ 302:31
live upon s. and bouille	SMOL 950:63
Macbeth slurping your s.	PAGE 749:31
never let his s. get cold	HOFF 484:58
s. in Ireland	WAUGH 1056:63
steam of the social s.	ACKR 4:54
thick giblet s.	JOYCE 538:53
soupkitchener Sao long, aol s.!	SHAW 923:82
sour fathers have eaten s. grapes	BIBLE 129:38
garden of cactus and s. grapes	MERR 672:21
gotta take the s.	GOLD 434:47
How s. sweet music is	SHAK 868:71
mixture of the sweet and the s.	LAFO 575:90
s. grapes and ashes	ASHF 41:69
s. misfortune's book	SHAK 870:22
s. offence	SHAK 895:46
sweet or s.	TRAV 1025:36
source as a s. of income	KEMB 549:36
backward motion toward the s.	FROST 407:88
chief s. of economic insecurity	ELLW 375:20
great s. of the holy river	SPEKE 955:61
inexhaustible s. of laughter	TOLS 1023:99
s. and end...of art	POPE 778:78
s....beyond all reason	HAMM 453:43
S. inexhausted of all	STER 970:28
s. of practically every good title	HEMI 470:16
sources from the most remote of s.	HEAT 465:45
invisible s. and echoes	HARR 459:35
s. of the Nile	ELIOT 366:33
ultimate s. of knowledge	POPP 784:25
sours world of sweets and s.	POE 776:48
souses night-clubbing s.	GERS 420:9
south a town in the S. of England	ORWE 742:96
fickle is the S.	TENN 997:5
full of the warm S.	KEATS 547:14
In the S., the war	TWAIN 1032:75
must s. of us remain	JOHN 524:60
niggars of de S.	TRUTH 1030:38
s., where there is no autumn	LAWR 586:89
The S. is avenged.!	BOOTH 178:4
the S. is hardly Christ-centered	OCON 735:85
travelling due s.	PEARY 763:36
wanton in the S.	TENN 997:6
South Africa people of S. A.	SMUTS 950:66
S. A., renowned...For politics	CAMP 227:14
When I left S.A.	WOODS 1092:50
South African S. A. police	SHAR 919:80
South America flow through S. A.	KIPL 560:25
South Pacific mask from the S. P.	ROSE 823:58

speaker (*contd.*):
S. of the House — GARN 415:*28*
What, Mr S.! — ROCHE 815:*41*
speakers observe the best s. — JONS 536:*23*
speakest howsome'er thou s. — SHAK 873:*87*
speaking before s., before — ROUS 827:*35*
ill s. between a fou man — SCOTT 855:*5*
it is I, your father, s. — BELL 85:*78*
prays without s. — FRIE 405:*57*
speaks every day S. a new scene — QUAR 796:*52*
She s. poniards — SHAK 879:*37*
s. holiday — SHAK 878:*19*
s. to us the same word — SCHW 852:*31*
spear boomerang No more s. — NOON 731:*25*
Bring me my s.! — BLAKE 168:*19*
cutteth the s. in sunder — BIBLE 116:*74*
deadly s. rests — ANON 21:*54*
fair Scotland's s. — SCOTT 853:*60*
knappeth the s. — BOOK 177:*74*
slander's venomed s. — SHAK 866:*38*
s. pierced his side — BIBLE 147:*72*
s. through the dead leaves — MANS 647:*5*
where the shield and s. — SPEN 958:*17*
spearmen stubborn s. — SCOTT 853:*59*
spears pruninghooks into s. — BIBLE 130:*56*
s. into pruninghooks — BIBLE 124:*57*
stars thrown down their s. — BLAKE 167:*96*
spec Just 'on s.', addressed as follows — PATE 760:*97*
special earth is nothing very s. — HOYLE 498:*2*
something s. about a poet — FROST 407:*90*
s. kind of man — GILL 426:*7*
still want to be s. — GRAY 440:*42*
specialist definition of a s. — MAYO 666:*9*
specialists All other men are s. — DOYLE 344:*17*
specialized s. but equally ordinary — GALB 412:*80*
s. form of art — PRIT 791:*65*
specials You can't trust the 's.' — COLL 276:*38*
species belonged to different s. — LAVER 584:*57*
certain s. of eternity — SPIN 960:*51*
Especially the male of the s. — LAWR 587:*1*
female of the s. — KIPL 565:*23*
human s....result of mistakes — MILL 679:*58*
human s., according to...theory — LAMB 577:*31*
No s. remains constant — OVID 747:*3*
of a superior s. — VINER 1045:*78*
one of the s. — ADDI 6:*7*
particular intelligent s. — HOYLE 498:*2*
s. of military instinct — HAYD 462:*88*
s. of person — WAUGH 1056:*72*
subordinate s. of Northumberland — SCOTT 856:*10*
specific apply to s. conditions — HUGO 501:*57*
comes forth the grand s. — BYRON 221:*9*
committing itself to anything s. — LODGE 609:*77*
facts, with the s. — ROTH 826:*22*
specimens s., lilies of ambition — DOUG 341:*59*
speck taking a s. for the whole — EDGE 361:*36*
speckled S. and white...and brown! — COLUM 278:*62*
spectacle duller s. this earth of ours — DEQU 316:*64*
great s. of life — ELIOT 366:*40*
national s. — LORCA 613:*40*
no s. so ridiculous — MACA 623:*1*
s. of nature — ROUS 827:*37*
s. that is now unfolding — CHUR 264:*19*
s. unto the world — BIBLE 150:*48*
spectacles gray-framed s. — GUNT 449:*87*
lewd, ungodly S. — PRYN 794:*11*
s. of books — DRYD 347:*59*
using old men's s. — DONNE 339:*30*
spectacular really a s. sight — SCHW 851:*30*
spectator artist is a s. — ERNST 379:*10*
atrocious to the s. — BIOY 162:*11*
participant or s. — GALL 412:*93*
S. of mankind — ADDI 6:*7*

spectator (*contd.*):
s. sport — GERG 420:*2*
think no more of the s. — DIDE 329:*27*
spectators actors or s.? — SHEL 931:*42*
gave pleasure to the s. — MACA 624:*27*
roars of infuriated s. — ORWE 745:*64*
too cold for the s. — SMITH 948:*26*
spectre s. is haunting Europe — MARX 660:*14*
spectres Four s. haunt the poor — LLOY 608:*57*
spectrum like the white ray of the s. — BLAV 169:*27*
speculate to s. is a gain — COUS 290:*87*
speculation from this top Of s. — MILT 693:*28*
mind against s. — RUSS 832:*17*
watches the s. — DICK 322:*74*
speculations s. of eternity or infinitude — ADDI 7:*19*
s. of lasting tranquillity — HAMI 453:*40*
speculator investor and s. — KEYN 554:*34*
speculators manipulators and s. — MAMET 644:*57*
S. may do no harm — KEYN 555:*35*
speech after-dinner s. — WAUGH 1057:*91*
as it does in one's s. — LARO 582:*29*
begin my s....'My husband and I' — ELIZ 374:*95*
concern was s. — ELIOT 372:*73*
controversy over freedom of s. — ORWE 745:*50*
deal by s. than by letter — BACON 59:*17*
era of free s. is closing — ORWE 742:*5*
essential form of economic s. — WRIS 1102:*21*
Fashion is free s. — LURIE 619:*42*
first people to demand free s. — BISS 164:*44*
free s., free passes — BETJ 100:*33*
freedom of s. — ROOS 822:*43*
freedom of s. means — BLACK 164:*47*
gave man s. — SHEL 930:*22*
given to extravagant s. and gestures — FERB 385:*7*
highest sense of human s. — STEV 974:*21*
integrity, plain s. — RODR 819:*88*
intelligible and rational s. — HUXL 508:*1*
joy of living s. — SPEN 957:*6*
killed...and make a s. — AUBR 45:*36*
learn the s. of the place — STEV 971:*50*
Let thy s. be short — BIBLE 132:*13*
loath to cast away my s. — SHAK 894:*4*
make a s. to maggots — CELI 247:*89*
neither s. nor language — BOOK 176:*66*
networks of dead s. — STARK 963:*96*
never taxed for s. — SHAK 901:*66*
no s. nor language — BIBLE 114:*44*
people of a strange s. — BIBLE 128:*35*
perfect plainness of s. — ARNO 38:*7*
political s. and writing — ORWE 744:*44*
power of reasoned s. — ARIS 34:*32*
Rude am I in my s. — SHAK 898:*5*
slow of s. — BIBLE 106:*58*
Speak the s. — SHAK 891:*32*
s. as...dignified as Latin — QUIL 797:*59*
s. be alway with grace — BIBLE 153:*23*
s. in that victorious brow — ARNO 36:*61*
s. is admirable — EUDA 380:*22*
s. is comely — BIBLE 124:*51*
s. is like a cracked kettle — FLAU 392:*38*
S. is often barren — ELIOT 366:*27*
s. is poetry: cadence — NOON 731:*22*
S. is the small change — MERE 671:*3*
s. of England has no name — BRYA 202:*19*
s. shall distil as the dew — BIBLE 108:*1*
s., that supremely human gift — MATH 663:*68*
s. they have resolved not to make — ELIOT 365:*24*
s. was rather like being savaged — HEAL 464:*28*
such is the s. — AELI 9:*51*
Thought could wed itself with S. — TENN 998:*28*
USA is the s. of a people — DOSP 340:*40*
Under all s. there lies a silence — CARL 235:*78*
verse is a measured s. — BACON 55:*15*
visible s....of the democracy — STEAD 964:*4*

speech (*contd.*):
what the dead had no s. for — ELIOT 372:*70*
speeches cannot be solved by s. — BISM 164:*38*
hodgepodge of all other s. — SPEN 957:*96*
leave it to men's charitable s. — BACON 60:*30*
preparing his impromptu s. — BIRK 163:*24*
S. in our culture — GALB 412:*87*
s. were prepared with...genius — ACHE 3:*38*
tries on s. — CURT 301:*23*
speed beauty of s. — MARI 651:*67*
forgetting the bright s. — ARNO 38:*98*
Full s. ahead — FARR 383:*74*
high s. toward the enemy — HALS 452:*35*
knee which contains all s. — YOUR 1108:*11*
little differences of s. — PRATT 789:*24*
riding at breakneck s. — BLAN 168:*22*
safety is in our s. — EMER 376:*41*
s. was faster than light — BULL 203:*56*
told at dictation s. — AMIS 17:*82*
with s. I cannot render — MIDD 673:*41*
speedboat bailing out of a s. — CAMP 226:*8*
spell sit and rightly s. — MILT 683:*16*
s. better than they pronounce — TWAIN 1032:*58*
s. it so abominably — SHAW 924:*1*
s. my name right — COHAN 272:*70*
s. of far Arabia — DELA 314:*28*
tyrant s. has bound me — BRON 191:*6*
went Thy s. through him — ROSS 824:*88*
spells s. into the spongy air — MILT 683:*23*
spend s., and s., and s.! — NICH 726:*56*
S. it, s. it; s. more — SHAK 878:*17*
S. not then his gifts — JONS 534:*85*
s. the rest of my life — JERO 521:*10*
whatever you have, s. less — JOHN 531:*22*
spending cut s. after he left office — DOLE 335:*53*
s. my children's inheritance — ANON 30:*52*
spendthrift true s. — GUIL 448:*78*
Spens Sir Patrick. S. — BALL 67:*49*
Spenser gentle S. fondly led — LAND 578:*59*
Immortal S., no frailty — NASHE 721:*79*
In S., and in Jonson, Art — DENH 315:*55*
spent s. some of my own money — KENN 552:*99*
s. your years and...s. yourself — BORG 179:*12*
sperm drop of s. — JIANG 522:*25*
milk and s. of kindness — MELV 668:*41*
spew s. thee out of my mouth — BIBLE 157:*6*
sphere British S. of Influence — ANON 25:*19*
direct an uncontrollable s. — CHUR 265:*45*
drown me in thy s. — DONNE 337:*87*
fit our s. — SCHR 850:*4*
gladdened once our humble s. — BRON 190:*86*
Let man's soul be a s. — DONNE 338:*16*
nobody has one exclusive s. — MARX 660:*10*
soul of every s. — HOLM 486:*98*
s. of complete abstraction — WHIT 1071:*58*
s. of leisure time — LOWE 617:*15*
s. With centric — MILT 691:*90*
than the moonës s. — SHAK 870:*35*
treat nature by...the s. — CEZA 248:*4*
spheres amongst th'eternal s. — SPEN 958:*16*
Driven by the s. — VAUG 1041:*20*
echo of the s. — BYRON 223:*63*
moving as the restless s. — MARL 652:*89*
music in the spacings of the s. — PYTH 796:*46*
Ring out, ye crystal s. — MILT 681:*90*
seems to shake the s. — DRYD 351:*68*
s. of existence — ELIOT 372:*66*
s. were formed in fright — MELV 667:*35*
start from their s. — SHAK 889:*74*
spice Variety's the s. of life — COWP 293:*56*
spider foul black cobweb to a s. — WEBS 1060:*49*
S., s., spin — MACN 637:*41*
s.'s touch, how exquisitely fine — POPE 780:*39*
What brought the kindred s. — FROST 407:*92*

square (*contd.*):
grows a glimmering s. — TENN 997:4
here is a little s. of blue — MONET 700:43
honest, so thoroughly s. — LERN 597:91
pointed out one corner of a s. — CONF 280:90
run quite out of s. — SPEN 959:36
slog to s. leg — JOYCE 538:55
thin trees in a city s. — LOWE 615:76
squares about the flowering s. — TENN 1000:50
squash S. is boxing — BARR 73:54
S....it's flagellation — COWA 291:8
squeaks Thin s. of radio static — CRANE 295:4
squeeze s. ourselves universally — MELV 668:41
squeezing in a s. of a lemon — GOLD 433:23
squire S.'s own daughter — GRAV 440:40
squires s. ride slowly towards the sea — CHES 259:36
squirrel joiner s. or old grub — SHAK 868:79
s.'s heart beat — ELIOT 366:37
St Francis I'm S. F. of Assisi — PARK 754:16
St John Awake, my S. J.! — POPE 780:32
Rev S. J. Froude put the phone down — SHAR 919:86
St Louis three girls from S. L. — STEIN 966:46
St Mary still S. M.'s Lake — WORD 1098:57
St Omer old man of S. O. — QUIL 797:62
St Pancras towers of S. P. — BEEC 82:15
St Paul didn't quite build S. P.'s — THOR 1017:4
I am designing S. P.'s — BENT 93:24
pray for you in S. P.'s — SMITH 949:59
stab I saw him s. and s. again — READ 803:51
noble Caesar saw him s. — SHAK 884:54
s. me in the back — LAMP 578:51
wound and s. us — KAFKA 540:84
stability s. or enlargement — JOHN 526:7
s. to a popular Government — WHIT 1069:17
stables s. are the real centre — SHAW 925:14
stack s. or the barn door — MILT 682:99
stadiums listen, at the s. — ABSE 1:9
staff break my s. — SHAK 917:40
cursing his s. — SASS 845:28
kamikaze ground s. — PARK 755:30
My s. of faith — RALE 800:13
rod and s. me comfort still — SCOT 856:19
rod and thy s. — BIBLE 115:50
s. in your hand — BIBLE 106:61
s. of honour for mine age — SHAK 862:36
s. of this broken reed — BIBLE 126:84
s. of this bruised reed — BIBLE 112:84
staffocracy 's.' has been created — SHUL 936:36
stag s. at eve had drunk — SCOTT 853:61
s. in the Priory coomb — DAVI 307:99
s. of warrant — DAVI 307:1
stage actor everywhere but...s. — CHES 257:84
All the world's a s. — SHAK 885:91
As large as is the s. — JONS 534:73
before we go quite off this s.? — POPE 780:26
daily s. of duty — KEN 549:47
Don't put your daughter on the s. — COWA 290:2
edge of the s. — DIDE 329:27
final s. — GARD 415:23
frets his hour upon the s. — SHAK 910:86
great s. of fools — SHAK 904:39
mellow glory of the Attic s. — ARNO 36:62
musty breezes of a bare s. — HART 459:47
On the s. he was natural — GOLD 433:29
On the s. of the universe — LAFO 575:96
played upon a s. — SHAK 895:31
putting up a s. set — WAITE 1048:30
science...has this tremendous s. — RABI 799:94
Self-pity in its early s. — ANGE 19:25
s. but echoes back — JOHN 526:80
s. of wisdom — SKIN 943:54
s. where every man must play — SHAK 872:77
s. where truth calls spade a spade! — BROW 200:96
to know the people...on the s. — PAGE 749:31

stage (*contd.*):
United Nations is...a s. — OBRI 734:65
Where's the s. — BOOTH 178:5
wonder of our s.! — JONS 535:8
stage-players S.-p. ...are sinfull — PRYN 794:11
stagecoach s. from London to Oxford — HAZL 463:4
travelling in a s. — IRVI 513:67
stagecoaches twice as fast as s.? — ANON 24:11
stages constantly and in their early s. — SHUL 936:31
stagflation sort of s. situation — MACL 634:91
staggered drinking have you s. — WEBS 1059:26
stagnate freedom to s. — STEV 973:81
stagnation not just inflation...or s. — MACL 634:91
too absolute a s. — BRON 191:93
stain after the rain...never a s. — SHEL 928:84
as with no s. — SHEL 930:38
bright s. on the vision — GRAV 440:34
sky is darkening like a s. — AUDEN 46:46
S. all your edges — SHAK 911:17
s....it can take out — GAY 416:54
s. like a wound — BURKE 207:32
s. the stiff dishonoured shroud — ELIOT 368:67
world's slow s. — SHEL 931:30
stains Innumerable of s. — KEATS 546:91
stair highest pavement of the s. — ELIOT 367:60
one pair of s. by the waterside — PEPYS 765:79
rising is by a winding s. — BACON 58:75
rising...by a winding s. — BACON 57:67
structure in a winding s.? — HERB 475:24
staircase S. wit — DIDE 330:38
steps of a s. — MALL 642:21
stairs Fallen Down S. — MORT 710:1
naked feet upon the s. — DOYLE 343:93
pushed her down the s. — DAVIS 308:26
rat-riddled s.? — BROW 198:53
see through a flight o' s. — DICK 320:28
Up s. and doun s. — MILL 679:59
up the s. of his concepts — STEI 966:52
stake burnt at the s. — SMITH 948:34
made life my common s. — VAUG 1041:23
paraboiled head upon a s. — MONT 703:93
reputation is at s. — SHAK 896:54
s....in such a glorious institution — BURKE 207:12
tied me to a s. — SHAK 910:87
Unless you s. your life — HEIS 467:78
what it is we have at s. — PITT 771:72
stale frizzled, s. and small — LOWE 617:96
nor custom s. — SHAK 905:71
s., a garment out of fashion — SHAK 916:6
s. is their gladness — HARP 458:23
Winter...hangs on until it is s. — CATH 244:42
Stalin If S. had learned...cricket — DOWN 343:80
S....lover of peace — NEHRU 722:94
that S. himself rose — TROT 1029:5
Stalinist nakedness of S. dictatorship — KENN 550:52
stalk With martial s. — SHAK 887:41
stalking s. in my chamber — WYATT 1103:30
stalking-horse folly like a s.-h. — SHAK 887:37
Stalky this was S.'s contribution — KIPL 562:68
stallion black s. on a field of snow — CAMP 227:19
watersmooth-silver s. — CUMM 299:79
stallions bared teeth of s. — CRANE 295:6
stalls Tank come down the s. — SASS 845:22
stalwart three stout and s. sons — BALL 68:60
stamina lowering a man's s. — DOUG 341:52
stamp but the guinea's s. — BURNS 213:42
indelible s. of his lowly origin — DARW 306:89
physics or s. collecting — RUTH 834:46
s. collection waits — BETJ 91:39
s. makes the current money — JONS 536:25
s. of his authority — LAMB 576:23
s. of university training — GERH 420:4
stand able to s. before thee — BIBLE 108:7
By uniting we s. — DICK 329:21

stand (*contd.*):
climb the rails into the Grand S. — SOME 952:1
cuspid's last s. — PERE 766:93
firm spot on which to s. — ARCH 33:14
If she can s. it, I can — EPST 379:98
light shadow never s. still — WEST 1067:76
makes a man s. straight — HELL 468:95
no time to s. — DAVI 308:20
not s. for — WAUGH 1057:84
s. a year or twa — BURNS 211:4
s. like greyhounds — SHAK 881:85
S. still, traveller and read! — ANON 30:67
S. Up!, S. Up For Jesus! — DUFF 354:23
s. up to anything — SHAW 921:18
therefore I hope to s. — WALP 1052:98
They that s. high — SHAK 863:52
who shall be able to s.? — BIBLE 157:13
standard advancing s. of religion — SMIL 945:76
her just s. — POPE 778:78
raise the scarlet s. — CONN 282:54
s. of ...Red Hugh — MACC 625:36
Truth is its own s. — SPIN 960:50
standardized he is s.; transformed — DOUG 342:68
standards Advance our s.! — SHAK 863:67
s. by which he lived — CHRI 261:72
s. of green unfurled — MOORE 706:33
standers-by not for any s.-b. — SHAK 916:99
standing heart of s. — EMPS 378:85
like to write s. up — HEMI 471:38
s. is slippery — BACON 57:70
s. on the edge — SALI 839:28
tired with s. — DONNE 336:71
standoffish Are they being s. — COLE 273:77
standpoint s. of what it attains — BURKE 208:53
stands No economy ever s. still — HARR 459:41
s. an instant in the sun — HYDE 509:14
s....for something younger — FIRB 389:71
strengthen whilst one s. — ROSS 823:68
Stanford S. Rivers lost me — LEVE 600:23
staple s. of his argument — SHAK 866:23
Stapleford osier-beds, S. Abbots — LEVE 600:23
star about its chilling s. — BERR 98:10
Being a s. has made it possible — DAVIS 309:32
birth to a dancing s. — NIET 728:79
catch a falling s. — DONNE 336:75
constant as the Northern S. — SHAK 883:38
curb a runaway young s. — BYRON 223:66
discovery of a s. — BRIL 188:52
don't want to sleep with the s. — CURT 302:24
dusk lit by one large s. — MERE 671:97
eve's one s. — KEATS 547:99
every s. that heaven — MILT 683:16
Fair as a s. — WORD 1095:8
grapples with his evil s. — TENN 999:44
great s. early droop'd — WHIT 1073:92
height, and at the s. — MERE 671:12
Hitch your waggon to a s. — EMER 377:74
Hope guides us by her s. — BRON 191:2
In heaven no single s. — THOM 1015:57
in his separate s. — KIPL 562:60
Jungle s. or jungle track — CULL 299:68
Knew you, and named a s.! — BROW 199:64
life hovers like a s. — BYRON 223:62
like a sinking s. — TENN 994:59
loftiest s. of unascended heaven — SHEL 930:25
love a bright particular s. — SHAK 901:3
merely the s.' tennis-balls — WEBS 1061:73
most auspicious s. — SHAK 916:20
My Lucky S. — FREED 403:29
No one ever leaves a s. — WILD 1079:16
not one s. of all — FROST 407:84
o'er the hill the eastern s. — BURNS 212:35
on the charge of a s.! — SHAK 902:2

state (*contd.*):

S. is the Church	SHAW 923:76
s. lottery as a public subsidy	QUINE 797:67
s. manifested by a specific syndrome	SELYE 858:41
s....master of money	BEVE 102:75
s. of innocency Adam fell	SHAK 876:64
s. of man	SHAK 918:61
s. of rut	GALS 413:3
s. of war by nature	SWIFT 986:6
s....takes no notice	CROM 298:51
s. where gun control	SIMP 939:90
s....withers away	ENGE 378:88
s. without...some change	BURKE 207:26
s. won't bother us anymore	MAO 648:17
storms of s.	SHAK 918:64
That is. is a s. of Slavery	GILL 426:6
The more the s. 'plans'	HAYEK 462:89
things o' the S.	NAIR 717:19
this isthmus of a middle s.	POPE 780:42
To preserve a trading s.	STEU 970:29
vital importance to the s.	SUN 982:30
voter...pernicious to the S.	WRIG 1101:2
we are the s.	WRIG 1102:12
When S. Magic fails	REED 805:88
When Venice sat in s.	BYRON 220:92
whole machinery of the s.	ENGE 378:90
whole worl's in a s.	OCAS 735:74
With wealth your s....improve	DONNE 337:79
women do not count in the s.	DAVI 309:42
worst s. of affairs	KLEE 566:47
worth of the S.	MILL 675:69
youth of a s.	BACON 59:24
state-controlled s.-c. ...echoes	DOUG 342:66
stately grow great and s.	STEV 975:40
more s. and admirable	WHIT 1073:86
one of the s. homos	CRISP 297:39
she is tall and s.	TENN 1001:82
S. as a galleon	GREN 446:51
s. homes of England	COWA 290:3
statement Every scientific s.	POPP 783:16
general s. is like a cheque	POUND 786:73
least cheering s.	LEBO 591:84
no s. which refers to a 'reality'	AYER 53:78
scientific s. speaks	POPP 783:22
sheer joy of felicitous s.	SCHL 848:74
s. and a metaphoric way	MALA 641:6
s. as an act of wilful defiance	SASS 845:21
statements apparent s. of fact	AYER 53:79
states attacks from outlaw s.	REAG 804:64
Have more s. perished	HOPE 490:71
In s. unborn	SHAK 883:42
independent or semi-independent s.	JAY 519:73
She's all s.	DONNE 337:78
s. of consciousness	MOORE 704:10
stinking s.	JOHN 525:76
thinking in terms of nation s.	ADEN 8:44
statesman abroad, you almost feel...a s.	
	MACM 635:7
agree with him, he is a s.	LLOY 609:67
business of a s.	STEU 970:30
constitutional. s. is in general	BAGE 62:66
definition of a constitutional s.	BAGE 62:65
first requirement of a s.	ACHE 3:35
politician is a s. who	STEV 973:88
rule...for a s., a courtier, or a lover	CHAR 252:81
speculative s.	ADDI 6:7
s.'s duty is to bridge	KISS 566:39
s. enamoured of existing evils	BIER 161:75
s. is a politician who	TRUM 1030:25
s. is preventing...plots	WALT 1052:10
Too nice for a s.	GOLD 433:28
statesmanship You call that s.	BEVAN 101:69
statesmen adored by little s.	EMER 376:33
Among modern s.	CHES 259:16

statesmen (*contd.*):

become s. and heroes	WARD 1053:14
some are born s.	SHAW 925:24
s....ignore at their peril	WILS 1086:55
s. of E.	TAYL 991:11
s....take on a science fictional way	ASIM 42:74
static A novel is a s. thing	TYNAN 1035:27
class people as s. and dynamic	WAUGH 1056:73
French...will never become s.	HUGO 501:61
Thin squeaks of radio s.	CRANE 295:4
station Eternity...as of a s.	DICK 328:16
honour is a private s.	ADDI 8:34
keep no rank nor s.	LOWE 617:96
towers of St Pancras S.	BEEC 82:15
Worked on Middleton's s.	LAWS 588:20
stationary All is flux, nothing is s.	HERA 473:82
stations train passes through s.	LEWIS 601:35
statistic exchange rate is only a s.	KRUG 570:6
statisticians sin With s.	AUDEN 49:6
statistics feed the hungry on s.	LLOY 608:53
lies, damned lies and s.	DISR 334:31
man of s.	HOLM 487:4
only tables and s.	OPPE 741:72
Politicians use s.	LANG 579:66
seemingly inanimate of s.	MAMET 643:53
s. for Manhattan Island	BART 75:87
S. triumph	BELL 88:21
unless s. lie	CUMM 300:87
statue s.'s brow	WALC 1048:42
s. inside every block	ORWE 743:9
s. of mystification	DICK 326:56
s. of one of our kings	APPL 32:98
walk around a s.	ROSSO 825:99
walking...with the S. of Liberty	CONR 285:16
statues like sepulchral s.	DONNE 337:95
Trees cut to S.	POPE 779:21
With s. on the terraces	KIPL 564:13
stature add one cubit unto his s.?	BIBLE 135:52
increased in s.	WHITE 1070:40
Jesus increased in wisdom and s.	BIBLE 142:80
Look not...on the height of his s.	BIBLE 110:36
Malice is of a low s.	HALI 452:29
man of giant s.	NEHRU 722:94
men of a great s.	BIBLE 107:82
mighty s.	MILT 687:98
persons of heroic s.	AMIS 17:96
status Bureaucracy defends the s. q.	PETER 767:7
economic s. of women	GILM 427:14
industrial and economic s.	SKEL 942:37
Policemen so cherish their s.	MAMET 643:45
restored the s. quo	HAMER 453:37
restored the s. quo	SQUI 961:65
s. and profits of war	TREV 1026:53
s. of a cathedral	RODR 819:89
s. of Galileo	GOULD 436:76
s. of 'native'	SART 844:20
the quo has lost its s.	PETER 767:7
statutes s. of the Lord are right	BIBLE 114:45
s. of usages therein obtained	MILL 674:57
staves aspen good for s.	SPEN 957:99
cement to me with s.?	BIBLE 110:41
stay My s., my guide, and lantern	SHAK 861:2
poor man's s.	WORD 1098:58
S., Frederic, s.!	GILB 424:64
s. in a concentration camp	JOHN 523:44
Will you not s.	HODG 483:49
Yet will not s.	GRAV 439:16
stays Old Hodge s. not his hand	RANS 802:37
s. there for years	HORA 493:27
steadiness s., self-control...courage	PEEL 763:44
steady how s. you hold your weapon	SIMP 939:90
s. and perpetual serenity	ADDI 7:17
s. and stolid-y	GILB 424:68
steak s. spread with butter	KURO 571:20

steak (*contd.*):

wanted s. and they offered spam	MALA 641:3
steaks smell of s.	ELIOT 367:56
steal most honourable...was to s.	RABE 799:88
poets...beg, borrow, or s.	POUND 785:57
silently s. away	KAUF 543:16
s. bread	FRAN 401:90
S. me awhile	SHAK 871:47
s. my Basil-pot away	KEATS 546:84
s. us from ourselves	DRYD 349:99
Thou shalt not s.	BIBLE 106:68
Thou shalt not s.	CLOU 271:49
When judges s. themselves	SHAK 897:74
steam powers of s.	WATT 1055:55
s. comes...navel	THOM 1011:89
s. of the social soup	ACKR 4:54
steamer This little s. ...is immortal	PRIE 790:37
steamers all you Big S.	KIPL 564:12
Daily the s. sidle up	AUDEN 46:53
steed s. and the shrill trump	SHAK 899:40
s. by Loc Suilig	MACC 625:36
s. was the best	SCOTT 853:54
waves bound...as a s.	BYRON 219:79
steeds curb thy fierce s.	BLAKE 165:58
mounting barbèd s.	SHAK 862:46
steel dew-like s.	BRAU 186:22
Give them the cold s.	ARMI 35:44
hand of s. in a velvet glove	WOOL 1093:83
him they feared to meet with s.	DAVIS 309:36
locomotive of s.	KAFKA 540:85
Meistersinger...set breath in s.	CRANE 295:5
red line tipped with s.	RUSS 834:44
s. my soldiers' hearts	SHAK 881:95
S. prices cause inflation	BLOU 170:39
s. rod runs right through	ANGE 19:23
though locked up in s.	SHAK 861:6
with hoops of s.	SHAK 888:63
wounded surgeon plies the s.	ELIOT 371:57
steel-true S.-t. and blade-straight	STEV 976:55
Steemie S. lecturing	SCOTT 855:1
steep s. and thorny way	SHAK 888:62
steeple Grand Sluice, and a high s.	ANON 24:6
in his own religious s.	CAMP 227:21
in s. hing	FERG 386:16
s. of my dreams	DEBU 311:66
steeplechase s. and gameboard	ELKIN 374:98
steeples s. far and near	HOUS 494:49
Till you have drenched our s.	SHAK 903:17
steering s. full speed ahead	GILM 427:20
Stein Gertrude S. said	STEIN 965:34
Gertrude S.'s prose song	LEWIS 602:63
Stella S., think not that I	SIDN 937:58
stem s. of the contained flower	ROET 819:93
stems gold is on the pine-s.	MERE 671:1
stench s. of appeasement	THAT 1008:27
stenches two and seventy s.	COLE 275:26
Stendhal fought two draws with S.	HEMI 471:37
step but one s. from...the horrible	DOYLE 344:19
dare not take a s.	SHAW 921:29
every individuality is...a false s.	SCHO 849:95
first s. that counts	DEFF 311:72
get up a s. that ain't there	JACO 515:93
isn't the first s.	KENN 552:4
look well to each s.	WHYM 1074:11
must go nowhere, s. out	LEWIS 602:64
new theory...a s. forward	POPP 783:23
One S. Forward	LENIN 595:49
small s. for a man	ARMS 35:49
small s. for mankind	BROD 189:71
s. in the wrong direction	LEVA 599:16
varies with every s.	THOR 1016:72
step-dame fled s.-d. Study's blows	SIDN 937:51
step-parents s.-p. ...disappointment	POWE 787:1
stepping s. where his comrade	SCOTT 853:59

steps by backward s. VAUG 1041:17
gentle odours led my s. SHEL 932:66
s. down the palate NABO 717:96
s. had well nigh slipped BIBLE 117:89
s. of a staircase MALL 642:21
s. take hold on hell BIBLE 120:61
thy lab'ring s. LUCR 619:35
treading the s. already marked SHEL 926:53
stereotype s. of rejected genius HUGH 499:29
stereotypes abandon established s. GORB 435:59
sterile seems to me a s. promontory SHAK 890:2
splendid and s. Dolores SWIN 987:33
Truths discovered...are s. FRAN 401:84
sterility victory of s. BELL 88:21
stern Kingly conclaves s. and cold SHEL 930:16
lantern on the s. COLE 275:27
solitary and most s. YEATS 1105:67
s., obdurate, flinty, rough SHAK 861:18
sterner s. stuff SHAK 884:49
Stetson Met S. COPE 287:50
Stevenson S.'s convictions LEHM 594:38
stew soporific s. of every living! SARD 843:94
steward backward s. for the poor POPE 780:29
lord commended the unjust s. BIBLE 143:3
Stewart land God gave to Andy S. SMITH 947:4
stewing no matter how much s. CURT 302:24
stewpan others again that it is a s. HUNT 505:33
stews Of s. and brothels only knew HERB 476:36
private sports the s. would blush MASS 662:56
stick coat upon a s. YEATS 1106:79
fell like a s. PAINE 750:50
give me my s. I'll face it LEAC 589:48
heard his s. thumping MANS 647:10
scratched with a s. KIPL 561:41
Speak softly and carry a big s. ROOS 822:45
s. and a string JOHN 532:43
s. I am about to cut BENT 92:16
water curves a s. LAFO 574:83
sticking-place courage to the s.-p. SHAK 908:35
sticks like s. of sealing-wax DICK 323:89
Nothing s. to him SCHR 850:8
S. nix hick pix ANON 26:41
take up pick-axes and s. HO 482:33
stiff-necked s.-n. people BIBLE 107:72
stiffen S. the sinews SHAK 881:84
time to s. ORWE 744:24
stile-a merrily hent the s.-a SHAK 911:27
still America...isn't standing s. CUMM 300:85
Be s., and know BIBLE 116:74
commune...and be s. BIBLE 114:33
No economy ever stands s. HARR 459:41
not keeping s. GUNN 448:86
said to my soul, be s. ELIOT 371:44
s. and quiet conscience SHAK 918:60
S. falls the Rain SITW 941:16
s. small voice BIBLE 111:69
Sunday...standing s. RHYS 808:29
they liked me 's.' DICK 328:2
stillness air a solemn s. holds GRAY 441:62
horrid s. first invades the ear DRYD 346:48
sense of rapacious s. BANKS 70:98
solemn s. of the buried foliage HOLM 485:72
s. can outlast SASS 845:38
s. in the midst of chaos BELL 88:26
s. where our spirits walk SASS 845:39
that s. ultimately best CRANE 294:98
stilts nonsense upon s. BENT 93:17
stimulus s. and object MANN 645:78
sting care not who they s. SHAK 861:5
death, where is thy s.? BIBLE 151:73
it is a s. PEELE 763:46
s. a stately horse JOHN 526:94
s. like a bee ALI 14:28
that inwardly doth s. SURR 982:41

stings s. in their tails BIBLE 157:18
stink earth shall have a foul s. ANON 22:77
stinker Outrageous S. KIPL 562:68
stinks stenches...and several s.! COLE 275:26
stint at pleasure s. their melody SHAK 862:43
stipple s. leaves with sun SACK 835:61
stir s. not up, nor awake my love BIBLE 124:48
stirk s. from a cottar SCOTT 854:70
stirks They gang in S. BURNS 209:59
stirred Shaken and not s. FLEM 393:59
S. for a bid HOPK 491:89
stirrup foot upon the s. DELA 314:27
sprang to the s. BROW 198:33
stirrup-pump simple s.-p. REED 805:84
stitch S.! s.! s.! HOOD 489:45
stoats rabbits ruled by s. ORWE 742:3
stock column of s. quotations DOSP 340:40
enslaved as farm s. SHAW 924:94
fight for that s. HOWA 497:92
If s. market experts AUGU 50:19
impoverished the public s. JOHN 531:13
waste its s. JUANA 539:64
stocking glimpse of s. PORT 784:31
stockings come to her in yellow s. SHAK 895:19
for the silk s. JOHN 525:87
her last...pair of s. CHAN 250:29
his s. fouled SHAK 889:86
pinking of thin s. DICK 322:66
Queen Elizabeth owned silk s. SCHU 851:19
s. were hung MOORE 704:4
Stockport rubbish was sent to S. ANON 30:66
stocks feet...hurt in the s. BOOK 177:90
reads 'storks' for 's.' FREUD 404:43
s. were sold BELL 87:9
stoic Every S. was a S. EMER 376:31
weakness for the s.'s pride POPE 780:42
with a s. calm SOME 952:1
stoicism Romans call it s. ADDI 8:29
Stoics Let the S. say what they please EMER 377:44
stole s. it fair and square HAYA 462:86
wonder where you s. 'em SWIFT 984:81
stolen horses may not be s. HALI 452:27
not wanting what is s. SHAK 899:39
revolution has been s. JIANG 522:26
S., s., be your apples HUNT 504:23
S. waters are sweet BIBLE 120:67
They'll say it's s. BRAD 184:1
stolid steady and s.-y GILB 424:68
stolidity cinder of s. CARL 233:29
stomach adventures on a drained s. BYRON 224:73
army marches on its s. NAPO 718:31
bring 'em off your s. LAMB 576:16
but a s., gentlemen, a s. HUNT 505:33
deepest loathing to the s. SHAK 871:41
good s. to a feast WEBS 1060:37
Had s. for 'em all SHAK 900:54
healthy s. is...conservative BUTL 218:45
heart and s. of a king ELIZ 373:90
If your s. disputes you PAIGE 750:41
in his s. more animated beings SMITH 949:46
little wine for the s.'s sake BIBLE 154:32
naturally have a weak s. BERN 96:74
no s. for such meat DOBS 334:35
no s. to this fight SHAK 881:98
pit of the s. HOUS 496:81
soul, or a s. SAKI 838:6
s. is not good ANON 23:85
s. sets us to work ELIOT 366:29
s. thinks her throat is cut RUNY 829:61
when you have a s. ache GORO 436:69
stomachs juries fill their s. SYNGE 988:63
stone At his heels a s. SHAK 892:61
blessed is the hard s. DARIO 305:77
bomb them into the S. Age LEMAY 595:43

stone (*contd.*):
carved in s. TENN 1001:78
creeping ivy clings...to s. COWP 292:46
cruelties of the S. Age CHUR 264:23
Here the s. images ELIOT 369:99
hurl a s. at MOOD 703:98
inside every block of s. ORWE 743:9
keeper of the s. DAVI 308:16
lay s. on s. ARNO 37:74
Leave not...a foot of s. POPE 783:2
let him first cast a s. BIBLE 145:47
Like a s. TAKU 990:85
lonely man...a s., a bone, a stick CHEE 255:52
massive sandal set on s. MILL 676:89
naked s. WORD 1101:94
nickname is the heaviest s. HAZL 464:21
no bigger than an agate s. SHAK 868:78
no s. unturned SHAR 919:80
Paris made of s. HUGO 501:65
Saturn, quiet as a s. KEATS 547:99
Sculpture in s. MOORE 705:13
see and imitate...in s. CUMM 299:75
seventy years of s. THOM 1010:61
shadow white as a s. ROET 819:98
sound of iron on s. DELA 314:27
s. and earth is closer to the truth HEAT 465:47
s. besmeared with sluttish time SHAK 913:65
s. commemorates...Ellis ANON 24:10
s. falls to the ground THOR 1017:93
s. fidelity They hardly meant LARK 581:5
s. flung into the water LEON 597:84
s. in my straw hat STEV 973:97
s. of our fortresses FAVRE 384:92
s. of stumbling BIBLE 125:64
s. of the heart YEATS 1106:73
s. remains, and the cross MACC 624:34
s. set in the silver sea SHAK 867:48
s. taken away from the sepulchre BIBLE 147:73
s. than with an axe JOHN 530:99
s. that puts the stars to flight FITZ 390:87
s. the tweny-first BROW 200:82
S. walls do not a prison LOVE 615:63
s. was cut out without hands BIBLE 129:45
s. which the builders refused BIBLE 118:27
swerd of this s. MALO 642:25
sword...out of the s. MUNRO 714:55
take away our hearts o' s. OCAS 735:75
take the s. from the s. ELIOT 370:34
The s.'s in the midst YEATS 1105:72
themselves as s. SHAK 914:81
things of bronze and s. RUNY 829:66
trunkless legs of s. SHEL 928:92
turn you like them to s. TATE 991:4
understanding of the S.-Age ARMEY 35:42
violet by a mossy s. WORD 1095:8
Virtue is like a rich s. BACON 59:13
water upon the s. STEAD 964:5
Wedding-Guest sat on a s. COLE 273:84
weight which is the s. HEPW 473:79
will he give him a s.? BIBLE 135:58
written of me on my s. FROST 407:97
stone-cutters S.-c. fighting time JEFF 519:80
stone-like Naked and s.-l. FREE 404:34
Stonehenge bring S. to Nyasaland BANDA 69:86
like a monogrammed S. RIVA 812:1
stones could aye peeble them wi' s. SCOTT 855:92
Dry s., sun and dust COPE 287:50
five smooth s. out of the brook BIBLE 110:40
houses are made of s. POIN 776:58
Inestimable s. SHAK 863:54
on thy cold, grey s. TENN 995:63
pavement s. are polished DICK 322:66
pavements fang'd with murderous s. COLE 275:26
people and the s. WILL 1082:86

strength (*contd.*):

triumphant conviction of s.	CONR 284:98
what is s. without	MILT 694:39
what s. I have's mine	SHAK 917:44
which by his s. and wit	HOBB 483:42
with my utmost s.	VAUG 1041:19
would but fain his s. renew	HERR 477:52

strengths make my s.   JONS 535:4

stress in times of s.   ORWE 742:94

Storm and s.	KAUF 543:22
s. and disorientation	TOFF 1022:85
S. is the state	SELYE 858:41
under s. of emotion	POUND 787:97

stresses s. of accent   SAND 842:80

stretch S. pants   ANON 27:70

stricken s. with most obstinate love   SIDN 936:44

stricture intensiveness as s.   BURKE 208:53

stride poet is allowed the s.   SAND 841:78

put the batter off his s.   SHAW 925:36

strife dull and endless s.   WORD 1094:2

Happiness is full of s.	ANOU 30:75
hear the silver s.	DICK 327:94
heavens free from s.	CORY 288:65
In Place of S.	CAST 244:30
internal friction and s.	ROTH 826:23
madding crowd's ignoble s.	GRAY 442:72
may be sturt or s.	DUNB 355:35
no s. can grow up there	MILT 688:12
no talebearer, the s. ceaseth	BIBLE 122:4
none was worth my s.	LAND 578:62
on the verge of s.	CORN 288:57
pleasures with rough s.	MARV 658:76
put an end To s.	BYRON 222:33
root of s.?	SURR 982:44
some to public s.	POPE 782:76
S. discorde and waistis wanis	ANON 23:88
The s. is o'er	POTT 784:43
the stern s.	SCOTT 853:60
With phantoms an unprofitable s.	SHEL 931:46

strike afraid to s.   POPE 781:65

By and by it will s.	SHAK 917:28
General S. taught working classes	BALF 65:18
I s. out three of them	BOIL 171:64
If you s. a child	SHAW 922:52
no right to s.	COOL 286:35
organise a formidable s.	HICKS 480:97
s. and sink and split	SHAW 925:16
s. it out	JOHN 529:64
s. sooner than speak	SHAK 875:47
s. with our spirit's knife	SHEL 931:46
that loves me s. me dead	SHAK 906:92
while the s. is hot	ANON 29:30

strikers longstaff sixpenny s.   SHAK 875:47

s. couldn't score in a brothel   DOCH 334:38

strikes narrow circle of s.   ENGE 378:89

string chewing little bits of s.   BELL 87:5

dullis on the s.	HENR 473:70
end of the golden s.	BLAKE 168:9
held together with s.	ACHE 3:44
Our eyes upon one double s.	DONNE 337:94
strangling in a s.	HOUS 494:43
s. along with you	DUBIN 353:3
s. to each side of its face	LEAC 588:29
walking on a s. across a gulf	DAVI 307:96
warbled to the s.	MILT 682:11

strings humming of the s.   PYTH 796:46

s....in the human heart	DICK 322:64
tied by th' s.	SHAK 905:80
When such s. jar	SHAK 861:1

strip Then s. lads   SCOTT 854:72

stripe s. for s.   BIBLE 107:69

stripes broad s. and bright stars   KEY 554:24

cut his s. away	KIPL 560:29
next week he's in s.	DAVI 308:11

stripes (*contd.*):

red and white s.	HATT 460:58
with his s. we are healed	BIBLE 127:1

stripling muzzled s.   STEP 968:80

strive may s. to be like them   GIBR 422:38

To s., to seek   TENN 995:62

strives s. for nothing so incessantly   DOST 341:47

striving rather than s. to arrive   HILL 480:5

s. evermore for these   GREN 446:52

stroke made at one s.   FRAN 402:97

s. of death is a lover's pinch	SHAK 906:7
s. of midnight ceases	HOUS 496:82
that s. of death	JOHN 531:13
This would, at a s.	HEATH 466:51
to the tune of flutes kept s.	SHAK 905:68

strokes better than bad s.   SHAK 884:62

Many s....with a little axe   SHAK 861:19

strong advantage of s. people   BONH 173:86

all the women are s.	KEIL 548:25
am s. and lusty	SHAK 885:82
battle to the s.	BIBLE 123:35
battle to the s.	DAVI 307:97
Be s. and of a good courage	BIBLE 108:8
Be s., and quit yourselves	BIBLE 109:30
be thou s. therefore	BIBLE 110:54
Come; and s. within us	KING 558:90
conquest for the s.	MASE 662:49
disarm the s.	FRAN 401:88
ever s. upon the stronger side	HAZL 463:9
every s. woman	FULL 409:34
grow s.	HUGH 499:14
If the fence is s. enough	SMITH 946:98
irrational and s. within us	WILS 1084:11
let the weak say, I am s.	BIBLE 130:56
man is s. before he is moral	FAUL 383:80
many are s. at the broken places	HEMI 470:19
Men's actions are too s.	EMER 377:60
minds that are not s. enough	SHAW 922:57
more s. than traitors' arms	SHAK 884:54
only the S. shall thrive	SERV 859:54
out of the s. came forth sweetness	BIBLE 109:17
pain is worse to the s.	JEFF 519:82
quit you like men, be s.	BIBLE 151:74
s. and dynamic	GAND 414:11
s. enough to bare the misfortunes	LARO 582:26
s. impulsive gravity of head	POPE 782:99
S. is the lion	SMART 944:69
S. without rage	DENH 315:53
too s....to succumb	HOFS 484:62
wants that little s.	HOLM 486:77
when I am weak, then am I s.	BIBLE 152:87

strong-men s.-m....rolled into one   SIEG 937:67

stronger at least the s.   GIBB 421:20

nothing s. than Necessity	EURI 380:24
s. by every thing you see, hear	STER 969:2
Swifter, higher, s.	ANON 25:27
unofficial magic becomes s.	REED 805:88
who is s. than death?	HUGH 500:44

strongest reason of the s.   LAFO 574:77

stronghold s. our God is still   LUTH 620:49

strongholds s. of...hypocrisy   GALL 412:91

structuralism theme defeats s.   GOLD 432:90

structure concept, s., and style   POUS 787:99

glittering s. of her cultivation	AUCH 46:40
kind of democratic s.	MO 698:10
s. of traditional stories	FRYE 408:21
style and s.	NABO 717:8
whole social s.	PARS 756:45

structures repairs its great public s.   HOWE 497:90

Those blessed s.   LOWE 617:13

struggle alarms of s. and flight   ARNO 36:65

as if it was quite a s.	FERB 385:9
delightful...after you cease to s.	FERB 385:11
living is a s.	WILD 1079:27

struggle (*contd.*):

Manhood a s.	DISR 332:82
not the triumph but the s.	COUB 289:71
perpetual s. for room and food	MALT 643:93
Say not the s. naught availeth	CLOU 270:32
s. against the impossible	HEDIN 466:61
s. between a set purpose	DOYLE 344:14
s. between the artist man	SHAW 921:26
s. for form only as long	KAND 541:95
s. for...my country's cause	OCON 735:81
s. for survival	ROTH 825:5
s....towards the heights	CAMUS 229:49
s. won by survivors	ANGE 19:20
thirty years of s.	LOOS 612:24
To see...is a constant s.	ORWE 744:41
unpitied sacrifice in contemptible s.	BURKE 206:1
variations on the eternal s.	LIN 604:96
What is s. to escape?	KEATS 547:7

struggles hope for our political s.   ROBB 813:11

Of all human s.	SHAW 921:26
s. and strives against nature	INNO 512:54
s. of Hector	HONO 488:32

strumpet Into a s.'s fool   SHAK 904:56

strut s. sitting down   REST 807:16

struts s. and frets his hour   SHAK 910:86

Stuart S. or Nassau go   PRIOR 790:49

Stuarts went out...with the S.   DISR 334:32

stubble like sparks among the s.   BIBLE 131:82

stubbornness s. is as iniquity   BIBLE 110:35

stucco s. houses   BETJ 100:40

student s. merely   THOR 1017:88

s. must remember	AGAS 9:61
S. of our sweet English tongue	FLEC 393:47

students s. on campus   NABO 717:99

teach s. how business is conducted   DEMI 315:44

studied s. as a branch of government   JAY 519:73

s. in his death   SHAK 907:23

studies After his s.   SHAK 864:80

air of delightful s.	MILT 685:54
He that in his s. wholly applies	CONF 280:91
inclines...to some particular s.	DRYD 347:57
s. in which the work that results dies	LEON 596:74
too much time in s. is sloth	BACON 59:21

studio go to my s. every day   GUST 449:93

s. is a torture area   LIBE 603:79

studious s. for their bellies   SAND 842:80

S. of laborious ease	COWP 293:59
S. to please	JOHN 525:75
There s. let me sit	THOM 1015:52

study dry air of the s.   HART 459:47

fled step-dame S.'s blows	SIDN 937:51
leisure of s.	GERB 420:98
most uncreative subject you can s.	ISSI 514:79
my first s. to obtain	WALP 1052:98
No social s.	MILLS 679:63
periphrastic s.	ELIOT 371:45
proper s. of mankind	HUXL 506:46
proper s. of mankind is man	POPE 780:42
proper s. of mankind is science	RABI 799:94
result of previous s.	AUST 51:36
s. distinct from science	RUSS 832:16
s. is a weariness of the flesh	BIBLE 124:43
S. is like the heavens	SHAK 865:5
s. of all these sciences	PLATO 774:24
s. of crime	MILL 678:40
s. of how to live well	GERB 419:96
s. of present pleasure	MONT 700:54
s. of public opinion	MERT 672:26
S. to be quiet	BIBLE 153:24

studying still s. verbs   SAND 841:73

what you learn while...not s.   CONA 279:82

stuff Ambition...sterner s.   SHAK 884:49

Brotherhood of the Right S.	WOLFE 1090:25
folks eat the s. thy raise	STEI 966:55

stuff (*contd.*):

It is frivolous s.	FORS 398:48
Nobody will see the s. again	HERB 474:96
s. that will do the trick	FORM 397:27
such s. As dreams are made	SHAK 917:37
stumble hands guiding where I s.	SASS 845:40
s. that run fast	SHAK 869:98
stumbling stone of s.	BIBLE 125:64
stump Blackened log and s.	LAWS 588:21
stumps roller, pitch, and s.	LANG 579:67
stunned like one that hath been s.	COLE 274:96
stunt s. our ambitions	SCHU 851:20
stupendous parts of one s. whole	POPE 780:40
stupid better the actor the more s.	CAPO 231:90
economy, s.!	ANON 29:37
If someone was s. enough	TAYL 992:16
more s. one becomes	MAO 649:32
not s., but…very dull	BEAV 80:80
people are too s. by three-quarters	MAJOR 640:99
pretend to be more s.	STARK 963:94
s. about some things	BELL 88:28
s. and ignorant	SMITH 946:91
s. enough to want it	CHES 259:34
s. man is doing something	SHAW 921:20
s., or sulky	HUNT 505:30
too s. to agree	TALL 990:90
Was man made s.	EBER 359:11
stupidity America—your s.	SNYD 951:86
confirmed in full s.	DRYD 348:82
intellect, a sweet s.	LISP 607:40
march of s.	DELI 314:38
profound s. of the inanimate	STER 968:82
struggle in vain against s.	SCHI 848:71
s. of the multitude	BAUD 77:28
the s. of its…propaganda	ORWE 743:20
sturdy filthy, s., unkillable infants	POUND 785:53
sturt may be s. or stryfe	DUNB 355:35
stutter feet began to s.	BURT 213:61
sty No better than a s.?	SHAK 906:95
Over the nasty s.	SHAK 892:56
pleasure in a sensual s.	MILT 683:19
style called this s. the Mandarin s.	CONN 283:66
colouring and s.	VASA 1040:9
concept, structure, and s.	POUS 787:99
debased of s., not individual	MAIL 639:81
Dressed in s., brand new tile	COLL 276:37
exercise of his own s.	JONS 536:23
eye on his s.	ARNO 38:5
first grace of s.	MOORE 705:18
form that my s. cannot discover	DARIO 305:76
forward in the old s.	WELL 1063:11
game is about…doing things in s.	BLAN 169:24
God…has no real s.	PICA 769:28
height of his own towering s.	CHES 259:22
inflated s. is…euphemism	ORWE 744:45
killed…in a high s.	AUBR 45:36
Latin…Spoils your s.	FLAU 393:46
Let others worry…about s.	ARET 33:17
most money on a s.	MING 695:63
Neither action nor s.	ACHE 3:37
newspaper needs…literary s.	PULI 795:21
Not their s. to say	NYE 733:47
one must first acquire a s.	SAIN 837:92
particularly high-class s.	WAUGH 1057:82
passage of good s.	FORD 396:4
process of adopting a new life s.	COWL 291:22
Salad…is a s.	LEBO 591:83
sense of s.	GREE 444:19
So is his s.	GIBB 422:33
s. and structure	NABO 717:8
S. is a fraud	DEKO 313:18
S. is beginning	NICH 726:53
s. is not a question of technique	PROU 793:8
S. is the dress of thoughts	CHES 257:79

style (*contd.*):

s., not compositions	MORT 710:98
s. of writing	THOR 1017:93
S. one must possess	CHASE 253:97
s. purely his own	THOR 1016:73
s. should be as a skein	JONS 536:27
s. to one's character	NIET 728:75
S.…too often hides eczema	CAMUS 229:56
that was the MGM s.	LEIS 595:42
true definition of s.	SWIFT 984:77
uninhibited was his s.	MEYER 673:32
what na s.	BURNS 210:87
what s. is to an artist	BUEC 203:41
When we see a natural s.	PASC 757:54
words—noble, the grand s.	ARNO 38:8
styles Different s. for…climes	BROD 189:65
two s. of portrait painting	DICK 321:47
styling S. is designing	ISSI 514:80
suaveness isn't born of confidence	HYDE 509:15
subconscious hole in the s.	HALE 451:21
Little s. mind, say I	ONEI 740:62
subdue attempt to s.	GILL 426:5
s. one single man	SWIFT 984:78
subject black because of its s.	MORR 709:89
British s., in whatever land	PALM 752:72
clicking with the s.	EISE 364:94
discussion of any s.	SHEL 927:56
do the same s. over again	DEGAS 312:90
elegantly adapted to the s.	DRYD 348:80
Every s.'s duty	SHAK 881:92
fickle, and unstable s.	MONT 701:61
I never s. myself to hours	RABE 799:85
individual s.	HORS 494:38
interested…not in its s.	SANT 842:89
introduce the s. of eating	HUNT 505:31
know a s. ourselves	JOHN 529:74
look like the s.	DALI 303:45
Math was my worst s.	TRIL 1026:55
no s. of England	PITT 771:68
no such thing as an uninteresting s.	CHES 258:94
see how the s. quakes!	SHAK 903:34
serious s.	ARNO 38:8
Spare…for his s. sake	COWP 292:43
Stick to your s.	CATO 245:54
s. …concept, structure	POUS 787:99
s. for this heroic song	MILT 692:98
s. full of natural error	PASC 757:55
s. is to the painter	RIVE 812:2
s. matter of the artist	WILDE 1076:46
s. that should never	THOM 1015:60
s. to the judgment	SCHI 847:66
s. …to this vice of lying!	SHAK 877:99
theory of the s. is complete	MILL 674:59
woman…a s. in marriage	STAN 963:90
worst mistakes…in his s.	HEIS 467:79
subject-matter nobility of s.-m.	WILDE 1076:32
subjection to woman's s.	STAN 963:89
attract Thy love, not thy s.	MILT 693:17
subjective begin from the s.	SART 844:13
subjectivity universe of human s.	SART 844:18
subjects best s. for artists	HEIN 467:75
ignorant, only on different s.	ROGE 821:45
model the minds of his s.	STEU 970:30
pray To several s.	SHAK 897:75
prosperous and happy s.	MORE 707:48
soujourners and passing s.	MUIR 712:32
S. choose me	MOORE 705:29
s. for a pair of…saints	SHAK 867:62
Talk about those s.	HOLM 486:90
tyrant has in common with s.	BROD 189:67
Unmarried men…not always best s.	BACON 57:59
were their s. wise	COWP 293:61
sublimation s. of the work instinct	LODGE 610:81
sublime dandy must aspire to be s.	BAUD 78:39

sublime (*contd.*):

Howls the s.	DICK 323:83
object all s.	GILB 425:90
science of the s.	CIXO 267:77
short from the S.	GRAH 437:86
step above the s.	PAINE 751:53
s. position but not a secure one	BERN 96:75
s., there yet lurks	MELV 667:36
'the s.' In the old sense	POUND 785:60
torture into aught of the s.	POE 775:41
submerged s. beneath the surface	GERH 420:5
submission coy s., modest pride	MILT 690:56
have an attitude for s.	ELIOT 366:31
starving them into s.	MANC 644:63
submissive Remember to be s.	AESC 9:60
subordinate all other ends are s.	PIUS 772:81
subsequence s. for consequence	JOHN 525:73
subsidy government s.	ANON 29:40
public s. of intelligence	QUINE 797:81
subsist enable the labourers…to s.	RICA 808:37
s. on ideas	BALZ 69:80
subsistence not any s. without a mind	BERK 95:51
S.…increases in arithmetical ratio	MALT 643:37
unlimited Means of S.	CANT 230:31
withdraw your means of s.	STEV 977:61
substance body and s. of his works	COLE 275:29
change of s.	MANN 645:80
Charisma without s.	CAMP 226:9
decision-making, not s.	KISS 566:38
Each s. of a grief	SHAK 867:50
empty of all human s.	SAIN 837:88
is the s. of men	SWIN 988:49
man of s.	ELLI 375:16
merchantis full of s.	DUNB 355:39
My s. was not hid from thee	BIBLE 120:50
one s. with the Father	BOOK 174:19
one that sucks his s.	LAMB 576:29
renews and varies its s.	OVID 747:3
set her foot upon thy s.	BIBLE 132:95
s. consisting in infinite attributes	SPIN 961:60
s. into that fat belly	SHAK 877:88
s. of my dreams	SASS 845:30
suck out the very s.	RABE 798:79
summed with all his s.	CHAP 252:68
wasted his s. with riotous living	BIBLE 143:98
worth, not s.	MILT 687:4
substances Even forms and s.	WORD 1096:30
substitute adequate s. for wit	PRIE 790:45
applied to some God's	RUNC 828:52
bloodless s. for life	STEV 974:17
excellent and nutritious s.	DOUG 341:60
in creating a s.	PAGE 749:32
most flawless proof…is no s.	EDDI 360:19
no s. for talent	HUXL 506:58
no s. for victory	MACA 621:73
offer abuse as a s.	GALL 412:94
Shouting is not a s.	STEV 972:78
s. for real experience	ALBEE 11:83
s. shines brightly as a king	SHAK 873:4
test is a mere s.	MUSS 716:86
substructure economic s.	FANON 382:59
subterfuge s. for hiding something	CALAS 225:94
subtle almost invariably s.	STRA 979:97
God is s.	EINS 363:61
know not well the s. ways	EMER 377:64
schoolman's s. art	POPE 781:69
serpent more s.	BIBLE 103:93
s., but savage	CAPO 231:85
subtlest s. and most poetic	FOWL 400:70
subtleties I do not deal with s.	BIRK 163:23
s., not made to rule	MILT 694:39
subtlety brother came with s.	BIBLE 105:33
s. of nature	BACON 55:27
subtraction that's s.	WEST 1067:81

suburban mowers on s. lawns — RICK 811:74
s. prejudice of anti-Semitism — POUND 787:90
suburbs Chekhov of the s. — LEON 596:68
Dwell I but in the s. — SHAK 883:30
subversion do not like s. or disloyalty — HELL 468:93
subversive funny is s. — ORWE 743:22
seen by dictators as s. — JONG 533:61
subway perspective of a s. tunnel — TOOLE 1023:4
succedaneum Science...a s. — WORD 1096:24
succeed all right if the talks s. — ZHOU 1109:23
If at first you don't s. — HICK 480:99
not enough to s. — VIDAL 1044:64
s. as his inheritor — SHAK 910:98
s. in being obscure — HORA 493:30
s. unconventionally — KEYN 555:40
succeeded only thing we haven't s. in — HUXL 507:72
succeeding just when they were s. — REST 807:17
success any chance of s. — KISS 566:34
argue...after...your technical s. — OPPE 741:71
Eighty percent of s. — ALLEN 14:51
For an actress to be a s. — BARR 73:56
gained for the universe by s. — JAMES 517:44
harness of their s. — HAMM 453:45
hope of s. — SMITH 949:59
howling commercial s. — GREE 444:23
If A is s. in life — EINS 363:72
it deifies s. — TWAIN 1034:11
May all s. — GILB 425:81
no s. without hard work — SOPH 953:20
not in mortals to command s. — ADDI 8:28
not solved by s. — WHITE 1070:41
owed his lack of s. to nobody — HELL 468:80
religion...is S. — BARR 73:50
S. and failure are both difficult — HELL 468:86
s. and miscarriage — JOHN 526:6
s. comes before work — KIMB 557:66
s. four flights — WRIG 1102:13
s. happens to an English writer — AMIS 17:89
S. hath made me — JONS 534:83
s. hide its emptiness — HAMM 453:48
S. in Circuit lies — DICK 328:11
s. in war — CHUR 264:17
S. instead of — MILL 677:8
S. is a great deodorant — TAYL 992:17
S. is counted sweetest — DICK 327:90
S. is disgraceful — MENC 669:68
S. is feminine — FAUL 384:87
S. is in the silences — CARM 236:4
S. is relative — ELIOT 371:37
S. is the American Dream — LEGU 594:29
s. isn't everything — HELL 468:95
S. never depended on pandering — BEAV 81:88
The play was a great s. — WILDE 1077:64
triumphant with far-ranging s. — COMM 278:66
true s. is to labour — STEV 974:17
vanquished by his own s. — SCHI 847:69
With his surcease s. — SHAK 907:31
successes important...as his s. — AGAS 9:61
pleasure at his own s. — RYLE 834:54
successful Horrible as s. artists — JONG 534:66
no matter how s. — JOHN 524:58
or s. without love — TROL 1028:97
S. crimes alone are justified — DRYD 350:40
s. in business — GILL 427:13
The more s. the villain — HITC 482:26
To be a s. father — HEMI 471:48
too lucky or too s. — JONG 534:69
succession interminable s. — EINS 363:63
s. and Horatio Alger in one — MAMET 644:57
successor science the s. — RUSS 832:21
succinct try my hardest to be s. — HORA 493:30
succour for s. flee — SPEN 957:92
succumb too...resourceful to s. — HOFS 484:62
suck s. melancholy out of a song — SHAK 885:87

suck (*contd.*):
s. out the very substance — RABE 798:79
sucker Never Give a S. — FIEL 388:60
s. born every minute — BARN 72:38
suckers green s. of youth — SHER 933:96
sucklings mouth of babes and s. — BIBLE 114:34
sucks s. us all up — SEXT 859:67
Where the bee s., there suck I — SHAK 917:41
Sudan at your 'ome in the S. — KIPL 560:34
sudden all of a s. it hits me — SIEG 937:67
s., and quick in quarrel — SHAK 885:92
s. with summer — SCOTT 852:37
suede blue s. shoes — PERK 766:99
Suez somewhere east of S. — KIPL 560:27
S. canal...flowing through — EDEN 360:24
suffer better to s. than to die — LAFO 574:79
Better one s. — DRYD 349:21
But doth s. a sea-change — SHAK 916:26
does not the woman always s. — BALZ 69:76
don't have to s. to be a poet — CIAR 266:52
have the courage to s. — TROL 1027:66
if he makes others s. — SZASZ 989:68
if so be that we s. with him — BIBLE 149:27
leaders who make them s. — SIHA 938:73
Life...makes us s. — ANOU 30:73
make them s. before I pack...in — CHAR 253:95
prepared to s. for it — BENN 91:90
s. for the Good — KIER 556:56
s. from the strangest sense — WELLS 1064:27
S. her self — WALL 1050:71
s. hym ...to wynne his spurres — EDWA 361:47
s. in one's whole self — LAWR 585:67
S. me to come to thee — WESL 1066:61
s. through no fault of their own — ELIZ 374:96
s. what is difficult to s. — HIRO 481:18
voice of those who s. — CESA 248:2
sufferance s. is the badge — SHAK 874:20
suffered greatly, have s. greatly — TENN 994:58
He who has s. much — ANON 21:62
s. at my side — SASS 845:31
s. in his spirit — HOMER 488:24
s....the neurotic ills — ISHE 513:73
women s. in the United States — FRIE 405:49
sufferers We have been the s. — BEVAN 101:62
suffering About s. ...never wrong — AUDEN 47:59
by s. even animals could — HEINE 467:70
Deep, unspeakable s. — ELIOT 365:11
Doing or s., — MILT 687:95
Give us back our s. — NIGH 729:96
good time for s. — GOLD 432:88
learn in s. — SHEL 927:69
likely to lead to s. — BERL 96:69
loved the s. many — BENT 93:19
s., and some risks — PEARY 762:35
s. from galloping consumption — GAND 414:12
s. from the particular disease — JERO 521:6
s., the agony, the tender words — WHIT 1071:61
tell of their s. — ACHE 2:19
the day you stop s. — WILL 1082:74
To each his s. — GRAY 441:48
victim of creative s. — KING 557:81
You can't avoid s. — COOP 287:46
suffers every observer necessarily s. — ORWE 745:50
one who does, not s. wrong — SHEL 929:14
suffice ice...would s. — FROST 407:85
sufficiency An elegant s. — THOM 1015:48
s. is of God — BIBLE 151:75
sufficient S. to have stood — MILT 689:34
Suffolk S. used to worship Sunday — BLYT 170:53
suffrage English have used to s. — CARL 236:85
Universal s. is counter-revolution — PROU 792:86
universal s. prevails — PARE 753:83
suffragists militant s. — WRIG 1101:99

sugar against a pound of s. — SPEN 956:87
honey a sauce to s. — SHAK 886:11
more eloquence in a s. touch — SHAK 882:11
suggestion s., by the imagination — RUSK 830:83
suggestions absorb whispered s. — KOES 568:70
suicide depression, neurosis and s. — HELL 468:86
except the s. — HEMI 470:25
excessive tolerance of s. — DURK 357:70
girls who have considered s. — SHAN 918:68
human race commit s. — ADAMS 5:71
not even s. — STEV 974:10
s. 25 years after his death — BEAV 81:83
s. is a great source — NIET 728:88
s. is not a very intelligent — KENT 553:8
s. kills two people — MILL 677:5
s. notes — PLOUT 775:35
S.: that mysterious route — HUGO 502:92
Twenty Volume S. Note — BARA 70:6
upright, or commit s. — MISH 696:75
war...it is s. — MACD 629:6
who have considered s. — WEBB 1058:16
suicides s. have a special language — SEXT 859:65
suit A silk s. — PEPYS 765:61
fresh s. of bright white linen — HERB 476:42
man in a large check s. — WELLS 1064:36
thousand dollar s. — ANON 29:47
suitcases s. are much better — SALI 838:23
suitor think that you are Anne's s. — SHAW 921:30
suits customary s. of solemn — TWAIN 1033:89
middle-aged men in dark s. — ABBO 1:1
s. of woe — SHAK 888:57
wear strange s. — SHAK 886:19
sulky s. Scottish spirit — SCOTT 856:11
sullen cope him in these s. fits — SHAK 885:79
genius was too s. — DRYD 347:63
I knew that s. hall — OWEN 748:15
s. cold Exhausted face? — SASS 845:32
Sullivan Gilbert to someone else's S. — RUSS 833:40
sulphur oat-cakes and s. — SMITH 949:49
Puffed its s. — BETJ 100:39
Sultan S.'s turret — FITZ 390:87
sultans Both S. of Swat — LARD 580:92
sultry where the climate's s. — BYRON 222:28
sum final s. never balances — MO 698:12
proportion to the s. involved — PARK 755:33
rolling up the s. — WILL 1082:88
s. and substance, of capitalist — MARX 660:21
s. of all the choices gone before? — DIDI 330:44
s. of the interests of...members — BENT 92:12
the s. of all matter is constant — OVID 747:3
worked out the s. themselves — KIER 556:54
Sumatra giant rat of S. — DOYLE 344:20
summer after many a s. — TENN 1003:21
all s. settled there and died — LARK 581:97
All through that s. — MUIR 712:28
chords of s. — DAYL 310:55
dark s. dawns — TENN 997:4
dead long s. days — BYRON 222:41
dream On s. eves — MILT 682:4
fantastic s.'s heat? — SHAK 866:47
grace a s. queen — SCOTT 854:67
guest of s. — SHAK 907:30
how costly s. was — SHAK 875:33
if it takes all s. — GRANT 439:8
In s., quite the other way — STEV 975:71
It was a s. evening — SOUT 954:31
last rose of s. — MOORE 706:35
last s. of its kind — HOLL 485:71
like a s. birdcage — WEBS 1059:30
Like s. tempest — TENN 997:8
live murmur of a s.'s day — ARNO 37:86
love in s.'s wonderland — NOYES 732:3
Made glorious s. — SHAK 862:45
mosquitoey s. night light — ASHB 41:57

summer (*contd.*):

no s. progress	ANDR 19:13
oldest griefs of s.	RICK 811:74
one swallow does not make a s.	ARIS 34:26
same winter and s.	SHAK 872:80
silent s. heaven	TENN 1004:56
Singest of s.	KEATS 547:13
studying all the s. night	MARV 658:79
sudden with s.	SCOTT 852:37
S. afternoon—s. afternoon	JAMES 517:31
s. all the year round	ORWE 743:10
s. droops, droop men	NASHE 721:81
S. in Winter	CRAS 295:18
s. is ended	BIBLE 128:23
s. is eternal	GUY 449:96
S. is icumen in	ANON 22:67
s.'s lease	SHAK 912:48
S. loves to sport	COLL 277:49
s. out of winter	DONNE 339:26
s. sang to me	MILL 676:88
s. soldier and the sunshine patriot	PAINE 750:42
s. winds that creep	SHEL 927:61
S....with its usual severity	COLE 275:23
sunlight of your s. day	ARLO 34:37
thou, O S.	BLAKE 165:58
thro endless s. days	DICK 328:96
through the s. is not heard	SHEL 927:63
through the s. suns	RICE 809:40
waken from his s. dreams	SHEL 928:88
way to ensure s. in England	WALP 1051:87
winter's big with s.	SACK 835:59

summer-dried s.-d. fountain   SCOTT 854:64
summer-fruits Beauty is as s.-f.   BACON 59:12
summer-gale sun and s.-g.   GRAY 443:89
summer-house S.-h. ...no shade   POPE 779:21
summers ninety s. had Death   EGAN 362:55

raw inclement s.	SWIFT 985:86
So many s. dry	SHAK 912:42
thousand s. are over	SWIN 986:20

summertime In s. in Bredon   HOUS 494:49
summit ascend to its s.   PAVL 761:19

at the s. of the world	PEARY 763:36
made to rest on its s.	NAPO 719:37
someone thought of s. meetings	ACHE 2:22
s. of these pyramids	NAPO 718:24

summits Nations touch at their s.   BAGE 61:58
   snowy s. old   TENN 997:98
summons s. thee to heaven   SHAK 908:41

Upon a fearful s.	SHAK 887:44
when fate s., monarchs must obey	DRYD 348:81

sums size of s. of money   HUXL 508:93
sun After the greatest clouds, the s.   ALAN 11:78

against a setting s.	SHAK 901:88
Aldershot s.	BETJ 100:35
all the s. that shines?	SHAK 916:10
And I will sing of the s.	POUND 785:47
And the s. went down	TENN 1005:58
apples of the s.	YEATS 1105:63
as the s. at noon	DONNE 339:26
beauty of the s.	SHAK 860:74
before you let the s. in	THOM 1011:82
beneath the S.	KIPL 563:98
between me and the s.	BLUN 170:46
black cloud carries the s. away	ELIOT 370:28
blessed s. himself	SHAK 875:36
Born of the s.	SPEN 956:72
bosom-friend of the maturing s.	KEATS 547:4
Bright as the s., her eyes	POPE 778:93
broad s. Is sinking down	WORD 1097:40
Busy old fool, unruly s.	DONNE 336:77
by the s. and candlelight	BROW 197:19
cannot make our s.	MARV 658:76
chambers of the s.	BLAKE 165:55
Close to the s.	TENN 1000:64

sun (*contd.*):

cock who thought the s. had risen	ELIOT 365:10
Copper s. or scarlet sea	CULL 299:68
countenance was as the s.	BIBLE 156:99
Cricket...worship in summer s.	BLUN 170:50
dawn upon them like the s.	RAND 801:25
description of the rising s.	SHER 934:9
Doubt thou the s. doth move	SHAK 889:91
earth is still going round the s.	ORWE 744:40
Education is another s.	HERA 473:83
enjoyed the s.	ARNO 36:67
eyes are nothing like the s.	SHAK 915:92
flakes burn in the sinking s.	SHEL 927:60
flush of a new-born s.	KIPL 561:40
from the searching s.	RALE 800:14
glory flames from s. and star	HOLM 486:98
Go out in the midday s.	COWA 290:97
going down of the s.	BINY 162:7
he beheld the s.	WORD 1100:79
heat of the s.	WHITE 1070:31
heavens' glorious s.	SHAK 865:5
in s. and shower	WORD 1095:6
in the s., in Regent's Park	WOOLF 1092:59
ivory s.	PIER 769:34
kiss of the s.	GURN 449:88
labour which he taketh under the s.?	BIBLE 122:14
land stares at the s.	SCOTT 852:37
Laughed in the s.	BROO 192:17
like a raisin in the s.?	HUGH 499:18
little window where the s.	HOOD 489:37
live by an invisible s.	BROW 196:4
London spread out in the s.	LARK 581:6
love that moves the s.	DANTE 305:73
love to all men 'neath the s.!	KIPL 564:4
maketh his s. to rise	BIBLE 134:45
meet the s. upon the upland lawn	GRAY 442:76
mix...the s. with punctuations	BRAU 186:19
Move him into the s.	OWEN 748:18
neither shall the s. light on them	BIBLE 157:15
Never did s. more beautifully steep	WORD 1097:46
no Cloud nor S.	DONNE 339:34
no homage unto the s.	BROW 196:93
no new thing under the s.	BIBLE 122:16
No s.—no moon!	HOOD 489:51
not a place in the s.	DULL 354:26
observations of the s.	STUA 980:8
on which the s. never sets	NORTH 731:30
our own place in the s.	BULOW 204:54
our place in the s.	WILH 1080:37
Ours. is one of 100 billion	BRAUN 186:21
over the fjord—the s.	MUNCH 713:51
pleasures Known under the s.	REID 806:98
proudest country under the s.	PARK 755:31
Quick-glancing with the s.	GRAY 441:58
quietest places Under the s.	HOUS 495:60
Rain, rain, and s.!	TENN 1003:35
rays of the s.	KIPL 563:80
robbed even the s.	MACM 636:24
ruin any pastime under the s.	MITF 697:93
sea escaping with the s.	RIMB 812:94
see the s. the other way round?	BISH 164:33
setting s.	GARL 415:27
shadow in the s.	ELIZ 373:89
shadow in the s.	SHAK 863:48
sitting in the s.	SOUT 954:31
softe was the s.	LANG 579:69
stand out of my s.	DIOG 331:60
stands an instant in the s.	HYDE 509:14
stipple leaves with s.	SACK 835:61
s. and moon to give them light	DICK 323:90
s. and moon Were in	MILT 683:25
s. and summer-gale	GRAY 443:89
s. and the rain are flying	STEV 976:56
s. behind the Downs	BETJ 100:51

sun (*contd.*):

s. came dazzling	TENN 993:43
s. climbs slow	CLOU 270:32
s. comes up with a word	CURN 301:13
s. could not be reproduced	CEZA 248:7
s. delights to peep	SHAK 913:54
s. doth parch the green	SURR 983:46
s. farthest off	ANDR 19:13
s. go down upon your wrath	BIBLE 152:1
s. has gane down	TANN 991:96
s. has gone in	SMITH 948:23
s. has gone to rest	LAUD 583:39
s. has left the sky	STEV 975:41
s. hums down	THOM 1011:88
s. is coming down to earth	MERE 671:1
s. is daily new and old	SHAK 914:75
s. is going down	SMITH 948:35
s. is lost	DONNE 338:11
s. itself is but the dark simulacrum	BROW 196:5
s. loste his hewe	CHAU 255:39
s., moon, and stars, brother	BORR 179:23
S. of righteousness arise	BIBLE 131:72
s. of suns	DICK 325:31
s. of the socialist revolution	LENIN 595:50
s....on the...Australian bush	LAWS 587:14
s. poured in like butterscotch	MITC 696:82
s. provides the moon	ANAX 18:99
s. Rises upon a world	HUGH 500:41
s. rose and set on their land	SITT 940:98
s. rose in your eyes	MACC 626:62
s. shall not smite thee	BIBLE 119:36
s. shines bright on Loch Lomond	ANON 24:1
s. that lights the ages	CASAL 243:24
s. that warms you	SHAK 866:2
s. that was seen by Whitman's eyes	BORG 179:12
s. was darkened	BIBLE 144:18
s. was shining on the sea	CARR 240:55
s. was up, they were scorched	BIBLE 137:97
s. went around the earth	ARNO 40:44
s. will not rise	HOMER 488:25
sweetheart of the s.	HOOD 489:39
The kind old s.	OWEN 748:19
the s. ...has gone down	ORAH 741:78
The s. has left the lea	SCOTT 855:3
the s. loves him	SMART 944:67
tired the s. with talking	CORY 288:63
to the rime-ringed s.	KIPL 565:19
too much i' th' s.	SHAK 888:47
under the s. and moon	GOLD 432:89
unwearied s. from day to day	ADDI 7:22
upon the quickening s.	DONNE 336:70
upper boulders in the s.	FROST 406:72
use of the s. and the planets	LEAC 588:34
Vermeer gave to the s.'s	LOWE 617:14
walks under the midday s.	MILT 683:28
wanton with the s.	MILT 681:86
watch the s. set again	RHYS 808:30
We make guilty...the s.	SHAK 902:2
When the s. goes down	BOND 172:79
where no s. shines	THOM 1010:52
where'er the s.	WATTS 1055:57
Wherever there is s.	BEAU 80:75
While the s....be not darkened	BIBLE 123:21
wind up the s. and moon	BYRON 223:66
With the dying s.	BOUR 181:48
with the s. to match	BROW 200:81
with the s.	KEN 549:60
woman clothed with the s.	BIBLE 157:20
worlds...circle round the s.	DICK 324:20

sun-girt S.-g. city, thou hast been   SHEL 927:71
sun-gods s.-g. and the like   FRYE 408:21
sunbeams extracting s.-b.   SWIFT 985:86

fatuous s. toil	OWEN 748:20
motes that people the s.	MILT 682:5

sunbeams (*contd.*):
s. dart through them — SHEL 927:60
sunbonnet s. as well as the sombrero — FERB 385:6
Sunday feeling of S. — RHYS 808:29
first drink on a S. morning — MACC 627:68
first S. in a new chariot — CONG 282:44
golf may be played on a S. — LEAC 589:42
Here of a S. morning — HOUS 495:50
married o' S. — SHAK 864:79
rainy S. in London — DEQU 316:64
smelt like S. afternoons — THOM 1012:95
than a pig on S. — TRUM 1030:21
worship S., not God — BLYT 170:53
sundial I am a s. — BELL 87:20
sundials mottoes on s. — POUND 785:61
sundown eldritch light of s. — DAYL 310:56
sodden towards s. — ELIOT 372:67
s. makes them mournful — BLUN 170:40
sundry s. contemplation — SHAK 886:16
sunflower s., weary of time — BLAKE 167:87
S., you were a s. — GINS 428:26
sung not worth being said is s. — BEAU 79:59
s. her first and last — GIBB 422:32
s. of Border chivalry — SCOTT 853:42
sunlight brooks the s. worse — JONS 536:16
fair s. of God — MACD 628:99
s. falls across the country — IHIM 510:30
S. is the best disinfectant — KENN 550:60
s. of your summer day — ARLO 34:37
s. on a stream — ROSS 823:67
s. streaming merciless — ATWO 44:17
superficial as a puddle in the s. — LEAC 589:38
upwards into hard s. — CUMM 299:76
weave the s. in your hair — ELIOT 367:60
will be s. later — MACN 637:43
sunny s. pleasure-dome — COLE 275:15
s. side of the street — FIEL 388:65
sunrise like s. from the sea — SHEL 932:63
Lives in Eternity's s. — BLAKE 166:82
s. brings back brightness — BLUN 170:40
suns gleam of a million…s.? — TENN 1005:69
light of setting s. — WORD 1094:98
process of the s. — TENN 996:79
remember through the summer s. — RICE 809:40
road to s. — SCOTT 852:36
sky cannot have two s. — CHIA 260:50
S. that set may rise — JONS 534:85
What other planets circle other s. — POPE 780:34
sunset sail beyond the s. — TENN 995:61
seen dawn and s. on moors — MASE 662:39
shadow that…loses itself in the s. — HAGG 450:5
sight of Etna at s. — WAUGH 1057:88
slow, exquisite coming on of s. — COOKE 286:32
sulphur to the s. — BETJ 100:39
S. and evening bell — TENN 1005:66
S. and silence! — COLUM 277:5
S. divides the sky — BYRON 220:94
s. fadeth in the west — SHAK 914:73
urine dump at s. — SCHW 851:30
sunset-touch there's a s.-t. — BROW 198:54
sunshades Sit around under s. — JOYCE 538:55
sunshine calm s. of the heart — CONS 285:18
Disgressions…are the s. — STER 969:96
into adventure and s. — FORS 398:30
Love comforteth like s. — SHAK 864:93
Scotsman…and a ray of s. — WODE 1089:1
shadows in a s. day? — MARL 653:4
s. patriot will…shrink — PAINE 750:42
the thunder and s. — TENN 995:61
sup s. upon myself — SHAK 911:13
s. with him, and he with me — BIBLE 157:7
superficiality discussed as s. — BURKE 208:53
superfluous s. in me to point out — ADAMS 4:64
s. to demand the time — SHAK 875:36

superfluous (*contd.*):
The s., a very necessary thing — VOLT 1046:99
trip to Europe would be s. — SAAR 834:55
superflux S. of pain — SWIN 987:30
superhuman s. undertaking — GIRA 428:42
superincumbent s. hour — SHEL 931:43
superior ask a s. to publish — HOPK 492:95
Justice is s. — PLATO 774:26
lawful power is still s. — DRYD 350:33
of the feudal s. — MILL 675:80
relieved to find a s. — TUCH 1031:47
rise s. to all considerations — STEV 973:92
s. creation — HARD 455:76
s. persons can remain s. — ORWE 742:92
s. to all …despotism — PITT 772:73
s. to any imaginative exercise — VIDAL 1044:58
that is sick Of his s. — SHAK 895:41
Titles…embarrass the s. — SHAW 922:50
superiority laugh of s. — GREE 445:28
s. of one man's opinion — JAMES 516:22
s. of the Greeks — FUSE 410:59
superiors councils of their s. — LEST 599:13
superlatives s.… worn shoddy — FITZ 391:21
superman between animal and S. — NIET 728:77
teach you the S. — NIET 728:76
supernatural by s. means — HOOK 489:55
case, was s. — MILL 675:73
evidence of s. beings — STEI 967:68
s. source of evil — CONR 285:8
superpower resources of a s. — SCHA 847:60
s. in the military and nuclear sense — WALE 1049:50
supersensitive s.…instrument — ERNST 379:11
superstition In all s. wise men — BACON 58:84
poison of enthusiasm and s. — SMITH 945:82
religion…true remedy for s. — BURKE 207:10
s. in avoiding s. — BACON 58:85
S. is the poetry of life — GOET 431:76
s. of an antiquated diplomacy — CECIL 247:85
S. religion of feeble minds — BURKE 208:37
S. sets the…world in flames — VOLT 1046:7
superstitions end as s. — HUXL 508:2
town whence s. comes — LESL 598:94
superstitious edge to the s. tale — PRIT 791:64
men of Athens…ye are too s. — BIBLE 148:1
must be benighted and s. — JAMES 518:51
superstructure dubiousness of…s. — DESC 317:81
economic substructure is also a s. — FANON 382:59
supped I have s. full with horrors — SHAK 910:85
supper After s. Pap took the jug — TWAIN 1033:83
Hope…is a bad s. — BACON 56:39
know s.'s ready — STEI 966:55
supple meets me soft and s. — FLET 394:75
suppliant thus the s. prays — JOHN 525:83
supplication s. of a dead man's hand — ELIOT 369:99
s. to the rose — FLEC 393:50
supplications voice of my s. — BIBLE 119:44
supply promise of s. — SHAK 877:86
see that s. is not tainted — SCOTT 852:43
steady s. of funerals — SHAW 926:43
support ask for your s. — NIXON 730:10
help and s. of the woman I love — EDWA 362:51
mutually s. one another — PARS 756:45
no invisible means of s. — BUCH 202:27
prepared to s. them — LAW 585:59
s. a flagging conversation — HUNT 505:31
s. my cat — GRAV 440:31
s. rather than illumination — LANG 579:66
to have everybody's s. — OLLI 738:33
what is low raise and s. — MILT 687:86
without nourishment and s. — SMOL 950:64
supporter no s. from the…earth — SHAK 872:64
supporters pregnant s. — BAIL 62:72
suppress easy to s.…the truth — CORN 288:61
s. one's vanity — JAMES 515:3

suppressed could not be generally s. — HOOV 490:61
must be s. — DENG 315:51
suppression no…accuracy of s. — BELL 88:22
supreme presuppose a S. Being — DOUG 342:70
sure Be s. your sin will find you out — BIBLE 108:88
grinds slow, but s. — HERB 476:40
hateth suretiship is s. — BIBLE 121:70
make s. he was dead — GOLD 434:49
surety s. for a stranger — BIBLE 121:70
surface crawl upon the s. — SWIFT 985:84
Errors…upon the s. flow — DRYD 348:85
in the lake…under the s. — ATWO 44:16
just below the s. — RUSS 832:15
mind…looks dingy on the s. — PIRS 770:56
monotony of a watery s. — MOORE 705:14
painting…is essentially a flat s. — DENIS 316:58
s. of articulate apprehension — GERH 420:5
thrown On the s. — WORD 1101:94
surfaces painterly s. — POPO 783:14
representation of s. and solids — PIERO 769:38
surfeit s. of the sweetest things — SHAK 871:41
s. with too much — SHAK 874:10
surge s. …In every Russian's…heart — PUSH 795:37
surgeon abilities of brain s. — BRES 187:36
Hand of the s. — MAP 649:33
intimacy of a s.'s scalpel — ANGE 20:31
Picasso studies…like a s. dissects — APOL 31:90
plastic s.…responsible for this face — CUOMO 300:4
poor s. hurts one person at a time — BOYER 183:68
way a s. operates — WHITE 1070:34
wounded s. plies the steel — ELIOT 371:51
surgeons S. must be very careful — DICK 327:92
surgical s. war — ASHD 41:62
Surinam Indians of S. represented — BEHN 85:71
surpassed pleasure of not being s. — HALI 452:24
surplus-value production of s.-v. — MARX 660:21
surprise perchance, with strange s. — THOM 1014:32
Sound of S. — BALL 68:65
sure of a big s. — BRAT 185:15
s. them out of — KIPL 563:88
Truth's superb s. — DICK 328:11
surprised Don't be s. — HEAN 465:38
s. by joy — WORD 1099:76
s. they had remembered — PRIT 791:66
s. to find it done at all — JOHN 528:39
surprises S. are foolish things — AUST 52:57
surrealism I am s. — DALI 303:49
surrealists Dali's…for the S. — SCHW 851:23
surrender daring of a moment's s. — ELIOT 369:96
Guards…do not s. — CAMB 226:7
never s. — CHUR 264:14
path of s. — KENN 551:73
see the s. of Quebec — MONT 702:76
shall never s. — CHUR 264:14
s. required, and deprivation inflicted — ELIOT 370:35
s.…was as honorable as resistance — ANGE 19:19
unconditional and immediate s. — GRANT 439:7
worst thing…is s. — ORWE 744:47
surrendered never s. before — NORM 731:27
Surrey full S. twilight! — BETJ 100:36
surroundings see only my s. — ELLI 375:16
surveillance keep me under s. — WANG 1052:13
survey exact s. of the land — DONNE 339:32
S. mankind — JOHN 525:81
s. of all the world — SHAK 876:75
survival insures the s. of the fittest — CARN 236:6
necessary for s. of the fittest — PALEY 751:60
struggle for s. — ROTH 825:5
s. had depended on…reading — ANGE 20:32
s. of the fittest — SPEN 955:66
s. of the fittest — SUMN 981:27
s. of the vulgarest — WILDE 1076:41
We are s. machines — DAWK 310:43
survive Can capitalism s.? — SCHU 851:18

survive (*contd.*):

continue to s.	TRUM 1030:22
fitted to s.	GOLD 432:87
s. with that equipment	DAVIS 308:27
those will s. whose functions	SPEN 955:66
To eat, to s.	STAN 963:92

survived Peanut butter has s.   KEIL 548:26

they who s. fought and drank	DAVIS 309:38

survivor lone s.   ANON 29:43

survivors are relentless s.   BUCK 203:37

more the s.'s affair	MANN 646:85
nuclear war s.	COUP 289:81
struggle won by s.	ANGE 19:20

suspect no matter how s.   VIDAL 1044:58

nothing makes a man s.	BACON 59:5

suspects Round up the usual s.   EPST 379:3

suspend s. my audience's power   HARD 456:80

s. the functioning of the imagination	HEMI 471:35

suspended Illinois...s. animation   OHARA 737:12

s. in me	ATWO 45:25
s. my religious inquiries	GIBB 421:27

suspenders must not forget the S.   KIPL 562:74

suspension willing s. of disbelief   COLE 275:20

suspicion banish squint s.   MILT 683:29

Caesar's wife must be beyond s.	CAES 225:85
Democracy is the recurrent s.	WHITE 1070:27
have a s. it's inevitable	LEAC 589:48
rich with s.	RICH 809:43
s. that electricity	THUR 1018:18
true loves without s.	SPEN 958:19

suspicions S. amongst thoughts   BACON 59:4

suspicious more s. of adjectives   SAND 841:73

Sussex bury my body in S. grass   BENET 90:62

S. by the sea!	KIPL 563:93
S. countryside	GRANT 438:4

sustenance S. for their helpless   SWIFT 985:97

sutlers sapient s. of the Lord   ELIOT 367:65

swaddled S. with darkness   ELIOT 368:69

swaddling-clothes him in s.-c.   BIBLE 142:77

swagman once was a s. camped   PATE 760:96

swain Be just, my lovely s.   BEHN 85:67

labouring s.	GOLD 432:8
no better than a homely s.	SHAK 862:22
with my dear s.	BALL -101:33

swains all our s. commend her?   SHAK 860:87

Muses sing of happy s.	CRAB 293:70

swallow Daffodils...before the s.   SHAK 911:30

flies with s.' wings	SHAK 863:60
O sister s.	SWIN 986:20
O tell her, S.	TENN 997:5
one s. does not make a summer	ARIS 34:26
s. a nest for herself	BIBLE 117:93
s. twitt'ring	GRAY 442:64
s. up death in victory	BIBLE 125:73

swallow-flights Short s.-f. of song   TENN 999:34

swallowed or be s.   TRUM 1030:32

swallows passage of s.   WHITE 1070:31

swam think you have s. in a gondola   SHAK 886:19

swamps bellowing across the...s.   WODE 1089:91

swan dies the s.   TENN 1003:21

every goose a s.	KING 558:94
full-breasted s.	TENN 1004:49
great pool a s.'s nest	SHAK 916:10
like a sleeping s.	SHEL 930:24
silver s.	GIBB 422:32
s. in the evening	COLUM 278:60
s. on...St Mary's Lake	WORD 1098:57
Sweet S. of Avon!	JONS 536:11
wild s. of a world	JEFF 520:85

swan-bosomed s.-b. tree   SITW 941:15

Swanee down upon the S. River   FOST 399:60

swanlike he makes a s. end   SHAK 872:79

swans Chuzzlewit suggested 'S.'   DICK 322:68

old ships sail like s.	FLEC 393:56

swans (*contd.*):

s. are geese	ARNO 39:22
take their geese for s.	BROO 193:45

swarm S. over, Death!   BETJ 99:31

swarming s. in Fords, in ocean liners   FERB 385:7

swastika Not God but a s.   PLATH 773:95

sway How fit he is to s.   MARV 657:67

s. of death	WORD 1100:90

swaying S. to and fro   HUGH 499:16

swear conscience... to s. by   STOWE 978:85

gentleman is disposed to s.	SHAK 916:99
man s. he loves me	SHAK 879:31
O s. not by the moon	SHAK 869:91
sin to s. unto a sin	SHAK 861:14
S. me, Kate	SHAK 876:62
S. not	BIBLE 155:72
s. to the Lord	HUGH 499:17

swearing cussin' and s.   STRA 979:94

take me up for s.	SHAK 915:98

swears Hardly ever s. a big, big, D—   GILB 423:55

sweat In the rank s.   SHAK 892:56

In the s. of thy face	BIBLE 103:2
Luck is a dividend of s.	KROC 569:97
miners s. their guts out	ORWE 742:92
none will s. but for promotion	SHAK 885:83
perfection's s.	WALC 1048:42
s. and blood and tears	DOUG 341:50
s. of my brow	FRAN 402:16
s. of one's brow	LIVI 607:47
s. pours down me	SAPP 842:92
wet with honest s.	LONG 611:98
wet with s.	GREE 444:4

sweating s. it out again   GREE 444:4

sweats the bloody s.   WILDE 1078:2

Sweden bold King of S.   LESL 598:94

Swedish sung by S. artists   WHAR 1068:3

sweep need of making a clean s.   DESC 317:81

s. him from my sight	SHAK 909:56

sweepings heap of random s.   HERA 474:89

sweeps Who s. a room   HERB 474:12

sweet All is not s.   JONS 535:89

buried in so s. a place	SHEL 930:33
day...never came so s.	SHAK 875:33
dead thing that smells s.	THOM 1012:8
Death is s.	ANOU 30:73
drink the s.	BIBLE 112:92
For thy s. love remembered	SHAK 913:57
Frivolity is s., in season	HORA 493:26
Heard melodies are s.	KEATS 547:8
how it was s.!	BROW 200:83
how s. and fair	WALL 1050:70
How s. are thy words	BIBLE 119:32
How s. the lily grows	HEBER 466:57
How s. the moonlight	SHAK 873:98
How sour s. music is	SHAK 868:71
if s., give thanks	SWIN 988:54
in my mouth s. as honey	BIBLE 157:19
make a s. lady sad	SHAK 895:46
mixture of the s. and the sour	LAFO 575:90
my own, my s.	TENN 1001:88
Naught so s. as melancholy	BURT 214:64
not so s. now	SHAK 893:91
not so short as s.	SHAK 868:69
shady leaves, their s. above	SPEN 958:19
So s. love seemed	BRID 187:42
So s., the sense faints	SHEL 928:88
Stolen waters are s.	BIBLE 120:67
S. and low	TENN 997:97
s. and seemly thing	HORA 493:22
s. as those	TENN 997:4
s. enemy, France	SIDN 937:54
s. full of bitterness	LYLY 620:59
S. is pleasure after pain	DRYD 351:69
S. is revenge	BYRON 222:32

sweet (*contd.*):

s. music is such art	SHAK 918:56
s. odour...doth in it live	SHAK 913:63
s. or sour	TRAV 1025:36
s. pea, that has run wild	STEV 972:65
s., s. is this human life	CORY 288:65
S. though in sadness	SHEL 928:90
Tell me not, S.	LOVE 615:66
That s. bondage	SHEL 927:58
'Tis s. to win	BYRON 222:33
would smell as s.	SHAK 868:85

sweet-apple Just as the s.-a. reddens   SAPP 842:93

sweeteners best s. of tea   FIEL 388:44

sweetest s. flower for scent   SHEL 930:30

s. music to a woeful mind	SIDN 937:49
s. way to me	KIPL 561:47

sweetheart Like the s. of the sun   HOOD 489:39

s. ran away with an actor	WINC 1086:58

sweetmeats pyramids of s.   DRYD 352:82

sweetness cannot write of s.   BELL 86:92

long s. of the simultaneity	ASHB 41:57
Love...is s.	WEBS 1061:59
no danger in s. and youth	ROCH 816:61
out of the strong came forth s.	BIBLE 109:17
passion for s. and light	ARNO 39:31
s. and light	ARNO 39:25
s. and light	SWIFT 984:58
s. fell from the air	MACL 634:81
s. fills the breast	CASW 244:35
s. never breedeth satiety	LYLY 620:61
s. of confession	FIRB 389:72
waste its s. on desert air	GRAY 442:69
where s. and light failed	FORS 398:45

sweets brought'st Thy s. along   HERB 474:11

only safe pleasure...boiled s.	CRIT 297:43
sing the s. I know	BARL 71:21
Stolen s. are always sweeter	HUNT 504:23
Stolen s. are best	CIBB 266:55
S. into your list	HUNT 505:29
s. of Burn-mill	WORD 1098:57
s. of life	CONG 281:31
S. with s. war not	SHAK 912:45
world of s. and sours	POE 776:48

swell And go to ev'ry s. affair   PORT 784:35

bones on the thrashed s.	LOWE 616:94
burnish, sprout, and s.	HERB 475:25
music...with its voluptuous s.	BYRON 219:84
peruked sea whose s.	SITW 940:2
unhurried Ground s.	ELIOT 372:59
Where the green s. is	HOPK 491:77
with its mighty s.	KEATS 544:42

swelling s. into bombast   DRYD 347:59

swerve s. neither to the right   CURZ 302:29

swerving most unnoble s.   SHAK 905:79

swift race is not to the s.   BIBLE 123:35

race is to the s.	DAVI 307:97
S. was the race	DRYD 350:29
True hope is s.	SHAK 863:60
With s., slow	HOPK 491:85

Swift S. is more Irish than Goldsmith   OBRI 733:61

swifter S., higher, stronger   ANON 25:27

Swiftian S. Lilliput   MACC 625:50

swim good night, or sink or s.   SHAK 875:44

s. to the Bermudas	WEBS 1060:57

swimmer excellence as a s.   BURKE 208:53

Like an unpractised s.	SHAK 866:35

Swinburne S. ...degenerates!   ONEI 740:59

S. is just emptiness to me	QUIL 797:63

swindler as if I were a s.   LAWR 586:92

swindles as all truly great s. are   OHEN 737:15

swine husks that the s. did eat   BIBLE 143:99

incompetent s.	SASS 845:28
men kill the fat s.	ANON 21:64
nation ruled by s.	THOM 1014:38

swine (*contd.*):
on a filthy s. — SPEN 957:3
pearls before s. — BIBLE 135:56
s. to show you — ALBEE 11:87
swine-drunk for he will be s.-d. — SHAK 901:81
swines blasted, jelly-boned s. — LAWR 585:63
swing if it ain't got that s. — ELLI 374:5
If it ain't got that s. — MILLS 680:66
swinger s. of birches — FROST 406:80
swinging keep s. after the music — HELP 469:9
swings we pulls up on the s.! — CHAL 248:11
swiped s. all the good ones — HEMI 470:16
Swiss operated by the S. — USTI 1038:80
S. are inspired hotel-keepers — MONT 701:60
S. clockmakers — STRA 979:4
switch We turned the s. — SZIL 989:71
Switzerland look upon S. — SMITH 949:43
S....had brotherly love — WELL 1063:1
S. is a small, steep country — HEMI 470:12
swivel crouch, s., tug — OBRI 734:71
swollen udder a s. wobble — RAINE 800:7
when rivers are s. — SOPH 953:18
swoop take away all at one s. — WEBS 1059:25
sword altar, s. and pen — WORD 1096:38
Arthur's s. snatched — MUNRO 714:55
brave man with a s. — WILDE 1078:98
came not to send peace, but a s. — BIBLE 136:79
carry fire and s. — PARN 756:40
caution of a s. — CLEV 269:13
China asked for a s. — BRID 188:45
could use the s. and pen — LAND 578:63
duty...to wield the s. of France — DEGA 301:47
fallen by the edge of the s. — BIBLE 132:9
father's s. he has girded — MOORE 706:34
flaming s. — BIBLE 103:3
gave them a s. — NIXON 730:16
Hold then my s. — SHAK 884:66
is that your s., or — WEST 1067:82
It is at once our s. — HUGH 501:54
let him who has a s. — HO 482:33
lightnings Thy s. — ELLE 374:1
man taketh his s. — BIBLE 131:75
may gyff you that s. — MALO 642:27
My S., I give to him — BUNY 205:74
Negro's s. — PHIL 768:23
never sheath the s. — ASQU 42:77
Nor shall my s. sleep — BLAKE 168:20
Norman arrow and s. — WILL 1080:44
oil can is mightier than the s. — DIRK 331:64
oyster...with s. will open — SHAK 878:13
peasants take up the s. — LUTH 620:48
pen is worse than the s. — BURT 214:68
pen mightier than s. — BULW 204:55
Plough...twin to the S. — COLUM 277:59
pulleth oute this s. — MALO 642:25
sharper than any twoedged s. — BIBLE 154:45
soldiers of the s. — RUSK 830:91
s. against s. — SHAK 905:83
s. has won in half a year — MOLT 699:37
s. of the Lord — BIBLE 109:15
s. of the Spirit — BIBLE 152:6
s. shall perish with the s. — BIBLE 140:52
threw the s. as farre — MALO 642:33
took his vorpal s. — CARR 239:47
Turning the word to s. — SHAK 877:2
two-edged s. in their hand — BIBLE 120:55
two-edged s. — WIEN 1074:7
watery if not faming s. — MARV 659:91
We draw the s. — WILH 1080:39
Wounds inflicted by the s. — RICH 810:69
sword-belt s.-b. upside down — LAWR 586:79
sword-pen raise my s.-p. — BURG 205:78
swords beat their s. into plowshares — BIBLE 124:57
Beat your ploughshares into s. — BIBLE 130:56

swords (*contd.*):
so we measured s. — SHAK 887:34
stout hearts and stout s. — BIRK 163:18
s., our law — SHAK 863:66
sworn I am s. brother — SHAK 868:66
s. to action — SASS 845:25
sycophancy between s. and rebellion — BAKER 63:83
sycophants surrounded by s. — HARD 455:76
syllable first s. of...advice — THOR 1016:80
last s. of recorded time — SHAK 910:86
one s. word — YOUR 1108:10
syllables number of s. — SAND 842:80
symbiosis s. of architecture — MURP 715:73
symbol education on the s. level — HUXL 508:90
In China the bat is a s. — LAWR 585:71
respect for the living s. — LABO 572:34
see nothing without a visible s. — BAGE 61:54
s. for America — ATWO 45:22
s. of an emerging middle-class — MACF 629:18
s. of Irish art — JOYCE 538:46
s. of national honor — KRUG 570:6
s. of the power — MOORE 705:25
what it is the s. of — JENK 520:99
symbolism handles s. rather like — NIGH 729:94
symbols cloudy s. of a high romance — KEATS 544:50
let us know as s. do — MACC 624:34
s. effortlessly shared — UPDI 1037:73
symmetry frame thy fearful s.? — BLAKE 167:95
Man is all s. — HERB 475:22
S. is boredom — HUGO 502:84
sympathetic s. unselfishness — SAKI 838:8
sympathies cosmopolitan s. — ROSE 823:61
sympathy awakened my maternal s. — PERE 766:90
failed to inspire s. in men — BEER 83:32
God-damned s. — WOOL 1093:84
never-failing s. and encouragement — WODE 1089:96
no intercourse and no s. — DISR 332:90
s. for the selfish — MUIR 713:40
s. with freedom — GLAD 429:53
tea and s. — ANDE 18:8
To s. with hopes and fears — SHEL 929:2
writer...universal in s. — BARN 72:31
symphonies five sweet s. — ROSS 824:83
fugues and s. have brought — SASS 845:31
symphony consort to th'angelic s. — MILT 681:90
orchestrating a s. of unhappiness — ROCK 817:73
philanthropy and s. concerts — WHAR 1068:95
s. must be like the world — MAHL 638:61
write a s. like that — DAMR 304:54
write his Ninth S. — ROY 827:41
You're a melody from a s. — PORT 784:33
symptom first s. of true love — HUGO 502:90
infallible s. — GIBB 421:21
s. of deficient vitality — STEV 974:19
s. of...emotional disturbances — VAND 1039:97
symptoms hundred good s. — POPE 783:13
s. are similar — BANKS 70:95
syndrome manifested by...s. — SELYE 858:41
Synge persons...out of S.'s plays — ONOL 734:68
synod general s. of the nation — BAIL 62:72
synonym Violation is a s. — DWOR 358:86
syntax mastery of vocabulary and s. — SAYE 846:51
shackled by the rules of s. — MACA 623:18
S. and vocabulary — MATH 663:69
synthesis Held in lunar s. — ELIOT 367:58
s. of forty-six years — STEIN 966:51
s. of hyacinths and biscuits — SAND 841:66
synthesizer Joyce was a s. — BECK 81:5
syphilis manage to avoid s. — SILVA 938:77
Syrian On arrival at a S. port — BAED 61:46
syrops lucent s. — KEATS 546:99
syrup pancake...when you pour s. — WRIG 1101:9
system Accepts into his playful s. — DUNN 356:58
American s. — HOOV 490:59

system (*contd.*):
automatic s. — MUMF 713:49
communications s. — HAYEK 462:90
empirical s. to be refuted — POPP 783:15
every computer in the human s. — GIBS 422:40
false s. of government — PAINE 750:46
got the North Pole out of my s. — PEARY 762:35
greater and more equitable s. — MACA 621:71
Love is just a s. — BARN 72:37
Observe how s. into system runs — POPE 780:34
patent s....added — LINC 605:1
science has...a s. of principles — PAINE 750:51
self...epicentre of the solar s. — PHIL 768:19
s. is benign — CRISP 297:41
s. of existence...with no eye — WIEN 1074:71
s. of soft enterprise — ARNO 40:45
s. of which they were the centre — DICK 323:90
s. that we live in — WILL 1082:71
s. which has no purpose — FROMM 406:70
tonic to the s. — LIVI 607:47
true s. of the world — ALEM 13:12
virtues of the s. — MACC 625:51
systems After that, we had s. — HOPP 493:15
are living s. — MONOD 700:45
Atoms or s. into ruin hurled — POPE 780:35
Away with s. — MERE 671:1
number of symbol s. — HUXL 508:90
Our little s. — TENN 998:17

ta thousand t.'s and Pardon's — BETJ 100:48
tabacco fumes of t. and liquors — LEWIS 602:61
going to leave off t. — LAMB 576:14
tabby Demurest of the t. kind — GRAY 441:50
tabernacle t. for the sun — BIBLE 114:44
t. of God with men — BIBLE 158:35
who shall abide in thy t.? — BIBLE 114:38
tabernacles holy place of the t. — BIBLE 116:73
How amiable are thy t. — BIBLE 117:93
t. of thy grace — SCOT 856:21
Tabitha T....called Dorcas — BIBLE 147:90
table behave mannerly at t. — STEV 975:33
clouds of the t. above — MONRO 700:48
In England...good t. manners — MIKES 674:52
gets down from the t. — SITW 940:3
Miss Bolo rose from the t. — DICK 321:29
patient etherized upon a t. — ELIOT 366:46
preparest a t. before me — BIBLE 115:50
reside at T. Mountain — HARTE 459:49
sit at the t. — HUGH 499:15
t. in a smoke-filled room — DAUG 306:93
t. in Barchester Towers — BROY 201:6
t. of brotherhood — KING 557:82
this thy T. — BOOK 175:30
Thou shalt prepare a t. — BOOK 176:67
thrown from the t. — TUTU 1032:54
table-talk Let it serve for t.-t. — SHAK 873:87
tableau t. of crimes and misfortunes — VOLT 1046:8
tablecloth Oedipus...over your t. — PAGE 749:31
tables creatures set upon t. — JOHN 529:76
furnish forth the marriage t. — SHAK 888:56
leave the word of God, and serve t. — BIBLE 147:86
My t....meet it is — SHAK 889:81
sit at rich men's t. — BROW 196:11
sitting at their dressing t. — OSBO 745:67
taboo t. birth control method — DALY 304:21
Tabor King Lear at the T. Grand — FIELD 387:40
tacit t., but constant and uniform — SMITH 946:89
tacks when you come to brass t. — ELIOT 370:12
tacky defines t. for all time — ANON 29:35
Toady, perhaps, even t. — ACHE 3:48
tact affection and t. — RUSS 832:25
tactful t. in audacity — COCT 272:62
tactics tolerate...only on t. — DULL 354:26
taedium vitae keep off the t. v. — JOHN 527:27

task (*contd.*):
Delightful t.!	THOM 1015:47
enormity of the t.	ACHE 3:34
fed your hunger like an endless t.	CRANE 294:98
Good life be now my t.	DRYD 350:50
good never will be our t.	MILT 687:95
morning sees some t.	LONG 611:99
one t. for all	KIPL 565:18
performance of the t. itself	SHIP 935:20
sets love a t. like that	HUNT 504:26
t. begun so often	MACN 637:41
t. is smoothly done	MILT 684:36
t. is trying to determine	BART 75:86
t. of science can never end	PEAR 762:32
t. which I am trying to achieve	CONR 284:88
too useless a t.	KEYN 545:29
what he reads as a t.	JOHN 527:30
What is our t.?	LLOY 609:62
Women have but one t.	COUB 289:70

tasks have been my t.   KOLL 568:76
independent thoughts, or even t.	MACL 635:96
sets us the t.	SCHW 852:31
t. could not be limited	AREN 33:16

tassels fluttering of…silk t.   DICK 322:66
tassie fill it in a silver t.   BURNS 210:97
taste a matter of t.   STEV 973:92
arbiter of t.	TACI 989:80
bad t. of the smoker	ELIOT 366:42
but not t. thee	HERR 477:58
difference of t. in jokes	ELIOT 366:43
Ghastly Good T.	BETJ 99:28
ghetto of good t.	KEIL 548:27
Good t. is better than bad t.	BENN 91:99
How sweet are thy words unto my t.	BIBLE 119:32
Impartiality is an acquired t.	RIFK 811:82
no t. for reading	SMOL 950:63
nowhere worse t.	JOWE 537:40
once they get the t.	HAZZ 464:27
pandering to the public t.	BEAV 81:88
questions of t.	ADAMS 5:75
sense of t.	BALL 68:66
splash of bad t.	VREE 1021:97
suspect his t. in higher matters	LAMB 576:20
t. and see that the Lord is good	BIBLE 115:61
t. as lightly as the Bee	JONS 536:13
t. for French clothes	SCHL 848:77
t. for simplicity cannot endure	DELA 314:22
t. my Anno Domini	FARQ 383:69
T. not when the wine-cup glistens	SCOTT 855:97
t. of codfish	GRIEG 447:59
t. of death but once	SHAK 883:33
t. the barley bree	BURNS 211:2
Though t., though genius bless	COLL 277:47
tolerate are those of t.	THUR 1019:49
undoubtedly wanted t.	WALP 1051:83
value is not in its t.	FULB 409:29
writer…must…create the t.	WORD 1099:75

taste-blind as a nation t.-b.   FISH 390:85
tastes t. greatly alter   JOHN 528:50
t. its own innocence	UPDI 1037:66
t. may not be the same	SHAW 923:66
t. no wiser book-maker	LUCAS 618:25

tattered t. coat upon a stick   YEATS 1106:79
tatters wallpaper…falling to t.   MILL 677:14
Tattle always despised Mr T.   CONG 281:19
tattoo t. soap bubbles   BROWN 194:55
tattooed Lydia The T. Lady   HARB 455:74
taught t. to be afraid   HAMM 454:56
what we call highly t.	ELIOT 366:40

tavern fear…the fist in the t.   ELIOT 370:35
good t.	JOHN 529:79
t. for his friends	DOUG 342:63

taverns sat in t. while the tempest   HOUS 496:70
tawny T. are the leaves   RANS 802:33

tax argue for t. increases   KRUG 570:5
Bats…pay no t.	BERR 98:15
hateful t.	JOHN 526:11
keeps armies of t. lawyers	WRIS 1102:20
lighten the t. burden	QUINE 797:67
put a t. on pianos	SITW 941:21
turned a t. into a diversion	STEE 964:16

taxation resists your t. in America   PITT 771:68
T. without representation	OTIS 746:75

taxed all the world should be t.   BIBLE 142:76
never t. for speech	SHAK 901:66

taxes certain as death and t.   DEFOE 312:87
death and t.	FRAN 402:12
Death and t.	MITC 697:90
no new t.	BUSH 215:87
only President who raised t.	DOLE 335:53
Only their little people pay t.	HELM 469:5
people overlaid with t.	BACON 59:3
true…as t. is	DICK 324:11

taxi empty t. arrived at 10   CHUR 265:44
going in a t.	SHAW 924:8

taxicab ears make him look like a t.   HUGH 499:13
Tay Bridge of the Silv'ry T.   MACG 630:24
Tayler Chesterton to…T.   WEST 1068:88
TB T. or not T.   ALLEN 14:37
Tchaikovsky Tell T. the news   BERRY 98:4
Tching T. prayed on the mountain   POUND 787:87
tea after t. and cakes and ices   ELIOT 367:48
afternoon or evening cup of t.	HOLM 486:3
ain't going to be no t.	MANS 647:1
assaying of t. is an art	MO 698:11
best sweeteners of t.	FIEL 388:44
ceremony known as afternoon t.	JAMES 516:14
Drinking the best t.	SNOW 950:70
give the boys a little t.	ANDE 18:8
My t. is nearly ready	STEV 975:41
Retired to their t. and scandal	CONG 280:5
singles we played after t.	BETJ 100:35
sometimes counsel…sometimes t.	POPE 778:97
sooner the t.'s out of the way	REED 805:86
Take some more t.	CARR 238:30
T., although an Oriental	CHES 259:30
T. for two	CAES 224:82
t. is brought at five	MONRO 700:47
T. is like the East	CHES 259:25
t. is not healthy	GORO 436:69
The way you sip your t.	GERS 420:10
we drink too much t.	PRIE 790:39
we'll all have t.	DICK 322:63
When I makes t. I makes t.	JOYCE 538:47
woman is like a t. bag	ROOS 821:33
your t. you sip	CRAB 294:81

tea-time every night at t.-t.   STEV 975:41
teabreaks t. and other manifestations   MISH 696:72
teach but t. high thought   TENN 1003:18
can easier t. twenty	SHAK 874:11
fool has a lot to t.	RABE 799:89
how can they t.?	DAVI 307:3
I can t. thee	SHAK 876:58
in order to t. himself	KAZIN 543:29
learn what it had to t.	THOR 1017:85
learn while they t.	SENE 858:46
t. him how to live	PORT 784:42
t. in song	SHEL 927:69
t. it round or flat	JOHN 524:59
T. me to feel another's woe	POPE 782:90
T. me, my God and King	HERB 475:13
t. that happiness	HARDY 456:96
T. the children under the…tree	QABO 796:47
t. the English how to talk	WILDE 1078:94
t. the rest to sneer	POPE 781:65
t. the sea what it may do	DONNE 337:87
t. thee in the way	BIBLE 115:59
t. this stuff	RUSS 834:45

teach (*contd.*):
T. us to care	ELIOT 369:10
t. us to forget our own	SHAK 910:97
t. you to drink deep	SHAK 888:55
to t. and delight	SIDN 937:62

teacher greatest t. of morals   HOOV 490:67
My greatest t.	SINA 940:94
Nobody loves a bad t.	WRAGG 1101:98
persuade the t.	TRIL 1026:55
poor t. hurts	BOYER 183:68
sea is a t. of truth	BELL 87:16
t. affects eternity	ADAMS 5:77
t., like every drill-sergeant	RYLE 834:54
t. who does not equip his pupils	PETE 767:8

teachers Believe false t.   SHAK 916:8
damage its t. did	STIG 977:66
Love and delight are better t.	DURER 356:67
more understanding than all my t.	BIBLE 119:31
mountains are stern t.	TILM 1020:65
rigorous t. seized my youth	ARNO 38:1
T.—a bunch of men	MISH 696:73

teaches He who cannot, t.   SHAW 922:48
High office t.	KISS 566:38
T. the time	TOML 1023:2

teaching environment and its t.   LAWR 587:9
follow mine own t.	SHAK 874:11
substituting indoctrination for t.	PETE 767:8
T. is not a lost art	BARZ 75:93

teachings no use for the t.   KHRU 556:51
team call it a t. game   ARLO 35:40
support their t.	BAIN 62:77
t. effort is a lot of people	WINN 1087:64
t. gave a whistle	MOORE 704:8
t. of little atomi	SHAK 868:78
t.'s up against it	GIPP 428:40
why should…your t. object?	HEND 472:54

teams two great t.   SHAN 919:75
teamwork more than t.   SIKO 938:75
teapot warming the t.   MANS 647:1
tear cannot t. out a single page   SAND 840:52
fallen a splendid t.	TENN 1001:88
furtive t.	ROMA 821:28
homage of a t.	BYRON 219:71
Of that divine t.	HUGO 503:93
shed one English t.	MACA 624:25
t. them up	TYSON 1035:31
t. to grace his obsequies	GRAY 443:85
unanswerable t.!	BYRON 221:14

tear-floods no t.-f. …move   DONNE 337:90
tearing t. up £5 notes   HEATH 466:54
tears bat with t. in your eyes   BRAD 184:95
Before my t. did drown it	HERB 475:28
bitter t. to shed	CORY 288:63
brings the t. into their eyes	CARR 241:76
cemented with t.	HERB 474:8
Come back in t.	ROSS 823:67
Creation's t. in shoulder blades	STEV 972:65
daffadillies fill their cups with t.	MILT 684:47
deal with your own t.	WYLIE 1104:47
Deep in heart-wrung t.	BURNS 212:24
delivered…mine eyes from t.	BIBLE 118:25
did I wash you with my t.	HERB 476:36
dip their wings in t.	TENN 999:34
Dismiss…your feign'd t.	SHAK 864:98
doesn't like them he t. them up	HITC 482:27
draw t. from me	HORA 493:31
Drew iron t.	MILT 682:11
Drops t. as fast	SHAK 900:64
eternal reciprocity of t.	OWEN 748:22
faded upholstey of t.	BROY 201:5
foolish t. upon my grave	TENN 998:14
fountains fraught with t.	KYD 571:26
frequently in t.	WEBS 1059:29
gift of t.	SWIN 987:26

Thames (*contd.*):
where the charter'd T. does flow — BLAKE 167:*92*
youthful T. — ARNO 39:*14*
thane T. of Cawdor lives — SHAK 907:*21*
T. of Fife — SHAK 910:*78*
Your face, my t. — SHAK 907:*28*
thank not please but t. you — DILL 331:*53*
only themselves to t. — SAYE 846:*51*
t. all those who made this possible — ANDR 19:*15*
t. me, love me, and reward me — SHAK 899:*23*
t. we all our God — WINK 1086:*59*
thankful must be t. — HAMM 453:*47*
t. that I am here to welcome you — STAN 962:*84*
thankless have a t. child — SHAK 902:*8*
thanks give solemn t. — COLU 278:*63*
give t. unto the Lord — BIBLE 119:*46*
give t. unto thee — BOOK 177:*94*
ta'en with equal t. — SHAK 891:*35*
T. for All the Fish — ADAMS 5:*68*
T. for tomorrow — ATKI 44:*3*
t. to you all — KENN 552:*3*
to give t. is good — SWIN 988:*54*
thanksgiving come…with t. — BIBLE 117:*6*
into his gates with t. — BIBLE 118:*9*
With proud t. — BINY 162:*6*
thatch fear…the fire in the t. — ELIOT 370:*35*
Thatcher better prospect than Mrs T. — HESE 479:*80*
father, except perhaps Mrs T. — WEST 1068:*92*
If Margaret T. wins — KINN 559:*12*
plutonium blonde…T. — SCAR 846:*55*
reappeared in the shape of…T. — HOGG 485:*68*
talk with Mrs T. — WEIG 1061:*77*
[T.] has been charging around — HEAL 464:*29*
[T.] has turned the…bulldog — STEEL 964:*10*
T. is a…tyrant — MACM 636:*17*
thawed t. and gone — KHAY 555:*42*
The Scream This became T. S. — MUNCH 713:*51*
theatre devotes himself to t. — BEAU 79:*62*
Execrable English T. — GOET 431:*69*
For the t. one needs long arms — BERN 97:*95*
go to the t. to be entertained — COOK 286:*27*
I left the t., dizzy and pale — QUIR 798:*72*
I like the t., but never come late — HART 459:*45*
in England nobody goes to the t. — AGATE 10:*65*
interview that turned towards the T. — PRIE 790:*45*
into the t. as a voyeur — FRIS 406:*68*
laughter in the rear of the t. — KAUF 543:*21*
most magical moment in the t. — CRON 298:*60*
only place…to construct a t. — GENET 418:*77*
only regret in the t. — BARR 73:*59*
people don't go to the t. — JOUR 537:*36*
quit going to the t. — SALI 839:*32*
remain in the t. — TYNAN 1035:*25*
talent…drained off into t. — RICH 810:*65*
t. a practice to scratch — MUSC 716:*81*
t. has always been essential — MAMET 644:*55*
t. has died in my lifetime — MILL 677:*11*
t. is irresistible — ARNO 39:*37*
t. is the primary evidence — THUR 1019:*37*
t. of man's life — BACON 55:*16*
we t. folk — MANK 645:*31*
what is happening in the t. — TYNAN 1035:*30*
what t. is all about — STOP 978:*80*
theatres books are t. — STEV 972:*63*
chain of moving picture t. — DOSP 340:*40*
t. have had their day. — BENN 92:*6*
towers, domes, t. — WORD 1097:*46*
theatricals game of private t. — JAMES 517:*44*
thee my little jokes on T. — FROST 407:*1*
Shakespeare—or t. — SCOTT 856:*15*
soul be required of t. — SMITH 948:*39*
theft Property is t. — PROU 792:*85*
there is a boundless t. — SHAK 902:*93*
what would be t. in other poets — DRYD 347:*60*

them Let's be getting at t. — GRACE 437:*84*
theme Fools are my t. — BYRON 218:*59*
imperfection in the chosen t. — WORD 1096:*19*
it is my t.! — DENH 315:*53*
must choose a mighty t. — MELV 668:*39*
My t. is alway humanistic — WILS 1084:*17*
so grave a t. — PRIOR 791:*62*
t., concept, structure — POUS 787:*99*
t. defeats structuralism — GOLD 432:*90*
t. too high doth seem — GURN 449:*91*
themes actions, and religious t. — POUS 787:*99*
leave great t. unfinished — MACB 624:*30*
muses on admired t. — MARL 653:*91*
no transcendent t. in life — FORD 397:*21*
t. in a new light — LUCAS 618:*32*
t. men always have loved — DAY 310:*46*
themselves him rather than t. — WINT 1087:*68*
ought to be doing for t. — JOHN 523:*52*
principal part of t. — HAZL 463:*3*
theologians if you believe the t. — SALI 839:*34*
invention of t. or priests — NIEB 727:*64*
theology hope of t. — INGE 511:*41*
keep history and t. apart — WELLS 1065:*43*
schools of t.…are to be overturned — DIDE 330:*36*
t., philosophy, history, art — ARNO 38:*6*
T., sir, is a fortress — MILL 676:*99*
theorem T.—The acquisition — SART 843:*5*
theories come to nature with your t. — RENO 807:*7*
't.' and 'goals' — KIPL 564:*5*
theorist half-baked t. — TRUE 1029:*14*
theorists armchair t. — ASHD 41:*62*
modern educational t. — RUSS 832:*26*
particularly economic t. — KNIG 567:*54*
talented economic t. — TOBIN 1021:*73*
t. who can ruin your game — BOTH 180:*34*
theorize mistake to t. — DOYLE 343:*84*
theorizing t. about music — HEINE 467:*71*
theory All t.…is grey — GOET 431:*74*
Democracy is the t. — MENC 668:*56*
in t. if genius had not proved — LESS 599:*9*
life without t. — DISR 332:*75*
new t. …a discovery — POPP 783:*23*
new t. is attacked — JAMES 517:*49*
no good t. of what it is — MELL 667:*25*
not apply t. to history — STIN 977:*69*
nothing in the t. to indicate — SIMON 939:*80*
Plato divined in t. — WHIT 1071:*60*
practical as the t. — OPPE 741:*75*
prop up their t. — TWAIN 1034:*20*
t. and methods of revolution — MAO 648:*20*
T. is a good thing — KAPI 542:*8*
t. of modern education — WILDE 1077:*82*
T. of Permanent Adolescence — CONN 283:*67*
t. of the Communists — MARX 660:*13*
t. of the subject is complete — MILL 674:*59*
t. that his wife is beautiful — MENC 669:*79*
without…a t. — POPP 783:*19*
wonders if it will work in t. — HELL 468:*90*
theosophy T. is the essence — BLAV 169:*26*
T., on earth, is like — BLAV 169:*27*
therapy form of t. — GREE 444:*25*
psychoanalytic t. of hysteria — FREUD 404:*41*
there not t., t. is no t. t. — STEIN 965:*41*
thermodynamics Second Law of T. — SNOW 950:*72*
thermometer t. had been longer — MOOD 703:*96*
Thermopylae old man of T. — LEAR 590:*69*
Thespian T. springs — DRAY 345:*39*
thick dashed through t. and thin — DRYD 350:*34*
grown t. — BIBLE 108:*3*
lay it on so t. — BUTL 217:*36*
T. and unwholesome — SHAK 892:*66*
t. as a plank — DIANA 319:*99*
thick-jewelled t.-j. shone — TENN 993:*21*
thick-skinned t.-s. grown-ups — SHAW 921:*27*

thick-skinned (*contd.*):
writers…become t.-s. — WAUGH 1057:*93*
thicker History gets t. and t. — TAYL 992:*13*
thicket t. of the world — JOHN 522:*29*
thief apparel fits your t. — SHAK 897:*88*
come as a t. — BIBLE 158:*26*
come like a t. in the night — POE 776:*44*
cries out stop t. — CONG 280:*14*
grand t. into God's fold — MILT 690:*51*
have a t. or two — SHAK 896:*66*
He that steals…is a t. — SCOTT 854:*70*
in what watch the t. would come — BIBLE 140:*40*
Jean Cocteau thinks I am a poor t. — GENET 418:*73*
not the mouse who is the t. — JACO 514:*91*
Opportunity makes a t. — BACON 54:*3*
Pleasure is a t. to business — DEFOE 312:*86*
rather have been the good t. — BROW 196:*2*
steals something from the t. — SHAK 898:*13*
t. breaks into my house — PAINE 750:*43*
t. cometh not, but for to steal — BIBLE 146:*53*
t. in the night — BIBLE 156:*87*
Upon a dwarfish t. — SHAK 910:*79*
what a deformed t. — SHAK 880:*55*
which is the t.? — SHAK 904:*44*
thieves Beauty provoketh t. — SHAK 885:*74*
best of t. — DRYD 349:*99*
fell among t., which stripped him — BIBLE 142:*89*
made it a den of t. — BIBLE 139:*31*
so much gained upon the t. — STEV 973:*94*
T. for their robbery — SHAK 897:*74*
T. for want of Work — SWIFT 985:*97*
T. out, profit in! — ANON 21:*48*
T. respect property — CHES 258:*10*
T. think I am a poor writer — GENET 418:*73*
Twenty Thousand T. — JOYCE 539:*63*
union of two t. — BIER 160:*67*
when t. cannot be true — SHAK 875:*49*
where t. do not break through — BIBLE 135:*50*
you are t. professed — SHAK 902:*93*
thigh bee with honied t. — MILT 683:*14*
happy dawning of her t. — HERR 477:*59*
on his t. a name written — BIBLE 158:*31*
smote them hip and t. — BIBLE 109:*19*
thimble silver t. lies cold — SITW 941:*25*
thimbles sought with t. — CARR 241:*87*
thin Enclosing every t. man — WAUGH 1057:*95*
how t. and clear — TENN 997:*99*
in every fat man a t. one — CONN 283:*75*
No matter how t. — SMITH 946:*97*
pallid and t. young man — GILB 424:*70*
t.…as a furled umbrella — EMERY 378:*80*
thine only call me T. — COLE 274:*2*
thing any manner of creeping t. — BIBLE 107:*78*
Being a t. immortal — SHAK 888:*72*
dear ravishing t. — BEHN 85:*70*
design…in a t. so small — FROST 407:*92*
do a t. in Israel — BIBLE 109:*29*
do only one t. at once — SMIL 945:*74*
excellent t. in woman — SHAK 904:*52*
far, far better t. that I do — DICK 326:*63*
fond t. vainly invented — BOOK 178:*98*
getting on with the bloody t. — EVANS 381:*38*
great To do that t. — SHAK 906:*98*
if a t. is worth doing — CHES 259:*17*
if they have a good t. — SHAK 877:*84*
it don't mean a t. — ELLI 374:*5*
It don't mean a t. — MILLS 680:*66*
least t. contains something — MAUP 665:*97*
life is the t. — SMITH 948:*22*
local t. called Christianity — HARDY 457:*10*
most important t. in life — PASC 758:*71*
most important t. in the world — SHAW 919:*88*
no new t. under the sun — BIBLE 122:*16*
one damned t. after another — HUBB 498:*3*

thing (*contd.*):

one t. we did right	ANON 28:*19*
palsy-stricken, churchard t.	KEATS 546:*90*
poor virgin…an ill-favoured t.	SHAK 887:*33*
prettier the kind of t.	LAMB 576:*22*
say that the t. is good	MOORE 704:*9*
sought to do the right t.	MACN 637:*34*
Technology…is a queer t.	SNOW 951:*75*
t. about girls	SALI 838:*21*
t. depicted is less stationary	LEGER 594:*22*
t. fall down in peace	MAYB 665:*6*
too much of a good t.?	SHAK 887:*22*
unlike any other t.…in the universe	STEI 966:*52*
what t. is love	PEELE 763:*46*
what to make of a diminished t.	FROST 406:*79*

things accept…the t. that cannot NIEB 727:*66*

all mortal t. doth sway	SPEN 959:*40*
all needful t.	WORD 1097:*43*
All other t. must	SCHI 847:*64*
All t. are artificial	BROW 195:*79*
all t. are become new	BIBLE 151:*80*
All t. are lawful for me	BIBLE 150:*56*
All t. are literally better	RUSK 830:*81*
all t. be done decently	BIBLE 151:*64*
All t. began in order	BROW 196:*7*
All t. bright and beautiful	ALEX 13:*17*
All t., by a law divine	SHEL 928:*85*
all t. come of thee	BIBLE 112:*86*
all t. work together for good	BIBLE 149:*29*
all the t. thou canst desire	BIBLE 120:*60*
By whom all t. were made	BOOK 174:*19*
do all t. through Christ	BIBLE 153:*17*
ear of jealousy heareth all t.	BIBLE 131:*79*
faculty of seeing t.	SPEN 956:*85*
fairest t. have fleetest	THOM 1014:*31*
fanatic for the externality of t.	LEWIS 602:*67*
habit…of correcting t.	BRADY 184:*4*
he that contemneth small t.	BIBLE 132:*5*
higher order of t.	MILL 678:*34*
impression of external t.	RUSK 830:*84*
In the nature of t.	SPIN 960:*48*
leave great t. undone	GLAS 430:*58*
Little t. affect little minds	DISR 332:*91*
Many t. are formidable	SOPH 953:*16*
Mind not high t.	BIBLE 149:*36*
more t. are shewed unto thee	BIBLE 132:*89*
more t. in heaven and earth	SHAK 889:*34*
mystery of t.	SHAK 904:*46*
new way of looking at t.	MILL 679:*52*
power in small t.	SOPH 953:*17*
present state of t.	BAGE 61:*49*
remembrance of t. past	SHAK 913:*58*
sad vicissitude of t.	STER 970:*18*
Say not soft t.	SORL 953:*23*
science…interested in t.	CURIE 301:*12*
secret t. belong unto the Lord	BIBLE 108:*98*
sort of t.	RYLE 834:*53*
These Foolish T.	MARV 659:*93*
t. are the sons	JOHN 526:*5*
T. fall apart	YEATS 1106:*77*
T. have dropped from me	WOOLF 1093:*79*
t. I can do without!	SOCR 952:*89*
t. I once read	SNYD 951:*80*
t. I'd be better without	PARK 754:*6*
T. in book's clothing	LAMB 577:*40*
t. in the world	RUSK 830:*78*
t. made matter very little	CUMM 299:*82*
t. people had once held against her	SCHL 848:*77*
t. people make fools of themselves	SHAW 920:*97*
T. that are seen	JOHNS 523:*40*
t. that are tender and unpleasing	BACON 58:*87*
t. which God hath prepared	BIBLE 150:*46*
t. which have never yet been done	BACON 56:*32*
T. without all remedy	SHAK 909:*57*

things (*contd.*):

t. you can do in a baseball game	STEN 968:*76*
think on these t.	BIBLE 153:*15*
thou hast created all t.	BIBLE 157:*10*
to whom such t. are nothing	SOPH 953:*22*
totality of facts, not of t.	WITT 1088:*74*
useful or pleasurable t.	RUSK 831:*95*
value of the world of t.	MARX 661:*26*
wanted to be three t.	SCHU 851:*16*
way of doing t. rightly	RUSK 830:*87*
What t. have we seen	BEAU 80:*66*
why and wherefore in all t.	SHAK 882:*7*

thingummy not…but t. DICK 323:*96*

think begin to t. about it HEYE 479:*88*

can't t. and hit	BERRA 98:*2*
can't t. for you	DYLAN 358:*92*
can't t. without his hat	BECK 81:*93*
cannot t. well, love well	WOOLF 1093:*68*
don't t. foolishly	JOHN 531:*26*
don't t. much of it	STRA 979:*99*
effort to t. clearly	JAMES 517:*37*
feel hot and t. cold	CARY 243:*17*
fellows whom it hurts to t.	HOUS 495:*63*
greatly t. or bravely die?	POPE 779:*5*
I am inclined to t.	DOYLE 344:*15*
if they t., they fasten	HOUS 496:*72*
If you can t.	KIPL 564:*8*
know more than you t.	SPOCK 961:*61*
might as well t. big	TRUMP 1030:*35*
more clearly than you t.	BAKER 63:*80*
never expect a soldier to t.	SHAW 921:*16*
not so t. as you drunk	SQUI 961:*66*
pains to t. otherwise	HUME 503:*2*
problem is not whether machines t.	SKIN 943:*52*
talk who never t.	PRIOR 790:*48*
t. and t. for months and years	EINS 363:*64*
t. back through our mothers	WOOLF 1093:*74*
T. before you speak	FORS 399:*54*
t. by fits and starts	HOUS 496:*72*
t. continually of those	SPEN 956:*71*
t.…exclusively of others	WAUGH 1057:*2*
t. he is growing old	IRVI 513:*65*
t. him so…t. him so	SHAK 860:*73*
t. is to be full	KEATS 547:*15*
t. like a man	SIMON 938:*79*
T. not of them	KEATS 547:*5*
t. perhaps even less	BROW 199:*56*
t. so highly	STEV 974:*21*
t. that science can do anything	RAY 803:*46*
t. that we t.	BIER 160:*72*
t., therefore I am	DESC 317:*79*
t. too little	DRYD 349:*22*
t. with them	BENN 92:*4*
t. you are doing nothing	JULI 539:*68*
try to t. it again	GOET 431:*75*
What I t., I utter	SHAK 911:*6*
What will Mrs Grundy t.?	MORT 710:*4*
When I t., I must speak	SHAK 886:*5*
When I would pray and t.	SHAK 897:*75*
when we t. of thee, O America!	WALP 1051:*88*
Whenever I t.	STEV 970:*32*

thinker incompleteness as a t. WEBB 1058:*14*

thinkers masses of wishful t. QUINE 797:*67*

thinking and then to t.! HAZL 463:*6*

cannot prevent people from t.	SCHI 847:*65*
employment for a t. man	ADDI 8:*41*
expedient in the way of our t.	JAMES 518:*50*
explicit in my t.	RUSS 833:*31*
feverish after so much t.	CARR 241:*80*
hearing, t., writing	HAZL 464:*19*
I, who was t. this	DESC 317:*78*
instead of t.	JOHN 532:*44*
inventory of unfinished t.	RAND 801:*22*
It ain't t. about it	TROL 1028:*80*

thinking (*contd.*):

left hand is my t. hand	HEPW 473:*81*
live no longer by t.	SHAK 887:*31*
modes of t. are different	JOHN 531:*19*
much drinking, little t.	SWIFT 984:*76*
not a substitute for t.	STEV 972:*78*
not merely as t.	PLATH 773:*90*
originality… manner of t.	MAUP 665:*94*
science…a refinement of everyday t.	EINS 363:*71*
science fictional way of t.	ASIM 42:*74*
T. is the great enemy of perfection	CONR 285:*11*
t. makes it so	SHAK 889:*98*
T. precisely and systematically	SOLOW 952:*93*
t. what nobody has thought	SZEN 989:*69*
t. what you really think	GINS 428:*34*
too busy t. about myself	SITW 941:*18*
usually a way of not t.	HELL 469:*2*
verbal t. is the most articulate	KOES 568:*70*

thinks person who reads or t. YOUR 1108:*5*

t. too much	SHAK 882:*23*
utter what he t. truth	JOHN 531:*14*
what his heart t.	SHAK 879:*52*

third deny that the T. Estate SIEY 938:*69*

nothing new in T. World	AUNG 50:*22*
the t. day he rose again	BOOK 173:*94*
There is no t.!	SAIN 837:*95*
t. day comes a frost	SHAK 918:*61*
t. kind of knowledge	SPIN 961:*59*
t. who walks always beside you?	ELIOT 369:*94*
To make a t., she joined the…two	DRYD 351:*58*

third-rate what in the world is t.-r.? HELL 468:*87*

thirst believeth…shall never t. BIBLE 145:*43*

hunger, t.…and death	GARI 415:*25*
man can raise a t.	KIPL 560:*27*
neither t. any more	BIBLE 157:*15*
nor a t. for water, but of hearing	BIBLE 130:*61*
pride which causes t.	DANTE 305:*11*
quench a country's t.	POPE 780:*29*
t. to be loved	RHYS 808:*25*
t. without quenching it	UPDI 1037:*57*
without the provocation of t.	SWIFT 985:*89*

thirsteth Ho, every one that t. BIBLE 127:*1*

thirstier t. than ever SALA 838:*17*

thirsty t., and ye gave me drink BIBLE 140:*44*

t. land springs of water	BIBLE 126:*82*
when I was t. they gave me vinegar	BOOK 177:*83*

thirteen clocks were striking t. ORWE 745:*54*

T. wasted years	ANON 27:*75*

thirty American women over t. FITZ 391:*16*

Between t. and forty	BENN 91:*98*
past t., and three parts iced	ARNO 37:*81*
t. pieces of silver	BIBLE 130:*68*
t. pieces of silver	BIBLE 140:*47*
t. years' experience	CARR 237:*12*

thirty-five between…t.-f. and forty DIOR 331:*62*

thirty-seventh t.-s. …situation JARRY 519:*70*

Thisbe Death of Pyramus and T. SHAK 870:*29*

love T. very tragical SHAK 871:*54*

thistle flew like the down of a t. MOORE 704:*8*

t., O my soul	MACD 627:*80*
t. yet'll unite	MACD 627:*77*

thistles t. blinterin' white MACD 627:*84*

thither transported hither and t. OVID 747:*3*

Thomas John T. says goodnight LAWR 586:*17*

T., because thou hast seen me	BIBLE 147:*77*
True T.	BALL 67:*52*

thorn Instead of the t.…the fir tree BIBLE 127:*8*

left the t. wi' me	BURNS 212:*23*
Oak, and Ash, and T.	KIPL 563:*98*
plant this t., this canker	SHAK 875:*43*
pricks like t.	SHAK 868:*75*
pull the t.	SCOTT 854:*68*
snail's on the t.	BROW 197:*25*
t. in the flesh	BIBLE 152:*86*

thorn (*contd.*):

without t. the rose	MILT 690:53

thorns crackling of t. under a pot | BIBLE 123:27 |

impious hand to Crown of T.	BRON 191:97
lily among t.	BIBLE 124:46
loops and t.	UPDI 1037:64
no t. go as deep	SWIN 987:35
pain…of their t.	BERN 97:88
received seed among the t.	BIBLE 137:98
some fell among t.	BIBLE 137:97
t. of life	SHEL 928:89

thorny life is t. | COLE 274:10 |

t. way to heaven	SHAK 888:62

thoroughfare t. ful of wo | CHAU 255:33 |

thou eternal T. | BUBER 202:21 |

t. wilt not often be mistaken	PENN 764:57
Thus far t. shalt go	PARN 756:41

thought Action…the enemy of t. | CONR 284:99 |

All t., all passions, all delights	COLE 274:3
beautiful clean t.	LAWR 585:70
become our own t. police	MAMET 643:44
bud of t.	DARIO 305:76
but teach high t.	TENN 1003:18
By t., word, and deed	BOOK 174:25
call in the stream of t.	JAMES 517:10
calmer of unquiet t.	WALT 1052:7
can to sight or t.	MILT 692:5
carving and colouring of a t.	SITW 941:28
ceases to move in t.	ELIOT 370:14
certain dimensions of t.	STEI 967:67
closer the expression is to the t.	FLAU 392:35
community of t.	ADAMS 5:78
deep t., reason, or imagination	DARW 306:88
different from what we t.	HAVEL 460:60
dress of t.	POPE 778:81
end of man is…not a t.	CARL 234:53
Eternity!…dreadful t.!	ADDI 8:35
eternity of t.	WORD 1095:14
Experience is the child of T.	DISR 332:71
great movements of human t.	BENN 92:6
greater cannot be t.	ANSE 31:82
habit of t.	SKEL 942:49
habits of metaphoric t.	FRYE 408:21
impartial in t. as well as in action	WILS 1086:46
in a general honest t.	SHAK 884:68
inward world of t.	ARNO 39:20
Language is called garment of t.	CARL 234:52
less permanent than t.	BUNT 204:56
liberty of t. perishes	ORWE 745:52
light of t.	SHEL 929:2
lived in pleasant t.	WORD 1097:43
loftiness of t.	DRYD 351:58
man of yearning t.	ROSS 825:95
mind of t. is drawn	KANT 542:7
Ministers of t.	SHEL 930:37
never could divine his real t.	BYRON 223:49
Not a t. in all my rest	VAUG 1041:19
not constant t. of sins	BLOOM 170:36
nothing more than your t.	BACH 54:96
odd t. strikes me	JOHN 532:36
once t. can never be unthought	DURR 357:80
optical form of t.	HUGO 501:60
Original t. is like original sin	LEBO 591:85
pale cast of t.	SHAK 890:21
Perish the t.	CIBB 266:54
possesses or possessed A t.	BYRON 219:71
reading of the history of t.	MERT 672:25
rear the tender t.	THOM 1015:47
revelation of T.	EMER 377:70
sensations rather than of t.!	KEATS 544:46
seven thousand years of human t.	LABR 572:35
shoots of green t.	WHITE 1070:40
sit alone with your t.	BOND 172:79
society in which t.	RUSS 832:28

thought (*contd.*):

songs…that tell of saddest t.	SHEL 929:5
spark of inextinguishable t.	SHEL 931:58
speech created t.	SHEL 930:22
splendour of sudden t.	BROW 199:78
strange seas of T.	WORD 1096:27
strive to express his t.	RYDER 834:51
sweet silent t.	SHAK 913:58
tease us out of t.	KEATS 547:11
t. frightens me greatly	SEVI 859:60
t. in the world	ARNO 38:11
t. is often original	HOLM 486:81
t. is viscous	ADAMS 5:83
t. it out with both hands	SAYE 846:49
t. it Pegasus	KEATS 544:40
t. moving in…complete abstraction	WHIT 1071:58
t. of before	GOET 431:75
t. of his name	ELIOT 371:40
t. of Thee wakes	KIER 556:58
t. raised to heaven	LESS 599:10
t. rationally, acted	LIPP 607:38
T. shall be the harder	ANON 21:60
T.…wed with T.	TENN 998:28
t. which could electrify	MILL 678:31
thousand minds in the same t.	TOCQ 1021:79
two people… hit upon the same t.	SHER 934:10
tyranny of conscious t.	BEEC 83:19
understandest my t.	BIBLE 119:48
unredeemed dreariness of t.	POE 775:41
unwholesome in their t.	SHAK 892:66
utmost bound of human t.	TENN 994:59
vehicle for the t. of our day	FORD 396:5
wait without t.	ELIOT 371:44
what you t. you came for	ELIOT 372:69
whistled…for want of t.	DRYD 352:84
works of t. and intelligence	PAST 759:88
world of t.	HAMI 453:41
wrought by want of t.	HOOD 489:50

thought-woven tall t.-w. sails | YEATS 1105:61 |

thoughtlessness t. is the weapon | CONN 283:70 |

thoughts appall your t. | MARL 652:85 |

As horrible t.	FULL 410:42
as thy t. in me	TENN 997:10
Beware t. that come in the night	HEAT 465:45
books…contain our very t.	CONR 285:3
censor one's own t.	WALEY 1049:51
Cleanse the t. of our hearts	BOOK 174:16
cocoon of its own t.	LOWE 616:87
dark soul, and foul t.	MILT 683:28
decided by a person's t.	KIM 557:65
deep t. can be winnowed	SAGAN 836:75
extreme t. take hold	DIDE 330:42
for my t. are not your t.	BIBLE 127:5
generate misleading t.	SPEN 956:67
give them your love but not your t.	GIBR 422:38
images of t. refined	KEATS 544:37
In ernistfull t. and in studying	HENR 473:70
in their barks my t.	SHAK 886:97
joy of elevated t.	WORD 1094:98
keep watch over my t.	HOUS 496:80
more offences…than I have t.	SHAK 891:25
Music is…your t.	PARK 753:87
My bloody t.	SHAK 899:42
my t. on white ships	COLUM 278:61
pained t. found	JEFF 519:79
pansies; that's for t.	SHAK 892:69
pleasant t. Bring sad t.	WORD 1095:4
pleasures which my t.	LANY 580:82
printing our t.	JOHN 528:52
propriety of t. and words	DRYD 348:80
pursue independent t.	MACL 635:96
recognize our own rejected t.	EMER 376:30
reveal their best t.	DESC 317:75
sad t. doth clear	VAUG 1041:22

thoughts (*contd.*):

shroud Of t.	BYRON 220:91
Style is the dress of t.	CHES 257:79
Suspicions amongst t.	BACON 59:4
than to his t.	HUGO 502:87
t. are my prostitutes	DIDE 330:34
t. are whirlèd	SHAK 860:90
t. began to burnish	HERB 475:25
t.…come crowding in so fast	DRYD 352:77
t. dally with false surmise	MILT 685:48
T. die and are buried	LIND 605:7
t. go blowing through them	BROO 192:18
t. have any relation to reality	CHES 258:6
t. have eyes	LYLY 620:59
t. may startle well	MILT 683:25
t. of men are widened	TENN 996:79
t. of other men	COWP 293:62
t. remain below	SHAK 892:49
t. shall be established	BIBLE 121:83
t. smothering ye	KELM 549:34
t. that arise in me	TENN 995:63
T., that breathe	GRAY 443:91
t. to an end	SMITH 948:37
t.…too deep for tears	WORD 1098:56
troubled t.	MILT 689:45
turn your t. to becoming his equal	CONF 283:78
United t. and counsels	MILT 687:92
whose second t. are good	BARR 73:48

thousand After a t. victories | SHAK 913:55 |

better than a t.	BIBLE 117:95
bound him a t. years	BIBLE 158:32
I feel like a t. dollars	OCON 736:88
If we could all live a t. years	BERG 94:42
Not in a t. years	SMITH 947:7
t. a week	ALGR 13:25
t. natural shocks	SHAK 890:21
t. roads lead to Rome	ALAN 11:80
t. shall fall at thy side	BIBLE 117:2
T. t. Saints attending	WESL 1066:65
t. years as one day	BIBLE 156:86
t. years in thy sight	BIBLE 117:98

thousand-year t.-y. conclusion | NIET 727:70 |

thousands But t. die | POPE 780:27 |

Saul hath slain his t.	BIBLE 110:42
T. of little kids	SALI 839:28
T. of miles of wheat	RICH 810:70

Thracian for the T. ships | SWIN 986:23 |

thraldom Europe from the t. | LLOY 608:60 |

highest step of t.	NASHE 721:84

thrall To none…I yield as t. | DYER 358:88 |

thrash t. the Spaniards too | DRAKE 345:29 |

thrashing t. your young woman | COOP 287:45 |

thread another t. in the web | PAGE 749:32 |

bind this line of scarlet t.	BIBLE 109:9
continuous t. of revelation	WELTY 1065:51
division is a t.	BUCH 202:22
Feels at each t.	POPE 780:39
found by the right t.	JONS 536:27
held together by a common t.	JACK 514:87
t. from life's frayed mantle	ABU 2:14
t. loosened from the sky	ROSS 824:87
t. of his verbosity	SHAK 866:23
t. to bind the heart	GILM 427:18
t. we follow from one day	AUST 52:71
With a silken t.	KEATS 544:43

threat every one did t. | SHAK 863:65 |

Whiles I t., he lives	SHAK 908:41

three Anyone who marries t. girls | STEIN 966:46 |

required t. necessaries	JONS 536:23
these t. have changed the whole face	BACON 55:30
T. be the things	PARK 755:23
T. days walking	SNYD 951:84
T. in One	ALEX 13:21
T. in One	DRYD 350:50

time (*contd.*):

antidote against the opium of t.	BROW 196:1
any convenient t. for	MITC 697:90
any given t. or place	WHIT 1071:62
Aphorisms…more for your t.	DUDEK 353:13
Art is long, and t.	LONG 611:95
As t. goes by	HUPF 505:34
as though for the first t.	SPEN 956:85
Ask him what t. it is	WYMAN 1104:52
at any t. upon the earth	WHIT 1072:73
At what t.	KELV 549:35
at whatever t.	PAZ 762:24
Bad girls don't have t.	BANK 70:92
bank and shoal of t.	SHAK 907:31
beat in T.	GINS 427:24
because it saves t.	LERN 597:92
besmeared with sluttish t.	SHAK 913:65
best means…of digesting t.	AUDEN 49:4
best t. to listen	WHITE 1071:47
beyond Space and T.	BROO 193:33
bid t. return	SHAK 867:56
births of t.	BACON 58:93
blowing the new direction of T.	LAWR 585:68
books of all t.	RUSK 831:96
both meeting at one t.	SPEN 958:19
bourne of t. and place	TENN 1005:66
Britain…on borrowed t.	CALL 225:98
burglar…takes his t.	OHEN 737:20
but for all t.!	JONS 536:10
but I am sick of T.	TENN 998:14
By the t. you say	PARK 754:7
camembert of t. and space	DALI 303:47
carried off by the wings of t.	LAFO 574:82
child of its t.	KAND 541:96
chronicles of the t.	SHAK 890:12
city of all t.	HAWT 462:82
closing t. in the gardens	CONN 283:79
comes a t.	TWAIN 1032:72
conversing I forget all t.	MILT 690:61
cormorant devouring t.	SHAK 865:4
Crafts which require the most t.	CANT 230:75
crying, I spent all my t.	LAB 571:33
cursed from the t. our mothers	SCHR 850:3
dark t. the eye	ROET 819:99
death of t.	GRAV 440:30
die…for such a long t.!	MOLI 698:16
do thy worst, old t.	SHAK 912:49
doing nothing until the right t.	BAKER 63:81
Doing t. is like climbing a mountain	DEAN 311:60
drifting, waiting its t.	MORG 707:62
dying…lasts so short a t.	JOHN 528:55
employment for his idle t.	WALT 1052:7
events of the t.	TIMES 1021:71
expiration of that t.	WARD 1053:16
face the man of the t.	STEV 971:50
Fate, T., Occasion, Chance	SHEL 930:23
feet in ancient t.	BLAKE 168:17
fighting t. with marble	JEFF 519:80
fill the t. available	PARK 755:32
Fire Next T.	BALD 64:1
fittest t. and place	RUSK 831:95
flaming bounds of place and t.	GRAY 443:90
fool all the people all of the t.	LINC 605:99
foot of t.	SHAK 901:85
Footprints on the sands of t.	LONG 611:96
For a long t.	UTTL 1038:82
for many a t.	KEATS 548:18
For technological man it was t.	MACL 635:51
for the t. remained	MILT 692:3
forefinger of all T.	TENN 996:92
foremost files of t.	TENN 996:82
full t. work	WELD 1062:94
give gratitude constantly all the t.	FAUL 383:79
Good T. was Had By All	SMITH 948:29

time (*contd.*):

great draughts of t.	BERR 98:10
great lie of our t.	POBE 775:40
Grown old before its t.	ROSS 823:70
gude t. coming	SCOTT 855:88
guest of one's t.	KENN 550:51
'half as old as T.'	BURG 206:95
half the t.	WHITE 1070:27
have not t. to say any more	MARL 652:81
having a more enjoyable t.	POWE 787:2
Health, Wealth, Love…and T.	ANON 30:68
hear t. sliding past you	RHYS 808:27
Heaven…is not a t.	BACH 54:94
high t. we relit the stars	APOL 32:96
hold back t.	GRASS 439:11
holy t. is quiet	WORD 1097:40
How slowly does sad T.	SPEN 959:32
Hurry up please it's t.	ELIOT 368:87
I…may be some t.	OATES 733:60
I spend all my t.	PLATO 773:3
in a t. out-worn	YEATS 1105:62
in his spare t.	GILL 426:6
in his t. plays many parts	SHAK 885:91
in love with the productions of t.	BLAKE 166:75
In our t. political speech	ORWE 744:44
In reality, killing t.	SITW 941:29
in t. leave the body	SMOL 950:64
in t. of affliction	PASC 758:72
In t. the savage bull	KYD 571:24
in t. t'will grow into	WEBS 1060:56
inconceivable in our t.	ROST 825:1
Is this a fit t.	STER 969:6
it was my t.	HOLL 485:71
keeps t., distance and proportion	SHAK 869:99
know the place for the first t.	ELIOT 373:78
laws of space and t.	CORY 288:66
length of t. that suggests	PRIE 790:41
let not T. deceive you	AUDEN 47:61
let the day be t. enough	DANI 304:62
litle t. while it is new	BALL 67:57
long past the t.	PETER 767:7
lot of t. to be a genius	STEIN 965:40
Love is space and t.	PROU 793:96
loved the t. too well	CLARE 267:84
made manifest in t.	MILL 679:48
make poor use of their t.	LABR 573:57
Make use of t.	SHAK 864:97
man is killing t.	LOWE 617:3
martyred slaves of T.	BAUD 77:30
masters…for a very long t.	SHAW 926:46
men of our t.	MACA 622:88
Men talk of killing t.	BOUC 180:38
mist of t.	THAT 1007:10
mock the t.	SHAK 908:37
moment in and out of t.	ELIOT 372:64
most isolated way of having a bad t.	CHER 256:68
Move in melodious t.	MILT 681:90
Nae man can tether t.	BURNS 211:16
neglects meditation, loses his t.	CONF 280:91
no account of T.	HOBB 483:40
no dividend from t.'s to-morrows	SASS 845:25
no enemy but t.	YEATS 1106:82
no precious t. at all	SHAK 913:66
no t. for eloquence	PASC 757:52
no t. for the fine graces	SMITH 946:2
no t. to bleed	SHAK 866:37
no t. to labour	ROGE 820:19
no t. to read	FOOT 396:94
no t. to stand and stare?	DAVI 308:20
nobody needs at any t.	WILD 1079:29
Not an easy t. for humorists	BUCH 202:31
not in earth or t. recoverable	PURDY 795:34
not redeemed from t.	ELIOT 373:80
not t. or opportunity	AUST 50:32

time (*contd.*):

now is the accepted t.	BIBLE 151:82
Old T. is still a flying	HERR 477:63
on t.—No, you were late	LERN 597:88
once our t. devour	MARV 658:75
out of key with his t.	POUND 785:60
out of t., out of space	WELLS 1064:27
own t. out of their work	MASE 662:52
pass away the t.	SHAK 863:48
passage of t.	WILL 1082:76
passed a hell of t.	SHAK 915:91
peace for our t.	CHAM 249:19
play the fools with the t.	SHAK 877:89
Plays…cut through t.	MILL 677:9
plenty of t. to win	DRAKE 345:29
point free in t.	DIDI 330:44
Popular in our t.	HUGH 499:29
pure clay of t.'s mud	MALA 641:9
puzzles me more than t. and space	LAMB 576:10
rags of t.	DONNE 336:77
really understands at the t.	THOM 1014:36
Redeeming the t.	BIBLE 152:2
remember'd for a very long t.	MACG 630:24
repair t.'s faults	MUIR 712:32
right notes at the right t.	BACH 54:92
saltness of t.	SHAK 877:81
same old druid T.	ROSE 823:60
same t. a thousand minds	TOCQ 1021:79
searched for myself across t.	CIXO 267:73
see the t.'s deformity	JONS 534:73
seeds of t.	SHAK 907:17
seen better faces in my t.	SHAK 902:11
sent before my t.	SHAK 863:47
sequence in t.	WELTY 1065:51
She's the original good t.	DAVIS 308:28
shipwreck of t.	BACON 55:11
shook hands with t.	FORD 397:13
short t.…does not make a man	ARIS 34:26
short the t. to run	DRYD 350:29
signs of our own t.	CARL 234:36
sing of T. or Eternity	TENN 1003:24
slap t. on their wrists	KINC 557:67
slow and still the t.	TWAIN 1033:84
small bridge in t.	STEI 966:60
something to do with t.	ROGE 820:15
somewhat before his t.	HARDY 456:2
soul of the whole Past T.	CARL 236:90
sounds in the movement of t.	BUSO 215:92
Space-ships and t. machines	KOES 568:69
speech is shallow as T.	CARL 235:78
spend t. and ink	GALS 413:3
sphere of leisure t.	LOWE 617:15
spoils of t.	GRAY 442:68
stars move still, t. runs	MARL 654:20
strain, T.'s eunuch	HOPK 492:9
strong necessity of t.	SHAK 905:63
sunflower, weary of t.	BLAKE 167:87
supreme cause of our t.	SPEN 957:91
Suspended in t.	ELIOT 372:67
Take a little t.	DICK 325:47
tasks…to fulfil for our t.	SCHW 852:31
That passed the t.	BECK 81:94
That T. could turn up	HEYW 480:92
that t. of night	GINS 428:34
Then while t. serves	HERR 477:62
there…existed at some t.	PALEY 751:65
there is t. for everything	BOLD 171:68
There was a t.	WORD 1097:48
They reject t.	FULL 410:43
think of having such a good t.	LOOS 613:31
this odd warpin t.	RICH 809:53
This t.…is a very good one	EMER 376:27
thoughts are spurred on by t.	LECO 592:2
through t. t. is conquered	ELIOT 370:27

time (*contd.*):

Through the cold t.	BIRN 163:26
tied to their t.	PISS 771:61
till t. and times are done	YEATS 1105:63
T., a maniac scattering dust	TENN 999:35
T.'s all-serving wave?	BRON 191:9
t. and chance happeneth	BIBLE 123:35
t. and death pinned human	FRAME 400:76
t. and energy from	MORE 707:52
T. and fevers burn away	AUDEN 47:74
T. and hour runs	SHAK 907:22
T. and the bell	ELIOT 370:28
t. appears to have been frozen	COUP 289:76
't.'s arrow'	EDDI 360:17
t.'s best jewel	SHAK 914:68
t. cannot destroy	MURP 715:71
t. changes people	PROU 793:6
t. Craves that we taste	GREE 445:32
t.'s deer is slain	MUIR 712:27
T.'s devouring hand	BRAM 185:8
t. enough for everything	GUNN 448:84
t. enough to sleep	HOUS 494:42
t.'s eternal motion	FORD 397:17
T. flies and takes me	SEVI 859:60
t. for such a word	SHAK 910:86
t.'s furrows I behold	SHAK 913:51
t. goes about its immemorial work	AMIS 17:93
T. goes on crutches	SHAK 879:44
T. goes…T. stays	DOBS 334:34
t. had come	PENI 764:55
t. has come…To talk of many things	CARR 240:57
T. has no divisions	MANN 646:84
T. has three dimensions	HOPK 492:97
T. has transfigured them	LARK 581:5
T. hath…A wallet	SHAK 896:51
T. hath set a blot	SHAK 867:57
T. held me green and dying	THOM 1010:66
T. hovers o'er	JOHN 525:83
t. in everybody's life	WILD 1079:32
T. in hours, days, years	VAUG 1041:20
T. is a great physician	DISR 332:77
t. is all I lacked	DOUG 341:59
t. is eating away my life	BAUD 77:18
t. is long	DU 353:10
T. is money	FRAN 402:4
t. is no healer	ELIOT 372:62
t. is now near at hand	WASH 1054:42
T. is on his side	BANKS 70:98
T. is on our side	GLAD 429:51
T. is our tedious s.	MILT 681:93
t. is out of joint	SHAK 889:85
T. is the 101st Senator	DODD 334:42
t. is the greatest innovator	BACON 58:94
t. is the longest distance	WILL 1081:97
t. is the medium of narration	MANN 646:86
T. is the metre	WALC 1048:38
t. is tied to the wrist	RAINE 800:9
T. kills us	SITW 941:29
T. like a serpent	CRANE 295:2
t. lost may nought recovered be	CHAU 254:12
T., Love, Beauty	MILL 677:15
t. may cease	MARL 654:20
T.'s most lethal weapon	SITW 941:23
T., not Corydon, hath conquered	ARNO 39:18
t. not to become a father	WHITE 1070:33
t. of a man or woman	WHIT 1073:84
t. of awakening consciousness	RICH 809:48
t. of life is short	SHAK 876:72
t. of their growth	ROSE 823:62
T. past and t. future	ELIOT 370:26
T. present and t. past	ELIOT 370:22
t. remembered	SWIN 986:2
T. rolls	SCOTT 854:63
T. seemeth…of the nature	BACON 55:10

time (*contd.*):

T. shall not lose	DONNE 336:70
T. shall turn those amber locks	DRAY 345:34
T. shall unfold	SHAK 902:98
t. sic causis has repairit	ANON 23:87
T. spent on any item	PARK 755:33
T.…strengthens friendship	LABR 572:41
T. that is moved	SLES 943:57
T., that takes survey	SHAK 876:75
T., that tireless gambler	BAUD 77:24
t. that we are living in	TOML 1023:2
t. that we love the best	LAUD 583:39
t.…the author of authors	BACON 54:5
T., the deer	MACL 633:70
T. the destroyer	ELIOT 372:61
T. the devourer	OVID 747:2
T., the world and the person	CIXO 267:72
T.'s thievish progress	SHAK 914:76
t. to cultivate modesty	SITW 941:18
t. to do divers…digging	LEAV 591:77
t. to every purpose	BIBLE 122:19
t. to get married	EPST 379:5
t. to make it shorter	PASC 758:80
t. to think about it	FONT 395:88
T. travels in divers paces	SHAK 886:6
T. turns the old days	SWIN 987:35
T. was away	MACN 637:44
t. was out of joint	STRA 979:93
T. we may comprehend	BROW 195:75
T. we shall not know	PEAC 762:31
T.'s wheels run back	BROW 199:76
t. when all men walk proudly	RAND 801:25
t. when the most powerful	MACA 623:9
t. when thou mayest be found	BIBLE 115:58
t. when too much seems to happen	COUP 289:75
t. when you have to let your clothes	MIDL 674:50
T., which takes…Our youth	RALE 800:16
t. will change it	BRON 192:12
T. will come when you will hear me	DISR 332:78
T. will not be ours	JONS 534:85
T. will run back	MILT 681:91
T.'s winged chariot	LINK 606:25
t. with a gift of tears	SWIN 987:26
T., you old gipsy man	HODG 483:49
t. you see him	RUNY 829:60
T., you thief	HUNT 505:29
'Tis t. to fear	SHAK 910:93
to be t.'s eunuch	HOPK 492:6
To choose t. is to save t.	BACON 58:95
to do with the t. of the day?	SHAK 875:36
to kill an admiral from t. to t.	VOLT 1046:1
to the end of t.	GAIN 411:69
tolling bell Measures t.	ELIOT 372:59
too much change in too short a t.	TOFF 1022:85
too much of the t.	THUR 1019:28
too much t. talking	THOM 1011:91
took t. to realize	HYDE 509:11
torments…may in length of t.	MILT 688:17
Torture and T.	BYRON 220:98
tower of my t.	NEME 722:4
ugly things…beautiful with t.	COCT 272:66
understood in t.	KIER 556:57
wake us T. and t. over	LARK 581:95
warn't no t. to be	TWAIN 1033:86
wastes her t.	WALL 1050:70
we shall die…'tis but the t.	SHAK 883:40
weak by t. and fate	TENN 995:67
weight of this sad t.	SHAK 904:50
what is t. but shadows	SASS 845:38
What t.'s the next one?	SLEZ 943:58
What, then, is t.?	AUGU 49:12
whatever is t. of your life	SPARK 955:52
when his t. is come	TWAIN 1034:5
When our t.'s come	DIBD 319:7

time (*contd.*):

When t. is broke	SHAK 868:71
When t. was open-eyed	LOWE 616:93
when we meet at any t. again	DRAY 345:40
whips and scorns of t.	SHAK 890:21
whirligig of t.	SHAK 895:37
whole t. the engine is at work	WATT 1055:55
wink of t.	BERR 99:19
witching t. of night	SHAK 891:44
world enough, and t.	MARV 658:72
writer's t. is spent	JOHN 529:72
wrong most of the t.	KURZ 571:23
time-honoured t.-h. bread-sauce	JAMES 516:24
time-lag t.-l. of fifty years	WELLS 1065:45
time-stricken t.-s. willow	CALL 226:4
timebo quem t.	BIBLE 159:41
timepiece human t.	ASLET 42:76
times aesthetic principle of our t.	ROGE 820:3
All t. are his seasons	DONNE 339:26
all t. I have enjoy'd	TENN 994:58
approaches recent t.	TAYL 992:13
at all t. and in all cultures	WEBER 1059:20
bad t. at Anfield	PAIS 751:54
best of t.…worst of t.	DICK 326:58
Different rhymes for different t.	BROD 189:65
different t. in the same country	RICA 808:32
discern the signs of the t.?	BIBLE 138:12
fatness of these pursy t.	SHAK 892:58
in all t. to come	SMITH 945:85
In t. of crisis	BALZ 68:72
live in oppressive t.	MAMET 643:44
mode of their t.	DAY 310:46
No t. were more dangerous	INOU 512:57
not for the fashion of these t.	SHAK 885:83
not for you to know the t.	BIBLE 147:79
old t.	GOLD 433:20
ruins of forgotten t.	BROW 196:94
Shall there be womanly t.?	MACE 629:13
sign of knowledge in our t.	WILL 1083:92
sundry t. and in divers manners	BIBLE 154:44
The T. They Are A' Changing	DYLAN 358:94
There are t. in politics	GALB 412:81
T. are changed	STEV 974:9
t. begin to wax old	BIBLE 131:77
t. have become vulgar	MOLI 698:19
t. long past	WORD 1098:57
t. of faith as best	SMITH 948:34
t. of preservation	SHAK 918:58
t. that try men's souls	PAINE 750:42
tincture from the t.	DEFOE 312:79
What t.!!	CICE 266:57
when the t. were not hard	EMER 377:75
Times The T. every morning	KING 558:96
The T. is…entitled	HAZL 463:7
timetable t. not necessarily	WELTY 1065:51
timetables imposed…by railway t.	TAYL 991:11
timid t. requests, invites denial	SENE 858:48
timidity in a young man is t.	HUGO 502:90
Timon Till I am T.	YEATS 1106:87
Timotheus Let old T. yield the prize	DRYD 351:74
TimothyWinters Timothy T.	CAUS 246:66
tin cat on a hot t. roof	WILL 1081:67
corrugated t. roof	BEEC 82:17
Gershwin keeps pounding on t.	GERS 420:9
opened a t.	STEV 973:97
tincture Actions receive their t.	DEFOE 312:79
tinge t. of tawny yellow	SALA 838:17
tingle ears of every one…shall t.	BIBLE 109:29
tinker do not matter a t. curse	SHIN 935:19
tinkering first rule of intelligent t.	EHRL 362:56
tinklings drowsy t.	GRAY 441:62
tinsel Titles are t.	SHEL 927:57
tint t. ends and the orange t. begins?	MELV 668:51
tinted in all his t. orders	FIRB 389:74

Tiny Tim none of us shall forget T. T. DICK 323:88
tip school-boy's t. THAC 1007:98
The t.'s a good one POUND 786:67
t. of every branch PLATH 773:91
tipped t. with gold for this JONS 535:87
tippenny Wi' t., we fear nae evil BURNS 211:17
tips loyal to the t. of his stubby fingers ACHE 3:39
tiptoe t. on the misty mountaintops SHAK 869:11
tired busy, and the t. FITZ 390:2
Give me your t., your poor LAZA 588:26
man is t. of London JOHN 530:92
soon get t. of them all SHAW 924:96
Thou art t. ARNO 39:22
T., above all GIRO 429:47
t. of being a woman SEXT 859:66
T. of knocking ARNO 37:87
t. of living WHITE 1070:29
t. of the truth ALBEE 11:84
tires rain never t. HUGH 500:49
Tiresias I T., old man ELIOT 369:89
tiresome Love…troublesom & t. FLEM 394:66
t. for children SAIN 836:83
Titan like thy glory, T. SHEL 930:27
T.'s painting VASA 1040:9
Titania moonlight, proud T. SHAK 870:34
Titanic deck of the T. MORT 710:3
Titans we are T. CARL 234:42
tithe Personality T.: A price paid COUP 289:85
tithes Bring ye all the t. BIBLE 130:70
Titian care much at heart about T. RUSK 830:88
title appropriate t. of 'agnostic' HUXL 508:97
courage prove my t. SHAK 906:6
does he feel his t. SHAK 910:79
friends could only read the t. WOOLF 1092:55
guarantee of a t. LISP 607:39
records prove the t. good ARLO 34:37
t. of…significance LEVE 599:18
vain t. of Trades Unions RUSK 831:10
whatever t. suit thee! BURNS 209:73
titles eskin-titles BENET
because there were no t. in it HEMI 470:16
hundred new t. of idiotism NASHE 720:75
T. are tinsel SHEL 927:57
T. distinguish the mediocre SHAW 922:50
titwillow Willow, t., t.! GILB 425:92
Tlön metaphysicians of T. BORG 178:10
toad should I let the t. work LARK 581:3
simply talked to T. GRAH 438:92
Squat like a t. MILT 690:66
t. beneath the harrow KIPL 559:14
t. in fun CRAS 296:28
t. or adder to catch MUIR 712:29
t., ugly and venomous SHAK 885:75
your arm, old t. LARK 581:10
toady T., perhaps, even tacky ACHE 3:48
toast faint flavour of t. TRAV 1025:21
let the t. pass SHER 933:97
milk and t. and honey MITC 696:82
my t. would be ADAMS 6:89
smell of buttered t. GRAH 438:92
t. of a' the town BURNS 212:39
t. with three times three GILB 425:83
Will Not Take this T. ANON 25:21
toasted t., and buttered on both sides JACK 514:85
toasted-cheese [called him], 'T.-c.' CARR 241:84
tobacco Beer, t., and music MANN 645:79
lives without t. MOLI 698:23
T., divine, rare, superexcellent t. BURT 214:73
tobacco-pipes dirty t.-p. ELIOT 366:42
Toby uncle T. would never offer STER 969:95
today All the poet can do t. OWEN 748:12
beat them t. STARK 963:99
down in the woods t. BRAT 185:15
Here t.—in next week tomorrow! GRAH 438:91

today (*contd.*):
here t., and gone to-morrow BEHN 85:68
Kind is my love t. SHAK 915:85
live t. MART 657:58
Living for t. LENN 596:57
Maybe not t., maybe not tomorrow EPST 379:2
Never do t. what you can put off PUNCH 795:25
person who lives for t. BELL 86:91
such a day tomorrow as t. SHAK 911:18
technology of t. GABOR 411:65
t. hidden by science! NIET 728:89
t. I am fifty-five REED 805:83
T. if ye will hear his voice BOOK 177:88
t. is no longer the news RUSK 830:73
T. shalt thou be with me BIBLE 144:17
T., t. unhappy day SHAK 867:56
T. we have naming of parts REED 804:80
vibrant and the beautiful t. MALL 641:13
Where are the warriors t.? SITT 940:98
wiser t. than he was yesterday POPE 778:73
toddle t. safely home and die SASS 845:27
toe t. of one shoe TRAV 1025:32
t. to t. PEEL 763:44
Washington Post…with your big t. LANCE 578:53
toenails makes my t. twinkle THOM 1011:73
toes Pobble who has no t. LEAR 590:52
stepping on your t. MOSS 711:7
t. grow big and black THOM 1011:89
tread in the bus on my t.? AUDEN 47:62
turn out your t. as you walk CARR 239:51
toff Me pal…does the t. DENN 316:61
toga Idealism is the noble t. HUXL 508:91
t., the kilt MURR 715:76
together able to sit t. KING 557:82
all hang t. FRAN 402:10
Both bound t. WALL 1050:74
looking t. in the same direction SAIN 836:80
toil cricket's manly t. BYRON 218:58
fatuous sunbeams t. OWEN 748:20
ferocious and endless t. GARL 415:27
Horny-handed sons of t. SALI 839:33
love and t. KIPL 564:3
mock their useful t. GRAY 442:66
more sweet than t. TENN 994:53
necessary…to be worn with t. EURI 380:29
Sleep after t. SPEN 957:8
smeared with t. HOPK 491:82
t. and trouble of acquiring it SMITH 946:93
T. conquered the world VIRG 1045:94
t., envy, want JOHN 525:82
t. in other men's extremes KYD 571:28
t. its desolation HAMM 453:48
t.'s obscure, and a' that BURNS 213:42
t. Of dropping buckets COWP 293:57
t. that is distroyed MACC 626:54
War…is t. and trouble DRYD 351:72
waste their t. SCOTT 853:47
Why t. to no avail? LI 603:77
with his t. he won DRYD 349:14
toiled forgot for which he t. SHAK 913:55
toilet can only be read on the t. MILL 677:19
toilette judged…through her t. DE 311:64
toils prudently their t. upbraid MARV 658:82
t., the conflicts, the sufferings SCHW 852:31
token sending…small cash t. CONN 283:60
told ate and drank as he was t. HOFF 484:58
not t. even the half POLO 777:67
the way it is t. here PACH 748:25
tolerable Not a t. woman's part AUST 51:47
scarcely t. and the…unbearable DAFOE 303:39
tolerance excessive t. of suicide DURK 357:70
to practice t. UNIT 1036:45
t. as uncertainty BURKE 208:53
tolerate cannot t. them DEGA 313:3

tolerate (*contd.*):
Louisianans don't t. corruption ANON 30:53
t. unlikely arguments FORD 397:14
We are not going to t. REAG 804:64
toll t. me back KEATS 548:19
Tolstoy in any ring with Mr T. HEMI 471:37
T., Hugo, Dostoevsky LESS 598:99
Tom Every T., Dick and Harry GOLD 434:40
his name was T. KING 558:92
more… than in all T. Jones JOHN 528:61
So T. went home with Ellie KING 558:99
T. bears logs SHAK 866:30
tomahawks t., wi' blude red-rusted BURNS 211:18
tomato You say t. GERS 420:12
tomatoes if I grew t. TREV 1026:50
tomb a t. and a dungeon HAWT 461:77
best-seller is the gilded t. SMITH 947:21
buried in the silent t. WORD 1099:76
Claret on my T. KEATS 545:66
erect…his own t. SHAK 880:66
fair Fidele's grassy t. COLL 276:42
ghost from the t. SHEL 928:84
graces…blossom on the t. CRAB 294:80
Kings for such a t. MILT 682:95
made our land a t. ORAH 741:78
Marriage is the grave or t. of wit CAVE 246:72
Pyramus, at Ninny's T. SHAK 871:43
smoking t. GINS 427:25
straight and narrow as a t. SMITH 948:31
this side the t. BYRON 219:83
This side the t. DAVI 308:21
t. remain uninscribed EMMET 378:81
totter towards the t. SAYE 846:53
toward the silent t. WORD 1100:86
world would smell…a t. SHEL 929:10
tombs Faith…feeds among the t. MELV 667:31
Nerves sit…like T. DICK 328:99
rose from these stone t. MORG 708:66
shovelled into the t. SAND 841:40
upon our brazen t. SHAK 865:4
tombstone The t. of capitalism STILL 977:67
t. white KIPL 561:45
tombstones t. where flowers BLAKE 167:91
Tommy O it's T. this KIPL 560:30
T. 'ows yer soul? KIPL 560:31
tomorrow Boast not thyself of t. BIBLE 122:5
building…with t. inside AKERS 10:74
die for him t. BALL -101:28
for t. we die BIBLE 151:69
For t. we shall die! PARK 754:9
here to-day, and gone t. BEHN 85:68
History…start again t. DURR 357:79
If scientists knew t.'s discovery ZUCK 1110:28
Kill me t. SHAK 900:55
put off till t. PUNCH 795:25
some good thing comes t. SHAK 877:3
such a day t. as today SHAK 911:18
Thanks for t. ATKI 44:3
T., and t., and t. SHAK 910:86
T. country then RICH 810:71
t. is another day MITC 697:92
T. is Saint Crispian SHAK 881:99
T. let us do or die! CAMP 227:31
t.'s life's too late MART 657:58
t. morning, We shall have REED 804:80
T. shall we strangers TU 1031:43
t. that is the object RUSK 830:73
t. we shall die BIBLE 125:71
t. we will run faster FITZ 391:7
t.…what he did today and yesterday LABR 572:41
T. when thou leav'st DONNE 336:74
what's going to happen t. QUINN 798:59
tomorrows time's t. SASS 845:25
no more t. PARF 753:84

tomtit little t. sang — GILB 425:*92*
tonality T. is a natural force — HIND 481:*12*
tone deep, autumnal t. — SHEL 928:*90*
ditties of no t. — KEATS 547:*8*
tones noble t. — GAUG 416:*38*
t. of a loved voice — ARNO 36:*70*
tongs t., and boniest doggerel — RUSK 831:*12*
tongue Before I taught my t. — VAUG 1041:*16*
bridleth not his t. — BIBLE 155:*62*
bury my t. at Champmédy — BENET 90:*62*
calls with a cockerel's t. — LEE 593:*15*
cannot endure my Lady T. — SHAK 879:*39*
citizens speaking the same t. — MAZZ 666:*13*
Confounds the t. — SHAK 861:*94*
daily changing t.? — WALL 1050:*74*
every t. should confess — BIBLE 153:*8*
eye to see nor t. — LENT 596:*67*
for mortal t. — GURN 449:*91*
hearing not my t. — SHAK 897:*75*
hidden even as a strange t. — DURER 356:*66*
hold your t. — DONNE 337:*79*
I have often given t. — YEATS 1105:*68*
In a neat's t. — SHAK 873:*89*
knot that would not yield to the t. — BIER 160:*70*
knoweth and yet holdeth his t. — BIBLE 132:*13*
Lends the t. vows — SHAK 888:*68*
Letting the rank t. blossom — BROW 200:*81*
lost my t. from — NICH 726:*51*
made our English t. — SPEN 957:*96*
More than that t. — SHAK 913:*53*
Murder, though it have no t. — SHAK 890:*17*
music of his own vain t. — SHAK 865:*10*
my t. freezes into silence — SAPP 842:*92*
my t. from…lying — BOOK 175:*37*
my t., the mystery — AQUI 32:*5*
mysmetre for defauts of t. — CHAU 254:*15*
never in the t. — SHAK 866:*29*
obnoxious to each carping t. — BRAD 184:*1*
of a slow t. — BIBLE 106:*58*
relation between the human t. — WAXM 1058:*12*
sad words of t. or pen — WHIT 1074:*5*
sharp t. in your head — PERE 766:*94*
sharp t. is the only — IRVI 513:*63*
shouldst give dust a t. — HERB 475:*31*
show you have a Scotch t. — SCOTT 855:*94*
snakes with double t. — SHAK 871:*40*
stick out your t. — MARQ 655:*36*
still the t. is wagging — SHER 933:*93*
stroke of the t. breaketh — BIBLE 132:*9*
sweet English t. — FLEC 393:*47*
thud of consonants in t. — BROY 201:*5*
t. acquire the Southern — STEV 976:*45*
t. and soul…be hypocrites — SHAK 892:*45*
t. cleaveth to my jaws — BIBLE 114:*49*
t. Could scarcely cry — BLAKE 166:*66*
t. could utter — TENN 995:*63*
t. Dropped manna — MILT 688:*14*
t. is a fire — BIBLE 155:*67*
t. is a little member — BIBLE 155:*66*
t. is the clapper — SHAK 879:*52*
t. like the tail of a dog — NASHE 721:*84*
t. seeking out…a sore tooth — BURU 215:*82*
t. shall sing aloud — BIBLE 116:*79*
t.'s sweet air — SHAK 870:*26*
t.…tipped with gold — JONS 535:*87*
t. taking a trip — NABO 717:*96*
trippingly on the t. — SHAK 891:*32*
truth in every shepherd's t. — RALE 800:*12*
use of my oracular t. — SHER 933:*83*
when he's holding his t. — JAMES 516:*15*
While I have a t. — OCON 735:*82*
with stammering lips and another t. — BIBLE 125:*75*
with your heart and t. — SHEL 927:*56*
words of t. and pen — HARTE 460:*53*

tongue (*contd.*):
Wounds…inflicted by the t. — RICH 810:*69*
write well in any t. — ASCH 40:*50*
you dried neat's t. — SHAK 876:*56*
Your hand, your t. — SHAK 907:*29*
tongue-tied t.-t.'s fighting — HARR 459:*36*
tongued t. with fire — ELIOT 372:*70*
tongueless t. vigil and all the pain — SWIN 986:*23*
tongues all nations…and t. — BIBLE 157:*14*
began to speak with other t. — BIBLE 147:*81*
clocks the t. of bawds — SHAK 875:*36*
Had I your t. and eyes — SHAK 904:*51*
keep your t. well-omened — HORA 493:*21*
silence envious t. — SHAK 918:*63*
sores on innocent t. — OWEN 748:*13*
terror…then to declare — ELIOT 373:*77*
though fallen, and evil t. — MILT 691:*82*
thousand several t. — SHAK 863:*63*
t. A dismal universal hiss — MILT 693:*17*
t. in trees — SHAK 885:*77*
t. of flame are in-folded — ELIOT 373:*81*
t. of men and of angels — BIBLE 150:*62*
t. of the French Council — SHAK 882:*11*
t. recant like beaten weather vanes — CRANE 295:*8*
t., that syllable men's — MILT 683:*24*
Walls have t. — SWIFT 985:*95*
we loose wild t. — KIPL 562:*62*
whispering t. can poison truth — COLE 274:*10*
tonic hatred is a t. — BALZ 68:*74*
t. to all save men — DOUG 342:*65*
tonight fixed it t. — SNYD 951:*83*
soul required of me t. — SMITH 948:*39*
T. she'll hae but three — BALL 67:*46*
T.—to you — NIXON 730:*10*
T. we sleep — MACN 637:*43*
tons saves t. of explanation — SAKI 838:*16*
weighs a hundred t. — MACC 625:*35*
took person you and I t. me for — CARL 233:*26*
tool basic t. for the manipulation — DICK 320:*13*
computer…only a t. — AMER 16:*65*
fashioned it with a graving t. — BIBLE 107:*71*
only edged t. — IRVI 513:*63*
T. Maker, Stacker of Wheat — SAND 841:*57*
worker uses a t. — MARX 661:*23*
tools filmmaker…afford his own t. — WELL 1063:*3*
Give us the t. — CHUR 264:*18*
persons using parties as t. — DISR 333:*20*
rudimentary t. to discover — PETE 767:*8*
secrets are edged t. — DRYD 346:*55*
Sin has many t. — HOLM 486:*87*
t. of their t. — THOR 1016:*79*
t. …painter's techniques — RENO 807:*10*
t. that go together with culture — REYES 807:*22*
want to know which t. — SEXT 859:*65*
Without t. he is nothing — CARL 234:*48*
tooth blue-black t. of sheer rock — BENU 94:*33*
drill to the t. of America — CLIN 269:*19*
like a broken t. — BIBLE 121:*99*
moral truth is a hollow t. — MAST 663:*64*
red in t. and claw — TENN 999:*32*
red in t. and claw — TENN 999:*41*
sharper than a serpent's t. — SHAK 902:*8*
tongue seeking out…a sore t. — BURU 215:*82*
t. for a t. — BIBLE 134:*42*
t. for t. — BIBLE 107:*69*
tooth-picker fetch a t.-p. now — SHAK 879:*38*
toothache endure the t. patiently — SHAK 880:*62*
Music helps not the t. — HERB 476:*39*
toothless t. terrier on Valium — SIKO 938:*74*
toothpicks pear on top of two t. — ACHE 2:*28*
top always room at the t. — WEBS 1059:*24*
carefully cleared at the t. — SHUL 936:*34*
dipped its t. — FROST 406:*80*
from the naked t. — WORD 1100:*79*

top (*contd.*):
from this t. Of speculation — MILT 693:*28*
I'm the bottom, you're the t. — PORT 784:*32*
On her ingrateful t.! — SHAK 902:*13*
on tap, but not on t. — CHUR 265:*42*
only way to get to the t. — ZATO 1109:*15*
started at the t. and worked down — WELL 1063:*4*
t. of admiration — SHAK 917:*31*
t. of the greasy pole — DISR 333:*9*
You're the t. — PORT 784:*33*
topaz gates of pearl and t. — LAUR 584:*45*
topee swell beneath a solar t. — HERB 476:*30*
toper poor t. whose untutored sense — CRAB 293:*65*
topic no ordinary t. — PLATO 774:*19*
conflicting…on the same t. — ALTH 15:*61*
constant t. — JOHN 528:*52*
most poetical t. in the world — POE 776:*50*
topics have but two t. — JOHN 530:*89*
tops like whipping t. — HODG 484:*52*
used to think their slender t. — HOOD 489:*38*
torch bear the t. of truth — LICH 604:*84*
king's t. throws its light — CYRA 302:*36*
lights the t. of war — HITL 482:*29*
Man is a t. borne in the wind — CHAP 252:*68*
science…the t. which illuminates — PAST 759:*40*
t. has been passed — KENN 550:*64*
torches as we with t. do — SHAK 896:*61*
O, she doth teach the t. — SHAK 868:*82*
one thousand burning t. — LAB 571:*33*
toreador t., en garde! — MEIL 666:*19*
Tories potential T. — ORWE 743:*12*
sensible T. — WALP 1051:*93*
T. own no argument but force — BROW 196:*9*
torment Christ perish in t. — SHAW 925:*25*
major writer…required major t. — BERG 95:*49*
More grievous t. — KEATS 546:*77*
more I feel T. within — MILT 692:*99*
smoke of their t. ascendeth — BIBLE 158:*2*
t. for our crimes — CHES 259:*26*
t. of the night's untruth — DANI 304:*62*
torments t.…may in length of time — MILT 688:*17*
will not have anybody's t. — CHES 257:*82*
Toronto T. is a kind of — USTI 1038:*80*
torpedoes Damn the t.! — FARR 383:*74*
torpor woke me from the t. — WARR 1054:*36*
torrent fiend for becoming a t. — LIGNE 604:*93*
torso background to a t. — AUDEN 46:*54*
t. which has no face — YOUR 1108:*11*
tortoise writing for the t. market — BROO 193:*36*
torture Behaviourism…t. — AUDEN 49:*2*
endure t.…for the national good — PANK 753:*82*
human cities t. — BYRON 220:*87*
T. and Time — BYRON 220:*98*
t. in the country of the mind — WHITE 1070:*42*
t. into aught of the sublime — POE 775:*41*
t. not again — SHEL 931:*47*
t. of a lingering…passion — ETHE 380:*18*
t.…of his fellow-creatures — FROU 408:*9*
t. one poor word — DRYD 348:*84*
Tory born a T. …die a T. — POWE 788:*18*
extinction of the T. Party — BEVAN 101:*62*
hatred for the T. Party — BEVAN 101:*64*
Let Whig and T. a' agree — SKIN 943:*55*
neither a Whig nor a T. — DISR 332:*88*
what is called the T. — CROK 297:*46*
wise T. and a wise Whig — JOHN 531:*16*
Toryism essence of T. — BAGE 61:*49*
tosh Never did I read such t. — WOOLF 1092:*57*
toss t. him to My breast — HERB 476:*35*
t. in the spray — ARNO 36:*54*
tossed t. and gored several persons — BOSW 180:*30*
totalitarian t. and corrupt tyrannies — MO 698:*10*
t. simplicities — LYND 621:*65*
totalitarianism friends of t. — ORWE 745:*51*

travels (*contd.*):

talk of my t. was to tarnish	THES 1009:40
t. fastest who t. alone	KIPL 560:20
treacherous none so t.	SHAW 921:26
treachers t. by spherical	SHAK 902:2
tread All that t.	BRYA 201:18
face with an undaunted t.	STEV 975:42
heavy is the t.	THOM 1012:13
so airy a t.	TENN 1001:88
tawny t. sublime	CRAIK 294:90
We t. upon	SHAK 896:67
treason feel the t. sharply	SHAK 916:7
hate traitors and the t. love	DRYD 351:56
he harbours t.	SHAK 861:3
last temptation is the greatest t.	ELIOT 370:33
Music is a t.	KHOM 555:45
popular humanity is t.	ADDI 8:32
T. and murder	SHAK 880:76
t. can but peep	SHAK 892:67
T. doth never prosper	HARI 457:17
T. has done his worst	SHAK 909:58
T. is but trusted	SHAK 876:71
t. is not owned	DRYD 350:40
t. to his country	JOHN 526:16
treasons From plots and t.	DRYD 350:31
t., stratagems, and spoils	SHAK 873:3
what care we For t.	WORD 1094:1
treasure covetous man all his t.	MILT 686:71
dig for hidden t.	TWAIN 1032:72
great t. and trouble therewith	BIBLE 121:80
he that has stolen the t.	CONG 280:14
If love be t.	OTWAY 746:85
layeth up t. for himself	BIBLE 143:51
Preserve it as your chiefest t.	BELL 86:94
purest t. mortal times afford	SHAK 866:40
Rich the t.	DRYD 351:69
She is your t.	SHAK 864:75
Thine be ilka joy and t.	BURNS 212:26
t. in earthen vessels	BIBLE 151:76
t. in heaven	BIBLE 139:24
t. is their only trust	DYER 358:89
t. may be hard to find	BRON 190:88
t. on which we should live	HERZ 479:77
Without glaidnes availis no t.	DUNB 355:37
treasures accumulated t. of age	IRVI 513:62
Better than all t.	SHEL 929:6
Not all the t. of the world	PAINE 750:43
opened their t.	BIBLE 133:24
Strange T. lodg'd	TRAH 1025:28
t. upon earth	BIBLE 135:50
treasury cast into the t.	BIBLE 141:70
If the T. were to fill	KEYN 555:36
well-filled t.	FRED 403:23
wonder sitting on the T. Bench	CHUR 263:7
treat always t. humanity…as an end	KANT 542:5
If you t. her gently	SNOW 951:78
must t. them carefully	HIND 481:14
Talk about a t.	COLL 276:37
way to t. her	FAUL 384:87
who gives a child a t.	MASE 662:46
treaties arising from t.	UNIT 1036:45
T. are like girls	DEGA 313:1
treatise T. of Human Nature	HUME 504:12
treatment diligent t.	PLATO 774:24
one sort of t. may serve for all	CARL 233:27
scientific t. for all diseases	SHAW 923:87
Suitable Case for T.	MERC 670:95
t. of a question is like	WITT 1088:78
treaty hand that signed the t.	THOM 1010:57
not a peace t.	FOCH 395:84
tree almost insensitive t.	DARIO 314:12
as a t. bears apples	EMER 377:67
billboard lovely as a t.	NASH 719:50
birds still hopping on the t.	STEV 975:32

tree (*contd.*):

bomb the knot off a t.	JENS 520:2
buss grew til a t.	YOUNG 1108:3
But a t. chiefly	THOM 1012:9
But there's a t., of many	WORD 1098:50
carve on every t.	SHAK 886:98
Christmas t. is lighted	MOYN 711:14
climbing a birch t.	FROST 406:80
desire…a t. of life	BIBLE 121:73
dew-bespangling herb and t.	HERR 477:61
each t.…a tranced woman	FREE 404:34
Eve, who tasted of the t.	LANY 579:77
evergreen t. of diabolical knowledge	SHER 933:79
every t. of the garden	BIBLE 103:90
form as a t. has form	POUND 787:94
fruit Of the forbidden t.	MILT 687:84
gave me of the t.	BIBLE 103:97
golden t. of actual life	GOET 431:74
Hast thou eaten of the t.	BIBLE 103:96
hewing down a t.	JOHN 530:99
land where the Bong-t.	LEAR 590:59
laughing leaves of the t.	SWIN 986:25
leaves grow on the t.	YEATS 1104:56
leaves to a t.	KEATS 544:51
lived on this Crumpetty T.	LEAR 590:65
loved a t. or flower	MOORE 706:38
make a right Rose T.	YEATS 1106:74
man, a madyn, and a t.	ANON 22:78
marked a t.	STUA 980:3
On a t. by a river	GILB 425:92
on the T. of Life	MILT 690:51
pine t. drops its dead	MERE 671:16
problems of a t.	MAMET 644:56
sat down under a juniper t.	BIBLE 111:68
sat under the T.	KIPL 561:40
shade of a Coolibah t.	PATE 760:96
shady cypress t.	ROSS 824:76
sings on yon, pom'granate t.	SHAK 869:10
smell thee on the t.	SHAK 900:53
some single herb or t.	MARV 658:82
somewhere in the Orange T.	NEIL 722:95
spoils the growth of the t.	SHER 933:96
stands the lonely t.	MILL 676:87
sticking in a t.	SCOTT 855:93
swan-bosomed t.	SITW 941:15
take a t. from the forest	SCOTT 854:70
Teach…under the nearest t.	QABO 796:47
that's why the t.	ANON 25:35
thocht it was a trustie t.	BALL 67:57
three ravens sat on a t.	BALL 67:54
t., a house, a field	MONET 700:43
t. Continues to be	KNOX 567:61
t. from which they spring	BIRD 163:16
t. of knowledge	BIBLE 103:89
t. of knowledge	BYRON 222:34
t. of knowledge is not that of Life	BYRON 221:19
t. of liberty must be refreshed	JEFF 520:90
t. of life	BIBLE 159:39
t. On fire by lightning	BYRON 220:88
t. planted by the rivers of water	BIBLE 113:29
t. that fantasies had planted	HERZL 478:75
t. to be desired	BIBLE 103:95
Under the greenwood t.	SHAK 885:86
Virginia's aged t.	RANS 802:32
Was there a t.	COWL 291:15
wisdom…is a t. of life	BIBLE 120:60
wish I were a t.	HERB 475:16
wither on the t.	JAY 519:74
trees all the t. are green	KING 558:94
among the gusty t.	NOYES 732:42
as fast as Arabian t.	SHAK 900:64
as winter changes t.	BRON 192:12
blasts the roots of t.	THOM 1010:51
childhood t. were green	MACN 637:45

trees (*contd.*):

country of birds and t.	WRIG 1101:10
cut down branches from the t.	BIBLE 139:30
daffodils…beneath the t.	WORD 1099:67
die when the t. were green	CLARE 267:84
filled the t. and flapped	HODG 483:50
fir t. dark and high	HOOD 489:38
ghostly t. all dead and dry	LAWS 588:21
Grass and t. wither	WU 1102:24
have fallen from the t.	WILH 1080:38
heavy t. they climb	SPEN 958:19
Ice-scratched slabs and bent t.	SNYD 951:82
in the end were the t.	WHITE 1070:40
Loveliest of t.	HOUS 494:39
lyke t. and erbys	MALO 642:32
music of its t. at dawn	ARNO 37:75
Of all the t.	KIPL 563:98
peopled by tribes and t.	WRIG 1102:11
procreate like t.	BROW 195:91
river in the t.	HEAN 465:40
see men as t., walking	BIBLE 141:67
Shade off the t.	CORY 288:67
shady t. cover him	BIBLE 113:25
snow fell, the t. stood	NEME 722:4
tall ancestral t.	HEMA 469:10
The t. and houses	THOM 1015:54
thin t. in a city square	LOWE 615:76
tongues in t.	SHAK 885:77
town among the t.	ROBI 815:31
T. cut to Statues	POPE 779:21
t. of noblest kind for sight	MILT 690:52
t. of the field shall clap	BIBLE 127:7
t.…resigned to the way	CATH 244:40
t. shall be my books	SHAK 886:97
t. that yield to the flood	SOPH 953:18
t. were surfaced like flesh	LEE 593:18
t. with black marching boots	HARR 459:31
under t. by the eldritch light	DAYL 310:56
vext garden t.	ARNO 39:16
walk, you lover of t.	BROW 199:62
with his lute made t.	SHAK 918:53
With rocks, and stones and t.	WORD 1095:7
trellises Through gilded t.	SITW 940:6
tremble And make me t.	TENN 1003:22
I t., I expire!	SHEL 931:55
Therefore t., and depart	SHAK 887:28
t. in this factory of books	SMITH 947:5
tremblers boding t. learned to trace	GOLD 433:12
trembling drink thy water with t.	BIBLE 129:37
trembly over t. and feverish	TWAIN 1033:88
tremulous the t. tide	YEATS 1104:58
trench t. warfare of World War I	NOON 731:21
trenches digging t. and trying on	CHAM 249:17
field between the t.	MACG 630:22
trepidation self-examination with t.	I 510:26
trespass cannot t. with impunity	AUDEN 48:88
t. there and go	HOUS 496:79
trespasses forgive us our t.	BOOK 173:91
trespassing without t. on others	BURKE 207:29
tresses bathe thy breathing t.	COLL 277:49
t. grey	SCOTT 853:42
trial Going to t.	THOM 1014:39
no office…is a t.	SHAW 920:90
t., and t. by what is contrary	MILT 685:63
t. by juries	JEFF 520:94
T. by jury	DENM 316:59
triangle lost its golden t.	MAIL 639:84
triangles Knights of Isosceles T.	ROOS 822:51
t. had made a god	MONT 702:81
tribal constructing t. lays	KIPL 561:48
For t. man space	MACL 635:92
tribalism t. and inquisitiveness	ALDI 12:7
tribe badge of all out t.	SHAK 874:20
customs of his t.	SHAW 921:19

tribe (*contd.*):

may his t. increase!	HUNT 505:27
of the t. of Tiger	SMART 944:67
our t.'s complicity	HEAN 465:37
purify the dialect of the t.	ELIOT 372:73
Richer than all his t.	SHAK 900:64

tribeless T., lawless, homeless   HOMER 488:21

tribes peopled by t. and trees   WRIG 1102:11

startled scaly t.	WORD 1100:84
t. have left off eating each other	THOR 1016:74
t....slumber in its bosom	BRYA 201:18
two mighty t., the Bores and Bored	BYRON 223:59

tribulation kept me in t.   MICH 673:36

out of great t.	BIBLE 157:15
ye shall have t.	BIBLE 146:66

tribunal new t. now   BROW 200:93

tributary how is she become t.!   BIBLE 128:29

tribute demands a heavy t.   INNO 512:55

feet thy t. bring	LYTE 621:66
Hypocrisy is a t.	LARO 582:27
t. of the current	FROST 407:88
t. to whom t. is due	BIBLE 149:39
vain t. of a smile	SCOTT 853:47

trice Change in a t.   SWIN 987:32

trick a confidence t.   WILS 1084:14

because of a t.	THUR 1019:31
conjuring t. with bones	JENK 520:99
served such another t.	SHAK 878:22
stuff that will do the t.	FORM 397:27
t. for t.	BEHN 85:67
T. is to Keep Breathing	GALL 413:95
t. of heaping obligations	SHAW 921:29
t. of making it appear	ORWE 744:25
t. of our English nation	SHAK 877:84
t. of that voice	SHAK 903:33
when the long t.'s over	MASE 661:34
wild t. of his ancestors	SHAK 876:71
win the t.	HOYLE 498:1

tricked t. and sold   SAND 841:67

trickling a t. Of heart   PATC 759:90

tricks all t. are either knavish   JOHN 530:1

an underdog new t.	STEV 973:86
no more mean t.	TWAIN 1033:87
old dog new t.	ONEI 740:66
Play such fantastic t.	SHAK 896:72
rare t. of a Machiavellian	WEBS 1060:43
shaped for sportive t.	SHAK 862:46
t. of sense	WILB 1075:21
t. that are vain	HARTE 459:50
Women are like t.	CONG 280:15

tried adherence to the old and t.   LINC 605:2

not been t. and found wanting	CHES 258:15
number of people have t.	KERR 553:17

trifle As 'twere a careless t.   SHAK 907:23

disregard love, as a t.	HUNT 504:20
never t. with nature	AGAS 9:62

trifles observance of t.   DOYLE 343:96

She who t. with all	GAY 416:51
t. away out of shamefaced	MORE 707:53
unconsidered t.	SHAK 911:26
with t. and jingles	BACON 59:8

trigger finger on the t.   MACM 635:9

Whose finger...on the t.?	ANON 26:53
Whose finger...on the t.?	DAILY 303:41

trillion ten, ten t.   LOWE 616:92

trilogy one-t. writer   ROTH 825:7

trim dress'd in all his t.   SHAK 915:83

trimmed If only t.   ROTH 826:25

trinity strong name of the T.   ALEX 13:21

thanks to the Holy T.   COLU 278:5

trinkets returned to your t.   KIPL 563:94

trip fearful t. is done   WHIT 1073:91

little t. to N.Y.	OHARA 737:11
long t. from all fours	THUR 1019:29

trip (*contd.*):

t., hack and push their opponents	FRY 408:10
t. to Europe would be superfluous	SAAR 834:55

tripe fat t. finely broiled?   SHAK 864:86

mercy of bankers and t. sellers	MENC 669:64
Painch, t. or thairm	BURNS 210:84

triple t. ways to take   KIPL 561:47

triple-towered t.-t. sky   DAYL 310:56

tripwire occasion, catalyst, or t.   ACKE 4:53

Trissotin Mithridates and half T.   MACA 624:21

triste jamais t. archy jamais t.   MARQ 656:42

tristesse Adieu t.   ELUA 376:25

Triton this T. of the minnows?   SHAK 911:10

T. blow his wreathèd horn   WORD 1099:72

triumph contact before we can t.   NAPO 718:32

enjoy their t.	HAMM 453:45
first t. over Libya	PLUT 775:37
meet with T. and Disaster	KIPL 564:8
no t. in it	TROL 1027:73
not the t. but the struggle	COUB 289:71
now is the Victor's t. won	POTT 784:43
pedestalled in t.?	BROW 200:91
Poor is the t.	THOM 1015:50
tiny grunt of t.	NIGH 729:94
To t., and to die	GRAY 443:88
t. is somehow clouded	COMM 278:66
t. of Enlightenment	BELL 88:30
t. of failure	RYAN 834:47
t. of his heart	ADDI 7:18
t. of hope over experience	JOHN 528:57
t. of the embalmer's art	VIDAL 1044:65
t. over death and sin	SPEN 958:24
t. over death and sin	SPEN 959:27
truth does not t.	PLAN 772:85
What t.!	ARNO 37:82
won a satisfaction and t.	WOLFE 1090:19
wrong would t.	BROW 200:2

triumphant militant and becomes t.   MORR 709:82

triumphs paints yet more glorious t.   CARL 234:35

t. of the Crusades   RUNC 828:53

trod Generations have t.   HOPK 491:82

T. beside me, close and dear   HOUS 495:59

Trojan left the T. shore   DRYD 352:76

never know what T. 'orses   BEVIN 102:77

trombone phrased on the t.   SINA 940:94

troop foreign t. ...in my country   PITT 771:70

over a t. of artists	WILL 1082:81
preposterous t. of sons	SOME 952:99
run through a t.	BIBLE 114:42

troops admires its shock t.   LECA 592:97

die with their t.	CHUR 264:22
Farewell the plumed t.	SHAK 899:40
lead the t. out	WALE 1049:50
T. always ready to act	FRED 403:23
t., and sweet societies	MILT 685:51
t. of friends	SHAK 910:81

trophies among a military one, t.   FUSE 410:60

Texas, the FBI, and hunting t.   KENN 552:94

trophy t. to magisterial interference   ANON 24:13

tropic between pole and t.   ELIOT 372:67

troth I wonder, by my t.   DONNE 336:73

thereto I plight thee my t.   BOOK 176:49

Trotsky done...by Lenin and T.   CHUR 263:98

trotter fastest t. in the Province   HALI 452:24

trouble Any wonder we're in t.?   DEMI 315:44

cause no t.	AESC 9:58
Double, double, toil and t.	SHAK 909:64
enough real causes of t.	ORWE 745:64
even I have t. doing it	BANK 70:93
full of t.	TWAIN 1032:64
great treasure and t. therewith	BIBLE 121:80
help when in t.	STEV 972:69
if you wanted to view t.	RIDGE 811:79
if you will only take the t.	SHAW 924:11

trouble (*contd.*):

In labour and t....more dignified	CHES 257:86
in time of t.	MARQ 656:46
Kindness in another's t.	GORD 435:61
Man...full of t.	BIBLE 113:9
man is born unto t.	BIBLE 112:2
may be t. ahead	BERL 95:61
repay the t. and expense	BELL 87:1
sit down with t.	GLAS 430:59
toil and t. of acquiring it	SMITH 946:93
t. enough of its own	WILC 1075:25
t. is that no devastating	GONC 434:51
T. t. and it will t. you!	TRAV 1025:39
t. with children	CRISP 296:33
t. with girls	SALI 839:26
t. with me	SALI 838:24
t. with Moore	FRY 408:18
very present help in t.	BIBLE 116:72
War...is toil and t.	DRYD 351:72
When in t., delegate	WAGN 1047:27
where all t. seems	SWIN 987:38

troubled Let not your heart be t.   BIBLE 146:60

t. on every side   BIBLE 151:77

troubles got over all its t.   JERO 521:10

help them through their t.	ALCO 12:2
take arms against a sea of t.	SHAK 890:21
t. of our proud and angry dust	HOUS 496:71
t. of the brain	SHAK 910:82
t. worse than your own	ALGR 13:24

trough slip with the gravy t.   MACB 624:32

t. between the two world wars   LEWIS 602:70

trousers asked me for my t.   KRUG 570:3

bottoms of my t. rolled	ELIOT 367:53
Chinese nurse with green t.	MANS 647:98
cloud in t.	MAYA 665:3
covered...with the t. of decorum	LICH 603:80
involve taking the t. off	BENN 91:76
men's t....great modern things	WARH 1053:22
Muses in striped t.	ORWE 744:36
never have your best t. on	IBSEN 510:21
t., jackets, shoes	LARI 581:93
t. of Winston Churchill	BREZ 187:39

trout find a t. in the milk   THOR 1016:70

portrait of a t.	HUGH 500:31
Where the grey t. lies	HOGG 485:67

trowel lays it on with a t.   CONG 280:8

Troy against our crumbling T.   MACN 637:37

fields where T. once was	OVID 747:96
Homer...chronicled the siege of T.	CUOMO 300:6
Priam's sons of T.	SURR 982:43
sail from the land of T.	VIRG 1045:79
Scare T. out of itself	SHAK 896:60
T.'s Chieftain	VIRG 1045:81
T.'s sacred citadel	HOMER 488:24
Was there another T.	YEATS 1105:67
Where's T.	BRAM 185:8

truant Biting my t. pen   SIDN 937:51

every t. knew	GOLD 433:12
t. in the law	SHAK 860:92

truce vacation, or a t.   WORD 1100:81

truck t., a producer or a critic   LEMM 595:45

t. passing by a factory   CAGE 225:89

truckload equipment by the t.   WELL 1063:3

trudged t. along unknowing   DRYD 352:84

true accept...as being t.   AYER 53:79

admitted to be t.	JAMES 517:49
always say what's t.	STEV 975:33
And is it t.?	BETJ 100:47
any less real and t.	SHAW 920:97
Art for the sake of the t.	SAND 840:55
as long as it isn't t.	CAPO 231:82
as t....as taxes is	DICK 324:11
be known to be t.	RUSS 832:17
Be so t. to thyself	BACON 58:89

true (*contd.*):

brew that is t.	PANA 752:75
But a t. man	INGR 511:44
called Faithful and T.	BIBLE 158:30
can the devil speak t.?	SHAK 907:20
Change proves t.	I 510:25
common reproach is t.	SOCR 951:87
dark and t.	TENN 997:5
don't know they're t.	BACH 54:99
equally happy, is not t.	JOHN 528:48
errors I had accepted as t.	DESC 317:81
Every t. work of art	FRIE 405:62
expected to go quite t.	JOHN 532:33
false or t.	YEATS 1105:60
friends are t.	BIER 161:84
Geometry is not t.	PIRS 771:57
hope's t. gage	RALE 800:13
Hope, art thou t.	SIDN 937:55
if I know what t. love is	TENN 1002:14
If it be t. that good wine	SHAK 887:38
keep on saying…it will be t.	BENN 91:92
kept him falsely t.	TENN 1002:15
let God be t.	BIBLE 148:14
Live pure, speak t.	TENN 1004:54
no matter how t.	VIDAL 1044:58
nothing is t. except the exaggerations	ADOR 9:50
Nothing is t.	ANOU 31:76
nothing more t.	LARK 582:19
old saying and a t.	SWIFT 984:76
remain t. to himself	KENN 552:87
ring in the t.	TENN 1000:56
rough appraisal, but curiously t.	ACHE 3:31
said t. things…by wrong names	BROW 199:58
say something t.	JAMES 517:34
Some t., some light	TENN 1003:38
something is t. that isn't	WILS 1084:14
supposing thou art t.	SHAK 914:79
sure they are t.	SHAK 912:38
that which was prov'd t. before	BUTL 217:22
'The t.'…is only the expedient	JAMES 518:50
to haue t. lufe agane	HENR 473:72
to thine own self be t.	SHAK 888:67
t. and honourable wife	SHAK 883:31
t. attribute of the soul	STAEL 962:77
T. eloquence has no time	PASC 757:52
T. Love…differs from gold	SHEL 931:53
t. love hath my heart	SIDN 936:47
t. lover of literature	SOUT 954:38
t. nature of poetry	RICH 809:52
t. that sin is the cause	JULI 539:69
t., wise friend called Piggy	GOLD 432:85
t. wood, of yew wood	DOYLE 343:94
t. writers have experienced this feeling	SARR 843:3
what a man would like to be t.	BACON 55:28
What I tell you three times is t.	CARR 241:82
what people say of us is t.!	SMITH 947:11
what we believe is not necessarily t.	BELL 86:85
whatever we conceive…is t.	DESC 317:80
whatsoever things are t.	BIBLE 153:15
when thieves cannot be t.	SHAK 875:49
which may be the t.	HAWT 461:71

truest those who paint 'em t. | ADDI 6:3

t. poetry is the most feigning	SHAK 886:10

truffle t. is not a true aphrodisiac | BRIL 188:54

truffles where the t. are | ALBEE 11:87

truism t. in technological | STER 968:83

truisms box of t. | MACN 637:49

Truman colleagues in the T. cabinet | REST 807:14

trump at the last t. | BIBLE 151:72

Lord with the sound of the t.	BOOK 177:75
t. of God	BIBLE 153:25

Trump T. is the price of progress | KRUG 570:5

trumpet Blow t. | TENN 1003:37

do not sound a t. before thee	BIBLE 134:47

trumpet (*contd.*):

great voice, as of a t.	BIBLE 156:98
if the t. give an uncertain sound	BIBLE 151:63
novel was not a t.	LESS 598:5
Pride…his own t.	SHAK 895:45
shifted his t.	GOLD 433:30
t. and the steady drum	MACC 625:40
t. is sounding	MACC 625:36
t. of a prophecy!	SHEL 928:91
t. shall sound	BIBLE 151:72
t. shrill hath thrice	SPEN 958:26

trumpets blow Your t., angels | DONNE 338:3

eagles and the t.?	ELIOT 368:73
eating…to the sound of t.	SMITH 949:57
never been amid the blare of t.	EUDA 380:22
priests blew with the t.	BIBLE 109:10
saith among the t., Ha, ha	BIBLE 113:23
silver, snarling t.	KEATS 546:86
thunderstorm or blare of t.	MANN 646:84
t., beat the drums!	MORE 707:59
T. sounded for him	BUNY 205:74
t. which sing to battle	SHEL 931:60

trumps If dirt were t. | LAMB 577:36

Let spades be t.!	POPE 778:99

truncheons extort their t. | COWP 293:61

trunk perish, t. and all | SOPH 953:18

Sin's rotten t.	COWP 292:46
So large a t.	BELL 87:98

trust absolute t. | SHAK 907:24

all power is a t.	DISR 332:72
brightness to hold in t.	SPEN 956:74
children of men put their t.	BIBLE 115:62
degree and quality of t.	SHAP 919:77
do I put my t.	BIBLE 117:88
don't t. anybody	KAIKO 541:92
don't t. him, we are friends	BREC 186:29
doth still my t. renew	BRID 187:43
empire is…power in t.	DRYD 349:20
equally faulty to t. everyone	SENE 858:44
gift or t.	MACC 625:48
If you can t. yourself	KIPL 564:8
In America few people will t.	MAIL 639:75
knowing…about whom they can t.	SHAP 919:78
man assumes a public t.	JEFF 520:95
men dare t. themselves	SHAK 901:86
never t. a woman who	WILDE 1077:69
never t. an expert	MAMET 643:54
Never t. the artist	LAWR 586:88
only two lawyers…who t. each other	DOLE 335:48
pains that conquer t.	TENN 999:35
Put not your t. in money	HOLM 486:84
put not your t. in princes	BOOK 177:95
Quhome ye may t.	HENR 473:72
Time, which takes in t.	RALE 800:16
treasure is their only t.	DYER 358:89
t. also in him	BIBLE 115:63
T. him as much as…a rattlesnake	ACHE 3:45
t. in Christ	WESL 1066:90
t. in God	DENN 316:60
t. in God	SMITH 949:48
t. in him	BIBLE 113:8
t. in the basic fairness	NIXON 730:14
T. in the Lord with all thine heart	BIBLE 120:57
t. man on his oath	SHAK 901:87
t. me not at all	TENN 1002:6
T. none, for oaths are straws	SHAK 880:78
T. not the physician	SHAK 902:94
t. that good shall fall	TENN 999:38
t. that somehow good	TENN 999:36
t. the very difference	JORD 537:30

trusted friend, in whom I t. | BIBLE 115:67

not to be t. when he does	HAMM 454:60
speaker is not to be t.	EUDA 380:22
To be t. is a greater compliment	MACD 628:4

trusted (*contd.*):

t. like the fox	SHAK 876:71

trustees t. of Posterity | DISR 332:92

trusting never extended to t. him | BULL 204:51

trusty T., dusky, vivid, true | STEV 976:55

truth a little beyond exact t. | STEE 964:23

absolute t.	HALD 451:18
absolute t. is not attainable	ORWE 745:51
Absolute t. is very rare	THOM 1014:37
absurd is…the first t.	CAMUS 228:45
accepted as t.	KING 558:85
according to t.	BURB 205:76
admitted the t.	LAUT 584:48
Americans polite by telling t.	BRAD 183:78
And love of t.	TENN 1003:81
And order, t., and beauty range	SMART 944:68
Art…cheating t.	RIDI 811:81
art is not t.	PICA 769:29
astray as a premature t.	ROST 825:2
authority and show of t.	SHAK 880:60
bear the torch of t.	LICH 604:84
Beauty is t., t. beauty	KEATS 547:12
before the t. has got its boots on	CALL 226:1
believe, falsely, to be the t.	HAMP 454:63
blaze of t. and liberty	MACA 622:90
books…contain our fidelity to t.	CONR 285:3
bright countenance of t.	MILT 685:54
burn sometimes with t.	DIDE 329:24
But it's the t.	KESEY 553:19
category of t. and falsehood	AYER 53:80
Celie, tell the t.	WALK 1049:58
certain basis of t.	HERZ 478:74
Church which abandons the t.	KUNG 571:16
closer to the t.	HEAT 465:47
cold as t.	RHYS 808:28
comfort of thy worth and t.	SHAK 913:60
Communist must grasp the t.	MAO 648:22
completely as too much t.	TWAIN 1035:24
concentrate to t. and liberty	SHEL 927:65
confirmation of t.	MILT 685:66
cult of t.	PIER 769:32
dared to speak the t.	TROL 1028:78
dearer still is t.	ARIS 34:36
Death cancels everything but t.	HAZL 463:12
distinguishing t. from falsehood	DESC 317:76
do not seek for the t.	BORG 178:10
doubt about the t.	MARG 650:60
Doubt t. to be a liar	SHAK 889:91
economical with the t.	ARMS 35:51
enemies of t. than lies	NIET 727:69
essence of all religion and absolute t.	BLAV 169:26
experience as our t.	LEGU 594:30
fear mortal t.	POIN 776:57
fight for freedom and t.	IBSEN 510:21
first casualty…is t.	JOHN 523:1
French t.	ROCH 816:48
full of grace and t.	BIBLE 144:27
function of t.	LIPP 607:36
further to discover the t.	BACON 54:5
God, the source of t.	DESC 318:82
golden heresy of t.	RUSS 833:38
good for testing the t.	PIRS 770:55
gospel t.	GREE 445:30
Granted we want t.	NIET 728:82
grope for t.	POPP 784:25
Habit…the test of t.	CRAB 294:82
habitually tells the t.	MENC 669:63
how one comes by the t.	MILL 678:22
I am the way, the t.	BIBLE 146:62
I have told you the t.	STEV 972:72
I never need catch up with the t.	MACG 630:29
in seeking for T.	PIUS 772:81
in t. must own	COWP 292:35
In t., the more I live	LACL 573:62

tug crouch, swivel, t.	OBRI 734:71
tulips t. bloom as they are told	BROO 192:25
tumble Gibraltar may t.	GERS 420:15
t. on the heather	SCOTT 854:72
tumbled t. off a bus	GRAH 437:86
tumbler Bring in…a clean t.	DICK 322:54
t. of London Water	SMITH 949:46
tumour confronts the t.	HALD 451:19
when it ripens in a t.	ABSE 1:6
Tumtum rested he by the T. tree	CARR 239:47
tumult sank in t. to a lifeless ocean	COLE 275:76
t. and shouting dies	KIPL 562:61
t. dwindled to a calm	BYRON 224:68
t. of the masses	ALCU 12:3
t. of thy mighty harmonies	SHEL 928:90
tune angels…singing out of t.	BYRON 223:66
average guy who could carry a t.	CROS 298:62
complain about the t.	BEVAN 101:68
dancers dancing in t.	TENN 1001:36
Every name is a t.	MOORE 705:22
forced to change their t.	BROD 189:65
good t. on old fiddle	BUTL 217:40
heavenly t. harsh sounding	SHAK 864:95
Hope…sings the t.	DICK 328:97
how it be in t.	SHAK 887:2
incapable of a t.	LAMB 576:25
lamentable t. is the sweetest music	SIDN 937:49
like a wayward t.	YEATS 1104:58
melody…sweetly play'd in t.	BURNS 212:40
Peter like a piper's t.	FARJ 383:63
sad raggy t.	HUGH 499:16
sudden springing of a t.	LOWE 615:76
Then murder's out of t.	SHAK 900:57
thunder to the t. of 'Greensleeves'	SHAK 878:24
we are out of t.	WORD 1099:73
tunes all the good t.	HILL 480:4
beat our t. for bears	FLAU 392:84
only know two t.	GRANT 439:10
slow old t. of Spain	MASE 662:39
t. at which he was…working	DICK 323:92
tunic closest, all-concealing t.	SHEL 928:95
tunnel between two points was a t.	MANC 644:63
end of the t.	LOWE 617:12
On leaving the t.	LEVIN 600:29
one t., dark and solitary	SABA 835:56
perspective of a subway t.	TOOLE 1023:4
some profound dull t.	OWEN 748:14
tunnels t. that re-wind themselves	CRANE 295:9
tuppence T. a Bag!	TRAV 1025:38
t. for all the rest!	FLAN 392:28
Wouldn't give you t.	COLL 276:37
turbid t. look and most profound	LAND 578:55
turbulent democracy…sometimes t.	CART 242:4
rid me of this t. priest?	HENR 472:63
turf At his head a green-grass t.	SHAK 892:61
blue ribbon of the t.	DISR 333:1
green t. beneath my f.	HAZL 463:6
pile of t. against the wall.	COLUM 278:62
shelving bank of t.	SHEL 932:66
t. such the honeyed showers	MILT 684:46
turf-dances t.-d. of…encounter	ALLEN 14:31
Turgenev beat Mr T.	HEMI 471:37
Turk In heathen, T. or Jew	BLAKE 166:65
malignant and a turbaned T.	SHAK 900:64
turkey It was a t.!	DICK 323:89
secure all the myrtle and t.	AUST 51:48
Turkey Christians that travel in T.	BUTL 216:1
In T. it was always 1952	THER 1009:44
T. carpet bears to a picture	MACA 623:98
turkish perpetual T. bath	SWET 983:52
Turks like those wicked T.	DICK 323:96
turmoil with ceaseless t.	COLE 275:14
turn could t., and live with animals	WHIT 1072:80
do not hope to t.	ELIOT 369:8

turn (*contd.*):	
painter must have a natural t.	DURER 356:67
requite thee with a shrewd t.	BIBLE 132:94
t. away thy face	SHAK 884:66
t. from Africa and live?	WALC 1048:31
t. of the road	FAWC 384:93
t. to little things	GIBS 422:39
wouldn't have left a t. unstoned	WIMP 1086:57
You t. if you want to	THAT 1007:15
turn-up t.-u. in a million	BEVIN 102:79
Turnball Mr T. had predicted	TROL 1028:83
Turner T. looks a bit shaky	JOHN 532:46
turning shadow of t.	BIBLE 155:60
take the wrong t.	CONN 283:71
The lady's not for t.	THAT 1007:15
T. and t. in the widening gyre	YEATS 1106:77
turnings all its narrow t.	DICK 325:35
t. intricate of verse	WORD 1096:30
turnip noises like a t.	MACD 628:92
turnips type your t.	CAMP 227:17
turpitude t. of incontinence	SCOTT 855:1
turret daily from the t. wall	MUIR 712:28
Sultan's t.	FITZ 390:87
washed me out of the t.	JARR 518:57
turrets gorgeous t.	MAHO 638:64
t. split the sky	LAND 578:63
turtle Behold the t.	ANON 29:39
traces of the t. soup	DICK 325:43
t. lives 'twixt plated	NASH 719:47
tutor nurse and t. of eccentric minds	LAWS 587:18
TV lecturers…should appear on T.	ZELD 1109:16
more interesting than T.	PIRS 770:53
T. licence	THOM 1015:59
T. soap operas?	UPDI 1037:62
twaddle better far write t.	MANS 648:13
twain go with him t.	BIBLE 134:43
never the t. shall meet	KIPL 560:23
Twain one book by Mark T.	HEMI 470:29
tweed thread of good-class t.	BENN 90:74
Tweed T. rins into the ocean	BURNS 212:31
Willie Wastle dwalt on T.	BURNS 212:29
Tweedledum T. and Tweedledee	CARR 239:53
Twelfth Night T. N. …a silly play	PEPYS 765:71
twelve in the sworn t.	SHAK 896:66
six nights when I was t.	THOM 1011:94
There are only t. notes	HIND 481:14
twelvemonth t. after The seven days	MUIR 712:35
twenties dead by their late t.	GRAV 440:36
twentieth horror of the T. Century	MAIL 639:85
t. will be happy	HUGO 502:91
twentieth-century t.-c. Russia	HELL 469:98
twenty cuts off t. years of life	SHAK 883:41
first t. years are the longest	SOUT 954:40
first t. years…still growing	THOM 1013:22
love…means t. things	BENN 91:86
one of the t.	SHAK 874:11
T. Thousand Thieves	JOYCE 539:63
T. Volume Suicide Note	BARA 70:6
T. will not come again	HOUS 494:40
twenty-four then we shall be t.-f.	HOUS 496:69
truth t.-f. times a second	GODA 430:63
twice gives the poor man t. as much	PUBL 794:13
victory is t. itself	SHAK 878:25
twice-told tedious as a t.-t. tale	SHAK 872:67
Twickenham T.…happy places	THOR 1017:2
twigs man bent some t.	RUDO 828:45
twilight grey t. poured	TENN 994:56
in the grey t.	YEATS 1105:62
lie…is a beautiful t.	CAMUS 229:62
pilots of the purple t.	TENN 995:77
Suspicions…fly by t.	BACON 59:4
t. from the lecture	STEV 971:53
t.'s last gleaming	KEY 554:24
twilights ancient shadow and t.	RUSS 833:37

twin ambition's ugly t.	KUSH 571:22
twinkle roguish t. in his eye	THOM 1015:53
t. of a fading star	ELIOT 369:99
twinkling in the t. of an eye	BIBLE 151:72
Jew in a t.	SHAK 874:25
twins threw the t. she nursed	GRAH 437:87
two t. cleaving together	MILT 685:58
twist Let him t.…in the wind	EHRL 362:58
pale death your vital t. shall sever	DAVI 307:7
twitch affected by every t.	TRUD 1029:12
twitter t. of sleeping canaries	GRAH 438:92
twlight love the t., flutter about	MILT 686:75
two being one and not t.	FLET 394:67
Can t. walk together	BIBLE 130:57
If ever t. were one	BRAD 184:2
must have t. you know	CARR 241:74
sin ye do by t. and t.	KIPL 561:46
think that t. and t. are four	HOUS 496:76
T. and t. is five	DOST 340:42
T. are better than one	BIBLE 123:23
t. for tea	CAES 224:82
t. ideas more inseparable	SMITH 949:44
t. kinds of Arctic problems	STEF 965:24
T. lads that thought	SHAK 911:18
t. plus t. make four	ORWE 745:58
t. shall withstand him	BIBLE 123:24
T. things are always the same	STEIN 966:42
T. women placed together	SHAK 917:48
went in t. and t.	BIBLE 104:10
two-faced not t.-f.	SNOW 951:74
Tyburn has a damned T.-Face	CONG 280:11
Tyne from the Severn to the T.!	KIPL 565:26
type grey paper with blunt t.!	BROW 197:28
highest t. of human nature	SPEN 956:69
megaphone of big t.	MAST 663:65
t. of the common man	ELIOT 370:31
T. of the wise	WORD 1100:88
types certain t. of society	PARS 756:45
device of moveable t.	CARL 234:47
only two t. of cases	BENN 91:76
T. and shadows have their ending	AQUI 32:6
typewriter acquires a new t.	AMIS 17:89
only needs a t. and paper	WINN 1087:63
t.…judged by…fingers	ANON 27:62
t. needs only paper	WELL 1063:3
typical hardly find a t. American	BARN 71:24
more t. and less exotic	ANON 27:60
typing isn't writing…it's t.	CAPO 230:78
tyrannical most t. and oppressive	CALH 225:96
tyrannies totalitarian and corrupt t.	MO 698:10
tyrannous love…so t. and rough	SHAK 868:74
tyranny Bolshevik t. is the worst	CHUR 263:98
burden of t.	SHAW 922:44
call it t.	HOBB 483:41
dark night of t.	MURR 715:78
equals, free from t.?	LANY 580:80
expresses its t. by reducing	MILL 679:47
liberty against t.	ROOS 822:52
modern democracy is a t.	MAIL 639:74
slow t. of moonlight	CRANE 294:96
Taxation…is t.	OTIS 746:75
t. begins	PITT 771:67
t. of conscious thought	BEEC 83:19
T. of Distance	BLAI 165:50
t. of 'the rat race'	THOM 1014:35
T. sets up…echo-chamber	CHAT 254:1
until this t. be over-past	BOOK 177:77
worst sort of t.	BURKE 207:22
yoke of t.	PITT 772:73
tyrant by force or like a t.	PASC 758:69
t. has in common	BROD 189:67
t. spell has bound me	BRON 191:6
t., t. Jealousy	DRYD 351:66
vengeful t. stricken	SULL 981:24

tyrants abject intercourse between t. and slaves

GOLD 432:6

all men would be t. ADAMS 4:61
As many councillors, so many t. SALV 839:41
barbarity of t. SMITH 949:42
blood of patriots and t. JEFF 520:90
Rebellion against t. DAVI 309:42
stuff of which t. are made BEAV 80:79
t. and sensualists are…right WOLL 1091:36
t. do defeat SHAK 883:25
t. from policy BURKE 207:34
t. of thy sex CONG 280:96
T. seldom want pretexts BURKE 208:43
when t. seems to kiss SHAK 910:93
tyre Roosevelt's spare t. GARN 415:28
tyres everything but the air in the t. CALD 225:95
tythe t. o' what ye waste at cartes BURNS 209:62

Ubu Mother U., you are very ugly JARRY 518:67
udder u. a swollen wobble RAINE 800:7
UFOs convinced that U. exist CART 242:1
ugliness march of material u. WHITE 1070:44
see beneath both beauty and u. ELIOT 370:16
u. has a thousand HUGO 501:55
u., vice and unhappiness BERN 97:87
ugly All Middlesex is u. COBB 271:54
Art produces u. things COCT 272:66
better to be good than to be u. WILDE 1076:53
Mother Ubu, you are very u. JARRY 518:67
not more u. SHAK 890:20
so very u. in persons of small means ELIOT 365:2
There is nothing u. CONS 285:20
toad, u. and venomous SHAK 885:75
tourist is an u. human being KINC 557:68
u. mathematics HARDY 456:82
u. woman is a blot BRON 191:94
wish he were not so u. BRON 190:89
UK enquiries about the U. climate SAMU 840:47
Ulster resistance to which U. LAW 585:59
U. will be right CHUR 263:92
Ulsterman armed Protestant U. REDM 804:75
ulterior free of u. motives JONG 533:63
ultimate u. mystery of nature PLAN 772:84
Ulysses Happy…like U. BELL 86:90
interest throughout U. BOWL 182:58
nature of the sickness found, U. SHAK 895:42
passages of U. MILL 677:19
U.…is a dogged attempt FORS 398:45
umbrella fatal forgotten u. MANS 647:1
good u. but a poor roof LOWE 616:90
neat as a furled u. EMERY 378:80
you have got…an u. FLET 394:78
umbrellas audience…put up its u. BEER 83:27
umpire Never argue with u. BOTH 180:35
perched like an u. AVIS 53:76
u., the pavilion cat LANG 579:67
umpiring come to see you u. GRACE 437:85
un-American Solitude is u.-A. JONG 534:64
un-birthday u.-b. present CARR 240:65
unable unwilling or u. WILL 1083:90
unacceptable u. face of capitalism HEATH 466:52
unadmitted u. desire to undress LIN 604:96
unapproachable u., the hard-bitten MACD 628:93
unarmed rode all u. SCOTT 853:54
unattainable flight after the u. WHIT 1071:56
unattended only the u. Moment ELIOT 372:64
unbalance world is…in dynamic u. BART 74:77
unbearable U. Lightness of Being KUND 571:15
expressing lightly the u. UPDI 1037:71
tolerable and the absolutely u. DAFOE 303:39
unbecoming nothing more u. CONG 280:6
u. for a cardinal JOHN 522:34
unbelief Because of your u. BIBLE 138:16
Blind u. is sure too err COWP 291:28

unbelief (*contd.*):
gained…by our u. BROW 199:55
help thou mine u. BIBLE 141:68
help thou my u. FORS 399:51
u., in denying them EMER 377:53
u. of what is false MACD 628:3
unbelievers money…has no u. GAUT 416:44
unborn possible to talk to the u. BARZ 75:95
Ventriloquizing for the u. GRAV 439:22
uncertain u. business of war GERB 420:98
U., coy, and hard to please SCOTT 853:58
uncertainties capable of being in u. KEATS 544:47
uncertainty distribution of u. STEIN 966:50
tolerance as u. BURKE 208:53
u.? Even ignorance? NIET 728:82
uncharitableness malice, and all u. BOOK 174:5
uncivilized very u. to invade HUNT 505:32
uncle her u. once taught her HEAN 465:43
Mine u.? SHAK 889:76
My u. was famous SPEN 956:87
real live nephew of U. Sam's COHAN 272:69
she wanted U. Tom LEE 593:17
U. Matthew was saying MITF 697:1
u. who could never walk down HOME 487:13
unclean all as an u. thing BIBLE 128:13
man of u. lips BIBLE 124:61
u. shall not pass BIBLE 126:83
unclubbable very u. man JOHN 528:43
uncomfortable when he is only u. SHAW 921:34
when it hardens does it become u. ANGE 19:25
uncommitted live free and u. THOR 1016:84
uncommon u. abilities BAGE 62:66
very u. cook SAKI 838:12
unconceptualisable concrete and u. KELM 548:31
unconcern looks with u. JOHN 526:99
unconcerned Thou u. canst hear POPE 781:61
unconscious u. in us warns us MOND 699:42
u.…interpreter—in the eye BRON 191:95
u. unity with life MILL 678:43
unconventional completely u. life BIRD 163:14
uncouth Nothing…more u DISR 333:22
U. unkist, said…Chaucer SPEN 957:95
undecided five who are u. STEN 968:75
undeniable u. pretensions PITT 771:71
under-belly u.-b. of the Axis CHUR 265:26
under-privilege u.-p. was over-used FEIF 384:97
undercurrent u. of emotion UPDI 1037:73
undercurrents imperceptible u. CUOMO 300:5
u., drifting, waiting MORG 707:62
u. of everlasting murmur RUSK 830:88
underdog can't teach an u. STEV 973:86
on the side of the u. PALEY 751:59
underdogs among the u. WAUGH 1057:90
undergarments old-fashioned u. LEWIS 601:50
undergraduate first modern u. LEVE 599:18
undergraduates with the u. HAZL 463:4
underground best part of him is u. ANON 29:44
Give me an u. laboratory PERE 766:91
might well be u. GILB 425:84
not rest from taking u. FRAME 400:76
underlings we are u. SHAK 882:20
underlip u. protruded a little MANS 647:2
underpants word means u. MURR 715:76
understand Adults never u. anything SAIN 836:83
believe so that I may u. ANSE 31:81
contempt for anything he didn't u. WOOL 1094:86
dogs who don't u. CALV 226:6
don't believe…won't u. AUGU 49:17
don't think I u. people FORS 398:40
hard to u. GORB 435:56
language I don't u. APPL 32:91
may not be made to u. it CONF 279:88
people…who u. pictures KIPL 561:44
really don't u. KENN 551:83

understand (*contd.*):
Sex…I really don't u. SALI 838:20
shewed unto thee than men u. BIBLE 132:89
striven…to u. them SPIN 960:46
talent is to u. a man HUGO 502:81
u. himself KAZIN 543:29
u. that a man TROL 1028:81
u. that you experience KAFKA 540:85
u. thy kisses SHAK 876:60
understood as to u. FRAN 401:91
we could not u. him WITT 1088:81
what they u. not SHEL 931:60
When I do not u. SOPH 953:21
wise enough to u. SCHW 851:28
Women…we should not u. CONG 280:15
understanding among men of u. PLATO 774:7
capable of u. each other BERL 96:70
declare, if thou hast u. BIBLE 113:17
experience and u. of life MILL 678:22
eye of my u. JULI 539:67
find you an u. JOHN 532:31
for the clearer u. of English WHAR 1068:3
for thy more sweet u. SHAK 865:11
good u. with a new mistress ETHE 380:15
in length of days u. BIBLE 113:7
lack of u. BIER 161:80
lean not unto thine own u. BIBLE 120:57
learn u., and to give answer BIBLE 132:93
more u. than all my teachers BIBLE 119:31
no occasion to exert his u. SMITH 946:91
pains toward creating u. NEWM 724:26
passeth all u. BOOK 175:33
patient, sardonic u. LESS 598:99
pleasing to…the u. ADDI 7:19
presume yourself ignorant of his u. COLE 275:19
problem of u. the world POPP 783:21
reputation of u. DRYD 348:78
too much u. GOLD 432:89
u. can intuit nothing KANT 541:98
u. unto the simple BIBLE 119:34
with all thy getting get u. BIBLE 120:59
woman of u. AUST 50:34
women's u. is freer and sharper CHRI 262:75
understatement That is an u. SAMU 840:46
understood have ye not u. BIBLE 126:90
life must be u. backwards KIER 556:57
never u. what music was FAURE 384:91
understudies slaughtered by their u. STOP 978:76
undertaker greeting give an u. BALD 64:5
undertaking no such u. CHAM 249:21
prepared to join…the u. MILL 675:78
prosecution of any u. JOHN 525:92
undertakings series of u. SART 844:17
will to desperate u. SHAK 889:87
undervalue conspiracy to u. them JAMES 516:12
underwater u. hazards MORT 710:92
underwear in the rain in your u. BRADY 184:3
like…skid-marked u. COUP 289:82
u. first, last and all the time BREC 186:26
Wearing u. is as formal HEMI 471:49
underwhelmed u. by the prospect JAY 519:76
underwood green u. and cover SWIN 986:24
underwrite u. it with their lives MILL 678:38
undisciplined U. squads of emotion ELIOT 372:53
undismayed go forth to meet him u. SHER 934:13
undoing u. of those human rights KENN 550:64
undone John Donne…U. DONNE 338:1
leave great things u. GLAS 430:58
Woe is me! for I am u. BIBLE 124:61
undoomed u. warrior ANON 21:53
undulate forms of pleasure, u. FUSE 410:81
undying his passion is Infinite, u. PARK 754:7
uneasy no u. feeling JOHN 527:27
U. lies the head SHAK 877:95

uneatable full pursuit of the u.   WILDE 1077:66
unemployed u. …do not have skills   CALL 226:99
unemployment creating u.   ROBI 814:20
  cure u. before Keynes   ROBI 815:37
  need be no more u.   KEYN 555:36
  reduce u.   HEATH 466:51
  u. only looks good   PASS 759:82
unexamined u. life is not worth   SOCR 952:90
unexpected By how much u.   SHAK 872:61
  expect the u.   HERA 473:88
unexplored hitherto u. country   SHIP 935:22
unexpressive the chaste, and u. she   SHAK 886:98
unfairnesses u. that were explained   GALL 413:96
unfaithful Confidence in an u. man   BIBLE 121:99
  ways of being u.   WYLIE 1104:48
unfashionable Fashion is…u.   CHAN 251:53
  u. is what other people wear   WILDE 1078:93
unfeathered u. two-legged thing   DRYD 349:14
unfed calls us, still u.   KIPL 561:54
unfeeling u. for his own   GRAY 441:48
unfit picked from the u.   HARK 457:19
  u. for a nation of shopkeepers   SMITH 945:84
  u. for power   FOOT 396:94
unfitness personal u.   GLAD 429:50
unfittest survival of the u.   SUMN 981:27
unforeseen contingent and the u.   FISH 389:82
unforgetful teach the u. to forget?   ROSS 824:92
unforgiveness an alp of u.   PLOM 775:33
unfruitful he becometh u.   BIBLE 137:98
  unwarranted as they are u.   AYER 53:77
ungartered U., and down-gyvèd   SHAK 889:86
ungodly counsel of the u.   BIBLE 113:29
  the hope of the u.   BIBLE 131:84
  u. in great power   BOOK 176:70
ungracious as some u. pastors do   SHAK 888:62
unhandsome she were u.   SHAK 879:32
unhanged not three good men u.   SHAK 876:54
unhappiest u. moment   SCHO 849:97
unhappiness cause of man's u.   PASC 757:58
  loyalty we all feel to u.   GREE 444:8
  Man's u.…comes of his greatness   CARL 235:56
unhappy each u. family   TOLS 1023:96
  guy gets too complicated he's u.   CHAN 250:36
  if it makes you so u.   CARR 239:52
  instinct for being u.   SAKI 838:6
  keeps the u. from thinking   DIBD 319:6
  making one another u.   MENC 670:83
  never as u. as one thinks   LARO 582:25
  some should be u.   JOHN 530:86
  speak when she is u.?   SMITH 948:36
  These u. people   SWIFT 985:87
  unhappiest moment of the u. man   SCHO 849:97
unhealthy u. for want of air   DICK 324:20
unheard those u. Are sweeter   KEATS 547:8
unholy Refrain from the u. pleasure   BELL 86:96
  sights u., Find out   MILT 682:96
unicorn Lion and the U.…fighting   CARR 240:71
  rarer than the u.   JONG 533:63
  u. and lion wild   SHAK 866:34
uniform gaunt u.   ADAMS 4:63
  good u. must work its way   DICK 321:30
  Should be more u.   HOOD 488:36
  talent like a u.   AUDEN 47:63
  u. 'e wore   KIPL 561:35
uniformity manageable u.   HUXL 508:90
  u. of their means   FUSE 410:59
uniforms buried in their u.   DOSP 340:40
unimaginable nothing was u.   DIDI 330:47
unimpeachable u. orthodoxy   RAHN 800:5
uninformed most unlearned and u.   AUST 51:51
uninstructed plain to u. people   HUXL 509:5
union impossible u.   ELIOT 372:66
  National U. of Mineworkers   MACM 635:14
  Only through their u.   KANT 541:98

union (*contd.*):
  proper u. of gin and vermouth   DEVO 318:89
  protesting against u.   GRAT 439:14
  remain in u. with England   SCOTT 856:10
  Sail on, O U.   LONG 611:8
  u., before his citizenship   LEWIS 601:49
  u. is perfect   DICK 329:22
  U. to be dissolved   LINC 604:98
  U. which never strikes   HICKS 480:97
  u. with the universe   RUSS 832:17
  war which saved the U.   WILS 1086:48
unionism u. is stronger than creed   LAWS 587:19
unions aggregations of trade u.   DOSP 340:40
  Hitler attacked the u.   NIEM 727:68
unique Murder is a u. crime   JAMES 517:35
  sonatas of Mozart are u.   SCHN 848:86
  u. to the level of the herd   MILL 679:47
uniqueness poet reminds…u.   COUS 290:87
unison in u. with this order   MILL 678:33
unit true middle class u.   SHAW 922:55
united country needs to be u.   JOHN 523:47
  reminded him of Sheffield U.   HATT 460:58
  u. by nothing   TOLS 1023:98
  u. in one person   HESS 479:84
United Kingdom Ireland and…U. K.   LLOY 609:63
United Nations If the U. N. once   EISE 364:86
  Peoples of the U. N.   UNIT 1036:45
  The U. N. cannot do anything   OBRI 734:65
  U. N. is not in a position   EDEN 360:22
  When we started the U. N.   HARR 459:39
United States defeat the U. S. aggressors   MAO 648:29
  friendship of the U. S.   GEOR 418:82
  have our U. S.-mania   RODO 818:87
  In the U. S.…more space   STEIN 965:37
  lies about the U. S.   STEV 972:71
  loyalty to the U. S.   ROOS 822:53
  mental illness of the U. S.   ATWO 45:20
  no major institution in the U. S.   FRIE 405:55
  politics in the U. S.   TOCQ 1021:76
  President of the U. S.   UPDI 1036:56
  problem with the U. S. economy   KRUG 570:5
  prominent as the U. S.   MUNCH 714:52
  so close to the U. S.   DIAZ 319:3
  test case of U. S. capacity   MACN 636:28
  U. S. and the British   CHUR 265:31
  U. S.…global gendarme   MACN 636:29
  U. S.…greatest poem   WHIT 1072:73
  U. S. imperialism   MAO 648:26
  U. S. is the best and fairest   BUSH 215:86
  U. S. is the biggest business   ROGE 820:6
  U. S. is…the great melting pot   MARS 656:55
  U. S. is the only country   ROGE 820:16
  U. S. …is warm-hearted   FERB 385:7
  U.S. must be neutral   WILS 1086:46
  U. S. of America   ROOS 822:44
  U. S.…the Jew among the nations   FERB 385:7
  U. S. to the Monroe Doctrine   ROOS 822:46
  U.S. will never again seek   WILS 1086:45
  Vice President of the U. S.   GARN 415:28
unity dwell together in u.!   BIBLE 119:45
  rich, dark, organic u.   HOMA 487:7
  unconscious u. of life   MILL 678:43
universal All partial evil, u. good   POPE 780:41
  and u. peace lie   TENN 996:90
  appetite, an u. wolf   SHAK 895:40
  books…of u. appeal   FORD 396:3
  He never listens is u.   MACK 632:50
  if it is not u.   TOLK 1022:91
  [man] is a u. machine   REDT 804:79
  maxim should become a u. law   KANT 542:4
  mirror of the u. elements   STEI 965:30
  old u. truths   FAUL 383:77
  particular and u.   BERG 94:44

universal (*contd.*):
  reach the u.   SART 844:7
  u. as sea sickness   SHAW 921:37
  u. darkness buries all   POPE 783:11
  u. frame is without a mind   BACON 57:64
  u. pollution and u. frustration   ILLI 511:32
  u. sickness   TRIL 1026:57
  u. suffrage prevails   PARE 753:83
  u. test of travel   GELL 417:71
  war tends to become u.   DUBO 353:9
universals Myth deals in false u.   CART 242:94
universe black hole of the u.   UMAS 1035:38
  boundless u.   TENN 996:85
  by which the u. is regulated   PAINE 750:51
  cement of the u.   SELF 857:37
  circumscribe This u.   MILT 691:85
  cold reaches of the u.   KENN 551:69
  come to esteem the u.   FONT 395:86
  corner of the u.   HUXL 507:78
  cover the u. with mud   FORS 398:45
  entire u.…is Pure Accident   OATES 733:54
  entities of which the u. is   KUHN 570:14
  explain the u.   BERL 96:68
  faintly through the u.   JOYCE 538:42
  galaxies populating the u.   BRAUN 186:17
  hell of a good u. next door   CUMM 300:93
  In this u.   WORD 1094:95
  kingdom is as wide as the u.   FLAU 392:34
  laws and nature of the U.   HARDY 457:9
  Life, the U. and Everything   ADAMS 5:66
  man said to the u.   CRANE 295:14
  many wonderful things…in the u.   COLT 277:58
  measure of the u.   SHEL 930:22
  Miss U.'s buttocks   BENE 89:58
  mock the u.   ARET 33:17
  no intention in the u.   MONOD 700:46
  no other u. except the human u.   SART 844:18
  Not for all the u. contains   OCON 735:81
  nothing dead in this U.   CARL 235:64
  nothing in the whole u.   OVID 747:3
  nothing is accidental in the u.   OATES 733:54
  of her myriad u.   TENN 1003:29
  On the stage of the u.   LAFO 575:96
  otherwise kindly u.   HARDY 456:91
  phenomenon of [the] u.   PEAR 762:32
  protons in the u.   EDDI 360:20
  Put back Thy u.   JONES 533:52
  stole a page from the U.!   MARTI 657:56
  sweet winds of the u.   MACD 628:99
  tinker with the u.   MILL 678:23
  transitory in the u.   GIRA 428:43
  u. appears as an infinite   MUIR 713:39
  u. had a beginning   MILL 675:73
  u. is arranged like a cithera   HONO 488:31
  u. is Copernican, not Ptolemaic   PHIL 768:19
  u. is not only queerer   HALD 451:17
  u. which philosophy contemplates   RUSS 832:17
  unlike any other thing…in the u.   STEI 966:52
  utmost limits of the u.   HUME 503:98
  vast order of the u.   PAGE 749:33
  Wisdom and Spirit of the u.!   WORD 1095:14
universities As to our u.   LODGE 610:83
  black market u.   ZELD 1109:16
  critics are like American u.   ALBEE 11:89
  escape our u.   OPPE 741:74
  u., and the public chair   MILL 675:67
university critic to the u.   BRAD 184:88
  dismissed from a German u.   TILL 1020:64
  fools at a u.   GERH 420:4
  no u. could pay   STIG 977:66
  of that famous u.   HAZL 463:4
  servant to be bred at U.   CONG 281:18
  this ancient U.   HOUS 495:67
  true U.…is a collection of books   CARL 236:91

university (*contd.*):
u. has failed you   GOHE 431:84
U. of Oxford   GIBB 421:26
u. of Oxtail   JOYCE 538:52
U. should be a place of light   DISR 333:17
u. where he didn't inhale   DOWD 342:77
u. where…the Jews are hosts   SACH 835:57
unjust abhor…the u.   CURZ 302:29
Every u. man   PLATO 774:13
u. in the least   BIBLE 143:5
unjustified course was u.   HIRO 481:19
unkillable filthy, sturdy, u. infants   POUND 785:53
unkind Midlands…sodden and u.   BELL 87:15
None…deformed but the u.   SHAK 895:35
position is admittedly u.   STEV 973:92
Thou art not so u.   SHAK 885:94
u. or irreverential word   HAWT 462:82
when givers prove u.   SHAK 891:22
unkindled u., uncoffined   BYRON 221:7
unkindness by my u. shaken   SHAK 915:91
unkist Uncouth, u., said…Chaucer   SPEN 957:95
unknown as One u.   SCHW 852:31
bird rising, unnamed, u.   REID 806:97
holier lot to be u.   HOPK 492:95
let nothing…be u. to you   RABE 799:93
route towards the u.   HUGO 502:92
She lived u.   WORD 1095:8
To that u. and silent shore   LAMB 576:9
tread safely into the u.   HASK 460:57
uncertain, u., arbitrary rule   LOCKE 609:70
u. Prime Minister by… U. soldier   ASQU 42:78
U., unkist, and lost   CHAU 254:5
ways that are still largely u.   REYES 807:22
unlearned most u. and uninformed   AUST 51:51
what we have u.   TWAIN 1034:12
unlessoned u. girl, unschooled   SHAK 873:84
unlucky u. to sound off   I 510:24
unmarried paid to them while u.   JOHN 529:81
U. men are best friends   BACON 57:59
unmask u. her beauty to the moon   SHAK 888:61
unmeaning u. thing it is   HAZL 463:10
unmentionable Everything was u.   DIDI 330:47
unmourned are all u. and unknown   HORA 493:25
unmoved u. this place leaves one   SNYD 951:84
U. though witlings sneer   JOHN 525:75
unmusical no…u. person   HENZE 473:74
Nothing can be more u.   DISR 333:22
unnatural both equally u.   GRAT 439:14
everlastingly being u.   MITC 696:83
foul, strange, and u.   SHAK 889:75
nothing so u. as the commonplace   DOYLE 343:98
U., he called them   SHAR 919:81
unnebulous u. train of words   BISH 164:32
unnecessary eliminate the u.   HOFF 484:57
often utterly u.   TOLS 1023:98
thou u. letter   SHAK 902:10
to do the u.   HARK 457:19
uncomfortable, u. and…useless   STEV 973:92
vain, u. things are men   ROCH 816:54
unnoble most u. swerving   SHAK 905:79
unnoticed that u. and that necessary   ATWO 45:27
unofficial u. magic becomes stronger   REED 805:88
unorthodox loopholes for an u.   ORWE 742:5
unpack u. my heart with words   SHAK 890:16
unpalatable disastrous and the u.   GALB 411:78
unparalleled lass u.   SHAK 906:8
u. elsewhere in our culture   SHAP 919:78
unpleasant enough u. things   RENO 807:12
face…is so peculiarly u.   SNOW 951:74
How u. to meet Mr Eliot!   ELIOT 361:9
u. way of saying the truth   HELL 468:91
unplumbed u., salt, estranging sea   ARNO 37:80
unpolished ignorant and u. people   DICK 327:79
unpopular safe to be u.   STEV 972:75

unpremeditated u. lay   SCOTT 853:43
unprincipled sold by the u.   CAPP 231:91
unprofitable most idle and u.   GIBB 421:26
weary, stale, flat, and u.   SHAK 888:52
unprovoked It seemed u.   STEV 976:60
unquestionable one u. truth   TOLS 1023:98
unquestioned u. law   WHAR 1068:3
unravel can devise, another can u.   WRIS 1102:20
unreal gunfire…sounded u.   USTI 1038:78
this story is u.   PACH 748:25
unreality general atmosphere of u.   QUEN 797:54
unreason woman…element of u.   WRIG 1101:3
unreasonable u. one persists   SHAW 922:56
unremarked legion of the u.   SAFI 836:72
unrequited Self-love…often u.   POWE 787:3
unrest root of the social u.   LECO 592:1
u. which men miscall delight   SHEL 931:47
unrighteousness cleanse…all u.   BIBLE 156:88
mammon of u.   BIBLE 143:4
unromantic u. poet   FROST 407:90
unsaid that which is u.   ANOU 31:76
unsatiable be not u.   BIBLE 132:11
unsatisfied leaves one u.   WILDE 1076:52
unscathed guilty never escape u.   BAIL 62:68
unscotch if you u. us   SCOTT 856:13
unscrupulous most u. kidney   FRY 408:10
unsearchable u. dispose Of highest   MILT 695:59
unseen all-seeing but u.   BYRON 220:99
Greet the u.   BROW 200:3
O friend u., unborn, unknown   FLEC 393:47
Of u. things above   HANK 455:70
unselfish u. are not the leaders   CONR 285:7
unselfishness u. of an oyster   SAKI 838:8
unsex u. me here   SHAK 907:27
unshackle u. …transient desires   EINS 363:63
unshorn presents the god u.   HERR 477:60
unsightly grotesque, if not u.   VEBL 1041:26
unsinkable u. air-craft carrier   MACA 621:72
unsophisticated u. can really go for   AMIS 16:74
unsorted u. stuff   GOLD 432:86
unsound notoriously u.   HOLM 486:83
unspeakable inedible raised to the u.   BASK 76:7
u. in full pursuit   WILDE 1077:66
unspiritual conditions that are u.   MARX 660:6
unspontaneous I am u.   KENN 550:58
unspotted keep himself u.   BIBLE 155:63
unstable U. as water   BIBLE 106:51
unstoned left a turn u.   WIMP 1086:57
unsubduable u. country   GILL 426:5
unsympathetic u. as butterflies   ELIOT 365:5
untalented product of the u.   CAPP 231:91
untell To u. the days   HEYW 480:92
unthinking Laughing…u. time   DRYD 352:95
painful process of U.   CUMM 299:75
untimely U. ripped   SHAK 910:89
untired against the new and u.   LINC 605:2
untouched expect to be u. by madness   BELL 88:23
untranslatable I too am u.   WHIT 1072:75
untrodden among the u. ways   WORD 1095:8
untrue blaming mirrors for being u.   LAFO 574:78
man who's u. to his wife   AUDEN 48:77
untruth torment of the night's u.   DANI 304:62
transfigured them into U.   LARK 581:5
why not rather u.?   NIET 728:82
untruths they have spoken u.   SHAK 880:64
untwist Not u.…these last strands   HOPK 492:1
unusual moved by what is not u.   ELIOT 366:38
unutterable looked u. things   THOM 1015:49
present u. things   THOR 1016:71
unvisionary u. language of farm   ENGLE 378:91
unwanted feeling of being u.   THER 1008:35
unwarrantable any u. belief   RICH 810:62
unwarranted u. as they are unfruitful   AYER 53:77
unwell begins to feel u.   KIPL 560:21

unwholesome u. in their thoughts   SHAK 892:66
unwieldiness cumbersome u.   DONNE 338:97
unwilling group of the u.   HARK 457:19
u. or unable   WILL 1083:90
unwise sight of the u.   BIBLE 131:81
unworldliness out of u.   MACC 625:46
unworthy opinion…is u. of him   BACON 58:83
U. was what he did   AESC 9:54
unwrung our withers are u.   SHAK 891:42
up cannot bear levelling u.   JOHN 527:37
curtain was u.   KAUF 542:15
more u. and down than sideways   HEMI 470:12
U., all of us   PEPYS 765:74
U. was the heartening   EMPS 378:85
upbringing result of my u.   DYSON 358:99
the u. a nun would envy   ORTON 742:85
upbringings u. that were so clean   COUP 289:82
upgrowth germ and first u.   KING 559:2
upharsin Mene, Mene, Tekel, U.   BIBLE 129:49
upholding u. all things by the word   BIBLE 154:44
upholstery dogs had eaten the u.   PERE 766:96
faded u. of tears   BROY 201:5
uplands thrilling over her u.   DAYL 310:55
upon Either with it or u. it   ANON 20:41
upper Have still the u. hand   COWA 290:3
no longer u. classes   TOCQ 1021:74
uprising knowest…mine u.   BIBLE 119:48
uproar amidst that joy and u.   CAMP 227:30
little u. as a jellyfish   WODE 1088:87
set all the city on an u.   BIBLE 148:97
upset not u., are you?   BANKS 70:95
upside autocracy turned u. down   HERZ 478:74
turned the world u. down   BIBLE 148:98
upstairs labour going u.   MUNDY 714:53
u. into the world   CONG 280:12
upstart curse…upon the sleek u.   RANS 802:34
u. crow   GREE 445:33
upwardly-mobile all pigs are u.-m.   THOM 1014:38
uranium nuclear reaction in u.   EINS 363:65
urban all u. and rural sounds   LAMB 577:33
Boston has become U. Renewal   MAIL 639:84
incomplete in the u. compound   MACL 635:95
urchin ribald, inspired u.   DAYL 310:57
urge absence of the u. to create   MAMET 643:49
something other than the u.   SAND 842:79
U. that impels women   THUR 1019:43
urgency fierce u. of now   KING 557:79
Life…having a sense of u.   BURT 214:63
urgent assurance…that nothing was u.   ACHE 2:25
Egyptians were u. upon the people   BIBLE 106:63
urgings felt sexual u.   COND 279:86
Uriah Set ye U. in the forefront   BIBLE 110:46
Uricon ashes under U.   HOUS 495:54
Urim U. and the Thummim   BIBLE 107:70
urinal burnt match skating in a u.   CRANE 295:9
urine Cannot contain their u.   SHAK 873:90
faintly scented u.   JOYCE 538:53
red wine of Shiraz into u.   BLIX 169:32
u. dump at sunset   SCHW 851:30
urn angel watching an u.   TENN 1001:78
bubbling and loud-hissing u.   COWP 293:60
dust falls to the u.   VAUG 1041:17
Lean on a garden u.   ELIOT 367:60
storied u.   GRAY 442:67
u. Of bitter prophecy   SHEL 932:65
urs strew your pathway…dreadful u.   HOLM 486:78
us before they get at u.   GRACE 437:84
usage dictionary of popular u.   GREE 444:17
usages statutes of u. therein obtained   MILL 674:57
usances my moneys and my u.   SHAK 874:20
use consumed by u.   GILL 427:13
designed its u.   PALEY 751:65
for the u. of his power   HOBB 483:38
how to make the best u. of it   SIMO 939:84

use (*contd.*):
keener with constant u. — IRVI 513:63
life is... given to all for u. — LUCR 619:36
little u. for contraceptives — SHAR 919:81
no u. for the teachings — KHRU 556:51
no u. save abuse — SIMO 939:87
Remains in u. with you — SHAK 905:63
skilled u. of blunt objects — PEAR 762:34
u. alone that sanctifies expense — POPE 779:24
U. every man — SHAK 890:31
u. him as he uses thee — SHAK 901:70
u. of a new-born child? — FRAN 402:13
u. of travelling — JOHN 532:44
value in u.! — SMITH 946:94
used let them be well u. — SHAK 890:12
shouldn't be much u. — HOLM 486:90
useful both viable and u. — HAYEK 462:91
extremely u. in life — SPIN 960:58
returns home wise and u. — BELL 86:90
science is said to be u. — HARDY 456:83
To be u....hideous — BAUD 78:40
what is u. to oneself — SPIN 960:55
useless as u....as possible — GALT 413:10
let me not live to be u.! — WESL 1066:69
Protestations...are always u. — COBB 271:53
speech they know to be u. — ELIOT 365:24
wars are u. — RICH 809:46
uses all the u. of this world! — SHAK 888:52
Usher's Well wife at U. W. — BALL 68:60
usquabae Wi' u., we'll face — BURNS 211:17
USSR Back in the U. — LENN 596:66
for the U. to reject Communism — KHRU 556:46
usury u. age-old — POUND 786:64
utensil every particle and u. — SHAK 894:5
utilitarian our u. world — STARK 963:95
utility foundation of morals, U. — MILL 675:71
immediate practical u. — HELM 469:4
neither gain nor loss of u. — JEVO 521:20
u. of some particular object — SMITH 946:94
view to future u. — JEVO 521:21
utopia u. remains forever closed — MAIL 639:81
view as an infernal U. — LEWIS 602:69
whatever U. of human virtue — HAWT 461:69
utopian U....romance — WEBB 1059:71
Utopias end all the static U. — INGE 511:39
U-turn catchphrase, the U.-t. — THAT 1007:15
utter ache to u. — SAND 841:56
Thou wilt not u. — SHAK 875:52
What I think, I u. — SHAK 911:6
utterance u. of the early Gods — KEATS 547:3
utterances by his own u. — PARN 756:40
Deathbed u. — PLOUT 775:35
uttered u. it a hundred times — HOLM 486:81
Uzza U. put forth his hand — BIBLE 112:85
Uzziah year that king U. died — BIBLE 124:60

vacancy aught of blinder v. — WORD 1100:78
chaos of v. — DELA 314:32
next v. for God — CIAR 266:51
v. which occupies the space — TOOLE 1023:6
which but for v. — SHAK 905:69
vacant v. into the v. — ELIOT 371:49
vacation v., or a truce — WORD 1100:81
vacations v. of the flesh — TZARA 1035:35
vaccinated v. with a phonograph — GOLD 433:33
vacuum cannot work in a v. — ROGE 820:4
nature hates a v. — WILL 1082:70
v. cleaner grazes over the carpet — RAINE 800:7
v. that fills a v. — GALB 412:87
vacuums role is...filling v. — CART 242:7
vagaries correct the v. — KEYN 554:34
v. of butlers — ACHE 2:26
vague woman's brain: v., slippery — RICH 810:64
vailèd with thy v. lids — SHAK 888:48

vain a' is done in v. — BURNS 213:48
Call it not v. — SCOTT 853:48
Destroy his fib...in v. — POPE 781:62
full as v. — DRYD 348:97
He is so v. — DISR 333:20
he seeks in v. — HELM 469:4
head grown grey in v. — SHEL 931:47
imagine a v. thing? — BIBLE 114:30
In v.—always in v. — DAVI 307:98
in v. decry'd and curst — POPE 782:91
name of the Lord thy God in v. — BIBLE 106:68
nothing is in v. — HERB 474:6
of Amber Snuff-box justly v. — POPE 779:2
role of the author is v. enough — DIDE 329:32
Say not...the wounds are v. — CLOU 270:32
soul...made first in v. — BROW 200:94
v. and doubtful good — SHAK 887:41
v. desire at last — ROSS 824:92
v., giddy, shallow, humorous youth — SHAK 881:79
v. in verse — SIDN 937:50
v. man,' said she — SPEN 959:28
V. matter is worse — BACON 55:9
V. thy onset! — ARNO 39:22
v. to mislike the current fashion — FULL 410:53
v., unnecessary things are men — ROCH 816:54
youth is v. — COLE 274:10
vainer role of the critic...is v. — DIDE 329:32
valanced Thy face is v. — SHAK 890:10
vale after I depart this v. — MENC 669:60
cool sequestered v. of life — GRAY 442:72
death's dark v. — SCOT 856:19
i'th'midst a horrid v. — MILT 687:98
Saimear's green v. — MACC 625:36
shady sadness of a v. — KEATS 547:99
v. in whose bosom — MOORE 706:32
v. of soul-making — KEATS 545:71
v. of tears — FERRE 387:28
v. of Tempe — RUSK 831:13
V., the three lone weirs — ARNO 39:14
violet-embroidered v. — MILT 683:26
Valentine Slander V. — SHAK 860:85
vales Making all the v. rejoice? — BLAKE 166:63
o'er v. and hills — WORD 1099:67
valet to his very v. seemed a hero — BYRON 221:21
valiant As he was v., I honour him — SHAK 884:47
makes e'en the v. more brave — DIBD 319:6
Ring in the v. man — TENN 1000:57
v. and martial — BACON 59:3
v., but not too venturous — LYLY 620:56
v. man and true — TENN 1005:60
v....taste of death but once — SHAK 883:33
validity If...God has any v. — BALD 64:99
Valium Cricket is baseball on V. — WILL 1081:54
toothless terrier on V. — SIKO 938:74
valley bicker down a v. — TENN 1002:97
Every v. shall be exalted — BIBLE 126:85
Green was my v. — LLEW 608:50
hill can't be a v. — CARR 239:49
in some such v. — SHIP 935:22
journeys through the v. — LEE 593:18
love is of the v. — TENN 998:12
paweth in the v. — BIBLE 113:22
V. and lowland, sing! — OAKL 733:52
v. between Buxton — RUSK 831:13
v. is his golden cup — MERE 671:13
v. of death — BIBLE 115:50
v. of Death — TENN 1000:71
v. sheep are fatter — PEAC 762:30
v. which was full of bones — BIBLE 129:41
world a v. so sweet — MOORE 706:32
valleys below them in the v. — TENN 994:52
descend into the v. again — LLOY 608:58
listening V. hear — BLAKE 165:57
Piping down the v. wild — BLAKE 166:1

valleys (*contd.*):
stranger strayed into...their v. — MONT 701:60
That v., groves, hills — MARL 655:31
thou who passest through the v. — BLAKE 165:58
Ye v. low where — MILT 684:46
valour better part of v. — SHAK 877:77
contemplation he and v. formed — MILT 690:55
fame, of v. — MARL 653:92
ideals, v. and the sacrifices — EISE 364:93
possess only strength and v. — BRON 191:94
report of v. — SHAK 895:28
So full of v. — SHAK 917:38
wonder at the desperate — JONS 534:80
valuable everything dear and v. — PITT 771:72
freedom is...supremely v. — HUXL 508:88
v. or even earnest — THOR 1016:80
valuation bias of v. — KEYN 554:34
superstitious v. of Europe — JAMES 516:10
value absolute v. — GREE 444:12
any v. at all in the world — LACL 573:62
consciousness of human v. — DEWEY 319:95
Diamonds are of most precious v. — WEBS 1060:50
economic v. of...women — GILM 427:16
enhance its v. — MANN 646:86
increase in v. of the world — MARX 661:26
lie...shows the v. of each object — CAMUS 229:62
loses its descriptive v. — LEGER 594:22
lost twenty-five percent of their v. — STEN 967:70
maximum v. which he can consume — HICKS 480:96
more permanent v. — LAWR 587:9
no influence on the future v. — JEVO 521:21
no more v. than their dress — HAZL 463:3
nothing has v. — FORS 398:43
nothing in the laws of v. — MILL 674:59
only a limited v. — ELIOT 371:46
Optimistic lies...therapeutic v. — SHAW 924:98
phonograph...commercial v. — EDIS 361:43
set a high v. — JOHN 531:20
v. depends on what is there — POUND 786:73
V....has two different meanings — SMITH 946:94
v. is not in its taste — FULB 409:29
v. judgments about the society — VAND 1039:94
v. not a v. — KOHL 568:75
v. of a liberal education — BREW 187:38
v. of a man — ANON 28:1
v., or worth of a man — HOBB 483:38
v. upon it we do ourselves — MONT 700:54
v. us what can be counted — WEIL 1062:81
very highest v. — RUSS 832:21
voice over wires...no practical v. — ANON 24:15
values human imaginative v. — BRON 190:78
lily-silver'd v. — POPE 783:6
sane balance of v. — POUND 786:80
the v. of art — OLSEN 739:37
v. and freedoms — THAT 1007:7
v. of women differ — WOOLF 1093:73
vampire like the v....dead — PATER 759:93
van Follow the v. — COLL 276:38
Vandyke V. is of the company — GAIN 411:70
Van Gogh My V. G. is better — HAMM 453:50
vanes like beaten weather v. — CRANE 295:8
vanished as rare things will, it v. — BROW 199:68
vanishest If thus thou v. — SHAK 906:7
vanitas V. vanitatum — BIBLE 159:50
vanities Guides us by v. — ELIOT 368:70
turn from these v. — BIBLE 148:95
vanity a foolish v. to be gratified — SHER 934:3
administering to the v. of others — AUST 52:65
day to find that it was v. — LAWR 587:13
drifted into sexual v. — WEBB 1058:14
Envy itself, and V. — MAND 645:71
getting old was about v. — OATES 733:56
pomps and v. — BOOK 175:36
Pull down thy v. — POUND 786:84

vanity (*contd.*):

speckled v. Will sicken	MILT 681:91
suppress one's v.	JAMES 515:3
v. doth very much corrupt	BAXT 79:51
v. of being seen	SMOL 950:63
v. of human hopes	JOHN 525:89
v. of person and of situation	AUST 52:66
v. of the writer	REES 805:92
v. of translation	SHEL 931:56
V. of vanities!	FRED 403:26
V. of vanities	BIBLE 122:14
V. of vanities	BIBLE 159:50
v., sets love a task	HUNT 504:26

Vanity-Fair name of V.-F. — BUNY 205:66
| only Rome v. Rome | BELL 86:87 |
| victor is often v. | SCHI 847:69 |

vans v. to beat the air — ELIOT 369:9
vantage from the v. point — PASS 759:82
vapour Floating, like a v. — FOST 399:61
life...even a v.	BIBLE 155:70
like v. over shrines	BROW 196:12
v. and fume	KIPL 561:42

vapours mystie v., cluddis and skyis — DUNB 355:42
| pestilent congregation of v. | SHAK 890:2 |
| v. or something worse | MONT 701:56 |

variable love prove likewise v. — SHAK 869:91
| v. as the shade | SCOTT 853:58 |

variation each slight v....preserved — DARW 306:83
| tunes...without any v. | DICK 323:92 |

varieties delineation of its v. — AUST 52:63
| What v. man has found out | AUGU 49:15 |

variety almost endless v. — LOCKE 609:72
democracy...admits v.	FORS 399:53
Her infinite v.	SHAK 905:71
Simplicity, without v.	HOGA 485:64
V. is the soul of pleasure	BEHN 85:63
V.'s the spice of life	COWP 293:56

variousness precise account of v. — TRIL 1026:56
varnishers v. and veneerers — MENC 670:68
vase like seeing a Sèvres v. — WAUGH 1058:9
opaque v. fills to the brim	ROET 819:93
took murder out of the Venetian v.	CHAN 251:50
water poured in to a v.	POUND 787:94

vasectomy v. of the vocal chords — ALTH 15:60
vassal God's silly v. — MELV 667:26
vassals his lithe bright v. tread — BLUN 170:41
Vassar old V. Girls — HEMI 470:16
vast wisdom, v., unwieldy — MILT 694:39
vat that it is a fermenting v. — HUNT 505:33
vaticination deal much in v. — CARL 233:34
vats ate the cheese out of the v. — BROW 197:32
| minces among bad v. | THOM 1011:89 |
| spirited purple of the v. | TENN 998:12 |

vaudeville Terrible V. — ACE 2:17
Vaughan Here V. lies dead — SASS 846:42
vault heaven's v. should crack — SHAK 904:71
| v. of the Temple of Peace | BRAM 185:7 |

vaunting V. aloud, but racked with — MILT 687:94
veal Bellamy's v. pies — PITT 772:76
Vega V. conspicuous overhead — AUDEN 46:50
vegetable adoption of v. diet — SHEL 927:59
Feminism...a catch-all v. drawer	PAGL 749:36
fruit Of v. gold	MILT 690:52
Mona Lisa of the v. world	HUGH 500:32
v., animal and mineral	GILB 424:62
v. love should grow	MARV 658:73

vegetables harvest...fruit and v. — MURR 716:79
| without eating her v. | ALTH 15:59 |
| your gods or your v. | GIRA 429:45 |

vegetarianism in favour of v. — INGE 511:35
vegetate v. in a village — COLT 277:57
vehicle v. for conveying ideas — MACB 624:31
| v. for the thought of our day | FORD 396:5 |

vehicles robot v. — DAWK 310:43
veil beautiful girl in a diaphanous v. — PERE 766:91
that transparent v.	WORD 1096:30
torn the v. of Europe	WARN 1053:26
unzips the v. from beauty	WHITE 1070:26
v. had been torn suddenly	MONET 700:44
v. of heaven	MARL 653:92
v. of the temple was rent	BIBLE 144:18
v. of the temple was rent	BIBLE 140:56
wrapped in a gauzy v.	SHEL 932:74

veils from the v. of the morning — YEATS 1104:57
| Religion blushing v. | POPE 783:10 |

vein not in the giving v. — SHAK 863:58
veins blood speaks to you in my v. — SHAK 873:85
bluest v. to kiss	SHAK 905:76
floweth in your v.	TRAH 1025:27
heats which my v. fill	DONNE 337:80
in its v. flows ink	KRAUS 569:87
love of...gardens is running in our v.	
	MACK 632:52
of human v.	YEATS 1106:84
v. are filled...with...carpet cleaner	CHEE 256:54
v. of rhyming mother-wits	MARL 652:84
v. that I may swim	MONT 703:93
v. that seemed to invite the lancet	SHER 933:88

velvet gold an' v. — ANON 24:12
hand of steel in a v. glove	WOOL 1093:81
In v. collar-rolls	KIPL 564:5
loll on v. and satin	FRAN 402:16
v. of her paws	GRAY 441:51

veneer all fantasy and v. — GALL 413:97
veneerers varnishers and v. — MENC 670:68
venerable Beautiful city! so v. — ARNO 38:10
| decrepit, without being v. | HAWT 461:75 |
| like a v. battlewagon | TIME 1020:66 |

Venetian plump V., fat, and lusty — FLET 394:75
vengeance but he's v. proud — SHAK 911:7
day of v. of our God	BIBLE 127:12
feeling of v.	DREN 346:42
instruments of v.	DONO 340:36
line a sudden v. waits	POPE 779:6
Tomorrow's v. on the head	SHAK 863:65
upon the Scots with a V.	FLET 394:67
V. is a personal reaction	RENO 806:4
V. is in my heart	SHAK 862:37
V. is mine	BIBLE 149:36
v. shall be taken...sevenfold	BIBLE 104:7
wreak their v.	TROL 1027:77

vengeances stored v. of heaven fall — SHAK 902:13
vengefulness fainted on his v. — MERE 671:5
veni V., vedi, vici — CAES 225:87
Venice any man in all V. — SHAK 874:9
cunning whore of V.	SHAK 900:48
in V. they did not learn to draw well	VASA 1040:9
Ocean's nursling, V.	SHEL 927:70
on the throat of V.	TOME 1023:1
V. is like...chocolate liqueurs	CAPO 231:79
V., on the Bridge of Sighs	BYRON 220:92
V. will linger in your mind	MORR 708:77

venison turtle soup, and v. — DICK 325:43
| v. pies and good wine | LOUI 613:45 |

venom of the reptile crew — BYRON 220:97
ventriloquist Facts are v.'s dummies — HUXL 507:80
ventriloquizing V. for the unborn — GRAV 439:22
venture drew a bow at a v. — BIBLE 111:72
each v....a new beginning	ELIOT 372:53
None wise dares hopeless v.	EURI 380:27
v. to hint	STEV 973:92

venturous valiant, but not too v. — LYLY 620:56
Venus blind boy, V.' baby — SPEN 959:29
embrace of the V. de Milo	DARIO 305:76
face of V.	BARR 73:56
Hero, V.' nun	MARL 654:25
Lady V. on the settee	SITW 940:99

Venus (*contd.*):
putting lipstick on the V. de Milo	PICK 769:31
V. here will choose her dwelling	DRYD 351:61
V. in her naked glory	MARL 654:24
V., take my votive glass	PRIOR 790:54

veracity tell us...with v. — GRAY 443:96
| v. of good men | EMER 377:57 |

verandahs houses there wear v. — MURR 715:75
verb God...is a v. — FULL 409:36
| noun and a v. | SHAK 861:15 |
| V. is God | HUGO 502:79 |

verbal v. contract — GOLD 434:43
verbatim v. I will quote it — PATE 760:97
verbosity exuberance of his own v. — DISR 334:24
| thread of his v. | SHAK 866:23 |

verbs mix...rain with v. — BRAU 186:19
| still studying v. | SAND 841:73 |

verdict every royal v. — WHIT 1069:16
| fearlessly challenge the v. | PALM 752:72 |
| Your v....will be less upon us | CLEM 269:3 |

verdure groves of ceaseless v. — MELV 668:42
verge ability to get to the v. — DULL 354:25
verges wanted your soft v. — HENRI 472:62
verifiability criterion of v. — AYER 53:79
verisimilitude do not seek...for v. — BORG 178:10
veritas v...attributa vino est — PLIN 775:31
verities old v. and truths of the heart — FAUL 383:77
verity in the cause of v. — BROW 195:68
Verlaine I'll stay off V., too — PARK 754:15
Vermeer V. gave to the sun's — LOWE 617:14
vermin humans...categorized as v. — CAREY 233:22
| Tory party...lower than v. | BEVAN 101:64 |

vermouth proper union of gin and v. — DEVO 318:89
vernacular in the v. — STEV 972:80
Vernon B. V. occupied her time — BROO 193:38
| impregnated by B. V. | QUIR 792:7 |

vers No v. is libre — ELIOT 371:42
Versailles V. of American — WOLFE 1091:32
verse Become a v. — HERB 475:24
bombast out a blank v.	GREE 445:33
book of v.	FITZ 390:88
by v. seek fame	SIDN 937:58
chime his childish v.	BYRON 219:64
could not v. immortal save	BYRON 219:73
give up v., my boy	POUND 786:66
in my v. ever live young	SHAK 912:49
incarnation of this v.	SHEL 928:91
Leave not a foot of v.	POPE 783:2
look upon this v.	SHAK 914:72
matter made for famous poet's v.	SPEN 958:17
now it's lyric v.	WAUGH 1057:91
publish a volume of my v.	HOPK 492:95
quire of bad v.	MACA 624:21
still thy v. has charms	SCOTT 853:53
turnings intricate of v.	WORD 1096:30
unmelodious v.	STEP 968:80
unpolished rugged v.	DRYD 350:41
unpremediated v.	MILT 692:98
vain in v.	SIDN 937:50
v. again shall gild	DRAY 345:34
v. be a glorious adventure	VERL 1042:39
V. calls them forth	LAND 578:57
V. hath a middle nature	DONNE 338:15
v. is a measured speech	BACON 55:15
V. is the optical form	HUGO 501:60
v. represents a handle	NASH 720:72
V. thus design'd	WALL 1050:76
v. you grave for me	STEV 975:31
whips my blood like v.	WILL 1083:4
Who only thinks in v.	VIAN 1043:48
Writing free v.	FROST 407:91
yet each v. of thine	HERR 478:72
you talk in blank v.	SHAK 886:19

verses false gallop of v. — SHAK 886:1

verses (*contd.*):

No one will get at my v.	WHIT 1073:1
raptures…made his v. clear	DRAY 345:39
v. and the prophecy	WALL 1050:74
v. from my heart	MARTI 657:57

vertebrate God…a gaseous v.   HAEC 450:2

vertue booste of conning nor v.   LYDG 620:54

vespers singing v. in the temple   GIBB 421:29

vessel In gallant trim gilded v.   GRAY 443:86

Launch your v.	TENN 1005:68
Let the Irish v. lie	AUDEN 47:71
like a potter's v.	BIBLE 114:32
make one v. unto honour	BIBLE 149:32
v. descending unto him	BIBLE 147:91
v. in which the powers of steam	WATT 1055:55
v., puffs her sail	TENN 995:61
wife…the weaker v.	BIBLE 156:81

vessels inclined plane of little v.   DICK 325:39

treasure in earthen v.	BIBLE 151:76
v. of a potter	BIBLE 157:4

vestals into their lives aciduous v.   STEV 974:3

vet v. can't catch his patient   HERR 478:70

veteran as a v. may differ   HUXL 509:4

veterans world its v. rewards   POPE 782:77

veto Mercury should not have my V.   LEST 599:13

   v. upon any mere aggression   LEES 593:20

vex tells me nothing that does not v.   AUST 52:64

   V. not thou   TENN 993:33

vexation added v. of prayers   TWAIN 1032:67

vexed knew by the blush…he was v.   SOME 952:98

viable both v. and useful   HAYEK 462:91

vials v. hermetically sealed   SWIFT 985:86

vibrant the v. and the beautiful   MALL 641:13

vibrations absolutely no v.   WILDE 1077:77

vicars hundred v. down the lawn   BROO 192:26

vice between virtue and v.   JOHN 527:31

bounds into a v.	DRYD 348:87
difficult and nerve-racking v.	MAUG 664:87
exalted person's fall into v.	CANM 230:65
Extremism…is no v.	GOLD 433:31
Far from being a v.	SADE 835:64
frequently regarded as v.	FORD 396:2
good old-gentlemanly v.	BYRON 222:39
greatest v. in an actor	HAZL 463:96
ill-natur'd, baneful V.	MAND 645:71
in v. their law's their will	SHAK 910:92
knowledge and survey of v.	MILT 685:66
lost by not being v.	WALP 1051:94
major v. and greatest pleasure	HEMI 471:43
moral restraint, v. and misery	MALT 643:38
Mutual forgiveness of each v.	BLAKE 166:81
nearer a v. than a virtue	JONS 535:97
no amusements…but v.	SMITH 949:58
no v. but beggary	SHAK 872:62
no v. so simple	SHAK 872:81
now called v.	SPEN 959:37
poverty, v., and misery	SUMN 981:26
prosperitie Upfostertis v.	BROWN 194:62
Prosperity that best discover v.	BACON 56:52
Punctuality is the v.	PATR 761:14
quotation is a national v.	WAUGH 1057:91
raptures and roses of v.	SWIN 987:32
sanction V., and hunt Decorum	BYRON 219:63
sensual pleasure without v.	JOHN 532:38
sole remaining v.	UPDI 1037:71
subject…to this v. of lying!	SHAK 877:99
V. came in…the door of necessity	DEFOE 312:82
v. in which no one boasts	NERV 723:11
V. is a monster	POPE 780:44
v.…lost half its evil	BURKE 207:32
v. of meanness	THOM 1014:43
v. pays to virtue	LARO 582:27
v. promises to her followers	MILT 685:65
v. to tiresome virtue	MOLI 699:26

vice (*contd.*):

v. with half its virtue	LOWE 617:10
Virtue itself turns v.	SHAK 869:96
Virtue…of v. must pardon beg	SHAK 892:58
When v. prevails	ADDI 8:34
whirled in folly and v.	TENN 1001:75

vice-presidency v.-p. isn't worth   GARN 415:29

vices discover his v. and virtues   CHAR 253:89

dishonour the v.	WILD 1079:31
dwelt upon her v.	BELL 87:12
Go very light on v.	PAIGE 750:41
hating v. too much	BURKE 208:39
mean between two v.	ARIS 34:27
Neither our v. nor our virtues	DUNC 355:45
nursed up in those v.	ASTE 43:89
of our pleasant v.	SHAK 904:47
v. and the follies of human kind	CONG 280:4
v.…fathered by our heroism	ELIOT 368:71
v. may be committed very genteely	BOSW 180:32
V.…never change	BEAU 79:62
v. of authority	BACON 58:74
v. of his ancestors	FAUL 383:76

vicious can't expect a boy to be v.   SAKI 837:3

Football…a v. game	BADE 60:45
never the truly v.	MARG 650:54
v.…to be a creative writer	LAWR 586:94

vicissitude no v. can find   WORD 1099:76

   sad v. of things   STER 970:18

victim fall v. to a big lie   HITL 482:28

first insults the v.	CRAB 293:75
not help it, I am also a v.	LESS 598:97
refuse to be a v.	ATWO 45:23
shell of his v.	ANNAN 20:35
unsavoury role of v.	YOUR 1108:8
v. and slave of his action	EMER 377:60
v. must be found	GILB 425:84
v. of creative suffering	KING 557:81

victimization safety in the state of v.   ANGE 19:27

victims Hibakusha, atomic v.   GEE 417:64

little v. play	GRAY 441:47
scrupulous and the just…are v.	CONR 285:7

victis Vae v.   BREN 187:35

   Vae v.   LIVY 608:48

victor Mighty v., mighty lord   GRAY 443:85

v. is often vanquished	SCHI 847:69
whichever side may call itself the v.	CHAM 249:16

Victoria admired…Queen V   WILDE 1079:13

Like Gladstone speaking to V.	MANC 644:67
Queen V. treats her prisoners	WILDE 1078:95
rises in the V. Nyanza	SPEKE 955:61

Victorian antagonist to the V. age   WILS 1084:23

hats, as in V. days	SITW 941:17
history of the V. age	STRA 979:92
lost sense of V. regard	PRIT 791:74

Victorianism inverted V.   FORS 398:45

Victorians V. expected   CASS 243:29

victories After a thousand v.   SHAK 913:55

victors are by v. undone	DRYD 352:88

victorious come off always v.   CARL 234:38

licensings to make her v.	MILT 685:64
show themselves v.	BALZ 69:75

victors History is written for the v.   DREX 345:43

v. are by victories undone	DRYD 352:88
v., they left…not a few	DAVIS 309:38

victory advantage is half the v.   DRAKE 345:28

authority of supreme v.	WHIT 1071:61
Dig for V.	DORA 340:38
fourth electoral v.	HESE 479:80
get anything by their v.	HALI 452:31
grave, where is thy v.?	BIBLE 151:73
great v. has been won	MACA 621:77
He judgement brings, and v.	OAKL 733:52
how to gain a v., Hannibal	MARH 650:61
In v.: magnanimity	CHUR 263:97

victory (*contd.*):

In v., one deserves it	POL 777:63
in v., there is no beauty	LAO 580:85
in v. unbearable	CHUR 265:47
judgment unto v.	BIBLE 137:89
lose Life…to discover V.	APOL 32:97
No force to win the v.	DYER 358:88
no substitute for v.	MACA 621:73
One more such v.	PYRR 796:45
Or to v.!	BURNS 212:37
swallow up death in v.	BIBLE 125:73
swept on to v.	PRIE 790:37
'twas a famous v.	SOUT 954:33
Truth beareth away the v.	BIBLE 131:74
valour, and of v.	MARL 653:92
V. at all costs	CHUR 264:12
v.…celebrated with the funeral rite	LAO 580:86
v. is twice itself	SHAK 878:25
V. of a cat	WILL 1081:67
V. of Samothrace	MARI 651:67
V. of sterility	BELL 88:21
v. of the children of light	BEND 89:57
v. sits on out helms!	SHAK 863:67
V. switches from man to man	HOMER 488:19
v. turns into a defeat	DE 311:65
what would be theft…is only v.	DRYD 347:60
where is thy V.?	BUNY 205:74

vie la v.…au pouvoir de la langue   CIXO 266:69

Viennesey waltz that is V.   GERS 420:9

viens fear thrills through my v.   SHAK 869:17

Vietnam Gay V. Veteran   MATL 664:71

government of V. is Communist	GELL 417:72
not an invasion of V.	NIXON 730:11
Patriotism in V.	NGUY 725:48
see V. as a war	PILG 770:42
so compelling since V. the War	WHITE 1069:21
to V. to take the train	THER 1009:42
To win in V.	SPOCK 961:62
V. is somewhere near Panama	ANON 27:88
V. is the place	KENN 551:67
V. was what we had instead	HERR 477:48
wrong people remember V.	HERR 477:49

view America is in my v.   SCHAW 847:61

best v. is on the right	LEVIN 600:29
distance lends enchantment to the v.	CAMP 227:25
each has his own v.	TERE 1005:74
if you wanted to v. trouble	RIDGE 811:79
illusion of a v. of life	ELIOT 369:5
never…see the same v. twice	STARK 963:97
point of v. of participant	GALL 412:93
point of v. sadly changed	MACA 622:81
Room with a V.	FORS 398:29
slow, firm, inflexible v.	PASC 757:47
soared quite out of reason's v.	DRYD 348:91
v. as an infernal Utopia	LEWIS 602:69
v. never changes	ANON 29:48
v. O'erlaid with black	MILT 682:6
v. On the clear hyaline	MILT 691:88
without any…purpose…in v.	PLAN 772:83

viewer modern v. is…overloaded   BELL 88:42

views false v.…do little harm   DARW 306:87

frightening v. of government	INOU 512:58
full of stately v.	KIPL 564:13
Hitler…held extreme v.	POUND 786:82
outdated v.	GORB 435:59
take short v.	SMITH 949:48
v. of the revolutionists	SCHL 848:73
Whenever you accept our v.	DAYAN 310:53

vigil yearly on the v.   SHAK 881:99

vigilance condition…is eternal v.   CURR 301:16

   not so much eternal v.   ORWE 742:95

vigilant Be sober, be v.   BIBLE 156:84

   v. as a cat   SHAK 876:65

vigilantes goose-stepping v.   LEWIS 601:48

voice (*contd.*):

The City's v.	SHEL 927:72
thundrous v.	WILL 1083:95
till thou obey my v.	BLAKE 168:10
Today if ye will hear his v.	BOOK 177:88
tones of a loved v.	ARNO 36:70
top of your v.	BAKER 63:81
transmit the v. over wires	ANON 24:15
trick of that v.	SHAK 903:33
true v. arose in me	FOX 400:74
tune her sacred v.	JOHN 525:77
tune thy jolly v.	BLAKE 165:59
utter forth a glorious v.	ADDI 7:23
v., a mystery	WORD 1097:39
v. as the sound of many waters	BIBLE 156:99
v. falls as they say love	LARK 581:99
v. in every wind	GRAY 441:46
v. in the darkness	LONG 612:18
v. is full of money	FITZ 390:4
v. less loud, through its joys	BROW 198:40
v.…like the sea	WORD 1096:38
v. of dolorous pitch	HOOD 489:45
v. of freedom	SCHA 847:60
v. of high midsummer's heat	ROBE 814:16
v. of him that crieth	BIBLE 126:85
v. of the archangel	BIBLE 153:25
v. of the Bard!	BLAKE 167:84
v. of the dead	TENN 1003:28
v., of the democracy	STEAD 964:4
v. of the people	ALCU 12:3
v. of the people	BACON 56:35
v. of the people	PITT 771:65
v. of those who suffer	CESA 248:2
v. said in mastery	BROW 196:14
v., so in a shapeless flame	DONNE 337:85
v., stunning as thunder	KINS 559:13
v. that tells him he is not	TRUM 1030:28
v. the word 'nature'	REDON 804:78
v. which failed to sound	MILNE 680:68
With a monarch's v.	SHAK 883:45
with cheerful v.	KETHE 554:23

voice-trained v.-t. to speak — WATE 1055:49
voiceless Science is v. — WEIL 1062:79
voices Ancestral v. prophesying war! — COLE 275:16

Bubble their colourful v.	HUGH 500:41
clatter of high v.	DOYLE 343:93
Clear Cymric v.	BUNT 204:59
drowning out of false v.	DELI 315:40
English don't raise their v.	HELL 469:1
hear v. in the air	KEYN 555:37
hearts and hands and v.	WINK 1086:59
Moans round many v.	TENN 995:61
Other V., Other Rooms	CAPO 230:77
soft v. die	SHEL 932:70
sounds of their v.	ANGE 20:32
Two v. are there	STEP 968:79
Two v. are there	WORD 1099:74
unbearable v. of its announcers	ORWE 743:20
v. are heard among them	BOOK 176:66
v. dying with a dying fall	ELIOT 367:49
v. elected me of all men	LEE 593:18
v. of liberty be mute?	CUMM 300:84
v. of young people	SMITH 947:15
v. telling him that	TRUM 1030:28

void All is without form and v. — HAZL 464:25

beating in v.	ARNO 40:38
decorations over a v.	YOUR 1108:6
No craving v. …in the breast	POPE 779:8
not enough…to be v.	BRAT 185:14
rubbish to the v.	TENN 999:37
shall not return unto me v.	BIBLE 127:6
terrors that flock to fill the v.	LEGU 594:25
v. in your life, fill it	NERVO 723:13
v. of noble rage	TENN 998:29

voids sins are attempts to fill v.	WEIL 1062:81
volcanic v. landscapes a poor girl	CHEE 255:51
volcano erupt like a v.	MACD 628:95
like a slumbering v.	WHITE 1071:48
volcanoes We are v.	LEGU 594:30
vole questing v.	WAUGH 1057:82
volley fine v. of words	SHAK 860:77
volleys make her hit backhand v.	KING 557:70
Volsces Cut me to pieces, V.	SHAK 911:17
Voltaire always like V.	TALMA 990:93
mock on, V. Rousseau	BLAKE 167:99
Rousseau, V.…united in one person	HESS 479:84
V., Rousseau…fools, and madmen!	ONEI 740:59
V. smiled	HUGO 503:93
volume iron-clasped v. of despair	POE 776:52
take in our hand any v.	HUME 504:10
Twenty V. Suicide Note	BARA 70:6
v. can ever be written on a flea	MELV 668:39
v.…so far above the average	WILDE 1076:32
world is a great v.	DONNE 339:33
volumes creators of odd v.	LAMB 577:32
Reticence, in three v.	GLAD 430:57
To their subsequebt v.	SHAK 895:43
voluntary faith…become as fully v.	CUPI 301:11
volunteers brave York V.	BROCK 189:64
voluptuous Lush, calm and v.	BAUD 77:22
vomit dog is turned to his own v.	BIBLE 156:85
dog returneth to his v.	BIBLE 122:2
Dog returns to his v.	KIPL 565:25
giant pool of crapulous v.	BOYD 182:62
vortex bisection of a v.!	OCON 735:82
into the v. of immensity	DICK 323:83
v. of our grave	CRANE 294:94
vote against giving women the v.	WRIG 1101:1
Fifty per cent…won't v.	VIDAL 1044:72
fighting for the v.	PANK 753:82
I cast only one v.	ONAS 739:43
man's decision on how to v.	SCHN 848:84
my hearty v.	SWIFT 984:80
one dollar, one v.	KRIS 569:96
One man shall have one v.	CART 243:13
v. for a woman	WATE 1055:49
v. somebody into office	GERG 420:2
women…trying for the v.	PANK 752:77
working classes…given the v.	WAUGH -101:5
voter v. who uses his money	SAMU 840:45
what the v. receives	PRICE 789:33
woman v.…pernicious to the State	WRIG 1101:2
voters v. have no contact	PRICE 789:2
votes asked men for v.	WEST 1068:90
giving v. to the most obscure	CHES 258:7
speeches and majority v.	BISM 164:38
voting It's not the v.	STOP 978:77
vow v.…made to her in marriage	SHAK 889:77
v. that is vowèd true	SHAK 901:77
v. that to-morne	MALO 642:31
v. to thee, my country	SPRI 961:63
vowels Only consonants and v.	RANS 802:38
Scrabble with all the v. missing	ELLI 374:3
shifting of v. and consonants	UNTE 1036:47
vows cancel all our v.	DRAY 345:40
constancy of its v.	SHAW 922:42
Dismiss your v.	SHAK 864:98
falser than v. made in wine	SHAK 886:14
he v. his passion	PARK 754:7
Lends the tongue v.	SHAK 888:68
V., oaths, and all	JONS 536:17
voyage long beautiful v.	TZARA 1035:35
v. and not harbour	TOYN 1024:18
v. is entirely imaginary	CELI 247:87
v. of their life	SHAK 884:60
v. of voyages	MUNDY 714:54
voyages v., such peregrinations	DONNE 339:24
voyeur into the theater as a v.	FRIS 406:68

vulgar called wicked than v.	LEWIS 601:45
Father is rather v.	DICK 326:53
Funny without being v.	GILB 426:98
More is v.	SPARK 955:53
rude remark or a v. action	WILL 1081:58
shallow and v. view	WEBB 1058:14
times has become v.	MOLI 698:19
v. love…v. man	DRYD 348:91
v. sort of capacities	BACON 55:7
v. to talk like dentist	WILDE 1077:79
work upon the v. with fine sense	POPE 779:14
vulgarest survival of the v.	WILDE 1076:42
vulgarities may have other v.	HELL 469:1
vulgarity mould of its v.	JEFF 519:77
singularity and v.	HAZL 463:1
vulgarizing succeeded in… v.	HUXL 507:72
vulnerable she is so v.	CURR 301:15
v. human beings	TURN 1031:51

wabe gyre and gimble in the w.	CARR 239:47
wad leave him a w.	BALL 67:51
waddle flounce at a w. away	THOM 1011:87
wade should I w. no more	SHAK 909:63
Wadman married to Mrs W.	STER 969:11
wag How now, mad w.?	SHAK 875:37
tail must w. the dog	KIPL 561:41
wage One man's w. rise	WILS 1085:37
w. against the enmity	SHAK 902:14
w. no war with women	SOUT 954:35
wage-earner status of the w.-e.	SKEL 942:37
wager w. that he does exist	PASC 757:63
wages better w. and shorter h.	ORWE 742:98
common w. of labour	SMITH 946:89
earneth w. to put it into a bag	BIBLE 130:64
floor under w. and a ceiling	WRIS 1102:16
Home…and ta'en thy w.	SHAK 916:16
labour and w. first	MANN 646:95
like rent and w.	SMITH 945:80
neither honours nor w.	GARI 415:25
never ta'en w. of her	WEBS 1060:54
rather than give them good w.	WEST 1067:87
rise of w.	RICA 808:33
took their w.	HOUS 496:77
w. may rise	MARX 660:16
w. of sin is death	BIBLE 149:22
w. should be left to…competition	RICA 808:34
waggon Hitch your w. to a star	EMER 377:73
Wagner like W.'s music better	WILDE 1076:47
W. had his good moments	ROSS 825:97
W.'s music is better	TWAIN 1034:21
write music like W.	GOLD 434:38
wags how the world was	SHAK 885:90
You w. that judge	OTWAY 746:77
wail suffice to w. their scorn	DANI 304:62
when I w.	SPEN 958:25
wailing fullers and their w.	ANON 21:49
in w. there's nought availing	CURR 301:18
wailsday tearsday, w.	JOYCE 538:61
waist from the w. They're centaurs	SHAK 903:35
waistcoat fourth w. button	LICH 603:30
open your w.	HUNT 504:18
yolk runs down the w.	DICK 321:50
waistcoats w. and…handkerchiefs	DICK 320:25
wait I can w.	LISZT 607:41
must w. until a shrimp	KHRU 556:14
to w. is life	HUGO 501:66
w. and not be tired	KIPL 564:8
w. on wrinkled age!	SHAK 866:32
w., seated in a chair	VALE 1038:84
w. until a man comes around	FULL 409:37
w. upon the Lord	BIBLE 126:91
You just w.!	THOM 1011:90
waited w. patiently for the Lord	BIBLE 115:66
waiter damn good head w.	GULB 448:82

war (*contd.*):
we prepare for w. like…giants — PEAR 762:33
weapon which will make w. — MORT 710:2
weapons of w. perished! — BIBLE 110:44
well that w. is so terrible — LEE 593:19
What if someone gave a w. — GINS 428:32
What makes w. interesting — DALL 303:50
What, then, was w.? — GRAV 439:21
When the w. broke out — WAUGH 1056:78
when there was w. — AUDEN 47:64
when w. is done — SASS 845:27
will not have another w. — GEOR 419:86
win a w. than win an earthquake — RANK 801:30
witnesses to the desolation of w. — GEOR 418:83
wonderful time—the W. — HUGH 499:21
world ruled and led to w.? — KRAUS 569:90
wrong w., at the wrong place — BRAD 184:94
war-cries w.-c. arise — MACC 625:36
war-drum w.-d. throbbed no longer — TENN 995:77
war-wolf Desmond the w.-w. — MACC 625:37
warbler Attic w. — GRAY 441:55
wardrobe body like a w. — THOM 1011:87
purple w. of thy side — CRAS 296:20
silken dalliance in the w. — SHAK 880:73
wards deftly in the oiled w. — KEATS 545:63
ware buy some other w. — BURNS 210:92
left that fancy w. — DICK 323:91
Scotland wants nae skinking w. — BURNS 210:85
wares w.…harder to get rid of — FROST 407:82
warfare general practice of w. — AUGU 49:16
mutual help…as often as w. — DOBZ 334:36
true method of w. — MAZZ 666:11
under the Borgias they had w. — WELL 1063:1
w. is based on deception — SUN 982:31
w. of men and machinery — WOLFE 1090:20
Warhol all about Andy W. — WARH 1053:20
Waring What's become of W.? — BROW 197:30
warlike altogether w. — LUTH 620:51
w. ironmongery — GILB 425:81
warm Be w., but pure — BYRON 219:61
Being black is w. and gay — RHYS 808:26
in the w. hedge — SHEL 932:93
neither w. nor cold — GREER 445:43
O, she's w.! — SHAK 912:43
whenever he was getting w. — SELL 858:39
yet so w. and yet so cold — LAWS 588:21
warmer cold war is getting w. — BARU 75:91
creatures in w. countries — GUY 449:96
warmonger w. put on my passport — BYRON 224:74
warmth key to human w. — ISHI 513:77
No w., no cheerfulness — HOOD 489:52
vigorous w. did…impart — DRYD 349:9
yearned for w. and colour — TENN 1003:19
warn w. you not to be ordinary — KINN 559:12
warned be w. by me — BELL 87:7
Warner I'd like to thank…Jack W. — ANDR 19:15
Working for W. Brothers — MIZN 697:6
warning by w. to avoid his fate? — SPEN 958:18
come without w. — DAVIS 309:41
solemn word of w. — WILS 1086:46
warp Weave the w. — GRAY 443:84
warped w. and cracked — CRANE 294:91
warping this odd w. time — RICH 809:53
warrant I signed my death w. — COLL 276:39
stag of w. — DAVI 307:1
Warren Miss W. is a great devotee — SHAW 920:10
warrior brought her w. dead — TENN 997:7
painful w. — SHAK 913:55
priest, w., poet — BAUD 78:43
This is the happy w. — READ 803:52
undoomed w. — ANON 21:53
w. eyes — HYDE 509:14
w. that is rapt with love — MARL 653:92
warriors pale w., death-pale — KEATS 545:74

warriors (*contd.*):
w. here do not seek out — ANDR 18:11
w. of Eternal Mind — RUSS 833:36
Where are the w. today? — SITT 940:98
wars All skilful in the w. — VAUG 1041:18
all their w. are merry — CHES 259:19
All w. are planned — RICE 809:39
brotherhood of men-at-w. — PAZ 762:24
divided by civil w. — MONT 702:79
from henceforth thou shalt have w. — BIBLE 112:89
getting them killed in w. — HUGH 499:23
History is littered with w. — POWE 788:16
holy w. — GUIB 448:77
maketh w. to cease — BIBLE 116:74
maketh w. to cease — BOOK 177:74
obviating of all future w. — FORD 396:6
sent to any foreign w. — ROOS 822:41
Since w. begin — UNES 1036:44
Soldiers find w. — DONNE 337:80
subsequent w. have been lost — ORWE 743:18
thought of earthquakes, and of w. — BYRON 222:30
thousand w. of old — TENN 1000:57
titanic w. had groined — OWEN 748:14
troops and the big w. — SHAK 899:40
w. and rumours of w. — BIBLE 139:37
W. are fought by children — LIVE 607:44
w. are useless — RICH 809:46
w. brought nothing about — DRYD 352:97
W. cannot be fought — MOUN 711:13
w. of the European powers — ADAMS 6:90
w. that are now afoot — GUST 449:92
We best avoid w. — EDEN 360:22
wear weapons and serve in the w. — BOOK 178:1
what care we…for w.? — WORD 1094:1
warship dark w. riding there below — SLES 943:57
wartime w. decisions — TRUM 1030:27
Warwickshire W. militia — EDGE 360:30
wary a lot to be w. about — WATE 1055:50
I can't help feeling w. — PRIE 790:43
Was-land furnishings of each W.-l. — FRAME 400:78
wash Gonna W. That Man — HAMM 454:55
Intellectually, most people never w. — DUDEK 353:17
may not w. it out — SIGO 938:71
never comes out in the w. — KIPL 563:95
shores by the w. — YEATS 1104:58
wash-out w.-o. of a cock up — ANON 29:33
washed w. in the brightness — RAND 801:26
w. me out of the turret — JARR 518:57
w. their robes — BIBLE 157:15
washing grows…only w. — THOM 1011:85
never…poured out my own w. — PU 794:14
seem thus w. her hands — SHAK 909:76
tattered w. on a line — MENC 670:91
Washington dependence…on W. — BENN 90:68
didn't come to W. — GRAMM 438:95
first came to W. — TRUM 1029:16
lawyers in W. who trust each other — DOLE 335:48
price on the W. Monument? — KENN 553:7
shorter than the W. monument — REST 807:15
spotlight of public life in W. — FOST 399:63
W. is a resigning town — SHUL 935:30
W. is a sieve — REAG 804:70
W. is a town — GERA 419:94
W. is awash — SCHR 850:9
W.…like dull diamonds — MAIL 639:84
W. Post over with your big toe — LANCE 578:53
wasps w. and hornets break through — SWIFT 984:63
Why stir the w. — RICK 811:76
waste applied without any w. — LEUP 599:15
dead w. and middle — TWAIN 1033:89
don't intend to w. any — ARMS 35:50
I love all w. — SHEL 927:66
in the w. howling wilderness — BIBLE 108:2
Life is too short to w. — SCOTT 852:41

waste (*contd.*):
utter w. is a coachload — HUNT 504:17
w. has thinly strayed — ADAMS 4:63
w. its stock — JUANA 539:64
W. of Blood — STUD 980:14
w. of seas — GALT 413:8
w. of white barren sand — SCHAW 847:61
w. remains and kills — EMPS 378:83
wasted Nothing is w. — HERB 474:6
presume to think her w. — EMPS 378:84
Thirteen w. years — ANON 27:75
wasteland observe a vast w. — MINOW 695:66
Wastle W. dwalt on Tweed — BURNS 212:29
watch as a w. in the night — BIBLE 117:98
as much a trade…to make a w. — LA 572:36
Care keeps his w. — SHAK 869:97
done much better by a w. — BELL 87:20
Either dead or my w. — MARX 659:1
fat gold w. — PLATH 773:98
gone by our w. — SHAK 887:43
If you w. a game — HOPE 491:74
repair a w. — THUR 1019:34
Set a w.…before my mouth — BIBLE 120:52
Suppose I had found a w. — PALEY 751:65
tell you how the w. was made — WYMAN 1104:52
ten tickings of thy w. — WORD 1095:11
tuppence for your old w. chain — COLL 276:37
universe…resembles a w. — FONT 395:86
w. a grass or a leaf — GRAV 439:15
W. and pray — BIBLE 140:51
w. each other w. each other — DURR 357:78
w. …hirelings kick a ball — PRIE 789:35
w. of his wit — SHAK 917:28
W. out w'en you'er gittin all — HARR 458:31
Wear your learning like your w. — CHES 257:76
watches Dictionaries are like w. — JOHN 532:33
famous soft w. — DALI 303:47
watchful W. as fowlers — OTWAY 746:81
watching I remember w. myself — RHYS 808:31
observe…just by w. — BERRA 98:1
watchmaker play the role of w. — DAWK 310:44
would have become a w. — EINS 363:74
watchman duty of a w. — STEAD 964:7
Like some melancholy w. — APOL 31:88
w. waketh but in vain — BIBLE 119:41
w. watches in vain — BIBLE 159:48
watchmen w. on the walls — KENN 552:92
w. shall lift up the voice — BIBLE 127:96
watchsprings like little w. — SPEN 956:83
watchword w. while he is here — CURZ 302:29
water about her, of dead w. — MACN 637:35
as w. spilt on the ground — BIBLE 110:49
asked for w.…brought him milk — BIBLE 109:14
back into the w. — ANON 28:3
barge-crowded w. — LARK 581:9
before it beat the w. — LONG 611:10
benison of hot w. — BROO 192:20
blade struck the w. — COKE 272:74
blood and w. — BIBLE 147:2
Blood may be thicker than w. — SOME 952:99
Brown bogs with black w. — COLUM 278:61
bubbles as the w. has — SHAK 907:19
built under the w. — STEW 977:65
Burned on the w. — SHAK 905:68
by land, or by w. — SWIFT 986:14
by w. and the word — STONE 978:73
conscious w. saw its God — CRAS 295:17
covered by useless w. — DOUG 342:64
daughter of Earth and W. — SHEL 928:84
dead still w. — WORD 1096:22
deeds Shall be in w. writ — BEAU 80:70
Differs…as much as wine and w. — MARL 655:17
drank rapidly a glass of w. — CUMM 300:84
Drink no longer w. — BIBLE 154:32

water (*contd.*):

drink thy w. with trembling	BIBLE 129:37
fall away Like w.	SHAK 917:50
farre into the w.	MALO 642:33
fields and the w. shout	MERE 671:1
Flowing like clean w.	MACD 628:94
flowing on Of w.	FARJ 383:63
fountain of the w. of life	BIBLE 159:36
give him w. to drink	BIBLE 122:1
go across salt w.	DICK 326:60
hands and feet in the w.	CONR 284:94
hart panteth after the w. brooks	BIBLE 115:68
hear time…like w. running	RHYS 808:27
hit the w. and become so much pulp	CAMP 226:8
Jesus…out of the w.	BIBLE 133:28
Lay a great w.	TENN 1004:42
lifted oars like w.	MANS 647:7
like w. in a well	SMITH 946:2
like wine through w.	BRON 191:10
little w. clears us of this deed	SHAK 908:50
make running w. talk	RAYB 803:48
Minnehaha, Laughing W.	LONG 611:11
moon Upon the w.	SHAK 912:34
moonlight on still w.	SCOTT 852:36
native habitat was hot w.	ANON 28:18
neither w. nor any other substance	WATT 1055:55
Not all the w.	SHAK 867:50
not to go into the w.	MACA 622:91
Nothing is more useful than w.	SMITH 946:94
one whose name was writ in w.	KEATS 548:22
only hot w.	GORO 436:69
patch of glassy w.	LAWS 588:21
poems have form…as w.	POUND 787:94
poured out like w.	BIBLE 114:49
pure air and w.	REES 805:92
rivers of w. in a dry place	BIBLE 126:81
Rivers…with w. broun	DOUG 341:54
run through fire and w.	SHAK 878:21
salt w. blinds them	SHAK 867:65
sight of salt w.	KIPL 563:90
skuttle fish…blackens all the w.	ADDI 7:25
slamming doors and slopping w.	MANS 647:97
Smooth runs the w.	SHAK 861:3
Smoothly the w. kissed	MILT 681:87
solidity of a w. buffalo	PERE 766:92
sound of w.	BASHO 76:1
sound of w.'s murmuring	SHEL 932:66
sports of the land And w.	REID 806:98
stone flung into the w.	LEON 597:84
stones with little w. drops	SHAK 866:34
struggling for life in the w.	JOHN 526:99
sullen w. far beneath	WORD 1096:31
tanks filled with w.	GILL 426:2
tears are but w.	SPEN 958:25
Too much of w. hast thou	SHAK 893:74
town surrounded by w.	MOORE 705:14
tumbler of London W.	SMITH 949:46
Unstable as w.	BIBLE 106:51
used to sing in the w.	DICK 322:68
vegetable diet and pure w.	SHEL 927:59
virtues We write in w.	SHAK 918:65
walk on running w.	WILK 1080:41
w. and the blood	TOPL 1023:7
w.'s care	YEATS 1105:61
w. carries all the things	LEON 597:78
w. comes ashore	FROST 407:89
w. curves a stick	LAFO 574:83
W., for Heaven's sake	THAC 1006:81
W. like a stone	ROSS 824:77
w. out of the wells of salvation	BIBLE 125:69
w. refreshes	HUME 503:2
w. shrank, and shuddered	ROBE 814:17
W. suggest her clear	DONNE 336:70
w. that was made wine	BIBLE 145:31

water (*contd.*):

w. this sorrow	SHAK 904:60
W. too pure breeds no fish	MAO 648:31
w. upon the stone	STEAD 964:5
W., w., everywhere	COLE 273:88
wetter w.	BROO 193:33
What is a wave without w.	PRAT 788:22
when I makes w. I makes w.	JOYCE 538:47
when she is in hot w.	ROOS 821:33
where no w. is	BIBLE 116:83
water-baby when he was a w.-b.	KING 558:99
water-bag leading a w.-b.	PATE 760:96
water-lily saw the w.-l. bloom	TENN 994:45
watercolorists pretty English w.	PISS 771:59
watercolour W. is not especially	PISS 771:59
watercolours etchings, w.	RODC 818:81
waterfall From the w. he named her	LONG 611:11
Waterloo From Marathon to W.	GILB 424:62
heart as big as W. Station	AGATE 10:66
W. House young man!	GILB 424:71
world-earthquake, W.	TENN 1000:69
waters as the w. cover the sea	BIBLE 125:68
beside the still w.	BIBLE 115:50
bosom the bright w. meet	MOORE 706:32
bread upon the w.	HAGG 450:4
By the w. of Babylon	WALP 1051:88
cast my bread on the w.	JACK 514:85
Cast thy bread upon the w.	BIBLE 123:40
come ye to the w.	BIBLE 127:3
crept by me on the w.	SHAK 916:24
depth Of w.	ROSS 824:79
different w. flow	HERA 473:85
effect of pent-up w.	SUN 982:34
Fades o'er the w. blue	BYRON 219:69
fen of stagnant w.	WORD 1096:38
floods of great w.	BIBLE 115:58
in the wilderness shall w. break out	BIBLE 126:82
knowledge of man is as the w.	BACON 55:13
luminous home of w.	ARNO 38:98
Many w. cannot quench love	BIBLE 124:55
mighty w. rolling evermore	WORD 1098:54
My native w. blue	OHAG 737:6
name is on your w.	SIGO 938:71
noise of w. in my ears	SHAK 863:54
Once more upon the w.!	BYRON 219:79
quiet w. by	SCOT 856:19
rolling w. go	TENN 997:97
see thee in our w.	JONS 536:11
spirit of God moved upon w.	BIBLE 102:82
still w. between walls	TENN 994:49
Stolen w. are sweet	BIBLE 120:67
troubled w. to whirlpool	LOWE 616:94
voice as the sound of many w.	BIBLE 156:99
w. aren't bound to anything	WINT 1087:67
w. murmuring	MILT 683:14
w. Of the River Lee	MAHO 638:65
w. shall overflow the hiding place	BIBLE 125:77
w. were abated from off the earth	BIBLE 104:12
When thou passest through the w.	BIBLE 126:93
While the nearer w. roll	WESL 1066:60
Who hath measured the w.	BIBLE 126:87
whore that sitteth upon many w.	BIBLE 158:27
wind makis w. overflow	ANON 23:87
yellow in the troubled w.	SALA 838:17
watershed prospect from the w.	STARK 963:97
waterside pair of stair by the w.	PEPYS 765:79
watersmooth-silver w.-s. stallion	CUMM 299:79
waterspouts noise of thy w.	BIBLE 116:70
watery w. noon	BROO 193:31
Watford woad began at W.	TALB 990:86
Watson Good old W.!	DOYLE 344:18
Wattle ever hear of Captain W.?	DIBD 319:5
wattles of clay and w.	YEATS 1104:57
waukin W. still and weary	BURNS 211:3

wave brooding on the charmèd w.

wave brooding on the charmèd w.	MILT 681:87
Churchill on top of the w.	BEAV 80:79
Cross alone has flown the w.	CRANE 294:91
disdainful w. of a white	ANGE 20:32
heard the w.'s splash	BYRON 222:44
lift me as a w.	SHEL 928:89
like a w. of the sea	BIBLE 155:59
off the crested w.	SIGO 938:71
Swiftly walk o'er the western w.	SHEL 932:72
Time's all serving w.?	BRON 191:9
w. glittered the dew	MANS 647:7
w.'s intenser day	SHEL 928:88
w. of all her waves	KIPL 561:54
w. on w.	CRANE 294:95
w. that echoes round	TENN 1002:4
What is a w. without water	PRAT 788:22
wind and w. and oar	TENN 994:53
wind, or swallowing w.	LOVE 615:64
Wish me luck, as you w.	PARR 756:42
Waverley continued to like W.	SCOTT 854:71
waves all thy w. and thy billows	BIBLE 116:70
Britannia, rule the w.	THOM 1015:46
dash of w.	ARNO 38:98
Him that walked the w.	MILT 685:49
Like as the w.	SHAK 914:67
lute-resounding w.	POPE 783:7
portly pusher of w.	UPDI 1036:50
proud w. be stayed	BIBLE 113:19
shines only on the w. behind us!	COLE 275:27
silver w. of thy sweet singing	SHEL 930:24
sparkling w.	WORD 1099:69
spent w.' riot	SWIN 987:38
successive w. of dissent	SCHO 848:87
tired w., vainly breaking	CLOU 270:32
w. bound beneath me	BYRON 219:79
w. upon the shore	SHEL 927:73
w.…washed it away	SPEN 959:45
w. were always saying	DICK 323:93
w. work less and less	SURR 982:41
Wealdstone turned to w.	BETJ 100:49
waving not w. but drowning	SMITH 948:33
wax didn't w. his moustache	KIPL 560:19
girls with w. faces	WILD 1079:26
heart is like w.	BIBLE 114:49
honey and w.	SWIFT 984:58
let virtue be as w.	SHAK 892:55
My faith shall w.	DANI 304:61
w. and wane	WATTS 1055:57
W. to receive	BYRON 221:22
waxwork be w. child at all?	DICK 322:59
way ain't got you one w.	NAUG 721:91
All the W. with LBJ	HOLT 487:6
always the w.	TWAIN 1033:93
best w. to suppose	HALI 452:30
catch the nearest w.	SHAK 907:25
certain w. to be wrong	STEI 966:59
cheer one on the tedious w.	ROSS 823:68
Commit thy w. unto the Lord	BIBLE 115:63
dirty, dangerous w.	GOLD 433:24
Every day, in every w.	COUE 289:72
Every w. of a man is right	BIBLE 121:92
except in such a w.	KANT 542:4
fall not out by the w.	BIBLE 106:49
go the longest w.	BUTL 217:37
going a long w.	TENN 1004:48
heavens wide pathless w.	MILT 682:9
here I go, on my w.	PARR 756:42
I am the w.	BIBLE 146:62
I don't know my w. about	WITT 1088:77
individual w. of just seeing	JAMES 517:46
it's the w. they say it	STEI 966:54
knows the w. but can't drive	TYNAN 1035:29
lead me in the w. everlasting	BIBLE 120:51

way (*contd.*):

Long is the w. And hard	MILT 688:22
lose their w.	THOM 1012:11
meet them on your w. down	MIZN 697:5
metaphoric w.	MALA 641:6
most difficult w.	MILL 679:49
My w. of life	SHAK 910:81
on our w. to the line	SASS 845:28
one certain w. for a woman	SPARK 955:46
pioneer a new w.	SHEL 926:53
plods his weary w.	GRAY 441:62
Rebellion lay in his w.	SHAK 876:66
safely by the middle w.	OVID 747:98
sees the world one w.	BARA 70:9
shortest w....commonly foulest	BACON 55:25
shortest w. to do many things	SMIL 945:74
take my endless w.	HOUS 495:56
That's the w. for Billy and me	HOGG 485:67
the end of the w.	PAST 759:83
This is the w.	BIBLE 126:80
this w. not to interfere	MURD 715:67
thorny w. to heaven	SHAK 888:62
up a sandy w.	BIBLE 132:8
War always finds a w.	BREC 186:31
w. guys yell when they're mad	STEI 966:55
w. is long	SENE 858:45
w. may be known upon earth	BIBLE 116:85
w. of a man with a maid	KIPL 561:47
w. of all the earth	BIBLE 109:11
w. of all the earth	BIBLE 110:54
w. of holiness	BIBLE 126:83
w. plain before my face	BOOK 176:1
w. that takes the town	HERB 475:14
w. to keep weeds	SHUL 936:31
w. to treat her	FAUL 384:87
w. was long	SCOTT 853:42
w. which seemeth right	BIBLE 121:75
w. you'd look at a chessman	JARR 518:61
whatsoe'er the w.	WORD 1100:92
women I...give w. to	PEPYS 765:78
you get in his w.	TOSC 1024:8

wayfaring w. men — BIBLE 126:83

ways acquainted with all my w. — BIBLE 119:48

all w. do lie open	SHAK 878:15
crooked winding w.	HERB 475:29
fly in different w.	HEMI 470:22
good...By all the w.	WESL 1067:75
great and gracious w.	PATM 760:4
Her w. are w. of pleasantness	BIBLE 120:60
know not well the subtle w.	EMER 377:64
learn her wanton w.	ROET 819:98
Let me count the w.!	BROW 197:19
look both w.	EDDI 360:18
maintain mine own w.	BIBLE 113:8
Most sure of all His w.	NEWM 724:32
neither are your w. my w.	BIBLE 127:5
nine and sixty w.	KIPL 561:48
the w. of God to man	POPE 780:33
w. are not as theirs	HOUS 496:73
w. deep and the weather sharp	ELIOT 369:3
w. of saying 'To hell with you'	FENW 385:4
whose w. are all discreet	PARK 753:90

weak arm the w. — FRAN 401:88

concessions of the w.	BURKE 206:5
entrust...freedom to the w.	EISE 364:82
eyesight has always been w.	GREG 446:47
flesh is w.	BIBLE 140:51
God hath chosen the w. things	BIBLE 150:45
How w. a thing	SHAK 883:37
let the w. say, I am strong	BIBLE 130:56
to be w. is miserable	MILT 687:95
w. alone repent!	BYRON 221:13
w. always have to decide	BONH 173:86
w. and feeble woman	ELIZ 373:90

weak (*contd.*):

w. and miserable men	CHOM 261:56
W. shall perish	SERV 859:54
w. spot or two in a character	HOLM 486:99
w., still tremulous	LEVE 600:25
when I am w., then am I strong	BIBLE 152:87

weaker One is never w. — OLLI 738:33

wife...the w. vessel — BIBLE 156:81

weakest w. in nature — PASC 758:66

weakness childish w. to lament — SHAK 862:32

felt only his w.	BELL 88:36
Marks of w.	BLAKE 167:92
means of w. and debility	SHAK 885:82
Power Girt round with w.	SHEL 931:43
sought her w. to reprove	LANY 580:79
strength and w. of human nature	MACA 624:21
strength is made perfect in w.	BIBLE 152:87
though it be a w.	JONS 535:97
w. for the stoic's pride	POPE 780:42
w. of our race	DELA 314:21
w. offered, strength	LANY 580:78
w. which impairs	ARNO 36:61

weaknesses pity...weakens our w. — BALZ 68:74

support two w. at the same time	WILD 1079:31
virtues out of their w.	MENC 670:80
w....into burnable energy	BELL 89:43

Wealdstone W. turned to waves — BETJ 100:49

wealth as their w. increaseth — MARL 653:98

all that w. e'er gave	GRAY 442:66
all w. alchemy	DONNE 337:78
Black love is Black w.	GIOV 428:36
born into w.	ROCK 817:68
by the acquisition of w.	MONT 703:87
cannot redistribute w.	TSON 1031:42
carry the w. of the Indies	JOHN 530:96
consume w. without producing it	SHAW 920:96
cunning purchase of my w.	JONS 534:75
distribution of w.	HARDY 456:83
distribution of w. and income	KEYN 555:38
everything yields to w.	BLEST 169:28
excessive w. a libel	SHEL 927:57
Health, W., Love...and Time	ANON 30:68
heroic w.	WORD 1096:38
how much w....in a country	SIDG 936:39
I have had w.	ALBE 31:91
insolence of w.	JOHN 530:97
Labour is the Father...of W.	PETTY 768:14
Large was his w.	DRYD 350:28
no w. but life	RUSK 831:94
Nor that content surpassing w.	SHEL 927:74
poor man's w.	SIDN 937:53
prevents the rule of w.	BAGE 61:55
prodigal of its w.	NORR 731:29
produce more w.	GILM 427:15
progress of society and w.	RICA 808:33
pursuit of w.	LUCR 619:35
representative of w.	MILL 674:60
Republics end by w.	MONT 702:85
rich man's w. is his strong city	BIBLE 120:68
road to w.	TROL 1027:64
Science...casts its w.	HERZ 478:72
the skill—the w.	ROOS 822:42
w. abides not	EURI 381:35
w. accumulates and men decay	GOLD 433:10
W. accumulates whatever	KEYN 554:30
w. and a good name	WALT 1052:2
W. cannot make a life	HERR 477:57
W. does not bring goodness	PLATO 773:3
W. has more and more increased	CARL 234:39
W. I ask not	STEV 976:52
W., in a commercial age	POUND 787:98
w. is distributed in...society	MILL 674:57
w. is health	DYER 358:90
w....makes them doubly poor	CRAB 293:73

wealth (*contd.*):

w. Of simple beauty	WHIT 1074:4
w. of steaming phrases	SCHU 851:17
w. with our wisdom	KENN 552:89
What w....to me had brought	WORD 1099:69
with w. and honour blest	DRYD 349:14
With w. your state...improve	DONNE 337:79
worker...poorer the more w.	MARX 661:26

wealthier To be w. or more powerful — HELO 469:7

wealthy healthy, w. and dead — THUR 1018:24

w. wife was she	BALL 68:60

weaned were we not w. till then? — DONNE 336:73

weans w. in their bed — MILL 679:59

weapon bayonet is a w. — ANON 26:43

how steady you hold your w.	SIMP 939:90
most deadly	PARK 756:37
nobler w. than a wound	CRAS 296:26
Nostalgia IS A W.	COUP 290:86
other hand held a w.	BIBLE 112:91
religious and political w.	LEWIS 602:60
thoughtlessness is the w. of the male	CONN 283:70
Time's most lethal w.	SITW 941:23
trusty shield and w.	LUTH 620:49
w. had none	SCOTT 853:54
w. is starvation	STEV 977:61
w. which will make war	MORT 710:2

weapons Clothes are our w. — CART 242:92

fought with nuclear w.	MOUN 711:31
hurt with the same w.	SHAK 872:80
into the cavity...cast all w.	DEKA 313:8
lawful...to wear w.	BOOK 178:1
not only with w.	MANC 644:66
prevent...nuclear w.	AMIS 17:91
w. against their capitalist exploiters	LENIN 595:50
W. grow rusty	HICKS 480:97
w. of mass extermination	RUSS 833:32
w. of war perished!	BIBLE 110:34
women...dropping their w.	OSBO 745:67
women's w., water-drops	SHAK 902:15

wearer merit of the w.! — SHAK 874:31

new w. of clothes	THOR 1016:82

weariest w....worldly life — SHAK 897:83

weariness Art thou pale for w. — SHEL 932:73

His W. the Prince	FIRB 389:74
hours of w.	WORD 1094:96
labour w.	LYLY 620:61
study is a w.	BIBLE 124:43
W. Can snore	SHAK 916:12
w., the fever, and the fret	KEATS 547:15
yet w. May toss him	HERB 476:35

wearing meals I...am w. — BUSH 215:85

wearisome monotonous and w. — THOR 1017:99

weary faint and be w. — BIBLE 126:91

fast asleep and w.	BIBLE 109:13
great rock in a w. land	BIBLE 126:81
How w., stale, flat, and unprofitable	SHAK 888:52
In me or, most w.	HOPK 492:1
lay his w. bones	SHAK 918:64
Let him be rich and w.	HERB 476:35
Let us not be w. in well doing	BIBLE 152:93
poor and the w. predominate	GARL 415:26
sae dowf and w.	BURNS 212:35
Say I'm w.	HUNT 505:29
Waukin still and w.	BURNS 211:3
w. be at rest	BIBLE 112:99
w. lot is thine	SCOTT 854:68
w. of these worldly bars	SHAK 883:25

weasel as a w. sucks eggs — SHAK 885:87

w. under the cocktail cabinet	PINT 770:47

weather Autumn's pleasant w. — BURNS 210:81

blue unclouded w.	TENN 993:44
calm or stormy w.	ROSS 823:68
Cricket w.	JOYCE 538:55
dry frigid w.	PIER 769:34

weather (*contd.*):

earthquakes preceded by bright w.	CARL 235:*61*
fair w.: for the sky is red	BIBLE 138:*12*
french wine and fine w.	KEATS 545:*67*
he is also part of the w.	TRIL 1027:*60*
Hillary…responsible for the w.	MACC 627:*69*
If it prove fair w.	SUCK 981:*23*
in clear w.	SURR 983:*46*
in red w.	STEV 971:*47*
it's fruitcake w.!	CAPO 231:*81*
Jolly boating w.	CORY 288:*67*
makes cold w.	SHAK 917:*48*
more w.…than anywhere else	SAMU 840:*47*
possible combination of w.	LODGE 609:*77*
promise of fair w.	DICK 323:*90*
protecting flat surfaces from the w.	BIER 161:*89*
sad or singing w.	SWIN 987:*44*
season of calm w.	WORD 1098:*54*
seven month of Arctic w.	ANON 25:*18*
sharp be the w.	SCOTT 854:*72*
talk is of the w.	JOHN 527:*19*
waiting for the w. to break	PINT 770:*46*
ways deep and the w. sharp	ELIOT 369:*3*
W. abroad	RICH 809:*41*
W. and rain	KIPL 564:*7*
w. sharp	ANDR 19:*13*
w. that bringeth no gain	DEKK 313:*9*
w. the cuckoo likes	HARDY 457:*13*
won't hold up the w.	MACN 637:*39*

weave So did I w. my self | HERB 475:*26*

tangled web we w.	SCOTT 853:*57*
W. the warp	GRAY 443:*84*

weaving w. and unweaving | ELIOT 365:*99*

web as little w. as this | SHAK 899:*20*

She left the w.	TENN 994:*45*
tangled w. we weave	SCOTT 853:*57*
w. do parents weave	NASH 720:*58*
w. of our grand illusion	PAGE 749:*32*
w. of our life	SHAK 901:*80*
wove a w. in childhood	BRON 190:*91*

webs Theoretical w., dirty w. | KELM 548:*31*

With swarthy w.	TENN 1004:*49*

Webster Like W. 's dictionary | BURKE 208:*51*

wed December when they w. | SHAK 887:*23*

w. a fair young man	CAMP 228:*40*
w. itself with Speech	TENN 998:*28*
w. ye to my youngest son	SCOTT 854:*78*
With this kiss I w. thee	HEYW 480:*93*

wedding barefoot on her w. day | SHAK 864:*75*

Be well ware of w.	ANON 22:*76*
bought her w. clothes	ADDI 7:*24*
face…like a w. cake	AUDEN 49:*7*
Let's have a w.	DICK 327:*74*
mouldering like a w. cake	RICH 809:*49*
till our w. day	COLUM 278:*60*
where a w. has been	LENN 596:*62*
white lies to ice a w. cake	ASQU 42:*81*

wedding-guest W.-G. stood still | COLE 273:*84*

weddings All w. are similar | BERG 94:*46*

wedlock together in holy w. | BOOK 176:*53*

W.…hath oft compared been	DAVI 307:*10*

Wednesday blue and white W. heart | HATT 460:*58*

He that died o' W.	SHAK 876:*70*
worked Monday…fired W.	ALGR 13:*25*

weed O thou w. | SHAK 900:*47*

on earth a vicious w.	DRYD 349:*19*
salt w. sways in the stream	ARNO 36:*55*

weeds all the idle w. that grow | SHAK 903:*32*

grubbing w. from gravel paths	KIPL 564:*14*
keep w. from overwhelming you	SHUL 936:*31*
Long live the w.	HOPK 492:*96*
smell far worse than w.	SHAK 914:*80*
w. of peace…triumphs	MILT 682:*3*
w. will overrun the fields	HOOV 490:*57*

weeds (*contd.*):

winter w. outworn	SHEL 932:*64*

week £1 per w. | ANON 25:*20*

accomplished in a w.	STEV 974:*23*
any crisis next w.	KISS 566:*37*
as much as a w.	TWAIN 1032:*57*
but a w. married	SHAK 879:*43*
Christian on a Pound a W.?	HARD 455:*77*
Englishman…there only a w.	FRAS 403:*19*
go a w. without a drink	LEWIS 601:*47*
lease for a w.	ANOU 30:*71*
Middle of Next W.	CARR 241:*89*
once a w. there should be	ORWE 744:*31*
takes the rest of the w.	WALK 1049:*56*
That Was The W.	ANON 27:*72*
tried…once a w.	JOHN 529:*83*
w., a natural day	MARL 654:*20*
w. is a long time in politics	WILS 1085:*32*

weekend the dirty w. | SMITH 946:*1*

weekends plumber on w. | ALLEN 14:*36*

weeks brief hours and w. | SHAK 915:*89*

w. of watching the roof leak	SNYD 951:*83*

weep better…to w. at joy | SHAK 878:*26*

blame thee now to w.	SHAK 864:*82*
No, I'll not w.	SHAK 903:*16*
not to w. at them	SPIN 960:*46*
O now you w.	SHAK 884:*55*
O, w. for Adonais!	SHEL 930:*34*
shepherds, w. no more	MILT 685:*49*
That he should w. for her?	SHAK 890:*14*
that I may not w.	BYRON 223:*51*
time to w.	BIBLE 122:*19*
To w. is to make less	SHAK 861:*20*
w. and know why	HOPK 492:*93*
w. for him	SHAK 884:*47*
W. If you can	HAMM 453:*47*
W. not for little Léonie	GRAH 437:*89*
w. on your own grave	GRAV 439:*22*
w. or she will die	TENN 997:*7*
w. with them that w.	BIBLE 149:*35*
w. with them that w.	SHAK 862:*39*
when I w.	SPEN 958:*25*
Why w. ye by the tide	SCOTT 854:*78*
you w. alone	WILC 1075:*25*

weeping doth that bode w.? | SHAK 900:*50*

full cause of w.	SHAK 903:*16*
Her little boy w. sought	BLAKE 166:*68*
joy at w.!	SHAK 878:*26*
prove the w. philosopher	SHAK 874:*15*
Rachel w. for her children	BIBLE 128:*28*
w. and gnashing of teeth	BIBLE 136:*65*
w. and gnashing of teeth	BIBLE 140:*42*
w. over sins…never committed	WILDE 1076:*34*

weeps before we know…why he w. | DUBOS 353:*11*

weigh But w. this song | YEATS 1105:*64*

number, w. and measure	HALES 451:*23*
'tis best to w.	SHAK 881:*80*

weighs W. heavily on me | KEATS 544:*36*

weight collapsed under the w. | CANN 230:*67*

counter-opinion of…same w.	SPEN 956:*87*
just w. is his delight	BIBLE 120:*69*
Number, W., or Measure	PETTY 768:*15*
'tis purchased by w.	SHAK 872:*82*
w. of the superincumbent hour	SHEL 931:*43*
w. of this sad time	SHAK 904:*50*
w. of womanhood	DANG 304:*59*
w. taken off the driving wheels	CANN 230:*68*

weights clock with w. and chains | COLUM 278:*62*

weighty drowneth that which is w. | BACON 55:*10*

weird home of the w. | LAWS 587:*18*

weirs grass grows on the w. | YEATS 1104:*56*

three lone w.	ARNO 39:*14*

welcome And W. To It | THUR 1019:*30*

Bear w. in your eye	SHAK 907:*29*

welcome (*contd.*):

effusive w. of the pier	AUDEN 46:*53*
rest may reason and w.	BROW 199:*74*
terrible events are w.	SHAK 906:*88*
thankful that I am here to w. you	STAN 962:*84*
W. to shuttle diplomacy!	SISCO 940:*96*
w. was not excessive	USTI 1038:*81*

welcomest often w. when…gone | SHAK 860:*91*

welfare goes with the w. | WILS 1084:*21*

highest w. of your souls	PLATO 773:*3*
most anxious for its w.	BURKE 206:*98*
W. is hated by those	GOLD 432:*94*
w. …of the Irish nation	REDM 804:*75*
W. should be a safety-net	ANON 30:*54*

welkin bow'd w.…doth bend | MILT 684:*36*

Hark! how all the w. rings	WESL 1066:*59*
let the w. roar	SHAK 877:*91*

well All manner of thing shall be w. | ELIOT 373:*81*

all shall be w.	JULI 539:*69*
And did it very w.	GILB 424:*76*
bed-time…and all w.	SHAK 876:*67*
being alive, but being w.	MART 657:*62*
cannot think w., love w.	WOOLF 1093:*68*
confident I can do w.	JOHN 526:*1*
dark w.	PRIC 789:*34*
do not feel quite w.	GALB 412:*85*
don't dress w.	SHAW 920:*4*
in some measure made me w.	SHAK 877:*79*
Is it w. with thee?	BIBLE 111:*76*
kingdom of the w.	SONT 953:*11*
knew too w.	FROST 407:*83*
like water in a w.	SMITH 946:*2*
looks w. enough on page	BUNT 204:*58*
man lives w.	KIPL 560:*21*
never speaks w. of me	CONG 280:*93*
One's country is where one does w.	ANON 20:*45*
valley of Baca make it a w.	BIBLE 117:*94*
w. as long as I live on h.	BIRD 163:*14*
when looking w. can't	SUCK 981:*17*
when things are going w.	BEAU 79:*61*
worth doing w.	CHES 257:*72*
Would all did so w. as I.!	DYER 358:*90*

well-appointed w.-a. three-deckers | PALM 752:*68*

well-being responsible for its w.-b. | PORT 784:*37*

well-bred w.-b. Captain | GILB 423:*55*

well-educated w.-e. young women | AUST 51:*39*

well-fed 60s face was w.-f. | WATE 1055:*50*

well-killed stab…A w.-k. Boche | READ 803:*51*

well-looking one of my w.-l. days | GOLD 433:*22*

well-off Awrish people are too w. | SHAW 923:*74*

well-rounded not a w.-r. person | BELL 88:*28*

well-spaced nothing is w.-s. | WILL 1083:*93*

well-to-do w.-t.-d. prosper | BRYAN 201:*14*

well-written w.-w. life almost as rare | CARL 235:*76*

Wellington shoot three W. College boys | KING 558:*96*

wells buckets into empty w. | COWP 293:*57*

go about and poison w.	MARL 653:*1*
w. of salvation	BIBLE 125:*26*

Welsh devil understands W. | SHAK 876:*61*

wench besides, the w. is dead | MARL 653:*2*

fair hot w.	SHAK 875:*36*
love w.	SHIR 935:*24*
O ill-stared w.	SHAK 900:*62*
stuff fit only for a w.	MASE 662:*40*
w.…strays so from her kind	DEKK 313:*13*

Wenonah called her the name W. | LONG 611:*9*

wept Caesar hath w. | SHAK 884:*14*

He w. to hear	BLAKE 166:*62*
I could have w.	HOLM 485:*11*
Jesus w.	BIBLE 146:*56*

Werther dies from excess…(like W.) | BART 75:*83*

W. had a love	THAC 1007:*1*

Wesen Mensch ist das W | SCHI 847:*64*

winter (*contd.*):

from w. going into w.	BEDE 82:8
furious w. blowing	RANS 802:35
furious w. rages	SHAK 916:16
heel Of limping w.	SHAK 868:76
How like a w.	SHAK 914:82
If W. comes	SHEL 928:91
In w. I get up at night	STEV 975:32
ninetieth w. came	EGAN 362:55
Now is the w.	SHAK 862:45
O W.! bar thine adamantine doors	BLAKE 165:60
People live within w.	MUNRO 714:60
poor as w.	SHAK 899:33
sad tale's best for w.	SHAK 911:23
same w. and summer	SHAK 872:80
severest w.,...the spring	COWP 292:49
Summer in W.	CRAS 295:18
summer out of w.	DONNE 339:26
through the perils of w.	TROL 1027:65
Thus in w. stands	MILL 676:87
Twice a week the w.	HOUS 494:48
very dead of w.	ANDR 19:13
was the w. wild	MILT 681:86
when rivers are swollen in w.	SOPH 953:18
w. evening settles down	ELIOT 367:56
W. is come and gone	SHEL 931:39
W. is for women	PLATH 773:99
w. is past	BIBLE 124:19
W. lies too long	CATH 244:42
w. long, I am one	NASH 720:70
w., plague and pestilence	NASHE 721:82
w.'s rains and ruins	SWIN 986:24
W. scourged the meadow	ROBE 814:17
w. weeds outworn	SHEL 932:64
w., when men kill the fat swine	ANON 21:64
w. wind is loud and wild	BRON 191:7
W., yelling through the troublous air	COLL 277:49
Would seem a w.'s day	ROCH 817:64
winters Four lagging w.	SHAK 866:43
green end of civilization's hardest w.	FOWL 399:67
Of those four w.	GREE 444:10
sixteen w. cannot blow away	SHAK 912:42
wipe Gives it a w.	HOOD 489:53
wire fine w. around our s.	STEV 972:79
high w. of his own making	FERL 386:20
wireless message came on the w.	PENI 764:55
wires Along the electric w.	AUST 52:72
transmit the voice over w.	ANON 24:15
w. that span the mountain stream	CRANE 295:99
wisdom acquire that kind of w.?	ATWO 45:30
age of w.	DICK 326:58
apply our hearts unto w.	BIBLE 117:1
attained the sum Of w.	MILT 693:30
beginning in w.	LOWE 617:4
beginning of w.	BIBLE 118:24
beginning of w.	FLAU 393:42
but not to our w.	BANKS 70:99
but w. lingers	TENN 996:80
cannot myself give birth to w.	SOCR 951:87
contrivance of human w.	BURKE 207:30
dispose Of highest w.	MILT 695:59
double share Of w.	MILT 694:39
evidence of our w.	TROL 1027:68
faith without w.	RUNC 828:53
famous then By w.	MILT 694:33
hard, ancient w.	WAUGH 1057:89
highest w. and...beauty	EINS 363:67
Homo ludens in his w.	DUNN 356:58
idea of elder w.	UPDI 1037:72
in much w. is much grief	BIBLE 122:17
in respect of w.	PLATO 773:1
infallible criterion of w.	BURKE 208:42
infinite goodness and w.	WALL 1049:61
Jesus increased in w.	BIBLE 142:80

wisdom (*contd.*):

make me to know w.	BIBLE 116:77
more than W., Art, or Nature	HERR 477:57
Music is...your w.	PARK 753:87
nor w., in the grave	BIBLE 123:34
Of such w.	PATER 759:95
only w. ever to be attained	PRAT 789:23
only w. we can hope to acquire	ELIOT 371:48
our pocket w.	STEV 974:13
palace of w.	BLAKE 166:73
pray we have the w.	ALLEN 14:50
privilege of w. to listen	HOLM 486:1
profoundest w.	HAWT 461:78
Raphael paints w.	EMER 377:72
reputation for w. and honour	BIBLE 123:36
run to conceits or w.	BART 74:72
Science robs men of w.	UNAM 1036:43
score of their w.	SWIFT 985:87
seek for knowledge and w.	SHEL 926:51
stage of w.	SKIN 943:54
staid W.'s hue	MILT 682:6
such w. as many of us have	TROL 1027:74
that hopeless w. of experience	ONEI 740:52
There is a w. that is woe	MELV 667:38
There's more of w.	WORD 1094:2
there's w. in women	BROO 192:18
those who love want w.	SHEL 930:17
thought...we had w.	BENET 90:64
turns W. to folly	MILT 691:83
utter words of w.	HUXL 507:80
We do not receive w.	PROU 793:92
what is bettre than w.?	CHAU 255:44
W. and policy dictates	NAPO 718:26
W. and Spirit of the universe!	WORD 1095:14
w. at one entrance quite	MILT 689:31
w. be put in a silver rod	BLAKE 166:61
W. begins at the end	WEBS 1060:51
w. can there be to choose	MILT 685:60
W. comes not from reason	GIDE 423:44
W. crieth out	BIBLE 120:56
W. denotes the pursuing	HUTC 506:41
W. hath builded her house	BIBLE 120:66
w. in discourse	MILT 692:96
W. in minds attentive	COWP 293:62
w. is a meditation	SPIN 960:57
W.'s heavenly Father	WORD 1100:92
W. is humble	COWP 293:63
W. is justified	BIBLE 137:87
W. is the principal thing	BIBLE 120:59
W....knowledge of good and evil	CHEE 255:50
w....lost in knowledge?	ELIOT 370:17
w....more precious than rubies	BIBLE 120:60
w. of a learned man	BIBLE 132:16
w. of God	BLAKE 166:78
w. of old men	ELIOT 371:47
w. of the crocodiles	BACON 58:92
w. of the sociologists	DYSON 358:99
W. say another	BURKE 208:49
W.'s self Oft seeks	MILT 683:28
w. shall die with you	BIBLE 113:6
w. teaches us	KEYN 555:40
w. to distinguish the one	NIEB 727:66
W. without honesty	JONS 536:18
With the ancient is w.	BIBLE 113:7
with w. well supplied	LUCR 619:35
world by w. knew not God	BIBLE 150:44
wisdoms w. of maturity	LIVE 607:45
wise A being darkly w.	POPE 780:42
all the rest, though fair and w.	SHEL 931:51
art of being w.	JAMES 517:42
as w. a snout on	FERG 385:15
as w. to cast a violet	SHEL 931:56
be lowly w.	MILT 691:91
Be not w. in your own conceits	BIBLE 149:36

wise (*contd.*):

Better is a poor and a w. child	BIBLE 123:25
better not to think ourselves w.	ELIOT 365:7
consider her ways, and be w.	BIBLE 120:63
cunning men pass for w.	BACON 58:58
discloses to the w.	BIER 161:80
folly to be w.	GRAY 441:48
fool doth think he is w.	SHAK 887:27
God only w.	SMITH 950:61
Great men are not always w.	BIBLE 113:15
heard a w. man say	HOUS 494:44
Histories make men w.	BACON 59:25
how vainly would the w.	ROCH 816:47
if you are w.	FOWL 399:65
in presence sad and w.	SURR 983:46
Is it the w. men or the fools?	IBSEN 510:20
liken him unto a w. man	BIBLE 135:63
make us happy make us w.	MASE 662:48
making w. the simple	BIBLE 114:45
manly w.	MARL 653:94
more fools than w.	GIBB 422:32
more of the fool than of the w.	BACON 58:77
Neither a w. man nor a brave man	EISE 364:79
No rules, however w.	RUSS 832:25
no w. man will undertake	CARL 234:45
None w. dares hopeless venture	EURI 380:27
Nor ever did a w. one	ROCH 817:66
nor talk too w.	KIPL 564:8
not w. to have either	GIRA 429:45
O w. young judge	SHAK 873:94
puzzle all the w.	DRYD 349:11
reputed w. For saying nothing	SHAK 873:1
returns home w. and useful	BELL 86:90
should be w.	SHAK 902:6
Sitting on a w. man's knee	HUXL 507:80
Some deemed him wondrous w.	BEAT 79:56
spirits of the w.	SHAK 877:35
teach a w. man	RABE 799:89
the mighty, the w.	WORD 1100:85
The w. want love	SHEL 930:17
think as w. men do	ASCH 40:50
to love and to be w.	BACON 55:21
What fool is not so w.	SHAK 865:19
wherefore thou be w.	TENN 1005:64
whether they be w. or simple	SCHW 852:31
wine can...the w. beguile	POPE 779:12
w. as serpents	BIBLE 136:76
w. course of prophilaxis	SILVA 938:77
w. enough to understand	SCHW 851:28
w. father that knows	SHAK 874:24
w., for cure, on exercise depend	DRYD 352:87
w. man keepeth it in	BIBLE 122:10
w. man proportions his belief	HUME 503:9
W. men come in all sizes	HERN 476:46
W. men fish here	STEL 967:69
w. men follow fools	BACON 58:84
w. men from the east	BIBLE 133:23
w. person is colour-blind	SCHW 852:32
w. shall shine	BIBLE 130:51
w. Tory and a w. Whig	JOHN 531:16
w. who soar	WORD 1100:88
wisest of the w.	TENN 1003:31
wise-cracking w.-c. and wit	PARK 754:17
wisely men and nations behave w.	EBAN 359:7
W. and slowly	SHAK 869:98
Wiseman wise-manned...By W.	BROW 200:86
wiseness let thy w. fear	SHAK 883:81
wiser and not the w. grow	POMF 777:68
be w. than ourselves	TROL 1027:68
ignorant man to be guided by the w.	CARL 235:31
looked w. when he was seated	KEYN 554:26
w....of the two sexes	GIBB 421:20
w. than their own	BROO 192:18
young man will be w.	TENN 1003:35

woke Happy till I w. again	HOUS 495:65
w. me from the torpor	WARR 1054:36
w. to black flak	JARR 518:57
Woking playing for W.	BETJ 99:32
wold clothe the w.	TENN 993:37
wolf appetite, an universal w.	SHAK 895:40
comrade with the w. and owl	SHAK 902:14
either a god or a w.	WEBS 1060:39
grim w. with privy paw	MILT 684:45
let the w. into the sheepfold!	INGR 512:50
man is a w.	PLAU 775:30
naked child against hungry w.	DAVI 307:96
seeth the w. coming	BIBLE 146:54
spotted w. of sameness	SOYI 954:45
w. also shall dwell with the lamb	BIBLE 125:68
w. and lamb shall feed together	BIBLE 128:16
w. and the lamb…united	ARIS 34:22
w. remains of a different opinion	INGE 511:35
W. that shall keep it	KIPL 561:52
w., the hyena, and the skunk?	BRYAN 201:15
wolves habitation for bears and w.	SCHAW 847:61
heard the w. scuffle	TATE 991:5
inwardly they are ravening w.	BIBLE 135:60
room in the west for w.	BABB 54:89
sheep in the midst of w.	BIBLE 136:76
there were w. in Wales	THOM 1012:95
w. whose gospel	MILT 686:80
woman advice…to any young w.	CURR 301:20
Although w. has performed much	STAN 962:88
Anon…was often a w.	WOOLF 1093:71
Any w. who understands	THAT 1007:12
Any w.'s death	RICH 809:51
anything done, ask a w.	THAT 1007:5
argument with men a w.	MILT 695:50
artist man and the mother w.	SHAW 921:26
As a w., I can't go to war	RANK 801:29
As to w.'s subjection	STAN 963:89
As w.'s love	SHAK 891:36
average man sees w.	MUIR 713:41
be a w. without thinking about it	CIXO 267:78
beautiful w. …qualities of a man	LABR 572:37
best w. painter	OKEE 738:22
better to love a w.	HARDY 457:4
bettre than a good w.?	CHAU 255:44
bettre than wisedom? W.	CHAU 255:44
between a man and a w.	GIBB 422:36
blessed with a w.'s brain	RICH 810:64
bloom on a w.	BARR 73:46
born of w.	TWAIN 1032:64
brawling w. in a wide house	BIBLE 121:93
broken-hearted w. tends the grave	HAYES 462:92
but a w.'s reason	SHAK 860:73
But yet a w.	SHAK 875:52
called a w. in my own house	WAUGH 1057:84
Can a w. forget her suckling child	BIBLE 126:95
cannot love a w. so well	ELIOT 366:41
cheeks of a young w.	DALI 303:46
child of our grandmother Eve…a w.	SHAK 865:11
civil and obliging young w.	AUST 50:29
clever w. to manage a fool	KIPL 560:16
constant w.	FORD 397:12
damnable w.'s trick	SHAW 921:29
Dear, dead w.	BROW 198:48
death…of a beautiful w.	POE 776:50
devil made himself a w.	HUGO 502:75
Did ever w., since the creation	STER 968:89
difference between one young w.	SHAW 923:84
dispassionate w….has yet to see	LABR 572:40
does not the w. always suffer	BALZ 69:76
don't know a w. until	LEVE 599:20
doors upon a w.'s wit	SHAK 887:24
driving…with a pretty w.	JOHN 530:90
each tree…a tranced w.	FREE 404:34
each w. thy fond flexible whore	DEKK 313:17

woman (*contd.*):	
either…your w.	WALK 1049:57
every strong w.	FULL 409:34
Every w. adores a Fascist	PLATH 773:95
Every w. should marry	DISR 333:13
excellent thing in w.	SHAK 904:52
Except the American w.	BARR 72:39
expect that W.	MERE 671:99
experience…of the w. writer	WITT 1088:62
fail as a w.	FRID 404:47
Farewell W.	ROCH 817:62
fashionable w. wears clothes	QUANT 796:49
fat white w.	CORN 288:58
feeling a w.'s pulse	STER 970:26
For a w. to have	GRAV 440:28
For a w., she has…talent	GOET 431:70
furious about W.'s Liberationists	LOOS 613:38
gentler sister W.	BURNS 210:83
Give not thy soul unto a w.	BIBLE 132:95
good w. if I had	THAC 1006:89
good-for-nothing w. on the streets	SHAW 923:69
government of a w.	BACON 60:37
greatest glory of a w.	PERI 766:98
ground is like a beautiful w.	SNOW 951:78
hard for a w. to define	HARDY 456:89
hate in a w.	SHAW 920:6
he seduces a w.	POMP 777:69
heart of man lodged in a w.	CONG 281:38
heart of w.	SHAK 883:37
help and support of the w. I love	EDWA 362:51
historical repugnance to w.	PAGL 749:34
I'm a w. I want things	MANS 647:98
if a w. have long hair	BIBLE 150:58
If I were a w.	VAND 1039:98
in a young w.	HUGO 502:90
in the shape of a w.	RICH 809:47
In w.'s eye the unanswerable tear	BYRON 221:14
is in w.…element of unreason	WRIG 1101:3
join together this man and this w.	BOOK 175:42
know that I am a w.?	SHAK 886:5
large-brained w.	BROW 196:10
lawful for a Catholic w.	MENC 670:81
Learn charity, w.	MILL 676:98
let not me play a w.	SHAK 870:31
Let still the w. take	SHAK 894:11
Let us have wine and w.	BYRON 222:42
Let w. share the rights	WOLL 1091:43
likes a w. in a skirt	HEPB 473:77
lips of a strange w.	BIBLE 120:61
look for the w.	DUMAS 354:28
looketh on a w. to lust after her	BIBLE 134:40
loose with the worst w.	EDWA 362:54
lovely w. in a rural spot	HUNT 504:21
lovely w. stoops to folly	AUST 52:59
lovely w. stoops to folly	ELIOT 369:90
lovely w. stoops to folly	GOLD 432:5
loving one unattainable w.	FROST 407:90
loyal and faithful w.	NATH 721:85
make love to every w.	KEEN 548:24
make love with a w.	ANOU 30:69
male…to accept a w.	PLATH 773:90
man and a w. in a garden	WILDE 1077:65
man and a w. looking at a girl	WOOLF 1093:66
Man delights not…nor w.	SHAK 890:3
man enough for a w.	DEKK 313:16
man or a w., old or young	WELTY 1065:49
Man that is born of w.	BOOK 176:56
man wants what a w. has—sex	DWOR 357:83
Man was by Nature W.'s cully	CONG 280:94
man's boots with a w.	MACC 624:33
man's commendation with w.	SHAK 895:28
Many a w. has a past	WILDE 1076:58
married w. is a slave	BALZ 68:69
masculine figure created by a w.	MENC 669:55

woman (*contd.*):	
masculine in the w.	KENT 553:9
mental relation with a w.	LAWR 586:93
middle-class w.	LURIE 619:41
millstone around a w.'s neck	GREER 445:38
misfortune to be born a w.	EDGE 361:32
more…sincere than a w. constant	CONG 281:28
most winning w. I ever knew	DOYLE 343:89
move a w.'s mind	SHAK 860:82
nakedness of the w.	BLAKE 166:78
need to possess this w.	LACL 573:59
never trust a w. who	WILDE 1077:69
never yet fair w.	SHAK 903:20
new w. is…above him	GRAND 438:98
Next to a w.	SHIR 935:24
no other purgatory but a w.	BEAU 80:72
no sane w. would marry	BIRD 162:12
No w. can be beauty	FARQ 383:73
No w. can look	TWAIN 1032:56
No w. has ever invented	FLAU 392:36
No w. has to prove herself	PAGL 749:35
No w. in my time	THAT 1007:3
No w. should have a memory	WILDE 1077:73
no w. ugly that has it	WYCH 1103:41
no w. who does not dream	ANON 26:36
none of w. born	SHAK 909:67
Not a tolerable w.'s part	AUST 51:47
not given to a w.	LISP 607:39
O W.!	SCOTT 853:58
occupation of a w. writer	WOOLF 1093:78
Old Testament makes a w.	STAN 963:90
old w. to outlive her dogs	WILL 1081:61
older w. knows	ATWO 45:30
one becomes a w.	DE 311:62
only comfort about being a w.	STARK 963:94
opinion is about a w.	JAMES 516:22
os cervix of a w.	SCHR 850:7
overmuch…in a w.	JUANA 539:66
paid for a w.	GREE 444:18
parent…a w. cannot	MUIR 713:42
passion for any w.	RIVE 813:3
pity any w. married to	WILDE 1077:77
place where w. never smiled	CLARE 267:83
play without a w.	KYD 571:29
prime truth of w.	CHES 259:17
print a w.'s age	CHRI 261:64
public is an old w.	CARL 235:60
questions…put to a defenceless w.	CHOP 261:63
rainy day and a contentious w.	BIBLE 122:8
recalls…a w.	AMADO 15:63
recently murdered w.	SHAR 919:86
responsibility…to be a w.	PALEY 751:63
restrictions on the w.	FULL 409:33
rich w. as a poor w.	THAC 1006:93
routinely silly w.	BYATT 218:54
roving w. gives rise to gossip	ANON 21:57
saw a w. flayed	SWIFT 984:62
scarce Another w.	JONS 534:84
scarce be a contented w.	ROCH 816:60
Self-development…w.'s motto	STAN 963:91
separates a man from a w.	ROBB 813:7
sex was something no w.	MUNRO 714:56
Sexually, W. is Nature's contrivance	SHAW 921:38
she is always the w.	DOYLE 344:2
She is only a w.	SIXT 942:31
sign of despair in a w.	WILDE 1078:91
Solitude …is a w.'s life	CART 242:93
soul-sides…One to show a w.	BROW 199:72
story of a w.'s life	STAEL 961:67
Success is…like a w.	FAUL 384:87
take some savage w.	TENN 996:81
tell a w.'s age	GILB 425:28
th' wonder of a w. wears off	OCAS 735:72
thanks of man and w.	PAINE 750:42

women (*contd.*):

make pale w. swoon	PISS 771:58
make w. more affectionate	BRIL 188:54
make w. unhappy	PUCK 794:16
Married w. are kept w.	SMITH 947:20
maternity to w.	MUSS 716:89
men and w. and the society	JAMES 517:34
men and w. are created equal	STAN 962:85
men and w. are not so…enslaved	SHAW 924:94
men and w. laughing	SAND 841:59
men and w. merely players	SHAK 885:91
men and w. of this generation	LLOY 608:58
Men don't know w.	TROL 1028:78
men like—not w.	NORR 731:28
men that w. marry	LONG 612:20
men, w., and clergymen	SMITH 949:51
menstruate and w. could not?	STEI 967:65
mettlesome w.	ANDR 18:11
middle-aged and elderly w.	LESS 598:1
mob of scribbling w.	HAWT 461:79
modern American w.	MACC 626:56
Monstrous Regiment of W.	KNOX 567:56
more w. are paid	FALU 382:56
Most w. are not so young	BEER 83:21
Most w. know that sex	WILB 1075:23
Music and w. I…give way to	PEPYS 765:78
must have w.	GAY 417:57
no place for w.'s plans	AESC 9:58
noticed how noisy w. are?	OSBO 745:67
Of all those young w.	POUND 785:59
of w. this I say	DUNB 355:36
offensive to many w.	LEWIS 602:61
one w. differs from another	MENC 669:73
owe nothing to W.'s Lib	THAT 1007:4
passing the love of w.	BIBLE 110:44
patriotism that has nerved w.	PANK 753:82
Plain w.…to be faced	ELIOT 366:34
portraits I paint of w.	LAUR 584:47
power over w.	LEGU 594:28
Priests, princes, w.	POPE 781:56
proper function of w.	ELIOT 365:22
rather second-rate w.	WEBB 1058:14
reduce w. of certain age	BROO 193:42
rights of w.	COPE 287:52
sadness of the w.'s movement	ANGE 19:26
save w. and girls	WEBB 1058:15
sayings are generally like w.'s letters	HAZL 464:17
secure the good conduct of w.	WOLL 1091:35
seventeen million French w.	GISC 429:48
She looks at other w.	FIRB 389:79
simple w. only fit	LEWIS 601:46
Single w.…propensity for being poor	AUST 52:61
sleep with w. we do not love	DIDE 330:37
society w. never serve chilli	RAYB 803:49
Solomon loved many strange w.	BIBLE 111:59
some w. govern their husbands	WOLL 1091:33
Some w.'ll stay	KIPL 563:96
strength in black w.	ANGE 19:23
such a place for wanton w.	BORR 180:25
Sweet is revenge—specially to w.	BYRON 222:32
taken for a ride by his w.	JOSE 537:33
there's wisdom in w.	BROO 192:18
though w. all above	SHAK 903:35
three w. I have admired most	WILDE 1079:13
through our mothers if we are w.	WOOLF 1093:74
tide in the affairs of w.	BYRON 223:54
to w. [I speak] Italian	CHAR 253:90
to w. lied like a Cretan	HARDY 456:88
trouble with w. like me	MANS 647:97
trumpet for W.'s Liberation	LESS 598:5
Two w. placed together	SHAK 917:48
values of w. differ	WOOLF 1093:73
wage no war with w.	SOUT 954:35
want w. to specialise in virtue	WEST 1068:88

women (*contd.*):

war between men and w.	THUR 1018:19
war… between men and w.	LYND 621:65
well-educated young w.	AUST 51:39
what all w. do	SHAW 921:29
Whatever w. do	WHIT 1074:10
when w. are free to make…decisions	FRIE 405:51
When w. kiss	MENC 669:72
when we are grown w.	SCHR 850:4
When will w. begin to have	JAMES 515:4
where w. are concerned?	SHAW 924:4
why God created w.?	WALL 1049:61
why young w. should marry	JOHN 529:81
Wine and w. will make men	BIBLE 132:6
Winter is for w.	PLATH 773:99
With many w.	TROL 1027:76
w. and gear are at the bottom	SCOTT 855:90
W. and Horses	KIPL 561:39
W. and men do not	VIAN 1043:47
W. are all in extremes	LABR 572:38
w. are brighter than men	LOOS 613:38
W. are expected to have weak	ELIOT 366:30
W. are from their very Infancy	ASTE 43:89
w. are in furious secret rebellion	SHAW 924:93
W.…are invisible people	FRIE 405:50
W. are like elephants	FIEL 388:58
W. are like tricks	CONG 280:15
W. are most fascinating	DIOR 331:62
W. are soft, mild, pitiful	SHAK 861:18
W. are strongest	BIBLE 131:74
W. are supposed to be very calm	BRON 191:93
W. are the only exploited group	JONG 533:62
W.…as looking-glasses	WOOLF 1093:70
w. become like their mothers	WILDE 1078:84
W.…behave like men	MACK 632:56
W.…born three thousand years old	DELA 314:36
w. breached the power structure	WOLF 1090:13
W. can't forgive failure	CHEK 256:59
W. cannot be expected	MILL 675:78
w. cannot escape it	GIBB 422:34
w. come out	KIPL 560:33
w. do not count in the State	DAVI 309:42
w. do the hod carrying	NEVI 723:15
W. enjoyed	SUCK 981:20
w.'s eyes this doctrine	SHAK 865:22
W. fond of dress	DE 311:63
w. for escape from this death	NIGH 729:98
W. had always fought for men	PANK 753:80
w.'s happiest knowledge	MILT 690:61
W. have but one task	COUB 289:70
w. have dominion over you	BIBLE 131:75
W. have no character	POPE 781:70
W. have no wideness in them	BOGAN 171:58
w. have read only the novel	GAUT 416:42
w. have taken it upon themselves	MARG 650:53
w. have walked past mirrors	ALLEN 14:33
w. highly hold in hate	SHAK 860:85
w. into a sex object	MORG 708:67
w. into darling little slaves	MILLS 679:64
W.…keep men from better company	
	WYCH 1103:36
W. know the damnation of charity	
	WEST 1067:87
W. like to sit down	GLAS 430:59
W.'s love is for their men	EURI 380:26
w. Must be half-workers?	SHAK 916:4
w. never took a single step forward	PANK 752:78
w. of her type	WAUGH 1056:69
W., of kynde, desiren	CHAU 255:38
w. offer our experience	LEGU 594:30
w.'s parts be acted by w.	CHAR 253:84
w. Passion, intellect	NIGH 729:95
w. prudes if they don't	MILL 679:61
w.…rendered systematically vicious	WOLL 1091:42

women (*contd.*):

w. rule us	CATO 245:52
w. see the relationship	FOWL 399:66
w. shall put on	TROL 1028:87
W. should be obscene	LENN 596:58
w. should be struck	COWA 290:96
W. should be trained	ANON 21:63
w. suffered…in the United States	FRIE 405:49
w.…Talking of Michelangelo	ELIOT 367:47
w., than to study household	MILT 692:2
w. the Pariahs	STAN 962:87
w., their rights and nothing less	ANTH 31:84
w. themselves help to make laws	ANTH 31:85
w. to bear rule	KNOX 567:57
w. today	PANK 753:81
W. try hard to save	HUGO 502:74
w. …trying for the vote	PANK 752:77
w., two almost divide	POPE 782:95
w.…remained thirty-five for years	WILDE 1078:90
w. understand by emancipation	GREER 445:40
w.'s unnatural, unsatiable lust	BURT 214:76
w.'s weapons, water-drops	SHAK 902:15
W. were brought up to believe	BARN 72:34
W. were ever things	VIRG 1045:87
W. who love the same man	BEER 83:31
w. who wear ankle socks	BENN 91:77
w. whom I really think	KEATS 545:64
W. Whose Lives Are Food	OATES 733:55
W. will love her	SHAK 912:41
w. within these marginal	RUET 828:47
w. won't buy anything	RUBE 828:43
W. would rather be	NASH 720:65
work its way with the w.	DICK 321:30
Yes, Sir…many w.	JOHN 527:28
You should be w.	SHAK 907:16
women-folk moo and coo with w.-f.	KIPL 564:5
won heaven on earth I have w.	SHAK 901:79
in the sun and have w. it	WILH 1080:37
life will not be w.	HEIS 467:78
not that you w. or lost	RICE 809:38
talk about who w.	KHRU 556:50
too quickly w.	SHAK 868:90
until they w. her	TENN 1003:18
woman in this humour w.?	SHAK 863:50
woman, therefore to be w.	SHAK 861:95
w. first prize in the lottery	RHOD 808:24
w. on the playing fields of Eton	WELL 1064:20
wonder all a w. and a wild desire	BROW 200:88
all knowledge and w.	BACON 54:4
all the w. that would be	TENN 995:77
capacity for w.	FITZ 391:6
common w. of all men	BROW 195:90
Hidden in w.	SCOTT 852:37
it is a w. what will be	PEPYS 765:76
longer the shoreline of w.	MACI 631:46
miles around the w. grew	HOUS 494:45
no longer w. and stand…in awe	EINS 363:67
sense of w.	LAWR 587:10
sense of w.	SOCR 952:88
sign or a w.	BIBLE 108:94
state of w.	GOULD 436:75
still the w. grew	GOLD 433:13
strangeness and w. lying	RUSS 832:15
struck with w.	LAWR 587:3
th' w. of a woman wears off	OCAS 735:76
through w. that men…philosophize	ARIS 34:24
with a sense of w.	JOVA 537:38
w. how long this is going	KEIL 548:29
w. of our stage!	JONS 535:8
w. what he meant by that	LOUIS 614:53
Worship is transcendent w.	CARL 236:88
wondered w. why young women	JOHN 529:81
wonderful after…it was w.	WILD 1079:15
most w. in the world	SIHA 938:73

wonderful (*contd.*):

name shall be called W.	BIBLE 125:66
O w., w., and most w.	SHAK 886:4
reality was no less w.	SHIP 935:22
What a w. boy he is!	HOGG 485:66
w. time—the War	HUGH 499:21
w. to listen to	HARDY 456:85
wondering w. what lay round	KAVA 543:27
w. whether it would take spin	HOME 487:13
wonders all W. in one sight!	CRAS 295:18
His w. to perform	COWP 291:27
left us surmising w.	QUIL 797:63
lost w. of the ancient world	AUCH 46:41
Of all the w.	SHAK 883:34
Seven W. of the World	ADDI 7:18
Signs are taken for w.	ELIOT 368:69
We carry with us the w.	BROW 195:76
w. in the deep	BIBLE 118:20
w. Of common things	MIDD 673:42
w. of the western world	SYNGE 988:63
wondrous we'll be w. rich	OTWAY 746:85
woo April when they w.	SHAK 887:23
cannot w. in festival terms	SHAK 880:65
Come, w. me, w. me	SHAK 886:20
forced to w.	WEBS 1060:55
So thou wilt w.	SHAK 868:90
were not made to w.	SHAK 870:38
when a married man doth w.	DONNE 337:86
w. not like a babe	SHAK 864:76
wood that piece of w.	MANN 646:94
bit about nudism in the w.	JOYCE 538:58
bows down to w.	KIPL 562:58
correct in cypress w.	PARK 754:10
courters'-and-rabbits' w.	THOM 1011:79
creeping ivy clings to w.	COWP 292:46
dark impenetrable w.	SCOTT 853:59
enclosing it in a case of w.	WATT 1055:55
Far off the w.	FREE 404:34
found myself in a dark w.	DANTE 305:67
goblets for a dish of w.	SHAK 867:62
harbour and neighbour w.	THOM 1010:68
Heap on more w.!	SCOTT 853:55
impulse from a vernal w.	WORD 1094:3
in the w. the furious winter	RANS 802:35
Land of…shaggy w.	SCOTT 853:50
maker of worn w.	UPDI 1036:50
piles of dry w. with red-hot coals	CISN 266:67
Proud Maise is in the w.	SCOTT 855:96
rooky w.	SHAK 909:60
Sit…in this w.	BRON 191:92
springth the w. nu	ANON 22:67
strange odours…of aromatic w.	CONR 284:96
Through w. and dale	COLE 275:16
true w., of yew w.	DOYLE 343:94
two pieces of w.	MITF 697:94
Two roads diverged in a w.	FROST 406:77
violin is w. and catgut	PRIE 789:35
Where no w. is…the fire goeth out	BIBLE 122:4
whiffling through the tulgey w.	CARR 239:47
w. a Piggy-wig stood	LEAR 590:59
w. found on the beach	ROSE 823:58
w.'s in trouble	HOUS 495:53
w. of Hallaig	MACL 633:70
wood-pigeons brassy w.-p.	HUGH 500:41
woodbine luscious w.	SHAK 870:39
well attir'd w.	MILT 684:47
w. spices are wafted	TENN 1001:85
woodcock Spirits of well-shot w.	BETJ 99:30
woodcocks springes to catch w.	SHAK 888:68
wooden W. legs are not inherited	CONK 282:49
W. Shoes	ANON 25:21
woodland stands about the w. ride	HOUS 494:94
woodlands about the w. I will go	HOUS 494:41
woods Enter these enchanted w.	MERE 671:11

woods (*contd.*):

Flow down the w.	SACK 835:61
for the w. against the world	BLUN 170:49
If you go down in the w.	BRAT 185:15
in the deep green w.	HOLM 485:72
in w. the noble savage ran	DRYD 347:69
let it loose in the w.	SHAW 924:95
Love-whispering w.	POPE 783:7
never knew the summer w.	TENN 998:29
ordered w. and gardens	MACK 632:52
pleasure in the pathless w.	BYRON 220:5
shepherd, thee the w.	MILT 684:40
shut the road through the w.	KIPL 564:7
The w. decay	TENN 1003:21
these hoary w. are grand	GALT 413:8
through the Wet Wild W.	KIPL 563:87
Tomorrow to fresh w.	MILT 685:52
went to the w.	THOR 1017:85
w. are lovely	FROST 407:86
w. as deep and cool	COWL 291:24
W., or steepy mountains	MARL 655:31
worked in the w.	SNYD 951:86
woodshed Something nasty in the w.	GIBB 422:35
wooed therefore to be w.	SHAK 861:95
We should be w.	SHAK 870:84
woman in this humour w.?	SHAK 863:50
wooer knight to be their w.	BALL 101:30
wooing won by w. thee	SHAK 901:79
Young men a w.	ANON 22:76
wool jeweller's cotton and fine w.	DICK 324:20
shall be as w.	BIBLE 124:56
Woolf afraid of Virginia W.?	ALBEE 11:85
woollen Odious! in w.!	POPE 781:57
rather lie in the w.	SHAK 879:33
word according to thy w.	BIBLE 118:29
according to thy w.	BIBLE 160:55
ages for the wrong w.	USTI 1037:75
ancient w. of courage	SHAK 863:67
At ev'ry w. a reputation	POPE 778:98
bad-weather kind of w.	BUFO 203:44
before thy uncreating w.	POPE 783:11
Bilbo's first w.	CONG 280:95
bring out of each w.	JAMES 517:48
By any other w.	SHAK 868:88
By thought, w., and deed	BOOK 174:25
by water and the w.	STONE 978:73
cannot utter a w.	SHAW 920:99
changed…to past Without a w.	LARK 581:7
choke the w.	BIBLE 137:98
Conscience is but a w.	SHAK 863:66
contempt of thy w.	BOOK 174:11
discouraging w.	HIGL 480:1
eaten thee for a w.	SHAK 866:24
every w. has its marrow	SMART 944:65
every w. she writes is a lie	MACC 626:59
every w. stabs	SHAK 879:37
every w. that proceedeth	BIBLE 108:92
falling cadence of the lovely w.	MAUG 665:89
final w., before I'm done	HALD 451:19
Fine w., 'legitimate'	SHAK 902:1
first w. on everything	HUGO 503:94
gone without a w.?	SHAK 860:76
Good isn't the w.	GILB 426:1
great actor or a household w.?	OLIV 738:27
great deal to make one w. mean	CARR 240:67
Greeks Had a W. for It	AKINS 10:75
hard, brown, nutlike w.	BART 74:72
hast kept my w.	BIBLE 157:1
have not the w.	ARNO 38:12
heareth the w.	BIBLE 137:99
horror of the w. 'flesh'	RENO 807:8
How the w. rolls—Leonora	CRAIK 294:90
If thou has heard a w.	BIBLE 132:7
In one w. he told me the secret	LEHR 595:40

word (*contd.*):

In one w.	PASC 758:74
In the beginning was the W.	BIBLE 144:24
In the beginning was the W.	ELIOT 367:65
kens a w. Burns	MACD 627:75
leave the w. of God	BIBLE 147:86
Let the w. go forth	KENN 550:64
lies in one little w.!	SHAK 866:43
Lord's First W.	FARJ 383:63
Love in search of a w.	LANI 579:76
Man's w. is God in man	TENN 1003:33
most important sense of the w.	MOORE 704:9
my most painted w.	SHAK 890:20
never will speak w.	SHAK 900:21
No man would set a w.	MILL 678:32
No simple w.	JONS 535:99
no w. in their language	SWIFT 985:89
No w. like 'Pardon'	SHAK 868:69
not one w. is said	STAN 963:89
Observant of the heavenly w.	DODD 335:46
ordinary sense of the w.	MILL 677:15
people answered him not a w.	BIBLE 111:63
pleynly, at a w.	CHAU 255:42
polite w. for dead…imagination	CUMM 300:95
Polyester…the most valuable w.	ANON 29:35
power of the written w.	CONR 284:88
power to speak another w.	SAPP 842:92
Preach the w.	BIBLE 154:40
precise meaning of a w.	BAND 69:87
proud Victorian w.	PRIT 791:74
run to and fro to seek the w.	BIBLE 130:61
say a w. against G.	SHAW 923:78
single w. even may be a spark	SHEL 931:58
So shall my w. be	BIBLE 127:6
solemn w. of warning	WILS 1086:46
speak the w. only	BIBLE 136:64
speaks to us the same w.	SCHW 852:31
spoken the foremost w.	BALL 67:40
sweeter…will be the w. lover	HELO 469:7
Take my w. for it	TENN 1004:51
take thy w. for faith	SHAK 910:96
tears wash out a w.	FITZ 390:89
Tell them…I kept my w.	DELA 314:26
that w. 'hummy', my darlings	PARK 754:94
The w. is life	SASS 845:39
The w. VALUE	SMITH 946:94
there is not a w. of fear	LAND 578:61
This is my final w.	BEAV 81:86
thru the nicht we spak nae w.	SOUT 954:26
torture one poor w.	DRYD 348:84
Turning the w. to sword	SHAK 877:2
unkind or irreverential w.	HAWT 462:82
unto me according to thy w.	BIBLE 141:74
upholding all things by the w.	BIBLE 154:44
use no w. …under stress	POUND 787:97
utter and see in a w.	SAND 841:56
voice of the w. 'nature'	REDON 804:78
What is honour?, A w.	SHAK 876:69
When I hear that w.	GINS 428:29
whose lightest w.	SHAK 889:74
whose w. one cannot believe	VICT 1043:51
with a flattering w.	WILDE 1078:98
without adding a w.	TROL 1028:89
w. alone shall fit	CHES 259:21
w.'s anguish is caused by people	FAUL 383:80
w. 'civilization' to my mind	MILL 679:55
W. climbs upward	DUNC 355:47
w. fitly spoken	BIBLE 121:98
w. for w. without book	SHAK 893:90
w. from the content	FLAU 392:35
W. has somehow got around	THUR 1020:52
w. have I hid in mine heart	BIBLE 119:30
w. is a lamp	BIBLE 119:33
W. is but wynd	LYDG 620:55

word (*contd.*):

w. is dead	DICK 328:*12*
w. is like a bell	KEATS 548:*19*
w. is the carving	SITW 941:*28*
w. is the Verb	HUGO 502:*79*
w....means just what I choose	CARR 240:*70*
w. means underpants	MURR 715:*76*
w. 'Now' is like a bomb	MILL 677:*4*
w. of Caesar	SHAK 884:*52*
w. of God is quick	BIBLE 154:*45*
w. of our God shall stand for ever	BIBLE 126:*85*
w. of worlds	CURN 301:*13*
w....out of a ladys lips	FLEM 394:*62*
w. spoken in due season	BIBLE 121:*81*
w. stung him	SITW 941:*7*
w. that may not be there	WILB 1075:*24*
W. was made flesh	BIBLE 144:*27*
w. within the w.	ELIOT 368:*69*
wordless set of w. symbols	UPDI 1037:*73*
words alms-basket of w.	SHAK 866:*24*
and aimiable w.	TENN 1003:*18*
any relation to the w.	ROSE 823:*58*
apt w. have power	MILT 694:*44*
ate and drank the precious W.	DICK 328:*14*
bad poet dwells...in a world of w.	ELIOT 368:*77*
Be not slave of w.	CARL 234:*51*
believed not the w.	BIBLE 111:*58*
bereft me of all w.	SHAK 873:*85*
better deeds than w.	SHAK 860:*76*
big w. to talk about dirty things	DOCT 334:*39*
But w. are w.	SHAK 898:*14*
callisthenics with w.	PARK 754:*17*
can drag, with w.	LOWE 615:*73*
can express in w.	NABO 717:*5*
coiner of sweet w.!	ARNO 38:*94*
comfortable w. our Saviour	BOOK 174:*26*
complete an incomplete self with w.	GASS 416:*36*
comprehending much in few w.	BIBLE 132:*13*
Dance, little w.	WORL 1101:*96*
danced on a plume of w.	DAYL 310:*57*
Deeds, not w.	EDGE 361:*35*
draftsman of w.	CUMM 300:*98*
embarrassed by the w.	HEMI 470:*17*
end to end w.	LODGE 610:*78*
entrance of thy w. giveth light	BIBLE 119:*34*
exchanged many frank w.	COOK 286:*28*
fair w....in foulest letters?	SHAK 878:*7*
few odd w. in Hebrew	DAY 310:*49*
few of the unpleasant'st w.	SHAK 873:*86*
fine volley of w.	SHAK 860:*77*
Fine w.!	SWIFT 984:*81*
food and not fine w.	MOLI 699:*32*
For w., like Nature	TENN 998:*19*
forgets w. as one forgets names	WAUGH 1057:*3*
four most dramatic w.	HART 459:*48*
frames in all but w.	FROST 406:*79*
fresh, usual w.	FORD 396:*4*
gave voice to three w.	LAMA 575:*3*
Give 'em w.	JONS 534:*78*
glorious sense of w.	ACHE 2:*24*
gloten of w.	LANG 579:*70*
God in whose w.	DONNE 339:*4*
Good w. are better	SHAK 884:*62*
grievous w. stir up anger	BIBLE 121:*78*
heaven hath my empty w.	SHAK 897:*75*
Hold fast the form of sound w.	BIBLE 154:*38*
house of w.	GALE 412:*88*
How often misused w.	SPEN 956:*67*
how you use proud w.	SAND 841:*44*
huffing of hyphenated w.	BROY 201:*5*
hundred and twenty w.	LINK 606:*23*
I have few w.	CIXO 267:*71*
If I write four w.	BOIL 171:*64*
if she respects not w.	SHAK 860:*82*

words (*contd.*):

Immodest w. admit of no defence	DILL 331:*56*
In W., as Fashions	POPE 778:*82*
language without w.	STEV 972:*55*
let thy w. be few	BIBLE 123:*26*
like others been all w.	MASS 662:*55*
long w. and exhausted idioms	ORWE 743:*19*
long w. Bother me.	MILNE 680:*74*
long w. to cover the errors	CHES 258:*1*
manipulation of w.	DICK 320:*13*
multiplieth w. without knowledge	BIBLE 113:*16*
my w. among mankind!	SHEL 928:*91*
my w. are my own	CHAR 253:*86*
mystery of w.	WORD 1096:*29*
never yet was put into w. or books	MELV 668:*40*
nor hear your w.	BIBLE 136:*75*
oaths are but w.	BUTL 217:*18*
of all w. of tongue and pen	HARTE 460:*53*
pain of history w. contain	WALC 1048:*34*
palm-oil with which w. are eaten	ACHE 2:*18*
play...some ten w. long	SHAK 871:*56*
Poets paint with w.	CARR 237:*17*
poets...write in w.	FOWL 400:*68*
power to master w.	SCAR 846:*54*
preoccupation with w.	CHAN 250:*44*
Proper w. in	SWIFT 984:*77*
propriety of thoughts and w.	DRYD 348:*80*
put my w. in thy mouth	BIBLE 128:*17*
quench the fire...with w.	SHAK 860:*81*
Read out my w.	FLEC 393:*47*
rhubarb w.	SIDN 937:*52*
roof in the w. deceiving	MILT 681:*92*
running tap of w.	MOORE 704:*1*
see and imitate...by w.	CUMM 299:*75*
shut up the w.	BIBLE 130:*51*
significations of their w.	HOBB 482:*36*
Some...find those w. mis-placed	CONG 280:*1*
sought out quaint w.	HERB 475:*25*
sounds called w. may be strung	FROST 406:*76*
spite and hard w.	MORR 709:*81*
still at the mercy of w.	THOM 1011:*74*
such a hail of w.	JONS 534:*84*
such abominable w.	SHAK 861:*15*
Such w. as 'chain' or 'train'	JAMES 517:*40*
Th' artillery of w.	SWIFT 983:*55*
that make up w.	UPDI 1037:*64*
Three unknown w.	GAUT 416:*41*
threw w. like stones	SPEN 956:*77*
Thy w. are too precious	SHAK 885:*73*
tune without the w.	DICK 328:*97*
two most beautiful w.	JAMES 517:*31*
two truly expressive w.	DERBY 316:*69*
unnebulous train of w.	BISH 164:*32*
unpack my heart with w.	SHAK 890:*16*
use w. as they are used	COMP 279:*74*
used big w. in dealing	RAMOS 801:*17*
using only comparative W.	PETTY 768:*15*
vital w. were once slang	GALS 413:*6*
weigh'st thy w.	SHAK 899:*30*
weighing w.	FLAU 392:*34*
What grows by the w.?	SIDN 936:*46*
which is saying, in other w.	POPE 778:*73*
wife full of w.	BIBLE 132:*8*
With high w., that bore	MILT 687:*4*
w. are a very fantastical banquet	SHAK 879:*47*
w. are beautiful things	MUSS 716:*87*
W. are...from a defunct language	CIXO 267:*74*
w. are idle	WEBS 1060:*33*
w. are images of thoughts	KEATS 544:*37*
W., are, of course	KIPL 565:*24*
w. are of less weight	BACON 58:*87*
w. are quick and vain	SHEL 930:*15*
w. are slippery	ADAMS 5:*83*
W. are the bugles	HANDY 455:*69*

words (*contd.*):

w. are the daughters	JOHN 526:*5*
w. are true and faithful	BIBLE 158:*35*
w. burst from him	SCOTT 856:*7*
w. came halting forth	SIDN 937:*51*
W. can keep people apart	MARC 649:*44*
w. can outlive us	PLOUT 775:*35*
w. clothed in reason's garb	MILT 688:*16*
w. come more readily	GREE 443:*99*
w. could never utter	THAC 1007:*1*
W. divested of their magic	MILL 679:*51*
w. divide and rend	SWIN 987:*28*
w. echo...in your mind	ELIOT 370:*23*
w. filling yer head	KELM 549:*34*
w. fly up	SHAK 892:*49*
w. in their best order	COLE 275:*24*
w. into ends of the world	BOOK 176:*66*
w. into life	SENG 858:*59*
W. just say what you want	KENN 550:*54*
w. left unsaid	STOWE 979:*89*
w., like children	NOON 731:*22*
w. most wonderful	NEWM 724:*32*
w. no virtue can digest	MARL 653:*91*
w. of learned length	GOLD 433:*13*
w. of my love	ROET 819:*96*
W. of the world	STEV 972:*67*
W. pay no debts	SHAK 896:*48*
w. prevail not	KYD 571:*25*
w. reign over ideas	SAND 840:*49*
w. seemed to them as idle tales	BIBLE 144:*21*
w. shall not pass away	BIBLE 140:*38*
W. should be an intense	WAUGH 1057:*92*
W. spoken on the road	MO 698:*8*
W. strain	ELIOT 370:*31*
w. tend to be blunt	MURR 716:*80*
w. that are only forms	WILS 1084:*19*
w., that burn	GRAY 443:*91*
w. that I speak...are life	BIBLE 145:*46*
W....the great foes of reality	CONR 285:*6*
W. the head does not shape	ANON 23:*82*
w. thou canst not understand	BIBLE 128:*35*
w. to the end of the world	BIBLE 114:*44*
W. to the heat of deeds	SHAK 908:*41*
w. which express	SHEL 931:*60*
w. which he of God	LANY 580:*79*
w. will follow	CATO 245:*54*
w. without knowledge?	BIBLE 113:*17*
W., w., mere w.	SHAK 896:*59*
W., w., w.	SHAK 889:*93*
worse than vain w.	BACON 55:*9*
worst...one can do with w.	ORWE 744:*47*
worth ten thousand w.	BARN 71:*22*
wrote the magnificent w.	KING 557:*78*
Wordsworth Let simple W. chime	BYRON 219:*64*
Mr. W.'s genius	HAZL 464:*15*
seen W. drunk	HOUS 495:*67*
what daffodils were to W.	LARK 582:*22*
W., both are thine.	STEP 968:*79*
W....crazed beyond all hope	BYRON 222:*38*
W. says somewhere	ARNO 38:*5*
work All buildings w.	JOHN 524:*1*
all hope of genuine good w.	BUTL 217:*41*
Art is the only w.	GRAY 440:*42*
being dead is hard w.	RILKE 811:*85*
Better the rudest w.	RUSK 830:*76*
break a man's spirit is devil's w.	SHAW 920:*98*
breed one w. that wakes	HOPK 492:*9*
buy his w.	RENO 807:*9*
Canst w. i'th' earth so fast?	SHAK 889:*83*
change from wives and w.	EWART 381:*44*
classical mind at w.	PIRS 770:*56*
composing a w.	PASC 757:*53*
continuous administrative w.	WEBER 1059:*22*
country safe to w. in	THAT 1007:*9*

world (*contd.*):

spoil…their toy the w.	COWP 293:61
squeeze a w. till it hurts	MACL 634:84
state of things throughout the w.	BACON 55:30
statements about the w.	BOYD 182:66
stay of the whole w.?	HOOK 489:54
still point of the turning w.	ELIOT 370:25
still point of the turning w.	ELIOT 370:29
stood against the w.	SHAK 884:52
Stop The W.	ANON 27:68
surrender the whole w.	BARB 71:11
survey of all the w.	SHAK 876:75
survive in this modern w.	GOLD 432:87
symphony must be like the w.	MAHL 638:61
taken a lead in w. affairs	THAT 1008:25
taketh away the sin of the w.	BIBLE 145:28
taste Brought death into the w.	MILT 687:84
teach the w. new love	PHIL 768:20
terror of the w.	GIBB 421:22
Than this w. dreams of	TENN 1004:47
that all the w. should be taxed	BIBLE 142:76
that ever happened in the w.	FOX 400:71
thick rotundity o' th' w.	SHAK 903:18
thicket of the w.	JOHN 522:29
things in the w.	RUSK 830:78
things that in the great w. be	WORD 1097:41
This gewgaw w.	DRYD 348:90
This great w. Shall so wear out	SHAK 904:36
this Is a w. of sweets	POE 776:48
this little w.	SHAK 867:48
This pendent w.	MILT 689:28
This various w.	SHEL 927:61
this vile w.	OTWAY 746:90
This w.…a thurghfare ful of wo	CHAU 255:33
This w.'s no blot	BROW 198:45
this w.'s ransoming	AQUI 32:5
this wicked w.	BOOK 175:36
Though we travel the w.	EMER 376:44
thought in the w.	ARNO 38:11
Thro' the w. we safely go	BLAKE 168:3
throw me off the w.	NASH 720:72
thrust me out to the wide w.	DRYD 348:98
Till the w. is wrought	SHEL 929:2
Time, the w. and the person	CIXO 267:72
To be honest, as this w. goes	SHAK 889:94
To save your w.	AUDEN 48:84
to seek a newer w.	TENN 995:61
to the ending of the w.	SHAK 882:3
Toil conquered the w.	VIRG 1045:94
top of the w.	CAGN 225:91
torch which illuminates the w.	PAST 759:88
torments in this w. or next	CHES 257:82
tragic a place this w.	LYND 621:64
tremendous w. in my head	HEWE 479:86
triple pillar of the w.	SHAK 904:56
trough between the two w. wars	LEWIS 602:70
true system of the W.	ALEM 13:12
Truth indeed came once into the w.	MILT 686:72
truth to go round the w.	SPUR 961:64
turned the w. upside down	BIBLE 148:98
two axes of the w.	FRAN 401:82
two divinest things this w. has	HUNT 504:21
two qualities in the w.	SHAW 923:75
unacknowledged legislators of the w.	SHEL 931:60
Undulate round the w.	WHIT 1073:93
unknown w. t'explore	WENT 1065:54
unreasonable silence of the w.	CAMUS 229:47
upstairs into the w.	CONG 280:12
value in my w.	GREE 444:12
vice is in this w. so necessary	MILT 685:66
visible w. seems formed in love	MELV 667:35
visible w. to love or reject	AUDEN 46:57
vision of the w.	TENN 995:77
wakes will move the w.	NAPO 718:25

world (*contd.*):

Walk cheerfully over the w.	FOX 400:75
war put the w. to sleep	MUIR 712:35
warm kind w. is all I know	CORY 288:65
warning to the w.	SHAK 914:72
way the w. ends	ELIOT 369:2
wears a mask in the w.	MARI 651:73
Well, W., you have kept faith	HARDY 457:14
What a w. is this	BOLI 172:70
What about the w., Mr Cummings?	CUMM 300:88
What Art was to the Ancient w.	DISR 332:84
what is happening in the w.	PRIT 791:71
What is this w.?	CHAU 255:32
what it does in the w.	KENN 552:93
what once it was, the w.	MARV 659:90
What would the w. be	HOPK 492:96
when all the w. dissolves	MARL 654:15
When all the w. is young	KING 558:94
when Rome falls—the W.	BYRON 220:3
When the w. was made	ANON 30:66
When the w. was young	BACON 59:7
When will the w. know	WALP 1051:91
Where in this small-talking w.	FRY 408:15
where the w. is quiet	SWIN 987:38
whole new democratic w.	CARL 234:47
whole wide w.	PAST 759:84
whole w. hallucinated	RUSS 833:41
whole w.'s in a state	OCAS 735:74
whole w. in his face	LONG 611:98
whole w. is a place of exile	HUGH 498:12
whole w. is frightened to death!	SHER 934:17
whole w. needs restructuring	GORB 435:57
wide in this w.	LANG 579:69
wildest beauty in the w.	OWEN 748:16
will leave to the w.	NASHE 721:77
window on the w.	UPDI 1037:69
Winds of the w.	KIPL 561:42
wiser w. doth greater thee confess	CAREW 232:8
Witness this new-made w.	MILT 691:88
woman of the w.	SHAW 924:11
wonders of the western w.	SYNGE 988:63
Words of the w.	STEV 972:67
words to the end of the w.	BIBLE 114:44
work shall with the w. remain	WALL 1050:74
working economy in the w.	MARS 656:53
w.'s a bubble	BACON 60:35
w.…a kind of kindergarten	ROBI 815:29
w.'s a scene of changes	COWL 291:13
w. a valley so sweet	MOORE 706:32
w.'s an inn	DRYD 352:93
w. as an honest man	LICH 604:86
w. be made fit and safe	WILS 1086:54
w. becomes stranger	ELIOT 372:55
w. being seldom visited	MONT 700:53
w. breaks everyone	HEMI 470:19
w. by wisdom knew not God	BIBLE 150:44
w. can only be richer for it	BRAD 184:97
w. continues to offer glittering prizes	BIRK 163:18
w. could become socialist	MAO 648:25
w. dawns on unrecognizing…eyes	REID 806:97
w.…does not owe us a living	EDIN 361:40
w. empty of people	LAWR 585:70
w. forgetting, by the w. forgot	POPE 779:11
w. goes on because	MILL 678:38
w. goes on out there	KRAM 569:84
w.'s going to be…one huge gallows	BRAU 186:20
w.'s great age begins anew	SHEL 932:64
w.'s great day	MUIR 712:36
w.'s great sorrows	RUSS 833:37
w.'s grown honest	SHAK 890:5
w. has grown grey	SWIN 987:40
w. has not to be put in order	MILL 678:33
w. has turned over	MACA 621:74
w. hath lost his youth	BIBLE 131:77

world (*contd.*):

w. haunted by the hydrogen	ROUS 827:30
w. holdith with Arthure	MALO 642:29
w. I never made	HOUS 496:74
w. in arms	MACA 624:21
w. in endlessly different ways	NUTT 732:46
w. in flames	VOLT 1046:7
w. in general knows	LEAR 590:62
W., in hounding me	JUANA 539:64
w. in its own image	NIET 728:84
w. in which children	DICK 326:67
w. in which he found himself	HOLM 485:74
w. in which this unconquerable	LAMB 576:14
w. into a welter of bloodshed	LLOY 608:60
w. is a comedy	WALP 1051:85
w. is a funny paper	WILL 1082:73
w. is a global campus	LODGE 610:80
w. is a great volume	DONNE 339:33
w. is all that is the case	WITT 1087:73
w. is an ever-living fire	HERA 473:86
w. is at the end of its tether	WELLS 1065:47
w. is bad enough	CLOU 270:34
w. is charged	HOPK 491:82
W. is crazier	MACN 637:36
w. is diminished by the experience	SHAW 926:48
w. is disgracefully managed	FIRB 389:69
w. is full of middle-class people	SHAR 919:87
w. is grievously given to lying	TWAIN 1034:15
w. is growing old	HAZL 463:13
w. is in flames today	WITTE 1087:71
w. is made up	BUCK 203:40
w. is more and more	TENN 996:80
w. is never the same	THOM 1011:93
w. is not black and white	GREE 445:29
w. is not thy friend	SHAK 870:21
w. is not with us	LEVE 600:24
w. is not yet prepared	DOYLE 344:20
w. is now as it was	BROW 195:71
w. is richer for a new beauty	MARI 651:66
w. is ruled by little else	KEYN 555:37
w. is run quite out	SPEN 959:36
w. is sagging	BART 74:77
w. is so full	STEV 975:39
w. is surely wide enough	STER 969:99
w. is weary of the past	MILL 677:20
w. is white with May	TENN 1003:37
w. is wounded	KELL 548:30
w. its veterans rewards	POPE 782:77
w. knew him not	BIBLE 144:26
w.'s last night?	DONNE 338:10
w. locks up its spoons	SHAW 921:39
w.'s magnificence	MARI 651:67
w. market… computers	WATS 1055:52
w. may perish	FERD 385:13
w. might gain	GREE 444:19
w. might now be a better place	DOWN 343:80
w.'s mine oyster	SHAK 878:13
w. mirrored in the newspapers	LESS 598:4
w. must be safe for democracy	WILS 1086:52
w. must reel	BERR 98:10
w.'s new fashion	SHAK 865:10
w. now stands on the brink	MOUN 711:13
w. Of all of us	WORD 1096:32
w. of emotions	COLE 276:32
w. of gammon and spinnage	DICK 324:12
w. of gutterals	STEV 971:37
w. of his own making	WRIG 1101:6
w. of objects…w. of words	ELIOT 368:7
w. of profit and delight	MARL 654:11
w. of the dead	FORS 398:49

world (*contd.*):
w. of thought	HAMI 453:*41*
w. of vile ill-favoured faults	SHAK 878:*20*
w. owes all its onward impulse	HAWT 461:*76*
w. pass behind him	FRIS 406:*65*
W.-politics stepped in	LEWIS 602:*68*
w. proletarian army	LENIN 595:*50*
w....ranged against an aggressor	ATTL 44:*8*
w.'s riches, which dispersèd lie	HERB 476:*34*
w. rolls under	HUGH 500:*35*
w. ruled and led to war?	KRAUS 569:*90*
w. seemed none so bad	HOUS 495:*65*
w. shall find this miracle	DANI 304:*61*
w.'s sharpness like	BROW 197:*17*
w. should listen then	SHEL 929:*7*
w.'s storm-troubled sphere	BRON 191:*8*
w., that grey-bearded...profligate	HAWT 461:*75*
w.'s tempestuous sea	EDME 361:*45*
w. that is ours no more	BINY 162:*9*
w. through him might be saved	BIBLE 145:*35*
w., to offer for their sin	MARV 657:*69*
w.'s tourists are coming here	WILS 1085:*36*
w. understands my language	HAYDN 462:*87*
w. was all before them	MILT 693:*29*
w. was before the creation	BROW 195:*88*
w. was headed	SZIL 989:*71*
w. was not worthy	BIBLE 154:*53*
w. we find terrifying	MAMET 643:*46*
w. well-tried and old	HUGH 500:*41*
w. where action is not sister	BAUD 77:*25*
w. where it is so easy to neglect	CORN 288:*61*
w. will disagree	POPE 780:*31*
w. will end in fire	FROST 407:*85*
w. will give thee credit	CHUR 262:*84*
w. will little note	LINC 605:*5*
w. without end	BOOK 173:*92*
w. without end	RHYS 808:*29*
w. without end. Amen	BIBLE 152:*99*
w. without our pain	LANY 580:*80*
w.'s work...done by men	GALB 412:*85*
W., w., I cannot get	MILL 676:*81*
w.'s worst son of a bitch	PARK 755:*26*
w. worth working for	MITC 696:*84*
w. would go round a deal faster	CARR 238:*25*
w. would have been	HALI 452:*26*
w. would smell...a tomb	SHEL 929:*10*
w. wrapped up in...jeweller's cotton	DICK 324:*20*
worst woman in the w.	EDWA 362:*54*
yearning for the wider w.	MUSC 716:*81*
your whole w. is bereft	LAMA 575:*1*
World Cup in the W. C. Final	RAMS 801:*19*
win the W. C. under...Labour	WILS 1085:*38*
world-earthquake w.-e. Waterloo!	TENN 1000:*69*
World War before W. W. II	HOPP 493:*15*
passing resemblance to W.W.II	BARR 72:*40*
warfare of W. W. I	NOON 731:*21*
worldkin world, or even a w.	CARL 235:*57*
worldly most loathèd w. life	SHAK 897:*83*
worlds best of all possible w.	CABE 224:*80*
best of all possible w.	VOLT 1046:*2*
Between two w. life hovers	BYRON 223:*62*
diverting and stimulating of w.	MENC 669:*78*
Dream not of other w.	MILT 691:*91*
so many w.	TENN 999:*45*
Wandering between two w.	ARNO 38:*2*
What w. delight	SPEN 957:*6*
w. not realized	WORD 1098:*53*
w. of wanwood leafmeal	HOPK 492:*93*
worst of both w.	MACL 634:*91*
worldview w. a compound of	TOOLE 1023:*4*
worm bird, insect, or w.	MILT 690:*63*
channerin' w. doth chide	BALL 68:*61*
Hast thou the pretty w.	SHAK 906:*3*
I am a w.	BIBLE 114:*48*

worm (*contd.*):
like a w. i' th' bud	SHAK 894:*15*
loss of a w.?	SIDN 937:*48*
Of man or w.	MILT 694:*40*
physicists could create a w.	KRUT 570:*8*
remorse, my w.	RIMB 812:*98*
The invisible w.	BLAKE 167:*88*
w. at one end	JOHN 532:*43*
w'en he fine a w.	HARR 458:*30*
w. of death	GRAV 440:*25*
w. sucking an envenomed sore?	DONNE 336:*68*
w. that hath eat of a king	SHAK 892:*62*
w. that never dies	BROO 193:*34*
worms among the hungry w. I sleep	BALL -101:*35*
exclusive w.	PARK 754:*10*
filled with the ends of w.	TOLK 1022:*89*
food for w.!	FRAN 402:*99*
gone into W.	LUTH 620:*47*
grubs, or w.!	POPE 781:*63*
have made w.' meat of me	SHAK 869:*4*
silk dresses out of w.	STEV 972:*61*
The more the w. writhe	BRON 192:*14*
the one the editor gives to the w.	MACH 630:*34*
vilest w. do dwell	SHAK 914:*72*
will surely become w.	MILL 678:*30*
w. destroy this body	BIBLE 113:*12*
w. have eaten them	SHAK 886:*21*
w. shall try	MARV 658:*74*
w. that are thy chambermaids	SHAK 870:*23*
wormwood end is bitter as w.	BIBLE 120:*61*
w. and the gall	BIBLE 128:*31*
worn necessary...to be w. with toil	EURI 380:*29*
w. some twenty yeare agoe	FLET 394:*77*
worried w. into being	FROST 407:*94*
worries leaving you with your w.	SAND 842:*81*
money has dissolved more w.	BLEST 169:*28*
worrisome night of this w. day	BERN 97:*89*
worry any one he wanted to w. about	HELL 468:*84*
cakes...looked green with w.	FIRB 389:*76*
don't need to w.	HUTC 506:*43*
friends are beginning to w.	EPST 379:*6*
nothing much to w. about	HERR 478:*70*
w. about is bad luck	TRUM 1030:*19*
w. incessantly	GREE 445:*37*
w. on the doorstep	FIEL 388:*55*
you don't have to w.	DENN 316:*60*
worse do w. than be a swinger	FROST 406:*80*
for better for w.	BOOK 176:*49*
from w. to better	JOHN 526:*3*
I follow the w.	OVID 747:*1*
inflicting one that is w.	BOIL 171:*65*
More will mean w.	AMIS 16:*76*
person for the w.	SWIFT 984:*62*
w. appear The better reason	MILT 684:*1*
w. case of woe	SHAK 916:*9*
w. occupations in this world	STER 970:*26*
w. than being talked about	WILDE 1076:*50*
w. things in life	SCOTT 854:*72*
w. when it comes late	JERR 521:*15*
worship condescend to w. her	FORS 398:*28*
even in the house of w.	PARN 756:*39*
find someone to w.	DOST 341:*47*
if thou wilt fall down and w. me	BIBLE 133:*31*
machines we w.	PRIE 790:*40*
not dressed for w.	UPDI 1037:*68*
O w. the King	GRANT 438:*5*
religion without...death w.	REED 805:*89*
traditional w. of progress	WIEN 1074:*13*
w. and great honoring	DUNB 355:*36*
w. her by...noble deeds	TENN 1003:*18*
w. him in spirit and in truth	BIBLE 145:*37*
W. is transcendent wonder	CARL 236:*48*
w. of God	WHIT 1071:*56*
w. of...second-rate women	WEBB 1058:*11*

worship (*contd.*):
w. the Caesars and Napoleons	HUXL 507:*75*
w. the Lord	BIBLE 117:*8*
w. this dull fool	SHAK 917:*43*
Your w. is your furnaces	BOTT 180:*37*
worshipful neither articulate nor w.	SNYD 951:*84*
worshipper Nature mourns her w.	SCOTT 853:*48*
priest is the w.	SHAW 923:*76*
worshippers without their w.	DURK 357:*72*
worships he w. in his way	SMART 944:*66*
worst At w., one is in motion	GUNN 448:*86*
best and the w. of this	SWIN 987:*43*
do thy w., old time	SHAK 912:*49*
exacts a full look at the w.	HARDY 457:*8*
favor of the w.	MILL 675:*74*
good to know the w.	BRAD 184:*92*
learn, at best and w.	RABAN 798:*74*
Let's reason with the w.	SHAK 884:*64*
No w., there is none	HOPK 492:*3*
only believe the w.	LAFO 574:*76*
This is the w.	SHAK 903:*29*
very best and the very w.	FORD 396:*3*
What America...does w.	FUEN 409:*27*
world's w. son of a bitch	PARK 755:*26*
w. are...passionate intensity	YEATS 1106:*77*
w. comes in the end	SYNGE 988:*62*
w. is better than any other person	HAZL 463:*14*
w. is better than none	JOHN 532:*33*
w. is death	SHAK 867:*58*
w. is yet to come	JOHN 524:*61*
w. of madmen	POPE 782:*87*
w. of prison life	STEN 967:*73*
w. of worse journeys	WOOD 1092:*47*
w. possible location in the world	ACHE 3:*52*
w. sin towards our fellow creatures	SHAW 920:*14*
w. thing is that we live in	HAVEL 460:*60*
w. time of the year	ELIOT 369:*3*
worsted though right were w.	BROW 200:*2*
worth been w. the whistling	SHAK 903:*31*
comfort of thy w. and truth	SHAK 913:*60*
for what they are w.	FORB 396:*97*
grow in w. and wit	TENN 996:*88*
honest w. must wait outside	CHAO 251:*63*
matter of more w.	SHAK 861:*97*
measured by his w.	SHAK 910:*91*
More w. than any man	SHAK 912:*41*
not w. going to see	JOHN 530:*5*
prove...their commercial w.	ROCK 817:*70*
Small is the w.	WALL 1050:*71*
two things w. aiming for	HIND 481:*13*
w. a great deal	WEBB 1058:*15*
w. doing well	CHES 257:*72*
w. of the State	MILL 675:*69*
worthier not necessarily to be w.	HELO 469:*7*
Worthington Mrs W.	COWA 290:*2*
worthwhile never does anything w.	CHAR 252:*78*
worthy he is also w.	PASC 758:*74*
not w. of me	BIBLE 136:*80*
Who is w. to open the book	BIBLE 157:*11*
world was not w.	BIBLE 154:*53*
w., O Lord, to receive glory	BIBLE 157:*10*
w. was what he suffered	AESC 9:*54*
Wotton W....a most dear lover	WALT 1052:*7*
wound always w. up and going	LOWE 616:*84*
bleeding in the bitter w.	SPEN 957:*99*
books that w.	KAFKA 540:*84*
heal me of my grievous w.	TENN 1004:*48*
later return to w.	MURR 716:*80*
Makes such a w.	SHEL 929:*12*
Most writers need a w.	AMIS 17:*90*
nobler weapon than a w.	CRAS 296:*26*
not the w. that caused the cream	ELTIT 375:*21*
purple, with love's w.	SHAK 870:*36*
Safe with his w.	SASS 845:*23*

wound (*contd.*):
stain like a w.   BURKE 207:*32*
taken an immortal w.   FROST 408:*7*
What w. did ever heal   SHAK 899:*28*
Willing to w.   POPE 781:*69*
w. for w.   BIBLE 107:*69*
w. is incurable   LACL 574:*68*
wounded Bury my heart at W. Knee BENET 90:*62*
forgive last the delicately w.   CIAR 266:*51*
When you're w.   KIPL 560:*33*
w. for our transgressions   BIBLE 127:*1*
w. surgeon plies the steel   ELIOT 371:*51*
wounding guardianship…against w. PATR 761:*15*
heart's deep-sore w.   SHAK 864:*95*
wounds Balm to fester's w.   MILT 694:*44*
balm to heal their w.   SHAK 862:*30*
Bind up my w.!   SHAK 863:*62*
bind up the nation's w.   LINC 605:*6*
bound up his w.   BIBLE 142:*90*
Faithful are the w. of a friend   BIBLE 122:*7*
Say not…labour and the w. are vain   CLOU 270:*32*
shall make my w. all sound   LAYA 588:*22*
the soldier lists his w.   PROP 792:*79*
too much attained by w.   HOFS 484:*62*
With balmy hands his w. to bind   COLL 277:*45*
w. are in his breast and face   DAVIS 309:*39*
w. I had on Crispin's day   SHAK 881:*1*
W. inflicted by the sword   RICH 810:*69*
w. of deadly hate   MILT 690:*50*
woven Joy and Woe are w. fine   BLAKE 168:*3*
w. and held together   JACK 514:*87*
wrath chariots of w.   GRANT 439:*6*
Envy and w. shorten the life   BIBLE 132:*10*
eternal w. Burnt after them   MILT 691:*81*
give place unto w.   BIBLE 149:*36*
in w. remember mercy   BIBLE 130:*63*
my w. did end   BLAKE 167:*93*
Nursing her w.   BURNS 211:*9*
provoke not your children to w.   BIBLE 152:*4*
soft answer turneth away w.   BIBLE 121:*78*
sun go down upon your w.   BIBLE 152:*1*
sware in my w.   BIBLE 117:*7*
Throw away thy w.   HERB 476:*37*
tygers of w.   BLAKE 166:*77*
warned you to flee from the w.   BIBLE 133:*27*
wine of the w. of God   BIBLE 158:*23*
w. and indignation against us   BOOK 174:*25*
W. brings…gravest hurt   EURI 380:*32*
W. is cruel   BIBLE 122:*6*
w. of the Lamb   BIBLE 157:*13*
w. of the lion   BLAKE 166:*78*
w. which thou condemnest   BLAKE 168:*10*
wreaths laurel w. entwine   HARTE 460:*52*
w. of fame and interest   MARV 658:*80*
wreck Amid the w. …of nations   PITT 772:*73*
decay Of that colossal w.   SHEL 928:*93*
From its own w.   SHEL 930:*27*
playing bowls upon a splitting w.   DAVI 307:*96*
rock on which thou art to w.   DRYD 350:*35*
worthless check, a total w.   PORT 784:*32*
w. and the story of the w.   RICH 809:*49*
w. of Paradise   SHEL 931:*54*
wreckage w. of men   WOOLF 1093:*72*
wrecks thousand fearful w.   SHAK 863:*54*
Vomits its w.   SHEL 929:*9*
w. of a dissolving dream   SHEL 932:*64*
w. will surface over the sea   EWART 381:*47*
wren Four Larks and a W.   LEAR 589:*50*
No, the w. goes to't   SHAK 903:*34*
robin-red-breast and the w.   WEBS 1060:*44*
Wren Sir Christopher W. said   BENT 93:*24*
wrest w. the ball from your neighbour ANON 25:*16*
wrestle w. not against flesh   BIBLE 152:*6*
w.…words and meanings   ELIOT 371:*45*

wrestling lay w. with…my God   HOPK 492:*2*
Light w. there incessantly with light CRANE 294:*95*
Texas w. match   WRIS 1102:*23*
wretch Excellent w.!   SHAK 899:*29*
My wife…poor w.   PEPYS 765:*9*
on a w. wilt thou be revenged?   SIDN 937:*48*
Perfidious w.!   TREI 1026:*45*
poor w. whose one d.   SHAW 921:*29*
Pulled the poor w.   SHAK 892:*72*
Saucy pedantic w.   DONNE 336:*77*
saved a w. like me!   NEWT 725:*42*
sharp-looking w.   SHAK 865:*3*
W., under a comfort   HOPK 492:*5*
w. who supports   JOHN 526:*15*
wretched All men hate the w.   SHEL 926:*54*
how w. I should be   ALBE 11:*91*
make every one w.   JAMES 515:*5*
man…a w. thing   DAVI 307:*9*
Most w. men   SHEL 927:*69*
O w. state of man   SIDN 936:*43*
This rortie w. city   SMITH 949:*60*
w. man that I am!   BIBLE 149:*24*
w.,rash, intruding fool   SHAK 892:*53*
wretchedness so bare and full of w. SHAK 870:*21*
w. is irremediable?   EDGE 361:*32*
wretches Poor naked w.   SHAK 903:*24*
w. hang   POPE 778:*89*
Wright W.'s limp sentences   WEST 1068:*91*
wring w. under the load of sorrow SHAK 880:*61*
wrinkle out…with the first w.   DRYD 347:*56*
What stamps the w.   BYRON 219:*78*
wrinkles let old w. come   SHAK 873:*88*
w. will devour   NASHE 721:*83*
wrist time is tied to the w.   RAINE 800:*9*
tread her w.   DUNC 355:*48*
wrists slap time on their w.   KINC 557:*67*
writ censure this mysterious w.   DRYD 351:*53*
One w. with me   SHAK 870:*22*
stol'n forth of Holy W.   SHAK 863:*53*
w. your annals true   SHAK 911:*17*
write allow them to sing and w.   MAZA 666:*10*
always w. of you   SHAK 914:*74*
as a man ought to w.   TROL 1028:*98*
as much of a labour to w.   HUXL 506:*57*
better to w. of laughter   RABE 798:*77*
cause to w. about me   GIOV 428:*36*
difficult not to w. satire   JUVE 540:*77*
Don't w. anything down   DOWD 342:*78*
Don't you like to w. letters?   HEMI 470:*15*
engender in those who w.   GOWE 437:*82*
few…as cannot w.   DENH 315:*54*
For a man to w. well   JONS 536:*23*
I w. because   GALL 413:*96*
If a man w. little   BACON 59:*24*
invoked, sit down to w.   SWIFT 985:*2*
isn't much to w. home about   HYDE 509:*13*
like to w. standing up   HEMI 471:*38*
look into thy heart, and w.   SIDN 937:*51*
make me w. too much   DANI 305:*66*
may w. at any time   JOHN 525:*86*
necessary to w. for oneself   FLAU 392:*40*
never w. another   WELD 1063:*97*
No man can w.   FAUL 384:*88*
not easy to w. well   JAMES 517:*34*
number who can w.   MACD 627:*35*
people who do not w.   GREE 444:*25*
those who cannot w.   POPE 782:*82*
to w. a really funny book   HEMI 470:*13*
To w. music is to   HONE 488:*29*
to w. or even to talk   THES 1009:*45*
took him seventeen years to w.   PRIE 790:*41*
try to w. as good   HEMI 471:*45*
watches over us when we w.   AMIS 17:*92*
What I feel most moved to w.   MELV 668:*47*

write (*contd.*):
When I do not w.   CIXO 267:*76*
when you w. or when you fight   HEMI 470:*30*
would have liked to w.   KAVA 543:*24*
w. about it if I like   STEIN 965:*41*
w. against your name   RICE 809:*38*
w. enough to sign contracts   GING 427:*21*
w.…exclusively of others   WAUGH 1057:*2*
w. for money or fame   MOORE 705:*23*
w. for the adults   WALK 1049:*53*
W.: for these words are true   BIBLE 158:*35*
w. his thoughts upon a slate   HOOD 489:*53*
W. me as one that loves   HUNT 505:*28*
w. music like Wagner   GOLD 434:*38*
w. of Hell   HERR 477:*50*
w. straight honest prose   HEMI 470:*28*
w. the beauty of your eyes   SHAK 912:*47*
w. …too early in your life   RILKE 811:*83*
w. whatever story   KELM 549:*32*
w. when I feel spiteful   LAWR 585:*64*
w. when there is something   HEMI 470:*27*
w. with no dinner   RANS 802:*38*
yet could w. of thee?   JONS 536:*15*
writer Aboriginal w. is a Janus-type NARO 719:*40*
advertisement w. uses his mastery   SAYE 846:*51*
art of the w.   APOL 32:*91*
as a w. or artist   STEV 977:*61*
ask the w. to censor   KELM 549:*32*
Asking a working w.   HAMP 454:*65*
basic material a w. works with   CATH 244:*47*
being a professional w.   ROST 825:*4*
being a w. here means nothing   GOLD 432:*91*
concealed beauties of a w.   ADDI 7:*15*
danger of its tricking the w.   SAND 842:*79*
Detach the w.   ROTH 825:*7*
duty of the w.   KENN 552:*87*
Every w. is a frustrated actor   STER 968:*85*
experience of the woman w.   WITT 1088:*82*
For the w. …as for the painter   PROU 793:*8*
function of a w.   CONN 283:*68*
good w. always works   STEI 966:*62*
good w. is not…a good book critic   BISH 164:*36*
great and original w.   WORD 1099:*75*
great w. … always the plodder   POUND 787:*95*
great w. creates a world of his own CONN 282:*57*
great w. does not…invent   PROU 794:*9*
greatest part of a w.'s time   JOHN 529:*72*
housewife or a complete w.   PLATH 773:*89*
If any w. thinks   SHAR 919:*87*
If I were a w.   DELI 314:*39*
if Mr Kissinger is a great w.   ANON 29:*45*
it is the w.   ASIM 42:*73*
lesser w. may entice…for a moment CONN 282:*57*
loopholes for an unorthodox w.   ORWE 742:*5*
major w.…required major torment   BERG 95:*49*
memorandum…to protect the w.   ACHE 3:*43*
modern hardback w.   MORT 710:*94*
No modern Irish w.   ORWE 744:*34*
No w. before the…19th century   WAUGH -101:*5*
No w., sacred or profane   PATM 760:*7*
occupation of a woman w.   WOOLF 1093:*78*
plain, rude w.   BURT 214:*65*
present or future w.   MILL 674:*59*
primarily a w.   GENET 418:*73*
primary requirement of a w.   STAEL 961:*74*
responsibility of the w.   ALGR 13:*26*
role of w. and critic divided   BRAD 184:*88*
stink…of the w.'s pride   SALI 839:*31*
success happens to an English w.   AMIS 17:*89*
To a w., madness is a final distillation DELI 315:*40*
Too much importance given to w.   BOWL 182:*53*
tragic w. does not have to believe   KRUT 570:*7*
true friend and a good w.   WHITE 1070:*32*
understand a w.'s ignorance   COLE 275:*19*

York (*contd.*):

by this son of Y.   SHAK 862:45
tumble…from London to Y.   KING 558:98
Yossarian hell kind of a name is Y.?   HELL 468:83
Y. was moved very deeply   HELL 468:82
you I'm afraid it's y.   COPE 287:54
Now that I know y.   GOET 431:83
see y. umpiring   GRACE 437:85
things perish, and, y. along   KEMP 549:42
young Alligators…eat their y.   MACD 629:8
an old man y.   TENN 995:66
Angry Y. Man   PAUL 761:17
apple that isn't y. anymore   GARBO 414:17
being y. until you retire   LARK 582:18
Bowls is a y. man's game   BRYA 201:17
call her a y. country   HOPE 490:72
can be y. without money   WILL 1082:68
compliment him about looking y.   IRVI 513:65
corrupting the minds of the y.   PLATO 773:2
crime of being a y. man   PITT 771:62
death of one so y.   SPEN 956:82
denunciation of the y.   SMITH 947:9
die so y.   AUDEN 47:63
dies married y.   SHAK 870:19
fashion for the y.?   CHAN 251:55
For to be y. I wald not   HENR 472:67
Go West, y. man   SOULE 953:24
granted to the aged or the y.   LAUR 584:44
have been y.   BIBLE 115:65
head bit off by it y.   SHAK 902:5
how y. the policemen look   HICKS 480:94
I, being y. and foolish   YEATS 1104:56
I was y.   FLEC 393:47
If…love were y.   RALE 800:12
in my verse ever live y.   SHAK 912:49
life-chances of the y.   MUSG 716:82
Like all the very y.   MITF 697:95
Like all y. men   SHAW 923:84
look y. till forty   DRYD 347:56
misery peculiar to the y.   LESS 598:98
most perish y.   ETHE 380:13
never an Angry Y. Man   AMIS 16:80
not so y. as they are painted   BEER 83:21
Now as I was y. and easy   THOM 1010:65
Old and y.   STEV 974:14
old heads on your y. shoulders   SPARK 955:51
old [might as well speak] to the y.   CATH 244:43
one so y.   FORD 397:18
persuade you, y. and old   PLATO 773:3
radical when y.   FROST 407:93
seventy years y.   HOLM 486:2
she died y.   WEBS 1061:71
Since we're not y.   RICH 809:53
So wise so y.   SHAK 863:56
still y. an' believing   WILL 1082:69
their y. dying for…oil   POWE 788:14
to be y., gifted and black   HANS 455:71
to be y. was very heaven!   WORD 1099:66
too y. to fall asleep   SASS 845:33
voices of y. people   SMITH 947:15
warn you not to be y.   KINN 559:12
We that are y.   SHAK 904:50
When I was a y. man   SCHU 851:14
When the world was y.   BACON 59:7
When thou wast y.   BIBLE 147:78
where she may lay her y.   BIBLE 117:93
whom the gods love dies y.   MENA 668:53
woman is as y. as her knee   QUANT 796:51
writers the y. like   BURG 206:87
you're only too y.   THOR 1017:96
y. and inexperienced house   JERO 521:10
Y., and so fair!   HOOD 489:48
y. girl's skin   RENO 807:8
y. have aspirations   SAKI 837:99

young (*contd.*):

y. man can bring off   UPDI 1037:63
y. man carbuncular   ELIOT 369:89
y. man not yet   BACON 57:62
y. men can possibly imagine   SMITH 947:14
Y. men have more virtue   JOHN 527:35
Y. men mend not their sight   DONNE 339:30
y. men shall see visions   BIBLE 130:55
y. men shall utterly fall   BIBLE 126:91
y. ones carry pistols   SHAW 920:93
y. things that marry for love   SHAW 924:91
y., too stupid   RYLE 834:54
Young Brigham Y. is dreadfully   WARD 1053:18
How gently…G M Y. deals   ACHE 3:46
younger something y. than she looks   FIRB 389:71
we do not get any y.   REED 805:83
y. than that now   DYLAN 358:93
youngling y. in the contemplation   MILT 685:65
youngman Let me die a y.'s death   MACG 630:27
youngster that y.'s throat   COWA 291:11
yourself looking out for y.   COOL 287:39
more interested in y.   GIDE 423:43
more interesting than being y.   GIEL 423:50
Nothing can bring you peace but y.   EMER 376:35
to y., that husband   JAMES 515:4
two topics, y. and me   JOHN 530:89
youth All the flattering y. defy   ROCH 817:65
anything to do with y. clubs   SPARK 955:49
bear the yoke in his y.   BIBLE 128:33
blessings of y.   DEMO 315:46
cased up…have y.   WEBS 1061:61
cheerful bird of y.   KHAY 555:44
corrupted the y. of the realm   SHAK 861:75
crudity of y., distaining   NORR 731:29
days of my y.   SOUT 954:30
days of our y.   BYRON 223:65
deeds of y.   SHAK 913:60
done it from my y.   CRAB 294:82
eagle mewing her mighty y.   MILT 686:75
Farewell y.!   FRANZ 403:17
full of unmannerly sadness in his y.   SHAK 874:15
giddy, shallow, humorous y.   SHAK 881:79
green suckers of y.   SHER 933:96
had been friends in y.   COLE 274:10
has the eyes of y.   SHAK 878:19
Her Aunt…from her Earliest Y.   BELL 87:10
Home-keeping y.   SHAK 860:71
hour of thoughtless y.   WORD 1094:98
Immortal y. to mortal maids   LAND 578:57
in my y. I never did apply   SHAK 885:22
in y. man is…depraved   MITC 696:78
In y. open your mind   ANON 23:82
infirmities…I had in my y.   WESL 1067:71
joy…in my y.   AUDEN 49:3
laugh uproariously in y.   BROO 192:29
less of an affair of y.   FITZ 391:9
Let age approve of y.   BROW 199:77
Let no man despise thy y.   BIBLE 154:31
misspent y. and middle age   THUR 1019:51
morn of y.   WORD 1100:85
no danger in sweetness and y.   ROCH 816:61
noble y. did dress   SHAK 877:90
not clean past your y.   SHAK 877:81
outlive Thy y., thy strength   MILT 693:24
pass over y.   CONG 281:31
poets in our y.   WORD 1097:44
rejoice with the wife of thy y.   BIBLE 120:62
Rejoice…in thy y.   BIBLE 123:41
rigorous teachers seized my y.   ARNO 38:1
rose Of y.   SHAK 905:82
roses for the flush of y.   ROSS 823:70
sign of an ill-spent y.   SPEN 956:70
sins of my y.   BIBLE 115:53
So long as y.   SHAK 913:51

youth (*contd.*):

sowed in y. a mustard seed   BRON 190:91
spirit of y. in everything   SHAK 915:83
strong disposition in y.   POWE 787:2
thoughtless y.…with vain desires   DRYD 350:50
Time, which takes…Our y.   RALE 800:16
To flaming y.   SHAK 892:55
to living y. denied   WORD 1100:90
transitory as your y.   THOM 1013:26
What one knows…in y.   ADAMS 5:79
Where y. grows pale   KEATS 547:15
whose follies cease with their y.   PITT 771:62
world hath lost his y.   BIBLE 131:77
y. and the feeling   CONR 284:98
Y. are boarded, clothed, booked   DICK 321:44
y. are long, long thoughts   LONG 612:12
Y., beauty, graceful action   DRYD 349:25
y., before I waxèd old   SPEN 959:29
y.'s eyes burned   ROSS 824:88
Y.…forgives itself nothing   SHAW 922:62
y. full of grace   WHIT 1073:98
y. had seemed to teach   HARDY 456:96
y., I do adore thee   SHAK 887:40
Y. is a blunder   DISR 332:82
y. is bent by…wintry fever   THOM 1010:51
y. is bliss   BETJ 100:51
y. is renewed like the eagle's   BIBLE 118:11
Y. is something very new   CHAN 251:54
y. is vain   COLE 274:17
y. may be forgiven   AUDEN 49:98
y. may wear and waste   CONG 281:31
Y. means love   BROW 200:87
y.'s most precious years   STUD 980:14
Y. of a Nation   DISR 332:92
y. of a state   BACON 59:29
y. of America   WILDE 1077:68
y. of England are on fire   SHAK 880:73
y. of frolics   POPE 782:77
y. of his own generation   FITZ 390:93
Y. on the prow   GRAY 443:86
y. pined away with desire   BLAKE 167:87
Y. shows but half   BROW 199:75
y. stone dead   SASS 845:27
y. to fortune unknown   GRAY 442:77
y. unkind   BAST 76:8
Y., what man's age is like   DENH 315:56
y.…who must travel   WORD 1098:51
youths Even the y. shall faint   BIBLE 126:91
two noble y., stand prisoners   WILDE 1075:26
y. at cricks did play   JOSE 537:32
Yukon law of the Y.   SERV 859:54
yuppies Y. as a class   ADLER 9:47

zany mountebank and his z.   WALP 1051:92
Zarathustra Z., sometime regius   JOYCE 538:52
zeal holy mistaken z. in politics   JUNI 540:73
with half the z.   SHAK 918:62
z. of the Lord of hosts   BIBLE 125:66
zealots murmur among the z.   HUME 504:12
zealous z. citizen   BURKE 208:40
zebra Stripid like a z.   KEATS 545:75
z. stripes along his jaw   ELIOT 367:66
Zembla gives to Z. fruits   POPE 782:93
zenith z. doth depend upon   SHAK 916:20
zephyr soft the z. blows   GRAY 443:86
Z. and Aurora   MILT 682:97
z. and khaki shorts   BETJ 99:32
zero Global double z.   ANON 28:21
z. and the infinite   JARRY 518:69
Zerubbabel word…unto Z.   BIBLE 130:67
zest tell with such high z.   OWEN 748:13
ziggurats later came z.   GILL 426:2
Zimbabwe play cricket in Z.   MUGA 711:20
Zimmermann Z. in bright lights?   MERM 672:19

Zion every one of them in Z. — BIBLE 117:*94*
  lay in Z. for a foundation — BIBLE 125:*77*
  Lord shall bring again Z. — BIBLE 127:*96*
  mount Z., on the sides — BIBLE 116:*75*
  shall be as mount Z. — BIBLE 119:*39*
  when we remembered Z. — BIBLE 119:*47*
  Z., city of our God! — NEWT 725:*43*
Zionism with criminal Z. — HUSS 505:*36*

zip remorseless Z. — CHRI 261:*71*
zipless z. fuck is absolutely pure — JONG 533:*63*
zodiac never give out my z. sign — PEACE 762:*26*
zombies political z. — WILS 1085:*40*
zone with the Heavenly z. — LOVE 615:*68*
  yesterdays, for the Canal Z. — PARF 753:*84*
zones dwellers in different z. — DISR 332:*90*
zoo may see at the Z. — KIPL 563:*76*

zoo (*contd.*):
  return the giraffes to the z. — NASH 720:*73*
  The Human Z. — MORR 708:*76*
zoological beings in the z. scale — CARB 231:*95*
Zoroaster Z., my dead child — SHEL 929:*13*
Zuleika Z., on desert island — BEER 83:*29*
Zurich little gnomes in Z. — WILS 1085:*28*